AUTHORS, LINGUISTIC EXPERTS, AND ACADEMICS ENDORSE

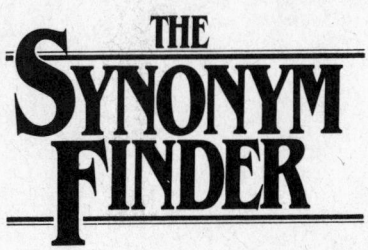

THE SYNONYM FINDER

"Thinking of a synonym is easy. Thinking of *the* synonym is what is hard. Lulliloo, then, to *The Synonym Finder*—in a class by itself for its staggering total of more than a million synonyms, but even more for its careful distinctions—distinctions that lead you arrow-straight to just the word or phrase you were trying to recall."

—Willard R. Espy

"Thank you for sending *The Synonym Finder*. I have been working it hard to test it out. I particularly like the fact that it saves me the extra step of consulting an index, which I must do with my Roget's. I like the print and the groupings, and expect to make this one of my regular working tools."

—Phyllis A. Whitney

"*The Synonym Finder* is a splendid tool for writers, both for professionals and those just beginning their long and arduous climb to precise prose."

—Irving Stone

"I compared the entries with those in comparable books that I own and found them unusually rich and useful. I know your book will be a great help in my work of simplifying legal documents."

—Rudolf Flesch, co-author of *A New Guide To Better Writing*

"Easily used . . . [a] large selection of synonyms for each listing."

—Dennis E. Morse, Ph. D., Medical College of Ohio at Toledo

THE SYNONYM FINDER

J. I. RODALE

Completely Revised
by
Laurence Urdang, *Editor in Chief*
and
Nancy LaRoche, *Managing Editor*

Editors
Faye C. Allen
Susan L. Duquès
Catherine A. Eckert
Adela Haberski French
Vincent D. Regan
Winifred vanRoden
Jack Vestali

Assistant Editors
Barbara W. Carlson
Janet S. Muller
Mary B. Redfield

Editorial Assistant
Marilyn Scott

Charles Gerras, *Project Development and Coordination for Rodale Press*

GRAND CENTRAL
PUBLISHING

NEW YORK BOSTON

Grand Central Publishing Edition

This Grand Central Publishing edition is published by arrangement with Rodale Press, Inc., 33 East Minor Street, Emmaus, Pennsylvania 18049

Grand Central Publishing
Hachette Book Group USA
237 Park Avenue
New York, NY 10017
Visit our Web site at www.HachetteBookGroupUSA.com.

Printed in the United States of America

First Hachette Book Group USA Edition: August 1986
25 24 23 22

Grand Central Publishing is a division of Hachette Book Group USA, Inc. The Grand Central Publishing name and logo is a trademark of Hachette Book Group USA, Inc.

Library of Congress Cataloging-in-Publication Data

Rodale, J. I. (Jerome Irving), 1898–1971.
The synonym finder.

1. English language—Synonyms and antonyms—Dictionaries. I. Urdang, Laurence. II. LaRoche, Nancy.
PE1591.R64 1986 423'.1 86-5599

ISBN 978-0-446-37029-5 (U.S.A.) (pbk.)
0-446-37030-4 (Canada) (pbk.)

INTRODUCTION

Those who work with language know that there is no such thing as a true "synonym." Even though the meanings of two words may be the same — or nearly so — there are three characteristics of words that almost never coincide: frequency, distribution, and connotation. *Panthera leo* and *lion*, *cucurbit* and *squash*, *sodium carbonate* and *washing soda* have quite different frequencies in English. We all know that a *house* is not a *home*, that not all *women* are *ladies*, that not all *men* are *gentlemen;* at a more subtle level, we soon learn the differences between *motherly* and *maternal*, *fatherly* and *paternal*, *brotherly* and *fraternal.* These are connotative differences.

It is a curiosity of English that it continuously acquires words from other languages to expand its lexicon. Observers have often noted that even if a new coinage or a loanword from another language starts out with "exactly" the same meaning as an existing word in English, the meanings begin to drift apart before very long, one acquiring quite different frequency, distribution, and connotation from the other. An incredible fact about English is that it retains many of the words developed in its lexicon. Some words do become obsolete and are dropped forever. Most, however, remain and develop nuances that expand for the writer and speaker the opportunities for expression and expressiveness.

For these reasons, a synonym dictionary must be used with caution. Even though two words may be quite similar in meaning, the substitution of one for the other may not always be appropriate, and the writer's intent may be ill served by his failure to select the *mot juste. The Synonym Finder* contains more words than any book of its kind — more than 1,500,000. Sometimes, it will be consulted to find a word that will lend variety to the user's language; other times it will be consulted to remind the user of the temporarily lost word or expression that was "right on the tip of his tongue." In either case, it should be used with understanding.

Every effort has been made to make this book as accurate, as complete, and as easy to use as possible. Inevitably, a user may disagree with the treatment given a particular word. In that case, he is urged to consult a major dictionary where he is likely to find fuller information on the word than *The Synonym Finder* can be expected to offer. The nature of language and the behavior of words defy precision in the preparation of a work like *The Synonym Finder*. The editors have often had to make admittedly arbitrary decisions on word inclusion and placement. It is to be hoped, however, that among the many related words offered, the user will find several that suit his subject and his context.

Laurence Urdang

Essex, Connecticut
July 28, 1978

A Note on the Style of
THE SYNONYM FINDER

The Synonym Finder follows dictionary format. Entries are arranged alphabetically, with all appropriate parts of speech included under a single headword. Homographs — words spelled identically but of different origins — are entered separately with an identifying superior number.

Word listings have been organized numerically according to definition and major semantic groups; further discriminations are shown within these groups by separating subgroups by semicolons.

Usage levels are indicated by appropriate labels, such as *Slang*, *Informal*, etc.; technical or specialized words are identified by a field label such as *Chemistry*, *Nautical*, etc. In addition, gist information (*enclosed in parentheses*) is often included to help the user avoid inappropriate choices.

All gist and usage information appears before the word to which it applies, and applies to that immediately following word only, unless otherwise clearly indicated (e.g., *Both Inf.*, *All Sl.*). Foreign words and phrases as yet unassimilated into English are appropriately labeled and italicized.

In most cases, usage or technical labels have been written in full (e.g., *Archaic*, *Literary*). Common and easily understood abbreviations that have been employed are listed below. The labels *Informal* and *Slang*, when written in full before an entire listing, refer to the entry headword, rather than to the synonyms that follow. When abbreviated (*Inf.* or *Sl.*), the labels, like others in *The Synonym Finder*, refer to the following word.

List of Abbreviations

Aeronaut.	Aeronautics
Anat.	Anatomy
Anthropol.	Anthropology
Archit.	Architecture
Astron.	Astronomy
Bacteriol.	Bacteriology
Biol.	Biology
Bot.	Botany
Brit.	British
Chem.	Chemistry
Ch.	Church
Civ. Eng.	Civil Engineering
Class. Myth.	Classical Mythology
Derog.	Derogatory
Dial.	Dialect
Eccles.	Ecclesiastical
Educ.	Education
Elect.	Electronics
Embryol.	Embryology
Entomol.	Entomology
Euph.	Euphemistic
Fig.	Figurative
Fort.	Fortifications
Fr.	French
Geom.	Geometry
Ger.	German
Gk.	Greek
Hist.	History
Hort.	Horticulture
Inf.	Informal
It.	Italian
Mach.	Machinery
Math.	Mathematics
Med.	Medicine
Metaphys.	Metaphysics
Mil.	Military
Naut.	Nautical
Obs.	Obsolete
Ophthalm.	Ophthalmology
Ornithol.	Ornithology
Parl.	Parliament
Parl. Proc.	Parliamentary Procedure
Pathol.	Pathology
Pharm.	Pharmacology
Philos.	Philosophy
Phonet.	Phonetics
Phys. Chem.	Physical Chemistry
Physiol.	Physiology
pl.	plural
Print.	Printing
Psychoanal.	Psychoanalysis
Psychol.	Psychology
Relig.	Religion
Rhet.	Rhetoric
Rom. Cath. Ch.	Roman Catholic Church
Rom. Hist.	Roman History
Scot.	Scotland/Scottish
Sl.	Slang
s.o.	someone
Sp.	Spanish
s.t.	something
Theat.	Theater
Theol.	Theology
U.S.	United States
usu.	usually
Vet. Med.	Veterinary Medicine
Zool.	Zoology

A

aback, *adv.* **1.** rearward, to *or* in the rear, back, toward the back, behind, backward, hindward; *Naut.* abaft, *Naut.* aft, *Naut.* astern, *Naut.* sternward; retrogressively, regressively, retrogradingly; *Fig.* aloof, *Fig.* at a distance.

2. taken aback surprised, startled, astonished, shocked, astounded, stupefied; flabbergasted, stunned, bewildered, amazed, thunderstruck, dumfounded; perplexed, confounded, nonplused, disconcerted, discomposed, discomfited, *Inf.* thrown off guard, *Inf.* thrown for a loss, *Inf.* floored.

abandon¹, *v.* **1.** forsake, desert, leave behind, throw over, jilt, run out on, *Inf.* leave flat, turn one's back on, *Sl.* give the deep six; ignore, cut off, neglect, ostracize; leave, depart, quit, go away from, vacate, evacuate.

2. discard, cast off, jettison, throw away, get rid of, toss out, throw out, (*of cards*) throw in, *Inf.* ditch, *Inf.* chuck, *Sl.* deep-six.

3. discontinue, give up, retire from, withdraw from, stop, end, cease, *Inf.* quit cold; throw up, lose hope of, despair of; forbear, desist from, drop; forgo, do *or* go without, dispense with, waive, lay aside.

4. repudiate, reject, disown, renounce, wash one's hands of; renege, forswear, disavow, disclaim, recant, (*usu. under oath*) abjure; bail out, bow out, pull out of, *Inf.* back out of, back-pedal, *Inf.* back away from *or* off on, *Inf.* cop out; betray, turn traitor, *Sl.* sell down the river, *Sl.* rat out *or* rat out on; defect, apostatize.

5. relinquish, abnegate, let go, deliver up, turn over to; surrender, concede, yield, submit, *Sl.* throw in the towel *or* the sponge; resign, abdicate, give up.

6. (*of oneself*) give way to, lose oneself in, yield to; indulge, gratify, wallow in, carouse, dissipate.

abandon², *n.* **1.** lack of restraint *or* self-control, unrestraint, lawlessness, surrender to impulse; licentiousness, wantonness, dissipation, profligacy; intemperance, incontinence, *Obs.* immoderation.

2. enthusiasm, spirit, élan, animation; verve, dash, life, vigor, ardor, *It. brio*; spontaneity, impetuosity, freedom.

abandoned, *adj.* **1.** forsaken, deserted, neglected; relinquished, given up, left behind, *Naut.* (*of a ship*) ahull; discarded, rejected, cast off *or* away *or* aside; shunned, scorned, outcast, forlorn, *Poetic.* lorn; bereft, adrift, alone, solitary, lonely, desolate; destitute, desperate, helpless, hopeless, wretched, mournful, unfortunate, friendless.

2. unrestrained, uncontrolled, unconstrained, licentious; shameless, dissolute, loose, wanton, dissipated, profligate, reprobate, depraved, lewd, impure, unchaste; immoral, wicked, accursed, flagitious, vicious, corrupt; sinful, bad, unprincipled, dishonorable, disreputable; lost, irreclaimable, irreformable, incorrigible, unrepentant, hardened.

abandonment, *n.* **1.** desertion, forsaking, rejection; defection, heresy, apostasy, recreance, recreancy; neglect, negligence, dereliction; departure, decampment, evacuation.

2. relinquishment, abnegation, resignation, abdication, *Archaic.* demission; renunciation, repudiation, disavowal, recantation, denial, (*under oath*) abjuration, backpedaling.

3. surrender, yielding, nonresistance.

abase, *v.* **1.** degrade, debase, vitiate, demean, discredit, demote, depose; devaluate, reduce, lower, depress; humiliate, humble, mortify, bring low, take down, bring *or* take down a peg.

2. disgrace, dishonor, shame; slander, calumniate, asperse, denigrate, malign, vilify, vituperate, revile, smirch, besmirch, smear, *Inf.* badmouth; belittle, deprecate, deflate, disparage, depreciate, downgrade, *Inf.* put down, *Inf.* playdown.

abasement, *n.* **1.** degradation, depravation, debasement, vitiation, deterioration, degeneration; devaluation, downfall, fall, descent, lowering, reduction, detrusion, depression; humiliation, humble pie, mortification, deflation; humility, humbleness, meekness, servility, lowliness, abjectness, submission, resignation, self-abasement, prostration.

2. disgrace, shame, dishonor, disrepute, obloquy, ingloriousness; infamy, ignominy, baseness, vileness, turpitude, meanness, despicableness, contemptibleness.

abash, *v.* disconcert, discomfit, take aback, ruffle, discompose; embarrass, chagrin, discountenance, put out of countenance, shame, put to shame, make ashamed, humiliate, mortify, humble, put down, take down, disgrace, cause to lose face; nonplus, confound, confuse, bewilder, astonish, dumfound, perturb; dismay, dishearten, daunt, intimidate, cow, browbeat, overawe, overwhelm.

abashed, *adj.* **1.** disconcerted, nonplused, taken aback, out of countenance, discomfited, dumfounded, chagrined; dismayed, daunted, cowed, intimidated, awestruck, overawed, subdued, timid, timorous.

2. embarrassed, ashamed, humiliated, mortified; shamefaced, shy, bashful, self-conscious, retiring, withdrawn.

abashment, *n.* awe, dismay, consternation, confusion, discomfiture; embarrassment, mortification, shame, humiliation, chagrin, vexation; shyness, bashfulness, self-consciousness.

abate, *v.* **1.** reduce, diminish, decrease, lower, lessen, attenuate, weaken, bate; alleviate, mitigate, allay, palliate, assuage, relieve; mollify, soften, pacify, appease; quiet, calm, tranquilize, soothe, *Sl.* simmer down; moderate, temper, *Archaic.* attemper; quell, slake, blunt, dull.

2. subside, let up, intermit, cease; decline, fall off, taper off, wane, fade away, ebb, slacken.

3. deduct, subtract, allow; discount, mark down, cut back; rebate, remit, pay back.

4. omit, leave out, skip, pass over, eschew, avoid.

abatement, *n.* **1.** reduction, lessening, letup, moderation, tempering; decrease, fall-off, diminution, remission; alleviation, mitigation, assuagement, relief, palliation, mollification, softening; waning, fading, ebb, decline, subsidence; weakening, attenuation.

2. suppression, check, control, curb, limitation, restraint; stoppage, termination, arrestment, abolition, eradication, elimination, extermination, extinguishment; quashing, quelling, crushing; prohibition, prevention, repression.

3. deduction, reduction, allowance; markdown, cutback, discount, write-off.

abattoir, *n.* slaughterhouse, slaughterpen, shambles, butchery, *Obs.* butcher-row.

abbé, *n.* ecclesiastic, clergyman, cleric, man of the cloth; abbot, prior, monk, friar, monastic, celibate; priest, padre; pastor, curate; minister, divine. See also **clergyman, ecclesiastic, priest.**

abbey, *n.* monastery, religious house, priory, cloister, cenoby, friary; convent, nunnery; seminary.

abbot, *n.* general, superior, head, officer, provincial, abbé, *Eastern Ch.* archimandrite; conventual, monk, monastic, cenobite, friar, brother; ecclesiastic, churchman, cleric, priest.

2. abbess, prioress, mother superior, mother general, mother vicar.

abbreviate, *v.* shorten, reduce, *Obs.* breviate; contract, cut, cut down, cut short, crop, clip; retrench, curtail, lessen; shrink, constrict, narrow, condense, compress; abridge, abstract, brief, synopsize, summarize, digest.

abbreviation, *n.* **1.** brief, abstract, synopsis, outline, sketch; précis, prospectus, résumé, syllabus, conspectus, compendium, epitome, survey, summary; digest, abridgement.

2. lessening, shortening, condensing, condensation, compressing, compression, contracting, contraction, curtailing, curtailment, reducing, reduction; decrease, cutting down *or* short, retrenchment, cropping, clipping, shrinking, narrowing; abstracting, abstraction, summarizing, summarization.

abdicate, *v.* **1.** resign, renounce, give up claim *or* right to, *Law.* disclaim, lay down, part with, retire from, vacate, abnegate, *Chiefly Scot.* demit; relinquish, let go, deliver up, hand over, turn over; surrender, yield, cede, give way.

2. abandon, forsake, desert, leave behind, turn one's back on, ignore, neglect; give up, quit, drop, throw over, cast aside.

3. repudiate, reject, disown, wash one's hands of; refuse, decline, forgo, do without.

abdication, *n.* **1.** resignation, resigning, renunciation, renouncing, retirement, retiring, abnegation, *Archaic.* demission.

2. relinquishment, abandonment, surrender, yielding, ceding, cession; transfer, transferral, transference, handing over.

3. repudiation, rejection, disowning, disclamation; deserting, desertion.

abdomen, *n.* **1.** belly, stomach, *Inf.* tummy, gut, *Sl.* breadbasket, *Scot. and North Eng.* wame; paunch, potbelly, *Inf.* bay window, *Inf.* corporation, *Sl.* pot, *Sl.* beerbelly, *Sl.* spare tire, *Obs.* gorbelly; colonic cavity, intestinal cavity; visceral cavity, *Anat., Zool.* venter, ventral region, ventricular cavity, *Anat.* epigastrium; pouch, (*of birds*) gizzard, (*of birds*) crop, craw, maw, ingluvies, (*of birds*) proventriculus, (*both of ruminating animals*) first stomach, rumen.

2. intestines, bowels, colons, (*of swine*) chitterlings; innards, inwards, insides, vitals, viscera, (*of animals*) entrails, *Inf.* gizzard, *Sl.* guts.

abdominal, *adj.* intestinal, visceral, splanchnic; gastric, stomachic, stomachal, stomachical, *Anat.* celiac, ventral, ventricular.

abdominous, *adj.* **1.** potbellied, round-bellied, big-bellied, *Sl.* beer-bellied, large-bellied, great-bellied, *Obs.* gorbellied; paunchy, *Inf.* bay-windowed, *Inf.* corporational; obese, fat, corpulent, overweight, *Scot.* fodgel; chubby, tubby, pudgy, plump; round, rounded out, rotund, portly.

2. full, bulging, protuberant, bloated, distended; swollen, turgid, tumid; puffy.

abduct, *v.* **1.** (*usu. of persons*) carry off, rape, seize, steal, make off *or* away with; kidnap, *Sl.* snatch, seize as hostage, hold for ransom; run off with, spirit away, steal away; lay hold of, lay hands on; (*usu. in reference to military service*) impress, press, conscript, *Naut.* shanghai, crimp.

2. commandeer, take over by force, hijack, skyjack, pirate; expropriate, appropriate, misappropriate, arrogate; wrest from, usurp, accroach; help oneself to, make free with.

3. *Usu. Physiol.* abduce, draw away, take away.

abduction, *n.* **1.** (*all of persons*) robbery, theft, capture, seizure, rape; man-stealing, kidnapping, child-stealing; impressment, conscription; (*both of animals*) petnapping, dognapping.

2. commandeering, hijacking, skyjacking, air piracy; expropriation, arrogation, misappropriation.

abductor, *n.* thief, robber, crook, rapist; kidnapper, petnapper; skyjacker, hijacker, air *or* sky pirate.

aberrant, *adj.* **1.** deviate, deviant, divergent, wayward, devious; erroneous, mistaken; deviating, diverging, departing, divagating, digressing, lapsing, wandering, rambling, straying, roving.

2. anomalous, anomalistic, abnormal, irregular, variable; odd, peculiar, curious, queer, incongruous, strange, errant, bizarre, weird; unconventional, uncommon, unusual, offbeat, out of the ordinary, eccentric, *Inf.* quirky, original, singular, exceptional, individual; extraordinary, egregious, remarkable, astonishing; monstrous, unnatural, freakish, *Inf.* freaky, heteroclite, heteroclitical, heteromorphic, heteromorphous, miscreated, malformed, deformed, misshapen, misshaped, teratoid, teratological, teratogenetic; epicene, androgynous, hermaphroditic, hermaphroditical.

3. perverse, perverted, corrupt, corrupted, twisted, *Inf.* kinky; depraved, degenerate, degenerated, deteriorated, vitiated, debased, abased.

4. vague, unsound, senile, *Sl.* not all there, *Sl.* not playing with a full deck.

aberration, *n.* **1.** deviation, divergence, departure, divarication, divagation, digression, declination, declension; lapse, irregularity, incongruity; waywardness, aberrance, aberrancy; wandering, straying, rambling, deviating, diverging, departing, divagating, digressing.

2. anomaly, abnormality, abnormity, variation; oddity, peculiarity, curiosity, quirk, eccentricity; nonconformity, unconformity, unconventionality, exception, singularity, singularness, bohemianism; strangeness, bizarreness, oddness, curiousness, queerness, freakishness, *Inf.* freakiness; freak, freak of nature, mutant,

deformity, abortion, malformation, miscreation, monster, monstrosity, teratogeny, *Biol.* teratism, heteroclite; hermaphrodite, epicene, androgyne.
3. untruthfulness, falseness, mendacity; misrepresentation, falsification, distortion, deception, subreption, fraud, sophistry; falsehood, fallacy, lie, untruth, sophism; falsifying, misrepresenting, lying, deceiving, twisting, distorting; perversion, corruption, depravity, depravation, degeneration, degeneracy, depredation, decadence, deterioration, vitiation, debasement, abasement.
4. derangement, mental disorder; vagary, unsoundness, senility; illusion, delusion, fancy, unreality, dream world, hallucination; monomania, alienation, self-deception; mania, craze, obsession, infatuation, fixation.

abet, *v.* **1.** encourage, prompt, urge, spur, goad, prod, egg on; incite, instigate, provoke, foment; stimulate, animate, whet, inspire, embolden; excite, arouse, inflame, fire, fire up, stir up, wind up, *Inf.* psych up.
2. support, advocate, patronize, back, endorse, sanction, approve, countenance; promote, further, forward, advance, favor, foster; help, aid, assist, subsidize, underwrite, second; uphold, maintain, sustain, succor; cooperate with, connive at, scheme at, befriend.

abettor, *n.* **1.** encourager, prompter, urger, spurer, inciter, instigator, provoker, fomenter; stimulator, animator, inspirer; exciter, arouser, rouser, rabble-rouser, enflamer, demagogue.
2. helper, aide, assistant, adjutant, coadjutant, coadjutor, coadjutress *or* coadjutrix, attendant, auxiliary; second, henchman, right hand, right-hand man; colleague, comrade, associate, consociate, companion, partner; cooperator, conniver, participant, participator; confederate, accomplice, accessory, partner in crime.
3. supporter, advocate, adviser, patron, patronizer, backer, endorser, upholder, sanctioner, approver; follower, disciple, adherent; agent, promoter, furtherer, advancer, favorer; subsidizer, underwriter, maintainer, sustainer.

abeyance, *n.* **1.** suspension, intermission, interruption, cease, cessation, discontinuation, remission; deferment, deferral, postponement, delay; lull, waiting period; waiting, reserve, reservation; inaction, dormancy, latency, quiescence.
2. in abeyance in cold storage, on ice, on a back burner, hanging fire, in a holding pattern, abeyant.

abeyant, *adj.* **1.** suspended, deferred, postponed, put off; tabled, shelved, set aside; inactive, static, stationary, resting, dormant, latent, quiescent; expectant, waiting.
2. See **abeyance** (*def.* **2**).

abhor, *v.* **1.** abominate, execrate, loathe, shudder at; despise, detest, feel aversion toward, hate, dislike; view with horror, shrink from; be nauseated by, not be able to stomach.
2. disdain, scorn, contemn, spurn, look down upon, shun.

abhorrence, *n.* **1.** loathing, abominating, execration, hatred, hate, detestation, odium; repugnance, aversion, hostility, enmity, animosity, animus, antipathy; horror, revulsion, disgust, noisomeness.
2. disdain, scorn, contempt.

abhorrent, *adj.* **1.** loathsome, abominable, execrable, heinous, atrocious, hateful, detestable, odious; repulsive, repellent, offensive, revolting, invidious; obnoxious, repugnant, disgusting, rank, noisome, distasteful, disagreeable; horrible, horrifying, hideous, shocking; nauseating, sickening; unpleasant, displeasing.
2. loath to; averse to, opposed to, against, resistant to.
3. remote from, distant from, removed from, outside of.

abidance, *n.* **1.** compliance, observance, acquiescence, submission, obedience; cooperation, assent, concession, consent.
2. conformity, conventionality, accordance, accord, congruity, harmony, affinity, similitude.
3. abidingness, perseverance, persistence, steadfastness, tenacity, pertinacity, *Inf.* stick-to-it-iveness; permanence, constancy.

abide, *v.* **1.** remain, continue, stay, stop, tarry, rest, sit, lie, keep.
2. live, dwell, reside, lodge, sojourn; *Archaic.* bide, house, take up quarters, pitch tent, settle, anchor, put down stakes, plant oneself.
3. last, endure, survive, outlive, persist, persevere, exist; be steadfast, be constant, be immovable, be immutable, be indestructible, be permanent.
4. await, expect, wait for, be in store for, stand in hand, anticipate, attend.
5. endure, bear, tolerate, stomach; put up with, stand, suffer, brook, bear with.
6. accept, acquiesce in, consent to, be in line with.
7. abide by a. comply with, observe, obey, acknowledge, agree to, submit to, conform to. **b.** discharge, carry out, fulfill; keep faithful to, persist in, hold to, stand by, adhere, stick to *or* with.

abiding, *adj.* eternal, unending, everlasting, immortal; unchanging, unchangeable, indestructible, indissoluble, immutable, changeless; durable, stable, lasting, constant, permanent; inherent, indwelling.

ability, *n.* **1.** capacity, capability, potential, potentiality; potency, power, strength; aptitude, intelligence, ingenuity, brilliance, cleverness, smartness, aptness, wit, mother wit, mind for, understanding; faculty, talent, gift, genius, facility, endowment, flair, bent, turn, knack, forte, strong point; inclination, proclivity, propensity.
2. competence, competency, adequacy, sufficiency, capableness, adeptness, proficiency, know-how, savoir faire; mastery, master hand, expertness, efficiency, efficacy; skill, skillfulness, dexterity, adroitness, address, deftness; qualification, readiness, knowledge.
3. abilities aptitudes, understandings, powers, strengths; faculties, talents, gifts, parts, *Obs.* intellectuals; skills, accomplishments, attainments.

abject, *adj.* **1.** degrading, debasing, humiliating, humbling, mortifying; poor, beggarly, paltry, sorry, sad, pathetic, pathetical, piteous, pitiful, pitiable; shabby, shoddy, dirty, scruffy, scrubby, scurvy; miserable, squalid, stark, destitute, hopeless, oppressed, brought-low.
2. base, base-spirited, base-minded, vile, low, low-minded, debased, depraved, degraded, unprincipled, immoral, profligate; evil, bad, wrong, ignoble; contemptible, despicable, reptilian, sordid, foul, infamous, ignominious, odious, opprobrious, obnoxious, detestable, execrable, rank, degenerate, corrupt, vicious, reprehensible, unmentionable, heinous, atrocious, flagitious, iniquitous, *Archaic.* facinorous.
3. obsequious, *Obs.* obsequent, slavish, servile, toadyish, sycophantic, sycophantical, sycophantish, flattering, fawning, truckling, ingratiating, *Sl.* bootlicking, *Sl.* brown-nosing; obeisant, prostrate, on one's knees; groveling, cringing, crawling, crouching, sniveling, cowering.

abjectness, *n.* **1.** humbleness, poorness, beggarliness, paltriness, patheticalness, pitifulness, pitiableness; shabbiness, shoddiness, dirtiness, scrubbiness, scruffiness, scurviness; miserableness, squalidness, starkness, hopelessness, oppressiveness; abjection, degradation, debasement, humiliation, humbling, mortification; misery, squalor, destitution, oppression.
2. baseness, vileness, lowness, depravity, unprincipledness, immorality, profligacy, profligateness; evilness,

badness, wrongness, arrantness, nefariousness; meanness, villainy, villainousness, ignobility, ignobleness; contemptibility, contemptibleness, despicability, despicableness, detestability, detestableness, sordidness, infamy, infamousness, ignominy, ignominiousness, odium, odiousness, opprobrium, opprobriousness, execrableness, degeneracy, degeneration, corruptedness, corruptness, corruption, viciousness, reprehensibility, reprehensibleness, heinousness, atrociousness, flagitiousness, iniquity, iniquitousness, *Archaic.* facinorousness.

3. obsequiousness, slavishness, servility, servileness, toadyishness, sycophancy, flattery, fawning, truckling, ingratiation, *Sl.* bootlicking, *Sl.* brown-nosing; obeisance, prostration, falling on one's knees; groveling, cringing, crawling, crouching, sniveling, cowering.

abjuration, *n.* **1.** renunciation, renouncement, retraction, disclamation, disclaiming; disavowal, denial, recantation, recall, taking back.

2. repudiation, *Law.* disaffirmation, reversal, revocation, repeal; rejection, discarding, disowning; abnegation, refusal, self-denial.

abjure, *v.* **1.** renounce, repudiate, disdain, forswear; abandon, desert, forsake, relinquish, give up, reject, discard, disown.

2. renege, take back, go back on, apostatize, depart from; recall, retract, recant, revoke, withdraw.

3. avoid, shun, eschew; forgo, *Inf.* swear off, stay away from, have nothing to do with, *Inf.* have no truck with.

ablaze, *adj.* **1.** burning, blazing, on fire, afire, fiery; flaming, aflame, flaring, ignited.

2. gleaming, glowing, aglow, glaring; brightly lit, lighted, alight, luminous, illuminated; radiant, brilliant, incandescent; shimmering, twinkling, flashing, flickering, glittering, sparkling, fluttering.

3. excited, exhilarated, enlivened, inspired, animated, enthusiastic, eager; stimulated, aroused, intensely desirous, intense; ardent, fervent, fervid, perfervid, impassioned, passionate, frenzied.

4. very angry, irate, wrathful, wroth, incensed; enraged, raging, infuriated, infuriate, furious; ranting, raving, vehement, fuming; heated, worked up, flared up; vexed, irritated, piqued, chafed, galled, riled, nettled, offended.

able, *adj.* **1.** competent, capable, adequate, equal to, *Inf.* up to, proficient, efficient; qualified, skilled, practiced, experienced, *Fr. au fait,* fit, fitted; powerful, potent, strong.

2. superior, expert, *Inf.* topnotch, topflight, top drawer, first-rate, *Inf.* crack, *Sl.* crackerjack, *Sl.* on the ball, *Inf.* whiz-bang, *Brit. Sl.* whizzo; talented, gifted, adept, skillful, dexterous, adroit, deft; smart, clever, ingenious, brilliant, inventive; intelligent, sagacious, learned, knowledgeable, versed.

3. apt, facile, accomplished, finished, polished, masterful, masterly; effective, striking, telling, revealing.

able-bodied, *adj.* healthy, in good health, fit, physically-fit, in good condition, sound, in fine fettle, able, athletic, *Inf.* in good shape, *Inf.* in shape; robust, vigorous, full of vigor, hearty, hardy, hale, hale and hearty, lusty, strong and healthy, bursting with health *or* vigor, *Scot., North. Eng. and Irish Eng.* sonsy; stout, staunch, stanch, firm, sturdy, burly, tough, iron, *Inf.* tough as nails, *Inf.* hard as rock; stalwart, rugged, hefty, husky, solid, well-knit; muscular, brawny, strapping, broad-shouldered, powerfully-built, *Derog.* muscle-bound; powerful, potent, mighty, all-powerful, herculean, *Literary.* puissant.

ablution, *n.* **1.** cleansing, purification, purifying, depuration, depurating, purge, purging, mundifying, epuration, lustration, lustrating; decontamination, decontaminating, depollution, depolluting, sanitization, sanitizing, antisepsis; baptizing, baptizement, *Eccles.* baptism, christening, aspersion, aspersing, *Rom. Cath. Ch.* Asperges, sprinkling, besprinkling, holy water sprinkle, morning star, affusion; immersion, submergence, dunking, *Archaic.* dipping.

2. holy water, *Eccles.* laver, *Eccles.* chrism; rinse, rinsings.

3. washing, wash, bathing, bath, lavation, lavage, *Archaic.* laving, cleaning, deterging, shampooing, shampoo, scrubbing, scrub, scrub-up; showering, shower, dousing, rinsing, rinse, flushing; abstersion, wiping, sponging, scouring.

abnegate, *v.* **1.** renounce, resign, abdicate; deny oneself, sacrifice, forgo, abstain from, forbear, refrain from; reject, refuse, decline, turn down, do *or* go without.

2. relinquish, give up, surrender, yield; concede, acquiesce, submit.

abnegation, *n.* **1.** renunciation, resignation, abdication; self-denial, sacrifice, abstinence, forbearance; rejection, refusal, declining, declination.

2. relinquishment, giving up, surrender, yielding; conceding, acquiescence, submission, submitting.

abnormal, *adj.* **1.** anomalous, anomalistic, irregular, variable; deviate, deviant, aberrant, divergent, heterodox, heretical, wayward; deviating, diverging, departing, digressing, lapsing, wandering, straying, rambling, roving.

2. strange, odd, peculiar, queer, offbeat, curious, quizzical, erratic, eccentric, weird, bizarre, *Inf.* quirky; unconventional, uncommon, unusual, unique, rare, extraordinary, exceptional, singular, individual; monstrous, unnatural, freakish, grotesque, heteroclite, heteroclitical, *Inf.* freaky.

3. huge, enormous, stupendous, colossal, immense, mammoth, gargantuan, gigantic, vast.

abnormality, *n.* **1.** anomaly, aberration, perversion; oddity, peculiarity, curiosity, rarity; monster, monstrosity, mutant, freak, heteroclite, malformation, miscreation, abortion, deformity.

2. deviation, aberrance, aberrancy, irregularity, variation, abnormity, divergence, digression, *Rare.* anomalism; unconformity, unconventionality, uncommonness, unusualness, uncommonality, singularity, singularness, exception; eccentricity, idiosyncrasy, quirk, hobby-horse; strangeness, oddness, queerness, bizarreness.

aboard, *adv.* **1.** on board, on deck, on ship, on board ship, on shipboard, all aboard, in *or* on the vessel, topside, before the mast; on; in, inside, inside of, within.

2. alongside, beside, along the side, by the side of, close to the side, to the side, off to the side, flush with, next to, right next to; abreast, side by side, cheek by cheek, cheek by jowl, board by board.

3. *Baseball Slang.* on base, on the basepaths, on, *Sl.* on the pond.

—prep. **4.** aboard of, on; in, into, to; inside, inside of, within.

abode, *n.* **1.** home, domicile, domicil, dwelling, dwelling place, dwelling home, residence, residency, habitation, habitancy, *Scot. and North Eng.* bigging, *Scot.* howff; lodging, lodgings, lodging place, lodgement *or* lodgment, nest, roost, perch; quarters, living quarters, rooms, accommodations, housing, roof over one's head, *Inf.* pad, *Inf.* crash pad, *Chiefly Brit. Inf.* diggings, *Brit. Inf.* digs; apartment, flat, tenement, walk-up, cold-water flat, *Brit.* chambers, *Chiefly Brit.* maisonette; penthouse, townhouse, condominium, *Sl.* condo; mobile home, motor home, camper, trailer; address, location, situation, whereabouts, place.

2. mansion, palace, palatial *or* stately dwelling, *Fr.*

hôtel, It. palazzo, villa, chateau, castle, *Chiefly Brit.* hall, *Brit.* court, *Archit.* folly, *Sl.* spread; manor, manor house, manor seat, estate, country estate, country home, country house, country seat, house and grounds, house and lot, *Brit. Dial.* toft, demesne, *Law.* messuage; farm, farmstead, grange, farmplace, *Archaic.* farmhold, *Brit.* farmery, *Brit.* croft, *Brit.* homecroft, *Scot. and North Eng.* steading; ranch, rancho, rancheria, hacienda; plantation.

3. cottage, cot, bungalow, bower, cabin, log cabin, blockhouse, *Brit. Dial.* cote, *Scot.* but-and-bend; hut, shed, shack, shanty, hutch, *Scot.* bothy; hovel, hole, dump, sty, pigsty, pigpen, tumbledown shack, wretched hut, mean dwelling, miserable quarters.

4. hearth, hearthstone, hearth and home, hearthside, fireside, fireplace, chimney corner, *Brit. Dial.* ingle, *Brit. Dial.* ingleside, *Chiefly Brit.* inglenook; homestead, household, family, family circle, domestic circle, bosom of one's family, seat of one's affections, home sweet home, *Inf.* place where one hangs one's hat.

5. residence, residency, habitation, habitancy, inhabitation, inhabitancy, commorancy, domiciliation; sojourn, sojournment, sojourning, stay, stay-over, stop, stop-over, stop-off, lay-over.

abolish, *v.* **1.** annul, nullify, disannul, disestablish, declare null and void, make void, quash; repeal, revoke, retract, rescind, abrogate; reverse, countermand, cancel, *Law.* nol-pros; invalidate, vacate, vitiate; do away with, cut out, remove, put an end to, terminate, make an end of, dispense with; supersede, overthrow, subvert, set aside, repudiate.

2. annihilate, eradicate, expunge, extirpate, obliterate; raze, demolish, exterminate, ravage, devastate, batter down, stamp out, crush out; extinguish, destroy, eliminate, quash, squelch, suppress.

abolition, *n.* **1.** annulment, nullification, disannulment, voidance, *Law.* defeasance, disestablishment, abolishment; revocation, repeal, rescinding, rescission, abrogation; recantation, retraction, withdrawal; reversal, countermand, counterorder, cancellation; invalidation, vitiation; termination, removal, dissolution; overthrow, subversion, repudiation.

2. annihilation, obliteration, eradication, extirpation, extinction; devastation, razing, ravaging, demolition, destruction; extinguishment, elimination, suppression.

abominable, *adj.* **1.** abhorrent, loathsome, execrable, despicable, heinous, odious, detestable, hateful; damnable, accursed, cursed, ignominious, reprehensible, deplorable, infamous.

2. repugnant, repulsive, revolting, repellent, offensive, noisome, obscene, frightful, disgusting, rank, atrocious; horrid, horrible, hideous, villainous; nauseous, nauseating, sickening; squalid, sordid; unpleasant, unlikable, disagreeable, *Brit. Inf.* beastly.

3. inferior, poor, bad, appalling, imperfect, defective, faulty, *Inf.* not up to snuff; vile, base, sorry.

abominate, *v.* abhor, loathe, execrate, despise, detest, hate, feel intense aversion toward, feel hostile toward, not be able to bear *or* abide; shudder at, shrink from, recoil from, blench from; feel repugnance toward, feel disgust toward, feel distaste for; dislike, mislike, disrelish, disfavor.

abomination, *n.* **1.** abhorrence, loathing, loathsomeness, execration, detestation, odiousness; hatred, hate, aversion, enmity, hostility, animosity, animus, antipathy; *Fr.* bête noire, bugbear; damnation, curse.

2. depravity, perversion, obscenity, atrocity; defilement, foulness, uncleanness; repugnance, disgust, repulsion, offense, torment, plague, annoyance, nuisance, infliction; ignominy, villainy, evil, wickedness; corruption, corruptness, pollution; disgrace, shame.

aboriginal, *adj.* native, indigenous, endemic, endemical, domestic, enchorial, autochthonous, autochthonal, autochthonic, primal, original, primordial; primeval, prehistoric, preadamic, noachian, noachic, noachical, antediluvian, antiquated, age-old, old; primary, prime, earliest, first, primitive, pristine, simple, elementary.

—n. **2.** autochthon, native. See **aborigine.**

aborigine, *n.* native, local, indigene, autochthon, aboriginal, *Australian Inf.* boong; primitive, original, settler, pioneer, *Australian.* bushman, original inhabitant, first resident; ancient, prehistoric man, antediluvian, preadamite, caveman, troglodyte.

abort, *v.* **1.** miscarry, deliver prematurely, develop incompletely.

2. fail, fall short, not reach, be deficient, be insufficient; terminate, end, cease, stop, check, arrest, quell, put down; frustrate, thwart, circumvent, contravene, obstruct, interfere, inhibit, hinder, intercept, prevent, preclude; checkmate, nullify.

abortion, *n.* **1.** miscarriage, premature birth, premature labor, untimely birth, premature delivery, unnatural birth, arrested development; aborticide, feticide, forced birth.

2. failure, nonsuccess, nonfulfillment, defeat, vain attempt; fizzle, fiasco, no-go, blunder, disappointment; frustration, thwarting, circumvention, contravention, obstruction.

3. monstrosity, miscreation, *Biol.* teratism; malformation, deformity, monster, freak, mutant, oddity, curiosity, lusus naturae.

abortive, *adj.* **1.** unsuccessful, vain, futile, useless, bootless, profitless, unavailing; worthless, nugatory; ineffective, inoperative, ineffectual; fruitless, unproductive, sterile, barren, impotent.

2. rudimentary, imperfectly developed; immature, incomplete, stunted; failing, miscarrying; not viable, untimely, premature.

abound, *v.* **1.** overflow, overflow with, flood, spill over, overspill, overbrim; exuberate, superabound, know no bounds; abound with, burst with, bristle with, throng with, be alive with; clutter, crowd, jam, pack.

2. flourish, luxuriate, thrive; be rich in, be well supplied, be well furnished, lack nothing.

3. teem, teem over, swarm, swarm over, overswarm, run over, overrun, run riot, run wild; overspread, spread over, overgrow, grow over; infest, plague, beset; multiply, increase, swell, proliferate, be prolific; stream, rain, flow, gush.

abounding, *adj.* **1.** rich, lavish, luxuriant, rank, profuse, prodigal, prolific, exuberant, superabundant; abundant, bountiful, bounteous, copious, plentiful, plenteous, fat, unstinted; ample, sufficient, enough, more than enough, *Inf.* plenty.

2. full, filled, abrim, *Archaic.* fraught; rife, replete, flush, well-supplied, abundantly-supplied; overflowing, overspilling, running over with, bursting, bristling, thick, thick with; teeming, teeming with, swarming, swarming with, crawling, crawling with, alive with. *Sl.* lousy with; crowded, crowding, thronged, thronging, jammed, packed, *Inf.* jam-packed.

about, *prep.* **1.** concerning, concerned with, touching, dealing with, regarding, in *or* with regard to, anent, respecting, with respect to, referring to, with reference to, of; relating to, in relation to, relative to, connected *or* associated with; engaged in, involved in, busy with.

2. near, nearby, nigh, close by; close to, neighboring, adjacent; in, inside, within; on, upon; with, beside, *Brit.* anenst.

3. around, surrounding, circumjacent, rounding, encircling, circling, encompassing, circumfluent; en-

folding, enwrapping, wrapped around, enveloping.
4. on the verge *or* brink of, ready to, readying to, prepared to, preparing to, soon to.
5. throughout, all over, in all parts, over, through.
—adv. **6.** approximately, roughly, generally, more or less, or so, all but, nearly, in the neighborhood of, in the vicinity of, close to; virtually, almost, well-nigh, nearing, approaching.
7. nearby, close by, hereabout, not far off.
8. in the reverse *or* opposite direction, halfway around, 180°, backwards.
9. to and fro, here and there, hither and thither, hither and yon, far and wide, helter-skelter.
10. around, in circumference, perimetrically, peripherally.
—adj. **11.** astir, stirring, up and around; moving, in motion, active.
12. in existence, existing, alive, living; happening, going on, going, in the air, current, prevailing, prevalent, widespread.

about-face, *n.* **1.** reversal, turnabout, turnaround, rightabout, switch, *Sl.* switcheroo, *Inf.* flip-flop, *Inf.* a 180°; backtracking, back-pedaling; change of heart, second thought, *Inf.* a different tune *or* song; tergiversation.
2. retraction, retractation, withdrawal, recantation, palinode, abjuration; repudiation, renunciation, defection, bolting, going over, apostasy.
—v. **3.** turn around, do an about face; back down *or* out of, renege, backtrack, backpedal, shift one's ground, *Inf.* flip-flop, do a flip-flop, do an about-face, *Inf.* do a 180°, sing a different song *or* tune; change one's mind, tergiversate.
4. retract, disavow, recant, unsay, withdraw, take back, *Inf.* eat *or* swallow one's words; deny, gainsay, renounce, forswear, abjure; repudiate, disclaim, disown.

above, *adv.* **1.** overhead, over one's head, on a higher place, at a higher place, in a higher place; atop, at the top, on the top; aloft, high up, up in the air *or* sky, far above the ground; skyward *or* skywards, toward the sky; in *or* to heaven, on high, in the firmament, in the celestial heights.
2. superior, upper, higher in rank *or* authority greater, mightier, more powerful; more elevated, loftier.
3. more, greater, larger, higher in quantity *or* number; more abundant, in excess, excessive, over and above, above and beyond.
4. before, earlier, foregoing, preceding, precedent; antecedent, prevenient, prior, anterior; aforementioned, aforesaid, aforestated, above-mentioned, above-stated; previously, formerly, in a former part.
—prep. **5.** atop of, on top of, aloft of, in a higher place than, to a higher place than, at a higher place than; over, on, upon, reaching higher than.
6. in excess of, exceeding, in surplus of, over and above, above and beyond; more than, greater than, larger than.
7. beyond, surpassing, exceeding, transcending, overpassing, superior in rank *or* standing to; higher in authority to, more elevated than, loftier than, greater than, mightier than, more powerful than.
8. not subject to, not liable to, not exposed to, not put through, not submitted to; not vulnerable to, not susceptible to, not in danger of; not open to, not amenable to, not willing to, not agreeable to; not capable of, not able to.
9. averse, opposed to, in opposition to, contrary to, counter to; against, versus, resistant to; disinclined to, unwilling to, reluctant to, loath to.
10. rather than, in preference to, in favor of.
11. north of, north from, northward of, northward from; toward the north; northwards, northerly, northwardly.
12. above all, first and foremost, in the first place, most important of all, before anything else, before anything; principally, chiefly, paramountly, supremely, pre-eminently; especially, particularly, peculiarly, expressly; mainly, primarily, essentially, mostly, predominantly.
—adj. **13.** written above, above-mentioned, above-stated, aforesaid, aforementioned, aforestated; aforenamed, aforegiven, aforecited; already stated, previously described, described above, indicated earlier, previously indicated *or* specified; earlier, foregoing, preceding, precedent, former; antecedent, previous, prevenient, prior, anterior.
—n. **14.** above-written, above-mentioned, above-stated, aforesaid, aforementioned, aforestated; aforenamed, aforecited, aforegiven.
15. heaven, firmament, sky, space, infinity; celestial expanse, the vault of heaven, the canopy of heaven; abode of God and angels, our Father's house, Abraham's bosom, heavenly kingdom, heavenly city; next world, world beyond the grave, happy hunting grounds, paradise.

aboveboard, *adv.* **1.** overtly, openly, in open sight, in the open, out in the open, in full view, in plain view, publicly, in public, in public view, for all to see; up front, on the table; before one's eyes, *Inf.* under one's nose; to one's face, face to face, man to man, heart to heart.
2. candidly, frankly, forthrightly, directly, straightforwardly; explicitly, unequivocally, undisguisedly, plainly, in plain words *or* English, with no nonsense, all joking aside; outspokenly, freely, boldly, unreservedly, unrestrainedly, unconstrainedly, uninhibitedly, unshrinkingly.
3. truly, truthfully, veraciously; guilelessly, ingenuously, sincerely, artlessly, naively, simply, undeceptively, undeceitfully, undeceivingly, without artifice.
4. honestly, uprightly, upstandingly; honorably, respectively, fairly, decently, justly.
—adj. **5.** open, open and aboveboard, straight, square, square-dealing, fair and square, square-shooting, straight-shooting; legitimate, up and up, *Sl.* on the up-and-up, up front, on the level, no-nonsense; honorable, respectable, reputable, creditable, estimable.
6. candid, frank, forthright, direct, straightforward, straight-from-the-shoulder, man-to-man, heart-to-heart; plain, plain-spoken, plain-speaking, downright, outright, explicit, unequivocal, unambiguous, undisguised, *Inf.* flat-footed; outspoken, free, free-spoken, free-speaking, unreticent, bold, unreserved, unrestrained, unconstrained, unchecked, unabashed, uninhibited, unshrinking.
7. guileless, ingenuous, sincere, genuine, artless, naive, simple, transparent, undeceptive, undeceitful, undeceiving, undissembling; true, truthful, veracious.
8. honest, upright, upstanding; fair, honorable, decent, just.

abracadabra, *n.* **1.** incantation, chant, magic formula, magic word, invocation, conjuration; mumbo-jumbo, hocus-pocus, open-sesame; charm, spell, rune, *Scot.* cantrip; sorcery, magic, apotropaism.
2. gibberish, jabber, Jabberwocky, chatter, prattle, cackle, gibber; babble, babblement, prate, tattle, twaddle, *Brit.* twattle; patter, gabble, blather, rapid and inarticulate talk; jargon, gobbledegook; nonsense, balderdash, balderal, babbling, *Fr.* bavardage; humbug, flummery, *Sl.* bunk, rubbish, *Inf.* rot, *Sl.* gar-

bage, *Sl.* horsefeathers; hogwash, stuff and nonsense, fudge, foolishness, rigmarole *or* rigamarole, amphigory; poppycock, *Inf.* fiddle-faddle, *Inf.* piffle, drivel, *Inf.* bosh, *Inf.* kibosh, *Inf.* flapdoodle.

abrade, *v.* **1.** erode, wear, wear down *or* away, wash away, corrode, fret, gnaw, fray, *Inf.* frazzle, graze, chafe; levigate, file, triturate, grind, whet, sand, sandpaper, pumice, rub, rub down, scour; smooth, polish, wax, burnish, buff, shine.

2. grate, rasp, scrape, scrape off, excoriate.

abrasion, *n.* **1.** rub, fret, fray, *Inf.* frazzle; scrape, scratch, graze, scuff, sore, *Both Path.* canker, ulcer.

2. erosion, eroding, wearing, wearing down *or* away, detrition, attrition, abrading, corrosion, corroding; fretting, gnawing, fraying, chafing; grinding, whetting, filing, sanding, pumicing; friction, rubbing, rubbing down, scouring; smoothing, polishing, burnishing, buffing, shining; grating, rasping, scrape, scraping, excoriation.

abrasive, *n.* **1.** abradant, emery, emery cloth, emery board, pumice, pumice stone, pumicer, rouge, sand, sandpaper, steel wool; file, rasp, whetstone, grindstone, millstone; cleanser, scouring powder, scouring pad, rubbing compound; polish, wax, burnisher, buffer, buff stick, buff wheel.

—adj. **2.** erodent, erosive, attritional, attritive, eroding, wearing, corrosive, abradant, abrading; fretting, gnawing, fraying, chafing; rough, coarse, ragged, jagged, sandpapery; harsh, grating, rasping.

abreast, *adv., adj.* **1.** beside, side by side, by the side of, adjacent to, next to, next door to, cheek by jowl, close at hand, aligned, in alignment, on a line with, in one line; bow to bow, stem to stem.

2. *Usu.* **abreast of** *or* **with, a.** equally advanced, alongside, up to the same plane, on a par, parallel, matched, even, tied, equal, alike. **b.** informed, knowledgeable, *Inf.* up on, *Inf.* on top of.

abridge, *v.* **1.** shorten, contract, cut down, abbreviate, condense, compress, concentrate; abstract, summarize, brief, synopsize, digest, epitomize.

2. reduce, retrench, decrease, diminish, lessen, shrink, narrow, bridge, subtract, subduct, curtail; truncate, cut, cut off, cut back, cut short, slash, clip, shear, shave, trim, prune, pare down, lop, lop off, dock.

3. deprive, cut off, divest, dispossess, debar, disinherit, shut off, shut out, bereave, despoil, strip.

abridgment, *n.* **1.** digest, epitome; compendium, survey, synopsis, abstract, summary, précis, conspectus, prospectus; syllabus, résumé, brief, outline, sketch.

2. shortening, contraction, contracting, cutting down, abbreviation, abbreviating, condensation, condensing, compression, compressing, concentration, concentrating; reduction, reducing, retrenchment, retrenching, decrease, decreasing, lessening, shrinkage, shrinking, narrowing, bridging, subtraction, subtracting, subduction, subducting, curtailing; obtruncation, detruncation, truncation, cut, cutting off *or* back *or* short, slashing, clipping, shearing, shaving, trimming, pruning, nipping, lopping, lopping off, docking.

3. deprivation, divestiture, dispossession, debaring, disinheriting, shutting off, cutting off, shutting out, bereavement, despoiling, stripping.

4. compactness, tightness, narrowness, narrow straits, squeeze, tight squeeze, bind, confined *or* restricted space, confinement; restriction, limitation, curtailment; loss, shortage, diminution.

abroad, *adv.* **1.** in foreign parts, out of the country, overseas, on the continent, *U.S.* in Europe, beyond seas; wandering, traveling, vacationing, on one's travels; distant, afar off.

2. away, about, out, out of doors, out of the house, not at home, in the open air, gone out; not present, absent, elsewhere, yonder.

3. spread around, in circulation, at large, astir, before the public, publicly.

4. broadly, widely, far and wide, expansively, extensively, unrestrainedly; everywhere, all over, ubiquitously.

5. wide of the mark, wide of the truth, in error, off the scent, off the course, without the last clue; puzzled, bewildered, at the end of one's wits, abstracted, preoccupied, perplexed.

abrogate, *v.* **1.** abolish, repeal, revoke, reverse, rescind; annul, disannul, nullify, declare null and void, render null and void, void, avoid; quash, invalidate, vitiate, vacate, disenact, disestablish; cancel, discharge; supersede, set aside, discontinue, *Law.* nol-pros, suspend, stop, cease.

2. recant, retract, abjure, unsay, recall; take back, withdraw, undo, renege; renounce, relinquish, abnegate, repudiate, deny, disclaim, disavow; countermand, counterorder, overrule, override; veto, negate.

3. terminate, dissolve, put an end to, bring to an end, do away with, destroy; throw overboard, write off, put aside, get rid of.

abrogation, n. 1. repeal, abolition, abolishment, revocation, reversal, rescinding, rescindment, rescission; annulment, annulling, disannulment, nullification, voidance, avoidance, *Law.* defeasance; quashing, invalidation, vitiation, *Obs.* vacatur, disenactment, disestablishment, setting aside; cancellation, discharge; suspension, *Law.* nolle prosequi, discontinuance, cessation.

2. recantation, retraction, retractation, abjuration, recall; taking back, withdrawal, undoing, *Cards.* renege; renouncement, renunciation, relinquishment; abnegation, repudiation, denial, disclaimer, disavowal; countermand, counterorder, overruling, overriding; veto, negation.

3. termination, dissolution, putting an end to, bringing to an end, doing away with, destruction; writing off, putting aside, getting rid of.

abrupt, *adj.* **1.** sudden, quick, hasty, instantaneous, rapid, swift, hurried; headlong, rash, precipitate, out-of-hand, unseasonable, ill-timed; unexpected, unforeseen, unanticipated, unlooked for, unannounced.

2. curt, brusque, blunt, gruff, short, broken off; rude, impolite, discourteous, uncivil, ungracious, unceremonious.

3. discontinuous, broken, disconnected, uneven, jerky, angular, rough, irregular, jagged, zigzag, cragged; cramped, harsh, stiff, (*as style*) inelegant.

4. steep, sheer, sharp, precipitous, declivitous, acclivitous.

abscess, *n.* ulcer, ulceration, noma, fester, festering, gathering, gumboil, parulis, tubercle, *Obs.* apostem *or* aposteme *or* apostume *or* aposthume, *Obs.* apostemation, *Archaic.* impostume *or* imposthume; canker, lesion, chancre, chancroid, soft chancre, simple chancre; boil, blain, furuncle, furunculus, carbuncle, pustule, pimple, papule, papilla, pock, wen, whelk, *Rare.* bleb, *Archaic.* botch; sore, open *or* running sore, gall, excoriation; whitlow, agnail.

abscond, *v.* **1.** flee, bolt, elope, escape, fly, take flight, take to flight, take wing, *Sl.* wing it, *Inf.* beat it, *Inf.* skip out, *Inf.* skip town, *Inf.* skedaddle, *Sl.* skidoodle, *Sl.* skidoo *or* skiddoo, *Sl.* vamoose *or* vamose, *Sl.* light out; run, run away, run off, take to one's heels, make a quick exit, *Rare.* fugitate, *Inf.* take off, *Inf.* clear out, *Inf.* make tracks, *Inf.* cut out, *Inf.* cut and run, *Inf.* fly the coop, *Sl.* split, *Sl.* scram, *Sl.* blow, *Sl.* hightail it, *Sl.* lam *or* take it on the lam;

retreat, withdraw, decamp, desert, abandon, take oneself, take French leave, quit the scene, make a getaway, beat a retreat, beat a hasty retreat, run for it, turn tail, show the heels, show a clean *or* extra-light pair of heels; leave, depart, exit, *Euph.* leave without saying good-bye, *Brit. Sl.* bugger off.

2. make off, pull out, absquatulate *or* absquotilate, give *or* take leg-bail, *Sl.* bail out, *Fig.* take the money and run; sneak off *or* away, creep off *or* away, steal off *or* away, slink off *or* away, slip away, slither away, skulk away, slide off, *Sl.* mooch off, *Sl.* duck off, *Brit. Sl.* mizzle; vanish, disappear, do the disappearing act, *Inf.* make oneself scarce, *Brit. Sl.* do a moonlight flit; evade, dodge, elude, bilk, give [s.o.] the slip, lose [s.o.], *Sl.* duck and run, *Sl.* dog it, *Sl.* ditch [s.o.], *Sl.* shake [s.o.] off.

absence, **1.** nonattendance, nonresidence, nonappearance.

2. unavailability, lack, need, want, deficiency, default; dearth, paucity, scarcity; privation, destitution; emptiness, negation, void, vacuum, vacuity, vacancy.

absent, *adj.* **1.** not present, out, off, away, abroad, elsewhere; nonattendant, nonresident, not at home; lost, astray, flown, missing, AWOL.

2. lacking, wanting, nonexistent, deficient.

3. inattentive, absent-minded, preoccupied, absorbed; unthinking, thoughtless, unconsidering, blank, oblivious, heedless; distracted, lost, listless, unconscious, unaware; woolgathering, musing, dreamy, faraway, removed.

— *v.* **4.** remove oneself, retire from, withdraw oneself, stay away from, decamp, abscond; play truant, skip, not show up, fail to appear, cut, ignore; shirk, evade, vacate, slip away.

absentee, *n.* deserter, truant, fugitive, exile, renegade, runaway; shirker, slacker, skulker, malingerer, quitter, backslider.

absenteeism, *n.* chronic absence, truancy, cutting, skipping, hooky *or* playing hooky; dereliction, delinquency, neglect, avoidance, evasion, shirking; desertion, sneaking out, French leave.

absently, *adv.* inattentively, abstractedly, distractedly; musingly, dreamily, listlessly; forgetfully, thoughtlessly, heedlessly, inadvertently; absent-mindedly, unmindfully, negligently; carelessly, sloppily, indifferently.

absent-minded, *adj.* **1.** musing, meditative, meditating, cogitative, cogitating; contemplative, contemplating, pondering, brooding, mulling over, ruminant, ruminative, ruminating, chewing, chewing one's cud, deliberating, reflective, reflecting; pensive, thoughtful, thinking, cerebrational, bemused, lost in thought, in a brown study, *Archaic.* museful; daydreaming, dreaming, dreamful, dreamy, stargazing, gazing out the window, in the clouds, in a trance, napping, sleeping, asleep; absent, withdrawn, remote, removed, distant, faraway, away, wandering, *Sl.* not at home, *Sl.* out to lunch, *Sl.* out of it.

2. abstracted, preoccupied, rapt, absorbed, immersed, engrossed, lost in, wrapped up, consumed, concentrating, occupied, busy; distracted, diverted, distrait, inattentive, unattentive, inadvertent, deaf, unheeding, unheedful, heedless; oblivious, unaware, unconscious, unmindful, insensible, blind; forgetful, forgetting, apt to forget, Lethied, amnesic, *Chiefly Southern U.S.* disremembering; scatterbrained, rattlebrained.

absolute, *adj.* **1.** perfect, complete, entire, whole, comprehensive, total, ideal, consummate; full, plenary; uncut, solid, undivided, exhaustive, undiminished; pure, clean, clear, faultless, flawless, unadulterated; uncorrupted, untinged, untainted, unblemished, unmixed, unmingled, unblended, uncombined, undiluted, unalloyed; genuine, unaltered, essential, real; plain, simple, regular, unadorned, stark.

2. outright, downright, out-and-out, straight-out, all-out, across-the-board; sheer, utter, unmitigated; unqualified, categorical, unconditional, unconditioned, unreserved, implicit; unrestricted, unlimited, total; unhampered, unimpeded, unbounded; free, self-determined, self-sufficing; irrepressible, uncontrollable.

3. autocratic, dictatorial, totalitarian, despotic; tyrannous, tyrannical, arbitrary, fascist; authoritative, magisterial, monarchal; sovereign, supreme, lordly, almighty, imperial; domineering, dogmatic, doctrinaire, controlling, commanding, peremptory; demanding, exacting, pressing, imperious, overbearing, imperative; unrestrained, self-willed, arrogant, haughty.

4. positive, determinate, certain, veritable, unequivocal, unambiguous, explicit, express; sure, confident, unquestionable, conclusive; official, confirmed, authoritative; demonstrable, demonstrated, apodictic, indubitable, undoubted; settled, fixed, definite, decided, decisive, pronounced; true, actual, factual, accurate, reliable.

5. ultimate, omnipotent, almighty, all-powerful, infallible, infinite; autonomous, self-existent, independent; self-evident, axiomatic, assumed, understood, accepted, given, manifest; intrinsic, inherent, essential, innate, ingrained, fundamental.

absolutely, *adv.* **1.** completely, wholly, fully, entirely; totally, nothing short of, unqualifiedly, utterly; categorically, unconditionally, unreservedly, implicitly; purely, clearly.

2. positively, certainly, veritably, unquestionably, unequivocally, unambiguously, explicitly; inalienably, officially, authoritatively, incontestably; demonstrably, demonstratedly, indubitably, undoubtedly, decidedly, decisively, perforce; definitely, precisely, exactly, surely, assuredly, conclusively, really, in reality, indeed; actually, factually, accurately, reliably; in fact, in truth, truly, verily; patently, manifestly; intrinsically, inherently, essentially, innately, fundamentally; ultimately, infinitely, infallibly.

—*interj.* **3.** naturally, of course, without a doubt, that's right, yes indeed, yes indeedy; to be sure, sure thing, *Inf.* you bet, *Inf.* you bet your life, *Inf.* roger, good enough, all right.

absoluteness, *n.* **1.** certainty, certitude, sureness, surety, assurance, assuredness, infallibility; positiveness, definiteness, actuality, substantiality, reality; accuracy, correctness, rightness; exactness, exactitude, preciseness, precision; perfection, faultlessness, flawlessness, ideality.

2. independence, self-determination, autonomy, supremeness, sovereignty; unlimitedness, unrestrained power, arbitrariness, despotism, absolutism. See **absolutism.**

absolution, *n.* **1.** forgiveness, forgiving, excuse, excusing, shriving, making allowances for; condonation, condoning, overlooking, disregarding, ignoring; acquittal, acquittance, acquitting, comburgation, exculpation, exculpating, clearance, clearing, proof of innocence, removal of guilt; pardon, pardoning, amnesty, remission, remitting, reprieve, reprieving, respite, exoneration, exonerating, warrant, warranting, justification, justifying, vindication, vindicating, righting, avenging.

2. liberation, liberty, liberating, freedom, freeing, setting free, letting go, letting out; emancipation, emancipating, deliverance, delivery, delivering, *Theol.* saving; loosening, disenthrallment, disenthralling, unbinding, unfettering; release, releasing, discharge, discharging, dismissal, dismissing; exemption, exempting, indemnity, immunity, impunity, *Rom. Cath. Ch.* dispensation, *Archaic.* franchise.

absolutism, *n.* sovereignty, supremeness, absoluteness; arbitrariness, imperiousness, domination, iron rule; authoritarianism, dictatorship, autocracy, autarchy, despotism, dictatorship, tyranny, totalitarianism, monarchy; Hitlerism, Stalinism, Caesarism, Bonapartism, imperialism, czarism, man on horsebackism, kaiserism.

absolve, *v.* **1.** forgive, excuse, shrive, make allowances for; condone, overlook, disregard, ignore, pay no attention to; acquit, exculpate, clear, prove innocent, uphold innocence, remove guilt; pardon, amnesty, remit, respite, reprieve, grant a stay of execution; exonerate, warrant, justify, vindicate, right.

2. liberate, emancipate, free, set free, let go, let out, deliver, ransom, *Both Theol.* save, redeem; loose, loosen, disenthrall, unbind, untie, unfetter, unshackle, unchain, unhandcuff, unbridle, unyoke, unmuzzle, *Archaic.* untruss; release, discharge, let off, dismiss, *Inf.* let off the hook; exempt, dispense with, except, exclude, *Rom. Cath. Ch.* dispense.

absorb, *v.* **1.** suck up, draw up *or* in, take up *or* in, osmose; drink up *or* in, imbibe; sponge, sponge up, soak up, blot up, sop up; *Physical Chem.* adsorb, gather *or* gather in.

2. consume, devour, swallow up, digest, engorge, eat up, gobble up; incorporate, assimilate, appropriate, embody, co-opt; engulf, inundate, deluge, swamp, submerge; destroy, overwhelm, whelm, overcome.

3. mesmerize, hypnotize, fix, arrest, rivet, fascinate, enwrap, enthrall, grip, hold, hold spellbound, *Sl.* grab; preoccupy, occupy *or* seize the mind, engross *or* engage wholly.

4. (*all of a person's time*) occupy, fill, fill up, take up, use up; monopolize, tie up.

5. understand, comprehend, apprehend, conceive, *Scot.* ken, fathom, follow, *Sl.* dig, *Sl.* savvy; grasp, seize, get the idea, *Inf.* get the picture, *Inf.* get the drift, *Sl.* get, *Inf.* catch on; master, learn; utilize, put to use, make use of, employ.

6. pay for, meet *or* cover the cost, bear the expense *or* cost, pay the bill, *Inf.* foot the bill.

absorbed, *adj.* **1.** rapt, engrossed, immersed, lost in, buried, deep into [s.t.], wrapped up, *Inf.* into [s.t.]; busy, involved, engaged, occupied, employed; concentrating, focusing, pensive, cerebrational, thoughtful, thinking, lost in thought, bemused, musing, *Archaic.* museful; meditative, meditating, contemplative, contemplating, cogitative, cogitating, reflective, reflecting.

2. preoccupied, obsessed, *Sl.* hung up; distracted, diverted, distrait; oblivious, absent-minded.

absorbent, *adj.* porous, spongy, spongiose, *Rare.* spongious, permeable, pervious; retentive, absorptive, *Physical Chem.* adsorbent; thirsty, bibbing, bibulous, imbibitory; recipient, receptive, assimilative, digestive; soaking, blotting, sponging, absorbing, sorbefacient, imbibing; resorbent.

absorbing, *adj.* **1.** fascinating, captivating, spellbinding, exciting, riveting; interesting, winning, pleasing, engaging, charming, amusing, entertaining, occupying, diverting, distracting; attention-getting, arresting, attracting.

2. preoccupying, obsession, obsessive, monopolizing; engrossing, immersing, enwrapping, deep.

absorption, *n.* **1.** sucking up, drawing up *or* in, taking up *or* in, osmosis; drinking up *or* in, imbibition; sponging, sponging up, soaking up, blotting up, sopping up; digestion, ingestion, ingurgitation; *Physical Chem.* adsorption.

2. consuming, consumption, devouring, engorgement, eating up, gobbling up; incorporation, incorporating, assimilation, assimilating, appropriation, appropriating, embodiment, embodying, inosculation; engulfment, engulfing, inundation, inundating, swallowing up; destroying, overwhelming, overcoming.

3. preoccupation, prepossession, obsession, engrossment, rapt *or* complete attention, deep *or* profound thought; concentration, occupation, monopolization; involvement, immersion; thoughtfulness, pensiveness, intentness, engagement; abstraction, abstractedness, musing, reverie, trance, brown study.

abstain, *v.* **1.** refrain from, forbear, desist from, restrain from, hold back from voluntarily; give up, *Inf.* swear off, quit, renounce, resolve *or* promise to give up; discontinue, stop, cease; let alone, keep one's hands off, turn aside from, hold off from, resist.

2. teetotal, fast, take the pledge, *Sl.* be on the wagon *or* water wagon.

3. keep in check, curb, curtail, control; withhold from, deny, abnegate, suppress, repress; refuse, decline, rebuff, reject, spurn; avoid, eschew, shun.

abstainer, *n.* teetotaler, nephalist, nondrinker, water-drinker, hydropot; temperance advocate, W.C.T.U. member, prohibitionist, *Inf.* dry, blue-ribboner, blue-ribbonist, blue-ribbonite; puritan, ascetic; Rechabite, Encratite.

abstemious, *adj.* **1.** habitually abstinent, nonindulgent, moderate, temperate; teetotal, nondrinking, sober, not intoxicated *or* drunk, prohibitionary, *U.S.* dry, blue-ribbon; continent, celibate, fasting, dieting; puritanical, puritanlike, austere, self-mortifying, self-depriving; ascetic, self-denying, self-abnegating; refraining, fore-bearing, desisting, self-restrained, self-controlled.

2. sparing, saving, frugal, thrifty, chary; conservant, conservational, careful, unwasteful, economical, prudent, provident; scrimping, penny-pinching, parsimonious, penurious; miserly, niggardly, stingy, cheap, tight, tight-fisted, close-fisted.

abstemiousness, *n.* **1.** teetotalism, nephalism, temperance, sobriety, soberness; prohibition, blue-ribbonism; Rechabitism.

2. habitual abstinence, abstention, nonindulgence, moderation, continence, celibacy, fasting; Puritanism, austerity, self-mortification, self-deprivation; asceticism, self-denial, self-abnegation; refrainment, refraining, forbearance, desistance; restraint, self-restraint, restraining from, control, controlling, self-control; holding off, resisting, resistance.

3. sparingness, frugality, frugalness, thrift, thriftiness, husbandry, careful management, conservation; conserving, saving, economizing, economy; scrimping, penny-pinching, parsimony, parsimoniousness, penuriousness; niggardliness, tightness, tight-fistedness, close-fistedness, stinginess, miserliness, cheapness.

abstention, *n.* holding off, refraining, abstinence. See **abstinence** (*defs.* **1-3**).

abstinence, *n.* **1.** teetotalism, nephalism, temperance, sobriety, soberness; prohibition, blue-ribbonism; Rechabitism.

2. abstention, nonindulgence, abstemiousness, moderation, continence, celibacy, fasting; Puritanism, austerity, self-mortification, self-deprivation; asceticism, self-denial, self-abnegation; refrainment, refraining, forbearance, desistance; restraint, self-restraint, restraining from.

3. giving up, *Inf.* swearing off, renouncing, renouncement, renunciation; letting alone, keeping one's hands off, turning aside from, holding off, resisting, resistance; checking, check, curb, curbing, curtail, curtailment, cutting down on; controlling, control, self-control, withholding; suppressing; suppression, repressing, repression; refusal, declining, rebuff, rejection, spurning; avoidance, eschewing, shunning.

4. frugality, frugalness, thrift, thriftiness; husbandry, careful management, conservation; conserving, saving, economizing, economy; sparingness, scrimping, penny-pinching; parsimony, parsimoniousness, penuriousness, niggardliness, stinginess, miserliness, cheapness.

abstinent, *adj.* abstemious, temperate, sparing. See **abstemious** (*defs.* **1-3**).

abstract, *adj.* **1.** theoretical, pure, unapplied; conceptual, ideational, notional, abstracted, metaphysical; ideal, transcendental, imaginary, visionary, immaterial, impractical, spiritual, intellectual, (*of art*) non-representational; general, non-particular, not concrete, indefinite.

2. difficult, abstruse, obscure, recondite, profound; enigmatical, mysterious, dark, hidden, remote, incomprehensible; subtle, refined, attenuated, rarefied.

—*n.* **3.** summary, epitome, synopsis, compendium, symposium, compilation, digest, conspectus; condensation, abridgement, reduction, compression, abbreviation; analysis, recapitulation; résumé, brief, précis; outline, *Fr. aperçu,* sketch, review, syllabus, prospectus; docket, bulletin, minute; extracts, fragments, cuttings, analects, clippings, citations.

4. essence, quintessence, pith, heart, core, kernel, marrow, substance; generality, universality; main, common run, average.

—*v.* **5.** remove, take away, draw away, detach, separate, disunite, dissociate, disjoin.

6. isolate, prescind, consider by itself; take out of context, view partially, look at one-sidedly; distinguish, discriminate, deduct, analyze.

7. divert, distract, engross, preoccupy.

8. steal, rob, appropriate, take away, seize, purloin, embezzle, plagiarize.

9. summarize, outline, epitomize, synopsize; abridge, abbreviate, shorten, condense, contract, compress, prune, curtail, cut down.

abstracted, *adj.* **1.** pensive, thoughtful, thinking, cerebrational, lost in thought, bemused; intent, concentrating, focusing; cogitative, cogitating, deliberative, deliberating, meditative, meditating, contemplative, contemplating, reflective, reflecting; musing, pondering, wondering about, *Archaic.* museful; ruminative, ruminant, ruminating, chewing, chewing one's cud, brooding, mulling over, in a brown study.

2. preoccupied, rapt, absorbed, immersed, engrossed, lost in, consumed, wrapped up, occupied, busy; oblivious, unaware, unconscious, unmindful, insensible, blind; distracted, diverted, distrait, inattentive, unattentive, inadvertent, deaf.

3. absent-minded, dreaming, dreamful, dreamy, napping, sleeping, asleep; daydreaming, stargazing, gazing out the window, in the clouds, in a trance; absent, withdrawn, remote, removed, distant, faraway, wandering, *Sl.* not at home, *Sl.* out to lunch, *Sl.* out of it.

abstraction, *n.* **1.** generality, concept, conception, idea, notion, presumption, supposition, hypothesis, theory; quixoticism, visionary notion, impractical notion, vague representation, daydream, pipe dream.

2. disconnection, isolation, disjunction, partial consideration, taking from context; withdrawal, separation, removal.

3. absent-mindedness, inattention, engrossment, preoccupation, inattentiveness, distraction, absorption; brown study, musing, pensiveness, thoughtfulness, raptness, reverie; aloofness, self-communing.

abstruse, *adj.* profound, deep, esoteric, recondite, abstract; impenetrable, incomprehensible, uncomprehensible, past *or* beyond comprehension, unknowable, inscrutable, unfathomable, incognizable, indecipherable, undecipherable, beyond understanding; mystic, mystical, cabalistic, occult, supernatural, preternatural, otherworldly, supermundane; mysterious, inexplicable, unexplainable, insolvable, insoluble, unaccountable, *Obs.* inextricable; puzzling, enigmatic, enigmatical; dark, obscure, dim, vague, nebulous.

abstruseness, *n.* profundity, profoundness, depth, deepness, esotericism, esoterism, esotery, reconditeness, abstrusity, abstractness; impenetrability, impenetrableness, incomprehensibility, incomprehensibleness, inscrutability, inscrutableness, unknowableness, unknowability, indecipherability, indecipherableness; mysticity, mysticality, mysticalness, cabalism, occultness, supernaturalness, preternaturalness, otherworldliness; mysteriousness, inexplicability, inexplicableness, unexplainableness, insolvability, insolubility, insolubleness; darkness, obscurity, obscureness, dimness, vagueness, nebulousness,; obfuscation, obscurantism.

absurd, *adj.* **1.** ridiculous, silly, foolish, *Sl.* cockeyed, childish, tomfoolish; ludicrous, nonsensical, senseless, poppycockish, amphigoric, *Sl.* cockamamie; asinine, idiotic, *Inf.* moronic, pointless, inane, fatuous, stupid; crazy, *Sl.* kooky, mad, wild, insane, demented, daft, *Inf.* daffy, peculiar, unusual, anomalous, strange, odd; empty-headed, harebrained, unintelligent, thoughtless, *Inf.* dumb, dull-witted; funny, laughable, risible, derisible, humorous, droll, comical, farcical.

2. unreasonable, irrational, illogical, meaningless, extravagant, preposterous; imaginary, fantastic, fabulous, illusory, illusive, chimerical; incredible, inconceivable, unimaginable, unthinkable; unbelievable, hard to believe, beyond belief, implausible, untenable, unheard of; doubtful, doubtable, dubitable, questionable.

3. untrue, fallacious, impossible, sophistic, incorrect, erroneous; self-contradictory, paradoxical, inconsistent.

4. inappropriate, improper, incongruous, impractical, unwise, ill-considered, ill-suited, ill-advised; egregious, glaring, flagrant, arrant.

absurdity, *n.* **1.** ridiculousness, ridiculosity, silliness, foolishness, folly, childishness, tomfoolery, absurdness; ludicrousness, nonsense, nonsensicalness, nonsensicality, senselessness; amphigory, bosh, poppycock, drivel, gibberish, balderdash, fiddle-faddle; babble, twaddle, prattle; pointlessness, inanity, fatuity, fatuousness, stupidity, bêtise; asininity, idiocy, imbecility; craziness, *Sl.* kookiness, madness, wildness, insanity, daftness; peculiarity, unusualness, strangeness, oddness; empty-headedness, unintelligence, *Inf.* dumbness, dullness; funniness, humor, joke, comicality.

2. unreasonableness, irrationality, illogic, illogicality, meaninglessness, extravagance, preposterousness; incredibleness, inconceivableness, unimaginableness, unbelievableness, implausibility, untenableness, questionableness.

3. untruth, lie, delusion, illusion; self-contradiction, paradox, inconsistency, incongruity, incongruousness; error, fallacy; sophistry, *Logic.* paralogism, *Logic.* hysteron proteron.

abundance, *n.* **1.** plenty, plenitude, bounty, cornucopia, horn of plenty, endless supply, *Scot.* scouth *or* skouth, *Scot. and North Eng.* routh; amplitude, ampleness, fullness, plenteousness, plentifulness, bountifulness, copiousness; richness, exuberance, luxuriance, lavishness; teemingness, rankness, prodigality.

2. quantity, quantities, volume, mass, fund, mine, store; lot, lots, heap, heaps, mountain, mountains, stack, stacks, pile, piles, load, loads, mess, slew, slews, whole slew, full measure, good *or* great deal, quite a little, *Sl.* scad *or* scads; *All Inf.* ton, tons, bag, bags, barrel, barrels, gob, gobs, oodles, *Chiefly Brit.* lashings *or* lashing.

3. excess, surplus, surfeit, oversupply, overflow, nimiety, superfluity; glut, plethora, overabundance, superabundance, supersaturation; riot, landslide, bonanza, flood, heap, profusion.

4. generosity, generousness, liberality, liberalism, liberalness, bountifulness, bounteousness, munificence.

5. affluence, wealth, wealthiness, prosperity, prosperousness; opulence, opulency, comfort; money, riches, fortune, treasure; means, resources, wherewithal.

abundant, *adj.* **1.** plentiful, plenteous, plenitudinous, *Inf.* plenty, fat, bountiful, bounteous, copious, ample, more than enough; big, large, great, huge, bumper; immeasurable, unmeasured, inexhaustible, bottomless, unstinted; much, many, numerous, *Inf.* dime a dozen; in quantity *or* quantities, in plenty, *Inf.* aplenty, *Inf.* galore.

2. rich, lavish, luxuriant, rank, thriving, profuse, prodigal, exuberant, superabundant; fruitful, fertile, fecund, productive, prolific, proliferous.

3. full, filled, chock-a-block, *Brit. Inf.* chocker, *Inf.* chock-full, jammed, packed, *Inf.* jam-packed, *Archaic.* fraught; rife, replete, well-supplied, well-provided, well-furnished, well-stocked; abounding, overflowing, overspilling, spilling over, running over, bursting, bristling, thick, thick with; rampant, teeming, teeming with, swarming, swarming with, crawling, crawling with, alive with, *Sl.* lousy with.

4. excessive, extravagant, superfluous, overabundant, oversufficient.

5. generous, liberal, munificent, beneficent.

6. affluent, wealthy, prosperous, fat; opulent, luxurious.

abuse, *v.* **1.** misuse, misemploy, misapply, misappropriate; wrong, aggrieve, *Inf.* shaft, *Inf.* give [s.o.] the shaft, disrespect, *Sl.* do [s.o.] dirty, *Sl.* kick [s.o.] around; profane, pervert, prostitute; exploit, impose upon, take advantage of, walk all over [s.o.].

2. mistreat, maltreat, mishandle, ill-use, ill-treat, bullyrag; manhandle, maul, batter, *Sl.* knock around *or* about; beat, beat up, pound, thrash, hit, strike, *Archaic.* belabor; harm, damage, bruise, wound, hurt, pain, injure; persecute, torment, agonize, torture, rack, *Sl.* give [s.o.] the works.

3. revile, vituperate, oppugn, assail, belabor, lash, rail against, inveigh against, *Inf.* sail into, *Inf.* jump down [s.o.'s] throat, *Archaic.* clapperclaw; tongue-lash, curse, execrate, imprecate, anathematize; upbraid, objurgate, excoriate, flay, fulminate against, lambaste; berate, censure, reproach, rebuke, reprove, *Sl.* strafe, *Sl.* chew out; vilify, traduce, asperse, calumniate, impugn, slur, malign, defame, denigrate, slander, libel, backbite, bespatter; denounce, decry, disparage, discredit, depreciate, deprecate, belittle, minimize, run *or* put down, *Inf.* knock, *Sl.* badmouth; scorn, deride, gibbet, ridicule, mock, lampoon, pasquinade, make fun of.

4. rape, ravish, outrage, violate, molest, deflower, *Obs.* devirginate, *Obs.* constuprate, *Obs.* stuprate, *Archaic.* harrow; assault, attack, *Archaic.* insult.

—n. **5.** misuse, misemployment, misapplication, misappropriation; exploitation, imposition.

6. revilement, vituperation, assailment, belaboring; curse, execration, imprecation, malediction, anathematization; ribaldry, scurrility, billingsgate; invective, railing, fulmination, upbraiding, objurgation, contumely, berating, scolding, tongue-lashing; censure, reproach, rebuke, reproval; vilification, impugnment, traducement, aspersion, calumniation, calumny, obloquy, slur; maligning, defamation, denigration, slander, libel, *Inf.* backbiting; diatribe, tirade, philippic, denunciation, disparagement, discrediting, depreciation, deprecation, insinuation, belittlement, minimization; scorn, derision, ridicule, mockery.

7. misusage, ill-use, ill-usage, mishandling, mistreatment, maltreatment, ill-treatment; manhandling, mauling, battery, beating, thrashing, child abuse, wife-beating; harming, damage, hurting, injury; persecution, tormenting, torturing.

8. corruption, wrongdoing, misdeed, fault, *Both Law.* malfeasance, misfeasance, *Chiefly Law.* malversation.

9. rape, ravishment, violation, molestation, defloration, deflowering, devirgination, *Obs.* constupration, *Obs.* stupration; assault, attack, *Archaic.* insult.

abusive, *adj.* **1.** affronting, insulting, offensive, off-putting, unbearable, insufferable, intolerable, *Brit. Inf.* beastly, *Archaic.* affrontive; fulminatory, objurgatory, objurgative, contumelious; indecent, vulgar, obscene, lewd, licentious; smutty, filthy, dirty, nasty, foul, vile; ribald, scurrilous, thersitical, foul-mouthed.

2. calumnious, calumnitory, aspersive, slurring, maligning, defamatory, denigrating, slanderous, libelous; vituperative, invective, denunciatory, denunciative, disparaging, depreciatory, depreciative, deprecative, deprecatory, deprecating, derogatory, derogative, belittling; derisive, scornful, mocking.

3. cruel, brutal, brutish, ruthless, mean, harsh, rough; injurious, harmful, hurtful, torturous, tormenting, persecutory.

4. corrupt, venal, crooked, *Law.* malfeasant; misapplied, inappropriate, improper, unauthorized, unjustified, unwarranted, undue; exploitative, exploitatory, taking advantage.

abut, *v.* **1.** join, adjoin, conjoin, connect, impinge; butt, touch, reach, kiss; juxtapose, meet end to end, border.

2. border on *or* upon, verge upon, lean on *or* upon *or* against; end at, finish at, stop at.

3. support, prop, prop up, bolster, bolster up, hold up, uphold, bear, bear up, upbear, keep up.

abutment, *n.* **1.** buttress, bulwark, support, stay, brace, prop, shore, shoulder; wall, retaining wall, supporting wall, thrust wall; jetty, breakwater, pier buttress.

2. junction, connection, apposition, joint; juxtaposition, adjacency, union, contact; contiguity, contiguousness, abuttal; conjunction, attachment, adhesion, cohesion.

abuttal, *n.* **1.** border, boundary, bound, confine; bourn, terminus, termination, limit; edge, fringe, skirt, verge; abuttals, boundaries, bounds, limits, confines, pale, perimeter.

2. adjacency, juxtaposition, contiguity, contiguousness; union, conjunction, convergence, confluence; meeting, joining, bordering, edging.

abutting, *adj.* adjacent, next to, *Inf.* right next to, *Inf.* next door; contiguous, bordering, edging, skirting; joining, adjoining, conjoining, touching, meeting, converging.

abysmal, *adj.* immeasurable, unfathomable, unfathomed, fathomless, bottomless, boundless, endless, infinite; deep, profound, abyssal; cavernous, yawning, gaping, plunging; great, vast, immense, enormous, huge, prodigious, stupendous.

abyss, *n.* **1.** void, gulf, gap, bottomless pit, abysm, yawning abyss; cavity, hole, pit, depth, shaft; gorge, canyon, ravine, chasm; cleft, fissure, crevice, crevasse; the deep, the depths, ocean depths, bottomless depths.

2. profundity, profoundness, *Archaic.* profound,

deepness; impenetrability, impenetrableness, incomprehensibility, incomprehensibleness, inscrutability, inscrutableness, unknowableness; mysticity, mysticality, mysticalness, cabalism, occultness.

3. (*all in ancient cosmogony*) **a.** chaos, primal chaos, pandemonium, discord, confusion. **b.** hell, inferno, infernal pit, Hades, perdition; netherworld, underworld, lower world, bowels of the earth.

academic, *adj.* **1.** educational, educatory, instructional, pedagogical, academical; collegiate, college, university, scholastic, school; formal, institutional.

2. *All U.S.* humanistic, classical, philosophical, scientific, cultural; humanities, liberal arts, literature, language, fine arts, philosophy, natural *or* social science.

3. theoretical, hypothetical, abstract, notional, ideational, speculative, *Archaic.* speculatory; unrealistic, impractical, ivory-towerish, utopian, visionary, starry-eyed, quixotic, chimerical; irrelevant, nongermane, beside the point, immaterial, inappropriate, useless, vain.

4. learned, scholarly, erudite, lettered, literary, well-read, studious, *Derog.* bookish; cultured, artistic, *Inf.* arty, *Sl.* artsy, *Inf.* longhair *or* longhaired; well-educated, conversant, versed, well-versed, knowledgeable; intellectual, cerebral, brainy, highbrow *or* highbrowed; pedantic, pedagoguish, professorial, donnish, pompous.

5. conventional, conforming, traditional, orthodox; standard, accepted, ordinary, usual; tradition-bound, rule-bound, uncreative, unimaginative, literal; prosaic, commonplace, trite, stale, hackneyed; vapid, empty, dull, boring.

—n. **6.** scholar, student, pupil, collegian, co-ed; professor, doctor, master, tutor, fellow, *Brit.* don, instructor, preceptor, lector, lecturer, docent, teacher, pedagogue, educator; schoolman, scholastic, academician, academe, gownsman.

7. savant, pundit, man of letters, one of the cognoscenti, one of the literati, member of the intelligentsia; intellectual, thinker, *Rare. Derog.* phrontist, literate, bibliophile; aesthete, *Inf.* longhair, bluestocking; pedant, pettifogger, hairsplitter; bookworm, highbrow, *Inf.* egghead, *Inf.* walking encyclopedia, *Inf.* know-it-all.

academician, *n.* fellow, scholar, savant, man of letters, artist, scientist, member of an academy. See **academic** (*def.* **6,7**).

academy, *n.* **1.** secondary school, high school, *Brit.* grammar school, (*in France*) lycée; preparatory school, *Inf.* prep school, *U.S.* private school, *Brit.* public school, boarding school, day school, seminary, institute, finishing school; classical school, Latin school, (*in Germany*) gymnasium.

2. school, college, university, educational establishment, *Disparaging.* phrontistery *or* phrontisterion; conservatory, polytechnic.

3. learned association *or* institution, athenaeum, fellowship of artists *or* scientists; club, coterie, circle.

4. cognoscenti, literati, intelligentsia, standard-setters, pace-makers, leaders, avant-gardists, trend-setters; *Usu. Disparaging.* the establishment, *Inf.* the powers-that-be.

accede, *v.* **1.** (*usu. fol. by* to) assent, consent, grant, allow, let, permit, approve of, go along with.

2. concede, acquiesce, yield, submit, comply, adhere, conform.

3. (*usu. of an office, title, or position*) attain, assume, succeed to, enter upon, inherit; arrive at, reach, come to.

accelerate, *v.* **1.** advance, promote, further, forward, help onward, facilitate; progress, succeed, thrive, prosper, flourish, grow; develop, improve, increase, add to, augment.

2. hasten, hurry, hustle, precipitate, antedate, *Archaic.* dispatch; expedite, speed *or* step up, quicken, urge on *or* forward, press *or* move forward; drive, incite, goad, spur, stimulate, energize, impel, compel, force, push on.

3. speed up, increase in speed *or* velocity, move *or* go faster, *Sl.* jazz up; pick up, *Sl.* open up, skyrocket, rise; (*all of an engine*) gun, *Sl.* give the gun, race, *Inf.* rev up, *Sl.* vroom, give the gas, feed gasoline to, *Sl.* step on the gas, *Sl.* floor it.

4. concentrate, intensify, compress, contract, compact; boil down, reduce, abbreviate, skim, gloss over, pass over.

acceleration, *n.* **1.** speeding up, speed-up, increase in speed *or* velocity, *Sl.* jazzing up; picking up, *Sl.* opening up, skyrocketing, rising; (*all of an engine*) gunning, *Sl.* giving the gun, racing, *Inf.* revving up, *Sl.* vrooming, *Sl.* giving the gas, *Sl.* stepping on the gas.

2. hastening, hurrying, hustling, precipitation, antedating; expedition, speed, promptness, dispatch; stepping up, quickening; urging on, pressing forward, driving; incitement, incitation, prompting, stimulation, energizing; advance, advancement, furtherance, promotion, movement forward, facilitation.

accent, *n.* **1.** emphasis, stress, accentuation, syllable stress, primary *or* secondary *or* tertiary stress, weak stress; attack, delivery, force of utterance; cadence, beat, rhythm, rhythm pattern, rhythmical emphasis, *Music.* rhythmical accentuation, *Music.* arsis *or* upbeat, *Music.* thesis *or* downbeat, *Pros.* ictus, prominent pulsation.

2. mark, accent mark, stress mark, character, symbol; diacritic, diacritical mark, tilde, circumflex, circumflex mark, cedilla.

3. pitch, timbre, tone, tone of voice, voice; intonation, intonation pattern, inflection, modulation; mood, tenor, significance.

4. pronunciation, articulation, enunciation, vocalization, utterance; speech pattern, manner of speaking, mode of expression.

5. regional accent, foreign accent; drawl, twang, brogue, burr, broad accent *or* speech; *Brit.* received standard, public school accent.

6. accents, language, speech, speaking, talk, talking, words, discourse; chatter, palaver, prattle, *Inf.* gab, *Sl.* yakkety-yak.

—v. **7.** accentuate, stress, emphasize, lay stress *or* emphasis upon, give emphasis to, punctuate; underline, underscore, point up, italicize, call attention to; feature, highlight, spotlight, give prominence to; intensify, strengthen, deepen, heighten.

accentuate, *v.* stress, emphasize, lay stress *or* emphasis upon, give emphasis to, punctuate; underline, underscore, italicize, point up, call attention to; feature, highlight, spotlight, give prominence to; intensify, strengthen, deepen, heighten.

accept, *v.* **1.** receive, take, gain, acquire, get, secure, come by.

2. accede to, acquiesce in, assent to, submit to, abide by, comply with, go along with, be in line with; agree to, take [s.o.] up on [s.t.], say "yes" to.

3. undertake, assume, take on, tackle, be willing to bear, become responsible for; begin, commence, enter upon, set about.

4. accommodate oneself to, reconcile oneself to, resign oneself to; suffer, endure, bear, tolerate, brook, take patiently, abide, accept, stand, withstand, submit to, put up with; swallow, digest, stomach, pocket; face the music, take one's medicine, take it.

5. adopt, avow, confirm, believe, acknowledge, *Inf.*

swallow, *Inf.* buy, go for; assume, credit, regard, esteem, value; understand, absorb, apprehend, perceive, penetrate, recognize; construe, interpret, put a sense upon.

acceptable, *adj.* **1.** worthy, deserving, competent, good enough; meritorious, estimable, praiseworthy, laudable, commendable, admirable, creditable; suitable, fit, seemly, proper, decorous; appropriate, apt, apposite, apropos; meet, due, just, right, fitting, befitting; timely, seasonable.

2. receivable, agreeable, welcome, gratifying, satisfying, pleasing; attractive, delightful, refreshing, pleasurable; inviting, desirable, likable, popular; impressive, prepossessing.

3. respectable, passable, tolerable, adequate, satisfactory, all right; presentable, admissible, fairly good, *Inf.* not that good, not too bad; fair, *Inf.* no great shakes, mediocre, middling, indifferent, so-so; barely adequate, minimal, minimum, lowest acceptable.

acceptance, *n.* **1.** accepting, taking, receipt, reception, recipience, acquisition.

2. approval, favor, approbation, affirmation, ratification, confirmation, recognition, acknowledgment, sanction; satisfaction, gratification.

3. assent to, belief in, compliance with, abidance by; submission to, acquiescence in, resignation to, tolerance of, toleration of.

4. *All Commerce.* bill, signed contract, endorsement, guarantee, agreement; order, draft, certification.

acceptation, *n.* **1.** approval, favorable regard, cordial reception, adoption, admission, assent; acclamation, acclaim, favor, support, accord, acceptance.

2. belief, conviction, view, opinion; expectation, assumption, conception, idea, notion, presupposition; hypothesis, theory; inference, judgment, conclusion, certitude, certainty.

3. meaning, sense, import, drift, significance; implication, explanation, interpretation, construction, understanding; connotation, denotation.

accepted, *adj.* **1.** approved, sanctioned, authorized, authentic; preferred, preferable; acceptable, allowable, allowed.

2. usual, customary, normal, expected, standard; conventional, traditional, time-honored; familiar, recognized, acknowledged, established, confirmed; fashionable, popular, current, in vogue.

access, *n.* **1.** approachability, approachableness, accessibility; admittance, admission, right of entry, permission to enter; entrance, entry, entrée, inlet, ingress; path, passage, adit, approach; way, means, road, route, course, avenue, street, highway.

2. attack, onset, fit, seizure, spasm, pang, *Path.* convulsion; spell, turn, bout, recurrence; outburst, outbreak, paroxysm, throe.

3. accession, succession, inheritance, assumption, taking on *or* over. See **accession** (*def.* **1**).

accessible, *adj.* **1.** approachable, getatable, *Inf.* come-at-able; easy, easy-going, familiar, informal; affable, genial, pleasant, cordial; sociable, friendly, companionable, congenial, complaisant; courteous, gracious, polite, civil; conversable, agreeable, obliging, compliant, bendable, willing.

2. reachable, attainable, obtainable, procurable; available, possible, conceivable, probable, likely; achievable, compassable, accomplishable.

3. open, wide-open, exposed, liable, subject, vulnerable, susceptible; defenseless, weak, assailable, attackable, unguarded, unprotected; easily influenced, influenceable, persuadable, manipulatable, manageable, passive.

accessibility, *n.* **1.** approachability, approachableness, getatableness, *Inf.* come-at-ableness; ease, convenience, familiarity, familiarness, informality; affability, affableness, geniality, genialness, pleasantness, cordiality, cordialness; sociability, sociableness, friendliness, companionableness, congeniality, congenialness, complaisance; courtesy, courteousness, graciousness, politeness, politesse, civility; conversableness, agreeableness, agreeability, acquiescence; obligingness, compliance, compliancy, willingness.

2. attainability, attainableness, availability, availableness; possibility, conceivability, conceivableness; probability, likelihood, likeliness.

3. openness, exposedness, liableness, liability, subjectedness; vulnerability, vulnerableness, susceptibility, susceptibleness; defenselessness, weakness, assailableness, unguardedness, unprotectedness; persuadableness, manageableness, passiveness, passivity.

accession, *n.* **1.** (*usu. of an office, title or position*) succession, inheritance, assumption, taking on *or* over; entering upon, arrival at, advent to; elevation, promotion, rise, coming to, reaching, attainment; induction, installation, initiation, inauguration, investiture.

2. increase, increment, gain, addition, augmentation, contribution; enlargement, expansion, aggrandizement, swelling, enrichment; extension, distention, spreading, widening.

3. consent, assent, giving in, acquiescence, yielding; agreement, accord, accordance, concord, concordance, concurrence; approval, acceptance, sanction, countenance.

4. approach, advance, advancement.

5. attack, onset, access. See **access** (*def.* **2**).

accessory, *n.* **1.** subordinate, subsidiary, auxiliary, adjunct, adjuvant, concommitant, subordinate part; minutiae *or* minutia, trivia, minor particular; supplement, supplementation, appendage, addition, appendix, appendant, attachment, accompaniment, appurtenance, appurtenant.

2. (*all of clothing*) frill, embellishment, spangle, tinsel, adornment, ornament, ornamentation, finery, decoration, embroidery, trim, trimming *or* trimmings, array, trapping *or* trappings; belonging, appropriate detail, fashionable accent.

3. accomplice, *Chiefly Law.* accessary, *Law.* accessory before *or* after the fact, *Law.* principal, partner in crime, *Sl.* gun moll *or* moll, *Law.* particeps criminis, socius criminis; confederate, abettor, aider, collaborator, cooperator, contributor, cohort, conspirator, fellow conspirator, conspirer, conniver, participant, participator; ally, partner, comrade, colleague, associate, consociate, socius, consort, confrère, sidekick, friend, *Chiefly Brit.* mate; helper, aid *or* aide, attendant, acolyte, deputy, ancilla, second, henchman, right hand, right-hand man, recruit, tool, *Sl.* stooge, *Sl.* gofer.

—adj. **4.** supplementary, supplemental, additional, appurtenant, accessorial, adscititious *or* ascititious; accompanying, attendant, collateral; contributory, contributional, helpful, aidful; belonging, privy; subsidiary, secondary, auxiliary, ancillary, subordinate, subservient, adjunct, adjuvant, *Obs.* adjutory, *Obs., Rare.* adjutorious; incidental, extra, extraneous, extrinsic, adventitious, of minor importance; unnecessary, unneeded, unessential.

accident, *n.* **1.** misfortune, mishap, misadventure, miscarriage, mischance, casualty; adversity, affliction, hurt, ruin, undoing, downfall, collapse; blow, nasty *or* staggering blow; disaster, tragedy, catastrophe, calamity, cataclysm; wreck, crash, collision, smash-up, crack-up, pile-up.

2. mistake, blunder, contretemps, *Inf.* slip-up, *Sl.* boo-boo, *Sl.* boner, oversight; leak; mischief.

3. fluke, freak accident, one in a million, twist of fate; shock; fortuity, happening, hap, hazard.

4. chance, mere chance, fortune, good fortune, luck, good luck, Lady Luck, happenstance, serendipity; fate; uncertainty, contingency; blind faith.

5. nonessential, inessential, unessential; incidental, accidental, contingent; extra, accessory, supplement, auxiliary; appendage, appurtenance, addition, addendum; secondary, subsidiary.

accidental, *adj.* **1.** unintentional, unintended, unpremeditated, unplanned, undesigned; unwitting, unthinking; unexpected, unforeseen, unanticipated, unlooked-for; chance, fortuitous, serendipitous, *Inf.* fluky; random, stray, haphazard, casual.

2. nonessential, unessential, inessential, incidental, extraneous, extrinsic, external, adventitious; extra, additional, supplementary, supplemental, adscititious; subsidiary, subordinate, secondary, accessory, collateral; circumstantial, contingent, dependent, conditional, provisional; irrelevant, beside the point, parenthetical, by-the-way; unnecessary, unneeded, superfluous, expendable, dispensable.

accidentally, *adv.* unintentionally, undesignedly, without design, by accident, by mistake; inadvertently, involuntarily, unwittingly, unconsciously, unthinkingly; randomly, haphazardly, casually, incidentally, unpredictably, whichever way the wind blows; fortuitously, by chance, as it chanced, as luck would have it, by a piece of luck, by a fluke, by good fortune *or* a piece of good fortune.

acclaim, *v.* **1.** applaud, cheer, celebrate; approve enthusiastically, hail; congratulate, felicitate, compliment, huzzah, rejoice in; praise, sound the praises of, extol, hosanna, bravo, cry up, laud, comment, *Archaic.* magnify; exalt, eulogize, glorify; pay tribute to, pay homage to, honor, crown.

2. announce, declare, call out; shout, noise about, bruit, rumor; salute, greet, welcome.

—*n.* **3.** applause, ovation, acclamation; praise, eulogy, citation; commendation, approbation; approval, endorsement. See **acclamation.**

acclamation, *n.* **1.** salutation, greeting, hail, welcome; applause, cheer, ovation, standing ovation, bravo, plaudits, *Inf.* hand, curtain calls, encore; hosanna, hurrah, huzzah; shouting, calling out, éclat, outcry, announcement, declaration; celebration, congratulation, rejoicing, triumph, jubilation, felicitation; paean, *Archaic.* gratulation.

2. acclaim, praise, extolment, laudation, *Archaic.* magnification, citation; eulogy, eulogization, exaltation, glorification, encomium, panegyric; tribute, homage, honoring, crowning; approval, endorsement, sanction, approbation, commendation.

acclimate, *v.* **1.** acclimatize, become accustomed to, get used to, become familiar with, *Inf.* learn the ropes, become acquainted with; adapt to, adjust to, naturalize; conform to, accommodate, become fitted *or* suited to; be attuned to, be in harmony *or* accord with.

2. accustom, familiarize, make used to, habituate, adapt; inure, harden, toughen, season, temper, anneal.

acclimation, *n.* acclimatization, acclimatation, *Rare.* acclimature, *Rare.* acclimatement, habituation, *Sociol.* acculturation; accustomedness, familiarity, familiarization, familiarness, acquaintance, acquaintanceship, acquaintedness; adaptation, adaptedness, adjustment, naturalization; inurement, inuredness, hardening, toughening, seasoning; conformity, accomodation, fittedness; harmony, accord.

acclivitous, *adj.* sloping upward, uphill, rising, ascending, inclining, mounting, climbing; heaving up, looming up, springing up, towering up; abrupt, sudden, sharp, bold.

acclivity, *n.* ascent, upward slope, grade, gradient, rise, incline, inclination, slant, pitch, cant, upgrade; elevation, glacis, bank, hill, hillside, hillock, eminence.

accolade, *n.* honor, award, tribute, testimonial, credit, recognition, crown; applause, cheering, clapping, encore, rooting for, plaudits, salvo; commendation, recommendation, good word, glowing words, honeyed words; compliment, flattery, puffery, adulation; eulogy, eulogium, eulogization, exaltation, glorification, encomium, panegyric; praise, extolment, kudos, acclaim, acclamation, prize, *Archaic.* magnification, citation; celebration, paean, congratulation, *Archaic.* gratulation; approval, approbation, endorsement, sanction, advocacy, espousal.

accommodate, *v.* **1.** aid, assist, help, abet, meet the wants of; oblige, favor, indulge, patronize; befriend, lend a hand, do a favor for, show kindness to, do right by; serve, do for, do a service for, cater to, make comfortable, attend to the convenience of; provide, supply, furnish; loan, lease, lend money to, advance, grant.

2. lodge, house, domicile, put up, quarter, board; provide with a roof, furnish room for, shelter, harbor; entertain, fete, wine and dine, regale.

3. adapt, attemper to, habituate, accustom; acclimate, acclimatize, conform to, comply with; become fitted *or* suited to, become attuned to, become in harmony *or* accord with, get used to.

4. adjust, modify, suit, fit; set straight, settle, compose, mend, patch, fix up; settle differences, arrange matters, heal the breach; reconcile, bring into agreement, make compatible, make consistent, make suitable; harmonize, restore harmony, level, balance, square; equalize, equate, even.

5. have capacity for, be capable of holding; contain, hold, receive, carry, seat; comprise, include, embrace, embody.

accommodating, *adj.* obliging, cooperative, indulging, patronizing, complaisant; adaptable, pliable, yielding, easy to deal with; helpful, suitable, favorable; pleasant, pleasing, gracious, benign, benignant; benevolent, kind, kindly, sympathetic; generous, humane, unselfish, charitable; conciliatory, placatory, appeasing, soothing; considerate, thoughtful, polite, tactful, concerned, courteous, attentive; agreeable, amicable, amiable, willing, well-disposed; friendly, neighborly, cordial, warm, warm-hearted.

accommodation, *n.* **1.** adaptation, habituation, orientation, reorientation; acclimation, acclimatization, conforming, complying; adjustment, modification, settlement, alteration, transformation, change, capitulation; reconciliation, harmonization, balancing, equalizing.

2. aid, assistance, help, abetment, abettal; service, benefit, advantage, profit; obligingness, favor, indulgence, patronage, support; kindness, generosity, courtesy, consideration, graciousness, hospitality.

3. **accommodations** arrangement, prearrangement, provision, groundwork, preparation; lodging, lodgment, home, abode, residence; quarters, dwelling, domicile, shelter; *Fr. pied-à-terre, Sl.* pad, *All Chiefly Brit. Inf.* diggings, digs.

4. allowance, grant, loan, advance, credit, mortgage; supply, stock, store, provisions, provender; blessing, boon, good turn, convenience, luxury.

accompaniment, *n.* **1.** accessory, complement, completer, concomitant, concurrent, affendant, *Astron.* comes; supplement, addition, extension, appendage, appurtenance, appurtenant, adjunct, appanage, annex, attachment.

2. (*all of music*) background, backup, obbligato, harmony, second part.

accompany, *v.* **1.** escort, squire, esquire, chaperon, take out, go out with, go along with, keep [s.o.] company, *Obs.* consort; companion, keep company with, associate with, take up with, go around with, *Inf.* go with, *Inf.* pal around with, *Inf.* hang around with, *Sl.* hang out with, *Archaic.* company; attend, be by one's side, convoy, protect, guard, support, back up, be behind; follow, go behind; usher, pilot, steer, guide, lead, conduct, direct, show the way.

2. coexist with, occur with, come with; belong to, be an appendage of, be an adjunct to, be an annex to, be part of.

3. associate, affiliate, syndicate, combine, unite, ally, marry, wed; join, link, connect, attach, couple, mate, partner, match, twin, pair up.

4. (*all of music*) back up, provide the background for, play piano *or* guitar for, harmonize, sing harmony to, chime in, *Jazz.* comp.

accompanying, *adj.* accessory, attendant, complementary, concomitant, concurrent, associate, fellow; related, connected, joint; subsidiary, subordinate, background; supplementary, supplemental, ancillary, auxiliary, added, additional, extra, appended, attached, annexed.

accomplice, *n.* accessory *or Chiefly Law.* accessary, *Law.* accessory before *or* after the fact, *Law.* principal, partner in crime, *Sl.* gun moll *or* moll, *Law.* particeps criminis, socius criminis; confederate, abettor, aider, collaborator, cooperator, contributor, cohort, conspirator, fellow conspirator, conspirer, conniver, participant, participator; ally, partner, comrade, colleague, associate, consociate, socius, yokefellow *or* yokemate, helpmate, helpmeet, *Obs.* helpfellow, coworker, co-aid, co-partner, consort, confrère, sidekick, friend, *Chiefly Brit.* mate; helper, aid *or* aide, attendant, acolyte, deputy, subsidiary, auxiliary, ancilla, second, henchman, right hand, right-hand man, recruit, tool, *Sl.* stooge, *Sl.* gofer.

accomplish, *v.* **1.** perform, do, execute, discharge, carry out, fulfill, realize; succeed in, manage, bring off, *Sl.* pull off, *Inf.* put over, *U.S. Sl.* swing, *U.S. Sl.* cut, *U.S. Sl.* hack; engineer, negotiate, work out; bring about, make happen, effect, effectuate; produce, turn out, achieve, attain; arrive at, compass, reach, gain, win.

2. finish, complete, carry through; dispose of, *Sl.* knock off, *Sl.* polish off, expedite, dispatch; conclude, close, wind up, clinch, clench, seal; perfect, crown, top, cap, put the last *or* finishing touch to, consummate; end, put an end to, terminate.

accomplished, *adj.* **1.** completed, effected, done, finished, ended, terminated; concluded, closed, clinched, sealed; established, consummated, fulfilled, realized, come true; achieved, attained, arrived at.

2. perfected, expert, proficient, adept, skillful, skilled; masterful, masterly, veteran, professional, *Fr. au fait;* topflight, top drawer, first-rate, exceptional, *Inf.* topnotch, ace, *Inf.* crack, *Sl.* crackerjack, *Sl.* on the ball, *Inf.* whiz-bang, *Brit. Sl.* whizzo.

3. talented, gifted, endowed, apt, clever; dextrous, adroit, deft, facile, ambidextrous, handy, neat, *Brit. Dial.* feat; good, finished, polished, practiced; experienced, ripe, mature; capable, able, competent, up to the mark, efficient, adequate, sufficient, qualified, trained.

4. cultured, refined, cultivated, polished, finished; genteel, well-bred, thoroughbred; elegant, graceful, fine, polite; urbane, suave, sophisticated, cosmopolitan; fashionable, stylish, high-class, *Sl.* classy.

5. learned, *Archaic.* studied, versed, knowledgeable; educated, lettered, intellectual, scholarly, erudite; well-educated, well-informed, well-read, literary.

accomplishment, *n.* **1.** fulfillment, realization, success, attainment, acquirement; completion, finishing, conclusion, closing; perfection, consummation, crowning, capping, topping; end, termination.

2. achievement, performance, production; deed, feat, act, exploit, *Archaic.* gest; action, maneuver, move, stroke, blow, coup; stroke of genius, tour de force.

accord, *v.* **1.** agree, concur, think alike, be of one mind; admit, permit, grant, allow, approve, accept, go along with, *Inf.* take to, *Inf.* cotton to, *Inf.* buy; yield, comply with, abide by, assent, accede, acquiesce, side with, concede, consent; acknowledge, recognize, *Archaic.* agnize, subscribe to, fall in with, *Sl.* string along with.

2. adapt, adjust, accommodate; harmonize, attune, coincide, correspond, conform to, tally with, comport with, gee with, jibe with, be in unison, chime in with; suit, fit, match, resemble, be appropriate, *Brit. Dial.* fadge; dovetail, square, equal, parallel.

3. grant, bestow, deign, vouchsafe; give, award, mete, bequeath, endow.

—*n.* **4.** harmony, correspondence, congruence, coincidence, conformation, symmetry; similitude, similarity, resemblance; coherence, consistency, uniformity.

5. agreement, mutual understanding, accordance, concord, concordance, concurrence, consonance; consensus, unanimity, unison; amity, harmony, communion, sympathy, rapport.

6. of one's accord voluntarily, of one's own free will, freely, determinedly, with choice.

accordance, *n.* **1.** agreement, conformity, concurrence (See **accord,** *def.* **5**).

2. bestowal, vouchsafement, endowment; granting, giving, confering, imparting; according, furnishing.

accordant, *adj.* agreeing, conformable, congruous, congruent; consonant, correspondent, complementary; fit, suitable, matching, meet, proper; harmonious, compatible, adapted, consistent.

accordingly, *adv.* **1.** correspondingly, conformably; compatibly, agreeably, compliantly; consistently; in accordance, in agreement.

2. consequently, in consequence, as a result, thus, hence, and so, in due course, *Obs.* thereafter; therefore, thence, so; then, in that case, in which case, in that event; that being the case, that being so, under the circumstances; as it is, as matters stand, *Inf.* as things stand.

according to, **1.** in accordance with, in accord with, accordingly; after the manner of, in keeping with, in line with, in step with.

2. consistent with, conformably to, conformable to, agreeably to; in conformity with, in compliance with, in agreement with, in harmony with; in correspondence to, correspondingly.

3. on the authority of, in the light of; as stated by; as maintained by, as believed by.

4. in proportion to *or* with, proportionately; commensurate with, commensurately, commensurable with, commensurably; proper to, suitable for.

5. contingent, contingent on, dependent, dependent on, depending on, hanging on, hinging on, revolving on; based on; depending on circumstances.

accost, *v.* **1.** assail, confront boldly, attack; assault, set upon, aggress, waylay; charge, storm, invade; bother, trouble, annoy, harass, molest, harry, bully; badger, nag, pester, pursue, importune; encounter, meet, face, meet face to face, front, affront, come face to face with; call to, appeal to, invoke.

2. approach, edge *or* sidle up to, draw near, near; overtake, meet up with, catch up to, *Inf.* nab; buttonhole, *Sl.* bend [s.o.'s] ear; address, say to, speak to, apostrophize; talk to, converse with; greet, salute, hail, welcome, bid *or* say hello, bid good day.

3. (*all usu. of prostitutes, procurers, etc.*) solicit, propose, suggest; lure, allure, tempt, sway, lead astray, obtain.

account, *n.* **1.** narrative, story, tale, sketch, relation; statement, description, delineation, portrayal, report, detail, recountal; recital, recitation, rehearsal, declamation, word; history, chronicle, record, memoir, tidings.
2. explanation, commentary, version, representation, exposition; unfolding, detailing, elaboration, *Sl.* megillah.
3. reason, cause, motive, consideration; sake, interest, advantage, benefit; basis, ground, score.
4. worth, value, esteem, regard, merit, honor; reputation, note, distinction, dignity, repute; concern, consequence, importance, rank.
5. estimation, judgment, opinion, valuation, point of view.
6. statement, invoice, charge, bill, *Brit., Inf.* tick, check, *Sl.* tab; count, tally, score; reckoning, computation, enumeration, calculation.
7. call to account blame, reprimand, reprove, rebuke, call down, call on the carpet, take to task.
8. on account of because of, for the sake of, on behalf of, in the interest of.
9. on no account never, absolutely not, *Sl.* not on your life; under no circumstances *or* conditions, *Sl.* no way.
10. take account of *or* **take into account** allow for, note, consider, give thought to.
—*v.* **11.** explain, show grounds, clear up, give a reckoning *or* an accounting, answer for; cause, be responsible for, be attributable to.
12. count, consider, believe, view, look upon; deem, judge, value, regard, esteem, rate.
13. assign, ascribe, attribute, credit; impute, charge, blame.

accountability, *n.* **1.** responsibility, liability, answerability, answerableness, chargeability, amenability, accountableness; obligation, bounden duty.
2. interpretability, interpretableness; intelligibility, understandableness, comprehensibility, comprehensibility, comprehensibleness.

accountable, *adj.* **1.** responsible, liable, answerable, chargeable, amenable; obligated, obliged, beholden, bound, duty-bound; subject, open to, exposed to.
2. explainable, explicable, interpretable; intelligible, understandable, comprehensible.

accountant, *n.* bookkeeper, auditor, comtroller, controller, certified public accountant, C.P.A., *Both Brit.* chartered accountant, C.A.; inspector, examiner, reckoner, analyst, *Insurance.* actuary, computer; clerk, registrar, recorder, agent; teller, cashier.

accouter, *v.* equip, furnish, supply, provide, *Obs.* appoint; outfit, fit out, fit, fit up, rig out, rig up, turn out, gear; deck, bedeck, deck out, caparison, trap, adorn, ornament; dress, clothe, garb, attire, apparel, habit, invest; *All Mil.* arm, munition, *Sl.* heel, *Archaic.* harness.

accouterments, *n.* **1.** equipage, outfit, outfitting, gear; dress, garb, apparel, attire, clothes, livery, *Archaic.* vesture; investiture, adornment, ornamentation.
2. equipment, furnishings, paraphernalia, appurtenances; appointments, trappings, fixtures, fittings, habiliments, trimmings, fixings, *Inf.* things; caparison, harness, tack, tackle, rigging.

accredit, *v.* **1.** (*usually fol. by* with) ascribe, assign, attribute, credit, give credit for, put down as, chalk up to *or* with; impute, charge with, blame, accuse.
2. associate, connect, link, tie in, couple, match *or* pair up, relate, think of together, consider jointly *or* in union; count, account, deem, hold, repute, esteem, refer, consider *or* regard as.
3. certify, endorse, back up; guarantee, vouch for, testify to, attest to.
4. sanction, approve of, accept, acknowledge, give one's stamp *or* seal of approval, pass judgement on, *Inf.* O.K.; authorize, warrant, legalize, validate, license, certificate; commission, qualify, empower, enable.
5. believe, give credence to, hold as true, put one's trust in, have faith *or* confidence in.

accredited, *adj.* **1.** certified, endorsed, guaranteed, vouched for, attested to.
2. sanctioned, approved, accepted, acknowledged, *Inf.* O.K.'d; authorized, warranted, legalized, legal, validated; licensed, qualified, commissioned.

accretion, *n.* **1.** increase, expansion, extension, augmentation, aggrandizement; addition, increment, supplement, gain, accession, access; growth, accrual, accruement, accumulation, piling up; enlargement, amplification.
2. consolidation, solidification, fusion, conglomeration, agglomeration; cohesion, coherence, adhesion, adherence; cementation, conglutination, agglutination; aggregate, aggregation.

accrual, *n.* **1.** accruement, accretion, accumulation, cumulation; amassing, collecting, gathering, heaping up, piling up; increase, growth, enlargement, augmentation, swelling, waxing, aggrandizement, acquirement; expansion, extension, rising, mounting up; *Both Finance.* maturing, maturation.
2. yield, gain, outcome, result.

accrue, *v.* **1.** accumulate, cumulate, amass, collect, gather, heap up, pile up; increase, grow, enlarge, augment, swell, wax, aggrandize; expand, extend, advance, rise, mount up.
2. result, redound; come from, emanate from, fall from, flow from, proceed from, derive from, ensue, arise in due course; yield, gain, bring in; *Both Finance.* mature, fall due.

accumulate, *v.* **1.** heap up, pile, pile up, roll up, stack up; collect, gather; assemble, mass, aggregate, bring together, congregate; amass, cumulate, agglomerate.
2. hoard, squirrel away, load up, stow away; garner, store up, stock up, lay by, lay up, lay in, *Inf.* stash away, reserve, set aside; save, save up, bank.
3. grow, augment, accrue, multiply; swell, enlarge, expand, extend, wax; rise, heighten, deepen.

accumulation, *n.* **1.** heap, pile, mass, bulk, drift; hoard, store, stock, stockpile, supply, fund; treasure, holdings, savings, *Inf.* loot.
2. collection, amassment, assemblage; aggregation, *Physical Chem.* coacervation; concentration, agglomeration, conglomeration, cluster, *Bot.* acervation.
3. increase, growth, build-up, accretion, accruement; backlog, pile-up.

accuracy, *n.* **1.** accurateness, exactness, exactitude, precision, preciseness; closeness, fidelity, faithfulness, conformity, accordance, agreement; rigorousness, strictness, severity, severeness; thoroughness, methodicalness, carefulness, painstakingness, exhaustiveness, minuteness, detailedness.
2. correctness, unerringness, rightness, rectitude, justness; truth, truthfulness, veracity, verity, veritableness; fact, actuality, factuality, literalness; definiteness, positiveness, absoluteness.
3. authenticity, soundness, validity, validness, integrity; flawlessness, faultlessness, perfection.

accurate, *adj.* **1.** exact, precise, close, faithful, in conformity, in accordance *or* agreement; correct, unerring, *Inf.* on the mark, on target, *Inf.* right on, *Sl.* spot on; right, just, proper; true, truthful, honest, veracious; factual, actual, literal; authentic, sound, valid; flawless, faultless, perfect, defectless, errorless.

2. careful, meticulous, punctilious, scrupulous, conscientious; particular, finical, finicky, picky, fussy; minute, detailed, thorough, nice; scientific, mathematical, severe, strict, rigorous.

accursed, *adj.* **1.** doomed, *Brit. Dial.* fey, damned, cursed, curse-laden, condemned, anathematized, *Archaic.* maledict; bedeviled, bewitched, hoodooed, voodooed, hexed; star-crossed, ill-fated, foredoomed; unsanctified, unblest, unholy, unconsecrated, unhallowed; ruined, undone, blighted, ravaged, despoiled; miserable, unfortunate, stricken, woeful, wretched, unhappy; desolate, woebegone, forlorn, abandoned.

2. damnable, diabolic, devilish, fiendish, satanic, demonic, demoniac, demoniacal, infernal, hellish; execrable, abominable, horrible, horrid, hideous, atrocious; base, vile, odious, obnoxious, wicked, sinful, iniquitous, evil, black-hearted, corrupt, depraved, villainous, sinister; reprobate, nefarious, flagitious, heinous; abhorrent, revolting, repulsive, repugnant, foul, rotten, offensive, loathsome, nauseous, nauseating; pernicious, pestilential, noxious, deadly, fell; malign, menacing, baleful, invidious, injurious, maleficent, malevolent, malicious, rancorous; hateful, detestable, despicable, infamous.

accusation, *n.* **1.** charge, *Law.* gravamen, indictment, *Law.* true bill, *Law.* plaint, *Law.* complaint, citation, summons; incrimination, crimination, recrimination, denunciation, *Scot. and North Eng.* threap; implication, inculpation, informing against, *Chiefly Scot.* delation; blaming, accusing; (*all in reference to wrongdoing*) imputation, attribution, ascription, assignment, allegation.

2. reproach, slur, innuendo, insinuation, animadversion, criticism; censure, rebuke, reproof, arraignment, reprehension.

accuse, *v.* **1.** charge, indict, *Law.* arraign, *Law.* impute, incriminate, criminate, recriminate, impeach, *Rare.* implead; denounce, implicate, (*of an innocent person*) *Inf.* frame, inculpate, inform against, *Chiefly Scot.* delate; cite, summon, serve with a summons *or* with papers, sue, libel, *Law.* prosecute; litigate, file charges, *Inf.* take it *or* [s.o.] to court.

2. blame, *Sl.* stick *or* pin [s.t.] on [s.o.], hold [s.o.] accountable *or* responsible, lay at [s.o.'s] door, finger, point the finger at [s.o.], *Chiefly Scot.* wite; (*all in reference to culpability*) allege, ascribe, attribute, assign, impute, lay.

3. fault, find fault with, censure, upbraid, reproach, rebuke, reprehend; reprove, tax, take to task, call to account; assail, revile, impugn, call into question; stigmatize, brand, gibbet, asperse, cast aspersions on, malign, slander, defame, vilify; attack, inveigh against, rail against, declaim against.

accuser, *n.* incriminator, criminator, recriminator, impeacher, charger, denouncer, *Chiefly Scot.* delator; informer, stool pigeon, *Sl.* fink, *Sl.* rat; blamer, assailer, attacker, reviler; adversary, opponent, opposer; *All Law.* plaintiff, prosecutor, petitioner, suitor, libelant.

accustom, *v.* **1.** familiarize, acquaint, expose to; make used to, habituate, naturalize, domesticate; break in, train, drill, ingrain, make routine, discipline; harden, toughen, inure, season, temper, anneal.

2. adapt, acclimate, acclimatize, get used to, become familiar with, *Inf.* learn the ropes, *Sl.* get the hang of, become acquainted with.

accustomed, *adj.* **1.** customary, habitual, set, fixed, rooted, established, traditional, consuetudinary, confirmed; usual, wonted, regular, daily, routine, normal, natural; ordinary, conventional, everyday, commonplace; general, prevailing, prevalent, common, frequent; well-known, popular, favorite, household; stock, well-worn, trite, hackneyed, cliché.

2. in the habit of, given to, wont to, prone to, in the practice *or* custom of; habituated, used to, addicted; acclimated, acclimatized, naturalized, familiar with, acquainted with; adapted, hardened, toughened, inured, seasoned, tempered, annealed.

ace, *n.* **1.** expert, master, proficient, adept, mavin, master hand, *Chiefly Brit. Inf.* dab hand, *Brit. Dial.* dabster; maestro, virtuoso, talent, genius, prodigy, standout, *Inf.* wizard, *Inf.* whiz, *U.S. Sl.* crackerjack, *Sl.* sharp, *Sl.* shark; professional, *Inf.* pro, journeyman, veteran, past master, past mistress, old hand, old stager; specialist, authority, connoisseur; (*both of martial arts*) black belt, dan.

—adj. **2.** excellent, first-rate, capital, *Inf.* tiptop, *Inf.* A-1, *Inf.* A number 1; exceptional, superior, standout, outstanding, striking; superlative, supreme, transcendent, sovereign, the best; matchless, peerless, nonpareil, perfect, sterling, classic, first-class; choice, prime, select, very good; fine, admirable, notable, noteworthy; remarkable, wonderful, marvelous, extraordinary.

3. masterful, masterly, proficient, expert; topflight, top drawer, *Inf.* topnotch, *Inf.* crack, *U.S. Sl.* crackerjack, *Sl.* on the ball, *Inf.* whiz-bang, *Brit. Sl.* whizzo; finished, polished, accomplished, practiced; experienced. *Fr. au fait,* professional, *Inf.* pro, veteran; adept, knowledgeable, skillful, talented, skilled, dextrous, adroit, deft, facile.

acerbate, *v.* **1.** embitter, bitter, exacerbate, envenom, sour, gall, rankle, poison.

2. exasperate, discompose, distress, ruffle, roil, pique, chafe, vex, grate, put out, try [s.o.'s] patience, *Sl.* drive [s.o.] nuts, *Sl.* get [s.o.'s] goat; anger, incense, enrage, infuriate, madden, raise [s.o.'s] ire, make [s.o.'s] blood boil.

3. irritate, aggravate, annoy, fret, hector, bother, nettle, perturb, disturb; torment, provoke, plague, badger, pester, persecute, harass, get on [s.o.'s] nerves.

—adj. **4.** embittered, bitter, galled, rankled, resentful; acrimonious, virulent, rancorous, acerbic, acerb.

5. angry, irate, incensed, *Inf.* mad, *Inf.* sore, *Sl.* hot, *Sl.* hot under the collar, *Sl.* teed-off, *Sl.* ticked-off; livid, enraged, infuriated, furious.

acerbity, *n.* **1.** (*all of taste*) sourness, bitterness, tartness, acidity, acidness, acridity, acridness, acidulousness; pungency, sharpness, unsavoriness, roughness, harshness.

2. (*all of expression or temperament*) acrimony, causticity, virulence, mordancy, trenchancy, astringency, asperity, venomousness, acrimoniousness; irritability, irritableness, irascibility, irascibleness, petulance, *Rare.* petulancy; short-temperedness, illtemperedness, testiness, edginess, touchiness, grouchiness, peevishness, crabbiness; snappishness, bearishness, currishness; brusqueness, gruffness, brashness, surliness; rudeness, churlishness, boorishness, gracelessness.

3. choler, rancor, spleen, ill humor, ill feeling, ill temper.

ache, *v.* **1.** pain, throb, hurt, smart, gnaw, twinge, pinch; be in pain, suffer pain, be sore.

2. suffer, sorrow, grieve, mourn; be distressed, be anguished, be disquieted; feel for, pity, feel sympathy.

3. be eager, yearn, long, hanker, hanker for, pine for; crave, desire earnestly, wish ardently.

—n. **4.** dull pain, continued pain, soreness, hurt, suffering, smarting; throb, pang, twitch, twinge, spasm, pinch, gripe; distress, affliction, woe, misery; heartache, anguish, grief, sorrow, dolor.

5. longing, craving, yearning, hankering, pining for; uneasiness, anxiety, angst.

achievable, *adj.* attainable, reachable, within reach, accessible; realizable, obtainable, procurable, compassable; accomplishable, doable, completable; practicable, workable, manageable, surmountable; reasonable, feasible, possible, conceivable, imaginable, thinkable, admissible; potential, likely, probable.

achieve, *v.* **1.** accomplish, carry out, perform, execute, do; bring off, manage, *Sl.* pull off, *Inf.* put over, *All U.S. Sl.* swing, cut, hack; make happen, cause, bring about, effect, effectuate, engineer, produce; realize, actualize, make real, make actual.

2. finish, complete, carry through; dispose of, *Sl.* knock off, *Sl.* polish off, expedite, dispatch; conclude, close, wind up, clinch, clench, seal, bring to a successful end; perfect, crown, top, cap, put the last *or* finishing touch to, consummate; end, put an end to, terminate.

3. get, obtain, procure, gain, win, earn, wrest; attain, reach, arrive at, realize, fulfill; succeed in, make good, *Inf.* make it, be successful, get ahead; set the world on fire, take the world by storm.

achievement, *n.* **1.** accomplishment, feat, deed, act, exploit, *Archaic.* gest; performance, production, action, maneuver, move, stroke, blow, coup; stroke of genius, tour de force.

2. fulfillment, realization, attainment, fruition, acquirement, success; completion, finishing, conclusion, closing; perfection, consummation, crowning, capping, topping; end, termination.

acid, *n.* **1.** acrimony, acrimoniousness, acerbity, causticity, mordancy; astringency, trenchancy, virulence, virulency, asperity, venomousness, venomness. *—adj.* **2.** (*all usu. of taste*) sour, vinegarish, vinegary, acetous, bitter, tart, harsh; acerb, acerbic, acidulous, acidulent, acescent, acidulated.

3. (*all usu. of expression or temperament*) astringent, severe, stern, harsh, *Obs.* asper, acerb, acerbic, austere, stringent; acrid, acrimonious, caustic, mordant, stinging, bitter, pungent; trenchant, cutting, sharp, biting, acute, keen, sarcastic, satirical, ironical; vitriolic, scathing, edged, double-edged, piercing, pricking; virulent, spiteful, malicious, vicious; peevish, petulant, cross, crabbed, testy, touchy, ill-tempered; scornful, sardonic, derisive, snide.

4. corrosive, corroding, eroding, wearing away, eating away, wasting; scalding, burning.

acidify, *v.* acidize, acidulate, acetify; ferment, turn, sour; embitter, envenom.

acidity, *n.* **1.** (*all usu. of taste*) sourness, bitterness, vinegariness, acidulousness; tartness, harshness, sharpness, acridity, acerbity.

2. (*all usu. of expression or temperament*) astringency, severity, sternness, harshness, acerbity, austerity, stringency; acrimoniousness, causticity, asperity, mordancy, bitterness, pungency, venomousness, venomness; trenchancy, keenness, sarcasm, satire, irony; virulence, spitefulness, maliciousness, malice, viciousness; peevishness, petulance, *Rare.* petulancy, crabbedness, testiness, touchiness, ill-temperedness, short-temperedness, edginess.

3. scorn, derision, spite, ill humor, ill temper, ill feeling.

acidulous, *adj.* **1.** sour, sourish, vinegarish, vinegary, acetous, citric, bitter, tart, harsh; acid, subacid, acerbic, acidulent, acescent, acidulated.

2. astringent, acerb, acerbic, austere, severe, stern, harsh, *Obs.* asper; acrid, acrimonious, caustic, mordant, stinging, bitter, pungent; trenchant, cutting, sharp, biting; acute, keen, sarcastic, satirical, ironical; vitriolic, scathing, piercing, pricking, edged, double-edged; virulent, spiteful, malicious, vicious; peevish, petulant, cross, crabbed, testy, touchy, ill-tempered, sour-tempered; scornful, sardonic, derisive, mocking, snide.

acknowledge, *v.* **1.** admit, grant, allow, accept, recognize, go along with, own, *Archaic.* agnize; avow, confess, profess, declare, subscribe to; certify, ratify, vouch for; concur, approve, yield, abide by, assent; accede, acquiesce, concede, consent, agree.

2. recognize, notice; address, greet, salute, hail, accost, beckon, nod to, signal to, extend the hand, doff the cap, smile upon.

3. thank, give thanks for, express gratitude for, show appreciation for; requite, recompense, compensate, reward, pay, settle.

acknowledged, *adj.* admitted, accepted, conceded; recognized, professed, declared, accredited; confessed, avowed, approved.

acknowledgment, *n.* **1.** admission, recognition, *Archaic.* recognizance; affirmation, avowal, profession; declaration, confession; endorsement, ratification, certification; acquiescence, accedence, assent, consent, abidance, concurrence.

2. expression of gratitude, show of appreciation, thanks; reward, tribute, honor; compensation, honorarium, gratuity, recompense, remittance, remuneration, pay, settlement.

3. greeting, salutation, salute, address.

4. response, answer, return, reply, replication.

acme, *n.* **1.** summit, apex, vertex, apogee, crest, heights, pinnacle, peak, spire, point, tip, tiptop; top, cap, crown, headpiece, head.

2. zenith, maximum, climax, culmination, crowning point, *Latin. ne plus ultra;* meridian, sublimity, supremacy, best, finest, perfection, consummation; extreme, utmost, uttermost, *U.S. Sl.* the most, *U.S. Sl.* the greatest; prime, heyday, bloom, full flower, blossom, efflorescence.

acquaint, *v.* *Usu.* **acquaint with** familiarize, make familiar, make conversant; introduce, make known, inform, clue in, advise, notify, apprise, make aware *or* cognizant, enlighten, let [s.o.] know [s.t.]; impart, communicate, mention, tell; disclose, reveal, divulge, let [s.o.] in on [s.t.].

acquaintance, *n.* **1.** colleague, confrère, associate, consociate, compeer, peer; teammate, co-worker, fellow worker; companion, comrade, copain, *Inf.* pal, *Inf.* buddy, chum, crony; friend, intimate, familiar; *Inf.* pickup.

2. social relationship, companionship, fellowship, friendship; affinity, association; intimacy.

3. familiarity, conversance, conversancy, cognizance, awareness, knowledge, understanding.

acquainted, *adj.* **1.** *Usu.* **acquainted with** apprised of, informed of, privy to, in on; aware of, alive to, conscious of, cognizant of; conversant with, familiar with, instructed in, knowledgeable in, versed in.

2. mutually known *or* recognized; sociable with, friendly with, on good terms with, comfortable with; known to say hello to.

acquiesce, *v.* (*often fol. by* in) assent, consent, concur, agree, accept, *Inf.* buy, accede; abide by, comply with, conform to; concede, admit, yield, *Inf.* come round; submit, bow to, give in, take it; acknowledge, recognize, grant, allow; subscribe to, fall in with, join in the chorus, go with the stream.

acquiescence, *n.* **1.** consent, assent, abidance, compliance, obedience; agreement, concurrence, accordance; acknowledgment, willingness, sufferance; surrender, resignation, capitulation, submission, yielding, giving in, accedence, concession, nonresistance.

2. subservience, servility, obeisance, ingratiation, subjection, slavishness, abasement, prostration, toadyism; cringing, fawning, bowing, scraping, cowering, truckling, *Sl.* bootlicking, bending; self-renunciation, self-surrender; self-effacement.

acquiescent, *adj.* **1.** assenting, consenting, concurring; agreeable, amenable; complying, compliant, obedient, *Rare.* morigerate, morigerous, conforming, abiding, faithful, dutiful, duteous; yielding, submitting, capitulating, conceding, acceding, willing; malleable, tractable, ductile; meek, timid, gentle, passive, docile.

2. subservient, servile, obsequious, ingratiating, obeisant, prostrate, *Archaic.* sequacious; truckling, bowing, scraping, fawning, cowering, cringing, crawling, toadying, toadyish, *Inf.* bootlicking; self-effacing, self-surrendering, self-abasing.

acquire, *v.* **1.** obtain, get, procure, secure; receive, inherit, fall into, come by, realize, make; take possession of, get one's hands on, get a hold of; capture, seize, grasp, net, bag; harvest, garner, reap, gather, collect, glean; buy, purchase, pick up, *Scot. Archaic.* coff.

2. earn, attain, win, gain, achieve; appropriate, assume, take on.

acquirement, *n.* **1.** *Usu.* **acquirements** attainments, accomplishments; endowments, gifts, attributes, talents, skills; abilities, capabilities, capacities, parts; learning, erudition, knowledge, culture.

2. acquisition, obtainment, gaining. See **acquisition** (*defs.* **1, 2**).

acquisition, *n.* **1.** obtaining, obtainment, getting, gaining, acquirement, securing, procurement, procuration; purchasing, buying, picking up; takeover, gain, annexation; seizure, appropriation, capture; inheritance, donation, gift, benefaction.

2. addition, accession, accretion; property, possession; purchase, *U.S.* buy, *Law.* acquest.

acquisitive, *adj.* greedy, grasping, grabbing, *Sl.* grabby, rapacious, ravenous, ravening, predatory, predacious; avaricious, covetous, eager for gain, mercenary; sordid, selfish, hoarding, possessive.

acquisitiveness, *n.* greed, graspingness, rapacity, perdaciousness, avarice, selfishness; ravenousness, voraciousness, insatiability, omnivorousness, covetousness; miserliness, penuriousness, parsimony, niggardliness.

acquit, *v.* **1.** exculpate, clear, prove *or* declare innocent, uphold innocence, pronounce *or* declare not guilty, remove guilt; absolve, forgive, shrive, excuse; exonerate, justify, warrant, vindicate, right; pardon, amnesty, remit, respite, reprieve.

2. free, release, set free, let go, liberate, emancipate, deliver; discharge, dismiss, let out of, let off, *Inf.* let off the hook.

3. satisfy, fulfill, fill, meet, answer, comply with; (*all of debts*) settle, pay up *or* off, liquidate, bring up to date, clear the books, close an account, *Accounting.* balance.

4. (*of oneself*) conduct, manage, bear, carry; comport, deport, demean, behave, act properly *or* right, *Archaic.* quit.

acquittal, *n.* **1.** exculpation, exculpating, clearance, clearing, compurgation, acquittance; absolution, absolving, forgiveness, forgiving, shriving, excusal, excusing; exoneration, exonerating, justification, justifying, warranting, vindicating; pardon, pardoning, amnesty, remission, remitting, respite, reprieve, reprieving; freedom, release, liberation, liberty, emancipation, deliverance, delivery; discharge, dismissal, letting out of, letting off, *Inf.* letting off the hook.

2. fulfillment, fulfilling, satisfaction, satisfying, compliance, complying; (*all of debts*) settlement, settling, payment, paying up *or* off, liquidation, liquidating, closing an account, clearing the books, *Accounting.* balancing.

acquittance, *n.* **1.** exculpation, exculpating, clearance, clearing, compurgation, acquittal; absolution, absolving, forgiveness, forgiving, shriving, excusal, excusing; exoneration, exonerating, justification, justifying, warranting, vindicating; pardon, pardoning, amnesty, remission, remitting, respite, reprieve, reprieving.

2. release, discharge, letting out of, letting off, *Inf.* letting off the hook, dispensation, *Commerce.* indulgence; fulfillment, fulfilling, making good, satisfaction, satisfying, compliance, complying; (*all of debts*) settlement, settling, payment, paying up *or* off, liquidation, liquidating, closing an account, clearing the books, *Accounting.* balancing.

3. warrant, warranty, discharge; receipt, voucher, chit, proof of payment, stamp, stub.

acrid, *adj.* **1.** (*all usu. of taste or smell*) bitter, biting, pungent; acid, tart, harsh, sour, subacid, acetous, vinegarish, vinegary; acerb, acerbic, acidulous, acidulent, acescent, acidulated; stinging, burning, smarting, irritating; disagreeable, unpleasant, nasty, unlikable; distasteful, unappetizing, unpalatable, unsavory.

2. caustic, mordant, acrimonious, bitter, acrid, acidulous, acid, pungent; trenchant, cutting, incisive, slashing, scathing; penetrating, piercing, stinging, pricking, nipping, biting; astringent, severe, stern, austere, stringent; harsh, keen, pointed, sharp, sharp-tongued.

3. sarcastic, satirical, ironic, ironical, cynical; double-edged, edged; contemptuous, contumelious, taunting, teasing; scornful, mocking, derisive, derisory, sardonic.

4. hostile, resentful, indignant, piqued, angry; peevish, petulant, crabbed, testy, splenetic, touchy, waspish, irascible, edgy; spiteful, virulent, malicious, venomous, vitriolic, vicious; antagonistic, rancorous, ill-disposed, malevolent, malign; ill-tempered, ill-humored, ill-natured, short-tempered; morose, surly, sullen, sour, moody; adverse, opposing, aggressive, belligerent, bellicose.

acrimonious, *adj.* **1.** caustic, mordant, bitter, acrid, pungent; astringent, severe, stern, austere, stringent; harsh, sharp, sour, acidulous, acid, tart; trenchant, keen, sarcastic, satiric, ironic, ironical; virulent, spiteful, malicious, venomous, vicious, malevolent, malignant; peevish, petulant, crabbed, testy, touchy, irascible, edgy; ill-tempered, ill-humored, ill-natured, short-tempered.

2. angry, resentful, hostile, indignant, piqued; morose, surly, moody; rude, churlish, boorish, bearish, graceless, unceremonious, rough; scornful, mocking, derisive, derisory, sardonic, unkind; abusive, corrosive.

acrimony, *n.* **1.** acrimoniousness, causticity, asperity, mordancy, acridness, acridity, pungency, venom, venomousness, venomness; astringency, severity, sternness, acerbity, austerity, stringency; harshness, sharpness, sourness, acidulousness, acidity, bitterness, tartness; trenchancy, keenness, sarcasm, satire, irony; virulence, spite, spitefulness, malice, maliciousness, viciousness; peevishness, petulance, *Rare.* petulancy, crabbedness, testiness, touchiness, irascibility, edginess; ill temper, ill-temperedness, short-temperedness, ill humor, ill-humoredness.

2. animosity, resentment, grudge, hostility, indignation, pique, dudgeon; moroseness, surliness, moodiness; rudeness, churlishness, boorishness, gracelessness, roughness; abusiveness, corrosiveness.

3. choler, rancor, anger, gall, spleen; contempt, haughtiness, disdain, scorn, derision, unkindness; malevolence, malignity.

acrobat, *n.* **1.** gymnast, tumbler, somersaulter, high vaulter; circus performer *or* artist; tight-rope walker, ropewalker, ropedancer, high-wire artist, slack-rope artist, funambulist, equilibrist, balancer; trapeze artist, man on the flying trapeze, aerialist, aerial gymnast *or* artist *or* performer; contortionist; stunt man, stunt girl.

2. tergiversator, tergiversant, Proteus, chameleon; timeserver, *Obs.* timepleaser, weathercock; temporizer, trimmer.

acrobatics, *n.* **1.** gymnastics, tumbling, athletics; calisthenics; acrobatic feats, trapeze *or* tightrope displays.

2. (*all of airplanes*) aerobatics, acrobatic maneuvers, *Inf.* stunt flying, *Inf.* stunting.

across, *prep.* **1.** opposite to, facing, fronting, confronting, in front of; on *or* to the other side of, beyond, past, over, the far side of.

2. in contact with, into the presence of, into, upon.

3. crosswise of, transversely to, athwart, thwart.

—adv. **4.** crosswise, crossways, cross, crisscross; transversely, transversally, transverse, thwartedly, *Obs.* traverse.

5. astride, astraddle, straddle, straddleback, straddle-legged; on.

6. on the other side, on the far side, opposite.

act, *n.* **1.** deed, turn, action; performance, proceeding, execution, consummation; conduct; doing, operation, transaction; undertaking, project, enterprise; work, task, job, commission.

2. exploit, feat, *Archaic.* gest, achievement, step, stride, advancement, progress; accomplishment, attainment, requirement, success.

3. maneuver, move, stroke, blow, coup, stunt, trick; stroke of genius, tour de force.

4. **in the act** in the process, in the middle, in the course; red-handed, *Latin. in flagrante delicto, Sl.* with one's pants down, *Inf.* with one's hand in the cookie jar.

5. formal decision, ruling, judgement, conclusion, determination, resolve, resolution; verdict, finding, arbitration, arbitrament; sentence, *Law.* award; declaration, pronouncement, decree, edict, proclamation; dictate, dictum, order, command, mandate; rule, regulation, law, *Law.* statute, ordinance; bill, enactment, measure, proposal, motion.

6. short performance, show, *Music.* gig, stand, appearance; routine, bit, skit, short play, *Theat.* one-acter, curtain raiser.

7. pretense, pretending, feigning, make-believe; sham, fake, counterfeit, dissimulation, dissemblance; affectation, show, insincerity, false appearance.

—v. **8.** do, go about, perform, execute, *Scot. and North Eng. Obs.* gar, discharge, carry out; be active, be employed, be busy.

9. decide, determine, resolve, judge, make up one's mind, reach *or* make a decision.

10. function, perform, operate; work, be effective, be efficacious.

11. (*all of oneself*) conduct, behave, comport, deport, demean; (*all of oneself*) manage, bear, carry, acquit.

12. pretend, feign, make believe; sham, fake, counterfeit, make a false show, dissemble, dissimulate; simulate, affect, put on, assume, *Inf.* do for effect.

13. perform, portray, play; represent, enact, act out, put on, produce, stage, give a show; tread the boards.

14. **act for** substitute, pinch-hit, fill in; do, serve, take the place of.

15. **act on** *or* **upon** **a.** follow, head, obey, comply with, yield to, conform to, act in accordance with. **b.** affect, influence; change, alter, transform, modify.

acting, *adj.* **1.** deputy, substitute, fill-in, temporary; representative, serving, practicing, performing.

2. functional, functioning, operational, operating, working, running, going, active; in action, in operation, at work.

—n. **3.** histrionics, dramatics, dramaturgy; play-acting, performing, enacting, enactment, playing; performance, rendition, theatrical, overacting, posturing, *Sl.* ham acting, *Sl.* hamming *or* hamming up.

4. portrayal, characterization, representation, projection; impersonation, personation; mimicry, mimicking, miming, *Rhet.* mimesis.

5. sham, posture, masquerade, show, false show, false front, façade; bluff, posing, feigning, pretending, making believe.

action, *n.* **1.** movement, motion; agency, operation, *Rare.* operance *or* operancy; performance, execution, enactment, discharge, dispatch; exercise, practice; working, operating, functioning.

2. act, deed, effort, endeavor, enterprise, transaction; feat, exploit, adventure, *Inf.* stunt; handiwork, doings, dealings, workings.

3. **actions** conduct, behavior, deportment, comportment, ways, manners; demeanor, mien, bearing, port, posture, guise, air, address.

4. vigor, vim, energy, spirit, *Inf.* snap; activity, goings-on, fun.

5. influence, power, potency; effect, result, consequence.

activate, *v.* **1.** actuate, energize, turn on, trigger, switch on, light; start, commence, begin, initiate, get going *or* started, set off, set in motion; motivate, induce, prompt, goad, prod, spur; impel, compel, force, push, drive.

2. excite, stimulate, awaken, arouse, rouse, stir up; kindle, incite, inspire, inflame, ignite, fire up, fuel; animate, enliven, invigorate.

active, *adj.* **1.** busy, on the go, occupied, engaged, employed, working, at it, *Inf.* on the move, *Inf.* up and doing; moving, kinetic, motive, on the wing, volitant, stirring, astir, up and about *or* around; bustling, hustling, restless, commotive, *Inf.* hyper; diligent, assiduous, industrious, hard-working, *Sl.* on the stick; zealous, sedulous, studious, persevering; indefatigable, tireless, untiring, unremitting, unwavering.

2. functioning, operative, working, running, ticking, in progress *or* motion, in operation, in effect, in force, in play; alive, existent, existing, extant, actual, ongoing; current, present, in the here and now, *Archaic.* instant.

3. energetic, energetical, vibrant, full of verve, vital, lively, full of life, *Chiefly U.S. Inf.* chipper; vivacious, sprightly, sprightful, jumping, hopping, swinging, vivid, animated, spirited, *Sl.* go-go; vigorous, robust, hardy, hearty, brisk, *Scot. and North Eng.* yauld; strenuous, exertive, laborious, physical.

4. nimble, agile, spry, volant, well-coordinated, *Brit. Dial.* wight, *Music.* volante; fleet, fleet-footed, rapid, quick, speedy, swift, ready, prompt, alert.

5. productive, producing, generative, creative, fertile, fecund, prolific; prosperous, thriving, flourishing, growing, booming; profitable, self-sustaining, in the black.

6. effectual, effective, efficacious, causative, potent, puissant, powerful, strong, forceful, forcible; influential, enterprising, up-and-coming; ambitious, aggressive, assertive, pushing, forward, officious, *Inf.* pushy.

7. reactive, eruptive, explosive, volatile, violent, drastic.

8. practical, applied, nontheoretical, nontheoretic,

functional, functionalistic, utilitarian, useful, down to earth; useable, serviceable, practicable, workable, feasible, operable.

activity, *n.* **1.** motion, movement, doing, action; stir, hustle, hustling, bustle, bustling, restlessness, commotion, tumult, fuss, flurry, pother, ado, *Inf.* to-do, *Sometimes Facetious.* do; busyness, occupation, employment, engagement; application, diligence, industriousness, industry, assiduousness, assiduity.

2. energy, vigor, vigorousness, vim, robustness, heartiness, briskness, nimbleness, agility, agileness, spryness; fleetness, rapidity, quickness, speediness, swiftness; alertness, readiness, promptness, promptitude.

3. enterprise, undertaking, venture, deed, work, labor, task, service, act; event, occurrence, happening, affair, *Inf.* goings on.

4. operation, function, process, working; performance, execution, effort, exertion, exercise.

5. vitality, liveliness, spirit, sprightliness; vibrancy, vivacity, vividness, animation.

actor, *n.* **1.** player, stage player, performer, stage performer, playactor, role player, trouper, *Sl.* ham; theatrician, thespian, Roscian, histrio, histrion, *Archaic.* histrionic; personator, impersonator, actress.

2. doer, executor, executant, executrix; worker, operator, operative, operant; architect, author, maker, creator, fabricator; agent, medium; promoter, mover, prime mover; participant, participator; practitioner.

actual, *adj.* **1.** real, true, *Brit. Dial.* gradely, *Both Archaic.* sooth, soothfast; factual, unimaginary, unfictitious, true-to-life, realistic; authentic, genuine, *Dial.* sure-enough, bona fide, veritable, valid, confirmed; rightful, legitimate, lawful, just, legal, licit, official.

2. absolute, positive, certain, sure, definite; unquestionable, indisputable, indubitable, undeniable.

3. present, current, existent, extant.

actuality, *n.* **1.** actualness, reality, realness; actualization, realization, entelechy; truth, verity, *Archaic.* troth, fact, *Archaic.* sooth.

2. physical existence, physicalness, corporeality, corporealness, substantiality, substantialness, materiality, materialness; tangibility, tangibleness, palpability, palpableness.

actualize, *v.* **1.** realize, make real, make actual; embody, make concrete, personify, externalize, objectify, exteriorize.

2. make happen, cause, bring about, effect, effectuate, work out, engineer, produce; bring off, manage, *Sl.* pull off, *Inf.* put over, *All U.S. Sl.* swing, cut, hack; accomplish, attain, achieve, reach, arrive at, compass; succeed in, make good, *Inf.* make it; fulfill, carry out, follow through, consummate.

actually, *adv.* really, in reality, in actuality, in fact, de facto, in essence, essentially, intrinsically, truly, in truth, truthfully, literally; indeed, verily, as a matter of fact, in point of fact.

actuate, *v.* **1.** incite, inspire, inspirit, kindle, inflame, ignite, fire up, fuel; stimulate, excite, awaken, arouse, rouse, stir up; motivate, induce, prompt, goad, prod, spur; draw, lead, urge, sway, persuade; impel, compel, force, push, drive.

2. energize, trigger, turn on, switch on, light; activate, animate, set in motion; initiate, instigate, start, commence, begin, get going *or* started, set off, bring about.

acumen, *n.* discernment, insight, perception, percipience, flair; perceptiveness, perspicacity, perspicaciousness, keenness, penetration, acuteness, sharpness, quickness; cleverness, astuteness, shrewdness, ingenuity, ingeniousness; resourcefulness, *Inf.* gumption; intelligence, knowledge, understanding, comprehension, discrimination, judgment; mother wit, wit, esprit; sense, intuition, brains, common sense, smartness; foresightedness, foreknowledge, farsightedness, longheadedness; sagacity, sagaciousness, wisdom.

acute, *adj.* **1.** pointed, sharpened, peaked, cuspated, cuspidate, acuate, *Bot.* apiculate; needle-shaped; acicular, aciculate, *Bot., Zool.* acuminate; barbed, prickly, spinous, acanthaceous, echinate, pectinated.

2. sharp, intense, cutting, piercing, excruciating, exquisite, fierce; poignant, distressing, distressful, painful, piquant, pungent.

3. abrupt, sudden, rapid, extreme, precipitous.

4. severe, critical, crucial, climactic, decisive, determining; momentous, major, great, profound, important, vital, essential, imperative; grave, drastic, serious, deep, urgent, pressing, exigent; dangerous, imminent, hazardous, precarious, dubious, ticklish; impending, threatening.

5. penetrating, astute, discerning, perceptive, intelligent, perspicacious; sharp-witted, clever, smart, bright, sharp, brainy, ingenious, brilliant; knowing, wise, sage, sagacious, sapient; keen, clear-witted; keen-sighted, discriminating, intuitive, judicious, comprehending; aware, wide-awake, on the ball; shrewd, calculating, cunning, artful, wily, foxy, crafty, hardheaded.

acutely, *adv.* **1.** sharply, intensely, piercingly, excruciatingly; poignantly, distressfully, painfully, piquantly, pungently.

2. severely, critically, crucially; profoundly, vitally, gravely, drastically, seriously, deeply.

3. keenly, incisively, penetratingly, astutely, perceptively, cleverly, ingeniously, shrewdly, cunningly, artfully.

acuteness, *n.* **1.** sharpness, keenness, pointedness; acumination, cuspidation, spinousness.

2. intensity, exquisiteness, fierceness; poignancy, piquancy, pungency.

3. abruptness, suddenness, rapidness, extremity, precipitousness.

4. severity, criticalness, cruciality, momentousness, greatness, profoundness, importance, imperativeness.

5. penetration, astuteness, discernment, perception, intelligence, perspicacity; wit, cleverness, smartness, brightness, acuity, sharpness, ingeniousness, brilliance; wisdom, sagacity; keenness, clear-wittedness, keen-sightedness, discrimination, intuitiveness, judiciousness; shrewdness, cunning, artfulness, wiliness, craftiness.

adage, *n.* **1.** proverb, *Archaic.* word, aphorism, gnome, apophthegm, *Archaic.* sentence, saying, moral; axiom, maxim, precept, dictum; principle, law, rule, golden rule, motto, byword; saw, hackneyed phrase, cliché, platitude, truism, *Inf.* bromide, commonplace.

2. epigram, mot, witticism, *Fr. jeu d'esprit,* quip, Atticism.

adamant, *adj.* **1.** flinty, stonelike, rock, rock-hard, hard as rock, adamantine; impenetrable; unbreakable, infrangible, imperishable, indestructable.

2. immovable, inflexible, rigid, stiff, firm, unshakeable, obdurate, inexorable, intractable, unyielding, unbending, uncompromising, intransigent; stubborn, tough, hard-nosed, hard-bitten; callous, inured, stoney, unfeeling, unmerciful, merciless, pitiless, hard-hearted, cold-hearted.

adamantine, *adj.* flinty, rock-hard; rigid, firm, immovable. See **adamant** (*defs.* **1, 2**).

adapt, *v.* **1.** adjust, make suitable, modify, moderate, limit, qualify, *Archaic.* attemper; conform, accommodate, comply, fit, suit; convert, change, alter, transform, metamorphose; fashion, shape, proportion, remodel.

2. acclimate, acclimatize, naturalize, become accustomed to, get used to, become familiar with, *Inf.* learn the ropes, become acquainted with; accustom, familiarize, make used to, habituate, assimilate; inure, harden, toughen, season, temper, anneal.

adaptability, *n.* **1.** adaptableness, adaptedness, adaptiveness, versatility, versatileness, many-sidedness; adjustability, changeability, changeableness, variability, variableness; alterability, alterableness, modification, modifiability, modifiableness, transformation, metamorphosis.

2. pliability, pliableness, pliancy, pliantness, flexibility, flexibleness, yieldingness, plasticity; malleability, malleableness, ductility, ductileness, tractility; conformability, conformableness, compliance, compliancy, accommodation, accommodativeness; amenability, amenableness, agreeability, agreeableness, obligingness; manageability, manageableness, submissiveness, docility, tractability, tractableness.

adaptable, *adj.* **1.** adjustable, changeable, variable, alterable, modifiable, transformable; acclimatable, acclimatizable, *Both Sociol.* acculturational, acculturative.

2. pliable, pliant, flexible, bendable, moveable, yielding, plastic; malleable, ductile, tractile; conformable, compliant, accommodative, adaptive; amenable, aggreeable, accommodating, obliging; manageable, submissive, docile, tractable.

adaptation, *n.* **1.** adjustment, modification, moderation, limitation, qualification; conformity, accommodation, compliance, yieldingness; fittedness, adaptedness, suitability, suitableness; conversion, change, variation, alteration, transformation, metamorphosis; fashioning, shaping, proportionment, remodeling.

2. acclimation, acclimatization, acclimatation, *Rare.* acclimature, *Rare.* acclimatement, naturalization, habituation, *Sociol.* acculturation; accustomedness, familiarity, familiarization, familiarness, acquaintance, acquaintanceship, acquaintedness; hardening, toughening, seasoning, inurement, inuredness.

adapted, *adj.* **1.** suitable, fit, fitting, befitting, appropriate, apt, becoming, seemly; proper, meet, correct, right; consonant, harmonious.

2. adjusted, acclimated, naturalized; accustomed, used to, habituated, assimilated; acquainted with, familiar with, familiarized; accordant, in agreement, conformable, compliant.

add, *v.* **1.** attach, adjoin, affix, append, suffix, annex, postfix, subjoin; join, unite, connect, adject, combine; tag, tag on, tack on, put on; superpose, superimpose, superadd.

2. total, sum, sum up, score up, (*on a cash register*) ring up; enumerate, number, count up, foot up, cast up, tot *or* tot up, figure up, cipher; count, compute, calculate, reckon.

3. **add to** increase, enlarge, aggrandize; extend, expand, lengthen, branch out, spread out; augment, supplement, complement; amplify, magnify, swell, raise; strengthen, reinforce, build, build up; aggravate, intensify, exacerbate, exaggerate.

4. **add up to a.** indicate, signify, mean, express, reveal; **b.** amount to, come to, mount up to, aggregate; comprise, contain, number.

addendum, *n.* **1.** addition, superaddition, extension, annex; appendage, attachment, appurtenance, appurtenant, adjunct, appanage.

2. appendix, supplement, codicil, *Law.* allonge; epilogue, postscript, p.s., P.S., subjoiner, subjunction, suffix, postfix, endpiece, tailpiece, tag.

adder, *n.* viper, asp, krait, poisonous snake; snake, serpent.

addict, *n.* **1.** *Inf.* fiend, *Inf.* hound, *Sl.* freak, *Sl.* nut, *Sl.* demon, *Sl.* bug; drug addict, drug abuser, drug user, *Inf.* user, *Inf.* junkie, *Sl.* hophead, *Sl.* dopefiend, *Sl.* dopenick, *Sl.* doper, *Sl.* mainliner, *Sl.* druggie, *Sl.* drughead; *Sl.* head, *Sl.* pothead; *Sl.* pill popper, *Sl.* pillhead, *Sl.* speed freak; *Sl.* tripper, *Sl.* acid head; alcoholic, drunkard, drunk, dipsomaniac; chain smoker; workaholic.

—*v.* **2.** give over to, give up to, submit to, surrender to; indulge in, contact *or* fall into a habit.

addicted, *adj.* devoted to, dedicated to, given to, given over to, prone to, in the habit of; dependent on, drug-dependent, *Inf.* hooked, *Inf.* strung-out, *Sl.* spaced-out.

addiction, *n.* dependence, drug dependence, physical dependence, psychological dependence, craving, drug addiction; (*of narcotics*) habit, *Sl.* monkey; alcoholism, dipsomania; habitual smoking, chain smoking, tobacco *or* nicotine addiction; habituation, indulgence, immersion; surrender, enslavement, subjugation.

addition, *n.* **1.** joining, uniting, combining; adding, tacking on, attaching, annexing, appending.

2. summation, totaling, adding up, counting up, enumerating; computation, calculation, reckoning.

3. increase, increment, accretion, accession, enlargement, augmentation; extension, expansion, continuation, prolongation.

4. additament, superaddition, affix, attachment, annexation; supplement, appendix, codicil, suffix, postscript, addendum, appendage, tailpiece; adjunct, appurtenance, accessory; insertion, interpolation, interjection, interposition.

5. *U.S.* annex, wing, ell.

6. **in addition** as well, besides, moreover, additionally, over and above.

additional, *adj.* **1.** supplementary, supplemental, additory, additamentary; extra, spare, fresh, new, reserved; further, other, more, over and above, superadditional.

2. added, appended, attached, annexed; augmented, increased, raised.

addle, *v.* **1.** baffle, confuse, mystify, *U.S. Inf.* buffalo, pose, *Sl.* cross up; muddle, obfuscate, befog; perplex, bewilder, nonplus, puzzle; stupefy, shock, disarm, discompose, *Inf.* discombobulate; disconcert, abash, embarrass, mortify, discomfit; disorient, unhinge, unbalance, throw off balance; upset, fluster, flutter, rattle, distract.

2. rot, decay, putrefy; go bad, sour, turn; mold, mildew, spoil, decompose, disintegrate, crumble; corrupt, pervert, contaminate, taint; foul, befoul, soil, sully, blacken, smudge, stain.

addlepated, *adj.* **1.** muddled, muddleheaded, addleheaded, addlebrained; dull, inexpressive, expressionless, stupid, *Inf.* dumb, *Inf.* dopey, empty-headed, *Inf.* fatheaded; dull-witted, *Sl.* dimwitted, slow-witted, half-witted, witless, unwitty; unthinking, unreasoning, incogitant, thoughtless; mindless, brainless, fatuitous, slow; dense, thick, thickheaded, wooden-headed, obtuse, stolid, oafish, cloddish, lumpish, blunt; blockheaded, dunderheaded, noodleheaded, boneheaded, thickskulled, blockish, doltish; weak-minded, simple, simple-minded, birdbrained, feeble-minded; harebrained, giddy, mercurial, reckless; absent-minded, scatterbrained, confused, bemused; featherheaded, featherbrained, rattleheaded, rattlebrained, light-minded, light-headed; empty, void, vacant, vacuous, blank, unoccupied; vapid, insipid, banal, bland.

2. absurd, silly, inane, pointless, fatuous, foolish; nonsensical, senseless, tom-foolish, *Sl.* cockeyed, *Scot. and North Eng.* glaikit; poppycockish, *Sl.* cockamamie, amphigoric; ridiculous, laughable, risible, derisible, ludicrous, *Sl.* for the birds; asinine, anserine, idiotic, *Inf.* moronic, imbecilic; childish, puerile, immature; crazy, crazed, *Scot.* doiled, *Sl.* kooky, *Inf.* half-baked, mad; daft, *Inf.* daffy, crackbrained, *Inf.* nutty; *All Slang.* balmy, dippy, batty, cuckoo, buggy, screwy, wacky, goofy, loony.

address, *n.* **1.** speech, oration, discourse, declamation, *Rhet.* apostrophe, salutation, eulogy, valedictory; lecture, talk, sermon, harangue, diatribe, philippic.
2. location, whereabouts, place, situation; house, home, residence, lodging, dwelling, domicile.
3. bearing, port, deportment, mien, demeanor, air, manner.
4. dexterity, adroitness, skillfulness, expertness; skill, ready skill, dispatch; facility, faculty, knack; cleverness, ingenuity; tact, discretion.
5. *Usu.* **addresses** courtship, courting, lovemaking, wooing, serenade, serenading, suit; attentions, blandishments.
—v. **6.** discourse, make a speech, give a talk, deliver an address, soapbox, platform, take the floor; declaim, hold forth, orate, lecture, sermonize, preach, pontificate; harangue, rant, *Inf.* spout, out-herod Herod.
7. salute, accost, hail, halloo, call to, greet; speak to, talk to, bespeak; approach, buttonhole.
8. solicit, importune, request, supplicate, call upon, apply to, invoke; implore, entreat, appeal to.
9. direct, superscribe, *Commerce.* consign.
10. woo, court, pay court to, make love to, serenade, *Inf.* spark, *Inf.* court and spark, *Sl.* hustle, *Sl.* put *or* slap the make on, *Sl.* put a move on; chase, chase after.

adduce, *v.* cite, point out, mention, instance, evidence, show clearly, illustrate, designate, name; propound, propose, produce; present, introduce, bring forward, advance, offer, proffer, give; affirm, declare, aver, assert; assign, attribute, ascribe; allege, claim, posit, maintain, indicate, contend; refer to, allude to, imply, suggest.

adept, *adj.* **1.** expert, masterful, masterly, topflight, top drawer, first-rate, *Inf.* topnotch, ace, *Inf.* crack, *Sl.* crackerjack, *Inf.* whiz-bang, *Brit. Sl.* whizzo; proficient, polished, finished, accomplished, versed, practiced, experienced, *Fr. au fait*; skillful, skilled, talented, good [at], *Sl.* on the ball; capable, able, competent, efficient, qualified.
—n. **2.** proficient, expert, master, master hand, *Chiefly Brit. Inf.* dab hand, *Brit. Dial.* dabster; maestro, virtuoso; genius, talent, prodigy, *Inf.* wizard, *Inf.* whiz, *U.S. Sl.* crackerjack, *Sl.* shark, *Inf.* sharp; connoisseur, authority, specialist; professional, *Inf.* pro, journeyman, veteran, past mistress, past master, old hand, old stager.

adequacy, *n.* sufficiency, sufficientness, adequateness; enough, no less, no more and no less, wherewithal; satisfaction, satisfactoriness, acceptability, admissibility, tolerability, tolerableness, contentment; completeness, thoroughness, extensiveness, plenty; competence, competency, ability, ableness, capacity, capability, capableness, fitness; efficiency, efficacy, utility, usefulness, serviceability, practicability.

adequate, *adj.* **1.** suitable, fit, due, commensurate, proportionate, equivalent, equal, (*of punishment*) condign; sufficient, enough, ample, plentiful.
2. satisfactory, competent, able, capable, up to scratch, *Inf.* up to snuff; passable, tolerable, acceptable, all right, unexceptional; respectable, presentable, admissible, allowable; fairly good, *Inf.* not that bad, not too bad; fair, *Inf.* no great shakes, mediocre, middling, indifferent, average, so-so, *Inf.* nothing to write home *or* brag about; minimal, minimum.

adhere, *v.* **1.** stick, cleave, accrete, cling, hold fast; fasten, attach, join, unite; coalesce, cohere; glue, agglutinate.
2. be attached, be faithful, be devoted, be constant, be loyal, be true; stand by, stick by, support, give support.
3. hold to firmly, comply with, abide by, fulfill; observe, respect, acknowledge; obey, follow, heed, mind.

adherence, *n.* **1.** attachment, devotion, constancy, faithfulness, fidelity, fealty, loyalty, allegiance; compliance, obedience, abidance, acquiescence, concurrence, observance, respect, acknowledgment, assent.
2. adhesion, cohesion, cohesiveness; cementation, concretion, accretion; tenacity, tenaciousness; glutinousness, viscosity, stickiness.

adherent, *n.* **1.** supporter, follower, disciple, pupil, sectary; devotee, fan, rooter, votary, upholder, backer, advocate, champion, patron; helper, attendant, assistant, acolyte; confidant, companion, ally, partner, partisan; accomplice, *Law.* accessory, confederate, abettor, henchman; retainer, vassal, satellite, hanger-on, parasite, sycophant.
—adj. **2.** sticking, clinging, adhering, tenacious; tacky, gummy, gluey, viscous, viscid, glutinous, mucilaginous, *Archaic.* sizy.

adhesion, *n.* **1.** association, union, alliance, adherence, strong connection, steady attachment; affinity, devotion, fidelity, faithfulness, loyalty, allegiance.
2. assent, concurrence, agreement, consent, acquiescence, approbation.
3. stickiness, clinginess, glutinousness, viscosity, viscidity, mucilaginousness.

adhesive, *adj.* **1.** clinging, adhering, sticking fast, tenacious; adhering, gummy, sticky, gummed, smeary, dauby, stringy, ropy; viscid, viscous, glutinous, agglutinant, agglutinative, mucilaginous.
—n. **2.** sticker, label, stamp, *Trademark.* Scotch tape; cellophane tape, gummed tape *or* label, adhesive tape *or* plaster, sticking plaster, court plaster, corn plaster.
3. glue, paste, rubber cement, musilage, library paste, *Inf.* stickum; sealing wax, solder, epoxy, mortar, plaster, cement.

adieu, *interj.* **1.** good-by, farewell, *Inf.* so long, *Inf.* bye-bye, see you later, fare thee well, God bless you; adios, *Latin. vale,* sayonara, *Fr. au revoir, It. arrivederci, Ger. auf Wiedersehen;* Godspeed, bon voyage, *Ger. gluckliche Reise,* have a nice trip.
—n. **2.** farewell, good-by, *Latin. vale,* sayonara; Godspeed, bon voyage; parting, separation, departure, leave, leave-taking, congé, valediction, valedictory.

adjacency, *n.* juxtaposition, adjacence, contiguity, contiguousness, abuttal; nearness, closeness, proximity, proximateness, proximation, approximation, propinquity.

adjacent, *adj.* **1.** juxtapositional, juxtaposed, next to, proximate, bordering; contiguous, abutting, meeting, tangential, tangent, touching, contactual, *Obs.* attingent; near, nearby, close, close by, nigh.
2. neighboring, next-door, vicinal, environmental; adjoining, conjoining, connecting, attached.
3. preceding, precedent, foregoing, anterior, antecedent, previous, prior, just before; next, following, ensuing, succeeding, just after; facing, opposite.

adjoin, *v.* **1.** border on *or* upon *or* against, abut on *or* upon, verge upon, impinge upon; lean on *or* upon *or* against; lie near to, lie close to, lie next to, lie *or* be adjacent to; end at, stop at, finish at.
2. touch, reach, butt, border, impinge, abut, meet, meet end to end; join, conjoin, connect, attach, unite, affix, annex.

adjoining, *adj.* contiguous, abutting, tangential, tangent, contactual, touching, joining, conjoining, connecting, meeting, *Obs.* attingent; adjacent, bordering, skirting, edging, proximate, juxtapositional, juxtaposed, next to, *Inf.* right next to, *Inf.* next door to; near, nearby, close, close by, nigh, neighboring, converging, vicinal.

adjourn, *v.* **1.** suspend, break off, break up, dissolve, discontinue, interrupt; prorogue, recess, intermit, *Law.* continue; stay, delay, *Parl. Proc. U.S.* table, lay aside, reserve; postpone, defer, shelve, put off.

2. repair, betake, resort; retire, withdraw, retreat, recede.

adjournment, *n.* suspension, breaking off, breaking up, interruption, discontinuation, dissolution; prorogation, recess, respite, intermission, *Law.* continuance; stay, delay, postponement, deferment, deferral.

adjudge, *v.* **1.** decree, ordain, rule, order, pronounce, proclaim; assign, ascribe, accredit, attribute, call.

2. award, present, bestow, grant, gift, endow; allow, dispense, distribute, deal out, pass out, dole out, mete out, apportion.

3. judge, try, hear, listen to, sit in judgment on; decide, determine, settle, adjudicate, arbitrate; sentence, destine, condemn, doom.

4. consider, regard, deem, hold, think of as; estimate, appraise, assess, evaluate, test, rate.

adjudicate, *v.* **1.** pronounce, decree, rule, ordain, order; judge, adjudge, determine, decide, settle.

2. try, hear, sit in judgment; arbitrate, umpire, referee.

adjudication, *n.* judgment, adjudgment, determination, decision, settlement, arbitration; pronouncement, ordainment, ruling, ordering, decreeing.

adjudicator, *n.* judge, justice, magistrate, (*in medieval England*) justiciar; arbiter, arbitrator, moderator, umpire, referee.

adjunct, . *n.* **1.** attachment, appendage, appurtenance, appurtenant, ancilla, appanage; annex, annexation, *Rare.* annexment, addition, extension, expansion, enlargement, augmentation, ell, wing.

2. supplement, supplementation, superaddition; appendix, addendum, codicil, *Law.* allonge; epilogue, postscript, p.s., P.S., subjoinder, subjunction, endpiece, tailpiece, suffix, postfix, tag; subsidiary, subdivision, branch, division, section, arm, part; complement, completer, accessory, accompaniment, concomitant, corollary, pendant, *Astron.* comes.

3. auxiliary, assistant, aide, helper, coadjutor, coadjutress, supplementary, appendant; affiliate, associate, fellow, sidekick; attendant, squire, equerry, courtier, gillie, page, footboy; attaché, aide-de-camp, *Mil.* orderly, *Obs.* waiter; subordinate, underling, small fry, *Inf.* small potatoes; servant, servitor, vassal, liegeman, *Hist.* retainer, *All Contemptuous.* flunky, lackey, satellite, slave, *Sl.* stooge.

—adj. **4.** subordinate, subsidiary, secondary, background, inferior, low-level, unimportant, unprivileged; appended, appendant, adjunctive, annexed, added; attached, allied, coalesced, coalescent, associate, associated, affiliate, affiliated.

adjure, *v.* **1.** charge, order, command, direct, bid; bind, oblige, obligate, require; enjoin, prescribe, decree, ordain; compel, press, drive, push, propel, prod; exhort, demand, insist.

2. entreat, implore, beseech, importune, beg, plead; request, solicit, petition, urge, ask; supplicate, pray, invoke, obtest; call on *or* upon, appeal to, conjure.

adjust, *v.* **1.** fit, adapt, accommodate, make correspondent *or* conformable; alter, modify, change; proportion, suit, measure, coordinate; fashion, frame, shape.

2. regulate, set, repair, fix, put in working order; right, set to rights, straighten, focus, tune in *or* up, attune, fine-tune; bring into line, synchronize, collimate, calibrate, align, balance.

3. settle, resolve, clear up, reconcile, make up, compose, harmonize; make peace, come to terms, agree, compromise, accommodate; arbitrate, negotiate, arrange terms, mediate; square, rectify, set right, redress, satisfy; make amends, mend, patch, heal.

4. adapt, acclimate, acclimatize, naturalize, become accustomed to, get used to, become familiar with; accustom, familiarize, make used to, habituate, assimilate; inure, harden, toughen, season, temper, anneal.

adjustable, *adj.* **1.** adaptable, changeable, variable, alterable, modifiable, transformable; acclimatable, acclimitizable, *Both Sociol.* acculturational, acculturative.

2. pliable, pliant, flexible, bendable, moveable, yielding, plastic; malleable, ductile, tractile; conformable, compliant, accomodative, adaptive; amenable, agreeable, accommodating, obliging; manageable, submissive, docile, tractable.

adjustment, *n.* **1.** adaptation, adaptedness, fit, fittedness; accommodation, conformity, compliance, yieldingness, correspondence, agreement; alteration, modification, change, conversion, transformation, metamorphosis; fashioning, shaping, proportionment, remodeling.

2. acclimation, acclimatization, acclimatation, *Rare.* acclimature, *Rare.* acclimatement, naturalization, habituation, *Sociol.* acculturation; accustomedness, familiarity, familiarization, familiarness, acquaintance, acquaintanceship, acquaintedness; hardening, toughening, seasoning, inurement, inuredness.

3. repair, regulating, tune-up; fixing, righting, setting right; straightening, focusing, tuning in, fine-tuning; bringing into line, coordination, synchronization, collimation, calibration, alignment, balancing.

4. settlement, agreement, compromise, accommodation, composition; reconciliation, *Music.* resolution, making up, making peace, coming to terms, harmonization; arbitration, negotiation, mediation; squaring, rectification, setting right, redress; satisfaction, amends, mending, patching, healing.

5. knob, lever, handle, grip, switch, button, instrument.

adlib, *n.* **1.** improvisation, extemporization, impromptu; (*all extemporaneous*) speech, remark, quip, retort; composition, piece, riff; performance, execution.

—adv. **2.** at one's pleasure, any way at all, any which way; freely, without restriction, without deliberation, impulsively, suddenly, on the spur of the moment; spontaneously, extempore, extemporaneously, offhand; without preparing *or* rehearsing.

ad-lib, *v.* **1.** improvise, extemporize, *Sl.* wing it, play it by ear; (*all extempore*) create, invent, originate, make up, fabricate; compose, perform, execute.

—adj. **2.** impromptu, improvised, makeshift, extemporaneous, extempore, offhand; unprepared, unplanned, unpremeditated, unrehearsed, off the top of one's head, *Sl.* off-the-cuff; spontaneous, impulsive, sudden, spur-of-the-moment.

administer, *v.* **1.** manage, control, conduct, direct, officiate; superintend, supervise, oversee, preside over, look after; govern, rule, head, lead, reign; execute, regulate, engineer, operate; implement, prosecute, carry out, effectuate, fulfill, bring to bear, put through, (*of an estate*) settle, arrange, dispose.

2. discharge, dispense, disburse; assign, allot, apportion, deal, mete; dole, measure, parcel; subscribe, tender, proffer, offer; furnish, accommodate, afford, provide; distribute, supply, equip, bestow.

3. apply, treat, attend, minister, doctor; medicate, dose, drug, physic.

4. help, aid, succor, assist; relieve, alleviate, comfort, assuage, console; support, abet, lend a hand, contribute; bestead, avail, serve, subserve; attend, wait on, care for.

administration, *n.* **1.** management, direction, control, regulation, conduct; superintendence, supervision, oversight, charge, command; jurisdiction, dominion, regime, rule, reign, government; directorship, leadership, headship, presidency, magistracy.

2. dispensation, dispensing, distribution, disbursement; furnishing, accommodation, supplying, bestowal; tendering, proffering, offering; application, ministration; (*of an estate*) settlement, disposal, arrangement, adjustment.

3. council, ministry, cabinet, department, chamber; parliament, congress, diet, duma, soviet, senate.

administrative, *adj.* managerial, directorial, supervisory, conductorial, regulatory; executive, executory, authoritative, official, directive, legislative; jurisdictional, governmental, gubernatorial, magisterial.

administrator, *n.* manager, director, executive, head, leader; supervisor, superintendent, overseer, foreman, boss; commander, commandant, president, intendant, chief, governor, ruler; organizer, controller, comptroller, factor, agent; guardian, custodian, trustee, *Law.* curator; steward, proctor, regent, dean; officer, official, speaker, chairman.

admirable, *adj.* **1.** estimable, valuable, valued, esteemed, worthy, deserving; respected, respectable, competent, creditable, reputable; honorable, honored, noble, venerable, revered; meritorious, laudable, praiseworthy, commendable; desirable, enviable, likable.

2. excellent, superior, superb, masterly, masterful, capable; perfect, supreme, transcendent, of the highest order; first-rate, first-class, of the first water, choice, prime; great, fine, wonderful, marvelous, glorious; rare, extraordinary, unusual, unique.

admiration, *n.* **1.** esteem, regard, high regard, high opinion, respect; approval, approbation, appreciation; honor, praise, veneration, reverence, awe, adoration; affection, fondness, liking, love.

2. delight, object of delight, wonder, pride and joy; sensation, marvel, rarity, phenomenon, miracle.

admire, *v.* **1.** esteem, respect, revere, venerate, look up to, think the world of, think highly of, approve; honor, extol, laud, praise, applaud.

2. appreciate, enjoy, delight in; love, be taken with, be enamored of, be smitten with, *Sl.* carry a torch for, adore, idolize, prize.

3. wonder at, marvel at, be amazed, be surprised.

admirer, *n.* **1.** enthusiast, fan, devotee, aficionado; reverencer, venerator, idolator; supporter, partisan, adherent, follower, votary, disciple.

2. suitor, beau, *Inf.* steady, sweetheart, truelove, wooer, lover; gallant, cavalier.

admissible, *adj.* **1.** allowable, permissible, legitimate, legal, lawful, licit; just, equitable, fair, reasonable, justifiable.

2. admittable, confessable, concessible, acknowledgeable, grantable, yieldable, giveable.

admission, *n.* **1.** entrance, access, entrée, entry, admittance; reception, welcome, greeting, introduction, acknowledgement, recognition; acceptance, inclusion, embracement, incorporation.

2. price of entry, fee, cost, charge, bill, receipts, tariff; cover charge, minimum; ticket, pass, credentials.

3. appointment, nomination, designation, assignment, commissioning; induction, installation, initiation, inauguration, investiture.

4. acknowledgement, confession, *Sl.* fessing up, *Inf.* owning up; profession, declaration, expression, utterance; disclosure, revelation, exposure, making known, *Inf.* letting on, divulgence.

5. recognition, admittance, admitting, allowance, granting; assent, accedence, consent, concession, acquiescence; agreement, approval, concurrence.

admit, *v.* **1.** let in, open the door to, allow to enter, give access to, give right of entry to, yield passage to, grant *or* afford entrance to, adhibit; take in, receive, welcome, greet; accept, include, embrace, incorporate; induct, install, initiate, inaugurate, invest, vest.

2. permit, allow, let, grant; admit of, be compatible with, tolerate, bear, stand, support.

3. approve of, accept, go along with, agree, concur with; allow as valid, concede, grant, recognize, see; assent to, accede to, yield to, submit to.

4. acknowledge, confess, *Sl.* fess up, *Sl.* come clean, *Inf.* own up, *Inf.* make no bones about; avow, profess, express, utter, declare, tell; make known, *Inf.* let on, divulge, let out, disclose, reveal, expose.

admittance, *n.* **1.** permission to enter, access, right of entry, admission; reception, welcome, greeting, introduction, acknowledgement, recognition; acceptance, inclusion, embracement, incorporation, induction, installation, initiation, inauguration, investiture.

2. entrance, entry, entrée, ingress; passage, adit, approach; entryway, portal, door, gate.

3. admitting, allowance, concession, granting; assent, accedence, consent, concession, acquiescence; agreement, approval, concurrence.

4. avowal, profession, expression, utterance, declaration; confession, *Sl.* fessing up, *Inf.* owning up; making known, *Inf.* letting on, divulgence, disclosure, revelation, exposure.

admittedly, *adv.* acknowledgedly, by acknowledgement, concededly, grantedly; confessedly, avowedly, declaredly, professedly.

admix, *v.* intermix, mix with, intermingle, mingle with, interlard; mix, mix in, blend, blend in, commix, combine, commingle, compound, mix *or* blend together; tinge with, sprinkle with, flavor with, season with.

admixture, *n.* **1.** mixture, commixture, intermixture, blend, mingling, commingling, intermingling.

2. combination, compound; medley, mélange, potpourri, olio; hodgepodge, mishmash, jumble, farrago, gallimaufry; hash, stew, ragout, salmagundi, olla-podrida.

3. spice, seasoning, flavoring, flavor, taste, twang; trace, tincture, smack, smattering, hint, suggestion, tinge; dash, pinch, touch, bit; sauce, condiment, relish.

admonish, *v.* **1.** caution, warn, forewarn, put on one's guard; advise, counsel against, *Archaic.* dissuade.

2. reprove, scold, rebuke, berate; censure, blame, take to task, call to account; chide, upbraid, reprehend, reproach, reprimand.

3. remind, notify, give notice to, inform, apprise, acquaint with; enlighten, make aware, make realize; jog, stir, jolt; urge, push.

admonition, *n.* **1.** counsel, advice, *Archaic.* dissuasion; caution, warning, monition, notice; forewarning, prediction.

2. reproof, reproval, remonstrance, expostulation; censure, blame, reprehension; scolding, chiding, rap on the knuckles, rebuke, upbraiding, reprimand, reproach.

admonitory, *adj.* warning, monitory, cautionary, precautionary, premonitory, forewarning; threatening, ominous, menacing, minatory.

ado, *n.* **1.** bustle, hustle, hurry, hurrying, flurry, flutter, buzzing *or* flitting about, scurry, hurry-scurry, running around, doing, *Inf.* to-do, *Sometimes Face-*

tious. do; busyness, stir, activity, action, motion, movement.
2. fuss, fuss and feathers, pother, trouble, travail, labor, bother, ceremony, fanfare; excitement, commotion, hubbub, agitation; confusion, upset, noise, babbling, splutter, hurly burly, ferment; tumult, disturbance, rabblement, rout, turmoil.

adolescence, *n.* **1.** youth, teens, teenage, teen years, pubescence; boyhood, girlhood, minority, nonage; heyday, rising generation, flower of youth, springtime of life, bloom *or* flower of life, golden season of life, dayspring of life.
2. immaturity, growing time, growing up; boyishness, girlishness, youthfulness, puerility, juvenescence, juvenility, prime of youth; juniority, pupilage, wardship.

adolescent, *adj.* **1.** teen-aged, in the teens, underage, minor; young, fresh, blooming, budding, unfledged, new-fledged.
2. youthful, juvenile, *Inf.* like a kid, boyish, girlish; inexperienced, tender, green, wet behind the ears, immature, unripe, callow; baby-faced, beardless, smooth-cheeked, downy-cheeked; juvenescent, pubescent.
—*n.* 3. teen-ager, teen, youth, youngster, juvenile, minor; girl, schoolgirl, young lady, lass, lassie, mademoiselle, damsel, maiden, maid, virgin, nymph, nymphet, slip, sprig, sprite; tomboy, hoyden, teenybopper, *Sl.* jail bait; boy, hobbledehoy, schoolboy, young man, scion, lad, junior, cadet, cub, stripling, fledgling, sapling, whelp, whippersnapper, juvenile delinquent, J.D.

adopt, *v.* **1.** choose for oneself, select for oneself; take to oneself, appropriate, arrogate; acquire, take on, assume, affect, put on; make one's own, embrace, espouse, accept.
2. affiliate, take in, receive, take as one's own child; foster, father, mother, take care of.
3. vote for, approve, sanction, ratify, confirm; support, sustain, endorse, back, uphold.

adoption, *n.* **1.** choosing for oneself, selecting for oneself; taking to oneself, appropriation, arrogation; acquirement, taking on, assumption, affectation; making one's own, embracement, espousal, acceptance.
2. fosterage, affiliation, taking in, taking as one's own child; fathering, mothering.
3. voting for, approval, approbation, sanction, ratification, confirmation; support, sustainment, endorsement, backing.

adorable, *adj.* **1.** lovable, dear, sweet, beloved; cherished, prized, treasured, idolized; enchanting, bewitching, engaging, charming, winsome, captivating, fascinating; attractive, alluring, appealing; lovely, fair, pretty, handsome; pleasing, enjoyable, winning; darling, precious, cute, pet.
2. holy, divine, hallowed, saintly, godly, godlike; angelic, pure, celestial, heavenly; sacred, venerable, blessed, consecrated, sanctified; honorable, respectable, admirable, estimable, worthy.

adoration, *n.* **1.** worship, veneration, reverence, homage; praise, glorification, blessing, exaltation, magnification; honor, respect, esteem, admiration; extolment, laudation, eulogization, panegyrization; deference, bowing down before, genuflection, kneeling before; supplication, invocation, prayer, orison, divine service, incense; idolatry, idolization, deification, apotheosis, hero-worship.
2. love, fondness, infatuation, passion, ardor, closeness; devotion, dedication, loyalty, faithfulness.

adore, *v.* **1.** love, cherish, hold dear, care for, dote on *or* upon; be in love with, wear one's heart on one's sleeve, be enamored of, have a crush on, carry the *or* a torch for; fancy, like, be fond of, be taken with; delight in, take pleasure in, enjoy, appreciate, relish, savor.
2. honor, respect, esteem, admire; praise, glorify, bless, exalt, magnify; extol, laud, eulogize, panegyrize; revere, reverence, venerate, hallow; worship, pay homage to; do service to, burn candles to, bow down before, kiss the feet of, prostrate oneself, fall at the feet of, genuflect before, kneel before; supplicate, invoke, pray to; look up to, put on a pedestal, defer to; idolatrize, idolize, deify, apotheosize.

adorer, *n.* **1.** worshiper, venerator, reverencer, reverer; idolater, iconolater; admirer, enthusiast, devotee, votary, aficionado, follower, fan; celebrant, communicant.
2. lover, paramour, sweetheart, truelove, inamorata, inamorato, boy friend, girl friend; swain, gallant, suitor, wooer, beau, cavalier, courtier.

adorn, *v.* **1.** decorate, embellish, trim, garnish, furbish, ornament, *Archaic.* dight, *Archaic.* ouch; embroider, elaborate, festoon, rubricate; array, bedizen, deck, deck out, bedeck, trap, trap out, caparison; dress, dress up, dress out, attire, accouter; spangle, bespangle, stud, bestud, beset; emblazon, blazon, bedaub, illuminate, paint, color; gild, varnish, trick out.
2. beautify, prettify, *Inf.* pretty up, primp up, fix up; *All Inf.* gussy up, doll up, spruce up, dude up, trick up, fig out, swank up.
3. enhance, enrich; glorify, intensify, brighten, deepen, heighten; set off, set off to advantage; dignify, grace, *Brit. Dial.* mense.

adorned, *adj.* **1.** decorated, embellished, trimmed, garnished, furbished, ornamented; embroidered, elaborated, festooned; arrayed, bedizened, bedecked, decked out, trapped out, caparisoned; spangled, bespangled, studded, bestudded, beset; emblazoned, blazoned, illuminated, painted, colored; gilt, gilded, begilt, varnished, tricked out.
2. beautified, prettified, primped up, fixed up; *All Inf.* prettied-up, gussied-up, dolled-up, spruced-up, duded-up, tricked-up, figged-out, swanked-out.
3. fancy, ornate, rococo, arabesque; busy, overwrought, overdone; inlaid, inwrought, filigreed, filigree, fretted.
4. rich, resplendent, brilliant, glittering, dazzling; florid, flowery; ostentatious, meretricious, showy, flamboyant, flashy, *Sl.* flash; gawdy, garish, tawdry; grandiose, high-flown, *Inf.* high-falutin.

adornment, *n.* **1.** ornament, decoration, frill, filigree, flourish, furbelow; tinsel, spangle, trinket, knickknack, gimcrack, bauble, gewgaw; accessory, attachment.
2. ornamentation, embellishment, trimming, garnish, garnishment, garniture, *Archaic.* ouch; embroidery, elaboration, trappings, festoons; array, bedizenment, enrichment, beautification, prettification; emblazonment, emblazonry, illumination; luster, flourish, veneer, gloss, gilt, gilding.
3. finery, frippery, frilliness, frills, frills and furbelows, folderol, trumpery, gaudery, fuss, *Inf.* foofaraw; ostentation, meretriciousness, showiness, show, flamboyance, flashiness, *Sl.* flash; gaudiness, garishness, tawdriness.
4. ornateness, fanciness, elaborateness, business; baroqueness, baroque, rococo, arabesque; richness, luxuriousness, luxuriance; brilliance, splendor, magnificence.

adrift, *adj., adv.* **1.** drifting, unanchored, unmoored, tide-borne, at the mercy of wind and tide; derelict, awash, *Naut.* ahull.
2. directionless, aimless, goalless, purposeless, rudderless, undirected; unstable, rootless, unsettled, insecure.
3. indecisive, uncertain, vacillating, wavering, fluctuating, shifting; fickle, inconstant, irresolute,

swayable.

4. lost, at a loss, at sea, confused, perplexed, puzzled; astray, stray, wandering, homeless.

adroit, *adj.* **1.** dexterous, ambidextrous, deft, handy, neat, *Brit. Dial.* feat; nimble, agile, active, quick, rapid, brisk, swift, lively; facile, ready, proficient, adept, skillful, skilled, experienced, *Fr. au fait.*

2. clever, ingenious, inventive, resourceful; shrewd, *Archaic.* parlous, *Inf.* cute; cunning, canny, guileful, subtle, artful, crafty, slick; sagacious, astute, keen, acute, sharp, sharp-witted, sharp as a tack, quick-witted; apt, smart, witty.

adroitness, *n.* **1.** dexterity, ambidexterity, deftness, sleight, sleight of hand, legerdemain; nimbleness, agility, quickness, rapidity, briskness, swiftness, liveliness; handiness, right-handedness, neatness; skillfulness, skill, faculty, knack, talent; finesse, felicity, readiness; artistry, craft, proficiency, adeptness, address, mastery, expertness.

2. cleverness, ingenuity, ingeniousness, inventiveness, resourcefulness; shrewdness, cunning, canniness, guile, subtleness, artfulness, craftiness, *Inf.* cuteness; sagaciousness, sagacity, astuteness, keenness, acuteness, sharpness, sharp-wittedness; aptness, smartness, wittiness.

adulate, *v.* **1.** worship, hero-worship, idolize, adore, worship the ground [s.o.] walks on, stand in awe of; deify, put on a pedestal; (*all to an excessive degree*) praise, glorify, exalt, extol.

2. fawn, toady, truckle, toadeat, flatter, puff, inflate, *Sl.* play up to, *Sl.* suck up to, *Sl.* shine up to, apple-polish, *Sl.* butter-up, *Sl.* brown-nose; lickspittle, *Sl.* bootlick, court, pay court to, curry favor, dance attendance upon.

3. kowtow, bow, bow and scrape, stoop, crouch; kneel, fall at the feet of, prostrate oneself; grovel, crawl, slither, worm, creep, squirm.

adulation, *n.* **1.** worship, hero-worship, idolization, adoration, deification; glorification, exaltation, extolment.

2. sycophancy, toadyism, toadeating, tufthunting, flattery, lip-homage, lip-service, *Rare.* blandation; cajolery, blandishment, blarney, palaver, *Inf.* soft-soap, *Inf.* sweet talk, *Inf.* honeyed words, *Sl.* line, *Sl.* snow job, *Archaic.* gloze.

3. servility, slavishness, obsequiousness, obsequence, subservience, *Obs.* vernility; prostration, obeisance, abjection, self-abasement.

adulator, *n.* toady, toadeater, sycophant, flatterer, fawner, fawning flatterer, truckler, tufthunter, courtier, backslapper, timeserver, apple-polisher, *Sl.* brown-nose, *Archaic.* pickthank; flunky, lackey, yes-man, jackal, bootlick, lickspittle, Uncle Tom, *Sl.* oreo; worshiper, hero-worshiper, idolizer, kowtower, groveler.

adulatory, *adj.* **1.** sycophantic, toadyish, toadeating, flattering, fawning, truckling, ingratiating, timeserving, *Sl.* bootlicking, *Sl.* apple-polishing, *Sl.* brown-nosing; unctuous, oily, buttery, candied, honey-mouthed, smooth-talking, smooth-tongued, sweet-talking.

2. servile, slavish, obsequious, subservient, *Obs., Rare.* vernile; submissive, docile, compliant, acquiescent, Uncle Tomish, tractable, mealy-mouthed; prostrate, obeisant, on one's knees; groveling, crawling, creeping, slithering; kowtowing, stooping, bowing and scraping.

adult, *adj.* **1.** mature, grown-up, full-grown, fully grown, grown; of age, at the age of consent, at the age of majority; ripe, ripened, fully developed.

2. (*of schools*) postgraduate, night, evening.

3. (*of movies and literature*) X-rated, pornographic, obscene.

—*n.* **4.** grownup, man, gentleman, woman, lady, twenty-one-year-old.

adulterate, *v.* alloy, tamper with, doctor, water down, thin out, *Sl.* cut; defile, make impure, deflower, contaminate, taint, pollute, infect; weaken, enfeeble, *Archaic.* extenuate, debilitate; impair, vitiate, spoil, mar, unfit, depreciate; degrade, debase, lower, deteriorate, warp, pervert, prostitute; corrupt, subvert, canker.

adulterated, *adj.* **1.** alloyed, doctored, adulterate, tampered with, watered down, mixed, *Sl.* cut; defiled, impure, contaminated, tainted, polluted, infected; weakened, enfeebled, debilitated; impaired, vitiated, spoiled, marred, depreciated; degraded, debased, lowered, deteriorated, warped, perverted, prostituted; corrupted, subverted, cankered.

2. adulterine, adulterous, ungenuine, spurious, unauthentic, meretricious.

adulteration, *n.* admixture, watering down, thinning out; defilement, contamination, pollution; impairment, vitiation, depreciation, disrepair, deterioration; degradation, debasement, perversion, corruption.

adulterous, *adj.* **1.** illicit, adulterate, unlicensed, unlawful, illegal; corrupt, immoral, impure, unchaste; dissolute, licentious, rakish; lustful, salacious, concupiscent, lecherous, prurient, lascivious, libidinous.

2. spurious, adulterine, ungenuine, unauthentic, mock, bogus.

adultery, *n.* fornication, *Law.* criminal conversation, infidelity, unfaithfulness, *Euph.* playing *or* fooling around, *Sl.* hanky-panky, cuckoldry; intrigue, liaison, affair, amour; libertinism, licentiousness, unchastity.

adumbrate, *v.* **1.** silhouette, outline, sketch, give a rough sketch of, trace; delineate, draft, diagram, chart; approximate, give a faint resemblance of, give an idea of; represent, portray, image, paint; explain, describe, tell about.

2. foreshadow, prefigure, forecast, predict, prophesy; portend, presage, prognosticate, warn, *Rare.* premonish; indicate, suggest, hint, give an idea of; denote, mark, emblem, symbolize, typify, allegorize.

3. overshadow, shadow, shade, overcast, cast a shadow over, becloud, cloud over; bedim, dim, darken, gloom, eclipse, opaque; cover, veil, conceal, hide; obscure, obfuscate, blur, confuse, muddle.

adumbration, *n.* **1.** silhouette, sketch, rough sketch, outline, delineation; draft, diagram, chart; approximation, resemblance, semblance, ghost, trace; representation, portrayal, picture, image; description, explanation.

2. foreshadower, prefigurement, forecast, prophecy; portent, presage, augury, omen, warning; indication, suggestion, hint, idea; prototype, archetype, type, model; symbol, sign, emblem, mark; parable, allegory, simile, metaphor, *Rhet.* parabole, *Rhet.* figure of speech.

3. shadow, penumbra, umbra, cloud; cover, veil, eclipse.

4. foreshadowing, prefiguration, prediction, premonition, prognostication; denotation, symbolization, typification, allegorization, parabolization.

5. overshadowing, shadowing, shading; obscuring, obfuscation, blurring, confusion, muddlement.

advance, *v.* **1.** send onward, push *or* bring forward, move *or* put forward; propel, shove, force toward the front *or* fore.

2. go forward, make headway, move on *or* onward, march *or* step forward; proceed, continue, keep going, press *or* push on, go *or* get on; make progress, gain ground, catch up; take the lead, get *or* go ahead; push forward, forge *or* move ahead, make way, clear the way; edge *or* inch along, move *or* go along.

3. suggest, propose, submit, recommend, present, bring up, introduce; call attention to, bring to mind, bring into consideration *or* notice; offer, proffer, tender, give, hold out, put forward, propound; adduce, allege, affirm, assert, bring forward.

4. promote, back, support, further, forward, help onward, facilitate; assist, aid, abet, foster, benefit; boost, raise, lift, increase, add to, augment, contribute to, conduce to; improve, strengthen, amend, make better, develop; progress, succeed, thrive, flourish, prosper, come on, grow.

5. move up, be promoted, improve in rank, rise to a higher position; strive for, work up to.

6. accelerate, speed up, pick up, step up, expedite; hasten, hurry, hustle, precipitate, antedate, *Archaic.* dispatch; quicken, stimulate, energize, *Sl.* open up, *Sl.* jazz up; drive, incite, goad, spur, impel, compel; force, push on, urge on *or* forward, press *or* move forward.

7. pay up front, make a down payment, make a deposit, buy on the installment plan, buy on the lay-away plan, retain, pay a retainer; supply, provide, produce, furnish, deliver, render; give, accord, contribute, donate, yield, afford; pay, lend, loan, accommodate.

—n. **8.** progress, movement forward, headway; gaining ground, pushing forward, forging ahead; moving along, going forward, pressing on, pushing ahead; inching ahead, edging along.

9. promotion, furtherance, improvement, advancement, rise, elevation; enhancement, ennoblement, aggrandizement, exaltation, honor, dignity.

10. breakthrough, step forward, major development; discovery, finding; invention, innovation, creation, production.

11. **advances** overtures, preludes, motions, gestures; offers, tenders, invitations, proposals, propositions.

12. price rise, price increase, markup, boost; addition, augmentation, increase, increment, gain.

13. down payment, deposit, retainer, payment up front.

14. **in advance** **a.** before, in front, ahead, prior, first, in the lead, forward. **b.** beforehand, previously, prematurely, early, before-time.

—adj. **15.** lead, first, precedent, antecedent.

16. preview, pre-examination; prepublication, preliminary *or* prior article.

advanced, *adj.* **1.** forward, placed in advance *or* at the front *or* forward, ranged at the front, set in the van.

2. improved, bettered, changed for the better; developed, perfected, refined, polished, honed-down.

3. precocious, early, far ahead, born before one's time; forward-looking, ahead of its time, progressive; avant-garde, ultramodern, way-out, far-out; original, unconventional, one of a kind.

4. old, aged, ancient, venerable, old as the hills; far on in years, far on in time, along in years, well-along, at an advanced age.

advancement, *n.* progress, movement forward, headway, promotion. See **advance** (*defs.* **8, 9**).

advantage, *n.* **1.** benefit, behoof, good, gain, profit; advancement, betterment, improvement; blessing, boon, prize, favor, help; privilege, vantage, convenience, comfort, easement, accommodation; use, utility, service, expediency; head start, favoring circumstance, favorable opportunity, superior situation.

2. power, authority, mastery, prestige; superiority, ascendancy, supremacy, preeminence, prerogative, right; leverage, hold, grip, purchase; odds, odds on one's side, upper hand, edge, whiphand, in; ace in the hole, trump card.

—v. **3.** serve, help, aid, benefit, avail, be of advantage to; further, promote, advance; profit, favor, prove beneficial to, yield gain to; get the best of, *Inf.* score on *or* off.

advantageous, *adj.* beneficial, good, favorable, helpful, of service, serviceable; convenient, expedient, fortunate, opportune, propitious, auspicious, salutary; valuable, profitable, gainful, lucrative, remunerative; to one's interest *or* best interest, to one's good, all to the good, all for the best.

advent, *n.* **1.** arrival, appearance, forthcoming; approach, access, accession, coming, coming near; approach of time, time drawing near.

2. (*usu. cap.*) coming of Christ, Incarnation; Second Advent, Second Coming, Parousia, Judgment Day.

adventitious, *adj.* extrinsic, external, extraneous, supervenient, foreign, alien; incidental, accidental, nonessential; chance, fortuitous, serendipitous, *Inf.* fluky; casual, random, haphazard.

adventure, *n.* **1.** risk, hazard, danger, peril, jeopardy; chance, fortune, fortuity.

2. enterprise, venture; speculation, gamble, plunge, stake, shot, *Inf.* flier; trial, essay, experiment.

3. exploit, feat, deed, tour de force; affair, episode.

—v. **4.** risk, jeopardize, hazard, venture; imperil, threaten, endanger.

5. dare, chance, wager, bet; stake, *Brit.* punt, sink, *Inf.* plunge; take a chance, run the risk, take a long shot, try one's fortune, play for, try one's luck.

adventurer, *n.* **1.** voyager, traveler, explorer, journeyer, globetrotter, landloper; wanderer, rover, roamer, wayfarer, itinerant, peripatetic; gadabout, vagabond, vagrant.

2. soldier of fortune, mercenary, professional soldier, legionary, legionnaire; knight-errant, swashbuckler, daredevil, madcap.

3. speculator, gambler, bull, wagerer, gamester, *Inf.* plunger.

4. trickster, sharper, swindler, rook, bamboozler; desperado, *Inf.* crook, thief, fleecer, *Inf.* hawk, *Sl.* stockateer, *Often Contemptuous.* stockjobber; impostor, pretender, deceiver; charlatan, quack, mountebank, con man; knave, rogue, scoundrel, cheat.

adventurous, *adj.* **1.** daring, audacious, bold; enterprising, adventuresome, venturesome; doughty, courageous, gallant, chivalrous; valorous, brave, valiant, heroic; undaunted, dauntless, intrepid, fearless; game, spirited, plucky, *Inf.* spunky, of sporting blood.

2. rash, foolhardy, reckless, temerarious, daredevil; brash, impetuous, hasty, incautious, headlong; imprudent, indiscreet, injudicious.

3. risky, dangerous, perilous, hazardous, jeopardous; uncertain, chancy, precarious, *Archaic.* parlous.

adversary, *n.* **1.** opponent, antagonist, enemy, foe, *Literary.* foeman, assailant, attacker; contestant, competitor, rival; opposer, disputant, debater.

2. **the Adversary** the devil, Satan, the archenemy.

adverse, *adj.* **1.** antagonistic, hostile, belligerent, bellicose, pugnacious; averse, unfriendly, uncongenial; antipathetic, antipathetical, repugnant, oppugnant, irreconcilable; injurious, inimical, pernicious, noxious, harmful, hurtful, afflictive, detrimental.

2. inauspicious, unpropitious, unfavorable, unlucky, unprovidential, untoward, sad; ominous, portentous, foreboding, bodeful; fatal, dire, black, star-crossed; disastrous, catastrophic, calamitous, ruinous, cataclysmic, cataclysmal.

3. opposed, opposing, oppositive, oppositional; opponent, adversary, adversative, conflicting, against, at loggerheads; counter, counteractive, counteracting, contrary, contradictory, contrapositive, (*of winds,* *etc.*) head.

4. opposite, other; confronting, facing; reverse, obverse, inverse, converse.

adversity, *n.* **1.** misfortune, affliction, hurt, harm, ruin, ruination; misery, woe, hardship, suffering, distress, bereavement, *Archaic.* bale, storm and stress, sea of troubles; infelicity, ill *or* bad luck, hard luck, ill *or* bad fortune, ambsace, evil eye, evil wind, dark cloud *or* star, storm clouds; trouble, the devil to pay; trial, tribulation, burden, weight, load.

2. mishap, mischance, miscarriage, misadventure, *Scot. and North Eng.* mishanter *or* mischanter, glitch, casualty, accident; shock, blow, nasty *or* staggering blow, buffet, stroke, stroke of bad luck *or* fortune; reverse, reversal, reverse of fortune, setback, bringdown, comedown, bitter pill; cross, check, checkmate; disaster, tragedy, calamity, catastrophe, cataclysm.

advert, *v.* **1.** remark, comment upon, mention, touch upon; refer to, allude to, hint at, suggest, insinuate, intimate, imply, indicate.

2. regard, look at, glance at, notice, see, view, watch, observe; pay attention to, heed, take heed of, mark, take note of, listen to; mind, see to, look after, keep an eye on, attend to, take care of.

advertise, *v.* publicize, bill, subserve; announce, blurb, broadcast, make known, publish; declare openly, promulgate, proclaim, herald, trumpet, ballyhoo, beat the drum; promote, advance, push, *Inf.* plug, *Inf.* hype, puff; call attention to, boast, brag, vaunt; post, display, blazon, placard, circularize; circulate, distribute, propagate, propagandize, spread, disseminate, disperse, scatter.

advertisement, *n.* **1.** ad, *Chiefly Brit. Inf.* advert, announcement, blurb, statement, broadcast, *Inf.* plug, *Sl.* pitch; *Radio and TV.* commercial, spot announcement, spot.

2. notice, placard, poster, display; circular, bulletin, bill, handbill, flyer, leaflet, throwaway, broadside.

3. advertising, publicity, promotion, publication, broadcasting; heralding, trumpeting, ballyhooing; propaganda, puffery, *Inf.* hype, *Inf.* plugging, pushing, hard sell; circulation, circularization, distribution, propogation, dissemination, dispersal, dispersion.

advertiser, *n.* adman, advertising man; publicist, promoter, publicity agent, PR man, *Usu. Disparaging.* flack; vendor, dealer, *Chiefly Brit.* monger, peddler, hawker; retailer, huckster, *Archaic.* hucksterer, trader; shopkeeper, tradesman, merchant, businessman.

advice, *n.* **1.** counsel, wisdom, guidance, instruction, teaching, *Chiefly Brit. Dial.* rede; recommendation, suggestion, word to the wise, tip, hint; plan, scheme, opinion, idea, what [s.o.] should do; principle, rule, law, doctrine, tenet, motto.

2. appeal, bidding, encouragement, persuasion, urging, exhortation; prescription, enjoiner, direction, command, charge, order, injunction; dissuasion, admonition, monition, caution, warning.

3. enlightenment, insight, knowledge, understanding; inside information, intelligence, data, facts; news, word, account, report, tidings, notice, notification, announcement; communication, message, memorandum, memo, letter, epistle.

advisability, *n.* **1.** recommendability, desirability, advisableness; expediency, expedience, practicality, usefulness, profitability, advantageousness, beneficialness; prudence, judiciousness, wiseness, sagacity.

2. correctness, rightness, propriety; properness, suitableness, suitability, seemliness, appropriateness, befittingness, fitness, meetness, aptness.

advisable, *adj.* **1.** recommendable, desirable, expedient, practical, useful; profitable, beneficial, advantageous, best; prudent, discreet, circumspect, politic, judicious, wise, sage, sagacious; sensible, reasonable, rational, intelligent; correct, proper, right, good; suitable, seemly, appropriate, befitting, fit, meet, apt, *Inf.* O.K.

2. counselable, consultable, helpable; open to *or* ready for advice, open-minded, treatable, undefensive.

advise, *v.* **1.** counsel, guide, instruct, teach, tutor, tell about, take under one's wing, *Inf.* steer; recommend, suggest, offer an opinion, give [s.o.] a tip *or* hint, tell [s.o.] what to do.

2. *Usu.* **advise with** consult, take counsel with, confer; deliberate, consider, weigh, discuss.

3. exhort, persuade, urge, coax, encourage, appeal to, make a bid to; prescribe, enjoin, direct, command, order; dissuade, admonish, caution, warn, *Archaic.* monish.

4. *Often* **advise of** inform, give news *or* word of, report, give an account of; enlighten, give insight, make known, impart, relate, communicate; apprise, acquaint [s.o.] with, let [s.o.] in on, notify.

advised, *adj.* **1.** (*usu. used in combination*) considered, weighed, pondered, contemplated, meditated, thought out; deliberated, arbitrated, mediated, discussed, debated.

2. deliberate, studied, circumspect, cautious, careful; prudent, judicious, sensible, reasonable.

3. informed, apprised, notified, acquainted, kept up *or* abreast, enlightened, let in on, in on, clued in.

advisedly, *adv.* deliberately, thoughtfully, after full consideration; prudently, discreetly, judiciously; cautiously, circumspectly, carefully, heedfully, guardedly, warily; slowly, painstakingly, methodically, systematically, with due process.

advisement, *n.* **1.** consideration, weighing, arbitration, contemplation, meditation; consultation, deliberation, debate, discussion.

2. counsel, guidance, supervision, care; instruction, teaching, tutorage.

adviser, *n.* **1.** counselor, guidance counselor, mentor, confidant, confidante, therapist; guide, coach, teacher, instructor, tutor, preceptor, director, pilot, *Inf.* steerer.

2. consultant, resource, professional, *Inf.* pro, expert; sage, wise man, Solomon, solon, fountain of knowledge, wealth of information, *Class. Myth.* Nestor; conferrer, *U.S.* conferee, arbitrator, arbiter, referee, umpire.

3. prompter, persuader, coaxer, urger, encourager; monitor, admonisher, admonitor, criticizer; meddler, interferer, backseat driver.

advisory, *adj.* **1.** counseling, helping, consulting, consultive, consultative, consultatory; professional, expert.

2. prudential, recommendatory, recommending, deliberative, conferring.

advocacy, *n.* **1.** support, backing, patronage, active espousal, maintenance, sustenance, *Obs.* advocation; countenance, favor, endorsement, subscription, sanction, recommendation, approval, approbation, blessing, grace, sponsorship, auspices *or* auspice, good offices, kind regard; defense, championship, relief, help, aid, assistance.

2. speaking for, pleading for, arguing for, speaking well *or* highly *or* warmly of, having *or* putting a good word in for; supporting, seconding, maintaining, sustaining, upholding, defending; espousing, favoring, countenancing, subscribing to, taking the side of, falling in with, joining oneself to, associating oneself with, lending one's name to; taking the part of, taking up *or* espousing *or* adopting the cause of, standing up for, siding with *or* taking sides with, standing behind; recommending, urging, propagating, endorsing, puffing,

singing the praises of, *Sl.* touting, *Sl.* hyping.

advocate, *v.* **1.** speak for, plead for, argue for, speak in favor of, speak well *or* highly *or* warmly of, have *or* put in a good word for; support, back, second, maintain, sustain, uphold; champion, defend, patronize, espouse, favor, countenance; subscribe to, take the side of, fall in with, join oneself to, associate oneself with, lend one's name to, take the part of, take up *or* espouse *or* adopt the cause of; stand up for, side with *or* take sides with, stand behind; recommend, urge, cry up, propagate, endorse, puff, sing the praises of, *Sl.* tout, *Sl.* hype.

—*n.* **2.** maintainer, sustainer, upholder, supporter; backer, second, seconder, abettor, patron, promoter; endorser, espouser, protagonist, propagator, propagandist, proponent, favorer, countenancer, exponent; defender, champion, vindicator; pleader, apologist, friend at court; activist.

3. intercessor, interceder, mediator, intermediator, intermediary, medium, intermedium, paraclete, middleman, go-between, interagent; moderator, arbitrator, negotiator *or* negotiant, umpire, referee; peace-maker, makepeace, pacificator, propitiator, conciliator, appeaser.

4. lawyer, attorney, attorney-at-law, counsel, counselor, counselor-at-law, councilor, barrister, solicitor, legal adviser, special pleader.

aegis, *n.* protection, guardianship, sponsorship, patronage, auspices; favor, championship, support, aid; safeguard, guard, defense, shelter, surety, guaranty.

aerate, *v.* **1.** air, hang out, dry out, ventilate, air out, freshen; oxygenate, oxygenize.

2. aerify, infuse air into, pass air through, permeate with air, fill with air, inflate; charge, charge with carbon dioxide, make effervescent, treat with gas.

aerial, *adj.* **1.** high, lofty; elevated, towering, soaring, aloft, sky-high; distant, remote, faraway, far reaching; skyward, heavenly, celestial, empyreal, empyrean, supernal.

2. airy, light, light as air, lighter than air, weightless; vaporous, thin, attenuated, invisible, see-through; atmospheric, aural, aeriform, gaseous, volatile.

3. ethereal, unsubstantial, incorporeal, imaginary, fanciful, flimsy, unreal, intangible, dreamy, dreamlike; visionary, ideal, idealistic, rarefied, spiritual, otherworldly; indistinct, faint, elusive, fugitive, tenuous.

4. ethereal, fairylike, delicate, fragile, graceful.

aerialist, *n.* trapeze artist, man on the flying trapeze, aerial gymnast *or* artist *or* performer; tight-rope walker, ropewalker, ropedancer, high-wire artist, slack-rope artist, funambulist, equilibrist, balancer; acrobat, gymnast, tumbler, somersaulter, high vaulter; circus performer *or* artist, stunt man, stunt girl.

aerie, *n.* **1.** eagle's nest, eyrie, nest.

2. retreat, asylum, haven, sanctuary, sanctum, sanctum sanctorum; hideout, hiding place, hideaway, refuge, cranny; stronghold, fortress, citadel, bastion, safehold, tower.

aeriform, *adj.* **1.** airy, light, light as air. See **aerial** (*def.* 2).

2. ethereal, unsubstantial, incorporeal. See **aerial** (*def.* 3).

aeronaut, *n.* pilot, balloonist, aerial navigator; aviator, airman, *Inf.* birdman, flier.

aeronautics, *n.* aerial navigation, aviation, flying, flight, volitation; ballooning, aerostatics; gliding, *Rare.* aerodonetics.

aesthete, *n.* **1.** connoisseur, virtuoso, aesthetician; epicure, epicurean, gourmet, gourmand; expert, authority, mavin, adept, savant, cognoscente; man *or* woman of taste, lover of beauty; critic, *Latin. arbiter elegantiae,* judge, arbiter.

2. dilettante, amateur, nonprofessional; eclectic, dabbler, hobbyist; pretender, fake; tyro, beginner, novice; devotee, votary, fan, follower.

aesthetic, *adj.* **1.** artistic, arty; tasteful, in good taste, to one's taste; beautiful, beauteous, exquisite, elegant, ornamental; well-composed, well-grouped, well-arranged; classic, simple, pure, chaste; fine, graceful, delicate, nice, dainty; attractive, charming, lovely, comely.

2. cultured, cultivated, refined, polished; discriminative, discriminating, particular, fastidious, critical.

3. sensitive, emotional, impressionable, responsive, receptive, susceptible; alive, conscious, open, vulnerable; aware, perceptive, sympathetic, empathetic.

afar, *adv.* **1.** (*usu. fol. by* off) far away, abroad, at a distance, a long way off, far off, far afield, far and wide, away, beyond range, out of range; remote, distant, beyond, yonder; over the hills and far away.

—*n.* **2. from afar** from a long way off, from a distance, from yonder.

affability, *n.* congeniality, friendliness, companionability, amicability; approachability, accessibility, conversableness, sociability; easiness, openness, unreservedness; amiability, agreeability, amenity, pleasantness, suavity; complaisance, benignness, gentleness, mildness, soft-spokenness, kindliness, obligingness; graciousness, cordiality, courteousness, courtesy, civility, comity, politeness, mannerliness.

affable, *adj.* congenial, friendly, companionable, amicable; approachable, accessible, communicative, conversible, sociable; easy, unreserved, open, familiar, free and easy, easygoing; amiable, agreeable, pleasant, suave; complacent, benign, gentle, mild, soft-spoken, kindly, obliging; cordial, gracious, courteous, civil, polite, mannerly, well-mannered.

affair, *n.* **1.** concern, business, matter, topic, interest, *Dial.* nevermind; transaction, undertaking, operation, action, proceeding; fact, thing, particular, point.

2. affairs concerns, matters, activities, business; transactions, finances, ventures, enterprises, undertakings.

3. event, incident, occasion; circumstance; occurrence, happening, phenomenon; episode, adventure, experience, case; performance, production, function, doings; party, soirée, reception.

4. amour, love affair, affair of the heart, amourette, *Fr. affaire d'amour, Fr. affaire de coeur;* intrigue, liaison, tryst, assignation.

affect[1], *v.* **1.** influence, sway, act on, play on, work on, impress upon, impact upon, effect; change, alter, modify, transform; concern, interest, be of interest to, be of importance to, apply to, relate to, pertain to.

2. touch, stir, move, soften, melt, tug *or* pull at the heartstrings; perturb, agitate, trouble, grieve, hurt; smite, pierce, penetrate, cut to the quick, *Inf.* sink *or* soak in, *Inf.* hit home, *Inf.* strike home, *Inf.* hit [s.o.] where it hurts; hit, wear, *Inf.* sit with, *Inf.* sit well with.

3. (*all of pain, disease, etc.*) strike, attack, inflict; grip, seize, take hold, lay hold.

—*n.* **4.** *Psychol.* emotion, passion, affection, sentiment; feeling, sensation, *Inf.* gut reaction.

affect[2], *v.* **1.** pretend, simulate, feign, fake, sham, counterfeit, *Sl.* make out like *or* make like.

2. put on airs, assume airs, assume, adopt, take on, put on, profess, pretend to; pose, posture, peacock; do for effect, make a show of.

affectation, *n.* **1.** pretension, pretentiousness, affectedness, unnaturalness, studiedness, artificial man-

ner; simulation, make-believe, artificiality, insincerity; posing, posturing, peacockery; foppery, dandyism, coxcombry.
2. pretense, show, false show, mere show, shallow display; sham, fake, fakery; pose, posture; airs, mannerisms, *Inf.* la-di-da.
3. (*all characterized by obvious artificiality*) trait, habit, characteristic, quirk; idiosyncrasy, peculiarity, mannerism, trademark.

affected[1], *adj.* **1.** influenced, swayed, acted upon, played upon, worked upon; changed, altered, modified, transformed; concerned, interested.
2. (*all as by climate, disease, etc.*) struck, attacked, afflicted; injured, impaired, hurt, harmed; seized, gripped, laid hold of.
3. (*all of the mind or feelings*) touched, stirred, moved, impressed, softened, melted; perturbed, agitated, troubled, distressed, grieved; smitten, pierced, penetrated, cut to the quick, *Inf.* hit where it hurts.

affected[2], *adj.* **1.** pretended, simulated, feigned, fake, faked, sham, counterfeit, spurious, bogus, *Inf.* phony; artificial, unnatural, make-believe, insincere; assumed, adopted, put on; empty, hollow, shallow.
2. pretentious, ostentatious, high-flown, *Inf.* high-hat, *Inf.* high-falutin; mannered, studied, worked-on, *Inf.* la-di-da, *Inf.* too-too; precious, overnice, *Chiefly U.S. Inf.* cute, *Sl.* cutesy, *Scot.* twee; hypocritical, sanctimonious, self-righteous, holier-than-thou, goody-goody.

affecting, *adj.* moving, touching, poignant, tender; pitiful, piteous, pathetic, saddening, heart-rending, heart-melting, heart-moving, heart-breaking; rueful, lamentable, deplorable, woeful, sorrowful; piercing, penetrating, acute, sharp, keen; impressive, overpowering, stirring, heart-stirring, soul-stirring.

affection, *n.* **1.** devotion, fond attachment, love, tenderness, endearment, caring, warmth, feeling, heart; fondness, liking, regard, favor, partiality, partialness, predilection, preference; kindness, good will, friendliness, solicitude, friendship, amity.
2. emotion, feeling, sentiment, passion, desire.
3. bent, disposition, predisposition, inclination, natural impulse; tendency, proneness, propensity, penchant, proclivity, leaning, bias.

affectionate, *adj.* **1.** loving, tender, warm, fond, caring, giving; devoted, attached, doting, lovesick, enamored, in love; amorous, cooing, spoony, *Sl.* lovey-dovey; passionate, fervent, ardent, amatory, erotic.
2. warm-hearted, cordial, sincere, earnest, friendly, solicitous, amiable; kind, nice, sweet, understanding, sympathetic, tender-hearted, soft-hearted.

affiance, *v.* betroth, engage, contract to, marry, agree to marry, promise to wed, plight one's troth, espouse.

affidavit, *n.* *Law.* sworn statement, attestation, deposition, voucher; oath, pledge, testimony, evidence, witness, affirmation.

affiliate, *v.* **1.** associate, unite, combine, conjoin, ally, wed, marry, yoke, bond *or* tie together; coalesce, league, club, team, herd together; syndicate, federate, confederate, incorporate; attach, couple, mate, partner, match, twin, pair up.
2. derive, trace, follow, research, look up.
3. favor, countenance, advocate, go along with, *Sl.* string along with; support, back, second, uphold, maintain; believe in, have faith *or* confidence in, hold as true; adopt, choose, select, pick out, cast one's lot with, take, receive; accept, vote for, approve, consent to, give one's assent to.
—*n.* **4.** subsidiary, subsidiary company, branch, arm, division, subdivision, section, part.
5. associate, fellow, ally, confrere, brother, sister, *Archaic.* peer; fellow member, compeer, consociate, condisciple; colleague, fellow worker, co-worker, yokefellow, yokemate, *Scot. and North England.* marrow; partner, counterpart, *Obs.* consort; auxiliary aide, helper, helpmate, assistant, ancilla, coadjutor, coadjutress; subordinate, underling, small fry, *Inf.* small potatoes.

affiliation, *n.* **1.** connection, connectedness, bond, link, tie, *Genetics.* linkage; relationship, relatedness, relation, affinity; association, alliance, coalition, union; membership, participation, cooperation, communication, intercourse, interchange, dealings.
2. companionship, fellowship, colleagueship, brotherhood, fraternity, fraternization, consociation; friendship, friendliness, comradeship, sociality, intimacy, *Inf.* chumminess.

affinity, *n.* **1.** natural liking, attraction, inclination; predilection, penchant, leaning, bent, proclivity, propensity; friendliness, sympathy, fondness, affection.
2. soul mate, other half, alter ego, second self; lover, suitor, beau, inamorato, flame; sweetheart, mistress, inamorata, ladylove.
3. relationship by marriage, kinship, kindred, alliance, propinquity; union, bond, attachment, association, connection, interconnection.
4. likeness, resemblance, similarity, similitude, homogeneity; correspondence, homology, parity, agreement, conformity; parallelism, symmetry, analogy, correlation.

affirm, *v.* **1.** state positively, assert, tell with confidence, aver, vouch, avouch; declare, proclaim, make known, enunciate, promulgate, profess, predicate, say, announce, pronounce; asseverate, depose, witness, bear witness to, attest, testify; claim, hold, contend, allege, propound.
2. ratify, approve, endorse, accept; establish, confirm, acknowledge; support, corroborate, sustain, back up, vouch for, guarantee, certify, warrant.

affirmation, *n.* **1.** assertion, avowal, word, vouchment, avouchment; testimony, deposition, predication, asseveration, averment; profession, acknowledgement, announcement, pronouncement; protestation, allegation.
2. ratification, approval, confirmation, corroboration; indorsement, certification, warranty.

affirmative, *adj.* assertive, assertory, affirmatory, affirming, assenting, asseverative, predicative; declaratory, declarative, positive, emphatic, categorical, insistent, dogmatic, absolute.

affix, *v.* **1.** connect, attach, fix, conjoin, subjoin; join, fasten, unite, tie, bind; tack, nail, staple, pin, hook.
2. add, add on, add to, annex, append, adjoin, *Inf.* tack on, *Inf.* hitch on, postfix; *All Grammar.* prefix, suffix, infix.
3. impress, agglutinate, glue on, paste on; tag, tab, ticket, label; stamp, seal, earmark, brand.
4. attribute, assign, ascribe, impugn; attribute to, ascribe to, assign to, impute to, charge to, credit *or* accredit with; fix on *or* upon, pin on, *Inf.* pinpoint, saddle on *or* upon, farther upon, blame for, *Inf.* hang on.
—*n.* **5.** addition, annexation, appendage, addendum, appendix; tailpiece, coda, epilogue, subscript; accessory, attachment, tag, tab; supplement, extension, (*of buildings*) wing.

afflatus, *n.* inspiration, genius, creative impulse, fire; revelation, divine communication; *Theol.* beatific vision, theopneusty.

afflict, *v.* **1.** vex, harass, torment, plague, beset, persecute; bother, perturb, disturb, agitate, discomfort, disquiet, irritate, inflame; grind, gnaw, gall, grate, fret, chafe, rasp, rub.

2. punish, scourge, visit, agonize, harrow, torture, rack, put on the rack, crucify, savage; hurt, harm, wound, pain, injure, damage, molest, scathe; strike, sting, stab, pierce, cut, lacerate.

3. trouble, burden, oppress; grieve, aggrieve, sorrow, embitter; anguish, break [s.o.'s] heart, make [s.o.'s] heart bleed, *Inf.* cut up; (*all of sickness*) sicken, disorder, derange, indispose; weaken, debilitate, enervate, enfeeble; disable, cripple, incapacitate, invalid.

afflicted, *adj.* **1.** vexed, harassed, tormented, plagued, beset, persecuted; bothered, perturbed, disturbed, agitated, flustered, irritated, inflamed.

2. punished, agonized, tortured, racked; hurt, harmed, wounded, pained, injured, damaged, molested; struck, stung, stabbed, pierced.

3. troubled, burdened, oppressed; grieved, aggrieved, saddened, embittered, heartbroken, *Inf.* cut up; weakened, debilitated, enervated, enfeebled; disabled, crippled, incapacitated.

affliction, *n.* **1.** adversity, hurt, harm, ruin, ruination, desolation; misery, wretchedness, agony, torture, torment, distress, suffering, *Archaic.* bale; woe, grief, dolor, sorrow, sadness, anguish, anxiety, unhappiness, heartache, heartbreak, heavy heart; trouble, hardship, sea of troubles, storm and stress; misfortune, infelicity, ill *or* bad luck, ill *or* bad fortune, ambsace, evil eye, evil wind, dark cloud *or* star, storm clouds; trial, tribulation, burden, weight, load, heavy load *or* burden.

2. mishap, mischance, miscarriage, misadventure, *Scot. and North Eng.* mishanter, glitch, casualty, accident; shock, blow, heavy *or* nasty *or* staggering blow, buffet, stroke, stroke of bad *or* ill luck *or* fortune; reverse, reversal, setback, comedown, bringdown, bitter pill; disaster, tragedy, calamity, catastrophe, cataclysm.

afflictive, *adj.* **1.** distressing, distressful, painful; tormenting, torturing, torturous, vexing, vexatious, plaguing, harassing, troubling.

2. sad, sorrowful, woeful, mournful, doleful, dolorous; grievous, sore, hard to bear *or* take; severe, hard, heavy, *Sl.* heavy-duty; unfortunate, unlucky, unhappy; wretched, miserable, deplorable, pitiful, pitiable, piteous, pathetic, pathetical.

3. dire, black, harrowing; disastrous, tragic, calamitous, catastrophic, cataclysmic, cataclysmal, ruinous.

affluence, *n.* **1.** wealth, opulence, riches; fortune, plenty, bounty; prosperity, *Sl.* easy street, wealthiness; money, gold, capital, substance, property, resources, wherewithal.

2. abundance, plenitude, amplitude, fullness, richness; excessiveness, luxuriance, profusion, copiousness, plethora; surfeit, repletion, nimiety, excess, exuberance; superabundance, superfluity, cornucopia, horn of plenty.

affluent[1], *adj.* **1.** wealthy, rich, opulent, pecunious, moneyed, flush; prosperous, well-to-do, flourishing, thriving, in clover; easy, comfortable, well-off, independent, *Sl.* on easy street; *Inf.* well-heeled, *Sl.* loaded, *Sl.* in the money, *Sl.* in the dough, rolling in riches, wallowing in wealth.

2. abundant, profuse, rife, brimming, teeming, full; plenteous, plentiful, bounteous, abounding, bountiful; copious, lavish, exuberant, luxuriant; superabundant, excessive, plethoric, inordinate, overfull.

affluent[2], *n.* tributary, confluent, branch, anabranch, feeder, ramification, arm.

afford, *v.* **1.** stand, bear, manage, support, have means for, have sufficient means for, meet the expense of.

2. yield, furnish, supply, provide; give forth, bring forth, generate, engender, beget.

3. give, confer upon, bestow, grant, award, accord, impart.

affray, *n.* fight, brawl, wrangle, *Inf.* set-to; quarrel, squabble, argument, dispute, disagreement, dissension, row, altercation, contention; disturbance, commotion, uproar, breach of the peace, fracas, rumpus; disorder, turbulence, tumult; struggle, scrimmage, clash, conflict, collision, strife, broil; scuffle, tussle, fray; encounter, brush; melee, fisticuffs, *Sl.* milling, combat, contest, duel, match; outbreak, riot, *Fr.* émeute; feud, vendetta; battle, action, skirmish, rencounter.

affront, *n.* **1.** insult, slight, slur, dig, barb, *Sl.* put-down; abuse, contumely, contempt, disdain, scorn; derision, ridicule, mockery; vilification, impugnment, traducement, aspersion, calumniation, calumny, obloquy; maligning, defamation, denigration, slander, libel, *Inf.* backbiting; impertinence, insolence, flippancy, *Inf.* cheek, impudence.

2. disrespect, rudeness, ill-treatment; indignity, discourtesy, incivility, dishonor, outrage; shame, disgrace, ignominy; degradation, humiliation, abasement, mortification; wound, blow, injury; offense, attack, as sault, aggression; provocation, vexation, irritation, annoyance.

—*v.* **3.** insult, slight, *Sl.* put-down, *Sl.* cut up, give offense to, disoblige; denounce, decry, disparage, discredit, vilipend, depreciate, minimize; disdain, contemn, scout, flout; scorn, deride, jeer, ridicule, scoff, mock, make a fool of, burlesque, guy, lampoon; abuse, wrong, vilify, impugn, traduce, slur, calumniate; malign, defame, denigrate, slander, libel, *Inf.* backbite; gibbet, drag through the mud; humiliate, belittle, put to shame, shame, chagrin, disgrace, degrade; offend, injure, hurt, hurt the feelings of, harm, ill-treat, smart, wound, damage.

4. irritate, nettle, chafe, gall, *Chiefly U.S.* rile, disturb; annoy, make [s.o.'s] blood boil, raise [s.o.'s] dander, anger; vex, provoke, aggravate, incense, inflame, exasperate, tease, *Inf.* rag, distress, fret; pique, *Inf.* miff, chafe, disgruntle, *Inf.* put [s.o.] off, give umbrage to, displease.

5. attack, assault, accost, assail, set upon, aggress; violate, transgress, trespass, infringe upon, encroach upon, intrude upon, step on the toes of; bother, trouble, annoy, harass, molest, harry, bully, badger.

6. embarrass, disconcert, abash, mortify, upset; confuse, fluster, ruffle, discountenance, distract, discompose, confound.

7. confront, come face to face with, meet face to face, meet, encounter; oppose, stand opposed to, stand in the way of, thwart, cross, counter, contradict, resist; dispute, challenge, threaten, call into question, oppugn; defy, face in defiance, stand up to.

aficionado, *n.* **1.** devotee, enthusiast, fan, rooter, *Inf.* buff, *Inf.* hound, *Sl.* bug, *Sl.* nut; addict, *Inf.* fiend, *Sl.* junkie, *Sl.* freak, *Sl.* head.

2. champion, votary, follower, disciple, satellite, adherent; zealot, partisan, bigot, fanatic; visionary, cultist, sectary.

3. promoter, supporter, *Inf.* pusher, *Inf.* booster, *Inf.* arm-waver; chauvinist, jingoist.

afoot, *adv., adj.* **1.** on foot, walking, pedestrially.

2. astir, about, abroad, up, up and about, out of bed; in progress, in motion, on the move, in existence.

aforesaid, *adj.* aforementioned, aforestated, aforenamed, aforegiven, aforecited; above-mentioned, above-stated; previously described, described above, indicated earlier, previously indicated, already said *or* mentioned; earlier, foregoing, preceding, precedent, former; antecedent, previous, prevenient, prior, anterior.

afraid, *adj.* **1.** frightened, fearful, fearsome, scared, *Archaic.* affrighted; terrified, panic-stricken, terror-stricken; apprehensive, alarmed, worried, uneasy, disquieted; distrustful, dreading, shrinking; tense, nervous, panicky, faint-hearted; tremulous, shaky, on edge, jumpy, jittery, edgy, anxious; aghast, shocked, overwhelmed, overcome; cowardly, craven, pusillanimous, white-livered, lily-livered.

2. timid, timorous, cautious, diffident, intimidated; hesitant, reluctant, disinclined, indecisive, unsure, tentative, unwilling.

3. sorry, apologetic, regretful, remorseful; guilty, conscience-stricken, penitent, heavy-hearted.

afresh, *adv.* again, anew, newly, freshly; once more, once again, encore, bis, over, over again, *Latin. de novo.*

aft, *adv. Naut.* toward the stern, astern, sternward, abaft, aback, backward, back, at the back, behind, in the rear, rearward.

after, *prep.* **1.** later, following, subsequent to, at the close of, in succession to, because of, in consequence of.

2. behind, following, in the rear of, *U.S.* in back of, *Inf.* back of, in the wake of.

3. (*in order or rank*) below, nearest to, next to.

4. in pursuit of, in search of, in quest of, in desire of, *Inf.* out to get.

5. in imitation of, in the style of, like, in the mannei of, on the model of, in the pattern of, after the nature of, according to; in compliance with, in harmony with, in conformity to, in agreement with.

6. concerning, about, regarding, relating to.

7. for, the same as, in honor of, in tribute to.

—adv. **8.** later, afterward, subsequently, next, following.

9. behind, in the rear, in back.

—adj. **10.** later, next, subsequent, succeeding, following, ensuing, consequent, resulting, latter.

11. *Chiefly Nautical.* hinder, posterior, back, hind, rearward, further rear, farther aft, sternward.

afterlife, *n.* **1.** afterworld, the hereafter, future world, future life, life after death, the great beyond, the sweet by-and-by; heaven, Zion, Abraham's bosom, the New Jerusalem, the Heavenly City, the Celestial City; Elysium, Elysian Fields, Islands of the Blessed, Valhalla, happy hunting grounds; nirvana, Paradise; immortality, perpetuity, deathlessness, eternity.

2. later life, subsequent life, ensuing years.

aftermath, *n.* **1.** results, consequences, end, end result; issue, outcome, upshot, turnout; sequel, outgrowth, follow-up; backwash, wake, fallout; side effect, by-product; development, effect, fruit, offshoot; repercussion, afterclap.

2. second growth, second crop, fog, rowen.

aftermost, *adj.* hindmost, last, furthest, rear, farthest back, *Obs.* hindermost, *Naut.* sternmost, *Naut.* aftmost.

afternoon, *n.* **1.** *Latin. post meridiem,* p.m., *Inf.* after; nap time, siesta time.

2. middle age, middle years, maturity; waning years, decline, ebb, wane.

afterthought, *n.* **1.** later thought, second thought, reconsideration, review; deliberation, meditation.

2. reflection, retrospection, reexamination, respeculation, *Inf.* second guess, rehash.

3. addition, supplement, extension; addendum, appendix, epilogue, postscript, P.S.

afterward, afterwards, *adv.* subsequently, after, then, next, in aftertimes, thereafter, thereupon, thereon, latterly, later, ultimately, posteriorly, ensuingly.

afterworld, *n.* afterlife, the hereafter, future world. See **afterlife** (*def.* **1**).

again, *adv.* **1.** once more, a second time, anew, afresh, newly, freshly; in addition, over, repeatedly, recurrently, reiteratively; another time, encore, bis, da capo, ditto, *Archaic.* anon.

2. moreover, besides, further, furthermore, as well as, in addition to.

3. on the other hand, on the contrary, *Fr. au contraire,* contrariwise, conversely.

4. back, in return, in reply, in answer, in response, in consequence, as a result, in restitution.

5. back again, in the opposite direction, to the same place, over the same course, on the same track.

6. again and again often, frequently, oftentimes; repeatedly, over and over, recurrently, reiteratively; regularly, habitually, time and time again, periodically, at short intervals; on and on, continuously, monotonously, incessantly, ceaselessly; persistently, insistently, harpingly, pertinaciously, perseveringly, doggedly, unremittingly; many a time and oft, ever and anon.

against, *prep.* **1.** in opposition to, opposed to, adverse *or* hostile to, at odds with, at cross-purposes with, in disagreement with, versus; in contempt of, in defiance of, contrary to, out of line with, not in keeping with.

2. opposite to, across, facing, fronting, confronting, in front of, close up to; toward, to, upon, on, in the direction of.

3. in contact with, up against, dead against, over against, athwart, nose-to-nose with, face-to-face with.

4. in preparation for, in provision for, in anticipation of, in expectation of; for, in order to.

5. in exchange for, in return for, in compensation for, in requital for; to match, to counterbalance, as a balance to.

6. in comparison with, by comparison with, in contrast with; compared to, compared with, taken with, vis-à-vis.

7. before, near, nigh, close to, close upon, hard upon; beside, next to, next door to, bordering on, verging on, on the brink of, on the verge of.

agape, *adv., adj.* **1.** open-mouthed, yawning, wide open, gaping, oscitant.

2. wonderstruck, spellbound, entranced, awestruck, thunderstruck; astonished, astounded, amazed, confounded, surprised; stupefied, dazed, dumbstruck.

age, *n.* **1.** lifetime, generation, duration, stage of life; year.

2. maturity, majority, seniority, adulthood; old age, agedness, oldness, elderliness, declining years; senescence, senectitude, senility, anility, caducity, dotage, decrepitude.

3. epoch, era, *Hindu.* kalpa, period; cycle, span, time, season, date; eon, aeon, chiliad, millenium, years, century, decade.

—v. **4.** mature, ripen, mellow, season; grow old, *Inf.* get on *or* get on in years, *Rare.* senesce, become senile.

aged, *adj.* **1.** old, olden, oldish, elderly, advanced; old as Methuselah, old as the hills, with one foot in the grave, over the hill; venerable, ancient, *Rare.* vetust, patriarchal, Noachian; senile, anile, senescent; gray-haired, gray-headed, hoary, gray, white-haired, white-headed.

2. antiquated, antique, time-worn, superannuated; worn-out, used, decrepit, run-down, broken-down, deteriorated.

3. mature, ripe, mellow, seasoned.

agency, *n.* **1.** company, concern, firm, house, organization, bureau, institution, corporation.

2. action, activity, operation, *Rare.* operance; performance, execution, discharge, dispatch, enactment, exercise, practice; employment, utilization, effectuation, manipulation, handling.

3. influence, effect, result, consequence; power, potency, force.

4. instrumentality, means, ways and means; intercession, intermediation, intervention, good offices.

agenda, *n.* program, schedule, outline, timetable, plan, recipe, itinerary; list, listing, laundry list, itemization, calendar, directory, catalog, bulletin; slate, record, register, *U.S.* docket; memorandum, reminder; tabulation, arrangement, scheme.

agent, *n.* **1.** representative, deputy, commissary; attorney, *Brit.* solicitor, *Law.* proctor, advocate; procurator, *Sl.* ten percenter; middleman, go-between, intermediary, negotiator, negotiant; substitute, proxy, vice-regent, *Govt.* chargé d'affaires ad interim; ambassador, emissary, envoy, deligate, messenger, minister; steward, syndic, factor, broker; functionary, civil servant, servant, factotum, comprador, diplomat, bureaucrat, commissioner; canvasser, traveling salesman; policeman, guard, detective, investigator, operative, spy.

2. cause, moving force, power, means, principle, elements, *Chem.* reagent; executor, perpetrator, doer, actor, principal, mover; practitioner, performer, operator, worker; promoter, organizer, developer; artificer, inventor, mechanic, artisan.

agglomerate, *v.* **1.** group, cluster, bunch up *or* together; mass, crowd, congregate; flock together, throng, herd, swarm, surge; collect, gather, accumulate, amass, cumulate; bring together, rally, muster, call up, round up, round in.

—adj. **2.** gathered, collected, accumulated; amassed, clustered, bunched up *or* together, massed; piled up, heaped up, jumbled.

agglomeration, *n.* pile, heap, stack, mass, accumulation, bulk; collection, amassment, assemblage, aggregation; concentration, conglomeration, congeries; cluster, clump, bunch, batch; assortment, variety, medley, miscellany, jumble, hodgepodge; clutter, *Inf.* mess.

agglutinate, *v.* **1.** adhere, glue *or* cement together, paste together, tape together; cohere, stick, grip, hold *or* cling fast; bond, fuse, weld, solder, join, attach, link, unite.

—adj. **2.** adherent, adhering, adhesive, cohesive, coherent, cohering; sticking, clinging, holding, tenacious; bonded, fused, joined, attached, linked, united, *Biol.* adnate; gummed, gummy, gummerous, sticky, gluey, cementitious, viscid, viscous, resiny, resinous, resiniferous, rosiny.

agglutination, *n.* **1.** adhesion, adherence, cohesion, coherence; gluing, cementation, pasting, sticking; fusion, bonding, attachment, juncture, conjunction, linkage, connection, adnation; grouping, union, coalescence.

2. conglomeration, conglomerate, agglomeration, aggregation, aggregate, cluster, group; mass, body, congeries, collage.

aggrandize, *v.* **1.** increase, enlarge, make larger, make bigger, make greater, *Chiefly Literary.* greaten; widen, thicken, broaden; lengthen, elongate, prolong, prolongate, protract; dilate, distend, inflate, swell, bloat, puff out, blow up.

2. augment, supplement, add to, superadd to; accrue, accumulate, cumulate, amass, pile up, heap up; multiply, double, redouble, treble, triple, quadruple.

3. magnify, amplify, enhance, enrich, deepen, heighten; escalate, step up, give a boost to, *U.S. Sl.* soup up, *Sl.* hop up, *Sl.* jazz up; accelerate, snowball, mushroom; intensify, strengthen, reinforce; exaggerate, maximize, concentrate; overstate, make much of, make the most of.

4. promote, advance, prefer, upgrade, boost; exalt, elevate, ennoble, dignify; honor, worship, crown; glorify, romanticize, glamorize.

aggrandizement, *n.* **1.** increase, enlargement, expansion, extension; widening, thickening, broadening; lengthening, prolongation, protraction; inflation, dilatation, dilation, waxing; growth, spread, swell.

2. addition, accretion, increment, accession, access; augmentation, supplement, annex, annexation, appendage, appendix, addendum, adjunct; accrual, accruement, accumulation, cumulation; multiplication, doubling, redoubling, trebling, tripling, quadrupling.

3. magnification, amplification, enhancement, deepening, coloring, heightening; escalation, acceleration, intensification; strengthening, reinforcement, concentration; exaggeration, overestimation, maximization, overstatement.

4. promotion, advancement, preferment, upgrading, boosting; exaltation, elevation, ennoblement, dignification; glorification, romanticization, lionization, glamorization.

aggravate, *v.* **1.** exacerbate, worsen, add insult to injury, rub salt in the wound, *Inf.* rub it in, pour oil on the fire; increase, heighten, deepen, intensify, add fuel to the flames *or* fire, fan *or* stoke *or* fuel the fire.

2. irritate, annoy, vex, peeve, nettle, chafe, get on [s.o.'s] nerves, tread on [s.o.'s] toes, go against the grain, *Chiefly U.S.* rile, *Inf.* miff, *Inf.* give [s.o.] a pain, *Inf.* rub [s.o.] the wrong way, *Inf.* get under [s.o.'s] skin; exasperate, ruffle, disturb, discompose, put out, try [s.o.'s] patience, *Inf.* put [s.o.'s] nose out of joint, *Sl.* get [s.o.'s] goat; set one's teeth on edge, stick in one's craw *or* crop, *Inf.* grate on one's nerves.

3. bother, pester, hector, harass, *Sl.* bug, *Sl.* hassle, *Sl.* drive [s.o.] nuts *or* bananas *or* crazy, *Sl.* drive [s.o.] up the wall.

4. anger, incense, irk, raise [s.o.'s] ire, get [s.o.'s] back up, *Inf.* get [s.o.'s] Irish *or* dander up, *Inf.* burn [s.o.] up, *Sl.* tick [s.o.] off, *Sl.* tee [s.o.] off; embitter, gall, rankle, envenom.

aggravation, *n.* **1.** exacerbation, intensification, magnification, amplification, increase; exacerbating, intensifying, magnifying, amplifying, increasing, aggravating, *Sl.* heating up.

2. irritation, annoyance, vexation, exasperation; displeasure, dissatisfaction, discontent, discontentment, disapproval, disapprobation.

3. anger, ire, dudgeon, high dudgeon, pique.

4. embitterment, bitterness, bitter resentment, resentment, hard feelings; spleen, choler, gall, bile, ill *or* bad humor; ill *or* bad temper, ill *or* bad feeling; virulence, acerbity, acrimony.

5. irritant, nuisance, bother, pest, bur, thorn in the side *or* flesh, pea in the shoe, salt in the wound, *Inf.* headache, *Inf.* pain, *Sl.* pain in the neck *or* rear, *Sl.* hassle; peeve, pet peeve, gripe, complaint, grievance; sore spot, sore point, *Inf.* touchy subject *or* matter; bore, crashing bore, *Sl.* drag, *Sl.* downer, *Sl.* bummer.

aggregate, *adj.* **1.** complete, entire, whole, total, all; added, combined, compound, composite; united, joined, grouped, agminate; massed, clustered agglomerate.

—n. **2.** whole, totality, entirety; total, sum, sum total; gross, net, summation; number, amount; *Sl.* whole bit, *Sl.* whole schmear.

3. assemblage, collection, accumulation, amassment; heap, pile, mass, cumulation; concentration, combination, composite, compound; agglomeration, conglomeration, group, knot, band, company; body, congregation, assembly, gathering; crowd, throng, aggregation, congeries; array, host, army, multitude; galaxy, con-

stellation.

4. accumulate, amass, sum, total, add up *or* together; group together, draw together, lump together; assemble, put *or* bring together, gather, gather together; compile, collate, collocate, colligate, unite, join together; anthologize, collect, garner, glean; organize, order, marshal; codify, methodize, systematize.

5. group, cluster, bunch up *or* together; mass, crowd, congregate, agglomerate; flock together, throng, herd, swarm.

aggregation, *n.* **1.** pile, heap, stack, mass, accumulation, agglomeration, bulk; collection, amassment, assemblage; number, composite, concentration, conglomeration; cluster, congeries; clump, bunch, batch; assortment, variety, medley, miscellany, jumble, hodgepodge; clutter, *Inf.* mess.

2. group, body; crowd, throng, mob, rout; bunch, gang, pack, herd, drove, swarm; congestion, press, crush; concourse, cumulation, confluence, convergence; galaxy, multitude, host.

aggress, *v.* (*in reference to hostilities*) start, initiate, begin, commence; offend, take the offensive, strike the first blow; attack, affront, assault, besiege; provoke, incite, foment, instigate, enkindle.

aggression, *n.* **1.** attack, assault, besiegement, beleaguerment; onslaught, onset, outbreak; sally, sortie, foray; raid, storming, offensive, *Mil.* blitz, *Mil.* blitzkrieg; thrust, charge, siege, barrage, investment.

2. encroachment, infringement, incursion, intrusion, inroad; transgression, trespass, offense; invasion, irruption, ingress.

3. belligerence, belligerency, bellicosity, aggressiveness; pugnacity, combativeness, militancy, jingoism.

aggressive, *adj.* **1.** offensive, invasive, intrusive, incursive; hostile, combative, belligerent, bellicose, pugnacious; warring, warlike, militant, martial, warmongering, jingoistic; contentious, quarrelsome, litigious, disputatious, argumentative.

2. assertive, self-assertive, forward; pushing, forceful, insistent, peremptory; vigorous, energetic, enterprising, go-ahead; bumptious, obtrusive, *Inf.* pushy, *Scot.* randy, obnoxious.

aggressor, *n.* provoker, initiator, instigator, beginner, mover, prime mover; attacker, assailant, assailer, assaulter, invader, offender; enemy, foe, adversary.

aggrieve, *v.* **1.** wrong, do an injustice to, *Sl.* do one dirty; abuse, mistreat, maltreat, ill-treat, mishandle, misuse, ill-use, bullyrag; oppress, persecute, torment, agonize; injure, hurt, bruise, harm, damage.

2. torture, rack, afflict, pain; distress, plague, vex, harass, harry; worry, trouble, upset, sadden; burden, weigh down *or* upon, load down, impose upon.

aggrieved, *adj.* **1.** wronged, abused, imposed upon, put upon, taken advantage of; offended, insulted, hurt, pained, maltreated, mistreated; injured, harmed, wounded, tormented, persecuted.

2. annoyed, plagued, bothered, disturbed; troubled, worried, distressed; unhappy, sorrowful, grieving, sad, saddened, woeful.

aghast, *adj.* **1.** horrified, terrified, horror-struck, panic-stricken; petrified, appalled, frightened, afraid, alarmed, dismayed, scared.

2. taken aback, surprised, startled, astonished, shocked, astounded, stupefied; flabbergasted, stunned, bewildered, amazed, thunderstruck, dumfounded; perplexed, confounded, nonplused, disconcerted, discomposed, discomfited, *Inf.* thrown off guard, *Inf.* thrown for a loss, *Inf.* floored.

agile, *adj.* **1.** well-coordinated, nimble, supple, sprightly, *Dial.* gainly, quick, lithe, yare; fleet-footed, fleet, swift, rapid, fast.

2. active, lively, alive, bustling, brisk, dapper; deft, dexterous; light-footed, spry, flitting, lightsome, winged, tripping, *Brit. Inf.* nippy.

3. smart, bright, alert, *Inf.* on the ball; quick-witted, keen sharp, acute.

agility, *n.* **1.** nimbleness, sprightliness, litheness, coordination, *Dial.* gainliness; quickness, fleet-footedness, fleetness, swiftness, rapidity.

2. activity, liveliness, aliveness, bustle, briskness, dapperness; suppleness, deftness, dextrousness; light-footedness, spryness, sprightliness; celerity, alacrity, legerity, *Brit. Inf.* nippiness.

3. smartness, alertness, wit, quick wit, quick-wittedness; acumen, perception, discernment.

agitate, *v.* **1.** disturb, shake, shake up, churn, churn up, (*of water, wine, etc.*) roil, (*of water, wine, etc.*) *Chiefly U.S.* rile; commove, convulse, upheave, heave; toss, wave, brandish.

2. perturb, disquiet, discompose, discountenance, ruffle, fluster, flutter, flurry, distract, unsettle, put out; alarm, trouble, upset; shock, jolt, jar, stagger, rock, rattle, pull one up short.

3. arouse, excite, suscitate, foment, impassion, stir up, work up, wind up, whip up, fire up, inflame, enkindle, ignite, touch off, light the spark; incite, instigate, provoke, sow the seeds of, stir the embers, fan the fire, add fuel to the flames, *Inf.* start something.

4. debate, discuss, moot, bandy words *or* opinions; canvass, talk over, go over, *Sl.* kick *or* knock around; argue, dispute, contend, controvert, wrangle, *Scot.* argle-bargle, *Sl.* hassle.

5. consider, weigh, deliberate; contemplate, muse, brood, reflect, ponder, meditate, excogitate; revolve, turn over, sort out, think out, puzzle out; plan, devise, plot.

agitated, *adj.* **1.** uneasy, ill-at-ease, restless, restive, shaky, jumpy, nervous, twitchy, jittery, fidgety.

2. disturbed, perturbed, distracted, unsettled, disquieted, discomposed, ruffled, flustered; aquiver, atwitter, wrought-up, worked-up, in an uproar, in a dither, in a titter, *Archaic.* in a pucker, *Inf.* in a tizzy, *Inf.* in a stew *or* sweat, *Inf.* steamed-up, *Sl.* worked up into a lather, *Sl.* lathered-up, *Sl.* in a lather, *Sl.* all shook up, *Sl.* all hot and bothered, *U.S. Sl.* hopped-up; frantic, frenzied, mad, maddened, corybantic, blue in the face.

3. aroused, excited, impassioned, stirred-up, wound-up, whipped-up, whipped into a frenzy, fired-up, inflamed.

agitation, *n.* **1.** arousal, excitation, fomentation, suscitation, inflammation; demagoguery, rabble-rousing, agitprop; incitement, instigation, provocation.

2. turbulence, turmoil, storm, upheaval, chaos; tumult, uproar, commotion, ado, to-do, hubbub, bother, stir, *Inf.* stew, *Inf.* tizzy, *Sl.* lather, *Archaic.* pucker.

3. disquiet, unrest, disturbance, excitement, distraction; trepidation, uneasiness, fear and trembling.

4. debate, open *or* public debate, discussion, argument, disputation.

agitator, *n.* **1.** demagogue, rabble-rouser, soap-box orator; inciter, instigator, provoker, fomenter, agitprop, labor baiter, *Fr. agent provocateur;* firebrand, incendiary, rebel, insurgent, insurrectionist, radical; troublemaker, mischief maker, stormy petrel, ringleader.

2. mixer, beater, blender, churn; shaker, jiggler, vibrator; whisk, eggbeater, paddle.

agnostic, *n.* **1.** skeptic, nullifidian, unbeliever, doubter, disbeliever, questioner, cynic, doubting Thomas, Pyrrhonist; empiricist, materialist, phenomenalist; freethinker, atheist; heretic, scismatic, backslider; infidel, pagan, heathen.

—adj. **2.** skeptical, doubting, nullifidian, unbelieving, incredulous, cynical, disbelieving, questioning, distrustful, Pyrrhonistic; free-thinking, atheistic, godless, faithless; pagan, heathen, heathenish, infidel; irreligious, irreverent, scoffing.

agnosticism, *n.* skepticism, unbelief, Pyrrhonism, doubt, disbelief; incredulity, incredulousness, cynicism; empiricism, materialism, phenomenalism; heresy, atheism, freethinking.

ago, *adj.* **1.** gone, gone by, bygone, past, *Archaic.* agone; former, quondam, earlier, previous, aforetime, prior, antecedent.

—adv. **2.** before now, before this time, heretofore, since; of old, of yore, aforetime, anciently, *Archaic.* agone; in the past, in time gone by, formerly, once, *Archaic.* erst *or* erstwhile.

agog, *adj.* **1.** eager, anxious, keen, expectant, anticipatory, breathless, desirous, *Sl.* itchy *Inf.* psyched *or* psyched up; agape, open-mouthed, *Inf.* ready and raring, on tiptoe, on pins and needles; excited, aroused, enthusiastic; ready, alert, vigilant, watchful, wakeful, open-eyed.

—adv. **2.** excitedly, eagerly, enthusiastically, keenly, agape, in eager anticipation, with bated breath, on the edge of one's seat; nervously, anxiously, impatiently.

agonize, *v.* **1.** suffer, writhe, bleed, go through hell, be in misery.

2. struggle, wrestle, grapple, fight with; labor, toil, strive, strain, exert oneself, exercise oneself, work on; pour over, worry over, trouble oneself over, lose sleep over, *Sl.* beat one's brains out.

3. torture, excruciate, rack, put someone on the rack, martyr, crucify; pain, hurt, scathe, lacerate, put someone through the wringer; torment, persecute, abuse, beat, *Sl.* work over, *Sl.* give someone the works, *Archaic.* belabor; anguish, distress, grieve, afflict, plague, harrow, rend, worry, trouble, disturb, *Scot.* fash.

agonizing, *adj.* torturous, excruciating, racking, tormenting, abusive; painful, hurtful, scathing, wringing, grievous; woeful, distressing, plaguing, harrowing, rending, troubling, disturbing.

agony, *n.* **1.** suffering, misery, wretchedness, martyrdom; pain, hurt, wound, sting, pang; anguish, distress, woe, harrowment, tribulation, trouble, hell.

2. rapture, ecstasy, raptus, bliss, beatitude; exaltation, elation, transport; paroxysm, throe, spasm, convulsion.

3. struggle, conflict, battle, fight, contest, agon; wrestle, wrestling, grappling.

agrarian, *adj.* **1.** landed, praedial, real.

2. agricultural, geoponic, agronomic, agronomical, pedological.

3. rural, country, nonurban, agrestic; georgic, pastoral, rustic, bucolic.

4. field, pastural, compestral, *Bot.* terrestrial; wild, feral, ferine, uncultivated, undomesticated, untamed.

agree, *v.* **1.** (*often fol. by* with) concur, accord, harmonize, think alike, be of one mind; admit, grant, allow, approve, accept, go along with, *Inf.* take to, *Inf.* cotton to, *Inf.* buy; yield, comply with, abide by, assent, accede, acquiesce, side with, concede, consent; acknowledge, recognize, *Archaic.* agnize, subscribe to, fall in with, *Sl.* string along with.

2. (*often fol. by* to) give consent, yield assent, promise; contract, bargain, compact, covenant, make an agreement; undertake, engage, stipulate for, bind oneself, pledge one's word, give assurance, take upon oneself.

3. (*often fol. by* with) coincide, correspond, conform to, tally, comport, *Inf.* gee, jibe, be in unison, stand, chime in; fit, suit, match, resemble, be appropriate, *Brit. Dial.* fadge; dovetail, square, equal, parallel.

4. compromise, reconcile, arrive at a settlement; come around, come to one mind, come to terms, come to an understanding, see eye to eye.

5. agree with (*usu. of foods or medicine*) suit, prove suitable, be good for; have a beneficial effect, be wholesome for, be healthful for, promote the health of.

agreeable, *adj.* **1.** pleasing, to one's liking, to one's fancy, to one's taste, after one's own heart, *Brit. Dial.* bonny; good, tasty, palatable, delectable, *Inf.* yummy, delicious, luscious; appealing, attractive, comely, handsome, good-looking, beautiful, elegant, graceful.

2. likeable, pleasant, good-natured, *Scot. and North Eng., Irish Eng.* sonsy; enjoyable, pleasurable, gratifying; delightful, charming, nice, sweet; amiable, kind, congenial, *Scot.* couthie, *Ger. gemutlich,* complaisant; amicable, friendly, neighborly, sociable.

3. willing, consenting, disposed, inclined; amenable, submissive, tractable, gentle, yielding, accommodating, gracious, genial, polite, cordial, courteous, mannerly, courtly.

4. suitable, appropriate, fitting, befitting, proper, meet, apt, seemly, becoming; congruous, consistent, compatible, consonant, correspondent, conformable, accordant; concordant, harmonious, pleasant, soothing, dulcet.

agreement, *n.* **1.** mutual understanding, accord, accordance, concord, concordance, concurrence; consensus, unanimity, unison; amity, harmony, communion, sympathy, rapport.

2. compact, contract, promise, word, covenant, treaty, concordat, cartel; deal, pact, bargain; conspiracy, collusion; proposal, stipulation, transaction, arrangement, acknowledgment; guarantee, warranty.

3. similitude, similarity, resemblance; congruence, correspondence, coincidence, symmetry, analogy; coherence, consistency, uniformity; harmony, compatibility; acquiescence, conformity, compliance, abidance; accommodation, adjustment, approval, acceptance, affirmation, corroboration.

agriculture, *n.* **1.** farming, geoponics, agribusiness, *Inf.* agric., *Inf.* ag., husbandry, animal husbandry, stock raising, pasturage; cultivation, tillage, horticulture, gardening, market gardening, *U.S.* truck farming, cropping, crop raising; viticulture, grapegrowing.

2. agronomy, *Inf.* agron., agronomics, pedology, soil science, soil conservation.

agriculturist, *n.* **1.** farmer, granger, husbandman, animal husbandman, *Fr. fermier, Sp. campesino;* cultivator, tiller, horticulturist, gardener, cropper, *U.S.* truck farmer, *Archaic. or Hist.* yeoman; viticulturist, viticulturer, grape grower.

2. agronomist, pedologist, soil scientist, agriculturalist.

aground, *adv., adj.* **1.** grounded, ashore, *Naut.* beached, *Obs.* graveled, stuck fast; shipwrecked, wrecked, cast away, swamped, foundering.

2. stranded, high and dry, deserted, abandoned, left in the lurch; straitened, in straits, in a fix, at a loss.

ague, *n.* chills, fever, chills and fever, malarial fever, *Path.* rigor; chill, chilliness, cold; shivering, shakes, quaking, trembling, tremor.

ahead, *adv.* **1.** in the front, at the head of; to *or* toward the front, in front of, in advance of, before.

2. onward, forward, on.

3. get ahead progress, gain ground, make headway, advance, move up in the world; make it, make good, be successful.

4. ahead of a. in front of, before. See *def.* **1. b.** superior to, outranking, more advanced than, beyond; on, up on, surpassing, outdistancing, outstripping, beating, winning out. **c.** in advance of, earlier than.

aid, *v.* **1.** help, assist, bestead, accommodate,

oblige, abet, befriend; contribute, join in, *Inf.* pitch in, *Inf.* chip in, lend a hand, lend oneself to, play *or* do one's part, boost, give a boost to, give a lift to; (*all usually negative*) lift a finger, lift a hand, raise a finger, raise a hand; (*all usually followed by with*) collaborate, cooperate, conspire, connive, coact, combine, join, unite, synergize, side, go *or* go along, team up, take part, join forces, *Inf.* hitch horses.

2. support, back, second, uphold, maintain, sustain, endorse, smile upon, *Inf.* go to bat for, *Inf.* stick up for, *Inf.* stick by, stand by; promote, further, advance, forward, advocate, cultivate, favor.

3. facilitate, ease, make easier, expedite, cut through red tape; speed, speed up, accelerate, hasten, quicken; intercede, pave the way, clear the way, open the way, run interference for, *Fig.* block for; disburden, disencumber, rid, disembarrass, deobstruct, lighten the load; bolster, elevate, prop up, enhance, tide over, put on one's feet, set up, set going.

4. meliorate, ameliorate, improve, better, profit, prosper, benefit, avail, advantage; subserve, stand in good stead, be useful *or* profitable to, *Inf.* come in handy; relieve, alleviate, mitigate, palliate, salve; comfort, sooth, solace, console, succor.

—*n.* **5.** help, assistance, benefit, avail; service, subvention, use, utility; facilitation, helping hand, lift, boost; relief, succor, protection, care, friendship; support, patronage, championship, backing, promotion, advocacy, countenance, upholding, sustenance, favor, blessing, grace, sponsorship, auspices *or* auspice, good offices, kind regard; fosterage, furtherance, advancement, advance, advantage, welfare; maintenance, ministry, ministration, restoration.

6. gift, subsidy, contribution, donation; kindness, beneficence, benevolence, benefaction, humanitarianism, altruism, philanthropy, charity, almsgiving; alms, dole, handout, allowance.

7. helper, aider, assistant, attendant, subsidiary, adjutant, coadjutant, coadjutor, coadjutress *or* coadjutrix, adjunct, adjuvant, adjutator, *Obs.* adjutor; acolyte, deputy, auxilliary, ancilla; second, man Friday, gal Friday, henchman, right hand, right-hand man, *Sl.* gopher; nurse's aid *or* aide, paramedic, orderly, paraprofessional, paralegal; partner, ally, comrade, colleague, associate, consociate; companion, helpmate, helpmeet, yokefellow *or* yokemate, *Obs.* helpfellow; co-worker, co-aid, co-partner, consort, confrere, sidekick, crony, *Inf.* buddy, *Chiefly Brit.* mate; satellite, sycophant, toady, yes-man, parasite; cooperator, collaborator, contributor, participant, participator; confederate, conniver, abettor, accomplice, accessory *or Chiefly Law.* accessary, *Law.* principal, *Law.* accessory before *or* after the fact, *Law.* particeps criminis, *Sl.* gun moll *or* moll, partner in crime.

8. supporter, advocate, adviser, patron, patronizer; sympathizer, backer, champion, endorser, upholder, sanctioner, approver; follower, partisan, disciple, adherent, devotee, sectary, votary; agent, promoter, furtherer, advancer, favorer; subsidizer, underwriter, financier, funder, angel, *Inf.* staker, *Inf.* grubstaker, *Sl.* meal ticket; maintainer, sustainer, benefactor, benefactress, benefiter, *Inf.* fairy godmother, sugar daddy; comforter, succorer, good Samaritan, ministering angel, friend in need.

aide-de-camp, *n.* attaché, *Mil.* adjutant, adjutant general, deputy, aide, staff *or* subordinate officer, camp assistant, *Chiefly U.S.* aid-de-camp, ADC.

ail, *v.* 1. pain, inflict pain, hurt, wound; bother, annoy, trouble, irritate; upset, worry, disturb; sicken, make [s.o.] ill, afflict, distress; attack, lay hold of, (*of pain, disease, etc.*) affect.

2. ache, hurt, smart, tingle; feel ill, feel awful, be unwell; suffer, agonize, labor under, writhe; be the matter with, be bothered by, be affected with, be in pain, be indisposed; decline, weaken, pine, languish, waste away, lose strength, droop, flag, dwindle, peak.

ailing, *adj.* **1.** sick, sickly, sickened, ill; unhealthy, unsound, unwell; diseased, morbid, pathological, poisoned; in a bad way, on the sick list, done for, on the shelf; out of sorts, under the weather, not up to snuff; aching, sore, pained, smarting, hurt, wounded; suffering, agonizing, miserable, down, complaining; delicate, faint, languishing, fading away, wasting away; weak, weakly, feeble, infirm; crippled, lame, paralytic, paralyzed, palsied; asthmatic, *Path.* phthisic, consumptive, tubercular.

2. indisposed, laid up, bedridden, confined; disordered, out of order, out of commission; invalided, valetudinarian.

3. afflicted, distressed, (*of pain, disease, etc.*) affected; bothered, annoyed, troubled, irritated; upset, worried, disturbed.

ailment, *n.* illness, sickness, indisposition, affliction; malady, disorder, complaint, disease, infection, morbidity, *Path.* affection; invalidism, valetudinarianism; weakness, feebleness, infirmity; pain, hurt, wound; disability, handicap; mental disorder, derangement, neurosis, psychosis, insanity.

aim, *v.* **1.** point, direct, draw *or* get a bead on, sight, focus, zero in on, beam, prepare to fire; position, mark, peg, level, train.

2. plan, design, propose, purpose, resolve; intend, tend toward, have in mind, have in view, mean.

3. strive toward, struggle toward, drive at, work toward, labor for; steer for, head for, be after, look after, seek; set one's sights, have an eye to, aspire to, head for, affect, hitch one's wagon to a star; endeavor, essay, attempt to reach, seek; want, wish, desire, crave; long for, yearn for.

—*n.* **4.** pointing, directing, sighting, focussing, beaming; positioning, marking, pegging, leveling, training.

5. target, mark, bull's-eye, destination.

6. goal, ambition; objective, object, end, determination; purpose, intention, intent, view, point, reason, resolution; design, scheme, plan; hope, dream, wish, desire, desideratum, aspiration; endeavor, undertaking, attempt, effort.

7. inclination, proclivity, tendency, drive, drift, bent; course, direction, bearing.

aimless, *adj.* **1.** purposeless, objectless, pointless, futile, inane, fatuous, to no avail; undirected, rudderless, blind; haphazard, accidental, hit *or* miss; random, chance, fortuitous, uncalculated, uncalculating.

2. drifting, wandering, stray, straying; unmotivated, uninspired, uninvolved; whimsical, capricious, flighty, frivolous; mercurial, volatile; reckless, careless, wanton.

3. erratic, fitful, desultory, unpredictable; irresolute, indecisive, undecided, unreasoning, unsure, vacillating; irregular, unsteady, wayward, inconstant; changeable, variable, mutable.

air, *n.* **1.** atmosphere, sky, aerospace, heavens, *Literary.* welkin, the open; ozone, oxygen, ether; breeze, zephyr, whiff, light wind, puff of wind, draft, ventilation.

2. circulation, dissemination, publication, *Archaic.* divulgation; revelation, publicity, exposure, vent, outlet.

3. climate, feel, aura, impression; appearance, demeanor, mien, semblance, cast, look, complexion, aspect, character; presence, attitude, style, bearing, carriage, deportment, conduct.

4. airs affectedness, posing, frills, pretense, pretension, *Inf.* swank; superciliousness, haughtiness, arrogance, pomposity.

5. **Music.** tune, melody, aria, song, descant, lay, ballad, carol; ditty, canzonet, cavatina, arietta; strain, theme.

6. **give [s.o.] the air** **a.** reject, turn down, refuse, rebuff, spurn. **b.** dismiss, discharge, fire, expel, oust.

7. **tread** *or* **walk on air** be elated, be happy, be exuberant, be exultant.

8. **up in the air** **a.** undecided, unsettled, unresolved, pending, indefinite. **b.** *Inf.* angry, perturbed, vexed.

—*v.* **9.** aerate, aerify, ventilate, oxygenate, fan, winnow; refresh, revivify, cool, freshen, purify.

10. display, exhibit, parade, flaunt; show off, vaunt, swagger.

11. publish, publicize, make public, disseminate, reveal, expose, *Archaic.* divulgate, vent; broadcast, televise.

aircraft, *n.* airplane, plane, glider, *Sl.* prop, jet, supersonic transport, SST, *Trademark.* Lear jet, *Trademark.* 747; helicopter, *Inf.* copter, *Sl.* bird, *Inf.* whirlybird, *Inf.* chopper, *Sl.* egg-beater; blimp, airship, dirigible, zeppelin; spaceship, rocket, sputnik, satellite.

airily, *adv.* **1.** breezily, lightheartedly, blithely, spritely, jauntily, lively; gaily, cheerfully, buoyantly, happily, gladly.

2. lightly, delicately, ethereally, daintily.

airiness, *n.* **1.** immateriality, incorporeality, bodilessness; unsubstantiality, tenuousness, illusoriness, unreality; ethereality, weightlessness, lightness, buoyancy.

2. delicacy, flimsiness, thinness; gauziness, diaphaneity, sheerness, transparency, limpidity, translucency, pellucidity.

3. liveliness, vivacity, sprightliness, jauntiness; breeziness, lightheartedness, levity, blithesomeness, gladsomeness, cheeriness, gaiety; joviality, jocundity, frivolity, flippancy, insouciance.

4. gracefulness, grace, light-footedness, nimbleness; agility, litheness, lissomness, suppleness, flexibility, pliancy.

airing, *n.* **1.** ventilation, aeration, aerification, fanning.

2. outing, promenade, walk, constitutional; jaunt, stroll, saunter, ramble; trek, hike, tramp, peregrination, wayfaring; excursion, drive, ride, motoring tour, circuit, turn.

3. circulation, dissemination, public exposure, publicity, *Archaic.* divulgation, showing, display, exhibition.

airplane, *n.* See **aircraft.**

airport, *n.* airfield, aerodrome, airdrome, airstation, hangar; field, runway, *Aeron.* airstrip.

airtight, *adj.* **1.** closed, shut tight, sealed, vacuum, impermeable.

2. indisputable, incontestable, incontrovertible, irrefutable, undeniable, irrefragable; impregnable, inexpugnable, unassailable, invincible.

airy, *adj.* **1.** breezy, windy, drafty; ventilated, open, exposed, alfresco.

2. immaterial, incorporeal, bodiless, weightless; unsubstantial, ethereal, tenuous; illusory, unreal, imaginary, visionary, phantasmal, spectral.

3. delicate, flimsy, thin; gauzy, diaphanous, sheer, gossamer, transparent, limpid, translucent, pellucid.

4. lively, animated, vivacious, sprightly, perky, jaunty; lighthearted, blithe, gladsome, cheerful, buoyant, gay; jovial, jolly, merry, sportive, jocund.

5. graceful, light-footed, nimble; agile, lithe, lissom, supple, flexible, pliant.

aisle, *n.* **1.** passageway, gangway, walkway, walk; corridor, alley, alleyway, lane, path; row, tier, section, box.

2. **in the aisle** (*of an audience, in reference to laughter*) convulsed, doubled up *or* over, hysterical, crying, splitting one's side, rolling in the aisle, *Sl.* splitting *or* busting a gut, *Sl.* wetting one's pants; roaring, guffawing.

ajar[1] *adj., adv.* partly open, open; unlatched, unclosed, unsecured.

ajar[2] *adj., adv.* at variance, in contradiction, incongruous, clashing, grating, discordant, inharmonious; *Inf.* out of kilter, *Sl.* out of whack, amiss.

akimbo, *adj., adv.* hand-on-hip; tilted, raised, angular, oblique, bent, crooked; askew, aslant, twisted, skewed, out of line.

akin, *adj.* **1.** related, cognate, consanguineous, kin, german, agnate, of one's own flesh and blood.

2. allied, similar, alike, like; analogous, parallel, correlative, corresponding, homologous, matching; germane, relevant, connected, associated, collateral.

3. kindred, of the same kind, homogeneous; cut from the same cloth, out of the same mold, in the same category; brothers under the skin.

alacrity, *n.* **1.** promptness, promptitude, willingness, readiness; eagerness, zeal, enthusiasm, avidity; swiftness, quickness, dispatch, expedition; haste, speed, celerity.

2. liveliness, briskness, sprightliness; animation, vivacity, vigor; effervescence, ebullience, vim; spiritedness, go, *Inf.* snap, get up, and go; cheerfulness, gaiety, glee, mirth, high spirits.

à la mode, fashionable, stylish, modish, popular, latest; chic, smart, all the go, all the rage; in fashion, in vogue, in style, in; rage, craze, fad, go; the thing, the latest thing, *Fr. dernier cri.*

alarm, *n.* **1.** fear, fright, scare, terror, affright, *Inf.* funk, panic, horror, dread; apprehension, consternation, dismay, trepidation, disquiet, discomfort, perturbation, misgiving, timidity, solicitude, concern, uneasiness.

2. hue and cry, war cry, call to arms, summons to arms, sound of trumpet, beat of drum.

3. alarm bell, siren, whistle, horn, warning *or* alarm gun, tocsin, alert, *Archaic.* alarum; signal light, red light, danger signal, cry of distress, SOS, May Day.

—*v.* **4.** frighten, scare, distress, terrify, affright, appall; shock, panic, throw into panic, startle, dismay, terrorize, intimidate, unnerve, daunt, consternate, disturb, agitate.

5. warn, alert, arouse, rouse, signal; sound an alarm, set off an alarm, ring a warning bell, send up a flare, *Inf.* blow out of bed; put on the alert, call to arms, summon to arms, call out the army, call out the troops, ring the tocsin.

alarmed, *adj.* fearful, afraid, frightened, scared; startled, terrified, affrighted, appalled, haunted with fear, shocked, panicky, thrown into panic; horrified, full of dread, apprehensive, anxious, full of trepidation, concerned; consternated, dismayed, distressed, troubled, disquieted, uneasy, unnerved, discomforted, disconcerted, disturbed; perturbed, full of misgivings, distrustful, suspicious; aroused, agitated, nervous, intimidated, daunted, timid, timorous, faint-hearted; aware, wary, alert, vigilant, watchful.

alarming, *adj.* dreadful, terrible, grievous, dire; threatening, hazardous, dangerous, perilous; terrifying, frightful, direful, appalling, ominous, portentous; disturbing, distressing, harrowing, rending; redoubtable, fearsome, fearful, formidable, awful; horrible, horrid, horrendous, monstrous; hideous, ghastly, eerie, grisly, gruesome, unspeakable; outrageous, shocking, amazing, startling, surprising.

alarmist, *n.* scaremonger, Cassandra, voice of doom, *Sl.* Chicken Little, croaker; worrywart, pessimist, gloom and doomer.

albeit, *conj.* although, even though, though, even if, notwithstanding that, in spite of the fact that.

album, *n.* **1.** portfolio, book, folder, scrapbook, memory book; file, depository, storage, record-keeper, organizer; compilation, catalog, collection, grouping.

2. record, phonograph record, recording, long-playing record, *Trademark.* LP, soundtrack, disk, disc, wax; cover, jacket, envelope, sheath, casing, case, binder, binding.

3. register, registry, guest book, sign-in book, autograph book, notebook; list, record, documentation, chronicle.

alchemy, *n.* magic, sorcery, witchcraft, witchery, wizardry; wonder-working, miracle-working, thaumaturgy; black magic, black art, voodoo.

alcohol, *n.* liquor, spirits, John Barleycorn, the demon rum, *Inf.* booze, *Inf.* hard stuff, *Sl.* likker, *Sl.* hooch, *Sl.* sauce, *Sl.* juice, *Sl.* medicine; moonshine, home brew, *Sl.* sneaky pete; firewater, *Sl.* red-eye, *Sl.* rot-gut, *Sl.* blue-ruin, *Sl.* mountain dew, *Sl.* white lightning; the bottle, the cup, the cup that cheers.

alcoholic, *adj.* **1.** intoxicating, intoxicant, *Archaic.* intoxicative, inebriant, inebriating, inebriative.

—n. **2.** *Pathology.* dipsomaniac, chronic alcoholic *or* drunk.

3. drunk, drunkard, inebriate, sot, soak, tosspot, toper, bibber, bibbler, *Obs., Rare.* biberon, barfly; drinker, hard drinker, serious drinker, problem drinker; *All Inf.* guzzler, swiller, soaker, sponge, lovepot; *All Sl.* boozer, boozehound, lush, souse, rummy, wino, alchy, dipso, juicer, juice-head, hooch hound, gin hound, swillbelly, swillpot, stew, stewbum, elbow-bender, elbow-crooker.

alcoholism, *n.* **1.** *Path.* dipsomania, crapulence, crapulousness, problem *or* heavy drinking, serious drinking, habitual *or* chronic drunkenness, chronic *or* acute alcoholism.

2. intoxication, insobriety, inebriety, inebriation, drunkenness, intemperance, *Inf.* tipsiness; drinking, imbibing, tippling, heavy drinking, toping, *Inf.* boozing, *Sl.* hitting the bottle *or* sauce *or* booze. *Brit. Sl.* bevying.

alcove, *n.* **1.** niche, nook, corner, cubbyhole, cubby; compartment, cubicle, stall, booth, carrel; grotto, cave, cavern, cove, *Chiefly Literary.* grot; recess, hollow, cavity, bay, indentation, concavity.

2. retreat, refuge, haven, shelter, burrow, hermitage; asylum, resort, sanctuary, sanctum sanctorum, ark, covert, hideaway, mew.

alembic, *n.* **1.** still, beaked vessel, *Metallurgy.* retort, crucible; cruet, beaker, carafe.

2. transformer, converter, refiner, purifier, distiller.

3. elixir, philosopher's stone, magic wand, magic potion, magic ingredient; magic formula, abracadabra, open sesame; magic answer, panacea, solution, missing link.

alert, *adj.* **1.** wide-awake, aware, *Inf.* heads-up, *Inf.* on the ball, *Inf.* on the stick, *Inf.* on one's toes; astir, up and about, up and doing, bright and early; smart, bright, sharp, keen, quick, *Inf.* quick on the trigger.

2. vigilant, watchful, Argus-eyed, attentive, on the qui vive; on the watch, on the alert, on the lookout; guarded, on guard, in readiness, prepared.

3. heedful, mindful, careful, cautious, wary, chary; precautious, circumspect, prudent, discreet.

4. swift, quick, speedy, rapid, fast, fleet; agile, nimble, spry, brisk, sprightly; lively, alive, vivacious, animated, spirited, frisky, active.

—n. **5.** vigilance, caution. See **alertness** (*def.* **1**).

6. alarm, *Archaic.* alarum, tocsin, siren, whistle, warning signal, warning; air raid drill, blackout, civil defense drill.

alertness, *n.* **1.** vigilance, watchfulness, wakefulness; caution, heedfulness, wariness; attention, lookout, guardedness; circumspection, precaution, prudence, discretion.

2. dispatch, alacrity, expedition, promptness, promptitude; celerity, quickness, haste, speed.

3. liveliness, sprightliness, friskiness, activity; animation, spirit, vivacity; nimbleness, agility, spryness, briskness.

alias, *n.* **1.** pseudonym, anonym, false name; assumed name, stage name, pen name, nom de plume, *Fr. nom de guerre,* allonym; nickname, sobriquet.

—adv. **2.** otherwise called, *Latin. alius dictus,* also called, also known as, a/k/a; otherwise, in other circumstances, elsewhere, in another place; at another time, previously, heretofore, formerly.

alibi, *n.* **1.** defense, plea, argument, apology, vindication, justification; excuse, reason, explanation.

2. *U.S. Informal.* cover-up, pretext, subterfuge, *Inf.* story, *Inf.* line, cock-and-bull story.

alien, *n.* **1.** foreigner, outsider, stranger, unnaturalized citizen; outlander, tramontane, barbarian; newcomer, immigrant, emigrant, *Often Disparaging.* wetback.

—adj. **2.** foreign, unnaturalized; tramontane, transmontane, ultramontane, transalpine, barbarian; ultramarine, transmarine, transatlantic, transpacific; exotic, strange, outlandish; distant, remote, faraway; nonterrestrial, unearthly, ultramundane.

3. adverse, hostile, opposed, inimical, antagonistic; conflicting, contrasting, contradictory, counteracting, contrary, opposite; unlike, dissimilar, differing; extrinsic, adventitious, outward, external.

alienate, *v.* **1.** estrange, turn away, keep at a distance, withdraw, wean away; make indifferent *or* averse, set against, oppose; separate, come between, divide, cut off *or* apart, sever, sunder, rupture; break up *or* off, part, disunite, disjoin.

2. turn away, transfer, divert, deflect.

alienated, *adj.* **1.** estranged, cut off, separated, divorced, disconnected, disengaged, disaffected; detached; segregated, shut out, shut off, sequestered, isolated; neglected, ignored, overlooked, disregarded, left behind; alone, solitary, separate, solo, friendless, companionless, rootless, homeless; uninvited, unaccompanied, unattended, unincluded.

2. self-contained, self-reliant, insular; private, guarded, cautious, noncommittal; secretive, close-mouthed, tight-lipped, buttoned-up, mum; withdrawn, detached, uncommunicative, taciturn, untalkative; undemonstrative, unresponsive, cool, cold, icy.

3. dissenting, disagreeing, opposed, clashing, conflicting, contradicting; nonconforming, revolutionary, radical, anarchic; hostile, resentful, revengeful, antagonistic, bellicose, belligerent.

alienation, *n.* estrangement, disaffection, coolness, turning away, withdrawal; separation, division, break, breach, rupture, sunderance, severance; breaking up *or* off, parting, disunion, disjunction.

alight[1], *v.* **1.** get off, disembark, debark, deplane, detrain, debus; pile off, pile out.

2. land, touch down, settle down, light upon, pitch

upon, descend upon, drop down on, come to rest upon; perch, lodge, settle, settle on, descend and settle.

3. chance upon, happen upon, hit upon, strike upon, come upon, fall upon, blunder upon, stumble over, come across, run across.

alight[2], *adj.* **1.** lighted, lit, bright, shining, illuminated, well-lighted; radiant, lambent, resplendent, brilliant, dazzling, ablaze, aflame, afire; fulgent, effulgent, refulgent; lustrous, lucid, lucent, *Rare.* relucent; glowing, aglow, luminescent, luminiferous, incandescent, phosphorescent; sparkling, glittering, twinkling, shimmering; glimmering, glistening, *Archaic.* glistering; gleaming, glaring, rutilant, fulgid; flashing, flickering.

align, *v.* **1.** straighten, collinate, parallel, range, rank, line up; adjust, arrange, regulate, sight, even, match up, fine-tune, calibrate; get in line, fall in, get in order.

2. *Usu.* **align with** affiliate, associate, ally, join; become one of, cast one's lot with, go along with, *Sl.* string along with; sympathize, believe in, have faith *or* confidence in; advocate, support, back, countenance, favor.

alike, *adv.* **1.** similarly, equally, in common; just the same, all the same, the same, in like manner, as one.

—adj. **2.** similar, akin, like, kindred, related, allied; correspondent, responding, resemblant, resembling, homologous; analogous, comparable, conformable; correlative, complementary, parallel, agreeing; synonymous, paronymous, cognate; equivalent, tantamount, equal, corresponding, matching; same, uniform, interchangeable; congeneric, consanguineous, homogeneous, consubstantial.

aliment, *n.* **1.** food, nourishment, nutriment, nurture; victuals, vittles, comestibles, eatables, edibles; commons, *Inf.* grub, *Sl.* eats, *Sl.* chow; bread, manna, staff of life, meat, viands, foodstuff; diet, fare, regimen; cheer, rations, provisions; repast, meal, board, keep; fodder, feed, forage, provender, pabulum; pasturage, pasture, herbage; pap, cereal, *Trademark.* Pablum.

2. sustenance, subsistence, alimentation, sustenation; support, maintenance, *Law.* necessaries; livelihood, living, *Inf.* bread and butter.

alimentary, *adj.* **1.** nourishing, nutritive, nutritious, wholesome; salutary, salubrious, healthful, good; sustenative, supportive, strengthening; eutrophic, eupeptic; digestive, peptic.

2. comestible, gustable, gustatory, alimental; eatable, edible, esculent, digestible; dietetic, dietary.

alimentation, *n.* food, nourishment, nutriment; sustenance, maintenance, support. See **aliment.**

alimony, *n.* **1.** *Law.* allowance, support payment, divorce settlement, child support.

2. maintenance, livelihood, keep, support, means; sustenance, subsistence, sustenation, aliment.

alive, *adj.* **1.** living, live, animate, breathing, respiring, undeceased, unexpired, unextinguished, alive and kicking, this side of the grave, above ground, with us, here, *Archaic.* quick; under the sun, on the face of the earth, in the world; corporeal, incarnate, embodied, bodily, fleshly, in the flesh, physical, palpable, tangible, material, substantial.

2. extant, existent, existing, in existence, unextinct; about, happening, going, going on, in the air *or* wind, prevalent.

3. operative, in operation *or* motion, effective, in effect *or* force, functioning, working, acting.

4. active, vigorous, robust, energetic, strenuous, dynamic, busy; astir, stirring, bustling, moving; lively, full of life, vital, vibrant; spirited, animated, brisk, frisky, sprightly, spry, *Inf.* peppy, *Inf.* snappy.

5. vivacious, vivified, effervescent, effervescing, bubbling, sparkling, breezy; vivid, viable, life-like, real, actual; stimulating, exciting.

6. **alive with** (all followed by with *or* of) swarming, thronged, crowded, stuffed, gorged, crammed; cloyed, glutted, surfeit, satiated, sated, overrun, overflowing; rife, teeming, abounding, abundant, rich; replete, filled, full.

all, *adj.* **1.** entire, whole, total, integral, the sum of, complete, full; every, each, each and every; any, any whatever, any and every; only, nothing but, nothing except.

—n. **2.** whole, total, aggregate, sum, sum total, entirety, integer; allness, comprehensiveness, universality; totality, everything, everyone, everybody.

3. (*often cap.*). universe, cosmos, macrocosm.

4. **after all** finally, at last, in the end, eventually, ultimately; nevertheless, notwithstanding, anyway.

5. **once and for all** finally, for the last time, at last, ultimately, at the last moment.

—adv. **6.** wholly, entirely, completely, altogether, quite, very, exceedingly; only, exclusively, solely, alone; each, apiece, to a man.

all-around, *adj.* **1.** versatile, many-faceted, adaptable, all-round; unspecialized, generalist.

2. inclusive, complete, out-and-out, thoroughgoing, thorough.

3. all-inclusive, comprehensive, blanket, umbrella, *Inf.* wall-to-wall.

allay, *v.* **1.** calm, lull, put to rest; quiet, still, silence, hush; soften, assuage, mollify, smooth over; soothe, compose, tranquilize, pacify, appease, *Sl.* simmer down; quell, lay, check, curb, suppress, repress.

2. lessen, relieve, moderate, temper, blunt, dull, slake, quench; lighten, ease, slacken, reduce, diminish; mitigate, alleviate, palliate.

allegation, *n.* **1.** affirmation, assertion, asservation, averment, avowal, avouchment, positive declaration, predication; testimony, attestation, certification; profession, imputation, insinuation, implication.

2. statement, sworn statement, deposition, affidavit, statement of facts.

3. accusation, charge, claim, complaint, bill of complaint; false claim, false witness, trumped-up charge, *Sl.* put-up job, *Sl.* frame up *or* frame.

allege, *v.* **1.** affirm, assert, asservate, aver, avow, avouch; state, declare, predicate, lay down; insist, maintain, contend, hold.

2. attest, testify, certify, vouch; depose, bear witness, give evidence, give one's word, warrant.

3. (*all without proof*) profess, claim, purport, pretend; impute, insinuate, imply; cite, name, attribute, assign, ascribe, *Sl.* finger *or* put the finger on.

4. adduce, advance, bring forward, produce, introduce, present, plead; offer, propose.

alleged, *adj.* **1.** asserted, asservated, averred, affirmed; stated, declared, predicated, announced, enunciated.

2. doubtful, dubious, unlikely, suspect, suspicious; supposed, assumed, presumed, reputed, inferred; professed, claimed, purported, avowed, pretended, so-called, in name only.

allegiance, *n.* loyalty, fidelity, faithfulness, *Archaic.* troth, constancy; devotion, homage, fealty, adherence, duty, obligation; obedience, compliance, deference, subservience, submission, subjugation.

allegorical, *adj.* figurative, not literal, metaphorical, tropical; representative, typical, significative, symbolic, emblematic, symbolizing, standing for.

allegorize, *v.* represent, stand for, symbolize, typify; shadow forth, image forth.

allegory, *n.* **1.** parable, fable, apologue, tale, story, illustration; fiction, fantasy, myth.

2. comparison, analogy, simile, metaphor, *Rhet.* parabole, *Rhet.* figure of speech, *Rhet.* trope, *Rhet.* image.

allergy, *n.* **1.** hypersensitivity, sensitivity; susceptibility, susceptibleness, susceptivity; vulnerability, weakness.

2. *Informal.* antipathy, natural aversion, incompatibility, personality clash *or* conflict; repugnance, revulsion, abhorrence, detestation; antagonism, hostility, animosity.

alleviate, *v.* mitigate, reduce, diminish, lessen, weaken; abate, let up, slacken, remit, relax; allay, assuage, *Rare.* lenify, palliate; appease, soothe, *Archaic.* attemper, relieve, ease, soften, cushion, mollify, lighten; smooth, calm, compose, tranquilize, still, quiet, lull; solace, console, succor, remedy; quell, slake, deaden, dull, blunt, take the edge off of; smother, check, curb, tame, subdue; moderate, temper, modify, qualify.

alleviation, *n.* assuagement, palliation, appeasement; soothing, relief, easing, easement; softening, cushioning, mollification, lightening; smoothing, calming, composing, tranquilizing, sedation, lulling; mitigation, abatement, remission; reduction, diminution, lessening, slackening, weakening, relaxation; subduing, subdual, slaking, deadening, dulling, blunting; tempering, moderating, moderation, qualifying; bettering, improvement, amelioration.

alley, *n.* back street, byway, lane, road, dirt road, dead-end; footway, footpath, walk, walkway, promenade, mall; path, aisle, corridor, passageway, passage.

alliance, *n.* **1.** coalition, entente, union, league, bloc, bund, federation, federacy, confederation, confederacy; partnership, co-partnership, affiliation; industry, enterprise, business, business establishment, commercial enterprise, concern, firm, company, house; corporation, incorporation, conglomerate, trust, syndicate, cartel, consortium, combine, machine, *Sl.* plunderbund; junction, fusion, combination, merger, merging; association, society, guild; pool, cooperative, cooperation, co-op; council, junta, conclave, assembly, convention, diet; faction, party, splinter group, ring, group, *Inf.* push, *Inf.* crew, *Inf.* gang.

2. marriage, matrimony *or* holy matrimony, bonds of matrimony, wedlock *or* holy wedlock, matrimonial union, marriage sacrament, sacrament of matrimony, wedding knot; mixed marriage, interfaith marriage, interracial marriage; intermarriage; kinship, nuptial tie *or* bind *or* knot, conjugal tie *or* bind *or* knot, connubial tie *or* bind *or* knot, marriage relationship, marital affinity, marriage *or* family connection.

3. pact, compact, treaty, covenant, concordat, contract, formal agreement; settlement, arrangement, understanding, cordial understanding, agreement, gentleman's agreement, deal, bargain, transaction.

4. affinity, affiliation, similarity, similitude, resemblance, correlation, relation, parallel, concurrence, correspondence; equivalence, parity, analogy, homogeneity, homology.

allied, *adj.* **1.** confederate, confederated, leagued, federate, federal, federated; joined, united, bound, connected, associated, organized, unionized; merged, combined, amalgamated, corporate, corporated, incorporated, syndicated, syndical, cooperative, cooperating, in cooperation.

2. related, kindred, akin, cognate, congeneric *or* congenerous; analogous, correlative, correlate, correlated, correlating, correspondent, corresponding, comparable, similar, resemblant, resembling, coordinated; equivalent, same, like, alike, of a piece, homogeneous, homologous, parallel, identical.

all-inclusive, *adj.* comprehensive, extensive, all-embracing, blanket, umbrella; full, total, complete, thorough; exhaustive, far-reaching, widespread, wholesale.

allocate, *v.* set apart, appropriate, designate, earmark, intend, specify; allot, apportion, divide up; assign, distribute, disperse, ration, mete out.

allocation, *n.* appropriation, allowance, grant, budget; apportionment, portion, share, ration; quota, stint, lot.

allot, *v.* **1.** parcel out, apportion, share, divide up, *Sl.* divy up, partition; distribute, dispense, dole out.

2. assign, hand over, render; grant, give, bestow, present; bequeath, leave, will.

3. appropriate, set apart, allocate, appoint; earmark, designate, design, intend, specify.

allotment, *n.* **1.** share, lot, part, portion; percentage, measure, quota, stint; apportionment, partition, division.

2. appropriation, allocation, allowance, grant, budget; dispensation, donation, ration, pittance, dole, handout.

all-out, *adj.* **1.** total, complete, thorough, thoroughgoing, exhaustive, unqualified, no-holds-barred.

2. vigorous, energetic, powerful, mighty; determined, resolute, decided; enthusiastic, ardent, fervent, keen.

allow, *v.* **1.** permit, give permission *or* leave to, let; authorize, approve of, go along with, give the green light, give the go-ahead; tolerate, put up with, bear, suffer, stand, brook, abide, endure; hear of, support, sanction, *Inf.* stand for.

2. grant, give, let have, accord; allot, allocate, ration, dole out, dispense; offer, donate, contribute; provide, endow, furnish, supply; bestow, confer, vouchsafe, impart, award, present.

3. admit, acknowledge, concede, acquiesce in, yield, cede; accede to, agree to, assent to, consent to, submit to, comply with, adhere to, conform to.

4. set apart, put aside, arrange for, plan for; consider, take into consideration, take into account, keep in mind, regard; provide for, make provision *or* concessions *or* allowances for.

allowable, *adj.* **1.** permissible, admissible, acceptable, all right; unforbidden, unprohibited; acknowledgeable, concessible, grantable; authorizable, warrantable, approvable, sanctionable; justifiable, vindicable, venial, excusable, pardonable.

2. legitimate, *Sl.* legit, lawful, legal, legalized, within bounds, *Inf.* kosher; proper, right, appropriate, apt, suitable, *Inf.* O.K.

allowance, *n.* **1.** amount, share, allotment, portion; given quantity, quota, ration, rate, stint.

2. grant, fellowship, scholarship, assistantship, stipend.

3. salary, pay, wages, hire, commission, sum, pittance, pin *or* pocket money; percentage, quarterage, expense account, viaticum; remittance, recompense, reward, renumeration; gratuity, tip, fee, douceur; annuity, pension, *Law.* alimony, maintenance; subsidy, subvention, subscription; aid, support, relief, help, dole, handout, alms.

4. endowment, contribution, donation; benefit, boon, benefaction, bestowal, bestowment; present, gift, *Fr. cadeau,* award, tribute, honorarium; offering, favor, largess, bounty.

5. addition, increase, margin, qualification, modification, limitation, restriction; discount, decrease, deduction, reduction, rebate, abatement.

6. acknowledgement, concession, consent, granting; assent, accedence, acquiescence; agreement, approval, concurrence; admitting, admittance, recognition.

7. sanction, sanctioning, tolerance, sufferance, brooking, abidance, endurance; support; authorization, authority, approval, countenance, approbation, going along with; permission, leave, consent, assent, *Law.* connivance; license, permit.

—*v.* **8.** diet, regulate, restrict, select, limit; allocate, ration, stint, allot, dole out, dispense.

alloy, *n.* **1.** compound, composite, hybrid, mongrel, amalgam; mixture, mix, combine, fusion, blend, coalescence, union, *Bot.* homogeny, *Archaic.* crasis; consolidation, conglomerate, agglomerate, aggregate; pinchbeck, sham, counterfeit, fake, imitation, synthetic.

2. admixture, commixture, minglement, interminglement; combination, conglomeration, agglomeration, aggregation, *Chem.* levigation; adulteration, debasement, pollution, contamination, vitiation.

3. karat, pureness, purity, fineness, quality; standard, grade, degree, level, criterion.

4. impurity, foreign *or* alien substance, pollutant, polluter, contaminant, debaser, vitiator.

—*v.* **5.** compound, admix, commix, mix, *Chem.* levigate; combine, interfuse, fuse, conjoin, incorporate, unite, unify, coalesce, merge; conglomerate, agglomerate, amalgamate, blend, homogenize, *Archaic.* temper; commingle, mingle, intermingle, intermix; synthesize, consolidate, compose, put together.

6. adulterate, debase, pollute, contaminate, vitiate; downgrade, depreciate, cheapen, lower in value; deteriorate, ruin, impair, harm.

all right, *adj.* **1.** safe, secure, whole, complete, unharmed, unhurt, uninjured, unimpaired, unbroken; sound, healthy, well, hale.

2. satisfactory, acceptable, allowable, permissible; warrantable, approvable, sanctionable, fine, *Inf.* okey-dokey, *Inf.* okle-dokle, *Inf.* O.K., *Inf.* kosher, *Sl.* hunky-dory, *Sl.* hunky.

—*adv.* **3.** yes, okay, very well, if you wish, why not?

4. satisfactorily, well, adequately, sufficiently, well enough, up to par; acceptably, admissibly, suitably, appropriately, aptly, properly, correctly.

5. certainly, assuredly, for sure, without a doubt, without fail.

allude, *v.* **1.** mention, mention in passing, touch upon; cite, refer to, advert to, point to, make an allusion to, *Dial.* signify.

2. hint, suggest, adumbrate; imply, implicate, intimate, insinuate, infer.

allure, *v.* entice, lure, bait, intrigue, beguile, inveigle; tempt, tantalize, seduce, ensorcell, bewitch, enchant; captivate, fascinate, charm, spellbind; entrance, enrapture, transport, enravish, transfix; titillate, tickle, interest, delight; arouse, rouse, incite, whet, stimulate; induce, persuade, prevail upon, bribe, suborn; attract, appeal, draw, magnetize, hypnotize, sway, mesmerize.

allurement, *n.* **1.** charm, magnetism, appeal, attraction; fascination, enchantment, entrancement, bewitchery, bewitchment; captivation, seduction, seducement, ensnarement, entrapment.

2. temptation, enticement, lurement, beguilement, tantalization, teasing, baiting.

alluring, *adj.* **1.** tempting, enticing, seductive, beguiling, tantalizing; inviting, stimulating, exciting, arousing; sensuous, *Inf.* sexy, voluptuous, beautiful.

2. fascinating, charming, engaging, winning, winsome, magnetic, appealing, attractive; enchanting, entrancing, bewitching, captivating, enrapturing, ravishing, irresistible.

allusion, *n.* casual reference, citation, quotation; hint, suggestion, intimation, inference.

allusive, *adj.* referential, indicative, inferential, suggestive, allusory.

ally, *v.* **1.** confederate, league, unite, unionize, unify, conjoin, join with, join forces *or* hands, band together, team up, *Inf.* gang up, side with, go *or* go along with, take part, *Inf.* hitch horses; join, combine, couple, yoke, pair, join together, bind together; wed, marry.

2. associate, interassociate, identify, relate, interrelate, correlate *or* corelate, parallel, draw a parallel; connect, interconnect, link, interlink, equate, tie.

—*n.* **3.** confederate, partner, comrade, comrade in arms, associate, consociate, socius, yokefellow *or* yokemate, companion, helpmate, helpmeet, *Obs.* helpfellow, co-worker, co-aid, co-partner, consort, confrere, sidekick, friend, *Chiefly Brit.* mate; conspirator, fellow conspirator, conspirer, conniver, abettor, accomplice, accessory *or Chiefly Law.* accessary, partner in crime, *Sl.* gun moll *or* moll; collaborator, cooperator, contributor, participant, participator; (*all of nations*) satellite, captive nation, puppet government *or* regime.

4. analogue, correspondent, coordinate, correlative, correlate, compliment, companion, mate, equivalent; relative, kin, fellow; twin, mirror image, duplicate *or* exact duplicate, close match, close imitation, reproduction, facsimile, copy, replica.

5. helper, aid *or* aide, attendant, acolyte, deputy, subsidiary, adjutant, coadjutant, coadjutor, coadjutress *or* coadjutrix, adjunct, adjuvant, adjutator, *Obs.* adjutor, auxiliary, ancilla, second, man Friday, henchman, right hand, right-hand man.

almanac, *n.* yearbook, calendar, register, registry, annual, annals, *Archaic.* annal; astronomical table, ephemeris.

almighty, *adj.* **1.** omnipotent, all-powerful, plenipotent; overpowering, overwhelming, overmastering, subduing, controlling; powerful, *Literary.* puissant, potent; dominant, predominant, commanding, forcible, telling; despotic, autocratic, dictatorial, lordly, masterful; authoritative, influential.

2. *Informal.* extreme, excessive, great, enormous; terrible, awful, bad.

—*n.* **3.** **the Almighty.** God, the Supreme Being, God Almighty; Supreme Goodness, Most High, Divine Being, the Deity, Divinity, Providence, the Godhead, Jehovah, Yahweh; God the Father, Divine Father, Father, Lord, Lord of lords, King of kings, King of glory; Creator, Author of all things, the Maker, the Maker of Heaven and Earth, the First Cause, the Light of the World; Ruler of Heaven and Earth, Sovereign of the Universe; the All-Powerful, the Omnipotent, the Omniscient, the All-knowing, the All-merciful, the All-wise; the Infinite, the Eternal, the Absolute.

almost, *adv.* virtually, as good as, *Inf.* just about, *Inf.* most; all but, for the most part, not quite, a little short of, barely, hardly, scarcely; nearly, near, next to, well-nigh, nigh, nigh upon *or* onto; close to, within an inch of, *Inf.* within an ace of, within a stone's throw, in the neighborhood *or* vicinity of; nearing, approaching, toward, verging on, on the brink *or* verge of, bordering on.

alms, *n.* **1.** charity, charitable donation, contribution, largess, bounty, benefaction, beneficence, offerings, maundy money; welfare assistance, welfare, dole, subsidy.

2. handout, gratuity, douceur, (*in India, Turkey, etc.*) baksheesh, (*in Chinese ports*) cumshaw.

almsgiving, *n.* charity, largess, benevolence, benefaction, munificence, liberality, open-handedness, generosity; altruism, humanitarianism, philanthropy, big-heartedness, public spiritedness.

aloft, *adv.* **1.** high up, up in the air *or* sky, in the clouds, far above the ground; skyward *or* skywards, toward the sky; in *or* to heaven, on high, in the firmament, in the celestial heights; overhead, over one's head, above, on a higher place, at a higher place, in a higher place; atop, at the top, on the top.

2. *All Nautical.* on the masts, at the masthead, in the upper rigging, overhead.

alone, *adj.* **1.** separate, single, lone, sole, individual, discrete; apart, cut off, isolated, solitary, by oneself, *Scot.* waff; unattended, unaccompanied, companionless, *Inf.* by one's lonesome.

2. lonely, lonesome, forlorn, bereft, forsaken; abandoned, deserted, derelict, desolate, out in the cold.

3. only, just, mere, simply, nothing but.

4. unique, unequaled, unparalleled, peerless, matchless, nonpareil; unexcelled, unsurpassed, incomparable; inimitable, unrepeated, freakish.

—adv. **5.** solitarily, solely, singly; separately, individually, distinctly, discretely.

6. unaided, unassisted, unhelped, by oneself, singlehandedly; under one's own steam; independently, on one's own, *Inf.* on one's lonesome.

7. only, exclusively, merely, simply, just.

along, *prep.* **1.** beside, by the side of, alongside, along the side of, *Obs. or Dial.* alongst, parallel with *or* to, close by; on the border of, on the boundary of, on the line of, on the edge of, on the fringe of; through, throughout, all through, throughout the course of, over, all over, roundabout; from one end to the other, throughout the length of; on.

2. during, in the course of, in the process of, in the middle of, in the midst of.

3. in accordance with, in conformity with, in keeping with, in harmony with, in line with, in step with, in agreement with, in compliance with, in uniformity with, in correspondence to; together with, right with, in there with; consistent with, congruent with, uniform with; comfortable to, according to.

—adv. **4.** lengthwise, lengthways, longwise, longways, by the length, in length, at length, in line with the length, longitudinally; parallel with *or* to the length, alongside, along the side, beside, by the side of, close to the side, next to, right next to; aside, on one side, to one side, to the side, off to one side, off to the side, on the side, sidelong; abreast, side by side, cheek by cheek, cheek by jowl, board by board.

5. onward, onwards, on, on ahead, ahead, forward, forwards, forth.

6. in company with, in agreement with, in association with, in conjunction with; together with, coupled with, paired with, partnered with, joined with, united with; with, plus, including, inclusive of, as well as, not to mention, to say nothing of, let alone; added to, linked to, with the addition of, in addition to, over and above; simultaneously, at the same time, in unison, together.

7. down the line, through the ranks, *Sl.* through the grapevine, from one person *or* place to another, from person to person, from place to place.

8. all along, all the time, all the while, from the start, from the beginning, throughout, at all times.

alongside, *adv.* **1.** along, along the side, beside, by the side of, parallel with *or* to the length, close to the side, next to, right next to; aside, at the side, on one side, to one side, to the side, off to one side, off to the side, on the side, sidelong; abreast, side by side, cheek by cheek, cheek by jowl, board by board.

—prep. **2.** along, beside, by the side of, along the side of, *Obs. or Dial.* alongst, parallel with *or* to, close by; on the border of, on the boundary of, on the line of, on the edge of, on the fringe of.

aloof, *adv.* **1.** apart, separately, by oneself; off, away, at a distance, at arm's length.

—adj. **2.** indifferent, apathetic, unconcerned, disinterested, incurious, uninquisitive; removed, detached, uninvolved, unresponsive, unsympathetic; distant, remote, unapproachable, unsociable, standoffish, *Inf.* offish; cool, chilly, frosty, icy, frigid; haughty, *Inf.* high-hat, above all that, Olympian.

3. reticent, reserved, shy, withdrawn; alone, solitary, isolated, insular, separate, apart, to oneself.

aloud, *adv.* **1.** audibly, distinctly, plainly, clearly; loudly, loudly and clearly, *Inf.* out loud, with a loud voice, sonorously, resoundingly.

2. noisily, lustily, uproariously, boisterously; at the top of one's lungs, deafeningly, ear-splittingly, thunderingly, stentoriously; obstreperously, clamorously, vociferously, blatantly, clangorously.

alphabet, *n.* **1.** letters, symbols, characters, signs, hieroglyphs, pictographs, ideographs; syllabary, rune.

2. ABC's, beginnings, first steps, first principles, fundamentals, basics, rudiments, mere beginnings.

alphabetize, *v.* arrange, put in order, put in alphabetical order, categorize, systematize, organize, codify, set-up, file, go from A to Z.

alpine, *adj.* mountainous, rangy, snow-clad, ice-peaked, cloud-capped; distant, remote, faraway; aerial, soaring, lofty, high-reaching, elevated, towering, very high.

already, *adj.* **1.** by this time, by that time, yet; previously, beforehand, before now, hitherto.

2. now, here and now, even now, just now, but now, as of now; so soon, so early.

also, *adv., conj.* in addition, additionally, too, besides, as well, to boot, ditto, yet; and, plus, as well as; furthermore, further, over and above, moreover, more than that; together with that, therewithal, *Archaic.* thereto; including, along with, together with; in conjunction with, conjointly.

altar, *n.* **1.** sacrificial table, elevated structure, platform, mound; *All Eccles.* Lord's table, holy table, communion table, God's board.

2. shrine, inner shrine, reliquary, adytum; sacred *or* holy place, sanctuary, holy of holies, sanctum sanctorum, inner chamber, penetralia; temple, church, place of worship.

alter, *v.* **1.** modify, adjust, qualify, (*both of clothing*) take in, let out; change, make different, commute; transform, transfigure, transmute, metamorphose, convert; mend, emend, amend, edit, correct, revise; fix, reform, better, ameliorate; reconstruct, remodel, recast, remold; shuffle, jumble together, shift, mix, interchange, exchange; diversify, vary; reverse, turn, invert, transpose.

2. castrate, geld, fix, emasculate, spay, *Surg.* hysterectomize, *Surg.* vasectomize.

alteration, *n.* **1.** modification, adjustment, qualification; (*both of clothing*) taking in, letting out; change, difference, variation, variance, vicissitude; innovation, revolution, divergence, deviation; transformation, transfiguration, transmutation, permutation, metamorphosis, conversion; mending, emending, emendation, amending, amendment, editing, correcting, correction, revising, revision; reformation, reforming, reconstruction, reconstructing, remodeling, recasting, remolding.

2. reversal, turn, inversion, transposition, transference; substitution, commutation; shuffle, shuffling, shift, shifting, mix, mixing, diversifying, diversification, interchange, interchanging, exchange, exchanging; transition, passage; reduction, lessening, lowering.

altercate, *v.* argue, quarrel, dispute, spar, have words; bicker, spat, tiff; debate, disagree, differ, dissent, fall out, contend; clash, struggle, be at variance, scrimmage, collide; fight, brawl, wrangle, jangle, row, squabble; expostulate, remonstrate, object.

altercation, *n.* **1.** argument, quarrel, dispute, disputation, sparring; bickering, spatting, jangling, jarring; debate, logomachy, disagreement, dissension, discord, fall out; difference, divergence, variance; controversy, war of words.

2. affray, fight, brawl, wrangle, *Inf.* set-to jangle, row, squabble, *Inf.* run-in; struggle, clash, conflict, collision, scrimmage, strife, contention, broil; scuffle, tussle, fray; disturbance, commotion, uproar, fracas, rumpus, scene; disorder, turbulence, tumult; outbreak, riot, feud; melee, fisticuffs, *Sl.* milling; combat, contest, duel.

alternate, *v.* **1.** rotate, change back and forth, change off, take turns, *Sports.* platoon; interchange, change places, transpose, reciprocate.

—adj. **2.** in rotation, one after another, consecutive, successive; reciprocal, mutual; every other, every second.

3. alternative, another. See **alternative** (*def.* **2**).

—n. **4.** *U.S.* substitute, understudy, backup, pinch hitter; deputy, vicar, proxy, representative, agent, *Chiefly Brit.* locum tenens; assistant, backer, second.

alternation, *n.* rotation, alternate succession, changing back and forth, changing off, taking turns; interchanging, changing places, transposition, reciprocation.

alternative, *n.* **1.** choice, option, selection, preference, pick, election; recourse, remaining choice, only other choice; substitute, backup, *Inf.* plan B.

—adj. **2.** alternate, another, different; other, additional.

although, *conj.* in spite of the fact that, despite the fact that, notwithstanding that, albeit that, for all of that, even though, though; admitting that, granting that, be that as it may; supposing that, be it that, even if.

altitude, *n.* **1.** height, elevation, stature, extent *or* distance upward, measurement.

2. *Usu.* **altitudes** heights, summit, peak, pinnacle, crest, point, spire, tip, top, tiptop; apex, vertex, apogee, extreme, *Latin. ne plus ultra;* acme, zenith, meridian, crown, culmination.

3. supremacy, ascendancy, ascendance, highness, loftiness, tallness; eminence, prominence, prominency, dignity, primacy.

altogether, *adv.* **1.** wholly, completely, entirely, totally, fully; in all, in all respects, with no exception, across the board, from A to Z, *Latin. in toto;* utterly, thoroughly, absolutely, out and out, perfectly; quite, clean, right, sheer, stark, *Inf.* plumb.

2. on the whole, in the main, by and large, all in all, in general, generally, in the long run; for the most part, for all practical purposes, virtually; all things considered, everything considered; chiefly, mainly, mostly.

altruism, *n.* **1.** philanthropy, humanitarianism, humaneness, humanity, public spirit; other-directedness, other-direction, *Psychol.* extroversion, unselfishness, disinterestedness.

2. bountifulness, munificence, generosity, charity, benevolence, beneficence, magnanimity, liberalness, open-handedness; large-heartedness, kind-heartedness, kindness.

altruistic, *adj.* **1.** philanthropic, humanitarian, humane, public-spirited; other-directed, *Psychol.* extroverted, non-egotistic, non-egotistical, non-egocentric, unselfish, disinterested.

2. bountiful, munificent, generous, charitable, benevolent, beneficent, magnanimous, liberal, open-handed; large-hearted, big-hearted, kind-hearted, kind.

alumnus, alumna, *n.* graduate, former student; disciple, apostle, pupil.

always, *adv.* **1.** every time, at all times, on every occasion, without exception; constantly, regularly, repeatedly; continually, incessantly, uninterruptedly, day in, day out; invariably, inevitably, unfailingly, infallibly.

2. forever, eternally, perpetually; ever, evermore, *Poetic.* aye, *Literary.* sempiternally, *Poetic.* for aye, forever and ever, forever and a day; everlastingly, endlessly, timelessly; unceasingly, ceaselessly, undyingly, interminably; till doomsday, without end, *Latin. in saecula saeculorum, Fr. toujours.*

amalgam, *n.* alloy, compound, composite, hybrid, cross-breed, mongrel; mixture, mix, combination, combine, admixture, commixture; blend, fusion, coalescence, union, *Archaic.* crasis; consolidation, conglomeration, conglomerate, agglomeration, agglomerate, aggregation, aggregate, *Chem.* levigation.

amalgamate, *v.* mix, commix, combine, blend, *Chem.* levigate, homogenize, *Archaic.* temper; fuse, interfuse, conjoin, incorporate, unite, unify, coalesce, merge; synthesize, consolidate, compose, put together; mingle, admix, commingle, intermingle, intermix; alloy, compound, conglomerate, agglomerate.

amalgamation, *n.* mixture, commingling, mingling, minglement, interminglement; blending, fusing, coalescence, union. See **amalgam.**

amanuensis, *n.* secretary, clerk, scribe, scrivener, stenographer, transcriber, transcriptionist, copyist, copier.

amass, *v.* **1.** gather, collect, hoard, squirrel away, load up, stow away; garner, store up, stock up, lay by, lay up, lay in, *Inf.* stash away, reserve, set aside; save, save up, bank.

2. heap up, pile, pile up, roll up, run up, stack up; assemble, mass, aggregate, bring together, congregate; cumulate, agglomerate.

amateur, *n.* **1.** nonprofessional, layman, do-it-yourselfer; dabbler, dallier, trifler, putterer, potterer, dilettante; beginner, novice, tyro, neophyte, learner.

2. fan, devotee, votary, aficionado, *Inf.* buff, *Sl.* freak, *Sl.* bug, *Sl.* nut; admirer, fancier, follower, groupie.

—adj. **3.** nonprofessional, avocational, (*of athletics*) sandlot.

4. amateurish, unprofessional. See **amateurish.**

amateurish, *adj.* **1.** unprofessional, unpolished, uneven, rough; unperfected, imperfect, faulty, flawed, deficient, wanting; inferior, second-rate, grubstreet, bush-league, minor-league; mediocre, unskilled, unskillful, incompetent, poor.

2. superficial, dilettante, dilettantish, shallow, meretricious, trashy; juvenile, jejune, insipid, dull, boring; unimaginative, uninspired, uncreative, unoriginal, imitative, derivative; hackneyed, trite, cliché, rehashed, warmed over.

amatory, *adj.* amorous, passionate, fervent, impassioned, rapturous, amatorious, Anacreonic; languishing, doting, lovesick, devoted, tender, fond; erotic, romantic, sentimental; *Archaic.* lovesome.

amaze, *v.* astound, astonish, dumfound, *Inf.* flabbergast; strike with wonder, stun, stagger, take aback, floor, shock, jar, jolt, *Inf.* bowl over, *Inf.* give [s.o.] a turn, *Inf.* catch [s.o.] up short; startle, surprise, disconcert, bewilder; dazzle, electrify, *Inf.* take one's breath away; unbalance, disorient, *Inf.* catch off guard, *Sl.* curl one's hair.

amazement, *n.* surprise, astonishment, stupefaction, wonderment, awe; bewilderment, befuddlement, perplexity, confusion; wonder, marvel, prodigy, miracle.

amazing, *adj.* surprising, astounding, astonishing, striking, remarkable; wonderful, fabulous, marvelous, stupendous; miraculous, prodigious, preternatural, incredible, unbelievable, inconceivable; unexpected, confounding, unprecedented; very strange, *Inf.* damnedest, highly extraordinary, very unusual, singular.

amazon, *n.* virago, termagant, spitfire, fury; castrator, emasculator; shrew, vixen, tartar, scold, Xanthippe.

ambassador, *n.* **1.** diplomat, emissary, legate, attaché, envoy, minister of state, dignitary, plenipotentiary, nuncio; representative, delegate, commissioner, official, agent.
2. messenger, courier, herald, harbinger; intermediary, go-between; announcer, proclaimer, spokesman.

ambience, *n.* environment, surroundings, setting, scene; atmosphere, milieu, mood, spirit, feeling, vibrations, *Sl.* vibes; climate, feel, air; complexion, cast, character, tone, flavor, color.

ambient, *adj.* **1.** surrounding, encompassing, encircling, circumambient; enclosing, enfolding, enveloping, environing; embracing, embosoming.
2. circulating, moving, swirling, whirling.

ambiguity, *n.* **1.** doubtfulness, dubiousness, uncertainty, vagueness, deceptiveness; obscurity, indistinctness, unintelligibility, abstruseness; equivocalness, ambivalence.
2. equivocation, doublespeak, double-talk, newspeak, duplicity, circumlocution, weasel words; double entendre, pun, irony; suggestiveness, figurativeness; richness.

ambiguous, *adj.* **1.** equivocal, *Logic.* amphibolous, paradoxical, duplicitous; ironic, two-edged, ambivalent, multi-leveled, figurative, suggestive, symbolic; misleading, roundabout, circuitous, ambagious, hedging, weasel-worded.
2. doubtful, dubious, left-handed, uncertain; vague, indefinite, indistinct, indeterminate, unclassifiable, anomalous; obscure, abstruse, unintelligible, incomprehensible; puzzling, mystifying, enigmatic, enigmatical, perplexing, problematic, problematical; cryptic, oracular, delphic.

ambition, *n.* **1.** aspiration, hoping, wishfulness, desire, covetousness; yearning, longing, want, need, craving; appetite, taste, hunger.
2. goal, aim, target, destination, end point, intent, purpose, design, plan, scheme; hope, dream, wish, ideal, raison d'être.
3. enterprise, drive, force, striving, *Inf.* push; energy, vigor, vim, verve; zeal, enthusiasm, eagerness, spirit, get up and go, *Dial.* gimp.
—*v.* **4.** aspire to, hope for, wish for, dream of; desire, covet, yearn for, long for, want, need, crave; hunger for, have an appetite *or* taste for.
5. aim for, shoot for, have an ideal *or* goal, scheme *or* plan toward, intend, purpose; seek, search for, look for, follow.

ambitious, *adj.* **1.** aspiring, hoping, dreaming, wishful, yearning, longing; desirous, craving, hungry, salivating; covetous, envious, green with envy, itching, discontent, discontented, dissatisfied.
2. avaricious, rapacious, voracious, greedy, acquisitive, grabbing, selfish, climbing, goal-oriented; exploitative, predatory, predacious, preying, taking advantage; scheming, planning, designing, *Inf.* on the make.
3. enterprising, go-ahead, striving, assertive, aggressive, driving, pushing, *Inf.* pushy; energetic, vigorous, forceful, full of vim and vigor; zealous, ardent, fervent, fervid, avid, earnest, enthusiastic, eager, spirited.
4. courageous, brave, audacious, bold, daring; ostentatious, pretentious, showy, show-offish, Icarian.

ambivalence, *n.* uncertainty, indecision, irresolution, unsettledness, inconclusiveness, incertitude, unsureness, infirmity of purpose, *Psychol.* ambitendency; doubt, hesitancy, hesitation; fluctuation, vacillation, tergiversation, changefulness, fickleness, caprice, capriciousness, second thoughts; instability, inconstancy; conflict, contradiction, opposition, antinomy, irreconcilability, paradox; confusion, ambiguity, equivocation, irony.

ambivalent, *adj.* uncertain, indecisive, irresolute, unsettled, inconclusive, unsure, infirm of purpose; doubtful, dubious, hesitant, hesitating, faltering, at loose ends, of two minds; fluctuating, vacillating, tergiversating, changing, mercurial, capricious, fickle, unstable, inconstant; conflicting, contradictory, opposite, opposing, irreconcilable, paradoxical, antinomic; confusing, ambiguous, equivocal, ironic.

amble, *v.* **1.** stroll, saunter; shuffle, *Inf.* mosey; ramble, meander, *Inf.* traipse; (*both of horses*) pace, rack.
—*n.* **2.** easy walk, easy pace, gentle pace; strolling *or* ambling gait; stroll, saunter, walk, ramble, jaunt.

ambrosial, *adj.* **1.** savory, delectable, palatable; delicious, tasty, tasteful, toothsome, flavory, flavorful; mouth-watering, appetizing, gustable; sweet, nectarous, sugary, honeyed.
2. fragrant, aromatic, balmy, perfumed, perfumy; amaranthine, redolent, sweet-smelling, rosy; odorous, odoriferous, olent.
3. divine, godly, heavenly, supernal; celestial, ethereal, elysian, empyreal, paradisiac; beatific, golden, glorious, exalted.

ambulate, *v.* **1.** walk, foot, *Sl.* hoof, *Sl.* take the shoe-leather express; step, pace, tread.
2. perambulate, stroll, promenade, saunter, amble; roam, rove, range, ramble; meander, circumambulate, straggle, gad about, gallivant, traipse, shuffle; peregrinate, traverse, trek, travel.

ambulatory, *adj.* **1.** walking, pedestrian, on foot; moving, mobile, shifting.
2. itinerant, peripatetic, wandering, wayfaring; nomadic, migratory, vagrant, vagabond; strolling, rambling, meandering.
3. *Law.* alterable, changeable, modifiable, mutable, permutable; revocable, reversible.

ambush, *n.* **1.** ambuscade, hiding-place, retreat, concealment, cover, screen, blind; trap, snare, pitfall, lure; lying in wait, lurking.
—*v.* **2.** ambuscade, lurk, skulk, lie in wait; waylay, entrap, ensnare, decoy, lure.

ameliorate, *v.* **1.** improve, better, make better, amend, meliorate; advance, promote, raise, elevate; straighten out, reform, revise, rectify, set *or* put straight, make *or* set right, fix, repair.
2. remedy, cure, mend, heal, doctor; relieve, ease, mitigate, lessen, assuage, alleviate.

amelioration, *n.* **1.** improvement, betterment, melioration; advancement, promotion, raise, elevation; straightening out, reform, revision, amendment, rectification, setting *or* making right.
2. remedy, cure, mending, healing, doctoring; relief, easing, mitigation, lessening, assuagement, alleviation.

amen, *interj.* **1.** it is so, so it is, so be it, be it so, so is it, so shall it be, let it be so, would that it were so; by all means, *Sl.* right on, *Sl.* way to go.
—*adv.* **2.** verily, truly, honestly, truthfully, precisely, assuredly, as a matter of fact, frankly, in truth, indeed, literally.
—*n.* **3.** assent, concurrence, approval, endorsement, backing, okay, O.K., commendation, approbation.

amenability, *n.* **1.** agreeableness, agreeability, reasonableness; compliancy, pliancy, flexibility, conformability, adaptability; yieldingness, acquiescence, submissiveness, deference, obedience; docility, manageability, manageableness, governability, tractability.

2. liability, accountability, accountableness, answerability, answerableness, chargeability, responsibility.

amenable, *adj.* **1.** agreeable, reasonable, persuadable; compliant, pliant, flexible, conformable, adaptable; yielding, acquiescent, submissive, deferential, obedient; docile, manageable, governable, tractable.

2. liable, accountable, answerable, chargeable, responsible; subject, obligated, obliged, bound.

amend, *v.* **1.** alter, modify, adjust, qualify; change, make different, commute; transform, transfigure, transmute, metamorphose, convert; reconstruct, remodel, recast, remold, reorganize; reverse, turn, invert, transpose.

2. mend, emend, edit, correct, revise; rectify, redress, set right, put right, reform, straighten out; repair, fix, fix up; better, ameliorate, improve; purify, cleanse, clean, purge; doctor, touch up, polish; heal, cure, remedy, restore; compensate, recompense, repay, make up for, redeem; relieve, mitigate, lessen.

3. attach, adjoin, affix, append, suffix, annex, postfix, subjoin; join, unite, connect, adject, combine; add, add to, tag, tag on, tack on, put on; superpose, superimpose, superadd.

amendment, *n.* **1.** alteration, modification, adjustment, qualification; change, difference, variation, variance, vicissitude; transformation, transfiguration, transmutation, metamorphosis, conversion; reconstruction, remodeling, recasting, remolding, reorganization; reversal, turn, inversion, transposition, transference; substitution, commutation; shuffle, shift, mix, diversification, interchange, exchange.

2. mending, emending, emendation, editing, correcting, correction, revising, revision; rectification, rectifying, redressing, setting right, putting right, reforming, reformation; repairing, reparation, fixing; amelioration, improvement, betterment; purification, cleansing, cleaning, purging, purgation; doctoring, touching up, polishing; healing, curing, restoring, restoration, remedying; compensation, recompense, repayment, redemption; relief, relieving, mitigation, mitigating, lessening, lowering, reducing, reduction.

3. attachment, addition, affixture, appendage; addendum, suffix, annex, postfix, postscript; joining, uniting, combining; adding, tacking on, tagging on, attaching, annexing.

amends, *n.* **1.** reparation, compensation, recompense, satisfaction; requital, quittance, payment, *Literary.* guerdon; indemnification, indemnity, restitution, restoration, remedy, redress; atonement, expiation; reward, retribution, return, salvage, consideration, acknowledgement; propitiation, conciliation; bribe, sop, damages, hush money, *Latin. quid pro quo,* douceur; apology, peace offering.

2. make amends compensate, recompense, make reparation, indemnify; propitiate, appease, conciliate; atone, atone for, expiate; apologize, beg pardon, be sorry for; make good, make right, make up for, set one's house in order; requite, repay, return, reimburse, remunerate, recoup.

amenity, *n.* **1.** pleasantness, pleasingness, pleasurableness, enjoyableness, agreeableness, agreeability, niceness; gentleness, softness, mildness, harmoniousness; delightfulness, gracefulness, sweetness; delectableness, tastiness, goodness, *Inf.* yumminess, palatableness.

2. affability, amiability, geniality, gentility, complaisance; politeness, refinement, graciousness, polish; gallantry, suavity, chivalry.

3. amenities civilities, urbanities, courtesies, comities, suavities, pleasantries, elegancies, urbanities; etiquette, social graces, manners; formalities, social procedures, proprieties, protocol, mores.

amiability, *n.* **1.** pleasantness, pleasingness, amenity, likeableness, good-naturedness, good-humoredness; delightfulness, sweetness, sweet-temperedness, lovableness; kindness, kindliness, complaisance, kindheartedness, benignancy; attractiveness, comeliness, handsomeness, beautifulness, beauty, elegance, loveliness.

2. amicability, friendliness, congeniality, neighborliness, sociability; affability, approachableness, accessibility, communicativeness; easiness, openness, unreservedness, familiarity, easygoingness.

3. agreeableness, willingness, amenableness, submissiveness, obligingness; graciousness, geniality, gentleness, mildness; politeness, cordiality, courteousness, mannerliness, courtliness, civility; urbanity, suaveness, sophistication.

amiable, *adj.* **1.** pleasant, pleasing, likeable, good-natured, good-humored, *Scot. and North Eng., Irish Eng.* sonsy; delightful, nice, sweet, sweet-tempered, lovable; kind, kindly, *Scot.* couthie, complaisant; sympathetic, understanding; kindhearted, warm-hearted, benignant; attractive, comely, appealing, handsome, good-looking, beautiful, elegant, lovely; engaging, winning, winsome, charming.

2. amicable, friendly, congenial; neighborly, sociable, fraternal, brotherly, sisterly, companionable, affable, approachable, accessible, communicative, conversive; easy, open, unreserved, familiar, free and easy, easygoing; affectionate, demonstrative, hearty.

3. agreeable, willing, consenting, disposed, well-disposed, inclined; agreeing, harmonious, concordant; amenable, submissive, tractable, yielding, accommodating, obliging, blank; gracious, genial, gentle, pacific, peaceable, benign; polite, cordial, courteous, mannerly, well-mannered, courtly, civil; urbane, suave, sophisticated.

amicable, *adj.* **1.** friendly, congenial, neighborly, sociable, fraternal, brotherly, sisterly, companionable; affable, approachable, accessible, communicative, conversive; easy, open, unreserved, familiar, free and easy, easygoing; affectionate, demonstrative, hearty.

2. agreeable, willing, consenting, disposed, well-disposed, inclined; agreeing, harmonious, concordant; amenable, submissive, tractable, yielding, accommodating, obliging, blank; gracious, genial, gentle, pacific, peaceable, benign; polite, cordial, courteous, mannerly, well-mannered, courtly, civil; urbane, suave, sophisticated.

3. pleasant, pleasing, likeable, good-natured, good-humored, amiable, *Scot. and North Eng., Irish Eng.* sonsy; delightful, nice, sweet, sweet-tempered, lovable; kind, kindly, *Scot.* couthie, complaisant; sympathetic, understanding; kindhearted, warm-hearted, benignant; engaging, winning, winsome, charming.

amicableness, *n.* **1.** friendliness, congeniality, neighborliness, sociableness; affability, approachability, accessibility, communicativeness, demonstrativeness, heartiness; easiness, openness, unreservedness, familiarity, easygoingness.

2. agreeableness, willingness, harmoniousness, concordance, gentleness, peaceableness; amenableness, submissiveness, obligingness; politeness, cordiality, courteousness, courtliness, civility; urbanity, suaveness, sophisticatedness.

3. amiability, pleasantness, pleasingness, likeableness; delightfulness, niceness, sweetness, sweet-temperedness; kindness, kindliness, complaisance, kindheartedness, warm-heartedness; sympathy, understanding.

amid, *prep.* **1.** mid, amidst, in the midst of, in the middle of; surrounded by, among, amongst, with; between, *Archaic.* betwixt, 'twixt.
2. during, in the course of.

amiss, *adv.* **1.** wrong, awry, astray, off, off the mark; improperly, wrongly, erroneously, falsely, fallaciously, mistakenly, incorrectly; inaccurately, inexactly, imprecisely, imperfectly, faultily; unsatisfactorily, poorly, badly, ill; inopportunely, inappropriately, unsuitably, unfavorably, unpropitiously.
—adj. **2.** wrong, awry, astray, off, off the mark; improper, erroneous, false, untrue, fallacious, mistaken, incorrect; inaccurate, inexact, imprecise, imperfect, faulty; out of order, out of whack, *Inf.* out of kilter, unsatisfactory, poor, bad, ill; inopportune, untimely, inappropriate, unsuitable, unfavorable, unpropitious.

amity, *n.* **1.** friendship, affinity, rapport, good *or* mutual understanding, goodwill, good feelings, peaceful relations, cordial relations; peace, concord, harmony, accord, accordance, agreement, unity, unanimity; fraternity, brotherhood, fellowship, comradeship; congeniality, cordiality, sociability, amicability, friendliness, neighborliness.

ammunition, *n.* **1.** weapons, arms, armament, firearms, munitions, *Mil.* matériel; guns, rifles, muskets, flintlocks, matchlocks; pistols, revolvers, six-shooters; shotguns, machine guns, howitzers, cannons, artillery.
2. bullets, shot, shrapnel, cartridges, shells, slugs, *Mil.* ball; gunpowder, powder, primers, fuzes; explosives, bombs, grenades, mines; missiles, rockets, torpedoes; chemicals, pyrotechnics.
3. *Informal.* information, instruction, advice, pointer, tip.

amnesty, *n.* **1.** pardon, pardoning, excuse, excusal, excusing, forgiveness, forgiving, absolution, absolving, remission, remitting, reprieve, reprieving; clemency, indulgence, indulgency, indulging, lenience, leniency, lenity; tolerance, forbearance, mercifulness, mercy, grace.
2. immunity, impunity, indemnity, exemption, exempting, exception, *Archaic.* franchise.
3. overlooking, disregarding, dispensation; oblivion, forgetting, ignoring.
—v. **4.** pardon, excuse, forgive, absolve, remit, reprieve; overlook, make allowances for, pass over, wink at, disregard; forget, ignore, look the other way, pay no attention to; dismiss, let off, *Inf.* let off the hook, *Inf.* let out of, *Law.* discharge; release, free, set free, liberate, emancipate, deliver.

among, *prep.* **1.** amid, mid, amidst, midst, in the midst of, in the middle of, in the thick of, amongst, mongst; surrounded by, encompassed by, enveloped by; in connection with, in association with, together with, with; between, *Archaic.* betwixt, *Archaic.* 'twixt.
2. out of, of; in the number of, in the class of, in the group of, in the company of, in the country *or* time of.
3. by all, by *or* with the whole of, with all, by most of, by *or* with many of; by the joint action of, by the reciprocal action of, by the mutual action of.
4. mutually, each with the other, with one another.

amorous, *adj.* **1.** loving, amatory, amatorious, amative, Anacreontic; passionate, impassioned, ardent, fervent.
2. sexual, lustful, concupiscent, salacious; lecherous, *Archaic.* lickerish, prurient, lascivious, wanton, cadgy, licentious, lewd, libidinous; sensual, voluptuous, erotic.
3. enamored, smitten, infatuated, taken with, *Inf.* sweet on, lovesick; devoted, doting, *Inf.* spoony; tender, fond, affectionate, *Sl.* lovey-dovey.

amorousness, *n.* **1.** passion, ardor, fervency; sexuality, lust, concupiscence, salaciousness; lecherousness, prurience, lasciviousness, lewdness, licentiousness, wantonness, libidinousness; sensuality, voluptuousness.
2. enamoredness, infatuation, lovesickness; devotion, dotingness; tenderness, fondness, affection, love, amativeness.

amorphous, *adj.* formless, unformed, unshapen, shapeless, structureless, unstructured; indeterminate, vague, nebulous, characterless, nondescript; unorganized, confused, jumbled, chaotic.

amount, *n.* **1.** total, grand total, sum, sum total, whole, aggregate, lot; *All Sl.* whole bunch, whole mess, whole deal, whole shebang, whole kit and caboodle, whole shooting match, the works, whole ball of wax.
2. quantity, number, count, *Scot and North Eng.* feck; deal, pack, mass, *Sl.* heap, *Sl.* mess; part, parcel, portion; measure, extent, reach, range, compass.
3. effect, significance, value, import, purport; result, sum and substance, harvest.
—v. **4.** equal, match, tally, correspond, agree, measure up to, *Sl.* stack up with *or* against; extend, reach, touch, approximate.
5. aggregate, total, add up to, come to, run to, mount up to, reckon up to; cost, sell for, fetch, bring, set one back.
6. become, develop into, grow, progress, advance, maturate, amount to something.

amour, *n.* love affair, romance, *Fr. affaire d' amour,* affair of the heart, *Fr. affaire de coeur;* affair, liaison, illicit love affair, fornication, adultery, *Law.* criminal conversation.

ample, *adj.* **1.** big, large, considerable, amplitudinous, *Scot.* wally; spacious, capacious, commodious, roomy; vast, great, immense, huge, boundless, voluminous; wide, broad, outspread, expansive, extensive.
2. plentiful, plenteous, plenitudinous, bountiful, bounteous, abundant, fat, copious; immeasurable, unmeasured, unstinted, inexhaustible, bottomless; much, many, numerous, *Inf.* dime a dozen; in quantity *or* quantities, in plenty, *Inf.* aplenty, *Inf.* galore.
3. profuse, abounding, overflowing, overspilling, spilling over, running over, exuberant, superabundant; rich, lavish, luxuriant; free, generous, liberal, handsome, munificent.
4. adequate, sufficient, enough, satisfactory; enough and to spare, enough and then some, more than enough, more than adequate, *Inf.* plenty.

amplification, *n.* **1.** increase, enlargement, *Archaic.* ampliation, aggrandizement; expansion, widening, thickening, broadening; extension, lengthening, prolongation, protraction; inflation, dilatation, dilation, waxing; growth, spread, swell.
2. addition, accretion, increment, accession, access; augmentation, supplement, annex, annexation, appendage, appendix, addendum, adjunct; multiplication, doubling, redoubling, trebling, tripling, quadrupling.
3. development, elaboration, fleshing out, stretching out; expatiation, descant, discourse; prolixity, verbosity; clarification, explication, explanation, detail, elucidation; illustration, demonstration, exemplification, typification.
4. exaggeration, overstatement, overcharging, overstressing; hyperbolization, overdrawing; magnification, enhancement, enrichment, deepening, heightening; romanticization, embroidering, stretching, straining; intensification, concentration, maximization; escalation, acceleration, aggravation.

amplifier, *n.* speaker, loudspeaker, *Inf.* amp, *Sl.*

squawk box; bull-horn, horn; megaphone, microphone, *Inf.* mike; tweeter, woofer, tweeter-woofer.

amplify, *v.* **1.** increase, enlarge, make larger, make bigger, make greater, *Chiefly Literary.* greaten; expand, widen, thicken, broaden; extend, lengthen, elongate, prolong, prolongate, protract; dilate, distend, inflate, swell, bloat, puff out, blow up.

2. augment, supplement, add to, superadd to; accumulate, cumulate, pile up, heap up; multiply, double, redouble, treble, triple, quadruple.

3. develop, enlarge on, flesh out, stretch out, elaborate, unfold; descant, expound on *or* upon, expatiate on *or* upon, dilate on *or* upon, discourse; clarify, make more explicit, explicate, explain, detail, go into detail, elucidate; illustrate, demonstrate, exemplify, typify.

4. exaggerate, make much of, overdo, overstate, overstress, overcharge, overcolor; hyperbolize, overdraw; magnify, enhance, enrich, deepen, heighten; romance, embroider, stretch, strain; intensify, concentrate, maximize; escalate, step up, give a boost to, aggravate; accelerate, snowball, mushroom.

amplitude, *n.* **1.** bigness, largeness, fulness, considerableness; spaciousness, capaciousness, commodiousness, roominess; vastness, greatness, immensity, immenseness, hugeness, boundlessness, voluminousness; width, wideness, breadth, broadness, latitude, expansiveness, extensiveness; size, extent, measure, volume, capacity, magnitude, dimensions.

2. abundance, ampleness, plentifulness, plenteousness, copiousness, bountifulness, bounteousness; plenitude, profusion, repletion, exuberance, superabundance; quantity, quantities, volume, mass, full measure.

amputate, *v.* cut off, sever, lop, lop off, clip, trim, prune; cut away, remove, excise; disjoint, mutilate, dismember, separate.

amuck, *adv.* frenziedly, crazedly, berserk, maniacally, *Sl.* like a nut, *Sl.* like a screwball, like a madman, with frenzied fury, with murder in one's eye, wildly; ferociously, violently.

amulet, *n.* charm, good luck charm, talisman; lucky piece, horseshoe, rabbit's foot, wishbone, *Brit.* merrythought; periapt, abraxas, phylactery, tefillin; scarab, apotropaic, swastika, triskelion; protector, preservative, safeguard.

amuse, *v.* **1.** please, charm, cheer, *Inf.* hand one a few laughs; gladden, gratify, tickle, take *or* tickle one's fancy, regale, exhilarate, enliven, rejoice.

2. interest, occupy, beguile, engross, absorb; divert, relax, do one's heart good, cheer up, solace; entertain, disport, recreate, dally.

amusement, *n.* **1.** pastime, entertainment, recreation, fun, cheer; pleasure, enjoyment, delight, gaiety; gratification, distraction, diversion, play, sport; relaxation, dalliance, merrymaking, pleasantry, merriment, joviality, jocoseness, jollity, jollification, drollery.

2. antic, lark, romp, gambol, spree, junket; prank, practical joke, escapade, revelry, tomfoolery, skylarking.

amusing, *adj.* **1.** pleasing, pleasurable, diverting, distracting, interesting, absorbing, engrossing, beguiling; recreative, lively, sportive.

2. laughable, funny, comical, witty, humorous, jolly; hilarious, sidesplitting, ludicrous, ridiculous, farcical; facetious, droll, salty, waggish; jocular, jocose, jovial, risible.

anachronism, *n.* **1.** archaism, antique, obsolete form; asynchronism, incongruity, discord, shock, jar.

2. misdate, misdating, prochronism, prolepsis, antedate, predating; parachronism, postdating; misplacing, misapplication, mislocation, contextual error.

analects, *n. pl.* passages, selections, extracts, excerpts, quotations, citations; sayings, pieces; collectanea, analecta; compilation, abstract, compendium, anthology, florilegium.

analgesic, *adj.* pain-relieving, pain-killing, anesthetic; palliative, alleviative, relieving, soothing, assuasive; sedative, calmative, lenitive, abirritant, anodyne; emollient, demulcent, softening.

analogous, *adj.* **1.** similar, comparable, like, not unlike; correspondent, corresponding, homologous, reciprocal, reciprocative, answering, matching, coinciding; kindred, akin, related, associated, allied, cognate.

2. equivalent, same; identical, alike, homogeneous, of a piece, of a kind, cast in the same mold.

analogy, *n.* **1.** comparison, compare, comparability, comparableness, comparativeness, parallelism, analogousness; likeness, resemblance, semblance, partial similarity; affinity, kinship, relation, relationship; connection, coincidence, likening, comparing.

2. agreement, accordance, correspondence, correspondency, concurrence, conformity, conformance; similarity, parity, parallel, equivalence, equivalency, similitude, alikeness; uniformity, oneness, sameness; coequality, mutuality.

analysis, *n.* **1.** dissection, breakdown, reduction, partition, dissociation, subdivision; disintegration, decomposition.

2. examination, investigation, study, inquiry; explication, explanation, interpretation, clarification; criticism, critique, review; summary, epitome, synopsis, abstract.

3. psychoanalysis, psychiatry, psychotherapy.

analyst, *n.* **1.** investigator, fact-sifter, inquisitor; examiner, assayer; evaluator, reviewer.

2. psychoanalyst, psychiatrist, alienist, *Sl.* headshrinker, *Sl.* shrink.

analytical, *adj.* resolving into first principles, treating of analysis, separative, inquisitive, questioning, investigative, critical, interpretative, explanatory, explicative.

analyze, *v.* **1.** separate, dissect, anatomize, break down; fractionate, decompose, distill, disintegrate.

2. examine critically, investigate, question, inquire into; criticize, critique, review; explicate, explain, interpret, clarify.

anarchic, *adj.* **1.** lawless, ungoverned, anarchical, anarchistic; Nihilist, Bolshevist, Bakuninist.

2. disorderly, disorganized, confused, deranged; tumultuous, turbulent, chaotic, riotous; rebellious, revolutionary, insurgent, mutinous; seditious, subversive, terroristic.

anarchist, *n.* **1.** Nihilist, Boshevist, Bakuninist; renegade, fifth columnist, *Archaic.* anarch, apostate.

2. revolutionist, revolutionary, rebel, mutineer, insurrectionary, insurgent, rabble-rouser; subverter, seditionist, terrorist; malcontent, radical, iconoclast.

anarchy, *n.* **1.** lawlessness, mobocracy, ochlocracy; Nihilism, Bolshevism, Bakuninism.

2. riot, chaos, disorder, disarray; disorganization, derangement, confusion, mess; tumult, turmoil, mayhem, bedlam, pandemonium; insurgence, insurrection, rebellion, revolution, uprising, mutiny; sedition, subversion, terrorism, apostasy.

anathema, *n.* **1.** curse, malediction, imprecation, execration; fulmination, commination, denunciation, censure; condemnation, proscription, sentence, *Theol.* damnation; interdiction, excommunication, banishment, *Eccles.* ban.

2. the damned, the doomed, fallen angel; abomination, abhorrence, aversion, antipathy, *Fr. bête noire.*

anathematize, *v.* **1.** curse, imprecate, execrate;

fulminate, comminate, denounce, censure; damn, condemn, proscribe, doom; excommunicate, banish, *Archaic.* ban.

2. swear, utter obscenities, use four-letter words; blaspheme, use profanities, take the name of the Lord in vain.

anatomize, *v.* **1.** dissect, vivisect, dismember, cut apart *or* up, skeletonize, lay open.

2. scrutinize, examine, analyze, study, pull apart, tear to pieces; probe, sift through, search through, investigate, research, inquire into, look into.

anatomy, *n.* **1.** biology, zoology, zoometry, botany, phytometry.

2. skeleton, bones, framework, frame, build, form, *Biol.* structure, *Inf.* body; construction, constitution, make-up, composition.

3. dissection, zootomy, vivisection, dismemberment, cutting apart *or* up.

4. scrutiny, study, analysis, examination; investigation, inquiry, research.

ancestor, *n.* **1.** forefather, forbear, progenitor, primogenitor, *Archaic.* predecessor; procreator, begetter; patriarch, parent, father, genitor.

2. forerunner, precursor; prototype, model, exemplar.

ancestral, *adj.* inherited, hereditary, lineal, patrimonial, patriarchal, patriarchic, patriarchical.

ancestry, *n.* ancestral line, lineage, descent, parentage, birth, derivation, extraction, filiation; family, dynasty, house, tribe; race, strain, stock, breed, bloodline, pedigree, stem, branch, stirps; heredity, genealogy, family tree; heritage, background, past, history, roots; nobility, noble *or* high birth, aristocracy, blue blood.

anchor, *n.* **1.** mooring, ground tackle, kedge, grapnel, grappling iron, killick; mushroom anchor, stockless anchor.

2. safeguard, mainstay, security, protection, support, strength, defense; prop, pillar, staff; refuge, asylum, haven, sanctuary.

—v. **3.** secure by anchor; fix, affix, fasten, attach, make fast, grasp, connect, bind.

4. drop anchor, ride at anchor, hold fast; rest, tarry, abide, stop, settle, remain, continue; dwell, reside.

anchorage, *n.* **1.** mooring, dock, landing, jetty, wharf, pier, quay; port, harbor, harborage, haven; shelter, refuge, asylum, sanctuary, port in a storm, *Scot.* bield.

2. wharfage, dockage, fee, toll, charge, fare, exaction.

3. tower, pillar, tower *or* pillar of strength, rock, rock of ages, *Inf.* rock of Gibraltar *or* Gibraltar.

anchorite, anchoret, *n.* eremite, hermit, solitary, recluse, *Islam.* marabout, *Islam.* santon; anchoress, ancress, hermitess, *Obs.* hermitress, nun; troglodyte, cave dweller, incluse; stylite, pillarist, pillar-saint; ascetic, celibate, monk, monastic, holy man.

ancient, *adj.* **1.** primeval, primal, prehistoric, preglacial, preadamic, Noachian, Noachiac, Noachical, antediluvian, before the Flood *or* Deluge; eolithic, Paleolithic, Mesolithic, Neolithic; pristine, early, earliest, primitive, primordial, primigenial.

2. antiquated, antique, fossilized, fossil-like, ancient, archaic; superannuated, oldest, age-old, immemorial, remote, old, old as the hills, timeworn, elderly, aged; venerable, gray, hoary, *Rare.* hoar, patriarchal.

3. atavistic, old-fashioned, old-fogyish, old-time, bygone, unmodern, quaint, old-world; out-of-date, outmoded, passé, obsolete, superseded, obsolescent.

—n. **4.** venerable, patriarch, elder; *Inf.* old-timer, Methuselah, *Inf.* oldster, *Sl.* relic.

5. ancients, *n.* antiquities, venerables, patriarchs, elders; aboriginals, aborigines; autochthons.

ancillary, *adj.* accessory, auxiliary, secondary, subordinate, subservient, subsidiary; secondary, adjunct, adjuvant, *Obs.* adjutory, *Obs., Rare.* adjutorious; incidental, extra, extraneous, extrinsic, adventitious; supplementary, supplemental, additional, appurtenant, accessorial, adscititious *or* ascititious; accompanying, attendant, collateral.

andiron, *n.* firedog, dog.

androgynous, *adj.* bisexual, epicene; *All Biol.* hermaphrodite, hermaphroditic, pseudohermaphrodite; *All Bot.* gynandrous, gynandomorphic, gynandromorphous, monoclinous.

anecdote, *n.* short story, sketch, narrative, relation, tale, *Inf.* yarn; fable, allegory, apologue, legend, myth; reminiscence, memoir; instance, illustration.

anecdotist, *n.* raconteur, storyteller, narrator, relator, yarn-spinner.

anemia, *n.* pallor, pallidness, paleness, wanness, colorlessness; weakness, feebleness, enervation, breathlessness, exhaustion, vigorlessness, powerlessness; *Pathol.* hemoglobin deficiency.

anemic, *adj.* pallid, pale, wan, ashen, colorless; weak, feeble, languishing, languid, enervated; exhausted, vigorless, powerless; ineffective, ineffectual, inefficacious, impotent.

anesthesia, *n.* insentience, insensibility, insensitivity, lack of feeling, numbness, deadness, dullness, *Med.* analgesia.

anesthetic, *n.* **1.** pain-killer, sedative, analgesic, drug, *Sl.* dope, opiate, narcotic.

—adj. **2.** analgesic, narcotic; deadening, dulling, numbing.

3. insensible, insensitive, insentient, insensate, numb, deadened.

anew, *adv.* again, newly, freshly, afresh; once more, once again, encore, bis, over, over again, *Latin. de novo.*

anfractuous, *adj.* winding, turning, sinuous, serpentine, snaky, tortuous, vermiculate; circuitous, meandering, devious; roundabout, ambagious, flexuous, curvy, curved; spiraling, circling, convoluted, volute, coiled; twisted, crooked, bent; mazy, labyrinthine.

angel, *n.* **1.** seraph, cherub, archangel; spirit, guardian angel, tutelary saint, messenger of God.

2. backer, patron, Maecenas, supporter, promoter; benefactor, helper, philanthropist, well-wisher, fairy godmother.

angelic, *adj.* **1.** heavenly, ethereal, elysian, empyrean, celestial; divine, godly, saintly, cherubic, seraphic, archangelic.

2. righteous, holy, pious, sanctified, good; virtuous, chaste, pure, sinless; unworldly, spiritual; beautiful, adorable, lovely, exquisite, delicate.

anger, *n.* **1.** ire, dudgeon, high dudgeon, *Scot.* birse, *Inf.* Irish, *Inf.* dander; wrath, passion, hot blood, hot temper, vials of wrath; rage, fury.

2. offense, indignation, umbrage; pique, huff, tiff, fume, *Inf.* slow burn.

3. embitterment, bitterness, resentment, bitter resentment, exacerbation, hard feelings; choler, spleen, gall, bile, ill *or* bad humor, ill *or* bad temper, ill *or* bad feeling; enmity, animosity, ill will, bad blood; virulence, acrimony, acerbity.

4. exasperation, irritation, annoyance, vexation, *Inf.* aggravation; displeasure, dissatisfaction, discontent, discontentment, disapproval, disapprobation.

—v. **5.** incense, raise [s.o.'s] ire or hackles, run afoul of [s.o.], get [s.o.'s] back up, *Inf.* get [s.o.'s] Irish *or* dander up, *Inf.* burn [s.o.] up, *Sl.* tee [s.o.] off, *Sl.* tick [s.o.] off; enrage, madden, infuriate, make [s.o.'s] blood boil, *Inf.* make [s.o.] see red; provoke, arouse, rouse, inflame, enflame, agitate, fire up, work

up, stir up; displease.

6. vex, pique, irritate, annoy, irk, peeve, nettle, chafe, *Chiefly U.S.* rile, *Inf.* aggravate, *Inf.* miff, *Inf.* give [s.o.] a pain, *Inf.* get under [s.o.'s] skin, *Inf.* get in [s.o.'s] hair, *Sl.* bug; exasperate, ruffle, roil, put out, get, *Sl.* get [s.o.'s] goat.

7. embitter, exacerbate, gall, rankle, envenom; affront, offend, insult; humiliate, mortify.

8. *All Inf.* burn up, do a slow burn, steam, steam up, freak, freak out.

angle[1], *n.* **1.** intersection, fork, Y, branch, crotch, division, *Archaic.* divide; bend, curve, crook, turn, twist, hook, elbow, knee; corner, nook, crevice, cranny, recess, niche.

2. viewpoint, standpoint, position, point of view, opinion, feeling, attitude, mind set; slant, approach, *Sl.* pitch, leaning, bias.

3. side, aspect, part, feature, phase, stage.

angle[2], *v.* **1.** fish, cast for, *Angling.* bob, troll, trawl; net, catch, draw in, hook, ensnare, entrap, capture, take alive.

2. fish, look for, hint at, beg for, try for, aim for, woo; scheme, plot, plan, contrive, devise; bait, lure, attract, decoy, trick, take in; manipulate, handle, manage, take care of.

angler, *n.* fisherman, fisher, piscator, troller, trawler; Izaak Walton.

angry, *adj.* **1.** wrathful, wroth, irate, ireful, incensed, horn-mad; enraged, raging, fuming, smoking, infuriated, *Rare.* infuriate, furious; livid, *Inf.* mad as a hornet, *Inf.* mad as hops, *Inf.* mad as a wet hen; inflamed, flaming, flaring, flared up, heated, red-hot, white-hot; distraught, overwrought, *Inf.* fit to be tied; upset, feverish, hysterical, *Inf.* blue in the face, not rational; violent, unrestrained, uncontrollable; ranting, raving, storming, foaming at the mouth, rabid, fanatical, frenzied; frantic, crazed, *Pathol.* delinious, mad, *Inf.* wild, out of one's mind, beside oneself, *Sl.* freaked out.

2. peeved, annoyed, put out, vexed, irritated; piqued, chafed, galled, riled, nettled; offended, affronted, *Inf.* sore; *Sl.* ticked off, *Sl.* teed off; displeased, on the outs with, indignant; worked up, *Inf.* hot under the collar, stirred up, kindled, enkindled; passionate, impassioned, impassionate, over-excited.

3. irritable, cross, surly, snappish, petulant, peevish; testy, *Sl.* uptight, choleric, touchy, huffy, peppery; splenetic, spleenful, bilious, cranky, ill-tempered, *Australian.* crook, bad-tempered; irascible, quick-tempered, short-tempered, *Inf.* short-fused; quarrelsome, contentious, belligerent, up in arms, pugnacious, bellicose; volatile, volcanic, explosive, hot-tempered, hot-headed, fiery, inflammable.

4. stormy, violent, strong, savage, tempestuous, turbulent, wild, rough; threatening, restless, agitated, foaming, boiling, seething, raging, howling, roaring; windy, blustering, blustery, gusty, blowing, squally, squallish.

angst, *n.* dread, terror, fear, fear and trembling, trepidation; apprehension, foreboding, fearfulness, anxiety; malaise, distress, disquietude, solicitude, worry; anguish, agony, suffering, torment, misery, dolor, sorrow, woe.

anguish, *n.* **1.** agony, torment, torture; pain, pang, throe, paroxysm; aching, suffering, misery, *Archaic.* bale, dolor; sorrow, heartache, heartbreak, grief, woe, ruth, sadness.

2. affliction, distress, *Med.* angor, disquiet, disquietude; anxiety, angst; remorse, regret, repentance, contrition, penitence, compunction.

—v. **3.** torture, torment, agonize, excruciate, wring; pain, injure, wound, hurt, make miserable, scathe, cut to the quick, cut to the heart; afflict, distress, disquiet, disturb, trouble, harry.

angular, *adj.* **1.** pointed, sharp-cornered, Y-shaped, V-shaped; forked, crotched, bifurcate, divaricate; jagged, scraggy.

2. bony, gaunt, rawboned, spare, lean, thin, lank, lanky, scrawny.

3. awkward, ungraceful, ungainly, uncouth, gauche, maladroit.

4. stiff, unbending, stern, austere, unyielding; abrupt, edged, sharp, crabbed.

animadversion, *n.* **1.** criticism, adverse *or* hostile criticism, *Inf.* flak, *Sl.* knock, *Sl.* swipe, *Sl.* slam; rebuke, reproof, reprimand, check.

2. censure, reproach, invective, reprehension, reflection, disapproval, disapprobation, stricture; aspersion, imputation, derogation, reprobation; chastisement, castigation, scolding, upbraiding, chiding.

animal, *n.* **1.** creature, beast, brute, *Dial.* critter, *Dial.* varmint; mammal, mammalian.

2. monster, fiend, demon, devil, mad dog; barbarian, savage, troglodyte, wild man; dog, cur, hound, swine, pig, ape.

—adj. **3.** animalistic, animalian, zooid, zooidal; instinctive, instinctual, nonrational.

4. physical, carnal, fleshly, bodily, sensual; coarse, vulgar, low, gross, obscene; inhuman, savage, bestial, beastly, beastlike, brutish; brutal, cruel, ferocious.

animate, *v.* **1.** create, breathe life into; vivify, quicken, vitalize; enliven, invigorate, energize, fortify, strengthen.

2. encourage, inspire, inspirit, buoy, hearten, enhearten, embolden; elate, gladden, cheer, *Inf.* pep up, *Inf.* buck up; delight, exhilarate.

3. actuate, activate, motivate, move, rouse, waken; incite, stimulate, arouse, rouse up; fire, kindle, enkindle, stir, goad, spur on, prod, prick; push, egg on, urge, impel, exhort; boost, promote, prompt, *Inf.* spark, *Inf.* sparkplug, instigate, foment, provoke; excite, work up.

—adj. **4.** alive, live, living, breathing; existing, existent; sensible, animal, self-moving, self-propelling.

5. lively, spirited, vivacious. See **animated** (*def.* **1**).

animated, *adj.* **1.** lively, full of life, vivacious, enlivened; inspirited, invigorated, energized, energetic, vivified, vitalized, reanimated, revived, revitalized, rejuvenated; vigorous, forceful, dynamic; inspired, eager, *Inf.* psyched *or* psyched up, hopeful; sunny, radiant, glowing, alive, *Inf.* bright-eyed and bushy-tailed; stimulated, excited, aroused, *Inf.* hot; intensely desirous, impassioned, passionate; zealous, ardent, vehement, fervent, fervid, perfervid; enkindled, kindled, sparkling, *Inf.* sparking, inflamed, fired up; stirred up, roused, awake; active, alert, quick, bright.

2. happy, blissful, beatific, pleased, delighted, *Inf.* tickled pink; blithe, blithesome, merry, gay, gleeful; glad, gladsome, joyful, joyous; ebullient, bubbling, bubbly, effervescent; charming, winsome, riant, laughing, smiling, happy as a lark, in good *or* high spirits; buoyant, cheerful, cheery, sprightly, pert, jaunty; airy, breezy, light-hearted, jolly, jovial, convivial; mirthful, playful, jocose, frolicsome, jocund, sportive, zestful; spirited, enthusiastic, enthused, exhilarated, rhapsodic, rhapsodistic; ecstatic, jubilant, over-joyed, elated, exultant, in seventh heaven; rapturous, enrapt, enraptured, enchanted, entranced, transported.

3. lifelike, animal-like, puppetlike; mechanical, automated, automatic, wind-up; moving, propelled.

animating, *adj.* **1.** vivifying, quickening, vitalizing; life-giving, heart-stirring, enlivening, invigorating, energizing, fortifying, strengthening; encouraging, in-

spiring, buoying, heartening, enheartening, emboldening.
2. actuating, activating, motivating, moving, rousing, wakening; inciting, stimulating, stirring, goading, prodding.

animation, *n.* **1.** liveliness, vivacity, spirit, animal spirits; dash, élan, zest, verve, flair, zing; fire, warmth, glow, fervency, ardor; dazzle, brilliance, *Music.* bravura; sprightliness, airiness, breeziness, buoyancy, cheer; ebullience, sparkle, effervescence; vigor, vim, *It. brio, Inf.* pep; vitality, life, energy; exuberance, enthusiasm, zeal, fervor, passion, intensity.
2. enlivenment, inspiritment, invigoration; encouragement, enheartenment, emboldening; urging, exhortation, instigation, stimulation, incitation, motivation, inspiration.

animosity, *n.* **1.** ill will, hostility, invidiousness, abhorrence, aversion, rankling aversion; opposition, vehement opposition, antipathy, rancor, antagonism, malevolence, malignity.
2. enmity, animus, loathing, hatred, detestation; virulence, spleen, acerbity, acrimony, gall, bitterness; anger, pique, umbrage, malice, spite, resentment; unfriendliness, dislike.
3. grudge, feud, bad blood, hostile relations, discord, contention.

animus, *n.* **1.** animosity, ill will, hostility, invidiousness; antipathy, rancor, antagonism, malevolence, malignity.
2. purpose, intention, will, mind, temper; inclination, disposition, spirit, animating nature.

annals, *n.* archives, chronicles, records, registers; annual reports, yearbooks, classbooks; journals, memoirs, diaries.

anneal, *v.* strengthen, toughen, temper, harden, firm up, indurate.

annex, *v.* **1.** attach, connect, affix, tack on; incorporate, include, take in, join, link, unite, consolidate, combine, merge; append, subjoin, suffix, postfix; supplement, superadd, add on to, enlarge, extend, expand, augment.
2. acquire, obtain, get, gain; take, procure, pick up; appropriate, arrogate, usurp, accroach, confiscate, expropriate, seize, take over, *Law.* sequester.
3. characterize, attribute, accredit, ascribe, credit, assign, impute, consider *or* regard as.
—n. **4.** attachment, appurtenance, appurtenant, adjunct, ancilla, appanage, annexation, *Rare.* annexment, ell, wing; supplementation, superaddition, addition, additament, extension, expansion, enlargement; complement, completer, accessory, accompaniment, concomitant.
5. affiliate, subsidiary, subdivision; branch, arm, division, section, part.
6. appendix, addendum, supplement, codicil, *Law.* allonge; epilogue, postscript, p.s., P.S., subjoinder, subjunction, endpiece, tailpiece, suffix, postfix, tag.

annexation, *n.* **1.** attachment, connection, affixation, affixture; incorporation, inclusion, consolidation, combination, merger, merge, merging; juncture, joining, linking, union, uniting; supplementation, superaddition, enlargement, extension, expansion, augmentation.
2. appropriation, procurement; arrogation, usurpation, accroachment; confiscation, expropriation, seizure, takeover, *Law.* sequestration.
3. appendage, appurtenance, appurtenant, adjunct, ancilla, appanage, *Rare.* annexment, ell, wing; supplement, addition, additament; complement, completer, accessory, accompaniment, concomitant.

annihilate, *v.* **1.** exterminate, obliterate, discreate, reduce to nothing, eradicate, erase, blot *or* wipe out, *Sl.* mop up, efface, dissolve, eliminate, extirpate, destroy totally, decimate, liquidate, massacre, kill off, slaughter, butcher, mow down; undo, cut off, put an end to, abolish, extinguish, quench, quash; raze, level, tear to the ground, ravage, gut, blast, devastate, ruin, desolate, demolish, wreck, smash, dismantle, lay in ruins; kill, murder, slay, *Sl.* rub out, cut down, put to death, execute, do to death, put to the sword, destroy, assassinate; uproot, root out, deracinate, *Obs.* overruncate.
2. invalidate, void, cancel, annul, nullify, retract, repeal, rescind, countermand, revoke, withdraw, abrogate, suppress.
3. trounce, trample, thrash, defeat thoroughly *or* utterly, rout, overwhelm, discomfit, humble, tread *or* trample underfoot, *Sl.* wipe the floor with, vanquish, conquer; crush, break, smash.

annihilation, *n.* **1.** butchery, carnage, slaughter, wholesale *or* general slaughter, wholesale killing, mass murder, mass homicide, mass slaying, mass execution, mass destruction, blood bath, decimation, liquidation, blotting *or* wiping out, genocide, pogrom, holocaust, *Euph., Hist.* Final Solution; murder, killing, slaying, cutting down, mowing down, *Sl.* mopping up, assassination, execution, deathblow, finishing stroke, killing blow; razing, gutting, leveling, blasting, smashing, dismantling.
2. extermination, obliteration, extinction, utter *or* total destruction, discreation, eradication, effacement, dissolution, disestablishment, elimination, extirpation, undoing, end, *Sl.* curtains, abolition, extinguishment; ravagement, devastation, ruination, desolation, demolition, wreckage.
3. invalidation, voidance, cancellation, annulment, nullification, retraction, repeal, rescindment, countermand, revocation, withdrawal, abrogation, suppression.

anniversary, *n.* **1.** birthday, red-letter day, *Fr. anniversaire;* centennial, centenary, bicentennial, *Chiefly Brit.* bicentenary.
2. jubilee, celebration, commemoration, fete.
—adj. **3.** annual, yearly, *Chiefly Brit.* twelvemonthly; centennial, bicentennial.

annotate, *v.* gloss, *Archaic.* gloze, note, footnote, interline, interlineate; elucidate, explain, illustrate, construe, expound; comment, remark upon, commentate, interpret.

annotation, *n.* **1.** notes, footnotes, gloss, glossary, appendix, scholium, marginalia, remarks; commentary, explanation, exegesis, exposition, elucidation, illustration, interpretation.
2. commenting, remarking on, making notes, supplying with notes.

annotator, *n.* glossarist, scholiast; commentator, explainer, expositer, expounder, interpreter.

announce, *v.* **1.** proclaim, promulgate, declare, *Scot. and North Eng.* kithe, call out; trumpet, herald, blazon, voice abroad, bruit; publish, print, *Archaic.* divulgate, reveal, disclose; publicize, placard, advertize, bill, bulletin, post; circulate, disseminate.
2. tell, state, inform, notify, give notice, apprise, signal; harbinger, usher in, state the approach of.

announcement, *n.* **1.** proclamation, pronunciamento, promulgation, declaration, annunciation; decree, ordinance, edict, rescript; statement, enunciation, recital.
2. publication, revelation, disclosure, *Archaic.* divulgation; broadcast, bulletin, report, communiqué, information, news, tidings, word; cable, wire, telegram; letter, missive, card.
3. message, commercial, advertisement, placard; broadside, leaflet, pamphlet, handbill, bill, brochure,

flier.

announcer, *n.* **1.** newscaster, reporter, anchor man; broadcaster, disk jockey, d.j., *Sl.* deejay; moderator, master of ceremonies, m.c., emcee.

2. messenger, harbinger, herald, forerunner; proclaimer, crier, trumpeter.

annoy, *v.* **1.** bother, pester, hector, harass, *Sl.* bug, *Sl.* hassle, *Sl.* drive [s.o.] nuts *or* crazy *or* bananas, *Sl.* drive [s.o.] up the wall; hound, dog, nag, pick on, pick at, *Sl.* ride, *Inf.* give [s.o.] a bad *or* hard time; bedevil, torment, tease, taunt, tweak, mock, *Inf.* needle; persecute, bully, bullyrag; trouble, plague, fret, worry, *Scot.* thraw, *Scot.* fash.

2. irritate, irk, pique, vex, provoke, peeve, nettle, chafe, get on [s.o.'s] nerves, *Chiefly U.S.* rile, *Inf.* aggravate, *Inf.* miff, *Inf.* give [s.o.] a pain, *Inf.* rub [s.o.] the wrong way, *Inf.* get under [s.o.'s] skin, *Inf.* get in [s.o.'s] hair; exasperate, ruffle, roil, disturb, perturb, disquiet, discompose, discountenance, put out, put off, try [s.o.'s] patience, *Inf.* get, *Sl.* get [s.o.'s] goat.

3. anger, incense, raise [s.o.'s] ire *or* hackles, get [s.o.'s] back up, *Inf.* get [s.o.'s] Irish *or* dander up, *Inf.* burn [s.o.] up, *Sl.* tick [s.o.] off, *Sl.* tee [s.o.] off; enrage, madden, infuriate, make [s.o.'s] blood boil, *Inf.* make [s.o.] see red; exacerbate, rankle, gall.

annoyance, *n.* **1.** irritant, nuisance, bother, pest, bur, thorn in the side *or* flesh, pea in the shoe, salt in the wound, *Inf.* headache, *Inf.* pain, *Sl.* pain in the neck *or* rear, *Sl.* hassle; trouble, problem, affliction; trial, ordeal, tribulation; weight, load, burden, heavy load *or* burden; bore, crashing bore; peeve, gripe, complaint, grievance.

2. provocation, incitement, incitation, excitation, agitation, deliberate aggravation.

3. irritation, vexation, exasperation, pique; irritating, annoying, vexing, exasperating, nettling, ruffling, disturbing; bothering, pestering, hectoring, harassing, *Sl.* bugging; hounding, dogging, nagging, *Sl.* riding; tormenting, teasing, taunting, persecuting, bullying.

4. displeasure, discontent, discontentment, dissatisfaction, disapproval, disapprobation; anger, ire, dudgeon, high dudgeon.

annoying, *adj.* **1.** bothersome, pestering, *Inf.* pesky, *Inf.* pestiferous, vexatious; troublesome, troubling, thorny, fretful, worrisome, worrying, *Dial.* plaguy; hectoring, harassing, hounding, dogging, nagging, tormenting.

2. nettlesome, nettling, irritating, *Inf.* aggravating, *Inf.* in one's hair; disturbing, perturbing, ruffling, disquieting, vexing.

3. unpleasant, disagreeable, distasteful; invidious, hateful, offensive, objectionable, obnoxious, odious, execrable; intolerable, unbearable, too much, *Inf.* a bit much.

4. angering, incensing, irksome, irking; maddening, infuriating, enraging; exacerbating, rankling, galling, embittering.

annual, *adj.* **1.** yearly, once a year, anniversary, (*of biological activity*) circannual; yearlong, perennial.
—n. **2.** yearbook, classbook; annals, *Archaic.* annal.

annually, *adv.* yearly, by the year, per annum, once a year, year after year, every year.

annul, *v.* **1.** nullify, disannul, abolish, declare null and void, render null and void, void, avoid; quash, invalidate, vacate, disenact, disestablish, cancel, discharge, supersede, set aside; repeal, revoke, reverse, *Law.* disaffirm, rescind, abrogate; *Law.* nol-pros, break off, stop, discontinue, suspend.

2. recant, retract, withdraw, recall, undo; go back on one's word, renege, back-pedal, eat one's words; renounce, abjure, repudiate, disclaim, disavow; countermand, counterorder, overrule, override, counteract, contravene; terminate, dissolve, put an end to, bring to an end.

3. eliminate, do away with, destroy, extinguish, efface, wipe out; obliterate, reduce to nothing, annihilate, eradicate, expunge, extirpate, exterminate; blot out, stamp out, crush out, sweep away.

annulment, *n.* **1.** nullification, annulling, disannulment, abolishment, abolition, voidance, *Law.* avoidance, *Law.* defeasance; quashing, invalidation, *Obs.* vacatur, disenactment, disestablishment, cancellation, discharge, setting aside; repeal, revocation, rescinding, rescission, abrogation, reversal; *Law.* nolle prosequi, cessation, discontinuance, suspension.

2. recantation, retraction, withdrawal, recall, undoing; renouncement, abjuration, repudiation, disclaimer, disavowal; countermand, counterorder, overruling, overriding; termination, dissolution, putting an end to, bringing to an end.

anodyne, *n.* **1.** painkiller, narcotic, opiate; laudanum, morphine, opium, poppy, mandrake, mandragora, nepenthe; sedative, tranquilizer, stupefacient; alleviative, palliative, lenitive; salve, ointment, balm, *Med.* calmative, *Med.* analgesic.

2. assuagement, relief, easing, easement, letup, respite, remission; abatement, mitigation, alleviation, palliation; softening, mollification, soothing, comfort.
—adj. **3.** pain-relieving, pain-killing, febrifuge, anesthetic; palliative, alleviative, relieving, soothing, assuasive; sedative, *Med.* calmative, lenitive, abirritant; emollient, demulcent, softening.

anoint, *n.* **1.** oil, embrocate, *Archaic.* salve; grease, lubricate, lard; smear, spread over, moisten, daub, slick on.

2. consecrate, sanctify, bless, hallow; dedicate, devote, *Archaic.* anele; ordain, crown, enthrone.

anomalous, *adj.* **1.** deviate, deviant, aberrant, divergent, heterodox, heretical, errant, wayward, devious; abnormal, irregular, variable, anomalistic; deviating, diverging, departing, digressing, lapsing, wandering, rambling, straying, roving.

2. strange, odd, peculiar, curious, queer, eccentric, offbeat, *Inf.* quirky; unconventional, uncommon, unusual, unique, extraordinary, exceptional, singular, individual; monstrous, heteroclite, heteroclitical, unnatural, freakish, *Inf.* freaky.

3. incongruous, incongruent, different, disparate, mismatched, ill-fitting, inharmonious, discordant, dissonant; inappropriate, inapplicable, inapropos, inapt, unsuited, unsuitable, inapposite, out of place; unfit, unacceptable, out of line, out of hand; contradictory, conflicting, contrary, inconsistent, discrepant.

anomaly, *n.* **1.** deviation, aberration, aberrance, aberrancy, divergence, digression, departure, divagation, divarication, *Rare.* anomalism; abnormality, abnormity, irregularity, variation.

2. nonconformist, deviate, deviant, deviator, radical, heretic, *Chiefly Brit.* punk; misfit, maverick, drop out, loner, lone wolf, solitary, solitary man, fish out of water, square peg in a round hole; character, card, original, pip, sport, exception, individual, nonesuch, nondescript, bohemian; crank, fanatic; crazy, flake, freak, three-dollar bill, crackpot, rare bird, queer fellow, queer duck, queer potato, *Inf.* fruitcake, *Inf.* dingbat, *Inf.* ding-a-ling; *All Sl.* weirdo, weirdy, weirdie, creep, oddball, screwball, nut, loony, looner, case, geezer, kook, odd duck, squirrel; monster, monstrosity, miscreation, malformation, abortion, deformity, mutant, freak, freak of nature, heteroclite, teratogeny.

3. oddity, peculiarity, curiosity, eccentricity, idiosyncrasy, idiocrasy, hobby horse, quirk; strangeness, oddness, queerness, curiousness, freakishness, bizarreness; uncommonness, uncommonality, unconventionality, unusualness, nonconformity, exception, singularity, singularness, individuality, individualness.

4. incongruity, incongruousness, difference, dissimilitude, variance, contrast, diversity, disparity; incoherence, inharmony, dissonance, discord, discordance, discordancy; inconsistency, discrepancy; incompatibility, unsuitability, unsuitableness, inaptitude, unfitness, inappropriateness, inapplicability.

anon, *adv.* **1.** soon, presently, in a little while, shortly, after a while; by and by, betimes, before long, *Archaic.* erelong, *Archaic.* eftsoons; early, ahead of time, beforehand.

2. later, at another time, then; afterward, afterwards, hereupon, thereupon.

3. immediately, at once, directly, straightway, straightaway; now, right now, right away, without delay, forthwith, forthright; presently, promptly, readily; instantly, right off, instanter, this moment.

4. ever and anon occasionally, now and again, now and then, at times; sometimes, intermittently, periodically, fitfully.

anonym, *n.* pseudonym, allonym, cryptonym, code name, ananym; alias, assumed name, false name, pen name, nom de plume, *Fr. nom de guerre*; professional name, stage name.

anonymous, *adj.* nameless, unnamed, innominate, anonymal; unknown, undesignated, unacknowledged, unspecified; pseudonymous, allonymous, cryptonymous, ananymous.

another, *adj.* **1.** a second, a further, an additional, an extra, a supplementary, a supplemental, one more.

2. a different, a distinct, a separate, some other; not the same, unidentical, dissimilar, variant.

answer, *n.* **1.** acknowledgment, confirmation, reply; response, rejoinder, return, replication, respondence; retort, repartee, riposte, *Sl.* comeback, retaliation, back talk, *Inf.* sass.

2. counterblast, countercharge, recrimination, counterstatement, counterclaim, refutation, rebuttal; *Both Law.* surrebuttal, surrejoinder; *Both Law.* plea, defense.

3. solution, explanation, interpretation, justification, reason; key, clue.

—*v.* **4.** make answer, acknowledge, confirm; reply, respond, field, rejoin, return; retort, riposte, *Sl.* come back; answer back, talk back, *Inf.* sass; retaliate, get back at.

5. solve, satisfy, explain, interpret, justify.

6. serve, fulfill, satisfy, serve the purpose; do, be adequate, be sufficient, be enough, pass, pass muster, measure up.

7. conform, correspond, correlate, be similar, be like.

8. answer for pay for, suffer for, atone for, make amends for, make reparation for, expiate; redeem, make good on, recompense, repay; redress, rectify, make *or* set right, put *or* set straight, settle.

answerable, *adj.* **1.** liable, accountable, responsible, chargeable, amenable; subject, obligated, obliged.

2. refutable, repudiable, rebuttable, disprovable, confutable.

3. correlative, proportionate, complementary; commensurate, commensurable, suitable, suited, corresponding, correspondent, accordant, agreeable.

ant, *n.* pismire, hymenopteron, hymenopter, *Chiefly Dial.* emmet, *Latin. formica, Fr. fourmi, Span. hormiga;* red ant, agricultural ant, harvester ant, leaf-cutting ant; foraging ant, army ant, driver ant, legionary ant; carpenter ant, white ant, termite.

antagonism, *n.* **1.** hostility, animosity, animus, hatred, enmity, ill will; antipathy, inimicalness, inimicality, unfriendliness.

2. opposition, oppugnancy, counterpressure, contrariety, antithesis, contradiction; conflict, rivalry, competition, *Obs.* emulation.

antagonist, *n.* enemy, foe, adversary, opponent, opposer; disputant, rival, vier; competitor, contender, contestant.

antagonistic, *adj.* **1.** opposing, opposed, adverse, antithetic, antithetical, oppugnant, counteractive, repugnant, thwarting; disputative, disputatious, contentious, argumentative, quarrelsome; rival, rivaling, competing, contrary, contradictory, renitent; discordant, dissonant, disharmonious, incongruous; disagreeing, incompatible, uncongenial, at odds.

2. hostile, antipathetic, inimical, unfriendly, at variance, on bad terms, on the outs; belligerent, bellicose, pugnacious, up in arms.

antagonize, *v.* **1.** embitter, set against, alienate, estrange, disaffect.

2. oppose, dispute, contradict, counteract, be contrary to, turn against, turn upon; rival, compete with, vie; oppugn, struggle with, contend with, go up against.

3. annoy, irritate, pester, anger. See **annoy**.

antecede, *v.* **1.** precede, come *or* go before, come first, go ahead of, go in advance; lead, head, *Inf.* head up, front.

2. outrank, outstrip, rate, have precedence.

3. usher in, herald, proclaim, announce, introduce; presage, anticipate; predate, antedate.

antecedence, *n.* precedence, precession, anteposition; priority, preference, preeminence; preexistence, anteriority, earliness, previousness.

antecedent, *adj.* **1.** preceding, precedent, prevenient, preliminary, anterior, forerunning, foregoing; earlier, former, preexistent; aforesaid, aforementioned.

—*n.* **2.** precursor, forerunner, front *or* lead runner; harbinger, herald, announcer, messenger, vaunt-courier.

3. antecedents a. ancestors, predecessors, antecessors, forefathers, fathers, progenitors, primogenitors. **b.** history, record, family history *or* record; ancestry, family, family tree, lineage, genealogy, stock, line, pedigree, house.

antedate, *v.* **1.** (*all with reference to age or time*) antecede, forerun, forego, precede, come *or* go before, come first.

2. anachronize, misdate, mistime, foredate, postdate; date back, backdate, assign to an earlier *or* previous date.

3. accelerate, precipitate, speed, speed up, hurry, hurry up, hasten, rush.

4. anticipate, foretaste, forestall.

antediluvian, *adj.* **1.** primeval, primal, prehistoric, preglacial, preadamic, Noachian, Noachic, Noachical; eolithic, Paleolithic, Mesolithic, Neolithic, before the Flood *or* Deluge; primary, prime, pristine, early, earliest, initial, first; autochthonal, autochthonous, aboriginal.

2. antiquated, antique, fossilized, fossil-like, ancient, archaic; superannuated, oldest, age-old, immemorial, old, old as the hills, time worn, elderly, aged; atavistic, old-fashioned, old-fogyish, old-time, bygone, unmodern, quaint, old-world; out-of-date, outmoded, passé, obsolescent, obsolete.

3. primitive, primordial, primigenial, elementary, simple, uncomplicated; rudimentary, rudimental, embryonic, undeveloped; crude, unrefined, coarse, rough, unpolished; uncivilized, barbaric.

—*n.* **4.** prehistoric man, Cro-Magnon, preadamite, cave man, ape-man, pithecanthrope, troglodyte; prim-

itive, autochthon, aboriginal, *Australian Inf.* boong.
5. ancient, venerable, patriarch, elder, old timer, granny, Methuselah, *Inf.* oldster, *Sl.* relic; old fogy, *Inf.* fuddy-duddy, *Inf.* stick-in-the-mud.

anterior, *adj.* **1.** advanced, forward, placed in advance *or* at the front *or* forward, ranged at the front, set in the van.
2. antecedent, preceding, precedent, prevenient, preliminary, forerunning, foregoing; earlier, former, preexistent; aforesaid, aforementioned.

anteriority, *n.* antecedence, precedence, precession, anteposition; priority, preference, preeminence; preexistence, previousness, earliness.

anteroom, *n.* **1.** antechamber, vestibule, lobby, foyer, parlor, locutorium; entranceway, entrance, narthex, propylaeum, propylon.
2. waiting room, lounge, reception room, outer room.

anthem, *n.* hymn, sacred song, psalm, song of joy, song of praise; paean, canticle, chant, plain song *or* plainchant, *Music.* motet, *Eccles.* antiphon, *Eccles.* responsory; chorus, chorale, *Eccles.* offertory, *Anglican Ch.* introit, recessional hymn.

anthology, *n.* collection, compendium, compilation, chrestomathy; digest, treasury, ana, collectanea, miscellany, album; garland, florilegium, spicilegium; selections, extracts, excerpta, citations, analects.

antic, *n.* **1.** *Usu.* **antics** caper, frolic, lark, romp, spree, gambol, frisk; sport, fun, merrymaking, playing; fooling around, foolishness, silliness, foolery, tomfoolery, horseplay; clowning, clownery, clownishness; buffoonery, buffoonism, buffoonishness, harlequinade.
2. *Usu.* **antics** prank, trick, joke, practical joke, *Inf.* dido; mischief, *Inf.* shenanigans, *Sl.* monkeyshines, *Sl.* monkey business, escapade, adventure; prankishness, *Inf.* hanky-panky, *Scot. and North Eng.* daffing.
—*v.* **3.** caper, frolic, *Inf.* skylark, romp, lark, gambol, frisk; play, sport, make merry, have fun; fool around, *Sl.* horse around, clown around, *Sl.* cut up; play tricks, play pranks, make mischief.

anticipate, *v.* **1.** foresee, foreglimpse, apprehend, antedate, foretaste; foreknow, precognize, preconceive, intuit; predict, foretell, forecast, prophesy.
2. expect, count on, reckon on, calculate upon, hope for, pin hope on; await, look forward to, look toward, look out for, watch out for, look for, *Sl.* lick one's chops over.
3. nullify, prevent, preclude, obviate, forestall, intercept; beat to the draw, *Inf.* get the jump on.
4. contemplate, consider, think about, have in mind, envisage, envision.

anticipation, *n.* **1.** foretaste, *Archaic.* antepast, foreglimpse, foreglance, foregleam, prior realization; contemplation, envisagement, envisionment.
2. expectation, prospect, thought; hope, hopefulness, faith, trust; confidence, assurance, certainty.
3. presentiment, premonition, preapprehension, foreboding, previous notion, vague idea, feeling, *Inf.* funny feeling, *Inf.* hunch; intimation, hint, suggestion.
4. intuition, foreknowledge, foresight, forefeeling, prescience, precognition, prevision, second sight, sixth sense.

anticipative, *adj.* **1.** expectant, expecting, in expectation, anticipating, anticipatory; hopeful, optimistic, sanguine.
2. precognitive, precognoscent, presentient; foreseeing, foreboding, prescient, foreknowing.

anticlimax, *n.* **1.** descent, drop, decrease, deflation, comedown; bathos, banality, triteness, triviality, commonplaceness.
2. disappointment, disillusionment, disenchantment, letdown; failure, fiasco, *Inf.* fizzle, *Inf.* dud, *Sl.* bomb.

antidote, *n.* **1.** counterpoison, counteracter, alexipharmic, theriac, theriaca; neutralizer, nullifier, *Old. Pharm.* mithridate; antiphogistic, counterirritant, antipyretic; cathartic, purgative, emetic, emetine, laxative.
2. antitoxin, antibody, antivenin, *Immun.* alexin, *Immun.* complement; preventive, preventive measure, protection, immunization, vaccination, vaccine, *Med.* prophylactic.
3. remedy, cure, curative, corrective, restorative, application, *Med.* specific; medicine, medication, medicament, drug, pharmaceutical, physic.

antipathetic, *adj.* **1.** abhorrent, odious, loathsome; antagonistic, invidious, hostile, hateful, averse, antipathetical.
2. offensive, disgusting, repugnant, aversive, distasteful, revolting, repulsive, repellent; obnoxious, nauseating, sickening, nauseous, *Inf.* allergic; unlikable, dislikable, unpleasant, displeasing; opposed, antithetical, antipodean, antipodal, clashing.

antipathy, *n.* **1.** abhorrence, loathing, detestation, hatred, hate; aversion, antagonism, hostility, enmity, animosity, animus, bad blood, ill will, *Archaic.* dyspathy; dislike, disrelish, disinclination, disfavor, uncongeniality, unfriendliness; incompatibility, contrariety, disagreement, clash.
2. opposition, antithesis; reluctance, unwillingness; disgust, revulsion, repugnance, distaste, *Inf.* allergy, nausea.

antiquary, *n.* **1.** antiquarian, archaist, paleologist, archaeologist; classicist, medievalist; dryasdust.
2. antiquer, antique dealer; curator, curatrix, collector.

antiquate, *v.* **1.** supersede, replace, retire; outmode, outdate, date, fossilize; superannuate, age.
2. antique, archaize.

antiquated, *adj.* **1.** obsolete, extinct, passé, outdated, out-of-date, outworn, outmoded, out of style, out; superseded, disused, out of use; bygone, past, *Archaic.* olden; obsolescent, dated, on the way out.
2. ancient, archaic, archaistic, fossil, fossilized, fossil-like, antique; superannuated, oldest, age-old, immemorial, remote, old, old as the hills, timeworn, elderly, aged; venerable, gray, hoary, *Rare.* hoar, patriarchal.
3. atavistic, old-fashioned, old-time, old-fogyish; unmodern, of the old school, quaint, old-world.

antique, *adj.* **1.** superannuated, oldest, age-old, old, old as the hills, timeworn, elderly, aged.
2. autochthonal, autochthonous, aboriginal, original; pristine, early, earliest, primitive, primordial, primigenial; primeval, primal, prehistoric, preglacial, preadamic, Noachian, Noachiac, Noachical, antediluvian, before the Flood *or* Deluge; ancient, archaic, archaistic, fossil, fossilized, fossil-like.
3. atavistic, old-fashioned, old-time, old-fogyish, of the old school; unmodern, quaint, old-world, colonial.
4. (*all of paper*) parchmentlike, parchmenty, uncalendered, uncoated, unglazed, rough.
—*n.* **5.** bibelot, curio, rarity, *Fr. objet d'art;* antiquity, relic, artifact, fossil, archaism.
—*v.* **6.** antiquate, archaize; emboss.

antiquity, *n.* **1.** ancientness, primordiality, primordialism; aboriginality, autochthonism, autochthonousness; oldness, elderliness, old age, agedness, *Archaic.* eld, venerableness.
2. eons ago, early ages, ancient times, time immemorial, distant past, days of old, olden days, *Obs.* yore.
3. **antiquities** *n.* **a.** relics, artifacts, fossils, archaisms; antiques, bibelots, curios; ruins, remains, remnants. **b.** ancients, aboriginals, aborigines,

autochthons; venerables, patriarchs, elders.

antiseptic, *adj.* **1.** disinfectant, germicidal, bactericidal.

2. sterile, germfree, uncontaminated, unpolluted; spotless, immaculate, clean, pure, scrubbed.

—n. **3.** disinfectant, germicide, bactericide; purifier, cleanser, *Eccles.* purificator.

antisocial, *adj.* unsociable, unfriendly, uncommunicative, reserved, closed, unsympathetic; antagonistic, hostile, menacing, threatening; opposed, conflicting, clashing, incompatible; misanthropic, man-hating, woman-hating, cynical; anarchic, revolutionary, radical, unpatriotic.

antithesis, *n.* **1.** opposition, contrast, contraposition, contrariety.

2. reverse, contrary, converse, inverse; opposite, antipode, other extreme, pole.

antithetic, *adj.* opposed, contrasted, opposite, antithetical, antipodian; counter, contrary, reverse, converse, inverse; diametrically opposed, polar, poles apart.

antitoxin, *n.* **1.** antibody, counteracter, antivenin, counterpoison, *Immun.* alexin, *Immun.* complement; neutralizer, nullifier, *Old Pharm.* mithridate.

2. vaccine, antiserum, serum, antidote, vaccinia, virus, *Med.* specific, *Vet. Pathol.* cowpox; preventive, protection, vaccination, inoculation, alexipharmic, theriac, theriaca, *Med.* prophylactic.

anxiety, *n.* **1.** uneasiness, disquiet, disquietude, inquietude, fretfulness; worry, trouble, concern, care, solicitude; nervousness, ants, *Inf.* butterflies, *Inf.* butterflies in one's stomach, *Sl.* heebie-jeebies, *Sl.* habdabs; misgiving, presentiment, foreboding; apprehension, fear, dread, angst; anguish, pain, suffering, torment, torture.

2. eagerness, avidity, intentness; desire, yearning, longing, aching.

anxious, *n.* **1.** distressed, disturbed, worried, troubled, carking, concerned, solicitous; uneasy, ill at ease, disquieted, unquiet, fretful, restless, itching; nervous, *Sl.* antsy, *Inf.* on pins and needles, on tenterhooks; on edge, perturbed, worked *or* wrought up; watchful, apprehensive, *Inf.* with one's heart in one's mouth, fearful, afraid; anguished, pained, suffering, tormented, tortured.

2. desirous, eager, avid, intent, keen, ardent.

any, *adj.* **1.** one, a, an, a single one, some; any one, *Inf.* any old, whatever, whichever; every, all.

—pron. **2.** anybody, anyone, somebody, someone.

—adv. **3.** somewhat, to some extent, to any extent, at all, in any degree, in the least, even a little bit.

anyhow, *adv.* **1.** in any way, anyway, *Dial.* anyways, anywise, in any manner, by any means.

2. in any case, at all events, in any event; no matter what, regardless, anyway, in spite of the fact that, notwithstanding; at any rate, nevertheless, nonetheless.

3. carelessly, haphazardly, any which way, negligently, sloppily; heedlessly, mindlessly, without thinking.

anytime, *adv.* **1.** at any time, whenever, at any moment, no matter when, whenever you like, at your convenience, when you will.

2. invariably, without exception, always, without fail, every time, consistently.

anyway, *adv.* in any way, anyhow, in any case, any which way. See **anyhow** (*defs.* **1-3**).

apace, *adv.* quickly, speedily, rapidly, swiftly, hurriedly; hastily, posthaste, with dispatch, expeditiously, readily; full speed, in full sail, *Inf.* lickety-split, *U.S. Army.* in double time, double-quick; at top speed, in high gear, hotfoot, zooming, full tilt; tantivy, at full gallop, hellbent, whip and spur, amain; headlong, hurry-scurry, pell mell.

apart, *adv.* **1.** separately, singly, alone, individually, independently; privately, secretly, exclusively; aloof, distant, away, afar; to the side, aside, by itself *or* oneself, to itself *or* oneself.

2. asunder, disjointly, *Archaic.* atwain, in pieces, to pieces, in two.

3. **apart from** besides, aside from, in addition to; other than, not counting, beyond that, excluding, except for.

apartment, *n.* **1.** flat, tenement, rent, walk-up, cold-water flat, *Brit.* chambers, *Brit.* apartments, *Chiefly Brit.* maisonette; penthouse, townhouse, suite, story, condominium, *Inf.* condo; chamber, room, stall, cell, nook, cabin, compartment.

2. apartment building, apartment house, apartment complex, apartment block, high rise, high riser, high-rise apartments, *Brit.* mansions.

3. quarters, living quarters, rooms, accommodations, housing, lodging, lodgings, lodging place, lodgment, housing, roof over one's head, *Inf.* pad, *Inf.* crash pad, *Chiefly Brit. Inf.* diggings, *Brit. Inf.* digs.

apathetic, *adj.* **1.** impassive, unemotional, emotionless, unfeeling, dispassionate, insentient, insensible, numb; cool, cold, frigid, frosty, icy; phlegmatic, lethargic, listless, languid, dull, stolid, bovine; inert, lifeless, torpid, inanimate, supine, spiritless, sluggish.

2. indifferent, unconcerned, unresponsive, uninterested, disinterested, incurious, uninquisitive; aloof, removed, detached, withdrawn.

apathy, *n.* **1.** impassivity, dispassion, lack of feeling *or* emotion, insentience, insensibility, unfeelingness, numbness; coolness, coldness, frigidity; phlegm, lethargy, languor, listlessness, dullness, stolidity, sluggishness, torpor; inertness, lifelessness, inanimation, supineness, spiritlessness.

2. indifference, unconcern, unresponsiveness, uninterestedness, disinterest, incuriousness, uninquisitiveness.

ape, *n.* **1.** monkey, gorilla, baboon, chimpanzee, chimp, orang-utan, gibbon, pongid, anthropoid, quadrumane.

2. imitator, mimic, *Inf.* copycat, parrot, echo, shadow, copyist.

—v. **3.** imitate, impersonate, *Inf.* take-off, *Inf.* do a take-off of, mimic, *Sl.* make like; mime, mirror, reflect, echo, parrot, take the appearance of; emulate, do like, follow suit, copy, affect, simulate, duplicate, reproduce, parallel; parody, caricature, burlesque, travesty, mock, sham, counterfeit, forge.

aperture, *n.* opening, hole, eye, eyelet, eyehole, peephole, pinhole, puncture, perforation, interstice, pore, bore, airhole, spiracle; slit, crack, gash, vent, slot, rent, foramen; chink, cleft, cranny, rift, crevice, fissure, *Archaic.* scissure; gap, break, breach, chasm, gulf, embouchure, open space, hiation; outlet, inlet, mouth, orifice, window, porthole, oriel; entrance, gate, hatch, door, portal, trap door, wicket, postern, vomitory, vomitorium; mousehole, keyhole, pigeonhole.

apex, *n.* **1.** summit, vertex, apogee, crest, heights, pinnacle, peak, spire, point, tip, tiptop; top, loft, aerie, cap, crown, headpiece, head.

2. acme, zenith, maximum, climax, culmination, crowning point, *Latin. ne plus ultra;* meridian, sublimity, supremacy, perfection, consummation, extreme, utmost, uttermost.

aphorism, *n.* proverb, apothegm, gnome, mot, adage, epigram, *Archaic.* word, *Archaic.* sentence; saw, pithy statement, sententious saying, saying; axiom, maxim, precept, dictum; epigram, witticism, *Fr. jeu d'esprit,* quip, Atticism; rule, golden rule, motto, moral, byword; cliché, hackneyed phrase, platitude, truism, *Inf.* bromide, commonplace.

aphrodisiac, *adj.* **1.** cantharidal, cantharidian, titillating, stimulating, exciting; seductive, enticing, alluring.

—n. **2.** cantharides, Spanish fly, philter, love potion; stimulative, stimulator, *Med.* stimulant, exciter, drug, turn-on.

apiarist, *n.* beekeeper, apaculturist, apiarian, bee breeder.

apiece, *adv.* each, for each one, for each, respectively; individually, separately, one by one, each to each; severally, distributively; seriatim, in a series, one after another.

aplomb, *n.* **1.** poise, assurance, confidence, self-assurance, self-confidence, self-possession, self-command; composure, steadiness, stability, self-restraint, self-control, collectedness; equanimity, calmness, equilibrium, balance, sang-froid, cool, imperturbability; sedateness, dispassion, staidness; level-headedness, common sense, rationality.

2. perpendicularity, verticality, uprightness, erectness, straightness.

apocalyptic, *adj.* revelatory, prophetic, fatidic, fatidical, vatic, vatical; predictive, prognosticative, augural, indicative; warning, signal, foreshadowing, forewarning; threatening, foreboding, ominous, portentious, oracular.

apocryphal, *adj.* **1.** unauthenticated, unverified, unconfirmed, unvalidated, unsubstantiated; unsanctioned, uncanonical; questionable, debatable, disputable, disputed, controvertible, controversial; dubitable, dubious, doubtful, uncertain, unsure, unknown.

2. false, spurious, unauthentic, not genuine; sham, *U.S.* bogus, mock, feigned, phony; untrue, fictitious, made-up, make-believe, unreal, imaginary.

apogee, *n.* **1.** summit, apex, vertex, crest, heights, pinnacle, peak, spire, point, tip, tip-top; top, head, headpiece, cap, crown, loft, aerie.

2. extremity, outer limit, farthest point; limit, bound, boundary, border, frontier; edge, rim, brim, brow, lip, ridge, verge, brink, margin; ultimate, terminal, terminus, termination, end.

apologetic, *adj.* **1.** sorry, regretful, remorseful, contrite, in sackcloth and ashes; expiatory, penitential, penitent, repentant; conscience-stricken, conscience-smitten, rueful, compunctious; self-reproachful, self-condemnatory, self-condemning, self-accusatory, self-accusing.

2. defensive, supportive, supporting; endorsing, sustaining, upholding, justificatory, justificative; vindicatory, vindicative, exonerative, exculpatory; mitigatory, palliatory, palliative, extenuatory, extenuating, excusatory; propitiatory, propitiative, conciliatory, conciliative.

apologist, *n.* **1.** defender, supporter, maintainer, seconder; pleader, arguer, advocate, vindicator, justifier, champion.

2. apologete, defender of the faith, evangelist.

apologize, *v.* **1.** beg pardon, ask pardon, make up; atone for, do penance, *Archaic.* shrive, expiate, make amends, eat humble pie; repent, regret, feel sorry, rue, lament.

2. defend, plead, argue, make a stand for, stand up for; support, bolster, uphold, maintain, sustain; endorse, second, advocate, espouse; vindicate, justify, excuse; palliate, propitiate, mitigate, extenuate.

apology, *n.* **1.** confession, expiation, lustration, purification, *Archaic.* shrift; amends, *Fr. amende honorable,* expression of regret *or* sorrow; penance, penitence, repentance; self-reproach, self-condemnation, self-accusation.

2. defense, plea, argument, claim, excuse, apologia; support, upholding, espousal, advocacy; vindication, exculpation, justification, explanation; palliation, extenuation, mitigation, propitiation.

3. makeshift, stopgap, excuse, poor excuse, poor specimen; pretext, pretense, semblance.

apostasy, *n.* **1.** (*all used in reference to allegiance or principles*) desertion, abandonment, forsaking, forswearing, relinquishment; rejection, rejecting, renunciation, renouncement, abjuration, repudiation.

2. withdrawal, secession; falling away, dropping out, *Sl.* copping out, turning one's back on; backsliding, recidivism, dereliction.

3. defection, treason, perfidy, betrayal; unfaithfulness, faithlessness, disloyalty, recreancy, recreance.

4. changeover, switchover, conversion; reversal, aboutface, turnabout, *Sl.* switcheroo, *Sl.* a 180°, *Inf.* flip-flop.

apostate, *n.* **1.** (*all used in reference to faith or principles*) deserter, renegade, recreant, defector, traitor; bolter, turncoat, retractor, recanter; tergiversator, straddler; renouncer, abjurer, repudiator, rejecter; dissenter, seceder; backslider, recidivist.

—adj. **2.** traitorous, treacherous, perfidious, recreant, renegade; disloyal, unfaithful, faithless, untrue, false.

3. heretical, schismatic, unorthodox, dissident, divergent; heathen, infidel, infidelic.

4. backsliding, recidivist, recidivous.

apostatize, *v.* **1.** (*all used in reference to faith or principles*) desert, abandon, forsake, forswear, reject, discard, relinquish; renounce, abjure, repudiate, disown; depart from, withdraw from, secede.

2. defect, change sides, go over, bolt, shift ground, change loyalties, turn traitor; tergiversate, veer round, do an aboutface, reverse oneself; recant, retract, disavow, disclaim; backslide, fall away, recidivate, lapse, relapse.

apostle, *n.* **1.** missionary, evangelist, proselytizer, propagandist, spreader of the faith, minister of the Gospel, missioner; revivalist, reformer, faith healer; witness, disciple; priest, minister, parson, divine.

2. pioneer, groundbreaker, originator, initiator; avant-gardist, experimenter; crusader, campaigner, promoter, *Inf.* pusher; advocate, supporter, champion, defender, apologist.

3. messenger, emissary, envoy; agent, representative, spokesman, deputy.

apostolic, *adj.* **1.** evangelical, evangelic, scriptural, biblical, patristic, apostolical.

2. canonical, orthodox, authorized, accepted; historical, traditional, doctrinal, dogmatic.

3. ecclesiastical, ecclesial, churchly, hierarchical; sacerdotal, hieratic, priestly; prelatic, episcopal; papal, pontifical, pontific, *All Disparaging.* papistical, papistic, popish.

4. founded by the Apostles; Christian.

apostrophe, *n.* *Rhetoric.* address, salutation, speech, oration, soliloquy; entreaty, appeal, supplication, invocation, solicitation, obtestation, imploration.

apothecary, *n.* **1.** druggist, pharmacist, pharmaceutist, pharmacologist, pharmaceutical chemist.

2. pharmacy, *U.S.* drugstore.

apotheosis, *n.* **1.** deification, godding, canonization; dignifying, ennoblement, enthronement, enthronization, enshrinement, elevation; exaltation, glorification, celebration; idealization, setting *or* putting on a pedestal, idolatry, worshipping, adoration, adulation, veneration, reverence.

2. deity, god, dignity, highness, loftiness, crown; idol, hero, venerable; ideal, exemplar, perfection, sublimity.

apotheosize, *v.* **1.** deify, god, canonize; dignify,

ennoble, enthrone, enshrine, crown.
2. elevate, exalt, glorify, celebrate; extol, laud, praise, *Archaic.* magnify; idealize, set *or* put on a pedestal, hero-worship, worship, idolize, adore, venerate, revere, bow down to.

appall, *v.* **1.** frighten, *Archaic.* affright, alarm, scare, intimidate; harrow, horrify, terrify, frighten out of one's wits, scare to death; shock, startle, astound, stun, stupefy, paralyze, petrify.
2. dismay, consternate, discourage, dishearten, deter; daunt, awe, overawe, unnerve, unman; abash, confound, disconcert, discomfit, put out, take aback.
3. disgust, sicken, revolt, nauseate, repel, make one sick, make one's stomach turn, *Sl.* gross out.

appalling, *adj.* **1.** frightening, alarming, intimidating, harrowing, terrifying, horrifying; frightful, fearful, dreadful, awful, dire, terrible, horrible; horrid, hideous, ghastly, grisly; shocking, startling, astounding, stunning, stupefying, paralyzing, petrifying.
2. discouraging, disheartening, daunting, awe-inspiring, unnerving, unmanning.
3. disgusting, sickening, revolting, repulsive, repelling; nauseating, loathsome, insufferable.

apparatus, *n.* **1.** equipment, instruments, tools, utensils, appurtenances; machinery, mechanism, machines, appliances, fixtures, plant; gear, stuff, tackle, outfit, paraphernalia.
2. system, organization; network, structure, hierarchy, chain of command.
3. contrivance, device, gadget, *Inf.* thingumbob *or* thingumabob, *Inf.* thingumajig, *Inf.* doohickey, *Inf.* gismo, *Sl.* whatayacallit, *Inf.* whoosis, *Sl.* whoosiwhatsis.

apparel, *n.* **1.** clothing, clothes, attire, wear, wearing apparel; raiment, garments, vestments, habiliments, *Inf.* gear, *Inf.* toggery, *Inf.* togs, *Inf.* duds, *Sl.* threads, *Sl.* rags; wardrobe, array, accouterments; livery, uniform, regalia; investment, investiture, vesture.
2. decoration, adornment, ornamentation; cover, covering, outer covering; plumage, feathers; coat; pelt, hide.
3. dress, garb, costume, habit, masquerade, disguise; guise, appearance, aspect, look, style; outfit, trappings, *Inf.* getup, *Inf.* rig, *Inf.* turnout.
—*v.* **4.** dress, clothe, garb, vest, attire, habit, *Sl.* dude up, *Sl.* swank up; array, bedizen, deck, deck out, deck up, bedeck; rig, rig up, rig out, trap, trap out, caparison; outfit, fit out, fit up, fit, gear, turn out, accouter.
5. adorn, ornament, decorate, trim, garnish, furbish, embellish, *Archaic.* dight, *Archaic.* ouch; prettify, beautify, fix up, prink, *Inf.* titivate, *Inf.* spruce up, *Inf.* doll up, *Inf.* gussy up, *Sl.* trick up, *Sl.* dude up, *Sl.* swank up, *Sl.* fig out.

apparent, *adj.* **1.** visible, seeable, discernible, perceivable, perceptible; open, in full view, unconcealed, public, overt; exposed, showing, unhidden, uncovered, unveiled, unshrouded, uncurtained, naked, bare.
2. plain, clear, obvious, evident, *Fr. en évidence,* manifest, patent; distinct, in focus, lucid, plain as day, plain as the nose on one's face; conspicuous, noticeable, prominent, unmistakable; striking, blatant, obtrusive, flagrant, glaring, egregious.
3. ostensible, seeming, presumable, *Archaic.* semblable; outward, external, superficial; likely, probable; possible, conceivable, plausible, specious; quasi, as it were; self-declared, avowed, professed, pretended, alleged.

apparently, *adv.* **1.** visibly, discernibly, perceivably, at a glance, to the eye, at first sight; openly, in full view, in plain sight, publicly, overtly.
2. plainly, clearly, distinctly, obviously, evidently, manifestly, patently; conspicuously, noticeably, prominently, unmistakably; strikingly, blatantly, obtrusively, flagrantly, glaringly, egregiously.
3. seemingly, ostensibly, on the face of it; outwardly, superficially, externally, in semblance, in show; presumably, likely, probably, possibly, conceivably, plausibly, speciously; avowedly, professedly, pretendedly, allegedly.

apparition, *n.* **1.** ghost, shade, shadow, revenant, Doppelgänger, doubleganger; spirit, presence, wraith, fetch, banshee; phantom, phantasm, specter, *Inf.* spook; fairy, fay, sprite, elf, goblin; vision, eidolon, sight, image, hallucination, spectacle; ignis fatuus, friar's lantern, will-o'-the-wisp; illusion, chimera, figment of the imagination, phantom of the mind; bogy, hobgoblin.
2. appearance, manifestation, materialization, epiphany, occurrence; revelation, disclosure, presentation; opening, unfolding, unfoldment; emergence, issuance; phenomenon, object, form, shape, figure, thing.

appeal, *n.* **1.** entreaty, supplication, suppliance, plea, imploration, invocation, prayer; solicitation, petition, suit, address, request, adjuration.
2. attraction, attractiveness, interest, engagingness; charm, allure, fascination.
—*v.* **3.** entreat, beg, beseech, plead, implore, invoke; solicit, petition, apply to, address, ask, request, adjure.
4. attract, engage, charm, fascinate; allure, entice, invite, tempt.

appear, *v.* **1.** emerge, rise, uprise, loom up, come into view, enter the picture; dawn, arise, come to light, come forth, break forth, burst forth.
2. seem, look, look like, look as if, seem as if; exhibit, wear the aspect, strike one as being; be obvious, be patent, be plain, be self-evident, be clear.
3. attend, arrive, turn up, crop up, show up, show one's face; turn out, *Sl.* make the scene.
4. perform, come on, be on stage, enter.
5. be created, be developed, be invented, come into being.

appearance, *n.* **1.** arrival, advent, coming, upcropping, rise, emergence; introduction, debut, exhibition, publication.
2. demeanor, mien, air, cast, look, aspect, character; presence, attitude, bearing, style, carriage, deportment; figure, visage, countenance, features.
3. semblance, face value, *Inf.* front, guise, show, pretense, presentment, image; face, outward form, exterior.
4. **appearances** indications, outward impressions, circumstances.
5. **make an appearance** come, arrive, show up, *Sl.* make the scene.

appease, *v.* **1.** pacify, quiet, calm, tranquilize, lull, soothe, compose, comfort; alleviate, relieve, palliate, allay, assuage, mitigate, abate, moderate, temper, lessen; take the edge off of, blunt, dull, deaden; stifle, still, silence, hush, smother; quench, slake, satisfy, *Sl.* shut [s.o.] up, keep [s.o.] quiet, give a sop to; subdue, suppress, put down, quell, quash.
2. placate, pacificate, *Archaic.* attemper; humor, dulcify, mollify, soften; reconcile, *Archaic.* accord, bring to terms, make peace, settle differences, defuse, pour oil on troubled waters; mediate, arbitrate, bridge the gap, negotiate, intervene, intercede; reunite, mend, patch, patch up, repair the breach, smooth over.
3. propitiate, conciliate, accommodate, adjust, compromise; yield, submit, surrender, concede, give in,

cave in, accede to demands.

appeasement, *n.* **1.** pacification, alleviation, palliation, allaying, assuagement; mitigation, abatement, moderation, tempering, lessening; blunting, dulling, deadening; slaking, quenching, satisfying, satisfaction; stifling, stilling, silencing, hushing, smothering.

2. placation, dulcification, mollification, softening; conciliation, propitiation, compromise, concession, accommodation, adjustment.

3. surrender, yielding, submission, acquiescence, accession; peace-offering, reparation, amends, sop, pacifier; calumet, peace pipe, olive branch; white flag.

appellation, *n.* **1.** name, title, honorific, style, designation; epithet, appellative, by-word, label, tag, *Sl.* handle, *Sl.* moniker; nickname, sobriquet, cognomen, agnomen, by-name, pet name, diminutive; pseudonym, anonym, allonym, alias, assumed name, pen name, nom de plume, *Fr. nom de guerre,* stage name, *Fr. nom de théâtre.*

2. denomination, naming, calling, dubbing, christening; identification, definition.

appendage, *n.* **1.** attachment, appurtenance, appurtenant, adjunct, appanage; appendix, addendum, codicil, *Law.* allonge; epilogue, postscript, p.s., P.S., subjoinder, subjunction, end piece, tail piece, suffix, postfix, tag; supplement, supplementation, superaddition, addition, extension, annexation, *Rare.* annexment, annex, wing, ell; subsidiary, subdivision, division, part, section, branch, arm; member, leg, limb, tentacle, extremity; complement, completer, accessory, accompaniment; concomitant, concurrent, pendant, counterpart, corollary, correlative, *Astron.* comes.

2. servant, servitor, domestic, menial, hireling, acolyte, vassal, liegeman, *Hist.* retainer; manservant, man, valet, butler, major-domo, seneschal, factotum, steward, footman, lackey, *Archaic.* groom; maid, handmaid, woman, *Fr. femme de chambre;* cupbearer, Ganymede; *All Contemptuous.* flunky, satellite, slave, *Sl.* stooge; subordinate, underling, small fry, *Inf.* small potatoes; attendant, assistant, auxiliary, ancilla, aide, helper, coadjutor, coadjutress, supplementary, appendant; squire, equerry, courtier, gillie, page, footboy, aide-de-camp, *Mil.* orderly, *Obs.* waiter; affiliate, associate, fellow, sidekick.

3. follower, pursuivant, shadow, groupie; dependent, parasite, sycophant, leech, sponge, toady, hanger-on, *Archaic.* trencherman.

appendant, *adj.* **1.** attached, appended, suffixed, subjoined, annexed, added; suspended, pendant, hanging *or* swinging from; additional, supplementary, supplemental, codicillary, adjunct; subordinate, subsidiary, secondary, auxiliary, ancillary.

2. accompanying, accessory, complementary, attendant, associated, affiliated; connected, related, relative, correlative, correlated, dependent, concomitant, concurrent; consequent, consequential, resultant, resulting, following *or* progressing from.

—n. **3.** attachment, appurtenance, appurtenant, adjunct, appanage, appendage; appendix, addendum, *Law.* allonge; supplement, supplementation, superaddition, addition, extension, annexation, *Rare.* annexment, annex, wing, ell.

4. complement, completer, accessory, accompaniment; concomitant, concurrent, pendant, counterpart, corollary, correlative, *Astron.* comes.

appendix, *n.* **1.** supplement, addendum, codicil, *Law.* allonge; epilogue, postscript, p.s., P.S., subjoinder, subjunction, suffix, postfix, endpiece, tailpiece, tag.

2. appendage, attachment, appurtenance, appurtenant, adjunct, appanage; supplementation, superaddition, addition, extension, annexation, *Rare.* annexment, annex.

appetence, *n.* **1.** desire, want, need, yearning, longing, wish, wishfulness; craving, appetite, hunger, taste *or* thirst for, appetency.

2. drive, instinct, passion, lust, aphrodisia, *Both Psychoanal.* libido, id; inclination, predilection, penchant, predisposition; tendency, propensity, proclivity, leaning, bent.

3. affinity, partiality, bias, liking, affection, fondness, love; attraction, magnetism, lure, allurement, pull.

appetite, *n.* **1.** hunger, thirst, craving, desire, want, need; appetency; voraciousness, ravenousness, edacity, gluttonousness, insatiability.

2. relish, taste, palate, sweet tooth; zest, gusto, partiality, bias, keenness; affinity, liking, affection, fondness, love; attraction, predilection, penchant; tendency, propensity, proclivity, leaning, bent.

appetizer, *n.* **1.** canapé, hors d'oeuvre, whet, *It. Cookery.* antipasto, *Hawaiian. pupu*; delicacy, dainty, tidbit, morsel, bite, *Fr. bonne bouche;* cocktail, apéritif, drink.

2. allurement, lure, enticement, temptation, teaser, tease, bait, *U.S. Sl.* come-on; invitation, attraction, *Inf.* eye-catcher.

appetizing, *adj.* **1.** savory, luscious, ambrosial, ambrosian, flavorous, flavorful, delectable, delicious, tasty; succulent, juicy, rich; nectarous, nectareous, nectarean, sweet; piquant, tart, spicy; palatable, toothsome, *Scot.* gustable.

2. appealing, enticing, alluring, inviting, attractive; tempting, seductive, tantalizing.

applaud, *v.* **1.** clap, cheer, hosanna, huzzah, bravo, root; encore, give [s.o.] a hand, make the rafters ring, whistle, stomp.

2. acclaim, praise, sound the praises of, sing the praises of, extol, cry up, laud, *Archaic.* magnify; approve enthusiastically, hail, commend; congratulate, felicitate, compliment, rejoice in; exalt, eulogize, glorify; pay tribute to, pay homage to, honor, crown.

applause, *n.* **1.** hand clapping, cheers, cheering, salvo, rooting, whistling, stomping; hosanna, huzzah, hurrah, bravo; ovation, standing ovation, encore, *Inf.* hand, plaudits, curtain calls; éclat, outcry, outburst; announcement, declaration.

2. acclaim, acclamation, praise, extolment, laudation, kudos, accolade, *Archaic.* magnification, citation; approval, approbation, endorsement, sanction, commendation; celebration, paean, congratulation, *Archaic.* gratulation, exultation, triumph, jubilation; eulogy, eulogium, eulogization, exaltation, glorification, encomium, panegyric; tribute, homage, honoring, crowning.

appliance, *n.* **1.** instrument, apparatus, mechanism, device, contrivance, gadget; tool, machine, equipment; (*all usu. pl.*) furnishing, accouterment, appointment, appurtenance.

2. application, applying, putting to use, putting into operation, practice, use, exercise.

applicable, *adj.* **1.** relevant, to the point, to the purpose, germane, pertinent, apposite, apropos, relative, related, bearing on; useful, well-adapted, compatible, convenient, adjustable, adaptable.

2. suitable, appropriate, proper, fitting, fit, befitting, right, seemly, due, timely, apt, pat, ready, *Sl.* on the button, *Sl.* right on.

applicant, *n.* candidate, office seeker, aspirant, postulant, suitor; job seeker, job hunter, interviewee, competitor; inquirer, solicitor, petitioner, claimant, suppliant, supplicant.

application, *n.* **1.** use, utilization, purpose, function, operation, appliance; exercise, practice.

2. relevance, bearing, aptness, suitability, pertinence; meaning, sense, significance, signification, import; purpose, intention, interpretation, tenor, drift.

3. attention, close attention, attentiveness; effort, persistent effort, persistence, perseverance, *Inf.* stick-to-it-iveness, resolution, tenacity; industry, diligence, dedication, devotion, constancy, assiduity, sedulity, sedulousness, intentness, addiction.

4. inquiry, request, resort, recourse, appeal, solicitation, petition, entreaty, suit; requisition, demand.

5. putting on *or* to, laying on *or* to, applying; installation, installing, putting in.

6. salve, lotion, balm, emollient, ointment, unguent, poultice, nard; plaster, pomade, pomatum.

apply, *v.* **1.** use, utilize, engage, employ, put to use, bring to bear, practice, exercise, bring into play, ply; execute, administer, direct, bring into effect, actualize, put into practice, carry out.

2. use for, assign, appropriate, allot, credit.

3. lay *or* spread on, rub on *or* in, put to *or* on, lay over, place over, cover over; touch to; install, deposit, put in place.

4. (*usu. of oneself*) devote, dedicate, give wholly to, be assiduous, persevere; work at, labor at *or* over, *Inf.* sweat over, buckle down to, *Inf.* knuckle down, put one's nose to the grindstone, study, concentrate.

5. make application, job seek, job hunt, put in for, put in a bid for, bid, try out for, audition; appeal, solicit, petition, sue, entreat, seek, look for, call upon, have recourse to.

appoint, *v.* **1.** name, designate, nominate, tab; assign, select, *Mil.* detail.

2. commission, delegate, deputize, depute; elect, vote in, place in office, install, invest, *Obs.* ordain.

3. determine, fix, settle, set, establish, prescribe, decide upon, arrange.

appointee, *n.* **1.** selectee, nominee, candidate; (*all resulting from a legal appointment*) beneficiary, legatee, *Law.* donee, *Law.* devisee, *Law.* grantee.

2. deputy, commissioner, commissary, agent, factor; representative, alternate, surrogate, proxy; delegate, legate, envoy, emissary; intermediary, mediator, middleman, go-between, medium, intermediate.

appointment, *n.* **1.** designation, assignment, nomination, naming, ordainment; deputation, delegation; election, selection.

2. office, position, post, place, berth, billet, station, *Sl.* gig.

3. engagement, meeting, interview, arrangement; tryst, rendezvous, assignation, date.

4. *Usu.* **appointments** equipment, furnishings, accouterments, appurtenances, fixtures, gear, apparatus; paraphernalia, fittings, habiliments, *Inf.* things; outfit, outfitting, turnout, rig.

5. **appointments** caparison, harness, trappings, tack, tackle, rigging; *All Mil.* arms, armaments, munitions, matériel.

apportion, *v.* allocate, allot, distribute, dispense; ration, measure out, measure off, admeasure; mete out, portion out, divide and assign, parcel out, deal out, dole out; cast out, disperse, scatter; divide up, *Inf.* divvy up, subdivide, share, partition, part, adjust; appropriate, designate, set apart, earmark, intend; specify, detail, list; assign, administer, award, grant, appoint.

apportionment, *n.* allocation, allocating, allotment, allotting, distribution, distributing, dispensation, dispensing; rationing, measuring out, measuring off, admeasuring; meting out, portioning out, parceling out, dealing out, doling out; dividing up, *Inf.* divvying up, subdivision, subdividing, sharing, partitioning, parting; appropriation, appropriating, designation, designating, setting apart, earmarking; specification, specifying, detailing, listing; assignment, assigning, administration, administering, awarding, granting, appointment, appointing.

apposite, *adj.* **1.** suitable, fitting, befitting, appropriate, meet, proper, becoming, seemly; suited, fit, well-suited, well-adapted, likely; agreeable, congenial, adapted, congruous; due, (*of punishment*) condign.

2. apt, pertinent, applicable, relevant, germane, relative to; apropos, to the point, to the purpose, well put, pat.

3. timely, felicitous, seasonable, convenient, opportune.

appraisal, *n.* **1.** estimated value, estimate, appraisement, price survey.

2. evaluation, valuation, assessment, appreciation; estimation, computation, calculation, approximation; counting, figuring, reckoning; gauging, rating, ranking, weighing, balancing; measuring, judging, sizing up, surveying; pricing, setting a price on, fixing the price of; ascertainment, determination.

appraise, *v.* **1.** evaluate, valuate, place *or* set a value on, assess, assay, *Obs.* apprise; price, set a price on, fix the price of; appreciate, value, prize, treasure.

2. estimate, compute, count, account, calculate, figure, reckon; gauge, rate, rank, weigh, balance, approximate; measure, *Archaic.* mete, judge, size, size up, survey; ascertain, determine, figure out.

appreciable, *adj.* **1.** perceptible, perceivable, recognizable, noticeable, discernible, distinguishable, detectable; cognizable, knowable, intelligible, comprehensible.

2. estimable, assessable, appraisable; computable, calculable, reckonable; determinable, ascertainable; sensible, material, measurable.

3. considerable, substantial, significant, pronounced; visible, apparent, evident; definite, undeniable, obvious.

appreciate, *v.* **1.** value, cherish, treasure, prize; enjoy, relish, savor, *Sl.* dig; like, love, care for, delight in, rejoice in, *Sl.* get a kick out of.

2. esteem, admire, honor, adore; respect, revere, reverence, venerate; hold in high regard, estimate justly, rate highly, realize the worth of; think highly of, think well of, think much of; attach *or* ascribe importance to, make much of, make a fuss over; applaud, acclaim, laud, praise.

3. perceive, note, detect, recognize, discern, feel, acknowledge; understand, comprehend, apprehend, realize, see the import of, fathom; know, have knowledge of *or* about, *Chiefly Scot.* ken; sympathize, be sensitive to, feel for; be conscious of, be aware of, be alive to, be cognizant of.

4. be grateful for, be obliged, be thankful, be appreciative, never forget.

5. increase, raise, boost, advance; escalate, multiply; grow, wax, gain, swell, spread, mount, boom.

6. improve, enhance the degree of, make of greater value; intensify, heighten, strengthen, fortify.

appreciation, *n.* **1.** evaluation, valuation, assessment, appraisal; estimation, computation, calculation, rating, ranking; measuring, judging, weighing, balancing.

2. cherishing, treasuring, prizing; enjoying, relishing, savoring, *Sl.* digging; liking, loving, caring for, delighting in, rejoicing in.

3. esteem, admiration, honor, adoration; respect, reverence, veneration.

4. perception, notation, detection, recognition, discernment; understanding, comprehension, apprehen-

sion, realization, cognizance; sympathy, sensitivity.
5. gratitude, gratefulness, thankfulness, thanks, thanksgiving; acknowledgment, obligation.
6. critical notice, review, opinion, commentary, critique; applause, acclamation, laudation, praise, tribute.
7. increase, raise, boost, advance; growth, spread, swell; escalation, multiplication.

appreciative, *adj.* **1.** understanding, comprehending, apprehending; realizing, cognizant of, conscious of, alive to, aware of, sensible of, *Sl.* hip; acquainted with, no stranger to, *Fr. au fait.*
2. grateful, thankful; obliged, under obligation, indebted, beholden.
3. sympathetic, sensitive; supportive, responsive, encouraging, reassuring; pleased, enthusiastic, praiseful.

apprehend, *v.* **1.** arrest, seize, take into custody, haul in; *Inf.* pick up, *Inf.* nab, *Inf.* pinch, *Sl.* bust, *Sl.* nail, *Sl.* run in, put the arm on [s.o.]; capture, catch, *Inf.* collar, take prisoner; detain, hold, secure; lock up, imprison, jail, incarcerate, immure.
2. comprehend, understand, take in, receive, *Chiefly Scot.* ken; apperceive, cognize, recognize, know, grasp, get, seize, *Inf.* get a fix on; fathom, penetrate, *Inf.* lay hold of; imagine, conceive, *Archaic.* hent; appreciate, *Sl.* dig, *Sl.* savvy, get the picture.
3. perceive, see, make out, discern, read, *Brit.* twig, *Inf.* make heads *or* tails of; intuit, sense, feel.
4. mistrust, distrust, suspect; anticipate, expect, forebode; dread, fear, funk, quail, shrink; cower, skulk, crouch, quake in one's boots, have cold feet.

apprehension, *n.* **1.** fear, foreboding, presentiment, premonition, prescience, presage; anxiety, dread, worry, disquiet, solicitude, care, concern; misgiving, uncertainty, suspicion, mistrust, distrust, qualm; uneasiness, apprehensiveness, *Inf.* butterflies, nervousness, queasiness; *Sl.* heebie-jeebies, the jitters, *Sl.* the willies, *Sl.* the creeps; alarm, perturbation, dismay, consternation, trepidation.
2. understanding, intellect, intelligence, mind, reason, *Gk. Philos.* nous; comprehension, apperception, grasp, insight, cognition, penetration; sense, intuition, feeling, imagination; perception, perspicacity, discernment; awareness, knowing, ken, knowledge; recognition, cognizance, realization, appreciation.
3. view, opinion, idea, sentiment; thought, impression, judgment, conjecture; belief, fancy, supposition, notion.
4. seizure, arrest, capture; detention, restraint, constraint, custody, taking into custody, *Sl.* bust; imprisonment, incarceration, durance, jailing.

apprehensive, *adj.* **1.** uneasy, anxious, qualmish, fretful; worried, alarmed, concerned, solicitous; disturbed, distressed, disquieted; fearful, afraid, scared; suspicious, mistrustful, distrustful, uncertain; nervous, *Sl.* uptight, queasy, jittery, skittish, jumpy; shaky, tremulous, trembling; quaky, fidgety, restless, restive, unquiet; hesitant, faltering, quavering, wavering; timid, cowardly, pusillanimous, timorous.
2. perceptive, discerning, penetrating, piercing; keen, sharp, acute, quick; percipient, perspicacious, discriminating, astute; sagacious, judicious, sapient, wise; sensitive, sensible, responsive, sentient, impressible; aware, cognizant, conscious, knowing, apperceptive, awake to; intelligent, understanding, comprehending; imaginative, inventive, thoughtful.

apprentice, *n.* **1.** novice, tyro, beginner, cub, greenhorn; neophyte, novitiate, newcomer, rookie, recruit, probationer; student, pupil, learner.
—*v.* **2.** article, bind, tie, contract, attach, associate; employ, enroll, place, position; train, instruct, coach, guide, teach the tricks of the trade.

apprise, *v.* notify, give *or* serve notice to, tell, inform, give word; report, announce, advertise, communicate; acquaint, brief, verse, familiarize, enlighten; advise, counsel, admonish, warn, point out, let know, give [s.o.] to understand, clue in, *Inf.* tip off; impart, disclose, divulge, reveal, break the news, come out with.

approach, *v.* **1.** near, come near *or* nearer, draw near *or* nearer, come close *or* closer, draw close *or* closer; draw nigh to, move closer to, *Inf.* belly up to, edge closer to; come within range, gain on, overtake, catch up to; hail, accost, confront, address, greet, salute, speak to.
2. approximate, nearly equal, come close to; resemble, be much like, be similar to, be comparable to.
3. present, offer, suggest, propose, recommend, advance, sound out; bring up, introduce, mention, broach; bring *or* put forward, propound, proffer, tender, hold out.
4. set about, begin, start, commence, make a start, take the first step, *Inf.* get the show on the road.
5. make advances to, make overtures to, proposition, solicit.
—*n.* **6.** nearness, close approximation, proximity, vicinity, neighborhood, propinquity.
7. access, entrance, entry, entryway, entrée, inlet, ingress; ramp, drive, driveway, lane, path, pathway, sidewalk; road, route, roadway, course, street, avenue, boulevard; highway, turnpike, pike, freeway, expressway, parkway, causeway, throughway; main road, highroad, thoroughfare, state highway, *U.S. Inf.* interstate, state highway, tollroad; speedway, autobahn, superhighway.
8. door, doorway, hatch, gate, gateway, postern, portal; threshold, stile, turnstile, wicket; hall, hallway, passage, passageway, arcade, gangway, walkway, corridor, gallery; lobby, foyer, vestibule, anteroom, waiting room; anteporch, porch, portico.
9. method, procedure, steps, course, mode, way, manner, style.
10. advance, overture, prelude, motion, gesture; offer, invitation, proposal, proposition.
11. presentation, offer, proposal, idea, thought, suggestion, recommendation.

approachable, *adj.* **1.** accessible, attainable, reachable, within reach, getatable, *Inf.* come-at-able.
2. (*all of a person*) open, agreeable, sociable, friendly, affable, congenial, genial; informal, low-key, easygoing; talkative, communicative, conversable.

approbation, *n.* approval, sanction. See **approval** (*defs.* **1, 2**).

appropriate, *adj.* **1.** suitable, fitting, befitting, meet, proper, becoming, seemly; suited, fit, well-suited, likely, agreeable, adapted, congruous; expedient, due, (*of punishment*) condign.
2. timely, felicitous, seasonable, convenient, opportune.
3. apt, pertinent, applicable, relevant, germane, apposite, apropos, to the point.
4. proper, particular, own, individual, separate, peculiar, characteristic, idiosyncratic.
—*v.* **5.** (*all usu. of funds*) set apart, assign, allot, apportion, appoint; allocate, disburse, dole out; authorize, legislate.
6. take possession of, avail oneself of, claim, confiscate, impound; seize, commandeer, expropriate, arrogate, usurp, accroach, assume; make free with, help oneself to, steal [s.o.'s] thunder.
7. steal, thieve, pilfer, purloin, finger, filch, *Inf.* snitch; peculate, embezzle, *Law.* defalcate, misappropriate, swindle, pocket; shoplift, palm, *Sl.* boost, walk off *or* away with; *Sl.* pinch, *Sl.* swipe, *Sl.* rip off, *Sl.* crook,

Sl. cop, *Sl.* lift.

appropriateness, *n.* suitability, suitableness, fitness, rightness, justness, seemliness; aptness, appositeness, expedience; felicity, congruity, becomingness; applicability, relevance, relevancy, pertinence; propriety, decorum, decorousness, covenance.

appropriation, *n.* **1.** takeover, seizure, capture; expropriation, arrogation, assumption, usurpation, accroachment; confiscation, impoundment.

2. theft, stealing, thievery, pilferage, pilfering, *Sl.* swiping, *Sl.* hustling, *Sl.* copping; peculation, embezzlement, misappropriation; shoplifting, palming, *Sl.* boosting; plagiarism, piracy, *Inf.* lifting.

3. (*all usu. of funds*) allotment, allocation, allowance, budget; dispensation, donation, dole, handout.

approval, *n.* **1.** approbation, countenance, favor, acceptance, adoption, stamp of approval, blessing; support, backing, patronage, advocacy; recommendation, commendation, acknowledgment, good word, good opinion, kudos; honor, respect, esteem, regard, consideration.

2. sanction, official sanction, formal approval, imprimatur, license; endorsement, ratification, confirmation, affirmation, certification, validation; consent, assent, concurrence, agreement, acquiescence, compliance; permission, leave, nod, *Inf.* the word, *Inf.* the OK, *Inf.* green light, *Inf.* go-ahead.

3. on approval on trial, on *or* under probation, without obligation to buy.

approve, *v.* **1.** appreciate, value, prize, cherish; respect, admire, esteem, like, think highly of; commend, praise, extol, speak well of.

2. sanction, allow, countenance, authorize, bless, *Inf.* OK, *Inf.* give the green light *or* go-ahead, *Inf.* say the word; accept, go along with, *Inf.* buy.

3. ratify, validate, certify, confirm, affirm, authenticate, homologate; recommend, advocate, support, back, second, uphold, sustain, maintain, favor.

approximate, *adj.* **1.** near, approaching, impending, forthcoming, coming, imminent.

2. rough, estimated, *Sl.* guesstimated; *Math.* interpolative, *Statistics.* extrapolative.

3. adjacent, juxtapositional, juxtaposed, proximate, next, next-door, neighboring; close together, close by, near, nearby, nigh, at hand, at close range; adjacent, contiguous, bordering, adjoining, abutting, tangential, tangent, touching, contactual.

4. similar, like, resemblant, connected, related, quasi; relative, analogous, comparative, corresponding.

—v. **5.** approach, come close, border on, neighbor, be on the brink of, be in the vicinity of; draw nigh, draw near, come together, close with, converge, come within a stone's throw; impend, verge, lean toward, move toward, *Archaic.* nigh.

6. estimate, make a rough guess, give a ball park figure, *Sl.* guesstimate, *Math.* interpolate, *Statistics.* extrapolate; gauge, reckon, figure, compute roughly.

7. simulate, look like, give the appearance of, *Inf.* be the spit and image of, resemble, bear a resemblance to, hint at; imitate, copy, duplicate, mimic, mock.

approximately, *adv.* **1.** about, just about, roughly, generally, estimatingly, in round numbers, more or less, or so; around, circa.

2. nearly, almost, *Inf.* most, all but, as good as, virtually; not quite, barely, hardly, scarcely; next to, close to, near, well-nigh, nigh, nigh upon *or* onto; nearing, approaching, toward, bordering on, verging on.

3. similarly, analogously, comparably, comparatively, relatively.

approximation, *n.* **1.** estimate, estimation, rough idea, ball park figure; reckoning, rough computation, *Math.* interpolation, *Statistics.* extrapolation; guess, guesswork, conjecture, *Sl.* guesstimate.

2. proximity, nearness, closeness, approach; propinquity, neighborhood, vicinity, vicinage; adjacency, adjacence, contiguity, abuttal.

appurtenance, *n.* adjunct, appanage, ancilla, auxiliary, appurtenant; attachment, appendage, annex; annexation, *Rare.* annexment; subordinate, small fry, *Inf.* small potatoes; subsidiary, subdivision, branch; supplement, supplementation, accessory, complement, accompaniment, concomitant, incidental, *Astron.* comes.

appurtenant, *adj.* **1.** belonging, appertaining, incident, part of; pertinent, pertaining, applicable, to the point; relevant, related, relating, relative, germane, connected; appropriate, apropos, apposite, apt; proper, felicitous, well-suited, suitable, fit, fitting, befitting, meet.

—n. **2.** adjunct, accessory, subordinate. See **appurtenance.**

a priori, **1.** deductive, inferential, from cause to effect.

2. presumptive, theoretical, postulational, suppositional, conjectural, hypothetical, speculative.

apropos, *adv.* **1.** opportunely, timely, seasonably, suitably, appropriately, aptly, pertinently, to the purpose.

2. apropos of with reference *or* regard *or* respect to, in respect of.

—adj. **3.** opportune, timely, seasonable; suitable, fitting, befitting, appropriate, applicable; apt, fit, meet, pat, to the point, pertinent, germane, relevant, apposite.

apt, *adj.* **1.** inclined, tending toward, leaning toward, of a mind to; disposed, liable, given, ready, prone, subject, likely, incident, *Archaic.* propense.

2. gifted, well-endowed, talented, intelligent, intellectual, sagacious; clever, ingenious, adroit, neat; brilliant, astute, bright, agile, quick, facile, ready, smart, acute, sharp; ace, topflight, top drawer, first-rate, *Inf.* topnotch, *Inf.* crack, *Sl.* crackerjack, *Sl.* on the ball, *Inf.* whiz-bang, *Brit. Sl.* whizzo; able, capable, competent, proficient, adept.

3. appropriate, proper, due, meet, becoming, felicitous; suitable, suited, congruous, fitting, befitting, well-adapted, apposite, pat; germane, relevant, pertinent, to the point, apropos, *Latin. ad rem.*

aptitude, *n.* **1.** ability, capability, proficiency; gift, talent, endowment, faculty, facility, flair, knack, forte; capacity, potential, the stuff, *Inf.* what it takes, *U.S. Inf.* the goods; predilection, proclivity, propensity; inclination, tendentiousness, proneness; penchant, bent, turn.

2. intelligence, intellect, genius, aptness, wit, mother wit, sagacity, head, brain, mind; ingenuity, astuteness, cleverness, brilliance, brightness, smartness, acuity, acuteness, sharpness, keenness; perspicacity, penetration.

3. aptness, fitness, qualification, preparedness, readiness; competency, adequacy, sufficiency, capableness.

aptness, *n.* suitability, suitableness, appropriateness, appositeness; applicability, relevance, relevancy, germaneness, relatedness; opportuneness, seasonability, timeliness, expedience, expediency, felicity, felicitousness; fitness, concordance, consonance, harmony, harmoniousness, congruousness.

aquarium, *n.* (*all for display of fish*) tank, bowl, tub; pond, pool, pound, reservoir; vivarium; marine museum.

aquatic, *adj.* **1.** marine, maritime, oceanic, pelagic, nautical, naval; littoral, shoreline; lacustrine, lake; fluvial, river.

—n. **2. aquatics** water sports, sea sports; natation,

swimming, diving, scuba diving; boating, sailing, yachting; water skiing, water polo; surfing, surfboarding.

aqueduct, *n.* **1.** conduit, channel, race, watercourse, artificial waterway; strait, seaway, river, tributary, estuary.

2. duct, pipe, main, tube, cylinder; passage, passageway, adit; sewer, culvert, cloaca, flume, trough, chute; spout, gutter, drain, gully, ditch.

3. *Anatomy.* artery, blood vessel, vessel, aorta; vein, capillary.

aqueous, *adj.* **1.** watery, waterish, serous, waterlike; soggy, boggy, dripping, wet; moist, damp, dewy.

2. watered down, diluted, thinned, adulterated, cut; insipid, tasteless, flat, vapid, dull; tame, feeble, weak, wishy-washy.

aquiline, *adj.* (*usu. of the nose*) eagle-like, beaked, hooked, curved; prominent, protruding, Roman.

arabesque, *n.* **1.** floral design, intricate pattern, ornamentation, Islamic decoration; anthemion, honeysuckle ornament.

2. *Fine Arts.* linear, motif, spiral, undulation, serpentine line, sinuosity.

arable, *adj.* plowable, tillable, farmable, cultivable, cultivatable; fertile, fruitful, productive, prolific, fecund.

arbiter, *n.* **1.** judge, determiner, decider, adjudicator, arbitress; moderator, umpire, referee, linesman; arbitrator, negotiator, reconciler, peacemaker, *Obs.* arbitrer; go-between, intermediary, mediator, intercessor.

2. authority, sovereign, master, lord, ruler, governor, controller; autocrat, dictator, director; the one with the final say.

arbitrament, *n.* **1.** arbitration, judgment. See **arbitration** (*def.* 2).

2. decision, sentence, verdict, decree, opinion, finding; umpirage; final say.

arbitrariness, *n.* **1.** capriciousness, whimsicalness, whimsicality, unreasonableness; willfulness, stubbornness, perverseness, mulishness, obstinacy, intransigence.

2. imperiousness, magisterialness, domineeringness, overbearingness, high-handedness, peremptoriness; superciliousness, haughtiness.

arbitrary, *adj.* **1.** discretionary, discretional, left to one's discretion, subject to one's judgment, judgmental; optional, done at one's pleasure, done by choice.

2. capricious, whimsical, fanciful, crotchety; unreasonable, irrational, unsupported, unsupportable, irresponsible.

3. despotic, tyrannical, tyrannous, autocratic; dictatorial, imperious, domineering, magisterial; overbearing, high-handed, peremptory, summary; supercilious, condescending, haughty, *Inf.* toplofty.

4. willful, stubborn, wayward, perverse, obstinate, mulish, opinionated; intransigent, unbending, unyielding; indocile, intractable.

arbitrate, *v.* **1.** decide, determine, settle; judge, adjudge, adjudicate, pronounce *or* pass judgment, decree, sentence; umpire, referee, *Inf.* ref; try, hear.

2. mediate, intervene, interpose, step in, come between; negotiate, bargain, bring to terms, parley; intercede, conciliate, placate, reconcile.

arbitration, *n.* **1.** mediation, negotiation, bargaining; peacemaking, bringing together, reconciliation, reconcilement, conciliation; intervention, interposition, intermediation, interference.

2. judgment, adjudication, decision, determination; settling, settlement, arbitrament.

3. hearing, trial; parley, conference, discussion.

arbitrator, *n.* negotiator, bargainer, reconciler, peacemaker, *Obs.* arbitrer; go-between, intermediary, mediator, intercessor; arbiter, arbitress, judge, determiner, decider, adjudicator; moderator, umpire, referee, linesman.

arbor, *n.* **1.** bower, grotto, alcove, recess, leafy shelter; trellis, lattice, pergola, pavilion, gazebo, (*in Turkey and Iran*) kiosk; pleasure-garden, promenade, pleasance.

2. retreat, refuge, haven, shelter, hermitage; asylum, resort, sanctuary, ark, covert, hideaway, mew.

arboreal, *adj.* treelike, arborescent, arboreous, dendroid, dendritic, dendriform, tree-shaped; branched, branchlike, ramose, ramous, ramiform.

arc, *n.* curve, bow, arch, bend, curved line, *Geom.* parabola, curvature, flexure, *Archit.* foil, arcuation; crescent, half-moon, lunula, meniscus.

arcade, *n.* **1.** gallery, roofed-in gallery, cloister, loggia, *Brit.* piazza, colonnade, peristyle, portico, porch.

2. passageway, covered passageway; market, shops, stalls, shopping mall *or* plaza.

arcane, *adj.* mysterious, enigmatic, enigmatical, inscrutable, unfathomable, incomprehensible, impenetrable; dark, deep, profound, abstruse, esoteric, recondite; obscure, secret, hidden, concealed, covert, veiled, masked, screened, cloaked; occult, cabalistic, cryptic, oracular, mystic, sphinxlike.

arcanum, *n.* **1.** *Often* **arcana** secret, mystery, cabala; enigma, conundrum.

2. secret remedy, alembic, elixir, magic potion; magic wand, panacea, nostrum.

arch[1], *n.* **1.** archway, arched doorway, arched gateway; span, vault, dome, cupola, cove, coved vault, cloistered vault; bow, bend, curve, arc, convexity, camber, curvature, horseshoe; camber piece, camber slip, *Anat.* fornix, *Math.* catenary, *Geom.* cycloid.

—*v.* **2.** arch over, vault, span, bridge; bow, bend, curve, camber.

arch[2], *adj.* **1.** chief, foremost, most important, principal, first; greatest, highest, consummate, extreme; first-class, first-rate, *Inf.* number one, top.

2. cunning, shrewd, adroit, sly, tricky, artful, designing, intriguing; waggish, roguish, saucy, mischievous; frolicsome, playful, prankish, tricksy, tricksome.

archaic, *adj.* antiquated, superannuated, antique, ancient, old, old as the hills; antediluvian, fossilized, prehistoric, primitive; obsolete, obsolescent, extinct; bygone, passé, out of date, old-fashioned, out of fashion, unfashionable, behind the times.

archaism, *n.* anachronism, throwback, atavism, relic, asynchronism; obsolete diction, archaic style, antiquated term.

arched, *adj.* vaulted, cambered, embowed, concave, forniciform, *Biol.* fornicate, *Heraldry.* enarched.

archer, *n.* bowman, longbowman, crossbowman, arbalester, toxophilite; Robin Hood, sagittary, *Astron.* Sagittarius.

archetype, *n.* **1.** prototype, original, protoplast, first form; ancestor, forerunner, precursor, predecessor.

2. pattern, paradigm, form, mold, model; standard, example, exemplar, paragon, ideal.

architect, *n.* **1.** designer, planner, city planner, building consultant, landscaper; draftsman, blueprinter, sketcher, artist; builder, constructor, maker, fashioner.

2. creator, author, inventor, former, originator; deviser, contriver, schemer, prime mover.

—*v.* **3.** design, plan, devise, contrive, scheme; create, invent, author, form, originate; blueprint, draft, sketch, draw up; construct, build, make, frame, fashion.

architecture, *n.* **1.** design, planning, architectonics; building, construction, making, framing, fash-

ioning; drafting, blueprinting, sketching.
2. buildings, edifices, structures, framework; physical environment, architectural ambience *or* milieu; fabric, constitution, make-up.
archives, *n.* **1.** records, annals, chronicles, historical documents *or* papers, memorabilia, memoranda, memorials; rolls, registers, statistics, lists, entries, ledgers; documents, public papers, government papers, *Law.* muniments.
2. registry, register office, chancery, *Brit.* muniment room; library, stack room, stacks, files; store, bank, museum.
archway, *n.* entrance, threshold, entrée, entry, entryway, ingress, approach; opening, door, doorway, hatch, gate, gateway, postern, portal; passage, passageway, walkway, gangway, arcade, corridor, gallery.
arctic, *adj.* polar, boreal, northern, septentrional; frigid, bleak, very cold, raw, hyperborean; icy, glacial, gelid, frozen, freezing, ice-cold; frosty, chilly, algid, wintry, brumal, hibernal, snowy, niveous; snowbound, icebound.
ardent, *adj.* **1.** passionate, impassioned, fervent, fervid, perfervid; zealous, eager, enthusiastic, spirited, high-spirited; emotional, emotive, excitable; volatile, fiery, hot-headed; heated, feverish, white-hot, inflamed, volcanic; overwrought, upset, hysterical, not rational; temperamental, high-strung, nervous, tense, touchy, testy, peppery.
2. lusting after, burning, *Sl.* hot for; infatuated, mad about, *Inf.* wild about; stimulated, excited, aroused; *Inf.* hot, *Inf.* turned on.
3. vehement, fierce, angry, rancorous, wrathful; burning, flaming, blazing, fiery; red-hot, flaring, flashing; malevolent, cruel, malicious, spiteful; waspish, hostile, inimical, severe, harsh; intense, intensified, strong, concentrated, consuming; deep, dark, profound, rich, vivid, brilliant.
ardor, *n.* **1.** fervor, fervency, warmth, glow, fire; devotion, devotedness, zeal, feverishness, passion, fanaticism.
2. enthusiasm, eagerness, earnestness, keenness, intentness, intensity, excitement; vigor, force, energy, determination, vehemence; relish, gusto, delight, elation, rapture, ecstasy, transport.
3. spirit, abandon, liveliness, vivacity; emotion, feeling, animation, exuberance, ebullience; vitality, life, buoyancy, bounce, zest, verve, zing, *Sl.* oomph.
4. heartiness, cordiality, affection, fondness, good will; desire, concupiscence, lust, libidinousness; sensuality, carnality, lechery, salacity, salaciousness; lasciviousness, licentiousness, wantonness.
arduous, *adj.* **1.** laborious, difficult, hard; onerous, burdensome, heavy, operose; exhausting, wearisome, tiresome, fatiguing; irksome, troublesome, trying.
2. energetic, vigorous, robust; forceful, forcible, emphatic, strenuous; herculean, mighty, powerful, strong, hefty; pushing, determined, earnest, assiduous.
3. steep, acclivous, acclivitous, uphill; sheer, bold, abrupt, precipitous, bluff, *Archaic.* headlong; upright, perpendicular, vertical, plumb.
4. severe, harsh, grim, bitter, tough; rigorous, cruel, fierce, ferocious; terrible, formidable, awful, extreme.
area, *n.* **1.** region, district, zone, quarter; locality, section, *U.S.* block; territory, realm, domain, province; department, precinct, arrondissement, canton, bailiwick; tract, stretch, terrain, field; expanse, sweep, reach, surface; compass, perimeter, range, extent, margin, scope, circuit; arena, ring, sphere, circle, orbit.
2. enclosure, close, *Fort.* parade, yard, court, backyard; plot, lot, plat, site, spot; patch, parcel, portion, part; clearing, square, plaza, *It. piazza;* esplanade, quadrangle, *Inf.* quad, (*in ancient Rome*) forum, (*in ancient Greece*) agora, marketplace.
arena, *n.* **1.** coliseum, hippodrome, amphitheater stadium, bowl, field; lists, circus, ring, cockpit; gymnasium, auditorium, stage, platform.
2. battlefield, field of conflict, scene of contest, theater of endeavor, sphere of action.
argosy, *n.* merchantman, merchant ship, cargo ship, trader, carrack, galleon; brigantine, brig, schooner; armada, flotilla, *Obs.* escadrille, fleet, *Archaic.* navy; oppulent supply, abundance, plentitude.
argot, *n.* idiom, *Inf.* lingo, jargon, slang, cant; dialect, patois, tongue, vernacular, parlance; terminology, vocabulary, nomenclature.
argue, *v.* **1.** debate, discuss, moot, bandy words, sift, *Inf.* kick around, *Sl.* hash over; quibble, cavil, nitpick, belabor a point, split hairs, chop logic; reason, ratiocinate, logicize, explain.
2. contend, dispute, disagree, contest, controvert, spar, cross swords, lock horns; wrangle, bicker, haggle, *Sl.* hassle, *Scot.* argle-bargle, *Scot.* sturt, *Scot. and North Eng.* threap, *Scot. and North Eng.* prig.
3. maintain, insist, hold, have, submit.
4. remonstrate, expostulate, plead with; persuade, dissuade, talk out of.
5. establish, demonstrate, show, prove; evince, evidence, manifest, illustrate, exhibit, display; indicate, attest, signify, point to, bespeak, tell, denote, mean, betoken; imply, suggest, connote.
arguer, *n.* debater, discusser, disputant, controversialist, contender, eristic, polemic, polemist; casuist, reasoner, logomachist; logician, dialectician.
argument, *n.* **1.** debate, discussion, polemic, logomachy, war of words; contestation, disputation, argumentation.
2. disagreement, contention, altercation, conflict, dispute, controversy, discord, clash, falling-out, *Inf.* hassle, *Inf.* barney; quarrel, row, squabble, dustup, spat, tiff, *Brit. Dial.* fratch, *Brit. Dial.* fratching; fracas, uproar, brouhaha, rumpus, *Inf.* ruckus; fight, tussle, donnybrook, *Scot.* sturt, *Scot. and North Eng.* threap, *Inf.* scrap, *Inf.* run-in, *Inf.* set-to, *Sl.* rhubarb; broil, embroilment, imbroglio; dissension, variance, difference of opinion, wrangling, bickering.
3. logic, ratiocination, reasoning, chain *or* course of reasoning.
4. case, evidence, ground, proof; plea, consideration, reason, pros and cons; answer, reply, response, riposte, counterstatement, rebuttal, refutation, *Sl.* sockdolager.
5. subject matter, thesis, theme, topic, gist, sum and substance, matter.
6. abstract, brief, summary, outline; synopsis, précis, conspectus, syllabus; digest, abridgment, compendium, epitome.
argumentation, *n.* **1.** logic, reasoning, chain *or* course *or* pattern of reasoning; polemics, dialectics.
2. debate, discussion, polemic, logomachy, war of words; disputation, disagreement, contention, altercation.
3. (*all in order to convince or persuade*) address, discourse, speech, argument.
argumentative, *adj.* **1.** quarrelsome, battlesome, contentious, combative, wranglesome, dissentient, exceptive; argumental, polemic, dialectic, eristic, logomachic.
2. cantankerous, irascible, irritable, dyspeptic, ill-humored, bad-tempered; petulant, peevish, cross, cranky, testy, *Inf.* mean, *Inf.* ornery.
3. controversial, debatable, moot, doubtful, dubious.

aria, *n.* air, melody, tune, song, chanson, *Music.* descant, lay, ballad, carol; ditty, canzonet, *Both Music.* cavatina, arietta; strain, theme.

arid, *adj.* **1.** parched, extremely dry, thirsty, moistureless, waterless, *Chem.* anhydrous; droughty, without rain, torrid, burning; baked, roasted, toasted, burnt; scorched, singed, charred, blistered; dried-up, withered, sere, shriveled, shrunken; dehydrated, evaporated, desiccated.

2. barren, unproductive, sterile, infertile, unfertile, unfruitful, fruitless, infecund, unfecund; uncultivable, uncultivatable, poor, deficient, lacking, impoverished, depleted, drained, devoid, empty, destitute; desert, desolate, bare, plain, stark, naked, stripped.

3. unimaginative, prosaic, prosy, commonplace; unsuggestive, sterile, pointless, purposeless; uninteresting, dull, flat, tasteless, bland; monotonous, boring, *Sl.* a drag, lifeless, drab, dreary; insipid, jejune, vapid, humdrum, tedious, tiresome, wearisome, soporiferous.

aridity, *n.* **1.** aridness, parchedness, extreme dryness, dehydration, evaporation, desiccation; torridity, torridness.

2. barrenness, unproductivity, unproductiveness, sterility, sterileness; infertility, infertileness, unfertility, unfruitfulness, fruitlessness, infecundity, uncultivation; poverty, poorness, deficiency, lack, impoverishment, destitution, depletion, drain; emptiness, desert, waste, desolation; bareness, plainness, starkness, nakedness.

3. prosaicness, prosiness, sterility; pointlessness, purposelessness, uselessness; dullness, lifelessness, flatness, tastelessness, blandness, drabness, dreariness; insipidity, insipidness, jejuneness, jejunity, vapidity, vapidness; monotony, monotonousness, humdrumness, tediousness, wearisomeness; boredom, ennui, fatigue, weariness, soporiferousness.

aright, *adv.* **1.** rightly, correctly, accurately, without error; exactly, truly, *Inf.* O.K., back to normal.

2. properly, fitly, well, in a proper manner, appropriately, suitably, aptly, duly.

arise, *v.* **1.** appear, show up, turn up, crop up, spring up, come to light, make an appearance; originate, commence, start, begin, open, dawn, come into existence.

2. *often* **arise from** result, proceed, emanate, turn out; issue, grow out of, flow, spring forth; follow, ensue, derive.

3. rise, ascend, climb, mount, scale, go up, come up; float, fly, soar, top, tower.

4. get up, stand up, stir, move around *or* about; awake, wake up, get out of bed, *Sl.* roll out.

aristocracy, *n.* **1.** nobility, *Fr. noblesse,* patriciate, (*in Britain*) peerage; elite, privileged class, dominant class, ruling class, oligarchy, the high and mighty; gentry, gentility, upper class, *Inf.* upper crust; meritocracy, the best and the brightest.

2. high society, *Fr. haut monde, Fr. beau monde,* fashionable society; social elite, clique, coterie, jet set, beautiful people, *U.S.* Four Hundred; F.F.V.'s, First Families of Virginia.

aristocrat, *n.* nobleman, noble, patrician, silk-stocking, *Inf.* blue blood, gentleman; peer, lord, duke, marquis, earl, count, viscount, baron; grandee, magnifico, don, hidalgo, *Fr. Hist.* chevalier.

aristocratic, *adj.* **1.** patrician, blue-blooded, silk-stocking, noble, gentle, genteel, wellborn, highborn; royal, princely, kingly, titled; (*all of animals*) thoroughbred, pedigreed, purebred.

2. elegant, graceful, *Scot.* genty, fine, delicate, exquisite; well-bred, polite, civil, mannerly, well-mannered, courteous; decorous, proper, *Fr. comme il faut,* fitting, becoming, seemly; gracious, ladylike, ladyish, courtly, gentlemanly, gentlemanlike; debonair, charming, chivalrous, chivalric, gallant, cavalier.

3. polished, finished, refined, cultivated; urbane, suave, sophisticated, cosmopolitan, worldly; fashionable, stylish, à la mode, modish, high-toned, *Sl.* tony, high-class, *Sl.* classy, *Inf.* swank.

4. affected, mannered, unnatural; pretentious, *Inf.* highfalutin, *Inf.* high-hat, on one's high horse; haughty, lordly, hoity-toity, arrogant, proud, snobbish, disdainful.

arm[1], *n.* **1.** forelimb, anterior limb, brachium; appendage, limb, branch, ramification, bough, offshoot, scion; handle, lever, crosspiece, axle.

2. inlet, estuary, mouth; cove, lagoon, bay, bight, gulf; fiord, frith, *Chiefly Scot.* firth, channel, strait, sound, *Scot.* kyle.

3. power, might, force, strength, potency, *Literary.* puissance; authority, command, sway; support, protection, defense.

4. with open arms cordially, graciously, warmly, friendly, kind-heartedly.

arm[2], *n.* **1.** *Usu.* **arms** weapons, armament, firearms, munitions, ammunition, *Mil.* matériel; guns, rifles, muskets, flintlocks, matchlocks; pistols, revolvers, six-shooters; shotguns, machine guns, howitzers, cannons, artillery, ordnance.

2. arms *Heraldry.* escutcheon, scutcheon, shield, armorial bearings; coat of arms, blazon, blazonment, blazonry, emblazonry, emblazonment, crest.

3. up in arms excited, keyed-up, wrought up, worked up, roused, indignant, angry, on one's high horse.

—*v.* **4.** equip, accouter, outfit, fit out, gird, array, furnish, provide; prepare, ready, prime, forearm; man, take up arms, muster one's forces.

5. fortify, strengthen, gird one's loins, brace, steel, reinforce, buttress; support, defend, guard, protect, cover.

armada, *n.* fleet, navy, argosy, squadron, flotilla, *Obs.* escadrille.

armament, *n.* weapons, arms. See **arm**[2] (*def.* **1**).

armed, *adj.* equipped, accoutered, outfitted, girded, arrayed, furnished; readied, primed, prepared; fortified, armed to the teeth, strengthened, braced, steeled, reinforced, buttressed.

armistice, *n.* **1.** truce, cease-fire, white flag, *Mil.* flag of truce.

2. reprieve, respite, rest, lull; interval, intermission, pause, stay, hitch, break, hiatus; stoppage, halt, cessation, stop; suspension, discontinuance, interruption, recess, abeyance, quiescence.

armor, *n.* **1.** covering, protection, wrapping, sheathing; mail, chain mail, coat of mail, armor plate, armature.

2. *Armor.* shield, buckler, *Archaic.* targe, *Class. Myth.* aegis; helmet, helm, armet, heaume, casque, sallet, sallade; morion, cabassett, comb morion, basinet, basnet, bascinet; visor, vizor, ventail, aventail; beaver, buffe, bever, wrapper, gorget; pauldron, epaulière, spaulder, monnion; rerebrace, cannon, couter, vambrace, cubitiere, elbow cop, gauntlet; cuirass, corselet, lorica, breastplate, backplate; fauld, culet, tasse, lame; cuisse, cuish, poleyn, genouillère, knee cop; greave, jamb, jambart, jambeau, sabaton, solleret; hauberk, byrnie, habergeon; allecret.

3. defense, safeguard, guard; bulwark, rampart, wall; shelter, cover, safety, protection; asylum, sanctum.

armory, *n.* **1.** depot, magazine, arsenal, ammunition dump; military storehouse, storehouse, depository, repository, warehouse.

2. National Guard headquarters, Guard headquarters, Reserve center, headquarters, H.Q., administration center, drill center; assembly center, hall, arena, auditorium, coliseum.

army, *n.* **1.** military, soldiers, soldiery, troops, regular army, standing army; armed forces, infantry, cavalry, artillery, militia; legion, battalion, garrison, detachment, brigade, regiment, division, company, corps, column, wing, phalanx, cohort.

2. multitude, host, galaxy, array, score; congregation, gathering, assembly, assemblage, meeting; group, body, swarm, hoard, crowd, throng, bunch, mob, rout; gang, band, troop; congestion, press, crush; concourse, cumulation, confluence, convergence.

aroma, *n.* **1.** odor, scent, fragrance, perfume, spicy smell, redolence, odoriferousness; bouquet, savor, trail, trace, breath.

2. character, quality, air, atmosphere, aura, exhalation, emanation, essence, spirit; flavor, complexion, tone.

aromatic, *adj.* fragrant, sweet-smelling, sweet-scented, scented, perfumed, balmy, redolent, odorous, odoriferous; spicy, savory, pungent, piquant, ambrosial.

around, *adv.* **1.** about, on all sides, right and left, in all directions; everywhere, throughout, all over, in all parts, over, through; to and fro, here and there, hither and thither, hither and yon, far and wide.

2. in circumference, perimetrically, peripherally.

3. near, nearby, proximately, close by, nigh, at close range; hereabout, not far off, at hand.

4. circuitously, in a round about way *or* fashion, indirectly.

5. recurrently, repeatedly, periodically, round, 'round; around the clock, again and again, over and over, indefinitely.

6. in the reverse *or* opposite direction, halfway around, 180°; in reverse, backwards, to the rear.

7. to an awareness, to one's point of view, to one's way of thinking, to one's senses; back to consciousness, into the waking world, back to life.

—prep. **8.** about, surrounding, circumjacent, rounding, encircling, circling, encompassing, circumfluent; enfolding, enwrapping, wrapped about, enveloping.

9. throughout, all over, in all parts of, over, through.

10. near to, nearby, nigh to, proximate to, close by, close to; neighboring with, next door to, next to, adjacent to, adjoined with, bordering on, beside; juxtaposed with, contiguous with, tangential with, tangent to.

11. approximately, circa, ca., about, just about, in the vicinity of, in the neighborhood of; roughly, generally, estimatingly, in round numbers, more or less, or so.

arouse, *v.* **1.** actuate, initiate, put in motion, sow the seeds of, start the wheels turning; stimulate, animate, reanimate, whet, invigorate, motivate, inspirit, inspire, galvanize, electrify, vivify, rally, revive, enliven, liven up, awaken, wake up, waken, rouse, shake up, jolt, jog; impel, induce, compel, constrain, move, press, drive, stir, fillip; alarm, startle, disturb, impress, strike, penetrate, touch to the quick; elicit, evoke, call forth, summon up, sound *or* raise the alarm.

2. incite, provoke, poke, prod, prick, goad, prompt, spur; encourage, urge, abet, egg on, put up to; instigate, look for trouble, *Inf.* start something; foment, agitate, suscitate, excite, impassion, stir up, work up, wind up, whip up, hype up, *Inf.* turn on, *Inf.* psyche up, fire up, inflame, enflame, enkindle, kindle, touch off, ignite the spark, build a fire under, stir the embers, fan the fire.

arraign, *v.* **1.** accuse, charge, indict, *Law.* impute, incriminate, criminate, recriminate, impeach, *Rare.* implead; denounce, implicate, (*of an innocent person*) *Inf.* frame, inculpate, inform against, *Chiefly Scot.* delate; cite, summon, serve with a summons *or* with papers, sue, libel, *Law.* prosecute; litigate, file charges.

2. criticize, fault, find fault with, censure, upbraid, reproach, rebuke, reprehend; reprove, tax, take to task, call to account, impugn, call into question, assail, revile; stigmatize, brand, asperse, cast aspersions on, malign, slander, defame, vilify; attack, inveigh against, rail against, declaim against.

arraignment, *n.* **1.** accusation, charge, indictment, *Law.* true bill, *Law.* gravamen; citation, summons; incrimination, crimination, recrimination, denunciation; implication, inculpation, blaming, accusing.

2. censure, blame; criticism, examination, finding fault, animadversion; calling into question, impugning; assailment, revilement.

arrange, *v.* **1.** order, dispose, array, assort, collocate; line, range, align, aline, straighten, trim; group, sort, classify, class, categorize, bracket; file, index, codify, tabulate; size, rank, grade, graduate; organize, systematize, coordinate, regulate, marshal, *Inf.* line up, set up; distribute, assign, allocate, apportion, allot, set out.

2. settle, decide, determine, adjust; agree to, fix on *or* upon, come to terms, compromise, conciliate, accommodate.

3. prepare, plan, ready, prime, prearrange, project; devise, form, design, block out, fix, contrive, prescribe; predetermine, premeditate.

4. orchestrate, compose, score, harmonize, instrument.

arrangement, *n.* **1.** order, ordering, disposition, ordination, grouping; array, assortment, collocation, set, series; mixture, miscellany, collection, selection; classification, categorization, category; graduation, grade, denomination, division; tabulation, codification, index; organization, systematization, coordination, regimentation, regulation; distribution, allocation, disposal, assignment, apportionment, allotment.

2. scheme, structure, design, frame, outline, system; policy, method, procedure, process; mode, form, style; make-up, composition, constitution, construction; configuration, interrelation, relationship, conformation, formation; formulation, combination, association, amalgamation.

3. arrangements preparations, plans, provisions, measures; groundwork, preliminaries; reservations.

4. settlement, adjustment, agreement, terms; contract, covenant, compact; compromise, conciliation, accommodation.

5. orchestration, adaptation, score, instrumentation, harmonization.

arrant, *adj.* **1.** downright, out-and-out, through and through, thorough, thoroughgoing, wholesale, all-out, *Inf.* flat-out; complete, total, outright, categorical, unequivocal, flat, dead; absolute, utter, profound, rank, gross; sheer, stark, brazen, bold; unmitigated, unqualified, unconditional, incontestable; perfect, positive, consummate, *Inf.* regular, *Inf.* plumb, *Brit.* proper; overt, undisguised, barefaced, unmistakeable, undeniable, evident, unconcealed, patent; pronounced, confirmed.

2. infamous, disreputable, ill-famed; scandalous, disgraceful, shameful, shocking, improper, ignominious, base, low, vile, wicked, foul; flagrant, egregious, glaring, heinous, flagitious, nefarious; atrocious, monstrous, outrageous; unscrupulous, shameless.

array, *v.* **1.** (*often of troops*) marshal, order, rank, muster, assemble, group, draw together *or* up, amass; range, arrange, line up, place, dispose.

2. clothe, attire, apparel, dress, habit, garb; dress up, prank, trick out *or* up, *Sl.* dude up, *Sl.* swank up; deck out *or* up, bedeck, bedizen, *Archaic.* bedight; caparison, *Inf.* doll up, *Inf.* gussy up, *Sl.* trick up; ornament, adorn, decorate, *Scot.* dink, embellish; accouter, equip, outfit, fit out, rig up *or* out.

—*n.* **3.** (*often of troops*) marshalling, muster, assembling, amassing, amassment, collection, agglomeration, aggregation, congregation; disposition, arrangement, line-up; display, parade, show, exhibition, exhibit.

4. apparel, attire, clothing, dress, wear, *Inf.* gear, *Inf.* toggery, *Inf.* duds, *Sl.* threads, *Sl.* rags; raiment, vestments, garments; finery, caparison, *Sl.* glad rags, *Sl.* heavy threads, *Sl.* Sunday-go-to-meeting clothes; regalia, outfit, ensemble, *Inf.* getup, *Inf.* rig.

arrear, *n.* **1.** *Usu.* **arrears** unpaid debt, payment outstanding, moneys owed, liabilities; arrearage, amount due *or* overdue, remaining balance; debt, financial obligation, debit, deficit, deficiency.

2. **in arrears** in debt, in default, in the hole, in the red; behind, late, overdue.

arrest, *v.* **1.** seize, take into custody, apprehend, haul in, *Inf.* pick up, *Inf.* nab, *Inf.* pinch, *Sl.* bust, *Sl.* nail, *Sl.* run in, put the arm on [s.o.]; capture, catch, detain; hold, secure, collar; take prisoner, imprison, jail, incarcerate.

2. attract, catch, hold the attention of, engross, engage, absorb, occupy, rivet.

3. stop, halt, check, abort, end; stay, stall, bring to a standstill; block, obstruct, prevent; hinder, inhibit, restrain, delay, interrupt, suspend, suppress; stunt, dwarf, nip in the bud.

—*n.* **4.** seizure, apprehension, police detention, legal restraint, constraint, capture; *Sl.* bust; taking into custody, imprisonment, incarceration, durance.

5. stoppage, cessation, check, stay; delay, suspension, interruption; hindrance, obstruction, prevention, suppression, restraining.

arresting, *adj.* attention-getting, striking, stunning; stimulating, exciting, electrifying, dazzling; impressive, noticeable, noteworthy, remarkable, conspicuous; unusual, out-of-the-ordinary, extraordinary, standout, singular.

arrival, *n.* **1.** advent, coming, appearance, forthcoming, approach, access, accession; return, reappearance, coming back.

2. landing, alighting, dismounting, debarkation, disembarkation, debusing, deplaning, detraining.

3. attainment, reaching, realization, actualization; consummation, fulfillment, fruition; completion, finishing, termination.

4. comer, incomer; newcomer, immigrant; visitor, visitant, guest; newborn, baby.

arrive, *v.* **1.** come, land, pull in, get here *or* there, get in; appear, show up, turn up, *Sl.* blow in, set in, present itself *or* oneself; arrive in, *Sl.* hit; alight, deplane, detrain, disembark, debark, debus, dismount; return, come back, get back.

2. succeed, *Inf.* make it, *Sl.* make the scene, *Inf.* get somewhere, get ahead, get ahead in the world, be somebody; thrive, prosper, flourish.

3. occur, happen, befall, come to pass, eventuate.

4. **arrive at** reach, attain, realize, get to, gain.

arrogance, *n.* **1.** haughtiness, loftiness, hauteur, self-importance; presumption, presumptuousness, overconfidence, fatuousness; pride, vanity, vainglory, conceit, snobbery, snobbishness, airs; pomposity, pompousness, egotism, superciliousness, contempt, contemptuousness, disdain, disdainfulness, scorn, scornfulness, contumely, contumeliousness.

2. insolence, impudence, brazenness, effrontery, audacity, defiance; impertinence, bumptiousness, *Inf.* pushiness; self-assertion, self-assuredness, self-assurance.

3. imperiousness, lordliness, overbearingness, high-handedness; pretension, braggadocio, bluster, swagger.

arrogant, *adj.* **1.** haughty, self-important, presumptuous, fatuous, proud, vainglorious; overconfident, overweening, conceited, high-and-mighty, snobbish, *Inf.* stuck-up, *Inf.* uppish, *Inf.* uppity, on one's high horse; pompous, egotistic, lofty, *Inf.* toplofty, condescending; disdainful, supercilious, cavalier, contemptuous, scornful, insulting, contumelious.

2. imperious, overbearing, domineering, arbitrary, high-handed; dictatorial, despotic, authoritative, dogmatic, magisterial.

3. brazen, impudent, insolent, defiant, rude, audacious, impertinent; swaggering, blustering, *Inf.* pushy; bumptious, self-assertive, self-assured, self-assuming.

4. excessive, exaggerated, immoderate, intemperate; extravagant, high-flown, *Inf.* highfalutin, preposterous; unconscionable, disproportionate, unreasonable, undue, unfounded, uncalled for, unwarranted.

arrogate, *v.* **1.** (*all in reference to oneself*) assume, appropriate, claim, avail oneself of, help oneself to, make free with; seize, take, commandeer, expropriate, usurp, confiscate.

2. (*all in reference to another; all falsely or unjustly*) impute, ascribe, attribute, assign, blame, charge to, lay to, lay at the door of; blame, accuse, *Inf.* finger, incriminate, inculpate.

arrogation, *n.* **1.** (*all in reference to oneself*) assumption, appropriation, undue claim, unwarranted seizure, expropriation, usurpation, confiscation.

2. (*all in reference to another; all falsely or unjustly*) attribution, ascription, imputation, charge, allegation, censure, blame, accusation, incrimination, inculpation.

arrow, *n.* **1.** feathered shaft, shaft, reed, flight, bolt, crossbow bolt, quarrel, *Astron.* Sagitta, dart, (*pl.*) quiver; missile, weapon.

2. pointer, indicator, directional signal, director, marker.

arsenal, *n.* depot, magazine, ammunition dump, military storehouse, storehouse; depository, repository, warehouse, entrepôt.

arson, *n.* incendiarism, malicious burning, firing, *Sl.* torching, *Sl.* torch job, *Sl.* match job; pyromania.

arsonist, *n.* incendiary, *Sl.* torch, *Sl.* match; pyromaniac, *Inf.* firebug.

art, *n.* **1.** skill, skillfulness, dexterity, adroitness, expertness, mastery, artistry; aptitude, facility, address, dispatch, ready skill, *Inf.* know-how; ingenuity, cleverness, talent, flair, knack, genius, way, touch, feel, hang, trick.

2. cunning, wiliness, slyness, foxiness, craftiness, guile, artfulness; deceit, deception, duplicity, trickery.

3. artiface, subterfuge, contrivance, device, expedient, craft, wile; scheme, plot, design, stratagem; ploy, maneuver, shift, dodge, tactic, ruse, red herring.

4. affectation, affectedness, unnaturalness, studiedness, artificial manner, airs, pretension, pretentiousness; simulation, make-believe, artificiality, insincerity; posing, posturing, peacockery.

artery, *n.* **1.** blood vessel, vessel, aorta; vein, capillary.

2. main road, highroad, thoroughfare, main street, *Inf.* drag, *Brit. Sl.* toby; throughway, avenue, boulevard, strip, concourse; route, highway, turnpike, pike, tollroad, state highway; freeway, *Brit.* clearway, expressway, parkway, causeway, *U.S. Inf.* interstate; speedway, autobahn, superhighway.

3. canal, artificial waterway, channel, race, conduit, watercourse; strait, aqueduct, waterway, seaway.

4. duct, pipe, main, tube, cylinder; passage, passageway, adit; conduit, sewer, culvert, cloaca, flume, trough, chute; spout, gutter, drain, gully, ditch.

artful, *adj.* **1.** cunning, crafty, sly, wily, subtle, foxy, *Sl.* crazy like a fox, *Scot. and North Eng.* pawky; shrewd, astute, canny, sharp, knowing.

2. insidious, guileful, disingenuous, scheming, plotting, calculating, contriving, designing; deceitful, tricky, crooked, dishonest, underhanded; false, false-hearted, double-dealing, two-faced, double-faced; shifty, slippery, smooth, slick.

3. ingenious, clever, resourceful, inventive; facile, deft, quick, ready, nimble-fingered; skillful, dexterous, adroit, adept.

arthritis, *n.* inflammation of a joint, stiffening of a joint, gout, rheumatism.

article, *n.* **1.** composition, essay, theme, paper; story, feature, write-up, layout; narrative, account, report, chronicle; review, study, critique, analysis, editorial, opinion, commentary, descant; discussion, disquisition, thesis, dissertation, discourse, homily, treatise, tract; piece, notice, note, spot, *All Journalism.* followup, sidebar, shirttail.

2. item, unit, one, individual, single, particular, particularity; piece, portion, particle, part, division, section, branch; element, component, constituent, ingredient.

3. thing, object, something, *Inf.* thingumajig, *Inf.* thingumbob, *Inf.* thingumabob, *Inf.* what-you-may-call-it; entity, being.

4. clause, paragraph, *Law.* covenant; provision, proviso, point, stipulation, term, condition.

—*v.* **5.** specify, list, name, mention individually; formulate, state in detail.

6. accuse, charge, impute, count, ascribe.

7. obligate, oblige, bind, pin down, tie; sign up, indenture, apprentice.

articulate, *adj.* **1.** clear, clear as day, crystal-clear, plain, manifest, lucid, obvious; distinct, definite, defined, well-defined, clear-cut; intelligible, understandable, comprehensible, apprehensible, fathomable; audible, hearable, loud and clear.

2. talkative, garrulous, loquacious, multiloquent, multiloquious, multiloquous, multi-loquacious, *Sl.* gabby; communicative, articulative, articulable; speaking, talking; (*all of speech*) unreticent, unreserved, unrestrained, unconstrained.

3. eloquent, well-spoken, silver-tongued, *Archaic.* facund, *Obs.* facundious; glib, slick, smooth, smooth-tongued, smooth-talking, smooth-spoken, fast-talking; (*all of speech*) fluent, flowing, facile, easy, graceful.

4. joined, united, unified, connected; coherent, cohesive, harmonious, congruous, congruent, agreeing, in agreement; uniform, consistent, of a piece.

5. *Zoology.* jointed, segmented, articulated.

—*v.* **6.** enunciate, pronounce, vocalize, voice, enounce; say, express, utter, breathe, give *or* let out, come out with.

7. clarify, clear up, make clear, make plain; explain, explicate, expound, elucidate; illuminate, shed *or* cast *or* throw light on.

8. unify, synthesize, combine, coalesce; integrate, incorporate, consolidate, merge; blend, fuse, flux; identify, make one.

9. joint, hinge, connect; (*all by joints*) join, unite, link, couple, fasten, splice; (*all by joints*) conjoin, subjoin, attach, fix, affix, annex.

articulation, *n.* **1.** enunciation, pronunciation, vocalization, utterance, phonation, voice, voicing; delivery, presentation, attack, force of utterance; elocution, diction, dialect, speech pattern, manner of speaking, mode of expression; articulating, pronouncing, vocalizing, enunciating; saying, expressing, uttering; delivering, presenting.

2. intonation, inflection, modulation; emphasis, accent, accentuation, stress, syllable stress.

3. verbalism, vocable, speech sound, phone, *Phonet.* consonant, *Phonet.* semivowel.

4. union, unification, connection, junction, conjunction, conjugation, joinder, jointure, linkage; joining, jointing, conjoining, bonding, linking, coupling, bracketing, yoking.

5. joint, juncture, intersection, nexus, connexus, point of union *or* contact; link, tie, bind, knot, yoke; coupler; miter, dovetail joint, rabbet, rabbet joint; pivot, hinge, elbow, knee.

artifice, *n.* **1.** stratagem, trick, wile, ruse; intrigue, plot, plan, scheme, strategy, machination; conspiracy, complot, cabal; device, contrivance, expedient, *Inf.* dodge, fetch, subterfuge, blind; maneuver, feint, deception, sleight, coup, blow, stroke; shift, move, evasion, shuffle.

2. cunning, ingenuity, inventiveness; cleverness, skillfulness, adroitness, dexterousness, adeptness, deftness; facility, facileness, quickness, readiness, aptness, brightness.

3. trickery, deceit, guile, craft, craftiness, shrewdness, wiliness, slyness; artfulness, subtlety, finesse; duplicity, doubledealing, cheating, cozenage; fraud, imposture, imposition, hoax.

artificer, *n.* **1.** inventor, creator, originator; deviser, contriver, machinator; designer, artist, architect; maker, builder, constructor, erecter, framer, fabricator, manufacturer.

2. craftsman, handicraftsman, artisan, artistic *or* skillful workman; operative, mechanic, machinist.

artificial, *adj.* **1.** man-made, manufactured, constructed; synthetic, ersatz, plastic, pseudo, simulated, imitated, imitation, ungenuine, *Inf.* phony; unauthentic, *Sl.* hyped-up, sham, make-believe, bogus, mock, fake, specious, brummagem; spurious, bastard, supposititious, false, counterfeit, fictitious, unreal; adulterate, adulterine, adulterous, alloyed.

2. factitious, feigned, so-called, pretended, assumed; forced, labored, strained, contrived, engineered, *Sl.* hokey, *Sl.* hoked-up; unnatural, affected, mannered, stilted; stagy, theatrical, overacted, overdone; insincere, hollow, meretricious, pretentious.

3. conventional, traditional, orthodox, rigid, arbitrary.

artillery, *n.* ordnance, cannon, mortars, howitzers, mounted guns; *Mil.* battery, enginery, *Mil.* fieldpieces; ballistae, catapults, culverins, falconets, jingals.

artilleryman, *n.* artillerist, gunner, cannoneer, *Hist.* bombardier, fusileer.

artisan, *n.* craftsman, handicraftsman, master craftsman, master, artificer, *Obs.* artist; skilled laborer *or* worker, journeyman.

artist, *n.* **1.** master, old master, past master; artiste, virtuoso, maestro; talent, genius, prodigy, giant, *Inf.* wizard *or* wiz.

2. artisan, craftsman, artificer; expert, adept, masterhand, proficient, *Sl.* no slouch.

3. trickster, deceiver, cheat, fraud, swindler, confidence man, *Sl.* con man *or* artist, bunco artist, *Inf.* shyster, *Inf.* flimflam man; fox, sly dog, sharpie, horse trader.

artistic, *adj.* **1.** beautiful, attractive, lovely, handsome, pleasing to the eye; exquisite, magnificent, of consummate art, in the grand style; harmonious, symmetrical, well-proportioned, well-composed, well-done, well-grouped, well-arranged.

2. virtuoso, brilliant, bravura; expert, masterful, masterly; talented, accomplished, skilled, good, proficient, excellent; skillful, clever, adept, adroit, apt, dexterous.

3. tasteful, in good taste, in the best taste, choice, well-chosen; aesthetic, sensitive, discriminative, art-minded, art-conscious, *Inf.* arty, *Sl.* artsy-craftsy; classic, elegant, restrained, subdued, understated; cultured, cultivated, polished, refined.

4. bohemian, unconventional, nonconforming, offbeat, original.

artistry, *n.* virtuosity, brilliance, genius; talent, skill, skillfulness, dexterity, adroitness, expertness, mastery; art, flair, knack, gift, way, touch, feel, hang.

artless, *adj.* **1.** open, open and sincere, open-hearted, ingenuous, guileless, genuine, sincere, undeceptive, undeceitful, undeceiving, unfeigning, undissembling, undissimulating; aboveboard, open and aboveboard, up front, up and up, on the level, no-nonsense; natural, uncontrived, unaffected, unassuming, unadorned, unpretentious, unpretending.

2. candid, frank, forthright, foursquare, straightforward, straight-from-the-shoulder; plain, plain-spoken, plain-speaking, downright, outright, explicit, unequivocal, unambiguous, undisguised, *Inf.* straight-out, *Inf.* flat-footed, *Inf.* matter-of-fact.

3. naive, simple, simple-minded, innocent, childlike; unsophisticated, undeveloped, unworldly, green, raw, born-yesterday, wet behind the ears; unsuspicious, trustful, trusting, unwary, unguarded.

4. inartistic, unartistic, unaesthetic; amateurish, crude, clumsy, awkward, badly *or* poorly made *or* constructed.

5. unskillful, inexpert, unproficient, unclever; undexterous, inadept, undeft, unfacile; unaccomplished, unskilled, untrained, untaught, untutored, unprepared; ungifted, untalented, unendowed.

artlessness, *n.* **1.** openness, openheartedness, ingenuousness, guilelessness, sincerity, sincereness, genuineness, undeceptiveness, undeceitfulness; naturalness, unaffectedness, unpretentiousness.

2. candor, candidness, frankness, forthrightness, straightforwardness, calling a spade a spade, *Sl.* telling it like it is; plain-speaking, plain-spokenness, downrightness, outrightness, explicitness, unequivocalness.

3. naiveté, naiveness, simpleness, simple-mindedness, innocence; unsophisticatedness, greenness, rawness, unworldliness; trustfulness, unsuspiciousness, unwariness, unguardedness.

4. unskillfulness, inexpertness, uncleverness; clumsiness, crudeness, awkwardness, undexterousness, undeftness, unfacileness; ungiftedness, untalentedness.

as, *adv., conj.* **1.** similarly, equally, to the same extent, in equal degree, no less than, in the same proportion; to such a degree *or* extent, to the degree that, in proportion to which.

2. for example, for instance, namely, to wit, *Latin.* *videlicet,* viz.; in a manner like that of, after the manner of, in the same manner with, of the same kind with; thus, in this way.

3. thought to be, considered to be, taken to be; viewed like, under the name of, in the idea *or* character of.

4. at the same time that, during the time that, while, when.

5. since, because, inasmuch as, forasmuch as, it being the case that; for the reason that, by reason of, on account of, in consideration of, considering that, on the score that.

6. though, even if, granting that.

7. **as for** with respect to, with regard to, with relation to; in reference to, in connection with, as regards; in the matter of, on the subject of, in point of, in that regard.

8. **as good as** **a.** equivalent to, equal to, tantamount to, the same as; of equal goodness with, up to the measure of. **b.** practically, almost, nearly, near, near to, close to. **c.** true to, faithful to.

9. **as if** as though, as it would be if, as might be; as it were, as if it were, so to speak, in a manner of speaking, quasi; just as, like; seemingly, supposedly.

10. **as it were** as if it were, so to say, so to speak; in a way, in a manner, in some sort; as it seems, as it would seem.

11. **as long as** provided that, assuming that, supposing that; since, because, as.

12. **as regards** with regard to, with reference to, with respect to, concerning, having to do with.

13. **as yet** up to the present time, until now; right now, at this moment, now.

—pron. **14.** that, who, which; being of the kind which, being of the class who.

—prep. **15.** in the role of, in the function of, in the status of.

ascend, *v.* **1.** rise, arise, uprise; levitate, float, lift off; shoot up, spring up, sprout, creep up, wing up; tower, extend upward, reach high; soar, fly aloft.

2. slope up, slant up, swerve up; heave, swell, expand; incline, lean, tilt, tip, list.

3. climb, go up, get up, mount, move upward, surmount; scale, scramble, clamber, work one's way up, shin, escalade; top, overtop, rise over *or* above; advance, increase, run up, escalate.

ascendancy, *n.* **1.** domination, dominance, predominance, hegemony, controlling influence, position of dominance, ascendant; dominion, rule, reign; control, sovereignty, mastery, prevalence, power. See **ascendant** (*def.* **1**).

2. superiority, preeminence, eminence; advantage over, pull, sway; importance, prestige, popularity.

ascendant, *n.* **1.** domination, dominance, predominance, hegemony, controlling influence, dominant position; supremacy, preeminence, superiority; mastership, lordship, chiefdom, seigniory, suzerainty, leadership; command, rule, control, hold, grasp; sway, prestige, weight, power, upper hand.

2. ancestor, forebear, forefather, sire; progenitor, primogenitor, procreator.

3. **in the ascendant** up-and-coming, flourishing, burgeoning; ascending, mounting, rising, on the rise, uprising, upcoming, on the way up; prevailing, winning, victorious, triumphant.

—adj. **4.** ascending, mounting, rising, uprising, upcoming, moving up; climbing, scandent, sprouting; raised, elevated, upturned, uplifted, curved upward; towering, extending above, reaching high.

5. superior, supreme, greater, higher, surpassing; eminent, preeminent, distinguished; predominant, dominant, ruling, controlling, prevalent; victorious, triumphant, prevailing, overcoming, in the ascendant.

ascension, *n.* rising, arising, uprising, ascent. See **ascent** (*defs.* **1, 2**).

ascent, *n.* **1.** rising, arising, uprising; levitating, floating; soaring, flying; shooting up, springing up, sprouting, creeping up.

2. climbing, mounting, moving upward, surmounting, traveling up; scaling, scrambling, clambering, shinnying, escalading.

3. advancement, increase, promotion, escalation; extension, heightening, augmentation.

4. gradient, steepness, elevation, height, eminence; ramp, hill, climb, rising ground, ascending path; acclivity, upgrade, upward slope, slope, incline, inclination; lean, tilt, list, grade.

ascertain, *v.* **1.** determine, establish, identify, pin [s.t.] down, *Sl.* peg, *Sl.* button down; verify, confirm, make certain of, make sure, determinate; conclude, resolve, settle, decide, come to a decision.

2. discern, figure, apprehend, grasp, understand, come to know; learn about, acquire knowledge of *or* information about; detect, discover, make out, get at; ferret out, dig out, unearth, uncover.

ascetic, *n.* **1.** abstainer, self-denier, celibate, puritan; penitent, *Islam.* fakir, *Islam.* dervish, *Islam.* Calender, *Hinduism.* yogi; self-punisher, self-tormentor, religious fanatic, flagellant, hair shirt wearer.

2. (*in the early Christian church*) monk, hermit, eremite, anchorite, anchoret, recluse, solitary, stylite; ancress, hermitess, *Obs.* hermitress, nun.

—adj. **3.** abstinent, abstemious, self-denying, self-mortifying, self-lacerating, self-punishing, self-tormenting, flagellant.

4. austere, strict, harsh, severe, rigorous, stern, puritanical, puritanic, frugal, plain.

5. continent, celibate, temperate, moderate, restrained, self-controlled, self-disciplined.

asceticism, *n.* self-denial, self-abnegation, self-mortification; mortification of the flesh, self-punishment, self-torment, self-laceration, flagellation, scourging, flagellantism; abstinence, fasting, penance, sackcloth and ashes, monasticism, self-renunciation; puritanism, abstemiousness, continence, celibacy; self-control, self-restraint, self-discipline.

ascribable, *adj.* **1.** attributable, assignable; imputable, chargeable, accusable.

2. explicable, explainable, accountable, traceable.

ascribe, *v.* **1.** attribute, assign, credit, accredit, give credit for, put down, chalk up to; impute, charge with, lay on, blame, accuse.

2. associate, connect, link, tie in, couple, match *or* pair up, relate, think of together, consider jointly *or* in union; count, account, deem, hold, repute, esteem, refer, consider *or* regard as.

ascription, *n.* **1.** attribution, attributing, assignment, assigning, adscription, creditation, accreditation, accrediting, chalking up to; imputation, imputing, charging, laying on, blaming, accusal, accusing.

2. exaltation, glorification, extolment, laudation; doxology, hosanna, hallelujah, alleluia, hymn; *Te Deum, Liturgy.* Gloria, Magnificat; tribute, eulogy, eulogization, commendation.

ash, *n.* **1.** cinder, ember, coal; slag, scoria, residue; lava, volcanic rock.

2. ashes paleness, ghastliness, pallor, sallowness, wanness.

3. ashes ruins, remains, vestiges, relics, *Archaic.* reliques; cremains, reliquiae; leftovers, bits, pieces, fragments.

ashamed, *adj.* **1.** embarrassed, humiliated, mortified, abashed, humbled, chagrined, chapfallen; distressed, discomforted, uneasy, disconcerted, out of countenance; discomposed, confused, perplexed, bewildered; put down, brought down, degraded. disgraced, dishonored; put to the blush, redfaced, *Inf.* red, sheepish, exposed, naked, stripped.

2. conscience-stricken, shamefaced, guilty, hangdog, remorseful, with one's tail between one's legs; disappointed *or* displeased in oneself.

3. unwilling, restrained, reserved, deterred, reluctant; bashful, modest, meek, shy, self-conscious, *Archaic.* verecund; decent, proper, innocent, chaste, virginal, pure; prudish, squeamish.

ashen, *adj.* **1.** gray, grayish, silver, silvery, grayish-white, ashy, ash-colored, light; blanched, bleached, whitened, hueless, colorless, faded, washed-out.

2. pale, pale-faced, ghastly, ghostly, ghostlike; pallid, sallow, sallowish, wan, deathlike, cadaverous.

3. cindery, cinderous, cinderlike, cinerous.

ashore, *adv.* on shore, on land, on the beach, aground; stranded, shoaled, beached, grounded.

ashy, *adj.* gray, grayish, cindery, cinderous; pale, ghastly. See **ashen**.

aside, *adv.* **1.** to *or* on the side, beside, alongside, abreast; laterally, next to, by, *Naut.* abeam, sideways, sidewise.

2. apart, away, separately, in reserve; out of the way, out of mind.

3. notwithstanding, albeit, howbeit, withal, despite, in spite of; however, yet, still, nevertheless; in any event, at all events, all the same, after all, just the same, even so.

4. aside from besides, apart from, in addition to; other than, not counting, beyond that, excluding, except for.

—n. **5.** apostrophe, by-play, whisper, soliloquy, monologue.

6. digression, departure, excursus, excursion.

asinine, *adj.* **1.** stupid, *Inf.* dumb, *Inf.* dopey, *Inf.* moronic, empty-headed, unintelligent, imbecilic, oxlike; dull, inexpressive, expressionless; addlepated, addleheaded, addlebrained, muddled, muddleheaded; dull-witted, *Sl.* dimwitted, slow-witted, half-witted, witless, unwitty; mindless, *Rare.* insulse, brainless, fatuitous; dense, thick, bovine, obtuse, Boeotian, stolid, oafish, loutish, cloddish, lumpish, blunt; doltish, blockish, asslike, blockheaded, dunderheaded, noodleheaded; boneheaded, wooden-headed, thick-headed, thickskulled; obstinate, stubborn, intractable, mulish, obdurate, unyielding, unbending.

2. idiotic, anserine, foolish; silly, absurd, inane, pointless, fatuous; nonsensical, senseless, crack-brained, *Scot.* doiled, *Sl.* cockeyed, *Scot. and North Eng.* glaikit; ridiculous, laughable, derisible, risible, ludicrous, *Sl.* for the birds; *All Sl.* balmy, dippy, batty, cuckoo, buggy, screwy, wacky, goofy, loony.

3. incautious, imprudent, indiscreet, irresponsible, injudicious; unwise, ill-considered, ill-suited, ill-advised, impolitic; impetuous, impulsive, hasty, short-sighted, heedless, unheeding; foolhardy, headlong, rash, brash, unwary; reckless, careless, thoughtless.

asininity, *n.* **1.** stupidity, stupidness, *Inf.* dumbness, *Inf.* dopiness, empty-headedness, unintelligence, dullness, fatuity; doltishness, oafishness, loutishness, obtuseness; obstinacy, obstinateness, stubbornness.

2. idiocy, *Inf.* moronity, *Inf.* moronism, imbecility; silliness, absurdity, absurdness, fatuousness, inanity, foolishness; nonsense, nonsensicality, nonsensicalness, senselessness, ridiculousness, ludicrousness; craziness, madness, lunacy, insanity; *All Sl.* balminess, dippiness, bugginess, screwiness, wackiness, goofiness.

3. incaution, imprudence, indiscretion; impetuousness, impulsiveness, hastiness, short-sightedness; foolhardiness, rashness, unwariness; recklessness, carelessness, irresponsibleness, thoughtlessness.

ask, *v.* **1.** inquire, question, query; quiz, catechize, probe, examine, test; interrogate, *Inf.* grill, pump, cross-examine, *U.S.* give the third degree.

2. request, appeal, petition, *Rare.* sue; interpellate, call on *or* upon, address, apply to, turn to; solicit, beg, plead, supplicate; beseech, pray to, entreat, impetrate, implore, adjure, obtest; cry for, clamor for.

3. demand, expect, count on, require, call for; urge, importune, dun, press; order, command, impose, requisition, *Brit. Mil.* indent.

4. invite, bid, summon, beckon, request one's presence.

5. **ask for** provoke, incite, inspire, encourage, instigate, induce; actuate, occasion, bring on *or* about, bring to pass.

askance, *adv.* **1.** suspiciously, mistrustfully, distrustfully, dubiously, doubtfully; disapprovingly, unapprovingly, disdainfully, scornfully, askew.

2. sideways, obliquely, indirectly, evasively, slyly, out of the corner of one's eye, with a side glance; askance, askant, asquint; at an angle, aslant, slantwise, at a slant, slantingly, crookedly.

askew, *adv.* **1.** awry, sideways, to one side, crookedly, out of line.

2. disapprovingly, unapprovingly, askance; disdainfully, scornfully, contemptuously, derisively.

—adj. **3.** crooked, awry, *Sl.* cock-eyed.

aslant, *adv.* **1.** slantwise, at a slant, slantingly, sideways, obliquely, at an angle; aslope, at a slope, diagonally, crossways, crosswise.

—adj. **2.** slanting, slant, slantwise, oblique, diagonal, sloping, aslope, at an angle.

—prep. **3.** slanting across, athwart, from side to side of.

asleep, *adv.* **1.** fast asleep, sound asleep, dead asleep, in *or* into a deep sleep, in *or* into a coma.

—adj. **2.** sleeping, resting, reposing, slumbering, dozing, drowsing, *Inf.* snoozing, *Sl.* logging z's; somnolent, soporose, soporous; dead to the world, *Inf.* out like a light, *Sl.* sacked out; dreaming, in the arms of Morpheus; napping, catnapping; comatose, unconscious, anesthetized; hypnotized, in a swoon, in a trance, in a faint.

3. dormant, inactive, passive, idle, latent; quiet, quiescent, still, stock-still, *Chiefly Brit.* stilly; unmoving, immovable, immobile, motionless, unstirring, calm, becalmed; stagnant, inert, sluggish.

4. numb, benumbed, insensible.

5. lifeless, inanimate, dead; deceased, departed, at rest.

asp, *n.* adder, European viper, Egyptian cobra, horned viper, *Archaeol.* uraeus, venomous snake *or* serpent, krait.

aspect, *n.* **1.** appearance, demeanor, mien, air, cast, look; countenance, visage, complexion, features, face, physiognomy, figure; bearing, attitude, presence, style, carriage, deportment.

2. nature, character, quality, property, attribute, feature; characteristic, trait, particularity, singularity.

3. view, viewpoint, standpoint, side, slant, angle, light, interpretation.

4. part, piece, segment, factor, phase.

5. outlook, prospect, exposure, direction; landscape, scene; side, surface.

asperity, *n.* **1.** acrimony, acrimoniousness, causticity, mordancy, bitterness, acridity, acridness, pungency, venom, venomousness, venomness; astringency, severity, sternness, acerbity, austerity, stringency; harshness, sharpness, sourness, acidulousness, acidity, tartness; trenchancy, keenness, sarcasm, satire, irony; virulence, spite, spitefulness, malice, maliciousness, viciousness; peevishness, petulance, *Rare.* petulancy, *Rare.* procacity, crabbedness, testiness, touchiness, edginess; irascibility, irritability, crossness; ill-temperedness, ill temper, short-temperedness, ill-humoredness, ill humor.

2. animosity, resentment, grudge, hostility; indignation, pique, dudgeon; moroseness, sullenness, surliness, moodiness; rudeness, churlishness, boorishness, gracelessness, discourtesy; abusiveness, corrosiveness.

3. choler, rancor, anger, gall, spleen, bile; contempt, disdain, contumely, scorn, derision, unkindness; malevolence, malignity.

4. hardship, burden, ordeal, trouble, tribulation, trial; difficulty, rigor, challenge, adversity.

5. roughness, unsmoothness, unevenness, irregularity; ruggedness, jaggedness, raggedness, cragginess; wrinkledness, corrugation, rugosity.

asperse, *v.* **1.** slander, libel, traduce, calumniate, falsify, accuse falsely, misrepresent, belie, impute, insinuate; injure, abuse, assail, stab, insult, backbite, *Sl.* badmouth, cast aspersions, attack; slur, sully, defile, smear, smirch, besmirch, soil, blacken, taint, tarnish, blemish, smudge, stain, spot, brand, stigmatize, drag through the mud *or* mire, heap dirt upon, fling dirt, throw mud on, *Sl.* dump on.

2. defame, denigrate, vituperate, vilify, vilipend, scandalize, run down, berate, revile, *Obs.* avile, malign, impugn, gibbet, criticize, pull to pieces, *Sl.* do a hatchet job on, cut up, shred, give a bad name, speak ill of, speak evil of, hold up to scorn, lampoon, pasquinade, sneer at, muckrake; denounce, rail, curse, execrate, animadvert, damn, imprecate, *Obs.* exprobrate, anathematize, censure, cry down, reproach; belittle, disparage, deprecate, decry, deflate, depreciate, derogate, devaluate, *Inf.* give a dog a bad name; humiliate, humble, mortify, *Sl.* put down.

3. sprinkle, besprinkle, spatter, bespatter, dot, speck, speckle, bespot, dapple, mottle.

aspersion, *n.* **1.** defamation, denigration, vilification, vituperation, scandal, yellow journalism, *Inf.* skeleton in the closet; censure, reproach, reflection, denunciation, curse, malediction, railing, invective, commination, revilement, animadversion, *Archaic.* exprobration; shame, disgrace, dishonor, ill-repute, obloquy, loss of face; belittlement, disparagement, deprecation, detraction, deflation, depreciation, derogation, devaluation, *Obs.* obtrectation; humiliation, humble pie, mortification; mockery, satirization, lampoon, pasquinade, squib.

2. slander, libel, calumny, calumniation, misrepresentation, false report, falsehood, lie, untruth, malicious falsehood, traducement, imputation, insinuation, *Inf.* brickbat, innuendo; abuse, injury, backbiting, mud-slinging; slur, blot, blot on the escutcheon, smear, smirch, taint, attaint, stain, tarnish, spot, black spot *or* mark, blemish, smudge, brand, stigma.

asphyxiate, *v.* choke, suffocate, smother, stifle; strangulate, throttle, garrote.

asphyxiation, *n.* choking, suffocation, smothering, stifling; strangulation, throttling, garroting.

aspirant, *n.* applicant, candidate, office seeker, postulant, suitor; job seeker, job hunter, interviewee, competitor; inquirer, solicitor, petitioner, claimant, suppliant, supplicant.

aspiration, *n.* **1.** desire, yearning, longing, want, need, craving.

2. ambition, goal, aim, objective; target, destination, mark, end point; intention, intent, purpose, design, plan, scheme; hope, heart's desire, dream, wish, ideal; high hopes.

3. enterprise, endeavor, drive, force, striving; zeal, enthusiasm, eagerness, spirit.

4. breathing, breathiness, breath, sigh, suspiration; respiration, inhalation, inspiration.

aspire, *v.* **1.** hope for, wish for, dream of; desire, covet, yearn for, long for, want, need, crave; hunger for, have an appetite *or* taste for.

2. aim for, shoot for, have an ideal *or* goal, scheme *or* plan toward, intend, purpose; seek, search for, look for, follow; hitch one's wagon to a star, shoot for the moon.

aspiring, *adj.* ambitious, hopeful, dreaming, wishful, yearning, longing; desirous, craving, hungry; enterprising, hard-working, enthusiastic; expectant, optimistic, sanguine, vaulting, high-flying; zealous, ardent, fervent, fervid, avid, earnest, eager, spirited.

asquint, *adv.* **1.** awry, askance, askew; sidelong, sideways, obliquely, deviously.

2. slyly, furtively, surreptitiously, secretively, shiftily, sneakingly, on the sly.

ass, *n.* **1.** donkey, burro, dickey, *Chiefly Scot.* cuddy, *Brit. Sl.* moke; jackass, jack, jenny, jennet; mule, hinny; beast of burden, pack *or* draft animal, *Archaic.* sumpter; wild ass, kiang, onager.

2. fool, tomfool, dope, nincompoop, ninny, lightweight; dunce, blockhead, lunkhead, bonehead, knucklehead, meathead, fathead, pinhead, numskull, addlepate; oaf, boor, lout, dolt, dullard, lummox, lubber, looby; idiot, simpleton, half-wit, lamebrain, pinbrain, moron, cretin, imbecile; *All Sl.* chump, sap, dumbbell, dingbat, ding-a-ling, jerk, booby, boob, noodle, nudnik, schmuck, schlemiel, *U.S.* schmo.

assail, *v.* **1.** attack, assault, raid, storm, charge; rush, blitz, blitzkrieg, set upon, descend upon, spring upon, pounce upon, begin hostilities, *Sl.* zap, *Sl.* jump, *Archaic.* insult; pelt, bombard, pepper, strafe, open fire upon; beset, besiege, importune, harass, harry; plague, molest, worry, trouble, *Scot.* fash.

2. revile, vituperate, abuse, belabor, lash, rail against, inveigh against, light into, *Inf.* sail into, *Inf.* tear into, *Inf.* rip into, *Inf.* lace into, *Inf.* jump down [s.o.'s] throat, *Archaic.* clapperclaw; scold, tongue-lash, rate, slate, harangue, rant, curse, execrate, imprecate, anathematize; upbraid, objurgate, excoriate, lambaste, flay, fulminate against; castigate, chastise, berate, censure, criticize, reproach, rebuke, reprove, *Inf.* jump on, *Inf.* dress down, *Inf.* slam, *Sl.* jump all over, *Sl.* strafe.

3. vilify, traduce, asperse, calumniate, impugn, slur, malign, defame, denigrate, slander, libel, backbite, bespatter; denounce, decry, disparage, discredit, depreciate, deprecate, belittle, minimize, run *or* put down, *Inf.* knock, *Sl.* badmouth; gibbet, scorn, deride, ridicule, scoff *or* jeer at, sneer at, mock, lampoon, pasquinade, make fun of.

4. affect, have an affect on, influence, make an impact *or* impression on, impinge upon, leave a mark on.

assailable, *adj.* attackable, assaultable, impugnable; vulnerable, weak, unsound, open to attack, lame; unsupportable, defenseless, unprotected.

assailant, *n.* assaulter, attacker, accoster, assailer, aggressor; antagonist, foe, enemy, opponent, adversary, challenger; accuser, reviler, maligner, slanderer, vilifier, abuser.

assassin, *n.* **1.** murderer, killer, slayer, manslayer, man-killer, cutthroat, thug, poisoner, strangler; liquidator, bravo, sniper, gunman, knifer, throttler, *Rare.* sicarian, *Euph.* silencer, *Euph.* dispatcher; *All Sl.* gun, hired gun, hit man, triggerman, torpedo, hatchet man.

2. executioner, executionist, *Sl.* Jack Ketch, garrotter, burker, burkist; butcher, slaughterer, Bluebeard, ripper, bloodspiller, bloodshedder, bloodletter.

3. homicide, patricide, matricide. See **murderer** (*def.* **2**).

assassinate, *v.* **1.** kill, slay, morganize, poison, do to death, liquidate, blot *or* wipe out, put an end to, get rid of, do away with, put away, put out of the way, silence, dispatch, finish, finish off, do for, fix, settle, lay [s.o.] out, lay [s.o.] low, *Inf.* put the kibosh on, *Inf.* nip in the bud; *All Sl.* off, hit, zap, waste, croak, eighty six, take off, rub out, bump off, knock off, polish off, give [s.o.] the works *or* the business; *All Euph.* send west, take for a ride, put [s.o.] out of his misery.

2. shoot, shoot down, riddle, *Inf.* blow [s.o.'s] brains out, *Sl.* pump [s.o.] full of lead; club, beat, batter, pound, hammer, brain, blackjack, *Sl.* knock *or* beat [s.o.'s] brains out; choke, strangle, throttle, stifle, garrote, *Sl.* scrag; knife, stab, cut [s.o.'s] throat, jugulate, cut, cut down, bayonet, pierce, run through, put to the sword, impale, spear, lance, *Euph.* let the daylight in; smother, suffocate, asphyxiate, burke; execute, put to death.

3. slaughter, butcher, cut to pieces, hew, hack, hack to pieces, chop, chop to pieces, dismember, draw and quarter, tear limb from limb, disembowel, mutilate, savage, maul, wade in blood, shed *or* spill blood.

4. (*all of character or reputation*) injure, abuse, assail, stab, blight, destroy, butcher, slaughter; defame, denigrate, vilify, vilipend, scandalize, run down, speak ill of, speak evil of, revile, malign, gibbet. See **defame** (*def.* **2**).

assassination, *n.* **1.** murder, homicide, manslaughter, killing, slaying, thuggee, murder most foul, bloody *or* foul murder, foul play, fatality, death, violent death, *Sl.* hit, dispatch, silencing, elimination, liquidation, blotting *or* wiping out; shooting, strangulation, strangling, choking, throttling, garrote, garroting, asphyxiation, suffocating, suffocation, smothering, burking, stabbing, knifing, impalement, poisoning.

2. (*all of character or reputation*) injury, abuse, destruction, butchery, slaughter; defamation, denigration, vilification, vituperation, scandal. See **defamation** (*def.* **2**).

assault, *n.* **1.** attack, offensive, onslaught, onset, rush, blitz, blitzkrieg, storming, *Fr. coup de main, Obs.* brunt; raid, foray, sortie, sally; invasion, aggression, incursion, escalade; siege, besiegement, besetment, investment; bombardment, strafing, air raid, peppering, salvo, fusillade, *Both Mil.* barrage, enfilade, *Navy.* broadside.

2. mugging, holdup; battering, beating, pounding, pummeling, pommeling, going over, *Sl.* pasting; hitting, striking, bastinado, *Scot.* dunt, *Scot. and North Eng.* paik.

3. molestation, violation, outrage; ravishment, rape, deflowering, *Obs.* devirgination, *Obs.* constupration, *Obs.* stupration.

—*v.* **4.** attack, raid, storm, charge, rush, blitz, blitzkrieg; set upon, pounce upon, descend upon, fall on, open fire upon, begin hostilities, light into, *Inf.* lace into, *Inf.* rip into, *Inf.* tear into, *Sl.* zap, *Sl.* let [s.o.] have it, *Sl.* lay into, *Archaic.* insult; pelt, bombard, barrage, pepper, strafe, fusillade, broadside, *Mil.* enfilade, *Inf.* gang up on.

5. mug, put the arm on [s.o.], *Sl.* jump; strike, hit, smite, knock, take a poke at, punch, pommel, pummel, batter, beat up, *Inf.* throw a punch, *Inf.* clout, *Inf.* slug, *Inf.* whack, *Inf.* wallop, *Inf.* crown, *Sl.* conk, *Sl.* belt, *Sl.* bash, *Sl.* plug, *Sl.* sock, *Sl.* bop, *U.S. Sl.* biff, *Scot.* dunt, *Scot. and North Eng.* paik.

6. assail, beset, besiege, siege, beleaguer; plague, molest, harass, harry, harrow, worry, trouble, *Scot.* fash, *Scot.* sturt.

assay, *v.* **1.** test, try out, experiment with; put to the test, prove, put to trial.

2. examine, analyze, inspect, scrutinize, look over carefully; investigate, check out, inquire into, search, probe, explore; study, consider carefully, give thought to, weigh; evaluate, assess, appraise, judge, pass judgement on.

3. attempt, try, undertake, endeavor, essay, make an effort, strive, exert oneself.

assemblage, *n.* **1.** collection, accumulation, amassment; number, aggregation, aggregate; concentration, mass; cluster, clump, batch; store, stock, pile, heap; medley, jumble; agglomeration, conglomeration, congeries, lump.

2. assembly, meeting, gathering; group, body, circle, knot, crowd, throng, bunch, gang, crew, company, band, troop, troupe; flock, pack, herd, drove, bevy, swarm, shoal; galaxy, multitude, host; congestion, press, crush; concourse, cumulation, confluence, convergence.

3. congregation, conclave, convocation; mustering, mobilization; association, union, combination; conference, convention; forgathering, conjunction, coalescence.

assemble, *v.* **1.** gather, convoke, summon, call together, bring together; rally, muster, call up, levy; round up, round in.

2. accumulate, amass; group together, draw together, lump together; compile, collate, collocate, colligate, unite, join together; anthologize, collect, garner, glean; organize, order, marshal; codify, methodize, systematize.

3. compose, put together, throw together, slap together; construct, set up, manufacture, make.

4. convene, forgather, come together; meet, *Inf.* gang up, huddle, go into a huddle, get together, rendezvous.

5. group, cluster, concentrate, bunch up *or* together; mass, crowd, congregate, agglomerate; flock together, throng, herd, swarm, surge.

assembly, *n.* **1.** gathering, assemblage, meeting; group, body, circle, knot; crowd, throng, bunch, mob, rout; gang, crew, company, band, troop, troupe; galaxy, multitude, host; congestion, press, crush; concourse, cumulation, confluence, convergence.

2. audience, congregation, community, flock; conclave, convocation, council, synod, consistory, conventicle; muster, mobilization; association, union, combination; conference, convention, congress; caucus, bloc, *Rom. Antiq.* comitia, junta; forgathering, conjunction, coalescence.

3. ball, dance; banquet, reception; soiree, salon.

assent, *v.* **1.** (*often fol. by* to) agree, concur, accord, harmonize, think alike, be of one mind; admit, grant, allow, approve, accept, go along with, *Inf.* take to, *Inf.* cotton to, *Inf.* buy; acknowledge, recognize, *Archaic.* agnize, subscribe to.

2. yield, acquiesce, concede, give in, submit; obey, comply with, abide by, consent to, defer to, conform to; side with, fall in with, *Sl.* string along with, go with the stream, join in the chorus, go with the current.

3. (*often fol. by to*) testify, endorse, uphold, sustain, corroborate, substantiate, verify, confirm, ratify, homologate; countersign, seal; check, visa, visé, clinch.

—*n.* **4.** agreement, concurrence, acceptance, accord, accordance; consent, approval, approbation, accedence; authorization, permission, go-ahead, *Inf.* green light; unanimity, unison, consensus; acknowledgment, recognition, confession, admission, avowal, affirmation.

5. compliance, abidance, conformity, obedience, morigeration, allegiance, observance; acquiescence, yielding, concession, submission, capitulation.

6. confirmation, corroboration, endorsement, verification, ratification; sanction, visa, visé, check.

assert, *v.* **1.** asseverate, aver, insist upon, proclaim, declare, predicate, allege; advance, propound, propose, offer, proffer, present, put forward, set forth, broach; emphasize, stress, pronounce, announce, enunciate, state, tell, say, utter.

2. assure, guarantee, promise, pledge, swear to; advocate, maintain, sustain, hold, press for, push for; defend, plead for, uphold, support, back up; attest to, testify to, avouch, vouch for.

3. affirm, postulate, protest, claim; profess, admit, avow, own, acknowledge.

assertion, *n.* **1.** declaration, proclamation, predication; averment, avowal, asseveration; assurance, promise, pledge, word, guarantee, say-so; affirmation, protestation, allegation, profession, acknowledgment.

2. statement, expression, utterance, representation; pronouncement, announcement, dictum, manifesto.

assertive, *adj.* **1.** emphatic, insistent, positive, decided, confident, certain, assured, sure; outspoken, mouthy, loudmouthed; dogmatic, dogmatical, peremptory, doctrinaire, opinionated.

2. aggressive, assertive, self-assertive, forward, bumptious, brash; driving, overbearing, domineering, pushing, *Inf.* pushy.

assess, *v.* **1.** appraise, value, rate, fix *or* determine value; tax, charge, levy, lay upon, impose, demand, exact, require, ask.

2. evaluate, judge, weigh, weigh the merits of; review, consider, investigate, look into; measure, gauge, take the measure of, look over, scan, *Inf.* give [s.o.] the once-over, *Inf.* size up, *Sl.* eyeball.

assessment, *n.* **1.** evaluation, review, consideration, examination, investigation, measurement, gauging, *Inf.* once-over, *Inf.* sizing up.

2. tax, taxation, levy, fee, charge, surcharge, rate; toll, duty, impost, exactation.

3. appraisal, appraisement, value, face value, assigned value, established value, market value; valuation, appreciation, price, worth.

asset, *n.* **1.** good quality, qualification, strength, virtue, power, talent, endowment, boon, blessing; resource, help, aid, benefit; boost, edge, advantage, plus, strong point, talking point, selling point.

2. possession, holding, item of property.

3. **assets** resources, property, goods, possessions, holdings, wealth, money, wherewithal; effects, estate, personal assets, chattel, belongings; real property, liquid assets, frozen assets, capital, cash, notes, accounts receivable, securities, bonds, equitable assets; inventories, *Commerce.* good will, fixtures, machinery, real estate.

asseverate, *v.* declare earnestly *or* solemnly, assert, affirm, state emphatically, say, aver, avow; avouch, assure, guarantee, certify, uphold, maintain; profess, propound, protest, pronounce, proclaim, predicate; depose, testify, attest, allege.

asseveration, *n.* emphatic assertion, affirmation, averment, avowal; avouchment, assurance, guarantee, certification; protestation, proclamation, predication; deposition, testimony, attestation, vow, oath, pledge.

assiduity, *n.* **1.** assiduousness, application, diligence, industry, exertion, labor; constancy, devotion, devotedness; care, pains, carefulness, attention, sedulity, sedulousness; tirelessness, indefatigability, perseverance, endurance, persistence, patience, intentness, zeal.

2. **assiduities** devoted attentions, vigilance, watchfulness.

assiduous, *adj.* **1.** constant, unremitting, continuous, *Inf.* without letup; tireless, untiring, indefatigable; persistent, determined, patient, plodding; busy, active, brisk, occupied, on the go, bustling, busy as a bee.

2. diligent, persevering, industrious, hard-working, working like a beaver; attentive, studious, careful, painstaking, sedulous; devoted, zealous, earnest; intent, engrossed.

assign, *v.* **1.** allocate, allot, distribute, pass out, dispense, give, grant, award; apportion, portion out, share, measure out, mete out, dole out, deal out, parcel out; appropriate, set apart, consign, relegate, authorize, legislate.

2. appoint, commission, charge, entrust, commit, depute, delegate; authorize, empower, enable; invest, induct, install, ordain; designate, name, nominate; specify, fix, set, determine, prescribe.

3. ascribe, attribute, accredit with, account to, chalk up to; adduce, bring forward, allege, point out; advance, offer, show, state.

assignation, *n.* **1.** appointment, meeting, date, rendezvous, tryst.

2. assignment, task, job, duty. See **assignment** (*def.* **1**).

assignment, *n.* **1.** task, job, duty, obligation, charge, responsibility, lesson, errand; stint, time, part, share.

2. post, position, appointment, commission.

3. allocation, allotment, distribution, dispensation, apportionment, meting out, doling out; allowance, share, part.

4. designation, naming, nomination; specification, fixing, setting, determination, prescription.

5. ascription, attribution, accreditation, accreditment; adduction, allegation, assertion; advance, offer, presentation.

assimilate, *v.* **1.** incorporate, take in, absorb, appropriate, make one's own; (*usu. of food*) digest, transform, convert, resolve into.

2. *Usu.* **assimilate to** *or* **with** adapt, adjust, accustom, acclimate, acclimatize, acculturize, *Sociol.* acculturate, naturalize; amalgamate, mingle, commingle, intermix, mix, combine with; homogenize, make similar *or* homogeneous; blend in, merge with, melt into; become one with, become similar, conform, fit, accommodate.

assimilation, *n.* **1.** (*often of food*) digestion, conversion, transformation, absorption, incorporation, *Both Biol., Physiol.* anabolism, constructive metabolism.

2. adjustment, accommodation, adaptation; naturalization, acclimation, acclimatization, *Sociol.* acculturation; homogenization, leveling, blending, merging, mingling, commingling, combining, mixing.

assist, *v.* **1.** help, aid, bestead, accommodate, oblige, abet, befriend; contribute, join in, *Inf.* pitch in, *Inf.* chip in, lend a hand, lend onself to, play *or* do one's part, boost, give a boost to, give a lift to; (*all usu. negative*) lift a finger, lift a hand, raise a finger, raise a hand.

2. *Usu.* **assist with** collaborate, cooperate, connive, conspire, coact; combine, join, unite, side, synergize, go *or* go along, team up, take part, join forces, *Inf.* hitch horses.

3. support, back, back up, second, uphold, sustain, maintain, endorse, smile upon, concur, stand by, *Inf.* go to bat for, *Inf.* stick up for; promote, further, advance, forward, advocate, cultivate, favor.

4. relieve, ameliorate, alleviate, mitigate, palliate, salve; comfort, soothe, solace, console, succor.

5. facilitate, ease, make easier, expedite, cut through red tape; speed, speed up, accelerate, hasten, quicken, lend wings to; intercede, pave the way, open the way, clear the way, run interference for, *Fig.* block for; disburden, disencumber, rid, disembarrass, deobstruct, lighten the load; bolster, prop up, enhance, tide over, put on one's feet, set up, set going.

6. attend, attend on *or* upon, be attendant on, dance attendance upon, tend; work for, labor in behalf of, serve, be of service to, render service to, do service for, *Obs.* adjuvate, minister to; cater to, pander to, wait on *or* upon, wait on hand and foot, be at [s.o.'s] beck and call.

7. (*all of gatherings or ceremonies*) attend, be present at, be at, go *or* come to, be on hand, *Inf.* be on deck, sit in *or* at, find oneself at, show one's face, make *or* put in an appearance, *Inf.* show up; visit, take in, haunt, frequent, *Inf.* do, *Inf.* catch, *Inf.* check out.

—n. **8.** lift, hand, helping hand, *Inf.* boost *or* boost up; contribution.

assistance, *n.* **1.** help, aid, use, utility, avail, service, subvention, benefit, facilitation, helping hand, lift, boost; relief, succor, sympathy, consolation, comfort; friendship, championship, protection; support, patronage, backing, promotion, advocacy, countenance, care, upholding, sustenance, maintenance, favor, blessing, grace, sponsorship, auspices *or* auspice, good offices, kind regard; fosterage, furtherance, advancement, advance.

2. gift, donation, subsidy, bounty, charity, alms; kindness, beneficence, benevolence, benefaction, humanitarianism, altruism, philanthropy, almsgiving.

assistant, *n.* **1.** helper, aid *or* aide, attendant, acolyte, deputy, auxiliary, second, man Friday, gal Friday, henchman, right hand, right-hand man, *Sl.* gopher; partner, ally, comrade, colleague, associate, consociate, yokefellow *or* yokemate, companion, helpmate, helpmeet, *Obs.* helpfellow, co-worker, co-aid, consort, confrère, sidekick, friend, *Chiefly Brit.* mate; cooperator, collaborator, contributor, participator, participant; confederate, conniver, conspirer, conspirator, abettor, accomplice, accessory, *Chiefly Law.* accessary, partner in crime, *Sl.* moll *or* gun moll; supporter, advocate, patron, patronizer, backer, endorser, upholder, sanctioner, approver; follower, disciple, adherent, partisan; satellite, sycophant, parasite, hanger-on, toady, yes-man.

2. subordinate, subsidiary, subaltern, clerk, underworker; servant, domestic, domestic servant, factotum, maid, maidservant, handmaiden *or* handmaid, *Archaic.* ancilla, butler, valet, (*in the British army*) batman; underling, inferior, menial, *Sl.* stooge; *All Chiefly Mil.* adjutant, coadjutant, coadjutor, coadjutress *or* coadjutrix, adjunct, adjuvant, adjutator, *Obs.* adjutor; *All Mil.* aide-de-camp *or Chiefly U.S.* aid-de-camp, ADC, attaché, adjutant general, staff *or* subordinate officer, camp assistant.

—adj. **3.** helpful, helping, aidful, aiding, assisting, obliging, accommodative, accommodating, cooperative, available, at-hand, handy; auxiliary, ancillary, adjuvant, subsidiary, accessory, attendant, subservient, adjunct, *Obs.* adjutory, *Obs., Rare.* adjutorious.

associate, *v.* **1.** relate, connect, link, think of together *or* at the same time; ally, bond *or* tie together, wed, marry, yoke; attach, couple, mate, partner, match, twin, pair up; unite, combine, conjoin, correlate; affiliate, coalesce, league, club, team, band together, herd together, syndicate, federate, confederate, incorporate.

2. *Usu.* **associate with** fraternize, socialize, mingle, mix; hobnob, take up with, go around with, rub elbows with, keep company with, *Inf.* pal around with, *Inf.* hang around with, *Inf.* go with, *Sl.* hang out with *Obs.* consort; accompany, companion, keep [s.o.] company, befriend, go along with, *Sl.* string along with, *Archaic.* company; escort, take out, go out with.

—n. **3.** colleague, affiliate, fellow, equal, *Scot. and North Eng.* marrow, *Archaic.* peer; fellow worker, coworker, yokefellow, yokemate; fellow member, compeer, consociate, condisciple; partner, counterpart, mate, teammate, helpmate, playmate, classmate, ship-

mate, messmate, housemate, roommate, *Inf.* roomie, *Inf.* other half, *Inf.* better half, *Obs.* consort; ally, confrère, brother, sister.

4. companion, comrade, crony, chum, *Fr. copain,* sidekick, shadow, alter ego, *Inf.* pal, *U.S. Inf.* buddy, *Sl.* cully, *Sl.* Siamese twin; bosom buddy, intimate, confidant, friend, amigo, *Fr. ami,* acquaintance.

5. confederate, accomplice, collaborator, cooperator, abettor; aide, assistant, coadjutant, coadjutor, coadjutress, ancilla, auxiliary, helper.

6. accompaniment, accessory, complement, completor; concurrent, attendant, concomitant, *Astron.* comes; supplement, appendage, adjunct, appanage, attachment, appurtenance, appurtenant, appendix.

—adj. **7.** fellow, companionate, related, connected, joint; allied, affiliated, coalescent.

8. concomitant, concurrent, attendant, accompanying, accessory, complementary; supplementary, supplemental, extra, additional, added, appended, appendant, adjunctive, attached, annexed.

9. subsidiary, subordinate, secondary, background; inferior, second-class, lower-level, unimportant, unprivileged.

association, **1.** alliance, league, coalition, union, guild, consortium, syndication, conspiracy, cabal; company, partnership, joint concern, corporation, amalgamation, combine, merger, monopoly, trust, alignment, bloc, cartel; society, organization, party, camorra; congregational, assemblage, group, band, team, troop; community, circle, club, fraternity, lodge, clan, set, clique.

2. friendship, friendliness, camaraderie, comradeship, sodality, intimacy, *Inf.* chumminess; companionship, fellowship, colleagueship, brotherhood, fraternization, consociation, esprit de corps.

3. affiliation, connection, connectedness, *Genetics.* linkage; relationship, relatedness, relation, kinship, affinity, similarity, likeness, resemblance, comparability, analogousness, analogy; membership, participation, cooperation, communication, intercourse, interchange, dealings, acquaintance with, knowledge of.

4. combination, compound, mixture, mingling, composite, whole; correlation, interdependency, interdependence, reciprocity, reciprocal relationship.

assort, *v.* classify, sort, type, group; rank, grade, graduate, rate, class, range; categorize, codify, bracket, index, tabulate, catalogue; file, list, alphabetize, number; segregate, sift, separate; distribute, parcel, allocate, assign, allot; array, marshal, dispose, place, position, arrange.

assorted, *adj.* **1.** varied, mixed, diverse, various, of different kinds; miscellaneous, heterogeneous, motley, mixed-bag, diversified, variegated; multifarious, manifold, omnifarious.

2. matched, suited, coordinated, compatible, harmonized; classified, grouped, arranged, selected, sorted.

assortment, *n.* **1.** collection, mixture, mélange, miscellany, medley, mixed bag, potpourri, olio, olla-podrida; salmagundi, stew, ragout, goulash, hash; conglomeration, hodgepodge, jumble, farrago, gallimaufry, Chinese menu.

2. group, batch, set, lot; category, class, type, sort, denomination; level, grade, rank.

3. classification, arrangement, grouping, sorting; distribution, parceling, allotment, allocation, assigning.

assuage, *v.* **1.** mitigate, relieve, ease, alleviate, palliate; moderate, temper, weaken, qualify; abate, lessen, diminish, lower, reduce.

2. appease, satisfy, slake, quench; indulge, gratify, sate, satiate; deaden, dull, blunt, obtund, take the edge off of; allay, lay, tranquilize, lull, put to rest; quell, still, quiet, silence, hush; smother, check, curb.

3. mollify, soften, *Rare.* lenify, soothe, *Brit., Australian.* dill, *Archaic.* attemper; pacify, calm, calm down, subdue, compose, comfort, solace, console; succor, remedy, heal; pour oil on troubled waters.

assuagement, *n.* **1.** relief, easing, easement, letup, respite, remission; abatement, mitigation, alleviation, palliation; softening, mollification, soothing, comfort; sedative, tranquilizer, alleviative, palliative, lenitive, balm, *Med.* calmative, anodyne, *Med.* analgesic.

2. satisfaction, appeasement, gratification, fulfillment, satiation; refreshment, refection, repast, collation.

assume, *v.* **1.** suppose, presuppose, premise, presume, take for granted; postulate, posit, predicate, theorize, hypothesize, hypothecate, speculate; suspect, imagine, surmise, guess; believe, fancy, think; infer, *Inf.* take it, understand, gather, conjecture, divine, intuit.

2. undertake, enter upon, begin, set about; take upon oneself, put on oneself, accept; try one's hand at, endeavor, venture, attempt; shoulder, take care of, attend to, take responsibility for, burden oneself with.

3. adopt, take on, take the part of, appear as, seem to be, pose as; impersonate, imitate, mimic, copy, ape, *Inf.* make like; affect, feign, simulate, counterfeit, sham; put on, don, endue, pretend to.

4. appropriate, arrogate, accroach, usurp; take over, adopt, seize, commandeer, expropriate, make free with.

assumed, *adj.* **1.** pretended, feigned, adopted; fictitious, make-believe, false, sham; counterfeit, spurious, bogus, so-called, pseudo.

2. taken for granted, supposed, presupposed, presumed; suppositional, hypothetical; given, granted, conceded, allowed.

3. usurped, accroached, appropriated, arrogated; seized, commandeered, expropriated, misappropriated, taken over, stolen.

assuming, *adj.* **1.** presumptuous, bold, audacious, brazen, impertinent; bumptious, forward, *Inf.* nervy, *Inf.* pushy, rude; impudent, insolent, *Inf.* cheeky, defiant; swaggering, boasting, blustering; overconfident, self-assertive, self-assured.

2. arrogant, imperious, overbearing, domineering, arbitrary, high-handed; dictatorial, despotic, authoritative, dogmatic, magisterial; self-important, conceited, vainglorious, vain, egotistic, pompous; condescending, disdainful, supercilious, cavalier; contemptuous, scornful, insulting, contumelious.

assumption, *n.* **1.** supposition, presupposition, premise, presumption; guess, guesswork, conjecture; surmise, inference, deduction, understanding; thesis, hypothesis, theory, postulate, postulation, axiom.

2. taking on *or* over, assuming, undertaking, adopting, adoption; entering into, beginning.

3. arrogation, appropriation, accroachment, usurpation; expropriation, commandeering, seizure, theft.

4. imperiousness, lordliness, pretension, presumption; presumptuousness; overconfidence, overbearingness, insolence, impudence, brazenness, boldness, audacity, effrontery; bumptiousness, impertinence, *Inf.* pushiness, *Inf.* nerve, *Inf.* gall, *Inf.* cheek; self-assertion, self-assuredness, self-assurance.

5. arrogance, self-importance, pompousness, pomposity; braggadocio, bluster, swagger; pride, vanity, vainglory, conceit, egotism; snobbery, snobbishness, airs, superciliousness, loftiness, hauteur; contemptuousness, contempt, disdainfulness, disdain, scornfulness, scorn, contumeliousness, contumely.

assurance, *n.* **1.** assertion, affirmation, averment, asseveration, profession, protestation, avouchment, declaration, statement.

2. pledge, promise, vow, oath, word of honor; guaranty, guarantee, warrant, warranty, contract, bond, security, surety; attestation, *Obs.* vouch, certification, confirmation, corroboration; testimony, *Law.* deposition, evidence, proof.

3. confidence, reassurance, reassurement, freedom from doubt, certainty, certitude; belief, conviction, persuasion, credence, faith, trust, reliance, dependence; security, secureness, assuredness, sureness.

4. self-confidence, self-possession, self-assurance, aplomb, poise; coolness, calmness, collectedness, composure, equanimity, self-control, restraint; courage, strength, fortitude, hardihood, spirit, pluck, *Sl.* guts; bravery, valor, intrepidity, intrepidness, daring, audacity, boldness, heroism, gallantry.

5. impudence, effrontery, gall, *Inf.* cheek, insolence, brashness, rudeness, *Sl.* lip, back talk, *Inf.* sass, *Sl.* mouth; impertinence, sauciness, *Inf.* sauce, pertness, *Inf.* nerve, audacity; boldness, *Inf.* face, presumption, presumptuousness, forwardness, *Inf.* freshness; self-assertiveness, chutzpah, bumptiousness, brazenness, brassiness, assertiveness, aggressiveness, *Inf.* pushiness; overbearingness, domineeringness, *Inf.* bossiness; arrogance, overconfidence, cocksureness; front, haughtiness, self-importance.

assure, *v.* **1.** assert, affirm, aver, asseverate, avouch, declare; state, inform, tell.

2. pledge, promise, vow, give one's word; guarantee, attest to, vouch for, certify, warrant; ensure, insure, make sure *or* certain, confirm, corroborate, make firm, stabilize, settle; secure, clinch, clench, *Sl.* cinch, seal, complete, consummate.

3. reassure, free from doubt, give confidence to, encourage; hearten, embolden, inspirit, strengthen, enliven, give [s.o.] a boost, *Sl.* give [s.o.] a shot in the arm, lift *or* raise [s.o.'s] spirits, gladden; cheer up, comfort, soothe, pacify, calm, solace, console, make [s.o.] feel better; relieve, mitigate, alleviate, palliate, assuage, ease, lessen, lighten.

assured, *adj.* **1.** guaranteed, sure, certain, secure, reliable, dependable, trustworthy, unfailing; definite, positive, absolute, infallible, unerring, inerrable; indubitable, undoubtable, unquestionable, indisputable.

2. confident, self-confident, self-possessed, sure of oneself, steady, unwavering, unhesitating, unflinching, unblinking; in control, self-controlled.

3. impudent, insolent, *Inf.* cheeky, brash, rude; impertinent, saucy, pert; bold, audacious, *Inf.* nervy, presumptuous, forward, *Inf.* fresh; self-assertive, bumptious, brazen, brassy, assertive, aggressive, *Inf.* pushy; overbearing, domineering, *Inf.* bossy, authoritarian; arrogant, overconfident, cocksure, haughty, self-important.

assuredly, *adv.* **1.** certainly, surely, definitely, no doubt, absolutely, positively; indubitably, without a doubt, doubtless, unquestionably, indisputably; truly, in truth, *Archaic.* in troth, actually, really; indeed, of course, to be sure, certes; infallibly, unerringly, inerrably; unfailingly, reliably, dependably; exactly, precisely, just so.

2. confidently, self-confidently, with surety, steadily, firmly; unwaveringly, unhesitatingly, unflinchingly, controllably, authoritatively.

astir, *adj.* **1.** moving, in motion, about; in circulation, abroach; active, stirring, bustling, lively.

2. roused, out of bed, unconfined, *Med.* ambulatory, *Med.* ambulant, walking, afoot, up and around, up and about.

astonish, *v.* amaze, astound, surprise, dumbfound, *Inf.* flabbergast. See **astound**.

astonished, *adj.* astounded, amazed, dumbfounded, *Inf.* flabbergasted; taken aback, floored, shocked, aghast, jolted, *Inf.* bowled over, *Inf.* caught up short; struck dumb, at a loss for words, stupefied, petrified, numbed; startled, surprised, disconcerted; round-eyed, wide-eyed, agape, open-mouthed, lost in wonder *or* amazement.

astonishment, *n.* **1.** amazement, wonderment, awe, great surprise; bewilderment, confusion, dismay, consternation, perplexity, stupefaction.

2. wonder, marvel, prodigy, miracle.

astound, *v.* astonish, surprise, amaze, *Inf.* flabbergast, dumbfound, dumbfounder, strike dumb, render speechless; stun, stagger, boggle, take aback, floor, shock, jar, jolt, *Inf.* bowl over, *Inf.* hit [s.o.] like a ton of bricks, *Inf.* give [s.o.] a turn, *Inf.* catch [s.o.] up short; stupefy, petrify, paralyze, benumb, incapacitate; strike with wonder, startle, surprise, disconcert; confuse, baffle, confound, nonplus, perplex, embarrass, pose; bewilder, dazzle, electrify, *Inf.* take one's breath away, *Sl.* blow one's mind; unbalance, disorient, *Inf.* catch off guard, *Sl.* curl one's hair.

astounding, *adj.* amazing, astonishing, wonderful; stunning, shocking, jarring, jolting, staggering; startling, surprising, disconcerting, benumbing, stupefying, dazing, numbing, paralyzing, petrifying, incapacitating; confusing, disorienting, baffling, confounding, perplexing, bewildering.

astraddle, *adv.* astride, pickaback, piggyback, straddleback, straddle-legged, straddlingly; on, across.

astral, *adj.* star-shaped, starlike, sidereal, sphery; starry, stellar.

astray, *adv., adj.* **1.** off the track, off, afield, off course, lost, stray; adrift, straying, wandering, drifting.

2. wrong, amiss, in error, abroad, at fault; wide of the mark, *Sl.* out in left field, erroneous, faulty, mistaken, incorrect; untrue, false, inexact, inaccurate.

3. misled, misguided, misdirected; deceived, deluded, fooled, befooled; beguiled, dazzled, seduced, captivated, hypnotized; confused, confounded, perplexed, disconcerted; bewildered, befuddled, befogged, bemuddled.

astringent, *adj.* **1.** *Medical.* astrictive, contracting, contractive, constrictive, constricting, constringent, styptic, binding.

2. severe, stern, rough, harsh, acerb, acerbic, austere, *Obs.* asper, acid, stringent; acrid, acrimonious, caustic, mordant, bitter, pungent; trenchant, cutting, sharp, acute, biting, keen, piercing, penetrating, pricking; sarcastic, satirical, ironic, ironical; vitriolic, scathing, double-edged; virulent, spiteful, malicious, vicious; peevish, petulant, cross, sour, crabbed, testy, touchy, ill-tempered, ill-humored; scornful, sardonic, derisive, snide, abusive.

astrologer, *n.* horoscoper, astromancer, Chaldean, star diviner, seer, soothsayer, astroalchemist, *Obs.* astrolog, *Obs.* astrologician, *Obs.* astrologaster, *Obs., Rare.* astrologomage.

astronomer, *n.* stargazer, astrographer, astrophysicist, astrochemist, astrophotographer; cosmographer, cosmologist, cosmogonist, uranographer, uranologist.

astute, *adj.* **1.** discerning, perceptive, penetrating, piercing; keen, sharp, acute, quick; eagle-eyed, hawk-eyed, lynx-eyed, sharp-eyed; perspicacious, percipient, discriminating, appercipient; sagacious, judicious, wise, sapient; discreet, politic, prudent, wary, chary, cautious; watchful, vigilant, Argus-eyed, mindful; clear-headed, thoughtful, sensible, intelligent, reasonable, sound; alert, quick-witted, nimble, bright, smart; long-sighted, far-sighted, far-seeing, long-headed.

2. clever, cunning, wily, tricky, crafty, arch; artful,

ingenious, astucious, Machiavellian, *Rare.* subdolous; shrewd, canny, *Inf.* cagey, shifty; sly, subtle, argute, foxy, vulpine; conniving, contriving, intriguing, designing.

astuteness, *n.* **1.** perception, discernment, penetration; perspicacity, percipience, appercipience, discrimination; acuteness, keenness, acumen, quickness, sharpness; sagacity, judiciousness, wisdom, sapience, mother wit, wits; intelligence, understanding, reason, sensibility, apperception, clear-headedness, soundness; discretion, prudence, wariness, chariness, caution; vigilance, watchfulness, mindfulness; common sense, good judgment, brains, sense, wit, mind; alertness, quick-wittedness, smartness, nimbleness.

2. cleverness, cunning, guile, wiliness, craftiness, trickery; artfulness, ingenuity, subtlety, astucity; shrewdness, canniness, slyness, foxiness, *Inf.* caginess, shiftiness.

asunder, *adv.* **1.** into pieces, to pieces, all to pieces, to bits, to shreds, *Inf.* to smithereens; in half, in two, in twain, into separate pieces *or* parts.

2. apart, far apart, wide apart, wide away, away, widely separated.

—adj. **3.** separated, disjoint, disconnected, disengaged, disunited, divided; severed, cleft, split, torn, torn apart, rent, cut, carved.

4. removed, remote, distant, far, far off, faraway.

asylum, *n.* **1.** hospital, sanatorium, sanitarium, *Fr.* hôtel-Dieu; home, old folks' home, old soldiers' home, sailors' rest, nursing home, convalescent home; mental institution, state hospital, psychiatric hospital, insane asylum, madhouse, bedlam, *Fr. maison de santé*, *Sl.* nuthouse, *Sl.* bughouse, *Sl.* loonybin, *Sl.* funny farm, *Sl.* laughing academy, *Sl.* booby hatch.

2. poor house, poor farm, almshouse, *Brit.* work house, charitable *or* eleemosynary institution; orphanage, foster home.

3. sanctuary, retreat, refuge, shelter, haven, hospice, harbor, harborage, port, port in a storm; sanctum, sanctum sanctorum, adytum.

4. covert, coverture, hideout, hideaway, hiding place; hole, lair, den, mew, abri, dugout, foxhole.

asymmetry, *n.* disproportion, misproportion, irregularity, unevenness; distortion, malformation, deformity; formlessness, amorphism, amorphousness.

at, *prep.* in, within; on, upon; near, in proximity to, in the vicinity of, about; toward, in the direction of; by, because of, in response to, with; at the point of, on the stroke of; by way of, by means of, through, from; up to, amounting to, to the extent of; engaged in, occupied with; in a state of, in a condition of.

atavism, *n.* *Biology.* (*in reference to an earlier type*) reversion, throwback, reappearance, recurrence; intermittent heredity, hereditary resurgence.

atelier, *n.* workshop, shop, workroom, studio, loft; garret, mansard.

atheism, *n.* **1.** denial, disbelief, unbelief, unbelievingness, incredulity, incredulousness; impiety, impiousness, ungodliness, irreligion, irreligiousness, irreverence, infidelity; apostasy, heresy.

2. skepticism, doubt, Pyrrhonism, nihilism; agnosticism, freethinking, rationalism, materialism, positivism; heathenness, heathenism, heathendom, paganism, idolatry.

atheist, *n.* **1.** nonbeliever, disbeliever, unbeliever, denier; irreligionist, infidel, heretic, iconoclast.

2. skeptic, doubter, Pyrrhonist, nihilist, nullifidian; agnostic, freethinker, rationalist, materialist, positivist; heathen, pagan, idolater, idolist.

atheistic, *adj.* **1.** disbelieving, unbelieving, nonbelieving, incredulous; infidel, infidelic, *Obs.* unfaithful, heretic, heretical, iconoclastic; impious, ungodly, irreligious, irreverent.

2. skeptical, doubting, Pyrrhonistic, nihilistic; agnostic, freethinking, rationalistic, materialistic, positivistic; heathen, pagan, unenlightened.

athirst, *adj.* **1.** desirous, longing, craving, covetous, *Philos.* orectic; eager, keen, avid, *Archaic.* fain, fervent, ardent, burning.

2. thirsty, parched, dry, *Dial.* droughty.

athlete, *n.* sportsman, sport, sporter, *Inf.* jock; player, games player, ballplayer; competitor, agonist; gymnast, acrobat.

athletic, *adj.* **1.** robust, vigorous, active, strong; hardy, hale, hale and hardy, lusty; firm, sound, sound as a dollar, stalwart, staunch, stout, solid, solid as rock.

2. able-bodied, well-knit, well-built, well-set; wiry, sinewy, thewy; muscular, muscled, well-muscled, *Usu. Derog.* muscle-bound; brawny, strapping, burly, thick-set, broad-shouldered, barrel-chested; ironmuscled, made of iron.

3. gymnastic, acrobatic, agonistic; sporting, sports.

athletics, *n.* **1.** sport, sports, games, sportsdom; *Brit.* track and field events; gymnastics, acrobatics, tumbling, somersaulting.

2. calisthenics, exercise, exercising, gymnastic exercises, isometric exercises, isometrics, *Brit.* physical jerks *or* jerks; drill, workout.

athwart, *adv.* **1.** across, crosswise, crossways, cross, crisscross, from side to side, transversely.

2. awry, askant, askew, obliquely, sidelong, sideways; perversely, wrongly, contrawise, crossgrained, across the grain, against the tide *or* wind; at cross purposes, in conflict, at odds, at variance, at issue; in confrontation, against, versus, *Sl.* eyeball to eyeball.

—prep. **3.** in opposition to, opposed to, adverse to, contrary to, counter to, dead against; in conflict with, at cross purposes with.

atmosphere, *n.* **1.** air, aerospace, aerosphere, space; sky, heaven, heavens, firmament, *Chiefly Literary.* welkin; biosphere, troposphere, stratosphere, ionosphere, exosphere, ozonosphere.

2. environment, medium, milieu, condition; background, setting, surroundings, sphere, element; tone, tenor, mood, aura, ambience; character, spirit, temper; feeling, *Sl.* vibrations, *Sl.* vibes.

atmospheric, *adj.* **1.** aerial, meteorological, climatic, pneumatic; aeriform, airy, gaseous, vaporous, ethereal, aerostatic.

2. muted, blurred, undefined, unpronounced, indistinct; hazy, cloudy, misty, foggy, smoky, shadowy.

atom, *n.* **1.** molecule, nucleus, proton, electron, neutron; monad, dyad, triad.

2. iota, jot, whit, mite, mote, *Archaic.* atomy; particle, corpuscle, bit, snippet; tittle, dot, point, *Inf.* smithereen; scintilla, spark, scrap, morsel, smidgen, shred, trace.

atomic, *adj.* **1.** molecular, nuclear.

2. microscopic, minute, infinitesimal, microbic, corpuscular; tiny, puny, wee, imperceptible, inappreciable.

atone, *v.* expiate, make amends, offset, countervail, redeem; pay, pay the penalty, make reparation, make up, recompense; conciliate, appease, propitiate; do penance, *Archaic.* shrive.

atonement, *n.* amends, expiation, redemption, compensation, indemnity, satisfaction; reparation, restitution, redress, remedy, repayment, requital; propitiation, appeasement, conciliation; penance, *Archaic.* shrift, purgation.

atrocious, *adj.* **1.** abominable, execrable, monstrous, horrible, horrid, horrendous; grievous, outrageous, shocking, enormous, flagrant; dark, black,

black-hearted, sinister, grim, dreadful, dire; hideous, grisly, gruesome, ghastly, unspeakable, unthinkable; vile, foul, base, mean, low, bad; wicked, sinful, evil, iniquitous, *Archaic.* facinorous, *Obs.* scelerous; nefarious, villainous, heinous, flagitious; infamous, notorious, odious; perfidious, treacherous, traitorous, insidious; damnable, damnatory, accursed, cursed; maleficent, malefic, malevolent, evil-minded; demonic, demoniac, devilish, fiendish, ghoulish, diabolical, satanic, hellish, infernal, unholy, ungodly, unblest.

2. brutal, inhuman, barbarous, barbaric, savage; brutish, murderous, slaughterous, bloodthirsty, sadistic; ferocious, ruthless, vicious, fell, truculent; wolfish, lupine, fierce, feral, ferine, bestial, *Obs.* belluine; pitiless, merciless, heartless, cruel, cold-blooded, hard-hearted, stony-hearted, marble-hearted.

3. tasteless, insipid, mawkish; vulgar, tawdry, cheap, gimcrack, brummagen, barbaric; meretricious, pretentious, ostentatious, gaudy; unpolished, inelegant.

atrocity, *n.* **1.** wickedness, evilness, fiendishness, heinousness, nefariousness, flagitiousness, blackness, atrociousness; cruelty, barbarity, savagery, brutality, bloodlust, murderousness, malignity; ferocity, fierceness, truculence, inhumanity, monstrousness, ruthlessness; horribleness, horridness, hideousness, dreadfulness, terribleness, outrageousness.

2. crime, offense, violation, injury, hurt, harm, evil, wrong; enormity, monstrosity, horror, outrage; abomination, disgrace, shame, scandal.

atrophy, *n.* **1.** degeneration, decline, wasting away, withering, weakening, enervation, emaciation; *Path.* marasmus, consumption, decay.

—*v.* **2.** waste away, wither, shrivel up, dry up; degenerate, decline, decay; exhaust, sap, weaken, enfeeble, enervate.

attach, *v.* **1.** fasten, affix, fix; join, connect, unite, wed, tie, bind, make fast to, hitch, pin, tack, rivet; stick, stick on, bond, cement, glue, solder, weld; append, add, annex, subjoin.

2. affiliate, associate, combine, join forces with; sign on, sign up, adhere to, belong to, conjoin.

3. assign, attribute, ascribe, accredit, adhibit; apply, pertain, tie in with, be incident, bear upon.

4. attract, charm, endear, enamor, fascinate, captivate; win, win over, conquer.

5. *Law.* entail, put a lien on, garnish, garnishee; seize, confiscate, appropriate, *Law.* distrain.

attachment, *n.* **1.** attaching, fastening, afixture, union, cohesion, joining, annexation; insertion, conjuncture, subjunction.

2. devotion, esteem, estimation, respect, admiration, loyalty, regard, affection, liking, fondness, endearment, tenderness, friendship, love, passion; predilection, leaning, affinity, inclination, penchant, partiality; adhesion, fidelity, devotedness.

3. junction, joint, connection, bond, binding, fastening, tie, link, nexus; binder, holder, clamp, connector, copula.

4. addition, accessory, adjunct, appurtenance, appendage, ornament, extra; extension, auxiliary, complement; rider, codicil, supplement.

5. *Law.* entailment, lien, garnish, garnishment; seizure, confiscation, appropriation, *Law.* distrainment, distrainor.

attack, *v.* **1.** assault, raid, storm, charge, rush, blitz, blitzkrieg; set upon, pounce upon, descend upon, fall on, open fire upon, begin hostilities; light into, *Inf.* lace into, *Inf.* rip into, *Inf.* tear into, *Sl.* zap, *Sl.* let [s.o.] have it, *Sl.* lay into, *Archaic.* insult; pelt, bombard, barrage, pepper, strafe, fusillade, broadside, *Mil.* enfilade, *Inf.* gang up on; beset, besiege, siege, beleaguer.

2. assail, vituperate, revile, rail against, inveigh against, lash, abuse, belabor, *Inf.* jump down [s.o.'s] throat, *Archaic.* clapperclaw; scold, tongue-lash, rate, slate, harangue, rant, curse, execrate, imprecate, anathematize; upbraid, objurgate, excoriate, lambaste, flay, fulminate against, *Inf.* slam; castigate, chastise, berate, censure, criticize, reproach, rebuke, reprove, *Inf.* jump on, *Inf.* dress down, *Sl.* jump all over, *Sl.* chew out, *Sl.* strafe.

3. vilify, traduce, asperse, calumniate, impugn, slur, malign, defame, denigrate, slander, libel, backbite, bespatter; denounce, decry, disparage, discredit, depreciate, deprecate, belittle, minimize, run *or* put down, *Inf.* knock, *Sl.* badmouth.

4. jump into with both feet, *Inf.* dig into; set about, go to work on, undertake, get started on, get going.

5. (*all of disease, destructive agencies, etc.*) seize, have in the clutches.

—*n.* **6.** assault, offensive, onslaught; rush, blitz, blitzkrieg, storming, *Fr. coup de main, Obs.* brunt; bombardment, strafing, air raid, peppering, salvo, fusillade, *Both Mil.* barrage, enfilade, *Navy.* broadside; encounter, conflict, battle, combat, *Mil.* skirmish; raid, foray, sortie, sally; invasion, aggression, incursion, escalade; siege, besiegement, besetment, investment.

7. onset, commencement, start, beginning.

8. (*of diseases*) seizure, fit, stroke, spell, *Pathol.* paroxysm.

attain, *v.* achieve, accomplish, compass, get, secure, obtain, procure; gain, win, *Inf.* walk off with, earn, wrest; reach, arrive at, come to, *Inf.* make it; finish, complete; realize, fulfill, actualize, make real, make actual; succeed in, make good, be successful, get ahead; set the world on fire, take the world by storm.

attainable, *adj.* achievable, reachable, within reach, accessible, at hand; realizable, obtainable, procurable, compassable; accomplishable, doable, completable; practicable, workable, manageable, surmountable; reasonable, feasible, possible, conceivable, imaginable, thinkable, admissible, within the realm *or* bounds of possibility; potential, likely, probable.

attainment, *n.* **1.** achievement, acquirement, fruition, fulfillment, consummation, realization, success; completion, finishing, termination.

2. accomplishment, feat, deed, act, exploit, *Archaic.* gest; performance, production, action, maneuver, move, stroke, blow, coup; stroke of genius, tour de force.

attempt, *v.* **1.** make an effort, try, work at, strive, aspire to, aim for, set one's sights on; undertake, take in hand, take upon oneself, try one's hand at; venture, essay, seek to, set out to, drive at, go about; do one's best, *Sl.* shoot one's bolt, strain every nerve, do all that lies in one; tackle, take on, take a whack *or* crack *or* stab at; *Sl.* give it a whirl, *Sl.* give it a shot.

2. attack, assault, assail, storm, take a shot at [s.o.].

—*n.* **3.** effort, endeavor, exertion, struggle, undertaking; try, *Inf.* the old college try, venture, aim, enterprise; trial, experiment, test, *Archaic.* emprise; *Inf.* stab, *Inf.* crack, *Inf.* whack.

4. attack, assault, onslaught, push, drive, pass, thrust.

attend, *v.* **1.** go to, be present at, sit in on, visit, frequent, haunt.

2. come with, occur with, coexist with; belong to, be an appendage of, be an adjunct to, be an annex to, be part of; result from, be consequent to, be a consequence of, follow from, flow from, issue from.

3. minister, nurse, take care of, care for, tend to; serve, wait on, squire, esquire, work for, be a slave to, dance attendance; assist, aid, help, succor.

4. accompany, companion, usher, go along with, keep [s.o.] company; escort, chaperone, matronize, convoy.

5. tend, shepherd, herd, watch over, look after, see after, keep an eye on; monitor, oversee, overlook; supervise, manage, superintend, direct, control, command, boss, take charge of, be in charge of; guard, protect, screen, shelter, flank, be by one's side.

6. heed, harken, listen, give ear; pay attention, look sharp, mind, take care, observe, notice, mark, note.

7. (*followed by* to) apply oneself, devote oneself, knuckle down *or* under, get to work, work on, think about, concentrate on.

attendance, *n.* **1.** ministration, care, tendance; service, assistance, aid, help; shepherding, herding, monitoring, overseeing; supervision, management, superintendence, direction.

2. assemblage, crowd, audience, number present, tickets sold, seats filled.

attendant, *n.* **1.** escort, accompanier, companion, comrade, crony, chum, *Fr. copain*, sidekick, shadow, *Inf.* pal, *U.S. Inf.* buddy, *Sl.* cully, *Sl.* Siamese twin; chaperon, matron, (*in Spain and Portugal*) duenna, governess, tutor, tutoress, nursemaid, nanny, sitter, baby-sitter, au pair girl; usher, guide, cicerone, pilot.

2. assistant, auxiliary, ancilla, helper, aide, aide-de-camp, *Mil.* orderly; squire, equerry, courtier, gillie, page, footboy, *Obs.* waiter; servant, servitor, pursuivant, follower, acolyte, vassal, liegeman, *Hist.* retainer; domestic, menial, hireling; manservant, man, valet, butler, major-domo, seneschal, factotum, steward, footman, lackey, *Archaic.* groom; maid, handmaid, woman, *Fr. femme de chambre;* cupbearer, Ganymede; *All Contemptuous.* flunky, satellite, slave, *Sl.* stooge.

3. consequence, result, effect, what follows; product, fruit, issue, upshot, outcome, conclusion, end, end product *or* result; corollary, byproduct, incidental; accompaniment, accessory, complement, completer, concomitant, concurrent, *Astron.* comes; supplement, appendage, appurtenance, appurtenant, adjunct, appanage, annex, attachment, addition, extension.

4. visitor, attender, frequenter.

—adj. **5.** present, in attendance.

6. accompanying, accessory, complementary; associated, associate, affiliated, allied, fellow; connected, related, relative, akin, affinitive, like, similar; consequent, consequential, resultant, resulting, following *or* progressing from, concomitant, concurrent.

attention, *n.* **1.** awareness, consciousness, mindfulness; heed, heedfulness, watchfulness, advertence; alertness, vigilance, circumspection, wariness.

2. observance, observation, notice, note, regard, *Dial.* nevermind, *Scot. and North Eng.* tent; consideration, reflection, contemplation; thoughtfulness, thought, deliberation; concentration, intentness, attentiveness; investigation, study, scrutiny; publicity, spotlight, public eye.

3. civility, politeness, courtesy; amenities, urbanities; deference, homage, service; respect, regard; care, ministration, tendance.

4. attentions courtship, address, wooing, courting.

attentive, *adj.* **1.** watchful, heedful, advertent, regardful, observant, noticing, *Archaic.* attent; aware, awake, wide-awake, conscious, mindful; alert, on the alert, on the lookout, on the qui vive, all ears, listening, sharp; wary, careful, circumspect, vigilant, on guard.

2. intent, concentrating, focused; occupied with, engrossed in, wrapped up in, absorbed in; rapt, enrapt, enraptured, taken up with; contemplative, reflective; painstaking, persevering, diligent, sedulous, assiduous, studious.

3. considerate, thoughtful, gracious, kind; polite, civil, courteous, courtly; respectful, deferential; accommodating, complaisant, obliging; gallant, debonair, chivalrous; devoted, persistent in attentions, wooing.

attenuate, *v.* **1.** thin, thin out, stretch out, spin out, extend, draw out, wiredraw; rarefy, etherealize, spiritualize, volatilize, vaporize, aerify; refine, subtilize, sublime.

2. weaken, reduce, lessen, decrease, diminish, lower; impair, invalidate, undermine, sap, undercut, enervate; dilute, adulterate, water down, *Inf.* cut.

—adj. **3.** attenuated, thin, thread-like, sheer, transparent; fine-spun, cobwebby, delicate, air-spun, airy, gossamer, gossamery; flimsy, insubstantial, ethereal; drawn-out, extended.

4. weak, enfeebled, frail, infirm.

5. slender, slim, emaciated, gaunt; slight, lean, lank, scraggy, scrawny.

attenuation, *n.* **1.** thinning out, rarefaction, etherealization, spiritualization, volatilization, vaporization; weakening, impairment, invalidation; diminution, lessening, dilution, adulteration.

2. thinness, tenuity, fineness, slenderness, leanness; flimsiness, delicateness, lightness, etherealness, airiness; refinement, subtlety, rareness.

attest, *v.* **1.** *Usu.* **attest to** testify, witness, bear witness, evidence, offer evidence, depone, swear to, state under oath, allege, plead; depose, certify, certificate, present an affidavit.

2. *Usu.* **attest to** guarantee, guaranty, insure, ensure, warrant, endorse, vouch for, stand behind *or* by, back up; promise, pledge, plight, give one's solemn word *or* promise; assure, offer assurance, asseverate, avouch, aver, affirm.

3. document, circumstantiate, manifest, show, exhibit, display, demonstrate; prove, confirm, bear out, verify, validate, establish, authenticate; corroborate, substantiate, sustain, uphold, vindicate.

attestation, *n.* **1.** testifying, witnessing, evidencing, declaration, testification, *Law.* exemplification; documentation, circumstantiation, demonstration, corroboration, substantiation; certification, confirmation, verification, validation, establishment, authentication; endorsement, vouching, recommendation; assurance, asseveration, averment, avouchment, affirmation.

2. testimony, evidence, information, witness, sworn statement, statement, document, *Law.* affidavit, *Law.* deposition; certificate, warrant, *Law.* acknowledgment; guarantee, guaranty, warranty, testimonial, *Obs.* vouch; promise, pledge, plight, oath, word.

attic[1], *n.* garret, monsard, dormer; loft, cockloft, crow's nest, *Archit.* clerestory.

attic[2], *adj.* **1.** classical, classic, ancient, antique, early; traditional, standard, typical.

2. elegant, cultured, polished, refined, dignified, tasteful, in good taste; pure, chaste, simple, delicate, subdued, nice; subtle, witty, clever, intelligent, incisive, penetrating.

attire, *v.* **1.** dress, clothe, garb, vest, apparel, habit, *Sl.* dude up, *Sl.* swank up; adorn, array, deck, deck out, bedeck, bedizen, dress up, trap, trap out, caparison; outfit, fit out, fit up, fit, rig, rig up, rig out, gear, turn out, accouter; *All Inf.* doll up, pretty up, gussy up, spruce up; *All Sl.* dude up, swank up, trick out *or* up, fig out.

—n. **2.** apparel, wearing apparel, wear, clothes, clothing; dress, garb, costume, guise, style; garments, vestments, raiment, habit, habiliments, *Inf.* gear, *Inf.*

toggery, *Inf.* togs, *Inf.* duds, *Sl.* threads, *Sl.* rags, (*of transvestites*) *Sl.* drag; investment, vesture, investiture; array, wardrobe, accouterment; livery, uniform, regalia.

3. finery, best clothes, best bib and tucker, *Inf.* Sunday clothes, *Inf.* Sunday best, *Inf.* Sunday-go-to-meetings, *Sl.* glad rags, *Sl.* heavy threads.

4. costume, outfit, ensemble, *Inf.* getup.

attitude, *n.* **1.** disposition, temperament, personality; feeling, view, opinion, thought, idea, frame of mind, mind-set, mental state, view, outlook; reaction, impression, interpretation, orientation; tendency, inclination, leaning, bent, turn, twist, bias, prejudice.

2. demeanor, bearing, appearance, guise, aspect; manner, mode, mood, air, mien, deportment, behavior; countenance, expression; position, posture, pose, stance, stand, carriage; figure, form, shape.

attitudinize, *v.* pose, strike a pose, assume an attitude, put on airs; camp, camp it up, behave affectedly, show off, put on an act; imitate, mimic, ape, pretend, feign, make believe.

attorney, *n.* **1.** lawyer, attorney-at-law, legal advisor, *Law.* counsel, counselor, counselor-at-law; advocate, *U.S. Inf.* barrister, solicitor, *Law.* proctor; pettifogger, Philadelphia lawyer, *Inf.* shyster.

2. agent, attorney-in-fact, factor, deputy, proxy, substitute.

attract, *v.* **1.** draw, pull, magnetize, drag.

2. allure, entice, invite, tempt, lure, inveigle; interest, catch [s.o.'s] eye, fascinate, charm, enamor, enchant, capture [s.o.'s] fancy, ensorcell; captivate, engage, win, seduce.

attraction, *n.* **1.** pull, traction, magnetism, draw, gravitation, gravity; affinity, inclination, tendency.

2. interest, appeal, attractiveness, fascination, charm; allure, enticement, temptation, inveiglement; enchantment, bewitchment, witchery, glamour, captivation, seduction.

3. lure, bait, *Sl.* come-on, teaser.

4. entertainment, feature, presentation, show, production, exhibition.

attractive, *adj.* **1.** pleasing, appealing, charming, engaging, winsome, winning, taking; interesting, fascinating, captivating, enchanting, bewitching; enticing, alluring, inviting, tempting, seductive, (*of a woman*) foxy.

2. delightful, pleasant, agreeable, sweet, *Inf.* cute, dainty; pretty, sightly, fetching, *Scot.* canny, fair; beautiful, lovely, stunning, *Inf.* eye-filling, striking, zingy; shapely, voluptuous, *Sl.* built, *Sl.* stacked, beddable, sexy; good-looking, handsome, comely, becoming, flattering; tasteful, elegant, artistic, aesthetic, picturesque.

attractiveness, *n.* **1.** pleasantness, delightfulness, pleasingness, eye appeal; prettiness, fairness, sightliness; beauty, loveliness, shapeliness, sexiness, comeliness, handsomeness; tastefulness, elegance.

2. attraction, charm, allure. See **attraction** (*def.* **2**).

attributable, *adj.* assignable, imputable. See **ascribable** (*defs.* **1, 2**).

attribute, *v.* **1.** *Usu.* **attribute to** ascribe, assign, credit, accredit, give credit for, put down, chalk up to *or* with; impute, charge with, lay on, blame, accuse.

2. associate, connect, link, tie in, couple, match *or* pair up, relate, think of together, consider jointly *or* in union.

—n. **3.** quality, property, distinction, note, mark, cachet; characteristic, character, feature, trait, grace, virtue; idiosyncrasy, idiocrasy, singularity; eccentricity, peculiarity, quirk, oddity.

4. endowment, gift, talent, genius; faculty, knack, ability, capability; specialty, bailiwick, stock in trade, trademark, forte, strong suit, *Sl.* bag, *Sl.* thing.

attrition, *n.* **1.** friction, rubbing, rubbing against; abrasion, whetting, sanding, pumicing, grinding, filing, chafing, fraying, fretting, corrosion, corroding, gnawing, eating out *or* away, consumption, consuming, devouring; scraping, scrape, excoriation, grating, rasping; erosion, eroding, wearing, wearing down *or* away, detrition.

2. debilitation, debilitating, enfeeblement, enfeebling, weakening, enervation, enerving, exhaustion, exhausting; undermining, sapping, harassment, harassing, harrying, badgering, pestering, nagging, hectoring; plaguing, persecution, persecuting, tormenting.

3. decrease, decreasing, reduction, reducing, abatement, diminution, diminishing, lessening; dwindling, shrinking, subsidence, ebbing; waning, decline, lowering.

attune, *v.* harmonize, coordinate, accord, assimilate, homologize; adapt, adjust, fit, tailor, measure, proportion; regulate, set, reconcile, synchronize.

auburn, *adj.* reddish-brown, copper, copper-colored, rust, rust-colored, bronze, bronze-colored, titian, henna, cinnamon; golden-brown, light-brown, russet, chestnut-brown, chestnut.

au courant, *French.* **1.** up-to-date, current, in the swim, enlightened, informed, well-informed, well-posted, in the know, *Sl.* hip, *Sl.* with it, *Brit. Sl.* suss; up on, abreast of.

2. stylish, modish, fashionable, in fashion, in style, in vogue, a la mode, all the rage, *Sl.* the thing; new, newfashioned, modern, up-to-the-minute, *Inf.* trendy, *Sl.* mod.

auction, *n.* public sale, vendue, *Scot and North Eng.* roup, *Chiefly Irish.* cant; tag sale, yard sale, garage sale.

audacious, *adj.* **1.** bold, venturesome, adventuresome, adventurous; daring, brave, courageous, valiant, valorous, lion-hearted, stout-hearted; fearless, dauntless, intrepid, undaunted, unshrinking, unflinching; stalwart, doughty, mettlesome, plucky, *Inf.* spunky, hardy; virile, manly, tough, *Sl.* gutsy, *Sl.* ballsy.

2. presumptuous, overconfident, impertinent, assuming, insolent, impudent, brazen, brassy, rude; unabashed, shameless, forward, *Inf.* fresh, bumptious, *Inf.* nervy, *Inf.* pushy; pert, *Archaic.* malapert, saucy, *Inf.* cheeky; rebellious, defiant, self-reliant, strong-willed.

3. foolhardy, rash, temerarious, reckless, desperate, wild; heedless, careless, harebrained, impulsive, hotheaded, madcap, headlong, daredevil, devil-may-care, death-defying, harum-scarum; injudicious, ill-considered, imprudent, indiscreet.

4. original, inventive, imaginative, unconventional, unorthodox; revolutionary, unprecedented, precedent-setting, radical, drastic, extreme; novel, untried, progressive, advanced.

5. lively, spirited, alert, alive, zesty, zestful, vivacious, *Inf.* zippy, peppy; ardent, fervent, hearty, keen; unrestrained, uninhibited, spontaneous, unconstrained, open, free.

audacity, *n.* **1.** boldness, courage, bravery, valor, hardihood, resoluteness, stalwartness; daring, derring-do, venturesomeness, adventurousness, fearlessness, intrepidity; backbone, grit, nerve, mettle, spirit, pluck, *Inf.* spunk, *Inf.* starch, *Inf.* guts; foolhardiness, rashness, temerity, recklessness, desperation; impetuosity, impetuousness, hot-headedness; imprudence, indiscretion, injudiciousness.

2. effrontery, impudence, *Inf.* cheek, *Inf.* brass, gall, bumptiousness; forwardness, chutzpah, assertiveness, *Inf.* pushiness; presumption, presumptuousness, insolence, impertinence; brazenness, brassiness, sauciness, rudeness, *Sl.* mouth, *Sl.* lip; self-importance, front, haughtiness, arrogance.

3. originality, inventiveness, invention, imagination, imaginativeness, creativity, creativeness; unconventionality, unorthodoxy, novelty, newness, uniqueness, unprecedentedness.

4. dash, zest, spirit, life, spark, pep, *Inf.* zip, zing; flair, panache, *Inf.* pizzazz.

audible, *adj.* hearable; heard; loud, out loud, distinct, clear, perceivable *or* perceptible to the ear.

audience, *n.* **1.** spectators, viewers, watchers, listeners, hearers, readers; attenders, attendants; assemblage, assembly, congregation; house, turnout.

2. public, following, regulars; fans, devotees, aficionados, *Inf.* buffs, *Inf.* nuts, *Inf.* freaks.

3. hearing, review, examination; trial, adjudication.

4. interview, reception, admission, access, entree; consultation, discussion, conference, parley, meeting, *Inf.* powwow.

audit, *n.* **1.** *Commerce.* examination, scrutiny, *Inf.* look at the books, investigation; review, check, analysis, inspection; accounting, verification, attestation, voucher.

2. statement, account, balance sheet.

—*v.* **3.** examine, scrutinize, *Inf.* look at the books, investigate; review, check, analyze, inspect; account, verify, attest, vouch.

4. *U.S.* listen in, sit in, observe.

audition, *n.* **1.** hearing, auscultation, listening, ear.

2. trial, test, tryout, hearing, audience.

auditor, *n.* **1.** hearer, listener, harkener, eavesdropper, audience.

2. accountant, certified public accountant, C.P.A., *Both Brit.* chartered accountant, C.A.; comptroller, controller, bookkeeper; inspector, examiner, reckoner, analyst, *Insurance.* actuary.

auditorium, *n.* **1.** assembly room, meeting space, multipurpose room; nave, auditory, durbar.

2. hall, assembly hall, house, basilica, gallery, lecture hall, concert hall, dance hall, casino; theater, parquet, amphitheater; coliseum, stadium, field house, arena.

augment, *v.* **1.** increase, enlarge, make larger, make bigger, make greater, *Chiefly Literary.* greaten, aggrandize; magnify, amplify, enhance, deepen, heighten; widen, thicken, broaden; lengthen, prolong, protract; expand, extend, spread, spread out; (*of writing or speech*) pad, stretch out, branch out; inflate, distend, puff out, dilate; wax, swell, grow larger.

2. supplement, add to, superadd to; accrue, accumulate, cumulate, amass, pile up, heap up; multiply, double, redouble, treble, triple, quadruple.

3. raise, elevate, boost, advance, exalt; rise, ascend, mount, skyrocket; burgeon, shoot up, spring up, sprout.

4. escalate, step up, give a boost to, *U.S. Sl.* soup up, *Sl.* hop up, *Sl.* jazz up; accelerate, snowball, mushroom; intensify, concentrate; exaggerate, maximize, make much of, make the most of, overstate; exacerbate, aggravate.

5. strengthen, reinforce, build up; grow, develop, mature, flourish.

augmentation, *n.* **1.** increase, enlargement, aggrandizement, expansion, extension; magnification, amplification, enhancement, deepening, heightening; widening, thickening, broadening; spreading out, (*of writing or speech*) padding, stretching out, branching out; lengthening, prolongation, protraction; inflation, distension, dilatation, dilation; waxing, swelling.

2. addition, accretion, increment, accession, access; supplement, annex, annexation, appendage, appendix, addendum, adjunct; accrual, accruement, accumulation, cumulation.

3. elevation, raise, boost, rise, advancement; multiplication, doubling, redoubling, trebling, tripling, quadrupling; mounting, ascending, skyrocketing; upsurge, upswing, upturn, step-up; burgeoning; shooting up, springing up, sprouting.

4. escalation, acceleration, intensification, concentration; exaggeration, maximization, overstatement; exacerbation, aggravation.

5. strengthening, reinforcement, build-up; improvement, upgrading, *Inf.* pickup; growth, development, maturation.

augur, *n.* **1.** seer, soothsayer, oracle, prophet, prognosticator, fortuneteller, foreteller, predictor, foreseer; diviner, divinator, geomancer, (*in ancient Rome*) haruspex.

—*v.* **2.** prognosticate, prophesy, predict, soothsay, vaticinate; foretell, forecast, divine, forewarn, *Rare.* premonish, *Obs.* auspicate.

3. foreshadow, forebode, presage, portend, omen, bode, foretoken, presignify; betoken, signify, mean, indicate, point to.

augury, *n.* **1.** prognostication, prophecy, prediction, prefigurement, vaticination, soothsaying, fortunetelling, foretelling; divination, geomancy, sortilege, (*in ancient Rome*) haruspicy; clairvoyance, second sight.

2. omen, sign, portent, token, prognostic, presage, bodement, soothsay; premonition, preindication, forewarning, foretoken, harbinger.

august, *adj.* **1.** majestic, grand, magnificent, stately, elegant, superb; glorious, admirable, noble; exalted, lofty, elevated; inspiring, awe-inspiring, impressive, solemn; sublime, transcendent; pompous, pretentious, ostentatious, showy.

2. venerable, of high birth, of high rank, *Chiefly Brit.* worshipful; imposing, dignified, glorious, admirable, noble; lordly, princely, royal, regal, kingly, imperial; supreme, paramount, eminent, preeminent; illustrious, renowned, noted, celebrated, distinguished.

aura, *n.* **1.** ambience, mood, character, quality, tone, feeling, feel, air; atmosphere, nimbus, environment, pervading influence; karma, *Inf.* vibrations, *Inf.* vibes; spirit, personality.

2. emanation, effluence, flow, outpouring; exhalation, expiration, effluvium, vapor; aroma, essence, perfume, scent, fragrance, odor.

aureole, *n.* **1.** halo, nimbus, aureola.

2. corona, circle of radiance, ring of light, crown of light, luminous cloud; effulgence, radiance, luster, luminosity, irradiation, light; luminescence, phosphorescence.

auspice, *n.* **1.** *Usu.* **auspices** patronage, support, sponsorship, protection, aegis; championship, advocacy, favor, approval, sanction, countenance; moral support, encouragement, assistance, aid, help, defense; security, safeguard, palladium; wardenship, guardianship, tutelage, guidance, care, responsibility, charge; leadership, control, authority, direction, supervision, superintendence, oversight.

2. divination, prognostication, augury; omen, sign, portent, bodement, warning, presage, prognostic; prophecy, forecast, indication, foreshadowing, prefigurement.

auspicious, *adj.* **1.** propitious, favorable, favonian, opportune, timely, seasonable; right, apt, appropriate, felicitous, suitable, convenient; promising, bright, sunny, fair, clear, cloudless; roseate, rosy, optimistic, hopeful, encouraging.

2. fortunate, lucky, providential; prosperous, flourishing, thriving, successful, golden, halcyon, palmy.

austere, *adj.* **1.** severe, harsh, strict, strait-laced, forbidding, hard, stern, grim; formal, aloof, cold, distant, stiff; inflexible, stilted, unbending, unyielding, rigid, tight; rigorous, relentless, unfeeling, inhuman, cruel; commanding, authoritative, authoritarian, peremptory.

2. abstemious, puritanical, puritan-like, abstinent, nonindulgent; moral, upright, righteous, right-minded, faultless, sinless; continent, chaste, celibate, virgin, virginal; restrained, self-restrained, controlled, self-controlled, self-disciplined, self-mortifying; ascetic, self-denying, self-abnegating.

3. serious, solemn, sober, formal; sedate, staid, conservative, reserved, dignified, poised; grave, important, consequential; significant, considered, concerned, responsible; momentous, weighty, heavy, ponderous, profound, intense.

4. subdued, quiet, soft, softened, mellow, toned down; gray, grayish, grayed, neutral; dull, dreary, mousy, drab; somber, dark, sad, gloomy, dun, heavy, leaden.

5. plain, simple, limited, unexaggerated, unembroidered, unvarnished, unadorned, unembellished; unornamented, undecked, ungarnished, unenriched; prosaic, ordinary, commonplace.

6 hard, harsh, severe, cold, realistic, practical; solid, substantial, firm, sound, real, tangible.

7. rough, harsh, strong, pungent, poignant; sharp, keen, biting, stinging, caustic, acrimonious; bitter, sour, tart, acid, acerb, vinegarish, astringent; distasteful, unpleasant, unpalatable, unsavory, disagreeable, nasty.

austerity, *n.* **1.** severity, harshness, asperity, strictness; hardness, sternness, grimness, seriousness, sobriety, soberness; formality, stiffness, inflexibility, unbendingness, rigidity, rigidness, tightness, rigor, rigorousness; relentlessness, unyieldingness, unfeelingness, inhumanity, cruelty; acrimony, acrimoniousness, acerbity, sharpness, keenness, commandingness, authoritativeness, peremptoriness.

2. abstemiousness, Puritanism, habitual abstinence, abstention, nonindulgence; continence, celibacy, chasteness, chastity, virginity; refrainment, refraining, forbearance, forbearing, desistance, desisting; holding off, resisting, resistance; restraint, self-restraint, control, self-control.

3. asceticism, self-denial, self-abnegation, self-deprivation; privation, hardship, suffering, affliction, trouble, burden, oppression.

4. **austerities** ascetic practices, repentance, contrition, penance, penitence, sack cloth and ashes, fasting; self-mortification, self-discipline, self-flagellation, scourging, whipping; hair shirt, scourge, whip, lash.

5. simplicity, plainness, unadornment, undecorousness; commonness, homeliness, unpretentiousness, ordinariness; bareness, spareness, baldness, nakedness.

authentic, *adj.* **1.** reliable, dependable, trustworthy, trusted, trusty; credible, believable, *Inf.* all right, *Inf.* O.K.; realistic, true-to-life, factual, actual, real, true; honest, truthful, veracious; exact, precise, accurate, close, faithful, strict; official, authoritative, unquestionable, indisputable, indubitable, *Sl.* from the horse's mouth.

2. genuine, real, *Dial.* sure-enough, simon-pure, sterling, the real McCoy; bona fide, veritable, *Sl.* real live, *Inf.* honest-to-goodness, *Inf.* kosher, *Archaic.* authentical, *Australian.* dinkum; legitimate, rightful, lawful, just, legal, licit; valid, authenticated, verified, confirmed; attested, vouched for, warranted, certified, guaranteed; standard, accepted, approved, conventional, orthodox.

authenticate, *v.* **1.** validate, certify, assure, confirm, seal; affirm, attest, corroborate, aver; vouch, accredit, endorse; guarantee, warrant, countersign, underwrite, insure.

2. verify, substantiate, support, prove, evidence, lend credence; sustain, back up, uphold, make good, justify.

authentication, *n.* **1.** certification, validation, confirmation; affirmation, assurance, attestation, corroboration; voucher, warranty, guarantee, guaranty, insurance.

2. verification, substantiation, support, proof, evidence.

author, *n.* **1.** writer, composer, scribe, inditer, scribbler, penman; belletrist, littérateur, man of letters; novelist, fictioneer, storyteller, narrator, spinner of yarns, romancer; dramatist, playwright, dramaturge, scenarist, screenwriter; tragedian, tragedist, comedian, comedist; poet, bard, versifier, skald, scop, poetaster; librettist, elegist, lyricist, fabulist; essayist, pamphleteer, epistoler; historian, chronicler, annalist, historiographer; publicist, biographer, memorialist; ghost writer, speech writer; journalist, reporter, newspaperman, *Archaic.* gazetteer; correspondent, contributor, paragrapher, *Brit.* paragraphist; editorialist, columnist, commentator, critic, reviewer; compiler, annotator, lexicographer, encyclopedist, anthologist; hack, *Chiefly Brit., Archaic.* penny-a-liner.

2. maker, creator, founder, originator, beginner, inventor; parent, father, begetter, sire, producer; framer, designer, planner, architect; deviser, former, contriver.

authoritative, *adj.* **1.** official, sanctioned, approved, validated, *Inf.* O.K.'d; valid, true, authentic, genuine, real, *Inf.* kosher; ruling, governing, dominant.

2. sound, weighty, heavy, grave; documented, certified, attested, *Sl.* from the horse's mouth; corroborated, evidenced, proven, supported, backed up.

3. positive, certain, sure, assured, self-assured, decided, self-confident, confident; assertive, insistent, emphatic, dogmatic, dogmatical; peremptory, arrogant, presumptuous; imperative, commanding, controlling, domineering, overbearing, pushing, *Inf.* pushy; authoritarian, masterly, stern, strict, dictatorial, imperious, despotic, autocratic, *Inf.* bossy.

authority, *n.* **1.** jurisdiction, dominion, domination, administration; sovereignty, dynasty, regency, prerogative, predominance, rule, reign, hegemony; control, sway, mastery, influence, guidance, leadership; authorization, permit, power, force, right, liberty, sanction.

2. sovereign, monarch, potentate, king, queen, regent, ruler, emperor, dictator, czar; head, president, governor, director, commander, controller, magistrate, official; arbiter, judge, adjudicator, decision-maker.

3. *Usu.* **authorities** government, legislature, lawmakers; law enforcers, police, policemen, gendarmerie, gendarmes.

4. source, document, reference; citation, quote, quotation, excerpt, passage.

5. expert, master, proficient, adept, ace, *U.S. Sl.* crackerjack; specialist, connoisseur, critic; pundit, scholar, sage, walking encyclopedia, *Inf.* brain.

6. precedent, ruling, decision, judgement, adjudication; statute, law, rule, principle, guide.

7. testimony, witness, evidence; attestation, certification, deposition, sworn statement; warrant, justification, credibility, *Inf.* O.K.

authorize, *v.* **1.** empower, invest, enable, entitle, depute, *Eccles.* ordain; certify, accredit, license, legalize, validate, notarize, visa; institute, establish, constitute, set up, make acceptable.

2. sanction, ratify, confirm, bind, accept, pass, approve, give one's nod of approval, set one's seal to, *Inf.* O.K., *Chiefly U.S.* approbate; permit, allow, *Inf.* give the green light *or* go-ahead; consent to, subscribe to, vouchsafe; agree to, give one's assent, concur with, accede to; endorse, underwrite, countersign, witness, acknowledge; countenance, support, uphold, back up, stand behind *or* by.

3. warrant, justify, excuse; explain, account for, defend, give grounds *or* reason for.

autobiography, *n.* memoirs, diary, journal, letters; personal history, personal narrative, one's own story, life, life story; adventures, experiences, fortunes.

autochthonous, *adj.* native, indigenous. See **aboriginal.**

autocracy, *n.* **1.** absolutism, despotism, totalitarianism, authoritarianism, monocracy, one-man rule, one-party rule, Caesarism, Stalinism; tyranny, uncontrolled *or* unlimited authority, complete control, absolute power *or* control, iron hand, iron fist, iron rule.

2. autarchy, dictatorship, totalitarian state, absolute monarchy.

autocrat, *n.* dictator, tyrant, despot, monocrat, autarch, overlord; absolute monarch, absolute ruler, supreme master.

autocratic, *adj.* **1.** absolute, unlimited, omnipotent, all-powerful; dictatorial, totalitarian, authoritarian, monocratic.

2. tyrannical, despotic, oppressive, iron-handed; imperious, domineering, overbearing, peremptory, high-handed, *Inf.* bossy.

autograph, *n.* **1.** signature, John Hancock, hand; *Sl.* handle, *Sl.* moniker; endorsement, inscription; mark, cross, X.

—*adj.* **2.** holography, holographic; signed, sealed, countersigned, endorsed, inscribed.

—*v.* **3.** sign, countersign, sign on the dotted line, initial, put one's John Hancock on; endorse, ratify, notarize, seal; inscribe, dedicate; mark, cross, X; validate, authenticate, accept, O.K.

automatic, *adj.* **1.** self-moving, self-acting, self-propelling, self-directing; mechanical, robotistic, robotlike, push-button, knee-jerk, habitual.

2. unconscious, instinctive, natural, spontaneous, unbidden; *Physiol.* involuntary, uncontrolled, *Physiol.* reflex.

automaton, *n.* robot, mechanical man; marionette, punchinello, fantocinno, puppet, pawn.

autonomous, *adj.* self-governing, self-legislating, self-ruling, self-directing, noncolonial; autonomic, allodial, independent, self-reliant, on one's own; free, unfettered, unrestricted, uncoerced.

autonomy, *n.* independence, freedom, liberty, self-determination, self-direction; self-government, self-rule, home rule, self-legislation; allodium, self-governing community.

autopsy, *n.* post-mortem examination, post-mortem, necropsy; dissection, anatomization.

autumn, *n.* fall, harvest time, harvest home, harvest.

auxiliary, *adj.* **1.** subsidiary, additional, supplementary, reserve, extra; accessory, ancillary, secondary, subordinate, subservient; helping, assisting, adjuvant, aiding, abetting; supportive, helpful, assistive, cooperative.

—*n.* **2.** helper, aide, assistant, right hand, right-hand man, girl *or* gal Friday, coadjutor, adjuvant; help, aid, support, adminicle; abettor, supporter, backer, patron; ally, confederate, comrade, partner, accomplice, collaborator, cooperator; accessory, subordinate, underling, employee, *Sl.* stooge, tool, cat's-paw.

3. colleague, confrere, associate, copartner, co-worker, mate; helpmate, companion, friend, chum, *Inf.* pal, *U.S. Inf.* buddy, sidekick, shadow.

avail, *v.* **1.** profit, benefit, help, get, serve, bestead, advantage, *Archaic.* boot; work, be effective, be efficacious, do, do the trick, succeed.

2. avail oneself of make good use of, make the most of, take advantage of, exploit, use, use to best advantage, turn to account, make capital out of.

—*n.* **3.** good, efficacy, effectiveness, use, usefulness, service, serviceableness; advantage, behoof, welfare, interest, benefit.

available, *adj.* **1.** usable, of use, of service, handy, at hand, to hand.

2. obtainable, accessible, attainable, reachable; on call, on hand, ready, present; in reach, on tap, at one's elbow, at one's finger tips; convenient, at one's service, at one's command, at one's disposal, at one's beck and call.

avalanche, *n.* **1.** snowslide, *Brit.* snow-slip, landslide, cascade, niagara.

2. disaster, cataclysm, catastrophe, calamity, devastation; debacle, *Fr. bouleversement,* upheaval, convulsion; inundation, deluge, flood.

avant-garde, *n.* **1.** (*usu. of the arts*) underground, counterculture; (*all collectively*) pioneer, experimenter, innovator, groundbreaker, modernist; precursor, forerunner, front *or* lead runner, predecessor; herald, harbinger, announcer.

2. new look, latest fashion, vogue, fashion; *All Inf.* the last word, the latest thing, *Fr. dernier cri,* in thing, what's in, what's happening.

—*adj.* **3.** experimental, exploratory, innovative, groundbreaking; advanced, progressive, ahead of its time, forward looking; original, novel, unique, new; imaginative, creative, unconventional, unorthodox, unusual; modern, ultramodern, modernistic, contemporary, present day, *Inf.* far-out, *Inf.* way-out; (*usu. of the arts*) underground, counterculture, radical, revolutionary.

avarice, *n.* **1.** greed, graspingness, acquisitiveness, *Sl.* grabbiness, avariciousness, rapacity, rapaciousness; selfishness, miserliness, penuriousness, parsimony, niggardliness; stinginess, meanness, close fistedness, tight-fistedness, mercenariness, venality.

2. ravenousness, voraciousness, gluttony, edacity, open-mouthedness, hoggishness, piggishness.

3. avidity, cupidity, yearning, craving, covetousness; eagerness, keenness, itch, appetite, stomach, *U.S. Dial.* big eye, appetence; anxiousness, breathlessness, impatience, longing; aspiration, hunger, ambitiousness.

avaricious, *adj.* **1.** greedy, covetous, eager for gain; acquisitive, grasping, grabbing, rapacious, ravenous, ravening, predatory, predacious; mercenary, venal, usurious; sordid, selfish, hoarding, possessive.

2. miserly, penurious, parsimonious, niggardly; stingy, mean, close-fisted, tight-fisted, close, *Inf.* tight, penny-pinching.

avenge, *v.* revenge, take revenge, take vengeance for, wreak vengeance, vindicate; settle a score, wipe out an old score, exact satisfaction for; retaliate, repay, requite, injure in return for, *Inf.* get back at, *Inf.* get even, *Sl.* get [s.o.], reward; punish, take the law into one's own hands.

avenue, *n.* **1.** boulevard, concourse, street, strip; main road, thoroughfare, *Inf.* drag, public road, roadway; drive, lane, terrace, circle, row; road, driveway, path, pathway, throughway.

2. means, way, channel, in; access, approach, admission, admittance; entrance, entry, entryway, entrée, inlet, ingress; passage, passageway, corridor, gangway, walk, walkway.

aver, *v.* (*all with confidence*) assert, asseverate, affirm, avow, avouch, vouch, certify, guarantee, give one's word; (*all in a positive or peremptory manner*) say, state, speak, speak up *or* out, have one's say, express, pronounce, profess; insist, maintain, submit, contend, hold, have, stand on *or* for.

average, *n.* **1.** norm, normal, mean, arithmetical mean, medium; medium grade, common run, standard, run, rule, normal state; mediocrity.

2. on the *or* **an average** usually, typically, generally, most of the time, more often than not, as often as not, for the most part.

—adj. **3.** typical, common, ordinary, usual, everyday, commonplace, garden-variety; normal, standard, on a par; fair, moderate, not bad, mediocre, middling, so-so, indifferent; passable, tolerable, decent, run-of-the-mill, *Sl.* no great shakes, *Sl.* not so hot; mean, medium, medial, median, middle, intermediate.

—v. **4.** equate, equalize, split the difference, strike a balance.

averment, *n.* **1.** affirmation, asservation, avowal, avouchment, profession, protestation; certification, attestation, guarantee.

2. assertion, declaration, pronouncement, statement, deposition, allegation; word, remark.

averse, *adj.* **1.** loath, hostile, inimical, antipathetical.

2. renitent, recalcitrant, obdurate, restive, reluctant, resistant, unyielding; adverse, unwilling, disinclined, indisposed, hesitant; opposed, against, counter, contrary, conflicting, protesting; backward, bashful, shy, shrinking, chary, wavering.

3. disgusted, repulsed, repelled, offended, nauseated, sickened.

aversion, *n.* **1.** antagonism, hatred, hate, hostility, antipathy, *Archaic.* dyspathy, enmity, animosity, animus, ill will; abhorrence, abomination, loathing, loathsomeness, execration, detestation, odiousness, rancor; dislike, disrelish, disfavor, disesteem, displeasure, disaffection.

2. opposition, prejudice, grudge, disinclination, reluctance, unwillingness; repugnance, repulsion, revulsion, disgust, distaste, nausea.

avert, *v.* **1.** ward off, prevent, forestall, debar, hinder, inhibit; preclude, obviate, avoid, circumvent, dodge; fend off, shield from, defend against, parry, stave off, *Archaic.* forfend; frustrate, eliminate, nip in the bud, arrest, stop.

2. turn away, turn aside, divert, deflect, draw off, sidetrack, detour.

aviary, *n.* birdhouse, birdcage, bird sanctuary, vivarium, dovecote, pigeon house *or* loft, *Rare.* volary.

aviation, *n.* **1.** flight, powered flight, jet flight, subsonic *or* supersonic flight, flying, volitation; gliding, sailing, soaring, sailplaning, volplaning.

2. military aircraft, warplane, battleplane, combat plane.

aviator, *n.* flier, airman, airplaner, air pilot, *Inf.* birdman, *U.S. Air Force Sl.* flyboy; aviatrix, airwoman, *Inf.* birdwoman; pilot, fighter pilot, ace.

avid, *adj.* **1.** desirous, greedy, cupidinous, avaricious, grasping, acquisitive, *Sl.* grabby, rapacious; selfish, hoarding, possessive; ravenous, ravening, voracious, devouring, gluttonous, gormandizing, cormorant, edacious; open-mouthed, hoggish, piggish, swinish; insatiable, insatiate, unquenchable, omnivorous, esurient.

2. enthusiastic, ardent, fervent, eager, keen, anxious, *Inf.* wild; breathless, impatient, longing, thirsty, athirst; ambitious, aspiring, hungry, craving; excited, *Inf.* all fired up, *Inf.* psyched *or* psyched up, *Sl.* hopped up, *Sl.* ape; heated, vehement, fervid, perfervid; burning, fiery, flaming, inflamed, glowing, white-hot.

3. earnest, wholehearted, devoted; zealous, agog, passionate, *Inf.* gung-ho, *Inf.* rah-rah; possessed, fanatic, fanatical, *Sl.* hung up, rabid, mad.

4. spirited, animated, vivacious, lively; vigorous, forceful, energetic, exuberant; ebullient, irrepressible, bubbling over, effervescent; demonstrative, emotive, expressive, effusive, gushing, *Inf.* gaga.

avidity, *n.* **1.** eagerness, earnestness, keenness, intentness, intensity, excitement; anxiousness, breathlessness, impatience, longing; enthusiasm, fervor, ardor, fervency, warmth, glow, fire; devotion, devotedness, zeal, feverishness, passion, fanaticism.

2. greediness, cupidity, yearning, craving, covetousness; avarice, graspingness; acquisitiveness, *Sl.* grabbiness, rapaciousness; itch, appetite, stomach, *U.S. Dial.* big eye, appetence; aspiration, hunger, ambitiousness.

avocation, *n.* **1.** hobby, pastime, interest, sideline, diversion, distraction; pleasure, relaxation, amusement, entertainment; enjoyment, fun, play, game, sport, toy.

2. vocation, calling, pursuit; occupation, profession, job, employment, work, trade, duty, task, function; business, office, line, concern.

avoid, *v.* evade, elude, dodge, shun; escape, avert, parry; eschew, abstain, refrain, forbear; *Inf.* give the go-by, stay away from, keep one's distance, steer clear of, go wide of, keep clear of; skirt, beat around the bush, hem and haw; shirk, funk, malinger, *Sl.* goldbrick; fight shy of, shy away from, blink at, flee from; *Inf.* make oneself scarce, *U.S. Sl.* vamoose, bolt, retreat, *Sl.* cut out, cut and run; bypass, circumvent, go around, circumambulate, detour.

avoidance, *n.* elusion, evasion, dodging, shunning; eschewal, abstinence, abstention, forbearance, refraining; shirking, *Sl.* goldbricking, malingering; go-by, bypass.

avouch, *v.* acknowledge, affirm, asseverate, aver, avow; assure, guarantee, certify, uphold, maintain; profess, propound, protest, pronounce, proclaim, predicate; depose, testify, witness, attest, allege.

avow, *v.* assert, affirm, state emphatically, declare earnestly *or* solemnly, say, aver; avouch, asseverate, assure, guarantee, certify, uphold, maintain; profess, propound, protest, pronounce, proclaim, predicate; depose, testify, attest, allege.

avowal, *n.* affirmation, assertion, averment, asseveration; avouchment, assurance, guarantee, certification; protestation, proclamation, predication; deposition, testimony, attestation; vow, oath, pledge.

avowed, *adj.* acknowledged, avouched, attested, certified, testified, deposed; divulged, disclosed, exposed; confessed, admitted, owned; declared, asseverated, averred, affirmed, alleged.

avowedly, *adv.* acknowledgedly, confessedly, admittedly, allegedly; openly, candidly, frankly, affirmatively.

await, *v.* **1.** wait for, expect, anticipate, watch for, look for, *Archaic.* attend; keep in view, have in prospect; tarry for, stay for, abide.

2. be ready for, be in store for, be prepared for; be in waiting for, sit up for, *Archaic.* bide; be reserved for, be contingent upon.

awake, *v.* **1.** rouse, wake up, waken. See **awaken.**

—adj. **2.** waking, conscious, astir, up and about; alert, on the alert, wide-awake, open-eyed, aware,

alive to, sharp; vigilant, watchful, circumspect, observant; attentive, heedful, mindful.

awaken, *v.* **1.** awake, wake up, waken, wake, rouse, get up; revive, become conscious, come to, come around, become aware.

2. arouse, animate, activate, vivify, enliven, quicken; stimulate, whet, prod; excite, work up, stir up, fire, kindle; spur, incite, fire up.

awakening, *adj.* **1.** rousing, arousing, vivifying, enlivening, quickening, stimulating; restoring, revivifying, *Med.* analeptic.

—n. **2.** waking up, rousing, stirring; consciousness, awareness, realization, recognition; revival, revivification, renewal, rebirth; arousal, animation, activation, vivification, quickening, invigoration.

award, *v.* **1.** present, bestow, gift, endow; assign, appoint, grant, allow, apportion, pass out, deal out, dole out.

2. decree, adjudicate, judge, adjudge, determine, decide in favor of.

—n. **3.** prize, trophy, medal, decoration, blue ribbon, citation; honor, laurels, wreath, palm, bay, crown; reward, recompense, remuneration, premium, payment, honorarium; gift, present, bestowal, endowment; grant, allotment, scholarship, fellowship.

aware, *adj.* **1.** conscious, sentient, alive to, *Archaic.* ware; cognizant, sensible of, familiar with, acquainted with, *Sl.* wise to; mindful, regardful, observant, awake, wide-awake; alert, cautious, wary, on the qui vive, on the beam *or* ball.

2. informed, in the know, apprised, enlightened, posted, up-to-date, *Fr. au courant;* knowledgeable, knowing, conversant, versed; sharp, quick, intelligent, percipient, discerning, discriminating; sophisticated, worldly-wise, urbane, *Sl.* hip, *Sl.* with it.

awareness, *n.* **1.** realization, recognition, discovery, awakening; intuition, insight, enlightenment; perception, apprehension, comprehension, appreciation, understanding.

2. consciousness, sentience, sensibility, sensitivity; observation, notice, note, regard; observance, consideration, mindfulness, regardfulness; alertness, watchfulness, wariness, cautiousness.

3. conversance, conversancy, knowledge, familiarity, acquaintance, ken; cognizance, percipience, discernment, discrimination; connoisseurship, sophistication, urbanity.

away, *adv.* **1.** from this place, off, abroad, absent, gone, from home, not at home, not present.

2. far, apart, at a distance, remote.

3. aside, in another direction, from contact.

4. out of possession, out of notice, out of use, out of existence, to an end, into extinction, into termination.

5. continuously, repeatedly, incessantly, uninterruptedly, relentlessly, interminably, unremittingly.

6. without hesitation, without delay, promptly.

7. **do away with** **a.** get rid of, abolish, stop, end. **b.** kill, murder, annihilate.

—adj. **8.** absent, not present, not at home, gone.

9. distant, remote, far off.

awe, *n.* **1.** reverence, veneration, adoration, respect, admiration, fear of the Lord; wonder, wonderment, amazement, astonishment, surprise, bewilderment, stupefaction, consternation.

2. dread, fear, anxiety, angst, apprehension, fright, affright, dismay; shock, alarm, horror; trepidation, quivering, quaking, trembling, fear and trembling.

—v. **3.** overwhelm, impress, affect, move, strike, stun, amaze, astonish, stupefy, bewilder, *Inf.* blow one's mind, *Inf.* hit like a ton of bricks.

4. intimidate, cow, daunt, dismay, abash; terrify, horrify, frighten, affright, scare.

awesome, *adj.* awe-inspiring, overwhelming, imposing, impressive, affecting, moving; majestic, sublime, solemn, august, venerable, stately, noble, regal, awful; formidable, redoubtable, portentous, marvelous, tremendous, fearsome, horrific, dreadful; terrible, ghastly, appalling, shocking, terrifying, horrible, horrendous; weird, fantastic, bizarre, supernatural, unearthly, uncanny, eerie.

awe-struck, *adj.* **1.** solemn, reverent, reverential, awed. See **reverent** (*defs.* **1, 2**).

2. dismayed, daunted, cowed, intimidated, overawed; overwhelmed, terrified, horrorstruck, appalled, abashed; stupefied, dumbfounded, struck speechless *or* mute *or* dumb with amazement, amazed, stunned, astounded, frozen, paralyzed with fear *or* wonder.

awful, *adj.* **1.** dread, dreaded, dreadful, direful, terrible, terrifying, spine-chilling.

2. bad, mean, petty, nasty, contemptible, base; distasteful, repulsive, grotesque, *Sl.* gross; unpleasant, unfortunate, terrible; inferior, shoddy, second-rate, poor.

3. reverential, reverent, devout, devotional. See **reverent** (*def.* **2**).

4. awesome, impressive, imposing, moving. See **awesome.**

—adv. **5.** *Informal.* very, extremely, extraordinarily, excessively, inordinately; *Inf.* like mad, *Inf.* something fierce.

awkward, *adj.* **1.** unskillful, unhandy, inexpert, inefficient, inept, incapable, inapt; clumsy, lubberly, left-handed, *Inf.* all thumbs; maladroit, bungling, blundering, bumbling, bunglesome, heavy-handed.

2. uncouth, agrestic, rustic, gauche, backward; ungraceful, ungainly, shuffling, slouching, lumbering; rude, coarse, rough, crude, boorish; loutish, churlish, vulgar, coarse; inelegant, indelicate, unrefined, homely, unpolished, dowdy; improper, untoward, uncourtly; stiff, uneasy, wooden, gawky, constrained.

3. unwieldy, unmanageable, cumbersome, cumbrous, incommodious, difficult to handle, ill-proportioned; bulky, hulking, massive, ponderous, weighty, hefty; unsuitable, unfit, ill-adapted.

4. hazardous, dangerous, risky, perilous; precarious, insecure, uncertain, chancy, threatening.

5. inopportune, untimely, unseasonable, malapropos, inconvenient; embarrassing, inappropriate, mortifying, disconcerting, humiliating; trying, unpleasant, uncomfortable, difficult.

awning, *n.* **1.** sunshade, covering, canopy, tilt, tarpaulin, *Inf.* tarp, baldachin.

2. shelter, cover, protection, refuge; haven, harbor, retreat, asylum, sanctuary.

awry, *adv.* **1.** askew, to one side, around, about; askance, askant, asquint, out of the corner of one's eye.

2. out of line, off-center, off balance, unevenly, crookedly, obliquely, at an angle, sideways; crossways, crosswise, traversely, diagonally.

3. amiss, wrong, off the mark, *Scot. and North Eng.* agley; athwart, perversely, wrongly, erroneously.

—adj. **4.** askew, crooked, tilted, to one side, sideways, off-center, uneven; slanted, slanting, slantwise, aslant, on a slant, diagonal, aslope, sloping, on a slope, at an angle, oblique.

ax, *n.* **1.** hatchet, broadax, maul, mattock, pickax, pick, adz, *Archaic.* celt; cleaver, hewer, chopper, cutter; battle-ax, poleax.

—v. **2.** chop, fell, split, cleave, cut up, hew, hack; shape, form, trim, pare.

axiom, *n.* **1.** self-evident truth, truth, truism;

postulate, rule, principle, theorem; assumption, presupposition, premise.

2. aphorism, apothegm, gnome, saying, proverb, adage, saw, byword; motto, maxim, precept, dictum.

axiomatic, *adj.* **1.** self-evident, apodictic, manifestly true, patently true, unquestionable, incontestable; manifest, certain, absolute; generally known, universally acknowledged, understood, granted, given, assumed, presupposed.

2. aphoristic, proverbial, gnomic, gnomical, apothegmatic, apothegmatical; terse, pithy, sententious.

axis, *n.* **1.** shaft, spindle, axle, bar, mandrel, *Machinery.* arbor; stem, trunk, pole, rod, pin; line of rotation, central line, vertical.

2. hinge, determiner, determinant, crux, decisive factor; foundation, base, basis, underpinning, undergirding, supports.

3. (*all usu. of nations*) alliance, coalition, compact, entente; league, confederation, union, combination.

aye, *adv.* **1.** yes, yea; pro, for, in favor.

—n. **2.** yes vote, vote for, favorable vote, yea.

3. advocate, supporter, backer, proponent, pro, yeasayer.

azure, *adj.* **1.** sky-blue, cerulean, deep-blue, cobalt blue, ultramarine, lapis lazuli, blue, purplish blue.

—n. **2.** sky, empyrean, firmament, vault of heaven, *Chiefly Literary.* welkin, azure deeps, heaven, the heavens.

B

babble, *v.* **1.** gibber, *Sl.* gibber-jabber, jargon; mutter, mumble, splutter, sputter; stammer, stutter.
2. chatter, chipper, prattle, cackle; twaddle, *Brit.* twattle, blather, drivel; talk nonsense, *Inf.* talk through one's hat; jabber, prate, bleat, *Inf.* gab; chit-chat, chitter-chatter, chaffer, bandy words; talk idly, *Sl.* shoot the breeze, *Sl.* gas, *Sl.* bull; palaver, clack, clatter, rattle, *Sl.* run off *or* on at the mouth; gush, blab, *Inf.* spout; gossip, buzz, tell tales, repeat everything one hears; be loquacious *or* talkative, ramble, maunder.
3. murmur, whisper, buzz; hum, drone, purr; purl, sough, rustle.
4. blab, blurt out, let slip, reveal foolishly; tattle, tattle-tale, tell on, inform on, *Sl.* squeal on, divulge secrets.
—n. **5.** gibberish, gibbering, *Sl.* gibber-jabbering. jargon; muttering, mumbling, spluttering, sputtering; stammering, stuttering.
6. prattle, prattling, chatter, chattering, chippering, cackle, cackling; jabber, Jabberwocky, prate, prating, twaddle, twaddling, *Brit.* twattle, *Brit.* twattling; patter, pattering, gabble, gabbling, blather, blathering, drivel, driveling; nonsense, *Fr. bavardage,* gobbledegook, hocus-pocus, mumbo-jumbo, abracadabra, open-sesame; humbug, flummery, *Sl.* bunk, rubbish, *Inf.* rot, *Sl.* garbage, *Sl.* horsefeathers; balderdash, hogwash, stuff and nonsense, *Inf.* bosh, fudge, foolishness, rigmarole *or* rigamarole; poppycock, *Inf.* fiddlefaddle, *Inf.* piffle, *Inf.* kibosh, *Inf.* flapdoodle; small talk, *Anglo-Indian.* bukh, chit-chat, chitter-chatter; gossip, *Inf.* scuttlebutt, buzz, idle talk, *Inf.* gab, *Sl.* bull; palaver, claptrap, *Sl.* hot air, *Sl.* gas.
7. murmur, murmuring, murmuration; whisper, whispering, buzz, buzzing; hum, humming, drone, droning, purr, purring; purl, purling, sough, soughing, rustle, rustling.
8. (*in reference to sounds*) medley, mélange, mixture, muddle, confusion; cacophony, jumble, hodgepodge, disorder.

babblement, *n.* babble, prattle, gibberish, chatter. See **babble** (*defs.* **5-7**).

babbler, *n.* prattler, prater, twaddler, *Brit.* twattler, driveler; patterer, patterist, rattlebrain, rattlepate; chatterbox, noisy chatterer, palaverer, magpie, popinjay, *Inf.* jay; excessive talker, jabberer, gabbler, blatherskite, *Sl.* windbag, *Sl.* windjammer, *Inf.* hot-air artist; blabber, blabbermouth, gusher, gossip; tattler, tattle-tale, tell-tale, tale-bearer, informer, *Sl.* squealer.

babbling, *n.* chatter, chattering, prattle, prattling, small talk, chit-chat, chitter-chatter; gossip, buzzing, *Inf.* gab, idle *or* foolish talk; palaver, *Sl.* hot air, *Sl.* gas, *Sl.* bull; nonsense, gibberish, jargon, gobbledegook; jabbering, jabber, Jabberwocky; cackling, cackle, gibbering, gibber; babbling, babble, babblement, *Fr. bavardage,* rambling, maundering; prate, prating, tattling, tattle, twaddling, twaddle, *Both Brit.* twattling, twattle; pattering, patter, gabbling, gabble, blathering, blather, driveling, drivel; blab, blabbing, gushing, *Inf.* spouting, *Sl.* running off *or* on at the mouth.

babe, *n.* **1.** baby, infant. See **baby** (*def.* **1**).
2. innocent, ingénue, greenhorn; beginner, neophyte, novice, novitiate; tyro, tenderfoot, abecedarian.
3. *Slang.* girl, woman, *Sl.* looker, *Sl.* dish.
4. babe in the woods gull, dupe, *Inf.* sucker; cat's-paw, simpleton.

baby, *n.* **1.** infant, newborn, neonate, babe, *It. bambino, Fr. enfant,* papoose, *Scot. and North Eng.* bairn; suckling, nursling, weanling; foundling, changeling; young child, toddler, tot, tiny tot, *U.S. Inf.* tad, pre-schooler; *Disparaging.* (*of an adult*) juvenile, adolescent.
—adj. **2.** newborn, neonatal.
3. infantile, childish, babyish. See **babyish.**
4. *Informal.* small, little, tiny, *Inf.* teeny, *All Baby Talk.* teeny-weeny, teensy-weensy, teentsy, teentsy-weentsy; diminutive, wee, *Inf.* peewee, miniature, mini, minute, pocket, pocket-sized; bantam, undersized, midget, dwarfish.
—v. **5.** pamper, pet, coddle, mollycoddle; dandle, cocker, cosset; spoon-feed, overprotect; spoil, humor, indulge, dote on.

babyish, *adj.* infantile, childish, baby, *Inf.* kiddish; immature, green, callow, adolescent; puerile, jejune, silly, foolish, inane.

bacchanal, *n.* **1.** reveler, carouser, wassailer, bacchant, bacchante, maenad, Thyiad; merrymaker, party-goer, masquerader, convivialist, frolicker, *Sl.* party girl, *Sl.* party boy.
2. bacchanalia, orgy, saturnalia. See **bacchanalia.**
—adj. **3.** bacchanalian, orgiastic, saturnalian. See **bacchanalian.**

bacchanalia, *n.* **1.** orgy, carousal, carouse, *Archaic.* rouse, carousing, saturnalia, Dionysia, bacchanal; debauch, spree, *Inf.* binge, fling, drinking bout, lost weekend, *Inf.* jag, *Inf.* toot, *Sl.* tear, *Sl.* bust, *U.S. Sl.* bender; compotation, wassail.
2. revelry, reveling, revels, frolic, merrymaking, partying, party, *Sl.* hot time, *Sl.* bash; carnival, festival, festivity, feast; jollification, conviviality, *Sl.* love-in,

Inf. goings-on.

bacchanalian, *adj.* orgiastic, saturnalian, bacchanal, bacchic, drunken, dissolute, debauched, dissipated; riotous, wild, frenzied, frenetic, mad; abandoned, wanton, licentious, intemperate, Dionysian, uninhibited, unrestrained, undisciplined; festive, gay, merry, jocund, sportive.

bachelor, *n.* **1.** single, stag, *Inf.* bach; celibate; misogynist, misogamist.

2. playboy, swinger, *Sl.* swingle, ladies' man, *Inf.* ladykiller, lover boy, Casanova. See **playboy.**

3. Bachelor of Arts, B.A., A.B.; Bachelor of Science, B.S., S.B.

bachelorhood, *n.* the single life, singleness, *Usu. Humorous.* single blessedness; bachelorism, bachelorship; celibacy, continence; misogyny, misogamy.

back[1], *n.* **1.** rear, end, tail end, heel, stern; posterior, breech, buttocks, rump, fundament, hindquarters, (*of animals*) loins, (*horse*) croup; (*of the neck*) nape, (*of the neck*) scruff, (*of the head*) *Anat.* occiput; reverse, reverse side, other side, flip side.

2. spine, vertebrae, backbone. See **backbone** (*def.* **1**).

3. behind one's back treacherously, falsely, faithlessly, disloyally, perfidiously; deceitfully, deviously, slyly, sneakily, furtively, secretly; insidiously, maliciously, venemously.

4. break [s.o.'s] back bankrupt, ruin, wipe out, *Inf.* break, *Sl.* bust; (*usu. financially*) cripple, defeat, vanquish, overcome, crush.

5. flat on one's back helpless, aidless, defenseless, beaten; destitute, friendless, abandoned, forlorn; incapacitated, powerless, impotent, weak, debilitated, strengthless, *Inf.* laid up.

6. get one's back up annoy, irritate, vex, irk, pique, provoke, exasperate, gall, anger.

7. turn one's back on forsake, abandon, leave behind, leave alone; reject, renounce, repudiate, disown, have done with; neglect, disregard, ignore, overlook, close one's eyes to, take no note of.

—*v.* **8.** support, help, aid, assist, succor, abet; encourage, promote, patronize, subsidize, sponsor, guarantee, warrant, ensure, countersign; endorse, approve, favor, sanction, countenance, recommend, maintain, affirm, advocate, argue *or* plead for.

9. sustain, hold up, uphold, bolster, strengthen, reinforce; corroborate, attest, validate, certify, substantiate, vouch for, second, back up, confirm, stand up for, take sides with, testify for, bear witness; *Racing.* bet on; *Music.* accompany.

10. (*all usually with* up) return, reverse, backtrack, back down, decline, retract; spring back, rebound, resile, recoil; revert, relapse, retrogress; pull *or* draw *or* fall back, retreat, beat a retreat, turn tail, ebb, recede, retrocede, *Rare.* regrade.

11. back down *or* **out** *or* **out of** abandon, withdraw from, retreat; renege, back-pedal, *Sl.* cop out.

12. back off back down; let up, stop, relent, forbear, hold back, refrain; discontinue.

—*adj.* **13.** hind, posterior, rear, hinder; *Anat.* dorsal, *Anat.* caudal, *Zool.* tergal, *Bot.* abaxial; hindmost, last.

14. removed, remote, out-of-the-way, secluded, isolated.

15. past, former, bygone, elapsed, expired, obsolete; overdue, late.

back[2], *adv.* **1.** backward, to the rear, behind. See **backward** (*def.* **1**).

2. earlier, prior, since, ago, heretofore.

3. back and forth to and fro, from side to side; (*of persons*) indecisive, uncertain, tentative, wavering, vacillating, undecided, fickle.

4. go back on betray, forsake, play false, break faith; repudiate, disavow, renege, contradict, deny, gainsay, take back, back-pedal, retract, weasel out, *Sl.* cop out.

backbite, *v.* **1.** defame, denigrate, vilify, vituperate, vilipend, scandalize, run down; berate, impugn, revile, blackguard, malign, gibbet, criticize, pull to pieces, *Sl.* do a hatchet job on, give a bad name, speak ill of, speak evil of, *Sl.* badmouth, gossip, engage in personalities; contemn, ridicule, despise, scorn, spurn, sneer at, jeer at, lampoon, pasquinade, muckrake; slur, sully, defile, smear, smirch, besmirch, soil, blacken, stain, tarnish, taint, attaint, smudge, blemish, spot, brand, stigmatize, drag through the mud *or* mire, heap dirt upon, fling dirt, throw mud on, *Sl.* dump on; injure, attack, abuse, assail, damage, hurt; dispraise, discommend, censure, cry down, reproach, execrate, denounce, fulminate, imprecate, damn, curse, comminate, delate.

2. belittle, disparage, detract, deprecate, deflate, devaluate, depreciate, derogate, decry; humiliate, humble, mortify; discredit, disprove, disfavor.

3. slander, libel, calumniate, traduce, falsify, accuse falsely, misrepresent, belie, asperse, impute, bear false witness against.

backbiting, *n.* **1.** defamation, denigration, vilification, vilipending, vituperation; yellow journalism, mud-slinging, muck-raking; slur, defilement, blot, blot on the escutcheon, smear, smirch, stain, taint, attaint, tarnish, spot, blackening, black spot *or* mark, blemish, smudge, brand, stigma; attack, assault, abuse, injury, *Inf.* brickbat, scurrility; censure, invective, railing, commination, reviling, obloquy, commination, curse, denunciation, contumely, malediction, animadversion, imprecation, delation, execration; belittling, disparagement, deprecation, deflation, derogation, depreciation, devaluation, discredit, disfavor; humiliation, humble pie, mortification.

2. slander, libel, calumny, calumniation, misrepresentation; falsehood, lie, untruth, malicious falsehood *or* untruth, traducement; aspersion, imputation, insinuation, innuendo, malicious gossip, dirt, scandalmongering.

backbone, *n.* **1.** spine, spinal column, vertebrae, *Anat.* spina, *Anat.* dorsum, (*of animals*) chine, (*of animals*) ridge, *Bot.* rachis.

2. character, integrity, soundness, manhood, manliness, quality, principles.

3. firmness, resolve, resolution, resoluteness, steadfastness, inflexibility; endurance, stamina, tenacity, indefatigability.

4. fortitude, courage, mettle, *Euph.* intestinal fortitude, *Sl.* guts; valor, daring, bravery, gallantry, hardihood; dauntlessness, intrepidity.

backer, *n.* **1.** supporter, upholder, champion, advocate, promoter, *Inf.* pusher; proponent, favorer, partisan, sympathizer, well-wisher; adherent, follower, disciple, votary.

2. sponsor, patron, (*of the arts*) Maecenas, financer, angel, subsidizer; guarantor, warrantor, endorser, ensurer, co-signer.

3. partner, sharer, mate, second, right hand, cooperator; aider, helper, assistant, coadjutor, coadjutrix, adjuvant, adjunct; abettor, accessory, accomplice, conspirator; ally, colleague, confrere, confidante, crony, sidekick.

backfire, *v.* **1.** explode, discharge, detonate, burst.

2. boomerang, come home to roost, backlash, recoil, rebound, spring back, resile, bounce back; ricochet; reverse, turn the tables.

background, *n.* **1.** rear, distance, offing, horizon, skyline.

2. antecedents, forebears, ancestors, parentage; upbringing, rearing, education; grounding, preparation, experience, work history, qualifications, credentials.

3. factors, conditions, circumstances, fabric, framework, backdrop; setting, stage, *Fr. mise en scene,* scene, environment, milieu.

4. in the background unobtrusive, unassertive, retiring; inconspicuous, unnoticed, unseen, behind the scenes, backstage, offstage; in the shadows, in the shade, in the wings, in the back seat, in the rear; out of sight, out of notice, out of the limelight, out of the spotlight, out of the public eye; in obscurity.

backhanded, *adj.* **1.** oblique, indirect, ambiguous, unclear; awkward, gauche, left-handed, maladroit, clumsy, heavy-handed, backhand; ill-contrived, ill-phrased, poorly put, tactless, inconsiderate, ungracious; improper, untoward, unsuitable, inappropriate, inapt.

2. sly, crafty, artful, cunning, insidious; underhanded, dishonorable, two-faced, Janus-faced, hypocritical, tartuffish, double-tongued, fork-tongued, deceitful, sneaking; untruthful, false, mendacious, unveracious; meaningless, hollow, insincere.

3. sarcastic, biting, caustic, cutting, trenchant, scathing; mordant, bitter, acrimonious, sardonic, derisive, ironic; insulting, mean, cruel, spiteful.

backing, *n.* **1.** aid, help, helping hand, abetment, abettal, relief, succor; assistance, cooperation, collaboration; boost, lift, strengthening, shot in the arm; support, propping, bracing, bolstering, sustenance, maintenance; sponsorship, patronage, advocacy, championing, promotion, furtherance, encouragement; endorsement, favor, commendation, approval, countenance, sympathy.

2. security, surety, collateral, assurance, guaranty, guarantee, warranty; protection, insurance, *Finance.* coverage, *Inf.* net.

3. supporters, boosters, sponsors, patrons, advocates, champions, following, followers; aides, helpers, assistants, second shift *or* string.

4. (*all of music*) background, back up, accompaniment; harmony, obbligato, second part.

backlash, *n.* **1.** (*all of machinery*) play, slip, allowance, liberty, freedom, extra space; slackness, laxity, laxness, looseness, wasted movement.

2. (*all of angling*) snarl, tangle, entanglement, snag, catch, hitch; knot, tie-up, obstruction, blockage, stoppage.

3. recoil, rebound, repercussion, reflex, reaction, response, kick, *Inf.* kickback; boomerang, reversal, turn around, about-face.

—v. **4.** recoil, rebound, bounce back, spring *or* snap back, kick, react, respond; boomerang, double back, reverse, turn around, about-face, make an about-face.

back-pedal, *v.* retract, take back, withdraw, recant, disavow, unsay, *Inf.* eat *or* swallow one's words; retreat, back up, backtrack, reverse oneself, renege, *Sl.* cop out, back down *or* out of; shift ground, change sides, tergiversate; about-face, do an about-face, *Inf.* flip-flop, do a flip-flop, *Inf.* do *or* pull a 180°, *Sl.* pull a switcheroo; deny, gainsay, renounce, forswear, abjure.

backset, *n.* **1.** setback, throwback, repulse, rebuff, reverse, reversal, turn for the worse, turning of the tide; discouragement, damper, *Inf.* cold water; relapse, fall, upset, misfortune, step backwards, worsening; defeat, loss, curb, check.

2. countercurrent, crosscurrent, undercurrent; ebb, backflow, reflux, refluence, regurgitation, *Naut.* backwash; eddy, whirlpool, vortex, maelstrom, swirl; restraint, variance, deflection, reflection, *Chiefly Brit.* reflexion.

backslide, *v.* **1.** relapse, recidivate, revert, regress, retrogress, retrograde, fall behind, slip, trip, slide, fall back into, take a step backwards; lapse, leave the straight and narrow, go wrong, go astray, break the faith, fall from grace, sin; worsen, take a turn for the worse, fail, weaken; decline, degenerate, deteriorate.

—n. **2.** relapse, recidivism, regress, regression, retrogression, retrogradation, reversion, step backwards, step in the wrong direction, reversal, about-face; lapse, straying, sinning, fall from grace; worsening, a turn for the worse, failing, weakening; decline, degeneration, deterioration.

backslider, *n.* relapser, recidivist, regressor; sinner, fallen angel, lost soul, lost sheep, apostate, heretic.

back talk, *n.* **1.** *Inf.* sass, *Sl.* mouth, *Sl.* lip, *Sl.* jaw, *Sl.* smart *or* wise talk, *Sl.* wisemouth, *Sl.* smart-mouth; retort, comeback, rejoinder, riposte; gibe, jeer, scoff, sneer, taunt, mockery, sarcasm.

2. impudence, audacity, effrontery, *Inf.* cheek, *Inf.* brass; impertinence, insolence, rudeness, *Inf.* freshness, flippancy; disrespect, insubordination, irreverence, contemptuousness; incivility, unmannerliness, discourtesy, impoliteness.

backward, backwards, *adv.* **1.** rearward, towards the back, in reverse, vice versa, upside down, topsy-turvy, inside out, back in front; crablike, retrocessively, retrogressively, regressively, *Scot. and North. Eng.* backlins; *Naut.* aback, *Naut.* abaft, *Naut.* aft, *Naut.* astern, *Naut.* sternward.

2. thoroughly wrong, totally confused, *Sl.* arsy-varsy, *Sl.* assbackwards, *Sl.* bassackwards.

3. backward and forward *Informal.* **a.** thoroughly, completely, perfectly, inside out, from A to Z, **b.** to and fro, back and forth, in and out. **c.** (*of persons*) wavering, vacillating, indecisive, undecided.

—adj. **4.** reversed, reverse, opposite, vice versa, topsy-turvy, upside-down, inside-out, inverse, mirror, counter-clockwise, *Brit.* anticlockwise; returning, recessive, receding, ebbing, refluent, retrocessive, retrograde, regressive, retrogressive, reversionary, counterproductive; retrospective.

5. lapsing, relapsing, recidivistic, recidivous, atavistic.

6. slow, laggard, tardy, late, behindhand, remiss, slack; undeveloped, underdeveloped, unprogressive, unsophisticated, rustic, backwoods, *Inf.* rinky-dink; inapt, inept, foolish, silly, fatuous, moronic, imbecile, idiotic, stupid, asinine, *Sl.* arsy-varsy, senseless, irrational; slow-witted, dull, simple, feeble-minded, witless, doltish, Boeotian, uncultured, unintelligent, *Sl.* soft, *Rare.* insulse.

7. bashful, shy, coy, demure, shrinking, retiring, timid, hesitant; disinclined, *Scot.* loathful, loath, averse, reluctant, chary, wavering; unconsenting, unwilling, opposed, antipathetical, protesting, balky, restive, uncomplying, noncompliant; perverse, refractory, unruly, unamenable, unyielding, recalcitrant, obdurate, stubborn, wayward, mulish, pigheaded, renitent, pervicacious, contumacious.

backwash, *n.* **1.** wake, wash, backflow, train, track, path; splashing, churning, concussion, disquietude, disturbance.

2. repercussion, reverberation, echo, remainder, leftover; aftermath, result, effect, fallout, consequence, outcome, upshot, outgrowth, issue, sequel, after effect, side effect, by-product, *Pathol.* sequela.

backwater, *n.* **1.** tidewater, marsh, swamp, bog; pool, water hole, pond, salt pond.

2. country, frontier, wilderness, bush; outpost, out of the way place, isolated area, no man's land, wasteland; wilds, hinterlands, woods, backwoods, *Sl.* the boondocks, *Australian.* outback.

3. retreat, refuge, seclusion, asylum; paradise, heaven, Shangri-la, utopia.

backwoods, *n.* **1.** hinterlands, wilds, wilderness, frontier, woods, bush, country, no man's land, *Sl.* the boondocks, *Australian.* outback, *U.S. Inf.* the sticks. —*adj.* **2.** *Also* **backwood** sequestered, secluded, isolated, lonely, remote, removed, inaccessible, *Australian.* outback; sylvan, woodsy, wild, frontierlike, unsettled; rural, agrarian, agrestic, country, countrified, provincial; rustic, pastoral, Arcadian, bucolic, georgic.

3. unsophisticated, unlearned, ignorant; naive, innocent, simple; unpolished, unrefined, uncultured, uncivil, unmannerly, artless, awkward, clumsy, inept; uncouth, hick, rude, boorish, gross.

bacterium, *n.* bacillus, schizomycete, germ, microbe, pathogen, microorganism, virus, *Inf.* bug.

bad, *adj.* **1.** virtueless, unrighteous, godless, impious, ungodly; immoral, amoral, nonmoral, unmoral, unprincipled, reprobate; corrupt, depraved, perverted, profligate, dissolute, libertine, abandoned, licentious; unscrupulous, dishonest, crooked, obliquitous, fraudulent, tricky; untrustworthy, disloyal, false, faithless, perfidious, treasonous, traitorous; treacherous, dangerous, insidious, deceitful, Machiavellian.

2. wicked, evil, sinister, dark, *Archaic.* facinorous, sinful, peccant, iniquitous; nefarious, malicious, vicious, spiteful, malevolent, black-hearted, evil-minded; diabolic, diabolical, satanic, demoniac, demoniacal, Mephistophelian; fiendish, hellish, infernal, Stygian.

3. villainous, criminal, flagitious, heinous, hateful, odious; cruel, brutal, brutish, inhuman, bestial, beastly; atrocious, terrible, awful, *Inf.* god-awful, horrible, horrendous, horrid, gruesome, grisly, hideous, grim; abominable, detestable, accursed, despicable, execrable, contemptible; vile, sordid, foul, base, low; dirty, filthy, scurvy, rotten, nasty, disgusting, undesirable; reprehensible, disgraceful, shameful, scandalous, opprobrious, disreputable, dishonorable.

4. defective, faulty, imperfect; below standard, under *or* below par, inferior, second-class, second-rate; unsatisfactory, inadequate, unacceptable, poor, weak, lacking, deficient; shoddy, cheap, no-good, miserable, wretched, *Inf.* lousy; useless, inutile, of no use, worthless, valueless; unsuitable, inappropriate, unapt; ineffectual, inefficient, inefficacious; inept, incapable, unable, incompetent, unqualified, unfit.

5. inaccurate, incorrect, inexact, imprecise, off the mark, off the beam, wrong, mistaken; false, erroneous, untrue, not true, invalid, not valid; faulty, unsound, fallacious, illogical, irrational, groundless, ungrounded, unfounded; unreliable, undependable, questionable, doubtful, dubitable, uncertain, unsure, unlikely.

6. injurious, harmful, noxious, unwholesome, unhealthy; hurtful, detrimental, deleterious, damaging, nocuous; destructive, ruinous, baneful, pernicious, baleful, malign; poisonous, venomous, deadly, fatal.

7. sick, ill, indisposed, *Inf.* under the weather, not well, unwell, ailing; sickish, nauseated, *Inf.* nauseous, queasy, qualmish, sick to one's stomach; unhealthy, in poor health, poor, poorly, *Inf.* lousy, miserable, wretched; sickly, weakly, invalid, valetudinarian, diseased, unsound, infirm; weak, feeble, faint, pale, white, pallid, wan, languid; failing, suffering, in pain.

8. tainted, spoiled, rotten, inedible, uneatable; rotted, decayed, carious, putrified, festered, putrefacient, putrescent, decomposed; infected, diseased, septic, blighted, (*of plants*) cankered; moldy, mildewed, mildewy, *Rare.* mucid, flyblown, maggoty; contaminated, impure, polluted, corrupted, defiled, vitiated; poisoned, envenomed.

9. unfavorable, unfortunate, untoward, unpromising, adverse, ill; unlucky, inauspicious, unpropitious, ill-fated, ill-starred, ill-boding, ill-omened; threatening, menacing, minatory, ominous, sinister, portentous; serious, dire, severe, terrible, horrible, dreadful, awful; fearful, frightful, appalling, ghastly, frightening, alarming, *Inf.* scary; dangerous, disastrous, devastating, calamitous, catastrophic, ruinous, desolating, ravaging; destructive, damaging, injurious, harmful, hurtful, detrimental, disadvantageous; unhappy, distressful, tragic, crushing, fatal, deadly; hopeless, incurable, immedicable, irremediable, irreparable, irrecoverable, irretrievable, irreversible, irrevocable.

10. discomforting, inconvenient, uneasy, hard, difficult, trying, rough, painful; disagreeable, unpleasant, distasteful, unpalatable, unsavory, sour, unappetizing, uninviting; unsatisfactory, disappointing, displeasing, offensive, objectionable, obnoxious; annoying, irritating, provoking, aggravating, irksome, vexatious, troubling, troublesome, bothersome; exasperating, infuriating, distressing, disturbing, upsetting, harrowing; disquieting, unsettling, unnerving, disconcerting; miserable, wretched, dreadful, awful, *Inf.* god-awful; disgusting, sickening, nauseating, revolting, repulsive, loathsome, repellent, odious, repugnant, abhorrent; unbearable, unendurable, intolerable, insufferable.

11. irascible, touchy, testy, peppery, short-tempered, fiery, volatile, choleric; irritable, impatient, fretful, petulant, snappish, peevish; cross, surly, ill-natured, bad-tempered; sullen, sulky, moody, sour; crabbed, grouchy, grumpy, churlish, cantankerous, cranky, crotchety; curmudgeonly, nasty, mean.

12. severe, grave, critical, serious, grievous, dangerous; acute, sharp, keen, penetrating, shooting, piercing, stabbing, cutting; biting, caustic, stinging, smarting, scathing, searing; strong, harsh, excruciating, horrible; consuming, enveloping, gripping, convulsive, spasmodic, gnawing, nagging; afflicting, punishing, tormenting, torturing, cruel; agonizing, racking, grating, grinding.

13. regretful, sorry, contrite, penitent, apologetic; sorrowful, rueful, mournful, doleful; dejected, down, downhearted, downcast; disconsolate, despondent, melancholy, sad; depressed, distressed, upset, disturbed, unhappy.

14. mischievous, naughty, disobedient, misbehaving, *Inf.* full of the devil; scampish, roguish, knavish, rascally, scoundrelly.

15. tragic, heartbreaking, anguishing, heart-rending; depressing, gloomy, dismal, discouraging, disheartening, disappointing; unfortunate, regrettable, lamentable, pathetic; somber, solemn, grave, heavy, oppressive; woeful, wretched, miserable, unhappy, distressful; painful, difficult, hard, trying, troubling.

16. inclement, severe, harsh, stormy, rainy, snowy, icy, foggy.

17. disagreeable, unpleasant, distasteful, unpalatable, unsavory, unappetizing; offensive, objectionable, noisome, disgusting; sickening, nauseating, nauseous, nasty, obnoxious; malodorous, mephitic, rank, foul, rancid, sour; rotten, spoiled, turned, putrid, putrefied, fetid, stinking, reeking; fusty, musty, moldy, *Rare.* mucid.

18. coarse, crude, rough, rude; filthy, foul, vile, nasty, gross, indelicate, fulsome; vulgar, obscene, indecent, pornographic, lewd, dirty; profane, irreverent, blasphemous; improper, not proper, ungrammatical, unconventional, unseemly, inappropriate, unacceptable.

19. unattractive, unshapely, unproportioned, uncomely, unlovely, homely, plain, undesirable; displeasing, unpleasant, ugly, unsightly.

20. counterfeit, not genuine, unauthentic, not real, spurious; false, sham, *U.S.* bogus, fraudulent; imitation, mock, fake, *Inf.* phony; forged, fabricated, simulated, unreal; pretended, feigned, fictitious, untrue; falsified, tampered with, misstated, misrepresented.

21. *Slang.* excellent, first-rate, first-class, capital, *Inf.* tiptop, *Inf.* A-1. See **excellent.**

—*adv.* **22.** *Informal.* badly, very much, a lot, in the worst way.

badge, *n.* **1.** crest, emblem, button, shield, chevron, brassard; device, escutcheon, coat of arms, *Heraldry.* achievement; insignia, ensign, sign, symbol, sigil, signet, representation, seal, stamp, brand, marker, *Archaic.* recognizance; decoration, award, token, medal, medallion, ribbon, cockade, rosette, braid, cordon, aiguillette, aglet.

2. identification, indication, signal, label, trademark, tab, earmark; trait, characteristic, distinction, diagnostic; uniform, shibboleth, livery, habit, weeper, phylactery.

badger, *v.* bait, provoke, torment, bedevil, plague; tease, taunt, tweak; bother, pester, hector, harass, *Sl.* bug, *Sl.* hassle; hound, nag, dog, *Sl.* ride; vex, pique, irritate, annoy, peeve, nettle, chafe, rile, *Inf.* aggravate; exasperate, ruffle, disturb, disquiet, discompose, discountenance, put out, try [s.o.'s] patience, *Inf.* put [s.o.'s] nose out of joint, *Inf.* get, *Sl.* get [s.o.'s] goat.

badinage, *n.* **1.** banter, raillery, repartee, wordplay, quiddity; teasing, *Inf.* kidding, *Inf.* ribbing, *Inf.* joshing; joking, jesting, pleasantry, drollery, jocularity, waggery; ridicule, mockery, *Inf.* ragging, *Brit.* quizzing, persiflage, derision.

—*v.* **2.** banter, tease, *Inf.* kid, *Inf.* rib, *Inf.* josh; chaff, rally, twit, *Inf.* pick *or* get on, *Inf.* needle; make fun of, mock, ridicule, jeer at, *Inf.* rag; laugh at, deride, fleer, taunt.

baffle, *v.* **1.** confuse, bewilder, perplex, nonplus, puzzle, confound, mystify, *Inf.* bamboozle, *Inf.* buffalo, stump, elude; disconcert, stagger, stun, daze, amaze, astonish, astound, dumfound, *Inf.* flabbergast; befog, bemuddle, mix up, fool, delude, trick, outwit, hoodwink, bluff, distract.

2. frustrate, thwart, foil; check, deflect, divert, obstruct, block; balk, bar, hinder, prevent; nullify, undo.

bag, *n.* **1.** pouch, sack, *Midland U.S. and Scot.* poke, *Southwestern U.S.* alforja, *Chiefly Scot.* pocket, *Obs.* budget; pack, packet, satchel, container, receptacle, reticule.

2. purse, (*in Scottish Highland costume*) sporran, change purse, money bag; pocketbook, handbag; grip, valise, carpetbag; ditty bag.

3. brief case, attache case, dispatch case; grip, carpetbag, valise; suitcase, case, luggage, trunk, portmanteau, Gladstone bag; vanity case, vanity bag, vanity box, cosmetic case, cosmetic bag.

4. backpack, knapsack, kitbag, haversack, rucksack; gunnysack, gunny-bag, duffel bag.

5. saddle bag, sabretache; mail bag, mail pouch.

6. feed bag, nose bag; doggie bag.

7. paunch, belly, abdomen, stomach, *Inf.* tummy, gut, (*both of ruminating animals*) first stomach, rumen, *Scot. and North Eng.* wame, *Sl.* breadbasket; potbelly, *Inf.* bay window, *Inf.* corporation, *Sl.* pot, *Sl.* beerbelly, *Sl.* spare tire, *Obs.* gorbelly; (*all of birds*) gizzard, crop, craw, maw, ingluvies, proventriculus.

8. cyst, *Both Anat., Zool.* sac, bursa; *All Bot.* sporangium, spore case, theca.

9. blister, bubble, bleb, bladder; *Anat.* saccule, sacculus, utricle; venter, ventricle; udder, teat, mammary gland; marsupium.

10. *Slang.* hag, crone, shrew. See **hag** (*def.* **1**).

11. *Slang.* hobby, diversion, pastime, amusement, avocation; partiality, predilection, preference, major interest, obsession.

12. *Slang.* mood, feeling, temper, humor, disposition, inclination, attitude, outlook.

13. **bag and baggage,** *Informal.* completely, entirely, totally, wholly, fully, altogether, perfectly, quite.

14. **in the bag,** *Slang.* certain, sure, assured, indisputable, definite.

—*v.* **15.** swell, swell up, swell out, *Brit. Dial.* plim, balloon, balloon up, balloon out, balloon forth; inflate, expand, puff up, puff out; fill out, belly, bulk, distend, enlarge, bloat.

16. put into, pocket, enclose, pouch.

17. (*usu. in hunting*) kill, catch, trap, shoot, snare, capture, *Inf.* land.

bagatelle, *n.* trifle, trinket, knickknack, gimcrack, gewgaw, toy, piece of junk; bauble, gaud, brummagem, kickshaw, *Inf.* doodad; tinsel, clinquant, ornament, spangle; pinchbeck, sham, imitation, simulation, fake, counterfeit.

baggage, *n.* **1.** luggage, suitcases, valises, trunks, bags, saddlebags, carpetbags; packages, pack, bundle, burden, load.

2. effects, things, paraphernalia, trappings, gear, viaticum, *Law.* movables; accouterment, equippage, equipment, supplies, apparatus.

3. prostitute, whore, strumpet, harlot, lady of pleasure, lady of the evening, street walker, *Sl.* hustler, *Archaic.* wench; courtesan, call girl.

4. hussy, trollop, slattern, slut, tramp; jade, vixen, harridan, hag, hoyden, minx; flapper, libertine, profligate, immoralist, debauchee, sensualist, *Sl.* bitch.

baggy, *adj.* **1.** puffy, puffed, plump, full, swollen, turgid, tumid, bloated, distended; bulging, bulgy, protuberant.

2. loose, slack, soft, limp, flabby, flaccid.

3. lumpish, lumpy, bulky, gross; shapeless, formless, amorphous.

bagnio, *n.* **1.** brothel, bordello, *Archaic.* bordel, *Obs.* stew, lupanar, *Obs.* kip, nunnery; house of ill-repute, house of ill-fame, house of prostitution, bawdyhouse, whorehouse, *Inf.* sporting house, *Inf.* call house; *All Sl.* call joint, pick-up joint, parlor house, cathouse, barrelhouse, honky-tonk.

2. hot-air bath, sudatorium, sudatory, Turkish bath, sauna, Finnish bath, Swedish bath; bathhouse, bathing house, bath, the baths, *Obs.* stew; (*all in ancient Greece or Rome*) thermae, tepidarium, caldarium.

bail¹, *n.* **1.** *Law.* surety, bond, bail bond, warranty, security, collateral, guarantee, deposit; pledge, plight, sponsorship.

2. bailor, bondsman, sponsor, backer, backup, custodian.

3. **go** *or* **stand bail for** bail out, bond, get [s.o.] out on bail, put up bail, post a bond, *Sl.* spring.

4. **jump bail** *Inf.* skip bail, *Inf.* skip out, *Inf.* run out, dodge bail, forfeit bail; *Sl.* blow town, *Sl.* fly the coop, *Brit. Sl.* do a moonlight flit; welsh, *Brit. Sl.* levant.

5. **on bail** out *or* free on bail, *Sl.* sprung, *Sl.* on the street.

—*v.* **6.** free *or* release on bail, grant bail, release in custody *or* charge, bond over, constrain.

7. bail out, post *or* go *or* stand bail, bond, post bond, guarantee, warranty, post collateral, make a deposit, give *or* pledge security *or* surety; sponsor, back, underwrite, assure, insure, *Sl.* spring, *Sl.* put on the street.

bail², *v.* **1.** dip, scoop, ladle, spoon; lade, empty, draw off, drain off.

2. **bail out** *Slang.* relieve, help out, aid, assist, indemnify, *Inf.* get [s.o.] out of hot water, *Inf.* help [s.o.] out of a spot *or* tight spot, *Inf.* give a hand *or* boost, lend a helping hand.

3. **bail out** *Slang.* give up, quit, get out, abandon, turn away from, evade responsibility, *Sl.* cop out; *Inf.* run out on, wash one's hands of, *Inf.* get out from under, *Inf.* get out while the getting is good, *Inf.* leave [s.o.] holding the bag.

bailiff, *n.* sheriff, deputy, deputy sheriff, constable; court officer, marshal, catchpole, tipstaff, *Brit.* magistrate.

bailiwick, *n.* **1.** jurisdiction, beat, circuit; diocese, parish; constituency, department, ward; estate, lands, region, pale; dominion, domain, sway, realm, empery.

2. ground, one's own ground, field, territory, field *or* realm of expertise, province, sphere, orbit; *Inf.* neck of the woods.

bait, *n.* **1.** lure, plug, troll, decoy; trap, snare, gin, springe, noose, trepan; pitfall, pit, net.

2. allurement, enticement, lurement, beguilement; temptation, tantalization, teasing, seduction, *Sl.* come-on; fascination, charm, enchantment, bewitchment, entrancement; captivation, ensnarement, entrapment; inducement, incitement, incentive, whet, bribe; attraction, magnetism, drawing, appeal, influence.

—*v.* **3.** entice, lure, allure, intrigue, beguile, inveigle; tempt, tantalize, seduce, ensorcell, bewitch, enchant; captivate, fascinate, charm, entrance, enrapture; titillate, tickle, interest; arouse, rouse, incite, whet, stimulate; induce, bribe, suborn; attract, appeal, draw, magnetize, hypnotize, sway.

4. badger, torment, hector, bedevil, plague; terrorize, persecute, molest, torture; harass, harry, beset, beleaguer; hound, dog, nag, pick on, pick at; be *or* get on [s.o.'s] back, *Brit.* chivvy, *Inf.* give [s.o.] a hard time, *Sl.* ride, *Sl.* needle, *Sl.* put the heat on.

5. tease, *Inf.* kid, *Inf.* rib, *Inf.* josh; badinage, chaff, rally, twit, *Inf.* pick *or* get on, make fun of, mock, ridicule, jeer at, *Inf.* rag; laugh at, deride, fleer, taunt.

bake, *v.* **1.** cook, roast, broil, grill, barbecue; sauté, braize, fricassee; fry, frizzle, pan, griddle, toast.

2. scorch, sear, burn, singe, char, scald; torrefy, kiln, dry, heat, parch, sun, fire; calcine, frit, anneal, harden, indurate, encrust; braze, vulcanize.

balance, *n.* **1.** scale, scales, steelyard, measure; beam, lever.

2. equilibrium, equipoise, equipollence, equipollency, equiponderance, equiponderancy; equivalence, equality, parity, par; equalization, uniformity, symmetry.

3. poise, composure, aplomb, steadiness, evenness, stability, consistency; assurance, confidence, self-assurance, self-confidence, self-possession, self-command; self-restraint, self-control, collectedness; equanimity, calmness, cool, coolness, sang-froid, imperturbability; sedateness, staidness, dispassion; level-headedness, prudence, common sense, discretion; sobriety, sanity, reason, presence of mind, rationality; sagacity, wisdom, sapience, judiciousness, judgment; perspicacity, discernment, acumen, long-headedness.

4. counterpoise, counterbalance, counterweight, countercheck; weight, stabilizer, equalizer, neutralizer, makeweight, ballast; compensation, offset, *Latin. quid pro quo,* recompense, requital, *Literary.* guerdon.

5. estimation, valuation, appraisal, assessment, appreciation, rating; weighing, consideration, ponderance, reckoning.

6. remainder, rest, difference, residue, residuum; surplus, extra, excess, overplus, superfluity; remains, remnants, relics, leavings.

7. **in the balance** at the turning point, at the crisis, at the critical point, at zero hour, in hinge, at the juncture.

—*v.* **8.** equalize, poise, stabilize, steady, level, even, square; countervail, counteract, countercheck, counterbalance, *Naut.* trim; compensate, offset, requite, *Literary.* guerdon; match, *Sports.* tie, equal, parallel, correspond, accord, harmonize.

9. arrange, adjust, proportion, align; range, order, array, *Mil.* dress; straighten, line up, collimate, draw up.

10. estimate, valuate, value, compare, assess, appraise, rate; weigh, ponder, consider, deliberate; reflect, muse, ruminate.

11. *Accounting.* total, tally, sum up, tot up, add up, count up; figure, compute, calculate, cipher, foot up; square, equate, settle, reckon.

12. waver, hesitate, sway, hover, falter, *Archaic.* demur; wobble, teeter, totter, rock, shake, quaver; vacillate, shilly-shally, dillydally, blow hot and cold, seesaw; oscillate, fluctuate, alternate, *Inf.* straddle, tergiversate.

balance sheet, *n.* ledger, account book, journal, register, log, cashbook, debits and credits; report, statement, account-current, running account; account, tally, reckoning, score, bill, total, sum total, bottom line.

balcony, *n.* **1.** porch, veranda, terrace, loggia, portico, *Chiefly New Eng. and Southern U.S.* piazza.

2. gallery, loge, boxes, upper circle; cheap seats, *Inf.* peanut gallery.

bald, *adj.* **1.** hairless, baldheaded, baldpated, *Scot.* beld, calvous, *Zool., Bot.* glabrous, smooth; shaven, depilated, tonsured, *Obs.* polled.

2. (*all of landscapes*) barren, stark, bleak, treeless; exposed, uncovered, coverless, naked, unsheltered.

3. (*all of prose styles, etc.*) plain, simple, bare, unadorned, unornamented, undecorated, unembellished, ungarnished, unvarnished, inornate, unelaborate; severe, austere, sober, ascetic, lean, spare, laconic, Spartan.

4. open, overt, undisguised, evident, obvious, manifest, clear; outright, downright, out-and-out, unmitigated; sheer, glaring, flagrant, arrant, blatant, notorious, baldfaced.

balderdash, *n.* nonsense, moonshine, gobbledegook; humbug, bunkum *or* buncombe, *Sl.* bunk, *U.S. Sl.* blah; flummery, *Inf.* hokum, *Sl.* applesauce, *Sl.* eyewash; rubbish, *Sl.* tripe, *Dial.* culch, refuse, chaff, trash, *Inf.* truck, trumpery; tommyrot, *Inf.* rot, *Sl.* garbage, *Sl.* crap, *Sl.* crock, *Sl.* bull; hogwash, swill, *Sl.* horsefeathers, stuff, stuff and nonsense, *Inf.* bosh, *Brit. Inf.* gammon, *Brit. Sl.* tosh; fudge, foolishness, folly, rigmarole *or* rigamarole, amphigory; footle, *Inf.* malarkey, *Sl.* bushwa, *Sl.* baloney, *Sl.* bilge *or* bilge water, *Sl.* meshugaas, *Scot. and North Eng.* haver; poppycock, *Inf.* fiddle-faddle, *Inf.* piffle, *Inf.* hooey, *Inf.* kibosh, *Inf.* flapdoodle; claptrap, rodomantade, fustian, bombast, rant; idle talk, froth, *Sl.* hot air, *Sl.* gas.

baldness, *n.* **1.** hairlessness, baldheadedness, baldpatedness, calvousness, *Pathol.* alopecia, *Zool., Bot.* glabrousness.

2. (*all of landscapes*) barrenness, bleakness, starkness, nakedness, treelessness.

3. (*all of prose styles, etc.*) plainness, simplicity, bareness, inornateness, unelaborateness; severity, austerity, soberness, leanness, spareness.

bale, *n.* bundle, *Archaic.* fardel, truss, pack, bunch, package, packet, parcel; load, lading, freight, cargo.

baleful, *adj.* harmful, injurious, nocuous, hurtful, afflictive; destructive, ruinous, calamitous, disastrous;

detrimental, pernicious, dangerous, hazardous, deleterious; pestilential, pestiferous, noxious, malicious, malign, malignant, menacing; malevolent, maleficent, malefic, evil, wicked, damnable, accursed; venomous, virulent, toxic, morbific; fell, baneful, mephitic, viperous, poisonous, *Archaic.* venenose; deadly, lethal, fatal, mortal, mortiferous, *Archaic.* lethiferous.

balk, *v.* **1.** refuse, be reluctant *or* unwilling, hesitate, pause, demur, object; stop, halt, freeze.

2. shy from, fight shy of, shun, avoid, eschew, steer clear of; evade, elude, dodge, shrink from, recoil, draw back, blench, flinch.

3. hinder, prevent, *Law.* estop, stop; thwart, foil, frustrate, disappoint, baffle; check, retard, slow down, obstruct, impede; restrict, restrain, bar, block, throw a bodyblock.

—n. **4.** hindrance, impediment, obstacle, obstruction, *Archaic.* remora, oppilation, interference, *Law.* estoppel; barrier, stop, stopper, block, barricade; curb, check, encumbrance, handicap; retardation, retardment, delay, postponement; restriction, stricture, limitation, inhibition.

5. disappointment, nonfulfillment, nonsuccess, failure, defeat; thwarting, foiling, setback.

balky, *adj.* **1.** stubborn, refractory, stiff-necked, restive, wayward, froward, willful, perverse, contrary; obstinate, mulish, pigheaded, bullheaded; recalcitrant, unbending, unyielding, inflexible; dogged, pertinacious, determined.

2. hesitant, disinclined, reluctant, unwilling, loath; constrained, restrained, reserved, timid, shy, backward, bashful.

3. unsure, doubtful, uncertain, indecisive, undecided, indefinite; wavering, hesitating, hovering, fluctuating, faltering; alternating, vacillating, oscillating, shilly-shallying; tardy, procrastinating, procrastinative; *Inf.* hot and cold; *Inf.* on-again, off-again.

ball[1], *n.* **1.** sphere, globe, orb, globule, conglobation, drop, glomeration, conglomeration; marble, clew, knot, *Sports Sl.* pill; ball game, baseball, football.

2. bullet, pellet, slug, *Archaic.* grapeshot, grape, shot, projectile, ammunition.

3. **on the ball** *Slang.* **a.** alert, awake, vital, stirring, astir. **b.** efficient, quick, adroit, able, competent, fit, qualified.

ball[2], *n.* dance, prom, *Inf.* hop; evening party, soiree, coming out party, debut; carnival, masquerade.

ballad, *n.* song, folk song, broadside, ditty, carole, noel, barcarole, boat song, chantey, fado; poem, lay, *Archaic.* fit, narrative poem, doggerel poem, fable, fabliau; hymn, anthem, chant, canticle; serenade, love song; blues, blues song.

ballast, *n.* **1.** stabilizer, *Aeron.* sandbag, weight, packing, filling.

2. balance, equilibrium, equilibration, steadiness, steadfastness, stability; counterbalance, counteraction, counterpoise, equiponderance, countercheck, compensation.

—v. **3.** balance, poise, equilibrate, equalize, *Aeron.* trim, level off; stabilize, steady, weight, weight down; counterbalance, counterpoise, offset, compensate.

balloon, *n.* **1.** aerostat, zeppelin, airship, dirigible, blimp, montgolfier, lighter-than-air craft.

—v. **2.** inflate, swell, swell out, bloat, belly, puff out, blow up, pump up, tumefy; dilate, distend, overdistend, *Obs.* sufflate; expand, overexpand, stretch, stretch out, outstretch; spread, spread out, outspread; grow, wax, fill out, fatten.

3. increase, enlarge, make larger, make bigger; multiply, augment, supplement, add to; magnify, amplify, deepen, heighten.

—adj. **4.** billowed, billowing, puffed out, ballooning; expanded, overexpanded, stretched, stretched out.

ballot, *n.* **1.** slate, ticket; voting ticket, *Brit.* voting paper, voting ball; show of hands, yeas and nays.

2. vote, voice, say, *Chiefly Brit.* plumper; suffrage, franchise; referendum, voting, election, poll, plebiscite; placet, *Inf.* the go ahead; vox populi.

—v. **3.** vote, cast a vote, elect, poll; choose, decide, pick, opt; draw lots, pick straws.

balm, *n.* **1.** ointment, salve, lotion, cream, oil, balsam, unguent; liniment, embrocation, demulcent, lenitive, *Med.* emollient, *Pharm.* cerate.

2. perfume, fragrance, scent, aroma, bouquet, incense, sweet smell, aromatic fragrance.

3. remedy, cure, cure-all, panacea; (*all in response to grief, sorrow, etc.*) comfort, condolence, consolation, commiseration, sympathy, soothing words.

balminess, *n.* **1.** fragrancy, aromaticness, redolence, odoriferousness, odorousness.

2. calmness, fairness, mildness, temperateness, pleasantness; gentleness, peacefulness, tranquility; clearness, brightness, sunniness, rosiness.

balmy, *adj.* **1.** mild, calm, fair, temperate, clement, pleasant; gentle, peaceful, tranquil, halcyon; clear, bright, sunny, rosy.

2. soothing, soft, lenitive, palliative, alleviative, mitigative, assuasive, sedative; healing, balsamic, demulcent, emollient, vulnerary.

3. fragrant, aromatic, redolent, odoriferous, odorous; ambrosial, sweet-smelling, sweet-scented, scented, perfumed.

4. Also **barmy** *Slang.* eccentric, queer, odd, peculiar. See **eccentric** (*def.* **2**).

baluster, *n.* **1.** post, spoke, spindle, rod, bar, pole; column, pillar, stanchion, pile, pier, upright, vertical; leg, support, prop.

2. **balusters** railing, rail, banister, *Archit.* balustrade, *Building Trades.* runner; handrail, guardrail, barrier.

bamboozle, *v.* **1.** *Often* **bamboozle into** delude, deceive, beguile, mislead, *U.S. Sl.* con; hoodwink, pull the wool over [s.o.'s] eyes, cozen, bluff, take in; fool, befool, dupe, hoax, humbug, *Brit. Inf.* gammon; seduce, charm, flatter, lie to; lure, allure, entice, induce, inveigle.

2. trick, spoof, outwit, overreach, circumvent, get around, put one over on; swindle, cheat, defraud, fleece, rook, gull, chouse, stack the deck, *Inf.* gyp, *Sl.* gaff; pluck, mulct, victimize, exploit, play on *or* upon, take advantage of, *Inf.* diddle, *Inf.* do.

3. perplex, puzzle, baffle, mystify; bewilder, befuddle, confuse, mix up.

bamboozler, *n.* **1.** deceiver, deluder, beguiler, hoodwinker; duper, hoaxer, humbugger; fraud, fake, phony, imposter, liar; pretender, charlatan, quack, mountebank, empiric.

2. trickster, prankster, joker, jokester, practical joker; swindler, cheat, cheater, defrauder, rook, fleecer, gyp, gypper; sharper, sharpie, shark, knave, scoundrel, rogue, villain.

ban, *v.* **1.** prohibit, forbid, interdict, outlaw, taboo, proscribe; disallow, reject, veto; prevent, preclude, make impossible, *Archaic.* forfend, inhibit; ostracize, exclude, shut out, debar, bar, segregate; banish, exile, expel, throw out, kick out, deport.

—n. **2.** prohibition, interdiction, interdict, forbiddance, outlawry, taboo, proscription, embargo; excommunication, banishment, exclusion, exception, ostracism, segregation, debarment, omission; disallowance, rejection, veto; prevention, preclusion, inhibition.

3. censure, condemnation, disapproval, reprehension, reprobation, reproof; denunciation, objurgation, *Sl.* put-down.
4. announcement, proclamation, pronouncement, notice; decree, ordinance, edict, decretal, *Roman Cath. Ch.* bull; formal order, *Law.* writ, *Law.* breve.
5. curse, malediction, execration, anathema, fulmination, imprecation, *Archaic.* malison.

banal, *adj.* hackneyed, trite, overdone, campy, *Inf.* bromidic, platitudinous, *Inf.* corny; conventional, humdrum, ordinary, commonplace, common, stock, old hat, stereotyped; unimaginative, unoriginal, stale, insipid, uninspired, flat, vapid, lifeless, unanimated; prosaic, prosy, dull, tedious, matter-of-fact; simple, fatuous, inane, jejune, feeble, wishy-washy.

banality, *n.* commonplace, triteness, triviality; platitude, *Inf.* bromide, truism, maxim, axiom, adage; saying, cliché, *Inf.* corn; inanity, jejunity, vapidity.

band[1], *n.* **1.** company, group, body, assemblage, assembly, aggregation; gathering, multitude, crowd, swarm, horde, host, throng, rabble, mob, crush.
2. set, coterie, clique, circle, gang, bunch, pack; society, association, club, order, sodality, fellowship; outfit, corps, troop, squad, team, crew; cabal, junto, secret society; league, confederation, alliance, tribe.
3. musical group, group, combo, ensemble, orchestra, *Brit.* waits.
—*v.* **4.** unite, confederate, ally, league together, join together, join forces *or* hands, team up, *Inf.* hitch horses; combine, merge, fuse, coalesce, consolidate, amalgamate, incorporate; gather, collect, assemble, mass, mobilize, muster.
5. affiliate, associate, fraternize, club *or* herd together; interact, coact, interface, cooperate, collaborate, work together *or* in unison *or* side by side, pull together, stand shoulder to shoulder.

band[2], *n.* **1.** bond, binding, tie, connection, link, nexus; strap, strop, withe, fascia, copula, vinculum; ring, hoop, ferrule.
2. belt, baldric, cord, cordon, braid, thong, (*for a horse*) surcingle; girdle, sash, waistband, cummerbund, cestus, *Archaic.* zone, *Archaic, Poetic.* cincture; headband, ribbon, frontlet, fillet; collar, collarband, neckband; hatband, sweatband; wristband, *Eccles.* maniple.
3. stripe, stripping, streak, streaking, striation; stroke, line, dash, bar; strip, tape, tag, label.

bandage, *n.* **1.** ligature, (*for the head*) galea, spica; dressing, *Surgery.* fascia; pledget, *Trademark.* Band-Aid, gauze pad, pad; *Med.* truss; *Med.* compress; *Surgery.* tourniquet.
2. headband, fillet, ribbon, band.
—*v.* **3.** swathe, dress; wrap, swaddle, bind, fillet; ligature, ligate, tie up; truss, gird, cincture.

bandit, *n.* **1.** brigand, highwayman, footpad, road agent, *Sl.* yegg *or* yeggman, *Sp. bandolero, Southwest U.S.* ladrone, *Australian.* bushranger, desperado, picaroon; outlaw, gangster, public enemy, criminal, mafioso, mobster, racketeer; thug, ruffian, rogue, tough, *Inf.* toughie, mugger, *Inf.* plugugly, rowdy, hoodlum.
2. pirate, rover, viking, corsair, buccaneer, privateer; freebooter, rapparee, (*in the Scottish Highlands*) cateran; rustler, hijacker, skyjacker, air *or* sky pirate; smuggler, contrabandist, runner, bootlegger; swindler, confidence man, con man, con artist; fleecer, trickster, bilker, sharper, *Inf.* hawk, blackleg.
3. pillager, plunderer, marauder, despoiler, depredator; ransacker, sacker, looter, vandal, rifler, forager, raider.
4. robber, burglar, thief, stealer, purloiner, *Inf.* crook; *Inf.* hold-up man, *Sl.* stick-up man, armed robber; safecracker, Jimmy Valentine; housebreaker, *Sl.* cracksman, *Brit.* picklock, Raffles, sneak thief, cat burglar, *Inf.* second-story man.
5. petty thief, *Sl.* ripoff, pilferer, filcher, shoplifter, *Sl.* ganef; pickpocket, cutpurse, purse-snatcher, *Sl.* dip.

bandy, *v.* **1.** throw, toss, toss about, pass, rally, shuffle; exchange, trade, swap, barter, chaffer, dicker; interchange, transpose, change hands, reciprocate.
—*adj.* **2.** bowed, curved, crooked, bent, twisted, askew, awry, misshapen; bowlegged, bowkneed.

bane, *n.* **1.** ruin, ruination, destruction, death, disaster, tragedy, evil; calamity, mishap, injury, harm; detriment, wrong, trouble, nuisance, pest, spoiler; plague, scourge, curse, nightmare, *Fr. bête noire.*
2. bale, misery, woe, sorrow, grief, dolor, anguish, despair; pain, distress, affliction, torment.
3. poison, toxicant, toxin, venom; contamination, pollution, taint, infection, virus.

baneful, *adj.* **1.** destructive, ruinous, pernicious, disastrous, calamitous; injurious, harmful, hurtful, damaging, detrimental, deleterious; tragic, evil, bad, sinister, threatening.
2. poisonous, toxic, venomous, noxious; lethal, deadly, morbific, fatal.
3. baleful, woeful, sorrowful, grievous, dolorous; anguished, pained, distressed, afflicted, tormented.

bang[1], *n.* **1.** explosion, boom, crash, report, shot, burst, discharge, salvo; clap, thunderclap, peal; whang, clangor, clang, clash; thump, plump, thud, *Inf.* whomp.
2. stroke, hit, smack, rap, knock, buffet, blow, cuff, box, *Inf.* wallop; slam, slap, whack, thwack, *Inf.* whop, *Inf.* bat, *Inf.* lick, *Sl.* smackeroo, *Sl.* sock.
3. energy, vitality, spirit, life, verve, pep; vigor, lustiness, virility, vim, *Inf.* zip.
4. *U.S. Slang.* thrill, excitement, joy, enjoyment, fun; boost, lift, *Inf.* kick, *Inf.* boot, *Inf.* clout, *Sl.* charge.
—*v.* **5.** strike, beat, pound, hammer, stroke, hit, whack, smite, thwack; bump, thump, plump, thud.
6. bat, slam, batter, lay on, pommel, pummel, *Sl.* paste, *Archaic.* belabor; punch, *Sl.* sock, *Sl.* punch out, *Sl.* slug; knock, cuff, buffet, drub, box, *Inf.* whop, *Inf.* clout, *Inf.* wallop, *Sl.* poke, *Sl.* take a poke at, *Sl.* conk, *Sl.* bash, *Sl.* belt, *U. S. Sl.* biff, *Sl.* bop, *Sl.* zap; cudgel, bludgeon, baste, club.
7. explode, burst, boom, report, shoot, shoot off *or* out, blow up, pop; implode, collapse, cave in; crash, smash, break, knock, thump; sound, clang, clangor, peal, clap, jangle, ring, resound, echo, reecho.
8. **bang up** damage, wreck, smash up, dent, *Sl.* total, bend, mar, flaw; maul, manhandle, rough up, *Inf.* give it to, *Sl.* knock around *or* about, *Sl.* give [s.o.] what for, *Sl.* work over, *Sl.* let [s.o.] have it, *Sl.* lay into, beat *or* beat up, slam around, beat [s.o.] black and blue.
—*adv.* **9.** suddenly, loudly, abruptly, violently; all of a sudden, quicker than a flash, without any warning; thump, crash, *Sl.* pow, *Inf.* slam-bang.
10. directly, precisely, *Inf.* smack, *Inf.* smack-dab, on the nose, on the spot, on the button, right on the button, on center, on target.

bang[2], *n.* fringe, forelock, cowlick, bangs.

bangle, *n.* bracelet, wristlet, circlet, anklet, armlet; ornament, trinket, gewgaw.

banish, *v.* **1.** exile, expatriate, proscribe, relegate, outlaw, deport, transport; unbrock, excommunicate, disfellow, disenfranchise; oust, eject, cast out, throw out, expel; discharge, drum out, cashier, *Sl.* bounch,

Sl. dump.

2. isolate, maroon, keep at arm's length, leave out in the cold; snub, *Inf.* cold shoulder, give [s.o.] the cold shoulder; shun, spurn, turn one's back on, set one's face against; neglect, disregard, ignore, refuse to associate with, send to Coventry; ostracize, exclude, shut out, bar, debar, segregate, blacklist; repudiate, disinherit, disown, cast aside; reject, discard, blackball.

banishment, *n.* **1.** exile, relegation, proscription, expatriation, deportation, transportation; expulsion, ejection, ouster, ousting; excommunication, disfellowship.

2. ostracism, exclusion, removal, separation, segregation; repudiation, rejection, abandonment.

banister, *n.* **1.** baluster, post, spoke, spindle, rod, bar, pole; column, pillar, stanchion, pile, pier, upright, vertical.

2. *Sometimes* **banisters** railing, rail, balusters, *Archit.* balustrade, *Building Trades.* runner; handrail, guardrail, barrier.

bank[1], *n.* **1.** heap, pile, stack, mass, accumulation, bulk, drift, cumulus; deposit, swell, mound, tumulus; ridge, knoll, dune; bundle, cock, shock, rick, mow.

2. embankment, dike, mole; terrace, parapet.

3. acclivity, ascent, upward slope, grade, gradient, rise, incline, inclination, slant, pitch, cant, upgrade; elevation, hillock, hill, hillside.

4. shore, rim, edge, coast, margin, marge, strand, beach; foreshore, littoral, *Law.* alluvion.

—*v.* **5.** heap up, pile, pile up, roll up, stack up; mass, aggregate, cumulate, drift.

6. slope, grade, incline, pitch; elevate, raise, heighten, deepen.

7. border, surround, embank, dike.

8. damp, dampen, bank *or* damp off, turn down, reduce to embers *or* coals; stifle, suffocate, extinguish.

bank[2], *n.* **1.** commercial bank, commercial house, *Brit.* clearing bank, savings bank, savings and loan, savings and loan association, Federal Reserve Bank; house of finance, savings *or* thrift institution, *Inf.* thriftie.

2. bank building, banking house, main bank, main branch, branch bank, branch, drive-in bank.

3. *Games.* draw pile, reserve; kitty, pot; dealer, croupier, house man; house, gambling house, casino.

4. storehouse, warehouse, depository, depot, repository; granary, silo, elevator, barn, garner; storeroom, loft, attic, cellar, stockroom; closet, cabinet, locker, crib, bunker, store, reservoir; cache, hold, armory, arsenal, magazine; treasury, coffer, strongbox, safe, piggy bank.

5. store, reserve, accumulation; hoard, stock, stockpile, supply, fund; treasure, holdings, savings, *Inf.* loot.

—*v.* **6.** save, save up, deposit; lay by, lay up, *Inf.* stash away; reserve, put aside, set aside, put by for a rainy day, *Inf.* salt away, feather one's nest; hoard, squirrel away.

7. *Games.* hold the stakes, be the banker, keep *or* hold the bank *or* kitty; deal, play for the house, run a game.

8. **bank on *or* upon** *Informal.* count *or* depend on, rely on, lean on; trust, have confidence in, pin one's hopes on, stake one's life on, swear by; credit, build on.

bank[3], *n.* **1.** line, tier, row, array, course, progression; file, rank, series, train, succession, string, chain, concatenation.

—*v.* **2.** align, line up, arrange in tiers *or* rows, put in order, array, rank, string, concatenate.

bankrupt, *n.* **1.** debtor, insolvent; pauper, beggar.

—*adj.* **2.** insolvent, financially ruined, wiped out, *Inf.* on the rocks, overdrawn, in debt, in the red; impoverished, destitute, poverty-stricken, penurious, impecunious, beggared, pauperized; indigent, poor, needy, pinched, straitened, distressed, *Inf.* strapped, *Inf.* up against it, *Inf.* on one's uppers, *Inf.* hard up, *Inf.* uptight; financially embarrassed, out of cash, *Inf.* short, *Brit. Sl.* skint, *All Inf.* broke, dead broke, flat broke, stone broke.

3. lacking, deficient in, wanting, without, sans; devoid of, deprived of, bereft of, bereaved of; in need of.

—*v.* **4.** impoverish, beggar, pauperize; drain, deplete, exhaust; *Inf.* break, *Sl.* bust, ruin, *Sl.* wipe out, break [s.o.'s] back, cripple financially.

5. **go bankrupt** *Inf.* take a bath, *Inf.* lose one's shirt, *Inf.* get wiped out; fail, fold *or* fold up.

bankruptcy, *n.* **1.** insolvency, liquidation, indebtedness, straitened circumstances; indigence, poverty, penury, destitution, impecuniousness, beggary, pennilessness, neediness; pauperism, pauperage, pauperdom, mendicancy, mendicity.

2. ruin, failure, disaster; ruination, downfall, undoing, collapse, debacle, breakup; destruction, corruption, vitiation, debasement.

3. depletion, deficiency, dearth, paucity, lack, want, absence, default; scarcity, insufficiency, inadequacy, short supply; scantiness, meagerness.

banner, *n.* flag, pennant, pennon, banderole, bannerol, streamer, burgee, jack, bunting; standard, gonfalon, vexillum, labarum, eagle; ensign, oriflamme, colors, insignia.

banquet, *n.* **1.** feast, repast, *Inf.* spread, refection, dinner, meal, treat; dinner meeting, symposium, dinner party, testimonial; entertainment, regalement, frolic, merrymaking; revelry, party, carnival, festival, festivity; carousal, wassail, compotation, bacchanalia.

—*v.* **2.** entertain, regale, treat, indulge; play host to, feed, wine and dine.

3. feast, dine, wine and dine, *Inf.* eat high off the hog; gormandize, gluttonize, gorge, stuff oneself, *Sl.* stuff one's face, overeat, indulge, eat one's fill; revel, carouse, frolic, make merry.

bantam, *n.* **1.** jackanapes, whippersnapper, puppy, *Inf.* cockalorum; popinjay, coxcomb, fop, dandy; braggart, gascon, boaster, swaggerer.

—*adj.* **2.** diminutive, wee, *Inf.* peewee, miniature, *Inf.* mini, minute, pocket, pocket-sized; small, tiny, *Inf.* teeny, little, baby, microscopic; undersized, stunted, dwarfish, midget, runty, puny, Lilliputian.

banter, *n.* **1.** raillery, repartee, wordplay, quiddity, badinage, persiflage; teasing, *Inf.* kidding, *Inf.* ribbing, *Inf.* joshing; joking, jesting, pleasantry, drollery, jocularity, waggery; ridicule, mockery, derision, *Inf.* ragging, *Brit.* quizzing.

—*v.* **2.** tease, *Inf.* kid, *Inf.* rib, *Inf.* josh; badinage, chaff, rally, twit, *Inf.* pick *or* get on; make fun of, mock, ridicule, jeer at, *Inf.* rag; laugh at, deride, fleer, taunt.

baptism, *n.* **1.** christening, pedobaptism, baptizement, liturgy, *Eccles.* sacrament; sprinkling, besprinkling, holy water sprinkle, morning star, aspersion, aspersing, *Rom. Cath. Ch.* Asperges, affusion; anointing, *Eccles.* chrism; immersion, submergence, dunking, *Archaic.* dipping; laying on of the hands, *Obs.* imposing; ablution, lustration, lustrating, cleansing, purification, purifying, decontamination, decontaminating.

2. ceremony, rite, ritual; anointment, anointing, dedication, dedicating, consecration, consecrating; initiation, initiating, (*of a ship*) launching, inauguration, commencement, beginning; naming, titling, entitling, entitlement, appellation, designating, designation, denominating, denomination, *Archaic.* nominating.

baptize, *v.* **1.** sprinkle, besprinkle, asperse, anoint; immerse, submerge, dunk, *Archaic.* dip; lay on the hands, *Obs.* impose.

2. cleanse, purify, lustrate, decontaminate; dedicate, consecrate, hallow, sanctify; initiate, (*of a ship*) launch, inaugurate, commence, begin.

3. christen, name, call, dub, title, entitle, style; term, designate, denominate, *Archaic.* nominate.

bar, *n.* **1.** rod, pole, shaft, stake, stick, sprag, *Archaic.* scape; crosspiece, *Naut.* crosshead, *Naut.* spar, *Naut.* boom, *Naut.* batten, *Naut.* fib.

2. (*all of gold or silver*) ingot, wedge, block, lump, nugget.

3. shoal, shallow, reef, coral reef *or* head; spit, tongue, sandbar, sandbank, gravel bank; ridge, ledge, shelf, flat.

4. obstacle, obstruction, barrier, barricade, blockade; stop, block, impediment, hindrance, check, deterrent, hurdle, stumbling block; constraint, restraint, trammel; snag, catch, hitch, rub, drawback, fly in the ointment; congestion, jamb, blockage, stoppage.

5. ban, prohibition, proscription, injunction, taboo, forbiddance, preclusion, disallowance; embargo, boycott, lock out.

6. diner, lunch counter, lunch room, luncheonette, grill room, cafeteria, canteen, cafe, restaurant.

7. tavern, saloon, barroom, taproom, alehouse, *Brit.* public house, *Brit.* pub, *Brit.* local; cocktail lounge, bistro, cabaret, nightclub; inn, hotel, hostel; *All Sl.* gin mill, watering hole, dive, barrel-house, honky-tonk, speakeasy, after-hours joint, *U.S., Obs.* blind tiger *or* pig.

8. counter, table, tray, buffet.

9. legal profession, legal fraternity, members of the bar; lawyers, attorneys, attorneys-at-law, solicitors, advocates, barristers, counselors; jurists, legists.

10. tribunal, court, judicatory, assize, inquisition, court-martial; board, commission, council, divan.

11. band, belt, strip; stripe, streak, striation; line, slash, dash, score.

12. rail, railing, balustrade, stile, pale, gunwale, guard.

13. crowbar, crow, iron crow, claw bar, pinch bar, wrecking bar; lever, pry, jimmy, handspike.

—*v.* **14.** bolt, latch, lock, lock up, padlock, secure, fasten.

15. obstruct, impede, hinder, deter, block, blockade, barricade, stand in the way; stop, stay, close, occlude, shut off, choke off; prevent, preclude, obviate, forestall, *Law.* enjoin, *Law.* estop; forbid, prohibit, ban, taboo, interdict, circumscribe, disallow, rule out, disqualify, draw the line; restrain, constrain, trammel, bridle, retard, frustrate, thwart.

16. exclude, omit, except, leave out, spurn, ostracize; isolate, separate, segregate, set apart, cut off *or* away; reject, refuse, repudiate, debar, lock out, shut out, blackball, eliminate, boycott; exile, relegate, banish, expatriate, outlaw, excommunicate, deport, cast aside, cast out, thrust out.

17. stripe, streak, striate, vein, marble; band, belt, crossbar.

—*prep.* **18.** except, excepting, except for, with the exception of; excluding, omitting, barring, precluding, leaving out; but, without, lacking, less, minus, save; besides, other than, apart from, *Inf.* outside of.

barb, *n.* **1.** prickle, pricker, sticker, thorn, barbule; pin, needle, bristle, spine, quill, spicule, *Zool.* spiculum; spur, gaff, spike, prong, tine; snag, jag, tooth, notch; cusp, nib, acumination, point, tip.

2. insult, affront, contumely; dig, cut, quip, slap in the face; gibe, jape, jeer, sneer, scoff.

3. *Also* **barbe** (*all of clothing*) dicky, bib, vestee, vest, waist, insert; scarf, cravat, muffler, necktie, neckband, *Obs.* neckcloth.

—*v.* **4.** spur, spike, prong; sharpen, acuminate, tip, *Brit.* nib.

barbarian, *adj.* **1.** primitive, rude, wild; rough, rugged, coarse, gross, vulgar; gruff, bearish, boorish, crass, rustic, ill-bred, churlish, clodhopping, *Archaic.* carlish; loutish, doltish, cloddish, oafish; uncivil, unrefined, uncouth, inurbane, unpolished; uncultivated, uncivilized, philistine, unmannered, ill-mannered, ungentlemanly, ungentle, uncourtly, inelegant, indelicate.

2. foreign, alien, peregrine; tramontane, transmontane, ultramontane, transalpine; ultramarine, transmarine, transatlantic, transpacific; exotic, strange, outlandish.

—*n.* **3.** brute, savage, hellkite; Yahoo, wild man, ogre, monster, troglodyte; Vandal, Goth, Hun, Tartar.

4. philistine, lowbrow, ignoramus; boor, rustic, churl, dolt, lout, clod, oaf, *Archaic.* carl; bumpkin, yokel, *Sl.* rube, *Sl.* hick, *Disparaging.* bogtrotter, hobnail, *Inf.* hayseed, kern, yahoo, *Sl.* lug.

5. foreigner, alien, outsider; stranger, tramontane, outlander; immigrant, emigrant, newcomer; heathen, pagan, gentile.

barbaric, *adj.* **1.** primitive, rude, wild, uncivilized. See **barbarian** (*def.* **1**).

2. ferocious, fierce, savage, ruthless, vicious, fell, truculent; untamed, wild, undomesticated, unbroken; feral, ferine, wolfish, lupine, beastly, bestial, *Obs.* belluine; brutal, inhuman, barbarous, hellish, Tartarian, Hunnish, Vandalic, Gothic; brutish, murderous, homicidal, slaughterous, bloodthirsty; sadistic, animalistic, cannibalistic, fiendish, ogreish; diabolical, demonic, demoniac, devilish; terrible, harsh, grim, severe; unrelenting, relentless, remorseless, implacable, inexorable, grinding.

3. pitiless, merciless, heartless, unkind, inhumane; cruel, hard-hearted, stony-hearted, marble-hearted, cold-blooded.

4. gaudy, ostentatious, showy, pretentious, meretricious, florid, ornate; flamboyant, flashy, garish, glittering, loud, conspicuous, boisterous; vulgar, bedizened, tawdry, specious, cheap, tinsel, gimcrack.

barbarism, *n.* **1.** crudity, coarseness, vulgarity; unenlightenment, uncivilizedness. See **barbarity** (*def.* **3**).

2. atrocity, outrage, enormity. See **barbarity** (*def.* **2**).

3. misuse, misusage, misapplication, error, infelicity, *Obs.* ill-usage; catachresis, solecism, *Rhet.* antiphrasis, cacology, caconym; anachronism, archaism, malapropism, spoonerism, slip, blunder, *Sl.* blooper; slang, vulgarism, corruption.

barbarity, *n.* **1.** cruelty, viciousness, ruthlessness; ferocity, fierceness, savagery, ferity, truculence, fellness; brutality, brutishness, barbarism, inhumanity; pitilessness, mercilessness, heartlessness, unkindness, hard-heartedness; relentlessness, remorselessness, implacability, inexorability; murderousness, bloodthirstiness, cold-bloodedness; harshness, severity, grimness, dreadfulness; flagrancy, heinousness, nefariousness, shamelessness; sadism, animalism, cannibalism, fiendishness; deviltry, diablery.

2. atrocity, outrage, enormity, depravity, *Archaic.* immaneness; slaughter, carnage, butchery, massacre, bloodletting; killing, murder, assassination, homicide; torture, torment, persecution, oppression; destruction, vandalism, pillage, depredation, ruination.

3. crudity, vulgarity, coarseness, grossness, rudeness, roughness, Gothicism; boorishness, crassness, bearishness, loutishness, churlishness; incivility, unrefinement, uncouthness, inurbanity; ungentlemanliness, inelegance, indecorum; impropriety; ungentility, ill-breeding, commonness, commonality, rusticity, plebianism.

4. ostentation, gaudiness, gaudery, tawdriness, meretriciousness, speciousness; pomposity, affectation, pretension, showiness; orotundity, coxcombry, peacockery, foppery; bombast, flatulence, fustian, rant; turgescence, turgidity, grandiloquence, sesquipedality, *Archaic.* tympany, altiloquence.

barbarous, *adj.* **1.** primitive, rude, wild, uncivilized. See **barbarian** (*def.* **1**).

2. ferocious, fierce, savage, vicious; brutish, murderous, slaughterous; remorseless, unrelenting. See **barbaric** (*defs.* **2, 3**).

3. discordant, dissonant, cacophanous, harsh; unmelodious, unmusical, inharmonious, tuneless, untuneful; jangling, jarring, rough, clashing; grating, strident, scraping, hoarse, raucous; screeching, shrill, screaky, shrieky.

4. foreign, alien, peregrine; exotic, strange, outlandish. See **barbarian** (*def.* **2**).

barbecue, *n.* **1.** *All U.S.* outdoor party, roast, picnic, cookout; feast, banquet, junket.

2. grill, griller, spit, grid, griddle, gridiron.

—*v.* **3.** broil, roast, grill, cook, toast, bake, torrefy.

barber, *n.* **1.** haircutter, hairdresser, beautician, *Fr. coiffeur.*

2. trim, cut, shave, shear, tonsure; dress, coiffure, arrange, style, comb.

bard, *n.* poet, poetess, poetizer, versifier, rhymer, sonneteer; minnesinger, scop, skald, trouveur, troubadour; rhymester, poetaster, balladmonger; minstrel, jongleur, singer, *Archaic.* gleeman, *Obs.* harper.

bare, *adj.* **1.** naked, stark naked, nude, *Inf.* in the buff, *Chiefly Brit.* starkers; uncovered, undressed, unclothed, undraped, unrobed, unclad, unappareled, unveiled; disrobed, stripped, bared, exposed, denuded, divested, peeled; bald, (of a young bird) callow, featherless; shaven, shorn, depilated, tonsured; (*all usu. of cloth)* napless, threadbare, worn, worn thin, worn out.

2. plain, simple, pure, severe, stark, austere, basic; lean, spare, laconic, Spartan; unadorned, unembellished, unornamented, unvarnished, inelegant; uncolored, colorless, monotonous, uninteresting, dull, prosaic; empty, unfurnished, barren, blank, void, hollow; unfinished, raw, unrefined, rough, unpainted.

3. unprotected, unshielded, unsheltered; verdureless, without vegetation; desolate, bleak, grim, gaunt.

4. mere, hardly enough, scarcely sufficient; inadequate, scanty, meager; deficient, deprived, jejune, wanting, lacking, devoid of, destitute of.

5. straightforward, undisguised, unconcealed, literal, hard, cold; revealed, disclosed, displayed, shown, exhibited; open, overt, manifest, clear; outright, downright, out-and-out, utter; sheer, glaring, flagrant, arrant, blatant, notorious, baldfaced.

—*v.* **6.** reveal, divulge, unmask, unfold, expose, disclose, bring to light; exhibit, display, show, evince.

7. uncover, undress, undrape, unrobe, unveil, unsheathe; disrobe, denude, denudate, divest, discase, uncase; dismantle, strip, deprive of.

8. shave, shear, depilate, tonsure; abrade, rub off, skin, erode, fret, bark, peel.

barefaced, *adj.* **1.** straightforward, undisguised, unconcealed, literal; frank, plainspoken, candid, bluff; open, overt, manifest, clear; revealed, disclosed, displayed, shown, exhibited; blatant, glaring, flagrant, arrant, notorious, baldfaced.

2. audacious, impudent, insolent, impertinent, assuming, presumptuous; overconfident, brazen, immodest, bold-faced, brassy, rude; shameless, unabashed, unblushing, unreserved, forward, outspoken, *Inf.* fresh, bumptious, *Inf.* nervy, *Inf.* pushy; bold, pert, *Archaic.* malapert, saucy, *Inf.* cheeky, flippant, defiant; indecorous, inappropriate, unseemly, indecent.

barefoot, *adj.* shoeless, unshoed, unshod, barefooted; (*usu. in regard to members of certain religious orders*) discalced.

barehanded, *adj.* **1.** ungloved, ungauntleted, unmitted, unmittened; unprotected, vulnerable.

2. unarmed, weaponless, powerless, helpless; unprepared, unequipped, untooled, unaided, unassisted, by oneself, *Sl.* all by one's lonesome.

barely, *adv.* **1.** only, just, only just, hardly; by the skin of one's teeth, with difficulty; scarcely, no more than.

2. openly, unconcealingly, revealingly, exposingly, nakedly.

bareness, *n.* **1.** nakedness, nudeness, nudity, undress; disrobement, divestment, divestiture; baldness, featherlessness.

2. plainness, simpleness, simplicity, pureness, purity; severity, starkness, austerity; brevity, laconism; unadornment, unembellishment, unornamentation, inelegance; colorlessness, uncoloredness, monotony, dullness, prosaism; rawness, roughness, unpaintedness; desolateness, desolation, bleakness, grimness, gauntness.

3. emptiness, barrenness, leanness, blankness, voidness, hollowness; insufficiency, meagerness, spareness, inadequacy, scantiness, deficiency.

4. straightforwardness, openness, literality, clearness, unequivocalness.

bargain, *n.* **1.** agreement, understanding, arrangement, stipulation; covenant, bond, compact, contract, concordat, convention, deed, indenture; transaction, deal; negotiation, settlement, treaty, mise, cartel, entente.

2. discount, reduction, *Inf.* a good deal, *Inf.* buy, *Inf.* giveaway, *Inf.* a steal.

3. in *or* **into the bargain** moreover, besides, over and above, additionally, in addition to, as well as.

—*v.* **4.** barter, haggle, *Scot.* argle-bargle, higgle, chaffer, dicker, bandy, *Inf.* beat down, *Offensive.* jew down; exchange, trade, swap, traffic, truck, peddle, vend, sell.

5. agree, settle, negotiate, come to terms, make terms; transact, deal, arrange, stipulate; covenant, contract, pledge, promise, plight.

6. bargain for anticipate, expect, count on, foresee, look for, reckon upon, think likely, surmise.

bargain-basement, *adj.* **1.** cheap, inferior, tatty, *Sl.* schlock, *Sl.* rinky-dink, *Sl.* crummy, *Inf.* chintzy, *Sl.* cheesy; second-rate, third-rate, *Inf.* dime-store; gaudy, gimcrack, tasteless, *Inf.* tacky.

2. reasonable, inexpensive, low-priced, moderately priced, priced to fit the pocketbook, priced to move, *Inf.* budget.

bargaining, *n.* barter, trade, exchange, traffic, dealing, interchange, business, commerce; peddling, vending, selling, swapping, trucking; dickering, higgling, haggling, chaffering, *Scot.* argle-bargle.

barge, *n.* **1.** flatboat, lighter, houseboat, transport, raft; canal boat, freighter, tanker, *Naut.* hoy; state barge, bucentaur.

—*v.* **2.** **barge in** intrude, break in, burst in on, enter forcefully, irrupt; interrupt, break in on, *Sl.* butt in, *U.S. Sl.* horn in.

3. **barge into** *Informal.* bump into, collide with, hit, *Inf.* plow into, crash into, smash into.

bark¹, *n.* **1.** bowwow, arf, yelp, yip, yap, cry; roar, bellow, *Obs.* bell, howl, bay, hoot, ululation.

2. blast, bang, report, crack, snap; boom, explosion, thunder.

3. snap, snarl, growl; shout, yell, outcry, bawl, *Inf.* holler; scream, screech, shriek.

—*v.* **4.** yelp, yip, yap, cry, roar, bellow, *Obs.* bell; howl, bay, hoot, ululate.

5. shout, yell, thunder, sound off, vociferate, bluster, bawl, *Inf.* holler; snap, snarl, growl; scream, screech, shriek; assail, rail at, revile, berate, lash out at, vituperate, *Inf.* bawl out.

6. **bark up the wrong tree** *United States.* follow the wrong scent, be on the wrong trail; blunder, err, be in error, make a mistake.

bark², *n.* **1.** skin, crust, peeling, rind, husk, shuck, pod, hide, shell, hull, integument, membrane, pellicle, involucre, *Anat., Zool.* cortex; cover, covering, coat, coating, case, casing, wrapping, wrapper, cloak, sheath, sheathing, envelope, enclosure, *Bot.* perigonium.

—*v.* **2.** peel, pare, skin, husk, shuck, hull, shell; strip, uncover, unwrap, unsheathe, uncloak; open, denude, denudate, bare; excoriate, scrape, shave, scale; abrade, rub, fret.

3. cover, enclose, envelop, encase, wrap, sheathe, cloak.

barmy, *adj.* **1.** frothy, spumy, spumous, spumescent, foamy, lathery; yeasty, fermenting, fermentative.

2. *Chiefly British Slang.* daft, eccentric, odd, peculiar, bizarre, *Inf.* different; addlepated, scatterbrained, featherheaded, simple-minded, muddled, confused; touched, not quite right, not all there, with a few loose screws, *Inf.* daffy, *Sl.* balmy, *Sl.* dippy, *Sl.* batty.

barn, *n.* stables, stalls, *Chiefly Brit.* mews; cowbarn, cowshed, cowhouse, *Brit.* byre, *Brit.* cowbyre.

barney, *n.* **1.** *Informal.* argument, altercation, dispute, clash, falling-out, wrangle, *Inf.* hassle; quarrel, bicker, disagreement, squabble, spat, tiff, *Inf.* words; contention, dissension, variance, difference of opinion.

2. prize fight, boxing match, sparring match, fisticuffs; pugilistic encounter; the ring.

3. brawl, fight, affray, fray, *Inf.* rough-and-tumble, tussle, scuffle, donnybrook; row, dustup, free-for-all, brannigan, *Inf.* scrap, *Sl.* rhubarb, *Inf.* knock-down-drag-out; turmoil, tumult, disturbance, uproar, clamor.

barnstormer, *n.* **1.** actor, player, stage player, performer, stage performer, playactor, role player, trouper, strolling player, *Sl.* ham; theatrician, thespian, Roscian, histrio, histrion, *Archaic.* histrionic; actress.

2. stunt pilot, stunt flier, stunt man.

baron, *n.* **1.** noble, nobleman, gentleman; aristocrat, patrician, blueblood, silk-stocking; peer, lord.

2. tycoon, magnate, power, king; business leader, top executive, big businessman, *Inf.* big boss; industrialist, captain of industry, financier.

baroque, *adj.* **1.** ornate, elaborate, involved, busy, fussy, frilly; overdone, overwrought, overworked, overlabored; rococo, arabesque, rocaille.

2. ostentatious, meretricious, flamboyant, showy, flashy, *Sl.* flash; gawdy, garish, tawdry, florid, flowery.

3. (*all to a ridiculous degree*) adorned, decorated, embellished, embroidered, elaborated, festooned.

4. extravagant, fantastic, outlandish, outrageous; odd, strange, peculiar, weird, queer, grotesque.

barracks, *n.* *Military.* billet, casern, cantonment, military quarters, quarters, *U.S. Sl.* the Q, *U.S. Inf.* bullpen; fort, garrison, camp, encampment.

barrage, *n.* **1.** bombardment, cannonade, shelling, battery, broadside, assault, salvo, volley; artillery fire, gunfire, drumfire, fire; barrier of fire, wall of fire, curtain of flame, deluge of steel.

2. superabundance, profusion, plethora; deluge, inundation, flood, avalanche, landslide, mountain, mass; storm, rash, riot, blitz.

barrel, *n.* **1.** cask, keg, hogshead, puncheon, butt, tierce, tun, rundlet; vat, tank, tub, firkin; container, vessel.

2. Often **barrels** lot, *Inf.* lots, *Inf.* oodles, *Inf.* tons; pile, heap, *Inf.* load, stack, mass accumulation, amassment; hoard, store, stock, stockpile, supply; abundance, volume, plenty, quantity, profusion, *Inf.* raft; storm, shower, ocean, sea; multitude, array, legion; scores, numbers, swarm, mob, *Sl.* slew, *Sl.* scad.

barren, *adj.* **1.** childless, sterile, infertile, unprolific, infecund, agenetic, unprocreant, *Bot.* acarpous, (*of cows*) farrow, impotent, effete.

2. unproductive, unyielding, unfructuous, unfruitful, fruitless; uncultivable, uncultivatable, fallow; exhausted, depleted, worn out, impoverished; meager, scanty, scarce, empty, lean, forlorn; poor, bare, dry, arid, bald, waste, desolate, dead, naked.

3. uninteresting, boring, unsuggestive, uninstructive, uninspiring; stale, dull, flat, inane, jejune, insipid, prosaic, tame.

4. dull, stupid, mentally deficient, unintelligent, moronic, idiotic, imbecilic, vacant; weak-minded, brainless, witless, fool-headed, foolish, simple, muddle-headed.

5. ineffective, ineffectual, incapable, inadequate, inefficient, incompetent, inept; useless, inutile, worthless, valueless, meritless, nugatory; futile, vain, bootless, unavailing, idle; unprofitable, profitless, unremunerative, unrewarding, unpaying, gainless; unsuccessful, *Inf.* no-go, to no avail, to no purpose, for naught.

6. (*usually fol. by* of) destitute, bereft, devoid , lacking, deficient, wanting.

barrenness, *n.* **1.** childlessness, sterility, infertility, unprolificness, infecundity, *Med.* agenesis, impotence, effeteness.

2. unproductiveness, unyieldingness, unfruitfulness, fruitlessness; exhaustion, depletion, impoverishment; meagerness, scarcity, poverty, emptiness; dryness, aridity, baldness, nakedness, bareness, waste, desolation, death.

3. dullness, staleness, flatness, inanity, prosaicness, tameness.

4. stupidity, dullness, mental deficiency, unintelligence, imbecility, simpleness; weakmindedness, brainlessness, witlessness, foolishness, muddle-headedness.

5. ineffectiveness, ineffectualness, inefficacy, inadequacy, inefficiency, incompetence, ineptness; uselessness, inutility, worthlessness, valuelessness, meritlessness, nugacity; futility, bootlessness, unavailingness, idleness; unprofitableness, profitlessness, nonsuccess, failure, defeat.

barricade, *n.* **1.** barrier, obstacle, hindrance; rampart, bulwark, protection. See **barrier** (*defs.* **1-3**).

—*v.* **2.** obstruct, block, blockade, bar; block up, close up, shut off, choke off; lock, padlock, bolt, secure, fasten, batten; shut in, fence in, defend, fortify.

barrier, *n.* **1.** bar, check, obstacle, hindrance, obstruction, impediment; barricade, barricado, blockade, block, roadblock, stopper; hurdle, difficulty, stumbling block.

2. wall, rampart, bulwark, circumvallation, *Fort.* breastwork, *Fort.* contravallation; railing, balustrade, *Fort.* parapet, fence, palisade, *Fort.* stockade; moat, ditch, dike, dam, breakwater, pier, mole; bank, *Fort.* parados, *Mil.* earthwork, *Fort.* glacis; cordon, chain, cable, rope, boom, hedge; abatis.

3. protection, safeguard, fortification, defense, redoubt.

4. limit, boundary, confine, pale, bourn; border, frontier, periphery, margin.

barrister, *n.* trial lawyer; attorney, attorney-at-law, lawyer, solicitor, advocate, *Law.* counsel, counselor, counselor-at-law; jurist, legist, member of the bar, *Sl.* legal beagle; pettifogger, Philadelphia lawyer, *Inf.* shyster.

barroom, *n.* tavern, saloon, bar, bar and grill, taproom, alehouse, groggery, *Brit.* grog shop, *Brit.* public house, *Brit.* pub, *Brit.* local; *All Sl.* gin mill, watering hole, dive, barrel-house, honkytonk, speakeasy, afterhours joint, *U.S., Obs.* blind tiger *or* pig.

barrow, *n.* handbarrow, wheelbarrow, dumpcart, pushcart, handcart, cart, truck, handtruck, dolly.

bartender, *n.* barkeeper, barkeep, barman, barmaid, bargirl; *Usu. Facetious.* mixologist.

barter, *v.* **1.** trade, exchange, swap, swop, bandy, commute, give and take.

2. bargain, deal, traffic, truck, dicker, haggle, *Scot.* argle-bargle, higgle, chaffer, negotiate.

—n. **3.** trade, traffic, commerce, buying and selling; business, marketing, merchandising, mercantilism, commercialism; dealing, transaction, exchange; bargaining, negotiation, truck.

4. goods, items, merchandise, stock, wares, articles, effects, stock in trade; commodities, produce, staples.

basal, *adj.* **1.** basic, fundamental, radical, basilar, elementary; primary, *Inf.* gut, nitty-gritty, meat-and-potatoes, underlying, substrative, substratal; intrinsic, innate, inherent; essential, indispensable, necessary, vital, sustentative, supporting.

2. *Physiology.* least, minimum, lowest, bottom, smallest.

base¹, *n.* **1.** stand, pedestal, rest, bed; support, prop, stay, brace; bottom, foot, *Fr. fond, Archit.* socle, *Archit.* plinth, *Bot.* caudex; foundation, principle, basis, footing, groundwork, substructure, substratum, understructure.

2. principal, essence, essentials, main ingredient, core, heart, element, component; root, radical, origin, source, stem.

3. camp, site, station, settlement, home; anchorage, mooring; starting point, point of departure.

—v. **4.** establish, found, form, build; ground, rest, root, fasten; hinge, depend, pivot, turn.

5. station, post, locate, place, install.

base², *adj.* **1.** low, mean, vile, sordid, bad, foul, wrong; depraved, debased, wicked, evil, iniquitous, sinful; debauched, degenerate, immoral, dissolute, demoralized, dissipated; abandoned, profligate, reprobate, incorrigible; corrupt, black-hearted, ignoble, sinister, miscreant, evil-minded; nefarious, flagitious, villainous, heinous, scandalous, flagrant, *Rare.* nefast, *Archaic.* felonious; disloyal, unfaithful, traitorous, treacherous, perfidious, unprincipled; disgraceful, shameful, contemptuous, discreditable, disreputable, dishonorable; reprehensible, blameworthy, culpable; scoundrelly, knavish, thievish, roguish; vicious, invidious, malicious, maleficent; contemptible, mean-spirited, *Inf.* low-down, currish; despicable, loathsome, abhorrent, odious, hateful, detestable, *Archaic.* caitiff; scurvy, insufferable, opprobrious, obnoxious.

2. dreadful, terrible, dire, grim, dark, black, baleful; accursed, cursed, damnable, damned; demonic, demoniac, diabolic, devilish, satanic, fiendish, hellish; execrable, abominable, horrible, horrid, gruesome, monstrous, atrocious.

3. offensive, unpleasant, objectionable, disagreeable; repulsive, repellent, revolting, repugnant.

4. cowardly, niddering, pusillanimous, dastardly, craven, recreant; chicken-hearted, milk-livered, lily-livered, yellow; faint-hearted, nervous, diffident, tremulous; timorous, timid, apprehensive, fearful, *Inf.* funky.

5. menial, lowly, servile, slavish, subservient; groveling, sniveling, cowering, cringing; obsequious, sycophantic, parasitical.

6. paltry, trivial, trifling, petty, slight, little, feeble; insignificant, inconsiderable, inappreciable, nugatory, worthless, trumpery; meager, scanty, measly, piddling, niggling, scrimpy, skimpy; niggardly, miserly, cheap, catchpenny.

7. counterfeit, fake, fraudulent, pseudo, pinchbeck; bogus, forged, bad, *Inf.* phony, flash, sham; spurious, supposititious, unauthentic, ungenuine, false, imitation; adulterated, alloyed, artificial, debased.

8. illegitimate, bastard, bastardly, baseborn; misbegotten, adulterine, natural, unfathered, spurious.

9. obscene, coarse, rude, vulgar, crude, gross, rough; profane, maledictory, blasphemous; smutty, foul-mouthed, scatalogical, filthy, dirty, pornographic, Fescinnine; bawdy, ribald, off-color, suggestive, unseemly, indelicate, indecorous, improper, indecent.

10. poor, wretched, sorry, abject, squalid, destitute; miserable, dismal, abysmal, dreary, *Literary.* drear; beggarly, shabby, scrubby, seedy, sleazy, abased.

baseborn, *adj.* **1.** lowborn, lowbred, vulgar, common; low, lowly, simple, humble, homely, homespun; plebian, proletarian, bourgeois; untitled, ungenteel, ungentle, unlanded; beggarly, poor, pauperish.

2. illegitimate, bastard, bastardly, base; misbegotten, adulterine, natural, unfathered, spurious.

3. contemptible, mean-spirited, currish. See **base²** (*def.* **1**).

baseless, *adj.* **1.** groundless, ungrounded, unfounded, unsubstantial, unsubstantiated, uncorroborated; unsound, erroneous, illogical, unreasonable, unreal, unjustifiable.

2. foundationless, bottomless; unsupported, free-standing.

basement, *n.* cellar, cellarage, wine cellar, storage room, *Naut.* hold.

baseness, *n.* **1.** vileness, meanness, lowness, viciousness, badness; sordidness, ignobility, foulness, sinisterness, darkness, black-heartedness; balefulness, dreadfulness, direness, direfulness, grimness; malice, maleficence, invidiousness; wickedness, iniquity, nefariousness, flagitiousness, heinousness; sinfulness, ungodliness, profanity, blasphemy; abomination, outrage, enormity, flagrancy, atrocity; damnableness, fiendishness, hellishness, devilishness; criminality, feloniousness, lawlessness; perfidy, treachery, recreancy, traitorousness, disloyalty, treason; villainy, knavery, roguery, miscreancy, rascality.

2. depravity, turpitude, degradation, depravation, debauchery; profligacy, reprobacy, reprobateness, degeneracy, dissipation; dissolution, immorality, obliquity, unchastity; wantonness, salaciousness, salacity, prurience; carnality, bestiality, perversity.

3. offensiveness, objectionableness, obnoxiousness,

disagreeableness; repulsiveness, repugnance, repellence, distastefulness; loathsomeness, odiousness, odium, hatefulness, despicability, despicableness, detestability; contemptibility, insufferableness, scurviness; opprobrium, ignominy, disgrace, obloquy; infamy, notoriety, disrepute, disreputableness; shamefulness, contemptuousness, discreditability.

4. cowardice, cowardliness, pusillanimity, poltroonery, unmanliness, *Inf.* yellow streak; dastardliness, dastardly, cravenness; faint-heartedness, diffidence, nervousness, tremulousness, *Inf.* cold feet; timidity, apprehension, dread, fearfulness, *Inf.* funk.

5. servility, subservience, lowliness, submissiveness, slavishness; obsequiousness, sycophancy, fawning, unctiousness.

6. paltriness, triviality, trivialness, pettiness; insignificance, inconsequentiality, inconsiderableness, worthlessness; meagerness, scantiness, skimpiness, slightness, feebleness.

7. obscenity, coarseness, vulgarity, crudity, grossness, rudeness; smuttiness, filthiness, dirtiness; ribaldry, *Archaic.* bawdry; unseemliness, indecorum, indecency, impropriety.

8. fraudulence, pretense, fraud, *Inf.* phoniness, speciousness, spuriousness; forgery, sham, fake, counterfeit, imitation, fabrication; adulteration, alloy, debasement, pinchbeck.

9. wretchedness, misery, abjectness; squalor, shabbiness, seediness, abasement; dreariness, dismalness, miserableness; beggary, poverty, destitution.

10. illegitimacy, bastardy.

bashful, *adj.* shy, timid, timorous, backward, hesitant, *Scot.* loathful, retiring, shrinking, unobtrusive, unostentatious; embarrassed, shamefaced, sheepish, blushing; diffident, abashed, modest, reserved, restrained, self-conscious, unconfident, *Archaic.* verecund, *Scot. and North Eng.* blate; coy, demure, meek, modest, unassuming.

bashfulness, *n.* shyness, diffidence, timidity, hesitation, timorousness; modesty, reserve, demureness, coyness, unobtrusiveness; embarrassment, sheepishness, constraint, self-consciousness.

basic, *adj.* **1.** fundamental, radical, basilar, basal; meat-and-potatoes, elementary, primary, *Inf.* gut; underlying, substrative, substratal; intrinsic, innate, inherent; essential, nitty-gritty, indispensable, necessary, vital, sustentative, supporting.

—*n.* **2. basics** fundamentals, ABC's, essentials, *Inf.* brass tacks, nuts and bolts, practicalities, hard facts, bedrock.

basically, *adv.* fundamentally, radically, basally; essentially, in substance, at heart, at bottom, *Fr. au fond;* intrinsically, inherently; primarily, firstly, for the most part, mostly, in the main.

basin, *n.* **1.** sink, tub, pan; bowl, dish, saucer, porringer, boat; receptacle, container, vessel.

2. pool, pond, puddle, reservoir; hollow, hole, cavity, dip, depression, indentation, crater.

3. bed, channel, bottom, foundation; bay, cove, inlet, harbor.

basis, *n.* **1.** base, foundation, bottom, ground, stand, support, footing; cause, grounds, occasion, warrant, right, reason, call.

2. groundwork, principle, fundamental, rudiment, radical, fundamental principle.

3. essence, core, heart, soul, heart and soul, substance, meat, pith; root, essential, principal constituent, fundamental ingredient.

bask, *v.* **1.** lie in, be exposed to; sunbathe, take a sun bath, sun oneself, tan oneself, brown oneself; warm oneself, toast oneself, *Scot. and North Eng.* beek.

2. luxuriate, indulge in, enjoy, revel, wallow, *Inf.* roll in; delight in, take pleasure in, rejoice in, be happy *or* glad of.

basket, *n.* hamper, creel, pannier, dosser, bassinet, punnet, scuttle, bucket; wicker, wickerwork; receptacle, container, holder, box, case, vessel.

bass, *adj. Music.* low, low-toned, low-pitched; deep, deep-toned, deep-pitched; sonorous, resonant, grave.

bastard, *n.* **1.** illegitimate child, bye-blow, *Brit. Sl.* get, *Archaic.* whoreson, natural child, love-child.

2. *Slang.* **a.** scoundrel, villain, rascal, cad, dog, blackguard. See **scoundrel** (*defs.* **1, 2**). **b.** failure, *All Inf.* loser, dud, washout.

—*adj.* **3.** illegitimate, misbegotten, misbegot, unlawfully begotten, baseborn, natural, unfathered.

4. spurious, adulterine, adulterous, adulterate, adulterated; feigned, faked, fake, artificial, contrived, factitious, simulated, imitation, make-believe; counterfeit, false, untrue, sham, bogus, mock, phony, ungenuine; supposititious, so-called; fraudulent, cheating, dishonest.

5. inferior, substandard, low-grade, second-rate, subnormal; imperfect, inadequate, deficient.

6. unwieldy, unmanageable, cumbersome, cumbrous, incommodious, difficult to handle, ill-proportioned; bulky, hulking, weighty, hefty; unsuitable, unfit, ill-adapted.

bastardize, *v.* **1.** illegitimatize, *Rare.* misbeget.

2. debase, degrade, devalue, demean, defile, cheapen, depreciate; adulterate, corrupt, pervert, vitiate, distort, pollute, prostitute; spoil, contaminate, ruin; dishonor, disgrace.

bastille, *n.* **1.** prison, confine, panopticon, jail, *Brit.* gaol; dungeon, oubliette, limbo; penitentiary, reformatory, house of correction, house of detention, detention home, *U.S.* workhouse.

2. keep, donjon, tower; citadel. See **bastion** (*def.* **1**).

bastion, *n.* **1.** citadel, fortress, fort, fortification, garrison; keep, donjon, stronghold, fastness; castle, chateau.

2. wall, bulwark, rampart, circumvallation, *Fort.* breastwork, *Fort.* contravallation; railing, balustrade, *Fort.* parapet, fence, palisade, *Fort.* stockade; barricade, barricado, blockade, block, barrier.

bat[1], *n.* **1.** stick, racket, mallet; club, shaft, staff, cudgel, bludgeon, truncheon, cane.

2. *Informal.* stroke, bang, hit, smack, rap, knock, buffet, blow, cuff, *Inf.* wallop, slam, swat, slap, whack, thwack, *Inf.* sock, *Inf.* whop, *Inf.* lick, *Sl.* smackeroo, *Sl.* zinger; strike, thump, tap, pat, poke, swipe, dab, jab.

3. *Slang.* spree, revel, debauch, *Inf.* binge, *Inf.* drunk, *Inf.* jag, *Inf.* bender, *Inf.* soak, *Inf.* souse, *Inf.* toot, lost weekend; orgy, party, romp, escapade, fling, caper, *Inf.* tear; wassail, carouse, carousal, bacchanalia.

4. go to bat for *Slang.* defend, stand up for, fight for, stick by; support, back up, advocate, champion, vouch for.

5. right off the bat immediately, quickly, at once, without delay, without hesitation, without another thought, *Inf.* off the top of one's head.

—*v.* **6.** strike, hit, batter, pound, lay on, pommel, pummel, *Sl.* paste; thrash, flog, switch, swat, birch, scourge, whip, horsewhip, thresh, flail; *Inf.* thump, *Inf.* lambaste, *Inf.* whale, *Sl.* whomp; smite, thwack, slap, smack; knock, cuff, buffet; *Inf.* clout, *Inf.* slug, *Inf.* slam, *Inf.* whack, *Inf.* knock [s.o.'s] block off, *Inf.* wallop, *Inf.* belt, *Sl.* sock; cudgel, bludgeon, baste, cane, bastinado, club, hammer; thrash, trounce, drub, *Inf.* wallop, *Sl.* clobber.

7. bat around *Slang.* **a.** roam, wander, ramble, drift, meander; prowl, *Sl.* mooch *or* hang around, *Sl.* fool around. **b.** ponder, debate, discuss, talk over, confer, *Inf.* kick around.

8. bat the breeze *Slang.* **a.** chat, chitchat, *Sl.* shoot the breeze, *Sl.* chin, palaver. **b.** exaggerate, brag, stretch the truth, talk nonsense; gossip, tittle-tattle, buzz.

bat², *v.* **1.** *Informal.* blink, flutter, flicker, twinkle, wink, nictitate, nictate.

2. not bat an eye *Informal.* show no emotion *or* surprise, remain unperturbed, maintain self-control, *Sl.* keep one's cool; be nonchalant, *Sl.* stay loose.

batch, *n.* **1.** grouping, bunch, group, cluster, mass, mess, aggregate; crowd, collection, set, array, assortment, conglomeration, agglomeration; combine, combination, mixture, conjunction.

2. quantity, measure, allotment, lot, amount, number, sum; volume, pan full, bowl full.

bath, *n.* **1.** wash, washing, cleaning, *Both Brit. Inf.* tub, tubbing; lavation, lavage, laving, cleansing, ablution; immersion, submergence, dunk, dunking, dip, dipping; soak, soaking, douse, dousing, rinse, rinsing, flush, flushing, shower, showering, sponge bath, sponging, douche, douching; sauna, steam bath, sitz bath, mundifying, deterging, (*of clothes*) laundering, shampoo, shampooing, lather, lathering, soaping; scrub, scrubbing, scrub-up, swabbing, mopping.

2. bath water, wash water; suds, foam; abluent, abstergent, detergent, shampoo.

3. bathtub, tub, shower, sitz bath; sink, washstand, washbowl, washbasin, basin, lavatory, lavabo, *Archaic.* laver; washtub, washbucket.

4. bathroom, washroom, wash-up, toilet, *Dial.* water closet, *Chiefly Brit.* w.c.

5. bathhouse, bagnio, steam bath, sauna, sudatorium.

6. baths spas, mineral springs, hot springs, warm springs, thermae, resorts.

7. solution, soak, preparation.

8. sweat, perspiration.

—*v.* **9.** wash, wash up, clean, clean up, scrub up, bathe, *Brit. Inf.* tub, lave, cleanse, *Chiefly Scot.* dight; lather, soap; shower, douse, rinse, flush, douche; foment, sponge, swab, wipe, mop, rub; immerse, submerge, dunk, dip; soak, steep, wet, irrigate, drench, imbue, saturate; mundify, deterge, (*of clothes*) launder, shampoo, *Brit. Dial.* buck.

bathe, *v.* **1.** wash, wash up, clean, clean up, scrub up, bath, *Brit. Inf.* tub, lave, cleanse, *Chiefly Scot.* dight; lather, soap; shower, douse, rinse, flush, douche; foment, sponge, swab, wipe, mop, rub; immerse, submerge, dunk, dip; soak, steep, wet, irrigate, drench, imbue, saturate; deterge, (*of clothes*) launder, shampoo, *Brit. Dial.* buck.

2. moisten, dampen, dew, bedew, humidify, mist; wash, suffuse, spread, overspread, overlay, screen, cover; coat, film, glaze, gloss, gelatinize, gelatinate; calcimine, whitewash, stain, tint, tinge, hue, dye.

3. splash, dash, wash against, break against, beat against, thrash against; roll, lap, undulate, surge, swell, wave, ripple; rush, flow, run, sweep.

4. surround, wrap, envelop, enfold, swaddle, cover; penetrate, pervade, permeate, smother.

5. sunbathe, take a sun bath, lie in the sun.

6. swim, float, play in the water.

—*n.* **7.** *All Brit.* swim, swimming, natation, dip, dipping, dunk, dunking; bath, bathing, soak, soaking.

bathos, *n.* **1.** anticlimax, comedown, letdown, bringdown, drop.

2. triteness, triviality, superficiality, shallowness; inanity, insipidness, emptiness, vacuity, vapidity, jejuneness; dullness, lifelessness, deadness, staleness; weakness, thinness, wishy-washiness.

3. sentimentality, oversentimentality, mawkishness, maudlinness, cloyingness, mushiness, soppiness, *Inf.* slushiness; bleeding heart, namby-pamby, mush, slush, *Inf.* goo, *Inf.* schmaltz, *Sl.* hearts and flowers.

bathroom, *n.* toilet, *Chiefly Dial.* jakes, *Sl.* john, *Sl.* can; *Chiefly Brit.* water closet *or* w.c., *Chiefly Brit.* convenience, *Brit. Sl.* loo; privy, outhouse, backhouse, stool, closet, *Chiefly New Eng.* necessary, *Brit. Sl.* bog; lavatory, latrine, rest room, wash room, comfort station, men's room, boys' *or* little boys' room, women's *or* ladies' room, girls' *or* little girls' room, powder room, lounge.

baton, *n.* staff, rod, staff of office, rod of authority, wand, truncheon, club, stick, bar; mace, scepter, crosier, crook, verge, fasces, *Class. Myth.* caduceus.

battalion, *n.* *Often Military.* army, troops, forces, garrison, phalanx, *Obs.* battalia; corps, legion, division, regiment, brigade, squadron, company, platoon, squad, section; detachment, contingent, column, formation, *U.S.* wing, square; body, group, force, unit, band, party; host, horde, multitude, mass, crowd, mob, herd, throng.

batten¹, *v.* **1.** grow fat, fatten, plump up *or* out, fill out, flesh out, round out.

2. glut, gormandize, *Archaic.* gluttonize, feast, banquet; cloy, gorge, cram, stuff, *Sl.* fill to the gills; overeat, overfeed, overstuff, overfill, overdo, overdose, *Sl.* o.d.; devour, eat greedily, raven, *Sl.* pig out, *Sl.* stuff one's face; bolt, force down, gobble, gulp, guzzle, drink like a fish, swill, *Inf.* swig; fill, surfeit, satiate, sate, satisfy, saturate, eat one's fill.

3. thrive, prosper, flourish; profit, gain, enrich oneself, feather one's nest, line one's pockets, increase one's riches, make one's pile, get all the gravy.

batten², *v.* fasten down, tie down, clamp down, screw down, nail down, cover up, board up; secure, tighten, make fast, fix; fasten, hook, latch, lock, padlock.

batter¹, *v.* **1.** beat, beat up, pound, lay on, pommel, pummel, thrash, trounce, pelt, *Sl.* paste, *Sl.* clobber, *Archaic.* belabor; maul, manhandle, rough up, *Sl.* knock around *or* about, *Sl.* give one the works; smite, hit, strike, slap, smack, cuff, buffet, punch, *Inf.* slug, *Inf.* whack, *Inf.* wallop, *Sl.* sock, *Sl.* belt; abuse, ill-use, mistreat, maltreat, ill-treat, mishandle, *Sl.* kick around.

2. bruise, wound, damage, mar, impair, injure, hurt, pain; smash, shatter, splinter, shiver, crush, crumble, fragment, disintegrate, break to pieces, pulverize.

batter², *n.* mixture, paste, *Inf.* goo, *Inf.* goop, semiliquid; base, starter.

batter³, *n.* batsman, cricketer, ballplayer, player; hitter, slugger, striker, man at the plate.

battery, *n.* **1.** series, suite, set, sequence, cycle; string, chain, ring; progression, succession, order.

2. battering, beating, pounding, pummeling, pommeling, going over, *Sl.* pasting; hitting, striking, bastinado, *Scot.* dunt, *Scot. and North Eng.* paik; whipping, thrashing, spanking, flogging.

3. assault, attack, offensive, onslaught, onset, rush, charge, blitz, *Fr. coup de main*, storming, *Obs.* brunt; raid, foray, sortie, sally; invasion, aggression, incursion, escalade; siege, besiegement, besetment, investment; bombardment, strafing, air raid, peppering, salvo, fusillade, *Both Mil.* barrage, enfilade, *Navy.* broadside.

battle, *n.* **1.** clash, struggle, strife, contention, tussle, scuffle; contest, war, bout, Armageddon; skirmish, action, brush; combat, warfare, fighting, hostilities; collision, conflict, meeting, engagement, encounter, rencounter; fight, donnybrook, *Scot.* sturt, *Inf.* scrap, *Inf.* run-in; duel, joust, tilt; confrontation, showdown; uprising, resistance, dissension, distraction; brawl, feud, affray, broil; slaughter, bloodshed, carnage, massacre, butchery; fracas, uproar, melee; campaign, crusade; tournament, tourney, competition.

2. assault, attack, offensive, onslaught; rush, blitz, blitzkrieg, storming, *Fr. coup de main, Obs.* brunt; bombardment, strafing, air raid, peppering, salvo, fusillade, *Both Mil.* barrage, enfilade, *Navy.* broadside; raid, foray, sortie, sally, invasion, aggression, incursion, escalade; siege, besiegement, besetment, investment.

3. argument, debate, discussion, polemic, logomachy, war of words; contestation, disputation, argumentation; disagreement, contention, altercation, dispute, controversy, discord; quarrel, row, squabble, dustup, spat, tiff, *Brit. Dial.* fratch, *Brit. Dial.* fratching; dissension, variance, difference of opinion, wrangling, bickering.

—*v.* **4.** contend, clash, conflict with, struggle, encounter, engage, meet; fight, give *or* do battle, combat, duel, joust, tussle, scuffle; brawl, feud, come to blows; war, make war, war against, go to war; pommel, beat, beat into the ground, batter; slaughter, massacre.

5. contest, confront, rise up against, resist, rail against, ride against; tourney, compete against.

6. assault, attack, raid, storm, charge, rush, blitz; set upon, pounce upon, open fire upon, begin hostilities, *Sl.* let [s.o.] have it, *Sl.* lay into, *Archaic.* insult.

7. argue, dispute, disagree, controvert, spar, cross swords, lock horns; wrangle, bicker, haggle, *Sl.* hassle, *Scot.* argle-bargle, *Scot.* sturt, *Scot. and North Eng.* threap, *Scot. and North Eng.* prig; quibble, cavil, nitpick, pettifog, belabor a point, split hairs.

battle cry, *n.* **1.** war whoop, war cry, Geronimo, cry of attack; yell, shout, cheer, rah.

2. slogan, motto, byword, catchword, catch phrase, buzz word, red flag, trigger word; watch word, shibboleth, pet phrase; expression, saying.

battlefield, *n.* battleground, arena, *Mil.* field, theater, theater of war, theater of operations, *Mil.* combat zone, no man's land; battle line, battlefront, *Mil.* front, *Mil. and Navy.* battle station.

battlement, *n.* **1.** wall, rampart, circumvallation, *Fort.* breastwork, *Fort.* contravallation; railing, balustrade, *Fort.* parapet, fence, palisade, *Fort.* stockade; outworks, *Fort.* ravelin, redoubt, *Fort.* redan.

2. stronghold, fastness, keep, donjon; bastion, fortification, fort, fortress, citadel, garrison.

battleship, *n.* warship, war vessel, man-of-war, floating fortress, ship of the line, destroyer, gunboat; cruiser, battle cruiser, *Inf.* battle wagon, corvette, *Naut.* monitor; dreadnought, superdreadnought, ironclad, frigate, sloop of war; torpedo boat, submarine, submersible, U-boat, submarine chaser; carrier, *U.S. Navy Inf.* flattop.

bauble, *n.* ornament, tinsel, clinquant, spangle, *Inf.* doodad; trifle, trinket, bagatelle, knickknack, gimcrack, gewgaw, toy, piece of junk.

bawdy, *adj.* **1.** obscene, pornographic, vulgar, filthy, dirty, smutty, *Sl.* raunchy, scatological; gross, crude, coarse; indecent, ribald, risqué, off-color, lewd; shameless, immodest, indecorous, unseemly, improper, indelicate, rude.

2. lustful, concupiscent, ruttish, carnal, voluptuous, bestial; salacious, libidinous, lascivious, prurient, lecherous, *Archaic.* lickerish; licentious, dissolute, unchaste, wanton, immoral, impure.

—*n.* **3.** obscenity, pornography, smut, *Sl.* raunch, dirt, filth, vulgarity, *Psychiatry.* coprolalia, coprology, scatology; coarseness, crudeness, grossness, nastiness, indelicacy, impropriety; indecency, lewdness, ribaldry, bawdry.

4. lustfulness, concupiscence, carnality, voluptuousness, bestiality; salaciousness, libidinousness, lasciviousness, prurience, lecherousness, *Archaic.* lickerishness; licentiousness, wantonness, unchastity, impurity.

bawdyhouse, *n.* brothel, bordello, *Archaic.* bordel, bagnio, *Obs.* stew, lupanar, *Obs.* kip, nunnery; house of prostitution, house of ill-fame, house of ill-repute, whorehouse, *Inf.* sporting house, *Inf.* call house; *All Sl.* call joint, cathouse, parlor house, barrelhouse, honky-tonk, pick-up joint.

bawl, *v.* **1.** shout, cry out, vociferate, exclaim, yell, whoop, *Inf.* holler; roar, bellow, blare, trumpet, bray, thunder; caterwaul, squall, screech, squeal; howl, ululate, hoot, yelp, bark, yap; hail, hallo, call out.

2. hawk, huckster, peddle, vend.

3. cry, wail, weep, lament, keen, *Scot.* greet, burst into tears, break down and cry; sob, blubber, whimper, snivel, whine, mewl.

4. bawl out *U.S. Informal.* upbraid, chastise, scold, reprimand, *Sl.* chew out. See **upbraid.**

—*n.* **5.** outcry, clamour, hubbub, hullabaloo; roar, bellow, scream, yell, shout, exclamation, ejaculation, *Inf.* holler; caterwaul, screech, cry, wail, squall, squeal; howl, hoot, whoop, yelp, yap, bark.

bay[1], *n.* **1.** harbor, cove, gulf, bight, basin, moorings; inlet, arm, sound, loch, fiord, *Chiefly Scot.* firth; estuary, mouth, *Dial.* creek.

2. hollow, valley, vale, dell, glen, dingle; recess, indentation, nook, enclosure.

bay[2], *n.* compartment, cubicle, carrel, carol, cell, stall, booth, closet, enclosure; alcove, niche, nook, cubbyhole, cubby, oriel, dormer, bay window, bow window, window seat, *Archit.* embrasure; recess, indentation, cavity, hollow, hole, space.

bay[3], *n.* **1.** howl, bark, help, bleat, baa, caterwaul, mew, ululation; wail, cry, boohoo, bawl, blubbering; vociferation, outcry, yell, shout, roar, clamor, squall, bellow, *Obs.* bell, *Inf.* hollering; snarl, growl, squawk, screech, scream, shriek, squeal.

2. at bay powerless, helpless, impotent; paralysed, motionless, frozen; cornered, trapped, treed, caught.

—*v.* **3.** howl, help, bark, bleat, baa, caterwaul, mew; wail, cry, boohoo, blubber; vociferate, yell, shout, roar, bellow, *Obs.* bell, clamor, *Inf.* holler; snarl, growl, squark, screech, scream, squeal.

4. assail, rail at, berate, revile, lash out at, vituperate, *Inf.* bawl out.

5. pursue, chase, follow; corner, trap, catch, tree; hold, keep, guard, maintain.

bay[4], *n.* **1.** reddish-brown, rust, russet, copper, bronze, auburn, hazel; terracotta, brick, ginger, henna, burnt orange.

2. roan, sorrel, chestnut; animal, horse, fox.

—*adj.* **3.** (*all horses or other animals*) roan, sorrel, chestnut, foxy; reddish-brown, auburn, hazel, rusty, rust-colored, russet, copper-colored, bronze; terracotta, clay-colored, brick-colored, burnt orange.

bayonet, *n.* **1.** blade, knife, dagger, dirk; poniard, poignard, skean, misericord.

—*v.* **2.** stab, jab, spear, knife, pierce, transpierce; lance, lancinate, spike, run through; stick, pink, plunge; impale, spit, gore, transfix; slash, gouge, tear.

bazaar, *n.* **1.** market place, market, mart, arcade; exchange, emporium, exposition; rialto, (*in ancient Rome*) forum, (*in ancient Greece*) agora.

2. fair, benefit, charity fair.

be, *v.* **1.** exist, live, be alive, have being; breathe, respire; prevail, obtain, inhere; seem, appear, look.
2. occur, happen, take place, come to pass, come about; crop up, spring up, arise, develop; hap, pass, come.
3. occupy, dwell, reside, inhabit; be located, be situated.
4. remain, stay, last, continue, stand, endure; abide, survive, persist.
5. attend, follow, escort, accompany; befall, betide, bechance.

beach, *n.* **1.** shore, seaside, water's edge, strand, sands, sand, *Chiefly Brit.* shingle; seashore, coast, seacoast, seaboard; foreshore, littoral, ground, land; rim, edge, margin, brink.
—*v.* **2.** *Nautical.* run *or* put ashore, run *or* put aground, ground, strand.

beachcomber, *n.* **1.** scavenger, forager, scrounge, scrounger; vagrant, tramp, derelict, human wreck; hobo, vagabond, *Sl.* stiff, *Sl.* bindlestiff, *Australian.* swagman, *Australian.* sundowner; rover, roamer, wanderer; loafer, shirker, *U.S. Inf.* bum; ragamuffin, tatterdemalion; outcast, pariah.
2. wave, comber, whitecap, white horse, breaker, surf; surge, swell, billow, ripple.

beached, *adj.* **1.** aground, grounded, ashore, *Obs.* graveled, stuck fast; shipwrecked, wrecked, cast away, abandoned.
2. stranded, high and dry, deserted, forsaken, left in the lurch; straitened, in straits, in a fix, at a loss; discarded, rejected, left behind; shunned, scorned, outcast, forlorn.

beacon, *n.* **1.** balefire, signal fire, smoke signal, watch fire, bonfire; torch, rocket, flare, firebrand, brand; pilot light, searchlight, flashlight; watchtower, lighthouse, pharos; warning, alarm, alert.
2. guide, guidepost, guideline, mile post, road sign, street sign, sign, signboard; mark, landmark, seamark, buoy; pointer, arrow, indicator.
—*v.* **3.** warn, alert; sign, signal, guide, direct, steer, pilot.
4. flash, glow, gleam, glimmer, beam, shine, glitter.

bead, *n.* **1.** globule, spherule, spheroid, oval; pellet, ball, shot, pea, pill; blob, bubble; dewdrop, pearl, tear; drop, droplet, glob, gutta; dab, lump, mass; particle, speck, dot, iota.
2. beads a. necklace, necklet, choker, pendant, lavaliere, chain. **b.** braid, cord; wampum, peag; trimming, passementrie. **c.** rosary, chaplet, devotions, prayers, Ave Marias, Aves, Hail Marys.
—*v.* **3.** (*all with beads*) decorate, embellish, ornament, adorn, trim, bedeck; string, thread.

beak, *n.* **1.** bill, nib, neb, pecker.
2. *Slang.* nose, snout, *Sl.* nozzle, *Sl.* schnozzola. See **nose.**
3. *Nautical.* **a.** ram, rostrum. **b.** prow, bow, stem, bowsprit.

beaked, *adj.* hooked, crooked, aquiline, pointed, sharp; hook-nosed, beak-nosed, Roman-nosed, crook-billed; beak-like, beak-shaped, bill-shaped.

beaker, *n.* glass, goblet, mug, stein; tankard, flagon, hogshead, horn, pot; cup, chalice.

beam, *n.* **1.** board, plank, timber, scantling, two-by-four; stick, strip, lath, furring, stud; rod, pole, *Naut.* spar, *Naut.* boom; girder, support, prop, brace, pile; rafter, crossbeam, tie beam, balk, joist, lintel; frame, trestle, transverse support.
2. ray, shaft, gleam, patch, spot, pencil; flash, streak, glare, lightning, coruscation, fulguration; glow, shine, shimmer, sparkle, flicker, twinkle; glitter, glint, glimmer, glistening; flutter, flare, spark, scintilla.
3. suggestion, impression, hint, indication, inkling, bit; glimmering, trace, vestige, faint glimpse, brief manifestation, evidence.
—*v.* **4.** shine, radiate, irradiate, glow, effulge, phosphoresce, incandesce; flash, streak, glare, glint, dart, fulgurate; glitter, twinkle, sparkle, flicker, flutter, scintillate, coruscate; glisten, *Archaic.* glister, glimmer, shimmer.

bear[1], *v.* **1.** (*all of animals*) give birth, bring forth, lay, drop; litter, hatch, spawn, cast; foal, lamb, calve, whelp, pup, kitten.
2. produce, yield, give forth, blossom, flower, bear fruit, fructify; breed, conceive, beget, engender, germinate, generate, reproduce, propagate.
3. support, hold up, sustain, uphold, shoulder, lift; bolster up, shore up, upbear, prop, underprop, underpin, underset, brace; cradle, pillow.
4. press, push, bear down, thrust; drive, compel, coerce, force, enforce, constrain; influence, affect.
5. behave, conduct, comport, act, deport, demean; carry oneself, manage oneself, govern oneself, regulate oneself; proceed, operate, function.
6. suffer, endure, undergo, experience, go through, pass through; encounter, live out, meet with, meet, taste, fare; support, weather, *Obs.* aby, forbear, *Chiefly Scot.* thole, *Scot. and North Eng.* dree; bear up, keep on, carry on, take it, brave it out, *Inf.* tough it out, *Inf.* stick it out, *Sl.* sweat it out, *Inf.* go through the mill, *Inf.* take it on the chin; *Inf.* hang in, *Inf.* keep the faith, keep one's chin up, *Sl.* stand the gaff.
7. hold out against, withstand, sustain without yielding, tolerate, take patiently, brook, submit to, abide, stand, put up with; permit, allow; swallow, digest, stomach, pocket.
8. warrant, signify, permit, admit, allow, be capable of, be worthy of.
9. carry, bring, tote, move; remove, conduct, haul, fetch, transport, displace, portage; (*in reference to gossip or tales*) transmit, spread.
10. (*as testimony*) render, afford, give; yield, furnish, supply; impart, bestow, confer.
11. lead, guide, take, escort, usher, conduct, pilot, direct, orientate; attend, accompany.
12. have, possess, be entitled to, contain, hold, be furnished with, be marked with; (*as authority*) use, exercise, utilize.
13. exhibit, show, display; put on, don, assume, accept, be marked with.
14. bear on *or* **upon** appertain, belong, pertain, touch upon; affect, concern, regard, refer, relate, be pertinent.
15. move, go, bend, turn, deviate, curve, fork, diverge; be directed at, be aimed at, be pointed at.
16. bear down on *or* **upon a.** press down, weigh down, burden, strain, encumber; coerce, compel, get after. **b.** strive toward, focus on, zero in on; approach, advance upon, move upon, draw near. **c.** rush upon, converge upon; attack, assail, march against. **d.** *All Naut.* approach, set in towards, veer towards, sail towards.
17. bear out substantiate, confirm, uphold, ratify, endorse, warrant; sustain, maintain, sanction, defend; authenticate, authorize, establish, verify, justify, vindicate, make good; support, circumstantiate, corroborate.

bear[2], *n.* **1.** churl, boor, curmudgeon, brute, barbarian, yahoo, *Inf.* goop, *Chiefly Scot.* tyke, *Brit. Sl.* mucker; lout, oaf, dolt, clod, clodhopper, clodpoll, gawk, looby, lubber, ox, *Chiefly Scot.* cuddy, *Inf.* lummox, *Sl.* klutz, *Sl.* galoot, *Sl.* lug, *Brit. Sl.* joskin.

2. grouch, crank, crab, sorehead, hothead, crosspatch, *Sl.* bitch.

3. *Stock Exchange.* shortseller, short, underseller, scalper, speculator.

bearable, *adj.* endurable, sufferable, tolerable, brookable, *Obs. Rare.* abideable; passable, admissible, supportable; experienceable.

beard, *n.* **1.** *Inf.* beaver, full beard, *Med.* barba; whiskers, mutton chops, burnsides, sideburns; goatee, Vandyke, imperial; stubble, bristles, five-o'clock shadow.

2. barb, point, spine, spur, jag, nib, prong, tine, cusp.

3. defy, brave, oppose, face, look in the face, confront, affront, stare down, stand up against, dare, double-dare.

—*v.* **4.** take the bull by the horns, bell the cat, pluck by the beard, slap [s.o.'s] face; tempt Providence, go in harm's way, skate on thin ice, dance on a razor's edge, march up to the cannon's mouth, beard the lion in his den.

bearded, *adj.* **1.** whiskered, bewhiskered, goateed; unshaven, stubbly, bristly.

2. tufted, *Bot.* awned, *Bot.* aristate, *Bot.* papose, *Zool., Bot.* barbate.

3. barbed, spined, tined, horned; sharp, pointed, sharp-pointed.

beardless, *adj.* **1.** clean-shaven, smooth-shaven, smooth-faced, glabrous-cheeked, whiskerless.

2. adolescent, immature, callow, green, inexperienced.

bearer, *n.* **1.** carrier, messenger, courier, postman, porter, bringer; envoy, herald, emissary, harbinger; estafette, postrider; transporter, conveyor, conductor; upholder, supporter, sustainer, maintainer.

2. holder, incumbent, occupant, occupier; resident, dweller, tenant.

bearing, *n.* **1.** manner, demeanor, air, attitude, temperament; carriage, gait, posture, pose, port; comportment, behavior, conduct, deportment; front, mien, aspect; appearance, look, cast, presence.

2. procreation, germination, propagation, reproduction; fructification, fecundation, conception; pregnancy, gestation, gravidity, fecundity; maturation, generation, incubation, breeding; (*all of animals*) heat, rut, berry.

3. spawning, genesis, giving birth, birth, childbirth, *Obs.* geniture; parturition, pullulation, producing, yielding; delivery, (*all of animals*) dropping, hatching, laying, casting.

4. enduring, sustaining, abiding, standing; withstanding, tolerating, weathering, suffering, braving, *Inf.* toughing, brooking, biding; putting up with, taking, swallowing, stomaching; undergoing, submitting to, *Chiefly Scot.* tholing, *Archaic.* forbearing, *Obs.* abying.

5. reference, relation, correlation; relevancy, pertinence, pertinency, germaneness, applicability, relativity; connection, association, respect, regard, concern; resemblance, affinity, correspondence, likeness, similitude, similarity; aptness, suitability, appositeness; dependency, contingency.

6. pivot, swivel, caster, ball bearing, ball, ball and socket; roller, trundle, wheel, trolley; pin, bolt, *Mach.* gudgeon, pintle.

7. **bearings** aim, direction, course, track, *Naut.* tack; set, inclination, bent, drift, trend; position, location, situation, placement.

bearish, *adj.* **1.** surly, cantankerous, irascible, crabbed, iracund, unfriendly, ill-natured, obnoxious, choleric; brusque, peppery, crusty, grumpy, grouchy, dyspeptic, snappish, waspish, snarling, growling; cross, feisty, huffy, irritable, peevish, cranky, bilious, testy, touchy, ill-tempered, bad-tempered, quick-tempered, short-tempered; fractious, contentious, quarrelsome, argumentative, caviling, disagreeable, *Inf.* ornery, *Inf.* bitchy, *Inf.* ugly; caustic, mordant, mordacious, sarcastic; sharp, uncivil, rough, harsh; abrupt, curt, short, terse, blunt.

2. churlish, boorish, loutish, oafish, doltish, cloddish, lubberly, loobyish, lumpen; crude, crass, beastly, bestial; rude, vulgar, uncouth, coarse, ill-bred, ill-mannered, unmannerly.

beast, *n.* **1.** creature, animal, mammal, quadruped.

2. brute, savage, heathen, pagan, hellkite; monster, ogre, troglodyte, wild man, Yahoo; barbarian, Vandal, Goth, Hun, Tartar; boor, rustic, churl, dolt, lout, clod, oaf, *Archaic.* carl; bumpkin, yokel, *Sl.* rube, *Sl.* hick, *Disparaging.* bogtrotter, hobnail, *Inf.* hayseed, kern, yahoo, *Sl.* lug; swine, pig, hog, glutton.

3. sensualist, voluptary, libertine, rake, profligate; satyr, lecher, goat, seducer, fornicator, adulterer, Bluebeard.

beastlike, *adj.* **1.** theroid, bestial, animalic, animalian, therimorphic.

2. primitive, wild, barbaric, barbarian, barbarous, uncivilized, heathen; rough, rugged, coarse, beastly, bearish, brutish; savage, fierce, ferocious, brutal; mean, vicious, cruel, ruthless.

3. boorish, churlish, loutish, oafish, doltish, cloddish, lubbery, loobyish, lumpen; crude, crass, rude, vulgar, lewd, wanton; uncouth, ill-bred, ill-mannered, unmannerly, uncivil.

beastly, *adj.* **1.** theroid, bestial, beastlike, animalic, animalian, therimorphic.

2. primitive, wild, barbaric, barbarian, barbarous, heathen; savage, fierce, brutal, inhuman; rough, rugged, coarse, bearish, brutish, boorish, churlish, loutish, oafish; swinish, boarish, piggish, hoggish, gluttonous, greedy; unclean, dirty, filthy, smutty, obscene, *Sl.* raunchy.

3. base, low, mean, sordid, bad; execrable, abominable, horrible, horrid, atrocious; vile, abhorrent, repulsive, loathsome, odious, hateful, detestable, despicable; offensive, nasty, unpleasant, objectionable, obnoxious, disagreeable; a beast of a.

4. carnal, sensual, lustful, libidinous, salacious; lascivious, licentious, lecherous, *Archaic.* lickerish, prurient; immoral, dissolute, profligate, unchaste, wanton, debauched, debased, dissipated, degenerate.

beat, *v.* **1.** batter, pound, lay on, pommel, pummel, *Sl.* paste, *Archaic.* belabor; thrash, flog, lash, switch, birch, scourge, flagellate, whip, horsewhip, curry, strap, thresh, flail, cowhide, spank, *Brit. Dial.* yerk, *Inf.* tan [s.o.'s] hide, *Inf.* trim, *Inf.* thump, *Inf.* lace, *Inf.* lambaste, *Inf.* whale, *Sl.* whomp; hit, strike, smite, thwack, slap, smack, *Australian.* ding; punch, knock, cuff, buffet, box, sandbag, *Scot. and North Eng.* paik, *Scot.* dunt, *Inf.* clout, *Inf.* slug, *Inf.* whack, *Dial.* hit [s.o.] up side the head, *Inf.* knock [s.o.'s] block off, *Inf.* wallop, *Inf.* crown, *Sl.* conk, *Sl.* bash, *Sl.* belt, *Sl.* sock, *Sl.* plug, *U.S. Sl.* biff, *Sl.* bop; cudgel, fustigate, bludgeon, baste, cane, bastinado, club, hammer, sledge hammer; maul, manhandle, rough up, *Inf.* give it to, *Sl.* knock around *or* about, *Sl.* give [s.o.] the business, *Sl.* give [s.o.] the works, *Sl.* give [s.o.] what for, *Sl.* work over, *Sl.* let [s.o.] have it, *Sl.* lay into.

2. (*all of water*) lap, wash, bathe, break against, dash against.

3. flutter, flap, flop, wave, undulate, vacillate, fluctuate; toss about, agitate, vibrate, quiver, shake, tremble, shiver; rotate, whirl, wheel, turn, revolve.

4. (*all of food*) stir, mix, blend; whip, whisk, froth.
5. shape, form, mold, forge, hammer; generate, create, fashion, model, manufacture, make, fabricate; produce, cause, effect, bring about, accomplish.
6. tread, trample, wear, groove, channel, make a way.
7. (*often fol. by* up) thrash, trounce, drub, *Inf.* wallop, *Inf.* whale, *Sl.* clobber, *Sl.* pin one's ears back.
8. defeat, trounce, rout, vanquish, worst, *Inf.* lick, *Sl.* shellac, *Sl.* pulverize; conquer, master, overthrow, overpower, overwhelm; break, subdue, quell, quench, thwart, check, stop; quash, destroy, crush, trample, do for, *Sl.* do in.
9. win over [s.o.], place first, get the better of, *Sl.* beat out; surpass, eclipse, exceed, excel, transcend, top, outdo, outstrip, do more for [s.o.]; overcome, prevail over.
10. throb, pound, thump; pulsate, pulse, palpitate.
—*n.* 11. stroke, blow, bastinado, *Scot.* dunt, *Scot. and North Eng.* paik, punch, box, knockout, *Both Boxing.* left, right, *Inf.* whomp, *Inf.* wallop, *Both Brit. Dial.* douse, yerk, *U.S. Sl.* biff, *Sl.* bop; buffet, cuff, strike, hit, thwack, slap, smack, *Inf.* whack, *Inf.* clout, *Sl.* conk, *Sl.* bash.
12. tap, click, clap, tick, ticktock.
13. throb, thump, pulsation, pulse, palpitation.
14. run, round, circuit, orbit, course, route, path, tack, tour, journey; assignment, duty, job, task, chore; zone, area, neighborhood.

beaten, *adj.* 1. trodden, well-trodden, trampled, much traveled; worn, well-used, over-used, threadbare, napless, smooth.
2. defeated, trounced, routed, vanquished, *Sl.* shellacked, *Sl.* pulverized; conquered, overthrown, overpowered, overwhelmed; broken, subdued, quelled, quenched; thwarted, checked, stopped, held back; quashed, destroyed, crushed.
3. exhausted, prostrate, prostrated, drained, spent, worn out, played out, *U.S. Inf.* tuckered, *Inf.* beat, *Inf.* done in, *Inf.* done for; fagged, jaded, depleted, used up; fatigued, tired, wearied, weary, drooping, ready to drop; toilworn, wayworn, footsore; haggard, emaciated, wasted, drawn, hollow-eyed; enervated, enervate, languid, debilitated, weakened, weak, enfeebled, feeble, faint, emasculated, emasculate, *Inf.* groggy.
4. (*all of food*) whipped, whisked, frothed; stirred, mixed, blended; pounded, tenderized.

beatific, *adj.* 1. blissful, heavenly, celestial, paradisical, paradisiac, Elysian; transcendent, transcendental, supernatural; divine, sacred, angelic, saintly.
2. rapturous, ecstatic, enchanting, enrapturing, transporting, enravishing; wonderful, glorious, delightful; happy, glad, joyful.

beatify, *v.* 1. enrapture, transport, enravish, enthrall, entrance, enchant, charm; gladden, make joyful, rejoice, *Archaic.* felicitate.
2. declare blessed, enshrine in the canon of saints; laud, venerate, revere; sanctify, hallow, bless, consecrate.

beating, *n.* 1. battering, pounding, pommeling, pummeling, pelting, going over, *Sl.* pasting; thrash, thrashing, flogging, lashing, flagellation, whipping, spanking, *Inf.* tanning; smacking, slapping, *Inf.* whacking; cudgeling, fustigation, bludgeoning, basting, flogging, clubbing, hammering.
2. defeat, trouncing, rout, vanquishment, *Sl.* shellacking; conquest, subjugation, overthrow, overpowering; repulse, rebuff, thwarting; perdition, destruction, ruin, deathblow.
3. pulsation, pulsating, pulse, pulsing, palpitation, palpitating, throb, throbbing.
4. (*all of water*) lapping, washing, bathing, breaking, dashing.

beatitude, *n.* 1. blessedness, sainthood, sanctity, saintliness; serenity, peace, heavenly peace, the peace that surpasses all understanding; bliss, heavenly bliss, blissfulness, joy, holy joy, joyfulness; delight, happiness, felicity; exaltation, elation, rapture, divine rapture.
2. blessing, benediction; encomium, eulogy; precept, commandment, moral; guide, teaching.

beau, *n.* 1. escort, squire, date, cavalier, partner; suitor, wooer, pursuer, admirer, adorer; lover, swain, inamorato, amorist, gallant; sweetheart, spark, *Inf.* flame, love, beloved, Romeo; fiancé, betrothed, young man, boy friend; paramour, intimate, *Fr. intime,* friend, *It. cicisbeo.*
2. dandy, jack-a-dandy, fop, coxcomb, popinjay; exquisite, *Sl.* swell, dude, blade, silk-stocking; puppy, jackanapes.
—*v.* 3. escort, squire, date, take out, go with see.

beautiful, *adj.* 1. comely, attractive, handsome, seemly, becoming, sightly, *Inf.* eye-filling, good-looking, pulchritudinous, *Chiefly Literary.* beauteous; fair, pretty, *Chiefly Scot.* bonny, shapely, well-proportioned, glamorous, sexy; charming, engaging, captivating, enthralling, enchanting, alluring, fascinating, winsome, winning, bewitching, enticing, tempting, seductive, ravishing.
2. personable, pleasant, lovely, *Inf.* divine; graceful, elegant, artistic; delicate, dainty.
3. excellent, superior, magnificent, gorgeous, fine; first-rate, first-class, prime, choice, select; exquisite, rare, superb, matchless, unequalled, nonpareil.
4. resplendent, dazzling, radiant, shining, lustrous, effulgent.

beautify, *v.* 1. adorn, prettify, grace, smarten, titivate, dress up, embellish, elaborate; enhance, heighten, set off, enrich, sweeten; bedeck, deck, deck out, array, ornament, fret, decorate, emblazon, garnish; spangle, bespangle, embroider, emboss, illuminate; paint, polish, burnish, gild, furbish, restore.
2. (*usu. of oneself*) dress, primp, prink, prank, preen, *Archaic.* prune, *Sl.* doll up, *Sl.* dude up.

beauty, *n.* 1. loveliness, comeliness, fairness, prettiness, pulchritude; attractiveness, eye appeal, allurement, glamour, charm, grace, winsomeness; gracefulness, elegance, artistry, delicacy, fineness; proportion, balance, symmetry.
2. belle, goddess, Venus, *Inf.* knockout, *Sl.* looker, *Sl.* dish, *Sl.* babe; siren, seductress, charmer, enchantress.
3. advantage, asset, strong point, strength; benefit, blessing, boon.

becalm, *v.* (*all of sailing vessels*) stop, halt, stall, bring to a standstill; take the wind out of one's sails.

because, *conj.* 1. since, as, whereas, inasmuch as, forasmuch as; due to the fact that, in view of the fact that, seeing that.
—*adv.* 2. on account, by reason, by virtue, through; due to, owing to, thanks to, for; as a result, consequently, therefore.

beck, n. nod, gesture, signal, summons. See **beckon** (*def.* 3).

beckon, *v.* 1. nod, gesture, gesticulate, crook the finger at; wave, signal, give a sign, call, summon, bid.
2. lure, attract, draw, intrigue, interest, tempt, invite, tantalize; allure, entice, decoy, lead astray, seduce; inveigle, induce, beguile, persuade, charm, coax.
—*n.* 3. nod, gesture, movement, gesticulation; sign,

signal, wave, summons, call; glance, look, wink.

becloud, *v.* **1.** cloud up *or* over, overcast, gray, darken, get dark, blacken; dim, bedim, fade, pale.

2. obscure, befog, eclipse, cloud, overshadow, adumbrate, cast a gloom over, shadow, shade; conceal, hide, screen, veil, shroud, shield, mask, cover, protect, cloak, curtain; overlay, overspread, blanket, envelop, enwrap, surround, enclose, shut in, close off.

3. confuse, obscure, obfuscate, befog, make indistinct, make unclear *or* fuzzy; muddle, mix up, bewilder, confound, perplex, puzzle, mystify, nonplus.

become, *v.* **1.** grow into, develop into, pass into, evolve into, ripen into, mature into; change into, turn into, alter into, convert into, transform into; mellow into, wax into; come to be, go, get, turn out to be.

2. happen, occur, come about, come to pass, turn out; befall, chance, *Archaic.* bechance, hap.

3. suit, fit, grace, enhance, enrich, adorn, garnish, embellish; behoove, befit, beseem.

4. become of happen to, come of, be the fate of.

becoming, *adj.* **1.** comely, attractive, handsome, *Chiefly Dial.* gainly, *Chiefly U.S. Inf.* cute; stylish, fashionable, chic, tasteful.

2. suitable, proper, fit, fitting, apt, appropriate, apposite, meet; decorous, seemly, graceful; right, decent, worthy, befitting; congruous, accordant, concordant, conformable, consistent, in keeping with.

bed, *n.* **1.** bunk, cot, *Brit.* lair, *U.S. Sl.* sack, *Brit. Sl.* kip; pallet, *Inf.* tick, mattress, sleeping bag, *Chiefly Brit.* palliasse couch, lounge, chaise longue, recliner, hammock, litter, stretcher; bedstead, bedframe, four-poster, high-riser, truckle *or* trundle bed, day bed, platform bed, bunk bed, water bed; crib, cradle, bassinet.

2. sleeping, sleep time, dreamland, land of Nod; good night, *Inf.* nighty night, *Mil.* taps.

3. lodging, lodgement, berth, roost, resting place, room, chamber, accommodation; *All Mil.* billet, quarters, quarterage, barracks *or* barrack, cantonment, casern *or* caserne, *Sl.* the Q; *All Mil.* camp, encampment, bivouac.

4. marriage, matrimony, wedlock, nuptials, espousal, connubiality, conjugality.

5. plot, grounds, plat, lot, space, *Hort.* flat; garden, tillage, planting; plants, flowers, foliage, seedlings, growth, *Bot.* cultivation.

6. base, basis, foundation, matrix, *Anat.* fundus, *Archit.* plinth, *Archit.* socle; groundwork, grounding, footing, support, prop, stand; platform, floor, surface; bottom, substructure, substratum, underneath; basin, channel.

7. layer, stratum, tier, level; band, belt, zone; seam, vein, lode, deposit.

—*v.* **8.** berth, sleep, billet, quarter, encamp; accommodate, make room for, lodge, provide lodging for, house, shelter, roof, put a roof over [s.o.'s] head; keep, have as a guest *or* lodger, *Inf.* put up.

9. tuck in, cover up, bed [s.o.] down, put [s.o.] to bed, show to one's room.

10. bottom, ground, found, base; set, fix, settle, establish, set up.

11. embed, inlay, insert, set into, fit into; immerge, immerse, implant, plant, bury, *Obs.* inter.

12. seduce, entice, allure, lure; take to bed, go to bed with, spend the night with, sleep with, bunk down with.

13. retire, turn in, bed down, *Sl.* hit the hay, *Sl.* hit the sack, *Sl.* sack out; recline, rest, nap, snooze, go to sleep, *Sl.* conk out.

14. sojourn, roost, spend the night, sleep over, stay, dwell at; room, camp, camp out, bivouac, *Inf.* bunk.

bedaub, *v.* **1.** besmear, smear, smirch, smudge; soil, stain, smutch, begrime; daub all over, blot, spot, blemish, splash, bespatter; blotch, mar, deface.

2. bedeck, deck out, bedizen, ornament gaudily *or* excessively; overdress, dress to the teeth, *Sl.* doll up, *Sl.* dude up, deck oneself out like Mrs. Astor's pet horse.

bedclothes, *n.* coverings, bedding, bedclothing; covers, coverlets, blankets, quilts, comforters, counterpanes, bedspreads; sheets, sheet blankets, pillowcases, pillowslips, pillow shams.

bedding, *n.* **1.** covers, blankets, sheets. See **bedclothes.**

2. litter, straw, hay, tick filling.

bedeck, *v.* **1.** deck out, bedaub, bedizen, overdecorate, decorate gaudily *or* excessively.

2. array, decorate, ornament, beautify, enhance.

bedevil, *v.* **1.** torment, agonize, distress, harrow, worry; harass, tease, pester, annoy, chaff, vex, provoke, irritate, *Sl.* bug.

2. possess, bewitch, seduce, entice; put *or* cast a spell on, becharm, mesmerize, hypnotize; witch, hex, *Inf.* spook.

3. confuse, muddle, confound, frustrate; befuddle, rattle, ruffle.

4. beset, hamper, cause trouble, *Sl.* trip up.

bedew, *v.* wet, dampen, moisten, sprinkle, besprinkle; humidify, spray, water; soak, drench, sop, imbue, make dank *or* muggy.

bedim, *v.* dim, cloud, becloud, overcast, blot out; shade, shadow, darken, cover, screen, veil, cloak; eclipse, overshadow, envelop; obscure, befog, obfuscate.

bedizen, *v.* bedaub, bedeck, dress gaudily. See **bedaub** (*def.* **2**).

bedlam, *n.* **1.** insane asylum, madhouse, *Sl.* crazy house, *Sl.* booby hatch. *Sl.* nut house, *Sl.* cuckoo's nest, *Sl.* loony bin; sanatorium, sanctuary, asylum, retreat.

2. uproar, pandemonium, confusion, clamor, commotion, hubbub, furor; disorder, disarray, chaos, anarchy; jumble, litter, clutter.

bedlamite, *n.* lunatic, madman, maniac, insane *or* crazy *or* deranged person, *Sl.* loony, *Sl.* nut, *Sl.* screwball, *Sl.* cuckoo; phrenetic, demoniac, energumen.

bedraggle, *v.* draggle, muddy, begrime, sully, soil, smutch, besmirch; soak, soak through, drench, wet, saturate, besot; muss, mess, mess up, stain, beslobber.

bedraggled, *adj.* draggled, muddied, grimy, sullied, soiled, smutched, besmirched, sloppy, filthy; soggy, dripping, soaking wet, wringing wet, drenched, drenched to the skin, sodden, splashed; slovenly, untidy, mussed messy, unkempt, stained, dirty, unclean.

bedrid, *adj.* **1.** See **bedridden.**

2. worn out, exhausted, tired, *Sl.* pooped, *Sl.* fagged out; decrepit, weakened, feeble, infirm; incapacitated, disabled, helpless.

bedridden, *adj.* confined, confined to bed, *Inf.* flat on one's back, *Inf.* down and out, encouched; homebound, shut-in, handicapped.

beefy, *adj.* **1.** brawny, muscular, strong, powerful, burly, sturdy, strapping, robust, stalwart, bouncing; thickset, stocky, solid, heavy, chunky; bulky, hulky, hulking; massive, massy, ponderous, gargantuan, elephantine.

2. obese, overweight, corpulent, gross; paunchy, potbellied, round-bellied, big-bellied, abdominous, *Inf.* bay-windowed, *Inf.* corporational, *Sl.* beer-bellied, *Obs.* gorbellied.

3. fat, plump, fleshy, rotund, buxom, well-fed; pudgy,

Chiefly Brit. podgy, chubby, portly, stout; dumpy, squab, lumpish; swollen, bloated, puffy; large, big, ample, full.

beeline, *n.* direct route, direct line, straight line, straight course, *Chiefly U.S.* air-line; short cut, cut, shortest distance, shortest way.

beer, *n.* malt, ale, porter, stout, *Brit. Inf.* swipes, *Sl.* suds, lager, bock, liquor.

beetle[1], *n.* **1.** hammer, beater, masher, smasher, masticator.

—*v.* **2.** beat, batter, pound, ram, lay on, pommel, pummel, crush, pelt, *Sl.* paste.

3. hammer, forge, shape, form, mold.

beetle[2], *adj.* **1.** overhanging, hanging over, leaning over, jutting over, pendent, swelling over; protruding, projecting, sticking out, poking out, shooting out, jutting out, bulging, prominent.

—*v.* **2.** project, protrude, jut out, stick out, poke out, shoot out, bulge, swell out, pout, belly, bunch; overhang, hang over, *Rare.* impend over, lean over, extend beyond, swell over, sag.

3. tower over, stand over, overtop, look down on.

befall, *v.* happen, *Archaic.* hap, occur, take place, supervene, betide, chance, *Archaic.* bechance, *Archaic.* arrive; transpire, intervene, crop up; become, come into being, come to pass, come about, fall, materialize; result, eventuate, turn out, prove; ensue, issue, arise, flow out, emanate; happen to, overtake.

befitting, *adj.* fitting, fit, meet, *Brit. Dial.* gradely, *Fr. comme il faut*; suitable, proper, becoming, seemly, decorous, decent; appropriate, apt, apposite, apropos; relevant, germane, *Latin. ad rem,* to the point, pertinent, pat.

befog, *v.* **1.** becloud, darken, obscure. See **becloud** (*def.* **2**).

2. confuse, obfuscate, make indistinct. See **becloud** (*def.* **3**).

befool, *v.* **1.** fool, dupe, hoax, humbug, *Brit. Inf.* gammon; bamboozle, delude, deceive, beguile, mislead; hoodwink, pull the wool over [s.o.'s] eyes, cozen, bluff, take in; seduce, charm, lie to; lure, allure, entice, induce, inveigle.

2. trick, spoof, outwit, overreach, circumvent, get around, put one over on; swindle, cheat, defraud, fleece, rook, gull, chouse, stack the deck, *Inf.* gyp, *Sl.* gaff; pluck, mulct, victimize, exploit, play on *or* upon, take advantage of, *Inf.* diddle, *Inf.* do.

before, *adv.* **1.** in front, up front, out front, in advance, in the van, in the lead, in the forefront, in the foreground; ahead, *Inf.* dead ahead, forward; first, foremost, headmost.

2. previously, formerly, hitherto, heretofore, ere, erenow, *Archaic.* beforetime; in the past, in times past, in days gone by, in the good old days.

3. earlier, sooner, *Dial.* afore; early, beforehand, ahead of time, with time to spare, betimes; in anticipation.

—*prep.* **4.** in front of, in advance of, ahead of, forward of.

5. previous to, prior to, earlier than; on the eve of, just before, right before.

6. in preference to, rather than, sooner than.

7. in the presence of, in the sight of, in plain sight of, in open sight of; in the regard of, in the face of, to one's face, before one's eyes, under the nose of, under the eyes of.

befriend, *v.* **1.** make friends with, acquaint, familiarize, make familiar, shake hands with; embrace, welcome, hail, receive with open arms, hold out a hand to, open the door to; take in tow, look after, keep an eye on, foster, protect, watch out for.

2. aid, assist, help, abet; serve, avail, bestead, accommodate, oblige; minister to, cater to, wait on *or* upon, attend; relieve, ameliorate, alleviate, mitigate, palliate, salve; comfort, soothe, solace, console, succor; contribute, boost, lend a hand, *Inf.* pitch in, *Inf.* chip in; give a boost, give a lift, do one's part, lift a hand, lift a finger; support, back, back up, second, uphold, stand by, *Inf.* stick up for, *Inf.* go to bat for; sustain, maintain, endorse, smile upon; promote, patronize, further, advance, forward, advocate.

befuddle, *v.* **1.** intoxicate, inebriate, besot, *Obs.* fuzzle; fluster, *Sl.* plaster, *Sl.* stew, *Sl.* sozzle.

2. stupefy, benumb, stun, daze; confuse, muddle, fuddle, jumble; confound, ruffle, rattle, boggle; obfuscate, befog, obscure, becloud, bedim; baffle, perplex, mystify, bewilder.

befuddled, *adj.* **1.** intoxicated, inebriated, inebrious, bibacious, crapulent, crapulous; drunk, drunken, sodden, besotted, sotted, awash, *Literary.* in one's cups; under the influence, the worse for liquor, under the weather; saturated, soused, full, *Scot.* fou; tipsy, grogged, *Archaic.* groggy, woozy, bleary-eyed, pie-eyed, glassy-eyed; punchy, *Inf.* punch-drunk, slap-happy, giddy; far-gone, staggering, staggering drunk, drunk as a lord, drunk as a piper, drunk as a fiddler, drunk as a skunk *or* owl; merry, happy, gay, jolly.

2. *All Inf.* boozy, tight, lit, lit up, lit to the gills, illuminated, liquored-up; half seas over, three *or* four sheets to the wind, under the sauce, off-color; pickled, lathered, high, high as a kite, fried to one's tonsils, full to the back teeth, primed to the sticking point; mellow, with a jag on, feeling good, feeling no pain; blind, blind drunk, dead drunk, paralyzed, out of it, out cold, out; under the table, helpless, passed out, in bed with one's boots on.

3. *All Sl.* loaded, lubricated, oiled, well-oiled; stewed, stewed to the gills, tanked, fried, boiled, *Brit.* pissed, *Brit.* bevied; primed, gassed, bombed, stoned, zonked, ripped, blitzed, scrooched, whiffed, whoozled; polluted, crocked, cocked, cocked to the gills, cock-eyed, canned, sloshed, squiffy, potted, plastered, sozzled, crocko; stiff, ossified, stinko, stinking, plotched, shellacked, swacked, screwed, blotto, smashed, skunk-drunk.

4. confused, muddled, fuddled, jumbled; dazed, stunned, numbed, benumbed; obfuscated, befogged, obscured, beclouded; baffled, perplexed, mystified, bewildered, puzzled, disconcerted; confounded, ruffled, rattled, boggled.

beg, *v.* **1.** ask for, apply for, seek, request, ask, call upon; appeal to, implore, beseech, entreat, plead, *Brit. Inf.* prig, pray, crave; petition, solicit, supplicate, obtest, adjure, conjure, *Rare.* sue; urge, press, importune, insist, demand.

2. seek alms, *Inf.* panhandle, pass the plate *or* cup *or* hat, *Sl.* bum, go from door to door; hustle, use, impose on; mooch off, sponge off, live off, cadge, *Scot.* sorn.

3. avoid, evade, beat around the bush, dodge, get around, escape.

beget, *v.* **1.** father, sire, procreate, generate, engender, get; breed, propagate, reproduce, spawn; impregnate, *Biol.* fecundate, *Biol.* fertilize.

2. cause, produce, effect, effectuate, make happen, bring about, bring to pass, give rise to, occasion.

beggar, *n.* **1.** cadger, *Inf.* panhandler, mendicant, beadsman, almsman, *Scot.* gaberlunzie; moocher, *Inf.* sponger, *Sl.* schnorrer, parasite, leech, hanger-on.

2. pauper, ragamuffin, tatterdemalion, hobo, *Sl.* bindle stiff; tramp, vagrant, beachcomber, vagabond, drifter; loafer, idler, *U.S. Inf.* bum, good-for-nothing, *Fr. vaurien;* derelict, castaway, outcast; rogue, knave, scamp, scoundrel; (*collectively*) trash, riffraff, rabble, canaille, scum, dregs of society, vermin, ragtag and bobtail, flotsam and jetsam.

—*v.* **3.** reduce to poverty, impoverish, pauperize, ruin, break, bankrupt, destroy financially.

beggarly, *adj.* **1.** mean, base, trashy, shabby, shoddy, dirty, filthy; miserable, wretched, vile, foul, sordid, scurvy, nasty; disgusting, contemptible,despicable, detestable.

2. inadequate, poor, sorry, sad, pitiful, pathetic; paltry, piddling, meager, mere, *Inf.* measly; small, puny, little, slight.

beggary, *n.* **1.** poverty, destitution, penury, indigence, impecuniousness, impecuniosity, pennilessness, neediness; insolvency, bankruptcy, liquidation; distress, straits, indebtedness; pauperism, pauperage, pauperdom, mendicancy, mendicity; lack, need, want, privation; paucity, dearth, shortage, deficiency, insufficiency, scarcity, default, absence.

2. beggars, rabble, riffraff.

begin, *v.* **1.** commence, start, go ahead, *Inf.* fire away, *Inf.* blast away; embark, set sail, set to *or* about, turn to, *Inf.* take off, *Inf.* jump off, *Inf.* kick off, *Inf.* blast off; take steps, get going, get a move on, get on the stick, start off, start out, move out, get the show on the road; start in, plunge in, *Inf.* pitch in, *Inf.* steam in, *Inf.* dive in, *Inf.* get one's feet wet, *Inf.* get down to it, *Inf.* get to it.

2. arise, rise, dawn, come into existence, come to be, take birth, see the light of day; issue forth, come forth, burst forth, break out; spring up, spring forth, crop up.

3. initiate, actuate, instigate, set in motion, start the ball rolling, take the first step, take the initiative, take the plunge, make a start, break the ice; open, pioneer, lead off; institute, inaugurate, found, establish, set up, organize, originate, break ground, lay the foundation, lay the first stone; introduce, launch, broach, usher in; create, beget, engender, father, conceive, give birth to, give rise to, sow the seeds of.

beginner, *n.* **1.** novice, novitiate, neophyte, tyro, amateur, rookie, greenhorn, tenderfoot, newcomer, new boy; student, pupil, freshman, learner, initiate, fledgling, apprentice, trainee; recruit, raw recruit, abecedarian, catechumen.

2. initiator, actuator, instigator, agent, originator, starter, mover, prime mover; founder, inaugurator, inventor, deviser, organizer; author, architect, conceiver, shaper, designer; creator, maker, producer, begetter, engenderer, parent, mother, father, sire.

beginning, *n.* **1.** initiation, actuation, instigation, creation, inception; institution, inauguration, introduction, constitution, establishment, origination, organization, foundation.

2. start, commencement, onset, outset, outbreak, dawn, conception, birth, genesis, exordium; *Inf.* kick-off, *Inf.* jump-off, *Inf.* send-off, *Inf.* take-off, *Inf.* blast-off; rise, arising, beginnings, emergence, incipience, nascence, infancy.

3. origin, source, first cause, starting point, square one; fountain, fountainhead, spring, mainspring; top, head.

—*adj.* **4.** initial, early, incipient, introductory, inaugural; prime, primary, primal, primeval; elementary, fundamental, basic, rudimentary.

begird, *v.* **1.** bind, belt, truss, gird; wrap, swathe, swaddle, bandage; buckle, tie, pinion, fasten, couple.

2. encompass, surround, circumvent, circumscribe, environ, encircle, ring; confine, hem in, hedge, limit, bound, enclose; contain, corral, fence, picket, pen, box in, shut in.

begrime, *v.* soil, dirty, blacken, tarnish; sully, befoul, defile, contaminate; smear, tar, grease, blur; draggle, drabble, bemire, *Archaic.* daggle, spatter, muddy, blotch; smudge, smutch, smirch, bedaub; spot, stain, maculate.

begrudge, *v.* envy, resent, grudge, be jealous; covet, crave, hanker for, desire, lust after.

beguile, *v.* **1.** mislead, delude, dupe, fool, befool; hoodwink, bamboozle, humbug, take in, pull the wool over [s.o.'s] eyes; deceive, cheat, gull, cozen, outwit, circumvent; defraud, fleece, swindle, pluck, rook, mulct, *Inf.* diddle, *Inf.* gyp.

2. divert, distract, delight, interest, regale; amuse, entertain, occupy, engross, absorb, engage; please, cheer, gladden, gratify, tickle.

3. (*usu. of time*) pass, while, spend, fritter, waste, idle.

behalf, *n.* **1. in** *or* **on behalf of** for, acting for, in place of, representing, as a representative of, in the name of, on the part of, under authority of, on orders of.

2. in *or* **on one's behalf** in the interest of, for the benefit of, for the advantage of.

behave, *v.* **1.** (*all of oneself*) deport, demean, conduct, comport, acquit; carry, bear; manage, govern, regulate.

2. act, perform, function, operate, run, work; respond, comply, adjust, conform.

3. (*all usu. imperative*) obey, mind, mind one's p's and q's; fly right, shape up, get on the stick, toe the line *or* mark.

behavior, *n.* **1.** demeanor, conduct, deportment, comportment, *Archaic.* havior; bearing, carriage, posture, gait, pose, port; manners, breeding, upbringing, rearing; habits, ways, dealings, customs, practice; morals, ethics, principles.

2. reaction, response, adaptation, adjustment; performance, function, operation.

3. misbehavior, disobedience, delinquency, misdeeds, *Inf.* cutting up, *Inf.* goings-on. See **misbehavior**.

behead, *v.* decapitate, decollate, sever the neck of, chop *or* cut *or* slice off the head of; guillotine, send to the ax, send to the headsman *or* headman; execute, kill, impose capital punishment on, inflict the death penalty on.

behest, *n.* **1.** command, commandment, order, decree, edict, fiat, precept, enjoiner, enjoinment, ordination, charge, word; dictate, mandate, rule, ruling, requirement, imposition, injunction, *Law.* writ; prescription, directive, direction, compulsion, instruction; volition, will, wish, desire, want, choice, pleasure; determination, fixation, fixture, decision, terms, appointment, establishment.

2. demand, exaction, ultimatum; exhortation, urge, urging, pleading, begging; solicitation, requisition, request, proposal, asking, petition; invitation, bidding, summons, call, beck, beckoning, nod.

behind, *prep.* **1.** *U.S.* in back of, at *or* on the heels of, in the wake of; beyond, on the other side of.

2. after, later than; off the pace of, out of step with.

3. supporting, promoting, backing, financing; instigating, causing, prompting, urging, goading.

—*adv.* **4.** in back, in the background, bringing up the rear, rearward.

5. afterwards, next, after, subsequently, close upon, hard at the heels.

6. slow, late, off the pace, off schedule; behindhand, in arrears, overdue, in debt.

behold, *v.* **1.** observe, look at, see, eye; notice, note, remark, mark, heed, pay attention to; witness, watch, view, survey; descry, discern, glimpse, gaze at, stare;

examine, inspect, discover; contemplate, peruse, scrutinize; consider, take cognizance of.

—interj. **2.** look! look at that! ecce!

beholden, *adj.* **1.** obligated, obliged, indebted, bound, owing; grateful, thankful.

2. answerable, accountable, responsible, liable, chargeable, amenable.

beholder, *n.* spectator, watcher, viewer, observer, witness, eyewitness; onlooker, bystander; inspector, examiner.

behoof, *n.* advantage, benefit, interest, good; well-being, *Archaic.* weal, welfare; betterment, improvement, furtherance, advancement, promotion; gain, profit, help, aid, service, avail.

behoove, *v.* **1.** be necessary, be essential, be requisite, be needful, be indispensable; be obligatory, be incumbent upon, be required of, be binding on, be bound; be proper, be due, be right, be correct; be suitable, be appropriate, be fitting, be meet; befit, become, beseem, suit, conduce.

2. be worthwhile, be advantageous, be gainful, be well, be to one's interests *or* advantage; be helpful, be useful, be beneficial.

being, *n.* **1.** existence, *Latin.* *esse*, life, living, animateness, animation; vital force, vital principle, elan vital, life blood, vitality, life force; actuality, reality, presence; ubiquity, omnipresence; truth, verity, veracity, fact.

2. substance, entity, *Metaphysics.* ens, principle; nature, essence, spirit, quiddity, haeccity, quintessence, essentialness; individuality, personality, character, temperament; particularity, singularity, peculiarity.

3. creature, beast, animal, thing; human being, human, person, fellow, man, earthling; body, soul, mortal, sentient; individual, personnage, one, someone, somebody, *Archaic.* wight.

4. Being God, the Absolute, the Creator, the Almighty, the Supreme Being.

belabor, *v.* **1.** beset, besiege, pelt, bombard, *Sl.* strafe; torment, beleaguer, harass, harry, hector, badger, hound, pester, bother, molest, be a thorn in [s.o.'s] side, *Brit.* chivy.

2. agonize, labor, toil, strain, strive, exercise oneself, overwork oneself, exhaust oneself; pore over, worry over, trouble oneself over, lose sleep over, *Sl.* beat one's brains out; overwork, beat to death.

belated, *adj.* **1.** tardy, late, behindhand, behind time, overdue; unpunctual, backward, slow.

2. delayed, detained, retarded; postponed, put off, deferred; adjourned, suspended, prorogued, remanded.

3. obsolete, out-of-date, archaic, behind the times, past, extinct; old-fashioned, oldfangled, outmoded, disused; forgotten, outdated, antiquated, antique, ancient, passé, old.

belch, *v.* **1.** eruct, *Inf.* burp, eructate; hiccup, hiccough.

2. eject, emit, issue, disembogue, pour out, outpour; throw out, expel, expectorate, spit; spew, discharge, vent, send forth, shoot, burst, blast; gush, hurl, blow, jet; spurt, squirt, spout, stream, *Geol.* extravasate; vomit, heave, retch, keck, disgorge; cast up, throw up, cough up, egest, puke, *Sl.* upchuck.

—n. **3.** eructation, *Inf.* burp, hiccup, hiccough.

beldam, *n.* hag, crone, harridan, witch; vixen, shrew, tartar, virago, scold, Xanthippe, termagent, spitfire; old woman, *Inf.* granny.

beleaguer, *v.* surround, encompass, circumscribe; environ, ring, encircle, circle, begird, girdle, engird; confine, hem in, gird, hedge, limit, bound; enclose, ensphere, contain, corral, fence, picket, pen, box in, shut in, blockade, block; siege, besiege, assail, bombard, invest.

belfry, *n.* bell tower, campanile, *Archit.* cupola, *Archit.* dome, steeple, spire; turret, minaret.

belie, *v.* **1.** misrepresent, falsify, distort, garble, pervert; disguise, color, varnish; understate, gloss over, minimize, belittle; stretch, exaggerate, magnify, amplify, overstate; deceive, mislead, misdirect, misguide, misinform.

2. contradict, deny, gainsay; oppose, contravene, counteract; renounce, repudiate, disavow; apostatize, desert, abandon, forsake, renege, *Inf.* go back on; backslide, regress, relapse, fail.

belief, *n.* **1.** credence, view, viewpoint, opinion, sentiment, mind; conviction, convincedness, persuasion, position; judgment, conclusion, deduction, inference, thinking; knowledge, understanding, comprehension.

2. feeling, intuition, divination, impression, fancy; attitude, way of thinking, experience; conjecture, guess, surmise, suspicion; apprehension, perception; notion, idea, concept, conception; assumption, supposition, presupposition, premise, presumption; hypothesis, thesis, theory, postulate, postulation.

3. faith, trust, reliance, dependence; confidence, assurance, certainty, freedom from doubt; security, secureness, assuredness, sureness; hope, expectation; acceptance, acquiescence, compliance, assent.

4. tenet, principles, teaching, rule, *Eccles.* catechism; doctrine, dogma, canon, axiom, theorem, maxim; sect, religion, denomination, affiliation, cult, leaning, fellowship, communion; creed, declaration, profession.

believe, *v.* **1.** maintain, assert, opine, hold, dare say; consider, regard, conceive, acknowledge, recognize; judge, deem, conclude, deduce, infer, think; posit, postulate, hypothesize, theorize.

2. understand, comprehend, know, realize, get through one's head; perceive, apprehend, feel, intuit, divine; guess, conjecture, surmise, suspect, fancy, imagine; assume, suppose, *Archaic.* trow, presuppose, presume.

3. trust, have faith in, confide in, put confidence in, *Inf.* take *or* put stock in, credit; accept, take it, *Inf.* buy, *Inf.* swallow, *Sl.* fall for; hope, expect.

4. believe in a. be persuaded of, be convinced, be sure of, swear by, take [s.o.] at his word. **b.** put faith in, pin one's faith on, repose in, build on, anchor on; count on, rely on, depend on, calculate on, lean on, cling to; be confident of, have confidence, be certain of, be assured of, be satisfied.

belittle, *v.* **1.** disparage, decry, deprecate, demean, detract, deflate, derogate, *Inf.* talk down; mitigate, bate, lessen, attenuate, decrease, diminish, boil down, wither, shrivel, subtract from, cheapen, devaluate, depreciate, downgrade, degrade, lower, reduce; shorten, shrink, abridge, contract, condense, compress, curtail, narrow, cut short, truncate, obtruncate; dwarf, bedwarf, overshadow, make small.

2. minimize, slight, underrate, undervalue, beggar, misprize, extenuate, underestimate, underreckon, think nothing of, set no store by, fail to count on; deemphasize, underplay, make light of, *Inf.* play down.

3. discredit, disfavor, disprove, make disreputable, injure *or* impair the credit *or* reputation of; criticize, pull to pieces, carp *or* cavil at; satirize, lampoon, pasquinade, caricature, ridicule, mock, poke fun at, laugh at, jibe at, sneer at, deride, disdain, contemn, scorn, scoff, spurn, pooh-pooh.

4. humiliate, humble, mortify, *Sl.* put down, make [s.o.] eat humble pie *or* crow *or* his words, make [s.o.] swallow his words; shame, disgrace, dishonor, abase, debase, vitiate; slur, sully, vilify, malign, blacken, impugn, traduce, falsify, scandalize, smear, smirch, besmirch, taint, defame, denigrate, impute, asperse, slander, libel, calumniate, *Sl.* dump on, drag through the mud *or* mire, heap dirt upon, fling dirt, *Sl.* dump on, *Sl.* badmouth, *Sl.* poormouth.

bell, *n.* tocsin, alarm, curfew, siren; carillon, chimes, gong; angelus; toll, ring, peal, chime, ding-dong; tintinnabulation, tinkling, tinkle, ting, ting-a-ling.

bellicose, *adj.* **1.** aggressive, antagonistic, combative, belligerent, pugnacious; hostile, unfriendly, inimical; contentious, quarrelsome, dissentious, wrangling, litigious, disputatious, argumentative; opposed, faultfinding, captious; contrary, perverse, stubborn.

2. militant, martial, warring, warlike, warmongering, jingoistic, *Inf.* on the warpath, unpeaceful; factious, chauvinistic, patriotic; contending, wrestling, battling, grappling, fighting; gladiatorial, pugilistic.

3. irritable, cantankerous, cross, surly, snappish, petulant, peevish; testy, fractious, *Sl.* uptight, choleric, touchy, huffy, peppery; splenetic, spleenful, bilious, cranky, ill-tempered, *Australian.* crook, badtempered; irascible, quick-tempered, short-tempered, *Inf.* short-fused.

4. violent, unrestrained, uncontrollable; volatile, volcanic, explosive, hot-tempered, hot-headed, fiery, inflammable; enraged, raging, fuming, irate, ireful, wrathful, wroth, angry; furious, livid, *Inf.* mad as a hornet, *Inf.* mad as a wet hen.

5. ranting, raving, storming, foaming at the mouth, rabid, fanatical, frenzied; frantic, crazed, *Pathol.* delirious, mad, *Inf.* wild, out of one's mind, beside oneself, *Sl.* freaked out.

belligerent, *adj.* **1.** militant, martial, warring, warlike, warmongering, jingoistic, unpeaceful; contending, wrestling, battling, grappling, fighting; gladiatorial, pugilistic.

2. aggressive, antagonistic, combative, bellicose. See **bellicose** (*defs.* **1-4**).

bellow, *v.* **1.** roar, blare, trumpet, bray, thunder; howl, ululate, hoot, yelp, bark, yap; caterwaul, squall, screech, squeal.

2. shout, cry out, vociferate, exclaim, yell, whoop, *Inf.* holler.

belly, *n.* **1.** abdomen, stomach, *Inf.* tummy, gut, *Sl.* breadbasket, *Scot. and North Eng.* wame; paunch, potbelly, *Inf.* bay window, *Inf.* corporation, *Sl.* pot, *Sl.* beer belly, *Sl.* spare tire, *Obs.* gorbelly; colonic cavity, intestinal cavity, visceral cavity, *Anat., Zool.* venter, ventral region, ventricle, ventricular cavity, *Anat.* epigastrium; pouch, (*of birds*) gizzard, (*of birds*) crop, craw, maw, ingluvies, (*of birds*) proventriculus, (*both of ruminating animals*) first stomach, rumen; intestines, bowels, colons, (*of swine*) chitterlings; innards, inwards, insides, vitals, viscera, (*of animals*) entrails, *Inf.* gizzard, *Sl.* guts.

2. appetite, appetence, appetency, hunger, thirst, craving, gluttony, *Pathol.* bulimia; relish, gusto, zest, eagerness; hankering, yearning, longing; lust, *Sl.* letch.

3. womb, uterus; hold, cavity, vault; interior, recess, recesses, penetralia; depth, depths, gulf, chasm, abyss.

4. underside, underpart, underbelly.

—*v.* **5.** swell, swell up, swell out, bag, *Brit. Dial.* plim; balloon, balloon up, balloon out, balloon forth; inflate, expand, puff up, puff out; fill out, bulk, distend, enlarge, bloat.

belong, *v.* **1.** *Usu.* **belong to** be a member of, be affiliated with, be associated with, be allied to, owe allegiance to; be a follower *or* adherent of, adhere to.

2. *Usu.* **belong to** be the property of, be owned by, be at the disposal of; be vested in, be occupied by, be held by, inhere in.

3. *Often* **belong to** be part of, be an adjunct to, be relevant to, be a concern of; pertain, appertain, relate, fit.

4. *Usu.* **belong in** have qualifications for, be suited for, be appropriate for.

belongings, *n.* **1.** effects, personal effects, chattels, possessions, personal possessions, property, properties, *Inf.* things, *Sl.* stuff, *Sl.* junk; baggage, bag and baggage, gear, impedimenta, dunnage, luggage, kit, duffel; *All Law.* personalty, choses, choses in possession *or* action, choses transitory.

2. paraphernalia, accouterments, appurtenances, appointments, appendages, accessories, trappings; goods, movables, movable articles *or* goods, furniture.

beloved, *adj.* **1.** loved, dearest, dear, precious, treasured, cherished, valued, prized; esteemed, revered, respected, admired, worshiped, idolized.

2. favorite, pet, favored, darling; doted on, pampered, spoiled, cosseted, babied.

—*n.* **3.** lover, inamorato, inamorata, sweetheart, spark, *Inf.* flame, love, Romeo, Juliet; fiancé, fiancée, betrothed, young man, boy friend, young lady, girl friend; paramour, intimate, *Fr. intime*, friend.

below, *adv.* **1.** under, beneath, underneath, *Dial.* neath; down, downward *or* downwards, netherward; low, on the ground; underlying, subjacent, on the bottom; underground, belowground, belowdecks, submerged, downstairs, *Chiefly Brit.* below stairs.

2. on earth, under the sun, in this world, here below, here; earthbound, earthly, worldly, terrestrial.

3. beneath, under, further down, underneath, lower than, lower down, *Dial.* neath.

—*prep.* **4.** lesser than, smaller than, cheaper than, lower than, inferior to; subordinate to, secondary to, subject to, subservient to.

5. unworthy of, undignified for, unbefitting, unbecoming, not behooving, unbeseeming; unsuitable, inapt, unfit, malapropos, unsuited, inappropriate, unmeet; degrading to, shameful to, discreditable to, unseemly to, indecorous to; distasteful to, unacceptable to, objectionable to, unattractive to.

belt, *n.* **1.** girdle, sash, waistband, cummerbund, cestus, *Archaic.* zone, *Archaic, Poetic.* cincture; baldric, cord, cordon, braid, thong, strap, (*for a horse*) surcingle.

2. band, headband, ribbon, frontlet, fillet; collar, collarband, neckband; hatband, sweatband; wristband, *Eccles.* maniple; stripe, stripping, streak, streaking, striation; stroke, line, dash, bar; strip, tape, tag, label.

3. zone, zonule, region, tract, area, district, circuit; circle, circlet, round, zodiac; circumference, periphery, perimeter; band, strip, layer, stratum, level.

—*v.* **4.** gird, girdle, begird, bind, truss; wrap, swathe, swaddle, bandage; buckle, strap, tie, pinion, fasten, couple, hook, snap.

5. encircle, encompass, cincture, surround, circumvent, environ, ring.

6. strap, beat, flog, whip, lash, flagellate, scourge, flail, thrash, wallop.

7. *Slang.* hit, sock, punch, *Inf.* slug, strike, smack. See **beat** (*def.* **1**).

bemire, *v.* **1.** muddy, spatter, bespatter, draggle, drabble, *Archaic.* daggle; smudge, smutch, smirch, bedaub; smear, slime, blur, tar, grease; spot, blotch, stain, taint, sully, maculate, defile, befoul; soil, dirty, muck, blacken, tarnish.

2. mire, swamp, bog, bury; plunge, sink, immerse, submerge, engulf.

bemoan, *v.* **1.** lament, mourn, grieve, sorrow, bewail, *Scot. and North Eng.* greet, express woe *or* distress, deplore, regret; suffer for, pine for, languish over, sigh, *Chiefly Literary.* suspire; anguish oneself, wring one's hands, tear one's hair out, beat one's breast; wail, weep, cry, sob, whimper, shed tears over; moan, groan, howl, bay, squall.

2. commiserate with, sympathize with, offer one's condolences; console, comfort, solace, soothe.

bemuse, *v.* **1.** confuse, addle, befuddle, muddy, mix up, muddle, bemuddle; perplex, puzzle, bewilder; discompose, disconcert, discomfit, upset.

2. stupefy, numb, benumb, stun, shock, overwhelm, knock over, *Inf.* bowl over; amaze, astound, astonish, surprise, knock [s.o.] off their feet.

bench, *n.* **1.** long seat, seat, stool, settle, pew, bleacher, grandstand seat, *Brit.* form, *Rowing.* bank, *Brit. Dial.* dickey.

2. workbench, worktable, table, trestle table, counter; stand, booth, stall, window.

3. court, bar, tribunal; judiciary, judicature; (*all collectively*) judges, jurists, adjudicators, legists, lawyers, advocates, counsel, barristers, solicitors.

bend, *v.* **1.** flex, bow, crook, twist, contort; curve, turn, swerve, veer, deviate, divagate, deflect, diverge; circle, coil, curl, spiral, loop; meander, worn, zigzag, wind, wind in and out, sinuate; hook, angle off, shoot off at an angle; arch, vault, camber, inflect.

2. mold, shape, determine, regulate; influence, sway, move, affect, dispose, predispose, warp, distort, prejudice, jaundice; compel, impel, induce, constrain, coerce, override, prevail over, gain the upper hand, wear down, soften up; master, dominate, predominate, domineer, rule, control, govern, boss, lead by the nose, twist around one's little finger.

3. subdue, subjugate, conquer, vanquish, suppress, overcome, overwhelm, overpower; crush, smash, humble, humiliate, bring one to his knees, bring to terms.

4. direct, point, aim, train, fix, set; incline, bear, head, steer; tend, trend, lean, bias; heed, mind, pay heed *or* attention, attend to, look after, turn to, set one's mind to.

5. stoop, crouch, squat, hunch, get down; bow, curtsey, genuflect, nod, bob, salaam, kneel; kowtow, bow and scrape, prostrate oneself, grovel, truckle to, cower, cringe.

6. yield, submit, acquiesce, concede, accede, agree, comply, concur, give way, give in; surrender, capitulate, succumb, give up, *Sl.* throw in the towel; relax, relent, soften, let up on, mellow.

7. bend over backwards go to great pains, go to great lengths, go to the trouble, go out of one's way, put oneself out, make a special effort.

—n. **8.** deviation, divergence, divagation, divarication, deflection, flecture.

9. curve, bow, turn, twist, bias, warp, veer, swerve, slue, skew; hook, crook, angle, dogleg, hairpin turn; meander, zigzag, *Chiefly Scot.* wimple.

beneath, *adv.* **1.** under, below, underneath, *Dial.* neath; underlying, subjacent, on the bottom, on the ground; underground, belowground, belowdecks, submerged, downstairs, *Chiefly Brit.* below stairs.

—prep. **2.** below, under, further down, underneath, lower than, *Dial.* neath, lower down.

3. less than, lesser than, inferior to, less important than, next to; subordinate to, secondary to, subject to, subservient to.

4. unworthy of, undignified for, unbefitting, unbecoming, not behooving, unbeseeming; unsuitable, inapt, unfit, malapropos, unsuited, inappropriate, unmeet; degrading to, shameful to, discreditable to, unseemly to, indecorous to; distasteful to, unacceptable to, objectionable to, unattractive to.

benediction, *n.* blessing, anointing, sign of the cross, *Archaic.* benison; prayer, invocation, grace, orison.

benefaction, *n.* **1.** good deed, good turn, favor, service, kindness, courtesy; bounty, generosity, charity, liberality, almsgiving; philanthropy, beneficence, benevolence, munificence, benignancy; patronage, countenance, championship; presentation, conferral, conferment, bestowment, endowment, dispensation, consignment.

2. present, gift, bestowal, largesse; gratuity, dole, *Fr. pourboire*, douceur, tip; bonus, prize, award; donation, alms, contribution, offering, offertory, oblation; benefit, boon, blessing, benediction; aid, assistance, help, succor; relief, comfort, solace; grant, subvention, honorarium, subsidy; devise, bequest, bequeathment, legacy.

benefactor, *n.* patron, helper, well-wisher, sympathizer, friend; philanthropist, supporter, backer, angel.

benefice, *n.* **1.** sinecure, office, preferment; rectorate, *Brit.* rectory, pastorate, pastorship; presbyterate, curacy, priorate, abbacy, chaplaincy, chaplainship, vicarate, vicarage, vicariage; bishopric, see, episcopate, archbishopric, primacy, cardinalate; provostship, deanery, professorship, lectureship.

2. stipend, prebend, emolument, revenue.

beneficence, *n.* **1.** kindness, goodness, graciousness, chivalry; humanitarianism, humaneness, humanity, love; altruism, unselfishness, consideration, considerateness; grace, mercy, pity, sympathy, forbearance; magnanimity, good will, brotherly love; generosity, charity, charitableness, bounty, liberality, almsgiving; philanthropy, benevolence, munificence, benignancy.

2. present, gift, bestowal, largesse, benefaction; donation, alms, contribution, offering, offertory, oblation; benefit, boon, blessing, benediction; aid, assistance, help, succor; relief, comfort, solace.

beneficial, *adj.* **1.** advantageous, helpful, serviceable, availing, valuable; favorable, propitious, auspicious, promising, benign; suitable, convenient, commodious, contributive, contributory, conducive; aidful, aiding, obliging, accommodative, accommodating, helping; profitable, gainful, rewarding, remunerative; lucrative, paying, moneymaking.

2. salutary, wholesome, efficacious, salubrious, salutiferous; healthful, healthy, nutritious, nourishing, *Inf.* good for; curative, healing, sanative, restorative; bracing, strengthening, invigorating, tonic; edifying, uplifting, improving; soothing, relieving, anodyne, comforting, calming, quieting, balsamic.

benefit, *n.* **1.** advantage, behoof, interest, good; well-being, *Archaic.* weal, welfare; betterment, improvement, furtherance, advancement, promotion; gain, profit, help, aid, service; avail, efficacy, use, usefulness, serviceableness.

2. *Usu.* **benefits** perquisites, *Inf.* perks, fringe benefits, *Inf.* fringes, *Inf.* extras; insurance, pension, vacation, paid holidays, sick days, earned days, personal days.

—v. **3.** do good to, be of service to, avail, bestead, serve, profit; get, aid, assist, help, advance, advantage; contribute to, improve, better, further, promote.

benevolence, *n.* **1.** kindness, goodness, graciousness, humanitarianism, humanity, love; tenderness, compassion, clemency, kindliness. See **beneficence** (*def.* **1**).

2. present, gift, largesse; contribution, donation. See **beneficence** (*def.* **2**).

benevolent, *adj.* **1.** kind, good, good-hearted, warm-hearted, humane, loving; altruistic, unselfish, considerate, thoughtful; kindly, kind-hearted, beneficent, benign, benignant; generous, charitable, bounteous, liberal, open-handed; magnanimous, philanthropic, big, humanitarian, munificent, big-hearted; merciful, pitying, ruthful, soft-hearted, compassionate, tender, gentle; clement, lenient, temperate, mild; fatherly, motherly, paternal, maternal, brotherly, sisterly; neighborly, friendly, amicable, amiable, cordial, gracious, chivalric, chivalrous; understanding, broad-minded, sympathetic, forbearant, tender-hearted; accommodating, accommodative, obliging, indulgent, well-meaning; helpful, helping, aiding, aidful.

2. charitable, nonprofit, eleemosynary.

benign, *adj.* **1.** kind, good, good-hearted, warm-hearted, humane, loving; kindly, kind-hearted, beneficent, benignant, benevolent; altruistic, unselfish, considerate, thoughtful; compassionate, tender, gentle, soft-hearted, merciful, ruthful; clement, lenient, temperate, mild, fatherly, motherly, paternal, maternal, brotherly, sisterly; neighborly, friendly, amicable, amiable, cordial, gracious, chivalrous; understanding, broad-minded, sympathetic, forbearant, tender-hearted.

2. favorable, propitious, auspicious, fair, promising; lucky, providential, timely, opportune; advantageous, beneficial, helpful, aidful, conducive.

3. (*of weather*) salutary, wholesome, salubrious, salutiferous, healthy; bracing, brisk, vigorous, strengthening, invigorating, animating; pleasant, pleasurable, balmy, refreshing, fair.

bent, *adj.* **1.** crooked, flexed, bowed, twisted, contorted; curved, coiled, circled, curled, spiraled, looped; arched, inflected, vaulted, cambered.

2. determined, insistent, set, resolved, fixed, directed; disposed, predisposed, inclined, prone, partial; moved, swayed.

—*n.* **3.** inclination, disposition, predisposition, temperament, affection, mind, turn, aptness; tendency, conatus, appetency, propensity, proclivity, leaning, penchant, proneness; direction, trend; predilection, partiality, prejudice, bias, ply, twist, feeling; prepossession, fondness, attraction.

4. gift, flair, knack, genius; ability, capability, capacity, aptitude, endowment, faculty; competence, skill, adroitness, proficiency.

benumb, *v.* numb, desensitize, anesthetize; drug, narcotize, deaden; dull, blunt, obtund, *Inf.* take the edge off; muddle, obfuscate, confuse, bewilder; stun, stupefy, daze; shock, stagger, electrify; paralyze, hypnotize, mesmerize, *Archaic.* magnetize, petrify; freeze, chill.

bequeath, *v.* **1.** will, dower, cede, leave to, make over to, *Law.* devise; consign, hand over, commit, entrust, turn over, transfer; apportion, allot, assign, distribute, dispense, pass out, dole out, mete out, deal out, divide, *Inf.* divvy up; endow, bestow, gift, present, give, donate, grant, confer upon, award, reward, render.

2. impart, hand down, hand on, pass on; send down, transmit, communicate.

bequest, *n.* **1.** inheritance, patrimony, bequeathal, *Law.* legacy, *Law.* dower, *Law.* will, *Law.* devise, *Civil Law.* fideicommissum, *Law.* hereditament, *Obs.* dowry, *Archaic.* heritance; endowment, bestowal, donation, disposition, gift, present.

2. heritage, bequeathment, ancestry; history, past, background.

berate, *v.* **1.** scold, chide, tongue-lash, rate, harangue, rant, curse, execrate, imprecate, anathematize; upbraid, objurgate, excoriate, lambaste, flay, fulminate against; castigate, chastise, berate, censure, criticize, reproach, rebuke, reprove, *Inf.* jump on, *Inf.* dress down, *Inf.* slam, *Sl.* jump all over, *Sl.* chew out, *Inf.* bawl out, *Sl.* strafe.

2. assail, revile, blackguard, vituperate, abuse, belabor, lash, rail against, inveigh against; attack, light into, *Inf.* sail into, *Inf.* tear into, *Inf.* rip into, *Inf.* lace into, *Inf.* jump down [s.o.'s] throat, *Archaic.* clapperclaw.

3. vilify, traduce, asperse, calumniate, impugn, slur, malign, defame, denigrate, slander, libel, backbite, bespatter; denounce, decry, disparage, discredit, depreciate, deprecate, belittle, minimize, run *or* put down, *Inf.* knock; pull to pieces, *Sl.* do a hatchet job on, cut up, shred, give a bad name, *Sl.* badmouth, speak ill of, speak evil of; gibbet, scorn, hold up to scorn, deride, ridicule, scoff *or* jeer at, sneer at, mock, lampoon, pasquinade, make fun of.

bereave, *v.* deprive, dispossess, divest, rob, strip, despoil.

bereavement, *n.* **1.** loss, dispossession, deprivation, privation, want; adversity, misfortune, hardship, trial, tribulation, trouble.

2. sorrow, grief, sadness, woe, mourning; anguish, travail, distress, heartache, misery.

berserk, *adj.* frenzied, mad, insane, maniacal, hysterical, frenetic; ranting, raving, storming, foaming at the mouth; enraged, raging, violent, fierce; out of one's head *or* mind; uncontrollable, unrestrainable.

berth, *n.* **1.** bed, bunk, billet, cot, pallet, *Sl.* the sack, *Sl.* the hay, *Brit. Sl.* kip, *Brit. Sl.* doss.

2. *Nautical.* anchorage, moorage, quayage; dock, dry dock, floating dock, graving dock, wharf, pier, landing pier, jetty, mole, quay, *Hist.* levee, landing space *or* place; harbor, port, haven.

3. *Chiefly British.* job, employment, living; post, position, place, situation, office, capacity; appointment, commission, charge, assignment.

—*v.* **4.** *Nautical.* moor, dock, land, warp, snub, tie up; anchor, drop anchor, cast anchor, lay anchor.

beseech, *v.* implore, entreat, obsecrate, importune, beg, plead, *Brit. Inf.* prig; appeal to, conjure, call upon; supplicate, pray, invoke, obtest, adjure; petition, *Rare.* sue, solicit, ask for, apply for, seek; urge, press, insist, demand.

beseem, *v.* befit, suit, become, accord with, match; be suitable, be appropriate, be fitting, be meet; behoove, be proper, be due, be right, be correct.

beset, *v.* **1.** assail, harass, attack; badger, bother, pester, hector, *Sl.* bug, *Sl.* hassle; hound, nag, dog, *Sl.* ride; bait, provoke, vex, *Sl.* needle; torment, bedevil, plague; tease, taunt, tweak.

2. surround, encompass, circumscribe; environ, ring, encircle, circle, begird, girdle, engird; besiege, siege, invest; enclose, ensphere, contain, corral, fence, picket, pen, box in, shut in.

3. stud, bestud, spangle, bead, embroider; deck, bedeck, array; decorate, ornament, embellish.

beside, *prep.* **1.** next to, by *or* at the side of, *Dial.* aside of, by, with, at one's elbow; alongside, side by side, abreast, cheek by jowl, next door to, adjacent to, in juxtaposition with; near to, close to, *Brit. Dial.* near-hand, close at hand to, nearby, close by; but a step from, on the edge of, bordering upon.

2. compared with, contrasted with, next to, in comparison with, in contrast with, against.

3. apart from, not connected with, not related to, irrelevant to, not relevant to, not applicable to, not pertinent to; off the point, off the subject.

4. besides, over and above, in addition to. See **besides** (*def.* **3**).

besides, *adv.* **1.** moreover, furthermore, further, in addition, additionally; also, too, likewise, still, yet, again; together with, along with, in conjunction with, conjointly; on top of everything else, to boot, into the bargain, as well; not counting, not to mention, not to speak of, to say nothing of.

2. otherwise, else, more, on the side.

—prep. **3.** over and above, above and beyond, in addition to; apart from, *U.S. Inf.* aside from, other than, except, excepting, *Inf.* outside of, with the exception of; excluding, barring, saving; exclusive of, without, sans.

besiege, *v.* **1.** siege, lay siege to, invest, contain, confine, cordon off, blockade; surround, encircle, encompass, hedge in, pen in, shut in.

2. importune, press, pressure, push, ply; pester, plague, bother, trouble, nag, hound, buttonhole; beset, beleaguer, hector, harass, harry.

besmear, *v.* smear, smirch, smudge, begrime, sully, soil, stain, smutch, draggle; daub all over, bedaub, blot, spot, blemish, splatter, spatter, bespatter; defile, blotch, mar, deface.

besmirch, *v.* soil, begrime, muddy, draggle, bedraggle, smutch, smear, besmear; blot, spot, blemish, stain, blotch; mar, defame, defile, sully, taint; tarnish, dull, discolor, oxidate.

besot, *v.* intoxicate, inebriate, stupefy. See **befuddle.**

bespatter, *v.* **1.** spatter, splatter, spot, blot, bedaub, stain, soil, sully, begrime, smudge, smirch, splash.

2. slander, defame, defile, blemish, blotch, mar; smear, besmear, muddy, tarnish, taint, blacken; mark, brand, stigmatize.

bespeak, *v.* **1.** ask for, ask for in advance, speak for, speak up for, solicit; prearrange for, order, engage, bid for, sue for; stipulate, requisition, reserve, secure, assure.

2. show, demonstrate, display, evince, exhibit, manifest, reveal, disclose, betray; indicate, imply, intimate; signify, import, point to, affirm, give a token *or* sign of, betoken; reflect, represent, savor of; tell of, proclaim, declare, express, testify, bear witness to, attest to; mean, denote, connote, suggest, purport.

besprinkle, *v.* **1.** sprinkle, scatter, strew, shower, dispense; dash, dust, powder, dredge, season, spice, flour, salt, sugar; dampen, moisten, spray, wet, water, bedew, spatter.

2. dot, spot, bespeckle, stipple, dapple, mottle; spread, disperse, broadcast, bestrew.

best, *adj.* **1.** excellent, unexcelled, unsurpassed, fine, *Inf.* super, *Inf.* superfine; first-class, first-rate, *Inf.* crack; superior, choice, select; top, paramount, capital; outstanding, foremost, preeminent; venerable, highest, peerless; perfect, superlative, consummate; pure, genuine, sterling, gilt-edged, sound, wholesome, *Inf.* tip-top.

2. auspicious, propitious, golden, advantageous; best-suited, right, correct, fitting, apt; most desirable, enviable, covetable.

3. largest, most, greatest, biggest, longest, most sizeable, substantial, preponderant, goodly.

—adv. **4.** excellently, most suitably, most advantageously, most fortunately, most happily.

5. greatly, extremely, most deeply, most highly, most fully.

6. as best one can try and try again, *Inf.* do one's darndest, fight the good fight, muddle through.

7. had best ought to, should, no doubt should.

—n. **8.** finest, first, leading, top, foremost; strongest, most powerful, most vigorous, healthiest.

9. finery, fine things, finest clothing, *Inf.* best bib and tucker, Sunday best. See **finery.**

10. peak, prime, zenith, apex, height, *Inf.* top of one's form.

11. hardest, utmost, *Inf.* darndest, *Inf.* damnedest.

12. regards, kindest regards, best *or* good wishes, greetings, love, *Sl.* the big hello.

13. get *or* **have the best of a.** benefit, win, *Inf.* come out ahead; have the upper hand *or* edge, *Inf.* hold the trump card. **b.** defeat, subdue, overpower, master, gain ascendancy *or* supremacy over, conquer.

14. make the best of manage, put up with, tolerate, make do, get by.

—v. **15.** defeat, beat, conquer, get the better of. See *def.* **13b.**

bestial, *adj.* **1.** theroid, animalic, animalian, beastly, beastlike, therimorphic.

2. primitive, wild, barbaric, barbarian, barbarous, heathen; savage, fierce, brutal, inhuman; rough, rugged, coarse, bearish, brutish; boorish, churlish, loutish, oafish; swinish, boarish, piggish, hoggish, gluttonous, greedy; unclean, dirty, filthy, smutty, *Sl.* raunchy, gross, obscene.

3. base, low, mean, sordid, bad; execrable, abominable, horrible, horrid, atrocious; vile, abhorrent, repulsive, loathsome, odious, hateful, detestable, offensive.

4. carnal, sensual, animalistic, lustful, libidinous, salacious; lascivious, licentious, lecherous, lewd, *Archaic.* lickerish, prurient; immoral, dissolute, profligate, unchaste, wanton, crude, debauched, debased, dissipated, degenerate.

bestir, *v.* **1.** stir, move, bustle, hurry, scurry, hasten, hustle, scramble, scurry, scuttle, exert oneself, *Inf.* get going *or* moving, get started; elicit, evoke, call forth, summon up; poke, prod, prick, goad, prompt, spur, work up, whip up; encourage, urge, egg on, press, drive; foment, agitate, excite, *Inf.* start something.

2. actuate, put in motion, start the wheels turning; stimulate, animate, motivate, inspire, vivify; liven up, arouse, awaken, wake up, waken, rouse, shake up, jolt, jog.

bestow, *v.* **1.** give, donate, present; assign, consign, impart, bequeath, render to, endow; award, confer, grant, favor, afford, vouchsafe; hand, pass, deliver, turn over to, yield, cede, commit, entrust; dispense, distribute, deal out, apportion, allot, divide.

2. apply, use, utilize, employ, dispense, dispose of, administer, adhibit; spend, expend, direct, devote, put to advantage *or* profit.

bestrew, *v.* scatter, disperse, strew, cast about, spread, broadcast, sow, impart, disseminate; diffuse, radiate, emanate, circumfuse.

bestride, *v.* **1.** straddle, bestraddle, ride *or* sit *or* stand astride of.

2. overstride, step over, pass over, cross, traverse.

3. stand over, tower over, arch over, rise above, overtop; command, dominate, overshadow; *Inf.* rule the roost.

bet, *v.* **1.** stake, put up collateral, put money on; cover, back up, pledge.

2. wager, gamble, lay a wager, *Brit.* punt; play the lottery, enter the sweepstakes, play the game, dice, shoot craps, play poker; take a chance, run a risk, take a long shot, stick one's neck out, *Inf.* risk it, *Inf.* chance it; risk, hazard, jeopardize.

—n. **3.** stake, collateral, security, surety, guaranty, pledge.

4. wager, gamble, chance, risk, long shot, *Sl.* shot in the dark.

5. lottery, sweepstakes, raffle; game of chance, fall of the dice, game of fortune *or* luck.

6. speculation, possibility, likelihood, uncertainty, pig in a poke, *Inf.* flier, hazard, risk; even odds, even chance, *Inf.* fifty-fifty chance, *Inf.* toss up, *Inf.* six of one and a half dozen of the other; venture, undertaking, enterprise, business.

betide, *v.* happen, *Archaic.* hap, occur, take place, supervene, befall, chance, *Archaic.* bechance, *Archaic.* arrive; transpire, intervene, crop up; become, come into being, come about, come to pass, fall, materialize; prove, eventuate, result, turn out; ensue, issue, emanate, flow out, arise.

betoken, *v.* **1.** indicate, show, signify, import, point to, denote. See **bespeak** (*def.* **2**).
2. portend, bode, forebode, promise, indicate, *Archaic.* bespeak, foreshadow, foretoken, foreshow, presage, augur; foretell, predict, forecast, prognosticate, prophesy.

betray, *v.* **1.** inform against, *Sl.* blow the whistle on, *Sl.* rat on; knife *or* stab in the back, *Sl.* do [s.o.] dirt; play Judas, give the Judas kiss to, *Inf.* sell out, deliver up, *Inf.* sell [s.o.] down the river; *Inf.* double cross, *Sl.* two-time; break faith with, let down, disappoint, break one's promise.
2. reveal, divulge, let the cat out of the bag, give away, blab, blurt out, let slip, disclose, *Archaic.* discover; violate a confidence, reveal the secrets of, whisper about; exhibit, display, vent, show, manifest, evince; unmask, uncover, unfold, bare, expose, bring to light, lay bare.
3. mislead, delude, dupe, fool, befool; hoodwink, bamboozle, humbug, take in, pull the wool over [s.o.'s] eyes; deceive, beguile, cheat, gull, cozen, outwit, circumvent; trap, ensnare.
4. (*all usu. in reference to sexual relations*) seduce, lead astray, entice, lure, trick; corrupt, pervert, debauch; violate, *Euph.* take advantage of, *Euph.* have one's way with, ravish, deflower, *Obs.* devirginate, *Obs.* constuprate, *Obs.* stuprate; defile, molest, outrage, desecrate.
5. abandon, walk out on, forsake, desert; leave behind, throw over, jilt, run out on, *Inf.* leave flat, turn one's back on, *Sl.* give the deep six; ignore, cut off, neglect, ostracize; leave, depart, quit, go away from, vacate.

betrayal, *n.* **1.** breach of faith, bad faith, disloyalty, perfidy, faithlessness, treachery; double-dealing, duplicity, falseness, chicanery; *Inf.* double crossing, subversion, undermining, corruption; *Inf.* double cross, Judas kiss; sedition, treason, mutiny, revolt, rebellion, revolution, insurrection.
2. revealing, divulging, blurting out, disclosing; giveaway, slip.

betrayer, *n.* traitor, renegade, apostate, recreant; conspirator, plotter, complotter, Catilinarian; Judas, false friend.

betroth, *v.* engage, affiance, plight, plight one's troth, espouse, bind, give one's hand, bestow one's hand upon, publish the banns, *Archaic.* handfast, *Obs.* affy; contract, covenant, settle, establish, make *or* strike a bargain, come to terms; agree, enter into, go in for.

betrothal, *n.* engagement, espousal, plighting, betrothment, sponsalia; vow, marriage compact, subarrhation, *Archaic.* affiance, *Archaic.* handfast; contract, compact, covenant, pact, settlement, agreement, understanding.

better, *adj.* **1.** superior, of a higher grade, preferable, more desirable, more acceptable; excelling, surpassing, exceeding, transcendent.
—*v.* **2.** improve, make better, amend, ameliorate, meliorate; advance, promote, raise, elevate; straighten out, reform, revise, rectify, redress, correct, put *or* set straight *or* right; repair, fix, remedy, cure, mend, heal, doctor, minister; relieve, ease, mitigate, lessen, assuage, alleviate.
3. enhance, heighten, strengthen, enrich, add to; renew, revive, revivify, give new life to; refresh, freshen up, brighten up, spruce up, smarten up, touch up; recondition, restore, renovate, remodel, redo, make over.
4. improve upon, surpass, exceed, excel, outdo, beat, outstrip, go [s.o.] one better.

bettor, *n.* gambler, gamester, player, wagerer, sharper, *Brit.* punter, *Inf.* sport, *Inf.* piker, *Inf.* tinhorn; speculator, *Inf.* plunger; bookmaker, *Inf.* bookie.

between, *prep.* **1.** amid, mid, in the middle of, amidst, midst, in the midst of, among, mongst; halfway from both, midway to both, *Archaic.* betwixt; intermediate to, interjacent to, intervening, intervenient to.
2. linking, connecting, joining, bonding; affiliating, associating, uniting, allying; involving, concerning, affecting, engaging, occupying.
3. distinguishing, differentiating, discriminating; characterizing, marking, featuring, peculiarizing.
—*adv.* **4.** intermediately, halfway, midway, in the middle, in between; in the midst, at intervals, intermittently.

bevel, *n.* **1.** oblique, cant, bezel, chamfer, miter; slant, angle, diagonal, bias, *Heraldry.* bend; incline, slope, tilt.
—*v.* **2.** cant, miter, cut at an angle, slant.
—*adj.* **3.** oblique, canted, mitered, beveled; slanted, diagonal, angled, at an angle; inclined, sloping, tilted.

beverage, *n.* drink, potable, thirst quencher; soda, soft drink; liquor, cocktail, draught, swill, *Inf.* swig, intoxicant, *Often Facetious.* libation; broth, soup, liquid.

bevy, *n.* **1.** flock, covey, gaggle, nest, brood, hatch; flight, swarm, horde, hive, cloud; pack, herd, drove, school, litter, farrow.
2. multitude, galaxy, sea, host, number, army, legion, lot, *Inf.* slew; crowd, throng, press, mob; assembly, assemblage, cluster, array, bunch, collection, contingent, body, mass; gathering, group, knot, company, tribe; gang, band, troupe, squad, crew, party.

bewail, *v.* **1.** lament, mourn, grieve, bemoan, *Scot. and North Eng.* greet, sorrow, express woe *or* distress over, deplore, regret; suffer for, pine for, languish over.
2. anguish oneself, wring one's hands, tear one's hair out, beat one's breast; wail, weep, cry, sob, whimper, shed tears, sigh, *Chiefly Literary.* suspire; moan, groan, howl, bay, squall.

beware, *v.* **1.** (*usu. imperative*) be careful, take heed, mind, watch out, look out.
2. be cautious, be wary, be on one's guard; keep out of harm's way, take precautions, be on the safe side, be prepared, think twice, count the cost; look before one leaps, be on the lookout, be on the alert.

bewilder, *v.* confuse, puzzle, perplex, baffle, mystify, stump, *Inf.* bamboozle, *Inf.* buffalo; nonplus, obfuscate, stun, daze, confound, stupefy, stagger; amaze, astound, astonish, muddle, bemuddle, mix up; befuddle, befog, becloud.

bewildered, *adj.* perplexed, baffled, confused, nonplused, mystified, buffaloed; uncertain, at sea, at a loss; stupefied, shocked, taken aback, thrown off balance, bowled over; discomposed, disconcerted, flustered, upset, *Inf.* discombobulated.

bewilderment, *n.* maze, labyrinth, network, confusion; tangle, entanglement, snarl, jumble, jungle, muddle, disorder; combination, mixture, medley, miscellany, melange, intermixture, conglomeration, botch, hodgepodge, wilderness, imbroglio.

bewitch, *v.* **1.** curse, hex, jinx, witch, becharm, cast a spell over, put a spell on, *Inf.* spook, *Sl.* put *or* slam the whammy on; demonize, bedevil, possess.
2. allure, lure, entice, charm, intrigue, beguile, inveigle; tempt, tantalize, seduce, enchant, ensorcell; captivate, fascinate, spellbind, entrance, mesmerize, hypnotize, transfix, enrapture, transport.

beyond, *prep.* **1.** on the farther side of, on the far side of, on the other side of; farther on than, more distant than, past, after, over, across, behind.
2. outside the reach of, outside the range of, outside the limitations of, above, too deep for, beyond the depth of; beyond the power of, beyond the control of.
3. over and above, above and beyond, in excess of, more than.
—adv. **4.** farther on, farther away, farther along, down the road, *Inf.* down the road a piece; far, far away, far off, afar, off, at a distance.
5. the great beyond hereafter, afterworld, otherworld, world to come, next world; future, ultimate future, destination, destiny; the unknown, the great unknown.

bias, *n.* **1.** angle, slant, tilt, cant, skew, list, slope, bevel.
2. tendency, inclination, proclivity, propensity, leaning, proneness; bent, warp, twist, partiality, prejudice, predilection; preconception, predisposition, fixed idea, preconceived notion; intolerance, bigotry, close-mindedness, narrow-mindedness, one-sidedness.
—v. **3.** predispose, dispose, incline, influence, sway, bend; warp, distort, prejudice, jaundice.

bib, *n.* chemisette, tucker, dickey; apron, pinafore; napkin.

Bible, *n.* **1.** Holy Writ, the Good Book, the Holy Scriptures. See **Scripture** (*defs.* **1-3**).
2. (*l.c.*) handbook, manual, vade mecum, enchiridion; guidebook, primer, text, textbook, authority.

bibliography, *n.* list, compilation, catalog, record, compendium; book list, bibliotheca.

bibliophile, *n.* booklover, bookworm, bibliophage; book collector, bibliopole; bibliotaph, bibliomaniac, bibliolater.

bibulous, *adj.* **1.** alcoholic, dypsomaniacal, bibacious, inebrious, crapulous, given *or* addicted to drink, *Sl.* on the sauce, *Sl.* on the bottle, *Sl.* on the booze, *Sl.* under the influence; drunken, sottish, besotted, awash, *Literary.* in one's cups, *Inf.* boozy, *Sl.* pifficated, *Sl.* pie-eyed, *Sl.* shit-faced; (*all with regard to alcoholic beverages*) intemperate, immoderate, excessive, inordinate, extreme. See also **drunk**.
2. absorbent, spongy, spongiose, porous, permeable, pervious; retentive, absorptive, *Physical Chem.* adsorbent; soaking, blotting, sponging, absorbing, sorbefacient, resorbent.

bicker, *v.* **1.** wrangle, argue, altercate, jangle, dispute; quarrel, have words, *Inf.* row, *Inf.* scrap, squabble, spat, tiff; conflict, clash, lock horns, fight, battle, spar, fence, cross swords; disagree, fall out, jar, be at loggerheads, be at variance, differ, dissent, oppose; contend, contest, litigate, haggle, *Sl.* hassle, *Scot.* argle-bargle, *Scot.* sturt, *Scot. and North Eng.* threap, *Scot. and North Eng.* prig; debate, question, discuss, controvert; bandy words, moot, sift, *Inf.* kick around, *Sl.* hash over; quibble, cavil, nitpick, belabor a point, split hairs, chop logic.
2. run rapidly, rush, hurry, hasten, move quickly *or* swiftly, scramble; race, speed, *Inf.* roar, *Inf.* barrel, tear, zoom, zip.
3. quiver, flicker, flutter, flit, dance; shiver, ripple, waver, sway, totter, stagger; flap, wave to and fro, oscillate, fluctuate, vacillate; quaver, shake, quake, tremble, twitter, shudder; undulate, vibrate, pulsate, throb; jerk, twitch, vellicate, jump.
4. twinkle, sparkle, glimmer, blink, shimmer; glint, glitter, glisten, *Archaic.* glister; spark, sputter, splutter, flash, flare; streak, gleam, fulgurate, glare, coruscate; glow, shine, stream, flow.
—n. **5.** wrangle, dispute, argument, altercation, controversy, tilt, jangle; quarrel, row, squabble, dust-up, spat, jar, tiff, *Inf.* hassle, *Inf.* barney; disagreement, falling-out, difference of opinion, discord, contention, strife, dissension, variance; conflict, clash, fight, *Inf.* scrap, brawl, battle; fracas, uproar, brouhaha, commotion, rumpus, *Inf.* rukus; struggle, tussle, donnybrook, *Scot.* sturt, *Scot. and North Eng.* threap, *Inf.* run-in, *Inf.* set-to, *Sl.* rhubarb; broil, embroilment, imbroglio.

bicycle, *n.* tandem, cycle, *Brit.* push-bike, *Inf.* bike, three-speed, *Inf.* a three, five-speed, *Inf.* a five, ten-speed, *Inf.* a ten, racer; highwheeler, penny-farthing, ordinary, boneshaker, velocipede, tricycle, *Inf.* trike; unicycle; safety bicycle, safety moped.

bid, *v.* **1.** command, order, adjure, dictate, charge, *Obs.* conjure, direct, enjoin; prescribe, set, appoint, ordain, decree, demand, require; summon, call, cite, beckon, invite.
2. propose, suggest, submit, advance, extend; offer, tender, proffer, pay.
—n. **3.** offer, proffer, proposal, proposition, suggestion, submission, motion; advance, ante.

bidding, *n.* command, commandment, order, ordinance, injunction, mandate, dictate, charge; summons, call, citation, convening; instruction, direction, prescription, enjoining; demand, requisition, request, behest, invitation; bid, offer, proffer, proposal, suggestion.

big, *adj.* **1.** large, huge, enormous, *Chiefly Brit. Inf.* whacking, prodigious, immense, colossal, monstrous; gigantic, giant, tremendous, Brobdingnagian, towering, tall, overgrown; great, vast, extensive, spacious, capatious, voluminous; grand, grandiose, majestic, august.
2. bulky, hulky, hulking; massive, massy, ponderous, gargantuan, elephantine; beefy, burly, brawny, muscular, strapping, robust, stalwart, bouncing, bouncy; thickset, stocky, solid, heavy, chunky.
3. obese, overweight, corpulent, gross; paunchy, potbellied, round-bellied, big-bellied, abdominous; fat, plump, fleshy, rotund, buxom, well-fed; pudgy, *Chiefly Brit.* podgy, chubby, portly, stout; swollen, bloated, puffy.
4. filled, brimming, overflowing; verging, bordering, on the brink.
5. important, salient, significant, consequential, weighty, influential, powerful; notable, noteworthy, esteemed, prominent, outstanding, famous, well-known, illustrious, renowned; eminent, distinguished, elevated, exalted, high, top; chief, head, leading, foremost, prime, supreme, paramount; main, principal, primary, capital, essential, radical.
6. boastful, bombastic, inflated, swell-headed; pretentious, haughty, arrogant, pompous.
7. magnanimous, generous, unselfish, altruistic; gracious, kindly, kindhearted, benevolent, beneficent, humane, forgiving; just, fair, impartial, unbiased, unprejudiced; noble, honorable, high-minded, lofty, sublime, princely, chivalrous, heroic; splendid, superb, glorious, magnificent.
8. loud, orotund, resounding, stentorian, booming, deafening.

bigot, *n.* intolerant, illiberal, *Inf.* little person, *Sl.* Archie Bunker; racist, anti-Semite; sexist, male chauvinist pig; superpatriot, ultranationalist, jingo, chauvinist.

bigoted, *adj.* intolerant, illiberal, close-minded, closed, narrow-minded, narrow; prejudiced, biased, warped, twisted, jaundiced, partial, one-sided; sexist, chauvinistic, jingoistic, racist, antiblack, anti-Semitic.

bilk, *v.* **1.** default, dishonor, refuse to pay, decline to redeem, *Sl.* welsh; abscond, *Sl.* skip town, *Brit. Sl.* levant, *Brit. Sl.* do a moonlight flit.

2. swindle, cheat, defraud, fleece, rook, gull, *Archaic.* chouse; stack the deck, *Inf.* gyp, *Sl.* chisel, *Sl.* gaff; pluck, mulct, victimize, exploit, play on *or* upon, take advantage of, *Inf.* diddle, *Inf.* do, *Sl.* burn.

3. bamboozle, delude, deceive, mislead, hoodwink, pull the wool over [s.o.'s] eyes; cozen, bluff, take in; fool, hoax, humbug, trick, outwit, circumvent, put one over on, *Brit. Inf.* gammon.

4. frustrate, thwart, balk, defeat, foil, cross.

5. vanish, disappear, do the disappearing act, *Inf.* make oneself scarce; elude, evade, escape, duck, dodge, give [s.o.] the slip, lose [s.o.], *Sl.* duck and run, *Sl.* dog it, *Sl.* ditch [s.o.], *Sl.* throw [s.o.] off the scent, *Sl.* shake [s.o.] off.

bill¹, *n.* **1.** invoice, statement, record, list of expenditures; account, check, tally, score, reckoning, tabulation, *Inf.* tab; liability, amount due, money spent, expenses, account payable, expenses, fee, charges, *Law.* cost.

2. note, treasury note, currency, money, paper money, legal tender, tender, greenback, *U.S.* certificate, *U.S.* silver certificate, *U.S.* gold certificate.

3. notice, bulletin, announcement, advertisement, ad, *Fr. affiche, Rom. Cath. Ch.* encyclical; leaflet, circular, folder, brochure, handbill, handout, dodger, throwaway, *U.S.* flier; broadside, broadsheet, billboard, poster, placard, card.

4. list, enumeration, particularization, specification, detailing, inventory, compendium; summary, summation, synopsis.

5. program, agenda, playbill; calendar, schedule, timetable, roster, *U.S.* docket; prospectus, syllabus, plan, outline, sketch, scheme, cadre, framework.

—*v.* **6.** invoice, charge for, send a statement to, put on one's check; total the expenses *or* cost, tabulate, list *or* tally expenditures.

7. announce, post, give notice, of; advertise, talk up, put up in lights; offer, present, pass off.

8. schedule, enter [s.t.] in the timetable, put [s.t.] on the calendar *or* agenda, include in the plan.

bill², *n.* beak, nib, neb, pecker.

billet, *n.* **1.** (*all in the military*) lodging, lodgings, lodging place, lodgment, quarters, living quarters, quarterage, housing, rooms, accommodations; barracks *or* barrack, cantonment, casern, military quarters, *Sl.* the Q; camp, encampment, bivouac.

2. *Military.* (*all for the provision of quarters*) order, ordinance, directive, dictation, direction, command, charge, imperative, requisition, requirement, precept, prescription; notification, notice, instruction, injunction.

3. place, station, post, position; bed, bunk, berth, cot, pallet, *Sl.* sack, *Brit. Sl.* kip; room, chamber, apartment, compartment, cabin, stall, cell, nook.

4. job, employment, employ, living; post, position, office capacity, situation; appointment, commission, charge, assignment.

—*v.* **5.** quarter, provide quarters for, bed, bunk, berth; house, shelter, give shelter to, lodge, provide lodging *or* lodgings *or* lodgment for, put up, have as a guest *or* lodger, roof, provide with a roof.

6. reside, live, live at, abide, *Archaic.* bide, dwell, dwell at, tenant, stay, stay at, remain, sojourn; domicile, domiciliate, establish oneself, take up residence, take up one's abode, make one's home, inhabit, occupy, settle, locate, ensconce, *Inf.* hang up one's hat.

billfold, *n.* wallet, folding purse, purse, pocketbook; card case, credit card container; money clip; money belt.

billowy, *adj.* surging, swelling, heaving, waving, undulating; rolling, rising, tossing; rippling, undulant, swirling; rising and falling, ebbing and flowing.

bimonthly, *adj., adv.* bimestrial, *Obs.* bimensal, every two months; semimonthly, fortnightly, twice a month.

bin, *n.* box, can, coffer, canister, case, casket, *Brit.* caddy; hutch, chest, cupboard; hamper, basket, crate, pannier; receptacle, container, hold; enclosure, stall, pen, crib.

bind, *v.* **1.** fasten, secure, tie, tie up, bundle, colligate, truss, wrap; join, unite, connect, encircle, gird, attach; lace, entwine, plait, interlace, weave, interlock; buckle, hook.

2. bandage, tape, dress, wrap, swathe.

3. strap, chain, moor, hitch, lash, tether, hobble, hopple, fetter, trammel, pinion, shackle, gyre; manacle, handcuff; leash, bridle, muzzle; chafe, choke, hamper.

4. hold, hold fast, grip, stick, stick together, adhere, glue, cement, paste, conglutinate, lute; cohere, consolidate, set, harden, solidify, congeal, gel, agglutinate, gum; clog, compact, fuse, coalesce; thicken, cake, clot, coagulate, curdle.

5. require, prescribe, assign; astrict, engage, oblige, obligate; restrict, constrict, constrain, force, compel, impel, press, enforce; inhibit, encumber, cumber, burden, yoke.

6. edge, border, hem, trim, purfle, purl.

—*n.* **7.** *Informal.* quandary, dilemma, predicament, *Inf.* double bind, *Inf.* catch-22, *Inf.* Hobson's choice, impasse, stand-off.

biography, *n.* life story, life, life history, *Inf.* bio; memoir, memoirs, recollections, adventures, fortunes; account, history, record; autobiography, filmography, psychobiography.

bird, *n.* **1.** flier, fledgling, cageling, fowl, bird of prey; songbird, warbler, songster.

2. *Slang.* eccentric, *Inf.* character, *Sl.* freak, *Sl.* nut, *Sl.* weirdo, *Sl.* whacko.

3. **birds of a feather** friends, cohorts, cronies, brothers, colleagues; gang, group.

4. **for the birds** *Slang.* ridiculous, absurd, preposterous, unbelievable, laughable; contemptuous, unworthy, reprehensible.

5. **the bird** *Slang.* disapproval, hissing, booing, scoffing, ridicule, *Inf.* Bronx cheer, *Inf.* raspberry.

birth, *n.* **1.** childbirth, bearing, delivery, parturition, confinement. See **bearing** (*def.* **2**).

2. background, parentage, line, lineage, descent, nativity, origin, race, extraction, derivation; ancestry, family, house, affiliation, blood, blood line, strain, stock; pedigree, genealogy, stirps; heritage, birthright, patrimony, legacy.

3. origin, beginnings, start, source, fountainhead. See **beginning** (*defs.* **2, 3**).

4. **give birth to a.** bear a child, bring forth, deliver. See **bear¹** (*def.* **1**). **b.** initiate, originate, discover, invent, spawn. See **begin** (*def.* **3**).

birthday, *n.* day of birth, natal day, anniversary; birthday party, celebration, commemoration.

birthmark, *n.* blemish, patch, discoloration, disfigurement, mole, nevus.

birthright, *n.* right, privilege, due, droit, *Law.* primogeniture; heritage, patrimony, legacy, inheritance, *Inf.* what's coming to one.

biscuit, *n.* bun, scone, *Brit.* cookie; cracker, soda cracker, saltine; rusk, cracknel, zwieback, wafer; hardtack; pretzel.

bisect, *v.* **1.** halve, divide in half, cut in two, dichotomize, *Obs.* dimidiate; split, cleave, sunder, cut down the middle.
2. intersect, intercross, decussate, cross, crisscross, crosscut, cut across.
3. fork, part, furcate, bifurcate, separate, subdivide; branch, ramify, stem, diverge, divaricate.

bisexual, *adj.* **1.** androgynous, epicine; *All Biol.* hermaphrodite, hermaphroditic, hermaphroditical, hermaphroditish, pseudohermaphrodite, pseudohermaphroditic; *All. Bot.* gynandrous, gynandromorphic, gynandromorphous, monoclinous.
2. bisexed, amphierotic, *Sl.* ac/dc, *Sl.* switch-hitting, *Sl.* hitting from both sides of the plate.
—n. **3.** androgyne, epicine; *All Biol.* hermaphrodite, pseudohermaphrodite, gynandromorph.
4. *All Sl.* switch-hitter, bi-guy.

bisexuality, *n.* **1.** androgyny, epicinism; *All Biol.* hermaphroditism, hermaphrodism, pseudohermaphroditism; *All Bot.* gynandry, gynandrism, gynandromorphy, gynandromorphism.
2. bisexualism, amphieroticism, *Sl.* swinging from both sides of the plate, *Sl.* switch-hitting, *Sl.* swinging *or* hitting both ways.

bishop, *n.* diocesan, prelate, archpriest, high priest, supervisor, overseer, *Ethiopian Ch.* abuna; patriarch, *Eastern Ch.* exarch, metropolitan, archbishop; coadjutor, auxiliary, suffragan; primate, pope, pontiff, Bishop of Rome. See also **ecclesiastic, clergyman.**

bishopric, *n.* episcopate, cathedral seat, cathedra, miter, see, diocese, office, territory, province, jurisdiction; archdiocese, archbishopric; prelacy, prelature, episcopacy, *Brit.* incumbency; primacy, pontificate, papal crown, Holy See.

bit[1], *n.* **1.** restrainer, harness, halter, yoke, rein; curb, check, restraint, brake.
2. take the bit in *or* **between one's teeth** rebel, break with, break away, revolt; resist, defy, disobey.
—v. **3.** hinder, impede, inhibit, curb; restrain, hold back, keep back, keep *or* hold in check, retard, hamper.

bit[2], *n.* **1.** piece, cantle, slice, *Brit. Dial.* collop, rasher, *Australian.* skerrick; part, cut, share, section, segment, moiety; particle, moit, mote; division, subdivision, fraction, hair; shaving, paring, sliver, shive, splinter, flake, scale, fragment, shard; morsel, crumb, grain, granule; chunk, lump, hunk, gob; portion, dose, installment; snatch, scrap, remnant, shred, fritter; cutting, snip, snippet; tab, stub, stump, butt, tatter; taste, sample, mouthful, sip, sup.
2. trace, touch, hint, trifle, tinge, suggestion, suspicion, tincture, *Archaic.* spice, shadow; spark, scintilla, gleam; mite, speck, smidgen, *Inf.* smitch, iota, molecule, atom, jot, whit, tittle; dot, point, dab, fleck, speck; minimum, pittance, modicum, driblet; item, article, particular, detail.
3. second, minute, little while, blink of an eye, flash; *Inf.* before you know it.
4. bit by bit by degrees, gradually, step by step, one step at a time; in time, slowly.

bitch, *n.* **1.** female dog, female canine.
2. *Slang.* prostitute, whore, harlot, call girl, hustler. See **whore.**
3. *Slang.* **a.** complaint, gripe, diatribe, lament. **b.** difficulty, unpleasantness, predicament, dilemma, knot, bind.
—v. **4.** *Slang.* complain, protest, object; grumble, *Sl.* bellyache, *Sl.* mouth off; deplore, lament, bewail.
5. *Slang.* spoil, bungle, botch up, ruin, wreck, *Inf.* make a mess of, *Inf.* mess up, *Sl.* screw up.

bite, *v.* **1.** nip, snap, snip, pinch, sting; eat, munch, crunch, nibble, gnaw, chew, masticate; grip, hold, clamp, sink one's teeth into; bite off, sever, chop off, cleave; separate, sunder, disunite, disjoin.
2. cut, tear, rip, slash, gash, slit, slice; wound, pierce, puncture, stab, knife; prick, stick, poke, gouge; bore, perforate, penetrate, drill; spear, impale, gore, run through.
3. eat into, corrode, burn, dissolve; eat away at, gnaw at, consume; erode, wear away, rust, deteriorate, rot, decay.
—n. **4.** wound, cut, bruise, scratch, incision, puncture, stab, lesion, laceration; tear, rip, slit, split, gash.
5. morsel, taste, mouthful, bit *or* piece of food; snack, nosh.

biting, *adj.* **1.** caustic, mordant, acrimonious, bitter, acrid, acidulous, acid, pungent; trenchant, cutting, incisive, slashing, scathing; penetrating, piercing, stinging, pricking, nipping. See **bitter** (*defs.* **4-6**).

bitter, *adj.* **1.** (*all usu. of taste*) acrid, biting, pungent; acid, tart, harsh, sour, subacid, acetous, vinegarish, vinegary; unsweet, unsweetened; acerb, acerbic, acidulous, acidulent, acescent, acidulated; distasteful, unappetizing, unpalatable, unsavory; disagreeable, unpleasant, nasty, unlikeable.
2. distressful, distressing, harrowing, heartbreaking, heart rending, tormenting; sad, unhappy, sorrowful, woeful, tearful, lamentable, mournful, regretful; poignant, moving, touching; acute, intense, severe; painful, smarting, agonizing, torturous, excruciating; grievous, crushing, deplorable, dreadful, brutal; oppressive, burdensome, consuming, racking, onerous; ruinous, calamitous, disastrous, tragic.
3. hostile, resentful, indignant, piqued, angry; adverse, opposed, opposing; aggressive, belligerent, bellicose; peevish, petulant, crabbed, testy, splenetic, touchy, waspish, irascible, edgy; spiteful, virulent, malicious, venomous, vitriolic, vicious; antagonistic, rancorous, ill-disposed, malevolent, malign; ill-tempered, ill-humored, ill-natured, short-tempered; morose, surly, sullen, sour, moody.
4. caustic, mordant, acrimonious, bitter, acrid, acidulous, acid, pungent; trenchant, cutting, incisive, slashing, scathing; penetrating, piercing, stinging, pricking, nipping, biting; astringent, severe, stern, austere, stringent; harsh, keen, pointed, sharp, sharp-tongued.
5. sarcastic, satirical, ironic, ironical, cynical; double-edged, edged; contemptuous, contumelious, taunting, teasing; scornful, mocking, derisive, derisory, sardonic.
6. insulting, excoriating, denouncing, berating, lashing; abusive, corrosive, corroding, erosive; cruel, mean, brutal; unkind, uncharitable, unbenevolent, uncordial, unamiable, unfriendly.

bitterness, *n.* **1.** (*all usu. of taste*) sourness, acidity, vinegariness, tartness, harshness, sharpness, acerbity.
2. resentment, grudge, animosity, hostility; indignation, pique, dudgeon; rancor, choler, anger, bile, spleen; gall, wormwood, gall and wormwood.
3. acrimoniousness, causticity, asperity, mordancy, acridness, acridity, pungency, venom, venomousness, venomness; virulence, spitefulness, maliciousness, malice, viciousness; trenchancy, keenness, sarcasm, satire, irony; peevishness, petulance, *Rare.* petulancy, crab-

bedness, testiness, touchiness, irascibility, ill-temperedness, short-temperedness, edginess.

bivouac, *n.* encampment, lodgment, castrametation; camp, cantonment, casern; quarters, lodgings, barracks, billet, berth.

biweekly, *adj., adv.* **1.** fortnightly, twice monthly, semimonthly, twice a month, every two weeks, every other week.

2. (*loosely*) semiweekly, twice weekly, twice a week.

bizarre, *adj.* strange, odd, unusual, uncommon; abnormal, irregular, unconventional, deviant, deviate, aberrant, erratic; queer, peculiar, curious, singular, off-beat, *Inf.* funny; quaint, eccentric, quizzical, pixilated; ludicrous, ridiculous, comical, droll; weird, freakish, grotesque, fantastic, baroque, outlandish; freaky, *Inf.* kinky, *Sl.* flaky, *Sl.* screwball, *Sl.* off the wall; *Sl.* screwy, *Sl.* buggy, *Sl.* squirrely, *Sl.* balmy, *Chiefly Brit.* barmy, *Sl.* wacky.

blab, *v.* **1.** blurt out, let slip, tattle, tell on, inform on, *Sl.* squeal on; gossip, buzz, babble, report, bruit.

2. chatter, prattle, chipper, cackle; prate, bleat, *Inf.* gab, jabber; chitchat, chaffer, talk idly, *Sl.* shoot the breeze, *Sl.* chew the fat, *Sl.* shoot the bull.

black, *adj.* **1.** dark, pitch-black, coal-black, jet, jetty; ebony, ebon, raven, sable; inky, pitchy, nigritudinous, atramentous; blackish, nigrescent, swarthy, swart, dark-skinned.

2. Negro, Negroid, colored, Afro-American, Afra-merican; Negrito, Papuan, Melanesian; African, Negrillo, Pygmy, Zulu, Bantu, Ibo, Ethiopian, Ethiopic, Nubian.

3. dirty, sooty, dingy, soiled, sullied; filthy, grubby, sloppy, unclean; grimy, begrimed, smudgy, smeared, smirched, besmirched; murky, mirky, turbid, muddy, oozy.

4. dusky, crepuscular, dark, tenebrous; shady, shadowy, umbrageous, obscure, dim; overcast, cloudy, overclouded, lowering; misty, hazy, nubilous, *Archaic.* caliginous; smoky, fuliginous, filmy, fumy; dull, blurred, indistinct, lacklustre, opaque; unilluminated, lightless, unlighted, moonless, night, nocturnal, Cimmerian.

5. gloomy, dismal, cheerless, Stygian; somber, sullen, dour, dreary, *Literary.* drear; downcast, desolate, pessimistic, melancholy; mournful, lugubrious, funereal, morose; disconsolate, dispirited, dejected, depressed, despondent, forlorn.

6. threatening, menacing, ominous, forbidding, minacious; unpropitious, unpromising, infelicitous, inauspicious; foreboding, portentous, ill-omened; impending, imminent, hanging over, over-hanging, looming, pregnant with, fraught with; sinister, grim, dire, direful, dreadful; baleful, fell, pernicious, harmful, nocuous.

7. evil, wicked, sinful, iniquitous; nefarious, villainous, flagitious, heinous, *Rare.* nefast; base, bad, vile, vicious, foul, low; black-hearted, arrant, ignoble, odious; abominable, execrable, atrocious, outrageous, horrible; ghastly, gruesome, grisly, hideous, unspeakable; damnable, accursed, maleficent, malevolent; demonic, diabolic, devilish, satanic, fiendish, infernal.

8. disgraceful, contemptible, shameful, scurvy, opprobrious; abhorrent, loathsome, hateful, detestable, despicable; perfidious, treacherous, insidious, traitorous; unscrupulous, unprincipled, blackguardly, scoundrelly, knavish; criminal, wrong, reprehensible, felonious; unpardonable, unforgiveable; corrupt, depraved, degenerate, *Rare.* turpid.

9. in black and white absolute, positive, categorical, unequivocal; plain, clear, distinct, unmistakeable; apparent, evident, explicit, marked.

blackball, *n.* **1.** rejection, disapproval, denial, nay, no vote, turn down, thumbs down; exclusion, ostracism, barring, banning; ouster, ejection, expulsion.

—*v.* **2.** reject, disapprove, vote against, say [s.o.] nay; exclude, ban, spurn, shut out, bar; turn one's back on, set one's face against; repudiate, cast aside, disown, discard; ostracize, shun, leave out in the cold, keep at arm's length, snub, *Inf.* cut, *Inf.* cold-shoulder, give [s.o.] the cold shoulder, refuse to associate with, send to Coventry, *Inf.* high-hat; oust, eject, throw out, expel, drum out, cashier, *Sl.* dump.

blacken, *v.* **1.** charcoal, blackwash, ink, cork; smudge, soot, smoke, begrime, *Brit. Dial.* colly; darken, obscure, obfuscate, dim; eclipse, black out; shade, shadow.

2. slander, libel, calumniate, impute, asperse, traduce, falsify; injure, abuse, assail, stab, backbite, *Sl.* badmouth; slur, sully, defile, smear, smirch, soil, taint, tarnish, stain, spot, drag through the mud *or* mire, heap dirt upon.

3. defame, denigrate, vilify, run down, berate, revile, malign, impugn, gibbet, give a bad name, *Sl.* do a hatchet job on.

blackguard, *n.* **1.** scoundrel, wretch, cur, cad, dastard, knave, rascal, wastrel, ne'er-do-well, rogue, devil, villain; *All Inf.* bum, jerk, rat, creep, stinker, louse, *Derog.* bastard, *Derog.* SOB; *All Brit. Sl.* rotter, bounder, blighter.

—*v.* **2.** vilify, berate, revile, defame, denigrate, vituperate, run down, malign, gibbet, impugn, speak ill of, hold up to scorn, give a bad name, scandalize, *Sl.* do a hatchet job on.

blacklist, *n.* **1.** denouncement, condemnation, proscription.

2. list of suspects *or* offenders *or* outcasts, enemies list; *Rom. Cath. Ch. Index Librorum Prohibitorum,* Index.

3. label, mark, put on one's list; denounce, condemn, proscribe; boycott, shun, spurn, turn one's back on, set one's face against; prohibit, forbid, taboo.

—*v.* **4.** exclude, shut out, lock out, bar from; repudiate, disown, cast aside, reject, discard, blackball; isolate, leave out in the cold, cut, refuse to associate with, send to Coventry.

5. banish, exile, relegate, expatriate, outlaw, deport, transport; excommunicate, disfellow, disenfranchise; oust, eject, throw out, expel; discharge, drum out, cashier, *Sl.* bounce, *Sl.* dump.

blackmail, *n.* **1.** ransom, tribute, exacted *or* enforced payment; bribe, hush money, *Inf.* protection, *Inf.* payola, graft.

2. extortion, *Sl.* shake-down, exaction, *Inf.* the squeeze; milking, *Inf.* bleeding, blood-sucking; wresting, wrenching, wringing, extraction, elicitation; badger game, skin game, *Sl.* murphy.

—*v.* **3.** extort, *Inf.* bleed, milk, squeeze, get out of, obtain by force; put the arm on [s.o.], *Sl.* lean on *or* against, put the screws to [s.o.]; mulct, *Sl.* shake down, *Inf.* put the bite *or* squeeze *or* shake on; wrest, wrench, tear from, extract.

4. compel, make, coerce, force, threaten; require, demand, insist on *or* upon, command, enjoin; call for, necessitate, tax, *Obs.* task, requisition.

black sheep, *n.* outcast, pariah, reprobate, apostate, recreant, renegade, *Archaic.* renegado, strayer, wanderer; idler, good-for-nothing, ne'er-do-well, *Chiefly Brit.* wastrel, *U.S. Inf.* bum, *Sl.* loser.

bladder, *n.* vescia, sac, bag, receptacle, pocket, pouch, bursa, capsule, theca; saccule, saccula, utricle, vesicle, cyst, blister, bleb.

blade, *n.* **1.** cutting edge, edge, cutter, opener; knife, scalpel, lancet, bistoury; razor, chisel, penknife, jacknife, bowie knife; sword, rapier, cutlass, sabre; spear, bayonet, dagger, poniard, stiletto, machete.

2. leaf, *Bot.* lamina, *Bot.* phyllome, *Bot.* sepal, needle, frond; leaflet, *Bot.* foliole, *All. Bot.* bract, bractlet, bracteole; stem, stalk, *Bot.* peduncle, leafstalk, *Bot.* petiole; shoot, twig, sprig, switch.

3. buck, playboy, ladies' man, man about town, *Sl.* lover boy, philanderer; dandy, fop, beau, dude, exquisite, *Sl.* swell.

blain, *n.* boil, furuncle, furunculus, carbuncle, pustule, pimple, papule, papilla, pock, wen, whelk, *Rare.* bleb, *Archaic.* botch; abscess, ulcer, ulceration, noma, fester, festering, gathering, gumboil, parulis, tubercle, *Obs.* apostem *or* apostemation, *Archaic.* impostume *or* imposthume; canker, lesion, chancre, chancroid, simple chancre, soft chancre; sore, open *or* running sore, gall, excoriation; whitlow, agnail.

blamable, *adj.* culpable, guilty, at fault, wrong, in the wrong; chargeable, answerable, responsible, liable, impeachable, accusable, imputable.

blame, *v.* **1.** accuse, hold [s.o.] accountable *or* responsible, lay at [s.o.'s] door, point the finger at [s.o.], *Sl.* pin *or* stick [s.t.] on [s.o.], *Chiefly Scot.* wite; (*all in reference to culpability*) allege, ascribe, attribute, assign, impute, lay.

2. fault, find fault, criticize, censure, reproach, reprove, reprehend, objurgate; berate, disparage, belittle; scold, chide, upbraid, reprimand, take to task, *Inf.* dress down, *Inf.* get *or* jump on.

—*n.* **3.** censure, animadversion, stricture, rebuke, complaint, criticism, reflection, castigation; reproof, admonition, reprehension, reproach, objurgation, chiding; disparagement, belittling; condemnation, disapprobation, disapproval, denunciation, reprobation, obloquy.

4. accusation, charge, indictment, *Law.* true bill, *Law.* plaint, *Law.* complaint; incrimination, crimination, recrimination, denunciation, *Scot. and North Eng.* threap; implication, inculpation, *Chiefly Scot.* delation; (*all in reference to wrongdoing*) imputation, attribution, ascription, assignment, allegation.

5. culpability, blamableness, blameworthiness, censurability; responsibility, *Inf.* rap, *Chiefly Scot.* wite, guilt, fault, sin, *Scot. and North Eng.* dirdum.

blameless, *adj.* inculpable, unblamable, uncensurable, unimpeachable, irreproachable, above reproach, above suspicion; innocent, clear, guiltless, sinless, stainless; uncorrupted, undefiled, untainted, unspotted, unsullied, unsoiled, unblemished, unmarred, untarnished; virtuous, good, moral, upright, upstanding; faultless, sterling, perfect, saintly, without fault, peerless, without peer, matchless; admirable, estimable, worthy.

blameworthy, *adj.* reprehensible, reproachable, condemnable; indefensible, inexcusable, unjustifiable; blameful, discreditable, disreputable, ignoble, shameful, immoral, unprincipled; wicked, nefarious, iniquitous, flagitious.

blanch, *v.* **1.** whiten, bleach, pale, gray, wash out; etiolate, achromatize, decolor, decolorize; dim, fade, cloud, grow dull, lose luster *or* brightness.

2. blench, go white, pale, grow pale, become pallid, *Archaic.* wan; droop, flag, sag, faint; *Inf.* pass out, swoon, black out, *Inf.* keel over.

bland, *adj.* **1.** gentle, agreeable, affable, amiable, suave, urbane; cool, composed, unemotional, undemonstrative; soulless, unanimated, casual, indifferent, uncaring, unresponsive.

2. benign, mild, nonirritating, calming, *Med.* calmative, assuasive, demulcent, lenitive, *Med.* abirritant.

3. nonstimulating, dull, boring, uninteresting, insipid, vanilla, nondescript; unexciting, unappealing, unappetizing, unattractive; uncolorful, gray, indistinct, ordinary, everyday, average, so-so, mediocre, *Sl.* blah, *Sl.* nothing.

blandish, *v.* flatter, cajole, wheedle, coax, *Inf.* sweet-talk, *Inf.* soft-soap; praise, overpraise, compliment, puff up, inflate [s.o.'s] ego, butter [s.o.] up, humor, indulge, pamper; fawn on, curry favor with, *Sl.* fall all over, toady to, truckle to, *Sl.* suck up to, *Inf.* apple-polish, *Sl.* brown-nose.

blank, *adj.* **1.** empty, void, vacant, unfilled; unornamented, unadorned, unembellished; barren, plain, desolate, bleak, austere.

2. indifferent, uninterested, apathetic, emotionless; expressionless, inexpressive, deadpan, poker-faced; vacuous, inane, fatuous, foolish, empty-headed; unthinking, unreflecting, unreasoning, brainless.

3. disconcerted, confused, perplexed, bewildered; confounded, nonplused, taken aback, shocked, dazed, dumbfounded, stunned, floored; speechless, dumb, frozen, paralyzed.

4. complete, absolute, unqualified, unmitigated; pure, unadulterated, unalloyed, perfect, consummate.

—*n.* **5.** emptiness, void, vacuum, vacancy; nothingness, nil, nothing, zero; space, gap, break, interruption.

blanket, *n.* **1.** cover, comforter, quilt, afghan, coverlet, bedspread, spread, bedcover, counterpane; bedding, bedclothes, bedclothing, linens.

2. covering, coverture, coat, cloak, mantle, (*for a horse*) housing; layer, sheet, carpet, coating, film, gloss, veneer, finish; overcoat, overcoating, overlay; wrapper, wrapping, envelope, lining, casing, padding.

—*v.* **3.** cover, overlay, overspread, envelop, enwrap, surround, enclose; conceal, obscure, eclipse, cloud, becloud, shadow, shade; hide, screen, veil, shroud, shield, mask, cloak, curtain.

blare, *v.* **1.** trumpet, blast, bang, clang, peal, ring, buzz, sound loudly; honk, toot, blow one's horn; screech, shriek, wail, howl, whine; clamor, cry out, shout, scream, yell, *Inf.* holler; roar, bellow, boom, thunder; resound, resonate, trill, vibrate, reverberate, echo.

2. proclaim, herald, trumpet, ballyhoo, beat the drum; declare loudly, promulgate, make known, announce, broadcast, advertise, promote.

blarney, *n.* **1.** cajolery, wheedling, blandishment, honeyed words, *Inf.* sweet talk, *Inf.* soft soap; *Inf.* spiel, *Sl.* line, *Sl.* pitch, *Sl.* snow job.

2. nonsense, twaddle, blather, drivel, gobbledegook; humbug, foam, froth, bunkum, *Sl.* bunk; flummery, rubbish, tommyrot, balderdash, *Sl.* horsefeathers, hogwash; claptrap, rodomantade, fustian, bombast, *Sl.* hot air.

blasé, *adj.* **1.** indifferent, apathetic, uninterested, nonchalant, pococurante; neutral, lukewarm, cool, unmoved, insensible, uncaring, careless, mindless of; listless, spiritless, flagging, phlegmatic; unastonished, unamazed, unattracted by; insouciant, carefree, unconcerned, devil-may-care, heedless.

2. bored, weary, tired, sick of; jaded, hardened, inured; spoiled, pampered, overindulged, sheltered, overprotected, catered to; surfeited, satiated, cloyed, glutted, gorged, overfed; saturated, full, replete, satisfied.

blaspheme, *v.* **1.** curse, execrate, damn, imprecate, anathematize, *Archaic.* ban, swear, *U.S. Inf.* cuss; profane, desecrate; denounce, excoriate, cry down, reproach, fulminate; criticize, censure, animadvert, *Sl.*

blast.

2. abuse, revile, vituperate, oppugn, assail, lash, rail against, inveigh against, *Inf.* sail into, *Inf.* jump down [s.o.'s] throat; vilify, traduce, asperse, calumniate, impugn, slur, malign, defame, denigrate, slander, libel, backbite; disparage, discredit, decry, depreciate, deprecate, belittle, minimize, run *or* put down, *Sl.* badmouth; scorn, deride, gibbet, ridicule, mock, lampoon, pasquinade, make fun of.

blasphemous, *adj.* sacrilegious, profane, irreligious, irreverent, maledictory; unholy, impious, undevout, ungodly, godless; unblest, unsanctified, unconsecrated, unhallowed; wicked, sinful, evil, iniquitous.

blast, *n.* **1.** gust, flaw, windflaw, flurry, high *or* stiff wind, whirlwind; squall, gale, blow, storm, tempest.

2. blare, honk, bellow, bray, blat, trumpet, toot; wail, shriek, screech, scream; peal, clang; noise, racket, din, clamor.

3. explosion, discharge, detonation, crash, roar, boom, burst, eruption; rumble, roll, thunder, fulmination; flash, flare, fulguration; shot, crack, report; volley, salvo, fusillade.

4. blight, curse, bane, scourge, visitation, stroke, affliction; plague, pestilence, pest, infestation.

—*v.* **5.** blare, trumpet, bugle, blat, bray; honk, toot, beep; shriek, screech, scream, wail; sound, peal.

6. ruin, destroy, blight, waste, lay waste, devastate, ravage; annihilate, exterminate, extirpate, eradicate, wipe *or* blot out.

7. demolish, blow up, blow to pieces, blow sky high; explode, detonate, discharge, go off, burst, boom, thunder, roar.

8. discredit, disprove, invalidate, belie, give the lie to, shoot *or* poke full of holes, knock the bottom out of.

9. curse, damn, confound, execrate, imprecate, curse up hill and down dale.

blatant, *adj.* **1.** obtrusive, flagrant, glaring, egregious; flaunting, brazen, shameless, arrant, notorious; overt, obvious, manifest, clear, bald, baldfaced; sheer, outright, out-and-out, unmitigated, hard-core.

2. noisy, clamorous, clamant, rackety, obstreperous, vociferous; tumultuous, boisterous, uproarious, roaring, rip-roaring, *Inf.* honky-tonk.

3. garish, gaudy, tawdry, loud, lurid, screaming; vulgar, coarse, tasteless, crude, crass, cheap, *Inf.* chintzy.

blather, *n.* **1.** drivel, driveling, blether, *Inf.* blithering; gushing, blabbing, *Inf.* spouting, excessive talk; babble, babbling, babblement, prate, prating, foolish talk; twaddle, twaddling, *Both Brit.* twattle, twattling; prattle, prattling, gibber, gibbering, gibberish; jabber, jabbering, Jabberwocky, *Sl.* gibber-jabbering; nonsense, moonshine, *Fr. bavardage,* gobbledegook, hocus-pocus, mumbo-jumbo, abracadabra, open-sesame; humbug, flummery, *Sl.* bunk, rubbish, *Inf.* rot, *Sl.* garbage, *Sl.* horsefeathers; balderdash, hogwash, stuff and nonsense, *Inf.* bosh, *Brit. Sl.* tosh, fudge, foolishness, rigmarole *or* rigamarole; poppycock, *Inf.* fiddle-faddle, *Inf.* piffle, *Inf.* kibosh, *Inf.* flapdoodle.

—*v.* **2.** blether, *Inf.* blither, babble; prate, bleat, twaddle, *Brit.* twattle; talk nonsense, *Inf.* talk through one's hat; drivel, gibber, *Sl.* gibber-jabber, jargon.

3. jabber, chatter, chipper, prattle, cackle, *Inf.* gab; chit-chat, chitter-chatter, make small talk, chaffer, bandy words; talk idly, *Sl.* shoot the breeze, *Sl.* gas, *Sl.* bull; palaver, clack, clatter, rattle, *Sl.* run off *or* on at the mouth; gush, blab, *Inf.* spout.

blaze, *n.* **1.** fire, flame, bonfire, *Brit. Dial.* ingle; conflagration, *Obs.* flagration, holocaust, wildfire, ring *or* sea of fire, wall *or* sheet of flames.

2. glow, gleam, glimmer, shimmer; flicker, blink, glint, glance, twinkle; flash, streak, fulguration.

3. outburst, outbreak, eruption, explosion, burst, blast, flare-up, spasm, convulsion; flood, torrent, deluge, rush.

—*v.* **4.** burn, flame, burst into flames, catch on fire, take fire.

5. shine, glow, gleam, glimmer, shimmer; blink, flicker, twinkle, glint, glance; flash, flare, glare; glitter, dazzle, bedazzle.

6. burn up, flare up, blaze up, *Inf.* see red, *Sl.* get hot under the collar; seethe, sizzle, smolder, boil, stew, simmer, fume, stir, *Inf.* do a slow burn, *Inf.* steam up, *Sl.* work oneself up into a lather *or* sweat *or* stew.

7. open fire, commence firing, fire away, *Sl.* blast away, *Sl.* open up on.

bleach, *v.* whiten, blanch, blench, wash out; etiolate, achromatize, decolor, decolorize; gray, pale, dim, cloud, fade; grow dull, lose luster *or* brightness.

bleachers, *n.* grandstand, tiers, stands; benches, long seats, seats, stools, settles, pews, *Brit.* forms.

bleak, *adj.* **1.** bare, barren, desolate, windswept, windy, exposed, open, unsheltered; desert, waste, poor, dry, arid, bald, empty, naked, dead; exhausted, depleted, worn out, impoverished, meager, scanty, scarce, lean; uncultivable, uncultivatable, fallow, unproductive, unyielding, unfruitful, fruitless, unfructuous.

2. rigorous, severe, bad, sharp, bitter, biting, cutting, nipping, piercing; frigid, very cold, raw, hyperborean, arctic; icy, glacial, gelid, frozen, freezing; ice-cold; frosty, chilly, algid, wintry, brumal, hibernal; snowy, niveous, stormy, inclement.

3. hopeless, depressing, discouraging, without promise; uninviting, dreary, *Literary.* drear, dismal, gloomy, cheerless, joyless; drab, dull, flat, monotonous; somber, melancholy, sad, mournful, forlorn, miserable, wretched.

blear, *v.* **1.** blur, tear, water, cry; dim, cloud. See **blur** (*def.* **2**).

—*adj.* **2.** blurred, blurry, dimmed, clouded, unclear, fogged, foggy.

—*n.* **3.** blur, cloudiness, dimness. See **blur** (*def.* **5**).

bleat, *v.* **1.** baa, blat, bray, whinny, cry, call; babble, prate, blather, blab.

—*n.* **2.** baa, whinny, bray, cry, call; babble, prating, blather.

bleed, *v.* **1.** shed blood, lose blood; flow, trickle, spout; exude, ooze, seep; run, diffuse, spread.

2. draw, take blood, *Med.* phlebotomize; drain, sap, deplete, exhaust, fag, weaken; exact, extort, extract, milk, squeeze, fleece.

3. anguish, ache, sorrow, grieve; suffer, pity, feel, sympathize, empathize.

blemish, *v.* **1.** mark, spot, speckle, stain, sully, tarnish, taint; injure, damage, impair, deface, mar.

—*n.* **2.** defect, fault, defacement, disfigurement, flaw, crack, scratch, mark; stain, blot, spot, speck, blur, smudge, smirch, smutch, taint; patch, blotch, discoloration, birthmark, nevus; mole, wart, pimple, wen, blain, bump, *Sl.* zit; scar, pock, cicatrix; bruise, *Sl.* hickey.

blench, *v.* flinch, wince, start, shy, recoil, blink; quiver, shiver, shudder, quake, tremble, shake, flutter; quail, cower, shrink, *Inf.* funk, crouch, retire, hang back, skulk; hesitate, falter, *Chiefly Brit.* jib; take to one's heels, turn tail, run away from, fly from, turn aside, swerve; evade, elude, shun, avoid, eschew, shirk, dodge.

blend, *v.* **1.** mix, admix, commix, intermix; mingle, commingle, scramble, intermingle, interlard; compound, combine, alloy, *Chem.* levigate, merge,

coalesce, melt together; unite, join, inosculate, fuse, amalgamate, incorporate; intertwine, interweave, link together; synthesize, homogenize, hybridize, mongrelize.
2. harmonize, go with, complement, suit, fit.
—*n.* **3.** combination, amalgamation, assimilation, incorporation; mixture, admixture, commixture, intermixture, mingling, intermingling, commingling; junction, union, fusion, synthesis; hybridization, mongrelization, homogenization; hybrid, mongrel, half-breed.

bless, *v.* **1.** consecrate, sanctify, hallow, dedicate; glorify, extol, praise, exalt, honor; canonize, *Rom. Cath. Ch.* beatify, make holy, baptize, anoint; make the sign of the cross, *Archaic.* sain, give benediction; absolve, pardon, acquit.
2. sanction, approve, be in favor of, support, endorse, countenance, smile upon; assent, consent, permit, allow.

blessed, *adj.* **1.** consecrated, sanctified, hallowed, sacred, holy, divine; venerated, reverenced, revered; glorified, extolled, exalted; sainted, canonized, *Rom. Cath. Ch.* beatified.
2. happy, joyful, joyous, exultant, blissful; elated, buoyant, sunny, cheerful, blithe; glad, pleased, contented.
3. fortunate, favored, lucky; endowed, granted, bequeathed, furnished, provided, supplied.

blessing, *n.* **1.** benediction, *Archaic.* benison, grace, thanksgiving, prayer, invocation; devotion, worship, praise, honor, glorification, exaltation; absolution, pardon, acquittal.
2. benefit, boon, advantage, profit, gain; favor, luck, good fortune, relief; bounty, gift, gratuity, alms, offering, benefaction.

blight, *n.* **1.** affliction, infliction, infestation, plague, scourge, bane; pestilence, disease, sickness, illness, *Pathol.* rot, *Plant Pathol.* dry rot, *Vet. Pathol.* worms; ulcer, canker, sore; fungus, mold, mildew, mucor.
2. curse, misfortune, bad luck, ill fortune, calamity; trouble, woe, tribulation, vexation, torment.
—*v.* **3.** blast, plague, scourge, afflict, inflict; destroy, ruin, devastate, kill.
4. wither, shrivel, ulcerate; mildew, rot, decay, die.

blind, *adj.* **1.** sightless, visionless, unsighted, unseeing, eyeless, stone-blind, amaurotic; purblind, partially sighted, blear-eyed, *Ophthal.* hemeralopic, *Ophthal.* nyctalopic.
2. obtuse, thick, dense, imperceptive, short-sighted; retarded, slow, dull, bovine, stolid, feeble-minded, weak-minded, weak-headed, slow-witted, stupid, *Sl.* dim-witted, *Inf.* dumb.
3. rash, impetuous, hasty, reckless, uncontrolled, unrestrained, wild, savage, violent, furious; irrational, unreasonable, unreasoning, mindless, senseless, unthinking, thoughtless, uncritical, undiscerning; unfathomable, incomprehensible, hard to see *or* understand.
4. ignorant, nescient, naive, unaware, unenlightened, unacquainted, unconversant, unversed; incognizant, unknowing, unapprised, uninformed; insensitive, insensible, unconscious, unfeeling; indifferent, insusceptible, unaffected, untouched, unmoved.
5. concealed, obscure, covered, hidden, hideaway, out of sight *or* view; undisclosed, unrevealed, unknown; anonymous, unidentified, unnamed.
6. closed, shut, sealed; obstructed, blocked, barred, blockaded, barricaded; impassable, dead-end, without exit.
—*v.* **7.** poke *or* put [s.o.'s] eyes out, gouge out the eyes of, render sightless, deprive of sight; cut off [s.o.'s] view, block [s.o.'s] line of vision, blindfold, get in [s.o.'s] way, *Archaic.* hoodwink.
8. conceal, hide, cover up, screen; obfuscate, obscure, cloud over, fog up, adumbrate, muddy.
—*n.* **9.** shade, cover, screen, shield, mantel, cloak, veil, curtain, drape, envelopment; mask, blinker, blinder, shutter.
10. concealment, hiding place, hideaway; subterfuge, cover, cloak, camouflage, masquerade, disguise, *Inf.* front.
11. affectation, pretense, deception, delusion, feint, fake, fraud; artifice, strategem, maneuver, chicanery, guile, wile, finesse, evasion, smoke screen; decoy, ruse, trick, trap, snare, net, catch, ambush, pitfall, *Inf.* dodge.
12. *Usu.* **the blind** the sightless, the visionless, the unsighted, the partially sighted.

blindfold, *v.* **1.** cover [s.o.'s] eyes, *Archaic.* hoodwink. See **blind** (*def.* **7**).
2. obfuscate, obscure, cloud over, fog up. See **blind** (*def.* **8**).
—*n.* **3.** mask, blinker, blinder, shutter. See **blind** (*def.* **9**).
—*adj.* **4.** rash, impetuous, irrational, unthinking. See **blind** (*def.* **3**).

blink, *v.* **1.** wink, nictitate, nictate; flutter, flicker.
2. squint, screw up the eyes, see with half an eye, look askance; glimpse, spot, espy, descry, spy, perceive, glance at.
3. wince, flinch, start, shrink, recoil, blench; quiver, shudder, quake, tremble, flutter; be startled, be shocked, be surprised, *Sl.* be freaked out.
4. ignore, overlook, bypass, disregard, pass over, neglect; slight, snub, ostracize, cut; shirk, evade, elude, shun, avoid, dodge.
5. twinkle, glisten, gleam, glimmer, glitter, coruscate, shimmer, sparkle, *Archaic.* glister; glow, blaze, radiate, shine, beam; flicker, flutter, waver, dance, glare; scintillate, bedazzle, flash, fulgurate; phosphoresce, be luminous.
—*n.* **6.** wink, flutter, flicker, waver, dance.
7. twinkle, gleam, glimmer, shimmer, sparkle, flash; glowing, shining, blaze.
8. **on the blink** *Slang.* in need of repair, *Sl.* on the fritz, in bad shape, not operating, out of order, *Inf.* out of whack *or* kilter, out of commission, broken; *Both Inf.* far gone, done for.

bliss, *n.* **1.** delight, happiness, felicity, enjoyment, delectation, pleasure, luxury; joy, joyousness, exaltation, elation, rapture, jubilation, ecstasy, ravishment; exhilaration, gaiety, jollity, gladness, cheer, glee, *Archaic.* joyance; enchantment, transport, captivation, fascination; gratification, fulfillment, contentment, glory.
2. heaven, Eden, seventh heaven, utopia, paradise; Elysium, Arcadia, sunshine, halcyon days; beatitude, serenity, peace, heavenly peace, blessfulness, blessedness.

blister, *n.* **1.** blain, boil, furuncle, carbuncle, pustule, pimple, papule, pock, wen, whelk, *Rare.* bleb, *Archaic.* botch. See **blain**.
2. swelling, bulging, bulge, bubble, protuberance, projection, prominence; growth, tumor, intumescence, tumefaction.
—*v.* **3.** vesicate, swell, tumefy.
4. thrash, whip, spank, batter, beat, beat up, punish.
5. excoriate, denounce, criticize, attack, assail, castigate, scathe; shame, disgrace, embarrass, mortify.

blithe, *adj.* **1.** cheerful, gay, jocund, jolly, merry, gleeful, blithesome; happy, pleased, contented, glad; ecstatic, joyful, elated, joyous, rejoicing, exultant, jubilant, overjoyed; enthusiastic, animated, spirited, flushed, buoyant, frisky, skittish; rollicking, playful, gamesome, frolicsome, sportive; jocular, jocose, joking, jesting, waggish; jovial, mirthful, delightful, gladsome, hilarious; sprightly, light-hearted, debonair, jaunty, lively, airy, brisk, spry.

2. genial, convivial, easygoing, amiable, friendly, outgoing; winsome, sunny, smiling, cheery, riant; optimistic, in good spirits, positive; bubbling, sparkling, effervescent.

3. carefree, free and easy, heedless, untroubled, unconcerned, happy-go-lucky; nonchalant, casual, indifferent, blase, devil-may-care; apathetic; dispassionate, detached, cool.

blizzard, *n.* snowstorm, snow squall, snow flurry, snow, snowfall; storm, squall, tempest, rainstorm, thunderstorm, hailstorm; hurricane, typhoon, tornado, whirlwind, *U.S. Inf.* twister, cyclone; gale, wind, blast, blow, windstorm.

bloat, *v.* swell, puff out *or* up, balloon, inflate, *Obs.* sufflate, pump up; expand, distend, stretch, dilate, spread out, fill up *or* out, round out; enlarge, get bigger, grow, gain, increase, pad.

blob, *n.* **1.** globule, drop, droplet, glob, gutta, bubble, dewdrop, pearl, tear; bead, spherule, spheroid, oval; pellet, ball, shot, pea, pill; lump, mass, dab, particle, dash, speck, dot, iota.

2. spot, mark, splotch, splash, dash, daub; stain, soil, smutch, blot, blotch, blemish; smudge, smear, dirty mark, finger print.

3. dullard, dolt, dunce, *Inf.* numskull, dope, booby, *Inf.* dummy, *Sl.* dumbbell; simpleton, Simple Simon, dimwit, nitwit, halfwit, *Sl.* zombie. See **fool** (*def.* **1**).

—*v.* **4.** spot, mark, splotch, splash, bespatter; bedaub, daub all over, blot, blotch, blemish; sully, stain, soil, dirty, smutch, begrime; smudge, smear, besmear, smirch.

bloc, *n.* **1.** alliance, coalition, union, league, entente, bund, federation, confederation; syndicate, cartel, combine, machine.

2. council, junta, conclave, assembly, diet, convention; party, faction, ring, group, splinter group, *Inf.* push, *Inf.* crew, *Inf.* gang; set, circle, coterie, clique; cabal, conspiracy, collusion, junto, plot, complot, camarilla, secret group *or* society.

block, *n.* **1.** chunk, brick, cake, cube, loaf, *Inf.* hunk; mass, lump, clod, clump, gob, wad; piece, wedge, bar.

2. scaffold, guillotine, maiden.

3. obstacle, obstruction, barrier, barricade, blockade; stop, impediment, hindrance, check, deterrent, hurdle, stumbling block; constraint, restraint, trammel; snag, catch, hitch, rub, drawback, fly in the ointment; congestion, jam, blockage, stoppage; dead end, blind alley, cul-de-sac, impasse.

4. mental block, psychological block, memory obstruction.

5. blockhead, dunce, nincompoop, half-wit. See **blockhead.**

—*v.* **6.** obstruct, impede, hinder, deter, bar, blockade, barricade, stand in the way; stop, stay, restrain, constrain, trammel, bridle, retard, frustrate, thwart.

7. fend off, ward off, stave off, beat off; parry, fend, counter.

8. shape, mold, form, fashion, tailor, frame.

9. plan, plan out, lay plans, lay out a plan, lay out, work out, sketch out, map out, hammer out, knock out; outline, delineate, schematize.

blockade, *n.* **1.** siege, besiegement, beleaguerment, investment, encirclement, envelopment, cutting off of supply lines.

2. barrier, barricade, obstacle, obstruction; stop, block, impediment, hindrance, check, deterrent, hurdle, stumbling block; congestion, jam, blockage, stoppage.

—*v.* **3.** besiege, siege, lay siege to, invest, contain, confine, cordon off; surround, encircle, encompass, hedge in, pen in, shut in.

blockhead, *n.* dunce, lunkhead, bonehead, knucklehead, fathead, pinhead, numskull, addlepate; fool, tomfool, dope, nincompoop, ninny, lightweight; oaf, boor, lout, dolt, dullard, *Inf.* chump, lummox, looby, *Sl.* klutz; idiot, simpleton, half-wit, lamebrain, pinbrain, moron, cretin, imbecile; *All Sl.* chump, sap, dumbbell, dingbat, ding-a-ling, meatball, meathead, jerk, booby, boob, noodle, blubberhead, nudnik, schmuck, schlemiel, *U.S.* schmo.

blond, blonde, *adj.* light, fair, light-colored, fair-skinned, light-toned; fair-headed, light-haired, tow-headed, whitish, *Archaic.* argent; golden-haired, flaxen.

blood, *n.* **1.** fluid, life fluid, *Class. Myth.* ichor, whole blood; grume, *Obs.* cruor, gore, plasma; juice, sap, latex, milk.

2. vital principle, vital force, *Fr. élan vital,* life-blood, life, being, vitality.

3. temperament, humor, nature, temper, state of mind, mood, spirit; disposition, character, makeup, mettle, constitution.

4. ancestry, lineage, heritage, genealogy, background, family, house; extraction, stock, pedigree, race; descent, derivation, origin, stirps, line; kinship, kindred, consanguinity, cognation, blood ties, blood lines.

5. in cold blood deliberately, premeditatively, intentionally, on purpose, knowingly, *Law.* with malice aforethought *or* malice prepense.

bloodless, *adj.* **1.** pale, wan, sickly, colorless, anemic; pallid, sallow, ashen, chalky, pasty; peaked, faint, faded, whey-faced; gaunt, haggard, drawn, emaciated; livid, deathly, deathlike, cadaverous; ghostly, ghastly, grim, white as a ghost *or* as a sheet.

2. spiritless, languid, dull, listless, sluggish, torpid; phlegmatic, apathetic, indifferent, lackadaisical.

bloodshed, *n.* slaughter, carnage, butchery, bloodbath, bloodletting; massacre, pogrom, mass-murder, genocide; destruction, decimation, extermination, *Rare.* trucidation, *Rare,* internecion; killing, slaying, homicide, murder, manslaughter.

bloodthirsty, *adj.* **1.** murderous, slaughterous, homicidal; ferocious, fierce, savage, ruthless, vicious, fell, truculent; brutal, inhuman, barbarous, barbaric, barbarian, hellish, brutish; sadistic, animalistic, cannibalistic, fiendish, ogreish; diabolical, demonic, demoniac, devilish.

2. harsh, grim, severe, unrelenting, grinding, remorseless; merciless, heartless, pitiless; cruel, hard-hearted, stony-hearted, marble-hearted; revengeful, vengeful, out for revenge, out for blood.

bloody, *adj.* **1.** bleeding, sanguinolent, *Med.* phlebotomical.

2. bloodstained, sanguinary, ensanguined, gory, blood-soaked.

3. slaughterous, murderous, homicidal; feral, brutal, cruel. See **bloodthirsty**.

4. hemal, hematal, hematic, sanguineous.

bloom, *n.* **1.** flower, blossom, inflorescence, floweret, floret; efflorescence, flowerage, *Bot.* anthesis; bud, burgeon, florescence, flowering, blossoming.

2. flush, glow, freshness; luster, gloss, sheen; health, soundness, vigor, strength, prime, heyday.

—*v.* **3.** flower, *Archaic.* blow, blossom; bud, burgeon, sprout, pullulate.

4. germinate, develop, grow, wax; flourish, prosper, thrive, luxuriate, batten.

blooming, *adj.* **1.** abloom, in bloom, flowering, blossoming, in blossom.

2. growing, waxing, flourishing, prospering, thriving, luxuriant; glowing, flushed, radiant; vigorous, healthy, sound.

blossom, *n.* **1.** bloom, flower, floweret. See **bloom** (*def.* **1**).

—*v.* **2.** flower, germinate, grow. See **bloom** (*defs.* **3, 4**).

blot, *n.* **1.** spot, speck, blotch, patch, dot, mark; smudge, smutch, smear, smirch, blur; stain, soil, dirt.

2. blemish, taint, flaw, mar; defect, fault, crack, scratch; imperfection, disfigurement, defacement.

—*v.* **3.** spot, smudge, smutch, mark, ink; speckle, bedaub, bespatter, draggle, drabble, *Archaic.* daggle; smirch, smear, slime; soil, dirty, sully, besmirch, muck, bemire; stain, tarnish, blacken, discolor, mar.

4. *Usu.* **blot out** obscure, shadow, adumbrate, darken, dim; obliterate, erase, expunge, rub out, delete, cancel, cross out, mark over *or* through, scratch out, *Print.* dele; annihilate, exterminate, extirpate, abolish, demolish, destroy, ruin, wipe out.

5. absorb, soak up, extract moisture from, dry out.

blotch, *n.* **1.** blob, glob, patch, globule, splash. See **blot** (*def.* **1**).

2. blemish, pimple, blackhead, eruption, *Sl.* zit, *Pathol.* wen; sore, pustule, blister, *Pathol.* blain, *Pathol.* cyst; bump, mole, wart, pock, bruise, birthmark, *Med.* nevus, *Sl.* hickey; scar, mar, taint, defect, fault, imperfection, discoloration, disfigurement, defacement.

—*v.* **3.** smear, smirch, stain. See **blot** (*def.* **3**).

blotter, *n.* record, register, list, day book, police blotter.

blow[1], *n.* **1.** slap, punch, hit, *Inf.* clout, *Inf.* buff, *Sl.* shot, *Sl.* slug, *Sl.* paste, *Sl.* bash, *Sl.* rap 'side the head. See **bat**[1] (*def.* **2**).

2. shock, calamity, reversal. See **calamity** (*def.* **2**).

3. **come to blows** fight, spar, grapple, scuffle, tussle, brawl, *Sl.* mix it up, engage in fisticuffs; dispute, skirmish, fall out, clash, row.

4. **without striking a blow** effortlessly, easily, without contest, *Inf.* hands down, *Inf.* walking away.

5. **strike the first blow** take the initiative, make the first move, lead off, start the ball rolling, meet [s.o.] head-on. See **begin** (*def.* **3**).

blow[2], *v.* **1.** breeze, flurry, puff; bluster, squall, blast; fly, soar, zoom, sail, float, drift; wave, flap, flutter, ruffle, flourish, undulate, waft, toss.

2. exhale, respire, expel, emit, spout, give off, vent; puff, pant, huff, wheeze, gasp, breathe hard; whistle, whiffle, wind, whoosh, sigh, suspire, exude.

3. sound, blast, blare, toot, toodle.

4. *Informal.* brag, boast, crow, bluff, *Inf.* talk big.

5. burst, explode, rupture, pop; break open, split open, crack, split; implode, pop in, collapse; blow up, shatter, burn out, blow out, puncture; destroy, demolish, detonate; erupt, burst forth.

6. *Slang.* lavish, spend freely, *Sl.* spend as if money is going out of style, *Inf.* throw one's money around; squander, waste, fritter away, misspend, run through, dissipate.

7. *Slang.* botch, bungle, muff, make a mess *or* hash of; mismanage, *Inf.* mess up, *Inf.* screw up.

8. **blow hot and cold** waver, vascillate, fluctuate, shift *or* go back and forth, *Inf.* shilly-shally.

9. **blow one's stack *or* top** lose one's temper, become enraged, flare up, lose control, *Sl.* flip one's lid, *Sl.* flip out; shout, yell, scream, bellow, roar.

10. **blow out** extinguish, snuff out, smother, stifle, douse, quash.

11. **blow over** cease, end, conclude, finish, terminate, come to an end; pass, pass away, come to rest, subside, settle down; sink into oblivion, be forgotten, go out of one's head, be gone, be buried in the past.

12. **blow up** exaggerate, enlarge on, overstate, embroider, color, stretch, heighten; enlarge, magnify, expand, amplify, distend, inflate, balloon.

—*n.* **13.** puff, breeze, zephyr, gust, flurry; wind, disturbance, turbulence, windstorm, storm, tempest, gale, blast; hurricane, tornado, whirlwind, cyclone, twister, squall, blizzard, northeaster; monsoon, simoom, sirocco.

14. sound, blast, blare; whine, wail, shriek; whistle, toot.

blowzy, *adj.* **1.** ruddy, red-faced, red, florid, rubicund, sanguine; bloated, puffy, swollen, pletoric, turgid, tumid.

2. disheveled, tousled, frowzy, uncombed, messed, mussy; unkempt, bedraggled, untidy, slipshod, slovenly, sloppy, slatternly.

blubber, *v.* **1.** cry, wail, whimper *Inf.* boohoo. See **bawl** (*def.* **3**).

—*n.* **2.** cry, caterwauling, bawl. See **bawl** (*def.* **5**).

bludgeon, *n.* **1.** club, cudgel, night-stick, *Inf.* billy, *Inf.* billy club, *Brit.* truncheon; blackjack, *Sl.* sap.

—*v.* **2.** club, cudgel, strike, hit, *Sl.* clout, beat, *Inf.* beat on; fell, knock down, beat up, beat senseless, *Inf.* clobber, *Sl.* sap. See **beat** (*defs.* **1, 7**).

3. coerce, bully. See **hector** (*def.* **3**) and **beat** (*def.* **8**).

blue, *n.* **1.** sky, blue skies, empyrean, firmament, vault of heaven, azure deeps, *Chiefly Literary.* welkin; the air, the atmosphere.

2. **out of the blue** suddenly, unexpectedly, all of a sudden. See **suddenly** (*def.* **1**).

—*adj.* **3.** sky-blue, baby-blue, powder-blue, deep-blue; azure, sapphire, cyan blue, aquamarine, turquoise, marine blue, ultramarine, lapis lazuli, navy, indigo.

4. depressed, despondent, morose, doleful, dispirited, unhappy, sad, downcast, glum; dismal, bleak, gloomy, depressing, dispiriting.

5. righteous, puritanical, moralistic, severe, strict, rigid, prudish.

6. *Informal.* indecent, risqué, bawdy, obscene, *Inf.* dirty; vulgar, coarse, offensive, improper.

bluff[1], *adj.* **1.** frank, open, honest, candid, plain-spoken, outspoken; direct, plain, straightforward, downright; crude, rough, unvarnished, burly, blustering.

2. steep, sheer, abrupt, sudden, precipitous; perpendicular, vertical; acclivitous, ascending, rising; bold, towering.

—*n.* **3.** cliff, palisade, scarp, ridge, escarpment; crag, peak; headland, promontory, foreland; wall, bank, slope, height, knoll.

bluff[2], *v.* **1.** mislead, delude, deceive, bamboozle, hoodwink, fake [s.o.] out, blind, pull the wool over [s.o.'s] eyes, throw dust in [s.o.'s] eyes; fool, trick, hoax, humbug, cozen, take in, put one over on, *Brit. Inf.* gammon.

2. pretend, feign, fake, sham, *Inf.* four-flush, *Inf.* bull; bluster, roister, puff, *Sl.* blow hard, *Sl.* talk big; brag, boast, hector, trumpet, bluster and bluff.

—*n.* **3.** sham, fake, show, false show, mere show, *Inf.* bull, *Inf.* four-flushing; bravado, braggadocio, bluster, fanfaronade.

4. fake, fraud, humbug, *Inf.* phony, *Inf.* fourflusher; blusterer, bluffer, blatherskite, *Sl.* blowhard, *Sl.* windbag; braggart, boaster, gascon, fanfaron.

5. call someone's bluff take one up on, take a dare, accept a challenge, take up the gauntlet.

blunder, *n.* **1.** mistake, error, flaw, fault, inaccuracy; botch, abortion, miscarriage, fiasco, fizzle, foozle, fumble, *Sl.* screwup; misunderstanding, misconception; inadvertence, omission, oversight, slip, *Inf.* slip-up, *Sl.* boo-boo, *Sl.* goof, *Sl.* boner; folly, stupidity, foolishness.

2. imprudence, impropriety, indiscretion, faux pas, gaffe, gaucherie, solecism; malapropism, spoonerism, howler, *Sl.* blooper, slip of the lip, slip of the tongue, slip of the pen, Freudian slip.

—*v.* **3.** flounder, stumble, bungle, slip, *Sl.* goof *or* goof up, *Inf.* flub; err, slip up, make a mistake; miscalculate, misjudge, misreckon, miscount, mistake; fail, miss, miscarry, abort, miss the mark; fumble, boggle, botch *or* botch up, mess up, hash up, *Sl.* screw up, muff, blow it, foozle, put one's foot in one's mouth.

blunt, *adj.* **1.** dull, rounded, not sharp, unpointed, edgeless, unsharpened, thick.

2. abrupt, curt, short, brusque; frank, candid, open, direct, outspoken, plain-spoken; plain, downright, unvarnished, straightforward; bluff, burly, brash, bold, brazen, barefaced, insolent, impudent; sharp, keen, trenchant, acrimonious, caustic, stinging, cutting, biting, piercing, stringent; brutal, cruel; churlish, bearish, gruff; inconsiderate, tactless, blustering; rude, uncivil, unceremonious, ungracious, discourteous, impolite, unmannerly.

3. dull, dim-witted, stupid, slow, thick, stolid, dense; insensitive, obtuse, unperceiving; unseeing, unobserving, inattentive.

—*v.* **4.** dull, round, soften, take the edge off of.

5. numb, stupefy, deaden, obtund; weaken, impair, devitalize; anesthetize, tranquilize, pacify, appease, soothe, mollify.

blur, *v.* **1.** smear, besmear, smirch, smudge; sully, dirty, soil, stain, smutch, begrime; bedaub, daub all over, blot, splotch, spot, blemish, splash, bespatter; blotch, mar, deface.

2. obscure, befog, obfuscate, make indistinct, dim, bedim; (*all of the eyes*) blur, tear, water, cry; cloud, becloud, overcast, overshadow, adumbrate, cast a gloom over, shadow, shade; eclipse, blot out, conceal, hide, screen, veil, shroud, mask, cover, cloak, curtain; overlay, overspread, blanket, envelop, surround, enclose.

3. dull, numb, anesthetize, make insensible, deaden, kill.

—*n.* **4.** smudge, smear, dirty mark, spot, stain, soil, smutch, blot, splotch, blotch, blemish; dirt, grime, filth.

5. blurredness, blear, indistinctness, dimness; cloudiness, fog, foginess, obscurity, obscureness, gloom, darkness, shadows, shade.

blurt, *v.* gush, blab, utter suddenly, ejaculate, exclaim, spout, call out; reveal, disclose, speak out of turn, let slip, give away the game, *Inf.* spill the beans, *Inf.* let the cat out of the bag. See **babble** (*def.* **4**).

blush, *v.* **1.** redden, color, flush, turn red *or* scarlet, crimson, mantle, glow.

—*n.* **2.** reddening, color, flush, rosiness, ruddiness; tint, hue, hint, suggestion.

bluster, *v.* **1.** spout, blast, roar, trumpet; gasp, wheeze, huff, puff, pant.

2. swagger, strut, roister, harangue, *Sl.* blow hard, *Sl.* blow, *Sl.* talk big; throw one's weight around, be overbearing, lord it over, give [s.o.] a hard time, bully, badger.

—*n.* **3.** racket, hubbub, hullabaloo, tumult, commotion, confusion; fanfaronade, bravado, bragging, braggadocio.

board, *n.* **1.** plank, beam, timber, scantling, two-by-four; strip, lath, panel, sheet, slab; clapboard, wallboard, siding, flooring, planking, lumber, wood.

2. room and board, lodging and meals; daily meals, food, *Sl.* eats, *Inf.* grub, victuals, provisions, rations; repasts, lunches, luncheons, dinners, suppers, breakfasts.

3. committee, council, cabinet, advisory group, panel; advisers, directors, trustees.

—*v.* **4.** *Often* **board up** *or* **over** close up, cover up, batten, fasten down, tie down, clamp down, screw down, nail down; secure, tighten, make fast, fix; fasten, hook, latch, lock, padlock.

5. feed, lodge, house, quarter, billet, accommodate, *Inf.* put up, bed; live in, *Inf.* room in, take one's meals, *Inf.* eat in.

6. go on board, go aboard, enter, go *or* get on, step aboard, come in *or* on.

7. come alongside, near, approach, close in on *or* upon, press in on, bear down on; attack, storm, assault, assail, beset.

boast, *v.* **1.** brag, crow, *Australian.* skite, beat the drum, draw the longbow, *Archaic.* vaunt, trumpet, blow one's own trumpet, toot one's own horn, sing one's own praises, *Sl.* shoot the bull, *Sl.* lay it on thick; bluster, roister, puff, *Sl.* blow hard, *Sl.* talk big; show off, strut, parade, swagger, flaunt, *Literary.* plume oneself; pat oneself on the back, flatter oneself; congratulate oneself.

2. brag about, make much of, celebrate, emblazon.

3. pride oneself on, possess, hold, have, enjoy.

—*n.* **4.** pride, pride and joy, treasure, gem; good thing, thing to be desired.

5. bragging, bravado, bluster, fanfaronade, gasconade, rodomantade, *Sl.* hot air, *Sl.* bunk; self-approbation, self-praise, vainglory.

boastful, *adj.* bragging, braggart, crowing, vaunting, blustering, vaporing, blowing, fanfaronading; proud, overproud, vain, vainglorious, egotistical, conceited, swell-headed, swollen, inflated, puffed-up; cocky, overbearing, overweening, *Scot.* vaunty; pretentious, pompous, arrogant, haughty, grandiloquent, magniloquent, *Inf.* high-hat.

boat, *n.* **1.** vessel, craft, yacht, houseboat, packet; sailboat, sloop, dory, pinnace; motorboat, speedboat, jet boat, shell, hydroplane, hydrofoil; rowboat, skiff, pram, punt, canoe, kayak, dugout, *Naut.* galley; tender, dinghy, yawl, lifeboat, tug.

2. ship, liner, steamer, ferry, ark, *Inf.* windjammer; slipper, schooner, galleon, cutter, *Naut.* ketch, *Naut.* brigantine, *Naut.* brig, *Naut.* bark; freighter, merchantman, carrack, barge, whaler, *Eastern U. S.* smack.

—*v.* **3.** float, sail, navigate, cruise, yacht, steam, drift; motorboat, hydroplane, row, paddle, oar.

4. ship, ferry, freight, barge; transport, convey, carry, send.

bob¹, *v.* **1.** jerk, twitch, jounce, weave, nod; oscillate, swing, vibrate, move back and forth, go up and down; quiver, quaver, shake, waggle, wiggle.

2. bob up emerge, appear, materialize, come up out of nowhere.

bob², *v.* cut short, trim, dock, clip, shear, prune, crop, lop.

bode, *v.* portend, augur, presage, import, point to, bespeak, betoken; indicate, signify, mean, imply, intimate, denote, connote, suggest, purport.

bodiless, *adj.* **1.** incorporeal, discarnate, disem-

bodied; spiritual, immaterial, unsubstantial, unfleshy; intangible, impalpable, imponderable, immeasurable.
2. extramundane, transmundane, supernatural, superphysical, hyperphysical; ethereal, airy, vapory; spectral, ghostly, phantom, wraithlike; shadowy, illusory, chimerical, visionary, fanciful, unreal.

bodily, *adj.* **1.** corporeal, corporal, fleshly, incarnate, carnal, somatic, physical; earthly, material, substantial, tangible, palpable; concrete, real, true, actual. *—adv.* **2.** as a body, as a group, collectively, en masse; wholly, as a whole, *Latin. in toto*; bag and baggage.

body, *n.* **1.** corporality, materiality, matter; corporeal structure, bulk, physique, build, figure, frame, form, shape; framework, skeleton, flesh and bones; trunk, torso.
2. carcass, corpse, cadaver, *Sl.* stiff, remains; cremains, ashes.
3. person, human being, human, being, individual, creature.
4. majority, bulk, most, major *or* greater part, lion's share, nearly all, preponderance; principal part, core, essence, heart, center, hub, kernel.
5. collectivity, aggregation, mass, corps; troupe, crew, team, band, party; group, bunch, gang, pack, herd; crowd, throng, mob.
6. consistency, consistence, density, solidity, firmness; richness, substance; shape, structure.

bog, *n.* marsh, *Brit.* fen, mire, quagmire, swamp, swampland, morass, wash, *Southeastern U.S.* pocosin, *Brit. Dial.* sump.

boggle, *v.* **1.** take alarm, take fright, *Inf.* push the panic button; start, jump, *Inf.* jump out of one's skin *or* pants; shy, fight shy.
2. hesitate, waver, falter, pause, hang back, shilly-shally, hem and haw; scruple, demur, object; shrink, recoil, blench, flinch, wince, pull back, *Inf.* funk.
3. dissemble, disguise, mask, camouflage, obscure, cloud; equivocate, prevaricate, hedge, sidestep, evade the issue, pussyfoot, weasel.
4. bungle, botch, muff, fumble, be all thumbs; *All Sl.* mess up, foul up, louse up, screw up, goof up, gum up, flub.
5. astound, astonish, amaze, overwhelm, *Inf.* flabbergast; startle, stagger, shock, bowl over.

bogus, *adj.* counterfeit, spurious, ungenuine, unauthentic, pseudo, quasi, apochryphal, sham, mock, make-believe, fake, *Inf.* phony.

bohemian, *adj.* **1.** nonconformist, unconventional, uncommon, unorthodox, *Fr. outré*; irregular, radical, left bank, avant-garde, way-out; original, eccentric, bizarre, curious, odd.
2. gypsy, nomadic, wandering, traveling, peregrinating, vagabond; itinerant, peripatetic, roaming, footloose.

boil¹, *v.* **1.** seethe, simmer, stew, steam, decoct, brew; cook, heat, parboil, poach.
2. foam, churn, froth, fulminate, spume, mantle; bubble, effervesce, burble, gurgle, guggle; fizz, fizzle, sputter.
3. rage, rave, bluster, storm, rant, roar, rampage; splutter, boil over, explode, *Sl.* blow one's top; fume, sizzle, chafe, smolder, bristle; fire up, burn up, flare up, flame up, fly into a passion, *Inf.* fly off the handle; ferment, quiver, stir up, arouse, rile.
4. **boil down a.** shorten, abridge, condense, digest, synopsize. **b.** come down, point, indicate, designate; mean, signify, denote.

boil², *n.* blain, furuncle, furunculus, carbuncle, pustule, pimple, papule, papilla, pock, wen, whelk, *Rare.* bleb, *Archaic.* botch; abscess, ulcer, ulceration, fester, festering, gathering, gumboil, parulis, tubercle, *Obs.* apostem *or* apostemation, *Archaic.* impostune *or* imposthume; canker, lesion, chancre, chancroid, soft chacre, simple chancre; sore, open *or* running sore, gall, excoriation; whitlow, agnail.

boisterous, *adj.* **1.** noisy, obstreperous, vociferous; agitated, disturbed, unquiet, restive; blustery, clangorous, rackety; loud, ear-splitting, booming, deafening; rowdy, rambunctious, brawling, disorderly, robustious, out of hand; clamorous, riotous, uproarious, rocking, wild; *Sl.* raising Cain, *Sl.* raising hell, *Sl.* raising the roof; rampageous, reckless, rampant, rollicking, swaggering; unrestrained, unruly, uncontrolled, uncontrollable.
2. (*of waves, wind, and weather*) stormy, raging, tempestuous, turbulent, tumultuous; rough, choppy, squally, swirling, whipping, gusty, *Archaic.* troublous; violent, vehement, furious, frenzied, cyclonic, typhonic.

bold, *adj.* **1.** courageous, fearless, daring, dauntless, unafraid; valiant, valorous, lionhearted, stouthearted, intrepid, audacious, *Scot.* bardy; heroic, stalwart, stout, sturdy, defiant, plucky, gritty; adventurous, venturesome; resolute, undismayed, unflinching, unalarmed, confident, assured; rash, daredevil, foolhardy.
2. barefaced, brazen, brassy, insolent, rude, impudent, impertinent, pert, saucy, fresh, *Scot. and North Eng.* crouse; immodest, unabashed, unreserved, shameless, cheeky, unblushing; presumptuous, forward, indecorous, unseemly; frank, candid, open, honest, direct, plainspoken, outspoken, straightforward.
3. conspicuous, prominent, eye-catching; ostentatious, obtrusive, pretentious; flashy, showy, garish, gaudy.
4. steep, sheer, bluff, abrupt, sudden, precipitous; perpendicular, vertical; acclivitous, ascending, rising, towering.

bolster, *n.* **1.** cushion, pillow, pad, hassock, *Brit.* woolsack; support, supporter, prop, brace, bracer, mainstay.
—v. **2.** cushion, pillow, cradle; support, prop, shore up, brace, underbrace, buttress; shoulder, lift, hold up, boost.

bolt, *n.* **1.** lock, latch, catch, holdfast, pin, fastener; spike, clamp, pawl, bar, tie, clinch; rod, skewer, spike, dowel, pin, peg; screw, nail, brad, rivet, staple.
2. dash, dart, sprint, bound, spring, rush, run; flight, escape, fleeing, hegira.
3. length, roll, coil; piece, section, portion.
4. arrow, dart, quarrel; missile, projectile, trajectile.
5. thunderbolt, lightning, sheet of lightning, flash, fulguration.
—v. **6.** fasten, make fast, secure; lock, latch, catch, pin; clamp down, *Mach.* batten, clinch, tie, pawl, bar.
7. shoot, discharge, fire, let fly, pour forth; detonate, set off.
8. gobble, gulp, swallow whole, devour, cram, stuff, gorge.
9. dash, fly, *Inf.* take off, *Sl.* tear off, scoot, speed, sprint, run; rush, hurry, hasten, spank, scud; flee, make a run for it, turn tail, escape.

bomb, *n.* **1.** explosive, fireball, *Inf.* blockbuster; grenade, Molotov cocktail, shell, torpedo, missile, projectile, trajectile; mine, land mine.
—v. **2.** bombard, *Brit. Sl.* prang, strafe, shell, torpedo, *Mil.* barrage, fusillade, blitz, blitzkrieg; shoot, fire on, open fire on, pepper, cannonade.

bombard, *v.* **1.** bomb, shell, fusillade. See **bomb** (*def.* **2**).
2. attack, batter, assault, raid, storm, charge, rush;

set upon, pounce upon, descend upon, fall on; light into, *Inf.* lace into, *Inf.* rip into, *Inf.* tear into, *Sl.* zap, *Sl.* lay into.
3. assail, vituperate, revile, rail against, inveigh against, lash, abuse, belabor, *Inf.* jump down [s.o.'s] throat, *Archaic.* clapperclaw.

bombardment, *n.* strafing, air raid, peppering, salvo, fusillade, *Navy.* broadside, *Both Mil.* barrage, enfilade; assault, offensive, onslaught; rush, blitz, blitzkrieg, storming, *Fr. coup de main, Obs.* brunt; battle, combat, *Mil.* skirmish; raid, foray, sortie, sally; invasion, aggression, incursion, escalade.

bombast, *n.* grandiosity, rodomontade, pomposity, magniloquence, grandiloquence; tumidity, turgidity, flatulence, *Archaic.* tympany; extravagance, rant, highflown language, sesquipedality; bravado, braggadocio, gasconade.

bombastic, *adj.* **1.** pompous, orotund, fustian, haughty, pretentious, ostentatious, flaunting, bombastical; grandiose, magniloquent, grandiloquent, Johnsonian, Ossianic, sonorous, sesquipedalian; high-sounding, high-flown, lofty, *Inf.* highfalutin, *Inf.* high-hat; inflated, swollen, bloated; flatulent, turgid, plethoric; impressive, euphuistic, periphrastic; extravagant, ranting, mouthy, declamatory; flamboyant, flashy, ornate, ornamental, showy, flowery, florid.
2. affected, mannered, studied, worked-on, acquired, assumed, adopted, put on; *Inf.* la-di-da; *Inf.* too-too.

bonanza, *n.* windfall, godsend, piece *or* stroke of luck, luck; find, discovery, lore, treasure-trove; boon, blessing, bonus.

bonbon, *n.* candy, fondant, confection, confectionery, sweet, sweetmeat, comfit, sugarplum, sugarcandy; chocolate, caramel, toffee, mint, peppermint, taffy, nougat, lollipop.

bond, *n.* **1.** tie, ligament, link, connection, nexus; band, binding, strap, belt; cord, cordon, braid, thong; restraint, constraint, check, control, reins; chains, fetters, shackles, trammels, manacles, handcuffs, harness, yoke.
2. agreement, compact, contract, promise, word, pledge; convenant, treaty, concordat, cartel, pact; transaction, *Inf.* deal, bargain; stipulation, arrangement, acknowledgment; guarantee, guaranty, warranty, surety.
—*v.* **3.** connect, bind, hold together. See **bind.**

bondage, *n.* slavery, enslavement, enthrallment, thralldom, captivity; prison, imprisonment, confinement, durance, duress; servitude, serfdom, vassalage, villeinage, indentureship, indention; oppression, repression, subjugation, subjection, subordination, control, restraint.

bone, *n.* **1.** ossicle, skeletal structure, cartilage, marrow, *Biochem.* ossein.
2. horn, ivory, tusk, whalebone, *Dentistry.* dentin, *Zool.* baleen.

bonus, *n.* **1.** reward, award, prize, gift, present, handsel, endowment, bestowal, largess, handout, *Sl.* freebie; dividend, extra, plus, surplus, gain, fringe benefit, perquisite, *Inf.* perk; compensation, recompense, remuneration, emolument, repayment payoff; gratuity, tip, douceur, honorarium, (*in Chinese ports*) cumshaw, (*in India, Turkey, etc.*) baksheesh, *Fr. pourboire.*
2. premium, bounty, inducement, encouragement, stimulation; bribe, bait, payment, *Inf.* payola, *Sl.* palm greaser.

book, *n.* **1.** opus, opuscule, work, tome, tract, treatise; publication, volume, writing, title.
2. notebook, looseleaf, pad, scratch pad; log, ledger, blotter, account book, day book; diary, journal.
3. by the book according to rule, according to Hoyle.
4. like a book completely, thoroughly, wholly, entirely, from A to Z; *Inf.* like the back of my hand, *Inf.* better than I know myself.
5. make book bet, gamble, wager, stake, *Brit.* punt.
—*v.* **6.** register, record, log, post, enter, enroll, insert, inscribe.
7. reserve, engage beforehand, charter.
8. schedule, slate, bill, program, *Inf.* line up.

bookish, *adj.* **1.** literary, lettered, literate, learned, erudite, educated, well-educated; conversant, knowledgeable, well-read, informed, well-posted, well-grounded, well-schooled, accomplished; intellectual, cerebral, brainy, highbrow *or* highbrowed; bibliophilistic, bibliophilic; studious, scholarly, diligent, sedulous, conscientious, industrious, assiduous.
2. academic, theoretical, hypothetical, abstract, notional, ideational, speculative; unrealistic, impractical, ivory-towerish, utopian, visionary.
3. pedantic, pedantical, scholastic, pedagoguish, donnish, precise, punctilious, exact, meticulous, fastidious, fussy, finicky, particular; stilted, formal, stiff, stuffy, dry; rigid, narrow, hidebound; platitudinous, unimaginative, unoriginal, uninteresting; boring, dull, tedious, tiresome.

bookkeeper, *n.* clerk, registrar, recorder, agent; accountant, certified public accountant, C.P.A., *Both Brit.* chartered accountant, C.A.; controller, comptroller, auditor; inspector, examiner, reckoner, analyst, *Insurance.* actuary, computer; cashier, teller.

bookworm, *n.* bibliophage, ardent reader; scholar, bookman, walking encyclopedia; student, overachiever, *Sl.* grind, *Brit. Sl.* swot. See also **bibliophile.**

boom, *v.* **1.** resound, resonate, vibrate, trill, reverberate, echo; bang, blast, blare, clang, peal, ring, buzz, sound loudly; screech, shriek, wail, howl, whine, cry; clamor, bellow, roar, rumble, thunder, clap; explode, burst, report, shoot, shoot off *or* out, blow up, pop, go off, detonate.
2. progress, prosper, thrive, flourish, luxuriate, burgeon, mushroom; spring up, burst forth, develop vigorously, sprout, shoot up, rise; grow, wax, increase, gain, add to.
3. promote, campaign for, advance, boost, build up, talk up; advertise, publicize, broadcast, announce, make known; declare openly, promulgate, proclaim, herald, trumpet, ballyhoo, beat the drum; push, *Inf.* plug, *Inf.* hype, puff, vaunt.
—*n.* **4.** booming, roaring, bellowing, rumbling, thundering; resonation, vibration, trilling, reverberation, echoing; banging, blasting, blaring, clamoring, clanging, pealing, ringing, buzzing; screeching, shrieking, wailing, howling, whining.
5. explosion, clap, bang, loud noise, report, shot, burst, pop, detonation.
6. increase, augmentation, addition, rise, gain, markup.

boomerang, *v.* come back, return, rebound, spring back, resile, bounce back; recoil, reverse, backfire, backlash, come home to roost; ricochet.

boon, *n.* benefit, advantage, plus, blessing, favor, good thing; reward, present, gift, handsel, endowment, bestowal, largess; perquisite, fringe benefit, *Inf.* fringe, *Inf.* extra, bonus, dividend; raise, increase, promotion, advancement, furtherance.

boor, *n.* **1.** churl, curmudgeon, brute, barbarian, yahoo, *Inf.* goop, *Chiefly Scot.* tyke, *Brit. Sl.* mucker; lout, oaf, dolt, clod, clodhopper, clodpoll *or* clodpole *or* clodpate, gawk, looby, lubber, ox, clown, slouch, *Chiefly Scot.* cuddy, *Inf.* lummox, *Sl.* klutz, *Sl.*

galoot, *Sl.* lug, *Chiefly Brit. Sl.* joskin; bungler, bumbler, fumbler, botcher, blunderer, boggler, *Inf.* butterfingers, *Inf.* stumblebum, *Inf.* duffer, *Sl.* slob; Philistine, vulgarian, vulgarist, ribald, low *or* vulgar *or* ill-bred fellow.

2. rustic, peasant, provincial, country cousin, countryman, farmer, plowman, plowboy, chuff, son *or* tiller of the soil, swain, kern *or* kerne, gaffer, hobnail, (*in Egypt*) fellah, (*in Russia*) muszhik *or* moujik *or* mujick *or* muzjik, (*in Spanish America and Southwestern U.S.*) peon, *Archaic.* hind, *Often Disparaging.* hillbilly, *Disparaging.* bogtrotter, *Fr. Sl. truffe, Inf.* chawbacon, *Inf.* cider squeezer; yokel, bumpkin, country bumpkin, hawbuck, *Dial.* lumpkin, *Sl.* hick, *Sl.* woodhick, *Sl.* rube, *Sl.* hayseed, *Sl.* hoosier.

3. (*all of peasants*) alien, foreigner, stranger, outsider, outlander, tramontane.

boorish, *adj.* **1.** rude, vulgar, uncouth, coarse, unmannerly, ill-mannered, ill-bred; churlish, brutish, barbaric, crude, crass, base, low, vile, contemptible; loutish, oafish, doltish, cloddish, stolid, clodhopping, gawkish *or* gawky, lubberly, lumpish, lumpen, clownish, *Sl.* klutzy.

2. rustic, rural, peasantlike, agrestic, agrarian; pastoral, bucolic, bucolical, sylvan *or* silvan, Arcadian; inurbane, backwoods, provincial, countrified *or* countryfied, country-bred, country-born, upcountry, from the sticks, yokelish, *Sl.* hickish, *Sl.* rube, *Sl.* hayseed; homespun, homebred, homey *or* homy, homely, homelike, homish, down-home, (*usu. of thought or philosophy*) cracker-barrel, *Inf.* folksy.

boost, *v.* **1.** lift, raise, raise up, cast up, hoist, heft, thrust up; elevate, exalt, upgrade, aggrandize.

2. promote, support, advance, further, forward, help onward, facilitate; publicize, *Sl.* plug, advertise, write, up, bring *or* drag into the limelight; commend, recommend, sanction, back, advocate, put in a good word for, pat on the back; assist, aid, abet, foster, benefit.

3. encourage, enhearten, praise, extol, acclaim, eulogize, laud, speak well of, have *or* say a good word for; inspire, inspirit, build up, buck up, uplift; animate, fire [s.o.'s] imagination, enliven.

4. increase, hike, inflate, jack up, add to, superadd to; enlarge, make greater, magnify, amplify, heighten.

—n. **5.** lift, raise, *Inf.* a leg up, hoist; thrust, heave, push, shove.

6. increase, hike, rise; enlargement, magnification, heightening, expansion.

7. refresher, *Inf.* pick-me-up, *Inf.* picker-upper, *Inf.* upper, *Inf.* shot in the arm, *Inf.* ego trip; peptalk, build-up, inspiration, uplifting; encouragement, praise, acclaim, laudation; upgrading, improvement.

8. promotion, support, advancement, furtherance; recommendation, commendation, sanction, backing, pat on the back; publicity, *Sl.* plug, advertisement, attention, write-up; assistance, aid, abettal.

boot, *n.* footwear, bootee, wellington, *Brit. Sl.* wellie; clodhoppers, combat boots, *Sl.* boondocker, *Sl.* gunboats; rubber, galosh, mukluk, overshoe.

booth, *n.* **1.** stall, stand, counter, table; compartment, cubicle, cubbyhole, cubby, bay, carrel, carol, cell; closet, room, enclosure.

2. shed, shack, lean-to, hut, outbuilding, outhouse; stable, pen, coop, hutch, cote; tent, awning, tepee, wigwam; shelter, covering, protection, roof.

bootless, *adj.* vain, unavailing, purposeless, useless, Sisyphean, futile, ineffective, inefficacious; worthless, valueless, nugatory; fatuous, inane, inconsequential; fruitless, unproductive, abortive, barren, effete, sterile, impotent; unprofitable, profitless, gainless, unremunerative; unsuccessful, *Inf.* no-go, to no purpose, to no avail, for naught.

booty, *n.* **1.** spoil *or* spoils, loot, plunder, pillage, *Archaic.* prey, *Archaic.* boot, *Scot. Obs.* reif.

2. prize, winnings, reward, recompense; profits, earnings, wages, salary, emolument, perquisites, *Inf.* perks; gain, grab, pickings, takings, *Inf.* haul.

3. stolen goods, *Inf.* steal, *Sl.* hot goods, *Sl.* boodle, *Sl.* the take, *Sl.* the goods, *Sl.* swag.

bordello, *n.* brothel, bagnio, *Obs.* stew, lupanar, *Obs.* kip, nunnery, *Archaic.* bordel; house of prostitution, house of ill-fame, house of ill-repute, bawdyhouse, whorehouse, *Inf.* sporting house, *Inf.* call house; *All Sl.* call joint, cathouse, parlor house, barrelhouse, honky-tonk, pick-up joint.

border, *n.* **1.** perimeter, periphery, edge, rim, fringe, verge, skirt; circumference, circuit, compass, ambit, margin, frame, outline, confine, confines; brink, brim, brow, hem; bound, limit, bourn, pale, extremity, termination; limits, city limits, outer limits.

2. frontier, frontier line, boundary, boundary line, bounding line, border line *or* borderline, partition, line, line of demarcation, line.

3. borderland, borderground, borders, bounds, march, marches, marchland; outpost; outskirts, purlieu.

4. edging, trimming, bordering, skirting, beading, selvage, welt, *Heraldry.* bordure, *Bot., Zool.* fimbria *or* fimbriae, *Bot., Zool.* fimbriation; binding, list; ruff, ruffle, flounce, flouncing, furbelow, galloon; frill, frilling, valance, orphrey, purfle, purfling.

—v. **5.** fringe, befringe, trim; bind; purfle, purl.

6. edge, skirt, verge, line; rim, hem; frame, march, bound, margin, marginate.

7. adjoin, abut on *or* upon, verge upon, impinge upon; neighbor, flank, side, lie near to, lie close to, lie next to, lie *or* be adjacent to; touch, reach, meet, butt, impinge, kiss; join, conjoin, connect, attach, unite, affix, annex, append.

bore¹, *v.* pierce, perforate, puncture, ream, trepan, riddle; penetrate, open up, reach into, tap, broach; drill, auger, mine, tunnel, burrow, lower into; cut out, dig out, gouge out; drive, punch, force, work; stab, pink, sink, stick, prick.

bore², *v.* **1.** weary, tire, wear on, wear out, fag out, exhaust, jade; buttonhole, *Inf.* bend [s.o.'s] ear, *Sl.* talk one's head off; set *or* send one to sleep, bore stiff, bore to tears, bore to death; annoy, trouble, irritate, irk, bother, exasperate, tax [s.o.'s] patience, *Inf.* get; pester, harp at, harass, burden, oppress.

—n. **2.** pest, bother, nuisance, pain, *Sl.* pain in the neck, *Sl.* headache, tiresome person; *Inf.* downer, *Inf.* drag, *Sl.* pill; *Inf.* drip, *Inf.* wet blanket, *Inf.* loser; *Sl.* dullsville, *Inf.* nowhere.

3. annoyance, irritation, aggravation, vexation, inconvenience.

bored, *adj.* **1.** weary, tired, sick of, worn out, fagged out, exhausted; buttonholed, bored stiff, bored to tears, bored to death; annoyed, irritated, irked, exasperated, *Sl.* fed to the gills, *Sl.* fed up; jaded, hardened, inured.

2. indifferent, uninterested, blasé, nonchalant, pococurante; listless, spiritless, flagging, phlegmatic.

boredom, *n.* **1.** ennui, *U.S. Sl.* the blahs, low spirits, doldrums, malaise; tedium, monotony, repetition, routine, schedule; dullness, humdrum, deadness, flatness; dreariness, stuffiness.

2. apathy, impassivity, dispassion, lack of feeling *or* emotion, insentience, insensibility, unfeelingness; lethargy, languor, listlessness, dullness, stolidity, sluggishness; indifference, unconcern, unresponsiveness, uninterestedness, disinterest.

boring, *adj.* **1.** tedious, monotonous, humdrum,

repetitious, routine, unvaried; dull, flat, dead, bland, insipid, *Sl.* blah, *Sl.* ho-hum; uninteresting, uninspiring, unanimated, unexciting, dry-as-dust; mediocre, *Inf.* nothing to write home about, *Sl.* nothing; long-winded, prolix, windy, wordy, drawn out, dragged out, long-drawn.

2. wearying, wearisome, tiring, tiresome, wearing, boresome; annoying, irksome, bothersome, exasperating.

borrow, *v.* **1.** ask for the loan of, use temporarily; scrounge, mooch, sponge, cadge, leech, freeload, *U.S. Inf.* bum.

2. appropriate, arrogate, purloin, usurp, commandeer, pirate; steal, snatch, filch, pilfer, pocket, grab, help oneself to; quote, cite, refer to, plagiarize; imitate, copy, paraphrase, abstract.

bosom, *n.* **1.** breast, mammary gland, tit, titty, *Sl.* boob, *Sl.* booby; *Anat., Zool.* mamma, teat, nipple, *Chiefly Dial.* pap, (*of animals*) dug, (*of cows*) udder; chest, bust, *Brit. Sl.* Bristols, *All Sl.* jugs, milk-jugs, set, lollapaloozas, mounds, globes, knockers, bings.

2. core, heart, center, soul; depths, bowels, interior, inside, recesses, womb, vault.

—adj. **3.** confidential, intimate, near and dear, faithful; cherished, dear, close, beloved, precious, darling.

boss, *n.* **1.** foreman, manager, superintendent, supervisor; director, leader, chief, head, executive; taskmaster, overseer, overlooker, overman; master, *Brit. Inf.* governor, employer, *Sl.* the man, *Sl.* honcho.

—v. **2.** manage, direct, control, order, command, take charge; preside over, oversee, supervise, superintend; domineer, dominate, push around, ride hard on, ride roughshod over, trample under foot, shove around.

botch, *v.* **1.** bungle, *Inf.* muff, *Inf.* flub; spoil, *Inf.* foul up, *Sl.* bitch, *Sl.* blow; hash, muddle, mangle, butcher, *Dial.* butch, *Sl.* screw up, *Sl.* mess up, *Sl.* louse up, *Inf.* bollix; gum up the works, make a hash of, make a mess of, make sad work of, *U.S. Inf.* throw a monkey wrench into; *All Sports.* boggle, fumble, foozle, boot.

2. blunder, stumble, flounder, slip, *Inf.* put one's foot in it, *Inf.* put one's foot in one's mouth.

both, *adj.* one and the other, the two, two together, *Scot. and North Eng.* baith.

bother, *v.* **1.** pester, hector, harass, *Sl.* bug, *Sl.* hassle, *Sl.* drive [s.o.] nuts *or* crazy *or* bananas, *Sl.* drive [s.o.] up a wall; hound, dog, nag, pick on, pick at, be on [s.o.'s] back, *Inf.* give [s.o.] a hard time, *Sl.* ride; torment, taunt, bedevil, tease, tweak, mock, heckle, *Inf.* needle; plague, trouble, fret, worry.

2. irritate, annoy, irk, vex, pique, provoke, peeve, nettle, chafe; get on [s.o.'s] nerves, tread on [s.o.'s] toes, *Chiefly U.S.* rile, *Inf.* aggravate, *Inf.* miff, *Inf.* give [s.o.] a pain, *Inf.* give [s.o.] fits, *Inf.* rub [s.o.] the wrong way, *Inf.* get in [s.o.'s] hair, *Inf.* get under [s.o.'s] skin; exasperate, ruffle, try [s.o.'s] patience, *Inf.* grate on *or* grate on [s.o.'s] nerves.

3. bewilder, confuse, baffle, perplex, confound; upset, perturb, disconcert, discomfit.

4. trouble, inconvenience, burden; impose upon, encroach upon, put out, discommode, incommode; put to the trouble, take the trouble, go to the trouble.

—n. **5.** nuisance, annoyance, vexation, *Inf.* headache, *Sl.* hassle, *Sl.* drag, *Sl.* bitch; inconvenience, imposition; disadvantage, handicap; problem, difficulty, affliction; irritant, burr, thorn, thorn in the side *or* flesh, pea in the shoe.

6. effort, exertion, energy, work; worry, pains, trouble, *Sl.* hassle.

7. dither, pucker, twitter, flutter, flurry, *Inf.* tizzy, *Inf.* stew, *Inf.* lather, *Inf.* sweat; commotion, fuss, to-do, ado, hubbub, tumult, stir, bustle.

8. bewilderment, confoundment, bafflement, puzzlement, perplexity, confusion, befuddlement.

9. pest, gadfly, buttonholer, *Inf.* pain, *Sl.* pain in the neck *or* rear, *Sl.* nudnik; nag, pesterer, annoyer, harasser, heckler, badgerer; tease, teaser, tormentor, persecutor; bore, frightful *or* dreadful bore, proser, twaddler, dryasdust.

bottle, *n.* container, glass, vial, phial, flasket, cruet; flask, decanter, carafe, pitcher, ewer, cruse; flagon, jar, carboy, demijohn.

bottom, *n.* **1.** foot, lowest point, lowest part, *Astron.* nadir, *Astron.* perigee; foundation, groundwork, understructure, substructure, substratum, understratum, underlayer; pedestal, footing, *Archit.* socle, *Archit.* plinth; support, prop, stay, brace; baseboard, dado, wainscot, underpinning.

2. underside, lower side, sole, undersurface, underpart, underneath, belly.

3. bed, ground, floor, bottoms; Davy Jones's locker.

4. buttocks, rump, posterior, hindquarters, haunches, fundament, nates, *Zool.* podex, *Anat.* gluteus maximus, (*both of a horse*) crupper, croup; seat, *Fr. derrière, Inf.* fanny, *Inf.* rear *or* rear end, *Brit. Inf.* bum, *Inf.* backside, *Inf.* behind. See **buttocks.**

5. basis, foundation, principle; essence, quiddity, substance; essentials, rudiments, main ingredient.

6. origin, cause, source, beginning, derivation, wellspring, fountainhead, spring; root, base, core, heart, *Inf.* nub.

bottomless, *adj.* **1.** baseless, foundationless, unsupported.

2. deep, unfathomed, unsounded, unmeasured; soundless, plumbless, immeasurable, abyssal, abysmal, fathomless, unfathomable, mysterious.

boudoir, *n.* bedroom, dressing room, sitting room, private room; chamber, sanctum, closet, retreat.

bough, *n.* branch, limb, twig, stem, stalk; bine, *Bot.* runner, *Bot.* sarmentum, tendril; shoot, sprout, switch, sprig, spray.

boulder, *n.* stone, rock, bowlder; sarsen, Druid stone, graywether.

boulevard, *n.* avenue, concourse, street, strip; main road, thoroughfare, *Inf.* drag, public road, roadway; drive, terrace, circle, row.

bounce, *v.* **1.** rebound, recoil, resile.

2. caper, gambol, frisk, prance, skip, trip, bob, romp.

3. bound, leap, jump, spring, hurdle, vault, clear.

—n. **4.** rebound, bound, recoil, spring; resilience, elasticity, give, snap, stretch.

5. vitality, energy, vivacity, go, get up and go, zing, *Inf.* zip, *Inf.* pep, *Inf.* pizzazz, *Sl.* oomph, *Brit. Sl.* stingo.

6. leap, lunge, jump, hurdle, vault.

bound[1], *adj.* **1.** tied, tethered, made fast, fastened, secured, fixed; in bonds, shackled, fettered, manacled, handcuffed; restrained, confined, restricted.

2. obligated, obliged, duty-bound; required, compelled, constrained.

3. destined, predestined, decreed, ordained, foreordained, fated, doomed; sure, certain, inevitable, unavoidable, inescapable; booked, scheduled; headed, routed.

4. determined, resolved, set on, decided, bound and determined.

bound[2], *v.* **1.** leap, spring, jump, hop, bob, curvet; skip, gambol, frolic, caper, romp, prance, dance; start, buck.

2. rebound, bounce, ricochet, boomerang; resile,

spring back, recoil.

—*n.* **3.** leap, spring, vault, saltation, *Dressage.* curvet, jump, hop, bounce; caper, antic, gambol, gambado, prance, flounce.

bound[3], *n.* **1.** *Usu.* **bounds** limits, boundaries; borders, outskirts. See **boundary** (*defs.* **1-3**).

2. out of bounds a. forbidden, prohibited, taboo, banned, off-limits. **b.** untoward, improper, uncalled for, unbecoming; disrespectful, irreverent, discourteous, impolite, rude.

—*v.* **3.** limit, confine, cramp, straiten, restrict, restrain; circumscribe, demarcate, delimit, hem in, wall in.

4. adjoin, abut, border, lie next to, be adjacent to, be contiguous with.

boundary, *n.* **1.** frontier, frontier line, boundary line, bounding line, border line, partition line, line of demarcation, line, fence.

2. border, perimeter, periphery, edge, rim, fringe, verge, skirt; circumference, circuit, compass, ambit, margin, frame, outline, confine, confines; brink, brim, brow, hem; bound, limit, butting, abuttal, bourn, pale, extremity, termination; limits, city limits, outer limits.

3. borderland, borderground, borders, bounds, march, marches, marchland; outpost, outskirts, purlieu, suburbs, *Fr. banlieue.*

boundless, *adj.* unbounded, unlimited, uncircumscribed, unrestricted, limitless, illimitable, shoreless; immense, vast, great, extensive; incalculable, undetermined, indeterminate, indefinite, undefined; immeasurable, measureless, innumerable, numberless, myriad, countless, untold, uncounted; infinite, endless, without end, unending, never-ending, interminable, inexhaustible; unceasing, constant, uninterrupted, perpetual, eternal; permanent, enduring, everlasting, perdurable.

bountiful, *adj.* **1.** generous, liberal, giving, munificent, princely, openhanded, free-handed; altruistic, free, unselfish, unsparing, unstinting, self-sacrificing; charitable, philanthropic, eleemosynary; kind, good, beneficent, benevolent, magnanimious, big-hearted, large-hearted.

2. rich, luxuriant, lavish, rank, prodigal, prolific, proliferous; profuse, rife, replete, abounding, overflowing, overspilling, spilling over, running over, exuberant, superabundant; full, filled, abrim, chock-a-block, *Brit. Inf.* chocker, *Inf.* chock-full, bursting, bristling, teeming, jammed, packed, *Inf.* jam-packed, *Archaic.* fraught.

3. ample, abundant, plentiful, plenteous, plenitudinous, bounteous, copious, fat, bumper; immeasurable, unmeasured, unstinted, inexhaustible, bottomless; much, many, numerous, *Inf.* dime a dozen; in quantity *or* quantities, in plenty, *Inf.* aplenty, *Inf.* galore.

bounty, *n.* **1.** generosity, liberality, munificence, open-handedness, free-handedness; charity, charitableness, philanthropy, almsgiving, giving, donating; altruism, unselfishness, self-sacrifice; kindness, goodness, beneficence, benevolence, grace, big-heartedness; grace, help, aid, assistance, relief, succor.

2. gift, largess, tribute, present, presentation, handsel *or* hansel; contribution, donation, offering, benefaction; grant, subsidy, subvention, endowment, bestowal, concession.

3. bonus, premium, gratuity, tip; reward, guerdon, honorarium, *Archaic.* meed; recompense, remuneration, rebate, solatium, *Inf.* kickback.

bouquet, *n.* **1.** nosegay, bunch of flowers, posy, corsage, boutonniere; spray, *Brit. Dial.* bough-pot; garland, wreath, festoon, chaplet.

2. aroma, odor, scent, fragrance, perfume, spicy smell; redolence, odoriferousness, savor; trail, trace, breath.

3. character, quality, air, atmosphere, aura, exhalation, emanation, essence, spirit; flavor, complexion, tone.

bourgeois, *adj.* **1.** middle-class, propertied, landed; working-class, proletarian, plebian.

2. conventional, common, ordinary, unimaginative; philistine, unrefined, uncultivated, uncultured.

3. materialistic, money-oriented, acquisitive; capitalistic, noncommunistic, nonsocialistic.

bourn, *n.* **1.** bound, limit, pale, extremity; frontier, boundary line, borderline, line of demarcation.

2. destination, goal, terminus, terminal point, finish, end, journey's end, end of the road, end of the line, last stop.

3. realm, domain, sphere, zone, range, ground, territory; area, vicinity, region, locale, locality.

bout, *n.* **1.** boxing match, prizefight, spar, fist-fight; trial, trial of strength, test, contest, duel; match, meet, tilt, joust; conflict, fight, clash, scuffle, tussle, scrap, fisticuffs, exchange of blows, *Inf.* set-to.

2. turn, round, inning, *Inf.* go, *Sl.* whack; shift, tour, stint, watch, time; period, spell, season, fit, stretch, run.

3. spree, fling, revel, carouse, debauch, drinking bout, drunk; *All Sl.* bender, binge, toot, tear, jag, bust, bat, bar-hop, *Brit.* pub-crawl.

bovine, *adj.* **1.** stolid, phlegmatic, torpid, hebetudinous, sluggish, spiritless, lifeless, inanimate.

2. dull, obtuse, dense, thick, thick-witted, slow-witted, dim-witted, dull-witted, dead between the ears, dead from the neck up; doltish, oafish, cloddish, lumpish, Boeotian.

bow[1], *v.* **1.** kneel before, salaam, genuflect, curtsey, nod, bob; prostrate oneself, fall on one's knees, lie prone, throw oneself at the feet of; bend the knee to, bend to, humble oneself to, defer to, stoop, get down.

2. bow and scrape grovel, truckle to, kowtow; lickspittle, lick [s.o.'s] shoes, like *or* kiss [s.o.'s] feet, kiss the hem of [s.o.'s] garment, *Sl.* bootlick; court, pay court to, curry favor, keep time to, dance attendance upon, be at [s.o.'s] beck and call, agree to anything; toady, toady to, fawn, fawn upon, *Sl.* fall all over; *All Sl.* shine up to, play up to, suck up to, apple-polish, butter-up, brown-nose.

3. submit, yield, surrender, give in, give way to; capitulate, succumb to, fall, bite the dust, lay down arms; resign oneself, acquiesce, throw in the towel, give up the ship, cease the struggle, grin and bear it.

4. subdue, subjugate, conquer, vanquish, suppress, overcome, overwhelm, overpower; crush, smash, humble, humiliate, bring [s.o.] to his knees; master, dominate, domineer, rule, control, govern, boss, lead by the nose; sway, influence, move, affect, dispose, predispose, warp, distort.

5. curve, bend, turn, swerve; flex, crook, twist, contort; arch, vault, camber, inflect.

—*n.* **6.** genuflection, prostration; bob, nod, curtsey, salaam, kowtow; greeting, salutation, salute, how-do-you-do.

bow[2], *n.* **1.** sling, slingshot, *Brit.* catapult, arbalest, longbow, crossbow.

2. bend, curve, curvature, sinus, *Math.* catenary, incurvation; arc, arch, arcuation, vault, camber, convexity, horseshoe; hook, crook, coil, spiral; crescent, half-moon, semi-circle, lune, meniscus; circle, wheel; wave, curl, crimp; parabola, hyperbola.

3. twist, bias, warp, veer, swerve, slue, skew; angle, inflection, dogleg; fold, flexune.

4. archer, bowman, toxophilite.

—*v.* **5.** curve, bend, turn, swerve; flex, crook; arch,

vault, camber, inflect.

bowel, *n.* **1.** (*often pl.*) *Anat.* intestine; intestines, large intestine, small intestine, colon, colons, (*of swine*) chitterlings.

2. **bowels** (*usu. pl.*) *Inf.* innards, inwards, insides; vitals, vital organs, vital parts; viscera, (*of animals*) entrails, *Inf.* gizzard, *Sl.* guts.

3. (*usu. pl.*) interior, interior part, interior space, inside, inside part, inner part, inner space; recess, recesses, penetralia; belly, depth, depths; hold, cavity, vault.

—*v.* **4.** disembowel, embowel, eviscerate, *Rare.* viscerate, exenterate.

5. devitalize, weaken, enervate; debilitate, enfeeble, deplete, sap, exhaust.

bower, *n.* **1.** arbor, grotto, alcove, recess, leafy shelter; retreat, refuge, haven, hermitage, asylum, resort, sanctuary, ark, covert, hideaway, mew.

2. cottage, hut, hutch, shack, shanty, *Scot.* bothy; cot, bungalow, *Brit. Dial.* cote, *Scot.* but-and-bend; cabin, log cabin, blockhouse, A-frame; lodge, ski lodge, chalet.

3. (*in medieval castles*) boudoir, private chamber, bedroom, dressing room.

—*v.* **4.** embower, shelter, shade, screen, protect, hide; surround, circle, encircle, encompass.

bowl[1], *n.* **1.** dish, saucer, porringer, boat, tureen, flagon; basin, sink, tub, pan; vessel, receptacle, container.

2. cup, mug, tankard, stein, toby, rummer, noggin, *Chiefly Scot.* tass, *Scot and North Eng.* stoup, *Chiefly Brit.* panikin; goblet, glass, tumbler, beaker, *Literary.* chalice.

3. drinking, tippling, imbibition; conviviality, merriment, joviality, festivity, partying, living it up.

4. crater, hollow, hole; dip, depression, indentation, valley.

5. stadium, coliseum, arena, field house; amphitheater, theater, arena stage, theater in the round.

6. **bowl game** football game, tournament, tourney, meet, play-off, championship, *Sports.* invitational.

—*v.* **7.** incline, pitch, slope, slant, lean, curve.

bowl[2], *v.* **1.** roll, trundle, troll; spin, reel, wheel, whirl, gyrate, revolve, rotate; pitch, hurl, fling, throw; knock, strike.

2. carry, convey, transport, move, tote, cart.

3. **bowl over** *Informal.* surprise, astonish, dumfound, flabbergast; disconcert, upset.

box[1], *n.* **1.** carton, package, pack, container, can, canister, skippet, *Gk. and Rom. Antiq.* pyxis; case, vasculum, receptacle, *Rom. Cath. Ch.* monstrance, shrine, reliquary; bin, crib, hutch, bunker; crate, trunk, coffer, casket, caddy, chest, file, cabinet; compartment, section, booth.

—*v.* **2.** package, pack, bundle, wrap; can, encase, seal up, bottle up; enclose, confine, impound, contain; hem in, shut in, fence, corral, picket, pen, cage, coop; imprison, lock up, incarcerate, immure, wall in.

box[2], *n.* **1.** blow, swat, *Inf.* whack, thwack, cuff, buffet; knock, hit, strike, stroke, *Inf.* sock, punch, jab.

—*v.* **2.** cuff, buffet, swat, *Inf.* whack, *Inf.* belt, *Inf.* sock, *Inf.* slam, *Inf.* slug, *Inf.* clout; strike, hit, knock, bat, batter, pound, lay on, pommel, pummel, *Sl.* paste; *Inf.* thump, *Inf.* lambaste, *Inf.* whale, *Sl.* whomp.

3. fight, spar, skirmish, scuffle, grapple, tussle, fisticuff; contend, contest, combat, battle.

boy, *n.* **1.** youth, youngster, stripling, sprig, lad, *Scot. and North Eng.* callant, *Irish Eng.* spalpeen, *Irish Eng.* gossoon; tyke, *Inf.* kid, *Inf.* little shaver, *U.S. Inf.* tad, *Inf.* small fry, junior; *Sl.* bub, *Sl.* gazabo; urchin, cub, puppy, whippersnapper, hobbledehoy.

2. page, young servant; waiter, *Fr. garçon.*

boycott, *v.* **1.** abstain from, refrain from, forbear, desist from, restrain from, hold back from voluntarily; refuse, rebuff, decline, reject, spurn; avoid, stay away from, eschew, shun; ignore, pass over, slight, disdain, scorn; blacklist, bar, exclude, debar; picket, keep out, shut out, lock out; ban, prohibit, proscribe, embargo; forbid, interdict, disallow, prevent.

—*n.* **2.** abstention, refrainment, forbearance, desistance, restraint, holding back; refusal, rebuff, rejection, spurn; avoidance, eschewal, shunning, slighting; blacklisting, barring, exclusion, debarment; picketing, prevention, disallowance, ban, embargo, prohibition, interdiction.

boyish, *adj.* youthful, young, juvenescent, juvenile; green, callow, inexperienced, immature, in the bud, unripe, unfledged, tender; puerile, childlike, childish, *Inf.* kiddish.

brace, *n.* **1.** clasp, clamp, vise, clincher, clip, hasp, holdfast, holder, stirrup; coupling, buckle, fastener, catch.

2. support, prop, stay, strut, truss, rib, beam, cantilever, stanchion; reinforcement, bracing, shore, buttress, *Building Trades.* raker; bracket, hook, hanger, guy, suspender, cable, *Naut.* mainstay, *Naut.* shroud; binder, bracer, splint, bandage, binding, band, fillet, tightener.

3. pair, couple, duo, dyad, twosome.

—*v.* **4.** strengthen, fortify, reinforce, support, prop up, hold up, shore up, stanchion; fasten, hook, clasp, buckle; bind, bandage, tie up, fillet.

5. steady, stabilize, secure, hold, make fast; tighten, tauten, tense, stretch; squeeze, constrict, compress, constringe, cramp.

bracelet, *n.* **1.** bracelet, band, circlet, wristlet, bangle.

2. **bracelets** handcuffs, cuffs, manacles, shackles.

bracing, *adj.* strengthening, fortifying, tonic, roborant; invigorating, stimulating, brisk, crisp; refreshing, reviviscent, restorative.

bracket, *n.* **1.** support, prop, buttress, *All Archit.* corbel, concole, cantilever.

2. clip, staple, clasp, hasp, coupling; fastener, clamp, tie, link.

3. grouping, class, status, classification, section, division, subdivision; genus, order, category, sort, kind; standing, station, rank, grade, degree, caliber.

—*v.* **4.** couple, connect, tie, join, bind, staple, link, unite; yoke, harness, pair, hook up; pinion, clip, clasp, fasten, attach, truss, affix.

brackish, *adj.* **1.** salty, briny, saline, saltish.

2. distasteful, unpleasant, unsavory, bitter, sharp, acrid.

brag, *v.* boast, crow, prate, vaunt, *Australian.* skite, *Anglo-Indian.* bukh, *Chiefly Dial.* crack; beat the drum, draw the longbow, trumpet, blow one's trumpet, toot one's horn, sing one's praises; bluster, roister, gasconnade, rodomontade; puff, bluff, vapor, *Sl.* blow hard, *Sl.* talk big, be windy; show off, strut, parade, swagger, flaunt, swash, flourish, *Literary.* plume oneself; pat oneself on the back, flatter oneself, glorify oneself, congratulate oneself; exaggerate, overstate, hyperbolize, color, enhance; *All Sl.* pile it higher and deeper, shovel it, shoot the bull, lay it on thick.

braggart, *n.* brag, braggadocio, boaster, bull-shooter, Thraso, Rodomonte; blusterer, gascon, fanfaron, trumpeter, tooter; blowhard, windbag, blatherskite, *Sl.* gasbag, *Sl.* loud mouth, *Sl.* big mouth; swaggerer, swasher, strutter, mummer, peacock, show-off; fop, coxcomb.

braid, *v.* **1.** weave, plait, plat, pleat, twill; interweave, interthread, interlace, *Brit. Dial.* raddle, *Brit. Dial.* wattle; entwine, intwine, knot, mat; interwind, interlock, interdigitate; twist, ravel, twine, tangle, entangle; wind, intort, coil, convolve, roll, cornrow; twirl, fold, infold, curl, wreathe, loop, knit, purl, thread.

2. trim, embroider, lace, frill.

brain, *n.* **1.** *Sometimes* **brains** intelligence, understanding, intellect, mind, reason, rationality, *Gk. Philos.* nous, intellectuality; aptitude, mentality, braininess, brain-power, *Inf.* gray matter, *Sl.* smarts; wisdom, sageness, sagacity, sapience, sapiency, wit, intellectualness; comprehension, apperception, grasp, insight, cognition, penetration; acumen, discernment, perspicacity, perception, percipience, judiciousness; recognition, cognizance, realization, appreciation, apprehension; astuteness, shrewdness, savvy, keenness, longheadedness, common sense; ingenuity, cleverness, aptness, parts; alertness, brilliance, brightness, acuity, sharpness.

2. *Slang.* planner, leader, designer; head man, boss, director, *Sl.* the man, *Inf.* kingpin.

3. *Informal.* genius, intellectual, intellect, thinker, *Inf.* an Einstein, mastermind, mental giant, *Inf.* wizard, *Inf.* whiz.

bramble, *n.* brier, brier bush, bramble bush, bush, shrub.

branch, *n.* **1.** limb, stem, bough, spray, switch, twig; shoot, sprout, runner, tendril.

2. section, division, subdivision, subgroup, member, affiliate, wing, arm, offshoot; chapter, lodge, post, office, local office, local.

3. tributary, feeder, spring, channel, stream, brook, runlet.

—*v.* **4.** fork, part, furcate, bifurcate, separate, divide, subdivide, bisect; ramify, stem, shoot off, angle off, go off on a tangent.

5. diverge, deviate, devaricate; spread, radiate, fan out.

6. **branch out** (*all of business activities, pursuits, etc.*) expand, extend, enlarge, increase, widen, broaden, develop.

brand, *n.* **1.** make, kind, type, sort, class, line; grade, quality.

2. trademark, stamp, label, name; symbol, sign, representation, seal, marker; identification, tab, tag, earmark; insignia, ensign, sigil, signet, badge, crest, emblem; motto, catch phrase.

3. mark, spot, blot, stain, slur; blemish, blotch, smudge, smirch, smutch, taint; stigma, mark of disgrace, discrediting, loss of reputation, disparagement, depreciation, defamation; imputation, false accusation, calumniation, slander, *Law.* libel.

—*v.* **4.** burn in, burn, scorch, singe, sear, cauterize; mark, put one's mark on, stamp.

5. stigmatize, disgrace, discredit, ruin [s.o.'s] reputation; spot, blot, stain, blemish, blotch, smudge, smirch, smutch, taint, spoil, sully, dirty; slur, disparage, depreciate, defame; *Law.* impute, accuse falsely, calumniate, slander, *Law.* libel.

brandish, *v.* **1.** wave, flourish, wield, raise, whisk; shake, jerk, swing, flap, move about, flap, wag.

2. flaunt, parade, display, disport, exhibit, show off, vaunt; swagger, strut, strut one's stuff, swashbuckle.

brash, *adj.* **1.** rash, hasty, precipitate, pell-mell; impetuous, impulsive, unrestrained, ungoverned, head-over-heels; reckless, risky, incautious, careless, unwary.

2. impertinent, rude, audacious; impudent, insolent, defiant, saucy, out of line, overweening, *Inf.* cheeky, *Inf.* fresh; blunt, tactless, undiplomatic; brazen, brassy, bold, shameless, barefaced.

3. *(all of wood)* brittle, rigid, hard; crisp, breakable, frangible, fragile.

brassy, *adj.* **1.** brass, coppery, golden; metallic, metalline.

2. harsh, grating, jangling, jarring, dissonant; shrill, strident, piercing; loud, noisy, blaring, thundering, deafening; raucous, clamorous, boisterous, uproarious, cacophonous.

3. brazen, bold, brash, loud-mouthed, mouthy, shameless, barefaced; impudent, insolent, out of line, saucy, *Inf.* cheeky, *Inf.* fresh.

brat, *n.* bantling, whelp, urchin, sprig, *Inf.* kid, child, youngster; cub, puppy, whippersnapper, jackanapes, imp, rascal, *Inf.* holy terror; chit, minx, hoyden.

bravado, *n.* braggadocio, gasconade, swagger; bragging, boasting, blowing, crowing, vaunting, name-dropping; fanfaronade, bluster, *Sl.* hot air, *Sl.* gas; bombast, pomposity, rodomontade, grandiosity, grandiloquence, magniloquence.

brave, *adj.* **1.** courageous, valiant, valorous, heroic, heroical, hero-like, stout-hearted, lionhearted, ironhearted, great-hearted; virile, manly, manful, gallant, chivalrous, chivalric; intrepid, fearless, dauntless, dreadless, aweless, nervy, *Sl.* gutsy, unafraid, unblenching, unblenched, undaunted, unalarmed, undismayed, unappalled; bold, bold-spirited, high-spirited, daring, dashing, adventurous; audacious, reckless, rash, foolhardy.

2. firm, resolute, resolved, determined, staunch, stanch, steadfast, stalwart, *Archaic.* stalworth, doughty, sturdy, hardy; indomitable, redoubtable, invincible, unconquerable, unyielding, unbending, unbowing, unshrinking, unfaltering, unhesitating, unswerving, unwavering, undeviating; mettlesome, plucky, gritty, game, red-blooded, spirited, *Inf.* spunky.

3. elegant, chic, smart, well-dressed, well-turned-out, dressed to kill, dressed to the teeth, dressed to the nines, *Sl.* all duded-up, *Sl.* all dressed up; natty, spruce, neat, sleek, trim; dapper, gay, rakish, jaunty, *Scot. or North. Eng.* braw; *All Inf.* posh, dressy, swank, swanky, ritzy; *All Sl.* classy, snazzy, sharp, nifty, spiffy, nobby, swell.

4. showy, ostentatious, gaudy, glittery, glittering, flash *or* flashy, flashing, flaunting, exhibitionistic, show-offish, *Inf.* show-offy.

—*n.* **5.** soldier, warrior, fighter, fighting man, fearless *or* dauntless soldier, intrepid warrior, good soldier, man-of-arms, man-at-arms; lion, tiger, bulldog, gamecock, fighting cock; common soldier, cannon fodder, GI *or* G.I., GI Joe, *U.S. Marine Sl.* leatherneck, *Brit.* Tommy, *Scot.* Jock, *Fr. poilu, Obs.* doughboy.

6. hero, heroine, champion, paladin, knight; stalwart, gallant, valiant, cavalier, chevalier, a man, brave man, man of courage *or* mettle.

—*v.* **7.** meet, face, brook, weather, sustain, undergo, endure, bear, suffer, *Inf.* take, *Inf.* stick, *Inf.* hang tough, *Inf.* hang in there; tolerate, stomach, abide, *Archaic.* bide, stand, stand for, put up with, bear with, *Inf.* lump it.

8. challenge, dare, outdare, *Sl.* double-dog-dare, defy, beard, brazen, outbrazen, look straight in the face *or* eye, throw down the gauntlet, show one's teeth, knock the chip off one's shoulder; confront, affront, front, encounter, oppose, stem, buffet, breast, stand up to *or* against, face up to, meet face to face, meet eyeball to eyeball, meet head-on, come face to face with, take the bull by the horns, bell the cat, *Inf.* bite the bullet, *Inf.* face the music.

bravery, *n.* **1.** courage, valor, valorousness, valiancy, valiance, heroism, prowess, stout-heartedness, lionheartedness *or* lion-heartedness, ironheartedness *or* iron-heartedness, great-heartedness *or* greatheartedness, high-heartedness; virility, manliness, manfulness, manhood, gallantry, chivalry, chivalrousness; intrepidity, intrepidness, fearlessness, dauntlessness, awelessness, dreadlessness; boldness, bold-spiritedness, high-spiritedness, daring, derring-do, audacity, audaciousness, rashness; dash, élan, panache, (*usu. negative*) bravado; assurance, self-assurance, self-reliance, confidence, pot-valor, pot-valiancy, pot-valiance.

2. fortitude, endurance, tenacity, determination, will, will-power; firmness, resoluteness, resolution, indomitableness, indomitability, invincibleness, invincibility, staunchness, stanchness, steadfastness, stalwartness, doughtiness, sturdiness, hardiness, hardihood, bulldog courage; mettle, pluck, pluckiness, spirit, backbone, gumption, blood, heart, nerve, grit, *U.S. Inf.* sand, *Inf.* starch, *Inf.* spunk, *Sl.* guts, *Sl.* moxie.

3. showiness, gaudiness, tawdriness, flamboyance, flashiness, frilliness, *Sl.* jazziness; gaiety, gaudery, trumpery, finery, frippery, frillery, superfluity, *Sl.* flash *or* flashery.

4. splendor, splendidness, splendiferousness, magnificence, grandeur, grandness, grandiosity, brilliance, gloriousness; elegance, luxuriousness, lavishness, sumptuousness, *Inf.* swankness *or* swankiness, *Inf.* poshness, *Inf.* plushness, *Inf.* ritziness.

brawl, *n.* **1.** fight, wrangle, affray, fray, rough-and-tumble, tussle, donnybrook, brannigan, *Inf.* scrap, *Sl.* rhubarb, *Scot.* sturt; fracas, rumpus, scramble, scuffle, brouhaha, free-for-all, *Inf.* ruckus; turmoil, tumult, clamor, uproar, commotion, disturbance; argument, quarrel, bicker, altercation, *Inf.* hassle, *Inf.* barney; disagreement, squabble, spat, tiff, *Brit. Dial.* fratch.

—*v.* **2.** fight, wrangle, tussle, wrestle, scuffle, lock horns, battle, spar, *Inf.* row, *Inf.* scrap; argue, quarrel, bicker, altercate, squabble, spat, tiff, *Inf.* hassle.

brawn, *n.* **1.** muscle, muscles, well-developed muscles, sinew, *Inf.* beef, muscularity; musculature, muscular development, physique; brawniness, huskiness, heftiness, *Inf.* beefiness.

2. power, potency, might, force, strength, muscular strength, *Literary.* puissance; mightiness, powerfulness, forcefulness.

brawny, *adj.* muscular, strapping, muscled, well-muscled, full-muscled, powerfully-muscled, well-developed, broad-shouldered, powerfully-built, *Derog.* muscle-bound; stalwart, rugged, hefty, husky, solid, well-knit; able-bodied, able, athletic, strong, wiry, sinewy, thewy; stout, staunch, stanch, firm, sturdy, burly, tough, iron, *Inf.* hard as rock, *Inf.* tough as nails; powerful, potent, mighty, all-powerful, herculean, *Literary.* puissant.

bray, *n.* **1.** whinny, neigh, bleat, blat, baa, cry, wail, call; blare, blast, honk, hoot.

—*v.* **2.** whinny, bleat, blat, baa, cry, wail, call; blare, trumpet, blast, honk, hoot.

brazen, *adj.* **1.** brass, brassy, coppery, golden; metallic, metalline.

2. bold, defiant, daring, brash, audacious; loud-mouthed, mouthy, outspoken, plainspoken, frank, candid; barefaced, shameless, immodest, indecent, indecorous, unseemly; impudent, insolent, bold-faced, out of line; saucy, *Inf.* cheeky, *Inf.* fresh, flippant, impertinent, pert, *Archaic.* malapert, rude; presumptuous, forward, familiar.

breach, *n.* **1.** break, rupture, fracture; cleft, split, cut, rent, rift; gap, opening, hole, gulf, void; chasm, crevice, fissure.

2. violation, transgression, contravention, infraction, infringement, nonobservance; offense, misdeed, misdemeanor, misfeasance, trespass.

3. schism, separation, disunion, falling-out, parting of the ways; discord, dissension, disagreement, friction, variance, conflict; hostility, antagonism, antipathy, enmity, ill will, bad blood; alienation, disaffection, estrangement.

—*v.* **4.** open, open up, make an opening, break open, lay open, break through, gap, burst, *Sl.* bust; cleave, crack, split, fracture, rupture.

5. violate, transgress, trespass, contravene, infringe; defy, flaunt, make a mockery of, take the law into one's own hands.

breadth, *n.* **1.** width, broadness, wideness, thickness; diameter, radius, caliber, bore; stretch, spread, reach, span; section, piece.

2. extent, magnitude, measure, degree, quantity, amount, fullness; capacity, volume, proportions, dimensions, size, gauge, bulk, content; scope, range, area, play, compass, swing, sweep.

3. expanse, space, extention, expansion, spaciousness, extensiveness, amplitude, vastness, immensity, capaciousness, largeness, roominess; open space, free space, clearing, opening.

4. liberality, liberalness, latitude, open-mindedness, broad-mindedness, magnanimity.

break, *v.* **1.** smash, shatter, batter, beat, crash; fracture, fragmentize, splinter, shiver, tear, chip, crack, snap; split, rend, reave, tear apart, wrench apart, pull to pieces; cleave, sunder, disjoint, cut off, break off, sever; crush, grind, pulverize, mash, granulate, hash, crumble, powder, pound; destroy, demolish, wreck, *Sl.* total, *Sl.* bust, ruin, knock to pieces; cut up, chop up, mince, hack up; mangle, lacerate, maim, make mincemeat of, mutilate; explode, burst, rupture, fulminate, blast.

2. infringe, breach, infract, commit a breach *or* infraction, violate, transgress, disobey, defy, contravene; oppose, act counter to, contradict, cancel out; ignore, disregard, neglect, pass over, disdain, scorn; fail to notice, take no note of, let slip *or* slide, forget, shirk, slight.

3. annul, nullify, disannul, abolish, declare null and void; quash, invalidate, vacate, disenact, cancel, discharge, set aside; repeal, revoke, rescind.

4. pierce, perforate, puncture; penetrate, reach into, tap, broach, open up; drill, mine, tunnel, burrow; drive, force into, work; stab, pink, sink, stick, prick.

5. interrupt, interfere, punctuate, *Sl.* butt in; interject, interpose, intrude, intervene; obstruct, get in the way of, choke off; discontinue, disconnect, break off, suspend, intermit; hinder, inhibit, impede, retard; stop, halt, arrest, restrain, check, cease, shut down, stay, stem.

6. overcome, overpower, overwhelm; crush, defeat, worst, beat down, put down, squelch; suppress, subdue, abort, extinguish, stamp out; humble, humiliate, bring [s.o.] to his knees.

7. decode, decipher, solve, figure out, unravel, untangle; translate, interpret, construe.

8. divide up, *Inf.* divvy up, subdivide, separate, partition, set apart; break up, scatter, disperse, disband, dismiss, dispel; disrupt, upset, unsettle.

9. betray, reveal, divulge, let the cat out of the bag, give away, blab, blurt out, let slip, disclose; violate a confidence, reveal the secrets of, whisper about; exhibit, display, vent, show, manifest, evince; unmask, uncover, unfold, bare, expose, bring to light, lay bare.

10. weaken, impair, invalidate, incapacitate, cripple, handicap, undermine; (*all usu. of health*) lose ground, take a turn for the worse, go downhill; (*all usu. of psychological or emotional health*) crack, let go, come apart at the seams, go to pieces, *Sl.* lose it, *Sl.* lose one's cool, break down.

11. initiate, begin, actuate, instigate, set in motion, start the ball rolling, take the first step, take the initiative, take the plunge, make a start, break the ice; break ground, institute, inaugurate, found, establish, set up.

12. **break down a.** See *def.* **10. b.** founder, collapse, topple down; come apart, break, go to pieces, fall to pieces; stop working, die out, *Sl.* conk out, *Sl.* go kaput.

13. break with a. depart from, separate from; break away, leave, escape. **b.** repudiate, renounce, disavow, disclaim, reject, wash one's hands of.

14. **break in a.** enter, go in *or* into, find one's way into, edge in, *Inf.* worm oneself into; burst in, barge in. **b.** train, initiate, show [s.o.] the ropes, condition, prepare. **c.** get used to, begin to wear *or* use. **d.** See *def.* **5. e.** burglarize, rob. See **rob** (*defs.* **1-3**).

15. **break someone's heart** disappoint, disillusion, let down; abandon, jilt, forsake, run out on, desert, turn one's back on.

16. **break up a.** (*of a personal relationship*) sever, break the ties, go separate ways; end, terminate, stop, cease, give up on. **b.** make [s.o.] laugh, amuse, entertain, divert; laugh, giggle, chuckle, roar, *Inf.* double up with laughter.

—*n.* **17.** crack, shatter, snap, smash; fracture, splinter, shiver, chip; explosion, burst, rupture, blast; split, tear, rent, flaw, fissure, cleft, *Archaic.* scissure; crevice, chasm, schism, cleavage, rift, breach, chink, slit, rip; gap, opening, hole, gulf, cavity, leak; slash, gash, cut.

18. altercation, difference, falling out, divergence, variance; parting of the ways, breaking up, breaking off, separation, disunion; discord, dissension, dissent, disagreement, friction, disruption, conflict, contention; dispute, tiff, argument, quarrel, misunderstanding.

19. interruption, interference, intrusion, punctuation; interjection, intervention, interposition; suspension, discontinuation, hiatus, lacuna; intermission, interlude, recess, rest, respite; pause, interval, lapse; division, *Class. Prosody.* caesura; stoppage, arrest, cessation; omission, space, gap.

breakable, *adj.* frangible, fragile, frail, brittle, easily broken; friable, crumbly, not shatterproof; shaky, tottering, wobbling, teetering; unstable, unsteady, *Inf.* jerry-built; weak, weakened, feeble, decrepit; delicate, flimsy, slight, dainty.

breakdown, *n.* **1.** collapse, foundering, toppling down, cave-in; malfunction, wearing out, *Sl.* conking out; (*all usu. of emotional or psychological health*) nervous breakdown, going to pieces, coming apart at the seams, cracking, *Sl.* losing it.

2. analysis, sorting out, division, organization, anatomization; rundown, review, summary.

breakwater, *n.* sea wall, mole, jetty, jutty, groin, barrier, embankment.

breast, *n.* **1.** chest, bosom, front; mammary gland, tit, *Sl.* boob; teat, mamma, nipple, *Chiefly Dial.* pap, (*of animals*) dug, (*of cows*) udder; bust, set. See **bosom** (*def.* **1**).

2. heart, soul, core; affections, feeling, emotion, sentiment, sensibility; conscience, compunction.

breath, *n.* **1.** respiration, breathing, wind, *Archaic.* halitus; inhalation, inspiration, exhalation, expiration; pant, wheeze, gasp, gulp.

2. life, life force, lifeblood, vital spark, breath of life, soul, anima.

3. pause, respite, break, breather, breathing spell, rest, recess, time-out, *Australian.* spell, *Inf.* letup.

4. murmur, whisper, sigh, undertone.

5. breeze, gentle breeze *or* wind, zephyr; puff, waft, whiff.

6. **take one's breath away** astonish, astound, amaze, stagger, startle, boggle; thrill, excite, galvanize.

breathe, *v.* **1.** respire, inhale and exhale, puff, pant, wheeze, gasp, gulp; inhale, inspire, exhale, expire, exhaust, expel.

2. whisper, murmur, sigh, aspirate; say, voice, utter, articulate, pronounce, enunciate, express.

3. infuse, instill, imbue, inject, transfuse.

4. break, take a break, take a rest, pause, recess, lay off, *Sl.* knock off, *Sl.* take ten *or* five.

5. **not breathe a word** be silent, keep one's mouth shut, hold one's tongue, seal one's lips, say nothing, keep mum, *Sl.* button up, *Sl.* muzzle.

breathless, *adj.* **1.** panting, choking, wheezing, gasping, gulping, out of breath; winded, blown, exhausted, wasted, spent.

2. amazed, astonished, astounded, thunderstruck, awestruck, openmouthed, *Inf.* flabbergasted.

3. eager, anxious, agog, all agog, *Sl.* psyched.

4. dead, lifeless, inanimate; still, motionless, calm, becalmed.

breeches, *n.* **1.** knickers, knickerbockers, shorts, smallclothes, plus fours, knee breeches; jodhpurs, riding breeches; pedal pushers, clam diggers, knee knockers; culottes, gauchos.

2. *Informal.* trousers, slacks, pants, jeans, corduroys; pantaloons, drawers.

breed, *v.* **1.** procreate, engender, father, beget, bear, give birth, bring forth; reproduce, propagate, multiply, pullulate; impregnate, fertilize; mate, copulate, couple.

2. raise, grow, develop, cultivate; rear, nurture, foster, mother, bring up.

3. cause, effect, bring about, give rise to; create, generate, produce, make.

breeding, *n.* **1.** procreation, engenderment, begetting, fathering, bearing, hatching, spawning; reproduction, propagation, pullulation, multiplication; mating, copulation, coupling, impregnation, fertilization.

2. development, cultivation, improvement; training, schooling, teaching, education; nurture, care, rearing, upbringing, bringing-up; background, extraction, parentage.

3. manners, courtesy, politeness, civility, gentility; behavior, conduct, bearing, comportment.

breeze, *n.* **1.** zephyr, gentle *or* light wind, *Naut.* cat's paw; breath, puff of air, whiff, whiffet; waft, current of air, draft, gust, *Rare.* flurry, blow; sea breeze, lake breeze, land breeze, onshore breeze.

2. *Slang.* **bat** *or* **shoot the breeze a.** chat, *Inf.* gab, *Sl.* chew the fat, gossip, *Sl.* jaw. **b.** talk nonsense, babble, *Inf.* talk through one's hat. See **babble** (*def.* **1**).

breezy, *adj.* **1.** airy, mild, gentle, light, soft, pleasant, cool; windy, blowy, blowing, blustery, blusterous; drafty, gusty, gusting, flawy; stormy, squallish.

2. fresh, sprightly, vivacious, animated, alive, lively, *U.S. Inf.* chipper, jaunty; spirited, dynamic, energetic, vigorous, active, spry; frisky, playful, frolicsome, *Inf.* full of pep, *Inf.* peppy, full of vim and vigor, bright-eyed and bushy-tailed; aglow, glowing, alight, lit up, bright, shining, shiny, sparkling; sunny, cheerful, cheery, glad, happy, mirthful, jolly, jovial; gay, blithe, blithesome, buoyant, light-hearted, free and easy, carefree; in good *or* high spirits, elated, overjoyed, thrilled, enthusiastic, enthused, excited.

brevity, *n.* **1.** briefness, shortness, shortlivedness, transcience, impermanence, ephemerality, caducity.

2. conciseness, succinctness, curtness, terseness, laconism; pithiness, pointedness, crispness, compactness, compression, compendiousness.

brew, *v.* **1.** steep, soak, ferment; cook, stew, boil, simmer, seethe, decoct; mix, concoct, stir up, blend, make, prepare, commix.

2. contrive, bring about, think up, hatch, spin, coin, forge; invent, design, shape, devise, plan, get up, *Inf.* cook up; start, organize, begin.

—*n.* **3.** mixture, concoction, fermentation, stew, potpourri; creation, formula; beer, ale.

bribe, *n.* **1.** graft, *Inf.* kickback, *Inf.* payola, *Inf.* plugola, *Inf.* hush money, *Inf.* protection *or* protection money, *Sl.* boodle; inducement, lure, reward, gift, gratuity.

—*v.* **2.** pay off, buy, buy off, suborn, corrupt, *Sl.* grease [s.o.'s] palm; fix, *Inf.* rig, *Inf.* square; induce, tempt, lure, entice, coax, influence.

bridal, *adj.* nuptial, wedding, marriage, matrimonial; conjugal, hymeneal; marital, spousal, connubial; nubile, marriageable.

bride, *n.* wife, spouse, *Inf.* better half, *Inf.* missis, *Inf.* little woman, *Scot. Inf.* wifey, *Rhyming Sl.* trouble and strife; mate, helpmeet, partner. See also **partner** (*def.* 3).

bridge, *n.* **1.** span, viaduct, *Scot.* brig; overpass, *Brit.* flyover.

2. connection, link, bond, tie.

—*v.* **3.** span, cross, traverse, go over, extend over, pass over, arch over; join, conjoin, connect, unite, link, tie.

bridle, *n.* **1.** halter, hackamore, headgear, headstall; governor, control, restraint, trammel, check, curb.

—*v.* **2.** restrain, check, curb, arrest, hold back, keep back; control, govern, keep in check.

3. bristle, raise one's hackles, get one's back up.

brief, *adj.* **1.** momentary, temporary, of short duration, short; impermanent, mortal, unenduring, fleeting, passing, fading; transitory, transient, fugacious, caducous, deciduous, monohemerous, monemerous, evanescent, ephemeral; mercurial, volatile, perishable, precarious; fast, swift, brisk, sudden, quick, fleet, meteoric; cursory, hurried, hasty.

2. concise, succinct, to the point, short and sweet; short-winded, straightforward, direct, pointed, emphatic; abbreviated, abridged, condensed, compressed, summarized, thumbnail, curtailed, curtate, contracted, *Obs.* breviate; compact, lean, compendious, packed, close, neat; comprehensive, summary, synoptic, *Inf.* meaty; pithy, sententious, epigrammatic, crisp, precise, exact, gnomic; laconic, terse, elliptical, breviloquent, *Rare.* pauciloquent; reticent, halting, sparing of words.

3. curt, sharp, abrupt, short-spoken, short; cutting, biting, sarcastic, acute, keen; caustic, acrimonious, virulent, mordant, trenchant; sullen, tart, sour, petulant, splenetic, choleric, acetose; testy, edgy, touchy, grouchy, irascible, short-tempered, short-fused; crabbed, crabby, peevish, snapping, snarling, growling, bearish, currish, waspish; brusque, brash, gruff, peppery, surly, crusty, thorny; unmannerly, rude, impolite, discourteous, ungraceful; stern, austere.

—*n.* **4.** outline, sketch, draft, analysis, abstract, résumé, syllabus; compendium, survey, synopsis, summary, précis, conspectus, prospectus; digest, epitome, extract, excerpt, minutes, pandect.

5. argument, demonstration, data, ground, proof, evidence; memorandum, memo, minute, entry, document, list of agenda, list of items; writ, warrant, summons, subpoena, injunction, *Rom. Cath. Ch.* decretal.

6. briefs underpants, underwear, underdrawers, drawers, *Sl.* skivvies, *Sl.* undies, *Trademark.* BVDs, *Trademark.* Fruit of the Looms, trunks, *Brit.* y-fronts, *Brit.* knickers.

7. briefing, once-over, running-over, going-over, rehash, review; rundown, *Sl.* lowdown, *Sl.* the word, sum and substance, gist.

8. *Theat. Brit.* free pass, pass, free ticket, free admission, complimentary ticket, courtesy card, *Sl.* freebie.

9. hold a brief for endorse, sanction, approve, favor, patronize, propound, promote, sing the praises of *or* sing [s.o.'s] praises; support, back up, side with, lobby for; defend, champion, second, stand by, stick up for.

10. in brief a. in short, in a word, in a few words, to put it briefly *or* concisely *or* succinctly, to be brief, for shortness sake, to come to the point, to cut the matter short, to make a long story short. **b.** in summary, in conclusion, *Inf.* in a nutshell, all in all, in all, in the final analysis.

—*v.* **11.** outline, sketch, abstract, epitomize, summarize, synopsize, digest.

12. instruct, inform, explain, enlighten, disclose, impart, communicate, acquaint.

briefly, *adv.* **1.** momentarily, temporarily, shortly, swiftly, briskly, suddenly, quickly; hastily, cursorily, perfunctorily, hurriedly.

2. concisely, succinctly, straightforwardly, emphatically, pointedly, directly; condensedly, compressedly, contractedly, abridgedly; compactly, closely, neatly; comprehensively, summarily, synoptically, compendiously; pithily, sententiously, epigrammatically, crisply, precisely, exactly, gnomically; laconically, tersely, elliptically, breviloquently; reticently, haltingly.

3. curtly, sharply, abruptly, cuttingly, bitingly, sarcastically, acutely, keenly; caustically, acrimoniously, virulently, mordantly, trenchantly, sullenly, tartly, sourly, petulantly, splenetically; testily, edgily, touchily, grouchily, irascibly, crabbily, peevishly, snappingly, snarlingly, growlingly, bearishly, waspishly, currishly; brusquely, brashly, gruffly, crustily; rudely, impolitely, discourteously, ungracefully, gracelessly, *Archaic.* unmannerly; sternly, austerely.

brigade, *n.* **1.** legion, corps, army, force, soldiers, troops, men, phalanx, garrison; division, section, battalion, *Obs.* battalia, regiment, company, squadron, squad, detachment, contingent, *U.S.* wing.

2. group, troop, tribe, band, party, unit, union, association, mass, body; host, horde, multitude, crowd, herd, throng.

brigand, *n.* **1.** outlaw, gangster, criminal, mafioso; thug, ruffian, *Inf.* mugger, hoodlum, *Sl.* hood, *Australian Sl.* larrikin; rogue, picaro, (*in India and Burma*) dacoit; highwayman, footpad, *Sl.* yegg *or* yeggman, bandit, bravo, *Sp. bandolero, Southwest U.S.* ladrone, *Australian.* bushranger, picaroon, desperado; pickpocket, pursesnatcher, shoplifter, thief, robber.

2. pirate, sea dog, sea wolf, viking, corsair, buccaneer, privateer, freebooter, rapparee, (*in the Scottish Highlands*) cateran.

3. kidnapper, abductor, (*usu. of cattle*) rustler; hijacker, skyjacker, air *or* sky pirate, terrorist.

4. smuggler, contrabandist, runner, bootlegger; *Inf.* poacher, deerjacker.

5. pillager, plunderer, marauder, despoiler, depredator, vandal; predator, ransacker, sacker, looter, rifler, forager, raider.

bright, *adj.* **1.** shining, illuminated, alight, light, lit; radiant, effulgent, lambent, resplendent, beaming, beamy, beamish; shiny, glossy, lustrous, sheenful; glowing, luminous, incandescent, phosphorescent; clear, transparent, translucent. See **brilliant** (*def.* 1).

2. splendid, splendrous, magnificent, rich, majestic, dazzling, beautiful; glorious, illustrious, distinguished.

3. clever, witty, quick, quick-witted; intelligent, brainy, intellectual; inventive, resourceful, ingenious,

proficient, accomplished; capable, competent, able. See **brilliant** (*def.* 3).
4. animated, alive, lively, spirited, sprightly; buoyant, airy, sunny, blithe, gay, cheerful, cheery; happy, joyous, joyful, glad, gladsome.
5. favorable, opportune, propitious, auspicious, providential, fortunate, lucky; promising, encouraging, rosy, rose-colored, roseate; fair, clement, mild, pleasant.

brighten, *v.* **1.** light, illumine, illuminate, *Archaic.* illume, irradiate.
2. shine, gloze, burnish, buff, polish, varnish, wax; glaze, gild, gloss, luster, mercerize; freshen, furbish, clean; enhance, adorn, *Sl.* jazz up, bedeck, beautify.
3. cheer, comfort, enhearten, uplift, encourage; lighten, cheer up, gladden, elate; enliven, animate, inspirit.

brilliant, *adj.* **1.** shining, bright, sunny, sunshiny; illuminated, alight, light, lit, lighted; white, golden, rutilant, aureate; radiant, irradiant, lambent, resplendent, beaming, beamy; dazzling, vivid, intense, ablaze, aflame, afire; fulgent, effulgent, refulgent, shiny, glossy, gleaming, agleam, glaring; lucid, lucent, *Rare.* relucent, luciferous; lustrous, (*both usu. of gems*) orient, oriental; sheenful, sheeny, nitid, polished, burnished; aglow, glowing, luminous, luminescent, luminiferous, incandescent, phosphorescent; sparkling, scintillating, scintillant, coruscating, twinkling, shimmering; glimmering, aglimmer, glistening, aglisten, *Archaic.* glistering, glittering, aglitter, fulgid.
2. magnificent, superb, rich, beautiful, gorgeous; sparkling, dazzling, splendid, splendrous, *Music.* bravura; glorious, illustrious, distinguished; renowned, famous, celebrated, eminent, prominent; august, admirable, majestic, honorable, noble, revered; exceptional, laudable, praiseworthy, worthy, remarkable; creditable, estimable, commendable, meritorious, deserving, exemplary; prime, choice, select, rare, best, sterling.
3. intelligent, bright, intellectual, cerebral, brainy; gifted, precocious, talented, apt; expert, adroit, dextrous, skillful, deft, handy; inventive, resourceful, ingenious, proficient, accomplished, masterful; capable, competent, able, efficient; quick, clever, alert, keen, sharp, alive; perceptive, percipient, perspicacious, discerning; astute, penetrating, acute, subtle; nimble-witted, sharp-witted, keen-witted, quick-witted; aware, observant, clear-eyed, far-sighted; sagacious, shrewd, long-headed, hard-headed; understanding, apprehending, comprehending, knowing, cognitive; sage, sapient, wise, profound, deep; scholarly, erudite, educated, learned, well-read; enlightened, enlightening, luminous.

brim, *n.* **1.** lip, rim, brink; edge, margin, perimeter.
2. visor, shade, shield, bill; promontory, headland, cliff, bluff.

brindled, *adj.* dappled, mottled, spotted, pied, piebald; speckled, freckled, flecked, blotched, streaked, variegated, marbled; pepper-and-salt, gray, tawny, dusky.

brine, *n.* **1.** salt water, saline solution, sea water, sea, ocean, *Archaic.* wave.
—*v.* **2.** pickle, marinade, steep, soak.

bring, *v.* **1.** carry, bear, take, convey, transport, deliver, transmit, send; conduct, escort, usher, guide, lead; fetch, get, gather.
2. attract, allure, lure, draw, pull; invite, encourage, invoke, court, prompt, ask for.

brink, *n.* **1.** brim, rim, lip, edge; margin, perimeter, apogee, extremity.
2. verge, point, moment; crisis, crossroads, juncture, turning point.

brisk, *adj.* **1.** active, lively, animated, spirited, vivacious; enlivened, invigorated, energetic, energized, vivified, vitalized, inspirited; vigorous, spry, sprightly, pert, *Inf.* peppy, *Inf.* snappy, *Music.* allegro; swift, quick, prompt, alacritous; airy, breezy, jaunty, zestful, sportive; full of life, full of get up and go, full of vim and vigor, in high spirits; eager, zealous, ardent, vehement, enthusiastic, fervent, *Inf.* sparking, fired up.
2. sharp, crisp, fresh, bracing, nipping; invigorating, refreshing, stirring, roborant; stimulating, revivatory, tonic, strengthening, beneficial; restorative, rejuvenating, revitalizing.

bristle, *n.* **1.** hair, whisker, nub, stubble, *Scot.* birse; prickle, *Zool.* seta, *Bot.* trichome, spicule, spine, quill, shoot; thorn, barb, barbule, point.
—*v.* **2.** prickle, horripillate, stand up, rise; start up, stir up, arouse; be angered, be infuriated, be maddened.

bristly, *adj.* prickly, stubbly, stubby, nubby, whiskered, bewhiskered; tipped, prickled, spined, quilled, pointed, barbed, pronged; rough, shaggy, hairy, bearded, comose; horrent, thorny, spiny; *All Zool., Bot.* trichomic, trichoid, barbellate, hispid, hispidulous, strigose, spicular, spiculate.

brittle, *adj.* **1.** fragile, frail, weak, infirm, delicate, feeble, rickety.
2. breakable, frangible, smashable, shivery, splintery, shattery, (*of wood*) brash; crumbly, friable, pulverulent, pulverable, pulverizable, powdery, triturable.

broach, *v.* suggest, mention, bring up, open; propose, offer, proffer, pose; introduce, submit, present, set forth, put before; throw out, bring to [s.o.'s] attention, place before, hold out; advance, put forward, propound, tender, move, make a motion.

broad, *adj.* **1.** wide, extensive, expansive, large; beamy, outspread, splay, spread out, thick, hippopotamic; spacious, capacious, roomy, ample, commodious, voluminous.
2. immense, vast, sweeping, far-reaching, far-flung; unlimited, illimitable, unbounded, boundless, measureless, infinite, interminable, endless.
3. full, entire, whole, complete, perfect; absolute, plenary, total, utter, thorough, all, out and out.
4. comprehensive, inclusive, encyclopedic, of great scope, compendious; all-inclusive, composite, exhaustive, all-embracing; general, universal, ecumenical, world-wide, catholic, latitudinarian, widespread.
5. plain, clear, direct, straightforward, sincere, candid, frank; undisguised, unconcealed, unquestionable, clear-cut; evident, visible, pronounced, apparent; striking, glaring, staring, bare, naked, well-marked.
6. broad-minded, liberal, good-hearted, good, fair, just. See **broad-minded**.
7. indelicate, indecent, improper, indecorous, infelicitous; unseemly, unbecoming, uncomely; unrefined, inelegant, ungentle, ungentlemanly, unladylike.
8. free, unrestrained, unconstrained, unconfined, unobstructed; open, untrammeled; uncontrolled, unbridled, unchecked, unfettered, unhindered, unimpeded.

broadcast, *v.* **1.** transmit, send out, cable, relay, radio; air, put on the air, televise, telecast.
2. scatter, disperse, strew, bestrew, sow, disseminate; spread, circulate, distribute, propagate, pass the word around.
3. advertise, announce, publish, voice; proclaim, herald, trumpet, blazon, blurb, ballyhoo, beat the drum, *Inf.* shout from the housetops *or* rooftops.
—*n.* **4.** show, program, telecast, radiobroadcast, radio program.

broaden, *v.* **1.** widen, enlarge, expand, extend; open,

open up, spread, spread out; stretch, distend, dilate, swell.

2. increase, develop; augment, supplement, add to.

broad-minded, *adj.* liberal, good-hearted, good, kind, fair, just, square, evenhanded; generous, charitable, considerate, thoughtful; big, magnanimous, philanthropic, munificent, benign, benevolent, beneficent; dispassionate, broad, impersonal, impartial, disinterested; unprejudiced, unbiased, unbigoted, unswayed; tolerant, forbearant, catholic, latitudinarian, understanding, sympathetic.

broadside, *n.* **1.** criticism, censure, critical review; attack, bombardment, battering, storming; assault, onslaught, assailment, besetment; cannonade, *Mil.* battery, *Mil.* barrage, discharge, volley, salvo.

2. placard, poster, bill, circular, *U.S.* flyer, brochure. See **brochure**.

brochure, *n.* pamphlet, booklet, leaflet, folder, chapbook; treatise, monograph, tractate, tract, essay; bulletin, notice, placard, poster, *Fr. affiche*, playbill, bill; advertisement, circular, handbill, *U.S.* flyer, broadside, broadsheet, handout, throwaway.

broil[1], *v.* **1.** grill, toast, barbecue, cook, heat, warm, roast, sear, toast, fry, griddle.

2. warm, heat, parch, burn, singe, sear, blister.

broil[2], *n.* **1.** quarrel, dispute, altercation, wrangle, embroilment, brouhaha; rumpus, uproar, tumult, outbreak, commotion; clash, scrimmage, scuffle, scramble, fracas, fray, brawl, scrap.

—*v.* **2.** brawl, scrimmage. See **brawl** (*defs.* **3, 4**).

broken, *adj.* **1.** shattered, smashed, crumbled, crushed, mangled, pulverized; fragmented, ruptured, torn, fractured, split, rent, cracked; damaged, destroyed.

2. interrupted, disrupted, unsuccessive, discontinuous, disjunct, disconnected, fragmentary, incomplete, discrete; spasmodic, intermittent.

3. defeated, beaten, overthrown, vanquished, overridden, conquered, overpowered, outdone, outmatched; quelled, suppressed, crushed, ruined, undone, *Inf.* licked, *Inf.* trimmed; fallen, subdued, weakened, reduced.

4. tamed, trained, broken in, gentled, domesticated, house-broken.

5. rough, irregular, not smooth, uneven.

6. weakened, unsteady, rundown, in poor health; disheartened, demoralized, dispirited.

7. ruined, bankrupt, impoverished.

8. **broken down** out of working order, in disrepair, not functioning, out of order, out of commission, gone haywire, *Inf.* on the blink, *Inf.* on the fritz, *Inf.* out of kilter, *Sl.* out of whack, *Sl.* gone kerflooie, *Sl.* kaput, *Sl.* on the bum, *Sl.* dead.

broken-hearted, *adj.* grief-stricken, sorrowful, mournful, disconsolate, comfortless, inconsolable; overcome, prostrated, stricken, heavy-laden, lamenting, forlorn, bowed down, spiritless; disappointed, dejected, heartbroken, crestfallen; dashed, crushed, despairing, in despair, hopeless; sad, melancholy, woeful, miserable, wretched, depressed, doleful, rueful, woebegone; gloomy, glum, cheerless, unhappy, long-faced.

broker, *n.* **1.** agent, factor, dealer, cambist; stockbroker, stockjobber.

2. middleman, wholesaler, distributor, jobber; medium, intermediary, go-between.

bronze, *adj.* metallic-brown, rust, rust-colored, copper, copper-colored, henna.

brooch, *n.* clasp, pin, stickpin, breastpin, chatelaine.

brood, *n.* **1.** litter, nest, furrow, fry, spawn, spat; young, offspring, get.

2. breed, line, strain, stock, kind, species.

—*v.* **3.** incubate, hatch, sit, set, cover.

4. ponder, meditate, muse, reflect, contemplate; consider, study, weigh, deliberate, ruminate, *Inf.* chew the cud.

brook[1], *n.* stream, streamlet, brooklet, creek, *Dial.* crick, *U.S. Dial.* kill, rivulet, rill, rindle, run, runnel, runlet *or Dial.* rundle, *Brit. Dial.* beck, *Brit. Dial.* gill *or* ghyll, *Scot. and North Eng.* sike *or* syke, *Scot. and North Eng.* burn; channel, waterway, watercourse; branch, tributary.

brook[2], *v.* suffer, endure, bear; tolerate, abide, accept, stand, withstand, take patiently, submit to, put up with; swallow, digest, stomach, pocket; undergo, experience, sustain, weather, forbear, *Obs.* aby, *Chiefly Scot.* thole, *Scot. and North Eng.* dree.

broom, *n.* sweeper, besom, whisk, *Archaic.* wisp; brush, duster.

broth, *n.* stock, consommé, bouillon; soup, pottage, *U.S.* chowder; liquid, water.

brothel, *n.* bordello, *Archaic.* bordel, bagnio, *Obs.* stew, lupanar, *Obs.* kip, nunnery; house of prostitution, house of ill-repute, house of ill-fame, bawdyhouse, whorehouse, *Inf.* sporting house, *Inf.* call house; *All Sl.* call joint, cathouse, parlor house, barrelhouse, honky-tonk, pick-up joint.

brother, *n.* **1.** sibling, sib, blood brother, identical twin; kin, kinsman, relative, relation.

2. associate, colleague, affiliate, fellow, comember, peer, compeer, confrere; mate, partner, helpmate, helpmeet, co-worker, yokefellow, yokemate; companion, friend, ally, comrade, crony, chum, *Fr. copain*, frater, amigo, *Fr. ami*.

brotherhood, *n.* **1.** kinship, relationship, relatedness, consanguinity, *Anthropol.* sib-ship.

2. fellowship, colleagueship, mateship, partnership, companionship, brotherliness, camaraderie, comradeship, esprit de corps; friendliness, amicability, sociability, clubbiness, *Inf.* chumminess, sodality; affability, kindliness, kind-heartedness, congeniality, geniality, cordiality, hospitality.

3. fraternity, club, lodge, clan, set, clique, community, society, circle, party; band, team, troop, group, congregation, assemblage; association, consociation, affiliation, consortium, conference; union, alliance, guild, league, coalition, organization.

brouhaha, *n.* clamor, uproar, hubbub, hullabaloo, din, commotion, *Inf.* to-do, disturbance, disruption, public sensation; turmoil, tumult, broil, brawl, struggle; pandemonium, bedlam, free-for-all, fracas, rumpus, scramble, scuffle, *Inf.* ruckus; tempest in a teapot.

brow, *n.* **1.** eyebrow, forehead, temple, front; visage, countenance, mien, appearance, aspect, air, bearing.

2. edge, brink, brim, verge, rim; top, summit, peak, apex, crown, tip.

browbeat, *v.* intimidate, cow, bully, bulldoze, bluster, dragoon; hector, badger, harass, taunt, threaten; dominate, domineer, overbear, subdue, beat down, terrorize; force, coerce, compel.

brown, *adj.* **1.** bay, chestnut, roan, sorrel; rust, brick, terra-cotta; cinnamon, ginger, hazel, maroon; chocolate, cocoa, coffee, puce; mahogany, walnut; henna, auburn, brunette, dark; dun, fawn, beige, ecru; tawny, musteline, dusky, fuscous, umber; tan, khaki, drab; bronze, copper, gold; tanned, sunburned.

—*v.* **2.** fry, sauté, grill, fricasse, cook.

browse, *v.* **1.** scan, peruse, skim, dip into, have a look at, look over, run over, check over; thumb through, flip through, leaf through, look through, glance through.

2. shop, shop around, window-shop, check out, *Inf.* poke around, *Sl.* nose around.

3. (*all of animals*) eat, eat from, nibble at, pick at, peck at; graze, pasture, feed, crop, batten.

bruise, *v.* **1.** contuse, injure, hurt, harm, do damage to, damage; discolor, blacken, mar, deface, *Inf.* mark up, spoil; scratch, scrape, bump, hit; cut, gash, slash, knife, wound; lacerate, mutilate, disfigure, maul, mangle, maim.

2. (*all of drugs or food*) crush, beat, pound, grind, pulverize, powder.

—*n.* **3.** contusion, black-and-blue mark, discoloration, spot, mark; blemish, blotch, *Sl.* hickey, disfigurement, scar; injury, hurt, bump, lump; scratch, scrape, abrasion, cut, *Sl.* boo-boo; rip, tear, slit, slash, gash, laceration, wound, mutilation.

brunette, *adj.* dark, dark-colored, darkish, swarthy, melanous, brown, brownish, browny; olive-skinned, brown-skinned, dark-skinned, dark-complexioned; dark-haired, brown-haired, black-haired, black-skinned, *Ethnol.* melanic.

brunt, *n.* shock, concussion, force, full force, violence, impact, percussion; strain, stress, pressure; effects, repercussions, consequences, results.

brush[1], *n.* **1.** broom, besom, whisk, whiskbroom; scrubber, scrub brush; hair brush.

2. encounter, engagement, action, skirmish, clash. See also **battle** (*def.* **1**).

—*v.* **3.** sweep, sweep up, broom, whisk; tend, groom, curry, rub down.

4. touch, graze, kiss, glance off; lick, scrape, skim.

5. brush aside disregard, ignore, dismiss, shrug off, have no time for, think no more of, forget about.

6. brush up on read up on, get up on; review, study, *Inf.* cram, *Sl.* bone up.

brush[2], *n.* **1.** thicket, scrub, wood, grove, copse, brushwood, *Brit.* bracken; undergrowth, underwood, underbrush, boscage, copsewood.

2. hinterland, backwoods, back country, up-country, the bush, *Australian.* outback, *Inf.* the sticks, *Inf.* the boondocks.

brusque, *adj.* abrupt, curt, blunt, short, hasty, rough; frank, forward, unreserved, plain-spoken, candid, downright, unvarnished, outspoken; bluff, burly, brash; harsh, stern, austere; sharp, keen, trenchant, acrimonious, caustic, virulent, stringent, brutal, cruel; churlish, bearish; rude, uncivil, unceremonious, ungracious, discourteous, impolite, unmannerly.

brutal, *adj.* **1.** pitiless, merciless, heartless, unkind, inhumane; unfeeling, uncompassionate, unsympathetic; cruel, hard-hearted, stony-hearted, marble-hearted, cold-blooded; cold, callous, insensitive, hardened, obdurate.

2. inhuman, barbarous, barbaric, savage, hellish, Tartarian, Hunnish, Vandalic; brutish, murderous, slaughterous, bloodthirsty; sadistic, bestial, beastly, animalistic, cannibalistic, fiendish, ghoulish, ogreish, *Obs.* belluine; diabolical, satanic, demonic, demoniac, devilish; terrible, harsh, grim, hard, severe; ferocious, ruthless, vicious, fell, truculent; wolfish, lupine, fierce, feral, ferine; tyrannical, Draconian, inquisitorial, oppressive; unrelenting, relentless, remorseless, implacable, inexorable, grinding.

3. gross, rude, coarse, vulgar, rough; gruff, bearish, boorish, crass, rustic, ill-bred, churlish, clodhopping, *Archaic.* carlish; loutish, doltish, cloddish, oafish; uncivil, unrefined, uncouth, inurbane, unpolished; uncultivated, unmannered, ungentlemanly, ungentle, uncourtly, inelegant, indelicate.

4. irrational, unthinking, unintelligent, unreasoning, uncomprehending; mindless, insensible, senseless, *Rare.* insulse, stupid.

brute, *n.* **1.** beast, creature, animal, *Dial.* critter.

2. barbarian, savage, hellkite, wild man; ogre, monster, troglodyte; Vandal, Goth, Hun, Tartar.

3. churl, lout, boor, oaf, rustic, dolt, clod, *Archaic.* carl; swine, devil, demon.

bubble, *n.* **1.** globule, glob, drop, droplet, bead, tear, blob, gutta; sphere, spherule, spheroid, ball, oval, *Geom.* ellipsoid; vacuum, air pocket, air hole, hole, opening, imperfection, defect.

—*v.* **2.** effervesce, percolate, boil, roll, foam, froth, spume; gurgle, guggle, fizz, burble; sparkle, glitter, glow, radiate.

buccaneer, *n.* **1.** pirate, sea robber, sea rover, sea dog, sea wolf; viking, corsair, privateer, freebooter, rapparee.

2. robber, bandit, bravo, *Sp. bandolero,* brigand, picaroon, desperado; outlaw, gangster, thug, ruffian.

3. pillager, plunderer, marauder, despoiler, depredator, vandal; predator, ransacker, sacker, looter, rifler, forager, raider. See also **pirate** (*defs.* **1-6**).

buck[1], *n.* **1.** stag, male deer, ram.

2. blade, playboy, ladies' man, man about town, *Sl.* lover boy, philanderer; dandy, jack-a-dandy, fop, popinjay, coxcomb, spark, beau, dude, exquisite, *Sl.* swell.

buck[2], *v.* **1.** leap, spring, jump, bound, vault; hop, skip, prance, gambol, frisk; bob, bounce, jerk; throw, dislodge, unseat.

2. resist, make a stand, contest, contend, oppose, object.

bucket, *n.* pail, scuttle, *Inf.* growler; barrel, cask, *Naut.* scuttlebutt; can, pan, tin, pot, basin, pitcher; vessel, container, holder.

buckle, *n.* **1.** clasp, clip, hook, catch, snap, hook and eye, button, fastener, fastening, hasp; brooch, pin, stickpin.

2. bend, bulge, fold, wrinkle, crumple, ripple, crinkle; knot, kink, crook, crimp, gnarl; twist, warp, contortion, curve, turn; curl, curlicue, screw, spiral, corkscrew, coil, loop, convolution, twirl, whorl, whirl.

—*v.* **3.** clasp, clip, pin, hook, catch, snap, button, hasp; fasten, tie, join, connect, hitch, yoke; link, bind, attach, tape, lash, lace, strap.

4. shrivel, shrink, warp, distort, contort; gnarl, knot, kink, crook, crimp; wrinkle, crumple, ripple, crinkle; twist, curl, spiral, screw, coil, loop, convolute, twirl, whirl; bend, curve, turn, bulge.

5. buckle down get down, concentrate, attend; set to work, start, begin, go at, proceed.

bud, *n.* **1.** sprout, burgeon, shoot, blade; stem, twig, spray, sprig; floweret, floret.

—*v.* **2.** bud, sprout, begin to grow, germinate, pullulate, send out shoots, put forth; bloom, blossom, open, flower, bear fruit, fructify; spring up, burst forth, shoot up, develop vigorously, mushroom, burgeon, boom; thrive, flourish, prosper, luxuriate.

3. nip in the bud stop, quash, quell, suppress, squelch, put down *or* out, stamp out, extinguish.

budge, *v.* **1.** move, stir, go; shift, move over, give way; nudge, push, shove; remove, dislodge.

2. yield, acquiesce, submit, bend, accede, concede, give in.

budget, *n.* **1.** estimate, statement, financial statement; costs, expenses, operating expenses, general expenses, overhead.

2. plan, blueprint, schedule, program.

3. allowance, ration, share, portion, part; allotment, allocation, percentage, quota.

4. stock, stockpile, reserve, reservoir, supply, store;

resources, means, assets, capital; funds, finances, moneys, purse.

—*v.* **5.** estimate, cost, cost out; plan, docket, schedule, program.

6. allow, allocate, allot, ration.

buff, *v.* **1.** polish, burnish, furbish, shine; wax, varnish, gloss; rub, rub up, smooth.

—*adj.* **2.** yellow, yellowish, gold, apricot, canary, sallow, citron, lemon.

buffer, *n.* **1.** shock absorber, bumper, fender; cushion, pillow, pad, mat.

2. guard, shield, screen; wall, dividing wall, partition, barrier, embankment, bulwark, rampart, levee, dike.

—*v.* **3.** absorb, cushion, pad, dull, deaden; ease, lessen, diminish, mitigate, alleviate.

buffet[1], *n.* **1.** blow, box, *Inf.* clip, cuff, poke, jab, dab, pat; thwack, slap, strike. See **blow** (*def.* **1**).

2. shock, concussion, shaking, jolt, jar; collision, clash, crash, bang.

—*v.* **3.** slap, punch, hit, *Inf.* clout, *Inf.* buff, *Sl.* slug, *Sl.* bash, rap; beat, pound, thump, thrash, *Inf.* wallop.

4. push, shove, thrust, butt, bunt; knock, brush, jostle, bump, ram, bang, hit, disturb.

5. contend against, clash, conflict with, struggle against; fight, battle, give *or* do battle, joust; brawl, feud, come to blows; pommel, beat, beat into the ground, batter.

buffet[2], *n.* **1.** sideboard, cabinet, cupboard, closet, locker, bureau.

2. lunch stand, stand, counter, shelf, table, board; cafeteria, lunchroom, snack bar, automat.

—*adj.* **3.** smorgasbord, potluck; mixed bag, assorted; help-yourself, do-it-yourself.

buffoon, *n.* jester, clown, fool, jokester; comedian, funnyman, wit, wag; mime, mimic, pantomimist, mummer; goliard, gracioso, pantaloon; acrobat, contortioner, juggler. See **fool** (*def.* **2**).

bugbear, *n.* **1.** bugaboo, bogy, *Inf.* bogyman; hobgoblin, ogre, spectre, phantom, scarecrow; monster, gorgon; nightmare.

2. anathema, abomination, hate, pet peeve, *Fr. bête noire;* annoyance, bane, irritation, thorn in the flesh *or* side.

bugle, *n.* cornet, horn, tooter; trumpet, clarion.

build, *v.* **1.** construct, assemble, set up; make, fabricate, manufacture, produce; erect, elevate, raise, rear, put up.

2. mold, form, fashion, model, shape, frame; create, invent, originate, devise, compose, put together; cast, block, hammer, forge, sculpture.

3. establish, found, originate, base.

4. develop, increase, strengthen; intensify, heighten, magnify, accelerate, speed up, pick up, quicken.

—*n.* **5.** manner, form, shape, configuration; physique, figure, body, frame.

building, *n.* **1.** structure, construction, erection, superstructure; edifice, fabric, pile; house, lodge.

2. construction, erection; making, manufacturing, framing, forming.

bulge, *n.* **1.** projection, protrusion, convexity, prominence, protruberance, (*of a bone*) tuberosity; nodule, node, knob, mass, lump, bump; swelling, intumescence, tumefaction, dilation, enlarging.

2. increase, augmentation, acceleration, intensification; surge, rise, boost.

—*v.* **3.** swell, swell up *or* out, puff up *or* out, tumefy; bag, belly, balloon, balloon up *or* out *or* forth; expand, distend, dilate, enlarge, bloat.

4. protrude, stick out, overhang, beetle, jut out, thrust forward.

bulk, *n.* **1.** magnitude, extent, mass, substance, matter; dimensions, density, thickness; quantity, volume, weight, heft, size, measure.

2. massiveness, immensity, hugeness, largeness, bigness; bulkiness, corpulence, corpulency, fatness, fleshiness, portliness.

3. greater part, better part, majority, body, nearly all, preponderance, lion's share.

bulky, *adj.* **1.** massive, immense, vast, ponderous; huge, enormous, colossal, mammoth, titanic, elephantine, monstrous, prodigious; large, big, great, substantial, goodly.

2. stout, thickset, full-figured; obese, fat, corpulent, overweight; chubby, tubby, pudgy, plump; rotund, portly, paunchy, potbellied, abdominous.

3. unwieldy, cumbersome, awkward, gross; hulky, hulking, clumsy, ungainly, ungraceful, lubberly, lumpish.

bullet, *n.* slug, pellet, ball, missile, projectile.

bulletin, *n.* **1.** news report, news, announcement, statement, flash; communication, notification, information, intelligence, tidings, word; communiqué, dispatch, telegram, aviso.

2. pamphlet, handbill, dodger, throwaway, flyer, leaflet; brochure, circular, folder, program; broadside, broadsheet, poster, placard.

3. summary, monograph, compendium, abstract; symposium, compilation, conspectus, analysis, recapitulation; outline, review, prospectus.

bully, *n.* **1.** browbeater, hector, ruffian, intimidator, *Sl.* bulldozer, *Inf.* terror, coercer, dictator, oppressor, despot, tyrant, hard taskmaster, Simon Legree.

2. blusterer, roisterer, vaporer, ranter, raver, rowdy, *U.S.* tough; (*all usually of women*) fury, hellcat, shrew, scold, vixen.

—*v.* **3.** intimidate, browbeat, overawe, cow, daunt, dismay, frighten, terrify, petrify, put the fear of the Lord into, scare, disconcert; domineer, overbear, lord it over, *Inf.* pull rank, override, ride roughshod over, *Inf.* push around, *Inf.* kick around, trample, tread on, *Inf.* walk all over [s.o.]; tyrannize, terrorize, threaten, coerce, exact, compel, lay down the law to, bulldoze, dragoon; hector, torment, harass, abuse, taunt, tease, bullyrag.

4. swagger, bluster, roister, bluff, rant, rave, rage, thunder, storm, *Sl.* showboat.

—*interj.* **5.** *Informal.* good, well done, great, neat, nifty, right on, boffo.

bulwark, *n.* rampart, redoubt, bastion, demilune, redan, ravelin; fortification, breastwork, outwork; wall, fence, palisade, barricade, barrier; abutment, embankment, bank, buffer, buttress, damn, dike, levee.

bum, *n.* **1.** *Informal.* derelict, drunkard, drunk, *Sl.* stiff, *Sl.* wino, *Sl.* rummy; beggar, mendicant, *Inf.* panhandler; vagabond, drifter, vagrant, hobo, tramp; loafer, idler, beachcomber, wastrel, good-for-nothing, ne'er-do-well; cadger, sponger, scrounger, parasite.

2. *Informal.* debauch, carouse, bacchanal, orgy, saturnalia. See also **carousal** (*def.* **1**).

—*v.* **3.** *Informal.* borrow, cadge, sponge, *Sl.* mooch, *Sl.* hit, *Sl.* hit up, *Sl.* touch, *Sl.* put the touch on; beg, scrounge; idle, laze, lounge, loaf, loaf around, *Inf.* bum around; wander, drift, tramp, hobo, vagabond; hitchhike, thumb.

—*adj.* **4.** *Slang.* bad, poor, unsatisfactory, inferior, worthless, *Sl.* crummy, *Sl.* cheesy; wretched, miserable, *Inf.* rotten, *Inf.* lousy.

5. *Slang.* false, untrue, spurious, bogus, counterfeit, fabricated, trumped-up; misleading, deceptive, fallacious.

bump, *v.* **1.** collide with, crash into, smash into, run into, *Inf.* plow into; butt, jar, jolt, jostle; strike, beat, rap, hit, bang, tap, smack, thwack, thump.

2. (*all by force of collision*) dislodge, displace, move, remove, shift; budge, nudge, shove, push.

3. bump into *Informal.* meet, encounter, chance upon. See **chance** (*def.* **9**).

4. bump off *Slang.* murder, kill, eliminate. See **murder** (*def.* **4**).

—*n.* **5.** collision, smash, crash, crack, smack, thud, clunk; blow, buffet, thwack, whack, lick, *Inf.* wallop.

6. swelling, lump, contusion, intumescence, tumescence; protuberance, node, nodule, knob, bulge.

bumpkin, *n.* rustic, peasant, provincial, country cousin, countryman; yokel, country bumpkin, hawbuck, hobnail, *Dial.* lumpkin, *Often Disparaging.* hillbilly, *Disparaging.* bogtrotter, *Inf.* chawbacon, *Inf.* cider squeezer, *Sl.* hick, *Sl.* rube, *Sl.* hayseed, *Sl.* hoosier, *Sl.* woodhick, *Fr. Sl. truffe;* clod, clodhopper, clodpoll *or* clodpole *or* clodpate, boor, oaf, lout, lubber, gawk, churl, ox, *Chiefly Scot.* cuddy, *Inf.* lummox, *Inf.* goop, *Sl.* galoot, *Sl.* lug, *Brit. Sl.* joskin.

bumptious, *adj.* aggressive, forward, obtrusive, self-assertive, *Inf.* pushy; arrogant, overbearing, overweening; cocky, overconfident, audacious, impertinent, insolent, impudent, brazen, brassy, *Inf.* nervy, *Inf.* cheeky, *Scot.* vaunty.

bunch, *n.* **1.** group, collection, assemblage, accumulation, gathering, concentration; bundle, cluster, fascicle, clump; bale, sheaf, wisp, tuft, fagot; lot, batch, family, set, series; quantity, stack, pile, heap, mass, array, assortment; agglomeration, conglomeration, galaxy, host, multitude.

2. bulge, knob, lump, protuberance. See **bulge** (*def.* **1**).

—*v.* **3.** group together, bring together, put together, amass; sort, assort, classify, class, bracket, lump together; line up, stack up, pile up, heap up; collect, gather, cluster, bundle.

4. *Usu.* **bunch up** crowd, herd, huddle, cram *or* jam together, squeeze up *or* in *or* together.

bundle, *n.* **1.** bunch, group, collection, assemblage. See **bunch** (*def.* **1**).

2. package, parcel, pack, packet, *Sl.* bindle, sack, knapsack, backpack; basket, hamper, bag, pouch, *Obs.* budget.

—*v.* **3.** tie, tie up *or* together, colligate, truss, wrap, package, bind, fasten; group, bunch, cluster, gather, categorize, bracket; classify, arrange, organize.

4. bundle off *or* **out** hurry off, hustle, rush off, scurry, scamper, *Inf.* vamoose, take off, *Sl.* split; decamp, abscond, depart, leave.

bungle, *v.* botch, mar, spoil, mismanage; *Inf.* muff, *Inf.* flub, *Inf.* foul up, *Inf.* screw up. See **botch** (*def.* **1**).

bungler, *n.* botcher, *Inf.* duffer, *Sl.* butcher, mismanager; fumbler, butterfingers, blunderer, stumbler, *Inf.* bull in a china shop; lubber, looby, lout, oaf, *Sl.* klutz, *Sl.* schlemiel; blockhead, dunce, ignoramus, *Sl.* bananahead, *Sl.* yo-yo.

bungling, *adj.* clumsy, awkward, bunglesome, gauche, maladroit; blundering, botching, stumbling, tripping; ungainly, lubberly, gawky, oafish, graceless, ungraceful; inept, unskillful, unaccomplished, inexpert, incompetent, stupid.

bunk[1], *n.* **1.** platform bed, bed, berth; cot, pallet, couch. See **bed** (*def.* **1**).

—*v.* **2.** *Informal.* bed down, sleep. See **bed** (*defs.* **8, 13, 14**).

bunk[2], *n.* *Slang.* See **bunkum**.

bunker, *n.* bin, box, chest, coffer. See **bin**.

bunkum, *n.* claptrap, humbug, pretense, foam, froth; insincere talk, empty promises, lies. See **nonsense** (*defs.* **2, 3**).

buoy, *n.* **1.** float, marker, guide, beacon, signal.

2. life preserver, life jacket *or* belt *or* vest, cork jacket, Mae West.

buoyancy, *n.* **1.** floatability; lightness, levity, weightlessness.

2. cheerfulness, cheer, joy, good humor, good *or* high spirits; liveliness, animation, spiritedness; resilience, *Inf.* bounce, *Inf.* pep, zing.

buoyant, *adj.* **1.** floatable, floaty, supernatant; light, weightless.

2. cheerful, gay, light-hearted, gleeful, mirthful, glad, happy, merry, jolly, jovial, bright, carefree, free and easy, in high spirits *or* humor; sprightly, vivacious, lively, full of life, animated, jaunty, resilient, *Inf.* bouncy, *Inf.* peppy.

3. invigorating, exhilarating, refreshing, bracing, stimulating.

burden, *n.* **1.** weight, onus, cross, millstone, albatross; duty, charge, obligation, responsibility, tax; strain, encumbrance, impediment, hindrance, handicap; trouble, care, anxiety, worry; hardship, difficulty, affliction, oppression; trial, tribulation, ordeal; woe, grief, misery, sorrow, *Archaic.* bale.

2. load, payload, charge, cargo, freight.

—*v.* **3.** weigh down, weight, load, load with, saddle with, charge, tax; encumber, cumber, impede, hamper, handicap; strain, overload, overburden, overtask, overtax.

4. trouble, distress, worry, torment, afflict, oppress; try, vex, perturb, disturb.

burdensome, *adj.* **1.** onerous, ponderous, oppressive, massive, backbreaking, crushing; cumbersome, cumbrous, unwieldy, bulky.

2. troublesome, distressing, bothersome, worrisome; vexatious, irksome, wearisome, tiresome.

bureau, *n.* **1.** chest of drawers, chiffonier, chest, dresser, commode, locker; chifforobe, wardrobe; cabinet, sideboard.

2. department, agency, office, post, portfolio; branch, division, subdivision.

burgeon, *v.* **1.** bud, sprout, begin to grow, germinate, pullulate, put forth, shoot out *or* up; bloom, blossom, flower, open, bear fruit, fructify.

2. grow, develop, proliferate, multiply; accelerate, quicken, snowball, mushroom, intensify, magnify; increase, augment, escalate, expand, spread.

burglar, *n.* **1.** housebreaker, *Brit.* picklock, Raffles, sneak thief, cat burglar, *Inf.* second-story man; *Inf.* hold-up man, *Sl.* stick-up man, mugger; safecracker, Jimmy Valentine; robber, thief, stealer, *Inf.* crook, *Sl.* yegg; felon, gangster, criminal.

2. pillager, plunderer, ransacker, sacker, looter, rifler, forager, raider, vandal. See also **robber**.

burglary, *n.* **1.** break-in, housebreak, housebreaking, breaking and entering, forced entry; robbery, theft, *Sl.* heist; *Inf.* hold-up, *Sl.* stick-up; *Inf.* mugging, *Sl.* jumping, *Sl.* rolling; safecracking.

2. stealing, thievery; larceny, felony.

3. looting, plundering, raiding. See also **robbery**.

burial, *n.* **1.** funeral, exequies, obsequies, rites *or* ceremonies; burying, interment, entombment, inhumation, sepulture.

2. grave, graveyard, cemetery. See **burial ground**.

burial ground, *n.* grave, graveyard, cemetery, God's acre, memorial park, necropolis, golgotha, potter's field; charnel house, (*of wild animals*) boneyard.

burlesque, *n.* **1.** satire, lampoon, farce, spoof; caricature, cartoon, parody, travesty; *Literature.* mock-heroic, mock-tragedy; mockery, imitation, exaggeration, take-off, macaronics.
2. *U.S. Theater.* peep show, striptease, girlie show, nudie; burletta, slapstick, harlequinade; follies.
—adj. **3.** satirical, farcical, caricatural, travestying, parodic, Hudibrastic; mock, mocking, mimic, apish; ludicrous, ridiculous, comic, mock-heroic, droll; exaggerated, put-on, overdone; sarcastic, ironical, derisive, ridiculing, quizzical; fantastic, bizarre, grotesque.
4. provocative, suggestive, exotic; bawdy, indecent, immodest, off-color, risqué.
—v. **5.** satirize, lampoon, caricature, parody, travesty; mock, mimic, imitate, exaggerate, take off, ape; ridicule, laugh at, make fun of, stultify.

burly, *adj.* **1.** stout, thickset, heavy, heavy-set, stocky; beefy, brawny, husky, sturdy, well-built, strapping; muscular, hefty, able-bodied, rugged, athletic, solid; hardy, manly, virile, tough, powerful, strong.
2. bluff, brash, churlish, bearish, surly; brusque, short, curt, abrupt; outspoken, forward, unreserved; unvarnished, rough.

burn, *v.* **1.** be on fire, flame, flare, blaze, deflagrate; smolder, smoke, go up in smoke; glow, radiate, phosphoresce, shine; flash, glare, beam; flicker, shimmer, twinkle, sparkle, spark.
2. set on fire, fire, ignite, light, *Inf.* put the match to; illuminate, kindle, enkindle, conflagrate, inflame; incinerate, reduce to ashes, cremate.
3. tingle, warm, glow, thrill, excite; arouse, inflame, animate, quicken; stir, stimulate.
4. swelter, perspire, sweat; be dying of the heat, be dripping wet.
5. hurt, sting, smart, throb, ache; injure, wound, pain, anguish, torment, grieve, sorrow; anger, annoy, irritate, vex.
6. desire, yearn, wish, long; crave, hunger, thirst, lust after, *Sl.* have the hots for, *Sl.* letch after.
7. consume, expend, use up, eat up, drain, exhaust; squander, run through, misspend, fritter away.
8. overcook, char, toast; sear, singe.
9. tan, suntan, sunburn, bronze, brown; redden, discolor.

burned, *adj.* **1.** cheated, swindled, taken, taken in, done in; fleeced, *Inf.* gyped, rooked, *Sl.* screwed, *Sl.* stung.
2. disillusioned, disappointed, disenchanted, disabused; hurt, wounded, injured.

burning, *adj.* **1.** blazing, ablaze, raging, on fire, afire, fiery; flaming, aflame, smoking, ignited; very hot, boiling, scalding, scorching, sizzling; smoldering, simmering, parching; roasting, broiling, grilling, baking, toasting.
2. gleaming, agleam, glowing, aglow, glaring; very bright, lighted, alight, luminous, illuminated; radiant, brilliant, incandescent; shimmering, twinkling, flashing, flickering, glittering, aglitter, sparkling, fluttering.
3. sharp, acute, cutting, biting, stinging, piercing; singeing, searing, cauterizing; strong, pungent, poignant, reeking, acrid; caustic, corroding; painful, excruciating, racking, tormenting, agonizing; smarting, prickling, irritating.
4. desperate, violent, tempestuous; very angry, *Inf.* burned up, irate, wrathful, wroth, incensed; enraged, raging, infuriated, infuriate, furious; ranting, raving, vehement, fuming, seething; heated, worked up, flared up; vexed, irritated, piqued, chafed, galled, riled, nettled, agitated; offended, disturbed, perturbed, unquiet.
5. excited, exhilarated, enlivened, inspired, *Inf.* psyched *or* psyched up; animated, enthusiastic, eager; stimulated, aroused, *Inf.* hot, intensely desirous, intense; ardent, fervent, fervid, perfervid, impassioned, passionate, frenzied.
6. crucial, critical, acute; pivotal, climacteric, decisive, vital, essential; urgent, pressing, compelling, primary, important.
—n. **7.** combustion, oxidation, fire, flame, blaze, conflagration; kindling, ignition, calefaction; incineration, cineration, cremation, incremation.
8. parching, roasting, scorching, torrefaction, scorification; singeing, cautery, cauterization, searing.
9. *Both Ceramics.* firing, baking.
10. (*all of ores and metals*) carbonization, calcination, cupellation.

burnish, *v.* **1.** buff, smooth, shine. See **polish** (*def.* **1**).
—n. **2.** gloss, luster; brightness, sparkle. See **polish** (*def.* **6**).

burrow, *n.* **1.** tunnel, furrow, groove, hole, excavation, hollow; den, lair, nook, niche; retreat, refuge, shelter, asylum.
—v. **2.** dig, tunnel, furrow; excavate, hollow out, gouge out, scoop out.

bursar, *n.* treasurer, purser, controller, holder *or* keeper of the purse strings; cashier; depositary.

burst, *v.* **1.** break open, split open, rupture, fly apart; burst open, dehisce, explode, detonate, fulminate, blow up, *Sl.* bust; crack, split, shatter.
2. issue forth, pour forth, discharge, emerge; rush, gush, jet, spout, surge.

bury, *v.* **1.** sink, submerge, immerge, immerse, inundate, engulf.
2. inter, inhume, sepulcher, lay away, *Inf.* lay to rest, consign to the grave, *Dial.* funeralize; entomb, ensepulcher, hearse.
3. cover, cover up, hide, conceal; secrete, hide away, stow away, lock up.

bush, *n.* **1.** shrub, shrubbery, scrub, bramble, brier.
2. undergrowth, underbrush; thicket. See also **brush**[2] (*def.* **1**).

business, *n.* **1.** occupation, profession, trade, line; vocation, avocation, career, following, calling, pursuit, craft, metier; employment, job, work, living, livelihood, means of support, *Inf.* bread and butter; station, place.
2. industry, enterprise, *Sl.* racket; trade, trading, barter, exchange; commerce, interchange, dealings, *Inf.* truck, intercourse, traffic, transaction, proceedings; affairs, ventures; negotiation, bargaining; merchandising, selling, promoting.
3. company, corporation, firm, house, establishment; shop, store; partnership, team.
4. concern, affair, problem, thing, point, point at issue; subject, matter, material, topic, thesis, theme, text, motif, *Inf.* proposition; question, problem, issue; case, facts, gist, pith.
5. duty, function, office, province; responsibility, obligation, charge.
6. **get down to business** stop beating around the bush, get to the point; get down to it, apply oneself, stop procrastinating; *Sl.* shape up.
7. **mind one's own business** keep one's nose out of, butt out of, steer clear of.

businesslike, *adj.* efficient, effectual, effective; systematic, orderly, regular, methodical, well-ordered, in order, thorough; practical, functional, pragmatic, matter-of-fact; diligent, painstaking, careful, sedulous, assiduous, industrious; correct, accurate, precise, shipshape; realistic, wordly-wise, down-to-earth;

workaday, routine, prosaic, unimaginative; conventional, formal, stiff, restrained, impersonal.

bust, *n.* **1.** portrait sculpture, sculpture, *Naut.* figurehead, head, carving; statue, statuette, figure, model; representation, image, effigy.

2. chest, breast, bosom, front. See **bosom** (*def.* **1**).

bustle, *v.* **1.** *Often* **bustle about** stir, move, fuss, fly, flutter, flit, buzz; hustle, run, rush, dash, dart, scramble, scamper, scuttle, hurry, lose no time.

2. *Often* **bustle with** abound, teem, swarm, be filled, be bursting, be overrun *or* thronged, be buzzing *or* humming.

3. hustle, hurry, rush, push, drive, compel; bestir, rouse, arouse, commove, agitate, excite.

—*n.* **4.** busyness, stir, fuss, flurry, pother, ado, *Inf.* to-do, *Sometimes Facetious.* do; briskness, robustness, fleetness, rapidity, quickness, speediness, swiftness; hustle, restlessness, commotion, tumult; activity, action, doing, motion, movement; occupation, engagement, employment.

busy, *adj.* **1.** occupied, engaged, employed, working, at work, on duty, at it; taken, in use, tied down *or* up; engrossed, absorbed, involved, intent, preoccupied, diverted; diligent, assiduous, industrious, laboring, toiling, grinding, drudging, slaving, hardworking, zealous, sedulous, studious, persevering.

2. active, energetic, energetical, vigorous, jumping, hopping, swinging, abuzz, never idle, on the go, *Inf.* on the move, *Sl.* go-go; vivacious, sprightly, sprightful, vivid, animated, spirited; vibrant, full of verve, vital, lively, full of life, *Chiefly U.S. Inf.* chipper; moving, kinetic, motive, volitant, on the wing, stirring, astir, up and about *or* around, *Inf.* up and doing; bustling, hustling, restless, commotive, hectic, on the fly, *Inf.* hyper; indefatigable, tireless, untiring, unremitting, unwavering.

3. officious, forward, aggressive, assertive, pushing, *Inf.* pushy; meddlesome, meddling, interfering, tampering, interposing, interloping, encroaching; intrusive, prying, pepping, peering, peeking, spying, curious, inquisitive, snooping, *Inf.* snoopy, *Inf.* nosy.

4. ornate, overelaborate, overdecorated, overadorned, overembellished, excessive, fussy, *Inf.* tacky; cluttered, overcrowded, overfilled, jammed; jumbled, muddled, chaotic, confused, disorganized.

—*v.* **5.** occupy, engage, engross, absorb, involve, take up [s.o.'s] time, divert, interest, preoccupy; employ, ply, use, exercise, put to work, keep [s.o.] going *or* active.

6. work at, toil, strive, labor, travail, slave; drudge, grind, hammer away, *Inf.* plug away *or* along.

busybody, *n.* meddler, snoop, pry, Paul Pry, eavesdropper, Dumbo; gossip, newsmonger, quidnunc, chatterbox, jabberer, gabbler, blatherskite, *Sl.* windbag; blabber, blabbermouth, tattler, tattle-tale, telltale, tale-bearer, informer, *Sl.* squealer; scandalmonger, muckraker, slanderer, backbiter, defamer.

but, *conj.* **1.** on the contrary, on the other hand, nevertheless, yet; except, save, notwithstanding, however; unless, if not, except that.

—*prep.* **2.** except, excepting, with the exception of, save, bar, barring.

—*adv.* **3.** only, just, singly, solely; merely, simply.

butcher, *n.* **1.** meat seller, meat-merchant, meat vendor, meat cutter.

2. slaughterer, mass-murderer, destroyer, liquidator, annihilator, exterminator; murderer, killer, slayer, manslayer, man-killer, homicide, Bluebeard, ripper, bloodspiller, bloodshedder, shedder-of-blood, cutthroat, executioner, executionist, *Sl.* Jack Ketch; scourge, fiend.

3. vendor, hawker, peddler. See **vendor** (*def.* **1**).

—*v.* **4.** (*all of meat*) slaughter, chop, hack, carve, cut, trim, slice, abattage; dress, prepare.

5. slaughter, massacre, kill off, annihilate, exterminate, liquidate, decimate, destroy, cut to pieces, maul, savage, dismember, disembowel, hew, hack, hack to pieces, chop, chop to pieces, mutilate, tear limb from limb, wade in blood, put to the sword, give no quarter, show no mercy, do to death; kill, slay, murder, cut down, execute, put to death, assassinate, shed blood, spill blood.

6. bungle, botch, make a mess *or* hash of, bosh, muff, blunder, foul up, *Sl.* mess up, *Sl.* blow, *Sl.* screw up, *Sl.* louse up, *Inf.* butch, *Inf.* flub, *Inf.* gum up the works, *Sl.* bitch, *Inf.* bollix.

butchery, *n.* **1.** slaughterhouse, slaughterpen, abattoir, shambles, *Obs.* butcher-row.

2. carnage, massacre, slaughter, wholesale killing, mass-murder, mass-homicide, mass-execution, mass-slaying, general slaughter, mass-destruction, bloodbath, effusion of blood, fusillade of blood, noyade, *Rare.* internecion, *Rare.* trucidation, decimation, annihilation, extermination, liquidation, pogrom, genocide; mutilation, dismemberment, disembowelment; killing, slaying, murder, manslaughter, homicide, assassination, bloodshed, bloodletting.

butt[1], *n.* **1.** end, extremity, tip, tail; bottom, base, support, foundation; handle, shaft, hilt, shank.

2. remnant, leftover. See **end** (*def.* **6**).

3. *Slang.* rear, rear end. See **buttocks**.

butt[2], *n.* victim, scapegoat, *Inf.* goat, *Inf.* the one on the receiving end, object, target; dupe, gull, cat's paw, *Sl.* sucker; laughingstock, gazingstock, byword.

butt[3], *v.* **1.** (*all with the head*) poke, jab, ram, bump; strike, rap, push, thrust, shove.

2. **butt in** meddle, intrude, *Sl.* horn in, interrupt, interfere, give one's two cents' worth, *Inf.* kibitz.

butt[4], *n.* cask, barrel. See **barrel** (*def.* **1**).

buttock, *n.* *Usu.* **buttocks** rump, posterior, dorsal *or* lumbar region, hindquarters, haunches, loins, fundament, nates, *Zool.* podex, *Anat.* gluteus maximus, (*both of a horse*) crupper, croup; seat, bottom, *Fr. derrière*, *Inf.* fanny, *Inf.* rear *or* rear end, *Brit. Inf.* bum, *Inf.* backside, *Inf.* behind, *Inf.* butt, *Inf.* can, *Inf.* duff, *Inf.* tail, *Inf.* beam, *Inf.* keister, *Inf.* prat, *Sl.* ass, *Brit. Sl.* arse, *Sl.* buns, *Sl.* cheeks, *Sl.* heinie.

button, *n.* **1.** stud, link, fastener; buckle, clasp, hook, hook and eye, snap.

2. disk, knob, dial, switch, tuner.

buttress, *n.* **1.** prop, support, reinforcement; stanchion, bar, beam, post, shore; strut, brace, bracket, rib, stay.

2. strengthener, upholder, sustainer, maintainer; mainstay, cornerstone, pillar.

—*v.* **3.** support, prop up, brace, shore up, undergird; strengthen, reinforce, uphold, defend, back up.

buxom, *adj.* (*used only of women*) full-bosomed, *Inf.* busty, *Sl.* top-heavy; healthy, robust, strapping, lusty, plump, chubby; rosy, rosy-cheeked, ruddy; lively, hearty, vigorous.

buy, *v.* **1.** purchase, pick up, pay for, get one's hands on, come by; invest in, put money into; acquire, obtain, get, procure, secure; hire, engage, take on.

2. bribe, suborn, pay off, buy off, *Sl.* grease [s.o.'s] palm; fix, *Inf.* rig, *Inf.* square.

—*n.* **3.** purchase, acquisition; *U.S. Inf.* bargain, *Sl.* steal. See **bargain** (*def.* **2**).

buzz, *n.* **1.** hum, murmur, bombination; drone, purr, whirring; sibilation, hiss, whizz; sigh, rustle, sough.

2. rumor, report, gossip, hearsay, *Inf.* scuttlebutt, scandal; small talk, chitchat.

—v. **3.** hum, murmur, bombilate, bombinate, whisper; whizz, whir, wheeze, sibilate, hiss, fizzle, sizzle.

4. gossip, spread rumors; talk idly, chitchat, chatter, palaver, prate, gabble, *Inf.* gab.

by, *prep.* **1.** near, next to, beside, abreast of, *Dial.* aside of; through, through the agency of, under the aegis *or* auspices of; by way of, via, over, along, on; not later than, before, at.

—adv. **2.** near, at hand, in the immediate vicinity; past, beyond; aside, to one side, away, out of the way.

3. by and large in general, for the most part, on the whole; as a rule, usually, most of the time.

bygone, *adj.* past, departed, dead, gone by, former, previous; old, ancient, obsolete, extinct; out of date, outdated, antiquated, passé, outmoded.

by-name, *n.* surname, cognomen, appellation; nickname, epithet, sobriquet. See **appellation** (*def.* **1**).

by-pass, *n.* **1.** detour, indirect route, circuitous route, roundabout way, roundabout; shortcut, side road, back road, by-path, byway.

—v. **2.** avoid, neglect, overlook, give [s.o. *or* s.t.] the go-by; circumvent, *Inf.* do an end run, *Inf.* short-circuit; miss, pass over, elude, evade, go over [s.o.'s] head.

by-path, *n.* byway, back road, side road, byroad; dirt road, footway, footpath, lane, alley.

bystander, *n.* onlooker, observer, witness, eyewitness; spectator, watcher, viewer, beholder, gazer, gaper, gawker; passer-by, looker-on.

byword, *n.* **1.** slogan, motto, catch phrase, battle cry. See **battle cry** (*def.* **2**).

2. proverb, maxim, apothegm, adage. See **adage** (*def.* **1**).

3. butt, victim, scapegoat. See **butt**[2].

C

cab, *n.* taxi, taxicab; carriage, cabriolet, brougham, hansom, hack, hackney, four-wheeler, fiacre, droshky, coach, vehicle, conveyance; driver's seat *or* compartment.

cabal, *n.* **1.** camarilla, junto, ring, gang, band, crew, party; faction, clique, coterie, set, *Inf.* push; union, coalition, combination, league, confederacy.
2. plot, complot, conspiracy, intrigue, connivance; plan, design, scheme, racket.
—*v.* **3.** plot, complot, conspire, intrigue, connive, machinate.

cabala, *n.* **1.** mysticism, occultism, cabalism; esoterics, esotericism, esoterism, esotery, hermetics, hermeticism; supernaturalism, transcendentalism; theosophy.
2. mystery, puzzle, enigma, question, question mark; secret, esoterica, arcanum, closed *or* sealed book; unknowable, unknown, deep *or* profound secret, mystery of mysteries.

cabalistic, *adj.* **1.** occult, mystic, mystical, supernatural, preternatural, transcendental.
2. secret, cryptic, perdu, private; concealed, hidden, veiled, shrouded, enshrouded; obscure, indefinite, dim, dark, vague, cloudy, nebulous.
3. impenetrable, incomprehensible, inscrutable, unfathomable, unknowable, incognizable, incognoscible, undiscoverable.

cabaret, *n.* **1.** nightclub, club, *Inf.* night spot, *Inf.* spot; dance hall, discotheque, *Inf.* disco, *Sl.* juke joint; casino; rathskeller, beer garden; tavern, bar, bistro, pub, public house, *Sl.* honky-tonk, *Sl.* dive, *Sl.* joint.
2. *British.* show, floorshow, entertainment; presentation, production.

cabin, *n.* **1.** cottage, cot, bungalow, bower, log cabin, blockhouse, *Brit. Dial.* cote, *Scot.* but and ben; hut, hutch, shack, shanty, *Scot.* bothy; lodge, ski-lodge, chalet.
2. room, chamber, compartment, apartment, cell, stall, nook; (*all on ships*) saloon, stateroom, house, deckhouse, cuddy.
—*v.* **3.** confine, constrict, squeeze, pinch, crowd, crush, pack, cram, ram, cramp, stuff, wedge.

cabinet, *n.* **1.** ministry, assembly, administration, senate; board, committee, council, advisory group, panel; advisors, directors, trustees.
2. commode, cupboard, china closet; chest, chest of drawers, set of drawers, bureau, chifforobe, chiffonier; receptacle, box, file, repository, safe.
3. chamber, compartment, booth, stall.

cable, *n.* **1.** rope, cordage, cord, strand, line, wire, guy; chain, mooring, *Naut.* hawser.
2. telegram, cablegram, telegraph; message, news.
—*v.* **3.** telegraph, wire, radio, radiograph.

cache, *n.* **1.** hiding place, dead drop, hole, hideout; crypt, vault, repository.
2. hoard, wealth, supply, store, garner; kitty, fund, collection, savings, nest egg; hidden treasure, loot.
—*v.* **3.** conceal, hide, secrete, cover, bury; store, put away, *Inf.* stash, squirrel *or* squirrel away, *Sl.* sock away, save.

cackle, *v.* **1.** cluck, chuckle, click, clack; crow, quack.
2. chuckle, chortle, giggle; titter, twitter, te-hee, snicker, snigger.
3. chatter noisily, prattle, jabber, gibber, *Sl.* gibber-jabber, jargon; babble, prate, tattle, twaddle, *Brit.* twattle; patter, gabble, blather, drivel; chit-chat, chitter-chatter, chaffer, bandy words; gossip, buzz; talk idly, *Sl.* shoot the breeze, *Sl.* gas, *Inf.* gab, *Sl.* bull; palaver, clack, clatter, rattle, *Sl.* run off *or* on at the mouth; gush, blab, *Inf.* spout, be loquacious *or* talkative.
—*n.* **4.** cackling, cluck, clucking, chuckle, chuckling, click, clicking, clack, clacking; crow, crowing, quack, quacking.
5. chuckle, chuckling, chortle, chortling, giggle, giggling, broken laughter; titter, tittering, twitter, twittering, *Inf.* te-hee; snicker, snickering, snigger, sniggering.
6. idle talk, small talk, chatter, chattering, *Anglo-Indian.* bukh; chit-chat, chit-chatting, chitter-chatter, gossip, blab, blabbing, *Inf.* gab; cackling, gibber, gibbering, *Sl.* gibber-jabbering; babble, babbling, babblement, *Fr. bavardage,* blather, blathering, rapid and inarticulate talk; twaddle, twaddling, *Brit.* twattle, *Brit.* twattling, drivel, driveling; prate, prating, tattle, tattling, excessive talk; gushing, *Inf.* spouting, *Sl.* running off *or* on at the mouth; rambling, maundering.

cacophonous, *adj.* harsh, grating, raucous, jarring, strident, screechy, screaky; absonant, dissonant, discordant, inharmonious, unmelodious.

cacophony, *n.* dissonance, discord, discordance, jar; stridency, grating, jangle, croaking, rasping, caterwauling.

cad, *n.* rascal, rapscallion, rogue, scamp; knave, scoundrel, *Inf.* heel, *Archaic.* caitiff, dastard, worm; boor, churl, bear, *Chiefly Brit. Sl.* bounder, vulgarian, miscreant; jilter, two-timer, double-crosser, cheater; buck, blade, playboy, ladies' man, man about town, *Sl.* lover boy, philanderer.

cadaver, *n.* corpse, dead body, *Sl.* stiff; carcass, remains.

cadaverous, *adj.* corpselike, deathlike; ghastly, ashen, chalky, pale, pallid, wan, blanched, sallow; gaunt, haggard, drawn, hollow-eyed, thin, emaciated; grim, sinister, hideous, horrible, revolting, sickening.

caddish, *adj.* ungentlemanly, unmannerly, ill-mannered, impolite, uncivil, uncouth, rude; ill-bred, low-bred, underbred; unrefined, coarse, raw, crude; base, vulgar, despicable, ignoble, contemptuous; obnoxious, obtrusive, presumptuous, presuming; jilting, *Sl.* two-timing, double-crossing, cheating.

cadence, *n.* **1.** flow, rhythmic flow, movement, lilt, swing, jingle.

2. beat, pulse, rhythm, rhythm pattern, rhythmical emphasis, *Music.* rhythmical accentuation, *Music.* arsis *or* upbeat, *Music.* thesis *or* downbeat, *Prosody.* ictus, prominent pulsation; accent, accentuation, stress, emphasis; meter, measure, rate, cadency.

3. intonation, intonation pattern, inflection, modulation; pronunciation, articulation, enunciation, vocalization; speech pattern, manner of speaking, mode of expression.

4. *Music.* flourish, cadenza, embellishment, bravura, concluding strain, *Inf.* big finish; trill, ornament, arabesque, falderal *or* folderol; run, roulade.

cadre, *n.* **1.** nucleus, core, hard core, key group, inner circle, central part.

2. framework, scaffold, skeleton, shell; outline, sketch, draft, plan, diagram.

café, *n.* coffeehouse, *Inf.* bistro, restaurant, eating house, diner, cafeteria, automat; bar, barroom, tavern, grogshop, wineshop, beer hall, beer garden, rathskeller; cabaret, night club.

cage, *n.* **1.** receptacle, box, enclosure, pound; pen, corral, crawl, crib, coop, aviary, mew; prison, cell, vault, dungeon, lockup.

2. framework, skeleton, scaffold, shell.

—v. **3.** confine, intern, impound, shut in; coop, mew, encage, pen, corral, fence; imprison, incarcerate, jail, lock up, immure; hem in, restrict, restrain.

cajole, *v.* wheedle, beguile, blandish, blarney, coax, palaver, gloze, *Inf.* sweet-talk, *Inf.* soft-soap; humor, jolly, pamper, pander to, cater to, *Inf.* stroke; flatter, fawn on, truckle, *Inf.* butter, butter-up, play up to, curry favor with.

cajolery, *n.* wheedling, beguilement, beguiling blandishment, blandishing, blarney, coaxing, palaver, *Inf.* soft soap, *Inf.* sweet talk, *Inf.* honeyed words, *Sl.* line, *Sl.* snow job; humoring, jollying, pandering to, catering to, *Inf.* stroking; flattery, *Inf.* butter, *Inf.* honey; fawning, playing up to, *Sl.* buttering-up, *Inf.* apple-polishing, currying favor.

cake, *n.* **1.** fritter, torte, pastry, sweet bread, sweet bun, cookie; pancake, griddlecake, flapjack; unleavened bread, wafer.

2. bar, piece, cube, block; floe, mass, crust.

—v. **3.** harden, indurate, solidify, coagulate, congeal, thicken; agglomerate, conglomerate, consolidate.

calamitous, *adj.* **1.** catastrophic, cataclysmic, cataclysmal, tragic, disastrous, ruinous; destructive, destroying, devastating, withering, demolishing, ravaging, desolating.

2. fatal, dire, black, ill-starred, ill-fated, star-crossed; inauspicious, unpropitious, unfavorable, unlucky, unprovidential, untoward; sad, miserable, wretched, woeful, baleful.

calamity, *n.* **1.** affliction, adversity, hurt, harm, ruin, ruination, desolation; misery, wretchedness, agony, torture, torment, distress, suffering, *Archaic.* bale; woe, grief, sorrow, dolor, sadness, anguish, anxiety, unhappiness, heartache, heartbreak, heavy heart; trouble, trouble and strife, sea of troubles, hardship, storm and stress; misfortune, infelicity, ill *or* bad luck, ill *or* bad fortune, ambsace, evil eye, evil wind, dark cloud *or* star, storm clouds; trial, tribulation, burden, load, heavy load *or* burden, weight.

2. catastrophe, cataclysm, disaster, tragedy; shock, blow, heavy *or* nasty *or* staggering blow, buffet, stroke, stroke of ill *or* bad luck *or* fortune; mishap, mischance, miscarriage, misadventure, *Scot. and North Eng.* mishanter; glitch, casualty, accident; reverse, reversal, reverse of fortune, setback, comedown, bringdown, bitter pill.

calculable, *adj.* **1.** computable, measurable, reckonable, countable; determinable, predictable, estimable, gaugeable, appraisable, assessable; ascertainable, discoverable.

2. reliable, dependable, to be counted on, trustworthy.

calculate, *v.* **1.** compute, count, figure, enumerate, work out, reckon; sum up; figure out, *Sl.* dope out, ascertain, determine; estimate, evaluate, gauge, measure, weigh, take into account; cast, forecast, predict.

2. design, intend, plan, set up; adapt, adjust, make suitable, fit.

calculating, *adj.* shrewd, sharp, scheming, designing, sly, crafty, contriving, *Sl.* sneaky; cautious, careful, wary, prudent; discreet, circumspect, politic, farsighted.

calculation, *n.* **1.** computation, reckoning, estimation, estimate, count; result, product, end product *or* result; expectation, forecast, prediction, prospect, anticipation.

2. forethought, foresight, planning, care, circumspection, deliberation; cautiousness, caution, wariness, discretion, prudence; design, craftiness, contrivance, scheme, expedient.

calculator, *n.* **1.** computer, arithmetician, mathematician; adding machine operator, computer operator, programmer, compilator.

2. calculating machine, adding machine, pocket calculator; abacus; computer.

calendar, *n.* **1.** menology, chronogram, *Obs.* ephemeris; almanac, chronology; chronicle, annals, record; log, register, daybook.

2. list, agenda, schedule, docket; bill, program, slate.

caliber, *n.* **1.** bore, diameter.

2. quality, merit, virtue, excellence; ability, capability, capacity, faculty, competence; gift, endowment; flair, talent, genius, knack.

calisthenics, *n.* exercise, physical training, athletics, gymnastics, slimnastics, aerobics, isometrics, daily dozen, *Brit.* physical jerks; jogging; drill, workout, warm-up, practice.

call, *v.* **1.** cry out, sing out, hail, halloo *or* hallo; cry, exclaim, shout, yell, *Inf.* holler, scream; clamor, vociferate; roar, bellow.

2. ask, invite, summon, signal; convoke, convene, muster, assemble, call together; telephone, phone, dial, dial up, ring, ring up, *Inf.* buzz.

3. announce, proclaim, order; name, christen, designate, style, dub, *Archaic.* clepe; consider, estimate, view as, judge, reckon.

4. call down a. invoke, appeal to, pray to, supplicate, petition, entreat. **b.** reprimand, chastise, reprove, rebuke, upbraid, chide.

—n. **5.** cry, outcry, clamor, shout, scream, *Inf.* holler; signal, cooee, sooey; animal note, caw, tweet, chirp.

6. summons, signal, alarm, tocsin; invocation, invitation, bidding, calling, appeal, notice, request.

7. visit, sojourn, stay, stopover; rest, pause, break.
8. lure, attraction, fascination, bewitchment, appeal, allurement.
9. need, occasion, cause, reason, justification; instigation, incitation.
10. phone call, *Inf.* ring, *Inf.* buzz.

call girl, *n.* prostitute, lady of the evening, woman of the profession, Mrs. Warren, *Fr. fille de joie;* demimondaine, demirep, loose woman, fallen woman, woman of ill repute, white slave; trollop, strumpet, *Archaic.* wench, trull, drab, quean; paramour, courtesan, mistress, concubine, kept woman, *Sl.* doxy. See also **prostitute** (*def.* **1**).

calling, *n.* **1.** vocation, pursuit, mission, office; profession, occupation, business, employment, work, job; trade, craft, line, specialty, forte, métier, field, area of specialization.
2. summons, invitation, call. See **call** (*def.* **6**).

callous, *adj.* hard, hardened, indurate, indurated; thickskinned, pachydermatous; inured, hard-boiled, case-hardened, hard-nosed; insensitive, unfeeling, obdurate, unsympathetic, hard-hearted, cold; indifferent, apathetic, uncaring.

callow, *adj.* immature, inexperienced, green; unsophisticated, uninitiated, naïve, innocent; sophomoric, juvenile, adolescent, childish, *Sl.* kiddish, puerile, infantile; undeveloped, unformed, unripe.

calm, *adj.* **1.** still, motionless, smooth, undisturbed, unagitated, quiet; windless, waveless, stormless; stationary, becalmed; tranquil, serene, restful, reposeful, placid, peaceful, halcyon.
2. composed, collected, *Inf.* together, self-possessed; cool, cool-headed, self-controlled, passionless, impassive, dispassionate; easy-going, relaxed, even-tempered, imperturbable, unexcitable, unflappable; unexcited, unmoved, unperturbed; unruffled, staid, sedate; undemonstrative, unemotional, stoical, philosophical.
—*n.* **3.** motionlessness, stillness, quietness, quietude, calmness; tranquillity, serenity, sereneness, placidness, placidity; repose, rest, reposefulness, restfulness, peace, peacefulness, harmony, harmoniousness.
4. composure, self-possession, coolness, dispassion; equanimity, poise, sang-froid; steadiness, self-control.
—*v.* **5.** soothe, allay, assuage, mollify, soften; quiet, still, compose, lull, hush; pacify, tranquilize, smooth, settle, *Inf.* cool [s.o.] off; sedate, opiate, narcotize, stupefy, dull, deaden; relax, loosen up, settle down; placate, mediate, reconcile.
6. defuse, depoliticize, devolatilize.

calmness, *n.* **1.** composure, self-possession. See **calm** (*def.* **4**).
2. motionlessness, stillness. See **calm** (*def.* **3**).

calumniate, *v.* **1.** slander, libel, impute, asperse, insinuate, traduce, falsify, accuse falsely, misrepresent, belie; injure, abuse, assail, stab, insult, backbite, *Sl.* badmouth, engage in personalities; slur, sully, defile, smear, smirch, besmirch, soil, blacken, taint, tarnish, attaint, blemish, smudge, stain, spot, brand, stigmatize, drag through the mud *or* mire, heap dirt upon, throw mud on, spatter, bespatter, *Sl.* dump on.
2. defame, denigrate, vituperate, vilify, vilipend, scandalize, run down, berate, revile, malign, impugn, gibbet, criticize, pull to pieces, *Sl.* do a hatchet job on, cut up, shred, give a bad name, speak ill of, speak evil of, hold up to scorn, sneer at, muckrake; belittle, detract, disparage, decry, deprecate, depreciate, derogate, devaluate, deflate; humiliate, humble, mortify, *Sl.* put down.

calumny, *n.* **1.** slander, libel, calumniation, false accusation, misrepresentation, falsehood, malicious falsehood, lie, untruth, traducement, aspersion, imputation, innuendo, *Inf.* brickbat, insinuation, reflection; abuse, injury, backbiting, mud-slinging; slur, blot, blot on the escutcheon, smear, smirch, taint, attaint, stain, tarnish, spot, black spot *or* mark, blemish, smudge, brand, stigma.
2. defamation, denigration, vilification, vituperation, scandal; censure, reproach, denunciation, curse, malediction, invective, commination, *Archaic.* exprobration, animadversion, revilement, obloquy; belittlement, deprecation, disparagement, detraction, derogation, deflation, depreciation, devaluation; humiliation, humble pie, mortification.

camaraderie, *n.* comradeship, companionship, brotherliness, esprit de corps, good-fellowship, clubbiness, *Inf.* groupiness; close friendship, intimacy, closeness, affinity, relationship, kinship, brotherhood; friendliness, amicability, sociability, congeniality.

camouflage, *n.* **1.** disguise, mask, screen, cloak, blind, covering, concealment; deception, trickery, ruse, artifice, subterfuge, dissimulation; pretense, guise, appearance, cover-up, show, window dressing, façade, front, false front.
—*v.* **2.** disguise, hide, conceal, cloak, mask, cover, cover up, cover over; deceive, misrepresent, falsify, gloss over, fudge; garble, muffle.

camp[1], *n.* **1.** encampment, bivouac, cantonment; military quarters, *Sl.* the Q; temporary lodgings, tents, shelters, barracks.
2. cabin, cottage, hut, summer home; resort, vacation spot, recreation area.
3. faction, sect, party, group, set, clique; cause, doctrine, persuasion.
—*v.* **4.** encamp, pitch camp *or* tent, tent, tent out, *Inf.* sleep out; hike, backpack; reside, lodge, stay over.
5. settle, put down roots, moor, anchor, become ensconced, move in and take over, carve a spot for oneself, inhabit.

camp[2], *n.* **1.** (*usu. deliberately exaggerated*) artificiality, affectation, affectedness, studiedness; ostentation, display, posing, posturing, peacockery; airs, mannerisms, gestures.
2. (*usu. conscious*) banality, inanity, vapidity, *Sl.* corniness *or* corn; egregiousness, blatancy; garishness, gaudiness, ugliness; crudeness, lack of subtlety *or* refinement.
—*v.* **3.** *Slang.* (*often in reference to homosexuality*) flaunt, display, show off, exult in, boast, announce; strut, flounce, prance, peacock.

campaign, *n.* **1.** battle, crusade, war; battle plan, course of action, strategy, tactics, maneuvers, operations.
—*v.* **2.** run for office, run, *Brit.* stand, *Inf.* throw one's hat in the ring; electioneer, canvass, barnstorm, *Inf.* take to the stump.

campus, *n.* college grounds, quadrangle, *Inf.* quad; college, university; academia, academe.

campy, *adj.* *Slang.* **1.** exaggerated, affected, mannered, studied; theatrical, extravagant, outlandish, ostentatious, showy; overdone, banal, egregious, blatant; garish, loud, crude, vulgar; trivial, trite, *Sl.* trashy, *Sl.* corny.
2. *All Derog.* (*of male homosexuals*) effeminate, queer, faggy, flitty, limp-wristed, *Sl.* swish.

can, *n.* **1.** container, receptacle, vessel; jar, tin; bucket, pail; drinking cup, tankard.
2. *Slang.* bathroom, toilet. See **bathroom.**
3. *Slang.* rump, buttocks. See **buttocks.**
—*v.* **4.** (*of foods*) preserve, put up, keep, make.
5. *Slang.* dismiss, discharge, fire. See **discharge** (*def.* **6**).

canal, *n.* **1.** artificial waterway, channel, race, con-

duit, watercourse; strait, aqueduct, waterway, seaway.
2. duct, pipe, main, tube, cylinder; passage, passageway, adit; conduit, sewer, culvert, cloaca, flume, trough, chute; spout, gutter, drain, gully, ditch.

cancel, *v.* **1.** void, avoid, declare null and void, render null and void, nullify, disannul, annul, quash, invalidate, vitiate, vacate, disenact, disestablish; set aside, call off, supersede, discharge; cease, *Law.* nol-pros, stop, discontinue, break off; countermand, counterorder, override, overrule; veto, negate.
2. revoke, rescind, abrogate, reverse, repeal, abolish; recant, retract, withdraw, take back, recall; renounce, relinquish, repudiate, abjure, forswear, abnegate; disavow, disclaim, disown, deny; unsay, go back on one's word, eat one's words, back-pedal, renege; tergiversate, apostatize, defect, change one's mind.
3. delete, *Print.* dele, blue-pencil, x out, cross out, strike out, scratch out, mark off; blot out, rub out, crush out, wipe out, erase, efface; expunge, eradicate, obliterate.
4. neutralize, nullify, expiate, compensate for, make up for, offset; counterbalance, counterpoise, counteract, countervail.
5. write off, absolve, clear, wipe the slate clean, eliminate.

cancellation, *n.* **1.** voidance, avoidance, cancel, disannulment, annulment, nullification, *Law.* defeasance; quashing, invalidation, vitiation, *Obs.* vacatur, disenactment, disestablishment, setting aside; cessation, *Law.* nolle prosequi, discontinuance, suspension; countermand, counterorder, overriding, overruling; veto, negation.
2. revocation, rescinding, rescindment, rescission, abrogation, reversal, repeal, abolishment, abolition; recantation, retraction, retractation, withdrawal, recall; renouncement, renunciation, relinquishment, repudiation, abjuration, abnegation; disavowal, disclaimer, disclamation, denial; apostasy, tergiversation, defection, change of mind.
3. deletion, *Print.* dele, crossing out, striking out, scratching out, marking off; blotting out, rubbing out, crushing out, wiping out, erasing, erasion, effacing; expunging, eradication, obliteration.
4. neutralization, nullification, expiation; counterbalance, counterpoise, counteraction.

cancer, *n.* **1.** tumor, malignancy, malignant growth, *Pathol.* carcinoma, *Pathol.* sarcoma, *Pathol.* metastasis.
2. evil, curse, calamity, trouble, tribulation, torment; blight, disease, sickness, illness, affliction; scourge, plague, pestilence, bane, infestation; corruption, rottenness, rot, foulness, pollution, putrefaction.

candid, *adj.* **1.** frank, forthright, direct, straightforward, straight-from-the-shouder, foursquare, man-to-man, heart-to-heart; plain, plain-spoken, plain-speaking, downright, outright, explicit, unequivocal, unambiguous, undisguised, *Inf.* flat-footed; outspoken, free, free-spoken, free-speaking, unreticent, bold, unreserved, unrestrained, unconstrained, unchecked, unabashed, uninhibited, unshrinking; blunt, bluff, brusque, tactless.
2. open, open and sincere, open-hearted, genuine, transparent; guileless, ingenuous, sincere, artless, naïve, simple, undeceptive, undeceitful, undeceiving, undissembling; aboveboard, open and aboveboard, up front, on the level, on the up and up.
3. informal, unposed, uncontrived, undesigned, unstudied; spontaneous, unpremeditated, uncalculated, undeliberated; extemporaneous, extemporary, impromptu, improvised, improvisational, unrehearsed, unprepared, ad-lib, *Inf.* off the top of one's head, *Inf.* off the cuff.
4. honest, honorable, just, fair, fair and square, square-dealing, square-shooting; impartial, equitable, objective, balanced, even, even-handed, *Inf.* level; unbiased, nonbiased, unprejudiced, nonprejudiced, nonprejudicial, unprepossessed, unjaundiced, open-minded.

candidate, *n.* **1.** office seeker, nominee, runner, front runner, seeker, aspirant, suitor; job seeker, applicant; contestant, competitor, entrant.
2. probationer, apprentice, journeyman, learner; postulant, novice, novitiate; *Eccles.* confirmand.

candied, *adj.* glacé, sugar-coated, sugared, honeyed; saccharine, sugary, sickeningly sweet; flattering, cajoling, ingratiating, blandishing.

candle, *n.* taper, tallow light, rush light, bougie, dip; paschal, vigil light; torch, flambeau, flare, flame.

candlestick, *n.* candleholder, standard, paschal, chandelier, luster; candelabrum; candlestand, torchère, girandole, sconce.

candor, *n.* **1.** frankness, forthrightness, straightforwardness, candidness, calling a spade a spade, *Sl.* telling it like it is; plain-speaking, plain-spokenness, downrightness, outrightness, explicitness, unequivocalness; outspokenness, freeness, free-spokenness, free-speaking, nonreticence, boldness, unreserve, unrestraint, unconstraint; bluntness, bluffness, brusqueness, tactlessness.
2. openness, open-heartedness, transparency; guilelessness, ingenuousness, sincerity, sincereness, artlessness, naïveté, naïveness, simpleness, undeceptiveness, undeceitfulness.
3. honesty, honorableness, justness, fairness, square-dealing, plain-dealing, square-shooting; impartiality, impartialness, equitableness, objectivity, objectiveness; open-mindedness, freedom from bias *or* prejudice.

candy, *n.* confectionery, confection, sweets, sweet, sweetmeat; bonbon, fondant, comfit, sugarplum, sugar-candy; taffy, butterscotch, praline, peanut brittle; fudge, cream, nougat, toffee, caramel, chocolate; mint, peppermint, kiss, lollipop, sucker; dainty, tidbit.

cane, *n.* **1.** stick, staff, walking stick, crutch; rod, alpenstock.
2. stem, reed, stalk, shoot.
—*v.* **3.** beat, strike, hit, smite, cudgel; slap, rap, thwack, smack, *Australian.* ding; flog, whip, switch, thrash, lash, scourge, knout, flagellate; horsewhip, curry, strap, thresh, flail; *Inf.* tan [s.o.'s] hide, *Inf.* lace, *Inf.* whale, *Brit. Dial.* yerk, *Inf.* trim.

canker, *n.* **1.** lesion, chancre, chancroid, soft chancre, simple chancre; abscess, ulcer, ulceration, noma, fester, festering, gathering, gumboil, parulis, tubercle, *Obs.* apostem *or* aposteme *or* apostume *or* aposthume, *Obs.* apostemation, *Archaic.* impostume; boil, blain, furuncle, furunclus, carbuncle, pustule, pimple, papule, papilla, pock, wen, whelk, *Rare.* bleb, *Archaic.* botch; sore, open *or* running sore, gal.
2. bane, curse, blight, scourge; plague, pestilence, infestation; cancer, disease; poison, venom; corruption, corrosion, moth and rust, worm in the apple *or* rose; torment, plight, woe, affliction, infliction, worry, grievance.
—*v.* **3.** ulcerate, sphacelate, suppurate, *Inf.* rankle; infect, blight, contaminate, pollute, poison, taint; corrupt, degenerate, debase, defile.
4. corrode, erode, deteriorate, wear away, destroy slowly; eat, eat away, eat into, gnaw, gnaw away, gnaw into, nibble away.
5. spoil, go *or* turn bad, go off; rot, rot away; fester; putrefy, putresce, decompose, mortify.

cannibal, *n.* man-eater, anthropophagite; ogre, ogress, monster, fiend, barbarian, wild man.

cannibalistic, *adj.* man-eating, hungry for flesh, flesh-eating, anthropophagical, *Class. Myth.* Thyestian; bestial, fiendish, ogreish, bloodthirsty.

cannonade, *n.* **1.** barrage, bombardment, shelling, battery, broadside, assault, salvo, volley, artillery fire; pounding, firing upon, attack.

—*v.* **2.** bombard, shell, patter, pound, fire upon, blast, pepper, attack with cannon.

canny, *adj.* **1.** careful, cautious, prudent. See **careful** (*def.* **1**).

2. astute, discerning, penetrating; shrewd, alert, keen, sharp, acute; knowing, sagacious, wise, sensible; quick-witted, bright, smart.

canoe, *n.* dugout, pirogue, kayak, outrigger.

canon¹, *n.* **1.** *Eccles.* rule, regulation, law, statute; decree, edict, order; doctrine, dogma, Decretals.

2. principle, standard, criterion, test; measure, norm, model, pattern, exemplar, bench mark; aesthetic, ethic.

3. Holy Writ, Scripture, inspired books, sacred writings. See **Scripture.**

4. catalogue, enumeration, list, *Inf.* laundry list, litany; roll, roster, muster, slate.

canon², *n.* prebendary, church dignitary, capitular, residentiary. See **clergyman, ecclesiastic.**

canonical, *adj.* **1.** authorized, orthodox, accepted, legitimate, approved, recognized, standard; legal, lawful.

—*n.* **2.** religious, novice; nun, sister, brother, monastic.

3. **canonicals** clerical garments, religious vestments, pontificals; attire, garb, habit, robes, *Archaic.* vesture; surplice, cassock, stole, alb, cope, maniple.

canonize, *v.* **1.** *Eccles.* declare a saint, enroll in the canon, accept as blessed, sanctify, beatify, affirm the salvation of, acknowledge as worthy of veneration, name capable of divine intercession.

2. glorify, magnify, elevate, exalt, extol, laud, honor; idolize, idolatrize, deify, apotheosize.

3. enshrine, consecrate, hallow, bless; venerate, worship; sing the praises of, esteem, revere, respect, awe, admire, put on a pedestal, think highly of.

4. (*usu. eccles.*) approve, sanction, endorse, authorize, validate, allow, permit, accept.

canopy, *n.* awning, tilt, tester, *Archit.* baldachin; cover, covering, cope, shade, tarpaulin, *Inf.* tarp.

cant, *n.* **1.** mummery, empty talk, lip service, *Archaic.* snuffling, *Inf.* bull, *Sl.* bunk; hypocrisy, insincerity, sanctimony.

2. jargon, terminology, shoptalk, *Inf.* lingo; argot, slang, patois, patter, vernacular; doublespeak, officialese, medicalese, businessese.

cantankerous, *adj.* surly, irascible, iracund, crabbed, crabby; unfriendly, ill-natured, obnoxious, choleric; brusque, peppery, crusty, grumpy, grouchy, dyspeptic, bearish, snappish, snarling; cross, feisty, huffy, irritable, cranky, peevish, bilious, testy, touchy, ill-tempered, bad-tempered, quick-tempered, short-tempered; argumentative, quarrelsome, fractious, contentious, disagreeable, *Inf.* ornery, *Inf.* bitchy, *Inf.* ugly; uncivil, sharp, abrupt, curt, short, terse, blunt, rough.

canteen, *n.* **1.** flask, flasket, wineskin; bottle, jug, jar.

2. shop, store, department store, commissary, *Both U.S. Army* post exchange, PX, *Both U.S. Air Force.* base exchange, BX.

canter, *n.* **1.** amble, saunter, gait, jog, trot, dogtrot, lope, gallop.

—*v.* **2.** amble, saunter, jog, trot, lope, gallop.

canvas, *n.* coarse cloth, sailcloth, duck, ticking, drill, denim, burlap, tarpaulin.

canvass, *v.* **1.** solicit votes, campaign, electioneer, poll, survey; request, ask for, bespeak, invite; apply for, appeal for, petition for, beg for, beseech, entreat, implore; press, urge, push.

2. investigate, inquire into, look into, *U.S.* check into *or* up on, inspect, go over; examine, scrutinize, explore, study, analyze, break down, take stock of; survey, scan, peruse, go *or* look through; consider, contemplate, think about, give thought to, evaluate, weigh; discuss, debate, discourse, talk about *or* over, air, ventilate; argue, dispute, reason, convince, persuade.

—*n.* **3.** solicitation, campaign, poll, survey; request, invitation, appeal, petition, suit; entreaty, plea, supplication, beseeching; urging, pressing, pushing.

4. investigation, inquiry, inspection, check, examination, scrutiny, exploration; study, analysis, breakdown, evaluation, weighing; consideration, deliberation, careful thought; discussion, debate, discourse, argument.

canyon, *n.* ravine, gulch, valley, gully; gorge, chasm, fissure, cleft, gap, water gap; opening, break, crack, cut, notch, split, divide.

cap, *n.* **1.** beanie, skullcap, zuchetto, calotte, beret, tam-o'-shanter, tam, calpac, toque, castor, montero, tuque, stocking cap, *Inf.* toboggan; nightcap, biggin; turban, tarboosh, fez, shako, barret, *Rom. Cath. Ch.* biretta; hat, bonnet, sombrero, ten-gallon hat; veil, net, snood, cover, covering, overlay; headscarf, mantilla, headcloth, wimple, hood; crown, crownpiece, mortarboard, headpiece, headgear, helmet, hard hat.

2. top, lid, capsule, plug, cork, stopper, stopple, bung, ferrule.

3. summit, apex, vertex, apogee, pinnacle, peak, tiptop, crest, heights, *Latin. ne plus ultra*; acme, zenith, meridian, crowning point, climax, culmination, maximum.

—*v.* **4.** top, crown, overlie, surmount, sit atop *or* on, pinnacle, tip, *Brit.* nib.

5. consummate, perfect, put the finishing touches on, round out *or* off, culminate, climax; complete, conclude, terminate, finish, end, top out.

6. surpass, transcend, excel, transcend, eclipse, overshadow, outdo, outstrip, outshine; best, better, beat, win over, prevail over; exceed, go beyond, rise above *or* over.

capability, *n.* **1.** capableness, competence, competency; efficacy, effectiveness, adequacy, sufficiency, readiness, qualification; capacity, potential, potentiality, potency, power, amplitude, magnitude, scope, extent, range, compass.

2. ability, faculty, talent, facility, mind [for]; flair, bent, turn, knack, forte, strong point; proficiency, adeptness, skill, skillfulness, dexterity, adroitness, deftness; aptitude, intelligence, intellect, cleverness, smartness, aptness, wit, mother wit, sagacity, head, brain, mind; acumen, penetration, perspicacity; sense, reason, judgment, understanding.

3. withstandingness, resistance, tolerance; endurance, strength.

4. **capabilities** potential, possibilities; aptitudes, gifts, endowments; abilities, faculties, powers, talents, skills; attributes, qualities, characteristics, features.

capable, *adj.* **1.** intelligent, apt, smart, clever, ingenious, brilliant; sagacious, learned, knowledgeable, versed, able, talented, gifted, adept, skillful, dexterous, adroit, deft; competent, proficient, efficient, adequate, equal to, *Inf.* up to; efficacious, effective, effectual; expert, masterful, masterly, accomplished;

skilled, experienced, *Fr. au fait,* practiced, qualified; adapted, suited, fitted.

2. capable of a. needing, in need of, wanting, requiring; receptive, impressionable, (*all usu. fol. by* of *or* to) susceptible, open, accessible, subject. **b.** predisposed to, inclined to, prone to, liable to, likely to, having a tendency for, tendentious, tendential, *Archaic.* propense.

capacious, *adj.* large, spacious, roomy, ample, commodious, voluminous; broad, expansive, wide, extensive, widespread; vast, immense, amplitudinous; huge, big, great, massive, gigantic, tremendous, mammoth.

capacitate, *v.* enable, empower, qualify; sanction, warrant, authorize; equip, endow, endue, supply, fit out, arm.

capacity, *n.* **1.** amplitude, ampleness, magnitude, largeness, sufficiency, room, *Naut.* burden; volume, dimensions, proportions, measure, space, size, scope, extent, range, compass.

2. aptitude, potential, capability, the stuff, *Inf.* what it takes, *U.S. Inf.* the goods; intelligence, intellect, aptness, wit, mother wit, sagacity, head, brain, mind; acumen, penetration, perspicacity; sense, reason, judgment, understanding; ability, gift, talent, endowment, forte; competence, adequacy, sufficiency, capableness, readiness.

3. withstandingness, resistance, tolerance; endurance, strength, power; susceptibility, vulnerability.

4. position, post, place, office; function, responsibility, job, duty, performance.

5. legitimation, authorization, empowerment; certification, license, warrant, sanction.

6. (*all of electricity*) capacitance, potential, output, yield, production.

caparison, *n.* **1.** trappings, housings; harness, tack, tackle, rigging.

2. finery, frippery, fancy dress, adornment, ornamentation, investiture, *Inf.* full *or* fine feather, *Brit. Inf.* full fig, *Sl.* fancy duds, *Sl.* glad rags, *Sl.* heavy threads; (*all of a sumptuous nature*) wardrobe, livery, dress, attire, apparel, *Archaic.* vesture.

3. (*all of a sumptuous nature*) equipment, equipage, apparatus, gear, accouterments, appurtenances, appointments; fixtures, fittings, habiliments, *Inf.* things; outfit, outfitting, turnout, rig.

—*v.* **4.** (*all with a caparison*) outfit, fit out, git up, fit, rig up, rig out, rig, turn out, gear; equip, furnish, supply, provide, *Obs.* appoint.

5. deck, deck out, bedeck, trap, adorn, array, ornament; (*all to a sumptuous degree*) dress, dress out, clothe, vest, garb, attire, apparel, habit, *Sl.* dude up; gown, robe, drape.

cape[1], *n.* cloak, capote, robe, dolan, domino, alsa, mantle, pelisse, pelerine, cope, burnoose, mantelet, *Rom. Cath. Ch.* mantelletta, (*in Spain and Spanish America*) manta, *Obs.* manteau; poncho, shawl, wrap.

cape[2], *n.* peninsula, chersonese, tongue, neck, *Archaic.* ness; promontory, headland, foreland, tip, point.

caper, *n.* **1.** frolic, frisk, romp, gambol; hop, skip, bounce, spring, prance, leap, jump, bound.

2. prank, trick, practical joke; antic, shenanigans, gambado, *Inf.* dido; fun, sport, jest, game; escapade, lark, spree, adventure.

—*v.* **3.** skip, hop, dance about; leap, jump, bound about; frolic, frisk, romp, gambol, cavort.

capital, *n.* **1.** seat of government, center of government, first city.

2. capital letter, majuscule, initial letter, *Inf.* cap, upper-case letter, uncial letter.

3. principal, assets, stock, investment; funds, moneys, finances, savings, hard cash, liquid assets; cash, reserve, means, wherewithal, working capital, supply, resources, revenue, ways and means; wealth, riches, treasure.

—*adj.* **4.** principal, chief, main, important; major, prime, paramount, ultimate, cardinal; first, primary, foremost, initial, front, head; dominant, predominant, preeminent, uppermost, topmost, utmost, master; crowning, leading, greatest, ruling, overruling; definitive, conclusive, determinative; key, vital, crucial, central, essential.

5. excellent, first-rate, first-class, fine, *Inf.* super, *Inf.* superfine, *Inf.* champion, *Sl.* class, *Sl.* supercalifragilisticexpialidocious; unexcelled, unsurpassed, unmatched, matchless, peerless, inimitable, incomparable; superior, choice, select, *Inf.* crack, *Inf.* of the first water; outstanding, preeminent, foremost, classic, best, top, *Inf.* topnotch, *Inf.* tiptop, *Inf.* A-1; highest, superlative, grand, perfect, supreme, consummate.

capitalism, *n.* free enterprise, laissez-faire; exploitation, dog-eat-dog.

capitalist, *n.* **1.** financier, investor, moneyman, banker, tycoon, baron.

2. rich man, man of means, moneybags, millionaire, multimillionaire, billionaire; plutocrat, nabob, *Sl.* fat cat, *Sl.* big fish.

capitalize, *v.* **1.** take advantage of, put to advantage, make the most of, turn to account, cash in on; seize the day, strike while the iron is hot, make hay while the sun shines; use, exploit, milk, bleed, drain, suck dry.

2. turn a profit, turn a penny, make a buck, realize on.

3. finance, back, fund, sponsor, pay for, *Inf.* angle, *Inf.* stake, *Sl.* bankroll, *Sl.* foot the bill.

capitol, *n.* Statehouse, legislative building; legislature.

capitulate, *v.* **1.** surrender, give up, lay down arms, raise the white flag, cry craven; yield, submit, succumb, fall, bite the dust; acknowledge defeat, come to terms; throw in the towel *or* the sponge, throw up one's hands; call it quits, *Sl.* pack it in, give up the ship.

2. acquiesce, comply, accede, give in, cry *or* say uncle; concede, accede, agree, concur; yield, cave in, bend, bow, relent, mellow, soften; back down, renege, retract, recant.

capitulation, *n.* **1.** surrender, submission, yielding; acquiescence, compliance, accedence, concession, nonresistance.

2. summary, summation, digest, abstract, résumé, synopsis, conspectus; enumeration, numeration, list, listing, catalogue.

caprice, *n.* **1.** vagary, notion, crank, impulse, brain wave; whim, whimsy, fancy, humor, crotchet, maggot; idiosyncrasy, idiocrasy, peculiarity, eccentricity, quirk, oddity; erraticism, turn, twist, fit; fad, craze.

2. whimsicality, capriciousness, fickleness, frivolity, volatility.

capricious, *adj.* whimsical, fanciful, impulsive, moody, crotchety; fickle, skittish, inconstant, moonish, changeable, changeful, variable, faddish; flighty, mercurial, volatile, undependable, unsteady, unstable; fitful, erratic, irregular, spasmodic, uneven; irresolute, uncertain, indecisive, undecided, vacillating, wavering, shilly-shallying, infirm of purpose; irresponsible, wayward, wanton, lawless; heteroclite, deviative, stray.

capsize, *v.* overturn, turn over, upend, keel over, knock over, tip over, *Inf.* turn turtle; upset, overset, overthrow.

captain, *n.* **1.** chief, leader, head, headman, *Inf.* number one, *Sl.* top banana; skipper, master, sailing master, officer, chief officer, ship's captain, *Inf.* old man; chieftain, commander, commandant, foreman, overlord, principal, governor.

—*v.* **2.** lead, command, head, boss, take charge, be in charge; steer, pilot, skipper.

caption, *n.* **1.** heading, title, legend, inscription, imprint; headline, banner, *Inf.* scarehead, *Journalism.* screamer.

—*v.* **2.** head, entitle, title, label, inscribe, imprint.

captious, *adj.* **1.** faultfinding, carping, nagging, caviling; scoffing, impugning, picking, *Inf.* picky; hard to please, hypercritical, critical, biting, cutting, belittling, deprecating; chiding, reproachful, censorious, disapprobatory, disapproving, derogatory; reprehensive, condemnatory, denunciatory, objurgatory, animadversional.

2. ensnaring, perplexing, entangling, entrapping; astute, pointed, clever, subtle, stealthy, crafty, calculating, artful; treacherous, arch, shrewd, *Inf.* loaded, *Inf.* tricky; sly, cunning, vulpine, *Inf.* foxy; invidious, scheming, conniving, perfidious, collusive, guileful, deceptive, delusive.

captivate, *v.* charm, delight, enchant, take the fancy of; fascinate, infatuate, enthrall, enrapture, enamor, bewitch, *Inf.* vamp, *Sl.* knock off one's feet, *Sl.* knock for a loop; attract, lure, catch, win, enchain, snare, ensnare, enslave; dazzle, transport, mesmerize, hypnotize, carry away, turn one's head; seduce, ravish, bedevil, becharm, inflame, tantalize, *Inf.* drive one crazy.

captive, *n.* prisoner, slave, hostage, bondman; convict, *Inf.* con, *Inf.* jailbird.

captivity, *n.* bondage, servitude, enslavement, slavery, thralldom, subjection; imprisonment, internment, detention, confinement, custody, committal, incarceration; durance, restraint, constraint.

capture, *v.* **1.** catch, take captive, take prisoner, arrest, apprehend, *Inf.* nab, *Inf.* corral, *Inf.* pinch, *Inf.* lay by the heels, *Inf.* collar, *Inf.* nail, *Inf.* bag; take into custody, seize, lay hold of, fasten on to, grasp, grab, wrest, snatch, carry off, *Inf.* cop; trap, ensnare, snare, snag.

—*n.* **2.** seizure, taking, taking prisoner, arrest, apprehension, *Inf.* collar, *Inf.* nailing, *Inf.* nabbing; trapping, snagging, bagging.

3. prize, trophy, gain, spoils, booty, loot, pickings, pillage, filchings, *Sl.* take, *Sl.* haul, *Sl.* swag.

car, *n.* **1.** vehicle, motorcar, *Both Chiefly U.S.* automobile *or* auto, *Inf.* bus, *Sl.* wheels; sedan, coupe, landau, limousine, *Inf.* limo, convertible, roadster, touring car, runabout; *Sl.* bomb, *Sl.* dragster, *U.S. Sl.* hot rod; wreck, rattletrap, *Facetious.* flivver, *Inf.* jalopy, *Inf.* clunker, *Inf.* crate, *Sl.* buggy, *Sl.* tin lizzie, *Sl.* heap, bucket of bolts.

2. cab, taxi, taxicab, hackney, *U.S.* hack; carriage, chariot, phaeton, hansom, cabriolet, wagon, cart, *Chiefly Brit.* trap, (*in Japan, the Philippines, etc.*) jinrikisha.

3. coach, diner, sleeper, smoker, caboose, *Brit.* van, *Trademark.* Pullman.

carafe, *n.* decanter, bottle, carboy, demijohn, flask, flasket; cruet, phial, vial, caster, jar; jug, cruse, flagon, pitcher.

caravan, *n.* convoy, wagon train, wagonage; procession, cavalcade, motorcade, parade, train, coffle; column, file, queue, line; band, troop, team, company, group; entourage, retinue, cortege, suite.

carcass, *n.* **1.** corpse, cadaver, dead body, remains, *Sl.* stiff; *All Fig.* body, *Sl.* bod, person, self.

2. frame, framework, skeleton; shell, hulk, wreck, ruins.

card, *n.* **1.** postcard, greeting card, sympathy card, mass card; identification, ID, badge, calling card; cards, playing cards.

2. bill, program, slate; calendar, schedule, docket, agenda, order of the day; menu, bill of fare; *Sports.* list, roster, batting order, line-up.

3. **in** *or* **on the cards** imminent, impending, near, at hand; likely, probable, apt, liable, in the wind *or* air, in the offing; destined, fated, ordained, in store.

cardinal, *adj.* **1.** main, chief, principal, prime, central, focal; essential, necessary, indispensable, primary, elementary, fundamental, basic, basal; first, foremost, headmost, leading, dominant, supreme, uppermost, highest, paramount, crowning, preeminent, top, greatest, vital, key, most important, important.

2. red, scarlet, crimson, vermilion.

—*n.* **3.** *Rom. Cath. Ch.* prelate, primate, hierarch, high priest, archpriest, *Eastern Ch.* exarch; archbishop, metropolitan, bishop, diocesan.

care, *n.* **1.** worry, anxiety, disquiet, disquietude, uneasiness, inquietude; distress, fretfulness, misgiving, qualm, apprehension; trouble, concern, regard, solicitude, cark; anguish, sorrow, dolor, grief, sadness, affliction, heartache; matter, ailment, ill, grievance; vexation, annoyance, nuisance, tribulation; strain, pressure, burden, onus; tax, cross, encumbrance, cumbrance, lead, handicap.

2. attention, carefulness, caution, prudence, pains; heed, heedfulness, watchfulness, advertence; alertness, vigilance, circumspection, wariness; awareness, consciousness, mindfulness; meticulousness, fastidiousness, conscientiousness, scrupulousness, punctiliousness, painstakingness; exaction, precision, preciseness, strictness, particularity, accuracy.

3. protection, charge, ward, keep; responsibility, safekeeping, safeguard, custody, guardianship, tutelage, guidance; surveillance, vigil, lookout.

4. ward, charge, dependent, minor, protégé.

—*v.* **5.** be concerned, be solicitous, be uneasy, worry, trouble; fret, fuss, fidget, be apprehensive; bother, mind, *Inf.* give a damn, *Inf.* give a hoot, *Inf.* give a hang, *Archaic.* cark.

6. **take care of** **a.** care for, sit, sit with, baby-sit, watch, look after. **b.** attend to, act on, deal with, see to, take action on, take up.

7. **care for** like, fancy, enjoy, be fond of, take to, be pleased with, *Inf.* be sweet on, *Sl.* have a crush on; prefer, rather, have a mind to, incline towards, hanker after; hope for, wish, want, desire; yearn for, long for, hunger for, thirst for, crave, covet; love, cherish, hold dear, be enamored of, treasure, prize.

careen, *v.* tilt, lean, cant, heel, incline, list, slope, slant; sway, bend, tend, lurch, pitch; tip, keel, turn over; veer, shift, swerve, deviate, diverge, sheer.

career, *n.* **1.** course, progression, progress, passage, line, movement, march; orbit, flowing, flow, flux, rush, onrush, run; journey, trip, trek; direction, road, route, track, beat, way; lap, round, circuit, ambit.

2. occupation, profession, trade, business, line; vocation, avocation, following, calling, pursuit, craft, metier; employment, job, work, living, livelihood; bent, inclination, set.

—*v.* **3.** run, hustle, bustle, rush, scramble, scamper, scuttle, bolt, dash, dart, fly, *Inf.* take off, *Sl.* tear off, scoot, speed, sprint, shoot; hurry, hasten, spank, scud.

carefree, *adj.* **1.** insouciant, free and easy, heedless, untroubled, unconcerned, unworried, happy-go-lucky, *Inf.* living the life of Riley; nonchalant, casual, indifferent, blasé, devil-may-care.

2. cheerful, gay, jocund, jolly, merry, mirthful, gleeful, blithe, blithesome; happy, pleased, contented, glad; ecstatic, joyful, elated, joyous, jubilant; sprightly, light-hearted, debonair, jaunty, lively, airy, brisk, spry; enthusiastic, animated, spirited, flushed, buoyant, frisky, skittish; rollicking, playful, gamesome, frolicsome, sportive; jocular, jocose, joking, jesting, waggish.

3. genial, convivial, easygoing; winsome, sunny, smiling, cheery, riant, laughing; optimistic, upbeat, in good spirits, positive; elastic, resilient.

careful, *adj.* **1.** cautious, wary, chary, canny, prudent; politic, discreet, judicious, circumspect; aware, alert, awake, observant; mindful, thoughtful, concerned, solicitous, considerate, regardful, heedful, attentive; watchful, vigilant, on guard, guarded; apprehensive, fearful, worried, uneasy; halting, hesitant, *Inf.* yellow-light.

2. meticulous, punctilious, scrupulous, conscientious; exact, precise, accurate, correct; particular, finical, finicky, picky, fussy, hard to please; critical, exacting, demanding, fastidious; painstaking, minute, detailed, fine, nice, thorough, searching; scientific, mathematical, severe, rigorous, strict, close.

careless, *adj.* **1.** inattentive, inadvertent, unmindful, unthoughtful, unthinking, nonobservant, disregardful; unwise, imprudent, injudicious, indiscreet, uncircumspect; unwary, incautious, off guard, unguarded, unheeding, heedless; reckless, rash, temerarious; inconsiderate, uncaring, tactless, uncivil, rude.

2. negligent, neglectful, remiss, slack, lax, loose; inaccurate, inexact, incorrect; disorderly, sloppy, untidy, *Inf.* messy, slovenly, slatternly, *Sl.* raunchy; unorganized, *Inf.* harum-scarum, hit-or-miss; casual, slapdash, slipshod, offhand.

3. nonchalant, casual, indifferent, perfunctory, blasé, devil-may-care, thoughtless, forgetful, absent-minded; lackadaisical, listless, apathetic; free and easy, untroubled, unconcerned, unworried, happy-go-lucky, insouciant.

4. sprightly, light-hearted, debonair, jaunty, lively, airy, brisk, carefree. See **carefree** (*defs.* **2, 3**).

caress, *v.* **1.** touch, brush, graze, lick, tongue; stroke gently, fondle, handle, pat, rub, massage; hold, hug, clasp, embrace, cuddle, snuggle, nestle, nuzzle; kiss, osculate, *Inf.* make out, *Inf.* neck, *Inf.* smooch; *Inf.* pet, *Sl.* canoodle, *Sl.* feel up, *Inf.* paw; toy with, play with, play footsie, *Both Euph.* fool around, mess around.

2. coddle, cosset, pamper, pet, baby, treat gently, favor.

—*n.* **3.** touch, brush, graze; stroking, fondling, handling, patting, rub, massage; hug, clasp, embrace, cuddle, nuzzle; kiss, osculation, *Inf.* smack.

caretaker, *n.* superintendent, *Inf.* super, supervisor, overseer, warden, manager, curator, steward; janitor, maintenance man, clean-up man, handyman; custodian, keeper, guardian, conservator, guard, watchman, warder.

careworn, *adj.* tired, weary, fatigued, haggard, drooping, faint, flagging, fagged, *Inf.* tuckered; weakened, worn, spent, exhausted, footsore; crushed, beaten, wasted, stricken, enfeebled, overwearied; overworked, heavy-laden, oppressed, toilworn, dispirited, sorry, life-weary, *Inf.* down and out; sorrowful, forlorn, bowed down.

cargo, *n.* lading, freight, freightage, haul; load, burden, charge, weight; contents, merchandise, goods, stuff; boatload, shipload, *Chiefly U.S.* carload, wagonload, truckload.

caricature, *n.* **1.** cartoon, portrait, sketch, drawing, representation, parody, spoof, farce, burlesque, takeoff; satire, lampoon, squib, pasquinade, travesty.

—*v.* **2.** mimic, imitate, ape, *Inf.* take off, *Sl.* make like; parody, satirize, lampoon, squib, burlesque, travesty; mock, ridicule, stultify, make fun of, laugh at.

carillon, *n.* bells, chimes, dingdong, tintinnabulation.

carnage, *n.* butchery, slaughter, wholesale *or* general slaughter, random *or* indiscriminate slaughter, massacre, blood bath, effusion *or* fusillade of blood, *Rare.* internecion, *Rare.* trucidation; pogrom, mass-murder, mass-slaying, mass-execution, noyade; genocide, mass-destruction, annihilation, extermination, liquidation.

carnal, *adj.* **1.** earthly, worldly, temporal, mundane, terrestrial; secular, profane, unspiritual, physical, corporeal.

2. sensual, voluptuous, fleshly, bodily; lustful, lascivious, libidinous, lubricous, lecherous, *Archaic.* lickerish, *Sl.* horny; concupiscent, sexual, erotic, lewd, prurient, salacious; unchaste, impure, unclean, indecent, wanton, wayward, prodigal; animal, animalistic, bestial, brutish, crude, coarse, gross.

carnality, *n.* **1.** worldliness, earthliness, temporalness, secularity, profaneness, unspirituality, corporeality.

2. sensuality, voluptuousness, fleshliness; lustfulness, lewdness, prurience, salaciousness, *Sl.* horniness; lust, lechery, concupiscence, *Sl.* hot pants, *Sl.* the hots; animality, bestiality, brutishness, coarseness, grossness.

carnival, *n.* **1.** amusement show, circus, extravaganza; sideshow, freak show, puppet show; merry-go-round, carrousel, Ferris wheel.

2. merrymaking, revelry, reveling, revels; frolic, partying, party; revel, masquerade, masque, ball; festival, festivity, fete, fiesta, Mardi gras; celebration, jubilee, *Inf.* jamboree, gala; funmaking, jollification, conviviality, whoopee, *Inf.* goings on; carousal, orgy, bacchanalia, saturnalia, *Sl.* love-in.

carnivorous, *adj.* flesh-eating, carnivoral, zoophagous, omophagous, omnivorous, ichthyophagous; anthropophagic, cannibalistic, man-eating; rapacious, predatory, predacious, raptorial.

carol, *n.* **1.** song, tune, melody, chant, ditty; noel, spiritual, hymn, canticle, anthem.

—*v.* **2.** sing, chant, lilt, melodize, chime in, *Music.* harmonize, *Music.* descant; warble, troll, trill, chirrup, chirp.

carousal, *n.* **1.** drinking bout, brannigan, drunk, potation, compotation, bouse, guzzle, drunken carouse *or* revel, bacchanal, bacchanalia; cocktail party, happy hour; spree, fling, carouse, revel, romp, bout, wassail; *All Sl.* binge, bender, hellbender, bust, toot, tear, jag, bat, barhop, bar-crawl, *Brit.* pubcrawl; revelry, merrymaking, jollification, *Inf.* goings on; celebration, gala affair, wing-ding; orgy, debauch, debauchery, saturnalia, *Scot.* randy.

2. a. carrousel, merry-go-round, roundabout. **b.** tournament, tourney, field day, gymkhana.

carouse, *n.* **1.** drinking bout, brannigan, bouse, compotation; spree, fling, carousal, revel. See **carousal** (*def.* **1**).

—*v.* **2.** revel, wassail, roister, bouse, make merry, cut loose, let loose, *Inf.* live it up, *Inf.* party, *Inf.* step out, whoop it up, *Sl.* make whoopee; go on a spree, make the rounds, *Sl.* tie one on, *Sl.* go on a drunk *or* binge *or* bender *or* toot *or* tear *or* bat *or* jag, *Sl.* paint the town red, *Sl.* bar-hop, *Sl.* bar-crawl, *Brit. Sl.* pub-crawl; debauch, dissipate, wanton, sow wild oats, have one's fling; overindulge, overdo, burn the candle at both ends, not know when to stop, not know when one has had enough.

carp, *v.* complain, faultfind, cavil, *Sl.* beef; quibble, wrangle, pull to pieces, *Sl.* nitpick; nag, pick on *or* at, peck at, jibe at; criticize, find fault, belittle, deprecate, disparage, impugn, decry, *Sl.* moan and groan; blame, chide, reproach, censure, rebuke, reprove, reprehend, sneer at, discredit, animadvert.

carpenter, *n.* woodworker, cabinetmaker, joiner, builder, hammerer.

carpet, *n.* rug, area rug, scatter rug, throw rug, mat, matting, runner; shag, Afghan, Oriental, Persian carpet *or* rug, Turkish rug *or* carpet.

carping, *adj.* faultfinding, nagging, caviling, captious; scoffing, impugning, *Inf.* picky; hard to please, hypercritical, critical, biting, bitter, cutting, belittling, deprecating; chiding, reproachful, censorious, disapprobatory, derogatory; reprehensive, condemnatory, denunciatory, objurgatory, animadversional.

carriage, *n.* **1.** coach, stagecoach, chariot, phaeton, hansom, landau, brougham, surrey, cabriolet, coupe, victoria, barouche, four-wheeler, hackney, rockaway, *U.S.* buggy, *Chiefly Brit.* tallyho; sulky, gig, calash, curricle, chaise, tilbury, (*in Japan, the Philippines, etc.*) jinrikisha; wagon, cart, tumbrel, *Chiefly Brit.* trap; car, vehicle, conveyance.

2. posture, stance, stand, pose, position; poise, bearing, presence, demeanor, appearance, attitude, guise, aspect, cast; manner, mode, mood, air, mien, deportment, behavior.

carrier, *n.* **1.** transporter, conveyor, vehicle, conveyance; bearer, bringer, messenger, runner; porter, *U.S.* bellboy, *U.S.* bellhop, delivery man; mail carrier, mailman; newsboy, newspaper boy.

2. frame, rack, roof rack, luggage carrier.

carrion, *n.* dead flesh, dead body, cadaver, corpse, remains, bones; offal, putrefying meat, rot, decay, decomposition; garbage, refuse, waste.

carry, *v.* **1.** convey, transport, *Inf.* tote; portage, haul, cart, lug, pull along, drag; move, shift, transfer, displace, transplant; take, deliver, give, bring, fetch, get, go get; transmit, send, dispatch, convey, communicate, bear, pass on *or* along; lead, impel, conduct; force, propel, push, press.

2. support, hold up, maintain, sustain, uphold; bear, take on, undertake, assume, shoulder, lift; buttress, brace, shore up, stay, prop up, underprop, underpin; strengthen, reinforce, fortify.

3. (*all of oneself*) behave, deport, demean, conduct, comport, acquit, bear; manage, govern, regulate.

4. extend, continue, take to; spread, distend, stretch, reach, expand.

cart, *n.* **1.** handcart, truck, handtruck, pushcart, wagon, dray; dumpcart, tipcart, barrow, handbarrow, wheelbarrow; carriage, tilbury, buggy, tumbrel, gig, dogcart, curricle, *Chiefly Brit.* trap.

—*v.* **2.** transport, convey, carry, bear, portage; dray, haul, lug, move, truck, tote; bring, conduct, transfer, transmit, transplant, convoy.

carte blanche, *n.* free license, license, free rein, blank check; run of the house, key to the city, full rights, pass key, passe-partout; permit, sanction, authority.

carton, *n.* box, package, packing box *or* case, crate, pasteboard *or* paperboard *or* strawboard case, corrugated paper *or* cardboard container.

cartoon, *n.* **1.** caricature, lampoon, pasquinade, burlesque, take-off, satire, parody; portraiture, portrait, representation, picture, portrayal; depiction, line drawing, sketch.

2. comic strip, comics, *U.S.* funnies; animated cartoon, *Motion Pictures.* short.

cartoonist, *n.* caricaturist, lampoonist, lampooner, pasquinader, burlesquer, satirist; artist, sketcher, drawer, animator.

cartridge, *n.* **1.** shell, cartouche, canister, canister shot, case shot, cap; bullet, ball, grenade, *Mil.* projectile.

2. capsule, cylinder, case, container; reservoir, magazine, cassette.

carve, *v.* **1.** cut, chisel, sculpt, sculpture, tool, block out, rough-hew; cast, form, mold, fashion, model, figure; hammer out, forge, roughcast, knock out; gouge out, gash, slash, hack, hackle; engrave, groove, cut in, trench, incise, grave, scrape, stipple; etch, notch, whittle, *Archaic.* insculp.

2. hew, saw, trim, prune, lop; detruncate, dismember, dislimb, disjoint, amputate, quarter; slice, cleave, chop, rive; sever, dissever, rend, halve, abscind, split, dissect.

3. divide, apportion, portion, partition; parcel, distribute, deal, dole, allot, allocate, assign; subdivide, split up, part.

cascade, *n.* waterfall, falls, cataract, chute, niagara; downpour, shower, deluge, flood; rush, slide, avalanche.

case[1], *n.* **1.** instance, occurrence, occasion; happening, phenomenon, event, adventure; affair, concern, matter, business; precedent, antecedent, exemplar; representative, prototype, type, standard, model, paradigm, norm; example, illustration, sample, exemplification, specimen.

2. situation, condition, state, circumstance, position, place; plight, problem, difficulty; predicament, *Inf.* fix, *Inf.* pickle, mess, pinch, turn, straits; dilemma, impasse, cul-de-sac, corner.

3. statement, presentation, postulation, plea; explanation, exposition, explication, reasoning, reason, rationale; argument, position, premise; thesis, assumption, hypothesis, supposition, presupposition, supposal; evidence, ground, testimony, proof, facts.

4. patient, sick person, invalid, valetudinarian, sufferer, victim, *Archaic.* sickling.

case[2], *n.* **1.** container, box, receptacle, can, canister, skippet; carton, package, crate, trunk, coffer, casket, caddy, bin, chest, cabinet; *Rom. Cath. Ch.* monstrance *or* ostensorium, pyx, *Gk. and Rom. Antiq.* pyxis; repository, reliquary, shrine; tray, vasculum; vessel, cask, hogshead, firkin, keg, tun, tub, vat, barrel; cartridge, cartouche, magazine, chamber.

2. covering, casing, sheathing, sheath, scabbard; envelope, wrapper, jacket, cover; boot, socket, holder, ferrule; integument, tegument, investment, *Bot.* involucre *or* involucrum, capsule, sac, wrapping, cloak; casement, housing, protection; pod, calyx, *Dial.* cod; rind, crust, peel, skin; shell, husk, bark, cortex, hull.

3. pair, couple, brace.

4. frame, framework, form, mold, cut; shape, structure, outline, contour.

casement, *n.* sash, frame, framing, framework, window frame, window sash, case, casing; wicket, oriel, dormer, bay window, bow window.

cash, *n.* **1.** legal tender, currency, coinage, specie, mintage, coin; lucre, money, hard money, change, *Sl.* dough, *Sl.* bucks, bill, bank note, note, *Sl.* scratch. See **money.**

—*v.* **2.** turn into money, realize in cash, liquidate assets, exchange, change.

cashier[1], *n.* teller, banker, *Finance.* cambist; treasurer, bursar, purser, depositary; accountant, comptroller, controller; (*of gambling houses*) croupier,

Sl. boxman.

cashier², *v.* **1.** dismiss, discharge, expel, fire, let go, lay off, send off *or* packing, *Mil.* drum out, *Inf.* kick upstairs, *Sl.* can, *Sl.* sack, *Sl.* give [s.o.] the boot; disbar, unfrock, suspend, strip of rank; depose, displace, oust, unseat, dethrone, disestablish, remove from office.
2. reject, discard, throw out, dispose of, get rid of, jettison, *Sl.* deep-six, *Sl.* eighty-six.

casino, *n.* **1.** gambling den *or* house, gaming house, betting parlor.
2. ballroom, dancehouse, discotheque, *Inf.* disco; tavern, roadhouse, nightclub, *Inf.* honky-tonk; clubhouse, club, resort, haunt, gathering *or* meeting place, rallying point, *Inf.* stomping ground, *Sl.* hangout.

cask, *n.* barrel, keg, hogshead, firkin, puncheon, pipe, tierce, tun, tub; vat, vessel, container, receptacle.

casket, *n.* **1.** coffin, pall, box, sarcophagus, *Scot. and North Eng.* kist, *Sl.* wooden overcoat *or* kimono.
2. chest, case, container, receptacle.

casserole, *n.* **1.** terrine, baking *or* covered dish, skillet, frying pan, saucepan.

cast, *v.* **1.** throw, toss, dart, shy, chuck, pitch; hurl, dash, sling, let fly, send, launch; fling, flirt, heave, jerk, cant, shoot, catapult.
2. disseminate, scatter, spread, bespread, strew, bestrew, sow, broadcast; distribute, disperse, circulate; sprinkle, spatter, bespatter.
3. emit, send forth, discharge, radiate; eject, throw forth, propel, project, spurt, squirt, jet, ejaculate; throw up, vomit, disgorge; expel, oust, exclude, bar, banish, remove, eliminate, exile.
4. lose, part with, misplace, mislay; shed, drop, doff, throw off, shake off; slough, peel, flake, molt, exuviate.
5. discard, reject, dismiss, set aside, throw out *or* away, toss out, get rid of, *Inf.* junk, *Inf.* trash, *Sl.* eighty-six.
6. bestow, award, impart, confer, commit; grant, present, give, bequeath; *All Theat.* select, choose, allot, assign.
7. arrange, shape, mold; plan out, make fit *or* suitable; form, sculpt, carve, model; work, knead, turn, twist, warp.
8. compute, calculate, reckon; figure; add, total, sum up.
9. forecast, predict, foretell, foresee, conjecture; prophesy, read the signs, interpret omens.
10. cast about search, seek, look for; grope about, ransack.
—*n.* **11.** throw, toss, *Chiefly Brit.* chuck, shy, pitch; hurl, sling, fling, flirt, heave, cant, jerk; shooting, launching, catapulting.
12. dissemination, sowing, broadcasting; scattering, spreading, strewing, sprinkling; distribution, dispersal, circulation.
13. emission, discharge, radiation; ejection, propulsion, projection, ejaculation; expulsion, elimination.
14. fortune, lot, portion, fate, destiny, doom, star.
15. arrangement, form, shape; mold, impression, casting; model, replica, reproduction.
16. *All Theat.* dramatis personae, performers, players, actors, actresses; company, troupe, repertory.
17. appearance, semblance, complexion, guise, aspect; carriage, mien, bearing, air; behavior, demeanor, deportment.
18. look, color, shade, hue, tint, tone; touch, dash, trace, twist, suggestion, suspicion, soupçon, hint; smack, flavor, taste.
19. sort, kind, style, type, stamp; spirit, vein, grain, streak, stripe; quality, nature.
20. tendency, inclination, leaning, propensity, proclivity; proneness, predisposition, bias; bent, direction, set, turn, predilection; disposition, humor, mood, temperament, constitution.
21. computation, reckoning, addition, calculation; sum, total, count.
22. forecast, prediction, prognosis, prophecy, foretelling; conjecture, guess, estimate.

castaway, *n.* **1.** discard, castoff, *Inf.* throw-out, (*of cards*) slough; reject, factory reject, second, irregular; hand-me-down.
2. outcast, pariah, Ishmael, unperson, nonperson; exile, expatriate, political refugee, outlaw, excommunicate; waif, stray, foundling; rejectee.
3. wanderer, vagabond, rover, itinerant, nomad, knight-of-the-road; beachcomber, vagrant, hobo, tramp; beggar, panhandler, scavenger; derelict, down-and-outer, *U.S. Inf.* bum.
—*adj.* **4.** adrift, cast adrift, shipwrecked, marooned, derelict, abandoned, forsaken, *Naut.* ahull; stranded, aground, grounded, stuck.
5. thrown away, discarded, rejected, unwanted, sloughed off, *Inf.* junked, *Inf.* trashed; second-hand, used, *Euph.* pre-owned, hand-me-down.

caste, *n.* class, rank, order, degree; position, standing, place, station, condition, status; sphere, affiliation, group, family, clan, lineage, descent, ancestry.

castigate, *v.* **1.** punish, discipline, chastise, chasten; spank, slap, strike, smite, baste, cuff, box, pummel; thump, beat, lace, drub, cane, birch, switch, trounce, thrash, strap, whip, horsewhip, flail, flog, lash, scourge, flagellate.
2. criticize, scold, blame, chide, reproach, censure, take to task, *Inf.* call on the carpet, *Inf.* haul over the coals, *Sl.* stick it to [s.o.]; correct, admonish, reprove, rebuke, reprimand, upbraid, berate, fustigate, objurgate, dress down, humble, *Inf.* tell [s.o.] off, *Sl.* put down; penalize, punish.

castle, *n.* **1.** stronghold, fortress, citadel, keep, tower, donjon, hold.
2. palace, manor house, hall, chateau, mansion, chalet.

castrate, *v.* **1.** asexualize, emasculate, ovariectomize, oophorectomize; alter, (*of horses*) geld, *Inf.* fix, *Inf.* cut, (*of female animals*) spay, (*of fowl*) capon, *New England* (*of animals*) deacon; eunuchize, unman, effeminize, womanize.
2. expurgate, purge, censor, bowdlerize, *Inf.* clean up; impoverish, weaken, debilitate, take the teeth out of, render ineffectual.

castration, *n.* asexualization, effeminization, *Surgery.* orchidectomy; ovariectomy, oophorectomy; altering, gelding, unmanning.

casual, *adj.* **1.** chance, fortuitous, serendipitous, *Inf.* fluky *or* flukey; unexpected, unanticipated, unforeseen, unforeseeable, unlooked-for.
2. offhand, offhanded, facile, easy, effortless, loose, smooth, slick; perfunctory, cursory, throwaway; nonchalant, blasé, cool, relaxed, at east, easy-going; informal, unceremonious, (*of clothes*) sporty.
3. indifferent, apathetic, unconcerned, uncaring, pococurante, uninterested, disinterested; listless, lackadaisical, half-hearted; dispassionate, inexcitable, lukewarm, tepid; carefree, free-and-easy, insouciant, devil-may-care.
4. random, haphazard, hit-or-miss, hit-and-miss, arbitrary, capricious, promiscuous, leaving much to chance; irregular, unsystematic, systemless, unmethodical, methodless, indiscriminate; orderless, un-

directed, aimless, indefinite, vague; careless, thoughtless; desultory, fitful, spasmodic, sporadic, erratic.

5. accidental, unintentional, unintended, unpremeditated, unmeditated, uncalculated, unplanned, undesigned; indeliberate, inadvertent, involuntary; unthinking, unwitting, unconscious; incidental, occasional, contingent, adventitious.

—*n.* **6.** temporary, temporary employee, *Inf.* temp, office temporary; casual laborer *or* worker, part-time laborer *or* worker *or* employee; (*of soldiers*) irregular.

7. almsman, almswoman, charity case, welfare case, welfare client.

casualty, *n.* **1.** *Military.* **a.** fatality, dead man; wounded man, injured man; missing in action, MIA. **b.** **casualties** fatalities, losses; dead, wounded, dead and wounded, missing in action.

2. victim, sufferer; unfortunate, poor unfortunate, wretch, miserable wretch, poor devil; loser, prey, fortune's fool.

3. accident, mishap, mischance, misfortune, misadventure, miscarriage, *Scot. and North Eng.* mishanter, glitch; shock, blow, nasty *or* staggering *or* heavy blow, buffet, stroke, fell stroke, stroke of bad *or* ill luck *or* fortune.

4. wreck, shipwreck; crash, car crash, plane crash; collision, smash-up, pile-up.

5. fluke, freak accident, one in a million, twist of fate; fortuity, happening, hap, hazard.

casuistry, *n.* sophistry, sophism, philosophism, speciousness; pettifoggery, quibbling, nitpicking, hairsplitting, *Derog.* jesuitism; subtlety, guile, deceit, chicanery, equivocation.

cat, *n.* **1.** feline, grimalkin, tabby; gib, tomcat, *Inf.* tom; kitten, pussy, *Archaic.* catling.

2. (*used only of women*) gossip, busybody, newsmonger, quidnunc; scandalmonger, muckraker, backbiter; shrew, virago, vixen, termagant, harridan, crone, *Sl.* bitch.

cataclysm, *n.* **1.** upheaval, violent upheaval, convulsion, spasm, eruption; violent change *or* disturbance, revolution, radical *or* total *or* sweeping change; subversion, overthrow, overturn, coup d'état; debacle, collapse, downfall, breakdown, breakup; ruin, ruination, desolation.

2. catastrophe, calamity, disaster, tragedy; shock, blow, staggering blow, buffet, stroke, stroke of ill luck; mishap, mischance, misfortune, miscarriage, misadventure, *Scot. and North Eng.* mishanter; acident, casualty, glitch.

3. flood, deluge, inundation, washout, engulfment, alluvion, alluvium; avalanche, landslide, mudslide; earthquake, quake.

catacomb, *n.* **1.** *Usu.* **catacombs** (*all underground*) cemetery, ossuary, burial ground; crypt, vault, sepulchre.

2. *Usu.* **catacombs** (*all underground*) tunnels, maze, labyrinth.

catalogue, *n.* **1.** list, enumeration, laundry list, beadroll, roll, slate, muster, directory; index, table, file, classification; inventory, record, register; schedule, calendar, docket; chartulary, archives.

2. bulletin, handbill, dodger, throwaway, flyer, leaflet; pamphlet, brochure, circular, folder; prospectus, syllabus.

—*v.* **3.** codify, classify, categorize, alphabetize; rank, group, bracket, sort, assort, arrange; list, enumerate, tabulate, enroll, chronicle, calendar, schedule, *Law.* docket.

catapult, *n.* **1.** sling, *Brit.* slingshot, trebuchet, ballista, mortar; crossbow, arbalest.

—*v.* **2.** let fly, send; launch, propel, hurl, fling, flirt, heave, jerk, cast, shoot; sling, dash, throw, toss, dart, shy, chuck, pitch.

cataract, *n.* **1.** cascade, waterfall, falls, sault; rapids, race.

2. niagara, debacle, avalanche, torrent, downpour; deluge, alluvion, inundation, washout, flood.

catastrophe, *n.* **1.** disaster, calamity, tragedy; blow, nasty *or* heavy *or* staggering blow, buffet, stroke, stroke of bad *or* ill luck *or* fortune, shock; mishap, mischance, misfortune, miscarriage, misadventure, *Scot. and North Eng.* mishanter *or* mischanter; accident, casualty, glitch; wreck, shipwreck, crash, car crash, collision, smash-up, crack-up, pile-up.

2. (*all usu. of an unfortunate nature*) end, finish, conclusion, terminus, termination, *Sl.* pay off; climax, consummation, culmination; end *or* final result, final event, last act, bitter end, finis, finale, curtain, final curtain, *Sl.* curtains.

3. failure, fiasco, *Inf.* flop, *Inf.* fizzle, *Inf.* dud, *Inf.* washout, *Sl.* bomb, *Sl.* turkey.

4. (*all in drama*) denouement, resolution, final solution; catastasis; epitasis; protasis.

5. cataclysm, convulsion, spasm, upheaval, eruption, avalanche, sudden violent change *or* disturbance; debacle, collapse, downfall, breakdown, breakup; ruin, ruination, desolation.

catcall, *n.* **1.** hoot, whistle, shout, cry, howl; gibe, jeer, hiss, boo, raspberry, *U.S.* Bronx cheer, *Sl.* the bird.

2. whistle, rattle, noisemaker, ticktock, clacker, clapper, catcaller.

catch, *v.* **1.** grasp, snatch, grab, claw, pluck; grip, clutch, clench, hold, *Basketball.* palm; receive, acquire, come into possession of.

2. seize, capture, take captive, apprehend, stop, arrest, take into custody, *Inf.* nab, *Sl.* cop; entrap, trap, ensnare, snare, entangle, trip up; corner, corral, lasso, rope, noose, bag, net, hook, pull in.

3. reach, get to, get in touch with, contact; intercept, cut off at the pass, overtake, catch up with.

4. understand, comprehend, fathom, savvy, *Inf.* get through one's head, *Inf.* figure out, *Inf.* catch on, *Inf.* get it, *Inf.* get a fix on, *Sl.* latch onto, *Sl.* get the drift of, *Sl.* get the hang of, *Brit.* lay hold of; perceive, discern, make out, *Inf.* make heads or tails of, *Brit.* twig; espy, see, see through, see the light, picture, read, recognize.

5. contract, get, break out with, *Inf.* come down with; be sick *or* ill with, become infected with, suffer from.

6. surprise, startle, take off guard, walk in on; detect, discover, find, come upon *or* across, *Inf.* spot.

—*n.* **7.** hook, clasp, clip, snap, hook and eye, buckle, button, fastener, fastening, pin; chain, link; latch, lock, bolt, hasp; click, clincher, pawl, holdfast, *Mach.* detent, *Mach.* dog.

8. take, pickings, *Inf.* haul, *Hunting.* bag; gain, winnings, prize, trophy; loot, booty, spoil, pillage, plunder, *Sl.* swag.

9. trick, snare, trap, springe; catch-22, *Sl.* hooker, *Inf.* small *or* fine point.

catching, *adj.* **1.** contagious, communicable, transmittable, transmissible, transferable, inoculable, infectious, spreadable, *Obs.* taking; epidemic, epidemical, miasmal, miasmatic, miasmatical, miasmic, pestilential.

2. fascinating, intriguing, interesting, charming, enchanting, entrancing, bewitching, hypnotizing, mesmerizing; captivating, winning, catchy; appealing, alluring, enticing, fetching, inviting, magnetic; appetizing, tantalizing, seductive.

catchword, *n.* slogan, refrain, motto, saying, byword, catch phrase, buzz word, battle cry, red flag, trigger word; signal, cue, cue word; watch word, password, formula, shibboleth, pet phrase, cliché; tag, epithet, name.

catechize, *v.* **1.** coach, tutor, instruct, train, teach, school, educate, initiate, nurture; edify, inspire; inform, show, familiarize, acquaint, enlighten; communicate, tell, impart, relate, preach, descant, discourse; inculcate, instill, indoctrinate, imbue, implant; ground, drill, discipline.

2. interrogate, cross-examine, examine, investigate, inquire, *Inf.* put through the third degree, interpellate, pump, drill; question, query, quiz.

catechumen, *n.* novice, novitiate, initiate, tyro, neophyte, amateur, rookie, greenhorn, tenderfoot, newcomer, new boy; beginner, abecedarian, student, pupil, freshman, learner, fledgling, apprentice, trainee; recruit, convert, proselyte, probationer.

categorical, *adj.* **1.** unqualified, unconditional, unconditioned, unrestricted, unreserved, unlimited, absolute, implicit, total; outright, downright, flat, out-and-out, straight-out, all-out, across-the-board; sheer, utter, unmitigated.

2. positive, determinate, certain, veritable, unequivocal, unambiguous, explicit, express; sure, confident, unquestionable, conclusive; official, confirmed, marked, emphatic, dogmatic, authoritative; demonstrable, demonstrated, apodictic, indubitable, undoubted; settled, fixed, definite, decided, decisive, pronounced; true, unmistakable, actual, factual, accurate.

category, *n.* **1.** class, classification, type, sort, kind, variety, family, genus, species, denomination; position, status, rank; designation, specification, heading; division, subdivision, department; province, sphere, *Inf.* bag, section.

2. arrangement, order, ordering, disposition, ordination, grouping; compilation, assortment, coordination, enumeration.

cater, *v.* **1.** provide, furnish, supply; purvey, mess, victual, forage; entertain, fête, wine and dine, regale.

2. cater to indulge, humor, favor, oblige; gratify, satisfy, please; give way to, yield to; pamper, coddle, spoil; serve, do for, do service for, work for; wait on *or* upon, attend, make comfortable, attend to the convenience of, minister to, pander to; curry favor, *Inf.* bootlick, fawn, toady to, *Inf.* butter up, *Inf.* sweet-talk, *Inf.* soft-soap, *Sl.* suck up to.

caterwaul, *v.* howl, screech, squall, shriek, wail, scream; squeal, yelp, bark, yap; miaow, mewl, whimper, whine, cry.

catharsis, *n.* purgation, purging, cleansing, cleaning out, ablution, abstersion; purification, purifying, depuration, epuration; lustration, *Roman Hist.* lustrum; expurgation, censoring, censorship.

cathartic, *adj.* **1.** purgative, purging, *Med.* lapactic, cleansing, cleaning, detergent, abstergent, abstersive; purifying, purificatory, depurative, ablutionary, lustrate, lustral; laxative, *Med.* aperient, carminative, emetic, vomitory; expurgatory, censorial.

—*n.* **2.** purgative, laxative, *Med.* aperient, physic, cleanser, purifier, depurative; carminative, emetic, vomitory.

cathedral, *n.* principal church, episcopal see, bishop's seat; bishopric, episcopate, diocese; bishop's chair, bishop's throne, cathedra.

Catholic, *n.* Roman Catholic; ultramontane; *All Disparaging.* papist, Roman, Romanist, Mariolater, *Brit. Sl.* left-footer.

catholic, *adj.* **1.** general, universal, ecumenical, widespread, world-wide, global; comprehensive, all-inclusive, all-encompassing, all-embracing.

2. liberal, broad-minded, open-minded, wide, broad; impartial, even-handed, fair, just, dispassionate, disinterested; unbiased, unprejudiced, unbigoted, unjaundiced, unprepossessed.

cattle, *n.* **1.** livestock, stock, domestic animals; cows, beef, neat, *Archaic.* kine.

2. *Disparaging.* rabble, rout, ruck, canaille, riffraff, rubbish, dregs, scum, scum of the earth, dregs of society.

caucus, *n.* assembly, assemblage, gathering; meeting, conclave, convention, council, conference, session.

cauldron, *n.* kettle, pot, crock, vat, boiler; pressure cooker; crockpot.

causation, *n.* **1.** origination, invention, creation, production, manufacture; inspiration, conception.

2. causality, cause and effect.

3. cause, reason, root, origin. See **cause** (*def.* **1**).

cause, *n.* **1.** occasion, source, root, origin, fountainhead, mainspring; agent, mover, prime mover; author, creator, producer, originator, parent, sire.

2. reason, reason why, why and wherefore, the why, *Inf.* what for; rationale, motive, explanation; inspiration, inducement, incentive, stimulus, determinant; base, basis, grounds, antecedents; right, call, warrant, ground, justification.

3. topic, question, matter, point, case, issue, problem, moot point, bone of contention.

4. ideal, principle, belief, tenet, conviction, guiding light; purpose, reason for being, raison d'être; end, aim, object, objection.

—*v.* **5.** effect, occasion, generate, bring about, bring on, bring to pass; begin, give rise to, raise, originate, found, institute; create, produce, author, father, sire.

6. compel, make, induce, force, coerce, constrain, *Scot.* gar, *Sl.* strongarm.

caustic, *adj.* **1.** acrimonious, mordant, bitter, acrid, pungent; trenchant, cutting, incisive, slashing, penetrating, piercing, stinging, nipping, biting; astringent, severe, stern, austere, stringent; harsh, keen, sharp, sharp-tongued; sour, acidulous, acid, tart; virulent, spiteful, malicious, maleficent, venemous, vicious, malevolent, malignant; invidious, hateful.

2. sarcastic, satirical, ironic, ironical, cynical; edged, double-edged; contemptuous, taunting, teasing; scornful, mocking, derisive, derisory, sardonic.

3. insulting, excoriating, denouncing, berating, lashing; abusive, corrosive, corroding, erosive; cruel, mean, brutal; unkind, uncharitable, unbenevolent, uncordial, unamiable, unfriendly.

4. peevish, petulant, crabbed, testy, touchy, waspish, irascible, edgy; ill-tempered, ill-humored, ill-natured, short-tempered; hostile, resentful, indignant, piqued, angry; morose, surly, moody.

5. rude, churlish, boorish, bearish, graceless, unceremonious, rough; unmannerly, uncivil, ill-bred, ungracious, impolite, discourteous; abrupt, brusque, blunt, curt, short, gruff, crusty.

cauterize, *v.* (*for curative purposes*) burn, sear, singe, scald, scorch, char, torrefy; (*by means of burning*) disinfect, sterilize, antisepticize, cleanse.

caution, *n.* **1.** alertness, prudence, care, wariness, circumspection, discretion, deliberation; watchfulness, vigilance, heed, attention, carefulness, heedfulness, guardedness; concern, thought, regard, mindfulness, attentiveness, calculation.

2. warning, caveat, admonition, monition, forewarning, alarm, *Inf.* yellow light, *Inf.* red flag; foreshadowing, indication, premonition.

—*v.* **3.** warn, admonish, dissuade, forewarn; advise, counsel, exhort, prescribe, enjoin; wag one's finger at, shake one's head, alert, put on one's guard, give a warning signal.

cautious, *adj.* careful, prudent, wary, *Archaic.* ware; shrewd, *Inf.* cagey, scrupulous, guarded, stealthy; precautionary, *Inf.* go-slow, *Inf.* yellow-light; watchful, vigilant, sleepless, wakeful. See **careful** (*def.* **1**).

cavalcade, *n.* procession, parade, array, spectacle; train, caravan, company, troop, retinue, cortege; file, column, march.

cavalier, *n.* **1.** horseman, knight, horse soldier, trooper, dragoon, lancer, hussar, cavalryman.

2. gentleman, gallant, man about town, blood, young blood, blade, beau, dandy, playboy.

—adj. **3.** haughty, disdainful, supercilious; proud, arrogant, contemptuous, patronizing, condescending, imperious, *Sl.* cocky.

4. offhand, *Inf.* flip, unceremonious, careless, casual, nonchalant, perfunctory, indifferent, blasé.

cavalry, *n.* mounted troops, horse, troopers, dragoons, lancers, hussars; mounted rifles, squadron, horse soldiers, horse marines.

cave, *n.* cavern, grotto, hollow, cavity; underground chamber, subterrane, den, dugout, tunnel, subway, cellar.

caveat, *n.* warning, caution, admonition, monition; forewarning, alarm, *Inf.* yellow light, *Inf.* red flag.

cavern, *n.* cave, grotto, subterrane. See **cave.**

cavernous, *adj.* **1.** deep-set, hollow, sunken, yawning, retreating, abysmal; concave, depressed, hollowed out, indented; pitted, crannied, furrowed, honeycombed, rimous, faveolate, alveolate.

2. hollow-sounding, rumbling, sepulchral; resonant, deep-toned, deep, reverberating, echoing, booming, thunderous.

cavil, *n.* **1.** carp, complain, quibble, pettifog, pull to pieces, *Sl.* nitpick; nag, pick on *or* at, fuss, *Inf.* hassle; jibe at, criticize, find fault, make mountains out of molehills; belittle, deprecate, disparage, impugn, decry, *Sl.* grouse, *Sl.* moan and groan; blame, chide, reproach, censure, rebuke, reprove, sneer at, discredit, animadvert.

—n. **2.** objection, criticism, *Inf.* brickbat; quibble, subtlety.

cavity, *n.* hole, hollow, cave, cavern; crater, cup, scoop, concavity; pit, shaft, chamber, mine, bore, tunnel, excavation; abyss, crevasse; opening, aperture, orifice, fissure, crack, cleft, chink, notch, gap.

cavort, *v.* prance, caper, frolic, romp, gambol; skip, hop, dance about; leap, jump, bounce, bound; hop, bob, trip, whirl, turn, caracole.

cease, *v.* **1.** stop, discontinue, desist, *Archaic.* surcease, quit, end, leave off, come to an end, finish, conclude, terminate; break off, pause, intermit, suspend, rest; take a break, take a breather; abate, lessen, lull, quiet down, let up, come to a halt *or* standstill.

2. put a stop to, halt, terminate, put an end to; check, quell, silence, suppress, *Archaic.* stanch; abandon, leave behind, drop, withdraw from, refrain from, abstain from, give up, forbear; bring to an end, complete, consummate.

—n. **3.** cessation, suspension, intermission, pause, letup. See **cessation.**

ceaseless, *adj.* **1.** unending, endless, never-ending, interminable, Sisyphean; eternal, perpetual, everlasting, lasting, enduring, perennial, permanent.

2. incessant, unceasing, nonstop, constant, uninterrupted, continual, continuous, unbroken; unremitting, unintermitting, relentless, persistent; recurrent, repeated, frequent, habitual.

3. untiring, indefatigable, unwearied, never-failing, unwavering, unfaltering, undiminished; invariable, fixed, stable, steady.

cede, *v.* yield, surrender, deliver up, turn over, part with; release, let go of, quit one's hold on, yield possession of; relinquish, renounce, forsake; transfer, give over, convey, make over, sign away, *Law.* demise; grant, give, donate, bequeath, tender, render.

ceiling, *n.* **1.** topside, upper side, roof, *Archit.* dome; cover, covering, covert, lid, top.

2. top limit, maximum, *Inf.* lid; limitation, restriction.

celebrate, *v.* **1.** observe, honor, keep, commemorate, memorialize, ceremonialize, solemnize, ritualize; consecrate, dedicate, hallow, make sacred, sanctify.

2. proclaim, herald, trumpet, ballyhoo, beat the drum; announce, make known, spread the word, broadcast, publicize, advertise, promulgate, *Sl.* hype.

3. praise, laud, eulogize, exalt, glorify; reverence, venerate, revere, adore, worship, crown, bless, pay homage *or* tribute to, honor; belaud, extol, *Archaic.* magnify, make much of, *Inf.* crack up; lionize, puff, swell, inflate, bloat, enlarge; hail, acclaim, cheer, congratulate, applaud; compliment, flatter, *Inf.* pat on the back, hand it to [s.o.], give [s.o.] credit.

4. paint the town red, *Inf.* go out on the town, *Inf.* do the town, *Inf.* kick up one's heels, make merry, *Inf.* raise the roof, *Sl.* whoop it up, *Sl.* party.

celebrated, *adj.* famous, famed, renowned, well-known, prominent, *Inf.* big-name; respected, venerable, distinguished, *Fr.* *distingué*, eminent, preeminent, notable, noted; illustrious, great, glorious, radiant, lustrous; honored, exalted, acclaimed, much touted, popular, well-liked; immortal, fabled, legendary, historical.

celebration, *n.* **1.** observance, keeping, honoring; ceremony, ceremonial, rite, ritual, procedure, formalities; remembrance, commemoration, memorialization, solemnization, ritualization; consecration, dedication, hallowing, sanctification.

2. holiday, religious feast day, holy day; event, occasion, red-letter day, birthday, anniversary, jubilee; festivity, festival, fête, carnival; party, gala, ball, dance, cotillion, extravaganza, happening, *Inf.* shindig, *Sl.* wing-ding, *Sl.* bash; gaieties, merrymaking, jollification, frolic, spree; revelry, saturnalia, carousal, Bacchanalia, bacchanal, wassail.

celebrity, *n.* **1.** personage, notable, dignitary, *Inf.* bigwig, *Sl.* big shot, *Sl.* biggie, *Sl.* big gun, *Sl.* big wheel, magnate; *Sl.* big cheese, *Fr.* *grand fromage, Sl.* fat cat, *Sl.* heavy, *Sl.* high-muck-a-muck; *Sl.* celeb, luminary, somebody, name, *Inf.* big name, lion; star, hero, superstar, toast of the town.

2. fame, renown, high repute, distinction, note, prominence. See **fame.**

celerity, *n.* **1.** swiftness, speed, rapidity, fastness, quickness, fleetness; hurry, haste, hastiness, precipitance; acceleration, velocity, pace.

2. dispatch, promptness, expedition; alacrity, briskness, sprightliness, spryness, liveliness; animation, vivacity, vim, vigor, bustle; ebullience, effervescence, spiritedness, go.

celestial, *adj.* **1.** heavenly, divine, godly, sublime, supernal, supernatural; ethereal, paradisiacal, Elysian, Arcadian, Olympian, utopian; angelic, seraphic, cherubic, saintly, blessed, blest, holy, hallowed; majestic, splendorous, blissful, glorious, golden, ambrosial.

2. astronomical, uranic, nebular, empyrean, empyreal; extraterrestrial, supramundane, extramundane, ultramundane, unworldly, unearthly; solar, heliacal, heliac, astral, sidereal, stellar, sphery, starry; planetary, asteroidal, lunar, selenological.

celibacy, *n.* **1.** (*all in reference to sexual relations*) continence, abstinence, self-restraint, asceticism, self-abnegation, self-denial; chastity, virginity, virtue, purity.

2. singleness, bachelorhood, spinsterhood, *Euph.* single blessedness; religious life, monasticism, priesthood, sisterhood, nunhood.

celibate, *adj.* **1.** single, unmarried, unwed, spouseless, wifeless, husbandless.

2. (*all in reference to sexual relations*) abstinent, continent, abstemious, restrained, self-disciplined, ascetic, austere.

3. chaste, pure, immaculate, virtuous, undefiled, virginal, unsullied, untouched, *Archaic.* honest.

—*n.* **4.** virgin, maid, maiden, spinster; bachelor, misogamist, misogynist.

5. priest, monk, brother, nun, sister.

cell, *n.* room, chamber, compartment, apartment, cabin; cubicle, stall, booth, berth, cubbyhole, *Brit.* snuggery; nook, recess, closet, hole in the wall, hole, cavity; cloister, hermitage, asylum, retreat; cage, enclosure, lockup, place of confinement, *Sl.* coop.

cellar, *n.* basement, vault, crypt, subbasement; downstairs, underground, *Chiefly Brit.* below stairs; storeroom, buttery, larder, cellerage.

cement, *v.* **1.** glue, paste, mortar, solder, braze, gum *or* stick together; bond, bind, join, fix, affix, unite, seal.

2. pave, concrete, asphalt, macadamize, plaster, stucco, parget; overlay, overspread, cover.

3. adhere, cohere, stick, hold, cling, cleave, take; congeal, harden, set.

cemetery, *n.* graveyard, burial ground *or* place, necropolis, golgotha, *Western U.S.* boot hill; churchyard, potter's field, memorial park, God's acre; charnel house, ossuary, (*of animals*) boneyard.

censor, *n.* **1.** examiner, reader, inspector, reviewer; expurgator, bowdlerizer, abridger, amender; Mrs. Grundy.

2. faultfinder, critic, criticaster, *Inf.* knocker; carper, complainer, caviler; castigator, chastiser, censurer, reprimander, chider, scold, scolder; denouncer, objurgator, berater; detractor, slanderer, backbiter, muckraker, defamer, libeler; calumniator, vituperator, vilifier, vilipender, reviler; abuser, traducer, disparager, depreciator, maligner; decrier, belittler, discreditor.

—*v.* **3.** examine, read, review, inspect; expurgate, bowdlerize, refine, purge; cut, delete, abridge, amend, edit.

censorious, *adj.* critical, faultfinding, captious, carping; complaining, animadversional, nagging, hair-splitting, querulous, caviling; caustic, biting, vitriolic, cutting, trenchant, severe; disparaging, berating, derogatory, disapproving, disapprobatory, hypercritical; objurgatory, denunciatory, fulminatory; condemnatory, comminatory, incriminatory, accusatory, damnatory; upbraiding, scolding, abusive; reproachful, censuring, reproving; vituperative, vilifying, invective, vilipending, blackening, opprobrious; calumniatory, scurrilous, defamatory, slanderous; maligning, aspersive, malicious, virulent.

censurable, *adj.* reproachable, reprovable, rebukable, impeachable, condemnable, damnable; reprehensible, blameworthy, guilty, culpable, faulty, at fault, imputable; answerable, chargeable, blamable, accountable, amenable; wrongful, wrong, amiss; discreditable, disgraceful, objectionable; uncommendable, illaudable.

censure, *n.* **1.** disapproval, disapprobation, reprobation, reprehension, objection; fulmination, denunciation, condemnation; criticism, animadversion, *Inf.* brickbat, aspersion, obloquy; tirade, philippic, diatribe.

2. reproof, reproach, rebuke, reprimand, stricture; upbraiding, castigation, objurgation, vituperation; scolding, dressing down, tongue-lashing, *Sl.* hell.

3. blame, accusation, accusal, charge; imputation, incrimination, crimination, inculpation.

—*v.* **4.** blame, accuse, charge, incriminate, criminate, inculpate.

5. criticize, arraign, animadvert on *or* upon, reprobate, condemn, denounce, denunciate, remonstrate, proscribe; decry, inveigh against, rail against, fulminate against, declaim against, attack; disapprove, deprecate, disparage, belittle.

6. upbraid, reproach, reprove, rebuke, reprehend; castigate, vituperate, reprimand, admonish; chide, scold, carp at, berate, *Inf.* take to task, *Inf.* call on the carpet, *Inf.* dress down; *All Sl.* blast, bawl out, yell at, give [s.o.] hell, lay [s.o.] out in lavender, read the riot act.

census, *n.* enumeration, poll, tally, count, head count, tabulation; statistics, figures, listing, statement; demography.

centenary, *adj.* **1.** hundredth, centurial; centuple, hundredfold.

—*n.* **2.** centennial, hundredth anniversary.

3. century, hundred years.

center, *n.* **1.** middle, middle point, navel, omphalos, midst; focus, focal point, focalization, point of concentration, point of convergence, cynosure; core, heart, marrow, gist, kernel, nucleus, crux; hub, nave, axis, pivot; *Biol.* centrosome.

—*v.* **2.** focus, focalize, bring into focus; converge, come together, unite, unify, meet; converge upon, centralize, concenter, concentrate, close on.

central, *adj.* **1.** middle, mid, median, medial, mesial, mean, intermediate, centric; midmost, middlemost, centermost.

2. internal, interior, inner, inside, inward, innermost; inland, midland.

3. pivotal, axial, key, focal; causal, basic, basal, fundamental; essential, indispensable, vital, *Inf.* gut.

4. cardinal, chief, main, principal, prime, primary, first, foremost, uppermost, paramount, most important.

centralization, *n.* **1.** consolidation, centralism, centering, focusing, focalization, concentration; convergence, confluence, congregation, aggregation.

2. unification, alliance, coalition, association, affiliation, confederation, federation; federalization, nationalization.

centralize, *v.* **1.** concentrate, concenter, converge, congregate, aggregate, come together, collect, gather; center, focus, focalize, consolidate, compact, streamline.

2. unify, unite, join, associate, affiliate, coalesce, ally, league, confederate, federate; federalize, nationalize.

centrifugal, *adj.* radial, radiating, outward, divergent, diverging, *Anat. and Physiol.* efferent.

century, *n.* **1.** centenary, one hundred years, ten decades; aeon, eternity, several lifetimes, five generations, what seems like forever.

2. period, era, age, time.

ceramics, *n.* pottery, earthenware, clay pots, crocks; porcelain, china, delft ware, stoneware, ironstone; tiles, mosaics.

cereal, *n.* **1.** grain, seed, kernal, meal, hominy,

Chiefly Southern U.S. grits; wheat, rye, oats, rice, corn, maize, barley, bran.

2. breakfast food, cold cereal, granola; oatmeal, *Trademark.* Cream of Wheat, farina, porridge, mush.

ceremonial, *adj.* **1.** formal, ritual, solemn, celebratory, triumphal, sacramental, ceremonious, commemorative; dignified, stately, imposing, impressive, lofty, august, majestic; conventional, customary, functional, ritualistic.

—n. **2.** rite, ritual, service, ceremony, observance; formality, duty, custom, practice, function; solemnity, sacrament, liturgy.

ceremonious, *adj.* **1.** ceremonial, formal, stately.

2. courteous, courtly, cavalier, polite; punctilious, exact, precise, just-so, particular, careful, scrupulous, fastidious, meticulous; correct, strict, rigid, stiff, rigorous, affected, fussy, finicky.

ceremony, *n.* **1.** rite, service, ceremonial. See **ceremonial** (*def.* **2**).

2. formalities, protocol, *Inf.* fuss, propriety, decorum, etiquette; conformity, conventionality, strictness, prescription; scrupulosity, nicety, punctilio.

certain, *adj.* **1.** confident, positive, sure; secure, free from doubt, believing, convinced, satisfied; assured, unshaken, unwavering, undeviating, *Inf.* cocksure.

2. destined, *Inf.* in the cards, bound to come, inevitable, inescapable, inexorable; *Inf.* in the bag.

3. unquestionable, indisputable, undeniable, evident, obvious, plain, clear, cogent; indubitable, incontestable, apodictic, irrefutable, incontrovertible; authoritative, beyond question, unequivocal, unqualified, absolute, conclusive, infallible, undisputed, unquestioned, past dispute; well-grounded, valid, unambiguous, unmistakable, irrefragable.

4. dependable, trustworthy, unfailing, reliable, *Inf.* foolproof, *Inf.* sure-fire; sound, steady, stable, solid, firm, fixed; constant, invariable, steadfast, changeless, unchanging, unaltering; settled, staid, unshakable, inviolate, unalterable.

5. agreed upon, definite, determined, predetermined.

6. special, specific, particular, express, precise, singular, especial, individual.

certainty, *n.* **1.** truth, fact, reality, actuality, factualness; conviction, belief, doubtlessness; reliance, assurance, confidence, trust, faith; unalterability, inexorability, unchangeability; inevitability, inescapableness, *Inf.* sure thing, *Sl.* cinch, *Sl.* shoo-in.

2. validity, conclusiveness, authoritativeness, unquestionableness, indisputability; absoluteness, infallibility, irrefutability, incontrovertibility, irrefragability, unimpeachability, incontestability; unequivocalness, indubitability.

certificate, *n.* **1.** document, testimonial, certification, *Law.* acknowledgment; statement, *Law.* affidavit, *Law.* deposition.

2. credential, diploma, *Inf.* sheepskin.

—v. **3.** document, depose, attest to, testify to, bear witness to, evidence, offer evidence for; confirm, verify, validate, authenticate, certify; corroborate, substantiate, support.

4. accredit, license, qualify, commission; authorize, warrant, legalize; sanction, approve of, give one's stamp *or* seal of approval, *Inf.* O.K.

certify, *v.* **1.** confirm, verify, validate, authenticate, testify to, attest to, certificate; corroborate, substantiate, sustain, uphold, support, prove, document, manifest, show, establish; depose, bear witness to, evidence, offer evidence for.

2. accredit, ratify, sanction, approve of, give one's stamp *or* seal of approval, pass judgment on, *Inf.* O.K.

3. assure, asseverate, avow, vow, give one's solemn word *or* promise, offer assurance, state on one's honor, pledge, swear to, state under oath, *Inf.* promise; avouch, affirm, assert, declare, state emphatically, say for certain *or* sure.

4. guarantee, warrant, insure, ensure, indemnify; endorse, vouch for, notarize, witness, underwrite, countersign, cosign for, back up, stand behind.

cessation, *n.* **1.** termination, ending, completion, finish, conclusion, close, desinence; discontinuance, breaking off, abruption; ceasing, stay, end, quitting, desisting, desistance; arrest, halt, stand, standstill, stoppage.

2. intermission, pause, cease, rest, break, *Inf.* breather, lull, respite, letup, recess, time out, leaving off; suspension, interruption, discontinuation, abeyance, remission.

cession, *n.* **1.** surrender, relinquishment, abnegation, abdication; transfer, transferal, transference, *Law.* conveyance; leasing, handing over, signing away, making over; release, quittance, acquittance, abandonment.

2. yielding, capitulation, submission; concession, conceding, acquiescence, compliance, agreement.

chafe, *v.* **1.** warm up, heat up, rub together, kindle, inflame.

2. wear, wear down *or* away, wear out, fray, ravel, unravel, shred, wear to shreds *or* pieces, tatter, *Inf.* frazzle, erode, waste away; abrade, rub, fret, rasp, grate, scratch, scrape, excoriate; scour, scrub.

3. irritate, rankle, exasperate, aggravate, exacerbate, rub the wrong way; annoy, vex, irk, peeve, gall, nettle, tease; harass, harry, ride, nag, get on one's back; plague, torture, torment, trouble; hector, pester, badger, *Archaic.* haggle, bother; disturb, agitate, shake, unsettle, ruffle, fluster, unnerve; pique, roil, rile, madden, anger, enrage, infuriate, inflame; arouse, excite, provoke, goad, spur, prod.

4. seethe, sizzle, simmer, foam, smoke, boil, burn; fume, rage, storm, rant, rave, go on, *Inf.* carry on; fret, fuss, make a fuss about *or* over, grumble, gripe, croak, complain, whine, *Inf.* grouse, *Inf.* stew, *Sl.* squawk, *Archaic.* pine, pout, frown, sulk, brood over *or* on, mope.

—n. **5.** irritation, aggravation, rub, vexation, torment, trouble, pain in the neck; annoyance, nuisance, bother, pest.

6. heat, hotness, caloric, warmth, warmness, burning; soreness, pain, ache, hurt; abrasion, rub, graze, scrape, scratch, sore; erosion, fret, fray, *Inf.* frazzle.

chaff¹, *n.* **1.** husks, shucks, hulls, glumes, pods, shells; cases, casings, outer coverings; peels, skins, rinds.

2. refuse, *Dial.* culch, rubbish, garbage, waste, *Brit.* wastrel, discarded matter; offal, carrion, rot, spoil; offscourings, dregs, draff, grounds, remains, leavings, leftovers; scraps, orts, hogwash, swill; remainder, residue, residuum, scum; scoria, dross, recrement, slag.

3. junk, worthless stuff, *Sl.* dreck, trumpery; trash, riffraff, *Brit. Dial.* raff, litter; filth, dirt, dust, sweepings; debris, detritus, rubble, stubble, wreckage; fragments, remnants, fag ends, bits and pieces, odds and ends; castoffs, rags, tatters, castaways, rejects, discards.

chaff², *v.* **1.** banter, josh, tease, twit, taunt, *Inf.* kid, *Inf.* ride, *Inf.* rail, *Inf.* rag; joke, jest, mock, make fun of, deride, ridicule good-naturedly; be playful *or* jocose, fool around, *Inf.* mess around, *Sl.* horse around, clown around.

—n. **2.** raillery, banter, bantering, badinage, persiflage; joshing, teasing, *Inf.* kidding, twitting, taunting; ribbing, *Inf.* riding, *Inf.* railing, *Inf.* ragging; joking,

jesting, mockery, good-natured ridicule; jocosity, jocoseness, jocularity, waggishness, waggery, drollery; levity, frivolity, frivolousness, giddiness, silliness, light-heartedness; humor, wit, witticism; repartee, quip, sally, *Inf.* wisecrack, clever *or* smart remark.

chagrin, *n.* **1.** vexation, annoyance, irritation, aggravation, perturbation, dismay; bitterness, resentment, chafing, rankling, smarting; bother, fret, worry, care, disquiet.

2. disappointment, frustration, sadness, sorrow, grief; unhappiness, depression, dejection, gloom, prostration, despondency.

3. humiliation, shame, mortification, abasement; embarrassment, discomposure, discomfiture, disconcertion.

—*v.* **4.** vex, annoy, irritate, irk, dismay, perturb, aggravate, exasperate, bother, chafe, rankle, ruffle, nettle.

5. disappoint, sadden, grieve; frustrate, thwart.

6. humiliate, shame, humble, mortify, abase, disgrace; embarrass, abash, disconcert.

chagrined, *adj.* vexed, annoyed, irritated, put out, irked, aggravated, exasperated, perturbed, dismayed, displeased, ruffled, nettled, bothered; disappointed, frustrated, dejected, downcast, sad, unhappy, despairing, desponding, despondent; humiliated, ashamed, embarrassed, mortified, disgraced, abashed, disconcerted, discomfited, nonplused.

chain, *n.* **1.** bond, binding, restraint, constraint, check, control; tie, interconnection, connection, joining; links, couplings, cable; fob, torque, catena; vinculum, nexus, copula.

2. **chains a.** bonds, fetters, shackles, manacles, handcuffs, trammels, bilboes, gyves. **b.** bondage, servitude, serfdom, helotry, slavery, enslavement; restraint, confinement, captivity, internment, detention, imprisonment, incarceration.

3. series, string, train, course, sequence; concatenation, succession, progression, range, file, line, row; procession, cavalcade, column, set, cycle.

—*v.* **4.** fasten, secure, lash, tie, string, bind, gird; enchain, shackle, manacle, handcuff, pinion, put in irons, fetter, tether, entrammel, gyve; hitch, make fast, moor, cable, belay, gird.

5. confine, restrain, encumber, restrict, limit, hamper, pin down, astrict; imprison, incarcerate, pen, cage, coop, entomb, immure.

chair, *n.* **1.** seat, bench, stool, sofa; armchair, fauteuil, Morris chair, easy chair, wing chair, rocking chair, *Inf.* rocker, Eames chair, (*in ancient Greece*) klismos; chairbed, chaise longue; wheelchair. See also **bench, stool, sofa, seat.**

2. pew, box, loge, stall.

3. throne, dais, bench, cathedra, stool, faldstool, see, office, *Brit.* woolsack, *Anglo-Indian.* gaddi.

4. professorship, professorate, instructorship, tutorship, tutorage, *Brit.* readership, *Brit.* lectureship.

5. chairman, chairwoman, chairlady, chairperson; presiding officer, speaker, leader, facilitator, moderator; toastmaster, master of ceremonies, *Inf.* emcee, *Inf.* M.C.

6. electric chair, *Sl.* hot seat, death seat; electrocution, execution.

—*v.* **7.** seat, install, swear in. See **seat** (*def.* 7).

8. (*usu. of meetings*) preside, moderate, lead, facilitate, direct, control, manage, oversee, supervise, govern; order, organize, co-ordinate; emcee.

chairman, *n.* chair, speaker; chairwoman, chairlady, chairperson; moderator, facilitator, leader, toastmaster, master of ceremonies, *Inf.* emcee; governor, executive, director, supervisor, manager, administrator.

chalk, *n.* **1.** blackboard crayon, marker, pastel, crayon, pencil.

—*v.* **2.** whiten, calcimine, whitewash; make pale, bleach, blanch, etiolate.

3. **chalk up to** ascribe, accredit, attribute, put down; lay, charge, impute.

chalky, *adj.* **1.** colorless, pale, pasty, wan, pallid, waxen, sallow, ashen, ghastly; blanched, bleached, milky, milk-white; white, albescent, snowy, niveous, marmoreal.

2. cretaceous, powdery, crumbly, pulverous, dusty, flaky, pulverulent; comminuted, triturable.

challenge, *n.* **1.** call, summons, invitation, bidding; notice, nod, beck, bid.

2. provocation, dare, gauntlet, glove, gage; confrontation, ultimatum, defiance, scorn, affront; menace, attack, countercharge, stand, opposition.

3. question, charge, allegation, imputation, denouncement; complaint, protest, objection, exception, disputation, dissension; expostulation, remonstration, reproach, contradiction, denunciation.

4. venture, hazard, risk; problem, puzzle, knot, perplexity, poser; obstacle, frustration, barrier, strait, crisis, *Inf.* tough job, *Inf.* hard row to hoe, *Inf.* hard nut to crack.

—*v.* **5.** dare, defy, brave, confront, encounter; face, affront, stand up to; accost, beard, breast, throw down the gauntlet; scorn, *Inf.* snap the fingers at.

6. call to question, question, dispute, protest, take exception, disagree, demur, object, dissent; retort, remonstrate, contradict, denounce, oppose, fulminate.

7. invite, arouse, stimulate, inspire; excite, spur on, goad, invigorate, jog, fan, propel.

chamber, *n.* **1.** room, apartment, stall, cabin, berth; bedroom, bedchamber, boudoir, dormitory, *Inf.* dorm; salon, drawing room, parlor, sitting *or* living room.

2. cell, cubicle, compartment, cubbyhole, *Brit.* snuggery; retreat, sanctum, cloister, study; nook, recess, closet, hole in the wall, cavity.

3. congress, diet, synod, soviet, divan, council; court, tribunal, judicature.

chameleon, *n.* fence-sitter, tergiversator, time-server, temporizer, trimmer, weathercock; quick-change artist, Proteus; *Inf.* all things to all people.

champ, *v.* **1.** bite, gnaw, grind, gnash; munch, chew, crunch, masticate, ruminate.

2. **champ at the bit** chafe, fret, fuss, fidget, squirm, be unable to sit still, pull at the leash, *Sl.* have ants in one's pants.

champion, *n.* **1.** winner, victor, leader, *Inf.* champ, *Inf.* shoo-in; conqueror, vanquisher, subjugator, subduer; avenger, vindicator, hero, paladin, knight.

2. defender, protector, guardian, friend in deed; helper, aider, abettor, protagonist, friend at court; supporter, upholder, maintainer, sustainer, advocate, backer, patron.

3. fighter, warrior, brave, man-of-arms, campaigner, veteran, old soldier.

—*v.* **4.** defend, protect, guard; help, aid, assist, speak for, fight for, stand up for; advocate, maintain, sustain, uphold, support, back, second; avenge, vindicate.

chance, *n.* **1.** fortuity, serendipity, happenstance, mere chance, happy chance; luck, Lady Luck, fortune *or* Fortune, Lady *or* Dame Fortune, wheels of fortune *or* chance, heads or tails, roll, *Inf.* cast *or* toss *or* throw of the dice; accident, coincidence, contingency, contingence; vicissitudes, ups and downs, fickle finger of fate, fate, way things fall, *Inf.* the breaks, *Inf.* how the cookie crumbles, *Inf.* how the ball bounces.

2. causelessness, purposelessness, randomness; unaccountability, unaccountableness, indemonstrability, unconfirmability; uncertainty, incertitude; unpredictability, unpredictableness, unforeseeableness; changeableness, capriciousness, fickleness; predestination, kismet, God's will, stars, planets.

3. prospect, possibility, the realm of possibility, conceivability, conceivableness; probability, probableness, likelihood, likeliness, liability.

4. opportunity, opening; time, occasion, turn, round, *Inf.* shot; sporting chance; advantage, good time, good chance, good opportunity; odds-on, sure bet, *Inf.* sure thing, golden opportunity.

5. risk, hazard, gamble; speculation, venture, *Inf.* flier, *Inf.* plunge, *Sl.* whack, *Sl.* crack; potshot, random shot, leap *or* shot in the dark, pig in a poke; potluck, blind bargain, sight-unseen transaction.

6. **by chance** accidentally, unintentionally, undesignedly, without design, by accident, by mistake; inadvertently, involuntarily, unwittingly, unthinkingly, unconsciously; randomly, haphazardly, casually, incidentally, unpredictably, whichever way the wind blows; luckily, fortuitously, as it chanced, as luck would have it, by a piece of luck, by a fluke, by good fortune *or* a piece of good fortune.

—v. **7.** occur, transpire, happen, hap, come, come about, come to pass, come off, *Sl.* come down, take place, betide; befall, fall, fall to one's lot, *Archaic.* bechance; result, come to, eventuate; turn up, crop up, *Inf.* show up, *Inf.* pop up.

8. *Informal.* risk, hazard, gamble; speculate, venture, *Inf.* plunge, *Inf.* go out on a limb; dare, jeopardize, tempt fortune, take *or* run the risk *or* hazard *or* chance; take a chance, try one's luck *or* fortune; leave *or* trust to chance, take a leap *or* shot in the dark.

9. **chance on** *or* **upon** happen upon, come on *or* upon, come across, stumble on *or* upon, hit upon, find; encounter, meet, meet with, run across, run into, cross the path of, *Inf.* meet up with, *Inf.* come *or* run up against, *Inf.* bump into, *Inf.* run smack into.

—adj. **10.** random, haphazard, casual, arbitrary, hit-or-miss; fortuitous, serendipitous, aleatory, unpredictable, *Inf.* fluky; unexpected, unanticipated, unforeseen, unlooked-for; accidental, unintentional, unintended, unpremeditated, undesigned, unplanned, uncalculated; indeliberate, inadvertent, involuntary; incidental, occasional, contingent, adventitious.

chandelier, *n.* luster, corona, light fixture, gasolier, electrolier; candelabrum, candlestick, candleholder, sconce.

change, *v.* **1.** substitute, shuffle, alternate, diversify, variegate; exchange, interchange, commute, switch, replace; bandy, barter, trade, swap.

2. alter, modify, permute, modulate, inflect, mutate; convert, transform, metamorphose, transfigure, transmute, transubstantiate, transmogrify; translate, transpose, metathesize; revolutionize, transshape, remodel, recast, reconstruct, restyle; shift, reorganize, reorder, permutate; distort, warp, bend, twist, denature, disguise.

3. vary, fluctuate, vacillate, tergiversate, *Inf.* blow hot and cold; reverse, turn, swerve, *Inf.* whistle *or* sing a different tune, *Inf.* be on the other side of the fence, *Sl.* do an about-face, *Sl.* do a 180°; move, evolve, grow, improve, better, reform; worsen, deteriorate, decline.

—n. **4.** alteration, modification, permutation, modulation, inflection, mutation; conversion, transformation, metamorphosis, evolution, transfiguration, transmutation, transubstantiation, transmogrification; translation, transposition, metathesis, transition; revolution, innovation, novelty, new idea *or* thing.

5. variation, fluctuation, vacillation, vicissitude; reversal, turnaround, turnabout, *Inf.* flipflop, *Sl.* a 180°, about-face; movement, growth, improvement, betterment, reformation; worsening, deterioration, decline.

6. coins, silver, pocket money, pin money, petty cash, *Sl.* smash.

changeable, *adj.* **1.** variable, protean, chameleonlike, chameleonic, changing, changeful; diversified, variegated, checkered, many-sided, many-faceted; inconstant, unsteady, unstable, uneven, irregular, unreliable, undependable; vacillatory, vacillant, vicissitudinary, vicissitudinous, fluctuant, varying, shilly-shallying; wavering, uncertain, unsure, indecisive, irresolute; fickle, skittish, faddish, flighty, mercurial, capricious, blowing hot and cold, lightsome.

2. alterable, modifiable, permutable, mutable, transformable, transmutable; commutative, substitutive, exchangeable, interchangeable, convertible, reversible.

changeless, *adj.* **1.** immutable, unchangeable, invariable, unalterable, incommutable, irreversible, inflexible; undeviating, unfaltering, unwavering, steadfast, steady, reliable, dependable; firm, fast, fixed, constant, durable, solid, stable, permanent.

2. enduring, abiding, lasting, persisting; indestructible, imperishable, perdurable, inextinguishable, indissoluble; perpetual, unfading, incorruptible, undecaying, amaranthine, perennial, *Bot.* (*of leaves*) indeciduous, (*of trees*) evergreen; deathless, undying, immortal, eternal, *Archaic.* eterne, everlasting.

channel, *n.* **1.** stream bed, floor, bottom, depths, basin.

2. strait, neck, narrows, fiord; estuary, inlet, lagoon, cove, *Naut.* roads; bight, bay, gulf, sound; watercourse, waterway, canal, creek, run; water gap, flume.

3. furrow, groove, rut, chase, ditch, dike, fosse, gully; gulch, ravine, *Western North Amer.* coulee, chasm, crevice, anfractuosity; conduit, culvert, *Civ. Eng.* aqueduct, duct, tube, pipe; trough, gutter, sluice, chute, shaft; trench, moat.

4. course, way, path, trail, approach; avenue, lane, road, route; artery, passage, passageway, pass, cut, fairway, runway; aisle, corridor.

—v. **5.** groove, furrow, flute, plow; trench, tunnel, burrow, hollow out, excavate, carve, cut.

6. convey, lead, conduct; aim, direct, guide.

chant, *n.* **1.** song, singing, melody, chanson, lied; carol, madrigal, glee, serenade, serenata, *Music.* cantata; spiritual, dirge, ballad; monody, homophony; aria, *Music.* arietta, chantey, *Music.* descant; lullaby, *Music.* berceuse; duet, *All Music.* catch, rondo, round, troll, movement.

2. tune, air, ditty, *Music.* cavatina, *Music.* cantilena, simple melody.

3. psalm, canticle, hymn, carol, spiritual, dirge, solemn *or* sacred song; Gregorian chant, plainsong, plainchant.

4. monotone, single tone, unvaried pitch, uniformity of tone.

—v. **5.** sing, chorus, choir, vocalize, *Music.* descant; carol, melodize, serenade; hum, croon, lullaby; lilt, troll, trill, warble, quaver, yodel, sing tremulously.

6. intone, cantillate, descant, *Archaic.* deacon, to sing a chant; psalm, hymn, sing hymns, carol.

chaos, *n.* confusion, disorder, upset; disunion, discord, disquiet, unrest, ferment, upheaval, storm; turmoil, tumult, tempest, broil, brawl, fray, row, struggle; clamor, uproar, hubbub, hullabaloo, din, commotion, flurry, *Inf.* to-do, disturbance, disruption; anarchy, pandemonium, bedlam, brouhaha, free-for-all, fracas, rumpus, scramble, scuffle, *Inf.* ruckus; bustle, hurry-scurry, ado, fuss, excitement, agitation; muddle, huddle, mess, tumble, jumble, litter, clutter, imbroglio, disarray, disarrangement.

chaotic, *adj.* **1.** confused, disordered, jumbled, muddled, harum-scarum, topsy-turvy, pell-mell; upset, scattered, askew, awry; desultory, disconnected, unordered, random; disorganized, unplanned, undirected, haphazard, unsystematic, unmethodical; formless, shapeless, aimless, purposeless, absurd; careless, slipshod, sloppy, untidy; littered, mussed, disordered, disarranged, hugger-mugger.

2. clamorous, uproarious, tumultuous, tumultuary, tempestuous; unrestrained, uncontrolled, unruly, boisterous, rampageous, wild, frantic, riotous, anarchal, lawless, orderless; unquiet, stirred-up, restless, agitated, hectic, frenzied, fermenting; seething, raging, turbulent, stormy.

chap, *v.* **1.** redden, roughen, chafe, make raw; split, cleave, crack, break, cut, open.

—n. **2.** crack, fissure, chink, cleft, rift, cranny, cavity; cut, slit, rent, split, break.

chapel, *n.* oratory, chantry, sacellum; church, house of God, place of worship.

chaperon, *n.* **1.** escort, matron, (*in Spain and Portugal*) duenna; guardian, shepherd, protector, protectress, tutelary, tutelar, houseparent, housemother, housefather, tutor, tutoress, governess, nursemaid; accompanier, companion, attendant.

2. headdress, turban, cap, hat.

—v. **3.** escort, accompany, companion, attend, go along with; guard, matronize, protect, shelter, shepherd, watch over, keep an eye on.

chaplain, *n.* priest, father, minister, rabbi, padre, *U.S. Mil. Sl.* sky pilot, *U.S. Mil. Sl.* Holy Joe; presbyter, residentiary; pastor, rector, vicar, parson, *Dial.* dominie, curate, curé, abbé; clergyman, cleric, ecclesiastic, churchman, reverend.

chapter, *n.* **1.** division, subdivision, branch, department; part, portion, section; clause, article, passage.

2. phase, stage, period, age, era, time; episode, occurrence, event, happening.

3. council, assembly, convocation, convention, conclave, synod, consistory; body, group, company, troop, troupe; gathering, assemblage, grouping, cluster, arrangement.

char, *v.* burn, cauterize, scorch, toast; carbonize, reduce to charcoal; fire, cremate, incinerate; sear, singe, scald, parch, roast, torrefy; calcine, oxidize, oxidate; scorify.

character, *n.* **1.** personality, individuality, ego; nature, disposition, temperament, temper, complexion; genius, idiosyncrasy; essential quality, *Hinduism, Buddhism.* dharma.

2. trait, feature, attribute, characteristic. See **characteristic.**

3. reputation, repute, status, standing, position, station, name; notability, note, glory, prestige, popular favor, éclat, fame, renown; distinction, esteem, regard, respect, worth, account.

4. integrity, honesty, honor; courage, strength, fortitude, backbone; respectability, rectitude, uprightness, morality, goodness; truthfulness, frankness, sincerity; conscientiousness, scrupulousness.

5. person, individual, being, human being, mortal, specimen, somebody, someone; man, woman.

6. eccentric, odd fellow, oddity, case, *Inf.* card, odd *or* queer fish, *Inf.* nut, *Inf.* poor soul. See **eccentric** (*def.* 5).

7. role, part, piece; portrayal, representation, characterization, personation, impersonation; actor, actress, dramatis persona.

8. insignia, ensign, sigil, signet, badge, crest, emblem; symbol, ideogram, sign, seal, mark, marker; trademark, idiograph, stamp, label, name, brand; notation, code, device; cipher, figures, numbers; letters, rune.

9. in character to be expected, as expected, as one might suspect *or* guess; just like one, one through and through; normal, proper, suitable.

10. out of character inappropriate, unfit, unsuitable; out of joint, out of tune; contrary to expectations.

characteristic, *adj.* **1.** typical, representative, indicative, illustrative, symptomatic, diagnostic; distinguishing, differentiative, distinctive, discriminative, diacritical; particular, specific, pointed, marked; special, unique, peculiar, singular; individualistic, individual, idiosyncratic; symbolic, emblematic.

—n. **2.** quality, nature, feature, attribute, property, trait; idiosyncrasy, idiocrasy, peculiarity, specialty, singularity, mannerism, quirk; personality, temperament, character, disposition; tendency, bias, leaning, propensity, proclivity, penchant, proneness, drift, predilection, predisposition, streak; complexion, tone, aspect, mood, cast, turn, bent, style; detail, particular, particularity, point, element, essential; badge, trademark, earmark, symptom, mark.

characterize, *v.* **1.** distinguish, specify, signalize, indicate; identify, show to be, define; label, tab, ticket, call; name, denote, designate, style; stamp, brand, put [s.o.] down as.

2. describe, portray, represent, depict, touch on; draw, sketch, paint, picture; analyze, evaluate, judge.

charge, *v.* **1.** fill, fill up, load, plug, pack, ram down, inject with; suffuse, pervade, permeate; spread over, overspread, overrun, saturate, diffuse; bathe, soak, steep; imbue, infuse, penetrate, interfuse.

2. command, bid, order, dictate, adjure, direct, *Obs.* conjure; ordain, decree, enact; prescribe, set, appoint; summon, beckon, invite, cite, call; enjoin, entreat, exhort, call upon, urge, incite, induce; require, demand, exact, requisition, *Brit. Mil.* indent.

3. impute, accuse, indict, arraign, impeach, cite, book; allege, assert, incriminate, implicate, criminate, point to, set down to, call to account; attribute, assign, ascribe, accredit, credit, invest with, chalk up to; refer, arrogate, appropriate, associate, connect with.

4. attack, assault, rush, storm, blitz; beset, beleaguer, besiege, siege; fall on, open fire on, pounce on, set upon, *Inf.* lace into, *Inf.* rip into, *Inf.* tear into; bombard, barrage, broadside, *Sl.* zap, *Sl.* let [s.o.] have it, *Sl.* lay into, *Sl.* give it to.

5. load, weigh, weigh down, weight, lade, saddle with, place on; burden, tax, encumber, cumber, superpose; impede, hamper, hinder, handicap; strain, overload, overburden, overtask, overtax, overwhelm, overcharge.

6. load, freight, fill, stow; stuff, pile, heap, stack, pack, *Rare.* implete.

7. impose, ask, expect, fix a charge, ask a price, price; levy, assess, appraise; fine, tax, exact.

8. defer payment, bill, debit, put on one's check *or* bill *or* tab; buy now, pay later; buy on the lay-away *or* installment plan; take on credit, take on account.

—n. **9.** duty, responsibility, office, trust; obligation, bounden duty, liability; oath, word, commitment, promise, pact; mission, calling, assignment, business.

10. care, custody, wardship, protection, keep, keeping, safekeeping, safeguard; auspices, aegis, patronage; guardianship, tutelage, guidance, chaperonage; supervision, superintendence, surveillance, management, direction; jurisdiction, control, rule, administration.

11. ward, dependent, minor, protégé.

12. command, commandment, order, ordinance; injunction, mandate, dictate, will; instruction, prescription, direction, bid; behest, bidding, request, demand, requisition; summons, summoning, call, invitation; enjoining, exhortation, entreaty, urging, incitement, inducement.

13. accusation, allegation, *Law.* gravamen, *Scot. and North Eng.* threap; indictment, arraignment, *Law.* true bill; imputation, implication, inculpation, attribution, assignment, ascription; citation, summons, *Law.* plaint, *Law.* complaint; incrimination, recrimination, crimination, blaming.

14. expense, outlay, expenditure, disbursement; cost, fare, amount; worth, value, valuation, quotation, assessment, appraisal, appraisement.

15. fee, price, exaction, payment, rent, dues; levy, tax, toll, rate, tithe, capitation, poll tax; excise, impost, tariff, customs, surtax, tribute, duty, *Hist.* scot; truckage, wharfage, towage, freightage, tollage; commission, brokerage.

16. attack, assault, onset, onslaught; raid, sally, sortie, foray, invasion; siege, besiegement, offensive, aggression, incursion, investment; blitz, blitzkrieg, storming, *Obs.* brunt; bombardment, strafing, *Mil.* barrage, *Mil.* enfilade, *Navy.* broadside.

17. load, burden, bale, payload, wagonload, carload; cargo, freight, shipment, portage; weight, onus, cross, millstone, albatross; encumbrance, cumbrance, impediment, hindrance, drag, handicap; vexation, annoyance, nuisance, tribulation; tax, strain, pressure, stress; affliction, sorrow, grief, anguish.

chargeable, *adj.* **1.** liable, responsible, accountable, answerable, amenable; indictable, arraignable, impeachable, blamable, imputable, accusable.

2. imposable, taxable, leviable, exactable, inflictable; dutiable, tithable, rateable, assessable.

charger, *n.* war-horse, cavalry horse, trooper, *Literary.* courser, *Archaic.* destrier; mount, steed, palfrey, riding horse.

charily, *adv.* **1.** carefully, with care, cautiously, with caution, heedfully, mindfully, guardedly, circumspectly, *Scot.* cannily; warily, leerily, suspiciously, distrustfully, askance.

2. sparingly, frugally, economically, thriftily; prudently, judiciously, providently.

chariness, *n.* cautiousness, carefulness, heedfulness, mindfulness, guardedness, watchfulness, circumspection, alertness, vigilance; wariness, leeriness, apprehension, suspiciousness, distrustfulness; prudence, care, discretion, solicitude, providence, forethought, foresight.

charitable, *adj.* **1.** generous, liberal, unselfish, bountiful, bounteous, munificent; free, free-handed, openhanded, giving, magnanimous, big-hearted; philanthropic, humanitarian, eleemosynary, almsgiving, altruistic; ungrudging, unsparing.

2. kind, beneficent, benignant, benevolent, caritative, benign, open-hearted; kindly, lenient, considerate, tolerant, humane, understanding, sympathetic; mild, easy, soft, soft-hearted, tender, merciful, clement, compassionate, indulgent, permissive; accommodating, agreeable, amiable, helpful, obliging, willing, easy-to-please; good-natured, well-disposed, friendly, well-meaning, well-intentioned, good.

charity, *n.* **1.** generosity, liberality, liberalness, bounty, munificence, munificentness; unselfishness, freehandedness, open-handedness, magnanimousness, bigheartedness; philanthropy, humanitarianism, altruism, almsgiving, giving, donating, self-sacrifice; love of mankind, Christian love, agape, *Latin. caritas*; kindness, beneficence, goodness, favor, service, courtesy; benignancy, benignity, benevolence, humanity, good will, open-heartedness, kindliness, kind-heartedness.

2. leniency, indulgence, permissiveness, easiness; tolerance, understanding, sympathy, considerateness, thoughtfulness, consideration; compassion, compassionateness, forgiveness, mercy; clemency, mercifulness; tenderness, soft-heartedness, softness, gentleness, mildness.

3. benefaction, donation, alms, contribution, offering, offertory, oblation; present, gift, bestowal, largess; gratuity, dole, *Fr. pourboire,* douceur, tip; bonus, plus, extra, prize, award; benefit, boon, blessing, benediction; aid, assistance, help, succor; relief, comfort, solace; grant, subvention, honorarium, subsidy; devise, bequest, bequeathment, legacy.

charlatan, *n.* quack, quacksalver, *Archaic.* empiric, pretender, imposter, humbug, mountebank; fraud, fake, *Inf.* faker, hypocrite, pharisee, *Inf.* fourflusher; cheat, deceiver, swindler, confidence man, *Inf.* con man; trickster, *U.S.* chiseler, hoaxer, defrauder, cozener; beguiler, decoy, allurer.

charm, *n.* **1.** attractiveness, appeal, allure, allurement, desirability, desirableness; pleasingness, engagingness, delightfulness, pleasantness, harmony, harmoniousness; beauty, beautifulness, pulchritude, loveliness, prettiness, comeliness; grace, gracefulness, elegance, refinement.

2. charms attractiveness, engagingness, appeal, allure, allurement; draw, pull, magnetism, irresistable attraction; beguilement, wiles, cajolery, blandishment, inducement, persuasion; enticement, lure, temptation, tantalization, seducement; bewitchment, enchantment, fascination, mesmerism, hypnotism, captivation.

3. trinket, small ornament, bauble, bit of jewelry, bijou; trifle, bagatelle, souvenir, memento, keepsake, token.

4. amulet, periapt, talisman, fetish; icon, sacred object, phylactery, scarab; hex sign, voodoo doll, apotropaion; lucky piece, safeguard, rabbit's foot, wishbone, *Ornith.* furcula, horseshoe.

5. chanting, chant, invocation, conjuration, conjuring, summoning, summons; magic formula, hocus-pocus, mumbo-jumbo, magic word, abracadabra, open-sesame, incantation.

—*v.* **6.** delight, please greatly, make happy, delectate; attract, appeal to, allure; draw, pull, engage; beguile, wile, cajole, blandish, coax, induce, persuade; entice, lure, tempt, tantalize, seduce; bewitch, enchant, fascinate, mesmerize, hypnotize, captivate.

charmer, *n.* **1.** enchanter, enchantress, bewitcher, beguiler, seducer, seductress, vamp, siren, temptress; ladies' man, lady-killer, Romeo, Valentino, Don Juan; con man *or* artist, smooth talker.

2. magician, *Archaic.* mage, wizard, witch, hex, warlock, sorcerer, sorceress, black magician, necromancer; conjurer, chanter, *Rare.* incantator, mesmerist, hypnotist, hypnotizer; exorcist, voodooist, theurgist.

3. miracle-worker, thaumaturge, medicine man, witch doctor, shaman, *Both Southern U.S. and West Indies.* root doctor, conjure man.

4. soothsayer, diviner, clairvoyant, prophet, prophetess; seer, fortuneteller, crystal-gazer, palmist, astrologer.

charming, *adj.* **1.** pleasing, delightful, delectable, enjoyable; attractive, appealing, *Inf.* fetching, *Inf.* eye-catching; winning, taking, engaging, winsome; sweet, agreeable, likeable; lovely, pretty, fair, handsome, prepossessing, beautiful, exquisite; graceful, elegant, refined.

2. enticing, alluring, tempting, tantalizing, titillating, thrilling; intriguing, diverting, beguiling, inducing, provocative, seductive, arousing; irresistible, magnetizing, electrifying, captivating, inflaming, enamoring; fascinating, catching, hypnotizing, mesmerizing; enchanting, bewitching, entrancing, enthralling, enrapturing, enravishing, transporting.

chart, *n.* **1.** graph, tabulation, table; diagram, blueprint, plan, scheme, outline, sketch, guide, map.
—*v.* **2.** graph, tabulate, draw, draw up, delineate; map out, chalk out; diagram, blueprint, plan, shape a plan, chart a course, steer, guide, pilot; draw up a scheme, outline, sketch, map, represent, picture.

charter, *n.* **1.** lease, permit, license, authority; franchise, concession.
2. covenant, agreement, contract, compact.
—*v.* **3.** establish, prescribe, ordain, constitute; grant, sanction, designate, commission, delegate, authorize; entitle, allot, assign, settle, license, legalize.
4. lease, hire, rent, engage.

chary, *adj.* **1.** careful, cautious, circumspect, mindful, heedful; guarded, on guard, alert, on the alert, on the qui vive, watchful; wary, leery, apprehensive, distrustful, suspicious, *Inf.* cagey.
2. shy, timid, bashful, self-conscious, skittish.
3. fastidious, particular, scrupulous, exacting, meticulous, punctilious, precise, difficult, hard to please; selective, fussy, finicky, picky, *Inf.* choosy.
4. frugal, thrifty, sparing, economical, conserving, unwasteful, *Scot.* canny.

chase, *v.* **1.** pursue, give chase, run after, fly after, follow after, make after, take off after, *Brit.* chevy; hound, dog, bedog; shadow, trail, haunt, *Inf.* tail; hunt, stalk, course, trace, track, run down.
2. suit, court, *Inf.* spark, *Inf.* court and spark, *Sl.* hustle, *Sl.* put *or* slap the make on, *Sl.* put a move on.
3. **chase out** run out, drive out, drive away, send away, send packing, put to flight.
—*n.* **4.** pursuit, hunt, hunting, sport, coursing, *Brit.* chevy, *Archaic.* venery.
5. game, quarry, prey, the hunted, kill.

chasm, *n.* **1.** gorge, canyon, ravine; void, abyss, cavity, hole, pit, bottomless pit; crevice, fissure, breach, break, rupture, fracture; cleft, split, rent, rift; gap, gulf, opening.
2. schism, separation, falling-out. See also **breach** (*def.* 3).

chassis, *n.* frame, framework, undercarriage, *Naut.* keel, skeleton.

chaste, *adj.* **1.** virtuous, good, innocent, modest; pure, *Archaic.* honest, virgin, virginal, vestal, maidenly, maidenish *or* maidish; untouched, undefiled, unused, uncorrupted, unadulterated, unsullied, unsoiled; pristine, fresh, clean, immaculate, snowy; spotless, unblemished, stainless, unstained, untainted, untarnished.
2. celibate, single, unmarried, unwed; spouseless, wifeless, husbandless, widowed.
3. continent, abstinent, abstemious, nonindulgent; self-restrained, self-controlled, reserved, self-disciplined, temperate, moderate, refraining, forbearing, desisting.
4. decent, clean, wholesome, pure; saintly, angelic, faultless, sinless; exemplary, meritorious, reputable, creditable; elevated, exalted, noble, honorable; moral, righteous, upright, right-minded, honest.
5. simple, subdued, unaffected, unpretentious; plain, unadorned, unornamented, unembellished, undecked, ungarnished, unenriched; neat, classic, elegant, attic; proper, prudish, seemly, tasteful, becoming; formal, decorous, sedate, strict, severe, precise; puritanical, puritan-like, austere, self-mortifying, self-depriving; ascetic, self-denying, self-abnegating.

chasten, *v.* **1.** discipline, correct, castigate; admonish, reprimand, reprove, scold, chide, criticize, censure, call down, call on the carpet, take [s.o.] to task, *Inf.* dress down, *Sl.* strafe, *Sl.* chew out, *Sl.* jump all over; objurgate, excoriate, upbraid, rebuke, flay, fulminate against, tongue-lash, lay [s.o.] out in lavender, *Inf.* jump down [s.o.'s] throat, *Archaic.* clapperclaw; punish, penalize, rap [s.o.'s] knuckles, slap [s.o.'s] wrists. See **chastise** (*def.* 1).
2. restrain, curb, check, stop, halt; subdue, tame, break, humble; temper, moderate, soften, tone down.
3. purify, refine, depurate; expurgate, purge, cleanse, deterge, *Med.* absterge; decontaminate, depollute, unsully.

chastise, *v.* **1.** spank, whip, thrash, flog, lash, switch, birch, scourge, flagellate, horsewhip, curry, strap, thresh, flail, cowhide, *Brit. Dial.* yerk, *Inf.* tan [s.o.'s] hide, *Inf.* trim, *Inf.* thump, *Inf.* lace, *Inf.* lambaste, *Inf.* whale, *Sl.* whomp, *Sl.* belt; beat, cuff, buffet, box, *Dial.* hit [s.o.] up side the head, *Inf.* whack, *Inf.* wallop, *Inf.* crown, *Inf.* give it to, *Sl.* knock around *or* about, *Sl.* give [s.o.] the business, *Sl.* give [s.o.] the works, *Sl.* give [s.o.] what for, *Sl.* let [s.o.] have it, *Sl.* lay into; fustigate, cudgel, bludgeon, baste, cane, bastinado.
2. discipline, correct, punish. See **chasten** (*def.* 1).

chastity, *n.* **1.** chasteness, virtue, virtuousness, goodness; innocence, innocency, modesty, *Rare.* pudicity; purity, pureness, untouchedness, uncorruptedness; freshness, cleanness, spotlessness, stainlessness, immaculacy, immaculateness.
2. celibacy, virginity, *Obs.* pucelage, maidenhood *or* maidhood; singleness, bachelorhood, spinsterhood, unmarried state, *Euph.* single blessedness.
3. continence, continency, abstinence, abstention, abstemiousness, nonindulgence; restraint, self-restraint, self-control; refrainment, refraining, forbearance, desistance.
4. Puritanism, austerity, self-mortification, self-deprivation; asceticism, self-denial, self-abnegation.

chat, *v.* **1.** talk, converse, palaver, *Inf.* rap, chitchat, coze, confabulate, chin, *Inf.* pass the time of day, *Inf.* beat one's gums, *Sl.* shoot the breeze *or* the bull, *Sl.* chew the fat *or* the rag, *Sl.* yak; chatter, clack, prattle, prat, rattle, babble; gossip, tittle-tattle, buzz.
—*n.* **2.** talk, conversation, palaver; tête-à-tête, coze, causerie, confabulation, *Inf.* confab, *Inf.* chin session, *Inf.* rap session; gossip, *Inf.* rap; chatter, prattle, clack, babble, rattle, *Brit.* natter.

chateau, *n.* **1.** castle, stronghold, fortress, citadel; keep, tower, donjon, hold.
2. palace, manor house, hall, mansion, country estate; vineyard estate, winery.

chattel, *n.* **1.** property, estate, estate and effects, holdings, possessions, what one has to one's name, what one can call one's own, *Law.* chose; movable, movable article; *Law.* acquest; *Law.* hereditament.
2. *Usu.* **chattels** belongings, personal belongings, effects, personal effects, personal estate, personal possessions, properties, *Inf.* things, *Sl.* stuff, *Sl.* junk; baggage, bag and baggage, gear, impedimenta, dunnage, luggage, kit, duffel; *All Law.* choses, choses in action *or* possession, choses transitory, personalty; paraphernalia, accouterments, appurtenances, appointments, appendages, accessories, trappings; goods, goods and chattels, movables, movable articles, furniture.
3. slave, bondsman, bondman, bond slave, chattel slave, indentured servant, servant, thrall, *Hist. or Archaic.* theow *or* thew; bondswoman, bondwoman, bondmaid.

chatter, *v.* **1.** jabber, prattle, cackle, gibber, *Sl.* gibber-jabber, jargon; babble, prate, tattle, twaddle, *Brit.* twattle; patter, gabble, blather, drivel; mutter, mumble, splutter, sputter, stammer; chit-chat, chitter-chatter, chaffer, bandy words; gossip, buzz, talk idly, *Sl.* shoot the breeze, *Sl.* gas, *Inf.* gab, *Sl.* bull; palaver, clack, clatter, rattle, *Sl.* run off *or* on at the mouth; gush, blab, *Inf.* spout; be loquacious *or* talkative, ramble, maunder.

—*n.* **2.** small talk, chit-chat, chitter-chatter, gossip, buzzing, *Inf.* gab, idle *or* foolish talk; palaver, *Sl.* hot air, *Sl.* gas, *Sl.* bull; nonsense, gibberish, jargon, gobbledegook, hocus-pocus, mumbo jumbo, abracadabra, open-sesame; humbug, flummery, *Sl.* bunk, rubbish, *Inf.* rot, *Sl.* garbage, *Sl.* horsefeathers; balderdash, hogwash, stuff and nonsense, *Inf.* bosh, fudge, foolishness, rigmarole *or* rigamarole; poppycock, *Inf.* fiddle-faddle, *Inf.* piffle, *Inf.* kibosh, *Inf.* flapdoodle.

3. chattering, jabbering, jabber, Jabberwocky; prattling, prattle, cackling, cackle, gibbering, gibber; babbling, babble, babblement, *Fr. bavardage*, rambling, maundering; prating, prate, tattling, tattle, twaddling, twaddle, *Both Brit.* twattling, twattle; pattering, patter, gabbling, gabble, blathering, blather, driveling, drivel; blab, blabbing, gushing, *Inf.* spouting, *Sl.* running off *or* on at the mouth.

chatterbox, *n.* excessive talker, jabberer, gabbler, blatherskite, *Sl.* windbag, *Sl.* windjammer, *Inf.* hot-air artist; blabber, blabbermouth, gusher, gossip; tattler, tattle-tale, tell-tale, talebearer; noisy chatterer, palaverer, magpie, popinjay, *Inf.* jay; prattler, babbler, prater, twaddler, *Brit.* twattler, driveler; patterer, patterist, rattlebrain, rattlepate.

chatterer, *n.* chatterbox, excessive talker, jabberer. See **chatterbox**.

chatty, *adj.* **1.** talkative, loquacious, voluble, garrulous, glib, wordy, *Inf.* gabby; effusive, bubbling, pattering, gushing; babbling, blathering, rambling; noisy, prattling, clacking, jabbering; buzzing, prating, tattling, tongue-wagging, *Sl.* windy.

2. friendly, cordial, warm, fond; companionable, amiable, affectionate; familiar, conversational, congenial, *Inf.* cozy, *Inf.* gossipy.

chauvinism, *n.* jingoism, partisanship, flag-waving, wrapping oneself in the flag, blind patriotism; machismo, male *or* female dominance *or* superiority; parochialism, provincialism, narrowness, ethnocentricity.

cheap, *adj.* **1.** inexpensive, reasonable, low-priced, moderately priced, economical; reduced, slashed, lowered, bargain *or* sale priced, marked down, discounted, cut-rate, wholesale, warehouse priced, priced to move, *Inf.* budget, *Inf.* bargain-basement.

2. mean, shabby, sorry, shoddy, tacky, tatty, schlock, *Sl.* rinky-dink, *Sl.* crummy, *Sl.* chintzy, *Sl.* cheesy; low, poor, indifferent, inferior, second-rate, gimcrack, *Inf.* dime-store, base, worthless, contemptible; meretricious, vulgar, trashy, tawdry, gaudy, sleazy.

3. stingy, niggardly, miserly, parsimonious, carking, skinflinty; penurious, mean, tight, tight-fisted, close-fisted; moneygrubbing, grasping, cheeseparing, scrimping, penny-pinching, grudging, begrudging, ungenerous, stinting; thrifty, frugal, sparing, chary; economical, prudent, saving, penny-wise, *Scot.* canny.

4. embarrassed, ashamed, humiliated, mortified; disconcerted, dismayed, abashed, uncomfortable, discomfited; degraded, low, dashed, crushed.

—*adv.* **5.** cheaply, inexpensively, reasonably; on sale, off the rack, at a discount, below cost, on clearance, *Inf.* for a song.

cheapen, *v.* **1.** lower, depreciate, drop in cost *or* value, reduce, discount, slash, cut, mark down, mark for clearance, *Inf.* budget-price; debase, adulterate, pollute, prostitute, demean.

2. belittle, humiliate, mortify, shame, disgrace, discredit; slight, scorn, misprize, spurn; detract from, pull to pieces, deprecate, decry, disparage, asperse, jibe at; vilify, calumniate, slander, traduce, malign, slur, brand, defame; satirize, lampoon, poke fun at, laugh at, mock, ridicule; scoff at, pooh-pooh, make light of.

cheat, *n.* **1.** cheater, swindler, fraud, confidence man, *Sl.* con man, *Sl.* flim-flam man, crook, chiseler; fake, phony, humbug, trickster, inveigler, bamboozler, dissembler, bluff, pettifogger; sharper, sharpie, shark, bilker, diddler; adventurer, rogue, picaroon, rascal, wolf in sheep's clothing, knave, deceiver, *Sl.* fourflusher; imposter, masquerader, pretender, mountebank, hypocrite, charlatan, *Inf.* quack.

2. cheating, fraud, swindle, confidence game, *Sl.* con game, *Sl.* flim-flam game, *Sl.* rip-off; deception, pretense, trick, hoax, imposture, artifice.

—*v.* **3.** swindle, defraud, fleece, rook, gull, *Archaic.* chouse; overcharge, *Sl.* soak, *Inf.* gyp, *Sl.* chisel, *Sl.* gaff, pluck, mulct; victimize, exploit, play on *or* upon, take advantage of, *Inf.* diddle, *Inf.* do, *Sl.* burn.

4. delude, deceive, beguile, mislead, hoodwink; pull the wool over [s.o.'s] eyes, cozen, bluff, take in, bamboozle, bilk, hornswoggle, cully, jockey, *Inf.* buffalo, *Inf.* finagle, *Sl.* con, *Sl.* flim-flam, *Sl.* flam, *Sl.* sting, *Sl.* put across; trick, spoof, outwit, overreach, circumvent, get around, put one over on.

5. plagiarize, crib, lift; rig, fix, throw; stack the deck, mark the cards, load the dice.

6. **cheat on** play around, fool around; deceive, betray, play false, be unfaithful *or* untrue to, cuckold, *Inf.* two-time.

check, *v.* **1.** stop, arrest, stay, stall, bring to a standstill; halt, pause, hesitate, balk, brake; put a stop *or* an end to, terminate, end, quash, quell, squash, *Inf.* put the kibosh on, nip in the bud; cut, cut back on, decrease, diminish, reduce, lessen, curtail, abridge.

2. restrain, hold back, control, limit, circumscribe, confine, restrict, *Law.* enjoin; hinder, hamper, block, obstruct, oppilate, inhibit; impede, retard, slow, handicap; curb, repress, constrain, contain, suppress, hold in, withhold; prevent, bar, debar, forbid, proscribe, *Law.* estop.

3. chain, fetter, shackle, hobble, trammel, bridle, rein, harness; choke, gag, muzzle, smother.

4. verify, corroborate, validate, authenticate, confirm, substantiate, support; investigate, research, *Archaic.* indagate, explore, survey, study; inquire into, probe, search into, look into; examine, inspect, test, scrutinize, peruse, look over.

5. **check out** *Informal.* take a look at, *Sl.* take a gander at, *Inf.* give [s.o.] the once-over; assess, *Inf.* size up.

6. correspond, agree, jibe, prove right, tally, check out; conform, harmonize, fall in with, dovetail.

7. **check up on** oversee, supervise, overlook, *Inf.* keep tabs on, monitor, regulate.

—*n.* **8.** stop, stay, prevention, preclusion, *Law.* estoppel; prohibition, forbiddance, disallowance, *Law.* injunction, *Law.* enjoinment; proscription, ban, embargo.

9. restraint, control, retardation, *Chem.* retardant; repression, inhibition, constraint; restriction, limitation, curb; damper, dampener, damp; bridle, bit, rein, checkrein, check line.

10. obstacle, deterrent, hindrance, impedient, trammel, balk; obstruction, oppilation, blockage, impediment, stopper; bar, barrier, barricade; block, stumbling block, catch, snag, hitch, drawback, liability;

dam, dike, retaining wall, wall, stone wall.
11. arrest, standstill, halt, stoppage; cessation, ceasing, discontinuation, discontinuance; suspension, abeyance; delay, holdover, deferment, deferral, postponement.
12. repulse, rebuff, rejection, setback, reverse, reversal; upset, checkmate, defeat, rout; impasse, dead end, stalemate, deadlock; difficulty, opposition, flak; disappointment, frustration, bafflement, nonplus.
13. test, test run, control test, trial, trial run, dry run, check-out; inspection, examination, exploration, search, probe, investigation; scrutiny, perusal, study, research, *Archaic.* indagation; verification, checkback, corroboration, validation, substantiation, authentication, confirmation.
14. criterion, standard, norm; measure, gauge, rule, yardstick; guideline, canon, principle; pattern, model, type, example, bench mark.
15. bill, tab; ticket, stub, receipt, scrip, coupon, token, tessera, *Chiefly Brit.* counterfoil; certificate, voucher, chit; label, *Brit.* docket; credentials, identification, ID, authorization, papers, pass.

checkered, *adj.* **1.** diverse, diversified, varied, versatile, many-sided.
2. variegated, multicolored, many-colored; checked, plaid, tartan.

checkmate, *n.* **1.** halt, stop, stoppage, arrest, check, stand, stay, *Chess.* mate; block, blockage, impasse; stalemate, deadlock, standstill, full stop, dead stop; stand-off, tie, draw, dead heat.
2. defeat, overthrow, rout, discomfiture; conquest, vanquishment, subjugation, victory, triumph, win; beating, drubbing, trouncing.
3. frustration, bafflement, thwarting, foiling; hindrance, obstruction, barrier, bar.
—*v.* **4.** rout, discomfit, trounce, drub, whip, crush, overwhelm, put to flight, floor, *Sl.* mop *or* wipe the floor with, *Inf.* make short work of; conquer, subjugate, vanquish, subdue, overpower, overthrow, master, overmaster; overcome, defeat, beat, worst, lick, win the day, prevail over, triumph over; outmaneuver, outgeneral, outwit, trump.
5. stop, arrest, check, *Chess.* mate; frustrate, foil, thwart, hinder, obstruct; ruin, spoil, upset, trip up.

cheek, *n.* **1.** jowl, chop, gill.
2. *Informal.* audacity, impudence, insolence. See **audacity** (*def.* **2**).
3. cheeks *Slang.* buttocks, rump, *Inf.* rear end. See **buttock.**
4. tongue in cheek facetiously, jokingly, jestingly, in jest, in fun, as a joke; mockingly, sarcastically, insincerely.

cheep, *v.* chirp, chirrup, peep, tweet, twitter, chatter; sing, carol, lilt.

cheer, *n.* **1.** shout, yell, hurrah, hurray, huzzah, rah.
2. encouragement, comfort, solace, consolation, relief; hopefulness, hope, faith, confidence, reassurance; inspiration, inspiritment, heartening, enheartenment, emboldening.
3. cheerfulness, gladness, gaiety, gayness; good *or* high spirits, blitheness, blithesomeness, light-heartedness, buoyancy, optimism, good nature; joy, sunshine, delight, pleasure, happiness, felicity, bliss; joyfulness, joyousness, jubilation, exhilaration, exultation, glee, elation; joviality, merriment, jollity, mirth, mirthfulness, hilarity; jubilance, jubilancy, rejoicing, jubilee, frolic, fun, enjoyment; revelry, revel, conviviality, festivity.
4. animation, liveliness, vivacity, vivaciousness, sprightliness; spirit, enthusiasm, exuberance, animal spirits; energy, life, vitality, vigor, vim, *Inf.* pep; ebullience, sparkle, effervescence, shine, glow.
—*v.* **5.** applaud, clap, salute; shout, yell, cry aloud, *Inf.* holler, root for; hurrah, hurray, huzzah.
6. cheer up be of good cheer, take heart, *Inf.* buck up, *U.S. Inf.* chirk; comfort, solace, make [s.o.] feel better, console, reassure; encourage, inspire, inspirit, *Inf.* pep up, buoy up, raise [s.o.'s] spirits, give [s.o.] a lift; gladden, hearten, enhearten, embolden; animate, vivify, quicken, vitalize, energize, enliven, brighten, invigorate, give new life to; fortify, strengthen, restore, revitalize, revivify, revive.
7. incite, stimulate, arouse, rouse up, awaken; fire, kindle, enkindle, stir, goad, spur on, prod, prick; push, egg on, urge, impel, exhort; boost, promote, prompt, *Inf.* spark, *Inf.* sparkplug, instigate, foment, provoke; excite, work up.

cheerful, *adj.* **1.** cheery, full of cheer, gay, sunny, in good *or* high spirits; blithe, blithesome, light-hearted, lightsome, buoyant, optimistic, positive, *Inf.* upbeat, beamish; debonair, free and easy, carefree, easygoing, breezy, airy, happy-go-lucky, untroubled; genial, convivial, amiable, good-natured, friendly; jovial, merry, jocund, jolly, mirthful, hilarious; riant, laughing, smiling, happy as a lark; joyful, joyous, jubilant, rejoicing, gleeful; exultant, in seventh heaven, elated, overjoyed, thrilled, exhilarated.
2. animated, alive, lively, *Chiefly U.S. Inf.* chipper, jaunty, vivacious, sprightly, fresh; spirited, dynamic, energetic, vigorous, active, spry; frisky, playful, frolicsome, sportive, zestful; enthusiastic, enthused, eager, excited; *Inf.* full of pep, *Inf.* peppy, full of vim and vigor, bright-eyed and bushy-tailed; aglow, glowing, flushed, alight, lit up, bright, enlivened, shining, shiny; sparkling, ebullient, bubbling, bubbly, effervescent; happy, glad, blissful, beatific, pleased, delighted, *Inf.* tickled pink.
3. hearty, ungrudging, generous, whole-hearted, heartfelt, genuine, sincere, earnest.

cheerfulness, *n.* cheer, good spirits, blitheness, gaiety, joyfulness, joyousness. See **cheer** (*defs.* **3, 4**).

cheering, *adj.* happy, good, pleasant, reassuring, comforting, encouraging, heartening, enheartening; promising, bright, sunny, auspicious, propitious, favorable; inspiring, inspiriting, revitalizing, revivifying, restoring; refreshing, stimulating, quickening, stirring, exciting.

cheerless, *adj.* **1.** gloomy, drab, dreary, dull, depressing, dismal; bleak, cold, comfortless, barren, grim, austere; desolate, lonely, deserted, empty, abandoned, uninviting; dark, somber, sunless, lightless, murky, dingy.
2. dejected, depressed, down, downcast, downhearted; disheartened, dispirited, discouraged, despondent, down in the mouth; sad, saddened, melancholy, sorrowful, plaintive, heavy-hearted; grievous, dolorous, doleful, mournful, rueful, lugubrious, funereal; morose, gloomy, saturnine, glum, joyless, sullen; unhappy, somber, solemn, grave, serious, tragic; miserable, wretched, woeful, woebegone, disconsolate, inconsolable; heartsick, heartsore, aching, grieving, mourning, lamenting, weeping, tearful, lachrymose; forlorn, hopeless, despairing, grief-stricken, afflicted, heartbroken, crushed.

cheery, *adj.* in good spirits, blithe, gay, cheerful, sunny. See **cheerful** (*defs.* **1, 2**).

chef, *n.* cook, food preparer; pastry chef, baker, confectioner; short-order cook, *Sl.* hash-slinger; gourmet, gastronome.

cherish, *v.* **1.** esteem, revere, venerate, idolize, idolatrize, adore; love, hold dear, fancy, dote on; hold, hold fast to, cling to, hang on to, cleave to, clasp.

2. harbor, shelter, support, defend, guard; aid, succor, foster, cultivate, sustain, preserve; nurse, care for, cradle, nurture, nourish, feed.

cherub, *n.* angel, seraph, *Fine Arts.* putto; innocent, darling; child, baby, babe, infant.

chest, *n.* **1.** thorax, front, breast; bust, bosom. See also **bosom** (*def.* **1**).

2. box, crate, trunk, coffer, casket, caddy, file; case, vasculum, receptacle, shrine, reliquary; bunker, bin, crib, hutch; carton, container, canister, *Gk. and Rom. Antiq.* pyxis; locker, strongbox, safe, repository; treasury, money-box, till, kitty.

3. chest of drawers, set of drawers, bureau, dresser; chifforobe, chiffonier, cabinet, cupboard.

chew, *v.* **1.** masticate, *Archaic.* manducate, grind, crush, crunch, craunch, munch, mumble; nibble, bite, gnaw, rend, damage, injure.

2. ruminate, meditate on, mull, consider, weigh, deliberate, cogitate.

chic, *adj.* **1.** stylish, fashionable, smart, natty, spruce, dapper, trim; modish, a-go-go, in the very latest style; in vogue, à la mode, in fashion, in style; popular, in, *Sl.* in the groove, all the rage; up-to-date, current, modern, mod, new; up-to-the-minute, *Inf.* trendy, *Sl.* cool, *Inf.* nifty, *Sl.* neat, *Sl.* hip, *Sl.* hep.

2. elegant, high-class, *Sl.* classy, high-toned, *Sl.* tony; silk-stocking, posh, luxurious, *Sl.* ritzy, fancy, *Inf.* swank, *Inf.* swanky, *Sl.* swell; dressy, flashy, *Sl.* snazzy, *Sl.* sharp, *Sl.* sharp as a tack; suave, urbane, sophisticated, chi-chi, cosmopolitan.

—n. **3.** style, stylishness, nattiness, spruceness, dapperness, trimness, neatness; fashionableness, modishness, elegance; dressiness, flashiness, *Sl.* snazziness, *Sl.* sharpness; flair, panache, pizazz, dash; fanciness, *Sl.* ritziness, *Inf.* swankiness, luxuriousness, *Sl.* class; polish, grace, refinement, culture; sophistication, cosmopolitanism, urbanity, urbaneness, suavity, suaveness.

chicanery, *n.* fraud, fraudulency, deceit, deception, chicane, duplicity, guile, double-dealing, *Sl.* monkey-business, *Sl.* dipsy-doodle; trickery, gulling, knavery, rascality, hoodwinking, duping, hoaxing, befooling; dishonesty, falseness, humbuggery, artifice, subterfuge; pettifoggery, bamboozling, cheating, cozenage, swindling, fleecing; wiles, sophistry, artfulness, craftiness, treachery; cajolery, beguilement, inveigling, blandishment, blarney.

chide, *v.* scold, tongue-lash, rate, upbraid, *Sl.* chew out, *Inf.* dress down, *Inf.* jump on; castigate, chastise, berate, censure, reproach, rebuke, reprove, reprimand, reprobate, blame; denounce, take to task, call to account, call down, lecture; admonish, caution, warn, forewarn, put on one's guard.

chief, *n.* **1.** head, leader, doyen, principal, *Inf.* boss, *Inf.* bossman, *Inf.* kingpin, *Inf.* number one, Mr. Big, *Sl.* top dog, *Sl.* head honcho, *Sl.* big cheese; superior, director, dean, chairman; manager, overseer, supervisor, superintendent, foreman, headman, *Brit.* gaffer.

2. chieftain, sachem, warlord, war chief, commander, commandant; ruler, lord, overlord, lord and master, suzerain, paramount.

—adj. **3.** supreme, head, first, foremost, headmost, premier, paramount, *Inf.* boss; ruling, reigning, commanding, controlling, directing, governing.

4. main, principal, cardinal, prime, primary, uppermost, most important; essential, necessary, indispensable.

chiefly, *adv.* **1.** principally, especially, particularly, essentially, first and last, first and foremost, above all.

2. mainly, in the main, mostly, for the most part, on the whole, by and large, predominantly; in general, generally, as a rule, usually.

chieftain, *n.* chief, sachem, commander. See **chief** (*def.* **2**).

child, *n.* **1.** youth, youngster, youngling, young one, *Archaic.* childe; juvenile, adolescent, tyke, *Inf.* kid, *Scot. and North Eng.* bairn, *Brit. Sl.* chavey, *Scot.* wean; boy, little boy, lad, stripling, sprig, *Scot. and North Eng.* callant, *Irish Eng.* spalpeen, *Irish Eng.* gossoon, junior; girl, little girl, lass, lassie, *Irish Eng.* colleen, miss, *Inf.* missy, *Inf.* junior miss; puppy, cub, kitten, chit, chick, *Inf.* small fry, *Inf.* shaver; baby, infant, babe, *It. bambino,* cherub, innocent; tot, toddler, *U.S. Inf.* tad, tiny tot, preschooler.

2. descendant, offspring, progeny; scion, heir, heiress; son, daughter, chip off the old block.

childbirth, *n.* accouchement, confinement, lying-in, labor, travail; bearing, childbearing, delivery, childbed, *Med.* eutocia, *Med.* dystocia; parturition, parturiency, pullulation; nativity, birth, genesis.

childhood, *n.* infancy, babyhood, tender age; youth, boyhood, girlhood, adolescence, puberty; juvenility, juvenescence, puerility, growing up; teens, school days, pupilage, flower of youth, springtime of life, dayspring of life; minority, nonage, juniority, immaturity.

childish, *adj.* **1.** infantile, childlike, *Rare.* childly, babyish, infantine, *Inf.* kiddish; boyish, girlish, youthful, young, juvenile, juvenescent, puerile, adolescent.

2. immature, undeveloped, unfledged, unfeathered, jejune; budding, tender, soft, unripe, delicate; inexperienced, green, tyronic, sophomoric, callow, unsophisticated, unwise; awkward, clumsy, inexpert.

3. silly, foolish, asinine, foolheaded; stupid, *Inf.* dumb, *Inf.* dopey, unintelligent; idiotic, imbecilic, inane, *Inf.* moronic; absurd, nonsensical, senseless, crackbrained; witless, halfwitted, *Sl.* dimwitted.

childlike, *adj.* **1.** infantile, babyish; boyish, girlish. See **childish** (*def.* **1**).

2. ingenuous, open, guileless, genuine, artless; sincere, honest, undeceptive, unfeigning, undissembling; natural, unassuming, unpretending; trusting, unsuspicious, unwary, unsuspecting; credulous, gullible, believing; frank, candid, forthright, straightforward; naive, simple, innocent, unsophisticated, unworldly; green, raw, wet behind the ears, born yesterday.

chill, *n.* **1.** cold, coldness, frigidity, gelidity, algidity, iciness; glaciation, *Physics.* regelation; briskness, chilliness, coolness; bitterness, rawness, bleakness; shivers, numbness, *Pathol.* algor.

2. influenza, flu, grippe, *Inf.* bug; fever, ague, cold, catarrh, rheum; cough, whooping cough, chin-cough, pertussis, bronchitis.

—adj. **3.** cold, frigid, icy, algid, gelid, freezing, ice-cold; nippy, cool, chilly, draughty, breezy; biting, bitter, nipping, brisk, sharp, snappy, penetrating, stinging; numbing, chilling, piercing, zippy; frosty, wintry, brumal, snowy, hibernal, hoary; glacial, arctic, hyperborean, Siberian, sunless, polar.

4. shivering, chattering, quivering, shaking; numbed, benumbed, frostbitten, frozen stiff, frost-nipped, chilled to the marrow *or* bone.

5. indifferent, aloof, apathetic, unconcerned, disinterested, incurious; unresponsive, unsympathetic, uncaring, unemotional, impassive; passionless, spiritless, unfeeling, inanimate, insensitive, cold-blooded; impervious, untouched, inured, unmoved, indurate; callous, hardened, obdurate, thickskinned.

6. unfriendly, unsociable, unwelcome, uninviting, standoffish, *Inf.* offish.

7. discouraging, depressing, disheartening, dispiriting, distressing; bleak, gloomy, dismal, sorry, woeful.

—*v.* **8.** refrigerate, freeze, cool, frigorify, *Rare.* infrigidate, *Rare.* frigidate; ice, glaciate, congeal, regelate; numb, benumb, petrify; nip, cut, pierce, pinch, bite, sting.

chilly, *adj.* **1.** cold, frigid; cool, nippy. See **chill** (*def.* **3**).

2. indifferent, unresponsive, impassive; unfriendly, unsociable. See **chill** (*defs.* **5, 6**).

chime, *v.* **1.** peal, toll, gong, dong, ring, clang, clangor; ding, ting, jingle, tinkle; sound, resound, reverberate; (*of time*) announce, indicate, mark, ring in, bring, usher in.

2. chime in a. harmonize, blend; complement, enhance. **b.** interrupt, break into, *Sl.* butt in, *Sl.* horn in, intrude into, add *or* put in one's two cents worth.

—*n.* **3. chimes** bells, carillon, glockenspiel; gong, Angelus, tocsin.

chimera, *n.* **1.** monster, monstrosity, Gorgon. See **monster** (*def.* **1**).

2. idle fancy, whim, humor, caprice, crotchet, bubble, vapor, maggot; daydream, dream, *Inf.* pipe-dream, castle in the air, pie in the sky, fool's paradise; figment of the imagination, hallucination, mirage, illusion; delusion, self-delusion, deception, self-deception, trick.

3. bugbear, bugaboo, bogy, *Inf.* bogyman; goblin, hobgoblin, ogre, spectre, phantom, nightmare.

chimerical, *adj.* **1.** unreal, imaginary, illusory, delusory; visionary, quixotic, romantic, starry-eyed, in the clouds; ethereal, unsubstantial, airy, vaporous, gossamery, spectral, dreamlike.

2. (*all to an extreme degree*) fanciful, notional, whimsical, unrealistic, fatuous; wild, fantastic, fabulous, outrageous, extravagant, preposterous, outlandish; gothic, bizarre, grotesque.

china, *n.* **1.** porcelain, eggshell porcelain, delft ware, majolica, faience, stoneware, ironstone, basaltware, Wedgwood ware, crackleware, gombroon.

2. pottery, crockery, ceramics, earthenware, ware, terracotta, *Both Ceram.* biscuit, bisque.

3. dishes, tableware, service.

chink[1], *n.* **1.** crack, chap, check, fissure, crevice, crevasse, cleft, stria, cranny, groove, sulcus, *Archaic.* scissure; break, fracture, rupture, split, rift, breach, scission, separation, division; slit, gash, scotch, rent, cut, incision.

2. hole, gap, cavity, opening, orifice, aperture; space, interspace, interval, interstice, narrow; chasm, gorge, ravine, gulch, gully, rut, furrow, ditch, trench.

—*v.* **3.** fill up, close up, stop up, plug up; cement, spackle, plaster.

chink[2], *n., v.* clink, clank, click, clack, rattle; jingle, tinkle, ting, ding, ring, clang, clangor, jangle.

chip, *v.* **1.** fragment, crumb, crumble, break up *or* off, crack off, chop *or* hack off; chisel, whittle, hew; nick, snick, notch, gash, scratch, mar.

—*n.* **2.** fragment, shard, chunk, snip, snippet; bit, morsel, gobbet, snatch, scrap, crumb; sliver, splinter, shive, shred, shaving, flake; slice, rasher, *Brit. Dial.* collop; piece, cantle, corner.

3. nick, snick, check, crack, break, fash, scratch, scotch, place, spot; imperfection, fault, flaw, defect, *Sl.* bug.

4. disk, wafer, slug, coin, *Obs.* plate; token, counter, marker, checker, man.

chipper, *adj. Chiefly U.S. Informal.* lively, cheerful, animated, vivacious, jaunty. See **cheerful** (*defs.* **1, 2**).

chirp, *v.* **1.** tweet, cheep, peep, chirrup; twitter, trill, warble, whistle; shrill, stridulate, crow.

2. carol, lilt, chime, sing, lift one's voice in song; rejoice.

—*n.* **3.** tweet, cheep, peep; twitter, trill, warble, whistle, song, call, cry; chirrup, stridulation, chatter, jabber.

chisel, *v.* **1.** sculpture, sculp, sculpt, carve, cut, hew; groove, furrow, chase, incise, engrave, grave; shape, fashion, form, model, figure.

2. *Slang.* cheat, swindle, bilk, bamboozle. See **bilk** (*defs.* **1, 2**).

chitchat, *n.* **1.** small talk, table talk, chatter, chitter-chatter, chin-chin; gossip, idle talk, talk; tittle-tattle, clatter, scandal, *Sl.* dirt.

—*v.* **2.** gossip, tattle, tittle-tattle, talk, *Inf.* dish the dirt.

chivalrous, *adj.* **1.** brave, courageous, valiant, valorous, heroic, stout-hearted, lionhearted; intrepid, fearless, dauntless, unafraid, undismayed, unappalled, unalarmed; bold, spirited, bold-spirited, high-spirited, daring, dashing.

2. firm, resolute, indomitable, invincible, steadfast, stalwart, doughty, unflinching, unyielding, unswerving, unshrinking; constant, dedicated, loyal, true, true-blue, faithful, reliable, dependable, steady.

3. courtly, gallant, gracious, courteous, gentlemanly, mannerly, well-mannered, well-bred; magnanimous, noble, liberal, charitable, merciful.

4. honorable, upright, upstanding, incorruptible; ethical, principled, high-minded, noble-minded; respectable, reputable, estimable, meritorious, highly-respectable; virtuous, righteous, uprighteous; just, fair, impartial, equitable, straight, fair and square, square-dealing.

chivalry, *n.* **1.** bravery, courage, valor, valiancy, heroism, prowess, stout-heartedness, lionheartedness; virility, manliness, manfulness, manhood; intrepidity, fearlessness, dauntlessness, awelessness; boldness, bold-spiritedness, high-spiritedness, daring, derring-do, audacity.

2. fortitude, endurance, tenacity, determination, will power; firmness, resoluteness, indomitableness, invincibleness, steadfastness, stalwartness, doughtiness; mettle, pluck, spirit, backbone, gumption, heart, nerve, grit, *Sl.* guts, *Sl.* moxie.

3. courtliness, gallantry, courteousness, mannerliness, gentlemanliness; magnanimity, nobleness, liberalness, charitableness, mercifulness.

4. virtue, virtuousness, righteousness, uprighteousness; honorableness, honor, uprightness, upstandingness, incorruptibility; high-mindedness, noble-mindedness; justness, fairness, impartialness, equitableness, straightness.

5. constancy, loyalty, fidelity, dedication, devotion; reliability, reliableness, dependability.

chock-full, *adj.* full, filled, filled to the top, filled to capacity *or* the utmost; rife, replete, abounding, overflowing, overspilling, bursting, ready to burst, *Sl.* fit to bust; dense, close, crammed, stuffed, crowded, packed, jammed, *Inf.* jam-packed, chock-a-block, *Brit. Inf.* chocker; packed like sardines, as full as a tick, standing room only, SRO.

choice, *n.* **1.** selection, eclecticism, adoption, acceptance, embracement, espousal, choosing; election, co-option, co-optation, *Law.* novation; appointment, assignment; nomination, vote, voice; determination, decision, commitment; judgment, opinion, discretion, volition, will, conclusion; discrimination, selectivity, differentiation, discernment.

2. alternative, *Dial.* druthers, option, possibility; answer, way out, solution; replacement, substitute, equivalent, surrogate.

3. pleasure, taste, preference, wish, desire; propensity, bias, inclination, prejudice, partiality, predisposition, predilection, prepossession; elect, elite, pick, select, best part, tidbit, prize, best, rarest, prime, treasure; gem, jewel, pearl, flower, cream of the crop; paragon, nonesuch, nonpareil, one in a million; champion, prodigy; excerpt, excerption, extract, extraction.
4. supply, store, fund, stock, surplus, accumulation; variety, alternative, selection; display, array, assemblage; profusion, large quantity, multitude, abundance, host.
—*adj.* **5.** superior, superlative, supreme, paramount, preeminent, exalted; unique, extraordinary, special, peculiar, unusual; rare, uncommon, scarce; best, first-rate, first-class, prime, *Inf.* champion, tiptop; consummate, perfect, excellent, ideal, sterling; precious, fine, superfine, exquisite, dainty; valuable, priceless, prize; exceptional, singular, particular; exclusive, restricted; preferred, preferable, preferential.
6. select, elect, singled out, chosen, hand-picked, elite, cream.

choke, *v.* **1.** strangle, strangulate, throttle, garrote, bowstring, gibbet, hang; asphyxiate, suffocate, burke, smother, stifle; gag, retch, gasp.
2. clog, dam up, plug, stop, cork, seal; congest, constrict, close, shut, occlude; obstruct, block, blockade, bar, prohibit; hinder, hamper, cramp, restrict, restrain, trammel, impede; check, inhibit, suppress, repress, curb, muzzle.
3. overload, overlade, surcharge, gorge; saturate, glut, satiate, cloy; engulf, submerge, flood, deluge, inundate, envelop; deaden, damp down, burn out, die out.

choleric, *adj.* irascible, quick-tempered, short-tempered, *Inf.* short-fused; testy, crusty, fractious, touchy, thin-skinned, edgy, on edge, *Sl.* uptight, huffy, peppery; splenetic, spleenful, bilious, atrabilious, cranky, ill-humored, ill-tempered, *Australian.* crook, bad-tempered; irritable, cross, surly, churlish, snappish, petulant, peevish; crabbed, grouchy, gruff, brusque, rude, impolite, discourteous; rancorous, acerbic, bitter; vixenish, shrewish, waspish, sharp; quarrelsome, contentious, belligerent, up in arms, pugnacious, bellicose; volatile, ignitable, volcanic, explosive, hot-tempered, hot-headed, fiery, wrathful.

choose, *v.* select, cull, pick, *Inf.* hand-pick, take, draw, check, x; prefer, favor, fancy, like, want, desire; single out, set apart, sort, separate, winnow, distinguish; balance, weigh, discriminate; determine, judge, decide, opt, see fit, think fit, resolve, make up one's mind; accept, adopt, espouse, embrace, take up, join, cast in one's lot; assign, appoint, elect, co-opt.

chop[1], *v.* **1.** *Often* **chop down** *or* **off** cut, hack, hew, hackle, haggle, fell, bring down; sever, split, cleave, sunder, rend; lop, prune, trim, shear, slip, crop, truncate.
2. *Often* **chop up** cut up, divide, partition, apportion; cube, dice, mince, hash, chip, splinter, shiver, crumb, crumble, fragment.
—*n.* **3.** cuff, buffet, knock, punch, box, *Inf.* whack, *Inf.* wallop, *Inf.* whomp, *Inf.* clout, *Sl.* plug, *Sl.* bop, *Sl.* sock, *Sl.* shot; blow, bastinado, *Scot.* dunt, *Sl.* conk, *Sl.* bash, *U.S. Sl.* biff, *Sl.* bop; strike, hit, smack, thwack, slap.
4. cutlet, rib, *Fr. côtelette*; piece, portion, slice, cut.

chop[2], *v.* **1.** jerk, bump *or* bounce along, start and stop, dart about; shift, shuffle, dodge, change, vary; swerve, veer, turn, whirl, swirl, whip around, reverse, *Naut.* jibe, *Naut.* tack; wave, undulate, fluctuate, vacillate.
—*n.* **2.** waviness, undulation, choppiness, roughness, unevenness; turbulence, storminess.

choppy, *adj.* **1.** (*of the sea, a lake, etc.*) wavy, undulating, rough, bumpy, uneven, irregular; blustery, turbulent, tempestuous, stormy.
2. (*of the wind*) gusty, squallish; variable, varying, fluctuant, protean, shifting, changeable, changeful, changing, swirling, whirling; inconstant, unstable, unsteady; capricious, mercurial, erratic, fitful, unreliable.

chops, *n.* **1.** jaw, muzzle; jaws, jowls, chaps; mouth, oral cavity, (*of an animal*) maw; *All Sl.* gob, *Scot.* gab, bazoo, kisser, mush, trap, yap.
2. lick one's chops *Slang.* anticipate, relish, savor.

choral, *adj.* choric, group, concert, in concert, in chorus, in unison; vocal, singing, operatic, hymnal, psalmic; harmonious, euphonious, concordant, accordant, symphonic.

chorale, *n.* **1.** hymn, hymn-tune, psalm, doxology, motet, canticle, cantata.
2. choir, chorus. See **chorus** (*def.* **3**).

chore, *n.* **1.** task, job, work, domestic work; routine, exercise, turn, stint.
2. assignment, duty, obligation, charge, care, responsibility; burden, nuisance, bother, trouble, inconvenience, *Sl.* drag.

chortle, *v.* **1.** chuckle, laugh gleefully; snicker, snigger; chant, sing exultantly; cackle, triumph, gloat, gloat over, crow, crow over.
—*n.* **2.** chuckle, giggle, snicker, cackle.

chorus, *n.* **1.** musical composition, *Music.* polyphony, *Music.* counterpoint, antiphony, antiphon, part music, part song, chorale; hymn, chant, plainsong, song, ballad, carol, descant, anthem; tune, air, melody, ditty, aria, arietta, lay, canzonet, cavatina.
2. refrain, *Music.* burden, *Music.* repetend, repetition, *Music.* coda, response, verse, strophe, antistrophe; ode, epode.
3. choir, choristers, chorale, choral group, glee club, *Ger. Kapelle*, ensemble, group of singers; carolers, street singers, *Brit.* waits.
4. (*all of sounds*) unison, accord, harmony, concert, one voice, unity, oneness; consonance, correspondence, agreement, assonance; concord, concordance, consensus, concurrence, unanimity.

christen, *v.* **1.** baptize, sprinkle, besprinkle, asperse, anoint; immerse, submerge, dunk, *Archaic.* dip; lay on the hands, *Obs.* impose.
2. name, call, dub, title, entitle, style; term, designate, denominate, *Archaic.* nominate.
3. dedicate, consecrate, hallow, sanctify.
4. initiate, (*of a ship*) launch, inaugurate, commence; begin using, break out, break in.

chronic, *adj.* **1.** inveterate, confirmed, habitual, hardened; set, settled, fixed, rooted, established; deep-rooted, deep-seated, ingrained, implanted, inborn, inbred.
2. persistent, constant, continual, continuous, incessant, unabating, unmitigating; lingering, continuing, lasting, abiding, enduring, unyielding, longstanding; lifelong, long-lived, of long duration, longevous; perpetual, eternal, permanent, ceaseless, endless, never-ending.
3. seasonal, perennial, cyclic, successive, frequent; intermittent, periodic, periodical, recurrent, recurring; repetitious, repeating, iterative, reiterative, repetitive.

chronicle, *n.* **1.** calendar, almanac, journal, log, record, memorandum, annal, archive; register, registry, docket, diary, document; roster, schedule, scroll; minutes, proceedings, transactions.
2. history, account, chronology; narrative, narration, recital, relation, story, legend, saga, epic, fortunes, adventures; memoirs, biography, autobiog-

raphy, life.

—*v.* **3.** record, put on record, set down, mark; document, register, calendar, *Law.* docket; enroll; chronologize, set forth in order; report, relate, recount, write an historic account of, take minutes, list, enter.

chronicler, *n.* historian, historiographer, chronologist, chronologer, annalist, documenter; registrar, recorder, clerk; autobiographer, biographer, memorialist; narrator, reporter.

chronological, *adj.* in sequence, sequential, sequent, consecutive, in order of time, measured in time, properly dated, ordered, progressive, serial; horologic, chronometric, chronographic, chronoscopic, temporal.

chubby, *adj.* **1.** tubby, pudgy, *Chiefly Brit.* podgy, plump, round, rounded out, rotund; fat, obese, corpulent, overweight, flabby, stout, portly, pursy, *Scot.* fodgel; fleshy, filled-out, well-fed; ample, substantial, full.

2. paunchy, potbellied, round-bellied, big-bellied, large-bellied, great-bellied, abdominous, *Inf.* baywindowed, *Inf.* corporational, *Sl.* beerbellied, *Obs.* gorbellied.

3. dumpy, stumpy, stubby, squabbish, squabby, squat, squatty; chunky, stodgy, thick, thickset.

chuck, *v.* **1.** pat, poke, tap, fillip; tweak, pinch, squeeze; fondle, caress.

2. toss, cast, throw, dart, shy, pitch, *Baseball.* peg; fling, flirt, jerk, cant, heave; hurl, dash, sling, let fly, send; propel, launch, catapult.

3. *Informal.* relinquish, give up, resign from, quit, drop, *Sl.* pack it in; abandon, desert, forsake.

—*n.* **4.** pat, poke, tap, fillip; tweak, pinch, squeeze; fondle, caress.

5. *Chiefly British.* toss, cast, throw, pitch, fling, jerk, cant.

chuckle, *v.* **1.** laugh quietly *or* to oneself, grin jovially *or* complacently, smile playfully, purr, grin like a Cheshire cat; chirp, chirrup, laugh gleefully, chortle good-humoredly.

—*n.* **2.** suppressed laughter, playful smile, jovial grin, Cheshire grin; good-humored chortle, gentle laughter; jollity, merriment, jocundity.

chum, *n.* **1.** companion, friend, comrade, *Obs.* copemate, crony, copain, *U.S. Inf.* buddy, *Inf.* pal; sidekick, shadow, alter ego, other self, *Scot. and North Eng.* marrow; playmate, schoolmate, schoolfellow, classmate; messmate, dinner companion, commensal.

2. confidant, familiar, *Inf.* bosom buddy, roommate, bunkmate, *Sl.* bunkie; cohort, collaborator, helper, helpmate; teammate, co-worker, fellow worker.

chunk, *n.* mass, lump, hunk; block, square, clump; wad, squab, *Inf.* hunch, nugget, clod; cut, slice, wedge, quantity, portion, chop, *Sl.* whack, *Inf.* gob; slab, rasher, *Brit. Dial.* collop; piece, fragment, bit, butt, bite, mouthful; dollop, blob, mound.

chunky, *adj.* **1.** stout, stodgy, stocky, thick, thickset; fat, obese, corpulent, overweight, flabby, portly, pursy, *Scot.* fodgel; fleshy, filled-out, well-fed.

2. dumpy, stumpy, stubby, squabbish, squabby, squat, squatty.

3. large, bulky, hulky, hulking; lumpy, lumpish, heavy, beefy, brawny, burly, sturdy; strapping.

church, *n.* **1.** place of worship, house of prayer, house of God, the Lord's house, meeting house, (*usu. in reference to Nonconformists*) conventicle; basilica, cathedral, minster; chapel, oratory, sacellum, chantry, shrine, vestry, bethel; sanctuary, tabernacle; pantheon, mosque, temple, synagogue.

2. public worship, religious exercises *or* services, prayer meeting, communion; devotions, office, benediction, mass, novena; matins, vespers, lauds, compline; ceremony, rite, ritual; camp meeting, revival meeting.

3. Christendom, body of believers, the elect, followers of Christ, disciples of Christ, the Mystical Body of Christ, the Church Militant; Holy Mother Church, the Bride of Christ.

4. community of worshipers, congregation, parish, Christian fellowship, communion, body, fold, flock.

5. religion, faith, creed, belief, doctrine; affiliation, persuasion, ism, denomination, sect, cult; faction, schism.

6. clergy, church officials, hierarchy, prelacy, episcopacy, papacy, the Vatican, popedom; presbytery, vestry, parish council, (*in some Reformed churches*) classis.

7. sacred calling, religious vocation, religion, clerical profession, priesthood, ministry, rabbinate; holy orders, the cloth, the pulpit, the desk; religious life, monasticism, celibacy, the convent.

8. (*usu. cap.*) pre-Reformation Christianity; the Roman Catholic Church.

churchman, *n.* ecclesiastic, clergyman, cleric, priest, minister, rabbi. See **clergyman, ecclesiastic**.

churl, *n.* **1.** rustic, peasant, provincial, country cousin, countryman, hobnail; farmer, plowman, plowboy, chuff, swain, gaffer, kern, son *or* tiller of the soil, (*in Egypt*) fellah, (*in Russia*) muszhik *or* moujik, (*in Spanish America and Southwestern U.S.*) peon, *Archaic.* hind; yokel, bumpkin, country bumpkin, hawbuck, *Dial.* lumpkin, *Often Disparaging.* hillbilly, *Disparaging.* bogtrotter, *Inf.* chawbacon, *Inf.* cider squeezer, *Sl.* hick, *Sl.* woodhick, *Sl.* rube, *Sl.* hayseed, *Sl.* hoosier, *Fr. Sl. truffe.*

2. boor, curmudgeon, brute, barbarian, yahoo, *Inf.* goop, *Chiefly Scot.* tyke, *Brit. Sl.* mucker; lout, oaf, dolt, clod, clodhopper, clodpoll *or* clodpole *or* clodpate, gawk, looby, lubber, ox, clown, slouch, *Chiefly Scot.* cuddy, *Inf.* lummox, *Sl.* klutz, *Sl.* galoot *or* galloot, *Sl.* lug, *Brit. Sl.* joskin.

3. wretch, cur, cad, scoundrel, dastard, knave, blackguard, rascal, wastrel, ne'er-do-well; bear, vixen, shrew, harpy; beast, hound, viper, skunk, polecat; vulgarian, vulgarist, ribald, Philistine, vulgar *or* low *or* ill-bred fellow; *All Inf.* jerk, rat, creep, stinker, louse, *Derog.* bastard, *Derog.* SOB; *All Sl.* bum, *Chiefly Brit.* rotter, *Chiefly Brit.* bounder, *Brit.* blighter.

4. miser, niggard, scrooge, skinflint, penny pincher, pinchpenny, moneygrubber, pinchfist, hunks, mucworm, *Obs.* lickpenny, *Archaic.* pinchgut, *Brit. Dial.* codger, *Sl.* tightwad, *Sl.* skin, *Chiefly Brit. Sl.* screw.

churlish, *adj.* **1.** rustic, rural, peasantlike, agrestic, agrarian; pastoral, bucolic, bucolical, sylvan *or* silvan, Arcadian; inurbane, backwoods, provincial, countrified, countrybred, country-born, upcountry, from the sticks, yokelish, *Sl.* hickish, *Sl.* rube, *Sl.* hayseed; homespun, homebred, homey, homely, homelike, homish, down-home, (*usu. of thought or philosophy*) cracker-barrel, *Inf.* folksy.

2. boorish, loutish, oafish, doltish, cloddish, clodhopping, lubberly, loobyish, clownish, lumpish, lumpen; crude, crass, brutish, barbaric, beastly, bestial, swinish, reptilian, contemptible, base, vile; rude, vulgar, uncouth, coarse, ill-bred, ill-mannered, unmannerly; arrogant, audacious, impudent, insolent, brash, brazen, bold, presumptuous, impertinent.

3. surly, cantankerous, irascible, crabbed, iracund, obnoxious, choleric, brusque, crusty, grumpy, peppery, grouchy, dyspeptic, thorny, bearish, snappish, waspish, snarling, growling, bristling; cross, feisty, huffy, huffish, irritable, peevish, cranky, bilious, testy, touchy, ill-tempered, bad-tempered, short-tempered; fractious, quarrelsome, caviling, disagreeable, *Inf.* ornery, *Inf.* bitchy, *Inf.* ugly; caustic, mordant, mordacious, biting, cutting, stinging, sarcastic, insulting; sharp, uncivil, rough, harsh; abrupt, curt, short, terse, blunt.

4. miserly, niggardly, penurious, parsimonious, chary, usurious, *Obs.* usurous, tight, tight-fisted, close, close-fisted, close-handed, *Inf.* stingy, *Inf.* cheap, narrow, illiberal, grudging, scrimping, pinching; beggarly, meager, paltry, shabby, *Sl.* two-bit, *Sl.* lousy, *Sl.* rotten; sordid, avaricious, greedy, rapacious, extortionate; covetous, venal, mercenary, grasping.

5. obstinate, stubborn, pertinacious, dogged; implacable, intractable, obdurate, resistant, defiant, unyielding, unbending, pig-headed, bullheaded, thick, mulish, hard-set, stiff-necked, stiff, rigid, hidebound, hard-bitten, stony; perverse, contrary, contumacious, untoward, balky, froward, willful, self-willed, cross-grained; rebellious, insubordinate, unruly, disobedient, fractious, refractory, incorrigible, ungovernable, unmanageable.

churlishness, *n.* **1.** rusticity, ruralism, agrarianism; pastoralism, pastorality, bucolicism; inurbanity, backwoodsiness, provincialism, provinciality, yokelism, *Sl.* hickishness; hominess, homeliness, hom'ishness, *Inf.* folksiness.

2. boorishness, loutishness, oafishness, doltishness, cloddishness, lubberliness, clownishness, lumpishness; crudeness, crassness, brutishness, barbarity, beastliness, bestiality, swinishness, contemptibleness, contemptibility, vileness, baseness; rudeness, uncouthness, coarseness, unmannerliness; arrogance, audacity, audaciousness, impudence, insolence, impertinence, brashness, brazenness, boldness, presumption, presumptuousness.

3. surliness, cantankerousness, irascibility, irascibleness, crabbiness, iracundity, obnoxiousness, choler, brusqueness, pepperiness, crustiness, grumpiness, grouchiness, dyspepsia, thorniness, bearishness, snappishness, waspishness, snarling, growling, bristling; crossness, feistiness, huffiness, huffishness, huff, irritability, irritableness, peevishness, crankiness, biliousness, testiness, touchiness, ill-temperedness, bad-temperedness, short-temperedness, chip on the shoulder; fractiousness, quarrelsomeness, cavil, disagreeableness, *Inf.* orneriness, *Inf.* bitchiness, *Inf.* ugliness; causticity, mordancy, mordacity, sharpness, sarcasm, insult; incivility, roughness, harshness; abruptness, curtness, shortness, terseness, bluntness.

4. miserliness, niggardliness, penuriousness, parsimony, parsimoniousness, usuriousness, *Obs.* usurousness, tightness, tight-fistedness, closeness, close-fistedness, close-handedness, *Inf.* stinginess, *Inf.* cheapness, narrowness, illiberalness, illiberality, grudgingness, scrimpingness, pinchingness; beggarliness, meagerness, paltriness, shabbiness; sordidness, avariciousness, avarice, greed, rapacity, rapaciousness, extortion; covetousness, venality.

5. obstinacy, obstinateness, stubbornness, pertinacity, doggedness; implacability, implacableness, intractability, intractableness, obdurateness, pigheadedness, bullheadedness, mulishness, stiffness, rigidity, rigidness, stoniness; perverseness, perversity, contrariness, contumacy, contumaciousness, untowardness, balkiness, frowardness, willfulness; rebelliousness, insubordination, unruliness, disobedience, factiousness, refractoriness, incorrigibleness, ungovernableness, ungovernability, unmanageableness, unmanageability.

churn, *n.* **1.** mixer, beater, blender; shaker, agitator, jiggler, vibrator; whisk, eggbeater, paddle.

—*v.* **2.** cream, whip, whip up; disturb, shake, shake up, (*of water, wine, etc.*) roil *or Chiefly U.S.* rile; commove, agitate, convulse, upheave, heave, toss.

chute, *n.* **1.** shaft, slide, funnel, gutter, channel, groove, *Mach.* race, *Mach.* raceway; course, way, waterway, conduit, culvert, *Civ. Eng.* aqueduct, duct; tube, pipe, main, hose, spout, gargoyle; flume, sluice, drain, *Naut.* scupper; ditch, dike, trench; trough, receptacle, hopper, sink.

2. waterfall, cataract; canyon, gorge, chasm, ravine, gulch, *Western North Amer.* coulee, watercourse, arroyo, couloir, gully.

cigarette, *n.* smoke, regular, king, king-size, filter, menthol; *Inf.* butt, *Inf.* cig, *Inf.* ciggy, *Sl.* weed, *Sl.* fag, *Sl.* coffin nail, *Sl.* gasper, *Sl.* cancer stick; (*all marijuana*) joint, reefer, *Sl.* stick. See **reefer**.

cinch, *n.* **1.** (*all of horses*) girth, girt, saddle band, surcingle; band, belt, girdle, strap. See **belt** (*def.* **1**).

2. *Informal.* tight grip, grasp, hold, clutch, grab, snatch.

3. *Slang.* something easy, *Inf.* snap, *Sl.* child's play, *Sl.* a breeze, duck soup, piece of cake, *Sl.* a picnic, pushover, *Inf.* shoo-in, a sure thing.

—*v.* **4.** gird, bind, girdle, begird, truss, belt. See **belt** (*def.* **4**).

cincture, *n.* **1.** circular border, band, tie, collar; belt, ring, skirt, ribbon, fillet, garland.

2. encompassment, encincture, circumjacence, circumambiance; walling in, hemming in, restriction, constriction, choking.

—*v.* **3.** encircle, circle, gird, begird, girdle, surround, encincture, ring, environ, encompass.

cinder, *n.* **1.** ash, spark, fleck; ember, coal, charcoal, clinker.

2. **cinders** remnants, remains, residue; soot, smut, dust, *Chiefly Scot. and Brit.* coom; sinters, scale, scoria, sphue.

cinema, *n.* **1.** motion picture, cine, film, movie, moving picture, picture show, photoplay, *Inf.* flick; silent film, talking picture, *Sl.* talkie; movies, films, pictures.

2. motion picture theatre, movie theatre, movie house, movie palace, cine, showcase, (*formerly*) nickelodeon.

cipher, *n.* **1.** zero, naught, nothing, nil, aught, *Sl.* goose egg.

2. number, numeral, integer, figure, digit; notation, symbol, sign.

3. nonentity, nobody, nonperson, unperson, obscurity, *Inf.* no account; nothing, naught, nullity, *Sl.* zilch, *Sl.* zip.

4. code, coded *or* secret message, secret writing; cryptograph, cryptogram, anagram, acrostic.

—*v.* **5.** figure, compute, calculate, do arithmetic *or* math, do sums; count, reckon, number, add, total, estimate.

6. code, decode, decipher, *Inf.* crack.

circle, *n.* **1.** disk, round, roundlet, roundel, wheel; ring, band, hoop, cordon, annulus; crown, coronet, diadem, halo, corona, aureole, wreath, garland; belt, *Archaic.* cincture, girth, cestus, baldric, cummerbund, sash; collar, necklace, neckband, fillet; bracelet, circlet, armlet; arena, rink, circus; orb, ball, globe, knob, bulb, pellet, globule, sperule.

2. realm, sphere, dominion, domain, province; field, bailiwick, hub, niche; circumference, perimeter, periphery, radius, compass; ambit, scope, capacity, extent, reach, stretch; zone, theatre, area, range, bounds; region, section, quarter, district, division, department, precinct; vicinity, vicinage, neighborhood, purlieus, pale.

3. group, set, coterie, knot, ring, *Inf.* bunch, *Inf.*

crowd, *Inf.* gang; clique, cabal, camarilla, faction; club, society, association, fraternity, school.

4. series, set, cycle; circuit, tour, lap, turn, sweep, swing.

5. revolution, full turn, twirl, gyration; spiral, rondure, coil, whorl, vortex.

—*v.* **6.** surround, encircle, ring; belt, girdle, gird, enclose, hedge in, hem in; ring round; circumnavigate, circumambulate, ensphere; encompass, compass, envelop, embrace.

7. rotate, revolve, whirl, twirl, reel; turn, wheel, spin, gyrate, pirouette, pivot, swivel; loop, coil, curl, eddy, gurge; circumrotate, circumvolve; move around, circulate.

circuit, *n.* **1.** round, lap, beat, ambit, cycle, compass; orbit, trajectory, revolution, turn, loop; circle, sphere, orb, globe; route, path, course, itinerary, run, track.

2. tour, voyage, journey, pilgrimage, trip, travels, wanderings; outing, excursion, expedition, peregrination, trek, hike, walk, stroll, perambulation.

3. frontier, frontier line, boundary, boundary line, bounding line, border line, partition line, line of demarcation, line.

4. border, perimeter, periphery, edge, rim, fringe, verge, skirt; circumference, compass, ambit, margin, frame, outline, confine, confines; brink, brow, brim, hem; bound, limit, bourn, pale, extremity, termination; limits, city limits, outer limits.

5. borderland, borderground, borders, bounds, march, marches, marchland; outpost; outskirts, purlieu, suburbs, suburbia, *Fr. banlieue.*

circuitous, *adj.* roundabout, circular, ambagious, meandering, tortuous, sinuous, serpentine, anfractuous, flexuous; turning, twisting, crooked, zigzag, helical, labyrinthine, mazelike; rambling, indirect, devious.

circular, *adj.* **1.** round, disklike, discoid, annular, ring-shaped, hooped; spherical, spheroidal, globular, globate, rotund, bulbous; cycloid, rotiform, orbicular, orbiculate, perimetric.

2. rounded, curved, curvilinear; arched, bowed, bent.

3. circuitous, roundabout, indirect. See **circuitous**.

—*n.* **4.** advertisement, handbill, *U.S.* flyer, broadside, broadsheet, handout, throwaway, advert; brochure, pamphlet, booklet, leaflet, folder; letter, bulletin, notice, announcement, release, press release, statement; placard, poster, bill.

circulate, *v.* **1.** spread, spread abroad, scatter, bestrew, strew, send out, disseminate, propagate, diffuse, disperse, intersperse, distribute; emit, give out, put forth, put forward; advertise, placard, publicize, make known, make public, publish, promulgate, run, *Archaic.* divulgate; proclaim, announce, declare, tell, utter, enunciate, give currency to; report, bring into the open, divulge, lay before the public, give to the world; blazon, blaze abroad, trumpet, broadcast, proclaim from the rooftops, proclaim at the crossroads, herald, noise abroad, hawk about; rumor, rumor about, bruit, whisper about, repeat, bandy about; air, ventilate, vent.

2. spread like wildfire, go the length and breadth of the land, course; get abroad, get out, come out, be published, become public, acquire currency; be diffused, permeate; drift, flit, blow about, scatter, disperse; emanate, flow, issue, go forth; meander, wander, pass around, travel; pass from mouth to mouth, change hands; go the rounds, circuit, shift about.

3. rotate, turn, circumrotate, revolve, circumvolve; move in a circle, circle, go around, compass; pirouette, gyrate, spiral, spin, pivot, swivel; whirl, swirl, gurge; wheel, roll, trundle; move around, pass around, round, make rounds; convolute, coil, twist, convolve; roll, curl, furl, involute; incurve, curve; reel, wind, unwind.

circulation, *n.* **1.** rotation, turn, circumrotation, revolution, circumvolution, volution; circling, compassing, rounding; gyration, gyre, spiral, pirouetting, spin, pivot, swivel, whirl, swirl, turbination; wheeling, rolling, trundling; convolution, coiling, twisting; circumvention, encircling, encompassing; rolling, curling, furling, involution; reeling, unwinding, winding.

2. flow, passage, circuit, round; orbit, tour, journey, excursion.

3. spreading, scattering, strewing, sprinkling, bestrewing; dissemination, dispersion, interspersion, distribution, propagation, diffusion; transmission, dispatch, conveyance; traveling, meandering; emanation, flowing, issuing, issuance.

4. advertisement, publicity, publication; publicizing, printing, publishing; proclamation, announcement, declaration, utterance, enunciation; reporting, divulging, repeating, repetition, bruiting; blazoning, trumpeting, broadcasting, heralding, notification; ventilation, venting, airing.

5. currency, acceptance, prevalence, vogue.

6. coinage, mintage, currency, coin, specie; paper money, legal tender, money, sterling, change.

circumference, *n.* perimeter, periphery, edge, rim, fringe, verge, skirt; circuit, compass, ambit, margin, frame, outline, confine, confines; brink, brow, brim, hem; bound, limit, bourn, pale, extremity, termination; limits, city limits, outer limits; border, frontier, frontier line, boundary, boundary line, bounding line, border line, partition line, line of demarcation, line.

circumjacent, *adj.* surrounding, circumscribing, circumscriptive, encircling, lying around, outlying, outlinear, peripheral, perimetric, circumferential; ambient, circumambient, encompassing, enveloping, enclosing, environing, circumfluent; enfolding, girding, engirding, encincturing.

circumlocution, *n.* **1.** periphrasis, periphrase, pleonasm, tautology, redundancy, *Inf.* circumbendibus; verbiage, verbosity, wordiness, prolixity, profuseness, diffuseness, long-windedness, longiloquence; repetition, repetitiveness, tediousness, battology; digressiveness, discursiveness, maundering, convolution, circuitousness, wandering, rambling, meandering, roundaboutness, indirection, *Archaic.* ambages; ambiguousness, vagueness, beating around the bush; newspeak, bureaucratese, gobbledegook.

2. digression, excursus, cloud *or* smokescreen of words, *Rare.* tautologism.

circumlocutory, *adj.* periphrastic, pleonastic, tautological, redundant; verbose, wordy, prolix, profuse, diffuse, long-winded, longiloquent; repetitive, tedious, battological; digressive, discursive, circuitous, roundabout, indirect, maundering, meandering, wandering, rambling; ambiguous, vague, obscure.

circumscribe, *v.* **1.** surround, encircle, circle, encompass, environ, outline, delineate; gird, engird, girdle, belt; circumvent, entrap.

2. bound, limit, confine, shut in, fence in, pen in, hem in, keep within bounds; restrict, curb, proscribe, prohibit, bar, forbid; restrain, check, bridle, trammel, bind, stay, hold in check; impede, hinder, hamper, tie one's hands.

3. demarcate, define, delimit, deliminate, mark off, rope off, stake out; determine, specify, fix, draw *or* mark boundaries.

circumspect, *adj.* **1.** careful, cautious, mindful, heedful; guarded, on guard, alert, on the alert, watchful, discreet; chary, wary, leery, apprehensive,

suspicious, *Inf.* cagey.
2. judicious, prudent, provident, politic, well-considered, well-judged, well-advised; acute, perceptive, percipient, perspicacious, discerning, discriminative.

circumspection, *n.* caution, care, prudence, discretion, solicitude, providence, forethought, foresight; cautiousness, carefulness, heedfulness, mindfulness; attention, attentiveness, watchfulness, alertness, vigilance; chariness, wariness, leeriness, apprehension, suspiciousness, *Inf.* caginess.

circumstance, *n.* **1.** detail, fact, factor, particular, point, item, element; feature, aspect, respect; part, attribute, accessory.
2. incident, occurrence, happening, event, instance, occasion, phenomenon, incidence; adventure, affair, case, episode; eventuality, contingency, possibility; fortuity, happenstance, coincidence, chance, accident; stipulation, proviso, provision, clause, qualification, specification.
3. **circumstances** condition, state, state of affairs, situation, position; plight, predicament, difficulty; crisis, exigency, emergency; vicissitudes, ups and downs, turn of events, course of events, the times; lot, fortune, welfare, well-being, *Archaic.* weal; standing, rank, grade, means, class, estate, status; footing, station, elevation, step, *Inf.* notch.

circumstantial, *adj.* **1.** indirect, evidential, deduced, presumed, implicative, inferential, implied, presumable; hearsay, interpretive, verisimilar; inconclusive, controvertible, conjectural, debatable.
2. secondary, incidental, contingent, dependent, conditional, provisional; nonessential, unessential, extraneous, extrinsic, external, adventitious, supervenient; accidental, fortuitous, serendipitous, chance.
3. particular, detailed, precise, exact, accurate, minute; explicit, specific, express, pointed, to the point; exhaustive, full, thorough, plenary, complete.

circumvent, *v.* **1.** entrap, ensnare; encircle, surround, encompass, circumscribe, ring around, box off; girdle, belt, loop; envelop, embrace, confine, hem in, pen in.
2. bypass, make a detour, circumnavigate, circumambulate, circle, skirt; avoid, shun, evade, elude, sidestep, *Inf.* do an end run, fight shy of, keep away from.
3. outwit, defraud, deceive, cheat, swindle; delude. beguile, hoodwink, befool; inveigle, gull, trick, bamboozle; baffle, confound, confuse, perplex, nonplus, disconcert, *Inf.* tree, *Inf.* discombobulate.
4. disappoint, frustrate, thwart, foil, check, abort; defeat, checkmate; cross, oppose, contravene.

circus, *n.* **1.** *Inf.* big top, cirque, carnival, rodeo; spectacle, exhibition, performance, entertainment, side show.
2. band, *Theat.* troupe, company, touring company.
3. ring, arena, hippodrome, amphitheater, coliseum, stadium, bowl, field; gymnasium, *Gk. Antiq.* palestra.
4. turmoil, commotion, uproar, hubbub, hullabaloo, three-ring circus; *Inf.* to-do, fracas, rumpus, *Inf.* ruckus; anarchy, chaos, confusion, bedlam, pandemonium, free-for-all.

cistern, *n.* reservoir, well, water barrel, tank, vat; basin, sink, tub; container, vessel, receptacle.

citadel, *n.* castle, keep, tower, donjon, fortress, fort, stronghold; safehold, fasthold, hold, bastion, rampart, battlement; fortification, buttress, bulwark, stockade, redoubt, palisade.

citation, *n.* **1.** citing, quoting, referring, alluding to, adducing; attesting, alleging, proving.
2. quotation, *Inf.* cite, extract, abstract, excerpt, passage, selection, clipping, reference, allusion; illustration, evidence, proof, documentation, witness, authority.
3. enumeration, mention, calculation, tally, inventory, record, register, schedule; roster, muster, roll call, poll, census.
4. summons, official call, bidding, charge, subpoena, writ of habeas corpus, arraignment, *Law.* venire facias *or* venire.
5. award, commendation, eulogy, honor, recognition; reward, decoration, medal, wreath, crown, laurels, blue ribbon.

cite, *v.* **1.** quote, allude to, adduce, refer to; excerpt, extract; exemplify, give as example, illustrate by; specify, name, mention, enumerate, present; manifest, make clear, denote; assemble, bring forward, display; attest, allege, prove, document, produce as witness.
2. summon, enjoin, subpoena, send for, bid appear, direct to appear, charge to appear, serve with a writ; arraign, implicate, involve, call for, *Law.* attach, *Law.* distrain.
3. recall, remember, recollect; revive, review, recover knowledge of, call to remembrance; evoke, remind, bring back, commemorate, retrace.
4. commend, recommend, praise, laud, support, accredit, pay tribute to; ratify, certify, guarantee, put in a good word for.
5. summon, call, rouse, arouse, awaken, inspire, motivate, animate, incite, stimulate.
—*n.* **6.** *Informal.* See **citation** (*def.* **2**).

citizen, *n.* burgher, voter, taxpayer, freeman, householder; townsman, oppidan, villager; inhabitant, burgess, dweller, indweller, resident, denizen; indigene, autochthon, native; civilian, lay person.

city, *n.* metropolis, metropolitan area, municipality, town, *Inf.* burg; megalopolis, urban sprawl; inner city, core city, asphalt jungle.

civic, *adj.* municipal, civil, metropolitan, urban, oppidan; community, town, burghal, village, neighborhood; communal, social, public.

civil, *adj.* **1.** civic, municipal, metropolitan. See **civic**.
2. domestic, internal, interior, intestine.
3. civilian, non-military, lay. See **civilian** (*def.* **2**).
4. civilized, well-behaved, well-bred, refined, cultured, cultivated, polished; genteel, gentle, ladylike, gracious; gentlemanly, gentlemanlike, courtly, gallant, chivalrous, chivalric; urbane, suave, sophisticated, elegant.
5. polite, courteous, well-mannered, mannerly, respectful, deferential, deferent; decorous, proper, formal, *Fr. comme il faut*; tactful, diplomatic, politic; cordial, genial, affable, pleasant; pleasing, charming, ingratiating, complaisant, agreeable, obliging.

civilian, *n.* **1.** non-military person, citizen, private citizen, layman, laic.
—*adj.* **2.** non-military, civil, lay, laic, laical, nonecclesiastical; secular, profane, worldly, temporal, nonreligious, unspiritual, mundane, everyday.

civility, *n.* **1.** courtesy, amenity, urbanity, comity, suavity, social graces, manners; social procedures, decorum, propriety, protocol.
2. courteousness, politeness, politesse, mannerliness, good behavior; respect, respectfulness, deference; decorousness, properness, formality, formalness, ceremony, ceremonialism; correctness, tact, diplomacy; cordiality, cordialness, graciousness, ladylikeness; gentlemanliness, courtliness, gallantry, chivalry; nicety, elegance, elegancy, refinement, culture, polish, sophistication.

civilization, *n.* **1.** culture, cultivation, refinement, polish; edification, enlightenment, sophistication,

worldliness; elevation, development, advancement, progress; taming, domestication, humanization, unbarbarizing, indoctrination, inculcation, socialization, citification, *Sociol.* acculturation; education, schooling, instruction, teaching.
2. customs, way of life, folkways, ways, habits, *Sociol.* mores.

civilize, *v.* **1.** tame, domesticate, humanize, unbarbarize, acculturize, acculturate, socialize, indoctrinate, inculcate; shape, mold, form; educate, school, instruct, teach, tutor, train, coach, break in, teach [s.o.] manners, show [s.o.] how to act.
2. cultivate, refine, polish, smooth the rough edges; enlighten, edify, inform, acquaint, sophisticate, citify; elevate, uplift, broaden, develop.

clack, *v.* **1.** clatter, clitterclatter, ticktack, click; snap, crack, rap, smack.
2. chatter, palaver, blab. See **chatter** (*def.* **1**).
3. cluck, chuck, cackle, gaggle, gabble, gobble.
—n. **4.** clatter, clitterclatter, ticktack, click; snap, crack, smack, rap.
5. rattle, rattlebox, clacker, clapper, cricket, noisemaker, bull-roarer, thunderstick; catcall, whizzer.
6. chatter, small talk, *Inf.* gab. See **chatter** (*def.* **2**).

claim, *v.* **1.** demand, require, command, have rights to, deserve, be entitled to, lay claim to, pretend, *Sl.* have dibs on; expropriate, requisition, commandeer, exact.
2. assert, declare, proclaim, predicate, allege, aver, asseverate; maintain, hold, profess, avow, affirm, acknowledge, admit, own; postulate, assume, take for granted, presume, premise.
3. challenge, call, summon, charge; sue, appeal, plea, petition, beg, pray, entreat.
—n. **4.** right, title, rights, droit, due, desert; request, demand, pretension, *Sl.* dibs; prerogative, privilege, franchise; power, authority, license, liberty; birthright, inheritance, heritage, legacy; grant, deed, lease, bill; tenure, proprietorship, ownership, domain, holding, leasehold, allodium, allod, freehold; share, stake, interest.
5. assertion, allegation, averment, asseveration; profession, avowal, acknowledgment; pronouncement, declaration, proclamation, predication; postulate, assumption, premise, presumption, supposition.
6. challenge, charge, summons, call; suit, appeal, plea, entreaty, petition.

claimant, *n.* applicant, petitioner, supplicant, suppliant, suitor; complainant, plaintiff, accusor, party, prosecutor, the prosecution, the state; candidate, postulant, pretender; heir, inheritor.

clairvoyance, *n.* **1.** extrasensory perception, ESP, clairaudience, second sight, crystal vision, sixth sense.
2. insight, perspicacity, percipience, discernment, discrimination, perception, clear-sightedness, penetration; intuition, sagacity, acumen, sapience.

clairvoyant, *adj.* **1.** psychic, second-sighted; telepathic, extrasensory, supersensible, pretersensual, telekinetic, psychokinetic; precognizant, foreknowing, prescient, foreseeing, foresighted.
2. insightful, perspicacious, percipient, discerning, discriminating, penetrating, perceiving, clear-sighted; intuitive, sagacious, sapient.

clamber, *v.* (*all with difficulty*) climb, mount, ascend; scramble, scrabble, crawl, claw, shin, shinny.

clammy, *adj.* **1.** sweaty, damp, moist, wet; rainy, drizzly, misty, vaporous, foggy; chilly, cold.
2. sticky, gummy, pasty, viscous, viscid, ropy, dauby, glutinous, adhesive; smeary, slimy, moldy, *Rare.* mucid.
3. morbid, sinking, sickly; uneasy, nervous, anxious, worried.

clamor, *n.* **1.** uproar, din, babel, racket, hue and cry, ballyhoo, hullabaloo; shouting, shout, yell, holler, outcry, vociferation; bray, bellow, blast, clangor, jangle; hissing, catcalls, caterwauling.
2. commotion, *Inf.* to-do, flurry, agitation, disruption, disturbance; discord, unrest, ferment, upheaval, storm; dissension, contention, strife, friction, clashing; turmoil, tumult, broil, brawl, struggle; anarchy, chaos, confusion, pandemonium, bedlam, brouhaha, free-for-all; fracas, rumpus, scramble, scuffle, *Inf.* ruckus.
—v. **3.** cry out, shout, yell, holler, vociferate, din; bray, bawl, bellow, whoop, hoot, yelp; hiss, catcall, caterwaul.
4. brawl, broil, struggle, wrangle; argue, quarrel, spat, squabble, tiff; dispute, contend, dissent, disagree.
5. demand, insist, press for, urge; drive, force, push, thrust, put.

clamorous, *adj.* **1.** uproarious, clamant, clangorous, rackety, blustering, noisy; loud, deafening, earsplitting, ear-piercing; bawling, bellowing, braying, howling, caterwauling, ululant, wailing, crying, hysterical.
2. brassy, bold, brash, loud-mouthed, mouthy, shameless, barefaced; unruly, boisterous, obstreperous, rampageous, wild, riotous; tumultuous, tumultuary, tempestuous, turbulent, stormy, raging.
3. urging, importunate, insistent, persistent, pressing, urgent; vehement, protesting.

clamp, *n.* **1.** vise, clasp, clincher, clip, hasp, holdfast, holder, stirrup, brace; coupling, buckle, fastener, catch.
—v. **2.** vise, press, squeeze, hold; secure, make fast, fasten, fix, brace, bracket; clinch, screw down, nail, bolt; grapple, grip, gripe, clip, clutch, clasp, grasp.

clan, *n.* **1.** tribe, family, house, gens, sept, dynasty, nation, race; line, lineage, ancestry, pedigree, breed, strain, stock, stirps, *Biol.* phylum, *Biol.* class, *Biol.* division.
2. clique, set, coterie, in-crowd, circle, knot, band, ring, gang, crowd; order, sect, faction, group, party, team, camorra; fraternity, brotherhood, fellowship, sodality, society, community, troop, club, lodge, organization; association, affiliation, consortium, company, alliance, league, coalition, federation, guild, union, *Inf.* outfit; confederation, syndication, conspiracy, cabal.

clandestine, *adj.* **1.** covert, undercover, stealthy, surreptitious, feline, nighttime, back-alley, CIA-type, Watergate, *Canon Law.* subreptitious; collusive, conspirative, conspiratory, furtive, underhand, underhanded, *Inf.* under the counter, backroom, sneaky, sneaking, sly, foxy, crafty, cunning; unethical, dishonorable, illegal, unlawful, unauthorized, *Canon Law.* obreptitious.
2. secret, hugger-mugger, dark, closed, unpublic, not open to the public, private, confidential, closed-door, closeted, *Archaic.* privy; hidden, concealed, ensconced, shrouded, cloaked, disguised, veiled, masked, screened, in the dark; undisclosed, unrevealed, unpublicized, silent; mysterious, arcane, intriguing.

clang, *v.* **1.** clank, clangor, reverberate; ring, knell, toll, chime, peal.
—n. **2.** clangor, clank, reverberation; ring, peal, dingdong, gong.

clangor, *n.* **1.** clang, ring, peal, reverberation.
2. clamor, din, racket, noise, uproar, tumult, hue and cry.

clank, *n.* **1.** dull clang, clangor, jangle, clink, *Sl.* clunk, chink.
—v. **2.** clang, clangor, jangle, clink, chink.

clannish, *adj.* **1.** akin, related, cognate, family, familial, lineal, fraternal; ethnic, ethnocentric, racial, tribal, cultural; leagued, allied, confederated.
2. cliquish, insular, closed, unmixing, exclusive, selective; narrow, parochial, provincial; haughty, snobbish, *Inf.* snooty, uppercrust, supercilious, disdainful, contemptuous.
3. prejudiced, bigoted, narrow-minded, close-minded, intolerant, illiberal.

clap, *v.* **1.** strike, smite, thwack, slap, smack, *Australian.* ding; punch, box, sandbag, *Inf.* slug, *Inf.* whack, *Inf.* clout, *Inf.* wallop, pound, thump, thrash, *Inf.* crown, *Sl.* conk, *Inf.* knock [s.o.'s] block off, *Sl.* bash.
2. buffet, cuff, tap, fillip; rap, bat, pat, dab, jab, poke, *Inf.* clip; hit, knock, bump, ram.
3. strike together, come together sharply, (*of wings*) flap *or* beat, snap; clatter, percuss; explode, fulminate, detonate; applaud, handclap.
4. put forcibly, place suddenly, set, bang, slam, dash, force, impose; thrust, push, sling, fling, hurl, rush, toss, pitch, cast; slap on, affix, put on, apply.
—*n.* **5.** blow, box, *Inf.* clip, cuff, poke, jab, dab, pat, tap, fillip; slap, punch, hit, *Inf.* clout, *Inf.* buff, buffet, *Sl.* slug, *Sl.* bash; thwack, slap, strike, *Inf.* whack; pound, thump, thrashing, *Inf.* wallop.
6. clapping, clatter, clack; applause, handclapping; bang, crack, slam, snap; peal, loud noise, sustained sound, discharge, report, shot; explosion, percussion, detonation, fulmination, burst.

clapper, *n.* **1.** tongue of a bell, tongue; rattle, clacker, noisemaker.
2. claqueur, paid applauder, *Sl.* hired rooter.

claptrap, *n.* **1.** bombast, rodomontade, rant, inflation, fustian, cant, jargon, empty words, hogwash; ostentation, sensationalism, frippery, gaudiness, tawdriness, glitter, gloss; pretentiousness, pretension, pretense, false show; bluster, fanfaronade, swaggering, peacockism, peacockery; cliché, banality, platitude, commonplace; sophism, sophistry, casuistry, jesuitism, speciousness, elenchus; untruth, hypocrisy, insincerity; humbug, bunkum, *Sl.* bunk; flattery, false praise, cajolery, blarney, palaver; nonsense, trumpery, twaddle, *Inf.* bosh, babble, prate, moonshine, gibberish, prattle, blather, drivel, *Sl.* bilge, rigmarole, tripe.
2. sham, fraud, deception, imposture, fabrication, stage effect, quackery, charlatanry; trick, hoax, mockery; pose, *Inf.* front, affectation, airs, attitude, veneer, display, parade.

claque, *n.* **1.** (*all usu. hired*) fans, followers, supporters, promoters, rooters, *Inf.* boosters, *Inf.* arm wavers; (*all usu. of adolescent girls*) bobbysoxers, teenyboppers, groupies.
2. sycophants, flatterers, toadies, toadeaters, tufthunters, timeservers, temporizers, *Archaic.* pickthanks.

clarification, *n.* clarifying, simplification, elucidation, explanation; description, definition, specification, explication, interpretation, annotation, comment, footnote; exposition, disclosure, revelation, *Archaic.* enucleation, uncovering, unveiling, unmasking; show, demonstration, manifestation, exhibition, presentation; solution, answer, light, illumination, enlightenment.

clarify, *v.* **1.** make clear, disambiguate, make plain, simplify, make simple, make understandable, render intelligible; make explicit *or* unequivocal, define, make precise, specify; show, point out, demonstrate, manifest, exhibit, present, set forth; elucidate, annotate, comment upon, footnote; explain, describe, explicate, interpret; solve, resolve, clear up, decipher, figure out, disentangle; shed *or* throw light on, illuminate, enlighten, fill in.
2. expose, bring to light, disclose, reveal, bring out, *Archaic.* enucleate; lay open, unfold, uncover, bare, unveil, unmask, make visible.

clarion, *adj.* **1.** brassy, shrill, stridulant, stridulous, strident; high-pitched, sharp, acute, penetrating, ear-piercing, earsplitting; loud, blaring, resounding, deafening.
2. clear, clear as a bell, distinct, on key *or* pitch; pure, true, sweet; full, rich, orotund, sonorous, resonant.

clarity, *n.* **1.** clearness, pellucidity, pellucidness, limpidity, limpidness, translucence, transparency, crystallinity, vitreousness, vitreosity, lucency; purity, simplicity, cleanness, severity; visibleness, visibility, brightness, brilliance, luminosity, radiance, effulgence, refulgence, refulgency, refulgentness.
2. lucidity, lucidness, perspicuity, plainness, unambiguousness, unambiguity, unmistakability; explicitness, preciseness, precision, exactness, definiteness, distinctness, clear-cutness; comprehensibility, comprehensibleness, understandability, understandableness, intelligibility, intelligibleness, penetrability; perceptibility, discernibleness, apprehensibility, decipherability, legibility; obviousness, apparentness, evidentness, manifestness, palpability, patentability.

clash, *v.* **1.** clang, clangor, clank, clatter, rattle.
2. bump into, collide with, crash into, smash into, run into, *Inf.* plow into; butt, jar, jolt, jostle.
3. conflict, contend, dispute, disagree, argue, contest, contravene, spar, cross swords, lock horns; squabble, quarrel, feud, bicker, have words, be at [s.o.'s] throat.
4. struggle, battle, encounter, engage, meet; fight, combat, give *or* do battle, duel, joust, tussle, scuffle, brawl, come to blows.
—*n.* **5.** clang, clangor, clank, clatter; din, racket, tumult, uproar, noise.
6. conflict, opposition, disagreement, discord, disaccord, dissension, friction, variance, strife; enmity, hostility, antagonism, antipathy, bad blood, ill will.
7. argument, altercation, dispute, row, quarrel, squabble, dustup, spat, tiff, *Brit. Dial.* fratch; encounter, meeting, engagement, confrontation, showdown; fight, battle, struggle, conflict, tussle, bout, donnybrook, *Scot.* sturt, *Inf.* scrap, *Inf.* run-in; skirmish, action, brush, fray, affray; melee, fracas, uproar, free-for-all.
8. collision, smash, crash, smash-up, crack-up, car crash.

clashing, *adj.* **1.** clanging, clangorous, clanking, clattering, rattling.
2. conflicting, opposing, disagreeing, discordant, dissenting, variant, differing; hostile, antagonistic, antipathetic.
—*n.* **3.** clang, clangor, clank, clatter; din, racket, tumult, uproar, noise.

clasp, *n.* **1.** hook, catch, clip, snap, hook and eye, button, fastener, fastening; pin, brooch, broach, buckle, agraffe; latch, lock, bar, bolt, hasp; click, clincher, pawl, holdfast, *Mach.* detent, *Mach.* dog; clamp, vise, brace.
2. grasp, handshake, grip, gripe, clutch, clench; hold, embrace, hug, squeeze.
—*v.* **3.** hook, catch, pin, clip, snap, button, buckle, fasten; secure, unite, couple, link; clinch, clamp, vise, brace, bracket; latch, lock, bar, bolt, hasp, shut.
4. seize, grapple, snatch, grab; clutch, clench, grip, grasp; hold, enfold, envelop, enclose, encircle, entwine; embrace, hug, squeeze, press, snuggle, cuddle, cherish.

class, *n.* **1.** category, division, section, branch, department, province, realm, domain, area; classification, arrangement, grouping; group, set, collection, selection; species, genus, breed, brood, genre; kind, sort, kidney, type, brand, name, variety; make, cast, cut, mold, form, style, manner; grain, feather, tone, color, stripe; stamp, designation, denomination, suit; character, constitution, make-up, composition, *Archaic.* crasis; temperament, temper, nature, humor, mood, persuasion.

2. level, stratum, position, place, state, caste; status, standing, rank, grade, estate, order, range; set, circle, sphere, coterie, clique; sept, clan, tribe, family; ancestry, lineage, stock, pedigree, descent, strain, derivation, extraction; origin, source, birth; connection, influence, power, weight, prestige, importance.

3. course, subject, curriculum; seminar, lecture, discussion; lesson, study; period, session.

—*v.* **4.** group, arrange, classify. See **classify**.

classic, *adj.* **1.** first-class, first-rate, excellent, superior, masterly, *Inf.* A one *or* A number one; consummate, quintessential, master; outstanding, remarkable, extraordinary; noteworthy, notable, of note, marked, exemplary.

2. standard, model, guiding, ideal; prototypical, paradigmatic, archetypal.

3. ancient; Archaic, Attic, Hellenistic. See **classical** (*def.* **1**).

4. basic, fundamental, rudimentary, elementary, primary.

5. ageless, timeless, deathless, immortal, undying, imperishable, eternal; enduring, lasting, abiding, perennial, perdurable.

6. traditional, customary, conventional, prescriptive, tried-and-true; legendary, venerable, hallowed, time-honored, longstanding; typical, characteristic, usual, normal, regular, regulation, stock, familiar, true-to-form, true-to-type.

7. definitive, authoritative; influential, weighty, prestigious.

—*n.* **8.** masterpiece, masterwork, *Archaic.* master, chef-d'oeuvre, great work, magnum opus.

9. standard, standard work, model, mirror, example, criterion; type, archetype, paradigm, prototype, original; ideal, paragon, exemplar, quintessence.

classical, *adj.* **1.** Greek, Hellenistic, Attic, Archaic; Roman, Augustan, Ciceronian; heroic, epic; ancient.

2. harmonious, symmetrical, balanced, proportioned, well-proportioned; concinnous, eurhythmic, regular; simple, plain, inornate, pure, restrained, understated; lucid, clear, clear-cut, eloquent; elegant, refined, polished, finished; stately, dignified, reposeful, grand, majestic; artistic, aesthetic, tasteful.

3. *Music.* art, serious, *Inf.* longhair, symphonic, concert.

4. standard, definitive, authoritative, influential, weighty, prestigious.

classicism, *n.* (*all in reference to art, literature, architecture, etc.*) proportion, balance, symmetry, order, harmony, concinnity, eurhythmy; simplicity, plainness, purity, restraint, understatement; lucidity, clarity, eloquence; elegance, refinement, polish, finish; stateliness, dignity, grandness, majesty.

classification, *n.* **1.** arrangement, grouping, ordering, collocation, categorizing, categorization, taxonomy; organization, systematization, codification, methodizing; designation, denomination, assignment, allocation, apportionment, distribution.

2. category, class, division, section, branch; group, set, collection, assortment, selection; kind, sort, type, genre, variety; order, range, rank, grade, gradation.

3. system, code, index, directory.

classify, *v.* arrange, range, order, dispose, place, group; organize, sort, assort, size; class, type, name, label, tag, ticket, brand; digest, index, file, codify, number, alphabetize; draw up, list, catalog; categorize, pigeonhole, *Sl.* peg, *Sl.* button-down, *Inf.* put [s.o. *or* s.t.] down as; associate, bracket; distinguish, rate, rank, grade, graduate; allocate, allot, assign, distribute.

clatter, *v.* **1.** rattle, clutter, racket, din; jangle, clang, clangor, echo, reverberate, resound.

2. hurtle, clank, crash, bang, clump, tramp, be heavy footed, *Inf.* stomp *or* thump around; clash, collide, bump.

3. chatter, jabber, cackle, clack; prate, rattle, gabble; gush, blab, *Inf.* spout; babble, prattle.

—*n.* **4.** rattling, clattering, clutter, racket, noise, din, clamor, raucousness, uproar; disturbance, tumult, pandemonium, commotion, hullabaloo, bedlam, *Inf.* shivaree; banging, thumping, clumping, crashing, clanking.

5. chatter, chattering, jabbering, jabber, prattling, prattle, cackling, cackle, gibbering, gibber; gabbling, gabble, babbling, babble, running on, rattling away.

6. gossip, buzzing, palaver, tittle-tattle, tattle, idle talk.

clause, *n.* **1.** sentence, paragraph, passage, section, division.

2. article, particle, provision, proviso, point, specification, particular, detail; stipulation, term, condition, qualification, exception, exemption, reservation, *Law.* covenant; rider, addendum, additament, addition, supplement, appendix, codicil.

claw, *n.* **1.** talon, pounce, curved nail, unguis, hoof, paw, *Fr. griffe, Ornith.* spur; pincer, nipper, chela, fang; hook, clamp, forceps, tongs; grapnel, grapple, grappling iron, cant hook.

—*v.* **2.** tear, scratch, pounce, *Archaic.* clapperclaw, scrape, dig; pierce, prick, puncture, punch, perforate, jab, poke, gouge; cut, gash, slash, rend, rip, lacerate, mangle; stab, knife, lancinate, wound.

3. seize, grab, pull, snatch, catch hold of, hook; grasp, grip, gripe, clench, clutch; grapple, clinch, hold fast, fasten upon.

clay, *n.* **1.** argillite, clay stone; clayey earth, loam, adobe, terracotta, brick; potter's clay, *Obs.* argil, *Ceramics.* slip, kaolin, bole, fire clay; clayware, pottery, earthenware, stoneware, ceramics, porcelain, china.

2. earth, ground, soil, *Archaic.* marl, *Archaic.* glebe; sod, turf, sward; mud, mire, wet earth.

3. human body, flesh, flesh and blood, mortal clay.

clayey, *adj.* clayish, claylike, argillaceous, argillitic, *Obs.* loamy, earthy; pasty, gummy, sticky, adhesive, gluey, viscid, viscous, viscoid; plastic, fictile, malleable, moldable, formable; tractable, yielding, pliant, flexible.

clean, *adj.* **1.** unsoiled, unspotted, spotless, speckless, white, snowy, immaculate; cleansed, washed, bathed, laundered, scrubbed, wiped, scoured; polished, dusted, swept, vacuumed, whisked; tidy, well-groomed, well-kept; fresh, fragrant, deodorized, sweet; wholesome, healthy, healthful.

2. pure, unstained, stainless, unblemished; perfect, flawless, faultless; virgin, untouched, unadulterated, unspoiled, untainted; unpolluted, uncontaminated, sanitized, disinfected, antisepticized.

3. clear, clarified, refined, distilled, unmixed; elutriated, *Chem.* edulcorated, purged, expurgated, defecated.

4. open, free, accessible, unobstructed, unblocked, passable; blank, void, vacant, empty; legible, readable, decipherable; distinct, definite, plain, unconfusing, uncomplicated.

5. regular, orderly, systematic; uniform, symmetrical, even, clean-cut; level, straight, flat; trim, well-made, shapely, neat, spruce, smart, dapper, *Chiefly. Brit.* trig; plain, simple, spare, frugal, economical; graceful, unornate, unembellished, unpretentious, unobtrusive.

6. innocent, chaste, vestal, virginal, lily-white; undefiled, undebased, unsullied, unfouled; honorable, reputable, fair, equitable, honest, just, judicious, sportsmanlike; virtuous, righteous, moral, good, upright, upstanding; decent, modest, decorous, demure, prudish, unobscene, unfoul, unobjectional, inoffensive; guiltless.

7. adroit, deft, dexterous, handy, neat, *Brit. Dial.* feat; proficient, adept, polished, finished, accomplished, skillful, skilled; masterful, masterly, expert.

8. complete, total, whole; decisive, conclusive, final; unqualified, unrestricted, unconditional; uninterrupted, undisturbed.

—adv. **9.** innocently, chastely, honorably, reputably; honestly, fairly, sportsmanly; virtuously, righteously, morally, uprightly, upstandingly; decently, modestly, decorously, demurely, prudishly; unobscenely, unfoully, unobjectionably.

10. regularly, systematically, uniformly, symmetrically, evenly, levelly, straightly; neatly, smartly, gracefully; simply, plainly, unornately, unpretentiously, unobtrusively.

11. cleanly, immaculately, tidily; freshly, fragrantly, sweetly; wholesomely, healthily; purely, stainlessly, clearly; antiseptically, sanitarily.

12. completely, fully, totally, wholly, thoroughly, entirely, inside and out, from cover to cover, from beginning to end; altogether, quite, utterly, to the utmost; decisively, conclusively, absolutely, finally; unqualifyingly, out and out, unrestrictedly, unconditionally.

—v. **13.** wash, bathe, lave, cleanse, *Chiefly Scot.* dight; deterge, (*of clothes*) launder, shampoo, lather, soap; scrub, swab, mop; shower, douse, rinse, flush, douche, sponge; absterge, scour, wipe, rub, polish; sweep, vacuum, whisk; tidy, neaten, order, do up.

14. dry-clean, lixiviate, leach.

15. purify, depurate, purge, expurgate, defecate, mundify, lustrate; freshen, ventilate, depollute, decontaminate, sanitize, sanitate, disinfect, antisepticize; clear, clarify, refine, distill; elutriate, *Chem.* edulcorate.

cleanly, *adj.* **1.** neat, orderly, tidy, well-kept, well-groomed, clean-cut; trim, compact, spruce, smart, dapper, *Chiefly Brit.* trig.

2. spotless, stainless, speckless, white, snowy, immaculate; fresh, fragrant, deodorized, sweet; unsoiled, unspotted, unblemished, unstained.

cleanse, *v.* **1.** clean, wash, bathe, lave. See **clean** (*def.* **13**).

2. purify, depurate, purge, expurgate. See **clean** (*def.* **15**).

cleanser, *n.* **1.** detergent, soap powder *or* flakes, abluent, abstergent, solvent, soap, shampoo, scouring powder; purifier, disinfectant, antiseptic; purgative, cathartic.

2. washer, dishwasher, washing machine; cleaner, launderer, laundryman, washerman, laundress, washerwoman, spotter; shampooer, sponger, wiper, douser; scrubber, swabber, mopper-up, scourer.

clear, *adj.* **1.** light, sunny, sunshiny; cloudless, fair, unclouded, fine, mild.

2. bright, shining, radiant, brilliant; illuminated, alight, lit, lighted; lambent, resplendent, beaming, irradiant, lucent, luciferous; aglow, glowing, luminous, luminescent, incandescent; lustrous, nitid, sparkling, glistening.

3. transparent, limpid, pellucid, translucent, crystalline, diaphanous; glassy, transpicuous, hyaline.

4. pure, even, perfect, unadulterated, unmixed, unalloyed; genuine, valid, true, real, authentic; unblemished, clean, unmarred, flawless, faultless, orient, stainless; unstained, unsullied, unpolluted, uncontaminated, untainted, uncolored.

5. defined, distinct, discernible, recognizable, well-defined, well-marked; visible, vivid, graphic; unhidden, undisguised, unconcealed; perceptible, distinguishable, audible, hearable; articulate, enunciated, enounced; (*of sounds*) clarion, silvery, sweet.

6. comprehensible, understandable, apprehensible, ascertainable; intelligible, legible, coherent, cogent; simple, plain-spoken, exoteric, straightforward; unambiguous, lucid, perspicuous, unconfused, luculent; perspicacious, perceptive, discerning, astute, penetrating, keen, sharp, quick.

7. evident, plain, obvious, palpable, manifest, apparent; unmistakable, unequivocal, unquestionable, incontrovertible; clear-cut, explicit, patent, express; pronounced, salient, prominent, marked, decided; undeniable, irrefutable, irrefragable, undubitable; incontestable, apodictic, indisputable; authoritative, absolute, downright, utter, sheer, thorough, out-and-out; unqualified, conclusive, undisputed, unquestioned, beyond question, beyond a shadow of a doubt.

8. positive, definite, assured, sure, certain; convinced, confident, secure, satisfied, free from doubt; unshaken, unwavering, undeviating, *Inf.* cocksure.

9. serene, calm, pacific, still, quiet; restful, stormless, windless; placid, tranquil, sedate, untroubled, unperturbed, undisturbed, unagitated; peaceful, halcyon, irenic, composed; quiescent, reposeful, comfortable, easeful.

10. excused, freed, loose, released, discharged, liberated, at liberty; manumitted, emancipated, disenthralled; free, rid, quit, scot-free; exonerated, vindicated, absolved, acquitted, *Inf.* let off, justified, forgiven.

11. open, wide, exposed, unobstructed, unimpeded, unembarrassed, untrammeled; unhampered, unencumbered, unburdened; unfettered, unyoked, unreined, unmuzzled, unshackled, unbridled, unchained; unrestrained, unchecked, unbound, unconstrained.

12. emptied, empty, unloaded, free, unpacked; exhausted, depleted, deflated.

—adv. **13.** clean, completely, entirely, totally; altogether, wholly, fully, utterly.

—v. **14.** lighten, brighten, break, clear up; clarify, enlighten, illuminate, shed light on; elucidate, explain, *Archaic.* enucleate; interpret, expose, bare, demonstrate, show, exhibit, lay open; define, make plain, make clear, disambiguate, simplify.

15. cleanse, purify, clean, expurgate, depurate, refine; wash, deterge, purge, expunge, *Med.* absterge; erase, wipe clean, wipe away; leach, lixiviate, filter, percolate, strain.

16. remove, evacuate, make vacant, get out; cut away, take away *or* off, sweep away *or* off; empty, flush, drain; exhaust, deplete, deflate, void, eliminate.

17. disentangle, free, extricate, disengage, disembarrass, disencumber; untie, unravel, untwist, unknot, loosen; detach, unfasten, unloose, separate, undo; unclog, unstop, unseal, unblock, dislodge.

18. exonerate, absolve, vindicate, excuse, exculpate; acquit, discharge, pardon, amnesty, reprieve, forgive, *Inf.* let off; release, liberate, free, set free, let go; emancipate, manumit, disenthrall, disenslave; unfetter, unshackle, unchain, unbind, unbolt, untie.

19. process, handle, expedite, dispatch, dispose,

reroute.

20. gain, profit, net, realize a profit, make a profit, earn, win, bring in; glean, reap, *Inf.* take off the top.

21. authorize, approve, pass, sanction, ratify, legalize; give one's nod of approval, set one's seal to, *Inf.* O.K., *Chiefly U.S.* approbate; permit, allow, consent to, *Inf.* give the green light to *or* go-ahead to.

22. settle, square, satisfy, liquidate, pay off, discharge; cancel debts, close an account, wipe off; balance, adjust, reckon.

23. pass over, skip over, leap over, hop over, jump over, vault over, bound over, bounce over, *Inf.* make.

clearance, *n.* **1.** clearing, opening, aperture, passage; space, hole, gap; separation, interspace, interval; slit, split, break, crack.

2. leeway, margin, allowance; headroom, headway, elbowroom, room to spare, *Naut.* berth.

clear-cut, *adj.* **1.** definite, explicit, detailed, precise, exact, fixed, distinct, well-defined, express; unambiguous, unmistakable, unconfused, unequivocal; lucid, clear, plain, perspicuous, understandable, intelligible, comprehensible, perceptible, discernible, apprehensible.

2. obvious, apparent, evident, transparent, *Inf.* baldfaced; manifest, palpable, patent; graphic, vivid, striding, conspicuous, salient; certain, sure, positive, unqualified, unconditional; absolute, categorical, downright, out-and-out, flat, undeniable.

clearheaded, *adj.* **1.** astute, discerning, perceptive, penetrating, piercing; perspicacious, percipient, discriminating, appercipient; bright, smart, sharp, shrewd, keen, quick, *Inf.* quick on the trigger; sagacious, sapient, wise.

2. alert, wide-awake, aware, *Inf.* heads-up, *Inf.* on the ball, *Inf.* on the stick, *Inf.* on one's toes, *Sl.* nobody's fool; observant, on the watch, on the alert, on the lookout; heedful, mindful, careful, cautious, wary, chary; attentive, vigilant, watchful, Argus-eyed, on the qui vive; eagle-eyed, hawk-eyed, lynx-eyed, sharp-eyed.

3. lucid, rational, sane, reasonable, sound, clear-thinking, clear-sighted, level-headed; judicious, prudent, wise, sober, circumspect; thoughtful, sensible, intelligent, reasonable; comprehending, thinking, knowing, cognitive; long-sighted, far-sighted, far-seeing, long-headed; resourceful, creative, imaginative.

4. composed, collected, calm, steady; untroubled, undisturbed, unperturbed, unshaken, unruffled, unexcited; poised, self-possessed, self-restrained, coolheaded, tranquil, serene, placid.

clearing, *n.* **1.** clearance, opening, passage; open space, open field, glade, cleared land; expanse, tract, patch of land, felled forest, tilled field.

2. extrication, disentanglement, disengagement, loosing, unraveling; acquittal, discharging, releasing; liberation, emancipation, freeing; vindication, exoneration, exculpation, justification.

3. clarification, refinement, purification; cleaning, flushing; brightening, becoming fair.

4. eradication, elimination, voidance, annulment; liquidation, settlement.

clearly, *adv.* **1.** distinctly, starkly, patently, palpably; noticeably, visibly, conspicuously, discernibly, apparently, recognizably, perceptibly, observably; manifestly, overtly, markedly, pronouncedly, prominently; in full view, in plain sight, before one's eyes, to the eye, obviously, evidently, to all appearances; transparently, openly, plainly; on the face of it, at the first blush, at first sight, prima facie, seemingly.

2. positively, determinately, certainly, veritably, unequivocally, unambiguously, explicitly, expressly; surely, confidently, assuredly, unquestionably, beyond question, conclusively, incontestably, irrefutably, uncontrovertibly, undeniably, irrefragably; demonstrably, indubitably, undoubtedly, beyond doubt, decidedly, definitely, decisively, admittedly; unqualifiedly, unconditionally, absolutely, totally, implicitly, utterly; officially, confirmedly, emphatically, dogmatically, authoritatively.

cleavage, *n.* **1.** cleaving, splitting, halving, chopping, cutting, slashing; fission, partition, section; cleft, split, slit, fissure, rent, line of division; severance, sunderance, bisection, bifidity, bifurcation, *Obs.* dimidiation.

2. division, separation, breach, scission; dichotomy, divergence, disjuncture, dissociation, divarication; rift, rupture, fracture, segmentation, fragmentation, disconnectedness, disjointure, disunion, divulsion, *Inf.* split in the ranks, *Inf.* parting of the ways.

cleave[1], *v.* **1.** stick, cling, clasp, hold close, hold fast, cherish; cohere, be united, be joined.

2. be true, be devoted, remain faithful, remain constant; stay close, stick together, *Inf.* stick with; grow together, coalesce; believe in, have faith in, uphold, sustain, support, stand by, upbear; embrace, grip, hold, hug.

cleave[2], *v.* **1.** split, divide, partition, halve, bisect, quarter, section; hack, hew, chop, slash, slit; part, rupture, open, lay open, gash, rive, rend, sunder; disjoin, separate, *Obs.* dimidiate, bifurcate; cut off, sever, shear off, detach, break off, abscind.

2. cut a passage, blaze a trail, make a path, make one's way, penetrate, breach the wilderness.

3. penetrate, pass through, sail through, plow, plow through, cut, cut through, tear, slice, slip, slide, move at a good clip.

cleaver, *n.* knife, butcher's knife, chopper; hatchet, ax, machete, tomahawk; blade, sword, broadsword.

cleft[1], *n.* **1.** space, opening, split, gap; scissure, fissure, crevice, crack, rift, chink, cranny; defile, gully, gulch, chasm, crevasse, ravine, flume, gorge, canyon, pass, *Brit. Dial.* clough; trench, ditch, trough, furrow, fosse.

2. cleavage, division, separation, divergence; rupture, rent, breach, break, fracture; fork, branch, bifurcation; cut, gash, slit, slot, nick, notch, chop; orifice, aperture, interstice, hiatus.

cleft[2], *adj.* split, divided, parted, separated, asunder; cut, gashed, slit, notched, slotted, cracked, crannied, fissured; cloven, rent, hewn, sundered, riven; halved, bisected, partitioned; branched, pronged, forked, bifurcate; ruptured, fractured, dissociated, divergent, disjointed.

clemency, *n.* **1.** mercy, leniency, quarter, humanity; mitigation, relief, easement, easing, softening, mollification, assuagement, lessening, alleviation, palliation; forgiveness, placability, exorability, indulgence; pity, sympathy, compassion, commiseration; consideration, kindness, kindheartedness, benignancy, benevolence, beneficence, charitability, magnanimousness, liberalness; forbearance, patience, tolerance, longanimity; gentleness, tenderness, easiness, softness, soft-heartedness, mild-heartedness.

2. (*of the weather*) mildness, moderation, temperance, balminess, warmth; calmness, tranquillity, peacefulness, stillness; favorableness, propitiousness, pleasantness, desirability.

clement, *adj.* **1.** merciful, lenient, humane, mitigative, mitigatory; forgiving, pardoning, placable, exorable, indulgent; pitying, sympathetic, compassionate, commiserative, commiserable, condolent, condolatory, truthful, *Rare.* pitiful; considerate, kind, kindly, kindhearted, benignant, benevolent, charitable, magnanimous, beneficent, liberal; forbearing, patient, tolerant, longanamous; gentle, tender, benign, easy, soft,

soft-hearted, mild-hearted.

2. (*of the weather*) mild, fair, moderate, temperate, balmy, warm; calm, tranquil, peaceful, halcyon, still, quiet; favorable, propitious, desirable, pleasant.

clench, *v.* 1. close, shut, seal, zipper, zip up, (*of the teeth*) grit.

2. grip, grasp, clasp, clutch, hold, hold fast *or* tight; grab, seize, lay hold of, lay hands upon, put an iron grip on.

3. clinch, nail, bolt, rivet, screw, hook, tack; (*all by nailing, screwing, etc.*) fix, fasten, secure, attach, join, connect, couple.

4. set, stiffen, tense, tighten, gird, brace, screw up, double up.

—*n.* 5. grip, hold, grasp, clutch, clamp, clinch; iron *or* tight grip, grip of steel, firm hold, strangle hold, hammer lock, bear hug.

clergy, *n.* 1. clergymen, ministers, rabbis, priests, preachers, clericals; churchmen, ecclesiastics, prelates, bishops, monsignori, cardinals.

2. priesthood, ministry, holy orders, the cloth, the pulpit; pastorate, prelacy, prelature, presbytery, episcopacy, hierarchy, *Rom. Cath. Ch.* the Church.

clergyman, *n.* 1. minister, priest, rabbi, ecclesiastic, churchman, cleric, clerical, clerk, parson, minister of the gospel, servant of God, man of the cloth, father, padre, *Brit.* blackcoat, reverend, cassock, abbé.

2. pastor, rector, dean, vicar, *Dial.* dominie; confessor, spiritual director, shepherd of souls; curate, curé, chaplain, *U.S. Mil. Sl.* sky pilot, *U.S. Mil. Sl.* Holy Joe; deacon, presbyter, elder.

3. preacher, evangelist, missionary, spreader of the Word, sermonizer, sermonist, *Obs. Rare.* sermoneer.

4. theologian, exegete, canonist, divine, Talmudist, hierophant. See also **priest**.

cleric, *n.* 1. clergyman, priest, minister, rabbi, parson, churchman, ecclesiastic. See **clergyman, ecclesiastic.**

—*adj.* 2. ecclesiastical, churchly. See **clerical** (*def.* 2).

clerical, *adj.* 1. secretarial, stenographic, typing, transcribing, transcriptional, scribal; filing, *Inf.* girl-Friday; bookkeeping, accounting, actuarial; white-collar, salaried, professional; clerkly, *Inf.* office, *Inf.* desk; *All U.S.* sales, selling, merchandising, marketing.

2. ecclesiastical, churchly, cleric, of the cloth; rabbinical, ministerial, pastoral, priestly, sacerdotal, hier atic; apostolic, monastic; prelatic, papal, pontifical, episcopal, canonical, hierarchic, hierarchical.

clerk, *n.* 1. office worker, record keeper, filer; secretary, typist, transcriber, transcriptionist; stenographer, recorder, notary, notetaker, shorthand writer, *Law.* prothonotary, (*in ancient Greece and Rome*) tachygrapher, *Obs.* brachygrapher, legographer; penman, copyist, scribe, scrivener, amanuensis; bookkeeper, accountant, calculator, reckoner, actuary; (*both used disparagingly*) pencil pusher, *Sl.* quill driver; *All U.S.* shopkeeper, salesman, saleswoman, salesperson, seller; assistant, researcher, leg-worker, legman, *Sl.* gofer, *Inf.* girl *or* man Friday.

2. clergyman, ecclesiastic, cleric; lay reader, lector, acolyte, sacristan, elder, presbyter. See also **clergyman, ecclesiastic.**

clever, *adj.* 1. bright, brilliant, luminous, keen, acute, sharp, sharp-witted, sharp as a tack; intelligent, gifted, well-endowed, precocious, talented; apt, smart, agile, quick, quick-witted, ready; able, capable, competent, efficient; adept, proficient, masterful.

2. facile, easy, graceful, *Inf.* nifty; glib, fluent, glowing, unconstrained; witty, epigrammatic, urbane, piquant; scintillating, sparkling, sprightly; jocular, waggish, whimsical, droll.

3. sagacious, cunning, guileful, shrewd, *Archaic.* parlous; canny, *Inf.* cute, subtle, artful, crafty, slick; sly, wily, foxy.

4. adroit, deft, dexterous, ambidextrous, nimble, handy, neat, *Brit. Dial.* feat.

5. ingenious, resourceful, inventive, Daedalian; original, originative, creative, imaginative.

cleverness, *n.* 1. brightness, brilliance, keenness, acuteness, sharpness, sharp-wittedness, braininess; gift, giftedness, endowment, genius, precocity, parts; talent, flair, bent, turn, forte; intelligence, aptness, smartness, agility, quickness, quick-wittedness; ability, capability, competence, competency, efficiency; adeptness, proficiency, mastery.

2. facility, ease, grace, finesse; wittiness, epigrammatism, urbanity, piquancy, piquantness; sprightliness, jocularity, waggishness, whimsy, drollness.

3. sagaciousness, sagacity, cunning, cunningness, guile, sleight, canniness, *Inf.* cuteness, shrewdness; subtleness, artfulness, craftiness, slyness, wiliness, foxiness.

4. adroitness, deftness, dexterity, dexterousness, ambidextrousness, nimbleness; handiness, neatness, knack.

5. ingenuity, ingeniousness, inventiveness, resourcefulness; originality, creativity, creativeness, imaginativeness, imagination, inspiration.

cliché, *n.* platitude, truism, saw, maxim, stereotype, *Inf.* bromide; prosaism, banality, commonplace, old story *or* song, familiar tune, old saw, *Inf.* chestnut.

click, *n.* 1. clack, snap, crack, cluck, clink, clank, clunk, chink; tick, tap, beat, clap, strike, hit; rattle, jingle, jangle.

2. pawl, *Mach.* detent, *Mach.* ratchet, toothed bar, *Mach.* dog; catch, latch, bolt, lock.

—*v.* 3. clack, snap, crack, cluck, clink, clank, clunk, chink; tick, tap, beat, clap, strike, hit; rattle, jingle, jangle.

4. *Informal.* **a.** succeed, make a hit, *Inf.* go over. **b.** fit well together, be synchronized, mesh; be compatible, get along, *Inf.* be on the same wavelength.

client, *n.* 1. customer, patron, patronizer, regular, *Fr. habitué*; buyer, purchaser, *Both Chiefly Law.* vendee, emptor; shopper, marketer; consumer, user.

2. dependent, follower, protégé, student, pupil, disciple; attendant, supporter, backer, adherent.

clientele, *n.* 1. clients, customers, trade, business, patronage; patrons, patronizers, regulars, *Fr. habitués*; buyers, purchasers, shoppers, marketers.

2. dependents, followers, protégés, students, pupils, disciples; following, attendants, *Obs.* attendance, cortege, retinue, supporters, backers, adherents.

cliff, *n.* precipice, crag, bluff, *Brit.* scar; ridge, ledge, shelf, palisade, crest, chine, escarpment; peak, pinnicale, summit, promontory, tor.

climacteric, *n.* 1. *Physiology.* menopause, change of life; crucial age, grand climacteric.

2. crisis, crux, crunch, crest; crossroads, turning point, critical moment *or* point, critical period, crucial moment, critical juncture, juncture, moment of truth, climax, zero hour; emergency, exigency; predicament, plight, dilemma, quandary, strait, extremity; pinch, rub, scrape, squeeze, push, *Inf.* hole, *Inf.* clutch, *Sl.* crunch.

climate, *n.* 1. weather, prevailing weather, *Literary.* clime.

2. region, area, zone, place, locale.

3. milieu, atmosphere, air, aura, ambience; spirit, feel, sense, tone, undertone, overtone; mores, norms, ethos, ideology, world view.

climax, *n.* 1. culmination, acme, zenith, meridian, high noon, pitch, orgasm, *Inf.* payoff; height, high point, extremity, maximum, max., crowning point, supreme moment; prime, heyday, maturity, fruition,

bloom, full flower; sublimity, supremacy, perfection, extreme, utmost, uttermost, *U.S. Sl.* the most, *U.S. Sl.* the greatest, *Sl.* the tops; summit, apex, vertex, apogee, *Latin. ne plus ultra*; pinnacle, peak, crest, heights; spire, point, tip, tiptop, top; crown, cap, headpiece, head, capper.
2. crisis, critical point, turning point, juncture, crossroads, turning of the tide; intensification, heightening, build-up, acumination, sharpening.
—*v.* **3.** culminate, peak, crest, heighten, intensify, come to a head; result, end, terminate; acuminate, sharpen, bring to a head, build up, increase; crown, cap, pinnacle, tip, top, top off, surmount, sit atop *or* on; consummate, perfect, put the finishing touches on, round out *or* off; complete, conclude, finish, top out, bring to a close.

climb, *v.* **1.** ascend, mount, scale, escalade, go up, get up; clamber, shin, shinny, struggle *or* scramble up, make *or* work one's way up; surmount, overtop, top; (*all of vines*) twine up, creep up, trail up.
2. rise, arise, lift, lift off; increase, shoot up, jump up, run up, advance, escalate, swell, tower; incline, lean, tilt, tip.
3. advance oneself, get ahead, make strides, work one's way up the ladder, improve one's position; achieve, succeed, make good, *Inf.* make it.
—*n.* **4.** ascent, mount, scaling; clamber, shinning, shinnying; surmounting, overtopping, topping.
5. hill, slope, mountain, elevation, height, peak, summit; incline, grade, gradient, acclivity.

clinch, *v.* **1.** attach, fasten, make fast, secure, fix, set; rivet, nail, screw, bolt, drive in; clamp, vise, brace; lock, bar, hasp; pinion, bind, tie, fetter.
2. seize, grab, *Inf.* collar, lay hold of; wrestle, grapple; grip, gripe, clench, clutch, clasp.
3. settle, dispose of, establish, complete, cap, conclude, culminate, crown; close, wind up, finish off, round out, *Sl.* sew up, *Sl.* put on ice; verify, confirm, guarantee, make sure, *Sl.* cinch, *Sl.* have in the bag.
—*n.* **4.** fastener, holdfast, fastening; hold, grip, *Inf.* cinch, gripe, clench, clutch, clasp.

clincher, *n.* **1.** fastener, holdfast, fastening; clamp, vise; nail, screw, rivet, bolt.
2. determining factor, *Inf.* cruncher, finisher, last straw, straw that broke the camel's back; crowning blow, finishing blow, *Fr. coup de grâce*, *Sl.* sockdolager, deathblow; finishing touch, last stroke, windup, close, finale, *Inf.* payoff, punch line; culmination, crown, crowning touch, cap, capper, capstone, *Fr. pièce de résistance*; end, end of the line, match point.

cling[1], *v.* **1.** adhere to, stick to, be attached to; stick together, cohere, fuse, coalesce, unite, join.
2. hold tight, cleave to, hug, embrace; hold fast, grapple, clinch; fasten upon, grip, gripe, grasp; clench, clutch, clasp, hang onto.
3. cherish, love, be attached to, be fond of; remain faithful to, remain constant to, be devoted to; be infatuated with, *Both Sl.* be hooked on, be stuck on.

cling[2], *v.* **1.** ring, ting, tinkle, tintinnabulate, chime, ding, ding-dong; clink, chink, clank, click, clack; clang, clangor, resound, twang, vibrate, jingle, jangle, rattle; knell, toll, strike, sound.
—*n.* **2.** ring, ringing, ting, tinging, tinkle, tinkling, tintinnabulation; chime, chiming, ding, ding-dong; clink, clinking, chink, chinking, clank, clanking, click, clicking, clack, clacking; clang, clanging, clangor, clangoring, resounding, twang, twanging, vibrating; jingle, jingling, jangle, jangling, rattle, rattling; knell, knelling, toll, tolling, striking, sounding.

clinic, *n.* infirmary, hospital, polyclinic, medical center; dispensary, outpatients' ward, emergency room.

clink[1], *v.* **1.** ring, ting, chink, ding. See **cling**[2] (*def.* **1**).
—*n.* **2.** ringing, tinging, chinking, ding, ding-dong. See **cling**[2] (*def.* **2**).

clink[2], *n.* *Slang.* jail, prison, lockup. See **jail**.

clip[1], *v.* **1.** cut off, bob, crop, snip, nip; shear, shave, fleece; trim, pare, prune; shorten, truncate, stunt, check the growth of, pollard.
2. curtail, cut short, reduce, diminish, retrench; shorten, abridge, condense, epitomize, abstract; boil down; cramp, constrict, contract, compress.
3. cut out articles, make clippings, extract, excerpt, quote, cite, cull, glean.
4. *Informal.* hit, punch, strike, swat, smack. See **smack**.
5. move swiftly, go rapidly, race, run, speed.
6. *Slang.* overcharge, cheat, swindle, rook, bilk. See **cheat**.
—*n.* **7.** clipping, cutting, snipping, bobbing; shearing, fleecing, shaving; cropping, trimming, paring, pruning; stunting, checking, docking, curtailment, retrenchment, truncation; abstraction, reduction, compression, abbreviation, condensation, epitome, contraction, abridgment.
8. piece, snip, snippet, snatch, chip, clip, shaving, sliver, slice, *Brit. Dial.* collop, paring, cut, cutting; shred, gleaning, scrap, sample, remnant, fragment.
9. *Informal.* hit, blow, crack, punch, swat, smack. See **smack**.
10. *Informal.* pace, rate, speed.

clip[2], *n.* **1.** metal clasp, hasp, fastener, hook, buckle, coupler, copula, vise; grip, gripper, snap; clinch, nail.
—*v.* **2.** fasten together, clamp, hasp, clinch, hold, hook, buckle, couple, grip, vise, press.
3. encircle, encompass, surround, enclose, enfold, circumscribe, envelop.

clipper, *n.* **1.** speeder, *Inf.* speedster, flier, *Inf.* speed demon, racer; fast-sailing vessel, corsair, frigate; sleigh, sled, bobsled, toboggan.
2. **clippers** shears, pruning tools, cutters, scissors; hair trimmer, razor.

clipping, *n.* **1.** excerpt, quotation, citation, literary gleaning, selection, abstract, cutting.
2. snip, piece, snippet, snatch, chip, lock of hair; remnant, fragment, scrap, sample, shred; shaving, sliver, slice, *Brit. Dial.* collop, paring, cut, cutting.

clique, *n.* set, coterie, in crowd, crowd, clan, circle, knot; band, ring, gang, troop, team, group, community; fraternity, sorority, brotherhood, sodality, society, club, lodge, organization; sect, faction, order, party, camorra.

cloak, *n.* **1.** cape, mantle, capote, robe, dolman, domino, aba, pelisse, pelerine, cope, burnoose, mantelet, *Rom. Cath. Ch.* mantelletta, (*in Spain and Spanish America*) manta, *Obs.* manteau; poncho, shawl, wrap, palatot, coat, overcoat, jacket, sweater; tunic, tabard, toga, gown, smock, blouse, frock, sacque, sack dress.
2. cover, screen, blind, mask, veil, shroud; disguise, incognito, camouflage, masquerade, misrepresentation; pretext, semblance, front, subterfuge, evasion.
—*v.* **3.** hide, conceal, ensconce, cover up, mask, veil, shroud, robe; obscure, obfuscate, adumbrate, cloud, becloud, befog, haze.

clock, *n.* **1.** horologe, watch, timekeeper, timer, timepiece, dial; chronometer, chronoscope, chronograph; speedometer, taximeter; time clock.
2. **around the clock** all day and night, without a break, nonstop; ceaselessly, perpetually, constantly, continuously, endlessly, incessantly.
—*v.* **3.** time, mark the time, keep time, measure

time, *Inf.* stopwatch.

clockwork, *n.* **1.** precision machinery, mechanism, inner workings, works, wheels within wheels, wheelworks, synchrony, perfectly timed *or* accurate operation.

2. **like clockwork** regularly, systematically, methodically, at regular intervals, on schedule, according to plan; smoothly, evenly, without a hitch, steadily, uniformly; invariably, without exception, every time.

clod, *n.* **1.** lump, mass, gob, glob, wad, ball; nugget, chunk, *Inf.* hunk, large piece; clump, cluster, bunch, pile, heap, mound; bulge, hump, node, bump, knob, bulb, protuberance.

2. earth, soil, ground, *Archaic.* loam, *Archaic.* glebe, field; sod, turf, sward, lawn, grass, green, greensward; subsoil, undersoil, clay, gumbo, mud, mire; marl, fertilizer, humus, mulch.

3. stupid person, blockhead, dolt, dunce, dope, *Inf.* dummy, *Inf.* knucklehead, *Sl.* nudnik, *Sl.* stupidhead, fool; oaf, lout, *Inf.* goop, *Sl.* jerk, *Sl.* creep, donkey, ass. See **fool** (*def.* **1**).

cloddish, *adj.* awkward, clumsy, inept, maladroit, heavy-handed, blundering, bungling, gawky *or* gawkish, like a bull in a china shop, *Inf.* butterfingered, *Sl.* klutzy; loutish, oafish, doltish, lumpish, lumpen, clodhopping, clownish, lubberly; obtuse, stolid, dull, dense, *Inf.* thick; rude, vulgar, uncouth, coarse, boorish, churlish, unmannerly, ill-mannered, ill-bred.

clodhopper, *n.* **1.** rustic, peasant, provincial, country cousin, countryman, hobnail; farmer, plowman, plowboy, chuff, son *or* tiller of the soil, swain, kern, gaffer, (*in Egypt*) fellah, (*in Russia*) muszhik *or* mujick, (*in Spanish America and Southwestern U.S.*) peon, *Archaic.* hind; yokel, bumpkin, country bumpkin, hawbuck, *Dial.* lumpkin, *Often Disparaging.* hillbilly, *Disparaging.* bogtrotter, *Inf.* chawbacon, *Inf.* cider squeezer, *Sl.* hick, *Sl.* woodhick, *Sl.* rube, *Sl.* hayseed, *Sl.* hoosier, *Fr. Sl. truffe.*

2. **clodhoppers** brogans, brogues, heavy shoes, clumsy footgear, work shoes *or* boots, construction boots, hiking shoes *or* boots, *Sl.* gunboats, *Sl.* combat boots.

clog, *v.* **1.** encumber, hamper, hinder, cumber, place an obstacle in the way of, balk; impede, incommode, embarrass, delay, *U.S.* filibuster, retard, slow up *or* down, brake; frustrate, thwart, cross, oppose, countercheck, counteract; complicate, make things difficult, interfere, get in the way, intervene, intercede, interpose, come between; interrupt, break off, cease, discontinue, suspend, put an end to, curtail; deadlock, bring to a standstill, bring to an impasse; checkmate, foil, defeat, crush, stamp *or* wipe out.

2. check, hold in check, hold back, restrain, constrain, cramp, trammel, bridle, curb; disadvantage, handicap, cripple, saddle, burden, load; hobble, hopple, tether, tie up, shackle, fetter, handcuff, chain, lock up; prevent, block, obstruct, *Obs.* intercept, deter; detain, stay, keep, halt, stop, arrest; bar, blockade, barricade, stand in the way; prohibit, forbid, disallow, debar, exclude, shut out.

3. crowd, stuff, cram, fill up, fill to overflowing, overfill, overstuff, overcrowd; clot, gum up, congest, choke up, stop up, dam up, close off, back up.

—*n.* **4.** encumbrance, hindrance, impediment, stumbling block; snag, catch, hitch, rub, drawback, fly in the ointment; difficulty, complication, embarrassment, cumbrance, trouble, bother, pain in the neck, inconvenience, incommodity; hobble, handicap, disadvantage, burden, load, saddle; restraint, constraint, cramp, trammel, bridle, curb, bit; tether, cord, chain, leash; shackle, handcuffs, fetter, lock, padlock; prevention, *Obs.* interception, prohibition, forbiddance, disallowance, debarring, exclusion.

5. block, obstacle, obstruction, remora, bar, barrier, hurdle, barricade, blockade; congestion, jam, blockage, stoppage; dead end, blind alley, cul-de-sac, impasse, stalemate, deadlock, checkmate.

6. check, balk, stay, deterrent, detention; stop, halt, pause, arrestment, end, curtailment, cessation; interruption, discontinuation, suspension; delay, *U.S.* filibuster, retardation, brake; frustration, thwarting, crossing, countercheck; interference, intervention, intercession, interposal.

cloister, *n.* **1.** covered walk, ambulatory, promenade, walkway, corridor; arcade, colonnade, gallery, piazza, archway; courtyard, quadrangle; portico, porch, stoa, *U.S.* veranda.

2. monastery, abbey, priory, friary, convent, nunnery, cenoby; novitiate, enclosure; cubicle, cell, closet, stall, carrel.

3. refuge, asylum, retreat, hermitage, haven, shelter, resort, sanctuary, sanctum sanctorum, (*in ancient worship*) adytum; ark, covert, hideaway, mew, arbor, bower; den, study, library, ivory tower.

4. religious life, *Inf.* religion, the contemplative life, monasticism, monachism, sisterhood, nunhood, convent, monastery.

—*v.* **5.** confine, shut up, immure, wall in, *Inf.* hole up, incarcerate, imprison; embower, coop up, pen in, fence in, hedge in, restrict, limit, enclose, closet.

6. seclude, set apart, isolate, separate, segregate, sequester, hide, conceal, shelter; retire, withdraw, hibernate.

cloistered, *adj.* **1.** secluded, sequestered, hidden, concealed, secreted; sheltered, protected, shielded, guarded; closeted, confined, immured, walled up, enclosed, holed up, incarcerated, imprisoned, shut up, penned in, cooped up.

2. recluse, reclusive, apart, aloof, remote; separate, separated, segregated, set apart; isolated, solitary, private, alone, solitudinarian, hermitic.

3. retired, withdrawn, monastic, monachal, conventual, cloistral, cloisterlike, claustral.

close, *v.* **1.** shut, close up, close off, seal, seal off, obturate; lock, padlock, bolt, latch; fix, fasten, secure, *Scot.* steek.

2. stop, clog, choke, jam, congest; block, obstruct, bar, occlude, barricade, blockade, stand in the way; impede, hinder, trammel, bridle, restrain.

3. join, unite, connect, articulate, bind, tie, splice, link, yoke, attach; coalesce, consolidate, merge, blend, come together, fuse.

4. complete, conclude, terminate, end, finish, adjourn, climax, culminate, wind up; settle, fix, establish, clinch, complete, decide, agree, come to terms *or* an agreement; arrange, adjust, work out.

5. grapple with, clench, embrace, lay hold of, clutch, grip, wrest, seize; do battle, join issue, come to close quarters, struggle with, tussle with, *Sl.* tangle with, lock horns, cross swords, join combat.

6. **close down a.** discontinue, suspend, cease, halt, stop, drop, break off, leave off, put an end to, have done with, dispatch. **b.** crack down, eliminate, exterminate, stamp out, make a clean sweep.

7. **close in on a.** approach, near, draw near, come close *or* closer, draw close *or* closer. **b.** surround, envelop, encircle, encompass, engird, box, bottle up, hem in, beseige, beleaguer, trap.

8. **close out a.** (*all of price*) reduce, lower, decrease, discount, mark down, cut, slash, cheapen. **b.** liquidate, dispose of, finish off, cancel, withdraw, *Inf.* put the kibosh on, *Sl.* eighty-six.

—*adj.* **9.** compact, condensed, dense, solid, crushed, pinched, squeezed, crowded, packed, *Inf.* jam-packed,

stuffed, packed like sardines.
10. near, proximate, approximate, in close proximity, immediate, within an ace of; vicinal, neighboring, bordering, abutting, contiguous, adjacent.
11. similar, like, alike, not unlike, much the same; analogous, comparable, parallel; correspondent, corresponding, reciprocal.
12. intimate, dear, familiar, *Scot.* pack, bosom; clubby, chummy, hob-and-nob, hand and glove, *Inf.* thick, *Inf.* thick as thieves, *Sl.* buddy-buddy, *Sl.* palsy-walsy; inseparable, indivisible, indissoluble, inseverable, fast.
13. confidential, privy, private, exclusive, special, personal; secret, top secret, inviolate, unrevealable, undivulgeable; screened, guarded, concealed, hidden.
14. tight, tight-fitting, skin-tight, snug, hugging.
15. intense, concentrated, strict, minute; constant, unremitting, unrelenting, assiduous, dogged, hands-on; intent, searching, vigilant, acute, attentive.
16. faithful, conscientious, true, accurate, literal, sound; scrupulous, exacting, stringent, particular, exact, precise.
17. well-matched, nearly equal *or* even, on equal *or* even terms, even-odds, *Inf.* fifty-fifty, *Sl.* anybody's; hard-fought, sharply contested, nip and tuck, neck and neck, nose to nose, photo finish, by a whisker, *Sl.* by a nose, *Sl.* by a hair.
18. shut, shut tight, closed, locked, latched, bolted, fixed, fast, secure.
19. enclosed, cloistered, closeted, secluded, shut in.
20. surrounding, enclosing, encompassing, enveloping, engulfing, engirding.
21. barred, blocked, barricaded, blockaded, obstructed, hindered, impeded, shut off.
22. narrow, tight, confined, confining, constricting, restricting, limiting, binding.
23. heavy, oppressive, muggy, humid, sweltering, thick, stagnant, stifling, suffocating; musty, stale, stuffy, fusty, moldy, mildewy.
24. reticent, taciturn, uncommunicative. See **close-mouthed**.
25. miserly, parsimonious, penurious. See **close-handed**.
—adv. **26.** almost, nearly, *Inf.* pretty near *or* close, closely, within a hair *or* eyelash; not quite, just about, all but, well-nigh, as good as.
27. near, nearby, near *or* close at hand, nigh, hard by, close by, at one's door, at one's heels.
—n. **28.** end, conclusion, termination, finish, finale, windup, coda, *Sl.* payoff, *Sl.* curtains.
29. enclosure, court, courtyard, piazza, plaza, plazza, arcade, cul-de-sac.

closefisted, *adj.* mean, stingy, mingy, tight, tight-fisted, close, miserly, niggardly, pinch-penny, penny-pinching, grudging, scrimping, ungenerous, illiberal, beggarly, penurious, parsimonious.

close-fitting, *adj.* tight, tight-fitting, skin-tight, snug, close, hugging; (*all of clothing*) constricting, restricting, limiting, confining, hampering, binding; glued, plastered, like paper on the wall.

close-mouthed, *adj.* reticent, taciturn, uncommunicative, reserved, retiring, quiet, close; silent, mute, mum, obmutescent, secretive, evasive; brief, terse, concise, laconic, *Rare.* pauciloquent.

closet, *n.* **1.** cabinet, cupboard, celleret, locker, cuddy, storage compartment, *Obs.* coin; wardrobe, press, clothes press, case; pantry, scullery, larder, buttery, ambry, store room, storage, cellar; repository, cache, vault, crypt, safe, *Chiefly Brit.* strong room.
2. cubicle, cubbyhole, cubby, booth, stall, bay, carrel, carol, cell; office, berth, cabin, chamber, camera; coop, pen, cage, confine; compartment, enclosure, room.
—v. **3.** confine, pen, cage, coop up, shut *or* close up, lock up; cloister, sequester, seclude.
—adj. **4.** private, secluded, sequestered, isolated, hidden, concealed; secret, covert, undercover, clandestine, furtive, unrevealed.
5. speculative, notional, theoretical, hypothetical; impractical, visionary, quixotic, romantic, unrealizable.

closure, *n.* **1.** stoppage, blockage, occlusion, obturation; locking, padlocking, bolting, latching, securing; plugging, stopping, corking, stanching, blocking, damming; strike, walkout, shutdown.
2. conclusion, termination, cessation, windup, *Rhet.* peroration, *Parl. Proc.* cloture; completion, culmination, consummation, fulfillment, perfection, realization.
3. lid, top, cover; plug, cork, stopper, stopple, bung; spigot, tap, faucet, valve; joint, joiner, juncture, union, connection, coupler, articulation; lock, padlock, latch, bolt; jam, congestion, impediment, barricade, blockade, barrier, obstruction, obstacle; bulwark, dam, levee, dike.

clot, *n.* **1.** lump, glob, knot, curd, precipitate, coagulum, coagulation, *Med.* grume, *Pathol.* thrombus; clump, gob, mass, concretion; obstruction, block, clog.
—v. **2.** coagulate, curd, cake, set; congeal, jell, jelly, thicken, curdle, (*of milk*) clabber; block, obstruct, clog, stop up, cut off.

cloth, *n.* **1.** woven fabric, textile, material, *Chiefly Brit.* stuff, dry goods; tissue, rag.
2. **the cloth** the clergy, the pulpit, the priesthood, the ministry, holy orders.

clothe, *v.* **1.** dress, garb, vest, attire, apparel, habit, *Sl.* dude up, *Sl.* drag; don, put on, slip on, slip into.
2. outfit, fit out, fit up, fit, rig up, rig out, rig, gear, turn out, accouter; array, bedizen, deck, deck out, bedeck, dress up, trap, trap out, caparison; *All Inf.* doll up, pretty up, gussy up, spruce up; *All Sl.* swank up, trick up, fig out.
3. cover, wrap, cloak, envelop, enwrap; muffle, swaddle; endow, endue *or* indue, invest.

clothes, *n.* **1.** apparel, wearing apparel, wear, dress, attire, garb, clothing; garments, raiment, vestments, habiliments, habit, *Inf.* gear, *Inf.* toggery, *Inf.* togs, *Inf.* duds, *Sl.* threads, *Sl.* rags, (*of transvestites*) *Sl.* drag; array, wardrobe, accouterment; livery, uniform.
2. costume, outfit, ensemble, *Inf.* getup.
3. finery, best clothes, best bib and tucker, *Inf.* Sunday clothes, *Inf.* Sunday best, *Inf.* Sunday-go-to-meetings, *Sl.* glad rags, *Sl.* heavy threads.
4. bedclothes, bedding, bedcovers, linens, sheets, blankets.

cloud, *n.* **1.** haze, vapor, mist, steam, fog, *Inf.* pea soup; nebula, nebulosity, smoke, smog, soot, dust, puff; smoke screen, dust storm.
2. pall, shroud, mantle, cloak, veil, screen, shade, shadow, cover.
3. blur, smudge, smear, smutch, smirch; blotch, spot, blurred spot, blot, macula, patch; stain, maculation; speck, speckle, daub; blemish, tarnish, imperfection, defect, flaw, fault, mar, taint; mark, stigma, brand; soil, dirt, grime.
4. despondency, despair, wretchedness, desolation, depression, dejection, prostration; oppression, hardship, misery, suffering; sorrow, distress, grief, woe; gloom, darkness, dimness; bewilderment, dilemma, confusion, perplexity; fogginess, obscurity, obscuration; occultation, eclipse; futility, uselessness, hopelessness, dark future; tragedy, disaster, ill fortune,

catastrophe, calamity; reverse, reversal, setback, comedown, bitter pill.

5. handwriting on the wall, ill omen, ill wind, evil star, gathering clouds, storm brewing, warning; skeleton in the closet, ghost, specter, scandal, bar sinister; trouble, affliction, ill fortune, thorn in the flesh, plague, pestilence, scourge, blight, bane; visitation, curse, evil dispensation, punishment; blot on one's escutcheon, disgrace, badge of infamy; premonition, doubt, suspicion, apprehension, damp, nightmare, incubus.

6. throng, crowd, congregation, flock; multitude, horde, host, legion, storm, army, vast number, vast assemblage, galaxy, shower; swarm, dense mass; volley, flight.

7. **in the clouds a.** absent-minded, faraway, abstracted, not all there; preoccupied, bemused, lost in a dream, lost in thought, dead to the world; dreaming, dreamy, woolgathering. **b.** impractical, unrealistic, unreasonable, irrational, starry-eyed.

8. **under a cloud** under suspicion, suspect, suspected, distrusted; in disgrace, in disrepute, *Sl.* in the doghouse, out of favor, unable to show one's face.

—v. **9.** overshadow, overspread, adumbrate, becloud, befog; darken, smoke, dim, bedim, dusk, blind, blacken; overcast, grow cloudy, gloom, darkle, promise rain; nebulize, fog, pale, mist, haze, shade, shadow; eclipse, hide, conceal, occult; frost, frost over; dull, blur, blear; shroud, cover, cloak, veil, screen, curtain.

10. depress, oppress, overwhelm, overcome; distress, upset, disturb, unbalance.

11. bewilder, confuse, perplex; disorient, muddle, mystify, baffle; obfuscate, obscure, complicate, confound.

12. put to shame, humiliate, mortify, discredit, expose, gibbet; denounce, anathematize, degrade, defile, defame, slander, vilify, vilipend; censure, criticize, reproach; malign, slur, give a bad name; doubt, mistrust, suspect; challenge, question; stigmatize, mark, brand; taint, sully, tarnish, stain.

cloudburst, *n.* shower, downpour, torrent, rainstorm, driving rain, pouring rain; raining cats and dogs; deluge, inundation, cataract, flood, flash flood.

cloudy, *adj.* **1.** overcast, overclouded, overshadowed, shadowy, gray; somber, lowering, heavy, leaden, darkened, eclipsed; sunless, starless, moonless; hazy, nubilous, foggy, misty, *Archaic.* caliginous, vaporous, murky; moist, damp, drizzly, drippy, wet; humid, muggy, steamy.

2. obscure, obfuscated, vague, indefinite, ambiguous, nebulous, undefined, ill-defined; indistinct, blurred, blurry, bleary, out of focus, unclear; incomprehensible, mysterious, occult, veiled, concealed, unrevealed; baffled, bewildered, confused, muddled, fogged.

3. gloomy, saturnine, dismal, dreary, depressed, oppressed, sullen, glowering; sorrowful, mournful, lugubrious; clouded, troubled, worried, anxious, unquiet, nervous.

4. milky, emulsified, opalescent, opaque, nontransparent; turbid, unsettled, stirred-up, agitated; thick, dense, viscous, viscid; muddy, sooty, smoky, fuliginous.

5. variegated, mottled, blotched, maculate, spotted; lackluster, lusterless, dull, dim, dingy, flat.

6. questionable, dubious, doubtful, suspect, distrusted, mistrusted; disgraced, in disrepute, discredited, denounced, defamed; defiled, maligned, stigmatized, tainted, sullied, stained, tarnished.

clown, *n.* **1.** buffoon, merry-andrew; jester, fool, harlequin, pantomime, mime; punch, pantaloon, Scaramouch; zany droll, wag, *Fr. farceur*; wit, comic, comedian, humorist, funnyman; joker, prankster, practical joker, *Inf.* cutup, *Inf.* card.

2. boor, churl, curmudgeon, brute, yahoo, *Inf.* goop; lout, oaf, dolt, clod, clodhopper, lubber, ox, slouch; *Inf.* lummox, *Sl.* klutz, *Sl.* galoot, *Sl.* lug; bungler, bumbler, fumbler, botcher, blunderer, boggler, *Inf.* butterfingers, *Inf.* duffer.

3. peasant, rustic, country cousin, provincial, gaffer, hobnail, *Often Disparaging.* hillbilly, *Inf.* chawbacon, *Inf.* cider squeezer; yokel, bumpkin, country bumpkin, hawbuck, *Sl.* hick, *Sl.* rube.

—v. **4.** jest, make fun, banter, chaff, joke, *Sl.* wisecrack; play pranks, *Inf.* cut up, trick, fool; pantomime, mime, burlesque, parody, lampoon, ridicule.

cloy, *v.* **1.** glut, stuff, cram, gorge, overfeed; surfeit, pall, overfill, overdo; satiate, sate, saturate, fill up, satisfy, suffice.

2. choke, gag, sicken, nauseate; dull, deaden, numb, benumb, blunt, obtund; weary, exhaust, tire, bore.

club, *n.* **1.** cudgel, bludgeon, bastinado, blackjack, bat, flail, billy, *Chiefly Irish Eng.* shillelagh, mace, *Archaic.* maul, *Obs.* truncheon; cane, baton, staff, stick, *Polo.* mallet.

2. society, organization, brotherhood, fraternity, sorority, fellowship, lodge, sodality, community, troop, team, group; clique, coterie, set, circle, knot, band, ring, gang, crowd, clan; association, affiliation, consortium, company, alliance, league, coalition, federation, guild, union, *Inf.* outfit.

3. headquarters, center, rendezvous, meeting place, house, clubhouse, haunt, casino, *Inf.* hangout; retreat, lodge, camp.

4. cabaret, night club, key club, *Inf.* night spot, *Inf.* spot; bistro, roadhouse, tavern, bar, pub, public house, rathskeller, beer garden, *Sl.* dive, *Sl.* joint, *Sl.* honky-tonk; dance hall, discotheque, *Inf.* disco, *Sl.* juke joint.

—v. **5.** cudgel, bludgeon, baste, bastinado, blackjack, flail, fustigate, *Archaic.* truncheon; beat, batter, maul, mall, flog, pommel, pummel.

6. coalesce, league, team, band, herd, pool; associate, affiliate, ally, syndicate, federate, confederate, incorporate; unite, combine, merge, conjoin, join together.

7. *Often* **club up** *or* **together** join forces, pull together, stand shoulder to shoulder, stand side by side, cooperate, concert, work *or* act together, act in concert; lump together, pool resources, make a joint contribution, make a common purse; share, apportion, split *or* divide the cost, *Inf.* divvy up the cost, *Inf.* go Dutch.

cluck, *v.* **1.** cackle, chuck, chuckle, click, clack; crow, quack; chirp, chirrup, chirk, coo.

—n. **2.** cackle, cackling, chuck, chucking, chuckle, chuckling, click, clicking, clack, clacking; crow, crowing, quack, quacking; chirp, chirping, chirrup, chirruping, chirk, chirking, coo, cooing.

clue, *n.* **1.** hint, tip-off, intimation, cue, suggestion; inkling, trace, note, glimmer, suspicion; insinuation, implication, inference; impression, feeling, idea, notion; direction, indication, indicator, pointer, guide, mark; sign, token, symptom, symbol, key.

—v. **2.** *Informal.* give [s.o.] a hint, tip off, intimate, cue, suggest; insinuate, imply, infer, give the impression; give a sign, indicate, direct, point out, guide.

3. **clue in** *Slang.* fill [s.o.] in, give [s.o.] the facts, *Inf.* give [s.o.] the low-down, give [s.o.] the details, inform [s.o.].

clump, *n.* **1.** cluster, group, bunch, aggregation, colony; thicket, shrubs, bushes, copse, *Chiefly Brit.*

spinney, *Bot.* aggregate; bundle, sheaf, pack, package, packet; collection, assembly, assemblage, pile, heap, stack, shock, mound, hill, mountain.
2. mass, agglutination, lump, clod; nugget, chunk, *Inf.* hunk, large piece; gob, glob, wad, ball; bulb, node, knot, gnarl, knur, knob, nodule; protuberance, projection, bump, bulge, hump, hunch.
3. clomping, stamp, stamping, *Inf.* stomp, *Inf.* stomping, heavy step *or* tread, stump; tramp, tramping, trudge, trudging, plod, plodding, lumbering, clamping; clumsy gait, stumbling, tripping, bump, bumping; plump, plumping, plop, plopping, *Inf.* plunk, *Inf.* plunking; thud, thudding, *Sl.* bonk, *Sl.* bonking, *Sl.* clunk, *Sl.* clunking, bang, banging.
—*v.* **4.** clomp, stamp, *Inf.* stomp, step *or* tread heavily, stump; tramp, trudge, plod, lumber, clamp; walk clumsily, stumble, trip, bump; plump, plop, *Inf.* plunk, thud, *Sl.* bonk, *Sl.* clunk, bang.
5. cluster, group, bunch, lump, mass, unite, agglutinate, stick together; bundle, pack, package, tie together, roll up, bind, sheaf; pile, heap, stack, shock; collect, assemble, congregate, aggregate.

clumsy, *adj.* **1.** awkward, ungraceful, ungainly; oafish, doltish, clodish, lumbering, heavy-footed, lubberly, bearish, bovine, lumpish, hulking; stiff, wooden, stodgy, stolid, heavy, unwieldly, ponderous.
2. unhandy, inept, bungling, bumbling, clownish, blundering; unskillful, left-handed, maladroit, bunglesome, ambisinister, like a bull in a china shop, *Inf.* all thumbs, *Inf.* butterfingered, *Inf.* klutzy.
3. rough, uncouth, gauche, unpolished, boorish; inelegant, graceless, coarse, gross, ill-conceived, crude, crass, thoughtless, insensitive, inconsiderate, tactless, untoward, inappropriate, unfitting.

cluster, *n.* **1.** clump, tuft, thicket, grove, truss, *Bot.* raceme, *Bot.* panicle; bouquet, posy, bunch, batch; wisp, shock, sheaf; fagot, bundle, bale; fascicle.
2. collection, group, knot, band, company; body, congregation, assembly, gathering; crowd, number, throng; bevy, covey, flock, swarm, hive, school, pack, drove, herd.
3. accumulation, heap, pile, cumulation; galaxy, constellation, mass, array, host, multitude; cloud, cumulus, drift; set, series, assortment, variety, medley, jumble, hodgepodge; clutter, *Inf.* mess.
4. amassment, assemblage, *Inf.* caboodle; aggregation, concentration, convergence, agglomeration, conglomeration.
—*v.* **5.** accumulate, collect, gather; group, bunch up *or* together; mass, crowd, congregate, aggregate, conglomerate, agglomerate; flock together, throng, herd, swarm, converge, surge; bring together, rally, muster, call up, round up, round in.
6. assemble, convene, forgather, come together, meet, mingle, *Inf.* gang up, huddle, go into a huddle, get together, rendezvous; convoke, summon, call together.
7. bundle, bunch; bind, tie, truss, swathe; colligate.

clutch[1], *v.* **1.** seize, snatch, grab, lay hold of, fasten upon; catch, capture, take, hook, snag, ensnare, *Sl.* nab.
2. grip, grasp, gripe, clasp, clench; hang on to, cling, hug, embrace, *Sl.* clinch.
3. grope for, claw at, snatch at, catch at, make a grab at, reach desperately for; pounce on, swoop down on.
—*n.* **4.** grasp, grip, gripe, clasp, embrace, clench; snatching, taking, seizure, capture, apprehension, *Sl.* nabbing.
5. power, control, grasp, grip, gripe, hold, clasp; hands, talons, claws, fangs; keep, custody, possession, retention; mercy, mastery, dominion, dominance.
6. hook, claw, talon, pounce; pincer, chela, nipper.
7. clip, clamp, vise, wrench, pliers; forceps, tongs, tweezers, pincers.

clutch[2], *n.* hatch, setting, nest, brood, incubation.

clutter, *v.* **1.** litter, mess, tumble, jumble, scatter, strew about; disarrange, disorder, unsettle, discompose; disorganize, shuffle, dishevel, make a shambles of, *Inf.* turn topsy-turvy, *Inf.* muss up.
2. clatter, rattle, racket; chatter, jabber, cackle, clack; prate, gabble, gush, blab, spout, sputter, gibber.
—*n.* **3.** heap, mess, jumble, huddle; confused medley, hash, patchwork, olla-podrida, gallimaufry, farrago, hodgepodge, mishmash; motley collection, odds and ends, lumber; litter, trash, *Inf.* garbage.
4. chaos, confusion, disarray, mix-up, muddle, tangle, tumble, minglement.
5. noise, racket, clatter, rattling, clamor, raucousness; chatter, jabber, prattle, cackle, gibberish, galimatias.

coach, *n.* **1.** stagecoach, carriage, phaeton, landau, brougham, surrey, cabriolet, coupe, victoria, barouche, four-wheeler, hackney, *U.S.* rockaway, buggy; gig, calash, curricle, chaise, tilbury; bus, motorcoach, omnibus; sedan, car, vehicle, conveyance; (*railroad*) day coach.
2. director, athletic director, *Inf.* gym teacher; manager, trainer.
3. tutor, private teacher; instructor, teacher, preceptor, mentor; voice *or* vocal instructor, dance teacher, ballet master.
—*v.* **4.** direct, teach, instruct, train, drill, excercise, *Inf.* whip into shape, *Inf.* put [s.o.] through the paces; tutor, guide, prompt, prime, *Inf.* prep, *Inf.* cram, *Inf.* brief.

coagulate, *v.* congeal, clot, gel, gelatinize, jell, jelly, jellify, thicken, *Obs.* incrassate; curdle, curd, *Scot. and North Central U.S.* lopper, *Pathol.* caseate; solidify, concrete, harden, cake, set, crystallize, compress.

coagulation, *n.* congelation, gelatinization, gel, clot, jellification, thickening, *Obs.* incrassation, *Pathol.* caseation; solidification, concretion, crystallization, compression, hardening, setting, caking.

coal, *n.* **1.** anthracite, hard coal, bitumen, soft coal, culm, jet; black diamonds, cobbles, slack; coke, fuel.
2. ember, clinker, cinder, ash; charcoal, briquette.

coalesce, *v.* **1.** unite, join, combine, connect, come together, converge, coincide; ally, league, confederate, join forces, band together; affiliate, associate, intermingle, commingle, mingle, mix; gather, cluster, muster, herd, throng, flock.
2. amalgamate, consolidate, incorporate, merge, blend, fuse.

coalition, *n.* **1.** unification, union, junction, conjugation, combination; fusion, amalgamation, consolidation, incorporation, conglomeration, integration, synthesis, merging, blending, fusing.
2. alliance, league, bloc, Bund, federation, confederacy, entente; partnership, copartnership, affiliation, association; corporation, conglomerate, trust, syndicate, cartel, consortium, combine, machine, *Sl.* plunderbund; council, junta, conclave, divan, assembly, convention, diet; cabal, conspiracy, junto, camarilla, clique, secret society; faction, party, splinter group.

coarse, *adj.* **1.** rough, uneven, bristly, setaceous, scratchy, prickly, bearded, whiskered; rough-grained, coarse-grained, sandpaper, linsey-woolsey; shaggy, hairy, wrinkled, *Bot.* rugose; scaly, jagged, broken, craggy, knobbed, knobby, nubbly, lumpy, bumpy; heavy, rugged, thick.
2. crude, unrefined, unmilled, unground, unpurified,

impure, unprocessed; flawed, imperfect, unperfected, rudimentary, undeveloped, primitive.

3. uncivil, uncouth, rude, crude, crass, unpolished; rough-hewn, homespun, homely, earthy; rustic, countrified, loutish, churlish, boorish, ignorant, unsophisticated; ill-mannered, ill-bred, impolite; unmannerly, ungentlemanly, unladylike, unwomanly; unseemly, unbecoming, indecorous; inharmonious, harsh, grating; gruff, bearish, boisterous, *Inf.* loud, brazen, brassy.

4. vulgar, obscene, lewd, lurid, scurrilous, Fescennine; ribald, bawdy, pornographic, smutty, *Sl.* raunchy; lascivious, prurient, base, foul, foul-mouthed, rank, filthy, dirty; indelicate, indecent, offensive, disgusting, revolting.

5. inferior, second-rate, faulty, low-class, raffish; mediocre, ordinary, prosaic, commonplace, common; sorry, trashy, tawdry, cheap, shabby, shoddy, paltry.

coarsen, *v.* roughen, thicken, densify, callous, harden, ossify; toughen, indurate, inure, desensitize, anesthetize, numb, benumb, blunt, dull, deaden.

coarseness, *n.* **1.** vulgarity, commonness, lowness, crudeness, rudeness; incivility, impropriety, unseemliness, ungentlemanly *or* unladylike behavior, bad manners; misconduct, rowdyism, ruffianism.

2. unrefinement, lack of polish, inelegance, parvenuism, lack of breeding, poor taste, Philistinism, gaucherie, tactlessness; boorishness, churlishness, brashness, brazenness.

3. indecency, indelicacy, offensiveness, scurrilousness; obscenity, foulness, filth, filthiness, lewdness, prurience, ribaldry, bawdiness, smuttiness, *Sl.* raunchiness.

4. cheapness, gaudiness, tawdriness, trashiness, shabbiness, shoddiness.

5. scratchiness, bristliness, prickliness; roughness, shagginess; hardness, callousness.

coast, *n.* **1.** seashore, shore, strand, seaside, seaboard, seacoast, littoral, water's edge; shoreline, coastline, strand line, high tide mark; beach, sands, sand, foreshore, inning, *Fr. plage, Chiefly Brit.* shingle, *Law.* derelict; waterside, edge, margin, rim, brink.

—*v.* **2.** slide down, sled, sledride, toboggan, bobsled, ski, skate; glide, glissade, volplane, float, drift, sail, waft, skim over the surface.

3. hug the shore, ply the coast, keep land in sight, stay near the coast, sail from port to port; border, skirt, rim, lie along the shore.

coastal, *adj.* seaboard, coastwise, shore, seaside, beachfront, littoral, waterside, riparian.

coat, *n.* **1.** overcoat, *Chiefly Brit.* greatcoat, surcoat, fearnought, dreadnought, maxim, midi, fur, mink, redingote; trenchcoat, mackintosh, raincoat, slicker; jacket, parka, machinaw, carcoat, blazer, sportcoat, spencer, windbreaker, *Chiefly Brit.* tunic, *All U.S. Mil.* battle jacket, combat jacket, Eisenhower jacket; wrap, sweater, shawl, stole, mantilla, poncho, haik, paletot, smock; cloak, cape, mantle, capote, robe, dolman, domino, aba, pelisse, pelerine, cope, burnoose, mantelot, (*in Spain and Spanish America*) manta, *Rom. Cath. Ch.* mantelletta, *Obs.* manteau.

2. fur, fleece, wool, pelage, pile, hide, pelt, fell; bark, crust, rind, peel, peeling, husk, shuck, pod, shell, hull, outside, exterior, *Bot.* epicarp; skin, membrane, pellicle, integument, derma, *Anat., Zool.* dermis, *Anat.* corium, scarfskin, *Anat., Zool., Bot.* epidermis, involucre, *Anat., Zool.* cortex, *Anat., Zool., Bot.* tunica; sac, cover, covering, case, casing, wrapping, wrapper, sheath, sheathing, envelope, enclosure, palea, *Bot.* periogonium, *Bot.* pericarp, *Anat.* pericardium, *Zool.* lorica.

3. layer, blanket, dusting, coating, film, sheet, leaf, foil, lamella, lamina; mask, screen, veil.

—*v.* **4.** cloak, mantle, jacket, fur, bundle [s.o.] up, wrap [s.o.] up; robe, gown, garb, clothe, dress.

5. cover, overlay, paint, enamel, gild, wash, whitewash, calcimine, plaster, parget; overcoat, varnish, lacquer, glaze, veneer, laminate.

coating, *n.* **1.** layer, blanket, dusting, film. See **coat** (*def.* **3**).

2. suiting, wool, tweed, worsted, flannel, gabardine, mackintosh; fabric, material, cloth.

coat of mail, *n.* hauberk, byrnie, habergeon; mail, chain mail, armor, suit of armor, armor plate, armature, panoply; cuirass, corselet, lorica, breastplate, *Armor.* brigandine; protection, covering, sheathing.

coax, *v.* **1.** wheedle, cajole, beguile, charm, inveigle; persuade, win over, palaver, induce, move; invite, lure, entice, wile; encourage, urge, entreat, importune, implore; blandish, flatter, *Inf.* sweet-talk, *Inf.* soft-soap, butter up, *Inf.* butter, *Inf.* honey up; humor, jolly, pamper, pander to, cater to; fawn on, play up to, curry favor with.

2. manipulate, work, manuever, guide, direct, steer, pilot, engineer.

coaxing, *n.* wheedling, cajolery, blarney, beguilement, charm, inveiglement; urging, entreaty, importunity, imploring; persuasion, palaver, *Inf.* sweet talk, *Inf.* soft soap, *Inf.* honeyed words, *Sl.* line, *Sl.* snow job; humoring, jollying, pandering to, catering to, pampering, *Inf.* stroking; flattery, blandishment, *Inf.* butter, *Inf.* honey; fawning, playing up to, *Sl.* buttering-up, *Inf.* apple-polishing, currying favor.

cobweb, *n.* **1.** spider's web, gossamer, thread, filament, fiber, fibril, fibrilla, *Biol.* membrane, *Zool.* webbing.

2. gossamer, cheesecloth, mosquito netting, gauze, tissue, tissue paper; sheer, chiffon, voile, organza, organdy, lace, filigree; ephemera, thin air, vapor, smoke, fog, dust; bubble, fizz, effervescence, suds, foam, froth, lather, spume, spray; feather, fluff, flue, down, thistledown; dream, fantasy, daydream, illusion; hallucination, phantom, shadow, ghost, spirit; ignis fatuus, will-o'-the-wisp.

3. plot, intrigue, scheme, machination, conspiracy, complicated plan; network, mesh, web; net, trap, snare, ensnarement; tangle, snarl, entanglement, involvement, involution, entwinement, intertwinement; lattice, latticework, fret, fretwork, meander; labyrinth, maze.

4. cobwebs confusion, indistinctness, fog, fogginess, vagueness, obscurity, dimness, cloudiness, unclarity; perplexity, uncertainty, bewilderment, bafflement, nonplus; paradox, puzzle, dilemma, quandary; disorder, disarray, disarrangement, disconcertment, muddle, jumble, mess.

cock[1], *n.* **1.** rooster, chanticleer, cockerel, male chicken; male bird *or* fowl, gander, drake, gobbler.

2. weathercock, weather vane, wind vane, vane.

3. leader, chief, captain. See **leader**.

4. stopcock, valve, faucet, tap, spigot.

cock[2], *v.* **1.** tilt, tip, incline, turn, twist, bend; set, position, pose.

2. stand up *or* upright, perk up, rise, stick up *or* out; bristle, stand on end, stiffen up.

3. *Dialect.* strut, swagger, swashbuckle, parade, put on airs, show off, flaunt oneself.

cockalorum, *n. Informal.* bantam cock, bantam, smart aleck, wiseacre, *Sl.* wise guy; jackanapes, whippersnapper.

cockeyed, *adj.* **1.** cross-eyed, strabismal, strabismic, strabismical, squinting, squint-eyed.

2. *Slang.* tilted, crooked, not straight, at an angle, twisted, slanted, sloped; awry, askew, to one side, sideways; slanting, aslant, slantwise, at a slant, sloping, aslope, at a slope.

3. *Slang.* foolish, absurd, crazy, *Sl.* cockamamie, nonsensical, senseless, insane, wild. See **foolish** (*def.* 2).

4. *Slang.* wrong, mistaken, erroneous, false, faulty; incorrect, off the mark, inaccurate, inexact, imprecise.

cocksure, *adj.* **1.** assured, self-assured, confident, self-confident, self-possessed, perfectly sure *or* certain of oneself; steady, unwavering, unswerving, unhesitating, unflinching, unblinking; in control, in charge, on top of everything, in command.

2. overconfident, too sure, cocky, arrogant, haughty, supercilious, self-important; conceited, *Inf.* stuck-up, snobbish, snobby, *Inf.* snotty, *Inf.* snooty, condescending, patronizing; overproud, inflated, puffed up, bloated, egotistic, egotistical, big on oneself, *Sl.* stuck on oneself, in love with oneself.

3. self-assertive, presumptuous, forward, assertive, aggressive, *Inf.* pushy; overbearing, domineering, *Inf.* bossy, authoritarian; bumptious, brazen, brassy, *Inf.* fresh, *Inf.* nervy, audacious, bold; impudent, insolent, *Inf.* cheeky, brash, rude, *Inf.* snippy, impertinent, saucy, pert.

coddle, *v.* **1.** pamper, cocker, cosset, dandle, mollycoddle, *Obs.* fondle; indulge, favor, humor, dote on, cater to, wait on hand and foot, pet, spoil, baby.

2. poach; simmer, stew, steep, brew, heat, cook gently.

code, *n.* **1.** digest, pandect, capitulary, body of law, corpus juris, civil code.

2. ethic, value system, morality; morals, principles, ethics; rule, law, principle, standard, criterion, canon, maxim, prescription, guideline, regulation.

3. cipher, cryptogram, cryptograph; cryptology, secret language *or* writing.

codicil, *n.* addition, addendum, supplement, rider, appendix, epilogue, coda, tail, back matter, subscript, postscript, PS, *Law.* allonge; afterthought, second thought, reconsideration.

codify, *v.* **1.** (*all of a set of laws*) digest, abstract, summarize, synopsize; condense, compress, concentrate, consolidate.

2. classify, group, arrange, pigeonhole; order, grade, graduate, rank, rate; catalogue, list, file, index, tabulate, alphabetize; organize, systematize, systemize, methodize, coordinate; standardize, formalize, regularize.

coequal, *adj.* **1.** equal, equipotent, equipollent, on equal *or* even terms, on the same footing; equivalent, tantamount, synonymous, all one, all the same, *Inf.* six of one, half a dozen of the other; equibalanced, equiponderant; uniform, of a kind, of a piece, cast in the same mold; level, even, parallel.

2. correspondent, corresponding, coordinate, complementary, complemental, complementing; correlative, correlational, correlated, reciprocal, reciprocative.

—*n.* **3.** peer, compeer, equal, rival; partner, colleague, confrere, associate.

4. counterpart, equivalent, match, twin, double, other half, alter ego, chip off the old block; alternate, pendant, companion, mate, fellow; correspondent, coordinate, correlative, parallel, analogue.

coerce, *v.* **1.** compel, force, drive, press, constrain, pressure, oblige, hustle, railroad; impel, urge, impress, provoke, extort, cause, require, exact, necessitate, make; draft, conscript, commandeer; persuade, induce, prevail upon, insist upon, *Inf.* shove *or* ram down one's throat; apply pressure, *Sl.* lean against *or* on, armtwist, twist [s.o.'s] arm, put the screws on *or* to, *Inf.* strong-arm, put the heat on, squeeze.

2. tyrannize, terrorize, threaten, exact, bulldoze, dragoon; bully, hector, torment, harass, abuse, taunt, tease, bullyrag; intimidate, browbeat, overawe, cow, frighten, terrify, petrify.

3. control, dominate, lay down the law to, supervise, direct, manage, boss, manipulate; domineer, overbear, boss around, bear down upon, lord it over, *Inf.* pull rank, override, ride roughshod over.

coercion, *n.* **1.** compulsion, pressure, duress, constraint, obligation; urge, provocation, requirement, necessitation; persuasion, inducement, insistence, armtwisting.

2. tyranny, terror, threat, force, enforcement; bullying, tormenting, harassment, abuse; intimidation, browbeating, frightening.

3. control, domination, supervision, manipulation; dominance, overriding; dictatorship, police state.

coeval, *adj.* contemporary, coexistent, coexisting, coetaneous, coeternal; contemporaneous, simultaneous, coinstantaneous, isochronal, isochronous, synchronous, synchronal; concurrent, concomitant, coincident, parallel; coextensive, conterminous, coterminous.

coexist, *v.* contemporize, coextend, happen together, exist together, exist side by side; concur, parallel, coincide, synchronize; accompany, go hand in hand with, keep pace with, keep in step with.

coexistence, *n.* concurrence, concurrency, simultaneity, simultaneousness, contemporaneity, contemporaneousness, coinstantaneousness, isochronism; coincidence, concomitance, concomitancy, coexistency; coevality, contemporariness, coetaneity, coetaneousness; coextension.

coexistent, *adj.* **1.** contemporary, coeval, coetaneous, coeternal, coexisting; simultaneous, contemporaneous, coinstantaneous, isochronal, isochronous, synchronous, synchronal; concomitant, coincident; concurrent, parallel, collateral, side-by-side; conterminous, coterminous, coextensive.

2. compatible, congenial, agreeable, cooperative, cooperating, symbiotic.

coffee, *n.* **1.** espresso, cappuccino, café au lait, *Sl.* java, *Sl.* mud; stimulant, *Inf.* pick-me-up *or* pick up.

2. coffee klatsch, kaffee klatsch, coffee party; social, gathering, social gathering, sociable, affair, *Inf.* get-together.

coffer, *n.* **1.** strongbox, money chest, locker, safe; box, chest, casket, case, jewelry case, coffret; can, cannister, container, receptacle, *Brit.* caddy.

2. coffers treasury, funds, capital, means, assets, moneys, finances, pecuniary resources.

coffin, *n.* casket, pall, box, sarcophagus, *Scot. and North Eng.* kist, *Sl.* wooden overcoat *or* kimono.

cog, *n.* **1.** sprocket, ratchet, tooth, gear tooth, sawtooth, jag.

2. *Informal.* pawn, nonentity, nothing, cipher, number; inferior, underling, subordinate, *Sl.* small fish.

cogent, *adj.* **1.** convincing, forceful, effective, telling, authoritative, weighty; influential, forcible, potent, powerful, puissant; clear, plain, certain, sure, positive, definite, evident, luculent; valid, sound, believable, proving, conclusive, unanswerable; persuasive, persuasory, efficacious.

2. to the point, at issue, relevant, pertinent, applicable, connected, tied in with; suited to, apropos, germane; consistent, corresponding, compatible.

cogitate, *v.* **1.** meditate, contemplate, think, cerebrate, put on one's thinking cap, be lost in thought, be abstracted, be absorbed, be immersed, be engrossed, concentrate, focus, put one's mind to; muse, ponder, brood, mull over, dwell on, be in a brown study; reflect, ruminate, chew over, chew one's cud, rack one's brains, cudgel one's brains.

2. deliberate, excogitate, take to heart, consider, *Archaic.* perpend; weigh, evaluate, study, revolve, review, turn over, examine, con; think about *or* over, have one's mind on, wonder about, consider, speculate, surmise, suppose, conjecture, theorize, hypothesize.

3. conceive, think up, imagine, fancy, have ideas about, *Inf.* dream up, envision, envisage, visualize; devise, contrive, machinate, cabal, plan, scheme, plot, design, *Obs.* consult, *Obs.* intrigue; frame, concoct, brew, invent, hatch.

cogitation, *n.* **1.** meditation, meditating, contemplation, contemplating, musing, pondering, brooding, mulling over, dwelling on; reflection, reflecting, cogitating, rumination, ruminating, chewing over, chewing one's cud, brown study; thought, thinking about *or* over, cerebration, cerebrating, being lost in thought; concentration, concentrating, focusing, having one's mind on, wondering about, lucubration, brainwork, headwork.

2. reason, rationality, thinking; intellect, mind, brains, brainpower; intelligence, sense, understanding.

3. thought, conception, concept, idea, conceit, notion; whim, whimsy, vagary, crotchet, fancy, hallucination; vision, dream.

4. design, plan, plot, scheme, stratagem; contrivance, device, intrigue, cabal, machination, expedient; concoction, invention, *Sl.* baby.

cognate, *adj.* **1.** related, kindred, akin, generic, congeneric, connatural, coordinal; uterine, enate, enatic, agnate, consanguine, consanguineous, german, sororal, fraternal.

2. allied, affiliated, associated, apposite, affined; similar, alike, common, correlated, corresponding, correspondent, comparative, relative.

cognition, *n.* **1.** perception, discernment, enlightenment, cognizance; intelligence, comprehension, understanding, notion, sensibility, apprehension, grasp.

2. wisdom, knowing, awareness, insight; conversance, conversancy, familiarity, acquaintance, ken.

cognizance, *n.* **1.** knowledge, familiarity, acquaintance, ken; percipience, discernment, discrimination; connoisseurship, sophistication, urbanity.

2. awareness, consciousness, sentience, sensibility, sensitivity; observation, notice, note, regard; observance, consideration, mindfulness, regardfulness; alertness, watchfulness, wariness, cautiousness.

3. realization, recognition, discovery, awakening; intuition, insight, enlightenment; perception, apprehension, comprehension, understanding, appreciation.

4. *Heraldry.* badge, label, sign, token; coat of arms, escutcheon; livery, uniform.

cognizant, *adj.* **1.** aware, conscious, sentient, alive to; sensible of, familiar with, acquainted with, *Sl.* wise to; mindful, regardful, observant, awake, wide-awake; alert, cautious, wary, on the qui vive, on the beam *or* ball.

2. informed, in the know, apprised, enlightened, posted, up-to-date, *Fr. au courant*; knowledgeable, knowing, conversant, versed; sharp, quick, intelligent, percipient, discerning, discriminating; sophisticated, worldly-wise, urbane, *Sl.* hip, *Sl.* with it.

cognize, *v.* perceive, discern, see; comprehend, understand, fathom, penetrate, apprehend, grasp, ken, seize; take in, make out, gain insight into, gain an impression of; know, realize, recognize; become conscious of, be cognizant of, be aware of, be sensible of; heed, attend, regard.

cognomen, *n.* surname, last name, family name, patronymic; name, title, honorific, style, designation, appellation; epithet, appellative, by-word, label, tag, *Sl.* handle; nickname, *Sl.* moniker, sobriquet, agnomen, by-name, pet name, diminutive; pseudonym, anonym, allonym, alias, assumed name, pen name, nom de plume, *Fr. nom de guerre*, stage name, *Fr. nom de théâtre*.

cohabit, *v.* live together, lodge together, reside together, abide together, stay together; bed down with, *Sl.* shack up with; room together, room with, *Sl.* buddy up.

cohere, *v.* **1.** stick, adhere, cleve, accrete, cling, clasp; fasten, attach, bind, fuse, seal, fix; conglutinate, join, conjoin, coalesce, unify, unite; combine, amalgamate, consolidate, connect, come together, converge; congeal, gel, gelatinize, gelatinate, jelly, set; thicken, coagulate, clot, clabber, curdle; solidify, harden, cake.

2. follow, make sense, be evident, stand to reason, be clear, be logical, be consistent, square with; hold good, hold water, hold up, stand; come together, be convergent; hang together, be unified, be organized.

coherence, *n.* **1.** cohesion, adherence, accretion, sticking; attachment, firm hold, fixity, agglutination; coalescence, union, junction, fusion; glutinousness, glutinosity, viscidity, viscosity, tenacity, inseparability, indivisibility; congelation, solidification, set, concretion, cementation; amalgamation, consolidation, connection, convergence.

2. logic, rationality, *Rhet.* concinnity, intelligence; comprehensibility, apprehensibility, understandability, intelligibleness, intelligibility, decipherability, penetrability.

3. consistency, congruity, accord, accordance, agreement, congruity, concord, concordance, conformity, unity; harmony, consonance, rapport, relation.

coherent, *adj.* **1.** adherent, adhering, sticking, cohering, accreted, conglutinate, agglutinate; glued, cemented, fixed; fused, joined, conjoined, indivisible, inseparable; tenacious, adhesive, cohesive, agglutinative, conglutinative, accretive, concretive, sticky; glutinous, viscid, viscous; curdled, congealed, *Archaic.* coagulative, *Obs.* coagulated, solidified, set; united, consolidated, combined, coalesced, coalescent, convergent, converging.

2. connected, unified, in agreement, accordant, concordant, congruent, congruous, concurrent; harmonious, consonant, in rapport.

3. consistent, logical, rational; cognizable, comprehensible, apprehensible, understandable, intelligible, decipherable, penetrable.

cohesion, *n.* coherence, adherence, accretion, sticking. See **coherence** (*def.* **1**).

cohort, *n.* **1.** troop, brigade, legion, squadron, squad, phalanx, platoon, column, unit, wing, battery, contingent, detachment; group, band, company, body, party, gang, crew, outfit, team.

2. following, cortege, retinue, entourage, suite, train, court.

3. partner, comrade, associate, companion; consort, confrere, sidekick, crony, friend, *Inf.* buddy, *Chiefly Brit.* mate.

coiffure, *n.* hairdo, haircut, blowcut, comb-out, permanent, permanent wave, *Inf.* coif; pixie, pageboy, bob, shag; upsweep, undo, pompadour, ducktail, beehive; bun, chignon; plait, braid, cornrows, *Archaic.* tress; afro, *Sl.* fro, natural.

coil, *v.* **1.** wind, spiral, curl, intort, twist, twirl, roll, intervolve, convolve, turn; clew, ball; curve, incurvate, sinuate; wrap around, entwine, twine, wreathe; reel, unwind, *Naut.* worm; rotate, revolve, wheel; interweave, *Both Chiefly Brit.* wattle, raddle; plait, braid, plat; screw, contort; meander, wander, ramble.

—*n.* **2.** helix, rings, circles, rondure, windings, *Bot.* tendril; spiral, gyration, whorl, vortex, twirl, twist, full turn, revolution, rotation; convolution, roll, curl; curlicue, kink.

coin, *n.* **1.** piece, specie, copper, peso, piece of eight, piaster, doubloon, escudo; change, silver, gold, mintage, coinage; pocket money, jingler, pin money, petty cash, chicken feed, rouleau; money, cash, currency, *Sl.* chink.

—*v.* **2.** mint, monetize, stamp out, die; issue, circulate.

3. invent, create, make up, compose, neologize, neoterize; devise, concoct, frame, hatch, formulate, design, conceive, germinate, think up *or* of, dream up; make, fabricate, manufacture, fashion, form, construct, produce; originate, initiate, begin, start, commence; introduce, inaugurate, launch, institute.

coinage, *n.* **1.** mintage, minting, monetization, monetizing, dieing, stamping; issuance, circulation.

2. change, coins, silver, gold, *Sl.* chink; pocket money, pin money, petty cash, chicken feed, rouleau; money, cash, currency.

3. invention, innovation, neologism, neology, neoterism; creation, original, composition, concoction, contrivance, fabrication.

coincide, *v.* **1.** synchronize, occur simultaneously, happen together; be correspondent, reciprocate; correspond, harmonize, comport, match, tally, equal; mesh, jibe, suit, go along with; be synonymous, be equivalent, be equal, be the same as; cohere, be congruous; conform, quadrate; accompany, be concomitant.

2. agree, concur, accord, see eye to eye, be at one with, fall along with *or* into.

coincidence, *n.* **1.** accord, harmony, concord, concordance, concert, rapport, unity, *Rhet.* concinnity; agreement, accordance, correspondence, conformity, conformation, conformance, congruity, congruence, congruency, consonance, consonancy; unanimity, consentience, consentaneity, consentaneousness, concurrence; equality, synonymity, identicalness, uniformity; similarity, affinity, connaturalness, consistency.

2. coexistence, contemporaneity, contemporaneousness, contemporariness, simultaneity, simultaneousness, concomitance, concomitancy, synchronism, synchronousness; coextension, coevality, coetaneity, coetaneousness; confluence, conflux; parallelism, correlation.

3. asynchronism, fluke, accident, chance, incidental occurrence, unpredictable event; serendipity, stroke of luck, *Sl.* good *or* lucky break, fortuitousness.

coincident, *adj.* **1.** agreeing, corresponding, correspondent, concurring, consentient, consentaneous, conforming, conformable, coinciding; accordant, concordant, congruent, congruous; harmonious, consonant; synonymous, equivalent, coordinate, alike; unanimous, in unison, in accord, in rapport, in harmony, at one, of the same mind, of one mind; comparable, similar.

2. simultaneous, concomitant, concurrent, parallel, collateral, side-by-side; contemporaneous, coinstantaneous, synchronal, synchronous, *Inf.* in sync, synchronized, isochronal, isochronous; coexistent, coexisting, contemporary, coeval, coetaneous; conterminous, coterminous, coextensive; joined, joint, conjoint, conjunct, copulate, united, linked, unified.

coincidental, *adj.* unpredictable, incidental, casual, chance, lucky, *Inf.* fluky, fortunate, fortuitous; asynchronous, accidental, unexpected, unforeseen.

coitus, *n.* sexual intercourse, coition, copulation, fornication, congress, consummation, commerce, union, conjugation, conjunction; coupling, mating, making love, going all the way, *Sl.* getting it on, *Sl.* doing it, *Sl.* going to bed.

cold, *adj.* **1.** heatless, sunless, cool, chill, chilly, nippy, unheated, unwarmed; frigid, icy, algid, gelid, freezing, ice-cold; frosty, wintry, brumal, hibernal, snowy, hoary, rimy; arctic, glacial, polar, hyperborean, hyperboreal, Siberian; bitter, biting, nipping, numbing, chilling; stinging, penetrating, piercing, blasting, zippy; sharp, brisk, keen, crisp, snappy; breezy, airy, draughty, windy.

2. chilled, numbed, benumbed, frostbitten, frostnipped, frozen stiff, frozen solid, chilled to the bone *or* marrow; shivering, chattering, teethchattering, quaking, shaking, shivery, aguish; refrigerated, cooled, iced; glaciated, frozen, icicled, frosted, congealed, regelated.

3. dead, gone, deceased, defunct; rigid, stiff, still, clay-cold; (*of fires*) extinguished, snuffed, choked.

4. unconscious, out, *Boxing.* knocked out, *Boxing.* k.o.'d, blacked out, *Inf.* passed out.

5. passionless, dispassionate, spiritless, unfeeling, coldblooded; insensitive, inanimate, insentient, unemotional, uncaring, heartless, soulless; unsympathetic, unresponsive, impassive; indifferent, aloof, apathetic, unconcerned, incurious.

6. frigid, passive, undesiring, supine, inert, inexcitable; phlegmatic, listless, lackadaisical, half-hearted; unexcitable, imperturbable, impervious, stony, flinty, steely; callous, hardened, obdurate, thick-skinned; unimpassioned, unperturbed, unruffled, stoical, stoic; reserved, reticent, uncommunicative; unmoved, indurate, inured, adamantine, untouched, unstirred.

7. unfriendly, unsociable, unwelcome, uninviting, forbidding; uncordial, ungracious, unamicable, inhospitable; unapproachable, inaccessible, distant, remote, standoffish, *Inf.* offish.

8. depressing, discouraging, dispiriting, disheartening, distressing; bleak, gloomy, stark, dismal, woeful, sorry.

9. uninteresting, uncompelling, uninspiring, unimaginative; lifeless, dull, vapid, insipid, prosaic; flat, zestless, drab, lackluster; tame, mediocre, bloodless; humdrum, commonplace, matter-of-fact, tedious, tiresome, wearisome, uninspired, boring.

10. faint, weak, slight, feeble, bare, meager, scarce, small, little; low, indistinct, faded.

—*n.* **11.** frigidity, chill, coldness, gelidity, algidity, iciness, frost, Jack Frost; glaciation, refrigeration, congelation, *Physics.* regelation; briskness, chilliness, coolness; bitterness, rawness, bleakness, sharpness; shivers, numbness, *Pathol.* algor; cold weather, cold snap, inclemency, severity.

12. influenza, flu, grippe, virus, *Inf.* bug; fever; ague, cold, catarrh, rheum; cough, whooping cough, chincough, pertussis, bronchitis, common cold; hay fever, rose fever, rose cold.

—*adv.* **13.** absolutely, completely, thoroughly, exactly, perfectly, precisely, pat, *Inf.* down.

14. without preparation, without training, unrehearsed, unready, unpracticed.

15. abruptly, suddenly, rashly, precipitously, on the spur of the moment, on the spot; unexpectedly, without warning *or* notice.

cold-blooded, *adj.* **1.** unemotional, dispassionate, spiritless, cold; insensitive, unfeeling, uncompassionate, uncaring, heartless; unkind, pitiless, merciless, hard-hearted, cold-hearted, marble-hearted, stony-hearted; unsympathetic, unresponsive, impassive, indifferent, aloof; unexcitable, imperturbable, frigid, chilly; impervious, stony, steely, flinty; hardened, obdurate, callous, thickskinned; unruffled, unperturbed, stoical, stoic; unmoved, unimpassioned, unstirred, untouched, indurate, inured.

2. cruel, brutal, inhuman, savage, barbarous; ferocious, fierce, wolfish, feral, ferine; harsh, severe, grim, hard, terrible; ruthless, vicious, fell, truculent; deliberate, calculating, cool, shrewd. See **cruel**.

coliseum, *n.* stadium, arena, bowl, circus, hippodrome, amphitheater, theater, colosseum.

collaborate, *v.* cooperate, coact, concur, conspire, connive, fraternize, work together *or* in unison *or* side by side, act jointly, stand shoulder to shoulder, pull together; join, unite, combine, synergize, team up, join forces *or* hands, *Inf.* hitch horses.

collaborator, *n.* **1.** cooperator, contributor, participant; confederate, conniver, conspirator, abettor, accomplice, accessory, partner in crime, *Sl.* moll *or* gun moll.

2. collaborationist, quisling, double-dealer, *Inf.* double-crosser, strikebreaker, scab, snake in the grass, *Sl.* rat, fink; turncoat, traitor, renegade, defector, subversive, fifth-columnist, fellow traveler.

collapse, *v.* **1.** cave in, tumble down, founder, give way, crumple, crumple up, fall down, fall inward *or* outward, come apart; crumble, fall into pieces, break into fragments, break apart, fall into ruin; be demolished, be torn down, be felled, be pulled down, be cut down.

2. break down, break, go to pieces; stop working, *Sl.* conk out, *Sl.* go kaput, *Inf.* peter out, *Inf.* fizzle out, die out; go to pot, *Inf.* go to the dogs, go to wrack and ruin; explode, blow up, fulminate, burst, detonate.

3. miscarry, abort, go wrong, misfire, fall through, not succeed, backfire, fall flat; flounder, falter, slip, trip, blunder, stumble; crash, smash up, crack up, meet with disaster, go up in smoke, shipwreck, run aground; go into a tailspin, *Inf.* nose-dive, decline rapidly; miss the mark, miss the boat, *Sl.* blow it, *Sl.* bomb, *Sl.* lay an egg, *Sl.* strike out, wash out, come to nothing; flunk out, *Inf.* not be up to snuff; fail, fall short, stop short of, fall by the wayside, *Sl.* flop; go amiss, go astray.

4. go out of business, go bankrupt, go to the wall, *Inf.* go on the rocks, go under, *Inf.* go broke, *Inf.* fold up, close down, default on payment, become insolvent, be ruined.

5. surrender, acknowledge defeat, suffer defeat, fall victim, fall prey; be overthrown, be checkmated, be impotent, be incapacitated, be hamstrung, be undermined; have the wind taken out of one's sails, have the ground cut out from under one, not have a leg to stand on.

6. sicken, take sick, become ill, be stricken; weaken, lose vigor, be on the ropes, be on one's last legs, *Sl.* be on the downslide, lose ground, take a turn for the worse, go downhill; faint, swoon, keel over, buckle, fall prostrate, pass out; dwindle, decline, decay, deteriorate; pine away, languish, fade away, droop, slump, bog down, sink; give out, give way, succumb, pass away, *Sl.* kick the bucket, lick *or* bite the dust.

7. (*all usu. of psychological or emotional health*) crack, let go, come apart at the seams, go to pieces, *Sl.* lose it, *Sl.* lose one's cool, break down, suffer a nervous breakdown.

—*n.* **8.** cave-in, breakdown, foundering, toppling down, falling into pieces, falling apart, breaking apart; calamity, catastrophe, cataclysm, disaster, devastation, desolation, deluge, havoc, destruction, demolition; prostration, leveling, felling, tearing down; smash, smash-up, crash, crack-up; explosion, fulmination, burst, detonation, rupture, break; malfunction, wearing out, *Sl.* conking out.

9. failure, fiasco, unsuccessfulness, *Inf.* comedown, reversal; abortion, miscarriage, vain attempt; *Inf.* flop, *Inf.* let down, *Sl.* washout; downfall, fall, debacle, overthrow, ruin; defeat, checkmate, discomfiture, rout; bankruptcy, insolvency.

10. sudden illness, attack, relapse, stroke, seizure; exhaustion, prostration, weakness, debility; dissolution, disintegration, decay, termination; tailspin, nose dive; (*all usu. of emotional or psychological health*) nervous breakdown, going to pieces, coming apart at the seams, cracking, *Sl.* losing it, surrender, giving in, giving way.

collar, *n.* **1.** neckpiece, neckband, collaret, gorget, wimple; ruff, rabato, ruche, bertha; boa, scarf, ascot, cravat.

2. **hot under the collar** *Slang.* angry, irate, upset. See **angry** (*def.* **1**).

—*v.* **3.** seize, grab, grasp, grip, grapple, clinch, clench, clasp, lay *or* take hold of, lay hands upon, fasten upon.

4. *Informal.* arrest, apprehend, capture. See **arrest** (*def.* **1**).

collate, *v.* compare, analogize, juxtapose, *Rare.* juxtaposit, appose; pair, partner, match, collocate; verify, confirm, check, crosscheck; sort, sort out, arrange, categorize.

collateral, *adj.* **1.** lateral, side, flanking, skirting.

2. parallel, side by side, cheek by cheek, cheek by jowl; concurrent, concomitant, coincident, simultaneous.

3. accompanying, attendant, associated, affiliated, relative; auxilliary, subordinate, subsidiary; additional, contributing, corroborating, sustaining, upholding, confirming, verifying, certifying, affirming; secondary, nonessential, unessential, incidental, accidental, dependent, contingent, indirect.

—*n.* **4.** security, insurance, assurance, surety; guarantee, pledge, warrant, gage, endorsement.

5. *Slang.* money, cash, *Sl.* dough, *Sl.* bread.

collation, *n.* **1.** comparison, juxtaposition, collocation, matching, pairing; confirmation, verification, validation; arrangement, ordering, grouping, distribution; organization, methodization, systemization, systematization.

2. light meal, snack, bite, nosh, tidbit.

colleague, *n.* **1.** associate, consociate, confrere, compeer, peer, mate; partner, copartner, cohort, collaborator, cooperator; ally, compatriot, confederate, accomplice, *Law.* accessory; assistant, adjunct, coadjutor, coadjutant, coadjutrix, coadjutress, adjuvant, aide.

2. teammate, co-worker, fellow worker; classmate, schoolmate, schoolfellow; messmate, dining companion, commensal.

3. friend, companion, sidekick, comrade, chum, crony, *Inf.* buddy, *Inf.* pal.

collect, *v.* **1.** accumulate, heap up, pile, pile up, roll up, stack up, pack; compile, amass, cumulate; hoard, squirrel away, load up, stow away.

2. gather, glean, take in, pull in, harvest, reap; garner, store up, stock up, lay by, lay up, lay in, *Inf.* stash away, reserve, set aside; save, save up.

3. group, cluster, bunch up *or* together; mass, crowd, congregate, agglomerate; flock together, throng, herd, swarm, surge; bring together, rally, muster, call up, round up, round in.

4. assemble, convene, forgather, come together, meet, *Inf.* gang up, huddle, go into a huddle, get together, rendezvous; convoke, summon, call together.

5. recover oneself, pull oneself together, compose oneself; regain one's poise *or* composure; *Sl.* get it all together, *Sl.* get one's head *or* act together, gather one's wits; come around, pick up the pieces, face the world again; screw up *or* renew one's courage, gather up *or* muster one's strength, rally one's forces.

6. call for, pick up, come to get; go to get, fetch; take away, haul, haul away.

7. earn, *Inf.* get paid, take in, *Sl.* pull down; get one's due, *Inf.* get what's coming to one, *Inf.* get paid off.

collected, *adj.* calm, composed, self-possessed, cool, *Inf.* together; nonchalant, at ease, unruffled, unexcited, undisturbed, unperturbed, undismayed, untroubled, sedate; self-controlled, poised, balanced, steady; imperturbable, inexcitable, unflappable, even-tempered, easy-going; peaceful, serene, tranquil, placid.

collection, *n.* **1.** accumulation, heap, pile, mass, cumulation; hoard, store, stock, stockpile, supply, fund; treasure, holdings, savings, *Inf.* loot.

2. amassment, assemblage; aggregation, concentration, agglomeration, conglomeration, cluster, clump; bouquet, posy; lot, pack, batch, bunch, *Inf.* raft.

3. set, series, array, assortment; variety, medley, jumble, hodgepodge; clutter, *Inf.* mess.

4. anthology, compilation, collected works, corpus; ana, analects, collectanea, garland.

5. assembly, group, body, congregation, muster, gathering; crowd, number, throng, host, multitude, confluence, concourse; drove, swarm, flock, herd.

6. offering, offertory, oblation, tithe; pledge, subscription, gift, contribution, donation, alms; drive, fund drive.

collective, *adj.* **1.** composite, aggregate, corporate, conglomerate; collected, gathered, compiled; accumulated, massed, clustered, agglomerate.

2. combined, compound, cumulative, agminate; joint, united, unified, coactive, concerted, cooperative, collaborative.

3. common, general, majority, representative; mutual, like-minded, concurrent, consonant.

—n. **4.** aggregate, assemblage, collection; body, congregation, assembly, gathering, crowd, throng, aggregation, multitude; company, band, group, crew, team, outfit.

collectivism, *n.* communalism, collective *or* public ownership, socialism, communism, Marxism; communization, socialization, nationalization, collectivization.

college, *n.* **1.** institution of higher learning *or* education, liberal arts college, four-year college; university, multiversity, *Derog.* education factory, *Derog.* phrontistery *or* phrontisterion; post-secondary school, junior college, two-year college, technical school, vocational school; academy, institute, polytechnic, conservatory; Alma Mater.

2. academia, academe, the groves of academe; the halls of ivy, college life, college years.

3. (*within a university or college*) department, division, discipline, area, field, faculty; school, professional school, specialized school, graduate school, postgraduate school.

4. learned association, athenaeum, cultural society, council, fellowship, academy; league, union, partnership, corporation, consortium.

5. company, assemblage, body, corporate body, conclave, community, congregation.

collide, *v.* **1.** crash, smash, bump, bang; meet, encounter, come into collision; crash into, smash into, run into, bump into, *Inf.* plow into, *Brit. Sl.* prang; butt, buffet, jar, jolt, jostle, dash.

2. clash, conflict, disagree, differ, disaccord, be at variance *or* cross-purposes.

collision, *n.* **1.** crash, impact, impingement, encounter, meeting; bump, shock, buffet; crash, smash-up, crack-up, pile-up, wreck; accident, casualty, automobile accident, car crash.

2. conflict, opposition, disagreement, discord, disaccord, dissension, friction, variance, clash.

collocate, *v.* **1.** assemble, gather, collect, amass, accumulate, muster, bunch, put *or* place together; juxtapose, collate, pair, partner, match.

2. arrange, range, order, dispose, place, group; classify, categorize, pigeonhole, *Sl.* peg; digest, index, file, codify, number, alphabetize, tabulate; organize, sort, sort out, assort; coordinate, systematize, systemize, methodize; grade, graduate, rank, rate, distinguish.

collocation, *n.* **1.** collection, assembly, assemblage, accumulation, amassment, gathering, mustering; collation, juxtaposition, matching, pairing.

2. arrangement, placement, distribution, allocation, allotment, disposal, situation, placing, ordering; classification, categorization, grouping, pigeonholing; tabulation, alphabetization, codification, indexing, filing, numbering; organization, assortment, sorting, sorting out; coordination, systemization, methodization; gradation, graduation, ranking, rating.

colloquial, *adj.* informal, casual, familiar, common, ordinary, unceremonial, everyday, workday, household; simple, plain, unadorned, unaffected, unstudied, unpretentious, unassuming, inartificial; conversational, confabulatory, interlocutory, chatty; vernacular, natural, native, dialectal, dialectical.

colloquialism, *n.* **1.** localism, regionalism, provincialism.

2. vernacular, idiom, parlance; spoken language *or* speech, everyday *or* workday *or* common speech, informal speech *or* language; (*all of speech*) informality, familiarity, commonness, simplicity, plainness, naturalness, inartificiality; chattiness, conversationalism.

colloquy, *n.* **1.** conversation, converse, talk, discourse, dialogue, interlocution, verbal exchange; chat, chitchat, palaver, confabulation, *Inf.* confab, little talk, causerie.

2. conference, discussion, debate, parlance; parley, powwow, huddle.

collude, *v.* **1.** conspire, connive, plot, complot, cabal, scheme, intrigue, maneuver, machinate; (*all in criminal activity*) cooperate, collaborate, unite, join, join forces *or* hands, band together, *Inf.* hitch horses.

2. (*all in reference to criminal activity*) abet, overlook, tolerate, ignore, disregard, wink *or* blink at, shut one's eyes to.

collusion, *n.* connivance, complicity, *Law.* covin, *Sl.* cahoots; conspiracy, cabal, plot, complot, intrigue, scheme, *Inf.* little game.

collusive, *adj.* conspirative, *Law.* covinous, conniving, conspiring, plotting, intriguing, scheming, designing, machinating, engineering; dishonest, deceitful, fraudulent; underhanded, double-dealing, treacherous.

colonial, *adj.* **1.** territorial, *Hist.* provincial, protectoral, mandated, imperial; daughter, dependent, subordinate, subject.

2. colonizing, settling, colonializing; early American, Pilgrim, Puritan, Anglo-American; frontier, pioneer, pioneering.

—n. **3.** colonist, colonizer, settler. See **colonist.**

colonist, *n.* colonial, colonizer, colonizationist, settler, *Hist.* planter, pioneer, *Chiefly U.S.* frontiersman, *U.S.* homesteader, squatter, habitant; forefather, founder, founding father, Pilgrim, Puritan, patriot; Anglo-American, immigrant, emigrant, émigré, *Amer. Hist.* redemptioner.

colonization, *n.* settling, peopling, establishing, founding, forming a colony; subjugation, conquest, dominion, rule, sovereignty.

colonnade, *n.* **1.** peristyle, columniation, peripteros, columnar building; portico, porch, veranda, gallery, *Chiefly Brit.* piazza, arcade, covered walk, cloister; columns, pillars, piers, posts, shafts, poles.
2. series, row, line, file, rank, string, sequence, succession, progression.

colony, *n.* **1.** settlement, *Hist.* plantation, *U.S.* homestead, frontier fort, stockade.
2. dependency, territory, province, dominion, possession, mandate, protectorate, daughter country, satellite.
3. village, town, hamlet; community, group, cluster, aggregation; section, district, quarter, neighborhood, block.

color, *n.* **1.** hue, tint, tinge, tinct, tincture; tone, shade, cast.
2. complexion, skin color *or* coloring *or* tone, coloring; bloom, glow, warmth, rosiness, brightness, ruddiness; blush, flush.
3. (*all in literary composition*) emphasis, force, strength, power, intensity; vividness, reality, sense, meaning, significance; life, vivacity, vibrancy, animation, vigor; brilliance, richness.
4. pigment, dye, paint, tint, colorant, crayon.
5. **colors a.** badge, insignia, rosette, ribbon. **b.** attitude, position, bent, bias, warp, slant, prejudice; personality, characteristics; aspects, stripe, vein, mold, grain, breed, strain, stamp. **c.** flag, standard, banner.
6. outward appearance, guise, semblance, show, mere show, facade, front, face; cloak, mask, disguise, masquerade.
7. plausibility, credibility, conceivability, possibility; probability, likelihood.
8. pretext, excuse, poor *or* lame excuse, likely story, *Inf.* alibi; justification, reason, grounds, defense, plea, protestation.
9. **change color a.** blush, flush, redden, crimson, glow, burn, flame, warm, color up. **b.** pale, turn *or* grow pale, turn white, whiten, blanch.
10. **flying colors** victory, triumph, success.
—*v.* **11.** tinge, tincture, temper, tint, shade, paint, dye, stain, daub, chalk; illuminate, brighten, blazon, emblazon; (*all with color*) imbue, infuse, suffuse, instill, breathe.
12. (*all of a narrative, report, explanation, etc.*) distort, twist, pervert, warp, slant, garble, slur, misconstrue, misstate, misquote, misrender, misrepresent, belie, falsify; torture, stretch, strain, exaggerate, overstate, overdraw, understate; disguise, mask, camouflage, gloss over, whitewash, varnish; embroider, embellish, adorn, ornament, titivate, dress up, paint in glowing colors *or* terms, deodorize.

colorable, *adj.* **1.** plausible, credible, tenable, believable, conceivable, feasible; specious.
2. deceptive, tricky, slippery, *Inf.* shady; ostensible, apparent, pretended, feigned, simulated, spurious, bogus, counterfeit, fraudulent, sham, false, fake, *Inf.* phony.

color blindness, *n.* achromatopsy, Daltonism, chromo-blindness, *Ophthalm.* monochromatism; *Ophthalm.* deuteranopia, green blindness; *Ophthalm.* protanopia, red blindness; *Ophthalm.* tritanopia, blue blindness, yellow blindness.

colorful, *adj.* **1.** multicolored, many-colored, variegated, kaleidoscopic, psychedelic; rich, brilliant, lustrous, luxuriant, intense, full-toned, bright-hued, high-colored, deep-colored; gaudy, garish, showy, loud, screaming, *Sl.* jazzy.
2. vivid, graphic, striking, impressive; vibrant, gay, bright, dynamic, inspirited, animated.
3. (*all of people*) eccentric, quaint, droll, flaky, offbeat, odd, *Inf.* quirky, *Sl.* balmy.

colorless, *adj.* **1.** hueless, toneless, uncolored, achromatic, achromous; drab, dreary, flat, mat, dingy, lusterless, lackluster, *Scot. and North Eng.* blae; bleached, blanched, washed-out, etiolated.
2. pallid, pale, pale-faced, anemic, sickly; waxen, sallow, wan, pasty, ashen, livid, ghostly.
3. dull, uninspired, spiritless, lifeless, dead, torpid, *U.S. Sl.* blah; boring, uninteresting, dry, dry-as-dust, *Inf.* ho-hum; weak, lukewarm, tepid; insipid, vapid, inane, empty, hollow; wooden, stiff, stodgy, stuffy.

colossal, *adj.* **1.** gigantic, monstrous, mammoth, gargantuan, titanic, Brobdingnagian, Cyclopean, Antaean; huge, vast, immense, massive, massy, ponderous; monumental, enormous, mountainous, magnitudinous; elephantine, dinosaurian, dinotherian, megatherine, jumbo.
2. herculean, mighty, powerful, strapping, strong; tall, towering, lofty, alpine, skyscraping.
3. tremendous, stupendous, extravagant, spectacular, wonderful, *Inf.* super, *Inf.* super-duper; prodigious, awe-inspiring, awful, terrible, commanding, imposing, overwhelming, overpowering, staggering; extreme, extraordinary, exceptional, inordinate, exorbitant, exceeding.

colossus, *n.* **1.** giant, titan, Gargantua, Goliath, Antaeus, giantess, Amazon; Hercules, Samson, Atlas, muscle man, Tarzan, Superman, man mountain; Cyclops, Polyphemus.
2. monster, behemoth, leviathan, whale, hippopotamus, elephant; dinothere, dinosaur, megalosaur, stegosaur, mammoth, megathere.
3. mountain, skyscraper, tower, monument; prodigy, wonder, marvel.

colt, *n.* **1.** foal, yearling, weanling, young horse.
2. youngster, shaveling, *Inf.* shaver, lad, *Chiefly Scot.* laddie, boy, youth, chap, *Inf.* kid; imp, rascal, brat, bantling, urchin; adolescent, *Contemptuous.* whelp, hobbledehoy, whippersnapper, jackanapes; scion, stripling, sprig, chip off the old block.
3. novice, beginner, neophyte, tyro, amateur, rookie, greenhorn, tenderfoot, newcomer; learner, apprentice, initiate, trainee, catechumen; fledgling, gosling, cub.

coltish, *adj.* **1.** playful, playsome, frivolous, jocular, jocose, roguish, prankish, mischievous; frolicsome, rompish, rollicksome, frisky; sportive, gamboling, lively, spirited, animated, skittish, feeling one's oats; perky, jaunty, debonair, lighthearted, blithe, blithesome; elated, ebullient, jubilant, mirthful, cheerful, *Inf.* chipper, merry, jocund, jolly; sunny, sparkling, breezy.
2. unruly, ungovernable, uncontrollable, intractable, indocile; wild, untamed, unbroken, undisciplined.

column, *n.* **1.** pillar, upright support, caryatid, atlas, telamon; columna caelata, pilaster, colonnade, peristyle; post, shaft, pier, pole, pylon; standard, stalagnite, spine, cylinder; *Naut.* mast, spar.
2. obelisk, monolith, pagoda; turret, minaret, tower, steeple, campanile, bell tower; totem pole.
3. (*all vertical*) list, row, line; queue, file, string, train, progression, formation.
4. editorial, commentary, essay, article; by-line article; syndicated column.

columnist, *n.* editorial writer, editorialist, editor, writer, analyst; correspondent, reporter, reviewer, critic; journalist, newsman, newswoman, gentleman *or* woman of the press, gentleman *or* woman of the Fourth Estate.

comatose, *adj.* **1.** unconscious, *Med.* soporose, insensible, *Psychiatry.* cataleptic, immobile, *Pathol.* narcoleptic; narcotic, stuporous, stupefied, drugged, hypnotized.

2. dull, sluggish, phlegmatic, lethargic, lymphatic, torpid, heavy, leaden, lifeless; languid, languorous, listless, spiritless; inactive, inert, supine, stagnant; lazy, otiose, idle, indolent, dronish.

3. insensible, unfeeling, impassible, blunt, callous; hardened, inured; anesthetic, numb, numbed, benumbed, deadened; cool, cold, frigid, icy, frozen; unresponsive, unsympathetic, unreceptive, passive; apathetic, indifferent, unconcerned, detached, withdrawn, oblivious, imperceptive, impercipient; passionless, unemotional, impassive; insensitive, thickskinned, pachydermatous; inanimate, insensate, insentient, exanimate.

4. sleepy, drowsy, somnolent, slumberous, oscitant, soporiferous, soporific; dormant, quiescent, inoperative.

5. unintelligent, slow-witted, dull-witted; stolid, obtuse, bovine, blockish, lumpish; dense, thickheaded, *Inf.* thick, slow, stupid.

comb, *n.* **1.** fine-tooth comb, serration, serrated edge, toothed strip; hair comb, hairbrush, brush, currycomb; card; rake, harrow.

2. cock's comb, crest, tuft, *Zool.* caruncle, topknot; growth, *Zool.* beard, outgrowth, ridge, spine; feather, plume, panache.

—*v.* **3.** arrange, fix, adjust, do, dress, adorn; put in order, smooth, disentangle, untangle, unsnarl, get the knots out; curry, groom, brush, rub, clean.

4. weed out, screen, sort through, sift through; discard, eliminate, get rid of.

5. (*all of wool fibers*) card, dress, separate.

6. sweep across, move across, extend across, reach across.

7. rake, search thoroughly, go over *or* through with a fine-tooth comb, look everywhere for.

8. break, break at the crest, roll over, curl over, form whitecaps.

combat, *v.* **1.** fight, contend, clash, conflict with, strive; encounter, engage, meet, join, face; battle, give *or* do battle, duel, joust, tussle, skirmish, scuffle, jostle; war, make war, war against, go to war, go to battle, wage war, take the field, take up arms; brawl, feud, come to blows; pommel, beat, beat into the ground, batter; box, spar, exchange fisticuffs, wrestle, grapple with; slaughter, massacre.

2. contest, confront, rise up against, *Obs.* militate against, rail against, ride against, struggle against, *Archaic.* reluct; oppose, defy, contradict, contravene, refute, confound; object to, protest, call in question, march against, make a stand against, dispute, oppugn; resist, repel, repulse, withstand, stand on one's ground; obstruct, thwart, hamper, traverse, interfere with, counteract; check, curb, hinder, impede, inhibit, restrict; restrain, constrain, barricade, bar, block, blockade; prevent, prohibit, forbid, interdict, proscribe, veto, embargo; frustrate, balk, foil, cross, play at cross purposes.

3. assault, attack, beset, assail, harass; raid, storm, charge, rush, tilt, blitz; set upon, pounce upon, bombard, open fire upon, engage in hostilities, *Sl.* let [s.o.] have it, *Sl.* lay into, *Archaic.* insult.

4. argue, dispute, disagree, controvert, run foul of, cross swords, lock horns, fall foul *or* afoul of; wrangle, bicker, haggle, *Sl.* hassle; quibble, cavil, nitpick, pettifog.

—*n.* **5.** fight, battle, duel, bout; contention, clash, conflict, struggle, strife; war, warfare, fighting, hostilities; assault, attack, offensive, harassment, assailment; siege, besiegement, besetment, investment; brawl, feud, affray, broil; collision, meeting, engagement, encounter, rencounter; contest, showdown, tournament, competition.

6. argument, debate, discussion, polemic, logomachy, war of words; controversy, dispute, disputation, discord, contestation; disagreement, quarrel, altercation; dissension, variance, difference of opinion, wrangling, bickering.

7. opposition, confrontation, defiance, contradiction, contravention, refutation, objection, protestation; uprising, resistance, dissension; obstruction, interference, counteraction.

combatant, *n.* **1.** fighter, battler, warrior, brave, soldier, man-at-arms, belligerent; attacker, assailant, assailer, assaulter, invader, aggressor, militant; adversary, opponent, antagonist, enemy, foe, opposition; rival, contestant, competitor, contender; duelist, swordsman, fencer, jouster, gladiator; champion, prize fighter, boxer, pugilist, wrestler, grappler; opposer, disputant, debater, arguer, wrangler.

—*adj.* **2.** combating, fighting, battling, warring; enemy, opposing, rival, opponent, adverse, antagonistic, hostile; combative, pugnacious, militant, looking for a fight. See **combative.**

combative, *adj.* pugnacious, quarrelsome, argumentative, contentious, agonistic; looking for a fight, antagonistic, opposing, adverse, opponent, rival; combatant, militant, hostile, unfriendly, ready for a fight.

combination, *n.* **1.** fusion, conjunction, admixture, blending, coalescence. *Bot.* homogeny; commingling, mingling, minglement, interminglement, intermixture.

2. aggregation, aggregate, assortment, medley, mélange, olio, potpourri, *Inf.* combo; collection, set, series, array, grouping, cluster; miscellany, miscellanea, salmagundi, hodgepodge, jumble, hash, gallimaufry, olla-podrida.

3. mixture, mix, conglomeration, agglomeration, combine, *Archaic.* crasis; amalgamation, blend, homogenization; compound, composite, hybrid, mongrel, amalgam, alloy, *Chem.* levigation; composition, synthesis, consolidation, mosaic, patchwork.

4. association, alliance, league, coalition, union, guild, consortium, syndication, conspiracy, cabal; company, partnership, joint concern, corporation, merger, monopoly, trust, alignment, bloc, cartel; society, organization, party, camorra; congregation, assemblage, assembly, convention, meeting, group, gathering, band, ring, gang, team, troop; community, circle, club, fraternity, brotherhood, lodge, clan, clique.

combine, *v.* **1.** mix, commix, admix, conglomerate, agglomerate; amalgamate, blend, homogenize; compound, alloy, *Chem.* levigate; commingle, mingle, intermingle, intermix, lump together; jumble, scramble, throw together; synthesize, consolidate, correlate, coordinate, compose, put together.

2. associate, affiliate, ally, marry, wed; bond, fuse, weld, yoke, bind, tie together; connect, join, link, chain, attach, inosculate; couple, mate, partner, twin, match, pair up, bring together; unite, conjoin, coalesce, league, club; team, band, herd, pool, merge, join forces; syndicate, federate, confederate, incorporate.

—*n.* **3.** combination, mixture, mix, conglomeration, agglomeration; amalgamation, blend, homogenization; compound, composite, hybrid, mongrel, amalgam, alloy, *Chem.* levigation.

4. commingling, mingling, minglement, interminglement, commixture, intermixture; aggregation, aggregate, assortment, medley, mélange, olio, potpourri, *Inf.* combo; collection, set, series, array, grouping, cluster; miscellany, miscellanea, salmagundi, hodgepodge, jumble, hash, gallimaufry, olla-podrida.

combustible, *adj.* **1.** inflammable, flammable, in-

flammatory, conflagratory, incendiary; fiery, combustive, explosive, ignitable, *Rare.* accendible, tindery; burnable, consumable.
2. excitable, nervous, high-strung, spirited, temperamental; touchy; testy, peppery, thin-skinned, edgy, on edge, *Sl.* uptight, choleric, snappish, irritable; irascible, quick-tempered, short-tempered, *Inf.* short-fused, impatient; hot-headed, hot-tempered, volatile, fiery, explosive, volcanic.

combustion, *n.* burning, *Chem.* oxidation, fire, flame, blaze, conflagration; kindling, ignition, calefaction; incineration, cineration, cremation, incremation; parching, roasting, scorching, torrefaction, scorification; singeing, cautery, cauterization, searing.

come, *v.* **1.** approach, near, draw near, close, close in, bear down upon; advance, make for, move toward, press upon.
2. arrive, enter, check in, clock in, punch in, ring in, sign in, pull in, roll in, *Inf.* hit town, *Sl.* blow in; appear, turn up, show up, make *or* put in an appearance; reach, gain, attain, arrive at, *Chiefly Naut. or Dial.* fetch, get to, *Inf.* make it.
3. extend, reach, stretch, run, go, range, cover.
4. occur, happen, transpire, take place, fall, come to pass, come about, *Sl.* come down; befall, betide, chance, *Archaic.* bechance; result, ensue, follow, eventuate, turn out, work out, *Inf.* pan out.
5. issue, emanate, flow from, emerge from, derive from, spring from, stem from, follow from, grow out of.
6. fare, manage, do, get on, get by, *Inf.* shape up, *Inf.* make out.
7. be born, take birth, become, enter into existence, come into the world, see the light of day, originate.
8. seem, seem like, appear, appear like, look, look like, sound, sound like, give one the feeling *or* impression of.
9. come across a. find, locate, discover; meet, encounter, run into, run across, *Inf.* bump into; chance upon, happen upon, fall upon, stumble upon. **b.** *Slang.* (*of debts*) settle, square, fix, discharge, make good; pay up, hand over, turn over, *Sl.* fork over, *Sl.* cough up. **c.** be communicated *or* conveyed; penetrate, sink in.
10. come along improve, show improvement, grow better, look up, pick up, perk up; rally, take a turn for the better, take a favorable turn; mend, recover, recuperate, get well, pull through.
11. come around a. relent, yield, bend, acquiesce, submit, mellow, soften; grant, concede, allow, accede; comply, agree, come to an agreement, come to terms *or* an understanding. **b.** come to, revive, regain consciousness. See **come to. c.** visit, pay a visit, look in, *Inf.* pop in, stop in *or* off *or* by, drop in *or* over, call on, look [s.o.] up.
12. come at charge, rush, rush at, dash at, fly at; attack, assail, assault, storm, beset, have at, close upon *or* with, pitch into, light into, *Inf.* go for; fall upon, set upon, descend upon.
13. come back a. return, turn back, go back, double back, retrace one's steps. **b.** *Informal.* rebound, spring back, *Inf.* bounce back, *Inf.* make a comeback. **c.** *Slang.* talk back, answer back, flash back, retort, rejoin, *Sl.* give [s.o.] some lip.
14. come between estrange, separate, alienate, divide, disunite, set at odds; sow dissension, stir up *or* make trouble, *Inf.* start something.
15. come by obtain, acquire, procure, get, secure, take possession, get hold of, lay hold of, get one's fingers *or* hands on; earn, win, score, come in for, net, bag, sack.
16. come down come to grief, run aground, fall on evil days, go downhill, deteriorate, degenerate, go to the dogs *or* the devil, *Inf.* go to pot, have seen better days, hit rock-bottom, *Sl.* be on the skids; (*all from a position of importance, distinction, etc.*) fall, descend, stumble, slide, slip, slump, plunge, plummet, flop, tumble, take a fall, *Inf.* come a cropper.
17. come down on a. oppose, voice opposition, protest; disapprove, disfavor, discountenance, take a dim view of; reject, veto, *Inf.* give thumbs down to. **b.** scold, reprimand, reprove, rebuke, chide, upbraid, admonish, berate, tongue-lash; *All Inf.* call down, dress down, tell off, tell a thing or two, jump on *or* all over; *All Sl.* bawl out, chew out, lambaste, give what-for.
18. come down with fall ill, take ill *or* sick, sicken, be stricken with; contract, catch, fall victim to, be stricken with.
19. come forward volunteer, step forward, offer one's services, offer *or* present *or* proffer oneself, not wait to be asked, need no invitation *or* prodding.
20. come in a. enter, step in, set foot in, cross the threshold, find one's way into, breeze in, *Inf.* barge in, *Sl.* bust in. **b.** penetrate, infiltrate, leak in, seep in, soak through; flow in, inflow, rush in, pour in, flood in. **c.** arrive, show up. See **come** (*def.* **2**).
21. come into a. acquire, obtain. See **come by. b.** inherit, *Chiefly Dial.* heir, come in for, step into a fortune; succeed to, step into the shoes of.
22. come off a. occur, happen, transpire; result. See **come** (*def.* **4**). **b.** acquit oneself, make one's mark, *Inf.* do oneself proud, *Inf.* do right by oneself.
23. come on a. also, **come upon** chance upon, happen upon, fall upon; find. See **come** (*def.* **9a**). **b.** progress, make progress, advance, proceed, get along, make steps *or* headway, make strides, forge ahead; develop, mature, ripen, age, fructify; flourish, thrive, bloom, blossom, fatten. **c.** (*all of the stage*) enter, make one's entrance, walk on, take the stage, *Inf.* hit the boards.
24. come out a. appear, be published, be released, be in print. **b.** manifest *or* reveal oneself, show one's true colors, break cover, *Sl.* blow one's cover, *Sl.* come out of the closet, come out into the open. **c.** stand revealed, be revealed, be seen in its true light, become known, become public *or* common knowledge, leak out, get out; circulate, spread, get around, *Inf.* go the rounds. **d.** end, finish, conclude, terminate. **e.** debut, enter society.
25. come out with a. confess, admit, acknowledge, own, *Inf.* own up, *Sl.* fess up, *Sl.* come clean, plead guilty; make a clean breast, take the load off one's mind, *Inf.* get it off one's chest, *Inf.* get it out of one's system; tell all, *Inf.* let it all hang out, *Sl.* sing, *Sl.* spill one's guts. **b.** disclose, divulge, make known, breathe, bring to light, shed light upon; expose, reveal, uncover, unmask; bring out, bring out into the open, open, lay open, let out, break the news, clear the air.
26. come over a. affect, happen to, bother, pester, annoy, irritate, *Sl.* bug, *Sl.* hassle, *Sl.* bite, *Sl.* eat. **b.** visit, drop by. See **come** (*def.* **11c**).
27. come through *U.S. Slang.* **a.** succeed, win, win out, triumph, prevail, weather the storm, *Inf.* beat the game *or* system; make the grade, rise to the occasion, *Sl.* cut the mustard, *Sl.* hack it; come off, *Inf.* make a hit, *Sl.* click, *Sl.* connect. **b.** meet expectations, fulfill requirements, justify hopes; bring [s.t.] off, *Inf.* pull [s.t.] off.
28. come to a. revive, regain consciousness, come around, recover, awaken, stir. **b.** total, total up to, add up to, amount to, mount up to, run to.
29. come up arise, rise up, turn up, crop up, spring up, *Inf.* pop up.
30. come up to a. approach, near. See **come** (*def.* **1**). **b.** compare, compare to *or* with, admit of comparison, measure up to, match up to, hold up against,

Inf. stack up against, *Inf.* hold a candle to.

31. come up with **a.** reach, approach, near, draw near, close in. **b.** produce, supply, furnish, provide, equip. **c.** present, submit, put forward, advance, hold out; propose, suggest, think of, think up, put up, offer.

comedian, *n.* **1.** comic, humorist, wit, funnyman, jokesmith; buffoon, clown, jester, harlequin, fool, merry-andrew, madcap; pantomime, mime, mimic, mummer, impersonator, vaudevillian, vaudevillist; Scaramouch, Columbine, Pantaloon, Punch, Punchinello; zany, droll, wag, *Fr. farceur.*

2. joker, prankster, jokester, practical joker, wisecracker, *Inf.* cut-up, chaffer, *Inf.* card; punster, epigrammist, caricaturist, burlesquer, quipster, *Fr. bel-esprit*; parodist, satirist, lampooner, comedist.

3. *Slang.* wiseacre, wise guy, smart aleck, wisenheimer, *Sl.* smart *or* wise ass; smarty, smartypants; Miss Tizzie Lish.

comedy, *n.* **1.** farce, comic opera, *It. commedia dell'arte*, comedy of manners, comedy of errors, musical, musical comedy; burlesque, *Theat.* burletta, commedietta, travesty, sock, skit; parody, satire, lampoon, gallows humor; harlequinade, pantomime, mimicry; vaudeville, slapstick, low comedy, high comedy.

2. fun, humor, wit, salt, Attic salt; drollery, wittiness, buffoonery, foolery, waggery, horseplay; banter, pleasantry, persiflage, raillery, chaffing, badinage; jesting, joking, japing, jocosity, jocularity; frivolity, jollity, joviality, jocundity; hilarity, levity, facetiousness, ludicrousness, ridiculousness, farcicality; tomfoolery, silliness, *Inf.* shenanigans; inanity, foolishness, giddiness.

comeliness, *n.* **1.** prettiness, loveliness, beauty, pulchritude, handsomeness; fairness, attractiveness, eye appeal, allurement; charm, grace, glamour, appeal, winsomeness, *Scot.* bonniness; wholesomeness, rosiness, blossom, flower, glow, radiance; sightliness, goodliness, agreeableness; gracefulness, elegance, delicacy, fineness; shapeliness, buxomness.

2. propriety, seemliness, decorum, decency, tastefulness, taste; correctness, refinement, polish; respectability, sedateness, mannerliness, modesty, demureness; suitableness, fittingness, meetness, fitness, aptness, appropriateness; harmony, concinnity, symmetry, balance, proportion.

comely, *adj.* **1.** pretty, handsome, beautiful, good-looking pulchritudinous; lovely, goodly, sightly, *Chiefly Literary.* beauteous, *Inf.* divine; pleasing, agreeable, appealing, attractive, *Scot.* bonny fair, wholesome, rosy, rosy-cheeked, blooming; healthy, glowing, radiant, bright-eyed; personable, nice, winsome, charming, alluring, engaging, winning; elegant, delicate, exquisite, fine, graceful; shapely, buxom, curvaceous, well-proportioned.

2. proper, seemly, becoming, befitting; decorous, tasteful, decent, modest; correct, refined, polished, cultivated; respectable, sedate, mannerly, demure, respectful, ladylike, polite; suitable, fitting, meet, apt, fit, appropriate, *Fr. comme il faut*; harmonious, concinnate, symmetrical, balanced, proportioned.

come-on, *n. Slang.* inducement, lure, enticement, allurement, temptation, tantalization. See **bait** (*def.* **2**).

comfort, *v.* **1.** console, solace, pacify, calm, compose, tranquilize, give respite to; relieve, ease, alleviate, soften, lighten one's burden, assuage, allay, palliate, ameliorate, mitigate, abate, reduce; reassure, encourage, hearten, enhearten, disburden, calm *or* quiet one's fears; support, sustain, bear up; cheer, gladden, divert, brighten one's outlook.

2. satisfy, gratify, pamper, warm, nourish, refresh; revive, restore, bolster up, put at ease; invigorate, rejuvenate, reanimate, revivify, inspirit.

—n. **3.** consolation, solace, condolence, commiseration, sympathy, soothing words; relief, easement, reassurance, rescue, deliverance; soothing, lightening, cheer, gladdening, diversion; source of comfort, friend in need, security blanket.

4. calm, calmness, composure, quiet, serenity, tranquillity, peace; respite, repose, rest, ease, contentment, well-being, happiness; enjoyment, pleasure, cheer, amusement; warmth, snugness, coziness, restfulness, peacefulness.

5. sufficiency, abundance, plenty, luxury, opulence, *Inf.* creature comforts, *Inf.* bed of roses.

comfortable, *adj.* **1.** habitable, homelike, *Inf.* homey, livable; cozy, warm, snug, *Inf.* water-tight; roomy, ample, loose, loose-fitting, commodious, luxurious, *Inf.* fit for a king.

2. at ease, at rest, relaxed, at one's ease; cheerful, contented, untroubled, without care; unmolested, undisturbed, unvexed, complacent, placid; quiet, restful, easeful, calm, tranquil, serene, peaceful; unafflicted, unplagued, free from pain *or* worry; prosperous, well cared for, well-off, well-to-do, free from want, *Inf.* on a bed of roses, *Inf.* in clover, *Inf.* sitting pretty.

3. likable, easy, amiable, congenial, genial, cordial; agreeable, enjoyable, pleasant, gratifying, satisfying, pleasing, pleasurable.

4. adequate, acceptable, sufficient, satisfactory.

comforter, *n.* **1.** sympathizer, consoler, mollifier, pacifier, peace-giver; helper, supporter, well-wisher, friend, *Inf.* friend in need.

2. *U.S.* quilt, down quilt, puff, eiderdown, *Chiefly Northern U.S.* comfortable; counterpane, bedcover, bedspread; *Inf.* security blanket.

comfortless, *adj.* **1.** dismal, inhospitable, drear, cheerless. See **cheerless** (*def.* **1**).

2. inconsolable, disconsolate, forlorn, woebegotten, sick at heart, wretched. See **cheerless** (*def.* **2**).

comic, *adj.* **1.** funny, droll, light, rich, humorous; zany, quizzical, comical, jocose, jocular; witty, facetious, waggish, Attic; punny, epigrammatic, *Rhet.* paronomastic; burlesque, (*of verse*) doggerel, vaudevillian, slapstick, farcical; nonsensical, absurd, ludicrous, ridiculous; amusing, laughable, risible, hilarious, side-splitting; silly, inane, foolish.

2. jocund, merry, blithe, blithesome, mirthful, jovial, jolly; gay, frolicsome, sportive, sporting, playful, prankish, puckish; frivolous, flippant.

—n. **3.** **comics** comic strip, funnies, cartoons, funny papers.

4. humorist, funnyman, jokesmith, wit. See **comedian** (*defs.* **1, 2**).

comical, *adj.* funny, droll, witty; amusing, entertaining. See **comic** (*defs.* **1, 2**).

coming, *n.* **1.** advent, approach, accession, access, nearing, afflux; arrival, landing, appearance, forthcoming, birth.

—adj. **2.** approaching, advancing, nearing, progressing; impending, looming, overhanging, threatening; close, near, at hand, close at hand, in view, on the horizon; imminent, forthcoming, momentary, about to happen, toward; prospective, anticipated, expected, due, in store, eventual; future, in the future, to come, in the wind, fated, written, foreseen.

3. up-and-coming, promising, ambitious, aspiring, hoping; enterprising, striving, assertive, aggressive, driving; climbing, progressing, go-ahead.

command, *v.* **1.** order, direct, charge, adjure, instruct, dictate; require, demand, exact, compel, make, coerce, force, task, inflict upon, lay on, obligate, impose upon; bid, tell, request, ask for, call upon, summon, call for, *Law.* subpoena, cite; enjoin, prescribe, lay down the law, give orders, determine; decree, ordain, enact, authorize, warrant, appoint, name, assign, designate.

2. rule, control, have control over, govern; boss, call the shots, *Inf.* call the tune, call the plays, run the show, have it all one's way; be in control, be in command, be in the driver's seat, be in the saddle, wear the pants *or* trousers, be in a position of authority; hold the purse strings, hold all the cards, be master of the situation, be on top of, have [s.o.] under one's thumb, have under control, have well in hand.

3. supervise, direct, superintend, oversee, preside over, officiate, head, lead, conduct, manage, administer, have *or* be in charge of; keep under control, hold in hand, hold in check, hold *or* keep in line; discipline, maintain order, regulate, regiment; dominate, rule the roost, wear the crown, occupy the throne, have the whip *or* upper hand, wield the scepter, wield the power *or* authority.

4. dominate, overlook, survey; tower above, loom over, stand over, bestride; overshadow, eclipse, overtop, rise above, be superior to; outshine, be in the ascendant, be supreme, crown, top, cap, beat; surpass, exceed, overrule, override, prevail over; dwarf, detract from, take away from.

—n. **5.** order, dictate, dictation, dictum, instruction, direction, directive, behest, *Archaic.* hest, imperative, ultimatum; exaction, imposition, requirement, demand, requisition, appointment, assignation, assignment; commandment, will, precept, prescript, prescription, enjoinment, ordainment; rule, regulation, ordinance, statute, act, law; mandate, decree, edict, proclamation, pronunciamento, manifesto; assertion, claim, statement, declaration, determination; admonition, injunction, charge, exhortation; bidding, summons, call, request, invitation, notification; authorization, warrant, *Law.* mittimus, citation, *Law.* writ, *Law.* subpoena, *Law.* mandamus.

6. control, mastery, power, authority, say-so, influence, sway; domination, sovereignty, supremacy, ascendancy; whip *or* upper hand, reins, helm, rudder; dominion, reign, rule, government, regulation, direction, lead; supervision, superintendence, oversight, management; leadership, captaincy, presidency, chieftaincy, chieftainship, headship; governorship, stewardship, charge, jurisdiction, protectorship; dictatorship, czarism, Caesarism, kaiserism, imperialism; tyranny, *U.S.* (*usu. of politics*) bossism, despotism, absolutism.

7. dominance, prominence, height, altitude, elevation, eminence, vantage point, advantage; view, outlook, prospect, eyeshot, eyesight, ken; expanse, extent, scope, sweep, range, reach, span, compass, limit, horizon.

commandeer, *v.* **1.** draft, induct, conscript, conscribe, impress, press, *Naut.* shanghai, crimp; recruit, enlist, *Archaic.* list, muster in, levy; activate, call up, mobilize.

2. seize, take possession of, expropriate, appropriate, misappropriate, arrogate, assume; requisition, confiscate, impound, *Law.* distrain; wrest from, take from, usurp, accroach; help oneself to, make free with.

3. abduct, take by force, carry off, steal, kidnap; hijack, skyjack; deerjack; pirate, plunder, rob, rape, pillage, ravage.

4. coerce, compel, force, pressure, *Inf.* strong-arm, dragoon; oblige, constrain; bulldoze, browbeat, bully, intimidate.

commander, *n.* **1.** manager, overseer, overlooker, overman, superintendent, taskmaster; supervisor, foreman, headman, boss, *Inf.* bossman, *Sl.* the man, *Sl.* head honcho, *Brit.* gaffer; leader, director, executive, administrator, dean, chairman, chairwoman, chairlady, chairperson, speaker; chief, head, principal, *Inf.* kingpin, *Inf.* number one, *Inf.* Mr. Big, *Sl.* top dog, *Sl.* big cheese, *Sl.* top banana.

2. officer, captain, ship's captain, skipper, commandant, *Inf.* old man; chieftain, sachem, warlord, war chief; ruler, governor, lord, overlord, lord and master, master, suzerain, paramount.

commanding, *adj.* **1.** imposing, impressive, majestic, august, noble, awesome; masterful, compelling, forceful, authoritative, self-assured, self-confident, positive; authoritarian, assertive, demanding, dictatorial, *Inf.* bossy, imperious, autocratic; domineering, overbearing, pushing, *Inf.* pushy, presumptuous, peremptory.

2. in command, chief, head, leading; directing, directorial, supervising, supervisory, superintending, overseeing; ruling, controlling, governing, administering, administrative, managing, managerial.

3. dominating, overlooking; wide, expansive, extensive, far-reaching.

commemorate, *v.* **1.** memorialize, celebrate, ceremonialize, solemnize, ritualize; observe, honor, mark, signalize; dedicate, sanctify, make sacred, consecrate, hallow; reverence, venerate, revere, pay tribute, pay homage; immortalize, preserve, keep, fix in memory.

2. recall, bring to mind, conjure up; remind one of, carry one's thoughts back to, serve as a memento of.

3. eulogize, panegyrize, extol, laud, *Archaic.* magnify, emblazon; glorify, bless, exalt, elevate, ennoble; praise, sound *or* sing the praises of, salute, cry up, *Inf.* crack up; compliment, flatter, acknowledge the merits of, lionize, aggrandize; commend, applaud, acclaim, cheer, congratulate; bestow honor upon, make honorable mention of, confer dignity upon, *Archaic.* distinguish.

commemoration, *n.* **1.** celebration, ceremony, ceremonial, commemorative, ritual, rite; dedication, sanctification, consecration; observance, keeping, honoring, hallowing.

2. eulogy, panegyric, eulogium, encomium, citation; testimonial, tribute, homage, honorable mention; public notice, recognition, acknowledgment; glorification, exaltation, elevation, ennoblement; praise, laudation, kudos, flattery, aggrandizement; commendation, applause, acclaim, acclamation; congratulation, toast.

3. memorial, commemorative service, wake, funeral; remembrance, recalling, reminiscence; memorialization, solemnization, ritualization.

4. holiday, feast day, holy day, saint's day; jubilee, anniversary, birthday; festivity, festival, fête, fiesta, carnival; revelry, merrymaking, rejoicing, carousal.

5. memento, souvenir, reminder; commemorative slab, gravestone, tombstone, marker, headstone.

commemorative, *adj.* **1.** memorial, celebrative, celebratory, celebrating, observing, honoring, marking, signalizing; recognizing, acknowledging; in honor of, in memory of, in commemoration of; kept in remembrance, perpetuating, preserving; reminiscent, reminding, recalling to mind.

—n. **2.** commemoration, ceremony, ceremonial, ritual, rite. See **commemoration.** (*def.* **1**).

commence, *v.* **1.** begin, start, go ahead, *Inf.* fire away, *Inf.* blast away; embark, set sail, get going, get a move on, *Inf.* take off, *Inf.* blast off, start off, start out, be off, move out, get the ball rolling, get [s.t.] off the ground, hit the trail, hit the road, get the show on the road; take up, turn one's hand to, venture on, turn to, set to *or* about, take steps; start in, plunge in, *Inf.* dive in, *Inf.* get one's feet wet, *Inf.* get down to, *Inf.* buckle down, *Inf.* get to, *Sl.* get on the stick.

2. initiate, actuate, instigate, set in motion, start the ball rolling; take the first step, take the initiative, take the plunge, make a start, make a beginning, break the ice; open, pioneer, lead off; institute, inaugurate, handsel; found, establish, set up, organize, originate, break ground, lay the foundation, lay the first stone; introduce, launch, broach, usher, *Sl.* ring in.

commencement, *n.* **1.** start, beginning, opening, dawn, genesis, advent; conception, origination, birth; rise, arising, emergence, incipience, nascence, infancy; *Inf.* kick-off, *Inf.* send-off, *Inf.* blast-off; starting point, threshold, square one; base, rudiments; first step, first stage, first move; début, *Inf.* coming out, unveiling; prelude, preface, introduction, preamble, proem, overture; fountain, fountainhead, spring, mainspring; top, head.

2. initiation, actuation, instigation, creation, inception; inauguration, establishment, foundation.

3. (*in universities and colleges*) graduation day, graduation services, graduation, baccalaureate services.

commend, *v.* **1.** recommend, promote, say a good word for, put in a good word for, stand up for, *Inf.* stick up for, stand by, uphold; endorse, back, advocate, sanction; approve enthusiastically, *Chiefly U.S.* approbate, preconize; encore, root for, applaud, clap.

2. praise, laud, extol, cry up, *Inf.* crack up, boost, *Archaic.* magnify, emblazon; acclaim, cheer, celebrate; congratulate, compliment, flatter, *Inf.* pat on the back, hand it to [s.o.], give [s.o.] credit; puff, swell, lionize, belaud, make much of.

3. entrust, trust, confide, delegate, depute, invest; consign, put into the hands of, hand over, transfer, deliver; commit, charge, assign.

commendable, *adj.* laudable, praiseworthy, meritorious, estimable, admirable, *Brit. Dial.* gradely; reputable, creditable, respectable, deserving, worthy; noble, sterling, exemplary, excellent, superior, good, above par; honorable, virtuous, righteous, upright, just, right-minded, principled; unimpeachable, irreproachable, blameless.

commendation, *n.* **1.** approval, approbation, endorsement, reference, sanction; recommendation, good word, glowing terms, pat on the back; acclaim, acclamation, extolment, laudation, kudos, *Archaic.* magnification; applause, cheering, clapping, plaudits, salvo, accolade.

2. tribute, testimonial, credit, recognition, citation; award, trophy, laurels, medal, ribbon; eulogy, eulogium, eulogization, encomium, panegyric; congratulation, compliment, flattery, puffery.

commendatory, *adj.* recommendatory, recommending, promoting, endorsing, advocating, sanctioning; approving, approbative, approbatory, preconizing, commending; praising, laudatory, acclamatory, celebrative, congratulant; complimentary, flattering, favorable.

commensurable, *adj.* proportionate, appropriate, adequate. See **commensurate** (*def.* **3**).

commensurate, *adj.* **1.** equivalent, equal, coequal, equidistant, cotaneous, commeasurable; coordinate, balanced, even, parallel, symmetrical; matching, fellow, same, identical.

2. corresponding, comparable, similar; counterpoised, counterbalancing, equiponderating; uniform, consistent, accordant, harmonious, coinciding, coincident, coextensive, synchronous, in agreement.

3. proportionate, proportional, proportioned, measured, to scale, on a proper scale, commensurable; appropriate, suitable, acceptable, meet, fit, due; adequate, ample, sufficient, satisfactory, enough, competent, passable.

comment, *n.* **1.** annotation, note, footnote, scholium, gloss, marginalia, *Latin.* adversaria; explanation, exegesis, expansion, exposition, elucidation, clarification, illumination, illustration, commentary; supplement, appendix, addendum, codicil, glossary, *Law.* allonge; postscript, p.s., P.S., subjoinder, epilogue, subjunction, endpiece, tailpiece, tag, postfix, suffix.

2. remark, word, statement, utterance; opinion, editorial, interpretation, observation, reaction; discussion, review, descant, criticism.

—*v.* **3.** annotate, make notes on, gloss, footnote; explain, expand upon, amplify, elucidate, clarify, illuminate, shed light, illustrate, exemplify.

4. remark, touch upon, say a word about, say something about; discuss, expound upon, descant, make a statement regarding; editorialize, opine, express one's views, interpret, give one's reaction to, give one's observations on, review, criticize.

commentary, *n.* **1.** annotation, notes, footnotes, scholia, gloss, marginalia; comments, remarks, *Latin.* adversaria.

2. essay, thesis, dissertation, exposition, exposé, study, tract, tractate, monograph, pamphlet, theme, composition, paper; discussion, discourse, lecture, speech, descant, disquisition, sermon, homily; review, opinion, interpretation, criticism; article, editorial, column, piece.

3. explanation, exegesis, elucidation. See **comment** (*def.* **1**).

4. *Usually* **commentaries** chronicle, record, history, archive, documentation, log, minutes, proceedings; journal, diary, memorandum, memoirs, commonplace book; narrative, narration, recital, account, report, chronology, detail, recapitulation, relation, recountal, description, delineation.

commentator, *n.* **1.** annotator, glossarist, scholiast; exegete, explainer, expositer, expounder, interpreter, commenter.

2. essayist, dissertationist, dissertator, monographer, monographist, pamphleteer, writer, author; lecturer, discourser, descanter, sermonizer, preacher, homilist, speaker.

3. editorialist, columnist, reviewer, critic, newsman, newspaperman, newspaperwoman, journalist; news analyst, newscaster, sportscaster, weatherman, broadcaster, *Brit.* newsreader, *Radio, Television.* anchor man.

commerce, *n.* **1.** trade, traffic, buying and selling, barter, truck; dealing, transaction, exchange, interchange, reciprocity; business, marketing, merchandising, mercantilism, commercialism; bargaining, negotiating.

2. social relations, conversance, association, fraternization, fellowship; communion, sympathy, harmony, union, connection, intimacy; communication, intercourse, interchange, dealings; interlocution, conversation, dialogue, colloquy, parley, discussion, debate; argument, disputation, logomachy, verbal contest.

3. coitus, coition, sexual intercourse, copulation, fornication, congress, consummation, conjugation, conjunction; coupling, mating, making love, *Sl.* doing it, *Sl.* getting it on, *Sl.* going to bed.

commercial, *adj.* **1.** mercantile, of business, of trade, of buying and selling; merchantable, marketable, saleable, vendible; mass-produced.

2. mercenary, avaricious, greedy, covetous, eager for gain; acquisitive, grasping, *Sl.* grabby, rapacious; selfish, hoarding, possessive.

—*n.* **3.** advertisement, ad, *Chiefly Brit. Inf.* advert, spot advertisement, spot; announcement, blurb, statement, broadcast, *Inf.* plug, *Inf.* pitch.

commingle, *v.* mix, admix, commix, intermix; blend, mingle, scramble, intermingle, interlard; combine, compound, alloy, *Chem.* levigate, merge, coalesce, melt together; unite, join, inosculate, fuse, amalgamate, incorporate; interweave, intertwine, link together; synthesize, homogenize, hybridize, mongrelize.

commiserate, *v.* pity, feel sorry for, compassionate; sympathize, condole, grieve, feel for, bleed for, empathize; solace, console, soothe, comfort.

commiseration, *n.* pity, compassion, fellow feeling, sympathy, empathy, condolence; solace, consolation, soothing, comfort, relief; charity, humanity, kindness, tenderness.

commissary, *n.* **1.** store, supply, outlet, exchange, commissariat, *U.S. Army.* post exchange, PX.

2. dining room, dinette, dining hall, mess hall, mess; refectory, *Fr. salle à manger, Rom. Hist.* triclinium, cafeteria.

3. deputy, agent, proxy, factor, attorney, attorney-in-fact, attorney-at-law, attorney general, solicitor general; legate, nuncio, ambassador, envoy, emissary; delegate, representative, consul, plenipotentiary, dignitary, diplomat, minister; alternate, surrogate, substitute, secondary; regent, provost, warden, chancellor, commissioner, vicar; broker, middleman, intermediary, instrument, lieutenant; steward, manciple, supplier, *Mil.* quartermaster, purser; provider, victualer, sutler, feeder.

commission, *n.* **1.** entrustment, entrusting, commitment, placing in charge, covenant, chargeship; investment, ordination, vesting; endowment, licensing, crediting, accrediting, accreditation; delivery, deliverance, placement, commending, *Feudal Law.* commendation; relegating, relegation, handing over, passing over, making over, consignment, bestowal.

2. order, direction, charge, command, commandment, ordinance; injunction, dictate, mandate, will; instruction, prescription, bid, bidding, behest, directive; request, demand, requisition, summons, exaction; authorization, warrant, grant, decree, writ, edict, exequator, *Rom. Cath. Ch.* bull, procuration; charter, document, certificate, diploma, papers.

3. authority, power, permit, sanction, license; force, right, prerogative; assignment, appointment, position, incumbency.

4. committee, delegation, deputation, legation, agency, board; council, consul, embassy, mission, proxy; congress, cabinet, chamber, legislature, senate, representatives.

5. task, duty, office, trust, responsibility, obligation, devoir; part, work, errand, *Inf.* bit; capacity, function, scope; post, station, berth, place, rank, role; service, job, occupation, employment, business.

6. perpetration, violation, committal, actuation, performance, execution, infliction, practice; malfeasance, wrongdoing, evildoing, lawbreaking; malpractice, misconduct, disobedience, misbehavior, insubordination; sinning, peccancy, trespass, transgression, transilience, transcursion; infringement, encroachment, intrusion, invasion, incursion.

7. crime, sin, wrong, wrongdoing, evil; deed, misdeed, offense, felony, malefaction, breach; infraction, misdemeanor, error, blunder, mistake.

8. compensation, share, cut, portion, piece, part; allotment, allowance, dividend; brokerage, percentage, fee, rake-off.

9. **in commission** in service, working, running, operable, operating, in operation, in use.

10. **out of commission** not working, in need of repair, out of kilter, *Sl.* out of whack, out of order, broken, disabled; injured, not playing, *Inf.* on the bench, *Sports.* on the sidelines, *Sports.* sidelined; out of action, in mothballs, mothballed, deactivated, inactive.

—*v.* **11.** authorize, command, bid, order, dictate, adjure, enjoin; ordain, decree, enact, institute, prescribe; set, appoint, assign, nominate, *Mil.* detail, name, station; sanction, charter, grant, warrant, privilege, enfranchise, license; ratify, approve, allow, permit, let; credit, accredit, qualify, legalize.

12. entrust, invest, endow, charge, vest, endue; entitle, brevet, promote; delegate, depute, deputize, empower, enable; consign, trust, place in charge of, deliver, make over, give over, hand over, turn over, relegate; commit, obligate, covenant, pledge, promise.

13. order, engage, contract for, indent, enlist; secure, hire, employ, book, retain; request, demand, requisition, impose, call for, ask for.

commissioner, *n.* **1.** official, agent, commissary, deputy, proxy, factor; attorney, solicitor, attorney general, solicitor general; representative, delegate, consul, envoy, emissary, ambassador, legate, nuncio; minister, dignitary, diplomat, plenipotentiary; negotiator, intermediary, middleman, broker.

2. magistrate, officer, public servant; governor, mayor, sheriff, marshal; regent, provost, warden, chancellor, vicar; exarch, (*all three Rom. Cath. Ch.*) vicar-apostolic, vicar-capitular, vicar-general; bey, dey, viceroy, pasha, tetrarch; burgrave, margrave, palatine, khedive; vice-chairman, vice-chancellor, vice-consul, vice-regent, vice-gerent.

3. authority, ruler, commander, director, head, chief, chairman.

commit, *v.* **1.** entrust, commend, confide, vest in, charge with; assign, relegate, appoint, commission, authorize, depute, delegate, invest, empower; send, dispatch, consign, hand over, give over, sign over, deliver, render, surrender, submit, yield; transfer, transmit, convey, forward; place, put, lay, deposit, reposit, store, save, bank, cache, *Inf.* salt down.

2. do, perform, practice, execute, *Inf.* pull; produce, effect, make, enact; perpetrate, pursue, continue, carry on; be a party to, participate in, have a hand in.

3. institutionalize, put away; hospitalize, confine, imprison, jail, incarcerate, put in custody; impound, intern, immure.

4. pledge, covenant, promise, swear, plight, vow, give one's word, assure; mortgage, hypothecate, impignorate; bind, obligate, engage, undertake; pawn, risk, stake; certify, guarantee, warrant, attest, vouch, answer for; compel, oblige, constrain.

5. (*usu. of oneself*) decide, make up one's mind, take a stand, fix upon, determine, choose; resolve, settle, conclude.

commitment, *n.* **1.** entrustment, entrusting, commending, confiding; assignment, assigning, relegation, relegating, placing in charge, appointing, appointment; commission, authorization, deputation, delegation, investment, empowering; sending, dispatching, consignment, committal; handing over, delivering, delivery, deliverance, rendering, surrendering, surrender, submission, submitting, yielding; transfer, transference, transmission, conveyance, forwarding; placement, placing, putting, laying away, depositing, deposit, repositing, storing, saving.

2. institutionalization, confinement, restraint, constraint, duress; detention, custody, imprisonment, incarceration, durance, internment, impoundment, immuring.

3. perpetration, pursuance, pursuing; doing, enacting, performing, performance, practice, practicing, executing, execution.

4. pledge, pledging, covenant, promise, vow, vowing, plighting, giving one's word, assurance, assuring; obligation, responsibility, undertaking; certification, guarantee, warrant, vouching, attesting.

5. decision, choice, stand, stance; determination, resolution, settlement, conclusion.

committee, *n.* council, board, cabinet, panel, chamber, advisory group, advisers, deliberative body, jury; commission, mission, task force, assignees, detail, work party *or* force.

commix, *v.* mix, admix, intermix, blend. See **commingle**.

commixture, *n.* mixture, mixing, admixture, intermixture, blend, blending; mingling, intermingling, commingling; intertwining, interweaving, interlarding; compound, compounding, alloy, alloying, *Chem.* levigation, merging, coalescence, uniting; junction, union, fusion, fusing, interfusion, synthesis; combination, amalgamation, assimilation, incorporation.

commode, *n.* **1.** buffet, sideboard, vitrine, china cabinet *or* closet, cabinet, cupboard, *U.S. Furniture.* lowboy, *Chiefly Brit.* dressing table; dresser, vanity, washstand; chest of drawers, chiffonier, clothespress, *U.S.* bureau.

2. toilet, potty, lavatory, outhouse, latrine, privy, *Sl.* john, *Naut.* head, *Chiefly Brit.* water closet, *Chiefly Brit.* w.c.

commodious, *adj.* **1.** spacious, capacious, roomy, loose, loose-fitting, big, large, huge, great, vast, extensive; comfortable, *Inf.* comfy, cozy, snug, homelike, *Inf.* homey, livable, habitable, pleasant, *Sl.* cushy; accommodating, convenient, conducive, appropriate, apt, suitable, well-suited, fitting, favorable.

2. ample, liberal, more than enough, abundant, plentiful, copious, profuse; commensurate, enough, adequate, sufficient, satisfactory.

commodity, *n.* **1.** thing, item, article, product, article of merchandise, ware, staple.

2. **commodities a.** goods, wares, stock in trade, vendibles, items of trade; produce, farm products. **b.** estate, belongings, chattels, capital, stock; resources, holdings, assets, property.

common, *adj.* **1.** mutual, collective, correlative, communal; reciprocal, interchangeable, interactive, correspondent, complementary, *Archaic.* commutal; joint, shared, parallel, twin, fellow; united, unified, consensual, concerted, unanimous.

2. public, community, civic, civil; state, national, international; social, societal, generic, racial.

3. widespread, general, universal, world-wide; ordinary, usual, conventional; prevailing, current, popular; customary, wonted, accustomed, habitual, routine, repeated, recurrent; established, acknowledged; ritual, traditional, orthodox, consuetudinary, *Inf.* according to Hoyle, *Inf.* S.O.P.; received, approved, understood; familiar, known, everyday, daily, average, normal, standard, *Inf.* G.I.

4. ordinary, plain, simple; native, domestic, homespun, garden-variety, run-of-the-mill, household, commonplace; homely, salt-of-the-earth, workday; vernacular, colloquial, informal, prosaic, pedestrian, plebeian, bourgeois, provincial; subordinate, minor, indistinguished, insignificant, inferior, of no value, worthless, low-bred, low-brow, ill-bred; nameless, ignominious, inglorious, ignoble, *Sl.* cottonpicking, *Sl.* no great shakes.

5. hackneyed, trite, stale, oft-repeated, oft met with, expected; overused, worn-out, well-trodden, in the beaten path; mediocre, indifferent, middling, indiscriminate, stock, unexceptional, *Inf.* dime-a-dozen.

6. mean, low, vile, cheap, base, lewd, depraved; indelicate, gross, trashy, tawdry; odious, low-minded, unseemly, of the street; coarse, vulgar, poor, shabby, ignoble; untutored, illiterate, uncouth, ill-mannered, uncultured, unrefined, unwashed, Philistine.

—*n.* **7.** green, square, village green *or* square; commons, quadrangle, mall, greensward, grassplot; park, campus.

commonalty, *n.* **1.** the public, the general public, the many, the great unnumbered; multitude, crowd, world at large; populace, citizenry, proletariat, hoi polloi, bourgeoisie, the masses, the humbler classes, rank and file; commoners, peasantry, salt of the earth; the lower classes, low life, dregs, underlings, riffraff, *Inf.* the great unwashed; mob, rabble, hoard, herd, rout.

2. society, community, commonwealth, state, body politic; stockholders, shareholders, participants, membership.

commoner, *n.* **1.** common person, one of the people, everyman, the common man, one of the crowd, *Inf.* one of the mob, *Inf.* John Q. Public, *Inf.* John Doe, *Inf.* John Smith, *Inf.* the man in the street; citizen, plebeian, pleb, proletarian, *Fr. roturier;* peasant, nobody, underling.

2. householder, townsman, burgher.

commonly, *adv.* **1.** without distinction, without originality, tritely, without inspiration, lacking spirit, indifferently, indiscriminately, without thought *or* effort, *Sl.* without a brain cell ticking; tolerably, ineffectually, perfunctorily, carelessly, negligently, idly, superficially, sloppily, *Inf.* any old way; badly, wretchedly, ignobly, unworthily; cheaply, meanly, negatively; with bad grace, rudely, uncivilly, sullenly, insolently, impudently; tastelessly, vulgarly, coarsely, showing ill breeding, lewdly, vilely, basely, contemptibly.

2. usually, generally, ordinarily, normally, in general; currently, popularly, conventionally, familiarly, universally; customarily, according to custom, in the usual way, in the natural order of things, by force of habit, habitually; as a matter of course, on an average, as a rule, most often, generally speaking, for the most part; daily, day by day, again and again, over and over, repeatedly.

commonplace, *adj.* **1.** ordinary, usual, general, undistinguished, unimpressive, mediocre, pedestrian, everyday, homely, workaday, *Inf.* run-of-the-mill; uninteresting, tame, dull, slow, sober; monotonous, boring, tedious, tiresome, wearisome, humdrum, unvaried.

2. trite, hackneyed, platitudinous, bromidic, familiar, stock, oft-repeated, stereotyped, tautological; trivial, prosaic, banal, dry, matter-of-fact, prosy; stale, tired, thin, threadbare, worn-out, not new, unimaginative, *Inf.* old-hat, *Inf.* moth-eaten, *Inf.* warmed-over; colloquial, popular, vernacular, provincial; unassuming, artless, unsophisticated, untutored, uncultured, vulgar, non-literary, uneducated, jargonal, *Inf.* jargony, *Inf.* slangy.

—*n.* **3.** cliché, platitude, *Inf.* bromide, old maxim, axiom, truism; prosaism, stereotype, hackneyed expression, trite saying, banality, triviality, common sentiment, twaddle, familiar tune, saw, *Inf.* same old song, *Inf.* chestnut.

common sense, *n.* practicality, sound judgment, good *or* plain sense; discernment, prudence, sound perception; native wit *or* intelligence, mother wit, intuition, *Inf.* horse sense; practical wisdom *or* knowledge, judiciousness, sound thinking, balanced judgment, worldly wisdom, *Inf.* the voice of experience; presence *or* coolness of mind, level-headedness, reasonableness, perspective, balance, ballast; composure, calmness, sang-froid; shrewdness, cleverness, resourcefulness.

common-sense, *adj.* sound, practical, sensible, commonsensible, commonsensical; wise, sagacious, judicious, just, prudent, intelligent; level-headed, cool, clearheaded, down-to-earth, matter-of-fact; logical, rational, sane, reasonable, dispassionate, cool and calm, sober; well-thought-out, solid, experienced, well-founded, soundly based, well-grounded, based on facts; sensible, shrewd, astute, hard-headed, expedient, politic; open-minded, unprejudiced, unbiased, unjaundiced; understandable, plausible, credible, believable.

commonwealth, *n.* **1.** empire, realm, state, nation, community.

2. commonalty, society, populace, citizenry, the body politic, the people, the general public.

3. republic, democracy, federation, federated states, representative government, constitutional government.

commotion, *n.* **1.** turmoil, tumult, turbulence, storm, storm and stress, squall, tempest, hurly-burly; disorder, chaos, confusion, upheaval; disquiet, unrest, disturbance, distraction, excitement, furor, agitation, disruption, perturbation, *Sl.* flap; bother, pother, trouble, fuss, fuss and feathers, *Inf.* to-do, *Inf.* foofaraw, *Inf.* stew, *Inf.* tizzy, *Sl.* lather, *Sl.* hoo-ha; ado, bustle, stir, activity, motion, movement.

2. uproar, racket, noise, hubbub, fracas, rumpus, *Inf.* ruckus; melee, hullaballoo, brouhaha, affray, brawl, broil, embroilment, imbroglio.

3. violence, fury, frenzy, rage; cataclysm, convulsion, eruption, outburst, explosion, fulmination.

4. sedition, insurrection, rebellion, insurgence; riot, revolt, revolution, uprising, mutiny.

communal, *adj.* public, common, collective, shared, mutual, joint, cooperative; community, town, burghal, village, neighborhood; civic, civil, social, societal; proletarian, plebeian, bourgeois.

commune[1], *v.* **1.** converse, talk, communicate, discourse, dialogue, discuss, *Sl.* rap; talk to, have a word with, speak with, confer with, parley; talk privately, have a tête-à-tête, confide in, tell secrets; chat, confabulate, coze, *Inf.* pass the time, *Sl.* chin; chatter, palaver, *Sl.* shoot the breeze *or* bull, *Sl.* chew the fat *or* the rag, *Sl.* yak, *Inf.* gab, *Sl.* gas, gossip, buzz.

2. meditate, think on, contemplate, muse, reflect; think about, consider, revolve, ponder, ruminate, think over.

—n. **3.** conversation, talk, discourse, exchange of ideas, dialogue, discussion, *Sl.* rap session, *Sl.* rap. See **communication** (*def.* **2**).

commune[2], *v.* partake of the Eucharist, communicate, receive communion, *Inf.* receive, take communion, go to communion, celebrate the Lord's supper, partake of the Lord's supper.

commune[3], *n.* **1.** collective, collectivity, co-operative, co-op, (*in Israel*) kibbutz; communalism, collectivism, joint *or* collective ownership.

2. community, town, (*in U.S. and Canada*) township, village, *U.S.* borough, (*in Scotland*) burgh; district, section, quarter, neighborhood, block.

communicable, *adj.* **1.** contagious, catching, transmittable, transmissible, transferable, inoculable, infectious, zymotic; spreadable, *Obs.* taking, spreading, carrying, *Vet. Med.* epizootic; epidemic, epidemical, pandemic, miasmal, miasmatic, miasmatical, miasmic, pestilential.

2. talkative, garrulous, loquacious, gabby, chatty. See **communicative** (*def.* **1**).

communicant, *n.* **1.** churchgoer, churchman, layman, parishioner, celebrant; Christian, believer, God-fearing man, worshiper, devotee, zealot, votary, venerator.

2. informant, source, *Inf.* tipster, *Inf.* leak, *Sl.* tout; reporter, communicator, publisher, announcer, annunciator, monitor, notifier; messenger, messenger boy, page, runner; spokesman, mouthpiece; press, media.

communicate, *v.* **1.** inform, tell, speak, advise, apprise, notify, give notice to, give word, mention to, point out, bring to one's attention, let know, have one to know, give one to understand, enlighten, clue in; *Inf.* open [s.o.'s] eyes; announce, publish, proclaim, declare, pronounce, set forth, put forth; convey, relate, put across, get across; say, utter, voice, breathe, enunciate, come out with, blurt out; disclose, reveal, divulge, bring out, make known, uncover, unmask, unveil, lay open.

2. impart, transmit, transfer, pass on *or* along, hand on, share; diffuse, disseminate, spread; confer, bestow, vouchsafe, grant, accord, allow; offer, extend, proffer, tender, deliver, present; infuse, suffuse, imbue, instill, implant, ingrain, inculcate; (*both of disease*) infect, afflict with.

3. intercommunicate, interface, interchange, exchange views *or* opinions *or* ideas; deal with, have dealings with, have commerce *or* intercourse with, *Inf.* have truck with, be in touch *or* contact with; commune, converse, talk, chat, confabulate, *Inf.* confab, *Sl.* chin, *Sl.* chew the fat, *Sl.* chew the breeze; raise, reach, come across, get [s.t.] across, get to, make contact with, *Inf.* contact, get in touch *or* contact with; correspond, write, epistolize, *Inf.* drop [s.o.] a line *or* note; telephone, *Inf.* phone, call, dial, *Chiefly Brit.* ring up.

communication, *n.* **1.** announcement, publication, declaration, pronouncement; disclosure, divulgement, revelation; enunciation, articulation, utterance, saying, speaking, voicing; impartation, transmission, transmittance, transference, transfer, conveyance, relation; diffusion, dissemination, spreading; conferral, bestowal, donation, endowment; delivery, presentation, extension, proffer, tender, proposal.

2. intercommunication, interplay, interface, interaction, interchange, intercourse, commerce, dealings, traffic, *Inf.* truck; conversation, discourse, discussion, colloquy, interlocution, confabulation; communion, community, fellowship, social intercourse; correspondence, contact, touch, connection.

3. information, *Inf.* info, data, facts, *Sl.* the dope, *Sl.* the scoop, *Sl.* the lowdown; report, account, statement, story; message, dispatch, word, communiqué, bulletin, flash; letter, missive, epistle, note, line.

4. communications the media, the news media; radio, television, TV, journalism, the press, the Fourth Estate; publishing, newspapers, magazines; film; advertising, publicity, public relations, PR.

communicative, *adj.* **1.** expansive, open, free, unreserved, unrestrained, unreticent, communicatory; frank, candid, straightforward, unsecretive; talkative, loquacious, garrulous, voluble, chatty, *Sl.* gabby; conversational, colloquial, interlocutory, confabulatory; accessible, approachable, conversable, receptive.

2. informative, instructive, educational, enlightening, *Inf.* eye-opening.

communion, *n.* **1.** sharing, exchange, give and take, cooperation, synergy, interaction, joint participation, collaboration; mutuality, reciprocity, interdependence, sympathy, rapport; harmony, consonance, concert, concord, concordance, accord, accordance, agreement, correspondence.

2. fellowship, togetherness, brotherhood, fraternization; companionship, friendship, friendliness, amity, clubbiness, *Inf.* chumminess; colleagueship, mateship, comradeship, camaraderie, esprit de corps, sodality; association, consociation, affiliation, alliance, alignment, connection, connectedness, *Genetics.* linkage; unity, union, unitedness, oneness, fusion.

3. intimacy, familiarity, closeness, relationship; intercommunication, communication, commerce, commune; intercourse, interchange, dialogue, conversation, interlocution.

communiqué, *n.* bulletin, announcement, statement, notice; report, news report, flash; dispatch, telegram, cable, wire, message, communication, aviso.

communism, *n.* Bolshevism, Marxism, Leninism, Sovietism; collectivism, communalism, communalization, state ownership; socialism, social democracy, phalansterianism, Fourierism, totalitarianism.

communist, *n.* **1.** Bolshevik, Bolshevist, Marxist, collectivist, communitarist, communalist; socialist, social democrat, Fourierist; *All Derogatory.* red, *Sl.* pinko, radical, leftist, revolutionary, totalitarian.

—adj. **2.** Bolshevistic, Marxist, collective, communal, state-owned, socialist; leftist, red, radical, revolutionary, totalitarian.

community, *n.* **1.** neighborhood, borough, district, township, parish; hamlet, town, *Archaic.* wick, *Archaic.* thorp, village, burg; municipality, city, metropolis; settlement, colony.

2. society, public, general public, commonalty, commonweal, body politic, nation, state; folk, people, *Ger. Volk,* populace, citizenry, family; habitancy, inhabitancy, population.

3. fellowship, sect, cult, school, denomination; commune, kibbutz, phalanx, phalanstery; convent, nunnery, cloister, priory, monastery, abbey, friary, lamasery, *Buddhism.* vihara, *Islam.* khankah, *Hinduism.* ashram; fraternity, sorority, sodality, brotherhood, sisterhood; company, association, congregation, band; circle, club, lodge, clan, set, clique, coterie; federation, union, alliance, coalition, combine; organization, guild, confederacy, league.

4. joint possession, common ownership, partnership, copartnership, joint tenancy, cotenancy, *Obs.* jointure; cooperative, co-op, communization, communion; communalism, communism, collectivism, phalansterianism, Fourierism.

5. agreement, accord, accordance, harmony, amity, unison, uniformity, unanimity; identity, similarity, likeness, homogeneity, affinity, kinship; conformity, concordance, concord, consonancy, concurrence, solidarity; affiliation, connection, relation, relatedness, relationship; comparability, analogousness, resemblance, analogy; correspondence, parallelism, complementariness, parity; unity, consentience, consentaneousness.

commutation, *n.* **1.** exchange, substitution, switch, surrogation, subrogation; interchange, counterchange, shuffling, transposition; bartering, trading, buying and selling, traffic; reciprocation, retaliation, recompense, compensation, indemnification, indemnity, replacement.

2. change, alteration, adjustment, adaptation, permutation, (*of currencies*) regulation.

3. (*all usu. of prison sentences or other penalties*) reduction, abridgment, diminution, curtailment, shortening; mitigation, relaxation, relieving, assuagement, alleviation, mollification; extenuation, palliation; compromising, plea bargaining; *Law.* compounding, remitting.

4. travel distance, distance, ride to work. See **commute** (*def.* **5**).

commute, *v.* **1.** exchange, substitute, change for, switch, put in place of, take the place of, surrogate, subrogate; supplant, succeed, supersede, interchange, counterchange, transpose, shuffle; barter, trade, *Inf.* swap, buy and sell, traffic; reciprocate, retaliate, give back, settle differences, atone; recompense, compensate, indemnify, requite, replace, repay, supply.

2. change, alter, adjust, adapt, permute, (*of money*) redeem.

3. (*all usu. of prison sentences or other penalties*) reduce, abridge, diminish, curtail, shorten; *Law.* compound, remit; mitigate, make less severe, relieve, assuage, alleviate, mollify, soften, allay; extenuate, palliate; compromise, plea bargain, *Sl.* cop a plea.

4. travel, drive back and forth, shuttle, take a bus, take a train.

—n. **5.** *Informal.* commutation, ride, ride to work, trip, journey; travel distance, distance.

compact[1], *adj.* **1.** dense, solid, firm, hard; close, tight, tight-knit, close-knit, impermeable, impassable, impenetrable; thick, heavy, thickset, stubby, squat, short, stocky; condensed, concentrated, compressed, packed together, squeezed together, crowded, overfilled, stuffed, cram-full, chock-full; bunched together, clustered together, clotted, stuck together, coherent, unified, as one; conjoined, conjunct, connected, combined, corporate, consolidated, united, solidified.

2. small, little, capsule, portable; tight, constricted, limited, narrow, close, snug; trim, tidy, neat, orderly, well-ordered, well-arranged, shipshape.

3. concise, succinct, summary, brief, short; capsule, summarized, condensed, compendious, synoptic; abridged, shortened, cut off *or* short; pithy, terse, tight, epigrammatic, laconic, pointed, to the point; curt, abrupt, short, cryptic, brusque, crisp, brisk, sharp.

—v. **4.** consolidate, condense, make dense, thicken, concentrate; pack together, press together, compress, tamp down, crowd together, squeeze together; reduce, shrink, shorten, abridge; constrict, narrow, lessen, limit, constringe, contract, draw in *or* together; join together, connect, unite, syncretize; combine, conjoin, knit together, interlace, intertwine; mingle, mix, blend, amalgamate, coalesce; fuse, alloy, melt into one; unify, merge; join forces, team up, become partners, corporate, associate, syndicate, confederate, ally.

5. cement, solidify, strengthen, reinforce, stabilize, make firm *or* stable; secure, affix, attach, link, clasp, hook, tie together, bind.

6. compose, make up, form, embody, incorporate, organize.

compact[2], *n.* **1.** formal agreement, contract, indenture, covenant, bond; concordat, treaty, alliance, pact, *Rare.* paction, convention; cease-fire, truce, cartel, entente, détente; mutual understanding, accord, accordance, concord, concordance, concurrence; conspiracy, collusion, league, confederacy, coalition, combination, union.

2. transaction, *Inf.* deal, bargain, arrangement, settlement; terms, conditions, stipulations.

3. promise, pledge, vow, oath, word of honor, parole, troth; gentleman's agreement, commitment, obligation, engagement; word, assurance, warrant, warranty, surety, security, guarantee, guaranty.

companion, *n.* **1.** comrade, crony, chum, copain, sidekick, shadow, alter ego, *Inf.* pal, *U.S. Inf.* buddy, *Sl.* cully, *Sl.* Siamese twin; partner, counterpart, mate, helpmate, classmate, shipmate, messmate, teammate, playmate, housemate, roommate, *Inf.* roomie, *Inf.* other half, *Obs.* consort; associate, colleague, compeer, affiliate, co-worker, yokefellow, yokemate, *Scot. and North Eng.* marrow, *Archaic.* peer; fellow, confrere, brother, sister; ally, friend, acquaintance, amigo, *Fr. ami.*

2. assistant, aide, squire, coadjutor, coadjutress, ancilla, auxiliary, helper, abettor; governess, matron, tutor, tutoress, nursemaid, nanny, *(in Spain and Portugal)* duenna; sitter, baby-sitter, au pair girl; guardian, tutelary, tutelar, shepherd, protector, protectress; escort, chaperon, attendant.

3. accompaniment, accessory, match, pendant, com-

plement, completer, concomitant, concurrent, *Astron.* comes; supplement, appendage, appurtenance, appurtenant, adjunct, appanage.
4. handbook, manual, reference book, vade mecum; guide, guidebook.
—*v.* **5.** accompany, escort, usher, squire, esquire, chaperon, go along with, *Obs.* consort; keep company with, associate with, go out with, *Inf.* go with, *Inf.* pal around with, *Inf.* hang around with, *Sl.* hang out with.
6. come with, coexist with; belong to, be an appendage of, be an adjunct to, be an annex to, be part of.

companionable, *adj.* congenial, amicable, friendly, affable, cooperative, easy to get along with; warm, affectionate, convivial, hearty, jolly, jovial, gregarious; sociable, social, clubby, *Inf.* chummy; brotherly, neighborly, genial, cordial, hospitable, kindly, kindhearted, polite, courteous; pleasant, agreeable, charming, ingratiating.

companionate, *adj.* **1.** associate, affiliated, allied, fellow, related, relative, akin, affinitive, like, similar; connected, joint, paired, matched, united, wedded, married; accompanying, attendant, accessory, concomitant, supplementary, supplemental, ancillary, auxiliary, appended, attached, annexed, added.
2. compatible, harmonious, accordant, concordant, consonant, concurrent; complementary, congruous, congruent, matching, hand in glove.

companionship, *n.* fellowship, colleagueship, mateship, brotherhood, fraternity, fraternization, togetherness, company; camaraderie, comradeship, esprit de corps, friendship, amity, *Inf.* chumminess; partnership, association, consociation, affiliation, alliance, union.

company, *n.* **1.** assemblage, group, body, circle, assembly; gathering, meeting, audience; concourse, rally, throng, number; entourage, cavalcade, drove, caravan; congregation, community, flock, host, lot; conclave, convocation, council, synod, consistory, conventicle; muster, mobilization, levy; association, union, convention, conference, congress; caucus, bloc, *Rom. Antiq.* comitia, junta; foregathering, conjunction, coalescence, convergence; concentration, aggregation, confluence, conflux.
2. companionship, fellowship, friendship, intimacy, intercourse, *Inf.* chumminess; association, consociation, sodality, society; comradeship, camaraderie, esprit de corps; fraternization, brotherhood, colleagueship.
3. guest *or* guests, visitor *or* visitors, caller, friends come to call; commensal, diner; habitué, frequenter; party-goers, partiers, celebrants, merrymakers, socialites.
4. business, firm, house, trust, establishment, institution, concern, *Fr. maison, Inf.* outfit; corporation, syndicate, association, holding company, partnership, copartnership, parent company, conglomerate.
5. guild, union, league, faction, fellowship; coalition, federation, alliance, *Ger. Bund*; organization, confederacy, combine.
6. crew, squad, team, detail, party; unit, detachment, division, band, outfit; posse, guard, patrol; column, wing, section, subdivision; brigade, regiment, garrison, troop, battery, contingent; squadron, battalion, platoon, force, corps; legion, cohort, phalanx.
7. cast, troupe, players, dramatis personae, actors, performers.
8. part company a. break up, part, disunite, separate, dissociate, fall out, become estranged. **b.** differ, disagree, dissent, conflict, oppose, vary, be of a different opinion *or* of a different mind. **c.** depart, withdraw, take leave, leave, exit, *Sl.* split.

comparable, *adj.* **1.** corresponding, proportional, proportionate, commensurable, similar, connatural, analogous, cognate; alike, like, near, akin, kindred, close, affinitive, relative, correlative; approximate, approaching, resembling, quasi; commensurate, equivalent, synonymous, same, identical, matching; balanced, parallel, symmetrical; uniform, consistent, accordant, harmonious, concordant, synchronous, in agreement.
2. equal to, coordinate, tantamount, on even ground with, on even terms with, on a par with, as good as, on a level with, in a class with, a match for.

comparative, *adj.* relative, comparable, near, close, approximate, proximate; limited, restricted, qualified, modified.

compare, *v.* **1.** collate, contrast, set side by side, juxtapose, oppose, set against, *Sl.* stack up; measure, weigh, balance; divide, separate, differentiate, discriminate; correlate, relate.
2. liken, equate, match, analogize, associate, identify with.
3. resemble, look like, be similar, have the earmarks of, take after, follow; correspond, parallel, approximate, approach; be a match for, hold a candle to, be as good as, be in a class with, be on par with, be on equal footing.

comparison, *n.* **1.** contrast, contrasting, setting side by side, collation, collating, apposition, juxtaposition, juxtaposing, setting against, *Sl.* stacking up; opposing, opposition, confrontation, confronting; measurement, measuring, weighing, balance, balancing; observation, close scrutiny, study; division, dividing, separation, separating, distinction, discrimination.
2. likening, equating, equation, match; analogy, parallel, association, identification; illustration, exemplification.
3. relation, correlation, ratio, proportion, commensurability, comparability; resemblance, likeness, similarity, affinity, filiation, kinship, propinquity, closeness, nearness, proximity, approximation; relationship, connection, cognation, alliance, comparativeness; consistency, agreement, concurrence, correspondence, homology; assonance, consonance, accord, unison; synonymy, equivalence, equipollence.

compartment, *n.* **1.** partition, section, part, division, department; area, sphere, space, place.
2. pigeonhole, cubbyhole, cubby, niche, nook; drawer, tray, well, till, box, bin, hold, receptacle, bunker.
3. booth, stall, bay, cubicle, carrel, carol, cell, cage, pew, alcove, corner; closet, locker, chamber, room, roomette, cabin, berth, apartment, enclosure.

compass, *n.* **1.** needle, magnetic needle, direction finder, radio direction finder, RDF, guide, loran, shoran, *Aeronaut.* earth inductor.
2. perimeter, periphery, border, edge, rim, fringe; circumference, ambit, margin, frame, outline, confine, confines; bound, limit, bourn, pale, extremity; limits, city limits, outer limits.
3. area, extent, range, scope; reach, stretch, spread, sweep, span, measure, width, breadth; section, region, zone, quarter; territory, realm, domain, province; premises, demesne.
4. scale, register, gamut, *Music.* diapason, range.
5. circuit, cycle, orbit, revolution; round, lap, turn, loop.
—*adj.* **6.** curved, rounded, bowed, crooked, hooked; arched, vaulted, cambered, embowed, forniciform.
—*v.* **7.** lap, go *or* move around *or* round, go the round, make the round of; circuit, circle, circumambulate.

8. surround, encircle, encompass, environ, outline, delineate; gird, engird, girdle, belt, ring; circumvent, bound, limit, confine, shut in, hem in, pen in, keep within bounds.

9. obtain, acquire, procure, get, get hold of, secure; achieve, accomplish, fulfill, carry out, carry off, bring off, *Inf.* pull off, *Sl.* come through, *Sl.* do *or* turn the trick; perform, do, discharge, execute, dispatch, *Inf.* take care of, *Sl.* polish off; effect, effectuate, bring about, bring to pass.

10. contrive, plot, complot, scheme, intrigue, collude, conspire, connive; maneuver, machinate, engineer.

11. understand, comprehend, fathom, read, follow, get the idea, *Inf.* get the picture, *Scot.* ken, *Sl.* savvy, *Sl.* dig; catch, grasp, seize, embrace, take in, apprehend, get hold of, *Inf.* catch on, *Inf.* catch *or* get the drift; see, perceive, discern, see the light.

compassion, *n.* pity, tenderness, heart, love, ruth, pathos, *Archaic.* bowels; clemency, lenity, leniency, mildness, easiness, gentleness; mercy, quarter, grace, exorability, placability, liberality; sympathy, commiseration, consolation, concern; kindliness, softheartedness, benignity, tender-heartedness, loving-kindness; charity, benevolence, magnanimity, kind-heartedness, beneficence, humanitarianism; sorrow, condolence, solace, fellow feeling, understanding, consideration, considerateness; forbearance, suffering, long-suffering, longanimity; tolerance, indulgence, patience, toleration, endurance; forgivingness, forgiveness, condonation; humanity, kindness, chivalry, goodness.

compassionate, *adj.* pitying, tender, ruthful, piteous, loving; clement, lenient, mild, easy, gentle, soft; merciful, liberal, gracious, exorable, placable, touched; sympathizing, sympathetic, commiserative, consoling; kindly, benign, benignant, soft-hearted, tender-hearted, humane; kind, good, chivalrous, forgiving, pardoning; charitable, benevolent, magnanimous, beneficent, kind-hearted, humanitarian; sorry, condolent, understanding, considerate; forbearing, tolerant, indulgent, patient.

compatibility, *n.* **1.** unanimity, consentience, consentaneity, consentaneousness, like-mindedness; concord, concordance, concurrence, consonance, concert; agreement, accord, accordance, compliance, conformity, conformance, conformation; unity, oneness, oneness of mind, single-mindedness.

2. affinity, friendship, rapport, good will, good feeling, amity, cordial relations; peace, peacefulness; congeniality, amicability, neighborliness; fraternity, brotherhood, brotherliness, fellowship, comradeship.

3. harmony, harmoniousness, proportion, balance, symmetry; coherence, cohesion, consistency; congruity, congruence, congruousness, mutual fitness.

compatible, *adj.* **1.** harmonious, in harmony, agreeing, in agreement, agreeable, accordant, in accord, concordant; concurring, concurrent, consentaneous, consentient; complying, compliant, complaisant, conforming, conformable; at one, in unison, in rapport, of the same mind, of one mind, like-minded.

2. coexistent, coexisting, coincident, coeval, concomitant, contemporary, contemporaneous, simultaneous, coinstantaneous; parallel, side-by-side; synchronized, in step, *Inf.* in sync.

3. consistent, coherent, cohesive, congruous, congruent; in line, in keeping.

compatriot, *n.* fellow countryman *or* countrywoman, countryman, brother, fellow citizen, countryfolk, countrypeople, *Sl.* paisano.

compeer, *n.* **1.** peer, equal, coequal, equivalent, equipollent; fellow, match, counterpart, like, twin, clone.

2. comrade, companion, chum, crony, copain, *U.S. Inf.* buddy, *Inf.* pal; sidekick, shadow, alter ego, other self; friend, confidant, familiar, intimate, *Inf.* bosom buddy.

compel, *v.* **1.** coerce, force, drive, press, constrain, pressure, oblige, hustle, railroad; impel, urge, impress, provoke, extort, cause, require, exact, necessitate, make; draft, conscript, commandeer; persuade, induce, prevail upon, insist upon, *Inf.* shove *or* ram down [s.o.'s] throat; apply pressure, *Sl.* lean against *or* on, armtwist, twist [s.o.'s] arm, put the screws on *or* to, *Inf.* strong-arm, put the heat on, squeeze.

2. tyrannize, terrorize, threaten, bulldoze, dragoon; bully, hector, torment, harass, abuse, taunt, tease, bullyrag; intimidate, browbeat, overawe, cow, frighten, terrify, petrify.

3. subdue, suppress, quash, quell, squash, crush; overpower, overwhelm, overcome; conquer, vanquish, defeat, override.

4. control, master, dominate, lay down the law to, supervise, direct, manage, boss, manipulate; domineer, overbear, boss around, lord it over, *Inf.* pull rank, ride roughshod over; curb, check, bind, repress, restrict; *Law.* distrain.

compendious, *adj.* concise, terse, succinct, brief, comprehensive, summary, packed, pithy, inclusive, elliptical, synoptic, compact, sententious; contracted, compressed, condensed, abridged, shortened, short.

compendium, *n.* **1.** treatise, dissertation, thesis, essay, theme, discourse, tract, study.

2. summary, epitome, synopsis, abstract, symposium, compilation, digest, conspectus; condensation, abridgment, reduction, compression, abbreviation; analysis, recapitulation; résumé, brief, précis; outline, aperçu, sketch, review, syllabus, prospectus, *Latin. multum in parvo*; docket, bulletin, minute; extracts, fragments, cuttings, analects, clippings, citations.

3. full list, inventory, account.

compensate, *v.* **1.** counterbalance, counterweigh, counterpoise, countervail, offset, be equivalent to; counteract, neutralize, nullify, cancel *or* cancel out; balance, equalize, handicap, even, square, equate; adjust, adapt, accommodate, *Naut.* (*of sails*) trim.

2. recompense, repay, reimburse, indemnify, refund; pay, remunerate, reward; make restitution, make amends, requite; satisfy, make up for, redress; atone, expiate, make good.

3. retaliate, pay back, get back, get even, even *or* settle the score, return like for like, give tit for tat, *Inf.* give [s.o.] a taste of his own medicine, *Euph.* return the compliment.

compensation, *n.* **1.** remuneration, payment, pay, *Brit. Sl.* get; salary, wages, emolument, consideration, hire; earnings, income, revenue, profits; charge, *Hist.* scot, fee, stipend, honorarium; reward, bonus, grant, benefaction; tip, gratuity, douceur, *Fr. pourboire*; bribe, hush money, payola, graft; commission, percentage, share, brokerage; cut, slice, *Inf.* rake-off, *Inf.* kickback.

2. repayment, reimbursement; satisfaction, damages, *Law.* solatium, indemnification, indemnity, recoupment; restitution, penalty, fine, (*in Anglo-Saxon and Germanic countries*) wergild; requital, quittance, return, redress; atonement, amends, expiation, reparation, retribution.

3. retaliation, reprisal, vengeance; reciprocation, tit for tat, quid pro quo, an eye for an eye, a Roland for an Oliver.

4. counterbalance, counterweight, counterpoise, offset, equivalent; neutralization, nullification cancellation; counteraction, reaction; equalization, balance, symmetry; adjustment, accommodation, handicap, adaptation.

compete, *v.* vie, contend, strive, struggle, fight, wrestle, tussle, grapple, jockey for position; combat, fight, battle, spar, joust, tilt, fence; meet, breast, lock horns, clash, collide, encounter, engage; participate, enter, throw *or* toss one's hat in the ring; rival, emulate, match, contest, oppose, challenge, play against, pit oneself against, try to beat [s.o.'s] time, defend one's title.

competence, *n.* **1.** fitness, fittedness, competency, qualification, eligibility, preparedness, readiness; capability, capableness, efficiency, commensurability, the stuff, *Inf.* what it takes, *U.S. Inf.* the goods; ability, ableness, efficacy, efficaciousness, effectiveness, effectivity; mastery, authority, expertness, expertise; proficiency, adeptness, address, finesse, facility, polish; practice, experience, know-how, savoir-faire; skillfulness, adroitness, deftness, dexterity, dexterousness; knowledgeability, understanding, *Sl.* savvy; conversance, familiarity.

2. adequacy, commodiousness, ampleness, substantialness; abundance, plenteousness, saturation, *Rare.* impletion; enough, fill, charge, full measure, plenty.

3. sufficiency, enough, sustenance, living, livelihood, support, subsistence; wherewithal, means; affluence, wealth, fortune, *Sl.* bundle.

4. responsibility, accountability; reasonableness, sensibleness, rationalness; saneness, soundness.

competent, *adj.* **1.** fit, fitted, qualified, eligible, prepared, well-grounded, trained, ready; capable, efficient, *Sl.* on the ball, commensurate, equal to, *Inf.* up to; able, efficacious, effective, effectual; masterful, expert, authoritative; proficient, adept, accomplished, polished, practiced, experienced, *Fr. au fait*; adroit, deft, dexterous, skilled, skillful; knowledgeable, versed, well-informed, *Inf.* knowing the ropes, *Sl.* savvy; conversant, familiar, up.

2. satisfactory, *Inf.* up to snuff; acceptable, adequate all right, *Inf.* O.K.; unexceptional, unremarkable, so so.

3. responsible, accountable; reasonable, sensible, rational; sane, mentally sound, *Latin. compos mentis.*

competition, *n.* **1.** contest, game, meet, match, one-on-one; bout, tournament, encounter, engagement, athletic event; race, run, sweepstakes, run for one's money; contention, challenge, opposition; strife, struggle, conflict, clash, fight, infighting, *Sl.* rat race.

2. rivalry, vying, emulation, *Inf.* one-upmanship, *Inf.* keeping up with the Joneses.

3. rival, challenger, competer. See **competitor** (*defs.* **1, 2**).

competitive, *adj.* **1.** rival, vying, emulative, competing, *Rare.* corival; striving, emulous, ambitious, aggressive, dog-eat-dog, cutthroat.

2. opposing, contentious, antagonistic, conflicting; combative, ready to fight, competitory.

competitor, *n.* **1.** rival, vier, opponent, *Rare.* corival; opposition, competition, enemy, foe, antagonist, other side.

2. emulator, challenger, contender, bidder, aspirant; contestant, participant, entrant, candidate.

3. fighter, battler, jouster, competer, *U.S. Inf.* go-getter.

compilation, *n.* **1.** compiling, gathering, accumulating, assembling, collecting, aggregating, drawing together, collating, colligating; gleaning, garnering, mustering; unifying, incorporating, marshalling; organizing, ordering, codifying, methodizing, systematizing.

2. collection, gathering, accumulation, assembly, assemblage; combination, assortment, aggregation, collocation, congeries.

3. anthology, thesaurus, ana, collectanea, album, miscellany, chrestomathy; corpus; compendium, synopsis, symposium, abstract, summary, review, digest; extracts, fragments, cuttings, analects, clippings, citations.

compile, *v.* accumulate, gather, amass; assemble, put together, group together, draw together, bring together; collate, collocate, colligate, unite; anthologize, compose; garner, glean; organize, order, codify, methodize, systematize.

complacency, *n.* **1.** self-satisfaction, self-content, smugness; ease, peace of mind, contentment, tranquillity, serenity.

2. joy, pleasure, delight, treat; comfort, help, relief.

complacent, *adj.* **1.** smug, self-satisfied, self-contented, pleased with oneself, like the cat that swallowed the canary; (*all with oneself, one's actions,* or *one's situation*) pleased, well-pleased, glad, delighted; content, at ease, placid, serene, tranquil.

2. pleasant, civil, affable, cheerful; complaisant, compliant, obliging, deferential, agreeable, amenable, conciliatory; gracious, decorous, chivalrous, courtly, gallant; suave, urbane, genteel, well-bred, cultivated, polished.

complain, *v.* grumble, growl, crab, gripe, fume, clamor, *Inf.* raise a fuss, *Inf.* yammer, *Sl.* grouse, *Sl.* grouch, *Sl.* kick, *Sl.* squawk, *Sl.* beef, *Sl.* bitch, *Dial.* holler; bewail, lament, moan, groan, kvetch, *Sl.* bellyache; criticize, censure, cavil, carp, nag, pick, *Inf.* give [s.o.] a hard time; find fault, deprecate, disapprove, deplore; murmur, whine, fret, repine.

complainant, *n.* plaintiff, claimant, accusor, accusatrix, suitor, prosecutor, the prosecution, the state.

complaint, *n.* **1.** criticism, animadversion, *Inf.* brickbat; cavil, quibble; lament, lamentation, jeremiad, wail, ululation, moan, groan, murmur, whimper, grumble; plaint, demur, objection, *Inf.* kick, *Inf.* gripe, *All Sl.* big stink, squawk, bellyache, beef.

2. reproach, reproof, reprimand, stricture, rebuke; tirade, harangue, diatribe, aspersion, obloquy, censure, castigation, objurgation, vituperation; disapproval, disparagement, disapprobation, reprobation, reprehension, condemnation; imprecation, fulmination, contumely, denunciation, detraction; protest, protestation, remonstrance, outcry; expostulation, deprecation, *Archaic.* dehortation; quarrel, dispute, disputation, apple of discord, disagreement.

3. sickness, illness, ailment, malady, indisposition, affliction; infirmity, disability, disorder, distemper; disease, infection, affection; invalidism, valetudinarianism, debility.

4. charge, suit, preferment, claim, *Law.* gravamen, grievance; crimination, blame, incrimination, accusation, indictment, imputation, inculpation.

complaisance, *n.* **1.** agreeableness, obligingness, amenability, reasonableness, pleasingness, willingness; compliance, compliancy, flexibility, conformability; deference, submissiveness, acquiescence, yieldingness, conciliation.

2. graciousness, geniality, complacence; amiability, likableness, good-naturedness, good-humoredness, pleasantness; amicability, neighborliness, friendliness, congeniality, sociability, affability; easiness, openness, unreservedness, familiarity, easygoingness; sweetness, niceness, delightfulness, lovableness; kindness, kindliness, kindheartedness, consideration, considerateness; charm, grace, engagingness, winsomeness; civility, cordiality, cordialness, courtesy, politeness, mannerliness, courtliness; urbanity, suavity, sophistication;

tact, address, diplomacy, finesse.

complaisant, *adj.* **1.** obliging, agreeable, accommodating, amenable, reasonable; deferential, respectful, submissive, acquiescent, yielding, conciliatory; compliant, pliant, flexible, pliable, conformable.

2. gracious, pleasant, complacent, genial; amiable, pleasing, likable, good-natured, good-humored, *Scot. and North Eng., Irish Eng.* sonsy; amicable, neighborly, friendly, sociable, congenial, affable; easy, open, unreserved, easygoing; delightful, nice, sweet, lovable; kind, kindly, kindhearted, considerate, *Scot.* couthie; engaging, winning, winsome, charming; civil, cordial, courteous, mannerly, courtly; urbane, suave, well-mannered, well-bred, civilized, sophisticated; tactful, diplomatic, politic, chivalrous, artful.

complement, *n.* **1.** crowning touch, finishing touch, final touch, *Inf.* clincher, *Inf.* topper; *All Fig.* icing *or* frosting on the cake, dessert.

2. balance, remainder, difference; filler, makeweight; supplement, addition, addendum, accessory.

3. counterpart, equivalent, match, twin, double, other half, alter ego; alternate, pendant, companion, mate, fellow; correspondent, coordinate, correlative, parallel, analogue.

4. aggregate, full amount *or* quantity, full number, full allowance, full measure; total, grand total, sum total, sum and substance, the whole, the entirety; the lot, one and all, all and sundry; load, capacity, full house; set, package, package deal; *All Sl.* the works, the whole works, the whole ball of wax, the whole kit and caboodle, the whole deal, the whole shooting match, the whole mess, the whole bunch, the whole shebang.

5. company, cast, troop; body, team, party, band, crew, outfit, *Inf.* bunch, *Sl.* mob.

—*v.* **6.** complete, set off; crown, cap, culminate, consummate, fulfill, *Inf.* top off.

7. correlate, reciprocate, correspond, coequal; supplement, add to, round off *or* out, fill out, make up, make good.

complementary, *adj.* **1.** complemental, completing, completory, completive, filling, fulfilling; perfecting, perfective, consummating, consummative, culminating, culminative.

2. correspondent, corresponding, parallel, analogous, answering, complementing; reciprocal, reciprocative, correlative, correlational, correlated; equivalent, coequal, tantamount; mutual, commutual, common, joint, respective, two-way.

3. interrelated, interconnected, interlinked, interassociated, interdependent; paired, mated, matched, doubled; companion, brother, sister, twin, fellow.

complete, *adj.* **1.** entire, whole, total, integral, comprehensive, plenary; self-contained, independent, autonomous, self-supporting; solid, undivided, unbroken, uncut, unshortened, unabridged, all in one; intact, sound; undiminished, unlessened, unreduced, unabated; full, filled, replete with, pregnant; cramfull, chock-full, jam-packed; stuffed, packed, *Inf.* wall-to-wall, crammed.

2. thorough, thoroughgoing, total, exhaustive, in-depth, A to Z, *Brit.* A to Zed, *Brit. Dial.* gradely; absolute, dyed-in-the-wool, full-fledged; utter, gross, rank, sheer, radical, sweeping; unqualified, unmodified, uncompromised, unconditional, unconditioned, unreserved, unmitigated; unrestricted, unlimited, unhampered, unimpeded, unbounded; unequivocal, clear, unambiguous, explicit, express.

3. categorical, flat, clear-cut; downright, out-and-out, outright, straight-out, all-but, through and through; fundamental, real, genuine, essential.

4. finished, ended, concluded, finalized, realized, fulfilled; accomplished, achieved, effected, effectuated, settled, executed; discharged, performed, enacted; terminated, ended, closed; culminated, capped, crowned; clinched, *Inf.* wrapped up, disposed of, *Sl.* polished off; mature, ripe, mellow, rounded out, rounded off, filled out.

5. perfect, ideal, exemplary, model; superlative, consummate, crowning, august; superb, exquisite, extraordinary; faultless, flawless, defectless; unblemished, spotless, unspotted, stainless, taintless, untainted, unsullied, unsoiled; untarnished, undefiled, unscathed, undefaced, unimpaired, uninjured, undamaged, unmarred.

6. developed, formed, disciplined, primed, cultivated, polished, bred.

—*v.* **7.** complement, supplement, fill in *or* out, implete, round out, round off; replenish, make up, refill; finish, conclude, finalize, realize, fulfill; accomplish, achieve, effect, effectuate, settle; execute, discharge, perform, bring about, enact; terminate, end, close; clinch, *Inf.* wrap up, dispose of, *Sl.* polish off, get through; consummate, cap, crown, culminate; mature, ripen.

8. perfect, make faultless, rectify, right, better, amend, ameliorate, improve; purge, cleanse, purify; correct, emend, edit, revise, clarify, mend; reform, regenerate, rehabilitate, repair; enrich, enhance, refine, retouch, remodel; elaborate, embellish, adorn; cultivate, develop; polish, shine, brighten, burnish, buff; restore, reclaim, revive, resuscitate, redo.

completely, *adv.* **1.** entirely, purely, wholly, stone, totally, comprehensively, plenarily, fully; into thin air, bag and baggage; solidly, soundly; throughout, altogether, nothing short of.

2. thoroughly, extensively, from the ground up, from A to Z, *Brit.* from A to Zed, absolutely; utterly, grossly, quite; unqualifiedly, unconditionally, unreservedly, *Sl.* all the way, to the nth degree, *Sl.* like mad, *Sl.* like crazy, *Inf.* hook, line, and sinker; enthusiastically, fervently, heart and soul, whole hog.

3. unequivocally, clearly, unambiguously, explicitly, expressly; fundamentally, actually, really, truly, verily, essentially, radically; categorically, flatly; downright, out-and-out, outright, all-out, straight-out; through and through, backward and forward.

completion, *n.* **1.** conclusion, finalization, realization, fulfillment; end, finish, finale, finis, close, *Sl.* mop-up, windup; termination, expiration; accomplishment, achievement, attainment, fruition, effectuation, settlement; execution, performance, enactment; consummation, culmination, maturation.

2. complementing, filling in *or* out, rounding out *or* off; replenishing, making up, refilling; finishing, concluding, finalizing, realizing, fulfilling; accomplishing, achieving, effectuating, settling; executing, discharging, performing, bringing about, enacting; terminating, ending, closing; clinching, *Inf.* wrapping up, disposing of, *Sl.* polishing off; consummating, capping, crowning, culminating.

3. perfecting, improving, rectifying, righting; purging, cleansing, purifying; correcting, emending, editing, revising, clarifying, mending; cultivating, developing.

complex, *adj.* **1.** compound, composite; elaborate, sophisticated, manifold, multifarious, multiple, multiplex; intricate, interwoven, involved, complicated, irreducible; inextricable, Gordian, knotted, snarled, tangled, entangled; mingled, mixed, motley, mosaic, multifaceted, variegated, compounded; conglomerate, aggregated, *Bot.* acervate, fascicular, multiform.

2. difficult, inscrutable, unfathomable, obscure,

deep, hidden, crabbed; undecipherable, enigmatic, cryptic, puzzling, perplexing, bewildering; impenetrable, mazy, labyrinthine, *Class. Myth.* Daedalian; roundabout, winding, circuitous, convoluted; tortuous, sinuous, meandering, anfractuous, flexuous.

—*n.* **3.** network, structure, organization, conglomerate, combination; totality, ensemble, conglomeration, aggregation, congeries; web, webwork, labyrinth, tangle, entanglement, complication, involution.

4. obsession, fixation, mania; fancy, notion, delusion; quirk, fixed idea, *Fr. idée fixe*, preoccupation.

complexion, *n.* **1.** tone color, coloration, coloring, pigmentation; cast, tinge, tint.

2. appearance, aspect, character, look, stamp; likeness, lines, carriage, bearing, outward show; face, mien, countenance, front, visage, semblance; color, nature, contour, angle, effect; tone, tenor, quality, presence; phase, manifestation, guise, favor, light, air, demeanor, expression.

3. viewpoint, attitude, posture, disposition, leaning, tendency; turn, mood, temper, spirit; figure, shape, image, composition, constitution, make-up, *Archaic.* crasis.

complexity, *n.* **1.** intricacy, network, complex, complicacy; web, webwork, tangle, tangled skein, sleave; coil, twist, involution, circuity, tortuosity, sinuosity, meander, ambagiousness, flexuosity.

2. complication, problem, perplexity, puzzle, riddle, bafflement, knot, Gordian knot; wilderness, jungle, labyrinth, maze; difficulty, entanglement, involvement, imbroglio; predicament, plight, quandary, dilemma, *Inf.* stew; kink, gnarl, knotty point, paradox; implication, ramification; wheels within wheels, Chinese boxes, incomprehensibility, unintelligibility, obscurity.

compliance, *n.* **1.** acquiescence, yielding, assent, abidance, submission; adaptability, agreeableness, complaisance, tractableness, tractability, malleability, malleableness, pliancy; respectfulness, dutifulness, faithfulness, biddableness, deference, capitulation; meekness, docility, timidity, passiveness.

2. subservience, servility, obeisance, ingratiation, subjection, slavishness, abasement, prostration, toadyism; cringing, fawning, bowing, scraping, cowering, truckling, *Sl.* bootlicking, bending; self-renunciation, self-surrender, self-effacement.

3. obedience, observance, conformity, abidance; accordance, concession, accedence; cooperation, collaboration, responsiveness.

compliant, *adj.* **1.** acquiescent, yielding, submissive, malleable, ductile, flexible, pliant; accommodating, agreeable, adapting, adaptable, tractable, disposed, inclined; dutiful, faithful, manageable, willing, capitulating, complying, obliging, obeying, nonresisting, unassertive, assenting; respectful, deferential; docile, timid, gentle, meek, passive, subdued.

2. subservient, servile, obsequious, ingratiating, obeisant, prostrate, *Archaic.* sequacious; truckling, bowing, scraping, fawning, cowering, cringing, crawling, toadying, toadyish, *Inf.* bootlicking; self-effacing, self-surrendering, self-abasing.

complicate, *v.* **1.** involve, make complex, make intricate; maneuver, scheme, contrive, manipulate, juggle; plan, plot, cast, frame, brew, hatch, concoct, devise.

2. embroil, entangle, snarl, tangle, muddle, mix up, jumble, *Sl.* mess up, *Sl.* screw up; clog, encumber, hinder, hobble, handicap, impede, hamper; confound, vex, bedevil, confuse; obscure, obfuscate, darken, conceal.

complicated, *adj.* **1.** complex, compound, elaborate, intricate, labyrinthine, Byzantine. See **complex** (*defs.* **1, 2**).

2. difficult, deep, profound, abstruse, recondite; obscure, indistinct, hidden, enigmatic, mysterious; incomprehensible, unclear, bewildering, paradoxical, ambiguous, unintelligible; involved, exacting, formidable, laborious, toilsome, operose; tangled, raveled, knotty, thorny, troublesome, problematic, beset with difficulties, perplexing, puzzling.

complication, *n.* complexity, intricacy; difficulty, entanglement. See **complexity** (*defs.* **1, 2**).

complicity, *n.* **1.** conspiracy, collusion, collusiveness, confederacy, complot; connivance, machination, intrigue; cabal, association, partnership, combination, alliance; collaboration, concurrence, abetment.

2. complexity, intricacy; complication, entanglement. See **complexity** (*defs.* **1, 2**).

compliment, *n.* **1.** praise, tribute, homage, honor, commendation, laudation, celebration, exaltation, extolment, glorification, adulation; eulogy, encomium, panegyric, good word, blurb; flattery, trumpetry, puffery, crying up, singing [s.o.'s] praises, praising to excess, overpraise, *Inf.* overdoing it, *Inf.* laying it on thick.

2. compliments good wishes, regards, respects; salute, salutation, greeting.

—*v.* **3.** praise, honor, salute, pay tribute *or* homage to, acclaim, laud, celebrate, exalt, extol, glorify, adulate; eulogize, panegyrize; commend, hand it to [s.o.]; flatter, puff, gratify, overpraise, praise to excess *or* to the skies, cry up, sing [s.o.'s] praises, *Inf.* slather, *Inf.* stroke, *Inf.* overdo it, *Inf.* lay *or* spread it on thick, *Inf.* pile it up *or* on.

4. favor, show regard for, pay regard to, do honor to; do a good turn, render a benefit, do [s.o.] a favor.

5. congratulate, felicitate, tender *or* offer one's congratulations *or* compliments; rejoice with, wish one well, wish one joy.

complimentary, *adj.* **1.** commendatory, laudatory, celebratory, acclamatory, adulatory; eulogistic, encomiastic, panegyrical; flattering, cajoling, wheedling, ingratiating, timeserving, *Sl.* bootlicking, *Inf.* applepolishing, *Sl.* brown-nosing, *Obs.* blandering, *Obs., Rare.* blandiloquous; unctuous, oily, buttery, candied.

2. free, free of charge, for free, for nothing, gratis, on the house, for love; free for the asking, free as the air, no strings attached.

complot, *n.* **1.** conspiracy, collusion; cabal, junto, camarilla, clique, secret society.

—*v.* **2.** collude, connive, conspire, plot, hatch a plot, cabal, scheme; maneuver, machinate, engineer; (*all in criminal activity*) collaborate, cooperate, unite, join, join forces *or* hands, band together, *Inf.* hitch horses.

comply, *v.* (*usu. fol. by* with) **1.** observe, obey, acknowledge, respect; adhere to, abide by, conform to; acquiesce in, submit to, consent to, agree to, concur, grant, accept; be faithful to, be regulated by, be subject to.

2. agree with, accord with, harmonize with, tally with, correspond, chime *or* fall in with; accommodate, adapt, adjust, suit, fit.

3. surrender, relent, give in, give way to, succumb; stoop, bend, bow, truckle to, knuckle under, do [s.o.'s] bidding.

4. perform, discharge, execute, carry out, carry into effect, come across with; meet, satisfy, fulfill, complete.

component, *adj.* **1.** constituent, composing, constituting, integral, integrant, forming; fragmentary, complementary, sectional, fractional, partial; elemen-

tary, fundamental, basic, underlying, primary, radical.
2. essential, intrinsic, inherent, constitutional, innate, inborn; indigenous, inbred, congenital, native, connate, inalienable, indivisible, inseparable; implanted, ingrained, infixed; indwelling, immanent, subsistent.
—n. **3.** constituent, part, element, fundamental, unit, module; integral part, part and parcel, integrant, member, organ; portion, section, fragment, complement, piece, parcel, segment, share, allotment; fraction, division, subdivision; item, detail, particular, feature; principle, factor, ingredient, material.

comport, *v.* **1.** (*all of oneself*) behave, conduct, deport, demean, acquit, *Archaic.* quit; carry, bear, hold; manage, govern, regulate.
2. agree, concur, go along with; accord, harmonize, attune; correspond, match, dovetail, coincide, tally, square, parallel, gee, jibe; conform, suit, fit, *Brit.* fadge.

compose, *v.* **1.** synthesize, combine, consolidate, put together, throw together, mix up, whip up; produce, form, make, manufacture, construct, erect, build; forge, fashion, fabricate, mold, form, weave.
2. constitute, comprise, make up, go into the making of, be a part *or* portion of, be an element *or* ingredient *or* component of, be an integral part of, be a constituent of.
3. arrange, array, align, line up, place, adjust, collocate; classify, coordinate, order, rank, grade, range, graduate; organize, correlate, systematize, group, assemble, collate, segregate; dovetail, fit together, fall into place.
4. (*of a literary, musical or choreographical work*) write, author, indite; create, coin, invent, make up; arrange, set to music, *Obs.* ditty; contrive, frame, devise, concoct, formulate, design, set up, think up.
5. settle, resolve, reconcile, conciliate; find a solution for, work out, come to terms on.
6. calm, becalm, quiet, hush, lull, quell, still, make tranquil, soothe, tame; dulcify, pacify, assuage, mollify, placate; calm down, pull oneself together, get hold of oneself.

composed, *adj.* calm, collected, self-possessed, cool, *Inf.* together; nonchalant, at ease, unruffled, untroubled, unperturbed, undisturbed, unexcited, undismayed; sedate, tranquil, serene, placid; self-controlled, poised, balanced, steady; imperturbable, inexcitable, unflappable, even-tempered, easy-going.

composer, *n.* **1.** creator, inventor, coiner; synthesizer, combiner, consolidator; contriver, deviser, concocter, framer, designer, architect; producer, maker, manufacturer, builder, forger, fabricator.
2. songwriter, songster, melodist, *Inf.* tunesmith, symphonist, lyricist, *Music.* arranger; maestro, musician.
3. author, writer, novelist, storyteller; playwright, dramatist, screenwriter. See **author** (*def.* **1**).

composite, *adj.* **1.** synthesized, consolidated, combined. See **compound**[1] (*def.* **1**).
—n. **2.** composition, synthesis, consolidation; combination, combine, mixture. See **compound**[1] (*def.* **2**).

composition, *n.* **1.** synthesis, consolidation, incorporation, integration; combination, union, conjunction, intermixture, commingling, mingling, minglement, interminglement, blending, *Bot.* homogeny; organization, correlation, systematization, grouping, assembly, collation, segregation.
2. creation, invention, innovation, origination; fabrication, manufacture, formulation, fashioning, forging, weaving.
3. compound, mixture, mix, composite, combine, concoction; alloy, admixture, amalgam, hybrid, mongrel, *Chem.* levigation; mosaic, patchwork, collage, pastiche; aggregation, aggregate, assortment, medley, melange, olio, potpourri, *Inf.* combo; miscellany, miscellanea, salmagundi, hodgepodge, jumble, hash, gallimaufry, olla podrida.
4. structure, build, form, framework, arrangement, layout; constitution, comprisal, contents, make-up, idiosyncrasy, *Archaic.* crasis; character, nature, fabric, texture, disposition, temperament, mettle, personality.
5. writing, literary technique, expository writing, creative writing, rhetoric, style, English, grammar; songwriting, lyricizing, hymnology; instrumentation, *Music.* arranging, *Obs.* dittying, setting to music.
6. essay, theme, article, paper, manuscript, draft; work, opus, masterpiece, masterwork, work of art, brainchild; novel, novelette, short story, book; piece, opuscule, melody, aria, air, song, jingle, ditty, arrangement.
7. settlement, resolution, solution, coming to terms; agreement, compromise, happy medium, middle ground.

compost, *n.* **1.** fertilizer, muck, manure, dung, ordure, guano, night soil, dressing.
2. compound, alloy, amalgam, combination, composition; blend, fusion, mixture, commixture, admixture; medley, potpourri, hodgepodge, mishmash.

composure, *n.* **1.** aplomb, sang-froid, poise, repose, self-possession, self-control, self-command; presence of mind, level-headedness, cool-headedness, coolness, equability, equanimity, equilibrium, *Inf.* cool; quiescence, quiet, stillness, calmness, peacefulness, peace, tranquillity, serenity; imperturbability, inexcitability, unflappability, even-temperedness.

compound[1], *adj.* **1.** composite, complex, intricate, involved, multiple, multiplex, compounded; manifold, multifarious, varied, diverse, multiform; synthesized, consolidated, incorporate, integrated; combined, mixed, hybrid, mongrel.
—n. **2.** composite, composition, synthesis, blend, merging, merger, consolidation; combination, combine, mixture, mix, commixture, intermixture, concoction, conglomeration, *Archaic.* crasis; mosaic, patchwork, collage, pastiche; alloy, admixture, amalgam, hybrid, mongrel, *Chem.* levigation.
—v. **3.** combine, synthesize, consolidate. See **compose** (*def.* **1**).
4. constitute, comprise, make up. See **compose** (*def.* **2**).
5. multiply, add on to, increase; augment, heighten, intensify, enhance; aggravate, exacerbate.

compound[2], *n.* **1.** court, courtyard, quadrangle, *Inf.* quad, square, enclosure, ring.
2. colony, settlement, village, kampong, *Law.* curtilage; quarters, residences, homes, camp, encampment; concentration camp, POW camp, prison.

comprehend, *v.* **1.** understand, apprehend, realize, take in, assimilate, absorb, receive, *Chiefly Scot.* ken; apperceive, cognize, recognize, know, *Sl.* savvy, grasp, get, get the picture, *Sl.* dig, *Brit. Sl.* suss out, seize, pick up, *Inf.* get a fix on; fathom, penetrate, *Inf.* lay hold of; imagine, conceive, *Archaic.* hent.
2. perceive, see, make out, discern, read, see through, *Brit.* twig, *Inf.* make heads or tails of; intuit, sense, feel.
3. comprise, include, contain; embrace, compass, cover, take into account *or* consideration; constitute, compose, make up, form.

comprehensible, *adj.* understandable, apprehensible, intelligible, coherent, articulate, unconfused, logical, consistent, explicable; recognizable, cognizable, cognoscible, knowable, graspable; imaginable, conceivable, realizable; fathomable, penetrable, perceivable, discernible; plain, obvious, clear, unambiguous, unequivocal; clear-cut, evident, overt, patent, palpable, manifest; lucid, pellucid, perspicuous, unclouded, translucent, unobscure, unhidden, unconcealed, unveiled; explicit, graphic, vivid, distinct.

comprehension, *n.* **1.** understanding, apprehension, intellect, intelligence; knowledge, *Sl.* savvy, *Inf.* fix, *Brit. Sl.* suss; wisdom, enlightenment; realization, insight, discernment, perspicacity, penetration; recognition, cognition, cognizance, apperception, perception, awareness; intuition, sense, imagination.

2. scope, extent, measure, range, breadth, latitude; embrace, compass, reach, sweep, limits, bounds; circuit, sphere, realm, orbit, area, province, field.

3. comprehensiveness, inclusiveness, extensiveness, thoroughness.

4. comprisal, comprising, inclusion, incorporation, containing; embracing, compassing, encompassing, covering, spanning; constituting, constitution, composition.

comprehensive, *adj.* **1.** inclusive, inclusory, all-inclusive, encyclopedic, blanket, umbrella; exhaustive, thorough, thoroughgoing, unqualified, radical, complete, all-around; extensive, extended, broad, wide, widespread, sweeping, far-reaching, expansive; voluminous, capacious, large, sizable, ample, substantial; universal, world-wide, ecumenical, catholic.

2. able, capable, intelligent; knowledgeable, wise, understanding, insightful, discerning, perspicacious; aware, perceptive, intuitive.

compress, *v.* **1.** condense, concentrate, consolidate, compact; press *or* force together, constrict, constringe, astringe, squeeze, pinch, crowd, crush, pack, cram, ram, tighten, stuff, wedge, cramp, *Obs.* constipate, bind, coarctate, wrap up, truss up; shorten, reduce, retrench, contract, curtail, cut down, cut back, cut off, cut short, decrease, diminish, subtract, subduct, narrow, bridge; abbreviate, abridge, abstract summarize, digest, epitomize, brief, synopsize; shrink, shrivel, wither, slim down, slenderize; restrict, straiten, constrain, astrict, confine, bound, limit, demarcate.

2. thicken, solidify, crystallize, harden, cake, set, gell, clot, coagulate, congeal, curdle, curd, *Obs.* incrassate; evaporate, dehydrate, desiccate, dissipate deliquesce, boil down; parch, dry up, inspissate.

compressed, *adj.* **1.** condensed, concentrated, consolidated, compacted, compact; constricted, constringed, astringed, squeezed, pinched, crowded, crushed, packed, crammed, tightened, rammed, stuffed, wedged, cramped, *Obs.* constipated, bound, wrapped-up, trussed-up; shortened, reduced, retrenched, contracted, curtate, curtailed, cut, cut down, cut back, cut short, cut off, decreased, diminished, subtracted, subducted, narrowed, bridged; abbreviated, abridged, abstracted, summarized, digested, epitomized, synopsized; shrunk, shrunken, shriveled, withered, sere, dried, slimmed-down, slenderized; restricted, confined, limited, demarcated.

2. thickened, solidified, crystallized, hardened, caked, set, gelled, clotted, coagulated, congealed, curdled; evaporated, dehydrated, desiccated, dissipated, boiled down, parched, dried-up, inspissated.

3. closed, shut, pressed *or* forced together, joined, united, unified, merged, coupled, connected, linked, incorporated, converged, coalesced.

4. flattened, leveled; collapsed, depressed, deflated.

compression, *n.* **1.** condensation, condensing, concentration, concentrating, consolidation, consolidating, amalgamating, incorporating; compaction, compacting, coalescence, cohesion, densification; thickening, hardening, concretion.

2. constriction, constricting, constringency, constringing, astringency, astringing, squeezing, pinching, crushing, crowding, packing, cramming, ramming, stuffing, wedging; binding, wrapping up, trussing up.

3. shortage, shortening, reduction, reducing, retrenchment, retrenching, contraction, contracting; curtailment, curtailing, cut, cutting down, cutting back, cutting short; decrease, decreasing, diminution, diminishing, subtraction, subtracting, subduction, subducting; narrowing, bridging; abbreviation, abbreviating, abridging, abstracting, summarizing, digesting, epitomizing, synopsizing.

4. shrinkage, shrinking, shriveling, withering; slimming down, slenderizing; restriction, restricting, constraint, constraining, astriction, boundary; *Gram.* ellipsis, *Gram.* syncope, *Gram.* hapology, *Phon.* elision, *Phon.* synaeresis.

5. density, denseness, consistency, consistence, impermeability, impenetrability, impenetrableness, solidity; compactness, closeness, tightness, narrowness; narrow straits, tight squeeze, bind, confinement; brevity, briefness, shortness, economy.

6. abridgment, survey, digest, epitome, compendium; synopsis, abstract, summary; précis, conspectus, prospectus; syllabus, résumé, brief, outline, sketch.

7. solidification, concretion, coagulation, congelation, clot, gel, curd, curds; evaporation, dehydration, desiccation, dissipation, deliquescence, inspissation.

comprise, *v.* include, contain, comprehend, embrace, subsume, take in, incorporate, embody; enclose, encircle, envelop, enfold, encompass, compass; cover, take into account *or* consideration, involve; span, extend, reach, pass over; hold, engross; consist of, be composed of, be compounded of, be resolvable into.

compromise, *n.* **1.** concession, trade-off, yielding, adjustment, modification, accommodation; reconciliation, reconcilement, conciliation, propitiation; making up, making peace, coming to terms, harmonization, rapprochement; arbitration, negotiation, mediation; squaring, rectification, setting right, redress, mending, patching, healing.

2. reparation, indemnification, atonement, compensation, satisfaction, amends; appeasement, pacification, placation; (*all usu. of prison sentences or other penalties*) commutation, *Law.* compounding, extenuation, alleviation, mitigation, abatement.

3. settlement, agreement, composition, conclusion; arrangement, understanding, terms, conditions, stipulations; truce, armistice, cease-fire, cartel, entente, détente; compact, formal agreement, contract, indenture, covenant, bond; treaty, alliance, pact, convention; mutual understanding, accord, accordance, concord, concordance, concurrence.

4. happy medium, golden mean, *Fr. juste-milieu, Latin. aurea mediocritas*; balance, mean, middle ground, middle of the road; moderation, temperance, reasonableness; mediocrity, half measures.

—*v.* **5.** settle, agree, compose, come to terms, come to an understanding, make the best of; arrange, make a deal, meet halfway, give and take, *Inf.* go fifty-fifty, bridge over; reciprocate, exchange, trade, trade off; concede, yield, adjust, modify, accommodate; arbitrate, negotiate, mediate.

6. rectify, square, set right, redress, mend, patch; appease, pacify, placate; compensate, indemnify, satisfy, make amends, atone; (*all usu. of prison sentences or other penalites*) commute, *Law.* compound, extenuate, alleviate, abate; reconcile, conciliate, propitiate; make peace, make up, come to terms, harmonize.

7. find a happy medium, strike a balance *or* mean, find the middle ground, steer a middle course, maintain a middle position; be noncommital, straddle, *Inf.* sit on the fence, serve two masters; (*of principles, ideals, etc.*) *Sl.* cop out, *Inf.* waffle, *Inf.* hedge, equivocate.

8. jeopardize, imperil, endanger; expose, lay open, risk, hazard; discredit, disparage, embarrass; implicate, involve unfavorably.

comptroller, *n.* accountant, certified public accountant, C.P.A., *Both Brit.* chartered accountant, C.A.; controller, treasurer, cashier, banker, bursar, purser, trustee, depositary; bookkeeper, reckoner, manager, inspector, examiner, analyst, *Insurance.* actuary; agent, steward, almoner; clerk, registrar, recorder.

compulsion, *n.* **1.** force, coaction, constraint, coercion, duress; will, pressure, press, stress, strain; control, domination, power, dint, strength, influence; oppression, suppression, physical coercion *or* violence, *Inf.* the strong arm; impressment, enforcement, forcing, compelling.

2. drive, urge, need, necessity, exigency, urgency; demand, requirement, obligation, duty, incumbency, task, imposition; impellent, goad, prod, spur, push, shove; provocation, urging, prodding, incitement, prompting, instigation; inducement, motivation, stimulus, stimulant, incentive.

compulsory, *adj.* **1.** coercive, forcing, forcible, compelling, constraining; controlling, commanding, authoritative, authoritarian, imperious, peremptory, *Inf.* bossy; dominating, overbearing, oppressive, crushing, forceful, violent, *Inf.* strong-arm.

2. mandatory, obligatory, requisite, required, prerequisite, necessary, needful; pressing, urgent, demanding, imperative, insistent, exigent, driving; compulsive, forced, enforced; binding, conclusive, final, inevitable, unavoidable, inescapable, unpreventable.

compunction, *n.* **1.** remorse, contrition, regret, penitence, repentance, contriteness, sorrow, sackcloth and ashes; pang of conscience, guilt, shame, embarrassment, self-humiliation, self-mortification; self-reproach, self-reproof, self-blame, self-accusation, self-condemnation.

2. uneasiness, hesitation, reluctance, unwillingness, disinclination; qualm, misgiving, apprehension, fear, worry, alarm, suspicion.

compunctious, *adj.* **1.** remorseful, contrite, regretful, penitent, repentant, penitential; sorrowful, grieved, sad, mournful, doleful, rueful, sorry, apologetic; self-reproaching, self-reproving, self-blaming, self-accusing, self-condemning, conscience-stricken, troubled, guilt-stricken, shamed, embarrassed, humiliated.

2. uneasy, hesitating, hesitant, reluctant, unwilling, disinclined, loath; conscience-stricken, qualmish, apprehensive, fearful, troubled, worried, alarmed, suspicious.

computable, *adj.* calculable, estimable, measurable, reckonable, countable, numerable; gaugeable, determinable, mensurable; appraisable, assessable, appreciable, ascertainable.

computation, *n.* **1.** calculation, estimation, figuring, reckoning, numeration; adding, counting, ciphering, footing; addition, summation, summing up, totaling, casting, enumeration.

2. measurement, gauging, mensuration, calibration, admeasurement, metage; appraisal, appraisement, evaluation, valuation, appreciation.

compute, *v.* **1.** calculate, reckon, estimate, figure, count; determine, work out, ascertain; add, cipher, sum, total, sum up, score up, (*on a cash register*) ring up; number, count up, enumerate, tot up, foot up, cast up.

2. measure, gauge, calibrate, admeasure, weigh, *Archaic.* mete; evaluate, value, appraise, assess, valuate, appreciate.

computer, *n.* **1.** adding machine, calculator, calculating machine; analog computer, digital computer, data processor.

2. mathematician, arithmetician, geometrician, geometer, algebraist; abacist, calculator, estimator.

comrade, *n.* **1.** companion, chum, crony, copain, *U.S. Inf.* buddy, *Inf.* pal, *Obs.* copemate; sidekick, shadow, alter ego, other self; playmate, schoolmate, schoolfellow, classmate; messmate, dining companion, commensal; teammate, co-worker, fellow worker.

2. friend, confidant, familiar, *Inf.* bosom buddy, roommate, bunkmate, *Sl.* bunkie; Achates; intimate, lover, bedfellow, soul mate, *Fr. intime.*

3. ally, compatriot, confederate; collaborator, cohort, cooperator, accomplice, *Law.* accessory; assistant, helper, helpmate; colleague, confrere, associate, consociate, compeer, peer, mate, comate.

con¹, *adv.* **1.** against, in opposition, in conflict; in confrontation, at odds, at variance.

—*n.* **2.** the negative, no, nay; argument, side, interest.

con², *v.* **1.** study, peruse, examine, scrutinize, pore over.

2. memorize, commit to memory, learn, learn by heart, learn word for word, learn by rote, master, *Sl.* get down; fix in the mind, ingrain, infix, inculcate, impress on the mind, get in one's head, hammer *or* drive into one's head.

con³, *v.* *U.S. Slang.* delude, deceive, mislead; bamboozle, hoodwink; cheat, swindle. See **bamboozle** (*defs.* **1, 2**).

concatenate, *v.* **1.** link, unite, catenate, connect, tie, bind, fuse; join, chain, conjoin, couple, hook, combine; string together, thread, lace, interlock, interlink.

—*adj.* **2.** linked, united, joined, chained, tied, bound; connected, interlocked, interlinked, interlocking, interlinking; successive, consecutive, sequent, seriatim; serial, sequential, consequent.

concatenation, *n.* **1.** link, linkage, connection, chain, tie, nexus, connexus; union, junction, juncture, conjugation, conjunction, conjuncture; joinder, joining, conjoining, connecting, interlinking, interlocking; coupling, accouplement, hookup, combination.

2. series, succession, sequence, course, catena, continuity, consecutiveness; string, line, queue, row, tier, column, train; file, cavalcade, procession, caravan.

concave, *adj.* **1.** incurvate, incurved, sunken, cupped, cup-shaped, scyphate, poculiform, calathiform, *Bot., Zool.* cyanthiform.

—*v.* **2.** hollow, hollow out, scoop, scoop out, gouge out; furrow, groove, trench.

concavity, *n.* **1.** incurvature, incurvation, incurvity; hollowness; impression, depression.

2. hollow, cavity, hole, sink, scoop, cup, bowl, crater, pit; indentation, indent, dent, dimple, concave.

conceal, *v.* **1.** hide, cover, secrete, ensconce, shelter; catch, bury, tuck away, keep away, keep out of sight, keep in the background; disguise, camouflage.

2. keep secret, keep dark, keep it all in, keep quiet about; hush up, hugger-mugger, *Inf.* cover up, *Sl.* keep the lid on; dissemble, cloud, becloud, befog, screen, mask, cloak, obscure, veil, curtain, enshroud, keep in the shade *or* the dark.

concealed, *adj.* hidden, secreted, hidden *or* tucked

away, buried; covered, sheltered, screened, masked, dissembled; secret, clandestine, hugger-mugger, unrevealed, unexposed, *Inf.* hush-hush; unseen, unperceived, latent, delitescent; obscured, invisible, imperceptible, indiscernible, inconspicuous, unapparent.

concealment, *n.* **1.** hiding, covering, sheltering, ensconcing; disguising, camouflaging, screening, enshrouding, veiling, masking; dissembling, cover-up, obscuring.

2. privacy, obscurity; inconspicuousness, imperceptibility, invisibility; quiescence, dormancy, latency.

3. secretion, burial; camouflage, disguise; hiding, cover, shield, blind, ambush, ambuscade; hiding place, hideaway, covert, coverture, *Inf.* hide-out; shelter, retreat, refuge, mew.

concede, *v.* **1.** acknowledge, recognize; admit, allow; yield, accede, agree, acquiesce, assent, accept, own, defer to, abide by, be persuaded, come over, come round.

2. deliver, grant, transfer, give, vouchsafe, bequeath, hand over, donate, tender, release, give up.

3. renounce, abandon, resign, surrender, relinquish, waive.

conceit, *n.* **1.** self-esteem, self-importance, self-approbation, self-admiration, self-love, self-worship, self-adulation; pride, vanity, vainglory, vaingloriousness, bovarism, egotism, *Inf.* ego trip, *Inf.* big head; self-praise, self-glorification, boastfulness, braggadocio, jactation, bluster, fanfaronade, gasconade; complacency, smugness, self-satisfaction, self-content.

2. thought, idea, notion, apprehension; concept, conception, conviction, sentiment, opinion; judgment, presumption, presupposition.

3. imagination, fancy, mind's eye.

4. fancy, whim, whimsy, caprice, fantasy; quirk, twist, kink, eccentricity, crotchet, maggot; daydream, dream, *Inf.* pipe dream, castle in the air, pie in the sky.

5. ornament, decoration, frill, filigree, flounce; gewgaw, gimcrack, *Inf.* doodad, *Inf.* fandangle.

conceited, *adj.* self-important, self-esteeming, self-admiring, self-worshiping, self-centered, egocentric, narcissistic, *Sl.* stuck *or* hung up on oneself; haughty, supercilious, disdainful, snobbish, *Inf.* stuck-up; proud, overproud, overweening, vain, vainglorious, egotistical, puffed-up, inflated, swollen, swell-headed, *Inf.* big-headed; smug, complacent, self-satisfied, self-contented, pleased with oneself; cocky, bumptious, overbearing, overweening, *Scot.* vaunty; boastful, bragging, crowing, blustering.

conceivable, *adj.* **1.** thinkable, imaginable, cogitable, supposable, fanciable, picturable, visualizable; knowable, understandable, comprehensible, apprehensible; cognizable, perceivable, cognoscible.

2. believable, credible, possible, tenable.

conceive, *v.* **1.** think, opine, conjecture, surmise, fancy; speculate, suppose, assume, presume, *Archaic.* trow; reckon, perceive, apprehend, understand, comprehend, see; contrive, devise, cogitate, concoct, excogitate; plot, plan, compass, design, purpose; fashion, fabricate, hatch, invent, scheme; create, formulate, form, frame, draft; coin, mint, neologize, neoterize.

2. imagine, envision, think up, dream up, make up, conjure up, *Inf.* feature; dream, picture, envisage, ideate, image, visualize.

3. think, believe, hold, maintain, dare say; consider, regard, look upon; acknowledge, deem, recognize; judge, conclude, deduce, infer; posit, postulate, hypothesize, theorize.

4. beget, procreate, father, sire; generate, engender, propagate, reproduce; become impregnated, become pregnant, become fertilized, come with child.

5. (*usu. in passive*) found, originate, give birth to, institute, establish, constitute; begin, initiate, start, occasion, bring about, set up.

concentrate, *v.* **1.** focus, center, concenter, converge, localize, centralize; compact, consolidate, contract, draw together, constrict, constringe, compress.

2. collect, gather, congregate, agglomerate, aggregate, amass, flock together; assemble, muster, rally, forgather; accumulate, cluster, conglomerate, bunch, pack, crowd, overcrowd, congest, swarm.

3. be engrossed in, be absorbed in, focus attention on, *Inf.* zero in on; think, ponder, meditate on, contemplate, ruminate, muse over, brood over; apply oneself, *Inf.* knuckle down, *Inf.* buckle down, *Sl.* knock one's brains out, cudgel one's brains; examine, scrutinize, analyze, study.

4. intensify, strengthen, condense, boil down, reduce; purify, *Chem.* rectify, refine; distill, vaporize, evaporate, extract; coagulate, clot, curdle, thicken, crystallize, concretize.

concentration, *n.* **1.** focus, centrality, convergence; consolidation, drawing together, constriction, compression.

2. collection, gathering, congregation, flock, assemblage, assembly, confluence, conflux; cluster, agglomeration, agglomerate, aggregation, aggregate, mass, amassment, heap, store, hoard; accumulation, clustering, conglomeration, bunching, packing, crowding, overcrowding, congestion, swarming; crowd, multitude, pack, horde, swarm, press, throng.

3. heed, absorption, engrossment, fixed regard, intentness, intensity; close attention, application, diligence, devotion; rumination, pondering, meditation, deep thought; deliberation, consideration, study, scrutiny, examination.

4. intensification, strengthening, condensation, boiling down, reduction; purification, *Chem.* rectifying, refinement; distillation, evaporation, extraction; coagulation, clotting, thickening, crystallization.

concept, *n.* idea, notion, conception, conceptualization, abstraction; opinion, belief, view, conviction, presumption, persuasion, apprehension, judgment, surmise; postulate, hypothesis, theory, conjecture; inference, conclusion, consideration.

conception, *n.* **1.** conceiving, originating, hatching, generating; inventing, innovating, initiating, creating; developing, devising, drafting; fashioning, building, forming, fabricating; planning, concocting, producing, evolving; launching, bringing forth.

2. fertilization, fecundation, inception of pregnancy, fertilizing.

3. beginning, origination, source, genesis; outset, inchoation, origin, inception, emergence, commencement, prime, start; introduction, inauguration, initiation; birth, nativity, nascence; incipience, dawn, opening, budding.

4. imagining, deliberating, philosophizing, meditating, speculating; musing, fancying, dreaming, envisaging, envisioning; cogitating, conceptualizing, considering, weighing, concentrating, communing; consideration, speculation, realization, meditation.

5. concept, notion, idea, thought, abstraction, conceptualization, principle; belief, view, opinion, conviction, assumption, supposition, persuasion; surmise, conjecture, hypothesis, theory, postulate; consideration, conclusion, inference, apprehension.

6. design, plan, draft; sketch, outline; scheme, proposal, proposition, projection, delineation.

concern, *v.* **1.** relate to, pertain to, appertain to, have to do with, regard; refer to, apply to, mean, go for; affect, touch, bear on *or* upon, have bearing on, be relevant to, be of importance *or* interest to, interest; be connected with, be affiliated with, be involved with.

2. be interested in, be involved in, have one's hand in, be engaged in; be busy with, be occupied with, be doing; make it one's business, busy oneself with, occupy oneself with, involve oneself with, engage oneself in, employ oneself in, devote one's time to.

3. trouble, worry, disquiet, make anxious, perturb, disturb, bother; pain, hurt, distress, cause [s.o.] grief.

—*n.* **4.** business, affair, matter, matter of interest, *Inf.* lookout; job, duty, charge, responsibility, chore, task, mission; department, field, subject, specialty, *Sl.* thing, *Sl.* bag.

5. regard, care, thought, consideration; attention, carefulness, caution, prudence, pains; heed, heedfulness, watchfulness, advertence; alertness, vigilance, circumspection, wariness; awareness, consciousness, mindfulness; meticulousness, particularity, fastidiousness, conscientiousness, scrupulousness, punctiliousness, painstakingness; exaction, exactness, preciseness, closeness, strictness, accuracy.

6. importance, bearing, relation, reference; connection, association, line, tie-in, interconnection; pertinence, relevancy, applicability, applicableness.

7. office, shop, store, house; partnership, business, company, firm, enterprise; establishment, organization, corporation, franchise.

concerning, *prep.* relating to, relative to, in relation to; regarding, in regard to, as regards, about, apropos of, anent; respecting, with respect to; referring to, with *or* in reference to, in re, re; in the case of, in the matter of.

concert, *n.* **1.** symphony, philharmonic, popular concert, pops; performance, show, *Sl.* gig; festival, rock festival; hootenanny, sing-along, sing-in; musicale; concerto; recital; *Inf.* jam session; serenade, aubade.

2. agreement, accordance, correspondence, conformity, conformation, conformance, congruity, congruence, congruousness; unanimity, consentience, consentaneity, consentaneousness, like-mindedness; accord, harmony, concord, concordance; unity, oneness, oneness of mind *or* purpose, single-mindedness; chorus, one voice, single voice; unison, consensus, joint *or* general agreement.

3. cooperation, collaboration, interaction, coaction, synergy, teamwork, give and take, pulling together, fraternization, *Chiefly U.S. Pol.* logrolling; joint action *or* operation, combined action *or* effort, coordinated *or* concerted effort *or* action, coadjuvant action *or* effort.

4. in concert together, jointly, in combination, in common, concurrently, coactively, concertedly; mutually, communally, collectively; cooperatively, cooperatingly, in cooperation, collaboratively, in collaboration, in partnership, in collusion, *Sl.* in cahoots; in union, in league, in association, corporately; unanimously, consentually, by mutual agreement *or* consent *or* assent; side by side, arm in arm, cheek by jowl, back to back, shoulder to shoulder, hand in hand; in unison, in close harmony, in close company with.

—*v.* **5.** arrange, prearrange, make arangements; contrive, devise, design, work out, work up, set up, *Inf.* hammer out; concoct, brew, *Inf.* cook up, hatch, hatch up; shape, cast, frame.

6. plan, lay plans, lay down a plan; conspire, collude, plot, complot, cabal; intrigue, connive, scheme.

7. cooperate, collaborate, unite efforts, pool interests, work together, pull together, hang together, stand together, *Sl.* play ball, *Sl.* do business; coact, cowork, synergize; associate, affiliate; unite, join, conjoin; confederate, league, band, ally; join forces, *Inf.* team up, *Inf.* hitch horses.

concerted, *adj.* **1.** arranged, planned, intended; prearranged, preplanned, premeditated, predetermined, forehand; well-laid, well-weighed.

2. concurrent, concomitant, parallel, collateral, side-by-side; mutual, joint, conjoint, conjoined, conjugate, conjunctive; synchronized, in step, *Inf.* in sync.

3. cooperative, cooperating, collaborative, collaborating, coactive, interactive, interactional, interacting, coordinated, synergetic, synergistic; coalitional, allied, leagued, confederated; associated, affiliated; amalgamated, consolidated, merged, incorporated, corporate; in league, in alliance, hand in glove with, *Inf.* in cahoots with.

concession, *n.* **1.** yielding, conceding, giving in; surrender, capitulation, abandonment, resignation, renunciation; acknowledgment, recognition, admission, apology; allowance, assent, compliance, acquiescence, agreement, accedence, accession.

2. compromise, adjustment, modification; extenuation, mitigation.

3. giving, granting, ceding, cession; bestowal, donation, conferment, conferral; grant, charter, gift, bequest, benefice.

4. privilege, exemption, exception; dispensation, indulgence, immunity.

5. franchise, authorization, warrant, license, permit; sanction, leave, permission; right, prerogative.

6. condition, reservation, qualification, provision, limitation, consideration.

conciliate, *v.* **1.** allay *or* alleviate the fears of, ingratiate oneself with, win over, gain the trust of, earn the confidence of, bring around; placate, appease, propitiate, pacify, pacificate, assuage, mollify, dulcify, soothe, *Brit., Australian.* dill, *Rare.* lenify, *Archaic.* attemper; humor, accommodate, oblige, make adjustments for, acquiesce, defer to, give in to.

2. reconcile, make the peace between, help to make up, settle *or* resolve differences between, bring to terms; reunite, unite, get back together; remedy, heal, mend, patch up, harmonize, restore harmony, put back on friendly terms, *Archaic.* accord; mediate, arbitrate, negotiate, intervene, bridge the gap.

conciliatory, *adj.* **1.** placatory, placative, appeasing, propitiative, pacifying, pacificatory, assuaging, conciliative; acommodative, obliging, deferential, obeisant; forbearing, forgiving, acquiescent, ready to give in; accordant, concordant, harmonious, compatible, agreeable, congenial, friendly, amiable, affable.

2. reconciliatory, peacemaking, pacific, pacifical, dovish.

concise, *adj.* **1.** succinct, pithy, terse, tight, epigrammatic; short, brief, small, thumbnail; cryptic, laconic, to the point, pointed, direct, straightforward; curt, abrupt, brusque, crisp, brisk, sharp, incisive, keen, trenchant; clear-cut, decisive, forceful, emphatic.

2. compact, capsule, summary, summarized, condensed, compressed, compendious, synoptic; abbreviated, abridged, shortened, curtailed, cut off *or* short.

conclave, *n.* **1.** conference, congress, parley, caucus, meeting, session, siting, huddle, *Inf.* powwow; assembly, gathering, congregation, forgathering, *Inf.* get-together.

2. council, convention, synod, diet, vestry, presbytery, convocation, consistory.

conclude, *v.* **1.** close, terminate, bring to an end, wind up, *Inf.* wrap up; clinch, clench, seal; perfect, consummate, culminate, round off; finish, complete, do; make short work of, dispose of, finish off *or* up,

Sl. polish off, *Sl.* knock off, dispatch; carry through, follow through, go through with, play out; expire, run out, run its course, be all over; stop, cease, halt, stay, hold, desist, give up; discontinue, suspend, drop, have done with, break off, leave off, quit, *Sl.* knock it off; postpone indefinitely, table, shelve, ring down the curtain on, call it a day, close *or* shut down shop.

2. settle, resolve, clear up, reconcile; make peace, come to terms, strike a bargain, agree, compromise, accommodate; arbitrate, mediate, negogiate, engineer, manage, arrange terms, work out, solve; bring about, cause, make happen, effect, effectuate, produce; bring off, *Sl.* pull off, *Inf.* put over, *All U.S. Sl.* swing, cut, hack; achieve, attain, accomplish, compass, arrive at, reach.

3. deduce, infer, construe, derive, put two and two together, *U.S. Inf.* figure out; calculate, compute, reckon, figure; gather, glean, get, arrive at; understand, realize, comprehend, perceive, see; assume, presume, take for granted, think; guess, conjecture, theorize, hypothesize, surmise; suspect, suppose, imagine.

4. decide, determine, fix upon; resolve, judge, make up one's mind, elect, prefer; choose, settle on, select.

conclusion, *n.* **1.** close, end, termination, finish, completion; finale, final act *or* scene, last part *or* stage; consummation, fruition, achievement, attainment, accomplishment, acquirement; realization, fulfillment, culminaton, climax, capper, denouement; expiration, death, bitter end; annihilation, extinguishment, eradication, abolishment; stopping, stoppage, cessation, discontinuance, halt; checking, arrestment, staying, holding back, desisting; suspension, breaking off, leaving off, quitting.

2. summary, summation, wrap-up, windup; résumé, synopsis, recapitulation, coda; epilogue, afterword.

3. result, issue, outcome, upshot; effect, consequence, repercussion, aftereffect, afterclap; aftermath, wake, train, trail; outgrowth, derivative, product, offspring, offshoot; fruit, yield, crop, harvest.

4. settlement, resolution, compromise, coming to terms; agreement, gentlemen's agreement, bargain, *Inf.* deal; pact, covenant, bond, compact, understanding; concordat, alliance, treaty; arrangement, contract, commitment.

5. final decision, judgment, determination, verdict, finding, arbitration, arbitrament; sentence, *Law.* award, declaration, decree; conviction, view, opinion, sentiments, impression, feeling; reasoning, reflection, observation, thought.

6. deduction, inference, construing, derivation; calculation, computation, reckoning, figuring, gathering, gleaning; understanding, realization, comprehension, perception; assumption, supposition, presumption; thinking, feeling, suspicion; guess, conjecture, theory, hypothesis, *Rare.* surmisal.

7. in conclusion finally, at last, at long last, at length, in the end; ultimately, eventually.

conclusive, *adj.* **1.** decisive, definitive, decided, settled, determining, determinative; final, ultimate, perfect, absolute, categorical, unqualified, unconditional; infallible, incontestable, unquestionable, indisputable, indubitable, incontrovertible, irrevocable; certain, sure, definite; undeniable, unrefutable, irrefragable; clear, defined, plain, apparent, obvious, evident, self-evident, manifest, patent, palpable; unavoidable, inescapable.

2. convincing, valid, authenticated, cogent, substantial, firm; confirmed, corroborative, established, fixed, set, habitual, chronic, inveterate; verifiable, verificative, confirmable; authoritative, strong, powerful; commanding, overwhelming, crushing, damning, telling, revealing; clinching, clenching, crowning, topping, capping.

3. concluding, closing, final, last, ending, terminal, terminative, *Rare.* conclusory; finishing, completing.

concoct, *v.* **1.** prepare, cook, cook up, make; compose, combine, mix, put together; get up, *Inf.* rustle up, muster up.

2. devise, contrive, cogitate, excogitate; think up, dream up, make up, conjure up, *Inf.* cook up; plot, compass, design, germinate; fashion, fabricate, hatch, invent, forge, scheme, *Sl.* hoke up; create, originate, formulate, form, draft, frame, shape; coin, mint, neologize, neoterize.

concoction, *n.* **1.** compound, mixture, combination, mix, composition, blend, admixture; brew, potion, drink.

2. creation, invention, formation, conception; fabrication, formulation, manufacture, production; contrivance, scheme, plot, plan, design, device; coinage, mintage, neologism, neoterism.

concomitant, *adj.* **1.** attendant, attending, accompanying, belonging; accessory, auxiliary, adjuvant, supplemental, supplementary; (*all usually in a subordinate capacity*) joint, joined, conjoint, conjoined, conjunctive, connected, tied, bound, linked; associated, affiliated; allied, united, leagued, confederated; amalgamated, merged, consolidated.

2. concurrent, parallel, collateral, side-by-side; coexistent, coexisting, coincident, coeval, contemporary, contemporaneous, simultaneous, coinstantaneous; synchronous, synchronal; synchronized, in time, in tempo, in step, *Inf.* in sync.

3. cooperative, cooperating, collaborative, collaborating, coactive, interactive, interactional, interacting, synergetic, synergistic.

—*n.* **4.** offshoot, corollary, side effect; side issue, accompanying circumstance, accessory fact; adjunct, addition, appendage, appendix, supplement, affix, attachment, tailpiece, coda; accessory, attendant, appurtenance, appurtenant; contemporary, coexistent, coeval.

concord, *n.* **1.** unanimity, consentience, consentaneity, consentaneousness, like-mindedness; concurrence, concordance, consonance; agreement, accord, accordance, compliance, conformity, conformance, conformation; unity, oneness, oneness of mind, single-mindedness; consensus, common consent, general consent; concert, chorus, one voice.

2. affinity, friendship, rapport, good will, good feeling, amity, cordial relations; congeniality, amicability, neighborliness; fraternity, brotherhood, brotherliness, fellowship, comradeship.

3. harmony, harmoniousness, proportion, balance, symmetry; coherence, cohesion, consistency; congruity, congruence, congruousness, mutual fitness; amalgamation, consolidation, merger, incorporation, unification; alliance, confederation, federation.

4. peace, peacefulness; quiet, quietude, serenity; tranquillity; order.

5. treaty, settlement, agreement, understanding; truce, armistice, cease-fire, cessation of hostilities; contract, compact, concordat, covenant, convention, pact.

concordant, *adj.* agreeing, in agreement, corresponding, correspondent, in correspondence, concurring, concurrent, consentient, consentaneous; harmonious, in harmony, consonant; accordant, in accord, complying, conforming, conformable; proportionate, balanced, symmetrical; coherent, cohesive, consistent, congruent; unanimous, in unison, at one, in rapport, of the same mind, of one mind, like-minded, single-minded.

concordat, *n.* formal agreement, contract, charter,

indenture, covenant, bond; compact, treaty, protocol, alliance, pact, *Rare.* paction, convention; mutual understanding, accord, accordance, concord, concordance, concurrence; settlement, arrangement, bargain, transaction, *Inf.* deal.

concourse, *n.* **1.** assemblage, gathering, forgathering, congregation, company; assembly, meeting, conference, rally; collection, cluster, crowd, group, throng, multitude, host, legion; crush, rout, swarm, horde, press.

2. esplanade, mall, promenade, grounds, turf; boardwalk, public walk, sidewalk, track, path; avenue, boulevard, causeway, highway, expressway, thoroughfare, road, land, driveway; terminal, waiting room, station, airport.

3. confluence, conflux, convergence, concurrence, junction, conjunction, joining; flocking together, concentration, focalization; accumulation, amassment, aggregation, aggregate, agglomeration, agglomerate, conglomeration, conglomerate.

concrete, *adj.* **1.** particular, specific, single, singular, certain, special, unique, sole, peculiar, individual, individualized; separate, isolated, distinct, discrete; exact, precise, direct, strict, minute; explicit, definite, express; plain, evident, manifest, obvious; pointed, marked, emphasized; restrictive, limiting, limited, bounded; determinate, well-defined, clear-cut, fixed, finite; determinative, determining, conclusive, decided; graphic, vivid, detailed, striking, telling.

2. actual, real, true, literal; factual, true-to-life, realistic, unimaginary; authentic, genuine, *Dial.* sure-enough, bona fide, veritable, valid, verifiable, confirmed, reliable, faithful; absolute, positive, certain, sure, unequivocal, unconditional.

3. physical, corporeal, bodily, substantial, material; non-abstract, tangible, palpable, sensible, perceptible; existing, existent, present.

4. solid, solidified, firm, consolidated; compressed, joined *or* packed together, compact, dense; conglomerated, agglomerated, agglomerative, compound, conglutinated, conglutinative; coalesced, coalescent, amalgamated; impenetrable, impervious, impermeable; coherent, cohesive, tight; petrified, petrificant, stonelike, lithoid, rocklike, *Archaic.* lapidific, *Physiol.* calcified, cement; hard, callous, indurate.

—n. **5.** instance, specific, specification, example; particularity, particular, item, feature, detail.

6. concretion, solid mass, conglomeration, agglomeration. See **concretion** (*def.* **1**).

7. pavement, paving, cement, mortar; asphalt, macadam.

—v. **8.** solidify, harden, indurate, densify, set; petrify, *Archaic.* lapidify; conglomerate, agglomerate, coalesce, amalgamate, cohere; conglutinate, agglutinate, stick together, adhere, weld, fuse; coagulate, thicken, congeal, clot, curdle; compress, join *or* pack together; cement, unite solidly.

9. concretize, actualize, realize, make real, make actual, embody, personify, make concrete; externalize, objectify, exteriorize; particularize, specify.

concretion, *n.* **1.** solidification, hardening, densification, induration, *Physiol.* calcification, firming, setting; petrification, *Archaic.* lapidification; conglomeration, agglomeration, coherence, cohering, cohesion; conglutination, agglutination, sticking together, adherence, adhering, adhesion, welding, fusion; brazing, soldering; coagulation, congelation, curdling; cementation, cementing, unification, unifying; consolidation, accretion, aggregation.

2. mass, lump, deposit, swell, mound, tumulus; cake, nugget, block, chunk, hunk; clot, coagulum, curd; knot, knob, node, nodule; stone, *Pathol.* calculus, rock.

concubine, *n.* mistress, paramour, kept woman, courtesan, odalisque, *Sl.* doxy.

concupiscence, *n.* **1.** (*all usually of a sensual nature*) desire, passion, ardor, longing, wanting, yearning, languishing, pining.

2. lust, lechery, *Sl.* the hots, *Sl.* hot pants; lustfulness, lasciviousness, libidinousness, lecherousness, lewdness, prurience, salaciousness, lubricity, *Sl.* horniness; animality, bestiality, brutishness, coarseness.

concupiscent, *adj.* **1.** lustful, lascivious, lewd, licentious, libertine, libidinous, lubricous, *Sl.* hot, *Sl.* horny; sexual, erotic, prurient, salacious; sensual, voluptuous, fleshly, bodily.

2. desirous, desiring, longing, wanting, *Archaic.* lickerish; craving, coveting, hungering, thirsting; itching to *or* for, dying for *or* to, devoured by *or* consumed with desire, *Sl.* hot to trot.

concur, *v.* **1.** agree, correspond, accord, conform; cohere, harmonize, chime.

2. assent, go along with; agree on *or* upon, come to an agreement *or* understanding, arrive at an agreement, come to terms, strike a bargain, covenant, *Inf.* get together; be of like *or* one *or* the same mind, see eye to eye; acquiesce, yield, submit, give in.

3. comply, accede, agree to, say yes to, echo, *Inf.* ditto; consent, grant; allow, countenance, sanction; approve, uphold, ratify, *Chiefly U.S.* approbate.

4. cooperate, collaborate, unite efforts, pool interests, work together, pull together, hang together, stand together, *Sl.* play ball, *Sl.* do business; coact, cowork, synergize; combine, merge, consolidate, amalgamate; associate, affiliate; unite, join, conjoin, coadunate; confederate, league, band; conspire, collude, connive, *Inf.* be in cahoots; join forces, *Inf.* team up, *Inf.* hitch horses.

5. coincide, synchronize, parallel; coexist, exist together, happen together, contemporize; accompany, keep in step, keep pace with; intersect, overlap.

concurrence, *n.* **1.** union, unification, conjunction, conjugation; joinder, accouplement, connection, *Inf.* hook-up; coherence, coalescence; concourse, confluence; amalgamation, merger, consolidation, incorporation; concurring, concurrency, agreeing, corresponding, correspondency, complying, conforming.

2. agreement, accordance, correspondence, conformity, conformation, conformance, congruity, congruence, congruency; unanimity, consentience, consentaneity, consentaneousness, like-mindedness; accord, harmony, concord, concordance, concert, rapport, unity; consensus, joint *or* general approval, unison.

3. assent, sanction, approval, approbation; compliance, concession, accession.

4. cooperation, collaboration, interaction, coaction, synergy, teamwork, give and take, pulling together, fraternization, *Chiefly U.S. Pol.* logrolling; joint action *or* operation, combined action *or* effort, coordinated *or* concerted effort *or* action, coadjuvant action *or* effort, gentleman's agreement.

5. coexistence, contemporaneity, contemporaneousness, simultaneity, simultaneousness; coincidence, concomitance, concomitancy; conjuncture, juncture.

concurrent, *adj.* **1.** parallel, collateral, side-by-side; synchronized, *Inf.* in sync; coexistent, coexisting, coincident, contemporary, contemporaneous, simultaneous, synchronous, synchronal; contiguous, adjacent, contingent, conterminous, coterminous, bordering, abutting.

2. cooperative, cooperating, collaborative, collaborating, coactive, coordinated, interactive, interactional, interacting, synergetic, synergistic; coalitional, united, allied, leagued, confederated; associated, affiliated; amalgamated, merged, consolidated, incorporated; joint, conjoint, conjoined, conjunctive; in league, in alliance, hand in glove with, *Inf.* in cahoots with; attendant, accompanying, concomitant.

3. agreeing, corresponding, correspondent, concurring, consentient, consentaneous; complying, conforming, conformable; accordant, concordant, congruent, congruous; coherent, cohesive, consistent; harmonious, consonant; unanimous, in unison, in accord, in rapport, in harmony, at one, of the same mind, of one mind, like-minded.

4. coincident, coinciding, intersecting, meeting, joining, connecting; confluent, convergent, converging; focal, centralized.

concussion, *n.* **1.** blow, bump, jolt, jolting, jar, jarring, jostle, jostling; impact, crash, crackup, smash, collision, clash, encounter.

2. shock, stun, daze, paralysis.

condemn, *v.* **1.** censure, reprobate, criticize, remonstrate, animadvert on; denounce, denunciate, objurgate, berate; blame, charge, accuse, impute, indict; incriminate, criminate, inculpate, implicate; disapprove, deprecate, disparage, discountenance; reproach, rebuke, reprove, reprehend, scold; castigate, vituperate, reprimand, upbraid, admonish; inveigh against, rail against, decry, declaim, run down, fulminate against; attack, assail, impugn; lash, vilify, curse, revile, vilipend.

2. proscribe, forbid, interdict, prohibit; ostracize, excommunicate, exile; ban, bar, outlaw, blackball, blacklist.

3. convict, find guilty, doom, damn; sentence, pass sentence, adjudge.

4. force, compel, command, coerce, enforce; press, impel, make; obligate, require, demand, necessitate; impose, order, bind, enjoin.

condemnation, *n.* **1.** censure,. reprehension, animadversion, criticism, remonstration, remonstrance; disapprobation, disapproval, objection, disparagement, deprecation; reproof, reproach, rebuke, reprimand, stricture; denunciation, denouncing, execration, invective; objurgation, berating, vituperation, contumely; reprobation, imprecation, fulmination, detraction, derogation; aspersion, obloquy, traducement, defamation, vilification, vilipending; castigation, upbraiding, scolding, admonishment, dressing-down; inveighing, declamation; blame, accusation, imputation, indictment; incrimination, crimination, inculpation, implication.

2. damnation, excommunication, banning, exile; proscription, ban, prohibition, outlawing, interdiction, blacklisting.

condemnatory, *adj.* **1.** incriminating, incriminatory, damning, damnatory, condemning, dooming; inculpatory, implicating, implicatory, implicative; imputative, accusatory, accusative, recriminatory, recriminative, criminatory, criminative.

2. denunciatory, denunciative, defamatory, fulminatory, comminatory, objurgatory, objurgative; reproachful, reprehensive, disapprobatory, objurgative; opprobrious, blaming, disparaging, scolding, disapproving, exprobatory; vituperative, critical, hypercritical, censorious, animadversional, faultfinding.

condensation, *n.* **1.** compression, compressing, concentration, concentrating, consolidation, consolidating, compaction, compacting, coalescence, cohesion, concretion, thickening, hardening, densification; constriction, constricting, constringency, constringing, astringency, astringent, squeezing, pinching, crowding, crushing, packing, cramming, ramming, stuffing, wedging, cramping, tightening; shortage, shortening, reduction, reducing, retrenchment, retrenching, contraction, contracting, curtailment, curtailing, cut, cutting down, cutting back, cutting short, decrease, decreasing, diminution, diminishing, subtraction, subtracting, subduction, subducting, narrowing, bridging; shrinkage, shrinking, shriveling, withering, slimming down, slenderizing.

2. density, denseness, impermeability, solidity; compactness, closeness, tightness, narrowness, narrow straits, tight squeeze, bind, confinement.

3. digest, epitome, compendium, survey, synopsis, abstract, summary, précis, conspectus, prospectus, syllabus, résumé, brief, outline, sketch.

4. abridgment, abridging, abbreviation, abbreviating, abstracting, summarizing, digesting, epitomizing, synopsizing.

5. solidification, coagulation, congelation, crystallization, cohesion, concretion, clot, gel, curd, curds; liquefaction, liquidization, distillation, evaporation, deliquescence, *Chem.* precipitation, fluidization.

condense, *v.* **1.** compress, concentrate, consolidate, compact; press *or* force together, constrict, constringe, astringe, squeeze, pinch, crowd, crush, pack, cram, ram, stuff, wedge, cramp, tighten, *Obs.* constipate; shorten, reduce, retrench, contract, curtail, cut, cut down, cut back, cut off, cut short, decrease, diminish, subtract, subduct, narrow, bridge; shrink, shrivel, wither, slim down, slenderize.

2. abbreviate, capsule, encapsulate, abridge, abstract, summarize, digest, epitomize, brief, synopsize.

3. thicken, solidify, crystallize, harden, cake, set, gel, clot, coagulate, congeal, curdle, curd, *Obs.* incrassate; liquefy, liquidize, *Rare.* liquesce, deliquesce, *Chem.* precipitate, fluidize, fluidify, flux.

condensed, *adj.* **1.** compressed, concentrated, consolidated, compacted; constricted, constringed, astringed, squeezed, pinched, crowded, crushed, packed, crammed, rammed, stuffed, wedged, cramped, tightened; shortened, reduced, retrenched, contracted, curtailed, curtate, cut, cut down, cut short, cut back, cut off, decreased, diminished, subtracted, subducted, narrowed, bridged; shrunk, shrunken, shriveled, withered, sere, dried, slimmed-down, slenderized.

2. abbreviated, encapsulated, compendious, abridged, abstracted, summarized, digested, epitomized, synopsized.

3. thickened, solidified, crystallized, hardened, caked, set, gelled, clotted, coagulated, congealed, curdled; liquefied, liquidized, deliquesced, *Chem.* precipitated, fluidized, fluidified.

4. thick, compact, close; solid, hard, concrete, cohesive, coagulate; liquid, *Chem.* precipitate, fluid.

condescend, *v.* **1.** deign, vouchsafe; humble oneself, lower oneself, unbend, stoop, descend; come down off one's high horse, come down a peg, sing small; yield, give in, back down, come around, come over, fall in with; acquiesce, comply with, accede, concede.

2. patronize, (*in speech*) talk down to, *Sl.* put down, set down, offend, humiliate.

condescending, *adj.* **1.** patronizing, scornful, disdainful, contemptuous, supercilious, despising; imperious, overbearing, high-handed, pompous, stilted, pretentious; snobbish, snobby, priggish, *All Inf.* snooty, snippy, snotty, high-hat, high-hatted; presumptuous, arrogant, haughty, lofty, lordly; inconsiderate, self-centered, tactless, uncharitable; offensive, humiliating, insulting, insolent.

2. humble, modest, lowly, self-effacing; deferring, submissive, yielding, complying, compliant; complaisant, gracious, courteous, civil.

condescension, *n.* **1.** deigning, stooping, condescending, condescendence; patronage, patronizing, looking down *or* upon; scorn, disdain, contempt, disrespect, underestimation; disparagement, discredit, slur, detraction; humiliation, dishonor, offense, insult, *Sl.* put-down; abuse, contumely.

2. snobbery, conceit, overbearingness, airs, assurance; audacity, insolence, brazenness, impudence, impertinence; sauciness, effrontery, gall, flippancy, *Rare.* procacity; presumption, arrogation.

3. deference, submission, yielding, compliance; toleration, tolerance, allowance, sufferance, permission, endurance; indulgingness, indulgence, humoring; humbleness, modesty, lowliness, self-effacement, self-abasement; complaisance, graciousness, civility; favor, courtesy, grace.

condign, *adj.* (*all usually of punishment*) just, fair, right, rightful, proper, meet, worthy, due; fitting, apt, appropriate, apposite, suitable; richly-deserved, well-deserved, merited; adequate, sufficient, ample, enough, satisfactory; proportionate, commensurate, correspondent, equivalent.

condiment, *n.* relish, sauce, dressing, chutney; seasoning, flavoring, spices, allspice, herbs and spices.

condition, *n.* **1.** state, stage, phase; situation, circumstance, state of affairs, kettle of fish; predicament, scrape, plight, quandary, dilemma, fix, corner, pinch, *Inf.* pickle.

2. shape, form, fitness, physical fitness, well-being, health, fettle; working order, *Inf.* kilter, *Sl.* whack.

3. position, place, station, estate; standing, footing, step, degree, rank, grade; status, stratum, level, class, caste.

4. qualification, restriction, limit, modification; consideration, allowance, exception.

5. requirement, necessity, essential, *Latin. sine qua non*; prerequisite, antecedent.

6. provision, proviso, contingency, contingent; stipulation, term, demand; article, clause, particular, point; premise, assumption, supposition, presupposition, hypothesis, postulate.

—*v.* **7.** prepare, equip, train, get ready, warm up, get in shape, shape up, work out, tone up; teach, instruct, tutor, coach; capacitate, enable, empower.

8. qualify, restrict, limit, set limits *or* boundaries; stipulate, require, demand, *Law.* provide.

conditional, *adj.* **1.** dependent, contingent, relative, subject to [s.t.], based upon [s.t.], *Inf.* iffy.

2. restrictive, restricted, qualified, with reservations, limitative, limiting; stipulatory, provisory, provisional, provisionary, probationary.

condole, *v.* grieve, lament, feel for, be *or* feel sorry for, bleed for, weep for, pity; sympathize, commiserate, compassionate.

condolence, *n.* commiseration, sympathy, feeling, fellow feeling, pity, compassion; consolation, solace, comfort, balm, soothing words; succor, relief, support, aid.

condonation, *n.* excusal, excusing, pardoning, forgiveness, forgiving, remission, remitting; overlooking, passing over, disregarding, dispensation, forgetting, oblivion, ignoring.

condone, *v.* **1.** excuse, pardon, forgive, remit, make allowances for.

2. overlook, pass over, wink at; disregard, dispense with, forget; ignore, look the other way, pay no attention to.

conduce, *v.* lead to, contribute to, add to; help, be of service to, aid, assist, abet, succor, support; promote, advance, forward, boost; influence, dispose, incline; arrange for, cause, effect, effectuate, bring about.

conducive, *adj.* contributive, contributing, contributory, accessory, ancillary; helpful, instrumental, useful; favorable, advantageous, convenient, good, in a fair way; leaning towards, tending towards, disposed towards.

conduct, *n.* **1.** behavior, demeanor, deportment, comportment, *Both Archaic.* havior, gest; bearing, carriage, posture, gait, pose, port; manners, p's and q's; breeding, upbringing, rearing; habits, ways, dealings, customs, practice; morals, ethics, principles.

2. reaction, responses, adaptation, adjustment; performance, function, operation.

3. misbehavior, disobedience, delinquency, misdeeds, *Inf.* cutting up, *Inf.* goings-on. See **misbehavior.**

4. direction, management, superintendence, supervision, oversight; regulation, running, operation, administration, government; control, command, charge.

5. orchestration, engineering, negotiation; execution, carrying out, performance, doing; accomplishment, discharge, fulfillment, consummation, completion.

6. conducting, leading, guidance, escort, tour.

7. direct, run, operate, manage, carry on; administer, govern, regulate, control, boss; superintend, supervise, oversee, preside over, look after; orchestrate, engineer, negotiate, work out.

8. execute, carry out, perform, do; succeed in, bring off, *Sl.* pull off, *Inf.* put over, *All U.S. Sl.* swing, cut, hack; accomplish, discharge, fulfill, complete, consummate; bring about, make happen, cause, effect, effectuate, produce.

9. lead, guide, take, show the way, escort, accompany.

—*v.* **10.** (*all of oneself*) behave, deport, demean, comport, acquit; carry, bear, manage, govern, regulate.

conductor, *n.* **1.** leader, chief, director, fugleman; head, marshal, drum major; chairman, president, executive; manager, supervisor, *Inf.* super, superintendent, overseer, *Inf.* boss; administrator, dean, functionary, bureaucrat, government official; captain, skipper, master, pilot, driver, steersman, helmsman; guide, cicerone, usher, escort, guard.

2. maestro, choir master, precentor, coryphaeus.

3. transmitter, carrier, conveyor, bearer.

conduit, *n.* **1.** duct, pipe, main, tube, cylinder; passage, passageway, adit; sewer, culvert, cloaca, flume, trough, chute; spout, gutter, drain, gully, ditch.

2. canal, artificial waterway, channel, race, watercourse; strait, aqueduct, waterway, seaway.

confabulate, *v.* chat, chitchat, palaver, converse, coze, talk together, pass the time of day, *Inf.* confab, *Sl.* rap, *Sl.* chin, *Sl.* chew the fat, *Sl.* shoot the breeze *or* bull, *Sl.* bull; talk *or* speak with, have a talk with, converse with, commune with, communicate with, visit with.

confection, *n.* **1.** composition, concoction, making; manufacture, production, preparation.

2. candy, sweet, sweetmeat, bonbon, comfit, dainty, confectionary; preserve, conserve, confect, confiture.

confederacy, *n* alliance, coalition, entente; union, league, bloc, bund, federation, federacy, confederation; partnership, corporation, incorporation, conglomerate, trust.

confederation, *n.* **1.** leaguing, unionizing, unification, union, allying, uniting, joining with, banding together, joining forces, teaming up, siding with, going along with, taking part, *Inf.* hitching horses; merging, blending, amalgamating, amalgamation, consolidating, consolidation, incorporating, incorporation; centralizing, centralization, federalizing, federalization, federating, federation.

2. interacting, interaction, coacting, coaction, interfacing, synergizing, synergy, combining, combination, cooperating, cooperation, collaborating, collaboration, working together *or* in unison *or* side by side, acting jointly *or* in concert, joint *or* concerted action, standing shoulder to shoulder, pulling together; conspiring, conspiracy, conniving, cabal, intriguing, intrigue, plotting, plot, complotting, complot, colluding, collusion; associating, association, consociation, fraternizing, fraternization, assembling, assembly, clubbing *or* herding together.

3. alliance, coalition; union, league, syndicate, cartel, combine.

confer, *v.* **1.** bestow, award, vouchsafe, accord, present; grant, yield, afford, allot, allow, render, donate; give; give out, deal out, dole out, mete out, *Inf.* dish out, *Inf.* hand out.

2. parley, palaver, deliberate, consult together, sit down together, hold conference, *Inf.* powwow, *Inf.* huddle, *Inf.* go into a huddle, *Inf.* put *or* lay heads together, *Inf.* talk turkey; consult with, discuss with, talk with, take up with, talk over; consult, call in, compare notes, exchange views.

conference, *n.* **1.** meeting, parley, palaver, colloquy, huddle, *Inf.* powwow; convention, council, caucus, session; talk, discussion, tête-à-tête, *Sl.* rap *or* rap session, *Sl.* bull session; forum, symposium, seminar, colloquium, round table; interview, audience, sitting.

2. consultation, deliberation, consideration, examination, study, analysis; dialogue, debate, conversation, communication, communion.

confess, *v.* **1.** acknowledge, admit, allow, grant, concede, avow, own, *Inf.* own up, *Sl.* fess up, *Sl.* come clean, *Sl.* cop a plea, plead guilty; disbosom, unbosom oneself, make a clean breast, take the load off one's mind, come out with, *Inf.* get it off one's chest, *Inf.* get it out of one's system; tell all, *Inf.* let it all hang out, *Sl.* sing, *Sl.* spill one's guts, *Sl.* spill the beans.

2. go to confession, make confession, receive absolution; shrive, hear confession, absolve, administer absolution.

3. declare, profess, make known, affirm, assert, asseverate; warrant, avouch, vow, swear.

confession, *n.* **1.** acknowledgment, admission, allowance, concession, *Inf.* owning up, *Sl.* fessing up; acceptance, recognition.

2. disclosure, revelation, divulgence, *Archaic.* shrift.

3. **confession of faith** profession, declaration, avowal, affirmation, assertion, asseveration, avouchment.

confidant, confidante, *n.* intimate, familiar, close friend, fast friend, *Latin. fidus Achates*, bosom friend, bosom buddy; bedfellow, bedmate, bunkmate, *Sl.* bunkie, roommate; chum, crony, pal, buddy, mate, comrade; alter ego, other self, second self, shadow, sidekick.

confide, *v.* **1.** trust, have faith, believe, take *or* put stock in, credit; depend on, rely on, put confidence in, swear by, count on, pin one's faith on; put one's trust in, be convinced, be satisfied, be assured of.

2. disclose, impart, reveal, tell, intimate; open one's heart, unburden, unbosom, get [s.t.] off one's chest, confess; whisper, pass on, breathe, breathe in the ear.

3. entrust, consign, turn over, make over; commit, put into the hands of, commend, give over; delegate, invest, assign, depute, empower.

confidence, *n.* **1.** trust, faith, reliance, dependence; security, sureness, assuredness, surety, positiveness.

2. self-reliance, assurance, self-assurance, self-confidence; aplomb, poise, coolness, calmness; pluck, spunk, spirit, gameness, heart, stamina, vigor; backbone, mettle, nerve, fiber; courage, fortitude, grit, *Sl.* guts.

3. presumption, presumptuousness, impertinence, impudence, effrontery; brashness, brazenness, cockiness, insolence, cocksureness, *Inf.* nerve, *Inf.* chutzpa; arrogance, overconfidence, audacity, assertiveness, bumptiousness; boldness, forwardness, pertness, *Inf.* freshness.

4. certitude, certainty, freedom from doubt, reassurance; conviction, belief, assurance, assertion, persuasion.

confident, *adj.* **1.** sure, certain, positive, absolute; assured, convinced, secure, satisfied; believing, undoubting, questionless; steady, unwavering, unhesitating, unflinching, unblinking; self-confident, self-assured, self-possessed.

2. presumptuous, impertinent, impudent, bold, forward; cocksure, brash, brazen, insolent, cocky, *Inf.* cheeky, *Inf.* fresh; audacious, assertive, bumptious, pert, *Inf.* nervy.

confidential, *adj.* **1.** secret, private, privy, restricted, eyes-only, personal, not public, *It. in petto*; not to be disclosed, not to be mentioned, not to be spoken.

2. intimate, familiar, bosom, close, dear, *Inf.* thick.

3. trusted, trusty, trustworthy, faithful; reliable, dependable, unfailing.

confidentially, *adv.* secretly, intimately, privately, in private; under the veil of secrecy, up one's sleeve, hugger-mugger, hush-hush, in strict confidence, in a whisper, *It. sotto voce*, under the rose, sub rosa, behind closed doors; under one's hat, off the record; between ourselves, *Fr. entre nous, Latin. inter nos*, between you and me, between you and me and the lamp post, aside.

configuration, *n.* external form, conformation, formation, structure, construction, construct; outline, contour, shape, build, figure, frame; cast, mold, type, set.

confine, *v.* **1.** restrict, hem in, hedge in; tie down, check, curb, limit; constrain, astrict, bind, bound, tie, restrain, trammel, hamper, cramp, straiten; fix, delimit, delimitate, demarcate; circumscribe, encircle, encompass, gird, begird, girdle, belt.

2. enclose, shut in, shut up, keep in, quarantine, isolate; cage, coop, pen in, rail in, fence, pale, picket, corral; box up, bottle up, seal up; bolt in, lock up, imprison, jail, incarcerate, impound, wall in, immure, put in irons.

—*n.* **3.** *Usu.* **confines** boundary, bound, limit, terminus, termination, *Archaic.* term; border, precinct, line of demarcation, frontier; margin, rim, skirt, edge, verge, brink.

confinement, *n.* **1.** restriction, hemming in, hedging in, tying down, check, curb, limitation; restraint, constraint, astriction, binding, tying; circumscription, encircling, encompassing, enclosure, enclosing, shutting in, keeping in, quarantine, isolation; caging, cooping, penning in, fencing; bolting in, locking up, imprisonment, limbo, incarceration, durance, custody, detention.

2. childbed, lying-in, *Fr. accouchement*, childbirth, parturition, labor, travail, delivery.

confirm, *v.* **1.** corroborate, verify, authenticate, validate, substantiate; bear out, prove, establish, evidence, give credence to; attest, certify, bear witness to, testify, vouch for; affirm, aver, assure, pledge, promise, guarantee, ensure, secure, insure; bind, seal, settle, clinch, clench, secure, fix, make certain *or* sure.

2. sanction, accredit, authorize, warrant; approve, ratify, endorse, support, underwrite; sustain, back up, uphold, make good, justify, vindicate; countersign, sign, subscribe, recognize, acknowledge; agree, con-

sent, accede, assent, concur, accord, acquiesce, comply.
3. strengthen, make firmer, reinforce, fortify, buttress, brace, steel.

confirmation, *n.* **1.** corroboration, verification, authentication, validation, substantiation; proof, evidence, attestation, certification, testimony, witness; affirmation, assertion, averment, assurance, positive declaration; pledge, promise, guarantee, guaranty, surety, security, warrant, warranty.
2. sanction, accreditation, authorization, approval, ratification, endorsement; support, sustainment, backing, defense, justification; signature, subscription, recognition, acknowledgment; agreement, consent, accedence, assent, concurrence, accord; acquiescence, compliance, accordance, conformity.

confirmed, *adj.* **1.** valid, true, factual, accurate, correct, right; corroborated, verified, authenticated, validated, substantiated, documented, certified, notarized; proven, demonstrated, shown, attested to.
2. settled, decided, clinched, sealed; certain, sure, definite, positive; firm, decisive, absolute, final, conclusive.
3. ratified, approved, accepted, recognized, acknowledged; authorized, official, licensed, sanctioned, warranted, accredited, endorsed.
4. genuine, real, bona fide, authentic; dyed-in-the-wool, through-and-through, complete; established, set, fixed, rooted; inveterate, chronic, habitual.

confiscate, *v.* **1.** seize, appropriate, expropriate, commandeer, arrogate, usurp, take possession of, claim.
2. dispossess, deprive, divest, *Law.* disseize, impound, *Law.* distrain.
3. steal, thieve, rob; plunder, despoil, pillage.

confiscation, *n.* **1.** appropriation, takeover, seizure, expropriation, arrogation, usurpation, accroachment, impoundment.
2. dispossession, deprivation, deprival, divestiture, bereavement, *Law.* disseizin.

conflagration, *n.* holocaust, wildfire, raging fire, ring *or* sea of fire, wall *or* sheet of flames, blaze, *Obs.* flagration.

conflict, *v.* **1.** clash, collide, jar, disagree, differ, disaccord, diverge, be at variance, be at odds; oppose, contradict, contravene.
2. contend, contest, argue, spar, cross swords, lock horns; squabble, quarrel, feud, bicker, wrangle, have words, be at [s.o.'s] throat; struggle, battle, do *or* give battle, encounter, engage, meet; fight, combat, duel, joust; tussle, scuffle, brawl, come to blows.
—*n.* **3.** battle, struggle, strife, tussle, scuffle; contest, war, bout, Armageddon; combat, warfare, fighting, hostilities; collision, meeting, encounter, engagement; fight, donnybrook, brawl, *Scot.* sturt, *Inf.* scrap, *Inf.* run-in.
4. controversy, infighting, feud; argument, altercation, dispute, row, quarrel, squabble, dustup, spat, tiff, *Brit. Dial.* fratch.
5. contention, opposition, *Literary.* agon; disagreement, discord, disaccord, dissension, friction, variance; enmity, hostility, antagonism, antipathy, bad blood, ill will.

confluence, *n.* **1.** flowing together, conflux; junction, union, meeting, concurrent; convergence, appulse, diffluence.
2. concourse, flocking together, concentration. See **concourse** (*def.* **3**).
3. crowd, throng, assemblage, concourse; shoal, covey, flock, bevy, drove, herd, mob, army, array, galaxy. See **concourse** (*def.* **1**).

confluent, *adj.* **1.** mingling, blending, commingling, flowing *or* running together, concurrent; joining, meeting, growing together, coalescent.
—*n.* **2.** tributary, branch, affluent, feeder; channel, stream, rivulet, brook, rill, creek, run, *Brit. Dial.* gill.

conform, *v.* **1.** (*usu. fol. by* to) comply, observe, obey, acknowledge, respect; adhere to, abide by, acquiesce in, submit to, yield to, consent to, agree to; concur, grant, accept; adapt to, adjust to, reconcile with; be conventional, be regular, be ordinary, run with the pack, swim with the stream, follow the crowd, follow the fashion, travel in a rut, do in Rome as the Romans do.
2. correspond, harmonize, tally, agree with, accord with; square, fit, suit, match.
3. adjust, adapt, accommodate; alter, modify, coordinate, assimilate, transmute; make conformable, bring into correspondence, reconcile, make similar, make harmonious; conventionalize.

conformable, *adj.* **1.** corresponding, like, resembling, similar; harmonious, agreeable, congruous, congruent, consonant, consistent with; appropriate, suitable, fit, befitting, proper, meet.
2. compliant, acquiescent, submissive, yielding; malleable, ductile, flexible, pliant; adaptable, tractable, manageable, governable, biddable; capitulating, willing, complying, obliging, obeying; docile, meek, timid, passive, unassertive.
3. dutiful, duteous, law-abiding, rule-abiding, loyal, faithful, respectful; conventional, customary, traditional, orthodox; habitual, usual, standard, common, ordinary.
4. subservient, servile, obsequious, ingratiating, obeisant, prostrate, *Archaic.* sequacious; truckling, bowing, scraping, fawning, cowering, cringing, crawling, toadying, toadyish, *Inf.* bootlicking; self-effacing, self-surrendering, self-abasing.

conformation, *n.* **1.** structure, form, manner of formation, make; shape, figure, configuration.
2. symmetry, correspondence, regularity, proportionality; balance, poise, equilibrium; congruity, consonance, agreement; harmony, compatibility, accord, accordance, concord, concordance; coherence, consistency, uniformity, conformity.
3. conformity, adaptation, adjustment; preparation, suiting, accommodation, acclimatization, assimilation.

conformity, *n.* **1.** correspondence, congruity, agreement, consonance, accord, accordance; concord, concordance, harmony, compatibility; likeness, similarity, similitude, resemblance, uniformity, homogeneity, unanimity; consistency, coherence; appropriateness, fitness, suitability.
2. compliance, obedience, morigeration, acquiescence, abidance; submission, subjection, yielding, surrender, capitulation; allegiance, observance, deference, respectfulness, dutifulness, faithfulness; conventionality, orthodoxy.

confound, *v.* **1.** perplex, nonplus, puzzle, mystify, bewilder, baffle, pose; amaze, astound, astonish, startle, stun, daze, dumfound, strike dumb, stupefy, petrify, paralyze, surprise, take by surprise; confuse, disconcert, dismay, unsettle, rattle, bother, muddle, embarrass.
2. contradict, refute, confute, disprove; rebut, counter; quash, void, annul, invalidate, upset, set aside, put down, explode, silence, *Inf.* shut up.
3. mingle, mix, blend, intermingle, jumble, make indistinguishable; mistake one thing for another, confuse, mix up.
4. damn, curse, denounce, imprecate, execrate, maledict.

confounded, *adj.* (*used euphemistically*) damned, damnable, execrable, cursed, accursed, blasted, infernal, diabolical; abominable, odious, hateful, detestable, dreadful, wretched; extreme, excessive, all-fired, monstrous, enormous, huge.

confront, *v.* **1.** oppose, stand opposed to, stand in the way of, thwart, cross, counter, contradict, resist; dispute, challenge, threaten, call into question, oppugn; defy, face in defiance, stand up to.

2. tackle, come to grips with, cope with; brave, meet head on, take the bull by the horns; face up to, face to face, come face to face with, meet, encounter; front, stand in front of, stand facing.

3. attack, accost, affront, assail; assault, set upon, aggress, waylay; charge, storm, invade; bother, trouble, annoy, harass, molest, harry, bully; badger, nag, pester, pursue, importune; call to, appeal to, invoke.

4. set face to face, bring face to face, set opposite, pit against; compare with, stand over against; set side by side, set in opposition.

confrontation, *n.* **1.** showdown, face-off; settlement, crisis, turning point; contest, battle, encounter, conflict.

2. opposition, counteraction, counter, contradiction, thwart, cross, confrontment; dispute, disputation, challenge, threat, dare; defiance, resistance, withstanding.

3. attack, assailment, assault; charging, storming, invading; bother, trouble, annoyance, harassment, molestation; badgering, nagging, pestering, importuning.

4. tackling, grappling, coping with, braving, taking the bull by the horns; meeting, facing, facing up to, meeting face to face.

confuse, *v.* **1.** blend, mix, intermix, combine, mingle, intermingle, commingle; blur, make unclear *or* indistinct, obscure, merge, lump together, tangle, entangle; mix up, transpose, interchange, juggle, switch.

2. mistake, confound, mix up, fail to see *or* make distinctions, *Inf.* compare apples with oranges.

3. disarrange, derange, disturb, disorder, disarray, disorganize; jumble, muddle, fuddle, *Brit. Sl.* muzz, snarl, *Sl.* ball up; bungle, spoil, upset, *Sl.* foul up, *Sl.* bollix up.

4. perplex, bewilder, baffle, nonplus, puzzle, mystify, pose, obfuscate, befog; buffalo, *Sl.* snow, *Inf.* cross [s.o.] up.

5. stupefy, shock, disarm, discompose, *Inf.* discombobulate; disorient, unhinge, unbalance, throw off balance, upset, fluster, flutter, rattle, addle, befuddle, distract, demoralize.

6. disconcert, abash, embarrass, mortify, shame; discomfit, dismay, consternate, irritate, chagrin.

confused, *adj.* **1.** blurry, foggy, unclear, indistinct, uncertain, hazy, obscure; mixed-up, transposed, interchanged, switched, confounded.

2. disorderly, in disorder, in disarray, hugger-mugger, disarranged, deranged, disorganized, jumbled, higgledy-piddledy; muddled, at sixes and sevens; tangled, snarled, *Inf.* fouled-up, *Inf.* balled-up, bungled, bollixed-up.

3. perplexed, bewildered, baffled, nonplused, mystified, buffaloed; uncertain, at sea, at a loss; stupefied, shocked, taken aback, thrown off balance; discomposed, flustered, upset, *Inf.* discombobulated, agitated, excited, aflutter, *Archaic.* bemazed.

4. disoriented, unhinged, unbalanced; fuzzy, in a fog, in a daze, in a stupor, *Inf.* muzzy, *Inf.* spaced out, *Inf.* out of it, *Inf.* flipped out, *Sl.* all wet.

confusion, *n.* **1.** disarray, disorganization, disarrangement, derangement, confusedness; jumble, mess, *Inf.* stew, huddle, *Scot. Inf.* guddle, mix-up, snafu, *Inf.* foul-up, *Sl.* ballup, *Brit. Sl.* balls-up.

2. disorder, upheaval, turmoil, moil, tumult, *Brit. Dial.* stour; anarchy, chaos, pandemonium, bedlam, babel, hugger-mugger, topsy-turvydom, three-ring circus; commotion, turbulence, brouhaha, uproar, pother, hurly-burly, convulsion; disturbance, trouble, to-do, row, riot, melee, fracas, rumpus, brawl, free-for-all, Donnybrook; agitation, stir, ferment, bustle, hubbub.

3. indistinctness, blurredness, obscurity; entanglement, complication, complexity, imbroglio, network, labyrinth, maze; ravelment, snarl, knot, coil, skein, tangle, congestion, tie-up; mixture, medley, jumble, jungle, wilderness, bewilderment, hodgepodge, clutter.

4. perplexity, bewilderment, bafflement, mystification, *Brit. Dial.* swither; stupefaction, uncertainty, demoralization, sixes and sevens; distraction, daze, fog, haze, *Psychiatry.* disorientation, unhingement.

5. embarrassment, mortification, humiliation, shame; abashment, chagrin, perturbation, consternation, discomposure, discomfiture, disconcertment.

confute, *v.* disprove, refute, rebut, invalidate, bring to naught; expose, show up, explode, scatter to the winds, discredit; belie, contradict, confound, controvert, gainsay, dispute; overthrow, subvert, overcome, defeat, upset, get the better of; squelch, silence, shut up.

congeal, *v.* **1.** solidify, harden, crystallize, concrete; freeze, ice, glaciate; refrigerate, chill, cool.

2. coagulate, thicken, condense, concentrate, compress, *Obs.* incrassate; stiffen, cake, set; curdle, curd, *Scot. and North Central U.S.* lopper, *Pathol.* caseate; gel, gelatinize, jell, jelly, jellify.

congenial, *adj.* **1.** compatible, correspondent, congruous, well-matched, suited *or* appropriate to each other; sympathetic, kindred, affinitive, related, cognate, like-minded, of the same mind, of one mind; concurrent, consentaneous, consentient, agreeing, in agreement, *Fr. en rapport*, at one, in unison; harmonious, concordant, accordant, in accord, consonant; synchronized, in step, *Inf.* in sync.

2. agreeable, amiable, companionable, cooperative, easy to get along with, *Scot.* couthie, *Ger. gemutlich;* easy-going, complaisant, compliant, conformable; likable, pleasant, good-natured, nice, sweet, kind, kindly, kind-hearted, cordial, hospitable, *Scot. and North Eng., Irish Eng.* sonsy; pleasing, favorable, to one's liking, to one's fancy, to one's taste, *Brit. Dial.* bonny; friendly, amicable, affable, neighborly, sociable. See **genial** (*def.* **1**).

congeniality, *n.* **1.** compatibility, congruity, congruence, congruousness, correspondence; sympathy, understanding, affinity, kindred, kindredness, like-mindedness, oneness, relationship, rapport; agreement, concurrence, consentaneousness, consentaneity; harmoniousness, harmony, accord, accordance, concord, concordance, consonance, concert.

2. amiability, affability, amity, good will, good feeling; pleasantness, pleasingness, likableness, likability, good-naturedness, good-humoredness; agreeableness, amenableness, amenity, sweetness, sweet-temperedness, *Ger. Gemutlichkeit*; geniality, graciousness, cordiality, hospitality, kindness, kindliness, kind-heartedness, warm-heartedness; friendliness, amicability, neighborliness, sociability.

congenital, *adj.* **1.** inborn, inbred, connate, connatural, natural, natural-born, ingenerate; native, hereditary, inherited, in the blood, in the family.

2. inveterate, rooted, deep-rooted, ingrained, engrained, inwrought, enwrought.

congeries, *n.* collection, assemblage, aggregation; pile, heap, mass, accumulation, amassment, agglomeration, bulk; number, composite, concentration, conglomeration; cluster, clump, *Bot.* sorus, bunch, batch, lot, crowd, pack; congestion, press, crush, cumulation;

jumble, hodgepodge, clutter.

congest, *v.* crowd, overcrowd, pack, cram, jam, stuff, wad, bunch; fill, overfill, plug, stop up, block, choke; inundate, flood, drench; gorge, glut, cloy, overfeed; overburden, overload, surcharge, overcharge.

congestion, *n.* **1.** crowding, overcrowding, packing, cramming, jamming, stuffing, wadding, bunching; filling up, plugging, stopping up, blocking, fullness, overfullness, repletion; plethora, profusion, superabundance, superfluity, nimiety, surfeit, excess.
2. obstruction, jam, tie-up, pileup, snarl.

conglomerate, *n.* **1.** agglomeration, agglomerate, aggregation, aggregate, conglomeration; corporation, multinational, multicompany; firm, company, partnership, joint concern, merger; trust, monopoly, cartel.
—adj. **2.** gathered, agglomerate, amassed, massed, clustered, agminate; grouped, combined, aggregate, mixed; united, joined, incorporated, merged.

congratulate, *v.* **1.** wish [s.o.] joy, rejoice with, felicitate, compliment, wish [s.o.] many happy returns, *Archaic.* gratulate, offer one's felicitations *or* compliments, bless; shake [s.o.'s] hand, *Inf.* pat on the back; hail, salute.
2. applaud, acclaim, cheer; praise, sound the praises of, sing the praises of, cry up, *Inf.* crack up; laud, extol, *Archaic.* magnify.

congratulation, *n.* **1.** wishing [s.o.] joy, rejoicing with, well-wishing, felicitation, complimenting, *Archaic.* gratulation, blessing.
—interj. **2. congratulations** best wishes, good wishes, bless you, take a bow, nice going, *Sl.* way to go; fine business, many happy returns.

congratulatory, *adj.* complimentary, felicitating, congratulant, congratulational, *Archaic.* gratulatory, gratulant; exultant, rejoicing, jubilant; celebrative, celebratory, favorable, positive; praising, praiseful, acclamatory, laudatory, commendatory.

congregate, *v.* **1.** gather, group, cluster, bunch up *or* together; mass, crowd, agglomerate; flock together, throng, herd, swarm; bring together, convoke, summon, call together, rally, muster, call up, mobilize; round up, round in, ingather.
2. assemble, convene, forgather, come together, converge, meet, *Inf.* gang up, huddle, go into a huddle, get together, rendezvous.

congregation, *n.* **1.** gathering, assembly, assemblage, meeting; group, body, circle, knot; crowd, throng, bunch, mob, rout; gang, crew, company, band, troop, troupe; galaxy, multitude, host; congestion, press, crush; concourse, cumulation, confluence, convergence.
2. conclave, convocation, council, synod, consistory, conventicle; muster, mobilization, association, union, combination; conference, convention, congress; caucus, bloc, *Rom. Antiq.* comitia, junta; forgathering, conjunction, coalescence.
3. community, flock, body, fold, parish; brethren, laity, fellowship, communion.

congress, *n.* **1.** legislature, Parliament, Duma; upper house, House of Lords, Senate; lower house, House of Commons, House of Representatives.
2. assembly, meeting, assemblage, gathering, concourse, *Inf.* powwow; conference, convention, muster; caucus, bloc, junta; conclave, convocation, council, synod, consistory, conventicle, soviet; forgathering, conjunction, coalescence; session, hearing, séance; interview, audience, sitting.
3. encounter, confrontation, counteraction; dealings, transaction, traffic, commerce, intercourse; conversation, discourse, converse.
4. coitus, intercourse, copulation, fornication. See **coitus.**
—v. **5.** assemble, congregate, convene, convoke; gather, collect, band.

congruity, *n.* **1.** agreement, accord, accordance, concord, concordance, correspondence, concurrence, consonance; unanimity, unison, unity, concert, uniformity, homogeneity; harmony, consistency, compatibility.
2. appropriateness, suitableness, fitness, aptness, appositeness; pertinence, relevance, relevancy, applicability, admissibility.

congruous, *adj.* **1.** agreeing, harmonious, compatible, accordant, consonant, congruent; correspondent, complementary, conformable, homogeneous.
2. proper, fit, fitting, befitting, becoming, seemly, meet; suitable, appropriate, expedient, apt, apposite; relevant, germane, applicable, admissible, apropos, *Latin. ad rem.*

conic, *adj.* conical, conoid, conoidal, cone-shaped; funnel-shaped, *Anat.* infundibular, *Bot.* infundibuliform; pyramid-shaped, pyramidal, tapering, pointed.

conjectural, *adj.* **1.** speculative, speculatory; suppositional, suppositive, presumptive; hypothetical, supposititious, theoretical, academic; referential, allusive.
2. guessed, surmised, suspected, imagined; assumed, reputed, supposed, putative; doubtful, uncertain, undetermined, hard to believe, questionable, problematic.

conjecture, *n.* **1.** guess, surmise, speculation, *Sl.* shot in the dark; assumption, supposition, presupposition, premise, presumption; hypothesis, thesis, theory, postulate, postulation; augury, forecast.
2. suspicion, inkling, feeling; intuition, divination, impression, fancy; attitude, way of thinking.
3. judgment, conclusion, deduction, inference, thinking; conviction, persuasion, position; belief, credence, view, viewpoint, opinion, sentiment, mind.
—v. **4.** guess, surmise, suspect; believe, think, fancy; imagine, envision, think up, dream up, make up, conjure up; infer, take it; assume, suppose, *Archaic.* trow, presuppose, presume, premise, take for granted; understand, gather, divine, intuit.
5. postulate, posit, predicate, theorize, hypothesize, hypothecate; hint, intimate, allude to; predict, augur, prognosticate.
6. maintain, assert, opine, hold, dare say; consider, regard, conceive, acknowledge, recognize; judge, deem, conclude, deduce.

conjoin, *v.* **1.** join, join together, unite, bind, bind together, tie, tie together, yoke, yoke together, hitch, hitch together, link, link together, concatenate, splice, couple; connect, bridge, span; combine, mix, commix, coalesce, commingle, blend.
2. ally, league, confederate, join forces *or* hands, team up, *Inf.* hitch horses; federate, federalize, centralize; associate, affiliate; incorporate, consolidate, amalgamate, merge.

conjoint, *adj.* **1.** joined, joined together, linked, linked together, tied, bound, coupled, spliced; conjoined, conjunct, conjugate; merged, combined, amalgamated, incorporated, consolidated; associated, confederated, federated; in union, in league, in alliance; in common, in conjunction, in association.
2. joint, concerted, coactive, hand in hand, arm in arm; mutual, common, communal, collective, shared; cooperative, cooperating, collaborative, collaborating, coordinated, coordinate, synergetic, synergistic; coalitional, conjunctive, corporate, corporative; federal, federate, confederate, league, union; concordant, agreeing, concurrent, consentual, consentaneous, consentient, concomitant, unanimous.

conjugal, *adj.* connubial, matrimonial, nuptial, hymeneal, epithalamic; marital, married, wedded; spousal, husbandly, wifely, bridal.

conjunction, *n.* **1.** combination, unification, accouplement, joinder; merger, incorporation, consolidation, amalgamation, conglomeration, engrossment; junction, juxtaposition, collocation; joining, linking, splicing, uniting, binding, bonding, yoking; connecting, conjoining, coupling; meeting, touching, bordering, edging, skirting, abutting.

2. union, association, affiliation, conjugation, conjuncture; cooperation, collaboration, coaction, united action; concurrence, concert, synergy; agreement, accordance, concordance; alliance, federation, confederation, league; conspiracy, collusion, *Inf.* cahoots.

3. coincidence, co-occurrence; simultaneity, simultaneousness; contemporaneousness, contemporaneity; coexistence, concommitance.

conjuncture, *n.* **1.** circumstances, state of affairs, set of conditions; context, environment, total situation, status quo, *Inf.* the picture *or* whole picture, *Inf.* the story.

2. coincidence, concurrence, co-occurrence; simultaneity, simultaneousness; contemporaneity, contemporaneousness; coexistence, concomittance.

3. crisis, crux, crunch; crossroads, turning point, critical moment *or* point, crucial moment, juncture, critical juncture, moment of truth, zero hour, *Mil.* H-hour; emergency, exigency; predicament, plight, dilemma, quandary, strait, extremity; pinch, rub, scrape, squeeze, push, *Inf.* hold, *Inf.* clutch.

4. combination, unification, union, connection, junction, conjugation, accouplement, joinder; merger, incorporation, consolidation, amalgamation, conglomeration, engrossment; joining, linking, splicing, uniting, binding, bonding, yoking; connecting, conjoining, coupling; meeting, touching, bordering, edging, abutting, skirting.

conjuration, *n.* **1.** invocation, evocation, calling up by incantation; calling upon, summoning, summons; petition, petitioning, suit, appeal; supplication, beseechment, beseeching, obtestation, obsecration; request, prayer, praying, orison, plea, pleading, intercession.

2. incantation, chant, magic formula, magic word, invocation; mumbo jumbo, hocus-pocus, abracadabra, open sesame.

3. spell, jinx, hex, negative influence; magic, charm, rune, *Scot.* cantrip, enchantment, bewitchment, bedevilment; trance, hypnosis, hypnotism, mesmerism, fascination, rapture; captivation, obsession, possession; entrancement, allurement, seduction.

4. magic, sorcery, wizardry, thaumaturgy, theurgy; black magic, black art, occult art, voodoo, hoodoo; witchcraft, witchery, necromancy, shamanism; divination, sortilege.

5. legerdemain, sleight of hand, artful trickery, skillful deception.

conjure, *v.* **1.** (*with the object as devil or spirit*) invoke, call upon, rouse, summon, beckon, command, order; call up, raise up, bring into existence, incorporealize.

2. cast a spell, enchant, bewitch, ensorcell, bedevil, entrance, spellbind; voodoo, hex, jinx, hoodoo.

3. *Usu.* **conjure up** recall, bring to mind, bethink, recollect, remember; call to mind, evoke, review, retrace.

conjurer, *n.* magician, conjurator, incantator, evocator, enchanter; sorcerer, wizard, warlock, theurgist; miracle-worker, thaumaturgist, wonder-worker, fairy godmother; witch, necromancer, shaman; medium, fortuneteller, diviner, dowser, soothsayer, astrologer, clairvoyant; voodoo, witch doctor, medicine man; Magus, Merlin, Wizard of Oz, Hecate, Circe.

connate, *adj.* **1.** inborn, inbred, native, natural, connatural, natural-born, ingenerate; congenital, hereditary, inherited, in the blood, in the family; innate, intrinsic, inherent, indigenous, indwelling, immanent.

2. cognate, related, kindred, akin, generic, congeneric; uterine, enate, enatic, agnate, consanguine, germane, sororal, fraternal; allied, affiliated, associated, apposite, affined; similar, alike, common, correlated, correspondent, comparative, relative.

connect, *v.* **1.** (*all often followed by together*) join, unite, splice, tie, bind, fasten, lash; chain, couple, link, concatenate; lace, string; knit, sew; gird, truss; hyphenate; bolt, lock, pinion, clamp; secure, anchor, moor; conjoin, subjoin, affix, fix, annex, attach, tack, staple, hook, nail, pin, rivet, screw; graft, ingraft; bridge, bridge over; (*of trains or buses*) connect up, continue, run; fuse, solder, weld; tape, glue, agglutinate, conglutinate, cement, paste; seal, concrete; clasp, button, buckle.

2. adjoin, abut, abut on *or* upon, verge upon, impinge upon; touch, reach, meet, kiss, butt, impinge; neighbor, border, flank, lie next to, lie *or* be adjacent to.

3. mix, combine, mingle, coalesce, blend; converge, come together, knit, grow together, cohere, adhere, stick together, hang *or* hold together; articulate, correlate, unify; amalgamate, consolidate, incorporate, merge.

4. associate, affiliate, join up with, join forces with, side with, go along with; league, ally, confederate, unionize, band together, join forces *or* hands, team up, *Inf.* hitch horses; associate with, deal with, treat with, have to do with, have connection with, *Inf.* tie in with.

5. relate, identify, ally, bracket, equate, parallel, draw a parallel; attribute, assign, ascribe, impugn; attribute to, assign to, ascribe to, impute to, charge to, credit *or* accredit with; fix on *or* upon, pin on, *Inf.* pinpoint, saddle on *or* upon, father upon, blame for, *Sl.* hang on.

6. (*all of ideas, fashions, art forms*) come off, go, *Inf.* make a go of it, succeed, prevail; *Inf.* catch on, *Inf.* take, *Inf.* make a hit, *Sl.* click.

connected, *adj.* **1.** joined, linked, tied, bound, spliced, fastened, lashed; chained, coupled, linked; secured, anchored, moored; conjoined, conjoint, subjoined, fixed, affixed, attached, annexed; tacked, stapled, hooked, nailed, pinned, riveted; fused, soldered, welded; taped, glued, cemented; sealed; clasped, buttoned, buckled.

2. merged, combined, associated, consociated, amalgamated, consolidated, incorporated; united, unified, leagued, allied, confederated, federated; in union, in league, in alliance; in common, in conjunction, in association.

3. mutual, shared, common, communal, collective; cooperative, cooperating, collaborative, collaborating, coordinated, coordinate, synergetic, synergistic; concerted, coactive, hand in hand, arm in arm; coalitional, conjunctive, conjugate, conjunct, corporate, corporative; concordant, agreeing, concurrent, consentual, consentaneous, consentient, concomitant.

4. related, affinal, affined, affinitive, agnate, cognate, *Gram.* paronymous; correlative, *Bot.* homogenous, alike; kindred, akin, sib; pertinent, relevant, appropos, germane, to the point, apt, apposite.

5. adjoining, joining, conjoining, contiguous, abutting, tangential, tangent, contactual, touching, meeting, *Obs.* attingent; adjacent, bordering, skirting, edging, proximate, juxtapositional, juxtaposed, next to,

Inf. right next to, *Inf.* next door to.

connection, *n.* **1.** union, junction, conjunction, juncture, conjuncture, conjugation, marriage, *Inf.* hookup; unification, accouplement, joinder; juxtaposition, collocation; joining, linking, uniting, binding, bonding, splicing, yoking; connecting, conjoining, coupling; meeting, edging, bordering, skirting, abutting.
2. intersection, nexus, connexus, point of union *or* contact; focus, focal point, focalization; coalescence, confluence; abutment, abuttal.
3. coherence, cohesion, adherence, adhesion; congruity, congruence, congruousness, harmony, harmoniousness, conformity, uniformity, consistency, connectedness; relevance, relevancy, pertinence, germaneness, applicability, appositeness; affinity, rapport.
4. link, tie, bond, knot, yoke; coupler, coupling, connective; joint, joiner, articulation, commissure; pivot, hinge, elbow, knee, dovetail joint, rabbet, rabbet joint; linkage, concatenation, chain; seam, suture, welt; clamp, clasp, latch, buckle, clip.
5. association, affiliation, relationship, relatedness, tie-in; attachment, dependence, mutual dependence.
6. merger, amalgamation, consolidation, incorporation; alliance, league, federation, confederation, bund, entente, combination; society, order, fraternity, sorority; cabal, conspiracy; coterie, set, circle, clique, cluster, *Inf.* bunch, *Inf.* gang, *Inf.* team, *Inf.* crew.
7. context, contextual relation, reference, frame of reference, bearing, *Archaic.* concernment.
8. relative, relation, blood relation, kinsman, sibling, sib, agnate, cognate; family, kin, kith and kin, kinsfolk, people, flesh and blood, *Inf.* folks; in-law, relative-in-law; kinship, relationship, blood relationship, consanguinity, family tie.
9. *Slang.* (*all of commerce in narcotics*) source, contact, *Sl.* main man; *Sl.* pusher, *Sl.* dealer.
10. *Usu.* **connections** pull, in, contacts; contact, go-between, middleman, intermediary, medium, friend at court.
11. sexual intercourse, sexual commerce *or* union *or* congress, sex, intercourse, mating; intimacy, carnal knowledge, sexual *or* marital relations, sleeping together *or* with; copulation, coitus, coition, *Archaic.* venery, sex act, act of love.

connivance, *n.* **1.** overlooking *or* purposely overlooking, ignoring, disregarding, paying no regard *or* heed to, paying no attention to, taking no notice *or* note of, being blind to, turning a blind eye to, closing *or* shutting one's eyes to, looking the other way, pretending not to notice, blinking the fact, winking *or* blinking at, feigning ignorance, hearing nothing, not hearing a word, *Inf.* taking, *Inf.* paying no mind *or* heed to; making light of, passing over, glossing over, letting pass, *Inf.* letting it go.
2. condoning, allowing for, making allowances for, being indulgent; suffering, countenancing, enduring, tolerating, bearing, bearing with, brooking, stomaching, putting up with, standing for; pardoning, excusing, forgiving, remitting, letting off.
3. conspiring, colluding, intriguing, plotting; (*all in criminal activity*) lending oneself to, being a party to, privately consenting, having a finger in the pie, *Inf.* being on the take; (*all in criminal activity*) interacting, coacting, interfacing, synergizing, combining, cooperating, collaborating, working together *or* in unison *or* side by side, acting jointly *or* in concert.
4. implied consent, tacit consent *or* approval *or* encouragement, secret approval, allowance, sufferance, tolerance, toleration, condonation *or* secret condonation; voluntary oversight, pretended ignorance; collusion, complicity, conspiracy, intrigue, corridor intrigue, jobbery, playing politics, *Chiefly U.S. Pol.* logrolling, indirect abetment *or* encouragement, remote participation; (*all in criminal activity*) interaction, coaction, synergy, cooperation, collaboration.

connive, *v.* **1.** overlook *or* purposely overlook, ignore, disregard, pay no regard *or* heed to, pay no attention to, take no notice *or* note of, be blind to, turn a blind eye, close *or* shut one's eyes to, look the other way, pretend not to notice, blink the fact, blink *or* wink at, feign ignorance, hear nothing, not hear a word, *Inf.* take, *Inf.* pay no mind *or* heed; make light of, pass over, gloss over, let pass, *Inf.* let it go.
2. condone, allow for, make allowances for, be indulgent; suffer, countenance, endure, tolerate, bear, bear with, brook, stomach, put up with, stand for; pardon, excuse, forgive, remit, let off.
3. conspire, collude, cabal, intrigue, plot, complot; (*all usually in criminal activity*) lend oneself to, be a party to, privately consent, play politics, have a finger in the pie; (*all usually in criminal activity*) interact, coact, interface, synergize, combine, cooperate, collaborate, work together *or* in unison *or* side by side, act jointly *or* in concert.

connoisseur, *n.* aesthete, epicure, (*both of food*) gourmet, gourmand; judge, critic, arbiter of taste, *Latin. arbiter elegantiae*; expert, authority, specialist, pundit, savant, maven, one of the cognoscenti.

connotation, *n.* **1.** suggestion, implication, signification, insinuation; allusion, reference.
2. subsense, undermeaning, undercurrent, undertone; nuance, touch, hint, intimation; inference, supposition, coloration; meaning, sense, significance, purport, import.

connotative, *adj.* suggestive, implicative, expressive, indicative, inferential, significative; allusive, referential; latent, underlying, under the surface, between the lines; implicit, tacit, understood, unspoken, unvoiced, unsaid, unuttered, unexpressed.

connote, *v.* suggest, imply, infer, hint at, intimate, insinuate, allude to; involve, include, implicate; mean, signify, indicate, import, purport, betoken, bespeak, point to.

connubial, *adj.* conjugal, matrimonial, nuptial, hymeneal, epithalamic; marital, married, wedded; spousal, husbandly, wifely, bridal.

conquer, *v.* **1.** (*all by force of arms*) acquire, obtain, win; overrun, occupy, annex; seize, take, take over, appropriate.
2. vanquish, subdue, subjugate, master, overmaster, overpower, overwhelm, overthrow, defeat; reduce, prostrate, flatten, crush, smash, break, humble, bring [s.o.] to his knees; suppress, quell, put down, beat down.
3. overcome, surmount, rise above, triumph over, prevail over, best, get the better *or* best of; prevail, triumph, succeed, win, *Inf.* come out on top.

conqueror, *n.* victor, victress, victrix; champion, hero, winner, triumpher; master, conquistador, subjugator, subduer, defeater, vanquisher.

conquest, *n.* **1.** vanquishment, subjugation, subjection, mastery, domination, overthrow, defeat; appropriation, seizure, *Inf.* takeover, occupation.
2. seduction, captivation, enchantment, allurement, enticement, inveiglement, enthrallment, fascination.
3. victory, triumph, success, win, walkaway, *Sl.* pushover, *Sl.* picnic; catch, captive, acquisition; feat, coup, feather in one's cap.
4. spoils, booty, plunder, loot, haul, take, prize, *Sl.* swag.

consanguinity, *n.* kinship, blood relationship, family tie *or* connection, common ancestry *or* lineage, cognation; filiation, enation, agnation, sibship; relationship, connection, association, affiliation.

conscience, *n.* **1.** sense of right and wrong, moral sense, inward monitor; the still, small voice; principles, scruples, morals, ethics, standards.
2. uprightness, honesty, probity, rectitude, integrity, conscientiousness.
3. **in all conscience** in all reason and fairness, in faith, in truth, truly, certainly, assuredly; honestly, upon my honor.

conscience-stricken, *adj.* contrite, pentitent, penitential, repentant; compunctious, remorseful, regretful, regretting, sorry, troubled, disturbed; guilt-ridden, self-accusing, self-reproachful; chastened, humbled, shamed, ashamed, embarrassed, chagrined.

conscientious, *adj.* **1.** scrupulous, principled, right-minded, ethical, moral, conscionable; upright, righteous, just, honorable, upstanding, high-minded; good, sincere, honest, true, all wool and a yard wide; earnest, hard-working, dedicated, devoted, faithful, loyal.
2. careful, cautious, prudent, politic, discreet, judicious, circumspect; mindful, thoughtful, regardful, heedful, attentive, solicitous; meticulous, punctilious, exact, precise, accurate; correct, proper, decorous, rigid, stiff, starched; particular, finical, finicky, picky, fussy, hard to please; critical, exacting, demanding, fastidious; painstaking, minute, detailed, fine, nice, thorough, searching; scientific, mathematical, severe, rigorous, strict, close.

conscious, *adj.* **1.** aware, sentient, alive to, *Archaic.* ware; cognizant, sensible of, familiar with, acquainted with, *Sl.* wise to; mindful, regardful, observant, awake, wide-awake, alert, on the beam *or* ball, thinking, reasoning; self-conscious, self-aware, knowing, percipient.
2. known, felt, perceived, apperceived, realized, experienced.
3. deliberate, intentional, on purpose, volitional, willed, willful; premeditated, designed, calculated.

consciousness, *n.* awareness, *Inf.* living daylights, sentience, sensibility, sensitivity; cognizance, familiarity, acquaintance; observance, consideration, mindfulness, regardfulness; wakefulness, alertness, watchfulness; perception, apperception, understanding, comprehension, apprehension, recognition, realization, intuition.

conscript, *v.* **1.** (*in reference to military service*) draft, induct, conscribe, impress, press, *Naut.* shanghai, crimp; recruit, enlist, *Archaic.* list, muster in, levy; activate, call up, mobilize.
2. recruit, procure, muster, gather up *or* together; secure, obtain, enroll, register; engage, take on, hire, employ.
3. commandeer, coerce, compel, force, pressure, *Inf.* strong-arm, dragoon; oblige, constrain, impel.
—*n.* **4.** (*all in reference to the military*) recruit, inductee, enlistee, draftee; cadet, plebe *or* pleb; buck private, private, P.F.C., seaman.

conscription, *n.* **1.** (*all in reference to military service*) draft, compulsory enrollment; enlistment, muster-in, levy, recruitment.
2. registration, sign-up; engagement, procurement, securing, hiring; gathering, assembling, mustering.

consecrate, *v.* **1.** sanctify, hallow, make holy, bless, anoint; canonize, *Rom. Cath. Ch.* beatify; deify, god, apotheosize.
2. devote, dedicate, pledge, promise, vow; commit, consign, assign, apply, give.
3. venerate, honor, esteem, revere, bow down to; glorify, extol, exalt, praise, laud, celebrate, *Archaic.* magnify.

consecration, *n.* sanctification, dedication, devotion, hallowing, blessing, anointing, *Eccles.* ordination; canonization, *Rom. Cath. Ch.* beatification; deification, godding, apotheosis.

consecutive, *adj.* **1.** successive, sequential, serial, seriate, seriatim, one after the other, progressive, step by step; continuous, uninterrupted, unbroken.
2. orderly, ordinal, consequent, sequent; logical, deducible, reasonable, rational.

consensus, *n.* common consent *or* assent, general agreement, unanimity, consentience, consentaneity, like-mindedness; concord, concordance, concurrence, consonance; agreement, accord, accordance, compliance, conformity, harmony; unity, oneness, oneness of mind, single-mindedness; concert, chorus, one *or* single voice.

consent, *v.* **1.** grant, permit, agree, allow, admit, approve; accept, go along with, *Inf.* take to, *Inf.* cotton to, *Inf.* buy; acknowledge, recognize, *Archaic.* agnize, subscribe to.
2. (*often fol. by* to *or an infinitive*) yield, acquiesce, concede, give in, submit; obey, comply with, abide by, defer to, conform to; side with, fall in with, *Sl.* string along with, go with the stream, join in the chorus, go with the current.
3. testify, endorse, uphold, sustain, corroborate, substantiate, verify, confirm, ratify, homologate; countersign, seal; check, visa, vise, clinch.
—*n.* **4.** permission, go-ahead, *Inf.* green light, approval, approbation.
5. agreement, acceptance, concurrence, accord, accordance; unanimity, unison, consensus; acknowledgment, recognition, confession, admission, avowal, affirmation.
6. compliance, abidance, conformity, obedience, morigeration, allegiance, observance; acquiescence, accedence, yielding, concession, submission, capitulation.
7. confirmation, corroboration, endorsement, verification, ratification; sanction, visa, vise, check.

consequence, *n.* **1.** result, effect, event, outcome, issue, upshot, sequel; aftermath, outgrowth, afterclap, turnout, aftereffect, fallout, wake; reaction, repercussion, reverberation.
2. inference, implication, conclusion, deduction, illation, corollary.
3. importance, significance, signification, portent, moment; weight, weightiness, greatness, import, force; magnitude, note, merit, value, substance; gravity, emphasis, stress, urgency; interest, concern, matter.
4. distinction, standing, elevation, grandeur; prominence, prestige, eminence, influence; notability, repute, fame, report; name, account, regard, esteem; mark, caliber, rank.

consequent, *adj.* **1.** resulting, consequential, resultant; owing to, due to, attributable to, ascribable to, derivable from; following, ensuing, subsequent, sequential, successive, sequent.
2. inferential, implicative, illative; deductive, derivative, educible, logical.

consequential, *adj.* **1.** resultant, resulting, following. See **consequent** (*defs.* **1, 2**).
2. important, significant, noteworthy, notable; momentous, eventful, epochal, weighty, portentous; considerable, substantial, big, impressive; grave, serious, pressing, urgent, critical; striking, salient, marked, signal.
3. self-important, proud, vainglorious, lordly; vain, conceited, egotistical; pompous, haughty, pretentious, *Inf.* uppity; arrogant, supercilious, bumptious, insolent, impudent; presumptuous, overweening, overconfident, *Inf.* uppish.

conservation, *n.* preservation, preserving, saving, reservation, protection; supervision, control, keeping, safe-keeping, care, charge, custody; maintenance, upkeep, support.

conservatism, *n.* **1.** traditionalism, conventionalism, orthodoxness, orthodoxy; preservation of the status quo, resistance to change, die-hardism; conservativeness, moderation, caution, prudence.

2. political conservatism, rightism, reaction, Hunkerism, Hunkerousness; ultraconservatism, Birchism, Bourbonism.

conservative, *adj.* **1.** opposed to change, diehard, reactionary, ultra-conservative; (*all of politics*) right-wing, rightist, Birchist, Birchite, Bourbonian, Hunkerous, Tory, Toryish.

2. cautious, prudent, careful, *Inf.* go-slow; moderate, temperate, sober, stable, unchanging, *Anthropol.* Apollonian; unprogressive, old-fashioned, *Sl.* square, *Sl.* straight, traditional, conventional, orthodox, standard; Ivy-league, *Inf.* button-down; middle-American, middle-class, bourgeois.

3. preservative, conservational, conserving, protective, protecting, saving.

—n. **4.** champion of the status quo, *Inf.* stick-in-the-mud, die-hard, *Inf.* hardhat; *Sl.* square, *Sl.* straight; political conservative, right-winger, rightist, reactionary, Bircher, Bourbon, Hunker, Tory.

conservator, *n.* guardian, custodian, keeper, caretaker, janitor, concierge, guard, watchman, warder; superintendent, *Inf.* super, supervisor, overseer, warden, manager, curator, steward.

conservatory, *n.* **1.** greenhouse, *Brit.* glasshouse, hothouse; nursery, arboretum, vinery; pleasure-garden, pleasure-grove, green court, viridarium; summerhouse, gazebo, pavilion.

2. conservatoire, music school, drama school, school of fine arts; institute, academy; studio, workshop, atelier.

conserve, *v.* **1.** preserve, keep, save, protect, guard, shield; take care of, maintain, keep up, support.

2. save, use sparingly, *Inf.* go easy on, reserve, set aside, spare, leave alone.

—n. **3.** *Often* **conserves** compote, fruit soup; preserves, jam, marmalade, jelly, julep; confiture, confection, comfit, sweetmeat, sugarplum, bonbon.

consider, *v.* **1.** contemplate, weigh, think over, turn over in one's mind, give thought to, mull over; ponder, *Archaic.* perpend, ruminate, cogitate, meditate on, brood over, muse on; deliberate, reflect upon, revolve, put one's mind to, give one's attention to, pay attention to, study, pore over, examine; chew over, talk over, discuss; envisage, envision, dream of; think about, kick around, tinker with, toy with, flirt with the idea.

2. heed, mark, note, observe; bear in mind, take into account, factor into, take into consideration, keep in view, make allowance for.

3. deem, adjudge, judge, think, believe, hold, opine, suppose; estimate, gauge, appraise, rate.

4. regard, respect, esteem, value, honor.

considerable, *adj.* **1.** sizable, *Inf.* tidy, *Inf.* pretty, substantial, appreciable; large, big, great; goodly, tolerable, fair, decent, reasonable.

2. distinguished, noteworthy, respectable, estimable, praiseworthy, remarkable, extraordinary; valuable, important, influential; illustrious, renowned, venerable.

considerate, *adj.* **1.** thoughtful, kind, kindly, kind-hearted, compassionate, tender, sympathetic, patient, forbearing; benevolent, beneficent, charitable, generous, unselfish; aware, sensitive, attentive, mindful, heedful, concerned, solicitous; friendly, neighborly, welcoming, gracious, obliging, accommodating.

2. considered, deliberate, deliberated, well-thought-out; prudent, careful, circumspect, circumspective.

consideration, *n.* **1.** attention, notice, heed, advertency; observation, examination, inspection, scrutiny, review; advisement, consultation.

2. deliberation, reflection, contemplation, speculation, thought; meditation, rumination, cogitation, musing; forethought, premeditation.

3. thoughtfulness, kindliness, kind-heartedness; compassion, sympathy, patience, forbearance; friendliness, benevolence, beneficence, generosity; attentiveness, concern, solicitude.

4. recompense, compensation, emolument, perquisite, remuneration, fee, payment; gratuity, tip, *Fr. pourboire.*

5. importance, import, significance, value; consequence, weight, moment.

6. estimation, esteem, honor, reverence, regard, respect, admiration.

considering, *prep.* bearing in mind, keeping in view, in view of, in light of, taking into consideration, taking into account, making allowance for.

consign, *v.* **1.** hand over, deliver, transfer, convey; remand, remit; give over, resign, yield; entrust, assign, delegate, relegate; bequeath, leave to, commend to, refer to, confide to; deposit with, commission, authorize.

2. *Commerce.* send, post, mail, ship, dispatch, freight, transmit.

consignment, *n.* delivery, transferal, giving over, relinquishment; entrustment, assignment, trust, delegation, relegation, bequest; commission, warrant, mandate; office, mission, errand, task.

consignor, *n.* merchant, vendor, seller; transmitter, shipper, dispatcher; shipping *or* freight company, transfer company.

consist, *v.* **1.** *Usu.* **consist in** be comprised in, be contained in, be constituted by; inhere in, lie in.

2. *Usu.* **consist of** be composed of, be made up of, be made from *or* with, be formed of; contain, hold, embrace, incorporate, involve, embody.

3. *Usu.* **consist with** harmonize, agree, accord with, conform; be compatible, be consistent, jibe, fit in with, go along with; accommodate, suit, befit, become.

consistency, *n.* **1.** coherence, holding together, retention of form, maintenance of solidity *or* firmness; density, firmness, thickness, viscosity.

2. adherence, attachment, devotion, constancy, faithfulness, fidelity, fealty, loyalty, allegiance; compliance, obedience, abidance, acquiescence, concurrence.

3. agreement, harmony, accordance, concordance; congruity, correspondence, consonance, compatibility, correlation, conformity.

consistent, *adj.* **1.** agreeing, accordant, concordant, compatible, congruous, consonant, harmonious, conformable.

2. undeviating, true to type, steady, dependable, regular; uniform, identical, selfsame, unchanging.

3. cohering, adhering, clinging, tenacious, persistent; devoted, faithful, loyal, *Inf.* tried and true.

consistently, *adv.* **1.** unswervingly, staunchly, firmly, faithfully, resolutely, unfailingly, without fail, dependably.

2. steadily, repeatedly, regularly, over and over, day in and day out, like clockwork.

consolation, *n.* **1.** comfort, pity, sympathy, compassion, commiseration, condolence, solace.

2. relief, easing, easement, soothing; softening, cushioning, mollification, lightening; smoothing, calming; mitigation, abatement, remission; reduction, diminution, lessening, slackening, weakening, relaxation; alleviation, assuagement, palliation, appeasement; slaking, deadening, dulling, blunting; tempering, moderating, moderation.

console, *v.* comfort, solace, afford consolation; share [s.o.'s] misery, lament with. See **comfort** (*def.* 1).

consolidate, *v.* **1.** unite, coalesce, league, incorporate, confederate, federate, syndicate; associate, affiliate, ally, pair up, correlate; pool, herd, flock, team, club, join forces, band together, pull together; unify, bring *or* draw together, grow together, ankylose, become one; concentrate, condense, compact, compress, streamline; centralize, federalize, nationalize.

2. combine, amalgamate, merge, blend, mix, conglomerate, agglomerate, lump together; connect, attach, join, conjoin, bind, tie together, bond, fuse; cohere, stick together, hold together.

3. solidify, congeal, harden, concrete, stiffen, set; strengthen, fortify, reinforce.

consolidation, *n.* **1.** unification, union, incorporation, confederation, federation, centralization, syndication, association, coalition; combination, amalgamation, conglomeration, agglomeration, connection, junction, conjunction, conjugation, fusion.

2. unity, unitedness, coalescence, oneness; connectedness, attachment, bondedness, coherence, cohesion.

3. solidification, concretion, hardening, stiffening; condensation, concentration, compression, compacting; strengthening, fortification, reinforcement.

consoling, *adj.* comforting, solacing, sympathetic, commiserative, compassionate, relieving, easing, assuasive, palliative, ameliorative, lenitive; queling, calming, peace-giving, restorative.

consonance, *n.* **1.** accord, concord, concordance, consonancy; agreement, accordance, conformity, conformance, conformation; correspondence, correspondency, congruity, congruence, congruousness; unanimity, consentience, consentaneity, consentaneousness, like-mindedness; unity, oneness, oneness of mind *or* purpose, single-mindedness; unison, consensus, joint *or* general agreement.

2. harmony, harmoniousness, euphony, symphony, homophony, monody, concert, concentus, *Rare.* unisonance, *Obs.* consort; tune, melody, diapason; chord, resonance, chime, chiming, attune, attunement; chorus, one voice, single voice.

3. rhyme, assonance, alliteration, crambo, *Archaic.* clink.

consonant, *n.* **1.** *Phonetics.* sonorant, sonant, sibilant; fricative, spirant; surd; stop; liquid.

—adj. **2.** agreeing, in agreement, agreeable, accordant, in accord, concordant, corresponding, correspondent, in correspondence; concurring, concurrent, consentient, consentaneous; complying, compliant, conforming, conformable; coherent, cohesive, consistent, congruent, congruous; unanimous, in unison, at one, in rapport, of the same mind, of one mind, like-minded, single-minded.

3. harmonious, in harmony, euphonious, symphonic, symphonious, homophonic, monodic; tuneful, in tune; melodious, melodic, musical, pleasant-sounding, pleasant to the ear; resonant, chiming.

4. consonantal, consonantic.

consort, *n.* **1.** spouse, husband, wife, better half, other half, *Humorous.* rib, squaw; helpmate, helpmeet, mate, partner.

2. companion, comrade, crony, chum, *Fr. copain,* sidekick, shadow, alter ego; friend, ally, *Inf.* pal, *U.S. Inf.* buddy, *Sl.* cully, *Sl.* Siamese twin.

—v. **3.** associate with, keep company with, hang out *or* around with, go around with, *Inf.* pal around with; fraternize, mingle with, mix with; couple with, pair off with.

4. agree, harmonize, blend, adapt, accommodate; correspond, jibe, tally.

conspicuous, *adj.* **1.** observable, recognizable, discernible, perceptible, distinguishable; defined, distinct, well-defined, well-marked; visible, vivid, graphic; unhidden, undisguised, unconcealed, unmistakable; unveiled, uncurtained, unshrouded, unscreened.

2. evident, plain, plain as day, plain as the nose on one's face, obvious, palpable, manifest, apparent; explicit, clear-cut, patent, express; pronounced, prominent, marked; unequivocal, unquestionable, incontrovertible.

3. blatant, obtrusive, flagrant, glaring, egregious; overt, bold, bald, baldfaced.

4. garish, gaudy, tawdry, loud, lurid, screaming; vulgar, coarse, tasteless, crass; showy, ostentatious.

5. striking, impressive, imposing, majestic, grand, august, stately, dignified; awesome, awe-inspiring, lofty, wondrous, marvelous, prodigious; distinguished, eminent, famous, famed, well-known, renowned; illustrious, glorious, brilliant, radiant, lustrous.

conspiracy, *n.* **1.** collusion, connivance, *Law.* covin; machination, manipulation, maneuvering, engineering, wire-pulling, foul play, sharp practice.

2. plot, complot, scheme, *Inf.* racket, *Inf.* little game; artifice, contrivance, stratagem, design, *Inf.* frame-up.

3. cabal, camarilla, junta, clique, secret society; coalition, alliance, confederacy.

4. concurrence, accord, agreement; collaboration, cooperation, coaction, affiliation; unification, combination, *Sl.* hookup, *Sl.* tie-in.

conspirator, *n.* confederate, collaborator, collaborationist, colluder, abettor, accomplice; cabalist, schemer, plotter, intriguer, conspirer, conniver; operator, machinator, engineer, *Inf.* finagler, *Inf.* wire-puller.

conspire, *v.* **1.** plot, complot, scheme, intrigue, cabal, be up to something *or* no good, *Dial.* collogue; machinate, maneuver, engineer, rig, operate, *Inf.* frame.

2. collaborate, cooperate, collude, concur, coact, *Sl.* play footsie with, *Sl.* be in cahoots with, *Sl.* be in bed with; unite, combine, join, join hands *or* forces, gang up on [s.o.], *Inf.* hitch horses.

constancy, *n.* **1.** faithfulness, fidelity, fealty, devotion, devotedness, abidingness, attachment, allegiance, loyalty; ardor, zeal, eagerness, earnestness; trustiness, trustworthiness, dependability, reliability; truthfulness, honesty, integrity, honor, principle.

2. steadfastness, steadiness, resolution, resoluteness, firmness, determination, decisiveness, purposiveness; perseverance, tenacity, *Inf.* stick-to-it-iveness; application, adherence, industry, diligence; fortitude, backbone, grit, mettle, pluck, *Inf.* sand; obstinateness, obstinacy, doggedness, stubbornness, *Inf.* cussedness, inflexibility, intransigence, obdurateness, contumacy, contumaciousness.

3. uniformity, regularity, similarity, sameness, invariableness; stability, permanence, fixedness; immutability, unchangeableness, unchangingness, incorruptibility, irreversibility.

constant, *adj.* **1.** uniform, regular, even, same, identical, systematic, methodical, invariable, fixed; firm, fast, solid, steady, stable; permanent, abiding,

enduring; immutable, unalterable, incommutable, unchanging, changeless, unchangeable, irreversible.
2. perpetual, endless, unending, never-ending, interminable, Sisyphean, eternal, everlasting; ceaseless, incessant, unceasing, nonstop, uninterrupted, continual, continuous, unbroken; unremitting, unintermitting, relentless, persistent; recurrent, repeated, frequent, habitual.
3. faithful, devoted, loyal, staunch, tried and true, trustworthy, true-hearted; steadfast, unwavering, unfaltering, undeviating, unswerving, reliable, dependable; resolute, determined, serious, decided, undaunted, indomitable; persevering, industrious, assiduous, sedulous; persistent, relentless, plodding, untiring, unflagging, unwearied, indefatigable; tenacious, dogged, strong-willed, grim, unshrinking; game, plucky, gritty; obstinate, stubborn, *Inf.* cussed, uncompromising, unbending, unyielding, inflexible, obdurate, contumacious.

constellation, *n.* **1.** *Astron.* configuration, *Astron., Rare.* asterism.
2. (*all of important or famous persons*) galaxy, pleiad, cluster, assemblage, gathering, group, body, company.

consternation, *n.* bewilderment, mystification, befuddlement, confusion; agitation, disquietude, perturbation; amazement, astonishment, surprise; panic, alarm, stupefaction, stupefiedness, paralysis; trepidation, dread, terror, horror, fear, fright; dismay, disheartenment, disillusionment.

constipated, *adj.* costive, *Pathol.* bound, blocked, impacted, *Euph.* in a bind.

constipation, *n.* costiveness, obstipation.

constituent, *adj.* **1.** component, integral, elemental. See **component** (*def.* **1**).
—*n.* **2.** part, element, unit. See **component** (*def.* **3**).
3. voter, elector, balloter.

constitute, *v.* **1.** compose, form, make, comprise, make up, consist of, compound; incorporate, embody.
2. appoint, nominate, name, deputize, depute, ordain; install, inaugurate, confirm, induct, commission.
3. establish, create, originate, develop; set up, found, institute, occasion, bring about, give rise to.
4. enact, draft, pass into law; legislate, ordain, decree.

constitution, *n.* **1.** composition, make-up, structure, *Archaic.* crasis; organization, synthesis, formation, configuration; arrangement, contexture, construction, conformation.
2. physique, build, body, physical nature; strength, vigor, health, power.
3. disposition, aspect, temperament, mood, mettle; character, nature, spirit, condition, state; essence, quiddity, idiosyncrasy, idiocrasy, singularity, particularity.
4. establishment, formation, founding, creation, foundation; institution, introduction, enactment, inception.
5. body of laws, *Latin. corpus juris*, code, charter, pandect, canon; rules, laws, principles.

constitutional, *adj.* **1.** inherent, inbred, intrinsic; inborn, innate, instinctive, congenital, connate, *Archaic.* ingenerate; indwelling, immanent, ingrained, infixed, implanted, instilled; indigenous, rooted, natural, native.
2. healthful, beneficial, salubrious, salutary, salutiferous; wholesome, hygienic, healthy, nutritious.
3. essential, fundamental, basic, elementary, basal; integral, component, constituent.
4. lawful, legal, legitimate, licit; statutory, chartered, vested; statuable, rightful, authorized, prescribed, permitted.
—*n.* **5.** walk, stroll, airing, amble, saunter, promenade, march; ramble, perambulation, hike, outing, tramp; trot, jog, jog trot, run.

constrain, *v.* **1.** coerce, compel, force, drive, press, pressure, oblige, hustle, railroad; impel, urge, impress, provoke, instigate, extort; cause, require, (*usu. used passively*) bind, exact, necessitate, make; draft, conscript, commandeer; persuade, induce, prevail upon, insist upon, pin [s.o.] down, *Inf.* shove *or* ram down one's throat; apply pressure, *Sl.* lean against *or* on, armtwist, twist [s.o.'s] arm, put the screws on *or* to, *Inf.* strong-arm, put the heat on, squeeze.
2. tyrannize, terrorize, threaten, bulldoze, dragoon; bully, hector, torment, harass, abuse, taunt, tease, bullyrag; intimidate, browbeat, cow, frighten, terrify, petrify.
3. confine, restrict, hem in, hedge in, tie down; check, curb, limit; bind, astrict, tie, bound; enclose, shut in, shut up, keep in, quarantine, isolate; cage, coop, pen in, rail in, fence, corral; box up, bottle up, seal up; lock up, imprison, jail, incarcerate, impound, wall in, immure, put in irons.
4. repress, inhibit, stifle; hamper, hinder, impede; restrain, hold back, hold in, control, suppress, swallow.

constraint, *n.* **1.** confinement, imprisonment, incarceration, durance, detention; captivity, chains, bonds; bondage, slavery, servitude, thralldom, subjugation, enthrallment.
2. repression, control, inhibition, stifling, restraint, suppression; diffidence, timidity, bashfulness, reserve, embarrassment.
3. restriction, limitation, check, curb, obstruction, deterrent.
4. coercion, compulsion, force, coaction; pressure, duress, obligation; persuasion, inducement, insistence, armtwisting; urge, provocation, requirement, necessitation, necessity.

constrict, *v.* **1.** cramp, squeeze, tighten, pinch, *Inf.* tighten up on, *Inf.* put the squeeze on, strangle, strangulate, draw *or* press in, bind, wrap up, coarctate, straiten, constringe, compress, astringe; contract, shrink, narrow, reduce, decrease, diminish, cut down *or* short, curtail.
2. impede, obstruct, block, clog, slow, stall, stop, arrest, reign, draw reign, *Inf.* pull back on, bring to a standstill, bring to an impasse, stalemate, checkmate, check, curb, retard, thwart, foil, prevent, inhibit, restrain, repress, constrain, hold, hamstring, delay, frustrate, bar, hold up, tie down, deter, detain, stay, *Inf.* clip one's wings; hinder, hamper, trammel, handicap, fetter, shackle, tie, tie one's hands, manacle; encumber, cumber, burden, saddle with; limit, restrict, confine, circumscribe, keep within bounds, bound, demarcate, define.

constriction, *n.* **1.** cramping, squeezing, tightening, pinching, strangling, strangulation, binding, wrapping up, coarctation, straitening, constringing, compression, compressing, astringing; contraction, contracting, shrinkage, shrinking, narrowing, *Obs.* angustation, reduction, reducing, decrease, decreasing, diminution, diminishing, cutting down *or* short, curtailment, curtailing.
2. tightness, contracture, stricture, inner pressure, astringency, strangulation, strangling, choking, squeezing, binding; cramp, crick, crimp, stitch, crink, pang, ache, throe; spasm, muscle spasm, convulsion.
3. knot, charley horse, gnarl, block; lump, bump, bulge, swell, swelling, tumescence, hump, knob, protuberance, node, nodule, nodulus.
4. impediment, obstruction, blockage, clog, clog-

ging, standstill, impasse, stalemate, checkmate, check, curb, curbing, retardation, thwarting, foil, prevention, preventing, inhibition, inhibiting, restraint, restraining, repression, repressing, constraint, constraining, hold, hamstring, delay, frustration, bar, deterrent, stay; hindrance, hampering, handicap, fetters, shackles, manacles, *Inf.* handcuffs; encumbrance, incumbrance, cumbrance, burden; limitation, limiting, restriction, restricting, circumscription, boundary, line of demarcation, pale.

5. *Phonetics.* (*all of the vocal tract*) closure, occlusion, stoppage, block, glottal stop, obstruction.

construct, *v.* **1.** build, frame, assemble, set up, put together; erect, elevate, raise, put up; manufacture, produce, fabricate, make.

2. form, fashion, mold, model, shape; forge, hammer out, sculpture, cast, block; create, invent, compose, devise, formulate, design.

construction, *n.* **1.** building, assembly, erection, elevation, architecture, tectonics; fabrication, manufacture, production; formulation, formation, fashioning, molding, shaping, forging.

2. structure, framework, build, form, make; composition, constitution, organization, configuration, arrangement, make-up; design, format, layout, style.

3. explanation, explication, clarification, exegesis, translation; interpretation, reading, rendering, analysis, commentary.

constructive, *adj.* **1.** helpful, advantageous, beneficial; productive, useful, practical.

2. structural, architectural, tectonic.

3. inferential, inferred, implied, implicit, deduced, derived; interpretive, interpretative, made up.

construe, *v.* **1.** explain, explicate, expound, interpret, translate; clarify, elucidate, spell out.

2. deduce, infer, gather, take, take to mean, understand by; diagnose, read, read into, read between the lines; decipher, unravel, resolve, figure out, make out, puzzle out, put two and two together.

consul, *n.* attaché, commercial attaché, consular agent, consul general.

consult, *v.* **1.** call in, seek the opinion of, confer with, seek *or* ask advice *or* information from, refer to.

2. take into account, have an eye to, regard, respect, have consideration *or* regard *or* respect for, be considerate of, be thoughtful of.

3. consider, deliberate, confer, parley, palaver, sit down together, hold conference, *Inf.* powwow, *Inf.* huddle, *Inf.* go into a huddle, *Inf.* put *or* lay heads together, *Inf.* talk turkey; discuss with, talk with, take up with, talk over, compare notes, exchange views *or* opinions.

consultation, *n.* **1.** conference, deliberation, consideration, examination, study, analysis; dialogue, debate, conversation, communication.

2. meeting, parley, palaver, colloquy, huddle, *Inf.* powwow; convention, council, caucus, session; talk, discussion, tête-à-tête, *Sl.* rap, *Sl.* rap session, *Sl.* bull session; forum, symposium, seminar, colloquium, round table; interview, audience, sitting.

consume, *v.* **1.** expend, use up, exhaust, drain, deplete, empty; finish, finish off, *Sl.* polish off, dispose of, get rid of, *Sl.* do in.

2. (*all of food or drink*) devour, absorb, eat up, swallow, gulp down, drink up, guzzle, gobble, bolt, wolf, *Inf.* put away *or* down, *Inf.* pack away *or* in.

3. devour, eat up, swallow up, envelop; engulf, inundate, deluge, swamp, submerge; drown, choke, smother, overcome; destroy, ruin, *Dial.* ruinate, ravage, wreak havoc upon; devastate, desolate, lay to waste, waste, *Sl.* kill; demolish, wipe out, wreck, *Sl.* total; raze, gut, fell, prostrate, level; wipe off the map, erase, obliterate, eradicate. See **destroy** (*defs.* **1,2,4,6**).

4. waste, dissipate, squander, fritter *or* fool away, lose, throw away, lavish, misspend, misuse, *Sl.* blow, spend foolishly.

5. absorb, engross, take up *or* in, draw in; preoccupy, occupy *or* seize the mind, engage wholly; mesmerize, hypnotize, fix, arrest, rivet; fascinate, enwrap, enthrall, grip, hold, hold spellbound, captivate.

6. disintegrate, break up, fall apart, wear out; decay, rot, spoil, rust, go bad; go, fail, quit, *Sl.* conk out, slow down, stop, die, give up, run out; waste away, fade away, ebb, weaken, tire, melt; dissolve, disappear, vanish, perish, evaporate, dissolve *or* disappear into thin air.

consumer, *n.* user, buyer, purchaser, *Both Chiefly Law.* vendee, emptor; shopper, marketer; customer, client, patron, patronizer, regular, *Fr. habitué.*

consummate, *v.* **1.** complete, perfect, crown, top, cap, put the last *or* finishing touch to; finish, carry through, conclude, close, wind up, clinch, clench, seal, bring to a successful end, terminate; fulfill, realize, actualize, achieve, reach, attain, gain; accomplish, compass, carry out, perform, execute, do.

—*adj.* **2.** complete, total, perfect; superior, supreme, transcendent, ultimate, best, matchless; superb, excellent, superlative, extraordinary; remarkable, notable, noteworthy, distinguished; highly accomplished, expert, proficient, adept, skilled, skillful; talented, gifted, endowed, apt; masterful, masterly, professional, veteran, experienced, practiced, versed, *Fr. au fait*; topflight, top-drawer, first-rate, *Inf.* topnotch, ace, *Inf.* crack, *Sl.* crackerjack, *Inf.* whiz-bang.

consummation, *n.* **1.** completion, perfection, final touch *or* stroke; close, end, termination, finish; conclusion, finale, final act *or* scene, last part *or* stage; culmination, climax, capper, denouement.

2. fulfillment, realization, actualization; accomplishment, attainment, acquirement, achievement, fruition, success.

consumption, *n.* **1.** use, expenditure, diminution, loss, reduction, depletion, exhaustion; waste, dissipation, dispersion, misuse; wear and tear, harm, damage; destruction, ruin, ruination, ravagement, devastation; demolition, wrecking, razing, gutting, leveling; wiping out, erasure, effacement, obliteration, eradication. See **destruction** (*defs.* **1, 2, 4, 6**).

2. tuberculosis, TB, white plague, pulmonary phthisis, black lung; gradual wasting away, wastage, decline, emaciation, tabes.

contact, *n.* **1.** touch, tangency, taction; union, juncture, junction, conjunction, association, meeting; connection, adhesion, cohesion.

2. collision, crash, concussion, impact, *Obs.* impingement.

3. adjacency, contiguousness, abuttal, abutment; apposition, juxtaposition; proximity, contiguity, nearness, closeness, propinquity; communication.

4. acquaintance, reference, referral, connection, *Sl.* in.

—*v.* **5.** communicate with, get in touch with, get hold of, reach, look up; approach, seek out; write, phone, call, notify; meet, see.

6. touch, meet, graze, brush, scrape; (*all usu. followed by* on, upon, *or* against) impinge, strike, dash, collide.

contagion, *n.* **1.** (*all usu. of disease*) communication, transmission, transmittal, transference.

2. infection, contamination, pollution, corruption.

3. spread, dispersion, dissemination, propagation, circulation; insinuation, suggestion.

contagious, *adj.* catching, communicable, transmittable, transmissible, transferable, inoculable, infectious, zymotic; spreadable, *Obs.* taking, spreading, carrying, *Vet. Med.* epizootic; epidemic, epidemical, pandemic, miasmal, miasmatic, miasmatical, miasmic, pestilential.

contain, *v.* **1.** hold, receive, admit, carry, seat; accommodate, have capacity for, be capable of holding.
2. comprise, include, comprehend, embrace, subsume, take in, incorporate, embody; enclose, encircle, envelop, enfold, encompass, compass; cover, take into account *or* consideration, involve.
3. restrain, control, keep under control, hold back, bind; repress, suppress, stifle; check, keep in check, *Both Sl.* keep the lid on, place the lid on, curb, halt, limit.

contaminate, *v.* defile, befoul, pollute, corrupt, foul, spoil; sully, taint, soil, besmirch, begrime; infect, poison, envenom, empoison, canker; vitiate, debase, adulterate; deprave, pervert, debauch, degrade, dishonor.

contamination, *n.* **1.** corruption, pollution, befoulment, defilement; infection, poisoning, contagion, septicity; vitiation, debasement, adulteration; degradation, perversion, depravation, debauchment.
2. uncleanness, foulness, impurity, filthiness; depravity, debauchery, dissipation.

contemn, *v.* **1.** disdain, scorn, despise, misprize, show contempt for, view with contempt, hold in contempt, snap one's fingers at, turn up one's nose at, spurn, slight, snub, shun.
2. deprecate, vituperate, disparage, reproach, censure, decry, condemn, vilify; consider beneath oneself, look down on *or* upon, *Sl.* put down.

contemplate, *v.* **1.** watch, keep an eye on, keep a vigil, rivet one's eye upon, stare at, gaze at, view, look at; attend, pay attention to, mind, heed; observe, regard, eye, peer, pry; survey, reconnoiter, scrutinize, scan, examine, inspect; witness, see, notice, note.
2. meditate, muse, ponder, brood, mull over, dwell on; reflect, cogitate, rack one's brains, cudgel one's brains, ruminate, chew over, chew one's cud, be in a brown study; think about *or* over, cerebrate, put on one's thinking cap, be abstracted, be lost in thought; concentrate on, focus on, put one's mind to, have one's mind on; consider, deliberate, excogitate, take to heart, *Archaic.* perpend; revolve, review, turn over, weigh, evaluate, study, con; wonder about, speculate, surmise, suppose, conjecture, theorize, hypothesize.
3. purpose, intend, aim, project, destine, mean; have in view, envisage, envision, visualize, dream of, aspire to, look forward to, imagine, fancy; conceive, think up, have ideas about, *Inf.* dream up; devise, contrive, plan, scheme, plot, design, *Obs.* consult; frame, concoct, invent, brew, hatch.

contemplation, *n.* **1.** watching, keeping an eye on, staring at, gazing at, viewing, looking at; attending, paying attention to, heeding; observation, observing, regarding, eyeing, peering, prying; surveyance, surveying, sighting, reconnaissance, reconnoitering, scrutinization, scrutinizing, scanning, examination, examining, inspection, inspecting; witnessing, seeing, noticing, noting, taking note.
2. meditating, musing, pondering, brooding, mulling over, dwelling on; reflecting, cogitating, ruminating, chewing over, chewing one's cud; thinking about *or* over, cerebrating, being lost in thought; concentrating on, focusing on, having one's mind on; considering, deliberation, deliberating, excogitation, excogitating, revolving, weighing, evaluation, evaluating, studying, conning; wondering about, speculation, speculating, surmising, supposing, conjecture, conjecturing, theorizing, hypothesizing.
3. meditation, reflection, cogitation, rumination, brown study; thought, cerebration, concentration, lucubration, brain work, headwork.
4. purpose, intention, aim, project, destination; proposal, plan, scheme, plot, design, concoction, idea, conception, contrivance.
5. prospect, potential, probability; vision, ambition, dream, aspiration, hope; anticipation, expectation, expectancy.

contemplative, *adj.* **1.** meditative, meditating, musing, pondering, brooding, mulling over; reflective, reflecting, cogitative, cogitating, ruminant, ruminative, ruminating, chewing, chewing one's cud; pensive, thoughtful, concentrating, intent, abstracted, rapt in thought, lost in thought, bemused, *Archaic.* museful; deliberative, excogitative, lucubrative.
—*n.* **2.** monk, *Rom. Cath. Ch.* friar, nun, sister, cenobite; yogi, yogin, yogini.

contemporary, *adj.* **1.** coexistent, coexisting, coeval, coetaneous, coeternal; contemporaneous, simultaneous, coinstantaneous, synchronal, synchronous, isochronal, isochronous; concurrent, concomitant, coincident, parallel; conterminous, coterminous, coextensive.
2. present, present-day, present-time, present-age, twentieth-century, of the here and now; extant, existing, living.
3. modern, modish, mod, fashionable, new-fashioned, newfangled; up-to-date, up-to-the-minute, in, *Inf.* now, *Sl.* hip, *Sl., Obs.* hep, *Sl.* with-it, *Sl.* together.

contempt, *n.* **1.** disdain, scorn, disregard, disrespect, mean *or* low opinion; disgust, loathing, abhorrence, revulsion, detestation; contemptuousness, haughtiness, arrogance, superciliousness, contumely.
2. dishonor, disgrace, shame, ignominy; humiliation, disfavor, disesteem, disrepute, discredit.

contemptible, *adj.* **1.** mean, abject, low, unworthy, base, inferior, loathsome, despicable, wretched, vile, scurvy, currish; shabby, trashy, sleazy, cheap, sordid, *Inf.* low-down, *Inf.* lousy, *Inf.* mangy, *Inf.* scummy.
2. ignominious, despised, miserable, lamentable, pitiful, *Sl.* stinking; worthless, trivial, paltry, sorry, petty, insignificant.

contemptuous, *adj.* **1.** haughty, lordly, pompous, arrogant, high and mighty; supercilious, cavalier, contumelious.
2. scornful, disdainful, insolent, impertinent; flouting, sneering, withering, insulting; cynical, derisive, jeering, scoffing.

contend, *v.* **1.** struggle, wrestle, grapple, tussle, scuffle; battle, fight, combat, war, wage war, skirmish; join battle with, set to, engage, encounter; clash, joust, tilt at, duel, cross swords with, fence; spar, brawl, scrap, box, fall to blows.
2. dispute, debate, argue, wrangle, altercate, *Archaic.* moot; squabble, quarrel, spat, be at loggerheads.
3. compete, vie, rival, contest; oppose, challenge, pit oneself against, play against, take on, face.
4. assert, maintain, hold, claim, profess; allege, affirm, state, aver, asseverate, predicate; declare, pronounce, enunciate.

content[1], *n.* **1. contents a.** insides, *Inf.* innards, inwards; constituents, components, ingredients. **b.** topics, subjects, themes, text, matter, subject matter; chapters, episodes.
2. significance, meaning, purport, intent, import, force; profundity, depth, pith, weight, substance, essence.
3. volume, capacity, mass, density; area, measure, compass; extent, scope, expanse, range, vastness; size,

bulk, magnitude, dimension, bigness, largeness.

content[2], *adj.* **1.** satisfied, gratified, pleased; happy, glad, sunny, cheerful; delighted, charmed.

2. peaceful, tranquil, quiescent, placid; comfortable, snug, at ease, at peace; easygoing, relaxed, complacent, calm, carefree; unworried, untroubled, unconcerned.

—v. **3.** appease, gratify, satisfy; please, delight, gladden, charm, cheer; placate, humor, pacificate; soothe, pacify, mollify, dulcify; pamper, coddle, mollycoddle.

—n. **4.** satisfaction, gratification, contentedness, contentment, complacency; happiness, pleasure, gladness, felicity, delight, cheer.

5. ease of mind, ease, comfort, well-being; quietude, respite, solace; serenity, peace, peacefulness, tranquillity.

contented, *adj.* satisfied, gratified, pleased. See **content**[2] (*defs.* **1, 2**).

contention, *n.* **1.** struggle, conflict, strife, hostilities, combat, war; fight, clash, skirmish, battle, fray, affray, fracas, melee, brawl, barroom brawl, scuffle, tussle; set-to, scrap, fisticuffs, slugfest.

2. rivalry, competition; contest, game, meet. See **contest** (*def.* **2**).

3. dispute, debate, argument, disagreement, dissension; controversy, disputation, contest, logomachy; squabble, altercation, wrangle, broil, quarrel, feud; spat, tiff, jangle, velitation, bicker, row, miff.

4. assertion, claim; opinion, view, belief.

contentious, *adj.* **1.** quarrelsome, argumentative, disputatious, litigious, controversial; dissentious, factious, at loggerheads, at odds, at variance, at issue; captious, fractious, bickering, peevish, querulous; cross, testy, snappish, petulant.

2. competitive, combative, agonistic, competitory, ready to fight; pugnacious, belligerent, bellicose, brawling; opposing, conflicting, antagonistic, hostile.

contentment, *n.* satisfaction, gratification, contentedness; happiness, gladness. See **content**[2] (*defs.* **4, 5**).

contest, *n.* **1.** battle, struggle, conflict. See **contention** (*def.* **1**).

2. competition, contention, rivalry; match, tourney, game, regatta, meet, joust, duel, tug of war; tournament, bout, round, encounter, engagement, *Fr. concours*, athletic event; race, run, dash, sprint; trial, heat, scrimmage; run-off, s lden death, showdown; sweepstakes, derby, handicap, steeplechase; Olympics, *(in ancient Greece)* agon, decathlon, pentathlon, marathon, *(in ancient Greece)* agonistics.

3. dispute, controversy, argument. See **contention** (*def.* **3**).

—v. **4.** struggle, battle, contend, fight, combat, war, wage war; wrestle, grapple, tussle, scuffle; set to, join battle with, engage, encounter; clash, skirmish, conflict; joust, tilt at, duel, fence, cross swords with; spar, brawl, scrap, box, fall to blows, *Sl.* duke.

5. dispute, argue, contend, litigate; oppose, controvert, challenge, impugn, counter; rebut, refute, deny, gainsay, confute; debate, call into question, question, *Rare.* discept.

6. compete, rival, strive against, vie; pit oneself against, play against, oppose, take on, face, challenge.

contestant, *n.* **1.** competitor, contender, rival, opponent, adversary; agonist, protagonist, antagonist.

2. disputer, disputant, litigant.

context, *n.* **1.** connection, contextual relation, relation, relationship, meaning; following words, next sentences; text, substance, subject, theme, topic, matter under discussion.

2. situation, circumstances, conditions, environment, milieu; qualifying factors, state of affairs, facts.

contiguity, *n.* **1.** adjacency, adjacence, juxtaposition, contiguousness, *Obs.* attingency *or* attingence, *Obs.* attiguousness; nearness, closeness, proximity, proximateness, proximation, approximation, propinquity, vicinage.

2. contact, abuttal, abutment; union, conjunction, intersection; meeting, joining, touching, abutting; connecting, conjoining.

3. continuum, continuous *or* unbroken mass *or* stretch, continuous *or* unbroken extent, expanse.

contiguous, *adj.* **1.** touching, meeting, joining, conjoining, connecting, contactual, abutting, tangential, tangent, *Obs.* attingent, *Obs.* attiguous; bordering, skirting, edging, juxtapositional, juxtaposed, proximate, in close proximity, next to, *Inf.* right next to, *Inf.* next door to.

2. adjacent, near, nearby, close, close by, hand by, nigh, neighboring, converging, vicinal.

continence, *n.* **1.** continency, chastity, celibacy, purity; virginity, virtue, innocence, innocency.

2. temperance, temperateness, moderation, moderateness, avoidance of extremes; restraint, self-restraint, self-control; refrainment, refraining, forbearance, desistance; abstention, abstinence, nonindulgence, abstemiousness.

3. Puritanism, austerity, self-mortification, self-deprivation, fasting; asceticism, self-denial, self-abnegation.

4. teetotalism, nephalism, sobriety, soberness; prohibition, blue-ribbonism; Rechabitism.

continent, *n.* **1.** mainland, main, *Latin.* terra firma.

—adj. **2.** chaste, celibate, virgin, virginal; pure, untouched, undefiled; virtuous, innocent, good; pristine, uncorrupted, unsullied, stainless.

3. temperate, moderate, self-restrained, self-controlled; refraining, forbearing, desisting; abstemious, abstinent, nonindulgent, dieting, fasting.

4. puritanical, puritan-like, austere, self-mortifying, self-depriving; ascetic, self-denying, self-abnegating.

5. teetotal, sober, not intoxicated *or* drunk; prohibitionary, *U.S.* dry, blue-ribbon.

contingency, *n.* **1.** chance, mere chance, happy chance, fortuity, serendipity, happenstance, luck, fortune; odds, run of luck; uncertainty, fortuitousness, casualness, randomness, haphazardness, arbitrariness, accidentalness.

2. possibility, likelihood, eventuality; event, circumstance, occasion, situation, case, juncture, conjuncture; casualty, accident, emergency, exigency, exigence; predicament, quandary.

3. fluke, chance event, chance occurrence, happening, hap; freak accident, one in a million, twist of fate; bad luck *or* fortune, stroke of bad luck *or* fortune.

4. incidental, detail, small detail, minor detail, minutia, particular, point; aspect, facet, factor; respect, regard.

5. nonessential, unessential, inessential; extra, accessory, appurtenance, supplement; auxiliary, subsidiary, secondary; addition, addendum, appendage.

contingent, *adj.* **1.** conditional, provisional, provisory, stipulatory; dependent on *or* upon, depending, depending on, hanging on, hinging on; circumstantial, depending on circumstances; subject to, incident to, incidental to.

2. likely, possible, probable, incident; in the cards, on the books, in the air, in the wind, afloat, astir, afoot.

3. uncertain, indefinite, undetermined, unsettled, unestablished; open, up in the air, touch-and-go, borderline, hanging in the balance, *Sl.* up for grabs; unpredictable, unforeseeable; unaccountable, undeterminable, unascertainable, undivinable.

4. chance, fortuitous, serendipitous, aleatory, *Inf.*

fluky *or* flukey; random, haphazard, casual, arbitrary, hit-or-miss; unexpected, unforeseen, unanticipated, unlooked-for; accidental, incidental, occasional, adventitious.

—*n.* **5.** share, quota, portion, lot, allotment, allocation, percentage, piece of the action, *Inf.* cut; part, parcel; measure, ration; dole, dividend, pittance.

6. (*all of troops*) detachment; reinforcements, reserves.

7. group, body, company, complement; party, faction, movement; coterie, clique, set, band, *Inf.* bunch, *Inf.* team, *Inf.* crew, *Inf.* crowd.

8. likelihood, probability, eventuality; possibility, contingency; event, circumstance, occasion, situation, case, juncture, conjuncture. See also **contingency** (*defs.* **1-3**).

continual, *adj.* **1.** uninterrupted, unbroken, unceasing, incessant, ceaseless, continuous; unremitting, ongoing, nonstop, constant; endless, eternal, everlasting, perpetual, sempiternal, infinite, boundless, *Inf.* no end, interminable, illimitable.

2. frequent, regular, persistent, repeated, habitual; around-the-clock, day-in and day-out, dawn-to-dusk, at every turn.

continuance, *n.* **1.** endurance, continuation, duration, lastingness, abidingness; permanence, constancy, perseverance, persistence; *Inf.* stay, staying power, stick-to-it-tiveness.

2. extension, prolongation, protraction, perpetuation; adjournment.

3. sequence, succession, addition, repetition; connection, concatenation.

continuation, *n.* **1.** extension, prolongation, continuance, perpetuation; line, sequence, continuity, succession, progression.

2. sequel, installment, addition, supplement, epilogue, postscript, appendix, peroration, *Music.* postlude; tail, train, wake; round, suite, series, chain, course; scale, rank, file, row, string, range.

continue, *v.* **1.** extend, keep on, endure, stick to; pursue, carry on, keep on, keep at, maintain course, go along; drag on, run on, wear on; be steadfast, persevere, persist.

2. resume, proceed, advance, further, add, pick up where one left off.

3. last, endure, survive, exist, remain, subsist, live on; be permanent, be constant, be durable.

4. abide, stay, rest, remain; tarry, linger, wait.

5. sustain, maintain, retain; prolong, protract, extend, perpetuate, preserve; support, uphold, bear up, hold up; follow up, stay on top of, stick with.

6. adjourn, postpone, delay, procrastinate; keep pending, carry over.

continuity, *n.* **1.** continuousness, uninterruptedness, unbrokenness; connection, linkage, union, cohesion, whole, coherence, interrelatedness, interrelationship; flow, duration, contiguity, continuum.

2. continuation, perpetuity, constancy, persistence; protraction, prolongation, extension.

continuous, *adj.* **1.** connected, entire, unbroken, uninterrupted; consecutive, progressive, serial, linear, successive.

2. ceaseless, unceasing, incessant, unremitting; endless, everlasting, eternal, sempiternal, interminable, infinite, boundless; ongoing, nonstop, constant, perennial, perpetual, continual.

contort, *v.* **1.** twist, wrench, turn, wrest; bend out of shape, warp, deform, put out of shape, misshape, disfigure; distort, screw up, make faces, grimace, pout, stick out one's lower lip, *Fr. faire la moue;* writhe, squirm, wriggle, wiggle.

2. shrivel, shrink, curl up, wrinkle, crumple, ripple, crinkle; gnarl, knot, kink, crook, crimp; curl, spiral, screw, coil, loop, convolute, twirl, whirl.

contortion, *n.* **1.** deformation, distortion, misshapenness, crookedness, lopsidedness; deformity, disfigurement, malformation, anamorphic formation; face, grimace, pout, *Fr. moue*.

2. twist, warp, curve, bend; bulge, fold, wrinkle, crumple, ripple, crinkle; knot, kink, crook, crimp, gnarl; curl, curlicue, screw, spiral, corkscrew; coil, loop, convolution, twirl, whorl, whirl.

contortionist, *n.* acrobat, gymnast, tumbler, exerciser; trapeze artist, trapezist, equilibrist, tightrope walker, ropedancer, funambulist.

contour, *n.* silhouette, profile, outline, lines, curves; form, shape, figure, mold, cast; feature, line, lineament, trait; configuration, conformation, structure, composition, make-up.

contraband, *n.* **1.** smuggling, illegal traffic, trafficking; black-marketeering, bootlegging, rum-running; dope-smuggling, drug traffic.

—*adj.* **2.** prohibited, illicit, unlawful, illegal, unlicensed, unauthorized; proscribed, restricted, forbidden, taboo, *Ger. verboten*, off-limits; smuggled, trafficked, brought in, sneaked in, bootleg, black-market, *Inf.* hot.

contract, *n.* **1.** compact, covenant, concordat, convention, pact, treaty, entente, alliance; settlement, arrangement, understanding, agreement, gentleman's agreement, deal, bargain, transaction; bond, indenture, commitment, obligation, *Sl.* hit, *Sl.* death warrant; warrant, warranty, guarantee, guaranty, pledge, word, promise, sponsion.

2. legal document, cartel, acknowledgment, written acknowledgment, written guarantee *or* guaranty, written warranty, written pledge *or* promise; written agreement, deed, lease.

3. betrothal, betrothing, betrothment, engagement, espousal, sponsalia, plighting, match, marriage compact, vow, subarrhation, *Archaic.* affiance.

—*v.* **4.** compress, condense, concentrate, abstract, synopsize, summarize, digest, brief, epitomize; constrict, straiten, constringe, astringe, squeeze, tighten, cramp, pinch, bind, wrap up, coarctate; reduce, retrench, shorten, lessen, curtail, decrease, diminish, cut, cut down, cut back, cut off, cut short, subtract, subduct, abbreviate, abridge, narrow, bridge, crop, clip, shear, trim, prune, pare down.

5. wrinkle, knit, crinkle, crease, ruffle, rumple, raddle, ruck, corrugate; purse, purse up, pucker.

6. (*all usually of disease*) catch, get, acquire, break out with, come down with, become infected with; expose oneself to.

7. incur, bring upon, fall into, lie under, bind oneself to, be obligated to; be liable, be responsible for, be answerable for, be chargeable for, be accountable for, be amenable to, be legally responsible for.

8. settle, establish, agree on, covenant, make *or* strike a bargain, come to terms; negotiate, make terms, adjust, work out, pound out, hammer out, bargain, dicker, haggle, higgle, *Sl.* hassle, *Scot.* argle-bargle; stipulate, limit, circumscribe, demarcate, bound.

9. enter into, assume, take on, take up, undertake, essay into, embark on *or* upon, set about, engage in, enter upon, agree, go in for, endeavor, try, tackle; form, develop, forge, generate, constitute, institute, fashion, organize, build, erect, engender, beget, breed, hatch; cultivate, solicit, *Inf.* tout; promote, propound, lobby, push; vow, vouch, indent, promise, commit oneself to.

10. betroth, engage, affiance, plight, plight one's troth, espouse, bind, give one's hand, bestow one's hand upon, publish the banns, *Obs.* affy.

11. shrink, become smaller, shrivel, wither, dwindle, decline, fall off, abate, subside, fall away, waste, wane, ebb.

contracted, *adj.* **1.** compressed, concentrated, drawn together, made smaller, constricted, straitened, constringed, astringed, squeezed, tightened, cramped, pinched, bound, wrapped-up; shrunken, shriveled, withered, dwindled, wasted; reduced, retrenched, shortened, curtate, lessened, curtailed, decreased, diminished, cut, cut down, cut back, cut short, cut off, subtracted, subducted, abbreviated, narrowed, cropped, clipped, shorn, trimmed, pruned.

2. condensed, abridged, digested; abstracted, synopsized, summarized, epitomized.

3. (*all of the mind or outlook*) narrow, narrow-minded, restricted, insular, isolated, isolationist, shallow, confined, short-sighted, near-sighted; prejudiced, bigoted, one-sided, partial, biased, opinionated, opinionative, self-opinionated, dogmatic, didactic; stiff, stiff-necked, rooted, immovable, set in one's ways; intolerant, illiberal, ultra-conservative, reactionary, strait-laced, puritanical.

contraction, *n.* **1.** compression, compressing, condensation, condensing, concentration, concentrating, abstracting, summarizing, digesting; constriction, constricting, confinement, confining, constringency, constringing, astringency, astringing, straitening, squeezing, tightening, pinching, cramping, binding, wrapping up; reduction, reducing, retrenchment, retrenching, shortening, lessening, curtailment, curtailing, diminishing, decrease, decreasing, cut, cutting down *or* back *or* short, subtraction, subtracting, subduction, subducting, abbreviating, bridging, abridging, narrowing, cropping, clipping, trimming, pruning, shearing.

2. abstraction, summarization, synopsis, digest, brief, epitome, abbreviation, compendium, résumé, précis, prospectus, survey, abridgment; narrow straits, squeeze, shortage, loss, diminution, compactness.

3. *Physiology.* (*all of muscle*) contracture, tension, tenseness, tensing, flexing, tightness, tightening, stretching.

4. restriction, control, limitation, regulation, protection, constraint; withdrawal, removal, extraction, taking out *or* away.

5. *Gram.* ellipsis, *Gram.* syncope, *Gram.* hapology; *Phon.* elision, *Phon.* synaerisis.

contractor, *n.* architect, builder, constructor, mason, manufacturer, maker, artificer; planner, deviser; worker, jobber, journeyman.

contradict, *v.* **1.** deny, disaffirm, gainsay, controvert, dispute; oppose, counter.

2. dissent, differ, challenge, impugn; rebut, refute; disprove, overthrow, negate, confute.

3. belie, disallow, thwart, counteract, contravene, run counter to; reverse, cancel, rescind, abrogate, annul, nullify.

contradiction, *n.* **1.** disaffirmation, gainsay, controversion, denial, denegation; contravention, refutation, negation, confutation.

2. response, rebuttal, rejoinder, impugnment, disputation, dissension; disagreement, difference of opinion.

3. inconsistency, variance, discrepancy, disparity, ambivalence, antithesis; incongruity, contrariety, antilogy, *Rhet.* antiphrasis; clash, controversiality, discordancy.

contradictory, *adj.* **1.** contradicting, inconsistent, paradoxical, ambivalent, antithetical, incongruous, inconsistent, discrepant; opposing, conflicting, antagonistic, irreconcilable, refutative, negational.

2. dissentient, dissenting, opposite, contrary, at odds, at variance; dissident, argumentative, disputative, unreconciled; negative, obstinate, perverse.

contradistinction, *n.* contrast, contrariety, contraposition, antithesis; difference, dissimilarity, dissimilitude, unlikeness, opposition, oppositeness; distinction, distinguishment, differentiation.

contraption, *n.* *Informal.* contrivance, device, gadget, invention, creation, artifice, makeshift, hickey, widget; mechanism, apparatus, rig, gear, tackle, equipment, machine, appliance, Rube Goldberg, *Archaic.* trangam; *All Inf.* whachamacallit, thingumajig, thingumabob, doohickey, do-hinkey, dingus, doodad, gismo, gimmick, fandangle, *Australian.* doover.

contrariety, *n.* **1.** contrast, contradistinction, contraposition, opposition, oppositeness, polarity, polarization; difference, dissimilarity, dissimilitude, unlikeness; distinction, differentiation, distinguishment.

2. perversity, contrariness, obstinacy, recalcitrance, noncooperation; hostility, antagonism, antipathy, friction, conflict, enmity, bad blood, ill will, repugnance, oppugnance.

3. the opposite, the antithesis, the contrary; the reverse, mirror *or* reverse image; the obverse, the other side, the other side of the coin, *Sl.* the flip side.

contrary, *adj.* **1.** opposite, counter, contradictory, contrapositive, converse, antithetical; incompatible, incongruous, irreconcilable, worlds apart, poles apart; discordant, clashing, discrepant, inconsistent.

2. averse, hostile, unfriendly, antagonistic, antipathetic, opposed, dead against, inimical, repugnant, oppugnant; warring, at odds, at variance, at cross purposes; unfavorable, untoward, adverse, inauspicious, unpropitious; ill, foul, inclement.

3. perverse, froward, unaccommodating, contumacious, cross-grained, refractory, *Scot.* thrawn; self-willed, willful, recalcitrant, wrong-headed; intransigent, intractable, obstinate, adamant, stubborn, stubborn as a mule, mulish, headstrong, pigheaded, bullheaded.

contrast, *v.* **1.** differentiate, discriminate, distinguish, make a distinction, mark, mark off *or* out; oppose, counterpose, set over *or* off against.

2. differ, vary, diverge, stand out *or* apart, form a contrast; diverge from, depart from, deviate from; counter, contradict, contravene, go contrary to, run counter to, fly in the face of.

—*n.* **3.** contrariety, contradistinction, contraposition, opposition, oppositeness, polarity, polarization; difference, dissimilarity, dissimilitude, unlikeness; distinction, distinguishment, differentiation.

contravene, *v.* **1.** oppose, be in conflict with, cross, clash with, run counter to; contradict, oppugn, countervail, refute, belie, confute, rebut; frustrate, foil, thwart, check, abort; obstruct, hinder, hamper, interfere, intervene; annul, nullify, abrogate.

2. violate, transgress, infringe, trespass, encroach upon; break, disobey.

contravention, *n.* **1.** counteraction, opposition, antagonism, oppugnancy, contradiction, rebuttal; frustration, thwarting, foiling, checking, aborting; obstruction, blocking, hindering, hampering, interference, intervention; annulment, nullification, abrogation.

2. violation, transgression, infringement, trespass, encroachment, disobedience.

contretemps, *n.* **1.** (*all of an embarrassing or inopportune nature*) mistake, error, blunder, botch, bungle, *Inf.* slip-up; *All Sl.* boner, boo-boo, goof, blooper, boggle, boot, dumb trick, fool mistake, screw-up, foul-up, louse-up.

2. (*all of an embarrassing or inopportune nature*) mishap, mischance, misadventure, miscarriage, glitch, accident.

3. faux pas, gaffe, social blunder *or* indiscretion, indiscretion, slip in conduct *or* manners, mistake in conduct *or* etiquette *or* propriety, breach of etiquette *or* manners; transgression, dereliction, misconduct, misdeed; false step, wrong step, misstep, wrong move, false move, bad move, trip, stumble; offense, peccadillo, oversight, omission, miss; leak, slip, lapse, lapsus.

contribute, *v.* donate, give, grant, bestow, accord, confer, present, endow, subsidize; provide, furnish, supply, equip, accommodate with; dispense, hand out; help, cooperate, *Inf.* pitch in, *Inf.* chip in, *Sl.* kick in, throw in, ante *or* ante up; influence, advance, forward, promote; have a hand in, bear a part, conduce to.

contribution, *n.* **1.** donation, gift, present, presentation, offering, alms; bestowal, bestowment, conferment; grant, endowment, subsidy, subvention, allowance; dispensation, hand out.

2. impost, levy, tax, tribute, duty; gratuity, tip, *Fr. pourboire.*

3. article, story, essay, critique, item.

contributor, *n.* **1.** donor, giver, presenter, bestower, conferrer; subscriber, supporter, backer, *Law.* grantor, subsidizer; patron, guardian angel, benefactor, fairy godmother, sugar daddy.

2. correspondent, reporter, journalist; columnist, reviewer, critic, free lance; writer.

contrite, *adj.* penitent, penitential, repentant, atoning, in sackcloth and ashes; remorseful, compunctious, regretful, regretting, sorry, sorrowful, troubled, disturbed; conscience-stricken, guilt-ridden, self-accusing, self-reproachful; chastened, humbled, shamed, embarrassed.

contrition, *n.* penitence, repentance, contriteness, sackcloth and ashes; remorse, compunction, regret, sorrow; pang of conscience, guilt, shame, embarrassment, self-humiliation, self-mortification; self-reproach, self-blame, self-accusation, self-condemnation.

contrivance, *n.* **1.** device, invention, creation, gadget, *Inf.* contraption; apparatus, mechanism, machine; instrument, implement, tool, utensil, *Inf.* thingumajig, *Inf.* thingumabob; rig, gear, outfit, tackle, equipment, makeshift, *Inf.* Rube Goldberg.

2. invention, inventiveness, ingenuity, ingeniousness, cleverness; creativeness, originality.

3. plan, plot, scheme, design; expedient, makeshift, fabrication, stratagem, machination, artifice, trick, stroke, coup; intrigue, conspiracy, complot, cabal.

contrive, *v.* **1.** devise, invent, imagine, originate, create, excogitate; design, plan, work out, think up, hit upon, dream up, spin; concoct, make up, fabricate, improvise; construct, work up.

2. plot, conspire, scheme, intrigue, complot; brew, hatch, trump up, fake, *Sl.* hoke up; machinate, maneuver, manipulate, *Inf.* finagle, *Inf.* wangle.

3. manage, cast, frame, coin, formulate, draft, sketch, block out, map out, shape out a course, bring about, effect, organize.

control, *v.* **1.** dominate, rule over, reign over, exercise control over, govern; command, order, dictate, have it all one's way, call the shots, call the plays, run the show; boss, lay down the law, hold the purse strings; be in control, be in the driver's seat, be in the saddle, wear the pants *or* the trousers, be in a position of authority; hold all the cards, have well in hand, have under control, be master of the situation, be on top of, have [s.o.] under one's thumb.

2. supervise, superintend, oversee, preside over, direct, manage, conduct, have *or* be in charge of; take the lead, lead, hold in hand, hold *or* keep in line, keep under control; discipline, maintain order, regulate, regiment; rule the roost, wear the crown, occupy the throne, have the whip hand; wield the scepter, wield the power *or* authority, sway, bend to one's will.

3. subdue, overpower, domineer, master, gain the upper hand, get the better of; browbeat, intimidate, bully, ride roughshod over, ride herd on; oppress, repress, suppress, rule with a high hand, rule with an iron hand, rule with a rod of iron, tyrannize; keep down *or* under, lord it over, break, humble, crush; subjugate, subject, subordinate, enthrall, enslave, reduce to slavery, hold captive, hold in bondage.

4. restrain, check, keep in check, curb, hold *or* keep back, contain, arrest; harness, bridle, rein in, hold in, leash; restrict, fetter, shackle; confine, limit, cramp, constrain; hold in, bottle up, cork up, box up, shut up, seal; block, clog, obstruct, stop; impede, inhibit, hinder, interfere, hamper, encumber, deter, dissuade; detain, keep in, hold, stay; prohibit, forbid, disallow, interdict, prevent, suppress; preclude, obviate, nip in the bud, *Inf.* put the kibosh on.

—*n.* **5.** rule, command, dictate, dictation, order; regulation, regulating, maintaining order, disciplining, discipline; regimentation, direction, directing, leading, lead, jurisdiction, charge; bossing, supervising, supervision, superintending, superintendence, overseeing, oversight, presiding over; conduct, conducting, calling the shots, calling the plays, managing, management.

6. domination, power, authority, influence, sway, ascendancy, reign; overpoweringness, overwhelmingness, mastery, the whip *or* upper hand; domineeringness, browbeating, intimidating, intimidation; bullying, riding roughshod over, riding herd on; oppression, repression, suppression, ruling with a high *or* iron hand, ruling with a rod of iron; tyranny, *U.S.* (*usu. of politics*) bossism, dictatorship, despotism, sovereignty, supremacy; subjugation, subjection, subordination; enthrallment, enslavement, slavery, captivity, bondage.

7. check, restraint, curb; constraint, cramp, limitation, restriction, ceiling; seal, block, clog, stopper, damper, brake, drag; inhibition, dissuasion, determent; leading string, leash, chain, rein, tether; yoke, halter, harness, bridle, collar, bit, snaffle, muzzle, gag; prevention, confinement, bar, bolt, lock, padlock, fetter, shackle; prohibition, forbiddance, embargo, disallowance, interdict, interdiction.

8. checker, controller, regulator; director, boss, foreman, manager, supervisor, overseer; restrainer, holder of the purse strings, treasurer.

9. controls instruments, devices, dials, knobs, buttons, handles, levers; switches, *Elect.* toggle switches, wheels, *Mach.* gears; panel, instrument panel, board, keyboard, dashboard.

controversial, *adj.* **1.** polemical, dialectic; dichotomous, factious, contradictory, discursive, litigious; eristic, pilpulistic.

2. debatable, disputable, argumentable, controvertible; moot, doubtful, questionable, open to discussion; disputed, unsettled, contended, at issue, under question, suspicious.

controversy, *n.* **1.** dispute, disagreement, altercation, war of words, contestation, verbal feud, difference of opinion, heated exchange, logomachy; debate, discussion, polemics, argumentation, disputation, pilpul; fine point, question at hand, moot point, debatable question; tug of war, hassle, political football, *Inf.* hot potato.

2. contention, strife, argument, quarrel, set-to, wrangle, squabble, spat, tiff, velitation, bicker, broil; row, brawl, rumpus, imbroglio.

controvert, *v.* **1.** dispute, altercate, wrangle, cross verbal swords; deny, gainsay, disaffirm, impugn; oppose, differ, traverse; argue against, challenge, contradict, protest, refute, rebut, counter.

2. debate, discuss, canvass; consider, examine, review, argue *or* talk about; threash out, talk it out, air, ventilate; join issue upon, put to the proof, *Rare.* discept.

contumacious, *adj.* contrary, perverse, froward, refractory, cross-grained, *Scot.* thrawn, wrong-headed; obstinate, stubborn, stubborn as a mule, mulish, pigheaded, bullheaded; willful, self-willed, intractable, headstrong, pervicacious, stiff-necked, dogged, obdurate; intransigent, uncompromising, unaccommodating, unbending, unyielding, unsubmissive, inflexible, adamant; tenacious, pertinacious, persistent; unruly, fractious, restive, unmanageable, ungovernable, uncomplying; recalcitrant, rebellious, opposed, recusant, resistant, factious; disobedient, insubordinate, disrespectful, insolent; heady, impetuous, rash.

contumacy, *n.* **1.** perverseness, perversity, perversion, contrariety, frowardness, refractoriness, wrongheadedness; obstinacy, stubbornness, mulishness, pigheadedness, bullheadedness; willfulness, intractableness, doggedness, obduracy; intransigence, inflexibility, immovability; tenacity, pertinacity, persistence, determination, resolution.

2. disobedience, insubordination, mutiny, sedition; recalcitrance, rebelliousness, rebellion, revolt, opposition, recusancy, resistance; fractiousness, restiveness, unmanageableness; headiness, impetuosity, impetuousness; infraction, violation, breach.

contumelious, *adj.* **1.** insulting, excoriating, denouncing, reproaching, berating, objurgating, objurgative, lashing; abusive, harsh, coarse; degrading, debasing, humiliating, mortifying; calumnious, slanderous, defamatory, opprobrious; cruel, mean, brutal; unkind, uncharitable, unbenevolent, uncordial, unfriendly; rude, churlish, boorish, bearish, rough; impolite, discourteous, uncivil, ungracious.

2. sarcastic, satirical, ironic, ironical, cynical, double-edged; contemptuous, scornful, disdainful, mocking, derisive, derisory; sardonic, caustic, acrimonious, bitter, biting, trenchant; taunting, teasing, flouting, sneering.

3. haughty, arrogant, high and mighty, overbearing, lordly, pompous, bumptious.

contumely, *n.* **1.** insult, affront, indignity, dishonor; contempt, scorn, derision, disdain, superciliousness; debasement, humiliation, degradation; abuse, scurrility, vituperation, invective, vulgarity; reproach, obloquy, calumny, opprobrium; sarcasm, cynicism, causticity, acrimony; impoliteness, discourteousness, discourtesy, incivility.

2. rudeness, churlishness, roughness, brusqueness, brusquerie; insolence, sauciness, pertiness, *Rare.* procacity; arrogance, haughtiness, overbearingness, pomposity.

contuse, *v.* bruise, make black and blue, blacken, discolor; injure, hurt, harm, damage; bump, hit, strike, beat up.

contusion, *n.* bruise, black and blue mark *or* spot, discoloration; blemish, blotch, mark, spot, *Sl.* hickey; injury, hurt, bump, lump, *Sl.* boo-boo.

conundrum, *n.* **1.** riddle, puzzle, puzzler, Chinese puzzle, poser, *Inf.* hard nut to crack, *Inf.* brain-teaser, *Inf.* mind-boggler, *Inf.* stumper, *Inf.* floorer; charade, rebus, anagram, logogriph, word game, acrostic, crossword puzzle.

2. enigma, mystery, secret, arcanum, crux, question, question mark; oracle, dark saying, riddle of the sphinx, obscure statement, ambiguity, equivocality.

convalescence, *n.* **1.** recuperation, recovery, restoration, improvement; rehabilitation, remediation, treatment, cure; revival, rejuvenation, rejuvenescence, rally, return to health.

2. hospitalization, institutionalization; incapacitation, bed rest.

convalescent, *adj.* **1.** recuperating, recovering, improving, getting well *or* better.

2. recuperative, recovery; for the ill, sick person's; rehabilitative, remedial, curative, treatment.

convene, *v.* **1.** assemble, congregate, meet, collect, gather, gather together, forgather, muster; sit, hold a meeting *or* session.

2. convoke, call together, bring together, round up, rally; summon, call for, send for; summons, cite, subpoena, serve.

convenience, *n.* **1.** expedience, utility, usefulness, serviceableness, adaptability, accessibility, handiness; suitability, appropriateness, fitness, fittingness; timeliness, seasonableness, opportuneness, favorableness, propitiousness.

2. leisure, ease, freedom; free time, spare time, spare moment, vacant hour, suitable opportunity.

3. advantage, accommodation, service, use, avail, profit.

4. facility, appliance, amenity, appurtenance, mechanical aid.

convenient, *adj.* **1.** expedient, advantageous, beneficial; useful, of use, helpful, serviceable, adapted, suitable; opportune, timely, well-timed, seasonable.

2. handy, at hand, within reach, at one's fingertips; nearby, propinquant, easily accessible, just around the corner.

convent, *n.* **1.** nunnery, motherhouse, novitiate; religious community, abbey, priory, cloister, cenoby; religious life, religion, sisterhood, nunhood, nunship.

2. See **monastery** (*def.* **1**).

convention, *n.* **1.** meeting, gathering, *U.S. Pol.* caucus; assembly, assemblage, congregation; congress, convocation, council; diet, synod, conclave; conference, parley, discussion.

2. contract, compact, agreement; treaty, covenant, concordat, entente; arrangement, understanding; bargain, deal, pact.

3. conventionality, custom, orthodoxy, tradition; propriety, etiquette, formality, protocol; punctilio.

conventional, *adj.* **1.** usual, customary, habitual, wonted; accustomed, normal, standard, regular, routine; traditional, tradition-bound, orthodox; formal, decorous, academic, methodical, rigid, uncompromising, canonical; conformist, conservative, *Sl.* uptight, *Sl.* button-down, *Sl.* square, *Sl.* straight, *Sl.* straight-arrow.

2. commonplace, common, ordinary, run-of-the-mill, prosaic; everyday, unoriginal, pedestrian, middlebrow; trite, cliché, stereotyped, hackneyed; bromidic, platitudinous.

converge, *v.* **1.** meet, intersect, join, blend together, flow into one another, unite, become one; focus, concentrate, collect, group; come together, merge, coincide, concur, correspond; approach, close in on, come closer to, draw together, center, focalize.

2. work towards a common goal, conspire, cooperate, combine efforts, work together.

convergence, *n.* convergency, coming together, merging, coincidence, concurrence, correspondence; concourse, conflux, confluence; meeting, intersection, corner, junction, juncture, joint; connection, joining, blending together, union, approach, centering, focalization, focus, concentration, collection, grouping.

convergent, *adj.* converging, intersecting, concurrent, merging, blending, flowing together, confluent; meeting, joining, connecting, connective, conjunctive, junctional, approaching, centering, centripedal.

conversable, *adj.* **1.** agreeable, obliging, accommodating, amenable, complaisant, complacent; acces-

sible, approachable, receptive.
2. communicative, expansive, open, free, unreserved, unrestrained, unreticent; frank, candid, up front, straightforward, unsecretive; talkative, loquacious, garrulous, voluble, chatty, *Sl.* gabby.
3. conversational, colloquial, interlocutory, confabulatory.

conversant, *adj.* **1.** *Usu.* **conversant with** acquainted with, familiar with, instructed in, knowledgeable in, versed in; learned, skilled, practiced, proficient; apprised of, informed of, privy to, in on.
2. acquainted, familiar, mutually known *or* recognized; sociable with, friendly with, on good terms with, comfortable with; known to say hello to.

conversation, *n.* **1.** talk, dialogue, discourse, colloquy, converse, interlocution, verbal exchange; chat, chitchat, palaver, confabulation, *Inf.* confab, little talk, causerie, table talk.
2. conference, meeting, parley, parlance, huddle, *Inf.* powwow; discussion, tête-à-tête, *Sl.* bull session, *Sl.* rap session, *Sl.* rap; interview, audience, sitting.
3. association, intimate acquaintance, familiarity, communion, community, fellowship, social intercourse; communication, correspondence, contact, touch, connection.

conversational, *adj.* **1.** colloquial, interlocutory, confabulatory, discoursive.
2. communicative, expansive, open, free, unrestrained, unreserved, unreticent, conversable; frank, candid, straightforward, unsecretive; talkative, loquacious, garrulous, voluble, chatty, *Sl.* gabby.

converse[1], *v.* **1.** talk, discuss, speak, chat, chitchat, confabulate, *Inf.* confab, coze, pass the time of day, *Brit. Dial.* tell, *Sl.* rap, *Sl.* chin, *Sl.* chew the fat *or* rag, *Sl.* shoot the breeze *or* bull, *Sl.* bull; talk *or* speak with, have a talk *or* little talk with, commune with, communicate with, visit with.
—*n.* **2.** conversation, talk, dialogue. See **conversation** (*def.* **1**).

converse[2], *adj.* **1.** transposed, reversed, turned round *or* around, contrary, opposite.
—*n.* **2.** the opposite, the antithesis, the contrary; the reverse, mirror *or* reverse image; the obverse, the other side, the other side of the coin *or* picture, *Sl.* the flip side.

conversion, *n.* **1.** transmutation, transubstantiation, transfigurement, metamorphosis, translation, transmogrification; change, alteration, adaptation, modification, permutation, mutation; reshaping, recasting, refashioning, remaking, redoing; restyling, remodeling, reconstruction, rebuilding.
2. proselytism, shift in belief *or* attitude, change of heart; spiritual growth, regeneration, rebirth, rebaptism.
3. transposition, metathesis, permutation, inversion, reversal; commutation, substitution, exchange, interchange; switch, trade, swap; shift, shifting, moving around, reordering, reorganization, rearrangement.
4. expropriation, taking without permission, stealing, embezzlement, peculation; misappropriation, misuse, diversion, deflection.

convert, *v.* **1.** transmute, transubstantiate, transform, transfigure, metamorphose, translate, transmogrify; change, alter, modify, permute, mutate, metabolize; transshape, reshape, recast, refashion, remake, redo; restyle, remodel, reconstruct, rebuild; make into, transform into, change into, adapt to *or* into.
2. proselytize, cause to change religion *or* belief; regenerate, create anew, give new life, cause to be reborn, rebaptize.
3. expropriate, take without permission, steal, *Sl.* lift, embezzle, peculate; misappropriate, misuse, divert, deflect.
4. transpose, metathesize, permutate, invert, reverse, turn around *or* about; change, exchange, substitute, interchange, commute, switch, swap, trade; shift, move around, reorder, reorganize, rearrange.
—*n.* **5.** proselyte, neophyte, catechumen; disciple, believer, follower.

convertible, *adj.* transmutable, transformable; changeable, alterable, modifiable, permutable, mutable; commutative, substitutive, exchangeable, interchangeable; invertible, reversible, adaptable, adjustable.

convex, *adj.* curved outward, rounded, *Astron.* gibbous, hemispheric; bossed, raised, protuberant, bulging, timid, salient; embowed, bent, arched.

convey, *v.* **1.** transport, carry, *Inf.* tote, bear; move, shift, transfer, displace, transplant; portage, haul, cart, lug, pull along, drag; take, deliver, give, bring, fetch, get; lead, impel, conduct, channel.
2. transmit, send, dispatch, pass on *or* along; communicate, impart, make known, tell, relate; disclose, reveal, divulge.

conveyance, *n.* **1.** transport, transportation, carrying, bearing, conveying, bringing; movement, shifting, transfer, transmission; portage, hauling, carting, lugging, dragging; freightage, ferriage, shipment, transshipment.
2. vehicle, van, lorry, truck, dray; cart, wagon, wain; carriage, equipage, hansom, hackney, hack, rig, coach, stagecoach; buggy, gig, surry, sulky, rickshaw; bus, cab, car, auto.

convict, *v.* **1.** declare guilty, prove guilty, find guilty; sentence, condemn, adjudge, doom.
—*n.* **2.** criminal, malefactor, felon, *Inf.* crook, lawbreaker, outlaw, gangster, public enemy; culprit, offender, guilty party; recidivist, transgressor, violator, *Law.* malfeasant, delinquent.
3. prisoner, captive, jailbird, *Sl.* con, lifer; trusty.

conviction, *n.* **1.** proof of guilt, sentence, judgment, adjudication, condemnation, penalty, punishment.
2. belief, certitude, certainty, assurance, trust; opinion, view, position; persuasion; faith, creed, doctrine, tenet, teaching, principle.

convince, *v.* *Often* **convince of** persuade, make [s.o.] see the light, bring [s.o.] to reason, talk [s.o.] into [s.t.], bring [s.o.] around *or* round, win [s.o.] over, sell [s.o.] on, *Inf.* jawbone; satisfy, assure, reassure, confirm [s.o.] of, prove to.

convivial, *adj.* **1.** jovial, gregarious, merry-making, anacreontic, social, party-loving, *Inf.* partying, *Sl.* whoop-it-up; hearty, jolly, cheerful, *Inf.* back-slapping.
2. festive, feastful, party, celebrative, holiday; merry, gay, joyful, joyous.
3. genial, cordial, hospitable; sociable, affable, friendly, amiable, amicable, congenial, agreeable.

convocation, *n.* **1.** assembling, gathering, collection, ingathering, forgathering, bringing together, rounding up *or* in; convening, summoning, calling together; muster, mobilization, marshalling, rallying, call up.
2. assembly, congregation, flock, gathering, levy, (*in Great Britain*) levee; convention, congress, conclave, diet, conference, meeting; council, committee, synod, *U.S.* caucus; legislature, parliament, Senate, House; assemblage, group, body, company; concourse, throng, crowd, mob.

convoke, *v.* **1.** assemble, collect, gather, ingather,

forgather, bring together, round up *or* in, group *or* herd together.
2. convene, summon, call together, call a meeting; muster, marshal, mobilize, call up, rally.
convolution, *n.* **1.** entanglement, involution, involvement, complication, complexity.
2. circumvolution, winding, twisting, coiling, turning, meandering.
3. whorl, sinuosity, roll, curl, coil, spiral, helix, curlicue, ringlet; kink, twirl, twist.
convoy, *v.* **1.** escort, chaperon, matronize, accompany, attend, companion; usher, guide, pilot, steer, conduct, lead, direct; guard, watch over, keep an eye on, look after, shepherd, screen, shelter, flank, be by one's side; protect, defend, back up, support, go *or* be behind.
—n. **2.** protection, defense, security, bulwark, shield, screen, cover, shelter, refuge, safety, safeguard; guidance, tutelage, custody, keeping, care.
3. escort, armed guard, bodyguard, contingent, *Navy.* escort carrier, *Mil.* escort fighter; entourage, retinue, cortege, suite.
4. train, file, row, line, queue; fleet, group, company, assemblage, aggregation.
convulse, *v.* **1.** agitate, disturb, unsettle, discompose, upset, shake, shake up, churn, churn up, swirl, roil, *Chiefly U.S.* rile; commove, heave, upheave, toss.
2. torture, torment, agonize, harrow, excruciate, wring, rack, twist.
3. amuse, *Inf.* crack [s.o.] up, *Inf.* break [s.o.] up; *All Sl.* wow, kill, slay, knock [s.o.] dead, knock [s.o.] out, knock *or* lay them in the aisles.
convulsion, *n.* **1.** spasm, paroxysm, throe; fit, seizure, stroke, attack, *Pathol.* ictus.
2. commotion, turmoil, tumult, turbulence, storm, storm and stress, hurly-burly; disorder, chaos, confusion, upheaval; furor, agitation, disturbance, disruption, unrest.
3. cataclysm, eruption, outburst, explosion, fulmination; violence, frenzy, fury, rage.
cook, *v.* **1.** bake, roast, broil, charbroil, grill, barbecue; sauté, braise, fricassee; fry, frizzle, pan, griddle, toast; boil, simmer, steam, stew, seethe, scald; precook, parboil; curry, devil.
2. heat, torrefy, parch, fire, kiln.
3. **cook up** *Informal.* concoct, prepare, make, make up, mix, brew; compose, combine, put together; fabricate, improvise, invent, create; contrive, scheme, plan, plot.
—n. **4.** chef, *Fr. Cookery.* chef à cuisine, kitchener.
cool, *adj.* **1.** chilly, chill, nippy, unheated, unwarmed, heatless, sunless; breezy, draughty, windy.
2. composed, collected, *Inf.* together, self-possessed, self-controlled; easy-going, relaxed, even-tempered, imperturbable, unexcitable, unflappable; unexcited, unmoved, unperturbed; unruffled, staid, sedate; undemonstrative, unemotional, stoical, philosophical; passionless, impassive, dispassionate.
3. passive, undesiring, unexcitable, frigid; phlegmatic, listless, half-hearted, lukewarm; stony, flinty, steely.
4. deliberate, intentional, purposeful, meant, willful, volitional, voluntary; premeditated, calculated, designed, planned, plotted, schemed, devised, contrived.
5. unfriendly, unsociable, unwelcome, uninviting, forbidding; uncordial, ungracious, unamicable, inhospitable; unapproachable, inaccessible, closed, tight; distant, remote, stand-offish, *Inf.* offish.
6. audacious, presumptuous, overconfident, impertinent, assuming, insolent, impudent, brazen, brassy, *Inf.* nervy, *Inf.* pushy; unabashed, shameless, forward, *Inf.* fresh, bumptious.
7. aloof, indifferent, apathetic, unconcerned, disinterested, incurious, uninquisitive; removed, detached, uninvolved, unresponsive, unsympathetic.
—v. **8.** chill, refrigerate, freeze, frigorify, *Rare.* infrigidate; ice, glaciate, congeal, regelate.
9. soothe, allay, assuage, mollify, soften; moderate, temper, *Archaic.* attemper; mitigate, abate, lessen, diminish, reduce; quiet, still, compose, lull, hush; pacify, tranquilize, smoothe, settle.
10. **cool it** *Slang.* **a.** take it easy, calm down, don't sweat it, go with the tide, roll with the punches, take it in stride, think nothing of it **b.** cut it out, drop it, lay off, knock it off, come off it.
11. **cool off** *Informal.* calm down, relax, loosen up, settle down, unwind, simmer down.
coop, *n.* **1.** cage, pen, corral, crawl, crib, aviary, mew; receptacle, box, enclosure, pound; *Slang.* prison, cell, vault, dungeon, lockup.
2. **fly the coop** *Slang.* escape, flee, *Inf.* make a getaway, break away, break jail, escape prison.
—v. **3.** cage in, pen up, encage, corral, fence; confine, intern, impound, shut in.
cooperate, *v.* **1.** (*all usually followed by* with) collaborate, coact, combine, concur, conspire, connive, fraternize, join, unite, synergize, interface, interact, team up, join forces *or* hands, work together *or* in unison *or* side by side, act jointly *or* in concert, stand shoulder to shoulder, pull together, *Inf.* hitch horses.
2. contribute, participate, take part, be a party to, share in, go *or* go along, play along, *Inf.* play ball, join in, *Inf.* pitch in, *Inf.* chip in, lend a hand, lend oneself to, play *or* do one's part, pull one's weight; (*all usually negative*) lift a finger, lift a hand, raise a finger, raise a hand; side *or* take sides with, cast in one's lot with, stand by, *Inf.* stick by; second, boost, give a boost to, give a lift to.
cooperation, *n.* **1.** interaction, collaboration, union, fusion, synergy, teamwork, give and take, pulling together, fraternization, *Chiefly U.S. Pol.* logrolling; joint action *or* operation, combined action *or* effort, coordinated *or* concerted *or* concurrent effort *or* action, coadjuvant action *or* effort, gentleman's agreement.
2. coaction, concurrence, concert, coadjuvancy, concord, accordance, harmony, agreement, unison, unanimity, consentience, consentaneity, consentaneousness.
3. help, aid, assistance, lift, boost, hand, helping hand; support, friendship, patronage, backing, advocacy, countenance, favor, blessing, grace, sponsorship, auspices *or* auspice, good offices, kind regard.
4. spirit, ardor, zeal, passion, fervidness, ferventness; enthusiasm, exuberance, exhilaration, animation, ebullience; esprit de corps, clanship, partisanship, fellowship, comradeship.
cooperative, *adj.* **1.** coactive, collaborative, collaborating, coordinated, interactive, interactional, interacting, synergetic, synergistic, consentient, consentaneous; mutual, joint, concurrent, concerted, coadjutant, united, unified, unanimous, harmonious, agreeing, accordant.
2. helpful, helping, aidful, aiding, assistant, assisting, obliging, accommodative, accommodating.
—n. **3.** company, pool, co-op, *Inf.* combine; commune, society, fraternity; partnership, alliance, entente, association, coalition, confederation.
cooperator, *n.* collaborator, contributor, participant, participator; confederate, conniver, conspirer, conspirator, abettor, accomplice, accessory *or Chiefly*

Law. accessary, partner in crime, *Sl.* gun moll *or* moll; helper, aid *or* aide, attendant, acolyte, deputy, adjutant, coadjutant, coadjutor, coadjutress *or* coadjutrix, adjunct, adjuvant, adjutator, *Obs.* adjutor, auxiliary, ancilla, second, man Friday, gal Friday, henchman, right hand, right-hand man, *Sl.* gofer; partner, ally, comrade, colleague, associate, consociate, socius, yokefellow *or* yokemate, companion, helpmate, helpmeet, *Obs.* helpfellow, co-worker, co-aid, co-partner, consort, confrere, sidekick, friend, *Chiefly Brit.* mate.

coordinate, *adj.* **1.** correspondent, complementary, complemental; correlative, correlational, reciprocal; equal, equipotent, on equal *or* even terms, on the same footing; equivalent, synonymous, tantamount, all one, all the same, of a kind, of a piece, cast in the same mold, *Inf.* six of one, half a dozen of the other.

—n. **2.** peer, compeer, equal, coequal, rival; partner, colleague, confrere, associate.

3. counterpart, equivalent, match, twin, double, other half, alter ego, chip off the old block; alternate, pendant, companion, mate, fellow; correspondent, correlative, parallel, analogue.

—v. **4.** arrange, range, order, dispose, place, group; classify, categorize, pigeonhole, *Sl.* peg; index, file, codify, collocate, number, alphabetize, tabulate; organize, sort, sort out, assort; systematize, systemize, methodize; grade, graduate, rank, rate, distinguish.

5. harmonize, adapt, adjust, attune; compose, balance, quadrate; fit, suit, match, mesh, square, parallel, correspond, tally with, jibe with, *Inf.* gee with.

6. cooperate, collaborate, coact, combine, concur, unite, synergize, interface, interrelate.

cope, *v.* **1.** manage, make do, make shift, get along *or* by; survive, subsist, eke out, scratch out; hold one's own, rise to the occasion, make the grade, *Sl.* cut the mustard, *Sl.* cut it, *Sl.* hack it, *U.S. Sl.* come through.

2. cope with treat, handle, dispatch, discharge, dispose of, take care of, deal with, do with; contend with, fight with, struggle with, wrestle with, grapple with, *Inf.* lock horns, *Inf.* bump heads, *Sl.* tangle with, *Sl.* mix it up.

copious, *adj.* **1.** plentiful, plenteous, plenitudinous, *Inf.* plenty, fat, bountiful, bounteous; big, large, great, huge, extensive; immeasurable, unmeasured, unstinted, inexhaustible, bottomless; much, many, numerous, *Inf.* dime a dozen; in quantity *or* quantities, in plenty, *Inf.* aplenty, *Inf.* galore.

2. ample, abounding, overflowing, overspilling, spilling over, running over; rich, lavish, luxuriant, thriving, exuberant, superabundant; fruitful, fertile, fecund, productive, prolific, proliferous.

3. full, filled, bursting, *Archaic.* fraught; chock-a-block, *Brit. Inf.* chocker, *Inf.* chock-full, jammed, packed, *Inf.* jam-packed; rife, replete, flush, well-supplied, well-stocked; rampant, teeming, teeming with, swarming, swarming with, crawling, crawling with, bristling, bristling with, alive with, *Sl.* lousy with.

4. excessive, extravagant, superfluous, overabundant, oversufficient.

copiousness, *n.* **1.** abundance, amplitude, ampleness, fullness, plenteousness, plentifulness, bountifulness, bounteousness; richness, exuberance, luxuriance, lavishness; teemingness, rankness, prodigality.

2. plenty, plenitude, bounty, cornucopia, horn of plenty, endless supply, *Scot.* scouth *or* skouth, *Scot. and North Eng.* routh; quantity, quantities, volume, mass, fund, mine, store; lot, lots, heap, heaps, mountain, mountains, stack, stacks, pile, piles, load, loads, mess, slew, whole slew, full measure, good *or* great deal, quite a little, *Sl.* scads *or* scad; *All Inf.* ton, tons, bag, bags, barrel, barrels, gob, gobs, oodles, *Chiefly Brit.* lashings *or* lashing.

3. excess, surplus, surfeit, oversupply, overflow, nimiety, superfluity; glut, plethora, overabundance, superabundance, supersaturation.

copper, *n.* penny, cent, *U.S. Inf.* red cent; *All Brit.* pence, p, twopence, tuppence, halfpenny, ha'penny, bawbee.

copse, *n.* thicket, grove, wood, scrub, boscage, copsewood, coppice, brush.

copulation, *n.* **1.** connection, combination, unification, accouplement, coupling, mating, joining.

2. sexual intercourse, *Inf.* sex, intercourse, sexual commerce, sex act, act of love, coitus, *Archaic.* venery. See **coitus**.

copulative, *adj.* linking, uniting, coupling, mating, joining, connecting, connective, conjunctive.

copy, *n.* **1.** imitation, reproduction, replica, ectype, transcript, apograph, replication, duplication; duplicate, carbon, facsimile, carbon copy, *Trademark.* Xerox; representation, semblance, likeness; counterfeit, forgery, fake, sham.

2. example, specimen, sample, piece.

3. manuscript, typescript, text.

—v. **4.** reproduce, duplicate, replicate, *Trademark.* Xerox; transcribe, rewrite; plagiarize, *Sl.* lift.

5. imitate, emulate, do like, simulate, follow suit, parallel, model after, copycat; mimic, ape, monkey, parrot, mirror, echo, reflect; impersonate, mock, parody, take off, caricature, burlesque.

6. counterfeit, forge, fake, sham.

copyist, *n.* **1.** transcriber, scribe, scrivener, *Judaism.* sopher; secretary, amanuensis.

2. imitator, copier, copycat, epigone; mimic, monkey, ape, parrot, echo, shadow.

coquet, *v.* flirt, vamp, trifle, toy, tease, dally, philander; look sweet at, make googoo eyes at, wink at, ogle; bill and coo, woo, *Inf.* spark, court, serenade; fondle, caress, *Inf.* spoon, pet, neck.

coquetry, *n.* flirtation, flirting, vamping, googoo eyes, sheep's eyes; trifling, toying, dallying, dalliance; wooing, *Inf.* sparking, courting, petting, *Inf.* spooning, necking.

coquette, *n.* flirt, vamp, belle, gold digger; hussy, *Chiefly Brit. Sl.* tart.

cord, *n.* **1.** string, twine, line, lanyard, cable; leader, gut, wire, strand, filament; braid, cordon, gimp, tape, ribbon, yarn; tendon, sinew, thew.

2. tie, bond, ligature, ligament, nexus, vinculum; link, connection, copula.

—v. **3.** bind, fasten, bundle, tie up, package; lace, thread, string.

cordial, *adj.* **1.** friendly, warm, courteous, gracious, affable, affectionate, genial, amiable, good-natured, pleasant; heartfelt, wholehearted, whole-souled, hearty, ardent, earnest, sincere, ingratiating.

2. stimulating, invigorating, cheering, restorative, fortifying, heartening, tonic, revivifying, refreshing.

—n. **3.** stimulant, exhilarant, tonic, *Med.* roborant, stomachic, *Inf.* bracer, *Inf.* pick-me-up, *Inf.* pickup.

4. liqueur, after-dinner drink.

cordiality, *n.* friendliness, warmth, graciousness, courtesy; affection, good will, fellow feeling, fraternization; heartiness, whole-heartedness, ardor, earnestness.

cordon, *n.* **1.** braid, cord, frog, *Heraldry.* riband; decoration, sash, ribbon, cordon bleu.

2. quarantine, cordon sanitaire, picket line; outposts,

guard posts, perimeter of defense.

core, *n.* center, heart, nucleus, germ, kernel, seed, nut; marrow, pith, gist, substance, essence, sum and substance, essential part, inner core, quintessence, heart of the matter, *Inf.* nub, *Inf.* nitty-gritty.

cork, *n.* **1.** stopper, stop, plug, stopple, bung, tampion; pin, peg, spill, spile, *Dentistry.* dowel; tap, spigot, cock, stopcock, faucet, valve.

2. cap, put the top *or* lid on, cover, close up, seal; plug, bung, stop.

corn, *n.* **1.** Indian corn, (*esp. technical and Brit.*) maize; butter and sugar corn, sweet corn, *U.S.* green corn; corn on the cob, roasting ears, ears.

2. cereal grain, (*in England*) wheat, (*in Scotland*) oats.

—*v.* **3.** brine, pickle, preserve *or* season *or* cure with salt, salt.

corner, *n.* **1.** angle, bend, curve, crook, turn, twist, hook, elbow, knee.

2. convergence, convergency, intersection, crotch, fork, junction, juncture, joint, connection, meeting.

3. end, edge, margin, rim; verge, brink, brim, brow, hem; border, periphery, perimeter, limit, extremity, termination.

4. nook, crevice, cranny, recess, niche, private spot, secret place.

5. tight spot, pickle, bind, hole, embarrassing *or* awkward situation; cul-de-sac, dead end, impasse, standstill, stalemate, deadlock.

6. region, part, area, place, quarter, district, section, *Inf.* neck of the woods.

—*v.* **7.** drive *or* force into a corner, back into a corner, push into a corner, bring to bay; prevent passage, obstruct, choke off, block off.

8. (*all of a stock or commodity*) gain exclusive control of, corner the market on, monopolize, keep all to oneself, *Sl.* hog, *Sl.* bogart.

corny, *adj.* *Informal.* old-fashioned, trite, banal, hackneyed, stale, platitudinous, *Inf.* bromidic, insipid; mawkish, sentimental, weak, feeble, poor, sick, *Sl.* sappy; simple, fatuous, inane, jejune; unsophisticated, *Sl.* hokey, naïve, amateurish, unsubtle, *Sl.* uncool.

corollary, *n.* conclusion, deduction, inference, illation; consequence, result, upshot, follow-up, fallout.

coronation, *n.* crowning, enthroning, enthronement, accession to the throne; investing, investiture, anointing, consecration, installation, inauguration.

coronet, *n.* crown, garland, wreath, chaplet; laurel, bay.

corporal, *adj.* bodily, corporeal, fleshly, incarnate, carnal, somatic, physical; earthly, material, substantial, tangible, palpable; concrete, real, true, actual.

corporation, *n.* company, trust, partnership, firm, house; merger, combine, conglomerate, multinational, multicompany; parent company, holding company.

corps, *n.* **1.** military unit, cohort, division, regiment, battery, battalion, brigade; detachment, platoon, column, squad; squadron, escadrille, phalanx, wing.

2. body, troupe, crew, team, band, party; group, bunch, gang, pack, herd; crowd, throng, mob.

corpse, *n.* cadaver, *Sl.* stiff, (*of animals*) carcass; skeleton, remains; earth, clay, dust, ashes; carrion.

corpulence, *n.* **1.** fatness, fleshiness, obesity, obeseness, *Fr. embonpoint, Pathol.* adiposis, adiposity, corpulency; chubbines, tubbiness, paunchiness, pudginess, plumpness, roundedness, rotundity; paunch, potbelly, *Inf.* bay window, *Inf.* corporation, *Sl.* pot, *Sl.* beerbelly, *Sl.* spare tire, *Obs.* gorbelly.

2. portliness, stoutness, burliness; hulk, bulk, bulkiness.

corpulent, *adj.* **1.** fat, obese, adipose, overweight, portly, pursy, *Scot.* fodgel; chubby, tubby, pudgy, *Chiefly Brit.* podgy, plump; round, rounded-out, rotund; fleshy, filled-out, well-fed, bouncing; ample, substantial, full; big, large, bulky, hulky, hulking.

2. dumpy, stumpy, stubby, squabbish, squabby, squat, squatty; chunky, lumpy, lumpish.

3. stout, stodgy, thick, thickset; heavy, heavy-set, stocky; beefy, brawny, burly, sturdy; strapping.

correct, *v.* **1.** set right, make right, set *or* put straight, redress, rectify; amend, emend, remedy, straighten out, fix, repair; doctor, cure, mend, touch up; improve, better, ameliorate, meliorate; reform, restore, rehabilitate, readjust; adjust, alter, change, modify.

2. scold, chide, rebuke, reprove, reprimand, *Inf.* dress down, berate; reprehend, take to task, call to account, blame, censure, criticize, lecture, warn; chasten, chastise, discipline, punish, castigate.

3. counteract, countervail, offset, counterbalance, counterpoise; compensate, make up for, neutralize, nullify, annul, cancel; undo, reverse, unmake.

—*adj.* **4.** accurate, exact, precise, close, faithful, strict; unerring, *Inf.* on the mark, on target, on the money, *Inf.* right on, *Sl.* spot on; on the button, on the dot, *Inf.* on the nose, *Sl.* on the beam; right, just, true, truthful, veracious; factual, actual, literal, true to life, true to form; authentic, real, sound, valid; flawless, faultless, perfect, defectless, errorless.

5. proper, *Fr. comme il faut*, suitable, fitting, befitting, meet, appropriate, apt; conventional, standard, prescribed, approved, accepted; established, traditional, consuetudinary, general, prevailing; normal, natural, usual, routine, customary.

correction, *n.* **1.** improvement, emendation, amendment, modification, alteration; remedy, redress, rectification, righting, reparation, repair.

2. punishment, chastisement, discipline; reproof, admonition, warning; reprimand, scolding, *Inf.* talking-to, *Inf.* dressing-down.

corrective, *adj.* **1.** remedial, therapeutic, medicinal, curative, healing; emendatory, *U.S.* amendatory, rectifying, counteractive; reparative, reparatory, restorative.

2. punitive, disciplinary, penal, castigative, castigatory, reformatory.

correctness, *n.* **1.** rightness, unerringness, inerrableness, infallibleness, unfailingness; absoluteness, certainty, sureness, positiveness, definiteness, fixedness.

2. accuracy, accurateness, exactness, exactitude, precision, preciseness; closeness, fidelity, faithfulness, conformity; truth, truthfulness, veracity, verity, veritableness; fact, actuality, factuality, literalness, authenticity, soundness, validity, validness, integrity; flawlessness, inerrancy, faultlessness, perfection.

3. properness, suitability, suitableness, seemliness, becomingness; fitness, fittingness, befittingness, meetness, appropriateness, aptness.

4. propriety, decorum, etiquette, customs, conventions; amenities, civilities, urbanities, graces, courtesies; good manners, good breeding, bon ton, good form.

correlate, *v.* **1.** bring together, relate to each other; compare, contrast.

2. correspond, interact, relate, connect, link, tie in; agree, jibe.

correlation, *n.* correspondence, equivalence; reciprocity, reciprocality, reciprocalness, mutual relationship, interrelationship, interdependence, mutuality; connection, relationship, tie-in.

correlative, *adj.* complementary, complemental, completing; corresponding, correspondent, analogous, similar; reciprocal, mutual, interrelated, interlinked, interconnected.

correspond, *v.* **1.** agree, comply, concur, conform, accord, go hand in hand, go along with; coincide, match, square, fit, fit together, go together; parallel, balance, equal, rival; tally, equate, follow; chime, harmonize, cohere, stand together.
2. reciprocate, complement, coequal, stand counter; relate, correlate, pertain, appertain, belong, answer; resemble, bear resemblance, mirror, look like; compare with, measure up against, *Inf.* stack up with.
3. (*all by letter*) communicate, keep in touch *or* contact, maintain connection; write, epistolize, exchange letters; write to, *Inf.* drop a line *or* note to; question, query; answer, reply, respond.

correspondence, *n.* **1.** similarity, analogy, likeness, resemblance, semblance; comparison, comparability; approximation, nearness, closeness.
2. agreement, accordance, conformity, concurrence; accord, harmony, concord, concordance, consonance, line, keeping; symmetry, balance, proportion, equilibrium; reciprocity, reciprocation, correlation, coequality, mutuality; uniformity, equivalence, equivalency, oneness, sameness.
3. counterpart, complement, correspondent, equivalent, coordinate; analogue, parallel; replica, copy, imitation; close match, close imitation *or* copy *or* replica; alternate, mate, fellow, companion; twin, alter ego; chip off the old block.
4. correspondency, corresponding, agreeing, complying, concurring, conforming; coinciding, matching; paralleling, equalling, rivaling; cohering, harmonizing; reciprocating, complementing, coequaling; relating, correlating; resembling, mirroring.
5. epistolography, epistolary intercourse *or* communication *or* exchange, letter writing, written correspondence *or* communication; (*both by writing*) commerce, intercourse; mail, *Brit.* post.
6. letters, epistles, missives, messages, favors, *Obs.* billets; notes, chits, lines; dispatches, bulletins; postcards.

correspondent, *n.* **1.** letter writer, pen pal; (*both by letter*) writer, communicator.
2. reporter, *Inf.* leg man; *Journalism.* stringer *or* string correspondent, *Journalism.* staffer, (*by letter*) contributor; foreign *or* special *or* war correspondent; journalist, newsman, newspaperman, newspaperwoman, newswriter, *Brit.* pressman, gentleman of the press, *Archaic.* gazetteer.
3. correlative, analogue, parallel; counterpart, equivalent, coordinate; reciprocator; replica, copy, imitation, close match; close replica, close copy, close imitation; alternate, mate, fellow, companion; twin, alter ego; chip off the old block.
—*adj.* **4.** analogous, comparable, parallel; similar, like, alike, not unalike; corresponding, reciprocal, reciprocative, answering.
5. agreeing, conforming, concordant, consonant, accordant; matching, coinciding; consistent, coherent, cohesive; synonymous, equivalent, *Inf.* six of one, half dozen of another; uniform, of a kind, of a piece, cast in the same mold.

corridor, *n.* **1.** passage, passageway, hall, hallway, aisle, walk, walkway, promenade, concourse; thoroughfare, causeway, thruway, channel, route, artery, driveway, path, lane, alley, alleyway, road, street, avenue, boulevard, highway, roadway.
2. arcade, gallery, loggia, colonnade, *Both Archit.* cloister, peristyle; piazza; lobby, foyer, vestibule, anteroom, antechamber; approach, entrance, entranceway, entryway, adit, way in.
3. narrow, defile, bridge, isthmus; outlet, way out, escape route.

corrigible, *adj.* **1.** reformable, correctible, remediable, emendable, reparable, improvable, curable, treatable; teachable, trainable, educable; changeable, amendable, flexible, adaptable.
2. amenable, tractable, pliant; submissive, acquiescent, yielding, agreeable, ready for; compliant, obedient, manageable, governable, docile.

corroborate, *v.* confirm, verify, prove right, validate, authenticate, certify, attest to; prove, establish, document, evidence, show, bear out, give credence to; sustain, uphold, substantiate, support, back up, endorse.

corroborative, *adj.* confirmatory, confirmative, verificative, verificatory, validatory, certificatory; substantiative, sustentive, upholding, supportive.

corrode, *v.* **1.** gnaw, eat out *or* away, fret, consume, devour, rust, *Both Chem.* oxidize, oxidate; erode, wear, wear down *or* away, waste away; abrade, rub away, chafe, fray; scrape, excoriate, grate, rasp, grind.
2. impair, deteriorate, ravage, waste, ruin, destroy; disintegrate, crumble, fragment, fractionate, decompose, decay; degenerate, worsen, canker, spoil, damage, harm, hurt, injure.

corrosion, *n.* **1.** gnawing, eating out *or* away, consumption, consuming, devouring, corroding, rusting, *Both Chem.* oxidation, oxidizing; erosion, eroding, attrition, detrition, wearing, wearing down *or* away, wear and tear, wasting away; abrasion, abrading, rubbing away, fretting, chafing, fraying; grating, rasping, grinding, scraping, excoriation.
2. impairment, impairing, deterioration, deteriorating, wear and tear, ravagement, ravaging, ruination, ruining, destruction, destroying; disintegration, disintegrating, crumbling, fragmentation, fragmenting, fractionization, fractionizing, decomposition, decomposing, decay, decaying; degeneration, degenerating, dilapidation, worsening; cankering, spoilage, spoiling, damage, damaging, harm, harming, hurt, hurting, injury, injuring.
3. rust, patina, calcification, film, deposit.

corrosive, *adj.* **1.** caustic, mordant, cauterant, escharotic, acrid, acrimonious, acid, acidic, cankerous; sharp, biting, gnawing, eating out *or* away, consumptive, consuming, devouring; corroding, rusting, *Both Chem.* oxidative, oxidizing.
2. erosive, erodent, wearing, wearing down *or* away, wasting away; abrasive, abrading, rubbing away, fretting, chafing, fraying; grating, rasping, grinding, scraping, excoriating.
—*n.* **3.** caustic, mordant, cauterant, escharotic, acid.

corrosiveness, *n.* causticity, causticness, mordancy, acridity, acridness, acrimoniousness, acidity, acidness, sharpness, bitingness; consumptiveness, devouringness, corrosivity, *Chem.* oxidizability; erosivity, erosiveness.

corrugate, *v.* **1.** furrow, groove, ridge, flute, striate; crease, seam, pleat, plicate, plait; wrinkle, crinkle, knit, pucker, cockle, ruffle, rumple.
—*adj.* **2.** furrowed, grooved, ridged, corrugated, fluted, wrinkled, creased.

corrugation, *n.* furrow, groove, channel, ridge, flute, stria; crease, seam, pleat, plication, plait; fold, wrinkle, crinkle, pucker, cockle, crumple; rugosity, unevenness, roughness, asperity.

corrupt, *adj.* **1.** dishonest, false, dishonorable, untrustworthy, underhand, deceitful, deceptive; crimi-

nal, knavish, crooked, villainous; base, faithless, recreant, traitorous; venal, bribable, mercenary, corruptible.
2. immoral, unprincipled, reprobate, unscrupulous, shameless, abandoned; depraved, wicked, evil, iniquitous, sinful, vicious; debased, debauched, degenerate, warped, perverted; dissolute, profligate, licentious, wanton, lascivious, lewd, lecherous, *Archaic.* lickerish, lustful, libidinous.
3. impure, adulterated, contaminated, defiled, tainted, polluted, infected; spoiled, rotten, decayed, rancid, fetid, putrid, putrescent, putrefactive; impaired, vitiated, marred, degraded, lowered, deteriorated.
—*v.* **4.** bribe, suborn, buy off, buy, pay off, grease [s.o.'s] palm; fix, *Inf.* rig, *Inf.* square; induce, tempt, lure, entice, coax, influence.
5. demoralize, deprave, debauch, degenerate, warp, pervert, seduce.
6. alter, adulterate, alloy, tamper with; debase, degrade, lower, prostitute; impair, vitiate, spoil, mar, blight; contaminate, defile, taint, pollute, infect, putrefy, poison, envenom.

corrupter, *n.* deceiver, knave, crook, villain, criminal; briber, tempter, enticer, wolf, coaxer; debaucher, debauchee, perverter; libertine, profligate, rake, roué; voluptuary, sensualist, seducer; lecher, satyr, goat.

corruption, *n.* **1.** depravity, vice, turpitude, wickedness, evil, iniquity, sinfulness, sin, viciousness; demoralization, perversion, degeneracy; laxity, looseness, immorality, shamelessness, abandon, fleshpots; dissolution, profligacy, wantonness, licentiousness, lasciviousness, lewdness, lustfulness.
2. dishonesty, baseness, falseness, underhandedness, deceit, deception; bribery, venality, mercenariness; jobbery, graft, *Law.* breach of trust; criminality, crookedness, villainy.
3. adulteration, debasement, impairment, vitiation, degradation, deterioration; contamination, defilement, tainting, pollution, infection; foulness, rottenness, rot, putrefaction, putrescence.

corsair, *n.* **1.** privateer, pirate, viking, buccaneer, freebooter, rapparee; raider, plunderer, marauder, depredator, looter, rifler.
2. privateer, armed ship, pirate ship, pirate, sea rover.

corset, *n.* stays, girdle, corselet, foundation, foundation garment, stomacher, *Obs.* bodice.

cortege, *n.* **1.** retinue, train, entourage; suite, staff, attendants, court.
2. procession, parade; column, string, line, file; cavalcade, caravan, coffle.

coruscation, *n.* gleam, flash, spark, glitter, *Archaic.* glister; ray, beam, flash, fulguration, glint, glance; sparkle, glimmer, scintillation, shiinmer, twinkling, glistening; radiance, brilliance, luster, luminescence, luminosity; glow, glare, phosphorescence, triboluminescence.

coruscation, *n.* gleam, flash, spark, glitter, *Archaic.* glister; ray, beam, flash, fulguration, glint, glance; sparkle, glimmer, scintillation, shimmer, twinkling, glistening; radiance, brilliance, luster, luminescence, luminosity; glow, glare, phosphorescence, triboluminescence.

cosmopolitan, *adj.* **1.** international, universal, global, world-wide, catholic, pandemic.
2. unprovincial, broadminded, liberal, cultivated, cultured; sophisticated, worldly, urbane, metropolitan, worldly-wise, wise in the ways of the world, *Inf.* jet-set.
—*n.* **3.** citizen of the world, world traveler, globetrotter, *Inf.* jet-setter, cosmopolite.

cosmopolite, *n.* See **cosmopolitan** (*def.* **3**).

cosmos, *n.* **1.** world, universe, creation, nature, wide world, *Inf.* the whole wide world; heavens, empyrean, vault of heaven, heavenly bodies, nebulae, galaxy, *Chiefly Literary.* welkin.
2. order, harmony, music of the spheres.

cosset, *v.* pamper, coddle, cherish, cocker; cuddle, nestle, nuzzle, hug; pet, fondle, caress, cover with kisses; dandle, pat on the cheek, chuck under the chin; make much of, fuss over, coo over, *Inf.* kill with kindness; coax, wheedle.

cost, *n.* **1.** price, value, worth, face value, market price *or* value; amount, figure, valuation, quotation, demand, asking price, appraisement, dollar value.
2. sacrifice, loss, penalty; damage, pain, suffering, detriment.
3. payment, outlay, expenditure, disbursement, expense; charge, rate, hire, fare, rent, *Inf.* what the traffic will bear.
—*v.* **4.** bring in, sell for, fetch, get; afford, yield, amount to, come to; (*all in relation to a given sum*) *Inf.* set [s.o.] back, *Inf.* run, *Inf.* put [s.o.] in the hole.
5. hurt, harm, injure, damage, do disservice to, overburden, weigh down, bear hard upon.

costly, *adj.* **1.** expensive, dear, high-priced, steep, stiff; exorbitant, extortionate, excessive, extravagant.
2. valuable, precious, priceless, inestimable; sumptuous, rich, opulent, lavish, magnificent, splendid, luxurious, gorgeous.

costume, *n.* livery, uniform, garb, habit, dress; clothing, clothes, attire; raiment, garments, vestments, *Inf.* gear, *Inf.* togs, *Sl.* rags, *Sl.* threads; ensemble, outfit, *Inf.* getup. See **apparel** (*def.* **1**).

cot[1], *n.* bed, bunk, berth, billet, pallet, *Naut.* hammock, *Sl.* the sack, *Sl.* the hay, *Brit Sl.* doss; *Brit.* crib.

cot[2], *n.* **1.** cottage, bungalow, bower, log cabin, blockhouse, *Brit. Dial.* cote, *Scot.* but and ben; hut, hutch, shack, shanty, *Brit.* bothy.
2. refuge, retreat, shelter, protection, hospice, hermitage, sanctuary, sanctum, sanctum sanctorum, haven; nest, hole, lair, den, cave.
3. sheath, casing, covering, sheathing, wrapper, wrapping, integument, involucre, involucrum.

coterie, *n.* **1.** club, fraternity, sorority, brotherhood, fellowship, sodality, society, community, troop, team, lodge, organization; sect, faction, order, group, party, camorra; association, affiliation, consortium, company, alliance, league, coalition, federation, guild, union, *Inf.* outfit.
2. clique, set, in crowd, circle; knot, band, ring, gang, crowd, clan.

cottage, *n.* hut, hutch, shack, shanty, *Brit.* bothy; cot, bungalow, bower, *Brit. Dial.* cote, *Scot.* but and ben; cabin, log cabin, blockhouse, A-frame, lodge, ski lodge, chalet.

couch, *n.* **1.** sofa, lounge, settee, divan, davenport, dais, ottoman, love seat, day bed, tête-à-tête, siamoise, vis-à-vis.
2. bed, cot, pallet, litter, *Sl.* sack, *Sl.* hay, *Brit. Sl.* kip, *Brit. Sl.* doss.
3. lair, den, burrow, tunnel, cave, hole, mew, covert.
—*v.* **4.** express, phrase, put into words, word, state, frame, style; infer, imply, suggest, hint at.
5. repose, recline, lounge, lie down, sprawl, loll, curl up, bed down; rest, *Inf.* take it easy.
6. crouch, squat, hunker down, stoop, bend, bow, dip; lie low, lie prone, hug the earth.
7. lurk, lie in wait, lie in ambush, *Inf.* lay for.

cough, *v.* hack, *Inf.* bark; choke, gag, gasp.

council, *n.* **1.** assembly, conclave, convocation,

synod, consistory, conventicle; conference, convention, congress, caucus; congregation, gathering; meeting, *Inf.* powwow, *Inf.* huddle.

2. cabinet, ministry, board, board of directors, directors; advisors, advisory board, brain trust, trustees; panel, committee, task force, study group.

counsel, *n.* **1.** advice, *Chiefly Brit. Dial.* rede, instruction, guidance, direction, teaching; opinion, suggestion, recommendation; warning, admonition.

2. consultation, deliberation, dialogue, discussion, consideration, conference; examination, study, analysis, advisement.

3. plan, design, deliberate purpose.

4. *Law.* legal advisor, attorney, lawyer. See **counselor** (*def.* **2**).

—*v.* **5.** advise, guide, instruct, direct; suggest, recommend, offer an opinion, tell [s.o.] what to do; urge, exhort, persuade, encourage; warn, caution, admonish.

counselor, *n.* **1.** advisor, guidance counselor, mentor, confidant; guide, coach, leader, teacher, tutor.

2. counselor-at-law, *Law.* counsel, trial lawyer, lawyer, *(in Britain)* barrister; legal advisor, advocate, attorney, solicitor, jurist, legist; pettifogger, Philadelphia lawyer, *Inf.* shyster.

count, *v.* **1.** enumerate, numerate, number; tell, count off, list, name.

2. calculate, compute, reckon up, tally, score, figure, give a figure to, put a figure on, quantify; add up, tally up, sum up, total up, figure up.

3. include, number among, reckon in *or* among, reckon with, take into account *or* consideration.

4. ascribe, impute, attribute, impute, assign, place, apply, attach.

5. consider, regard, esteem, deem, hold, judge, look upon.

6. matter, have worth, weigh, carry weight, rate, amount, *Inf.* cut ice, *Inf.* have clout.

7. **count on** *or* **upon** depend on, lean on, rely on, reckon on, calculate on, figure on; trust, take on trust, be sure of, take for granted; believe in, swear by.

—*n.* **8.** enumeration, numeration, calculation, computation, numbering, tallying, counting.

9. total number, total, sum total, grand total, tally, score, *Inf.* the whole story, *Inf.* the bottom line; whole, aggregate, lot, measure.

countenance, *n.* **1.** appearance, look, expression, complexion, mien, air; image, cast, semblance, form.

2. visage, face, *Sl.* pan, *Sl.* mug, *Sl.* kisser; profile, contour, features, lines, physiognomy.

3. sanction, approval, approbation, favor, acceptance, adoption, blessing, grace, *Inf.* O.K., advocacy, patronage, sponsorship, championship, support, backing, endorsement; encouragement, moral support, succor, assistance, aid, help.

—*v.* **4.** permit, allow, have, let [s.o.] get away with; tolerate, stand for, put up with.

5. approve, sanction, condone, hold with, favor; support, endorse, back up, second, stand up for, stand behind *or* beside, take the side of, be a part of, go along with; patronize, maintain, sustain, uphold; assist, aid, help, abet, succor, lend a hand, lend oneself to; encourage, promote, further, foster, forward, advance.

counter[1], *n.* **1.** table, chopping block, work surface; stand, stall, booth, window, display case; check-out area, cash register, cashier.

2. token, marker, man, checker; disk, wafer, coin, slug, *Obs.* plate.

counter[2], *n.* **1.** enumerator, numberer, abacist; figurer, reckoner, estimator; arithmetician, mathematician, adder.

2. calculator, calculating machine, adding machine, abacus; computer, data processor.

counter[3], *adv.* **1.** in the reverse direction, in the wrong way, against the grain, against the current *or* tide, downstream; contrary, in opposition, against, versus.

—*adj.* **2.** opposite, contrasting, different, another; reverse, return, second; oppositional, diametrically opposed, converse, inverse; contrary, antithetical, antithetic, polar, antipodal, oppositive, adversative.

—*n.* **3.** rebuttal, retaliation, return, comeback, answer; opposition, disputation, argument, denial.

—*v.* **5.** meet, answer, come back with, return, rebut, retaliate; oppose, controvert, offset; combat, contend with, dispute, argue against, deny.

counteract, *v.* **1.** act against, go *or* act counter to, oppose, contravene; run counter to, traverse; cross, antagonize, thwart, obstruct, frustrate, impede, hinder, interfere with; check, repress, restrain; resist, *Obs.* militate against, withstand; clash with, conflict with, work at cross purposes.

2. counterbalance, offset, counterpoise, countervail; neutralize, destroy the effect of, undo; annul, nullify, cancel.

counteraction, *n.* **1.** opposition, resistance, contravention, contradiction, contrariety, reaction; antagonism, obstruction, frustration, hindrance, interference, friction; check, repression, restraint; clash, conflict, collision.

2. counterbalance, counterpoise, neutralization; annulment, nullification, cancellation.

3. counterattack, counterblast, countermove, countermeasure; counterblow, counterpunch, counterthrust, counterstroke.

counterbalance, *n.* **1.** balance, counterpoise, counterweight, equilibration.

—*v.* **2.** balance, counterpoise, equilibrate; equalize, make up for, compensate.

3. offset, countervail; neutralize, destroy the effect of, undo.

counterfeit, *adj.* **1.** forged, fraudulent, imitation, fake, *Inf.* phony; not genuine, bogus, spurious, supposititious, bastardly, *Australian.* bunyip.

2. pretended, feigned, simulated, make-believe, sham, flash; unreal, false, insincere, mock, ersatz, synthetic; artificial, factitious, contrived, fictitious; assumed, put-on, pseudo; specious, meretricious, theatrical.

—*n.* **3.** imitation, reproduction, forgery, fake, *Inf.* phony, sham; falsification, fraud; *Jewelry.* paste; *Masonry.* scagliola; (*of literary works*) plagiarism.

4. pretense, deception, feigning, make-believe.

—*v.* **5.** forge, *Brit. Inf.* coin; (*all fraudulently*) imitate, copy, plagiarize, falsify, reproduce.

6. resemble, mirror, look like, favor; duplicate, replicate, match, echo.

7. simulate, assume, take on, affect, ape, mimic.

8. feign, dissemble, pretend, fake, act, put on, sham, malinger.

counterfeiter, *n.* **1.** forger, *Fr. faux-monnayeur, Brit. Inf.* coiner.

2. falsifier, imitator, copier, plagiarist; pretender, feigner, malingerer; imposter, mountebank, charlatan, quack, empiric, *Australian.* bunyip.

countermand, *v.* **1.** revoke, rescind, abrogate, reverse, repeal, abolish; annul, disannul, nullify, declare null and void, render null and void, void, avoid; quash, invalidate, vitiate, vacate, disenact, disestablish; cancel, discharge; supersede, set aside.

2. retract, recall, withdraw, take back; counterorder, override, overrule.

—*n.* **3.** counterorder, overriding, overruling, veto.

countermarch, *n.* **1.** reversal, about-face, turnabout; backlash, recoil, reaction, boomerang, rebound.
—*v.* **2.** do an about-face, veer round, wheel about; turn tail, take to one's heels, retrace one's steps; retreat, retire, draw back; revert, retrogress, fall back; withdraw, recede, retrocede, retrograde.

counterpart, *n.* **1.** copy, duplicate, duplication, *Inf.* ditto; model, reproduction, replica, fascimile; representation, reflection, likeness, effigy; Photostat, *Inf.* stat, Xerox copy, *Inf.* Xerox.
2. parallel, analogue, coordinate, correlative, correlate, reciprocator, correspondent, corresponding part.
3. equivalent, match, twin, double; alternate, pendant, companion, mate, fellow; imitation, close imitation, close copy, close match; complement, supplement; reverse, obverse.
4. equal, coequal, peer, compeer, rival; partner, opposite number, sidekick, alter ego, *Australian.* cobber; associate, colleague, confrere.
5. chip off the old block, the very image, the spitting image, spit and image.

counterpoise, *n.* **1.** counterbalance, balance, counterweight; equilibration, equalization, equivalence, equilibrium, equanimity.
—*v.* **2.** counterbalance, balance, equilibrate; equalize, make up for, compensate, square.
3. counteract, offset, countervail; neutralize, destroy the effect of, undo.

countrified, *adj.* rustic, rural, farm, country, agrestic, agrarian, bucolic; backwoods, provincial, inurbane, country-bred, country-born, upcountry, *Sl.* from the sticks, *Sl.* from the boonies, yokelish, *Sl.* hickish, *Sl.* rube, *Sl.* hayseed; homespun, homebred, homey, homely, homelike, down-home, (*usually of thought or philosophy*) cracker-barrel, *Inf.* folksy.

country, *n.* **1.** region, district, territory, tract of land, land, terrain; section, quarter, area, place; parts, neighborhood, *Inf.* neck of the woods.
2. nation, power, state, commonwealth, city-state; kingdom, realm, royal domain *or* territory; union, confederation, confederacy.
3. people, public, population, inhabitants, residents, dwellers; members, membership, citizens, citizenry; nation, society, community; nationality, race, tribe, stock, ethnic group.
4. native land, homeland, fatherland, *Latin. patria,* mother country; land of one's birth, ancestral home, roots.
5. rural districts, provinces, countryside, *U.S. Inf.* the sticks, *Sl.* the boondocks, *Sl.* the boonies, *Australian.* outback; backwoods, hinterlands, back country, woods, bush, *Sl.* the bushes; wilds, wilderness, frontier, no man's land, the middle of nowhere.
—*adj.* **6.** rural, agrarian, agricultural, agrestic; countrified, provincial, rustic, pastoral, Arcadian, bucolic, georgic, sylvan, *U.S.* woodsy, woodland, woody, wooded; back-wood, backwoods, sequestered, secluded, out-of-the-way; isolated, lonely, remote, removed, *Australian.* outback; sparsely populated, frontierlike, uninhabited.
7. backward, unlearned, ignorant; unpolished, unrefined, uncultured, unsophisticated, unworldly; naive, simple, innocent, artless; awkward, clumsy, inept, *Sl.* klutzy, hobnail, loutish, oafish; rude, uncivil, impolite, uncouth, hick, boorish, gross; unmannerly, wild, *Inf.* woolly, rough, hard, tough.

countryman, *n.* **1.** native, indigene, native inhabitant *or* resident; compatriot, fellow citizen, fellow countryman *or* countrywoman.
2. rustic, yokel, country bumpkin, peasant, *Inf.* hayseed, *Inf.* hick, *Sl.* rube, (*in the Southern U.S.*) redneck, bogtrotter; clodhopper, *Sl.* klutz, clumsy boor, churl, lout, oaf.
3. farmer, husbandman, *Brit.* yeoman; farm laborer, *Archaic.* hind, plowman; swain, country boy *or* lad, plowboy.

countryside, *n.* **1.** rural district, provinces, country, *U.S. Inf.* the sticks, *Sl.* the boondocks. See **country** (*def.* **5**).
2. rustics, countryfolk, countrymen. See **countryman** (*def.* **2**).
3. landscape, scenery, scene, panorama, tableau, picture, sight; view, vista, prospect, outlook.

county, *n.* shire, canton; province, state, region, territory.

coup, *n.* (*all of a highly successful nature*) stroke, move, maneuver, act, action, deed, feat, exploit, stunt; master stroke, *Fr. coup de maître,* stroke of genius, tour de force.

coup de grace, *n.* deathblow, mortal blow, decisive blow, killing blow, final stroke, finishing touch, quietus, end-all; the kill, the clincher, the settler, the equalizer, the finisher; knockout, knockout blow, KO, *Inf.* kayo *or* kayo punch, *Inf.* Sunday punch, *Inf.* haymaker, *Sl.* sockdolager.

coup d'état, *n.* (*all of political power*) seizure, grab, power grab, coup, putsch, overthrow, overturn; revolt, revolution, rebellion, mutiny, insurgence, uprising; (*all in reference to power or government*) violent change, radical *or* total *or* sweeping change, clean sweep.

couple, *n.* **1.** pair, duo, dyad, twosome, binary, couplet, doublet, matched set; brace, span, yoke, team; two, both, *Archaic.* twain.
2. twins, *Astron.* Gemini; partners, lovers, man and wife, husband and wife.
—*v.* **3.** partner, twin, double, pair *or* match up, mate; unite, join, bond, fuse, weld, glue, cohere, stick together, hold together; yoke, bind, tie together, bracket; connect, attach, link, chain, shackle; associate, affiliate, ally.
4. marry, wed, lead [s.o.] to the altar, walk [s.o.] down the aisle, give away, hook up, join in holy wedlock *or* matrimony, *Sl.* hitch.
5. copulate, have sex, have relations; fornicate, have an affair.

coupon, *n.* certificate, check, stub; ticket, *Sl.* freebie, *Sl.* Annie Oakley; advertisement, label, tag.

courage, *n.* **1.** bravery, valor, valorousness, valiancy, valiance, heroism, prowess, stout-heartedness, lionheartedness, iron-heartedness, great-heartedness, high-heartedness; virility, manliness, manfulness, manhood, gallantry, chivalry, chivalrousness; intrepidity, intrepidness, fearlessness, dauntlessness, awelessness, dreadlessness; boldness, bold-spiritedness, high-spiritedness, daring, dash, élan, panache, derring-do, audacity, audaciousness, rashness, (*usually negative*) bravado; assurance, self-assurance, self-reliance, confidence, pot-valor, pot-valiance, pot-valiancy.
2. fortitude, endurance, tenacity, determination, will, will power; firmness, resoluteness, resolution, indomitableness, indomitability, invincibleness, invincibility, staunchness, stanchness, steadfastness, stalwartness, doughtiness, sturdiness, hardiness, hardihood, bulldog courage; mettle, pluck, pluckiness, spirit, backbone, gumption, blood, heart, nerve, grit, *U.S. Inf.* sand, *Inf.* starch, *Inf.* spunk, *Sl.* guts, *Sl.* moxie.

courageous, *adj.* **1.** brave, valiant, valorous, heroic, hero-like, stout-hearted, lionhearted, iron-hearted, great-hearted; virile, manly, manful, gallant, chivalrous, chivalric; intrepid, fearless, unafraid, dauntless, dreadless, aweless, nervy, *Sl.* gutsy, unblenching, unblenched, undaunted, unalarmed, undismayed, unappalled; bold, bold-spirited, high-spirited, daring, dashing, adventurous, audacious, rash, reckless; assured, self-assured, self-reliant, confident, pot-valorous, pot-valiant.

2. firm, resolute, indomitable, unconquerable, invincible, staunch, stanch, steadfast, stalwart, *Archaic.* stalworth, doughty, sturdy, hardy; unflinching, unyielding, undeviating, unswerving, unfaltering, unshrinking, unbending, unhesitating; mettlesome, plucky, gritty, game, spirited, red-blooded, *Inf.* spunky.

courier, *n.* messenger, carrier, postman, mailman, letter carrier, mail carrier; bearer, porter, bringer; harbinger, herald, runner, forerunner, (*in Turkey*) kavass; envoy, emissary, legate, nuncio; postrider, rider, estafette, pony express rider; transporter, conveyor, conductor; Pheidippides, Hermes, Mercury, Iris, Ariel.

course, *n.* **1.** progression, headway, progress, march, advance, furtherance; proceeding, development, rise.

2. route, way, run, road, lane, avenue, passage, track, trail; direction, channel, tack, cut, pass; runway, fairway, approach; path, line, trajectory, career, arc; round, beat, circuit, ambit, circumference, orbit; trend, tenor, drift, bearing.

3. passage, passing, lapse, duration; span, spell, space, stretch; term, time, period, stage, phase, season; progress, flow, sweep, current, tide, flight.

4. procedure, process, way, wise; manner, mode, method; scheme, plan, system, regimen; policy, conduct.

5. conduct, behavior, comportment, deportment; carriage, bearing, presence; demeanor, mien, air, aspect; manners, ways, actions, dealings; customs, habits, practice, wonts, conventions, praxis.

6. series, sequence, succession, concatenation, catenation, chain; cycle, circle, continuity, regularity; set, order, ordering, turn, array, arrangement.

7. program, study, curriculum, schedule; class, lesson, lecture, instruction, seminar.

8. in due course eventually, in time, in the course of time, sooner or later; ultimately, in the end, at length.

9. of course certainly, surely, definitely, assuredly, by all means; indubitably, undoubtedly, without a doubt, no doubt.

—*v.* **10.** run through *or* over, pass through *or* over, cover, traverse, cross; wander over, travel over, roam over.

11. chase, pursue, follow, run after, hound, mouse, dog, be at one's heels; hunt, stalk, trail, shadow, track, follow the scent of; search out, ferret out, scout out, look for.

12. run, race, rush, surge, gush; speed, hie, hasten, hurry, post; scamper, scud, sprint, scurry; gallop, charge, bolt, dash.

court, *n.* **1.** courtyard, yard, enclosure, close, quadrangle, *Inf.* quad, *Fort.* parade; peristyle, patio, veranda, cloister; square, plaza, esplanade, *It. piazza, Fr. place.*

2. lane, way, drive, circle; alley, row, *Chiefly Brit.* mews, *Chiefly Brit.* terrace; road, avenue, street.

3. palace, mansion, castle, chateau, royal residence; hall, manor house.

4. retinue, cortege, train, entourage; suite, staff, royal household, attendants.

5. attention, homage, deference, respects, regards; amenities, urbanities, civilities, courtesies; address, courtship, wooing, attentions, blandishments, suit.

6. bench, bar, judiciary, judicature, judicatory; tribunal, forum, chancery; assizes, trial, session; Areopagus, King's Bench, Queen's Bench; Star Chamber, Inquisition.

—*v.* **7.** curry favor with, flatter, cajole, coax, wheedle, blandish; fawn upon, toady, pander to, *Inf.* soft-soap, *Inf.* honey up; *Inf.* butter up, *Inf.* bootlick, *Inf.* apple-polish, *Sl.* brown-nose.

8. woo, address, pay addresses to, pay suit to, serenade, bill and coo, make love to, *Archaic.* sue; go with, keep company, go steady with; take out, date, *Brit.* walk out with.

9. invite, solicit, attract, draw; ask for, leave the door open to; induce, sway, prompt; provoke, whet, inspire, engender; make, motivate, actuate, generate; cause, lead to, elicit, bring on *or* about.

courteous, *adj.* **1.** mannerly, well-mannered, polite, civil, respectful, deferential, deferent; decorous, proper, formal, *Fr. comme il faut*, ceremonious; tactful, diplomatic, politic; cordial, genial, affable, good-humored, pleasant, sociable; pleasing, winning, charming, ingratiating, complaisant, agreeable, obliging, attentive.

2. well-behaved, well-bred, refined, polished, civilized; genteel, gentle, ladylike, gracious, kind; gentlemanly, gentlemanlike, courtly, gallant, chivalrous, chivalric; urbane, suave, debonair, sophisticated, elegant.

courtesan, *n.* prostitute, harlot, whore, woman of ill repute, trollop, strumpet, quean; lady of the evening, call girl, *Fr. fille de joie*, Cyprian; woman of the profession, member of the oldest profession, Mrs. Warren; paramour, concubine, mistress, kept woman, odalisque, hetaera, white slave, *Sl.* doxy; temptress, siren, seductress, Delilah, Jezebel.

courtesy, *n.* **1.** mannerliness, politeness, politesse, civility, good manners, good behavior, courteousness; respect, respectfulness, deference; decorousness, properness, formality, formalness, ceremony, ceremonialism; correctness, tact, diplomacy; cordiality, cordialness, amenity, geniality, affability, amiability, sociability, friendliness, agreeability; helpfulness, complaisance, obligingness, *Fr. prévenance.*

2. gentility, gentleness, graciousness, kindness, ladylikeness; gentlemanliness, courtliness, gallantry, chivalry; urbanity, suavity, social graces, manners; nicety, elegance, elegancy, refinement, culture, polish, sophistication; social procedures, decorum, propriety, protocol.

3. respects, devoirs, regards; welcome, reception, greeting, salutation.

4. consent, agreement, acquiescence, indulgence; generosity, beneficence, munificence; favor, help.

5. curtsy, bow, genuflection, nod, handshake.

courtier, *n.* **1.** attendant, servitor, squire, pursuivant, seneschal, steward, major-domo, chamberlain; liegeman, vassal, subject, cupbearer, train-bearer; henchman, supporter, follower.

2. flatterer, blandisher, wheedler, cajoler; fawner, sycophant, *Archaic.* pickthank, toady, *Inf.* bootlicker, *Sl.* brown-noser, *Inf.* apple polisher, yes man, truckler; parasite, hanger-on.

courtliness, *n.* **1.** politeness, politesse, civility, mannerliness, courteousness, courtesy; respect, respectfulness, deference; decorousness, properness, formality, formalness, ceremony, ceremonialism; correctness, tact, diplomacy, savoir-faire; gentlemanliness, gallantry, chivalry; elegance, elegancy, bon ton, refinement, gentility, etiquette, culture, polish, sophistication; social procedures, decorum, propriety, protocol.

2. flattery, blandishment, blarney, wheedling, cajolery; obsequiousness, sycophancy, fawning, toadying, playing up to, *Sl.* buttering-up, *Inf.* apple-polishing, currying favor.

courtly, *adj.* **1.** gentlemanly, gentlemanlike, gallant, chivalrous, chivalric; refined, well-bred, polished, sophisticated, elegant, suave, debonair, urbane; polite, civil, mannerly, well-mannered; respectful, deferential, deferent; decorous, proper, formal, *Fr. comme il*

faut, ceremonious; tactful, diplomatic, politic.
2. flattering, blandishing, wheedling, cajoling, fawning, sycophantish, obsequious, toadying, *Inf.* bootlicking, *Inf.* apple-polishing, *Sl.* brown-nosing.

courtship, *n.* wooing, courting, dating, suit, serenading.

courtyard, *n.* court, quadrangle, *Inf.* quad, *Archit.* peristyle, *Archit.* cloister; patio, yard.

cousin, *n.* kinsman, kinswoman, kin, congener, *Inf.* coz.

cove, *n.* **1.** bay, bight, inlet, *Chiefly Brit.* creek, *Both Chiefly Scot.* firth, frith; arm of the sea, fiord, estuary.
2. nook, recess, niche; cave, cavern, grotto, hollow, cavity; hideaway, shelter, refuge, retreat.
3. narrow pass, passage, defile; trail, lane, course, corridor; channel, strait.

covenant, *n.* **1.** contract, compact, concordat, convention, pact, treaty, entente, alliance; bond, indenture, commitment, obligation; agreement, arrangement, understanding, settlement, gentlemen's agreement, deal, bargain, transaction; pledge, word, promise, sponsion.
2. legal document, cartel, acknowledgment, deed, lease; warrant, warranty, guarantee, guaranty.
—*v.* **3.** pledge, promise, avow; settle, establish, agree on, make *or* strike a bargain, come to terms; negotiate, make terms, adjust, work out, pound out, bargain, *Scot.* argle-bargle; stipulate, limit, circumscribe, demarcate, bound.

cover, *v.* **1.** protect, shield, shelter, place under cover; conceal, hide, house, secrete, ensconce, cache, bury.
2. overlay, overspread, blanket, mantle, canopy, carpet, pave, film, coat, layer; overgrow, overrun, envelop; overlie, overlap, extend over *or* beyond, imbricate.
3. clothe, outfit, equip, gear up, garb, robe, invest, gird, accouter; cover oneself, wrap up, enwrap, bundle up, muffle up, swaddle; encase, sheathe, case, jacket; don *or* put on one's hat.
4. **cover oneself with** collect, heap up, earn, work for; secure, acquire, pick up, glean, harvest; win, receive, attain, achieve, realize.
5. defend, protect, guard, keep safe; attend, watch over, safeguard, secure; tend, escort, conduct, convey; flank, bulwark, fortify, reinforce.
6. take over, take charge *or* responsibility, relieve, act for, double for; substitute, replace, stand in for, take [s.o.'s] turn, back [s.o.] up, *Sl.* pinch-hit; take the blame for, *Sl.* take the rap for, *Sl.* be the goat.
7. screen, curtain, shade, cloak, shroud, veil, mask, hood; hedge, camouflage, disguise; shadow, obscure, cloud, fog, overcast, overshadow, darken, dim, eclipse.
8. **cover up** hide, conceal, keep secret, repress, *Inf.* hush up, *Inf.* keep mum, *Inf.* put *or* keep the lid on; *Inf.* stonewall, *Inf.* keep under one's hat, *Inf.* keep one's lips buttoned; dissemble, hugger-mugger, feign, pretend; cloud, obscure, obfuscate, *Inf.* lay down a smokescreen; falsify, misrepresent, equivocate, play false, *Sl.* put on an act.
9. lay on, spread with, slather, go heavy with, be generous with, *Sl.* slap on, *Sl.* pile on, *Sl.* slobber on; coat, smear, besmear, daub, bedaub; paint, varnish, plaster, incrust; plate, gild, enamel, lacquer.
10. include, contain, incorporate; deal with, embrace, take in, comprise, embody, subsume; provide for, admit, refer to, take into account; review, view, survey, study, take stock of; explore, examine, peruse, consider, investigate, inquire into; report on, write up, describe, tell of.
11. flood, overflow, wash over, inundate, submerge, overrun, engulf.
12. counterbalance, compensate, offset; make good for, be good for, settle up, square with, requite, *Inf.* square; remit, recoup, adjust, satisfy.
13. pass over, travel over, pass through, traverse, cross over, range over, track over, tramp *or* wander over.
—*n.* **14.** lid, top, cap; ceiling, roof, overhead; head covering, hat, headdress, scarf, hood, cowl; binding, jacket, wrapper, wrap, case, sheathe, envelope; haze, film, coating, layer; blanket, mantle, canopy, carpet.
15. pretense, feigning, dissembling, shamming, putting up a front, surface, empty show, disguise, camouflage; façade, false front, smokescreen, window dressing, faking, hoodwinking; hugger-mugger, *Inf.* cover-up.
16. woods, underbrush, undergrowth; thicket, vegetation, shrubbery, ground cover; break, bosket, copse, grove.
17. retreat, refuge, haven, lair, den, covert, coverture; hiding, blind, ambush, ambuscade.
18. veil, screen, cloak, shroud, mask, curtain, shadow, shade.
19. **break cover** emerge, come out of hiding, come into the open, come forth, step forward, *Inf.* come out of the closet.
20. **take cover** hide, seek shelter *or* safety, run for cover, burrow in, *Inf.* run for the hills; conceal oneself, get out of sight, lie low, *Inf.* hide out.
21. **under cover** secretly, covertly, clandestinely, incognito; furtively, stealthily, on the sly, conspiratorially, confidentially, in the dark.

covering, *n.* **1.** protection, shield, shelter, housing; roof, ceiling, overhead, thatch, canopy, awning, marquee, baldachin; pavilion, tent, tarpaulin, tarp, tilt; parasol, umbrella, sunshade; paving, carpet, rug, flooring, linoleum.
2. lid, top, cover; hat, cap, headdress, bonnet; hood, cowl, shawl, kerchief, handkerchief, scarf, mantilla.
3. screen, curtain, shade, veil, facade, false front, smokescreen, mask; shadow, cloud, haze, overcast, fog; pall, darkness, obscurity, swaddling, shroud.
4. blanket, mantle, robe, cloak, wrap, clothing, gear, garb; envelope, sheathe, chase, jacket, binding, wrapper.
5. capsule, pod, casing, tegmen, integument, theca; film, coating, layer, crust.

coverlet, *n.* bedspread, counterpane, bedcover; quilt, comforter, eiderdown, blanket.

covert, *adj.* **1.** covered, clandestine, surreptitious, underground, behind the scenes, in the background, behind the curtain; out of sight, unseen, invisible, unapparent, latent, dormant, delitescent; unknown, unsuspected, undiscovered; unspoken of, untold, unbreathed, sub rosa; muffled, clouded, dark, mysterious, obscure; furtive, underhanded, stealthy, sly, sneaking, *Inf.* sneaky; deceitful, insidious.
2. sheltered, concealed, hidden, private, secluded, secret, disguised, camouflaged, incognito; screened, veiled, masked.
—*n.* **3.** shelter, cover, protection, refuge, harbor, haven, asylum, sanctuary; hiding place, retreat, resort; lair, den, snuggery, cell, closet, *Latin. sanctum sanctorum*, *Inf.* hide-out; cave, hole, nest, abri.
4. concealment, disguise, camouflage; screen, veil, mask; shield, defense.

covet, *v.* **1.** desire, want, long for, wish for, have an appetite for; fancy, have an eye on, ogle, set one's heart on, yearn for, hanker for, sigh for, pine for; aim after, aspire to, set one's sights on, dream of.
2. be bent upon, thirst after, crave, eye greedily, hunger for, itch for, have a passion for, lust after; envy, begrudge, grasp after.

covetous, *adj.* **1.** desirous, greedy, avaricious, grasping, acquisitive, *Sl.* grabby, rapacious; selfish, hoarding, possessive; miserly, penurious, parsimonious, grudging, niggardly; stingy, mean, close fisted, tight-fisted, close, *Inf.* tight, penny-pinching; mercenary, venal, usurious.

2. ravenous, ravening, voracious, devouring, gluttonous, gormandizing, cormorant, edacious; open-mouthed, hoggish, piggish, swinish; insatiable, insatiate, unquenchable, omnivorous.

3. eager, avid, cupidinous, fain, *Archaic.* lickerish; anxious, breathless, impatient, longing, thirsty, athirst; ardent, agog, zealous, fervent, burning; ambitious, aspiring, hungry, craving, esurient.

4. lustful, lecherous, libidinous, lascivious, salacious, concupiscent, carnal, prurient.

covetousness, *n.* **1.** desire, greed, graspingness, acquisitiveness, *Sl.* grabbiness, avariciousness, rapacity, rapaciousness; selfishness, self-seeking, egocentricity, self-interest, self-indulgence; miserliness, penuriousness, parsimony, niggardliness; stinginess, meanness, closefistedness, tight-fistedness, mercenariness, venality, usurious, sordidness.

2. eagerness, cupidity, avidity, yearning, craving; keenness, itch, itching, appetite, stomach, *U.S. Dial.* big eye, appetence; anxiousness, breathlessness, impatience, longing, thirst, ardor, zeal, fervency, passion, mania; hankering, aspiration, hunger, lust, ambitiousness.

3. ravenousness, voraciousness, gluttony, edacity, open-mouthedness, hoggishness, piggishness, swinishness; insatiability, insatiateness, omnivorousness, gulosity.

covey, *n.* brood, bevy, flock, *Rare.* nide; group, company, body, set, outfit, gang, crew.

cow[1], *n.* bovine, heifer, *U.S.* bossy, *Dial.* critter, *Sl.* moo-cow.

2. till the cows come home for a long time, forever, forever and a day. See **forever**.

cow[2], *v.* intimidate, overawe, awe, daunt, dismay, dishearten; terrify, petrify, frighten, affright, scare; threaten, domineer, buffalo, browbeat, bulldoze, bully, push around, bullyrag; subdue, overcome, break.

coward, *n.* poltroon, dastard, craven, recreant, *Archaic.* caitiff, *Archaic.* niddering; yellowbelly, mouse, baby, big baby, wheyface, invertebrate, *Inf.* jellyfish, *Inf.* fraidy-cat, *Inf.* scaredy-cat, *Inf.* nervous nellie, *Sl.* chicken, *Sl.* weak sister; sissy, weakling, milksop, Milquetoast, mollycoddle, *Inf.* pantywaist.

cowardice, *n.* pusillanimity, timidity, timorousness, faint-heartedness, weak-heartedness, *Inf.* chicken-heartedness; poltroonery, dastardliness, recreancy, cravenness, cowardliness; faint heart, weak knees, white feather, *Inf.* chicken heart, *Inf.* funk, *Sl.* cold feet, *Sl.* yellow streak.

cowardly, *adj.* craven, poltroon, dastardly, base, recreant, *Archaic.* niddering, *Archaic.* caitiff; pusillanimous, timorous, timid, fearful, afraid, frightened, afraid of one's shadow, not having the heart, unmanly, faint-hearted, lily-livered, white-livered, *Inf.* chicken-hearted, *Inf.* chicken-livered, *Inf.* pantywaist, *Inf.* yellow, *Sl.* yellow-bellied, *Sl.* candy-assed.

cowboy, *n.* cowpuncher, cowpoke, cow hand, bronco, *Western U.S.* buckaroo, *Southwestern U.S.* vaquero, gaucho; drover, cowherd, cattle-herder, *Chiefly Brit.* grazier, *Brit.* cowman, *Obs.* neatherd.

cower, *v.* **1.** cringe, shrink, flinch, wince, quail, recoil, blench, *Inf.* funk, *Sl.* mooch; shake, tremble, quiver, *Inf.* shake in one's boots *or* shoes; kowtow, bow, bow before, bow to, bow and scrape.

2. skulk, slink, slither, sneak; grovel, wallow, welter.

3. *All Brit. Dial.* stoop, squat, hunch, crouch, slouch.

coxcomb, *n.* dandy, jack-a-dandy, fop, dude, beau, spark, popinjay; blade, *Chiefly Brit.* blood, buck, jackanapes, whippersnapper; *Fr. petit maître*, Beau Brummel, macaroni, *Archaic.* princox; exquisite, *Sl.* peacock, prinker, preener, show-off; fashion plate, male clotheshorse, silk-stocking, *Brit. Inf.* toff, snob.

coy, *adj.* **1.** shy, modest, demure, prudish, *Archaic.* verecund; meek, submissive, tame, gentle, unassuming, unpretentious; bashful, diffident, retiring, reserved, demurring; self-conscious, sheepish, shamefaced, blushing, embarrassed; constrained, reluctant, hesitant, backward, skittish; unconfident, unsure, timid, timorous; shrinking, withdrawn, distant, *Inf.* introverted, quiet, unsocial, unsociable.

2. coquettish, flirtatious, flirty, philandering, playing hard-to-get.

cozen, *v.* cheat, deceive, beguile, inveigle; double-cross, play one false, dupe, *Sl.* take [s.o.] for a ride; take advantage of, *Inf.* have [s.o.] eating out of one's hand, *Inf.* wrap [s.o.] around one's little finger. See **cheat** (*defs.* **3**, **4**).

cozenage, *n.* deception, deceit, trickery; hoaxing, deluding, fooling, hoodwinking; swindling, fraudulency, misrepresentation, chichanery, pettifoggery, *Inf.* hocus-pocus, *Inf.* hanky-panky; double-dealing, circumvention, bluffing, feinting, *Inf.* pulling the wool over [s.o.'s] eyes, guile, wile, imposition; victimization, treachery, knavery, duplicity, machination, artful dodging.

cozy, *adj.* **1.** snug, warm, comfortable, homelike, *Inf.* homey; easy, relaxing, cheerful; sheltered, ensconced, *Inf.* snug as a bug in a rug, *Inf.* comfy, *Inf.* comfy-cozy.

2. (*usually as a result of dishonesty*) expedient, convenient, beneficial, advantageous, profitable; gratifying, self-serving, of mutual benefit.

crabbed, *adj.* **1.** grouchy, ill-natured, ill-humored, cross, peevish, splenetic, cantankerous, crotchety, crusty; irritable, touchy, testy, out of sorts; bitter, sour, caustic, churlish, snappish, waspish, surly, acrimonious; petulant, sulky, sullen, morose.

2. perverse, contrary, obstinate, stubborn; captious, sarcastic, contumelious, virulent; growling, snarling, harsh.

3. intricate, obscure, hard to understand, trying, difficult, confusing, cryptic, *Inf.* clear as mud.

4. illegible, scribbled, undecipherable, hieroglyphical; squeezed, cramped, labored.

crabbedness, *n.* grouchiness, ill nature, ill humor, peevishness, spleen, gruffness; irritability, crotchetiness, *Inf.* crabbiness; bitterness, churlishness, snappishness, surliness, acrimoniousness; petulance, moodiness, sullenness, moroseness; acerbity, asperity, acrimony, harshness.

crabby, *adj.* grouchy, irritable, ill-humored. See **crabbed** (*def.* **1**).

crack, *v.* **1.** snap, pop, clap, go bang; boom, crash, clash, explode, thunder, detonate, fulminate.

2. break, crackle, craze, chap; fracture, fragmentize, chip, break off, splinter, shiver, shatter, smash, burst; break *or* snap in two, split, cleave, sunder, sever, rend, reave, disjoint; damage, impair, *Sl.* bust, *Sl.* total.

3. succumb, fall to, yield, give way, lose ground, go downhill; collapse, topple, break down, come apart at the seams, go to pieces, let go, *Sl.* lose one's cool, *Sl.* crack up; founder, fail, die out, *Sl.* conk out, *Sl.* go kaput.

4. move, touch, stir, upset, break [s.o.] up, shake [s.o.] up, get to.

5. strike, hit, slap, smack, thwack, *Inf.* whack, *Inf.* clip, *Dial.* hit up side the head; knock, thump, box, buffet, punch, jab, cuff.

—*n.* **6.** snap, clap, pop, clack; bang, shot, report, sounding; boom, burst, crash, explosion, detonation.

7. blow, hit, strike, slap, slam, thwack, *Inf.* whack, *Inf.* clip, *Inf.* clout; knock, thump, punch, fillip, jab, cuff.

8. fissure, crevice, crevasse, chink, cleft, stria, cranny, interstice, groove, sulcus, *Archaic.* scissure; fracture, break, chap, check, rupture, split, rift, breach, scission, slit, separation; hole, gap, cavity, opening, orifice, aperture; space, interspace, interval, interstice, narrow.

cracked, *adj.* **1.** broken, crackled, fractured, chipped, chinky, rimose; fissured, split, cloven, reft, rent, agape, dehiscent; holey, foraminous, pervious, leaky.

2. damaged, injured, marred, impaired; faulty, imperfect, defective.

3. *Informal.* mad, insane, *Sl.* nuts, *Sl.* off one's nut. See **crazy** (*defs.* **1, 2, 9**).

crackle, *v.* **1.** snap, clap, click, crepitate, decrepitate; pop, burst, go bang, shoot off.

2. crack, break, fracture; fragmentize, craze, chap, shiver, shatter, smash.

cradle, *n.* **1.** crib, bassinet, baby's bed; bed, cot, litter.

2. hotbed, breeding place, nursery; infancy, nascence, beginnings, origins, incunabula; source, fountainhead, mainspring, birthplace, origin.

—*v.* **3.** rock, rock to sleep; calm, pacify, quiet, lull, soothe; nestle, tuck in, put to bed.

4. nurture, foster, nourish, mother, tend, care for, take care of, watch over; nurse, wet-nurse, suckle.

craft, *n.* **1.** skill, skillfullness, dexterity, adroitness, expertness, mastery, artistry; aptitude, facility, address, dispatch, ready skill, *Inf.* know-how; ingenuity, cleverness, talent, flair, genius, art, knack.

2. cunning, wiliness, slyness, foxiness, artfulness, guile, subtlcty, craftiness, shrewdness; deceit, deception, duplicity, trickery.

3. artifice, subterfuge, contrivance, wile; scheme, plot, design, stratagem.

4. trade, occupation, vocation, calling, metier.

5. guild, union, society, association, organization, fraternity, brotherhood.

6. ship, boat, vessel, bark, skiff.

craftsman, *n.* **1.** artisan, handicraftsman, master craftsman, artificer, mechanic; skilled laborer, journeyman.

2. artist, master, old master, past master; talent, genius, prodigy, giant, *Inf.* wizard *or* wiz.

crafty, *adj.* **1.** cunning, artful, sly, wily, subtle, foxy, *Sl.* crazy like a fox, *Scot. and North Eng.* pawky; shrewd, astute, canny, sharp, knowing, *Inf.* cagey.

2. insidious, guileful, disingenuous, scheming, plotting, designing, calculating, contriving; deceitful, tricky, crooked, dishonest, underhanded, *Inf.* left-hand; false, false-hearted, double-dealing, two-faced, Janus-faced; shifty, slippery, smooth, slick.

crag, *n.* steep rock, cliff, bluff; ridge, *Phys. Geog.* arête, scarp, escarpment, palisade; peak crest, aiguille, pinnacle, tor; *Chiefly Brit.* pike, *Scot. and North Eng.* brae.

craggy, *adj.* **1.** full of crags, cragged; rocky, jagged, gnarled, scraggy, broken, uneven, anfractuous; steep, abrupt, precipitous.

2. rough, harsh, rugged; blunt, brusque, bluff; bearish, surly, churlish; unrefined, unpolished, inurbane.

cram, *v.* **1.** stuff, fill, fill up, overfill, overstuff, overcrowd, fill to overflowing, stuff to the gills, fill to the brim.

2. force down *or* in, ram down, pack in, push in, shove in, press in; jam, squeeze, compress, condense.

3. overfeed, overeat, overdrink, overindulge, overdo; glut, gorge, cloy, satiate, surfeit, eat one's fill; gormandize, *Archaic.* gluttonize, eat greedily, *Sl.* pig out, *Sl.* munch out, put down *or* away, pack in; devour, raven, consume, eat up, drink up, absorb, swallow; bolt, gobble, *Inf.* wolf down, gulp, guzzle, swill, swig; drain, empty, finish, finish off, *Sl.* polish off, *Sl.* knock off, make short work of.

cramp[1], *n.* **1.** (*often pl.*) muscular contraction, spasm, convulsion, crick, stitch, crink, throe, pang.

—*v.* **2.** convulse, affect with spasms; incapacitate, cripple, paralyze, lame, maim; hamstring, undermine, unfit, invalidate.

cramp[2], *n.* **1.** clamp, staple, clasp, fastening.

2. obstruction, block, check, barrier, damper, stopper; restriction, hindrance, stoppage, preclusion, restraint.

—*v.* **3.** secure, fasten, clamp, staple.

4. confine, restrict, restrain, hamper, hinder, impede, bridle; check, arrest, abort; obstruct, handicap, encumber, clog, saddle with, tie the hands.

5. steer, direct, drive.

6. **cramp one's style** *Informal.* thwart, frustrate, inhibit, foil, balk; restrain, restrict, hamper, hinder, impede, obstruct.

—*adj.* **7.** indecipherable, illegible, difficult to understand, knotty.

8. contracted, narrow, close, crowded, confined, incommodious, tight, limited, convulsive.

cramped, *adj.* **1.** stiff, abrupt, dry, harsh, blunt, crabbed; formal, labored, ponderous, forced, artificial; ungraceful, awkward, graceless, unpolished.

2. indecipherable. See **cramp[2]** (*def.* **7**).

3. narrow. See **cramp[2]** (*def.* **8**).

crane, *n.* derrick, winch, hoist, tackle, halyard, davit; lift, elevator, dumbwaiter; windlass, capstan, gin, pulley.

cranium, *n.* skull, brainpan, sconce, *Anat.* pericranium; head, crown, pate, poll, *Archaic.* costard, *Archaic.* mazard; *Inf.* noggin, *Inf.* noddle, *Sl.* bean, *Sl.* noodle, *Sl.* nob, *Sl.* nut.

crank, *n.* **1.** lever, arm, bar, shaft, spindle, crankshaft; handle, *Print.* rounce; pulley, gin, windlass, capstan.

2. grouch, crab, bear, churl, *Inf.* sourpuss; scold, nag, shrew, virago; scowler, snarler, frowner, wasp, *Inf.* crosspatch.

3. zealot, fanatic, bigot, maniac, monomaniac; fan, enthusiast, devotee, buff, *Inf.* nut; eccentric, character, oddity, *Inf.* crackpot, Don Quixote, *Sl.* bird.

4. whim, notion, fancy, caprice, whimsy; quirk, quiddity, quip, crotchet, kink, vagary.

—*v.* **5.** start, turn over, get going, rev, spin.

cranky, *adj.* **1.** grouchy, crabby, surly, sour, moody, crotchety; sulky, morose, sullen, whining; irascible, waspish, gruff, churlish, bearish; cross, ill-tempered, ill-natured, ill-humored; irritable, splenetic, fretful, choleric; testy, petulant, snappish, peevish, captious, perverse; cantankerous, querulous, quarrelsome, contentious.

2. eccentric, odd, queer, bizarre, pixilated; capricious, whimsical, fickle; erratic, inconsistent, impulsive, flighty.

3. shaky, rickety, tottering, teetery; unsteady, precarious, unsound.

4. crooked, bent, curved, hooked, zigzag, angular; tortuous, sinuous, serpentine, winding.

cranny, *n.* **1.** chink, chip, crack, chap, check, fracture, break; fissure, crevice, crevasse, groove, furrow, rut, bergschrund; cleft, split, slit, rift, breach, stria, rupture, sulcus, scission, *Archaic.* scissure, separation; gash, rent, scotch, cut.
2. hole, gap, cavity, opening, orifice, aperture; space, interspace, interval, interstice, narrow.

crapulous, *adj.* **1.** drunk, intoxicated, inebriated, inebriate, inebrious, bibacious, crapulent; drunken, sodden, besotted, sotted, sottish, awash, *Literary.* in one's cups; saturated, soused, full, *Scot.* fou; tipsy, grogged, fuddled, muddled, obfuscated, woozy, bleary-eyed, pie-eyed, glassy-eyed.
2. *All Inf.* boozy, tight, lit, lit up, lit to the gills; three *or* four sheets to the wind, under the sauce, pickled, high.
3. gluttonous, edacious, devouring, gormandizing, cormorant, voracious; open-mouthed, hoggish, piggish, porcine, swinish, gross, self-indulgent.
4. greedy, insatiable, insatiate, unquenchable, omnivorous.

crash, *v.* **1.** smash, shatter, break, batter, dash to pieces, wreck, destroy; fracture, fragmentize, splinter, shiver; chip, crack, snap.
2. bump into, collide with, smash into, run into, *Inf.* plow into, drive into; butt, jar, jolt, jostle.
3. fall, tumble, topple; collapse, fail, fold, give way, crumble.
4. clash, clang, clank, clatter; bang, boom, thunder, roar, explode, fulminate.
5. *Informal.* come uninvited, invade, intrude, *U.S. Sl.* horn in; sneak in, slip in.
—n. **6.** clatter, clangor, clang, bang, racket, din; boom, thunder, blast, detonation, explosion.
7. smash, smash-up, wreck, crack-up, collision.
8. bankruptcy, financial disaster, collapse, failure, downfall, fall, ruin, ruination.

crass, *adj.* **1.** crude, coarse, vulgar, rude; impolite, unmannered, ill-mannered, uncouth, ill-bred, uncivil, uncourteous; boorish, backward, rustic, countrified, unsophisticated, inurbane; unrefined, unpolished, indelicate, insensitive.
2. obtuse, dull, slow-witted, stolid, bovine, blockish, stupid, dense, thick, obtuse; loutish, oafish, doltish, lumpish.
3. gross, unsubtle, blatant, glaring, undisguised, open, naked, outright, downright, out-and-out.

crate, *n.* box, case, container, holder, receptacle; basket, hamper, pannier, dosser, wickerwork.

crater, *n.* cavity, hollow, depression, dip; hole, pit, cleft, opening; abyss, chasm, gulf.

cravat, *n.* necktie, tie, bow tie, bolo tie, four-in-hand; ascot, foulard, stock, neckerchief, neckcloth, scarf, bandana, dickey.

crave, *v.* **1.** desire, covet, want, want with all one's heart, want in the worst way, be dying for; long for, yearn for, hunger for, thirst for, pant for, lust for, hanker for, *Inf.* yen for.
2. require, need, demand, necessitate, dictate, call for, cry out for.
3. beseech, entreat, implore, supplicate, pray, sue, solicit, call on *or* upon; beg for, plead for.

craven, *adj.* **1.** cowardly, poltroon, dastardly, base, recreant, *Archaic.* niddering, *Archaic.* caitiff; pusillanimous, timorous, timid, fearful, afraid, frightened, afraid of one's shadow, faint-hearted, lily-livered, white-livered, *Inf.* chicken-hearted, *Inf.* chicken-livered, *Inf.* pantywaist, *Inf.* yellow, *Sl.* yellow-bellied, *Sl.* candy-assed.
—n. **2.** poltroon, coward, dastard, recreant, base fellow, *Archaic.* caitiff, *Archaic.* niddering; yellowbelly, mouse, baby, big baby, wheyface, invertebrate, *Inf.* jellyfish, *Inf.* fraidy-cat, *Inf.* scaredy-cat, *Inf.* nervous nellie, *Sl.* chicken, *Sl.* weak sister; sissy, weakling, milksop, Milquetoast, mollycoddle, *Inf.* pantywaist.

craving, *n.* **1.** desire, *Inf.* yen, hunger, thirst; longing, yearning, hankering; concupiscence, lust.
2. (*all of narcotics*) addiction, dependence, physical *or* psychological dependence, habit, *Sl.* monkey.

craw, *n.* (*all of a bird, insect or animal*) crop, maw, gullet, esophagus, throat, pharynx; stomach, gizzard, ventriculus; belly, venter, *Fr. ventre*; intestines, guts, insides, entrails.

crawl, *v.* **1.** creep, crawl on all fours; worm, inch along, go at a snail's pace, advance slowly, drag oneself along, pull oneself along; trail, lag behind, follow behind.
2. skulk, slink, move stealthily, sneak; sneak up on, creep up on, come up on, come up from behind.
3. be overrun with, be overgrown with, be filled with, be full of, swarm with, be swamped with, be overwhelmed with *or* by.
4. cower, crouch, cringe; grovel, toady, fawn.

craze, *v.* **1.** madden, *Obs.* dement, derange, *Archaic.* bedlamize, distemper; drive insane, drive crazy, drive mad, drive wild; unsettle, unbalance, distract, unhinge; enrage, frenzy, inflame, excite.
2. crack, check, (*of ceramic glaze*) crackle, split, chap, fissure, fracture, shatter.
—n. **3.** fad, vogue, fashion, mode, rage; the thing, last word, *Fr. dernier cri*; mania, furor, enthusiasm; whim, fancy, crotchet, quirk, caprice, vagary; passion, infatuation, obsession, fixation, fascination, preoccupation.

crazy, *adj.* **1.** insane, mad, demented, lunatic, deranged, crazed; of unsound mind, *Latin. non compos mentis*; daft, *Inf.* daffy, *Chiefly Brit. Inf.* potty, *Inf.* dotty, *Inf.* crackpot; unbalanced, touched, *Inf.* half-baked, *Brit. Sl.* bonkers, unhinged; brainsick, *Sl.* kooky, *Sl.* meshuga; *All Sl.* balmy, dippy, batty, bats, cuckoo, buggy, bughouse, bugs, screwy, wacky, wacko, goofy, loony, squirrelly, bananas, nuts, nutty, nutty as a fruitcake.
2. out of one's head, out of one's mind, *Sl.* loco, mad as a hatter, mad as a March hare; not all there, not quite right, not right upstairs, *Inf.* out in left field, *Inf.* off the wall; stark raving mad, *Inf.* cracked, *Inf.* mental, *Sl.* schizo, *Inf.* off one's rocker, *Inf.* off one's trolley, *Brit. Sl.* off one's chump; *All Sl.* have bats in one's belfry, have a few buttons missing, have a few loose screws.
3. maniacal, wild, *Archaic.* wood, raving, hysterical, madding, frantic, frenzied, delirious; out of control, *Inf.* haywire, berserk; beside oneself, at one's wit's end.
4. absurd, silly, inane, fatuous, foolish; crack-brained, *Scot.* doiled, *Sl.* cockeyed, *Scot. and North Eng.* glaikit; ridiculous, laughable, risible, derisible, ludicrous, *Sl.* for the birds; asinine, anserine, idiotic, *Inf.* moronic, imbecilic; childish, puerile, immature.
5. stupid, simple-minded, bird-brained, feeble-minded, dull-witted; harebrained, light-minded, light-headed, giddy; scatterbrained, absent-minded, confused; muddled, muddlepated, bemused.
6. impractical, injudicious, unsensible; unfounded, groundless, unsound; haphazard, unconnected; irrational, illogical, unreasonable; preposterous, extravagant, excessive; unrealistic, half-baked; senseless, nonsensical, pointless; irrelevant, inconsequential, purposeless; inappropriate, inept, improper, incongruous, inconsistent; imprudent, indiscreet; unwise, ill-considered, ill-suited, ill-advised; short-sighted, careless, unwary, irresponsible; reckless, rash, harum-scarum.

7. enthusiastic, excited, avid, eager, zealous; ardent, fervid, fervent, passionate, impassioned; fanatical, *Inf.* wild, dithyrambic; intense, rabid, vehement.

8. infatuated, enamored by *or* with, *U.S. Sl.* ape over *or* for, keen on *or* about, wild about, mad about *or* after, fond of, *Inf.* gone on; *U.S. Sl.* all hopped up about, *Sl.* hepped up *or* over, *Sl.* hot about *or* for *or* on, *Sl.* steamed up about, *Sl.* nuts about *or* on, desirous, avid for *or* of, covetous.

9. peculiar, strange, offbeat, queer, odd, flighty, eccentric; fantastic, fabulous, imaginary, illusory, illusive, chimerical; incredible, inconceivable, unimaginable, implausible.

10. like crazy *Slang.* ardently, fervently, passionately, intensely; devotedly, devoutly; enthusiastically, madly, furiously, excitedly; wildly, impetuously, hastily, hurriedly, recklessly.

creak, *v.* grate, grind, grit, jar, jangle, clank; scrape, scratch, rasp, stridulate; squeak, screak, screech, shrill, shriek, scream.

cream, *n.* **1.** lotion, emollient, cosmetic, emulsion; *Pharm.* ointment, unguent, liniment, salve; pomade, pomatum.

2. best *or* choicest part, flower, quintessence; elite, *Fr. crème de la crème*, salt of the earth, *Inf.* cream of the crop, pick of the litter; aristocracy, upper class, *Inf.* upper crust, the best and the brightest; social elite, jet set, beautiful people, *U.S.* Four Hundred.

—adj. **3.** cream-colored, yellowish-white, off-white, buff.

crease, *n.* **1.** ridge, groove, furrow, corrugation, crimp; fold, dog-ear, plication, plicature, ruck; wrinkle, line, crow's feet; rimple, crinkle, crankle, crumple, rumple; gather, ruffle, pucker, tuck, pleat, plait; ripple, bump, bulge, roll, protrusion, protuberance, lump, hump, hunch.

—v. **2.** put a crease in, fold, ruck, wrinkle, furrow; groove, ridge, corrugate, crimp; fold down *or* back, dog-ear; rimple, crinkle, crimple, crankle, crumple, rumple; gather, ruffle, pucker, tuck, pleat, plait; ripple, bulge, protrude, hump.

create, *v.* **1.** engender, generate, beget, sire, father, spawn, procreate; bring into being, bring to life, give life to, call into existence, cause to exist.

2. originate, invent, innovate, coin; make, produce, fashion, fabricate, frame; design, contrive, devise, develop, construct, build, rear, erect; shape, form, mold, forge; imagine, conceive, *Inf.* dream up, *Inf.* hatch; visualize, envisage.

3. invest, constitute, appoint, install, elevate.

4. found, institute, establish, initiate, give rise to, occasion, break ground, sow the seeds of.

5. bring about, arrange, inaugurate, start, launch, incept; *Inf.* start the ball rolling, *Inf.* take the first step, *Inf.* make the first move.

creation, *n.* **1.** generation, siring, fathering, spawning, procreation.

2. origination, invention, innovation; beginning, start, inception, genesis, engenderment; embodiment, formulation, realization, establishment, constitution, institution.

3. formation, development, production, construction, fabrication; design, contrivance, conception; idea, concept, notion, fancy, product of one's imagination; plan, dream, vision.

creative, *adj.* **1.** inventive, imaginative, visionary, inspired; talented, accomplished, artistic, endowed; original, fanciful, ingenious, resourceful; clever, adept, adroit, skilled.

2. formative, shaping, making; godlike, divine, demiurgic; life-giving, life-breathing, quickening.

creator, *n.* **1.** author, originator, generator, initiator, prime mover, founder, father, architect; inventor, framer, maker, designer; artist, craftsman, producer.

2. (*usu. cap.*) God, the Deity, the maker of Heaven and Earth; demiurge. See **Deity**.

creature, *n.* **1.** being, body, thing, object, living thing, entity, something.

2. animal, beast, brute, *Dial.* varmint, *Dial.* critter; mammal, mammalian, vertebrate, invertebrate, quadruped; reptile, bird, fish.

3. person, human being, human, man, woman, fellow, earthling; body, soul, mortal, sentient; personnage, individual, character, one, someone, somebody, *Archaic.* wight.

4. dependent, hireling, puppet, parasite, hanger-on; minion, subordinate, ward, vassal, subject, liegeman; servant, serf, slave, lackey, flunky, *Archaic.* yeoman; chamberlain, *Hist.* retainer, squire, page.

5. wretch, miscreant, scoundrel, rascal, cur, *Archaic.* caitiff; brute, monster, ogre.

credence, *n.* belief, faith, trust, security; confidence, credit, creditability, trustworthiness; reliance, reliability, dependence, dependency, assurance.

credential, *n.* certificate, document, deed, title, *Law.* muniment; diploma, record, degree; authority, warrant, *Chiefly Brit.* docket; card, passport, pass, visa, safe-conduct; authorization, exequatur, permit, license; attestation, testimonial, testament, voucher.

credibility, *n.* reliance, reliability, believability, believableness, plausibility; dependence, dependability, constancy; trustworthiness, veracity, integrity, faithfulness, scrupulousness; confidence, belief, faith, assurance.

credible, *adj.* **1.** believable, imaginable, conceivable, supposable; plausible, ostensible, specious; tenable, maintainable, well-grounded, well-founded.

2. reliable, trustworthy, trusty, dependable; honest, veracious, truthful, forthright, straightforward, scrupulous, ethical.

credit, *n.* **1.** trustworthiness, faithfulness, integrity, honor; rectitude, probity, veracity, honesty, good faith; credibility, reliability, dependability, solvency; constancy, loyalty, firmness.

2. commendation, praise, acclaim, tribute, regard; good word, citation, laudation; honor, esteem, merit, respect, favor, veneration.

3. pride, boast, joy, glory, gem, pearl, flower, feather in the cap.

4. acknowledgment, creditation, accreditation, charging; ascription, attribution, assignment, adscription; imputation, blame, laying on.

5. repute, reputation, good name, estimation, prestige, influence; standing, status, rank, caliber.

6. sum, debt, due, debit, score, account, tally.

7. on credit by deferred payment, on a charge account, on a charge, on layaway, *Chiefly Brit. Inf.* on tick, *Sl.* on the cuff; on one's tab, on one's bill, on one's account.

—v. **8.** believe, trust, have faith in, put confidence in, put trust in, *Inf.* put *or* take stock in, *Inf.* buy; confide in, depend on, rely on, take on credit.

9. bring honor *or* esteem to, reflect credit upon, redound to, do honor to.

10. credit to *or* with ascribe, attribute, accredit, assign; chalk up to, put down to, give credit for; impute, lay on, charge with, blame, accuse.

creditable, *adj.* reputable, respectable, respected; honorable, honored, noble, venerable, revered, admirable; estimable, esteemed, worthy, deserving, valuable, valued; meritorious, laudable, praiseworthy, commendable; trustworthy, reliable, dependable; excellent, superior, above par, up to the mark, good.

creditor, *n.* lender, loaner, dun, money-lender, *Obs.* moneyman; usurer, moneymonger, Shylock, *Inf.* loan shark.

credulity, *n.* gullibility, gullibleness, credulousness, will to believe, blind faith, trustfulness, unsuspiciousness.

credulous, *adj.* trusting, trustful, believing, undoubting, unsuspicious, uncritical, unskeptical, overtrustful, easy of belief, easy, soft; gullible, deceivable, dupable, foolable, deludable, exploitable; naive, unsophisticated, green, born yesterday, *Inf.* wet behind the ears.

creed, *n.* **1.** tenet, principles, articles, teaching, rule, *Eccles.* catechism; doctrine, dogma, canon, formula; axiom, theorem, maxim.

2. sect, religion, denomination, affiliation, cult, fellowship, communion; faith, belief; persuasion, position, leaning, conviction, opinion, view.

creek, *n.* **1.** watercourse, stream, streamlet, brook, brooklet, rivulet, run, runnel, burn, rill, rindle, *Dial.* crick; channel, strait; branch, tributary.

2. *Chiefly British.* inlet, bay, cove, bight, *Both Chiefly Scot.* firth, frith; fjord, estuary.

3. **up the creek** *Slang.* in a predicament, in a bind, in trouble; perplexed, off balance, taken by surprise.

creep, *v.* **1.** crawl, crawl on all fours; squirm, wriggle, wiggle, writhe; worm, inch along, go at a snail's pace, advance slowly, drag oneself along, pull oneself along; trail, lag behind, follow behind.

2. skulk, slink, move stealthily, steal; sneak up on, come up on, come up from behind.

3. cower, crouch, cringe; grovel, *Inf.* bootlick, toady, fawn.

4. slip, slide, shift, move, dislocate.

5. **make one's flesh creep** frighten, scare, terrify, horrify, make one's hair stand on end; repel, repulse, revolt, turn one's stomach.

creeping, *adj.* **1.** crawling, crawling on all fours; vermicular, squirming, wriggling, wiggling, *Zool.* reptant.

2. slow, dragging, plodding, snail-like, dawdling; lagging, trailing, tardy, dilatory.

3. cowering, crouching, cringing; groveling, reptilian, fawning, obsequious, sycophantish, servile, truckling.

cremate, *v.* burn, incinerate, consume by fire, reduce to ashes; inurn.

cremation, *n.* burning, incineration, consumption by fire, reduction to ashes; inurnment.

crematory, *n.* crematorium, incinerator, pyre, furnace, burning place.

crescent, *n.* **1.** demilune, lune, lunette, lunula, meniscus, half-moon; semicircle, half circle, hemicycle; sickle, scythe.

—adj. **2.** sickle-shaped, falcate, falciform, bicorn; lunate, lunar, lunular, lunulate, luniform; curved, bow-shaped, convexo-concave; semi-circular, crescentic.

3. increasing, increscent, crescine, growing, waxing.

crest, *n.* **1.** comb, cockscomb, *Zool.* caruncle, *Obs.* coxcomb; tuft, cluster, mane, tassel, top-knot; panache, plume, pompon.

2. spine, chine, fin, spinal *or* vertebral column, *Anat.* backbone; protuberance, projection, excrescence, outgrowth, bulge, bump, swelling, *Anat.* knot, *Anat.* promontory.

3. regalia, regale, badge, emblem, device, arms, *Heraldry.* charge, *Heraldry.* bearing, *Archaic.* armory; symbol, design, ornament, ornamentation, embellishment, adornment, decoration, garnish, trim.

4. head, pate, *Anat.* sinciput, skull, poll, *Inf.* noggin, *Sl.* noodle, *Sl.* block; headpiece, headgear, cap, crown, crownpiece, helmet; top, tip, tiptop, point, spire, apex, vertex, *Latin. ne plus ultra*; acme, zenith, meridian, apogee, crowning point, climax, culmination.

5. summit, pinnacle, peak, needle, tor, alp, mountain top, heights; ridge, reef, ledge, range, chain, line, *Geol.* hogback, *Phys. Geog.* arête.

6. best, finest, prime, utmost, uttermost, extreme, *U.S. Sl.* the greatest, *U.S. Sl.* the most, *Sl.* the tops; sublimity, supremacy, consummation, perfection.

—v. **7.** crown, cap, top, top out, pinnacle, tip, *Brit.* nib; surmount, climb, mount, ascend, scale.

8. peak, rise, spire, tower, culminate, climax; jut, beetle, protrude, protuberate, bulge, stick out *or* up.

crestfallen, *adj.* depressed, in the doldrums, down in the dumps, dejected, low-spirited, chapfallen, mopish; sad, unhappy, despondent, disconsolate, downcast, cast down, downhearted; melancholy, blue, dispirited, woebegone, heavy-hearted; moody, gloomy, glum, sullen, morose, saturnine; oppressed, weary, spiritless; discouraged, disheartened, out of heart.

crevasse, *n.* chasm, gorge, ravine, bergschrund; gulch, gully, rut, furrow, ditch, trench. See **crevice** (*def.* **2**).

crevice, *n.* **1.** fissure, cleft, crack, chap, check, stria, cranny, groove, sulcus, *Archaic.* scissure; break, fracture, rupture, split, rift, breach, scission, separation; slit, gash, scotch, rent, cut.

2. chasm, gorge, ravine, crevasse, bergschrund; gulch, gully, rut, furrow, ditch, trench; hole, gap, cavity, opening, orifice, aperture; space, interspace, interval, interstice, narrow.

crew, *n.* **1.** company, squad, team, corps; group, assemblage, band, troupe, party, gang; posse, force, body; throng, mob, pack; multitude, mass, crowd, horde, herd, host.

2. *Nautical.* sailors, bluejackets, mariners, seamen, seafarers, gobs, *Inf.* tars, seadogs, shellbacks, hands, *Brit. Sl.* matelots.

crib, *n.* **1.** child's bed, bassinet, cradle.

2. hovel, hut, hutch, shack, shanty, *Brit.* bothy.

3. enclosure, stall, pen, cage, coop; bin, box, rack, manger.

4. *Informal.* translation, key, *U.S. Sl.* trot, *Sl.* pony.

—v. **5.** enclose, shut in, shut up, keep in, quarantine, isolate; confine, cage, coop, pen in, rail in, fence, pale, picket, corral; box up, bottle up; imprison, incarcerate, wall in.

6. *Informal.* plagiarize, palm off as one's own, pirate; pilfer, steal, lift, filch, purloin, misappropriate.

crick, *n.* kink, hitch, cramp, pain; spasm, throe, twitch, tremor, twinge, pang.

crier, *n.* **1.** herald, announcer, proclaimer, bellman, town crier.

2. hawker, peddler, vendor, huckster, cheap-jack, costermonger, colporteur.

crime, *n.* **1.** offense, transgression, violation, injury, hurt, harm, wrong, malfeasance, malefaction, misdeed; felony, *Law.* tort; atrocity, monstrosity, enormity, horror, outrage; disgrace, abomination, shame, scandal.

2. iniquity, wickedness, unrighteousness, evil, sin; depravity, corruption, dereliction, vice.

criminal, *adj.* **1.** felonious, larcenous, homicidal, murderous, burglarious; unlawful, illegal, lawless, illicit, law-breaking; delinquent, derelict; malfeasant, misfeasant.

2. nefarious, iniquitous, wicked, flagitious; evil, immoral, sinful, unrighteous, errant, wrong, bad; degenerate, depraved, corrupt, vile, foul, black, villainous.

3. heinous, abominable, monstrous, atrocious, vicious; outrageous, flagrant, gross; disreputable, notorious,

infamous.
4. guilty, culpable, condemnable, censurable; blameworthy, opprobrious, reproachful, reprehensible.
5. *Both Informal.* **a.** senseless, foolish, frivolous; inappropriate, illogical. **b.** exorbitant, usurious, extortionate, overpriced; unconscionable, preposterous.
—n. **6.** felon, larcener, larcenist, misdemeanant, lawbreaker; convict, *Sl.* jailbird, parolee; ex-convict, *Inf.* ex-con, recidivist, repeat offender, *Inf.* chronic crook; transgressor, trespasser, offender, culprit, miscreant; malefactor, evildoer, wrongdoer, sinner; malfeasant, misfeasor; perjurer; *Inf.* scofflaw.
7. gangster, mobster, racketeer, mafioso, desperado, terrorist; thug, tough, *Inf.* toughie, mugger, ruffian, *Inf.* plugugly, rowdy, hoodlum, *Sl.* hood, *Inf.* goon, hooligan, *Inf.* roughneck, *Inf.* baddy, *Sl.* bad actor, *Sl.* gunsel, *Sl.* mug, ***Australian Sl.*** larrikin, *Brit. Hist.* Mohock, (*in Paris*) apache.
8. assassin, murderer, killer, slayer, sniper; strangler, cutthroat, garroter; liquidator, *Euph.* silencer, *Euph.* dispatcher; gunman, *All U.S. Sl.* gun, hired gun, hit man, triggerman, hatchet man, torpedo.
9. bandit, hold-up man, *Sl.* stick-up man, armed robber; robber, burglar, thief, stealer, purloiner, *Inf.* crook, shoplifter; pickpocket, purse-snatcher, cutpurse, embezzler, peculator, *Law.* defalcator.
10. extortionist, extortioner, blackmailer, usurer, loan shark, *Sl.* bleeder; smuggler, runner, bootlegger, contrabandist, white-slaver; swindler, confidence man, con artist, con man; forger, counterfeiter, *Fr. faux-monnayeur, Brit. Inf.* coiner.
11. kidnapper, abductor, rapist; sodomist, pervert, degenerate, child molester, *Sl.* short eyes.
12. arsonist, incendiary; rioter, bomb-thrower, bomb-planter.
13. villain, blackguard, scoundrel, knave, *Sl.* no-good, *Sl.* bad guy.

criminality, *n.* crime, lawbreaking, wrongdoing, evildoing, misconduct, malefaction; evilness, wickedness, sinfulness, depravity, corruption, villainy, turpitude.

crimp, *v.* **1.** flute, ruffle, scallop, bend; wave, ripple, curl, friz, frizzle, crimple; corrugate, furrow, groove, ridge, striate; press, crease, seam, pleat, plicate, plait; wrinkle, crinkle, cockle, crumple, knit, pucker, gather, smock, tuck.
2. hinder, hamper, frustrate, restrict, inhibit, thwart, get in the way, hold back, slow down; check, arrest, stop, curb.
—n. **3.** flute, ruffle, scallop, wave, curl, bend; corrugation, furrow, groove, channel, ridge, stria; crease, fold, seam, pleat, plication, plait; wrinkle, crinkle, cockle, pucker, crumple.

crimson, *adj.* carmine, cramoisy, magenta, fuchsia, claret, claret-red, alizarin, deep purplish red, deep purple; burgundy, wine, vinaceous, maroon, blood-red, ruddy, sanguine, rubicund, *Archaic.* rubric; red, rose, rosy, roseate, cardinal, cerise, ruby, scarlet, cranberry, vermilion.

cringe, *v.* **1.** cower, shrink, quail, blench, flinch, wince, start, recoil, shy, *Inf.* funk, *Sl.* mooch; shake, tremble, quiver, *Inf.* shake in one's boots *or* shoes, kowtow, bow, bow before, bow to, bow and scrape, bend, bend before, stoop, squat, crouch, slouch, hunch; kneel, kneel before, fall on one's knees; lie prone, lie low, prostrate oneself, throw oneself at the feet of.
2. grovel, crawl, creep, creep before, slither, sneak, sneak along, steal, steal along, worm, worm along, worm one's way.
3. fawn, fawn upon, *Sl.* fall all over, truckle, truckle to, toady, toady to; lickspittle, lick [s.o.'s] shoes, lick *or* kiss [s.o.'s] feet, *Inf.* be a yes man to, agree to any thing, *Sl.* bootlick, court, pay court to, curry favor, keep time to, dance attendance upon, be at one's beck and call; flatter, wheedle, slaver, puff, puff up, inflate, blow up; *All Sl.* shine up to, play up to, suck up to, apple-polish, brown-nose, earn brownie points.

cringing, *adj.* **1.** cowering, shrinking, quailing, blenching, flinching, wincing, starting, recoiling, shying, *Inf.* funking, *Sl.* mooching; shaking, trembling, quivering, *Inf.* shaking in one's boots *or* shoes.
2. servile, slavish, obsequious, *Obs.* obsequent, subservient, menial, *Obs., Rare.* vernile; submissive, docile, unassertive, compliant, acquiescent, deferential, tractable, mealy-mouthed, Tomish, Uncle Tomish; prostrate, obeisant, on one's knees, lying prone, lying low, prostrating oneself, throwing oneself at the feet of; kneeling, on one's knees, falling on one's knees; kowtowing, bowing, bowing before, bowing and scraping, bending, bending before, stooping, squatting, crouching, slouching, hunching; groveling, crawling, creeping, slithering, sneaking, worming.
3. sycophantic, sycophantical, sycophantish, toadyish, toadying, flattering, fawning, truckling, wheedling, slavering, puffing, puffing-up; courting, paying court to, currying favor, timeserving, keeping time to, dancing attendance upon, being at one's beck and call, *Sl.* bootlicking, *Sl.* footlicking, *Inf.* apple-polishing, *Sl.* brown-nosing, *Obs.* blanding, *Obs., Rare.* blandiloquous, *Rare.* blandiloquent.

crinkle, *v.* **1.** turn, bend, crankle, buckle; wind, coil, twist.
2. wrinkle, crimple, cockle, crumple, knit, shrivel, pucker, gather, smock, tuck; crimp, flute, ruffle, scallop; corrugate, furrow, groove, ridge, striate; ripple, wave, curl, friz, frizzle.
3. rustle, swish, whoosh, whish; murmur, whisper, sibilate, hiss.

crinkly, *adj.* **1.** wrinkly, crimpled, cockled, buckled, creped, shriveled; gathered, smocked, puckered, knit; corrugate, corrugated, furrowed, grooved, ridged; fluted, crimpy, ruffled, scalloped; wavy, curly, ripply, frizzy, kinky.
2. curvy, winding, twisty, sinuous, serpentine, anfractuous.
3. rustling, swishing, swooshing, whooshing; murmuring, whispering, sibilant, hissing.

cripple, *n.* **1.** lame person, paralytic, amputee; invalid, convalescent, valetudinarian.
—v. **2.** lame, becripple, hamstring, hock, amputate; disable, incapacitate, debilitate; maim, mangle, mutilate, scar; hurt, abuse, injure, maltreat, misuse, do violence to; impair, damage, mar, vitiate, spoil; weaken, enfeeble, enervate, prostrate, paralyze.

crisis, *n.* **1.** turning point, point of no return, Rubicon, conjuncture, juncture, pass; climax, climacteric, moment of truth, *Inf.* zero hour.
2. emergency, exigency, extremity; disaster, calamity, catastrophe; deadlock, standstill, impasse; strait, pinch, *Inf.* crunch, *Inf.* clutch, rub, push; trouble, difficulty, fix, hot water; predicament, plight, dilemma, quandary, *Inf.* pickle, scrape; entanglement, mess, muddle, kettle of fish, stew, imbroglio.

crisp, *adj.* **1.** brittle, crumbly, friable, breakable, frangible.
2. fresh, green, unwilted, unwithered, firm, flavorous.
3. sharp, tart, blunt, abrupt, straightforward, candid; decided, resolved, unhesitating, unwavering; pithy, concise, succinct, terse.
4. lively, animated, spirited, vivacious, enthusiastic, *Inf.* sparkling, eager; sprightly, vigorous, invigorated, energetic.
5. clean, neat, spruce, trim, trig, well-groomed, well-

pressed, *Inf.* snappy, smart.
6. brisk, bracing, nipping, chilly; invigorating, refreshing, stirring, roborant; stimulating, revivatory, tonic, strengthening, beneficial; restorative, rejuvenating, revitalizing.
7. crinkled, wrinkled, crumpled, puckered, gathered; rippled, waved, wavy, curly, frizzy, frizzled.

criterion, *n.* measure, gauge, scale, barometer, yardstick, guide, guideline, test; standard, norm, touchstone, benchmark, point of comparison; model, example, exemplar, precedent, lead; original, prototype, archetype, type, classic example; pattern, paradigm; rule, law, canon, maxim, code.

critic, *n.* **1.** commentator, reviewer, essayist, expositor, expounder, editor, editorialist, criticaster; censor, Mrs. Grundy, Grundyist, *Rare.* aristarch.
2. connoisseur, esthete, epicure; judge, arbiter, arbiter of taste, *Latin. arbiter elegantiae;* expert, authority, specialist, pundit, savant, maven, one of the cognoscenti.
3. faultfinder, carper, caviler, quibbler, pettifogger, momus, smellfungus, *Inf.* nitpicker; censurer, detractor, derogator, backbiter, *Inf.* knocker.

critical, *adj.* **1.** captious, censorious, severe, hypercritical, overcritical, faultfinding, carping, caviling, quibbling, pettifogging, hairsplitting, niggling, *Inf.* nitpicking.
2. judicial, astute, perspicacious, perceptive, discerning; fastidious, particular, meticulous, exacting, conscientious, punctilious, fussy, discriminate, discriminating, difficult, hard to please; precise, accurate, exact, correct, scrupulous; acute, keen, fine, subtle, delicate, nice; minute, detailed.
3. crucial, decisive, pivotal, momentous, eventful, climacteric; important, all-important, essential, of the essence, vital, heartbeat, *Inf.* gut; urgent, pressing, compelling, imperative, exigent, high-priority; serious, grave.
4. dangerous, hazardous, perilous; uncertain, risky, touchy, touch-and-go, ticklish, *Inf.* chancy, *Inf.* hairy.
5. explanatory, explicative, clarifying, illuminating, elucidative; glossarial, annotative, editorial, scholiastic; commentative, expository, discursive.

criticism, *n.* **1.** evaluation, judgment, assessment, appraisal, appreciation, estimation, analysis.
2. censure, reproof, reproach, animadversion, stricture, disapproval, condemnation, derogation, denunciation, disparagement; exception, objection, disagreement, disaccord; brickbat, flak, bad press, bad notices.
3. captiousness, censoriousness, hypercriticism, overcriticism, faultfinding, carping, caviling, quibbling, pettifoggery, niggling, hairsplitting, *Inf.* nitpicking.
4. critique, review, commentary. See **critique**.

criticize, *v.* **1.** judge, adjudge, appraise, assess, evaluate, estimate; treat, examine, analyze, survey, comment upon.
2. attack, flay, light into, *Inf.* lace into, *Inf.* pan, *Inf.* slam, shoot down, *Sl.* blast, *Sl.* let [s.o.] have it with both barrels, *Sl.* let [s.o.] have it right between the eyes; cavil, carp, find fault, *Inf.* nitpick, pick apart, pick to pieces, *Inf.* pick holes in, *Inf.* knock, *Sl.* cut up *or* to pieces, haul over the coals; get on [s.o.'s] back, *Inf.* jump on, *Inf.* jump all over, *Sl.* get on [s.o.'s] case.
3. condemn, denounce, blame, censure, reprove, reproach, animadvert upon; disapprove, frown upon, take exception to, take offense; castigate, fustigate, berate, tongue-lash; vilify, malign, gibbet, vituperate, run down, put down.

critique, *n.* review, notice, critical notice; report, article, editorial, essay, blurb, commentary, analysis, *Inf.* write-up; rave, *Inf.* pan, *Inf.* slam, *Inf.* swipe, *Inf.* hit.

croak, *v.* **1.** talk hoarsely, speak thickly, grunt, groan, murmur.
2. grumble, complain, grouse, mutter, maunder; cry down, disparage, depreciate, belittle.
3. *Slang.* die, perish, *Sl.* kick the bucket.

crock, *n.* **1.** (*all earthenware*) pot, jar, vessel, container, pitcher, ewer, flagon, *Gk. and Rom. Antiquity.* amphora, piece of crockery.
2. *Slang.* nonsense, rubbish, garbage, *Sl.* bullroar, *Sl.* bull; bunkum, *Sl.* bunk.

crockery, *n.* crocks, earthenware, clay ware, terra cotta, pottery, stoneware, ceramics, porcelain, china.

crone, *n.* hag, beldam, *Sl.* old bag, *Sl.* old bat; shrew, virago, vixen, nag; old woman, grandam, *Brit.* gammer.

crony, *n.* comrade, companion, chum, *Fr. copain, U.S. Inf.* buddy, *Inf.* pal, *Obs.* copemate; sidekick, shadow, alter ego, other self; friend, Achates, confidant, familiar, *Inf.* bosom buddy, roommate, bunkmate, *Sl.* bunkie; teammate, co-worker, fellow worker; ally, compatriot, confederate, cohort, collaborator, cooperator, accomplice, *Law.* accessory; assistant, helper, helpmate; colleague, confrere, associate, consociate, compeer, peer, mate, comate.

crook, *n.* **1.** hook, angle, dogleg, hairpin turn; curve, curvature, incurvature, incurvation, bow, arc, turn, twist, tortuosity; bend, bending, flexion, flexure, fold, inflection.
2. *Informal.* swindler, thief, embezzler, confidence man, *U.S. Sl.* con man, robber. See **swindler** (*def.* **1**).
—*v.* **3.** bend, flex, bow, twist; curve, incurvate, turn, deflect; circle, coil, curl, spiral, loop; arch, vault, camber, inflect.
4. meander, worm, zigzag, wind, wind in and out, sinuate; hook, angle off, shoot off at an angle, bear off; swerve, veer, deviate, divagate, diverge, slue.

crooked, *adj.* **1.** bent, bending, flexed, bowed, hooked, twisted, contorted; curved, incurvated, angular, coiled, circled, curled, spiral, looped; arched, arcuate, inflected, vaulted, cambered.
2. winding, flexuous, sinuous, tortuous, serpentine; meandering, worming, zigzag; swerving, veering off, deviating.
3. awry, askew, tilted, to one side, sideways, off-center, uneven, *Brit. Sl.* squint; slanted, slanting, slantwise, aslant, diagonal, aslope, sloping, oblique.
4. deformed, misshapen, disfigured, distorted, gnarled, warped; irregular, asymmetric.
5. deceitful, tricky, dishonest, fraudulent, underhanded, *Inf.* left-handed; insidious, guileful, disingenuous, scheming, plotting, designing, calculating, contriving; false, false-hearted, double-dealing, two-faced, shifty, slippery, smooth, slick; crafty, cunning, artful, sly, wily, subtle, foxy; shrewd, astute, canny, sharp, knowing, *Inf.* cagey; unscrupulous, unprincipled, Machiavellian.
6. loaded, fixed, rigged, doctored, marked, weighted, predetermined.

crop, *n.* **1.** harvest, yield, gathering, garner, gleaning, reaping, cutting, season's growth; production, product.
2. supply, collection, selection, assortment, batch, lot.
3. craw, gullet, maw, throat.
—*v.* **4.** clip, cut short, trim; top, lop, mow; graze, nibble, browse.

cross, *n.* **1.** crucifix, crux, rood, crosslet.
2. crossing, crosswalk, corner; crossroad, crossway, intersection, junction, juncture; convergence, convergency, point of meeting.
3. thwarting, frustration, stumbling block, impediment, encumbrance, hindrance, pain in the neck; trouble, problem, difficulty, embarrassment, trying situa-

tion; snag, catch, hitch, rub, drawback, fly in the ointment.
4. misfortune, mishap, mischance, adversity, evil, ill, calamity, disaster, catastrophe; affliction, grief, misery, woe; harm, injury, pain, suffering, trial, tribulation, ordeal; blow, stroke, bitter cup.
5. burden, responsibility, weight, load, albatross.
6. crossbreed, hybrid, half-breed, mongrel, *Sl.* mutt.
7. **cross out** *or* **off** cancel out, scratch out, draw a line through, strike out, blue-pencil, delete, *Print.* dele, x out, mark off; remove, erase, rub out, wipe out, sponge out, blot out, obliterate.
—v. **8.** intersect, meet, join, converge, come together; lie *or* pass across, crisscross, zigzag, weave, interlace, lace; interweave, intermingle, combine, interlink, interlock, fit together; intertwist, twist together, entwist, entwine, braid, plait, pleat, fold across; intertwine, entangle, enmesh, ensnarl, ensnare.
9. traverse, span, bridge, extend across, stretch *or* reach across; pass over, ford, ply, travel over *or* across, go across *or* through, cut across.
10. transport, carry across *or* over, take across *or* over.
11. *Slang.* betray, *Inf.* double-cross; inform on, *Sl.* squeal on, tell on, *Sl.* rat on, *Sl.* blow the whistle on.
12. baffle, confuse, *Sl.* cross up, thwart, frustrate; oppose openly, foil, contradict; interfere, get in the way, impede, hinder, retard, check, slow up *or* down; block, obstruct, stop, prevent, keep back *or* down.
13. interbreed, intercross, crossbreed, hybridize, cross-fertilize, cross-pollinate; mix, intermix, blend, fuse, interfuse.
—adj. **14.** athwart, across, intersecting, crosswise, crossways, transverse, from side to side, oblique, at an angle.
15. reciprocal, mutual.
16. contrary, opposing, opposite, at odds; differing, disagreeing, dissenting; adverse, unfavorable, disadvantageous.
17. crossbred, hybrid, mixed, mongrel.
18. annoyed, bothered, *Inf.* put-out, peeved, irritated, vexed, griped, piqued, *Inf.* ticked off, *Sl.* pissed off, angry, upset.
19. snappish, snappy, impatient, irritable, short, touchy, testy, thin-skinned, waspish, peevish, petulant; irascible, choleric, ill-tempered, ill-humored, splenetic; cranky, grouchy, grumpy, cantankerous, crotchety, crusty.

cross-examine, *v.* **1.** cross-question, interrogate, quiz, *Inf.* grill, pump, catechize.
2. examine closely, scrutinize, look at carefully; investigate, *Inf.* check out, probe, explore thoroughly, go over with a fine-tooth comb.

cross-grained, *adj.* stubborn, pigheaded, mulish, obstinate, obdurant, unyielding, unbending; perverse, contrary, opposed, resistant; refractory, recalcitrant, unmanageable, intractable, contumacious; headstrong, willful, strong-willed, wayward.

crossing, *n.* **1.** crosswalk, corner, point of crossing; crossroad, crossway, intersection, junction, juncture; traffic circle, rotary, cloverleaf, interchange, underpass, overpass.
2. thwarting, frustration, foil, balk; contradiction, opposition, interference, intervention; stumbling block, problem, difficulty; snag, catch, hitch, rub, drawback, fly in the ointment; deterrent, hindrance, impediment, encumbrance; check, retardation, slowing up *or* down; block, stop, obstruction.
3. hybridization, crossbreeding, interbreeding, intercrossing, cross-fertilization, cross-pollination.

crosswise, *adv.* **1.** across, crossways, athwart, thwart, cross, crisscross; transversely, from side to side, sideways, awry, askant, obliquely, at an angle.
2. contrarily, perversely, wrongly, contrariwise, contradictorily, opposingly; at cross purposes, at odds, at variance, at issue; in confrontation, against, versus, *Sl.* eyeball to eyeball.

crotch, *n.* fork, bifurcation; corner, angle, bend; divarication, division; groin.

crotchet, *n.* odd fancy, vagary, whim, whimsy, notion, kink, maggot; bias, twist, warp; eccentricity, quirk, peculiarity, idiosyncrasy.

crotchety, *adj.* **1.** grouchy, crabby, crabbed, ill-humored, irritable, cranky, cross; irascible, churlish, curmudgeonly, dyspeptic, disagreeable.
2. eccentric, freakish, queer, strange, odd, *Sl.* cracked.
3. capricious, whimsical, erratic, fitful, mercurial, changeable, fickle.

crouch, *v.* **1.** stoop, bend, bend down, squat, hunker, hunker down, hunch, hunch over.
2. cringe, cower, crawl, creep; grovel, truckle, bootlick, toady, fawn, flatter, *Inf.* apple-polish, *Sl.* suck up to; kneel to *or* before, bow, bow and scrape, be at [s.o.'s] beck and call.

crow[1], *n.* raven, chough, rook, jackdaw, daw, grayback, *Astron.* Corvus; grackle, starling.

crow[2], *v.* **1.** boast, brag, beat the drum, *Inf.* toot one's own horn *or* trumpet, trumpet; sing about, exult, glory in, gloat, gloat over; show off, strut, swagger, parade, flaunt; bluster, roister, gasconade, bluff, puff, *Sl.* talk big.
2. cock-a-doodle-doo; cackle, cluck, caw.

crowd, *n.* **1.** throng, horde, concentration, mass, concourse, confluence, conflux, covergence; herd, pack, swarm, flock, drove, bevy, shoal; congestion, jam, press, crush, rush, flood, deluge, *Inf.* mob scene.
2. assemblage, collection, amassment, cumulation; array, galaxy, multitude, force, host; congregation, association, league, assembly, conference, convention; forgathering, conjunction, coalescence.
3. group, company, party, body, gathering; set, circle, clique, faction, coterie; knot, bunch, gang, crew, band, troop, *Inf.* caboodle; team, troupe, squad; sisterhood, brotherhood, sorority, fraternity, sodality, guild, club.
4. commonalty, the public, the general public, the masses; populace, citizenry, proletariat, hoi polloi, bourgeoisie, rank and file; commoners, peasantry; the lower classes, low life, dregs, riffraff, *Inf.* the great unwashed; mob, rabble, rout.
5. audience, spectators, viewers, watchers, listeners, hearers, attenders, attendants; attendance, house, turnout; followers, regulars, fans, devotees, aficionados, *Inf.* buffs, *Inf.* nuts, *Inf.* freaks.
6. collection, accumulation, heap, pile, mass, cumulation; hoard, store, stock, stockpile, supply, fund; agglomeration, conglomeration, clump; lot, pack, batch, bunch, *Inf.* raft; array, assortment, variety, medley, jumble.
—v. **7.** throng, swarm, herd, group, cluster, huddle, concentrate, bunch up *or* together; mass, congregate, agglomerate; flock together, surge, stream; convene, forgather, come together, meet, *Inf.* gang up, go into a huddle, get together.
8. shove, press forward, push, make one's way, squeeze through, *Inf.* elbow *or* shoulder one's way, jostle, *Inf.* pile in, *Inf.* stumble over one another.
9. pack, squeeze, cramp, cram, jam; lump together, compress, congest, bunch, bundle, serry, *Inf.* pack as tight as sardines.
10. fill, heap, pile on, load, lade; pack, stuff, wad, implete, lumber; choke, gag.

crowded, *adj.* **1.** filled, full, packed, congested, serried; thronged, populous, teeming, swarming, overflowing, *Inf.* jammed to the rafters.
2. close, tight, squeezed in, pressed together, jammed, cramped, compressed, compact; dense, thick, solid, *Inf.* packed in like sardines, *Inf.* breathing down each others' necks; *Inf.* close as pages in a book, *Inf.* hanging from the ceiling.

crown, *n.* **1.** diadem, coronet, coronal, tiara; garland, chaplet, wreath, festoon, circlet, circle, ring, ringlet; adornment, ornamentation, decoration.
2. bay, laurel, palm, award, reward, prize, trophy, token, memento; kudos, praise, distinction, honor.
3. sovereign, ruler, monarch, potentate, king, *Latin.* *rex*, queen, emperor, empress, His *or* Her Majesty, His *or* Her Highness; majesty, sovereignty, royalty, rule, rulership, power, authority; regality, dominion, kingdom, territory, jurisdiction.
4. regalia, regale, emblem, design, symbol.
5. cap, hat, crownpiece, headpiece, headgear, helmet.
6. summit, pinnacle, peak, tor, mountaintop, heights; alp, promontory, headland, cliff, precipice, crag, bluff; spire, needle, point, tip, tiptop, top; apex, vertex, apogee.
7. pate, sinciput, forehead, brow; skull, head, poll, *Inf.* noggin, *Sl.* noodle, *Sl.* block; comb, crest, ridge, antler, *Botany.* corolla; tuft, cluster, tassel, topknot.
8. acme, zenith, meridian, climax, culmination, crowning point, *Latin. ne plus ultra*; sublimity, supremacy, consummation, perfection; best, finest, utmost, uttermost, extreme, *U.S. Sl.* the greatest, *U.S. Sl.* the tops, *U.S. Sl.* the most; prime, heyday, bloom, full flower, blossom, efflorescence.
—*v.* **9.** inaugurate, royalize, king, make [s.o.] a king *or* queen; induct, install, invest, empower; decorate, adorn, festoon, dignify, honor, reward, award, make a presentation.
10. cap, top, top out, surmount, pinnacle, tip, *Brit.* nib; consummate, perfect, put the finishing touches on, round out *or* off, culminate, climax; accomplish, fulfill, achieve, attain, compass; complete, conclude, terminate, finish, end.
11. *Informal.* hit, strike, cuff, beat, buffet, *Dial.* hit [s.o.] up side the head, *Inf.* knock [s.o.'s] block off, knock, punch, box, *Inf.* wallop, *Inf.* slug, *Inf.* whack, *Sl.* conk, *Sl.* bop, *Sl.* bash, *Sl.* belt, *Sl.* sock, *U.S. Sl.* biff.

crucial, *adj.* **1.** decisive, determining, pivotal, critical; essential, of the essence, vital, heartbeat, *Inf.* gut; climactic, momentous, eventful, major, profound; all-important, important, high-priority.
2. acute, severe, serious, grave; perilous, hazardous, dangerous, life-threatening, precarious, *Sl.* hairy; trying, difficult, demanding, urgent, pressing, compelling, imperative, exigent.
3. cross-shaped, cruciform; transverse, intersecting, secant; latticed, fretted, interlaced.

crucible, *n.* **1.** vessel, beaked vessel, still, alembic, *Metallurgy.* retort; mortar, cauldron, vat; cruet, beaker, carafe.
2. test, acid test, proof; trial, ordeal, trial *or* ordeal by fire; tribulation, hardship.

crucify, *v.* **1.** persecute, torment, torture, rack, wring, excruciate; harrow, distress, agonize, trouble.
2. (*of oneself*) practice self-discipline *or* self-denial, mortify the flesh, subdue the passions.
3. put to death, execute, nail to the cross, hang on the cross.

crude, *adj.* **1.** raw, coarse, unrefined, unmilled, unground, unprepared, undressed, unprocessed; natural, original, pristine, untouched.
2. primitive, rudimentary, unformed, undeveloped, unevolved; sketchy, drawing-board, outline.
3. faulty, flawed, sloppy, shoddy, poor; incomplete, unfinished, unpolished, incondite; unperfected, imperfect, inartistic.
4. uncouth, rude, crass, coarse, unpolished, uncivil; rough-hewn, homespun, homely, earthy; rustic, countrified, loutish, churlish, boorish; ignorant, awkward, clumsy, oafish; gruff, bearish, boisterous, *Inf.* loud, cheap, tatty, brazen, brassy, brash, ill-bred, ill-mannered, unmannerly, impolite; indecorous, improper, unseemly, unbecoming.
5. vulgar, obscene, lewd, lurid, ribald, bawdy, smutty, *Sl.* raunchy; foul, foulmouthed, dirty; indelicate, indecent, offensive, disgusting, revolting.
6. undisguised, blunt, bare, naked, open; blatant, glaring, outright, downright.

crudity, *n.* **1.** vulgarity, coarseness, commonness, lowness, crudeness; rudeness, incivility, impropriety, unseemliness, bad manners; boorishness, churlishness, boisterousness, brazenness, brassiness.
2. lack of polish, lack of breeding, unrefinement, inelegance, inurbanity, inurbaneness; parvenuism, poor taste, garishness, loudness, Philistinism, gaucherie, tactlessness.
3. indecency, indelicacy, offensiveness, scurrilousness; obscenity, foulness, filth, filthiness, lewdness, prurience, ribaldry, bawdiness, smuttiness, *Sl.* raunchiness.

cruel, *adj.* **1.** barbarous, barbaric, bloodthirsty, ferocious, savage, truculent; vicious, brutal, brutish, inhuman, animalistic, beastly; sadistic, masochistic; evil, malevolent, maleficent, fiendish, diabolical, hellish, infernal.
2. stern, strict, rigid, severe, unrelenting; harsh, grim, relentless, remorseless, implacable; pitiless, merciless, ruthless, heartless; hard-hearted, flinty, stony-hearted, cold-blooded, unfeeling.

cruelty, *n.* **1.** barbarity, barbarousness, viciousness, ruthlessness, ferocity, fierceness, savagery, truculence; brutality, brutishness, inhumanity; murderousness, bloodthirstiness, cold-bloodedness; harshness, severity, grimness; sadism, masochism; fiendishness, deviltry, diablery.

cruet, *n.* bottle, decanter, vessel, *Eccles.* ampulla; vial, caster, beaker, carafe; alembic, crucible; ewer, pitcher; cup, mug, noggin.

cruise, *v.* **1.** sail, navigate, coast, traverse the seas, ride the bounding main; travel, voyage, journey.
2. meander, wander, rove, range, prowl, drift; ramble, saunter, peregrinate.
3. *Informal.* solicit, pander, pimp; be on the make, look for a pick-up.
—*n.* **4.** boat trip, freighter trip, sail; voyage at sea, vacation at sea.

cruiser, *n.* **1.** ship of war, warship, battle cruiser, armored cruiser, light cruiser, corvette; battleship, ship of the line, man-of-war, dreadnought, capital ship, *Inf.* battle wagon.
2. squad car, cruise car, police car, *Inf.* black and white, *Sl.* Smoky, *Sl.* Smoky Bear.

crumb, *n.* bit, fragment, particle, mite, morsel; nip, pinch, nibble, bite, snatch; speck, trifle, scrap, shred, fritter, little crumb, tiny bit, *Baby Talk.* teensy-weensy bit; snip, snippet, sliver, splinter, seed, grain; dot, dab, soupçon, minim; atom, molecule.

crumble, *v.* **1.** fragment, break up, crumb, crack, splinter, shred, fritter; crush, break, shiver, powder, pulverize, triturate, comminute.
2. disintegrate, fall to pieces, fall apart, break down; collapse, tumble down, give way, break up, go to wrack

and ruin, come to dust; decay, deteriorate, fall into decay, rot *or* waste away, molder, decompose, degenerate; disappear piecemeal, fall off, vanish, fade away, decline, perish.

crumbly, *adj.* friable, apt to crumble, soft; brittle, shivery, fragile, frail, breakable, frangible, fissile.

crumple, *v.* **1.** rumple, wrinkle, crinkle, pucker, crimple, rimple; ruffle, corrugate.

2. collapse, fall, topple, tumble, break up, shatter; give way, break down, go *or* fall to pieces, *Inf.* go to smash; shrink, shrivel, crush, squash.

crunch, *v.* **1.** chew noisily, munch, gnaw, champ, chump, *Dial.* chomp, *Inf.* scrunch, *Dial.* chaw, craunch; chew, masticate.

2. crush, grind, grate, rasp; pulverize, shatter, smash, pound.

crusade, *n.* **1.** campaign, holy war; cause, movement; march, struggle, push.

—*v.* **2.** march on *or* against, move on; campaign, struggle, do battle, take up arms, take up the gauntlet; take up a cause, fight *or* work for, lobby, canvass; stump, stump the countryside, *Inf.* beat the drum, *Inf.* take to the streets, *Inf.* fight the good fight, *Inf.* go on the warpath; knock on every door, go door to door, go to the people, barnstorm, *Inf.* take to the stump.

crusader, *n.* campaigner, fighter, battler; reformer, visionary, dreamer, idealist; advocate, champion, enthusiast, zealot, fanatic, partisan; liberal, progressive, radical.

crush, *v.* **1.** squash, mash, press down, compress, cramp, constrict, tighten; squeeze, pinch, bruise, contuse; crumple, rumple, wrinkle.

2. pound, grind, smash, shiver, splinter, shatter, pulverize, granulate, powder, triturate, comminute, reduce to powder; crumble, fragment, break up; trample, stomp, crush under foot.

3. press, squeeze, force, force out, extract, express.

4. embrace, hug, enfold, clutch, grip, hold tight, *Inf.* squeeze the life out of.

5. destroy, demolish, raze, level, ruin, wreck, topple, flatten; erase, blot out.

6. oppress, persecute, browbeat, ride roughshod over; suppress, subdue, quell, quash, put down, squelch, scotch; vanquish, overcome, overpower, conquer.

7. shame, abash, degrade, abase, disgrace, mortify, humiliate, chagrin.

crust, *n.* **1.** cover, coat, layer, blanket, mantle, topping; skin, coating, film, haze, scale, slough; scab, incrustation, cake.

2. shell, casing, hull, husk, rind, bark, cortex.

crusty, *adj.* harsh, surly, rude, curt, brusque, short; sour, bitter, caustic; testy, prickly, touchy, fretful; crabbed, grouchy, ill-natured. See **crabbed** (*defs.* **1, 2**).

cry, *v.* **1.** weep, shed tears, boohoo, sob; bawl, blubber, whimper, mewl, pule, whine, snivel; moan, wail, groan, ululate; lament, mourn, bewail, keen.

2. shout, yell, *Inf.* holler, squall, yowl, bellow, whoop; roar, rend the air, howl; scream, shriek, screech, *Scot. and North Eng.* skirl; sing out, vociferate, ejaculate, voice, utter; bruit, broadcast, proclaim, exclaim, announce; blazon, clamor, blare, hawk; call out, hail, address, call to, hallo, halloo, halloa, *Fox Hunting.* tallyho; yo-ho, *Inf.* yoohoo, hello, hi, hey; cheer, huzza, hurrah, bravo, *Sl.* hubba.

3. bark, yelp, bay, bowwow, woof; meow, miaow, purr, caterwaul; whinny, neigh, bray, moo; caw, crow, cock-a-doodle-doo; cluck, cackle, hoot, gabble, quack, squawk; chirp, cheep, peep, witter, coo, cuckoo; bleat, baa, squeal, oink.

4. implore, beg, plead, beseech, solicit, entreat, appeal; supplicate, adjure, pray, obtest, obsecrate.

5. cry down disparage, belittle, berate, debase; decry, run down, denigrate, underrate, cheapen.

—*n.* **6.** weeping, sob, sobbing, lament, lamentation, wail, moan, groan, keen, ululation, whimper, mewl.

7. shout, *Inf.* holler, squall, yell, roar, howl; scream, shriek, screech, *Scot. and North Eng.* skirl; clamor, outcry, calling, exclamation, hue and cry; uproar, hubbub, hullabaloo; proclamation, announcement, declaration, annunciation; enunciation, utterance, ejaculation, acclamation, vociferation, voice; hail, ahoy, hi, hello; hallo, halloo, halloa, ho, hey, *Inf.* yoohoo, yo-ho; cheer, huzza, hurrah, bravo, *All Fox Hunting.* yoicks, tallyho, huic.

8. entreaty, appeal, plea, supplication, imploration, solicitation; request, prayer, orison.

9. slogan, keynote, shibboleth, password, key work; battle cry, signal, banzai.

10. bark, yelp, bowwow; meow, miaow, purr, caterwaul; whinny, neigh, bray, moo; caw, crow, cock-a-doodle-doo; cluck, hoot, cackle, gabble, quack, squawk; chirp, cheep, peep, coo, cuckoo; bleat, baa, oink, squeal.

11. a far cry a. a long way, quite some distance, faraway, a country mile, remote, distant; **b.** remotely related, very different, discrepant, incongruous.

crypt, *n.* tomb, vault, mausoleum, sepulcher, burial chamber, grave.

cryptic, *adj.* **1.** occult, esoteric, arcane, perdu, hermetic; secret, hidden, veiled, top secret, *Inf.* hush-hush; obscure, indistinct, indefinite, unclear, nebulous, vague; inscrutable, oracular, sphingine, sphinxian; mystic, cabalistic, supernatural; unutterable, ineffable, inviolable, undisclosable, unrevealable, unspeakable.

2. mysterious, inexplicable, insolvable, unaccountable, *Obs.* inextricable; puzzling, enigmatic; strange, weird, bizarre.

3. terse, short, brief, elliptical; abrupt, curt.

cub, *n.* **1.** pup, puppy, whelp, colt.

2. youth, youngster, younker, *Dial.* young'un; boy, lad, hobbledehoy; fledgling, stripling, slip, scion, sprig, chit.

cube, *n.* hexahedron, six-sided body, solid, *Sl.* die.

cuddle, *v.* **1.** hug, embrace, embosom, enfold; caress, fondle, pet, coddle, *Sl.* canoodle; dally, nuzzle, make love, bill and coo, *Inf.* neck, *Inf.* smooch, *Sl.* make out, *Sl.* mess *or* fool around.

2. snuggle, nestle, curl up, bundle.

—*n.* **3.** hug, embrace, squeeze.

cudgel, *n.* **1.** club, bludgeon, bat, bastinado, *Brit.* truncheon, *Chiefly Irish Eng.* shillelagh; night stick, *Inf.* billy, *Inf.* billy club; blackjack, rubber hose, *Sl.* sap.

—*v.* **2.** beat, bludgeon, pummel, bastinado, strike, *Inf.* clobber, *Sl.* clout; thrash, drub, baste, lambaste.

cue, *n.* **1.** reminder, prompt, catchword, key word; indication, signal, nod, wink.

2. hint, intimation, implication, insinuation, innuendo; suggestion, tip, pointer, word to the wise.

3. role, part, function, office, position, place.

4. stimulus, incentive, impetus, fillip, motive; goad, prick, jog, jolt, spur.

—*v.* **5.** signal, indicate, nod, *Inf.* give the nod, wink; prompt, remind, feed lines, jog *or* refresh the memory, set back on the track.

6. (*all of a musical or dramatic performance*) insert, introduce, put in, stick in.

cuff[1], *n.* **1.** handcuff, manacle, hand-fetter, fetter, shackle, chain, bond, trammel, gyve, bilboe, *Sl.* bracelet.

2. off the cuff *Slang.* **a.** extemporaneously, impromptu, ad lib, offhand, on the spur of the moment. **b.** informally, unofficially, off the record; confidentially, in confidence.

3. on the cuff *Slang.* **a.** on credit, on account, on trust, *Chiefly Brit. Inf.* on tick. **b.** free, free of charge, on the house, for nothing.

—*v.* **4.** handcuff, *Sl.* slap the bracelets on [s.o.]; manacle, shackle, put in irons; chain, enchain, tether, fetter, gyve.

cuff², *v.* **1.** buffet, slap, strike, hit, smite, punch, rap, box, box [s.o.'s] ears, whack, bat.

—*n.* **2.** buffet, blow, slap, punch, rap, swat, thwack, whack, *Inf.* bat.

cuirass, *n.* corselet, breastplate, backpiece, aegis, coat of mail; armor plate.

cuisine, *n.* cookery, cooking; menu, bill of fare; table, board, *Inf.* feed.

cul-de-sac, *n.* impasse, bottleneck, pocket, blind, *Inf.* blind alley, *Inf.* deadend; trap, snag, quandary, predicament.

cull, *v.* choose, select, pick over, winnow, sift, sort out, separate the wheat from the chaff; collect, pick up, gather, garner, harvest, reap, crop; pluck, glean, single out, pick out, fix upon.

culminate, *v.* **1.** *Usu.* **culminate in** climax, peak, crest, heighten, come to a head; result, end, come to an end, terminate, run its course.

2. complete, conclude, finish, top out, bring to a close; consummate, perfect, put the finishing touches on, top off, round out *or* off; crown, cap, pinnacle, tip, top, surmount.

culmination, *n.* **1.** consummation, perfection, completion, conclusion, closing, termination, ending.

2. climax, acme, zenith, meridian, high noon, orgasm, high point, supreme moment; sublimity, supremacy, perfection, utmost, uttermost; height, extremity, extreme, maximum, max.; summit, apex, vertex, apogee, *Latin. ne plus ultra*; pinnacle, peak, crest, heights; spire, point, tip, tiptop, top; crown, crowning touch, cap, capper, capstone, keystone, headpiece, head; finishing touch, last stroke, windup, close, finale, *Inf.* payoff, punch line; end, end of the line, terminus, terminal.

culpability, *n.* blame, blameworthiness, censurability; responsibility, guilt, fault; delinquency, dereliction.

culpable, *adj.* blameworthy, blamable, censurable, reprehensible, reproachable, reprovable; at fault, guilty, sinful, transgressive, peccant, found wanting.

culprit, *n.* offender, guilty party, malefactor, miscreant; rascal, reprobate, wrong-doer, evil-doer, *Sl.* the heavy, *Sl.* the bad guy; felon, criminal, delinquent, lawbreaker, transgressor, sinner.

cult, *n.* **1.** affiliation, faith, denomination, school, persuasion, belief; faction, party, scism, ism.

2. worshipers, believers, members, followers; devotees, enthusiasts, zealots, fanatics; claque, fan club, hero-worshipers.

3. adoration, veneration, worship, homage, reverence, hero worship.

cultivate, *v.* **1.** dress, till, till the soil, farm, work, work the land; plow, spade, dig, delve, hoe, harrow, rake; fertilize, manure, compost.

2. civilize, develop, improve, improve [s.o.'s] mind, enlighten, educate, school; train, discipline; refine, polish, finish, perfect.

3. (*all of an art, science, etc.*) promote, foster, advocate, support, patronize; encourage, abet, further, advance, uphold, back; help, aid, assist.

4. (*all of an art, science, etc.*) pursue, follow, keep abreast of; study, investigate, delve into, search into, devote oneself to.

5. woo, court, pay court to, pay addresses to; seek [s.o.'s] friendship, seek [s.o.'s] company, make advances, break the ice; ingratiate oneself with, curry favor, dance attendance upon, *Sl.* shine up to, *Sl.* suck up to, *Sl.* play up to, *Sl.* butter up.

cultivation, *n.* **1.** agriculture, agronomy, geoponics, farming, husbandry, tillage, tilth; tilling, dressing, working; aquaculture, aquiculture, hydroponics.

2. civilization, development, improvement, training, preparation, conditioning, grooming; education, instruction, teaching, tuition; enlightenment, edification, illumination.

3. (*all of art, science, etc.*) promotion, fosterage, advocacy, support, patronage; encouragement, abetment, furtherance, advancement, backing; help, aid, assistance.

4. (*all of art, science, etc.*) pursuit, following, study, investigation; devotion.

5. culture, refinement, polish, manners, good breeding; taste, good taste; savoir-faire, tact, discretion, discernment, discrimination.

culture, *n.* **1.** cultivation, refinement, polish; edification, enlightenment, sophistication, urbanity, worldliness; elevation, development, advancement, progress; attainment, accomplishment, learning, erudition, knowledge, education; manners, breeding, good breeding, gentility, civility; elegance, grace, courtliness, savoir-faire; taste, good taste, discernment, discrimination.

2. civilization, way of life, customs, folkways, ways, habits, life style, *Sociology.* mores.

3. agriculture, agronomy, geoponics, farming, husbandry, tillage, tilth; tilling, dressing, working; aquaculture, aquiculture, hydroponics.

—*v.* **4.** cultivate, dress, till, till the soil, farm, work, work the land; plow, spade, dig, delve, hoe, harrow, rake; fertilize, manure, compost.

cultured, *adj.* **1.** cultivated, civilized, refined, polished, finished; genteel, well-bred, thoroughbred, aristocratic, blue-blooded; elegant, graceful, fine; polite, mannerly, courteous, gracious, chivalrous, chivalric, gallant, cavalier, urbane, suave, sophisticated, cosmopolitan; fashionable, stylish, high-class, *Sl.* classy.

2. enlightened, superior, high-brow, accomplished; learned, *Archaic.* studied, versed, knowledgeable; educated, lettered, intellectual, scholarly, erudite; well-educated, well-informed, well-read, literary.

culvert, *n.* drain, channel, sewer, cloaca; conduit, duct, trough, gutter, ditch, gully, *Brit.* sough; water-course, waterway, canal.

cumbersome, *adj.* **1.** burdensome, onerous, oppressive; tiresome, irksome, vexatious, troublesome, worrisome, inconvenient.

2. unwieldy, clumsy, awkward, unmanageable, incommodious; ponderous, hefty, heavy, massive, bulky.

cumulative, *adj.* increasing, growing, adding, totaling, *Inf.* piling up; crescent, waxing, swelling, enlarging; accumulative, additive.

cunning, *n.* **1.** craft, craftiness, guile, wiliness, slyness, foxiness, artfulness, subtlety, shrewdness; deceit, deception, duplicity, trickery.

2. skill, skillfullness, dexterity, adroitness, expertness, mastery, artistry; aptitude, facility, address, dispatch, ready skill, *Inf.* know-how; ingenuity, cleverness, talent, flair, genius, art, knack.

—*adj.* **3.** ingenious, clever, resourceful, imaginative, inventive, creative.

4. crafty, artful, sly, wily, subtle, foxy, *Sl.* dumb *or* crazy like a fox, *Scot. and North Eng.* pawky; shrewd, astute, canny, sharp, knowing, *Inf.* cagey.

5. insidious, guileful, disingenuous, scheming, plotting, designing, calculating, contriving; deceitful, tricky, crooked, dishonest, underhanded; shifty, slippery, smooth, slick.

cup, *n.* **1.** teacup, demitasse, *Fr. tasse*; *Literary.* chalice, goblet, wine glass; glass, beaker, tumbler, cannikin; can, mug, stein, tankard; wineskin, drinking horn *or* gourd, rhyton; bowl, *Gk. and Rom. Antiquity.* kylix; punch bowl, jorum, *Gk. and Rom. Antiquity.* kyathus.

2. cupful, 8 fluid ounces, 16 tablespoons, 240 milliliters; teacupful, 4 fluid ounces, 120 milliliters.

3. pan, basin, depression, crater, hollow, concavity; furrow, groove, trough; hole, cavity, excavation, pit.

cupboard, *n.* sideboard, buffet, china closet, cabinet, commode, *Obs.* ambry; pantry, cuddy, closet, storeroom.

Cupid, *n.* **1.** god of love, Amor, Eros, amoretto.

2. matchmaker; marriage broker, *Yiddish.* shadchan *or* schatchen.

cupidity, *n.* **1.** greed, graspingness, acquisitiveness, *Sl.* grabbiness, avariciousness, rapacity, rapaciousness; selfishness, miserliness, penuriousness, parsimony, niggardliness; stinginess, meanness, close-fistedness, tight-fistedness, mercenariness, venality, sordidness.

2. eagerness, avidity, yearning, craving, covetousness; keenness, itch, itching, appetite, stomach, *U.S. Dial.* big eye, appetence; anxiousness, breathlessness, impatience, longing, thirst, ardor, zeal, fervency, passion, mania; hankering, aspiration, hunger, ambitiousness.

3. ravenousness, voraciousness, gluttony, edacity, open-mouthedness, hoggishness, piggishness.

cupola, *n.* belfry, bell tower, campanile, steeple, spire; lantern, lookout, tower, turret; dome, onion dome, polygonal vault.

cur, *n.* **1.** mongrel, mongrel dog, bitch, lurcher, *Sl.* mutt.

2. wretch, cad, scoundrel, dastard, knave, blackguard, villain, wastrel, ne'er do well; beast, hound, viper, skunk, polecat; *All Inf.* jerk, rat, creep, stinker, louse; *All Sl.* bum, *Vulgar.* bastard, *Vulgar.* SOB, *Chiefly Brit.* rotter, *Chiefly Brit.* bounder, *Brit.* blighter.

curable, *adj.* healable, treatable, remediable, reparable; mendable, fixable, restorable; recoverable, retrievable, reclaimable; corrigible, reformable, improvable.

curate, *n.* assistant priest, parish priest, *Brit.* deputy rector *or* deputy vicar; chaplain, padre, *U.S. Mil. Sl.* sky pilot, residentiary; priest, parson, minister, presbyter, abbé, curé, *Brit.* incumbent; ecclesiastic, clergyman, cleric, churchman, *Brit.* blackcoat, reverend, man of the cloth.

curative, *adj.* **1.** therapeutic, medicinal, *Rare.* medical, curing, healing, sanative, sanatory; remedial, corrective, reparative, reparatory; mending, restorative, restoring, recuperative, recuperatory; beneficial, advantageous, helpful, salutary, healthy, good, wholesome.

—*n.* **2.** remedy, cure, cure-all, panacea. See **cure** (*def.* 2).

curator, *n.* keeper, guardian, custodian, conservator, caretaker, janitor, concierge; guard, watchman, warder, defender, protector, preserver; steward, administrator, manager, overseer, superintendent, *Inf.* super, supervisor; foreman, director, warden, boss, man in charge.

curb, *n.* **1.** border, edge, margin, skirt, rim, lip, periphery, verge; brow, brink, ridge, ledge; curbstone, *Brit.* kerb.

2. frame, framework, enclosure, boundary; confines, bounds, limits, sides; wall, fence, railing, rail, post, picket, palisade, barrier, barricade.

3. restraint, self-restraint, check, checking; curbing, holding back, control, controlling, self-control; curtail, curtailment, cutting down on, moderation, temperance; slackening, slack, leniency, looseness, *Inf.* letting up on, *Sl.* laying off of; slowing up *or* down, deceleration, braking.

4. hindrance, retardant, damper, damp, wet blanket; repression, suppression, withholding; constraint, confinement, bar, bolt, lock, padlock; restriction, limitation, leading string, leash, chain, rein, tether; yoke, halter, harnass, bridle, collar, stay; bit, snaffle, muzzle, gag.

5. abstention, abstinence, nonindulgence, abstemiousness, moderation, continence, celibacy, fasting; Puritanism, austerity, self-mortification, self-deprivation; asceticism, self-denial, self-abnegation; refrainment, forbearance, desistance.

—*v.* **6.** restrain, check, keep in check, hold back, contain, control; withhold, deny, abnegate, suppress, repress; curtail, cut down on, moderate, be temperate, *Inf.* let up on, *Sl.* lay off of, be lenient, be slack *or* loose with; slow up *or* down, decelerate, brake; stop, *Sl.* cheese, hold, stay, cease, arrest, halt; pull up, stop short, come to a halt; discontinue, interrupt, let up, pause, suspend, intermit; drop, have done with, let alone, let be, leave well enough alone, keep one's hands off, turn aside; desist, resist, abstain, forbear, restrain; forgo, do without, sacrifice; give up, *Inf.* swear off, quit, leave off, break off; renounce, relinquish, put aside.

curd, *n.* clabber, curdled milk, bonnyclabber, casein; yogurt, custard, flummery; coagulum, clot, cake, film, crust, scab; sponge, dough.

curdle, *v.* curd, clabber; coagulate, congeal, solidify, thicken; sour, ferment, spoil, *Inf.* turn.

cure, *n.* **1.** remedial treatment, therapy, therapeutics; healing, reparation, restoration; recuperation, recovery, convalescence.

2. remedy, restorative, antidote, counteractive, neutralizer, corrective, preventive, prophylactic; cure-all, panacea, elixir, cure for all ills, nostrum; medicine, medicament, medication, *Med.* prescription, *Pharm.* drug, *Bio-chem.* antibiotic, physic, germicide; healing substance, *Pharm.* lotion, *Pharm.* ointment, unguent, salve, balm, liniment; tonic, *Physiol., Med.* stimulant.

3. (*all of meat or fish*) preservation, smoking, salting, drying, kippering; pickling, brining, corning; marinading, marinating.

—*v.* **4.** heal, restore to health, make well *or* whole, *Inf.* bring around, put one back on one's feet; treat, doctor, apply remedies to, give medicine to, medicate, drug, dose, physic; attend to, take care of, minister to, nurse; palliate, mitigate, alleviate, relieve, lessen, ease, free from pain.

5. remedy, fix, repair, set right *or* straight, correct.

6. (*all of meat or fish*) preserve, smoke, salt, dry, kipper; pickle, brine, corn; marinade, marinate.

curfew, *n.* **1.** evening bell, eleventh hour, bedtime; nightfall, close of day, sundown, sunset, *Brit. Dial.* cockshut; evening, eventide; dusk, twilight, *Literary.* gloaming.

2. ban, prohibition, proscription, forbiddance, interdict; preventive measure.

curiosity, *n.* **1.** inquisitiveness, inquiringness, inquiring, acquisitiveness, investigativeness, investigating, interrogating, querying, questioning, search, searching, scrutinizing, study, studying, interest, research, researching.
2. intrusiveness, officiousness, meddlesomeness, meddling, business, interference, interfering, intermeddling, prying, intruding, interposing, *Inf.* kibitzing; obtrusiveness, forwardness, audacity, impertinence; snooping, *Inf.* snoopiness, prowling, peeping, peering, eavesdropping, mousing, *Inf.* rubbernecking, *Inf.* nosiness.
3. peculiarity, idiosyncrasy, idiocrasy, eccentricity, hobby-horse; aberration, aberrance, aberrancy, deviation, anomaly, *Rare.* anomalism.
4. curio, oddity, rarity, novelty, freak; wonder, marvel, miracle, phenomenon, prodigy; spectacle, spectacular, sight, eye-opener, *Sl.* mind-boggler, *Sl.* mind-blower.

curious, *adj.* **1.** inquisitive, inquisitorial, inquiring, investigative, investigatory, investigating; interrogative, interrogatory, interrogating, querying, questioning, searching, scrutinizing, studying, *Rare.* zetetic, *Rare.* percontatorial.
2. meddlesome, meddling, intermeddling, intrusive, prying, interfering, intruding, interposing, *Inf.* kibitzing, officious, busy; obtrusive, forward, audacious, impertinent; snooping, prowling, peeping, peering, eavesdropping, mousing, *Inf.* rubbernecking, *Inf.* ñosy, *Inf.* long-nosed, *Inf.* snoopy; overcurious, burning with curiousity, agape, agog, all agog.
3. odd, peculiar, queer, oddish, offbeat, quizzical, cranky, *Inf.* funny, baffling; strange, weird, bizarre, erratic, freakish, grotesque, *Sl.* rum, *Sl.* far out; unusual, uncommon, unconventional, unique, unorthodox, unwonted, rare, exotic, out of the ordinary, novel, singular, exceptional; extraordinary, remarkable, astonishing, phenomenal, prodigious.
4. (*all of books*) indelicate, coarse, gross, vile, offensive, fulsome; obscene, pornographic, smutty, prurient, foul, dirty, filthy, lurid, unclean, salacious, licentious; sexy, erotic, sensual, bawdy, ribald, lewd, indecent, suggestive, risqué.

curl, *v.* **1.** coil, twist, turn, twist and turn, wind, spiral, loop, hook, crook; meander, snake, slink, worm.
—*n.* **2.** ringlet, curlicue, tress, lock; coil, whorl, spiral, helix, volute, gyre; screw, corkscrew.
3. curvature, curvation, curving; convolution, circumvolution, winding, turning, meandering.

curly, *adj.* wavy, curled, kinky, frizzy; whorled, spiraled, volute; corkscrew.

curmudgeon, *n.* crab, bear, *Inf.* crank, *Inf.* crosspatch, *Inf.* grouch, *Inf.* grouser, *Inf.* sorehead, *Sl.* bellyacher; churl, boor, brute, barbarian, yahoo, *Inf.* goop, *Chiefly Scot.* tyke, *Brit. Sl.* mucker.

currency, *n.* **1.** money, cash, hard *or* cold cash, legal tender, greenbacks; coin, specie; paper money, bills, banknotes, *Inf.* folding money; *All Sl.* dough, bread, moolah, jack, long green, shekels, spondulicks, *U.S.* bucks, *U.S.* kale.
2. prevalence, acceptance, popularity, commonness, generality, reign, run; vogue, fashion, style, mode, prevailing taste.
3. exposure, publicity, fame, notoriety, public eye *or* consciousness, *Inf.* spotlight, *Inf.* limelight.
4. circulation, communication, transmission, transference; diffusion, dissemination, spreading.

current, *adj.* **1.** present, immediate, instant, imminent, now-passing, happening, occuring, ongoing, going on, present-day; existent, extant, actual, being, coincident, concomitant, coeval, coexistent, simultaneous, contemporaneous, synchronous.
2. well-known, widely-known, commonly-known, common knowledge, familiar; reported, rumored, circulated, in circulation, in the news, in the air, going around, making the rounds, all over town; talked-of, talked-about, in everyone's mouth, on everyone's lips *or* tongue.
3. prevalent, prevailing, dominant, predominant, ruling, reigning; widespread, general, universal, rife, rampant, epidemic; common, commonplace, everyday, usual, ordinary, customary, normative, conventional, regular, habitual, standard, average.
4. popular, in fashion, in style, in vogue, à la mode, all the rage, *Sl.* the thing; new-fashioned, modern, *Inf.* trendy, *Sl.* mod, *Sl.* now; fashionable, stylish, modish.
5. new, present, latest, most-recent, fresh; up-to-date, up-to-the-minute, in the swim, *Fr. au courant*, enlightened, informed, well-posted, in the know, *Sl.* hip, *Sl.* with it, *Brit. Sl.* suss; up on, abreast of.
—*n.* **6.** flux, flow, flowing; tide; progress, ongoing.
7. waterway, watercourse, channel, stream, river, brook, creek.
8. draft, updraft, downdraft, wind, air current, crosscurrent, undercurrent, thermal; jetstream.
9. trend, drift, direction, course, bearing, aim, turn, set, tenor, tone, swing, line; bent, inclination, tendency, general tendency, main course, mainstream, main current, the way the wind blows *or* river flows, the way things go; spirit, spirit of the age, *Ger. zeitgeist*.
10. electricity, direct current, DC, alternating current, AC, power, *Sl.* juice.

curse, *n.* **1.** imprecation, execration, fulmination, malediction, denunciation, proscription, abomination, damnation, excommunication.
2. charm, incantation, conjuration, invocation, magic formula, voodoo, hoodoo, jinx, evil eye, *It. malocchio*, *Inf.* Indian sign, *Sl.* whammy, *Sl.* double-whammy, *Archaic.* wanion.
3. abuse, cursing, vituperation, vilification, invective; profanity, oath, blasphemy, expletive, *Inf.* cuss, *Inf.* bad *or* dirty word, *Sl.* swear.
4. evil, misfortune, calamity, trouble; bane, scourge, plague, affliction, torment; harm, evil days *or* times, bitter pill, cross to bear, thorn in the side, crown of thorns; annoyance, vexation.
—*v.* **5.** anathematize, comminate, execrate, maledict, fulminate, excommunicate; blast, damn, denounce, proscribe, vituperate, thunder against, badger; call down, *Inf.* cuss out; give [s.o.] the evil eye, *Sl.* give [s.o.] the whammy *or* double-whammy, *Sl.* put the whammy on [s.o.].
6. blaspheme, swear, use God's name in vain.
7. plague, blight, scourge, injure, harm, destroy, doom; jinx, vex, trouble, beset, annoy, harass, distress.

cursed, *adj.* **1.** doomed, accursed, *Brit. Dial.* fey, damned, curse-laden, condemned, anathematized, *Archaic.* maledict, bedeviled, bewitched, hoodooed, voodooed, hexed; star-crossed, ill-fated, foredoomed; unsanctified, unblest, unholy, unconsecrated, unhallowed; ruined, undone, blighted, ravaged, despoiled; miserable, unfortunate, stricken, woeful, wretched, unhappy; desolate, woebegone, forlorn, abandoned.
2. damnable, diabolic, devilish, fiendish, satanic, demonic, demoniac, demoniacal, infernal, hellish; execrable, abominable, horrible, horrid, hideous, atrocious; base, vile, odious, obnoxious, wicked, sinful, iniquitous; evil, black-hearted, corrupt, depraved, villainous, sinister; reprobate, nefarious, flagitious, heinous; abhorrent, revolting, repulsive, repugnant, foul,

rotten, offensive, loathsome, nauseous, nauseating; pernicious, pestilential, noxious, deadly, fell; malign, malevolent, malicious, rancorous; hateful, detestable, despicable, infamous.

cursory, *adj.* hasty, superficial, perfunctory, desultory; rapid, hurried, quick, summary, unreflected, precipitate; shallow, ephemeral, discursive, slight; transient, fleeting, passing; careless, immethodical, unmeditated, slapdash, loose.

curt, *adj.* **1.** short, shortened, abbreviated, abridged, condensed.
2. brief, concise, succinct, terse, laconic, pithy, crisp; summary, compact, compendious.
3. short-spoken, abrupt, brusque, blunt, gruff; rude, uncivil, unceremonious, ungracious, impolite; snappish, tart, petulant; harsh, bluff, sullen, hostile, crusty.

curtail, *v.* reduce, decrease, retrench, diminish, cut, cut short, cut down, cut back, cut off, subtract, subduct, lessen, shorten, contract, abridge, abbreviate, narrow, shrink, compress, *Obs.* breviate, dock, crop, clip, shear, trim, prune, pare down, shave, nip; *All Inf.* pull back on, tighten up on, put the squeeze on; limit, restrict, tie down, rein, draw rein, constrict, confine; stub, stunt, truncate, obtruncate, detruncate, lop, lop off; slim down, slenderize, shrivel, wither, dwarf.

curtailment, *n.* reduction, reducing, decrease, decreasing, retrenchment, retrenching, diminution, diminishing, cutting short, cutting off, cutting down, cutting back, subtraction, subtracting, subduction, subducting; loss, lessening, shortage, shortening, contraction, contracting, abridgement, abbreviation, narrowing, shrinkage, shrinking, compression, compressing; docking, cropping, shearing, trimming, clipping, pruning, shaving, nipping; limitation, limiting, restriction, restricting, constriction, constricting, confinement, confining; stubbing, stunting, truncation, obtruncation, detruncation, lopping, lopping off; slimming down, slenderizing, shriveling, withering.

curtain, *n.* **1.** window curtain, window shade; hanging, drapery, tapestry, dosser, portiere, valance, lambrequin; backdrop, drop, scrim; arras; firescreen.
2. screen, shutter, blind, shade, drape; cover, cloak, veil, purdah.
—*v.* **3.** screen, hide, shield, drape, cover, conceal, veil.

curtsy, *n.* bow, bob, nod, salute, greeting, how-do-you-do; genuflection, kowtow, salaam.

curvature, *n.* arcuation, incurvation, incurvature, curvation, *Pathol.* cyrtosis, curve, camber, bend, bending, flexure; aduncity, hook, crook; sinuosity, anfractuosity, winding, curl.

curve, *n.* **1.** arc, arch, vault, *Archit.* extrados; incurve, camber; crescent, lunule, lune, meniscus, half moon; bend, turn, horseshoe, *Phys. Geog.*, *U.S.* oxbow; *Geom.* parabola, *Geom.* epicycloid, *Geom.* ellipse.
2. trick, deception, cheat, swindle, ruse, wile.
—*v.* **3.** bend, arch, *Archit.* embow, bow, round; incurve, camber; crook, hook, turn, inflect, deflect; wind, curl, coil, spiral.

cushion, *n.* **1.** pillow, bolster, upholstery; hassock, mat, pad, pillion, *Brit.* woolsack; seat, rest; buffer, shock absorber, fender.
—*v.* **2.** pillow, bolster, cradle; support, prop, shore up, brace, underbrace, buttress.
3. check, forestall, quieten, mollify; soften, lessen, allay, mitigate.

cusp, *n.* point, pointed end, nib; tip, apex, peak, top; corner, angle.

custodian, *n.* **1.** keeper, guardian, caretaker, conservator, protector, preserver, defender; guard, warder, watchman, watchdog.
2. janitor, concierge, clean-up man, maintenance man, handyman.
3. steward, administrator, curator, manager, overseer, superintendent, *Inf.* super, supervisor; foreman, director, warden, boss, man in charge.

custody, *n.* **1.** keeping, care, guardianship, ward, wardship, protection, *Law.* trusteeship; keep, safekeeping, safeguard; tutelage, guidance, chaperonage; supervision, superintendence, surveillance, direction, control.
2. holding, possession, retention, *Law.* seizin.
3. imprisonment, confinement, detention, incarceration, durance; constraint, restraint, duress, fetters.

custom, *n.* **1.** practice, way, fashion, procedure, policy, rule, use; habit, convention, wont, praxis, usage, observance, habitude, second nature; consuetude, tradition, *Law.* presciption, routing, course; conventionality, matter of course, conventionalism, formality, form.
2. tax, toll, duty, levy, impost; rate, tariff, excise, assessment, exaction.

customary, *adj.* accustomed, habitual, set, fixed, rooted, established, traditional, consuetudinary, confirmed; usual, wonted, regular, daily, routine, normal, natural; ordinary, conventional, everyday, commonplace; general, prevailing, prevalent, common, frequent; well-known, popular, favorite, household; stock, well-worn, trite, hackneyed, cliché.

customer, *n.* patron, client, (*collectively*) clientele; buyer, *Law.* emptor, *Law.* vendee; purchaser, shopper, marketer, patronizer.

cut, *v.* **1.** gash, slash, lance, slit, slice; notch, ridge, *Cookery.* score; sever, abscind, split, carve, cleave, sunder; rend, rive, tear, rip; divide, section, apportion; dissect, cut apart, anatomize, disjoint, quarter; disjoin, disunite, dismember.
2. wound, hurt, pain, grieve, aggrieve, distress, lacerate; afflict, trouble, injure, discomfort; insult, slight, affront, offend; touch, move, affect.
3. shun, scorn, snub, slight, spurn, rebuff; ignore, turn one's back on, freeze [s.o.] out, take no note of, cold-shoulder, look right through [s.o.].
4. strike, crack, whip, lash, scourge, flog, flagellate; birch, switch, stripe; mutilate, mangle.
5. hew, saw down, fell; chop, hack, splinter; reap, mow, harvest, gather; lop off, truncate, amputate, detach, remove; trim, clip, dock, snip, nip, snap; shear, crop, (*of the hair*) bob; pare, shave, prune.
6. intersect, decussate, cross, bisect.
7. abridge, shorten, abbreviate, condense; contract, epitomize, summarize, abstract; curtail, retrench, cut back; edit, eliminate; reduce, diminish, lower, abate, mitigate, cut down on, ease up on.
8. dissolve, dilute, thin, water *or* water down; adulterate, degrade, debase, pollute; vitiate, weaken, doctor.
9. sculpture, sculpt, sculp, chisel; carve, whittle, incise, engrave; shape, form, fashion, mold.
10. excavate, hollow out, scoop out, gouge; dig, burrow, tunnel, *Archaic.* delve.
11. (*usu. of engines*) stop, halt, turn off, switch off; *Informal.* discontinue, desist, cease, *Sl.* knock off, *Sl.* cut out.
12. record, make a recording *or* record of, put on disc; tape, taperecord, put on tape; film, photograph.
13. (*usu. with* across) pass, go, come, roam, ramble, trek; cross over, travel over, traverse.
14. swerve, veer, tack, yaw, turn, change direction *or* course, *Naut.* jibe.

15. *Informal.* decamp, *Inf.* vamoose, *Inf.* split, *Inf.* take off, *Sl.* cut out, abscond.
16. **cut across** transcend, go beyond, rise above.
17. **cut in** interpose, interrupt, *Sl.* butt in.
18. **cut off** **a.** intercept, seize en route. **b.** interrupt, obstruct, hinder, thwart, stop. **c.** disinherit, disherit, disown, renounce.
19. **cut up** **a.** lacerate, wound, injure. **b.** misbehave, *Inf.* fool around, *Sl.* horse around, disobey, play pranks *or* jokes. **c.** ridicule, criticize, vilify, slander, *Inf.* bad-mouth.
—adj. **20.** detached, severed, broken off, separated, *Bot.* incised, *Bot.* cleft.
21. apportioned, divided, sectioned.
22. reduced, lowered, marked down, diminished; diluted, watered, watered down, adulterated.
23. castrated, gelded, caponized, eunuchized, emasculated, effeminized.
24. **cut and dried** **a.** fixed, settled, predetermined, automatic. **b.** unoriginal, uninspiring; trite, hackneyed; dull, boring, plodding, wearisome.
—n. **25.** gash, slash, slit, cleft, rift; incision, groove, opening, indentation; wound, laceration; nick, tear, rip.
26. slice, piece, portion, quantity, sliver, shaving, *Dial.* collop; snip, snippet, snatch, chip; sample, fragment, remnant.
27. percentage, *Inf.* share; graft, *Inf.* kickback, *Inf.* rake-off.
28. style, fashion, mode, manner; shape, form, configuration; type, sort, kind, ilk.
29. strip, swath; passage, course, channel; furrow, trench, tunnel, burrow, ditch, hole, dugout; belt, avenue, corridor, aisle.
30. excision, omission, deletion; excerpt, selection, quotation; cutting, clipping, analects.
31. reduction, cutback, slowdown, diminution; curtailment, abbreviation, abatement, mitigation.
32. insult, affront, offense; sarcasm, taunt, dig, jibe, jeer, slap in the face; rebuff, snub, slight, cold shoulder, deep freeze.
33. woodcut, print, *Fine Arts.* block print; engraving, etching; impression, illustration, picture, design.

cutaway, *n.* morning clothes, morning dress, swallow-tailed coat, tail coat, *Inf.* tails, *Inf.* tie and tails, white tie, formal, *Sl.* monkey suit, *Sl.* soup-and-fish; tuxedo, *Inf.* tux. See **tuxedo**.

cuticle, *n.* epidermis, scarfskin, skin, *Anat.* derma; integument, membrane, pellicle.

cutpurse, *n.* pickpocket, pickpurse, lightfingers; purse snatcher, mugger; thief, robber, crook, bandit.

cutthroat, *n.* **1.** thug, killer, murderer, slayer; assassin, liquidator, bravo, gunman, executioner, *Euph.* dispatcher, *Euph.* silencer; *All Sl.* gun, hired gun, hit man, triggerman, torpedo, hatchet man.
—adj. **2.** murderous, killing, homicidal, death-dealing, lethal, fatal, mortal; savage, barbarous, cruel, brutal, fiendish, bloodthirsty, sanguinary; ferocious, violent, wild, berserk, maniacal.
3. ruthless, merciless, unmerciful, pitiless, unfeeling; dog-eat-dog, every man for himself.

cutting, *n.* **1.** severance, disseverance, sunderance; splitting, cleaving, cleavage, slitting; rending, tearing.
2. piece, part, particle, bit; slice, *Inf.* clip, clipping; (*all usu. of a plant*) cut, slip, scion.
—adj. **3.** sharp, sharpened, edged, honed, razor-sharp; lancinating, stabbing; keen, pointed.
4. numbing, freezing, frigid, chilling, raw; cold, chilly, algid, bitter; piercing, penetrating, biting, nipping, stinging, pricking.
5. caustic, mordant, mordacious, acrimonious, acrid, acidulous, acid, pungent; trenchant, incisive, slashing, scathing; astringent, severe, sharp, sharp-tongued, acerb, acerbic, stern, harsh, austere, stringent; spiteful, virulent, malicious, malificent, venomous, vicious, malevolent, malignant; invidious, hateful.
6. sarcastic, sardonic, scornful, mocking, ridiculing, derisive, derisory; satirical, ironic, ironical, double-edged, cynical; contemptuous, contumelious, disparaging, sneering, disdainful, supercilious, depreciatory; critical, captious, carping, censorious, faultfinding.

cycle, *n.* **1.** round, revolution, rotation; series, succession, run, sequence.
2. eon, age, period, epoch, era.
3. bicycle, bike, monocycle, tricycle; motorcycle, quadricycle, scooter, tandem, velocipede.
—v. **4.** recur, reoccur, return, reappear; come again, roll again.
5. ride, go for a ride, drive; motorcycle, bicycle.

cyclone, *n.* windstorm, storm, gale, gust, squall, blast, simoon, sirocco, whirlwind; tornado, hurricane, typhoon, tempest, twister; monsoon.

cynic, *n.* pessimist, gloom and doomer, *Inf.* gloomy Gus, naysayer, *Sl.* crapehanger; misanthrope, man-hater, misogynist; scowler, sneerer, snarler, growler, grumbler; critic, complainer, faultfinder, detractor; scoffer, satirist, carper, caviler, *Inf.* knocker; skeptic, nullifidian, doubter; killjoy, *Sl.* partypooper, spoilsport, damper.

cynical, *adj.* **1.** skeptical, doubting, doubtful, suspicious, distrustful, disbelieving, unbelieving; critical, captious, hypercritical, carping, caviling, censorious, faultfinding; sarcastic, sardonic, scornful, mocking, ridiculing, derisive, derisory; satirical, ironic, ironical, double-edged; pessimistic, misanthropic, negative; contemptuous, contumelious, disparaging, sneering; disdainful, supercilious, haughty, arrogant.
2. caustic, mordant, mordacious, acrimonious, bitter, acrid, acidulous, acid, pungent; trenchant, cutting, incisive, slashing, scathing; penetrating, piercing, stinging, pricking, nipping, biting; keen, pointed, sharp, sharp-tongued; astringent, severe, acerb, acerbic, stern, harsh, austere, stringent; spiteful, virulent, malicious, malificent, venomous, vicious, malevolent, malignant; insulting, excoriating, denouncing, berating, abusive, scurrilous, offensive, vituperative; mean, brutal, unkind, uncharitable, unbenevolent.
3. abrupt, brusque, blunt, curt, short, gruff, snappish, crusty; peevish, petulant, crabbed, testy, touchy, waspish, irascible, edgy; ill-tempered, ill-humored, ill-natured, short-tempered; hostile, resentful, indignant, piqued, angry; morose, surly, sour, moody.

cynicism, *n.* **1.** misanthropy, antisociality, hatred; pessimism, defeatism, malism; skepticism, suspicion, disbelief, distrust.
2. derision, ridicule, scorn, mockery; satire, irony, lampoon, burlesque; contempt, disparagement, disdain, superciliousness, haughtiness, arrogance; criticism, censure, hypercriticalness, captiousness; taunt, fleer, gibe, jeer, flout, scoff, sneer, wipe, quip, nip; abuse, contumely, barb, slur, vituperation, aspersion.
3. acrimony, acrimoniousness, causticity, asperity, mordancy, acridness, acridity, pungency, venom, venomousness, venomness; trenchancy, keenness, incisiveness; virulence, spite, spitefulness, malice, maliciousness, viciousness; astringency, severity, sternness, acerbity, austerity.
4. peevishness, petulance, *Rare.* petulancy, crabbedness, testiness, touchiness, irascibility, edginess; ill temper, ill-temperedness, short-temperedness, ill humor,

ill-humoredness.

cynosure, *n.* **1.** focal point, focus, focus of attention, center of attention, center of interest, polestar.

2. lodestar, guiding light, leader, paragon, hero, mirror, shining example; ideal, beau ideal, acme, apotheosis.

cyst, *n.* bladder, sac, vesicle, bag, blister, bleb; saccule, saccula, utricle, *Bot.* theca.

czar, *n.* tsar, autocrat, king, emperor, kaiser, Caesar, khan, shah; crowned head, potentate, monarch, sovereign, majesty; dictator, despot, absolute monarch, tyrant, autarch, *Ger. Fuhrer, It. duce, Span. caudillo*; ruler, leader, chief, overlord, suzerain.

D

dab, *v.* **1.** bedaub, besmear, smear, smudge, blot, spot; coat, plaster, tar, paint, varnish.
2. pat, tamp, tap, poke, jab; rap, swat, hit, strike, whack, slap, *Inf.* swipe, thump, flap.
—n. **3.** pat, tap, poke, jab, light blow, peck; rap, knock, fillip, stroke, smack, *Inf.* swipe, whack.
4. bit, mite, speck, *Inf.* smidgen, *Inf.* smitch, nip, spot; trace, touch, hint, trifle, tinge, suggestion; pinch, dash, drop, sprinkling, driblet, crumb, modicum.

dabble, *v.* **1.** splash, splatter, slosh, swash; sprinkle, spray, asperge; moisten, dampen, damp, wet, wet down.
2. splash about, paddle, (*in water*) play.
3. potter, putter, tinker, fiddle, *Inf.* fool around; trifle, dally, dillydally; half know, know a little, smatter, scratch the surface, toy with, flirt with.

dabbler, *n.* putterer, potterer, smatterer, trifler, dallier, piddler, *Inf.* dabster; dilettante, sciolist, half scholar; amateur, nonprofessional, layman, do-it-yourselfer.

daft, *adj.* **1.** crazy, crazed, *Sl.* bughouse, *Sl.* kooky, *Inf.* potty, *Sl.* nuts, *Inf.* nutty, *Inf.* daffy; insane, mad, demented, lunatic, deranged; of unsound mind, *Latin. non compos mentis*; unbalanced, touched, *Inf.* half-baked, unhinged; not all there, not quite right, not right upstairs, *Inf.* mental, *Inf.* cracked; out of one's head, out of one's mind, mad as a hatter, mad as a March hare; maniacal, wild, raving, hysterical, frenzied, delirious, berserk; *All Sl.* balmy, dippy, batty, cuckoo, buggy, screwy, wacky, goofy, loony.
2. dazed, moonstruck, possessed, infatuated; peculiar, strange, odd, eccentric, pixilated; irrational, illogical, unreasonable; unreasoning, unthinking, incogitant, thoughtless.
3. simple-minded, simple, bird-brained, weak-minded, weak-headed, feeble-minded; harebrained, giddy, mercurial, reckless; absent-minded, scatter-brained, confused, bemused; featherheaded, feather-brained, rattleheaded, rattlebrained, light-minded, light-headed; empty, void, vacant, vacuous, blank, unoccupied.
4. addlepated, addleheaded, addlebrained, muddled, muddleheaded; dull, inexpressive, insensate, expressionless; stupid, *Inf.* dumb, *Inf.* dopey, empty-headed; dull-witted, *Sl.* dimwitted, slow-witted, half-witted, fat-witted, witless, unwitty; mindless, brainless, fatuitous; dense, thick, thickheaded, wooden-headed; obtuse, *Inf.* cretinous, Boeotian, stolid, oafish, cloddish, lumpish, blunt; blockheaded, dunderheaded, noodleheaded, boneheaded, thickskulled, blockish, doltish.
5. silly, absurd, inane, pointless, fatuous, foolish; nonsensical, senseless, crackbrained, *Scot.* doiled, *Sl.* cockeyed, *Scot. and North Eng.* glaikit; poppycockish, *Sl.* cockamamie, amphigoric; ridiculous, laughable, risible, derisible, ludicrous, *Sl.* for the birds; asinine, anserine, idiotic, *Inf.* moronic, imbecilic; childish, puerile, immature.

dagger, *n.* dirk, poniard, misericord, stiletto, stylet, *Obs.* bodkin; knife, skean, sheath knife, bowie knife, jackknife, pocketknife, switchblade; short sword, blade, rapier, *Fencing.* foil; saber, yataghan, falchion, creese, anelace, kukri; machete, bolo, butcher knife, cleaver, barong.

daily, *adj.* **1.** diurnal, quotidian, circadian, day-to-day.
2. everyday, ordinary, common, commonplace; usual, regular, habitual, customary, wonted.

dainty, *adj.* **1.** exquisite, delicate, fine; beautiful, lovely, pretty, fair, goodlooking, handsome, comely, becoming, flattering; tasteful, refined, elegant, graceful, artistic, aesthetic; neat, petite, smart, trim, minion, fine, natty, spruce, *Chiefly Brit.* trig; attractive, appealing, *Inf.* fetching, *Inf.* eye-catching, enticing, charming, taking, engaging, winsome.
2. delicious, delectable, tasty, appetizing, savory, luscious, ambrosial, ambrosian, flavorful, epicurian; succulent, juicy, rich; nectarous, nectarean, sweet, tender; palatable, toothsome, *Scot.* gustable.
3. particular, discriminating, painstaking, meticulous, fastidious, scrupulous; fussy, *Inf.* pernickety, finical, finicky, squeamish, overnice, overrefined; exacting, difficult, hard to please.
—n. **4.** delicacy, sweetmeat, comfit, treat; morsel, tidbit, kickshaw, hors d'oeuvre; candy, bonbon, confection, sugarplum; ambrosia.

dale, *n.* valley, river valley *or* basin, *Scot.* strath; dell, vale, *Brit. Dial.* clough, *England.* combe; glen, dingle, *Brit. Dial.* gill; cleft, ravine, defile, gap.

dalliance, *n.* **1.** dawdling, dillydallying, shilly-shallying, procrastination; delay, *Archaic.* tarriance, loitering, lingering, *Sl.* hanging around; idling, loafing, *Inf.* lallygagging, *Sl.* goofing-off.
2. trifling, toying, fiddling, playing, tinkering, pottering, puttering, dabbling.
3. flirtation, coquetry, come-hither looks, *Sl.* goo-goo eyes; lovemaking, billing and cooing, *Inf.* spooning, *Inf.* necking, *Inf.* smooching, *Sl.* making out, *Sl.* messing *or* fooling around; cuddling, coddling, dandling, petting, *Sl.* canoodling.

dally, *v.* **1.** sport, play, *Sl.* mess *or* fool around; caress, cuddle, coddle, pet, *Sl.* canoodle; nuzzle, make love, bill and coo, *Inf.* spoon, *Inf.* neck, *Inf.* smooch, *Sl.* make out.

2. trifle, toy, flirt; potter, putter, smatter, tinker, fiddle, *Inf.* fool with.

3. dawdle, loiter, linger, dillydally, shilly-shally, take one's time, take one's own sweet time, *Inf.* lallygag; delay, tarry, kill time, waste time, while away the time *or* hours.

damage, *n.* **1.** injury, harm, loss, suffering, misfortune; hurt, wound, bruise, blow, accident; disaster, destruction, devastation, havoc, ruin; wrong, evil, mischief, grievance, outrage.

2. fault, blemish, scar, scratch; erosion, corrosion, dryrot, blight; dilapidation, disintegration, disrepair, wear and tear; defacement, defilement, vandalism, defoulment.

3. damages *Law.* cost, expenses, exactment, fine, penalty, mulct, amercement; compensation, satisfaction, indemnity, reparation.

—v. **4.** injure, harm, wrong, wound, deal a blow to, abuse; impair, incapacitate, maim, cripple; tamper with, break, wreck, *Sl.* do a job on; split, crack, rend, tear; mar, deface, vandalize; disfigure, mutilate; gnaw, erode, eat, rust, corrode, wear away; undermine, ravage, wreak havoc on, destroy.

5. spoil, despoil, defile, blemish, stain, taint, pollute, contaminate; pervert, corrupt, blight, debase.

dame, *n.* peeress, aristocrat, blueblood, baroness, noblewoman, *Fr. grande dame*; dowager, matron, matriarch.

damn, *v.* **1.** condemn, denounce, denunciate, objurgate, berate; castigate, fustigate, tongue-lash, reprimand, reprove, upbraid; censure, reprobate, criticize, remonstrate, animadvert on; vilify, gibbet, vituperate, run down, put down.

2. attack, flay, light into, *Inf.* lace into, *Inf.* pan, *Inf.* slam, shoot down, *Sl.* kill, *Sl.* blast, *Sl.* let [s.o.] have it right between the eyes; cavil, carp, find fault, *Inf.* nitpick, pick apart, pick to pieces, *Inf.* pick holes in, *Inf.* knock, *Sl.* cut up *or* to pieces.

3. proscribe, forbid, interdict, prohibit; ostracize, excommunicate, exile.

4. curse, *U.S. Inf.* cuss, anathematize, comminate, execrate, maledict, fulminate, blast; blaspheme, swear, use God's name in vain.

5. convict, declare guilty, prove guilty, find guilty; sentence, pass sentence on, condemn, adjudge, doom, sign the death warrant.

—interj. **6.** confound it, hang it, *All Euph.* darn, dang, gosh-darn, doggone, drat, blame.

—n. **7.** trifle, *Sl.* cent, *Sl.* red cent, *Sl.* two cents; *Inf.* hoot, tinker's damn; drop in the ocean, *Inf.* hill of beans.

8. give a damn *Informal.* care, be concerned, mind, *Sl.* give a hoot, take interest in, have taste for.

damnable, *adj.* **1.** abominable, execrable, horrible, horrid, hideous, atrocious, accursed; base, vile, odious, obnoxious, wicked, sinful, iniquitous, blackhearted; dark, evil, depraved, corrupt, villainous, sinister; diabolic, devilish, fiendish, satanic, demonic, demoniac, demoniacal, infernal, hellish.

2. nefarious, flagitious, heinous; revolting, repulsive, outrageous, repugnant, foul, rotten, offensive, nauseous, nauseating; pernicious, pestilential, noxious, deadly, fell; malign, menacing, baleful, invidious, injurious, maleficent, malevolent, malicious, rancorous, venomous; detestable, hateful, abhorrent, loathsome, infamous, despicable.

damnation, *n.* **1.** condemnation, denunciation, commination, objurgation; censure, criticism, castigation, reproval.

2. excommunication; bell, book, and candle; proscription, exile, ban.

3. curse, *U.S. Inf.* cuss, oath, *Archaic.* malison, anathema, execration, imprecation, malediction, fulmination.

damnatory, *adj.* See **damning.**

damned, *adj.* **1.** doomed, accursed, cursed, *Brit. Dial.* fey, curse-laden; condemned, anathematized, *Archaic.* maledict; bedeviled, bewitched, hoodooed, voodooed, hexed; star-crossed, ill-fated, foredoomed; unsanctified, unblest, unholy, unconsecrated, unhallowed; ruined, undone, blighted, ravaged, despoiled.

2. detestable, hateful, infamous, despicable; loathsome, abhorrent, revolting, repulsive, repugnant; foul, rotten, offensive, nauseous, nauseating.

—adv. **3.** extremely, very, *Inf.* awfully, *Inf.* terribly, excessively, greatly, exceedingly; superlatively, remarkably *U.S. Inf.* darned, downright, quite, *Sl.* hell of a, *Sl.* heck of a; absolutely, utterly, completely, entirely, wholly, fully, altogether.

damning, *adj.* **1.** incriminating, incriminatory, damnatory, condemnatory, condemning, dooming; inculpatory, implicating, implicatory, implicative; imputative, accusatory, accusative, recriminatory, recriminative, criminatory, criminative.

2. denunciatory, denunciative, defamatory, fulminatory, comminatory, objurgatory, objurgative.

damp, *adj.* **1.** moist, dewy, wettish, watery, aqueous; dank, steamy, clammy, muggy, humid; foggy, vaporous, misty, drizzly, dripping, rainy; swampy, marshy, boggy, fenny, miry; soggy, spongy, sodden.

2. unenthusiastic, lukewarm, indifferent, apathetic; dejected, depressed, despondent, spiritless, listless, lifeless.

—n. **3.** moisture, humidity, dampness. See **dampness.**

4. check, barrier, obstacle; discouragement, wet blanket, cold water. See **damper** (*defs.* **1, 2**).

—v. **5.** moisten, bedew, humidify. See **dampen** (*def.* **1**).

6. check, restrain, retard, dull, deaden. See **dampen** (*def.* **2**).

7. stifle, suffocate, smother, choke, extinguish, quench.

dampen, *v.* **1.** moisten, bedew, humidify, vaporize, damp; wet, sodden, soak, saturate.

2. check, restrain, deter; slacken, slow, retard, inhibit; lessen, diminish, abate, moderate, allay, temper; dull, deaden, depress, deject, dispirit, cast a pall over; discourage, dishearten, put a damper on, lay a wet blanket on.

damper, *n.* **1.** barrier, obstacle, stumbling block, impediment, hindrance, stay, stop, difficulty; snag, hitch, knot, check, discouragement; load, drag; pall, cold water.

2. wet blanket, *Sl.* party pooper, kill-joy, *Sl.* crapehanger.

dampness, *n.* moisture, dew, damp, wetness, wateriness, sogginess; humidity, steaminess, dankness, mugginess, clamminess; fog, mist, vapor.

damsel, *n.* maiden, maid, girl, schoolgirl, lass, lassie, *Irish Eng.* colleen; miss, mademoiselle, young lady, demoiselle, *Archaic.* damoiselle; young unmarried woman, virgin.

dance, *v.* **1.** step to the music, shuffle one's feet, *Sl.* shake your booties, *Sl.* hoof *or* hoof it, *Sl.* boogie, trip the light fantastic, *Sl.* cut a rug; move to the music, rock, reel, sway, swing; whirl, twirl, spin, turn around, pirouette; glide, slide.

2. wiggle, wriggle, *Sl.* wiggle one's hips; jig, bob up

and down, bounce, hop; skip, leap, jump about; prance, caper, gambol, romp, frolic.
—*n.* **3.** ballroom dance, round dance, one-step, two-step, polka, waltz, foxtrot; square dance, Virginia reel, quadrille, cotillion, hoedown; folk dance, jig, Highland fling; belly dance, danse du ventre; tap dance.
4. ball, fancy-dress ball, *Fr. bal travesti,* formal, *U.S. Inf.* prom, promenade; dancing party, *Inf.* shindig, social, *Inf.* hop.
5. the dance ballet, toe-dance; interpretive dance, interpretation, improvisational dance, improvisation, eurhythmics; modern dance, jazz, jazz-ballet.
6. choreography, dance notation, composition.

dancer, *n.* **1.** ballet dancer, toe-dancer, figurant, coryphee; danseur, premier danseur, premier danseur noble; danseuse, ballerina, prima ballerina, prima ballerina assoluta.
2. square dancer, *Inf.* heel-kicker, *Sl.* hoofer, *Sl.* boot-stomper; jigger, belly dancer; tap-dancer.

dander, *n. Informal.* anger, ire, temper, passion. See **anger** (*defs.* **1-4**).

dandle, *v.* **1.** dance on the knee, ride on the knee, toss up and down.
2. pet, pamper, coddle, cosset, mollycoddle, cocker; cuddle, nestle, nuzzle, hug, caress.

dandy, *n.* **1.** fop, coxcomb, *Sl.* peacock, Beau Brummell, fancy Dan, popinjay; fashion plate, exquisite, clotheshorse, prettyboy; jack-a-dandy, blade, gay blade, *Chiefly Brit.* blood, buck; dude, silkstocking, spark, *Sl.* swell, *Brit. Inf.* toff; man-about-town, beau, boulevardier, fashionable, the glass of fashion and the mold of form, gallant, ladykiller, ladies' man; zoot suiter, sharp dresser, macaroni.
2. gem, beauty, *Inf.* beaut, *Inf.* daisy, *Sl.* humdinger, *Sl.* killer, *Sl.* lollapalooza.
—*adj.* **3.** foppish, dandified, coxcombical, natty, spruce, *Inf.* all duded up, *Inf.* all gussied up; dapper, gay, rakish, jaunty, *Scot. and North Eng.* braw; *Inf.* swank, *Inf.* swanky, *Sl.* spiffy, *Sl.* snazzy.
4. excellent, fine, swell, first-rate, *Inf.* jim-dandy.

danger, *n.* **1.** risk, peril, chance, hazard, jeopardy; vulnerability, liability, susceptibility endangerment, imperilment; instability, unsafety, insecurity, unsoundness, precariousness.
2. menace, threat, minacity, dark clouds; imminence, gathering storm, clouds on the horizon, storm brewing.

dangerous, *adj.* **1.** perilous, hazardous, jeopardous, *Archaic.* parlous; risky, chancy, uncertain, *Sl.* hairy, *Chiefly Scot.* unchancy; vulnerable, exposed, unsheltered, assailable, defenseless; unsafe, unsound, insecure, shaky, rickety, precarious.
2. threatening, dire, menacing, ominous, alarming, minacious, fraught with danger; imminent, impending, looming.

dangle, *v.* **1.** hang, hang down, depend, droop, sag; drag, draggle, trail; swing, sway, oscillate, librate.
2. flaunt, flourish, wave, brandish, hold up.
3. follow, follow at heel, hang about *or* around, hang on the skirts *or* sleeve of, attach oneself to, pin oneself on, fasten oneself upon.

dank, *adj.* humid, steamy, clammy, muggy; moist, damp, dewy, wet, watery, chilly.

dapper, *adj.* **1.** (*all usu. in reference to dress*) neat, trim, smart, natty, spruce, sleek; gay, rakish, jaunty, *Scot. and North Eng.* braw; chic, elegant, well-dressed, well-turned-out, dressed to kill, dressed to the teeth, dressed to the nines, brave, out of a band box, *Inf.* all gussied-up, *Sl.* all duded-up, *Sl.* all dressed-up; *All Inf.* posh, dressy, swank, swanky, ritzy; *All Sl.* classy, snazzy, sharp, nifty, spiffy, nobby, swell.
2. spry, sprightly, agile, nimble, quick, pert, lively.

dapple, *adj.* **1.** spotted, marked, blotchy, mottled, particolored, variegated; pied, piebald, pinto.
—*v.* **2.** dot, spot, bespeckle, stipple, mottle, fleck, bedaub.

dare, *v.* **1.** brave, meet, face, brook, weather, sustain, undergo, endure, bear, *Inf.* take, *Inf.* stick, *Inf.* hang tough, *Inf.* hang in there; adventure, attempt, risk, hazard, stake, run the gauntlet; pluck up courage, take heart, stand one's ground; presume, make bold, present a bold front, show fight, fly in the face of.
2. challenge, defy, beard, brazen, outbrazen, look straight in the face *or* eye, throw down the gauntlet, show one's teeth; confront, affront, front, encounter, oppose, taunt, provoke; meet, meet defiantly, hurl defiance at, stand up to *or* against, *Inf.* face the music; meet face to face, meet eyeball to eyeball, meet head-on, square off against, take the bull by the horns, bell the cat, twist the lion's tail.
—*n.* **3.** challenge, taunt, confrontation, ultimatum, provocation; gauntlet, glove, gage; defiance, scorn, affront, stand, opposition.

daredevil, *n.* **1.** adventurer, man of courage, blood, brave, soldier-of-fortune, hotspur, *Fr. enfant perdu;* stuntman, stunt driver, Evel Knievel, *Inf.* hellcat; ace, *Inf.* flying fool; wildcat, madcap, harebrain, fool; glory hog, exhibitionist, show-off.
—*adj.* **2.** daring, rash, heedless, reckless, death-defying, fearless, intrepid, dauntless, unshrinking, unafraid; venturesome, adventurous, bold, audacious, brave, courageous, nervy, *Sl.* gutsy; headlong, breakneck, impulsive, impetuous, precipitate, imprudent, incautious, wild, desperate; madcap, foolhardy, harebrained.

daring, *n.* **1.** bravery, boldness, courage, valor, hardiness, resoluteness, stalwartness; audacity, derring-do, venturesomeness, adventurousness, fearlessness, intrepidity; enterprise, valor, heart, defiance; nerve, mettle, spirit, grit, pluck, *Inf.* spunk, *Inf.* guts; foolhardiness, rashness, temerity, recklessness, desperation; impetuosity, impetuousness.
—*adj.* **2.** bold, venturesome, adventuresome, adventurous; audacious, brave, courageous, valiant, valorous; fearless, dauntless, intrepid, undaunted, unshrinking, unflinching, plucky, *Inf.* spunky.
3. impudent, brazen, brassy; unabashed, forward, *Inf.* fresh, bumptious, *Inf.* nervy, *Inf.* cheeky; flagrant, arrant, barefaced.
4. foolhardy, rash, temerarious, reckless, heedless, careless, harebrained; impulsive, madcap, headlong, daredevil, devil-may-care, death-defying, wild.

dark, *adj.* **1.** lightless, aphotic, opaque, black, black as ink, inky, pitch-dark, pitchy, jetblack, jetty; unilluminated, unlit, shady, shadowy, *Literary.* darkling; murky, foggy, misty, tenebrous, *Archaic.* caliginous; dull, dim, faint, pale, feeble, weak, ill-lighted, poorly-lit.
2. swarthy, swart, dusky, ebony, sable, dark-complexioned, dark-skinned.
3. dismal, dreary, bleak, grim, funereal; somber solemn, grave, heavy; gloomy, melancholy, blue, depressed, dejected, cheerless, joyless, sad, sorrowful, disconsolate, doleful, dolorous, *Inf.* down in the dumps, *Inf.* down in the mouth.
4. sullen, dour, glum, morose, sulky, long-faced crestfallen, chapfallen, moody, brooding; frowning, scowling, glowering, black-browed.
5. evil, wicked, villainous, infamous, iniquitous, black-hearted, flagitious, base, vile; ominous, foreboding, threatening, menacing, sinister.

6. ignorant, unenlightened, unlearned, inerudite, uneducated, unschooled, untutored, untaught; uncultured, uncultivated, unrefined.
7. recondite, abstruse, profound, deep, esoteric; impenetrable, incomprehensible, unfathomable; difficult, hard, over one's head, *Inf.* tough; complex, complicated, intricate, *Inf.* tricky.
8. occult, hidden, secret, cryptic, perdu, concealed, veiled; obscure, vague, nebulous, ambiguous, *Rare.* imperspicuous; mysterious, arcane, inexplicable, enigmatic, puzzling, baffling, perplexing, confounding, bewildering.
9. reticent, taciturn, uncommunicative, reserved, retiring, quiet, close-mouthed, close; silent, mute, mum, obmutescent, secretive, evasive.
—n. 10. darkness, lightlessness, blackness, opacity; gloom, gloominess, murk, murkiness, obscurity, tenebrosity, semidarkness.
11. night, nighttime, nightfall, dead of night, witching hour.
12. **in the dark a.** benighted, in darkness, in ignorance; ignorant, uninformed. See also **dark** (*def.* 6). **b.** in secrecy, secret, closed, concealed, obscured, veiled, sealed.

darken, *v.* 1. blacken, black, opaque; shade, shadow, overshadow; eclipse, occult, black out, blot out; smudge, smirch, blotch, soot, begrime.
2. cloud, becloud, obscure, obfuscate, obumbrate.
3. dull, deaden, mat, tone down, take the color out of.
4. dim, grow dim, grow dark, dusk.
5. gloom, begloom, depress, deject, dishearten, dispirit, discourage, oppress, cast down, cast a pall *or* gloom over, take the heart out of [s.o.] *Inf.* get [s.o.] down, *Sl.* bum [s.o.] out.
6. blind, strike blind, put [s.o.'s] eyes out.
7. (*all usu. from anger*) change *or* turn color, look black, turn blue in the face.

darling, *n.* 1. beloved, love, truelove, ladylove; dear one, sweetheart, sweet, honey, precious, jewel; pet, apple of one's eye; favorite, minion, toast.
—adj. 2. loved, beloved, dear, precious, treasured, cherished, valued, prized; favorite, favored, pet.
3. *Informal.* lovely, charming, engaging, enchanting, captivating, alluring, bewitching; lovable, adorable, cute, sweet, winsome.

dart, *n.* 1. arrow, quarrel, *Archery.* flight, barb, barbule, sting.
2. dash, rush, drive, scramble, scurry.
—v. 3. start, spring, leap, bolt, shoot; dash, whisk, whiz, tear, rush, fly, flit; bound, run, sprint, race, speed, hie, hasten, hurry, post; scoot, scud, scuttle, *Inf.* skedaddle.
4. thrust, hurl, jaculate, heave, let fly, fling, sling; throw, pitch, toss, cast; project, propel, push, launch.

dash, *v.* 1. smash, shatter, crash, *Brit. Dial.* pash; strike, break, split, cleave, rive, rend; shiver, fragment, splinter, crack, split, snap; crush, destroy; beat, batter, slam, ram, hit, smite.
2. throw, hurl, catapult; fling, cast, sling, shy, pitch; propel, shoot, drive, thrust; heave, chuck.
3. splash, besplash, slosh, swash, plash, dabble; spatter, bespatter, splotch; sprinkle, besprinkle, dot, speckle, spangle; daub.
4. mix, admix, blend, commingle; adulterate, debase, pollute, contaminate, taint, alloy; dilute, weaken, thin, *Sl.* cut; strengthen, lace, *Inf.* spike.
5. ruin, blight, spoil; frustrate, thwart, check, balk, foil, bring to naught; defeat, overthrow.
6. depress, dispirit, deject, cast down, sadden, prostrate; dishearten, discourage, dismay, daunt, unman, undo; disappoint, dampen, throw a damper on.
7. confound, baffle, confuse, disconcert, discomfit; abash, humiliate, mortify, embarrass, chagrin.
8. rush, dart, bolt, bound, spring; run, sprint, fly, hasten, speed, take off; scud, *Inf.* scoot, *Inf.* skedaddle.
—n. 9. (*all usu. of water*) splashing, crashing, smashing, clashing, colliding; breaking against, beating, striking, hitting, battering.
10. bit, little, pinch, grain, *Inf.* smidgen, *U.S. Inf.* tad; shade, touch, tinge, tincture; trace, suggestion, suspicion, soupçon, hint, smack, flavor, taste; sprinkle, sprinkling.
11. rush, run, *Track.* race; bolt, flight, stampede, escape; advance, sally, onset.
12. élan, vigor, style, flair, flourish, panache, *Inf.* pizzazz, *Sl.* oomph; bounce, zing, zest, verve; spirit, life, buoyancy, briskness, *Inf.* snap; enthusiasm, eagerness, ardor, fervor; abandon, exuberance, vitality, exuberance, vitality, vivacity, *It. brio.*
13. mettle, pluck, courage; gallantry, boldness, daring, intrepidity, fearlessness.

dashing, *adj.* 1. impetuous, spirited, lively, buckish; energetic, active, *Inf.* peppy, *Inf.* snappy; dynamic, vigorous, forceful, go-go, swinging; animated, exuberant, spritely, airy, brisk, breezy.
2. high-spirited, mettlesome, game, plucky; gallant, brave, valiant, valorous, courageous; hearty, stouthearted, stout, stalwart; daring, fearless, dauntless, venturous, venturesome, adventurous, adventuresome.
3. showy, ostentatious, pretentious, swashbuckling; florid, flamboyant, dazzling, brilliant, vivid, bright, bright-colored, colorful, gay.
4. dapper, jaunty, neat, trim, crisp, smart, *Inf.* sharp; stylish, chic, modish, voguish, fashionable, elegant.

dastard, *n.* 1. coward, craven, poltroon, recreant; cur, *Inf.* meany, base fellow, worm, *Archaic.* caitiff, *Archaic.* niddering; sneak, shirker, yellow belly, mouse, baby; weakling, milksop, Milquetoast, mollycoddle.
—adj. 2. cowardly, craven, mean, dastardly. See **dastardly**.

dastardly, *adj.* 1. cowardly, craven, poltroon, recreant, dastard; pusillanimous, timorous, timid, fearful, afraid, frightened, afraid of one's shadow, cowering, faint-hearted, chicken-livered, shy, skittish, *Inf.* yellow.
2. base, mean, mean-spirited, low, vile, abject, despicable, *Archaic.* niddering, *Archaic.* caitiff; sneaking, sneaky, deceitful, underhanded, insidious.

data, *n.* 1. facts, figures, statistics, input, materials; information, *Inf.* info, *Sl.* dope, *Sl.* poop.
2. memoranda, documents, abstracts, notes, papers, dossier.
3. evidence, grounds; assumptions, premises.

date, *n.* 1. day, point in time; period, time, season, cycle; month, lunation, quarter, semester; year, lustrum, decade, generation, century; age, epoch, era, eon.
2. interval, space, span, length of time, duration.
3. appointment, engagement, assignation, meeting, rendezvous, tryst.
4. escort, squire, beau, boyfriend, man, *Inf.* old man, swain, lover; girlfriend, girl, *Inf.* steady; woman, lady, *Sl.* baby, *Inf.* old lady; *Inf.* pick-up.
5. **up-to-date** current, up-to-the-minute, modern, contemporary.
6. **to date** up to the present, up to now, as of now;

yet, so far, up to this point.
—*v.* 7. (*all of a particular period*) belong to, originate in, come from.
8. show one's age; become obsolete, obsolesce, pass out of use *or* style, be dated.
9. make a date with, make an appointment with; escort, squire, take out; go out with, go with, go steady with; go around together, keep company with, *Sl.* hang out together.
10. fix the period of, determine the date of, assign a date to.

dated, *adj.* out-of-date, back-number, passé, outmoded, out-of-style, old-fashioned, *Inf.* old hat; obsolete, obsolescent, no longer used, gone by the boards, forgotten.

daub, *v.* 1. smear, besmear, bedaub, cover, coat, plaster, *Inf.* slapdash, *Inf.* slap on.
2. begrime, soil, dirty, sully, bedraggle, draggle, muddy; smudge, smirch, spatter, splatter, slop, spot, stain; defile, deface, befoul.
—*n.* 3. smear, smudge, smirch, spot, patch, *Inf.* mess, *Inf.* splot.

daunt, *v.* 1. intimidate, unnerve, dismay, petrify, frighten, affright, scare, *Archaic.* amate; overawe, terrorize, threaten, browbeat, bully, bulldoze, cow; disconcert, alarm, appall, take aback, *Inf.* take the fight out of, shake up.
2. dishearten, discourage, dispirit, unman, tame; deter, set back, put off, check, thwart, shake, take the heart out of, *Inf.* take the starch out of; bring low, deject.

daunted, *adj.* 1. dismayed, intimidated, cowed, unnerved, unmanned, disheartened, overawed, subdued, overcome, demoralized, *Inf.* broken, *Inf.* psyched out; fearful, afraid, frightened, terrified, timid, timorous, cowardly, appalled, alarmed.
2. deterred, put off, set back, *Inf.* thrown for a loss, checked, frustrated, blocked; reluctant, hesitant, without the heart for [s.t.].
3. abashed, disconcerted, discomfited, disappointed, discouraged, disillusioned, deflated, dispirited, spiritless, dejected, downcast, depressed, sad.

dauntless, *adj.* intrepid, daring, venturesome, bold, audacious, *Rare.* impavid; fearless, undaunted, Spartan, brave, valorous, courageous, unafraid, unaffrighted; indomitable, unconquerable, stout-hearted, lion-hearted, valiant, heroic; resolute, doughty, unflinching, unshrinking, unappalled; stalwart, plucky, game, hardy, high-spirited, gritty, *Inf.* spunky, mettlesome; manly, manful, chivalrous, gallant; confident, self-reliant.

dawdle, *v.* 1. waste time, take one's time *or* one's own sweet time, kill time, fritter time away; idle, trifle, finick, potter, fiddle, piddle, *Inf.* fiddle-faddle; dally, dilly-dally, procrastinate, *Inf.* diddle, shilly-shally, vacillate.
2. loiter, poke, loll, hang around, mill around; slouch, loaf, daydream, *Inf.* lallygag; lounge, vegetate; lag behind, move at a snail's pace, work bankers' hours.
3. shirk, *Sl.* goof off, lie down on the job; fool around, mess around, *Sl.* screw around, do nothing.

dawdler, *n.* laggard, lingerer, loiterer; lie-abed, slugabed, layabout, dreamer, lotus-eater, drone, lounger; snail, slowpoke, tortoise, afternoon farmer, lazybones; loafer, fainéant, do-nothing, sluggard, sloth, idler, trifler; shirker, *Sl.* goof-off, goldbrick, slouch; lubber, clod.

dawn, *n.* 1. daybreak, sunrise, sunup, aurora, cockcrow, daylight, daypeep; break of day, peep of day, crack of dawn, dawning, early light, *Archaic.* dayspring; morning, morn, prime, morningtide.
2. beginning, birth, start, inception, commencement; advent, appearance, arrival; unfolding, onset, nascency, rise, emergence, outset, awakening; inauguration, initiation, foundation, incipience.
—*v.* 3. grow light, lighten, break, gleam, brighten.
4. originate, begin, commence, start, enter upon, arise, give birth; initiate, inaugurate, set in, come into existence; appear, rise, open.
5. occur to, appear, come to mind, enter one's mind, pass through one's mind, flash across one's mind, flash upon the inner eye; strike, hit, break, come to one's knowledge.

day, *n.* 1. daylight, daytime, *Poetic.* daytide; light of day, broad daylight, full sun; sunlight light, sunshine, dayshine, sun.
2. 24 hours, mean solar day, solar day, *Archaic.* sun.
3. feast day, holyday, saint's day; anniversary, birthday, natal day, jubilee; fete, holiday, red-letter day.
4. period, time, age, epoch, era, generation, cycle.
5. heyday, prime, ascendancy, height, zenith; best, greatest strength *or* influence, height of one's power, full flowering.
6. date, point of time, point in time, time, set time, particular day, appointed time.
7. **call it a day** quit, break off, stop work, finish up, *Sl.* knock off, *Sl.* call it quits, close up shop.

daybreak, *n.* dawn, sunrise, cockcrow; morning, morn. See **dawn** (*def.* 1).

daydream, *n.* 1. reverie, castle in the air, castle in Spain, dream, musing; fancy, flight of fancy, whim, whimsy, vagary, crotchet, notion, imagination; conceit, thought, idea, conception, concept.
2. fantasy, phantasm, fantasm, phantasma, *Lit.* fantasia, *Inf.* pipe dream; figment, figment of the imagination, fiction, invention, fabrication; vision, visualization, envisagement, hallucination, mirage.
—*v.* 3. stargaze, gaze out the window, dream; imagine, fantasize, phantasize, *Rare.* phantasy; hallucinate.

daylight, *n.* 1. light, sunshine, sunbeam, sun, luminosity; daylight hours, daytime, day.
2. openness, publicity, the light of day; full knowledge, understanding, comprehension; intelligibility, clearness, clarity, lucidity, perspicuity.
3. dawn, Aurora, crack of dawn; daybreak, morning. See **daybreak.**
4. space, opening, gap; passage, passageway.

daze, *v.* 1. amaze, astonish, astound, boggle, stagger, startle, surprise, overpower, *Inf.* bowl over, *Inf.* floor, *Sl.* blow one away, *Sl.* blow one's mind; stun, stupefy, petrify, paralyze, benumb, dumfound, strike dumb; dazzle, blind.
2. confuse, bewilder, perplex, confound, baffle; befuddle, muddle, addle, mystify, puzzle, nonplus.
—*n.* 3. stupor, trance, trancelike state; muddle, fluster, confusion.

dazzle, *v.* 1. blind, bedazzle; stun, daze, stagger, overpower.
2. amaze, astonish, astound, *Inf.* bowl over, *Inf.* floor, *Sl.* blow one away, *Sl.* blow one's mind; stupefy, dumfound, strike dumb, overawe; confuse, bewilder, muddle, befuddle, addle, mix up; confound, perplex, baffle, puzzle, mystify, nonplus; fluster, flurry, rattle, ruffle, discompose, disconcert, discomfit, *Inf.* discombobulate.
—*n.* 3. splendor, brilliance, magnificence, wonder, wondrousness; sparkle, glitter, flash, *Inf.* razzle-dazzle, *Inf.* razmatazz.

dazzling, *adj.* bright, brilliant, vivid, splendent,

splendiferous, resplendent; stunning, overpowering, blinding, bedazzling, fulgent, foudroyant; radiant, glowing, gleaming, beaming, sparkling; (*all usu. of a woman*) beautiful, gorgeous, ravishing.

dead, *adj.* **1.** deceased, extinct, defunct, perished; departed, gone, no more, still, asleep, *Sl.* cold, *Brit. Sl.* potted head, lifeless, inanimate, exanimate, inorganic.
2. numb, numbed, benumbed; unconscious, comatose, impassive.
3. insensible, insensitive, insentient, insensate; unemotional, emotionless, unfeeling, dispassionate; apathetic, indifferent, lukewarm, unconcerned, unresponsive, unsympathetic; uninterested, unimpressible, disinterested, incurious, uninquisitive; cool, cold, frigid, frosty; callous, hardened, inured.
4. dull, sluggish, phlegmatic, lethargic, torpid, heavy; languid, listless, spiritless; lazy, oscitant, drowsy.
5. extinguished, quenched, smothered, suffocated, stifled, choked; ended, terminated, dissolved, checked; quashed, quelled, suppressed, squelched, crushed; finished, finished off, *Sl.* eighty-sixed.
6. obsolete, obsolescent, outmoded, passé; extinct, no longer in existence; expired, lapsed, passed; disused, discontinued, fallen into desuetude.
7. tired, tired out, exhausted, fatigued, worn out, played out, spent, *Sl.* pooped, *Sl.* dished.
8. barren, infertile, unproductive, unprofitable, unyielding, unfructuous, unfruitful, fruitless; depleted, used up, worn out, impoverished; poor, bare, dry, arid, bald, desolate, naked; stale, washed-up, useless.
9. stagnant, standing, motionless, still, stationary, static; inactive, inert; quiet, quiescent, dormant, calm; not working, out of commission.
10. tedious, tiresome, boring, boresome, wearisome, uninteresting, dry, dry-as-dust; tasteless, bland, insipid, jejune, flat, vapid, *Sl.* nothing, *Sl.* blah; uneventful, humdrum, monotonous, ordinary, run-of-the-mill, commonplace, prosaic, matter-of-fact.
11. complete, absolute, total, entire; outright, downright, out-and-out, straight-out, all-out, across-the-board; sheer, utter, thorough, unmitigated; unqualified, categorical, unconditional, unconditioned, unreserved, unrestricted.
12. abrupt, sudden, quick, hasty, instantaneous, rapid, swift, hurried; unexpected, unforeseen, unanticipated, unannounced.
13. accurate, exact, precise; correct, unerring, unfailing, *Inf.* on the mark, on target; direct, straight; sure, certain, crack.
14. unresounding, without resonance; without resilience, without elasticity; heavy, without bounce.
—n. **15.** silence, soundlessness, noiselessness; quiet, stillness, hush, peace; dark, darkness, blackness; depth, midst.
—adv. **16.** completely, absolutely, totally, entirely; utterly, thoroughly, unqualifiedly, categorically, unconditionally; directly, exactly, diametrically.

deaden, *v.* **1.** press, dampen, blunt, obtund, hebetate; weaken, subdue, moderate; soothe, assuage, mitigate, abate, lessen, diminish, reduce, buff; repress, suppress, restrain, retard; choke, stifle, check, damp; muffle, mute, quiet, smother.
2. devitalize, enfeeble, impair, incapacitate; desensitize, paralyze, numb, benumb, anesthetize, drug, dope.

deadlock, *n.* **1.** stalemate, impasse, standstill; quietus, halt, stop, stoppage, full stop, dead stop, cessation; stand, stay, check, checkmate, mate; block, blockage; stand-off, tie, draw.
2. dilemma, perplexity, nonplus; predicament, hole, *Inf.* fix, corner; dead end, blind alley, cul-de-sac.
—v. **3.** stop, halt, cease, bring to a standstill; stand, stay, curb, check, checkmate; forestall, preclude, obviate, intercept; block, blockade, bar, debar; thwart, trump.
4. prostrate, paralyze, incapacitate, disable, render helpless, make ineffective; undermine, spike, *Inf.* put the kibosh on.
5. hinder, impede, obstruct, clog, trammel; cramp, bind, shackle, inhibit; corner, run *or* drive into a corner, drive *or* push to the wall, *Inf.* tree.
6. confuse, confound, perplex, bewilder, stump, embarrass, nonplus, *Inf.* flummox.

deadly, *adj.* **1.** fatal, mortal, lethal, mortiferous, deathful, *Archaic.* lethiferous; pernicious, dangerous, hazardous, deleterious, detrimental; harmful, injurious, nocuous, hurtful, nocent, baleful, noisome; destructive, ruinous, calamitous, disastrous; pestilential, pestiferous, noxious, malicious, malign, malignant, menacing; venomous, virulent, toxic, morbific; fell, baneful, mephitic, viperous, poisonous, *Archaic.* venenose; infective, infectious, pestilent, contaminative, contagious, leprous, septic.
2. murderous, homicidal, slaughterous, bloodthirsty, sanguinary, internecine; brutal, violent, vicious, inhuman, barbarous, barbaric, hellish; ferocious, ruthless, savage, truculent, fierce, feral, ferine; terrible, harsh, severe, grim, dreadful, dire; unrelenting, relentless, remorseless, implacable, inexorable, unappeasable; pitiless, merciless, heartless, cruel, cold-blooded, cold-hearted, hard-hearted, marble-hearted, stony-hearted.
3. deathlike, deathly, pallid, wan, pale; livid, sallow, ashen, ghostly, white; cadaverous, corpse-like, skeletal, emaciated; gaunt, haggard, hollow-eyed.
4. excessive, inordinate, great, immoderate; overmuch, needless, undue, unnecessary, superabundant.
5. true, unerring, accurate, precise, correct, unfailing, on target, on the mark, *Inf.* in the bull's-eye.
6. dull, boring, tiresome, humdrum, tedious, uninteresting; fatiguing, wearisome, monotonous, *Fr. ennuyant;* lackluster, dry, jejune; heavy, ponderous, irksome.

deaf, *adj.* **1.** hard of hearing, unhearing, stone-deaf.
2. unmoved, unwavering, unswerving; insensitive, unconcerned, indifferent, inattentive, refusing to listen; unmindful, regardless, heedless.

deafen, *v.* make deaf; split the ears, stun with noise, din; drown out, muffle, stifle, hush, quiet.

deal, *v.* **1.** distribute, dispense, mete out, allocate, allot, bestow, assign; apportion, share, divide, parcel out, dole out.
2. (*usu. fol. by* with *or* in) occupy oneself in, engaged in, practice, have to do with, have concern, concern; attend to, take care of, see to, reckon with.
3. trade, traffic, do business, buy and sell, exchange; bargain, barter, dicker, haggle, higgle, chaffer, palter; negotiate, arrange, come to terms.
4. deliver, administer, give, direct, cast, launch.
—n. **5.** uncertain amount, quantity, lot, extent, degree.
6. *Informal.* **a.** business transaction, dealings, arrangement, negotiation; pact, contract, compact, agreement, concordat. **b.** bargain, price, *Inf.* buy.

dealer, *n.* wholesaler, jobber, merchant, salesman, trader, tradesman, *Chiefly Brit.* monger; retailer, shopkeeper; vendor, chandler, sutler, peddler, *Brit.* chapman, hawker, huckster, *Chiefly Brit.* costermonger; trafficker, middleman, (*in stolen goods*) *Sl.* fence.

dealings, *n.* **1.** business, commerce, buying and sell-

ing, exchange, trade, traffic, jobbing, agiotage; barter, bargain, negotiation.
2. management, relations, doings, action; proceeding, policy, practice, behavior, treatment.

dean, *n.* **1.** (*in schools and colleges*) official, officer, dignitary; faculty head, department *or* section head, registrar, secretary, provost, regent, president; counselor, advisor, personnel placement director, student services officer.
2. (*within a class or category*) senior member, senior, elder, elder statesman, ranking member, chief, leader, grand old man, principal, patriarch; first, foremost, most respected, most venerable, paramount, preeminent.
3. (*of religious bodies*) chapter head, capitular, *Rom. Cath. Ch.* vicar forane; pastor, rector, vicar; clergyman, ecclesiastic, cleric, priest, minister.

dear, *adj.* **1.** loved, beloved, darling, precious, treasured, cherished, valued, prized; favorite, favored, pet; respected, admired, highly esteemed, honored, venerated.
2. expensive, high-priced, costly, valuable; rich, sumptuous; excessive, overmuch, high, *Inf.* steep.
—n. **3.** beloved, love, truelove, ladylove, darling; sweetheart, sweet, honey, precious, jewel; pet, apple of one's eye, favorite.

dearth, *n.* **1.** scarcity, scarceness, lack, want; deficiency, shortness, shortage, insufficiency, stint; scantiness, paucity, exiguity, meagerness, rareness; sparseness, seldomness, fewness, poorness, barrenness; depletion, exhaustion, emptiness, vacuity.
2. famine, starvation, drought, famishment, inanition; destitution, poverty, indigence, need; privation, deprivation, half rations, *Chiefly Brit.* short-commons; fast, diet, xerophagy, Lent, *Obs.* Quadragesima.

death, *n.* **1.** decease, demise, passing, expiration, departure, release, exit; end, cessation, dissolution, termination; brain death, *Biol.* biolysis, necrosis; rest, eternal rest, quietus, *Sl.* curtains, *Euph.* the great adventure.
2. angel of death, Grim Reaper, Azrael, (*in ancient Greece*) Thanatos, (*in ancient Rome*) Mors; skeleton, skull and crossbones, death's head, the number 14, (*Hebrew letter*) nun, the black horse.
3. extinction, extermination, eradication, extirpation, liquidation, obliteration; destruction, annihilation, ruin, ruination.
4. bloodshed, bloodletting, carnage, slaughter, butchery; murder, massacre, slaying, killing.

deathless, *adj.* **1.** immortal, undying, imperishable, never-dying.
2. unceasing, perpetual, eternal, everlasting; lasting, *Latin. aeres perennius,* constant; never-ending, endless, interminable, unending, unfading, without end.
3. timeless, memorable, historic, unforgettable; venerable, eminent, distinguished, illustrious.

deathlike, *adj.* cadaverous, skeletal, corpse-like, emaciated; pale, wan, ghostly, ghastly, pallid; livid, bloodless, anemic, white, etiolated; grim, gaunt, deathly, haggard, hollow-eyed; wasted, withered, shriveled.

debacle, *n.* **1.** downfall, collapse, breakdown, disintegration; breakup, dispersion, disruption, dissolution; overthrow, ruin, demolishment, devastation, wreck, havoc, disaster; tumult, turmoil, overturning, *Fr. bouleversement,* upsetting.
2. ice breakup, torrent, cataclysm, cataract; inundation, deluge, flood, rush of water.

debar, *v.* **1.** shut out, exclude, preclude, bar, keep out; except, leave out, omit, delete, eliminate, remove, take *or* cut out; expel, eject, reject, *Inf.* kick out, oust; get rid of, discard, throw out.
2. delay, retard, slow up *or* down, impede; restrain, inhibit, repress, constrain, keep back; hinder, hamper, obstruct, get in the way; thwart, forestall, frustrate, foil, balk; block, check, abort, halt, stop, arrest; prevent, prohibit, proscribe, disallow, veto, forbid, taboo.

debase, *v.* **1.** devaluate, depreciate, deteriorate, vitiate, depress, lower, impair, level, reduce, degrade, demote, depose; demean, deprecate, disparage, belittle; shame, disgrace, dishonor, discredit; humble, humiliate, mortify.
2. adulterate, pollute, contaminate, spoil, mar, taint, dilute, weaken, mix, admix, thin, alloy, *Inf.* doctor; deprave, pervert, corrupt, desecrate, debauch, abase; defile, foul, befoul, soil, sully, smirch, besmirch, blacken, smear, smudge, stain, spatter, bespatter.

debased, *adj.* **1.** devalued, devaluated, depreciated, reduced, vitiated, lowered, impaired, deteriorated; adulterated, impure, mixed, polluted, fouled, befouled, tainted, soiled, contaminated, stained, tarnished, besmirched, desecrated, sullied, *Inf.* doctored.
2. depraved, debauched, degenerate, degraded, sordid, corrupt, abandoned; base, vile, low, lapsed, fallen, vicious, despicable, contemptible; shameful, disgraceful, dishonorable, disreputable; abject, groveling, ignoble; inferior, worthless.

debasement, *n.* **1.** devaluation, depreciation, deterioration, descent, fall, reduction, lapse, impairment; adulteration, pollution, contamination.
2. degradation, degeneration, abasement, depravation, debauchery, baseness, decadence, corruption, perversion, defilement, desecration; disgrace, shame, dishonor, humiliation, ignominy, mortification.

debatable, *adj.* **1.** controversial, polemical, in dispute; subject to discussion, moot, open to question, in question, questionable, problematic, open to doubt, doubtful, dubitable, dubious; uncertain, unsure, unsettled, undecided, borderline.
2. discussable, disputable, contestable, arguable, controvertible.

debate, *n.* **1.** discussion, dispute, disputation, argumentation, polemic, logomachy, war of words; verbal controversy, altercation, wrangle, heated argument, disagreement, dissension, variance, difference of opinion.
2. deliberation, consideration, careful thought, meditation, reflection, contemplation, cogitation.
3. contest, contention, competition, struggle, strife.
—v. **4.** discuss, moot, bandy words, sift, *Inf.* kick around, *Sl.* hash over; argue, argue the pros and cons, dispute, contend, contest, question; disagree, dissent, differ, controvert, oppose; spar, cross swords, lock horns, altercate, wrangle.
5. deliberate, consider, think over *or* on, meditate, reflect on, contemplate, cogitate, ponder, examine a question; think [s.t.] through, reason [s.t.] out, ratiocinate, logicize, explain.

debauch, *v.* **1.** seduce, pervert, subvert, demoralize, lead astray, lead away; (*all toward immorality*) tempt, allure, entice, inveigle; (*all into immorality*) trap, entrap, snare, ensnare, pull under.
2. corrupt, vitiate, debase, abase; pollute, contaminate, infect, poison, taint, befoul, soil, sully; defile, desecrate, deprave, deflower, profane; violate, abuse, ravish, rape, ruin.
3. dissipate, wanton, sow wild oats, live hard, live fast, have one's fling; overindulge, overdo, burn the candle at both ends, not know when to stop, not know when one has had enough; carouse, revel, wassail,

roister, bouse, make merry, cut *or* let loose, *Inf.* party, *Inf.* live it up, *Inf.* step out, *Sl.* make whoopee; go on a spree, make the rounds, *Sl.* tie one on, *Sl.* go on a binge *or* bender *or* toot, *Sl.* paint the town red, *Sl.* bar-hop, *Brit. Sl.* pub crawl.

—*n.* **4.** intemperance, debauchery. See **debauchery**.

5. orgy, saturnalia; spree, fling, bout, carouse, revel, wassail; drinking bout, drunk, brannigan, bouse, guzzle, compotation, bacchanal; *Inf.* binge, *Inf.* booze, *Sl.* bender, *Sl.* hellbender, *Sl.* bust, *Sl.* toot, *Sl.* tear, *Sl.* jag, *U.S. Sl.* bum, *Sl.* bar-hop, *Brit. Sl.* pub-crawl.

debauchee, *n.* rake, rakehell, roué, profligate, wanton, libertine, playboy, *Inf.* rip, *Sl.* swinger, Don Juan, Casssanova, Lothario; sensualist, sybarite, pleasure-seeker; carouser, wassailer, rounder, wastrel, ne'er-do-well.

debauchery, *n.* profligacy, dissoluteness, licentiousness, rakishness, libertinism, dissipation; whoring, wenching, womanizing, *Sl.* leching; intemperance, self-gratification, self-indulgence, overindulgence, unrestraint, incontinence, immoderation; revelry, carousal, *It. dolce vita,* wild *or* riotous *or* free living, *Inf.* high living, killing pace.

debilitate, *v.* weaken, enfeeble, make feeble, enervate, deprive of strength; exhaust, fatigue, tire, tire out, *Sl.* poop *or* poop out, wear out *or* down; unbrace, unman, emasculate, undo, incapacitate, cripple, impair; deplete, diminish, reduce, undermine, vitiate.

debility, *n.* **1.** weakness, feebleness, enfeeblement, lack of strength, *Pathol.* asthenia, *Pathol.* adynamia; infirmity, exhaustion, prostration, enervation; decrepitude, caducity, senility; emasculation, castration, unmanning, impotence, impuissance.

2. languor, lassitude, listlessness; frailty, faintness, *Inf.* wooziness; weariness, fatigue.

3. atrophy, *Pathol.* atony, flaccidity, flabbiness, limpness; degeneration, decline.

debonair, *adj.* **1.** gay, jaunty, merry, vivacious; light-hearted, smiling, cheery, sunny, sprightly, lightsome, gay as a lark, spry, lithe; breezy, buoyant, free and easy, sportive, jocund.

2. gracious, courteous, mannerly, polite, gentlemanly, affable, obliging; urbane, suave, refined, well-bred, genteel, elegant, graceful, dapper; gallant, chivalrous, civil.

debris, *n.* **1.** ruins, wreckage, remains, fragments, detritus, shards, brash, *Naut.* mush; flotsam and jetsam, odds and ends, this and that.

2. junk, rubble, trash, rubbish, litter, sweepings, scourings, leftovers; dross, dregs, refuse, waste, waste matter; mess, slush, garbage, *Sl.* dreck, *Sl.* crap.

debt, *n.* **1.** obligation, indebtedness, incumbrance, accountability, responsibility; liability, claim, account, score, due; deficit, arrears, debit.

2. in debt owing, accountable, liable, responsible, answerable for; beholden, bound, bounden; in arrears, in the red, *Sl.* in hock; in difficulties, in dire straits, straitened, encumbered, *Inf.* owing everyone in town, *Inf.* over one's head, *Inf.* in up to one's ears.

debut, *n.* **1.** initial performance, premiere, first appearance, first time up *or* on *or* out; introduction, coming out.

2. launching, entrance, undertaking, beginning, first step, first attempt, trial, *Inf.* first shot, *Inf.* first time anywhere *or* on stage, *Inf.* first time around.

—*v.* **3.** launch, undertake, plunge into, enter upon, venture, go into, begin, take up, set about, *Sl.* tackle; enter society, come out.

decadence, *n.* **1.** decay, corruption, perversion, debasement, retrogression, recession; decline, wane, ebb, declension, fall; deterioration, degeneration.

2. dissolution, dissipation, moral decay, wild living, self-indulgence, *It. dolce vita.*

decadent, *adj.* **1.** decaying, declining, on the wane, falling off, falling into ruin, withering; deteriorating, degenerating, spoiling, rotten, tainted.

2. dissolute, dissipated, wasted, worn out; sensuous, hedonistic, epicurean, carnal; perverted, depraved.

decamp, *v.* **1.** flee, mosey, run off, make off, take off, make tracks, take flight; fly, bolt, run, show a clean *or* light pair of heels; escape, abscond, *Jocular.* absquatulate, take the money and run; take to one's heels, cut and run, *Inf.* hightail it, *Inf.* hotfoot it, *Inf.* skedaddle, *Inf.* scram, *Sl.* split, *Sl.* cut out, *Sl.* vamoose, *Sl.* light out.

2. skip, run out, *Inf.* go AWOL, desert; take French leave, *Brit. Sl.* do a moonlight flit; slip away, sneak off, steal away, slink away, *Brit. Sl.* mizzle.

3. depart, leave, go away, go off, be off, *Inf.* shove off, *Inf.* make oneself scarce, *Brit. Sl.* bugger off.

4. break camp, strike tents; march off *or* away, move off *or* on; vacate, evacuate.

decapitate, *v.* behead, guillotine, decollate, ax, bring to the block; lop *or* chop off, top, truncate, put under the ax.

decapitation, *n.* beheading, decollation, putting under the executioner's ax; lopping *or* chopping off, truncating, topping.

decay, *v.* **1.** decline, sicken, fail, waste away, atrophy, ebb, wane, dwindle; wither, degenerate, deteriorate, molder, crumble, fall to pieces, disintegrate, wear away, corrode.

2. spoil, rot, go bad, putrefy, decompose.

—*n.* **3.** decline, failing, weakening, labefaction, collapse, downfall, ruin, ruination; decadence, retrogradation, corruption; degeneration, deterioration, disintegration, dissolution; impairment, disrepair, dilapidation, decrepitude; corrosion, erosion, crumbling, *Plant Pathol.* dry rot; falling off, wasting away, weakness, atrophy, frailty, caducity, senescence.

4. spoilage, rot, rottenness, rotting, cariosity, putrefaction, putrescence, putridity, decomposition.

decease, *n.* **1.** death, demise, passing, expiration. See **death** (*def.* **1**).

—*v.* **2.** die, perish, expire. See **die** (*def.* **1**).

deceased, *adj.* dead, defunct, late. See **dead** (*def.* **1**).

deceit, *n.* **1.** deception, dissimulation, hypocrisy, duplicity, dark and crooked ways, evil ways; fraud, cheating, chicane, trickery; jugglery, trumpery, dupery, hocus-pocus, fraudulence, shenanigan; craft, wiles, guile, finesse, *Inf.* razzle-dazzle, cozenage, double-dealing; cunning, slyness, wiliness, duping, circumvention, *Sl.* jive, *Sl.* hype; intrigue, sophistry, subtlety, collusion; treachery, betrayal, tergiversation, disloyalty; chicanery, knavery, *Inf.* hanky-panky, *Sl.* funny business, *Sl.* monkey business.

2. trick, strategem, ruse, Trojan horse, artifice, pretense, *Obs.* cog; contrivance, wile, subterfuge, misrepresentation; fake, sham, hoax, swindle, shuck, feint, blind; fraud, imposture, imposition, *Law.* covin, humbug, *Inf.* flimflam, *Inf.* flam; falsehood, lie, fib, untruth, prevarication.

3. falseness, untruthfulness, deceptiveness, dishonesty, insincerity, trickiness; deceitfulness, underhandedness, indirection, mendacity.

deceitful, *adj.* **1.** insincere, disingenuous, false, mendacious, untruthful, hollow; dishonest, underhanded, untrustworthy, crooked; wily, tricky, designing, scheming, guileful, double-dealing; artful, crafty, Machiavellian, cunning, sly, snaky, foxy; subtle, insidious, collusive, circumventive, prevaricative; two-faced, Janus-faced, hypocritical, *Sl.* jive; perfidious, treacherous, traitorous, Punic, treasonable.

2. misleading, fallacious, illusory, illusive, spurious, factitious; fraudulent, deceptive, catchy; evasive, dodgy, elusive, slippery, shifty; specious, sham, bogus, counterfeit, mock, pseudo; make-believe, delusive, feigned, pretended, unreal, imaginary.

deceive, *v.* mislead, misinform, misguide, sail under false colors; delude, fool, take in, throw dust in the eyes of, pull the wool over the eyes of, *Inf.* slip *or* pass [s.t.] over on, slip *or* pass one over on; cozen, dupe, gull, defraud, cheat; rook, victimize, *Archaic.* chouse, defraud, bilk, swindle; steal a march on, cog, *Sl.* take, *Sl.* snooker; pass off, palm off, impose upon, pull a fast one on, *Inf.* throw a curve; humbug, gammon, bluff, juggle, have [s.t.] up one's sleeve, *Inf.* flimflam; hoodwink, trick, outwit, bamboozle, overreach; entrap, ensnare, enmesh; beguile, seduce, bait, decoy; lead on, take for a ride, *Inf.* fake [s.o.] out, *Inf.* rope [s.o.] in, *Inf.* string along; *All Inf.* fast-talk, flam, hype, jive, buffalo, bulldoze; *All Sl.* con, snow, suck in, sucker in, murphy; betray, play false, double-cross, two-time, *Sl.* shaft, *Sl.* cross [s.o.] up.

deceiver, *n.* cheat, cheater, duper, fraud, deluder, cozener, outwitter; hypocrite, dissimulator, tartuffe, Pecksniff, *Inf.* used-car salesman, tricky dick; bamboozler, hoodwinker, swindler, sharper, defrauder, bilker, fleecer, Uriah Heep; knave, scoundrel, rogue, mountebank, Fagin, snake in the grass, cockatrice; impostor, pretender, charlatan, quack, confidence man, *Sl.* con man, wolf in sheep's clothing, ass in lion's skin; trickster, hoaxster, humbug, juggler, prestidigitator; traitor, betrayer, Judas, informer, Benedict Arnold, quisling, *Sl.* stool pigeon; liar, dissembler, perjurer, prevaricator, circumventor; dodger, weasel, fox, Artful Dodger.

decelerate, *v.* **1.** slow up *or* down, wind down, de-escalate; put the brakes on, throttle down, check *or* reduce speed, brake; come to a stop *or* halt.

2. let up on, ease up on, go easy on; relax, take it easy, take it slow, loosen up.

decency, *n.* **1.** propriety, good taste, decorum, dignity, respectability; appropriateness, seemliness, fitness, suitability, suitableness, becomingness; etiquette, formality.

2. virtue, goodness; chastity, purity, modesty, pudency, continence; kindness, generosity, niceness, pleasantness; amenity.

decent, *adj.* **1.** fitting, befitting, appropriate, *Fr. comme il faut*, proper, mannerly, decorous, dignified; tasteful, in good taste.

2. modest, chaste, pure, virtuous; prudish, nice-nelly.

3. respectable, worthy, upright, honest, honest as the day is long; honorable, trustworthy, dependable.

4. attractive, comely, fair, good-looking, of seemly appearance; wholesome, like the girl next door.

5. adequate, sufficient, passable, fairly good, good enough, not bad, tolerable, reasonable; mediocre, indifferent, moderate, ordinary, so-so.

6. kind, obliging, accommodating, generous; courteous, thoughtful.

deception, *n.* **1.** dissimulation, duplicity, hypocrisy, deceit. See **deceit** (*defs.* **1, 3**).

2. ruse, strategem, artifice, wile. See **deceit** (*def.* **2**).

deceptive, *adj.* fallacious, illusory, illusive, spurious, factitious; deceiving, misleading, evasive, elusive, dodgy, shifty, slippery; fraudulent, false, deceitful, hollow; catchy, sophistical, casuistic; specious, bogus, sham, counterfeit, pseudo, mock; chimerical, delusive, visionary, unreal, imaginary; feigned, fancied, pretended, make-believe.

decide, *v.* **1.** determine, settle, arbitrate, umpire, referee, *Inf.* ref; try, hear; evaluate, weigh, consider, think over; reach *or* come to a decision, form an opinion, hold, deem; judge, adjudge, adjudicate, rule, decree, order, *Inf.* call the tune, pass *or* pronounce judgment, sentence.

2. mediate, intervene, interpose, step in, come between, intercede; negotiate, arrange terms, bargain, parley; bring to terms, reconcile, conciliate; placate, appease, satisfy; adjust, make *or* set right, set straight, remedy, fix; solve, work out, conclude, end, terminate, finish off.

3. take it into one's head, *Inf.* take a notion; make up one's mind, *Inf.* fish or cut bait, *Inf.* if you can't take the heat get out of the kitchen; make a decision, resolve, settle on, fix on *or* upon; choose, pick *or* pick out, select.

decided, *adj.* **1.** definite, unmistakable, marked, pronounced, clear, obvious, evident; clearcut, unambiguous, unequivocal; emphatic, categorical, absolute, unqualified, unconditional; flat, firm, fixed, definitive; final, conclusive, determinate, determinative; positive, absolutely sure *or* certain, unquestionable, undeniable, indisputable, incontrovertible, incontestable.

2. settled, sewed up, *Sl.* in the bag, clinched, clenched, sealed.

3. resolute, strong-willed, determined, dogged; decisive, unhesitating, unwavering, unswerving.

decipher, *v.* make out, read, understand, get [s.t.] out of it; decode, translate, interpret, render, explain, construe; solve, work out, figure out, unravel, disentangle.

decision, *n.* **1.** determination, resolution, settling, settlement, arbitration, arbitrament, *Law.* award, *Sports.* call; judgment, adjudication, sentence; finding, conclusion, verdict, ruling, decree, edict, order, command.

2. evaluation, weighing, consideration, making up one's mind.

3. firmness, resolution, resolve, determination; grit, pluck, spirit, purpose, strength, will-power; perseverance, tenacity, persistence; steadfastness, unswervingness; decisiveness, finality, conclusiveness, definitiveness.

decisive, *adj.* **1.** determining, determinative, deciding, settling; determinate, definite, firm, flat, fixed, definitive; unqualified, unconditional, absolute, categorical, emphatic; conclusive, crushing, final.

2. resolute, determined, decided. See **decided** (*def.* **3**).

deck, *v.* outfit, deck out, *Archaic.* bedight, array, bedeck, bedizen, emblazon, *Inf.* trick out; adorn, decorate, embellish, ornament, garnish, enhance, trim, spangle; furbish, refurbish, preen, *Inf.* spruce up; beautify, enrich, elaborate, grace.

declaim, *v.* **1.** speak, orate, perorate, proclaim, hold forth; make a speech, sermonize, lecture; soliloquize, pronounce, enunciate.

2. denounce, inveigh *or* speak against, decry, attack, criticize, censure, rebuke, reproach, *Inf.* rap; harangue, rant, rail, spout, *Inf.* sound off.

declamation, *n.* **1.** speechmaking, speaking, orating, *Inf.* stumping; haranguing, ranting, spouting, mouthing.

2. speech, oration, address, discourse, lecture, sermon, recitation; tirade, harangue, *Inf.* stump speech; oratory, delivery, eloquence, rhetoric, style, grandiloquence, magniloquence, bombast.

declamatory, *adj.* **1.** oratorical, rhetorical, theatrical, *Inf.* stagy; stilted, turgid, tumid, high-sounding, pretentious, pompous.

2. bombastic, high-flown, grandiose, grandiloquent, magniloquent, fustian, orotund, inflated, overblown.

declaration, *n.* **1.** announcement, annunciation, publication; averment, asseveration, assertion, affirmation, avowal, avouchment; revelation, disclosure, divulgement, manifestation.

2. proclamation, pronouncement, manifesto, pronunciamento, promulgation, statement, formal *or* authoritative statement *or* announcement; notice, formal notice, notification.

declarative, *adj.* affirmative, assertive, positive, emphatic, decided; expressive, communicatory, declaratory; publicational, promulgatory, propagatory, proclamatory, annunciatory, enunciative; explanatory, expository.

declare, *v.* **1.** announce, annunciate, publish, broadcast, herald, cry, blare, blazon, trumpet; pronounce, rule, decree, proclaim, promulgate.

2. state, aver, assert, asseverate, affirm, avow, avouch, set down, lay down, speak up *or* out, have one's way; maintain, contend, have, hold, insist, submit; allege, profess, claim; swear, predicate, attest, testify; certify, validate, ratify, confirm.

3. disclose, divulge, tell, give out, come out with, let out, make known, manifest, reveal.

decline, *v.* **1.** deny, turn down, reject, refuse; frown upon, turn thumbs down on, negative, veto; resist, rebuff, repel, repudiate; spurn, shun, avoid; abstain from, forgo, do without.

2. dissent, demur, balk, protest; withhold consent, refuse, not budge, remain adamant, put one's foot down.

3. descend, drop off, slope, slant, sink, dip; incline, lean, tilt; depress, bend down, turn down.

4. wane, decrease, diminish; abate, let up, taper off, subside, ebb; fade away, evanesce, vanish, die out; approach an end, come to a close, *Inf.* peter out, wind down; obsolesce, be on the way out; dwindle, shrink, contract.

5. deteriorate, degenerate, decay; languish, flag, droop, sink, fail, weaken, die; shrivel, wither, molder, rot; waste away, melt away, fade away *or* out.

—*n.* **6.** declivity, downward slope. See **declivity**.

7. failing, weakening, weakness, debility; worsening, retrogression, regression, degeneration; deterioration, declination, decay, atrophy, wasting away; enfeeblement, senility, senescence, caducity, (*of women*) anility, decrepitude, dotage.

8. diminution, lessening, lowering; wane, subsidence, ebb, recession, fall-off, downturn, downtrend, downslide, downswing; slump, fall, drop-off, plunge, nosedive.

declivity, *n.* downward slope *or* slant, *Scot. and North Eng.* brae, hillside; decline, declension, descent, downgrade; drop, fall, dip; pitch, grade, angle; incline, hill, mount, rise.

decompose, *v.* **1.** disintegrate, divide, atomize, dissolve, break up, fractionate; distill, reduce, resolve, separate, *Physical Chem.* electrolyze, *Chem.* hydrolyze; analyze, anatomize, dissect, take apart.

2. decay, rot, addle, putrefy; spoil, go bad, turn, sour; crumble, fall apart, fall to pieces.

decomposition, *n.* **1.** disintegration, fractionation, division, atomization; distillation, reduction, resolution, separation, *Physical Chem.* electrolysis, *Chem.* hydrolysis, *Biochem.* proteolysis; analysis, anatomization, dissection.

2. decay, rot, rottenness, caries, cariosity, cariousness; spoilage, putrefaction, putrescence, putrescency, putridity, putridness.

decorate, *v.* **1.** adorn, ornament, embellish, trim, garnish, furbish, *Archaic.* ouch, *Archaic.* dight; embroider, elaborate, festoon, rubricate; array, bedizen, deck, deck out, bedeck, *Scot.* dight; dress, dress up, attire, accouter, caparison, trap out; beautify, prettify, fix up, prink, *Inf.* spruce up, *Inf.* pretty up, *Inf.* trick up.

2. spangle, bespangle, stud, bestud, beset; emblazon, blazon, illuminate, paint, color, bedaub; gild, varnish, trick out.

3. cite, honor, do *or* pay honor, pin a medal on.

decoration, *n.* **1.** adornment, ornamentation, embellishment, garnishment; embroidery, elaboration; bedizenment, enrichment, beautification, prettification; emblazonment, emblazonry, illumination.

2. ornament, frill, filigree, flourish, flounce, furbelow; tinsel, spangle; trinket, bauble, knick-knack, gimcrack, gewgaw, *Archaic.* ouch, *Inf.* doodad, *Inf.* fandangle; finery, frippery, folderol, fuss, *Inf.* foofaraw, *Sl.* jazz, *Sl.* flash.

3. colors, order, badge, medal, ribbon, laurel, wreath, cordon, garter, star.

decorous, *adj.* **1.** proper, seemly, decent, becoming; tasteful, in good taste, dignified, refined, polished, elegant, genteel; polite, mannerly, well-behaved, gentlemanly, ladylike; respectful, deferential, conventional; formal, ceremonial, ceremonious, strict, staid, stilted.

2. suitable, appropriate, apt, apposite, apropos; fit, fitting, befitting, meet, *Fr. comme il faut*; just, right, in keeping, in character.

3. sedate, calm, serene, composed, unruffled; subdued, reserved, modest, demure, quiet, unobtrusive; solemn, grave, sober; settled, steady.

decorum, *n.* **1.** etiquette, protocol, punctilio, good form, the thing to do; politeness, good manners, mannerliness, best behavior; gentility, breeding, gentlemanliness, ladylikeness, dignity, sedateness, respectability, decency.

2. propriety, properness, correctitude, correctness, conformity; suitability, suitableness, appropriateness, seemliness, becomingness, fitness, congruity.

decoy, *n.* **1.** bait, lure, stool pigeon, magnet, loadstone; enticement, allurement, seduction, attraction; trap, gin, snare, ensnarement, pitfall; smoke screen, camouflage, cover-up, pretense; phony, fake, sham.

—*v.* **2.** lure, bait; attract, magnetize, entice, allure, seduce; entrap, ensnare.

decrease, *v.* **1.** diminish, lessen, reduce, lower, abate, bate; contract, shrink, constrict, narrow; cut, pare, prune, truncate, crop, lop, dock, clip; condense, cut down, compress, shorten, abridge, scale down, boil down; abbreviate, curtail, cut short.

2. mitigate, alleviate, allay, assuage, *Rare.* lenify, palliate; quell, slake, deaden, dull, blunt, take the edge off of; modify, temper, qualify; minimize, extenuate, make light of, soft-pedal, play down, downplay.

3. subside, ebb, recede, retrocede; dwindle, *Inf.* peter out; slacken, let up, wind down, slow down, deescalate; fall off, taper off, wane, fade away, die out.

—*n.* **4.** diminution, reduction, lessening, diminishing, decrement, abatement, retrenchment, cutback; contraction, shrinking, shrinkage, constriction, constricting, narrowing; condensation, compression, shortening, abridgment, abbreviation, curtailment.

5. mitigation, alleviation, assuagement, palliation; quelling, relieving, easing, softening; loosening, relaxation, slackening.

6. subsidence, ebb, recession; decline, downturn, drop-off, fall-off, declension, decrescence, wane; sinking, falling off, fading away, dwindling, dying out; weakening, attenuation, loss, attrition, wearing away, erosion, wasting away; retardation, slowdown,

deescalation.

decree, *n.* **1.** ordinance, edict, *Law.* writ, rescript, assize; dictate, dictum, order, injunction, command; fiat, sanction, prescript, mandate, firman; proclamation, pronunciamento, manifesto, ukase; ruling, verdict, judgment, *Law.* award, finding, sentence; rule, regulation, law, canon, enactment, *Law.* statute, act; warrant, authorization.

—*v.* **2.** ordain, rule, adjudge, order, command, dictate, pronounce, proclaim; charge, bid, enjoin, direct, prescribe, instruct; enact, appoint, authorize, establish; decide, determine, arbitrate, adjudicate, settle, set; exact, demand, require, tax with; sentence, *Law.* award, find.

decrepit, *adj.* **1.** feeble, enfeebled, infirm, weak, weakened, weakly, emasculate, effete; aged, old, elderly, ancient; senile, anile, senescent, doddering, tottering; disabled, crippled, palsied, laid up, laid on one's back, bedridden, sickly, valetudinarian.

2. dilapidated, rickety, broken-down, tumbledown, rundown, worn, worn-out, weatherbeaten, faded; deteriorated, decayed, wasted, the worse for wear, on its last legs; withered, wilted; antiquated, antique, timeworn, superannuated.

decrepitude, *n.* **1.** feebleness, enfeeblement, infirmity, weakness; debility, invalidity, palsy, disablement, incapacity, helplessness; old age, caducity, senescence, senility, anility, dotage, hoary age.

2. dilapidation, decay, deterioration, degeneration, decadence, retrogression, wasting, falling off, superannuation.

decry, *v.* **1.** detract, disparage, demean, deprecate, belittle, deflate, depreciate, devaluate, damn with faint praise, *Inf.* talk down; discredit, disfavor, make disreputable, injure *or* impair the credit *or* reputation of; criticize, dispraise, cut up, shred, pull to pieces, *Sl.* do a number on, *Sl.* do a hatchet job on, carp at, cavil at, peck at, *Inf.* knock, *Inf.* rap; minimize, slight, underestimate, underrate, undervalue, beggar, extenuate, underreckon, misprize, think nothing of, set no store by, fail to count on; deemphasize, underplay, make light of, make little of, *Inf.* play down; lampoon, pasquinade, caricature, satirize; ridicule, mock, poke fun at, laugh at, sneer at, jeer at, jibe at; disdain, deride, contemn, scoff, spurn, scorn, pooh-pooh.

2. denounce, rail, curse, condemn, anathematize, *Obs.* exprobate, cry down; censure, reproach, impeach, bring to book, call to account, slate, inveigh against, clamor against, remonstrate against, reprove, recriminate, reprehend, reprobate, pass strictures, perstringe, animadvert upon.

3. defame, denigrate, vilify. See **detract** (*def.* 3).

dedicate, *v.* **1.** devote, bless, hallow, sanctify, consecrate, make holy, deify, apotheosize, enshrine; set apart, signalize; (*of oneself*) give, offer, surrender.

2. inscribe, preface, address, name.

dedication, *n.* **1.** enshrinement, deification, apotheosis, consecration, canonization, ordination.

2. devotion, faithfulness, fidelity, fealty, allegiance, adherence; surrender, relinquishment.

3. inscription, preface; message, address.

deduce, *v.* conclude, infer, gather, glean, understand, figure, *Sl.* dope out; presume, assume, suppose, opine, *U.S. Dial.* reckon, surmise, guess.

deducible, *adj.* inferable, derivable, traceable; consequent, sequent; conceivable, logical, reasonable.

deduct, *v.* **1.** subtract, withdraw, take away, abstract, remove, take out, take from, *Archaic.* subduct; discount, take off, *Inf.* lop off, *Sl.* knock off.

2. detract, devalue, devaluate; weaken, reduce, diminish, lessen, abate, bate, lower, curtail.

deduction, *n.* **1.** subtraction, removal, withdrawal, abstraction, *Archaic.* subduction; diminution, lessening, abridgment, curtailment, retrenchment, reduction.

2. discount, *U.S.* cut rate, markdown, cutback, rollback; rebate, refund; *Math.* subtrahend; allowance, exemption, (*in reference to taxes*) *Sl.* deduck.

3. inference, conclusion, corollary, illation; induction, derivation, implication; consequence, result, demonstration, proof; presumption, assumption, understanding; reasoning, ratiocination.

deed, *n.* **1.** act, turn, action; proceeding, performance, execution, doing; undertaking, project, enterprise; work, task, job, commission.

2. exploit, feat, *Archaic.* gest; achievement, step, stride, advancement, progress; accomplishment, attainment, acquirement, success.

3. maneuver, move, stroke, blow, coup, stunt, trick; stroke of genius, tour de force.

deem, *v.* think, judge, believe, imagine, presume; consider, estimate, calculate, hold, set down as; regard, view, look upon, see; suppose, surmise, fancy, take it, opine, *Archaic.* ween, count, reckon.

deep, *adj.* **1.** immeasurable, bottomless, fathomless, depthless; extensive, broad, wide, far-reaching, vast, massive; retreating, yawning, cavernous, abysmal; submerged, sunk, sunken, on the bottom; buried, in the bowels of the earth, subterranean; deep-seated, deep-rooted, inmost, out of sight, *Inf.* way down.

2. sagacious, sage, wise, learned, knowing; penetrating, discerning, perspicacious, shrewd, astute; artful, subtle, designing, scheming, devious, cunning.

3. profound, extreme, intense, great; grave, pressing, urgent, critical, vital, important, significant, *Inf.* heavy.

4. difficult, unclear, obscure, abstruse, esoteric, recondite; impenetrable, inexplicable, incomprehensible; secret, hidden, mysterious, unfathomable, concealed; enigmatic, mystical, sphinxlike, occult.

5. absorbed, engrossed, preoccupied, rapt, intent, involved, entangled; immersed, plunged into, lost in, swallowed up, occupied, engaged.

6. rich, full, big, strong, powerful, heavy, solid; full-toned, resonant, sonorous, bass, basso; rumbling, booming, resounding; guttural, growly; dark, intensified, vivid, vibrant, vigorous, full-bodied.

7. earnest, sincere, serious, sober, somber; philosophical, thoughtful, reflective; heartfelt, poignant, fervent, ardent, impassioned; intense, deep-felt.

—*n.* **8.** bottom, depths, deepest reaches, bottommost point; depth, profundity, extent, vastness, abyss.

9. culmination, central point, midpoint, middle, midst; silence, still, stillness, fastness, recesses, remotest point.

10. the deep *Chiefly Literary.* the ocean, the sea, the seas, the high seas, the seven seas, main, the ocean blue, the waves; briny deep, Davy Jones's locker, Neptune's kingdom.

—*adv.* **11.** profoundly, intensely, deeply. See **deeply**.

deepen, *v.* **1.** excavate, dredge, scoop out, dig out, dig; dig, burrow, sink, cut out, mine, sap.

2. intensify, strengthen, increase, enhance, add to, magnify, amplify, augment; reinforce, redouble, expand, broaden, darken; heighten, elevate, advance.

deeply, *adv.* **1.** deep, far down, far below the surface, at a great depth, out of reach, *Inf.* way down, *Inf.* deep deep down.

2. profoundly, strongly, formidably, powerfully, urgently, intensely, acutely, keenly, vividly; extensively, greatly, immeasurably, vastly, abysmally; to a great extent, very much, in high degree.

3. passionately, with feeling, with depth, movingly, impressively, without reservation; penetratingly, piercingly, sharply.

4. soundly, thoroughly, completely, entirely; gravely, seriously, severely; in deep, beyond *or* out of one's depth, over one's head, *Inf.* out of one's league *or* ballpark.

5. intricately, mysteriously; cunningly, skillfully, subtly, artfully.

6. sonorously, resonantly, richly, fully, boomingly.

deface, *v.* **1.** disfigure, disfeature, deform, mar, spoil, ruin, flaw, blemish, uglify, blotch; vandalize, trash, damage.

2. efface, expunge, erase, eradicate, obliterate, blot *or* wipe out, rub *or* sponge out; delete, cancel, strike out, cross out, rule out.

defacement, *n.* **1.** disfigurement, deformation, distortion, impairment, uglification; vandalism, destruction, damage; erosion, wear and tear, discoloration, oxidation.

2. effacement, erasure, eradication, expunction, obliteration; deletion, cancellation.

de facto, **1.** in fact, in reality, in actuality, in effect, in point of fact, as a matter of fact; really, actually; accepted, recognized; behind-the-scenes.

2. real, actual, existing, existent, extant.

defamation, *n.* **1.** denigration, vilification, vituperation, scandal, *Inf.* skeleton in the closet; censure, reproach, denunciation, railing, curse, malediction, invective, commination, *Archaic.* exprobration, revilement, obloquy; belittlement, deprecation, disparagement, detraction, deflation, derogation, depreciation, devaluation; humiliation, humble pie, mortification.

2. calumny, slander, libel, false accusation, misrepresentation, falsehood, malicious falsehood, lie, abuse, injury, traducement, mud-slinging, backbiting; aspersion, muckraking, imputation, insinuation, innuendo, *Inf.* brickbat, reflection; slur, blot, blot on the escutcheon, smear, smirch, taint, attaint, stain, tarnish, spot, black spot *or* mark, blemish, smudge, brand, stigma, badge of infamy.

defamatory, *adj.* **1.** denigrating, vituperative, vilipenditory, critical, condemnatory, denunciatory, disapprobatory, disapproving, imprecating, maledictive, maledictory; scandalous, shocking, flagrant, notorious, outrageous; shameful, disgraceful, reproachable, dishonorable, discreditable, disfavorable, disreputable; humiliating, humbling, mortifying; belittling, disparaging, detractory, depreciatory, deprecatory, derogatory, deflating, devaluating.

2. slanderous, calumnious, calumniatory, traducent, aspersive, imputative, false, untrue, maliciously false *or* untrue, misrepresentative, abusive, injurious, contumelious, insulting, backbiting; defiling, sullying, staining, tainting, tarnishing, soiling, blemishing, smearing, smirching, smudging, branding, stigmatizing.

defame, *v.* **1.** denigrate, vituperate, vilify, vilipend, scandalize, run down, berate, revile, malign, impugn, criticize, pull to pieces, *Sl.* do a hatchet job on, cut up, shred, give a bad name, speak ill of, speak evil of, gibbet, hold up to scorn, sneer at, muckrake; denounce, rail, curse, execrate, damn, imprecate, *Obs.* exprobate, anathematize, censure, cry down, reproach; discredit, disprove, disfavor; belittle, disparage, detract, decry, deprecate, depreciate, derogate, devaluate, deflate; humiliate, humble, mortify, *Sl.* put down.

2. calumniate, slander, libel, asperse, impute, insinuate, traduce, accuse falsely; falsify, misrepresent, belie; injure, abuse, assail, stab, insult, backbite, *Sl.* badmouth, engage in personalities; slur, sully, defile, smear, smirch, besmirch, soil, blacken, blemish, tarnish, taint, attaint, smudge, stain, spot, brand, stigmatize, drag through the mud *or* mire, heap dirt upon, *Sl.* dump on.

default, *n.* **1.** neglect, negligence, inadvertence, dereliction, fault, oversight; shortcoming; lapse, failure, omission, nonfulfillment, nonfeasance, nonperformance, *Sports.* forfeiture.

2. nonpayment, nonremittal, delinquency, *Commerce.* dishonor.

3. want, lack, absence; shortage, deficit, deficiency.

—*v.* **4.** bilk, *Sl.* welsh, cheat, *Commerce.* dishonor, refuse to accept a bill *or* charge, refuse to honor by payment, decline to pay *or* redeem, *Inf.* rip off, *Sl.* skip town, *Brit. Sl.* levant, *Brit. Sl.* do a moonlight flit.

5. fail, lapse, be negligent, *Sports.* forfeit; fall short, come short, run short, be found wanting, not measure up, *Inf.* not make the grade, *Sl.* not hack it.

defaulter, *n.* delinquent, nonpayer, cheat, *Sl.* welsher, *Brit. Sl.* levanter; tax evader, *Inf.* tax dodger.

defeat, *v.* **1.** conquer, vanquish, subdue, subjugate, oppress; rout, discomfit, overwhelm, *Sl.* mop *or* wipe the floor with, overrun, trample, *Inf.* run into the ground; crush, overthrow, smash, thrash, trounce, trim, whip, drub, floor; worst, hash, *Sl.* skin, *U.S. Sl.* skunk, *Inf.* settle [s.o.'s] hash, *Inf.* lick, *Sl.* cream, *Sl.* shellac, *Sl.* pulverize; break, quell, quench, quash, destroy, *Sl.* zap, clobber, polish off, *Sl.* do in; beat, get the better of, best, upset, upend, *Inf.* whomp.

2. master, overpower, overcome, surmount, outsmart, triumph over; control, dominate, gain the upper hand over; humble, bring down, have at one's beck and call; have eating out of one's hand, *Inf.* have wrapped around one's little finger.

3. frustrate, thwart, foil, balk, check, stop, abort; arrest, stay, stall, bring to a standstill; put a stop *or* an end to, terminate, end, *Inf.* put the kibosh on, nip in the bud; annul, disannul, nullify, cancel.

4. hinder, hamper, block, obstruct, oppilate, inhibit; confound, baffle, disconcert; prevent, bar, debar, forbid, proscribe.

—*n.* **5.** conquest, vanquishment, subjugation; rout, discomfiture, overwhelming, trampling, overcoming, overpowering, overthrow, upset; beating, drubbing, trouncing.

6. downfall, breakdown, collapse; destruction, ruin, perdition; failure, fiasco, miscarriage.

7. frustration, thwarting; rebuff, check, checkmate; reverse, undoing; nonsuccess, no go, abortion, disappointment; loss, setback.

defecate, *v.* **1.** void excrement, excrete, egest, *Physiol.* evacuate; have a bowel movement *or* B.M.; *All Euph.* go potty, relieve oneself, do number 2; move, pass, empty.

2. purify, clarify, refine, cleanse, depurate, purge.

defecation, *n.* **1.** voiding excrement, excretion, egestion, *Physiol.* evacuation, *Physiol.* dejection; diarrhea, dysentery, *Sl.* the runs.

2. purification, cleansing, purge, depuration.

defect, *n.* **1.** fault, error, mistake; imperfection, failing, weakness, infirmity, frailty; drawback, liability, weak point; blemish, birthmark, blot, stain, scar, cicatrice, deformity; flaw, scratch, crack, spot, tear, blotch; vice, foible; (*all usu. pl., often of machinery*) bugs, snags, kinks, rough spots.

2. want, loss, lack, absence, default, omission, deficiency; failure, shortcoming; insufficiency, inadequacy, shortage, shortfall, dearth.

—*v.* **3.** abandon allegiance, desert, change sides, break faith, go over, bolt, apostatize; shift ground, change loyalties, turn traitor; tergiversate, veer round, do an aboutface, reverse oneself; renege, back out, bail out, bow out, *Sl.* cop out.

4. forsake, forswear, reject, discard, relinquish; renounce, abjure, repudiate, disown; depart from, withdraw from, secede; revolt, mutiny, disobey, rebel.

defection, *n.* **1.** (*used in reference to allegiances*) forsaking, forswearing; rejection, rejecting, renunciation, renouncement, abjuration, repudiation.

2. treason, perfidy, betrayal; unfaithfulness, faithlessness, disloyalty, recreancy, recreance; apostasy, heresy.

3. secession, withdrawal, falling away, dropping out, *Sl.* copping out, turning one's back on; backsliding, recidivism, dereliction.

4. conversion, changeover, switchover; reversal, aboutface, turnabout, *Sl.* switcheroo, *Sl.* a 180°, *Inf.* flip-flop.

5. failure, lack, loss, deficiency. See **defect** (*def.* **2**).

defective, *adj.* **1.** faulty, imperfect, incomplete, lacking, wanting, deficient; inaccurate, incorrect, erroneous, unsound, infirm, weak, poor, inefficient, sloppy; marred, flawed, impaired, bruised, blemished, broken, disfigured, injured, mutilated, warped, deformed; in disrepair, inoperative, inoperable, not working, out of order, out of commission, *Inf.* on the blink, *Sl.* on the fritz, *Sl.* on the bum.

2. *Psychology.* mentally deficient *or* incompetent *or* unsound, feeble-minded, retarded, simple; dim-witted, half-witted, imbecilic, idiotic, moronic, *Sl.* not all there; *Euph.* exceptional, *Euph.* special.

defend, *v.* **1.** *Usu.* **defend from** *or* **against** protect, shelter, screen, shield; fight for, take up the cudgels for; guard, safeguard, ward off, fend off, parry; garrison, fortify, arm, secure, hold the fort, preserve, keep, save.

2. support, bolster, advocate, endorse, stand behind *or* beside, stand up for, make a stand for, stick up for, go to bat for; represent, make a case for, argue for, speak in behalf of, hold a brief for, *Law.* plead; uphold, maintain, sustain, vindicate, justify; (*of oneself*) rationalize, give reasons for, apologize, palliate, extenuate, make excuses.

defender, *n.* **1.** protector, guard, bodyguard, escort, convoy; guardian, watchman, caretaker, warder, warden, keeper, preserver.

2. supporter, bolsterer, endorser, seconder, backer, advocate, champion; upholder, maintainer, sustainer, vindicator, justifier; (*all of law*) lawyer, attorney, counselor, counsel, pleader, *Brit.* barrister, *Brit.* solicitor.

defense, *n.* **1.** protection, shelter, shield, buckler, aegis, screen, armor, mail, cover, *Rare.* muniment; guard, watch, ward, custody, care, safekeeping; fortification, fortress, stronghold, garrison, fort, tower of strength; bulwark, bastion, rampart, parapet, redoubt; barricade, buttress, palisade; security, safeguard, palladium.

2. vindication, justification, argument, plea, apologia; apology, extenuation, palliation, excuse.

defenseless, *adj.* **1.** unprotected, unguarded, unsheltered; unfortified, unarmed, weaponless, weak, helpless, powerless, impotent; insecure, unsafe, dangerous, perilous, precarious.

2. vulnerable, uncovered, exposed, naked, wide open; open to attack, pregnable, penetrable, invadable, attackable, assaultable, assailable.

defensible, *adj.* **1.** invulnerable, impregnable, impenetrable, secure, safe, holdable; unattackable, unassaultable, unassailable; fortified, armed, ironclad, bulletproof, shellproof, bombproof.

2. justifiable, vindicable, defendable, supportable; tenable, maintainable, sustainable; pardonable, forgivable, venial, excusable, allowable, permissible.

defer[1], *v.* **1.** delay, postpone, suspend, table, shelve, *Sl.* put on the shelf, pigeonhole, prorogue; hold off, hold up, lay over, refrain from further action, hold in abeyance, put in cold storage, put on ice, put on a back burner, hang fire, put in a holding pattern; procrastinate, wait, put off, cunctate, temporize, dally, gain time, *Inf.* drag one's feet, *Inf.* foot drag; *Inf.* stall, stave off, *U. S.* filibuster; respite, stay, reprieve.

2. adjourn, recess, discontinue, interrupt, intermit, break off; pause, break, breathe, *All Inf.* take a break, take a breath, take a breather, catch one's breath, take five.

defer[2], *v.* **1.** yield, submit, bow, bow to; give way to, give ground to; give in, surrender, acquiesce, comply, assent, capitulate; accede, cede.

2. refer, relegate, consign, entrust, deliver, hand over.

deference, *n.* **1.** submission, acquiescence, compliance, resignation, acceptance, yielding; nonresistance, passivity, complaisance; obeisance, obsequiousness, obsequence, servility, slavishness, abjection, self-abasement, prostration; docility, submissiveness, unassertiveness, tractability, Uncle Tomism.

2. regard, respect, consideration, thoughtfulness; courtesy, civility, politeness.

deferential, *adj.* **1.** respectful, regardful, considerate, thoughtful; obedient, dutiful; polite, courteous, civil.

2. submissive, acquiescent, compliant, complaisant, passive, nonresisting, docile, tractable, mealy-mouthed, Uncle Tomish; obeisant, prostrate, on one's knees, groveling; servile, slavish, obsequious, *Obs.* obsequent, subservient, menial, *Obs., Rare.* vernile.

deferment, *n.* **1.** delay, holdup, postponement, suspension, moratorium, abeyance, prorogation; procrastination, tardiness, cunctation; *Inf.* stall, *U. S.* filibuster, Fabian policy; wait, waiting period; adjournment, break, breath, breather, pause, recess, time-out.

2. reprieve, respite, stay, moratorium.

defiance, *n.* **1.** resistance, combativeness, confrontation, antagonism, opposition; declaration of hostilities, throwing down *or* taking up the gauntlet *or* glove, throwing down the gage, facing down.

2. bearding, threatening, intimidation, provocation; challenge, threat, insult, despite.

3. disregard, contempt, scorn, indifference, noncompliance, waywardness; recalcitrance, stubbornness, intransigence; contumacy, rebelliousness, recusancy, disobedience, insubordination, insurgency; mutiny, sedition, revolt, rebellion, riot, strike, sabotage; war cry, war whoop, taking up arms.

4. bravado, gutsiness, daring, derring-do; audacity, boldness, braveness, intrepidity.

defiant, *adj.* **1.** resistant, antagonistic, bellicose, belligerent, hostile, pugnacious, provocative, threatening, in opposition; audacious, bold, *Scot.* bardy, headstrong, hard-headed, devil-may-care, gutsy.

2. unruly, contumacious, disobedient, insubordinate, rebellious, mutinous; stubborn, mulelike, obstinate, unyielding, adamant, recalcitrant; insubmissive, recusant, restive, refractory; insolent, snippy, scornful, dissentient, contemptuous, disregardful.

deficiency, *n.* **1.** lack, want, absence, default, dearth, paucity, destitution; scarcity, insufficiency, short supply; scantiness, meagerness, inadequacy, incompleteness.

2. failing, defect, frailty, flaw. See **defect** (*def.* **1**).

3. shortage, shortfall. See **deficit**.

deficient, *adj.* **1.** lacking, wanting, incomplete, unfinished; defective, flawed, impaired, imperfect; infirm, weak, faulty, unsound, inferior, poor, bad; not up to par, not up to snuff.

2. inadequate, insufficient, unsatisfactory; short, scarce, sketchy, skimpy; scanty, meager, exiguous.

deficit, *n.* monetary deficiency, shortage, shortfall; loss, arrears, indebtedness; red ink.

defile, *v.* **1.** pollute, taint, dirty, soil, poison, befoul, make filthy, begrime; spot, smear, blot, blur, smudge, smirch, draggle, spatter, besmear, daub; maculate, stain, tarnish.

2. ravish, rape, deprive of virginity, deflower; assault, attack, force, mistreat, abuse; debauch, deprave.

3. desecrate, profane, debase, treat sacrilegiously; contaminate, infect, make impure, vitiate.

4. sully, dishonor, disgrace, asperse, blacken; deprecate, defame, denigrate.

defilement, *n.* **1.** pollution, contamination, filth, taint, foulness, maculation; smudging, spotting, smearing.

2. rape, sexual abuse, forced sexual intercourse, attack; defloration, violation, incest, depravity.

3. desecration, profaning, debasement, corruption; degradation, vitiation, wickedness.

4. sullying, denigration, deprecation, disgracing.

definable, *adj.* **1.** determinable, fixable; ascertainable, perceptible, appreciable, visible, evident; describable, explicable.

2. definite, finite, fixed; clear-cut, precise, exact, specific.

define, *v.* **1.** explain, expound, spell out, elucidate, throw light on; construe, interpret, translate, literalize.

2. demarcate, mark out, limit, delimit, bound, circumscribe, compass, encompass; determine, fix, establish, lay down, prescribe.

3. describe, delineate, outline, set out; characterize, specify, represent, depict, render; exemplify, illustrate; entitle, designate, denominate, label.

definite, *adj.* **1.** specific, particular, definitive, defined, determinate, determined, fixed; limited, bound, circumscribed, encompassed, delineated.

2. clear, clear-cut, sharp-cut, unambiguous, unequivocal; explicity, graphic, obvious, manifest, plain, express; precise, exact, accurate, correct; indisputable, well-grounded, established, confirmed; well-founded, valid, substantial, solid, concrete.

3. positive, certain, sure, decided, settled; conclusive, decisive, final.

definitely, *adv.* clearly, plainly, obviously, explicitly; unequivocally, indisputably, absolutely; positively, certainly, surely, to be sure; finally, decidedly, conclusively, once and for all.

definition, *n.* **1.** demarcation, delineation, delimitation, circumscription, encompassment; determination, fixing, settlement, settling.

2. explanation, elucidation, expounding, exposition; illustration, exemplification, commentary.

3. distinctness, sharpness, clearness, clarity; discernibleness, apparentness, perceptibility, visibility.

definitive, *adj.* exhaustive, thorough, complete, consummate, most reliable, perfect; absolute, unqualified, categorical, exact, accurate; decisive, conclusive, terminative, final, crowning, ultimate; determinate, determined, settled, positive, unquestionable; defining, settling, limiting.

deflate, *v.* **1.** let the air out, release the air from, collapse, blow out, flatten, wind, take the wind out of; exhaust, empty, void, deplete; shrink, constrict, contract; compress, squeeze, press.

2. reduce, lower, decrease, diminish; devalue, depreciate, depress.

3. depress, dispirit, let down, lower the spirits, discourage, dishearten; puncture, plunge into despair, puncture *or* prick one's balloon, take the wind out of one's sails, rain on one's parade; dash, knock down, sink, *Sl.* bring down; humble, mortify, humiliate, bring down from one's high horse.

deflect, *v.* **1.** turn aside, diverge, shy, incline; avert, shunt, sidetrack, turn away, divagate, divaricate; bend, swerve, curve, crook, twist, flex, buckle; refract, divert, switch, glance off.

2. (*usu. in a nautical sense*) shift, jibe, jib, gybe, gibe, alter course, change direction; yaw, deviate, sheer, veer, tack, go about, wear; slew, slue, wheel round, swing, sweep; cant, heel, warp, tilt, bear down, edge, bear off, sidle.

deflection, *n.* **1.** deviation, declination, divagation, divarication, *Aeron.* drift; divergence, diversion, swerve, bend, curve, crook, twist; refraction, flection, deflexure, refringence.

2. (*usu. in a nautical sense*) jibe, gybe, yaw, shift, sheer; slew, slue, round, swing, sweep; veer, tack, wear, cant, tilt, heel, warp.

deflower, *v.* **1.** violate, rape, ravish, molest, take, steal [s.o.'s] maidenhead, deprive of virginity, *Obs.* devirginate, *Obs.* constuprate, *Obs.* stuprate; force, attack, assault, abuse; *Euph.* take advantage of, *Euph.* have one's way with, ill-treat, ill-use, maltreat, mistreat; debauch, seduce, corrupt, pervert, dishonor.

2. despoil, spoil, mar, harm; desecrate, defile, outrage.

deform, *v.* **1.** disfigure, mar, uglify, deface, distort, contort, malform, misshape; twist, bend, gnarl, warp, mutilate; cripple, mangle, maim, damage, hurt.

2. metamorphose, transform, transmogrify, change the form of.

deformed, *adj.* **1.** misshapen, malformed, distorted, ill-proportioned, misproportioned; irregular, unnatural, grotesque; contorted, curved, awry, askew, crooked, gnarled; crippled, lame, humpbacked, hunchbacked, *Pathol.* kyphotic, bowlegged, bandylegged, knock-kneed, clubfooted, splayfooted, taliped, snub-nosed; stumpy, stunted, dwarfed.

2. hateful, vile, depraved, loathsome, gross; offensive, repulsive, revolting; hideous, monstrous, ugly, unsightly; warped, twisted, perverted.

deformity, *n.* **1.** deformation, disfigurement, malformation, misshapenness, defacement, distortion, disfiguration; contortion, crookedness, twisting, *Pathol.* kyphosis, warp; ugliness, unsightliness, eyesore, blemish, imperfection; monstrosity, abortion.

2. hatefulness, depravity, vileness, grossness; loathsomeness, repulsiveness, offensiveness.

defraud, *v.* cheat, rook, victimize, chouse, skin, fleece, bilk, swindle; steal a march on, cog, *Sl.* take, *Sl.* snooker; fool, cozen, dupe, delude, take in, throw dust in the eyes of, pull the wool over the eyes of, *Inf.* slip *or* pass [s.t.] over on; hoodwink, trick, bamboozle, outwit, overreach; humbug, gammon, bluff, juggle, *Inf.* flimflam; pass off, palm off, impose upon, pull a fast one on, *Inf.* throw a curve, take for a ride, *Inf.* rope [s.o.] in; mislead, misguide, misinform, *Inf.* fast-talk, *Inf.* flam, *Inf.* hype, *Inf.* jive, *Sl.* con, *Sl.* sucker in.

defray, *v.* pay for, bear the expense *or* cost, stand the cost, *Inf.* foot the bill, *Inf.* pick up the check *or* tab; pay off, *Inf.* pay up, settle, square, discharge, liquidate, clear, *Finance.* amortize.

defrayal, *n.* payment, defrayment, discharge, settlement, clearance, liquidation, *Finance.* amortization.

deft, *adj.* **1.** dexterous, ambidextrous, adroit, handy, neat, *Brit. Dial.* feat; nimble, light, agile, active, quick, rapid, brisk, swift, lively; skillful, skilled, adept, proficient, facile, ready, experienced, *Fr. au fait.*

2. clever, shrewd, *Archaic.* parlous, *Inf.* cute; cunning, canny, guileful, subtle, artful, crafty, slick; ingenious, inventive, resourceful; sagacious, astute, keen, acute, sharp, sharp-witted, sharp as a tack, quick-witted; apt, smart, witty.

defunct, *adj.* **1.** deceased, dead, extinct. See **dead** (*def.* **1**).

2. obsolete, obsolescent, outmoded, passé; expired, dead; not operating, not functioning. See **dead** (*def.* **6**).

defy, *v.* **1.** disregard, ignore, flout, fly in the face of, disobey; slight, set at naught, scoff at, thumb one's nose at, snap one's fingers at; disdain, spurn, deride, contemn, despise.

2. challenge, dare, double-dare, *Sl.* double-dog-dare; confront, front, face, meet face to face, meet head-on, meet eyeball to eyeball, square off.

3. withstand, stand, endure, hold up, hold out, bear up.

degeneracy, *n.* corruption, turpitude, decadence, immorality, depravity, depravation, dissoluteness, profligacy, abandon; baseness, vileness, wickedness, evilness, sinfulness, low-mindedness.

degenerate, *v.* **1.** deteriorate, decline, sink, worsen, take a turn for the worse, slip; go downhill, go to pieces, go to ruin, *Inf.* go to pot, *Inf.* go to the dogs, *Sl.* hit the skids; fall, fail, lapse, retrogress, retrograde, let oneself go; go wrong, err, go astray, leave the straight and narrow.

—adj. **2.** deteriorated, degraded, debased; corrupt, decadent, depraved, debauched, dissolute, fallen, vice-ridden; mean, base, vile, ignoble, base-minded, low-minded, *Inf.* low-down.

—n. **3.** wretch, beggar, derelict, drunkard, vagrant, *Sl.* bum, *Sl.* low-life, *Sl.* bag lady, *Sl.* stiff.

4. (*all in reference to sexual activity*) pervert, deviate, fiend, maniac, psychopath; sadist, masochist, fetishist, voyeur, scotophiliac, erotomaniac, nymphomaniac; sodomist, sodomite, bugger; pederast, pedophiliac, child-molester; catamite, *Sl.* gunsel, *Sl.* chicken, *Sl.* punk; coprophiliac; necrophiliac; zoophiliac.

degeneration, *n.* **1.** deterioration, vitiation, degradation, decline, declination, declension, descent, drop, fall; retrogression, retrogradation, regression, lapse, atrophy; corruption, depravation, debasement, demoralization, dissolution, dissipation.

2. degeneracy, turpitude, immorality. See **degeneracy.**

degradation, *n.* **1.** demotion, deposition, reduction in *or* stripping of rank, removal *or* dismissal from office; fall from repute, removal from standing, obloquy, loss of face, deprival of honor; disgrace, dishonor, disrepute, discredit, derogation, shame, ignominy, humiliation, mortification, *Inf.* comedown.

2. depravity, degeneration, decadence, abasement, corruption, perversion, deterioration, vitiation, meanness, baseness, turpitude.

3. *Geology.* erosion, abrasion, wearing away.

degrade, *v.* **1.** demote, downgrade, lower *or* reduce in rank, dismiss *or* remove from office, declass, break *or* strip of rank, disrate, cashier, *Mil.* drum out, *Mil. Sl.* bust, *Inf.* kick upstairs, disbar, defrock *or* unfrock; depose, unseat, dethrone, *Rare.* disenthrone.

2. debase, abase, defame, vitiate, deprave; discredit, devalue, detract, lower, reduce, depress; shame, disgrace, dishonor; humble, humiliate, mortify; belittle, demean, deprecate, disparage, deflate, derogate, (*of oneself*) bemean.

3. dilute, weaken, mix, water *or* water down, (*of alcohol or drugs*) *Inf.* cut, thin, admix, alloy, *Inf.* doctor; pollute, contaminate, adulterate; defile, corrupt, pervert, vulgarize, debauch, soil, sully, dirty *or* soil one's hands.

degraded, *adj.* **1.** depraved, degenerate, debased, base, contemptible, despicable, corrupt, sordid, vicious, vile, mean, scurvy, rascally, fallen, lapsed, *Inf.* low-down; dishonorable, disreputable, shameful, abandoned; vulgar, coarse, gross, shabby, indelicate, low-minded, crude.

2. abject, ignoble, groveling; inferior, worthless.

degree, *n.* **1.** stage, grade, gradation, scale; step, rung, stair, peg, notch; point, mark.

2. status, rank, standing; standard, grade; position, station, class, caste; worth, value, merit, quality; situation, condition, lot, estate.

3. extent, measure, magnitude, quantity, amount, fullness; shade, strength, intensity; capacity, volume, proportions, dimensions, size, gauge, bulk, content; breadth, width, depth, broadness, wideness, height, length; scope, range, play, compass, swing, sweep; spread, reach, span.

dehydrate, *v.* dry up *or* out, desiccate, exsiccate, evaporate, sun-dry, parch; remove the moisture from, drain, draw off water from.

deification, *n.* **1.** immortalization, apotheosis, *Archaic.* canonization; exaltation, glorification, dignifying, ennoblement, enthronement, putting on a pedestal; elevation, raising up, lifting up; transfiguration, transformation, enhancement, intensification, magnification, heightening, enlargement, aggrandizement.

2. idolization, adoration, worship, celebration; honor, homage, tribute, reverence, awe, veneration; idealization, admiration, respect, esteem, estimation.

deify, *v.* **1.** make a god of, immortalize, apotheosize, *Archaic.* canonize; exalt, glorify, dignify, ennoble, enthrone, put on a pedestal; elevate, raise, upraise, raise up, make lofty; lift, uplift, lift up, cast up; promote, advance, boost, upgrade, improve, ameliorate, better; transfigure, transform, renew, change; enhance, intensify, magnify, heighten, increase, add to, enlarge, make bigger than life, aggrandize.

2. idolize, regard as a deity, adore, worship, celebrate; honor, pay homage to, pay tribute to; reverence, venerate, revere, hold in awe; idealize, look up to, admire, respect, value, esteem.

deign, *v.* condescend, stoop, think fit, see fit, deem worthy; vouchsafe, assent, yield, concede.

deity, *n.* **1.** (*cap.*) God, God Almighty, the Almighty, the Godhead, Divine Being, the Deity, Providence, Holy One; God the Father, Divine Father, Our Father; Jehovah, Yahweh, Allah; the Supreme Being, Supreme Goodness, the All-Powerful, the Omnipotent, the All-Merciful, the All-Wise, the All-Knowing, the Omniscient; the Infinite, the Eternal, the Absolute; Lord, Lord of Lords, King of Kings, King of Glory; Creator, Author of all things, the Maker, the Maker of Heaven and Earth, the First Cause, the Prime Mover, the Light of the World, Ruler of Heaven and Earth, Sovereign of the Universe, Most High.

2. god, goddess, divine being, demiurge, *Rom. Relig.* lares and penates, *Hinduism.* avatar, joss; idol, golden calf, graven image, icon.

3. divinity, numen, spirit, genius.

deject, *v.* dispirit, dishearten, daunt, take the heart out of, *Inf.* take the starch out of, *Sl.* bring down, *Dial.* take the tuck out of; discourage, dampen, put a damper on one's spirits, *Inf.* put a wet blanket on, *Inf.* throw cold water on; sadden, dismay, cast a gloom *or* pall on *or* over; *Inf.* break one's heart; depress, put [s.o.] down in the dumps *or* the doldrums, make [s.o.] despondent, weigh [s.o.] down, lie heavy on, oppress, crush, prostrate, *Sl.* bum [s.o.] out; enervate, weaken, weary, tire, dull, deaden.

dejected, *adj.* disheartened, dispirited, low-spirited, downhearted, downcast, down, *Inf.* down in the dumps; discouraged, daunted, dismayed, distressed, disappointed, crestfallen, brokenhearted, heartsick, *Inf.* broken up; unhappy, cheerless, glum, gloomy, under a cloud, doleful, *Archaic.* wan; saddened, sad, blue, forlorn, melancholy, mopey, mopish, long-faced, chap-fallen, *Inf.* down in the mouth, *Sl.* off one's feed; miserable, morose, heartbroken, woebegone, heavy-hearted, disconsolate, sorrowful, mournful, lachrymose, funereal; depressed, weighed down, burdened, crushed, prostrate, *Inf.* broken, *Sl.* bummed out; despondent, hypochondriac, hypochondriacal, *Brit.* hipped, spiritless, lifeless, exanimate, enervated, weakened, weary, tired, drained.

dejection, *n.* disheartenment, dispiritedness, low-spiritedness, downheartedness, low spirits, downcastness; discouragement, disappointment, crestfallenness, broken-heartedness, heartsickness; unhappiness, cheerlessness, glumness, gloominess, dolefulness, mopishness, mopiness; sadness, melancholy, sorrowfulness, mournfulness, lachrimosity; miserableness, moroseness, heartbrokenness, forlornness, woebegoneness, disconsolateness, disconsolation, despair, hopelessness; depression, blues, blue devils, doldrums, *Inf.* dumps, *Inf.* funk, *Sl.* blue funk, *Both Psychiatry.* hypochondria, hypochondriosis, *Archaic.* vapors; despondency, spiritlessness, lifelessness, enervation, exanimation.

delay, *v.* **1.** defer, postpone, suspend, table, shelve, *Sl.* put on the shelf, pigeonhole, prorogue; hold off, hold up, lay over, refrain from further action, hold in abeyance, put in cold storage, put on ice, put on a back burner, hang fire, put in a holding pattern; procrastinate, wait, put off, cunctate, temporize, gain time; prolong, protract, lengthen, extend; *Inf.* stall, stave off, *U.S.* filibuster; respite, stay, reprieve.

2. impede, hinder, hamper, encumber, obstruct, hold up; detain, retard, hold back, set back, check, hold in check; confine, arrest, restrict, restrain, slow up, *Sl.* hang up, inhibit, deter, prevent; stay, stop, halt.

3. linger, loiter, lag, dally, dillydally, dawdle, (*often fol. by* along) poke, *Both Inf.* drag one's feet, footdrag.

4. adjourn, recess, discontinue, interrupt, intermit, break off; pause, break, breathe, *All Inf.* take a break, take a breath, take a breather, catch one's breath, take five.

—n. **5.** procrastination, tardiness, dilatoriness, cunctation; protraction, prolongation, extension; postponement, deferment, deferral, abeyance, prorogation.

6. lag, lagging, drag, dragging, *Inf.* footdragging; tarrying, lingering, loitering; dalliance, dallying, dillydallying, dawdling.

7. discontinuation, cessation, hiatus, adjournment, recess, interruption; wait, waiting period, interstice, interval, interim, intermission, intermittency, intermittence; break, pause, rest, halt, stop, breath, time-out, breathing space, breathing spell, breather; hold, hold-up, hesitation, hesitancy; waiver, suspension, moratorium; reprieve, respite, stay.

8. stall, *U.S.* filibuster, Fabian policy.

delectable, *adj.* **1.** delightful, enjoyable, pleasing, pleasurable, pleasant, agreeable; gratifying, satisfying; charming, enchanting, ravishing; exciting, titillating.

2. delicious, tasty, appetizing, *Inf.* scrumptious; savory, luscious, ambrosial, ambrosian, flavorful; palatable, toothsome, *Scot.* gustable.

delectation, *n.* **1.** delight, enjoyment, pleasure, agreeableness; gratification, satisfaction; excitement, titillation, exhilaration, exultation, ecstasy, rapture, transport; gladness, elation, jubilation, joy, bliss, felicity, contentment; enchantment, charm, gaiety; diversion, entertainment, *Inf.* thrill, *Inf.* kick.

2. refreshment, refection; treat, snack, tidbit, morsel, dainty.

delegate, *n.* **1.** representative, deputy, commissary, appointee, spokesperson; middleman, go-between, diplomat, intermediary, negotiator, negotiant; substitute, alternate, proxy, vice-regent, regent, viceroy, surrogate; functionary, commissioner, bureaucrat; ambassador, emissary, envoy, legate, minister; agent, messenger, operative; consul, plenipotentiary.

—v. **2.** commission, deputize, depute; elect, vote in, place in office, install, invest, induct, ordain; appoint, name, designate, nominate; charge, authorize, commit, entrust, empower, enable; assign, appropriate, consign, relegate, pass on, devolve.

delegation, *n.* **1.** deputizing, deputation; appointment, designation, nomination; installation, investiture, induction, ordination; authorization, entrusting, empowering, charging; assignment, appropriation, relegation, devolvement.

2. delegates, deputies, embassy, legation; committee, subcommittee.

delete, *v.* cross out, strike out, scratch, x out, mark off, blue-pencil, *Print.* dele, *Inf.* bleep out; erase, remove, take out, cancel, blot out, rub out, crush out, wipe out, efface, destroy; expunge, eradicate, obliterate.

deleterious, *adj.* pernicious, injurious, baneful, mischievous; harmful, hurtful, noxious, nocuous, noisome; baleful, menacing, malignant, bad; unwholesome, unhealthy, insalubrious; poisonous, venomous, virulent, toxic, mephitic, pestilential, pestiferous; detrimental, disadvantageous, damaging, destructive, ruinous; malicious, vicious, wicked, evil, malevolent; deadly, fell, fatal, mortal, lethal, killing; murderous, suicidal.

deliberate, *adj.* **1.** intentional, purposeful, meant, destined, willful, volitional, voluntary; premeditated, preconceived, preconceptional, aforethought, predeterminate, predetermined, prepense; meditated, studious, studied, considered, weighed; preconcerted, prearranged, predesigned, preplanned, preplotted, predevised, precontrived; calculated, cold-blooded, designed, planned, plotted, schemed, devised, contrived, *Obs.* intrigued, *Obs.* consulted.

2. considerate, thoughtful, determined, decided, resolute, resolved, unwavering; methodical, methodic, systematic, orderly; cool, calm, collected, composed, unexcited, dispassionate; painstaking, thorough, meticulous, scrupulous, accurate, exact, precise; punctilious, fastidious, finicky, finical, particular; circumspect, cautious, careful, prudent, discreet; chary, wary, guarded, watchful, vigilant.

3. steady, even, regular, balanced; stable, solid, firm, secure, sure, confident, unhesitating, unhesitant, unhesitative, unfaltering; leisurely, unhurried, slow, slow-paced, tortoise-like, snail-like; measured, gradual, paced; lingering, plodding, trudging, laborious, labored.

—v. **4.** excogitate, consider, speculate, take to heart, *Archaic.* perpend; ponder, muse, think about; weigh, evaluate, revolve, review, study, scrutinize, examine, inspect, con.

5. contemplate, meditate, cogitate, rack one's brains, cudgel one's brain, trouble one's head; reflect on, think over, ruminate, chew, chew one's cud, brood, mull over, dwell on, be in a brown study; concentrate, focus, have one's mind on, put one's mind to; cerebrate, put on one's thinking cap, be abstracted, be lost in thought.

6. consult with, take counsel, confer with, advise with; discuss, debate, argue, reason.

deliberately, *adv.* **1.** intentionally, purposefully, on purpose, willfully, of one's own free will, volitionally, voluntarily, on one's own; premeditatedly, premeditatingly, with aforethought, predeterminately; meditatedly, meditatively, studiously, considerately; preconcertedly, designedly, calculatedly, wittingly, knowingly, with one's eyes wide open, in cold blood.
2. thoughtfully, determinedly, decidedly, resolutely, unwaveringly; methodically, systematically, in an orderly manner; coolly, calmly, collectedly, composedly, dispassionately; painstakingly, thoroughly, meticulously, scrupulously; circumspectly, cautiously, carefully, prudently, discreetly; charily, warily, guardedly, watchfully, vigilantly.
3. steadily, evenly, regularly; stably, solidly, firmly, surely, confidently, unhesitatingly, unhesitantly, unhesitatively, unfalteringly; unhurriedly, in a leisurely manner, slowly, measuredly, gradually, lingeringly; ploddingly, trudgingly, laboriously.

deliberation, *n.* **1.** excogitation, excogitating, consideration, advisement; speculation, speculating, taking to heart, pondering, musing, thoughtfulness, thinking over, weighing, revolving, review, reviewing, study, studying, scrutinization, scrutinizing, examination, examining, inspection, inspecting, conning; contemplation, contemplating, meditation, meditating, reflection, reflecting, rumination, ruminating, brooding, mulling over, concentration, concentrating, focusing, cerebration, cerebrating.
2. consultation, consulting, conference, conferring, discussion, discussing, debate, debating, argument, arguing, reasoning.
3. intention, intentionality, purposefulness, willfulness, volition, determination, deliberateness; premeditation, forethought, aforethought, calculation, cold-bloodedness.
4. methodicalness, systematicness, orderliness, painstakingness, thoroughness, meticulousness, scrupulousness; circumspection, caution, cautiousness, carefulness, prudence, discretion; chariness, wariness, guardedness, watchfulness, vigilance; steadiness, evenness, stability, solidness, firmness, sureness, confidence; leisureliness, slowness, ploddingness.

delicacy, *n.* **1.** lightness, fineness, slightness, slenderness, fragility, daintiness; translucency, tenuity, diaphaneity, transparence, etherealness, flimsiness; tenderness, softness.
2. tidbit, appetizer, dainty, bonbon, sweetmeat, luxury.
3. refinement, finesse, nicety, grace, sensibility; fastidiousness, exactness, accuracy, precision, scrupulosity, carefulness; subtlety, sensitivity, sensitiveness.
4. criticalness, precariousness, ticklishness; difficulty, arduousness.
5. frailty, frailness, infirmity, feebleness.

delicate, *adj.* **1.** dainty, fine, sheer, transparent, translucent; smooth, silken, soft, thin, gauzy, gossamer; elegant, exquisite, choice, tender.
2. fragile, frail, perishable; slender, slight, attenuated, small; feeble, weak, ailing, unwell, infirm, sickly.
3. faint, muted, subdued, pastel, subtle.
4. difficult, ticklish, critical, precarious, *Sl.* hairy, dangerous.
5. perceptive, sensitive, tactful, politic, diplomatic, considerate; careful, exact, accurate, painstaking.
6. discriminating, refined, discerning, fastidious; squeamish, prudish, finical, finicky.

delicious, *adj.* **1.** delectable, tasty, dainty, appetizing, luscious, ambrosial, ambrosian, flavorful, epicurean; succulent, juicy, rich; nectareous, nectarean, sweet, tender; palatable, toothsome, *Scot.* gustable.
2. fragrant, odoriferous, aromatic, perfumy, perfumed, scented; sweet, sweet-smelling.
3. delightful, enjoyable, pleasing, pleasurable, pleasant, agreeable; gratifying, satisfying; charming, enchanting, ravishing; exquisite, delicate, nice; exciting, titillating.

delight, *v.* **1.** gratify, gladden, please, cheer, suit; thrill, excite, tickle, *Inf.* tickle pink; titillate; please highly, afford pleasure to, fill with joy, ravish; captivate, charm, enchant, entrance; transport, enrapture, enthrall, fascinate, bewitch, ensorcell; entertain, amuse, divert, refresh.
2. *Usu.* **delight in** enjoy, appreciate, love, like; relish, savor, revel in, indulge in, feast on, delectate, *Inf.* smack one's lips over, *Inf.* get a kick from, *Inf.* eat up; bask in, luxuriate in, wallow in.
—*n.* **3.** pleasure, joy, gratification, *Inf.* paradise, *Inf.* heaven, *Inf.* thrill, *Inf.* kick; gladness, happiness, bliss, rejoicing, felicity, content; elation, jubilation, exhilaration, exultation; ecstasy, transport, ravishment, rapture, delirium; enchantment, charm, gaiety.

delighted, *adj.* pleased, happy, gladdened, elated, joyous, jubilant, ecstatic, thrilled; beaming, blooming, overjoyed, gladsome, content, *Inf.* in clover, *Inf.* jumping for joy, *Inf.* pleased as punch, *Inf.* tickled pink, *Inf.* feeling high *or* good; enraptured, ravished, transported, in heaven *or* paradise, carried away; charmed, enchanted, captivated, entranced.

delightful, *adj.* **1.** delectable, delicious, enticing, tempting, inviting; joyous, cheering, enjoyable, pleasurable, welcome, gratifying, pleasure-giving.
2. thrilling, titillating, exciting; fascinating, enchanting, captivating, ravishing, enrapturing, transporting.
3. attractive, charming, prepossessing, engaging, winning; agreeable, congenial, amiable, winsome; lovely, heavenly.

delineate, *v.* **1.** sketch, draft, outline roughly, block in *or* out; trace, figure, contour, draw the lines of; draw, design, diagram, draw a diagram of, chart, map *or* map out.
2. portray in words, depict, define, describe, *Archaic.* limn; outline verbally, paint a mental picture, set forth in words.

delineation, *n.* **1.** chart, diagram, design, plan, map; sketch, tracing, rough draft, outline; lines, contour, shape, figure, form, profile, silhouette; drawing, portrait, picture, depiction, representation, rendition.
2. description, depiction, mental image *or* picture; verbal outline, account, report, relation, narration, story, tale.

delinquency, *n.* **1.** dereliction, negligence, *Law.* nonfeasance, omission, failure, default; remissness, faithlessness, carelessness; wrongdoing, malefaction, malfeasance, misfeasance, *Chiefly Law.* malversation.
2. guilt, blame, fault; culpability, reprehensibility, criminality; crime, lawbreaking, wrong.
3. misdeed, misstep, offense, indiscretion, misdemeanor, infraction, violation; misconduct, misbehavior, disobedience, mischievousness; sin, transgression, trespass, wrong, peccadillo, venial sin.

delinquent, *adj.* **1.** negligent, neglectful, derelict, faithless, careless, remiss, slack; guilty, culpable, blameworthy, reprehensible.
2. overdue, past due, due, in arrear; behind, back, late, tardy; unsettled, unpaid, owing, outstanding.
—*n.* **3.** juvenile delinquent, misdemeanant, malefactor, misdoer; culprit, criminal, offender, youthful offender, wrongdoer, lawbreaker; hooligan, rascal, ruffian, hoodlum; roughneck, rowdy, *Sl.* hood, tough, bully, *Sl.* hard guy, *Australian Sl.* larrikin; truant, rapscallion, *Inf.* scalawag, *Inf.* scofflaw; urchin, scamp, mischief-maker, bad boy.

delirious, *adj.* **1.** deranged, unhinged, mad, *Inf.* out of *or* off one's head; irrational, incoherent, raving, ranting, babbling.
2. wild, wild-eyed, distracted, beside oneself, out of one's wits, frantic, frenzied, rabid, hysterical; hot, feverish, in a fever, febrile, flushed, burning; ecstatic, transported, carried away.

delirium, *n.* **1.** (*all usu. temporary*) insanity, madness, derangement; incoherence, ranting, raving, ranting and raving, babbling.
2. passion, fever, frenzy, fury, rage, furor; craze, hysteria; ecstasy, transport, rapture, abandon, intoxication.

deliver, *v.* **1.** transfer, turn over, hand over, pass-over, *Inf.* fork up, *Inf.* fork out *or* over, present; convey, send, transmit, remit, forward; make over, bequeath; yield, surrender, cede, concede, grant, relinquish, waive.
2. utter, voice, speak, enunciate, recite; express, declare, pronounce; communicate, impart, announce, proclaim, promulgate, publish.
3. direct, deal, put forth, project, launch; throw, pitch, cast, hurl; discharge, fire, shoot, eject, expel, emit.
4. liberate, emancipate, manumit, set free, release; disburden, unload, disencumber, disentangle, extricate, free; rescue, save, redeem, ransom; preserve, keep, protect, help, succor.
5. *Informal.* come through, do as expected; finish successfully, produce the promised results.

deliverance, *n.* **1.** liberation, emancipation, manumission, setting free, release, extrication, escape; rescue, salvation, redemption, ransom; absolution, pardon, acquittance; reprieve, respite, armistice, truce.
2. pronouncement, declaration, proclamation, formal statement, announcement, report; judgment, sentence, verdict.

delivery, *n.* **1.** transferal, transference, transmission, conveyance, dispatch, shipment; intrusting, handing over, giving over, giving up, surrender, rendition, relinquishment, resignation.
2. distribution, allotment, allocation, apportionment, dispensation, issuance.
3. utterance, speech, elocution; intonation, articulation, enunciation, pronunciation; style, manner, expression, execution, performance, presentation.
4. liberation, emancipation, deliverance. See **deliverance** (*def.* **1**).
5. parturition, childbirth, giving birth; childbed, accouchement, lying-in, confinement, labor, travail, throes; midwifery, obstetrics.

delude, *v.* deceive, mislead, misguide, misinform; fool, take in, throw dust in [s.o.'s] eyes, pull the wool over [s.o.'s] eyes, *Inf.* slip *or* pass [s.t.] over on, *Inf.* lead [s.o.] up the garden path; cozen, dupe, gull, defraud, cheat; rook, victimize, *Archaic.* chouse, bilk, swindle; pass off, palm off, impose upon, pull a fast one, *Inf.* throw a curve; humbug, gammon, bluff, juggle, have [s.t.] up one's sleeve, *Inf.* flimflam; hoodwink, trick, outwit, bamboozle, overreach; entrap, ensnare, enmesh; beguile, seduce, bait, decoy, lead on, take for a ride, *Inf.* fake [s.o.] out, *Inf.* rope [s.o.] in, *Inf.* string along; *All Inf.* fast-talk, flam, hype, jive, buffalo, bulldoze; *All Sl.* con, snow, suck in, sucker in, murphy; betray, play false, double-cross, two-time, *Sl.* shaft, *Sl.* cross [s.o.] up.

deluge, *n.* **1.** flood, flash flood, inundation, *Brit.* spate, overflow, freshet; downpour, drenching rain, cloudburst.
2. avalanche, cataclysm, catastrophe, disaster, calamity, debacle.
—*v.* **3.** flood, inundate, overrun, overflow; swamp, submerge, engulf, drown, bury, overwhelm.

delusion, *n.* **1.** misconception, misapprehension, misunderstanding, misinterpretation, misconstruction, misbelief; fallacy, error, mistake; self-deception, fool's paradise; illusion, false impression, myth, ignis fatuus, will-o'-the-wisp, bubble; hallucination, vision, mirage, dream; apparition, chimera, fancy, phantasm, phantasmagoria, specter.
2. deception, trick, stratagem, ruse, artifice, pretense, *Obs.* cog; contrivance, wile, subterfuge, misrepresentation; fake, sham, hoax, swindle, shuck, feint, blind; fraud, imposture, imposition, *Law.* covin, humbug, *Inf.* flimflam, *Inf.* flam; falsehood, lie, fib, untruth, prevarication.
3. magic, conjuring, legerdemain, prestidigitation, sleight of hand, trickery; jugglery, trumpery, dupery, hocus-pocus, shenanigan.

delusive, *adj.* **1.** deceptive, misleading, fallacious, illusory, illusive, spurious, factitious; evasive, dodgy, elusive, slippery, shifty; specious, sham, bogus, counterfeit, mock, pseudo, artificial; false, unreal, make-believe, feigned, pretended; imaginary, fancied, fantastic, chimerical, visionary.
2. deceitful, untrustworthy, underhanded, crooked, dishonest, fraudulent; insincere, disingenuous, mendacious, untruthful, hollow; double-dealing, artful, crafty, cunning, sly, snaky, foxy; two-faced, Janus-faced, hypocritical.

delve, *v.* search, research, investigate, search out; unearth, dig up, hunt up *or* out, ferret out; pursue, track, trail, follow the trail, trace; explore, probe, penetrate, sound, fathom, look into, go deeply into; peer, pry, look behind the scenes, make inquiry, fish for; rummage, ransack, turn upside down.

demagogue, *n.* rabble rouser, agitator, firebrand, haranguer, soapbox orator; wrangler, malcontent, troublemaker.

demagoguery, *n.* **1.** demagogism, rabble rousing; agitation, fomentation, incitation, exhortation, instigation, provocation, trouble making.
2. fanaticism, dogmatism, bigotry, jingoism, chauvinism; red scare, McCarthyism.

demand, *v.* **1.** claim, lay claims to, claim as a right; solicit, order, requisition; dun, extort; inquire for *or* after, seek, make inquiry.
2. ask, call for, insist on, importune, clamor, cry; supplicate, entreat, obtest, adjure, impetrate; invoke, press, urge; exact, impose, sue.
3. require, need, want, lack, stand *or* be in need of; call for, ache for.
—*n.* **4.** request, requirement, order, direction, command, charge, bidding, behest, call; requisition, draft, application; inquiry, suit, petition, ultimatum, mandate, injunction, precept, decree; exaction, imposition.
5. want, need, requirement, necessity, essentiality, exigency.
6. **in demand** popular, sought after, fashionable, celebrated, admired, in vogue, *Inf.* the people's choice, *Inf.* the in thing.

demarcation, *n.* **1.** border, boundary, bound, bourn; pale, line, limit, frontier; distinction, differentiation.
2. separation, delimitation, definition, marking off; division, partition.

demean, *v.* **1.** degrade, debase, vitiate, lower in dignity *or* standing *or* rank, reduce, depreciate, devalue, demote, depose, discredit; shame, disgrace, dishonor, humble, humiliate, mortify, *Inf.* put down; belittle, deprecate, disparage, decry, deflate.
2. (*all of oneself*) comport, deport, bear, conduct, carry, act, acquit, steer, manage, maintain; behave, play *or* do one's part.

demeanor, *n.* **1.** conduct, behavior, deportment. See **deportment** (*defs.* **1, 2**).
2. physiognomy, facial expression, countenance, visage.

demented, *adj.* **1.** insane, crazy, crazed, mad, lunatic, lunatical, deranged; of unsound mind, *Latin. non compos mentis*, mentally ill; psychotic, schizophrenic, *Sl.* schizo; daft, *Inf.* daffy, unbalanced, touched, *Inf.* unglued, *Inf.* half-baked, *Brit. Sl.* bonkers, unhinged, distracted; dazed, moon-struck, possessed, infatuated; odd, peculiar, queer, bizarre, *Chiefly Brit. Inf.* potty, *Inf.* dotty, *Inf.* crackpot; brainsick, *Sl.* kooky, *Sl.* meshuga; *All Sl.* balmy, dippy, batty, bats, cuckoo, buggy, bughouse, bugs, screwy, wacky, wacko, goofy, loony, squirrelly, bananas, nuts, nutty, nutty as a fruitcake.
2. out of one's head *or* mind *or* senses *or* wits, *Scot.* redwood, *Sl.* loco, mad as a hatter, mad as a March hare, far-gone, stark raving mad; not all there, not quite right, not right upstairs; *Inf.* out in left field, *Sl.* in outer space, *Sl.* in orbit, *Inf.* off the wall; *Inf.* cracked, *Inf.* mental, *Sl.* off one's rocker, *Sl.* out of one's tree, *Sl.* off one's trolley, *Brit. Sl.* off one's chump; *All Sl.* have bats in one's belfry, have a few buttons missing, have a few loose screws.
3. maniacal, hysterical, madding, *Archaic.* wood, delirious; frantic, frenzied, frenetic; ranting, raving, storming, foaming at the mouth, convulsing; beside oneself, at one's wit's end; out of control, uncontrollable, unrestrainable, corybantic, *Inf.* haywire, berserk, rabid, wild; violent, stormy, fierce, turbulent.
4. absurd, silly, inane, fatuous, crackbrained, foolish; irrational, wild-eyed, illogical, unreasonable; senseless, nonsensical, pointless; ridiculous, laughable, ludicrous; asinine, anserine, idiotic, *Inf.* moronic, imbecilic; childish, puerile, immature.
5. stupid, simple-minded, bird-brained, feeble-minded, dull-witted; harebrained, light-minded, light-headed, giddy; scatterbrained, absent-minded; confused, muddled, bemused.

demimondaine, *n.* **1.** demirep, cocotte, loose woman, fallen woman, harlot, whore, hussy, slut, slattern, tramp, vamp, wanton, white slave, *Sl.* bitch, *Sl.* broad, *Sl.* chippy.
2. prostitute, lady of the evening, woman of the profession, Mrs. Warren, *Fr. fille de joie*; trollop, strumpet, *Archaic.* wench, trull, drab, quean, painted woman, woman of the streets, streetwalker, bar girl, *Inf.* pick-up, call girl, Cyprian; *All Sl.* cat, tart, hustler, bim, moll, hooker, floozie, working girl, *Brit. Sl.* bird, *Mexican Sl.* caliente; madam, bawd, procuress, pander.
3. paramour, courtesan, mistress, concubine, kept woman, *Sl.* doxy.
4. temptress, siren, seductress, Jezebel, Delilah; flirt, coquette, minx; adventuress, hetaera.

demise, *n.* **1.** death, decease, expiration; end, termination. See **death** (*def.* **1**).
2. *Law.* transfer, transference, conveyance, alienation, abalienation; making over, transmission, quitclaim, cession, transposition; bequeathal, legacy.

democracy, *n.* republic, government by the people, representative government, constitutional government, popular government, self-government, commonwealth.

democratic, *adj.* representative, Jeffersonian, republican, popular, Populist, proletarian, of the people; of, by, and for the people.

demolish, *v.* **1.** raze, tear down, pull down, take down, bring down, break down, throw down, beat down, batter down; cast down, knock down, fling down, hurl down, precipitate, *Inf.* spill, tumble, topple; fell, lay level, prostrate, level, bulldoze, flatten; cut down, chop down, hew down.
2. devastate, desolate, lay waste; ravage, wreak havoc upon, destroy, ruin, *Dial.* ruinate, bring to ruin, lay in ruins; wreck, *Sl.* total, knock to pieces, dash to pieces, smash, waste, *Sl.* trash, reduce to nothing; undo, unmake, unbuild, dismantle, disassemble, take apart.
3. pulverize, crush, squelch, *Sl.* smush, mash; crash, shatter, batter, break; fracture, splinter, tear, crack, split, rend, tear apart, wrench apart; mutilate, mangle, maim, make mincemeat of; mar, damage, spoil, mark, spot, stain; disfigure, scar, deface, blemish.
4. annihilate, discreate, exterminate, extirpate, extinguish; erase, efface, eradicate, expunge, cancel, obliterate; excise, cut, cut out, cut off; blot out, strike out, stamp out, crush out, wipe out, rub out; kill, kill off, slay, slaughter; murder, finish, finish off, *Sl.* do in, *Sl.* zap, sacrifice, mow down.
5. purge, get rid of, leave no vestige *or* trace of, liquidate, remove, dispose of; terminate, dissolve, bring to an end, put an end to, do away with; explode, burst, blast, blow up.
6. quash, quell, suppress, squelch, crush, vanquish, squash; nip, nip in the bud, *Inf.* put the kibosh on; overthrow, overturn, overwhelm, subvert, cause the downfall of, defeat, conquer.
7. devour, swallow up, gobble up, consume, gorge, eat away, bolt, stuff; guzzle, gulp, drown.

demolition, *n.* **1.** razing, tearing down, pulling down, taking down, bringing down, breaking down, throwing down, beating down; casting down, knocking down, flinging down, hurling down, precipitation; felling, leveling, prostration; cutting down, chopping down, hewing down.
2. devastation, desolation, laying waste, gutting, wipe-out; ravagement, havoc, holocaust, destruction, dilapidation, ruination, bringing to ruin, laying in ruins; wrecking, wreckage, knocking to pieces, dashing to pieces, smashing; dismantling, disassembly, taking apart.
3. pulverization, crushing, squelching, *Sl.* smushing, mashing; crashing, shattering, battering, breaking, breakup; fracturing, tearing apart, wrenching apart, cracking, splitting; mutilation, mangling, making mincemeat of; marring, damage, spoilage, mark, spotting, stain; disfigurement, scarring, defacement.
4. annihilation, discreation, extermination, extirpation, extinguishment, extinction; erasure, erasion, effacement, eradication, expunction, cancellation, obliteration; excision, cutting out, cutting off; blotting out, striking out, stamping out, crushing out, wiping out, rubbing out; killing, slaying, slaughter; murder, finishing off, *Sl.* zapping, sacrifice, mowing down.
5. purgation, getting rid of, leaving no vestige *or* trace of, liquidation, removal; termination, dissolution, bringing to an end, putting an end to, doing away with.
6. quashing, quelling, suppression, squelching, crushing, vanquishment, squashing; nipping, nipping in the bud, *Inf.* putting the kibosh on; overthrow, overturn, subversion, defeat, conquest.

demon, *n.* **1.** devil, evil spirit, cacodemon, *Arab. Myth.* afreet, *Islamic Myth.* genie *or* jinn *or* djinn, *Class. Myth.* Alastor, Astarotte; fiend, ogre, ghoul, monster, vampire, harpy; werewolf, wolfman, lycanthrope, *Fr. loup-garou*; incubus, succubus, nightmare, siren, nymph, *Slavic Myth.* rusalka; troll, sprite, *Ger. Folklore.* nix, elf, *Irish Folklore.* leprechaun; pixy, brownie, imp, dwarf; goblin, host, *Irish Folklore.* banshee, barghest; hobgoblin, bogy, Puck, boogeyman, boogey, spook.
2. brute, savage, beast, monster, hellhound, bar-

barian; Hun, Goth, Vandal, Mongol, Tartar; blackguard, rogue, scoundrel, knave, villain, thug, Mohock; hooligan, hoodlum, roughneck, rowdy, bully, *Sl.* hood; lecher, goat, hog, swine, wolf, tiger.

3. human dynamo, hard-worker, pusher, hustler, go-getter, *Inf.* eager beaver; man of action, powerhouse, *Inf.* live wire, *Inf.* busy bee, Stakhanovite, overdoer, doer.

4. daemon, eudemon, guardian angel, fairy godmother, tutelary saint *or* deity, numen, genius, familiar spirit.

demoniac, *adj.* See **demonic.**

demonic, *adj.* **1.** possessed, daemonic, demon-ridden, lycanthropic; bewitched, bedeviled, hoodooed, voodooed, hexed, accursed, cursed; maddened, moonstruck, crazed, demented, raving, rabid; delirious, maniacal, lunatic, mad, stark raving mad, stark staring mad; deranged, *Fr. aliéné, Fr. fou*; frenzied, corybantic, frenetic, fanatical, dithyrambic.

2. diabolic, diabolical, devilish, fiendish, ghoulish; satanic, Mephistophelian, demonian, demoniac, demoniacal, cacodemonic; infernal, hellish.

3. damnable, execrable, abominable, horrible, horrid, hideous, monstrous, atrocious; base, vile, odious, obnoxious, villainous, sinister; wicked, iniquitous, evil, sinful, impious, *Obs.* scelerous, black-hearted, corrupt, depraved, *Archaic.* facinorous; reprobate, nefarious, flagitious, unspeakable, heinous; profligate, immoral, dissolute, vitiated, perverted, perverse; pestilential, malevolent, malicious, malign, maleficent, venomous, virulent; dire, black, dreadful, baleful.

demonstrable, *adj.* provable, evincible, attestable, confirmable, substantiable, establishable, verifiable; inferable, deductable, self-evident, axiomatic; conclusive, decisive, positive, certain, undeniable, unquestionable, indubitable, indisputable, irrefutable, incontestable; real, actual, factual.

demonstrate, *v.* **1.** prove, substantiate, sustain, *Inf.* go to show; fix, settle, set at rest; establish, determine, ascertain.

2. describe, illustrate, show how, give an idea of; explain, explicate, expound.

3. manifest, exhibit, evidence, evince, display, show, exemplify, *Scot. and North Eng.* kithe; cite, name, document, bring home to.

4. protest, sit-in, rally, march; strike, picket, boycott.

demonstration, *n.* **1.** proof, substantiation, conclusive evidence, sure sign; verification, confirmation, certification, authentication, validation, affirmation.

2. description, explanation, elucidation, exposition, clarification.

3. display, exhibit, exhibition, manifestation, show, showing, presentation; retrospective.

4. example, demo, representation, illustration, exemplification; citation, reference; instance, item, case, particular.

5. protest, sit-in, teach-in; rally, march, parade.

demonstrative, *adj.* **1.** open, expressive, unreserved, unrestrained, unreticent, communicative; emotional, feeling, loving, affectionate, tender, warm.

2. illustrative, evincive, indicative, designative, exhibitive, significant, symptomatic; explanatory, explicative, expository, clarifying, illuminating, elucidative.

3. material, telling, convincing, overwhelming, damning; decisive, certain, sure, absolute, incontrovertible, indisputable, irrefutable, incontestable.

demoralization, *n.* **1.** destruction of morale, disheartenment, taking the fight *or* heart out of, *Inf.* taking the spunk out of; crushing, breaking down, unmanning, subdual; paralysis, crippling, devitalization, enervation, weakening, loss of courage.

2. bewilderment, confusion, fluster, ruffle, disturbance, perturbation, disconcertment, discomfiture; agitation, upset, *Inf.* dither, *Inf.* tizzy; fright, fear, trepidation, panic, rout.

3. corruption, debauchedness, perversion, depravedness, depravity, depravation, vitiation, lowering, debasement; adulteration, contamination, pollution, spoiling, defilement.

demoralize, *v.* **1.** destroy the morale of, take the fight out of, take the heart out of, take the spirit out of, *Inf.* take the spunk out of, *Inf.* take the starch out of, *Dial.* take the tuck out of; dispirit, dishearten, daunt, subdue, break down, unman; crush, render powerless, paralyze; cripple, devitalize, enervate, weaken, enfeeble; depress, deject.

2. bewilder, confuse, fluster, ruffle, disturb, perturb, shake *or* shake up, disconcert, unnerve, discomfit; agitate, upset, frighten, panic, throw into a panic, rout.

3. undermine the morals of, corrupt, debauch, pervert, deprave, vitiate, lower, debase; adulterate, contaminate, pollute, spoil, defile.

demoralized, *adj.* **1.** spiritless, dispirited, disheartened, *Archaic.* heartless; daunted, subdued, broken, unmanned, crushed; powerless, paralyzed, crippled, devitalized, enervated, weakened; depressed, dejected, downcast.

2. bewildered, confused, flustered, ruffled, disturbed, perturbed, shaken, disconcerted, unnerved, discomfited; agitated, upset, *Inf.* in a dither, *Inf.* in a tizzy; frightened, afraid, scared, panicked, routed.

3. corrupt, bad, sinful, wicked, immoral, dissolute, profligate; debauched, perverted, depraved, reprobate; vitiated, debased, base, low, degenerate, degraded; adulterated, contaminated, polluted, spoiled, defiled.

demote, *v.* downgrade, lower *or* reduce in rank, degrade, humble, *Inf.* take *or* knock down a peg or two; declass, break *or* strip of rank, disrate, cashier, *Mil.* drum out, *Mil. Sl.* bust, *Inf.* kick upstairs; depose, unseat, dethrone, *Rare.* disenthrone, uncrown, defrock *or* unfrock; oust, dispossess, displace, disbar, expel, exile; dismiss *or* remove from office, discharge, *Inf.* rif, *Inf.* fire, *Sl.* get rid of, *Sl.* can, *Sl.* sack, *Sl.* give the boot, give the pink slip, *Inf.* give [s.o.] his walking papers, *Sl.* turn out, *Sl.* bounce.

demulcent, *adj.* soothing, mollifying, appeasing, pacifying, calming, sedative, comforting; emollient, softening, relaxing, easing; relieving, alleviative, alleviatory, assuasive, mitigative, mitigatory, lenitive; mild, gentle, soft.

demur, *v.* **1.** object, take exception, be unwilling, dissent, disapprove; protest, remonstrate, expostulate, wrangle, dispute, contest.

2. hesitate, scruple, boggle, cavil, hang back, doubt; waver, waffle, fudge, dodge, duck; hold fire, shrink from, shy at, pause.

—n. **3.** objection, dissent, remonstrance, demurral; hesitation, doubt, unwillingness, qualm, scruple, misgiving.

demure, *adj.* **1.** shy, meek, modest, reserved, retiring, diffident, bashful, coy; reticent, taciturn, quiet; timid, timorous, fearful, shrinking, like a shrinking violet, blushing.

2. undemonstrative, impassive, indifferent; unpresumptuous, introverted, withdrawn, self-effacing, constrained.

3. puritanical, prim, priggish, prudish, goody-goody, prissy, finicky, overmodest, self-righteous, affected; chaste, virtuous, virginal, strait-laced.

4. sober, sedate, staid, grave, serious, solemn; austere, stoic, uncomplaining.

den, *n.* **1.** lair, cave, hollow, dugout, hole, grotto; niche, nook, nest, recess; covert, aerie, roost, hive, nidus.

2. den of iniquity, *Inf.* dive, *Sl.* joint; roadhouse, speakeasy, *U.S. Sl.* barrelhouse; bawdy-house, house of ill-repute.

3. study, library, sanctum sanctorum, snuggery; hermitage, retreat, cubicle, cell, cloister.

denial, *n.* **1.** contradiction, gainsay, disaffirmation, negation, denegation; disavowal, unsaying, repudiation, disclaimer, disclamation, *Rhet.* apophasis; retraction, recantation, (*usu. under oath*) abjuration.

2. refusal, rejection, turndown, declination; rebuff, repulse; forbiddance, veto, disallowance, prohibition, proscription, disapproval, *Inf.* no-go; thumbs down, deaf ear.

3. renunciation, renouncement, disowning; disinheriting, disinheritance, disheriting.

4. refutation, answer, disproof, confutation; protest, objection, contravention; disagreement, dissent, demur, demurral.

5. disbelief, unbelief, skepticism, doubt, distrust.

denigrate, *v.* **1.** defame, vituperate, vilify, vilipend, scandalize, run down, revile, malign, impugn, gibbet; criticize, pull to pieces, cut to pieces, cut up, shred, give a bad name, speak ill *or* evil of, *Sl.* do a hatchet job on; slander, calumniate, libel, asperse, impute, traduce; injure, abuse, assail, stab, backbite, *Sl.* badmouth, engage in personalities; slur, sully, defile, smear, smirch, besmirch, soil, drag through the mud *or* mire, heap dirt upon, *Sl.* dump on.

2. black, blacken, darken; shade, shadow, overshadow, overcast.

denizen, *n.* inhabitant, habitant, resident, dweller, occupier, occupant, householder, addressee, *Archaic.* inhabiter.

denomination, *n.* **1.** name, title, style, appellation, designation; epithet, appellative, by-word, label, tag, *Sl.* handle, *Sl.* moniker.

2. variety, genus, species, class; kind, sort, ilk, type; nature, character, stamp, breed, brand, color, stripe, grain; make, mark, cast, shape, form.

3. sect, school, persuasion, communion, ism, faith, church; body, group, association, order, society, fellowship, fraternity, brotherhood.

4. identification, definition, denotation, specification, signification; naming, calling, dubbing, christening.

denote, *v.* **1.** indicate, show, point out; signify, mark, note; symbolize, betoken, represent, stand for, typify.

2. mean, denominate, designate, name; connote, allude, bring to mind; imply, suggest, intimate.

denouement, *n.* **1.** final resolution, solution, conclusion, finale, final act *or* scene, last part *or* stage, capper; final touch *or* stroke, consummation, perfection, completion; close, end, termination, finish.

2. climax, culmination, high point, peak.

3. outcome, upshot, final issue, result, effect, consequence.

denounce, *v.* **1.** criticize, condemn, denunciate, arraign, animadvert on *or* upon, reprobate, remonstrate, proscribe; decry, inveigh against, rail against, fulminate against, declaim against, attack, assail; disapprove, deprecate, disparage, belittle.

2. upbraid, reproach, reprove, rebuke, reprehend; castigate, vituperate, reprimand, admonish; chide, scold, carp at, berate, *Inf.* dress down, *Sl.* blast; revile, impugn, call into question; stigmatize, brand, gibbet, asperse, cast aspersions on, malign, slander, defame, vilify; blacklist, blackball, ostracize.

3. accuse, charge, indict, *Law.* arraign, *Law.* impute, incriminate, criminate, impeach, *Rare.* implead; implicate, inculpate, inform against, (*of an innocent person*) *Inf.* frame, *Chiefly Scot.* delate; cite, summon, serve with a summons *or* with papers; file charges, bring to justice, take [s.o.] to court.

dense, *adj.* **1.** thickset, closely packed, crowded, stuffed, crammed, jammed together, compressed, pushed together, consolidated; compact, tight, close, close-knit, tight-knit, cohesive; condensed, concentrated, soupy, thick, heavy; solid, massive, impenetrable, impermeable, impassable.

2. thick-headed, *Inf.* thick, thick-witted, slow, stupid, slow-witted, dull, dull-witted; stolid, obtuse, crass, gross, Boeotian, bovine, blockish, lumpish.

3. intense, concentrated, powerful, strong, extreme.

4. opaque, nontransparent, not translucent.

density, *n.* **1.** denseness, compactness, crowdedness, tightness, closeness, cohesiveness; thickness, richness, substance, body; bulk, massiveness, heaviness, weight, mass, solidity, solidness; impenetrability, impenetrableness, impermeability, impermeableness, impassability, impassableness.

2. thick-headedness, thick-wittedness, *Inf.* thickness, stupidity, slowness, slow-wittedness, dullness, dullwittedness; obtuseness, stolidness, stolidity, bovinity, crassness.

dent, *n.* **1.** dint, hollow, depression, dip, trough, crater, concavity; hole, cavity, excavation, pit.

2. dimple, indentation, indent; cut, scratch, scrape, mark, flaw, chip; notch, nick, deep recess, groove, furrow.

—*v.* **3.** make a dent in, dint, indent, push in *or* down, press in *or* down, depress.

4. cut, chip, scratch, scrape, mark, flaw; notch, nick, groove, furrow.

denude, *v.* strip, denudate, nakedize, bare, lay bare, expose; divest, uncover, disrobe, unclothe, undress, unsheath.

denunciation, *n.* **1.** fulmination, condemnation, criticism, censure; disapproval, disapprobation, reprobation, reprehension, objection; animadversion, *Inf.* brickbat, aspersion, obloquy; tirade, philippic, diatribe.

2. reproof, reproach, rebuke, reprimand; upbraiding, castigation, objurgation, vituperation; scolding, dressing down, tongue-lashing, *Sl.* hell.

3. accusation, accusal, charge, blame; imputation, incrimination, crimination, inculpation; informing against, squealing, finking, *Sl.* ratting, (*both of an innocent person*) *Inf.* framing, *Inf.* frame-up.

denunciatory, *adj.* censorious, reproachful, condemnatory, fulminatory; damnatory, maledictory, comminatory; accusatory, imputative, incriminatory, recriminatory.

deny, *v.* **1.** dispute, gainsay, controvert, naysay, disbelieve; contradict, traverse, nullify, negate, disaffirm; disprove, confute, refute, discredit; protest, oppose, contravene; object, demur, refuse assent, disagree.

2. refuse, reject, turn down, decline, disallow; forbid, prohibit, proscribe, veto, disapprove; negative, say no to, turn thumbs down, turn a deaf ear.

3. disavow, forswear, disclaim; retract, unsay, recant, take back, back-pedal.

deodorant, *n.* deodorizer, antiperspirant, *Sl.* odoreater; air freshener, air conditioner; disinfectant, fumigator.

deodorize, *v.* ventilate, aerate, air, aerify; freshen, sweeten, refresh, air-condition; disinfect, fumigate, sanitate, sanitize, purify.

depart, *v.* **1.** leave, go away, go off, be off, (*usu. imperative*) *Inf.* beat it, *Inf.* run along, *Inf.* scram, *Inf.* buzz along, (*usu. imperative*) *Inf.* buzz off, *Inf.* make oneself scarce, *Inf.* shove off, *Sl.* split, *Sl.* cut out, *Brit. Sl.* bugger off, *Sl.* vamoose.

2. go forth, issue forth, set off, set out, *Inf.* hit the road, start out, sally forth, march out; get going, get under way, entrain, embus, enplane, embark, set sail, ship out, weigh anchor.

3. exit, make an exit, take oneself off, take one's departure *or* leave; bid farewell, bid adieu, say good-by, bid godspeed, decamp, break camp, pull out.

4. flee, escape, abscond, fly, bolt, run, take to one's heels, cut and run, *Sl.* light out, *Inf.* hightail it, *Sl.* hotfoot it; skip, run out, *Brit. Sl.* do a moonlight flit.

5. recede, retrocede, ebb, return, go back; fall back, retire, retreat, withdraw.

6. diverge, branch, fork, deviate, digress; swerve, veer; turn aside, move away; differ.

7. pass away, expire, vanish, disappear, *Sl.* go poof; evanesce, fade away, melt away, dissolve; die, decease, give up the ghost, *Euph.* pass on.

department, *n.* **1.** division, section, compartment, segment; group, head, class; branch, subdivision, bureau, office, agency.

2. region, territory, province, state, (*in the Soviet Union*) oblast; shire, county, duchy, wapentake, canton; ward, diocese, parish; quarter, zone, precinct, arrondissement, commune, district, township; bailiwick, neighborhood, purlieus; circuit, orb, area, scene, beat, terrain, *Sl.* turf.

3. sphere, sphere of activity *or* influence, realm, circle, domain; control, authority, jurisdiction, responsibility, sway, empery; line, field, walk of life, station, berth; theater, arena, field of action.

departure, *n.* **1.** leaving, going away, starting out, setting out *or* off; takeoff, embarkation, sailing; exit, leave, parting, separation, farewell, adieu, good-by, congé.

2. flight, escape, running off, running away, *Sl.* splitting, taking off; retreat, withdrawal, retirement.

3. divergence, branching off, forking off; deviation, veering, swerving, declination, declension, aberration; variation, change, shift, difference, novelty, innovation; digression.

4. death, demise, decease, dying; *All Euph.* passing, passing away *or* on.

depend, *v.* **1.** dangle, pendulate, hang, hang down, droop, draggle, overhand, swing, flap.

2. turn, hinge, be dependent on, be subject to, be contingent upon.

3. depend on trust in, rely on, count on, lean on; swear by, bank on, pin one's faith on, have full confidence in; build upon, support oneself by, earn a living at.

dependable, *adj.* trustworthy, honest, honorable, aboveboard, as good as one's word, honest as the day is long; reliable, trusty, sure, unfailing, strong, abiding, steady, firm, *Inf.* all-right, *Inf.* O.K.; established, reputable, secure, safe, stable; responsible, principled, conscientious; faithful, true, steadfast, true-blue, devoted, *Inf.* Johnny-on-the-spot.

dependence, *n.* **1.** connection, attachment, contingency, reference, bearing, relevancy, relationship; interconnection, interdependence, mutual dependence.

2. subordination, subservience, deference, submission; subjugation, subjection, servility, servitude, yoke, vassalage.

3. reliance, trust, faith, belief; confidence, assurance, expectation, hope.

4. support, mainstay, stay, truss, buttress, pillar; shore, prop, staff, crutch, anchor.

5. helplessness, weakness, defenselessness, vulnerability.

dependency, *n.* **1.** dependence, connection; subordination, subjection; reliance; helplessness. See **dependence** (*defs.* **1-3, 5**).

2. appendage, attachment, auxiliary, subsidiary, adjunct, subject.

3. colony, province, subject territory, protectorate; fief, fee, duchy, dukedom, margravate, seigniory.

dependent, *adj.* **1.** pendent, hanging down, pensile, pendulous; dangling, drooping, hanging, suspended.

2. clinging, leaning, relying, counting on; helpless, weak, vulnerable, defenseless, poor, indigent; minor, youthful, immature, *Inf.* tied to one's mother's apron strings.

3. conditional, conditioned, provisory, provisional, contingent; concomitant, corollary, ancillary, accessory to.

4. subordinate, subject to, subservient; at the disposal of, in the hands of; sustained by, held up by, supported by.

—n. **5.** child, youth, youngster, minor, *Inf.* deduction, *Inf.* just a kid, *Inf.* mamma's boy, charge; apprentice, protégé, pupil, student, *Inf.* teacher's pet.

6. pensioner, grantee, retainer; follower, satellite, hanger-on, henchman, puppet, creature, lackey, flunky, *Sl.* stooge; parasite, sycophant, *Inf.* camp-follower; subordinate, underling, hireling, mercenary; subject, bondsman, serf, liegeman, thrall, slave; minion, vassal, yeoman, churl; servant, servitor, menial.

depict, *v.* **1.** delineate, sketch, draft, outline roughly; trace, figure, contour, draw the lines of; draw, design, diagram, chart, map *or* map out; portray, paint, represent.

2. portray in words, describe, characterize, define, detail, *Archaic.* limn; outline verbally, paint a mental picture, picture, set forth in words; narrate, relate, recite, recount, romance; record, chronicle.

deplete, *v.* exhaust, use up, consume, spend, run out of; evacuate, empty, unload; drain, bleed; weaken, enervate, impoverish; reduce, decrease, lessen.

depleted, *adj.* exhausted, used up, consumed, spent, worn out, drained, bled; evacuated, emptied, empty, vacant; bare, naked, barren; bereft of, deprived of, devoid of, short of, out of; in want, without resources; reduced, lessened, decreased, at low ebb; weakened, enervated, impoverished.

depletion, *n.* exhaustion, consumption, using up, expenditure, spending; evacuation, emptying, voidance, purgation, purging, unloading, elimination, removal; reduction, decrease, lessening; impoverishment, drain, decrement, dissipation.

deplorable, *adj.* **1.** lamentable, regrettable, pathetic, pitiable, miserable; mournful, depressing, upsetting, disturbing, distressing; troublesome; afflicting, tormenting, woeful, wretched, unhappy, hopeless, desperate; unfortunate, tragic, unforeseeable; calamitous, heinous, outrageous, grievous, disastrous; heartbreaking, anguishing, heart-rending; somber, solemn, grave, heavy, oppressive; painful, difficult, hard, trying, troubling.

2. reprehensible, disgraceful, shameful, scandalous, opprobrious, disreputable, dishonorable; abominable, detestable, despicable, execrable, contemptible; vile, sordid, foul, base, low.

deplore, *v.* lament, mourn, grieve, sorrow, bemoan, bewail, express woe *or* distress over; suffer for, pine for, languish over; weep over, cry for, wail for, keen, shed tears for, sigh for; regret, rue, repent of.

deport, *v.* **1.** expel, banish, exile, eject, proscribe, expatriate; extradite; dislodge, evict, throw out, ship

out, kick out, *Sl.* bounce out; ostracize, blackball, send to Coventry; carry off, transport, transplant, displace, remove, relegate.
2. (*of oneself*) bear, conduct, behave, demean, comport, carry, manage; act, play one's part, steer one's course, mind one's p's and q's.

deportation, *n.* expulsion, exile, banishment, proscription, sequestration, expatriation, relegation; transplantation, ostracism, rogue's march; extradition, transportation, displacement, outlawry; removal, dislodgement, eviction.

deportment, *n.* **1.** demeanor, conduct, comportment, gest; actions, manners, behavior, etiquette; obedience, observance.
2. bearing, carriage, port, posture, stance; air, mien, manner, style, attitude; appearance, aspect, semblance, cast, guise, look, expression.

depose, *v.* **1.** remove from office, unseat, dethrone, *Rare.* disenthrone, uncrown, defrock *or* unfrock; demote, downgrade, lower *or* reduce in rank, degrade, humble, *Inf.* take *or* knock down a peg or two; declass, break *or* strip of rank, disrate, cashier, *Mil.* drum out, *Mil. Sl.* bust, *Inf.* kick upstairs.
2. oust, dispossess, displace, disbar, expel, exile; dismiss, discharge, *Inf.* rif, *Inf.* fire, *Sl.* get rid of, *Sl.* can, *Sl.* sack, *Sl.* give the boot, give the pink slip, *Inf.* give [s.o.] his walking papers, *Sl.* turn out, *Sl.* bounce.
3. give sworn testimony, declare *or* state under oath, *Law.* make a deposition, *Law.* make an affidavit; testify, bear witness to, attest to, certify; swear, affirm, aver, asseverate, assert, allege.

deposit, *v.* **1.** put, place, set, lay, (*of coins*) insert, *Archaic.* repose; put down, set down, lay down.
2. precipitate, settle, dump.
3. bank, save, hoard; store, stow, reposit, lay in, lay away, put away, squirrel away.
—*n.* **4.** silt, alluvium, precipitation, deposition, sinter, loess; moraine, scree, detritus, *Geol.* diluvium; sediment, dregs, lees; *Chem.* sublimate, *Metallurgy.* dross.
5. ore bed, quarry, dike, mineral deposit; run, vein, lode, mother lode; mine, gold mine, bonanza.
6. depository, warehouse, repository. See **depository** (*def.* **1**).

depositary, *n.* **1.** trustee, guardian, steward, *Law.* fiduciary; treasurer, banker, cashier, bursar, purser, *Rom. Hist.* quaestor.
2. depository, repository, warehouse. See **depository** (*def.* **1**).

depository, *n.* **1.** warehouse, storehouse, storeroom, depot, repository, magazine, repertory, reservoir, (*in the Orient*) godown; bank, treasury, safe, vault, safety-deposit box, coffer, locker, chest, money chest.
2. depositary, trustee; treasurer. See **depositary** (*def.* **1**).

depot, *n.* **1.** bus station, railroad station, train station, *Fr. gare, Ger. Bahnhof,* terminal, terminus; station house, stopping-place, stop.
2. storehouse, warehouse, depository, repository, magazine, cache.

deprave, *v.* corrupt, make bad, debauch, seduce, pervert, subvert, demoralize, lead astray, lead away; make worse, corrode, undermine, eat away at; vitiate, debase, abase, lower, degrade, degenerate, deteriorate; adulterate, pollute, contaminate, infect, poison; taint, stain, soil, sully, dirty; spoil, defile, desecrate, profane; abuse, violate, deflower, ravish, rape, ruin.

depraved, *adj.* **1.** corrupt, immoral, unprincipled, reprobate; perverted, warped, misguided, distorted; wicked, evil, iniquitous, sinful, vicious; villainous, miscreant, vile, foul, base, low; demoralized, deteriorated, degenerate, debased, abased, vitiated, degraded, lowered; adulterated, contaminated, polluted; defiled, desecrated, violated, unchaste, impure, unclean; tainted, stained, soiled, sullied, spoiled.
2. dissolute, profligate, licentious, abandoned, wanton, libertine, intemperate, debauched; lewd, obscene, dirty, indecent, immodest, shameless; lascivious, lecherous, *Archaic.* lickerish, lustful, libidinous; animal, animalistic, carnal, sensual.

depravity, *n.* **1.** corruption, corruptness, corruptedness, perversion, depravation; demoralization, deterioration, corrosion, degradation, debasement, abasement, vitiation, degeneration, degeneracy, degenerateness; adulteration, pollution, contamination, defilement, desecration, violation; unchastity, unchasteness, impurity, uncleanness; foulness, baseness, vileness, turpitude; criminality, wickedness, sinfulness, iniquity; wrong-doing, sin, evil-doing, crime.
2. immorality, vice, dissoluteness, profligacy, profligateness, licentiousness, license; lechery, debauchery, debauchment, intemperance, libertinism, prostitution; animalism, carnality, sensuality, lustfulness; libidinousness, lewdness, lecherousness, prurience, pruriency; obscenity, indecency, vulgarity, low-mindedness.

deprecate, *v.* **1.** censure, reproach, impeach, bring to book, call to account, cry down, slate, inveigh against, perstringe, animadvert upon, reprove, recriminate, reprehend, reprobate, pass strictures; denounce, deplore, rail, curse, condemn, anathematize, *Obs.* exprobrate; berate, upbraid, castigate, objurgate, chastise, chasten, reprimand, scold, chide, admonish, rebuke, take to task, *Inf.* dress down, lecture, *Inf.* bawl out; disapprove, disfavor, dislike, frown upon, look askance; criticize, *Inf.* knock, carp at, cavil at, peck at.
2. expostulate, remonstrate, dissuade, divert, *Archaic.* dehort, deter, discourage, demur, dishearten; warn, caution, advise *or* counsel against; protest, enter a protest, dispute, argue, *Scot.* argle-bargle, wrangle, haggle, hassle, altercate, challenge, oppose, object to, conflict with, take exception to, join issue upon.
3. belittle, detract, disparage. See **disparage** (*def.* **2**).

deprecatory, *adj.* **1.** censuring, reproachful, opprobious, impeaching, slating, inveighing, reproving, recriminating, reprehensive, reprobative, reprobating; denunciatory, denunciating, railing, cursing, condemnatory, maledictory, anathematizing; berating, upbraiding, castigating, objurgatory, objurgative, objurgating, chastising, chastening, reprimanding, scolding, chiding, admonishing; disapproving, disapprobatory, disapprobative, disfavoring; criticizing, carping, caviling; protestant, protestive, protesting, disputatious, disputative, disputing, contentious, argumentative, altercating, challenging, opposing, objecting, conflictive, conflictory, conflicting.
2. deprecative, belittling, disparaging, demeaning, deflating, derogatory, derogative, derogating, detractory, detractive, detracting; depreciatory, depreciating, devaluating, cheapening, lessening, decreasing, diminishing, bating, attenuating, mitigating; minimizing, underestimating, underrating, undervaluing, beggaring, extenuating, underreckoning, deemphasizing, underplaying; lampooning, caricaturing, ridiculing, mocking, jeering, sneering, jibing; disdainful, derisive, derisory, deriding, snide, contemptuous, scornful.
3. apologetic, regretful, compunctious, sorry, penitent, penitential, contrite, humble, expiatory, propitiatory, supplicatory, remorseful, rueful, self-condemnatory, self-reproachful.

depreciate, *v.* **1.** devaluate, devalue, deflate, depress, cheapen; reduce, decrease, lessen, lower, cut, slash, subtract from, mark down, put on sale.

2. belittle, minimize, underrate, undervalue, underestimate, underreckon; slight, make light of, think nothing of, set no store by, underplay, *Inf.* play down; derogate, detract from, discredit, disparage, decry, deprecate, *Inf.* talk down.

3. decline, fall, tumble, slide, slip, go down; sink, drop, slump, fall off, lose value.

depreciation, *n.* **1.** devaluation, deflation, depression, cheapening; reduction, decrease, lowering, lessening, diminution, shrinkage; decline, fall, falling off, drop, slump.

2. belittlement, minimization, underestimation; derogation, pejoration, discrediting, disparagement, deprecation, detraction.

depredate, *v.* **1.** plunder, rob, despoil, *Archaic.* spoil, spoliate, pillage, *Chiefly Scot.* reive; ravage, harry, rape, carry off, maraud, devastate; ransack, sack, loot, gut, fleece, strip, rifle; raid, foray, forage, prey on *or* upon; lay waste, desolate, wreak havoc upon, ruin, lay in ruins.

2. pirate, freeboot, buccaneer, privateer, filibuster; seize, capture, steal, thieve.

depredation, *n.* **1.** plunder, plundering, plunderage, rapine, pillage, spoliation, despoliation, despoilment, *Obs.* direption, raven *or* ravin; preying upon, ravaging, ravage, harrying, marauding, *Archaic.* maraud, sacking, *Rare.* sackage; laying waste, devastation, desolation; raid, inroad, razzia, foray; foraging, looting, ravishment, seizure, grag, rape; kidnapping, hijacking, skyjacking, air piracy, commandeering.

2. brigandage, piracy, buccaneering, freebooting, banditry, highway robbery, *Obs.* latrociny, privateering, filibustering, *U.S. Inf.* (*usu. of cattle*) rustling; robbery, theft, thievery, *Law.* larceny, stealing.

depredator, *n.* **1.** pillager, plunderer, marauder, despoiler, ransacker, sacker, rifler, looter, forager, raider; ravager, destroyer.

2. pirate, rover, viking, corsair, buccaneer, privateer; freebooter, rapparee, (*in the Scottish Highlands*) cateran; kidnapper, abductor, rustler, hijacker, skyjacker, air *or* sky pirate.

3. robber, burglar, thief, stealer, *Inf.* crook, housebreaker; highwayman, footpad, *Sl.* yegg or yeggman, bandit, *Sp.* bandolero, *Southwest U.S.* ladrone, *Australian.* bushranger, brigand, picaroon, outlaw, desperado.

depress, *v.* **1.** dispirit, dishearten, discourage, put [s.o.] down in the dumps *or* the doldrums. See **deject.**

2. weaken, enfeeble, debilitate, enervate; exhaust, sap, drain, weary, tire; dull, deaden, kill.

3. devaluate, devalue, depreciate, cheapen; diminish, lessen, lower, reduce, cut, slash; degrade, downgrade, demote, break; humble, abase, take [s.o.] down a notch *or* peg or two, humiliate, mortify.

depressant, *n.* sedative, tranquilizer, soporific, hypnotic, sleeping-pill; alcohol, liquor, spirits, *Inf.* booze; analgesic, painkiller, aspirin; opiate, opium, codeine, morphine; barbiturate, *Sl.* barbs, *Inf.* down *or* downer, quaalude, *Sl.* lude, *Brit.* mandrax, *Brit. Sl.* mandy, *Pharm., Trademark* Seconal, *Sl.* red; heroin, *Sl.* H, *Sl.* horse, *Sl.* smack, *Sl.* crank, *Sl.* junk, *Sl.* scag.

depressed, *adj.* **1.** dispirited, disheartened, crestfallen; unhappy, sad, blue, melancholy. See **dejected.**

2. sunken, hollow, recessed, set back, pushed *or* poked in; concave, indented, dented, dimpled.

3. devaluated, devalued, cheapened, depreciated, degraded, downgraded; diminished, lessened, reduced, lowered, cut, slashed.

4. destitute, poverty-stricken, poor, strapped, bad off, *Inf.* hard up; lacking, needy, in need, in want.

depressing, *adj.* dejecting, discouraging, daunting, damping, disappointing, disheartening, dispiriting, depressive, depressant; saddening, cheerless, sad, melancholy, blue, heartbreaking; sorrowful, woeful, mournful, lachrymose, dolorous; distressing, painful, afflictive; dreary, bleak, gloomy, dismal, hopeless; black, somber, grave, heavy.

depression, *n.* **1.** indentation, dent, dint, dimple, recess; hollow, concavity, cavity, pit, hole; dip, bowl, sink, sink hole, swallow, swallow hole.

2. downheartedness, low spirits, crestfallenness; sadness, melancholy, blues, doldrums. See **dejection.**

3. (*of the economy*) recession, decline, slump, bad times, hard times; inactivity, slowdown, dullness, stagnation, paralysis, standstill; stagflation.

deprivation, *n.* **1.** withholding, deprival, denial; dispossession, expropriation, *Law.* disseizin, appropriation, confiscation, seizure, taking away, *Law.* attachment; divesture, stripping, despoliation, spoliation.

2. privation, want, need, lack; loss, bereavement, hardship, distress.

3. removal, deposition, dismissal, ousting, expulsion.

deprive, *v.* **1.** withhold, deny, refuse, debar, shut out.

2. remove, divest, strip, denude, despoil; dispossess, *Law.* disseize, expropriate, appropriate, confiscate, *Law.* attach, seize, commandeer; bereave, wrest from, wring from, take away; mulct, rob.

depth, *n.* **1.** deepness, profoundness, profundity; complexity, intricacy, obscurity, abstruseness, reconditeness, esotericism.

2. gravity, weight, moment, importance, significance; seriousness, solemnity, sobriety.

3. sagacity, wisdom, understanding; awareness, perception, insight, intuition, sensitivity; discernment, perspicacity, astuteness, acumen, acuity, shrewdness, artfulness, subtlety.

4. pit, bottomless pit, bowels, bowels of the earth; gulf, abyss, chasm, cavity, hole, crevasse.

5. intensity, vividness, brilliancy, brightness; richness, strength, darkness.

6. depths a. midst, middle, innermost part, remotest part, womb; **b.** deep, deeps, ocean bottom, floor, bed, ground, Davy Jones's locker.

7. in depth thoroughly, extensively, comprehensively.

deputation, *n.* **1.** appointment, designation, nomination; installation, investiture, induction, ordination; authorization, entrusting, empowering, charging; assignment, appropriation, relegation, devolvement.

2. delegates, delegation, embassy, legation; committee, subcommittee.

deputize, *v.* depute, commission, delegate; appoint, name, designate, nominate; charge, authorize, commit, entrust, empower, enable; consign, relegate, pass on, devolve.

deputy, *n.* **1.** representative, delegate, commissary, surrogate; appointee, provost, spokesperson; ambassador, emissary, envoy, legate, agent, factor, messenger, minister; middleman, go-between, diplomat, intermediary, negotiator, negotiant; substitute, alternate, proxy, vice-regent, viceroy; lieutenant, assistant, operative, right hand person; functionary, commissioner, bureaucrat; consul, plenipotentiary.

—adj. **2.** assistant, second-in-command, subordinate, associate; elected, appointed, designated, ordained.

derange, *v.* **1.** disarrange, disorder, throw into disorder, disorganize, turn topsy-turvy, disjoint, disarray; upset, muss *or* muss up, mess *or* mess up; misarrange, put out of place, misplace, displace, dislocate; dishevel, rumple, ruffle, tousle, *Chiefly Scot. Dial.* touse; clutter, litter, scatter, shuffle; jumble, muddle, entangle.

2. unsettle, discompose, perturb, disconcert; agitate, distress, disturb, trouble; confuse, confound.

3. incapacitate, throw out of gear, indispose; weaken, devitalize, disable; enfeeble, debilitate; invalid, sicken.

4. craze, madden, *Obs.* dement, *Archaic.* bedlamize, distemper; drive insane, drive crazy, drive mad, drive wild; unbalance, unsettle, distract, unhinge; enrage, frenzy, excite, inflame.

deranged, *adj.* **1.** disordered, disarranged, disorganized, disjointed, disarrayed; misarranged, out of place, misplaced, displaced, dislocated; disheveled, rumpled, ruffled, tousled; upset, topsy-turvy, messy; cluttered, littered; jumbled, muddled, entangled.

2. incapacitated, indisposed; weakened, devitalized, disabled; enfeebled, debilitated.

3. unsettled, discomposed, perturbed, disconcerted; agitated, distressed, disturbed, troubled; confused, confounded.

4. insane, crazy, crazed, mad, lunatic, lunatical, demented; of unsound mind, *Latin. non compos mentis,* mentally ill; psychotic, schizophrenic, *Sl.* schizo; daft, *Inf.* daffy, unbalanced, touched, *Inf.* unglued, *Inf.* half-baked, *Brit. Sl.* bonkers, unhinged, distracted; dazed, moon-struck, possessed, infatuated; odd, peculiar, queer, bizarre, *Chiefly Brit. Inf.* potty, *Inf.* dotty, *Inf.* crackpot; brainsick, *Sl.* kooky, *Sl.* meshuga; *All Sl.* balmy, dippy, batty, bats, cuckoo, buggy, bughouse, bugs, screwy, wacky, wacko, goofy, loony, squirrelly, bananas, nuts, nutty, nutty as a fruitcake.

5. out of one's head *or* mind *or* senses *or* wits, *Scot.* redwood, *Sl.* loco, made as a hatter, mad as a March hare, far-gone, stark raving mad; not all there, not quite right, not right upstairs; *Inf.* out in left field, *Sl.* in outer space, *Sl.* in orbit, *Inf.* off the wall; *Inf.* cracked, *Inf.* mental, *Sl.* off one's rocker, *Sl.* out of one's tree, *Sl.* off one's trolley, *Brit. Sl.* off one's chump; *All Sl.* have bats in one's belfry, have a few buttons missing, have a few loose screws.

6. maniacal, hysterical, madding, *Archaic.* wood, delirious; frantic, frenzied, frenetic; ranting, raving, storming, foaming at the mouth, convulsing; beside oneself, at one's wit's end; out of control, uncontrollable, unrestrainable, corybantic, *Inf.* haywire, berserk, rabid; wild violent, fierce.

7. absurd, silly, inane, fatuous, crackbrained, foolish; irrational, wild-eyed, illogical, unreasonable; senseless, nonsensical, pointless; ridiculous, laughable, ludicrous; asinine, anserine, idiotic, *Inf.* moronic, imbecilic; childish, puerile, immature.

8. stupid, simple-minded, birdbrained, feeble-minded, dull-witted; harebrained, light-minded, lightheaded, giddy; scatterbrained, absent-minded; confused, muddled, bemused.

derangement, *n.* **1.** disarrangement, disorder, disorganization, disarray; upset, muss, mess; misarrangement, misplacement, displacement, dislocation.

2. incapacitation, weakening, devitalization, disablement, invalidation; enfeeblement, debilitation.

3. discomposure, perturbation, disconcertion, disconcertment; agitation, distress, disturbance, trouble, confusion.

4. insanity, insaneness, madness, lunacy, *Psychiatry.* dementia, dementedness; distraction, disorientation, unbalance, unsoundness; mental illness, loss of reason, unsound mind, diseased mind; craziness, *Sl.* kookiness, *Inf.* nuttiness, daftness, brainsickness; infatuation, possession; eccentricity, oddness, queerness; *All Sl.* balminess, bugginess, screwiness, wackiness, goofiness.

5. psychosis, neurosis, psychoneurosis; schizophrenia, *Psychiatry.* dementia praecox, monomania, automania, dipsomania, pyromania, delusion of grandeur; senility, anility, dotage, *Psychiatry.* amentia; *Psychol.* kleptomania, *Psychol.* split personality; *All Psychiatry.* melancholia, hypochondria, paranoia, mania, lyssophobia, fugue, alienation, delusion.

6. frenzy, franticness, furor, delirium, phrenitis, anoesis, hysteria; *Pathol.* delirium tremens, blue devils, *Sl.* the horrors, *Sl.* jimjams; ranting, raving, storming, foaming at the mouth; wildness, fierceness, violence.

derelict, *adj.* **1.** abandoned, forsaken, deserted, neglected; relinquished, given up, left behind, *Naut.* (*of a ship*) a hull; discarded, rejected, cast off *or* away *or* aside; shunned, scorned, outcast, forlorn; bereft, adrift, alone, solitary, lonely, desolate; destitute, desperate, helpless, hopeless, wretched, mournful, unfortunate, friendless.

2. negligent, neglectful, remiss, delinquent, *Inf.* asleep at the wheel *or* at the switch *or* on the job; indolent, lazy, slothful, laggard, shiftless, do-nothing, fain'eant; slack, loose, lax, sloppy, slipshod; dilatory, delaying, procrastinative, cunctatious, cunctatory.

—n. **3.** vagrant, beachcomber, tramp, hobo; beggar, scavenger, parasite, leech, scrounge, scrounger; outcast, pariah; degenerate, deviate, *Sl.* lowlife; down-and-outer, *Inf.* bum, *Sl.* stumblebum, *Sl.* stewbum.

4. delinquent, do-nothing, shirker, slacker, loafer, malingerer; dawdler, dallier, time-killer; idler, ne'er-do-well, *Sl.* goof-off, *Sl.* goldbrick, *Both Chiefly Brit.* good-for-nothing, wastrel.

dereliction, *n.* **1.** negligence, negligency, neglect, delinquency, remissness, *Obs.* indiligence; laxity, slackness, looseness, *Fr. laissez-aller;* slovenliness, sloppiness, shoddiness; carelessness, inaccuracy, inexactitude, inexactness.

2. disregard, omission, oversight, inattention, default, *Law.* laches; disregardfulness, inattentiveness, forgetfulness, neglectfulness; incaution, incautiousness, heedlessness, inadvertence, inadvertency.

3. languor, languidness, inexertion, indolence, otiosity, otioseness, laziness, idleness, sloth; dilatoriness, procrastination, delay, cunctation; nonchalance, insouciance, improvidence, imprudence, imprudency, indiscretion.

4. noninterference, laissez-faire, passiveness, passivity, faineance; nonobservance, nonperformance, noncooperation.

5. fault, wrongdoing, shortcoming; infraction, violation, transgression.

6. abandonment, desertion, forsaking; rejection, renunciation, abdication, disavowal, relinquishment; defection, heresy, apostasy, recreance, recreancy.

deride, *v.* **1.** scoff at, mock, jeer, ridicule, knock, gird at; fleer, laugh at, guy, *Australian.* chiack; taunt, gibe, twit, rag; tease, rally, *Inf.* roast, banter, chaff, rib, kid, *Sl.* razz; flout, scorn, sneer at, disdain, pooh-pooh; scout, contemn, curl one's lip at; hiss, boo, hoot at, heckle, catcall, whistle at, rail at, cry down; *Inf.* thumb one's nose at, *U.S.* give [s.o.] the raspberry *or* Bronx cheer.

2. make fun of, lampoon, satirize, parody, pasquinade; make sport of, poke fun at, make a fool out of, make the butt of, *Sl.* make an ass of; insult, detract, belittle, run down, disparage; slur, slander, abuse, vilify, harass.

derision, *n.* **1.** ridicule, mockery, sarcasm, scoffing; scorn, disdain, contempt, disrespect, cheek; lampoon, satire, parody, burlesque; pasquinade, pasquil, travesty, caricature.

2. jeer, jibe, fleer, raillery, chaff, *Inf.* roast; poke, dig, cut, rub; boo, hiss, hoot, catcall, cry, *U.S.* Bronx cheer, raspberry, *Sl.* bird; taunt, quip, contumely, lip; slight, spurn, insult, slur, detraction, affront.

3. butt, goat, joke, laughingstock, monkey; fool, dupe, gull, gudgeon; target, mark, *Inf.* jay, *Sl.* sucker, *Sl.* john.

derisive, *adj.* scornful, derisory, jeering, disdainful; contemptuous, supercilious, arrogant, insolent; mocking, taunting, flouting, jesting, insulting, contumelious; sarcastic, sardonic, parodistic, satirical.

derivable, *adj.* traceable, ascribable, attributable, imputable, assignable; accountable, referable, explicable; deducible, inferable, educible, concludable; obtainable, evolvable, elicitable, extractable.

derivation, *n.* **1.** drawing, accounting, deriving, inferring, deducing, concluding; acquisition, obtainment, borrowing, procurement.

2. origin, source, spring, wellspring; fountainhead, head, fountain, fount, springhead; foundation, origination, beginning, commencement; cause, causation, *Latin. fons et origo;* development, rise, evolution, growth; formation, root, etymology.

3. derivative, illation, induction; conclusion, inference, deduction; consequence, corollary.

derivative, *adj.* **1.** derived, acquired, borrowed, gotten, obtained, procured; derivational, illative, inferential, eductive, deductive, extractive.

2. secondary, unoriginal, imitative; warmed-over, rehashed, thinly disguised.

derive, *n.* **1.** extract, obtain, procure, secure, get, gain; bring forth, evolve, evoke, elicit, educe; glean, winnow, cull, reap, harvest, collect, gather.

2. trace, track, follow back, etymologize, root out.

3. infer, deduce, presume, suppose; guess, deem, opine, esteem, reckon; conclude, surmise, reason, draw an inference *or* conclusion, arrive at.

4. originate, arise, spring from, flow from; proceed, come, steam, hail.

derogate, *v.* **1.** discredit, disfavor, make disreputable, injure *or* impair the credit *or* reputation of; censure, reproach, inveigh against; reduce, lower, degrade, downgrade, debase, abase, vitiate; shame, disgrace, dishonor; humiliate, humble, mortify, *Sl.* put down.

2. belittle, disparage, demean, deprecate, deflate, detract, decry, *Inf.* talk down; devaluate, depreciate, cheapen, lessen, decrease, diminish, bate, abate, attenuate, boil down, shrivel, wither, mitigate; minimize, slight, underestimate, underrate, undervalue, beggar, extenuate, underreckon, misprize, think nothing of, set no store by, fail to count on; deemphasize, underplay, make light of, *Inf.* play down; lampoon, pasquinade, caricature, satirize; ridicule, mock, poke fun at, laugh at, sneer at, jeer at, jibe at; disdain, deride, contemn, scoff, spurn, scorn, pooh-pooh.

3. defame, denigrate, vilify, vituperate, vilipend, scandalize, malign, gibbet, run down, impugn, berate, revile, *Inf.* knock, *Inf.* rap, speak ill of, speak evil of, *Sl.* badmouth, *Sl.* poor mouth, backbite; slander, libel, calumniate, traduce, falsify, accuse falsely, impute, asperse, insinuate; injure, abuse, insult, attack, assail, stab, *Sl.* dump on, *Sl.* trash; criticize, pull to pieces, cut up, shred, *Sl.* do a number on, *Sl.* do a hatchet job on.

4. (*all of oneself*) degenerate, deteriorate, decline, sink, worsen, retrogress, retrograde, run to seed, go to pot, go bad, lapse, fail, crumble, disintegrate; deprave, defile, corrupt, pervert.

5. grovel, crawl, creep, slither, worm, wallow; lie prone, stoop, bow, crouch, slouch; cringe, cower, quake, shake, tremble; be servile, behave abjectly, lick [s.o.'s] feet *or* boots; (*all of oneself*) degrade, abase, prostrate.

derogation, *n.* **1.** discredit, disfavor, obloquy, loss of face; censure, reproach, invective, reflection, animadversion, disapproval, disapprobation, criticism, stricture; curse, denunciation, condemnation, execration, revilement, commination, fulmination, malediction; degradation, debasement, abasement, vitiation, reduction, lowering; shame, disgrace, dishonor; humiliation, humble pie, mortification.

2. defamation, denigration, vituperation, vilification, scandal, scandalization, scandalmongering, abuse, injury, attack, scurrility, running down, gibbeting, backbiting, *Sl.* badmouth, *Sl.* poormouth; slander, libel, calumny, calumniation, traducement, falsification, misrepresentation, false accusation, slur, imputation, aspersion, insinuation, innuendo, *Inf.* brickbat.

3. belittlement, disparagement, deprecation, deflation, detraction, *Inf.* talking down; depreciation, devaluation, diminution, decrease, abatement, attenuation, mitigation, bating, cheapening, lessening; minimization, dispraise, underestimation, extenuation, undervaluing, underrating, underreckoning, beggaring; lampoon, pasquinade, squib, caricature, satirization; sarcasm, ridicule, mockery, jeer, jibe, scoff, sneer; disdain, derision, contempt, scorn, contumely.

4. degeneration, deterioration, decline, retrogression, retrogradation, lapse, failure, disintegration; depravation, defilement, corruption, perversion.

5. servility, abjection, abjectedness, abjectness, prostration, self-abasement.

derogatory, *adj.* **1.** discrediting, disfavorable, unfavorable, disapproving, disapprobatory, disapprobative; censuring, reproachful, opprobrious, impeaching, slating, inveighing, reproving, recriminating, reprehensive, reprobative, reprobating.

2. belittling, disparaging, demeaning, deflating, derogative, derogating, detractory, detractive, detracting; depreciatory, depreciative, depreciating, devaluating, cheapening, lessening, decreasing, bating, diminishing, attenuating, mitigating; minimizing, underestimating, underrating, undervaluing, beggaring, extenuating, underreckoning, deemphasizing, underplaying, *Inf.* downplaying; humiliating, humbling, mortifying; lampooning, caricaturing, ridiculing, mocking, jeering, sneering, jibing; disdainful, derisive, derisory, deriding, snide, contemptuous, scornful; satirical, sarcastic, biting, caustic, vitriolic, acrimonious, scathing.

3. defamatory, denigrating, vituperative, vilifying, vilipenditory; slanderous, libelous, calumnious, calumniatory, traducent, false, untrue, maliciously false *or* untrue, misrepresentative, aspersive, imputative, insinuating; abusive, hurtful, scurrilous, injurious, contumelious, insulting, foulmouthed, backbiting.

descant, *v.* **1.** sing, warble, croon, trill, peal.

2. comment on, discourse, relate; elaborate, expatiate, dilate, amplify, dissertate, expand, enlarge, spell out; harp on, dwell on, hammer away at, beat into the ground, insist, yammer; digress, deviate, wander, ramble, branch out, go off on a tangent; speechify, perorate, orate, harangue, rant, spiel.

descend, *v.* **1.** come down, go down, move down, climb down; drop, fall, subside, slope, gravitate, settle on, land on; decline, set; plummet, plunge, sink, dip, dive, submerge, founder, immerse; tumble, slump, topple, droop; trip, stumble, lurch, careen; hit the

deck, take the long count.
2. dismount, light, alight, get down *or* off, pile out *or* off; debark, disembark, deplane, detrain; land, arrive.
3. condescend, stoop, grovel, toady, bootlick, prostrate onself, kowtow; sprawl, crawl, kneel, crouch; degrade, debase, demean, adulterate, deprave, debauch, pervert, sully.
4. degenerate, deteriorate, go downhill, hit bottom, *Sl.* hit the skids; ride *or* head for a fall.
5. spring, derive, issue; be the product *or* offspring *or* descendant of; be passed down *or* on through generations, be handed down.
6. attack, assault, assail, pounce, raid, invade, swoop, charge.

descendants, *n. pl.* **1.** offspring, offshoots, progeny, issue, seed, posterity, scions; family, children, sons, daughters, brood; spawn, breed, race, lineage, strain.
2. adherents, disciples, followers, protégés, pupils.

descent, *n.* **1.** drop, fall, plunge, sinking, downrush; subsidence, settling; droop, slip, trip, stumble, tumble, lurch, careen.
2. slope, grade, gradient; decline, declivity, declension, declination, downgrade; incline, inclination; ramp, chute, slide, down-stairway, *Mining.* downcast.
3. ancestry, parentage, origin, roots; lineage, genealogy, paternity, heredity, family tree; succession, filiation, sonship; pedigree, stock, line, blood, strain, extraction, derivation, breed.
4. moral decline, deterioration, degradation, debasement, abasement, debauchery; lapse, backslide, fall from grace, recidivism; downfall, comedown, setback.
5. assault, attack, pounce, swoop, onslaught, incursion; foray, sortie, raid, invasion.

describe, *v.* **1.** give an account of, narrate, tell, recount, relate, recite, pronounce, express; report, set out, chronicle; explain, define, elucidate; specify, detail, flesh out, footnote, annotate; indicate, denote, connote, signify; epitomize, characterize, label.
2. depict, portray, picture, illustrate; delineate, draw, paint, *Archaic.* limn, sketch, trace, reproduce.

description, *n.* **1.** portrayal, portraiture, depiction, sketch, delineation, characterization; detailing, specification, elaboration, *Sl.* megillah; account, narrative, story, tale; relation, recountal, recital, recitation, rehearsal, statement, report; record, chronicle, history, commentary, memoir.
2. sort, kind, brand, kidney, variety, type; breed, brood, species, genus, class, category, genre, denomination, suit, designation; grain, stripe, feather, tone, color, hue; make, cast, cut, stamp, mold, form; character, constitution, makeup, composition, *Archaic.* crasis; nature, manner, temperament, temper, humor, mood, persuasion.

descriptive, *adj.* depictive, delineative, illustrative, describing, detailed, particularized; graphic, vivid, striking, picturesque; portraitlike, lifelike, true to life, realistic.

descry, *v.* notice, discern, espy, sight; distinguish, make out, recognize; perceive, discover, ken, detect, determine; recognize, find out, ferret out.

desecrate, *v.* defile, profane, unhallow, treat sacrilegiously, commit sacrilege; blaspheme, curse, swear; debase, degrade, befoul; contaminate, infect, make impure, vitiate, pollute; misuse, corrupt, violate.

desecration, *n.* defilement, profaning, profaneness, blasphemy, sacrilege, impiety; debasement, degradation, dishonoring; contamination, infection, vitiation, befoulment, pollution; misuse, abuse, violation, outrage.

desert[1], *n.* **1.** barrens, Sahara, dust bowl; wasteland, waste, wilderness, wild, no man's land; moor, heath, tundra, veldt, steppe, savanna, plain.
—*adj.* **2.** desolate, barren, bare, devoid, empty, destitute, poor, deficient; uncultivable, uncultivatable, sterile, infertile, unfertile, unproductive.
3. arid, dry, moistureless, waterless, droughty, without rain, thirsty, *Chem.* anhydrous; dehydrated, desiccated, dried up; parched, baked, roasted, toasted, burnt, scorched, hot, burning, torrid.
4. camellike, cactuslike, cactoid, succulent; oasitic, oasal, oasean.

desert[2], *v.* **1.** abandon, forsake, leave behind, throw over, jilt, run out on, *Inf.* leave flat, *Inf.* leave in the lurch, turn one's back on; ignore, cut off, neglect, ostracize.
2. betray, turn traitor, *Sl.* sell down the river, *Sl.* rat out *or* rat out on; apostatize, defect; repudiate, abjure, reject, disown, renounce; renege, bail out, *Inf.* back out of, back-pedal, *Inf.* back away from, back off on, *Inf.* cop out.
3. leave, depart, quit, go away from, vacate, evacuate; secede, withdraw from; flee, fly, bolt, take to one's heels, turn tail, cut and run.
4. relinquish, abdicate, give up, yield, let go, resign.
5. (*usu. in reference to military duty*) run away, *Inf.* run, go AWOL; make off, sneak off, abscond, decamp, take French leave.

desert[3], *n.* **1.** *Often* **deserts** just reward, due, right, birthright, *Literary.* guerdon, *Archaic.* meed; requital, recompense, compensation; just punishment, *Inf.* comeuppance, *Inf.* what's coming to one, *All Sl.* (*usu. with get*) his, hers, yours, theirs.
2. merit, worth, excellence, value, quality, virtue, integrity; guilt, culpability, blamability; responsibility, accountability, answerability.

deserted, *adj.* **1.** forsaken, abandoned, neglected; cast off, rejected, shunned, ignored, outcast; forlorn, *Poetic.* lorn, woeful, wretched, unfortunate, friendless, unfriended; destitute, bereft, bereaved.
2. untenanted, tenantless, uninhabited, unoccupied, vacant, empty; unfrequented, in a backwater, out of the way, secluded, sequestered; desolate, godforsaken, isolated, lone, lonely, solitary.

deserter, *n.* **1.** runaway, fugitive, escapee, *Archaic.* runagate; truant, delinquent, derelict; absconder.
2. traitor, betrayer, forsaker, *Sl.* ratter, *Sl.* fink; backslider, heretic, apostate, renegade, recreant, turncoat; abdicator, abdicant.
3. shirker, slacker, malingerer, *Inf.* quitter, *Sl.* copout, *Brit.* skulker.

desertion, *n.* **1.** abandonment, forsaking, defection, betrayal; heresy, apostasy, recreance, recreancy; neglect, negligence, dereliction.
2. flight, escape, evasion, elusion; departure, decampment, evacuation.
3. relinquishment, abnegation, resignation, abdication, *Archaic.* demission; secession, withdrawal, retirement; renunciation, disavowal, recantation, denial.
4. desolation, desertedness, deprivation, bereavement; solitude, isolation, loneliness; separation, separateness, alienation, estrangement.
5. (*usu. in reference to military duty*) running away *or* off; absence without leave; going AWOL.

deserve, *v.* merit, be worthy of, be qualified for; earn, be entitled to, have a right to, have a claim to; have [s.t.] coming to one.

deserved, *adj.* merited, earned; just, rightful, right, due, equitable, fair; fitting, (*of punishment*) condign, suitable, appropriate, meet, reasonable, justified, justifiable.

deserving, *adj.* worthy, qualified; laudable, praiseworthy, commendable, admirable; estimable, meritorious, creditable; virtuous, righteous, upright, dutiful, good; exemplary, sterling, excellent.

desideratum, *n.* hope, dream, wish, heart's desire, desire, aspiration, ideal; need, want, lack; essential, *Latin. sine qua non;* aim, goal, ambition; objective, object, end, mark, determination.

design, *v.* **1.** plan, plot, scheme, draw up plans, work out, block out, map out, shape out a course; organize, arrange, set up; contrive, devise, develop; fashion, fabricate, frame, make, effect, produce; shape, form, mold, forge; construct, build, rear, erect.

2. depict, delineate, sketch, draft, outline roughly, lay out; trace out, figure, draw the lines of; portray, paint, represent; define, detail, *Archaic.* limn.

3. originate, invent, innovate; coin; imagine, conceive, *Inf.* dream up, *Inf.* hatch; visualize, envisage.

4. intend, purpose, mean, have in mind to do, have in view, aim at, aspire to.

—*n.* **5.** delineation, depiction, drawing; preliminary sketch, rough draft, draft; outline, blueprint, plan, layout; chart, diagram, map, study.

6. arrangement, organization, configuration; composition, make-up, constitution, construction; structure, formation, system.

7. motif, pattern, style, *Fine Arts.* cartoon; model, prototype, *Archaic.* copy, archetype; form, shape, figure.

8. scheme, schema, proposal, program, project, scenario, script; contrivance, expedient, stratagem, device, artifice, shift, invention.

9. plot, intrigue, conspiracy, cabal; machination, wirepulling, manipulation; designs, evil intentions, hostile *or* aggressive conniving.

10. intention, purpose, intent, view, point, drift, reason, resolution; objective, object, purport, determination; end, destination, target, mark, bull's-eye; thought, cogitation, expectation; hope, dream, wish, desire, desideratum, aspiration; goal, ambition.

designate, *v.* **1.** indicate, signify, denote, signal; mark *or* point out, show, make known, express, formulate, mention, note; specify, state in detail, stipulate, particularize, individualize, pinpoint; earmark, set aside.

2. characterize, depict, represent, illustrate; describe, define, delineate, outline.

3. name, denominate, call, term, style, nickname, dub; entitle, address; christen, baptize; identify, label.

4. appoint, nominate, delegate; select, choose; elect, vote in, place in office, induct, ordain; assign, appropriate, consign, relegate, allot.

designation, *n.* **1.** indication, signification, denotation, pointing out, showing; expression, formulation, notation; specification, stipulation, particularization, individualization.

2. appellation, name, title, honorific, style; epithet, appellative, by-word, label, tag; nickname, *Sl.* moniker, sobriquet, cognomen, agnomen, by-name, pet name, diminutive; pseudonym, anonym, allonym, alias, pen name, stage name.

3. appointment, nomination, delegation; selection, choice, election; induction, ordination; assignment, appropriation, consignment, relegation, allotment.

4. nature, character, condition; sort, kind, class, ilk, variety, type.

designedly, *adv.* intentionally, purposefully, on purpose, willfully, of one's own free will, volitionally, voluntarily on one's own; premeditatedly, premeditatingly, with aforethought, predeterminately; meditatedly, meditatively, studiously, considerately; preconcertedly, deliberately, calculatedly, wittingly, knowingly, with one's eyes wide open, in cold blood.

designer, *n.* **1.** creator, inventor, deviser, artificer, fashioner, craftsman, artist; founder, originator, author, producer; architect, draftsman, drawer, delineator, sketcher, pattern maker; styler, decorator; molder, sculptor, carver; engraver, chaser, painter, limner, illustrator, cartoonist, caricaturist.

2. schemer, intriguer, machinator, conspirator, conniver, plotter, planner, contriver.

designing, *adj.* **1.** scheming, calculating, intriguing, conspiring, plotting, conniving; guileful, doubledealing, tricky, wily; sharp, shrewd, politic, artful, crafty, Machiavellian, cunning, sly, snaky, foxy; subtle, insidious, collusive, circumventive, prevaricative; stealthy, treacherous, feline; deceptive, dishonest, underhanded, untrustworthy, crooked; deceitful, insincere, disingenuous, false, mendacious, untruthful.

2. provident, cautious, prudent, careful, heedful, mindful.

desirable, *adj.* **1.** agreeable, pleasing, attractive, inviting, charming, winning, taking, captivating; admirable, estimable, valuable, worthy; excellent, superior, superb, fine, goodly; first-rate, first-class, prime; popular, in demand, eligible.

2. advisable, recommendable; fitting, proper, meet, seemly; expedient, profitable, remunerative, gainful, advantageous, beneficial.

desire, *v.* **1.** wish for, long for, desiderate, want; yearn for, hope for, care for, pine for, sigh for; hanker after, have a yen for, covet, fancy, have a fancy for; have an eye to, be attracted to, have a mind to, have at heart, be bent upon; be inclined towards, be prone to, be predisposed towards, prefer; aspire to, emulate, set one's heart on; crave, hunger, thirst, relish; lust after, burn for, *Inf.* be wild *or* mad about, *Sl.* have the hots for, *Inf.* letch after; eye, eyeball.

2. ask for, request, summon, solicit, importune; petition, entreat, urge, plead; beseech, beg, implore, supplicate, adjure; endeavor to obtain, appeal for, apply to; requisition, order, demand, require.

—*n.* **3.** longing, wish, wishing, desideration, want, wanting; yearning, hope, hoping, pining, sighing, hankering, *Inf.* yen, *Sl.* itch, fondness, liking; attraction, aspiration, emulation, ambition; inclination, predilection, preference, propensity, proclivity; predisposal, predisposedness, bent, leaning, disposition; fancy, fancying, coveting, covetousness, eagerness, ardor, craving; appetency, appetite, hunger, thirst, ravenousness; relish, rapaciousness, voracity, voraciousness; avidity, greed, greediness, cupidity, avarice, graspingness; frenzy, mania, craze, rage.

4. request, solicitation, importunity; petition, entreaty, adjuration, urge, urging; pleading, beseeching, beseechingness, begging, imploring, imploringness, imploration; supplication, prayer, appeal; application, requisition, demand, call, summons, order, requirement.

5. lust, lustfulness, concupiscence, libido, sexual appetite *or* urge, aphrodisia; lewdness, bawdiness, *Archaic.* bawdry, wantonness; lasciviousness, salaciousness, salacity, lubricity, libidinousness; carnal passion, prurience, pruriency, *Pathol.* satyriasis, *Pathol.* nymphomania; lechery, lecherousness, *Sl.* letch, *Sl.* the hots, burning; (*all of animals*) heat, rut, estrus; eroticism, erotism, sensuality, sexuality.

desired, *adj.* **1.** yearned for, longed for, pined for, wished for, hoped for; aspired, emulated; coveted, hankered after, fancied, envied, craved, lusted after.

2. correct, proper, precise, exact, accurate, right, true; specific, particular, express; required, necessary, appropriate, characteristic, individual; selected, chosen, picked, preferred, decided upon.

desirous, *adj.* **1.** desiring, eager, fain, longing, yearning, desiderative; wishing, wishful, pining, hoping, hopeful; partial to, inclined, prone to, ready, willing, impatient, *Sl.* itchy, anxious, overanxious.
2. enthusiastic, enthused, *Inf.* wild, agog, *Inf.* psyched *or* psyched up; stimulated, excited, aroused, *Inf.* hot; lusting after, *Sl.* hot for, mad about, *Inf.* dying for, *Inf.* wild about, infatuated; inflamed, fired up, burning, impassioned, passionate; fervent, fervid, perfervid, ardent, zealous, spirited.
3. ambitious, emulous, aspiring; enterprising, up-and-coming, pushing, *Inf.* pushy, aggressive.
4. avid, greedy, craving; appetitive, hungry, thirsty, ravenous, voracious, omnivorous; covetous, avaricious, rapacious.

desist, *v.* **1.** stop, *Sl.* cheese, hold, stay, cease, arrest, halt; pull up, stop short, come to a halt; discontinue, interrupt, suspend, intermit; drop, have done with, let alone, let be, leave well enough alone, keep one's hands off, turn aside; resist, abstain, forbear, restrain, hold back voluntarily; forgo, do without, sacrifice; give up, *Inf.* swear off, quit, leave off, break off, let up, pause; renounce, relinquish, put aside.
2. keep in check, hold back, curb, curtail; control, *Sl.* lay off, *Inf.* let up on, contain; withhold, deny, abnegate, suppress, repress; refuse, decline, take no part in, have nothing to do with, stand *or* hold aloof; rebuff, reject, spurn; avoid, eschew, shun.

desolate, *adj.* **1.** devastated, laid waste, desolated, barren; ravaged, gutted, wrecked, ruined, destroyed.
2. deserted, uninhabited, unpeopled, depopulated, untenanted, unoccupied; desert, waste, wild, bare, empty, destitute; unvisited, unfrequented, inhospitable; solitary, lonely, isolated, remote, secluded, out-of-the-way.
3. forlorn, *Poetic.* lorn, bereft, abandoned, forsaken; outcast, excluded; alone, lonely, lonesome, lost; estranged, alienated, companionless, friendless, unfriended, homeless.
4. disconsolate, unconsolable, sad, cheerless, joyless, spiritless, hopeless, despondent; dejected, downcast, low-spirited, downhearted, discouraged, depressed; melancholy, doleful, sorrowful, mournful; miserable, wretched, woebegone, woeful, heavy-hearted; broken-hearted, bereaved.
5. dreary, *Literary.* drear, dismal, gloomy, bleak, somber, dark, funereal, tenebrous.
—*v.* **6.** devastate, lay waste, waste; despoil, *Archaic.* spoil, ravage, harry, pillage, plunder, depredate; ransack, sack, strip, rifle; destroy, blast, wreck, ruin, lay in ruins; demolish, raze, level, gut, obliterate, annihilate, extirpate.
7. depopulate, unpeople; make desolate, eject, drive out, expel, evict, dispossess.
8. depress, discourage, daunt, dishearten, dispirit; sadden, deject, weigh down, burden, oppress, trouble; distress, grieve, wound, pain.
9. forsake, abandon, desert, quit, leave, leave in the lurch, turn one's back on, repudiate, *Inf.* drop, renounce, reject, disown, disinherit.

desolation, *n.* **1.** destruction, ruination, holocaust, demolition, ruin, havoc; spoliation, despoliation, despoilment, ravage, pillage, plunder, sack; rapine, ravishment, predation, depredation; depopulation, unpeopling.
2. devastation, waste, wreckage, ravagement; extermination, extirpation, obliteration, annihilation; nothingness, void, non-being, nullity, nonexistence, absolute, absence.
3. dreariness, barrenness, gloom, gloominess, dismalness, dismality, desolateness; bleakness, emptiness, darkness, blackness, bareness.
4. loneliness, lonesomeness, forlornness; solitude, solitariness, isolation, sequestration, seclusion.
5. disconsolateness, despondency, despair, dejection, depression; sorrow, grief, dolor, affliction, tribulation; woe, anguish, misery, wretchedness, agony, suffering; sadness, melancholy, dolefulness.
6. vastness, *Archaic.* vastity, emptiness, wilderness, desert, wasteland.

despair, *n.* **1.** hopelessness, disheartenment, dismay, discouragement; dejection, depression, despondency, slough of despond; defeatism, pessimism; resignation, resignedness.
2. gloom, melancholy, melancholia, misery, miserableness, wretchedness, distress, broken-heartedness; grief, sorrow, dolor, anguish; desperation, disconsolateness, unconsolability.
3. tribulation, trial, ordeal; heartache, pain, suffering, burden, cross; incubus, nightmare; extremity, anxiety; nemesis, bane, scourge, curse, plague, bother, nuisance.
—*v.* **4.** lose hope of, despond, give up, surrender, quit, *Sl.* pack it in, give up the ship, cry quits, cry craven, throw in the towel, throw in the sponge; resign oneself to, grin and bear it, lie down and die; take one's own life, commit suicide *or* hari-kari, *Inf.* overdose, *Sl.* O.D., *Sl.* brodie, *Sl.* take the gas, *Sl.* take a powder.

despairing, *adj.* **1.** despondent, disconsolate, inconsolable, comfortless, suicidal; dejected, depressed, melancholy, forlorn, downcast, *Inf.* down; wretched, miserable, broken-hearted, heartbroken; grieving, sorrowing, lamenting; grief-stricken, cheerless, sad; plaintive, woeful, woebegone, rueful, sorrowful, dolorous, funereal; discouraged, disheartened, daunted, intimidated; concerned, worried, anxious.
2. desperate, yielding, giving up, grasping at straws; reckless, rash, impetuous, foolhardy, harebrained; incautious, imprudent, injudicious; dangerous, risky, hazardous, daring, bold; frantic, mad, violent, wild, passionate, frenzied.

desperado, *n.* **1.** terrorist, gunman, gangster, criminal, mafioso, (*in Paris*) apache; thug, tough, mugger, ruffian, rowdy, hoodlum, *Sl.* hood, *Inf.* goon, hooligan, *Inf.* roughneck, *Inf.* baddy, *Australian Sl.* larrikin, *Brit. Hist.* Mohock.
2. highwayman, footpad, *Sl.* yegg *or* yeggman, bandit, *Sp.* bandolero, outlaw, *Southwest U.S.* ladrone, *Australian.* bushranger, bravo, brigand; picaroon, rogue, (*in India and Burma*) dacoit.
3. pirate, rover, viking, corsair, buccaneer, privateer; freebooter, rapparee, (*in the Scottish Highlands*) cateran; pillager, plunderer, marauder, despoiler, depredator, ransacker, sacker, looter, rifler, forager, raider.
4. malefactor, miscreant, villain, hellhound, fiend, knave, blackguard; lawbreaker, felon, cutthroat, murderer, robber, thief.

desperate, *adj.* **1.** reckless, rash, precipitate, hasty, overhasty, impetuous; ill-conceived, headlong, breakneck, madcap, foolhardy, harebrained; incautious, imprudent, indiscreet, injudicious; dangerous, risky, hazardous, death-defying, daring, bold; frantic, mad, violent, wild, passionate, frenzied, frenetic; furious, infuriated, rabid, rampant, raging, turbulent, tumultuous.
2. urgent, compelling, pressing; acute, critical, crucial; perilous, hazardous, precarious.
3. beyond hope, hopeless, despaired of, lost, irredeemable; beyond recovery, irrecoverable, irrevocable, past cure, incurable, irremediable, remediless; beyond repair, irreparable, irretrievable, irreclaimable; serious, grave, fatal, deadly.

4. shocking, outrageous, intolerable, bad; deplorable, lamentable, distressing, woeful.
5. great, intense, extreme, excessive, extravagant; supreme, monstrous, prodigious, all-out; final, ultimate, last-ditch, do-or-die; futile, useless.
6. despairing, yielding, giving up, grasping at straws; despondent, inconsolable, wretched, suicidal; downcast, forlorn, broken-hearted.

desperation, *n.* **1.** recklessness, rashness, foolhardiness, impetuosity, imprudence, boldness; frenzy, passion, rage, madness, fury.
2. urgency, pressure, compulsion; acuteness, criticalness, crucialness; seriousness, gravity, graveness, importance.
3. hopelessness, despair, despondency, slough of despond, depression; dejection, discouragement, disheartenment; defeatism, pessimism; disconsolateness, unconsolability, gloom, melancholy, misery, wretchedness, distress.
4. irredeemableness, irredeemability, irrecoverableness, irrevocability, irrevocableness, incurability, incurableness, irremediableness, irreparability, irreparableness, irretrievability, irretrievableness.

despicable, *adj.* **1.** contemptible, worthy of scorn, worthy of disdain, reptilian, stinking, *Inf.* lousy, scurvy; abhorrent, abominable, execrable, loathsome, hateful, odious, detestable, heinous; evil, ugly.
2. ignominious, sordid, vile, *Inf.* scummy, ignoble, beneath contempt, base, base-spirited, mean, mean-spirited, miserable, villainous, wretched, sorry, *Archaic.* caitiff; paltry, low, abject, cheap, shabby, groveling, servile, beggarly, worthless, nameless, *Inf.* no-account; disgusting, rank, distasteful, disreputable, shameful, disgraceful, unadmirable.

despise, *v.* **1.** scorn, disdain, contemn, spurn, misprize; show contempt for, scout, flout, consider beneath oneself, look down on *or* upon, look down the nose at, have a low opinion of; deride, scoff at, sneer at, jeer at, mock, ridicule, laugh at; slight, snub, shun.
2. feel disgust toward, feel distaste for; dislike, feel aversion toward, hate, detest, loathe, abominate, execrate, abhor.

despite, *prep.* **1.** notwithstanding, regardless of, in spite of, in defiance of, in contempt of, in the face of, in the teeth of, against.
—*n.* **2.** insult, antagonism, abuse, malignity; contempt, defiance, contumacy, insolence.

despoil, *v.* **1.** plunder, pillage, rob, spoliate, *Archaic.* spoil, *Chiefly Scot.* reive; ravage, harry, rape, maraud, ravish, depredate; raid, forage, ransack, sack, loot, gut, fleece, rifle; desecrate, defile, outrage, violate.
2. devastate, lay waste, desolate, wreck havoc upon, wreck, destroy, damage, ruin, vandalize.
3. strip, dispossess, deprive, denude, divest, bereave, *Law.* disseize, wring from, wrest from, wrench from, confiscate, seize.
4. commandeer, make off with, carry off, snatch; steal, thieve, filch, *Sl.* lift; pirate, rustle, poach.

despoliation, *n.* **1.** pillage, plunder, plundering, plunderage, rapine, depredation, spoliation, despoilment, *Obs.* direption, raven *or* ravin; ravaging, pillaging, harrying, marauding, sacking, *Rare.* sackage; raid, foray, razzia, inroad; foraging, looting, ravishment, seizure, grab, rape.
2. devastation, ravage, waste, desolation, destruction, ruin, havoc, damage, wreckage; burning, razing, leveling, demolishing; desecration, defilement, outrage, violation, vandalism; injury, harm, hurt, impairment, loss, scathe; collapse, breakdown, downfall.
3. brigandage, piracy, buccaneering, freebooting, banditry, highway robbery, *Obs.* latrociny, privateering, filibustering; robbery, theft, thievery, stealing.
4. dispossession, deprivation, deprival, divestiture, bereavement, *Law.* disseizin; confiscation, appropriation, expropriation.

despond, *v.* be depressed, be cast down, despair; lose hope of, lose heart, give up, surrender, quit, *Sl.* pack it in, give up the ship, cry quits, cry craven, throw in the towel, throw in the sponge; falter, give way, sink, droop, pine away; mope, mourn, lament, grieve, sorrow.

despondency, *n.* **1.** dejection, depression, mopishness, *Psychiatry.* hypochondria; slough of despond, doldrums, dumps, blues; hopelessness, disheartenment, dismay, discouragement; defeatism, pessimism.
2. gloom, melancholy, melancholia, misery, miserableness, wretchedness, distress, broken-heartedness; grief, sadness, sorrow, dolor, anguish; disconsolateness, unconsolability, desperation.

despondent, *adj.* dejected, depressed, *Sl.* bummed out, weighed down, burdened, *Inf.* broken, hypochondriac, hypochondriacal; disheartened, dispirited, low-spirited, *Brit.* hipped, downhearted, downcast, down, *Inf.* down in the dumps; discouraged, daunted, distressed, crestfallen, broken-hearted, heartbroken, heartsick, *Inf.* broken-up; cheerless, glum, gloomy, doleful, *Archaic.* wan; saddened, sad, blue, forlorn, melancholy, mopey, mopish; miserable, morose, woebegone, heavy-hearted, disconsolate, sorrowful, mournful, lachrymose, funereal.

despot, *n.* autocrat, dictator, tyrant, oppressor; monocrat, autarch, absolute *or* supreme ruler, monarch, soverign, emperor; lord, master, overlord.

despotic, *adj.* **1.** tyrannical, tyrannous, oppressive, despotical; iron-handed, strict, harsh, severe, hard, stern, authoritarian; monarchical, lordly, haughty, arrogant, overbearing, domineering; imperious, dictatorial, peremptory, high-handed, *Inf.* bossy.
2. autocratic, absolute, unlimited, omnipotent, all-powerful, totalitarian, monocratic.

despotism, *n.* **1.** absolutism, totalitarianism, autocracy, monocracy, one-man rule, one-party rule; czarism, Caesarism, kaiserism, Stalinism, imperialism; *U.S.* (*usu. of politics*) bossism.
2. supremacy, sovereignty, absolute power *or* control, uncontrolled *or* unlimited authority, complete control, domination; iron hand *or* fist, iron rod, iron rule; tyranny, oppression, repression, suppression.
3. autocracy, autarchy, dictatorship, totalitarian state, absolute monarchy, sovereignty, sovereign state.

destination, *n.* **1.** place *or* point of debarkation, where [s.o.] is going *or* bound, where [s.o.] gets off, journey's end; stop, stopping place, landing place, station, port of call; terminus, last stop, end of the line, end of the road, *Railroads.* terminal.
2. purpose, intent, intention, design; reason, motive, motivation, raison d'être; goal, objective, object, end, aim.

destine, *v.* **1.** design, intend, purpose, mean, resolve, determine, set; designate, dedicate, allot, *Obs.* appoint; mark, earmark, tag, set apart *or* aside; consecrate, devote; reserve, *Brit.* bespeak; plan, project.
2. fate, ordain, doom, *Rare.* destinate; predetermine, predestine, *Obs.* predestinate, preordain, foreordain, foreordinate, predecide, foredoom, *Inf.* have in store for.

destined, *adj.* **1.** bound for, on the way to *or* towards, *Inf.* headed for; routed, booked, scheduled.
2. designed, intended, meant, determined, set; designated, dedicated, alloted; engaged, reserved, *Brit.*

bespoken.

3. fated, fatal, ordained, doomed, *Rare.* destinated, *Obs.* destinal, *Obs.* destinable; written, in the cards, on the books; predetermined, predestined, predestinate, predestinated, preordained, foreordained, foredoomed, predecided.

4. certain, sure, sure as death, sure as death and taxes, fateful; inevitable, unavoidable, inescapable, ineluctable, ineludible.

5. liable to, bound to; planning to, intending to, meaning to, aiming to; planning on, counting on, figuring on; plotting to, scheming to, conspiring to, contriving to.

destiny, *n.* **1.** fate, fortune, lot, cup, portion, die, doom, *Archaic.* foredoom, *Chiefly Scot.* weird, writing on the wall, *Brit. Inf.* cup of tea; karma, kismet, *Obs.* destin *or* destine.

2. destination, future, ultimate future; hereafter, otherworld, world to come, next world; the beyond, great beyond; the unknown, great unknown; the grave, eternal home.

3. predetermination, predestination, God's will, Fortune's wheel, wheel of fortune; stars, planets, chance, happenstance, fortuity, serendipity; accident, coincidence, contingency, contingence; uncertainty, potluck, luck, fortune; heads or tails, roll *or* cast *or* toss *or* throw of the dice; vicissitudes, ups and downs, fickle finger of fate, way things fall, *Inf.* the breaks, *Inf.* how the cookie crumbles, *Inf.* how the ball bounces.

4. Chance, Fortune, Lady *or* Dame Fortune, Fortuna, Luck, Lady Luck.

5. the Destinies Fates, Weirds, Weird Sisters, (*Greek*) Moerea, (*Roman*) Parcae, (*Scandinavian*) Norns.

destitute, *adj.* **1.** poverty-stricken, impoverished, penurious, impecunious, beggared, pauperized; indigent, poor, needy, necessitous, bad off, badly off; pinched, straitened, distressed, *Inf.* strapped, *Inf.* up against it, *Inf.* on one's uppers, *Inf.* hard up; financially embarrassed, out of cash, *Inf.* short, *Brit. Sl.* skint, *All Inf.* broke, dead broke, flat broke, stone broke; bankrupt, ruined, wiped out, *Inf.* on the rocks, insolvent, overdrawn, in the red; down and out, out at the elbows, down at the heels, seedy.

2. *Usu.* **destitute of** devoid, deprived, deficient, bereft, bereaved; lacking, wanting, in need; without, sans.

3. helpless, stranded, high and dry, *Sl.* up the creek, *Inf.* over a barrel; defenseless, unprotected, unprovided, unsupplied; exposed, naked, vulnerable.

destitution, *n.* **1.** poverty, penury, indigence, impecuniousness, impecuniosity, beggary, pennilessness, neediness; insolvency, bankruptcy, liquidation; distress, straits, indebtedness; pauperism, pauperage, pauperdom, mendicancy, mendicity.

2. lack, want, need; absence, default, scarcity, insufficiency; paucity, dearth, shortage, deficiency; exhaustion, depletion, scantiness, meagerness; deprivation, starvation, famine, drought.

destroy, *v.* **1.** demolish, wipe out, pulverize, wreck, *Sl.* total, knock to pieces; raze, gut, fell, prostrate, level; pull down, tear down, take down, bring down, break down, throw down, cast down, beat down, knock down; shatter, crash, smash, batter, break; fracture, splinter, tear, crack, split, rend, tear apart, wrench apart; explode, burst, fulminate, implode; blast, blow up, bomb; mutilate, mangle, maim, make mincemeat of; mar, damage, spoil, mark, spot, stain; disfigure, scar, deface, blemish.

2. devastate, desolate, lay waste; ravage, work havoc upon, ruin, *Dial.* ruinate, bring to ruin, bring to naught, lay in ruins; despoil, rob, plunder, gut, pillage, ransack; vandalize, waste, *Sl.* trash.

3. quash, crush, subdue, quell, stifle, suppress, squelch, vanquish, squash; cut short, shoot down, *Inf.* cook one's goose, *Inf.* put the kibosh on, nip, nip in the bud; terminate, check, put an end to, dissolve, stop; overthrow, overwhelm, overturn, overcome; subvert, topple, cause the downfall of, upset, defeat, conquer; damn, seal the doom of, curse; annihilate, discreate, exterminate, extirpate.

4. erase, efface, eradicate, expunge, obliterate; blot out, sponge out, wipe out, rub out, cancel, strike out; scratch out, blue-pencil, delete, *Print.* dele, x out, cross out, mark off.

5. undo, unmake, unbuild, dismantle, disassemble, take apart.

6. kill, kill off, slay, slaughter, end, put an end to, make an end of, bring an end to; murder, sacrifice, dispose of, finish, finish off, *Sl.* do in, *Sl.* zap; assassinate, get rid of, mow down, do away with, put out of the way, *Inf.* wipe out, remove, massacre, liquidate, decimate; extinguish, quench, snuff out, put out, stamp out, smother, stifle, choke; devour, swallow up, consume, eat away; drown, strangle, set fire to, shipwreck, submerge, shoot, garrote, hang, knife, decapitate.

7. annul, nullify, disannul, declare null and void, render null and void, void, avoid; quash, invalidate, vitiate, vacate, disenact, disestablish; cancel, discharge; supersede, set aside; repeal, revoke, rescind, reverse, abrogate, abolish; suspend, *Law.* nol-pros, stop, discontinue, break off, countermand, counterorder, override, overrule; veto, negate.

8. disprove, refute, confute, rebut; dispute, deny, oppose, controvert, counter; contradict, belie, negate; overturn, overthrow, subvert; expose, reveal, unmask; discredit, disparage, demean, debase.

9. weaken, undermine, enfeeble, debilitate; enervate, exhaust, sap, devitalize; disable, cripple, paralyze.

10. neutralize, frustrate; counterpoise, counterbalance, counteract, overbalance, outweigh.

destroyer, *n.* **1.** demolisher, desolator, despoiler; wrecker, mutilator; robber, plunderer, ransacker, vandal; effacer, eliminator, eradicator, expunger.

2. annihilator, exterminator, killer, slayer, manslayer, slaughterer, dealer of destruction; murderer, Cain, assassinator, assassin, cutthroat, strangler, butcher, poisoner; executioner, gunman, hangman, decapitator, guillotiner, lyncher, *Inf.* hatchet man, *Sl.* hit man; incendiary, arsonist.

3. savage, cannibal, barbarian, Goth, Hun.

4. iconoclast, nihilist, anarchist.

5. plague, pestilence, epidemic, pandemic, scourge; explosive, submarine, warship, torpedo, bomb.

destruction, *n.* **1.** demolition, wipe-out, pulverization, wrecking, wreckage, rack and ruin; razing, gutting, felling, prostration, leveling; pulling down, tearing down, taking down, bringing down, breaking down, throwing down, casting down, beating down, knocking down; shattering, crashing, crack-up, collision, smashing, battering, breaking; fracture, splintering, tear, crack, split, rending, tearing apart, wrenching apart; explosion, (*of a rocket*) destruct, burst, fulmination, implosion, blast; mutilation, laceration, damage, spoil, marking, spotting, stain; disfigurement, scarring, defacement, blemish.

2. devastation, desolation, ravagement, havoc, holocaust, ruination; despoilment, robbing, spoliation, plundering, depredation, pillage, gutting, ransacking; vandalism, vandalizing, wasting, *Sl.* trashing.

3. quashing, crushing, quelling, subduing, stifling, suppression, squelching, vanquishment, squashing; cutting short, shooting down, *Inf.* putting the kibosh

on, nipping, nipping in the bud; termination, checking, putting an end to, dissolution, stopping; overthrow, overturning, overwhelming, overcoming; subversion, toppling, upsetting, defeat, conquering; damnation, sealing the doom of, cursing; annihilation, discreation, extermination, extirpation.
4. erasure, erasion, effacement, eradication, expunging, obliteration, blotting out, sponging out, wiping out, rubbing out, cancellation, striking out; scratching out, deleting, crossing out, *Print.* dele, marking off.
5. undoing, unmaking, unbuilding, dismantling, disassembling, taking apart.
6. killing, killing off, slaying, slaughter, putting an end to, making an end of, bringing to an end; murder, sacrifice, immolation, disposing of, finishing off, *Sl.* doing in, *Sl.* zapping, assassination, getting rid of, mowing down, doing away with, putting out of the way, *Inf.* wiping out, removal; massacre, liquidation, butchery, carnage, decimation; extinguishing, extinction, quenching, snuffing out, putting out, stamping out, smothering, choking; devouring, swallowing up, consumingness, eating away; drowning, strangling, setting fire to, shipwreck, submerging, shooting, garroting, hanging, knifing, decapitation.
7. annulment, nullification, disannulment, voidance, avoidance; quashing, *Law.* defeasance, invalidation, vitiation, *Law.* vacatur, disenactment, disestablishment; cancellation, discharge, setting aside; repeal, revocation, rescission, rescinding, reversal, abrogation, abolition; suspension, *Law.* nolle prosequi, cessation, discontinuance, breaking off; countermand, counterorder, overruling, overriding; veto, negation.
8. disproof, refutation, confutation, rebuttal; disputation, denial, opposition, countering; contradiction, belying, negation; overturning, overthrowing, disparagement, demeaning, debasing.
9. weakening, undermining, enfeeblement, debilitation, enervation, exhaustion, sapping, devitalization; disablement, breakdown, paralyzation.
10. neutralization, frustration; counterpoise, counterbalance, counteraction, contravention; overbalancing, outweighing.
destructive, *adj.* **1.** ruinous, disastrous, dire, dreadful, calamitous, catastrophic, cataclysmic; devastating, wasting, ravaging; disruptive, troublesome, distracting, obstreperous, unruly, subversive; annihilative, eradicative, extirpative, incendiary, conflagrative.
2. pernicious, injurious, deleterious, baneful, mischievous; harmful, hurtful, noxious, noisome; malicious, vicious, wicked, evil, malevolent; detrimental, disadvantageous, damaging; baleful, menacing, malignant, bad; unwholesome, poisonous, toxic, pestilential, pestiferous, virulent.
3. deadly, fell, fatal, mortal, lethal, killing; murderous, suicidal.
4. adverse, negative, contrary, contradictory, opposed, opposing, opposite, antithetical, conflicting; disproving, refuting, confuting, discrediting, invalidating; derogatory, disparaging, disapproving; unfavorable, unpropitious, inauspicious; unfriendly, antagonistic, clashing, hostile.
desultory, *adj.* inconsistent, inconstant, irregular, chaotic, haphazard; orderless, disorderly, unmethodical, unsystematic; changeable, capricious, shifting; unconnected, disconnected, random; unsteady, erratic, spasmodic, fitful; discursive, digressive, rambling, aimless, wandering, errant, roving.
detach, *v.* **1.** unfasten, uncouple, disengage, disconnect, unfix, unhitch, disjoin, disunite; disentangle, loosen, free; separate, dissociate, abstract, cut off, isolate, segregate.
2. *Military.* send on a special mission, detail.
detachment, *n.* **1.** disconnection, separation, severing, disseverance, disengagement, disjoining; loosening, unfixing; division, disunion, dissociation, segregation, abstraction.
2. aloofness, unconcern, indifference; preoccupation, absent-mindedness, inattention; faineancy, donothingness.
3. impartiality, freedom from prejudice, objectivity, disinterestedness, dispassion; tolerance, broadmindedness.
4. party, detail, force, body, division, men; squadron, garrison, regiment, brigade, battalion, squad, corps, platoon.
detail, *n.* **1.** item, particular, fact, point, factor, element, circumstance; aspect, feature, respect, attribute; unit, component, part, member, accessory.
2. **details** particulars, minutiae, niceties, fine points, fine print; counts, items, petty *or* minor details, trivialities, trivia.
3. attention, devotion, fidelity, faithfulness; conscientiousness, meticulousness, method, punctiliousness, scrupulousness; exaction, exactitude, exactness, precision, accuracy, correctness, nicety.
4. appointment, assignment, mission, errand; duty, charge, commission, task, chore, stint, job, part.
5. party, squad, group, detachment, company, body, force.
—*v.* **6.** specify, spell out, delineate; relate, recount, narrate, set forth; describe, depict, portray, mention; cite, cite chapter and verse, note, mark, point out, designate, indicate; list, enumerate, tabulate, codify, catalogue; itemize, particularize, differentiate; dot one's i's and cross one's t's.
7. appoint, assign, delegate, charge, commission; name, select, nominate, elect.
detailed, *adj.* **1.** involved, complex, complicated, intricate; convoluted, embarrassed, entangled.
2. itemized, particularized, individualized; exhaustive, comprehensive, thorough, plenary, complete, all-inclusive; particular, precise, minute, circumstantial; specific, pointed, explicit, express, exact, to the point.
detain, *v.* **1.** retard, slow, stay, buttonhole, check, delay, hinder; impede, inhibit, keep back, withhold.
2. stop, arrest, *Inf.* collar, retain, restrain, confine, secure, lock up, incarcerate, imprison, impound; pen, coop up, put behind bars, immure.
detect, *v.* **1.** discover, find, ferret out, dig up, unearth; sleuth, track down, turn up; catch, come across *or* upon, stumble across *or* upon, light *or* happen upon, chance upon.
2. ascertain, determine, establish, get to the bottom of; uncover, unmask, unveil, lay open, bring to light, bring out; expose, disclose, reveal.
3. descry, espy, observe, spy, spot, see, make out; discern, apprehend, perceive, learn of, *Brit.* twig; intuit, sense, feel, read, become aware of, get wind *or* scent of, smell out.
detection, *n.* **1.** discovering, finding out, ferreting out, unearthing, tracking down, smelling out; observation, espial.
2. discovery, find; ascertainment, determination, establishment; apprehension, perception, sighting.
detective, *n.* investigator, private investigator, *Sl.* private eye, FBI agent, G-man, *Inf.* sleuth, *Inf.* bird dog, *Inf.* sherlock, shadow, *Inf.* tail, *U.S. Sl.* dick, *U.S. Sl.* fuzz, *Sl.* narc; policeman, police officer, *Chiefly Brit.* constable, *Inf.* cop, *Sl.* copper, *U.S. Sl.* gumshoe, *Sl.* flatfoot, *Sl.* bull.
detention, *n.* **1.** restraint, detainment, retention; confinement, durance, duress, imprisonment, incarceration, quarantine.

2. retardation, delay, stopping, staying, checking, delaying; hindrance, withholding, retaining, arrest.

deter, *v.* **1.** daunt, intimidate, frighten *or* scare off *or* away; dishearten, dismay, dispirit, damp, cool, chill, throw cold water on, throw a wet blanket on, take the wind out of [s.o.'s] sails; discourage, dissuade, disincline, indispose, advise against, warn, frighten *or* scare out of, *Inf.* talk out of.

2. check, arrest, prevent, bar, obstruct, block, hold up; stall, stymie; thwart, frustrate, foil, balk, cross, *Sl.* stonewall; hinder, impede, restrain, constrain, bridle, trammel, hold back.

detergent, *adj.* **1.** cleansing, cleaning, detersive, abstergent, washing, bathing, laving; scrubbing, swabbing, mopping; purifying, depurative, purificatory; purging, purgative, cathartic.

—*n.* **2.** cleanser, cleaner, detersive, solvent, abstergent; scouring powder, soap powder *or* flakes, soap; purifier, depurative, purgative, cathartic.

deteriorate, *v.* **1.** degenerate, decline, sink, worsen, take a turn for the worse, slip, slide; go downhill, go to pieces, go to ruin, *Inf.* go to pot, *Inf.* go to the dogs, *Sl.* go *or* run to seed, *Sl.* hit the skids; fall, fail, lapse, weaken, retrogress, retrograde, let oneself go.

2. corrupt, vitiate, debase, abase; pollute, contaminate, infect, poison, taint, soil, sully, befoul; debauch, seduce, pervert, subvert, demoralize, lead astray *or* away.

3. disintegrate, crumble, break up, fall apart; erode, ablate, wear away, weather; decay, decompose, crumble into dust.

deterioration, *n.* **1.** degeneration, vitiation, declination, declension, atrophy; retrogression, retrogradation, regression, lapse; corruption, depravation, degradation, debasement, demoralization, dissolution, dissipation, perversion, subversion, seduction; disintegration, dilapidation, erosion, corrosion, wear and tear; decay, decomposition, moth and rust.

2. decline, drop, fall, descent, slump, downturn, downtrend, turn for the worse.

determination, *n.* **1.** decision, solution, adjudication, adjudgment, arbitrament, arbitration.

2. ascertainment, verification, finding, learning; establishment, confirmation; discovery, uncovering, unearthing.

3. settlement, verdict, judgment, opinion, decree; diagnosis, prognosis; upshot, conclusion, result, final issue, end, outcome.

4. firmness, resoluteness, steadfastness, tenacity; resolve, fortitude, will power, will; mettle, backbone, courage, grit, nerve, boldness; spunk, pluck, stamina, spirit, zeal, ardor; drive, push, persistence, pertinacity, perseverance, doggedness; stability, steadiness, constancy; indomitability, obduracy, intransigence; obstinacy, stubborness, pigheadedness.

5. intention, purpose, reason, motive, basis, ground, rationale; design, project, plan, purport, intentionality, ulterior motive; wherefore, *Fr. raison d'être,* reason why, the why and wherefore.

6. direction, aim, end, goal, mark, objective; propensity, tendency, proclivity, leaning; bent, drift, bearing, course, tenor, tack.

determine, *v.* **1.** settle, decide, resolve, fix; adjudge, judge, arbitrate, decree, ordain; adjust, reckon, come to an agreement; clinch, settle once and for all, *Inf.* sew up, *Inf.* nail down, *Inf.* wrap up, *Inf.* put the bow on, *Inf.* put the cap *or* lid on, *Inf.* put on ice.

2. conclude, find, opine; ascertain, make certain of, verify, establish; make out, detect, tell, descry; find out, discover, pin down, get.

3. affect, influence, condition, work upon, act on, qualify, modify; control, govern, regulate, direct, rule, command; cause, give form to, shape, designate, effect; prescribe, set, order, impose, dictate.

4. impel, induce, influence, prompt, sway; give direction to, lead, decide, turn the scales; incline, bend, dispose, turn; give a push to, give a push in the right direction, show the way, put on the right track, set straight.

5. lead, bring to, conduce to, redound to, contribute to, predispose to; forward, advance, promote.

6. decide, choose, elect, select; will, purpose, resolve; make up one's mind, fix upon, settle upon, make a d-cision, make a resolution.

determined, *adj.* **1.** resolute, firm, steadfast, purposeful; staunch, constant, persevering, stanch; earnest, intent, fixed; game, plucky, spunky, *Inf.* scrappy; dogged, tenacious, gritty, relentless, bent on, *Inf.* hellbent, do-or-die; unfaltering, unhesitating, unflinching, unwavering, unyielding; unflagging, indomitable, intransigent, obdurate; obstinate, stubborn, inflexible, mulish.

2. settled, decided, resolved, fixed, confirmed; agreed, set, sealed, *Inf.* sewed up, *Inf.* signed, sealed and delivered.

determining, *adj.* decisive, deciding, definitive; crucial, pivotal, critical, essential; important; chief, supreme; determinate, determinative, concluding, conclusive, settling; final, authoritative, absolute, peremptory, positive.

deterrent, *n.* block, stumbling block, catch, snag, hitch, rub, fly in the ointment, drawback, liability; check, hindrance, balk, impedient; obstacle, obstruction, oppilation, blockage, impediment, stopper; bar, barrier, barricade.

detest, *v.* abhor, loathe, execrate, despise, abominate, hate, feel aversion toward, feel hostility toward; not be able to bear *or* abide, shudder at, shrink from, recoil from, blench from; feel repugnance toward, feel disgust toward, feel distaste for; dislike, mislike, direlish, disfavor, disesteem.

detestable, *adj.* **1.** abhorrent, loathsome, execrable, odious, heinous, despicable, abominable, hateful; dislikable, unlikable, unpleasant, *Brit. Inf.* beastly, displeasing, disagreeable.

2. repugnant, aversive, disgusting, rank, repulsive, repellent, revolting, distasteful, obnoxious, noisome; vile, sordid, putrid, rotten, foul; sickening, nauseaing, nauseous, noxious; ugly, scurvy, ignoble, mean, base, abject, low.

detestation, *n.* abhorrence, loathing, abomination, execration, odium, hatred, hate, detesting; antipathy, aversion, animosity, animus, enmity, hostility; *Fr. bête noire,* bugbear; offense, repugnance, revulsion, disgust, distaste, nausea; dislike, disrelish, disfavor, disesteem, displeasure.

detested, *adj.* hated, loathed, despised, abhorred, execrated, abominated, held in abomination, held in contempt; disliked, unliked, disfavored, unfavored, disrelished; ostracized, shunned, blackballed; scorned, contemned, ridiculed, sneered at, laughed at, scoffed at; booed, hissed, *Sl.* raspberried, *Sl.* given the Bronx cheer.

detester, *n.* **1.** hater, loather, abhorrer, despiser; execrator, abominator, curser, vilifier; detractor, disparager, derogator.

2. misanthrope, misanthropist, misogynist, manhater, woman-hater, sexist, male chauvinist pig; racist, bigot, anti-Semite, *Inf.* Archie Bunker; chauvinist, jingo, jingoist, xenophobe; Timon, Alceste.

dethronable, *adj.* **1.** impeachable, oustable, deposable, unseatable, displaceable; uncrownable, discrownable, *Rare.* disenthronable, debarrable, unbarrable; defrockable, unfrockable, *Rare.* unchurchable, excommunicable, expellable, divestable; (*all from power, political office, etc.*) removable, replaceable, dispensable, expendable, unessential.

2. demotable, downgradable, degradable, disratable; *Sl.* bumpable, *Sl.* firable, *Sl.* breakable, *Mil. Sl.* bustable.

dethrone, *v.* **1.** depose, uncrown, *Rare.* disenthrone; remove from office, unseat, force to abdicate, *U.S.* impeach, drive out of office, oust, dispossess, displace, disbar, expel, exile.

2. demote, downgrade, lower *or* reduce in rank, degrade, humble, *Inf.* take *or* knock down a peg or two; defrock *or* unfrock, declass, *Inf.* strip of rank, disrate, cashier, *Mil.* drum out, *Mil. Sl.* bust, *Inf.* kick upstairs.

detonate, *v.* **1.** explode, go off, fulminate, blow up, *Archaic.* displode; burst, *Inf.* bust, break open, fly apart; bang, blast, boom, roar, thunder, clap.

2. set off, *Obs.* detonize; discharge, shoot, fire.

3. ignite, kindle, light, spark; start, give rise to, cause, produce, engender.

detonation, *n.* **1.** explosion, blow-up, blast, fulmination, *Archaic.* displosion; burst, *Inf.* bust, bursting, breaking open, flying apart, dissiliency, dissilience; bang, report, boom, roar, thunder, clap.

2. setting off, *Obs.* detonization; discharge, firing, volley.

3. ignition, kindling, lighting; sparking, spark, start, engenderment.

detour, *n.* indirect course, roundabout way, roundabout, *Inf.* circumbendibus; byway, byroad, bypath, by-pass.

detract, *v.* **1.** divert, deflect, shift, avert; withdraw, draw away, turn aside, turn off, turn away, diverge, swerve; (*of the mind or attention*) distract, sidetrack, draw off, divide.

2. belittle, disparage, demean, deprecate, derogate, deflate, decry, *Inf.* talk down, depreciate, devaluate; humiliate, humble, mortify, *Sl.* put down; lampoon, pasquinade, caricature, satirize.

3. defame, denigrate, vilify, vituperate, vilipend, scandalize, malign, gibbet, run down, impugn, berate, revile, *Inf.* knock, *Inf.* rap, speak ill of, speak evil of, *Sl.* badmouth, *Sl.* poormouth, backbite; slander, libel, calumniate, traduce, falsify, misrepresent, accuse falsely, impute, asperse, insinuate; injure, insult, abuse, assault, attack, assail, stab, *Sl.* dump on, *Sl.* trash.

detraction, *n.* **1.** belittlement, disparagement, deprecation, derogation, deflation, decrial, *Inf.* talking down, depreciation, devaluation; humiliation, humble pie, mortification; lampoon, squib, pasquinade, caricature, satirization; sarcasm, ridicule, mockery, jibe, jeer, scoff, sneer; disdain, derision, contempt, scorn, contumely.

2. discredit, disfavor, obloquy, loss of face, disapproval, disapprobation, criticism, stricture.

3. defamation, denigration, vituperation, vilification, scandal, scandalization, scandalmongering, abuse, injury, attack, scurrility, running down, gibbeting, backbiting, *Sl.* badmouth, *Sl.* poormouth; slander, libel, calumny, calumniation, traducement, falsification, misrepresentation, false accusation, slur, imputation, aspersion, insinuation, innuendo, *Inf.* brickbat.

detractive, *adj.* **1.** belittling, disparaging, demeaning, deflating, derogatory, derogative, derogating, detractory, detracting, depreciatory, depreciative, depreciating, devaluating; humiliating, humbling, mortifying; lampooning, caricaturing, ridiculing, satirizing, mocking, jeering, jibing, sneering; satirical, sarcastic, caustic, biting, vitriolic, acrimonious, scathing; disdainful, derisive, derisory, deriding, snide, contemptuous, scornful.

2. discrediting, disfavorable, unfavorable, disapproving, disapprobatory, disapprobative, critical.

3. defamatory, denigrating, vituperative, vilifying, vilipenditory; slanderous, libelous, calumniatory, calumnious, traducent, false, untrue, maliciously false *or* untrue, misrepresentative, aspersive, imputative, insinuating; abusive, hurtful, scurrilous, injurious, contumelious, insulting, backbiting, foulmouthed.

detractor, *n.* **1.** belittler, disparager, deprecator, derogator, depreciator; lampooner, satirist, muckraker, hack; defamer, vilifier, vilipender, denigrator, scandalizer, impugner, asperser, backbiter, maligner, evil-speaker, carper, caviler, *Inf.* knocker; censor, censurer, reviler, castigator, inveigher, reprover, disapprover, denouncer, railer, curser, execrator, imprecator, anathematizer, critic.

2. slanderer, libeler, calumniator, traducer, falsifier, liar; mud-slinger, dirt-flinger.

detriment, *n.* injury, impairment, damage, hurt, harm, wrong, ill, evil; disadvantage, drawback, liability.

detrimental, *adj.* harmful, hurtful, baneful, pernicious, noisome, mischievous; injurious, deleterious, damaging, prejudicial, destructive; disadvantageous, adverse, unfavorable, untoward, inimical.

detrition, *n.* erosion, abrasion, friction. See **attrition** (*def.* 1).

detritus, *n.* **1.** rock fragments, drift, sediment, alluvium, moraine; pebbles, gravel, grit, pulverulence, sand, powder, dust.

2. debris, flotsam and jetsam, wreckage, ruins, remains, fragments, shards; rubble, rubbish, litter, junk, trash.

devastate, *v.* **1.** lay waste, waste, desolate; despoil, *Archaic.* spoil, spoliate, ravage, harry, pillage, plunder, depredate; ransack, sack, strip, rifle; destroy, blast, wreck, ruin, lay in ruins; demolish, raze, level, gut, obliterate, annihilate, extirpate.

2. (*often used figuratively*) overwhelm, overpower, vanquish, overmaster, subdue, conquer; destroy, crush, overcome, rout, undo, discomfit.

3. disconcert, take aback, floor; confound, nonplus, discompose, abash; fluster, ruffle, *Inf.* discombobulate; embarrass, chagrin, mortify, humiliate.

devastating, *adj.* **1.** destructive, desolating, ruinous, ravaging; plundering, vandalizing, pillaging; extirpative, annihilative, annihilatory.

2. harmful, deleterious, pernicious, baleful, menacing, malign; wasting, enervating, weakening, debilitating; deadly, fatal, lethal.

3. satirical, ironic, caustic, sarcastic, acerbic; biting, cutting, trenchant, stinging; mordant, sardonic, derisive.

4. keen, incisive, sharp, piercing, penetrating.

devastation, *n.* **1.** destruction, ruination, holocaust, demolition, ruin, havoc; spoliation, despoliation, despoilment, ravage, pillage, plunder, sack; rapine, ravishment, predation, depredation.

2. desolation, waste, wreckage, ravagement; extermination, extirpation, obliteration, annihilation.

develop, *v.* **1.** grow, evolve, increase, fill out, expand, enlarge, swell, wax, become greater *or* larger; mature, maturate, ripen; bloom, blossom, flower, bear fruit, fructify; sprout, germinate, pullulate, bud,

shoot, burst forth, burgeon; extend, distend, stretch, spread, widen.
2. advance, further, promote, exploit; get ahead, go up in the world, progress, make headway, fare well, get *or* go along; become, come to be, get to be, work up to.
3. elaborate, amplify, magnify, add to, augment, supplement, reinforce.
4. generate, breed, propagate, hatch; bring up, rear, foster, cultivate; invent, fashion, coin; institute, establish, organize; constitute, compose, form, erect, build.
5. explicate, unfold, lay open, uncover, reveal, disclose, make known; be disclosed, become manifest, become evident, appear, dawn, come to light, come out, creep.

development, *n.* **1.** growth, evolution, increase, increment, expansion, aggrandizement, enlargement, dilatation, swell; maturity, maturation, ripeness, unfolding, opening, blooming, blossoming, flowering.
2. improvement, build-up, strengthening; amplification, magnification, extension, augmentation, elaboration; progress, advancement, furtherance, promotion.
3. event, occurrence, happening, circumstance, item, issue.

deviant, *adj.* **1.** aberrant, deviate, divergent. See **deviate** (*defs.* **5-7**).
—n. **2.** noncomformist, deviator, radical. See **deviate** (*defs.* **8-10**).

deviate, *v.* **1.** veer, straggle, turn aside; wander, ramble, meander, stray, drift, rove, divagate, *Scot. and North Eng.* sklent; err, miss, go astray, lose one's way.
2. depart, diverge, deflect, vary, differ, change, step aside, steer clear of; curve, turn, bend, swerve, tack, slue, slew, yaw, bear off, wheel, wheel about, swing about; shy, back off, *Chiefly Brit.* jib; sidle, edge.
3. digress, maunder, descant, be diffuse, rhapsodize, wax longwinded, go off on *or* at a tangent, beat around the bush.
4. divert, sidetrack, shift, switch, shunt.
—adj. **5.** aberrant, deviant, divergent, errant, heretical, heterodox, wayward, devious; unacceptable, out of line, out of hand; erroneous, mistaken; deviating, diverging, divagating, departing, digressing, lapsing, wandering, rambling, drifting, straying, roving.
6. anomalous, anomalistic, abnormal, irregular, variable; odd, peculiar, curious, queer, strange, bizarre, weird, freakish; eccentric, idiosyncratic, *Inf.* quirky; unconventional, uncommon, unusual, offbeat, out of the ordinary, singular, exceptional, individual, individualistic, unorthodox; monstrous, unnatural, heteroclite, heteromorphic, heteromorphous, malformed, deformed, misshapen, misshaped, miscreated; epicene, androgynous, hermaphroditic, hermaphroditical, transsexual.
7. perverse, perverted, corrupt, corrupted, twisted, *Inf.* kinky; wanton, depraved, degenerate, degenerated, deteriorated, vitiated, debased, abased; licentious, lascivious, lewd, suggestive; sadistic, masochistic; homosexual, homoerotic, homophile, *Inf.* gay, *Inf.* bent, *Derog.* queer, lesbian, sapphic, tribadistic, *Derog.* butch; bisexual, bisexed, *Sl.* switch-hitting, *Sl.* hitting *or* swinging from both sides, *Sl.* ac/dc, amphierotic; autoerotic.
—n. **8.** anomaly, deviant, *Rare.* anomalism, abnormality, abnormity, irregularity, variation.
9. nonconformist, deviator, radical, heretic, *Chiefly Brit.* punk; misfit, maverick, drop out, loner, lone wolf, solitary, solitary man, fish out of water, square peg in a round hole; character, card, original, pip, sport, exception, individual, nonesuch, nondescript, bohemian; crank, fanatic; crazy, flake, freak, three-dollar bill, crackpot, rare bird, queer fellow, queer duck, queer potato, *Inf.* fruitcake, *Inf.* dingbat, *Inf.* ding-a-ling; *All Sl.* weirdo, weirdy, weirdie, creep, oddball, screwball, nut, loony, loner, case, geezer, kook, odd duck, squirrel.
10. homosexual, homosexualist, homophile, third sex, invert; transvestite, drag queen; *All Sl.* queen, gunsel, chicken, punk, limp-wrist, three-dollar bill, *Brit.* ginger, ginger beer, *Brit.* poof, *Brit.* poofter, *All Derog.* homo, queer, faggot, fag, fruit, flit, fairy, pansy, nance, auntie; bisexual, *Sl.* bi-guy, *Sl.* switch hitter; lesbian, sapphist, tribade, *Sl.* butch, *Sl.* femme, *Derog.* dyke, *Derog.* bull dyke, *Archaic.* fricatrice.
11. (*all with reference to sexual relations*) pervert, fiend, brute, deviant, degenerate, maniac, criminal, psychopath; sadist, masochist, fetishist, voyeur, scatophiliac, erotomanic, narcissist, nymphomaniac; sodomist, sodomite, bugger; pederast, pedophiliac, catamite; coprophiliac; necrophiliac; zoophiliac.

deviation, *n.* **1.** veer, veering, curve, curving, turn, turning, swerve, swerving, bend, bending; tacking, wheeling, wheeling about, swinging about; shift, shifting, switch, switching, shunting, straying, drifting, roving, divagating; digression, digressing, maundering.
2. departure, divergence, declension, declination, deflection, stepping aside, steering clear; change, difference.
3. aberration, waywardness, deviousness, unacceptableness; anomaly, abnormality, irregularity, variable, variableness; strangeness, oddness, incongruousness, peculiarity, curiousness, queerness, eccentricity, quirk, *Inf.* quirkiness; unconventionality, uncommonness, uncommonality, unusualness, exception, singularity, singularness, individuality.
4. unnaturalness, freakishness, *Inf.* kinkiness; perversion, corruption, wantonness, depravity, depravation, degeneracy, degeneration, decadence, deterioration, vitiation, debasement, abasement; licentiousness, lasciviousness, lewdness, erotomania; homosexuality, homosexualism, homoeroticism, sexual inversion, lesbianism, sapphism, tribadism *or* tribady, *Inf.* gayness, *Derog.* faggotry, *Derog.* faggism; bisexuality, bisexualism, amphieroticism, *Sl.* swinging *or* hitting both ways; autoeroticism.
5. (*all with reference to sexual relations*) perversion, fiendishness, deviance, abnormality, psychopathy, pathology, criminality; sadism, masochism, sadomasochism, *Sl.* s-m, algolagnia, algolagny; fetishism, voyeurism, scatophilia, narcissism, exhibitionism; sodomy, buggery; pederasty, pedophilia; coprophilia; necrophilia; zoophilia; incest, incestuousness.
6. division, departure, disunion, secession, desertion, underground movement; separation, falling out, breach, split, rupture, break, rent.
7. monstrosity, heteroclite, freak, mutant, hermaphrodite, epicene.

device, *n.* **1.** appliance, instrument, apparatus, mechanism, contrivance, *Inf.* contraption, invention, gadget, hickey, *Sl.* gimmick; implement, utensil, tool, machine, equipment, gear, outfit, tackle, rigging; means, wherewithal, resources, expedient, agent, medium.
2. design, plan, project; strategem, *Inf.* wrinkle, artifice, trick, *Inf.* flimflam, wile, ruse, trap; intrigue, plot, scheme, strategy, machination; conspiracy, complot, cabal; subterfuge, blind, *Inf.* dodge, fetch; maneuver, feint, deception, sleight, shift, move, evasion, shuffle; fraud, imposture, imposition, hoax.
3. pattern, figure, motto, slogan, legend; mark, trademark, hallmark, *Numismatics.* countermark;

symbol, token, emblem, seal, signet, coat of arms, insigne, badge.

devil, *n.* **1.** (*sometimes cap.*) Evil One, Wicked One, Spirit of Evil, prince of darkness, prince of sinners, monarch of hell, prince of liars; Lord of the Flies, Lord of Vermin, the Serpent, the dragon, the goat, seirizzin, the dickens, the deuce; Adversary, Tempter, Foul Fiend, Archfiend, Archdemon; Old One, Old Bogy, Old Boy, Old Scratch; Old Harry, Old Davy, Nick, Old Nick; *All Scot.* the Auld Ane, the Deil, Auld Clubfoot, Auld Nick.

2. Lucifer, Satan, Mephistopheles, Beelzebub, Satan, Sathanas; Moloch, Belial, Clootie, Samael, *Scot.* Hornie, *Japanese Myth.* Oni, *Jewish Myth.* Asmodeus; Abaddon, Apollyon, Diabolus, Azazel, *Islamic Myth.* Elbis, Iblis.

3. evil spirit, cacodemon, genie, djinn. See **demon** (*def.* **1**).

4. brute, savage, beast, monster, barbarian; witch, shrew, hag, hellcat, vixen, Xanthippe; virago, crone, ogress, *Sl.* battle-ax. See **demon** (*def.* **2**).

5. fox, sly dog, slyboots, dodger, Artful Dodger, reynard; trickster, *Sl.* shyster, *Inf.* slick *or* smooth operator, *Inf.* Philadelphia lawyer, horse-trader; sweet talker, charmer, confidence man, *Sl.* con man, *Sl.* smoothie.

6. wretch, unfortunate, beggar; bum, tramp, hobo, vagabond; ragamuffin, urchin, tatterdemalion, ragpicker.

devilish, *adj.* **1.** diabolic, diabolical, fiendish, ghoulish; satanic, Mephistophelian, demonic, demonian, demoniac, demoniacal, cacodemonic; infernal, hellish.

2. damnable, accursed, execrable, abominable, horrible, horrid, hideous, monstrous, atrocious; base, vile, odious, obnoxious, villainous, sinister; wicked, iniquitous, evil, sinful, impious, *Obs.* scelerous, blackhearted, corrupt, depraved, *Archaic.* facinorous; reprobate, nefarious, flagitious, heinous; profligate, immoral, dissolute, vitiated, perverted, perverse; pestilential, malevolent, malicious, malign, maleficent, venomous, virulent; dire, black, dreadful, baleful.

3. merciless, heartless, hard-hearted, stony-hearted, unkind, unfeeling, cruel; relentless, unrelenting, unsparing, remorseless.

4. impish, mischievous, elfish, prankish; vexatious, troublesome, naughty, annoying.

5. *Informal.* excessive, great, enormous; terrible, awful. See **excessive, enormous.**

devil-may-care, *adj.* **1.** reckless, careless, heedless, wanton, rash, foolhardy; temerarious, headlong, impetuous, impulsive, madcap, breakneck.

2. rollicking, swaggering, roistering, swash-buckling; sporty, jaunty, gay, saucy, pert; raffish, rakehell, profligate, prodigal, dissolute, disreputable; shameless, barefaced, unabashed; impudent, impertinent, forward, fresh, audacious.

3. indifferent, cavalier, offhand, nonchalant; easy-come-easy-go, easygoing, lackadaisical, casual; carefree, insouciant, pococurante, unconcerned, unworried; flippant, frivolous, shallow.

deviltry, *n.* **1.** mischievousness, mischief, foul play, devilry, *Inf.* goings-on; villainy, knavery, rascality, roguery.

2. wickedness, diabolicalness, fiendishness, satanicalness, hellishness, infernality; evil, iniquity, improbity, vice; maliciousness, villainousness, malevolence, viciousness, nefariousness, flagitiousness, heinousness.

3. black magic, black art, witchcraft, sorcery, diablerie.

devious, *adj.* **1.** indirect, roundabout, circumventive, dodging, evasive, deviating; circuitous, winding, curvy, worming, flexuous, sinuous, anfractuous, tortuous, serpentine, zigzag; vagrant, wandering, meandering, unsettled, unstable.

2. tricky, cunning, crafty, sly, wily, foxy, snaky, artful, subtle; insidious, guileful, scheming, designing, contriving, plotting, calculating, Machiavellian; shifty, slippery, smooth, slick; sneaky, stealthy, furtive, secretive, secret, surreptitious; deceitful, deceptive, delusive, misleading, prevaricative, subreptitious; crooked, dishonest, insincere, disingenuous, underhanded, *Inf.* left-handed.

devise, *v.* **1.** concoct, scheme, contrive, arrange, project, design, work out, plan, plan for; originate, invent, create, compose, excogitate; design, draft, frame, coin, mint, shape, construct, work up; think up, *Sl.* dope out, hit upon, dream up, spin, make up; fabricate, fashion, hatch, put together, order; improvise, plot, conjure up, neologize, neoterize, germinate, formulate, form.

—*n.* **2.** *Law.* will, bequeath, bestow, confer, hand down, convey, transfer.

devoid, *adj.* void, destitute, bare, barren, bald, denuded; lacking, wanting, deficient; depleted, short, empty, out; without, sans.

devote, *v.* **1.** assign, apply, commit, consign; allot, allocate, set aside, set apart.

2. (*often of oneself*) give, offer, pledge, surrender, dedicate; bless, sanctify, hallow, consecrate, make holy.

devoted, *adj.* **1.** faithful, true, true blue, loyal; unremitting, untiring, indefatigable, persistent, persevering, tenacious, determined; earnest, attentive, eager, ardent, zealous; addicted, hooked.

2. intimate, fond, loving, amorous, affectionate, admiring, infatuated; tender, warm, close, cordial.

3. dedicated, pledged, promised, vowed; consecrated, sanctified, hallowed, holy, sacred, blessed.

devotee, *n.* **1.** votary, champion, follower, disciple, satellite, adherent; zealot, partisan, bigot, fanatic; visionary, cultist, sectary; believer, religionist, pietist.

2. enthusiast, fan, aficionado, *Inf.* buff, *Inf.* hound, *Sl.* bug, *Sl.* nut; addict, *Inf.* fiend, *Sl.* junkie, *Sl.* freak, *Sl.* head; (*all usu. of adolescent girls*) (*in the 40s*) bobbysoxer, (*in the 60s*) teenybopper, (*in the 70s*) groupie.

3. promoter, supporter, *Inf.* pusher, *Inf.* booster, *Inf.* arm-waver; chauvinist, jingoist.

devotion, *n.* **1.** prayer, religious worship, worship, homage, reverence, veneration, adoration, laudation, glorification; thanksgiving, grace, blessing, benediction; dedication, consecration, sanctification; service, observance, prayer meeting, mass, vespers, matins.

2. piety, devoutness, godliness, saintliness, spirituality, holiness, sanctity, religiousness; religiosity, pietism.

3. loyalty, faithfulness, fidelity, constancy, fealty, steadfastness; respect, deference, obeisance.

4. ardor, fervor, passion, fanaticism, fire; zeal, enthusiasm, eagerness, earnestness, willingness, readiness; diligence, perseverance, assiduity, sedulousness, *Inf.* stick-to-it-iveness.

5. love, strong affection, devotedness, attachment, adherence; idolization, infatuation, enchantment; esteem, fondness, liking, regard, admiration, inclination, fancy, yearning.

devotional, *adj.* **1.** devout, pious, reverential, religious, worshipful, prayerful; godly, saintly, spiritual.

2. holy, sacred, sanctified, blessed, consecrated; solemn, dedicated, hallowed, ceremonial.

devour, *v.* **1.** swallow, gulp, eat up, swallow up, gulp down, gobble, bolt, wolf, raven, *Inf.* put away *or* down, *Inf.* pack away *or* in; banquet, feast, gobble up, gormandize, gluttonize, gorge, stuff, cram, make a pig of oneself, eat greedily, *Sl.* eat like there's no tomorrow,

Sl. pig in, *Sl.* stuff one's face, *Sl.* tuck in.
2. consume, dispatch, finish, finish off, dispose of, get rid of, *Sl.* polish off, *Sl.* do in, *Sl.* kill; destroy, ruin, ravage, wreck havoc upon; devastate, lay to waste, waste; demolish, wipe out, wreck, *Sl.* total; wipe off the map, erase, obliterate, eradicate.
3. engulf, swallow up, envelop, swamp; overcome, overwhelm, conquer, subjugate; triumph over, whip, drub, rout; overturn, vanquish, overpower; thrash, trim, break.
4. take in, drink in, absorb; ogle, fix on, stare, gape, *Inf.* gawk, *Inf.* give [s.o.] the once over, *Sl.* eyeball, *Sl.* slobber over, *Sl.* drool over.

devout, *adj.* **1.** pious, reverent, religious, worshipful, prayerful, church-going, faithful; heaven-minded, holy, godly, saintly, seraphic; angelic, pure in heart; pietistic, righteous, solemn, serious.
2. sincere, earnest, heartfelt; fervent, fervid, ardent, intense, vehement.

dexterity, *n.* **1.** adroitness, deftness, sleight, sleight of hand, legerdemain; nimbleness, agility, quickness; handiness, right-handedness, neatness, skillfulness, skill, faculty, knack, talent; finesse, felicity, ambidexterity, facility, readiness; artistry, craft, proficiency, adeptness, address, mastery, authority, expertness.
2. cleverness, shrewdness, *Inf.* cuteness, artifice, cunning, cunningness, guile, canniness, subtleness, artfulness, craftiness; ingenuity, ingeniousness, inventiveness, resourcefulness; astuteness, keenness, acuteness, sharpness, sharp-wittedness; sagaciousness, sagacity, aptness, smartness, wittiness.

dexterous, *adj.* **1.** adroit, deft, ambidextrous, handy, neat, *Brit. Dial.* feat; nimble, agile, quick; facile, ready, skilled, skillful; proficient, adept, experienced, *Fr. au fait.*
2. clever, shrewd, *Archaic.* parlous, *Inf.* cute; ingenious, inventive, resourceful; cunning, canny, guileful, subtle, artful, crafty, slick; astute, keen, acute, sharp, sharp-witted, sharp as a tack, quick-witted; sagacious, apt, smart, witty.
3. masterful, masterly, expert, artistic; excellent, polished, finished, well executed; workmanlike, workmanly, practiced, accomplished.

diabolic, *adj.* **1.** damnable, accursed, execrable; abominable, horrible, horrid, hideous, monstrous, atrocious; base, vile, odious, obnoxious, villainous, sinister; wicked, iniquitous, sinful, evil, impious, *Obs.* scelerous, black-hearted, corrupt, depraved, *Archaic.* facinorous; reprobate, nefarious, flagitious, heinous; profligate, immoral, dissolute, vitiated, perverted, perverse; pestilential, malevolent, malicious, malign, maleficent, malefic.
2. devilish, diabolical, fiendish, ghoulish; satanic, Mephistophelian, demonic, demoniac, demoniacal, cacodemonic; infernal, hellish.

diadem, *n.* **1.** crown, coronet, tiara, mitre.
2. wreath, garland, laurel, bays; circlet, headband, fillet, chaplet.

diagram, *n.* **1.** drawing, line drawing, sketch, draft; picture, view, illustration, representation; outline, delineation, skeleton, figure, profile.
2. chart, graph, plot, table, scheme, schema, blueprint.

dial, *n.* **1.** sundial, horologe, clock, timepiece.
—*v.* **2.** telephone, *Inf.* phone, call, call up, *Brit.* ring up, *Inf.* buzz, *Inf.* give [s.o.] a ring *or* buzz.

dialect, *n.* **1.** tongue, speech, speech pattern, idiom, regionalism, localism, provincialism, accent; vernacular, colloquialism, patois, pidgin, pigeon, lingua franca.
2. jargon, cant, argot, parlance, lingo, slang.

dialectic, *adj.* **1.** dialectical, logical, rational, rationalistic, reasoned; analytic, deductive, inductive; argumentative, controversial, polemical, contentious.
2. dialectal, dialect, regional, provincial, vicinal, areal; idiomatic, vernacular, local, native; colloquial, conversational, spoken, informal, used, in use *or* usage, common, popular, of the people; jargonal, jargonistic, jargonish, jargonesque, slangy, cantish, argotic.
—*n.* **3.** discussion, debate, argument, polemic, war of words, search for truth, *Rare.* disceptation.
4. *Often* **dialectics a.** logic, reasoning, ratiocination; argumentation, disputation, polemics, controversy, contention. **b.** philosophy, metaphysics, rationalism; doctrine, rationale, system *or* body of thought.

dialectician, *n.* logician, rationalist, reasoner, casuist; philosopher, metaphysician; arguer, polemist, polemic, debater, discusser, controversialist.

dialogue, *n.* **1.** conversation, converse, talk, interlocution, duologue, verbal exchange; chat, chitchat, small talk, table talk, causerie, confabulation, *Inf.* confab.
2. (*of a play*) lines, words, speaking, spoken part.
3. discussion, discourse, communication, exchange of ideas *or* opinions; debate, argument, polemic, dialectic, search for truth, *Rare.* disceptation; conference, colloquy, palaver, parley, parlance; meeting, huddle, tête-à-tête, *Inf.* powwow, *Fr. pourparler, Sl.* bull *or* rap session, *Sl.* rap.

diameter, *n.* breadth, width, thickness, length *or* distance through the center, outside diameter; inside diameter, caliber, *Mach.* bore.

diametrical, *adj.* direct, complete, absolute, exact, extreme; diametrically opposite *or* opposed, antipodal.

diaphanous, *adj.* sheer, light, thin, translucent, transparent, see-through; delicate, fine, silken, chiffon, gossamer, gauzy, cob-webby.

diary, *n.* **1.** journal, daily record, log, logbook; daybook, datebook, appointment book.
2. history, chronicle, annals.

diatribe, *n.* tirade, invective, philippic, screed, curse, jeremiad, vituperation, denunciation, stream of abuse, bitter harangue, verbal onslaught; reproof, rebuke, reprimand, upbraiding, *Inf.* tongue lashing, *Sl.* dressing down, *Sl.* bawling out, *Sl.* chewing out.

dicker, *v.* **1.** bargain, drive a bargain, negotiate, higgle, haggle, chaffer, *Scot.* argle-bargle, *Inf.* talk down, *Inf.* beat down, *Offensive.* jew *or* jew down.
2. trade, barter, swap, swop, bandy, commute, give and take, sell, vend, peddle, deal, traffic, truck, huckster, hawk.

dictate, *v.* **1.** prescribe, impose, set, lay down, lay down the law, *Inf.* call the shots, *Inf.* call the tune; ordain, decree, promulgate.
2. command, order, charge, direct, enjoin; constrain, oblige, necessitate.
—*n.* **3.** command, order, charge, direction, imperative, bidding, behest; edict, caveat, mandate, decree.
4. guiding principle, principle, rule, law, code; dictum, precept, axiom, maxim.

dictation, *n.* **1.** arbitrary direction, command, charge, order, injunction, enjoining; mandate, caveat, ukase, prescription; behest, admonition, exhortation; counsel, advice, suggestion, word to the wise, recommendation, guidance.
2. transcription, typescript, *Latin. verbatim et literatim,* shorthand, notehand; business letter.
3. utterance, pronouncement, fiat, dictum, assertion, *Inf.* the word.

dictator, *n.* despot, autocrat, tyrant, absolute monarch, autarch; czar, kaiser, Caesar, *Ger. Fuhrer, It.*

duce, Span. caudillo; shah, khan, rajah, mogul, sultan, emir, caliph, sheik; chief, ruler, leader, headman, sachem; overlord, lord, oppressor, master; disciplinarian, martinet, commander, taskmaster; pasha, bashaw, sirdar.

dictatorial, *adj.* **1.** absolute, unlimited, unrestricted, arbitrary, omnipotent, all-powerful; autocratic, totalitarian, monocratic, authoritarian.

2. tyrannical, despotic, oppressive, iron-handed; imperious, overbearing, peremptory, positive, authoritative, high-handed, *Inf.* bossy; haughty, arrogant, supercilious, lordly, high-and-mighty.

dictatorship, *n.* **1.** autarchy, totalitarian state, absolute monarchy.

2. autocracy, absolutism, despotism, totalitarianism, authoritarianism, monocracy, one-man rule, one-party rule; tyranny, uncontrolled *or* unlimited authority, complete control, absolute power *or* control, iron hand, iron fist, iron rule; reign of terror.

diction, *n.* **1.** writing style, language, vocabulary, usage, word choice, wording, phraseology, phrase, phrasing, verbalism; idiom, terminology, *Inf.* lingo, jargon, argot, cant; dialect, patois.

2. accent, stress, inflection, intonation, *Linguistics.* prosody; enunciation, pronunciation, elocution, delivery; fluency, articulateness, eloquence, silver tongue, oratory, rhetoric.

3. command of language, word sense, feel for words, *Ger. sprachgefühl.*

dictionary, *n.* wordbook, lexicon, Webster, glossary, gloss; encyclopedia, cyclopedia.

dictum, *n.* **1.** axiom, maxim, precept, dictate; proverb, adage, aphorism, gnome, apothegm, moral, saying, *Archaic.* word, *Archaic.* sentence; cliché, saw, platitude, truism, *Inf.* bromide.

2. command, order, charge. See also **dictate** (*def.* **3**).

didactic,, *adj.* **1.** instructive, instructional, propaedeutical, preceptive, educational, educative, informational, informative; moralistic, moralizing, homiletic, homiletical, *Inf.* preachy.

2. didactics art *or* science of teaching, pedagogics, pedagogy; teaching; instruction, schooling, tuition.

die, *v.* **1.** expire, decease, meet death, cease to live, lose one's life, lay down one's life, *Sl.* bite the dust, *Sl.* kick the bucket, *Sl.* kick in; give up the ghost, breathe one's last, draw one's last breath, *Sl.* croak; pass away, pass on, be no more, go the way of all flesh, pay the debt of nature, pay Charon, *Sl.* cash in, *Sl.* cash in one's chips, *Sl.* turn up one's toes, *Inf.* push up daisies, be numbered with the dead; go to one's reward, go to one's resting place, go to one's last home, leave this world, *Euph.* go west, cross the Styx.

2. end, come to an end, come to nothing, die away; vanish, disappear, be gone, be heard of no more, leave no trace, be lost to view; melt away, dissolve.

3. stop, come to a full stop, halt, *Sl.* conk out, *Sl.* go dead, *Inf.* fizzle out, peter out, break down.

4. weaken, lose strength, languish, sink, droop, fade, waste away, lapse, fail, faint; wane, ebb, evanesce; decline, deteriorate, degenerate, fall off, *Chief. Biol.* retrograde, wear away, disintegrate, crumble, molder; wither, go to seed, go bad, rot.

5. pine for, long for, hunger for, crave, hanker after, be bent on, want, desire, covet.

6. die down fade away, recede, lull, wane, let up, abate, subside, become calm or quiet, pass, cease.

die-hard, *n.* **1.** *Inf.* bitter-ender, intransigent, irreconcilable, resister; extremist, fanatic, zealot; reactionary, ultraconservative, radical.

—*adj.* **2.** intransigent, irreconcilable, uncompromising, adamant, steeled; resisting, unyielding, inflexible, rigid, cast-iron, indomitable, tenacious, determined, resolved.

diet[1], *n.* **1.** food and drink, food, foodstuffs, victuals, comestibles, edibles, viands; fare, rations, commons, provisions, cheer, board; nutrition, nourishment, nutriment, aliment, subsistence, sustenance.

2. regimen, dietary, regime; abstinence, fasting, fast, limitation of food consumption.

—*v.* **3.** eat sparingly, fast, abstain.

4. feed, nourish, eat, nurture, fare.

diet[2], *n.* **1.** assembly, convocation, convention, conventicle, conclave; session, meeting, plenum.

2. council, congress, parliament, senate, house of representatives, legislature, House of Lords, House of Commons; states-general, synod, cortes, divan, soviet, duma.

differ, *v.* **1.** contrast, vary, diverge, be dissimilar, be unlike, be different; stand out *or* apart, deviate from, depart from; contradict, run counter to, counter, contravene.

2. disagree, disaccord, fail to agree, be at variance; conflict, oppose, clash, think differently, stand in opposition, stand in opposite corners.

3. fall out, part company, go separate ways; have a difference, have a difference of opinions; quarrel, quibble, squabble, wrangle, altercate; bicker, spat, argue, tiff.

difference, *n.* **1.** dissimilarity, unlikeness, dissimilitude, contrast, confliction; contrariety, opposition, antithesis, contradiction, contradistinction; inconsistency, discrepancy, inconformity, nonconformity; disparity, inequality, imparity, imbalance, incongruity; variation, divergence, deviation, departure; oppositeness, contrariness, adverseness.

2. idiosyncrasy, peculiarity, particularity, differentia, individuality; singularity, idiocrasy, mannerism, eccentricity, oddity; kink, quirk, quip.

3. discrimination, distinguishment, judgment, discernment, distinction, differentiation, discreteness.

4. disagreement, disaccord, antagonism, contention; controversy, contest, conflict; dissension, dissidence, dissent, variance; discord, division, strife.

5. dispute, debate, disputation, logomachy, quarrel, wrangle, jangle, set-to; altercation, clash, brawl, *Inf.* scrap; falling out, parting of ways, misunderstanding, sixes and sevens; squabble, spat, tiff, miff, bickering, row, broil; feud, breach, vendetta, faction; rupture, schism.

6. cause, issue, question, point, ground, *Latin. casus belli,* apple of discord, bone of contention, seed of discontent.

7. remainder, rest, residue, residuum, balance, excess, *Inf.* what's left.

different, *adj.* **1.** dissimilar, unlike, disparate, contrary, contrastive, contradistinct; diverse, divergent, discrepant; incongruous, incompatible, inharmonious, inconsonant; deviant, variant, altered, changed, modified.

2. distinct, unidentical, nonidentical, (*of twins*) fraternal; separate, exclusive, not the same, a horse of a different color; another, other.

3. several, some, not a few; many, numerous, abundant; manifold, multifarious, assorted, motley, variegated, mixed, varied; various, sundry, divers, miscellaneous, certain.

4. unusual, peculiar, unique, singular, distinctive; out of the ordinary, extraordinary, remarkable, off the beaten track; novel, new, noteworthy, exceptional; unheard-of, something else, another story; unfamiliar, unaccustomed, unwonted.

differential, *adj.* **1.** distinctive, distinguishing, diacritical, discriminative; characteristic, peculiar, special, unique, particular, singular.

—n. **2.** discrepancy, disparity, difference, amount of difference.

differentiate, *v.* **1.** distinguish, discriminate, see *or* tell the difference, make a distinction; tell apart, *Inf.* tell which is which *or* who's who, separate, set off *or* apart.

2. change, alter, make different, modify, adapt, adjust. See **change** (*def.* **2**).

difficult, *adj.* **1.** hard, laborious, arduous, strenuous, rough, *Sl.* hell of a; toilsome, wearisome, troublesome, bothersome, irksome; tough, Herculean, Augean, demanding, formidable; trying, uphill, exhausting, painful; burdensome, oppressive, onerous, hampering.

2. hard to understand, abstruse, recondite, abstract, profound, obscure; complex, intricate, puzzling, perplexing, complicated, involved, inexplicable, knotty, thorny, ticklish; pathless, trackless, labyrinthine.

3. hard to manage, intractable, unmanageable, perverse, refractory; obdurate, obstinate, stubborn, *Inf.* cussed, flinty, stony; unaccommodating, uncompliant, unyielding, uncompromising, inflexible, rigid.

4. hard to satisfy, fastidious, perfectionist, fussy, critical, hypercritical, difficile; finical, finicky, particular, squeamish.

5. disadvantageous, unfavorable, inconvenient, ill-timed.

6. hard-pressed, hard up, pinched, straitened.

difficulty, *n.* **1.** laboriousness, arduousness, strenuousness, formidableness, formidability; labor, strain, struggle, hard sledding, rough going, tough job, hard row to hoe.

2. troublesomeness, bothersome, irksomeness, burdensomeness, oppressiveness, onerousness; trouble, bother, annoynace, *Inf.* hassle, *Inf.* hard time.

3. quandary, predicament, straits; plight, hot water, pickle, fix, pass, rub; embarrassment, deep water, mess, muddle, jam, scrape; quagmire, slough, swamp, bog.

4. trial, tribulation, ordeal, hardship; crisis, emergency, exigency, urgency.

5. dilemma, problem, perplexity, bafflement, puzzle, poser; tough nut to crack.

6. reluctance, unwillingness, indisposition, disinclination, refusal; demur, objection, protest, squawk, kick, gripe, complaint, *Sl.* beef, *Sl.* bitch; cavil, qualm, scruple.

7. impediment, hindrance, obstacle, barrier, obstruction, roadblock; opposition, *Inf.* flak, stumbling block, hurdle; snag, hitch, tie-up, hold-up, delay.

diffidence, *n.* timidity, timorousness, apprehension, faint-heartedness, diffidentness; bashfulness, shyness, abashment, coyness, demureness; embarrassment, sheepishness; lack of self-confidence, insecurity, reluctance, hesitancy, doubtfulness, backwardness; modesty, humility, unobtrusiveness, self-effacement; self-consciousness, constraint, self-awareness; reserve, restraint, aloofness, distance, stand-offishness.

diffident, *adj.* shy, bashful, abashed, coy, demure, *Inf.* introverted, *Archaic.* verecund; timid, timorous, apprehensive, insecure, fearful, faint-hearted, unconfident; constrained, reluctant, hesitant; self-conscious, self-aware, quiet, uncommunicative, unsocial, unsociable; sheepish, embarrassed, blushing; meek, modest, shrinking, self-effacing, unassuming, unobtrusive, unpretentious, restrained, reserved, retiring, withdrawn, in a shell, distant, aloof, stand-offish.

diffuse, *v.* **1.** disperse, dissipate, dispel, circumfuse, spread; scatter, strew, bestrew, sow; disseminate, broadcast, propagate, distribute, dispense, circulate, cast forth; effuse, radiate, shed, give forth.

—adj. **2.** wordy, verbose, prolix, profuse, long-winded, loquacious, lengthy, long, unending, endless; pleonastic, tautological, repetitive, redundant; discursive, digressive, rambling, wandering, maundering, meandering; circumlocutory, periphrastic, circuitous, roundabout, ambagious, indirect; pointless, aimless, ambiguous, vague, obscure.

3. spread out, sidespread, scattered, dispersed; sparse, thin, scanty, meager.

diffusion, *n.* **1.** dispersion, dissipation, dissipativity, circumfusion, spreading; scatteredness, scattering, strewing, bestrewing, sowing; dissemination, propagation, distribution, dispensation, circulation; effusion, effusiveness, radiation.

2. verbosity, verboseness, wordiness, prolixness, prolixity, profuseness, long-windedness, loquaciousness, loquacity; pleonasm, tautology, repetitiveness, redundancy; discursiveness, discursion, digressiveness, digression, diffusiveness, rambling, wandering; circumlocution, periphrasis, circuitousness, ambagiousness, indirectness; aimlessness, pointlessness, ambiguousness, ambiguity, vagueness.

dig, *v.* **1.** (*all in reference to earth*) work, loosen up, break up, turn over, prepare, dress; hoe, till, cultivate, harrow, plow; shovel, spade, dibble; toil, grub, *Inf.* work pick and shovel; excavate, hollow out, scoop, gouge; tunnel, burrow, channel, mine, undermine, sap.

2. thrust, force in, prod, poke, insert, push into, plunge, plunge into, force into, thrust into.

3. delve, dig down, search, research; investigate, probe; persevere, leave no stone unturned.

4. *Slang.* **a.** appreciate, enjoy, esteem, prize, like, love, rate high. **b.** understand, comprehend, grasp, *Inf.* get, *Inf.* catch on; realize, discern, perceive, make out, recognize.

5. dig up a. unearth, exhume, quarry, bring to the surface. **b.** *Informal.* come across, discover, find, bring to light, expose; research, study, search out, sift out, plod, grind, *Inf.* go the spade work.

—n. **6.** poke, thrust, push, punch, thump, jab.

7. *Informal.* taunt, gibe, cutting remark, insult, hoot, jeer, sneer, slur, quip, twit, sly remark, insinuation, *Inf.* slap in the face, *Inf.* needle, *Inf.* wisecrack, *Inf.* low blow.

digest, *v.* **1.** (*of food*) break down, dissolve, transform; absorb, assimilate.

2. comprehend, understand, master, absorb, take in; ponder, reflect, think over, mull over; study, contemplate, weigh, consider, meditate upon.

3. endure, bear, tolerate, brook; submit to, suffer, abide, stand; swallow, stomach, pocket.

4. classify, order, codify, methodize, systematize.

5. condense, abridge, summarize, shorten, compress, edit, epitomize, abbreviate; sketch, review, outline.

—n. **6.** summary, epitome, synopsis, abstract; compendium, pandect, symposium, compilation, conspectus; condensation, abridgment, reduction, compression, abbreviation; analysis, recapitulation; résumé, brief, précis; outline, aperçu, sketch, review, syllabus, prospectus; docket, bulletin, minute; extracts, fragments, cuttings, analects, clippings, citations.

digestion, *n.* **1.** (*of food*) absorption, assimilation; conversion, transformation; eupepsia, eupepsy; dyspepsia, dyspepsy.

2. comprehension, understanding, mastery.

dignified, *adj.* stately, grave, solemn, formal; noble, honorable, distinguished, distingué, impressive, imposing; august, grand, majestic, splendid, regal, sublime, exalted, lofty.

dignify, *v.* **1.** honor, ennoble, exalt, glorify; crown, enthrone, deify, make into a god, immortalize, apotheosize, *Archaic.* canonize; idolize, make bigger than life, idealize, put on a pedestal; elevate, raise, upraise, raise up, make lofty; lift, uplift, lift up, cast up; promote, advance, boost, upgrade, improve, ameliorate, better; enhance, intensify, magnify, heighten, increase, enlarge, aggrandize.

2. title, entitle, confer a title upon, confer honors upon, give an honorary degree.

dignitary, *n.* chief *or* head of state, high official, notable, personage, *Inf.* V.I.P., *Archaic.* dignity; *Sl.* big shot, *Sl.* biggie, *Sl.* big gun, *Sl.* big wheel, magnate; *Sl.* big cheese, *Fr. grand fromage, Sl.* fat cat, *Sl.* heavy, *Sl.* high-muck-a-muck; celebrity, *Sl.* celeb, luminary, somebody, name, *Inf.* big name, lion; star, hero, superstar, toast of the town.

dignity, *n.* **1.** stateliness, noble bearing, distinguished air, gravity, reserve, solemnity, formality, formalness, ceremoniousness; class, impressiveness, imposingness, presence; greatness, augustness, grandness, grandeur, magnificence, majesty, splendor; sublimity, exaltedness, elevation, height, loftiness; eminence, high station *or* rank, high standing, honorable position.

2. nobility, nobleness, honorableness, worthiness, worth, respectability, respectableness, reputability, reputableness.

digress, *v.* **1.** maunder, descant, be diffuse, be episodic, rhapsodize, wax longwinded, go off on *or* at a tangent, beat around the bush.

2. (*all of writing or speaking*) deviate, divagate, deflect, diverge, depart, excurse, run off; veer, straggle, turn aside; wander, ramble, meander, stray, drift, rove, lose one's way.

digression, *n.* **1.** maundering, descanting, being diffuse, being episodic, rhapsodizing, waxing longwinded, circumlocution, going off on *or* at a tangent, beating around the bush; (*all of writing or speaking*) deviating, divagating, deflecting, diverging, departing, running off; (*all of writing or speaking*) veering, straggling, turning aside, wandering, rambling, meandering, straying, drifting, roving, losing one's way; (*all of writing or speaking*) deviation, divagation, deflection, divergence, departure, aberration, ramification, divarication, variation, alteration, declination, elongation, diversion, swerve.

2. excursus, excursion, rhapsody, incidental passage *or* excursion, *Fig.* side trip, *Fig.* trip to the country, *Inf.* side street; *All Rhet.* apostrophe, ecbole.

digressive, *adj.* diffuse, episodic, rhapsodic, excursive, discursive, desultory, deviate, deviant, divergent, deflective; circumlocutory, circumlocutional, circumlocutionary; veering, straggling; deviating, divagating, rambling, straying, wandering, meandering, drifting, roving.

dike, *n.* **1.** dam, breakwater, pier, mole; embankment, bank, *Phys. Geog.* levee.

2. ditch, trench, channel, moat, fosse.

3. wall, rampart, bulwark, *Fort.* breastwork; railing, balustrade, *Fort.* parapet, *Mil.* earthwork, fence, palisade, *Fort.* stockade.

4. causeway, *Brit. Dial.* causey, raised path, viaduct, bridge.

5. barrier, bar, check, obstacle, hindrance, obstruction, impediment, barricade.

dilapidate, *v.* **1.** disintegrate, crumble, break up, fall apart; erode, ablate, wear away, weather; decay, decompose, crumble into dust; deteriorate, degenerate, decline, sink, worsen, fall into disrepair *or* ruin.

2. destroy, ruin, upset, disrupt, pull down; deface, mar, injure, spoil.

dilapidated, *adj.* **1.** ruined, in ruins, broken-down, gone to wrack and ruin; in disrepair, unimproved, *Sl.* sleazy, run-down; tumble-down; falling to pieces, crumbled, crumbling; ramshackle, rickety, shaky.

2. deteriorated, decadent, decayed; disintegrated, decomposed, broken up, fallen apart, *Scot.* disjaskit; eroded, worn away, weathered, wasted; worn-out, time-worn, decrepit; moth-eaten, mildewed, moldy, moldering.

3. destroyed, battered, *Inf.* beat up; defaced, marred, spoiled; injured, impaired, damaged.

dilapidation, *n.* disintegration, erosion, corrosion, wear and tear; deterioration, decay, decadence; decomposition, moth and rust; disrepair, decrepitude; downfall, collapse, disorganization, disruption; destruction, impairment, injury.

dilate, *v.* **1.** enlarge, make larger, increase; widen, thicken, broaden; lengthen, prolong, protract.

2. expand, extend, spread, outspread, spread out, branch out; distend, inflate, bloat, puff out, blow up, dome; swell, intumesce, tumefy; fill out, fatten.

3. develop, enlarge on, detail; expound on *or* upon, descant, discourse, expatiate on *or* upon; magnify, amplify, spin a long yarn; dwell on, talk about at length.

dilation, *n.* **1.** enlargement, increase, widening, thickening, broadening, dilatation; lengthening, prolongation, protraction.

2. expansion, extension, spread; distention, inflation, *Both Pathol.* aneurysm, varix; swelling, bloating, intumescence, tumefaction.

3. expatiation, descant, discourse; magnification, amplification; prolixity, verbosity; tautology, redundance; periphrasis, circumlocution.

dilatory, *adj.* **1.** procrastinating, postponing, deferring, tabling, shelving; slow, lagging, laggard, sluggish, backward; dallying, dillydallying, shillyshallying, idling; lingering, loitering, dawdling, tarrying, *Chiefly Brit.* pottering; lackadaisical, indolent, lazy, slothful, otiose; tardy, not prompt, late, behindhand.

2. delaying, temporizing, *Inf.* stalling, *U.S. Cong.* filibustering; prolonging, protracting, retarding, slackening; forestalling, preventing, staving off, obstructing, blocking, avoiding; Fabian.

dilemma, *n.* **1.** predicament, plight, *Inf.* pickle, *Inf.* fix, difficulty, trouble, *Inf.* hot water, scrape; corner, tight spot, *Sl.* box, bind, double bind, catch-22, vicious circle; strait, *Inf.* squeeze, pinch, push; cul-de-sac, dead end, blind alley; impasse, standstill, stalemate, deadlock.

2. difficult choice, *Fr. embarras de choix,* tough question, hard nut to crack, poser, puzzle; complicated problem, knot, entanglement, intricacy.

3. quandary, perplexity, uncertainty, confusion, bewilderment; muddle, mess, botch, jumble, hodgepodge.

dilettante, *n.* **1.** dabbler, *Inf.* dabster, smatterer, sciolist, half scholar, amateur, nonprofessional, layman; do-it-yourselfer, putterer, potterer, trifler, dallier, piddler.

2. art lover, person of taste, connoisseur, *Latin. arbiter elegantiae*; member of the intelligentsia *or* cognescenti.

diligence, *n.* assiduity, assiduousness, application, exertion, labor, industry, industriousness; perseverance, persistence, pertinacity, tenacity, constancy, sedulousness, doggedness, intentness, earnestness, *Inf.* stick-to-it-iveness.

diligent, *adj.* **1.** industrious, assiduous, sedulous,

hard-working; intense, intent, concentrated, steady, earnest, zealous; busy, busy as a bee *or* beaver, active, employed, engaged, occupied, hard at it, eager-beaver.
2. painstaking, thorough, thoroughgoing; persistent, pertinacious, dogged, plodding, slogging, plugging; persevering, unremitting, unrelaxing, unfaltering, untiring, tireless, indefatigable.

dillydally, *v.* vacillate, fluctuate, waver, hover, hem and haw, blow hot and cold; trifle, toy, flirt, potter, putter, *Inf.* piddle, *Sl.* futz; dally, dawdle, loiter, linger, shillyshally, take one's time, take one's own sweet time, *Inf.* lallygag; delay, tarry, waste time, fritter away time, kill time, while away the time *or* hours.

dilute, *v.* **1.** weaken, attenuate, extenuate, thin, rarefy; mix, adulterate, *Inf.* water *or* water down, (*of alcohol or drugs*) *Inf.* cut.
—adj. **2.** weak, weakened, thin, thinned, attenuated, diluted; adulterated, *Inf.* doctored, *Inf.* watered *or* watered down, (*of alcohol or drugs*) *Inf.* cut.

dim, *adj.* **1.** faint, weak, pale, imperceptible, hardly noticeable, indiscernible; vague, undefined, fuzzy, confused; nebulous, mysterious, unfathomable, incomprehensible.
2. ill-defined, unclear, indistinct, blurred, blurry, clouded, obscured; obfuscated, muffled, bleared.
3. shadowy, dark, gloomy, somber, tenebrous; gray, leaden, cloudy, hazy, misty, foggy, overcast, lowering; obscure, dusky, crepuscular, *Archaic.* caliginous.
4. lusterless, darkened, tarnished, dulled; dingy, sullied, smudgy, smirchy, dirty, dun; lurid, dismal, murky, muddy, opaque.
5. obtuse, dull-witted, slow-witted, dense, doltish, stupid.
6. take a dim view of disapprove of, view with disfavor, be displeased by; look askance at, reject, withhold sanction, refuse to accept; take exception to, set one's face against, turn one's nose up at.
—v. **7.** darken, shade, shadow, bedim, turn down, lower, *Inf.* douse; eclipse, cloud, cloud over, becloud, obscure, obfuscate, shroud.
8. fade, grow dim, pale, blur; flutter, waver, flicker, glimmer, blink.

dimension, *n.* **1.** measure, extent, expanse, range; length, extension, reach, stretch; compass, gauge, caliber, bore.
2. dimensions a. magnitude, size, volume, capacity; field, range, scope, extent, spread, span, sweep. **b.** importance, greatness, weight, bigness; significance, momentousness, import; seriousness, gravity, urgency.

diminish, *v.* **1.** lessen, reduce, lower, abate, decrease, bate; contract, shrink, constrict, narrow; cut, pare, prune, truncate, crop, lop, dock, clip; condense, cut down, compress, shorten, abridge, scale down, boil down; abbreviate, curtail, cut short.
2. mitigate, alleviate, allay, assuage, *Rare.* lenify, palliate; appease, soothe, relieve, ease, soften, cushion, mollify; quell, slake, deaden, dull, blunt, take the edge off of; modify, temper, qualify; minimize, extenuate, make light of, soft-pedal, play down, downplay, underestimate, underrate.
3. subside, ebb, recede; dwindle, *Inf.* peter out; slacken, let up, wind down, slow down, de-escalate; fall off, wane, fade away, die out.
4. disparage, discredit, detract from; degrade, downgrade, debase, abase, vitiate; belittle, deprecate, demean, derogate; devaluate, depreciate, cheapen, attenuate; humble, humiliate, mortify, *Sl.* put down.

diminution, *n.* **1.** reduction, cutback, lessening, diminishing, decrement, abatement, decrease, retrenchment; contraction, shrinking, shrinkage, constriction, constricting, narrowing; condensation, compression, shortening, abridgment, abbreviation, curtailment.
2. mitigation, alleviation, assuagement, palliation; soothing, quelling, relieving, relief, easing, softening, cushioning, mollification; minimizing, minimization, extenuation, soft-pedaling, playing down.
3. subsidence, ebb, recession; decline, downturn, declension, decrescence, wane; sinking, fall-off, falling off, fading away, dwindling, dying out; weakening, attenuation, loss, attrition, wearing away, erosion, wasting away.

diminutive, *adj.* small, little, *Inf.* baby, bantam, slight, featherweight; wee, tiny, Lilliputian, elfin, miniature, minute, microscopic, animalculous, infinitesimal; short, *Inf.* half pint, undersized, puny, runty; homuncular, midget, dwarfish, *Med.* nanoid, pygmy, stunted, shrunken; small-scale, compact, limited, vest-pocket, pocket-sized; portable.

din, *n.* **1.** uproar, clamor, babel, racket, hurly-burly, hue and cry, ballyhoo, hullabaloo; shouting, shout, yell, holler, outcry, vociferation; bray, bellow, roar, blare, blast, thunderclap, peal, fanfare, tintinnabulation; crash, clash, clangor, clang, jangle, clattering, rattling; hissing, catcalls, caterwauling.
2. commotion, *Inf.* to-do, flurry, agitation; turmoil, tumult, broil, brawl; anarchy, chaos, pandemonium, bedlam, brouhaha, free-for-all; fracas, rumpus, scramble, scuffle, *Inf.* ruckus.
—v. **3.** clamor, cry out, shout, roar, yell, holler; bray, bawl, bellow, whoop, hoot, yelp; hiss, catcall, caterwaul; blare, blast, crash, clash, clang, clatter, rattle; drone, drum in the ears, ring in the ears, deafen, split the ears.

dine, *v.* sup, have dinner, breakfast, lunch, take sustenance, break bread, refresh the inner man, eat; fall to, play a good knife and fork, *Sl.* tuck in; banquet, feast, *Sl.* eat high off the hog, gourmandize, gluttonize, gorge, stuff, *Sl.* stuff one's face, *Sl.* pig out, *Inf* eat [s.o.] out of house and home; regale, fete, treat, feed.

dingy, *adj.* dark, dull, dim, dun, grayish brown, lackluster, dusky; drab, dismal, dreary, cheerless, *Scot. ourie*; shadowy, gloomy, tenebrous, obscure; murky, hazy, smoggy; sooty, smoky, fuliginous, smudgy, smeared; smutchy, dirty, grimy, soiled, muddy; shabby, seedy, worn, rundown, sloppy, crumby.

dining room, *n.* dining hall, cafeteria, mess, mess hall, chow hall; refectory, triclinium; dinette, breakfast nook.

dinner, *n.* main meal, repast, refection; feast, banquet; supper, collation; table d'hôte.

dint, *n.* **1.** force, power, potency, puissance; strength, might, energy, drive; ability, capability, capacity; means, virtue, efficacy; effort, will, determination.
2. dent, indentation, depression, concavity; pit, hollow, dimple, pock; crater, basin; impression, scar.

diocese, *n.* ecclesiastical district, bishopric, episcopate, cathedral seat; see, territory, province, jurisdiction; archdiocese, archbishopric; prelacy, prelature, prefecture, episcopacy, benefice, *Brit.* incumbency.

dip, *v.* **1.** duck, dunk, lower, plunge, immerge, immerse, souse, sink, submerge, submerse, put *or* push under; douse, drench, soak, steep, bathe.
2. wet slightly, sprinkle, spray, asperge, dabble, moisten, dampen, damp, wet, wet down; wash, lave, splash, splatter, swash, slosh, slop.
3. raise, take up, scoop *or* scoop up, ladle, bail, cup up, shovel.
4. dive, duck, take a plunge, plunge into, fall for-

ward *or* headlong, pitch.

5. **dip into** reach into, put one's hand into, go into.

6. sink, set, go down, drop down, lower, descend; fade, disappear, drop out of sight, duck behind, hide.

7. decrease slightly, lower, fall *or* fall off, decline, wane, drop *or* drop off; descend, go down, sink, gravitate; incline, decline, slope downward, bend *or* slant down, droop.

8. dabble in, smatter, scratch the surface, engage in slightly; skim, browse, look through, glance at, go *or* run through.

diploma, *n.* **1.** graduation certificate, parchment, *Inf.* sheepskin, degree, academic title.

2. title, deed; public *or* official document, charter, constitution.

diplomacy, *n.* **1.** statesmanship, statecraft, politics; Machiavellianism, intrigue, machination, maneuvering, wirepulling.

2. tact, tactfulness, discretion, prudence, judiciousness, sense, common *or* good sense.

diplomat, *n.* **1.** ambassador, envoy, emissary, legate, plenipotentiary; consul, attaché, chargé d'affaires.

2. negotiator, arbitrator, mediator, intermediary, middleman, go-between; peacemaker, make-peace, pacifier, reconciler, conciliator, appeaser.

diplomatic, *adj.* **1.** tactful, discreet, politic, prudent, judicious; sensitive, discerning, perspicacious.

2. ambassadorial, consular, ministerial, plenipotentiary; political, governmental, statesmanlike.

dipper, *n.* ladle, ladler, scoop, spoon, shovel; bail, bailer, pail, bucket.

dipsomania, *n.* alcoholism, crapulence, problem *or* heavy *or* serious drinking, habitual *or* chronic drunkenness, chronic *or* acute alcoholism; intoxication, inebriety, insobriety, drunkenness, intemperance, *Inf.* tipsiness; drinking, tippling, imbibing, heavy drinking, toping, *Inf.* boozing, *Sl.* hitting the bottle *or* booze *or* sauce, *Brit. Sl.* bevying.

dipsomaniac, *n.* drunk, drunkard, alcoholic, sot, soak, inebriate, tosspot, toper, bibber, barfly; drinker, hard drinker, serious drinker, problem drinker; *All Inf.* guzzler, swiller, soaker, sponge, lovepot; *All Sl.* boozer, boozehound, hooch hound, gin hound, lush, souse, rummy, wino, alchy, dipso, juicer, juicehead, swillbelly, stew, elbow-bender.

dire, *adj.* **1.** dreadful, terrible, grievous, grim, baleful, dark; terrifying, frightful, dread, terrific, appalling; alarming, distressing, harrowing, rending; redoubtable, fearsome, formidable, awful; horrible, horrid, horrendous, monstrous, atrocious; hideous, ghastly, eerie, grisly, gruesome, unspeakable; outrageous, shocking, enormous, flagrant; nefarious, heinous, flagitious, villainous; infamous, notorious, odious; wicked, evil, vile, sinful, iniquitous, *Archaic.* facinorous; maleficent, malefic, malevolent, demonic, diabolic, devilish; abhorrent, revolting, repulsive, repugnant, loathsome, despicable; pernicious, pestilential, noxious, deadly, fell.

2. ominous, direful, sinister, fearful; fateful, portentous, premonitory, augural; inauspicious, unpropitious, ill-boding, unfavorable, unpromising, untoward; ill-fated, ill-starred, ill-omened, doomed, accursed, cursed.

3. urgent, desperate, pressing, exigent, compelling, crying, imperative; critical, crucial, vital; earnest, serious, grave, important.

direct, *v.* **1.** administer, engineer, orchestrate, quarterback, *Inf.* call the plays, run the show, make decisions, dispose, *Inf.* call the shots; manage, superintend, run, operate, carry out, handle, manipulate; supervise, oversee, preside, counsel, advise; boss, be master over, dominate, domineer, push *or* shove around, ride herd on, ride roughshod over.

2. command, instruct, dictate, order, give orders, charge, adjure; bid, tell, enjoin; ordain, decree, enact, authorize, warrant, lay down the law, wield one's power *or* authority.

3. control, have control over, regulate, rule, rule the roost, govern, be on top of, be master of; be in control, be in command, be in the driver's seat *or* saddle, wear the pants *or* trousers, have the upper hand, have under control, have well in hand, hold the purse strings, hold all the cards.

4. steer, drive, pilot, navigate, hold the reins, be at the helm; guide, lead, conduct, usher, escort, accompany; point, aim, steer [s.o. *or* s.t.] toward, head [s.o. *or* s.t.] toward, orient *or* position toward, put on the right track, show the way, point out the way, give directions to, *Chiefly Scot.* airt; intend *or* destine for, address, send, mail.

—adj. **5.** straight, straightaway, undeviating, unswerving, unwinding, uncircuitous; shortest, nearest, as the crow flies.

6. unmediated, immediate, noninterventional; first hand, from the horse's mouth, personal, face to face, vis-à-vis, head-on.

7. exact, accurate, correct, precise, verbatim, word for word.

8. explicit, clear, plain, simple, unequivocal; absolute, categorical, unqualified, unconditional, unambiguous, unmistakable; straightforward, forthright, uncircumlocutory, unperiphrastic, straight to the point, *U.S. Inf.* straight-out, *Inf.* flatfooted, nononsense, point blank; frank, candid, outspoken, bluff, blunt, plain-spoken, matter of fact, shirtsleeve, open, unreserved, uninhibited, honest, truthful, sincere, ingenuous, aboveboard, artless, undesigning.

direction, *n.* **1.** way, route, course, path, track, road, line, run; orientation, relative position, heading, bearing, *Chiefly Scot.* airt; drift, tack, movement, trend, tenor, pattern; inclination, disposition, tendency, bent, set.

2. instruction, prescription, recipe; command, order, dictate.

3. administration, government, ministry, statecraft, decision-making; management, supervision, superintendence, conduction, operation; ministration, care, oversight, eye, surveillance; guidance, care, oversight, eye, surveillance; guidance, leadership, steerage, pilotage, navigation; control, mastership, regulation, handling, manipulation, disposal, charge, rule.

directly, *adv.* **1.** straight, right, forthright, forthrightly, without swerving, without deviation, uncircuitously; in a beeline, as the crow flies, by the shortest route, in a straight line.

2. immediately, at once, instantly, without delay, without hesitation, now, straightaway, right away; soon, momentarily, in a moment, instantaneously, in an instant, in a second; promptly, quickly, speedily; as soon as possible, ASAP, next; presently, shortly, in a little while.

director, *n.* **1.** administrator, executive, bureaucrat, functionary, official, marshal; president, head, chief, principal, *Inf.* kingpin, *Inf.* number one, *Inf.* Mr. Big, *Sl.* top dog, *Sl.* big cheese, *Sl.* top banana; governor, minister, regent, dean, chairman, chairwoman, chairlady, chairperson.

2. manager, superintendent, *Inf.* super, foreman, fugleman; supervisor, overseer, overlooker, overman, headman, boss, *Inf.* bossman, *Sl.* the man, *Sl.* head honcho, *Brit.* gaffer; master, commander, overlord, taskmaster; ruler, suzerain, paramount.

3. captain, skipper, commandant, *Inf.* old man; pilot, steersman, helmsman, driver, guide, leader, quarterback, cicerone; (*all of an orchestra, chorus, etc.*) conductor, maestro, choirmaster, precentor, coryphaeus.

dirge, *n.* funeral song, burial hymn, elegy, requiem, *Rom. Cath. Ch.* trental, *Dies Irae*; lament, keen, threnody, threnode, epicedium, monody, ululation, jeremiad, *Scot., Irish.* coronach; knell, toll, passing bell.

dirt, *n.* **1.** filth, grime, squalor, squalidness; smudge, stain, tarnish, rust; dust, soot, ashes, cinders; smoke, smog, pollution, particulate matter, contaminant, adulterant; mud, muck, mire, ooze, sludge, slime, *Sl.* crud, *Inf.* gook, *Sl.* yuk; foulness, slop, excrement; refuse, garbage, trash, rubbish, waste, junk; sweepings, leavings, chaff, dross.

2. earth, ground, soil, loose soil, loam, sand, clay, silt, residue.

3. obscenity, vileness, corruption, foulness, indecency, evil-mindedness; smut, pornography, profanity, ribaldry, bawdiness; sordidness, coarseness.

4. gossip, scandal, talk, news, story, scoop; divulgence, revelation, expose; rumor, hearsay, scuttlebutt, supposition.

dirty, *adj.* **1.** unclean, soiled, grimy, stained, spotted, smudged; unwashed, filthy, muddied, bedraggled, dirt-encrusted; foul, begrimed, besmeared, smirchy, befouled, polluted; sleazy, squalid, slovenly, slatternly, *Inf.* sloppy, *Inf.* scruffy, *Sl.* crumby, *Sl.* grungy, *Sl.* yucky; tarnished, defiled, ruined, spoiled.

2. contemptible, mean, base, low, scurvy, ignominious, *Inf.* low-down; vile, despicable, nasty, sordid, ignoble, infamous; shabby, beggarly, abject, paltry, pitiful.

3. obscene, indecent, suggestive, off-color, bawdy, smutty, prurient, salacious, risqué, ribald, pornographic, blue, *Sl.* raunchy; lewd, lascivious, perverted, lecherous, libidinous, licentious, lustful, *Archaic.* lickerish; loose, wanton, coarse, concupiscent, carnal, unchaste.

4. (*of weather*) foul, stormy, squally, gusty, disagreeable, sloppy; misty, rainy, sleety; cloudy, overcast, murky, gloomy, leaden, threatening, lowering.

5. unfortunate, inauspicious, untimely, inopportune, unseasonable; unlucky, unpropitious, infelicitous, unhappy, disastrous.

6. unsportsmanlike, unfair, dishonorable, unscrupulous; crooked, villainous, dishonest, deceitful, corrupt, fraudulent; treacherous, two-faced, back-stabbing.

7. resentful, bitter, angry, wrathful, scorching, smoldering; indignant, offended, annoyed, peevish.

—*v.* **8.** soil, stain, spot, smudge, muddy, sully, pollute; splash, spatter, *Inf.* slop up, *Inf.* foul up; bedraggle, draggle, begrime, besmear, smear, smirch; defile, besmirch, foul, befoul; blacken, tarnish.

disability, *n.* **1.** incapacity, inability, incapability, inherent lack; unfitness, impotence, helplessness, powerlessness, weakness, ineptitude, incompetence, disqualification.

2. disablement, defect, affliction, infirmity, handicap, impuissance, inanition; decrepitude, senility, superannuation, caducity; paralysis, collapse, exhaustion.

disable, *v.* **1.** incapacitate, indispose, cripple, lame, prostrate; mutilate, mangle, impair, mar, spoil, ruin; damage, break, put out of gear, put out of whack.

2. make harmless, scotch, make incapable *or* ineffective, paralyze, choke up; unman, disarm, emasculate, take the teeth out of; tie the hands of, clip the wings of, pull the rug out from under; enfeeble, weaken, enervate, debilitate.

3. disqualify, invalidate, disenable.

disabuse, *v.* undeceive, disillusion, disillusionize, unbeguile, disenchant; open the eyes of, wake [s.o.] up, clue [s.o.] in, make [s.o.] see the light; set straight, set right, correct; burst [s.o.'s] bubble, shatter [s.o.'s] illusions, make [s.o.] see the real world.

disadvantage, *n.* **1.** disadvantageousness, deprivation, privation, loss, lack, *Archaic.* discommodity; drawback, liability, handicap, weakness, weak spot, flaw, defect, fault, minus; inconvenience, trouble, pain in the neck; stumbling block, impediment, obstacle, hindrance, barrier, hurdle.

2. prejudice, disservice; detriment, harm, damage, injury, mischief.

3. **at a disadvantage** with one arm tied, behind the eightball; in a tight spot, cornered, in a corner, boxed in, between a rock and a hard place, between Scylla and Charybdis; up a tree, at bay.

disadvantageous, *adj.* **1.** unfavorable, inopportune, inauspicious, unpropitious; unseasonable, ill-timed, ill-starred; unfortunate, unlucky, hapless; inconvenient, discommodious, troublesome, bothersome, annoying, obnoxious, offensive; burdensome, onerous, awkward.

2. inadvisable, inexpedient, injudicious, imprudent, unwise.

3. detrimental, deleterious, baleful, harmful, hurtful, injurious; damaging, destructive, disastrous, calamitous; noxious, unhealthy, pernicious, poisonous, baneful.

disaffect, *v.* alienate, estrange, divide, disunite, come between; antagonize, set against, set at odds *or* variance; anger, incense, provoke, heat up, *Chiefly U.S.* rile, madden, infuriate, enrage; exacerbate, aggravate, embitter, envenom.

disaffected, *adj.* alienated, estranged, divided, disunited, separated, torn; implacable, irreconcilable, inexorable; bitter, vindictive, revengeful, spiteful; hostile, antagonistic, inimical, antipathetic, unfriendly, averse; dissatisfied, discontented, disgruntled, displeased, *Inf.* fed up; seditious, mutinous, rebellious, up in arms.

disaffection, *n.* alienation, estrangement, separation, division, disunion; disloyalty, infidelity, inconstancy, unfaithfulness, unsteadfastness; hostility, antagonism, antipathy, enmity, animosity, ill will, bad blood; anger, dudgeon, high dudgeon, spleen, rancor, bitterness; resentment, umbrage, offense, pique; dissatisfaction, discontentment, displeasure, disapproval, disapprobation; aversion, dislike, disinclination, disfavor, disgust, abhorrence, repugnance, loathing.

disagree, *v.* **1.** differ, fail to agree, disaccord, be at variance, be at odds; think differently, stand in opposition, stand in opposite corners, diverge, deviate; part company, go separate ways, have a difference of opinion.

2. conflict, oppose, clash; contrast, vary, be dissimilar, be unlike, be different; contradict, run counter to, counter, contravene.

3. altercate, argue, quarrel, dispute, spar, have words, fall out; bicker, spat, tiff; quibble, squabble, wrangle; debate, dissent, contend, take issue with, contest, object, *Scot.* thraw.

4. offend, sicken, nauseate; disturb, trouble, bother, discommode, jar, interfere.

disagreeable, *adj.* **1.** unpleasant, unpleasing, displeasing, distasteful; nauseating, nauseous, sickening, unpalatable, unsavory; disgusting, noisome, *Sl.*

yukky, *Sl.* gross; repugnant, offensive, obnoxious, shocking, nasty; repulsive, repelling, repellent, revolting, objectionable; abominable, odious, heinous, detestable.

2. unfriendly, unamiable, alienating, offish; abrupt, blunt, brusque, curt, austere, stern; sharp, trenchant, acrimonious, caustic, sarcastic, biting, piercing, stringent; brutal, cruel.

3. discourteous, impolite, uncivil, bad-mannered; indelicate, uncourtly, ungallant, indecorous.

4. sulky, morose, sullen, ill-tempered, ill-humored; grouchy, peevish, petulant, splenetic, thorny, cross.

disagreement, *n.* **1.** difference of opinion, discord, lack of agreement, discord, misunderstanding; parting of the ways, break up, divergence, deviation.

2. conflict, opposition, contradiction, contrariety, strife; dissimilarity, dissimilitude, unlikeness, difference, disparity, inequality; discrepancy, variance, incongruity, dissonance; diversity, nonconformity; disunity, disunion, division.

3. altercation, argument, quarrel, dispute, disputation, controversy, contention; sparring, bickering, spatting, jangling, jarring, clashing; dissension, dissent, dissidence, discord, falling-out; debate, logomachy, war of words; vendetta, feud, rivalry.

disallow, *v.* **1.** forbid, veto, interdict, proscribe, negative, say no to, ban, *Law.* disaffirm; prohibit, restrain, restrict; bar, debar, exclude, except.

2. reject, rebuff, repel, repulse, set aside; ignore, slight, disregard, shun, neglect, avoid; have no regard *or* use for, place no value on, set no store by, set at naught.

3. disclaim, disavow, forswear; repudiate, (*usu. under oath*) abjure, disown, throw over, turn one's back on.

disannul, *v.* **1.** declare null and void, render null and void, annul, nullify, void, avoid; quash, invalidate, vitiate, vacate, disenact, disestablish; cancel, discharge; supersede, set aside; repeal, revoke, rescind, reverse, abrogate, abolish; suspend, *Law.* nol-pros, stop, discontinue, break off.

2. recant, retract, abjure, unsay, withdraw, recall; renounce, repudiate, relinquish, abnegate, deny, disclaim, disavow, disown; take back, undo, renege; countermand, counterorder, overrule, override; veto, negate.

3. terminate, dissolve, cast aside, cast behind, put an end to, do away with, bring to an end; eliminate, destroy, extinguish, efface, x out, wipe out; obliterate, reduce to nothing, annihilate, eradicate, expunge, extirpate, exterminate; blot out, stamp out, crush out, sweep away.

disappear, *v.* **1.** vanish, leave no trace, dematerialize, vanish from sight, disappear off the face of the earth, vanish into thin air, be lost to sight; be swallowed up, go down the drain, go by the board; evaporate, dissipate, disperse, volatilize, vaporize; fade, evanesce, fade away, melt away, dissolve, *Sl.* go poof; recede, recede from view, retrocede, ebb, wane; withdraw, retire, retreat, repair; depart, leave, go, go away, quit, vacate; flit away, fly away, *Brit. Sl.* mizzle, up and go, take wing, *Sl.* vamoose, *Jocular.* absquatulate, decamp.

2. pass away, cease to exist, die out, cease to be; pass on, die, expire, perish; be no more, come to an end, become extinct, pass into oblivion, become obsolete.

disappearance, *n.* **1.** vanishment, evanescence, dematerialization; eclipse, occultation; evaporation, vaporization, dissipation, dispersal; fading away, melting away, dissolution; recession, retrocession, wane, ebb; withdrawal, retirement, retreat; exit, departure, vacation, leave.

2. passing away, death, expiration, passing on, dying out; obsolescence, extinction, extinguishment.

disappoint, *v.* **1.** fail [s.o.], dissatisfy disillusion, disenchant, let [s.o.] down; delude, mislead, deceive; abandon, leave in the lurch, stand [s.o.] up.

2. defeat, frustrate, thwart, foil, balk; hinder, hamper, impede, interfere, interrupt, intervene; baffle, disconcert, dumfound.

disappointed, *adj.* discouraged, depressed, disillusioned, dissatisfied, disenchanted, discontented; frustrated, thwarted, foiled, balked; abandoned, failed.

disappointment, *n.* **1.** nonfulfillment, nonsuccess, failure, defeat, inefficacy; thwarting, foiling, setback, balk; miscarriage, abortion; fiasco, *Inf.* washout, fizzle, flash in the pan, *Inf.* no-go, shipwreck.

2. disillusionment, letdown, dissatisfaction, discontent; mortification, chagrin, frustration, bafflement; regret, rue, sorrow, pain; bitter pill, *Inf.* body blow, *Inf.* comedown.

disapproval, *n.* **1.** disapprobation, objection, exception, disparagement, discountenance; deprecation, declamation, detraction; dislike, disfavor, displeasure, dissatisfaction; censure, animadversion, criticism; condemnation, denunciation, objurgation, berating; reprehension, reproach, rebuke, reproof; remonstration, expostulation, admonition.

2. boo, hiss, hoot, jeer, whistle, catcall, *U.S.* Bronx cheer, raspberry; frown, scowl, glower, glare, black look, dirty look; nay, veto, thumbs down, rejection, denial, negation, refusal, disallowal; protest, demonstration, sit-in, boycott.

disapprove, *v.* **1.** disfavor, deprecate, protest against, object to; remonstrate, expostulate, be against, come out against; disparage, discountenance, look dimly upon, take exception to, think ill of, dislike; frown upon, take a dim view of, look askance at, *Literary.* set one's face against; censure, denounce, deplore, animadvert on, curse, objurgate, berate, *Obs.* exprobate; condemn, criticize, reprobate, cry down, declaim, decry; inveigh against, rail against, run down, put down, *Inf.* knock down; reproach, rebuke, reprove, reprehend; admonish, chide, scold, castigate, upbraid.

2. veto, disallow, vote down, turn down, turn thumbs down; refuse to sanction, withhold assent, say no to, disaffirm; refuse, reject, deny, negate, negative, spurn.

disarm, *v.* **1.** unarm, unman, disable, render defenseless *or* helpless *or* powerless, take the teeth out of.

2. lay down arms, sheathe the sword, turn swords into plowshares; demobilize, demilitarize, deactivate, disband.

3. set at ease, put [s.o.'s] mind at ease; calm, calm [s.o.] down, mollify, appease, conciliate, propitiate, reconcile.

disarmament, *n.* demobilization, demilitarization, deactivation, disbanding, mustering out; weapons control, arms limitation.

disarrange, *v.* **1.** disorder, put out of order, displace, dislocate, move out of place; disorganize, unsettle, disturb, shake *or* shake up, discompose, derange; throw into disorder, disarray, dishevel, tumble, tousle; mess *or* mess up, *Inf.* muss *or* muss up, rumple *or* rumple up; turn upside down, *Inf.* turn topsy-turvy, make a shambles of; clutter, litter, scatter *or* strew objects about.

2. mix *or* mix up, shuffle, jumble, scramble; confuse, muddle, shake, fuddle, *Brit. Sl.* muzz, snarl, *Sl.* ball up; bungle, spoil, upset, upset the apple cart, *Sl.* foul up, *Inf.* bollix up, *Sl.* screw up.

disarray, *v.* **1.** disorder, dishevel, mess *or* mess up, disarrange. See **disarrange**.

2. undress, take one's clothes off, disrobe, strip.
—*n.* **3.** disorder, displacement, dislocation, disarrangement, disorganization, unsettledness, discomposure, derangement; dishevelment, untidiness, clutter, mess, heap, pile, huddle; confusion, confusedness, muddle, *Inf.* guddle; hash, hodge-podge, mishmash; jumble, tangle, knot, snarl; mix-up, snafu, *Inf.* foul-up, *Sl.* ball-up, *Brit. Sl.* balls-up.
4. disorderly *or* sloppy dress, dishabille, undress, careless *or* loose dress.

disaster, *n.* **1.** catastrophe, calamity, tragedy, terrible accident *or* occurrence, *Sl.* curtains; shock, blow, heavy *or* staggering *or* nasty blow, buffet, stroke, fell stroke, stroke of ill *or* bad luck *or* fortune; mishap, mischance, misfortune, miscarriage, misadventure, *Scot. and North Eng.* mishanter *or* mischanter; accident, casualty, glitch; reverse, reversal, reverse of fortune, setback, comedown, bringdown, bitter pill.
2. cataclysm, convulsion, spasm, upheaval, eruption, sudden violent change *or* disturbance; debacle, collapse, downfall, breakdown, break up.
3. flood, deluge, inundation, washout, engulfment, alluvion, alluvium; avalanche, landslide, mudslide; earthquake, quake; typhoon, hurricane: tidal wave, tsunami; cyclone, tornado, *Inf.* twister.
4. (*all of performances, entertainment, etc.*) failure, fiasco, *Inf.* flop, *Inf.* fizzle, *Inf.* dud, *Inf.* washout, *Sl.* bomb, *Sl.* turkey.
5. affliction, adversity, hurt, harm, ruin, ruination, wrack and ruin, desolation; trouble, trouble and strife, sea of troubles, hardship, storm and stress; infelicity, ill *or* bad luck, hard luck, ill *or* bad fortune, ambsace, evil eye, evil wind, dark star *or* cloud, storm clouds.

disastrous, *adj.* **1.** catastrophic, calamitous, cataclysmic, cataclysmal; ruinous, destructive, destroying, devastating, demolishing; ravaging, desolating, blighting, withering; harrowing, dire, black, fatal.
2. crushing, disheartening; grievous, sore, hard to bear *or* take; severe, hard, heavy, *Sl.* heavy-duty.
3. appalling, shocking, frightful, horrendous, dreadful, sinistrous; wretched, miserable, deplorable, pitiful, pitiable, piteous, pathetic, pathetical; unfortunate, unhappy, unlucky.

disavow, *v.* **1.** disclaim, deny, gainsay, contradict, disaffirm; retract, recant, recall, unsay, take back; repudiate, renounce, (*usu. under oath*) abjure, forswear; defect, apostatize.
2. disown, reject, cast off; disinherit, disherit, *Rare.* exheredate, cut off; wash one's hands of, turn one's back on, have nothing further to do with.

disavowal, *n.* **1.** denial, disaffirmation, retraction, recantation, recall; contradiction, gainsay; disclaimer, disclamation.
2. repudiation, renunciation, renouncement, (*usu. under oath*) abjuration; disowning, discarding, rejecting, rejection, disinheriting, disheriting.

disband, *v.* break up, dissolve, disorganize, dismiss, let go; disperse, scatter, separate; muster out, release, demobilize, send home, inactivate; retire, fold, close, put in mothballs.

disbelief, *n.* **1.** unbelief, incredulity, distrust, discredit, nonconviction; skepticism, doubt, dissent, questioning, challenge; rejection, scorn, repudiation, denial, negation, nihilism.
2. irreverence, free thought, irreligion; paganism, Pyrrhonism, godlessness, infidelity; agnosticism, atheism.

disbeliever, *n.* unbeliever, skeptic, doubter; atheist, agnostic. See **unbeliever.**

disburden, *v.* **1.** disencumber, unburden, lighten one's load, relieve, alleviate, unload; free, extricate, disengage, disembarrass, disentangle, unsnarl, disembroil; set at ease, set one's mind at ease *or* rest, take a load off one's mind.
2. discharge, discard, dispose of, cast off; dump, fling away, jettison.

disburse, *v.* **1.** spend, expend, pay out, outlay, *Inf.* lay out, *Sl.* fork out, *Sl.* shell out, *Sl.* dish out.
2. distribute, parcel out, portion out, dole out, deal out, mete out; dispense, administer, issue.

disbursement, *n.* expenditure, payment, outlay, spending; distribution, disposal, dispersion, dispensation, issuance, administration.

discard, *v.* **1.** reject, throw away, throw out, (*of cards*) slough; eject, toss out, dismiss from use, thrust aside, lay aside, cast aside, have done with, *Inf.* junk, *Inf.* trash, *Sl.* eighty-six, eliminate, *Sl.* scratch; abandon, relinquish, forsake; dispense with, get rid of, drop.
2. repudiate, rescind, recall, retract, revoke; abolish, nullify, declare null and void, cancel.
—*n.* **3.** castaway, *Inf.* throw-out, (*of cards*) slough; distress merchandise, factory reject, reject, second, irregular, *Inf.* markdown; (*pl.*) rejectamenta; hand-me-down; outcast, derelict.

discern, *v.* see, behold, perceive, cognize; observe, notice, espy, descry, detect, discover; make out, decipher, figure out, ascertain, determine; distinguish, pick out, recognize; differentiate, make a distinction, discriminate, judge.

discernible, *adj.* visible, seeable, apparent, perceivable, perceptible; open, in full view, revealed, unconcealed, exposed, showing, unhidden, uncovered, unveiled, naked, bare; conspicuous, observable, noticeable; distinguishable, recognizable, well-marked, detectable, discoverable; distinct, in focus, lucid, plain as day, plain as the nose on one's face; plain, clear, evident, obvious, manifest, patent, palpable.

discerning, *adj.* astute, perceptive, clear-eyed, penetrating, piercing; keen, sharp, acute, quick; eagle-eyed, hawk-eyed, lynx-eyed, sharp-eyed; perspicacious, percipient, appercipient, discriminating, critical; sagacious, judicious, wise, sapient, knowing, aware, sensitive; discreet, politic, prudent, cautious, watchful, Argus-eyed, mindful; clear-headed, thoughtful, sensible, intelligent, reasonable, sound; alert, quick-witted, bright, smart, clever, shrewd, subtle; long-sighted, far-sighted, far-seeing, long-headed.

discernment, *n.* **1.** acumen, perceptiveness, insight, perspicacity, perspicaciousness, penetration, awareness; discrimination, distinguishment, acuteness, keenness, sharpness; cleverness, astuteness, shrewdness, ingenuity, ingeniousness; perception, *Psychol.* apperception, percipience, notice, observance; ascertainment, determination, discrimination, *Inf.* good eye.
2. apprehension, understanding, *Obs.* skill, comprehension; intelligence, knowledge, profundity, depth; sagacity, sagaciousness, wisdom; intuition, divination, clairvoyance; foresightedness, farsightedness, longheadedness; mother wit, wit, esprit; sense, common sense, good sense, judgment, prudence, brains, smartness, brightness.
3. descrying, espial, beholding, detection, discovery, seeing, discerning.

discharge, *v.* **1.** unload, unburden, disburden, free, relieve, remove.
2. fire off, shoot, detonate, explode, burst; let off, let fly, set off; deliver a charge, give vent to.
3. emit, pour forth, send forth, send out, eject; gush, disembogue, cast forth; void, teem, empty; excrete, exude, ooze, leak.

4. exonerate, absolve, acquit, pardon, reprieve, exculpate, clear; exempt, relieve, release; liberate, set free, manumit, emancipate, allow to go.

5. fulfill, perform, execute, carry out, accomplish; observe, abide by, conform to, acquiesce in, consent to.

6. dismiss, oust, get rid of, discard, cashier, deprive of office; fire, *Sl.* sack, *Sl.* bounce, *Sl.* can, *Euph.* terminate; give [s.o.] walking papers, send packing, *Sl.* give the boot to, *Sl.* boot out, let the axe fall, *U.S. Gov't, Inf.* rif.

7. pay, settle, liquidate, satisfy.

8. *Law.* cancel, abolish, rescind, void, annul, make void, nullify, invalidate; expel, clear from, banish, put away.

—*n.* **9.** emptying, unloading, disburdening.

10. firing off, shooting, detonation; explosion, fusillade, salvo, volley, blast, pop, shot, report, burst, crash.

11. emission, ejection, projection, expulsion, vent, flowing forth; voidance, emptying, disemboguement.

12. *Law.* exoneration, exculpation, acquittal, pardon, acquittance, clearance, absolution; liberation, release, setting free, manumission, emancipation; respite, reprieve.

13. *Law.* annulment, nullification, invalidation, voidance; abolition, destruction, banishment.

14. payment, liquidation, satisfaction, settlement.

15. fulfilment, performance, execution, accomplishment, achievement; observance, abidance.

16. dismissal, ouster, displacement, congé, riddance; *Sl.* bounce, *Sl.* sack, *Sl.* the gate, *Inf.* the axe, *Inf.* walking papers.

disciple, *n.* **1.** pupil, scholar, student, educatee; learner, apprentice.

2. votary, devotee, follower, satellite; adherent, partisan, sectary; supporter, promoter, booster; proponent, advocate, defender, apologist; successor, upholder, representative.

3. convert, proselyte; apostle, evangelist, missionary, emissary; *Relig.* follower of Christ, Christian.

disciplinarian, *n.* martinet, drill sergeant, hard master, formalist, stickler; taskmaster, trainer, coach, teacher, authoritarian, tyrant, despot, dictator.

discipline, *n.* **1.** drilling, training, coaching, exercise; development, preparation, instruction, schooling; inculcation, indoctrination, systematization; drill, routine, method, practice, procedure.

2. direction, rule, government, subjection; control, regulation, check, restriction, limitation, restraint, curb, reins; compulsion, coercion.

3. correction, chastisement, reprimand, reproof, rebuke; punishment, castigation, penalty.

4. branch of knowledge, course of study, curriculum, subject, course, specialty, major.

—*v.* **5.** drill, train, coach, exercise; instruct, teach, tutor, give lessons, school, edify; inform, enlighten, inculcate, indoctrinate; ground, prepare, prime, qualify; rear, bring up, form, guide; inure, accustom, familiarize, habituate, toughen, harden, break in, put through paces.

6. control, ride herd on, direct, govern, supervise, oversee, preside over, manage, conduct; lead, hold in hand, hold *or* keep in line, regulate, regiment; restrain, check, curb, hold *or* keep back, contain, arrest; harness, bridle, rein in, hold in, leash, muzzle; restrict, constrain, confine.

7. correct, chastise, reprimand, reprove, rebuke, criticize, make an example of; punish, castigate, penalize.

isclaim, *v.* **1.** repudiate, renounce, (*usu. under oath*) abjure, forswear; deny, gainsay, contradict, disaffirm; disavow, retract, recant, recall, unsay, take back.

2. disown, cast off, disinherit, disherit, *Rare.* exheredate, cut off; wash one's hands of, turn one's back on, have nothing further to do with.

3. reject, refuse, decline, turn down; ignore, be deaf to, turn a deaf ear to, turn thumbs down, say no to.

disclaimer, *n.* **1.** disavowal, denial, disaffirmation; retraction, recantation, recall; contradiction, gainsay, disclamation.

2. repudiation, renunciation, renouncement, (*usu. under oath*) abjuration; disowning, discarding, rejecting, rejection, disinheriting, disheriting.

disclamation, *n.* disavowal, renunciation. See **disclaimer** (*defs.* **1, 2**).

disclose, *v.* **1.** make known, reveal, tell, impart, inform, relate, utter, *Archaic.* discover, declare, break the news; divulge, let slip, leak, let the cat out of the bag, spill the beans, blow the lid off, blurt out, blab; release, break, report, publish, *Archaic.* divulgate, print, broadcast, air, communicate; tell tales, tattle, betray, blow the whistle on, *All Sl.* squeal, squeak, rat, fink, stool, peach.

2. expose, uncover, bare, show, strip; unmask, unveil, take off the chadri, come out of the closet; bring to light, unearth, exhume, exhibit.

disclosure, *n.* revelation, enlightenment, exposure, divulgence, uncovering, unveiling, exposition; exposé, publication, broadcast, report, communication; leak, admission, avowal, confession.

discolor, *v.* **1.** stain, tinge, tint, tone, streak, *Archaic.* distain; wash, fade, pale, bleach, blanch, wash out, weather; tarnish, rust, oxidize; soil, mark, mar, blur, sully.

2. distort, misrepresent, color, varnish, doctor, warp, *Inf.* stretch.

discoloration, *n.* stain, spot, blotch, patch, mark, blemish, flaw, taint; bruise, contusion, maculation, macula.

discomfit, *v.* **1.** rout, trounce, drub, whip, crush, overwhelm, put to flight, floor, *Sl.* mop *or* wipe the floor with, *Inf.* make short work of; conquer, subjugate, vanquish, subdue, overpower, overthrow, master, overmaster; overcome, defeat, beat, worst, lick, win the day, prevail over, triumph over; outmaneuver, outgeneral, outwit, checkmate, trump.

2. frustrate, foil, thwart, hinder, obstruct; ruin, spoil, upset, trip up, shipwreck.

3. disconcert, confuse, confound, perplex, baffle, floor, take aback; discompose, ruffle, abash, nonplus, fluster, *Inf.* discombobulate; embarrass, chagrin, perturb, disturb, demoralize.

discomfiture, *n.* **1.** rout, beating, drubbing, trouncing; defeat, repulse, conquest, vanquishment, overthrow; subjugation, subdual.

2. frustration, rebuff, ruination, undoing, spoiling, miscarriage, abortion; disappointment, failure, nonsuccess.

3. confusion, discomposure, chagrin, embarrassment, disconcertion, bafflement, abashment, shame, humiliation, demoralization.

discomfort, *n.* **1.** uneasiness, disquietude, anxiety, worry, concern, care, trouble; hardship, distress, *Archaic.* misease; mild hurt, uncomfortableness, malaise, aches and pains.

2. ache, pain, pang, throb, twinge, smart, sting, burn; nuisance, pest, bother, *Inf.* headache, *Sl.* hassle, *Sl.* pain in the neck *or* rear, vexation, annoyance; irritant, burr, thorn in the side *or* flesh, pea in the shoe; inconvenience, disadvantage, handicap; problem, affliction, difficulty; trial, tribulation, ordeal; load, burden, weight.

discommode, *v.* inconvenience, trouble, put [s.o.] to the trouble, incommode, put [s.o.] out, impose upon, encroach upon, burden; bother, disturb, *Sl.* hassle, *Sl.* bug.

discompose, *v.* **1.** disarrange, disorder, unsettle, disturb, upset, confuse, disorganize, derange; unhinge, throw into confusion *or* chaos, disarray, dishevel, tousle, rumple, *Inf.* muss up; mix up, muddle, jumble, mess up.

2. disturb, agitate, ruffle, discomfit, disconcert, disquiet; chagrin, perturb, vex, irritate, nettle; confound, fluster, rattle, flurry, unbalance, disorient; abash, embarrass, nonplus; daunt, dishearten.

discomposure, *n.* **1.** disorder, disarray, confusion, dishevelment, disorganization, derangement; chaos, jumble, tangle, mess, *Inf.* muss; dislocation, misplacement.

2. agitation, flurry, fluster, disorientation; chagrin, perturbation, irritation, vexation; anxiety, worry, uneasiness, malaise, disquiet, disquietude, discontent, inquietude, restlessness; embarrassment, humiliation, mortification.

disconcert, *v.* **1.** discompose, discomfit, abash; unsettle, agitate, disquiet, perturb, ruffle, rattle, fluster, *Inf.* bowl over; trouble, upset, annoy, worry, *Inf.* shake up; confound, confuse, nonplus, bewilder, demoralize, perplex, baffle, puzzle; daunt, *Inf.* faze, *Inf.* throw off balance, *Inf.* throw for a loss.

2. disarrange, confuse, disorder, unhinge, upset, *Inf.* discombobulate; frustrate, foil, spoil, ruin, thwart, hinder; undo, undermine, deflate, *Inf.* take the wind out of one's sails, *Sl.* throw out of whack *or* kilter.

disconcerted, *adj.* confused, confounded, perplexed, bewildered, taken aback, nonplused; abashed, discomfited, out of countenance, embarrassed, mortified; unhinged, disorganized, ruffled, rattled, *Sl.* shook up, *Sl.* shook, *Inf.* discombobulated, caught off balance, flustered, *Inf.* in a dither, *Inf.* in a tizzy; uneasy, ill-at-ease, uncomfortable, discomposed, disquieted, anxious, upset, disturbed, perturbed, vexed, put out.

disconnect, *v.* **1.** sever, break *or* cut off, abscind, dissever; break, sunder, rend, tear apart, divide, split, cleave, rive; separate, part, break up, dissolve, split up.

2. interrupt, discontinue, suspend; halt, stop, quit, cease.

3. detach, unfasten, undo, unhook, unlink, unhinge, uncouple, disengage; unfix, unhitch, disjoin, disunite, take apart; disentangle, loosen, loose, free; dissociate, remove from, abstract, cut off, isolate, segregate.

disconnection, *n.* **1.** severence, cut-off, disseverance, disseverment, disseveration; division, *Archaic.* divide, partition, part, split, cleave; breaking up *or* off, parting, separation, split-up, divorce.

2. discontinuity, gap, break, hiatus, disruption, interruption, discontinuation, suspension; halt, stop, stoppage, cessation, cease; breach, rent, schism, rift; opening, fissure, slit, cleft, chink, crack, fracture, flaw.

3. detachment, disengagement, dissociation, abstraction, cutting off, segregation, isolation; disunion, disjunction, disjointedness, incoherence, unrelation, unrelatedness.

disconsolate, *adj.* **1.** inconsolable, heartbroken, forlorn, grief-stricken, comfortless, wretched, miserable; sad, unhappy, woeful, heavy-hearted, dispirited, low-spirited; depressed, dejected, despondent, melancholy, woebegone, discouraged, downcast; blue, *Sl.* down, down in the mouth, in *or* down in the dumps.

2. gloomy, dark, dreary, *Literary,* drear, dismal; somber, depressing, saddening, sad, funereal.

discontent, *adj.* **1.** dissatisfied, discontented, disaffected, displeased; fretful, complaining, querulous, pettish, testy, petulant, cranky; chafed, annoyed, piqued, vexed, exasperated, angry.

—n. **2.** dissatisfaction, disquiet, inquietude, discontentment; envy, displeasure, distaste; uneasiness, restlessness, impatience, fretfulness; irritation, pique, annoyance, vexation, exasperation, umbrage, anger.

discontinuance, *n.* cessation, termination, stoppage, adjournment, stop, stay; disruption, delay, postponement; interruption, discontinuation, suspension, recess, pause; intermission, recess, lull, interval; respite, rest, break, letup.

discontinue, *v.* **1.** terminate, put an end to, end, put a stop to, halt, stay, *Inf.* cut out, *Sl.* can.

2. abandon, quit, leave off, cease, desist from, stop, drop; (*usu. of work*) shut up shop, call it a day, *Inf.* call it quits, *Sl.* knock off; cancel, cease to take, let [s.t.] expire *or* run out.

3. interrupt, suspend, intermit, break off, pause; abstain from, refrain from, give up, quit.

discontinuity, *n.* lack of unity, lack of coherence, disunion, incoherence, disjunction, disjointedness, disconnectedness; discontinuation; disruption, disconnection, interruption, severance, rupture, breach, fissure, rift; division, separation, cleavage, divorce, split.

discontinuous, *adj.* **1.** interrupted, broken, broken off, punctuated; disconnected, unconnected, disjointed, incoherent.

2. intermittent, fitful, spasmodic; on and off, alternate, periodic; random, irregular.

3. discrete, distinct, separated, separate; disjoined, disjunct, detached.

discord, *n.* **1.** disharmony, dissonance, din, jangle, cacophony.

2. incompatibility, variance, diversity, disunity; rupture, breach, break, split, falling out; controversy, argument, dispute, contention, dissension; conflict, strife, friction, wrangling, clashing; hostility, animosity, war, warfare.

discordant, *adj.* **1.** incongruous, disparate, inconsistent; contrary, disagreeing, divergent, opposed, adverse, opposite; paradoxical, contradictory, incompatible, inimical, conflicting; different, differing, dissimilar.

2. dissonant, absonant, inharmonious, tuneless, unmusical, unmelodious, untuneful, *Music.* atonal; cacophonous, harsh, strident, shrill, screechy, grating, jangling, jarring, clashing.

discount, *v.* **1.** deduct, take off, *Inf.* lop off, *Sl.* knock off; reduce, mark down, cut back, roll back.

2. disregard, ignore, overlook, pass over, gloss over; leave out of account *or* consideration, pay no attention to, take no note of; brush off, blink at, wink at.

—n. **3.** reduction, deduction, markdown, cut rate, cutback, rollback; rebate, refund; allowance, exemption, (*in reference to taxes*) *Sl.* deduck.

discountenance, *v.* **1.** embarrass, shame, chagrin, abash, humiliate, put down, cause to lose face, humble; disconcert, nonplus, discompose, perturb, annoy, put out of countenance; dishearten, discomfit, daunt, discourage, dispirit.

2. disapprove, disfavor, discourage, frown upon; reject, object to, condemn, veto, turn thumbs down on, take exception to; resist, oppose, have nothing to do with, wash one's hands of, refuse to condone.

discourage, *v.* **1.** dishearten, dispirit, dampen one's spirits, cast a pall, blunt; disenchant, damp, throw cold water on, throw a wet blanket over, put a damper on; daunt, dismay, intimidate, overawe, cow, abash, appall; unnerve, prostrate, unman.

2. divert, sidetrack, switch, shift, shunt; deter, hold back, restrain, curb, rein in.

3. hinder, prevent, dash one's hopes, repress, suppress, squelch, *Inf.* bulldoze, *Inf.* put the kibosh on; obstruct, oppose, obviate, stop short.

4. caution, warn, advise against; expostulate, urge against, dehort, remonstrate, admonish, dissuade, talk out of; deprecate, deplore, *Inf.* talk down, *Inf.* put down.

discouragement, *n.* **1.** dejection, disheartenment, lack of spirit; depression, low spirits, gloom, melancholy, despondency, despair; dismay, frustration, consternation, hopelessness, prostration; loss of confidence, cold feet, hesitation, fearfulness, mistrust.

2. opposition, resistance, antagonism, contravention; dissuasion, intimidation, expostulation, remonstrance, prohibition.

3. damper, wet blanket, cold water; deterrent, hindrance, impediment, obstacle, barricade, preclusion, interference, *Inf.* setback; curb, check, control, rein, restraint, constraint; repression, restriction, inhibition; rebuff, slap in the face, *Inf.* put-down.

discourse, *n.* **1.** conversation, talk, dialogue, colloquy, converse, interlocution, verbal exchange; chat, chitchat, palaver, confabulation, *Inf.* confab, table talk.

2. address, speech, oration, declamation, *Rhet.* apostrophe, salutation, valedictory; lecture, sermon, screed, harangue, diatribe, philippic; treatise, study, thesis, dissertation, descant, essay.

—*v.* **3.** converse, talk, discuss, speak, chat, chitchat, confabulate, *Inf.* confab, coze, pass the time of day, *Brit. Dial.* tell, *Sl.* rap, *Sl.* chin, *Sl.* chew the fat *or* rag, *Sl.* shoot the breeze *or* bull, *Sl.* bull.

4. address, deliver an address, make a speech, give a talk, soapbox, platform, take the floor; declaim, hold forth, lecture, sermonize, preach, pontificate; harangue, rant, rave, rant and rave, *Inf.* spout, outherod Herod.

discourteous, *adj.* rude, impolite, uncivil, unceremonious, unmannerly, bad-mannered, ill-bred, disrespectful, misbehaved; indelicate, uncourtly, ungallant, indecorous, ungracious; ungentlemanly, unladylike, brash, bold, hoydenish, *Scot.* randy; brazen, barefaced, insolent, impudent, insulting, impertinent, pert, saucy, fresh; bluff, surly, sullen, bearish, gruff; inconsiderate, tactless, *Scot. and North Eng.* misleared; abrupt, blunt, brusque, curt, clipped, short; rough, crude, boorish, churlish, loutish, vulgar, coarse.

discourtesy, *n.* **1.** rudeness, impoliteness, incivility, unmannerliness; inconsideration, tactlessness, disrespectfulness, misbehavior; ungraciousness, indecorum, uncourtliness, ungentlemanliness, hoydenism; brashness, boldness, brazenness, insolence, impudence, impertinence, pertness, tartness, sauciness, freshness; flippancy, arrogance, cheek, lip, effrontery, presumption; surliness, sulkiness, bearishness, churlishness; abruptness, bluntness, brusqueness, curtness, shortness, harshness; uncouthness, coarseness, crudeness, crudity, vulgarity; boorishness, loutishness.

2. snub, insult, affront; rebuff, come back, snide remark, short answer, hard words; sulks, scowl, frown, black looks.

discover, *v.* **1.** discern, detect, descry, espy, notice, make out, perceive, distinguish, recognize, catch a glimpse of, catch sight of, *Inf.* spot; see, behold, observe, view, *Brit.* twig, *Archaic.* ken.

2. locate, find, determine, ascertain, put one's finger on; uncover, unearth, bring to light, turn up, dig up, root out, ferret out, smoke out, search out.

3. conceive, contrive, devise, design, invent, patent; concoct, make up, *Inf.* cook up; innovate, pioneer, originate; chance upon, stumble upon, happen upon, light upon; find out, hear of, learn of, catch wind of.

discovery, *n.* **1.** apprehension, detection, discernment, espial, perception, recognition, realization; ascertaining, determining, locating, uncovering, unearthing; introduction, origination, coinage.

2. find, finding, treasure, lucky strike, serendipity; invention, innovation, contrivance, concoction, neologism; conception, idea; breakthrough, leap, new phase.

discredit, *v.* **1.** detract, degrade, censure, reproach, make disreputable, bring into disfavor, injure *or* impair the credit *or* reputation of, tear down; disparage, decry, demean, deprecate, deflate, devaluate, depreciate, belittle; defame, slur, asperse, malign, calumniate, libel, slander, traduce, denigrate, sully, smear, blacken, stain, tarnish, taint, smirch, besmirch, smudge; humiliate, humble, mortify.

2. disprove, invalidate, refute, undermine credibility, destroy belief in, shake one's faith; lampoon, mock, ridicule.

3. disbelieve, deny, misbelieve, refuse credence to, give no credit to, *Inf.* give no ear to; challenge, dispute, raise objections; doubt, question, distrust, mistrust, place no confidence in, put no faith in; hesitate, waiver, have one's doubts.

—*n.* **4.** disbelief, unbelief, incredulity, loss of belief, loss of credence; disproval, invalidation, refutation; doubt, doubtfulness, skepticism, question, dubiety, dubiousness, dubiosity, suspicion, distrust, mistrust; lack of confidence, uncertainty, hesitation, indecision; qualm, scruple, compunction.

5. disrepute, disfavor, obloquy, disesteem, loss of face; detraction, derogation, degradation, devaluation, depreciation; shame, disgrace, dishonor, scandal, reproach, ignominy, infamy, odium, opprobrium, baseness, debasement, vitiation, turpitude, ill-repute; humiliation, humble pie, mortification.

6. aspersion, slur, imputation, slander, reflection, denigration, defamation, smear, smirch, blot, stain, taint, attaint, tarnish, spot, blemish, smudge, brand, stigma; lampoon, mockery, squib, pasquinade.

discreditable, *adj.* **1.** blameworthy, blamable, culpable, censurable, chargeable, accusable, impeachable, imputable; undutiful, delinquent, negligent; improper, unseemly, unbecoming, unworthy, objectionable, uncommendable, reprovable, peccable, illaudable.

2. disgraceful, shameful, dishonorable, reprehensible, unprincipled, scandalous; degrading, ignoble, inglorious.

discreet, *adj.* careful, prudent, wise, sagacious; cautious, precautious, judicious, sensible; guarded, circumspect, wary, chary; aware, awake, alert, heedful, watchful, vigilant, *Inf.* on one's toes; diplomatic, tactful, politic, strategic; reserved, noncommital.

discrepancy, *n.* **1.** inconsistency, variance, dissimilarity, deviation, divergence; disparity, incongruity, contrariety; difference, disagreement, discordance, misunderstanding, credibility gap, cross purposes.

2. moot point, disputed point, question at issue, vexed question, knotty point, point in dispute, bone of contention.

discrepant, *adj.* differing, disagreeing, at variance; discordant, clashing, jarring, conflictory; inconsistent, contradictory, opposite, contrary, paradoxical, incongruous.

discrete, *adj.* separate, distinct, detached; disconnected, disjunct, disjunctive, discretive, discontinuous.

discretion, *n.* **1.** prudence, judiciousness, wisdom, sagacity, caution, forethought; sound *or* mature judgment, good sense, thoughtfulness, deliberation, discrimination, *Inf.* good eye, discernment, tact; moderation, sophrosyne, *Brit. Dial.* mense.

2. freedom of choice, liberty, volition, option, will; preference, pleasure, election, inclination; mind, disposition, liking, wish, desire, purpose, intent.

discretionary, *adj.* optional, elective, open, unrestricted, unqualified, unconditioned; voluntary, volitional, volitionary, unrestrained.

discriminate, *v.* distinguish, discern, differentiate; split hairs, mince matters; divide, separate, segregate, isolate, set apart, set off, separate the sheep from the goats, separate the wheat from the chaff; prejudge, presuppose, presume.

discrimination, *n.* **1.** discernment, astuteness, penetration, acumen, perspicacity, keenness, sharpness, acuteness, shrewdness; sagacity, judgment, wisdom, insight; discretion, prudence, caution, carefulness, forethought, longheadedness.

2. racism, sexism, chauvinism; bias, prejudice, bigotry, intolerance, narrow-mindedness.

3. taste, good taste, finesse, grace, polish, refinement, culture; fastidiousness, finicality, meticulosity, hypercriticism.

discriminative, *adj.* **1.** distinctive, diacritical, characteristic, particular, peculiar, special, typical.

2. distinguishing, disjunctive, differentiating, differential, discriminating, analytical, critical; discerning, perceptive, perspicacious, percipient, clear-eyed, keen; aesthetic, artistic, tasteful, cultivated, cultured, refined, polished.

3. preferential, prejudicial; racist, sexist, chauvinistic.

discursive, *adj.* digressive, excursive, desultory, episodic, rhapsodic; circumlocutory, circumlocutional, circumlocutionary, circuitous, roundabout; rambling, roving, wandering, meandering, drifting, straggling, veering; diffuse, wordy, long-winded, prolix, verbose.

discuss, *v.* **1.** talk over, debate, moot, bandy words, *Inf.* kick around, *Sl.* hash over; argue the pros and cons, argue for and against, argue, dispute, contend, contest, question; disagree, dissent, differ, controvert, oppose; spar, cross swords, lock horns, altercate, wrangle, bicker; haggle, dicker, *Sl.* hassle out, fight out, thresh *or* thresh over, *Inf.* hash out, *Inf.* iron out, come to a decision.

2. confer, parley, *Inf.* compare notes, get together on; go over, review, look at; talk about, exchange views, *Inf.* talk turkey, talk seriously; talk, converse, *Sl.* rap, chat, *Sl.* chew the rag *or* fat, *Sl.* shoot the bull, *Sl.* bat *or* shoot the breeze, pass the time of day, *Inf.* gab, gossip. See **chat.** (*def.* **1**).

3. discourse, converse on, speak on, talk on *or* about, treat, deal with, handle; present, bring up, air, ventilate, open up for discussion; study, examine a question, deliberate, consider, weigh.

discussion, *n.* **1.** debate, dispute, disagreement, contention, dissension, variance, difference of opinion; disputation, argumentation, polemic, logomachy, war of words; verbal controversy, altercation, wrangle, heated argument, *Sl.* hassle.

2. conference, meeting, parley, *Inf.* powwow; tête-à-tête, private talk *or* conference, review; conversation, discourse, palaver, talk, chat; coze, causerie, confabulation, *Inf.* confab; *Inf.* chin session, buzz session, gossip session; exchange of ideas, *Sl.* rap, *Sl.* rap session, *Sl.* bull session, airing, ventilation.

3. study, examination, deliberation, consideration, careful thought; ratiocination, reasoning; inquiry, investigation, examination, close inspection, canvass; review, survey, check, search, probe, exploration; scrutiny, scrutinization, analysis, dissection.

disdain, *v.* **1.** scorn, contemn, hold in contempt, revile; misprize, consider beneath oneself, spurn, spit upon, curl one's lip at; despise, hate, detest, loathe, abhor; reproach, deprecate, disparage; deride, ridicule, laugh at, poke fun at, make fun of.

2. belittle, pooh-pooh, look down upon, set at naught, *Sl.* put down; disregard, slight, snub, shun, cut, *Inf.* high-hat, upstage, give a cold shoulder to, turn up one's nose at, ostracize, rebuff; ignore, have nothing to do with, disown, cut off, disavow, have no use for, wipe one's feet on, brush aside.

—*n.* **3.** scorn, contempt, contemptuousness, scornfulness, contumely, opprobrium; deprecation, disparagement, belittling; hate, detestation, loathing, abhorrence.

4. insolence, arrogance, haughtiness; superciliousness, *Inf.* toploftiness, hauteur, airs; aloofness, indifference.

5. derision, sneering, scoffing, jeering, mockery, mocking, taunting, flouting, gibing, twit, hissing, booing, catcall; ridicule, laughter.

disdainful, *adj.* contemptuous, scornful, insolent; sneering, derisive, insulting, jeering, scoffing, flouting; proud, haughty, lordly, pompous, arrogant, superior, supercilious, contumelious.

disease, *n.* malady, illness, sickness, ailment, *Inf.* bug, pathology, morbidity, distemper, *Pathol.* affection; unhealthiness, ill-health, abnormality, unsoundness, disorder, derangement; affliction, complaint, *Inf.* mulligrubs, indisposition; infirmity, disability, invalidism; infection, *Inf.* virus, fever, *Inf.* temperature, contagion, plague, pestilence; idiopathy, cachexia, dyscrasia, *Plant Pathol.* canker.

diseased, *adj.* **1.** pathological, morbid, afflicted, affected, infected; poisoned, tainted, corrupted, contaminated, corroded; deranged, abnormal.

2. sick, sickly, ailing, ill; unhealthy, unsound, unwell, unwholesome, *Sl.* germy; laid up, out of sorts, off one's feed, down with a bug, indisposed.

disembark, *v.* land, debark, deplane, detrain, step out of, leave; unload, put *or* go ashore, *Inf.* pile out; climb down from, get down *or* off, descend the gangplank, dismount, alight, light.

disembarrass, *v.* **1.** relieve, ease, put at ease, make comfortable, relax, allay, soothe; mollify, appease, assuage, mitigate.

2. rid, free, liberate, release, extricate, disentangle; unclog, unstop, open, clear, remove, unseal; unburden, unload, unhamper, discharge, disburden, disencumber, lighten the load; get rid of, get off one's hands, get off one's back, wash one's hands of.

disembodied, *adj.* **1.** bodiless, incorporeal, discarnate; spiritual, immaterial, unsubstantial, unfleshly; intangible, impalpable, imponderable, immeasurable.

2. airy, ethereal, vapory; spectral, ghostly, phantom, wraithlike; extramundane, transmundane, supernatural, superphysical, hyperphysical.

disembowel, *v.* eviscerate, exenterate, gut, draw, cut out, cut open, embowel, gralloch, *Rare.* paunch.

disembroil, *v.* clear up, unclutter, unsnarl, unscramble; restore order, free up. See **disentangle**.

disenable, *v.* disable, unfit, impair, enfeeble, weaken, enervate, devitalize; emasculate, unman, effeminize; handicap, debilitate, cripple, paralyze, lame, maim; disqualify, invalidate, undermine; prevent, impede, hinder, obstruct, hamstring, hobble; tie one's hands, clip one's wings, put a spoke in one's wheel; put out of gear, put out of commission, put out of action, lay [s.o.] up, *Sports.* sideline.

disenchant, *v.* disillusion, disillusionize, disabuse, undeceive, open [s.o.'s] eyes, set [s.o.] straight, make [s.o.] see the real world, make [s.o.] grow up; disentrance, unhypnotize, break the spell, snap [s.o.] out of it. See **disillusion**.

disencumber, *v.* unload, unhamper, unburden, discharge. See **disembarrass** (*def.* **2**).

disengage, *v.* loosen, loose, unfasten, detach, unhook, unattach; unbuckle, unclinch, unhitch, unclasp, uncouple; disjoin, disunite, divide, divorce; unloose, free, liberate, set free, disinvolve, disentwine; unbolt, unbar, unlock, unlatch; unpin, unfix, unbind, unlace, untie; unleash, unfetter, unchain; extricate, get out, cut loose, break out, get free of, get quit of; get out of, get rid of, throw off, shake; part, separate, dissever, sever, sunder, disconnect, break, cleave, ax; pull the plug, cut the wire, cut the knot, sever the ties, break the connection.

disengaged, *adj.* **1.** unattached, released, free, loose, unconnected, out of gear; liberated, freed, unhitched, disjoined, disentangled; apart, asunder, separate.

2. unoccupied, free, at leisure, unengaged, unemployed, doing nothing; at ease, not busy, idle, inactive, *Inf.* laying about *or* around.

disengagement, *n.* **1.** disconnection, separation, loosening, detachment, unfastening, unhitching; disjunction, disunion, divorce, severance, disseverance; parting, breaking, splitting, disruption; dissociation, breaking up, division, fission; disentanglement, disinvolvement, extrication, extraction, removal.

2. leisure, freedom, liberty, *It. dolce far niente*; free time, spare time, own time, ease, relaxation; breather, spell, *Inf.* let-up, lull, rest, relief, respite, pause, break, time-out, breathing spell.

disentangle, *v.* **1.** unravel, unwind, undo, untwist, untie, unknot, unbind; unfold, unroll, untangle, unweave, unthread, unbraid; comb, card, dress, separate; uncurl, unkink, unsnarl, straighten, smooth, groom.

2. clear up, solve, answer, resolve, figure out, work out, find out, *Sl.* dope out; unscramble, disembroil, make out, decipher, decode, *Inf.* crack.

3. simplify, disinvolve, clarify, sort out, get to the core *or* heart.

disenthrall, *v.* free, liberate, emancipate, manumit, enfranchise, affranchise, franchise; deliver, rescue, ransom, redeem, *Theol.* save; release, set free, loose, loosen, let loose, turn loose, set loose, let go, unpen, unmew, disimprison; unbind, untie, unfetter, unshackle, unchain, unhandcuff, unbridle, unyoke, unmuzzle, *Archaic.* untruss.

disfavor, *n.* **1.** disrespect, disregard, low regard, disesteem, low esteem, low *or* poor opinion, low estimation, dim view; dislike, discontentment, unhappiness, displeasure, dissatisfaction; disapproval, disapprobation, discountenance.

2. discredit, dishonor, disgrace, shame, disrepute, ill repute; obloguy, odium, opprobrium, ignominy, infamy; alienation, estrangement, disaffection, ostracism, *Sl.* the doghouse.

3. disservice, ill turn, bad deed, *Sl.* raw deal; insult, affront, offense, slight, discourtesy, slap in the face; aspersion, jeer, taunt, gibe, *Inf.* brickbat, *Sl.* put-down.

disfigure, *v.* deface, deform, disfeature, blemish, mar, spoil, ruin, flaw, scar, blotch, uglify; injure, impair, maul, damage, vandalize, trash.

disfigurement, *n.* **1.** defacement, deformation, distortion, disfeaturement, impairment, injury, uglification; vandalism, destruction, damage.

2. ugliness, unsightliness, unattractiveness; hideousness, horribleness, horridness, frightfulness, repulsiveness.

3. blemish, blotch, stain, spot, blot, smudge; defect, flaw, fault, imperfection; eyesore, fright, mess, monstrosity; deformity, malformation, mutilation; scar, pit, pockmark, *Med.* cicatrix, (*both usu. resulting from drug abuse*) *Sl.* track, *Sl.* crater; birthmark, mole, port-wine stain *or* mark, *Med.* naevus.

disgorge, *v.* **1.** spit out, spew out, vomit forth, burst forth; spew, jet, spurt; vomit, regurgitate, heave, throw up, be sick, *Sl.* puke, *Sl.* barf, *Sl.* upchuck, *Sl.* blow lunch.

2. (*all usu. in reference to something illicitly obtained*) surrender, yield, cede, relinquish, give up, turn over, *Inf.* hand over, *Sl.* fork up *or* over, *Sl.* cough up, render up; release, let go, forgo, renounce, abandon, *Sl.* kiss good-bye; return, replace, give back.

3. discharge, eject, expel; jettison, cast off *or* away, throw out *or* off *or* away.

disgrace, *n.* **1.** dishonor, shame, degradation, scandal, debasement, vitiation, ill-repute, reproach, ingloriousness; ignominy, infamy, odium, opprobrium, condemnation.

2. slur, imputation, aspersion, defamation, denigration, slander, libel, vilification, smear, smirch, blot, blot on the escutcheon, stain, taint, attaint, tarnish, spot, black spot *or* mark, blemish, smudge, brand, stigma, *Inf.* skeleton in the closet.

3. discredit, disrepute, disfavor, disrespect, obloquy, disapproval, disapprobation, disesteem, loss of face, downfall, fall, descent; humiliation, humble pie, mortification; belittlement, disparagement, deprecation, deflation, derogation, detraction, depreciation, devaluation.

—*v.* **4.** shame, dishonor, degrade, abase, debase, vitiate, reproach; sully, impute, slur, asperse, vilify, scandalize, blacken, smear, smirch, besmirch, taint, attaint, tarnish, stain, smudge, spot, bespatter, brand, stigmatize, *Sl.* dump on, drag through the mud *or* mire, heap dirt upon; slander, calumniate, libel, denigrate, defame.

5. discredit, disfavor, derogate, disprove, depreciate, devaluate, lower, reduce, detrude, depress; demean, belittle, detract, disparage, decry, deprecate, deflate; humiliate, humble, mortify.

disgraced, *adj.* **1.** shamed, dishonored, reproached, ill-famed; disfavored, *Sl.* in the doghouse; humiliated, mortified, humbled.

2. discredited, invalidated, refuted; belittled, disparaged, decried, derogated, deprecated, depreciated, deflated.

3. libeled, slandered, aspersed, slurred, denigrated, defamed, scandalized, smirched, besmirched, smeared, smeared, stained, tarnished, tainted, blemished, smudged, branded, stigmatized.

disgraceful, *adj.* **1.** shameful, dishonorable, degraded, inglorious; infamous, ignominious, odious, contemptible, despicable, opprobrious, detestable, sordid, degenerate, depraved, horrible, heinous, vicious, atrocious, flagitious; corrupt, reprehensible, unprincipled, debased, base, vile, evil, sinful, bad, wrong, low, arrant, nefarious, *Obs.* scelerous; mean, villainous, ignoble.

2. libelous, slanderous, defamatory; shocking, scandalous, notorious, flagrant, shameless, outrageous; improper, unseemly, unbecoming, *Obs.* indign, unworthy, undutiful, delinquent, objectionable, uncommendable, reprovable, peccable, illaudable; indecent, lewd, obscene, perverse.

3. disreputable, discreditable, disfavorable; censurable, blameworthy, blamable, culpable, chargeable, accusable, impeachable, imputable; humiliating, mortifying; belittling, deflating, derogatory, disparaging, deprecating.

disgruntled, *adj.* discontented, discontent, malcontent, dissatisfied, displeased, unhappy; disappointed, dejected, disheartened, let down; sulky, sullen, poutful, resentful; cranky, grumpy, grouchy, surly, churlish, ill-humored, in a bad mood; vexed, annoyed, irritated, exasperated, disgusted, *Inf.* fed up.

disguise, *v.* **1.** camouflage, costume, put into a costume, change the appearance *or* looks of, dress [s.o.] up; cloak, mask, veil, shroud, ensconce, cover up; cover, cover over, conceal, hide.

2. misrepresent, falsify, deceive, give a false picture of *or* appearance to; fake, fudge, feign, masquerade as, simulate, act, put on; dissemble, dissimulate, gloss over, varnish, muffle, garble.

—n. **3.** camouflage, mask, cloak, incognito; covering, concealment, blind, screen, veil; costume, masquerade, outfit, *Inf.* getup.

4. guise, pretense, appearance, semblance, cover, cover-up; show, window dressing, veneer, facade, false front, *Inf.* front; deception, trickery, ruse, smoke screen, artifice, subterfuge, dissimulation.

disguised, *adj.* **1.** camouflaged, costumed, masquerading, incognito; cloaked, shrouded, veiled, masked, screened, ensconced; hidden, concealed, undercover, covert, secret, clandestine.

2. varnished, glossed over, muffled, dissembled, garbled; deceptive, illusory, unreal, tricky; false, fake, counterfeit, feigned, pretend, make-believe.

disgust, *v.* **1.** nauseate, sicken, *Inf.* turn one's stomach; satiate, glut, surfeit; offend, repel, repulse, *Sl.* turn [s.o.] off, *Inf.* put [s.o.] off, displease; outrage, scandalize, shock, *Sl.* gross out; cause aversion, dissatisfy, annoy.

—n. **2.** distaste, disrelish; satiety, surfeit, glut, repletion; fulsomeness, noisomeness, nausea, sickness, queasiness.

3. odium, abhorrence, abomination, loathing, detestation, hatred, dislike, disaffection; aversion, disapprobation, antipathy, animosity, animus, antagonism, enmity, hostility; repugnance, revulsion, offense, repulsion; dissatisfaction, disapproval, displeasure, annoyance.

disgusted, *adj.* nauseated, sickened, sick and tired, sick of, *Sl.* fed to the gills *or* teeth, *Inf.* fed up; offended, repelled, repulsed, *Sl.* turned off, displeased; outraged, scandalized, shocked, *Sl.* grossed out.

disgusting, *adj.* **1.** nauseating, nauseous, sickening, fulsome, noisome; distasteful, unpalatable, unsavory, unappetizing, insipid; odious, abhorrent, abominable, execrable, anathematic, loathsome, detestable, hateful, unlikable; antipathetical, antagonistic.

2. repugnant, aversive, repellent, revolting, repulsive, offensive, objectionable, off-putting; obnoxious, nasty, unpleasant, displeasing, disagreeable, insufferable; outrageous, scandalous, reprehensible, ignominious, shocking; gross, vile, foul, vulgar, shameless, stinking.

dish, *n.* **1.** container, receptacle, bowl, vessel, utensil; plate, platter, paten, saucer; tureen, crock, cup, porringer; pan, skillet, tray, salver; carafe, bottle.

2. serving, sampling, helping.

—v. **3.** ladle, scoop, spoon, shovel, dig.

4. dish it out *Informal.* lay it on, come down on, give [s.o.] the business, work [s.o.] over, lambast.

5. dish out *Informal.* deal out, dole out, mete out, distribute, measure out, parcel out.

dishabille, *n.* **1.** undress, informal dress, casual attire; disarray, disorderly dress.

2. housecoat, dressing gown, kimono, muumuu; robe, negligee, peignoir, nightgown.

dishearten, *v.* **1.** daunt, dismay, unnerve, unman, intimidate, cow; appall, frighten, affright; disconcert, *Inf.* shake up, abash.

2. discourage, dispirit, take the heart out of, *Inf.* take the starch out of, *Dial.* take the tuck out of; depress, deject, sadden, *Inf.* break one's heart, distress, cut up, lie heavy on, weigh [s.o.] down, crush, prostrate.

3. dampen, put a damper on, damp, cast a gloom *or* pall on *or* over, *Inf.* put a wet blanket on, *Inf.* throw cold water on; deaden, dull, enervate, weaken, weary, tire.

disheartened, *adj.* **1.** discouraged, disappointed, depressed, dejected, downcast, saddened, brokenhearted, *Inf.* broken-up; distressed, burdened, weighed down, crushed, *Inf.* broken, prostrate.

2. dismayed, unnerved, unmanned, daunted; terrified, intimidated, cowed, frightened, horrified, appalled, aghast; disconcerted, abashed.

3. spiritless, dispirited, exanimate, weakened, drained, enervated, weary, tired.

dished, *adj.* concave, incurvate, incurved, cupped, cup-shaped, scyphate, poculiform, caluthiform, *Bot., Zool.* cyanthiform; scooped, scooped out, hollow, hollowed out, sunken, depressed, pushed in.

disheveled, *adj.* unkempt, untidy, disordered, disarranged; tousled, mussed, rumpled, blowzy; windblown, uncombed, every which-way; disarrayed, confused, beat up; messy, frowzy, slovenly, slatternly.

dishonest, *adj.* **1.** untruthful, false, mendacious, lying, speaking with forked tongue; deceitful, two-faced, hypocritical, insincere, disingenuous; crooked, cheating, underhanded, shady; rascally, roguish, knavish, thievish, Fagin-like.

2. fraudulent, phony, spurious, counterfeit, fake, *U.S.* bogus; charlatanic, quackish; deceptive, misleading, tricky, shifty, slippery.

3. unscrupulous, unprincipled, conscienceless; dishonorable, on the take, corrupt, contemptible, wrongful, immoral; unlawful, illegal, criminal, felonious.

4. untrustworthy, faithless, falsehearted, treacherous, perfidious; unjust, unfair.

dishonesty, *n.* **1.** falsity, mendacity, untruthfulness, lying, prevaricating; duplicity, double-dealing, hypocrisy; disingenuousness, insincerity, improbity; deceit, cheating, crookedness, deviousness, knavery, roguery, rascality, villainy; dirty pool, dirty tricks, foul play.

2. fraud, *Archaic.* covin, deception, humbug, chicanery, trickery, throwing a curve ball, swindle, con game, shell game; sharp practice, shiftiness, dealing from the bottom of the deck, stacking the deck, loading the dice.

3. thievery, larceny, stealing, robbery, highway robbery, holdup; tapping the till, hiking checks, robbing the blind; venality, jobbery, graft, corruption.

4. malpractice, malfeasance, misconduct, illegality, criminality; wrongdoing, wickedness, immorality, unrighteousness, unscrupulousness, unfairness; faithlessness, infidelity, betrayal, perfidy, treachery.

dishonor, *n.* **1.** disgrace, shame, reproach, ignominy, ill-repute, public disgrace *or* contempt; scandal, degradation, shameful conduct, dishonorableness, ingloriousness; abasement, debasement, vitiation, fall, downfall, descent; infamy, odium, opprobrium, condemnation; humiliation, mortification.

2. disrepute, disfavor, discredit, obloquy, disapproval, disapprobation, disesteem, low estimation, loss of face; belittlement, disparagement, devaluation, depreciation, derogation, detraction, deflation, deprecation.

3. indignity, disrespect, contumely, ill-treatment, maltreatment, insult, affront, abuse, outrage; slight, discourtesy.

4. slur, imputation, aspersion, defamation, denigration, vilification, slander, libel; smear, smirch, blot, blot on the escutcheon, brand, stigma, spot, black spot *or* mark, *Inf.* black eye, blemish, smudge, taint, attaint, attainder.

—*v.* **5.** disgrace, shame, reproach, degrade, abase, debase, vitiate; humiliate, humble, mortify.

6. discredit, disfavor, disprove, depreciate, devaluate, lower, reduce; demean, belittle, derogate, detract, disparage, decry, deprecate, vilipend, deflate.

7. insult, affront, injure, abuse, illtreat, maltreat, outrage; slight, be discourteous.

8. slur, impute, asperse, denigrate, defame, vilify, slander, libel, smear, smirch, besmirch, blot, taint, attaint, tarnish, spot, smudge, brand, stigmatize.

9. *Commerce.* bilk, welsh, cheat, default, refuse to accept a bill *or* charge, refuse to honor by payment, decline to pay *or* redeem, *Inf.* rip off, *Sl.* skip town, *Brit. Sl.* do a moonlight flit, *Brit. Sl.* levant.

10. rape, ravish, debauch, seduce, deflower, abuse sexually, assault, *Obs.* devirginate, *Obs.* construpate; violate, pollute, defile.

dishonorable, *adj.* **1.** shameful, disgraceful, degraded, inglorious; infamous, ignominious, odious, opprobrious, sordid, despicable, contemptible, detestable, degenerate, depraved, reprehensible, foul, heinous, debased, corrupt, base, vile, evil, bad, arrant; mean, low, villainous, ignoble.

2. shameless, unprincipled, unscrupulous, unfair, unjust; disreputable, discreditable, *Inf.* shady.

3. shocking, outrageous, notorious, scandalous, unmentionable, flagrant; indecent, ribald, lewd, lowminded; improper, unseemly, unbecoming, unworthy, undutiful, delinquent, unconscientious, objectionable, uncommendable, reprovable, peccable, illaudable.

4. treacherous, perfidious, false-hearted, traitorous, untrustworthy, venal, crooked.

dishonored, *adj.* **1.** shamed, disgraced, reproached, ill-famed; disfavored, *Sl.* in the doghouse; humiliated, mortified, humbled.

2. discredited, invalidated, refuted; belittled, disparaged, deprecated, depreciated, derogated, deflated, decried.

3. affronted, insulted, slighted, abused, ill-treated, maltreated; shocked, outraged, scandalized.

4. raped, ravished, debauched, seduced, deflowered, abused sexually, assaulted; violated, polluted, defiled.

5. libeled, slandered, aspersed, slurred, denigrated, defamed, smirched, besmirched, smeared, stained, tarnished, tainted, blemished, smudged, branded, stigmatized.

disillusion, *v.* disillusionize, disenchant, disabuse, undeceive, unbeguile; open [s.o.'s] eyes, make [s.o.] see the light, wake [s.o.] up, disentrance, unhypnotize, break the spell, snap [s.o.] out of it; burst [s.o.'s] bubble, shatter [s.o.'s] illusions, make [s.o.] see the real world, make [s.o.] grow up; tell [s.o.] the truth about [s.t.], clue [s.o.] in, set [s.o.] straight, set [s.o.] right, correct [s.o.].

disinclination, *n.* reluctance, hesitance, lack of desire, indisposition, unwillingness, averseness, loathness; objection, demur, opposition, recalcitrance, recalcitrancy, resistance, renitence, renitency.

2. distaste, dislike, disrelish, aversion, repugnance, antipathy, disgust, loathing, abhorrence.

disinclined, *adj.* reluctant, not in the mood, indisposed, unwilling, loath; averse, antipathetic, opposed, recalcitrant, resistant, renitent.

disinfect, *v.* antisepticize, free from infection, sterilize, sanitize, sanitate, rid of germs; fumigate, deodorize; decontaminate, cleanse, clean, purify, depurate, purge.

disinfectant, *n.* bactericide, antiseptic, sterilizer, sanitizer; fumigant, deodorizer, deodorant; decontaminator, cleanser, cleaner, purifier, depurative, purger.

disingenuous, *adj.* insincere, uncandid, unfrank, mealy-mouthed; deceitful, dishonest, underhanded, crooked, tricky, double-tongued; false, false-hearted, double-dealing, two-faced, mendacious, lying, untruthful; artful, insidious, guileful, scheming, plotting, calculating, contriving, designing; cunning, crafty, sly, wily, foxy; shifty, slippery, smooth, slick.

disinherit, *v.* cut off, cut off without a penny; expropriate, deprive, dispossess, divest; oust, evict, turn out, *Inf.* send out into the storm; disown, repudiate, renounce, turn [s.o.'s] picture to the wall.

disintegrate, *v.* crumble, fall apart, fall to pieces, go to wrack and ruin, decompose, decay, rot, molder, dissolve, erode; break up, disperse, disband.

disinter, *v.* **1.** exhume, disinhume, dig up, disentomb.

2. unearth, uncover, bring to light, disclose, expose, discover, root out; resurrect, revive, bring back.

disinterested, *adj.* **1.** unbiased, impartial, impersonal, neutral; unprejudiced, open-minded, fair, equitable, just, dispassionate; candid, honest, generous, magnanimous, unselfish.

2. unconcerned, detached, aloof, uninterested, lukewarm.

disjoin, *v.* separate, divorce, detach, dissociate, segregate, isolate, abstract; disunite, disconnect, uncouple, disentangle, disengage; dismember, dissect, anatomize, disjoint; sever, dissever, sunder, rend, tear, rive, split, break; divide, partition, break up, split up, interrupt, disrupt.

disjoint, *v.* **1.** dislocate, displace, throw out; dismember, dissect, anatomize; disconnect, dissociate, separate, uncouple. See **disjoin** and **anatomize** (*def.* **1**).

2. part, come apart, break in two, fall apart, disintegrate.

3. derange, disarrange, disorder, put out of order, disorganize; disarray, unsettle, disturb, discompose.

disjointed, *adj.* **1.** dislocated, displaced, thrown out; dismembered, dissected, skeletonized, vivisected, cut apart *or* up, pulled apart, in pieces; separated, separate, disconnected, divided, disunited, disjunct; split, severed, cleft, torn apart, rent, asunder.

2. incoherent, noncohesive, ununified, without unity; loose, unconnected, broken, choppy, discontinuous, unsmooth; rambling, wandering, aimless, directionless; disorganized, disordered, disorderly, out of order.

disjunction, *n.* separation, disseverance, disseverment, disseveration, disconnection, detachment, division, disjuncture; severance, cleavage, cleft, breach, rent, split, break, breakage, fracture, crack; disunion, disunity, noncohesion, noncohesiveness, disassociation, dissociating, divorce, disengagement; incoherence, incoherency, looseness, brokenness, discontinuity, choppiness.

disjunctive, *adj.* **1.** separating, dividing, disconnective, dissociative, disjoining.

2. distinguishing, discriminative, discriminating, distinctive, differentiating, differential, diacritical.

disk, *n.* **1.** disc, plate, *Mil.* sabot, flan; circle, *Archaic.* orb, face, roundel; ring, discus, quoit.

2. phonograph record, record, recording, wax.

dislike, *v.* **1.** regard with displeasure, mislike, disrelish, disfavor, disesteem; hold as disagreeable, feel repugnance toward, not be able to bear *or* abide, *Sl.* get turned off by, be disinclined toward, shrink from, recoil from; turn up the nose at, object to, mind; have no stomach *or* use *or* taste for, not be able to stomach.

2. feel hostility toward, antipathize; feel *or* bear malice toward, hold *or* bear a grudge against; have an aversion to, hate, despise, detest, loathe, abominate, execrate, abhor.

—*n.* **3.** disrelish, disfavor, disesteem, disaffection, displeasure, dissatisfaction; disinclination, distaste, disgust, repugnance, revulsion, repulsion, nausea; ill will, animosity, invidiousness, enmity, antagonism; aversion, antipathy, hostility, hatred, animus, detestation, loathing, odium, abomination, execration, abhorrence.

dislocate, *v.* **1.** misarrange, put out of place, misplace, displace; derange, disarrange, disorder, throw into disorder, disorganize, turn topsy-turvy, disjoint, disarray; upset, mess *or* mess up, muss *or* muss up, disturb, discompose; dishevel, rumple, ruffle, tousle, *Chiefly Scot. Dial.* touse; clutter, scatter, litter, shuffle; jumble, muddle, entangle.

2. disarticulate, put out of joint, luxate; disconnect, unhinge, disengage.

dislocation, *n.* **1.** misarrangement, misplacement, displacement; disarrangement, derangement, disorder, disorganization, disarray, irregularity; disturbance, disruption; upset, mess, *Inf.* muss, jumble.

2. disarticulation; luxation; disconnection, unhinging, disengagement.

dislodge, *v.* **1.** displace, delocalize, dismount, *Obs.* displant, cut loose, knock loose, kick out, tear loose, extricate.

2. oust, expel, eject, evict, put out, turn out of doors; drive out, force *or* press out, extrude, thrust out; dispel, scatter, disperse; remove, dismiss, discharge, bump, fire, *Sl.* sack; unseat, depose; expatriate, exile, banish, dispossess, deport.

disloyal, *adj.* unfaithful, faithless, untrue, false, false-hearted; two-faced, Janus-faced, double-tongued, deceitful, untrustworthy; apostate, traitorous, treasonable, treacherous, perfidious, recreant, renegade; heretical, schismatic, unorthodox, dissident, divergent.

disloyalty, *n.* unfaithfulness, faithlessness, infidelity, falseness, false-heartedness; apostasy, traitorousness, Iscariotism, treason, perfidy, recreancy; deceit, double-dealing, duplicity; disaffection, breach, estrangement.

dismal, *adj.* **1.** gloomy, cheerless, melancholy, depressing, somber, morose; dark, black, grim, solemn, funereal, bleak, lugubrious; blue, joyless, sad, unhappy, doleful, sorrowful, dolorous; drab, dull, cold, chilly; barren, desolate, austere, empty; comfortless, uninviting, inhospitable, dreary, *Literary.* drear; miserable, woeful, wretched, woebegone, forlorn; dingy, murky, sunless, rayless, lightless, Cimmerian, tenebrous.

2. inept, unskilled, unhandy, undeft, undexterous; amateurish, incompetent, inexpert, inexperienced, untaught; bungling, blundering, butterfingered, *Inf.* all thumbs; maladroit, clumsy, lubberly, awkward, oafish.

dismantle, *v.* **1.** strip, disfurnish, deprive of, remove from, disencumber.

2. take apart, take to pieces, disassemble, tear down, break down, raze, level, demolish, destroy, ruin, fell.

dismay, *v.* **1.** dishearten, daunt, appall, terrify, horrify, frighten, affright, petrify, panic, scare, *Archaic.* amate; intimidate, cow, overawe, unman, unnerve, enervate, disconcert, abash, consternate; discourage, depress, deject, dispirit, sadden.

2. disillusion, disenchant, chagrin, shock, startle, surprise, take aback; alarm, perturb, disturb, unsettle, discompose, jar, jolt, upset, *Inf.* shake up.

—*n.* **3.** disheartenment, consternation, terror, panic, horror, fear, funk, fright, affright, trepidation, *Inf.* cold feet; dread, apprehension, awe, intimidation; agitation, perturbation, alarm, anxiety, concern, fear and trembling.

4. disillusionment, disenchantment; mistrust, misgiving, qualm; scare, shock; chagrin, discouragement.

dismember, *v.* **1.** disjoint, dissect, anatomize, skeletonize, vivisect, cut apart *or* up; dislimb, amputate, remove a limb, cut off a limb. See **disjoin.**

2. mutilate, dilacerate, lacerate, mangle, chop up, cut into pieces, tear *or* rip *or* pull apart; disfigure, deface, mar, damage, injure, maim, cripple, disable.

dismiss, *v.* **1.** discharge, send away, disband, adjourn, dissolve, disperse, demobilize; release, free, liberate, give leave to go, *Inf.* let out; send away, turn out, send about one's business, turn away; banish, oust, expel, cashier; break off with, *Inf.* give [s.o.] the air; *Sl.* brush off.

2. fire, put out of a job, let go, lay off, give one one's walking papers, drop, deselect; shelve, send packing, *Inf.* bounce, *Inf.* sack, *Inf.* give [s.o.] the sack, *Inf.* send down the road, *U.S. Gov't. Inf.* rif, *Sl.* can; dislodge, set adrift, ship, pack off.

3. put away, reject, set aside, lay aside; think no more of, put out of one's mind, have done with, write off, *Inf.* turn thumbs down.

dismissal, *n.* **1.** adjournment, dissolution, end, close; permission to go, congé; release, freedom to depart; freedom, liberation, manumission.

2. firing, expulsion, removal, displacement; discharge, walking papers, *Inf.* bounce, *Inf.* sack, *Sl.* boot, *Sl.* pink slip; *Sl.* the bum's rush, *Sl.* heave-ho.

dismount, *v.* **1.** get off, alight, disembark, debark, deplane, detrain, debus; come down, get down, descend from; drop down, fall down.

2. unhorse, unmount, unseat, unsaddle; throw down *or* off, buck off, push off.

3. delocalize, displace, dislodge, *Obs.* displant.

4. dismantle, unrig, unmake, unbuild; take apart, take down.

disobedience, *n.* **1.** noncompliance, nonobservance; intractableness, indocility, insubmission; stubbornness, perverseness, contumacy, obstinacy; waywardness, unruliness, forwardness; defiance, insubordination, disregard, indiscipline; neglect, negligence, dereliction, delinquency; recusancy, opposition, recalcitrance; neglect of duty, undutifulness.

2. violation, infraction, infringement, transgression; mutiny, revolt, rebellion, insurgence, revolution, treason; outbreak, uprising, insurrection, sedition, strike.

disobedient, *adj.* insubordinate, noncompliant, nonobservant, defiant, disregardful; naughty, mischievous; undutiful, remiss, derelict, delinquent, negligent; unruly, wayward, fractious, restive, unmanageable, ungovernable, uncomplying, indisciplined; intransigent, uncompromising, unaccommodating, unsubmissive.

2. contumacious, contrary, perverse, froward, refractory, cross-grained, wrong-headed; stubborn, obstinate, willful, intractable, indocile, headstrong, pervicacious, obdurate; recalcitrant, rebellious, opposed, dissentient, recusant, resistant, factious; mutinous, revolting, rebellious, insurgent, riotous, revolutionary; anarchistic, lawless.

disobey, *v.* defy, disregard, ignore, flout, fly in the face of, kick over the traces; counter, go counter to, oppose, resist, contravene, contradict; infringe, violate, transgress, break rules; slight, set at naught, scoff at, thumb one's nose at, snap one's fingers at; mutiny, revolt, rebel, strike, take the law into one's own hands; riot, rise in arms.

disoblige, *v.* **1.** refuse to oblige, not cooperate with, fail to accommodate, neglect, slight; offend, affront, insult, *Sl.* put down. See **affront** (*def.* **3**).

2. disappoint, let down, fail to live up to expectations; dissatisfy, displease, discontent, disgruntle.

3. inconvenience, incommode, put out, discommode; trouble, bother, annoy, disturb.

disobliging, *adj.* unobliging, unaccommodating, uncooperative; disagreeable, unpleasant, ill-natured, ungracious, discourteous, uncivil, rude, offensive; unkind, unsympathetic, unfriendly, ill-disposed, hostile.

disorder, *n.* **1.** disorderliness, disarray, displacement, dislocation, disarrangement, disorganization; dishevelment, untidiness, clutter, mess, heap, huddle; hash, hodge-podge, mishmash, jumble, scramble, tangle; mix-up, snafu, *Inf.* foul-up, *Sl.* ball-up, *Brit. Sl.* balls-up.

2. confusion, confusedness, muddle, *Inf.* guddle, imbroglio; unsettledness, discomposure, disconcertment, agitation, perturbation, upset; discord, disunion, disquiet, unrest, ferment, upheaval, storm; turmoil, tumult, tumultuousness, turbulence, tempest; breach of peace, public disturbance, disruption, minor uprising, riot; chaos, confusion, anarchy, pandemonium, bedlam, brouhaha, melee, free-for-all, fracas, rumpus; broil, brawl, fray, row, struggle, fight, scuffle, *Inf.* ruckus; clamor, uproar, hubbub, hullabaloo, din, fuss, excitement, commotion, flurry, *Inf.* to-do.

3. ailment, malady, complaint, illness, sickness, indisposition, affliction, disease; derangement, mental disorder, neurosis, psychosis, insanity.

—*v.* **4.** missarrange, put out of place, misplace, displace, dislocate, move out of place; throw into disorder, disarray, dishevel, tumble, tousle, *Chiefly Scot. Dial.* touse; mess *or* mess up, muss *or* muss up, ruffle *or* ruffle up, rumple *or* rumple up; turn upside down, *Inf.* turn topsy-turvy, make a shambles of; clutter, litter, scatter *or* strew objects about.

5. unsettle, discompose, shake *or* shake up, disconcert, perturb; upset, agitate, distress, trouble; disturb, disrupt; confuse, mix *or* mix up, shuffle, jumble, scramble; muddle, snafu, fuddle, *Brit. Sl.* muzz, snarl, tangle, *Sl.* ball up; bungle, spoil, upset the apple cart, throw a monkey wrench into the works, sabotage, *Sl.* foul up, *Sl.* bollix up, *Sl.* screw up.

6. derange, incapacitate, throw out of gear, indispose; weaken, devitalize, disable, invalidate; enfeeble, debilitate, invalid, sicken.

disorderly, *adj.* **1.** confused, chaotic, all mixed-up, upside down, *Inf.* topsy-turvy; at sixes and sevens, muddled, jumbled, hugger-mugger, scrambled, tangled; disordered, out of order, out of place, disarranged, in disarray, deranged; untidy, cluttered, messy, disheveled, *Inf.* mussed up, messed up, ruffled up, rumpled, tousled, *Chiefly Scot. Dial.* toused; unkempt, slovenly, sloppy, shoddy, careless, slip-shod, poor.

2. unorganized, disorganized, unmethodical, unsystematic; irregular, indiscriminate, haphazard, random, aimless, pell-mell, helter-skelter.

3. unruly, undisciplined, disobedient, misbehaving; unmanageable, uncontrollable, ungovernable, intractable; rebellious, mutinous, lawless; violent, wild, unrestrained, rough, rough-and-tumble, rowdy, rowdyish, boisterous, noisy; tumultuous, riotous, uproarious, turbulent; distraught, upset, disturbed, turbid, perturbed, agitated, worked up, wrought up, *Inf.* in a stew.

disorganization, *n.* **1.** disunion, disruption; dishevelment, disarray, derangement, disarrangement, misarrangement; unconnectedness, disjointedness, incoherence.

2. disorder, chaos, confusion, tohubohu; anarchy, lawlessness, disorderliness, unruliness, turmoil; mess, scramble, tumble, muddle, morass, snafu, *Inf.* mix-up, *Sl.* screw-up.

disorganize, *v.* disorder, derange, disarrage, misarrange; confuse, muddle, jumble, put out of order, throw into confusion *Inf.* disorder, mix up, *Inf.* raise hell with, disarray, dishevel, *Inf.* mess up, *Inf.* make a mess of, make a shambles of.

disown, *v.* **1.** repudiate, reject, disclaim, disavow; renounce, forsake, cast off, abandon; deny, recant, retract, take back.

2. disinherit, disherit, *Rare.* exheredate, cut off; wash one's hands of, turn one's back on, have nothing further to do with.

disparage, *v.* **1.** discredit, disfavor, make disreputable, injure *or* impair the credit *or* reputation of; censure, reproach, inveigh against; reduce, lower, degrade, downgrade, debase, abase, vitiate; shame, disgrace, dishonor; humiliate, humble, mortify, *Sl.* put down.

2. belittle, deprecate, demean, deflate, detract, decry, derogate, *Inf.* talk down; devaluate, depreciate, cheapen, lessen, decrease, diminish, bate, abate, attenuate, boil down, shrivel, wither, mitigate; minimize, slight, underestimate, underrate, undervalue, beggar, extenuate, underreckon, misprize, think nothing of, set no store by, fail to count on; de-emphasize, underplay, make light of, *Inf.* play down; lampoon, pasquinade, satirize, caricature; ridicule, mock, poke fun at, laugh at, jeer at, sneer at, jibe at; disdain, deride, contemn, scoff, spurn, scorn, pooh-pooh.

3. defame, denigrate, vilify, vituperate, vilipend, scandalize, malign, gibbet, run down, impugn, berate, revile, speak ill of, speak evil of, *Sl.* badmouth, *Sl.* poormouth, backbite; slander, libel, calumniate, falsify, accuse falsely, traduce, impute, asperse, insinuate; injure, abuse, assail, stab, insult, *Sl.* dump on, *Sl.* trash; criticize, pull to pieces, cut up, shred, *Sl.* do a hatchet job on, *Sl.* do a number on.

disparagement, *n.* **1.** belittlement, deprecation, derogation, deflation, detraction, *Inf.* talking down; depreciation, devaluation, diminution, decrease, abatement, attenuation, mitigation, bating, cheapening, lessening; minimization, dispraise, underestimation, extenuation, undervaluing, underrating, underreckoning, beggaring; sarcasm, ridicule, mockery, jeer, gibe, scoff, sneer; disdain, derision, contempt, scorn, contumely.

2. discredit, disfavor, obloquy, loss of face; censure, reproach, invective, reflection, animadversion, disapproval, disapprobation, criticism, stricture; curse, denunciation, condemnation, execration, revilement, commination, fulmination, malediction; degradation, debasement, abasement, reduction, lowering, vitiation; shame, disgrace, dishonor; humiliation, humble pie, mortification; defamation, denigration, vilification, vituperation, scandal, scandalization, scandalmongering, abuse, injury, attack, scurrility, running down, gibbeting, backbiting, *Sl.* badmouth, *Sl.* poormouth; slander, libel, calumny, calumniation, traducement, falsification, misrepresentation, false accusation, slur, imputation, aspersion, insinuation, innuendo, *Inf.* brickbat.

3. indignity, insult, affront, slight, ill treatment, maltreatment, outrage, disrespect; discourtesy, rudeness, incivility, hissing, cat call, Bronx cheer, raspberry; snub, rebuff, home thrust, reprimand, reproof, rebuke, reprehension, castigation, scolding, chiding, *Inf.* dressing down, scowl, frown, black look.

disparity, *n.* inequality, imparity, unevenness, incongruity, disproportion; discrepancy, inconsistency; difference, dissimilarity, dissimilitude, unlikeness, contrast, contrariety.

dispassion, *n.* **1.** inexcitability, imperturbability, unflappability; tranquillity, serenity, placidity; composure, collectedness, equanimity, poise, aplomb, sang-froid, presence of mind, self-possession, self-control, level-headedness, calmness, coolness, cool-headedness, *Sl.* cool; nonchalance, insouciance, casualness, off-handedness.

2. impartiality, neutrality, disinterestedness, dispassionateness.

dispassionate, *adj.* **1.** calm, composed, collected, self-possessed, cool, *Inf.* cool as a cucumber, *Inf.* together; unemotional, unexcitable, unflappable, imperturbable, even-tempered, easygoing; poised, balanced, steady, self-controlled; nonchalant, matter-of-fact, at ease, unruffled, unexcited, undisturbed, unperturbed, undismayed; placid, tranquil, serene, peaceful.
2. impartial, fair, just, equitable, objective, even-handed, disinterested, neutral; straight, square, fair and square, square-dealing, plain-dealing, square-shooting, straight-shooting; unbiased, unprejudiced, unjaundiced, unprepossessed, open-minded.

dispatch, *v.* **1.** dismiss, send off, send forth, send on one's way; release, let go, free, send away, give leave.
2. transmit, forward, consign, remit; send, post, mail, ship, freight, express.
3. kill, put to death, take the life of, execute, slay, do away with, slaughter; electrocute, gas, asphyxiate, shoot; put to the sword, do to death, finish, put an end to; hang, gibbet, string up, garrotte, crucify; behead, decapitate, guillotine, axe, bring to the block; murder, *All Sl.* erase, rub out, blot out, knock off, 86, ice, hit, zap, do in, waste, take for a ride; *All Sl.* gun down, get, fix, silence, take care of.
4. expedite, push through, *Inf.* ram through, *Sl.* railroad; hurry, quicken, hasten, accelerate; dash off, *Inf.* zip off, dispose of, make short work of.
—*n.* **5.** promptness, speed, quickness, haste, expedition, celerity, expeditiousness; swiftness, rapidity, fastness, hurry, hastiness, precipitance, quick riddance.
6. execution, killing, slaying; electrocution, gassing, asphyxiation, shooting, hanging, crucifixion, garrotting, decapitation, beheading.
7. missive, rejoinder, note, reply; letter, epistle, report, instruction; telegram, bulletin, flash; communiqué, communication, word, *Brit.* express.

dispel, *v.* scatter, disperse, spread out, scatter to the four winds; strew, bestrew, disseminate, overspread; dissipate, dissolve, diffuse, vanish, evanesce, disappear; disband, dismiss, demobilize, break up; rout, drive away, chase away, shoo, send running in all directions, send flying, drive off.

dispensable, *adj.* **1.** not necessary, unnecessary, unessential, nonessential, needless, superfluous; useless, unrequired, uncalled-for, gratuitous; expendable, replaceable, disposable, throwaway, removable.
2. distributable, apportionable, allottable, divisible.

dispensation, *n.* **1.** distribution, disbursement, apportionment, allocation, allotment, assignment, assignation; furnishing, accommodation, supplying, bestowal.
2. administration, management, direction, control; execution, regulation, operation, conduct; supervision, superintendence, oversight, charge, command; arrangement, system, order, disposal; organization, disposition, classification; administering, ministration, application, discharge; implementation, prosecution, effectuation.
3. doing away with, abolition, repeal, revocation, rescinding; cancellation, abrogation, nullification, annulment, *Law.* defeasance.
4. relaxation, loosening, slackening, lessening; exemption, release, exception, reprieve, discharge; remission, absolution, quittance; pardon, amnesty, acquittal, exoneration, clearance.

dispense, *v.* **1.** deal out, distribute, disburse, apportion, allot, dole out; mete out, allocate, award, assign, detail; parcel out, divide, share, measure, *Inf.* dish out, *Inf.* spoon out; supply, equip, bestow, furnish, grant.
2. administer, discharge, apply, minister; implement, prosecute, carry out, effectuate, bring to bear; execute, regulate, operate, engineer; direct, prescribe.
3. grant a dispensation, exempt, except, release, free, reprieve, let off; relax, loosen, lessen, bend the rules; remit, absolve, acquit, pardon, excuse, exonerate, clear.
4. **dispense with a.** forgo, do without, not touch, abstain, forswear, forbear, refrain from; waive, relinquish, give up; cede, yield, renounce, disclaim, reject. **b.** rid of, do away with, abolish, repeal, revoke, rescind; abrogate, nullify, annul, cancel; dispose of, shake off, clear.

dispenser, *n.* **1.** distributor, giver, dealer, allotter, apportioner; vendor, peddler, seller, salesman, trader, wholesaler, merchant; donor, presenter, contributor, bestower, grantor; druggist, pharmacist, apothecary, *Brit.* chemist.
2. container, holder, box, package, canister, carton; vending machine, candy machine, cigarette machine, soda machine.

disperse, *v.* **1.** scatter, broadcast, scatter to the winds, sow, bestrew, sprinkle, spatter; spread, circulate, disseminate, dissipate, diffuse.
2. disband, dissolve, dismiss; dispel, drive away *or* off, rout, separate, break up, eject, banish.
3. disappear, vanish, clear out, melt away, run off, evanesce.

dispersion, *n.* scattering, broadcast, distribution; spread, circulation, dissemination; divergence, separate, disjunction; dissipation, diffusion; apportionment, allocation, allotment.

dispirit, *v.* dishearten, throw cold water on, damp, dash, wither one's hopes; discourage, deter, disincline; deject, cast down, sadden, depress; knock down, prostrate, unman; tire, weary.

dispirited, *adj.* discouraged, disheartened, dejected, downcast, down-hearted, crestfallen; in the doldrums, mopish, weary, out of sorts, *Inf.* down in the dumps; glum, forlorn, cheerless, sad, *Inf.* down in the mouth, heartsick, unhappy; depressed, despondent, unconsolable, disconsolate, *Scot.* sackless.

displace, *v.* **1.** disturb, disarrange, disorder, derange, unsettle, confuse; move, relocate, shift, transfer, transpose; misplace, mislay, put in the wrong place.
2. replace, supplant, supersede, succeed, take the place of, crowd out, *Inf.* bump.
3. remove, depose, dislodge, unseat, disestablish; oust, eject, expel, dispossess, uproot, evict, export, exile, banish; discharge, dismiss, cashier, fire, *Inf.* bounce, *Inf.* sack.

display, *v.* **1.** exhibit, present, set forth, expose, air, uncover, disclose, demonstrate; show, evince, manifest, betray; advertise, publicize, post, placard, blazon; array, arrange, place, dispose.
2. unfold, unfurl, extend, open out, spread out, stretch out.
3. flaunt, *Sl.* put on the ritz, flourish, parade, vaunt, show off, boast.
—*n.* **4.** exhibition, exhibit, show, presentation, airing, exposition; advertisement, publication, posting; array, arrangement, staging, window dressing.
5. evincement, manifestation, revelation, disclosure, uncovering, exposure, divulgence.
6. ostentation, pretension, ritz, splash; blazon, spectacle, parade, pageant, pageantry, ceremony; pomp, magnificence, grandeur, splendor, glitter, flourish.

displease, *v.* **1.** anger, incense, raise [s.o.'s] ire, *Sl.*

tick [s.o.] off, *Sl.* tee [s.o.] off; exacerbate, gall, rankle, envenom, embitter.

2. irritate, annoy, irk, pique, vex, peeve, nettle, chafe, *Chiefly U.S.* rile, *Inf.* aggravate, *Inf.* miff, *Sl.* bug, *Sl.* hassle; exasperate, ruffle, roil, disturb, perturb, disquiet, discompose, put out, *Sl.* get [s.o.'s] goat.

3. hurt, pain, offend, affront, insult; slight, humiliate, mortify, slap [s.o.] in the face.

displeasure, *n.* **1.** dissatisfaction, discontentment, disfavor, dislike, distaste, unhappiness; disapproval, disapprobation, discountenance.

2. irritation, annoyance, vexation, pique, chagrin, exasperation, *Inf.* aggravation; anger, ire, dudgeon, high dudgeon; offense, pain, hurt, ache; umbrage, indignation, huff, tiff, fume, *Inf.* slow burn.

3. embitterment, bitterness, exacerbation, resentment, hard feelings; spleen, choler, rancor, gall, bile, ill *or* bad feeling.

disport, *v.* **1.** divert, entertain, amuse, delight, regale, titillate, enliven; cheer, gladden, rejoice; recreate, refresh.

2. sport, game, play, frolic, make merry, revel; frisk, gambol, romp, caper, junket; sow wild oats, paint the town red, carouse.

—*n.* **3.** entertainment, pastime, amusement, diversion, divertissement, distraction; recreation, sport, play, fun, pleasure; relaxation, dalliance, merrymaking, pleasantry, merriment, joviality, jocoseness, jollity, drollery.

4. antic, lark, romp, gambol, spree, junket; escapade, revelry, tomfoolery, skylarking.

disposable, *adj.* **1.** throwaway, non-returnable; plastic, paper.

2. available, free for use, accessible, obtainable.

disposal, *n.* **1.** array, arrangement, placing, disposition; order, ordering, grouping, distribution, assortment, collocation; organization, classification.

2. dispensation, bestowal, transference, transfer; assignment, settlement, determination; transaction, sale, auctioning off.

3. power, command, control, decision, discretion; conduct, direction, management, administration, government, regulation.

dispose, *v.* **1.** arrange, order, array, assort, collocate; line, range, align, place; group, classify, class, categorize, rank; organize, systematize, coordinate, regulate, marshal, *Inf.* line up, set up.

2. incline, bend, move, lead, direct, induce, tempt; prompt, actuate, motivate; influence, bias, predispose.

3. ready, prepare, prime, make fit, equip, arm.

4. dispose of a. decide, determine, settle, end, finish with, find a place for. **b.** discard, throw away, get rid of, cast forth, dump, unload; dismiss, fire, *Inf.* kick out, remove; work off. **c.** distribute, deal out, dispense, assign, allocate, apportion, allot; transfer, make over, bestow, give away, part with, sell, vend, peddle off, auction. **d.** destroy, do away with, finish off, *Sl.* knock off, kill; finish, *Sl.* polish off, eat up.

disposed, *adj.* inclined, tending toward, leaning toward, of a mind to, predisposed; apt, liable, given, ready, prone, subject, likely, incident, *Archaic.* propense; constituted, conditioned, molded, formed.

disposition, *n.* **1.** nature, humor, spirit, temperament, temper, grain, mood, vein; outlook, mind-set, frame of mind; character, make-up, inner man, qualities, constitution, idiosyncrasy.

2. inclination, bent, bias, leaning, tendency, turn, direction; predisposition, *Path.* diathesis, subjectability, liability, proclivity, propensity; readiness, willingness, weakness, predilection, liking, affection, penchant, appetite.

3. arrangement, grouping, organization, disposal. See **disposal** (*def.* **1**).

4. settlement, conclusion, resolution; determination, decision, outcome, result, upshot.

5. bestowal, transference, transaction, disposal. See **disposal** (*def.* **2**).

6. control, direction, management, disposal. See **disposal** (*def.* **3**).

dispossess, *v.* **1.** strip, deprive, divest, bereave, *Law.* disseize; disinherit, disown, unhouse; depose, unseat, turn out, dethrone, dismiss, displace, dislodge; supplant, supersede, take the place of; demote, unfrock, disbar.

2. expropriate, commandeer, confiscate, impound, *Law.* distrain; wrest from, take from, seize; rob, plunder, despoil, pillage.

3. oust, eject, drive out, expel, evict, *Inf.* throw out, *Inf.* kick out, *Sl.* bounce; exclude, blackball, blacklist, ostracize, excommunicate; banish, exile, deport, expatriate.

dispossessed, *adj.* **1.** evicted, ousted, expelled, ejected, cast out, *Sl.* bounced; uprooted, unhoused, banished, exiled, deported, expatriated; excluded, shut out, blackballed, blacklisted, ostracized, banned, outlawed.

2. displaced, rootless, homeless, outcast, disenfranchised; wandering, vagrant, nomadic, vagabond, itinerant, unsettled.

3. disinherited, disaffiliated, alienated, lost, abandoned; demoralized, debilitated, disoriented, confused, purposeless, goalless, guideless; shaken, unstable, unsteady, uncertain, floundering, *Inf.* at sea.

dispossession, *n.* **1.** deprivation, deprival, divestiture, bereavement, *Law.* disseizin; deposition, dislodgement, dismissal, displacement, demotion; removal, loss.

2. expropriation, confiscation, appropriation, abduction; spoliation, stripping, plunder, pillage, ravaging.

3. ouster, eviction, ejection, ejectment, expulsion; banishment, exile, expatriation, deportation; exclusion, excommunication, blacklisting, blackballing.

dispraise, *v.* **1.** censure, reproach, animadvert on *or* upon, criticize, arraign, reprobate, condemn, denounce, remonstrate; disparage, discredit, disfavor; belittle, deprecate, demean, detract, decry, derogate, *Inf.* talk down.

—*n.* **2.** censure, disapproval, disapprobation, reprobation, reprehension; criticism, animadversion, *Inf.* brickbat, aspersion, obloquy, loss of face; curse, denunciation, condemnation, execration, commination, malediction; belittlement, disparagement, deprecation, derogation, detraction.

disproof, *n.* **1.** invalidation, refutation, confutation, negation, denial, disproval, *Inf.* squelch, *Archaic.* redargution.

2. rebuttal, answer, proof to the contrary, *Inf.* squelcher.

disproportion, *n.* asymmetry, unbalance, nonconformity, nonuniformity, inconsonance, incoherence; irregularity, unevenness, unequalness, lopsidedness; disparity, imparity, difference, dissimilarity, dissimilitude, unlikeness; discrepancy, inconsistency, incongruity.

disproportionate, *adj.* **1.** asymmetrical, unbalanced, ill-balanced, lopsided, top-heavy, out of proportion, disproportional; uneven, unequal, irregular, disparate; discrepant, inconsistent, inconsonant, inharmonious, incongruous.

2. extreme, excessive, extravagant, inordinate, too

much, overmuch, uncalled-for, unnecessary, blown out of proportion.

disprove, *v.* invalidate, negate, deny, refute, confute, controvert, contradict, prove to the contrary; rebut, parry, answer; discredit, belie, give the lie to, expose, show up; explode, *Inf.* blow sky-high, puncture, *Inf.* shoot full of holes, *Inf.* knock the bottom out of; defeat, overturn, overthrow, throw out, squash, *Inf.* squelch.

disputable, *adj.* debatable, open to discussion, moot, controvertible, contestable, arguable, problematic; questionable, doubtful, dubious, uncertain; unsettled, undecided, undetermined.

disputant, *n.* debater, disputer, controverter; adversary, opponent, antagonist, contender, litigant, plaintiff, agonist; polemicist, hair-splitter, dissenter, pilpulist, logomachist; arguer, wrangler, brawler.

disputation, *n.* debate, dispute, polemics, argumentation, *Rare.* disceptation; altercation, wrangle, verbal controversy, dissidence, dissension.

disputatious, *adj.* argumentative, dissentious, contentious, disputative; fractious, captious, discordant; logomachical, polemical, controversial; testy, hotheaded, irascible; quarrelsome, querulous, cantankerous, bickering; litigious.

dispute, *v.* **1.** debate, discuss, argue, ventilate, air, *Rare.* discept; oppose, controvert, refute, confute, argue against; quarrel, wrangle, differ, disagree, altercate, clash, fight about, brawl, row, bicker, squabble, have words, fall out, riff, spat, *Brit. Archaic.* brangle.
2. question, gainsay, impugn, challenge, call into question; disagree, differ, dispute, take exception to; deny, object to, contradict, resist, struggle against; contend, contest, litigate.
—*n.* **3.** controversy, contest, strife, conflict; debate, discussion, disputation, argument, altercation, war of words, imbroglio, agon; quarrel, wrangle, donnybrook, brawl, broil, rumpus, row, fracas, squabble, bickering, *Obs.* brabble, hassle, tiff, spat.
4. disagreement, difference, contestation, dissension; friction, feud, open rupture, disturbance, discord, scrimmage, litigation.

disqualification, *n.* **1.** incapacitation, disablement, crippling, debilitation; enfeeblement, enervation, prostration, paralyzation; incapacity, disability, unfitness; woundedness, lameness, injuredness; debility, weakness, prostrateness, paralysis.
2. rejection, exclusion, debarment, elimination, removal, expulsion, ejection, ouster; disenfranchisement, disentitlement, disenablement, deprivation of rights; ineligibility, unqualifiedness, incompetence, ineptness, ineptitude.

disqualify, *v.* **1.** incapacitate, disable, unfit, indispose, lay up, put in bed *or* the hospital; cripple, becripple, maim, wound, lame, invalid; injure, hurt, damage, impair.
2. reject, declare ineligible *or* unqualified, turn down; disfranchise, disenfranchise, disentitle, disenable, deprive [s.o.] of rights, *Law.* disbar; exclude, shut *or* keep out, debar, bar, prevent [s.o.'s] participation; eliminate, remove, take *or* put out, expel, eject, throw out, oust, *Inf.* kick out.

disquiet, *n.* **1.** unquietness, uneasiness, unease, disquietude, inquietude, restlessness, unrest; fretfulness, distress, worry, concern, alarm; anxiety, anguish, angst, fear, dread, foreboding; nervousness, ants, *Inf.* butterflies, *Inf.* butterflies in one's stomach, *Sl.* heebie-jeebies, *Sl.* habdabs, *Sl.* creeps.
2. disturbance, disconcertion, discomposure, agitation, perturbation, upset, unsettlement; confusion, fuss, turmoil, tumult, commotion, fuss, excitement, hubbub. See **commotion** (*defs.* **1, 2**).
3. interruption, disruption, disturbance; annoyance, bother, irritation, vexation; trouble, inconvenience, discomfort, disadvantage, discommodity, incommodity.
—*v.* **4.** interrupt, disrupt, disturb [s.o.'s] peace, bother, pester, *Sl.* bug; inconvenience, incommode, discomfort, discommode, put out; fret, annoy, vex, irritate, roil; agitate, perturb, upset, shake *or* shake up, unsettle; distress, concern, trouble, worry, alarm; unquiet, make uneasy, inquiet, disturb, disconcert, ruffle, discompose.

disquisition, *n.* **1.** dissertation, treatise, thesis, essay, exposition, exposé, commentary; discussion, excursus, study; tract, tractate, monograph, pamphlet; theme, composition, paper; article, editorial, column, piece; review, opinion, interpretation, criticism, critique.
2. address, speech, oration, declamation, salutation, valedictory; discourse, lecture, descant, sermon, homily; harangue, diatribe, tirade, philippic.

disregard, *v.* **1.** overlook, ignore, take no notice of, close the eyes to, blink *or* wink at, neglect, forget, skip, never mind, let be, let alone; not trouble oneself about, dismiss from one's thoughts, let in one ear and out the other, leave out of consideration, turn a deaf ear to; gloss over, pass by *or* over, let pass, skip *or* skim over, pretermit, give a miss; pass up, waive, push aside, set aside.
2. slight, turn up one's nose at, turn one's back upon, *Sl.* brush off, snub, *Sl.* ritz, high-hat; cut, give the cold shoulder to, *Inf.* cold-shoulder, *Inf.* put the freeze on, look coldly upon, give [s.o.] the go-by; keep at arm's length, avoid, shun, stand *or* hold aloof; reject, rebuff, slam the door in [s.o.'s] face; insult, affront, disdain, scorn.
3. minimize, slight, underrate, undervalue, beggar, misprize, underestimate, underreckon, think nothing of, set no store by, fail to count on; make light of, take no account of, pay no attention *or* regard *or* heed to, sneeze at; de-emphasize, underplay, *Inf.* play down.
—*n.* **4.** inattention, nonobservance, oversight, pretermission, omission, preterition; neglect, negligence, carelessness, heedlessness; slight, indifference, cold shoulder, coldness, the go-by.
5. contempt, disdain, disparagement, repudiation; disesteem, disfavor, low regard; belittlement, depreciation, underestimation, undervaluation.
6. affront, insult, injury, indignity, dishonor; incivility, discourtesy, impoliteness, rudeness; slur, dig, *Sl.* cut, snub, spurn, *Sl.* put-down, slap in the face.

disrelish, *v.* **1.** dislike, disfavor, turn up one's nose at, *Sl.* be turned off by. See **dislike** (*def.* **1**).
—*n.* **2.** distaste, dislike, disinclination. See **distaste**.

disrepair, *n.* dilapidation, unrepair, deterioration, decay, ruination, collapse; damage, injury, wreckage, havoc, ravage, dry-rot; shabbiness, raggedness, rags and tatters, decrepitude.

disreputable, *adj.* base, low, unsavory, unworthy, abject, ignominious, low-down; vile, iniquitous, wicked, bad; heinous, shocking, outrageous, scandalous; discreditable, disgraceful, shameful, opprobrious, unbecoming; despicable, sneaking, slippery, unscrupulous, corrupt, crooked; dishonorable, unprincipled, nefarious, arrant, rascally, knavish, villainous; disgraced, dishonored, notorious, infamous, shady, questionable, under a cloud *or* shadow, disreputable.

disrepute, *n.* disgrace, dishonor, ill-repute, ignominy, bad name, bad character, ill-favor, unpopularity; disfavor, discredit, disesteem, degradation, debasement, abasement; shame, odium, infamy, stigma, brand, stain, blot, slur, taint, shadow.

disrespect, *n.* discourtesy, rudeness, impoliteness, incivility, unmannerliness; inconsideration, disregard, tactlessness, disrespectfulness, irreverence, misbehavior; indecorum, ungraciousness, uncourtliness, ungentlemanliness, hoydenism; impudence, insolence, impertinence, pertness, tartness, sauciness, brashness, brazenness, boldness, *Brit. Sl.* side; arrogance, flippancy, effrontery, back talk, *Inf.* cheek, *Sl.* lip, *Sl.* mouth; surliness, churlishness, bearishness; uncouthness, coarseness, crudeness, vulgarity, bad taste; boorishness, loutishness, cloddishness.

disrespectful, *adj.* rude, impolite, uncivil, ill-bred, bad-mannered, misbehaved, irreverent, out of line, out of order, unruly; brash, bold, brazen, hoydenish, *Scot.* randy; insolent, impudent, impertinent, pert, saucy, fresh, *Inf.* cheeky; inconsiderate, tactless, indiscreet, *Scot. and North Eng.* misleared; rough, crude, vulgar, tasteless; boorish, loutish, churlish, cloddish, lumpish; contemptuous, disdainful, scornful, sneering, flouting, insulting.

disrobe, *v.* undress, take off one's clothes, shed, doff, remove, cast off, strip, strip down, *Euph.* do a strip tease, *Sl.* drop one's drawers, *Sl.* drop trow; unclothe, undrape, unveil, divest.

disrupt, *v.* **1.** disorder, disorganize, derange, disarrange, disarray, dislocate, displace, move out of place; shuffle, mix up, jumble, scramble, tangle, snarl, *Sl.* ball up; agitate, confuse, disturb, upset, disconcert, unsettle, discompose, shake up.

2. interrupt, interfere with, break up *or* into; suspend, discontinue, intermit; stop, arrest, halt, block, *Inf.* throw a monkey wrench *or* a wrench into.

3. sever, dissever, cleave, sunder, rend, rive, split, break apart; separate, detach, dissociate, disconnect, divide, disjoin; disunite, disassociate, divorce, uncouple, disengage.

disruption, *n.* **1.** breakup, severance, cleavage, scission, schism, fissure, cleft, rupture, rift, breach, sundering, rending, splitting, parting; separation, disconnection, detachment, division, dissociating, disjunction, disjuncture; disunion, disunity, disassociation, divorce, disengagement, disentanglement.

2. disorder, disorderliness, disorganization, disarray, disarrangement; dishevelment, scramble, tangle, jumble, clutter, mess, untidiness.

dissatisfaction, *n.* **1.** discontent, unhappiness, displeasure, sorrow, nonfulfillment; uneasiness, disquiet, inquietude, *Ger. weltschmerz*, restlessness, malaise, *Pathol.* dysphoria.

2. disappointment, chagrin, dismay, distress; anger, vexation, annoyance, exasperation, irritation, edginess, chafing.

3. disapproval, disapprobation, dislike, distaste; resentment, bitterness, spleen, wormwood.

dissatisfied, *adj.* **1.** displeased, unhappy, unsatisfied; discontent, discontented, ungratified, unfulfilled, frustrated, disturbed; offended, rubbed the wrong way; irked, annoyed, ticked off, teed off, *Sl.* pissed; mad, angry, angered, *Inf.* hopping; in a snit, feeling bitchy, disgruntled.

2. disappointed, dejected, let down, left with a sour taste in one's mouth; regretful, sorry, repining, morose, glum, in a funk; restless, ill-at-ease, uneasy, weary, uncomfortable.

dissect, *v.* **1.** anatomize, vivisect, dismember, cut up *or* apart, lay open, perform an autopsy.

2. analyze, take apart, examine, scrutinize, inspect, look at closely, go over with a fine-tooth comb; study, research, inquire into, look into, *Inf.* check out, investigate; sift, probe, search, explore.

dissection, *n.* **1.** anatomy, anatomization, zootomy, vivisection, dismemberment, cutting up *or* apart, autopsy, post-mortem examination, *Inf.* post-mortem.

2. analysis, examination, scrutiny, scrutinization, inspection, check; inquiry, investigation, probe, study, research, sifting, search, exploration.

dissemble, *v.* **1.** dissimulate, cover up, screen, mask, veil, shroud, conceal, disguise, camouflage.

2. feign, pretend, simulate, affect, sham, fake, playact, put on an act, make a show of, *Inf.* make like.

dissembler, *n.* hypocrite, dissimulator, tartuffe, Pecksniff, *Inf.* used-car salesman; cheat, cheater, fraud, deceiver; knave, scoundrel, mountebank, snake in the grass; imposter, pretender, quack, charlatan, confidence man, *Sl.* con man, wolf in sheep's clothing; trickster, humbug, prestidigitator; liar, perjurer, prevaricator, circumventor. See also **deceiver**.

disseminate, *v.* spread, circulate, broadcast, publish; promulgate, propagate, teach, distribute, dispense, diffuse, disperse; dissipate, scatter, sow; give out, give to the world, publicize, make public, drag into the open; bandy about, blaze about, hawk, rumor, bruit.

dissemination, *n.* circulation, broadcasting, publication; promulgation, propagation, distribution; propagandism, indoctrination, proselytism; dispersal, emission, scattering.

dissension, *n.* **1.** discord, strife, contention, wrangle. See **dispute** (*defs.* **3, 4**).

2. dissent, disagreement, variance, conflict of opinion, discordance; nonconformity, noncompliance, protest, protestation; demur, demurral, objection.

dissent, *v.* **1.** disagree, differ, dispute. See **dispute** (*defs.* **1, 2**).

2. reject, repudiate, disavow, renounce, abjure, apostatize, forswear, discard; forsake, abandon, secede, withdraw, defect.

—*n.* **3.** dispute, dissension. See **dissension** (*def.* **2**).

4. dissentience, discordance, noncompliance, disaffection, disaffiliation; sectarianism, schism, recusancy, heterodoxy, apostasy, heresy.

dissenter, *n.* dissident, nonconformist, objector; protestant, separatist, sectarian, schismatic, apostate, recusant, heretic.

dissentient, *adj.* unorthodox, dissident, dissenting, iconoclastic; antipathetic, contradictory, adverse, noncompliant, contrary; heterodox, recusant, apostate; schismatic, sectarian, denominational; antagonistic, hostile, irreconcilable.

dissertation, *n.* treatise, thesis, disquisition, essay, exposition, commentary; discourse, lecture, descant, sermon, homily; address, speech, oration. See **disquisition**.

disservice, *n.* disfavor, unkindness, bad turn, ill turn, dirty trick; abuse, harm, injury, damage, pain, kick in the face; wrong, injustice, grief.

dissever, *v.* sever, cleave, sunder, rend, rive, split, break apart, cut *or* hack up *or* apart, tear *or* rip apart; separate, detach, dissociate, disconnect, disjoin, disjoint; disunite, disassociate, uncouple, unfasten, disengage, disentangle; divide, *Inf.* divvy up, cut into pieces, chop up; apportion, section, quarter, halve.

dissidence, *n.* nonagreement, difference of opinion, disagreement, discordance, rupture, feud, dispute, dissent. See **dissent** (*def.* **4**).

dissident, *n.* See **dissenter**.

dissimilar, *adj.* unlike, different, disparate. See **different** (*defs.* **1, 2**).

dissimilarity, *n.* unlikeness, difference, dissimilitude. See **difference** (*def.* **1**).

dissimulation, *n.* feigning, pretending, pretense, hypocrisy, deception, misrepresentation; simulation, affectation, act, show, semblance, sham.

dissipate, *v.* **1.** scatter, disperse, strew, bestrew; dispel, broadcast, sow, disseminate; diffuse, spread abroad, throw to the winds, distribute; sprinkle, spatter.

2. squander, misspend, lavish, indulge oneself, spend money as though there's no tomorrow, not know the value of a dollar; waste, deplete, drain, pour money down the drain; burn up, fritter away, use up, throw away.

3. vanish, disappear, evanesce, fade away; ebb, subside, shrink away, die away; evaporate, melt, melt into thin air, vaporize, disintegrate, fall apart, break up, *Inf.* peter out, decay; atomize, crumble, fragmentize.

4. revel, roister, wallow; party, make merry, whoop it up, make whoopee, live it up, have a ball; sow wild oats, go to hell in a handbasket, overdo, play the night away, burn the candle at both ends; debauch, wanton, *Sl.* lech, womanize, wench, swing, *Inf.* sleep around; carouse, get blitzed, get tight as a hoot-owl, go on a spree *or* bender *or* toot *or* whooper-dooper; get high, fly, blast.

dissipated, *adj.* dissolute, debauched, rakish, rakehell; licentious, promiscuous, wanton, profligate, abandoned; intemperate, incontinent, self-indulgent, free-living, Saturnalian; drunken, sottish, crapulous, Bacchanalian. See also **dissolute**.

dissipation, *n.* **1.** dispersion, diffusion, dissemination, scattering, emission; disintegration, dissolution, decay, fragmentation; disappearance, evaporation, evanescence, fading away.

2. squandering, wastefulness, misuse; prodigality, extravagance, lavishness, indulgence.

3. dissoluteness, profligateness, profligacy, immorality; abandonment, wantonness, corruption, depravity, wickedness; voluptuousness, sybaritism, dolce vita, hedonism, self-indulgence, self-gratification; high *or* fast living, materialism; sensualism, libertinage, carnality, debauchery; libidinousness, lasciviousness, licentiousness, license, lewdness, animalism, rakishness; *Path.* satyriasis, *Path.* nymphomania, womanizing, *Sl.* leching, wenching, whoring; prostitution, pimping; intemperance, winebibbing, *Sl.* boozing, drunkenness, inebriation, carousel; alcoholism, dipsomania, crapulousness; overindulgence, eating the whole thing, *Sl.* pigging out, gourmandism, gluttony; drug abuse, pill popping, getting high, flying, freaking out.

4. amusement, diversion, distraction, change of pace; entertainment, enjoyment, pleasure, delight.

dissociate, *v.* **1.** disunite, separate, sever, dissever, disjoin; detach, divorce, abstract, disconnect, disengage; sunder, cut off; segregate, set apart, isolate, insulate.

2. withdraw oneself, part company, take leave, quit, go away, tune out; disband, disperse, scatter.

dissociation, *n.* disunion, separation, division; severance, disjunction, dissevering; disconnection, detachment; sundering, parting, splitting, dividing; divorce, break, cleavage, rupture, rift, split.

dissoluble, *adj.* **1.** soluble, dissolvable, leachable, percolable; liquefiable, meltable, liquescent, deliquescent.

2. separable, severable, divisible, detachable, disjoinable, dissociable.

3. terminable, endable, concludable, discontinuable, closeable.

dissolute, *adj.* **1.** licentious, libertine, lascivious, debauched, dissipated, wasted, rakish, rakehell; lecherous, lubricous, satyric, satyrical, satyrlike, goatish, *Sl.* horny, *Archaic.* lickerish; concupiscent, prurient, lustful, libidinous, salacious; ruttish, beastly, bestial, swinish; obscene, lewd, Fescennine, Cyprian, indecent, dirty, foul, indelicate; loose, wanton, wild, profligate, abandoned; promiscuous, whorish, of easy virtue, unchaste, impure; coarse, gross, crude.

2. lawless, unrestrained, unbridled, unchecked, ungoverned; intemperate, incontinent, self-indulgent, free-living, Saturnalian; drunken, sottish, crapulous, Bacchanalian.

3. degenerate, depraved, corrupt, perverted; vicious, foul, vile, base; wicked, iniquitous, nefarious, heinous, flagitious, atrocious; immoral, sinful, peccant, evil-minded, vice-ridden; unregenerate, unredeemable, unprincipled, shameless, unscrupulous, reprobate; shameful, disgraceful, rascally, worthless; notorious, infamous, scandalous, disreputable.

dissolution, *n.* **1.** separation, resolution, severance, disseverance, disseverment, disseveration, disconnection, detachment, division, parting, disjunction, disjuncture; divorce, disengagement, disassociation, disunion, break-up, *Inf.* bust-up; untying, unbinding, undoing, unfettering, loosening.

2. dismssal, disbandment, adjournment, recess, prorogation, suspension; discontinuation, discontinuance, stoppage, halt; termination, end, ending, finish, conclusion, closing, wind up, wrap-up.

3. disintegration, collapse, crumbling, decomposition, decay; destruction, ruin, devastation, annihilation; dispersal, diffusion, dissipation, scattering *or* spreading out.

4. disappearance, evaporation, vanishment, departure.

dissolve, *v.* **1.** solvate, (*in prescriptions*) solvere, macerate, put into a solution; liquefy, melt, thaw, thaw out, deliquesce, fuse.

2. disbond, untie, unbind, resolve into; separate, sever, dissever, break up, divide, disconnect, detach, disjoin, dissociate; disunite, divorce, disassociate.

3. terminate, end, put an end to, discontinue, bring to an end *or* conclusion, wind up, finish up, close, call to a close, break off; adjourn, recess, prorogue, suspend, break up, dismiss, disband.

4. disintegrate, crumble, collapse, fall to pieces, fall apart, decompose, decay, rot; disperse, diffuse, dissipate, scatter *or* spread out.

5. abolish, nullify, cancel, void, invalidate; veto, countermand; annul, abrogate, rescind, revoke, repeal, call off.

6. wane, fade, dim, weaken, evanesce, dwindle, shrink, diminish, decline, decrease, lessen, slack off; fade away, waste away, erode, *Sl.* conk out, *Inf.* peter out; disappear, evaporate, vanish, go up in smoke, die out, perish.

dissonance, *n.* **1.** discordance, inharmoniousness, unmelodiousness; cacophony, stridency, jangle, jarring, clashing, grating, croaking, rasping, hoarseness.

2. disaccord, disagreement, difference of opinion; discord, dissension, dissent; discrepancy, inconsistency, variance, incongruity; dissimilarity, dissimilitude, unlikeness, difference, disparity.

dissonant, *adj.* **1.** discordant, absonant, inharmonious, unmelodious, tuneless, out of tune; cacophonous, strident, harsh, grating, raucous, jarring, jangling, clashing, screechy, screaky; disagreeable, unpleasant, displeasing.

2. disagreeing, differing, opposed; dissimilar, different, divergent, irreconcilable; discrepant, inconsistent, at variance, incongruous, contradictory, opposite.

dissuade, *v.* discourage, disincline, stop, hold in leash, harness, pull in, turn aside from, talk out of, persuade not to. See **discourage**.

dissuasion, *n.* discouragement, *Archaic.* dehortation, rein, squelch, *Inf.* kibosh. See **discouragement** (*defs.* **3, 4**).

dissuasive, *adj.* discouraging, cautionary, warning, monitory, admonitory, expostulatory, remonstrative, *Archaic.* dehortatory; deprecatory, repressive, suppressive.

distance, *n.* **1.** remoteness, farness, farawayness, far-offness; remove, interval, interspace, interstice, gap, space; span, reach, stride, range, span, length, width; circuit, circumference, perimeter; commute.

2. area, field, expanse, stretch, spread, sweep.

3. reserve, reservation, coolness, aloofness, offishness, haughtiness; constraint, restraint, stiffness, unresponsiveness.

4. foreign parts, distant quarter, outer reaches, antipodes, ultima Thule.

—*v.* **5.** pass, leave behind, outdistance, outrun; surpass, excel, outdo, outstrip, outreach, outrange.

distant, *adj.* **1.** (*often fol. by* from) remote, far, far-off, far-away, afar, abroad, yon, yonder, out-of-the-way, outlying, inaccessible, at a distance; ultramundane, transatlantic, transalpine, antipodean.

2. separate, apart, distinct, disparate, not joined.

3. faint, obscure, indistinct, uncertain, not obvious, not plain, slight.

4. reserved, reticent, withdrawn; formal, stiff, aloof, cool, frigid, icy; uncordial, unfriendly, unneighborly, unsociable, unapproachable, uncommunicative, unresponsive; haughty, high-hat, condescending.

distaste, *n.* dislike, disinclination, disrelish, disfavor; aversion, disgust, abhorrence, loathing, revulsion, repugnance, detestation, horror; dissatisfaction, discontentment, disaffection, displeasure; disapproval, disapprobation, disesteem.

distasteful, *adj.* **1.** unpleasant, displeasing, disagreeable, unfavorable, undesirable, nasty; obnoxious, offensive, objectionable, off-putting, uninviting; repugnant, aversive, disgusting, fulsome, noisome, atrocious; unlikable, hateful, detestable, loathsome, abominable, abhorrent, hostile, antipathetic.

2. unpalatable, unsavory, unappetizing, insipid; brackish, bitter, sour, rancid, turned, curdled; sickening, nauseating, nauseous, *Med.* nauseant, bilious.

distend, *v.* expand, extend, enlarge, spread, outspread; dilate, inflate, bloat, puff out, blow up, balloon; swell, intumesce, tumefy; fill out, fatten.

distention, *n.* expansion, extension, enlargement, spread; dilation, dilatation, inflation, *Path.* aneurysm, *Path.* varix; intumescence, tumefaction, swelling, bloating, ballooning.

distill, *v.* **1.** condense, vaporize, gasify, sublimate, fractionate; brew, press out, squeeze, *U.S.* bootleg.

2. trickle, dribble, drip, drop, leak.

distinct, *adj.* **1.** separate, discrete, individual, various, unjoined, unconnected, unassociated; different, dissimilar, unlike, disparate.

2. clear, clear-cut, crystal-clear, well-defined, vivid, graphic; plain, plain as day, plain as the nose on one's face, evident, apparent, manifest, obvious, patent, palpable, tangible, evident, self-evident; definite, unmistakable, explicit, pointed, certain, lucid, unambiguous, unequivocal, loud and clear.

3. unusual, uncommon, rare, unique, notable; singular, exceptional, one of a kind.

distinction, *n.* **1.** discrimination, differentiation, distinguishment; perception, discernment, penetration; contradistinction, separation, division.

2. difference, otherness, discreteness, dissimilarity, dissimilitude; nicety, subtlety, subtle difference, fine point, nuance.

3. note, mark, importance, consequence, significance, account, rank; eminence, prominence, repute, reputation, prestige, dignity; fame, glory, renown.

distinctive, *adj.* characteristic, distinguishing, particular, individual, singular; unusual, uncommon, peculiar, idiosyncratic; noteworthy, remarkable, *Inf.* spanking.

distinctness, *n.* **1.** separatenesss, discreteness, individuality, unconnectedness; difference, dissimilarity, dissimilitude, unlikeness, disparateness.

2. clearness, vividness, graphicness, manifestness, obviousness, plainness; certainness, lucidity, pointedness, unmistakableness, unambiguousness.

3. unusualness, uncommonness, rareness, uniqueness, notableness; singularity, singularness, peculiarity, exceptionalness, exceptionality.

distinguish, *v.* **1.** single out, set apart, mark off, point out, signalize; demarcate, delimit, fix, circumscribe.

2. differentiate, discriminate, judge, ascertain, decide, determine; tell, tell the difference, tell apart, tell between, tell which is which *or* who's who.

3. perceive, discern, see, note, make out; descry, detect, notice, espy; recognize, identify, apprehend, observe.

4. make famous, dignify, celebrate, honor, ennoble; memorialize, immortalize, solemnize, commemorate, glorify; salute, bestow honor upon, applaud, commend; extol, lionize, praise, acclaim.

5. classify, categorize, group, grade, size, rate; specify, characterize, particularize, individualize, stigmatize; define, denote, detail, indicate, designate, point to, tag, name, label; segregate, separate, docket.

distinguishable, *adj.* evident, plain, clear, manifest, well-marked; noticeable, perceivable, recognizable, conspicuous, discernible.

distinguished, *adj.* **1.** conspicuous, marked, distinct, salient, pointed; striking, staring, stark, outstanding, signal; flagrant, in bold print, in bold relief, right in front of one's eyes, standing out like a sore thumb, at the tip of one's nose; eye-catching, eye-filling, well-defined, explicit, articulate.

2. noted, eminent, famous, well-known, celebrated, esteemed; renowned, illustrious, prominent, preeminent, notable, *Archaic.* eximious; legendary, immortal, fabled, memorable; honorable, venerable, revered, respected.

3. dignified, distingué, grand, stately, august; imposing, majestic, magnificent, exalted, imperious; lordly, noble, kingly, imperial, princely, magisterial; aristocratic, well-bred, genteel, gentle, to the manner born, blue-blooded.

distort, *v.* **1.** deform, misshape, twist, turn awry, wrench; mangle, wring, wrest, writhe; contort, gnarl, screw, knot, warp; buckle, wrinkle, curl, crumple, bend, crook; grimace, snarl, pout, screw up one's face, mow, make a face; disfigure, mutilate, deface, mar, blemish.

2. pervert, misrepresent, falsify, fabricate, invert, *Scot.* thraw; torture, doctor, tamper with; color, varnish, slant, bias; exaggerate, stretch, overdraw, strain; embroider, embellish, dress up; misinterpret, belie, misquote, misconstrue, misstate, misrender, misreport; garble, slur, mutter, mumble.

distortion, *n.* **1.** deformation, contortion, misshapement, anamorphosis, anamorphism; wryness, crookedness, twistedness; asymmetry, disproportion, lopsidedness; deformity, curvature, bend, malformation, *Path.* kyphosis; disfigurement, defacement, mutilation.

2. twist, wrench, wrest, wring; gnarl, knot, knar, warp; curl, buckle, wrinkle; grimace, snarl, rictus, *Fr. moue*, pout, mow.

3. misrepresentation, perversion, falsification, fabrication, inversion, confabulation; misstatement, misinterpretation, misconstruction; exaggeration, embellishment, embroidery; coloring, false coloring, bias, slant.

distract, *v.* **1.** divert, draw away, turn aside, deflect, sidetrack, shunt; avert, switch, change course, *Naut.* jibe.
2. amuse, entertain, beguile, delight, gratify, interest, regale; occupy, engross, absorb, engage, abstract; relax, refresh, enliven; exhilarate, charm, inspirit, raise a smile, excite laughter, cheer, gladden, rejoice.
3. perplex, bewilder, confound, puzzle, confuse, complicate, befuddle; disconcert, discompose; dazzle, daze, mystify; annoy, harass, torment, tantalize; worry, agitate, embarrass, flurry, fluster, rattle; disturb, put out of one's head, make frantic, trouble, craze, madden, derange, disorder.
4. alienate, estrange, disaffect, make inimical, make unfriendly; disunite, divide, rend by dissension *or* strife; separate, part, put asunder.

distracted, *adj.* **1.** confused, perplexed, bewildered, confounded; lost, absent-minded, in a brown study, mystified; pensive, thoughtful, engrossed, preoccupied, reflecting, ruminative, deliberating; abstracted, inattentive, unheeding, heedless, unheedful, oblivious, unaware, unconscious, insensible, blind.
2. overwrought, distraught, wild, irrational, troubled, beside oneself; worked up, frantic, aflutter, frenzied, feverish, excited, phrenetic, delirious; mad, raving, deranged, insane, crazed.

distraction, *n.* **1.** confusion, befuddlement, bewilderment, puzzle, perplexity, mystification, quandary; disconcertion, discomposure, consternation; preoccupation, abstraction, absent-mindedness; mental distress, derangement, aberration, desperation, alienation; raving, hallucination, delirium, incoherence, rage, fury; madness, lunacy, craziness, insanity, mania.
2. diversion, amusement, pastime, entertainment, divertissement, beguilement; recreation, relaxation, refreshment, enlivenment; solace, comfort, consolation, restorative, easement; hobby, interest, play, sport, game; fun, delight, merriment, festivity, exhilaration, joy, jubilation; gratification, pleasure.
3. disturbance, tumult, agitation, perturbation, commotion, disorder; stir, hurly-burly, pother, stew, bustle, fuss, ado, to-do, flurry, helter-skelter; discord, dissension, contention, opposition, friction, disunity, conflict, squabble, row, feud; hullabaloo, din, rumpus, bedlam, pandemonium.

distraught, *adj.* **1.** distracted, bewildered, confused, disturbed, troubled; perturbed, agitated, upset, worked up, wrought up, *Inf.* in a stew; overwrought, beside oneself, at one's wit's end, frantic, aflutter, frenzied, feverish, excited, phrenetic; wild, raving, maniacal, hysterical, delirious, irrational; out of control, *Inf.* haywire, berserk.
2. mentally deranged, crazed, crazy, out of one's mind *or* head, insane, mad, demented, lunatic; unsound, *Latin. non compos mentis*, unbalanced, unhinged, *Inf.* off one's rocker, *Inf.* off one's trolley, *Sl.* loco. See **crazy** (*defs.* **1, 2**).

distress, *n.* **1.** anguish, misery, *Archaic.* bale, dolor, grief, sorrow, *Archaic.* dole; sadness, woe, ruth, heartache, heartbreak; ache, hurt, pain, suffering; torture, torment, agony; bereavement, mourning; woefulness, wretchedness, heaviness of heart, desolation, dejection, depression, oppression; uneasiness, worry, anxiety, angst.
2. repentance, contrition, penitence, regret, remorse, compunction.
3. affliction, grievance, tribulation, trouble; annoyance, vexation, perturbation, aggravation, thorn in one's side.
4. misfortune, adversity, straits, difficulties, sea of troubles; hardship, austerity, need, necessitude, privation, lack, want; poverty, pennilessness, destitution, penury, wolf at the door, pauperism, beggary, impecuniosity.
5. danger, peril, imperilment, precariousness, liability, jeopardy; disaster, calamity, catastrophe.
—*v.* **6.** pain, sadden, aggrieve, make one's heart bleed, break one's heart; deject, dishearten, make miserable, depress; injure, wound, hurt, cut up, cut to the quick, cut to the heart, scathe.
7. afflict, grieve, perturb, disturb, harrow; trouble, worry, bother, harry, vex, annoy; persecute, plague, harass, oppress; torment, torture, agonize, inflict suffering upon.
8. encumber, overburden, overload; tax, strain, sap, weaken, enervate, wear out.

distribute, *v.* **1.** deal out, allot, dole out, mete out, parcel out, *Inf.* dish out, *Inf.* spoon out; dispense, award, allocate, apportion; administer, discharge, minister, apply; assign, issue, give out, detail; divide, *Inf.* divvy, partition, prorate, quarter; share, measure, admeasure, portion out.
2. disperse, dispel, spread, scatter, strew, bestrew; disseminate, overspread, sprinkle, spatter, circumfuse; sow, diffuse, propagate, broadcast.
3. pass out, deliver, circulate, convey, transmit; pass around, hand out, hawk.
4. classify, class, arrange, order, assort, compart; methodize, systematize; catalogue, tabulate, codify; divide, break into, break down, separate, set apart.

distribution, *n.* **1.** allotment, allocation, disbursement, assignment, dole; apportionment, portion, prorating, partition, repartition, quarter; lot, parcel, share, slice, cut, bit, *Inf.* divvy; administration, issuance, ministration, application.
2. dissemination, propagation, diffusion, dispersion, dispersal; circumfusion, scattering, strewing; circulation, spread, dispensation, broadcast; delivery, giving out, posting, shipment, transference.
3. arrangement, classification, organization, ordering, gradation; system, method, way; formulation, assortment, array, collation, collocation; tabulation, codification, cataloguing; division, breakup, separation.
4. frequency, rate of occurence *or* recurrence, prevalence, incidence, oftenness.
5. placement, location, deployment, disposition, situation; emplacement, fixation, localization, installation, establishment.
6. marketing, selling, merchandising, trafficking, retailing, trading; handling, transporting, dealing, exchange.

district, *n.* **1.** division, section, precinct, constituency, prefecture, department, arrondissement, ward; borough, province, state, canton, county, city; town, community, commune, parish; quarter, neighborhood.
2. region, area, domain, realm, sphere; zone, pale, demesne, territory, tract of land, *Literary.* clime; country, parts, place, locale, locality, *Inf.* neck of the woods.

distrust, *v.* **1.** mistrust, suspect, be suspicious of, be wary *or* leery of; shy away from, shrink from, watch out for; doubt, be skeptical of, disbelieve, have one's doubts, have misgivings, wonder about, question.
—*n.* **2.** mistrust, credibility gap, lack of confidence *or* trust; suspicion, doubt, doubtfulness, dubiety, dubiosity, dubiousness; disbelief, unbelief, incredulity, incredulousness; watchfulness, wariness, leeriness, shyness; hesitation, uncertainty, misgiving, *Sl.* bad

vibes; qualm, question, second thought.

distrustful, *adj.* mistrustful, doubtful, dubious, suspicious; skeptical, disbelieving, unbelieving, incredulous; watchful, wary, leery, chary, shy, hesitating, uncertain, not sure, wondering, questioning; qualmish, uneasy, nervous.

disturb, *v.* **1.** disquiet, discompose, ruffle, *Inf.* shake up; discommode, incommode, inconvenience, put out, put off.

2. interrupt, interfere with, bother, pester, plague, hector, harass, *Sl.* bug, *Sl.* hassle, *Sl.* drive [s.o.] nuts *or* crazy *or* bananas, *Sl.* drive [s.o.] up the wall; irritate, annoy, irk, vex, pique, provoke, peeve; get on [s.o.'s] nerves, *Chiefly U.S.* rile, *Inf.* aggravate, *Inf.* miff, *Inf.* give [s.o.] a pain, *Inf.* get in [s.o.'s] hair, *Inf.* get under [s.o.'s] skin.

3. agitate, churn up, (*of water, wine, etc.*) roil; disorder, disarrange, misarrange, unsettle, disorganize; go against the grain, buck the system, rock the boat, make waves, make *or* cause trouble.

4. trouble, bewilder, confuse, perplex, baffle, confound, upset, disconcert, discomfit.

disturbance, *n.* **1.** disorder, disarrangement, derangement, misarrangement, disorganization, disarray, dishevelment, disruption.

2. inquietude, agitation, perturbation, flurry, flutter, restlessness, uneasiness, *Sl.* flap; confusion, perplexity, bewilderment, bafflement, mystification, *Brit. Dial.* swither; uncertainty, stupefaction, demoralization, sixes and sevens, disorientation.

3. commotion, uproar, racket, noise, hubbub, fracas, rumpus, *Inf.* ruckus, *Scot.* stramash; melee, hullaballoo, brouhaha, brawl, broil, imbroglio, to-do, row, free-for-all, Donnybrook, *Brit.* turn-up; bother, pother, trouble,fuss, fuss and feathers, *Inf.* foofaraw, *Inf.* stew, *Inf.* tizzy, *Sl.* lather, *Sl.* hoo-ha.

4. upheaval, turmoil, moil, tumult, turbulence, storm, hurly-burly; unrest, distraction, furor, excitement; riot, revolt, revolution, uprising; sedition, insurrection, insurgence, rebellion.

5. nuisance, annoyance, vexation, interruption, pain, *Sl.* pain in the neck, *Inf.* headache, *Sl.* hassle, *Sl.* drag, *Sl.* bitch; inconvenience, imposition; irritant, bur, thorn in the side *or* flesh, pea in the shoe.

disturbed, *adj.* **1.** agitated, ruffled, flustered, perturbed, flustered, troubled, upset, discomposed, *Sl.* all shook-up, *Sl.* all hot and bothered; uneasy, anxious, restive, apprehensive, on pins and needles.

2. annoyed, irritated, vexed, piqued, peeved, *Chiefly U.S.* riled, roiled, *Inf.* aggravated, *Inf.* miffed; pestered, bothered, hectored, harassed, harried.

3. confused, bewildered, perplexed, baffled, disconcerted, mixed-up.

4. neurotic, psychoneurotic, disordered, unbalance; psychopathic, psychotic, mentally-ill, *Sl.* screwed-up, *Sl.* messed-up.

disunion, *n.* **1.** severance, disjunction, disconnection, separation, division, abstraction; partition, detachment; interruption, disruption.

2. dissension, disunity, dissidence, discord; alienation, estrangement, variance; breach, schism, split, rupture, feud, spat, disagreement. See **disunity**.

disunite, *v.* **1.** separate, disjoin, sever, split, dissever, dispart; dissociate, abstract, detach, part, divide, rend, divorce; interrupt, disrupt; disengage, unfasten, loosen; dismember, disjoint; disband, scatter.

2. alienate, estrange, set at varience, set at odds, put discord between, split wide open, widen the breach; embroil, entangle, pull different ways, render inharmonious, pit against, stir up dissension.

disunity, *n.* dissension, discord, discordance, dissidence; disagreement, dissent, nonconcurrence; alienation, estrangement, variance; breach, schism, split, rupture; feud, spat, squabble, quarrel, wrangling, tiff, clashing, bickering, contention, strife, friction, controversy, altercation.

disuse, *n.* nonuse, nonemployment, discontinuance, cessation; desuetude, want of practice, neglect; relinquishment, abrogation, forbearance, abstinence.

ditch, *n.* **1.** trench, dike, *Fort.* escarp, *Fort.* scarp; excavation, pit, dugout, abri, foxhole, manhole, hole, furrow; fosse, moat, canal; drain, sewer, gutter, cloaca; conduit, culvert, main, pipe, duct; passage, channel, race, waterway, watercourse.

—*v.* **2.** dig, excavate, burrow, hollow out; scarp, escarp.

3. derail; force *or* run off the road, sideswipe; crash-land.

4. *Slang.* **a.** discard, jettison, throw away, get rid of. **b.** escape, evade, elude, shake.

diurnal, *adj.* **1.** daily, quotidian, circadian, day-to-day, everyday.

2. day, daytime, nonnocturnal.

divan, *n.* **1.** sofa, couch, lounge, chaise lounge, settee, davenport, dias, ottoman, musnud, love seat, day bed, tête-à-tête, siamoise, vis-à-vis.

2. council, cabinet, ministry, congress, committee, commission.

dive, *v.* **1.** plunge, sound, submerge, go underwater, go deep; descend, fall, nose-dive, dip, swoop, pitch, lurch; leap, dart, spring, lunge, dash, scoot, whisk.

—*n.* **2.** plunge, *Inf.* header, jump, cannonball, flip, belly-flop; *All Fancy Diving.* half twist, full twist; dash, lunge, spring, leap.

diverge, *v.* **1.** spread, spread apart, come apart, open, open up, radiate, fly off, go asunder, divaricate, branch off; divide, separate, subdivide, fork, part, ramify, disunite, divorce; sever, dissever, cleave, rive, split, sunder, bisect, dissect, disconnect.

2. depart, deflect, vary, differ, change, step aside, steer clear of; curve, turn, bend, swerve, tack, slue, slew, yaw, bear off, wheel, wheel about, swing about; divert, sidetrack, shift, switch, shunt.

3. deviate, digress, veer, straggle, turn aside; wander, ramble, meander, stray, drift, rove, divagate, *Scot. and North Eng.* sklent.

divergence, *n.* **1.** spreading, spreading apart, coming apart, opening, opening up, radiating, flying off, divaricating, forking, parting, branching off; dividing, separating, subdividing, ramifying, disuniting, divorcing; severing, dissevering, cleaving, riving, splitting, sundering, bisecting, dissecting, disconnecting; spread, radiation, divarication; division, subdivision, separation, fork, part, disunion, ramification, divorce; severance, disseverance, dissection, disconnection.

2. departing, deflecting, varying, differing, changing, stepping aside, steering clear of; curving, turning, bending, swerving, tacking, bearing off, wheeling, wheeling about, swinging about; diverting, sidetracking, shifting, switching, shunting; departure, deflection, variation, difference, change; curve, turn, bend, swerve; diversion, shift, switch.

3. deviating, digressing, veering, straggling, turning aside; wandering, rambling, meandering, straying, drifting, roving, divagating; divergency, deviation, digression, divagation.

divergent, *adj.* **1.** centrifugal, radial, spreading, spreading apart, coming apart, opening, opening up, radiating, flying off, divaricating, branching off; dividing, separating, subdividing, forking, parting, branching, branched, furcate, bifurcating, ramifying, ramiform, disuniting; severing, dissevering, cleaving, riving, splitting, bisecting, dissecting, disconnecting.

2. different, conflicting, dissimilar, diverse, variant; departing, deflecting, varying, differing, changing; curving, turning, bending, swerving; diverting, shifting, switching, shunting.

3. deviate, deviant, aberrant; deviating, diverging, digressing, veering, straggling, wandering, rambling, meandering, straying, drifting, roving, divagating.

divers, *adj.* several, sundry, various, numerous, many; different, varied, assorted, mixed, miscellaneous, multifarious, manifold.

diverse, *adj.* unlike, different, dissimilar, varying; separate, apart, distinct; multiform, diversiform, diversified, varied, variant, manifold, divergent, differing; various, miscellaneous, motley, heterogeneous, mixed, assorted, variegated, checkered.

diversify, *v.* vary, change, transform, alter, modify; variegate, streak, stripe, striate, fleck, dapple, dot, spot, mottle, checker.

diversion, *n.* **1.** deflection, turning aside, digression; divergence, deviation, variation, detour.

2. distraction, amusement, pastime, entertainment; recreation, relaxation, refreshment, enlivenment; solace, comfort, consolation, restorative, easement, rest; divertissement, hobby, beguilement, interest; play, sport, game, frolic, fun, delight, merriment, festivity; exhilaration, joy, jubilation; gratification, pleasure.

3. *Mil.* feint, ruse, blind, stratagem.

diversity, *n.* **1.** unlikeness, difference, dissimilarity, dissimilitude, contrast, confliction; contrariety, opposition, antithesis, contradiction, contradistinction; inconsistency, discrepancy, inconformity, nonconformity; disparity, imparity, inequality, incongruity; variation, divergence, deviation, departure; disagreement, dissension, dissidence, dissent, variance, contrariety.

2. nonuniformity, unevenness, irregularity, disproportion; multiformity, multifariousness, manifoldness, multiplicity; miscellany, variety, heterogeneity, assortment, medley; variegation, diversification.

divert, *v.* **1.** turn aside, deflect, draw away, avert, switch, change course, *Naut.* jibe, shift; shunt, sidetrack, swerve; separate, part, go asunder; branch off, ramify, fork, divaricate.

2. distract, entertain, amuse, delight, gratify, beguile, interest, regale; occupy, engross, absorb, engage; withdraw, abstract, preoccupy; relax, refresh, enliven; charm, inspirit, exhilarate; cheer, gladden, rejoice, raise a smile, excite laughter.

divest, **1.** unclothe, disrobe, dismantle, undress; remove, put off, take off, doff; strip, lay bare, bare, uncover, expose, lay open, denude, denudate.

2. despoil, deprive, dispossess, bereave.

3. rid, free from, disencumber, relieve of, disabuse; purge, dispose of, get rid of, do away with, debunk.

divide, *v.* **1.** cut, sever, dissever, split, rend, sunder, dispart, cleave, rive; bisect, halve, quarter, intersect; subdivide, compart, partition, repartition, demarcate.

2. separate, part, disconnect, detach, disjoin; diverge, branch, fork, open, divaricate.

3. estrange, cause to disagree, sow dissension, set *or* pit against one another, make hostile *or* discordant, set at variance *or* odds, alienate, disaffect; come between, widen the breach, *Inf.* split wide open, *Inf.* break up.

4. share, assign, portion out, apportion, allocate, allot, *Inf.* divvy *or* divvy up; distribute, dispense, dole, deal *or* mete *or* parcel out.

5. classify, catalog, label, categorize; segregate, group, grade, rate, assort, dispose.

dividend, *n.* **1.** share, portion, quantum, *Inf.* cut, *Inf.* split, *Archaic.* meed; surplus, gain.

2. bonus, extra, lagniappe, plus, fringe benefit, perquisite, *Inf.* perk, *Sl.* freebie.

divination, *n.* **1.** augury, prophecy, soothsaying, *Obs.* hariolation, forecasting, foretelling, prediction, prognostication, oracle, vaticination, *Obs. Rare.* fatidicency, *Obs. Rare.* mantology.

2. sortilege, astrology, horoscope, haruspicy, haruspication, geomancy, hydromancy, rhabdomancy, auspice, ornithomancy, arithmancy, necromancy, bibliomancy, belomancy, spodomancy, graptomancy, gyromancy, lithomancy, halomancy, hieromancy, hieroscopy, (*usu. jocular*) pedomancy.

3. magic, sorcery, thaumaturgy, necromancy, witchcraft, incantation, spell, charm; omen, presage, sign, portent.

4. intuition, foreknowledge, prescience, prevision, instinctive foresight, clairvoyance, discernment; presentiment, presage, premonition, forewarning, foreboding; surmise, conjecture, supposition, presumption, assumption, speculation, guesswork.

divine, *adj.* **1.** godly, godlike, deiform, deified; sacred, religious, holy, saintly, sainted, venerable, angelic, seraphic, blessed, blest, sanctified, hallowed, consecrated.

2. heavenly, celestial, spiritual, ethereal, supernal; beatific, blissful, rapturous, ecstatic; supreme, exalted.

3. supernatural, preternatural, superhuman; transcendent, supermundane, hyperphysical, immaterial.

4. *Informal.* superlative, *Inf.* super, admirable; lovely, charming, stunning, striking; fashionable, chic.

—n. **5.** theologian, canonist, decretist, exegete, hierophant, rabbi, religious scholar, hierologist, Doctor of the Church, Talmudist, Talmudic scholar.

6. clergyman, ecclesiastic, churchman, cleric, clerk, *Brit.* blackcoat; priest, father, padre, abbé, confessor; minister, parson, *Dial.* dominie, curate, curé, chaplain, *U.S. Mil. Sl.* sky pilot; pastor, shepherd, vicar, canon, rector; high priest, bishop, prelate, hierarch; preacher, evangelist; presbyter, elder.

—v. **7.** prophesy, discover by divination, foretell, predict, foresee, foreknow, forecast, forewarn, prognosticate, vaticinate, *Obs.* hariolate.

8. presage, augur, portend, foreshow, foreshadow, bode, forebode, foretoken, betoken, shadow forth, signify, point to, *Obs.* auspicate.

9. conjecture, surmise, guess, speculate, suspect, suppose, assume, presume, theorize, hypothesize; intuit, discern, perceive, fancy, imagine, dream; understand, fathom, apprehend, grasp, comprehend.

diviner, *n.* **1.** prophet, soothsayer, seer, clairvoyant, oracle, augur, fortuneteller, prognosticator, Chaldean, astrologer, geomancer, (*in ancient Rome*) haruspex; prophetess, sibyl, witch; sorcerer, conjurer, wizard, magician, necromancer.

2. conjecturer, surmiser, guesser, theorizer, theorist, hypothesizer, hypothesist; interpreter, reader, expounder, explainer.

divinity, *n.* **1.** uncreated being, godhood, God, the Deity, the Godhead, Omnipotence, Omniscience, Providence, the Absolute, the Infinite, the Eternal, the First Cause, the Unmoved Mover.

2. deity, god, goddess, genius, spirit, guardian, *Class. Myth* daemon, *Hindu Myth.* diva, angel, seraph.

3. theology, Scripture, Torah, Talmud; canon law, religion, theosophy, hierology, hagiography, hagiology.

4. godliness, excellence, perfection, supreme virtue.

divisible, *adj.* dividable, separable, cleavable, severable, splittable, fragmentary.

division, *n.* **1.** separation, partitionment, segmentation; disconnection, detachment, disjunction, splitting, scissure; severance, parting, disunion, dismemberment; partition, split, break, breach, rupture.
2. section, part, slice, piece, component, segment; fraction, bit, fragment, scrap, chunk; portion, share, parcel, sector, apportionment, allotment; room, compartment; member; cutting.
3. dividing line, boundary, boundary line, border line, partition line, line of demarcation; line, fence, border, margin.
4. disagreement, difference of opinion. See **disagreement** (*defs.* **1, 2**).
5. section, sector, branch, arm, department.
6. classification, category, group, class, family, subdivision.

divorce, *n.* **1.** disunion, disjunction, disconnection, dissolution, separation; severance, breach; split, *Sl.* split-up, division, detachment, partition; interruption, disruption.
—*v.* **2.** separate, disunite, disjoin, sever, split, split up, dissever, dispart; dissociate, detach, part, divide, rend; interrupt, disrupt; disengage, unfasten, loosen.
3. (*all of the marriage contract*) dissolve, break, break up; annul, cancel, declare null and void, wipe out.

divulge, *v.* disclose, reveal, make known, tell, impart, inform, relate, utter, declare, break the news; release, break, report, publish, communicate, broadcast, *Archaic.* divulgate; come out with, let slip, leak, let the cat out of the bag, spill the beans, blow the lid off, *Inf.* let it all hang out, *Sl.* sing, *Sl.* spill one's guts; expose, uncover, unmask, unveil, bring out, bring out into the open, lay open, bring to light.

dizzy, *adj.* **1.** light-headed, vertiginous, *Inf.* woozy; befuddled, muddled, in a stew, bewildered, puzzled, confused, distraught.
2. *Informal.* fickle, capricious, inconstant, vacillating; featherheaded, scatterbrained. See **flighty**.

do, *v.* **1.** perform, execute, *Scot. and North Eng. Obs.* gar, discharge, carry out, fulfill, realize; succeed in, manage, bring off, *Sl.* pull off, *Inf.* put over, *U.S. Sl.* swing, *U.S. Sl.* cut, *U.S. Sl.* hack; engineer, negotiate, work out; bring about, make happen, effect, effectuate; produce, turn out, achieve, attain.
2. accomplish, finish, complete, carry through; dispose of, *Sl.* knock off, *Sl.* polish off, expedite, dispatch; conclude, close, wind up, clinch, clench, seal; perfect, crown, top, cap, put the last *or* finishing touch to, consummate; end, put an end to, terminate.
3. render, afford, give, bear, pay, put forth; observe, keep, practice.
4. serve, suffice for, be enough, be adequate, measure up, pass muster; answer, satisfy, suit, content, appease.
5. make, prepare, fix, make ready, get ready, arrange.
6. create, originate, form, design, fashion, fabricate; develop, shape, mold.
7. *Informal.* wear out, exhaust, do in, tire, fatigue; overcome, ruin, conquer, defeat.
8. *Informal.* cheat, trick, deceive, cozen, dupe, take advantage of; swindle, defraud, do out of, fleece, bilk.
9. act, conduct, comport, behave; carry oneself, manage onself, bear oneself.
10. proceed, continue, go ahead; get along, fare, manage, make out; do well, succeed in, make good.
11. happen, transpire, take place, occur, go on; arise, appear, chance, turn up, crop up, come up.
12. **do away with** **a.** abolish, put an end to, repeal, revoke, rescind; cancel, invalidate, nullify, annul, make void. **b.** kill, slay, murder, shoot, put to death; do in, get rid of, put away, remove, finish off; liquidate, erase, blot *or* wipe out, *Sl.* rub out, *Sl.* bump off, *Sl.* knock off, *Sl.* snuff out.
13. **do without** forgo, dispense with; give up, abstain from, eschew, refrain from, forbear, desist.
—*n.* **14.** action, activity, commotion, excitement; bustle, hustle, flurry, fuss, *Inf.* to-do, bother; hubbub, racket, tumult, disturbance, ferment, uproar.
15. *Chiefly Brit.* party, affair, occasion, soirée, fête.
16. **do's and don'ts** customs, rules, regulations; standard, code, policy, guide, precept, formula.

docile, *adj.* **1.** manipulate, manipulable, tractable, malleable, ductile, pliable, pliant, manageable, *Scot.* tawie; passive, timid, gentle, meek, mild, subdued; compliant, complying, amendable, cooperative, accommodating, agreeable, willing, disposed, inclined, assenting; nonresistant, obedient, dutiful, biddable, responsive; acquiescent, capitulating, submissive, yielding, deferential, obsequious.
2. teachable, educable, instructible, schoolable; trainable, coachable, drillable, disciplinable.

docility, *n.* **1.** manageability, manageableness, tractability, tractableness, malleability, malleableness, ductility, ductileness, pliability, pliableness; passiveness, timidity, timidness, meekness, gentleness, mildness; acquiescence, compliance, cooperativeness, agreeableness, willingness; obedience, dutifulness, biddability, biddableness, responsiveness, submissiveness, obsequiousness.
2. teachability, teachableness, educability, educableness, instructability, schoolability; trainability, trainableness, coachability, disciplinability, disciplinableness.

dock[1], *n.* **1.** pier, quay, wharf, dockage, marina, basin, (*in the Far East*) bund; jetty, jutty, mole.
—*v.* **2.** bring in, lay up, land, put in, tie up; anchor, moor, berth, cast *or* lay *or* drop anchor.

dock[2], *v.* **1.** cut short, cut off the end, shorten; crop, bobtail, snip, lop, nip; pare down, prune, shear, pollard, poll; truncate, abridge, curtail, retrench, *Rare.* obtruncate.
2. deduct, subtract, take out; lessen, reduce, diminish, decrease.

doctor, *n.* **1.** physician, medical practitioner, M.D., medical doctor, medical man, healer, *Sl.* pill peddlar, *Sl.* doc; allopath, osteopath, homeopath; surgeon, *Sl.* sawbones, specialist, consultant; resident, intern; dentist, orthodontist; veterinarian, *Inf.* vet.
—*v.* **2.** minister, treat, attend, administer; medicate, prescribe for, remedy; heal, make better, cure, care for.
3. repair, mend, correct, fix, patch up; improve, ameliorate, meliorate, get better; restore, rebuild, make over, rehabilitate, reconstruct; set to right, put in order.
4. falsify, misrepresent, pervert, misstate, misreport, misrender, belie; twist, distort, color, *Scot.* thraw; tamper with, invert, misconstrue, misconstruct.
5. adulterate, water down, dilute, thin out, weaken, *Sl.* cut; doctor up, add to, strengthen, mix with, blend, *Inf.* spike.

doctrinaire, *adj.* **1.** dogmatic, dogmatical, doctrinal; authoritarian, domineering, imperious, overbearing, pushing, *Inf.* pushy; assertive, insistent, emphatic, imperative, authoritative; opinionated, bigoted, prejudiced, biased, one-sided, narrow-minded, intolerant, fanatical.
2. impractical, unpractical, unpragmatic, unrealistic;

theoretical, hypothetical, ideologic, ideological, speculative, visionary.
—*n.* **3.** impractical theorist, non-realist, ideologist, ideologue; pundit, authoritarian, *Inf.* know-it-all, dogmatist, dogmatizer, bigot, zealot, fantic.

doctrine, *n.* **1.** theory, opinion, belief, conviction; principle, precept, maxim, dictum, axiom; tenet, dogma, teaching, doxy; postulate, proposition, thesis.
2. creed, credo, canons, articles of faith, body of teachings, gospel; The Word.

document, *n.* official paper, certificate, instrument, charter, record, chronicle; legal paper, *Law.* testament, *Law.* deed, *Law.* writ; credential, voucher, diploma.

dodder, *v.* shake, shiver, tremble, teeter, totter; shamble, stagger, shuffle, sway; twitch, quiver, quaver, quake; bob, reel, falter, flounder; vacillate, dither, oscillate, fluctuate, hesitate, waver.

doddering, *adj.* **1.** senile, aged, decrepit, (*of women*) anile, superannuated; feeble, *Inf.* dotty, infirm, shaky, unsteady, shivering, trembling, teetering, tottering; shambling, staggering, shuffling, swaying; twitching, quivering, quavering, quaking; bobbing, reeling, faltering, floundering; vacilliating, oscillating, fluctuating, hesitating, wavering.
2. weak-minded, foolish-minded, foolish, silly, ineffectual; in one's dotage, in one's second childhood.

dodge, *v.* **1.** shift, move *or* dart aside, jump away, parry; duck, bob, bob and weave, veer, swerve, jib; whiffle, sidestep; shy, recoil, draw back.
2. avoid, elude, evade, give [s.o.] the slip; hide from, stow away, escape, skulk; bolt, run away, decamp, abscond, elope, take off, scram; shun, stay clear, make oneself scarce, sneak off, sneak out the back way; stay out, play truant, shuffle off to Buffalo, malinger, call in sick.
3. prevaricate, quibble, equivocate, *Sl.* waffle, fudge; hedge, qualify; doubletalk, palter, backtrack, back-pedal, sidetrack; tergiversate, vacillate, shilly-shally.
—*n.* **4.** sidestep, dart, swerve, swerving; elusion, evasion, avoidance, escape.
5. *Informal.* trick, ruse, wile, ploy, feint; stratagem, scheme, contrivance, maneuver, artifice, subterfuge, machination, expedient, shift; ingenuity, adroitness, slyness, cunning, sharp practice; chicane, deception, prevarication, equivocation, double talk, sophistry.

dodger, *n.* shifty one, slippery one, trickster, evader, deserter, runaway, *Archaic.* runagate, AWOL; malingerer, truant, shirker, slacker, renegade, goldbrick, *Sl.* goof-off; chiseler, sharpie, sly boots, *Sl.* cutie, one who plays fast and loose.

doer, *n.* executer, accomplisher, effector, performer, worker; enterpriser, entrepreneur, *U.S. Inf.* go-getter; *Sl.* operator, *Sl.* wheeler-dealer.

doff, *v.* **1.** (*all of clothing*) take off, remove, shed, throw off, toss off, cast off *or* away, get rid of; disarray, disrobe, undress, strip, bare, denude, nakedize.
2. (*all of a hat*) tip, raise, lift, take off, remove.

dog, *n.* **1.** canine, hound, *Sl.* pooch, *Fr. chien*; female dog, bitch; cur, tyke, mongrel, *Sl.* mutt; doggy, pup, puppy, whelp.
2. dingo, wild dog, wolf, fox, jackal, coyote, hyena.
3. *Slang.* scoundrel, knave, rogue, wretch, scamp, scapegrace, rascal, rapscallion, miscreant, villain.
4. *Informal.* fellow, man, boy, *Inf.* guy, *Sl.* dude, *Fr. type.*
5. *Slang. Inf.* lemon, *Inf.* dud, piece *or* hunk of junk.
6. **go to the dogs** *Informal.* deteriorate, degenerate, go to ruin, go to pot, go to hell in a handbasket, fall apart.
7. **put on the dog** *U.S. Slang.* affect *or* put on airs, put on a show, show off; (*all of oneself*) display, exhibit, parade, flaunt.

dogged, *adj.* **1.** determined, earnest, fixed, intent; steadfast, firm, purposeful, deliberate; constant, persevering, staunch, stanch; game, spunky, plucky, gritty; tenacious, relentless, bent on, *Inf.* hellbent, do-or-die; unhesitating, unfaltering, unflinching, unwavering, unflagging; indomitable, indefatigable, untiring.
2. stubborn, mulish, obstinate, set, pigheaded, bull-headed, stubborn as a mule *or* ox; inflexible, unmovable, unyielding, unbending, obdurate, impervious; intractable, intransigent, refractory, perverse, willful, recalcitrant, headstrong; resistant, difficult, forward, opinionated, opinioned.

dogma, *n.* **1.** creed, credo, doctrine, teachings; tenet, tenent, maxim, precept, axiom; code, canon, rule, principle, article *or* principle of faith, credendum.
2. conviction, belief, firm belief, fixed opinion; theory.

dogmatic, *adj.* dogmatical, doctrinaire, doctrinal; assertive, insistent, emphatic, imperative, authoritative; authoritarian, domineering, imperious, overbearing, pushing, *Inf.* pushy; opinionated, bigoted, prejudiced, biased, one-sided, narrow-minded, intolerant, fanatical.

dogmatism, *n.* presumption, positiveness, peremptoriness, opinionatedness; arrogance, imperiousness, high-handedness; bigotry, intolerance, closed-mindedness.

doing, *n.* **1.** action, performance, execution, effectuation, implementation, enactment; accomplishment, achievement, realization; act, deed, work, handiwork, exploit, enterprise, feat, stunt.
2. affair, concern, matter, business, *Inf.* job.
3. **doings** deeds, actions, exploits, handiwork; affairs, matters, concerns, dealings; accomplishments, achievements; events, happenings, proceedings, transactions, *Inf.* goings-on.

dole, *n.* **1.** share, portion, allotment, lot, parcel, quota, moiety; modicum, pittance, pinch, mite, driblet, drop in the bucket, *Inf.* smidgen.
2. apportionment, allocation, distribution, division, disposal; dispensation, issuance, administration.
3. alms, charity, *Sl.* handout; subsidy, stipend, allowance; unemployment, unemployment compensation, workmen's compensation, *Sl.* unem, *Brit. Sl.* the brew; welfare, food stamps; social security, medicare, medicaid.
—*v.* **4.** donate, present, give, give away.
5. **dole out** ration, allot, deal out, mete out, parcel out, portion out; distribute, dispense, issue, administer.

doleful, *adj.* sorrowful, mournful, disconsolate, depressed, dejected, cheerless, joyless, dolorous; gloomy, melancholy, sad, blue, *Inf.* down in the dumps, *Inf.* down in the mouth; pathetic, pitiable, pitiful, piteous, wretched.

doll, *n.* **1.** figure, figurine, *Baby Talk.* dolly; toy soldier, puppet, muppet, marionette; toy, plaything.
2. *Usu. Offensive.* woman, girl; *All Sl.* gal, dame, chick, broad, dumb broad, babe, tomato, skirt, jill, cutie, filly, *Brit.* bird, *Brit.* lemon.

dollar, *n.* *All Sl.* buck, smacker, smackaroo, greenback, fish, frogskin, skin.

dolor, *n.* sorrow, grief, *Archaic.* dole, sadness, ruth, heartache, heartbreak; anguish, misery, *Archaic.* bale; bereavement, lamentation, mourning; ache, pain, hurt, suffering, *Archaic.* teen; torture, torment, agony; wretchedness, desolation, heaviness of heart, despondency, despair, slough of despair, moroseness, depression, oppression; melancholy, disconsolateness, unhappiness, infelicity.

dolorous, *adj.* grievous, painful, rending, harrowing; mournful, woeful, melancholy, sad; sorrowful, rueful, doleful; tearful, lachrymose, lugubrious.

dolt, *n.* blockhead, thick head, *Inf.* chump, dunce, *Inf.* dummy, *Sl.* dope, *Sl.* dumbbell, *Sl.* meatball *or* meathead; dullard, fathead, numskull, beetlehead, bonehead, dunderhead, dunderpate, chucklehead, *Sl.* dumbhead, *Sl.* lunkhead, *Inf.* knucklehead, *Sl.* stupidhead, *Sl.* goon; simpleton, idiot, *Inf.* moron, imbecile, lamebrain, dim-wit, nit-wit, half-wit; pinhead, *Sl.* birdbrain, *Sl.* flake, *Sl.* dingbat, *Sl.* ding-a-ling; fool, ninny, nincompoop, ninnyhammer; *All Slang.* jerk, boob, booby, noodle, nudnik, blubberhead.

doltish, *adj.* blockheaded, boneheaded, blockish, thick, thick-headed, thick-skulled, dense; obtuse, stolid, lumpish, blunt, dull; *Inf.* dopey, *Inf.* dumb, dull-witted, dim-witted, slow, slow-witted, half-witted; stupid, unintelligent, simple, simple-minded, weak-minded, bird-brained, feeble-minded, deficient; idiotic, *Inf.* moronic, imbecilic, foolish; mindless, brainless, empty-headed, blank, vacant, vacuous.

domain, *n.* **1.** realm, empire, kingdom; sultanate, archduchy, duchy, principality, palatinate.
2. region, area, zone, territory; province, precinct, department; district, quarter, section; field, pale, arena; bailiwick, dominion, jurisdiction.
3. academic discipline, discipline, specialty, concern, branch *or* field of study, department of knowledge.

dome, *n.* **1.** rotunda, cupola, onion dome, (*in classical architecture*) tholos.
2. *Slang.* head, pate, poll, crown, sconce, *Sl.* noodle, *Sl.* noggin, *Sl.* bean, *Usu. Disparaging.* skull.

domestic, *adj.* **1.** household, home, family; residential, domiciliary.
2. tame, domesticated, broken, housebroken.
3. native, indigenous, aboriginal, autochthonous; home-grown, home-raised, homebred, homemade, native-grown.
—n. **4.** servant, help, hired help; butler, footman, *Brit.* boots, *Chiefly Brit.* buttons; majordomo, steward, housekeeper; driver, chauffeur, coachman; valet, groom, gentleman's gentleman, man, (*in the British army*) batman; factotum, do-all, slavey, man *or* maid of all work; maid, handmaiden, chambermaid, maidservant, upstairs maid, au pair *or* au pair girl, betweenmaid, *Brit. Inf.* tweeny; cook; charwoman, laundress, scullion, menial, drudge.

domesticate, *v.* **1.** tame, gentle; train, housebreak; break, *Sl.* bust.
2. familiarize, naturalize, habituate, orient, break in; habituate, accustom, assimilate, acclimate; domiciliate.

domicile, *n.* **1.** home, abode, residence, residency, dwelling, dwelling place, dwelling home, habitation, habitancy, *Scot. and North Eng.* bigging, *Scot.* howff, lodging, lodgings, lodging place, lodgement *or* lodgment, nest, roost, perch; quarters, living quarters, rooms, accommodations, housing, roof over one's head, *Inf.* pad, *Inf.* crash pad, *Chiefly Brit. Inf.* diggings, *Brit. Inf.* digs; apartment, flat, tenement, walk-up, cold-water flat, *Brit.* chambers, *Chiefly Brit.* maisonette *or* maisonnette; penthouse, townhouse, condominium, *Sl.* condo; mobile home, motor home, camper, trailer; address, location, situation, whereabouts, place.
2. mansion, palace, palatial *or* stately dwelling *or* home *or* residence, *Fr. hotel, It. palazzo*, villa, chateau, castle, *Chiefly Brit.* hall, *Brit.* court, *Archit.* folly, *Sl.* spread; manor, manor house, manor seat, estate, country estate, country home, country seat, country house, house and grounds, house and lot, *Brit. Dial.* toft, demesne, *Law.* messuage; farm, farmstead, farmplace, *Archaic.* farmhold, grange, *Brit.* farmery, *Brit.* croft, *Brit.* homecroft, *Scot. and North Eng.* steading; ranch, rancho, rancheria, hacienda; plantation.
3. cottage, cot, bungalow, bower, cabin, log cabin, blockhouse, *Brit. Dial.* cote, *Scot.* but-and-ben; hut, hutch, shed, shack, shanty, *Scot.* bothy; hovel, hole, dump, sty, pigsty, pigpen, tumbledown shack, wretched hut, mean dwelling, miserable quarters.
4. hearth, hearthstone, hearth and home, hearthside, fireside, fireplace, chimney corner, *Brit. Dial.* ingle, *Brit. Dial.* ingleside, *Chiefly Brit.* inglenook *or* ingle nook; homestead, household, family, family circle, domestic circle, bosom of one's family, seat of one's affections, home sweet home, *Inf.* place where one hangs one's hat.
—v. **5.** domicil, domiciliate, establish oneself, take up residence, take up one's abode, make one's home, inhabit, occupy, settle, locate, ensconce, *Inf.* hang up one's hat; take *or* strike root, plant oneself, anchor, come to anchor, drop anchor, moor; nest, nestle, perch, roost, squat, burrow, hive; lodge, rent, room, berth, bunk, bed, quarter *or* billet at, put up at, *Inf.* hang out, *Sl.* crash, *Brit. Sl.* doss down; camp, camp out, bivouac, pitch one's tent.

dominant, *adj.* **1.** ruling, controlling, governing, regnant, reigning; supreme, superior, surpassing, preeminent, paramount.
2. commanding, prominent, most important *or* influential; predominant, main, chief, principal, head, leading, strongest; prevailing, prevalent, most widespread.

dominate, *v.* **1.** control, rule over, reign over, exercise control over, govern; command, order, dictate, have it all one's way, call the shots, call the plays, run the show; boss, lay down the law, hold the purse strings; be in control, be in the driver's seat, be in the saddle, wear the pants *or* trousers, be in a position of authority, hold all the cards, have well in hand, have under control; rule the roost, wear the crown, occupy the throne, have the whip hand; wield the scepter, wield the power *or* authority, sway, bend to one's will.
2. subdue, overpower, domineer, master, gain the upper hand, get the better of; be master of the situation, be on top of, have [s.o.] under one's thumb; browbeat, intimidate, bully, ride roughshod over, ride herd on; oppress, repress, suppress, rule with a high hand, rule with an iron hand, rule with a rod of iron, tyrannize; keep down *or* under, lord it over, break, humble, crush; subjugate, subject, subordinate, enthrall, enslave, reduce to slavery, hold captive, hold in bondage.
3. tower above, loom over, stand over, bestride; overlook, survey; project, jut over, hang over, beetle over.
4. overshadow, eclipse, overtop, rise above, be superior to; outshine, be in the ascendant, be supreme, crown, top, cap, beat; surpass, surmount, exceed, outweigh, preponderate; overrule, override, prevail over, take precedence over; dwarf, detract from, take away from.
5. predominate, prevail, be widespread, permeate, pervade, overrun, overspread; characterize, distinguish, designate, define, describe, denominate.

domination, *n.* **1.** control, rule, command, authority; power, influence, sway, ascendancy, supremacy, reign; overpoweringness, overwhelmingness, mastery, the whip *or* upper hand; domineeringness, browbeating, intimidating, intimidation; bullying, riding roughshod over, riding herd on.

2. oppression, repression, suppression, ruling with a high *or* iron hand, ruling with a rod of iron; tyranny, despotism, sovereignty, absolutism; dictatorship, czarism, Caesarism, kaiserism, imperialism, *U.S.* (*usu. of politics*) bossism; subjugation, subjection, subordination; enthrallment, enslavement, slavery, captivity, bondage.

domineer, *v.* **1.** tyrannize, rule with a rod of iron, rule with an iron *or* high hand; boss *or* boss around; browbeat, intimidate, bully, ride roughshod over, trample, ride herd on; oppress, suppress, repress, keep down *or* under, lord it over; break, humble, crush, overpower, get the better of; subdue, subjugate, subject, subordinate, enthrall, enslave, reduce to slavery, hold captive, hold in bondage.

2. dominate, master, control, rule, govern; command, order, lay down the law, call the shots *or* plays, *Inf.* wear the pants; run the show, rule the roost, wear the crown, occupy the throne, have the whip hand; have the upper hand, be master of the situation, be on top of, have [s.o.] under one's thumb; wield the scepter, wield the power, sway, bend to one's will.

3. dominate, tower above, loom over, stand over, bestride; overshadow, eclipse, dwarf, detract from, take away from; prevail over, overtop, rise above, surmount, surpass, top, crown, cap, beat.

domineering, *adj.* overbearing, imperious, magisterial, lordly, high and mighty; high-handed, arbitrary, presumptuous, peremptory, arrogant, haughty, insolent; commanding, imperative, willful, forceful, coercive, aggressive, pushing, *Inf.* pushy; masterful, authoritarian, authoritative, *Inf.* bossy, dictatorial; despotic, autocratic, tyrannical, iron-handed; oppressive, hard, harsh, strict, severe, tough.

dominion, *n.* **1.** supremacy, primacy, preeminence, upper *or* whip hand, sway, hegemony; reign, sovereignty, suzerainty, empery, (*in India*) raj; kingship, lordship, mastership, leadership, seignority; authority, jurisdiction, power, *Inf.* say *or* say-so.

2. rule, command, mastery, control, domination; hold, grasp, grip, clutches.

3. territory, region, area, country, domain, kingdom. See also **domain** (*def.* **1**).

don, *v.* put on, slip on, slip into, assume; (*all usu. oneself*) dress, dress up, clothe, vest, garb, attire, apparel, habit, *Sl.* dude up; robe, gown, drape; outfit, fit out, rig up, accouter, turn out, gear.

donate, *v.* **1.** present, bestow, confer, allot, render, award, impart; allow, grant, yield, vouchsafe, afford; proffer, offer, tender, extend, issue; bequeath, will, leave, pass down.

2. contribute, give, subscribe, pledge, put oneself down for, do one's part, *Inf.* chip in, *Sl.* kick in.

donation, *n.* **1.** presentation, bestowal, conferral, allotment, rendition, proffer, tender.

2. contribution, gift, present, offering, benefaction; gratuity, tip, douceur, *Fr. pourboire*; bonus, lagniappe; handout, alms, charity, dole.

done, *adj.* **1.** completed, through, finished, *Fr. fini*; finished up, concluded, ended, terminated.

2. worn out, exhausted, *Inf.* dog-tired, prostrate, prostrated, *Fr. épuisé*; very tired, fatigued, *Fr. fatigué*, tired out, *U.S. Inf.* tuckered out, fagged out, *Sl.* pooped out; played out, used up, spent, depleted, drained, *Inf.* bushed; done for, beaten, *Inf.* beat, *Inf.* done in, worn to a frazzle; worn, toilworn, wayworn, footsore; jaded, wearied, weary, drooping; on one's last legs, ready to drop, dead, more dead than alive; haggard, emaciated, wasted, drawn, hollow-eyed; enervated, enervate, languid, debilitated, weakened, weak, enfeeble, feeble; faint, *Inf.* woozy, *Inf.* groggy.

3. done for a. tired, exhausted, played out. See **done** (def. **2**). **b.** beaten, *Inf.* beat, *Inf.* done in, washed up, lost, finished; ruined, undone, broken, destroyed, dashed; defeated, foiled, frustrated, thwarted.

donkey, *n.* **1.** ass, burro, dickey, *Chiefly Scot.* cuddy, *Brit. Sl.* moke; jackass, jack, jenny, jennet; mule, hinny; beast of burden, pack *or* draft animal, *Archaic.* sumpter.

2. fool, dope, nincompoop; dunce, dolt, blockhead, knucklehead; oaf, boor, lout; idiot, simpleton, halfwit. See also **ass** (*def.* **2**).

donor, *n.* giver, donator, grantor, contributor, benefactor, benefactress, supporter, backer, angel; fairy godmother.

do-nothing, *n.* **1.** idler, fainéant, loafer, drone, *Inf.* bum, sluggard, slugabed, lazybones; laggard, loiterer, lounger, lingerer, trifler, dawdler, dallier; daydreamer, lotus-eater; shirker, goldbrick, *Sl.* goof-off; good-for-nothing, ne'er-do-well, *Fr. vaurien*, worthless person.

—adj. **2.** idle, fainéant, lazy, slothful, sluggard, otiose, indolent; sluggish, laggard, slow-moving, torpid, lethargic; inactive, inert, passive, supine.

doom, *n.* **1.** (*all usu. of an adverse nature*) fate, fortune, destiny, lot, cup, portion, die, *Archaic.* foredoom, *Chiefly Scot.* weird, *Brit. Inf.* cup of tea; karma, kismet, *Obs.* destin.

2. ruin, ruination, rack and ruin, destruction, dissolution, extinction, annihilation, bane; death, death knell, end, finish, terminus, quietus.

3. condemnation, damnation, guilty verdict; sentence, judgment, pronouncement, *Sl.* rap.

—v. **4.** fate, ordain, destine, *Rare.* destinate; predetermine, predestine, preordain, foreordain, predecide, foredoom, *Inf.* have in store for.

5. condemn, damn, consign to damnation, sign [s.o.'s] death warrant; sentence, pass sentence.

doomed, *adj.* **1.** destined, fated, ordained; predestined, foreordained, preordained, predetermined, predesigned.

2. damned, accursed, cursed, curse-laden; condemned, *Brit. Dial.* fey, anathematized, *Archaic.* maledict; bedeviled, bewitched, star-crossed, ill-fated, foredoomed.

3. ruined, wrecked, overwhelmed, crushed, undone, *Inf.* done for, destroyed; lost, washed up, wiped out; down the drain, gone to pot, shot, *Sl.* kaput, *Fr. fini*, all over, finished, *Sl.* have had it.

door, *n.* **1.** opening, aperture, hatch, doorway, *Fr. porte*; trapdoor, hidden *or* secret door; gate, gateway, postern, portal; threshold, stile, turnstile, wicket; hall, hallway, passage, passageway, arcade, gangway, walkway, corridor, gallery; lobby, foyer, vestibule, anteroom, waiting room; anteporch, porch, portico.

2. entrance, entry, entryway, entrée, inlet, ingress; approach, ramp, drive, driveway, lane, adit; path, pathway, route, road, roadway, course, way, means.

doorkeeper, *n.* **1.** porter, *Inf.* doorkeep, doorman, gatekeeper, ostiary; guard, turnkey, sentinel, sentry, watchman, warder, watchdog.

2. guardian, keeper, warden, conservator, caretaker, custodian, concierge, janitor.

dope, *n.* **1.** paste, *Inf.* gook, *Sl.* goop; glue, rubber cement, epoxy; lubricant, oil, grease.

2. narcotic, drug; *Inf.* opiate, sedative, soporific, barbiturate, *Inf.* down *or* downer; amphetamine, stimulant, *Inf.* up *or* upper, *Sl.* speed; hallucinogen, psychedelic; marijuana, *U.S. Sl.* Mary-Jane, *Sl.* pot, *Sl.* grass, *Sl.* reefer, *Sl.* weed.

3. *Slang.* news, word, story, data, facts, *Inf.* score, scoop, *Sl.* deal; inside information, *Inf.* info, *Inf.*

lowdown, *Sl.* poop.

4. *Slang.* dolt, blockhead, *Inf.* chump, dunce, *Inf.* dummy, *Sl.* dumbell. See **fool** (*def.* **1**).

dormant, *adj.* **1.** sleeping, asleep, resting, at rest; hibernating, (*of land*) fallow, dormient; inactive, lifeless, inert, still, stock-still, silent; motionless, immovable, immobile; unmoving, stationary, becalmed.

2. dull, sluggish, passive, lethargic, stagnant; sleepy, somnolent, slumberous, torpid, torpescent, comatose.

3. latent, implicit, undisclosed, unexpressed, quiescent; potential, undeveloped, unrealized; veiled, hidden, unapparent.

4. suspended, deferred, postponed, in obeyance; pausing, stopping, breaking, waiting, hesitating, hesitant, delaying, abeyant.

dose, *n.* **1.** quantity, portion, measure, draught; swallow, gulp, *Inf.* shot, *Inf.* slug, (*of dope*) *Sl.* hit; daily dose, medicine, medicament; lethal dose, toxic dose, overdose, o.d.

2. *Slang.* venereal disease, *Inf.* V.D., gonorrhea, *Sl.* clap.

—*v.* **3.** administer, dispense, dole out, give, apportion; medicate, treat.

dot, *n.* **1.** spot, point, speck, mark, jot; period, decimal point, polka-dot; particle, mote, mite, iota, atom; freckle, pinprick.

2. on the dot on time, precise, punctual, exact, prompt, *Inf.* on the button; opportune, well-timed; scrupulous, conscientious, careful, meticulous, accurate, literal.

—*v.* **3.** spot, sprinkle, bespeckle, speckle, fleck, stipple, stud, bestud; scatter, distribute, disperse; mark, punctuate, pepper, accent, point up *or* out, emphasize; pit, pock, freckle, maculate.

dotage, *n.* **1.** senility, old age, superannuation, caducity; decrepitude, infirmity, declining years; second childhood, childishness, anility.

2. foolish fondness, predilection, leaning, fatuity; indulgence, coddlement, pampering.

dote, *v.* **1.** *Usu.* **dote on** idolize, hold dear, prize, treasure, adore, be stuck on; make much of, indulge, spoil, coddle, pamper, lavish on.

2. be in one's second childhood, be feebleminded, be in one's dotage, show one's age; ramble, wander.

doting, *adj.* **1.** indulgent, overgenerous, lavish, extravagant, liberal, obliging, pampering; easygoing, soft, tenderhearted, forbearing, lenient, yielding, lax.

2. senile, anile, infirm, weak, unsound, *Inf.* dotty; childish, foolish, feeble-minded.

double, *adj.* **1.** equal, equaled, matched, correspondent, comparable; equivalent, commensurate, again as much.

2. duplicate, twin, identical; paired, in pairs, coupled, mated, geminate; dual, duplex; twofold, binal, binate, replicate.

3. folded, bent over, doubled; bifold, biform, biformed, two-ply.

4. deceitful, insincere, two-faced, Janus-faced, hypocritical; double-dealing, false, dishonest, equivocal, guileful, knavish.

—*adv.* **5.** twice, by twos, two-by-two, doubly, encore, bis.

—*n.* **6.** duplicate, twin, copy, replica, clone, facsimile, look-alike; counterpart, match, equal.

7. substitute, *Inf.* sub, proxy, alternate, fill-in, secondary, locum tenens; stand-in, understudy, *Inf.* pinch hitter, stunt person.

8. on the double quickly, losing no time, with haste, posthaste; briskly, at full speed, in double-quick time, at full gallop, tantivy; without delay, straightway.

—*v.* **9.** multiply *or* increase by two; enlarge, magnify; duplicate, copy, geminate; match, mate, pair, couple, associate.

10. fold, turn, turn back, turn again, redouble, make two thicknesses, plait.

11. double back, go back, go round, sail round, backtrack, return; elude, evade.

double-dealing, *n.* duplicity, equivocation, dissimilation, cant, lip-service, mouth-honor; treachery, foul play, betrayal, Judas kiss, disloyalty, bad-faith, infidelity, faithlessness, perfidy, breach of trust, *Inf.* two-timing; dishonesty, hypocrisy, mendacity, deception; guile, artifice, trickery, Machiavellism, deceit, improbity; knavery, roguery, rascality, fraud.

double entendre, *n.* ambiguity, double meaning, suggested *or* hidden meaning; pun, word play, play on words, anagram; paradox, equivocation, dubiousness, indefiniteness, vagueness.

doublet, *n.* **1.** vest, jerkin, waistcoat, jacket.

2. pair, set, couple, two.

doubly, *adv.* two-fold, in double measure, double; twice, again, once more, over again, bis.

doubt, *v.* **1.** suspect, distrust, be uncertain, entertain doubts, be in a state of uncertainty, not know what to think, *Inf.* not know which way to turn, waver; mistrust, fear, be in suspense, harbor suspicions, *Inf.* take with a grain of salt, *Inf.* smell a rat.

2. lack confidence in, have doubts about, scruple, stickle, shy at, be apprehensive of; lack conviction, lack faith, waver, hesitate to believe, discredit; question, query, challenge, object, dispute, contradict, deny, disbelieve, demur; float in a sea of doubt.

—*n.* **3.** uncertainty, hesitation, indecision, undecidedness, irresolution, vacillation, unsettled opinion; suspense, distrust, mistrust, suspicion; question, faltering, lack of conviction, indefiniteness; incertitude, dubiety, dubiousness, lack of certainty; disbelief, incredulity, skepticism, dissent.

4. perplexity, quandary, dilemma, confusion; ambiguity, problem, question, open question, difficulty.

doubter, *n.* skeptic, disbeliever, questioner, doubting Thomas; scoffer, iconoclast, nonconformist; dissenter, freethinker, apostate.

doubtful, *adj.* **1.** uncertain, wavering, undecided, hesitating, irresolute, vacillating, indecisive; perplexed, confused, in suspense, *Inf.* up in the air; wondering, skeptical, distrustful, suspicious, incredulous, disbelieving, from Missouri.

2. questionable, debatable, disputable, dubious, equivocal, ambiguous; apocryphal, problematic, enigmatical, puzzling; undetermined, indeterminate, nebulous, obscure, vague, muddy; precarious, indefinite, conjectural, incredible, unbelievable.

doubtless, *adv.* **1.** unquestionably, truly, without doubt, undoubtedly, of course, assuredly; certainly, for certain, surely, positively, beyond a shadow of a doubt, incontestably, indisputably, irrefutably; really, actually, to a certainty, and no mistake, no doubt, in truth, to be sure, for sure, without fail.

2. probably, apparently, in all probability; presumably, most likely, seemingly, ostensibly; supposedly, perhaps, mayhap.

doughty, *adj.* brave, resolute, game, valorous. See **brave** (*defs.* **1, 2**).

dour, *adj.* **1.** hard, inflexible, unyielding, rigorous, austere, Spartan, unsparing; ironhanded, strict, harsh, stern, severe; uncompromising, rigid, stringent, obdurate.

2. sullen, gloomy, inclement, morose, sour.

douse, *v.* **1.** drench, souse, imbue, saturate; immerse, submerge, dunk, duck, dip; soak, steep, swash, slosh; flood, deluge, inundate; wet, rinse, sprinkle, sparge; plunge, dive, immerge.

2. splash, flush, flush out, irrigate, hose down, shower, sprinkle.

3. *Informal.* extinguish, quench, blow out, put out, out, smother, snuff, snuff out, stamp out.

4. *Informal.* remove, take off, doff, tip.

dovetail, *v.* **1.** mortise, tenon, join, fit, fit together, intersect, unite, splice, link.

2. tally, conform, correspond, fit *or* go together, match; agree, accord, jibe, fall in with, concur, go hand in glove, see eye to eye; equal, balance, square, parallel; harmonize, coincide.

dowdy, *adj.* slovenly, untidy, tacky, frowzy, dumpy, frumpy, looking like Tugboat Annie; carelessly dressed, sloppy, messy, unkempt; bedraggled, draggletailed, slatternly, sluttish; ill-dressed, unfashionable, out-of-date, old-fashioned; shabby, worn-out, rag-tag, drab, dull.

dower, *n.* **1.** estate, widow's inheritance, property, substance; inheritance, legacy, heritage, bequest; provision, trust, settlement, maintenance, pension, annuity.

2. See **dowry**.

3. endowment, natural gift, gift, talent, faculty, genius, bent, knack, forte.

down[1], *adv.* **1.** at the lowest point, at a low rate *or* degree, to a low point, below par, minimally, at a low ebb; at ground level, to the ground, underground, below the horizon; underfoot, on the ground *or* floor, underneath, under, beneath, below, *Archaic.* adown.

2. downstairs, downtown, down home, downstate, downstream, down the line, down the way *or* road.

3. in check, under control, penned in, hemmed in, in adversity, *Inf.* in a tight spot, *Inf.* between a rock and a hard place; in disgrace, in disfavor, *Inf.* on the list.

4. confined to bed, in bed, abed, laid up; sick, ailing, prostrate.

5. from a former time, onward in time, through the ages *or* years, down the corridors of time.

6. (*all of payment*) as downpayment, as retainer, up front, in advance, as earnest; in cash, on the counter, into the hand, on the barrelhead; at once, without delay, now, immediately, forthwith.

7. **down with** away with, get rid of, *Fr. à bas*; oust, push out, *Inf.* kick out; stamp out, squelch, put an end to; abolish, repeal, do away with, revoke, invalidate, terminate; overthrow, overcome, pull down, bring down, upset, supplant, defeat, destroy, wipe out.

—prep. **8.** from top to bottom, along the way, on the way down, from a higher to a lower point.

—adj. **9.** descending, going down, coming down, downward; tumbling, sliding, dropping, falling, plunging.

10. dejected, downcast, sad, blue, disconsolate. See **downcast**.

11. **down and out** destitute, impoverished, *Sl.* broke *or* flat broke; derelict, forsaken, forgotten, lost, adrift, *Inf.* on the skids, *Sl.* on the bum.

12. **down on** hostile to, antagonistic, unsympathetic, antipathetic, set against.

—n. **13.** descent, reverse, decline, falling, falling off, coming down, sinking; lapse, drop, plunge; fall, sink, droop, sag, slip.

—v. **14.** overthrow, conquer, subdue, win over, beat, put down; fell, floor, knock down, knock out, KO; bring down, shoot down, bag, tally, rack up.

15. drink, swallow, gulp, toss off; drain, drain to the dregs, drain to the bottom, *Inf.* swill.

down[2], *n.* fluff, baby feathers, fuzz, undergrowth; bloom, peach fuzz; nap, pile, shag; wool, thatch, fur; beard, whiskers, 5 o'clock shadow, chin fur; filament, cobweb, gossamer, thistledown.

downcast, *adj.* dejected, disheartened, dispirited, low-spirited, downhearted, down, *Inf.* down in the dumps; discouraged, daunted, dismayed, distressed, disappointed, crestfallen, broken-hearted, heartsick, *Inf.* broken up; unhappy, cheerless, glum, gloomy, under a cloud, in the doldrums, doleful, *Archaic.* wan; saddened, sad, blue, forlorn, melancholy, mopey, mopish, long-faced, chapfallen, unsmiling, *Inf.* down in the mouth; miserable, morose, heartbroken, woebegone, heavy-hearted, disconsolate, sorrowful, mournful, lachrymose, funereal; depressed, weighed down, burdened, crushed, prostrate, *Inf.* broken, *Sl.* bummed out; despondent, *Psychiatry.* hypochondriac *or* hypochondriacal, *Brit.* hipped, spiritless, lifeless, exanimate, enervated, weakened, weary, tired, drained.

downfall, *n.* **1.** collapse, debacle, breakdown, break up; drop, fall, descent, crash, smash, tailspin *or* tail spin, nose dive; defeat, overthrow, overturn, labefaction, coup d'état; undoing, ruin, ruination; debasement, abasement, degradation; shame, disgrace, humiliation, mortification.

2. mistake, blunder, botch, bungle, error, *Inf.* slip-up; transgression, dereliction, dereliction of duty, misconduct, misdeed; false step, wrong step, misstep, false move, wrong move, bad move, trip, stumble; offense, peccadillo, oversight, omission; leak, slip, lapse, lapsus; *All Sl.* boner, goof, dumb trick, fool mistake, screw-up, foul-up, louse-up.

3. downpour, downrush, spate, cascade, flood, deluge; cloudburst, thunderstorm, thundershower, scud, *Brit. Dial.* brash.

downgrade, *n.* **1.** slope, grade, slant, pitch, inclination; descent, decline, declivity; dip, drop, fall, slip.

2. **on the downgrade** declining, weakening, sinking, failing, going down *or* downhill, sliding, slipping; falling, falling off, losing ground, going to pot *or* seed, going to the dogs, hitting the skids, going into a tailspin; off, depressed, slumping, sagging.

—v. **3.** demote, degrade, humble. See **demote**.

4. minimize, belittle, understate, gloss over, soft-pedal, whitewash, make light of; denigrate, detract from, run down, criticize, *Sl.* badmouth.

downhearted, *adj.* sad, depressed, downcast, broken-up, atrabilious. See **downcast**.

downpour, *n.* deluge, inundation, torrent, torrential *or* driving rain, pouring *or* drenching rain, cloudburst, *Inf.* cats and dogs; flood, flash flood, washout.

downright, *adj.* **1.** complete, total, outright, out-and-out, categorical, dead, flat, unequivocal, unmitigated, unqualified, unconditional, incontestable; thorough, thoroughgoing, wholesale, all-out, *Inf.* flat-out; absolute, utter, profound, sheer, stark, arrant, rank; perfect, positive, consummate, *Inf.* regular, *Inf.* plumb, *Brit. Inf.* proper.

2. clear, manifest, distinct, palpable, evident, self-evident, conspicuous, definite, unmistakable, undeniable.

3. candid, frank, forthright, foursquare, straightforward, straight-from-the-shoulder; plain, plain-spoken, plain-speaking, explicit, unambiguous, undisguised, *Inf.* straight-out, *Inf.* flat-flooted, *Inf.* matter-of-fact; outspoken, free-spoken, free-speaking, free-tongued, free, unreticent, bold, unreserved, unrestrained, unconstrained, unchecked, unabashed, uninhibited, unsparing, unshrinking; blunt, bluff, brusque, brash, tactless.

—adv. **4.** completely, totally, categorically, dead, unequivocally, unconditionally, incontestably, *Inf.*

plumb; absolutely, utterly, profoundly, sheerly, starkly, arrantly, rankly; perfectly, positively, consummately.
5. clearly, manifestly, distinctly, evidently, conspicuously, definitely, unmistakably, undeniably.
downtrodden, *adj.* oppressed, burdened, weighed down, troubled, laden; plagued, afflicted, abused, mistreated, harassed, distressed, beset; languishing, weak, feeble, wasted, haggard, prostrate, in subjection to, overcome, overwhelmed, helpless, powerless, laid low, beaten to a frazzle; poor, ignominious, sorry, pitiful, low, miserable, wretched; tyrannized, under the lash, under the heel of, in the power of, enslaved; downtrod, ground down, downfallen, at the mercy of, trodden under foot, trodden down, *Inf.* walked all over.
downward, *adj.* **1.** heading down, descending, going down, moving down, sliding, slipping.
—adv. **2.** in descending order, from the source *or* beginning, from the top, toward the extremities, down, downwards.
downy, *adj.* **1.** fluffy, feathery, plumose, furry; fleecy, fleece-like, lanuginose *or* lanuginous; soft, smooth, silken, silky, satiny, velvety, vultinous.
2. hairy, pubescent, *Bot., Entomol.* tomentose, *Bot.* villous *or* villose.
3. soft, gentle, soothing, comforting, calm, restful, tranquil; comfortable, pleasurable, commodious, cozy, easy, luxurious.
4. light, airy, ethereal; fragile, delicate, gossamer, gossamery, filagree; thin, rare, fine, unsubstantial.
dowry, *n.* dower, marriage portion, jointure, dot, *Scot. and North Eng.* tocher; property, marriage settlement.
doze, *v.* **1.** sleep, slumber, drowse, nap, catnap, take a nap, *Inf.* snooze, *Inf.* snatch forty winks, *Inf.* catch some shut-eye, *Sl.* zizz, *Brit. Sl.* doss.
—n. **2.** nap, cat nap, siesta, slumber, *Inf.* snooze, *Inf.* forty winks.
drab[1], *adj.* **1.** dun, dun-colored, dull brown, dull-gray, mouse-colored, *Inf.* mousy.
2. dull, dreary, dingy, flat, mat, lusterless, lackluster, *Scot. and North Eng.* blae; dark, dismal, cheerless, *Scot.* ourie.
3. dead, lifeless, spiritless, uninspired, *U.S. Sl.* blah, *Sl.* nothing; boring, uninteresting, dry, dry-as-dust, *Inf.* ho-hum; weak, lukewarm, tepid.
drab[2], *n.* **1.** slattern, slut, trollop, sloven, draggletail; frump, dowdy; hag.
2. prostitute, harlot, whore, hussy, loose woman, wanton, fallen woman, woman of the streets, streetwalker, trull, quean, painted woman, bar girl, *Inf.* pick-up, *All Sl.* tart, cat, hooker, floozie, working girl. See also **prostitute** (*def.* **1**).
—v. **3.** wanton, wench, womanize, *Sl.* sleep around, lecher, *Sl.* lech.
draft, *n.* **1.** drawing, sketch, line drawing, delineation, picture; design, chart, diagram, blueprint.
2. preliminary form, rough sketch, outline, skeleton; plan, survey, overview, conspectus; formulation, framing, plot, strategy, *Inf.* game plan; composition, inditement.
3. conscription, levy, induction; lottery, selection. See **conscription** (*def.* **1**).
4. air current, flow, inflow, influx, stream; breath, puff, whiff; breeze, wind; chill.
5. (*often* draught) drink, swallow, dose, quaff, potation, potion; sip, nip, *Inf.* swig, *Inf.* bracer.
6. check, *Brit.* cheque, money order, bill of exchange; debenture, *Commerce.* drawback.
7. drawing out, drawing from, taking; requisition, demand, order, claim; drain, outflow, withdrawal, depletion.
8. haulage, force; pull, tug, heave; haul, load, burden, baggage, freight, cargo, lading.
9. air regulator, damper, movable plate, check, stop, hindrance; vent, ventilator.
10. beast of burden; donkey, mule, ox.
—v. **11.** draw, *Archaic.* limn, sketch, delineate; etch; trace, outline, diagram, design.
12. write, compose, put together, draw up; formulate, frame, plan, block out.
13. conscript, impress. See **conscript** (*def.* **1**).
14. draw, pull, haul, drag, tow, tug, yank.
—adj. **15.** tentative, proposed, preliminary, trial, provisional, temporary, speculative; flexible, adaptable, unsettled, unfinished, incomplete, undeveloped; outline, skeletal, sketchy, rough, diagrammatic.
16. (*usu. of beer*) on tap, cask-drawn, from a cask.
17. (*usu. of animals*) drawing, hauling, pulling.
draftsman, *n.* **1.** sketcher, planner, designer, drafter, drawer, delineator; artist.
2. (*of documents or speeches*) writer, author, framer, composer, formulator, planner.
3. *Brit.* (*in the game*) checker, draughtsman.
drag, *v.* **1.** haul, hale, lug, draw, pull, strain; tow, take in tow, tug; trawl, troll, trail.
2. dredge; rake, harrow, grade.
3. (*all usu. in reference to irrelevant matter*) introduce, insert, bring in, put in, stick in, pop in, slip in, work in, worm in, squeeze in, foist in.
4. crawl, creep, go at a snail's pace; trudge, plod; shamble, shuffle, limp along, poke along, *Inf.* mosey.
5. protract, prolong, lengthen, extend, draw out, spin out, stretch out; expatiate, amplify, dilate, expand, enlarge upon; perorate, speak at length, spin a long yarn, go on and on, never finish.
6. draggle, straggle, lag behind, trail behind; linger, loiter, dillydally, dally, shillyshally, *Inf.* lallygag.
—n. **7.** *Slang.* bore, dryasdust; *Sl.* drip, *Sl.* pill. See **bore** (*def.* **2**).
8. *Slang.* (*all of transvestites*) attire, apparel, dress. See **attire** (*def.* **2**).
draggle, *v.* **1.** drabble, bedrabble, bedraggle, *Archaic.* daggle; (*all by dragging through mud, dirt, etc.*) soil, dirty, muddy, begrime, bemire.
2. straggle, drag *or* trail *or* lag behind, dally, dillydally, shillyshally, *Inf.* lallygag.
dragoon, *n.* **1.** cavalryman, trooper, mounted soldier, cavalier, cuirassier, horseman, equestrian; chasseur, hussar, uhlan.
—v. **2.** force, coerce, compel, impel, drive, put the screws on *or* to; crush, ride roughshod over, trample, ride herd on; tyrannize, rule despotically, oppress, suppress, repress, browbeat.
drain, *v.* **1.** draw off, sluice, pump off, withdraw, remove, take away; extract, milk, tap, broach; filter, filtrate, percolate.
2. deprive, impoverish, pauperize, ruin; consume, empty, expend, deplete, exhaust; tax, sap, bleed, enervate, devitalize; reduce, wear, degenerate, debilitate, cripple, impair.
3. flow out, well out, effuse, shed; leak, discharge, exude, ooze, seep, trickle.
—n. **4.** pipe, conduit, culvert, sewer, cloaca, tube; gutter, *Brit.* sough, trench, ditch; outlet, channel, watercourse.
5. expenditure, disbursement, outflow, outgo; withdrawal, reduction, strain, depletion, exhaustion.
drainage, *n.* **1.** piping, tubing, guttering, sewage system.

2. sewage, seepage, bilge water, waste water.

drama, *n.* **1.** play, stage play, dramatic play; screenplay, photoplay, theatricals, stage show, show; theatrical piece, piece, work, vehicle.
2. dramatury, stagecraft, dramatic art, histrionic *or* thespian art; dramatics, histrionics, histrionism, theatrics, theatricalism, showmanship; representation, portrayal, depiction, delineation; stage business.

dramatic, *adj.* **1.** theatrical, theatric; dramaturgical, dramaturgic; scenic, stagy; operatic; thespian, histrionic, histrionical, Roscian, *Sl.* hammy.
2. vivid, graphic, expressive, meaningful; moving, touching, affecting, emotive; powerful, potent, forceful; telling, cogent, effective.
3. striking, impressive, sensational, spectacular; startling, sudden, surprising; thrilling, exciting, stirring, breathtaking, electrifying, nerve-shattering.

dramatist, *n.* playwright, dramaturge, dramaturgist, screenwriter; tragedian; comedian; melodramatist; dramatic poet; *Theat.* play doctor.

dramatize, *v.* **1.** stage, mount, put on, produce; theatricalize; melodramatize.
2. emote, emotionalize, tug the heartstrings; rant, spout, roar, declaim, out-Herod Herod; act, enact, perform, play a part, play to the gallery; affect, play-act, put up a front; overact, make a show *or* production of, *Sl.* ham it up; overdo, *Inf.* lay it on, *Inf.* lay it on thick, *Inf.* pile it on.

drape, *v.* **1.** cover, blanket, overspread, overlay, mantle; overlie, cloak, curtain, fold, veil, shroud; envelop, swathe, enwrap, swaddle, wrap, sheathe; dress, festoon, adorn, array, deck; bedight, bedeck, prink.
2. hang, let fall, drop, lean over; droop, dangle; suspend, depend, pend, swing.
—n. **3.** curtain, hanging, tapestry. See **drapery**.

drapery, *n.* covering, hanging, curtain, mantle; tapestry, dosser, portiere, valance, lambrequin; window shade, window curtain, drop, backdrop, scrim, arras; blind, shade, drape; cover, cloak, veil, shroud, fold, purdah, screen.

drastic, *adj.* **1.** violent, forceful, powerful, forcible, rigorous; fierce, strong, potent, puissant, effective, efficacious; emphatic, imperative, telling, striking.
2. severe, harsh, intensive, keen, acute, poignant, sharp.
3. extensive, extreme, draconian, far-reaching, considerable, broad, enormous, inordinate, egregious.

draw, *v.* **1.** pull, tug, magnetize, *Physiol.* adduct; tow, haul, lug, drag, yank, hale; take in tow, lead, *Naut.* warp, *Naut.* kedge.
2. pull out, take out, extract, bring out; unsheathe, bare, produce, pull a gun.
3. attract, allure, invite, lure, entice; tempt, persuade, influence; interest, fascinate, catch [s.o.'s] eye, capture [s.o.'s] fancy, captivate, win, seduce; engage, elicit, call forth, invoke.
4. sketch, trace, mark out, lay out, outline, contour, scratch, map out, chart; depict, delineate, *Archaic.* limn, portray, represent, picture, diagram.
5. compose, create, frame, formulate, design, devise; form, fashion, shape, fabricate; envision, contrive, plan, plot.
6. inhale, suck in, breathe in, inspire, respire, *Obs.* sufflate, *Literary.* suspire.
7. deduce, infer, conclude, reason, derive; gather, glean, get; guess, presume, opine, reckon, suppose, think.
8. receive, get, obtain, accept; procure, secure, pick up; bring in, produce, gather, reap, cull; take in, acquire, earn, gain.
9. drain, empty, sluice, siphon, filtrate; milk, sap, bleed; tap, pump off.
10. choose, pick, select, elect, single out; take, decide on, make a choice of, fix upon; favor, prefer, fancy.
11. shrink, contract, wrinkle, shrivel, knit, compress, constringe; dwindle, decrease, diminish, reduce, decline.
12. approach, come near, advance, near, draw nigh, move towards, gain on, edge close.
13. draw out a. pull out, root out, uproot, deracinate, remove, extract, withdraw; pluck out, tear out, wrench, wrest. **b.** prolong, lengthen, make longer, prolongate, protract; extend, stretch out, elongate, continue, filibuster.
14. draw up a. write up, compose, draft, prepare; indite, pen, write, redact, put in writing; dash off, scribble down, put down, throw on paper, knock off. **b.** arrange, put into position, set, arrange, sort; marshal, order, rank. **c.** halt, bring to a stop, stop, rein in; pull up to, sidle up to.
—n. **15.** attraction, drawing power, magnetism, charisma; pull, influence, gravity.
16. tie, stalemate, parity, dead heat, *Inf.* photo finish.

drawback, *n.* hindrance, impediment, obstacle, stumbling block, hurdle, encumbrance; obstruction, *Archaic.* remora, oppilation, interference, *Law.* estoppel; discouragement, deterrent, damper; bar, barrier, stop, stopper, block, barricade; curb, check, balk, catch, hitch, snag; disadvantage, detriment, difficulty, problem, trouble; inconvenience, pain in the neck, nuisance; liability, handicap, weakness, weak spot, flaw, defect, fault, minus.

drawing, *n.* **1.** sketch, tracing, picture, copy; diagram, design, outline, composition; representation, depiction, portrait, portrayal, delineation, figure; cartoon, caricature, black and white, pen and ink.
2. raffle, lottery, draw, lot, sweepstakes, *Sl.* sweep; the numbers.
3. selection, pick, picking, choice, choosing, extraction, withdrawal.

drawing room, *n.* reception room, reception hall, salon, parlor, living room, sitting room.

drawl, *v.* **1.** twang; prolong syllables, linger over one's words; (*all of speech*) lengthen, extend, protract, stretch, prolong, prolongate, elongate, drag *or* draw *or* stretch *or* spin out.
—n. **2.** regional accent, accent, broad accent *or* speech, twang.

drawling, *adj.* twanging, twangy, drawly; (*all of speech*) monotonous, monotone, singsong, humdrum, droning, longsome; slow, slow-paced, tardigrade, snail-paced, snail-like; lagging; leisurely, languid, dreamy; lazy, otiose.

dread, *v.* **1.** fear, be afraid, worry, *Inf.* funk, mistrust, distrust, suspect, anticipate, expect, apprehend, forebode; hesitate, falter, have second thoughts, have cold feet; quail, flinch, recoil, shy, shrink; cower, skulk, crouch; shiver, shake, shudder, quiver, shake in one's boots, tremble.
—n. **2.** fear, fearfulness, fright, *Inf.* funk; terror, horror, panic; alarm, perturbation, dismay, consternation, trepidation; worry, disquiet, disquietude, concern; apprehension, misgiving, uncertainty, suspicion, mistrust, distrust, qualm; angst, fear and trembling, anguish, anxiety; uneasiness, apprehensiveness, *Inf.* butterflies, nervousness, queasiness; cowardice, timidity, diffidence; hesitation, cold feet, second thoughts; *Sl.* heebie-jeebies, the jitters, *Sl.* the willies, *Sl.* the creeps; bugaboo, bugbear, bogy, *Fr. bête noire*, nightmare.
—adj. **3.** frightful, terrible, dreadful, dire. See

dreadful (*defs.* **1, 2**).

dreadful, *adj.* **1.** terrible, grievous, grim, dire, baleful, dark; terrifying, frightful, direful, dread, terrific, appalling; alarming, distressing, harrowing, rending; redoubtable, fearsome, formidable, awful; horrible, horrid, horrendous, monstrous, atrocious; hideous, ghastly, eerie, grisly, gruesome, unspeakable; outrageous, shocking, enormous, flagrant; nefarious, heinous, flagitious, villainous; infamous, notorious, odious; wicked, evil, vile, sinful, iniquitous, *Archaic.* facinorous; maleficent, malefic, malevolent, demonic, diabolic, devilish, fiendish; abhorrent, revolting, repulsive, repugnant, loathsome, despicable; pernicious, pestilential, noxious, deadly, fell.

2. awe-inspiring, awesome, imposing, impressive, inspiring; venerable, august, reverential, revered, respected, reverenced.

3. unpleasant, disagreeable, unpleasing, offensive, distasteful, displeasing; unwelcome, uninviting; ugly, unsightly, uncomely, homely, *Inf.* God-awful; unpalatable, uneatable, unsavory, unappetizing, undelectable, undelicious.

dream, *n.* **1.** vision, nightmare; apparition, will-o'-the-wisp, ignis fatuus, chimera, fairy; phantom, shade, specter, ghost, wraith, incubus, succubus, bugbear; fantasy, phantasm, phantasma, *Lit.* fantasia, *Inf.* pipe dream, romance; figment, figment of the imagination, fiction, invention, fabrication; visualization, envisagement, hallucination, mirage, illusion, delusion; shadow, vapor, nothingness.

2. daydream, castle in the air, castle in Spain, musing; fancy, flight of fancy, whim, whimsy, vagary, crotchet, notion, imagination; conceit, thought, idea, conception, concept; design, plan, scheme; aspiration, goal, aim, mark.

—*v.* **3.** have dreams, have nightmares, hallucinate; see in a vision, visualize, envisage, rhapsodize, idealize; daydream, stargaze, gaze out the window, fall into reverie, be preoccupied, be abstracted; imagine, fantasize, phantasize, *Rare.* phantsy; fancy, muse, build castles in the air, suppose, conceive, dream up, conjure up, think.

dreamer, *n.* visionary, fantast, castle-builder, romancer, daydreamer; idealist, Pollyanna, Pangloss; somnambulist, sleepwalker.

dreamland, *n.* dream world, land of dreams, cloudland, land of Nod, never-never land, fairyland, land of make-believe; unreality, illusion, fantasy.

dreamy, *adj.* **1.** notional, fanciful, whimsical, quixotic, romantic, poetic, rapt; visionary, idealistic, utopian.

2. thoughtful, speculative, pensive; abstracted, in a brown study, absent-minded, preoccupied; featherheaded, featherbrained, scatterbrained, *Inf.* dizzy, *Sl.* out to lunch, *Sl.* out in left field.

3. vague, dim, indistinct, faint, shadowy; ethereal, aerial, airy, vaporous, diaphanous, gossamer; insubstantial, immaterial, incorporeal, asomatous, discarnate, bodiless; spectral, chimerical, dreamlike, intangible, impalpable; illusory, fictitious, fantastic, imaginary.

4. drowsy, sleepy, somnolent, lethargic; lackadaisical, listless, dull, torpid, comatose.

5. soothing, calming, quieting, refreshing; restful, tranquil, peaceful.

6. *Informal.* wonderful, marvelous, terrific, fabulous, heavenly.

dreary, *adj.* **1.** gloomy, cloudy, dismal, dim, bleak, *Literary.* drear, *Both Scot. and North. Eng.* dowie, dree; gray, shadowy, dark, obscure; uninviting, cheerless, joyless.

2. dull, flat, drab, arid, dry, dry-as-dust, uninteresting, vapid, lifeless, *Sl.* nothing, *Sl.* blah, *Sl.* dead; monotonous, singsong, repetitive, unvaried, boring, boresome, tedious, tiresome, wearisome, humdrum, routine, ordinary, run-of-the-mill, commonplace, prosaic, uneventful.

3. glum, downcast, dispirited, disheartened, dejected; unhappy, sad, melancholy, blue, depressed, despondent; doleful, somber, sullen, sorrowful, mournful, lugubrious, funereal; forlorn, miserable, wretched.

dreg, *n.* **1. dregs** lees, grounds, sediment, deposit, settlings, draff, heeltap, *Chem.* sublimate, *Chem.* precipitate; residue, residuum, debris, detritus, fecula, remnants, leftovers, remainder, remains, rest; refuse, garbage, trash, rubbish, offal, offscourings, recrement, dross, scoria.

2. *Usu.* **dregs** riffraff, scum, rabble; deadbeats, bums, *Inf.* good-for-nothings, *Inf.* washouts, *Sl.* losers.

3. scrap, piece, particle, mite; bit, little, smidgen, *Chiefly Brit., Inf.* spot; pittance, modicum, moiety, minimum, *Inf.* minim.

drench, *v.* soak, bathe, wash, steep, infuse; tincture, macerate, marinate; saturate, imbue, permeate, souse, drown, inundate, flood; douse, swash, wash, slosh, splash, wet; immerse, immerge, dip, dunk, submerse, submerge, plunge.

dress, *n.* **1.** frock, gown, robe; outfit, suit, ensemble, costume, *Inf.* getup.

2. clothing, clothes, apparel, wearing apparel, garb, attire; raiment, vestments, habit, habiliments, *Inf.* gear, *Inf.* toggery, *Inf.* togs, *Inf.* duds, *Sl.* threads, *Sl.* rags; wardrobe, array, accouterment; livery, uniform.

3. formal attire, formal wear, formals, elegant attire, dress clothes; evening wear, evening dress, evening clothes; evening gown, dinner gown *or* dress; full dress; tuxedo, *Inf.* tux, black tie, white tie and tails, *Inf.* tails, *Sl.* monkey suit, *Sl.* soup and fish; finery, best clothes, best bib and tucker, *Inf.* Sunday clothes, *Inf.* Sunday best, *Inf.* Sunday-go-to-meetings, *Sl.* glad rags, *Sl.* heavy threads.

4. cover, covering, outer covering; skin, outer skin *or* layer; plumage, feathers; coat; pelt, hide.

5. appearance, guise, aspect, look; outfit, trappings, *Inf.* getup, *Inf.* rig, *Inf.* turnout; costume, habit, masquerade, disguise.

—*v.* **6.** clothe, vest, garb, attire, apparel, habit, *Sl.* dude up; robe, gown, drape; outfit, fit out, fit up, fit, accouter, turn out, gear; don, put on, slip on, slip into.

7. array, bedizen, deck, deck out, bedeck, trap, trap out, caparison; beautify, prettify, fix up, prink, *Inf.* titivate, *Inf.* spruce up, *Inf.* doll up, *Inf.* gussy up, *Sl.* trick up, *Sl.* dude up, *Sl.* swank up, *Sl.* fig out.

8. adorn, ornament, decorate, trim, garnish, furbish, *Archaic.* dight, *Archaic.* ouch; spangle, bespangle, stud, bestud, beset; emblazon, blazon, illuminate, bedaub; gild, varnish, trick out.

9. prepare, *Inf.* prep, ready, get *or* make ready, *Inf.* fix.

10. cultivate, till, till the soil, work, work the land; plow, spade; fertilize, manure.

11. comb, comb out, comb out and do up, do up, card; groom, preen, plume.

12. bandage, poultice, plaster, dress [s.o.'s] wounds; splint, strap; treat, doctor, minister to, care for.

13. align, line up, bring into line; straighten, straighten out, adjust, put into order.

14. dress down *Informal.* reprimand, scold, berate. See **reprimand**.

dresser, *n.* bureau, chest of drawers, chest, chiffonier, commode, locker; dressing table, vanity *or* vanity table; wardrobe, chifforobe; sideboard, cabinet.

dressing, *n.* **1.** condiment, relish, sauce, chutney, flavoring.
2. bandage, ligature, (*for the head*) galea, spica, *Surgery.* fascia; pledget, *Trademark.* Band-Aid, gauze pad, pad; *Med.* truss; *Med.* compress; *Surgery.* tourniquet.
3. fertilizer, compost, manure, muck, dung, ordure, guano, night soil.

dressmaker, *n.* seamstress, tailoress; tailor, *Hum.* sartor; clothier, haberdasher, hosier, outfitter; modiste, couturier, couturière.

dribble, *v.* **1.** trickle, drip, drop, fall in drops; sprinkle, drizzle; leak, ooze, exude, seep, filter, filtrate, distill, percolate.
2. purl, gurgle, flow; squirt, spurt, spout, gush, issue, well out *or* forth.
3. drivel, drool, drip saliva, slaver, slobber, slabber; sputter, splutter; snivel, run at the nose.

driblet, *n.* **1.** morsel, bite, mouthful, scrap, small portion *or* part; particle, mite, modicum, minimum, moiety; bit, little, piece, *Inf.* smidgen, minim, *Chiefly Brit., Inf.* spot; speck, splotch, daub, dash, pinch, dab, trace, sprinkling.
2. pittance, small *or* petty sum.

drift, *n.* **1.** impulse, impetus, drive, driving force; pressure, push, urge, rush, sweep, controlling influence; current, flow, run, movement, motion.
2. tendency, direction, bias, trend; course, gravitation, bearing; inclination, bent, leaning, proclivity, propensity, penchant.
3. meaning, intent, purport, tenor, tone, vein; implication, connotation, significance, signification; sense, import, spirit, gist, essence, core, pith.
4. heap, pile, mass, accumulation; mound, bank, dune.
—v. **5.** wander, ramble, rove, roam, meander; deviate, digress, stray, go off the track; peregrinate, tramp, nomadize, *Sl.* bum around.
6. be carried along, be borne, be swayed, go with the wind *or* tide, go with the current.

drill, *n.* **1.** cutting instrument, boring tool, rotary tool.
2. calisthenics, exercise, physical training; gymnastics, slimnastics, aerobics; workout, warm-up.
3. teaching, instruction, grounding, training, coaching, drilling; inculcation, indoctrination, initiation, discipline.
—v. **4.** pierce, bore a hole, bore, puncture, gore, perforate; penetrate, pass through, transpierce.
5. teach, instruct, tutor, school; question, catechize, beat into, cram; indoctrinate, inculcate, instil, infuse; coach, train, initiate, ground.

drink, *v.* **1.** imbibe, quaff, sip, sup, *Archaic.* bib, *Inf.* swig, *Inf.* belt, *Inf.* pull; drain, wash down, toss off; gulp, swallow, *Sl.* guzzle *or* guzzle down, *Sl.* swill *or* swill down.
2. (*all of alcoholic beverages*) tipple, tope, bouse *or* bowse, *Inf.* booze, bibble, nip, *Archaic.* dram; drink like a fish, drink hard, drink seriously; get drunk, *Sl.* get plastered *or* pickled, *Brit. Sl.* get bevied; *All Inf.* gargle, wet *or* moisten one's whistle, take a drop, chug, chug-a-lug, lap, lap up, commune with the spirits, drown one's sorrows; *All Sl.* hit the sauce *or* bottle *or* booze, scoop a few, knock a few back, liquor up, souse, dip the beak, exercise *or* crook *or* bend *or* raise the elbow; overindulge, carouse, revel, wassail, go on a spree, make the rounds, *Sl.* tie one on, *Sl.* go on a binge *or* bender *or* drunk, *Sl.* paint the town red, *Brit. Inf.* pub-crawl.
3. toast, toast to, drink a toast to, drink to, pledge, drink *or* pledge the health of.
4. absorb, suck up, draw up *or* in, take up *or* in, drink up *or* in; sponge, sponge up, soak up, blot up, sop up; ingest.
—n. **5.** beverage, potable *or* potables, drinkable *or* drinkables, liquid, liquid refreshment; soft drink, nonalcoholic beverage; cold drink, thirst quencher.
6. intoxicant, alcoholic beverage, potation; liquor, alcohol, spirits, John Barleycorn, the demon rum, *Inf.* booze, *Inf.* hard stuff, *Sl.* likker, *Sl.* hooch, *Sl.* sauce, *Sl.* red-eye, *Sl.* medicine; *Sl.* rot gut, *Sl.* poison, *Sl.* blue ruin; moonshine, firewater, *Sl.* mountain dew, *Sl.* white lightning; mixed drink, cocktail, highball, *Inf.* chaser; stimulant, bracer, *Inf.* eye-opener; nightcap, *Brit. Inf.* sundowner; the bottle, the cup, the cup that cheers; parting cup, stirrup cup, *Scot.* doch-an-dorrach *or* -dorris *or* wee doch-an-dorrach.
7. intoxication, insobriety, inebriety, inebriation, drunkenness, intemperance, *Inf.* tipsiness; alcoholism, dipsomania, problem *or* heavy drinking, serious drinking, habitual drunkenness, bibulousness, crapulence *or* crapulency, crapulousness; drinking, imbibing, heavy drinking, tippling, toping, bibition, bibation, bibbing, bibbling, *Rare.* bibbery, *Inf.* boozing, *Inf.* swilling, *Sl.* hitting the bottle *or* sauce *or* booze, *Brit. Sl.* bevying.
8. draft, quaff, bumper, potation, libation, *Brit. Sl.* bevy; nip, spot, tot, jigger, *Inf.* finger *or* two; sip, sup, *Inf.* swig, *Inf.* swill, *Inf.* pull, *Inf.* snort, *Inf.* jolt; swallow, *Inf.* slug, *Inf.* guzzle, *Inf.* gargle; lap, slurp.
9. ocean, sea, the deep, the brine, the briny deep, *Inf.* the briny, *Sl.* the big drink.

drinkable, *adj.* **1.** potable, potatory, fit to drink; drinking.
—n. **2.** beverage, potables, drinkables, liquid, liquid refreshment, liquids.

drinker, *n.* **1.** imbiber, bibber, bibbler, *Obs., Rare.* biberon, tippler, quaffer, social drinker.
2. drunkard, drunk, inebriate, sot, soak, tosspot, toper, barfly; alcoholic, chronic alcoholic *or* drunk, dipsomaniac; hard drinker, serious drinker, problem drinker; *All Inf.* guzzler, swiller, soaker, sponge, lovepot; *All Sl.* boozer, boozehound, lush, souse, rummy, wino, alchy, juicehead, hooch hound, gin hound, swillbelly, swillpot, stew, stewbum, elbow-bender *or* elbow-crooker; carouser, reveller, wassailer.

drinking bout, *n.* spree, fling, carouse, carousal, revel, revelry, wassail, celebration, *Scot.* randy; orgy, debauch, saturnalia; drunk, potation, compotation, guzzle, drunken carousal *or* revelry, bacchanal, bacchanalia; *All Sl.* binge, bender, bust, toot, tear, bat, jag, *Brit.* pub-crawl.

drip, *v.* **1.** drop, fall in drops, dribble, trickle; sprinkle, drizzle; leak, ooze, exude, seep, filter, filtrate, distill, percolate.
—n. **2.** *Slang.* bore, *Sl.* drag, *Sl.* deadbeat, *Sl.* pill, damper, *Sl.* downer, wet blanket, kill-joy, *Sl.* party-pooper.

drive, *v.* **1.** hurl, propel, expel, repel, rout, drive away, drive off.
2. task, tax, work; overwork, overtask, overtax, drive into the ground.
3. impel, urge, press, push, thrust, shove; move, actuate, set going, set in motion; spur, prod, prick, goad, poke, lash, whip; induce, compel, coerce, make, force, *Inf.* pressure *or* high-pressure, *Inf.* lean on, *Inf.* squeeze, *Inf.* put the screws on *or* to; constrain, oblige, necessitate, require, demand, leave no option *or* choice.
4. herd, shepherd, ride *or* tend herd, drove, punch cattle, wrangle, round up.
5. chauffeur, taxi, bus, *Inf.* give [s.o.] a lift *or* ride, *Inf.* run [s.o.] [somewhere]; take *or* go for a drive, *Inf.*

take *or* go for a spin *or* whirl, *Sl.* take *or* go for a tool; ride, motor, tour, journey.

6. **drive at** allude to, refer to, suggest, imply, infer, intimate, hint at, mean, have in mind.

7. **drive a hard bargain** bargain, negotiate, haggle, chaffer, dicker, *Inf.* hack *or* hammer *or* work out a deal, *Scot.* argle-bargle.

—n. 8. ride, Sunday drive, *Inf.* spin, *Inf.* whirl, *Inf.* joyride, *Sl.* tool; (*all in a motor vehicle*) trip, quick trip, run, journey, peregrination, excursion, tour; jaunt, outing, junket.

9. energy, vigor, vim, verve, spunk, *Inf.* pep, *Inf.* zip, *Inf.* pizzazz, *Inf.* snap, *Inf.* punch, *Inf.* get-up-and-go; initiative, enterprise, industry; ambition, ambitiousness, aggressiveness, hustle.

10. road, roadway, route, scenic route, alternate route; private road, byway, driveway.

drivel, *v.* 1. drool, drip saliva, slaver, slobber, slabber; sputter, splutter; snivel, sniffle.

2. babble, gibber, *Sl.* gibber-jabber, jargon; twaddle, *Brit.* twattle, blather, blether, *Inf.* blither, drool; talk nonsense, *Inf.* talk through one's hat; ramble, maunder, meander, talk idly, *Inf.* gab, *Sl.* gas; jabber, prate, patter, gabble; clack, clatter, rattle, *Sl.* run off *or* on at the mouth; chatter, prattle, chipper, cackle; chit-chat, chitter-chatter, make small talk.

3. fritter away, squander, idle away, fool away, waste; trifle, loiter, putter, dally, dilly-dally, *Inf.* lallygag, dawdle, pass time idly *or* frivolously; lavish, throw away, misspend, burn, *Sl.* blow, spend recklessly *or* extravagantly; scatter, dissipate, spill, lose; deplete, go *or* run through, consume, exhaust, run out of.

—n. 4. drool, drooling, dripping saliva, slaver, slavering, slobber, slobbering, slabber, slabbering; sputter, sputtering, splutter, spluttering; saliva, spit, spitting, spittle; sputum, mucus, *Vulgar.* snot; snivel, sniffle; runny *or* stuffed nose.

5. nonsense, falderal, gibberish, Jabberwocky; babble, babbling, babblement, *Fr. bavardage*; twaddle, twaddling, *Both Brit.* twattle, twattling; blather, blathering, drool, drooling; rambling, maundering, meandering; jargon, *Sl.* jive, Greek, *Chiefly Southern U.S.* Choctaw; hocus-pocus, mumbo jumbo, abracadabra, open sesame, fiddle-de-dee; moonshine, gobbledegook, foolish humbug, foam, froth, bunkum *or* buncombe, *Sl.* applesauce, *Sl.* eyewash; rubbish, *Sl.* tripe, refuse, *Dial.* culch, chaff, trash, *Inf.* truck, trumpery; tommyrot, *Inf.* rot, *Sl.* garbage, *Sl.* crap, *Sl.* crock, *Sl.* bull; balderdash, hogwash, swill, *Sl.* horsefeathers.

6. stuff, stuff and nonsense, *Inf.* bosh, *Brit. Inf.* gammon, *Brit. Sl.* tosh; fudge, foolishness, folly, rigmarole *or* rigamarole, amphigory; footle, *Inf.* malarkey, *Sl.* bushwa, *Sl.* baloney, *Sl.* bilge *or* bilge water, *Sl.* meshugaas, *Scot. and North Eng.* haver; poppycock, *Inf.* fiddle-faddle, *Inf.* piffle, *Inf.* hooey, *Inf.* kibosh, *Inf.* flapdoodle; idle talk, *Inf.* gab, *Sl.* gas, *Sl.* hot air; jabber, prate, patter, gabble; clack, clatter, rattling, *Sl.* running off *or* on at the mouth; chatter, prattle, chippering, cackle; chit-chat, chitter-chatter, small talk, *Anglo-Indian.* bukh.

driveler, *n.* 1. drooler, slaverer, slobberer, slabberer; splutterer, sputterer, spitter; sniveler, sniffler.

2. babbler, prattler, prater, twaddler, *Brit.* twattler; maunderer, rambler, patterer, patterist, rattlebrain, rattlepate; chatterbox, noisy chatterer, palaverer, magpie, popinjay, *Inf.* jay; excessive talker, jabberer, gabbler, blatherskite, *Sl.* windbag, *Sl.* windjammer, *Inf.* hot-air artist; blabber, blabbermouth, gusher, gossip.

3. fool, ninny, nincompoop, nitwit; simpleton, idiot, *Inf.* moron, imbecile, ignoramus; dunce, dolt, *Inf.* dummy, *Inf.* numskull, *Sl.* dope, jackass.

driver, *n.* 1. chauffeur, coachman, reinsman, whip, *Irish Eng.* jarvey; busdriver, motorman; taxidriver, cabdriver, cabman, *Inf.* cabby, *Inf.* hack *or* hackie, *U.S.* hackman; truck driver, trucker, teamster; wagoner, muleteer, *Sl.* mule skinner.

2. motorist, automobilist, Sunday driver, *Inf.* joyrider, *Sl.* road hog.

3. cowboy, cowpuncher, cowpoke, cow hand, bronco buster, *Western U.S.* buckaroo, *Southwestern U.S.* vaquero, gaucho; drover, cowherd, cattle-herder, *Chiefly Brit.* grazier, *Brit.* cowman, *Obs.* neatherd.

drizzle, *v.* sprinkle, spray, mist, *Chiefly Dial.* mizzle; spray, wet, dribble.

droll, *adj.* 1. funny, humorous, clownish, comic, comical; laughable, ridiculous, facetious, jocular, joking, witty, waggish; amusing, diverting, entertaining, sportive, jocose, merry; farcical, ludicrous, zany.

2. bizarre, quaint, whimsical, queer, strange, odd, eccentric; outlandish, grotesque, *Sl.* rum.

drollery, *n.* jest, joke, witticism, waggery; mummery, buffoonery, zanyism, farce, absurdity, burlesque; humor, wit, dry wit, esprit; prank, tomfoolery, shenanigan, monkeyshine.

drone[1], *n.* parasite, leech, sponger, *Inf.* sponge, *Inf.* deadbeat; do-nothing, idler, fainéant, loafer, *Inf.* bum, sluggard, slugabed, lazybones; laggard, loiterer, lounger, lingerer, trifler, dawdler, dallier; daydreamer, lotus-eater; shirker, goldbrick, *Sl.* goof-off; good-for-nothing, ne'er-do-well, *Fr. vaurien*, worthless person.

drone[2], *v.* 1. buzz, hum, murmur, bombilate, bombinate, whisper; whizz, whir, wheeze, sibilate, hiss, fizzle, sizzle; sigh, rustle, sough.

—n. 2. buzz, hum, murmur, bombination; purr, whirring; sibilation, hiss, whizz; sigh, rustle, sough.

drool, *v.* 1. water at the mouth, drivel, dribble, drip saliva, slaver, slobber; sputter, splutter.

2. babble, gibber, *Sl.* gibber-jabber, blather, blether, *Inf.* blither. See **drivel** (*def.* **2**).

—n. 3. drivel, slaver, slobber, slabber. See **drivel** (*def.* **4**).

droop, *v.* 1. sag, hang down, give way; bend, bow, (*of trees, flowers, etc.*) nod; slouch, crouch, stoop; dip, lean, curve; sink, slump, settle, drop; hang loosely, swag, depend from, dangle, loll.

2. languish, *Dial.* dwine, flag, fade, faint, weaken; wither, wilt, shrivel, decay, molder, rot; decline, wane, ebb, fall off; fail, deteriorate, degenerate; waste away, melt away, fade away *or* out.

3. despond, falter, give in *or* way, lose hope, lose heart, give up, surrender, quit, *Sl.* pack it in, cry quits, throw in the towel, throw in the sponge; pine away, mope, mourn, lament, grieve, sorrow.

drop, *n.* 1. globule, glob, droplet, bead, gutta; blob, bubble; dewdrop, pearl, tear; spheroid, oval; earring, ornament, pendant.

2. (*usu. all of liquid*) small quantity, bit, little, *Inf.* smidgen, minim, *Chiefly Brit., Inf.* spot; speck, trickle, splotch, daub, dash, pinch, dab, trace, sprinkling; driblet, particle, mite, modicum, minimum, moiety; (*all usu. of alcohol*) swallow, dram, toast, sip, draught, *Inf.* nip, *Inf.* bracer, *Inf.* swig.

3. confection, candy, hard candy, sweet, bonbon, *Trademark.* life-saver; lozenge, cough drop, glycerine tablet.

4. fall, descent, declivity, slope, sloping; incline, inclination, declination, declension; precipice, abyss, chasm.

5. decline, fall-off, drop-off; depreciation, devaluation; deterioration, downgrade, downturn, downslide; diminution, decrease, lessening; reduction, cutback, fall-back.

6. trapdoor, gallows, gibbet, swing, scaffold, platform.

—*v.* **7.** fall in drops, drip, trickle, dribble; distill, sprinkle; leak, ooze, seep, filter, percolate.

8. sink, fall, descend, precipitate; dive, plunge, plummet, swoop; plop, fall plump.

9. fall down, faint, swoon, be stricken, collapse; die, fall dead, drop dead.

10. abandon, forsake, desert, leave behind, throw over, jilt, run out on, *Inf.* leave flat; discard, cast off, jettison, throw away, get rid of, toss out, *Inf.* ditch, *Inf.* chuck.

11. discontinue, give up, retire from, withdraw from, stop, end, cease, *Inf.* quit cold; throw up, lose hope of, despair of; forbear, desist from; forgo, do *or* go without, dispense with, waive, lay aside.

12. repudiate, reject, disown, renounce; renege, forswear, disavow, disclaim, recant; bail out of, pull out of, bow out of, *Inf.* back out of.

13. squat, crouch, lie low; cringe, cower.

14. sink, fall lower, drop off, fall off, decline; diminish, lessen, subside, slacken, dwindle, taper off; decrease, depreciate.

15. reduce, curtail, cut, slash; bring down, lower, depress; demote, degrade.

16. discharge, unload, set down, leave off, let off; let go of, release, ungrip; shed, slough off, cast off, doff, discard.

17. omit, leave out, eliminate, deselect; (*usu. in reference to speech or writing*) elide, slur, blend, contract.

18. fell, floor, bring down; shoot, kill, murder, (*of game*) bag. See **kill**.

19. dismiss, discharge, oust, *Sl.* bounce; fire, let go, *Sl.* sack, *Inf.* give [s.o.] his walking papers.

20. (*all of animals*) give birth to, bear, bring forth, litter, spawn; foal, lamb, calve, whelp, pup, kitten.

21. drop off a. fall asleep, doze, doze off, drowse, *Inf.* snooze, nap, nod. **b.** decline, decrease. See *def.* **14** above.

drought, *n.* **1.** aridity, aridness, parchedness, extreme dryness, thirstiness, waterlessness, droughtiness; dehydration, evaporation, desiccation; torridity, torridness.

2. dearth, scarcity, scarceness, lack, want; deficiency, shortness, shortage, insufficiency, stint; scantiness, paucity, exiguity, meagerness, rareness; sparseness, barrenness, emptiness, vacuity; depletion, exhaustion.

drove, *n.* **1.** herd, pack, flock, gaggle; bevy, covey, flight; brood, hatch, litter; school, swarm, shoal.

2. band, company, group, body, assemblage, assembly, aggregation; multitude, gathering, crowd, swarm, horde, host, throng, rabble, mob, crush.

drown, *v.* **1.** go down, go under, sink, descend to Davy Jones' locker, perish at sea, descend to a watery grave.

2. submerge, submerse, immerse, engulf; flood, inundate, deluge, drench, swamp.

3. overpower, overwhelm, overcome; deaden, stifle, muffle, silence, mute; swallow up, engulf; extinguish, obliterate, wipe out; suppress, quash, quench.

drowse, *v.* **1.** be in a trance *or* daze, walk around half asleep; drag oneself around, be sluggish *or* listless; languish, droop, flag.

2. *Often* **drowse away** doze, nap, catnap, nod off, drop off, take a siesta, *Inf.* snooze, *Inf.* catch forty winks; sleep, slumber, count sheep, visit the sandman, go to the land of Nod, *Sl.* log Z's, *Sl.* catch some Z's, *Sl.* catch a little shut-eye, *Brit. Sl.* doss; rest, repose, recline, relax, lie back.

drowsy, *adj.* **1.** groggy, sleepy, half asleep, somnolent, slumberous, slumbery; dozy, nodding, dozing, heavy-eyed, yawning, oscitant.

2. sluggish, torpid, lethargic, listless; otiose, lazy, slow, lackadaisical, indolent; dull, drugged, dazed, *Inf.* dopey; lifeless, sleeping, asleep, dormant, comatose.

3. somniferous, somnific, somnifacient, soporific, sleep-inducing, hypnotic; sedative, narcotic, opiate, opiatic, drugging.

drub, *v.* **1.** club, cane, birch; cudgel, flog, bludgeon, baste, bastinado; strap, switch, lash, scourge, whip, horsewhip, flagellate, flail; sandbag, blackjack, *Brit.* cosh, sledgehammer, hammer; beat, batter, thrash, curry, *Brit.* towel, *Inf.* lace; fustigate, *Dial.* larrup, give [s.o.] a fat lip; pound, pummel, pelt, paste, wallop; beat the bejesus out of, beat [s.o.'s] brains bloody, beat to a pulp, beat black and blue; work over, *Sl.* waste, stomp, do a job on, clobber; wipe up the floor with, mutilate, brutalize; hit, sock, strike, smite, punch; cuff, whack, thwack, knock, strike; buffet, bop, *Sl.* whump, *Sl.* biff, thump, bop; spank, tan [s.o.'s] hide.

2. defeat, overcome, best, worst; ace, knock out, K.O., floor; win over, beat out, trim; eclipse, surpass, outdo, outstrip, top, prevail over, stop; rout, vanquish, lick, *Sl.* shellac; trounce, blitz, cream, trample; demolish, make mincemeat of, pulverize, crush, destroy, wipe out, kill, ravage.

drubbing, *n.* beating, thrashing, bludgeoning, workover, *Law.* battery; clubbing, caning, bastinado, flogging; walloping, pummeling, fustigation, pounding, thumping, stomping; whipping, defeat, knockout, trip to dreamland; trouncing, vanquishment, loss.

drudge, *n.* **1.** plodder, toiler, *Sl.* grind, plugger; common laborer, slave, factotum, scrubwoman, scullion, dishwasher; menial, flunky, fag, hack.

—*v.* **2.** work hard, toil, moil, labor, *Brit.* fag; slave, plod, grub, *Inf.* plug *or* plug along, *Inf.* grind; keep one's nose to the grindstone, work in a sweatshop, work in a saltmill; sweat and strain, get rock-pile duty, scrub, pound away.

drudgery, *n.* hard work, toil, moil, travail, *Brit.* fag, slave labor; sweatshop work, sweat of one's brow; treadmill, hack work, assembly line, *Sl.* the pits; meniality, slavery, bondage, serfdom.

drug, *n.* **1.** medicine, medication, medicament, remedy, physic, cure; cure-all, panacea, wonder drug.

2. narcotic, *Inf.* opiate, depressant, sedative, tranquilizer, soporific, hypnotic; barbiturate, *Sl.* barbs. *Inf.* down *or* downer, quaalude, *Sl.* lude, *Sl.* red; heroin, *Sl.* H, *Sl.* horse, *Sl.* smack, *Sl.* junk, *Sl.* scag, *Sl.* crank; stimulant, antidepressant, energizer, amphetamine, *Inf.* up *or* upper, *Sl.* white cross, *Sl.* black beauty, *Sl.* bennie *or* benzie, *Sl.* dexie, *Sl.* speed, *Sl.* meth, *Sl.* pep pill; cocaine, *Sl.* coke, *Sl.* C, *Sl.* snow, *Chiefly Brit. Sl.* charlie; *Sl.* dope, marijuana, *U.S. Sl.* Mary-Jane *or* MJ, *Sl.* pot, *Sl.* grass, *Sl.* weed, *Sl.* reefer; hashish, *Sl.* hash, THC, *Sl.* killer weed, *Sl.* angel dust, *Sl.* thai stick *or* finger, opium; hallucinogen, psychedelic, LSD, *Sl.* acid, *Sl.* orange sunshine, *Sl.* windowpane, *Sl.* blotter, *Sl.* purple haze, STP; mescaline, peyote, mescal buttons, *Sl.* buttons, *Sl.* mushrooms; belladonna, deadly nightshade, jimson weed, *Sl.* loco weed. See **stimulant** (*def.* **1**) and **depressant**.

—*v.* **3.** stupefy, poison, narcotize, put under the influence, benumb, numb, blunt, dull, anesthetize, render insensible, deaden.

4. dope, administer a drug, dose, medicate, treat.

drugged, *adj.* **1.** doped, *Inf.* dopey, sluggish, befuddled, dazed, stupefied, narcotized, numbed, benumbed, anesthetized, under, under the influence.

2. turned on, *Sl.* stoned, *Inf.* high, *Sl.* up, *Sl.* off, *Sl.*

high as a kite, *Sl.* flying; hyperactive, *Sl.* hyper, *Sl.* charged up, *Sl.* hopped up, *Sl.* speedy, *Sl.* buzzed; *All Slang.* spaced out, spacey, tripped out, out, gone, out of it, bombed, zonked, blown out, ripped, wasted, wrecked, blitzed, wiped out, knocked out.

druggist, *n.* apothecary, pharmacist, pharmaceutist, pharmacopolist, pharmaceutical chemist.

drum, *n.* **1.** tambour, tympanum, tabor, taboret; kettledrum, bass drum, side drum, tom-tom, snare-drum, traps, tambourine, Oriental drum, war drum; *Anat., Zool.* tympanic membrane *or* eardrum.

—*v.* **2.** beat, tap, sound, thrum, resound; reiterate, drive home, harp on, hammer at.

3. drum out expell, dismiss, disown, outlaw; oust, dismiss, discharge, cashier, fire, *Sl.* bounce, *Sl.* sack; demote, rip the buttons off of.

4. drum up obtain, create, canvass, solicit, petition; round up, scare up, bid for, beat the bushes for.

drunk, *adj.* **1.** intoxicated, inebriated, inebriate, inebrious, bibacious, crapulent, crapulous; drunken, sodden, besotted, sotted, sottish, awash, *Literary.* in one's cups; under the weather; saturated, soused, full, *Scot.* fou; tipsy, grogged, *Archaic.* groggy, fuddled, muddled, obfuscated, woozy, bleary-eyed, pie-eyed, glassy-eyed; far-gone, stupefied, staggering, staggering drunk, drunk as a lord, drunk as a piper, drunk as a fiddler, drunk as a skunk *or* owl; merry, happy, gay, jolly; maudlin.

2. *All Inf.* boozy, tight, lit, lit up, lit to the gills, illuminated, liquored-up; half seas over, three *or* four sheets to the wind, under the sauce, off-color; pickled, lathered, high, high as a kite, fried to one's tonsils, full to the back teeth, primed to the sticking point; mellow, have a jag on, feeling good, feeling no pain; blind, blind drunk, dead drunk, paralyzed, out of it, out cold, out, under the table, helpless, passed-out, in bed with one's boots on.

3. *All Sl.* loaded, lubricated, oiled well-oiled, stewed, stewed to the gills, tanked, fried, boiled, *Brit.* pissed, *Brit.* bevied; primed, gassed, bombed, stoned, zonked, ripped, blitzed, scrooched, whiffed, whoozled; polluted, crocked, cocked, cocked to the gills, cockeyed, canned, sloshed, squiffy, potted, plastered, sozzled, crocko; stiff, ossified, stinko, stinking, plotched, shelacked, swacked, screwed, blotto, smashed, skunk-drunk.

4. excited, breathless, exuberant; exhilarated, invigorated, stimulated, animated, inspirited; ecstatic, enraptured, transported, abandoned; fervid, fervent, ardent, impassioned, passionate; inflamed, enflamed, fired-up, heated, hot, red-hot; flushed, feverish, delirious.

—*n.* **5.** drunkard, inebriate, sot, soak, tosspot, toper, bibber, bibbler, *Obs., Rare.* biberon, barfly; alcoholic, chronic alcoholic *or* drunk, dipsomaniac; drinker, hard drinker, problem drinker, serious drinker; *All Inf.* guzzler, swiller, soaker, sponge, lovepot; *All Sl.* boozer, boozehound, lush, souse, rummy, wino, alchy, juicehead, juicer, hooch hound, gin hound, swillbelly, swillpot, stew, stewbum, elbow-bender, elbow-crooker.

6. drinking-bout, compotation, guzzle, drunken carousal *or* revelry, bacchanal, bacchanalia; spree, fling, carouse, carousal, revel, revelry, wassail, *Scot.* randy; *All Sl.* binge, bender, bust, toot, tear, bat, jag, *Brit.* pub-crawl.

drunkard, *n.* drunk, inebriate, sot, soak, tosspot, toper, bibber, bibbler, *Obs., Rare.* biberon, barfly; alcoholic, chronic alcoholic *or* drunk, dipsomaniac; drinker, hard drinker, serious drinker, problem drinker; *All Inf.* guzzler, swiller, soaker, sponge, lovepot; *All Sl.* boozer, boozehound, lush, souse, rummy, wino, alchy, dipso, juicehead, juicer, hooch hound, gin hound, swillbelly, swillpot, stew, stewbum, elbow-bender, elbow-crooker.

dry, *adj.* **1.** dried, dehydrated, desiccated, exsiccated, evaporated, *Chem.* anhydrous; juiceless, sapless, undampened, unmoistened, dried up, dried out, arid, sear, parched, rainless, droughty; thirsty, unwatered, waterless, bare, barren, fruitless, sterile, unproductive; (*all food*) stale, hard, hardened.

2. dull, uninteresting, boring, tedious, tiresome, wearisome; dry-as-dust, dull-as-dishwater; flat, stale and unprofitable; commonplace, prosaic, prosy; meager, plain, unadorned, bald.

3. droll, witty, waggish, humorous; satirical, sarcastic, cynical.

4. severe, unemotional, indifferent, cold, impersonal, aloof, remote.

—*v.* **5.** dehydrate, exsiccate, desiccate, parch, make dry; preserve, cure.

6. wither, wilt, shrivel, dry up, harden.

7. sponge, wipe off, wipe away; swab, towel, drain, blot.

—*n.* **8.** *Informal.* prohibitionist, teetotaler. See **teetotaler**.

dual, *adj.* double, twofold, duplicate, duplex, dualistic, binary, biform, bioform, bifold; twin, matched, paired, coupled, geminate.

duality, *n.* twoness, doubleness, duplexity, biformity, dichotomy, dualism.

dub, *v.* **1.** knight, confer knighthood upon; name, call, confer, entitle; designate, style, term, label, tag; baptize, christen, denominate, nominate, nickname; invest, instate, induct, inaugurate.

2. dress, smooth, plane, face, shave, pare; planish, mill, even, level; rub, burnish, furbish, scrub, scour.

dubiety, *n.* doubtfulness, doubt, dubiosity, skepticism, dubitation; incertitude, uncertainty, hesitation, reluctance; suspicion, mistrust, distrust, disbelief, incredulity; misgiving, qualm, scruple; unbelief, agnosticism, Pyrrhonism.

dubious, *adj.* **1.** doubtful, equivocal, ambiguous, unsure, indeterminate, dubitable; unclear, obscure, vague, hazy, foggy, nebulous, indefinite, imprecise; enigmatic, cryptic, mysterious, apocryphal.

2. questionable, shady, *Inf.* fishy, rotten in Denmark; untrustworthy, unreliable, debatable, moot, disputable, controvertible.

3. undetermined, unsettled, undecided, unresolved; problematic, indecisive, speculative, open, tentative, pending.

4. wavering, hesitant, uncertain, fluctuating; irresolute, vacillating, variable, oscillatory, inconstant; bewildered, puzzled, perplexed, confused.

duck, *v.* **1.** immerse, plunge, throw in, dive, dip, wet; souse, submerge, douse, drench; plunk, drown, *Inf.* dunk.

2. bow, bob, drop; stoop, bend, squat, hunker down, hunch down, get *or* fall down, hit the deck, hit the dirt, *Sl.* hit it.

3. avoid, evade, elude, shun; dodge, parry, turn aside; swerve, pull away, recoil, shy away *or* off, steer clear of.

duct, *n.* pipe, tube, conduit, *Anat., Zool., Bot.* vessel; flue, chimney, smokestack, funnel; drain, culvert, sewer; channel, canal, passage.

ductile, *adj.* **1.** malleable, moldable, shapeable, formable, flexible, bendable, pliant, pliable, plastic, soft; elastic, stretchable, tensible, tensile, extensible, *Chiefly Zool., Anat.* extensile; (*of people and animals*) lissome, limber, supple, lithe, willowy, double-jointed.

2. tractable, manageable, manipulatable, manipulable, docile, facile, easy, *Scot.* tawrie; susceptible, disposed, inclined, amenable, compliant, complying, cooperative, agreeable, accommodating, willing, assenting, nonresistant, passive; teachable, educable, instructible, schoolable; trainable, coachable, disciplinable.

ductility, *n.* **1.** malleability, moldability, flexibility, pliability, pliableness, pliancy, pliantness, plasticity, softness; elasticity, tensibility, tensibleness, tensility, tensileness, stretchability, extensibility, extensibleness, ductileness; (*all of people and animals*) lissomeness, limberness, suppleness, litheness, willowiness.

2. tractability, tractableness, manageability, manageableness, docility, facility, easiness; susceptibility, amenability, compliance, cooperativeness, agreeableness, willingness, non-resistance, passivity, passiveness; teachability, teachableness, educability, educableness, instructibility, schoolability; trainability, trainableness, coachability, disciplinability, disciplinableness.

dude, *n.* dandy, jack-a-dandy, fop, Beau Brummell, fancy Dan, popinjay, coxcomb, *Sl.* peacock; exquisite, fashion plate, the glass of fashion and the mold of form, macaroni, sharp dresser, zoot suiter, silkstocking; blade, gay blade, buck, man about town, boulevardier, *Chiefly Brit.* blood; beau, gallant, ladies' man, lady-killer, spark, *Sl.* swell, *Brit. Inf.* toff.

due, *adj.* **1.** payable, immediately payable, mature, outstanding, receivable; owed, unpaid, in arrears.

2. rightful, right, proper, right and proper, correct, fitting, appropriate, apposite, apt, lawful, meet; adequate, sufficient, enough, satisfactory, ample, plenty; commensurate, proportionate, corresponding.

3. worthy, meriting, meritorious, deserving, entitled to, coming to; warranted, merited, deserved, richly deserved, well-earned, justified, (*usu. in reference to punishment*) condign.

4. scheduled, slated, booked, billed; expected, awaited, anticipated, look-for.

5. **due to** attributable, assignable, ascribable, imputable, chargeable, accountable; owing to, assigned *or* referred to, derivable from.

—*n.* **6.** right, rightful *or* lawful claim, birthright, natural *or* divine right, prerogative; desert, just deserts, *Inf.* comeuppance.

7. **dues** fee, membership fee, charge, charges.

duel, *n.* shoot-out, affair of honor, *Fr. affaire d'honneur,* monomachy.

dugout, *n.* **1.** shelter, hovel, lean-to; cave, excavation; intrenchment, trench, ditch, foxhole; fortification, barricade.

2. dory, canoe, kayak.

dulcet, *adj.* **1.** melodious, canorous, lyrical, musical, tuneful; harmonious, euphonious, symphonious, mellifluous, mellifluent; silvery, silver-toned, clear as a bell.

2. pleasant, agreeable, soothing, solacing; peaceful, tranquil, halcyon, calm, mellow; lovely, attractive, charming, enchanting, ravishing; delightful, winsome, sweet.

dull, *adj.* **1.** unintelligent, witless, slow-witted, dull-witted; stolid, obtuse, crass, Boeotian, bovine, blockish, lumpish; dense, thick-headed, *Inf.* thick, slow, stupid, *Brit., Australian Inf.* dill, *Scot. and North Eng.* dowf; backward, doltish, *Sl.* birdbrained, simple; empty-headed, vacuous; unimaginative, undiscerning.

2. insensible, unfeeling, numb; callous, hardened, inured; unresponsive, insensitive, unsympathetic, unreceptive; passionless, indifferent, uncaring.

3. sluggish, phlegmatic, lethargic, torpid, heavy, lifeless; languid, listless, spiritless, apathetic; inactive, inert, stagnant; lazy, oscitant, drowsy.

4. tedious, tiresome, boring, boresome, wearisome, uninteresting, *Sl.* dead, dry, dry-as-dust; tasteless, bland, insipid, jejune, flat, vapid, *Sl.* for the birds, *Sl.* nothing, *Sl.* blah; uneventful, humdrum, monotonous, ordinary, run-of-the-mill, commonplace, prosaic, matter-of-fact.

5. dreary, dismal, *Scot. and North Eng.* dowie, bleak, drab, somber; murky, lowering, gloomy, dark, sunless; cheerless, sad, melancholy.

6. cloudy, dim, indistinct, blurred, blurry, gray, opaque; lackluster, lusterless, colorless, *Optics.* achromatic; tarnished, faded, washed out; deadened, dulled, muted, muffled, stifled, softened.

7. blunt, unsharpened, dulled, pointless, edgeless.

—*v.* **8.** blunt, take the edge off of, obtund; lessen, allay, assuage, alleviate, palliate; appease, soothe, relieve, ease, soften, cushion; slake, quench, deaden; decrease, diminish, reduce; modify, moderate, temper.

9. stupefy, benumb, hebetate, besot; sedate, narcotize, opiate, drug, tranquilize, lethargize.

10. fade, blanch, bleach, whiten, gray, wash out; etiolate, achromatize, decolor, decolorize.

11. obscure, cloud, becloud, blur; darken, dim, bedim, bedull; tarnish, sully, stain.

12. depress, deject, dishearten, dispirit, discourage; damp, dampen, throw cold water on, throw a wet blanket on, cast a pall over.

dullard, *n.* dolt, dunce, *Inf.* deadhead, blockhead, *Sl.* dummkopf, oaf, clod; loggerhead, thickhead, *Inf.* chump, *Inf.* coot, *Inf.* dummy, *Sl.* dodo, *Sl.* dope, *Sl.* dumbbell, *Sl.* meatball *or* meathead; fathead, numskull, beetlehead, bonehead, dunderhead, dunderpate, chucklehead, *Sl.* dumbhead, *Sl.* lunkhead, *Sl.* lardhead, *Inf.* knucklehead, *Sl.* stupidhead; donkey, ass, *Sl.* goon, lubber, lout; simpleton, Simple Simon, saphead, noodle, idiot, cuckoo, *Inf.* jay; idiot, *Inf.* moron, *Sl.* retread, imbecile, mooncalf, lamebrain, dim-wit, nit-wit, half-wit, *Sl.* zombie, goose; pinhead, *Sl.* birdbrain, scatterbrain, *Sl.* flake, rattlehead, rattlebrain, harebrain, *Sl.* dingbat, *Sl.* ding-a-ling, featherbrain, addle-brain, addle-head; fool, ninny, nincompoop, ninnyhammer, *Sl.* yo-yo, tomfool; *All Sl.* jerk, schmuck, boob, booby, noodle, nudnik, blubberhead; ignoramus, know-nothing, schlep, *Inf.* lightweight, lowbrow.

duly, *adv.* **1.** in a due manner, properly, as is proper, seemly, suitably, fitly, fittingly, befittingly, as is fitting, rightly; becomingly, decorously.

2. in due season, in due time; regularly, punctually.

dumb, *adj.* **1.** mute, speechless, silent, noiseless, soundless, mum, aphonic; voiceless, non-vocal, wordless, pantomimic; reticent, taciturn, quiet, uncommunicative, reserved, tongue-tied.

2. *Informal.* stupid, slow-witted, featherbrained, dull. See **dull** (*def.* **1**).

dumfound, *v.* astound, astonish, amaze, *Inf.* flabbergast, strike dumb, render speechless, dumfounder; stun, stagger, take aback, floor, shock, jar, jolt, *Inf.* bowl over, *Inf.* give [s.o.] a turn, *Inf.* catch [s.o.] up short; stupefy, petrify, paralyze, benumb, incapacitate; startle, surprise, disconcert; confuse, baffle, confound nonplus, perplex, embarrass, pose; bewilder, dazzle, electrify, *Inf.* take one's breath away; unbalance, disorient, *Inf.* catch off guard.

dumfounded, *adj.* astounded, amazed, astonished, *Inf.* flabbergasted, taken aback, floored, *Inf.* bowled over; stunned, shocked, startled, surprised, disconcerted, dazed, speechless, dumb, numb, paralyzed, frozen, petrified, incapacitated; confused, disoriented, baffled, confounded, nonplused, perplexed, bewildered; *Inf.* shaken, *Sl.* shook, *Inf.* caught up short, *Inf.* caught off guard, *Inf.* thrown for a loss, *Sl.* knocked for a loop.

dummy, *n.* **1.** copy, sample, representation, reproduction, reprint; substitute, imitation, counterfeit, sham.
2. mannequin, model, lay figure, dressmaker's dummy.
3. *Informal.* dolt, blockhead, numskull, dullard. See **dullard.**
4. scapegoat, *Inf.* goat, straw man; agent, representative, alternative, double.
5. *Slang.* mute, deaf-mute, dumb person.

dump, *v.* **1.** drop, fling down, let fall, deposit; throw away, dispose, discharge, cast off.
2. empty out, pour out, unload, rid, unburden, disburden, *Naut.* break bulk.
3. fire, dismiss, expel, oust, *Inf.* give [s.o.] his walking papers; *All Sl.* sack, can, give [s.o.] the boot, bag, bump, bounce.
—*n.* **4.** junkyard, wasteyard, trash pile *or* dump, rubbish heap, refuse heap, *Brit. Dial.* midden.

dun[1], *v.* (*usu. for payment of debts*) importune, press, urge, tax, solicit, beset, buttonhole; ply, push, besiege, *Inf.* work on; plague, pester, nag, *Sl.* bug.

dun[2], *adj.* **1.** greyish-brown, swarthy, dusky, umber, drab; khaki, sallow, tawny, muddy.
2. dark, gloomy, somber, dim, tenebrous, shadowy; murky, pitchy, coaly, dirty, sooty; cloudy, overcast, leaden, fuliginous, crepuscular.

dunce, *n.* dolt, numskull, simpleton, dullard. See **dullard.**

dune, *n.* sand hill, sand ridge, mound, moor, barrow, *Scot.* brae; knoll, swell, hillock, hummock, monticule, molehill, anthill.

dung, *n.* manure, excrement, muck, fertilizer, ordure, guano; dressing, night soil, droppings, cow *or* buffalo chips, *U.S. West* cow pies, coprolites, coproliths, *Sl.* flops; feces, stools, waste, feculence.

dungeon, *n.* **1.** oubliette, black hole, *Sl.* the hole, *Inf.* solitary; cell, cage, enclosure, lockup, place of confinement, *Sl.* coop.
2. (*all in a castle*) donjon, keep, hold, stronghold, safehold.

dupe, *n.* **1.** gull, gudgeon, *Brit. Dial.* cull, *Archaic.* cully, *Inf.* chump, *Sl.* sap, *Sl.* schnook, *Sl.* schlemiel, *Sl.* boob; greenhorn, sitting duck, easy *or* soft mark *or* target, *Inf.* sucker, *Inf.* cinch, *Sl.* patsy, *Sl.* pigeon, *U.S. Sl.* fall guy, *Sl.* softie *or* soft touch, *Sl.* pushover; laughing-stock, butt, fair game, fool, everybody's fool, *Inf.* goat, *Brit. Sl.* mug.
2. pawn, puppet, tool, instrument, flunky, lackey, cat's paw, creature, minion, dummy, *Sl.* stooge.
—*v.* **3.** delude, deceive, fool, take in, throw dust in the eyes of, pull the wool over the eyes of, *Inf.* slip *or* pass one over on; gull, cozen, defraud, cheat; rook, victimize, defraud, bilk, swindle, cog, *Archaic.* chouse, *Sl.* take, *Sl.* snooker; pass off, palm off, impose upon, pull a fast one on, *Inf.* throw a curve; hoodwink, trick, outwit, bamboozle, overreach; lead on, take for a ride, *Inf.* fake [s.o.] out, *Inf.* rope [s.o.] in, *Inf.* string along; *All Inf.* jive, fast-talk, flam, hype, buffalo, bulldoze; *All Sl.* con, snow, suck *or* sucker in, murphy.

duplicate, *v.* **1.** copy, replicate, clone; reproduce, repeat, double, make twofold, perform again; copy, run off, *Trademark.* Mimeograph, mimeo, *Trademark.* Xerox.
—*n.* **2.** copy, facsimile, replica, reproduction, replication, clone; twin, double, likeness, match, mate, fellow, counterpart, look-alike, ringer, dead ringer; carbon, carbon copy, transcript.
—*adj.* **3.** corresponding, matching, twin, exactly alike; similar, alike, the same, Tweedledum and Tweedledee, *Inf.* like two peas in a pod, *Inf.* spitting image, *Inf.* spit and image; duplex, bifold; double, twofold, doubled.

duplicity, *n.* guile, chicanery, double-dealing, ambidexterity; artificed, trickery, Machiavellianism, Machiavellism, deceit, improbity; equivocation, dissimilation, cant, lip-service, mouth-honor; treachery, foul play, betrayal, Judas kiss, disloyalty, bad-faith, infidelity, faithlessness, perfidy, breach of trust, *Inf.* two-timing; dishonesty, insincerity, hypocrisy, mendacity, deception; knavery, roguery, rascality, fraud.

durability, *n.* durableness, endurance, lastingness; everlastingness; perpetualness; persistence, perdurability, imperishability, incorruptibility; longevity, duration, continuance; immutability, changelessness, invariability, incommutability; permanence, stability, steadfastness, reliability, dependability, firmness, fastness, constancy.

durable, *adj.* **1.** enduring, abiding, persisting, continuing; resistant, stout, long-lasting, strong, substantial, sound, holding up well; imperishable, perdurable, unfading, undecaying, incorruptible, amaranthine, perennial.
2. endless, everlasting, longstanding; established, firm, fast, fixed, stable, constant, permanent; immutable, changeless, unchangeable, unalterable, incommutable, invariable; undeviating, unfaltering, unwavering, steadfast, steady, reliable, dependable.

duration, *n.* extent, extension, continuance, endurance, perpetuation, continuum; period of time, period, time; age, life, lifetime, existence; term, space, course, span, spell, stage, stretch, sentence.

duress, *n.* **1.** compulsion, coaction, coercion, force; constraint, oppression, control, arm-twisting, pressure, exaction, extortion; power, dint, discipline, enforcement, strength.
2. restraint, imprisonment, incarceration, immurement, jailing; detention, confinement, captivity; quarantine, isolation; arrest, custody, care, keeping, guardianship; bondage, thralldom; shackles, manacles, fetters, bonds, irons, stocks.

during, *prep.* throughout, through, for the time of, while, over; in, within, until; continuing, pending.

dusk, *n.* **1.** twilight, crepuscule, *Literary.* gloaming; late afternoon, evening, eventide, evenfall, eve, *Archaic.* even, *Archaic.* evensong, sundown, sunset, moonrise, day's end, edge of night, nightfall.
2. shade, shadiness, shadow, shadowiness, dimness, cloudiness, fogginess, mistiness, haziness, murk, murkiness; semi-darkness, darkness, gloom, gloominess, tenebrousness, somberness, obscurity.

dusky, *adj.* **1.** shadowy, shady, dim, dark, unlit, unilluminated, *Literary.* darkling; gray, cloudy, foggy, misty, hazy, murky; overcast, gloomy, somber, lowering, tenebrous, obscure.
2. darkish, dark-colored, grayish, dingy, sooty, smoky, fuliginous, charcoal; ebony, sable, black, inky, pitchy, pitch-dark, pitch-black, jetblack, jetty; (*of the skin, complexion, etc.*) swarthy, swarth, swart, olive, olive-skinned, dark-skinned, dark-complexioned, dark-complected.

dust, *n.* **1.** powdery dirt, sawdust, filings; soot, smut.
2. earth, ground, land, soil, dirt; turf, sward, sod, clay.
3. rubbish, riffraff, rubble, trash; junk, worthless stuff, *Sl.* dreck; remains, leavings, leftovers, scraps; filth, dirt, offscourings; dregs, remnants, odds and ends.
4. commotion, turmoil, tumult, turbulence; disorder, chaos, confusion, upheaval; disruption, distraction, disturbance, uproar, racket, fracas, rumpus.
5. bite the dust a. die, drop dead, *Sl.* croak, perish, pass away, expire. **b.** lose, fail, suffer defeat,

go down, go under.

6. **lick the dust** a. See *def.* **5a.** b. grovel, demean oneself, kowtow, toady, truckle, bootlick.

7. **throw the dust in [s.o.'s] eyes** deceive, mislead, delude, fool, take in, *Sl.* con, *Sl.* put [s.o.] on, pull the wool over [s.o.'s] eyes.

—*v.* 8. clean, cleanse, wipe off, sweep out, mop.

9. powder, sprinkle, spray, spread, strew.

dutiful, *adj.* respectful, regardful, deferential, reverent, filial; moral, virtuous, ethical, righteous; conscientious, responsible, punctilious, reliable; considerate, thoughtful, polite, courteous, civil; compliant, obedient, faithful, manageable, willing, capitulating, obliging; accommodating, agreeable, nonresisting, unassertive, acquiescent, yielding, submissive, malleable, flexible, pliant, adapting, adaptable, docile, tractable.

duty, *n.* 1. obligation, function, business; responsibility, trust, office, charge, care; requirement, burden, onus, devoir; assignment, commission, chore, work, task, routine, job; engagement, occupation, service; mission, calling; part, role, bit.

2. deference, obedience, respect, homage, reverence; allegiance, fealty, faithfulness, fidelity, loyalty.

3. tax, levy, tariff, charge, excise, custom, impost; dues, fee, toll, rate.

4. **do duty** substitute for, stand in for, take the place of.

5. **off duty** at liberty, free, off work, off, on vacation.

6. **on duty** engaged, occupied, busy, at work, *Sl.* on the job, tied up.

dwarf, *n.* 1. midget, homunculus, little man, pygmy, manikin, chit, fingerling, dapperling, cock-sparrow, hop-o'-my-thumb, Tom Thumb, Lilliputian, *Chiefly Scot.* wee fellow *or* lad *or* one, *Obs.* pigwidgin, *Archaic.* dandiprat; shrimp, runt, pee-wee, squirt, pipsqueak, half-pint, small-fry, *Inf.* shorty; imp, elf, fairy, sprite, goblin, (*in German Folklore*) kobold, *Irish Folklore.* leprechaun, *Chiefly Brit.* little person.

—*v.* 2. stunt, arrest, atrophy, check, bedwarf.

3. overshadow, overtop, rise above; dominate, bestride, tower over *or* above.

dwarfish, *adj.* runty, pygmy, undersized, squat, stunted, atrophied, stubby, dumpy, truncated, scrubby, wizened, (*of trees or shrubbery*) pollard; short, little, small, miniature, miniscule, minikin, diminutive, tiny, half-pint, elfin, bantam, slight, Lilliputian, *Chiefly Scot.* wee, *Scot.* cutty, *Inf.* Tom Thumb, *Sl.* pint-sized, *Sl.* pocket-sized, *Sl.* sawed-off, *Sl.* knee high to a grasshopper.

dwell, *v.* 1. reside, domicile, live; (*with* on *or* upon) inhabit, people, populate; abide, *Archaic.* bide, sojourn, stay, tarry, remain, *Sl.* crash; room, bunk, lodge, tenant; quarter, take up quarters, settle, be settled, keep house, establish oneself, plant oneself, put down stakes, anchor; pitch tent, encamp, bivouac; nestle, roost, burrow, perch, tabernacle, put up at.

2. (*often fol. by* on *or* upon) continue, linger, pause, tarry; ponder, be absorbed in, be engrossed in, be in a brown study; emphasize, expatiate, expound, elaborate; descant, harp on, insist upon.

dweller, *n.* resider, habitant, inhabitant, *Archaic.* inhabiter, *Law.* commorant; abider, sojourner; denizen, occupier, occupant, addressee, incumbent; lodger, renter, boarder, roomer, tenant, paying guest; householder, cottager, homesteader, settler, lessee; villager, citizen, townsman, oppidan, burgher, burgess; indigene, native, compatriot, autochthon.

dwelling, *n.* 1. residence, abode, home, house, homestead, household; domicile, dwelling house, lodgings, quarters, diggings, *Chiefly Brit., Inf.* digs; mansion, castle, palace, manor house; villa, chateau, chalet, country seat, hall; hacienda, plantation, farmstead, grange; condominium, townhouse, suite, apartment house, apartment, *Inf.* pad, tenement, flat, *Chiefly Brit.* maisonette; inn, hotel, motel, hostelry, hospice; cabin, cottage, bower, log house, bungalow, hut, shanty, shack, hovel, lean-to; barracks, bivouac, camp; tent, wigwam, tepee, igloo; (*in Turkey and Iran*) kiosk.

2. den, cave, hole, cell, lair; coop, hutch, byre, barn, stable; hive, eyrie, nest, nidus, rookery, perch, roost.

3. hiding place, hermitage, retreat, refuge, asylum, haunt, *Inf.* hangout.

dwindle, *v.* 1. wane, fade, diminish, lessen, fritter; shrink, contract, become smaller; condense, compact, reduce, shorten, abridge, abbreviate, curtail, cut short.

2. decline, fall, sink, flag, droop, drop; degenerate, go downhill, decay, rot, deteriorate, wither, shrivel, dry up, *Brit. Dial.* wizen; waste away, ebb, wear away, erode; disappear, vanish, evanesce, evaporate, die off *or* out, *Inf.* peter out.

dye, *n.* 1. pigment, color, coloring, colorant, tint, *Chem.* aniline dye, *Obs.* tincture, *Obs.* taint; stain, paint, wash, solution.

2. hue, shade, tone, cast, tinge, *Literary.* tinct.

—*v.* 3. color, pigment, tint, tinge, tincture, shade; stain, paint, wash, overspread; (*all of the hair*) lighten, frost, streak, bleach; (*all with color*) imbue, ingrain, infuse, suffuse, instill, impregnate.

dying, *adj.* moribund, expiring, going, slipping, sinking, fading *or* fading fast; near death, at death's door, knocking on heaven's door, on one's deathbed, at the last breath, in the death throes, in the jaws of death, with one foot in the grave, *Inf.* on one's last leg, *Latin. in extremis.*

dynamic, *adj.* 1. energetic, vigorous, active, alive, electric, aggressive, *Inf.* peppy; lively, spry, spirited, eager, zealous; emphatic, forcible, forceful, mighty, powerful, strong; brisk, strenuous, potent, puissant, high-powered; effective, effectual, efficacious, efficient, trenchant.

2. propulsive, propelling, driving, impelling, impulsive, galvanic, electrifying.

dynamo, *n.* hustler, pusher, demon, hard-worker, go-getter, *Inf.* eager beaver; man of action, powerhouse, *Inf.* live wire, *Inf.* busy bee, *Inf.* fire-ball, *Inf.* ball of fire, *Inf.* crackerjack; Stakhanovite, overdoer, doer; workaholic, work horse.

dynasty, *n.* rule, house, ascendancy, suzerainty, regime, regnancy, sovereignty; dominion, authority, sway, reign, control, command, mastership; administration, regency, governance, government, jurisdiction, direction; kingship, crown, autocracy, monarchy, imperialism; leadership, master, hegemony, predominance, prerogative; tyranny, dictatorship, despotism, absolutism.

dysentery, *n.* diarrhea, loose bowels, *Physiol.* flux, *Physiol.* dejection, *Pathol.* licentery; *All Sl.* the bug, the runs, the trots, the green-apple two-step, tourist's lament, turistas, the G.I.'s, Montezuma's revenge, Delhi belly, Gyppie tummy.

E

each, *adj.* **1.** every, any, respective, separate, individual, personal, particular.
—*pron.* **2.** each one, every one, one and all, each and all, all and sundry.
—*adv.* **3.** apiece, per, a person, *Inf.* a head, *Sl.* a shot; per capita, per diem, per annum; respectively, separately, singly, severally, individually.

eager, *adj.* **1.** desirous, hoping, hopeful, wishing, wishful; yearning, longing, craving, emulous, desiring, anxious, itching, *Sl.* itchy, solicitous, keen; zestful, alive, full of life, energetic, lively, bright-eyed and bushy-tailed; wide-awake, awake, active, alert, quick, bright; sparkling, *Inf.* sparked, kindled, enkindled; inflamed, fired up, stirred up; spirited, enthusiastic, enthused, *Inf.* psyched, psyched up, exhilarated, ecstatic; inspired, enlivened, inspirited, invigorated, energized; vivified, vitalized, animated, sanguine; reanimated, revived, revitalized, rejuvenated; stimulated, excited, aroused, *Inf.* hot; intensely desirous, fain, impassioned, passionate; zealous, *Inf.* gung-ho, ardent, vehement, fervent, fervid, perfervid; frenzied, frantic, crazed, mad, *Inf.* wild, infatuated.
2. earnest, intense, sincere, heartfelt; wholehearted, profound, serious; diligent, hard-working, industrious, studious; persevering, sedulous, resolute; ambitious, aspiring, up-and-coming, enterprising, pushing, *Inf.* pushy, aggressive; impulsive, impetuous, impatient, hasty; overeager, overanxious, greedy, avid, ravenous, voracious.

eagerly, *adv.* **1.** ardently, keenly, enthusiastically, avidly, zealously; zestfully, lively, with zest, with relish, with gusto, *Inf.* to beat the band, *Sl.* up a storm; quickly, swiftly, expeditiously, with dispatch; promptly, readily, willingly, at the drop of a hat.
2. vehemently, vigorously, fervently, passionately, perfervidly; impatiently, anxiously, longingly, desirously, yearningly.
3. heartily, warmly, with open arms, cordially, earnestly, sincerely, gladly. cheerfully.

eagerness, *n.* **1.** enthusiasm, ardor, avidity, keenness, fervor, intensity; zeal, willingness, readiness, promptness, gameness; anxiousness, solicitude, intentness; impatience, fluster, ruffle, *Inf.* itchy feet, *Sl.* ants; desire, longing, yearning, wishing.
2. zest, appetite, spirit, relish, gusto, élan, animation, life; verve, vitality, vigor, vim, liveliness; *Inf.* go, *Inf.* snap, *Inf.* pluck, stir, dash, bustle, flurry; dispatch, expedition, sharpness, briskness, quickness; enterprise, diligence, industry, assiduousness, studiousness, sedulity, perseverance.
3. cordiality, warmth, heartiness, earnestness, sincerity, *Fr. empressement*; alacrity, cheer, agreeability, agreeableness, amiability.

eagle-eyed, *adj.* sharp-sighted, quick-sighted, keen-sighted, hawk-eyed, lynx-eyed; all-seeing, far-seeing, all-observant, not missing a thing; clear-sighted, perspicacious, discerning, discriminating, perceptive; insightful, intuitive; keen, acute, wide awake, sharp, sharp as a tack, alert, bright; Arguseyed, watchful, vigilant, on the watch for; on the alert, on the qui vive, on guard, on the lookout; wary, prudent, discreet.

ear, *n.* **1.** hearing organ, auditory apparatus, *Fr. oreille*; internal ear, middle ear, external ear.
2. hearing, sense of hearing, audition.
3. attention, heed, observance, observation, notice, note, regard; heedfulness, attentiveness, concentration, thought, consideration.

early, *adv.* **1.** initially, at the start, early in the game, *Chiefly Brit.* early on, *Scot.* timeously.
2. at daybreak, matutinally, at the break *or* crack of dawn, with cock's crow, with the birds.
3. prematurely, precociously, too soon; untimely, ahead of time, beforehand, before the appointed time, *Brit. Dial.* rathe.
4. long ago, in the old days, in bygone days, in the past; remotely, previously, heretofore, erenow, *Scot.* air; originally, primarily.
—*adj.* **5.** primary, prime, primal, initial, initiative, premier, first, opening, antecedent, *Scot.* air.
6. premature, precocious, *Inf.* previous, untimely, early-bird; advanced, anticipatory, eager, precipitate.
7. primeval, pristine, earliest; original, aboriginal, autochthonal, autochthonous; primitive, primordial, primigenial; ancient, antique, antiquated, archaic, archaistic; prehistoric, preglacial, preadamic, antediluvian.
8. timely, *Scot.* timeous, prompt; immediate, undelayed; expeditious, quick, fast, speedy, rapid, alacritous.

earmark, *n.* **1.** identifying mark, tag, label, band, crop, brand, trademark, stamp; fold, dog-ear.
2. characteristic, trait, sign, symptom, feature, attribute, property; quality, nature, personality, temperament, character, disposition. See **characteristic** (*def.* **2**).
—*v.* **3.** tag, label, brand, stamp, crop, band, identify; mark, fold, dog-ear.
4. set aside, put away, hold, reserve, keep in reserve.

earn, *v.* **1.** gain, acquire, obtain, secure; get, profit, benefit, avail; procure, gather, garner, glean, reap.
2. (*all usu. of wages*) make, clear, *Sl.* pull down, pocket, bag; gross, net, *Inf.* take home; make a pretty

penny, bring home the bacon, keep the wolf from the door, keep the pot boiling, be the breadwinner.

3. bring about, cause, effect; produce, yield; merit, deserve, win, be worthy of, be qualified for, be entitled to, have a right to, have a claim to, have [s.t.] coming to one.

earnest[1], *adj.* **1.** fervent, fervid, perfervid, ardent, zealous, passionate, impassioned, intense; assiduous, diligent, intent, concentrated; firm, resolute, determined, *Inf.* bound and determined, decided, purposeful; serious, sincere, in earnest, *Inf.* for real; devoted, dedicated, committed, wholehearted; thoughtful, solemn, grave.

2. heartfelt, deep-felt, strongly *or* keenly felt, *Archaic.* homefelt, profound, deep; warm, hearty, cordial, friendly.

3. crucial, critical, decisive, pivotal, eventful, momentous, climacteric; important, all-important, essential, of the essence, vital, heartbeat, *Inf.* gut; urgent, imperative, pressing, compelling, exigent, high-priority.

earnest[2], *n.* downpayment, deposit, binder, handsel, installment, stake; pledge, pawn, gage, security, surety, promise, *Sl.* hock; *Law.* escrow, *Law.* earnest money, *Old Eng. Law.* God's penny; retainer, advance, payment up front.

earnestness, *n.* fervor, fervency, fervidity, ardor, zeal, passion, vehemence, intensity; resolution, firmness, determination, steadfastness, iron-will, purposefulness; seriousness, gravity, sobriety, solemnity, thoughtfulness; diligence, assiduity, intentness, concentration, *Inf.* stick-to-it-iveness; devotion, dedication, commitment, wholeheartedness.

earnings, *n.* **1.** wages, salary, emolument, *Brit. Sl.* get; compensation, pay, payment, hire, consideration; stipend, fee, honorarium; income, revenue, profit, returns, interest, yield; net, bottom line, *Inf.* take home; perquisites, *Inf.* perks, fringe benefits, benefits, *Inf.* fringes, *Inf.* extras.

2. profits, *Sl.* take, winnings, *Sl.* velvet, proceeds, *Sl.* clean-up, pickings, *Sl.* gravy.

3. remuneration, recompense, reward, *Archaic.* meed, *Literary.* guerdon, deserts.

earring, *n.* ornament, bauble, jewel; hoop, dangle, pendant, eardrop, *Dial.* earbob, stud.

earth, *n.* **1.** globe, sphere, planet, world, biosphere, terrene.

2. dry land, terra firma, terra, solid ground.

3. ground, soil, topsoil, subsoil; dirt, clay, gravel, loam, humus, mud; turf, clod, sod.

4. mankind, people, all the peoples of the world, the whole world, the wide world, the world at large; humanity, the human race, race of man, one world.

earthborn, *adj.* **1.** earthly, worldly, physical, natural, corporal, corporeal; from the earth, of earthly origin, sprung from the earth, terrigenous; autochthonous, indigenous.

2. mortal, human, born of woman; perishable, ephemeral, transient, transitory, fleeting, passing.

earthen, *adj.* **1.** made of earth, mud, dirt, clay, terraqueous.

2. baked, formed, fictile, terra-cotta.

earthenware, *n.* pottery, crockery, crocks, clay ware, ceramics, stoneware, basaltware, ironstone, terra cotta, gombroon, faience, *Ceramics.* biscuit.

earthly, *adj.* **1.** terrestrial, terrene, telluric, tellurian, subastral, sublunary.

2. worldly, mundane, temporal, physical, natural, corporeal, material.

3. mercenary, venal, money-grubbing, materialistic, pragmatic; vile, low, fleshly, sensual, earthy.

earthquake, *n.* seism, seismism, microseism, earth tremor, shock, upheaval, cataclysm.

earthy, *adj.* **1.** sensual, funky, carnal, sexy, voluptuous, virile, lush, sensuous; robust, lusty, hale, hardy.

2. ribald, bawdy, indecorous, shameless, wanton, unblushing, abandoned, coarse, crude, vulgar, common, dirty, filthy, *Sl.* raunchy, smutty, indecent, obscene; unpolished, unrefined, untutored, uncultured, provincial, peasant, lower-class; rude, churlish, cloddish, boorish, brash, crass.

3. direct, open, natural, artless; unpretentious, unaffected, unsophisticated, unassuming, down-home; rustic, homey, work-a-day, salt-of-the-earth, comfortable.

4. earth-like, terrene, clayey, cloddy, muddy, sandy, dusty.

5. realistic, basic, practical, pragmatic, unidealistic, down-to-earth, matter-of-fact, hard-boiled.

ease, *n.* **1.** comfort, relaxation, well-being, complacency; repose, rest, restfulness, peace, peacefulness; serenity, calm, calmness, tranquillity, stillness; peace of mind, security, contentment, content.

2. facility, dexterity, adroitness, skill, skillfulness, address, deftness; expertness, proficiency, masterfulness, finesse, grace; readiness, easiness, quickness, adeptness, aptness; capability, ability, knack, flair, turn, bent.

3. plenty, prosperity, prosperousness, abundance, affluence, wealth; luxury, lavishness, opulence, opulency; bed of roses, life of Riley, *Sl.* easy street.

4. unaffectedness, naturalness, artlessness, ingenuousness; unconstraint, unreservedness, unrestraint; informality, casualness, unceremoniousness; affability, complaisance, familiarity, easygoingness, relaxedness; lightness, unconcern, carelessness, indifference, nonchalance, insouciance.

5. easiness, simpleness, facileness; simplicity, plainness, clearness, clarity, lucidity; effortlessness, facility.

—*v.* **6.** comfort, tranquilize, soothe, relax; quiet, quieten, still, calm, pacify; solace, console, cheer; relieve, disburden.

7. mitigate, abate, lessen, lighten, diminish, reduce; alleviate, assuage, allay; appease, palliate, mollify, soften; sweeten, sugar-coat, smooth, ameliorate.

8. maneuver, guide, steer; edge, sidle, inch, squeeze.

9. facilitate, simplify, uncomplicate, clear, smooth, expedite, speed up; aid, assist, forward, advance.

easeful, *adj.* comfortable, agreeable, pleasant, pleasing; quiet, undisturbed, unruffled, untroubled, calm; peaceful, placid, serene, tranquil, still; restful, reposeful, relaxed, relaxing.

easily, *adv.* **1.** effortlessly, with ease, with no trouble at all, handily, hands down, without even trying, (*both usu. jocular*) with one's eyes closed, no hands; smoothly, skillfully, facilely, dexterously, adroitly.

2. by far, far and away, beyond question, unquestionably, without a doubt, doubtlessly, undisputably, obviously, patently.

3. be apt to, likely, well.

easiness, *n.* **1.** simpleness, facileness. See **ease** (*def.* **5**).

2. unaffectedness, unconstraint, casualness. See **ease** (*def.* **4**).

eastern, *adj.* **1.** easterly, eastward, east.

2. (*usu. cap.*) Oriental, Asian, Levantine.

easy, *adj.* **1.** simple, plain, obvious, *Scot.* eath; readily comprehensible *or* learnable; effortless, *Inf.* hands-down, clear *or* plain *or* smooth sailing, *Sl.* gut, *Sl.* cushy, *Sl.* cinchy, easy as pie, easy *or* simple as 1, 2, 3; a pushover, a piece of cake, *Inf.* a snap, *All Sl.*

cinch, picnic, breeze, duck soup, child's play, no sweat.

2. comfortable, contented, satisfied, well-pleased, at ease; secure, tranquil, quiet, untroubled, relieved.

3. easygoing, carefree, casual. See **easygoing**.

4. lenient, indulgent, light, undemanding, unexacting; gentle, mild, soft; unoppressive, unburdensome.

5. compliant, tractable, docile, manageable; accommodating, amenable, agreeable; complaisant, acquiescent, submissive; susceptible.

6. smooth, unconstrained, free; clear, limpid, lucid, fluent, flowing, graceful, natural, unforced; loose, unconfining, unrestricting, roomy, ample.

7. informal, casual, unceremonious, down-to-earth; unaffected, natural, homey, *Sl.* just-folks; unreserved, unrestrained, open; suave, urbane, sophisticated.

8. leisurely, unhurried, moderate, temperate, regular, steady, even, jog trot.

easygoing, *adj.* **1.** unworried, calm, carefree, careless, without a care in the world, nonchalant, happy-go-lucky, cheerful; unconcerned, insouciant, uninvolved, indifferent, pococurante, apathetic.

2. relaxed, laid-back, casual, placid, serene, cool, composed, unruffled, *Inf.* together; even-tempered, mild-tempered, unexcitable, imperturbable; patient, tolerant, understanding, uncritical, accepting.

eat, *v.* **1.** take a meal, fare, break bread, dine, sup, lunch, breakfast, *Sl.* put *or* tie on the feedbag, snack, nosh; feed, take sustenance, take in nourishment, refresh the inner man, ingest, consume; masticate, chew, munch, champ, crunch, bite, nibble; devour, tuck in, fall to, gobble up, gulp down, bolt, wolf, *Inf.* put away *or* down, *Inf.* pack away *or* in, *Chiefly Brit. Sl.* scoff *or* scoff up, *Sl.* scarf down, *Sl.* garbage *or* garbage down; feast, banquet, gormandize, fress, gorge, engorge, glut, *Sl.* pig out, *Sl.* stuff one's face.

2. corrode, wear away, waste away, rust, decay, rot, crumble, molder; gnaw through, bore into; ravage, devastate, destroy, demolish, ruin.

3. eat one's heart out long for, hunger for, pine for, hanker after, want, desire, crave; lament, sorrow, grieve, despond.

eatable, *adj.* edible, comestible, esculant; dietetic. See **edible**.

eater, *n.* diner, luncher, breakfaster, nosher, nibbler, snacker; consumer, devourer, gorger, glutton, gourmand, *Inf.* pig, *Inf.* hog; gourmet, epicure.

eavesdrop, *v.* overhear, bend an ear, listen in, prick up one's ears, harken; wiretap, *Inf.* tap, *Sl.* bug; prowl, pry, *Inf.* snoop.

eavesdropper, *n.* big ears, Dumbo, listener, hearer, auditor; wiretapper; gossip, *Chiefly Scot.* delator, Paul Pry, Peeping Tom, spy, *Inf.* snooper.

ebb, *n.* **1.** reflux, refluence, flowing back, receding, recession, retrocession; outflow, outflux; ebb tide, low tide, low water, neap tide, neap.

2. decline, wane, fall-off, subsidence; decay, erosion, wasting away, dying out, weakening, falling; deterioration, degeneration, regression, retrogression.

3. lowest point, nadir, rock bottom; worst possible state, *Sl.* the pits.

—*v.* **4.** recede, retire, flow back, withdraw, draw back, retrocede; subside, abate, fall away, fall back.

5. decline, sink, flag, droop, wane; decay, deteriorate, degenerate, crumble, wither, shrivel; languish, fade away, waste away; decrease, dwindle, die out, *Inf.* peter out.

ebony, *n.* **1.** black, jet, ink, coal, pitch, soot, charcoal.

—*adj.* **2.** ebon, jet, black, jet-black, coal-black, inky, pitchy, sooty, fuliginous, dusky, sable; dark, swarthy, swart.

ebullience, *n.* **1.** boiling up, ferment, fermentation, bubbling over, effervescence, effervescing, overflow, ebullition.

2. high spirits, exhilaration, buoyancy, breeziness, vivacity; exuberance, enthusiasm, zest, spirit; excitement, agitation.

ebullient, *adj.* high-spirited, exhilarated, buoyant, breezy, vivacious, sparkling, aglow; exuberant, enthusiastic, zestful, irrepressible, excited, agitated; boiling up, bubbling up, effervescent, foamy, foaming, frothy, yeasty; gushing, overflowing, effusive.

ebullition, *n.* **1.** (*usu. of feelings*) outburst, outbreak, overflowing, seething; fit, storm, explosion, rage, passion; paroxysm, spasm, throe.

2. high-spirits, exhilaration, enthusiasm, ebullience. See **ebullience** (*def.* **2**).

3. boiling up, fermentation, bubbling over, ebullience. See **ebullience** (*def.* **1**).

eccentric, *adj.* **1.** unconventional, uncommon, unique, unusual, unorthodox, uncustomary, unwonted, rare, out of the ordinary; atypical, original, singular, exceptional, individual, lone, sole, solitary; unexampled, unparalleled, unprecedented, unfamiliar, uncomfortable; extraordinary, egregious, astonishing.

2. deviate, deviant, aberrant, stray, wayward, erratic, anomalous, anomalistic, abnormal, irregular, variable; peculiar, curious, queer, odd, oddish, offbeat, quizzical, cranky, *Inf.* funny, *Inf.* kinky, off-center, incongruous; quaint, droll, comical, laughable, *Inf.* quirky, idiosyncratic, flaky, *Sl.* balmy, *Chiefly Brit.* barmy; strange, weird, bizarre, freakish, grotesque, *Sl.* rum, *Sl.* far out; fanciful, whimsical, notional, crotchety, maggoty, capricious, fickle, waggish.

3. mad, demented, unbalanced, daft, touched, crackbrained, mad as a hatter *or* March hare; *All Inf.* cracked, dotty, daffy, *Brit.* potty, over the top, not all there, have bats in one's belfry, have a screw loose, have a few buttons missing, not playing with a full deck, have rooms to let; *All Sl.* screwy, screwball, mental, kooky, bugs, bughouse, squirrely, wacko, wacky, nuts, loony, loco, nutty, bananas, bats, batty, bonkers, cuckoo *or* coo-coo, dippy, off one's rocker, off the wall, out in left field, *Brit.* off one's chump.

4. *All Geom.* parabolic, hyperbolic, decentered; *Astron.* elliptic.

—*n.* **5.** character, card, original, pip, sport, exception, individual, nonesuch, nondescript, bohemian; crank, fanatic; crazy, flake, freak, three-dollar bill, crackpot, rare bird, queer fellow, queer duck, queer fish, queer potato, *Inf.* fruitcake, *Inf.* dingbat, *Inf.* ding-a-ling; *All Sl.* weirdo, weirdy, weirdie, creep, oddball, screwball, nut, loony, looner, case, geezer, kook, odd duck, squirrel.

6. curiosity, curio, oddity, peculiarity, rarity; aberration, aberrance, aberrancy, deviation, anomaly, *Rare.* anomalism.

eccentricity, *n.* **1.** oddity, curiosity, rarity; irregularity, incongruity, variation, abnormality, discrepancy, difference, variance, dissimilitude, disparity, inconsistency; exception, singularity, particularity; idiosyncrasy, idiocrasy, mannerism, quirk, twist, kink, hobby-horse; quip, crotchet, whim, caprice, flight of fancy; aberration, aberrance, aberrancy, deviation, anomaly, *Rare.* anomalism.

2. oddness, strangeness, queerness, bizarreness, curiousness, quirkiness, incongruousness; uncommonness, uncommonality, unconventionality, unusualness, uniqueness, exception, exceptionalness, singularity, singularness, individuality, individualness, distinctiveness; whimsicality, fancifulness, waggishness, capriciousness; outlandishness, preposterousness, extravagance.

ecclesia, *n.* **1.** (*usu. of Christians*) congregation, church, assemblage, meeting, gathering, community; fellowship, communion, body, fold, flock, parish; worshipers, followers, believers, brethren, laity.

2. (*in ancient Greece*) assembly, council.

ecclesiastic, *n.* **1.** clergyman, churchman, cleric, clerk, *Brit.* blackcoat; minister, parson, divine, reverend, priest, father, rabbi; padre, abbé, curate, cure, chaplain, *U.S. Mil. Sl.* sky pilot, *U.S. Mil. Sl.* Holy Joe; pastor, rector, vicar; dean, canon, prebendary, presbyter; lector, reader, gospeler, deacon, acolyte, sacristan, *Eastern Ch.* ecclesiarch.

2. patriarch, primate, pope, pontiff, archbishop, bishop, prelate, cardinal, archpriest, high priest, hierarch; capitular, provincial; (*both usu. used as titles*) eminence, reverence.

3. monastic, conventual, religious, cenobite; monk, friar, brother, abbot, prior; nun, sister.

4. preacher, evangelist, revivalist, spreader of the Word, missionary, sermonizer, sermonist, (*both usu. used disparagingly*) pulpiteer, gospel-monger.

5. theologian, canonist, exegete, divine, Talmudist, Doctor of the Church, hierophant, hierologist. See also **priest, clergyman**.

ecclesiastical, *adj.* churchly, hierarchical, hierarchic, ecclesial; religious, spiritual, nonsecular; clerical, cleric, ministerial, pastoral; priestly, sacerdotal, hieratic, prelatic, episcopal, apostolic, papal, pontifical.

echo, *n.* **1.** reverberation, repercussion; iteration, repetition.

2. imitation, reproduction, copy, replica, replication, duplication; mimicking, aping; representation, semblance, likeness; reflection, twin, counterpart, counterfeit, fake, sham.

3. sympathy, empathy, affinity, harmony; unanimity, accord.

—*v.* **4.** reverberate, resound, ring; repeat, reecho; reflect, return, give back.

5. imitate, emulate, do like, simulate, copy, follow suit, parallel, model after, copycat; mimic, ape, monkey, parrot, mirror; impersonate, mock, parody, take off, caricature.

éclat, *n.* **1.** glory, renown, fame, famousness, eminence, celebrity, celebratedness; prestige, high repute, reputation.

2. acclamation, acclaim, ovation, standing ovation, plaudits, round of applause, applause, *Inf.* hand; praise, kudos, approval.

3. flourish, splendor, lavishness, pomp, pageantry, showiness, ostentation; show, exhibition, display, *Inf.* production; hurrah, fuss, fuss and feathers, *Inf.* to-do, *Sl.* big deal.

eclectic, *adj.* **1.** selective, selecting, picking and choosing; drawing on all sources, touching all bases, all over the place.

2. multiform, complex, compound, synthesized, synthetic, pieced *or* pulled together; multifaceted, manifold, multifarious, multiple, many-sided, heterogeneous; diverse, diversified, varied, grab bag; comprehensive, broadly based, well-rounded, liberal, catholic; unstructured, open, free, nondoctrinaire, nondogmatic.

eclipse, *n.* **1.** obscuration, obfuscation, concealment, occultation, blockage, hiding, covering; darkening, shadowing, shading, adumbration, beclouding, overclouding, overcasting, bedimming, dimming.

2. overshadowing, outshining, outstripping, outdoing, outrivaling, outvying; transcendence, surpassing, excelling, excellence.

—*v.* **3.** block, obscure, obfuscate, conceal, hide, cover, cloak, veil, enshroud; darken, shadow, shade, adumbrate, becloud, overcloud, cloud, overcast, dim, bedim.

4. overshadow, outshine, outstrip, outdo, outrival, outvie; transcend, surpass, excel.

economic, *adj.* budgetary, pocketbook, money, monetary, pecuniary, financial, fiscal; bread-and-butter, meat-and-potatoes.

economical, *adj.* **1.** economizing, thrifty, saving, sparing, chary; provident, prudent, careful, unwasteful, conservative, conservant, conservational; frugal, scrimping, penny-pinching, parsimonious, penurious; miserly, niggardly, stingy, tight, stinting, tight-fisted, closefisted, cheap.

2. money-saving, cost-effective, high-yield; economy, low-cost, budget, low-budget, low-income.

economize, *v.* **1.** conserve, save, use sparingly, *Inf.* go easy on.

2. save, put [s.t.] aside, save for *or* against a rainy day.

3. scrimp, skimp, pinch pennies, cut corners, tighten one's belt, be sparing *or* frugal, make both ends meet; be penurious, be parsimonious, be stingy *or* cheap, stint, *Inf.* pinch a penny till it squeaks.

4. (*all of expenses*) cut, trim, cut down on, reduce, diminish, retrench; cut back, curb, curtail, straiten, restrict, limit.

economy, *n.* **1.** husbandry, thrifty management, conservation; conserving, saving, economizing; thrift, thriftiness, frugality, frugalness, sparingness; scrimping, skimping, penny-pinching, cutting corners, tightening one's belt, making ends meet; parsimony, parsimoniousness, penuriousness; miserliness, niggardliness, stinginess, tightness, tight-fistedness, closefistedness, cheapness.

2. (*all of expenses*) cut, trimming, cutdown, reduction, decrease, diminution, retrenchment, cutback; control, check, curb, curtailment, straitening, restriction, limitation.

3. conservation, preservation, preserving, saving, reservation, protection; supervision, control, keeping, safe-keeping, care, charge, custody; maintenance, upkeep, support.

4. national income, national earnings, net national product, gross national product, GNP.

ecru, *adj.* light brown, tan, beige, brownish; unbleached, off-white, fawn, tawny, sandy; fuscous, dusky.

ecstasy, *n.* **1.** exaltation, elation, exhilaration, thrill, ravishment; paroxysm, orgasm, excitement, excitation; sensation, emotion, enthusiasm, élan.

2. rapture, transport, bliss, elysium; euphoria, happiness, joy, gladness, felicity; delight, delectation, seventh heaven, swinging on stars; relish, enjoyment, pleasure, gratification; spell, trance, reverie, psychedelia.

3. afflatus, inspiration; jubilation, exultation, rejoicing; radiance, beatitude, paradise.

ecstatic, *adj.* **1.** exalted, exhilarated, thrilled, ravished; transported, blissful, rhapsodic, rapturous, orgastic; excited, enthusiastic, elated; joyful, glad, felicitous, beaming; happy as a clam at high tide, bouncing with joy, up in the air, beside oneself, overjoyed; in orbit, delirious, on cloud nine; flying, walking on air, floating.

2. exultant, rapt, entranced, enchanted, enraptured; beatific, radiant, glorious.

eddy, *n.* **1.** countercurrent, counterflow, counterflux, backwater, backflow, back stream.

2. whirlpool, gurge, swirl, whirl.

edge, *n.* **1.** border, rim, margin, lip, fringe, periphery, perimeter, skirt; circumference, circuit, compass, ambit, outline, frame; bound, limit, bourn, pale, extremity, outer limits, apogee; brink, brow, verge, brim.

2. cutting-edge, knife-edge, razor-edge, feather-edge.

3. (*all of tone of voice, appetite, etc.*) sharpness, keenness, acuteness, pointedness; harshness, severity, vehemence; virulence, causticity, acrimony, trenchancy.

4. *Informal.* advantage, handicap, head start, *Inf.* jump; upper hand, whip hand. See also **advantage** (*def.* **2**).

5. on edge **a.** nervous, on tenterhooks, *Inf.* on pins and needles, *Sl.* antsy; tense, uneasy, ill at ease, apprehensive, *Inf.* with one's heart in one's mouth. **b.** impatient, eager, avid, intent, keen, ardent, desirous, champing at the bit, *Inf.* raring to go, *Sl.* psyched.

—*v.* **6.** sharpen, acuminate, put an edge on; whet, hone, strop, strap, file.

7. border, fringe, befringe, trimp; blind; purfle; purl.

8. sidle, veer, skew, sidestep, sideslip, go sideways.

9. creep, crawl, inch along, worm along; slink, pad, prowl, snake.

edgy, *adj.* irritable, testy, touchy, prickly, sensitive, grouchy, crabbed, irascible, peevish, bearish, snarling, growling; tense, *Inf.* uptight, under a strain; nervous, high-strung, all nerves, a bundle of nerves. See also **edge** (*def.* **5**).

edible, *adj.* eatable, comestible, esculant, fit to eat; nutritive, nutrient, dietetic; delicious, good, succulent, *Inf.* yummy, *Archaic.* gustable.

edict, *n.* proclamation, pronouncement, declaration, manifesto; bull, fiat, decretal, ukase, firman, capitulary; order, command, injunction, mandate, decision, dictum, rescript, prescript, decree; mittimus, indiction, ban; public notice, caveat, assize, enactment, act, law, statute, regulation, ordinance.

edification, *n.* **1.** uplifting, enlightening, teaching, instructing, guiding, leading, steering.

2. uplift, improvement, benefit, enlightenment; instruction, education, guidance; inculcation, indoctrination, initiation; salvation, rebirth.

edifice, *n.* mansion, palace, hall, temple, cathedral; skyscraper, high-rise, condominium, *Inf.* condo; building, structure, pile, megastructure.

edify, *v.* instruct, educate, teach, school, give lessons, tutor, coach, direct, guide, inculcate, prepare; benefit, uplift, raise up, raise [s.o.'s] consciousness, open [s.o.'s] eyes, show [s.o.] the way *or* the light, show, inform, enlighten.

edit, *v.* **1.** revise, rewrite, amend, rephrase; rectify, modify, correct, emend, redact, copy-edit, annotate; adapt, polish, touch-up; select, compile, compose, prepare, *Inf.* prep; delete, blue-pencil, *Inf.* clean up, *Both Television.* blip, bleep.

2. compose, put together, bring out; direct, run, manage, head up, be chief of.

3. expurgate, bowdlerize; delete, excise, expunge.

edition, *n.* **1.** issue, number, printing, press run.

2. volume, version, impression, exemplar.

editor, *n.* reviser, rewriter, blue-penciler, copy editor, redactor, emender; compiler, collector, annotator; lexicographer; journalist, writer, columnist, editorial writer.

editorial, *v.* essay, article, piece, opinion piece, think piece, column, policy *or* position statement; op-ed article.

educate, *v.* teach, instruct, tutor, school, inform, enlighten, edify; train, coach, break in; initiate, ground, prepare; ready, prime, harden, inure; exercise, practice, drill, discipline; nurture, foster, nourish, breed, rear, bring up; cultivate, develop, broaden, civilize, humanize; indoctrinate, inculcate, instil, infuse; govern, direct, guide, lead; mold, shape, form; preach, lecture, moralize.

educated, *adj.* **1.** learned, scholarly, erudite; literate, lettered, literary, well-read, *Usu. Derog.* bookish; knowledgeable, informed, conversant, versed, well-versed, well-grounded; accomplished, skilled, masterly.

2. cultivated, refined, cultured, artistic, *Inf.* arty, *Sl.* artsy, *Inf.* longhair or longhaired; enlightened, broad-minded, open-minded, aware, sensitive; articulate, well-spoken, fluent; intellectual, cerebral, brainy, highbrow *or* highbrowed; pedantic, pedagogish, professorial, donnish.

3. trained, schooled, instructed, tutored, coached, drilled, disciplined; prepared, readied, primed, hardened, inured; shaped, formed.

education, *n.* **1.** teaching, instruction, tuition, tutelage; direction, guidance, nurture, breeding, development; inculcation, indoctrination, initiation, discipline.

2. learning, knowledge, lore, information, skill; preparation, schooling, training, initiation, apprenticeship; erudition, scholarship, wisdom, study, *Usu. Derog.* bookishness; enlightenment, edification, culture, cultivation, refinement.

3. didactics, pedagogics, pedagogy. See **pedagogy** (*def.* **2**).

educational, *adj.* **1.** academic, academical, scholastic, school, educatory; collegiate, college, university; learning, teaching, pedagogic, pedagogical.

2. educative, informational, informative, instructive, instructional, propaedeutic; didactic, moralistic, homiletic, homiletical, *Inf.* preachy, disciplinary; cultural, humanistic, scientific; broadening, edifying, uplifting.

educator, *n.* pedagogue, educationist, *Educ.* methodologist, teacher, schoolteacher, schoolmaster, *Chiefly Scot.* dominie, schoolmistress, schoolmarm; professor, doctor, master, tutor, fellow, *Brit.* don, instructor, preceptor, lector, lecturer, *Brit.* reader, docent; mentor, counselor, guide; schoolman, scholastic, academician, academe, gownsman.

educe, *v.* **1.** draw forth *or* out, bring forth *or* out, elicit, evoke, call forth, summon; develop, derive, evolve.

2. infer, deduce, conclude, surmise, reason; suppose, guess, esteem, reckon, opine; arrive at, draw an inference *or* conclusion.

eerie, *adj.* uncanny, weird, unnatural, macabre, unearthly, preternatural, mysterious; *Inf.* spooky, *Inf.* scary, creepy, eldritch; chilling, witching, scaring, alarming; ghostly, spectral, wraithlike, phantasmal; awful, dreadful, strange, odd, *Scot. and North Eng.* unco.

efface, *v.* **1.** expunge, obliterate, wipe out, blot out, stamp out, crush out, snuff out, strike out; eradicate, extirpate, destroy, annihilate, discreate, exterminate, abolish; remove, eliminate, get rid of, do away with, leave no vestige *or* trace of, put an end to, extinguish, bring to an end; terminate, dissolve, check, stop, cut short; expel, cast off, throw over.

2. erase, cancel, rub out; delete, cross out, scratch, x out, black out, mark off, blue-pencil, *Print.* dele.

3. withdraw, shy, draw back, recoil; be inconspicuous, blend into the scenery, be a wallflower.

effect, *n.* **1.** consequence, result, outcome, conclusion, issue, end, upshot, event, sequel; aftermath, outgrowth, afterclap, turnout, aftereffect, fallout, backwash, wake; side effect, by-product, offshoot; repercussion, reaction, feedback.

2. efficacy, capacity, potentiality, capability, ability; power, potency, *Inf.* punch, force, vigor, strength, value, weight; validity, soundness, reliability.

3. impact, influence, impingement; impression, sensation, feeling.

4. execution, accomplishment, fulfillment, realization, success; achievement, performance, production, operation.

5. purport, meaning, import, sense, tenor, bearing; gist, drift, implication, significance; intent, intention, purpose, object.

6. **in effect** **a.** for practical purposes, virtually, so to speak. **b.** basically, essentially; really, actually, truly, verily; no buts about it, any way you look at it.

7. **take effect** go into operation, begin to function, start to work.

—*v.* **8.** cause, bring about, make happen, effectuate. See **effectuate**.

effective, *adj.* **1.** effectual, efficacious; capable, competent, efficient; adequate, sufficient, fit.

2. functioning, useful, serviceable, operative, in order; practical, current, actual, real, valid.

3. striking, impressive, telling, pointed, moving, arousing; noticeable, attractive, conspicuous, standout, remarkable; forcible, powerful, potent, influential, cogent.

effectual, *adj.* **1.** adequate, competent, able, capable, qualified, up to scratch, *Inf.* up to snuff; satisfactory, sufficient, passable, tolerable, acceptable.

2. effective, efficient, efficacious, operative, functional; powerful, influential.

3. valid, sound, solid, substantial; binding, legal, lawful; cogent, convincing, forceful, authoritative.

effectuate, *v.* **1.** cause, bring about, make happen, effect; accomplish, realize, achieve, fulfill, reach; make certain, ensure, secure.

2. execute, carry out, bring to pass; do, perform, act out, implement.

effeminacy, *n.* unmanliness, invirility, milksopism, sissiness; (*of men*) femininity, womanishness, effeminateness; androgyny.

effeminate, *adj.* unmanly, emasculate, emasculated, milksoppy, pansyish, *Inf.* pantywaist; (*all of men*) feminine, womanish, ladylike, female, sissyish, campy, *Sl.* faggy, *Sl.* limp-wristed; androgynous, hermaphrodite, hermaphroditic.

effervesce, *v.* **1.** bubble, burble; foam, froth, fizz, fizzle, hiss, sputter; pop, snap; spume, spew forth; ferment, boil.

2. rejoice, delight, laugh, show excitement, sparkle; exhibit happiness, exult, be in good *or* high spirits, be happy, be gay.

effervescence, *n.* **1.** bubbling, burbling; foaming, frothing, fizzing, fizzling, hissing, sputtering; popping, snapping.

2. ebullition, seething, overflowing, outburst; ebullience, high spirits, exhilaration, enthusiasm, exuberance; animation, vivacity, liveliness, excitement; delight, gaiety, happiness.

effervescent, *adj.* **1.** effervescing, bubbling, burbling; foaming, frothing, fizzing, fizzling, hissing, sputtering; popping, snapping; boiling, fermenting.

2. ebullient, exhilarated, enthusiastic, exuberant; overflowing, demonstrative, animated, vivacious, lively, breathless, excited; delighted, gay, happy.

effete, *adj.* **1.** weakened, enfeebled, enervated, devitalized, drained, worn-out, used-up, played-out, burned-out, spent; weak, feeble, powerless.

2. decadent, degenerate, corrupt, dissolute, dissipated, depraved, debauched, deteriorated, degraded, debased.

3. barren, sterile, infertile, unprolific, infecund, *Med.* agenetic, unprocreant, impotent; unproductive, unyielding, unfructuous, unfruitful, fruitless.

efficacious, *adj.* **1.** effective, effectual, operative, prevailing, productive, efficient, *Archaic.* prevalent; competent, proficient, adept, masterful, expert, masterly, *Fr. au fait*; skillful, adroit, deft.

2. powerful, potent, sovereign, forceful, forcible, strong, weighty; dynamic, vigorous, energetic, active, *Archaic.* virtuous; sound, valid, reliable, believable; capable, able, qualified, adequate, sufficient.

efficacy, *n.* **1.** effectiveness, effectualness, productiveness, efficiency, *Scot. and North Eng.* feck, *Archaic.* prevalent; competence, competency, proficiency, adeptness; mastery, expertise, expertness, know-how, savoir-faire.

2. capacity, potentiality, capability, capableness, ability, ableness; power, potency, virtue, force, vigor, strength, value, weight; validity, soundness, reliability, believability.

efficiency, *n.* **1.** competence, competency, fitness, fittedness, qualification, eligibility, preparedness, readiness; capability, capableness, commensurability, the stuff, *Inf.* what it takes, *U.S. Inf.* the goods; mastery, authority, expertness, expertise; proficiency, adeptness, address, finesse, facility, polish; practice, experience, know-how, savoir-faire; skillfulness, adroitness, deftness, dexterity, dexterousness.

2. productiveness, productivity, generation, efficaciousness, effectiveness, causativeness; potency, power, high-poweredness, *Literary.* puissance, energy, vigor, dynamism.

3. apartment, room, flat.

efficient, *adj.* **1.** efficacious, effectual, effective, effecting, valid, active, operative, operant; causative, productive, producing, generative, generating, assembly line; potent, powerful, high-powered, puissant, energetic, vigorous, dynamic.

2. competent, fit, fitted, *Sl.* on the ball, qualified, eligible, prepared, well-grounded, trained, ready; capable, commensurate, equal to, *Inf.* up to; expert, masterful, masterly, *Inf.* crack, *Sl.* crackerjack, *Inf.* whizbang, *Brit. Sl.* whizzo; proficient, adept, accomplished, polished, practiced, experienced, *Fr. au fait*; clever, adroit, slick, deft, skillful, talented, dexterous.

3. economical, thrifty, saving.

effigy, *n.* image, likeness, representation, resemblance; icon, idol; figure, figurine, doll, straw man, scarecrow.

effluence, *n.* **1.** discharge, emission, efflux, effusion, exhalation, *Obs.* vent.

2. outflow, outflowing, outpour, outpouring, emanation, effluent.

effluvium, *n.* fume, exhalation, exhaust; miasma, mephitis, *Archaic.* malaria; gas, vapor; reek, stench, odor.

efflux, *n.* See **effluence** (*defs.* **1, 2**).

effort, *n.* **1.** exertion, striving, impulse, conatus, nisus; struggle, strain, stress, application, exercitation; trouble, pains, grind, push; work, labor, toil, travail, industry; sweat of one's brow, *Inf.* elbow grease, muscle, back; practice, discipline, training, exercise, drill.

2. attempt, venture, endeavor, essay, *Fr. coup d'essai*; try, aim, trial, test; *Inf.* go, *Inf.* pull, *Inf.* the old college try, *Sl.* crack, *Sl.* whack.

3. achievement, feat, exploit, attainment, deed, act; bold stroke, tour de force, opus.

effortless, *adj.* **1.** easy, facile, simple, *Scot.* eath, downhill, like taking candy from a baby, easy as 1,2,3 *or* A,B,C, easy as pie; a piece of cake, a pushover, *Inf.* a snap, a cinch, smooth *or* clear sailing; *All Sl.* gut, cushy, cinchy; no sweat, child's play, a breeze, duck soup; nothing to it.

2. smooth, flowing, fluid, unforced, unconstrained; limpid, cogent, lucid, natural, free-flowing.

3. passive, inactive, inert, lifeless, otiose; languid, sluggish, supine, recumbent; indifferent, apathetic, slack.

effrontery, *n.* audacity, impertinence, impudence, gall, nerve, *Inf.* cheek, *Inf.* brass, *Sl.* moxie; insolence, brassiness, brazenness, rudeness, *Sl.* mouth, *Sl.* lip; temerity, foolhardiness, rashness, brashness, boldness; imprudence, injudiciousness, indiscretion; arrogance, haughtiness, front, self-importance, self-assertion; assertiveness, bumptiousness, *Inf.* pushiness, forwardness, *Sl.* chutzpah; shamelessness, sauciness, pertness.

effulgence, *n.* brilliance, radiance, iridescence, resplendence, shine, refulgence, *Archaic.* fulgor; fire, blaze, flame; twinkle, twinkling, sparkle, sparkling, shimmer, scintillation, coruscation, glistening; flash, beam, ray, fulguration, glint, glance; gleam, glitter, glimmer, flicker, *Archaic.* glister; nimbus, aureola, halo; luminescence, luminosity, nitidity, phosphorescence, incandescence, fluorescence, illumination; sheen, luster, splendor, glow.

effulgent, *adj.* radiant, brilliant, shining, resplendent, iridescent, fulgent; sunny, bright, sunshiny, light, lit, alight; dazzling, vivid, ablaze, aflame, afire; blazing, fiery, burning, flaming; sparkling, gleaming, scintillating, glistening, coruscating, fulgid; twinkling, lambent, flickering, shimmering, glimmering, rutilant; glowing, refulgent, luminous, luminescent, nitid; incandescent, phosphorescent, fluorescent; lustrous, shiny, glossy, sheen, (*of gems*) orient; lucent, luciferous, *Rare.* relucent, lucid

effuse, *v.* **1.** spill, dispense, pour out, send forth, emit, secrete; shed, disseminate, open the sluices, turn on the tap, disembogue.

2. exude, diffuse, emanate, well out, issue forth, flow out, gush, spout, spurt; seep, filter, ooze, *Pathol.* extravasate.

3. prattle, gabble, chatter, rattle, prate, jabber, blather, babble.

effusion, *n.* **1.** outpouring, gush, stream, emission, efflux, effluence, emanation; outflow, diffusion, dispersion; discharge, shedding, spilling, extravasation.

2. outburst, eruption, explosion, paroxysm; profusiveness, exuberance, bubbling over, ebullition, boiling over.

effusive, *adj.* **1.** poured out, diffused, spread widely, overflowing, streaming.

2. demonstrative, unreserved, unrestrained, emotive; expansive, lavish, generous, profuse, copious; exuberant, rhapsodic, enthusiastic, ebullient, hearty, ardent, fervent, warm, sentimental, gushing, *Sl.* gooey; pleonastic, wordy, verbose, long-winded.

egest, *v.* void, evacuate, excrete, discharge, eject, expel.

egg[1], *n.* ovum; embryo, nucleus, cell; germ, seed.

egg[2], *v.* *Usu.* **egg on** urge, encourage, prod, push, goad, spur; instigate, induce, trigger; set on, rouse to, prick, stimulate; start up, get going, hurry on, actuate, animate; wheedle, coax, inveigle, prevail upon, exhort; incite, inspire, persuade, sway, tempt, entice, lure.

egghead, *adj.* *Informal.* pedant, bookworm, highbrow, *Inf.* longhair, *Inf.* know-it-all, *Inf.* walking encyclopedia. See **intellectual** (*def.* **5**).

egg-shaped, *adj.* oval, ovate, ovoid, oviform, elliptical, ellipsoid; obovate, pear-shaped, bell-shaped.

ego, *n.* **1.** the I, the self, oneself.

2. egotism, self-importance, conceit. See **egoism** (*def.* **2**).

3. self-esteem, self-respect, feelings, sensibilities, *Fr. amour propre*; self-image, self-concept, self-identity, identity, picture *or* image of oneself.

egoism, *n.* **1.** selfishness, self-indulgence, self-gratification, self-satisfaction, self-serving; self-consideration, self-interest, self-aggrandisement, *Inf.* looking out for number one; personalism, privatism, individualism.

2. egotism, self-conceit, self-esteem, self-regard, self-importance, self-approbation, self-admiration, self-love, self-worship, self-adulation; conceit, pride, vanity, vainglory, vaingloriousness, bovarism, *Inf.* ego trip, *Inf.* big head; self-praise, self-glorification, boastfulness, braggadocio, jactation, bluster, fanfaronade, gasconade.

egoist, *n.* **1.** egocentric, narcissist; self-server, self-seeker, self-pleaser; individualist.

2. egotist, *Inf.* swellhead; braggart, braggadocio, boaster, *Inf.* bullshooter, *Sl.* blowhard, *Sl.* windbag, *Sl.* gasbag, *Sl.* loud mouth, *Sl.* big mouth.

egoistic, *adj.* egocentric, self-centered, self-absorbed, narcissistic, introverted, egotistical, wrapped-up in oneself; selfish, self-serving, self-seeking, self-indulgent, self-interested.

egotism, *n.* See **egoism** (*def.* **2**).

egotist, *n.* See **egoist** (*def.* **2**).

egotistic, *adj.* **1.** conceited, self-important, self-centered, self-admiring, self-worshiping, self-esteeming, *Sl.* stuck *or* hung up on oneself; vain, vainglorious, proud, overproud, overweening, puffed-up, inflated, swollen, swellheaded, *Inf.* big-headed; boastful, bragging, braggart, crowing, vaunting, blustering; cocky, bumptious, overbearing, *Scot.* vaunty.

2. egoistic, self-absorbed, narcissistic. See **egoistic**.

egregious, *adj.* glaring, flagrant, notorious, infamous; striking, blatant, obtrusive, conspicuous, prominent; out in the open, overt, bold, bald, baldfaced, undisguised; loud, crying, screaming, sensational, lurid; scandalous, startling, shocking, outrageous, gross, appalling, disgraceful.

egress, *n.* **1.** egression, going out, exit, going away, leaving, departure, parting; escape, slipping out *or* away; issue, issuance, flowing *or* passing out; emergence, emanation, coming forth, *Phys. Geog.* debouchment.

2. exit, outlet, issue, vent, means of escape, *Archaic.* escapement; way out, door out, passage out; door, doorway, gate, gateway, postern, back door, window, hole, opening, aperture, mouth.

either, *adj.* **1.** one or the other, one of two, either one.

2. both, each, the one and the other.

—pron. **3.** one or the other, either one.

—adv. **4.** also, too, as well.

ejaculate, *v.* **1.** exclaim, blurt out, cry out, yell out, call out, vociferate, *Inf.* spout off, *Inf.* holler out, *Sl.* pop off; utter, speak, say, voice.

2. discharge, emit, spurt, spout, squirt, release, vent; expel, eject, shoot off *or* out, fire off, send off, let fly; spew, expectorate, spit out *or* up, throw up, egest, vomit, puke, regurgitate, *Sl.* upchuck; (*all of semen*) climax, have an orgasm, *Sl.* come, *Sl.* finish.

ejaculation, *n.* **1.** exclamation, blurt, utterance; cry, yell, call, vociferation.

2. discharge, emission, spouting, squirting, release, *Obs.* vent, (*both of semen*) climax, orgasm; expulsion, ejection, shooting off *or* out; expectoration, spitting out *or* up, throwing up, egestion, vomit, *Med.* vomitus, regurgitation; emptying, voidance, disemboguement, unloading.

eject, *v.* **1.** expel, oust, exclude, remove, get rid of, drive away *or* out, force out, thrust out, *Inf.* throw out, *Inf.* kick out; deport, transport, banish, exile, expatriate, ostracize; evict, displace, turn out, put [s.o.] out in the street, deprive *or* strip [s.o.] of property, dispossess, divest, take away [s.o.'s] home; discard, cast out *or* off, throw away, toss out, eliminate, jettison.

2. dismiss, cashier, drum out, fire, give [s.o.] his walking papers *or* a pink slip, lay off; send [s.o.] packing, *Inf.* give [s.o.] the axe, *Sl.* sack, *Sl.* bounce, *Sl.* can, *Sl.* dump, *Sl.* give [s.o.] the boot, *Sl.* boot out, *U.S. Govt. Inf.* rif, *Euph.* terminate.

3. throw, thrust, propel, project, impel; emit, exude, excrete, discharge, throw off, give off, send out *or* forth.

ejection, *n.* **1.** expulsion, ouster, ousting, riddance, exclusion, ejectment; deportation, transportation, banishment, exile, expatriation, ostracism; eviction, displacement, dispossession, deprivation, devestment; discard, discarding, elimination, throwing away, jettison.

2. dismissal, firing, conge, layoff; *Inf.* the axe, *Sl.* the sack, *Sl.* the bounce; *Sl.* the gate, *Sl.* the boot, *Sl.* the heave-ho, *Sl.* the bum's rush.

3. discharge, emission, excretion, exudation.

eke out, *v.* **1.** supplement, add to, round out, fill in, complete; increase, enlarge, extend, stretch out.

2. (*usu. in reference to one's living*) manage, get by, keep the wolf from the door, keep one's head above water, make ends meet, scrimp, economize; live from hand to mouth.

elaborate, *adj.* **1.** detailed, thorough, complete, comprehensive, exhaustive, complicated; painstaking, intricate, precise, minute; skillful, masterly; finished, perfected, elegant.

2. labored, laborious, operose, studied; decorated, ornamented, ornate, baroque, rococo, precious; fussy, dressy, showy, ostentatious.

—*v.* **3.** develop, flesh out, add to, amplify, enlarge, increase; work up, fashion, devise, concoct, prepare, produce; perfect, consummate, complete, accomplish, effect, achieve, compass.

4. improve, better, amend, ameliorate, meliorate; refine, cultivate; beautify, enhance, heighten, strengthen, enrich; touch up, smarten up, spruce up, brighten up, polish, finish; decorate, bedeck, adorn, embellish, garnish.

elaboration, *n.* **1.** development, amplification, enlargement, increase; working up, devising, concoction, preparation, production, formation; perfection, consummation, completion, accomplishment.

2. improvement, betterment, amendment, amelioration, melioration; refinement, cultivation, polish; beautification, touching up, enhancement, elevation, heightening, strengthening, enrichment, addition.

élan, *n.* dash, vigor, style, flair, flourish, panache, *Inf.* pizzazz, *Sl.* oomph; bounce, zing, zest, verve; spirit, life, buoyancy, briskness, *Inf.* snap; enthusiasm, eagerness, wholeheartedness, ardor, excitement; abandon, exuberance, animal spirits, vitality, vivacity, vivaciousness, *It. brio*; freedom, spontaneity, spontaneousness.

elapse, *v.* (*of time*) intervene, transpire, lapse; slip by, slip away, pass by, pass away, slide by, glide by, steal by, roll along, go by; expire, be sent, be lost, be past, end.

elastic, *adj.* **1.** flexible, bendable, pliable, springy, supple, rubbery, plastic, ductile; tensible, stretchable, dilatable, extensible, extensile, contractive, contractile; resilient, rebounding, recoiling, recuperative.

2. adaptable, adjustable, accommodating, yielding, responsive; tolerant, compliant.

elasticity, *n.* **1.** flexibility, springiness, suppleness, rubberiness; plasticity, ductility, tensibility, tensileness, extensibility, dilatability, contractibility, contractility, resilience, recuperation.

2. adaptability, adjustability, accommodation, response; tolerance, agreeability, compliance, acquiescence.

elate, *v.* gladden, cheer, delight, thrill, please, hearten, make happy; exhilarate, elevate, lift up, *Inf.* turn on, make proud.

elated, *adj.* exhilarated, jubilant, exultant, euphoric, exalted, ecstatic; triumphant, happy, overjoyed, rejoicing, gleeful, joyful, delighted, excited; pleased, pleased as Punch, tickled, *Inf.* tickled pink; *Sl.* turned on, in high spirits, on top of the world, crowing, thrilled; transported, blissful, in paradise, carried away, treading *or* walking on air, on cloud nine, *Dial.* in hog heaven, *Dial.* in high cotton.

elation, *n.* euphoria, joy, cloud nine, exhilaration, jubilance, exaltation, ecstasy; thrill, rapture, transport, pleasure, delectation, delight, enjoyment, gratification, beatitude, happiness; jubilation, seventh heaven, rejoicing; enthusiasm, excitement, ebullition, high spirits.

elbow, *n.* **1.** bend of the arm, ancon, funny bone, crazy bone; bend, fluxure, fold, sharp turn, right angle, corner, crook.

2. at one's elbow nearby, close by, at hand, within reach, handy; at one's finger tips, under one's nose.

3. bend, lift *or* **crook an elbow** drink, imbibe, *Sl.* souse, *Inf.* swig, *Inf.* booze.

4. out at the elbows a. poorly dressed, shabby, disheveled, shoddy, *Inf.* seedy, in rags, down at the heels. **b.** impoverished, poverty-stricken, needy, in want, pauperized, beggarly.

5. rub elbows with mingle with, associate with, hobnob, fraternize, socialize, mix, *Inf.* hang out *or* around with.

6. up to one's elbows very busy, engrossed, occupied, absorbed, engaged; up to one's ears in, head over heels in, immersed in, wrapped up in, all wound up in.

—*v.* **7.** jostle, shoulder, hustle, scuffle, scramble; push, bump, shove, plow, bulldoze.

elbowroom, *n.* ample room, spare room, enough space; growing room, breathing room, *Ger. Lebensraum*; latitude, margin, free play; sweep, range, swing; open space, free space, clearing, expanse; opportunity, freedom.

elder, *adj.* **1.** older, senior, of greater years, more advanced in age.

2. higher ranking, ranking, superior, chief, preeminent, paramount, foremost, primary, prime, principal.

3. earlier, former, prior, previous, bygone.

—*n.* **4.** senior, superior, master, first-born; parent, forefather, ancestor, forebear; predecessor.

5. elderly person, aged person, oldster, veteran, *Inf.* old-timer, graybeard, *Rare.* grisard, retiree, senior citizen, *Euph.* golden-ager, *Derog.* old fogy; sexagenerian, septuagenarian, octogenarian, nonagenerian, centenarian.

6. chief, ruler, patriarch; dean, elder statesman, grand old man.

7. presbyter, governing layman, assistant pastor, preacher.

elderly, *adj.* **1.** old, rather old, oldish, on in years, along in years, advanced in years, past one's prime, *Inf.* over the hill, *Derog.* long in the teeth; late middle-aged, *Fr. d'un certain age*; gray-haired, gray-headed; aged, hoary, venerable, patriarchal; ancient, senile, (*of women*) anile, decrepit, senescent, aging; retired, superannuated.

—n. **2. the elderly** (*used collectively*) elderly persons, aged persons, the aged, retired persons, retirees, oldsters, *Inf.* oldtimers, senior citizens, *Euph.* goldenagers. See also **elder** (*def.* **5**).

elect, *v.* **1.** select by vote, vote, give one's vote, ballot, cast one's ballot, poll; co-opt, appoint, designate.

2. pick *or* pick out, *Inf.* hand-pick, select, single out, choose; decide upon, make up one's mind on, settle on, fix on *or* upon. See **choose.**

—adj. **3.** picked out, *Inf.* hand-picked, chosen, selected; appointed, designated, elective.

4. select, choice, prime, quality, fitst-rate, first-class, grade-A, A-1, A number 1, the best.

election, *n.* **1.** selection by vote, co-optation, cooption, appointment, designation, nomination; preliminary election, *U.S. Politics.* primary.

2. public *or* popular vote, referendum, plebiscite, direct vote.

3. electing, voting, balloting, poll; vote, voice, *Latin. vox populi*, say, opinion, choice. See **choice** (*def.* **1**).

electioneer, *v.* campaign for, canvass for, solicit votes for, *Inf.* stump for, barnstorm for; plump for, support, back, promote, advance; talk up, ballyhoo, beat the drum for, push, *Inf.* plug, *Inf.* hype.

elective, *adj.* **1.** electoral, electing, selecting, selective, choosing.

2. elect, appointed, designated; picked *or* picked out, *Inf.* hand-picked, selected, chosen.

3. optional, not required, unrequired, voluntary, discretionary.

elector, *n.* voter, balloter, constituent; selector, chooser.

electric, *adj.* **1.** galvanic, *Elect.* voltaic, *Elect.* faradaic, *Physics.* charged; electrified, electric-powered, battery-powered, cordless.

2. stimulating, galvanizing, electrifying, jolting, jarring; thrilling, exciting, breathtaking; stirring, moving, rousing, soul-stirring.

electrify, *v.* **1.** galvanize, energize, dynamize, charge.

2. startle, stun, stagger, shock, jolt, jar, take one's breath away, pull one up short, *Inf.* bowl over, *Inf.* give one a turn; thrill, excite, flush, *Inf.* give one a kick *or* charge.

3. invigorate, animate, vitalize, enliven, exhilarate, stimulate, fire, rouse, arouse.

electrocute, *v.* execute, put to death, *Fig.* pull the switch on, *Euph.* send to the hot seat, *Sl.* burn, *Sl.* fry.

eleemosynary, *adj.* **1.** charitable, philanthropic, altruistic, benevolent, beneficent, almsgiving.

2. funded, supported, sponsored, subsidized, financed, non-profit, not for profit.

elegance, *n.* **1.** fineness, luxuriousness, sumptuousness, opulence; grandeur, richness, choiceness; the good life, high style, exquisiteness, gracefulness; pulchritude, beauty, comeliness, finery, *Fr. haute couture*, swankiness.

2. refinement, grace, gentility; dignity, distinction, class, courtliness, old-world charm, polish, culture; correctness, politeness, propriety.

3. intelligence, discernment, discrimination, Atticism, taste; harmoniousness, proportion, felicity; purity, fastidiousness.

elegant, *adj.* **1.** luxurious, posh, sumptuous, grand, fine; rich, swank, gorgeous, ornamental, ornate; excellent, choice, superior, select; exquisite, tasteful, in good taste, nice; well-done, well-made, finished.

2. urbane, Chesterfieldian, polished, suave, top-hat; sophisticated, chi-chi, stylish, fashionable; cultured, cultivated, well-bred, to the manner born, courtly; debonair, dapper, charming; polite, courteous, genteel, gracious, correct; minion, delicate, fastidious, recherché; lovely, comely, well-coiffed, dressed to the nines, dainty; beautiful, shapely, handsome.

3. discriminating, refined, intelligent, Attic, classical; well-proportioned, appropriate, balanced, harmonious, concinnous; aesthetic, artistic.

elegiac, *adj.* elegiacal, sorrowful, plaintive, mournful; sad, *Fr. triste*, melancholy; lugubrious, maudlin, emotional; epicedial, dirge-like, threnodic, funereal, somber.

elegy, *n.* dirge, threnody, (*in Scotland and Ireland*) coronach, requiem, monody; song of lamentation, lament, plaint, keen, Kaddish.

element, *n.* **1.** component, constituent, ingredient, part, unit, module; member, integrant, part and parcel; portion, section, fragment, complement, piece, parcel, segment; item, detail, feature, particular.

2. habitat, medium, native state, domain; lair, ground, locus, resort, haunt; sphere, field, circle, realm, quarter, zone.

3. elements a. weather, climate, clime, atmospheric forces *or* conditions, environment. **b.** principles, rudiments, fundamentals, foundations; outline, synopsis.

elementary, *adj.* **1.** primary, rudimentary, rudimental, abecedarian; inchoate, imperfect; embryonic, embryonal, germinal, genetic, genetical, nascent, undeveloped; incipient, beginning, original; introductory, preparatory, proemial, preliminary, prefatory; fundamental, basic, basal, radical, root, underlying; primitive, primordial, primigenial.

2. simple, simplex, uncompounded, uncomplex, uncomplicated, easy, facile, *Inf.* soft, understandable, clear, plain.

3. elemental, component, constituent, factorial, essential; natural, naturelike.

elephantine, *adj.* **1.** huge, big, mammoth, jumbo, gargantuan, massive, enormous; monumental, immense, large, massy, Brobdingnagian, Cyclopean; towering, monstrous, titanic; mighty, stupendous, *Inf.* whopping, *Inf.* thumping.

2. ponderous, pachydermal, hippopotamic, bulky, weighty, gross, heavy.

3. clumsy, ungraceful, awkward, ungainly, oafish; hulking, lubberly, lumbering.

elevate, *v.* **1.** lift up, raise, move up, thrust up, heave, hoist; rear, raise aloft, erect, uprear, escalate; boost, uplift, upthrust, upheave, upthrow, upcast; jerk up, hike up, pull up.

2. exalt, magnify, heighten, aggrandize; dignify, ennoble, enthrone, crown; extol, glorify, esteem, greaten; enshrine, immortalize, lionize, deify.

3. promote, advance, prefer, *Sl.* kick upstairs; upgrade, improve, ameliorate, meliorate, enhance, enrich, better.

4. cheer, cheer up, elate, gladden, brighten, put in a good mood; hearten, buoy, revive, vitalize; inspirit, inspire, animate, raise the spirits, *Inf.* give a lift; regale, refresh, exhilarate, enliven.

elevated, *adj.* **1.** raised, upturned, lifted, upraised, upcast, upright; high, up, high up, aloft, above; conspicuous, salient, distinct, articulate, marked, in bold relief.

2. noble, lofty, sublime, magnificent, majestic, splendid, imposing, impressive; exalted, grand, glorious, august, stately; dignified, distinguished, magnified; prominent, eminent, illustrious, notable, preeminent; high-minded, honorable, admirable, estimable; principled, righteous, sterling, meritorious.

3. grandiloquent, high-flown, stilted, pretentious; pompous, affected, magniloquent, orotund; high-sounding, *Inf.* high-falutin, overdone, showy.

4. elated, animated, overjoyed, rejoicing; joyful, cheerful, gleeful, glad, blithe; in good *or* high spirits, of good cheer, *Sl.* high.

elevation, *n.* **1.** height, altitude, ceiling; tallness, stature.

2. eminence, height, prominence, salience; hill, hillock, mount, mountain, plateau, mesa; acclivity, ascent, rise, levitation, lift, rising ground, upslope.

3. loftiness, exaltation, grandeur, majesty, imperialness; dignity, distinction, solemnity, gravity; nobleness, nobility, sublimity, stateliness, splendor, impressiveness; refinement, cultivation, grace.

4. promotion, advancement, preferment, furtherance; improvement, enhancement, enrichment, amelioration; heightening, aggrandizement, magnification; escalation, upping, raising, lifting.

elevator, *n.* hoist, *Chiefly Brit.* lift, *Fr. ascenseur*; dumbwaiter, spout, chute; escalator, moving stairs.

elf, *n.* imp, brownie, leprechaun, dwarf, gnome, troll; nixie, puck, kobold; sprite, pixie, fairy, peri, fay, undine; goblin, hobgoblin, incubus, succubus, banshee.

elfin, *adj.* **1.** elf-like, small, little, dainty; bantam, diminutive, wee, Lilliputian, pint-sized, dwarfish.

2. elfish, elvish, mischievous, tricksy, prankish; arch, impish, playful, frolicsome.

elicit, *v.* evoke, call forth, fetch *or* draw out; educe, deduce, derive, develop, bring out, bring to light; extract, draw forth, wrest, wring from, extort, wrench, *Inf.* pump.

elide, *v.* omit, delete, leave out, *Gram.* syncopate; slide over, blend, slur.

eligibility, *n.* eligibleness, worthiness, suitableness, desirability, fitness, qualification, utility.

eligible, *adj.* **1.** fit, proper, qualified, appropriate, suitable, acceptable, worthy of choice, desirable, worthwhile.

2. single, unwed, unmarried, *Inf.* available.

eliminate, *v.* **1.** discard, get rid of, get clear of, remove, cast away, cast aside, reject; dismiss, discharge, fire, *Sl.* sack; expel, cast out, force out, eject, evict; drive out, thrust out, extrude, throw out, oust, *Sl.* bounce; exclude, shut out, shut the door upon, debar; segregate, set apart, set aside, put aside; ostracize, blackball; banish, relegate, exile, expatriate, proscribe, deport, maroon; purge, do away with, liquidate, leave no vestige *or* trace of; terminate, dissolve, bring to an end, put an end to, check, stop, cut short, suspend; nip, nip in the bud, *Inf.* put the kibosh on.

2. obliterate, annihilate, extinguish, expunge, extirpate, discreate, eradicate, exterminate, abolish; blot out, strike out, stamp out, crush out; quash, quell, squelch, crush, vanquish, squash; overthrow, overturn subvert, topple, defeat, conquer.

3. omit, exclude, drop, leave out, disregard, by-pass, ignore, overlook; erase, rub out, scrape out, scratch out; wash out, sponge out; delete, *Print.* dele, blue-pencil, edit, edit out; cross out, x out, cancel, black out, mark off; excise, cut, cut out.

4. *Physiol.* void, egest, defecate, urinate, pass, empty, evacuate.

elimination, *n.* **1.** discard, removal, getting rid of, casting away, casting aside, rejection; omission, exclusion, by-pass; erasure, erasion, rubbing out, scraping out, scratch out; washing out, sponging out; deletion, *Print.* dele, editing; crossing out, cancellation, blacking out, marking off; excision, cutting, cutting out.

2. dismissal, discharge, casting out, forcing out, ejection, expulsion, eviction; extrusion, throwing out, driving out, ouster; debarment, segregation, ostracism, separation; banishment, relegation, exile, proscription, expatriation, deportation; purgation, liquidation, leaving no vestige *or* trace of; termination, dissolution, check, suspension.

3. obliteration, annihilation, extinguishment, extinction; extirpation, discreation, eradication, extermination, abolition, abolishment; blotting out, striking out, stamping out, crushing out; quashing, suppression, squelching, vanquishment, squashing; overthrow, overturn, subversion, defeat.

4. *Physiol.* voidance, egestion, excretion, defecation, urination, evacuation.

elite, *n.* **1.** privileged class, dominant class, ruling class, establishment; upper class, *Inf.* upper crust, gentry, gentility, aristocracy, nobility, silk-stockings, blue bloods; meritocracy, the best and the brightest, the high and the mighty; notables, personages, bigwigs, men of mark, grandees.

2. high society, cream of the crop, *Fr. crème de la crème, Fr. haut monde*, beau monde, fashionable society, jet set, the beautiful people, celebrities, stars, *U.S.* Four Hundred; F.F.V.'s, First Families of Virginia.

3. good life, high life, *Sl.* the big time, *Inf.* the major leagues.

4. choice, best, first water, first-class, nonpareil, nonesuch, paragon; pink, pearl, sterling.

elixir, *n.* **1.** extract, tincture, compound; cordial, invigorator; panacea, catholicon, nostrum, cure-all, cure for all ills, wonder drug, miracle drug.

2. quintessence, essence, pith, heart, core, kernel; principle, basis.

elliptical, *adj.* **1.** oval, ovate, ovoid, egg-shaped, curved.

2. (*all of speech and writing*) economic, terse, laconic, concise, succinct, concentrated, compact, neat.

3. (*all of speech and writing*) ambiguous, abstruse, cryptic, obscure, recondite, mysterious.

elocution, *n.* manner of speaking, utterance, delivery; articulation, enunciation, pronunciation; diction, wording, phrasing, parlance, phraseology; oratory, rhetoric, declamation.

elongate, *v.* lengthen, extend, *Anat.* protract, draw out, stretch, *Scot. and North Eng.* rax; increase, grow longer, trail out.

elope, *v.* **1.** (*all in order to marry*) run off, run away; sneak off *or* away, steal off *or* away, slip off *or* away.

2. abscond, flee, bolt, escape. See **abscond** (*defs.* **1,2**).

eloquence, *n.* power of speech, forcefulness, expressiveness, cogency; elocution, diction, address, articulation, enunciation; gift of gab, command of words, way with words, *Archaic.* facundity; (*all of speech*) fluency, facility, ease, gracefulness, glibness, slickness, smoothness; oratory, rhetoric, declamation.

eloquent, *adj.* **1.** articulate, well-spoken, silver-tongued, *Archaic.* facund, *Obs.* facundious, Ciceronian; oratorical, rhetorical, declamatory; (*all of speech*) poetic, graceful, easy, facile, flowing, fluent, glib, slick, smooth, smooth-tongued.

2. (*all of speech*) expressive, cogent, telling; forceful, emphatic, spirited, vigorous, impassioned, trenchant, vehement, burning; striking, vivid, graphic; effective, persuasive, impressive; concise, succinct, pointed, pithy, meaty.

3. (*of looks*) meaningful, significant, revealing, suggestive.

elsewhere, *adv.* in *or* to some other place, somewhere else, anywhere else, another place, not here; not present, away, absent, abroad, hence.

elucidate, *v.* **1.** shed *or* throw light on, make lucid *or* clear, illuminate; clarify, make plain, simplify, render intelligible; make explicit *or* unequivocal, define, make precise, spell out, specify; show, point out, demonstrate, manifest, exhibit, present, set forth; annotate, gloss, comment upon, margin, footnote; explain, describe, explicate, interpret; delineate, depict, portray, picture, illustrate; solve, resolve, clear up, decipher, figure out.

2. expose, disclose, reveal, bring out, *Archaic.* enucleate; lay open, unfold, uncover, bare, unveil, unmask, make visible.

elucidation, *n.* **1.** elucidating, throwing light on, making lucid *or* clear, illumination; clarification, making plain, simplification; defining, definition, specifying, spelling out; demonstration, manifestation, exhibition, presentation, exemplification; exposure, disclosure, revelation; delineation, depiction, portrayal, illustration; explanation, description, explication; interpretation, version, rendition, deduction, inference; diagnosis, solution.

2. commentary, comment, critique, exegesis, exposition; annotation, gloss, footnote, note, scholium, marginalia.

elude, *v.* **1.** evade, avoid, dodge, bilk, duck, give [s.o.] the slip, lose [s.o.], *Sl.* duck and run, *Sl.* dog it, *Sl.* ditch [s.o.], *Sl.* throw [s.o.] off the scent, *Sl.* shake [s.o.] off; vanish, disappear, do the disappearing act, *Inf.* make oneself scarce.

2. escape, get away, get free, get clear of, make *or* effect one's escape, make good one's escape, *Archaic.* scape.

elusive, *adj.* **1.** evasive, elusory, slippery, shifty, hard to pin down, *Inf.* cagey.

2. intangible, impalpable, imponderable, undefinable, inexplicable.

Elysium, *n.* heaven, paradise, eternity, glory, kingdom of heaven, *Inf.* kingdom come, happy hunting ground, Nirvana, Valhalla, Elysian Fields, Bower of Bliss.

emaciate, *v.* atrophy, wither, shrivel, dry up, *Brit. Dial.* wizen; shrink, reduce, contract, dwindle, attenuate; waste, consume, erode, wear away, eat away; weaken, enfeeble, enervate; starve, undernourish, underfeed.

emaciated, *adj.* gaunt, drawn, haggard, pinched, hollow-eyed, withered, shriveled, shrunken, dried up, wizened, *Brit. Dial.* wizen; scrawny, scraggy, spare, skinny, thin, lean, lanky, lank, slim, slender, attenuate, attenuated, tenuous; atrophied, atrophic, tabescent, wasted, phthisic, phthisical, worn, eroded, decayed, *Pathol.* marasmic, *Pathol.* marasmoid; frail, weak, feeble, enfeebled, enervated, infirm; undernourished, underfed, starved.

emaciation, *n.* **1.** gauntness, haggardness, witheredness, shrunkenness, boniness; scrawniness, scragginess, spareness, skinniness, thinness, leanness, lankness, lankiness, slimness, slenderness, attenuation, tenuity; *Psychiatry.* anorexia.

2. atrophy, atrophia, withering, shriveling; consumption, consumptiveness, phthisis, phthisic, wasting away, erosion, decay, degeneration, *Pathol.* marasmus, *Pathol.* tabes; weakening, enfeebling, enfeeblement, impairment, enervation, invalidation; undernourishment, malnutrition, inanition, starvation.

emanate, *v.* **1.** arise, appear, spring, effuse, exude, effervesce, *Phys. Geog.* debouch, discharge, ooze, filter, percolate; surge from, stem from, trickle from, flow from, proceed from, take rise from, result from, originate.

2. emit, issue, send forth, radiate, give off, project, exhale, disembogue; give out, send out, put out, waft out, fling out, throw out.

emanation, *n.* **1.** discharge, emission, effusion, effluent, efflux, efflorescence, exhalation, effluvium, mephiles; proceeds, issue, discharge, drainage, leakage, percolation, disemboguement; karma, aura, vibrations, *Inf.* vibes.

2. flowing, arising, emerging, springing, welling; issuance, emergence, escape, outflow, oozing, gushing, outpouring, effluence, *Phys. Geog.* debouchment.

emancipate, *v.* free, liberate, enfranchise, affranchise, franchise, manumit; release, loose, loosen, let loose, turn loose, set loose, set free, let go, disimprison, unmew; disenthrall, unfetter, unbind, untie, unbridle, unyoke, unshackle, unchain, unhandcuff, unmuzzle, *Archaic.* untruss; deliver, rescue, ransom, redeem, *Theol.* save.

emancipation, *n.* freedom, freeing, liberation, liberty, liberating, enfranchisement, enfranchising, affranchisement, affranchising, franchisement, franchising, manumitting; release, releasing, loosing, loosening, disimprisoning; disenthrallment, disenthralling, unfettering, unbinding, untying, unbridling, unyoking, unshackling, unchaining; deliverance, delivery, delivering, rescue, rescuing, ransom, ransoming, redemption, redeeming, *Both Theol.* salvation, saving.

emancipator, *n.* liberator, deliverer, rescuer, preserver; freer, manumitter, enfranchiser, releaser; breaker of bonds, *Both Theol.* Savior, Redeemer.

emasculate, *v.* **1.** castrate, asexualize, alter, demasculinize, effeminize; unman, eunuchize, (*both of fowl*) capon, caponize, (*of horses*) geld, *Inf.* fix, *Inf.* cut; maim, cripple, mutilate.

2. weaken, soften, debilitate; render harmless, render ineffectual, pull the teeth from, take the teeth out of, remove the sting *or* bite of; (*all of literature*) expurgate, bowdlerize, censor, *Inf.* clean up, purge.

emasculation, *n.* **1.** castration, asexualization, alteration, demasculinization, effeminization; unmanning, eunuchizing, (*of fowl*) caponization, (*of horses*) gelding, *Inf.* fixing, *Inf.* cutting; maiming, crippling, mutilation.

2. weakening, softening, debilitation; expurgation, bowdlerization, censoring, *Inf.* cleaning up, purging.

embalm, *v.* **1.** (*all of a corpse*) preserve, mummify, anoint, treat with aromatics, prepare for burial, lay out.

2. (*all of memories*) keep in mind, remember, cherish, enshrine, immortalize; reminisce, look back on, go over, relive, reexperience.

3. stunt, dwarf, stop *or* slow the development of.

4. perfume, scent, give fragrance to, aromatize.

embank, *v.* bank, bank up, mound, dike; fortify, secure, protect, defend, guard, shield.

embankment, *n.* **1.** bank, mound, elevation of earth, *Phys. Geog.* levee; dike, dam, breakwater, mole; pier, jetty, quay, wharf.

2. causeway, *Brit. Dial.* causey, raised road *or* path, viaduct, bridge.

3. wall, rampart, bulwark, *Fort.* breastwork; railing, balustrade, *Fort.* parapet, *Mil.* earthwork, fence, palisade, *Fort.* stockade.

embargo, *n.* restriction, restraint of commerce *or* trade, restraint, impediment, hindrance, check, barrier, inhibition; standstill, stoppage, shut down, quarantine, prohibition, proscription, interdiction, ban.

embark, *v.* **1.** board ship, go aboard, take ship; sail, set sail, put to sea, weigh anchor, get under way, hoist the blue peter.

2. begin, commence, undertake, go into, enter upon, venture into, set about; launch into, plunge into, broach, institute, start, take the first step; take up, tackle, turn one's hand to, assume.

embarrass, *v.* **1.** disconcert, chagrin, make uncom-

fortable, discomfort, discountenance, discomfit, make self-conscious; abash, shame, humiliate, mortify, cause to lose face, put down, humble; discompose, disturb, upset, fluster, agitate, bother, distract, derange; confound, perplex, nonplus, confuse, pose.
2. complicate, make intricate, entangle, tangle, snarl, muddle, involve.
3. impede, hamper, hinder, obstruct, frustrate, thwart; encumber, burden, handicap, clog; plague, vex, annoy, harass, trouble, distress.
4. straiten, *Rare.* indebt; (*all financially*) beset, beseige, beleaguer, burden.

embarrassed, *adj.* **1.** abashed, chagrined, nonplused, humiliated, mortified, put down, humbled; disconcerted, discomforted, uncomfortable, ill-at-ease, discomfited, discomposed, upset, flustered; ashamed, shamefaced, blushing, flush, flushed, red-faced, red in the face, *Inf.* red, [have] egg on one's face; self-conscious, awkward, clumsy, sheepish, shrinking, timid.
2. confused, at a loss, on the horns of a dilemma, between the devil and the deep blue sea, in a bind; *Inf.* between a rock and a hard place, *Inf.* in a fix, *Inf.* in a scrape, *Inf.* in a pickle, *Inf.* in hot water, squirming, wriggling, pinned to the wall, *Sl.* in for it.
3. (*all financially*) straitened, in debt, in the red, insolvent, impecunious, *Inf.* hard-up, *Inf.* broke, *Inf* pinched, *Inf.* short.

embarrassment, *n.* **1.** chagrin, shame, abashment, disconcertment, disconcertion, discomposure, discomfort, uncomfortableness, uneasiness, self-consciousness, awkwardness, bashfulness, clumsiness, perturbation, bewilderment.
2. predicament, dilemma, bind, no-win situation, quandary, plight, scrape, imbroglio, straits, pass, difficulty, rub, *Archaic.* hobble; trouble, mess, *Inf.* hot water, *Inf.* pickle, *Inf.* fix, *Inf.* stew; entanglement, confusion, perplexity, muddle.
3. blemish, stain, smudge, wart, skeleton in the closet, *Inf.* dirty linen; blunder, *Sl.* blooper, *Sl.* boner, faux pas, gaucherie; sore spot, touchy subject.
4. hindrance, impediment, obstacle, stumbling block, rub, snag, hitch; encumbrance, burden, handicap.
5. overabundance, superabundance, superfluity, excess, surplusage, profusion; surfeit, glut, repletion; oversupply, deluge, flood, inundation, avalanche.

embassy, *n.* **1.** consulate, legation, ministry, residence, *Archaic.* embassade.
2. delegation, legation, deputation, representation, staff; ambassadors, envoys, emissaries.
3. mission, commission, errand.

embattle, *v.* **1.** arm, equip, prepare, outfit, fit out; fortify, strengthen, brace, buttress, shore up.
2. crenellate, circumvallate.

embed, *v.* fix, bed, set, locate, base, root, establish, deposit; inlay, lay in, install, insert, plant, implant, press in, impact; pop in, thrust in, drive in, ram in, stuff in; graft, ingraft, dovetail.

embellish, *v.* **1.** adorn, decorate, ornament, trim, furbish, *Archaic.* dight, *Archaic.* ouch; elaborate, festoon, rubricate; array, bedizen, deck, deck out, bedeck, trap, trap out, caparison; dress, dress up, attire, accouter; spangle, bespangle, stud, bestud, beset; emblazon, blazon, illuminate, bedaub; gild, varnish, trick out.
2. beautify, prettify, fix up, prink, *Inf.* titivate, *Inf.* spruce up, *Inf.* pretty up, *Inf.* trick up.
3. (*all usu. of a statement or narrative*) embroider, garnish; exaggerate; color, paint, paint in glowing colors, tell in glowing terms, *Inf.* play up; set off, set off to advantage; enhance, enrich; deepen, heighten, intensify, brighten; glorify; grace, dignify; gloss, gloss over, whitewash, *Inf.* fudge.

embellishment, *n.* **1.** ornament, decoration, frill, filigree, flourish, flounce, furbelow, *Archaic.* ouch; tinsel, spangle; bauble, trinket, knickknack, gimcrack, gewgaw, *Inf.* doodad, *Inf.* fandangle; accessory, attachment.
2. adornment, decoration, ornamentation, trimming; trappings, festoons; array, bedizenment, enrichment, beautification, prettification; emblazonment, emblazonry, illumination.
3. (*all usu. of a statement or narrative*) embroidery, garnish, garnishment, garniture; exaggeration; coloration, coloring, *Inf.* razzle-dazzle; enhancement, enrichment; deepening, heightening, intensifying, brightening; glorifying; glossing, glossing over, whitewashing, *Inf.* fudging.

embers, *n.* live coals, smouldering remains; cinders, brands; dross, clinkers, slag, ash, scoriae; residue, remnants, fag ends.

embezzle, *v.* misappropriate, peculate, *Law.* defalcate, misapply, misuse; steal, rob, purloin, abstract; dip into the public purse, *Inf.* rob the till, *Inf.* have one's hand in the till; defraud, swindle, thieve, filch, cheat; pluck, fleece, rook, bilk.

embezzlement, *n.* fraud, peculation, misappropriation, *Law.* defalcation, abstraction; theft, thievery, robbery, stealing, pilfering, swindle; larceny, *Chiefly Law.* malversation, *Law.* malfeasance.

embezzler, *n.* peculator, *Law.* defalcator, thief, robber; swindler, highbinder, fleecer, trickster, bilker, sharper, *Inf.* hawk; confidence man, con artist, flimflam artist; defaulter, *Sl.* welsher; racketeer, criminal, lawbreaker.

embitter, *v.* **1.** (*all of taste*) sour, acidulate, acidify, acetify; (*all of feelings*) envenom, gall, rankle, acerbate, exacerbate, poison.
2. irritate, aggravate, annoy, bother, fret, nettle, vex, plague, disturb, perturb, plague, harass, *Chiefly U.S.* rile, *Inf.* rub [s.o.] the wrong way, *Sl.* drive [s.o.] nuts, *Sl.* get [s.o.'s] goat; anger, incense, enrage, infuriate, madden, raise [s.o.'s] ire, make [s.o.'s] blood boil.

emblazon, *v.* **1.** paint, color, illuminate, blazon; decorate, ornament, adorn, embellish; array, bedizen, deck, bedeck, deck out.
2. proclaim, publish, herald, trumpet; praise, celebrate, extol, exalt, laud, glorify, sing *or* ring [s.o.'s] praises.

emblem, *n.* **1.** symbol, representation, insignia, regalia, token, sign, badge, totem; effigy, image, figure, design, attribute, character; mark, memento, reminder, example, type, motto; metaphor, allegory, figuration, allusion; indication, indicium, *Heraldry.* cognizance, evidence.
2. flag, pennant, standard, banner, ensign, oriflamme, eagle; monogram, cartouche, signet, seal; coat of arms, escutcheon, crest; throne, crown, scepter; cockade, epaulet, chevron, stripes, *Mil. Sl.* scrambled eggs, stars.

emblematic, *adj.* symbolic, symbolical, representative, significative, metaphorical, figurative, allegorical; suggestive, indicative, indicant, denotative, allusive.

embodiment, *n.* **1.** incarnation, corporealization, materialization, substantiation, personification, concretization, reification, externalization, exteriorization; fusion, amalgamation, consolidation, coalescence; combination, unification; comprisal, composition, constitution, inclusion; encompassment, incorporation, assimilation, comprehension.
2. materiality, corporeality, substantiality, physical-

ness, concreteness, flesh and blood.

embody, *v.* **1.** incarnate, corporealize, materialize, concretize, substantiate, reify, externalize, exteriorize.
2. fuse, merge, amalgamate, consolidate, coalesce; combine, unite, join.
3. comprise, compose, constitute, hold, contain; embrace, encompass, incorporate, assimilate, admit, take in, comprehend.

embolden, *v.* encourage, enhearten, hearten, reassure, assure, raise hope, cheer, root, bear up, buoy, buoy up, *Inf.* chirk, *Inf.* pat on the back; stimulate, animate, whet, motivate, inspire, inspirit, nerve, pluck up, build up, buck up, rally, revive, boost, boost up, invigorate, awaken, pep up, *Inf.* peptalk, *Sl.* give a shot in the arm to; impel, induce, compel, constrain, press; excite, arouse, rouse, inflame, enflame, fire up, stir up, *Inf.* psyche up.

embosom, *v.* **1.** enfold, wrap up, enwrap, envelop; enclose, surround, encircle, encompass; bury, hide, conceal, secrete.
2. embrace, hug, snuggle, clutch, cuddle, caress; take in one's arms, hold close, hold.
3. cherish, hold dear, value, prize, appreciate; foster, nurse, nurture, take care of, shelter, protect.

emboss, *v.* ornament in relief, boss, chase, enchase, engrave, raise, fret, tool; sculpture, carve.

embrace, *v.* **1.** take into one's arms, hug, squeeze, clasp, press to one's bosom, embosom, enfold; hold in one's arms, caress, cuddle, snuggle, nestle, nuzzle; *Sl.* clinch, grab, snatch, clutch, grasp, hold onto, grip, cling to.
2. welcome, receive warmly, take in, accept, adopt.
3. avail oneself of, use, make use of, employ; take, grab, grasp, seize, jump at.
4. survey, scan, see, take in, drink in, absorb, understand, comprehend.
5. encircle, surround, encompass, gird, girdle, enclose, hem in; envelop, engulf, enfold, enwrap, wrap, swathe.
6. include, hold, contain, comprise, comprehend, embody, incorporate; cover, deal with, provide for.
—n. **7.** hug, squeeze, clasp, bear hug, tight embrace, *Sl.* clinch; hold, grasp, grip, clutch, grab, snatch.

embroider, *v.* embellish, elaborate, enlarge on, exaggerate, overstate, stretch, heighten, puff; dress up, adorn, color, paint, varnish, gild; blow up, *Inf.* pile it on; fabricate, invent, prevaricate, lie, fib.

embroidery, *n.* **1.** needlework, needlepoint, cross-stitch; tatting.
2. elaboration, embellishment, exaggeration, expansion, amplification, hyperbole, overstatement; stretching the imagination *or* the truth, coloring, distortion, strain; yarn, tall story, *Inf.* fish story, *Inf.* whopper.

embroil, *v.* **1.** trouble, disturb, agitate, vex, rankle, discompose, discommode; rouse, ferment, ruffle, unsettle, upset; estrange, disunite, split up, set at variance *or* odds, pit one against another, set at sixes and sevens.
2. confuse, perplex, confound, muddle, befuddle, entangle, enmesh, mix up, complicate, ensnarl; involve, implicate, inculpate, incriminate, embarrass, compromise, *Inf.* get into hot water, *Inf.* get into trouble, *Inf.* put [s.o.'s] head in the noose *or* on the block.

embroilment, *n.* **1.** discord, strife, quarrel, difference of opinion, dissension; contention, disturbance, squabble, squall, commotion, imbroglio, uproar; rumpus, fracas, scrimmage, donnybrook, tumult.
2. confusion, perplexity, distraction, disorder, derangement; complication, trouble, muddle, mix up; implication, involvement, embranglement, entanglement, *Inf.* mess, *Inf.* a heap of trouble.

embryo, *n.* **1.** germ, fetus; nucleus, egg, ovum; seed, seedling, sprout.
2. origin, genesis, incipience; square A, rudiments, beginnings; start, commencement.

embryonic, *adj.* fetal, rudimentary, undeveloped; initial, beginning, incipient, primary, elementary, inchoate; immature, unfinished, developing, imperfect.

emend, *v.* edit, revise, redact; correct, amend, alter; ameliorate, improve, polish, touch up; rewrite, reform; blue-pencil, clean up; delete, abridge, tighten; expurgate, cross out, scratch, slash, cut, kill.

emendation, *n.* editing, redaction, revision, *U.S.* rewrite; alteration, correction, amelioration, improvement, polishing; deletion, abridgement, expurgation.

emerald, *n.* **1.** beryl, precious stone, gem, jewel.
—adj. **2.** green, kelly green, grass-green, verdant, viridescent, *Heraldry.* vert.

emerge, *v.* **1.** come forth, emanate, issue, flow, stream forth, effuse; egress, discharge, emit, pour out, disembogue, come out; grow out of, proceed, ensue; originate, eventuate, derive from.
2. come up, arise, crop up, spring up, *Inf.* pop up; come, materialize, surface; reveal itself, show itself, present itself, *Astron.* emerse, come out of hiding; appear, become visible, rise, come into view *or* notice, uprise, come to light, come to the fore; peep out, peer out, fade in, stick one's head out.
3. commence, come into existence, begin, start, spring forth; open, set in, come to pass, come about, happen, occur; develop, grow, evolve, unfold.

emergence, *n.* **1.** emanation, issue, issuance, emission; egress, egression, outflow, outflowing, discharge, outpour, outpouring; efflux, effusion, effluence.
2. coming into view, rise, appearance, apparition, materialization, *Astron.* emersion; coming, advent, eventualization; disclosure, exposure, presentation, showing, unfolding; evolution, development, growth.

emergency, *n.* exigency, crisis, urgency, juncture, conjuncture, extremity, pinch; accident, contingency; unforeseen circumstance, befalling; fix, mess, bind, *Inf.* pickle, *Inf.* stew; *All Inf.* hole, clutch, crunch, tight squeeze; straits, pass, difficulty, hot water, trouble, rub; quandary, dilemma, perplexity; plight, predicament, impasse, cul-de-sac, imbroglio, corner.

emigrant, *n.* **1.** emigre, defector, political refugee, fugitive; displaced person, D.P.; expatriate, immigrant, colonist, foreigner, alien.
2. migrant, trekker, *Derog.* Okie; itinerant, peregrinator, wanderer, vagrant.

emigrate, *v.* **1.** (*usu. from one country to another*) move, resettle, relocate; immigrate, expatriate oneself; migrate, trek; depart, leave, abandon, forsake, quit, renounce, repudiate, reject.
2. uproot, dispace, dispossess, drive out, force out.

emigration, *n.* **1.** (*usu. from one country to another*) moving, resettling, relocation; immigration, expatriation; migration, trekking; departure, withdrawal, exodus.
2. displacement, removal, dispossession.

eminence, *n.* **1.** repute, distinction, eminency, note, mark; standing, station, rank, position; fame, celebrity, report, figure; consequence, importance, significance, account; reputation, prestige, dignity, glory, honor, esteem.
2. loftiness, grandeur, majesty, exaltation, excellence, greatness, preeminence; sublimity, nobility, stateliness, imperialness, augustness, nobleness, splendor.
3. height, altitude, ceiling; loftiness, tallness, stature.
4. prominence, salience, projection, protrusion, ex-

trusion; protuberance, tumescence, excrescence, nodulation; excurvation, swell, swelling, convexity, convexness.

eminent, *adj.* **1.** distinguished, famed, esteemed, exalted; celebrated, illustrious, renowned, preeminent, outstanding, *Archaic.* eximious, *Archaic.* egregious; honorable, venerable, revered, respected, honored; grand, glorious, important, great; august, stately, noble, imperial, sublime, kingly, princely.

2. conspicuous, marked, noticeable, considerable, great; noteworthy, notable, noted, signal, foremost; memorable, unforgettable, remarkable, momentous.

3. lofty, high, tall, high-reaching, towering, aerial; raised, elevated, perched.

4. protruding, projecting, protuberant, sticking out, jutting out, standing out; salient, protrusive, extrusive, projective; in relief, raised, embossed, bossed.

emissary, *n.* **1.** agent, envoy, attaché, diplomat, ambassador, plenipotentiary; representative, commissioner, delegate, legate, nuncio, internuncio, *Rom. Cath. Ch.* vicar; deputy, proxy, substitute; intermediary, go-between, middleman, mediator; messenger, courier, herald, (*in Turkey*) chiaus.

2. spy, secret agent, undercover agent, intelligencer, informer, *Sl.* stool pigeon.

emission, *n.* **1.** discharging, emanation, ejaculation, sending forth, pouring forth, outpour, effusion; exudation, excretion, secretion, oozing, leaking; throwing out, extrusion, ejection; eruption, bursting forth, eructation, disgorgement, egestion, voidance, evacuation.

2. discharge, drainage, ejecta; egesta; semen.

3. issuance, issue, publication; distribution, circulation.

4. utterance, expression, vocalization, declaration, pronouncement.

emit, *v.* **1.** discharge, expel, ejaculate, pour forth, outpour, send forth, emanate, send out, give off; squirt, spurt, shoot, jet; excrete, exude, secrete, ooze, leak, perspire; spill out, gush, disembogue, cast forth, throw out, extrude, eject; erupt, burst forth, *Geol.* extravasate, eruct, eructate, belch forth, spew, vomit, cast up, expectorate, spit; purge, evacuate, void, egest.

2. issue, publish, get out; distribute, circulate, give out.

3. utter, voice, vocalize, articulate, express, give vent to, declare, pronounce.

emollient, *adj.* **1.** lenitive, soothing, assuasive, demulcent; mitigative, allaying, relieving, anodyne, alleviative, palliative, mildening; softening, making supple, making pliable, relaxing; healing, remedial, restorative, balsamic, therapeutic.

—n. **2.** *Medicine.* lenitive, salve, balm, ointment, cerate, oil, lubricant, lotion, liniment, embrocation; mustard plaster, *Med.* sinapism, poultice, *Med.* cataplasm.

emolument, *n.* **1.** remuneration, payment, pay, *Brit. Sl.* get, compensation, consideration; salary, wages, earnings; perquisites, *Inf.* perks, fringe benefits, *Inf.* fringes, *Inf.* extras; hire, fee, stipend, honorarium, allowance; profit, proceeds, revenue, income; return, interest, yield, gain.

2. tip, gratuity, douceur, *Fr. pourboire,* (*in India and Turkey*) baksheesh, remembrance; bribe, graft, boodle, blackmail, hush money; percentage, cut, share, *Inf.* kickback, *Inf.* rake-off.

emote, *v.* **1.** gush, sentimentalize, make a fuss over, make a show over, put on a show; affect *or* feign emotion, put [s.o.] on, playact, pretend, *Sl.* fake it; enthuse, get excited, get all worked up, show excessive emotion, go on, *Inf.* carry on, *Inf.* take on, tear one's hair out.

2. overact, exaggerate, melodramatize, dramatize, behave theatrically; act, perform, play a role; rant, rave, out-Herod Herod.

emotion, *n.* feeling, sentiment, sensation, passion; *Psychol.* affect; chord, response, reaction.

emotional, *adj.* **1.** emotive, noncognitive, *Psychol.* affective.

2. sensitive, sentient, sensuous, feeling, sympathetic, compassionate, warm, tender, affectionate, loving; sentimental, melodramatic, mawkish, maudlin, misty-eyed, dewey-eyed, gush, *Australian.* soony.

3. impassioned, impassionate, feelingful, passionate, ardent; moving, poignant, pathetic, heartfelt, heart-rending, soul-stirring; expressive, demonstrative, dramatic, electric, thrilling, sensational.

4. excitable, easily excited, high-strung, susceptible, quick to tears, tense, nervous; temperamental, hot-tempered, inflammable, volatile, volcanic, fiery, hot-headed, hot-blooded.

5. hysterical, ranting, raving, frantic, overwrought; rapturous, rapt, ecstatic, carried away.

emotionalism, *n.* **1.** sentimentality, gushiness, mawkishness, maudlinism, maudlinness, play on *or* appeal to one's emotions, emotiveness, emotivity; melodrama, melodramatics, dramatics, theatrics, playacting, tears and laughter; sensationalism, showiness, demonstrativeness.

2. excitability, excitableness, nervousness, tenseness; temperamentalness, inflammableness, inflammability, volatileness, hot-headedness, hot-bloodedness; hysteria, hystericalness, ranting, raving, franticness.

emotionalize, *v.* impassion, move, affect, touch, reach, strike a chord, kindle a feeling, play on [s.o.'s] feelings *or* heartstrings; excite, agitate, upset, work up, disturb; rouse, inflame, fire up, enkindle, fan the flame.

empathize, *v.* identify with, sympathize, respond, react, understand, be in tune, *Sl.* be hip to, *Sl.* be into [s.t.], *Sl.* dig, *Sl.* be turned on to; imagine, project, experience vicariously, put oneself into another's place *or* shoes, *Inf.* tune in.

emperor, *n.* sovereign, ruler, rex, king of kings, crowned head, czar, kaiser, Great Mogul, (*in ancient Rome*) imperator, (*in Incan empire*) Inca, (*in medieval China*) khan, (*in Japan*) mikado, (*in Ethiopia*) Negus.

emphasis, *n.* **1.** stress, accent, italics, underlining, underscoring; significance, consequence, consideration, moment, import, note, mark; importance, priority, preeminence; weight, gravity, ponderosity; seriousness, solemnity; urgency, exigency, tension; pressure, insistence; affirmation, assurance, averment.

2. vital concern, matter of concern, matter of importance, matter of life and death; object of note, something special, *Inf.* big deal, *Inf.* one for the books, *Inf.* something to write home about.

3. (*all of expression*) intensity, power, strength, force, force of utterance; energy; accentuation, strong accent, vigorous enunciation, attack; clamor, uproar, outburst, outcry; exclamation, ejaculation, vociferation, vociferance; powerfulness, forcibleness; vociferousness; positiveness, decidedness; peremptoriness, imperativeness, dogmatism.

4. (*all of form or outline*) prominence, distinctness, plainness, clearness, clarity, definiteness, definition; visibility, visibleness, perceptibility, discernibleness *or* discernableness; conspicuousness, conspicuity, salience, saliency.

emphasize, *v.* **1.** stress, lay stress *or* emphasis on, give emphasis to, punctuate, accent; underline, underscore, point up, italicize, call attention to, mark, bring home, press home; feature, highlight, spotlight, play up, give prominence to, bring to the fore, bring into relief, *Inf.* headline; intensify, strengthen, deepen, heighten.

2. dramatize, overemphasize, overstress, overaccentuate, make a mountain out of a molehill, make a big thing out of nothing, make a federal case of; belabor, rub in, harp on, dwell on, hammer away, pound away.

emphatic, *adj.* **1.** stressed, emphasized, accentuated, accented, punctuated, underlined, underscored; (*all of speech*) passionate, impassioned, vehement, ardent, fervent, fiery, fired-up, burning; enthusiastic; animated, spirited, lively.

2. forceful, forcible, insistent, high-pressure; determined, earnest, intense, intensive; urgent, pressing, compelling, critical, crucial, exigent; peremptory, imperative, absolute, dogmatic; crying, clamorous, vociferous; affirmative, assertive, positive, definitive; pronounced, decided, explicit, express; unequivocal, flat, broad, round, categorical, *Inf.* in no uncertain terms; cogent, telling, incisive, effective; trenchant, pointed, marked, barbed, cutting, biting, piercing, penetrating.

3. striking, impressive, strongly marked, forcibly significant; vivid, graphic, distinct, plain, clear, manifest; definite, unmistakable, not to be mistaken.

4. prominent, eminent, outstanding, in relief, in bold *or* high relief; conspicuous, salient, bold, boldly *or* clearly outlined, well-defined; noticeable, sticking *or* hanging out.

empire, *n.* **1.** domain, realm, kingdom; *All Fig.* region, area, zone, territory; province, precinct, quarter, district; bailiwick, dominion, jurisdiction.

2. empery, supremacy, primacy. See **dominion** (*def.* **1**).

empirical, *adj.* experiential, experimental, empiric; seen, observed, heard, felt, sensed.

employ, **1.** hire, enlist, enroll, take on, bring aboard; sign up, sign, engage, retain; commission, contract for, indenture; put to work, put on the payroll, put on salary; try out, apprentice.

2. use, utilize, apply; wield, ply, operate, work; handle, manipulate, put to use; occupy, devote, spend, exercise.

employee, *n.* worker, staffer; hand, hired hand, hireling; workingman, workman, laborer; job-holder, wage-earner; helper, assistant.

employer, *n.* boss, proprietor, manager, director, *Brit. Inf.* governor; leader, owner, president; contractor, entrepreneur; skipper, *Inf.* old man, *Inf.* top dog, top man; patron.

employment, *n.* **1.** work, job, employ, service; station, situation, post, position; appointment, berth, billet, assignment, commission; charge, mission, duty, task; stint, errand, chore, drudgery; occupation, business, profession; vocation, undertaking, calling, pursuit; craft, trade, metier, skill, line.

2. hiring, engaging, taking on, putting to work.

3. use, utilization, application, operation, exercise.

emporium, *n.* **1.** trading center, commercial resort, center of trade; fair, bazaar, market, open market, market place, chief mart, forum, shopping quarter.

2. department store, store, shop, establishment; entrepot, warehouse, storehouse, magazine.

empower, *v.* **1.** authorize, warrant, license, certify, certificate, validate, document, accredit, qualify, *Eccles.* ordain; invest, entrust, entitle, commission, depute, delegate authority to, constitute, *Archaic.* appoint; franchise, charter, legalize, formalize, establish, set up.

2. permit, allow, give the go ahead *or* green light, consent to, vouchsafe; sanction, confirm, ratify, pass, vote for; approve, give one's nod of approval, countenance, *Chiefly U.S.* approbate, *Inf.* O.K.; enable, capacitate, endow, endue, equip, outfit, arm; potentiate, strengthen, invigorate, energize.

empress, *n.* **1.** female sovereign, queen, regina.

2. consort of an emperor, sultana, maharanee, czarina.

emptiness, *n.* **1.** voidness, vacuity, vacancy, vacantness, hollowness; bareness, blankness, barrenness; depletion, exhaustion, inanition.

2. vacuum, void; interruption, hiatus, interim, interval, interlude.

3. destitution, lack, want, need, necessity, requirement; deficiency, scarcity, deprivation.

4. futility, ineffectiveness, uselessness; vanity, insignificance, meaninglessness, unimportance, worthlessness; unreality, delusion, falseness, insubstantiality; folly, sham, mockery.

5. inanity, fatuousness, foolishness, silliness; thoughtlessness, senselessness, brainlessness, dullness, stupidity, unintelligence.

6. verbosity, prolixity, wordiness; loquaciousness, loquacity, garrulity, volubility.

empty, *adj.* **1.** void, vacant, without contents, unfilled, hollow, *Scot. and North Eng.* toom; unfurnished, bare, barren, blank, unadorned; depleted, (*of alcoholic beverage containers*) *Inf.* dead, exhausted, drained, spent.

2. unoccupied, untenanted, tenantless, uninhabited; abandoned, deserted, unclaimed, available, *Inf.* up for grabs.

3. unburdened, unencumbered, unloaded, unsupplied; unfilled, unfed, hungry.

4. devoid of, destitute of, lacking, wanting, bereft of; without, sans, out of, short of, deficient, deprived.

5. futile, ineffectual, ineffective, idle, useless, unavailing, profitless, bootless; vain, insignificant, meaningless, valueless, unimportant, worthless; unreal, delusive, without substance, insubstantial; unsatisfactory, unsatisfying.

6. blank, clear, expressionless, inexpressive, deadpan, poker-faced; vacuous, inane, fatuous, foolish, silly; empty-headed, thoughtless, unthinking, unreflecting, unreasoning, brainless; dull, dense, stupid, unintelligent.

7. verbose, prolix, long-winded, wordy; loquacious, garrulous, talkative, voluble; babbling, blabbing, chattering.

—*v.* **8.** unload, unburden, disburden, free, relieve, remove; emit, pour forth, pour out, teem, send forth, send out, eject; gush, disembogue, cast forth; discharge, exude, ooze, seep, trickle; void, evacuate, make vacant, vacate.

9. deplete, exhaust, use up, consume, spend, run out of; drain, bleed, tax, sap, enervate, devitalize.

empyreal, *adj.* empyrean, celestial, heavenly, uranic, astronomical; extraterrestrial, otherworldy, supramundane, extramundane, ultramundane, unworldly, unearthly; cosmic, solar, heliacal, heliac, nebular, astral, sidereal, stellar, sphery, starry; planetary, asteroidal, lunar, selenological.

empyrean, *n.* **1.** highest heaven, seventh heaven.

2. visible heavens, firmament, vault of heaven, sky, ether, the blue, the wild blue yonder, the azure, *Chiefly Literary.* welkin.

emulate, *v.* **1.** imitate, pattern *or* model after, reflect, mirror, echo; look up to, follow, take after, follow as an example, do like, walk in the footsteps of.

2. equal, match, parallel, keep pace with, come up

to, measure up to, compare to, run abreast of; strive to excel, challenge comparison, vie with, compete with.

emulation, *n.* **1.** effort to equal, attempt to match, imitation; effort to excel, competition, rivalry, vying.

2. high regard, high opinion, honor, veneration, reverence, esteem, respect.

emulous, *adj.* competitive, competing, contending; admiring, reverential.

enable, *v.* **1.** capacitate, qualify, endow, endue, equip, outfit, arm; potentiate, strengthen, invigorate, energize.

2. authorize, warrant, accredit, license, certify, certificate, validate, document; invest, entrust, entitle, commission, delegate, depute, constitute; franchise, charter, legalize, formalize, establish, set up.

3. sanction, approve, give the go ahead *or* green light, give one's nod of approval, countenance, *Chiefly U.S.* approbate, *Inf.* O.K.; agree to, give one's assent, concur with, go along with, accede to; confirm, ratify, pass, vote for; facilitate, ease, assist, aid, help.

enact, *v.* **1.** make into law, establish as law, legislate, pass into law, ratify, sanction, approve; decree, ordain, rule, adjudge, pronounce, proclaim.

2. act, play the part of, portray, represent on the stage, personate, impersonate, personify.

enactment, *n.* **1.** legislation, making *or* passing into law, ratification, sanctioning, approval.

2. motion, proposal, measure, bill, legislation; law, statute, ordinance, rule, regulation; act, decree, edict, proclamation, declaration, pronouncement.

3. provision, condition, stipulation, proviso, clause.

enamel, *n.* **1.** lacquer, varnish, japan, glaze, glossy finish *or* surface, coating, coat of paint; veneer, inlay, overlay, decoration, ornamentation.

2. gloss, polish, luster, sheen, shine, glow.

3. nail polish, nail enamel, nail lacquer, nail paint, nail gloss.

—*v.* **4.** lacquer, japan, varnish, glaze, coat, finish, paint; veneer, overlay, inlay, decorate, ornament.

5. gloss, polish, shine, buff, burnish.

enamor, *v.* captivate, enthrall, enrapture, bewitch, ensorcell, infatuate, charm, allure, fascinate, enchant, sweep off one's feet.

encage, *v.* confine, immure, pen, coop, corral, impound; coop up, pen in, shut in, fence in, wall in; imprison, incarcerate, embar.

encamp, *v.* bivouac, camp, set up camp, tent, pitch camp, pitch one's tent; camp out, sleep out, rough it; (*all in a camp*) lodge, quarter, billet, bed, bunk, berth.

encampment, *n.* **1.** camp, campsite, campground, camping ground, (*in the Near East*) caravansary, bivouac, *Mil.* casern, *Mil.* cantonment.

2. (*both in a camp*) lodgment, settlement; laying out of camp, *Mil.* castramentation.

encase, *v.* box, box up, case, crate, carton; pack, package, parcel; enclose, envelop, wrap, sheathe.

enchain, *v.* **1.** fetter, enfetter, shackle, pinion, trammel, entrammel; handcuff, manacle, put in bilboes, put in irons; restrain, confine, secure; bind, truss; hamper, hobble, immobilize.

2. hold fast, rivet, captivate, engross; mesmerize, magnetize, enchant, hold rapt.

enchant, *v.* **1.** cast a spell upon, spellbind, bewitch, charm, mesmerize, hypnotize, ensorcell; bind by incantations, hoodoo, hex.

2. captivate, allure, delight, enrapture, fascinate; enamor, transport, entice, enthrall, infatuate; catch, win, lead captive, enchain.

enchanter, *n.* magician, sorcerer, wizard, conjurer, mesmerist, thaumaturgist, necromancer; witch doctor, medicine man, shaman; seer, soothsayer.

enchanting, *adj.* charming, captivating, intriguing, entrancing, attractive, prepossessing, engaging, winning; agreeable, winsome, enrapturing, ravishing, irresistible.

enchantment, *n.* **1.** sorcery, witchcraft, magic. See **magic** (*defs.* **1-3**).

2. charm, fascination, delight, entrancement, allurement, glamor; bliss, rapture, transport, ecstasy; captivation, mesmerism, hypnotism.

enchantress, *n.* **1.** sorceress, witch, hex, fairy; siren, Circe, Lorelei.

2. charmer, fascinating woman, *Fr. femme fatale*, seductress, *Inf.* mankiller, *Inf.* vamp; Jezebel, Salome.

encircle, *v.* **1.** surround, encompass, hoop, gird, girdle, engird; embrace, span, belt; wind, wreathe, enwreathe; ring, environ, circumscribe; beset, hedge, besiege; enclose, hem in, confine. See **enclose**.

2. make a circuit, compass, circle, revolve *or* rotate around.

enclose, *v.* **1.** hem in, shut in, close in; pen, pen in, fence in, corral, *Archaic.* pound, impound; confine, immure, wall in, imprison, embar, cage; encompass, surround, girdle, picket; sheathe, encase, cloak, cocoon, enwrap, embosom; bracket.

2. insert, enfold, enter; hold, contain, include.

enclosure, *n.* **1.** pen, sty, fold, corral, paddock, pound; ring, arena; precincts, *South African. kraal,* yard; prison yard, compound, stockade, concentration camp; court, close, cloister; circumvallation, enceinte, pale.

2. fence, fencing, railing; paling, boarding, palisade; barbed wire, hedge, hedgerow, barrier, barricade, ropes; girdle, mantle, jacket, wrapper, envelope, boundary; insertion.

encomium, *n.* eulogy, eulogization, laud, laudation, *Archaic.* magnification, citation; exaltation, glorification, panegyric; tribute, homage, honoring, crowning; extolment, praise, acclaim, acclamation; applause, plaudits, *Inf.* hand, hosanna, hurrah; paean, *Archaic.* gratulation; approbation, commendation, approval, endorsement, sanction.

encompass, *v.* **1.** encircle, circle, circumscribe, surround, ring, ring around, environ, compass; belt, girdle, gird, engird, begird, enclose, hedge in, hem in, ensphere.

2. envelop, enfold, embrace; contain, comprise, include, take in, cover, comprehend, incorporate.

encore, *interj.* **1.** again, once more, once again, bis, a second time, another time.

—*v.* **2.** call back, recall, ask a repeat *or* return.

—*n.* **3.** repeat, repeat performance, replay, return; ovation, standing ovation, bows, curtain calls.

encounter, *v.* **1.** come upon, meet, accost, confront, face, come into contact, cross one's path; run into, *Inf.* bump into, fall across, run across; happen upon, chance upon, stumble upon, light upon, hit upon; come face to face with, front, stand in front of, stand facing.

2. meet with, experience, suffer, endure, undergo, bear; brave, brook, meet head on, come to grips with, tackle; befall, be one's lot, happen to.

3. contend, confront, clash, conflict with, skirmish, struggle; engage, meet, join, face; battle, do battle, war, make war, wage war; grapple, wrestle, spar, box, fight; tussle, scuffle, brawl, duel, shoot it out with, feud.

—*n.* **4.** meeting, joining, junction, coming together, confrontation, facing; presentation, introduction, greeting, salutation.

5. combat, battle, skirmish, conflict; fight, contest,

duel, bout, feud, *Sl.* scrap, joust, tilt; clash, contention, struggle, war; scuffle, tussle, brawl, fray, affray; broil, melee, fracas, *Inf.* run-in, *Inf.* set-to, *Inf.* mix-up; collision, engagement, rencounter, rencontre, *Fr. rencontre.*

encourage, *v.* **1.** enhearten, hearten, reassure, assure, cheer, root, bear up, buoy, buoy up, *Inf.* chirk, *Inf.* pat on the back; stimulate, animate, whet, motivate, embolden, inspire, inspirit, nerve, build up, buck up, rally, boost, invigorate, *Sl.* give a shot in the arm to, *Inf.* peptalk; prompt, urge, urge on, exhort, spur, goad, prick, egg on; impel, induce, incline, dispose, prevail upon, persuade, influence, sway; incite, instigate, actuate, provoke, foment; excite, arouse, rouse, inflame, enflame, fire, fire up, stir, stir up, wind up, *Inf.* psyche up.

2. abet, assist, help, aid, second, succor, relieve, lend oneself to, subsidize, underwrite; uphold, maintain, sustain; support, advocate, patronize, lobby, back, recommend, endorse, sanction, approve, countenance; promote, further, forward, advance, favor, foster.

encouragement, *n.* **1.** enheartening, heartening, reassuring, assuring, cheering, rooting, buoying, buoying up, *Inf.* chirking; stimulating, animating, motivating, emboldening, inspiriting, nerving, nerving up, building up, bucking up, rallying, boosting, invigorating; prompting, urging, urging on, exhorting, spurring, goading, prodding, pricking, egging on; impelling, inducing, inclining, disposing, prevailing upon, influencing, persuading, swaying; inciting, instigating, actuating, provoking, fomenting; exciting, arousing, rousing, enflaming, firing, firing up, stirring, stirring up, winding up, *Inf.* psyching up.

2. abetting, assisting, helping, aiding, subsidizing, underwriting, seconding; upholding, maintaining, sustaining, succoring; supporting, advocating, patronizing, lobbying, backing, endorsing, sanctioning, approving, countenancing; promoting, furthering, forwarding, advancing, favoring, fostering.

3. hope, enheartenment, cheer, lift, boost, build up, buoyancy, reassurance, assurance, pat on the back; promise, good omen, good auspices, clear sky, bright prospect; inspiration, stimulation, stimulus, motivation, incentive, inducement, instance, pep talk; instigation, urge, urging, prompting, goad, prick, spur; excitement, arousal, inflammation; influence, persuasion, exhortation, advice.

4. help, aid, assistance, security, aegis, protection, championship; relief, refreshment, succor, solace, consolation, comfort; support, backing, sponsorship, patronage, advocacy, auspice *or* auspices, countenance, favor, approval, approbation, sanction, blessing; furtherance, promotion, advance, advancement.

encroach, *v.* **1.** intrude, obtrude, interlope, irrupt, move in on, *Inf.* muscle in, *Inf.* tread on [s.o.'s] toes; trespass, infringe, impinge, entrench, trench, invade, infiltrate.

2. overstep, transgress, overstep the bounds, know no bounds, go too far; presume on *or* upon, impose on *or* upon, take liberties, abuse one's privileges.

encroachment, *n.* trespass, infringement, impingement, entrenchment, invasion, incursion, inroad, influx, infiltration; intrusion, obtrusion, irruption; arrogation, usurpation, seizure, overrunning; transgression, violation.

encumber, *v.* **1.** impede, hamper, hinder, retard, cumber, handicap, cramp, constrain; restrain, bridle, trammel; bar, stay, obstruct, check.

2. clog, block up, fill up, congest, stuff, pack, jam.

3. burden, weigh down, weight, load down, charge, tax; oppress, strain, overload, overburden, overtask, overtax.

encumbrance, *n.* **1.** impediment, hindrance, handicap, disadvantage, cumbrance, strain; burden, weight, onus, cross, millstone, albatross; duty, obligation, responsibility, tax.

2. dependent, charge, ward, protégé, child, son, daughter.

encyclopedia, *n.* cyclopedia, book of knowledge, yearbook, annual, almanac, reference book; dictionary, wordbook, thesaurus, lexicon, glossary.

encyclopedic, *adj.* extensive, vast, broad, wide-ranging, diversified, universal; comprehensive, all-inclusive, exhaustive, complete, thorough.

end, *n.* **1.** termination, conclusion, expiration, cessation, abruption, stoppage, close, finish, wind-up; completion, fulfillment, attainment, accomplishment, culmination, consummation; ending, finale, finis, denouement, peroration, epilogue, period.

2. extremity, furthermost part, terminus, terminal, pole, point, nib, tip, top, head, horn; limitation, bound, boundary, limit, pale, bourn; border, confine, margin; acme, apogee, ultimate, utmost, uttermost, extreme.

3. purpose, aim, object, objective, goal, reason, motive, motivation, intent, intention, design; destination, final cause, raison d'etre.

4. result, outcome, consequence, upshot, effect, issue, fruit, flower.

5. destruction, ruin, ruination, dissolution, extermination, annihilation, death, *Sl.* curtains; deathblow, *Fr. coup de grâce, Sl.* finisher, *Sl.* sockdolager; doom, doomsday, day of wrath, Judgment Day.

6. remnant, fragment, scrap, stub, fag end, butt, heel.

7. share, part, portion, segment, sector, province, field, area, responsibility, *Inf.* load.

8. at loose ends unsettled, drifting, dallying; confused, uncertain, wavering, *Inf.* betwixt and between, *Sl.* not together.

9. make both ends meet economize, husband, live within one's means, endure, survive, subsist, *Inf.* get by, *Inf.* scrape by.

10. no end *Informal.* very much, considerably, *Inf.* a lot.

11. on end continuously, successively, consecutively, serially.

—*v.* **12.** conclude, terminate, settle, close; complete, accomplish, consummate, achieve; finish, finish off, put an end to, make an end of, bring to an end; adjourn; (*all usu. with* in) reach, arrive, culminate, climax.

13. cease, stop, discontinue, drop, cut, cut short, bring down the curtain; die, die out, expire, vanish, pass, pass away, peter out, wind up *or* down, run down *or* out, blow over, run its course; quit, desist, abandon, leave off, break, break off, call it quits, call it a day.

14. kill, destroy, do in; annihilate, exterminate, eradicate, get rid of, wipe out, extinguish, abolish, dissolve; quell, arrest, check, squelch, put down, *Inf.* put the kibosh on.

endanger, *v.* imperil, expose to danger, jeopardize, put in jeopardy; hazard, expose, risk, venture, take a chance, tempt fate; put on a spot, commit, involve, sail too near the wind; call attention to, bring into the open.

endear, *v.* **1.** evoke love *or* affection, charm, captivate, win, win over, attach, attract; warm the cockles of one's heart.

2. lose one's heart to, be enamored of, smile upon, dispose *or* incline toward, fold to the heart; hold in affection *or* love, hold dear, esteem, prize, value, treasure, enjoy, admire.

endearment, *n.* **1.** affection, fondness, attachment, tie, bond.

2. fondling, petting, necking, spooning, *Sl.* canoodling, lovemaking, *Inf.* making out; caress, hug, cuddle, squeeze, embrace; osculation, kiss, buss, *Inf.* smack, *Inf.* smacker, *Inf.* big fat kiss; making eyes, *Inf.* making goo-goo eyes; winning ways; loving *or* honeyed words, pet name, sweet talk, baby talk, billing and cooing.

endeavor, *v.* **1.** strive, struggle, labor, try hard, do one's best, set at [s.t.] with a will; try, make an effort, take pains, bestir oneself; attempt, tackle, take on, try one's hand, *Inf.* have a go, *Inf.* take a crack *or* whack *or* shot at; essay, undertake, work at, go about; aspire, aim, *Inf.* shoot for; seek to, venture, make a bold push, *Inf.* dream the impossible dream, *Inf.* take one's chances; tempt fortune, adventure; feel *or* pick one's way, grope, *Inf.* make a stab at, *Inf.* give it the old college try.

—*n.* **2.** striving, struggle, try, attempt, effort, conatus, *Inf.* crack, *Inf.* whack, *Inf.* shot; essay, undertaking, venture, enterprise, quest, aim, nisus.

endless, *adj.* **1.** infinite, limitless, unlimited, boundless, illimitable, termless; countless, numberless, untold, innumerable; unmeasured, measureless, unmeasurable, indeterminable, incalculable.

2. eternal, enduring, undying, immortal, deathless; everlasting, *Literary.* sempiternal, perdurable; unfading, perpetual, imperishable, amaranthine, perennial.

3. unceasing, incessant, ceaseless, unending, interminable; constant, nonstop, unremitting, recurring.

4. continuous, unbroken, continual, uninterrupted, without end, never-ending, entire.

endorse, *v.* **1.** approve, give one's stamp *or* seal of approval, set one's seal to, seal, *Inf.* O.K.; sanction, warrant, authorize, confirm, ratify, pass, vote for.

2. support, vouch for, give one's word, give testimonial to, testify to, attest to, back up, stand behind *or* by; sustain, uphold, corroborate, substantiate, document, prove; aid, assist, patronize, encourage, favor, recommend.

3. sign for, sign on the dotted line, subscribe, undersign; assign, docket, sign *or* make over, note, receipt; autograph, *Inf.* put one's John Henry *or* John Hancock on [s.t.]; countersign, cosign for, underwrite, witness; validate, legalize, notarize, visa.

endorsement, *n.* **1.** approval, approbation, sanction, acceptance, warrant, authorization; seal *or* stamp of approval, stamp, seal, signet, sigil, cachet, *Inf.* O.K.; confirmation, ratification, passage.

2. assurance, guarantee, testimonial, testimony, attestation, promise, word, *Obs.* vouch; recommendation, advocacy, support, patronage, assistance, commendation, encouragement.

3. countersignature, subscription, underwriting; transfer, transference, docketing, *Law.* assignment; signature, signing, autograph, *Inf.* John Hancock, *Inf.* John Henry.

endow, *v.* **1.** bestow, present, give, gift, confer, proffer, *Archaic.* propine; will, leave, pass down, *Law.* bequeath, *Law.* devise, dower; grant, allot, subsidize, award; benefact, largess, donate, contribute, offer.

2. enrich, invest, endue, furnish, provide, supply, accommodate; equip, appoint, fit out, arm, rig; array, adorn, grace, clothe, dress out, deck out; enable, empower, qualify.

endowment, *n.* **1.** bestowal, presentation, gift, conferment, conferral; benefaction, donation, contribution; endowing, granting, subsidizing.

2. foundation, grant, aid, allowance, allotment, stipend, subsidy, subvention; benefaction, bounty, largess, donation, conative, contribution, offering, altarage; *Law.* bequest, *Law.* acquest, *Law.* legacy, *Law.* devise, heritage, inheritance, dowry, *Civil Law.* dot; gift, present, *Scot.* propine; benefit, blessing, boon.

3. endowments attributes, properties, qualities, characteristics, features; gifts, talents, faculties, dowers, parts; aptitudes, understandings, powers, strengths.

endurable, *adj.* tolerable, bearable, brookable, livable, supportable, maintainable, sustainable, sufferable, *Obs. Rare.* abideable.

endurance, *n.* **1.** perseverance, tolerance, toleration, maintenance, sufferance, sustainment, abidingness; forbearance, acceptance, long-suffering, patience, stoicism, resignation; dispassion, composure, equanimity, even temper, sang-froid; stamina, hardihood, backbone, pluck, mettle, spunk, *Sl.* guts.

2. duration, continuance, lastingness, permanence, durability, durableness; persistence, perseverance, continuing power, *Inf.* stick-to-it-iveness; soundness, solidity, stability, fixedness, changelessness, immutability, immovableness.

3. trial, hardship, trouble, tribulation, distress; calamity, misfortune, torment, ordeal.

endure, *v.* **1.** undergo, experience, bear, go through, pass through; encounter, live out, meet with, meet, taste, fare.

2. hold out against, withstand, sustain without yielding, support, bear, weather, *Archaic.* forbear, suffer, *Chiefly Scot.* thole, *Scot. and North Eng.* dree; take it, brave it out, *Inf.* tough [it] out, *Inf.* stick [it] out, *Sl.* sweat [it] out, go through the mill, *Inf.* take it on the chin; *Inf.* hang in, *Inf.* keep the faith, keep one's chin up, *Sl.* stand the gaff.

3. tolerate, take patiently, brook, submit to, bear without resistance; abide, stand, withstand, put up with, permit, allow; swallow, stomach, digest, pocket.

4. last, continue to exist, persist, perdure, be permanent, be durable, wear well; abide, *Archaic.* bide, stay, remain, tarry, rest, hold, hold on, hold one's ground.

enemy, *n.* **1.** antagonist, adversary, attacker, assailant, hostile party, foe, *Literary.* foeman; opponent, opposer, rival, vier, competitor, contestant, contender.

2. the opposition, hostile nation *or* state, the other side, them.

3. the Enemy the devil, Satan, the archenemy, the Adversary.

energetic, *adj.* **1.** energetical, vigorous, dynamic, electric; active, alive, full of energy, *Inf.* full of pep, *Inf.* peppy, *Inf.* snappy, *Inf.* on one's toes, full of vim and vigor; eager, ready to go, bright-eyed and bushy-tailed; lively, spirited, *Sl.* go-go, full of life, animated, vibrant, vital; sprightly, sprightful, spry, *Chiefly U.S. Inf.* chipper; robust, hardy, hale, brisk, strenuous, exertive, laborious, physical.

2. jumping, hopping, cracking, busy, on the go *or* move; zealous, industrious, diligent, devoted, hardworking, determined; ambitious, enterprising, pushing, driving, aggressive; forcible, forceful, emphatic, powerful, mighty, strong, potent, puissant, high-powered; effective, effectual, efficacious, efficient, trenchant.

energetically, *adv.* vigorously, dynamically, with might and main, briskly, strenuously, actively, *Inf.* hammer and tongs, zealously, eagerly, ardently; full tilt, *Inf.* to beat the band, *Sl.* up a storm, with all one's might, with everything one's got, heart and soul; determinedly, pointedly, diligently, industriously, with a vengeance; ambitiously, enterprisingly, aggressively; strongly, emphatically, forcefully, forcibly, powerfully, mightily, potently, puissantly; effectually, efficaciously, efficiently.

energize, *v.* **1.** enliven, invigorate, liven up, pep up; stimulate, animate, reanimate, whet, motivate, inspirit, inspire, *Inf.* sparkplug, galvanize, electrify; vivify, quicken, vitalize.

2. actuate, activate, move, rouse, waken; incite, arouse, rouse up, instigate, provoke; fire, kindle, enkindle, *Inf.* spark, stir, goad, spur on, prod, prick; push, egg on, urge, impel, exhort; boost, promote, prompt, foment; excite, work up.

3. be in operation, be active; put forth energy, do one's utmost, spare no efforts; struggle, labor, strain; buckle to, grind, plod, slave; toil, drudge, sweat.

energy, *n.* **1.** vigor, vitality, birr, *Inf.* starch, stamina, get up and go; intensity, force, power, puissance, might, *Sl.* guts, nerve; potency, potentiality, efficacy, effectiveness, efficiency, cogency; virility, forcefulness, elbow grease, muscle; drive, push, *Psychol.* conation; initiative, ambition, enterprise.

2. animation, liveliness, vivacity, spirit; dash, elan, zest, verve, flair, zing; fire, warmth, glow, fervency, ardor; sprightliness, airiness, buoyancy, bounce, cheer; ebullience, sparkle, effervescence; vigor, vim, *Inf.* zip, *It. brio*, *Sl.* oomph, *Inf.* pep; exuberance, enthusiasm, zeal, fervor, passion; alertness, *Chiefly Scot.* smeddum.

enervate, *v.* **1.** weaken, enfeeble, debilitate, devitalize, deprive of strength; exhaust, deplete, sap, impoverish; tire, strain, fatigue, *Inf.* take it out of [s.o.]; demoralize, defeat, *Inf.* take the starch out of, break, shatter; unbrace, unnerve, unman, emasculate, effeminize.

2. impair, invalidate, disable, incapacitate, cripple, paralyze, handicap, undermine; dilute, adulterate, debase, water, water down, *Inf.* cut; thin, attenuate; lessen, diminish, lower, reduce, minimize.

enervation, *n.* **1.** weakness, enfeeblement, feebleness, infirmity, debilitation, debility, devitalization, *Both Pathol.* asthenia, adynamia; exhaustion, depletion, impoverishment; impotence, impuissance, powerlessness, helplessness, inability; tiredness, weariness, fatigue, strain, lassitude, languor; demoralization, defeat, collapse; emasculation, castration, effeminization.

2. impairment, invalidation, disablement, incapacitation, crippling, paralysis, undermining; dilution, adulteration, debasement; reduction, minimization, lessening, diminishing, lowering.

enfeeble, *v.* weaken, enervate, debilitate, devitalize, deprive of strength; exhaust, deplete, sap. See **enervate** (*defs.* **1,2**).

enfold, *v.* **1.** envelop, wrap up, enwrap, lap, entwine, swathe, muffle up, swaddle, shroud; surround, encircle, encompass, enclose; clasp, enclasp, embosom, embrace, hug.

2. fold, drape, double, pleat, plait, gather, ruffle, pucker.

enforce, *v.* **1.** implement, put into effect *or* force, bring to bear, *Inf.* clamp down, *Inf.* crack down, get tough, toughen *or* tighten up; prosecute, follow up, back up, carry through; carry out, execute, perform, discharge; complete, accomplish, put through, fulfill, realize.

2. administer, manage, control, conduct, direct, boss; officiate, preside over, watch over, supervise, superintend, oversee, look after, see that [s.t.] is done.

3. force, compel, coerce, press, pressure, make, dragoon; necessitate, cause, drive, railroad, *Inf.* shove *or* ram down one's throat; impel, urge, impress, lay stress upon, insist upon, demand, impose upon, require, exact, extort; apply pressure, *Sl.* lean against *or* on, armtwist, twist [s.o.'s] arm, put the screws on *or* to, squeeze, *Inf.* strong-arm, put the heat on; threaten, intimidate, bulldoze, browbeat, bully, give [s.o.] a hard time, hector, harass.

enforcement, *n.* **1.** implementation, putting into effect, bringing to bear, *Inf.* clamping down, *U.S. Inf.* crackdown; prosecution, carrying out *or* through, execution, discharge, completion, fulfillment, realization.

2. control, domination, supervision, manipulation; force, compulsion, coercion, pressure, duress, constraint, obligation; necessitation, requirement, press, urging, prompting, prick, provocation, goad, spur, boot, shove, push; insistence, demand, exaction, extortion, threat; intimidation, armtwisting, bulldozing, browbeating, bullying; a hard time.

enfranchise, *v.* **1.** naturalize, admit to citizenship; grant [s.o.] voting rights.

2. authorize, license, privilege, warrant; charter, empower, sanction, qualify.

3. emancipate, affranchise, liberate, manumit, disenthrall, free, set free; release, disimprison, unfetter, unshackle.

enfranchisement, *n.* **1.** naturalization, admission to citizenship; the vote, the right to vote.

2. authorization, accordance; license, privilege, warranty, charter; sanction, grant, concession, carte blanche; permission, leave.

3. emancipation, affranchisement, liberation, manumission, disenthrallment, deliverance; release, disimprisonment.

engage, *v.* **1.** occupy, employ, busy, engross, absorb; entertain, divert, amuse; hold, secure, tie up.

2. employ, hire, enlist, enroll, take on, *Inf.* take on board, bring aboard, put to work, put on the payroll; sign up, sign, retain, book, reserve; commission, appoint, delegate; contract for, indenture; choose, select, secure.

3. attract, draw, pull, magnetize; allure, entice, invite, tempt, lure, inveigle; interest, fascinate, charm, enamor, enchant; captivate, win, catch.

4. bind, require, prescribe, assign; astrict, oblige, obligate, commit; pledge, promise, covenant, agree; stipulate, contract, bargain; betroth, affiance, speak for, plight one's troth, espouse, give one's hand, *Eccles.* publish the banns.

5. join battle with, set to, encounter, enter into conflict with, give battle to, take the field; contend, struggle, wrestle, grapple, tussle, scuffle; battle, fight, combat, war, wage war, skirmish; clash, joust, duel, cross weapons.

6. occupy oneself, become involved, be occupied, take part; take up, undertake, embark on, set *or* go about; throw oneself into, launch into, tackle, plunge *or* dive into.

engaged, *adj.* **1.** occupied, preoccupied, employed, busy, *Inf.* tied up, *Inf.* hung up; engrossed, absorbed, caught up in, wrapped up in, lost in, immersed in; entertained, diverted, amused.

2. pledged, promised, committed, bound; contracted, covenanted, stipulated; betrothed, affianced, spoken for, plighted, espoused.

3. battling, fighting, combatting, warring; contending, struggling, wrestling.

engagement, *n.* **1.** promise, word, word of honor, parole, pledge, vow, oath; guarantee, warranty, compact, contract, covenant, treaty; obligation, commitment; deal, pact, bargain; agreement, arrangement, acknowledgment, stipulation.

2. betrothal, betrothment, *Archaic.* troth, plighting, espousal, sponsalia, subarrhation, *Archaic.* affiance.

3. employment, business; post, station, rounds; period, stint.

4. appointment, meeting, interview, arrangement; tryst, rendezvous, assignation, date.

5. fight, battle, duel, bout; collision, meeting, encounter, rencounter; contention, clash, conflict, struggle, strife; war, warfare, fighting, hostilities; assault, attack, offensive, assailment; siege, besiegement, besetment; brawl, feud, affray, broil.

engaging, *adj.* **1.** pleasing, delightful, enjoyable; charming, attractive, appealing, *Inf.* fetching, *Inf.* eye-catching; winning, taking, winsome; sweet, agreeable, likeable; lovely, pretty, fair, handsome, prepossessing, beautiful, exquisite; graceful, elegant, refined.

2. enticing, alluring, tempting, tantalizing, titillating; intriguing, diverting, beguiling, inducing, provocative, seductive, arousing; irresistible, magnetizing, electrifying, captivating, inflaming; fascinating, catching, hypnotizing, mesmerizing; enchanting, bewitching, entrancing, enthralling, enrapturing.

engender, *v.* **1.** cause, produce, effect, effectuate, bring about, bring to pass, give rise to, occasion; excite, provoke, rouse, arouse, work up.

2. beget, create, procreate, father, sire, sow the seeds of, conceive, give birth to; breed, propagate, reproduce, spawn.

3. arise, rise, dawn, come into existence, come to be, take birth, see the light of day, begin.

engine, *n.* **1.** motor, turbine, dynamo, generator, transformer, transducer.

2. machine, mechanism, apparatus, device, contrivance, *Inf.* contraption; tool, utensil, implement, appliance, convenience, facility, utility, mechanical aid.

engineer, *n.* **1.** operator, handler, conductor, driver, pilot; (*on a streetcar or subway*) motorman, (*on a cable car*) gripman, *Brit.* engine driver, *Inf.* Casey Jones, *Railroad Sl.* hogger *or* hog head.

2. combat engineer, pioneer, *U.S. Navy.* Seabee, *Brit.* sapper.

—*v.* **3.** plan, devise, lay out, orchestrate, mastermind; manage, superintend, direct, conduct, handle, run, *Inf.* quarterback, *Inf.* call the shots; produce, perform, do, achieve, accomplish, effectuate, bring about.

4. arrange, negotiate, put through, *Inf.* swing, *Sl.* put over; scheme, intrigue, conspire, connive, plot; maneuver, machinate, manipulate, pull strings *or* wires, jockey, finesse, rig, *Inf.* wangle, *Inf.* finagle.

engird, *v.* encircle, circle, surround, encompass, environ, outline, circumscribe, delineate; gird, begird, girdle, belt; circumvent, beset, entrap, trap.

engorge, *v.* devour, raven, bolt, gobble, gulp down, wolf down, ingurgitate; glut, gorge, cram, stuff; gluttonize, gormandize, guttle, play a good knife and fork.

engrave, *v.* **1.** cut, carve, incise, grave, etch, chisel; chase, enchase, hatch, stipple; ornament, mark, blaze; print, imprint, stamp.

2. impress, fix, set, lodge, embed, infix, stamp, brand.

engraver, *n.* lithographer, graver, etcher; lapidary, lapidarist, chalcographer, glyphographer, wood-engraver, xylographer, cerographist; carver, sculptor.

engraving, *n.* **1.** cutting, chiseling, incising, graving, chasing, hatching, stippling, ornamenting, marking, carving, sculpting; lithography, chromolithography, etching, drypoint; anaglyphy, chalcography, zincography, xylography; photoengraving, *Obs.* hiliogravure, glyphography.

2. device, relief, anaglyph, intaglio, cameo; *Trademark.* Graphotype, tailpiece.

3. plate, block, copperplate, cerograph.

4. print, impression, pull; lithograph, etching, drypoint, aquatint, mezzotint, chromolithograph, vignette, cut, woodcut, xylograph; half-tone, photogravure, rotogravure, illustration, picture, proof, positive, negative.

engross, *v.* **1.** absorb, immerse, preoccupy, obsess, consume, devour, take all one's time; keep one busy, engage, involve, occupy, employ, hold, hold one's attention; amuse, divert, distract; rivet, fix, fixate, arrest, attract.

2. inscribe, letter, superscribe, transcribe, *Rare.* scribe; engrave, imprint.

3. buy up, forestall, corner, corner the market; monopolize, have all to oneself, control the market.

engrossing, *adj.* **1.** absorbing, immersing, enwrapping, deep; preoccupying, obsessing, obsessive, monopolizing; fascinating, captivating, spellbinding, interesting; riveting, attention-getting, arresting, attracting; engaging, occupying, amusing, charming.

2. monopolizing, controlling, having all to oneself, having a corner on the market.

engrossment, *n.* **1.** absorption, absorbing, immersion, immersing; preoccupation, preoccupying, obsession, obsessing, consumption, consuming, devourment, devouring, *Inf.* bag, *Sl.* hang-up; involvement, involving, occupation, occupying, engagement, engaging, employment, employing, business, busying; abstraction, raptness, intensity, concentration, pensiveness, musing, thoughtfulness.

2. inscription, superscription, transcription, transcript, copy.

engulf, *v.* **1.** swallow up, gulf, gulp, consume, engorge; submerge, whelm, submerse, sound; sink, send to the bottom, go down; inundate, flood, deluge, overwhelm; drown, swamp, entomb, bury.

2. plunge, dive, pitch, leap, fall headlong, jump; immerse, absorb, engross, bury in, engage.

enhance, *v.* **1.** intensify, magnify, amplify, heighten; increase, make greater, *Chiefly Literary.* greaten; enrich, strengthen, deepen, darken; reinforce, double, redouble.

2. augment, elevate, aggrandize, raise, boost, escalate, *Inf.* jack up, hike.

enhancement, *n.* **1.** intensification, magnification, amplification, heightening; strengthening, enrichment, deepening, darkening; reinforcement, doubling, redoubling.

2. increase, increment, accretion, raise; elevation, escalation, aggrandizement, augmentation, boost, hike.

enigma, *n.* **1.** mystery, puzzle, riddle, conundrum, question, question mark; problem, dilemma, quandary, plight, predicament, skeleton in the closet, *Inf.* pickle, *Inf.* jam, *Inf.* fix; maze, labyrinth, tangle, knot; secret, arcanum, closed *or* sealed book; unknown, unexplored ground *or* territory, *Latin. terra incognita*; unknowable, deep *or* profound secret, mystery of mysteries.

2. oracle, dark saying, hidden meaning, obscure statement, riddle of the sphinx; puzzler, poser, *Inf.* hard nut to crack, *Inf.* brain-teaser, *Inf.* mind-boggler, *Inf.* stumper, *Inf.* floorer.

enigmatic, *adj.* **1.** puzzling, baffling, bewildering, perplexing, confounding, mystifying, enigmatical; inexplicable, unexplainable, insoluble, insolvable, unaccountable, *Obs.* inextricable; strange, weird, bizarre.

2. mysterious, arcane, cryptic, esoteric, occult, perdu, hermetic, hermetical; secret, hidden, veiled, masked, screened; obscure, indistinct, indefinite, unclear, shadowy, nebulous, vague; inscrutable, oracular, sphingine, sphinxian, sphinxlike; mystic, mystical, transcendental, cabalistic.

3. abstruse, recondite, abstract, heavy; impenetrable, unfathomable, incomprehensible, uncomprehensible, past *or* beyond comprehension *or* understanding.

4. ambiguous, equivocal, noncommittal; secretive, covert, clandestine, under-the-table, under-the-counter; evasive, shifty, circuitous.

enjoin, *v.* **1.** direct, order, command, charge, bid; enact, decree, ordain, summon; adjure, dictate, instruct, call upon; require, exact, call for, ask for; bind, force, set, saddle with, impose.

2. prescribe, recommend, advise, counsel, advocate, suggest, move; caution, admonish, exhort; urge, persuade, prompt, press, encourage.

3. prohibit, proscribe, ban, interdict, prelude, disallow, forbid; restrict, inhibit, bar, hinder, obstruct; restrain, constrain, prevent, hold back.

enjoy, *v.* **1.** take pleasure in, be pleased with, take satisfaction in, derive pleasure from; delight in, relish in, rejoice in, revel in, riot in, *Sl.* groove on; luxuriate in, bask in, indulge in, swim in, wallow in; feast on, savor, appreciate, gloat over, *Inf.* smack one's lips over, eat up; like, love, fancy, take to, *Sl.* dig.

2. have a good time, have a time of it, *Inf.* have the time of one's life, *Inf.* have a ball, *Inf.* eat [s.t.] up; *Sl.* get a bang *or* kick *or* boot out of, *Sl.* get a charge *or* lift out of, *Sl.* get high off of, *Sl.* get off on.

3. benefit from, profit from, reap the benefits of; make good use of, avail oneself of, make the most of; make use of, use, put to use, utilize, use to one's advantage.

enjoyable, *adj.* delightful, pleasant, pleasing, agreeable, pleasurable, gratifying, satisfying; lovely, nice, good, great, *Sl.* swell, *Sl.* fine; fun, amusing, entertaining, diverting; delectable, delicious, palatable, tasty, toothsome, savory.

enjoyment, *n.* delight, pleasure, joy; delectation, gratification, satisfaction; zest, relish, gusto, exhilaration, transport, ecstasy; gladness, cheer, mirth, glee, merriment, jollity, gaiety; happiness, elation, elevation, felicity, bliss; contentment, ease, comfort, cakes and ale, wine and roses, bed of roses, creature comforts; treat, feast, banquet, regalement, revelment, revel, revelry; good time, fun, *Sl.* kick, *Sl.* bang, thrill; amusement, diversion, entertainment, recreation, divertissement.

enkindle, *v.* **1.** fire, ignite, torch, deflagrate, burn, kindle, burn up *or* down, set aflame *or* alight *or* on fire, set fire to, put to the torch, put *or* apply a match to, *Obs.* accend, *Obs.* flagrate.

2. incite, provoke, actuate, poke, prod, prick, goad, prompt, spur; encourage, urge, abet, egg on, put up to; instigate, look for trouble, *Inf.* start something; foment, agitate, suscitate, excite, impassion, intensify; arouse, madden, craze, stir up, wind up, work up, whip up, lash into a frenzy, *Inf.* psych up, heat up, *Obs.* calefy *or* calify, fire up, inflame, enflame, touch off, ignite the spark, stir the embers, stoke *or* fuel *or* fan the fire, add fuel to the flames *or* fire.

3. stimulate, animate, reanimate, whet, invigorate; motivate, inspirit, inspire, galvanize, electrify, *Inf.* spark; energize, activate, vivify, rally, revive, enliven; liven up, pep up, awaken, wake up, waken, shake up, jolt, jog; push, drive, press, force, force along, propel; hound, whip, lash, flog; impel, induce, compel, constrain, move, stir, fillip; evoke, elicit, call forth, summon up, raise *or* spread the alarm.

enlarge, *v.* **1.** increase, augment, add to, supplement; double, triple, treble, quadruple, multiply; magnify, amplify, make greater *or* larger *or* bigger, aggrandize, *Chiefly Literary.* greaten; expand, extend, distend, stretch, spread; widen, broaden, heighten, lengthen, elongate, deepen, thicken, increase the capacity of.

2. dilate, distend, inflate, blow up, swell, tumefy, intumesce, bloat, puff out, bulge, protuberate; grow, wax, become greater *or* larger *or* bigger; develop, mature, maturate, sprout, shoot up; mushroom, snowball, burgeon, spread out, outspread, branch out, sprawl.

3. expatiate, expound, descant, dissertate, perorate, discourse, dwell on, talk at great length; elaborate, detail, make more comprehensive, give wider scope *or* greater breadth to; prolong, prolongate, protract, draw out, spin out, drag out, go on, drone on.

enlargement, *n.* **1.** increase, increment, augmentation, supplementation; multiplication, doubling, tripling, trebling, quadrupling; amplification, magnification, aggrandizement, *Archaic.* ampliation; expansion, extension, distension, inflation, blowing up, swell, swelling, intumescence, tumefaction, bloating, bulging, protuberation; growth, growing, waxing, development, maturation, sprouting *or* shooting up.

2. larger *or* bigger copy *or* print, giant-sized picture, *Photography.* blow-up.

3. addition, extension, wing, ell, annexation, annex, *Rare.* annexment; supplementation, appendage, appurtenance, appurtenant, adjunct, appendage, attachment; supplement, appendix, addendum, codicil, *Law.* allonge.

enlighten, *v.* **1.** instruct, teach, tutor, school, educate, inform, apprise; edify, uplift, open [s.o.'s] eyes, make [s.o.] see the light; indoctrinate, inculcate, instil, infuse; train, coach, initiate, ground, prepare, ready; counsel, advise, guide, preach, lecture, moralize, sermonize; civilize, cultivate, refine, polish.

2. explain, illustrate, illumine, illuminate, clarify, clear up, elucidate, spell out; indicate, show, show how, demonstrate; describe, point out, tell; acquaint with, familiarize with, introduce to, apprise of.

enlightened, *adj.* **1.** aware, insightful, sensitive, broad-minded, open-minded, reasonable, rational; wise, understanding, comprehending; intellectual, cerebral, brainy, highbrow *or* highbrowed; articulate, well-spoken, fluent; civilized, cultivated, refined, cultured, artistic, *Inf.* arty, *Sl.* artsy, *Inf.* longhair *or* longhaired.

2. educated, learned, scholarly, erudite; literate, lettered, literary, well-read, knowledgeable, informed, conversant, versed, well-versed, well-grounded; sensible of, apprised of, acquainted with, familiar with.

3. trained, schooled, instructed, tutored, coached; prepared, readied, primed.

enlightenment, *n.* **1.** understanding, wisdom, sapience, (*usu. cap.*) *Buddhism.* prajna; comprehension, awareness, insight, perception, sensitivity; open-mindedness, broad-mindedness, freedom of thought, appreciation; learning, knowledge, lore, information, skill; preparation, schooling, training, initiation, apprenticeship; erudition, scholarship, study, *Usu. Derog.* bookishness; edification, culture, cultivation, refinement.

2. education, teaching, instruction, tuition, tutelage; direction, guidance, nurture, development; inculcation, indoctrination, initiation, discipline; explanation, illustration, elucidation, illumination, clarification.

enlist, *v.* **1.** (*usu. in reference to military service*) enroll, sign up, *Inf.* join up; volunteer, volunteer for the draft.

2. (*in reference to military service*) draft, impress, press, recruit, induct, levy, conscript, conscribe, *Archaic.* list, muster in, *Naut.* shanghai, crimp; activate, call up, mobilize.

3. recruit, procure, muster, gather up *or* together; secure, obtain, enroll, register; engage, take on, hire, employ.

enlistment, *n.* **1.** term, period, incumbency, *Chiefly Mil.* tour, tour of duty, *Inf.* time, stint, *Mil. Sl.* hitch.

2. enrollment, registration, sign-up; engagement, procurement, mustering, securing.

3. conscription, recruitment, levy, drafting.

enliven, *v.* **1.** invigorate, stimulate, inspirit, exhilarate; energize, animate, raise, vivify, vitalize; reanimate, revive, revivify, revitalize, rejuvenate; kindle, enkindle, *Inf.* spark, waken, awaken, stir; rouse, arouse, whet, quicken, make active, incite; fire *or* fire up, *Inf.* light a fire under, inflame, inspire; excite, thrill, tingle.

2. brighten, warm, make cheerful, make sprightly *or* gay; perk up, *Inf.* pep up, bolster *or* bolster up; refresh, give freshness to, cheer *or* cheer up, give a lift to, uplift; enhance, beautify, prettify, grace; spruce up, make smart, smarten up, *Sl.* jazz up, *Sl.* soup up; add to, improve, ameliorate, meliorate, show off to advantage.

enlivenment, *n.* jauntiness, sprightliness, pertness, friskiness, playfulness, sportiveness; energy, spirit, élan, dash, ardor; passion, zeal, gusto, vigor; eagerness, animation, *Inf.* ginger, enthusiasm; sparkle, ebullience, excitement; ecstasy, thrill, *Inf.* rush, tingling; exhilaration, liveliness, alacrity, briskness; vivacity, effervescence, bubbling; gladsomeness, joyousness, cheerfulness, levity; high spirits, good spirits, gaiety, merriment, lightheartedness; blithesomeness, airiness, sunniness, breeziness, buoyancy; hilarity, mirth, mirthfulness, elation; glee, gleefulness, exultation, jubilation; merrymaking, rejoicing, laughter; jocundity, jocularity, joviality, conviviality, jollity.

en masse, in a mass, in a body, all together, as a group, as a whole, as one, ensemble.

enmesh, *v.* net, catch, capture, trap, entrap, snare, ensnare, *Obs.* illaqueate; mesh; entangle, tangle, trammel, snarl, intertwine.

enmity, *n.* animosity, animus, hostility; odium, hatred, hate, dislike, unfriendliness; malignity, malevolence, malice, spite, venom, grudge, ill will; rancor, acrimony, bitterness, hard feelings; antagonism, invidiousness, antipathy, bad blood, aversion; alienation, estrangement; contention, opposition, repugnance.

ennoble, *v.* **1.** exalt, glorify, lionize, aggrandize, magnify; raise, elevate, uplift; honor, dignify, grace, adorn.

2. confer *or* bestow honor upon, pin a medal on, knight; distinguish, signalize, look up to.

ennoblement, *n.* exaltation, glorification, lionization, aggrandizement, magnification, elevation, dignification.

ennui, *n.* boredom, world-weariness, *Ger. Weltschmerz*; lackadaisicalness, languor, listlessness, lethargy, sluggishness, *Inf.* the blahs, *Inf.* blue Monday; doldrums, melancholy, *Archaic.* spleen.

enormity, *n.* **1.** atrociousness, wickedness, evilness, fiendishness, heinousness; cruelty, barbarity, savagery, brutality, murderousness; ferocity, fierceness, truculence, inhumanity, monstrousness, ruthlessness; horribleness, hideousness, dreadfulness, terribleness, horridness.

2. atrocity, outrage, monstrosity, horror; abomination, disgrace, scandal; crime, offense, violation, transgression; injury, hurt, harm, evil, wrong.

3. immensity, hugeness, greatness, vastness, massiveness, stupendousness, prodigiousness, enormousness.

enormous, *adj.* **1.** huge, immense, vast, stupendous, massive, *Archaic.* enorm, *Archaic.* immane; gargantuan, colossal, tremendous, prodigious, mammoth, titanic, gigantic, *Sl.* gigando.

2. atrocious, abominable, execrable, monstrous, horrible, horrid, horrendous; grievous, outrageous, shocking, flagrant; vile, base, foul, low, mean; wicked, sinful, evil, iniquitous, *Archaic.* facinorous; nefarious, villainous, heinous, flagitious; infamous, notorious, odious, ignominious; opprobrious, shameful, disgraceful.

enough, *adj.* **1.** sufficient, adequate, *Archaic.* enow; ample, abundant, plenteous, plentiful, *Inf.* plenty.

—n. **2.** sufficiency, adequacy, competency; amplitude, full measure, *Latin. quantum sufficit*; abundance, copiousness, plenty, plenitude, plenteousness, profusion; repletion, surfeit, satiety, fill.

—adv. **3.** sufficiently, satisfactorily, tolerably, passably, adequately; abundantly, plentifully, plenteously, *Inf.* aplenty; without stint, with no effort spared, with no expense spared, to one's heart's content, ad libitum.

enrage, *v.* infuriate, madden, lash into a fury, whip into a frenzy, make [s.o.'s] blood boil, *Inf.* make [s.o.] see red; anger, incense, irk, raise [s.o.'s] ire *or* hackles, get [s.o.'s] back up, *Inf.* get [s.o.'s] Irish *or* dander up, *Inf.* burn [s.o.] up, *Sl.* tee [s.o.] off, *Sl.* tick [s.o.] off, *Brit. Sl.* put [s.o.'s] monkey up; provoke, agitate, inflame, enflame, fire up, work up, wind up, whip up; exasperate, exacerbate, acerbate.

enrapt, *adj.* transported, entranced, enchanted, spellbound, fascinated, captivated, charmed; enraptured, rapt, overjoyed, ecstatic, *Sl.* turned on.

enrapture, *v.* transport, entrance, enchant, fascinate, captivate, charm, bewitch, spellbind, enthrall; overjoy, gladden, gratify, thrill, rejoice, delight, excite, *Sl.* send, *Sl.* blow [s.o.'s] mind, *Sl.* turn [s.o.] on.

enrich, *v.* **1.** endow, make rich, provide for; set up for life, feather one's nest; satiate, sate.

2. enhance, appreciate, upgrade, aggrandize; improve, ameliorate, better, restore, furbish, revalue.

3. adorn, decorate, embellish, garnish; ornament, deck, bedeck; beautify, gild, grace; bedizen, array, prink; garland, festoon, enamel.

4. refine, polish, brighten; uplift, elevate, develop, mature; hone, sharpen.

enrichment, *n.* **1.** endowment, satiation, appreciation, aggrandizement, enhancement; improvement, betterment, advancement, furtherance.

2. adornment, embellishment, beautification, ornamentation, decoration; refinement, cultivation, development.

enroll, *v.* **1.** register, matriculate, sign up; enlist, join, *Inf.* join up, volunteer, recruit.

2. note, mark *or* put down, record, list, catalogue, chronicle; enter, insert.

3. roll, coil, ball, roll into a ball, wrap up *or* around.

enrollment, *n.* **1.** registration, matriculation, sign-up; enlistment, joining, recruitment.

2. list *or* listing of members, roster, register, record.

en route, *adv.* on the way, on the road, in transit.

ensconce, *v.* **1.** cover, shelter, seclude, hide, conceal, keep out of sight; screen, camouflage, veil, shroud.

2. settle, nestle, snuggle up, cuddle up, curl up; seat, locate, set, put, place, install, lodge, entrench.

ensemble, *n.* **1.** whole, entirety, totality, whole thing, total, sum, *Sl.* whole bit, *Sl.* whole schmear; aggregate, composite, combination, agglomeration, conglomeration; collection, assemblage, accumulation, cumulation, mass, pile, heap.

2. outfit, matched set, costume, coordinates, getup; apparel, attire, garb, garments, clothing, clothes.

3. *Music.* act, show, performance, number, piece, routine, *U.S. Sl.* bit, *Sl.* thing.

4. trio, quartet, chamber orchestra, chorus, choir; troupe, troop, company, band, circle; group, association, affiliation, union.

—adv. **5.** together, all together, en masse, as a group *or* whole, in concert; simultaneously, at the same time, at once, all at once.

enshrine, *v.* **1.** sanctify, dedicate, consecrate; beatify, hallow; deify, apotheosize, exalt, idolize.

2. cherish, hold sacred, immortalize, revere, venerate, adore; esteem, prize, value, preserve.

enshroud, *v.* shroud, cover, conceal, cloak, bury, obscure, cloud, becloud; veil, mask, envelop, wrap, hide.

ensign, *n.* **1.** flag, standard, pennant, pennon, banneret, banner, insigne, insignia, streamer; banderole, oriflamme, labarum, gonfalon, tricolor, jack, blue

peter, burgee, cornet; Stars and Stripes, Union Jack.
2. badge, shield, badge of office, coat of arms; escutcheon, crest, armorial bearings, hatchment; eagle, star, crown, anchor; brassard, sash, stripe, chevron, bar, tab, epaulette; cockade, *Mil. Sl.* garbage, *Mil. Sl.* scrambled eggs, ribbons.
3. sign, seal, signet, token, emblem, device, figurehead; logo, symbol, brand, brand name, cipher, sigil, signet, signature; type, index, criterion.

enslave, *v.* **1.** overcome, conquer, subjugate, subject, yoke, fetter, trammel, shackle, enchain; capture, trap, ensnare, snag, catch, lay by the heels, lead captive; take prisoner, kidnap, abduct, carry off.
2. captivate, fascinate, enrapture, enthrall; infatuate, inflame; bewitch, becharm, enchant; mesmerize, hypnotize, carry away, transport.
3. lay hold of, get a hold on, addict, habituate, *Inf.* hook.

enslavement, *n.* **1.** slavery, bondage, enthrallment, thralldom, captivity; subjugation, subjection, subordination, control, restraint, oppression, repression; confinement, durance, duress; servitude, serfdom, vassalage, indenture.
2. capture, seizure, taking, ensnarement, conquest.
3. addiction, dependence, (*of narcotics*) habit; alcoholism, dipsomania; habituation, surrender.

ensnare, *v.* **1.** snare, trap, entrap, tangle, entangle, enmesh, snarl, embroil, *Archaic.* entoil, *Archaic.* trepan.
2. inveigle, take in, dupe, gull, hoax; bamboozle, beguile, mislead, hoodwink; get around, put one over on; seduce, allure, captivate.

ensue, *v.* **1.** follow, come afterward, succeed, come next; attend, happen, occur, chance, come to pass, turn out; present itself, turn up, crop up.
2. result, eventuate, transpire; proceed, arise, emanate, flow, spring, come out of.

ensure, *v.* **1.** secure, attain, win, confirm, lock in, nail down; bring surely, bring about, bring round, effect, set up; clinch, bag, net, *Inf.* cinch.
2. assure, make sure *or* certain, dismiss all doubt; warrant, guarantee, underwrite, certify.

entail, *v.* involve, require, necessitate, occasion; give origin to, bring on *or* about, produce; set up, institute, inaugurate, open the door to; cause, predetermine, preordain, impose.

entangle, *v.* **1.** tangle, snarl, ensnarl, ravel, knot, kink; twist, intertwist, twine, intertwine, mat; disorder, disarrange, tumble, jumble, rumple, muss.
2. ensnare, enmesh, entrap, snag, catch, catch up; seduce, lure, allure.
3. embroil, tie up, encumber, involve; confuse, perplex, nonplus, discompose, ruffle; confound, bewilder, muddle, befuddle; mix up, complicate, *Sl.* foul up.
4. implicate, inculpate, incriminate, *Inf.* suck in; embarrass, compromise, *Inf.* get into a mess, *Inf.* get into trouble, *Inf.* get into hot water.

entanglement, *n.* **1.** tangle, snare, complication, problem, perplexity, puzzle, knot, Gordian knot; complexity, intricacy, network, complex, complicacy, web, webwork; coil, twist; wilderness, jungle, labyrinth, maze.
2. difficulty, involvement, imbroglio; predicament, fix, plight, quandary, dilemma; kink, gnarl, knotty point, frustration.
3. confusion, bewilderment, distraction, disorder, derangement; trouble, muddle, mix up, *Sl.* snafu, *Sl.* foul-up; implication, involvement, embarrassment, embranglement, *Inf.* mess, *Inf.* a heap of trouble; obstruction, obstacle, quagmire, quicksand, slough.

entente, *n.* **1.** rapprochement, conciliation, peacemaking; pact, compact, treaty, covenant, concordat, contract, formal agreement; settlement, arrangement, understanding, cordial understanding, agreement, deal; fraternization, camaraderie, concord, accord, concert, harmony.
2. alliance, coalition, union, league, bloc, bund, federation, federacy, confederation, confederacy; partnership, co-partnership, affiliation.

enter, *v.* **1.** come in *or* into, go in *or* into, pass into, flow into, move through; approach, set foot on, board, embark.
2. break in, force one's way in, intrude, irrupt, trespass; interrupt, break in on, burst in upon, *Sl.* butt in, *U.S. Sl.* horn in; infiltrate, invade, penetrate.
3. admit, enroll, sign up, register, matriculate; be admitted, obtain entrance *or* entrée, get in, be accepted.
4. begin, start, undertake, commence; break ground, launch, get underway, *Inf.* get off the ground, start off, forward; set out on, start out, take the first step; get going, set sail, hit the road *or* trail, be off; depart, leave, sally forth, venture out *or* forth, *Inf.* take off, *Inf.* push off.
5. penetrate, pierce, perforate, stick, prick; puncture, punch, stab, wound, lancinate.
6. insert, put in, introduce, inject, inset, place in; stick in, shove in, push in, drive in, hammer in, infix; thrust in, force in, ram in, cram in, stuff in, wedge in, put between.
7. join *or* join up, enlist in, become a member, sign up with, enroll in; unite with, associate oneself with, become connected with, belong to.
8. engage in, become involved in, occupy oneself with, be concerned with, take an interest in; share in, participate in, partake of; undertake, take upon oneself, assume responsibility; commit oneself, pledge oneself, bind oneself, promise, give one's word.
9. record, register, document; put *or* set down, keep minutes, note, jot down, take down; list, tally, tabulate, keep score, inventory; index, file, chronicle, schedule, catalogue, calendar.
10. put forward, submit, register, offer, proffer, tender, hold out; bring up, broach, introduce, propose, suggest, volunteer; maintain, assert, claim, declare, avow, insist.
11. **enter into a.** participate in, engage in. See **enter** (*def.* 7). **b.** investigate, consider, check up *or* up on, look into, analyze, study, examine, scrutinize, probe. **c.** sympathize with, empathize with, share in, feel for, have compassion for.

enterprise, *n.* **1.** plan, scheme; venture, undertaking, *Archaic.* emprise, project, task; campaign, crusade, cause.
2. work, effort, attempt, essay, endeavor, struggle.
3. boldness, readiness, go-ahead, push, initiative, ambition; intensity, force, power, puissance, might, courage, *Sl.* guts, nerve; energy, go, vigor, *Inf.* starch, vitality, get up and go; dash, élan, zest, vim, *Inf.* zip, snap, *It. brio*, *Sl.* oomph, *Inf.* pep; animation, liveliness, vivacity.
4. industry, business, *Sl.* racket; company, corporation, firm, house, establishment; shop, store; partnership, team.

enterprising, *adj.* **1.** venturous, venturesome, adventurous; courageous, bold, caring, audacious, fearless, dauntless; spirited, mettlesome, plucky; energetic, vigorous, strenuous, forceful, full of vim and vigor, indefatigable; zealous, ardent, fervent, fervid, avid, enthusiastic, eager; alert, wide-awake, sharp, keen, smart, resourceful, self-reliant.
2. ambitious, aspiring, climbing, up-and-coming, goal-oriented; earnest, resolved, resolute, determined,

intent; striving, go-ahead, assertive, aggressive, driving, pushing, *Inf.* pushy; efficient, brisk, *Inf.* snappy, quick, ready; industrious, diligent, hard-working, assiduous, sedulous, persevering, painstaking.

3. initiative, imaginative, creative, inventive; productive, constructive.

entertain, *v.* **1.** divert, interest, occupy, beguile, engage, engross, absorb; amuse, please, charm, cheer, *Inf.* hand one a few laughs; gladden, gratify, tickle, exhilarate, enliven, rejoice.

2. disport, recreate, dally; clown, joke, jest, cut up, burlesque, mimic, impersonate, sing and dance.

3. host, receive guests, welcome; give a party, *Inf.* throw *or* toss a party, have people over, have company; regale, wine and dine, fete, banquet, treat.

4. consider, take into consideration, weigh, contemplate, ponder; mind, heed, attend.

5. (*of thoughts and feelings*) harbor, shelter, foster, nurture, cherish; hide, conceal; hold, possess.

entertainer, *n.* **1.** host, hostess; master of ceremonies, M.C., emcee.

2. actor, actress, thespian, tragedian, tragedienne; night club performer, comic, comedian, comedienne, impressionist, mime; speaker, lecturer, reader, monologist, reciter; musician, singer, chanteuse, *It., Fr. cantatrice,* diva; dancer, ballerina; circus performer, *Sl.* kinker, clown, acrobat, animal trainer.

entertaining, *adj.* **1.** amusing, pleasing, pleasurable; diverting, interesting, distracting, absorbing, engrossing, beguiling; recreative, lively, sportive.

2. laughable, funny, comical, witty, humorous, jolly; hilarious, sidesplitting, ludicrous, farcical; jocular, jocose, jovial, risible.

entertainment, *n.* **1.** amusement, diversion, divertissement, distraction, pastime; recreation, play, sport, fun, cheer; pleasure, enjoyment, gratification, delight, gaiety; relaxation, dalliance, merrymaking, pleasantry, merriment, joviality, jocoseness, jollity, jollification, drollery.

2. antic, lark, romp, gambol, spree, junket; prank, practical joke, escapade, revelry, tomfoolery, skylarking.

3. celebration, gala, fete, soiree, party; dance, ball, prom; pageant, parade, spectacle, extravaganza; festival, carnival, circus; exhibition, presentation, performance, concert, show, play, movie, film; night life.

4. hospitality, welcome, reception, accommodation; refreshment, refection, collation, tea, cocktails; repast, dinner, banquet, feast.

enthrall, *v.* **1.** charm, attract, captivate, take one's fancy; fascinate, allure, enrapture, infatuate, hold spellbound, spellbind; enamor, inflame, excite, thrill, ravish; bewitch, becharm, enchant, mesmerize, hypnotize, carry away, transport.

2. subjugate, enslave, master, subdue; overpower, overcome, vanquish, trample under foot; enchain, keep in bondage, hold in thralldom, weigh down, keep under.

enthrallment, *n.* **1.** possession, subjection, bondage, captivity; slavery, thralldom; fetters, chains.

2. enchantment, charm, spell, witchery, bewitchment; fascination, entrancement, infatuation, passion, obsession, fixation, mania, absorption, preoccupation, prepossession.

enthrone, *v.* **1.** imperialize, ennoble, episcopize, king, give sovereignty to; enthronize, seat *or* place upon a throne, crown; empower, authorize, entitle.

2. exalt, glorify, dignify; deify, apotheosize, canonize; elevate, raise, upraise, make lofty, aggrandize; honor, revere, respect, admire, look up to, pay homage to; worship, adore, idolize, idealize, romanticize, glamorize, put [s.o.] on a pedestal.

enthuse, *v.* **1.** effervesce, bubble over, emote, gush, be effusive *or* ebullient, overflow with enthusiasm; get *or* become excited, get *or* be all worked up, wax enthusiastic, grow eager *or* zealous *or* ardent; *Inf.* get psyched *or* psyched up, *Inf.* get all fired up; become interested in, get involved *or* absorbed in, get into, get caught up in, be possessed with, be taken with.

2. excite, make exuberant, work up, *Inf.* psych *or* psych up; impassion, inflame, *Inf.* fire up; interest, get the attention of, involve, absorb, possess.

enthusiasm, *n.* **1.** eagerness, earnestness, keenness, intentness, intensity, excitement; fervor, ardor, fervency, warmth, glow, fire; devotion, devotedness, zeal, feverishness, passion, fanaticism.

2. spirit, abandon, liveliness, vivacity; emotion, animation, exuberance, ebullience; vitality, life, buoyancy, bounce, *It. brio,* zest, verve, zing, *Sl.* oomph; vigor, force, energy, determination, vehemence; relish, gusto, delight, elation, rapture, ecstasy, transport.

3. optimism, assurance, confidence; sanguineness, hope, hopefulness.

enthusiast, *n.* **1.** devotee, fan, aficionado, *Inf.* buff, *Inf.* hound, *Sl.* bug, *Sl.* nut, addict, *Inf.* fiend, *Sl.* junkie, *Sl.* freak; (*all usu. of adolescent girls*) (*in the 40s*) bobbysoxer, (*in the 60s*) teenybopper, (*in the 70s*) groupie.

2. votary, champion, disciple, follower, satellite, adherent; zealot, partisan, bigot, fanatic; visionary, cultist, sectary.

3. promoter, supporter, *Inf.* pusher, *Inf.* booster, *Inf.* arm-waver; chauvinist, jingoist.

enthusiastic, *adj.* **1.** ardent, fervent, eager, keen, anxious, *Inf.* wild; excited, *Inf.* all fired up, *Inf.* psyched *or* psyched up, *Sl.* hopped up, *Sl.* ape; heated, vehement, fervid, perfervid; fiery, flaming, inflamed, glowing, white-hot.

2. earnest, wholehearted, devoted; zealous, passionate, *Inf.* gung-ho, *Inf.* rah-rah; possessed, fanatic, fanatical, *Sl.* hung up, rabid, mad.

3. spirited, animated, vivacious, lively; vigorous, forceful, energetic, exuberant; ebullient, irrepressible, bubbling over, effervescent; demonstrative, emotive, expressive, effusive, gushing, *Inf.* gaga.

enthusiastically, *adv.* **1.** ardently, fervently, eagerly, keenly, *Inf.* in a big way, anxiously; vehemently, fervidly, desperately, excessively, extremely, *Inf.* all-fired; devotedly, earnestly, in earnest, wholeheartedly, *Inf.* with bells on; zealously, passionately, *Inf.* like mad, *Inf.* like crazy, fanatically, rabidly, madly.

2. vigorously, forcefully, energetically, with might and main, with a vengeance, *Inf.* hammer and tongs, *Inf.* for all one's worth, *Inf.* to beat the band, *Sl.* up a storm; fiercely, tooth and nail.

3. spiritedly, animatedly, exuberantly; ebulliently, irrepressibly, effervescently; demonstratively, emotively, expressively, effusively, gushingly.

entice, *v.* allure, lure, tempt, inveigle, beguile, seduce, tantalize, pique, *Archaic.* trepan; bait, bait the hook, lead on, draw on, *Sl.* give [s.o.] the come-on, *Sl.* bat one's eyes at; wheedle, cajole, *Inf.* sweet-talk, coax, blandish, *Sl.* soft-soap; ensnare, draw in, *Sl.* rope in, *Sl.* suck in.

enticement, *n.* **1.** allurement, allure, temptation, invitation, beguilement, inveiglement, tantalization, seduction, baiting; cajolery, blandishment, coaxing, wheedling.

2. lure, decoy, bait, snare, trap, forbidden fruit, *Sl.* come-on; honeyed words, *Inf.* soft soap.

entire, *adj.* **1.** whole, complete, total, aggregate, integral, plenary, full; extensive, extended, wholesale; comprehensive, universal, inclusive, all-inclusive; unbroken, undivided, indivisible, undividable, uncut, unshortened, unabridged, all in one, unitary; intact, sound, indissoluble, hale, solid; self-contained, independent, autonomous, self-supporting.

2. thorough, thoroughgoing, exhaustive, in-depth, A to Z, *Brit.* A to Zed, *Brit. Dial.* gradely; absolute, dyed-in-the-wool, full-fledged, *Inf.* teetotal, complete; utter, gross, rank, sheer, radical, sweeping; unqualified, unmodified, uncompromised, unconditional, unconditioned, unreserved, unmitigated; unrestricted, unlimited, unhampered, unimpeded, unbounded; unequivocal, clear, unambiguous, explicit, express.

3. unimpaired, undamaged, unharmed, uninjured, unscathed, unmutilated, undecayed; pure, unmixed, unmingled, unblended, unalloyed; undiminished, unlessened, unreduced, unabated.

—*n.* 4. See **entirety** (*defs.* 1, 2) and **whole** (*defs.* 7, 8).

entirely, *adv.* 1. wholly, purely, fully, *Latin. in toto, Latin. in extenso*, completely; totally, plenarily, aggregately, every whit, every inch, nothing short of, 100%; comprehensively, extensively, from the ground up, universally, inclusively; soundly, substantially, solidly; as a whole, all in all, in the main; throughout, at length, altogether; en masse, in a body.

2. thoroughly, in all respects, in every respect, exhaustively, arrantly, absolutely; from first to last, from head to foot, cap-a-pie, from top to toe, from A to Z, *Brit.* from A to Zed; utterly, sheerly, quite, root and branch; downright, out-and-out, outright, all-out, straight-out; through and through, backward and forward; radically, fundamentally, essentially.

3. unqualifiedly, uncompromisingly, unconditionally, unreservedly, unmitigatedly; *Sl.* all the way, to the nth degree, *Sl.* like mad, *Sl.* like crazy, lock, stock and barrel, *Inf.* hook, line, and sinker; enthusiastically, fervently, heart and soul, bag and baggage, whole hog; unequivocally, positively, clearly, unambiguously, explicitly, expressly.

entirety, *n.* 1. wholeness, completeness, totality, allness, aggregate, assemblage, collective, ensemble, *Fr. tout ensemble*; integrity, integrality, fullness, plenitude, entireness; comprehensiveness, universality, *Rare.* omnitude, inclusiveness; undividedness, indivisibility; intactness, soundness, solidarity, solidity.

2. all, the whole, alpha and omega, beginning and end, length and breadth; entire amount, sum total, gross amount; everything, everybody.

entitle, *v.* 1. title, give [s.o.] a title, *Archaic.* entitulate; give [s.o.] a right *or* claim to, authorize, legalize, warrant, sanction, license; empower, qualify, enable, capacitate, fit for.

2. christen, baptize, name, call, address; designate, term, dub, nickname, label, style; characterize, qualify.

entity, *n.* 1. thing, real thing, *Metaphys.* ens, object, article; creature, person, being.

2. being, existence, *Philos.* subsistence, life; essence, inner being, essential nature, quiddity.

entomb, *v.* ensepulcher, sepulcher; bury, inter, inhume, inurn; lay away, *Inf.* lay to rest, *Sl.* put six feet under, consign to the grave, *Dial.* funeralize.

entombment, *n.* sepulture, burial, burying, interment, inhumation, inurnment.

entourage, *n.* 1. attendance, train, retinue, cortege, suite, court, following, followers; escort, bodyguard, convoy, staff, attendants.

2. environment, environs, surroundings, circumstances, ambience; milieu, purlieus, ambit, precincts.

entrails, *n. pl.* 1. viscera, body organs, internal organs, internals, insides, inwards, *Inf.* innards, *Inf.* gizzard, *Sl.* guts, liver and lights; vital parts, vital organs, vitals.

2. alimentary canal, bowel, bowels, colon, colons, (*of swine*) chitterlings, intestine, intestines.

entrance[1], *n.* 1. admission, admittance, permission to enter, access, right of entry; entry, entryway, entree, inlet, ingress; approach, ramp, drive, driveway, lane, adit; path, pathway, route, road, roadway, course, way, means; street, avenue, boulevard, highway; opening, aperture, hatch, door, doorway, gate, gateway, postern, portal; threshold, stile, turnstile, wicket; hall, hallway, passage, passageway, arcade, gangway, walkway, corridor, gallery; lobby, foyer, vestibule, anteroom, waiting room; anteporch, porch, portico.

2. accession, succession, inheritance, assumption, taking on *or* over; entering upon, arrival at, advent to; elevation, promotion, rise, coming to, reaching, attainment; induction, installation, initiation, inauguration, investiture.

3. beginning, start, outset, dawn, birth; debut, commencement, prelude, overture.

4. coming in, inflow, influx; invasion, incursion, inroad, irruption; break-in, intrusion, trespassing, infiltration, penetration.

entrance[2], *v.* 1. enrapture, fascinate, bewitch; enchant, spellbind, magnetize; captivate, enamor; delight, please, transport, ravish; charm, allure, attract; interest, intrigue.

2. hypnotize, mesmerize, cast a spell on, hex; bewilder, bedazzle, dazzle.

entrant, *n.* 1. new member, arrival, novice, neophyte, tyro, beginner; freshman, plebe; kindergartener, first grader, catechumen; pledge, initiate, probationer, proselyte, convert; newie, cub, greenhorn, babe in the woods.

2. contestant, player, lottery player; candidate, applicant, petitioner, seeker; competitor, rival, opponent.

entrap, *v.* 1. ensnare, snare, net, mesh, bag, sack, gin, trap, *Archaic.* entoil, *Archaic.* trepan.

2. entice, inveigle, allure, lure, beguile, tempt; bait, bait the hook, lead on, draw on; involve, implicate, entangle, enmesh, draw in, drag *or* hook into, make a party to, *Sl.* rope in, *Sl.* suck in.

3. embarrass, show up, expose, reveal; trip, trip up, catch, catch off guard, catch napping, catch out; *Inf.* corner, *Inf.* tree, *Inf.* have [s.o.] on the ropes, *Sl.* put [s.o.] on the spot, *Sl.* have the goods on [s.o.].

entrapment, *n.* enticement, allurement, allure, temptation, invitation, beguilement, inveiglement, tantalization, seduction.

entreat, *v.* 1. beseech, implore, invoke, enjoin, impetrate, appeal, obtest; pray, plead, crave, supplicate; sue, solicit, petition; invoke, call on *or* upon, call to, cry to.

2. request, ask, apply to; importune, urge, press, ply.

entreaty, *n.* appeal, bid, suit, prayer, call, cry, clamor; solicitation, suppliance, beseechment, impetration, obtestation, invocation, petition, adjuration.

entrée, *n.* 1. entrance, entry, entryway, inlet, ingress; approach, drive, driveway, lane, adit; path, pathway, route, road, roadway, course, way, means; street, avenue, boulevard, highway; opening, aperture, hatch, door, doorway, gate, gateway, postern, portal; threshold, stile, turnstile, wicket; hall, hallway, passage, passageway, arcade, gangway, walkway, corridor, gallery; lobby, foyer, vestibule, anteroom, waiting room; anteporch, porch, portico.

2. access, admission, admittance, permission to enter, right of entry.

3. means, way, channel, avenue, approach; in, influence, *Sl.* pull.

4. main course, principal dish, *Fr. pièce de*

résistance; meal, dinner, supper.
5. side dish, side order, entremets.

entrench, *v.* **1.** dig in, fortify, solidify, establish; embed, fix, ground, plant, root; wall, fence, bulwark, barricade, embattle; brace, buttress, shore up, reinforce, stiffen.
2. trench, encroach, trespass, infringe, impinge; invade, ingress, make inroads, infiltrate; overstep, overrun, advance; intrude, obtrude, interlope.

entrenchment, *n.* **1.** fortification, bulwark, rampart, bastion, *Fort.* vallation; trench, ditch, foxhole, dugout, sap, moat, fosse; nest, bunker, pill box, abri; beachhead, bridgehead, line, *Mil.* hedgehog; bank, parados, wall, embankment, mound; fence, defense, outwork, *Rare.* muniment; *All Fort.* work, redan, breastwork, earthwork, redoubt, lunette, tenaille.
2. encroachment, infringement, impingement, invasion; trespass, transgression, violation; intrusion, obtrusion, irruption; overstepping, overrunning, advance; inroad, ingress, incursion, infiltration.

entre nous, between ourselves, between you and me, *Latin. inter nos*, between us, between you and me and the lamppost; confidentially, in strict confidence, off the record, under one's hat, under the rose, sub rosa; secretly, privately, in private, intimately, under the veil of secrecy, hush-hush, hugger-mugger.

entrepreneur, *n.* **1.** businessman, enterpriser, businesswoman, entrepreneuse; executive, *Sl.* exec, financier, industrialist; magnate, tycoon, *U.S.* baron, captain of industry.
2. contractor, employer, hirer; manager, director, producer, conductor, impresario.

entrust, *v.* delegate, depute, deputize, put or place in [s.o.'s] hands; confide, commit, hand over, turn over, deliver; make over, assign, consign.

entry, *n.* **1.** entrance, entree, inlet, ingress, approach, access, admittance. See **entrance[1]** (*def.* **1**).
2. statement, item, brief, record, minutes, account, bulletin, description; note, memorandum, *Inf.* memo, jotting, thought.
3. contestant, competitor, rival; opponent, adversary.

entwine, *v.* intertwine, weave, interweave; wattle, thatch, lace, interlace, knit; splice, link, interlink, intertwist; braid, plait, crisscross, entangle.

enumerate, *v.* **1.** list, specify, name, cite; estimate, check, check off, go over, run over, take account of; catalogue, detail, mark, take stock of; recount, narrate, relate.
2. count, compute, calculate, reckon, numerate, number, tally, add; call roll, poll.

enumeration, *n.* **1.** listing, naming, citing, cataloguing, detailing, marking; recounting, narrating, relating.
2. computation, calculation, reckoning; tally, poll, census, nosecount; statistic, *Inf.* stats.
3. list, catalogue, roster, checklist, *Inf.* laundry list; recapitulation, narration, litany.

enunciate, *v.* **1.** articulate, pronounce, modulate, intone, intonate, vocalize, accentuate; say, express, utter, voice, breathe, give *or* let out, come out with; deliver, present.
2. affirm, assert, asseverate, avow, avouch, aver; insist, maintain, contend, hold, stand for *or* on; propound, propose, put forward; allege, claim, set forth; depose, testify, attest, swear.
3. proclaim, promulgate, state, give notice; declare, pronounce, profess, enounce; announce, publish, publicize, broadcast, herald, make known; signal, annunciate, knell; cry, blare, blazon, trumpet.

enunciation, *n.* **1.** delivery, presentation, attack, force of utterance; speech pattern, manner of speaking, mode of expression; emphasis, accent, accentuation, stress, syllable stress; articulating, pronouncing, modulating, intonating, vocalizing, enunciating; saying, expressing, uttering, voicing; delivering, presenting.
2. articulation, pronunciation, vocalization, voice, voicing, phonation; intonation, inflection, modulation; vociferation, exclamation, *Rhet.* ecphonesis.
3. announcement, proclamation, promulgation, annunciation, broadcast, statement, formal statement *or* announcement; notice, formal notice, notification; declaration, pronouncement, profession, enouncement; affirmation, asseveration, averment, avowal, avouchment, acknowledgment; allegation, accusation; protest, formal protest.

enunciative, *adj.* **1.** vocal, oral, verbal, spoken, phonetic, phonetical; voiced, vocalized, articulated, pronounced; intoned, intonated, inflected, modulated; stressed, accented, accentuated, emphatic, emphasized; articulate, intelligible, distinct, clear, plain.
2. expressive, declarative, declaratory, enunciatory, enunciable; affirmative, affirmatory, assertive.

envelop, *v.* **1.** enfold, enwrap, wrap, sheathe, case, cover; hide, conceal, embosk, shroud, enshroud, clothe, overlay; hood, cloak, shield, screen; protect, shelter.
2. encompass, enclose, encase, encircle, enwreathe, surround; clasp, embrace.

envelope, *n.* wrapper, wrapping, wrap; cover, covering, capsule, case, casing, container, holder, receptacle; skin, sheathe, condom; cod, *Dial.* pod, pocket; *Biol.* integument, *Biol.* theca.

envenom, *v.* **1.** poison, empoison; infect, taint, pollute, contaminate, foul, befoul; vitiate, corrupt, debase.
2. embitter, exacerbate, acerbate, gall, rankle, bitter, sour; anger, incense, enrage, madden, infuriate, make [s.o.'s] blood boil.

enviable, *adj.* covetable, desirable, to be desired, much to be desired, worth having; appetizing, relishable, mouth-watering, tempting; excellent, fine, good, pleasing, after one's own heart, worthy of emulation.

envious, *adj.* begrudging, jealous, resentful, green-eyed, green with envy, *Obs.* emulous; covetous, desirous, itching, yearning, hankering; discontent, malcontent, dissatisfied, displeased, unhappy.

environ, *v.* surround, encircle, ensphere, rim; gird, begird, girdle, engird, loop around; circumscribe, compass; encompass, enclose, envelop, hem in, embrace.

environment, *n.* **1.** surroundings, milieu, conditions, influences, circumstances, *Fr. mise en scène*; habitat, medium, element; entourage, ambience, atmosphere, mood, aura; setting, scene, background.
2. encirclement, surrounding, encompassment.

environmentalist, *n.* **1.** ecologist, naturalist; city planner, urbanist.
2. conservationist, preservationist, eco-activist, *All Inf.* clean-air freak, econut, anti-pollutionist, nonuker; Thoreauvian, nature lover.

environs, *n.* outskirts, suburbs, faubourgs, purlieus, *Fr. banlieue*, precincts; surroundings, circumjacencies; vicinage, vicinity, neighborhood, *Fr. alentours*, street, district; exurbs, *Sl.* boonies, city limits, outer limits.

envisage, *v.* contemplate, visualize, envision, picture; daydream about, dream of, aspire to, look forward to, imagine, fancy; conceive, think up, have ideas about, *Inf.* dream up.

envoy, *n.* **1.** diplomat, envoy extraordinary, minister, plenipotentiary, legate; ambassador, consul, attaché, chargé d'affaires.

2. emissary, agent, representative, delegate, deputy; nuncio, internuncio; messenger, herald, courier, runner; go-between, middleman, intermediary, mediator.

envy, *n.* **1.** jealousy, resentment, grudge, begrudging, heartburn, green-eyed monster, enviousness; discontentment, malcontentedness, dissatisfaction, unhappiness, heartburning; rivalry, cupidity, *Obs.* emulation.

2. covetousness, desire, wanting, longing *or* wishing for, yearning *or* hankering after, sighing *or* pining for, *Inf.* yen, *Sl.* letch; craving, relish, taste, appetite, appetence, hunger, thirst; fancy, eye, *U.S. Dial.* big eye; itch, passion, lust.

—*v.* **3.** begrudge, be jealous of, resent, grudge, be envious of; covet, desire, want, wish for, long for, yearn for, hanker after, sigh for, pine for, *Inf.* have a yen for; crave, relish, have an appetite *or* taste for, hunger *or* thirst for; fancy, have an eye on, ogle, eye greedily; have an itch for, have a passion for, lust after, *Sl.* letch after.

eon, *n.* age, ages, years on end, a long time, an eternity; *Inf.* forever.

ephemeral, *adj.* short-lived, momentary, temporary, brief, of short duration; impermanent, mortal, unenduring, fleeting, passing, fading; evanescent, transient, transitory, fugacious, caducous, deciduous, monohemerous.

epic, *adj.* **1.** epical, Homeric, Vergilian; narrative, descriptive, detailed, graphic; legendary, historic, historical, mythical, fabulous, fantastic; heroic, great, superhuman; grand, majestic, impressive, imposing, grandiose.

2. colossal, huge, vast, very large, voluminous; overdone, excessive, exaggerated, inflated; bombastic, fustian, pompous, high-sounding, high-flown, pretentious, grandiloquent, rhetorical; lofty, elevated, exalted, sublime.

3. epic poem, epopee, epos; narrative, chronicle, history, saga; legend, myth, story, tale.

epicure, *n.* **1.** connoisseur, aesthete, epicurean; gourmet, gourmand, gastronome, gastronomist; deipnosophist, conversationalist.

2. voluptuary, sensualist, *Fr. bon vivant,* hedonist, sybarite, cormorant; glutton, hog, belly-god, wine bibber; libertine, roué, debauchee, lecher, Paphian.

epicurean, *adj.* **1.** sybaritic, sensual, carnal, voluptuous; orgiastic, wild, unrestrained; self-indulgent, intemperate, free-living, Saturnalian.

2. dissolute, licentious, libertine, lascivious, debauched, dissipated, wasted; concupiscent, prurient, libidinous, salacious; beastly, bestial, swinish, porcine, piggish; drunken, bibulous, sottish, crapulous, gluttonous, Bacchanalian.

3. refined, cultivated, polished, cultured, civilized, well-bred, genteel, courtly; pampered, indulged; finished, fine, urbane; aesthetic, tasteful, in good taste, graceful, delicate, exquisite; noble, gentle, pure.

4. meticulous, punctilious, discriminating, fastidious; overscrupulous, overcritical; formal, proper, dainty, strict, overnice; squeamish, fussy, finicking, finicky.

—*n.* **5.** voluptuary, sensualist, *Fr. bon vivant, Inf.* high liver, sybarite, epicure. See **epicure** (*defs.* **1, 2**).

epicureanism, *n.* **1.** epicurism, sybaritism, hedonism, luxuriousness, voluptuousness, sensuality, sensuousness; gourmanderie, gastronomy.

2. intemperance, self-gratification, self-indulgence, overindulgence, unrestraint, incontinence, immoderation; revelry, carousal, dolce vita, wild *or* riotous *or* free living, *Inf.* high living; crapulence, gluttony, greediness, gulosity, edacity.

3. carnality, voluptuousness, fleshiness; lustfulness, lasciviousness, libidinousness, lecherousness, lewdness, prurience, salaciousness, *Sl.* horniness; lust, lechery, concupiscence; debauchery, profligacy, dissoluteness, rakishness, libertinism, dissipation.

epidemic, *adj.* **1.** prevalent, widespread, extensive, prevailing, predominant, pandemic; wide-ranging, far-reaching, general; rampant, sweeping, rife; endemic; epizootic.

—*n.* **2.** plague, pestilence, pest, disease, *Obs.* murrain; contagion, infection; endemic, pandemic; visitation, scourge; illness, sickness, ailment, malady.

3. increase, raise, boost, rise, elevation; mounting, skyrocketing; upsurge, upswing, shooting up, upturn, step-up; burgeoning, flourishing.

epidermis, *n.* skin, scarfskin, integument, outerskin, cuticle; *Anat.* derma, *Anat.* dermis, *Anat.* corium, cutis.

epigram, *n.* **1.** witticism, quip, mot, bon mot, turn of thought, *Fr. jeu d'esprit,* Atticism; pleasantry, jest, pun, *Fr. jeu de mots, Fr. calembour*; equivoque, play on words, double entendre.

2. adage, aphorism, gnome, proverb, moral, apothegm; saw, saying, words of wisdom, *Archaic.* word, *Archaic.* sentence; axiom, maxim, precept; motto, byword, catchword.

epigrammatic, *adj.* **1.** terse, tight, compact, succinct, concise; brief, short, to the point, pointed, pithy; exact, precise, sharp, neat, keen; ingenious, witty, crisp, well-turned, *It. ben trovato*; laconic, lean, elliptical, breviloquent, *Rare.* pauciloquent.

2. aphorismatic, aphoristic, gnomic, sententious, moralistic, proverbial; axiomatic, apothegmatic, preceptive.

epilogue, *n.* afterword, postscript, PS, coda, excursus, tail, tailpiece, *Music.* postlude, (*in poetry*) envoy; supplement, addendum, appendix, back matter; conclusion, peroration, codicil, swan song, last *or* final words.

epiphany, *n.* **1.** incarnation, theophany, *Hindu Myth.* avatar; (*all esp. of a deity*) appearance, manifestation, revelation, apparition, embodiment, materialization.

2. *Literature.* perception, insight, inspiration, *Fr. apercu*; recognition, cognizance, realization, identification; understanding, awareness, comprehension, conception, apprehension.

3. Epiphany Three Kings' Day, Twelfth Day, Twelfth Night, Twelfthtide.

episcopacy, *n.* **1.** *Eccles.* government by bishops; Episcopalianism.

2. (*all of a bishop*) incumbency, office, episcopate, bishopric, archbishopric, prelacy; canonry, prebendary.

3. bishops collectively, body of bishops.

episcopal, *adj.* **1.** hierarchical, ecclesiastical, clerical; prelatical, canonical, capitular; apostolic, sacerdotal, priestly, hieratic; pontifical, papal.

—*n.* **2.** (*cap.*) *Informal.* See **Episcopalian**.

Episcopalian, *n.* member of the Protestant Episcopal Church, *Inf.* Episcopal; member of the Church of England, Anglican, Anglo-Catholic, High Churchman, *Inf.* C of E, Low Churchman.

episcopate, *n.* **1.** (*all of a bishop*) incumbency, office, term, appointment, calling, benefice. See **bishopric** and **episcopacy** (*def.* **2**).

2. diocese, see, bishopric, ecclesiastical district *or* jurisdiction. See **diocese** and **see**[2].

3. bishops collectively.

episode, *n.* **1.** incident, occurrence, event, happening; circumstance, occasion; experience, adventure; affair, action, thing; a link in the chain, a slice in the loaf of life; interlude, digression, excursus.

2. chapter, installment, sequel; scene, story, narrative; vignette, sketch.

episodic, *adj.* rambling, jumpy, digressive, discursive; intermittent, spasmodic, sporadic; sequential, consequent, *Fr. en suite.*

epistle, *n.* **1.** letter, missive, communication, correspondence, *Rom. Cath. Ch.* encyclical, favor; line, note, *Obs.* billet; dispatch, *Brit.* post; message, bulletin, postcard, *Inf.* postal, wire, telegram; billet-doux, love letter, *Sl.* mush note.

2. didacticism, lesson, moral.

epitaph, *n.* inscription, tombstone marking, *Latin. hic jacet*; motto, saying.

epithet, *n.* **1.** appellative, by-word, label, tag; nickname, pet name, *Sl.* handle, *Sl.* moniker; appellation, designation, name, title, honorific, style.

2. curse, oath, expletive, obscenity, *Inf.* swearword, *Sl.* dirty word.

epitome, *n.* **1.** summary, abstract, synopsis, compendium, symposium, compilation; digest, conspectus; condensation, abridgment, reduction, compression, abbreviation; analysis, recapitulation; résumé, brief, précis; outline, aperçu, sketch, review, syllabus, prospectus; docket, bulletin, minute; extracts, fragments, cuttings, analects, clippings, citations.

2. representation, typification, archetype, prototype, model, example.

epitomize, *v.* **1.** summarize, outline, compress, abridge, shorten, condense, contract, curtail, abbreviate; diminish, lessen, reduce; digest, recapitulate, review, sum up, restate.

2. represent, typify, exemplify.

epoch, *n.* era, age, date, period; interval, space, span, stretch; cycle, season.

equable, *adj.* **1.** uniform, identical, always the same, regular, consistent; unvarying, unchanging, invariable, constant; steady, stable, level, even.

2. just, equitable, fair, impartial, unbiased, unprejudiced, neutral, uninvolved, dispassionate.

3. even-tempered, imperturbable, calm, cool, collected, composed, unruffled, smooth; serene, tranquil, peaceful.

equableness, *n.* **1.** uniformity, sameness, regularity, regularness, consistency; unchangingness, constancy, invariability, invariableness; steadiness, stability, stableness, levelness, evenness.

2. justness, equitableness, fairness, impartiality, impartialness, neutrality, dispassionateness.

3. imperturbability, imperturbableness, calmness, coolness, collectedness, unruffledness, smoothness, serenity, tranquillity, peace, peacefulness.

equal, *adj.* **1.** coequal, equipotent, equipollent; on equal *or* even terms, on the same footing, on a par with; identical, selfsame, alike, homogeneous, of a piece, of a kind, cast in the same mold; interchangeable, all one, all the same, much the same, neither more nor less, *Inf.* six of one, half a dozen of another; duplicate, match, twin, *Inf.* ditto.

2. correspondent, coordinate, commensurate, equivalent, proportionate, tantamount; synonymous, analogous; similar, comparable, like.

3. balanced, proportioned, symmetrical, harmonious.

4. even, regular, constant, steady, level, invariant, unvarying, unchanging, unfluctuating.

5. adequate, sufficient, satisfactory, ample, enough, good enough; suited, fitted, up to, up to the mark; competent, able, capable.

—n. **6.** coequal, peer, compeer, rival; partner, confrere, colleague, associate, brother; match, mate, fellow, pendant, companion; twin, double, counterpart, equivalent, other half, alter ego, chip off the old block.

—v. **7.** match, correspond, parallel, commeasure; emulate, vie, rival, keep pace with, keep step with, run abreast; come up to, measure up with, *Inf.* stack up against.

equality, *n.* **1.** parity, coequality, equivalence, equipollence, parallelism; identity, par, oneness, sameness, unity; symmetry, proportion, balance, equilibrium.

2. correspondence, agreement, accordance, concurrence, conformity, coincidence; similarity, similitude, analogy, likeness, resemblance, semblance; comparison, comparability, analogousness.

3. justice, impartiality, fairness, fair play, fair treatment, fair field and no favor.

equalize, *v.* **1.** equate, even up, square, *Archaic.* equal; handicap, compensate, countervail, counterpoise; adapt, fit, tailor, measure; adjust, set, regulate, accommodate, synchronize, *Inf.* sync.

2. level, level off, even, smooth, plane; regularize, symmetrize, harmonize; poise, balance.

equanimity, *n.* calmness, composure, peacefulness, tranquillity, serenity, placidity, peacefulness; imperturbability, inexcitability, unflappability, even-temperedness; presence of mind, level-headedness, coolheadedness, coolness, equability, equilibrium, *Inf.* cool; aplomb, sang-froid, poise, repose, self-possession, self-control, self-command.

equate, *v.* **1.** equalize, balance, strike a balance, poise, parallel, draw a parallel, compare, set side by side; contrast, offset, juxtapose, pit one against the other.

2. reduce, boil down, simplify, streamline.

3. relate, ally, associate, connect, link, tie, bracket, throw *or* toss together, identify.

equatorial, *adj.* tropic, tropical, torrid, hot, sizzling, steaming, humid, sultry, sweltering, sudorific; baking, stifling, suffocating, oppressive; torpid, torporific; lush, jungled.

equestrian, *n.* **1.** horseman, rider, postilion, skilled rider; bareback rider, circus rider, stunt rider; cowboy, gaucho, vaquero.

2. mounted soldier, horse guard, dragoon, trooper, cavalryman, hussar, cossack, knight; horse soldier, horse marine.

—adj. **3.** mounted, up, on horseback, in the saddle.

equilibrist, *n.* tightrope walker, ropewalker, ropedancer, high-wire artist *or* performer, slack-rope artist *or* performer, *Circus Sl.* ballet broad; funambulist, balancer; aerialist, aerial gymnast *or* artist *or* performer; circus performer, *Sl.* kinker.

equilibrium, *n.* **1.** balance, equipoise, equipollence, equipollency, equiponderance, equiponderancy; equivalence, equality, parity, par; equalization, uniformity, symmetry.

2. equanimity, calmness, cool, coolness, sang-froid, imperturbability; sedateness, staidness, dispassion; level-headedness, common sense, discretion; sobriety, sanity, reason, presence of mind, rationality; poise, composure, aplomb, steadiness, evenness, stability; assurance, confidence, self-possession, self-command, self-restraint, self-control, collectedness.

equip, *v.* **1.** furnish, supply, provide, purvey, gird, *Archaic.* dight, *Obs.* appoint; ready, prepare, store, stock; outfit, fit out, fit up, fit, accouter, rig, rig up, rig out, turn out, gear; *All Mil.* arm, forearm, munition, *Sl.* heel, *Archaic.* harness.

2. array, deck, bedeck, deck out, caparison, trap,

adorn, ornament; dress, dress out, clothe, garb, attire, apparel, habit, invest, endue; robe, gown, drape.

equipage, *n.* **1.** carriage, rig; coach and four, coach and six; fourwheeler, barouche, brougham, landau, phaeton, victoria; twowheeler, chaise, *Chiefly Dial.* shay, one hoss shay, sulky.

2. outfit, outfitting, turnout, gear; chattels, belongings, effects; bags, baggage, bag and baggage, luggage.

3. equipment, furnishings, furniture, accouterments, appurtenances, appointments; apparatus, fixtures, fittings, paraphernalia, habiliments, *Inf.* things; caparison, harness, trappings, tack, tackle, rigging; *All Mil.* arms, munitions, materiel.

equipment, *n.* **1.** apparatus, gear, accouterments, furnishings, furniture, appurtenances, appointments; tools, contrivances, machinery; implements, appliances, utensils, conveniences; fixtures, fittings, paraphernalia, habiliments, *Inf.* things; outfit, outfitting, turnout, rig; supplies, material, wherewithal; caparison, harness, trappings, tack, tackle, rigging; *All Mil.* arms, armaments, munitions, materiel.

2. belongings, effects, chattels; kit, duffel; bags, baggage, bag and baggage, luggage.

3. provision, providing, supply, supplying, accouterment, furnishing, furnishment; outfitting, fitting out; arrangement; preparation, preparing, readying.

4. knowledge, expertise, technique, *Inf.* know-how, *Sl.* savvy; experience, background, qualifications; ability, capability, capacity, makings, *Sl.* the stuff, *Sl.* the goods, *Sl.* what it takes; talent, flair, gift, knack, instinct, faculty, genius.

equipoise, *n.* **1.** balance, equilibrium, equipollence. See **equilibrium** (*def.* **1**).

2. counterpoise, counterbalance, counterweight, countercheck; weight, stabilizer, equalizer, neutralizer, makeweight, ballast; compensation, offset, *Latin. quid pro quo*, recompense, requital, *Literary.* guerdon.

equitable, *adj.* **1.** just, fair, impartial, fairminded, even, even-handed; unbiased, disinterested, dispassionate, unprejudiced, open-minded, broad-minded, tolerant, neutral; unswayed, unbigoted, unwarped, undistorted.

2. rightful, right, lawful, legitimate, *Inf.* kosher, legal, licit, constitutional; justifiable, defensible, warrantable, supportable, reasonable; judicious, well-advised, sensible, wise.

3. upright, righteous, honorable, upstanding, noble; ethical, proper, moral, conscionable; principled, high-minded, right-minded, uncorrupt; good, sincere, true, scrupulous; honest, truthful, veracious, straight, *Inf.* square, *Inf.* fair and square, meet.

equity, *n.* **1.** justice, fairness, fair play, impartiality, impartialness, fair-mindedness, evenness, even-handedness, equitableness; unprejudicedness, objectivity, disinterestedness, dispassionateness, open-mindedness, broad-mindedness, tolerance, neutrality.

2. rightfulness, lawfulness, justness, legitimacy, legitimateness, legality, constitutionality; justifiability, defensibility, warrantableness, supportability, supportableness; reasonableness, reasonability, judiciousness, sensibleness.

3. uprightness, righteousness, honorableness, upstandingness, nobility, nobleness; honor, integrity, probity, virtuousness, virtue, rectitude; ethicalness, ethicality, propriety, morality, rightness, conscionableness; high-mindedness, right-mindedness, uncorruptedness; goodness, sincerity, conscientiousness, scrupulousness; honesty, truthfulness, veracity, openness, *Inf.* straightforwardness.

equivalence, *n.* **1.** parity, coequality, parallelism, equipollence, equipollency; equality, identity, par, oneness, sameness; reciprocity, reciprocation, correlation, mutuality.

2. correspondence, correspondency, agreement, accordance, concurrence, conformity, conformance; coincidence, connection; similarity, similitude, analogy, likeness, resemblance, semblance; comparison, comparability, comparableness, comparativeness, compare, analogousness.

3. same, equivalent, opposite number, match, double, twin; alternate, companion, mate, fellow, pendant.

equivalent, *adj.* **1.** equal, tantamount, synonymous, commensurate, equiparent, *Inf.* so much; identical, alike, homogeneous, of a piece, of a kind, cast in the same mold; interchangeable, all one, all the same, much the same, neither more nor less, *Inf.* six of one, half a dozen of another.

2. coequal, equipotent, equipollent, on equal terms *or* footing, on even terms, on the same footing.

3. correspondent, corresponding, coordinate, complementary, complemental, complementing; correlative, correlational, correlated, reciprocal, reciprocative.

—*n.* **4.** same, equivalence, opposite number, match, double, twin; alternate, companion, mate, fellow, pendant.

equivocal, *adj.* **1.** ambiguous, amphibolic, *Logic.* amphibolous, paradoxical, duplicitous; ambivalent, two-edged, multi-leveled, changing, uncertain, wishy-washy; misleading, roundabout, circuitous, ambagious, hedging, weasel-worded, double-tongued; doubtful, dubious, left-handed, questionable, suspicious, shady.

2. vague, hazy, indefinite, indistinct, indeterminate, unclassifiable, anomalous, undetermined; puzzling, mystifying, enigmatic, enigmatical, perplexing, problematic; obscure, abstruse, unintelligible, incomprehensible; mysterious, cryptic, oracular, delphic.

equivocate, *v.* prevaricate, quibble, *Sl.* waffle, fudge, lie; evade, dodge, elude, weasel out, shuffle; shift, hedge, fence, beat around the bush; qualify, compromise, cop out; doubletalk, *Inf.* talk out of both sides of one's mouth, palter; backtrack, back-pedal, sidetrack; tergiversate, vacillate, shilly-shally; mislead, deceive, mystify, dissemble.

equivocation, *n.* prevarication, evasion, quibble, dodge, elusion, avoidance; shuffling, shifting, hedging, beating around the bush; qualification, compromise, cop-out; ambiguity, amphibology, vagueness, indefiniteness, indistinctness, indeterminateness; ambivalence, uncertainty, vacillation, tergiversation; double-speak, double talk, palter, weasel words, sophistry, deception, deceit, speciousness, chicane, chicanery, fraud; lie, falsehood, untruth, *Inf.* fib.

era, *n.* **1.** age, epoch, eon, period, time *or* times, day *or* days, date, division of history, *Hinduism, Buddhism.* kalpa; stage, cycle, season, generation; interval, span, space, spell, stretch.

2. dynasty, reign, rule; administration, presidency, government.

eradicate, *v.* **1.** extirpate, destroy totally, annihilate, discreate, exterminate, abolish; expunge, obliterate, efface; strike out, blot out, stamp out, crush out, snuff out, wipe out; remove, eliminate, get rid of, liquidate, purge; do away with, leave no vestige *or* trace of, put an end to, extinguish, bring to an end; terminate, dissolve, check, stop, cut short; expel, cast off, throw over; quash, quell, squelch, crush, vanquish, squash; overthrow, overwhelm, overturn, subvert, topple, cause the downfall of, defeat, conquer.

2. demolish, raze, ravage, devastate, lay waste, desolate; ruin, *Dial.* ruinate, bring to ruin, lay in ruins.

3. erase, cancel, rub out, scrape out; delete, *Print.* dele, blue-pencil, black out, cross out, mark off, x out.
4. uproot, unroot, pull out by the roots, pull up, pluck up, root out, outroot, deracinate; pull out, draw out, tear out, take out, extract; unearth, excavate, dig up *or* out, grub up *or* out; weed out, rake out.

eradication, *n.* **1.** extirpation, total destruction, annihilation, discreation, expunction, extermination, abolition, abolishment; obliteration, effacement; removal, elimination, liquidation, purgation; extinguishment, extinction, putting an end to, bringing to an end, leaving no vestige *or* trace; termination, dissolution, check; quashing, suppression, squelching, crushing, vanquishment, squashing; overthrow, overturn, overwhelming, subversion, defeat, conquering.
2. demolition, ravagement, devastation, desolation; ruin, ruination.
3. erasure, erasion, cancellation, rubbing out, scraping out; deletion, *Print.* dele, blacking out, marking off.
4. uprooting, unrooting, pulling up, plucking up, pulling out by the roots, rooting out, outrooting, deracination; pulling out, drawing out, wrenching out, tearing out, avulsion, taking out, extraction, evulsion; extrication, disengagement, dislodgment, disentanglement; unearthing, excavation, digging up *or* out, grubbing up *or* out; weeding out, raking out.

erase, *v.* **1.** expunge, eradicate, rub *or* wipe off, rub *or* scrape out; delete, cancel, scratch, cross out, strike out, blot out, mark over *or* through, draw through, edit out, blue-pencil, *Print.* dele.
2. obliterate, efface, destroy, extirpate, remove, dissolve, eliminate, get rid of, do away with, *Inf.* bleep out.

erasure, *n.* **1.** eradication, expunction, rubbing *or* wiping off, rubbing *or* scraping out; deletion, cancellation, cassation, crossing out *or* through; effacement, extirpation, obliteration, elimination, removal.
2. void, blank *or* empty space, *Inf.* bleep; rub, abrasion, attrition; blot, spot, mark, blue mark, *Print.* dele, strikeover.

erect, *adj.* **1.** upright, stand-up, standing up, unrecumbent; at attention, stiff-backed; raised, elevated, rampant, reared up; vertical, perpendicular, plumb, straight.
—*v.* **2.** build, construct, raise, put up, pitch; assemble, put together, hammer together; fabricate, make.
3. upright, lift up, upraise, raise aloft, pry; heave, upheave, rear, uprear; straighten, right, stand up; hoist, mount, elevate.
4. establish, set up, found; institute, constitute; create, form, organize.

erection, *n.* **1.** construction, fabrication, raising.
2. building, structure, framework, edifice, house.
3. *Physiol.* tumescence, tumidity, turgescence, turgidity; distention, swelling.

eremite, *n.* **1.** anchorite, anchoret, hermit, recluse, solitary, *Islam.* marabout, *Islam.* santon, *Obs.* beadsman; nun, anchoress, ancress, hermitess, *Obs.* hermitress; troglodyte, cave dweller, incluse; stylite, pillarist, pillar-saint; ascetic, celibate, monk, monastic, holy man.
2. loner, isolate, isolato, solitudinarian, *Inf.* introvert, *Inf.* lone wolf.

eremitic, *adj.* **1.** hermitic, hermitical, *Rare.* hermitish, anchoritic, stylitic, troglodytic.
2. isolated, recluse, reclusive, sequestered; solitary, lone, single, solitudinarian.
3. ascetic, austere, self-disciplined, hermitlike, celibate, puritanical.
4. outcast, desolate, forlorn, lonely.

ergo, *conj., adv.* therefore, thus, so, then, consequently, accordingly; hence, thence, whence; wherefore, for that reason, on that account, this being the case, as a result.

erode, *v.* **1.** wear, wear down *or* away, waste away, wash away; corrode, fret, gnaw, consume, devour, eat out *or* away; abrade, rub down, chafe, fray, *Inf.* frazzle; grate, rasp, grind, scrape, excoriate.
2. canker, deteriorate, ravage, despoil.
3. channel, gutter, groove, rut, furrow.

Eros, *n.* **1.** Cupid, Amor, god of love, amoretto.
2. (*l.c.*) sexual desire, passion, aphrodisia, lust, sexual appetite *or* urge, libido; eroticism, erotism, concupiscence, *Sl.* letch, *Sl.* the hots, burning, *Psychiatry.* erotomania, *Pathol.* satyriasis, *Pathol.* nymphomania. See **desire** (*def.* **5**).

erosion, *n.* **1.** wearing, wearing down *or* away, wear and tear, wasting away, washing away, wash out, eroding, detrition, attrition; corrosion, corroding, fretting, gnawing, consumption, consuming, devouring, eating out *or* away; abrasion, abrading, rubbing down, chafing, fraying, grating, rasping, grinding, scraping, scrape, excoriation.
2. cankering, deterioration, deteriorating, ravagement, ravaging, despoilment, despoiling.
3. channeling, guttering, grooving, rutting, furrowing.

erosive, *adj.* wearing, washing, erodent, eroding, attritional, attritive; corrosive, corroding, caustic, fretting, gnawing, consumptive, consuming, eating; abrasive, abrading, chafing, fraying, scraping, excoriating, grating, rasping, grinding; cankering, deteriorating, ravaging, despoiling.

erotic, *adj.* **1.** amatory, Anacreontic, amorous, lovesome, fond, enamored, infatuated; passionate, rapturous, fervent, ardent; tempestuous, impetuous, burning, fiery.
2. aphrodisiac, venereal, seductive, inflammatory, titillating, enticing, alluring, ravishing; entrancing, bewitching, enchanting.
3. lustful, lusty, carnal, voluptuous, sensuous, *Inf.* sexy; wanton, lascivious, prurient, lecherous, libidinous, lubricous, *Archaic.* lickerish; concupiscent, adulterous, shameless, dissolute, debauched, unchaste; ribald, obscene, salacious, bawdy, risqué, *Inf.* blue.

err, *v.* **1.** be mistaken, be in error, be incorrect, be in the wrong, be at fault, fly in the face of; misbelieve, lose faith; misjudge, misreckon, miscalculate, misestimate; misunderstand; be out of line, be off the mark, be wide of the mark, *Inf.* be off base, *Inf.* be way off base, *Sl.* bark up the wrong tree; delude *or* deceive *or* trick oneself.
2. make a mistake, blunder, bungle, botch, muff, flub, fumble, *Inf.* slip up, *Inf.* drop the ball, *Inf.* put one's foot in one's mouth, *Inf.* put one's foot into it, *Sl.* goof, *Sl.* make *or* pull a boner, *Sl.* make a boo-boo, *Sl.* boot one, *Sl.* boot it.
3. sin, commit sin, transgress, trespass, do wrong; fall *or* lapse into sin *or* error, go astray, go wrong, go amiss; degenerate, go bad, go to the bad, *Inf.* go to the deuce *or* devil, *Inf.* go to pot, *Inf.* go to the dogs, *Sl.* go to hell.
4. stray, veer, swerve, deviate, digress, turn aside, turn away; wander, ramble, rove, straggle, go out of line, leave the straight and narrow; drift, go adrift, lose one's way; nod, trip, stumble, slip, lapse.

errand, *n.* **1.** trip, journey, jaunt, *Brit.* message.
2. commission, mission, duty, charge; entrustment, commitment, task, assignment, consignment, trust; undertaking, job, chore, work.

errant, *adj.* **1.** roaming, wandering, traveling,

journeying, rambling, roving, ranging; gallivanting, *Inf.* traipsing, flitting, strolling; straying, wayward, shifting, meandering; vagrant, bohemian, nomadic, transient, vagabond, footloose, itinerant, peripatetic.
2. erring, deviant, deviating. See **erring** (*def.* **1**).
3. aimless, directionless, undirected, haphazard, loose, free, stray; discursive, divagatory, digressive, excursive, tangential, maundering; indirect, roundabout, circuitous, ambagious; desultory, episodic, random, intermittent, sporadic, fitful.

erratic, *adj.* **1.** eccentric, queer, unusual, abnormal, odd, quaint; peculiar, singular, curious, unique; bizarre, extraordinary, strange, outlandish, unorthodox, unconventional.
2. irregular, inconsistent, anomalous, aberrant; fitful, sporadic, spasmodic, intermittent, unsteady; capricious, whimsical, fanciful, notional; flighty, fickle, mercurial, volatile, changeful, changeable.
3. wandering, meandering, unfixed, unanchored, unsettled. See **errant** (*defs.* **2, 3**).

erratically, *adv.* **1.** capriciously, whimsically, fancifully, without rhyme or reason; aimlessly, haphazardly, directionlessly, indirectly, circuitously; discursively, digressively, tangentially.
2. irregularly, inconsistently, aberrantly; desultorily, sporadically, intermittently; randomly, episodically, fitfully, spasmodically; by fits and starts, off and on, now and then, here and there.

erratum, *n.* misprint, typographical error, *Inf.* typo, printer's error, typist's error, (*of printed or written words*) omission, corrigendum; slip of the pen, *Lat. lapsus calami.*

erring, *adj.* **1.** in error, wrong, incorrect, inaccurate, erroneous, faulty; straying, devious, on the wrong track *or* path, wide of the mark; wayward, deviant, erratic, aberrant.
2. sinning, transgressive, peccant, peccable; bad, wicked, iniquitous, felonious; criminal, lawless, reprehensible, objectionable, censurable; shameless, corrupt, profligate, abandoned, wanton, dissolute.

erroneous, *adj.* **1.** mistaken, incorrect, amiss, wrong, all wrong, *Sl.* all wet, *Sl.* full of beans *or* prunes, *Sl.* full of hot air; false, fallacious, untrue, not true, devoid of truth, not right; spurious, counterfeit, fictitious, bogus; apocryphal, groundless, unfounded.
2. inaccurate, inexact, imprecise, unprecise; faulty, flawed, unsound, illogical, *Sl.* cockeyed.
3. in error, erring, in the wrong; astray, wide of the mark, *Inf.* off base, *Sl.* off the beam, *Sl.* at sea, *Sl.* out in left field; deceived, deluded.

error, *n.* **1.** mistake, inaccuracy, *Sports.* miscue; misprint, corrigendum; fault, flaw, human error; oversight, omission; blunder, botch, bungle, flub, muff; leak, slip, slip of the tongue *or* pen, *Inf.* slip-up; *All Sl.* pratfall, fool mistake, dumb trick, foul-up, louse-up, screw-up, boner, boo-boo, goof, blooper, clinker, clunker.
2. misunderstanding, misconception, misapprehension; misidentification; miscalculation, misestimation; misjudgment, error in judgment, misreckoning; misconstruction, misreading, misinterpretation, wrong impression.
3. fallacy, false *or* mistaken belief, heresy, false doctrine; illusion, delusion, self-delusion, deception, self-deception, mirage, hallucination.
4. erroneousness, falsity, fallaciousness, untrueness, incorrectness, uncorrectness; faultiness.
5. sin, moral offense, lapse from virtue; misdeed, misstep, transgression, trespass; crime, criminal offense *or* act, felony; offense, breach; misdemeanor, impropriety, indiscretion, misconduct, peccadillo, venial sin; wrongdoing, evil, wrong, bad, iniquity.
6. *Baseball.* misplay, fumble, *Inf.* booble, *Sl.* boot, *Sl.* E, *Sl.* the big E.
7. *Philately.* freak, variety; misprint, erratum, printer's error.

ersatz, *adj.* synthetic, man-made, plastic; artificial, simulated, imitated, imitation; spurious, counterfeit, sham, *U.S.* bogus, *Inf.* phony.

erstwhile, *adj.* former, late, quondam, once, *Inf.* ex; old, past, gone, bygone, forgotten.

eructation, *n.* belch, belching, *Inf.* burp, *Inf.* burping, bringing up gas, bringing [s.t.] up; emission, ejection, vomiting, disgorgement; expulsion, extrusion, egestion, voidance.

erudite, *adj.* **1.** learned, scholarly, punditic, wise, sage, profound, deep; well-versed, knowledgeable, literate, literary, well-read, lettered; educated, well-educated, well-instructed, well-tutored, well-schooled, well-posted, well-grounded.
2. academic, scholastic, intellectual, highbrow, highbrowed, *Inf.* long-haired, pedantic, bookish.
3. cultured, refined, polished, sophisticated, worldly, worldly-wise, *Sl.* savvy, knowing, *Sl.* in the know, enlightened, aware, cognizant, conscious, alive to; acquainted, familiar, intimate, at ease *or* home, conversant; expert, proficient, very good, adept, skillful, skilled; experienced, practised, accomplished.

erudition, *n.* **1.** knowledge, learning, scholarship, wisdom; information, facts, data, lore; teachings, doctrines, precepts, concepts, theories; letters, *Archaic.* literature, book learning, formal education, schooling, instruction, tuition.
2. refinement, culture, cultivation, polish, sophistication; enlightenment, awareness, cognizance, consciousness; understanding, ken, knowledge, knowing; familiarity, intimacy, ease, proficiency, adeptness, skill, expertise, expertness.

erupt, *v.* **1.** burst forth *or* open, break open, split open, rupture, gape, dehisce, *Sl.* bust; detonate, fulminate, explode, blow, blow up, go off; (*of a volcano, geyser, etc.*) eject, emit, expel, hurl *or* throw forth, discharge, send out *or* up; spout, squirt, spurt, spew *or* spit out, belch forth; gush, jet, boil over, pour forth *or* out, spill over, overflow.
2. explode, blow up, unleash one's temper *or* anger, fly off the handle, blow one's top, hit the ceiling *or* the roof.

eruption, *n.* **1.** outburst, outbreak, splitting open, dissilience, dissiliency, rupture, gape, dehiscence; earthquake, quake, tremor, *Chiefly U.S.* temblor, upheaval, *Phys., Geog.* cataclysm; explosion, detonation, fulmination, blast, blowing up.
2. (*of a volcano, geyser, etc.*) ejection, emission, expulsion, discharge, ebullition; spouting, squirt, spurt, outpour, spewing *or* spitting forth, belching; gushing, boiling over, spilling over, overflow.

escalator, *n.* moving staircase, moving stairway; elevator, lift, conveyor.

escapade, *n.* **1.** prank, trick, caper, stunt; mischief, *Fr. boutade*, practical joke; reckless *or* wild *or* madcap adventure; antics, tomfoolery, *Inf.* shenanigans, *Sl.* monkey shines, horseplay; gambado, lark, frolic; romp, gambol, skylarking.
2. escape, flight, giving the slip, pulling a Houdini.

escape, *v.* **1.** get away, get free, get out, get clear of, break away, make *or* effect one's escape, make good one's escape, get away safely, *Archaic.* scape *or* 'scape, *Inf.* jump, *Inf.* skip, *Inf.* make a getaway *or* clean getaway, *Inf.* fly the coop; *All Sl.* break jail *or* prison, break out, break loose, cut loose, bust out, bust loose, go *or* leap over the wall, lam *or* take it on

the lam; free oneself, break one's chains, slip the collar, shake off the yoke.
2. elude, evade, bilk, dodge, slip through [s.o.'s] hands *or* fingers, give [s.o.] the slip, lose [s.o.], throw [s.o.] off the scent.
3. abscond, flee, bolt, elope, fly, take flight, take to flight, take wing, *Sl.* wing it, *Inf.* beat it, *Inf.* skip out, *Inf.* skip town, *Inf.* skedaddle, *Sl.* skidoodle, *Sl.* skidoo *or* skiddoo, *Sl.* vamoose *or* vamose; run, run away, run off, take to one's heels, make a quick exit, *Rare.* fugitate, *Inf.* take off, *Inf.* clear out, *Inf.* make tracks, *Inf.* cut out, *Inf.* cut and run, *Sl.* split, *Sl.* scram, *Sl.* blow, *Sl.* hightail it; retreat, withdraw, abandon, desert, take oneself off, take French leave, quit the scene, beat a retreat, beat a hasty retreat, run for it, make a run for it, turn tail, show the heels, show a clean *or* extra-light pair of heels; leave, depart, exit, *Euph.* leave without saying good-bye, *Brit. Sl.* bugger off.
4. make off, pull out, absquatulate, give *or* take legbail, *Sl.* bail out, *Fig.* take the money and run; sneak off *or* away, steal off *or* away, creep off *or* away, slink off *or* away, slip off *or* away, slither away, slide off, skulk away, *Sl.* mooch off, *Sl.* duck off, *Brit. Sl.* mizzle; vanish, disappear, do the disappearing act, *Inf.* make oneself scarce, *Brit. Sl.* do a moonlight flit, *Sl.* duck and run, *Sl.* dog it.
5. leak, leak out; drain, seep; emanate, issue forth, pour forth, flow out; stream, gush, spurt, flood.
—*n.* **6.** flight, departure, *Archaic.* scape *or* 'scape; running away, bolt, decampment, desertion, abandonment, elopement, absquatulation, French leave, retreat, hasty retreat, *Sl.* disappearing act, *Sl.* skedaddle, *Sl.* skedaddling, *Sl.* scramming.
7. getaway, jailbreak, prisonbreak, *Inf.* break, *Inf.* breakout; exodus, hegira, migration; deliverance, delivery, release, freedom.
8. evasion, elusion, avoidance, dodge, duck, sidestep; narrow escape, hairbreadth escape, near miss, tight squeeze, *Inf.* close call, *Inf.* close shave, *Inf.* close one.
9. opening, outlet, exit, egress, way out; escape hatch, hole to crawl out of; loophole, escape clause, pretext, *Inf.* out.
10. fantasy, fantasizing, escape into fantasy, oblivion, escape into oblivion; dreaming, daydreaming, wishful thinking; escapism, *Psychol.* autism, *Psychol.* dereism.
11. leakage, leaking, leak; seepage, drainage; discharge, effluence, efflux, effluxion, outflow; outpour, outgush, outburst, outrush.

escapist, *n.* non-realist, dreamer, daydreamer, woolgatherer; optimist, cockeyed optimist, Pollyanna; avoider, ostrich, evader; fugitive, vagabond, rover.

eschew, *v.* shun, avoid, steer clear of; have nothing to do with, refuse to touch with a 10-foot pole; let well enough alone, shirk; abstain from, refrain from, forgo, forbear; evade, elude, shy away from, shrink from, keep one's distance; escape, keep out of the way of, flee from; snub, ignore, disdain, turn up one's nose at; renounce, set one's face against, shudder at, disrelish.

escort, *n.* **1.** chaperon, accompanier, companion; attendant, squire, assistant, aide, aide-de-camp; usher, guide, pilot, conductor, leader; guardian, shepherd, protector, protectress, matron, tutelary, tutelar, tutor, tutoress, governess, nursemaid, (*in Spain and Portugal*) duenna.
2. entourage, retinue, cortege, train, suite, company; bodyguard, armed guard, convoy, contingent, *Navy.* escort carrier, *Mil.* escort fighter.
3. date, partner, cavalier, beau, boyfriend, sweetheart, *Inf.* steady.
4. protection, defense, security, bulwark, shield, screen, cover, shelter, refuge, safety, safeguard; guidance, tutelage, custody, keeping, care.
—*v.* **5.** chaperon, matronize, accompany, companion; attend, squire, esquire, wait upon, assist, aid; usher, conduct, pilot, steer, guide, lead, direct.
6. convoy, guard, watch over, shepherd, keep an eye on, look after; protect, screen, shelter, flank, be by one's side; defend, back up, support, go *or* be behind.
7. date, take out, *Inf.* go with, *Inf.* go steady with.

escutcheon, *n.* **1.** shield, heraldic shield, scutcheon, *Chiefly Brit.* hatchment, *Heraldry.* lozenge.
2. blot on one's escutcheon shame, disgrace, dishonor, disrepute; stigma, stain, tarnish, smirch, smudge, spot, blot; skeleton in one's closet.

esoteric, *adj.* **1.** abstruse, recondite, deep, profound, abstract; impenetrable, incomprehensible, unfathomable, inscrutable, indecipherable.
2. occult, cryptic, perdu, hidden, veiled; obscure, dark, dim, vague, nebulous, *Rare.* imperspicuous; mysterious, arcane, inexplicable, insolvable, insoluble, unaccountable, *Obs.* inextricable; puzzling, enigmatic, enigmatical.
3. private, privy, secret, acroamatic, *Obs.* acroamatical, undisclosed, untold; confidential, privileged, auricular, *Sl.* inside; inner, inmost, intimate, personal, subjective, solipsistic.

especial, *adj.* **1.** special, extra special, extraordinary, out of the ordinary, exceptional, unusual, uncommon; superior, preeminent, eminent, outstanding, striking, noteworthy, notable, marked, remarkable, signal, *Inf.* spanking.
2. particular, certain, specific; distinctive, unique, singular; individual, personal, own, peculiar to.

especially, *adv.* **1.** particularly, in particular, specially, exceptionally, extraordinarily, uncommonly, unusually; singularly, uniquely, distinctively, peculiarly.
2. chiefly, mainly, principally, primarily, firstly, first of all, first off, first and foremost, first and last, above all, more than any other; predominately, mostly, for the most part, on the whole, by and large.
3. outstandingly, strikingly, noticeably; markedly, notably, signally, noteworthily.

espial, *n.* **1.** detection, discernment, discovery, perception, recognition, spotting.
2. observation, surveillance, reconnaissance, notice, regard; following, shadowing, trailing, *Inf.* tailing; espionage, spying, intelligence, *Inf.* cloak and dagger work.

espionage, *n.* spying, undercover work; prying, probing, digging; surveillance, following, tailing; reconnaissance, reconnoitering; eavesdropping, bugging, wiretapping, breaking codes; deception, foxiness, pretension.

esplanade, *n.* **1.** promenade, walk, boardwalk, sidewalk, mall, parade; alley, lane, road, highway, parkway, freeway.
2. patio, terrace, piazza, green, square, quadrangle, circus; close, yard, lawn, parterre, slope, glacis, sward.

espousal, *n.* **1.** advocacy, adoption, patronage, championship, defense; furtherance, promotion, support, aid, assistance; auspices, subvention, countenance.
2. betrothal, betrothment, affiancing, engagement rite, match; marriage, wedding, bridal, nuptials, *Sl.* tying the knot.

espouse, *v.* **1.** adopt, embrace, take up, assume, make one's own; elect, choose, opt for, enlist under the banners of; champion, advocate, defend, stand up for, stick up for, side with; support, uphold, maintain, sustain, back up, second; work for, abet, lend oneself to, lend aid to, finance, back, hold out a helping hand to, *Inf.* angel; further, forward, advance, promote, take in hand, favor, patronize, smile upon, befriend.
2. marry, lead to the altar, give one's hand to, wive, wed.

esprit, *n.* wit, mother wit, intuition, sense, common sense; brains, *Inf.* gray matter, smartness; cleverness, astuteness, shrewdness, ingenuity, ingeniousness; sprightliness, initiative, drive, resourcefulness, *Inf.* gumption; perceptiveness, perspicacity, perspicaciousness, keenness, acuteness, sharpness, quickness; acumen, discernment, insight, perception, percipience, flair; intelligence, understanding, comprehension; sagacity, sagaciousness, wisdom.

esprit de corps, *n.* solidarity, group interest, group feeling, togetherness, party spirit, sense of union, high morale; teamwork, cooperation, coordination; unanimity, mutual interest; fellowship, comradeship, sodality, companionship.

espy, *v.* discern, perceive, detect, descry, discover, notice, make out, distinguish, recognize, catch a glimpse of, catch sight of, *Inf.* spot; see, behold, observe, view, *Brit.* twig, *Archaic.* ken.

essay, *n.* **1.** theme, article, paper, photo-essay, manuscript; commentary, *Journalism.* think piece, editorial, article, piece; thesis, dissertation, disquisition, tract, treatise, discourse; work, opus, masterpiece, work of art, brainchild.

2. attempt, effort, endeavor, exertion, struggle, undertaking; try, venture, enterprise; trial, experiment, test, *Inf.* stab, *Inf.* crack, *Inf.* go-around *or* go-round.

—v. **3.** attempt, try, make an effort, endeavor, strive, work at, aim; undertake, take in hand, take upon oneself, set *or* turn one's hand to, try one's hand at, try one's fortune at; venture, set out to, go about; tackle, take on, take a crack *or* whack *or* stab at; *Sl.* give it a whirl, *Sl.* give it a shot, *Sl.* have a go at; strain, put one's back to it, do one's best.

4. put to the test, put to trial, try out, experiment, test, assay.

essayist, *n.* writer, author, littérateur, penman; newspaperman, newspaperwoman, scribe, journalist, columnist, editorialist.

essence, *n.* **1.** essential part, quiddity, quintessence, essentiality, inmost substance, central nature, vital element, necessary constituent, *Latin. sine qua non*, *Metaphys.* hypostasis; principle, entity, inwardness, being, actuality, reality, essentialness, suchness; pith, heart, core, soul, marrow, kernel, gist; sum and substance, sum total; life, lifeblood, spirit; truth, purport, verity; tenor, import, drift, sense, significance.

2. extract, concentrate, concentration, distillate, abstraction, elixir.

3. perfume, scent, attar, fragrance, pleasing odor, aroma; pungency, sachet, incense, bouquet, balminess, redolence, musk, civet.

essential, *adj.* **1.** indispensable, necessary, requisite, vital, important; fundamental, constitutional, characteristic, inherent, basic, intrinsic; indigenous, inward, organic, ingrained; absolute, cardinal, principal, leading, main, capital; substantial, material, *Sl.* nitty-gritty.

—n. **2.** fundamental, rudiment, cornerstone; indispensable, element, chief point, main ingredient, primary constituent, vital part; crux, *Sl.* nitty-gritty, brass tacks, bare bones, bottom line; quality, attribute, characteristic, peculiarity, trait, feature, mark.

establish, *v.* **1.** create, give rise to, bring into being, start, found; institute, set up, organize; make, form, fashion, build, construct; coin, make up, compose, fabricate, contrive.

2. install, settle, ensconce, lodge, entrench; secure, ground, root, plant, place, put, seat, station, locate.

3. prove, show to be true, substantiate, evidence, support, back up; authenticate, validate, certify, confirm, verify; attest to, affirm, corroborate, aver.

4. enact, appoint, ordain, decree; rule, adjudge, order, command, dictate, pronounce, proclaim; authorize, legalize, warrant, sanction, license, entitle.

establishment, *n.* **1.** formation, organization, constitution; construction, erection; creation, commencement, start, origin, foundation, founding, beginning, inception, initiation; installation, appointment, ordainment; proof, confirmation, substantiation, verification, demonstration, settlement; validation, certification, authorization.

2. system, constituted order *or* system, officialdom; power structure, pecking order, *Inf.* totem pole; hierarchy, power elite, ruling class *or* circle, *Inf.* the powers that be; *All Inf.* higher-ups, the brass, VIP's, bigwigs, big shots, big fish.

3. home, abode, domicile, dwelling, residence, habitation; homestead, household, *Inf.* place where one hangs one's hat; estate, manor, house and grounds.

4. business, firm, concern, company; corporation, trust, syndicate, combine, cartel; association, society, guild, brotherhood.

5. shop, store, emporium; market, mart, marketplace.

6. building, structure, edifice; place, location, *Inf.* spot; *Sl.* joint, *Sl.* dive, *Sl.* hole, *Sl.* dump.

7. institution, institute, organization, foundation.

estate, *n.* **1.** property, real property, real estate, land, piece of property; place, residence, abode, home.

2. assets, holdings, resources, wealth, fortune, worth; possessions, properties, personal property, personal assets, belongings, effects, chattels, *Inf.* things, *Law.* choses, *Law.* personalty.

3. station, position, place, standing, social standing, status, social status, dignity; class, caste, stratum, level, grade.

4. situation, circumstance, condition, state; period, stage, cycle, time, age.

esteem, *v.* **1.** value, appreciate, prize, cherish, hold dear, treasure; honor, revere, reverence, respect, venerate, pay respect to, defer to; admire, think highly of, look up to, hold a high opinion of; like, love, be fond of, hold in affection, adore, care for; commend, speak well of, praise, extol, exalt.

2. regard, consider, deem, reckon, fancy, opine; view, take for, see, recognize; judge, adjudge, think, hold.

—n. **3.** respect, regard, favor, estimation, high regard, high opinion; admiration, approval, approbation, appreciation; honor, reverence, veneration; awe, homage, deference; affection, liking, love, fondness.

estimable, *adj.* **1.** worthy, deserving, valuable, valued, esteemed; respected, respectable, competent, creditable, reputable; honorable, honored, noble, venerable, admirable; meritorious, laudable, praiseworthy, commendable; trustworthy, reliable, dependable, unimpeachable, incorruptible; excellent, good.

2. assessable, appraisable; computable, calculable, reckonable; determinable, ascertainable.

estimate, *v.* **1.** calculate approximately, reckon, figure, compute roughly, approximate, make a rough guess, make an estimate, give a ball park figure, *Sl.* guesstimate.

2. gauge, rate, rank, weigh, measure, *Archaic.* mete, judge, size, size up; appraise, evaluate, valuate, place *or* set a value on, assess, fix the price of, price, assay, *Obs.* apprise.

—n. **3.** educated guess, approximation, rough guess, ball park figure, *Sl.* guesstimate; estimation, reckoning, figure, rough computation *or* calculation.

4. judgment, opinion, estimation. See **estimation** (*def.* **1**).

5. appraisal, estimated value, appraisement, evaluation, valuation, assessment, price.

estimation, *n.* **1.** judgment, opinion, thinking, sentiment, feeling, mind; belief, point of view, viewpoint, position, persuasion, conviction; conclusion, deduction, inference, guess, conjecture, surmise.

2. esteem, respect, regard, admiration. See **esteem** (*def.* **1**).

3. estimate, rough guess, approximation, ball park figure. See **estimate** (*def.* **3**).

estrange, *v.* **1.** alienate, disaffect, harden the heart, make indifferent *or* averse *or* hostile, destroy one's affections; antagonize, set *or* pit against, set by the ears, set at odds *or* variance; separate, come between, divide, cut off *or* apart, disunite, sever, sunder, rupture; widen the breach, cause to break with; anger, incense, provoke, heat up, *Chiefly U.S.* rile, madden, infuriate, enrage; exacerbate, aggravate, embitter, envenom.

2. turn away, keep at a distance, hold at arm's length; withdraw, wean away from, keep aloof, keep away, keep oneself at a distance; part company, separate, leave, take leave, go away, quit.

estrangement, *n.* **1.** disaffection, alienation, separation, division, disunion; break, breach, split, severance, falling-out, breaking up *or* off; parting, withdrawal, pulling away, backing off.

2. hostility, antagonism, antipathy, enmity, animosity, ill-will, bad-blood; resentment, umbrage, displeasure; aversion, dislike, disinclination, unfriendliness; discord, disagreement, difference.

estuary, *n.* inlet, cove, reach, arm, armlet, *Scot.* loch; firth, fjord, bay, bayou, mouth.

et cetera, and so on, and so forth, and more of the same, and the rest, and the like, *Inf.* what have you, *Inf.* whatnot, *Inf.* and all that; and others, et al.

etch, *v.* **1.** engrave, eat *or* burn into, corrode; bite in, carve, scrape, furrow; impress, imprint, infix.

2. grave, incise, enchase, chase, hatch, crosshatch, stipple, drypoint; outline, sketch out, draw, depict, design.

eternal, *adj.* **1.** infinite, timeless, always existing; *Archaic.* eterne; unbegotten, self-originated, self-existent, self-active; absolute, almighty, boundless, illimitable.

2. perpetual, endless, unending, never-ending, interminable, Sisyphean; ceaseless, incessant, unceasing, nonstop, constant, uninterrupted, continual, continuous, unbroken; unremitting, unintermitting, relentless, persistent; recurrent, repeated, frequent, habitual.

3. enduring, lasting, abiding, everlasting, *Literary.* sempiternal, aeonian, amaranthine, perennial; immutable, constant, unwavering, unfaltering, undiminished; invariable, fixed, durable, stable, steady, permanent.

4. *Metaphys.* unchangeable, changeless, unchanging, immutable, imperishable, perdurable, indestructible; immortal, undying, never-dying, ever-living, deathless.

eternally, *adv.* forever, evermore, *Poetic. or Dial.* ay, *Poetic. or Dial.* for ay, for everlasting, *Latin. in saecula saeculorum*; everlastingly, timelessly, interminably, through all the ages, world without end, to the end of time, till the crack of doom, till doomsday, forever and a day; constantly, perpetually, ceaselessly, incessantly, continually; morning, noon and night; day in and day out, day and night.

eternity, *n.* **1.** eternalness, everlastingness, infinite duration, timelessness; unendingness, interminableness, unceasingness; perpetuity, perdurability; illimitableness, boundlessness, infinity.

2. immortality, hereafter, afterlife, everlasting life, futurity; next world, world to come, heaven, *Amer. Ind.* happy hunting grounds, *Buddhism.* nirvana.

3. duration, age, eon, seeming endlessness, ages and ages.

ethereal, *adj.* **1.** airy, vaporous, gaseous, pneumatic; tenuous, rarefied, subtle, chimerical, shadowy.

2. delicate, fine, thin, frail; gossamer, gossamery, insubstantial, diaphanous, wispy, misty.

3. heavenly, celestial, unearthly, otherworldly; Elysian.

ethereality, *n.* **1.** airiness, gaseousness, vaporousness, etherealness; immateriality, unsubstantiality, incorporeity; tenuousness, rarity, subtileness.

2. delicateness, fineness, thinness, fragility, frailty; sheerness, diaphanousness.

3. heavenliness, celestialness, unearthliness, otherworldliness.

etherealize, *v.* **1.** spiritualize, disembody, dematerialize.

2. refine, attenuate, rarefy, subtilize, thin, thin out.

ethical, *adj.* moral, righteous, just; upright, faithful, honest, open, straightforward; virtuous, pure, good, decent, fair; noble, high-minded, lofty, honorable, principled, magnanimous, conscientious; right, correct, proper, seemly, decorous; deontological.

ethics, *n.* conscience, principles, high standards; morality, righteousness, justness; integrity, honesty, uprightness, rectitude; probity, virtue, conscientiousness, propriety, seemliness, decency; deontology, *Judaism.* Pirke Aboth, Ten Commandments, decalogue, golden rule.

etiolate, *v.* blanch, blench, whiten, make white *or* pale; achromatize, bleach, wash out; grow white *or* pale, pale, fade, lose color.

etiolated, *adj.* blanched, blenched, white, colorless, light-colored, chalky; bleached, whitened, faded, paled; achromatic, hueless; milky-white, snow-white; pale, blond, albinic, albinal.

etiquette, *n.* manners, good manners, politeness, proper *or* good behavior, propriety, decorum, seemliness; rules, code, convention, form, ceremony, custom, customs, established conventions, formality, protocol; good form, conventionality, fashion, mode, accepted forms, style.

Eucharist, *n.* **1.** Holy Communion, sacrament of the Lord's Supper; Sacrifice of the Mass, Holy Sacrifice; offering, offering of the host, oblation; *Theol.* transubstantiation, *Theol.* impanation, the body of our Lord, real presence.

2. communion bread *or* wafer, *Eccles.* Host; wafer, consecrated wafer, holy bread, bread of life, bread of angels, *Latin. panis angelicus*; *Eccles.* viaticum; spiritual food, manna.

eugenics, *n.* **1.** racial improvement, generic amelioration *or* betterment; genetic counseling.

2. genetics, selective breeding, stirpiculture, genetic engineering, genetic control, genetic adaptation, controlled *or* planned evolution.

eulogize, *v.* **1.** praise, sound the praises of, sing the praises of, cry up, *Inf.* crack up; extol, laud, *Archaic.* magnify, emblazon, panegyrize; say a good word for, put in a good word for, *Inf.* tout, promote, boost; glorify, bless, exalt, elevate; pay homage to, pay tribute to, crown, honor.

2. applaud, acclaim, cheer, celebrate, congratulate, *Archaic.* gratulate; approve enthusiastically, hail, commend, sanction; compliment, flatter, appreciate; blandish, belaud, puff.

eulogy, *n.* **1.** panegyric, eulogium, encomium, citation; testimonial, declaration, announcement, oration.

2. praise, extolment, laudation, kudos, *Archaic.* magnification; commendation, celebration, congratulation, *Archaic.* gratulation, paean, laud; exaltation, glorification, tribute, homage, honor, crown; acclaim, acclamation, applause, plaudits, salvo, accolade; hosanna, huzzah, hurrah.

eunuch, *n.* castrato, gelding; *Fig.* sissy, *Inf.* pantywaist, mama's boy, *Sl.* fairy, *Sl.* fag.

euphemism, *n.* (*all of language*) nice-nellyism, newspeak; substitution, milder equivalent, metaphor, trope, figurative extenuation; mollification, mitigation, lessening, softening, cushioning, padding.

euphemistic, *adj.* (*all of language*) extenuatory, softened, mild, inoffensive, vague, indirect; euphemistical, euphemious, metaphorical, figurative, tropical.

euphonious, *adj.* melodious, dulcet, tuneful, harmonious, symphonious, canorous, lyrical, lyric, musical; mellifluous, mellifluent, sweet-sounding, pleasant-sounding, pleasing, agreeable; smooth, soothing, soft, mellow, golden-toned, rich; flowing, fluid, rhythmical, fluent, eloquent, silver-tongued; silvery, silver-toned, clear as a bell.

euphony, *n.* melody, melodiousness, harmony, harmoniousness, dulcetness, tunefulness, canorousness, lyricalness, musicality, musicalness, music; mellifluousness, sweetness, pleasantness, pleasingness, agreeableness; smoothness, soothingness, softness, mellowness, goldenness, richness; rhythmicity, fluency, fluidity, fluidness, eloquence; silveriness, clearness, clarity.

euphoria, *n.* elation, joy, jubilance, jubilation, exaltation; transport, rapture, bliss, ecstasy; elevation, cloud nine, seventh heaven, nirvana; high, *Sl.* trip.

euphuism, *n.* (*of writing style*) **1.** affectation, mannerism, Gongorism; fastidiousness, finicalness, delicacy.

2. high-flown language, inflation, bombast, orotundity, fustian, rant, turgidity; grandiloquence, magniloquence; floridness, floweriness, ornateness, sesquipedalism; periphrasis, circumlocution.

euthanasia, *n.* mercy killing, putting [s.o.] out of misery; painless death, easy death.

evacuant, *adj.* **1.** cleansing, emptying, evacuating; eliminant, ejective, evacuative.

2. cathartic, purgative, abstergent; diuretic; emetic.

—n. **3.** purgative, cathartic, laxative, *Trademark.* Ex-lax, eliminant; emetic, nauseant; diuretic.

evacuate, *v.* **1.** empty, make empty, remove; drain, exhaust, deplete, deprive.

2. vacate, abandon, desert, relinquish, forsake, leave empty, withdraw from, retire from, go away.

3. *Physiol.* eliminate, defecate, void; expel, discharge, eject, emit; throw out, clean out.

evacuation, *n.* **1.** discharge, ejection, expulsion, elimination; purgation, catharsis; emptying, depleting, exhausting, draining off.

2. departure, retreat, flight, exodus, pulling out, withdrawal, abandonment; clearance, removal; retirement, pulling back.

3. defecation, excretion, voidance, urination; bowel movement, stool, feces, excrement, egesta, *Med., Physiol.* dejection.

evade, *v.* **1.** avoid, dodge, whiffle, sidestep, elude, weasel out, give [s.o.] the slip; avert, parry, escape, *Inf.* shake off, get rid of, *Sl.* beat the rap; sneak off, sneak out the back way, make oneself scarce, take off, scram; shun, stay away from, stay clear of, keep clear of, go wide of, keep one's distance, *Inf.* give the go-by; stay out, play truant, shuffle off to buffalo, malinger, call in sick; shirk, funk, *Sl.* goldbrick; ignore, close one's eyes to, look the other way; neglect, skip, omit.

2. prevaricate, quibble, equivocate, *Sl.* waffle, fudge; hedge, shuffle, shift, fence, skirt, beat around the bush, hem and haw; qualify, cop out; give [s.o.] the runaround, talk one's way out of, do an end run, maneuver, baffle; doubletalk, *Inf.* talk out of both sides of one's mouth, palter, backtrack, back-pedal, sidetrack; tergiversate, vacillate, shilly-shally, straddle the fence.

evaluate, *v.* **1.** appraise, *Obs.* apprise, assess, assay, valuate; price, set a price on, fix the price of.

2. gauge, rate, rank, weigh, balance, approximate; test, test-drive, measure, *Archaic.* mete, judge, size, *Inf.* size up, survey; ascertain, determine, figure out; estimate, compute, count, account, calculate, figure, reckon.

evanesce, *v.* vanish, disappear, vanish *or* disappear into thin air, leave no trace, be lost to view; evaporate, melt, dissolve; fade away, peter out, dissipate, disintegrate.

evanescence, *n.* fading away, vanishing, *Poetic.* evanishment, disappearance, occultation; evaporation, dissipation, disintegration, dissolving, melting; ephemerality, ephemeralness, fugacity, transcience, transientness, volatility, impermanence.

evanescent, *adj.* fading, passing away, vanishing, disappearing; momentary, brief, fleeting, ephemeral, short-lived, fugacious, fugitive, transient, transitory, volatile, temporary, impermanent, mortal, perishable; on the way out, obsolescent.

evangelical, *adj.* **1.** scriptural, biblical, evangelic; textual, textuary, evangelistic, according to *or* based on the Gospels *or* New Testament; orthodox, canonical; divine, inspired.

—n. **2.** (*often cap.*) textualist, fundamentalist, Biblicist; Pentecostal, charismatic, born-again Christian, witness for Christ *or* the Lord; *Derog.* Jesus freak.

evangelist, *n.* **1.** preacher, missionary, missioner, minister of the Gospel, proselytizer, propagandist, catechist, evangel; revivalist, reformer, saver of souls *or* sinners, preacher of repentance, faith healer.

2. crusader, campaigner, advocate, champion, promoter, defender, apologist.

evangelistic, *adj.* **1.** proselytistic, propagandistic, preaching, witnessing, testifying, missionary, hortatory, hortative.

2. zealous, ardent, devoted, impassioned, enthusiastic, fervid, fanatical, fiery, rabid.

evangelize, *v.* (*usu. in reference to Christianity*) proselytize, convert, christen, baptize; preach, indoctrinate, catechize, instruct, inculcate; spread the faith *or* the Word *or* the Gospel; witness, bear witness, testify, speak in tongues.

evaporate, *v.* **1.** vaporize, volatilize; exhale, mist, steam, fume, reek.

2. dehydrate, dry, dry up *or* out, desiccate, exsiccate, sun-dry, parch, sear; remove the moisture from, drain, draw off water from, wring out.

3. disappear, vanish, leave no trace, dematerialize, vanish from sight, vanish into thin air, be lost to sight; dissipate, disperse, dispel; fade, evanesce, fade away, melt away, dissolve.

evaporation, *n.* **1.** vaporization, vaporescence, volatilization; exhalation, misting, steaming, boiling away, fuming, reeking.

2. dehydration, drying up *or* out, desiccation, exsiccation, parching, searing; draining, wringing.

3. disappearance, vanishment, dematerialization; dissipation, dispersion, dispelling; fading, evanescence, fading away, melting away, dissolution.

evasion, *n.* **1.** avoidance, dodge, dodging, elusion, slip; shake, go-by, bypass, escape; flight, retreat; shunning, shirking, *Sl.* goldbricking, malingering; ignoring, neglect, omission.

2. prevarication, quibble, quibbling, equivocation; roundabout, shuffling, hedging, shift, skirting, beating around the bush, hemming and hawing; qualification, cop-out; tergiversation, vacillation, shilly-shally, ambivalence; ambiguity, amphiboly, doublespeak, double talk, palter, weasel words; sophistry, deception, deceit, chicanery.

evasive, *adj.* prevaricative, quibbling, equivocating, shuffling; tergiversating, vacillating, wavering; ambiguous, amphibolic, elusive, slippery, evanescent, fleeting; misleading, roundabout, circuitous, ambagious, hedging, weasel-worded, double-tongued; shifty, deceptive, deceitful, duplicitous, tricky.

eve, *n.* **1.** vigil, night before, day before, time *or* period before.

2. verge, point, brink, edge; threshold, *Psychol.* limen, doorsill, doorstep.

even, *adj.* **1.** level, plane, flat, smooth, complanate; horizontal, linear, rectilinear; flush, straight, true, plumb; balanced, right, equalized; symmetrical, proportionate, proportional, commensurate, correlative.

2. parallel, collateral, coextensive, equidistant, parallelistic, parallelogrammatical; abreast, alongside, *Inf.* neck and neck, tie.

3. regular, equable, orderly, systematic, methodical; stable, steady, unchanging, constant, set; harmonious, rhythmical, measured, metrical, consistent; monotonous, unbroken, unvaried, uniform; uninterrupted, swerving, unfluctuating, unvarying, in step, in line.

4. equal, same, all one, like, identical, similar; coordinate, coequal, to the same degree, of the same rank; on an equal footing, equally advantaged, evenly matched, on even terms, *Inf.* even-steven; on a par, as good as, the same as.

5. square, paid, quits, equal, adjusted, on par, clear, *Inf.* clean.

6. calm, placid, serene, tranquil; unexcitable, imperturbable, undisturbable; unruffled, even-tempered, composed, cool; calm, cool, and collected.

7. equitable, impartial, fair, just, honest, upright, reputable, fair and square; aboveboard, straightforward, on the level, *Sl.* on the up and up; disinterested, unbiased, unprejudiced, unbigoted, dispassionate.

—adv. **8.** evenly, regularly, equably, uniformly, smoothly; uninterruptedly, unbrokenly, monotonously, like clockwork.

9. still, yet, notwithstanding, nonetheless, albeit; but, all the same, however, nevertheless, be that as it may, even so, however that may be, whatever.

10. directly, exactly, squarely, square, expressly; straight, just, right, dead, point-blank, plumb.

11. indeed, yea, ever so, more than ever, all the more.

12. at all, hardly, scarcely, barely, not quite, so much as, no more than.

13. break even neither gain nor lose, *Inf.* come out O.K; win a few, lose a few.

14. get even avenge, revenge, pay back, repay, reciprocate; retaliate, bear malice, strike back; give tit for tat, give an eye for an eye, give quid pro quo, return like for like.

—v. **15.** level, smooth, equalize, align, flush; flatten, lay level, plane, planish.

16. make uniform, balance, equilibrize, proportion; harmonize, symmetrize, regulate, coordinate.

even-handed, *adj.* impartial, equitable, neutral, taking no sides; scrupulous, honorable, incorrupt. See **even** (*def.* 7).

evening, *n.* **1.** even, eventide, close of day, fall of day, decline of day, *Archaic.* vesper, *Archaic.* evensong; sunset, sundown, nightfall, shank of the evening, *Brit. Dial.* cockshut; twilight, crepuscule, dusk, grayness, *Literary.* duskingtide, *Archaic.* gloam, *Archaic.* gloaming, *Dial.* cocklight, *Dial.* owllight; curfew, bedtime, taps, lights out.

2. declining period, latter portion, last part, last act, close, end, epilogue; old age, elderliness, oldness, years, vale of years, autumn of life; decay, decrepitude, caducity, infirmity, senility, anility.

—adj. **3.** twilight, crepuscular, dusky, vesper, vespertine, nightly.

evening star, *n.* Venus, Vesper, Hesper, Hesperus, star light, star bright.

evensong, *n.* vespers, evening prayer, evening service, *Eccles.* compline; *Rom. Cath. Ch.* Angelus.

event, *n.* **1.** occurrence, incident, occasion; affair, happening, *Archaic.* hap, episode, action; deed, act, experience; case, matter, circumstance; eventuality, phenomenon, fact; exploit, feat; accident, chance, happenstance.

2. outcome, result, consequence, issue, upshot; sequel, subsequence, aftermath.

3. at all events in any event, in any case, at any rate; regardless, *Nonstandard.* irregardless, irrespective, willy-nilly; no matter what, come what may, happen what may, whatever is the case; anyhow, anyway, at least.

even-tempered, *adj.* calm, cool-headed, cool, composed; calm, cool and collected; unruffled, self-possessed, untroubled, unagitated, unexcited; placid, tranquil, serene, peaceful, halcyon; sober, sober-minded, staid, impassive; unexcitable, imperturbable, undisturbable.

eventful, *adj.* **1.** fraught with happenings, busy, filled.

2. momentous, consequential, significant, epochal; important, memorable, notable, outstanding, signal; striking, remarkable, impressive, interesting.

eventual, *adj.* **1.** future, coming, prospective, impending; ensuing, succeeding, consequent; inevitable, preordained, destined; ultimate, final, last; concluding, closing, ending, terminating.

2. contingent, conditional, dependent, possible.

eventually, *adv.* finally, ultimately, in the end; at last, at the final whistle, at the showdown, when all is said and done; at some time, in the course of time, in time; sooner or later, in the long run.

eventuate, *v.* result, issue, ensue, follow; end, conclude; come about, come to pass, befall, *Archaic.* bechance, betide, happen, occur.

ever, *adv.* **1.** always, forever, at all times, eternally, everlastingly; in all ages, to the end of time, till the crack of doom, till doomsday, to the last syllable of recorded time.

2. continuously, incessantly, constantly, perpetually, endlessly; relentlessly, unremittingly, persistently, recurrently, repeatedly, frequently, habitually.

3. at any time, at any period, at any point, on any occasion; by any chance, in any possible case, at all.

everlasting, *adj.* **1.** eternal, timeless, *Archaic.* eterne; infinite, boundless, illimitable; almighty, absolute; immortal, deathless, undying, ever-living; imperishable, indestructible, perdurable; immutable, changeless, unchanging, unchangeable.

2. enduring, lasting, abiding, *Literary.* sempiternal, aeonian, amaranthine, perennial, (*of trees*) evergreen; immutable, constant, unwavering, unfaltering, undiminished; invariable, fixed, durable, stable, permanent.

3. recurrent, repeated, repetitious, frequent, habitual; incessant, ceaseless, unceasing, nonstop, constant, uninterrupted, continual, continuous, unbroken; unremitting, unintermitting, relentless; perpetual, endless,

unending, never-ending, interminable, Sisyphean.
4. monotonous, tedious, wearisome, tiresome, boring, dreary, humdrum; ponderous, sluggish, stolid, plodding, routine.

evermore, *adv.* **1.** always, forever, eternally, everlastingly, *Poetic.* for ay, to the end of time, through all the ages, till the crack of doom, till doomsday, to the last syllable of recorded time; perpetually, constantly, continually, endlessly, unceasingly.
2. henceforth, hereafter, ever again, in the future, from now on, from this moment on, from this time forward.

everyday, *adj.* **1.** daily, diurnal, quotidian; circadian.
2. ordinary, common, commonplace, household, garden-variety, average; familiar, customary, conventional, usual, regular, routine, run-of-the-mill; normative, habitual, stock, wonted, accustomed; plain, simple, nondescript, prosaic, matter-of-fact, workaday; vernacular, colloquial, informal, conversational, spoken.

everyone, *pron.* everybody, all, one and all, each and every one, to a man, *Inf.* every man-jack, *Inf.* every mother's son; the whole world, tout le monde, everybody under the sun, *Inf.* everybody and his uncle; every Tom, Dick, and Harry.

everything, *n.* **1.** the whole, the aggregate, the entirety, the package, the corpus, the lot, *Inf.* everything but the kitchen sink; *All Sl.* whole deal, whole bunch, whole mess, whole kit and caboodle, whole megillah, whole shooting match, whole shebang, whole ball of wax, whole schmear.
2. be-all, be-all and end-all, all that matters, all; raison d'etre.

everywhere, *adv.* in all places, in every place, in every part, all over; omnipresently, ubiquitously, extensively; far and wide, right and left, high and low, hither and yon, in every nook and cranny; throughout the length and breadth of the land; here, there, and everywhere; under the sun, from pole to pole, the world over, at all points of the compass, on the face of the earth, to the four winds, in all climes, throughout the world.

evict, *v.* oust, expel, dislodge, turn out, turn out of house and home, kick *or* boot out, run out; dispossess, expropriate, foreclose, *Law.* disseize.

eviction, *n.* ejection, expulsion, dislodgment, removal; dispossession, repossession, foreclosure, expropriation, ouster, *Law.* disseizin.

evidence, *n.* **1.** proof, confirmation, verification, validation, authentication, certification; corroboration, substantiation, ground, support, warrant, *Obs.* vouch; documentation, document, exhibit, certificate, *Law.* certification, *Law.* exemplification; testimony, witness, attestation, statement, sworn statement, *Law.* deposition, *Law.* affidavit; data, information, facts, body of facts, (*of guilt*) the goods, *Inf.* ammunition, *Sl.* ammo.
2. indication, sign, signal, token, mark, denotation; demonstration, illustration, display, exhibition.
—*v.* **3.** manifest, evince, denote, make clear *or* plain, make obvious; demonstrate, show, display, exhibit.
4. testify, give testimony, attest, witness, bear witness, offer evidence; document, establish, circumstantiate, certify, certificate, depose, give a sworn statement, state under oath; sustain, uphold, vouch, warrant, support, endorse, back up, stand behind *or* by; corroborate, substantiate, bear out, prove right, vindicate; prove, verify, confirm, validate, authenticate, give credence to.

evident, *adj.* **1.** manifest, apparent, obvious, patent, palpable, express; clear, clear-cut, plain, plain as day, plain as the nose on your face, *Fr. en evidence*; conspicuous, salient, visible, seeable, recognizable, distinguishable, unmistakable; transparent, exposed, bald, unhidden.
2. understandable, comprehensible, cognizable, apprehensible, ascertainable, intelligible; discernible, perceivable, perceptible.

evidently, *adv.* apparently, so it looks, as far as one can see, seemingly, so it seems, as far as one can tell; clearly, plainly, visibly, manifestly, obviously, patently, palpably; unquestionably, undeniably, undoubtedly, without a doubt, indubitably, certainly.

evil, *adj.* **1.** wicked, sinful, iniquitous, *Archaic.* facinorous, *Obs.* scelerous; nefarious, villainous, flagitious, heinous, infamous, *Rare.* nefast; blackhearted, sinister, arrant, ignoble; bad, base, vile, foul, low, mean, odious, obnoxious; abominable, execrable, horrible, horrid, atrocious, grievous; ghastly, grim, dire, dark, black, dreadful; hideous, grisly, gruesome, unspeakable; damnable, damnatory, accursed, cursed; maleficent, malefic, malevolent, evil-minded; demonic, demoniac, diabolic, devilish, fiendish, satanic, hellish, infernal; unholy, unrighteous, unblest, unsanctified, unhallowed, unconsecrated.
2. perfidious, treacherous, insidious, traitorous; unscrupulous, unprincipled, crooked, dishonorable; blackguardly, scoundrelly, thievish, knavish; criminal, wrong, reprehensible, felonious, lawless; unregenerate, unrepentant, impenitent, obdurate, incorrigible; unpardonable, unforgivable; degenerate, corrupt, depraved, *Rare.* turpid; immoral, dissolute, profligate, reprobate, abandoned, dissipated; opprobrious, disgraceful, shameful; contemptible, scurvy, abhorrent, loathsome, hateful, detestable, despicable.
3. pernicious, harmful, injurious, nocuous, hurtful, mischievous; detrimental, deleterious, baleful, fell; pestilential, pestiferous, noxious, malicious, menacing, malignant, malign; venomous, virulent, baneful, toxic, mephitic, viperous, poisonous, *Archaic.* venenose; destructive, ruinous, damaging.
4. unfortunate, unlucky, unpropitious, unpromising, infelicitous; adverse, inimical, ill, unhappy, woeful; disastrous, calamitous, catastrophic, cataclysmic.
5. irascible, irritable, petulant, cross, testy; ill-natured, ill-tempered, cantankerous, crabby, crabbed, sour, crusty; morose, sulky, surly, churlish, sullen.
—*n.* **6.** wickedness, iniquity, vice, improbity, sin, sinfulness, deviltry, unholiness, ungodliness; nefariousness, flagitiousness, heinousness; vileness, viciousness, badness, baseness, foulness, meanness; opprobrium, ignominy, disgrace, infamy; atrocity, outrage, abomination, enormity; crime, malefaction, wrongdoing, feloniousness, lawlessness; unregeneracy, impenitence, incorrigibility; maleficence, malignancy, malevolence, malignity, rancor, maliciousness; perfidy, treachery, foul play; villainy, knavery, delinquency.
7. depravity, turpitude, degradation, degeneracy, corruption; profligacy, reprobacy, immorality; debauchery, lewdness, lasciviousness, licentiousness, lust; salacity, prurience, wantonness, carnality; unchastity, promiscuity, concupiscence; perversity, bestiality; obscenity, profanity, indecency, ribaldry, vulgarity.
8. harm, mischief, injury, hurt, *Archaic.* bale, perniciousness, harmfulness; destruction, damage, ruin; disaster, calamity, catastrophe, debacle, cataclysm; misfortune, affliction, misery, suffering, woe, ill; sorrow, unhappiness, infelicity, adversity; disease, sickness, illness, ailment, malady, disorder, infirmity; infection, contagion, virus.

evildoer, *n.* **1.** malefactor, villain, criminal,

wrongdoer, delinquent; offender, recidivist, malfeasant, miscreant, culprit, jailbird, convict, felon; crook, hoodlum, ruffian, hooligan, roughneck, tough; desperado, outlaw, gunman, gangster; murderer, assassin, cutthroat, rapist; hijacker, pirate, footpad, burglar, safecracker, forger; Vandal, Goth, Hun, Apache, Nazi, Fascist, nihilist; oppressor, tyrant, terrorist; incendiary, anarchist, firebrand; saboteur, marplot.

2. sinner, wretch, *Archaic.* caitiff, fiend, demon, Loki, devil, devil incarnate; monster, witch, ghoul, ogre, beast, hellhound, vulture, snake, serpent, viper; cur, brute, bully; scoundrel, blackguard, black sheep, ne'er-do-well, good-for-nothing; reprobate, debauchee, libertine, wanton; scamp, scrapegrace, mischief-maker.

evil-minded, *adj.* **1.** salacious, depraved, lewd, lascivious, licentious, lecherous, *Archaic.* lickerish; foulmouthed, dirty, smutty, obscene.

2. wicked, cruel, truculent, vicious; malicious, malevolent, malign, spiteful, bitter; ruthless, hateful, rancorous, nasty; fiendish, demoniac, devilish, diabolical, satanic, hellish, infernal; cold-blooded, inhuman, untamed, barbarous, savage, feral; depraved, atrocious, felonious, fell; destructive, venomous, poisonous, malignant.

evince, *v.* **1.** prove, manifest, make manifest, make clear, evidence, make evident, establish, certify; display, exhibit, show, indicate, demonstrate.

2. tell, make known, disclose, divulge; reveal, betray, expose, show up, shine the light on, bring to light.

eviscerate, *v.* **1.** disembowel, embowel, bowel, exenterate, *Rare.* viscerate.

2. devitalize, weaken, enervate; debilitate, enfeeble, deplete, sap, exhaust.

evocative, *adj.* reminiscent, suggestive, remindful, educative; stimulating, exciting, awakening, reawaking, arousing, stirring, kindling, rekindling; provocative, striking, penetrating, sensitive.

evoke, *v.* elicit, educe, call, summon, invite; provoke, cause, bring about, induce; suggest, remind, recall, reawake, rekindle; conjure up; stimulate, excite, awaken, rouse, arouse, stir, kindle; call forth, invoke, adjure, obtest.

evolve, *v.* develop, grow, become, become more complex *or* sophisticated; grow out of, turn into, derive from, result, emerge; progress, go forward, increase, expand, snowball; produce, construct, formulate, build up; unroll, unfold, uncoil, open.

evolution, *n.* **1.** evolvement, unfolding, flowering, ripening, unrolling, succession, fruition; development, elaboration, growth, production, creation.

2. rotation, turn, turning, convolution, circuition, gyration, *Dressage.* curvet.

ewer, *n.* pitcher, carafe, cruet, cruse, urn; jug, decanter, flagon, crock, ampulla; vessel, container.

exacerbate, *v.* **1.** aggravate, worsen, add insult to injury, rub salt into the wound, *Inf.* rub it in, pour oil on the fire; sharpen, intensify, heighten, deepen, add fuel to the fire *or* flames, fan *or* stoke *or* fuel the fire *or* flames.

2. embitter, envenom, gall, rankle, acerbate, sour, poison.

3. exasperate, discompose, distress, ruffle, roil, pique, chafe, grate, put out, try [s.o.'s] patience, *Sl.* get [s.o.'s] goat, *Sl.* drive [s.o.] nuts *or* up the wall; anger, incense, enrage, infuriate, madden, raise [s.o.'s] ire, make [s.o.'s] blood boil.

4. irritate, annoy, bother, pester, fret, nettle, vex, plague, disturb, perturb, harass, hector, torment, provoke, badger, *Chiefly U.S.* rile, rub [s.o.] the wrong way.

exacerbation, *n.* **1.** aggravation, intensification, heightening, deepening, sharpening, worsening.

2. embittering, envenoming, acerbating, galling, rankling, souring, poisoning.

3. exasperation, exasperating, ruffling, chafing, putting out; angering, infuriating, maddening.

4. irritation, irritating, annoying, bothering, pestering, fretting, plaguing, vexing, disturbing, perturbing, harassing, hectoring, tormenting, provoking, badgering.

exact, *adj.* **1.** accurate, precise, close, faithful, in conformity, in accordance *or* agreement; correct, unerring, *Inf.* on the mark, on target, on the money, *Inf.* right on, *Sl.* spot on, on the button, on the dot, *Inf.* on the nose, *Sl.* on the beam; right, just, true, truthful, veracious; factual, actual, strict, literal, true to life; authentic, real, sound, valid; flawless, faultless, perfect, defectless, errorless.

2. careful, meticulous, punctilious, scrupulous, conscientious; particular, finical, finicky, fussy; minute, detailed, thorough, nice, scientific, methodical, mathematical; critical, demanding, fastidious; strict, rigorous, severe, rigid, unbending, unyielding, ungiving.

—*v.* **3.** demand, require, compel, insist on *or* upon, command, enjoin; call for, necessitate, tax, *Obs.* task; requisition, request, ask.

4. wring, wrest, *Law.* extort, *Inf.* bleed, extract, squeeze, get out of, take forcibly; elicit, draw out, pry out; shake down, *Inf.* put the bite *or* squeeze *or* shake on, put the arm on [s.o.], *Sl.* lean against *or* on.

exacting, *adj.* **1.** severe, strict, rigorous, hard, tough, difficult, firm, stern; demanding, exigent, fastidious, critical, *Rare.* exactive; rigid, unbending, unyielding, ungiving; harsh, unsparing, oppressive, burdensome; peremptory, imperious, imperative, commanding, dictatorial, tyrannical.

2. difficult, painstaking, close, strict, searching; arduous, laborious, toilsome, operose; trying, troublesome, tough, uphill.

3. extortionate, blood-sucking, greedy, covetous, avaricious; grasping, rapacious, voracious, ravenous, insatiable.

exaction, *n.* **1.** extortion, blackmail, *Sl.* shakedown, *Inf.* the squeeze, milking, *Inf.* bleeding, bloodsucking; skin game, badger game, *Sl.* murphy.

2. wresting, wrenching, wringing, extraction; demand, requirement, claim, requisition, elicitation.

3. duty, tax, impost, levy, tariff, toll, excise, custom, dues, fee; ransom, tribute, exacted *or* enforced payment; bribe, douceur, hush money, *Inf.* protection, *Inf.* payola, graft.

exactitude, *n.* **1.** exactness, precision, preciseness, accuracy, accurateness; closeness, fidelity, faithfulness, conformity, accordance, agreement; minuteness, detailedness, rigorousness, strictness, severity, severeness; thoroughness, methodicalness, carefulness, painstakingness, exhaustiveness.

2. correctness, unerringness, rightness, rectitude, justness; truth, truthfulness, veracity, verity, veritableness; fact, actuality, factuality, literalness; definiteness, positiveness, absoluteness.

3. authenticity, soundness, validity, validness, integrity; flawlessness, faultlessness, perfection.

exactly, *adv.* **1.** precisely, accurately, closely, faithfully, strictly, to a hair, to the letter; literally, word for word, verbatim, line for line; perfectly, just so, just right, to a T, to a tee, to a turn; explicitly, in detail, minutely, completely, absolutely, fully, quite.

2. just, right, on the dot, *Inf.* right on, *Sl.* spot on, on the button, on the money, *Inf.* on the nose, *Inf.* on the mark, on target; directly, squarely, *Inf.* plunk, *Inf.*

plumb, *Inf.* smack-dab *or Dial.* smack-to-dab.

3. quite so, quite right, as you say; indeed, truly, definitely, positively, unquestionably, absolutely, undeniably, unequivocally; certainly, surely, *Archaic.* certes, of course.

exactness, *n.* exactitude, precision, preciseness, accuracy, accurateness. See **exactitude** (*defs.* **1,3**).

exaggerate, *v.* **1.** overstate, overdo, make much of, overstress, overcharge, overcolor, make a mountain out of a molehill, make much ado about nothing; hyperbolize, overdraw; romance, embroider, stretch, stretch the point, strain; color, paint, paint in glowing terms, oversell, *Inf.* play up, *Inf.* build up *or* on; *Inf.* pile it on, *Inf.* lay it on, *Inf.* lay *or* spread it on thick, *Sl.* bull, *Sl.* shoot the bull, *Sl.* shoot off one's mouth; embellish, overdevelop, enlarge on, elaborate; magnify, enhance, enrich, deepen, heighten.

2. brag, boast, puff, bluff, *Sl.* blow hard, *Sl.* talk big; show off, *Sl.* ham it up, out-Herod Herod, swagger, flaunt, flourish; set off, set off to advantage; whitewash, gloss over, *Inf.* fudge; overrate, overestimate, overvalue, overshoot the mark.

3. inflate, swell, blow up, bloat, dilate, distend; increase, enlarge, make larger, make bigger, make greater; intensify, concentrate, maximize; aggravate, give a boost to, step up.

exaggerated, *adj.* **1.** overstated, overdone, overstressed, overcharged; hyperbolized, overdrawn; extravagant, inflated, blown-up, bouncing; colored, embroidered, embellished, magnified, enhanced, enriched; intensified, aggravated, maximized; stretched, far-fetched, improbable, *Inf.* fishy; preposterous, outrageous, egregious.

2. bombastic, pompous, fustian, pretentious, flaunting; grandiose, magniloquent, grandiloquent; high-sounding, high-flown, vaulting, lofty, *Inf.* highfalutin, *Inf.* high-hat; flamboyant, flashy, showy, flowery, ornamental.

exaggeration, *n.* **1.** overstatement, *Rhet.* hyperbole; tall tale, *Inf.* fish story, old wive's tale, yarn; *Sl.* hot air, *Inf.* bull, *Inf.* bunk, *Sl.* gas; tempest in a teapot, much ado about nothing; caricature, take-off, distortion.

2. embellishment, magnification, enhancement, deepening, heightening; embroidery, fringe; puffery, flattery, *Sl.* snow job.

3. bombast, grandiosity, rodomontade, pomposity, magniloquence, grandiloquence; bravado, braggadocio, gasconade; braggardism, boasting, rant.

4. intensification, concentration, maximization, overkill; overestimation, overvaluation; inflation, swelling, enlargement, *Inf.* whopper.

exalt, *v.* **1.** glorify, dignify, ennoble, enthrone, canonize; honor, adore, worship, crown, bless, idolize, pay tribute to, pay homage to; reverence, venerate, revere, consecrate, sanctify; deify, apotheosize, idealize, romanticize; appreciate, value, esteem, respect, admire, look up to.

2. elevate, raise, upraise, raise up, make lofty; lift, uplift, lift up, cast up; promote, advance, boost, upgrade; improve, ameliorate, meliorate, better.

3. praise, sound the praises of, sing the praises of, extol, cry up, *Inf.* crack up, *Archaic.* magnify, emblazon; encore, root for; approve enthusiastically, hail, commend, sanction, endorse; recommend, say a good word for, put in a good word for; compliment, flatter, puff, boost, swell, lionize, belaud, make much of; applaud, acclaim, cheer, celebrate, congratulate, *Archaic.* gratulate; eulogize, panegyrize.

4. inspire, fire [s.o.'s] imagination, exhilarate; inspirit, enliven, animate; stimulate, incite, arouse, stir up, work up, provoke.

5. enhance, intensify, magnify, heighten, strengthen; increase, enlarge, aggrandize, extend, widen.

exaltation, *n.* **1.** glorification, ennoblement, enthronement, canonization; adoration, worship, crowning, blessing; reverence, veneration, consecration, sanctification; deification, apotheosis, idealization, romanticization.

2. glory, dignity, grandeur; elevation, loftiness; eminence, prestige, fame, celebrity, notability.

3. praise, extolment, acclamation, *Archaic.* magnification, citation; approval, approbation, endorsement, sanction, commendation, recommendation, advocacy, espousal; celebration, congratulation, *Archaic.* gratulation; appreciation, respect, regard.

4. elation, exultation, jubilation, rhapsody; excitement, happiness, joy, delight; rapture, ecstasy, bliss, transport, inspiration.

exalted, *adj.* **1.** glorified, glorious, dignified, grand, magnificent, honorable; eminent, prestigious, celebrated, notable; illustrious, distinguished, renowned, famous, famed; imposing, august, commanding, striking, towering, stately; aristocratic, noble, kingly, regal, royal, lordly, princely, imperial, majestic; sublime, elevated, lofty; transcendent, *Inf.* out of this world, celestial, ethereal.

2. raised up *or* aloft, high, uplifted; promoted, advanced, upgraded, improved, ameliorated, bettered.

3. enhanced, intensified, magnified, heightened, strengthened; increased, enlarged, aggrandized, extended, widened.

4. inspired, exhilarated; inspirited, enlivened, animated; stimulated, incited, aroused, stirred-up, worked-up, provoked.

5. elated, exultant, triumphant, jubilant; excited, happy, joyous, delighted; rapturous, ecstatic, blissful, transported; rhapsodic, inspired.

examination, *n.* **1.** scrutiny, scrutinization, inspection, canvass, close observation *or* watch; investigation, inquisition, inquiry, study, analysis; research, exploration, probe, search; sifting, going through *or* over, survey, review, checkout, audit; assessment, appraisal, *Inf.* once-over, *Sl.* casing.

2. interrogation, the third degree, cross-examination, cross-questioning, *Inf.* grilling; *Eccles.* examen, examination of conscience.

3. test, checkup, quiz, catechism, set of questions, questionnaire.

examine, *v.* **1.** scrutinize, analyze, take apart, audit; investigate, look into, inquire into, canvass, check into; research, explore, probe, search, go over with a fine-tooth comb; sift, go through, go over, review, take stock of; study, pore over, think on, consider, weigh.

2. check out, take a look at, inspect, survey, appraise, assess, *Sl.* case; watch, observe, keep an eye on.

3. test, sound out, quiz, question closely, catechize; interrogate, give [s.o.] the third degree, cross-examine, cross-question, *Inf.* grill, pump.

examiner, *n.* **1.** questioner, tester, quizzer, catechizer; inquirer, inquisitor, investigator, researcher, researchist.

2. inspector, auditor, reviewer, censor, critic, analyst, scrutinizer.

example, *n.* **1.** sample, sampling, specimen, piece, *Archaic.* ensample; test, experiment, *Inf.* pilot.

2. exemplar, model, pattern, paradigm, mirror; ideal, pink, paragon, phoenix; standard, norm, bench mark, rule, criterion; precedent, parallel case.

3. instance, *Inf.* for instance, case in point, specific; typical situation, representative illustration.

4. problem, question, exercise, lesson.

exanimate, *adj.* **1.** dead, deceased, extinct, defunct, no more, *Sl.* eighty-sixed; lifeless, inanimate, inorganic.

2. disheartened, dispirited, spiritless, dejected, downcast, *Inf.* down in the dumps, *Sl.* bummed *or* bummed out.

exasperate, *v.* **1.** anger, incense, elite, *Chiefly U.S.* rile, raise [s.o.'s] ire, *Sl.* tick [s.o.] off, *Sl.* tee [s.o.] off; enrage, madden, infuriate, make [s.o.'s] blood boil, lash into a fury, whip into a frenzy; (*all to a maddening degree*) provoke, goad, prod, taunt, tease.

2. discompose, disquiet, disturb, perturb, ruffle, roil, vex, pique, chafe, put out, try [s.o.'s] patience, *Inf.* get, *Sl.* get [s.o.'s] goat.

3. irritate, annoy, irk, peeve, bother, pester, harass, hector, plague, torment, badger, *Inf.* miff, *Inf.* give [s.o.] a pain; rub [s.o.] the wrong way, get under [s.o.'s] skin, get in [s.o.'s] hair, *Sl.* bug.

4. exacerbate, aggravate, worsen, add insult to injury, rub salt into the wound, *Inf.* rub it in, pour oil on the fire; sharpen, intensify, heighten, deepen, add fuel to the fire *or* flames, fan *or* stoke *or* fuel the fire.

5. embitter, envenom, gall, rankle, acerbate, sour, poison.

exasperation, *n.* **1.** provocation, fomentation, incitement, incitation, instigation, excitation, agitation, inflammation, deliberate aggravation; provoking, fomenting, inciting, instigating, agitating, inflaming; infuriation, enragement; infuriating, angering.

2. irritation, vexation, annoyance; irritating, annoying, bothering, exasperating, pestering, vexing, disturbing, harassing, hectoring, badgering.

3. exacerbation, aggravation, intensification; exacerbating, aggravating, intensifying, heightening, deepening, sharpening, worsening.

4. displeasure, discontent, dissatisfaction, disapproval, disapprobation; anger, ire, dudgeon, pique, huff, tiff; indignation, umbrage, offense; rage, fury, vehemence.

5. embitterment, bitterness, bitter resentment, resentment, resentfulness, hard feelings, animosity; virulence, acrimony, acerbity; choler, rancor, spleen, ill *or* bad humor, ill *or* bad feeling, ill *or* bad temper.

6. irritant, nuisance, pest, bother, problem, trouble, *Inf.* headache, *Sl.* pain in the neck, pea in the shoe; salt in the wound.

ex cathedra, *Latin.* from the seat of authority, from the authorities, from the powers that be, *Inf.* from the top, *Sl.* from the horse's mouth; with authority, authoritatively, imperatively, commandingly, officially; authoritative, imperative, commanding, preeminent, supreme, autocratic, dictatorial, arbitrary.

excavate, *v.* **1.** dig out, scoop out, hollow out, gouge, pit, cut out, channel; quarry, mine, sink a mine, stope, sap, tunnel, *Inf.* work pick and shovel; backhoe.

2. unearth, dig up, bring to the surface, exhume, disinter; shovel out, lay bare, uncover.

excavation, *n.* hole, hollow, cavity, pit, crater; quarry, mine, cellar, foundation; earthwork, *Inf.* dig; burrow, cavern, dugout; ditch, trench, trough, cut, groove, sap, furrow; opening, cutting, shaft, stope; depression, indentation, dent, dint.

exceed, *v.* **1.** transcend, surmount, surpass, go beyond, outdo, cap, top, go over the top; overshadow, minimize, reduce, eclipse, tower above, dominate; outrank, come first; run over, overflow, slop over; overshoot, go by the mark, overstep, overplay, overdo, overact; overtax, overburden, overextend, overload; oversupply, glut.

2. go by, pass, overtake, run down; excel, shoot ahead of, outrun, outpace, outdistance, outstrip, *Inf.* leave in the dust, *Inf.* get the jump on; beat, prevail over, overwhelm; take precedence over, overrule, override.

exceedingly, *adv.* extremely, especially, amazingly, astonishingly; beyond measure, immeasurably, excessively, surpassingly, superlatively, incomparably; vastly, enormously, highly, eminently, greatly, supremely; notably, over and above, by far, to a great *or* unusual degree, *Inf.* no end, *Inf.* in the worst way, *Inf.* to pieces.

excel, *v.* **1.** dominate, tower above, be head and shoulders above, stand out in the crowd, hold sway; lead, take the lead, lead the pack.

2. surpass, exceed, outshine, eclipse, shadow, throw into the shade; beat, outdo, outstrip, distance, outdistance; outclass, *Inf.* beat hollow, come out on top, top, trump, outplay; break the record, take the cake *or* prize, win the crown *or* laurel wreath.

3. outrank, outweigh, take precedence, come first, have the advantage, have the ball in one's court, call the shots, be in the driver's seat, hold the upper hand.

excellence, *n.* **1.** superiority, eminence, preeminence, distinction, greatness, nobility, transcendence, majesty, exaltation; worth, value, fineness, quality; supremacy, perfection.

2. merit, virtue, asset, advantage, plus, strong point, talking *or* selling point; feature, quality.

excellent, *adj.* **1.** first-rate, of the first order, capital, *Inf.* tiptop, *Inf.* A-1, *Inf.* A number 1, *Northwest U.S. and Canada.* skookum; extraordinary, very remarkable, *Sl.* bang-up, *Inf.* smashing, marvelous, wonderful, splendid, *Brit. Sl.* ripping; *Inf.* great, *Inf.* super, *Sl.* tuff, *Sl.* bad, *Sl.* cool, *Inf.* dandy, *Inf.* jim-dandy.

2. exceptional, superior, standout, outstanding,striking; superlative, supreme, transcendent,sovereign, the best; matchless, peerless, nonpareil, perfect, sterling, classic, first-class; choice, prime, select, very good, *Australian Sl.* bosker, *Scot. and North Eng.* braw; fine, admirable, worthy, estimable, notable, noteworthy; distinguished, eminent, *Archaic.* eximious.

except[1], *prep.* **1.** excluding, with the exclusion of, barring, leaving out, omitting, not counting, less, minus; but, save, saving, excepting, with the exception of; other than, apart from, besides, *Inf.* outside of.

—*conj.* **2.** *Usu.* **except that** with the exception, but, save, saving, *Archaic.* excepting.

except[2], *v.* exclude, bar, debar, lock out, shut out, keep out; reject, spurn, ostracize, blackball, block acceptance of; eliminate, remove, weed out; omit, leave out, pass over.

exception, *n.* **1.** exclusion, barring, debarment, blockage, lockout, shutout; rejection, spurning, ostracism, blackball; omission, leaving out, noninclusion.

2. anomaly, rarity, irregularity, special *or* uncommon *or* unusual case; oddity, quirk, freak, rare bird; *Inf.* pip, one for the books.

3. **take exception to** object, demur, raise *or* make an objection, cavil; challenge, question, call into question; disagree with, oppose, be in opposition to, dissent.

exceptional, *adj.* **1.** special, especial, unusual, uncommon, out of the ordinary; rare, unique, singular, individual, anomalous, anomalistic, exceptive; abnormal, irregular, deviant, divergent, out of the way, aberrant; strange, odd, peculiar, curious, queer, unheard of, *Inf.* quirky, *Inf.* freaky; eccentric, offbeat, unconventional.

2. extraordinary, extraordinaire, phenomenal, prodigious, *Inf.* out of this world; superior, outstanding, excellent, above average; inimitable, incomparable, unparalleled, unmatched, unprecedented.

excerpt, *n.* **1.** extract, pericope; citation, quotation, quote; selection, portion, scrap, cull; passage, section, chapter, paragraph, phrase; scene, frame; measure, bar.

—*v.* **2.** extract, abridge, quote, cite; cull, select, pull out; pluck, pick out, cut out.

excess, *n.* **1.** overabundance, superabundance, overplus, nimiety, surplus, surplusage, superflux; profusion, surfeit, glut, plethora, overflow, overload, more than enough, enough and to spare, enough and then some; superfluity, redundancy, supererogation, oversufficiency, overkill, overdose, too much of a good thing.

2. extravagance, inordinateness, unrestraint, prodigality, overdoing.

3. intemperance, immoderation, overindulgence; inebriety, insobriety, drunkenness, alcoholism, dipsomania; dissipation, dissoluteness, fast *or* free living, *Inf.* life in the fast lane.

—*adj.* **4.** extra, surplus, spare, leftover, over and above.

excessive, *adj.* immoderate, extravagant, lavish, beyond all bounds, *Inf.* devilish, *Chiefly U.S. Inf.* all-fired; unreasonable, disproportionate, undue, inordinate, uncalled-for, unwarranted, unneeded, needless, unnecessary; exorbitant, extreme, too much, unconscionable, outrageous, preposterous, monstrous, rank, egregious, *Inf.* criminal; superabundant, overabundant, copious, profuse, plethoric, overfull; redundant, superfluous, oversufficient, *Inf.* too much, *Inf.* a bit much.

excessively, *adv.* **1.** immoderately, extravagantly, unreasonably, disproportionately, unduly, inordinately; amazingly, extraordinarily, damn, damned, *All Euph.* confoundedly, dad-blasted, dad-blamed, dad-burned, blasted, *U.S. Sl. and Dial.* blamed.

2. extremely, exceedingly, exorbitantly, outrageously, preposterously, *Inf.* criminally, *Sl.* hell of a, *Inf.* devilishly, *Inf.* all-fired; superabundantly, overabundantly, profusely, copiously; redundantly, superfluously, needlessly, unnecessarily.

exchange, *v.* **1.** trade, barter, swap, substitute; interchange, bandy, toss around, pass, return, reward, reciprocate, return the compliment, requite, echo; seesaw, trade off, alternate, shuttle, swing.

—*n.* **2.** barter, trade, interchange, commutation, swap, switch, trade-off, shuffle, substitution, change; brokerage, jobbing, *Inf.* middlemanning, speculating.

3. reciprocation, reciprocity, transposal, *Latin. quid pro quo,* tit for tat; revenge, retribution, retaliation, reprisal, requital, counterattack, an eye for an eye, a tooth for a tooth; retort, rejoinder, comeback.

4. (*all of securities exchange*) stock market, stock exchange, Wall Street, the Exchange, the Board, the Big Board, the Market, Bourse.

5. central office, central exchange, switching point *or* station.

exchangeable, *adj.* returnable, replaceable, tradable, swappable, switchable; commutable, convertible, substitutive.

excise, *v.* **1.** expunge, delete, erase; strike out, cross out, x out; scratch, cut, kill; expurgate, bowdlerize, clean.

2. cut out, curette, curet, *Surgical.* resect; extirpate, remove, eradicate.

excision, *n.* removal, deletion, extirpation, elimination; abscission, *Surgical.* resection, extirpation; excommunication, expulsion.

excitable, *adj.* **1.** nervous, high-strung, emotional, flappable, fidgety, skittish, restless, restive; inflammatory, inflammable, volcanic, explosive, ebullient, stormy, tempestuous, turbulent; wrathful, violent, fierce; fiery, passionate, vehement, hot-blooded, high-spirited, fervid, fervent; demonstrative, enthusiastic, *Sl.* psyched; frantic, frenzied, furious, wild, feverish, rabid, hysterical, delirious.

2. impulsive, impetuous, precipitate, precipitative, impatient, hasty, rash, brash, heedless, reckless; uncontrollable, uncontrolled, ungovernable, irrepressible; mobile, quick, active, lively, spry, sprightly, mercurial.

3. testy, edgy, short, short-tempered, quick-tempered, short-fused, hot-headed; irascible, irritable, choleric, acerbic, cantankerous; moody, temperamental, sensitive, petulant, waspish, peevish.

excite, *v.* **1.** incite, provoke, prod, poke, prick, goad, spur, prompt; instigate, look for trouble, *Inf.* start something; encourage, urge, abet, egg on, put up to; foment, agitate, commove, suscitate, impassion, *Brit. Dial.* kittle, arouse, stir up, work up, wind up, whip up, lash into a fury, *Inf.* psych up, fire up, heat up, *Obs.* calefy, enflame, enkindle, kindle, touch off, ignite the spark.

2. stimulate, animate, reanimate, whet, *Inf.* turn on, invigorate, motivate, inspirit, inspire, *Inf.* spark, galvanize, electrify, energize, rally, revive, enliven, liven up, hype up, awaken, wake up, waken, rouse, shake up, jolt, jog; activate, generate, affect, initiate, occasion, give rise to, start, *Inf.* get going; impel, induce, compel, constrain, move, press, drive, stir, fillip; elicit, evoke, raise, call forth, summon up, raise *or* sound the alarm; touch, impress, strike, penetrate, touch to the quick, rivet the attention, *Inf.* groove on, *Sl.* get off on.

3. ruffle, fluster, flurry, flutter, perturb, disturb, disquiet, discompose, disconcert, upset, make nervous; torment, persecute, needle, harass, bully, bullyrag.

4. exasperate, exacerbate, roil, pique, chafe, vex; annoy, irritate, aggravate, hector, nettle, plague, badger, pester.

excited, *adj.* **1.** agitated, aroused, inflamed, enflamed, keyed-up, high-strung, temperamental, feverish, overwrought, wrought-up, wound-up, worked-up, stirred-up, whipped-up, beside oneself, *Inf.* hot and bothered, *Inf.* hot under the collar, *Sl.* hopped-up; disturbed, perturbed, upset, discomposed, disconcerted, distracted, ruffled, flustered, fluttered; nervous, edgy, on edge, apprehensive, tense, uneasy, restless, restive, fidgety, skittish; frantic, frenzied, wild, seething, maddened, crazed, delirious, hysterical, *Sl.* zonkers, *Sl.* out of one's skull *or* gourd.

2. impassioned, fervid, fervent, ardent, zealous, vehement, fiery, red-hot, hot; eager, enthusiastic, enthused, elated, intoxicated, ebullient, *Sl.* psyched; stimulated, animated, *Inf.* turned-on, invigorated, motivated, inspired, *Inf.* sparked, galvanized, electrified, energized, rallied, revived, enlivened, hyped-up, roused, jolted, jogged.

3. angry, incensed, vexed, exasperated; furious, outraged, blustering, foaming, fuming, raging, flaming; irritated, annoyed, aggravated, hectored, nettled, plagued, badgered, pestered, tormented, persecuted, needled, harassed, bullied.

4. brisk, active, lively, animated, energetic, spry, sprightly, dynamic, busy, spirited, bustling, smart, *Inf.* snappy, *Inf.* peppy, *Inf.* frisky; stormy, tumultuous, turbulent, volcanic, explosive.

excitement, *n.* **1.** agitation, perturbation, excitation, violence, tension, unrest, trepidation, trepidity, disquiet, disquietude, ferment, fermentation, restlessness, fever, malaise, *Archaic.* conturbation; commotion, brouhaha, hurly-burly, hubbub, row, fuss, flurry, flutter, fluster, bustle, ado, to-do, stir, activity, scene, flare-up,

Inf. fireworks, *Brit. Dial.* swither; turbulence, tumult, tumultation, turmoil, tempest, storm, churn, swirl, furor, whirl, frenzy, fit, paroxysm, maelstrom.
2. stimulus, stimulant, urge, motive, impulse, desire, itch, fillip, provocative, incentive, *Physiol.* excitant; drive, push, press, goad, spur, prick, prod, jolt, jog, poke, thrust, dictate, call; lure, allure, charm; thrill, kick, action, *Sl.* rush, feeling, sensation; passion, ardor, fervor, zeal, warmth, flush, fire, heat; eagerness, enthusiasm, ebullition, elation; explosion, outburst, outbreak, riot.
3. stimulation, animation, invigoration, motivation, infection, vivification, exhilaration, galvanization, electrification; incitation, incitement, instigation, encouragement; provocation, fomentation, actuation, suscitation, inflammation, infuriation, disturbance; temptation, allurement, seduction, beguilement, inveiglement; fascination, intoxication, enravishment, entrancement.

exciting, *adj.* **1.** thrilling, electrifying, galvanizing, galvanic, spine-tingling, hair-raising, *Inf.* far out, *Inf.* rip-roaring, *Inf.* rip-snorting; stimulating, stirring, bracing, rousing, inspiring, invigorating, excitant, excitative, excitatory; moving, impelling, compelling, affecting, soul-stirring, heart-stirring, heart-moving; overpowering, overwhelming, overcoming, startling, astonishing, *Sl.* mind-boggling, *Sl.* mind-blowing, *Sl.* trippy.
2. alluring, inviting, enticing, tempting, tantalizing, irresistible; charming, captivating, provocative, intriguing, fascinating, entrancing, beguiling, intoxicating, bewitching, enrapturing; attractive, interesting, appealing, piquant; seductive, sensuous, desirable, toothsome, mouth-watering, *Inf.* sexy; ravishing, voluptuous, glamorous, luxurious.

exclaim, *v.* cry out, ejaculate, vociferate, rap out; burst out, spit out, let loose; clamor, shout, squall, holler, bawl; yell, yell bloody murder, rend the air, make the welkin ring, bellow.

exclamation, *n.* outcry, vociferation, *Rhet.* ecphonesis, ejaculation; cry, bellow, yowl, yell, hoot; yelp, screech, squall, shriek, scream; roar, clamor, squawk; protest, interjection.

exclude, *v.* **1.** debar, shut out, shut the door on, lock out; bar, stand in the way, prevent; ban, disallow, prohibit, forbid, embargo.
2. eliminate, count out, rule out, preclude; forget, pass over, skip, except, omit, leave *or* keep out; spurn, reject, refuse, deny, repudiate; ostracize, blackball; isolate, separate, segregate, set apart, cut off *or* away.
3. expel, eject, oust, depose, remove, get rid of, drive away *or* out, force out; evict, turn out, put out, thrust out, toss out, *Inf.* throw out, *Inf.* kick out, excommunicate; exile, banish, relegate, deport, expatriate.

exclusion, *n.* **1.** debarment, shutout, barring, bar; ban, disallowance, forbiddance, injunction, embargo, prevention.
2. elimination, counting out, ruling out, preclusion; passing over, exception, omission, cut; spurning, rejection, refusal, denial, repudiation; ostracization, blackballing; isolation, separation, segregation, cut-off.
3. expulsion, ejection, ejectment, ouster, ousting, deposition, removal, riddance; eviction, *Inf.* throwing out, *Inf.* kicking out, excommunication; exile, banishment, deportation, expatriation.

exclusive, *adj.* **1.** mutually exclusive, incompatible; antithetical, inimical.
2. complete, entire, total, all.
3. single, individual, one, sole, only.
4. select, particular, picky, choosy, selective; limited, restrictive, closed, tight, clannish; cliquish, snobbish, snobby, *Inf.* snotty, *Inf.* snooty, *Inf.* uppity, haughty, arrogant, aloof, cold, unfriendly.
5. posh, elegant, luxurious, fancy, swanky, *Sl.* ritzy; expensive, high-priced, *Inf.* steep.

excogitate, *v.* **1.** think out, devise, contrive, figure out, invent, design; make up, hatch, create, coin, fabricate, frame, concoct, brew; think up, conceive, imagine, fancy, have ideas about, *Inf.* dream up, envision, envisage, visualize.
2. deliberate, ponder, weigh, evaluate, study, review, examine, check out; consider, *Archaic.* perpend, think on *or* about, contemplate, turn over in one's mind, reflect on, cogitate, meditate, ruminate, chew over, brood on, mull over, dwell on.

excommunicate, *v.* unchurch, expel, *Inf.* kick out, cut off, exclude. See **exclude** (*defs.* **2, 3**).

excommunication, *n.* unchurching, expulsion, ejection, ouster, exclusion. See **exclusion** (*defs.* **2, 3**).

excoriate, *v.* **1.** strip, peel, skin, scalp, bark, husk, shuck, shell, decorticate; scrape, grate, rasp, file, grind, whet, sand, abrade, scour.
2. denounce, blame, accuse, condemn, censure; upbraid, reprove, reproach, rebuke, criticize; chastise, punish, discipline, reprimand, scold, chide; berate, objurgate, vituperate, castigate, inveigh against, rail against.
3. vilify, calumniate, malign, asperse, traduce, slander, defame, libel, blacken; disparage, depreciate, belittle, put down, stigmatize, brand; abuse, attack, flay, flog, scourge.

excrement, *n.* feces, fecal matter, excreta, egesta, waste matter, stools, *Sl.* do, waste, feculence; dung, manure, muck, fertilizer, ordure, guano; droppings, night soil, dressing, cow *or* buffalo chips, *U.S. West* cow pies, coprolites, coproliths, *Sl.* flops.

excrescence, *n.* **1.** growth, excretion, tumor, lump, intumescence, tumefaction; swelling, protuberance, protrusion, prominence; blister, blain, boil, carbuncle, pimple, pustule, pock, whelk.
2. outgrowth, offshoot, branch, extension, appendage.

excrete, *v.* egest, defecate, void, pass, urinate; discharge, expel, eject, evacuate, eliminate, throw off; exude, emit, perspire, sweat.

excretion, *n.* **1.** defecation, voidance, urination; discharge, ejection, evacuation, elimination, extrusion, exudation, secretion.
2. perspiration, sweat; urine, excrement; smegma. See **excrement**.

excruciate, *v.* agonize, torture, rack, put [s.o.] on the rack, wring, crucify, martyr; pain, wound, hurt, scathe, pierce, stab, lacerate, put [s.o.] through the wringer; torment, persecute, abuse; anguish, distress, afflict, plague, harrow, rend.

excruciating, *adj.* agonizing, tortuous, torturing, racking, wringing, painful; (*all of pain*) raw, sharp, cutting, acute, severe, intense, insufferable, unbearable, unendurable; anguishing, distressing, poignant, afflictive, plaguing, harrowing, rending; tormenting, persecuting, abusive.

excruciation, *n.* agony, torture, racking, wringing; torment, persecution, abuse; pain, anguish, distress, woe, harrowing, tribulation, hell; wretchedness, misery, suffering, martyrdom.

exculpate, *v.* acquit, clear, clear one's name, prove *or* declare innocent, uphold innocence, pronounce *or* declare not guilty, remove guilt, free from blame; exonerate, vindicate, right, set *or* put right, justify, warrant, defend; release, free, set free, let go, liberate, emancipate, deliver; dismiss, let off, *Inf.* let out of, *Inf.* let off the hook, *Law.* discharge; absolve, forgive, pardon, amnesty, excuse, remit, reprieve, respite.

exculpation, *n.* acquittal, acquittance, acquitting, compurgation, clearance, clearing, clearing of one's name, proof *or* declaration of innocence, upholding of innocence, removal of guilt, freeing from blame; exoneration, exonerating, vindication, vindicating, righting, justification, justifying; freeing, release, releasing, liberation, emancipation, deliverance, dismissal, *Law.* discharge; absolution, absolving, forgiving, pardon, pardoning, amnesty, excuse, excusing; remission, remitting, reprieving.

exculpatory, *adj.* **1.** acquitting, compurgatory, exonerative, exonerating, vindicatory, vindicative, vindicating, exculpating; absolutory, absolvent, absolving, forgiving, pardoning, excusatory, excusing, remissive, remitting.

2. clement, lenient, indulgent, forbearing, sparing; merciful, humane, compassionate.

excursion, *n.* **1.** outing, airing, drive, ride; jaunt, junket, stroll, ramble; walk, hike, trek, tramp, peregrination, pilgrimage; expedition, trip, tour, voyage, sail, cruise; globe-trotting, sightseeing.

2. deviation, digression, divagation, wandering off, excursus.

excursive, *adj.* (*all of speech*) discursive, digressive, wandering, roaming, roving, peripatetic, errant; rambling, aimless, desultory, unconnected, disconnected, random.

excusable, *adj.* forgivable, pardonable, condonable, understandable; allowable, permissible; venial, minor, slight.

excusatory, *adj.* exculpatory, exonerative, vindicatory, vindicative; apologetic, justificatory; extenuating, mitigating.

excuse, *v.* **1.** forgive, absolve, shrive, remit; forbear, spare, judge with leniency; pardon, amnesty, reprieve, exculpate, exonerate, vindicate; acquit, clear, prove innocent, uphold innocence, remove guilt; condone, make allowances for, overlook, pass over, wink at, disregard, forget, ignore, look the other way, pay no attention to.

2. apologize, repent, explain, extenuate, palliate, make excuses; defend oneself, rationalize, tell one's story, *Inf.* alibi, *Inf.* do a song and dance; justify, warrant, sanction, approve, allow, permit.

3. release, relieve, dismiss, discharge, free, liberate, let off, *Inf.* let off the hook; exempt, dispense with, except, exclude, leave [s.o.] out, keep [s.o.] out, *Rom. Cath. Ch.* dispense.

4. remit, waive, release from, let out of, *Commerce.* indulge, clear the books, wipe the slate clean.

—n. **5.** explanation, story, apology, apologia, rationalization, argument, allegation, claim, assertion, *Law.* rejoinder, *Law.* deraignment, *Inf.* song and dance, *Inf.* alibi; reason, basis, grounds, support, justification, plea; extenuation, palliation, *Law.* demurrer, *Law.* rebutter, *Law.* essoin.

6. forgiveness, forgiving, absolution, absolving, shriving, remission, remitting; pardoning, reprieve, reprieving, respite, exculpation, exculpating, exoneration, exonerating, vindication, vindicating, acquittal, acquittance, acquitting, clearance, clearing; forbearance, sparing, judging with leniency, *Both Rom. Cath. Ch.* indulgence, indulgency; condonation, condoning, excusal, overlooking, disregarding, ignoring.

7. pretext, ostensible reason, pretense, feint; subterfuge, escape, way out, out, loophole; evasion, elusion, means of avoiding, *Inf.* cop-out, *Inf.* stall.

8. makeshift, poor specimen, pitiful example, substitute.

execrable, *adj.* **1.** abominable, abhorrent, heinous, loathsome, odious, invidious, hateful, detestable, despicable, deplorable; offensive, atrocious, disgusting, rank, distasteful, repulsive, obnoxious.

2. cursed, accursed, *Archaic.* maledict, damned, plagued, anathematized, imprecated, excoriated, inveighed against, railed against, fulminated against; condemned, censured, denounced.

3. inferior, poor, bad, horrible, appalling, imperfect, defective, faulty, *Inf.* not up to snuff.

execrate, *v.* **1.** abhor, abominate, loathe, despise, detest, hate; have an aversion to, feel hostility toward, be hostile to, not be able to bear *or* abide.

2. curse, *Archaic.* accurse, damn, swear at, anathematize, revile, imprecate, invoke evil upon, excoriate, plague, inveigh, rail against, fulminate; vituperate, condemn, proscribe, censure, denounce.

execration, *n.* **1.** curse, imprecation, malediction, anathema, damnation, excoriation, fulmination, plague; vituperation, condemnation, censure, denunciation.

2. abhorrence, abomination, detestation, animosity, animus, hatred, hostility, abhorring, abominating, loathing, despising, detesting, hating; cursing, imprecating, anathematizing, damning, excoriating, fulminating; vituperating, condemning, proscribing, censuring, denouncing, denunciating.

3. the condemned, the damned, the cursed, the accursed; anathema, *Fr. bete noire*, bugbear, bogeyman.

execute, *v.* **1.** carry out, accomplish, perform, do, discharge, fulfill, consummate; succeed in, manage, bring off, *Sl.* pull off, *Inf.* put over, *U.S. Sl.* swing, *U.S. Sl.* cut, *U.S. Sl.* hack; mastermind, engineer, negotiate, work out; bring about, make happen, cause, effect, effectuate; put through, produce, turn out, achieve, attain, realize; carry through, complete, finish; dispose of, *Sl.* knock off, *Sl.* polish off, expedite, dispatch.

2. put to death, behead, decapitate, guillotine, decollate; hang, gibbet, lynch, *Sl.* string up, *Sl.* stretch, crucify; stone, lapidate; burn at the stake, electrocute, send to the electric chair; gas, poison, drown; kill, murder, slay, shoot, strangle; put an end to, get rid of, put away, remove, silence, finish off, dispatch; *All Sl.* rub out, bump off, knock off, snuff out. See **kill** (*defs.* **1, 2**).

execution, *n.* **1.** accomplishment, fulfillment, realization, success, attainment, acquirement; achievement, performance, production; completion, consummation, finishing, conclusion.

2. capital punishment, judicial murder; hanging, lynching, *Euph.* necktie party; decapitation, decollation, guillotining; electrocution, gassing, poisoning; crucifixion, impalement, lapidation, stoning; burning, burning at the stake; killing, murder, slaying, shooting, strangling, strangulation. See **killing** (*defs.* **1, 2**).

3. (*all of performance*) mode, style, manner, touch, technique, technical skill; rendition, rendering, interpretation, representation, version.

executioner, *n.* executionist, *Sl.* Jack Ketch, hangman, lyncher, garroter; decapitator, headsman, beheader; gasser, exterminator, annihilator; firing squad; crucifier, killer, murderer, slayer; bloodspiller, bloodshedder, bloodletter. See **killer** (*def.* **1**).

executive, *n.* **1.** administrator, director, manager, leader, head, chief, principal; supervisor, superintendent, *Inf.* super, overseer, boss; master, commander, taskmaster, overlord; *Inf.* kingpin, *Inf.* number one, *Inf.* Mr. Big, *Sl.* top dog, *Sl.* top banana, *Sl.* big cheese.

2. president, premier, ruler, governor, intendant, mayor, *Inf.* (*collectively*) brass.

3. dignitary, personage, *Inf.* V.I.P., *Inf.* bigwig, *Sl.* biggie, *Sl.* big shot; celebrity, luminary, somebody, *Inf.* big name.

—adj. **4.** administrative, managerial, directorial, supervisory, conductorial, regulatory; executory, au-

thoritative, official, directive, legislative, front-office; jurisdictional, governmental, gubernatorial, mayoral, magisterial.

executor, *n.* guardian, custodian, trustee, *Law.* curator; regent, steward, factor; administrator, agent, enforcer, operator, performer.

exegesis, *n.* hermeneutics; (*all usu. of Scripture*) explication, explanation, exposition, interpretation, elucidation; clarification; criticism, critique, comment; annotation, gloss, marginalia, scholia.

exegete, *n.* Biblical scholar, textualist, Talmudic scholar, Talmudist; divine, religious scholar, hierophant, hierologist, theologian, patrist; expounder, interpreter, annotator, scholiast.

exegetical, *adj.* hermeneutic, hermeneutical; explicatory, explicative, explanatory, expository; interpretative, interpretive, elucidative, illustrative; annotative, annotatory, scholiastic.

exemplar, *n.* **1.** paragon, ideal, standard of perfection *or* excellence, beau ideal, *Latin. ne plus ultra*; model, pattern, paradigm, *Inf.* pilot, form, mold, die; standard, norm, measure, measurement, benchmark, point of reference.

2. example, exemplification, illustration, demonstration; epitome, representative, sample, specimen, instance, *Inf.* for instance, typical instance *or* case, case, case in point, *Archaic.* ensample.

3. archetype, prototype, original, first of its kind, protoplast, first form; forerunner, precursor, predecessor, ancestor.

exemplary, *adj.* **1.** model, worthy of imitation, admirable, commendable, praiseworthy, laudable, meritorious, worthy; superior, outstanding, noteworthy, notable, above average; noble, quality, excellent, sterling, topflight, first-rate, *Inf.* topnotch; supreme, consummate, superb, perfect, faultless, ideal.

2. warning, admonitory, monitory; example-setting, lesson-teaching, point-making, precedent-setting.

3. illustrative, exemplifying, demonstrative; experimental, pilot; epitomic, epitomical, typical, representative, sample.

exemplification, *n.* illustration, example, instance, case; embodiment, personification, incarnation. See **exemplar** (*def.* **2**).

exemplify, *v.* **1.** illustrate, instance, give an example, give an instance *or* case of, cite a case in point, tell a story *or* anecdote about, *Rare.* example; model, show, demonstrate, exhibit, display.

2. epitomize, typify, represent, embody, personify; be a sample *or* specimen of, be a case *or* an instance of, serve as an example of, give an idea of.

exempt, *v.* **1.** free from, release from, absolve, excuse from, dismiss from, relieve of, dispense with; let out of, let off, *Inf.* let off the hook, dispense; except, make an exception, spare from, exclude from, leave [s.o.] out, keep [s.o.] out, pass over *or* by.

—adj. **2.** immune, not subject to; free, freed, scot-free, released, absolved, excused, dismissed from, relieved of, *Inf.* off the hook; excepted, spared, excluded, left out, kept out, passed over *or* by.

—n. **3.** immune, indemnitee; exception, favorite, pet.

exemption, *n.* immunity, impunity, indemnity, freedom, freeing, release, releasing, absolution, excusal, excusing, exempting, *Rom. Cath. Ch.* dispensation, *Archaic.* franchise; exception, excepting, exclusion, excluding; privilege, favoritism, special treatment; (*in ref. to taxes*) deduction, *Sl.* deduct.

exercise, *n.* **1.** workout, warm-up, limbering up; exertion, exercitation, effort, work; calisthenics, gymnastics, aerobics, isometrics, sports, yoga; action, movement; deed, act, activity; practice, drill, training, discipline, studying.

2. operation, employment, utilization, use; application, appliance, adhibition, functioning.

3. feat, performance, recitation, recital; composition, etude, study, scales.

4. **exercises** ceremony, ritual, rite, observances, formalities; service, worship.

—v. **5.** warm up, limber up, work out, work up a lather, exert, flex one's muscles; practice, drill, train; school, indoctrinate, inculcate, develop.

6. employ, apply, use, utilize; execute, perform, discharge; display, exhibit, show, indicate.

7. effect, produce, effectuate, bring about, impart.

8. worry, make uneasy, agitate, stir up; perturb, disturb, trouble, distress; annoy, vex, *Inf.* drive up the wall.

exert, *v.* **1.** exercise, use, employ, put to use, utilize; wield, bring into play, set in motion, put to work; put forth, expend, spend, put out.

2. **exert oneself** strive, endeavor, attempt; struggle, strain, push, drive, go all out, knock oneself out, *Sl.* bust a gut, *Sl.* bust one's butt; apply oneself, concentrate, beat one's brains out, cudgel one's brains; give [s.t.] one's all, do one's best *or* utmost *or* damnedest, spare no effort, take pains; toil, labor, plod, drudge, grind, sweat, slave.

exertion, *n.* **1.** effort, struggle, strain, stress, push, drive, *Inf.* muscle, *Inf.* elbow grease; endeavor, attempt; industry, diligence, assiduity, sedulity.

2. exercitation, application, adhibition; use, employ, utilization, practice, exercise.

exfoliate, *v.* scale, peel, flake, flake off, shell, fall off, *Pathol.* desquamate; shed, cast off, molt, mew; depilate, decorticate, pare, husk, skin; splinter, shiver, slice.

exfoliation, *n.* **1.** scaling, flaking, molting, mewing, *Pathol.* desquamation; depilation, paring, husking, decortication.

2. integument, pellicle, skin, outerskin, shell, husk, coat.

exhalation, *n.* **1.** breath, respiration, expiration, exsufflation; evaporation, vaporization, emanation, volatilization, gasification, dissipation.

2. vapor, steam, gas, air; puff, huff, whiff, gasp, blast; sigh, sough, suspiration.

exhale, *v.* **1.** breathe, respire, expire, exsufflate; blow, puff, huff, bluster, pant, gasp, wheeze; sigh, sough, whisper, whistle, whiff, whiffle.

2. breathe out, expel, emit, eject, belch; blow off, give off, emanate, spout, send off, pass off, pour off; smoke, fumigate, fume, reek; vent, exhaust, evacuate.

3. evaporate, draw off, vaporize, vapor, volatilize, escape; rise in vapor, go up in smoke, steam, gasify, dissipate.

exhaust, *v.* **1.** use up, consume, eat up, finish; expend, spend, dissipate, *Sl.* blow; waste, squander, fritter away, fool away, run through; *Inf.* scrape the bottom of the barrel.

2. drain, wear out, fatigue, weary, tire, tire out, enervate, lethargize; wind, fag, *Inf.* tucker, *Inf.* bush, *Inf.* take it out of, *Sl.* poop, *Sl.* poop out, *Sl.* knock out, burn out, do in; sap, overtire, overwork, burn the candle at both ends; overtask, tax, strain; prostrate, debilitate, disable, devitalize.

3. draw out, extract, root up, take out, extricate; dig up, comb through, treat thoroughly, go over, go over with a fine-toothed comb, cover all the ground.

4. empty, drain off, pour out, discharge, spill, run out; deplete, deflate, collapse; clean out, clear out, sweep off.

5. pass out, escape, vent, emit; spurt, stream, gush, belch, spew out; flow out, blow off, give off, spout, send off, pour off, pass off.

—n. **6.** escape, release, outflow, outpour, efflux, effluence; outburst, outrush, outgush, running out.

7. steam, smoke, gas, fumes, carbon monoxide, carbon dioxide.

exhausted, *adj.* **1.** tired, tired out, *Inf.* dog-tired, dead tired, *Sl.* dead, dead on one's feet; overtired, done in, all in, ready to drop; fatigued, weary, worn out, *Inf.* tuckered out, *Inf.* bushed, fagged out, played out, burned out, wiped out, spent, *Archaic.* forspent; drowsy, sleepy, half-asleep, groggy, *Sl.* dopey, *Sl.* drugged; *All Sl.* shot, beat, pooped, pooped out, (*with have*) had it.

2. toilworn, wayworn, footsore; winded, panting, out of breath, breathless, gasping for breath *or* air; haggard, feeble, weak, faint, prostrate, *Pathol.* atonic.

3. consumed, drained, depleted, used up; emptied, bare, dry.

exhausting, *adj.* laborious, arduous, strenuous, back-breaking, *Sl.* ball-busting, hard, difficult; tedious, wearisome, tiresome; tiring, fatiguing, weakening, enervating, debilitating.

exhaustion, *n.* **1.** weakness, faintness, swoon, faint, *Pathol.* syncope; feebleness, lassitude, lethargy, inanition; fatigue, weariness, tiredness, prostration, collapse, burnout; debilitation, enervation, enfeeblement, debility, *Pathol.* asthenia.

2. depletion, consumption, draining, emptying; dispersion, wasting, prodigality, dissipation, wastefulness.

exhaustive, *adj.* comprehensive, encyclopedic, all-inclusive; in-depth, profound, thorough; thoroughgoing, extensive, far-reaching.

exhibit, *v.* **1.** display, show, demonstrate, set forth, present, offer; expose, air, unveil, unfurl, extend, spread out; place, arrange, array, dispose, set up; flaunt, parade, brandish, show off.

2. indicate, express, manifest, make plain *or* clear, betray, give away; evince, evidence, exemplify, *Scot. and North Eng.* kithe; reveal, disclose, produce, bring forward, bring out, roll out, *Inf.* trot out.

3. explain, explicate, expound; describe, illustrate, show how, give an idea of.

—n. **4.** display, show, showing. See **exhibition** (*def.* 2).

5. evidence, proof, grounds, facts, data; example, demonstration, *Inf.* demo, illustration, representation, exemplification; item, instance, case, particular.

exhibition, *n.* **1.** demonstration, manifestation, representation, evincement, indication, expression, exemplification; revelation, disclosure, divulgence; explanation, explication, description, illustration.

2. exhibit, show, showing, display, presentation, unveiling, airing; mounting, staging, stage show, production, performance; review, retrospective; exposition, *Inf.* expo, fair.

exhibitionist, *n.* **1.** show-off, extrovert, *Sl.* grandstander, *Sl.* hot dog, *Sl.* hotshot, *Sl.* showboat; dandy, fop, clotheshorse.

2. deviant, pervert, sex deviant *or* pervert, *Sl.* flasher.

exhilarate, *v.* **1.** cheer, gladden, uplift, make merry, make happy *or* joyous; delight, elate, exalt, brighten; warm, move, inspire, enthuse; hearten, enhearten, encourage, nerve, embolden; fortify, build up, nourish, restore; reassure, confirm, comfort, solace; improve, ameliorate, meliorate; aid, assist, support, sustain; strengthen, buttress, brace, reinforce.

2. enliven, invigorate, stimulate, inspirit, energize; animate, raise, vivify, vitalize; reanimate, revive, revivify, revitalize, rejuvenate; fire, *Inf.* light a fire under, inflame; enkindle, *Inf.* spark, stir, quicken, awaken, make active; arouse, tingle, thrill; *Inf.* pep up, perk up, bolster *or* bolster up, cheer, refresh, give a lift to.

exhilaration, *n.* high spirits, good spirits, gaiety, merriment, lightheartedness; blithesomeness, airiness, sunniness, breeziness, buoyancy; liveliness, alacrity, briskness, vivacity, effervescence, bubbling; gladsomeness, joyousness, cheerfulness, levity; hilarity, mirth, mirthfulness, elation; glee, gleefulness, exultation, jubilation; merrymaking, rejoicing, laughter; jocundity, jocularity, joviality, conviviality, jollity; jauntiness, sprightliness, pertness, friskiness, playfulness, sportiveness; energy, spirit, elan, dash, ardor; passion, zeal, gusto, vigor; eagerness, animation, *Inf.* ginger, enthusiasm; sparkle, ebullience, excitement; ecstasy, thrill, *Inf.* rush, tingling.

exhort, *v.* urge, persuade, sway, prompt, prevail upon; press, peptalk, *Inf.* sparkplug, encourage, move, animate, stimulate; impel, instigate, induce, incite, inspire, provoke; rouse, goad, egg on, spur, fillip; inflame, fire up, spark, stir, push, quicken, hasten; advise, counsel, recommend, prescribe; caution, warn, alarm, expostulate; admonish, advise against, forewarn, dissuade; enjoin, entreat, charge, adjure, implore; impress, instruct, preach, lecture.

exhortation, *n.* **1.** persuasion, prompting, urging, urge, insistence; encouragement, stimulation, incentive, inducement, instigation; inspiration, incitement, impulse, instance, provocation; prick, goad, spur, stimulus, fillip; pep talk, rally, call to arms; advice, counsel, word to the wise, recommendation, prescription, warning, caution; admonition, monition, forewarning, injunction, expostulation, remonstrance; entreaty, charge, adjuration, enjoining, imploration.

2. lecture, preachment, instruction, homily, sermon, evangelization; harangue, tirade, *Inf.* fire and brimstone.

exhume, *v.* **1.** dig up, unearth, disinter, excavate; unbury, disinhume, disentomb, exhumate, unsepulcher.

2. resurrect, restore, regenerate, revive, reanimate; bring to life, bring to light, bring back, recall, reincarnate.

exigency, *n.* **1.** urgency, exigence, need, needfulness; imperativeness, imperative, importunity, importunateness, solicitousness, clamorousness; insistence, instance, pertinacity, pertinaciousness, pressure.

2. exigencies demands, needs, wants, requirements, urgencies, necessities, essentials, requisites.

3. emergency, crisis, juncture, conjuncture, crossroads; extremity, pinch, dire circumstance, contingency; strait, difficulty, rub, trouble, *Inf.* hot water; predicament, plight, impasse, imbroglio, corner, cul-de-sac; fix, bind, pass, mess, *Inf.* pickle, *Inf.* stew; *All Inf.* hole, clutch, clinch, crunch, tight squeeze.

exigent, *adj.* **1.** urgent, pressing, imperative, high-priority; critical, acute, crucial, pivotal, climacteric; demanding, insistent, importunate, compelling, instant, pertinacious; crying, clamoring, clamorous, loud, clamant, solicitous.

2. taxing, exacting, draining, exorbitant, extortionate; austere, harsh, severe, dire, Spartan, lenten, abstemious; rigorous, rough, stringent, stiff, hard, stern.

exiguous, *adj.* scanty, scant, meager, sparse, bare, mere, slight; trifling, piddling, negligible, inconsiderable, *Inf.* skimpy, *Inf.* scrimpy; slender, slim, thin, lean; frugal, sparing, poor, impoverished; miserly, niggardly, mean, parsimonious, stingy, *Inf.* chintzy;

small, wee, tiny, puny, petty, diminutive, paltry.

exile, *n.* **1.** separation, displacement, dislocation, expatriation, uprooting, exilement.

2. displaced person, D.P., expatriate, alien, émigré; outcast, expellee, outsider, deportee, Ishmael, Hagar; pariah, leper, nonperson, unperson.

3. expulsion, ostracism, banishment, deportation, relegation, excommunication; proscription, outlawry, prohibition, banning, barring; exclusion, segregation, isolation, sequestration, quarantine; ejection, eviction, ouster.

—*v.* **4.** expatriate, dislocate, displace, separate, export; scatter, unsettle, uproot; expel, banish, ostracize, excommunicate, deport; run out, drive out, cast out, thrust out, send away, relegate; proscribe, outlaw, ban, bar, prohibit; eject, exclude, oust, evict; isolate, cut off, quarantine, sequester, seclude, maroon.

exist, *v.* **1.** be, have being; live, breathe, draw breath, respire; have life, have animation, have vitality, be viable; subsist, vegetate.

2. continue, remain, endure, abide, last, stay; survive, *Sl.* get along.

3. occur, happen, obtain, prevail; take place, ensue, result, eventuate, befall, betide, come off, crop up, bechance.

existence, *n.* **1.** being, existing, subsistence, *Latin. esse*; actuality, reality, presence, fact, living.

2. continuance, duration, abidingness, endurance, lastingness, permanence, persistence.

3. mode of being, lifestyle, manner, fashion.

4. life, vital principle, animation, vitality, nature.

5. entity, being, thing, creature, *Metaphys.* ens; essence, quiddity.

exit, *n.* **1.** way out, passage out, doorway, door, gate, mouth; outlet, opening, aperture, porthole, loophole, window; hatch, *Naut.* booby hatch, trapdoor, postern.

2. departure, going out, taking off, leaving; withdrawal, retreat, retirement; egress, debouchment; emanation, issuance, issue, discharge, vent; escape, evacuation, flight, exodus, hegira; abandonment, vacation, desertion.

—*v.* **3.** leave, go out *or* away, depart, quit, take off; withdraw, retire, repair, retreat; issue, emanate, discharge, vent; escape, flee, fly, evacuate; vacate, decamp, break camp, abandon, forsake, desert.

exodus, *n.* flight, escape, move, migration, emigration; hegira, fleeing; exit, departure, leaving, going out, sallying forth; retreat, withdrawal, recession.

exonerate, *v.* **1.** acquit, clear, vindicate. See **exculpate**.

2. release, discharge, free. See **excuse** (*def.* **3**).

exoneration, *n.* **1.** acquittal, acquittance, vindication. See **exculpation**.

2. excusal, release, relief, dismissal, discharge, freedom, liberty, liberation, emancipation, deliverance, delivery; exemption, exception, exclusion, indemnity, immunity, impunity, *Rom. Cath. Ch.* dispensation.

exorbitance, *n.* **1.** excessiveness, nimiety, extravagance, immoderateness, unreasonableness, undueness, inordinateness; outrageousness, preposterousness, monstrousness, rankness, egregiousness; redundancy, superfluity, supererogation, oversufficiency, overkill, overdose, too much of a good thing.

2. expensiveness, costliness, dearness, highness, *Inf.* steepness, *Inf.* stiffness.

exorbitant, *adj.* **1.** excessive, unreasonable, immoderate, disproportionate, undue, inordinate, uncalled-for, unwarranted, unnecessary; extreme, too much, unconscionable, outrageous, preposterous, monstrous, rank, egregious, *Inf.* criminal.

2. expensive, costly, dear, high-priced, *Inf.* steep, *Inf.* stiff; overpriced, prohibitive, priced out of the market; extortionate, cutthroat, gouging, usurious.

exorcise, *v.* (*in reference to evil spirits*) expel, cast out, drive out, deliver from, exsufflate; unspell, disenchant.

exorcism, *n.* **1.** (*usu. in reference to evil spirits*) casting out, driving out, expulsion, deliverance from; exsufflation, disenchantment.

2. incantation, conjuration, invocation, countercharm, hocus-pocus.

exoteric, *adj.* **1.** public, plebian, proletarian, vulgar, common, vulgate; open, unexclusive, nonexclusive, communal, community; unreserved, available, accessible, obtainable.

2. popular, commonplace, widespread, general; simple, clear, pat, literal; intelligible, comprehensible, explicit; plain, undisguised, unconcealed, unhidden; express, manifest, apparent, evident, conspicuous, in broad daylight, clear as a bell.

3. exterior, external, outside, extrinsic, extraneous; superficial, surface, outer, outward, outermost.

exotic, *adj.* **1.** foreign, unnative, alien; outlandish, barbarian, ultramontane, tramontane, out of the way; new, novel, different, unheard-of; external, extraneous, extrinsic.

2. striking, outrageous, incredible, fabulous, astonishing; remarkable, out of the ordinary, extraordinary, marvelous, wondrous; unusual, strange, peculiar, singular, unique, unexpected; exciting, glamorous, extravagant, sensational, electrifying; thrilling, impressive, *Inf.* big-city, colorful.

3. topless, bottomless, striptease, go-go, disco; racy, *Inf.* sexy, risque, titillating, voluptuous.

expand, *v.* **1.** increase, enlarge, make larger, make bigger, make greater, *Chiefly Literary.* greaten, aggrandize; magnify, amplify, enhance, deepen, heighten; widen, thicken, broaden; lengthen, prolong, protract; extend, spread, outspread, spread out, branch out, *Mil.* deploy; unfold, unfurl, stretch out, open; wax, grow larger.

2. dilate, distend, inflate, bloat, puff out, blow up; swell, intumesce, tumefy; fill out, fatten.

3. augment, supplement, add to, superadd to; accrue, accumulate, cumulate, amass, pile up, heap up; multiply, double, redouble, treble, triple, quadruple.

4. escalate, step up, give a boost to, *Sl.* soup up, *Sl.* hop up, *Sl.* jazz up; accelerate, snowball, mushroom; exacerbate, aggravate.

5. develop, enlarge on, overstate; descant, expound on *or* upon, detail; intensify, concentrate; exaggerate, maximize, make much of, make the most of.

6. strengthen, reinforce, build up; grow, mature, flourish.

7. raise, elevate, boost, advance, exalt; rise, ascend, mount, skyrocket; burgeon, shoot up, spring up, sprout.

expanse, *n.* **1.** space, extension, expansion; spaciousness, amplitude, vastness, immensity, capaciousness, largeness; open space, free space, clearing, opening; leeway, margin, elbowroom; open country, wilderness, waste, desert, wild region, desolate country.

2. infinity, infinitude, unlimitedness, boundlessness; abyss, chasm, gulf; emptiness, void.

3. magnitude, measure, degree, quantity, amount, extent, fullness; capacity, volume, proportions, dimensions, size, gauge, bulk, content; period, duration, term, continuance; breadth, depth, width, broadness, wideness, height, length; arena, sphere, region, territory; field, tract, distance; stretch, spread, reach, span; district, circuit, area; scope, range, compass, sweep; latitude, longitude.

expansion, *n.* **1.** enlargement, extension, aggrandizement, increase; magnification, amplification, enhancement, deepening, heightening; widening, thickening, broadening; lengthening, waxing, prolongation, protraction; unfolding, unfurling, opening; spreading out, stretching out, branching out, *Mil.* deployment; diffusion, dissemination, dispersion, dispersal.
2. inflation, distension, dilatation, dilation, *Physiol.* diastole; bloating, puffing out, blowing up; swelling, intumescence, tumefaction, puffiness.
3. addition, accretion, increment, accession, access; augmentation, supplement, annex, annexation, appendage, appendix, addendum, adjunct; accrual, accruement, accumulation, cumulation.
4. elevation, raise, boost, rise, advancement; upsurge, upswing, upturn, step-up; mounting, ascending, skyrocketing; multiplication, doubling, redoubling, trebling, tripling, quadrupling; burgeoning, shooting up, springing up, sprouting.
5. development, explanation, expounding on *or* upon, detailing; intensification, concentration, escalation, acceleration; maximization, overstatement; exacerbation, aggravation.
6. strengthening, reinforcement, build-up; improvement, upgrading, *Inf.* pickup; growth, maturation.
7. expanse, space, spaciousness, amplitude, vastness, immensity, largeness; open space, free space, clearing, opening, open country; wilderness, waste, desert, wild region, desolate country; infinity, infinitude, unlimitedness, boundlessness; abyss, chasm, gulf; emptiness, void.

expansive, *adj.* **1.** expanding, enlarging, enhancing, deepening, heightening; extending, spreading, unfolding, unfurling, stretching out, opening; dilatable, inflatable.
2. strengthening, reinforcing; growing, maturing, flourishing; burgeoning, sprouting.
3. comprehensive, inclusive, all-inclusive, all-including, all-embracing; thorough, thorough-going, exhaustive, complete; entire, out-and-out, radical; extensive, *Inf.* wall-to-wall; universal, catholic, worldwide, nationwide, global, cosmopolitan; wide-reaching, far-reaching; infinite, unlimited, unbounded, unrestricted, boundless.
4. large, large-scale, big, bulky, great; substantial, considerable, sizeable, generous, liberal; immense, vast, massive; gigantic, huge, enormous, colossal, stupendous.
5. spacious, extended, expanded; ample, capacious, voluminous, roomy, commodious; broad, wide, widespread, spread out, outspread, stretched out, outstretched.
6. (*of a person's character or speech*) effusive, ebullient, overflowing; demonstrative, communicative, talkative, loquacious; outgoing, uninhibited, extroverted, outspoken; free, open, frank; unrestrained, unreserved, unreticent.

expatiate, *v.* (*all of speech*) descant, perorate, discourse, dissertate; expand, enlarge, amplify, protract, prolong; harp on, dwell on; digress, wander, rove, roam, maunder, ramble.

expatriate, *v.* **1.** exile, banish, proscribe, outlaw, deport; expel, cast out, oust, dismiss; relegate; ostracize, blackball, exclude, isolate, maroon, seclude.
2. emigrate, migrate, leave the country.
—*n.* **3.** exile, displaced person, D.P., expellee, emigrant, emigre; castaway, outcast, pariah, outlaw.

expect, *v.* **1.** anticipate, await, abide, *Archaic.* attend; look ahead to, watch for, have in prospect, look forward to, keep in view; contemplate, foresee.
2. rely upon, hope for, calculate upon, count upon, reckon upon, bargain for; trust, look for; require, exact, demand.
3. suppose, surmise, conjecture, believe, presume, *Archaic.* ween.

expectant, *adj.* **1.** expecting, awaiting, abiding; ready, eager, anxious; in suspense, on tiptoe; apprehensive, on tenterhooks *or* pins and needles; open-eyed, vigilant, open-mouthed, agape; with bated breath.
2. prospective, expected, future, potential, likely, destined, imminent, eventual; threatening, looming, brewing.
3. pregnant, expecting, enceinte, gravid, with child, in the family way.

expectation, *n.* **1.** anticipation, expectancy, prospect, contingency; contemplation, looking forward to, expecting, awaiting, abiding.
2. presumption, reckoning, calculation, anticipatory desire; hope, assurance, trust, reliance, dependence, confidence; suspense, apprehension, anxiety.
3. probability, likelihood, chance, possibility; susceptibility, liableness, liability.
4. *Usu.* **expectations** prospects, outlook, speculation, high hopes; good fortune, profit.

expectorate, *v.* spit, discharge, expel, eject; cough up, hawk.

expediency, *n.* **1.** suitability, suitableness, seemliness, appropriateness, fittingness; properness, correctness, rightness, goodness; judiciousness, wisdom, sagacity; sensibleness, reasonableness, rationality, intelligence.
2. advisability, desirability, desirableness, practicality, usefulness, utility; advantage, advantageousness, beneficiality, helpfulness, serviceability, favorability, timeliness; convenience, opportunism, propitiousness, auspiciousness, fortunateness, salutariness; valuability, profitableness, profit, gain, gainfulness, lucrativeness, remunerativeness.

expedient, *adj.* **1.** suitable, seemly, appropriate, befitting, fitting, fit, meet; proper, correct, right, good, essential; prudent, discreet, circumspect, politic, judicious, wise, sage, sagacious; sensible, reasonable, rational, intelligent.
2. advisable, recommendable, desirable, practical, useful; advantageous, beneficial, helpful, of service, serviceable, favorable; convenient, opportune, propitious, auspicious, fortunate, salutary; valuable, profitable, gainful, lucrative, remunerative; to one's best interest, to one's good, all to the good, all for the best.
—*n.* **3.** device, tool, contrivance, means, agency, measures, shift, resort, resource; plan, plot, scheme, design; makeshift, stopgap, fabrication, invention; stratagem, machination, artifice, trick, ruse, stroke, coup, maneuver, feint.

expedite, *v.* **1.** hasten, hurry, precipitate, antedate, quicken, speed *or* step up, accelerate; urge on, press forward, push, shove, drive, railroad.
2. advance, promote, forward, further; encourage, boost, build up, support, patronize; facilitate, enable, make easy for; assist, aid, help, abet, succor, lend a hand, give a leg up.
3. dispatch, accomplish promptly, make short work of, *Inf.* whip off, *Inf.* dash off, finish *or* complete quickly.
4. issue, put forth, give out; dispatch, send off, mail; distribute, circulate, promulgate.

expedition, *n.* **1.** excursion, trip, tour, journey, voyage, sail, cruise; exploration, search; circuit, round trip, turn, whirl; jaunt, junket, stroll, ramble; outing, airing, drive, ride; walk, hike, trek, tramp, peregrina-

tion, pilgrimage; campaign, crusade, mission; march, invasion, raid.
2. group, crowd, company, party, body, gathering; crew, band, troop, team, squad.
3. alacrity, promptness, promptitude, readiness; swiftness, quickness, fastness, dispatch; haste, speed, celerity, rapidity, velocity.

expeditious, *adj.* prompt, immediate, instant, instantaneous; direct, summary, fast; rapid, fleet, meteoric, quick, swift, brisk; timely, seasonable, punctual, early, in good time.

expel, *v.* **1.** drive out, force out, thrust out, extrude, eject, *Sl.* bounce, run [s.o.] off *or* out, evict, put out, dispossess; suspend, *Sl.* kick out; dismiss, fire, *Sl.* sack, show the door, cashier, drum out; disown, repudiate, reject, discard; exile, expatriate, banish, proscribe, outlaw, relegate, deport; excommunicate, unchurch; ostracize, blackball, exclude, isolate, maroon.
2. discharge, excrete, eliminate, egest, void, evacuate.

expend, *v.* **1.** disburse, spend, pay out, outlay, *Inf.* lay out, *Sl.* fork out, *Sl.* shell out, *Sl.* dish out, ante up; squander, dissipate, burn up, waste, lavish; fritter away, run through.
2. consume, use up, exhaust, drain, sap, deplete, empty; finish, finish off, *Sl.* polish off.
3. use, exert, wield, apply, adhibit, employ.

expenditure, *n.* **1.** disbursement, outlay, expense; cost, charge, price, fee; overhead, general costs, outgo; payment, compensation, recompense, settlement; remuneration, reward, pay.
2. consumption, exhaustion, drain, depletion.

expense, *n.* **1.** cost, charge, price, quotation, quoted price, fee; amount, rate, fare, figure; outlay, amount expended.
2. expenditure, disbursement; consumption, exhaustion, drain, depletion.
3. **expenses** reimbursement, payment, compensation, recompense, settlement; expense account, allowance, per diem.
4. **at the expense of** at the sacrifice of, at the cost of; to the detriment of, to [s.o.'s] loss.

expensive, *adj.* **1.** high-priced, costly, dear, high, *Inf.* steep, *Inf.* stiff; exorbitant, extortionate, excessive, unreasonable; running into money, in the upper price brackets, beyond one's means.
2. valuable, precious, priceless, inestimable; sumptuous, rich, opulent, lavish; prodigal, wasteful, extravagant.

experience, *n.* **1.** affair, episode, ordeal, event, incident, occurrence, happening; encounter, transaction, adventure, *Sl.* trip; circumstance, case.
2. involvement, encountering, meeting, facing; exposure, observing, observation, perceiving, perception, impression; trials, vicissitudes, ups and downs.
3. life, existence, background, lifework; *U.S. Inf.* school of hard knocks.
4. wisdom, common sense; sophistication, enlightenment, knowledge, learning, cognizance, ken; know-how, savoir-faire.
—*v.* **5.** encounter, meet, face; observe, perceive, apprehend; taste, sample, test, try; sense, feel; undergo, go through, get [s.t.] under one's belt; live through, endure, suffer through.
6. understand, learn about, become knowledgeable about, become familiar with, find out about; realize, discover, become enlightened, appreciate; know, cognize, *Chiefly Scot.* ken; assimilate, absorb, take in.

experienced, *adj.* **1.** accomplished, practiced, skillful, polished, proficient, adept, good [at], *Fr. au fait*; knowledgeable, versed, prepared, qualified, well-grounded, trained, primed, ready; competent, fit, fitted, capable, able, efficient, *Sl.* on the ball; veteran, professional, *Inf.* knowing the ropes, *Sl.* savvy; expert, master, masterful, masterly.
2. mature, ripened, seasoned, salted; weathered, hardened, toughened, battle-scarred, *Inf.* through the mill, *Inf.* through the wringer; sophisticated, knowing, *Sl.* in the know, worldly, worldly-wise, *Sl.* wise, *Inf.* been around, initiated.
3. undergone, lived through, gone through, endured, suffered through; contacted, met, faced, observed, perceived; tasted, sampled, tested, tried; sensed, felt.

experiment, *n.* **1.** trial, test, demonstration, examination, investigation, inquiry, questioning, research, experimentation; venture, endeavor, effort, attempt, essay, go; tryout, feeler, trial balloon, speculation; trial and error, process of elimination, tentative procedure, shot in the dark, random shot.
2. test procedure, *Inf.* pilot, operation; observation, analysis, touchstone, assay.
3. evidence, verification, confirmation, corroboration, substantiation, authentication, proof.
—*v.* **4.** try, test, demonstrate, examine, probe, investigate, inquire, question, speculate; try out, sample, try and try again, make trial of, conduct an experiment; put to the test, analyze, assay; verify, prove, demonstrate.
5. venture, endeavor, attempt, essay, have a go at; approach, look at, take a fresh look at, begin work on, take preliminary steps, set about, break with tradition, explore new avenues, enter virgin territory, *Inf.* give something a whirl, *Inf.* fool around with; feel one's way, put out feelers, send up a trial balloon, feel the pulse; grope for, fish for, grasp at straws.

experimental, *adj.* **1.** tentative, hypothetical, speculative, probationary, on approval, pending; conjectural, theoretical, questionable, indefinite; assumptive, empirical, experiential.
2. exploratory, pilot, under examination *or* consideration, on trial, theoretic, provisional, untried; in the trial stages, full of kinks, not perfected, probative, probatory; under observation, in the spotlight, under the microscope.

expert, *n.* **1.** specialist, authority, pundit, scholar; one of the cognoscenti, connoisseur, critic; (*both of martial arts*) black belt, dan.
2. master, proficient, adept, mavin, master hand, *Chiefly Brit. Inf.* dab hand, *Brit. Dial.* dabster; maestro, virtuoso, talent, genius, prodigy, standout, *Inf.* wizard, *Inf.* whiz, *U.S. Sl.* crackerjack, *Sl.* sharp, *Sl.* shark; professional, *Inf.* pro, journeyman, veteran, past mistress, past master, old hand, old stager.
—*adj.* **3.** masterful, masterly, standout, topflight, top-drawer, first-rate, ace, *Inf.* topnotch, *Inf.* crack, *U.S. Sl.* crackerjack, *Inf.* whiz-bang, *Brit. Sl.* whizzo.
4. proficient, adept, finished, polished, accomplished, practiced, experienced, *Fr. au fait, Inf.* knowing the ropes; skillful, skilled, dexterous, adroit, deft, facile; knowledgeable, learned, well-versed, well-informed.
—*v.* **5.** counsel, advise, consult with, confer, recommend, suggest; enlighten, educate, acquaint, apprise, inform, notify.

expiate, *v.* atone, make amends, make up for, offset, redeem; do penance, shrive, pay, pay the penalty, pay the piper; recompense, make reparation; redress, right, remedy; go to confession, wash away one's sins; put on sackcloth and ashes, beat one's breast, cry mea culpa.

expiation, *n.* amends, compensation, indemnity, reparation, restitution, redress, repayment, requital, quittance; redemption, satisfaction, remedy, righting;

penance, taking one's punishment, *Archaic.* shrift, purgation.

expiration, *n.* **1.** conclusion, termination, end, coming to an end; finish, finis, culmination; close, stoppage, cessation, dissolution, breakdown; omega, death, demise, bitter end, *Sl.* taps; finale, final act *or* scene *or* chapter, coda; wind-up, last hurrah.

2. breathing out, exhalation, respiration; gasping, puffing, panting.

expire, *v.* **1.** end, come to an end, terminate; stop, discontinue, cease, stop working, fail, wither on the vine; close, come to a close, complete, finish, conclude; run out, run its course, go up in smoke; die out, burn out, be extinguished, burn up.

2. die, perish, decease; fade away, waste away, pass, pass away; go to sleep, give up the ghost; depart, go away, ride into the sunset, go west; write the last chapter, take the full count, go to the last round-up; meet one's Maker, go to heaven, go to the great beyond; join the Heavenly Host, join the invisible *or* angelic choirs; cross the Great Divide, cross the River Styx, say hello to Charon, pay one's fee; say the last goodby, breathe one's last; *Sl.* drop dead, *Sl.* conk out, *Sl.* kick the bucket; exsanguinate, overdose.

3. breathe out, exhale, respire; gasp, puff, pant; sigh, blow, wheeze.

explain, *v.* **1.** define, interpret, explicate, expound, comment on, point out; simplify, make plain, unfold, delineate, put across, spell out, get across; decipher, decode, render intelligible, untangle, unravel; clarify, elucidate, clear up, resolve, solve, reveal; illustrate, throw *or* shed light on, expose, demonstrate, show, make manifest, bare.

2. describe, account for, give an account of, lay open, set forth, give the facts, tell the whole story; justify, warrant, account for, tell one's side of the story, apologize.

explainable, *adj.* See **explicable**.

explanation, *n.* **1.** explication, clarification, definition; interpretation, exegesis, commentary, note; exposition, unfoldment, elucidation, illustration; deduction, conclusion, hypothesis, theory, conception.

2. solution, answer, key, secret, signification, meaning; description, accounting, reason, background; warrant, justification, vindication, mitigation, rationalization; defense, excuse, apology, cover, gloss, alibi.

explanatory, *adj.* descriptive, justificatory, explicative; elucidative, commentarial, illustrative, expressive; interpretive, expository, exegetic.

expletive, *adj.* **1.** unnecessary, unneeded, needless, nonessential, gratuitous.

—n. **2.** filler, filling, padding, wadding; embellishment, ornament, decoration, frill.

3. exclamation, ejaculation, outburst, blurt; curse, oath, obscenity, epithet, *Inf.* swearword, *Inf.* dirty word, *Inf.* cuss word, *Inf.* four-letter word, *Sl.* dirty name.

explicable, *adj.* accountable, definable, solvable, soluble, resolvable, determinable, ascertainable, explainable; understandable, interpretable, intelligible.

explicate, *v.* **1.** develop, evolve, work up *or* out, construct, build, assemble, put together; devise, conceive, construe, concoct, think up, dream up.

2. explain, expound, elucidate, clarify, clear up, make clear; interpret, untangle, unriddle; simplify, put into plain words *or* English, *Inf.* spell out.

explication, *n.* **1.** explanation, exposition, clarification, resolution; description, illustration; interpretation, exegesis; (*of an idea, theory, etc.*) development, formation.

2. key, gloss, note, annotation, word of explanation; critique, criticism, commentary, essay, pandect; treatise, dissertation, thesis, paper, study.

explicit, *adj.* **1.** express, specific, definite, precise, exact, positive, pointed; unequivocal, unambiguous, unqualified, downright, outright, out-and-out, *Sl.* no-nonsense; categorical, unconditional, absolute, fixed, final, peremptory; clear, crystal-clear, manifest, plain, obvious, unmistakable, distinct, well-defined.

2. outspoken, free-spoken, free-speaking, free, bold, unreticent, unrestrained, unreserved, unabashed, uninhibited, unsparing, unshrinking; open, candid, frank, forthright, direct, straightforward, straight-from-the-shoulder, foursquare; plain, plain-spoken, *Inf.* straight-out, *Inf.* flat-footed, *Inf.* matter-of-fact; blunt, bluff, brusque, point-blank.

explode, *v.* **1.** burst, blow up, detonate, fulminate, fly apart, fly into pieces; discharge, blast, go off, report, sound, boom, thunder, roar, bang, pop; let off, set off, fire off, shoot, let fly.

2. rant, rave, rant and rave, rage, bellow, storm; bluster, splutter; fly into a passion, *Inf.* fly off the handle, go into hysterics, have *or* throw a tantrum *or* fit, *Inf.* have a conniption *or* conniption fit, *Inf.* hit the ceiling *or* roof, *Sl.* have a hemorrhage; *All Sl.* blow one's cool, blow a fuse *or* gasket, blow one's top *or* stack, flip, flip one's wig *or* lid, freak *or* freak out.

3. disprove, invalidate, refute, repudiate; discredit, belie, give the lie to, shoot *or* poke full of holes, knock the bottom out of, blow to pieces, blow sky high; mock, lampoon, ridicule.

exploit[1], *n.* **1.** (*all usu. extraordinary*) deed, feat, *Archaic.* gest, act, action; achievement, step, stride, advancement, progress; accomplishment, attainment, acquirement, success.

2. maneuver, move, stroke, blow, coup, stunt, trick; stroke of genius, tour de force.

exploit[2], *v.* **1.** utilize, put to use, use to good advantage, maximize, make the most of; capitalize on, turn to one's advantage, profit from, milk, *U.S. Inf.* cash in on.

2. use, abandon, misuse, walk all over [s.o.], take advantage of; impose upon, trade upon, play on *or* upon; deceive, delude, beguile, trick, hoodwink, cozen, dupe, gull, gudgeon, fool, *Inf.* put something over on, *Inf.* work, *Sl.* take for a ride.

3. promote, further, advance, improve.

exploration, *n.* investigation, inquisition, inquiry, study, analysis, review; survey, *Civ. Eng., Geol.* reconnaissance; research, probe, search; examination, scrutiny, scrutinization, inspection, canvass, close observation *or* watch.

explore, *v.* **1.** traverse, range over, travel over, wander over; check out, take a look at, inspect, survey, reconnoiter; search, prospect.

2. scrutinize, examine, plumb, analyze, take apart, dissect; investigate, look into, pry into, inquire into, canvass, check into; research, probe, go over with a fine-tooth comb; sift, go through, rummage through; go over, review, take stock of; study, pore over, think on, feel out.

explosion, *n.* **1.** blast, discharge, detonation; bang, boom, burst, eruption, crash; rumble, roll, thunder, fulmination; shot, crack, report; salvo, volley, fusillade.

2. outburst, outbreak, burst, flare-up, eruption, upheaval; fit, tantrum, convulsion, spasm, seizure, paroxysm, *Chiefly Brit.* wax, *Brit. Inf.* paddy-whack, *Sl.* wing-ding.

3. sudden increase, acceleration, speedup; mushrooming, burgeoning; population explosion.

explosive, *adj.* **1.** fulminant, fulgurous; eruptive, volcanic, inflammable; loaded, primed; dangerous,

perilous, serious, critical, bad, ugly.
—*n.* **2.** dynamite, TNT, blasting cap, percussion cap; powder, gunpowder; nitroglycerine, cordite, melinite, gelignite, lyddite.

exponent, *n.* **1.** interpreter, explainer, expounder, expositor; advocate, upholder, defender.
2. illustration, representation, exemplification; exemplar, model, paradigm, mirror; symbol, token, indication, index; instance, example, sample, specimen. type.

export, *v.* ship overseas, send abroad; market abroad, sell overseas.

expose, *v.* **1.** endanger, imperil, jeopardize, put in jeopardy, lay open *or* subject to danger; hazard, risk, venture, chance, take a chance, tempt fate, sail too near the wind, fly too close to the sun.
2. uncover, bare, unveil, unsheathe, discase, uncase; divest, strip, undress, unrobe, disrobe, denude, denudate.
3. present to view, exhibit, display, show, indicate, point out, evince, make manifest; take the wraps off, come out of the closet, unveil, unmask, show up; discover, descry, detect, find, uncover, unearth, exhume, dig up, smoke out.
4. bring to light, bring out, make known, reveal, disclose, divulge; tell, impart, inform, relate, utter, *Archaic.* discover, break the news; release, break, report, publish, *Archaic.* divulgate, print; advertise, broadcast, air, vent, ventilate, communicate; blurt out, blab, leak, let out, let slip, let the cat out of the bag, spill the beans; betray, *Inf.* blow the whistle on, *Sl.* blow the lid off, *Sl.* pull the plug on; tattle, tattletale, *All Sl.* squeal, squeak, rat, fink, stool, peach.
5. desert, abandon, forsake, turn one's back on; run out on, strand, *Inf.* ditch, *Sl.* give the deep six, leave high and dry, *Inf.* leave flat; turn out, put out, turn into the street.

exposé, *n.* exposure, revelation, uncovering, unveiling. See **exposure** (*def.* **1**).

exposition, *n.* **1.** fair, bazaar, staple, market, mart, *Inf.* expo; exhibit, exhibition, show, showing, presentation, unveiling, unfurling; mounting, staging, stage show, production, performance; review, retrospective.
2. explanation, explication, illustration, description; clarification; interpretation, exegesis.
3. treatise, discourse, dissertation, thesis, paper, study; critique, commentary, criticism, essay, pandect; key, gloss, note, annotation, word of explanation.
4. display, demonstration, *Inf.* demo, manifestation, representation; revelation, disclosure, divulgence.
5. abandonment, desertion, forsaking, leaving out in the cold, turning one's back on.
6. exposure, openness, nakedness, unprotectedness, defenselessness, helplessness.

expositor, *n.* expounder, explainer, interpreter, exponent; commentator, scholiast; demonstrator, exhibitor.

expository, *adj.* explicative, explanatory, declarative, elucidative; essayistic, expounding, discursive; interpretive, exegetic, hermeneutic; descriptive, illustrative.

expostulate, *v.* remonstrate, plead in protest, argue, reason against, object, protest; admonish, warn, forewarn, caution, exhort, put on one's guard; advise, counsel against, *Archaic.* dissuade, *Archaic.* dehort; reproach, rebuke, disapprove of, complain of.

expostulation, *n.* remonstration, remonstrance, objection, protest, complaint, argument; admonition, warning, caution, exhortation; advice, counsel, *Archaic.* dissuasion, *Archaic.* dehortation; reproach, rebuke; disapproval, disapprobation, deprecation.

exposure, *n.* **1.** disclosure, revelation, exposé, uncovering, unmasking, unveiling, baring, laying open; airing, publication, broadcast, report, communication; divulgement, leak, admission, confession, avowal.
2. endangerment, jeopardy, hazard, risk, openness to danger, subjection to peril; vulnerability, vulnerableness, susceptibility, liability.
3. exposition, turning out, abandonment, desertion, forsaking.
4. frontage, facing, setting, location; aspect, direction, view, outlook.

expound, *v.* **1.** discourse, discuss, descant, make a statement regarding; remark, touch upon, say a word about, say something about; teach, instruct, inform; editorialize, opine, comment, commentate, express one's views, give one's reaction to, give one's observations on, review, criticize, critique.
2. explain, define, interpret, explicate, comment on, point out; delineate, put across, spell out, get across; clarify, elucidate, clear up; solve, resolve, unriddle, reveal.

express, *v.* **1.** verbalize, put into words, word, say, utter, voice, give voice to, breathe, give vent to, enunciate, come out with, blurt out; announce, proclaim, declare, herald, pronounce, set forth, put forth; communicate, inform, tell, speak, give word, mention, point out, bring to [s.o.'s] attention, let [s.o.] know, have one know, give one to understand; explain, define, explicate, comment on; describe, account for, give the facts.
2. state, assert, discourse, discuss, descant, make a statement regarding; remark, say a word about, say something about; editorialize, opine, express one's views, interpret, give one's reaction to, give one's observations on, review, criticize.
3. show, manifest, make manifest, demonstrate, exhibit, evidence, evince, embody; reveal, expose, bare, make known; present, set forth, offer; illustrate, throw *or* shed light on.
4. symbolize, stand for, represent; designate, signify, indicate, delineate, depict.
5. press out, squeeze out, extract.
6. emit, emanate, send forth, give out, exude.
7. **express oneself** air one's views *or* opinions, speak one's mind *or* piece, *Sl.* put in one's two-cents worth; do one's thing, let it all hang out, let it happen, be oneself, be true to oneself.
—*adj.* **8.** explicit, clear, crystal-clear, manifest, plain, obvious, unmistakable, distinct, well-defined; specific, definite, precise, positive, pointed; unequivocal, unambiguous, unqualified, downright, outright, out-and-out, *Sl.* no-nonsense; categorical, unconditional, absolute, fixed, peremptory.
9. duly *or* exactly formed, vivid; accurate, precise, exact, true; faithful, close.
10. quick, fast, direct, summary; rapid, fleet, meteoric, swift, brisk; expeditious, prompt, immediate, instant, instantaneous.
—*n.* **11.** direct train, nonstop train; courier, carrier, runner; dispatch, telex, telegram.

expression, *n.* **1.** verbalization, utterance, enunciation; announcement, proclamation, declaration, pronouncement; communication, informing, mentioning, telling; explanation, definition, explication, description.
2. statement, assertion, discourse, discussion, descant; remark, comment, opinion, editorial, interpretation, observation, criticism.
3. word, term, saying, turn of speech; phrase, idiom,

locution, metaphor, simile, *Rhet.* trope; wording, phrasing, phraseology, choice of words; language, diction, style.
4. manifestation, show, demonstration, illustration, exhibition, evidence, embodiment; presentation, offering; sign, symbol, token, representation; indication, signification.
5. aspect, air, mien, appearance, countenance, look, carriage.
6. tone, intonation, *Grammar.* modulation, enunciation, accent; shading, nuance; interpretation, touch.
7. feeling, emotion, ardor, zeal; pathos, passion, pervading spirit; depth, intensity, power, force.

expressionless, *adj.* **1.** blank, empty, vacuous; dull, dry, unimaginative, boring; wooden, deadpan, poker-faced, straight-faced; unresponsive, undemonstrative, apathetic, unimpassioned.
2. inscrutable, inexplicable, incomprehensible, hidden, mysterious.

expressive, *adj.* **1.** indicative, suggestive, allusive; informative, telling, demonstrative; designative, denotative, denominative, descriptive, representative, delineative.
2. meaningful, fraught with meaning, pregnant, significant, significative, thoughtful; pointed, forceful, direct, emphatic, pithy.
3. sympathetic, full of feeling, emotional, passionate; poignant, moving, evocative, artistic; eloquent, vivid, graphic; deep, intense, powerful.

expropriate, *v.* **1.** seize, commandeer, take possession of, appropriate, misappropriate, arrogate, assume; confiscate, impound, *Law.* distrain; (*all of persons*) abduct, impress, conscript, *Naut.* shanghai, kidnap; wrest from, take from, usurp, accroach; help oneself to, make free with.
2. dispossess, strip, divest, deprive of, *Law.* disseize, bereave; oust, evict, eject, expel, remove, dislodge.
3. steal, plagiarize, copy, *Inf.* lift, *Inf.* crib, forge, counterfeit, pirate, *Euph.* borrow; rob, despoil, thieve; filch, pilfer, purloin, snatch, make off with, walk off with, *Euph.* remove.

expropriation, *n.* **1.** forceful seizure, takeover, appropriation, confiscation, impoundment, (*usu. of persons*) abduction; (*all usu. in reference to military service*) impress, conscript, *Naut.* shanghai, crimp; arrogation, usurpation, accroachment, assumption.
2. dispossession, deprivation, deprival, divestiture, bereavement, *Law.* disseizin; deposition, dislodgment, dismissal, displacement, demotion.
3. theft, thievery, stealing; plagiarism, piracy, pirating, forgery, counterfeiting; robbery, rapine, pillaging, plunder, spoliation, stripping.

expulsion, *n.* **1.** discharge, ejection, pushing out; elimination, excretion, voiding, voidance, evacuation, dislodgment.
2. exile, banishment, expatriation, deportation, transportation; banning, ostracization, excommunication, proscription, marooning, isolation, segregation, outlawing.
3. eviction, rejection, repudiation; *Sl.* the boot, *Inf.* the old heave-ho, ouster, dismissal, removal, firing, sacking, bouncing; cashiering, disbarment, drumming out.

expunge, *v.* **1.** obliterate, extirpate, eradicate, exterminate, annihilate, abolish, discreate; blot out, strike out, stamp out, snuff out, crush out; devastate, destroy, demolish, ravage, desolate, ruin, *Dial.* ruinate, raze; efface, wipe out, do away with, remove, liquidate, purge, leave no vestige *or* trace of; eliminate, put an end to, get rid of, extinguish, bring to an end, dispose of; quash, quell, squelch, crush, vanquish, subdue, squash.
2. erase, rub out, scrape out, scratch out; delete, *Print.* dele, blue-pencil, edit, edit out; cross out, x out, cancel, black out, mark off; wash out, sponge off *or* away; excise, cut, cut out.

expurgate, *v.* censor, purge, cleanse, *Inf.* clean up, sanitize, delete expletives, bowdlerize; weaken, soften, refine, debilitate; castrate, emasculate, pull the teeth from, take the teeth out of, *T.V.* blip.

exquisite, *adj.* **1.** beautiful, attractive, handsome, good-looking, *Scot.* bonny, comely; striking, showy, smart, chic, elegant; small, fragile, delicate, graceful, subtle, ethereal.
2. admirable, excellent, fine, rare, consummate, precious, perfect; choice, select, superior, outstanding, matchless, peerless, incomparable; ornate, splendid, wonderful.
3. intense, acute, keen, piercing, excruciating, sharp, poignant.
4. discriminating, fastidious, sensitive, appreciative; discerning, knowing, educated, trained, refined.

extant, *adj.* existing, existent, in existence, subsistent; surviving, living, alive, present.

extemporaneous, *adj.* **1.** improvised, improvisatory, off-the-cuff, ad-lib, unprepared, unstudied, extempore; impromptu, on-the-spot, spur-of-the-moment, informal; impulsive, unexpected, sudden.
2. makeshift, temporary, impermanent, occasional.

extempore, *adv.* spontaneously, offhand, impromptu, extemporaneously; freely, without restriction, without deliberation, impulsively, suddenly, on the spur of the moment, at a moment's notice; ad lib, off the top of one's head, off the cuff, on the spot.

extemporize, *v.* improvise, ad-lib, play it by ear, wing it, think on one's feet; (*all improvisational*) create, invent, originate, make up, fabricate; compose, perform, execute.

extend, *v.* **1.** spread, outspread, spread out, branch out, *Mil.* deploy; unfold, unfurl, stretch out, draw out, straighten out, open; stretch, spread, sprawl; reach, run, range.
2. offer, proffer, submit; grant, give, bestow, confer, impart, present; hold forth, hold out, reach out, put forth, carry forward, yield.
3. expand, increase, enlarge, make larger, make bigger, make greater, *Chiefly Literary.* greaten, aggrandize; widen, thicken, broaden; dilate, distend, inflate, bloat, puff out, blow up, swell, intumesce, tumefy; fill out, fatten.
4. lengthen, elongate, place at full length; prolong, prolongate, protract, spin out; continue, perpetuate, keep up, string on, carry on, drag on, drag out; maintain, preserve, sustain.
5. develop, enlarge on, expound on *or* upon, detail; magnify, amplify, enhance, deepen, heighten; intensify; concentrate; exaggerate, maximize, make much of, make the most of, overstate.
6. augment, supplement, add to, superadd to; accrue, accumulate, amass; multiply, double, redouble, treble, triple, quadruple.
7. escalate, step up, give a boost to, *Sl.* soup up, *Sl.* hop up, *Sl.* jazz up; accelerate, snowball, mushroom; exacerbate, aggravate.

extension, *n.* **1.** spread, spreading out, branching out, *Mil.* deployment; unfolding, unfurling, stretching out, drawing out, straightening out, opening; stretch, spread, sprawl; diffusion, dissemination, dispersion, dispersal.
2. lengthening, elongation, prolongation, protraction; continuation, perpetuation, stringing on, carrying on, dragging on, dragging out; postponement, de-

ferment, prorogation.

3. expansion, increase, enlargement, aggrandizement; widening, thickening, broadening; dilatation, dilation, distension, inflation; bloating, puffing out, blowing up; swelling, intumescence, tumefaction, puffiness.

4. addition, accretion, increment, accession, access; accrual, accruement, accumulation, cumulation; multiplication, doubling, redoubling, trebling, tripling, quadrupling.

5. augmentation, supplement, annex, annexation; appendage, appendix, addendum, adjunct; branch, wing, ell.

6. magnification, amplification, enhancement, deepening, heightening; intensification, concentration, escalation, acceleration; exaggeration, maximization, overstatement.

7. extent, magnitude, measure, degree, quantity, amount, fullness; capacity, volume, proportions, dimensions, size, gauge; breadth, width, depth, broadness, wideness, height, length; stretch, spread, reach, span; scope, range, play, compass, swing, sweep.

extensive, *adj.* **1.** spacious, extended, expanded, expansive; ample, capacious, voluminous, roomy, commodious; broad, wide, widespread, spread out, outspread, stretched out, outstretched.

2. comprehensive, inclusive, all-inclusive, all-including, all-embracing; thorough, thoroughgoing, exhaustive, complete; out-and-out, entire, radical, *Inf.* wall-to-wall; universal, catholic, worldwide, nationwide, global, cosmopolitan; wide-ranging, far-reaching; infinite, unlimited, unbounded, unrestricted, boundless; wholesale, indiscriminate.

3. lengthy, protracted, prolonged, elongated, sustained; long, longish, overlong, long-drawn; drawn out, dragged out, spun out, strung out; prolix, diffusive, diffuse; interminable, without end.

4. large, large-scale, big, bulky, great; substantial, considerable, sizeable; generous, liberal; immense, vast, massive; gigantic, huge, gargantuan, enormous, colossal, stupendous.

extent, *n.* **1.** magnitude, measure, degree, quantity, amount, fullness; capacity, volume, proportions, dimensions, size, gauge, bulk, content; period, duration, term, continuance; breadth, width, depth, broadness, wideness, height, length; arena, sphere, region, territory; field, tract, distance; stretch, spread, reach, span; district, circuit, area; scope, range, play, compass, swing, sweep; limit, limitation, bounds, borders; latitude, longitude.

2. expanse, space, extension, expansion; spaciousness, amplitude, vastness, immensity, capaciousness, largeness; open space, free space, clearing, opening.

extenuate, *v.* **1.** make less serious, play down, downplay, gloze, smooth over; gloss over, whitewash, cover up, varnish; paint a better picture of, palliate, mitigate, soften; temper, moderate, tone down; attenuate, weaken, lessen, diminish; reduce, decrease, dilute, minimize; make allowances for, apologize for, excuse; rationalize, justify, qualify; refine, rarefy.

2. underestimate, underrate, make light of, *Inf.* kid about; disregard, condone, overlook, downgrade.

extenuation, *n.* mitigation, palliation, tempering, softening, gloss, playing down; varnish, whitewash, coverup; underestimation, downgrading; explanation, interpretation, rationalization.

exterior, *adj.* **1.** outer, external, outside; extrinsic, outward, outdoor, outlying; peripheral, superficial, surface; extraneous, foreign, aline.

—n. **2.** appearance, aspect, demeanor, mien, face; surface, integument, skin, covering, shell, façade; outside, externals, superficiality.

exterminate, *v.* **1.** annihilate, obliterate, eradicate, erase, blot *or* wipe out, *Sl.* mop up, efface, eliminate, extirpate, destroy totally, decimate, liquidate, massacre, kill off, slaughter, butcher, mow down; undo, cut off, put an end to, abolish, extinguish, quench, quash, overthrow; raze, level, tear to the ground, ravage, gut, blast, devastate, ruin, despoil, desolate, demolish, lay in ruins; kill, murder, slay, cut down, put to death, execute, do to death, put to the sword, destroy, assassinate.

2. uproot, root out, deracinate, *Obs.* overruncate.

external, *adj.* exterior, outside, outer. See **exterior** (*def.* **1**).

extinct, *adj.* **1.** non-existing, died out, dead, defunct, gone without a survivor, disappeared from the face of the earth; ended, terminated, finished; gone, lost, evaporated, vanished, departed, abolished; annihilated, wiped out, exterminated, eradicated, extirpated, liquidated.

2. obsolete, out-moded, passé, antiquated, out-of-date.

3. quenched, extinguished, burned out; put out, snuffed out, reduced to ashes.

extinction, *n.* **1.** coming to an end, terminating, dying out; death, nonexistence, nonsurvival.

2. annihilation, extermination, eradication, extirpation, obliteration, destruction.

extinguish, *v.* **1.** snuff out, put out, quench, *Inf.* douse, *Inf.* dinch, blow out, (*of a light*) turn off, (*of a cigar, cigarette*) *Sl.* snub out; smother, suffocate, stifle, damp, choke.

2. extirpate, obliterate, expunge, eradicate, exterminate, annihilate, discreate, abolish; blot out, strike out, stamp out, crush out; devastate, destroy, demolish, ravage, desolate, ruin, *Dial.* ruinate, raze; efface, wipe out, do away with, remove, liquidate, purge, leave no vestige *or* trace of; eliminate, put an end to, get rid of, bring to an end, dispose of; terminate, dissolve, check; quash, quell, suppress, squelch, crush, vanquish, subdue, put down, nip, nip in the bud, *Inf.* put the kibosh on; overthrow, overturn, overwhelm, subvert, topple, defeat, conquer.

3. kill, kill off, slay, slaughter; murder, finish, finish off, *Sl.* do in, *Sl.* zap, sacrifice, mow down.

4. erase, rub out, scrape out, scratch out; wash out, sponge out; delete, *Print.* dele, blue-pencil, edit, edit out; cross out, x out, cancel, black out, mark off.

5. obscure, eclipse, darken, throw into the shade, overshadow, *Inf.* show up, outdo.

6. *Law.* annul, nullify, disannul, declare null and void, render null and void, void, avoid, elide; quash, invalidate, vitiate, vacate, disenact, disestablish; cancel, discharge; suspend, cease, nol-pros, stop, end, discontinue, break off.

extirpate, *v.* **1.** obliterate, exterminate, expunge, eradicate, annihilate, discreate, abolish; blot out, strike out, stamp out, snuff out, crush out; devastate, destroy, demolish, ravage, desolate, ruin, *Dial.* ruinate, raze; efface, wipe out, do away with, remove, liquidate, purge, leave no vestige *or* trace of; eliminate, put an end to, get rid of, extinguish, bring to an end, dispose of; terminate, dissolve, check; quash, quell, squelch, crush, vanquish, subdue, squash; overthrow, overwhelm, overturn, subvert, topple, defeat, conquer.

2. uproot, unroot, pull out by the roots, pull up, pluck up, root out, outroot, deracinate; pull out, draw out, tear out, take out, extract; excise, cut, cut out; unearth, excavate, dig up *or* out, grub up *or* out; weed out, rake out.

extirpation, *n.* **1.** obliteration, extermination, expunction, eradication, annihilation, discreation, abolition, abolishment; devastation, total destruction, demolition, ravagement, desolation, ruin, ruination; effacement, wipe out, removal, liquidation, purgation, leaving no vestige *or* trace of; elimination, putting an end to, extinguishment, extinction, bringing to an end, disposing of; termination, dissolution, check; quashing, suppression, squelching, crushing, vanquishment, squashing; overthrow, overturn, overwhelming, subversion, defeat, conquering.

2. uprooting, unrooting, pulling up, plucking up, pulling out by the roots, rooting out, outrooting, deracination; pulling out, drawing out, wrenching out, tearing out, avulsion, taking out, extraction, evulsion; excision, cutting, cutting out; unearthing, excavation, digging up *or* out, grubbing up *or* out; weeding out, raking out.

extol, *v.* praise, sound the praises of, sing the praises of, cry up, laud, *Archaic.* magnify; approve enthusiastically, hail, commend; eulogize, panegyrize, glorify, bless; exalt, elevate, compliment, flatter; pay tribute to, pay homage to, honor, crown; applaud, acclaim, cheer, celebrate, congratulate, *Archaic.* gratulate.

extoller, *n.* **1.** praiser, applauder, lauder, laudator, exalter, eulogist, encomiast, panegyrist; *Inf.* tout, *Inf.* touter, booster, promoter, fan, devotee, publicist.

2. timeserver, temporizer, *Inf.* back-scratcher; toady, sycophant, tufthunter, claquer, *Inf.* bootlicker; fawner, flatterer, wheedler, cajoler, smooth-talker, *Inf.* soft-soaper.

extort, *v.* **1.** wrest, wrench, tear from, wring, extract; blackmail, milk, squeeze, get out of, *Inf.* bleed, pry out, obtain by force; *Sl.* shake down, *Inf.* put the bite *or* squeeze *or* shake on, put the arm on [s.o.], *Sl.* lean on *or* against [s.o.], put the screws to [s.o.]; take away from, deprive of, bereave of, despoil, fleece, *Sl.* skin.

2. compel, make, coerce, force, threaten; require, demand, insist on *or* upon, command, enjoin; call for, necessitate, tax, *Obs.* task, requisition; request, ask, elicit, draw out.

extortion, *n.* **1.** blackmail, shakedown, exaction, *Inf.* the squeeze; milking, *Inf.* bleeding, bloodsucking; wresting, wrenching, wringing, extraction, elicitation; badger game, skin game, *Sl.* murphy.

2. tribute, ransom, exacted *or* enforced payment; bribe, hush money, *Inf.* protection, *Inf.* payola, graft.

extortionate, *adj.* **1.** exorbitant, expensive; excessive, outrageous. See **exorbitant** (*defs.* **1, 2**).

2. usurious, bloodsucking, wringing, exacting; avaricious, rapacious, ravening, voracious, greedy; sordid, mean, venal.

extortionist, *n.* extortioner, blackmailer, shakedown artist; bloodsucker, *Sl.* bleeder, leech, vampire, vulture; exacter, wrester, wrencher, wringer; rack-renter.

extra, *adj.* **1.** additional, accessory, auxiliary, ancillary, supplemental, supplementary, adventitious; secondary, subsidiary, collateral, nonessential, incidental; more, new, fresh, plus, further, farther, other; odd, spare, reserve, surplus, leftover, unused.

—n. **2.** addition, accessory, appendage, appurtenance; coda, supplement, addendum, appendix; bonus, premium, dividend, tip, gratuity, lagniappe.

3. surcharge, markup, added cost, unexpected cost *or* expense.

4. tabloid, special, special edition.

5. supernumerary, *Inf.* super, walk-on, walking gentleman *or* lady, *Inf.* spear-carrier.

—adv. **6.** additionally, in addition, also, as well, besides, too, to boot, into the bargain; beyond, plus, on top of, over and above.

7. unusually, uncommonly, incredibly, unexpectedly, uncustomarily; exceptionally, markedly, notably, remarkably, strikingly.

extract, *v.* **1.** get out by force, draw forth, draw out, pull out, pry out, drag out, take out; wrest, extort, extricate; remove, exact, eliminate; tear out, pluck out, wring from, wrench, root up, extirpate, deracinate, eradicate; distill, squeeze out, express, press out.

2. deduce, elicit, derive, obtain, get; evolve, evoke, bring forth.

3. excerpt, quote, cite, cull, glean.

—n. **4.** excerpt, quotation, quote, citation, selection, abstract; analect, clipping, cutting, note, minute.

5. distillation, distillate, concentrate, concentration, solution, *Pharm.* decoction; essence, quintessence.

extraction, *n.* **1.** pulling out, drawing out, removal, elimination; extrication, eradication, extirpation, deracination.

2. ancestry, lineage, descent; parentage, family, genealogy; race, breed, stock, strain, blood, stirps, pedigree; origin, birth.

3. extract, distillate. See **extract** (*def.* **5**).

extraneous, *adj.* **1.** extrinsic, external, adventitious, accidental, incidental, unessential; ulterior, outlying; outlandish, foreign, alien, strange, exotic.

2. irrelevant, immaterial, inapplicable, inapt, inapposite, inappropriate, impertinent, unrelated, unconnected, off the subject; nothing to do with it; superfluous, redundant, unnecessary, needless, nonessential, beside the point *or* mark, beside the question.

extraordinary, *adj.* **1.** uncommon, unusual, rare, unique, exceptional, special, singular, signal, one of a kind; strange, curious, odd, peculiar, bizarre, abnormal, paranormal.

2. striking, remarkable, surprising, amazing, astonishing, extraordinaire; glorious, grand, sublime, miraculous, wondrous, sublime; impressive, breathtaking, fantastic, fabulous, *Inf.* unreal, *Inf.* far out, *Inf.* super, *Sl.* the greatest, *Sl.* too much.

3. unfamiliar, unheard of; unparalleled, unprecedented, unexpected, *Sl.* bang-up; unbelievable, preposterous, *Inf.* damnedest, *Sl.* hell of a; out of the way, unconventional, *Inf.* way out.

4. lofty, majestic, august, huge, vast, enormous; monstrous, grotesque, prodigious.

5. important, eminent, illustrious, famous, prominent, renowned; distinguished, noteworthy, noted, notable.

extravagance, *n.* **1.** prodigality, lavishness, profligacy, wastefulness, recklessness, spendthrift ways, folly, excess, exorbitance.

2. excessiveness, immoderateness, unreasonableness, undueness, inordinateness; outrageousness, preposterousness, monstrousness; absurdity, flightiness, capriciousness, wildness, fantasy, *Inf.* craziness; superfluity, supererogation, oversufficiency, too much of a good thing, overkill, *Inf.* too much, *Inf.* over the top.

extravagant, *adj.* **1.** excessive, extreme, inordinate, profuse; prodigal, improvident, wasteful, spendthrift, thriftless, penny wise and pound foolish; spending lavishly, squandering, unthrifty, imprudent.

2. unreasonable, outrageous, unrestrained, wild, immoderate, preposterous; irregular, foolish, flighty, impracticable, exceeding the bounds of reason, absurd, irrational.

3. exorbitant, expensive, overpriced, dear, high, costly, *Inf.* steep, *Inf.* stiff.

4. ethereal, fanciful, quixotic, romantic, imaginary, visionary; high-flown, fantastic, fabulous, legendary.

extravaganza, *n.* spectacle, spectacular, *Inf.* spec, pageant; production, exposition, review, stage show; panorama, glitter and tinsel, splurge, phantasmagoria, *Inf.* wild show, *Inf.* circus, *Inf.* three-ring circus, *Inf.*

sideshow; farce, burlesque, comic opera, opera buffa, opéra bouffe, opéra comique, operetta.

extreme, *adj.* **1.** exceptional, extraordinary, out of the ordinary, notable, outstanding, remarkable, *Sl.* hell of a; unusual, abnormal, unconventional, different, offbeat, exotic, foreign, strange, odd, bizarre, weird, eccentric, *Inf.* way-out, *Sl.* far-out; egregious, flagrant, glaring.

2. maximum, maximal, max., greatest, most, utmost, uttermost; supreme, paramount, superlative, *Inf.* almighty; highest, uppermost, upper, topmost, top, tiptop, summital, apical.

3. lowest, least, slightest, smallest, minimal, minim.

4. farthest, remotest, outermost, outlying, outer, apogeal, apogean, marginal, peripheral; distant, remote, far-off, faraway; last, hindmost, rearmost, endmost, ultimate, *Fr. dernier*; final, terminal, terminating, ending, finishing, closing, concluding, culminating.

5. radical, drastic, complete, total, thorough, thoroughgoing; sheer, utter, downright, out-and-out, unqualified, unmitigated, arrant; excessive, extravagant, exorbitant, outrageous, inordinate, undue, unnecessary, uncalled for, disproportionate; unlimited, beyond the bounds, *Inf.* steep, *Fr. outré*; immoderate, intemperate, overindulgent, uncontrolled, unrestrained, unbridled, violent, severe; unreasonable, irrational, uncompromising, fanatical, zealous, rabid, *Inf.* all-fired.

—n. **6.** maximum, max., most, uttermost, utmost, *Math.* extremum; apex, vertex, apogee, acme, zenith, *Latin. ne plus ultra*; summit, pinnacle, peak, height, top, tip, tiptop; best, finest, prime, *U.S. Sl.* the most, *U.S. Sl.* the greatest, *Sl.* the tops.

7. opposite, pole, contrary, counter, contradiction, antonym, the other end of the scale.

8. excessiveness, excess, extravagance, exorbitance, outrageousness, inordinance, disproportion; immoderation, intemperance, overindulgence; unreasonableness, irrationality, fanaticalness, radicalness, zealousness, rabidity, rabidness.

9. extremity, crisis, emergency, exigency, pressing situation; adversity, pinch, plight, quandary, dire strait *or* circumstance, time of stress.

10. last resort, *Fr. dernier resort*, risk, chance, going out on a limb; ultimatum.

extremely, *adv.* **1.** exceptionally, extraordinarily, unusually, uncommonly, abnormally; remarkably, notably, damned, danged, *U.S. Inf.* darned, *Sl.* hell of a.

2. very, exceedingly, excessively, inordinately, disproportionately, to a degree, *Sl.* almighty; immoderately, intemperately, overindulgently, uncontrollably, unrestrainedly; exorbitantly, to the nth degree, outrageously, drastically, radically; zealously, rabidly, fanatically, *Both Chiefly U.S. Inf.* all-fired, all-firedly.

extremist, *n.* radical, ultra, ultraist, immoderate, sansculotte, *Politics.* Jacobin; zealot, fanatic, raver, *Sl.* crazy; leftist, left-winger, radical, Communist, *Derog. Sl.* commie, Bolshevik, Red, *Sl.* pinko, *Sl.* pink, *Inf.* Wobbly; reactionary, rightist, right-winger, conservative, ultraconservative, champion of the status quo, diehard, Bircher, Birchite, Bourbon, Hunker, Tory; *Inf.* hard-hat.

extremity, *n.* **1.** limit, outer limit, farthest point, horizon, the end of the earth; ambit, bound, boundary, border, frontier; periphery, margin, edge, rim, brim, brow, lip, ridge, verge, brink; ultimate, end, finale, termination, terminal, terminus.

2. limb, appendage, arm, leg, hand, foot; finger, toe, fingertips, digits.

3. crisis, emergency, exigency, pressing situation; pinch, plight, quandary, time of stress; adversity, hard luck, dire strait *or* circumstance, misfortune, setback, hardship, destitution, indigence, trouble, disaster.

4. maximum, max., most, uttermost, utmost, extreme, *Math.* extremum; apex, vertex, apogee, acme, zenith, *Latin. ne plus ultra*; summit, pinnacle, peak, height, top, tiptop; best, finest, prime, *U.S. Sl.* the most, *U.S. Sl.* the greatest, *Sl.* the tops.

5. risk, chance, going out on a limb, heroic act, valor above and beyond the call of duty; last resort, *Fr. dernier resort;* ultimatum.

6. excessiveness, excess, extravagance, exorbitance, outrageousness, inordinance, disproportionateness; immoderation, intemperance, overindulgence; unreasonableness, irrationality, fanaticalness, radicalness, zealousness, rabidity, rabidness; abnormality, unusualness, exceptionality, exceptionalness; unconventionality, differentness, foreignness, strangeness, oddness, bizarreness, weirdness, eccentricity.

extricate, *v.* disentangle, untangle, disembarrass, get [s.o.] off the hook, disencumber, relieve; extract, remove, withdraw, pull *or* get [s.o.] out of; disengage, disconnect, disjoin, detach, separate from; disenthrall, disimprison, rescue, ransom, free, liberate, set free, set *or* turn loose, deliver, emancipate, save; release, let loose, untie, unbond, unfetter, unyoke, unshackle, unchain, unmanacle, *Archaic.* untruss.

extrinsic, *adj.* **1.** unessential, unnecessary, unneeded, dispensable; irrelevant, impertinent, unrelative, unrelated, nonrelative, nonrelated; foreign, alien, adventitious.

2. external, outside, outward, environmental; extrinsical, uninherent, uninnate.

extrovert, *n.* socializer, outgoing person, mingler, *Inf.* mixer, everybody's buddy *or* friend; hail-fellow, hail-fellow well met, *Inf.* glad-hander, *Inf.* backslapper.

extroverted, *adj.* outgoing, outwardly directed, unself-centered, unselfish, giving of one's self; extrovert, extrovertish; sociable, socializing, social, people-oriented; friendly, amicable, congenial, hail-fellow; hearty, exuberant, effervescent, bubbly.

extrude, *v.* **1.** expel, oust, force out, press *or* push out, eject, thrust out, *Inf.* throw out, *Inf.* kick out. See **expel (*def.* 1)**.

2. protrude, stick out, poke out, hang out; project, extend, jut out, beetle.

exuberance, *n.* **1.** exuberancy, lavishness, extravagance, prodigality, unlimitedness, unreservedness, whole-heartedness; generosity, generousness, liberality, liberalism, liberalness, bountifulness, bounteousness, munificence.

2. ebullience, yeastiness, high-spiritedness, exhilaration, buoyancy, bounce; liveliness, vivacity, animation, sparkle, effervescence; enthusiasm, zest, energy, *Inf.* zip, vitality, animal spirits.

3. profusion, luxuriance, lushness, richness, rankness, teemingness, prodigality; abundance, plenty, plenitude, bounty, cornucopia, horn of plenty; plentifulness, plenteousness, copiousness, superabundance.

exuberant, *adj.* **1.** lavish, extravagant, prodigal, unlimited, unreserved, wholehearted; generous, liberal, bountiful, bounteous, munificent.

2. ebullient, yeasty, high-spirited, exhilarated, buoyant, bouncy; animated, sparkling, effervescent, enthused, enthusiastic, irrepressible; zestful, energetic, full of life, lively, vivacious.

3. profuse, luxuriant, lush, thriving, rank; abundant, plentiful, copious, prolific; rich, flush, abounding, overflowing, teeming, superabundant.

exude, *v.* **1.** sweat, perspire, ooze out, secrete, excrete, discharge; send out, give off, emit, send forth; emanate, issue, well out *or* forth; flow out, pour out, outpour, gush, spurt, squirt, shoot, jet.

2. ooze out, seep, filter, filtrate, leak; trickle, drizzle, dribble, drip, drop.

exult, *v.* rejoice, jubilate, triumph, glory; glory in, sing about, crow; jump for joy, skip, dance, make merry, revel; be elated, be exhilarated, be in high spirits, be in transport, be in ecstasy; be glad, be delighted.

exultant, *adj.* rejoicing, triumphant, jubilant, joyous, overjoyed; exhilarated, excited, elated, delighted, gleeful; transported, ecstatic, euphoric, exalted, walking *or* treading on air, in seventh heaven, on cloud nine, *Dial.* in hog heaven, *Dial.* in high cotton.

exultation, *n.* triumph, glory; rejoicing, jubilation, joyousness, delight, gladness; excitement, exhilaration, elation, joy, cloud nine, seventh heaven, exaltation; rapture, transport, ecstasy; reveling, revelry, paean.

eye, *n.* **1.** oculus, orb, *Sl.* peeper, *Sl.* glim, *Sl.* lamp; eyeball, iris, white of the eye.

2. sight, vision, perception, discernment, ken; look, glance, gaze, glimpse.

3. regard, view, aim, intention, respect; viewpoint, judgment, estimation, opinion; appreciation, awareness, sensitivity.

4. watch, observance, observation, lookout, surveillance, vigilance; regard, notice, survey.

5. hole, perforation, foramen; aperture, peep, peephole; buttonhole, eyelet, loop.

6. center, middle, midst, thick; hub, heart, kernel, core.

7. see eye to eye agree, concur, coincide, stand with; accord, harmonize, jibe with, chime in with, be in unison.

—*v.* **8.** view, see, behold, catch sight of, look at, *Inf.* lay eyes on, *Inf.* eyeball, *Sl.* lamp; watch, keep in view, keep an eye on; observe, look on, survey, scan; scrutinize, inspect, pour over, peer at; stare at, goggle, gawk at, ogle, make eyes at, give [s.o.] the eye, leer at.

eye doctor, *n.* ophthalmologist, oculist, optometrist.

eyesight, *n.* sight, vision, perception, discernment; range of vision, gaze, glance, view; observation, contemplation, regard, survey; inspection, scrutiny.

eyesore, *n.* defacement, disfigurement, deformity, impairment, mar, scar; defect, blemish, blot, blight, contamination, pollution, ugliness; offense, atrocity.

eyewitness, *n.* testifier, witness; observer, onlooker, bystander; spectator, watcher, viewer, beholder, gazer, gaper, gawker; passer-by, looker-on.

F

fable, *n.* **1.** apologue, allegory, parable, moral, bestiary; nursery rhyme, fairy tale, ballad, rhyme, song.
2. fiction, tale, tall tale *or* story, *Inf.* yarn, story, adventure.
3. legend, myth, tradition, old wives' tale; lay, epic, saga, chronicle, *Fr. roman-fleuve*, annal, history.
4. untruth, lie, falsehood, fib, prevarication, white lie, *Inf.* taradiddle; fabrication, invention, figment, concoction, *Inf.* whopper, fish story; canard, cock and bull story, mare's nest.
—*v.* **5.** lie, fib, prevaricate, misstate, misrepresent, misreport; make up, concoct, invent, fabricate; make believe, pretend, affect, sham; spin a yarn, tell a tall tale.
6. repute, suppose, imagine, think, believe; take for, assume, presume, presuppose, consider, regard.

fabled, *adj.* **1.** legendary, storied, fabulous, mythical; chimerical, imaginary, figmental, fanciful; romantic, idealistic.
2. fictitious, made-up, make-believe, invented, imagined; unreal, notional, unfounded; assumed, supposed, reputed; feigned, contrived, concocted, conjured.

fabric, *n.* **1.** cloth, textile, weave, loom, dry goods, broadcloth; stuff, material, piece, bolt; jute, burlap, gunny, sackcloth; tapestry, towelling, cambric, linen, lawn; mohair, alpaca, vicuña, Angora, wool, worsted; jersey, homespun, duffel, canvas, khaki, khadi, khaddar, kersey; tweed, serge, baize, shalloon; felt, frieze, velvet, velour, corduroy; flannel, cotton, muslin, drill, mull, nainsook, jaconet; calico, fustian, moleskin, sharkskin; dimity, voile, gingham, madras, poplin, seersucker; chintz, silk, cretonne, foulard, damask, grosgrain, brocade; satin, taffeta, ninon, chiffon, sarcenet, lace, chenille.
2. texture, nap, tissue, pile, weaving, weave; intertexture, contexture, crossing, conformation; grain, surface, granulation, feel, touch, denier, make.
3. framework, structure, outline, scheme, cadre, frame, contour, profile; make-up, build, organization, constitution, configuration, formulation.
4. building, edifice, structure, erection; tower, dome, house, skyscraper.

fabricate, *v.* **1.** construct, build, frame, fashion, figure; manufacture, produce, put out, make.
2. assemble, set up, compose, compile; erect, elevate, raise, put up, rear.
3. devise, formulate, design, mint, coin, hatch; invent, make up, think up; create, concoct, imagine, think, originate.
4. forge, fake, counterfeit, contrive, falsify; rig, set up, trump up, hatch, spin, concoct, *Inf.* pull out of a hat, *Inf.* cook up, *Sl.* hoke up; prevaricate, lie, fib.

fabrication, *n.* **1.** construction, manufacture, production, assemblage, composition, formation, building; structure, organization, complex, architecture, fabric, erection, frame, mold, build, physique, skeleton.
2. origination, invention, creation, concoction, devisal, contrivance; formulation, design, original work.
3. forgery, fake, counterfeit, sham, falsification, minting, coinage; falsehood, lie, fib, untruth, prevarication, mendacity, untruthfulness; fiction, figment, fable, yarn, tall tale *or* story, fish story, cock and bull story, *Inf.* song and dance.

fabulous, *adj.* **1.** incredible, unbelievable, inconceivable; amazing, astounding, astonishing, prodigious, *Scot.* unco; stupendous, tremendous, extraordinary, phenomenal, wondrous, miraculous; remarkable, exceptional, *Australian.* bonzer, *Inf.* out of this world.
2. marvelous, superb, great, wonderful, *Inf.* super, *Inf.* neat, *Sl.* cool, *Sl.* keen, *Sl.* boss; *Sl.* the bee's knees, *Sl.* the cat's meow, *Sl.* the cat's pajamas, *Sl.* far out, *Sl.* fab; whopping, thumping, thundering, rattling, howling, *Brit.* father and mother of.
3. fabled, storied, celebrated, traditional, legendary, mythical, mythic; chimerical, figmental, fanciful, imaginary, fantastic, fantastical; visionary, dreamy, quixotic, extravagant, eidetic; romantic, idealistic, storybook, fairytale, Cinderellaesque.
4. fictitious, fictional, made-up, make-believe, *Inf.* just pretend, pretended, feigned; invented, contrived, concocted, coined, fabricated; unreal, unfounded, notional, suppositional, hypothetical, suppositious.

façade, *n.* **1.** front, face, forefront, frontage, exterior.
2. illusion, pretense, false impression, affectation; disguise, mask, masquerade, *Sl.* put-on, false colors, camouflage, veneer, fake veneer.

face, *n.* **1.** countenance, visage, physiognomy, features, lineaments; *Sl.* mug, *Sl.* pan, *Sl.* phiz, *Sl.* puss, *Sl.* kisser; silhouette, profile; makeup, cosmetics, war paint.
2. expression, look, mien, aspect, air, demeanor; smile, grin, grimace, smirk, sneer, frown, pout, *Fr. moue.*
3. prestige, repute, good repute, dignity, family honor.
4. mask, camouflage, veneer, façade, covering; illusion, false impression, pretense, disguise, masquerade; appearance, semblance, surface.
5. *Informal.* audacity, effrontery, boldness, impudence, nerve, self-assurance; brass, gall, unmitigated

gall, *Inf.* cheek, *Sl.* lip, sauciness, *Inf.* sauce, chutzpa.
6. exterior, outside, front, forepart, frontage, frontal; vital *or* right side, working surface, facet.
7. **face to face** opposite, confronting, conflicting, vis-à-vis; intimately, à deux, tête-à-tête, eyeball-to-eyeball, face-on.
—*v.* **8.** contemplate, look at, gaze at, observe, view, survey, eye.
9. front on, front toward, stand opposite to.
10. encounter, meet, confront; brave, buck, dare, challenge, duel, defy, beard; oppose, resist, withstand, grapple with, keep at bay.
11. coat, cover, superimpose, incrust; envelop, encase, veneer, wash; (*all of stone*) surface, polish, dress, level, sand, smooth, finish.
12. **face up to** acknowledge, admit, face the music; confront, meet head on, deal with, cope with, brazen out *or* through.

facet, *n.* aspect, phase, characteristic, side, angle, slant, twist; factor, particular, item, detail, point, element.

facetious, *adj.* **1.** tongue-in-cheek, unserious, not serious, joking, jesting, *Inf.* joshing, *Inf.* kidding, *Inf.* fooling around.
2. funny, humorous, comical; jocular, jocose, waggish, witty, *Archaic.* facete; droll, humorsome, whimsical.
3. frivolous, flighty, giddy, dizzy; merry, mirthful, jovial; playful, sportive.

facile, *adj.* **1.** adept, proficient, expert, artful, masterful, masterly; deft, adroit, dexterous, ambidextrous, handy, skillful, skilled, *Brit. Dial.* feat.
2. easy, simple, elementary, snap, *Sl.* cinchy.
3. fluent, flowing, free, smooth; complaisant, easygoing, bland, mild; unconstrained, affable, agreeable, gracious, graceful, suave; urbane, glib, superficial.
4. influenceable, acquiescent, responsive, obedient, obeyant; compliant, cooperative, willing; flexible, pliant, pliable, manageable, tractable, ductile, malleable; yielding, submissive, deferential, docile.

facilitate, *v.* **1.** ease, smooth, simplify, uncomplicate, clear; relieve, assuage, disburden, disencumber; alleviate, allay, mitigate, lessen, abate, reduce, lighten.
2. assist, aid, help, befriend; forward, advance, promote, encourage, further, foster, open the door for, pave the way for, make way for, clear the way for; support, back, abet, sustain.

facility, *n.* **1.** edifice, building, structure, plant; complex, system, network.
2. easiness, simpleness, conducibleness, conduceability, conduciveness; feasibility, feasibleness, practicability, practicableness.
3. benefit, aid, means, resource, advantage, convenience, opportunity.
4. gift, talent, endowment, aptness, aptitude; ability, ableness, faculty, capability, capableness; adeptness, proficiency, address, expertness, masterfulness, readiness; deftness, adroitness, skillfulness, skill, dexterity, ambidexterity, knack, turn, bent.
5. ease, fluency, smoothness, suaveness, suavity, flowingness; affability, complaisance, easygoingness; finesse, grace, graciousness, urbanity.

facing, *n.* **1.** decoration, veneer, coating, protection; front, false front, façade.
2. lining, interfacing, reinforcement.

facsimile, *n.* copy, replica, reproduction, representation, likeness, portrait, photograph; image, semblance, resemblance, reflex; duplicate, carbon, photocopy, *Trademark.* Xerox copy, *Trademark.* Mimeograph, *Inf.* mimeo, *Inf.* ditto, *Inf.* dup., *Inf.* fax; reprint, transcript, apograph; simulation, imitation, (*of jewels*) paste; forgery, counterfeit, fake, sham.

fact, *n.* **1.** detail, item, particular, point, component, element, feature, contingency, factor; circumstance, deed, act, *Fr. fait accompli*; phenomenon, incident, event, affair, occurrence, happening, experience, episode.
2. certainty, certitude, truth, verity, reality, actuality, factuality; naked truth, unvarnished truth, gospel, scripture, *Sl.* the God's-honest truth.
3. *Often* **facts** information, data; the whole *or* straight story, *Inf.* the inside info *or* dope, *Inf.* low down, *Inf.* the score, *Inf.* the scoop, *Sl.* the straight goods.

faction, *n.* **1.** contingent, sector, section, division, side, splinter party; bloc, caucus, party, group, coalition, band, ring, gang, *Inf.* crowd, crew; clique, coterie, clan, set, circle, *Inf.* push; camorra, cabal, camarilla, junto, junta, confederacy.
2. infighting, dissension, discord, strife, contention, quarrelling, factiousness; clash, clashing, jar, disharmony, controversy, disagreement, variance, difference of opinion; upheaval, tumult, turbulence, storminess, fighting; rebellion, revolt, insurrection, mutiny; disruption, rupture, division, split, schism, splintering.
3. intrigue, stratagem, plot, complot, conspiracy; connivance, scheme, design.

factious, *adj.* dissentious, discordant, contentious, quarrelsome, at loggerheads; dissident, disharmonious, disagreeing, disputatious, at odds, at variance, at sixes and sevens; disruptive, disrupting, divisive, troublemaking; rebellious, revolting, insurrectionary, mutinous, insubordinate.

factitious, *adj.* **1.** artificial, contrived, affected, insincere, ungenuine, unauthentic, supposititious; faked, simulated, assumed, put-on, pretended, unnatural, forced; fake, bogus, sham, mock, counterfeit, pinchbeck; engineered, rigged, set-up.
2. made, man-made, manufactured, crafted, fabricated, built, constructed.

factor, *n.* **1.** element, part, component, constituent, ingredient; particular, item, detail, point, facet, aspect, thing, consideration.
2. agent, instrument, consignee, functionary; representative, proxy; middleman, intermediary, medium, go-between.
3. financier, backer, supporter, sponsor, patron, moneyman, angel.

factory, *n.* plant, shop, workshop, sweatshop, manufactory, mill, foundry, metalworks; works.

factotum, *n.* do-all, general servant, chief servant, man *or* maid of all work, *Brit. Inf.* slavey; jack of all trades, handyman, *Inf.* Mr. Fix-it.

factual, *adj.* **1.** true-to-life, realistic, credible, believable, natural; accurate, exact, precise, close, faithful, honest, strict; literal, verbatim, word-for-word, line-for-line.
2. correct, right, objective, straight; unbiased, unprejudiced, undistorted, unwarped; unexaggerated, unembellished, unvarnished, unadulterated, pure, gospel.
3. actual, true, real, veracious, *Obs.* veritable, *Brit. Dial.* gradely, *Both Archaic.* sooth, soothfast; authentic, genuine, bona fide; valid, sound, confirmed; unimaginary, unfictitious.

faculty, *n.* **1.** ability, facility, aptitude, genius, wits; gift, talent, flair, bent, turn, knack; skill, technique, skillfulness, dexterity; adroitness, deftness, proficiency; inclination, proclivity, propensity.
2. capacity, capability, potentiality; power, potency, force; function, operation, process; endowment, gift, attribute, property, characteristic, feature, virtue; sense.

3. staff, teacher, schoolmasters, *Chiefly Brit.* masters, (*in the English universities*) dons, instructors, coaches, tutors, academics; professors, professorate, professoriate, academicians, lecturers, pedagogues.
4. profession, occupation, vocation, calling, métier; discipline, area, field, branch.
5. power, prerogative; license, right, privilege; permission, authorization, sanction.

fad, *n.* vogue, fashion, style, trend, ton, mode, *Inf.* last word, *Fr. dernier cri, Sl.* the thing, *Sl.* latest or newest thing; craze, mania, rage, furor; whim, fancy, crotchet.

fade, *v.* **1.** blanch, blench, bleach, pale, whiten, gray, wash out; dim, cloud, grow dull, lose luster *or* brightness; etiolate, achromatize, decolor, decolorize.
2. languish, waste away, *Dial.* dwine, droop, flag, sag, faint; wither, wilt, shrivel, decay, molder, rot; decline, wane, ebb, fall off; fail, deteriorate, degenerate.
3. dissolve, melt away, deliquesce; disappear, evanesce, vanish, vanish into thin air, leave no trace, perish, die.
4. lessen, abate, diminish, decrease, slacken; subside, let up, intermit, cease; taper off, drop off, obsolesce, die out.

fag, *v.* **1.** tire, tire out, exhaust, weary, jade; fatigue, prostrate, *Inf.* tucker out, wear out, knock out, *Sl.* poop, do in; spend, strain, droop, flag.
—*n.* **2.** menial, slave, flunky, *Inf.* gofer; drudge, plodder, moiler, laborer.
3. *Slang.* homosexual. See **homosexual** (*def.* **2**).
4. *Slang.* cigarette, *Inf.* butt. See **cigarette**.

fagot, *n.* **1.** bundle of sticks, firewood, kindling; branches, twigs, fascine.
2. bundle, *Sl.* bindle, bale; bunch, cluster; pack, packet, parcel.

fail, *v.* **1.** go wrong, abort, miscarry, not succeed, be defeated, be frustrated; flounder, falter, slip, trip, stumble, blunder; shipwreck, run aground, come to grief, meet with disaster, *Inf.* come a cropper; miss the mark, miss the boat, *Sl.* blow it, *Sl.* flush it, *Sl.* bomb, *Sl.* lay an egg, *Sl.* strike out, wash out, labor in vain, come to nothing; fizzle, fink out, *Inf.* flop, *Sl.* bite the dust, lose the day, end in smoke, fall flat, go to wrack and ruin, have had it.
2. fall short, stop short of, not reach, fall by the wayside; be deficient, be insufficient, be defective, be wanting, be lacking; not pass muster, not make the grade, *Sl.* not cut the mustard, flunk; disappoint, prove inadequate, turn out badly.
3. dwindle, decline, decay, deteriorate; pine away, languish, fade away, disappear, cease, pass away; wane, give out, droop, ebb, sink, collapse; sicken, weaken, flag, lose vigor, crumble, be on the ropes, *Sl.* be on the downslide, be on one's last legs.
4. go out of business, go bankrupt, go under, *Inf.* fold *or* fold up, close down, drown in red ink, go to smash, default on payment, not pay.
5. forsake, desert, omit to perform, neglect to observe; ignore, slight, evade, cut, give the go-by to, shut one's eyes to; avoid, escape, renounce, forswear.

failing, *n.* **1.** failure, nonsuccess, nonfulfillment; miscarriage, abortion; no-go, vain attempt; fizzle, fiasco, botch, blunder, washout, flash in the pan.
2. shortcoming, fault, imperfection, defect, weakness; frailty, foible, flaw, blemish, infirmity, blind side.
3. delinquency, dereliction, negligence, inadvertency, omission; indiscretion, offense, peccadillo, mistake, slip, error; recreancy, backsliding, apostasy.
4. wasting away, languor, decline, decay, deterioration, debilitation; collapse, decrepitude, *Pathol.* atony *Pathol.* asthenia, *Pathol.* cachexia.

failure, *n.* **1.** lack of success, nonsuccess, nonfulfillment, defeat, frustration, inefficacy; mishap, misfortune, mischance; miscarriage, abortion; blunder, error, slip, trip, stumble, faux pas; botch, muff, mess, muddle; fizzle, fiasco, *Inf.* washout; vain attempt, wild-goose chase, sleeveless errand; checkmate, deathblow, tragedy, debacle, sinking ship; rebuff, repulse, overthrow, discomfiture, beating, drubbing, *Inf.* body blow.
2. delinquency, dereliction, negligence, inadvertency; nonobservance, omission, default, oversight, pretermission; indiscretion, peccadillo, mistake; recreancy, backsliding, apostasy.
3. insufficiency, deficiency, want, lack, dearth, scarcity.
4. deterioration, decline, decay, wasting away, failing, languor, debilitation; collapse, decrepitude, *Pathol.* atony, *Pathol.* asthenia, *Pathol.* cachexia.
5. bankruptcy, insolvency, financial disaster; crash, wreck, ruination, downfall.
6. unsuccessful person *or* thing, also-ran, lead balloon, *Inf.* flop, *Sl.* bomb, *Sl.* brodie, *Inf.* clunker, *Inf.* lemon, *Inf.* dud, *Sl.* clinker, *Inf.* bummer, *Sl.* bust; down-and-outer, loser, schlemiel, *Sl.* dog.

faint, *adj.* **1.** pale, dim, distant, obscure, faded, weak, feeble, thin, faltering, trembling; low, soft, gentle, dulcet, whispered, muted, stifled, muffled; dull, indistinct, unclear, inaudible, imperceptible.
2. dizzy, *Inf.* woozy, vertiginous, lighthearted, giddy; weak, exhausted, tired, worn out, limp, drooping, about to drop.
3. cowardly, timorous, timid, fearful, afraid, frightened, afraid of one's shadow; unmanly, faint-hearted, lily-livered, white-livered, *Inf.* chicken-hearted, *Inf.* chicken-livered, *Inf.* pantywaist, *Inf.* yellow, *Sl.* yellow-bellied, *Sl.* candy-assed.
—*v.* **4.** lose consciousness, swoon, pass out, black out, *Pathol.* suffer syncope; limpen, go limp, crumple, succumb, give way, keel over, drop, collapse, *Sl.* conk out, die, faint dead away.
5. grow weak, lose strength, languish, droop, fade, flag, diminish, fall off; fail, decline, go downhill, sink.
—*n.* **6.** unconsciousness, blackout, swoon, fainting spell, *Pathol.* syncope, *Chiefly Scot.* dwalm.

fair[1], *adj.* **1.** unbiased, unprejudiced, impartial, uncolored; disinterested, dispassionate, detached; even-handed, equitable, just, *Inf.* square, objective.
2. proper, legitimate, straightforward, aboveboard.
3. ample, sufficient, adequate, OK, enough; moderate, middling, so-so, *Fr. comme ci, comme ça,* indifferent; mediocre, ordinary, common, pretty good, not bad; decent, goodish; passable, tolerable, respectable, reasonable, satisfactory.
4. sunny, bright, cloudless, clear, pleasant; fine, calm, halcyon.
5. unblemished, untarnished, spotless, unstained; impeccable, pure, good, clean, virtuous.
6. blonde, blondish, light brown, pale; creamy, peaches-and-cream, strawberry-blonde.
7. good-looking, comely, pretty, bonny, attractive, well-favored, lovely; beautiful, *Chiefly Literary.* beauteous, pulchritudinous, handsome; dainty, delicate; charming, sweet, enchanting.
8. courteous, gracious, polite, civil, fair-spoken; affable, friendly, agreeable, personable; civilized, suave.

fair[2], *n.* **1.** exhibition, show, showing, display, exhibit; livestock show, farm show, horse show; county fair, state fair, harvest fair, country fair, 4-H fair, Grange fair; exposition, *Inf.* expo.
2. market, mart, flea market, bazaar, exchange,

marketplace, open-air market, farmer's market, antique show, dealers' show.

fairly, *adv.* **1.** equitably, justly, impartially, dispassionately; rightly, legitimately, properly, honestly, candidly, reasonably.

2. moderately, tolerably, passably; amply, sufficiently, adequately; somewhat, sort of, rather, pretty well.

3. actually, completely, totally, fully; positively, decidedly, absolutely.

4. clearly, obviously, evidently, distinctly, plainly, openly.

fairness, *n.* **1.** justice, justness, equity, equitableness, impartiality; probity, uprightness, integrity, honesty, veracity, rectitude; good faith, *Latin. bona fides*, scrupulousness, conscientiousness.

2. handsomeness, comeliness, attractiveness; beauty, pulchritude, loveliness; charm, winsomeness.

fairy, *n.* fay, pixy, peri, sylph, nymph; sprite, nix, nixie, kelpie; Puck, Oberon, Mab, Titania, Tinkerbell; elf, brownie, leprechaun, troll, kobold.

fairyland, *n.* dreamland, cloudland, Cloud Cuckooland, Land of Nod, Oz, never-never land, the Hundred Acre Wood, Middle Earth, forest of Arden, happy valley, enchanted forest; paradise, Shangri-la.

faith, *n.* **1.** belief, credence, conviction; trust, reliance, dependence; confidence, sureness, assuredness, certainty, certitude; expectation, aspiration, hope, hopefulness, optimism, buoyancy.

2. religion, persuasion, denomination, sect; belief, doctrine, teaching, dogma, creed; tenet, principle, position, policy; opinion, feeling, intuition.

3. duteousness, obedience, compliance; devotedness, devotion, dedication, consecration, allegiance, single-heartedness, patriotism; loyalty, loyalness, faithfulness, fidelity, fealty, trueness, true-heartedness; steadfastness, steadiness, unchangingness, constancy, abidingness, lastingness, enduringness, permanence.

faithful, *adj.* **1.** loyal, allegiant, true, *Scot.* leal, true-hearted; devoted, patriotic, dedicated, steadfast, steady-going, unchanging, incorruptible; staunch, true-blue, yeomanly, unwavering, unswerving, firm, stable, supportive.

2. conscientious, scrupulous, punctilious, meticulous, careful; particular, finical, finicky, fussy; thorough, minute, detailed, scientific, methodical, nice, mathematical; critical, demanding, fastidious; strict, severe, rigorous, rigid, unbending, unyielding, ungiving.

3. reliable, trusted, dependable, good, trustworthy, trusty, tried and true; honest, sincere, truthful, veracious, true to one's word; upright, moral, virtuous, high-principled.

4. close, accurate, exact, precise; correct, unerring, *Inf.* on the mark, on target, on the money, *Inf.* right on, *Sl.* spot on, on the button, on the dot, *Inf.* on the nose; right, just, true, factual, actual, strict, literal, true to life; authentic, real, sound, valid; flawless, faultless, perfect, defectless, errorless.

—n. **5. the faithful** believers, loyal members, congregation, *Fr. les fidèles*, brethren.

faithless, *adj.* **1.** unbelieving, disbelieving, skeptical, incredulous, doubting; freethinking, agnostic, atheistic.

2. disloyal, unfaithful, untrue, traitorous, treacherous, perfidious; false, false-hearted, double-tongued, untrustworthy, dishonest, dishonorable, unscrupulous, unprincipled; deceptive, deceitful, two-faced, fraudulent, hypocritical, lost to shame, dead to honor; unstable, unsteady, fickle, inconstant, shifting, unreliable, mercurial, vacillating, wavering, fluctuating.

faithlessness, *n.* **1.** infidelity, unfaithfulness, disloyalty, inconstancy, recreancy, dereliction; breach of trust, dishonesty, fraudulence, double-dealing, perfidy; betrayal, treachery, traitorousness, treason.

2. doubt, skepticism, incredulity, uncertainty, dubiety, dubiosity; mistrust, distrust, suspicion, unbelief, freethinking, Pyrrhonism; irreligion, impiety, blasphemy; agnosticism, atheism.

fake, *v.* **1.** counterfeit, invent, forge, fabricate, manufacture, *Brit.* coin; concoct, hatch, create, make up; lie, fib, tell a lie *or* fib *or* story.

2. falsify, alter, modify; whitewash, disguise, color, paint a rosy picture, doctor up, gloss *or* varnish over.

3. pretend, feign, sham, malinger, dissemble, act, make believe, play the role of; affect, put on, assume, take on; (*all fraudulently*) simulate, imitate, copy, duplicate, mimic, ape.

—n. **4.** counterfeit, two-dollar bill, wooden nickle, brummagem; fraud, imposture, imposition, hoax, artifice, ruse, delusion.

5. faker, imposter, deceiver, mountebank, charlatan, quack, empiric, *Inf.* phony, *Australian.* bunyip; feigner, pretender, malingerer, imitator; falsifier, counterfeiter, copier, plagiarist.

6. fabrication, fiction, contrivance, concoction, *Inf.* story; falsehood, lie, white lie, fib, untruth, half truth.

—adj. **7.** counterfeit, fraudulent, imitation, not genuine, *Inf.* phony; bogus, spurious, supposititious, pinchbeck, bastardly, *Australian.* bunyip.

8. false, unreal, insincere, mock, ersatz, synthetic, plastic, *Sl.* hokey; artificial, factitious, contrived, fictitious; assumed, put-on, pseudo; specious, meretricious, theatrical; pretended, feigned, simulated, make-believe, sham, flash.

fakir, *n.* mendicant monk, dervish, religious ascetic, holy beggar.

falderal, *n.* **1.** nonsense, gibberish, Jabberwocky, babble, babbling, babblement, *Fr. bavardage*; twaddle, twaddling, *Both Brit.* twattle, twattling; blather, blathering, drivel, driveling, drool, drooling; jargon, *Sl.* jive, Greek, *Chiefly Southern U.S.* Choctaw; hocus-pocus, mumbo-jumbo, abracadabra, open-sesame, fiddle-de-dee; moonshine, gobbledegook, humbug, foam, froth, bunkum *or* buncombe, *Sl.* bunk, *U.S. Sl.* blah; flummery, *Inf.* hokum, *Sl.* applesauce, *Sl.* eyewash; rubbish, *Sl.* tripe, refuse, *Dial.* culch, chaff, trash, *Inf.* truck, trumpery; tommyrot, *Inf.* rot, *Sl.* garbage, *Sl.* crap, *Sl.* crock, *Sl.* bull; balderdash, hogwash, swill, *Sl.* horsefeathers; stuff, stuff and nonsense, *Inf.* bosh, *Brit. Inf.* gammon, *Brit. Sl.* tosh; fudge, foolishness, folly, rigmarole *or* rigamarole, amphigory; footle, *Inf.* malarkey, *Sl.* bushwa, *Sl.* baloney, *Sl.* bilge *or* bilge water, *Sl.* meshugaas, *Scot. and North Eng.* haver; poppycock, *Inf.* fiddle-faddle, *Inf.* piffle, *Inf.* hooey, *Inf.* kibosh, *Inf.* flapdoodle; idle talk, *Inf.* gab, *Sl.* gas, *Sl.* hot air; jabber, prate, patter, gabble; clack, clatter, rattling, *Sl.* runningoff *or* on at the mouth; chatter, prattle, chippering, cackle; chit-chat, chitter-chatter, small talk, *Anglo-Indian.* bukh.

2. trifle, trinket, gewgaw, bagatelle, kickshaw; gimcrack, whim-wham, knickknack; bauble, small ornament, charm, bit of jewelry, bijou; frippery, gimcrackery, trumpery.

fall, *v.* **1.** descend, come *or* go down, drop down, gravitate, sink; slip, slide, backslide; trip, trip over one's own feet, stumble, fall down, take a spill, tumble; go head over heels, pitch, plunge, plummet, dive, take a nosedive; drop, plop, plump, *Inf.* plunk; topple, fall over, keel over, collapse, slump, crumple, fall into a heap.

2. decline, depreciate, fall off, drop off, dip, lower, go down, decrease, slump; diminish, flag, wane, ebb, recede, give way; subside, abate, let up, lessen; dwindle, waste away, languish, droop, faint, fade, fail, deteriorate, go downhill, die.

3. slope, slant, incline downwards, tilt; hand down, reach *or* extend downward, droop.

4. sin, err, transgress, offend, trespass, go astray, fall from grace; lapse, falter, slip, backslide, go downhill, deteriorate, degenerate, go to pot *or* to the dogs; be degraded, be demoted, be reduced, be humbled.

5. succumb, give in *or* up, submit, yield, cry quits, surrender, capitulate; be taken, be defeated, be overthrown, be taken over.

6. drop dead, die, perish; be slain, be killed.

7. come, fall on *or* upon, descend upon, envelop.

8. come to pass, happen, *Archaic.* arrive, chance, come about, befall, occur, take place; turn out, result, issue, stem from, arise.

9. (*all of trees and animals*) fell, chop down, cut down, knock down, strike down, shoot down.

10. **fall back on** *or* **upon a.** fall back to, retreat to, withdraw to, retire to, draw back to. **b.** have recourse to, resort to, take to, make use of, use, employ, call into action, call into play, call upon; rely on, depend on, count on *or* upon, trust in.

11. **fall down** *Informal.* disappoint, fail, fall short.

12. **fall for** *Slang.* **a.** be deceived by, be fooled by, be taken in by, be duped by. **b.** fall in love with, become infatuated with.

13. **fall in** sink inward, cave in, collapse, come down about one's ears, crash in; break down, fall apart, crumble.

14. **fall off a.** separate from, withdraw, retreat, back away, back off *or* down; retire, step aside *or* down, yield, give way. **b.** deteriorate, decline, decrease, diminish. See **fall** (*def.* **2**).

15. **fall on** *or* **upon a.** assault, attack, assail, set upon, rush upon, go for, swoop down on. **b.** experience, encounter, run into, bump into, meet with, come upon *or* into. **c.** chance upon, happen upon, light on *or* upon, hit upon *or* on, discover.

16. **fall out a.** quarrel, disagree, squabble, argue, fight, dispute, bicker, wrangle, altercate. **b.** happen, occur. See **fall** (*def.* **8**).

17. **fall to** begin, go to, start, start in on, commence, set about, go about, get the ball rolling, get the show on the road, get under way; tackle, take on, undertake; apply oneself, put one's shoulder to the wheel, put one's nose to the grindstone.

—n. **18.** drop, plop, plump, *Inf.* plunk; descent, falling, sinking, gravitation; slip, slide, backslide; trip, stumble, spill, tumble, plunge, dive, nosedive; plummeting, pitching, toppling, falling over, keeling over.

19. decline, depreciation, falling off, drop-off, dip, lowering, decrease; diminution, flagging, wane, ebb, recession; subsidence, abatement, lessening, letup; dwindling, drooping, fading, deterioration, going downhill, slipping; faint, slump, collapse.

20. **falls** waterfall, cataract, cascade.

21. downward slope, declivity, downhill, downgrade, descent, decline; incline, inclination, slant, grade, slope; angle, pitch, tilt.

22. sin, error, transgression, offense, trespass; the Fall, original sin, fall from grace, aboriginal catastrophe; downfall, lapse, slip, backslide; deterioration, degeneration, depravation, debasement, abasement, degradation; demotion, setback, comedown, humbling.

23. surrender, capitulation, giving up *or* in, submission, yielding; capture, overthrow, taking, seizure.

fallacious, *adj.* **1.** false, untrue, not true, devoid of truth, not right; erroneous, mistaken, incorrect, *Sl.* all wet, all wrong; spurious, counterfeit, fictitious, *U.S.* bogus.

2. delusive, deceptive, deceiving, underhanded, illusory, illusive; deceitful, insidious, guileful, fraudulent.

3. illogical, *Sl.* cockeyed, unsound, faulty, flawed; inaccurate, inexact imprecise, unprecise, inconsistent; unsubstantial, unfounded, ungrounded, groundless, untenable, invalid.

fallacy, *n.* **1.** false *or* mistaken notion, misconception, misbelief, misapprehension, misjudgment, miscalculation; error, mistake, solecism, heresy; illusion, delusion, bubble, chimera, fantasy.

2. sophistry, sophism, casuistry, *Logic.* paralogism, *Latin. non sequitur.*

3. erroneousness, mistakenness, wrongness, fallaciousness.

fallibility, *n.* imperfection, errability, errancy, liability to error.

fallible, *adj.* imperfect, errable, errant, error-prone, liable *or* open to error.

fallout, *n.* **1.** settling, radioactive fallout, *Inf.* radioactive snow *or* rain.

2. aftermath, aftereffect, afterclap, outgrowth; consequence, effect, result, outcome, event, issue; wake, backwash, trail, reaction, turnout, repercussion, reverberation.

fallow[1], *adj.* uncultivated, unplowed, untilled, unseeded, unplanted, unsown, unsowed; empty, neglected, unused, idle, dormant, resting, inactive, inert; barren, unproductive, unyielding, unfructuous, unfruitful, fruitless; uncultivable, uncultivatable, exhausted, depleted, worn out, impoverished; poor, bare, bald, arid, dry, waste.

fallow[2], *adj.* pale-yellow, sallow, light-brown, pale-brown, dun, grayish-brown.

false, *adj.* **1.** untrue, untruthful, unveracious, mendacious, devoid of truth, not right; lying, fibbing, perjured, forsworn; fabricative, fabricated, trumped up.

2. erroneous, mistaken, incorrect, amiss, wrong, all wrong, *Sl.* all wet, *Sl.* full of beans *or* prunes, *Sl.* full of hot air; inaccurate, inexact, imprecise, unprecise; faulty, flawed, unsound, illogical, *Sl.* cockeyed; in error, erring, in the wrong; astray, wide of the mark, *Inf.* off base, *Sl.* off the beam, *Sl.* at sea, *Sl.* out in left field; off key, off pitch, not in tune.

3. treacherous, traitorous, treasonous, disloyal, perfidious, unfaithful, faithless, inconstant, recreant; insincere, disingenuous, false-hearted, affected, two-faced; dishonest, dishonorable, untrustworthy; Machiavellian, cunning, conniving, double-dealing, wily, sly; cantish, pharisaic, tartuffish, hypocritical.

4. deceptive, deceitful, fallacious, delusive, disappointing; misleading, roundabout, circuitous, hedging, double-tongued; artful, tricky, meretricious, shifty, duplicitous; evasive, ambiguous, equivocal, questionable, dubious, suspicious.

5. counterfeit, forged, fraudulent, imitation, fake, faked, *Inf.* phony; not genuine, bogus, spurious, suppositious, bastardly; pretended, feigned, simulated, make-believe, sham, flash; unreal, mock, ersatz, synthetic; artificial, factitious, contrived, *Sl.* hokey, fictitious; assumed, put-on, pseudo; specious, theatrical.

falsehood, *n.* **1.** lie, fib, untruth, false statement, mendacity, inveracity; fabrication, fiction, make-believe; canard, false story, hoax; false swearing, perjury; exaggeration, distortion, false coloring; perversion, misstatement, misrepresentation, falsification.

2. deception, deceit, deceptiveness, craftiness, artifice; guile, duplicity, trickery; evasion, ambiguity, concealment; untruthfulness, mendaciousness.

3. prevarication, equivocation; dissimulation, feigning, dissembling; malingering, faking, pretending.
4. hypocrisy, pharisaism, casuistry, double-talk; double-dealing, two-facedness, dishonesty; perfidy, disloyalty, treachery, bad faith, Judas kiss; lip service, cant, insincerity; cajolery, flattery, false praise.
5. pretense, show, hollowness, fraud, sham; deception, trick, humbug, *Inf.* flimflam, *Inf.* flam; counterfeit, imitation, reproduction, fake, *Inf.* phony.

falsetto, *n.* artificially high voice, squeak, squeal; soprano, counter-tenor.

falsify, *v.* **1.** misrepresent, misstate, misquote; pervert, distort, adulterate; overstate, overdo, overstress, overcharge, overcolor; hyperbolize, overdraw, exaggerate, stretch, stretch the point, strain, (*of writing or speech*) pad; color, paint, paint in glowing terms, doctor, dress up; oversell, *Inf.* play up, *Inf.* build up *or* on; equivocate, prevaricate, hedge; trump up, hatch, spin, concoct, cook up.
2. dissemble, dissimulate, conceal; feign, pretend, fake, act, put on, sham, malinger; counterfeit, forge, *Brit. Inf.* coin.
3. disprove, show to be false, prove unsound, confute; refute, rebut, contradict, oppose.

falter, *v.* **1.** hesitate, waver, hover, hang in the balance, vacillate, oscillate; fluctuate, blow hot and cold, alternate, go back and forth between; be undecided, *Inf.* straddle the fence, dilly-dally, shilly-shally; hem and haw, delay, waste time, trifle, dawdle, take one's time; tarry, loiter, linger, lag behind, hang back, drag one's feet, shuffle, shamble.
2. break, give way, halt, pause, stop briefly; stammer, stutter, lisp, speak haltingly *or* brokenly.
3. stumble, trip, fall down, slip, slide; move unsteadily, stagger, reel, sway, totter, teeter, teeter-totter; dodder, tremble, shake, quiver; limp, hobble, hitch.
4. lose strength, weaken, deteriorate, go downhill, fail, slip, backslide, lapse, relapse, regress, worsen; wane, flag, ebb, diminish, fade, faint, die away.

fame, *n.* **1.** renown, bays, celebrity, stardom, illustriousness, greatness, preeminence, superiority, supremacy; eminence, notability, note, distinction, mark; prominence, rank, standing, prestige, weight, importance, account.
2. honor, laurels, glory, praise, kudos, éclat, acclamation, acclaim; popularity, vogue, favor, esteem, high regard, admiration, respect.
3. reputation, repute, name, notoriety; public regard, estimation, regard, opinion, judgment.

familiar, *adj.* **1.** known, well-known, common, frequent, repeated; habitual, accustomed, customary, wonted, traditional, conventional; usual, ordinary, everyday, commonplace, trite, stock, cliché, hackneyed.
2. *usu.* **familiar with** conversant with, acquainted with, instructed in, knowledgeable in, versed in; apprised of, informed of, privy to, in on; aware of, alive to, conscious of, cognizant of.
3. informal, unceremonious, natural, casual, simple; unconstrained, free, open, unreserved; easy, free-and-easy, relaxed, comfortable, at ease, at home.
4. intimate, close, *Scot.* pack, dear, confidential, bosom; clubby, chummy, hob-and-nob, hand and glove, *Inf.* thick, *Inf.* thick as thieves, *Sl.* buddy-buddy, *Sl.* palsy-walsy; friendly, neighborly, amicable, sociable.
5. overfamiliar, disrespectful, taking liberties; forward, intrusive, presumptuous; bold, impudent, saucy.
6. domesticated, acclimatized, broken, tame; housebroken; domestic, familial, household; docile, tractable, gentle, meek.
—*n.* **7.** close friend, Achates, sidekick, constant companion, shadow, alter ego, other self, *Scot. and North Eng.* marrow; comrade, *Obs.* copemate, chum, crony, *U.S. Inf.* buddy, *Inf.* pal; confidant, *Inf.* bosom buddy, roommate, bunkmate, *Sl.* bunkie; lover, soulmate, bedfellow, intimate, *Fr. intime.*
8. colleague, confrere, associate, consociate, cohort, compeer, peer, mate; teammate, co-worker, fellow worker, *Sl.* benchie, *Sl.* benchmate.

familiarity, *n.* **1.** knowledge, mastery, comprehension, understanding, grasp, handle, hold, *Sl.* fix; acquaintance, conversance, personal knowledge, experience, association; recognition, realization, cognizance, awareness.
2. friendliness, affablity, agreeableness; sociability, sociableness, neighborliness; courtesy, kindness, kindliness, good will, benevolence.
3. friendship, companionship, fellowship; acquaintanceship, association; intimacy, closeness, affinity.
4. informality, unceremoniousness, unreservedness; openness, candor, candidness, frankness; naturalness, casualness, ease, freedom.
5. overfamiliarity, liberties, disrespect; presumption, presumptuousness, impudence, impertinence, boldness; impropriety, indecorum, unseemliness.

familiarize, *v.* **1.** acquaint, make familiar with, make conversant with; initiate in, indoctrinate in, enlighten, inform; educate, teach, instruct, tutor, school; prime, prepare, coach, advise.
2. habituate, accustom, make used to; inure, harden, toughen, season, temper, anneal; adapt, acclimate, acclimatize, naturalize, domesticate; break in, train, drill, ingrain, make routine, discipline.
3. introduce, present, bring forward, bring into notice, bring before the public, make well-known, bring into common knowledge *or* use.

family, *n.* **1.** parents and children, household, ménage; children, *Inf.* kids, brood, generation; relatives, relations, *Inf.* folks, people, kin, kinsmen, kinfolk, next of kin, kith and kin; descendants, offspring, offshoots, progeny, issue, seed, posterity, scions.
2. ancestry, ancestral line, lineage, descent, parentage, birth, derivation, extraction, filiation; dynasty, house, tribe, clan; race, strain, stock, breed, bloodline, pedigree, stem, branch, stirps; heredity, genealogy, family tree; heritage, background, past, history, roots; nobility, noble *or* high birth, aristocracy, blue blood.
3. class, genus, species, kind, type, order.

famine, *n.* **1.** scarcity of food, large-scale food shortage, bare subsistence.
2. hunger, starvation, inanition, *Rare.* famishment; fast, diet, xerophagy, Lent; privation, deprivation, half rations, *Chiefly Brit.* short-commons, *Psychiatry.* anorexia.
3. dearth, scarcity, scarceness, lack, want; deficiency, shortness, shortage, drought, insufficiency, stint; scantness, paucity, exiguity, meagerness, rareness; sparseness, seldomness, fewness, poorness, barrenness; depletion, exhaustion.

famished, *adj.* hungry, ravenous, famishing, starving, starved; voracious, edacious, craving; empty, malnourished, undernourished; hollow.

famous, *adj.* famed, renowned, celebrated, well-known, prominent, *Inf.* name, *Inf.* big-name; noted, notable, eminent, preeminent, esteemed, respected, venerable, distinguished, *Archaic.* eximious; illustrious, great, grand, glorious, radiant, brilliant, lustrous; honored, exalted, acclaimed, much-touted, big-time, on the map, popular, well-liked; immortal, fabled, legendary, historical, memorable.

fan[1], *n.* **1.** blower, air conditioner, air cooler, ventilator, aerator; palm leaf, flabellum, (*both esp. in India*) punkah, thermantidote.

—*v.* **2.** ventilate, air, aerate; air-condition, air-cool; cool, chill, refrigerate; winnow, blow upon, stir up a breeze; refresh, freshen, revive, revitalize.

3. arouse, agitate, excite, stimulate, suscitate, foment, impassion, move, stir up, work up, whip up, fire up; inflame, enkindle, ignite, touch off; incite, instigate, provoke, stir the embers, add fuel to the flames.

4. spread, spread out, outspread, lay out, open up; unfurl, unfold, stretch out.

fan[2], *n.* **1.** devotee, enthusiast, aficionado, *Inf.* buff, *Inf.* hound, *Sl.* bug, *Sl.* nut; addict, *Inf.* fiend, *Sl.* junkie, *Sl.* freak; satellite, claqueur, (*all usu. of adolescent girls*) (*in the 40s*) bobbysoxer, (*in the 60s*) teenybopper, (*in the 70s*) groupie.

2. votary, champion, follower, disciple, adherent; zealot, partisan, bigot, fanatic; visionary, cultist, sectary.

3. promoter, supporter, *Inf.* pusher, *Inf.* booster, *Inf.* arm-waver; chauvinist, jingoist.

fanatic, *n.* **1.** zealot, partisan, bigot, sectarian; extremist, radical; devotee, votary, champion, disciple. See **fan** (*defs.* **1, 3**).

—*adj.* **2.** fanatical, zealous, extremist; frenzied, frenetic, phrenetic, *Sl.* off the wall. See **fanatical**.

fanatical, *adj.* **1.** partisan, biased, partial, prejudiced; narrow-minded, intolerant, dogmatic, stubborn, obstinate; uncompromising, extreme, radical, unreasonable.

2. enthusiastic, ardent, fervent, eager, keen, anxious, *Inf.* wild; heated, vehement, fervid, perfervid; *Inf.* all fired up, *Inf.* psyched *or* psyched up, *Sl.* hopped up, *Sl.* ape; zealous, agog, passionate, *Inf.* gung-ho, *Inf.* rah-rah; possessed, fanatic, *Sl.* hung up, rabid; frenzied, frenetic, phrenetic, hysterical, *Sl.* off the wall.

fanaticism, *n.* **1.** devotion, devotedness, fetishism; monomania, single-mindedness, infatuation; enthusiasm, zeal, zealotry, feverishness, passion; insanity, frenzy, hysteria.

2. dogmatism, bigotry, intolerance, close-mindedness, narrow-mindedness; prejudice, bias, partiality.

fanciful, *adj.* **1.** capricious, whimsical, frivolous, extravagant, flighty, irresponsible, unstable; unpredictable, erratic, irregular, eccentric, odd; strange, bizarre, queer, outlandish, freakish, freaky; ridiculous, fantastic, crazy.

2. imaginative, original, inventive, creative; visionary, impractical, impracticable, quixotic, romantic, poetic.

3. fancied, imaginary, unreal, illusory, visionary; imagined, made-up, make-believe, mythical, fairytale.

fancy, *n.* **1.** imagination, creativity, originality; conception, origination, generation, creation, invention, fabrication, formation.

2. mental image, visualization, picture; conception, concept, thought, notion, idea, abstraction, conceptualization; perception, view, opinion, understanding, belief, impression, sentiment, feeling.

3. daydream, reverie, fantasy, fiction, make-believe, fable, myth, unreality; illusion, figment, vision, mirage, hallucination; phantom, phantasm, apparition, ghost, specter, eidolon, chimera.

4. caprice, whim, whimsy, *Archaic.* megrim, vagary, humor; odd notion, crotchet, kink, *Archaic.* maggot; quirk, peculiarity, eccentricity.

5. inclination, set, bent, leaning, tendency; predilection, propensity, proclivity, predisposal, predisposedness, disposition; preference, partiality, attraction, liking, fondness, taste, penchant; desire, wish, longing, yearning, hankering, *Inf.* yen, *Sl.* itch, *Sl.* letch.

6. critical judgment, taste, sense, eye, perception, discernment, discrimination.

7. trend, rage, fad, craze, mania, latest thing; style, fashion, *Brit.* twig, mode, vogue, look.

—*adj.* **8.** choice, prime, select, quality, grade A, A number 1, the best; custom, special, deluxe, luxury, luxurious, sumptuous, elegant, posh, *Sl.* classy, *Sl.* snazzy, *Sl.* ritzy.

9. ornamental, decorative; decorated, adorned, embellished, embroidered; elaborate, rich, lavish, ornate, baroque, rococo, gingerbread; florid, showy, ostentatious, overdone.

10. whimsical, capricious, flightly, irregular, fanciful. See **fanciful** (*def.* **1**).

—*v.* **11.** picture, visualize, envisage, envision, imagine, image, ideate, think, dream, daydream, fantasize; conceive, think up, *Inf.* dream up, make up, conjure up, *Inf.* feature.

12. think, suppose, imagine, suspect, surmise, guess, conjecture, infer; presume, assume, take for granted.

13. take a liking to, like, go for, be attracted to; be inclined towards, be prone to, be disposed *or* predisposed toward, prefer; have a fancy for, have an eye for, have a desire for, have a yen for; hanker after, yearn for, long for, wish for, desire, want, covet; lust after, burn for, *Inf.* be wild *or* mad about, *Sl.* have the hots for, *Inf.* lech after.

fanfare, *n.* **1.** flourish, fanfaron, trumpet blast, trumpet-call, sound of horn, horn blowing; din, blare, blast.

2. show, display, do, stir, commotion, hullabaloo, *Inf.* whop-de-do, *Sl.* hoopla, *Sl.* ballyhoo, *Sl.* hype; hubbub, brouhaha, ruckus, rumpus, tumult; bustle, fuss, *Inf.* to-do.

fanfaron, *n.* **1.** braggart, swaggerer, gascon, braggadocio, trumpeter, blowhard, *Inf.* windbag, *Sl.* gasbag, hot air merchant, *Fr. soi-disant*, blatherskite.

2. See **fanfare** (*def.* **1**).

fanfaronade, *n.* bragging, braggadocio, swaggering, boasting; bravado, bluff, bluster, bombast, rant; nonsense, tommyrot, *Inf.* flapdoodle, balderdash, *Inf.* bosh, *Inf.* bunkum, *Sl.* bunk.

fantasize, *v.* dream, daydream, build castles in the air, ride a magic carpet, see things, have visions, hallucinate, *Sl.* trip; imagine, envision, speculate, consider, let the mind roam, give free rein to the imagination; star gaze, muse, mull, reflect, ponder, wonder about.

fantastic, *adj.* **1.** imaginary, visionary, romantic; unreal, unsubstantial, illusive, illusory, farfetched, *Inf.* far out.

2. whimsical, capricious, absurd, ridiculous, ludicrous; odd, strange, queer, eccentric, peculiar, quaint, freakish; extravagant, rococo, baroque, showy, ostentatious; grotesque, bizarre, outlandish, fabulous; phantasmagoric, nightmarish, Kafkaesque; irrational, mad, wild, crazy.

fantasy, *n.* **1.** imagination, originality, creativity, resourcefulness, inventiveness, fancy.

2. image, conception, conceptualization, perception, reflection; vision, dream, fancy, daydream; hallucination, illusion, phantasmagoria, mirage, vapor, delusion; phantasm, shadow, specter, chimera, hobgoblin, phantom; aberration, haunt, *Archaic.* maggot, fear, horror, haunting fear, nightmare.

3. whimsy, whim, caprice, figment, flight, flight of fancy, notion, vagary, conceit; drollery, craziness, crazy notion *or* idea, *Inf.* screwball *or* wacky idea; implausibility, unlikelihood, peculiar notion.

4. myth, legend, romance, mystery, adventure, fairy tale; horror story, ghost story, spooky tale, *Inf.* chiller,

Inf. thriller, *Sl.* hair-raiser, *Inf.* spine-tingler; science fiction; farce, absurdity, nonsense, wild story, tall tale, whopper, folk story; *All Music.* fantasia, potpourri, medley.

far, *adv.* **1.** afar, far off, far away, a long way off, *Inf.* a good way off.

2. by far a. incomparably, immeasurably, inimitably; very much, by a great deal, by a long way, *Inf.* by a long shot, far and away. **b.** plainly, clearly, obviously, manifestly, visibly; definitely, positively, decidedly, beyond the shadow of a doubt, beyond doubt.

3. far and wide broadly, widely, extensively, far and near; abroad.

4. far out *Slang.* **a.** unconventional, uncommon, unusual, unique, unorthodox, *Sl.* kinky; marching to a different drummer. **b.** radical, extreme, ultra, out of this world, *Inf.* way out, *Inf.* too much. **c.** recondite, esoteric, abstruse.

5. go far advance, progress, go places, make headway, rise in the world, get on, *Inf.* get ahead; make a name for oneself, cut a swath, set the world on fire, *Inf.* make a noise in the world.

—adj. **6.** remote, distant, removed, far-off, faraway; far-flung, way-off, out of the way, Godforsaken, back of beyond; inaccessible, out of reach.

7. farther, further, thither, yonder, yon, ulterior.

8. few and far between infrequent, uncommon, unusual; rare, scarce, seldom seen, seldom met with, almost unheard of, *Inf.* hard to come by.

farce, *n.* **1.** comedy, low comedy, broad *or* raw comedy, slapstick, *Theat.* farcetta; burlesque, lampoon, satire, parody, travesty, caricature.

2. foolery, tomfoolery, buffoonery, clownishness; ridiculousness, nonsense, absurdity.

3. mockery, sham, child's play, joke, jest, *Sl.* goof.

farcical, *adj.* absurd, ludicrous, ridiculous, preposterous; foolish, silly, nonsensical, asinine; funny, comical, humorous, laughable; droll, amusing, facetious.

fare, *n.* **1.** price, fee, charge, cost, exaction, payment; hire, rental, fee.

2. food, nutriment, aliment, viands, edibles, bread; victuals, provisions, rations, commons, comestibles; meals, board, sustenance, nourishment; diet, regimen, menu, table.

—v. **3.** eat, feed, partake, break bread; breakfast, lunch, sup; dine, feast, banquet, *Sl.* eat high off the hog.

4. get on, get along, do; make out, make it, live through [s.t.], come out of [s.t.], land.

5. (*used impersonally*) proceed, go, happen; turn out, end up, finish up.

farewell, *interj.* **1.** good-by, Godspeed, God be with you, adios, adieu, sayonara, aloha; bye, *Inf.* bye-bye, see you later, *Inf.* so long, *Inf.* toodle-oo, *Chiefly Brit.* ta ta, *It. Inf. ciao*; until we meet again, *Fr. au revoir, It. arrivederci, Ger. auf Wiedersehen, Span. hasta la vista, Latin. Vale, Latin. vive valeque*; bon voyage, have a good *or* nice trip.

—v. **2.** good-by, aloha, sayonara, *Latin. Vale*; swan song, valedictory, *Inf.* send-off.

3. departure, parting, leave-taking, going away, congé; adieu, valediction.

far-fetched, *adj.* improbable, implausible, unlikely, remote; unbelievable, incredible, doubtful, *Inf.* hard to swallow, *Inf.* fishy, *Sl.* smelly; strained, labored, remotely connected, forced, unnatural, artificial, affected, *Inf.* hokey, unheard of, *Inf.* far out, *Inf.* bull; quaint, strange, fantastic, *Inf.* hard to take.

farm, *n.* **1.** grange, homestead, farmstead, farmplace, *Archaic.* farmhold, *Brit.* farmery, *Brit.* croft, *Brit.* homecroft, *Scot. and North Eng.* steading; ranch, rancho, rancheria, hacienda; plantation, manor, manor farm, *Inf.* spread.

—v. **2.** cultivate, dress, till, till the soil, work, work the land; plow, spade, dig, delve, hoe, harrow, rake; fertilize, manure, compost.

3. rent, rent out, lease, lease out, *Brit.* let *or* let out, hire out; sublease, sublet; job *or* job out.

farmer, *n.* **1.** agriculturalist, agronomist, granger, yeoman, landsman, husbandman; plowman, plowboy, sodbuster, chuff, gaffer, swain, kerne, son *or* tiller of the soil, (*in Egypt*) fellah, (*in Russia*) muzhik, (*in Spanish America and Southwestern U.S.*) peon, *Archaic.* hind; rustic, peasant, country cousin, hobnail, yokel, bumpkin, hawbuck, *Dial.* lumpkin, *Sl.* hick, *Sl.* rube, *Sl.* hayseed.

2. taxman, tax collector, publican, revenuer, *Brit.* exciseman.

farming, *n.* agriculture, agronomy, agribusiness, geoponics, husbandry, tillage, tilth; cultivation, tilling, working, dressing, fertilizing.

farrago, *n.* hodgepodge, mishmash, jumble, gallimaufry; medley, mélange, mixture, potpourri, salmagundi, miscellany, olla-podrida.

far-sighted, *adj.* **1.** long-sighted, *Ophthalm.* hypermetropic, *Obs.* presbyopic.

2. prescient, foresighted, far-seeing, anticipatory; wise, sagacious, shrewd, acute, discerning; sensible, thoughtful, provident, prudent, discreet, judicious, cautious, watchful.

farther, *adv.* **1.** further, further on *or* off, at *or* to a greater distance, beyond, past.

2. further along, at *or* to a more advanced point; more deeply involved, more intense, more accelerated, more advanced.

3. more, to a greater extent *or* degree, longer.

—adj. **4.** further, further away, ulterior, more distant *or* remote, more inaccessible; yon, yonder, over there, beyond *or* past here.

5. more extended, longer, increased, lengthier, additional, supplementary.

farthest, *adj.* remotest, utmost, uttermost, outermost, furthest, farthermost; ultimate, extreme, final, last; longest, most extended.

fascinate, *v.* attract, appeal to, allure, lure, draw, pull, engage, engross, absorb; delight, charm, enchant, enamor, infatuate; entice, tantalize, intrigue, beguile, tempt, seduce; bewitch, ensorcell, captivate, spellbind, entrance, mesmerize, hypnotize, transfix; enrapture, enravish, transport.

fascination, *n.* attractiveness, charm, appeal, allure, allurement, engagingness, delightfulness; attraction, draw, pull, magnetism; engrossment, absorption, infatuation; enchantment, bewitchment, entrancement, enravishment, mesmerism, hypnotism, captivation; enticement, lure, temptation, tantalization, seduction.

fascism, *n.* totalitarianism, dictatorship, autocracy, absolutism; extreme nationalism, regimentation, racism; white supremacy, apartheid.

fascist, *n.* **1.** fascist party member, follower of Mussolini, Black Shirt; Nazi, Bundist.

2. dictator, totalitarian, suppressor, autocrat, authoritarian, regimentator; extreme nationalist, racist, white supremacist.

fashion, *n.* **1.** style, *Brit.* twig, mode, vogue, look; trend, rage, fad, craze, latest thing; practice, custom, convention, general tendency; etiquette, decorum, protocol; proprieties, amenities, urbanities, civilities, courtesies, graces; good manners, good breeding, bon ton, good form.

2. high society, *Fr. haut monde*, beau monde, fashionable society; social elite, clique, coterie, jet set, beautiful people, *U.S.* Four Hundred.

3. manner, mode, *Archaic.* guise, method, taste; system, approach, way; type, kind, sort; make, cut, line, design, pattern; form, shape, texture, quality; mold, stamp, cast, conformation, structure, configuration.

—v. **4.** shape, form, mold, pattern, design, structure; make, create, forge, carve, hew; construct, build, fabricate, mint; invent, originate, contrive, devise, make up, compose.

5. accommodate, adapt, adjust, acclimate; suit, fit, conform to, comply with; be attuned to, be in harmony *or* accord with, be compatible with.

fashionable, *adj.* **1.** stylish, smart, natty, spruce, dapper, trim; chic, modish, a-go-go, in the very latest style; in vogue, à la mode, in fashion, in style; popular, in, *Sl.* in the groove, all the rage; up-to-date, current, modern, mod, new; up-to-the-minute, *Inf.* trendy, *Sl.* cool, *Inf.* nifty, *Sl.* neat, *Sl.* hip, *Sl.* hap.

2. elegant, high-class, *Sl.* classy, high-toned, *Sl.* tony; silk-stocking, *Sl.* ritzy, fancy, *Inf.* swank, *Inf.* swanky, *Sl.* swell; dressy, flashy, *Sl.* snazzy, *Sl.* sharp, *Sl.* sharp as a tack; suave, urbane, sophisticated, chichi, cosmopolitan.

3. polished, refined, finished, cultured, cultivated; genteel, well-bred, thoroughbred, aristocratic, blueblooded, gentle; gracious, graceful, *Scot.* genty, ladylike, ladyish, fine; polite, civil, courteous, mannerly, well-mannered; courtly, gentlemanly, gentlemanlike, chivalrous, chivalric, gallant, cavalier, debonair, charming.

4. customary, usual, general, prevailing; conventional, accepted, approved, traditional.

fast[1], *adj.* **1.** quick, rapid, swift, speedy, express, expeditious, accelerated, *Music.* mosso; fleet, nimble, light-footed, spry, brisk.

2. wild, dissipated, rakish, unconventional, unrestrained, loose; immoral, wanton, promiscuous, licentious, lecherous, lustful, lewd; libidinious, pleasure-seeking, sybaritic, carnal; intemperate, drunken, sottish; self-indulgent, dissolute, profligate.

3. fastened, tied, tight, taut, knotted; closed, secure, secured, adhering, stationary, immovable, firm, firmly fixed, indissoluble; inextricable, trapped, caught; fortified, resistant, impregnable, impervious, strong, rigid, invulnerable, invincible.

4. loyal, steadfast, devoted, faithful; permanent, enduring, lasting, abiding, durable; unchangeable, ineradicable, sure.

5. pull a fast one delude, deceive, mislead; *Sl.* con, bamboozle, hoodwink, cheat, swindle, defraud, trick, put one over on [s.o.].

—adv. **6.** tightly, firmly, securely, fixedly, immovably, tenaciously, closely.

7. quickly, swiftly, speedily, rapidly, hastily, posthaste, expeditiously, with dispatch, *Inf.* lickety-split.

8. wildly, uncontrollably, recklessly, prodigally, profligately, unrestrainedly, loosely, extravagantly, wantonly.

fast[2], *v.* **1.** abstain, go hungry, starve, famish; reduce, diet, lose weight, *Med.* bant; live on air, eat nothing, give up.

—n. **2.** abstinence, starvation, famishment, *Psychiatry.* anorexia; xerophagy, bread and water, short commons, iron rations; dieting, *Med.* banting, *Med.* Bantingism; hunger-strike.

3. fast day, Lent, day of abstinence, day of fasting, Quadragesima; fish-day, meatless day, Friday.

fasten, *v.* **1.** attach, affix, fix; hook, clasp, clip, snap, button, buckle, catch; join, connect, colligate, unite, wed, secure, couple, link; tie, bind, tether, make fast, hitch, pin, tack; latch, lock, bar, bolt, rivet, hasp; clinch, clamp, vice, brace, bracket; cotter, dowel, miter; stick, stick on, bond, cement, glue, solder, weld, fuse.

2. enclose, envelop, encircle; box in, hem in, shut in, case in, cage, confine; coop up, pen up, bolt *or* bar in.

3. aim, point, direct, draw *or* get a bead on; sight, focus, zero in on, beam; position, mark, train.

4. seize, take hold, catch hold, snatch, grab; cling, cleave, hold onto for dear life; clutch, clench, grip, grasp.

fastening, *n.* clasp, hook, catch, clip, snap, hook and eye, button, fastener; latch, lock, padlock, bar, bolt, hasp; pin, buckle, agraffe; clamp, vise, brace; tie, link, bond, vinculum, nexus; hinder, holder, connector, copula, yoke; rope, chain, tether; nail, dowel, tack, screw, clincher, rivet, staple, holdfast, peg, spike.

fastidious, *adj.* **1.** hard to please, critical, difficult; overcritical, hypercritical, overdemanding, overexacting; fussy, finicky, overparticular, finical, meticulous; picky, *Inf.* choosy, dainty, *Inf.* fuddy-duddy, *Inf.* pernickety.

2. overfastidious, overnice, overdelicate; affected, coxcombical, foppish, dapper, dandy.

fat, *adj.* **1.** obese, overweight, flabby, stout, portly, pursy, corpulent, *Scot.* fodgel; chubby, tubby, pudgy, plump; round, rounded out, rotund; fleshy, well-fed; paunchy, potbellied, roundbellied, big-bellied, large-bellied, great-bellied, abdominous, *Inf.* baywindowed, *Inf.* corporational, *Sl.* beer-bellied, *Obs.* gorbellied.

2. large, bulky, hulky, hulking; massive, gross, ponderous, gargantuan, elephantine; lumpy, lumpish; heavy, beefy, brawny, burly, sturdy.

3. fatty, greasy, suety, tallowy; blubber, blubbery, adipose, pinguid, lardaceous, sebaceous; oily, oleaginous, unctuous; buttery, butyraceous; soapy, saponaceous.

4. fertile, rich, lush, productive, teeming, fruitful; plentiful, abundant, plenteous, copious, flush; bountiful, well-stocked, well-supplied, well-furnished, replete.

5. well-paying, profitable, lucrative, remunerative.

6. wealthy, prosperous, affluent, moneyed, comfortable, well-to-do, well-off, *Inf.* well-heeled.

7. thick, broad, extended, extensive, expanded, voluminous; big, ample, immense.

8. dull, stupid, sluggish, obtuse, doltish, weak-minded, thickheaded, slow-witted, dull-witted, fat-witted.

—n. **9.** fat cell, fatty tissue, adipose tissue; fatness, obesity, obeseness, corpulence, corpulency, *Fr. embonpoint, Pathol.* adiposis; chubbiness, tubbiness, paunchiness, pudginess, plumpness, roundedness, rotundity; portliness, stoutness, burliness; hulk, bulk.

10. riches, wealth, fortune, affluence, plenty, plenitude, bounty, abundance; opulence, splendor, luxury, lavishness; superfluity, overabundance, excess, overplus, surplus, surplusage, redundancy.

11. lard, tallow, suet, *Zool.* blubber; butter.

—v. **12.** fatten, batten, increase; plump, fill out. See **fatten** (*defs.* **1, 3**).

fatal, *adj.* **1.** deadly, lethal, mortal, mortiferous, deathful, *Archaic.* lethiferous; venomous, virulent, toxic, morbific; fell, baneful, mephitic, viperous, poisonous, *Archaic.* venenose.

2. destructive, ruinous, annihilative, calamitous, disastrous, catastrophic, cataclysmic, extirpative; killing, slaughtering, slaughterous, suicidal, murderous, death-dealing, internecine, internecive; pernicious, dangerous, hazardous, deleterious, detrimental; harmful, injurious, nocuous, hurtful, nocent, baleful, noisome; noxious, malicious, malign, malignant, menacing; pestilential, pestiferous, infective, infectious, pestilent, contaminative, contagious, leprous, septic.

3. fateful, critical, crucial, pivotal; decisive, determinating; momentous, eventful, climacteric.

4. inevitable, ineluctable, inescapable, unpreventable; unavoidable, ineludible, inevasible; fated, destined, fixed, predestined, foreordained, predetermined.

fatalism, *n.* **1.** *Philos.* predeterminism, necessitarianism, necessarianism; Calvinism.

2. stoicism, resignation, resignedness, acceptance, acquiescence.

fatality, *n.* **1.** disaster, calamity, catastrophe, terrible accident *or* occurrence, fatal accident, violent death, *Sl.* curtains; (*all resulting in death*) wreck, crash, car crash, plane crash, collision, head-on collision, smash-up, crack-up, pileup.

2. death, casualty; dead, casualties, fatalities.

3. deadliness, mortality, lethality, fatal influence; malignance, malignancy, virulence.

4. accident, mishap, mischance, misfortune, misadventure, miscarriage; shock, blow, heavy *or* nasty *or* staggering blow, buffet, stroke, fell stroke, stroke of ill *or* bad luck *or* fortune; failure, collapse, debacle, breakdown, break up.

5. destiny, destination, ultimate future; fortune, lot, cup; predestination, predetermination. See **fate** (*defs.* **1, 3**).

fate, *n.* **1.** fortune, lot, cup, portion, die, doom, *Archaic.* foredoom, *Chiefly Scot.* weird, *Brit. Inf.* cup of tea, writing on the wall; destiny, karma, kismet, predetermination, predestination, God's will, Fortune's wheel, wheel of fortune, whatever comes; stars, planets, astral influence; *All Inf.* the way it goes, the breaks, the way the ball bounces, the way the cookie crumbles.

2. destination, ultimate future; hereafter, afterworld, otherworld, world to come, next world; the beyond, great beyond; the unknown, great unknown; the grave, eternal home.

3. inevitability, inevitableness, certainty, sureness; inescapableness, unavoidableness; uncontrollability, unpreventability.

4. death, death knell, deathblow, quietus, bane; end, finish, conlusion, terminus, termination, windup, *Inf.* payoff; end *or* final result, final event, last act, bitter end, finis, finale, curtain, final *or* last curtain, *Sl.* curtains; ruin, ruination, destruction; downfall, debacle, undoing, collapse; disaster, catastrophe.

5. **Fates** Providence, Lady *or* Dame Fortune, Fortuna; Weirds, Weird Sisters, (*Greek*) Moerae, (*Roman*) Parcea, (*Scandinavian*) Norns; Destinies.

—*v.* **6.** predetermine, predestine, *Obs.* predestinate, preordain, foreordain, foreordinate, predecide, doom, foredoom, *Inf.* have in store for.

7. destine, ordain, mark, *Obs.* appoint; determine, set, assign, ascribe, allot.

fated¹, *adj.* **1.** destined, determined, ordained, doomed; written, in the cards, in store; predetermined, predestined, predestinate, predestinated, preordained, foreordained, foredoomed, predecided.

2. certain, sure, sure as death, sure as death and taxes, fatal, fateful; inevitable, unavoidable, inescapable, ineluctable, ineludible.

fated², *adj.* **1.** momentous, decisive, major, significant, consequential, earth-shaking; weighty, heavy; crucial, critical, pivotal; of moment, of importance, of consequence, of weight.

2. fatal, deadly, lethal, mortal, feral, killing, deathdealing; disastrous, ruinous, destructive, destroying, devastating, demolishing; harrowing, dire, black.

3. destined, determined, ordained, fated; certain, inevitable. See **fated** (*defs.* **1, 2**).

4. prophetic, prophetical, fatidic, fatidical, apocalyptic, apocalyptical; ominous, portentous, foreboding, bodeful, threatening, ill-boding, ill-omened; inauspicious, unpropitious, unfavorable, unpromising, unlucky, ill-starred, evil-starred.

father, *n.* **1.** male parent, paterfamilias, *Brit. Inf.* pater, *Inf.* dad, *Inf.* daddy, papa, *Inf.* pop, *Sl.* old man, *Sl.* gaffer, *Brit. Inf.* governor, *Fr. père, Archaic.* sire.

2. ancestor, forefather, forebear, progenitor, primogenitor, *Archaic.* predecessor.

3. (*usu. cap.*) God, the Deity, the maker of Heaven and Earth, the first person of the Trinity. See **Deity**.

4. *Ecclesiastical.* priest, abbé, curé, padre, pastor, parson, shepherd, clergyman, *Coptic Ch.* anba.

5. procreator, begetter, maker; creator, author, originator, generator, initiator, prime mover, founder, architect; inventor, framer, designer.

6. patriarch, elder, leader; provider, protector, patron.

7. precursor, forerunner; prototype, model, exemplar.

—*v.* **8.** beget, sire, procreate, generate, engender, get; breed, propagate, reproduce; bring into being, bring to life, give life to, call into existence, cause to exist.

9. originate, be the author of; make, produce, fashion, fabricate, frame; imagine, conceive, *Inf.* dream up, *Inf.* hatch.

10. provide for, support, care for, take care of; take charge of, look after, take the responsibility of; act as a father to, adopt.

fatherhood, *n.* **1.** paternity, fathership, progenitorship; parenthood, parentage.

2. fatherliness, paternalness, protectiveness.

fatherland, *n.* native land *or* soil, motherland, mother country, natal place; home, homeland, country; the old country.

fatherly, *adj.* paternal, parental, like a father, befitting a father; kind, kindly, caring, beneficent, benevolent, benign; affectionate, tender, demonstrative; sympathetic, understanding, indulgent, obliging, forbearing, well-meaning; protective, shielding, sheltering.

fathom, *v.* **1.** sound, plumb; measure, mark, ascertain.

2. understand, comprehend, grasp, *Sl.* dig, catch, be hip to; know, see, perceive; sense, divine, intuit; penetrate, probe, search out; get to the bottom of, ferret out, root out, delve.

fathomless, *adj.* **1.** bottomless, soundless, unsounded, unfathomed, plumbless, measureless; abysmal, cavernous, plunging; deep-sea, deep as the sea *or* ocean, deep as a well.

2. impenetrable, incomprehensible, uncomprehensible, past *or* beyond comprehension, unknowable, inscrutable, unfathomable, incognizable, indecipherable, undecipherable, beyond understanding; obscure, dark, dim, vague, nebulous; mysterious, arcane, inexplicable, unexplainable, insolvable, insoluble, unaccountable, *Obs.* inextricable; puzzling, enigmatic, enigmatical.

fatigue, *n.* **1.** weariness, tiredness, exhaustion, *Obs.* fatigation; lassitude, lethargy, *Inf.* the blahs, languor, listlessness, sluggishness; debility, enervation, prostration; ennui, boredom, tedium, drowsiness, heaviness.

2. exertion, strain, labor, toil, drudgery, *Sl.* drag; hardship, trouble, difficulty.

—*v.* 3. tire, weary, exhaust, *Obs.* fatigate, *Inf.* take it out of, *Sl.* poop, wear out, tucker out, do in; enervate, jade, fag; debilitate, drain, deplete, prostrate; lethargize, stupefy, bore.

fatigued, *adj.* wearied, tired, worn out, done in, all in, exhausted, enervated, run-down; bushed, *Sl.* pooped, like a dishrag, heavy-lidded, *Inf.* beat.

fatness, *n.* 1. corpulence, portliness, stoutness, *Fr. embonpoint*; obesity, *Sl.* fat city, pursiness, Falstaffian girth; fleshiness, chubbiness, plumpness, rotundity; bigness, bulkiness, capaciousness, massiveness, grossness; adiposity, fattiness, greasiness.

2. richness, fertility, fecundity, fruitfulness, prolificacy, productivity, lushness, profuseness.

fatten, *v.* 1. make fat, enlarge, stuff, pad, distend; feed, feed up, bloat, cram; beef up, batten.

2. enrich, enhance, refine, *Archaic.* lard; fertilize, nourish, nurture, mellow.

3. grow fat, pinguefy, thicken, widen, broaden; put on weight, get fat, gain weight, put on pounds, spread.

fatty, *adj.* adipose, tallowy, suety; blubbery, lardy, lardaceous; marbled, rich, greasy.

fatuitous, *adj.* silly, inane, absurd, pointless, foolish, fatuous; asinine, idiotic, *Inf.* moronic, imbecilic. See **fatuous** (*defs.* **1, 2**).

fatuity, *n.* 1. silliness, absurdity, absurdness, *Archaic.* insipience, foolishness, fatuousness, infatuation; unreasonableness, irrationality, illogicalness, illogicality; asininity, idiocy, idioticalness, *Inf.* moronism, *Inf.* moronity, imbecility; craziness, *Sl.* kookiness, madness, daftness, *Inf.* nuttiness; *All Sl.* balminess, bugginess, screwiness, goofiness, wackiness, looniness.

2. stupidity, *Inf.* dopiness, empty-headedness, dullness, hebetude, inexpressiveness; weak-mindedness, simple-mindedness; unintelligence, unintellectualness, thoughtlessness; dull-wittedness, *Sl.* dim-wittedness, slow-wittedness, half-wittedness, witlessness, unwittiness; mindlessness, brainlessness, slowness; density, denseness, thickness, thickheadedness, obtuseness, stolidness, lumpishness, bluntness; emptiness, voidness, vacancy, vacuousness, blankness; vapidity, insipidness, banality, blandness.

fatuous, *adj.* 1. silly, inane, absurd, pointless, foolish; ridiculous, ludicrous, laughable; senseless, nonsensical, *Scot. and North Eng.* glaikit, cockeyed; unreasonable, irrational, illogical; groundless, unconnected, driftless, aimless; preposterous, extravagant, excessive; amphigoric, poppycockish, *Sl.* cockamamie, *Inf.* piffling; childish, puerile, immature; asinine, idiotic, *Inf.* moronic, imbecilic; crazy, crazed, *Sl.* kooky, *Scot.* doiled, mad; daft, *Inf.* daffy, crackbrained, *Inf.* nutty; *All Sl.* balmy, dippy, batty, cuckoo, buggy, screwy, wacky, goofy, loony.

2. dull, inexpressive, expressionless, stupid, *Inf.* dopey, empty-headed; weak-minded, simple, simple-minded; unthinking, unreasoning, incogitant, thoughtless; unintelligent, unintellectual; dull-witted, *Sl.* dim-witted, slow-witted, half-witted, witless, unwitty; mindless, brainless, fatuitous, slow; dense, thick, thick-headed, obtuse, stolid, lumpish, blunt; empty, void, vacant, vacuous, blank, unoccupied; vapid, insipid, banal, bland.

3. unreal, illusory, imaginary, fantastic, fanciful, fabulous, illusive, chimerical; deceptive, misleading, delusive, delusory, false.

faucet, *n.* spigot, cock, tap, valve; petcock, stopcock, drain cock, sea cock.

fault, *n.* 1. defect, flaw, imperfection, *Sl.* bug; blemish, taint, spot, stain; frailty, weakness, infirmity, foible, shortcoming, failing.

2. error, mistake, inaccuracy; omission, oversight, slip-up, slip, lapse; blunder, botch, fumble, foozle, *Sl.* boo-boo, *Sl.* goof, *Sl.* boner; gaffe, gaucherie, faux pas.

3. misdeed, misdemeanor, transgression, offense, wrong; misconduct, misbehavior; sin, vice, indiscretion, peccadillo.

4. responsibility, blamability, blameworthiness, answerability, accountability.

5. **at fault** blameworthy, censurable, culpable, blamable; responsible, answerable, accountable; guilty, wrong, in the wrong.

6. **find fault** complain, criticize, carp; cavil, quibble, *Inf.* nitpick, pettifog; frown upon, take exception to, pick holes in.

7. **to a fault** excessively, immoderately, unreasonable, unduly, overmuch, too much; extremely, exceedingly, needlessly, out of all proportion, preposterously.

—*v.* 8. blunder, fumble, boggle, botch *or* botch up, mess up, hash up, muff, foozle, *Inf.* flub, *Sl.* goof *or* goof up, *Sl.* screw up; flounder, stumble, bungle, slip; err, slip up, make a mistake, miscalculate, misjudge, misreckon, mistake.

9. find fault with, censure, upbraid, reproach, rebuke, reprehend; reprove, tax, take to task, call to account; impugn, assail, revile, call into question; stigmatize, brand, asperse, cast aspersions on, malign, slander, defame, vilify; attack, inveigh against, rail against, declaim against.

10. blame, accuse, *Sl.* stick *or* pin [s.t.] on [s.o.], hold [s.o.] accountable *or* responsible, lay at [s.o.'s] door, point the finger at [s.o.]; (*all in reference to culpability*) allege, ascribe, attribute, assign, impute, lay.

faultfinder, *n.* carper, caviler, quibbler, pettifogger, fussbudget, momus, smellfungus, *Inf.* nitpicker; critic, censor, Mrs. Grundy, *Inf.* fuddy-duddy, *Rare.* aristarch; censurer, detractor, derogator, backbiter, *Inf.* knocker; crab, bear, curmudgeon, *Inf.* crank, *Inf.* crosspatch, *Inf.* grouch, *Inf.* grouser, *Inf.* sorehead, *Inf.* squawker, *Sl.* bellyacher.

faultfinding, *n.* 1. pettifoggery, carping, caviling, quibbling, niggling, hairsplitting, *Inf.* nitpicking; hypercriticism, overcriticism, criticism, captiousness, censoriousness.

—*adj.* 2. captious, censorious, severe, hypercritical, overcritical, critical; querulous, contentious, carping, caviling, quibbling, pettifogging, hairsplitting, niggling, *Inf.* nitpicking; bad-tempered, ill-tempered, ill-disposed, cross, crabby, *Inf.* grouchy, *Inf.* sore, *Sl.* bellyaching.

faultless, *adj.* perfect, letter-perfect, ideal, impeccable, absolute, flawless, *Brit. Inf.* spot on; innocent, blameless, guiltless, inculpable, unimpeachable, above reproach *or* suspicion; immaculate, pure, sinless, spotless, unblemished, untainted.

faulty, *adj.* 1. defective, imperfect, unsound, *Inf.* on the blink, *Inf.* on the fritz; incomplete, insufficient, inadequate, deficient, lacking, wanting; unfinished, partial, sketchy, uneven.

2. wrong, incorrect, inaccurate, erroneous, untrue, fallacious; illogical, invalid, flawed, fallible, *Logic.* paralogical.

3. blameworthy, reprehensible, censurable, impeachable, reproachable, reprovable, indictable.

faux pas, *n.* 1. gaffe, social blunder *or* indiscretion, slip in conduct, mistake in conduct *or* etiquette *or* propriety, breach of etiquette *or* manners; transgression, dereliction, misconduct, misdeed; false step, wrong step, misstep, trip, stumble, bad move, wrong move, false move; offense, peccadillo, oversight, omission, miss; leak, slip, lapse, lapsus.

2. mistake, error, blunder, botch, bungle, *Inf.* slip-up; *All Sl.* boner, boo-boo, goof, boot, bobble, blooper, dumb trick, fool mistake, screw-up, foul-up, louse-up.

3. (*all of an embarrassing or inopportune nature*) mishap, mischance, misadventure, miscarriage, accident.

favor, *n.* **1.** kind act, good deed, kind deed, good turn, labor of love, courtesy, *Fr. beau geste*; blessing, boon, grace, grant, *Theol.* dispensation; benefaction, *Archaic.* benefit, *Archaic.* benignity, benevolence.

2. kindness, generosity, consideration, graciousness, hospitality, friendliness; good will, *Archaic.* gree, compassion, sympathy; aid, assistance, help, abetment, abettal.

3. approval, approbation, sanction, countenance, endorsement; patronage, fosterage, tutelage, sponsorship, guidance, auspices, aegis, care; advocacy, championship, espousal, encouragement, backing; obligingness, accommodation, indulgence; support, protection, cover.

4. good terms, good understanding, good footing, good graces; good opinion, favorable regard; harmony, rapport, friendly relations; privilege, advantage, special interest, immunity; license, *Inf.* pull, in, connections, weight; preference, partiality, prejudice, bias, favoritism, leaning, nepotism.

5. present, gift, memento, remembrance, souvenir, memorial; token, trophy, keepsake, relic.

6. letter, epistle, message, communication, dispatch, missive, *Obs.* billet; reply, answer, acknowledgment, rescript.

7. **favors** (*all usu. in regard to sexual intimacy*) permission, consent, allowance, leave; liberty, license; compliance, acquiescence, agreement.

8. **in favor of** **a.** on *or* in behalf of, in the name of, on account of, for the sake of. **b.** on the side of, for, all for, pro.

9. **in one's favor** to one's credit, in one's interest; approving, well-disposed; beneficial, helpful.

—*v.* **10.** approve, approbate, sanction, countenance, endorse, commend, recommend; foster, sponsor, advocate, espouse, smile upon, encourage, back; defend, support, champion; oblige, patronize, indulge, accommodate.

11. prefer, single out, select, elect; go in for, go for, be all for; opt for, fancy, pick; have a preference for, treat with partiality, side with; esteem, respect, have regard for, fawn upon.

12. facilitate, expedite, precipitate; accelerate, forward, advance, promote; ease, make easier, lighten, smooth; palliate, extenuate, spare.

13. treat tenderly, deal with gently, tend indulgently, handle with care, take care of; indulge, pamper, coddle, baby; gratify, satisfy; protect, cover, guard.

14. aid, assist, help, succor, abet, meet the wants of; befriend, lend a hand, do a favor for, show kindness to, do right by; serve, do for, do a service for, cater to, make comfortable, attend to the convenience of; provide, supply, furnish.

15. *Informal.* resemble, look like, take after, be the image of, mirror, echo; duplicate, parallel, approximate, correspond.

favorable, *adj.* **1.** advantageous, profitable, valuable, *Archaic.* available; beneficial, helpful, comfortable, wholesome, salutary; useful, handy, appropriate; convenient, serviceable, suitable, fit, applicable, conducive; rewarding, gainful, constructive; good, positive; effective, productive, effectual.

2. eager, in the mood, willing, *Archaic.* fain; enthusiastic, ardent, zealous; inclined, *Archaic.* propense, disposed, predisposed, minded; agreeable, amicable, amiable, well-disposed; approving, commendatory, praising; friendly, sympathetic, congenial, understanding, kind.

3. propitious, auspicious, promising, benign, reassuring, encouraging; opportune, lucky, timely, fortunate, providential; pleasing, fair, looking up.

favored, *adj.* **1.** preferred, pet, favorite, choice, chosen, selected; recommended, liked, *Inf.* highly touted. See **favorite** (*def.* **3**).

2. privileged, advantaged, prosperous, well-off, affluent; elite, noble, elect, cream of the crop; preeminent, dominant, prevailing, on top, influential; licensed, exempt, immune, unliable, unaccountable.

favorite, *n.* **1.** preference, choice, predilection; idol, god, hero, star; apple of [s.o.'s] eye, man *or* woman after one's heart, fair-haired boy *or* girl, jewel; darling, dearest, beloved, dear, *Inf.* duck, honey, sweetheart; minion, yes-man, apple polisher, *Inf.* sweet-talker, *Inf.* bootlicker, pet, cosset; spoiled person, brat.

2. (*all usu. sports*) front-runner, choice, probable winner, overdog.

—*adj.* **3.** chosen, choice, preferred, favored, especially liked, selected, welcomed, pet; popular, lionized, in; ideal, utopian, fair-haired; to one's liking, to one's taste, to one's heart.

favoritism, *n.* **1.** partiality, bias, prejudice, prepossession; one-sidedness, unilateralism, unilaterality; partisanship, partisanry, partisanism, nepotism; inequity, unfairness, unjustness, injustice.

2. preference, predilection; inclination, bent, leaning, penchant, proclivity, weakness for; undispassionateness, undetachment.

fawn, *v.* kowtow, bow, bow before, bow and scrape, stoop, crouch; kneel, fall on one's knees, fall at the feet of, prostrate oneself; grovel, crawl, creep, creep before, slither, *Sl.* Tom; cringe, cower, squirm; toady, toady to, truckle, truckle to, toadeat, fawn upon, *Sl.* fall all over, wheedle, puff, puff up, inflate, blow up, *Sl.* suck up to, *Sl.* play up to, *Sl.* shine up to, *Inf.* apple-polish, *Sl.* butter up, *Sl.* brown-nose, *Sl.* earn brownie points; lickspittle, lick [s.o.'s] shoes, lick *or* kiss [s.o.'s] feet, *Inf.* be a yes man to, agree to anything, *Sl.* bootlick, court, pay court to, curry favor, dance attendance upon.

fawner, *n.* toady, toadeater, sycophant, flatterer, fawning flatterer, truckler, tufthunter, courtier, wheedler, puffer, backslapper, backscratcher, timeserver, *Inf.* apple-polisher, *Sl.* brown-nose, *Sl.* brownnoser, *Sl.* brownie, *Obs., Rare.* blander, *Archaic.* pickthank; parasite, leech, sponge, sponger, hanger-on; flunky, lackey, yes-man, jackal, spaniel, bootlick, bootlicker, footlicker, lickspit, lickspittle, kowtower, Uncle Tom, Tom, *Sl.* oreo, cringer, groveler, sniveler.

fawning, *adj.* **1.** servile, slavish, obsequious, *Obs.* obsequent, subservient, menial, *Obs., Rare.* vernile; submissive, docile, unassertive, compliant, acquiescent, deferential, Tomish, Uncle Tomish, tractable, mealy-mouthed; groveling, crawling, creeping, slithering; kowtowing, crouching, stooping, bowing, bowing and scraping; whining, whimpering, sniveling.

2. sycophantic, sycophantical, sycophantish, toadyish, toadying, toadeating, flattering, truckling, wheedling, ingratiating, timeserving, *Sl.* bootlicking, *Sl.* footlicking, *Inf.* apple-polishing, *Sl.* brown-nosing, *Obs.* blanding, *Obs., Rare.* blandiloquous; buttery, candied, unctuous, oily, honey-mouthed, smooth-talking, sweet-talking, smooth-tongued, *Rare.* blandiloquent.

—*n.* **3.** servility, servileness, slavishness, obsequiousness, obsequence, subservience, *Obs.* vernility; submissiveness, docility, unassertiveness, compliance, acquiescence, deference, tractability, tractableness, Tomishness, Uncle Tomishness; prostration, obeisance, abjection, abjectness, self-abasement; groveling, crawling, creeping, slithering; kowtowing, crouching, bowing, bowing and scraping; squirming, cringing, cowering; whining, whimpering, sniveling.

4. sycophancy, sycophantism, toadyism, toadeating, tufthunting, lip-homage, mouth-honor, unctuousness, fawningness, flattery, *Inf.* butter, *Inf.* oil, *Inf.* honey, *Sl.* banana oil, *Sl.* goo, *Rare.* blandiloquence, *Obs.* blanding, *Obs., Rare.* blandation, *Obs., Rare.* blandiloquy; truckling, *Sl.* falling all over, toadying, slavering, *Inf.* buttering, *Inf.* soaping, *Inf.* oiling, *Inf.* honeying, *Inf.* apple-polishing; *All Sl.* shining up to, sucking up to, playing up to, buttering-up, brownnosing; courting, paying court to, currying favor, dancing attendance upon, licking [s.o.'s] shoes, kissing [s.o.'s] feet, *Sl.* bootlicking.

5. cajolery, wheedling, beguilement, beguiling, blandishment, blandishing, blarney, coaxing, palaver, palavering, *Inf.* soft soap, *Inf.* sweet talk, *Inf.* honeyed words, *Sl.* line, *Sl.* snow job, *Archaic.* gloze; humoring, jollying, pampering, coddling, petting, pandering to, catering to, *Inf.* stroking.

fay, *n.* fairy, sprite, pixy, sylph, peri, nixie, nix; elf, brownie, leprechaun, gnome; kobold, genie.

faze, *v.* *Informal.* daunt, intimidate, unnerve, dismay, petrify, frighten, affright, scare, *Archaic.* amate; overawe, terrorize, threaten, cow; disconcert, alarm, appall, take aback, *Inf.* take the fight out of, abash, *Inf.* shake up.

2. dishearten, discourage, dispirit, unman; deter, set back, put off, check, thwart, shake, take the heart out of, *Inf.* take the starch out of.

fear, *n.* **1.** dread, fright, *Inf.* funk, fearfulness; terror, horror, panic; alarm, perturbation, dismay, consternation, trepidation; apprehension, misgiving, uncertainty, suspicion, mistrust, distrust, qualm; worry, disquiet, disquietude, solicitude, concern.

2. angst, fear and trembling, anguish, anxiety; trembling, shaking, quaking, quivering, palpitation; uneasiness, apprehensiveness, *Inf.* butterflies, nervousness, queasiness; cowardice, timidity, diffidence; hesitation, cold feet, second thoughts; *Sl.* the creeps; bugaboo, bogy, *Fr. bête noire*, nightmare; phobia.

3. awe, amazement, reverence, veneration, respect.

—*v.* **4.** dread, be afraid, be scared, take fright, be alarmed; mistrust, distrust, suspect, anticipate, expect, apprehend, forebode; hesitate, falter, have second thoughts, *Sl.* have cold feet; quail, flinch, recoil, shy, shrink, blench, *Inf.* funk; cower, skulk, crouch; shiver, shudder, quiver, shake in one's boots, tremble.

5. worry, be anxious, be concerned about, be solicitous, be disquieted.

6. revere, reverence, venerate, stand in awe of.

fearful, *adj.* **1.** dreadful, dread, terrifying, frightful, direful, appalling; terrible, grievous, grim, dire, baleful, dark; alarming, distressing, harrowing, rending; redoubtable, fearsome, formidable, awful; horrible, horrendous, monstrous, atrocious; hideous, ghastly, eerie, grisly, gruesome, unspeakable; abhorrent, revolting, repulsive, repugnant, loathsome, deadly, fell.

2. afraid, scared, frightened, *Archaic.* affrighted, fearsome; terrified, panic-stricken, terror-stricken; apprehensive, alarmed, worried, uneasy, disquieted; distrustful, dreading, shrinking; tense, nervous, panicky; tremulous, shaky, on edge, jumpy, jittery, edgy, anxious; cowardly, craven, pusillanimous, white-livered, lily-livered, chicken-hearted.

3. timid, timorous, faint-hearted, cautious, diffident, intimidated; hesitant, reluctant, unsure, unwilling.

4. awe-inspiring, awesome, imposing, impressive, inspiring; venerable, august, reverential, revered, respected, reverenced.

fearless, *adj.* dauntless, undaunted, Spartan, brave, valorous, courageous, unafraid, unaffrighted; unshrinking, unflinching, unblenching, unapprehensive; intrepid, daring, venturesome, bold, audacious, *Rare.* impavid; indomitable, unconquerable, stout-hearted, lion-hearted, valiant, heroic; resolute, doughty, unappalled; stalwart, plucky, game, hardy, high-spirited, gritty, *Inf.* spunky, mettlesome; manly, manful, chivalrous, gallant.

feasibility, *n.* **1.** workability, workableness, practicability, practicableness, feasibleness; usability, usableness, usefulness, practicality, practicalness, reasonableness; realizability, realizableness, attainability, attainableness.

2. applicability, applicableness, appropriateness, suitability, suitableness.

feasible, *adj.* **1.** workable, doable, effectible, accomplishable; practicable, usable, useful, practical, reasonable, within reason, realistic, based on reality, within available means; completable, achievable, attainable, realizable, obtainable, reachable, within reach.

2. applicable, appropriate, suitable, suited, fitting, *Inf.* O.K.; advisable, recommendable, worthwhile, expedient, desirable, advantageous.

3. probable, likely, expectable; possible, within the realm of possibility, admissible, conceivable, imaginable, thinkable.

feast, *n.* **1.** celebration, ceremony, rite, ritual, observance; memorialization, ritualization, commemoration, remembrance, solemnization; occasion, event, holiday, holy day, feast day, saint's day; gala day, red-letter day, anniversary, birthday, jubilee; festivity, festival, fete, revel, wassail; carnival, Mardi Gras, mi-carême, fair, fun-fair.

2. banquet, repast, collation, meal, fare; *Inf.* spread, picnic, treat, garden party, *Fr. fête champêtre, Brit.* bump-supper, *Chiefly Brit. Sl.* beanfeast *or* beanfest; barbecue, cookout, clambake, *Inf.* feed, *Sl.* blow-out, *Sl.* bust, junket; feasting, eating and drinking, *Rare.* epulation; festal cheer, good table, festive board, groaning board.

3. merrymaking, *Brit.* holiday-making, jollification, revelry, party; frolic, spree, whirl, lark; refreshment, entertainment, regalement, *Inf.* whoopee, fun, fast and furious; saturnalia, carousal, orgy, debauch, bacchanalia, bacchanal.

—*v.* **4.** dine, wine, wine and dine, banquet, partake; gormandize, gorge, engorge, glut, play a good knife and fork; indulge, cram, stuff, eat one's fill, *Sl.* pig out.

5. entertain, treat, banquet, regale, wine and dine, dine, take out; give *or* throw a party for, hold a reception for; honor, do the honors, kill the fatted calf, ring the bell for; toast, salute, drink to, raise *or* tilt glasses to, celebrate.

6. revel, make merry, *Inf.* make whoopee, celebrate; carouse, wassail, roast, roister, quaff; have a good time, make it a party, paint the town red, *Inf.* go out on the town, *Inf.* do the town, *Sl.* whoop it up, *Sl.* do it up, *Brit. Sl.* beat it up, have fun.

7. gratify, delight, please, make happy, charm, gladden; cheer, thrill, entertain, amuse, refresh.

8. admire, relish, savor, revel in, luxuriate in, take delight in.

feat, *n.* **1.** (*all usu. extraordinary*) deed, exploit, *Archaic.* gest, act, action; achievement, step, stride, advancement, progress; accomplishment, attainment, acquirement, success.

2. maneuver, move, stroke, blow, coup, stunt, trick; stroke of genius, tour de force.

feather, *n.* **1.** plume, quill, pinion, *All Ornithol.* plumule, penna, covert, tectrix; (*collectively*) panache, hackle, tuft, crest, tussock; plumage, down, *Ornithol.* scapular, *Ornithol.* mantle, (*of a hawk*) mail.

2. condition, state, temperament, mood, humor, spirit; temper, disposition, way.

3. kind, type, species, order, variety, sort, nature; character, mark, brand, grade, quality; metal, kidney, color, stamp, mold, shape.

4. fluff, *Inf.* fluffy, flake, flurry, featherweight; fuzz, floss, lint, mote, dust; gossamer, cobweb, spider web.

5. **a feather in one's cap a.** honor, honors, kudos, laurels, wreath, bays, garland, ribbon, medal, battle honors, blushing honors; distinction, glory, dignity, izzat, prestige. **b.** accomplishment, deed, feat, exploit.

feathery, *adj.* **1.** feathered, fledged, plumose, plumed, pennaceous, tufted; downy, fluffy, flossy, fleecy.

2. light, lightweight, featherweight, featherlight, light as air, light as a feather, gossamer, gossamery; unsubstantial, imponderous, weightless; ethereal, airy, floaty, buoyant.

feature, *n.* **1.** **features** face, countenance, visage, physiognomy, *Sl.* mug, *Sl.* kisser, *Sl.* puss; looks, lineaments.

2. (*all of the face*) cast, form, turn, shape, figure, configuration, *Inf.* cut of one's jib; appearance, expression, look, lineament, aspect; profile, silhouette.

3. mark, hallmark, earmark, trademark, specialty, keynote; trait, characteristic, attribute; property, quality; peculiarity, quirk, mannerism, idiosyncracy, idiocrasy.

4. special attraction, main *or* special feature, drawing card, leading card, headliner, top of the bill, main bout; special, leader, loss leader, lead item, main item, number one seller.

5. highlight *or* high light, outstanding *or* distinctive feature; high spot, high point, memorable part, best part, cream, cream of the crop; focus, focal point, main focus; cynosure, center of attention, center of attraction, center of interest.

—*v.* **6.** characterize, distinguish, mark, earmark, differentiate, set apart, *Inf.* keynote; define, describe, symbolize, typify, stand for, sum up; indicate, signify, identify, betoken, symptomize, signalize.

7. highlight, spotlight, play up, set off, give prominence to, bring to the fore, bring into relief; star, *Inf.* headline; emphasize, stress, lay emphasis *or* stress upon, give emphasis to, punctuate, accent, accentuate; underscore, underline, italicize, point up, call attention to.

8. depict, picture, portray, represent, draw, paint, sketch; delineate, outline, silhouette, contour, profile, circumscribe.

9. *Informal.* imagine, conceive of, dream of; visualize, picture to oneself.

feces, *n.* **1.** waste matter, excrement, excreta, stools, waste, dirt; dung, manure, compost, ordure, guano, droppings, *Inf.* do, *Sl.* load, *Sl.* doo-doo; cow *or* buffalo chips, *Brit.* cow-pat, *U.S. West* cow pies, *Sl.* flops, coprolites, coproliths.

2. dregs, sediment, residue, grounds, lees, heeltap; dross, scum, off-scum, skimmings, slag, sprue, scoria, sludge, bilge; detritus, loess, debris, drift, moraine; chaff, clippings, trimmings, garbage, slough, scurf; refuse, waste, sewage, drainage; slops, swill, pigswill, hogwash, draff; feculence, muck, filth, dirt, mud, offal.

feculence, *n.* sediment, residue, scum; muck, filth. See **feces** (*def.* **2**).

feculent, *adj.* muddy, turbid, foul, befouled, messy, mucky, roily; marshy, miry, quagmiry, fenny, boggy, swampy; dreggy, scummy, grimy, dirty, smudgy; fecal, excrementitious, filthy, slimy, putrid, *Physiol.* stercoraceous.

fecund, *adj.* **1.** fruitful, productive, fructuous, fruit-bearing, fructiferous, feracious, frugiferous; fertile, potent, generative, propagative, fructificative.

2. prolific, profuse, bounteous, teeming; alive with, pullalating, *Inf.* crawling with, swarming; proliferous, proliferating, spawning, multiparous; abundant, plenteous, full, copious, *Rare.* uberous, exuberant, luxurious, lush, rank, rich, rife; flush, thick, close, dense.

fecundity, *n.* **1.** fruitfulness, fertility, fructiferousness, prolificacy, prolificality; productiveness, generativeness, uberty, *Rare.* feracity.

2. abundance, wealth, luxuriance, lushness, exuberance, copiousness, bounty.

federal, *adj.* federated, confederate, in league, leagued, allied, in alliance; united, linked *or* banded *or* bound together.

federation, *n.* **1.** fusion, uniting, allying, confederating.

2. confederation, confederacy, league, *Ger. Bund*, alliance, coalition; amalgamation, combination, syndicate, combine; union, *Ger. Verein*, society, association, fraternity, brotherhood.

fee, *n.* **1.** charge, bill, toll, fare; expense, price, *Brit.* tariff, cost, *Inf.* damages, admission.

2. payment, pay, emolument, salary, stipend; wage, wages, hire, paycheck, *Inf.* weekly insult; remuneration, recompense, compensation; commission, allowance, honorarium, perquisite.

3. gratuity, tip, baksheesh, *Fr. pourboire, Ger. Trinkgeld*, douceur, handout, *Sl.* beer money; gift, present, bonus, premium; reward, bounty, *Archaic.* meed, *Literary.* guerdon.

—*v.* **4.** pay, remunerate, recompense, compensate; requite, reimburse; tip, leave a little something.

feeble, *adj.* **1.** weak, frail, fragile, delicate, slight, puny, *Pathol.* asthenic, anemic; weakly, sickly, not strong, unhealthy, *Scot.* shilpit, ailing; infirm, unsteady, *Inf.* dotty, shaky, trembling, tottering, doddering; impotent, powerless, impuissant, helpless; decrepit, old, senile, invalid, unsound, weakened, enfeebled, debilitated; enervated, enervate, languid, languishing, drooping, fading, failing, declining, dying.

2. feeble-minded, weak-minded, simple, simple-minded. See **feeble-minded**.

3. low, soft, gentle, dulcet, whispered, muted, stifled, muffled, inaudible, imperceptible; weak, thin, tiny, small, faltering, trembling; faint, dim, pale, dull, faded, distant, obscure, far-away; indistinct, unclear, blurred, blurry, vague, nebulous, hazy, misty, misted, foggy, fogged.

4. ineffective, ineffectual, unavailing, futile, useless, hopeless; feckless, incompetent, inefficient, poor, unsatisfactory, half-baked, *Sl.* half-assed; lame, insufficient, inadequate, unconvincing, flimsy; wishy-washy, thin, weak, watery, watered-down; lax, loose, careless, slipshod, shoddy, sloppy; miserable, *Inf.* lousy, meager, mere, paltry, insignificant, unimportant, *Archaic.* seely.

feeble-minded, *adj.* feeble, *Inf.* weak in the head, weak-minded, deficient, subnormal, retarded, slow;

slow-witted, dull, dull-witted, stupid, *Inf.* dumb, foolish; empty-headed, blank, vacant, vacuous, *Sl.* having nobody home, *Sl.* empty upstairs. See **foolish** (*def.* **3**).

feebleness, *n.* weakness, debility, *Pathol.* asthenia, infirmity, lack of strength, deficiency, invalidness; decrepitude, senility, incompetence, disability, incapacity, inability, incapability; impotence, powerlessness, impuissance, helplessness; frailty, frailness, delicateness, delicacy, fragility, fragileness.

feed, *v.* **1.** nourish, nurture, foster, sustain, maintain, support, board; browse, fodder, graze, crop; subsist, exist, survive, live on; eat, fare, dine, wine and dine, break bread, partake, *Inf.* tie on the feed bag, *Inf.* pitch *or* steam in; devour, engorge, wolf, *Sl.* stuff *or* fill one's face.
2. satisfy, gratify, do one's heart good, warm the cockles of one's heart; sate, satiate, appease, slake, allay, assuage.
3. cater, purvey, provision, provender, victual; supply, provide, furnish, accommodate, equip.
—*n.* **4.** forage, fodder, pasture, pasturage; food, foodstuff, provisions, provender, edibles, victuals, *Inf.* vittles, comestibles, viands, board.
5. *Informal.* feast, repast, banquet, meal, *Inf.* spread.

feel, *v.* **1.** touch, palpate, finger, thumb, handle, palm, paw; brush, graze; stroke, caress, pet, fondle, *Sl.* feel up.
2. sense, intuit, have a feeling, *Inf.* have a funny feeling, *Inf.* feel in one's bones, *Inf.* have a hunch, *Inf.* get *or* have the impression, just know; apprehend, perceive, know, discern, see, note, understand, comprehend, *Brit. Sl.* suss.
3. probe, grope, grabble, scrabble, fumble, poke around, feel *or* pick one's way.
4. condole, grieve, lament, be sorry for, bleed for, weep for, pity; sympathize, empathize, commiserate, compassionate.
5. experience, have, know, sustain, undergo, go through; bear, endure, brook, abide, brave, withstand, stand, suffer.
6. seem *or* seem like, appear *or* appear like, look *or* look like, sound *or* sound like, strike one as.
—*n.* **7.** texture, surface, finish.
8. atmosphere, climate, air, milieu, ambience, vibrations, *Sl.* vibes; quality, sense, note, tone, overtone, undertone.
9. knack, way, art, hang, trick; genius, flair, talent, faculty.
10. touch, sense of touch, tactile sense.

feeler, *n.* proposal, offer, advance, overture, approach, leak; trial balloon, pilot balloon, *Fr. ballon d'essai*, probe, barometer, weathervane, straw vote, straw to the wind; sample, random sample, experiment.

feeling, *n.* **1.** touch, sense of touch, tactile sense, feel.
2. sensation, sense, sense impression, impression; intuition, inkling, vague feeling, *Inf.* funny feeling, suspicion, *Inf.* sneaking suspicion, *Inf.* hunch; hint, intimation, foreboding, presentiment, premonition; tingle, quiver, throb, palpitation.
3. emotion, affection, *Psychol.* affect; passion, fervor, ardor, vehemence, heat, fire, warmth; response, reaction, *Inf.* gut reaction.
4. consciousness, awareness, sentience, sensibility, perception; sensitivity, consideration, discrimination, tact, tactfulness.
5. compassion, commiseration, pity; tenderness, tenderheartedness, heart, soul; sympathy, empathy, fellow feeling, identification; echo, chord, vibration, *Inf.* vibe.
6. sentiment, notion, idea, conception, thought, estimation, theory; opinion, outlook, viewpoint, point of view; attitude, stance, position, posture, way of thinking.
7. **feelings** sensibilities, susceptibilities, sympathies, sentiments, emotions, passions.
—*adj.* **8.** sensitive, sentient, sensible, intuitive; emotional, demonstrable; warm, tender, tenderhearted, softhearted, soft; sympathetic, compassionate, responsive, receptive.
9. passionate, impassioned, intense, ardent, fervent, fervid, vehement; hot, red-hot, heated, fiery.

feign, *v.* **1.** affect, simulate, fake, sham, give the appearance of; adopt, assume, take on, put on, pretend to be [s.t.] one is not; impersonate, personate, pose as, pretend to be [s.o.], pass oneself off as, sail under false colors, (*all deceptively*) allege *or* claim *or* profess to be, *Sl.* make like; (*all deceptively*) imitate, copy, ape, mimic; dissemble, dissimulate, misrepresent, disguise, falsify.
2. pretend, make believe, malinger, playact, act; put on airs, assume airs, posture, do for effect.
3. fabricate, make up, forge, counterfeit; think *or* dream up, invent, concoct, devise, create; lie, tell a lie *or* a white lie, tell a story, make excuses.

feigned, *adj.* **1.** fake, counterfeit, sham, bogus, fraudulent, false, spurious, meretricious, flash; pretended, make-believe, acted, theatrical, affected, put-on, mock, insincere, ungenuine, *Sl.* hokey; pseudo, imitation, simulated, synthetic, ersatz, specious, unauthentic.
2. assumed, adopted, taken on, borrowed, someone else's, not one's own; stolen, taken, appropriated, usurped.
3. disguised, camouflaged, dissembled, dissimulated, misrepresented, misleading, deceptive; fabricated, forged, made up, factitious, fictitious, untrue; (*all fictitiously*) invented, created, concocted, devised, contrived.

feint, *n.* **1.** dodge, maneuver, false *or* deceptive move, mock attack, distraction; jugglery, sleight of hand, legerdemain, prestidigitation; trick, wile, ruse, artifice, deception, pretext, subterfuge, blind; bait, decoy, lure, trap, snare, *Sl.* plant.
2. disguise, camouflage, mask, cloak, wolf in sheep's clothing; sham, fake, hoax, fraud, humbug, imposition; pretense, make-believe, show, mere show, affectation, affectedness, put-on; pose, posture, semblance, air, appearance.

felicitate, *v.* congratulate, wish [s.o.] joy, rejoice with, wish [s.o.] many happy returns, offer one's felicitations *or* compliments; salute, hail, toast, drink to, wish well to; pay one's respects to.

felicitation, *n.* *usu.* **felicitations** congratulations, joy, compliments, blessings, good wishes, best wishes, wish for happiness; greetings, salutations; toasts, cheers.

felicitous, *adj.* well-suited, apt, appropriate, suitable, accordant, apropos, apposite, germane, pertinent, to the point, *Latin. ad rem*; becoming, graceful, gainly, seemly, fitting, *Inf.* just right; neat, pat, *Inf.* on the button *or* mark, *Inf.* on target; well-put, well-said, well-expressed, well-chosen, inspired; seasonable, timely, well-timed, opportune, propitious, auspicious, of good omen; harmonious, happy, meet, congenial, fortunate, lucky, successful, prosperous.

felicity, *n.* **1.** happiness, joy, joyfulness, bliss, blissfulness, ecstasy, rapture; delight, pleasure, gladness, enjoyment, satisfaction, gratification, contentment, harmony.
2. appropriateness, suitability, suitableness, fitness,

rightness, justness, seemliness; aptness, appositeness, expedience; congruity, becomingness; applicability, relevance, relevancy, pertinence; propitiousness, auspiciousness.

feline, *adj.* **1.** catlike, lynxlike, leonine; graceful, slinky, seductive, sensual.

2. cunning, crafty, canny, sly; artful, designing, wily, tricky; subtle, insidious, treacherous, stealthy, sneaking, sneaky, pussy-footing.

fell[1], *v.* cut down, hew, mow, level, raze, demolish; shoot, wound, strike down, prostrate; overthrow, kill.

fell[2], *adj.* **1.** fierce, savage, ferocious, vicious, truculent; bestial, brutish, feral, ferine, tigerish, wolfish, lupine; brutal, violent, inhuman, barbarous, barbaric, hellish, Tartarian, Hunnish, Gothic, Vandalic; murderous, homicidal, slaughterous, bloodthirsty, sanguinary; sadistic, animalistic, cannibalistic, fiendish, ogreish; diabolical, demonic, demoniac, devilish; terrible, harsh, dire, dreadful, grim, severe; unrelenting, relentless, remorseless, implacable, inexorable, grinding.

2. pitiless, merciless, heartless, cruel, ruthless; hard-hearted, cold-hearted, stony-hearted, marble-hearted, cold-blooded.

3. deadly, lethal, fatal, mortal, *Archaic.* lethiferous; pestilential, pestiferous, noxious, malicious, menacing, malignant, malign; maleficent, malefic, malevolent, damnable, accursed; venomous, virulent, toxic, baneful, mephitic, viperous, poisonous, *Archaic.* venenose; detrimental, deleterious, pernicious, baleful; harmful, injurious, nocuous, hurtful; destructive, ruinous, calamitous, cataclysmic, catastrophic, extirpative.

fellow, *n.* **1.** man, male, *Inf.* chap, *Inf.* guy, *Inf.* dad, *Sl.* joe, *Sl.* dude, *Sl.* cat, *Sl.* gazabo, *Sl.* bozo, *Sp. hombre*; gentleman, squire, esquire, don, hidalgo, caballero; gaffer, *Inf.* codger; boy, *Inf.* kid, *Scot.* chield; individual, person, *Inf.* customer.

2. good-for-nothing, *Inf.* no-account, *Inf.* no-count, *Sl.* skate, *Archaic.* knave, *Archaic.* yeoman, *Chiefly Scot.* geck.

3. companion, comrade, crony, chum, *Fr. copain*, sidekick, shadow, alter ego, *Inf.* pal, *U.S. Inf.* buddy, *Sl.* cully, *Sl.* Siamese twin; friend, acquaintance, amigo, *Fr. ami*; associate, ally, colleague, affiliate, coworker, yokefellow, yokemate, *Scot. and North Eng.* marrow, *Archaic.* peer; partner, helpmate, helpmeet, classmate, shipmate, messmate, teammate, playmate, housemate, roommate, *U.S. Inf.* roomie, *Obs.* consort.

4. equal, peer, compeer, confrere, brother, sister.

5. mate, twin, double, counterpart, one of a pair, bird of a feather, *Astron.* comes; duplicate, copy, facsimile; match, complement, completer, accessory, concomitant, concurrent.

—*v.* **6.** equalize, uniform, bring up to par, even up, match up.

—*adj.* **7.** associate, associated, affiliate, affiliated, allied, coalescent, united, joint, bonded, connected; comparable, related, akin, similar, like, resemblant.

fellowship, *n.* **1.** companionship, colleagueship, mateship; comradery, camaraderie, comradeship, esprit de corps, togetherness, fraternization, brotherhood, friendship, amity.

2. community, circle, society, party, camorra; congregation, assemblage, group, band, team, troop.

3. communion, intercommunication, communication, exchange, intercourse, interchange; mutuality, reciprocity, sharing, interdependence.

4. friendliness, amicability, sociability, clubbiness, *Inf.* chumminess, sodality, intimacy; affability, geniality, cordiality, hospitality, kindliness, kind-heartedness, congeniality.

5. association, consociation, partnership, affiliation, joint concern; consortium, syndication, conspiracy, cabal; fraternity, club, *Ger. Gemeinschaft*, lodge, clan, set, clique; company, alliance, coalition, league, union, guild; organization, corporation, amalgamation, combine, merger, monopoly, trust, alignment, bloc, cartel.

felon, *n.* **1.** larcener, larcenist, malfeasant, misfeasor, perjurer; lawbreaker, criminal, convict, *Sl.* jailbird, parolee; ex-convict, *Inf.* ex-con, recidivist, repeat offender, *Inf.* chronic crook; transgressor, trespasser, offender, culprit, miscreant; malefactor, evildoer, wrongdoer, sinner.

2. gangster, mobster, racketeer, mafioso, desperado, terrorist; thug, tough, *Inf.* toughie, mugger, ruffian, rowdy, hoodlum, *Sl.* hood, *Inf.* goon, hooligan, *Inf.* roughneck, *Inf.* baddy, *Sl.* bac actor, *Sl.* gunsel, *Sl.* mug, *Australian Sl.* larrikin, (*in Paris*) apache.

3. assassin, murderer, killer, slayer, sniper; strangler, cutthroat, garroter; liquidator, *Euph.* silencer, *Euph.* dispatcher; gunman, *All U.S. Sl.* gun, hired gun, hit man, trigger-man, hatchet man, torpedo.

4. bandit, hold-up man, *Sl.* stick-up man, armed robber; robber, burglar, thief, stealer, purloiner, *Inf.* crook; embezzler, peculator, *Law.* defalcator.

5. extortionist, extortioner, blackmailer, usurer, loan shark, *Sl.* bleeder; smuggler, runner, bootlegger, contrabandist, white-slaver; forger, counterfeiter, *Fr. faux-monnayeur, Brit. Inf.* coiner.

6. kidnapper, abductor, rapist; sodomist, pervert, child molester, *Sl.* short eyes.

feminine, *adj.* **1.** soft, delicate, gentle, tender; docile, submissive, amenable, deferential; lady-like, refined, genteel.

2. (*of men*) effeminate, womanish, unmasculine, unmanly, effete; sissy, sissyish, *Sl.* faggy.

fence, *n.* **1.** railing, rail, paling, boarding, balustrade, palisade, *Fort.* stockade; enclosure, confine, boundary, periphery, border, margin; barrier, barricade, wall, circumvallation; hedge, hedgerow.

2. fencing, swordplay, swordsmanship.

3. **on the fence** *Informal.* uncommitted, undecided, unsettled, irresolute; neutral, impartial, nonpartisan.

—*v.* **4.** enclose, circumscribe, surround, encircle, encompass; corral, pen, box, case, encase, shut in.

5. defend, protect, shelter, screen, shield; guard, safeguard, ward off, fend off.

6. hedge, beat around the bush, qualify, prevaricate, quibble, equivocate, *Inf.* waffle, fudge; doubletalk, *Inf.* talk out of both sides of one's mouth, palter, backtrack, back-pedal, sidetrack; tergiversate, vacillate, shilly-shally; parry, elude, evade, dodge, shuffle.

fencing, *n.* **1.** swordplay, swordsmanship, fence.

2. hedging, beating around the bush, qualification, prevarication, quibble, equivocation; evasion, dodge, elusion, avoidance; tergiversation, vacillation; double-speak, double-talk, palter, weasel words.

fend, *v.* **1.** *Often* **fend off** ward off, keep off, divert; deflect; avert, prevent, forestall, debar, hinder, inhibit; shield from, defend against, parry, stave off, *Archaic.* forfend; protect, guard, safeguard, shelter, screen, shield.

2. **fend for oneself** take care of oneself, provide for oneself, get along, get by, scrape along, make do, shift.

fender, *n.* defender, protector, shielder, guardian; guard, shield, buffer, bumper, screen, fence, bulwark; shelter, defense, safeguard, security; mudguard, splashguard, cowcatcher, pilot.

feral, *adj.* **1.** bestial, beastlike, beastly, brutish, ferine, *Obs.* belluine; untamed, wild, undomesticated, unbroken; rapacious, ravenous, ravening, predatory,

predacious, raptorial.
2. fierce, savage, ferocious, vicious, fell, truculent; tigerish, wolfish, lupine; brutal, violent, inhuman, barbarous; murderous, slaughterous, bloodthirsty, sanguinary; cruel, ruthless, cold-blooded.

ferment, *n.* **1.** yeast, mold, bacteria, leaven, mother, mother of vinegar, *Brit. Inf.* barm; pepsin, enzyme.
2. fermentation, working, raising, transformation; effervescence, bubbling, boiling, seething, foaming.
3. tumult, commotion, hubbub, hurly-burly, racket, uproar, imbroglio, turbulence, turmoil, embroilment, confusion, stew, brouhaha, fuss, *Inf.* to-do; agitation, state of unrest, *Inf.* a fine state of affairs, *Inf.* a fine mess, *Inf.* a can of worms; sound and fury, *Inf.* barrel of trouble; heat, glow, fever, furor, frenzy.
—*v.* **4.** leaven, raise; work, turn, rise, foam, bubble, effervesce, boil, seethe; pickle, sour, clabber.
5. excite, inflame, foment, incite, provoke, arouse, stir up, agitate, bring to a head *or* to the boiling point; start trouble, *Sl.* raise Cain.

ferocious, *adj.* **1.** bestial, brutish, beastly, beastlike, *Obs.* belluine, feral, ferine; untamed, wild, undomesticated, unbroken; predatory, predacious, raptorial; rapacious, ravenous, ravening.
2. fierce, savage, vicious, fell, truculent; tigerish, wolfish, lupine; brutal, violent, inhuman, barbarous, barbaric, hellish, Tartarian, Hunnish, Vandalic, Gothic; murderous, homicidal, slaughterous, bloodthirsty, sanguinary; sadistic, animalistic, cannibalistic, fiendish, ogreish; diabolical, demonic, demoniac, devilish; terrible, harsh, dire, grim, severe; unrelenting, relentless, remorseless, implacable, inexorable, grinding.
3. pitiless, merciless, heartless, cruel, ruthless; hardhearted, stony-hearted, marble-hearted, cold-blooded.
4. extreme, great, grave; intense, acute, sharp, poignant; flaming, vivid.

ferocity, *n.* fierceness, ferociousness, brutality, viciousness, truculence, ferity, brutishness; cruelty, inhumanity, savagery, ruthlessness, blood-thirstiness, fiendishness, barbarity.

ferret, *v.* **1.** *Usu.* **ferret out** drive *or* hunt out, smoke out, search out, track down, *Inf.* bird-dog; smell out, sniff out, grub up, *Inf.* nose out; bring to light, unearth, disinter, exhume, dig out, run down, trace down, look up, root out; fish out, worm out; pry into, nose around, search about, look into; fathom, *Inf.* get at, *Inf.* see daylight.
2. harry, annoy, badger, hound, tease, harass, persecute, drive from pillar to post; distress, worry, plague, nettle, afflict; torment, trouble, fret, bother, pester; incommode, disturb, exhaust, wear down, *Inf.* get to [s.o.]

ferry, *v.* come and go, go back and forth, shuttle; play, run, traverse, beat, pass; convey across, carry over, pilot, taxi, chauffeur.

fertile, *adj.* **1.** fecund, fruitful, productive, fructuous, fruit-bearing, feracious, fructiferous, frugiferous; generative, potent, virile, reproductive, propagative, fructificative, progenerative.
2. prolific, teeming, profuse, bounteous; pullulating, alive with, *Inf.* crawling with, swarming; proliferous, proliferating, spawning, multiparous; abundant, plenteous, full, copious, *Rare.* uberous; exuberant, luxurious, lush, rank, rife, rich, fat, flush.
3. creative, inventive, resourceful, ingenious; original, ideaful, visionary, constructive, formative.

fertility, *n.* **1.** fecundity, fruitfulness, *Bot.* proliferous, prolificacy, prolificality, fruitiferousness; productiveness, *Rare.* feracity; luxuriance, lushness, exuberance, richness, *Rare.* uberty; copiousness, fullness, rankness, profusion, profuseness.
2. productivity, inventiveness, creativity, creativeness, originality; resourcefulness, imagination, imaginativeness, ingenuity.

fertilize, *v.* **1.** fecundate, impregnate, *Sl.* knock up, inseminate, pollinate.
2. fructify, enrich, feed, dress, treat the soil, manure.

fertilizer, *n.* manure, plant food, compost, dressing, side-dressing; marl, bone meal, yesterday's gardenias; guano, droppings, dung.

fervent, *adj.* **1.** earnest, eager, animated, enthusiastic, excited; ardent, zealous, *Inf.* gung-ho, impassioned, passionate; fervid, perfervid; emotional, emotive, temperamental, high-strung; nervous, tense, excitable, touchy, testy, peppery; spirited, high-spirited, volatile, fiery, hot-headed; heated, feverish, white-hot, inflamed, volcanic; frenzied, frantic, crazed, mad, *Inf.* wild; overwrought, upset, hysterical, not rational; headstrong, stubborn, impetuous, impatient, hasty; sensitive, feeling, sentient, demonstrative, responsive; sensuous, warm, sentimental, deep-feeling; poignant, touching, moving; transported, rapt, enraptured, rapturous, ecstatic.
2. burning, blazing, ablaze, raging, on fire, afire, fiery; flaming, aflame, smoking, ignited; very hot, boiling, scalding, scorching, sizzling; smoldering, simmering, parching; glowing, aglow, gleaming, glaring; very bright, lighted, alight, luminous, illuminated; radiant, brilliant, incandescent.

fervid, *adj.* **1.** fervent, enthusiastic, ardent. See **fervent** (*def.* **1**).
2. burning, very hot, glowing. See **fervent** (*def.* **2**).

fervor, *n.* **1.** fervency, ardor, fervidness, zeal, intensity, passion; enthusiasm, ebullience, exuberance, excitement, elation, elan; eagerness, gusto, delight, relish; verve, vehemence, spirit, vigor, zest, zing, *Sl.* pizzazz; earnestness, intentness, seriousness, devoutness, heartiness, wholeheartedness, sincerity.
2. heat, fire, glow, feverishness.

fester, *v.* **1.** suppurate, gather, matter, maturate, come *or* draw to a head; run, drain, discharge.
2. ulcerate, sphacelate; mortify, necrose, gangrene, putrefy, putresce.
3. rot, rot away, decay, decompose, disintegrate; corrupt, corrode, canker; spoil, go *or* turn bad, go off.
4. (*all of feelings*) rankle, rile, gall, irk, get, get to one, get one's goat; anger, inflame, enflame, stir, stir up, work up; irritate, annoy, torment, vex, plague, bother, fret, chafe, exacerbate, exasperate.
—*n.* **5.** abscess, ulcer, ulceration, noma, festering, gathering, gumboil, parulis, tubercle, *Obs.* apostem *or* aposteme *or* apostume *or* aposthume, *Obs.* apostemation, *Archaic.* impostume *or* imposthume; canker, lesion, chancre, chancroid, soft chancre, simple chancre; boil, blain, furuncle, furunculus, carbuncle, pimple, pustule, papule, papilla, pock, wen, whelk, *Rare.* bleb, *Archaic.* botch; sore, open *or* running sore, excoriation; whitlow, agnail.

festival, *n.* **1.** saint's day, holy day, feast day, *Rom. Cath. Ch.* holy day of obligation, (*in ancient Rome*) feria; rite, ritual, ceremony, celebration, observance, keeping; remembrance, memorialization, commemoration.
2. gala day, red-letter day, banner day, field day; holiday, day of rejoicing, occasion, event, birthday, anniversary, jubilee.
3. activities, doings, festivities, fun and games; entertainment, divertissement, refreshment, amusement, regalement.
4. feast, repast, banquet, revel, fete, wassail, festivi-

ty; carnival, fair, fun-fair, kermis, Mardi Gras, mi-carême; social gathering, get-together, reunion, social, après-ski; soiree, levee, reception, symposium, housewarming; party, dance, ball, *Inf.* hop, square dance, *Inf.* shindig, *Sl.* bash; *Inf.* high jinks, *Inf.* do, *Sl.* jamboree, *Sl.* wingding; junket, *Sl.* blow-out, *Sl.* bust; frolic, spree, whirl, lark; treat, spread, barbecue; saturnalia, carousal, orgy, debauch, Bacchanalia, Bacchanal.

5. merrymaking, *Brit.* holiday-making, jollification, revelry, revels, *Brit. Inf.* mafficking; gaiety, merriment, festivity, conviviality; hilarity, mirth, glee, jollity, sport; joyousness, rejoicing, joyfulness, felicity; fun, funmaking, *Inf.* whoopee, *Inf.* whoop-de-doo, *Inf.* hoopla, fun fast and furious.

festive, *adj.* **1.** convivial, joyous, merry, mirthful, gleeful; gay, sportive, fun-making, uproarious; rollicking, rompish, romping; jovial, jolly, good-time, festal, festival, holiday, in holiday spirits, Christmassy.

2. hospitable, hearty, back-slapping, hail-fellow-well-met; cordial, social, genial; after-dinner, postprandial, unbuttoned.

festivity, *n.* **1.** celebration, regalement. See **festival** (*defs.* **2-4**).

2. gaiety, merriment, revelry. See **festival** (*def.* **5**).

festoon, *n.* **1.** (*all usu. looped or draping*) garland, wreath, lei, chaplet.

—*v.* **2.** wreathe, enwreathe, string flowers; decorate, adorn, ornament, embellish, garnish, array, bedizen, deck, deck out, bedeck, dress, dress up.

fetch, *v.* **1.** get, go for *or* after, go get, *Hunting.* retrieve; capture, seize, grasp, bag, snatch; grip, grab, lay hold of, collar; catch, entrap, ensnare.

2. bring, deliver, conduct, escort, usher, guide, lead; convey, transport, carry.

3. sell for, cost, bring in, bring as a price, yield, afford.

4. *Informal.* captivate, fascinate, enchant, bewitch, allure; delight, titillate, tantalize, carry away.

5. perform, execute, carry out, accomplish, effect, achieve, do; discharge, fulfill, consummate.

6. fetch and carry do the dirty work, perform menial tasks, do service, wait on *or* upon.

—*n.* **7.** extent, expanse, reach, stretch, area, range, span.

8. trick, wile, ruse, artifice, stratagem; device, contrivance, expedient, *Inf.* dodge, subterfuge, blind; maneuver, feint, deception, sleight, coup; shift, move, evasion, shuffle.

fetching, *adj.* *Informal.* charming, fascinating, captivating, enchanting; alluring, provocative, tantalizing, titillating. See **charming.**

fete, *n.* **1.** feast, feast day, holy day. See **festival** (*def.* **1**).

2. holiday, occasion. See **festival** (*def.* **2**).

3. festivity, doings; fair, carnival. See **festival** (*defs.* **3, 4**).

—*v.* **4.** entertain, treat, banquet, regale, wine and dine, dine, welcome, give *or* throw a party for, hold a reception for; honor, do the honors, kill the fatted calf, ring the bell for; roast, toast, salute, drink to, raise *or* tilt glasses to, celebrate.

fetid, *adj.* malodorous, smelly, noisome, stinking; rank, rancid, foul, strong-smelling, musty, moldy; tainted, rotten, putrid, strong, gamy, mephitic.

fetish, *n.* **1.** talisman, charm, amulet, periapt, phylactery, wishbone, scarab, swastika, magic symbol; idol, graven image, golden calf, joss, totem.

2. *Psychiatry.* compulsion, erotic fixation, sexual compulsion.

fetter, *n.* **1.** *Usu.* **fetters** chains, shackles, gyves, trammels; irons, bonds, pinions; manacles, handcuffs, *Sl.* bracelets, *Brit. Sl.* darbies; hampers, clog, governor.

—*v.* **2.** shackle, gyve, manacle, handcuff, put in irons; chain, enchain, truss, bind, bind hand and foot, tie up, tie down; trammel, entrammel, hobble, hamper, clog, pinion.

3. restrain, detain, cage, confine, constrain, lock up, put away, incarcerate, imprison; impound, enclose, pen up, hold captive.

fettle, *n.* condition, order, shape, form, *Inf.* kilter, *Sl.* whack; health, fitness, physical fitness, well-being; state, position, place, situation, circumstance, state of affairs, way, fix, kettle of fish.

fetus, *n.* embryo, fertilized egg; unborn baby.

feud, *n.* **1.** vendetta, rivalry, cold war; hostility, antagonism, animosity, enmity, opposition; acrimoniousness, bitterness, ill will, bad blood, hard feelings, unfriendliness; schism, faction, breach, estrangement, falling out.

2. quarrel, argument, altercation, contention; fight, row, squabble, bickering, spat, tiff, dustup, *Brit. Dial.* fratch; dissension, strife, discord, jar, clash, conflict, factiousness; disagreement, difference of opinion, controversy, contest, variance.

fever, *n.* **1.** fever, heat, *Inf.* temperature, *Sl.* temp; feverishness, febricity, *Pathol.* pyrexia; fire, inflammation, redness, flush, glow; *All Pathol.* scarlet fever, scarlatina, yellow fever, yellow jack, typhus fever, typhoid fever, malaria, ague, delirium, calenture.

2. feverish excitement, restlessness, unrest, agitation, disquiet, unquiet, turmoil, ferment; upset, confusion, fluster, *Inf.* dither, *Inf.* tizzy, frenzy, panic.

3. desire, ardor, passion, intensity, fervency, eagerness, zeal, zealousness, enthusiasm.

feverish, *adj.* **1.** febrile, fevered, feverous, *Pathol.* pyretic, *Pathol.* pyrexic *or* pyrexical, fever-ridden; red, flushed, glowing, inflamed, fiery, hot, red-hot, burning, parched; sudorific, sweating; *Pathol.* delirious, hectic.

2. excited, agitated, restless, nervous, unquiet, wrought up, worked up, frenzied; upset, flustered, confused, *Inf.* in a dither, *Inf.* in a tizzy, frantic.

3. intense, strong, burning, ardent, fervent, impassioned, passionate, desirous, zealous, eager, enthusiastic.

few, *adj.* not many, hardly any, scarcely any; *Inf.* a couple of, a handful of, a sprinkling of, one or two; scant, skimpy, meager; rare, scarce, few and far between; occasional, infrequent, sporadic.

fiancé, fiancée, *n.* betrothed, intended, sweetheart; girlfriend, boyfriend, bride-to-be, husband-to-be.

fiasco, *n.* failure, miscarriage, frustration, nonsuccess, nonfulfillment, inefficacy, *Sl.* no-go, flash in the pan; lead balloon, *Inf.* flop, *Sl.* bomb, *Sl.* brodie, *Inf.* clunker, *Inf.* dud, *Sl.* clinker, *Inf.* bummer, *Sl.* bust; fizzle, botch, blunder, foozle, abortion; muddle, mess, scrape, jam; complete disaster.

fiat, *n.* decree, edict, act, (*in the Middle East*) firman, ukase; ordinance, rule, law, assize; dictum, dictate, command, commandment, order, precept, prescript, mandate, admonition, injunction; proclamation, pronunciamento, manifesto; warrant, sanction, authorization.

fib, *n.* **1.** lie, falsehood, falsity, untruth, prevarication; white lie, misrepresentation, fabrication, invention; fiction, fairy tale, story, tall tale, cock and bull story.

—*v.* **2.** lie, prevaricate, misspeak, palter; equivocate, fudge, sidestep, *Inf.* waffle; withhold, make a mental reservation, talk with one's fingers crossed.

fiber, *n.* **1.** filament, fibril, tendril, strand, thread; web, cobweb, gossamer.
2. character, nature, quality, stripe, streak, grain; constitution, composition, makeup, mold, cast, frame; spirit, disposition, temperament.

fibrous, *adj.* threadlike, stringy, wiry, fibroid, filamentous, filamentary, filiform, fibrillar, fibrilliform, fibrillose.

fickle, *adj.* **1.** capricious, whimsical, fanciful, flighty, giddy, dizzy, frivolous, facetious; changeable, variable, mutable, moody, unpredictable, unaccountable; volatile, mercurial, quicksilver; impulsive, impetuous, erratic, spasmodic, fitful, irregular.
2. indecisive, undecided, uncertain, unsure, irresolute, unresolved; wishy-washy, blowing hot and cold, wavering, fluctuating, vacillating, shilly-shallying.
3. inconstant, unfaithful, faithless, disloyal, unsteady, unstable, unsteadfast; tricky, slippery, shifty, double-dealing, treacherous, perfidious; unreliable, undependable, untrustworthy, fly-by-night, fickle-minded; unrestrained, undisciplined, uncontrolled, fast and loose.

fickleness, *n.* **1.** capriciousness, fancifulness, giddiness, facetiousness; changeableness, mutability, moodiness; impulsiveness, impetuosity, erraticalness.
2. indecision, uncertainty, irresolution, wishy-washiness.
3. inconstancy, unfaithfulness, disloyalty; treacherousness, perfidiousness, shiftiness; unreliability, undependability, untrustworthiness, fickle-mindedness.

fiction, *n.* **1.** story, tale, romance, novel, antinovel, *Archaic.* gest; myth, legend, fable, parable, allegory, saga, epic; mystery, *Inf.* whodunit, *Inf.* thriller, *Inf.* shocker; science-fiction story, sci-fi story, *Inf.* space opera.
2. fabrication, invention, concoction, tall tale *or* story, cock and bull story, fish story, *Inf.* song and dance; lie, prevarication, falsehood, fib, canard, *Inf.* whopper; fancy, whimsy, *Archaic.* maggot, crotchet; fantasy, vapor, imagining, hallucination, figment of the imagination.

fictitious, *adj.* **1.** feigned, simulated, pretended, affected, assumed, put-on, faked; disingenuous, insincere, supposititious; false, spurious, counterfeit, sham, ungenuine, unauthentic, pseudo, bogus, fake, *Inf.* phony; artificial, synthetic, made out of whole cloth.
2. fabricated, invented, manufactured, concocted, made-up, trumped-up; imaginary, fictive, unreal, nonfactual, make-believe, figmental, fictional; fabulous, legendary, mythical, mythological.

fiddle, *n.* **1.** violin, viol, viola, cello; crowd *or* crwth.
2. **fit as a fiddle** healthy, in good health, sound, fit, robust, in fine fettle, *Inf.* in shape *or* in good shape.
—*v.* **3.** twiddle; fuss with, fool with, toy with, play with, fidget with, finger; (*of a dial, knob, etc.*) adjust, tune.
4. trifle, toy, play, *Inf.* mess around, *Inf.* monkey around; dally, dillydally, dawdle, *Inf.* diddle.

fiddle-de-dee, *interj.* nonsense, stuff and nonsense, balderdash, hogwash, pish, pish and tush, pshaw, humbug, bah, poppycock, fiddle-faddle, tommyrot, *Inf.* rot; *All Sl.* garbage, bunk, bosh, *Brit.* tosh, baloney, bushwa, bilge water, horsefeathers, moonshine, *Vulgar.* bullshit.

fiddle-faddle, *n.* *Informal.* nonsense, balderdash, bunkum. See **nonsense** (*def.* **2**).

fidelity, *n.* **1.** duteousness, obedience, compliance; devotedness, devotion, dedication, consecration, allegiance, single-heartedness, patriotism; loyalty, loyalness, faithfulness, fealty, trueness, true-heartedness; steadfastness, steadiness, unchangingness, constancy, abidingness, lastingness, enduringness, permanence; staunchness, unswervingness, firmness, resoluteness; stability, stableness, solidity, solidness, strength, incorruptibility, incorruptibleness.
2. trustworthiness, trustiness, reliability, reliableness, dependability, dependableness, responsibility, responsibleness; sincerity, sincereness, earnestness, conscientiousness, scrupulousness; uprightness, integrity, probity, righteousness, honorableness, upstandingness.
3. accuracy, exactness, exactitude, precision, preciseness, closeness, faithfulness, strictness; correspondency, correspondence, similarity, agreement, accordance, conformity; honestness, truthfulness, credibility, credibleness, authenticity, genuineness, realness.

fidget, *v.* **1.** twiddle, twiddle one's thumbs, jitter, move by fits and starts, *Scot.* fidge, twitch, jerk; play around, fool around; wiggle, wigwag, squirm, itch, scrabble, *Sl.* have ants in one's pants.
2. agitate, irritate, annoy, bother; fluster, ruffle, upset, discombobulate.
—*n.* **3.** *Usu.* **fidgets** fidgetiness, restlessness, dither, stew, uneasiness, skittishness; jitters, nervousness, fantods, *Sl.* willies, *Sl.* heebie-jeebies, *Inf.* whim-whams, *Sl.* jimjams, *Inf.* screaming-meemies.

fidgety, *adj.* restless, restive, jittery, skittish, jumpy, *Sl.* antsy; impatient, unquiet, uneasy, itchy, nervous, tremulous; flustered, flurried, ruffled, fussed, in a pother.

field, *n.* **1.** pasture, clearing, *Archaic.* glebe; meadow, *Archaic.* mead, lea; sward, green, lawn, lot, common, campus.
2. playing field, the turf, track, hippodrome; ballfield, diamond, gridiron, arena, lists; parade ground, *Sl.* grinder, drill field; battleground, theater of operations.
3. sphere, scope, domain, realm; territory, province, bailiwick, bounds, department; expanse, stretch, extent, area, space, range, reach; limits, confines.
4. discipline, specialization, forte, expertise.

fiend, *n.* **1.** Satan, demon, devil. See **devil** (*defs.* **1-3**).
2. savage, monster, ogre, beast, brute; sadist, Genghis Khan, Attila the Hun, Bluebeard, Jack the Ripper; malefactor, badman, *Brit.* bad hat, *Sl.* bad news, *Sl.* bad actor, *Sl.* rotter; hit man, gunslinger, *Inf.* plugugly, *U.S.* tough; barbarian, ruffian, rowdy, *Inf.* meanie, *Sl.* creep, ghoul; scoundrel, villain, Iago, *Sl.* rat, blackguard; cad, *Inf.* heel, *Sl.* no-goodnik, *Sl.* bastard.
3. mischief-maker, imp, brat; pain in the neck, annoyance, nuisance, pest; jackanapes, whippersnapper.
4. addict, *Sl.* freak; *Inf.* hound, *Sl.* hophead, *Sl.* druggie; chain smoker, *Sl.* nicotine nut; alcoholic, *Sl.* boozer.
5. fan, enthusiast, aficionado, devotee, follower, *Inf.* buff; *Sl.* nut, *Sl.* bug, monomaniac.

fiendish, *adj.* **1.** inhuman, barbarous, barbaric, savage, Tartarian, Hunnish, Vandalic; brutal, brutish, murderous, slaughterous, bloodthirsty, sanguinary, sadistic, ogreish; terrible, harsh, fell, truculent; ferocious, ruthless, vicious, feral, ferine; pitiless, merciless, heartless, unkind, unfeeling, cruel, hardhearted, stony-hearted, cold-blooded; unrelenting, relentless, remorseless, inexorable.
2. demonic, diabolic, diabolical, devilish, ghoulish; satanic, Mephistophelian, demonian, demoniac, demoniacal, cacodemonic; infernal, hellish, hellborn.

3. damnable, execrable, accursed, abominable, horrible, horrid, hideous, monstrous, atrocious; base, vile, odious, obnoxious, villainous, sinister; wicked, iniquitous, evil, sinful, ungodly, impious, *Obs.* scelerous, black-hearted, corrupt, depraved, *Archaic.* facinorous; nefarious, flagitious, unspeakable, heinous; profligate, immoral, dissolute, vitiated, perverted, perverse; pestilential, malevolent, malicious, malign, maleficent, malefic, venomous; dire, black, dreadful, baleful.

fierce, *adj.* **1.** wild, savage, ferocious, vicious, fell, truculent; brutish, feral, ferine, tigerish, wolfish, lupine; brutal, inhuman, barbarous, barbaric, hellish, Tartarian, Hunnish, Gothic, Vandalic; murderous, homicidal, slaughterous, bloodthirsty, sanguinary; terrible, harsh, grim; unrelenting, relentless, remorseless; pitiless, merciless, heartless, cruel, ruthless, cold-blooded.

2. violent, furious, raging, frenzied, furibund, vehement; turbulent, tempestuous, tumultuous, tumultuary, uproarious, stormy; clamorous, rampant, boisterous, blustery, blusterous, blasty, gusty; cyclonic, typhonic.

3. keen, intense, fervent, fervid; eager, earnest, avid, zealous; ardent, passionate, impassioned, fiery; enthusiastic, spirited, high-spirited, animated, hearty; unrestrained, unbridled, uncurbed, unchecked, uncontrolled.

4. *Informal.* bad, severe, grave; formidable, awful, dire, dreadful; bitter, biting, racking, tearing, gnawing.

fiery, *adj.* **1.** on fire, afire, in flames, flaming, conflagrant; burning, blazing, ablaze; igneous, volcanic; intensely hot, red-hot, white-hot, candent; tropical, sweltering, *Archaic.* calid, torrid, parching; heated, thermal, calorific.

2. glowing, aglow, lurid, incandescent, incalescent; gleaming, glaring, brightly lit, alight; luminous, illuminated, radiant, brilliant; shimmering, twinkling, flashing, flickering, glittering, sparkling, fluttering.

3. zealous, ardent, vehement, eager, intensely desirous; *Inf.* hot, stimulated, aroused; passionate, impassioned, fervent, fervid, perfervid, frenzied, frantic; excited, exhilarated, *Inf.* psyched *or* psyched up, enthusiastic; enlivened, inspired, animated.

4. excitable, nervous, high-strung, spirited, temperamental; touchy, testy, peppery, emotional, volatile, volcanic; impetuous, impulsive, hasty, agitated, irritated, irritable, vexed, galled, riled, piqued, chafed, nettled; offended, disturbed, perturbed; very angry, wrathful, incensed, irate; enraged, infuriated, furious.

5. flammable, inflammable, inflammatory, conflagratory, conflagrative; combustible, explosive, incendiary; ignitable, *Rare.* accendible, tindery; burnable, consumable.

6. inflamed, feverish, fevered, feverous, febrile, *Pathol.* pyretic, *Pathol.* pyrexic *or* pyrexial, fever-ridden; hot, red-hot, burning, parched; flushed, sudorific, sweating; *Pathol.* delirious, hectic.

7. spicy, tangy, zesty, piquant; savory, rich, aromatic, fragrant; pungent, sharp, keen, strong, hot; racy, peppery, nippy, *Inf.* zippy, *Inf.* snappy.

fiesta, *n.* **1.** saint's day, holy day, feast day, *Rom. Cath. Ch.* holy day of obligation, anniversary; celebration, observance, keeping, honoring; remembrance, memorialization, commemoration, ritualization, solemnization.

2. festival, fete, gala, feast, revel, wassail; carnival, fair, fun-fair, Mardi Gras.

fight, *n.* **1.** battle, combat, duel, bout; contention, clash, conflict, struggle, *Scot.* sprattle, strife; war, warfare, fighting, hostilities; assault, attack, offensive, harassment, assailment; siege, besiegement, besetment, investment; collision, meeting, engagement, encounter, rencounter; brawl, feud, affray, wrangle, *Inf.* set-to; row, *Scot.* collieshangie, free-for-all, donnybrook, rumble, broil; contest, show-down; melee, fisticuffs, boxing, *Sl.* milling, match; outbreak, riot, *Fr. émeute;* scuffle, tussle, fray.

2. disagreement, squabble, difference of opinion, disaccord, discord, misunderstanding; parting of the ways, break up, divergence; altercation, argument, quarrel, *Sl.* mix-up, dispute, disputation, contention; sparring, bickering, spatting, jangling; dissension, dissent, dissidence, discord, *Inf.* blow-up, falling-out.

—*v.* **3.** battle, give *or* do battle, contend; clash, conflict with; encounter, engage, meet; duel, joust, tussle, skirmish, scuffle, jostle; war, make war, war against, go to war, go to battle, wage war, take the field, take up arms; brawl, feud, go at it tooth and nail, come to blows; pommel, beat, beat into the ground, batter; box, spar, exchange fisticuffs, slug it out, wrestle, grapple with; slaughter, massacre, butcher.

4. assault, attack, beset, assail, harass; raid, storm, charge, rush, tilt, blitz; set upon, pounce upon, bombard, open fire upon, engage in hostilities, *Sl.* let [s.o.] have it, *Sl.* lay into, *Archaic.* insult.

5. contest, confront, rise up against, *Obs.* militate against, rail against, ride against, struggle against, *Archaic.* reluct; oppose, defy, contradict, make something of, contravene, refute, confound; object to, protest, call in question, march against, make a stand against, dispute, oppugn; resist, repel, repulse, withstand, stand one's ground; frustrate, balk, foil, cross, play at cross purposes.

6. disagree, differ, fail to agree, disaccord, be at variance, be at odds; think differently, stand in opposition, diverge, deviate; part company, go separate ways, have a difference of opinion.

7. altercate, argue, quarrel, dispute, spar, have words, fall out; bicker, spat, tiff; quibble, squabble, wrangle; debate, dissent, contend, take issue with, contest, object, *Scot.* thraw.

8. conduct, carry on, wage, maneuver.

fighter, *n.* **1.** warrior, brave, combatant, soldier, militarist, redcoat, janissary, Tommy Atkins, private, cavalryman, dragoon, man-at-arms, belligerent; attacker, assailant, assailer, assaulter, invader, aggressor, militant; rival, contestant, competitor, contender.

2. duelist, swordsman, fencer, jouster, gladiator; sharpshooter, rifleman, fusileer, musketeer, grenadier; archer, bowman; wrangler, brawler, affrayer; mercenary, soldier of fortune, free lance, adventurer; infantryman, foot soldier; artilleryman, gunner, cannoneer.

3. *All Boxing.* boxer, champion, prize fighter, *Inf.* slugger, pugilist; wrestler, grappler.

4. trouper, *Inf.* scrapper, die-hard, fanatic.

figment, *n.* fabrication, concoction, invention, illusion, delusion, product of the imagination; fiction, story, fable; falsehood, canard.

figurative, *adj.* metaphorical, tropical, not literal; allegorical, parabolic, anagogic, ironic, satirical; representative, descriptive, imagistic, illustrative, pictorial, graphic; significative, emblematic, symbolic, symbolizing, standing for.

figure, *n.* **1.** number, numeral, cipher, digit.

2. sum, total, aggregate, amount, price, cost.

3. **figures** arithmetic, mathematics; statistics, *Inf.* stats., numerical data.

4. form, shape, outline, cast, cut; configuration, conformation, structure, frame, build, body.

5. representation, image, picture, icon; effigy, sculpture, statue, bust, mold, cast; illustration, drawing, diagram; design, pattern, device; emblem, symbol, type, representative, sign.

6. character, personality, personage, somebody notable, worthy.

7. *Usu.* **figures of speech** metaphor, simile, conceit, trope, personification, image, imagery; *All Rhet.* antithesis, metonymy, synecdoche, antonomasia, enallage.

—*v.* **8.** compute, calculate, reckon, cipher, work out; count, numerate, enumerate; total, add up, sum up; appraise, assess.

9. adorn, ornament, bedeck, embellish; variegate, diversify, mark.

10. portray, impersonate, take the part of, appear as; perform, act.

11. metaphorize, personify, allegorize, fable; symbolize, signify, emblemize; represent, stand for.

12. outline, trace, sketch, adumbrate; draw, delineate, limn, depict, portray, picture; shape, form, image.

13. *Informal.* reason, think about, ponder over; conclude, judge, opine; surmise, conjecture, suppose, believe.

figurehead, *n.* **1.** titular head, nominal head, assumed head, acting head.

2. (*on prow of a ship*) sculpture, carving, bust, statue, image.

figurine, *n.* statuette, carving, china figure; knickknack, trinket, gimcrack, ornament.

filament, *n.* fiber, fibril, fibrilla, strand; string, thread, floss, twist, yarn; twine, packthread, cord, rope, cable, wire; hair, tendril, cilia, lash, cobweb, gossamer, *Biol.* membrane, *Zool.* webbing.

filch, *v.* **1.** steal, thieve, rob, pilfer, purloin, finger, pick, *Inf.* snitch, cabbage, abstract, *Chiefly Brit.* prig, *Brit. Sl.* snaffle, *Euph.* borrow, *Archaic.* nim; peculate, embezzle, *Law.* defalcate, misappropriate, convert; shoplift, palm, *Sl.* boost, walk off *or* away with, *Euph.* remove; *All Sl.* heist, pinch, hook, swipe, hustle, rip off, frisk, crook, cop, lift.

2. appropriate, expropriate, arrogate, usurp; pirate, plagiarize, copy, *Inf.* lift, *Inf.* crib, forge, counterfeit.

3. swindle, defraud, mulct, shark, cheat, fleece, *Inf.* flimflam, rook, bilk, *Inf.* welsh, *Inf.* do [s.o.] out of, *Inf.* gyp, *Sl.* pluck, *Sl.* chisel, *Sl.* clip.

4. mooch, scrounge, scavenge, freeload, sponge, *Sl.* bum.

file[1], *n.* **1.** dossier, organized collection *or* assortment, arrangement; folder, organizer, envelope, container, holder; filing cabinet, cabinet, drawer, box, pigeonhole, receptacle, repository, compartment.

2. line, queue, row, rank; string, chain, range, series.

—*v.* **3.** organize, categorize, systematize, classify, set up; arrange, put *or* place in order, alphabetize; pigeonhole, interfile, insert, put in place, replace.

4. march *or* walk in a line *or* row, parade, pass in formation, follow the leader.

5. file for, apply, make application, fill out *or* turn in an application, put in for, put in *or* make a bid for, make a claim for; register, sign up, get one's name on the list.

file[2], *n.* **1.** rasp, emery board, nail file, abrasive.

—*v.* **2.** rasp, scrape, grate, shred; grind, whet, sand, sandpaper, pumice; abrade, rub, rub down, scour; polish, burnish, buff, smooth, wax, shine; trim, cut down, reduce, shave, plane, shape.

filial, *adj.* **1.** sonly, daughterly, sonlike, daughterlike.

2. devoted, dutiful, respectful; affectionate, loving, fond.

filibuster, *n.* **1.** *U.S.* (*all in reference to legislation*) obstruction, hindrance, impediment, prevention, postponement, delay; (*all in reference to formal discourse, to accomplish the preceding*) exhortation, declamation, harangue, spiel, tirade, bombast; dissertation, oration, peroration, endless discourse; monologue; tangent, digression, rambling, wandering, irrelevancy, excursus.

2. freebooter, buccaneer, pirate, viking, corsair, privateer. See **pirate** (*defs.* **1-4**).

—*v.* **3.** *U.S.* (*all in reference to legislation*) impede, obstruct, hinder, prevent, delay, postpone, put off; (*all to accomplish the preceding*) hold forth, expound, expatiate, rant, rave, discourse interminably, go on at length; maunder, blather, ramble, digress, go off on a tangent, wander, meander, stray.

4. pirate, buccaneer, privateer, freeboot. See **pirate** (*defs.* **7, 8**).

filigree, *n.* **1.** wirework, fretwork, fret, scrollwork, grillwork, latticework, lattice; lacework, lace, network, netting, net, mesh, crochet, tatting; ornamentation, decoration, arabesque.

2. gossamer, sheer, chiffon, voile, organza, organdy, tissue, tissue paper; ephemera, whim, vagary, caprice, fancy, daydream, dream, illusion.

—*adj.* **3.** delicate, fine, finely-wrought, fragile, dainty.

fill, *v.* **1.** fill up, fill to the brim, fill to overflowing, overfill, stuff, overstuff, crowd, overcrowd, congest; load *or* load down, lade, burden, overburden; cram, force down *or* in, ram down, pack in, push in, shove in, press in, jam, squeeze, pack like sardines.

2. supply, furnish, provide, outfit; store, lay in *or* by, stock, restock, refill, replenish, renew.

3. feed fully, satiate, content, eat one's fill, satisfy, sate, cloy, pall; surfeit, glut, gorge, stuff, cram; overfeed, overeat, overdrink, overindulge, overdo; gormandize, *Archaic.* gluttonize, eat greedily, *Sl.* pig out, *Sl.* munch out, put down *or* away, pack in.

4. pervade, penetrate, infuse, inject, charge; permeate, spread throughout, overspread, suffuse, impregnate, imbue, soak, saturate.

5. occupy, serve, act, function, perform, execute, do, discharge, carry out *or* through, complete, fulfill.

6. meet *or* fulfill the requirements, *Inf.* fill the bill.

7. stop up, clog, stuff, block; close, close off, caulk, seal, plug, bung, cork.

8. fill in a. complete, fill out, fill in the blanks, **b.** substitute for, sub for, stand in for, replace, take the place of. **c.** *Slang.* inform, advise, notify, tell, let in on, share with.

9. fill out a. fill in, complete, fill in the blanks. **b.** round out, fatten, pad, enlarge, make bigger, inflate, blow up, puff up; swell, grow, expand, extend, stretch, spread *or* spread out, diffuse, widen, dilate, dilatate.

fillip, *n.* **1.** snap, flip, flick, click, tick, tap, crack.

2. stimulus, urge, incentive, inducement, encouragement, provocation, incitement, motivation; spur, goad, prod, stick, whip, lash; push, shove, jab, sting, prick, shot.

—*v.* **3.** stimulate, urge, induce, encourage, provoke, incite, motivate, spur, goad, poke, prod, prompt, prick, push, egg on; jar, jolt, inspire, fire, whet, sharpen, keen, awaken, arouse, animate, quicken, get going.

film, *n.* **1.** skin, membrane, pellicle, integument, peel, caul; covering, cover, layer, coat, coating, blanket, dusting, sheet; mask, screen, veil, gauze, web, gossamer; scum, foam, froth; slick, oilslick, spill.

2. haze, cloud, mist, blur, milkiness, pearliness, murkiness; vapor, steam, fog, smoke, smog, smoke screen, dust storm.

3. motion picture, movie, *Inf.* flick, cinema, cinematography, movies, films, pictures, *Inf.* pix; feature, short, short subject, episode, serial, *Inf.* chapter; filmstrip, slide show, videotape, tape; microform, microfilm, microfiche, fiche, filmcard; *Inf.* instant replay, *Inf.* playback; rerun, revival, *Inf.* oldie.

—*v.* **4.** cover, coat, varnish, glaze, veneer, slick *or* spill over; shade, mist, shadow, cloud, haze, dull, blur, blear, screen; hide, conceal, mask, veil, shroud, robe; obscure, obfuscate, adumbrate.

5. photograph, put on film, preserve on film, make a movie, do a take, shoot, shoot a scene; videotape, tape, microfilm.

filmy, *adj.* **1.** gauzy, gossamer, gossamery, sheer, diaphanous, fine, thin, delicate, flimsy, unsubstantial, see-through, translucent, transparent; light, airy, floaty.

2. hazy, misty, dull, blurred, bleary, cloudy; milky, pearly, opalescent, frosted; coated, murky, vaporous, opaque, obfuscated.

filter, *n.* **1.** strainer, strain, screen, sieve, sifter, colander, riddle; leaching field, drainage, field; net, netting, gauze, cheesecloth.

—*v.* **2.** strain, filtrate, clear, clarify; purify, refine.

3. percolate, leach, run through, pass through, filter through; find, vent, escape, flow out, effuse; exude, seep, transude, ooze, drain, leak.

filth, *n.* **1.** refuse, trash, garbage, slop; sewage, discharge, dregs, lees, slime; sediment, silt, sludge, muck, mire, mud, dirt, slush; decay, rot, putrescence, putridity, carrion, offal, foul matter; leavings, excrement, feces; excreta, manure, dung, ordure, night soil, guano; grime, smudge, smoke, soot, dust, ashes; nastiness, filthiness, uncleanness, squalor.

2. defilement, pollution, contamination, taint, foulness, maculation; corruption, adulteration, debasement, degradation, deterioration, rottenness.

3. obscenity, pornography, smut, *Sl.* raunch; grossness, vulgarity, vileness, nastiness, indecency; foul language, *Inf.* dirty talk.

filthy, *adj.* **1.** foul, dirty, unclean, slimy, mucky, feculent, fecal; defiled, polluted, tainted; musty, smelly, rotten, fetid, gone bad, flyblown, maggoty, putrid, purulent, *Sl.* cruddy, muddy, soiled, stained, grimy, begrimed, smeared, dirtsmeared, sooty, smoky, dusty.

2. unwashed, bedraggled, slovenly, unkempt, piggish, sloppy, sleazy; squalid, wretched, shabby, deteriorated, ramshackle; miserable, uncared-for, dingy, *Sl.* slummy.

3. low, contemptible, despicable, base, mean; vile, scurvy, ignominious, trashy, sordid.

4. depraved, corrupt, obscene, impure, indelicate, indecent, gross, offensive, objectionable; nasty, coarse, shameless, vulgar, nasty-minded, foul-mouthed, loose; lewd, smutty, pornographic, bawdy, ribald, suggestive, risqué, *Sl.* raunchy.

final, *adj.* **1.** concluding, completing, terminating, ending, finishing, closing; terminal, endmost, last, *Inf.* tail-end; last-ditch, extreme; last-minute.

2. ultimate, eventual, coming, unavoidable, inevitable.

3. conclusive, decisive, determinate, definitive, complete, thorough, exhaustive; fixed, finished, decided, irrevocable, unappealable; incontrovertible, indisputable, irrefutable, sure, certain, absolute.

finale, *n.* end, finish, conclusion, terminus, termination, windup, *Sl.* pay off; climax, culmination, consummation; end *or* final result, final event *or* scene, last act, bitter end, finis, curtain, final curtain, *Sl.* curtains, catastrophe.

finality, *n.* **1.** conclusiveness, decisiveness, definitiveness, irrevocableness; terminality; completeness, wholeness, totality, entirety; ultimateness, eventuality, unavoidableness, inevitableness.

2. end, finish, finale. See **finale**.

finally, *adv.* **1.** in the end, after all, at last, at long last, lastly, at length; ultimately, eventually, in the long run, when all is said and done.

2. conclusively, decisively, convincingly, absolutely, definitely, once and for all.

finance, *n.* **1.** money management, investment, investment theory, fiscal matters, pecuniary matters; economics, banking, accounting.

2. finances revenue, resources, capital, holdings, assets, stock, wealth, cash, money; treasury, bank accounts; personal finances, wherewithal.

—*v.* **3.** furnish credit, back, *Inf.* angel, set [s.o.] up in business, capitalize, be a silent partner of [s.o.], underwrite.

financial, *adj.* pecuniary, fiscal, money, monetary, economic, bread-and-butter.

financier, *n.* banker, treasurer, cambist, broker, moneyman, money-lender; capitalist, rich man, large-scale investor, plutocrat, millionaire, *Sl.* fat cat, *Sl.* one of the big boys.

find, *v.* **1.** come upon *or* across, chance upon, happen upon, light upon, hit upon, stumble on *or* upon; run into, bump into, fall on *or* upon, meet with, encounter, experience.

2. earn, win, gain, get, procure, acquire, obtain, reach, attain, succeed.

3. discover, locate, place, lay one's hand on, put one's finger *or* hand on; ascertain, find out, hear of, get wind of, learn of; determine, figure out, solve, get at, unriddle, decode, decipher; make out, discern, detect, descry, espy, notice, perceive, remark, note, distinguish, recognize, catch a glimpse of, catch sight of, *Inf.* spot; see, behold, observe, view, *Brit.* twig, watch, *Archaic.* ken.

4. recover, recoup, recuperate, regain, get *or* make back, repossess, take back.

5. provide, furnish, supply, outfit.

6. find fault complain, grumble, mutter, gripe, *Sl.* bitch, *Sl.* squawk, object to, take exception; carp, cavil at *or* about, *Inf.* nitpick, pick *or* pull apart, pick to pieces, *Inf.* pick holes in, *Sl.* cut up *or* to pieces; criticize, *Inf.* knock, *Inf.* pan, shoot down, put down, *Sl.* dump on, *Inf.* slam; disparage, depreciate, belittle, laugh *or* scoff at, make fun of, ridicule; attack verbally, *Inf.* light into, lace into, *Sl.* lay into, assail, *Inf.* tear into, *Inf.* rip into; *Sl.* blast, *Sl.* let [s.o.] have it, *Inf.* jump on, *Inf.* jump all over, get on [s.o.'s] back, *Sl.* get on [s.o.'s] case, *Sl.* get down on, come down on, land on hard; berate, tongue-lash, dress down, lay out in lavender, tear apart, rake over the coals; call down, rebuke, scold, admonish, chide, shake the head *or* finger at, reprehend, reprove, reproach; blame, censure, disapprove, frown upon, denounce, condemn.

7. find out **a.** discover, ascertain. See **find** (*def.* **3**). **b.** detect, expose, show up, bring out into the open; bring to light, turn up, uncover, unearth, disinter, dig up, root out, ferret out, smoke out, search out; track down, pursue, follow, trail, stalk, hunt down.

8. find, finding, discovery, hit, strike; catch, deal, bargain, good buy; lucky hit, bonanza, jackpot, windfall, godsend, boon.

finding, *n.* **1.** discovery, find. See **find** (*def.* **8**).

2. decision, award, verdict, conclusion, judgment, sentence, pronouncement, decree, order.

fine[1], *adj.* **1.** good, satisfactory, acceptable, all right, *Inf.* O.K., *Sl.* copacetic, *Sl.* hunky-dory, *Chiefly Brit. Inf.* tickety-boo, *Archaic.* rum; quality, superior, high grade, choice, select; splendid, *Inf.* splendiferous, superb, magnificent, *Sl.* swell, *Sl.* cool, *Brit. Sl.* ripping; excellent, first-rate, first-class, prime, top drawer, *Inf.* out of this world.

2. pure, solid, sterling, twenty-four carat, one hundred percent; unadulterated, unpolluted, clear.

3. ground, powdered, crushed, pulverized, comminute, triturated, particled; grated, minced, chopped.

4. fragile, delicate, frail, dainty, slight, small, tiny, *Inf.* teeny; thin, tapered, attenuated, slender; filamentary, filamentous, filamented, fibriform, fibrillar, fibrilliform, threadlike, hairlike, fibratus, tendrillar, tendrilous.

5. gossamery, gossamer, gossamered, chiffon, sheer, tissuey, tissuelike, finely woven; gauzy, gauzelike, light, lightweight, flimsy, cobwebby, filmy, diaphanous, transparent, translucent, pellucid, airy, ethereal.

6. refined, cultured, polished, finished; tasteful, discerning, discriminating, fastidious, nice, precious; elegant, exquisite, high-fashion, fashionable, stylish, modish, chic, smart, *Inf.* nifty, *Brit. Sl.* nobby; elaborate, lavish, ornate, gaudy, garish, ostentatious, showy, flashy.

7. subtle, elusive, fine-drawn, finespun, finely honed; witty, clever, urbane, suave, sophisticated; keen, acute, sharp, perspicacious, quick, intelligent, apt.

8. good-looking, handsome, pleasing to the eye, seemly, *Scot.* wally; gorgeous, beautiful, *Chiefly Literary.* beauteous, pretty, lovely, fair, comely, becoming, attractive, *Chiefly U.S. Inf.* cute, *Chiefly Scot.* bonny.

—interj. **9.** all right, okay, *Inf.* O.K., *Inf.* okey-dokey; agreed, very well, good enough, good, you bet, suits me, sure.

fine², *n.* **1.** mulct, amercement, penalty, settlement, *Law.* damages; forfeiture, forfeit, confiscation, *Law.* sequestration; fixed fee, fee, charge, cost.

—v. **2.** mulct, amerce, impose a fine upon; confiscate, *Law.* sequestrate; penalize, punish, exact punishment.

finery, *n.* **1.** frippery, best clothes, best bib and tucker, *Inf.* Sunday clothes, *Inf.* Sunday best, *Inf.* Sunday-go-to-meetings, *Inf.* gear, *Sl.* glad rags, *Sl.* heavy threads.

2. frilliness, frills, frills and furbelows, falderal, trumpery, gaudery, fuss, *Inf.* foofaraw, *Sl.* jazz.

finespun, *adj.* **1.** sheer, delicate, fine, tissuey, flimsy, gauzy, gauzelike, cobwebby; light, filmy, diaphanous, transparent, translucent; gossamer, lacy, lacelike, filigree; filamentary, filamentous, filamented, fibriform, fibrillar, fibrilliform, threadlike; hairlike, fibratus, tendrillar, tendrilous; thin, tapered, slender.

2. refined, subtle, nice, precise, exact, hairsplitting.

finesse, *n.* **1.** delicacy, subtlety, subtleness, artfulness, craftiness, shrewdness, *Inf.* cuteness; skillfulness, skill, ability, knack, talent; adroitness, proficiency, adeptness, mastery, expertness; facility, facileness, quickness, aptness, brightness.

2. savoir-faire, tact, discretion, diplomacy, worldly wisdom, know-how; taste, refinement, polish, elegance, grace.

3. artifice, stratagem, trick, wile, ruse; scheme, strategy, machination, plot, plan, intrigue; device, contrivance, expedient, *Inf.* dodge, fetch, blind; maneuver, feint, deception, sleight, coup, blow, stroke; shift, move, evasion, shuffle, juggle; trickery, deceit, guile, craft.

—v. **4.** maneuver, *Inf.* finagle, manipulate, gerrymander, intrigue; live by one's wits, contrive.

5. cheat, delude, deceive, beguile, mislead, hoodwink; trick, outwit, overreach, circumvent, get around, put one over on; pull the wool over [s.o.'s] eyes, bluff, take in, *Inf.* buffalo, *Sl.* con, *Sl.* flimflam, *Sl.* flam.

finger, *n.* **1.** digit, pointer, arrow, index.

2. **have a finger in** meddle in *or* with, stick *or* poke one's nose in, have a hand in, get involved in; snoop, pry, nose; tamper with, monkey with, mess around with.

3. **keep one's fingers crossed** wish for good luck, hope for the best, be hopeful, *Inf.* think positive; knock on wood.

4. **lay** *or* **put one's finger on** **a.** remember, recall, bring to mind, bring back. **b.** discover, find, find out; locate, put one's hands on, identify, place, *Sl.* peg; signify, point out.

5. **lift a finger** make an attempt, do something, help out, do one's part, contribute.

6. **put the finger on** *Slang.* inform on *or* against, tell on, *Inf.* snitch on, tattle, *Sl.* squeal on; betray, *Sl.* double cross, *Sl.* sell out, *Sl.* blow one's cover, testify *or* bear witness against.

7. **slip through one's fingers** pass by, slip by, escape, go unchecked, become elusive.

8. **twist around one's little finger** manipulate, use, misuse, lead by the nose; have influence over, control, keep under one's thumb.

—v. **9.** touch, feel, handle, palpate, thumb, palm, paw; stroke, caress, pet, fondle; tickle, toy with, play with, meddle; brush, graze; massage, knead, rub; manipulate, twiddle.

10. steal, purloin, pilfer, filch, seize, rob, pick, cabbage, *Brit. Sl.* snaffle, *Euph.* borrow; shoplift, palm, *Sl.* boost, walk off *or* away with, *Euph.* remove; *All Sl.* heist, pinch, swipe, hustle,rip off, frisk, cop, lift.

11. *Informal.* point out, identify, put the finger on. See **finger** (*def.* **6**).

finicky, *adj.* **1.** fussy, overparticular, finical, meticulous; picky, *Inf.* choosy, dainty, *Inf.* fuddy-duddy, *Inf.* pernickety; fastidious, hard to please, difficult, critical; overcritical, hypercritical, overdemanding, overexacting.

2. overfastidious, overnice; affected, coxcombical, foppish, dapper, dandy.

finis, *n.* conclusion, close, end, termination, finish, completion; finale, final act *or* scene, final curtain, last part *or* stage; summary, summation, wrap-up, wind-up; result, issue, outcome, upshot; *Fr. fait accompli,* completed act; *All Inf.* that's it, that's that, that's all folks; expiration, death, bitter end; deathblow, K.O., *Fr. coup de grâce.*

finish, *v.* **1.** complete, do, carry through, play out, go *or* follow through with; carry out, fulfill, realize, achieve, attain, accomplish, compass; bring to an end, settle, resolve, terminate, end; conclude, close, wind up, *Inf.* wrap up, clinch, clench, seal; perfect, consummate, culminate, round off; crown, top, cap, put the last *or* finishing touch to.

2. dispose of, deal with, get out of the way, *Inf.* get out from under; make short work of, finish off *or* up, *Sl.* polish off, *Sl.* knock off, expedite, dispatch; have done with, give up, stop, cease, discontinue, suspend.

3. **finish off** overcome, overwhelm, overpower, defeat, conquer; destroy, kill, consume, put an end to, *Inf.* wipe out, *Sl.* rub out; dispose of, *Sl.* do in, get rid of, do away with, put out of the way.

4. varnish, lacquer, glaze, gild, veneer, put a finish on; polish, glow, burnish, rub down, give a shine; dress, face, smooth.

5. refine, culture, cultivate, polish; educate, inform, teach, make knowledgeable *or* learned.
—*n.* 6. conclusion, termination, end, completion, closing, last stage, final act *or* scene; fulfillment, realization, attainment, acquirement, accomplishment; perfection, consummation, culmination, crowning, capping, topping; wrap-up, summary.
7. culture, refinement, cultivation, polish, shine; genteelness, elegance, grace; politeness, politesse, urbanity, urbaneness, suavity, suaveness; sophistication, worldliness, cosmopolitanism; fashionableness, fashionability, stylishness, *Sl.* class; knowledge, learning, learnedness, wisdom, sagacity; education, scholarliness, erudition.
8. surface, texture, grain, veneer; coating, varnish, lacquer, glaze; polish, gloss, shine, luster, burnish, smoothness.

finished, *adj.* 1. ended, completed, played out, *Inf.* over with, done; fulfilled, realized, achieved, accomplished; settled, resolved, terminated; concluded, closed, clinched, clenched, sealed; perfected, consummated, culminated, rounded off; crowned, topped, capped; whole, complete, entire, full.
2. polished, ideal, perfect, faultless, impeccable, flawless; elegant, refined, graceful, beautiful; classic, choice, prime.
3. highly accomplished, expert, proficient, skillful, skilled; masterful, masterly, veteran, professional, *Fr. au fait*; talented, gifted, endowed, apt, dexterous, adroit, deft, facile, clever; topflight, top drawer, first-rate, exceptional, *Inf.* topnotch, ace, *Inf.* crack, *Sl.* crackerjack, *Sl.* on the ball, *Inf.* whiz-bang, *Brit. Sl.* whizzo.
4. condemned, doomed, damned; *Inf.* washed up, done for, lost, ruined, gone.

finite, *adj.* bounded, limited, restricted, terminable; measurable, definable; demarcated, delimited, delimitated.

fiord, *n.* bay, inlet, *Scot.* firth, frith, estuary, arm of the sea, finger of the sea; gulf, bight; cove.

fire, *n.* 1. combustion, ignition, spark, flame, blaze, conflagration, holocaust; cooking fire, bonfire, wildfire, forest fire.
2. light, flashing light, glow, luminosity, luminous appearance, illumination; incandescence, fiery display, sparkle, scintillation; brilliance, luster, splendor, radiance.
3. energy, enthusiasm, liveliness, vivacity, alacrity, *Fr. empressement*, eagerness; power, driving power, potency, strength, vehemence, force, might; vigor, dash, gusto, vim, verve, élan, pep, punch, spirit, life; earnestness, intensity, fervor, fervency, ardor, burning passion.
4. imaginativeness, inspiration, creativity, creativeness, inventiveness; genius, talent, flair, knack.
5. trial, trouble, affliction, stress, ordeal; persecution, torture, abuse.
6. fusillade, volley, barrage, broadside, salvo; flak, anti-aircraft fire.
7. **hanging fire** delayed, put off, postponed, undecided, unsettled, pending; up in the air, on a back burner, on the back of the stove, awaiting action; abeyant, in abeyance.
—*v.* 8. ignite, light, kindle, enkindle, put a match to, set on fire, burn, set burning.
9. heat, bake, smelt, dry, toast; singe, cauterize, brand, sear, cremate.
10. inflame, arouse, fill with ardor; quicken, animate, enliven, trigger, instigate; stir, stimulate, whet, urge, goad, spur; foster, incite, rouse, stir up, breathe life into, put life into; electrify, galvanize, inspire, motivate, *Inf.* sparkplug.
11. shoot, fire off, let off, discharge; detonate, explode; bombard, shell, snipe at, pepper, torpedo, pull the trigger.
12. dismiss, discharge, cashier, oust, depose, get rid of, let [s.o.] go, *Euph.* terminate; give [s.o.] his walking papers, *Sl.* give [s.o.] the ax, *Sl.* sack, *Sl.* bounce, *Sl.* can.

firearm, *n.* gun, weapon; rifle, musket, shooting iron, fusil, carbine; shotgun, blunderbuss, sawed-off shotgun; matchlock, flintlock, firelock; harquebus, hackbut, arquebus; breechloader, muzzleloader, smoothbore; pistol, revolver, *Trademark.* Colt *or* Colt .44, handgun; repeater, derringer, six-shooter, automatic, *Sl.* Saturday-night special, zipgun; *U.S. Sl.* rod, *Sl.* gat, *Sl.* equalizer; .45, .38, .22, .357 magnum; machine gun, submachine gun.

firebrand, *n.* 1. brand, live coal, torch, light, flambeau, match, cresset, linstock; ember, coal, faggot; kindling, tinder, touchwood, spunk, punk, amadou.
2. agitator, instigator, *Fr. agent provocateur*, factionary; rabble-rouser, seditionary, incendiary, *Brit.* tub-thumper, anarchist, terrorist; troublemaker, mischief-maker, ill-wisher, wreck.

fireman, *n.* 1. fire fighter, fire extinguisher, *Sl.* smokey, *Sl.* hotshot.
2. fire tender, stoker; *Sl.* bilge rat.

fireplace, *n.* 1. hearth, hearthside, fireside, fire, hearthstone, chimney corner, *Brit. Dial.* ingle, *Brit. Dial.* ingleside, *Scot.* ingle cheek, *Chiefly Brit.* inglenook *or* ingle nook.
2. firebox, grate, grill, griller, hob, hub.

fireproof, *adj.* unburnable, incombustible, uninflammable; fire resistant, flame resistant, flame retardant.

fireside, *n.* 1. hearth, hearthside, fireplace, fire, hearthstone, chimney corner, *Brit. Dial.* ingle, *Brit. Dial.* ingleside, *Scot.* ingle cheek, *Chiefly Brit.* inglenook *or* ingle nook.
2. home, abode, domicile, domicil, residence, residency, dwelling, dwelling place, dwelling home, habitation, *Scot. and North Eng.* bigging, *Scot.* howff.
3. homestead, home sweet home, hearth and home, hearthstead, household, family, family circle, domestic life.
—*adj.* 4. informal, casual, low-key, low-pitch, natural, easy, easy-going, free and easy, *Inf.* laid-back; friendly, neighborly, amiable, amicable, genial, congenial, social, sociable, cordial.

fireworks, *n.* 1. pyrotechnics, illuminations, thunderflash, Greek fire, *Fr. feu d'artifice, Fr. feu de joie*; sparkler, fizgig, cherry bomb, firecracker, Roman candle, Catherine wheel, rocket, star shell.
2. tantrum, temper, outburst, paroxysm, fit, explosion; rage, furor, dander, hysterics, fire and fury, storm, frenzy.

firm[1], *adj.* 1. hard, stiff, rigid, solid, hardened, solidified; compressed, compact, indurated, condensed; congealed, frozen, impermeable, impenetrable; stony, adamantine, steely, iron; osseous, ossified, bony, horny.
2. fixed, fast, set, close, taut, secure, stationary; immovable, unmovable, irremovable; anchored, moored, tied, rooted, grounded; established, riveted, nailed, bolted.
3. steady, stable, balanced, even, constant; unchangeable, unalterable, changeless, immutable, invariable; irrevocable, irreversible, indissoluble, irrepealable; abiding, enduring, durable, deep-rooted, deep-seated, longstanding.
4. steadfast, unwavering, unswerving, unflinching; unfaltering, undeviating, unhesitating, true; unflag-

ging, dogged, indomitable, relentless, inexorable, plodding; tenacious, gritty, *Inf.* hellbent, *Inf.* stick-to-it-ive; invincible, invulnerable, unassailable, impregnable.

5. determined, resolute, decided, set upon, resolved, confirmed, staunch, stanch; earnest, intent, serious, sober, purposeful, thoughtful, deliberate; obstinate, stubborn, hard-line, obdurate, intransigent; inflexible, unmalleable, unbending, unyielding; irresilient, inelastic, impliant, unimpressive.

firm², *n.* company, business, concern, house, *Fr. maison, Inf.* outfit; trust, establishment, institution; corporation, syndicate, association, holding company, conglomerate; partnership, co-partnership, co-operation.

firmament, *n.* sky, heaven, heavens, vault of heaven, vault, *Dial.* lift, *Chiefly Literary.* welkin; empyrean, air, ether, celestial sphere, starry host; infinity, space, the void, universe, stratosphere; azure, the blue, cerulean, blue sky, the wild blue yonder, outer space.

firmness, *n.* **1.** hardness, rigidity, solidity, resistance; toughness, callosity, callousness, durity; petrification, ossification, density, compactness; adamant, steel, iron; irresilience, inelasticity.

2. stability, steadiness, constancy, balance; fixedness, immovableness, soundness, fastness; establishment, rootedness.

3. immutability, unalterability, unchangeableness, invariability, fixity; irrevocability, irreversibility, indissolubility, irrepealability; durability, durableness, endurance, changelessness; abidingness, lastingness, continuance, perdurability, survival, duration.

4. determination, resolution, steadfastness, tenacity, *Inf.* stick-to-it-ive-ness; resolve, fortitude, will, will power; mettle, backbone, courage, intrepidity, grit, nerve; drive, push, persistence, pertinacity, perseverance, doggedness; iron will, indomitability, relentlessness, inexorability; intransigence, obstinacy, stubbornness, obduracy.

first, *adj.* **1.** premiere, initial, initiative, opening; antecedent, anterior, preceding, precedent, in the front; primary, prime, primal; earliest, pristine, primeval, primigenial; elementary, fundamental, rudimentary, rudimental; original, incipient, beginning, germinal, embryonic, embryonal, genetic, genetical, nascent; oldest, eldest, primogenital, primogenitary, senior.

2. principal, capital, chief, cardinal, paramount main, major, meat-and-potatoes, head; first-rate tops, top-drawer, topflight, *Inf.* topnotch, *Inf.* tiptop, *Inf.* crack, *Inf.* whiz-bang, *Brit. Sl.* whizzo; first-class, ace, grade A, *Brit. Sl.* top-hole, *Inf.* dandy, second to none; supreme, superlative, best, top, highest, crowning, acmic, summital; greatest, maximal, nonpareil, unparalleled, matchless, peerless, utmost, uppermost; supereminent, preeminent, star, sovereign, ruling; prevailing, hegemonic, predominant; ranking, leading, foremost.

—adv. **3.** earliest, before anything else, initially; originally, primarily; firstly, in the first place, right off the bat, to begin with, from the start, at the outset.

4. rather, in preference to [s.t.], more willingly *or* readily; sooner, before.

—n. **5.** beginning, origin, genesis, alpha, prime, dawn, dawning; incipience, inception, commencement, start, outset, the word "go"; germ, seed, conception, germination, embryo, birth, nativity.

6. first place, victory, win, defeat, triumph, success, blue ribbon.

first-rate, *adj.* **1.** first-class, ace, grade A, *Inf.* A-1; tops, top-drawer, topflight, *Inf.* topnotch, *Inf.* tiptop, *Brit. Sl.* top-hole, second to none, *Inf.* crack, *Inf.* whiz-bang, *Brit. Sl.* whizzo.

2. supreme, superlative, best; superb, excellent, exceptional, superior, extraordinary, meritorious, *Inf.* dandy; highest, top, crowning, acmic, summital; greatest, maximal, nonpareil, unparalleled, matchless, peerless, utmost, uppermost, unsurpassed, transcendent; fine, outstanding, great, admirable, remarkable, estimable, noteworthy, worthy.

fiscal, *adj.* financial, economic, monetary, money, pecuniary, sumptuary, capital; bread-and-butter.

fish, *v.* **1.** angle, troll, flycast, cast, bob, jig, spin, *Inf.* plug; net, trawl, seine.

2. look for, search for, hunt for, cast *or* beat about for, grope for; dig for, delve for.

fisherman, *n.* angler, fisher, piscator, piscatorian; Izaak Walton.

fishery, *n.* **1.** fishing, angling. See **fishing**.

2. fishing rights, *Law.* piscary.

fishing, *n.* angling, fishery, trolling, casting, *Inf.* plugging; trawling, netting; rod and reel, halieutics, *Rare.* piscatology.

fishy, *adj.* **1.** fishlike, piscine, piscatorial.

2. *Informal.* improbable, unlikely, hardly possible; farfetched, extravagant, exaggerated, hyperbolical; colored, embroidered, embellished.

3. *Informal.* questionable, dubious, doubtful, suspicious, not kosher, *Inf.* shady; devious, evasive, slippery, tricky, *Inf.* cagey.

4. expressionless, inexpressive, vacant, empty, blank, deadpan, wooden, *Inf.* poker-faced; dull, lackluster, lusterless, glassy, glassy-eyed.

fission, *n.* splitting, disjuncture, parting, division, scission, cleaving; rupture, break, cleavage, severance.

fissure, *n.* crevice, crevasse, chink, cleft, chasm, stria, cranny, interstice, groove, sulcus, *Archaic.* scissure; crack, fracture, flow, break, chap, check, rupture, split, rift, breach, scission, slit, slot, gash, hole, cavity; space, interspace, interval, interstice, narrow.

fist, *n.* **1.** clenched hand, *Sl.* (*usu. pl.*) duke, *Brit. Dial.* nieve; *Inf.* hand, *Sl.* mitt, *Sl.* paw.

—v. **2.** clench, grip, grasp, clasp, clutch; grab, seize, put an iron grip on.

fistic, *adj.* pugilistic, gladiatorial, fighting; combative, pugnacious, contentious, bellicose.

fisticuff, *n.* **1.** blow, clout, thump, pelt, knock, rap, smack, slam, whack, bang, swipe, *Sl.* whang, *Sl.* shot; punch, hook, jab, thrust, lunge; pummel, thump, buffet, thwack.

2. fisticuffs boxing, prize fighting, pugilism; bout, event, fist fight, prize fight, boxing match; fist fighting, free-for-all, battle royal, set-to, brawl, broil, donnybrook, scrap, fracas, melee; spar, go-around, mill, round, scuffle, tussle, scrimmage; shindy, rumpus, row, fray, affray.

fit¹, *adj.* **1.** suitable, well-suited, well-adapted, fitted; correspondent, corresponding, corresponsive, analogous, coherent; conforming, consonant, congruous, harmonious.

2. proper, due, meet, seemly, decorous, right, correct, fitting, befitting; apt, appropriate, apropos, apposite, pat, applicable; relevant, germane, pertinent, to the point, *Latin. ad rem*; becoming, felicitous, occasional.

3. competent, efficient, *Sl.* on the ball; commensurate, equal to, *Inf.* up to; capable, able, capacitated; qualified, eligible, satisfactory, *Inf.* up to snuff *or* par, acceptable, adequate, *Archaic.* sufficient; worthy of *or* to, deserving of *or* to.

4. prepared, readied, primed, trained, well-grounded, up to grade; equipped, furnished, outfitted, fitted out, fitted up, suited up.

5. hardy, stalwart, sturdy, muscular, strong; robust,

strapping, hearty, vigorous, in good shape *or* condition; hale, healthy, well; sane, mentally sound, *Latin. compos mentis.*

—*v.* **6.** suit, befit, correspond to, analogize, tally, match, equal, go, *Inf.* click, *Brit. Dial.* fadge.

7. become, harmonize, jibe, conform, coincide, mesh, synchronize, *Inf.* sync, dovetail.

8. concur, meet, connect, come together, cohere, fuse, contact; join, adjoin, reach.

9. adjust, join together, accommodate, fashion; adapt, modify, regulate, calibrate, graduate.

10. qualify, endow, endue; capacitate, enable, empower, entitle; *Inf.* bring up to snuff *or* par.

11. prepare, ready, get ready, prime, condition; ground, train, instruct, coach, teach, educate.

12. provide, supply, furnish, accouter, outfit, fit out, fit up; equip, rig, arm, forearm, fledge, *Archaic.* harness; apparel, attire, array, caparison, deck out; garb, clothe, robe, drape, dress, invest, vest.

13. affix, arrange, dispose, situate, station, position, place, put; deposit, seat, locate, set, lay, *Archaic.* impose.

—*n.* **14.** trying-on, fitting, sizing, measure, tailoring, alteration, altering; regulating, regulation, calibrating, calibration, graduating, graduation.

fit², *n.* **1.** convulsion, spasm, paroxysm, throe, qualm; attack, seizure, spell, stroke, *Pathol.* ictus; outbreak, outburst, tantrum, storm, explosion, eruption; agitation, *Inf.* dither, *Inf.* tizzy, *Inf.* stew, ferment, fume.

2. **by** *or* **in fits and starts** fitfully, intermittently. See **fitfully**.

fitful, *adj.* **1.** intermittent, sporadic, coming in spells; unsteady, unstable, uncertain, uneven; inconstant, mutable, variable, changeable, vicissitudinous, erratic, fluctuating, flickering.

2. convulsive, spasmodic, paroxysmal; agitated, disturbed, discomposed, unsettled, upset, shaken; feverish, fretful, churned up, restless, tossing and turning; anxious, nervous, worried, *Sl.* in a sweat.

fitfully, *adv.* intermittently, off and on, sporadically, irregularly, interruptedly, occasionally, by fits and starts, spasmodically.

fitness, *n.* **1.** health, physical fitness, well-being, salubrity; soundness, good shape, fine fettle, fine feather, tone, bloom, *Inf.* tiptop condition; robustness, rosiness, vigor, haleness, heartiness, lustiness.

2. appropriateness, applicability, suitableness, aptness, meetness; aptitude, suitability, propriety; eligibility, competency, qualification, preparation.

3. relevancy, relevance, pertinence, good example, case in point, good point; expedience, the very thing, congruity, correspondence; admissibility, compatibility.

4. preparedness, readiness, ripeness, mellowness.

fitting, *adj.* **1.** befitting, fit, meet, *Brit. Dial.* gradely, *Fr. comme il faut*; suitable, proper, becoming, seemly, decorous, decent; appropriate, apt, apposite, apropos; relevent, germane, *Latin. ad rem*, to the point, pertinent, pat.

2. suited, adapted, compatible, consistent; congruent, congruous, harmonious, consonant, accordant, agreeing, conformable; agreeable, congenial, likely, acceptable, reasonable; favorable, commodious, convenient; opportune, seasonable, timely, felicitous; to the purpose, useful, applicable, practicable, feasible.

—*n.* **3.** **fittings** furnishings, furniture, trappings, accouterments, equipment, paraphernalia, appurtenances; appointments, fixtures, trimmings, fixings, extras.

fix, *v.* **1.** fasten, secure, clinch, make fast; attach, connect, couple, link, pin, clasp; rivet, nail, screw, bolt, drive in; cement, solder, weld, fuse; clamp, vise, brace, stay, prop; lock, bar, hasp; gird, buckle, tie, bind, truss, hitch; tether, yoke, fetter, pinion.

2. set, solidify, congeal, harden, stiffen, rigidify.

3. establish, institute, organize, found; stabilize, ground, plant, implant, install; settle, determine, decide, conclude, seal; define, limit, delimit; purpose, resolve, will.

4. (*usu. of eyes or attention*) direct, level at; attract, hold, magnetize.

5. repair, mend, restore, doctor, fix up; patch, patch up, touch up, renovate, renew; correct, amend, rectify, remedy, better, ameliorate; adjust, arrange, straighten, place.

6. *Informal.* get even with, retaliate, wreak vengeance, take retribution.

7. *Informal.* castrate, asexualize, eunuchize. See **castrate** (*def.* **1**).

8. **fix up** *Informal.* **a.** arrange for, plan for, provide with, furnish. **b.** smooth out *or* over, clear up, solve, resolve, reconcile.

—*n.* **9.** *Informal.* predicament, dilemma, plight, *Inf.* pickle, difficulty, trouble, *Inf.* hot water, scrape; corner, tight spot, *Sl.* box, bind, double bind, catch-22, vicious circle; strait, *Inf.* squeeze, pinch, push, hole, quagmire; cul-de-sac, dead end, blind alley; impasse, standstill, stalemate, deadlock; quandary, perplexity, uncertainty, confusion, muddle, mess, botch.

fixation, *n.* obsession, monomania, mania, complex, *Sl.* hang-up; compulsion, fixed idea, *Fr. idée fixe*, preoccupation, fetish; delusion, fancy, notion, crotchet; quirk, oddity, eccentricity.

fixed, *adj.* **1.** fastened, secured, clinched, made fast; attached, connected, coupled, linked, pinned, clasped; tied, bound, nailed down, cemented, welded.

2. firm, settled, stable, rooted; unwavering, unbending, unpliant, rigid; stationary, motionless, immovable; set, permanent, inveterate; definite, constant, steady.

3. set upon, intent upon, resolved, resolute, determined, persistent, stubborn.

4. repaired, mended, restored, renewed; rectified, corrected, adjusted, put in order.

fixity, *n.* stability, constancy, unchangingness, permanence, endurance, durability; preservation, conservation, maintenance; persistence, determination, perseverance, doggedness.

fixture, *n.* attachment, appurtenance, accessory, appliance, equipment; appendage, addition, appendix; apparatus, contrivance, instrument, device, tool, gadget.

fizz, *v.* **1.** hiss, sibilate, sputter, fizzle, swish, sizzle, rustle, buzz, whiz; effervesce, ferment, bubble, sparkle, froth, fume.

—*n.* **2.** hissing sound, sibilation, sputter, fizzle, swish, sizzle, rustle, buzz, whiz; effervescence, fermentation, sparkling, bubbling, froth, fume, spray, foam.

3. *All U.S.* soda water, club soda, soda, tonic water, tonic, quinine water, quinine, seltzer water, seltzer.

4. *Brit. Inf.* champagne, *Sl.* bubbly.

fizzle, *v.* **1.** hiss, sibilate, sputter, fizz, swish, sizzle, rustle, buzz, whiz; effervesce, bubble, sparkle, aerate, foam, froth, spume.

2. *Informal. Often* **fizzle out** fail, miscarry, abort, founder; misfire, collapse, cave in, come to nothing, fall short, fall through, miss the mark, miss the boat, come to grief, end in smoke.

—*n.* **3.** hissing sound. See **fizz** (*def.* **2**).

4. *Informal.* failure, miscarriage, nonsuccess, nonfulfillment, vain attempt, *Sl.* no-go, flash in the pan;

fiasco, *Inf.* washout, *Inf.* flop, *Sl.* bomb; botch, blunder, foozle, abortion; muddle, jam, mess, scrape.

flabbergast, *v.* *Informal.* astound, amaze, dumbfound, strike dumb, render speechless; overcome, stun, stagger, boggle, take aback, floor, shock, jar, jolt, *Inf.* bowl over. See **astound**.

flabbiness, *n.* flaccidity, unfirmness, pendulousness, droopingness, limpness, quagginess.

flabby, *adj.* **1.** flaccid, unfirm, out of tone; drooping, pendulous, quaggy, limp, *Dial.* limpsy, *Inf.* out of shape.

2. weak, feeble, impotent, powerless, strengthless; nerveless, spineless, *Sl.* gutless, *Sl.* chicken.

flaccid, *adj.* flabby, unfirm; drooping, pendulous; soft, quaggy, limp, *Dial.* limpsy.

flaccidity, *n.* flabbiness, unfirmness, softness, pendulousness, droopiness, limpness, quagginess.

flag[1], *n.* **1.** ensign, colors, standard, banner, banneret, pennant, pennon, streamer, banderole; jack, Union Jack, *Naut.* blue peter, bunting; Stars and Stripes, Old Glory, The Star-Spangled Banner, Stars and Bars; tricolor, oriflamme, gonfalon, vexillum.

—*v.* **2.** flag down, signal, wave down, hail; motion, gesture.

flag[2], *v.* **1.** droop, sag, hang down; hang loosely, dangle, loll, sway; swag, sink down, slump, settle, drop.

2. languish, *Dial.* dwine, fade, faint, weaken, lose one's strength; fail, go downhill, deteriorate, degenerate, waste away, pine away, fade away *or* out, die.

3. decline, wane, ebb, fall off, drop off, diminish, decrease; taper off, abate, subside, lessen, ease up, let up.

flagellate, *v.* whip, scourge, flog, lash; horsewhip, strap, switch, give the cat-o'-nine-tails, make [s.o.] run the gauntlet; birch, cane; cudgel, fustigate, bastinado; thrash, beat, drub.

flagellation, *n.* whipping, scourging, flogging, lashing; horsewhipping, strapping, switching; beating, pounding; punishment, gauntlet.

flagon, *n.* bottle, decanter, carafe, jug; cruet, cruse; ewer, pitcher, amphora; crock, jar, pot; vessel, container; canteen, flask.

flagrant, *adj.* **1.** glaring, egregarious, conspicuous, flaming, crying; noticeable, evident, obvious; barefaced, impudent, loud, open; forward, bold, brazen, audacious, defiant, obtrusive; ostentatious, flaunted, paraded, displayed.

2. scandalous, shocking, outrageous, disgraceful, shameless; gross, enormous, rank, smelling to high heaven, coarse, reproachful; notorious, arrant; infamous, flagitious, heinous, nefarious, atrocious, monstrous; wicked, *Archaic.* facinorous, iniquitous, villainous.

flagstone, *n.* flag, flat stone slab, paving stone.

flail, *v.* thrash, thresh; whale, whip, horsewhip, flog; strike, beat, batter, buffet, drub.

flair, *n.* **1.** gift, endowment, dowry, genius, talent, faculty; knack, bent, turn, forte; propensity, proclivity, disposition, tendency; ability, ableness, capability, capableness, facility; skill, skillfulness, dexterity, ambidexterity, adroitness, deftness, finesse, felicity; aptitude, capacity, aptness, mother wit, mind [for].

2. panache, flamboyance, showiness, style; verve, vivaciousness, liveliness, animation, enthusiasm, vigor, spirit; smartness, spruceness, dapperness, trimness, neatness, *Inf.* niftiness.

3. discernment, acumen, perspicacity, acuteness, acuity, keenness, sharpness; perception, percipience; shrewdness, astuteness, sagacity, sagaciousness, savvy.

flak, *n.* **1.** anti-aircraft fire, *Sl.* ack-ack.

2. *Informal.* criticism, hostile *or* adverse criticism, bad press, bad notices, *Inf.* knock, *Inf.* rap, *Inf.* swipe; censure, disapproval, disapprobation; aspersion, imputation, animadversion, brickbat; opposition, disagreement, conflict, friction.

3. *Informal.* argument, altercation, clash, falling-out, *Inf.* hassle; quarrel, row, squabble, dustup.

flake, *n.* **1.** scale, scurf, floc, floccule; peel, pellicle, membrane, skin; chip, shaving; snowflake, snowcrystal, crystal.

—*v.* **2.** peel, peel off, scale, scale *or* flake off, desquamate, exfoliate.

flambeau, *n.* torch, flaming torch, brand, firebrand, link, cresset.

flamboyant, *adj.* **1.** brilliant, bright, dazzling, splendid, resplendent; showy, gaudy, flashy, *Sl.* flash; ostentatious, meretricious.

2. dashing, swashbuckling, gay, colorful; jaunty, rakish, brave, *Scot.* braw.

3. ornate, elaborate, fancy, high-wrought; florid, flowery, fussy, frilly, rich, luxurious; baroque, rococo, arabesque.

flame, *n.* **1.** *Often* **flames** burning gas *or* vapor, blaze, fire, bonfire, *Brit. Dial.* ingle; conflagration, *Obs.* flagration, holocaust, wildfire, ring *or* sea of fire.

2. glow, glare, gleam, flash, coruscation; glimmer, shimmer; spark, scintilla, glint, flicker; flash, streak, fulguration.

3. brilliant light, luster, brightness, luminosity, phosphorescence; scintillation, sparkling; effulgence, radiance, refulgence.

4. bright coloring, streak of color, bright reddish-orange color.

5. ardor, fervor, fervency, warmth, fire; devotion, devotedness, zeal, feverishness, passion, fanaticism; enthusiasm, eagerness, intensity, excitement.

6. *Informal.* sweetheart, lover, girlfriend, inamorata, boyfriend, inamorato, beau, heart's desire.

—*v.* **7.** burn, blaze, fire, be on fire, flare, deflagrate; burst into flames, catch on fire, take fire, go up in smoke.

8. glow, radiate, phosphoresce, shine; flash, glare, beam; flicker, shimmer, twinkle, sparkle, spark, glitter, dazzle.

9. **flame up or out** burn up, flare up, blaze up, *Inf.* see red, *Sl.* get hot under the collar; seethe, sizzle, fume; burn with passion, be fervid.

flaming, *adj.* **1.** blazing, burning, ablaze, raging, on fire, afire, fiery, aflame; ignited, sizzling, smoldering.

2. gleaming, agleam, glowing, aglow, glaring; very bright, lighted, alight, luminous; radiant, brilliant, incandescent; shimmering, twinkling, flashing, flickering, glittering, aglitter, sparkling, fluttering.

3. ardent, fervent, fervid, perfervid, impassioned, passionate, frenzied; stimulated, aroused, *Inf.* hot, intensely desirous, intense; animated, enthusiastic, eager, excited, exhilarated.

4. egregious, blatant; flaunty, conspicuous, flagrant.

flange, *n.* rim, ridge, lip, brim, projecting edge, skirt, border; rib, collar, shoulder.

flank, *n.* **1.** side, quarter, loin, haunch, flitch, *Entomol.* pleuron.

—*v.* **2.** border, edge, bound, fringe, skirt, wing, verge, curb, wall, limit, confine.

3. outflank, outmaneuver, loop, circle, ring, surround, hem in; go around, elude, detour, avoid, evade.

flap, *n.* **1.** tab, tail, lap, lug; leaf, skirt, apron, overhang, loop.

2. flapping, swinging, flutter; wave, undulation.

3. slap, whack, swat, smack, thwack, thump, bump;

hit, swipe, flail, rap, pat, clap, tap.

—*v.* **4.** slap, swat, bat, whip, lash, lambaste, lick, lace; bump, beat, whack, tamp; smack, bang, clip, click, thump, thwack, wallop.

5. flutter, oscillate, wave, wave about, toss; wag, waggle, move to and fro, swing; fly, flow, flop, hang, dangle, slacken.

flapdoodle, *n. Informal.* nonsense, bosh, rubbish, twaddle, balderdash, stuff and nonsense, rot, fiddle-faddle, fiddlesticks. See **nonsense** (*def.* **2**).

flapjack, *n.* griddlecake, pancake, hotcake, battercake, flapcake, flannel cake, buckwheat cake; crepe, blini, blintz, tortilla, (*in India*) chapati; fritter, fried cake.

flare, *v.* **1.** burn unsteadily, blaze, flame; flash, sparkle, scintillate, coruscate, gleam, fulgurate, glitter twinkle, flicker, glisten, *Archaic.* glister, glimmer, flutter, shimmer; glow, phosphoresce, incandesce; radiate, illuminate.

2. burst forth, erupt, break out, boil over; blow up, go off, pop; explode, displode, fulminate; detonate, detonize, set off.

3. spread outward, splay, expand, dilate, extend, mantle, stretch; broaden, widen, enlarge; increase, augment, aggrandize; amplify, project, magnify.

4. flaunt, show off, *Inf.* put on the dog; display, air, exhibit, disport; vaunt, boast, brag; parade, swagger, strut, swashbuckle.

5. signal, direct, indicate, guide, light; flag, warn, command.

6. **flare out** *or* **up** *Informal.* vent one's anger, become enraged, *Inf.* blow one's top, *Inf.* lose one's cool, lose one's temper; *Inf.* fly off the handle, throw a tantrum, *Sl.* throw *or* have a fit, lose one's grip *or* grasp; go beserk, boil over with rage, fly into a passion.

—*n.* **7.** unsteady light, flame, spark, scintilla; shimmer, flicker, twinkle, glitter, sparkle, flutter; flash, fulguration, gleam, coruscation, glare; glow, incandescence, brilliance, radiance; luminosity, phosphorescence, shine, refulgence.

8. signal, beacon, light; torch, flambeau, link, taper, candle, flashlight; guide, direction, orientation; indication, command; alarm, warning.

9. outward spread, extension, expansion; broadening, widening, enlargement, aggrandizement.

10. outward curvature, convexity, arcuation; dilation, bulge, protrusion; curve, arc, crescent.

flash, *n.* **1.** streak, patch, glint, lightning; shaft, ray, beam; gleam, glare, fulguration, coruscation; brightness, dazzle, dazzling, bedazzlement, bedazzling, blinding; blaze, flame, flare, spark, scintilla, scintillation; shimmer, flicker, twinkle, glitter, sparkle; glimmer, blink, glistening, glistering, flutter, fluctuation, oscillation, vacillation; brilliance, resplendence, splendor, resplendency, radiance; effulgence, refulgence, refulgency, vividness, intensity; luminosity, illumination, luminance, luster, gloss, sheen; glow, incandescence, phosphorescence, iridescence.

2. show, showing, manifestation, demonstration, brief outburst *or* outbreak; emission, voicing, declaration, statement, observation; affirmation, assertion, expression, communication, indication, sign; display, exhibit, exhibition, exposition, representation; presentation, unfoldment, disclosure, revelation, divulgence.

3. instant, moment, minute, second, split second; twinkling, twinkle, breath, trice, *Inf.* jiffy; eyewink, wink of the eye, *Fr. coup d'oeil*; twinkling of an eye, *Inf.* bat of an eye, two shakes of a lamb's tail.

4. showiness, flauntiness, floridness, showy appearance; pomp, pomposity, pompousness, fanfare, *Inf.* razzle-dazzle; gaudiness, garishness, ostentation, parade, pageantry, spectacle; flashiness, *Sl.* pizzazz, vividness, brightness, gayness, colorfulness; loudness, cheapness, tawdriness, meretriciousness; display, exhibit, exhibition, disporting; swaggering, strutting, peacockery, swashbuckling; boasting, bragging, vaunting.

5. flashing, flaming, flaring, blazing, burning; blast, violent outburst *or* outbreak, ebullition, paroxysm, dissilience, dissiliency; explosion, *Obs.* displosion, fulmination, detonation; eruption, cataclysm, upheaval; outpouring, volley, discharge.

6. lock, sluice, penstock, sluice gate; floodgate, head gate, tide gate; dam, weir.

—*v.* **7.** flame, blaze, burn, conflagrate; flare, spark, scintillate; gleam, glare, effulge, fulgurate, coruscate; streak, stream, beam; glitter, glimmer, glisten, *Archaic.* glister, glint; shimmer, shine, flicker, sparkle, twinkle; flutter, fluctuate, oscillate, vacillate; glow, phosphoresce, incandesce, make radiant; brighten, dazzle, bedazzle, blind; illuminate, illumine, *Archaic.* illume, *Obs.* enlumine, light *or* light up.

8. dart, dartle, dash, *Inf.* scoot, scuttle, *Inf.* skedaddle; run, sprint, scud, tear; rush, hasten, hurry; fly, run like the wind, race; bolt, bound, spring, leap, start quickly, *Sl.* tear off, *Inf.* take off; streak, *Inf.* go hell-bent, bolt like lightning *or* greased lightning, go like a shot.

9. *Informal.* show off. See **flare** (*def.* **4**).

—*adj.* **10.** showy, ostentatious, *Inf.* sporty. See **flashy** (*def.* **2**).

11. counterfeit, forged, fraudulent, imitation; fake, not genuine, bogus, spurious; pretended, feigned, simulated, make-believe, sham; unreal, mock, ersatz, synthetic; artificial, factitious, contrived, fictitious; assumed, put-on, pseudo.

12. brief, momentary, temporary, of short duration, short; impermanent, mortal, unenduring, fleeting, passing, fading; transitory, transient, fugacious, evanescent, ephemeral; fast, swift, brisk, sudden, quick, fleet, meteoric; cursory, hurried, hasty.

flashy, *adj.* **1.** sparkling, coruscant, scintillating, glittering; brilliant, magnificent, superb, rich, dazzling, *Music.* bravura; splendid, splendrous, celebrated, distinguished; admirable, exceptional, laudable, praiseworthy, worthy, remarkable; commendable, meretorious, deserving, exemplary; prime, choice, select, rare, best, sterling.

2. showy, flamboyant, gaudy, ostentatious, pretentious, flash, *Inf.* sporty; bedizened, tricked out *or* up, flaunting, garish; tawdry, loud, *Inf.* tacky, cheap, meretricious; obtrusive, pompous, glaring; bright, gay, florid, gorgeous, colorific, colorful, chromatic; *All Sl.* snazzy, ritzy, jazzy, classy.

flask, *n.* **1.** bottle, flagon, decanter, carafe, pitcher, jug; cruet, cruse.

2. flat bottle, canteen, wineskin; flasket, vial.

flat, *adj.* **1.** level, plane, horizontal; even, smooth, unbroken.

2. horizontal, lying down, stretched out, spread out, spread-eagle; prostrate, lying flat, prone, supine, reclining, recumbent.

3. deflated, collapsed, blown out, ruptured, punctured.

4. outright, direct, downright, out-and-out, straight-out; unqualified, categorical, unconditional, total, complete; absolute, conclusive, unquestionable, positive, definite, firm, set, final.

5. lifeless, spiritless, prosy, prosaic, vapid, dull, tedious, tiresome; boring, monotonous, bland, insipid, jejune, uninteresting, pointless.

6. stale, unpalatable, unsavory, unappetizing; vapid, insipid, dead, tasteless, flavorless, *Fr. fade*; weak, thin, watery, watered-down.

—*n.* 7. **flats** low shoes, loafers, pumps; espadrilles, sandals, *Brit.* plimsolls, sneakers.
8. level ground, lowland, plain, steppe, tundra, champaign, flat *or* open country; prairie, grassland, savannah, *Brit.* heath, *Chiefly Brit.* moor, (*both in South America*) pampas, campo; plateau, tableland, mesa.
9. marsh, morass, bog, swamp; shoal, shallow, sandbank, sand bar.
10. *Informal.* flat tire, blow-out.
11. tenement, apartment, room *or* rooms, efficiency, studio, place, *Sl.* pad.
—*v.* 12. flatten, make flat, level. See **flatten** (*def.* 1).
—*adv.* 13. horizontally, levelly.
14. flatly, positively, absolutely; completely, utterly.
15. exactly, precisely.

flat-footed, *adj.* 1. splay-footed.
2. *Informal.* firm, explicit, definite, uncompromising, determined, resolute, unwavering.

flatten, *v.* 1. make flat, flat, level, level off *or* out, plane, even out *or* off, smooth, smooth out.
2. go flat, lose fizz, become stale.
3. raze, tear down, demolish, destroy, ruin, smash; fell, chop down, cut *or* mow down, knock down, floor; overcome, overthrow, prostrate; step on, squelch, squash, quash, crush, put down; shoot down, put a pin in [s.o.'s] balloon, burst [s.o.'s] bubble, puncture, deflate.

flatter, *v.* 1. compliment, salute, praise, laud, belaud, extol, exalt, celebrate, glorify, eulogize, panegyrize, adulate, trumpet, cry up, ring *or* sing [s.o.'s] praises; puff, puff up, inflate, magnify, blow up, overpraise, praise to excess, praise to the skies; *All Inf.* slather, overdo it, lay it on, lay *or* spread it on thick, pile it on *or* up.
2. fawn, fawn upon, *Sl.* fall all over, truckle, truckle to, toady to, toadeat, slaver, *Inf.* butter, *Inf.* honey, *Inf.* soap, *Inf.* oil; *All Sl.* shine up to, suck up to, play up to, butter up, *Inf.* apple-polish, *Sl.* brown-nose, get brownie points; court, curry favor, pay court to, dance attendance upon, lickspittle, lick [s.o.'s] shoes, kiss *or* lick [s.o.'s] feet, *Sl.* bootlick, *Inf.* run after, *Inf.* be a yes man to, agree to anything.
3. cajole, wheedle, beguile, blandish, blarney, coax, palaver, gloze, *Inf.* soft-soap, *Inf.* sweet-talk; humor, jolly, pamper, coddle, pet, pander to, cater to, *Inf.* stroke.
4. delude, deceive, seduce, trick, hoax, fool, hoodwink, mislead, string along.

flatterer, *n.* 1. complimenter, saluter, praiser, lauder, laudator; extoller, exalter, celebrator, glorifier, encomiast, eulogizer, eulogist, panegyrist, adulator, trumpeter.
2. sycophant, toady, toadeater, fawner, truckler, tufthunter, courtier, wheedler, puffer, backslapper, backscratcher, timeserver, *Inf.* apple-polisher, *Sl.* brown-nose, *Sl.* brown-noser, *Sl.* brownie, *Obs., Rare.* blander, *Archaic.* pickthank; parasite, leech, sponge, sponger, hanger-on; flunky, lackey, *Inf.* yes man, jackal, spaniel, bootlick, bootlicker, footlicker, lickspit, lickspittle, kowtower, Uncle Tom, *Sl.* oreo, cringer, groveler, sniveler.
3. cajoler, beguiler, blandisher, coaxer, palaverer, palaverist; humorer, coddler, pamperer, panderer, caterer, *Inf.* stroker.

flattery, *n.* 1. compliment, salute, praise, laudation; tribute, extolment, exaltation, celebration, glorification; eulogy, eulogium, eulogization, encomium, panegyric, adulation; trumpetry, crying up, ringing *or* singing [s.o.'s] praises, puffery, puffing up, inflation, inflating, magnification, magnifying, blowing up; overpraise, overpraising, excessive praise, praising to the skies; *All Inf.* slathering, overdoing it, laying it on, laying *or* spreading it on thick, piling it up *or* on.
2. sycophancy, sycophantism, toadyism, toadeating, tufthunting, lip-homage, mouth-honor, unctuousness, fawningness, *Inf.* butter, *Inf.* oil, *Inf.* honey, *Sl.* goo, *Sl.* banana oil, *Rare.* blandiloquence, *Obs.* blanding, *Obs., Rare.* blandation, *Obs., Rare.* blandiloquy; truckling, truckling to, *Sl.* falling all over, toadying, slavering, *Inf.* buttering, *Inf.* soaping, *Inf.* oiling, *Inf.* honeying, *Inf.* apple-polishing, *Sl.* shining up to, playing up to, *Sl.* sucking up to, *Inf.* buttering-up, *Sl.* brown-nosing; courting, paying court to, currying favor, dancing attendance upon, licking [s.o.'s] shoes, kissing *or* licking [s.o.'s] feet, *Sl.* bootlicking.
3. cajolery, wheedling, beguilement, beguiling, blandishing, blarney, coaxing, palaver, palavering, *Inf.* soft soap, *Inf.* sweet talk, *Inf.* honeyed words, *Sl.* line, *Sl.* snow job, *Archaic.* gloze; humoring, jollying, pampering, coddling, petting, pandering to, catering to, *Inf.* stroking.

flatulence, *n.* 1. intestinal gas, wind, *Sl.* burps, belches, eructation, abdominal rumblings, *Med.* borborygmus.
2. empty talk, idle words, mere words, twaddle, babble, idle chatter, fustian, fanfaronade, boasting; humbug, claptrap, *Sl.* hot air, *Sl.* bull, *Sl.* crap.

flatulent, *adj.* 1. gassy, gas-producing, windy.
2. pompous, pretentious, vain; long-winded, *Archaic.* ventose, wordy, verbose, prolix, tedious; bombastic, boastful, *Brit.* waffling, turgid, diffuse, discursive.

flaunt, *v.* 1. parade, display, *Inf.* sport, exhibit, air, hold up, flash; put forth *or* forward, emphasize, spotlight, draw attention to, show off; splash, make a splash, splurge, make a splurge; make a show, cut *or* make a figure, *Sl.* cut a dash, *Sl.* cut a shine, *Sl.* cut a feather; swagger, swank, swashbuckle, strut, *Sl.* strut one's stuff, peacock; boast, brag, vaunt, talk up; put on airs, put up a front, *U.S. Sl.* put on the dog, *Sl.* put on, *Sl.* put on the ritz.
2. wave, dangle, brandish, flourish, wield, raise.

flaunty, *adj.* showy, ostentatious, vain, pretentious; flamboyant, flashy, gaudy, garish. See **flashy** (*def.* 2).

flavor, *n.* 1. taste, tastiness, savor, savoriness; tang, piquancy, sapidity, palatability, palatableness.
2. essence, spirit, soul, nature; aspect, property, characteristic; touch, vein, style.

flavorful, *adj.* 1. tasty, delicious, flavorsome, flavorous, palatable, sapid, appetizing, toothsome; delectable, luscious, *Sl.* yummy, ambrosial, ambrosian, *Archaic.* gustable, *Fr.* *délicieux*; gourmet, epicurean; sweet, piquant, spicy.
2. enjoyable, satisfying, pleasing, agreeable, pleasant, nice.

flavorless, *adj.* tasteless, savorless, unpalatable, stale, mild, bland; dull, insipid, vapid, jejune, mawkish, flat; wishy-washy, milk and water.

flaw, *n.* 1. fault, defect, imperfection, defacement, disfigurement; blemish, blotch, mark, scratch, scar, macula, macule; blot, spot, speck, blur, stain, smudge, smirch, smutch, taint, discoloration.
2. loophole, way out, catch, hooker; lapse, slip, slip-up, oversight, omission; weakness, weak spot, frailty, infirmity, foible, shortcoming, failing, *Sl.* bug; mistake, error, *Sl.* boo-boo, *Sl.* goof, *Sl.* boner.
3. chink, crack, cranny, check, chip, chap, crevice, crevasse; break, fracture, fissure, split, rupture, cleft, breach, rift, scission, *Archaic.* scissure; rent, tear, gash, scotch, slit, cut, puncture; opening, cavity, gap, hole, aperture, orifice.

flawless, *adj.* 1. defectless, unmarred, unimpaired,

uninjured, undamaged, unflawed; unblemished, stainless, taintless, unsullied, unsoiled, untarnished; virgin, chaste, clean, snowy, spick-and-span. See **faultless.**

2. sound, legally valid; loophole-proof, catch-proof, foolproof; strong, unbreakable, unescapable.

3. uncracked, unbroken, unchipped, uncrannied, unchecked; whole, solid, complete.

flaxen, *adj.* golden, aureate, buff; yellow, yellowish, pale-yellowish, xanthous, cream-colored; sandy, fulvous, tawny, yellowish-brown; saffron, saffron-colored, saffron yellow, yellow-orange; blond, *Inf.* blondish, reddish-blond, strawberry blond.

flay, *v.* **1.** strip, strip off, excoriate, peel, *Pathol.* desquamate, pare, skin, *Inf.* skin alive, scalp, bark, husk, shuck, shell, decorticate; shave, shear, depilate, tonsure; erode, rub off, wear away, eat away.

2. criticize, attack, light into, *Inf.* lace into, *Inf.* pan, *Inf.* slam, shoot down, *Sl.* blast, *Sl.* let [s.o.] have it right between the eyes; cavil, carp, find fault, *Inf.* nitpick, pick apart, pick to pieces, *Sl.* cut up *or* to pieces; get on [s.o.'s] back, *Inf.* jump on, *Sl.* get on [s.o.'s] case; castigate, fustigate, berate, tongue-lash.

3. fleece, swindle, defraud, mulct, shark, cheat, *Inf.* flimflam, rook, bilk, *Inf.* welsh, *Inf.* do out of, *Inf.* gyp, *Inf.* bunko, *Inf.* diddle, *Inf.* take, *Inf.* take [s.o.] for a ride, *Sl.* clip.

fleck, *n.* **1.** spot, mark, speck, speckle, dot; freckle, mole, macula; blemish, *Sl.* boo-boo, zit, blackhead.

2. dash, scintilla, spark, bit, *Inf.* itty-bitty thing, jot, whit, tittle.

—*v.* **3.** spot, speckle, dot, dapple; spatter, sprinkle, salt and pepper; spangle, bespangle, stud, star; stipple, mottle, freckle; checker, variegate, freak; marble, striate, stripe, streak.

flecked, *adj.* spotted, speckled, dappled, dotted, Seurat-like; spattered, sprinkled, powdered; mottled, stippled; starred, freckled, pimpled; spangled, bespangled, studded; marbled, striated, veined, variegated; parti-colored, pied, piebald, (*usu. of horses*) skewbald.

flee, *v.* **1.** run, run away *or* off, take to one's heels, make a quick exit, *Rare.* fugitate, *Inf.* take off, *Inf.* clear out, *Inf.* make tracks, *Inf.* cut out, *Inf.* cut and run, *Inf.* fly the coop, *Sl.* split, *Sl.* scram, *Sl.* blow, *Sl.* hightail it, *Sl.* lam *or* take it on the lam; abscond, bolt, elope, escape, take flight, take to flight, take wing, *Sl.* wing it, *Inf.* beat it, *Inf.* skip out, *Inf.* skip town, *Inf.* skedaddle, *Sl.* skidoodle, *Sl.* skidoo, *Sl.* vamoose; retreat, withdraw, decamp, abandon, desert, take oneself off, take French leave, quit the scene, make a getaway, beat a retreat, beat a hasty retreat, run for it, make a run for it, turn tail, show the heels, show a clean *or* extra-light pair of heels; leave, depart, exit, *Euph.* leave without saying good-bye, *Brit. Sl.* bugger off.

2. make off, pull out, *Jocular.* absquatulate, give *or* take leg-bail, *Sl.* bail out, take the money and run; vanish, disappear, do the disappearing act, *Inf.* make oneself scarce, *Brit. Sl.* do a moonlight flit.

3. fly, speed, speed off, hasten off, move swiftly *or* quickly *or* briskly, waste *or* lose no time.

fleece, *n.* **1.** coat, coating, covering, hide; pelage, fur, hair, plumage, feathers; wool, down, fluff, fuzz; shag, pile, nap; *Bot., Zool.* pubescence, *Bot.* tomentum, *Bot.* villus; *Biol.* (*usu. of newborns*) lanugo.

—*v.* **2.** shear, clip, poll, flay; shorten, trim, pare, cut off; strip, bare, denude.

3. swindle, defraud, mulct, shark, cheat, *Inf.* flimflam, rook, bilk, *Inf.* welsh, *Brit. Sl.* levant, *Inf.* do out of, *Inf.* gyp, *Inf.* bunko, *Inf.* diddle, *Inf.* take, *Inf.* take [s.o.] for a ride, *Inf.* take [s.o.] to the cleaners, *Sl.* pluck, *Sl.* chisel, *Sl.* clip; overcharge, *Sl.* soak, *Sl.* sting, *Inf.* rip off.

4. rob, steal, thieve, pilfer, purloin, filch; peculate, embezzle; shoplift, *Sl.* boost; extort, blackmail, *Sl.* bleed.

5. plunder, despoil, pillage, ravage, rape; maraud, ransack, sack, loot, gut, strip, rifle; raid, foray, forage.

6. overspread, shroud, cloud, becloud, mantle; coat, cover, film; fleck, dapple, dot.

fleecy, *adj.* **1.** downy, fleece-like, soft, smooth, lanuginose, lanuginous, velvety, velutinous; fluffy, feathery, flurry, nappy, shaggy.

2. woolly, lanate, lanose, flocculent, flocky, *Bot.* floccose.

3. hairy, pubescent, *Bot., Entomol.* tomentose, *Both Bot.* villous, villose.

fleer, *v.* horselaugh, heehaw; mock, deride, taunt, make fun of; ridicule, twit, pull [s.o.'s] leg; jeer, sneer, scoff, gibe, give [s.o.] the business.

fleet¹, *n.* flotilla, armada, argosy, naval force, task force; squadron, division, *Obs.* escadrille.

fleet², *adj.* swift, fast, rapid, quick, double-quick, expeditious, speedy; arrowy, winged, cometary, meteoric; agile, nimble, nimble-footed, light-footed, swift-footed, light of heel.

fleeting, *adj.* passing, flitting, flying, unenduring, here today—gone tomorrow; transient, transitory, temporary, impermanent; brief, short-lived, momentary; ephemeral, evanescent, vanishing.

fleetness, *n.* swiftness, rapidity, quickness, speediness; speed, lightning *or* blazing speed, velocity; expedition, dispatch, promptitude, promptness; agility, nimbleness, nimble-footedness, quick-footedness, light-footedness.

flesh, *n.* **1.** muscle, tissue, fat; meat, beef, mutton, veal, pork; substance, matter, pith, marrow, gist, core.

2. fatness, weight, corpulence, obesity. See **fleshiness.**

3. body, materiality, corporeality, corporality, physicality; corporeity, *Biol.* soma, flesh and blood, man.

4. physical nature, animal nature, animality, libido; carnality, sensuality, sensualism, earthiness; voluptuousness, luxuriousness, sybaritism, fleshpots, hedonism.

5. mankind, man, humanity, humankind, womankind, creaturehood; mortality, the living, ourselves, human race, human species, human beings, homo sapiens, earthlings.

6. kin, family, kinship, relatives, relations; kindred, kith and kin, brethren, blood.

7. surface, skin, epidermis, scarfskin, coat, *Sl.* hide, integument.

8. **in the flesh** present, before one's eyes, in person, here, in front of one.

—*v.* **9.** **flesh out** fill out, fill, color, give dimension, substantiate, draw out, incorporate, embody.

fleshiness, *n.* fatness, obesity, obeseness, corpulence, corpulency; pursiness, *Inf.* avoirdupois, *Fr. embonpoint,* adiposity, *Pathol.* adiposis; paunch, potbelly, *Sl.* beer belly, *Obs.* gorbelly, tubbiness, chubbiness, pudginess, plumpness, chunkiness, paunchiness, stumpiness, lumpiness, dumpiness; roundedness, rotundity, portliness, stoutness, bulkiness.

fleshly, *adj.* **1.** bodily, physical, corporal, corporeal, somatic, incarnate; material, substantial, palpable, tangible.

2. sensual, carnal, erotic, sensuous, hot, earthy; lusty; animal, bestial, beastly, brutish; lustful, lascivious, lecherous, lewd, licentious.

3. worldly, unspiritual, mundane, earthly, terrestrial, secular, lay.

fleshy, *adj.* fat, obese, corpulent, overweight; chubby, tubby, pudgy, chunky, *Brit.* podgy, plump; paunchy, potbellied, *Obs.* gorbellied; bouncing, well-fed, ample, filled-out; meaty, beefy, brawny, strapping, *Brit. Inf.* chopping; bosomy, *Inf.* top-heavy, buxom.

flexibility, *n.* **1.** pliability, pliancy, flexility, bendability; suppleness, litheness, softness, limberness, lissomness; malleability, plasticity, tractility, ductility, flaccidity; elasticity, stretch, stretchability; give, spring, springiness, resilience.

2. adaptability, conformability, adjustableness; tractableness, compliancy, compliance; docility, obedience, submissiveness, manageability; willingness, readiness, agreeability.

flexible, *adj.* **1.** bendable, pliable, pliant, flexile, snappy, whippy; tractile, ductile, malleable, plastic, mollescent, flaccid; elastic, springy, resilient, stretchable, extensile, tensile; supple, limber, lithe, lissome, double-jointed, loose-limbed.

2. adaptable, conformable, adjustable, malleable; tractable, compliant, cooperative, docile, biddable, obedient, submissive; manageable, easy, facile, mild, complaisant, affable.

3. willing, yielding, ready; amenable, agreeable, acquiescent, receptive, predisposed.

flexure, *n.* **1.** bending, flexing, curving, incurvation, sinuosity, *Anat.* flexion.

2. bend, crook, hook, elbow, horseshoe; arcuation, bow, arc, crescent, meniscus, lunula; turn, curvature, sweep, curve; fold, loop, festoon, curl, twist.

flick, *n.* **1.** snap, flip, fillip, tap, click.

—*v.* **2.** flutter, bat, flicker, flap, wag, waggle, whip, switch.

flicker, *v.* **1.** twinkle, sparkle, glimmer, blink, shimmer; glint, glitter, glisten, *Archaic.* glister, burn unsteadily; spark, scintillate, flame, flare *or* flare up; flash, fulgurate, gleam, streak, glare, coruscate; glow, shine, luminesce, incandesce, phosphoresce.

2. waver, sway, wave to and fro; quiver, shiver, ripple; oscillate, fluctuate, vacillate; quaver, shake, quake, tremble, twitter, shudder; undulate, vibrate, pulsate, throb; jerk, twitch, vellicate, jump.

3. flutter, hover, flit, flirt, dance; glint, flash, whisk, skin; glide, wing, fly; dart, dartle, move quickly.

—*n.* **4.** flame, spark, scintilla, scintillation, unsteady *or* tremulous light; shimmer, shimmering, glimmer, glimmering, flickering, blink, glitter, glittering, glint, glinting; twinkle, twinkling, sparkle, sparkling, glistening, *Archaic.* glistering; flash, fulguration, gleam, gleaming, glare, coruscation; glow, incandescence, brilliance, refulgence, radiance; luminosity, luminance, phosphorescence, refulgence; shine, sheen, gloss, luster.

5. glimmering, inkling, glint; trace, vestige, scintilla; indication, evidence, impression; brief occurrence *or* appearance, apparition; emergence, rise, coming, advent; happening, incident, incidence, circumstance, situation, event.

flier, flyer, *n.* **1.** aviator, airman, air pilot, aeronaut, airplaner, aeroplaner, pilot, *Sl.* flyboy, *Inf.* barnstormer; ace, fighter pilot; aviatrix, aviatress, airwoman.

2. speeder, thunderbolt, flash, rocket, cannonball, streak, *Inf.* blue-streak; *All Inf.* scorcher, hummer, sizzler, hustler, goer, hell-driver, speed demon, speed maniac, speed merchant; express, express train, lightning express, *Inf.* cannonball express.

3. *Informal.* standing *or* running *or* flying leap *or* jump; leap, jump, vault; lunge, spring, pounce.

4. *Informal.* (*all of business ventures*) experiment, speculation, venture, feeler; random shot, leap *or* shot in the dark, *Sl.* plunge; risk, hazard, gamble, chance.

5. *U.S.* handbill, leaflet, leaf, bill, circular, notice, folder; handout, throwaway, dodger; advertisement; placard, poster, broadside, broadsheet, proclamation, bulletin.

flight[1], *n.* **1.** soaring, sailing, zooming, cruising; gliding, planing, volplaning, sailplaning; aviation, volitation, *Rare.* volation.

2. distance, extent, length, span, range, reach; course, route, direction, trajectory.

3. flock, bevy, covey, gaggle; swarm, swarming, cloud.

4. trip, run, crossing, crossover; shuttle, *Inf.* hop, *Inf.* jump.

5. unit, tactical unit, squadron, wing, escadrille, formation.

6. dart, dash, sprint, speed, swoop, scud, clip, race, career; scoot, scamper, scurry, scuttle.

7. *Archit.* stairway, staircase, stairs, steps.

flight[2], *v.* **1.** fleeing, bolting, absconding, running, running away, running off, eloping, taking to one's heels, *Inf.* taking to the woods, *Inf.* heading for the hills, *Inf.* skedaddling, *Sl.* scramming, *Sl.* splitting; evacuation, desertion, abandonment, decampment; bolt, hasty retreat, French leave, *Jocular.* absquatulation, fugitation, *Sl.* disappearing act, *Sl.* skedaddle.

2. departure, *Archaic.* scape *or* 'scape; exodus, hegira, migration; getaway, jailbreak, prison break, *Inf.* breakout, *Inf.* break, *Sl.* lam.

3. **put to flight** rout, stampede, discomfit, panic; disperse, scatter, scatter to the winds.

4. **take to flight** retreat, withdraw, decamp; flee, bolt, abscond. See also **flee** (*def.* **1**).

flightiness, *n.* capriciousness, changefulness, fickleness, inconstancy, volatility, mercurialness; frivolity, whimsicality, giddiness, light-headedness; flippancy, lightness, levity.

flighty, *adj.* **1.** changeful, capricious, whimsical, fanciful, impulsive; fickle, skittish, inconstant, moonish, changeable, variable, faddish; mercurial, volatile, undependable, unsteady, unstable; delirious, lightheaded, rattlebrained, harebrained, half-witted, mad, crazy, unbalanced, eccentric, wild, extravagant; giddy, frivolous, flyaway, fitful, erratic, irregular, spasmodic, uneven; irresolute, uncertain, indecisive, undecided, vacillating, wavering, shilly-shallying, infirm of purpose.

2. irresponsible, wayward, wanton, reckless, thoughtless, heedless, lawless, abnormal, heteroclite, deviative, stray.

flimflam, *n.* **1.** *Informal.* nonsense, twaddle, bosh. See **nonsense** (*def.* **2**).

2. trick, deception, humbug, fraud, swindle, *Inf.* the old army game, confidence game, *Sl.* con game, *Inf.* flimflam game, *Sl.* rip-off; pretense, hoax, imposture, artifice.

—*v.* **3.** trick, delude, humbug, cheat, *Inf.* pull a fast one. See **cheat** (*defs.* **3, 4**).

flimsy, *adj.* **1.** thin, light, slender, slight, delicate, filmy, diaphanous, airy, ethereal; sheer, silken, gossamer, cobwebby, gauzy.

2. weak, feeble, frail, fragile, unsubstantial; trivial, frivolous, immaterial, superficial, shallow, lacking force, vain, transparent, ineffectual; inadequate, poor, worthless, paltry, niggling, piddling; foolish, idle, puerile, petty, trifling, meager.

3. cheap, shabby, ramshackle, rickety, tumbledown, dilapidated, jerry-built, gimcrack; sorry, scrubby, sleazy, wretched.

flinch, *v.* **1.** blench, recoil, start, withdraw, crawl *or* pull back *or* away; swerve, turn away from, dodge, get out of the way, flee, run away, retreat.

2. shrink, shy away from, cringe, quail, wince; cower,

crouch, *Inf.* funk; quake, tremble, quiver, shudder, shake, *Inf.* shake in one's boots *or* shoes, shiver, show fear.

flinders, *n.* splinters, slivers, shives, shreds, shavings, parings, flakes, scales; fragments, shards, chips, chunks, hunks, snippets, particles, bits, *Inf.* smithereens; pieces, morsels, crumbs, grains, granules, fritters, scraps.

fling, *v.* **1.** hurl, sling, flirt, jerk, cant, pitch, toss, cast, throw, heave; propel, project, jaculate, catapult, launch, shoot, fire, send, let fly.

2. flounce about, dance *or* hop around, jig, throw oneself around; jerk, throw a fit *or* tantrum.

3. *Usu.* **fling out** lash out, fulminate, explode, *Inf.* blow up, *Inf.* blow off steam.

flint, *n.* stone, rock, silica; adamant, granite.

flinty, *adj.* **1.** adamantine, impenetrable, unyielding, hard as flint, firm, durable; stony, rocky, granitic; callous, horny.

2. indurate, hardened, inured; unfeeling, unimpressible, stony-hearted, cold-hearted; cruel, unmerciful, merciless, pitiless, hard-hearted; stubborn, obstinate, obdurate, inflexible, firm, rigid, stiff, unbending; inexorable, unyielding, unalterable.

flip, *v.* **1.** toss, fling, sling, pitch, cast, hurl, heave, chuck, throw.

2. jerk, twist, turn, flop, flounce.

3. turn over, turn upside down; turn around, twirl, spin.

4. flick, tap, fillip, rap, pat, dab, strike; snap, crack.

5. **flip out** *Slang.* go berserk, go crazy, lose one's cool, *Sl.* lose it, *Sl.* freak out, *Sl.* flip one's lid.

6. (*all with* over) *Sl.* go wild, rave, get excited, enthuse, jump up and down; be infatuated, be enchanted.

—*n.* **7.** flick, tap, rap, pat, dab, fillip, strike, stroke; swat, thwack, cuff, blow; snap, crack.

8. jerk, twist, turn, flop, flounce.

flippancy, *n.* impudence, insolence, impertinence, pertness, tartness, sauciness, *Inf.* sauce, brashness, brazenness, boldness, *Brit. Sl.* side; arrogance, effrontery, back talk, *Inf.* cheek, *Sl.* lip, *Sl.* mouth; discourtesy, rudeness, impoliteness, incivility, unmannerliness; inconsideration, disregard, tactlessness, disrespectfulness, irreverence, misbehavior; indecorum, ungraciousness, uncourtliness, ungentlemanliness, hoydenism.

flippant, *adj.* **1.** brash, bold, brazen, hoydenish, *Scot.* randy; insolent, impudent, impertinent, pert, *Archaic.* malapert, saucy, *Inf.* flip, fresh, *Inf.* cheeky; *Sl.* smart-mouth; bumptious, cocky, overconfident, audacious, *Inf.* nervy, *Scot.* vaunty; aggressive, forward, obtrusive, *Inf.* pushy; rude, impolite, uncivil, ill-bred, bad-mannered, misbehaved, out of line, out of order, unruly.

2. superficial, frivolous, shallow, thoughtless; free and easy, devil-may-care, carefree, insouciant, pococurante.

flirt, *v.* **1.** coquet, vamp, tease, dally; entice, tantalize, lead on; look sweet at, make googoo eyes at, *Inf.* play footsie, wink at, ogle, make a play for, throw oneself at [s.o.], cast sheep's eyes at, make calf eyes at; play at love, pretend love, (*of a man*) philander, play fast and loose; whistle at, wolf-whistle at; bill and coo, woo, *Inf.* spark, court, serenade; undress with a glance.

2. trifle, toy, entertain, consider, give a thought to, *Inf.* try out, *Inf.* try on.

3. jerk, dart about, flit, skim along.

4. wave, flutter, twirl, whirl, whisk.

5. toss, fling, flip, sling, pitch, cast, hurl, heave, chuck, throw.

—*n.* **6.** coquette, vamp, belle, gold digger; hussy, *Brit. Sl.* tart, jilt, wanton.

7. philanderer, fast man, playboy, gallant, *Sl.* lounge lizard, lady killer, *Sl.* masher, *Sl.* wolf, *Sl.* sheik.

8. throw, toss, fling, flip, sling, pitch, heave; jerk, darting motion.

flirtation, *n.* **1.** coquetry, flirting, vamping, affectation of love, gallantry; trifling, toying, dallying, dalliance, philandering; wooing, *Inf.* sparking, courting, billing and cooing, necking, petting, *Inf.* spooning, serenading; googoo eyes, sheep's eyes, wolf-whistle, wink, ogle, side glance, double take.

2. affair, amour, romance, intrigue.

flirtatious, *adj.* flirty, coquettish, coy, dallying; wanton, loose, fast-and-loose; philandering, *Sl.* wolfish.

flit, *v.* **1.** dart, flirt, hop, volitate; fly, soar, sail, zoom, sweep, skim, skim along.

2. flutter, flitter, flap, beat, wave; flick, flicker, dance; quiver, quaver.

3. (*all of time*) fly by, pass swiftly, pass by *or* away quickly, fleet; elapse, lapse, slip, slide, glide; fade, melt; vanish, disappear, evaporate, go up in smoke.

—*n.* **4.** flutter, flicker, flitter, flap, beat, beating; waver, quiver, quaver, dance.

5. *Slang.* homosexual, homophile, homosexualist; *All Derog. Sl.* homo, queer, faggot, fag, fruit, pansy, fairy.

flitting, *adj.* **1.** darting, flirting, skimming, fleeting, passing; fast, rapid, fleet, quick, brisk, meteoric, mercurial.

2. transient, transitory, momentary, ephemeral, short-lived, temporary, brief.

3. fluttering, flittering, flapping, beating, waving, flickering, dancing; quivering, quavering.

float, *v.* **1.** buoy, ride, swim, rest on, waft; be buoyant, be buoyed up, be suspended on.

2. drift, sail, glide, slip along; hover, move lightly, move gracefully.

3. launch, instigate, initiate, get going, push off; promote, sell, purvey.

4. vacillate, oscillate, fluctuate, tergiversate, shilly-shally.

5. wander aimlessly, mill around *or* about, meander, *Sl.* bum around, *Sl.* hang out.

—*n.* **6.** raft, pontoon, buoy; life preserver, lifesaver.

7. parade display, pageant unit, spectacle, show, diorama.

floating, *adj.* **1.** buoyant, buoyed up, natant, swimming, afloat; drifting, borne along, suspended.

2. unfixed, movable, unsettled, migratory, wandering, circulating; shifting, variable, fluctuating.

3. *Finance.* in circulation, in use, reachable, accessible.

flock, *n.* **1.** fold, herd, drove, pack; bevy, flight, gaggle; brood, litter, hatch; school, shoal; swarm.

2. multitude, host, horde, throng; crowd, press, crush, mass; mob, rabble, ruck, rout.

—*v.* **3.** gather, foregather, meet, assemble, collect, come together, congregate; crowd, throng, swarm, mill; cluster, bunch, clot; flock together, herd together, band together, club together, *Sl.* gang up with.

flog, *v.* whip, horsewhip, flail, thrash, thresh, flagellate, *Inf.* leather, *Inf.* hide, *Inf.* tan [s.o.'s] hide; strap, belt, switch, make [s.o.] run the gauntlet; birch, *Inf.* whale, *Inf.* welt, cane, club, cudgel, fustigate, bastinado; beat, pound, buffet, pummel, belabor, lay on, *Inf.* lick, *Inf.* larrup, *Inf.* wallop, *Sl.* lambaste, *Sl.* clobber.

flogging, *n.* whipping, horsewhipping, thrashing, flailing, flagellation, forty lashes, lashing, switching, the gauntlet, *Inf.* hiding, *Inf.* tanning.

flood, *n.* **1.** deluge, inundation, alluvion; freshet, flash flood, spate; overflow, spillover; torrent, cataract; tidal wave, high tides, tsunami; cloudburst, downpour; gullywasher, *Inf.* gully-whomper, monsoon.

2. outpouring, tide, flow, stream, flush; waves, cas-

cade, waterfall; copiousness, plenteousness, *Obs.* galore, profusion; overabundance, superabundance, plethora, excess, nimiety; superfluity, surplus, a bit of muchness, more than enough; satiety, glut, *Sl.* enough to choke a horse; *All Inf.* tons, barrels, heaps.
—*v.* **3.** overflow, break the bounds, surge, swell; pour forth, disembogue, debouch; deluge, inundate, pour over; submerge, cover, bury, drown; drench, saturate, soak.
4. overwhelm, overpower, overburden, crush, break [s.o.'s] back; sate, glut, choke, fill up to [s.o.'s] ears; bog down, mire down, swamp.

floodgate, *n.* **1.** water gate, sluice, sluice gate, lock gate; faucet, tap, cock.
2. barrier, obstacle, obstruction, barricade, barricado; dam, weir, dike, embankment; moat, tank trap, dragon teeth, Maginot line; fence, barbed wire; gate, door, turnstile.

floor, *n.* **1.** flooring, planking, boarding, parquet; pavement, paving, flagging; foundation, support, groundwork, footing; flat, bed, bottom, ground, earth; story, deck, level.
2. platform, stage, rostrum, stand, scaffold.
3. (*of prices or wages*) base, base rate, minimum, bottom.
—*v.* **4.** plank, parquet, pave, flag, deck.
5. knock down, fell, prostrate; defeat, conquer, vanquish, quell, subdue; rout, discomfit, overwhelm, *Sl.* mop *or* wipe the floor with, overrun, trample, *Inf.* run into the ground; crush, overthrow, smash, thrash, trounce, trim, whip, drub; worst, hash, *Inf.* lick, *Sl.* cream, destroy, beat, best.
6. *Informal.* confound, nonplus, perplex, bewilder, baffle; amaze, astound, astonish, startle, stun, daze, dumfound, surprise, confuse, disconcert.

flop, *v.* **1.** *Often* **flop down** fall down, collapse, plump down, *Inf.* plunk down, drop down, plop down, throw oneself down.
2. *Informal.* fail, fall flat, miss the mark, *Sl.* bomb. See **fail** (*def.* **1**).
3. flap, flutter, oscillate, wave, toss, move to and fro, fly; swing, hang, dangle.
—*n.* **4.** thud, thump, clump; fall, jar, jolt, jerk.
5. *Informal.* failure, fiasco, no-go, fizzle, *Inf.* washout; lead balloon, *Sl.* dog, *Theat.* turkey, *Sl.* bomb, *Sl.* brodie, *Inf.* clunker, *Inf.* lemon, *Inf.* dud, *Sl.* clinker, *Sl.* bust.

floral, *adj.* flowery, abloom, blooming, blossoming; botanical, herbaceous; woodsy, sylvan, arboreous; verdant, verduous, green, grassy, mossy.

florescence, *n.* blossoming, flowering, flowerage, *Bot.* anthesis, efflorescence; bloom, blossom, flower, inflorescence, bud, burgeon; development, outgrowth, fruition, maturation.

florid, *adj.* **1.** reddish, ruddy, rubicund, blowzy; high-colored, erubescent, rubescent, blushing; rosy, flushed, glowing, blooming, radiant.
2. flowery, frilly, fussy, busy, ornate, baroque, elaborate, involved, *Music.* bravura; adorned, decorated, embellished, embroidered, festooned; overdone, overwrought, rococo, arabesque, rocaille; ostentatious, flamboyant, showy, flashy, *Sl.* flash; gaudy, garish, tawdry; (*of writing*) high-flown, bombastic, rhetorical, figurative, tropical, euphuistic.

flossy, *adj.* **1.** silky, silken, satiny, smooth, velvety, velutinous; downy, fluffy, feathery, plumose; fragile, delicate, gossamer, gossamery, ethereal, airy, light.
2. *Sl.* fashionable, chic, stylish, mod; fancy, dolled-up, dressy.

flounce, *v.* **1.** (*all in reference to bodily movement*) twist, turn, jerk, fling, toss, bounce; preen, exhibit, parade.
—*n.* **2.** trimming, frill, furbelow, ornament; ruffle, fringe, valance, edging, skirting, hemming.

flounder, *v.* **1.** struggle, wallow, welter, flop; stagger, stumble, tumble, tumble about, toss about, plunge around, thrash.
2. blunder, bungle, muddle; fail, come to grief, meet with disaster, take a bad turn, collapse, *Inf.* come a cropper.
3. hesitate, waver, vacillate, falter; lose one's way, drop out.

flour, *n.* **1.** meal, ground *or* bolted meal, ground *or* bolted wheat, bran, farina.
—*v.* **2.** pulverize, mill, grind and bolt.
3. powder, dust, sprinkle, speckle.

flourish, *v.* **1.** grow, grow like a weed, increase, develop, wax; burgeon, mushroom, boom, spring up, burst forth; sprout, bud, germinate, pullulate; bloom, blossom, flower, bear fruit, fructify; mature, maturate, ripen; luxuriate, abound, superabound.
2. be in one's prime, feel good, burst with health, *Inf.* feel like a million *or* million bucks; be vigorous, have energy, feel one's oats, *Inf.* be full of pep *or* zip *or* beans.
3. thrive, prosper, succeed, do well, fare well, make good, go great guns, *Brit. Dial.* fadge; advance, progress, make headway, get ahead, get on *or* along, rise in the world.
4. brandish, wave, wield, swing, shake.
5. parade, flaunt, vaunt, prance, peacock, strut, swagger, swashbuckle, *Inf.* show off, *Inf.* parade one's wares, *Sl.* strut one's stuff, *Sl.* grandstand, *Sl.* hotdog; puff, boast, brag, bluster, *Inf.* talk big, *Sl.* blow-hard.
6. decorate, ornament, embellish, adorn, trim, garnish; embroider, elaborate, festoon.
—*n.* **7.** parade, show, exhibition; flaunt, vaunt, blazon, *Inf.* dash, *Inf.* splash.
8. decoration, ornamentation, adornment, embellishment; frill, embroidery, elaboration, *Rhet.* purple passage *or* patch; verve, style, flair, panache.

flourishing, *adj.* thriving, booming, prospering, in full swing, *Inf.* going strong; growing, waxing, developing, burgeoning, mushrooming; (*of vegetation*) luxuriant, lush, rank, exuberant.

flout, *v.* **1.** disdain, contemn, scorn, misprize, spurn, scout; disparage, discredit, denounce, decry, vilipend, depreciate, minimize; ridicule, mock, deride, jeer, scoff, laugh in *or* up one's sleeve at, sneer; burlesque, lampoon, satirize; taunt, fleer, guy, twit, gibe at; poke fun at, snicker, snigger; tease, *Inf.* rag, chaff.
2. malign, defame, denigrate, slander, libel, *Inf.* backbite; belittle, humiliate, make a fool of, disgrace, degrade; insult, affront, *Sl.* put down, *Sl.* cut up; blaspheme, profane, take [s.o.'s] name in vain.
—*n.* **3.** insult, affront, *Sl.* cut, *Sl.* put-down, slap in the face; slur, dig, barb; abuse, contumely, contempt, disdain, scorn; repudiation, disparagement, belittlement, depreciation; humiliation, degradation, abasement, mortification; ridicule, derision, mockery, scoffing, sneering; gibe, jeer, taunt, fling, quip, wipe; hoot, hiss, catcall, sibilation; obscenity, vulgarity, blasphemy, profanity, scurrility.

flow, *v.* **1.** run, stream, proceed, drift, glide, slide, move, go along; roll, purl, ripple, gurgle, bubble, trickle; rush, cascade, fall; circulate, move around *or* through, pass through.
2. *Usu.* **flow from** issue, emanate, grow, arise, result, follow, derive; originate, begin, come from, start, be born at.
3. gush, surge, swell, well *or* rush forth; effuse, spout, spurt, jet, ejaculate.
4. overflow, flood, brim over. well over, run over,

spill over *or* out, slosh *or* slop over, leak out, seep, ooze, drip; abound, teem, be rich in, be full of, run over with, be overrun with.

—*n.* **5.** current, drift, course, tide, ebb; stream, streamlet, brook, brooklet, creek, *Dial.* crick, *U.S. Dial.* kill, river, rivulet; channel, sluice, canal, waterway, watercourse; torrent, cascade, cataract, falls, rapids.

6. issuance, emanation, afflux, flux, outflow, outpour, outpouring, efflux, effluence; trickle, dribble, seepage, oozing; spout, spurt, jet, spring, geyser.

7. overflowing, flood, deluge; affluence, abundance, plenty; copiousness, plethora, excess.

flower, *n.* **1.** blossom, bloom, nosegay, bouquet; bud, floweret, floret; perennial, annual.

2. prime, acme, zenith, heyday, height, maturity, efflorescence, *Latin. floruit*; youth, early vigor, springtime of life, salad days.

3. ornament, adornment, embellishment, ornamentation, decoration; floral design, *Print.* fleuron, rosette, acanthus.

4. best, pick, choicest, best part, finest; elite, cream, *Fr. crème de la crème*; the least expendable.

—*v.* **5.** blossom, produce flowers, bud, burgeon, bloom, effloresce; come out, unfold, open, dehisce; develop, mature, come to full bloom.

flowery, *adj.* **1.** flower-covered, blooming, bloomy, blossomy, blossoming; flowering, floral, florescent, efflorescent, floriferous; floriated.

2. (*usu. of language*) ornate, florid, high-flown, euphuistic, showy, elaborate; figurative, highly-wrought, overwrought; rhetorical, redundant, pleonastic; bombastic, grandiloquent, inflated.

flowing, *adj.* **1.** streaming, running, drifting, gliding, sliding, moving along; circulating, moving around, passing through; rolling, purling, rippling, gurgling, bubbling, trickling; gushing, surging, effusive; rushing, cascading, falling.

2. fluent, smooth, free-flowing, continuous, unbroken, uninterrupted; graceful, facile, effortless, easy.

3. abounding, teeming, rich, lush; overflowing, brimming over, swollen; flooded, overrun.

fluctuate, *v.* **1.** vacillate, waver, yo-yo, seesaw, teeter-totter; equivocate, shilly-shally, hem and haw, blow hot and cold, tergiversate, straddle the fence.

2. wave, undulate, oscillate, pendulate.

fluctuation, *n.* **1.** vacillation, wavering, instability, unsteadiness; change, variation, alternation; hesitation, ambivalence, irresolution, indecision, undecisiveness, uncertainty, infirmity of purpose; fickleness, capriciousness, changeableness.

2. undulation, oscillation, rising and falling; rise and fall, ebb and flow, flux and reflux.

flue, *n.* duct, passage, air passage, air hole, airway, vent, venthole; chimney, smokestack, smokeshaft, stack, funnel, stovepipe, *Naut. Sl.* Charley Noble.

fluency, *n.* **1.** facility, command, control; ease, felicity; grace, gracefulness, smoothness.

2. eloquence, articulateness, silver tongue, well-spokenness; volubility, verbosity, prolixity, long-windedness, *Inf.* gift of gab; profuseness, wordiness, verbiage, *Rare.* multiloquence; glibness, slickness.

3. flow, flowing, flux, fluxion, afflux, affluence.

fluent, *adj.* **1.** eloquent, articulate, well-spoken, silver-tongued, *Archaic.* facund, *Obs.* facundious; glib, slick, smooth, smooth-tongued, smooth-talking, smooth-spoken, fast-talking; voluble, verbose, prolix, long-winded, *Rare.* multiloquent.

2. smooth, easy, graceful, fluid, facile; mellifluous, tripping, euphonious, smooth-sounding, pleasing to the ear; harmonious, balanced, proportioned.

3. flowing, streaming, running, coursing, racing, pouring rushing, gushing.

fluff, *n.* **1.** down, thistledown, flue; flake, feather, fuzz, floccule, floss; fur, wool, nap, pile; lint, mote, wisp, dust; fuzzball, furball, dustball.

2. trifle, frivolity, triviality; fribbling, frippery, bagatelle, nothing.

fluffy, *adj.* **1.** downy, pillowy, flossy, cottony, lanuginose, lanuginous; fleecy, woolly, furry, lanate, lanose, flocculent; feathery, fuzzy, flaky; nappy, pilose, velvety, peachy; pubescent, wispy, *Bot.* tomentous, *Bot.* pappose.

2. light, featherweight, featherlight, gossamer, gossamery, light as air, light as a feather; airy, ethereal, floaty.

3. frivolous, trifling, unimportant, insignificant, inconsequential; slight, inconsiderable, piddling, of little value; airy, superficial, light, idle, shallow.

fluid, *n.* **1.** liquid, water; gas vapor, ether.

2. rheum, lymph, sap, juice, milk, latex, chyle; blood, *Sl.* claret, ichor, gore, grume, *Obs.* cruor, *Pathol.* sanies; pus.

—*adj.* **3.** liquid, aqueous, fluxional, fluxionary; liquefacient, solvent, fluidal, fluxive, uncongealed, unclotted; gaseous, vaporous, volatile, steamy, gassy, vaporific, flatulent.

4. fluent, running, flowing; runny, watery, rheumy, phlegmy; juicy, sappy, pussy, mattery; hemal, sanguineous, bloody, sanguinary, gory, *Pathol.* sanious, lymphatic.

5. shifting, deviating, changing, unstable; changeable, fickle, inconstant.

fluidity, *n.* **1.** liquidity, liquidness, liquefaction, fluxility, fluxion, gaseousness, volatility.

2. flow, fluency, smoothness, evenness; facility, ease.

3. adaptability, flexibility, pliancy; versatility.

4. instability, unstableness, fickleness, inconstancy, changeableness, flightiness; shifting, flux.

fluke, *n.* **1.** lucky stroke, stroke of luck *or* fortune, stroke of good luck *or* fortune; windfall, blessing, accidental advantage, piece of good luck *or* fortune; lucky chance, *Inf.* big chance, *Sl.* break, *Sl.* lucky *or* good *or* big break; chance, fortuity, fate, luck, good luck *or* fortune, serendipity, potluck.

2. random shot, lucky shot, chance hit, one in a million, long odds, *Sl.* lucky strike, *Sl.* scratch hit; gamble, risk, *Inf.* flier, leap *or* shot in the dark, pig in a poke.

3. chance event, chance occurrence, happenstance, happening, hap; accident, freak accident, casualty; bad luck *or* fortune, stroke of bad luck *or* fortune, hard luck.

flummery, *n.* **1.** oatmeal, gruel, *U.S.* mush, hot cereal, *Chiefly Brit.* porridge, farina; fruit custard, blancmange, white pudding.

2. nonsense, moonshine, gobbledegook; foolish humbug, bunkum *or* buncombe, *Sl.* bunk, *U.S. Sl.* blah; balderdash, *Inf.* hokum, *Sl.* applesauce, *Sl.* eyewash; rubbish, *Sl.* tripe, refuse, *Dial.* culch, chaff, trash, *Inf.* truck, trumpery; tommyrot, *Inf.* rot, *Sl.* garbage, *Sl.* crap, *Sl.* crock, *Sl.* bull; hogwash, *Sl.* horsefeathers, stuff, stuff and nonsense, *Inf.* bosh, *Brit. Inf.* gammon, *Brit. Sl.* tosh; fudge, foolishness, folly, rigmarole *or* rigamarole, amphigory; footle, *Inf.* malarkey, *Sl.* bushwa, *Sl.* baloney, *Sl.* bilge *or* bilge water, *Sl.* meshugaas, *Scot. and North Eng.* haver; poppycock, *Inf.* fiddle-faddle, *Inf.* piffle, *Inf.* hooey, *Inf.* kibosh, *Inf.* flapdoodle; claptrap, rodomontade, fustian, bombast, rant, *Sl.* hot air, *Sl.* gas.

3. flattery, empty compliment, excessive *or* insincere

praise, *Inf.* slathering, overdoing it, spreading *or* laying it on thick; sycophancy, sycophantism, toadyism, toadeating, tufthunting, lip-homage, mouth honor; unctuousness, excessive smoothness *or* suaveness, *Inf.* oil, *Inf.* butter, *Inf.* honey; toadying, toadying to, *Inf.* buttering up, *Inf.* soft-soaping, *Inf.* oiling, *Inf.* honeying, *Inf.* apple-polishing, *Inf.* boot-licking; currying favor, kissing *or* licking feet, *Inf.* being a yes-man to, agreeing to anything; adulation, fawning, fawningness; *All Sl.* shining up to, playing up to, sucking up to, brown-nosing, snow job, line.

4. cajolery, wheedling, blarney, blandishment, blandishing, *Rare.* blandishments; palaver, palavering, palaverment, beguiling, beguilement; coaxing, *Inf.* sweet talk, honeyed words, *Archaic.* gloze.

flunky, *n.* **1.** lackey, servant, male servant, valet, butler, gentleman, manservant, *Archaic.* varlet; footman, *Fr. valet de pied*, groom, equerry, livery, servitor, retainer, yeoman; footboy, boy, page, bellboy, *Brit.* boots, *Brit.* buttons; menial, *Inf.* gofer.

2. toady, yes-man, bootlicker. See **toady** (*def.* **1**).

flurry, *n.* **1.** snow shower, snow squall, light snowfall, dusting; flake, snowflake, fluff, fluffy.

2. fluster, ferment, bustle, whirl, fuss, *Inf.* tizzy; hurry, haste, flush, hurry-scurry, pell-mell; upset, pother, stir, *Inf.* to-do, ado, hubbub, commotion; excitement, din, hustle, flutter; agitation, disturbance, perturbation, trepidation.

—*v.* **3.** fluster, confuse, bewilder, confound, bedevil, perplex; rattle, disconcert, perturb, ruffle; put on edge, unsettle, upset.

flush[1], *n.* **1.** blush, redness, rosiness, bloom; reddening, rubescence, rubicundity; glow, freshness, radiance, gleam, sparkle, glimmer.

2. overspreading, overflow, overflowing; inundation, flood, flooding, drenching, deluge.

3. thrill, excitement, throb, tingle, tingling, quiver; palpitation, pulsation, titillation, excitation, electrification.

4. vigor, health, hardihood, vim, vitality; freshness, healthiness, haleness, heartiness, robustness; lustiness, full-bloodedness, wholesomeness.

5. fever, fire, heat, warmth, febricity, *Pathol.* pyrexia; inflammation, ague, *Pathol.* calenture.

—*v.* **6.** redden, color, blush, crimson, turn red, mantle, incarnadine; suffuse, flame, burn.

7. flood, drench, spray, wash, douse, wash away, drain, empty, evacuate, discharge, clean out, clear out.

8. flow, rush, gush, stream, pour forth; overspread, cover, spread over, inundate, flood, flow over, deluge.

9. animate, excite, impassion, inflame, work up; rouse, instigate, stir, kindle; elate, elevate, hearten, inspirit, cheer, encourage, gladden, delight.

flush[2], *adj.* **1.** even, level, smooth, flat, plane, complanate; plumb, straight, true.

2. contiguous, adjacent, conterminous, adjoining, next to; touching, in contact, contactual, abutting, meeting, *Obs.* attingent.

3. well-supplied, well-equipped, well-to-do, well-heeled; affluent, prosperous, wealthy, rich, moneyed; on easy street, in the chips, in the money, *Sl.* rolling in dough.

4. abundant, plentiful, copious, replete, full, plenteous, bounteous; fecund, fertile, fruitful, rife, lush, luxuriant, exuberant.

5. blushing, glowing. See **flushed** (*def.* **2**).

6. vigorous, lusty, hearty, hale, robust, hardy; full of life, spirited, fresh, lively.

7. full, full to overflowing, overflowing, overbrimming; spilling over, running over, teeming over, chock-full, brimful.

—*adv.* **8.** on the same level, in a straight line, squarely, square, evenly, even, dead, plumb, directly.

—*v.* **9.** make flush, even, square, level, even off, smooth, flatten, lay level, plane, planish; equalize, align, balance.

flushed, *adj.* **1.** excited, aroused, impassioned, quickened; enthused, inspired, possessed, animated; feverish, febrile, hot, burning, in a fever, ablaze; aquiver, aflutter, atwitter, *Inf.* in a tizzy, in a ferment, hectic, overwrought.

2. blushing, ablush, red, glowing, warm, rosy, reddened, rubicund, scarlet; ruddy, blowzy, sunburned, burnt.

3. cheerful, gay, light-hearted, insouciant, carefree, happy, happy-go-lucky; airy, jaunty, buoyant; vivacious, lively, brisk, allegro, sportive, *Inf.* chipper; elated, exultant, exhilarated, in high spirits, in high feather.

4. enthusiastic, sanguine, expectant, anticipative, anticipatory; hopeful, optimistic, heartened; assured, confident, certain.

fluster, *v.* **1.** excite, flutter, agitate, *Inf.* give the heebie-jeebies *or* willies *or* jimjams, flurry; shake, upset, *Inf.* discombobulate, discompose, disquiet; perturb, disturb, bother; stagger, shock, startle, boggle, take aback.

2. confuse, rattle, disconcert, *Inf.* faze, confound, discomfit; bewilder, distract, baffle, throw off, puzzle, perplex, nonplus, *Inf.* blow one's mind; addle, muddle, fuddle, befuddle; dumfound, daze, dazzle.

flutist, *n.* flautist, flute player; fifer, piper, Pied Piper, Pan; piccoloist, *Inf.* piccolo Pete, oboist.

flutter, *v.* **1.** wave to and fro, sway, undulate, flap, flop; toss about, oscillate, fluctuate, vacillate; swish, swing loosely, flourish; wag, dangle, pendulate; waver, ripple, quiver, shiver, quaver, shake, vibrate, tremble, twitter, shudder; jerk, twitch, vellicate, jump.

2. beat, pulse, expand and contract, palpitate, pitapat; throb, thump, alternate, pound, reverberate; vibrate, agitate, quiver.

3. flit, flirt, dance, hover; glint, flash, whisk, skim; glide, wing, fly, soar; dart, dartle, move quickly.

4. fluster, flurry, confuse, confound, bewilder; baffle, pose, befuddle; perplex, puzzle, nonplus; befog, make muddled *or* unclear, mystify, bamboozle; obscure, obfuscate, disorient, disorientate; embarrass, disconcert, discompose, unsettle, agitate, perturb; upset, rattle, unhinge, unbalance.

—*n.* **5.** swaying, undulating, undulation; flap, flapping, flop, flopping; tossing about, oscillating, oscillation, fluctuating, fluctuation, vacillating, vacillation; swish, swishing, loose swinging, swing, flourish, flourishing; wag, wagging, dangling, pendulating; waver, wavering, ripple, rippling, quiver, quivering, shiver, shivering; quaver, quavering, shake, shaking, vibrating, vibration; tremble, trembling, twitter, twittering, shudder, shuddering; jerk, jerking, twitch, twitching, vellicating, vellication, jump, jumping.

6. fluster, nervous excitement, flurry, *Inf.* dither; confusion, disorder, bewilderment, bafflement; befuddlement, perplexity, puzzledness, puzzlingness; muddledness, muddlement, disorientation; mystification, bamboozlement, obscureness, obfuscation; embarrassment, disconcertingness, disconcertion, disconcertment, discomposure; mental agitation, perturbation, perturbedness, perturbment; turmoil, tumult, unsettlement; unhingement, unhinging, upset, unbalance, unbalancing.

7. sensation, stir, commotion, convulsion, turmoil, tumult; confusion, flurry, ado; hubbub, bustle, activity, *Inf.* to-do; agitation, excitement, fermentation; furor, uproar, disorder; turbulence, storm, squall; outbreak, outburst, ebullition.

flux, *n.* **1.** flow, stream, course, current, run; ebb and flow, tide; surge, swell, sweep.
2. movement, motion, stir; passage, process; change, mutation, alteration; transition, modulation, adaptation.
3. instability, fluctuation, swinging, swaying, oscillation; vacillation, wavering, shifting, indecision, irresolution.

fly¹, *v.* **1.** take wing, wing one's way, take off, take to the air, become airborne; soar, sail, zoom, cruise, coast, sweep, skim, *Inf.* kite; glide, plane, volplane, sailplane; dart, flit, flirt, hop, volitate.
2. float, hover, drift, hang, poise, float in the air; flutter, flicker, quiver, quaver; flap, wave, waver, undulate, toss, wag, wigwag.
3. aviate, jet, take *or* make a flight, be airborne, ride the skies *or* friendly skies; rocket, skyrocket.
4. dash, bolt, tear, tear along, bowl along, make time, cover ground, make strides *or* rapid strides; run, sprint, whiz, whisk; zip, career, rip, scour, scud, scorch, outstrip the wind, race like the wind, go *or* be off like a shot, *Chiefly Brit.* hare, *Inf.* clip, *Inf.* roar, *Inf.* barrel; hasten, make haste, race, speed, speed up, accelerate, hustle, hurry, post, hie, rush, move swiftly, move quickly; scamper, scurry, scoot, trip, skip.
5. flee, abscond, escape, take flight, take to flight, *Sl.* wing it, *Inf.* beat it, *Inf.* skip out, *Inf.* skedaddle, *Sl.* skidoodle, *Sl.* skidoo, *Sl.* vamoose; run, run away, run off, elope, take to one's heels, make a quick exit, *Inf.* clear out, *Inf.* cut out, *Inf.* cut and run, *Inf.* fly the coop, *Sl.* split, *Sl.* scram, *Sl.* blow, *Sl.* hightail it, *Sl.* lam *or* take it on the lam; retreat, withdraw, decamp, take oneself off, take French leave, quit the scene, make a getaway, beat a retreat, beat a hasty retreat, run for it, make a run for it, show the heels, show a clean *or* extra-light pair of heels, make a beeline for, *Inf.* take to the woods, *Inf.* head for the hills. See also **flee** (*def.* **2**).
6. (*all of time*) elapse, lapse, pass, pass by, pass swiftly, pass away, go by, move swiftly, slip, slide, glide; flow, advance, roll *or* press on; fade, melt, vanish, disappear, evaporate, go up in smoke; expire, run out, run its course.
7. pilot, control, be at the controls, fly left seat; copilot, fly right seat; solo, *Inf.* barnstorm; operate, drive, maneuver, manipulate.
8. hoist, hoist aloft, hoist up, raise, raise aloft, raise up, rear, rear up, lift, lift up, uplift, upraise, uprear, uphoist, *Inf.* sky.
9. transport, convey, send, dispatch; ship, freight, air-freight, express, air-express; post, mail, airmail.
10. elude, evade, escape, avoid, bilk, dodge, sidestep.
11. **fly at** *or* **into** attack, assault, assail, strike, strike at, strike out at, hit, have at, have a go at, lay about at, lay into, light into, pitch into; attack suddenly, charge, rush, rush at, rush upon, fall upon, pounce upon, swoop down upon, descend on *or* upon.
12. **fly in the face of** defy, flout, ignore, disregard, slight, treat with contempt, scoff at, thumb one's nose at; oppose, act in opposition to, go against; cross, contradict, contravene, controvert, counter, run counter to, go contrary to.
13. **fly off the handle** *Informal.* lose one's temper, explode, fly into a passion *or* rage *or* temper, have a tantrum, *Inf.* blow up, *Inf.* blow one's top *or* stack, *Inf.* hit the ceiling, *Sl.* go nuts, *Sl.* blow a gasket *or* fuse, *Sl.* flip, *Sl.* flip out, *Sl.* flip one's wig *or* lid, *Sl.* have a hemorrhage; get excited, get into a dither *or* tizzy, lose one's composure, *Sl.* blow one's cool.
14. **go fly a kite** *Slang.* split, scram, drag, beat it, get lost, take off, take a hike *or* walk, hit the road; buzz off, bug off, shove off, push off, go jump in a lake, drag your ass; mind your own business, keep your nose out of this, butt out, go peddle your fish.
15. **let fly** **a.** hurl, propel, fling, throw, pitch, toss, heave, chuck, lob, cast, hurtle, *Inf.* peg; shoot, shoot off, fire, fire off, let off, launch. **b.** (*all of emotions*) erupt with, burst forth *or* out *or* into, break out into; let go with, hold nothing back, give free reign; emit, discharge, vent, give out *or* off, *Fig.* open the sluices *or* floodgates.
—n. **16.** zipper, flap, lap, fly front.
17. tent fly, flap, lap, overlap, overlay, overlayer.
18. flying, volitation, *Rare.* volation; soaring, sailing, zooming, cruising; gliding, planing, volplaning, sailplaning; flight, trip, run, crossing, *Inf.* hop, *Inf.* jump.
19. *Baseball.* fly ball, pop fly, Texas leaguer, high fly, pop up.
20. *Theat.* flies, fly loft, fly gallery, fly floor, loft, gallery.
21. **on the fly** **a.** during flight, in the air, before reaching *or* hitting ground, off the ground. **b.** hurriedly, in a hurry, hastily, with haste, with a rush, in a sweat; quickly, speedily, swiftly; on the run, on the move, on the go, on the wing, in motion, *Inf.* on the hop *or* jump.

fly², *n.* **1.** housefly, true fly; gadfly, horsefly, bluebottle.
2. *Angling.* spinner, wobbler, popper; lure, hook, fishhook; jig, squid, plug.
3. **fly in the ointment** problem, snag, drawback, hitch, rub, *Inf.* catch; inconvenience, *Inf.* little problem, *Inf.* one small problem; flaw, kink, worm in the apple *or* rose, *Sl.* bummer.
4. **no flies on** *Slang.* alert, sharp, smart, knowing, wide-awake, nimble-minded, *Brit. Sl.* fly; dry behind the ears, not born yesterday, *Inf.* nobody's fool, *Inf.* no fool, *Inf.* no dumbbell; *Inf.* with it, *Inf.* together, *Inf.* hip, *Brit. Sl.* suss.

fly-by-night, *adj.* **1.** unreliable, irresponsible, unstable, unsteady, inconstant; disreputable, discreditable, dishonorable; shifty, shady, sharp, jackleg, dishonest, crooked.
2. brief, momentary, transitory, ephemeral, short-lived; impermanent, not lasting, like the shifting sands; transient, fleeting, *Inf.* here-today-gone-tomorrow.
—n. **3.** bad credit risk, debt-skipper, *Sl.* welsher, check-bouncer; confidence man, *Inf.* con man, swindler, fleecer.

flying, *adj.* **1.** soaring, sailing, zooming, cruising, coasting, sweeping, skimming; gliding, planing, volplaning, sailplaning; darting, flitting, flirting, hopping; taking wing, winging, winging one's way, taking off, taking to the air; airborne, volant, volitant, volitational.
2. floating, hovering, drifting, hanging; fluttering, flapping, waving, wavering, undulating, tossing, wagging; flowing, streaming, blowing.
3. fast, rapid, swift, fleet, mercurial; quick, speedy, express, double-quick, winged; agile, nimble, *Brit. Sl.* fly.
4. hasty, hurried, rushed; brief, fleeting, passing, fading; transitory, transient, momentary, short-lived, ephemeral, temporary, impermanent; here today, gone tomorrow; fly-by-night; evanescent, vanishing, disappearing.
5. fleeing, bolting, running, eloping, escaping; retreating, deserting, withdrawing, abandoning, decamping; running away, taking *or* making flight, fugitive.

—*n.* **6.** flight, aviation, volitation, *Rare.* volation.

foal, *n.* colt, filly, young horse; pony, *Archaic.* hobby.

foam, *n.* **1.** bubbles, head, froth, spume, yeast, *Brit. Inf.* barm; lather, suds, soap bubbles; foaminess, frothiness, spumescence; fizz, effervescence, sparkle.

—*v.* **2.** froth, cream, spume, lather, soap, soap up, suds up.

foamy, *adj.* **1.** foamlike, frothy, spumous, spumy, spumescent, yeasty, barmy; lathery, sudsy, soapy.

2. foaming, bubbling, bubbly, fizzing, fizzy, effervescing, effervescent, sparkling, *Fr. mousseux.*

focus, *n.* **1.** center, central point, focal point, focalization, point of concentration, point of convergence; nucleus, *Biol.* centrosome; core, heart, marrow, kernel, navel, middle, crux.

2. hub, nave, axis, pivot, pole; headquarters, clubhouse, rendezvous, haunt, gathering *or* meeting place; magnet, center of attention, attractor, allurer, lure, cynosure.

—*v.* **3.** focalize, bring into focus, clear up, line up; center, centralize, bring together, unify; converge, concenter, come together, meet, unite; concentrate, direct one's thinking to, zero in on.

fodder, *n.* forage, ensilage, silage, provender, stock, store; feed, food, rations; roughage, grain, herbage, hay, grass, pasture, pasturage.

foe, *n.* **1.** enemy, *Literary.* foeman, opponent, antagonist, adversary, attacker, combatant; rival, contestant, contender, competitor.

2. ill-wisher, backbiter, slanderer, vilifier, traducer, calumniator.

fog, *n.* **1.** vapor, cloud of vapor, haze, mist, brume, smog, *Sl.* soup, *Sl.* pea soup; drizzle, dankness, dampness.

2. murkiness, obscurity, overcast, cloudiness, mistiness, dirty weather.

3. bewilderment, confusion, perplexity, bafflement; vagueness, haziness, indefiniteness, uncertainty; stupor, daze, haze, stupefaction; distraction, *Psychiatry.* disorientation, unhingement.

—*v.* **4.** mist over, cloud up, becloud, obscure, befog, eclipse, cast a pall over; conceal, hide, screen, veil, shroud, shield, mask, cover, cloak, curtain; blanket, envelop, enwrap, close *or* shut in, close off.

5. bewilder, perplex, confuse, muddle, mix up, confound, puzzle, nonplus.

foggy, *adj.* **1.** hazy, misty, overcast, gray, damp, murky, lowering, brumous, *Sl.* soupy; smoky, smoggy, dirty; vaporous, steamy, humid; cloudy, beclouded.

2. obscure, vague, dim, indistinct, dark, dusty, shadowy; confused, dim, unclear.

fogy, *n.* *Usu.* **old fogy** conservative, *Inf.* mossback, one behind the times, anachronism, *Inf.* fossil, one who lives in the past *or* the dark ages, fogram, *Inf.* fuddy-duddy, *Inf.* antique, *Inf.* stick-in-the-mud, *Sl.* dodo, *Sl.* dodo bird.

foible, *n.* **1.** weakness, frailty, infirmity, minor failing, fault, shortcoming, deficiency, weak side *or* point, failing; flaw, chink, blemish, defect.

2. peculiarity, quirk, idiosyncrasy, crotchet, eccentricity, whimsy, *Inf.* blind spot, *Sl.* hang-up, *Sl.* kink, *Sl.* flake.

foil¹, *v.* frustrate, thwart, impede, hamper, balk, baffle, contravene, counter, circumvent, checkmate, cut the ground from under [s.o.], pull the rug out from under [s.o.]; override, knock down, *Inf.* shoot down; discomfit, daunt, *Inf.* faze, disconcert, rattle, hinder, cripple, *Inf.* trip up, *Sl.* screw up, *Sl.* mess up [s.o.'s] plans, *Sl.* spoil [s.o.'s] game; defeat, vanquish, overthrow, subdue, *Sl.* put down; repulse, set back, check, prevent, *Inf.* clip [s.o.'s] wings; outwit, outsmart.

foil², *n.* **1.** sheet, layer, leaf, scale, flake, wafer; film, lamina, ply, coating, membrane.

2. contrast, striking difference, antithesis, contrariety; setting, background, staging.

3. dupe, gull, puppet, tool, butt, fall guy, *Inf.* cat's paw, *Inf.* straight man, *Inf.* stooge, *Inf.* second banana.

foil³, *n.* rapier, blade, fencing sword, épée, steel.

foist, *v.* **1.** force upon, impose upon, thrust upon, lay on *or* upon, unload upon; take advantage of, palm off, pass off, fob off.

2. drag in, work in, insert in, fudge in, lug in, worm in, squeeze in, edge in, wedge in, throw in, toss in, thrust in, stick in.

fold¹, *v.* **1.** double, double over *or* up, turn up *or* under, dog-ear, infold, crease; tuck, gather, crimp; pleat, plait.

2. wrap, wrap up, enwrap, enclose, envelop; clasp, embrace, hug, embosom, press, *Inf.* squeeze.

3. go out of business, fail, collapse, close, shut down, *Inf.* fold up; go bankrupt, be ruined, lose everything, *Inf.* go broke, *Inf.* go under; (*all of theatrical performances*) *All Sl.* flop, bomb, lay an egg, go over like a lead balloon.

—*n.* **4.** crease, wrinkle, *Chiefly Scot.* wimple, *Zool., Anat.* plica; layer; tuck, gather; furrow, pucker, crinkle; crow's feet.

fold², *n.* **1.** (*all usu. for sheep*) enclosure, close, confine, corral, coop, pen.

2. congregation, assembly, *Fig.* flock; people, brethren, parishioners, churchgoers, *Fig.* sheep.

foliage, *n.* leafage, leaves, frondescence, foliation, foliature, *Bot.* vernation; flora and fauna, vegetation.

folk, *n.* **1.** nation, society; race, clan, tribe; populace, population, public, general public, citizenry.

2. folks *Informal.* relatives, relations, kin, kinfolk, kith and kin, kinsmen, flesh and blood, family; parents.

folklore, *n.* legends, fables, myths, mythology, lore; oral history, traditions; superstitions, old wives' tales.

follow, *v.* **1.** succeed, come next *or* after, take the place of, replace, supplant.

2. go after, go behind, walk behind, tread behind, tread on the heels of, bring up the rear, *Sl.* string along, *Inf.* tag along.

3. obey, give allegiance to, adopt, conform to, comply with, yield to, be guided by, accept as an authority; observe, mind, heed, regard, note; imitate, emulate, do like, simulate, model after, copy, copycat; mimic, ape, mirror, echo, reflect.

4. result from, ensue, supervene, arise; emanate, issue, flow.

5. attend, accompany, companion, escort, squire, go along with.

6. chase, pursue, run after, take off after, *Brit.* chevy; hound, dog, bedog; trail, *Inf.* tail, haunt, shadow, breathe down one's neck; hunt, stalk, course, trace, track, run down.

7. attain to, try for, aim at, strive for; cultivate, devote oneself to, dedicate oneself to.

8. attend to, be concerned with, keep up with, engage in; understand, comprehend, catch on, grasp.

follower, *n.* **1.** pupil, student, apprentice, protégé; disciple, adherent, partisan, sectary, votary; convert, proselyte; supporter, promoter, booster; proponent, advocate, defender, apologist; successor, heir, upholder, representative.

2. imitator, emulator, epigone, copyist, *Inf.* copycat.

3. attendant, servant, page, steward, henchman, squire, *Hist.* retainer; admirer, devotee, aficionado.

4. fan, rooter, groupie, claqueur; sycophant, parasite, satellite, hanger-on, dangler, toady; faddist, *Brit. Sl.* trendy, sheep.

following, *n.* **1.** attendants, retinue, train, suite, entourage; dependents, clientele, clientage.

2. adherents, patrons, supporters, advocates; devotees, admirers, fans, claque.

—adj. **3.** next, ensuing, succeeding, successive, sequent, sequential, subsequent, consequent, resulting.

folly, *n.* **1.** absurdity, absurdness, inanity, pointlessness, fatuousness; senselessness, nonsense, nonsensicalness, nonsensicality, meaninglessness, *Archaic.* insipience; unreasonableness, irrationality, illogicalness, illogicality; preposterousness, extravagance, excessiveness; poppycock, amphigory, bosh, drivel, gibberish, balderdash, fiddle-faddle; babble, twaddle, prattle; ridiculousness, ridiculosity, laughableness, ludicrousness; comicality, comicalness, funniness, humor, humorousness, drollness; asininity, idiocy, idioticalness, *Inf.* moronism, *Inf.* moronity, imbecility; craziness, *Sl.* kookiness, madness, wildness, insanity, dementedness; daftness, *Inf.* nuttiness, peculiarity, strangeness, erraticism, eccentricity, oddness, oddity; *All Sl.* balminess, bugginess, screwiness, goofiness, wackiness, looniness.

2. weak-mindedness, simple-mindedness, featherheadedness, rattleheadedness; light-mindedness, lightheadedness, feeble-mindedness, *Inf.* dizziness; muddleheadedness, absent-mindedness, bemusement, confusion, confusedness; dullness, *Inf.* dopiness, *Inf.* dumbness, insensateness; dull-wittedness, slow-wittedness, half-wittedness, unwittingness; hare-brainedness, giddiness, mercurialness, recklessness, unstableness, instability; stupidness, stupidity, unintelligence, mindlessness, fatuity, brainlessness, slowness; denseness, density, thickness, thickheadedness, obtuseness, stolidness, lumpishness, bluntness; blockheadedness, boneheadedness, doltishness; empty-headedness, blankness, vacancy, vacuousness.

3. triflingness, frivolousness, frivolity, shallowness; unimportance, inconsiderableness, insignificance; pettiness, picayunishness, triviality, paltriness; smallness, scantiness, meagerness.

4. antic, antics, caper, *Inf.* shenanigans, *Sl.* monkeyshines, *Sl.* monkeybusiness; mischief, prankishnesss, *Inf.* hanky-panky, *Scot. and North Eng.* daffing, prank, trick, practical joke; farce, mockery, mummery; fooling, tomfoolery, horseplay; clowning, clownery, clownishness, zanyism; buffoonery, buffoonism, buffoonishness, harlequinade; joking, jesting, jocosity, jocoseness, jocularity, waggishness, waggery, drollery; levity, facetiousness; silliness, childishness, immaturity, puerility, juvenility.

5. inappropriateness, ineptness, ineptitude, improperness, impropriety, incongruousness, incongruity, inconsistence, inconsistency; indiscretion, imprudence, unwiseness, irresponsibility; impetuousness, impetuosity, impulsiveness, hastiness, short-sightedness; foolhardiness, incaution, heedlessness, rashness, brashness, recklessness, unwariness; mistake, blunder, false move, *Sl.* goof, faux pas.

foment, *v.* **1.** instigate, incite, provoke, actuate, initiate, put in motion, sow the seeds of, *Inf.* start something, look for trouble; encourage, urge, abet, spur, goad, prompt, egg on, put up to; agitate, excite, suscitate, impassion, arouse, rouse, brew, stir up, work up, wind up, whip up, *Inf.* psych up, fire up, inflame, enkindle, kindle, touch off, ignite the spark, stir the embers, fan the fire; stimulate, animate, reanimate, invigorate, motivate, galvanize, electrify, inspire, inspirit, vivify, rally, enliven, liven up, awaken, wake up, shake up, revive; promote, foster, further, forward, advance, favor; support, advocate, patronize.

2. poultice, embrocate, plaster, stupe, *Obs.* stive; heat, warm; bathe, wash.

fomentation, *n.* **1.** instigation, incitement, incitation, provocation, actuation, initiation; encouragement, urge, urging, abetment, abetting, spurring, goading, prompting; agitation, excitement, excitation, suscitation, arousal, inflammation; stimulus, fillip, incentive, provocative, *Sl.* shot in the arm; stimulation, animation, invigoration, motivation, galvanization, inspiration, vivification, rallying, enlivening, livening up, awakening, waking up, shaking up, reviving; promotion, furtherance, advancement, advance; support, advocacy, patronage.

2. embrocation; bathing, washing; heating, warming.

3. poultice, counterirritant, mustard plaster, plaster; liniment, ointment, salve, liquid, oil, lotion.

fond, *adj.* **1.** *Usu.* **fond of** partial to, having a liking for, having a taste for, having a fancy for; in love with, *Inf.* sweet on, enamored of, infatuated with, *Sl.* stuck on, *Sl.* hooked on, addicted to.

2. loving, adoring, affectionate, tender, warm, caring.

3. overindulgent, doting, overfond, excessively attached *or* devoted, uxorious.

fondle, *v.* caress, stroke gently, pet, pat; hold, hug, clasp, embrace, cuddle, snuggle, nestle, nuzzle; kiss, osculate, *Inf.* make out, *Inf.* neck, spoon, *Inf.* smooch; *Inf.* pet, *Sl.* canoodle, *Sl.* feel up, rub, massage, handle, *Inf.* paw; toy with, play with, play footsie with, *Both Euph.* fool around, mess around.

fondness, *n.* **1.** affection, affectionateness, tenderness, love, *Fr. amour*; kindness, care, devotion, attachment.

2. liking, like, taste for, eye for, weakness; partiality, preference, inclination, leaning, tendency toward; penchant for, desire, fancy.

3. overindulgence, dotingness, excessive devotion *or* attachment, uxoriousness.

food, *n.* **1.** nourishment, nutriment, sustenance, subsistence; aliment, viands, bread, foodstuffs, solids, edibles, *Inf.* grub, *Sl.* eats, *Sl.* chow, *Chiefly Brit. Sl.* scoff; victuals, provisions, rations, commons, comestibles, *Western U.S. Sl.* chuck, *Brit. Sl.* prog; board, fare, meals, menu, table,diet, regimen; mess, swill, *Inf.* glop, *Sl.* slop.

2. See **fodder**.

fool, *n.* **1.** ninny, nincompoop, silly, silly billy, *Sl.* yo-yo, tomfool; simpleton, Simple Simon, saphead, noodle, idiot, cuckoo, *Inf.* jay, *Sl.* jerk, imbecile, mooncalf, *Inf.* moron; dimwit, nitwit, half-wit, *Sl.* zombie, goose; scatterbrain, *Sl.* birdbrain, *Sl.* flake, rattlehead, rattlebrain, rattlepate, harebrain, *Sl.* dingbat, *Sl.* ding-a-ling; featherbrain, addle-brain, addlehead, addle-pate, pinhead; dolt, clod, oaf, dunce, *Inf.* chump, *Inf.* coot, dullard, *Inf.* numskull; dope, booby, *Inf.* dummy, *Sl.* dumbbell, *Sl.* meatball *or* meathead; blockhead, beetlehead, bonehead, dunderhead, dunderpate, chucklehead, *Sl.* dumbhead, *Sl.* lunkhead, *Inf.* knucklehead, *Sl.* stupidhead; donkey, ass, lubber, lout; ignoramus, know-nothing, lowbrow, illiterate.

2. jester, clown, *Archaic.* antic, zany, buffoon, droll, jokester, *Inf.* stooge, wiseacre, merry-andrew; scaramouch, punchinello, pierrot, harlequin, punch.

3. dupe, gull, *Brit. Dial.* cull, *Sl.* pigeon; butt, sap, gudgeon, tool, cat's paw; sucker, victim, easy mark, fall guy, sitting duck, *Inf.* goat; pushover, cinch, greenhorn.

4. **be nobody's fool** be wise, be sagacious; be shrewd,

be astute, be sharp, be canny; be sly, *Sl.* savvy, be cunning, be crafty; be perceptive, be discerning, be perspicacious.

—*v.* **5.** befool, make a fool of, spoof, play a trick on, play a joke on, kid; trick, deceive, humbug, delude, con, cheat, beguile, cozen, do, take in; hoodwink, blindfold, bluff, throw dust into the eyes, pull the wool over [s.o.'s] eyes, bamboozle; mislead, misguide, misdirect, lead astray, give a bum steer, misinform; swindle, defraud, finagle, pluck, fleece, bilk; victimize, hoax, dupe, gull, pigeon, *Sl.* hornswoggle, *Inf.* flimflam, *Inf.* diddle; circumvent, get around, overreach.

6. jest, joke, banter, tease, trifle with, spoof, josh, jive, put [s.o.] on; gibe, jeer, mock, deride, scoff, taunt; act the fool, play the monkey.

7. pretend, make believe, feign, act, play; stage, simulate, sham, counterfeit, fake.

8. **fool around** squander, waste, run through, throw away, fritter away; dissipate, deplete, exhaust, expend, misspend.

9. **fool with** toy with, trifle with, meddle with, tamper with, mess in *or* with, monkey around *or* with, dabble with *or* in, palter with, dally with, fiddle with.

foolery, *n.* **1.** antic, antics, caper, *Inf.* shenanigans, *Sl.* monkeyshines, *Sl.* monkeybusiness. See **folly** (*def.* **4**).

2. absurdity, inanity, pointlessness, fatuity, fatuousness, foolishness, folly. See **folly** (*def.* **1**).

foolhardy, *adj.* reckless, rash, brash, temerarious, desperate, hotheaded; harebrained, thoughtless, regardless, careless, short-sighted, daring, venturous, venturesome, adventurous, dare-devil, devil-may-care; impetuous, impulsive, hasty, madcap, heedless, unheeding, *Inf.* trigger-happy, unwary; headlong, unexpected, unforeseen; spontaneous, unpremeditated, sudden, abrupt, precipitate; audacious, bold, fearless; incautious, imprudent, indiscreet, irresponsible, injudicious; unwise, ill-considered, ill-suited, ill-advised, impolitic.

foolish, *adj.* **1.** incautious, imprudent, indiscreet, irresponsible, injudicious; unwise, ill-considered, ill-suited, ill-advised, impolitic; impetuous, impulsive, hasty, short-sighted, heedless, unheeding; foolhardy, headlong, rash, brash, unwary; thoughtless, careless, reckless; spontaneous, unpremeditated, sudden, abrupt, precipitate.

2. absurd, inane, pointless, fatuous, senseless, nonsensical, *Inf.* damfool, *Inf.* damfoolish, tomfoolish, *Scot. and North Eng.* glaikit, *Sl.* cockeyed; poppycockish, *Sl.* cockamamie, amphigoric; ridiculous, derisible, risible, laughable, ludicrous, *Sl.* for the birds; comical, funny, farcical, humorous, droll; asinine, anserine, idiotic, *Inf.* moronic, imbecilic; childish, puerile, green, immature; crazy, crazed, *Sl.* kooky, *Scot.* doiled, mad, wild, insane, demented; daft, *Inf.* daffy, crackbrained, *Inf.* nutty; peculiar, strange, odd; *All Sl.* balmy, dippy, batty, cuckoo, buggy, screwy, wacky, goofy, loony.

3. weak-minded, simple, simple-minded, birdbrained; featherheaded, featherbrained, rattleheaded, rattlebrained; light-minded, light-headed, *Inf.* dizzy, *Inf.* footling; muddled, muddleheaded, addlebrained, addlepated; absent-minded, scatterbrained, confused, bemused; feeble-minded, deficient, subnormal, retarded; dull, vapid, *Inf.* dopey, insensate, *Inf.* dumb; dull-witted, dim-witted, slow-witted, half-witted, witless, unwitty; harebrained, giddy, mercurial, reckless, erratic, unstable, harum-scarum; stupid, unintelligent, mindless, fatuitous, brainless, slow; dense, thick, thickheaded, thick-skulled, thick-witted, obtuse, stolid, lumpish, blunt; blockheaded, boneheaded, blockish, doltish; empty-headed, blank, vacant, vacuous.

4. unreasonable, irrational, illogical, meaningless; preposterous, extravagant, excessive; haphazard, aimless, driftless, unconnected, groundless; inappropriate, inept, improper; incongruous, inconsistent.

5. trifling, petty, nugatory, frothy, frivolous, shallow; unimportant, inconsequential, immaterial, inconsiderable, insignificant; petty, picayune, trivial, measly, paltry; small, minor, slight, meager.

foolishness, *n.* **1.** senselessness, meaninglessness, thoughtlessness, shallowness, vacantness, blankness, vacuousness, emptiness; vapidity, vapidness, insipidity, insipidness, flatness, dullness, tediousness; stupidity, asininity, imbecility, idioticalness, insensateness, dumbness, doltishness; slowness, moronity; illogic, illogicalness, illogicality, irrationality, irrationalness; idiocy, lunacy, madness, craziness, *Sl.* screwiness.

2. folly, unwiseness, imprudentness, imprudency, *Archaic.* insipience; indiscretion, indiscreetness, ineptitude; unreasonableness, foolhardiness, *Sl.* foolheadedness, hastiness, impulsiveness, impetuousness; impracticality, impracticalness, pointlessness, wild-goose chase, extravagance; ridiculousness, ridiculosity, ludicrousness, preposterousness; absurdity, absurdness, nonsensicalness, nonsensicality.

3. nonsense, moonshine, gobbledegook; foolish humbug, bunkum *or* buncombe, *Sl.* bunk, *U.S. Sl.* blah; flummery, *Inf.* hokum, *Sl.* applesauce, *Sl.* eyewash; rubbish, *Sl.* tripe, refuse, *Dial.* culch, chaff, trash, *Inf.* truck, trumpery; tommyrot, *Inf.* rot, *Sl.* garbage, *Sl.* crap, *Sl.* crock, *Sl.* bull; balderdash, hogwash, *Sl.* horsefeathers; stuff, stuff and nonsense, *Inf.* bosh, *Brit. Inf.* gammon, *Brit. Sl.* tosh; fudge, folly, rigmarole *or* rigamarole, amphigory; footle, *Inf.* malarkey, *Sl.* bushwa, *Sl.* baloney, *Sl.* bilge *or* bilge water, *Sl.* meshugaas, *Scot. and North Eng.* haver; poppycock, *Inf.* fiddle-faddle, *Inf.* piffle, *Inf.* hooey, *Inf.* kibosh, *Inf.* flapdoodle; claptrap, rodomontade, fustian, bombast, rant, *Sl.* hot air, *Sl.* gas.

4. antic, antics, caper, *Inf.* shenanigans, *Sl.* monkeyshines, *Sl.* monkeybusiness; prankishness, mischief, *Inf.* hanky-panky, *Scot. and North Eng.* daffing; prank, trick, practical joke; fooling, foolery, tomfoolery, horseplay; clowning, clownery, clownishness; buffoonery, buffoonism, buffoonishness, harlequinade; joking, jesting, jocosity, jocoseness, jocularity, waggishness, waggery, drollery; levity, frivolity, facetiousness; silliness, inanity, childishness, puerility, juvenility, *Inf.* sappiness.

foot, *n.* **1.** trotter, hoof, paw, pad; *Inf.* tootsy, *Anat.* pes, kicker, (*usu. pl.*) dog.

2. base, foundation, principle, basis, footing, groundwork, substructure, substratum, understructure; support, pedestal, stand, rest, prop, stay, brace; bottom, *Archit.* socle, *Archit.* plinth, *Bot.* caudex.

3. end, edge, boundary, extremity, limit, border, margin, rim.

4. **get off on the right foot** get a good start, begin auspiciously, get out of the right side of the bed, *Rare.* auspicate.

5. **on foot** **a.** afoot, by foot; walking, running, skipping, jogging, sprinting. **b.** in play, in progress *or* operation, going on.

6. **put one's best foot forward** **a.** make a good impression, get on the good side of; be on one's best behavior. **b.** hurry, proceed with haste, hasten, accelerate.

7. **put one's foot down** stand fast, stand *or* hold one's ground, hold one's own, stick to one's guns; lay down the law, insist, not take "no" for an answer, have the last word.

8. **put one's foot in one's mouth** *Informal.* blunder, make a faux pas, make *or* pull a boner; make a fool of oneself, be tactless *or* inconsiderate.

—*v.* **9. foot it** walk, go on foot, traverse on foot, *Sl.* hoof, *Sl.* take the shoe-leather express; step, pace, tramp, march; perambulate, stroll, promenade, saunter, amble, take a walk, go for a walk.

10. foot the bill pick up the check *or* tab, treat; settle a bill, pay a bill, discharge an obligation, *All Sl.* cough up, shell out, fork over.

footfall, *n.* **1.** footstep, step, tread, stride, gait.

2. sound of footsteps, tramp, plod, plunk.

foothold, *n.* place to stand on, *Gk. pou sto*, footing, standing, purchase; base, foundation, support; grip, hold, toehold; vantage, position, bridgehead, beachhead.

footing, *n.* **1.** foothold, established *or* secure position. See **foothold**.

2. basis, base, foundation, ground, groundwork, substructure; principle, fundamental, rudiment.

3. stability, settlement, equilibrium, even keel, status quo.

4. position, condition, situation, station, estate, place; status, stratum, level, class, caste; step, degree, rank, grade.

5. terms, standing, relations.

footle, *v.* **1.** caper, prance, frisk, gambol, be playful *or* jocose; fool around, *Inf.* mess around, *Sl.* screw around, *Sl.* horse around, act childish; get into mischief, *Inf.* pull shenanigans, play a prank *or* trick; be silly, joke, jest, clown, play the buffoon; giggle, titter, twitter, *Inf.* teehee.

2. gibber, *Sl.* gibber-jabber, blather, *Inf.* blither, drivel, drool; twattle, *Brit.* twattle, prate, talk nonsense, *Inf.* talk through one's hat; jabber, jargon, *Sl.* jive; chatter, chipper, prattle, cackle.

—*n.* **3.** nonsense, foolishness, silliness. See **foolishness** (*defs.* **3, 4**).

footpath, *n.* path, pathway, *Brit.* footway, walkway, garden path; trail, track, lane; bypath, byway; bypass, shortcut.

foot soldier, *n.* infantryman, *Rare.* footman, sepoy, peltast; enlisted man, G.I., G.I. Joe, doughboy, *Sl.* grunt, Tommy, Tommy Atkins, cannon fodder; regular, private, *Inf.* non-com, legionnaire; mercenary.

footstep, *n.* footfall, step, tread; plod, plunk; pace, stride; footprint, footmark, track; trail, trace, *Archaic.* vestige, mark.

footstool, *n.* ottoman, hassock, stool; taboret, bench; faldstool, kneeler, prie-dieu.

fop, *n.* dandy, beau, jack-a-dandy, coxcomb; spark, dude, *Sl.* swell, *Brit.* toff; Beau Brummel, fancy Dan, *Sl.* peacock, *Sl.* bantam cock, *Sl.* glamor puss; exquisite, *Hist.* macaroni, silk-stocking, clotheshorse; poseur, popinjay, la-di-da, strutter; pompous ass, cock of the walk; prig, prinker, pretty-boy, *Archaic.* carpet knight; blade, sophisticate, gallant, cavalier; ladies' man, lady killer, *Sl.* lounge lizard.

foppery, *n.* foppishness, dandyism, *Sl.* peacockery; conceit, vanity, *Fr. amour-propre*, affectation.

foppish, *adj.* showy, dandyish, overdressed, dapper, natty, swank, *Inf.* swell-elegant; fastidious, finicky, finical, prinking, preening; pompous, vainglorious, self-glorifying; vain as a peacock, self-satisfied, *Sl.* stuck up, *Inf.* stuck on oneself, conceited, in love with oneself, blinded by one's own glory; affected, la-di-da, pretentious.

for, *prep.* **1.** for the purpose of, in order to, with the object *or* goal of, so as to become, with a view *or* eye to, in quest of, seeking, looking for; destined for, in destination of, toward, to.

2. concerning, belonging to; appropriate to, fitting for, suited to, adapted to, fit to, to be used with.

3. instead of, in place of, as a replacement for, in exchange for, as the equivalent of; in return for, in payment for.

4. as regards, with regard *or* respect to, respecting, with reference to, proportionate to, in proportion to.

5. during, in the space *or* time of, throughout, through, over the extent of.

6. in favor of, favorable to, in support of, supportive of, in championship of; on the side of, with, associated with.

7. in the interest of, contributive to, on *or* in behalf of; for the sake of, in the honor of.

8. by reason of, because of, on account of; caused by, as a result of, resultant to, due to.

—*conj.* **9.** since, as, inasmuch as, forasmuch as, whereas; due to the fact that, in view of the fact that, seeing that; because, for the reason that.

forage, *n.* **1.** fodder, provender; coarse food, dry food, grain, hay, oats, grass; herbage, pasture, pasturage.

2. raid, sack, plundering, ravaging, looting, rifling; foray, assault, invasion, incursion.

—*v.* **3.** search about, seek, look around, fish for, hunt, track down; rummage, ransack, rake through; (*all usu. in reference to food*) scavenge, *Brit. Sl.* prog, scrape up, scratch around for, scrounge *or* scrounge around.

4. raid, plunder, pillage, loot, sack, rifle, gut, strip; (*usu. of cattle*) rustle, *Inf.* poach; invade, intrude, encroach, trespass.

foray, *n.* **1.** raid, incursion, invasion, razzia, inroad, irruption; charge, thrust, sortie, sally.

2. attack, assault, encounter, offensive, onset, onslaught, skirmish; intrusion, encroachment, trespass.

—*v.* **3.** raid, attack, assault, assail, rush, storm; invade, set upon, fall upon, swoop down upon, descend upon.

4. ravage, pillage, forage, ransack; sack, loot, gut, fleece, strip, rifle.

forbear, *v.* **1.** refrain from, abstain from, desist from, cease; stop, hold, stay, leave off, break off, let up, pause.

2. forgo, sacrifice, renounce; quit, give up, do *or* go without, *Inf.* cut out; avoid, shun, eschew.

3. keep back, withhold, restrain oneself, refrain, hold back, abstain; tolerate, suffer, endure, abide, brook, put up with, bear with; be patient, be self-controlled, be tolerant, be lenient.

forbearance, *n.* **1.** abstinence, restraint, self-restraint, self-control, self-denial; refraining, forbearing, desisting, desistance; avoidance, eschewal; temperance, moderation.

2. patience, endurance, tolerance, toleration; sufferance, longanimity, long-suffering; submission, resignation.

3. leniency, permissiveness, indulgence; clemency, mercy, pity; lenity, mildness, meekness.

forbid, *v.* **1.** prohibit, proscribe, outlaw, interdict, taboo, put off limits, ban, place an injunction on; disallow, say no to, refuse, veto, nix, turn thumbs down, turn down, reject.

2. hinder, impede, slow up *or* down; restrain, hold back, check, curb; deter, get *or* stand in the way, block, prevent; stop, halt, arrest.

3. exclude, eliminate, count out, rule out, preclude; debar, shut out, lock out, keep out, bar.

forbiddance, *n.* interdiction, interdict, taboo, prohibition, proscription, outlawry, ban, injunction, embargo; disallowance, veto, rejection, refusal.

forbidden, *adj.* not allowed, prohibited, proscribed, outlawed, *Ger. verboten, Fr. interdit*, taboo, out-of-bounds, off-limits; disallowed, vetoed, nixed, turned down, rejected, refused.

forbidding, *adj.* grim, unfriendly, hostile, surly, harsh, hard, stern, tough; bad, nasty, ugly, mean, cruel, vicious, evil; dangerous, sinister, dark, threatening, menacing, ominous, portentous, foreboding.

force, *n.* **1.** vigor, life, vitality, power, potency, *Literary.* puissance, strength; stamina, energy, animation, birr; violence, dint, shock, impact, striking ability, *Inf.* punch, *Inf.* zip, *Sl.* pizazz.

2. compulsion, coercion, arm-twisting; duress, constraint, enforcement, coaction; impulse, stimulus.

3. ability, agency, effectiveness, efficacy, binding effect.

4. meaning, significance, signification, weightiness, weight, value; emphasis, stress, import, vehemence; validity, cogency, virtue, caliber.

5. troops, army, host, legion, squadron, regiment, battalion, detachment, division, phalanx; patrol, convoy; armament, artillery, weaponry.

—v. **6.** necessitate, oblige, compel, constrain, coerce; effect, enforce, push through, *Inf.* railroad, *Sl.* shove down [s.o.'s] throat; exact, extort, twist from, wrest, wring.

7. impel, urge, push, press; propel, thrust, obtrude; elbow, shoulder.

8. strain, pressure, pull, stretch, tense, intensify, tax, overburden, distort.

9. break open, snap, crack, pry, jimmy, *Sl.* blow, *Sl.* blast.

forced, *adj.* **1.** enforced, required, obligatory, compulsory, involuntary; committed, obliged, constrained, compelled.

2. strained, unnatural, artificial, false, feigned, *Sl.* phony; overdone, stagey, far-fetched, catachrestic; affected, stilted, *Inf.* put on; studied, calculated, mannered, recherché; labored, self-conscious, stiff.

3. driving, pressing, necessary, emergency, unavoidable, inescapable.

forceful, *adj.* vigorous, dynamic, energetic; virile, lusty, strong, robust, mighty, powerful; potent, effective, moving, gripping; intensive, vehement, emphatic, definite, positive; cogent, persuasive, telling, convincing, weighty.

forcible, *adj.* **1.** impressive, striking, urgent, irresistible, forceful. See **forceful**.

2. compulsory, obligatory, required, binding, incumbent, imposed, forced, coercive.

3. violent, drastic, intense, unrestrained.

forcibly, *adv.* **1.** compulsorily, by force, coercively, under protest, against one's will, willing or unwilling, willy-nilly, *Fr. bon gré, mal gré, Inf.* come hell or high water; necessarily, of necessity, needs must, *Fr. coûte que coûte*.

2. vehemently, fiercely, ferociously, without restraint, emphatically, intensively, violently; vigorously, energetically, with might and main, with herculean effort; powerfully, effectively, efficaciously, convincingly.

fore, *adj.* **1.** frontal, in *or* at the front, at the head, at *or* on top, ahead, above.

2. first, foremost, headmost, most advanced, highest, best, top, leading, lead, head, chief.

3. former, earlier, previous, preceding, foregoing, prior, antecedent, anterior.

4. fore and aft front and rear, at both ends, coming and going; stem to stern, top to bottom, head to toe *or* foot.

—n. **5.** front, forefront, foremost part, top, head.

6. to the fore a. to *or* toward the front, forward up, to the surface; out, into the open, into the spotlight, to the forefront. **b.** at head, within reach, ready, available.

forebear, *n.* *Usu.* **forebears** ancestors, forefathers. See **forefather**.

forebode, *v.* **1.** augur, presage, portend, foreshadow, foreshow, foretoken, presignify, omen; betoken, signify, mean, indicate, point to.

2. sense, intuit, feel, have a feeling, *Inf.* have a funny feeling, *Inf.* feel in one's bones.

3. prognosticate, prophesy, predict, soothsay, vaticinate; foretell, forecast, divine, forewarn, *Rare.* premonish, *Obs.* auspicate.

foreboding, *n.* **1.** augury, prediction, prognostication, prophesy, prefigurement, forecast, handwriting on the wall; premonition, prognostic, preindication, forewarning; foretoken, portent, omen, sign, token, harbinger.

2. presentiment, feeling, vague feeling, *Inf.* funny feeling, suspicion, *Inf.* sneaking suspicion, intuition; anxiety, misgiving, apprehension, apprehensiveness, boding; dread, fear, ill-feeling, chill along the spine.

—adj. **3.** premonitory, forewarning, foreshadowing, foretokening, preindicative; ominous, portentous, bodeful, threatening, menacing, lowering; inauspicious, unpropitious, unfavorable, unpromising, ill-omened.

forecast, *v.* **1.** predict, prognosticate, prophesy, augur, soothsay, vaticinate; foretell, forebode, forewarn, divine, *Rare.* premonish, *Obs.* auspicate.

2. guess, conjecture, estimate, speculate, hazard a guess, *Inf.* go out on a limb.

3. prearrange, predetermine, project, plan ahead, set up, work out; (*all beforehand*) plan, devise, contrive, design.

—n. **4.** guess, conjecture, estimate, estimation, *Inf.* shot, *Inf.* shot in the dark, *Inf.* stab.

5. prediction, prognostication, prophecy, prefigurement, augury, foreboding, divination.

6. divination, geomancy, sortilege; soothsaying, fortunetelling, foretelling; forecasting, (*of weather*) meteorology; guesswork, speculation.

foreclose, *v.* **1.** exclude, shut out, bar, debar; reject, refuse, lock out, shut out.

2. obstruct, block, blockade, barricade, stand in the way; prevent, hinder, impede, deter.

forefather, *n.* ancestor, forebear, grandfather, progenitor, primogenitor, *Archaic.* predecessor; procreator, begetter; patriarch, parent, father, genitor; author, maker, creator, originator.

foregoing, *adj.* preceding, precedent, prior, prevenient, preliminary, antecedent, anterior, forerunning; earlier, former; aforesaid, aforementioned.

foregone, *adj.* **1.** previous, past, prior, earlier, former.

2. predetermined, predecided, prejudged, preestablished, preordained; fixed, set, cut-and-dry.

forehead, *n.* brow, front.

foreign, *adj.* **1.** alien, peregrine; tramontane, ultramontane, transalpine; ultramarine, transmarine, transatlantic, transpacific.

2. irrelevant, impertinent, inappropriate, inapt, inapposite, unrelated, unconnected; extraneous, extrinsic, external, adventitious, ulterior, outside, outlying; remote, removed, distant.

3. unfamiliar, strange, peculiar, odd, curious, *Scot.* fremd; exotic, outlandish, barbarian.

foreigner, *n.* alien, non-native, outlander, outsider,

tramontane, stranger, barbarian; immigrant, emigrant, newcomer, *Brit.* new boy.

foreknowledge, *n.* prescience, foresight, precognition; foreboding, presentiment, premonition, presage, prior feeling.

foreland, *n.* cape, promontory, headland, head, *Scot.* mull, point, hook, spur.

foreman, *n.* **1.** superintendent, *Inf.* super, manager, line manager, fugleman; supervisor, overseer, overlooker, overman, chief, headman, boss, *Inf.* bossman, *U.S. Inf.* straw boss, *Sl.* the man, *Sl.* head honcho, *Brit.* gaffer; master, commander, director, taskmaster.

2. foreman of the jury, (*in Scotland*) jury-chancellor.

foremost, *adj.* primary, prime, principal, paramount, chief, cardinal, main, uppermost, most important, central, focal; first, leading, headmost, supreme, premier, top, crowning, preeminent, number one, *Inf.* numero uno, *Inf.* boss.

forensic, *adj.* rhetorical, polemical, polemic, controversial, argumentative, eristic; dialectic, dialectical, litigious, pilpulistic.

foreordain, *v.* **1.** destine, design, intend, mean, purpose, resolve, determine, set; designate, dedicate, allot, *Obs.* appoint; mark, earmark, tag, set apart *or* aside; consecrate, devote; reserve, *Brit.* bespeak.

2. fate, ordain, doom, *Rare.* destinate; predetermine, predestine, *Obs.* predestinate, preordain, foreordinate, predecide, foredoom, *Inf.* have in store for.

forerun, *v.* **1.** come before, precede, go before, forego, antecede, run ahead, go first; go in advance, cut in, *Brit.* jump the queue, run in front of, take the lead; herald, usher in, lead the way, blaze the trail, take the lead, show the way.

2. prefigure, foreshadow, foretoken, give signs of, presage; point to, signalize, indicate, betoken.

3. anticipate, foretell, forecast; preview, foresee, foreglimpse, look ahead; scent, feel in one's bones, foreknow.

forerunner, *n.* **1.** predecessor, precursor, foregoer, antecedent; ancestor, forbear, progenitor, forefather, father, genitor; pathfinder, pioneer, explorer; vanguard, apostle, missionary, man from Cook's.

2. omen, sign, portent, symptom, token; premonition, presage, augury, forewarning; foretoken, prefigurement, preview.

3. herald, harbinger, advance man, usher, announcer, crier, towncrier; advance guard, avant-courier, courier, outrider.

foresee, *v.* **1.** foreknow, divine, forecast, prognosticate, foretell; predict, prophesy, vaticinate, forebode, augur; look into the future, gaze into the crystal ball.

2. see beforehand, preview, get a glimpse of, foreglimpse, see ahead, forerun, *Inf.* get a sneak preview; expect, look ahead, anticipate, look forward, watch for.

3. beware, take care, be prudent, exercise caution, give heed to, pay attention to; keep an eye out for, keep one's eyes open, keep one's ears open, be on guard, look before leaping; stop, look and listen.

foreshadow, *v.* forebode, foretoken, foreshow, presage, prefigure, presignify, augur, portend, bode, omen; betoken, signify, mean, indicate, point to.

foresight, *n.* **1.** prudence, care, judgment, discretion, discrimination; sagacity, perspicacity, judiciousness, presence of mind; caution, readiness, preparation, precaution, heed, watchfulness; farsightedness, long-sightedness, circumspection.

2. prevision, prescience, preview, prefigurement, foreglimpse; glimpse, prospect, vision; foretaste, anticipation, handsel.

3. foreknowledge, precognition, clairvoyance, clairvoyancy, second sight; preconception, prenotion, apprehension, presentiment.

4. sight, bead, sighthole, peep sight, aim.

forest, *n.* **1.** wood, woods, woodland, wooded area, timberland, *Brit.* plantation, *Brit.* chase; grove, sylvan thicket, copse, covert, *Archaic.* bosk; bush, virgin forest, greenwood, wildwood; chaparral, underbrush, brake, canebrake.

2. cluster, large number, myriad; herd, flock, bunch, multitude, multiplicity, mass, profusion, accumulation.

forestall, *v.* **1.** preclude, prevent, hinder, thwart, frustrate; obviate, intercept, obstruct, sidetrack, avert, ward off, stave off, fend off, parry, divert, avoid; nip in the bud, squelch in its infancy.

2. anticipate, be beforehand, get ahead of, steal a march on, get the start on, beat to the draw.

3. buy up ahead, monopolize, corner, get a corner on; engross, *Sl.* hog, get control of, get an exclusive on.

forestry, *n.* forest management, forest planting, tree growing, tree planting; woodcraft, forestation, afforestation, *Bot.* dendrology, silviculture.

foretaste, *n.* prelibation, handsel, first taste, *Archaic.* antepast; anticipation, intuition, foreknowledge, presentiment, premonition.

foretell, *v.* **1.** predict, prognosticate, prophesy, augur, soothsay, vaticinate; forecast, forewarn, divine, *Rare.* premonish, *Obs.* auspicate.

2. forebode, foreshadow, foreshow, foretoken, portend, presage, presignify, prefigure, bode, omen; betoken, signify, indicate, mean, point to.

forethought, *n.* **1.** provision, prudence, providence, precaution, foresight, long-sightedness, farsightedness, wisdom.

2. anticipation, prior consideration *or* thought, premeditation; presurmise, preconception, prenotion.

foretoken, *n.* **1.** sign, signal, indication, harbinger, token, augury, omen, portent, prognostic; presage, foreboding, forewarning, warning, premonition, handwriting on the wall.

—*v.* **2.** foreshadow, prefigure, foreshow, presage, portend. See **foreshadow**.

forever, *adv.* always, ever, evermore, *Poetic.* ay, *Latin. in saecula saeculorum*; till the end of time, till hell freezes over, till the cows come home, till Niagara Falls; eternally, world without end, everlastingly, perpetually, undyingly; constantly, ceaselessly, continually, incessantly, unremittingly, unceasingly, endlessly; for good and all.

forewarn, *v.* precaution, prewarn, *Rare.* premonish; alert, warn, give warning *or* fair warning, put on guard, put on the qui vive, *Sl.* give the high sign to; caution, admonish, advise, say a word to the wise; clue in, tip off, *Inf.* put a bug in [s.o.'s] ear.

foreword, *n.* preface, preamble, proem; introduction, exordium, prelude, prologue, prolegomenon; epigraph, inscription, dedication.

forfeit, *n.* **1.** fine, penalty, penalization, mulct, amercement, *Law.* sequestration; fixed fee, fee, charge, cost.

—*v.* **2.** relinquish, hand over, give over, give up, default, *Law.* escheat.

forfeiture, *n.* **1.** fine, penalty, mulct, forfeit. See **forfeit** (*def.* **1**).

forge[1], *n.* **1.** (*all for heating metal*) fireplace, furnace, hearth, bloomery, chafery.

2. smithy, smithery, stithy, blacksmith's workshop; ironworks, foundry.

—*v.* **3.** beat, hammer out, *Fig.* extund; form, shape, fashion, mold, found, cast.

4. conceive, invent, devise, create, frame, coin, compose; fabricate, manufacture, produce.

5. (*all usu. of handwriting; fraudulently*) imitate, copy, reproduce, simulate, duplicate, replicate, mimic, ape; falsify, alter, modify.

6. (*both of money*) counterfeit, *Brit. Inf.* coin.

forge², *v.* (*usu. used with* ahead) push on, plod along, press on; progress laboriously, drudge, drive, shove; move forward slowly, inch, make one's way.

forger, *n.* **1.** counterfeiter, faker, *Fr. faux-monnayeur*; coiner, *Brit.* coin-clipper.

2. copyist, falsifier, plagiarist.

forgery, *n.* **1.** (*all in reference to handwriting; all fraudulent*) alteration, modification; simulation, imitation, copying, reproduction, duplication, replication.

2. counterfeit, imitation, reproduction, fake, *Inf.* phony, sham; falsification, fraud; *Jewelry.* paste; *Masonry.* scagiola; (*of literary works*) plagiarism, pirated manuscript.

forget, *v.* **1.** cease to remember, *Chief. South. U.S.* disremember, draw a blank, fail to think of; lose, lose sight of, have [s.t.] slip one's mind, have [s.t.] escape one; overlook, pass over, pass by, jump over, miss, skip, omit; leave behind, omit to take.

2. let be, let alone, let bygones be bygones, never mind; disregard, ignore, take no notice of, close the eyes to, blink *or* wink at, neglect; let in one ear and out the other, turn a deaf ear to; write off, let pass, dismiss from one's thoughts.

3. forget oneself misbehave, misconduct oneself, be improper, be indiscreet, act unseemly; offend, trespass, transgress, err, deviate, go astray, go amiss.

forgetful, *adj.* **1.** amnesic, Lethied, apt to forget; absent-minded, abstracted, distracted, preoccupied, rapt, absorbed, wrapped up; daydreaming, dreamy, absent, remote, faraway, *Sl.* not at home, *Sl.* out to lunch, *Sl.* out in left field, *Sl.* out of it.

2. disregardful, inattentive, inadvertent, unheeding, unheedful, heedless; oblivious, unaware, unconscious, unmindful, mindless; neglectful, negligent, careless.

forgetfulness, *n.* **1.** amnesia, lapse of memory, oblivescence; oblivion, waters of oblivion, Lethe, nepenthe.

2. absent-mindedness, woolgathering, preoccupation, remoteness, dreaminess; obliviousness, unawareness, unconsciousness, unmindfulness, mindlessness; disregard, inattention, inadvertence, nonobservance, oversight; neglect, negligence, carelessness, heedlessness, thoughtlessness.

forgive, *v.* **1.** absolve, shrive, excuse, make allowances for; condone, overlook, pass over, disregard, ignore, look the other way, pay no attention to.

2. remit, waive, dispense with, abolish, do away with, *Commerce.* indulge; release from, let off, exempt, *Inf.* let off the hook, *Inf.* let out of; cancel, void, nullify, delete, erase, clear the books, wipe the slate clean.

3. pardon, amnesty, reprieve; acquit, exculpate, exonerate, vindicate, clear, prove innocent, uphold innocence, remove guilt.

4. harbor no grudge, bear no malice, bury the hatchet, let bygones be bygones, make up, make peace.

forgiveness, *n.* **1.** absolution, absolving, shriving, excusal, excusing, making allowances for; pardoning, reprieve, reprieving, remission, remitting, amnesty; acquittal, acquittance, acquitting, compurgation, exculpation, exculpating, exoneration, exonerating, vindication, vindicating, clearance, clearing; condonation, condoning, overlooking, disregarding, ignoring.

2. mercifulness, mercy, grace, compassion, humanity; clemency, forbearance, lenience, leniency, lenity, *Both Rom. Cath. Ch.* indulgence, indulgency.

forgiving, *adj.* **1.** absolutory, absolvent, absolving, shriving, excusive, excusing, condoning, remissive, remitting; acquitting, exculpatory, exculpating, exonerative, exonerating.

2. merciful, compassionate, humane, clement, forbearing, sparing, lenient, indulgent; placable, conciliative, conciliatory, reconcilable.

forgo, *v.* **1.** abstain from, refrain from, do *or* go without, sacrifice, offer up; renounce, forswear, forsake, abandon, quit, discard, part with, eliminate, *Inf.* cut out, *Inf.* swear off; shun, avoid, eschew, pass up, turn down, decline, refuse.

2. resign, abdicate, give up claim *or* right to, *Law.* disclaim; retire from, vacate, relinquish, hand over, surrender, yield.

forgotten, *adj.* unremembered, out of mind, past recollection; gone, bygone, past, buried in the past, irrecoverable, irretrievable, lost; overlooked, passed over, passed by, missed, skipped, left behind.

fork, *n.* **1.** pronged *or* tined utensil, piece of silverware; trident, pitchfork, pronged instrument *or* tool.

2. branching, bifurcation, crotch, crutch, divarication, furcation; split, division, dividing, separation, scission, divergence, parting of the ways; angle, angulation, turn, bend, elbow, knee, hook; corner, intersection, crossroads, junction.

3. branch, limb, *Bot., Zool., Anat.* ramus; tributary, offshoot.

—*v.* **4.** branch, divaricate, bifurcate; branch off, furcate, diverge, ramify; divide, bisect, split up, separate, go in different directions, go separate ways; angle, turn, bend, hook.

forked, *adj.* **1.** branched, bifurcate, biforked, divaricate, two-pronged, crotched, Y-shaped, V-shaped; branching, furcate, ramiform, pronged, tined, forficate, scissorlike; divided, split, bisectional.

2. zigzag, angular, sharp-cornered, full of turns; serpentine, sinuous, winding, curved.

forlorn, *adj.* **1.** miserable, wretched, abject, pitiful, pitiable, piteous, pathetic, pathetical, woebegone, woeful, *Archaic.* woesome, *Obs.* baleful; desolate, dreary, *Literary.* drear, dismal, gloomy, lugubrious, funereal; depressed, dispirited, dejected, despondent, down, melancholic, glum, somber, low-spirited, disheartened, discouraged; sad, unhappy, infelicitous, sorrowful, bereaved, doleful, dolorous, dolorific, grieved, mournful, lachrymose, lachrymal, lachrymatory, comfortless, joyless, cheerless, inconsolable.

2. abandoned, deserted, forsaken, forgotten, neglected, shunned, scorned, outcast, cast out, *Poetic.* lorn; lost, homeless, friendless, companionless, helpless, alone, solitary, isolated, lone, lonely, lonesome.

3. hopeless, without hope, desperate, in desperate straits, despairing, in despair; crushed, broken, vanquished, overcome, overwhelmed.

4. destitute, indigent, bereft, deprived, beggared, beggarly, *Inf.* hard-up, down and out, high and dry, out at the elbows, down at the heels, down on one's luck; poor, ill-off, badly *or* poorly off, needy, in need, wanting, in want, lacking, ill-provided, unprovided, unsupplied, ill-supplied.

form, *n.* **1.** configuration, figuration, conformation, formation, arrangement, disposition, organization, order; structure, construction, construct, frame, framework, exterior, outward form.

2. figure, physique, build, skeletal structure, body, person; shape, contour, silhouette; appearance, aspect, look, complexion; countenance, visage, feature, face, physiognomy; pose, presence, attitude, bearing, carriage.

3. mold, cast, matrix, shaper; pattern, prototype, guide, model; manikin, mannequin, dummy.

4. format, setup, layout, blueprint, outline, sketch, adumbration, *Inf.* getup; design, plan, scheme, idea.

5. species, breed, brood, order, class, genus; type, kind, genre, sort, kidney, variety; stamp, designation, denomination, name, suit; description, grain, feather, fabric, texture, tone, color, stripe; make, cast, cut, style, manner, nature; character, make-up, idiosyncrasy, *Archaic.* crasis.

6. method, formula, formulary, set order, system, manner, mode; formality, ceremony, rite, ritual, *Eccles.* ordinance; procedure, motions, steps.

7. blank, questionnaire, questionary, application *or* entry blank; document, paper.

8. etiquette, protocol, decorum, propriety, properness, punctilio, conventionality; deportment, conduct, behavior, *Inf.* what's expected.

9. condition, state, fettle, *Inf.* kilter; fitness, physical fitness, health, well-being.

—*v.* 10. make, fabricate, manufacture, produce, mint, turn out, put out; construct, build, assemble, set up, put together; erect, elevate, raise, rear, put up.

11. formulate, frame, forge, devise, contrive, think up; conceive, visualize, envision, imagine, image, *Inf.* dream up, *Inf.* hatch; design, pattern, outline, sketch, trace, adumbrate, draw, delineate, limn; create, compose, invent, coin, originate, start, engender, incept, beget, innovate, initiate, inaugurate; institute, found, establish, generate, bring about.

12. constitute, comprise, make up, go into the making of, be a part *or* portion of, be an integral part of, be an element *or* ingredient *or* component of, be a constituent of.

13. organize, systematize, coordinate, correlate, collate, group, assemble; order, rank, grade, range, graduate; arrange, array, dispose, align, line up, adjust, collocate, place, position.

14. contract, acquire, incur, get; develop, grow into, pick up.

15. shape, fashion, mold, model, knead; cast, stamp, block, block out, hammer, chisel, hew, roughhew, sculpture.

16. discipline, drill, exercise, shape up; train, coach, get in shape; teach, instruct, educate, school.

17. materialize, take shape *or* form, come into being *or* existence, appear, show up.

18. dovetail, fall *or* settle into place, fit together, make a design *or* pattern.

formal, *adj.* 1. conventional, standard, regular, customary; proper, seemly, decorous; ceremonial, ritual, solemn; observant, strict, rigid, inflexible, uncompromising; set, fixed, exact, precise, punctilious; stiff, stilted, prim, stuffy, stand-offish, reserved, aloof; starched, strait-laced, prudish, puritanical.

2. ceremonious, elaborate, *Sl.* veddy-veddy proper, fancy, elegant; bombastic, overblown, pretentious, pompous.

3. perfunctory, routine, indifferent; unspontaneous, methodical, orderly; nominal, apparent, external, superficial, *Latin. pro forma.*

formality, *n.* 1. convention, form, observance; usage, practice, custom, wont, *Inf.* the way it's done, protocol, *Inf.* S.O.P.; ceremony, ritual, rite, service, liturgy.

2. rigidity, inflexibility, stiffness; strictness, exactness, punctilio, precision.

3. ceremoniousness, excessiveness, overinflation; red tape, *Inf.* fiddle-faddle.

4. convenance, propriety, etiquette; gesture, empty compliment.

format, *n.* 1. form, shape, contour; frame, framework, structure; size, dimensions, measurements, thickness; appearance, look, aspect.

2. organization, arrangement, setup, order, grouping; composition, make-up, contents, constitution, comprisal.

3. layout, blueprint, outline, sketch, adumbration; pattern, guide, model; design, plan, scheme, formula, *Inf.* getup.

4. style, mode, manner, make, cast, cut; variety, type, kind, genre, suit.

formation, *n.* 1. manufacture, making, fabrication, production, generation; construction, building, framing; creation, invention, origination, genesis, innovation; institution, founding, establishment.

2. materialization, development, emergence, appearance.

3. configuration, layout, design, pattern, format, shape, contour, figure, outline, silhouette, outward appearance, look, aspect; composition, make-up, constitution, contents, comprisal; organization, order, arrangement, setup; structure, construct, build, frame, framework, exterior.

formative, *adj.* 1. forming, shaping, molding, forging, fashioning; developmental, developing.

2. formable, moldable, shapable, malleable, tractable, pliable, pliant, supple, ductile, fictile, plastic; impressionable, susceptible, teachable, educable.

former, *adj.* 1. prior, earlier, previous, foregone; preceding, precedent, foregoing, antecedent, anterior; erstwhile, whilom, last; preexistent, preliminary; quondam, one-time, *Archaic.* sometime.

2. past, long past, bygone, long-ago, ancient; antediluvian, antebellum, primitive, pristine; gone, long gone, departed, old, lapsed, late, over and done with.

formerly, *adv.* 1. previously, aforetime, heretofore, *Archaic.* erst, at one time, once; hitherto, ere now.

2. in days of yore *or* old, in the old days, in times past, once upon a time; back then, long ago, when the world was young; in the dim, dark ages.

formidable, *adj.* 1. feared, dreaded, dread, dreadful; awesome, redoubtable, frightful, frightening; threatening, menacing, alarming, intimidating; petrifying, terrifying, horrifying, *Inf.* scary; appalling, horrible, terrible, awful; demoralizing, discouraging, dismaying.

2. strong, forceful, powerful, mighty, robust, indomitable, invincible; difficult, arduous, tough, *Inf.* rough; cogent, effective, convincing, telling.

3. huge, tremendous, great, superior, exceptional, extreme; unusual, impressive, terrific, fantastic; mind-boggling, *Inf.* wild, incredible, *Inf.* mind-blowing, *Sl.* socko.

formless, *adj.* 1. shapeless, unshaped, unshapen, unformed, without form, not formed, embryonic, undeveloped; unhewn, uncarved, rough, unfashioned; misshapen, ill-fashioned, ill-made, distorted, deformed.

2. amorphous, indeterminate, indefinite, vague, nebulous, characterless, nondescript; unorganized, confused, jumbled, chaotic, structureless, unstructured; free-form, unconventional, nontraditional, experimental.

formula, *n.* 1. recipe, receipt, rule, formulary, prescription; set of word, set of symbols, set expression, code, cliché, shibboleth, password.

2. conventional method *or* procedure, ritual, order,

set order, established order; formality, formal model, procedural dictate, etiquette, protocol, rubrics, rules of order, rules of procedure.

3. baby food, milk and water, milk mixture; special diet, diet.

4. religious doctrine, discipline, creed, credo, canon.

formulate, *v.* **1.** state, state clearly, define, articulate; particularize, specify, itemize, indicate, designate; determine, denote, systematize, formularize.

2. devise, conceive, think of, think up, excogitate; create, invent, originate, hit upon, coin; compose, make up, dream up, imagine, improvise, plot out, draw up; plan, design, map out, block out, plan, prepare.

fornication, *n.* **1.** copulation, coition. See **coitus.**

2. *Bible.* adultery, infidelity, unfaithfulness, cuckoldry.

3. *Bible.* idolatry, idol worship, worship of false gods, worship of graven images.

forsake, *v.* **1.** desert, abandon, quit, leave in the lurch, *Inf.* leave flat, jilt, throw over, *Inf.* give [s.o.] the air; flee, depart, vacate; reject, cast off, discard, dispose of, jettison, fling away; isolate, maroon.

2. renounce, repudiate, disown; resign, abdicate; revoke, recant, forswear, disclaim, disavow, deny, go back on, go back on one's word; yield, surrender, waive, forgo, relinquish, give up.

forsaken, *adj.* deserted, abandoned, neglected; cast off, rejected, shunned, ignored, outcast; forlorn, *Poetic.* lorn, desperate, wretched, woeful, unfortunate, friendless; lonely, alone, solitary, godforsaken, isolated, marooned, derelict; destitute, bereft, bereaved.

forswear, *v.* **1.** reject, renounce, (*usu. under oath*) abjure; forgo, sacrifice, go *or* do without, quit, relinquish, give up, *Inf.* swear off, *Inf.* cut out; avoid, shun, eschew; forsake, abandon, desert.

2. deny, retract, take back; recant, disavow, disclaim, renege; repudiate, disown.

3. perjure oneself, lie under oath, swear falsely.

fort, *n.* **1.** fortress, citadel, stronghold, defense, fastness, garrison, acropolis; castle, tower, donjon, keep, turret, hold; refuge, shelter, safeguard, palladium.

2. fortification, battlement. See **fortification** (*def.* **2**).

3. hold the fort **a.** defend, uphold, make a stand for, stand by, stand up for. **b.** carry on, maintain, maintain the status quo, *Inf.* keep things going *or* moving, keep things on an even keel.

forte, *n.* strong point, specialty, long suit, technique; talent, skill, métier, aptitude, faculty; gift, genius, endowment; bent, turn, *Inf.* baby, *Inf.* cup of tea, *Sl.* bag, *Sl.* thing.

forth, *adv.* **1.** forward, forwards, outward, outwards, onward, onwards, ahead, along.

2. hence, thence, whence; on, out, onward, therefrom, thereof.

3. out, into view, into the open, into notice, into prominence, *Inf.* on the table, *Inf.* out of the bag.

4. away, abroad, from home, off, yonder.

forthright, *adj.* **1.** outspoken, free-spoken, free-speaking, free, unreticent, bold, unreserved, unrestrained, unconstrained, unchecked, unabashed, uninhibited, unshrinking; blunt, bluff, brusque, tactless.

2. frank, candid, direct, straightforward, straight-from-the-shoulder, man-to-man, heart-to-heart; plain, plain-spoken, plain-speaking, downright, outright, explicit, unequivocal, unambiguous, undisguised, *Inf.* flat-footed.

3. direct, straight, straightforward, straightaway; unswerving, unveering, undeviating, unstraying.

—adv. **4.** direct, directly, right, straight, straightforward, straightforwards, straightly, straight ahead, dead ahead; unswervingly, unveeringly, undeviatingly; in a direct *or* straight line, in a line for, in line with, *Inf.* in a bee line, *Inf.* as the crow flies, *Inf.* straight as an arrow.

5. outspokenly, freely, boldly, unreservedly, unrestrainedly, unconstrainedly, uninhibitedly, unshrinkingly.

6. candidly, frankly, forthrightly, directly, straightforwardly; explicitly, unequivocally, undisguisedly, plainly, in plain words *or* English, with no nonsense, all joking aside.

7. immediately, instantly, instanter, in a moment, at once, straightaway, then and there, right away, right off, *Inf.* right off the bat; in a glance, at a moment's notice.

forthwith, *adv.* immediately, at once, without delay, *Jocular.* immediately if not sooner, right away, instantly, instanter; at once, this very minute *or* moment, this instant, right off the bat, pronto, now; directly, straightway, presently, *Archaic.* anon; promptly, speedily, summarily, posthaste; instantaneously, in the wink of an eye, in the same breath, *Inf.* in a jiffy, in a tick, in a moment, at the drop of a hat, on the spot.

fortification, *n.* **1.** strengthening, reinforcement, buttressing, bracing, backing, redoubling; augmentation, addition, magnification, aggrandizement, intensification.

2. battlement, rampart, protection, bastion, *Fort.* vallation; parapet, blockhouse, *Fort.* machicolation, gallery, vault, *Fort.* casemate; barricade, buttress, buffer, palisade, abatis, stockade, enceinte; embankment, wall, parados, bank, mound; fence, defense, outwork, *Rare.* muniment, *Fort.* circumvallation; entrenchment, trench, moat, ditch, foxhole, dugout; bunker, nest, pill box, abri, *Mil.* hedgehog; *All Fort.* work, earthwork, breastwork, fieldwork, hornwork, lines; redan, redoubt, ravelin, lunette, demilune, tenaille; scarp, escarp, vallum, counterscarp, glacis.

fortify, *v.* **1.** defend, protect, *Fort.* circumvallate; garrison, shelter, safeguard, cover, guard.

2. brace, shore up, buttress, reinforce; back, line, underline; harden, stiffen, stuff; temper, steel, indurate.

3. strengthen, embolden, empower; quicken, energize, invigorate, vivify, revive; encourage, cheer, hearten, buoy; assure, reassure, make confident.

4. augment, increase, heighten, redouble, enhance, *Inf.* spike; amplify, intensify, aggrandize, magnify; supplement, add, superadd, enlarge, *Literary.* greaten; build up, bump up, boost.

5. confirm, prove, validate, authenticate, verify; establish, substantiate, circumstantiate; corroborate, back up, uphold, bear out, make good; endorse, attest, certify, warrant.

fortitude, *n.* patience, endurance, sufferance; tolerance, forbearance, long-suffering, longanimity; strength, moral strength, trepidity, courage, backbone; heart, grit, mettle, nerve, *Sl.* guts, *Inf.* intestinal fortitude; tenacity, pertinacity, perseverance, resoluteness.

fortress, *n.* **1.** fort, citadel. See **fort** (*def.* **1**).

2. haven, refuge, shelter, asylum, sanctum, sanctuary, safeguard, palladium; retreat, covert, hiding place, abri, port in a storm; hermitage, cloister, resort, home.

fortuitous, *adj.* **1.** chance, serendipitous, *Inf.* fluky *or* flukey; unexpected, unanticipated, unforeseen, unlooked-for; casual, random, haphazard, hit-or-miss, arbitrary.

2. accidental, unintentional, unpremeditated, unplanned, undesigned; indeliberate, inadvertent, involuntary; incidental, occasional, contingent, adventitious.

3. lucky, fortunate, happy, felicitous, providential; blessed, favored, in luck, born under a lucky star, born with a silver spoon in one's mouth, blessed with luck.

fortuity, *n.* **1.** chance, mere chance, happy chance, happenstance, serendipity; accident, coincidence, contingency, contingence; uncertainty, potluck, blind faith; luck, good luck, Lady Luck, fortune *or* Fortune, good fortune, wheels of fortune, heads or tails, cast *or* throw *or* toss of the dice; fate, destiny; vicissitudes, ups and downs, fickle finger of fate, way things fall, *Inf.* the breaks, *Inf.* how the cookie crumbles, *Inf.* how the ball bounces.

2. fluke, chance event, chance occurrence, one in a million, long shot, twist of fate; happening, *Archaic.* hap, hazard; freak accident, casualty.

fortunate, *adj.* **1.** lucky, fortuitous, happy, felicitous, *Scot. and North Eng., Irish Eng.* sonsy; favored, blessed, blessed with luck, in luck, born under a lucky star, born with a silver spoon in one's mouth; successful, crowned with success, prosperous, halcyon, rich, well-off; flourishing, thriving, booming, succeeding, out in front, ahead of the game, on top, *Sl.* on top of the heap.

2. auspicious, propitious, providential, favorable, advantageous, ripe; opportune, seasonable, timely, well-timed, just in time, convenient; encouraging, promising, full of promise, of promise; rosy, bright, fair, golden, benign, benignant.

fortune, *n.* **1.** (*all as determined by wealth*) position, place, situation; station, status, standing, footing, rank; level, grade, class; conditions, circumstances.

2. capital, assets, worth; income, money, revenue; stock, substance, possessions, means; estate, property; wealth, material wealth, treasure.

3. riches, great wealth; affluence, opulence, opulency, easy circumstances, *Sl.* easy street; mint, gold mine.

4. chance, mere chance, happy chance, happenstance, fortuity, serendipity; accident, coincidence, contingency, contingence; uncertainty, potluck, blind faith; luck, wheels of fortune *or* chance, Fortune's wheel, heads or tails, cast *or* toss *or* throw of the dice; vicissitudes, ups and downs, fickle finger of fate, way things fall, *Inf.* the breaks, *Inf.* how the cookie crumbles, *Inf.* how the ball bounces.

5. *Often* **fortunes** prospect, promise, expectation, anticipation; story, life, life story, story of one's life, biography, memoir; adventures, escapades, experiences.

6. destiny, fate, lot, cup, portion, die, doom, *Chiefly Scot.* weird; predestination, kismet, God's will, stars, planets; end, destination, final lot.

7. Chance, Fortune, Lady *or* Dame Fortune, Fortuna, Luck, Lady Luck.

8. success, successfulness, prosperity, prosperousness; felicity, good luck, good fortune, happy fortune; fortunateness, luckiness.

fortuneteller, *n.* seer, soothsayer, oracle, prophet, prognosticator, augur, foreteller, foreseer; diviner, geomancer, (*in ancient Rome*) haruspex; prophetess, sibyl, witch; astrologer, horoscoper, astromancer, astroalchemist, Chaldean, *Obs.* astrolog, star diviner, stargazer.

fortunetelling, *n.* augury, prognostication, prophecy, prediction, prefigurement, vaticination, soothsaying, foretelling, forecasting, *Obs.* hariolation, *Obs., Rare.* fatidency, *Obs., Rare.* mantology; chiromancy, palmistry, palm-reading; divination, geomancy, sortilege, (*in ancient Rome*) haruspicy; astrology, stargazing. See also **divination** (*def.* **2**).

forum, *n.* **1.** town meeting, assembly, symposium, round-table discussion, conference, talk, colloquy; debate, argument.

2. court, tribunal, *Law.* chancery, judiciary, judicatory, judicature, bench, bar.

forward, *adv.* **1.** toward, towards, to; onward, onwards, forth, ahead, along, outward, outwards.

2. hence, thence, whence; on, out, onward, therefrom, thereof.

3. toward the front, in front, toward the bow, fore; frontwards, in the van, in the forefront.

4. out, into view, forth, into the open, into notice, into prominence, on the table, *Inf.* out of the bag.

—*adj.* **5.** onward, advancing, progressing, progressive, forward-looking, forward-moving.

6. advanced, well-advanced, early, *Bot.* rare-ripe, premature, precocious; over-early, in advance, immature, abortive; untimely, unseasonable, inopportune; anticipative, anticipatory, precipitate, unexpected.

7. ready, prompt, eager, game, earnest, keen, avid, fervent; willing, prone, well-disposed, amenable, agreeable; glad, pleased, *Archaic.* fain.

8. presumptuous, impertinent, insolent, officious; bold, brash, rash, brazen, audacious; impudent, rude, unmannerly, *Archaic.* malapert, unabashed; brassy, *All Inf.* cocky, cheeky, flip, fresh, smart, smart-alecky.

9. front, fore, face, anterior; frontal, foremost, headmost, at the front, at the fore.

10. future, coming, later, subsequent; prospective, eventual, to come, to be.

11. radical, extreme, ultra, *Fr.* outré; liberal, freethinking, left, leftist, left wing, revolutionary, unconventional, progressive.

—*v.* **12.** transmit, send, send on, pass along, mail, post, deliver, express, ship, freight; consign, remit.

13. advance, promote, further, second; help, aid, assist, abet, succor; patronize, back, foster, nourish; encourage, favor, give a lift, lend a hand.

14. hasten, quicken, expedite, hurry; speed, accelerate, step up, move along, dispatch; shove, move, push, drive, job.

forwardness, *n.* **1.** overreadiness, overconfidence, arrogance, chutzpa; presumption, presumptuousness, impertinence, insolence, officiousness, effrontery; boldness, brashness, audacity, brazenness; pertness, sauciness, brass, *Inf.* cheek, *Inf.* nerve, *Sl.* lip, snooks; impudence, rudeness, unmannerliness.

2. readiness, promptness, willingness, earnestness; eagerness, gameness, enthusiasm, zeal, ardor, fervor; amenability, agreeability, alacrity.

fossil, *n.* **1.** remains, reliquiae, relics, bones, skeleton; petrified remains, petrifaction, *Archaic.* lapidification; part, piece, surviving trace, impression, footprint, track, spoor.

2. *Inf.* fogy, *Inf.* fuddy-duddy. See **fogy**.

foster, *v.* **1.** further, encourage, stimulate, boost, promote, foment, advance, forward, push *or* push for, advocate; sanction, approve, countenance; support, back, contribute to, conduce to, patronize; help, aid, abet, succor, assist, lend a hand, give a leg up; favor, smile upon, facilitate, enable, make easy for, clear the way for.

2. bring up, rear, raise; care for, take care of, cherish, nurture, nourish, cultivate, breed; nurse, harbor, keep, hold, preserve, sustain, maintain.

foul, *adj.* **1.** contaminated, polluted, infected, adulterated, impure, defiled, tainted; spoiled, rotten, moldy, decayed, decomposed, carious, fetid, putrid, putrescent, putrefactive; ill-smelling, evil-smelling, *Sl.* funky, rancid, stinking, stinky, rank, mephitic, noisome, musty.

2. dirty, unclean, unwashed, soiled, dusty, lutose,

grimy, grubby; stained, tarnished, spotted, sullied, smudged, smeared; filthy, dirt-encrusted, bedraggled, begrimed, besmeared, smirchy; muddied, muddy, miry, turbid, feculent.
3. (*of weather*) stormy, squally, gusty, blasty, blustery, disagreeable, sloppy; misty, foggy, rainy, drizzly, sleety, wet; cloudy, overcast, bleak, murky, gloomy, leaden, threatening.
4. unsportsmanlike, unfair, dishonorable, dishonest, deceitful, deceptive; crooked, criminal, villainous, knavish, rascally, corrupt, fraudulent; venal, bribable, mercenary, corruptible; unscrupulous, immoral, unprincipled, shameless; treacherous, two-faced, backstabbing, underhanded; slippery, tricky, *Inf.* shady, sinister.
5. abominable, abhorrent, loathsome, execrable, despicable, contemptible, heinous, scurvy, odious, detestable, hateful; obnoxious, offensive, disgusting, revolting, repulsive, repugnant; nauseous, nauseating, sickening; infamous, ignoble, scandalous, disgraceful; base, low, abject, mean, vile, sordid, wicked; flagitious, nefarious, iniquitous, atrocious, vicious.
6. obscene, vulgar, coarse, gross, smutty, risqué, indelicate, indecent, improper, immodest, suggestive, off-color, *Inf.* blue; lewd, salacious, pornographic, scatologic, *Sl.* raunchy; scurrilous, ribald, abusive, blasphemous, thersitical, irreverent, profane, Fescennine; insulting, offensive, slighting, outrageous.
—adv. **7. run foul** *or* **afoul of** come into conflict *or* controversy *or* collision with, get in trouble with, run into trouble with, *Sl.* have a hassle with, run up against.
—n. **8.** violation, infraction, infringement, transgression.
—v. **9.** soil, stain, spot, smudge, muddy, sully, pollute; splash, spatter, *Inf.* slop up; bedraggle, draggle, begrime, besmear, smear, smirch, besmirch, befoul; blacken, tarnish.
10. contaminate, defile, taint, pollute, infect, putrefy, poison, envenom.
11. collide with, crash into, smash into, run into, bump into *Inf.* plow into *Brit. Sl.* prang.
12. dishonor, disgrace, shame, reproach, degrade, abase, debase, vitiate; discredit, depreciate, devaluate; demean, belittle, derogate, disparage, decry; denigrate, slur, impute, asperse, defame.
13. foul up *Sl.* bungle, botch, *Inf.* flub, *Inf.* muff, spoil, *Sl.* bitch, *Sl.* blow; hash, muddle, mangle, *Sl.* screw up, *Sl.* mess up, *Sl.* louse up, *Inf.* bolix, gum up the works, *U.S. Inf.* throw a monkey wrench into.

foulmouthed, *adj.* **1.** profane, blackguardly, *Obs.* blackguard, Fescennine, rough-spoken; scurrilous, *Archaic.* scurrile, thersitical, ribald.
2. vulgar, obscene, indecent, gross, vile, filthy, dirty, smutty, nasty, scatologic, scatological, *Sl.* raunchy; crude, crass, rude, boorish, loutish, brutish; coarse, rough, base, lowly.
3. abusive, affronting, insulting, *Archaic.* affrontive; vituperative, contumelious, objurgatory, objurgative.

foul play, *n.* **1.** treachery, perfidiousness, perfidy, duplicity, guile, double-dealing; sharp practice, *Inf.* dirty trick, underhanded dealing; villainy, roguery, knavery; fraud, deception, chicanery, skulduggery; assault, attack, outrage; murder, manslaughter, assassination, homicide.
2. unfair conduct, unfairness, *Sl.* dirty pool, unsportsmanliness, low blow, a hit below the belt; violation, transgression.

found, *v.* **1.** establish, start, give rise to, create, originate, bring into being, bring about; institute, set up, organize, develop.
2. build, construct, frame; lay the foundation, lay the lowest part of; erect, elevate, raise, put up, rear.
3. base, ground, root, rest, set, locate.

foundation, *n.* **1.** basis, groundwork, principle, fundamental, rudiment, radical, fundamental principle, underlying principle; root, source, *Fr. fond*; grounds, rationale, reason why, reason, cause, wherefore; purpose, motive, occasion.
2. base, bottom, ground; substructure, substratum, understructure, basement, cellar, underpinning; stand, support, footing, foothold.
3. establishment, founding, setting up, settlement, institution; creation, commencement, installation, origination.

founder[1], *n.* builder, organizer, establisher, institutor; inventor, discoverer, framer, maker, designer, architect; creator, author, originator, generator, initiator, prime mover, father; producer, artist, craftsman.

founder[2], *v.* **1.** sink, go down, go to Davy Jones' locker, swamp; run aground, split upon a rock, shipwreck, capsize; roll, toss, heave, welter, wallow, tumble about, thrash, flounce; pitch, make a plunge, take a header, lurch, reel.
2. settle, subside, decline, descend.
3. fail, not succeed, go wrong, abort, miscarry; flounder, falter, collapse, fall through, *Inf.* come a cropper; come to grief, meet with disaster, turn out badly, end in smoke, come to nothing, never get off the ground.
4. stumble, stagger, sprawl, trip, fall, topple down *or* over; break down, go lame.

foundling, *n.* abandoned infant, waif, orphan, parentless child, outcast, castaway; changeling.

fountain, *n.* **1.** source, spring, well, fountainhead, wellspring, springhead, head.
2. jet, spray, spout, spurt; reservoir, fount, *Archaic.* font; water fountain, water cooler.
3. cause, origin, beginning. See **fountainhead**.

fountainhead, *n.* origin, source, head, rise, spring, well, wellspring, springhead; beginning, primary cause, *Latin. fons et origo*, causation, genesis, birth; first cause, prime mover, creator, author, agent, generator; inspiration, influence, fire, Castalia, Pieria; root, mainspring, derivation, *Embryol.* primordium; occasion, reason, ground, base; inception, impulse, determinant, determining condition, first factor.

fourflusher, *n.* *Informal.* bluffer, sham, faker, pretender, poseur, fraud. See **fraud** (*def.* **3**).

four-handed, *adj.* quadrumanous.

foursquare, *adj.* **1.** square, quadrangular, rectangular, equiangular, tetragonal, *Math.* orthogonal, quadriform, *Rare.* quadrate, *Rare.* quadratic, *Rare.* quadratical, *Rare.* quadrantile, *Obs.* quadrant, *Obs.* quadran *or* quadren, *Obs., Rare.* quadrantal.
2. firm, immovable, unswerving, unwavering, unflinching, undeviating, unshrinking, unfaltering; resolute, resolved, tenacious, inexorable, inflexible, uncompromising, unyielding, intransigent, determined, decided, fixed, settled; steady, steadfast, staunch, constant, dedicated, true, true-blue; trustworthy, *Inf.* trusty, reliable, dependable, sure.
3. candid, frank, forthright, direct, straightforward, straight-from-the-shoulder; plain, plainspoken, plainspeaking, downright, outright, explicit, unequivocal, unambiguous, undisguised, *Inf.* flat-footed, *Inf.* straight-out, *Inf.* matter-of-fact; outspoken, freespoken, free-speaking, unreticent, free, bold, unreserved, unrestrained, unconstrained, unchecked, uncurbed, unabashed, uninhibited; blunt, bluff, brusque, brash, tactless.
—adv. **4.** candidly, frankly, forthright, forthrightly, directly, straightforward, straightforwards, straight-

forwardly; explicitly, unequivocally, undisguisedly, plainly, in plain words *or* English, with no nonsense, all joking aside; outspokenly, freely, boldly, unreservedly, unrestrainedly, unconstrainedly, without reserve *or* restraint *or* constraint, unabashedly, uninhibitedly; bluntly, bluffly, brusquely, brashly, tactlessly.

—*n.* **5.** square, quadrangle, rectangle, quadrate, *Rare.* tetragon, *Obs.* quadran.

fowl, *n.* **1.** hen, brood hen, mother hen, old hen, biddy, chicken; rooster, cock, bantam, chanticleer.

2. domestic fowl, barnyard birds, poultry, ducks, turkeys, geese, peahens, peacocks; birds, pheasants, quail, partridge, guinea hens; waterfowl.

foxy, *adj.* **1.** cunning, crafty, artful, sly, wily, subtle, *Sl.* dumb *or* crazy like a fox, *Scot. and North Eng.* pawky; shrewd, astute, canny, sharp, knowing, *Inf.* cagey; foxlike, vulpine.

2. ingenious, clever, resourceful, imaginative, inventive, creative; discerning, penetrating, wise, knowing, intelligent; alert, wide-awake, vigilant.

3. deceitful, tricky, crooked, dishonest, underhanded; shifty, slippery, smooth, slick; stealthy, sneaky, deceptive, designing, intriguing; insidious, guileful, disingenuous, scheming, plotting, designing, calculating, contriving.

4. discolored, yellowed, foxed, stained, streaked, spotted, blotted, mildewed.

5. reddish-brown, yellowish-brown, tawny, roan, rust-colored, rusty, ruddy, rufous, fuscous.

6. *Sl.* good-looking, attractive, alluring, fascinating; inviting, sensuous, stirring, voluptuous, sexy.

foyer, *n.* lobby, entrance hall, anteroom, antechamber, reception room; vestibule, hall, loggia.

fracas, *n.* **1.** uproar, commotion, disturbance, tumult, turmoil; brawl, fight, wrangle, rough-and-tumble, tussle, donnybrook, brannigan, *Inf.* scrap, *Sl.* rhubarb, *Scot.* sturt; rumpus, scramble, scuffle, brouhaha, free-for-all, fray, affray, *Inf.* ruckus; hubbub, hullabaloo, pandemonium, outbreak, broil, imbroglio, melee, riot, disorder.

2. dispute, contention, discord, noisy quarrel, argument, altercation, vociferation, wrangle, row, *Inf.* hassle, *Inf.* barney; disagreement, squabble, spat, tiff, *Brit. Dial.* fratch.

fraction, *n.* **1.** piece, segment, part, portion, division, subdivision, slice.

2. fragment, bit, particle, mite, trifle; morsel, crumb, chip, chunk, scrap, snip, snippet, shaving.

fractious, *adj.* **1.** peevish, irritable, testy, captious, snappish, quarrelsome, pettish, waspish, touchy; out of sorts, crabbed, grouchy, ill-natured, ill-humored, cross, splenetic; churlish, acrimonious, bitter, sour, caustic; petulant, sulky, sullen, morose, fretful; irascible, huffy, peppery, feisty.

2. rebellious, unruly, insubordinate, perverse, contrary, obstinate, stubborn, pigheaded, mulish, obdurate, unyielding, unbending, cross-grained; opposed, resistant, refractory, recalcitrant, unmanageable, intractable, contumacious; headstrong, willful, strong-willed, wayward.

fracture, *n.* **1.** break, rupture, breach, separation, division, cleavage.

2. split, crack, rift, slit; fissure, cleft, chink; gap, opening, aperture, crevice, rime, chasm; chap, notch, gash, cut, flaw.

fragile, *adj.* **1.** delicate, frail, dainty, fine, elegant, exquisite; brittle, easily broken, breakable, frangible, smashable, shivery, splintery, shattery; crumbly, friable, pulverulent; shaky, rickety, tottering, wobbling, teetering; unsteady, weak, weakened, feeble, decrepit; flimsy, slight, unsubstantial; trivial, frivolous, immaterial, superficial, shallow, lacking force, transparent, ineffectual.

2. ailing, unwell, infirm, unsound, sickly.

fragility, *n.* **1.** delicacy, frailness, brittleness, frailty, breakableness, frangibility, crumbliness, friability; flimsiness, ricketiness, shakiness, unstableness, unsteadiness, decrepitude.

2. frailness, weakness, infirmity; caducity, transitoriness, tenuousness, shallowness, hollowness, precariousness.

fragment, *n.* **1.** part, particle, piece; chip, chink, shard, smithereen, splinter, sliver; scrap, bit, snip, snippet, wisp, tatter, corner; morsel, crumb, ort; modicum, iota, whit, mite, trifle.

2. remnant, fraction, section, segment, remainder; snatch, shred, sample, specimen, dose, taste; bits and pieces, dribs and drabs.

fragmentary, *adj.* **1.** broken, imperfect, disconnected, detached, disjunct, interrupted, spasmodic; discontinuous, intermittent, uneven; incomplete, unfinished, sketchy, rough, perfunctory, truncated, cut short.

2. scattered, piecemeal, odd, separate, discrete.

fragrance, *n.* **1.** aroma, fragrancy, redolence, balm, balminess, bouquet; odor, smell.

2. cologne, eau de cologne, toilet water, sachet; perfume, scent, attar, extract.

fragrant, *adj.* aromatic, sweet-smelling, sweet-scented, odoriferous, odorous, redolent, spicy, balmy, ambrosial, perfumed.

frail, *adj.* **1.** fragile, brittle, perishable. See **fragile** (*def.* **1**).

2. delicate, ailing, unwell, infirm, unsound, sickly; thin, slender, thin as six o'clock, thin as a shadow, slender as a reed *or* rail; slight, puny, wispy, ethereal, unsubstantial, shadowy.

3. weak, susceptible, impressionable, malleable, plastic, unresisting, easily led, vulnerable, unguarded.

frailty, *n.* **1.** delicacy, fragility, weakness, infirmity, caducity; thinness, puniness; susceptibility, suggestibility, impressionability.

2. fault, failing, flaw, imperfection, defect, deficiency; foible, weak side, moral weakness, fallibility, peccability.

frame, *n.* **1.** structure, construction, scaffolding, casing, framing, framework; support, substructure, foundation, groundwork, underpinning; beams, rafters, girders; skeleton, shell, body, chassis, hull; backbone, spine, chine.

2. shape, size, build, figure, physique; contour, outline.

3. state of mind, mood, humor, spirit; temperament, temper, disposition, nature, character.

4. form, fabric, texture, make, mold, stamp; constitution, make-up, composition, configuration; order, scheme, plan, grid.

—*v.* **5.** construct, build, assemble, set up, put together; erect, elevate, raise, rear, put up; make, fabricate, manufacture, produce; form, fashion, mold, model, shape; forge, carve, hew.

6. create, invent, concoct, hatch, originate, coin; contrive, devise, formulate, put together; compose, indite, draft, draw up, redact; set up, establish, constitute, institute; plan, scheme, project, organize, systematize, block out, map out, sketch, design; conceive, imagine.

7. encase, enclose, box.

framer, *n.* constructor, builder, assembler; maker, fabricator, manufacturer; creator, inventor, originator, former, founder, planner, organizer; composer, inditer, author, artist, designer, sketcher.

framework, *n.* **1.** structure, skeleton, scaffolding, frame. See **frame** (*def.* **1**).

2. form, fabric, constitution, frame. See **frame** (*def.* 4).

franchise, *n.* **1.** right to vote, the vote, suffrage, enfranchisement.

2. warrant, warranty, charter; permission, grant, license, leave, consent; privilege, prerogative.

frangible, *adj.* breakable, fragile, frail, brittle, rickety; friable, crumbly, not shatterproof; flimsy, splintery, slivery, discerptible, fissile; shaky, tottering, wobbling, teetering; unstable, unsteady, *Inf.* jerry-built; weak, weakened, feeble, decrepit.

frank, *adj.* **1.** candid, forthright, direct, straightforward, straight-from-the-shoulder, man-to-man, heart-to-heart; plain, plain-spoken, plain-speaking, downright, outright, explicit, unequivocal, *Inf.* flatfooted; outspoken, free, free-spoken, free-speaking, unreticent, bold, unreserved, unrestrained, unconstrained, unchecked, unabashed, uninhibited, unshrinking; blunt, bluff, brusque, tactless.

2. open, open and sincere, openhearted, genuine; guileless, ingenuous, sincere, artless, naive, simple, undeceptive, undeceiving, undeceitful, undissembling; aboveboard, open and aboveboard, up front, on the level, on the up and up, no-nonsense.

3. obvious, patent, transparent, see-through; clear, manifest, distinct, undisguised, unambiguous, perspicuous, unmistakable, not to be mistaken; clear-cut, crystal-clear, as plain as day, as plain as the nose on one's face; evident, apparent, visible, noticeable, perceptible, discernible; express, avowed.

—n. **4.** stamp, postmark, postage, postage stamp; signature, inscription, mark, initial *or* initials; seal, imprint.

—v. **5.** stamp, dispatch, postmark; sign, inscribe, initial, mark; seal, imprint.

6. send, convey, dispatch; post, mail, send by *or* by the *or* through the mail.

7. facilitate, ease, make easier, cut through red tape; accelerate, speed, speed up, quicken, hasten.

frankincense, *n.* olibanum, gum resin, incense, fragrance, perfume.

frantic, *adj.* overexcited, overwrought, all worked-up, wild, frenzied, hysterical, at one's wit's end, at the end of one's rope; distraught, distracted, *Inf.* in a dither, *Inf.* in a tizzy, upset, extremely agitated; furious, in a furor, beside oneself, out of control, delirious; unglued, unhinged, unstuck, unstrung, *Inf.* haywire; berserk, crazy, insane, crazed, mad, stark raving mad, maniac, maniacal; raving, raging, rabid, foaming at the mouth.

fraternal, *adj.* devoted, loyal, true, close, *Inf.* thick, *Sl.* tight; affectionate, loving, caring, concerned; friendly, kind, sympathetic, understanding.

fraternity, *n.* **1.** brotherhood, kinship, propinquity, relationship, relatedness, consanguinity, *Anthropol.* sibship.

2. *U.S.* club, lodge, *Inf.* frat; clan, set, group, clique, coterie, circle, community, society.

3. organization, union, federation, federacy, confederacy, alliance, guild, league, coalition; association, consociation, affiliation, consortium, conference; assemblage, congregation, group, band, team.

4. fellowship, colleagueship, partnership, companionship, friendship; brotherliness, camaraderie, comradeship, esprit de corps; closeness, *Sl.* tightness, clubbiness, clannishness.

fraternize, *v.* associate, socialize, mingle, mix, hobnob; take up with, fall in with; go around with, keep company with, consort with, rub elbows with, *Inf.* pal around with, *Inf.* hang around with, *Inf.* go with, *Sl.* hang out with.

fraud, *n.* **1.** deceit, trickery, sharp practice, double-dealing, cozenage, *Law.* barratry, *Canon. Law.* obreption, *Scots. Law.* subreption, *Archaic.* covin; chicanery, knavery, *Inf.* hanky-panky, *Sl.* monkey business, *Sl.* funny business; imposture, imposition, humbug, *Inf.* flimflam.

2. wile, ruse, sham, shuck, trick, deception, hoax, subterfuge, artifice, stratagem, *Sl.* scam, *Scot.* brogue; cheat, swindle, *Sl.* gyp, *Inf.* rip-off; dirty deal, dirty trick.

3. impostor, pretender, masquerader, mountebank, quack, charlatan, fake, *Inf.* phony; bluff, bluffer, *Inf.* fourflusher; cheat, cheater, swindler, confidence man, *Sl.* con man, *Inf.* flimflammer, *Sl.* flimflam man; trickster, inveigler, bamboozler, dissembler.

fraudulent, *adj.* **1.** dishonest, crooked, criminal; treacherous, false, falsehearted, two-faced; deceitful, guileful, insidious, sharp, shifty, tricky, *Inf.* shady; dishonorable, unscrupulous, unprincipled.

2. fake, bogus, pinchbeck, spurious, counterfeit, ungenuine, unauthentic, *Inf.* phony.

fraught, *adj.* full of, pregnant with, replete with, abounding in, teeming with, *Inf.* chock-full of, *Inf.* jam-packed with; involving, attended with, accompanied by.

fray[1], *n.* fight, brawl, wrangle, tussle, scuffle, melee, *Inf.* set-to, *Sl.* milling; quarrel, row, argument, dispute, squabble, altercation; fracas, rumpus, *Inf.* ruckus, disturbance, breach of the peace; conflict, clash, struggle, strife, battle, action; encounter, brush, skirmish.

fray[2], *v.* **1.** ravel, unravel, unweave, shred, wear to shreds, wear to pieces, tatter, *Inf.* frazzle; abrade, rub, chafe, fret, erode; wear, wear down *or* away, wear out, waste away.

2. decompose, discompose, abash, disconcert, discomfit, ruffle, fluster, unnerve; agitate, shake, unsettle; addle, muddle, confuse, bewilder, nonplus, perplex; trouble, perturb, upset, disturb, bother; annoy, irritate, rankle, exasperate, aggravate, rub the wrong way; vex, irk, peeve, gall, nettle, tease; strain, overwear, tax, overtax, burden, overburden, overload, overtask, overwork; fatigue, *Obs.* fatigate, tire, weary, overweary.

—n. **3.** erosion, fret, *Inf.* frazzle; rub, abrasion, scrape, graze, scratch, scuff.

frazzle, *n.* **1.** *Informal.* exhaustion, enervation, debilitation, prostration, incapacitation, collapse.

2. remnant, shred, tatter, tag end, rag.

freak, *n.* **1.** caprice, capricious notion, whim, vagary; crotchet, quip, quirk, kink, maggot; eccentricity, idiosyncrasy, peculiarity; humor, fancy, whimsy, whimsicality, capriccio; fad, fantasy, craze; turn, twist.

2. aberration, anomaly, abnormality, irregularity; curiosity, oddity, rara avis; monster, monstrosity, miscreation, *Biol.* teratism, malformation; abortion, mutant, deformity, freak of nature, lusus naturae; hermaphrodite, two-headed person.

3. chimera, cockatrice, kraken, dragon, *Heraldry.* wyvern, *Arabian Myth.* roc; Cyclops, mermaid, sagittary, ogre; *All Class. Myth.* hydra, hippocampus, basilisk, griffin, centaur, Harpy, Minotaur.

4. *Sl.* enthusiast, fan, devotee, *Inf.* buff, *Sl.* nut; addict, drug addict, hippie, *Sl.* head, *Sl.* acid-head, *Sl.* pillhead, *Sl.* dopenik, *Sl.* doper. See **addict**.

freakish, *adj.* **1.** capricious, whimsical, notional, *Archaic.* maggoty; quixotic, erratic, wayward, fitful; fanciful, humorsome, crotchety; outlandish, queer.

2. freaky, grotesque, monstrous, bizarre; abnormal, unnatural, aberrant, anomalous, incongruous, preternatural, exceptional, peculiar; fantastic, strange, wild.

freckle, *n.* *Med.* lentigo; blemish, mark, spot, speck.

free, *adj.* **1.** independent, self-governed, self-governing, self-directing, inner-directed; sovereign, autonomous, unsubject, uncolonial; enfranchised, freeborn.

2. unconfined, at liberty, at large, loose, on the loose; freed, liberated, released, let out, let go; emancipated, manumitted, unenslaved, enfranchised; ransomed, delivered, rescued, saved; unensnared, *Inf.* off the hook, unentangled, in the clear, unencumbered, scot-free.

3. at leisure, idle, not busy; unengaged, unoccupied, not tied down *or* up.

4. unbound, untied, unchained, unshackled, unfettered, untrammeled; unimpeded, unhampered, unbridled, unrestrained, uncurbed, unmuzzled; unregulated, ungoverned, unrestricted, laissez-faire, no-holds-barred, catch-as-catch-can; rampant, wild.

5. voluntary, unforced, uncoerced, uncompelled; spontaneous, unprompted, unbidden, unasked for, unsolicited; absolute, unqualified, unconditioned, unconditional, no-strings-attached.

6. clear of, devoid of, destitute of, lacking, wanting, deficient in; without, sans.

7. exempted, exempt from, released, excepted; relieved of, rid of, immune from, safe from, not liable.

8. open, empty, void; vacant, available, unclaimed, untaken, *Inf.* up for grabs; unoccupied, untenanted, tenantless, uninhabited.

9. uninhibited, relaxed, informal, unceremonious, casual, familiar, free and easy; unreserved, unconstrained, natural, artless, ingenuous; open, candid, frank, sincere, outspoken, free-spoken.

10. overfamiliar, presumptuous, assuming, arrogant; forward, aggressive, *Inf.* pushy, assertive; impudent, cocky, bold, brash, audacious.

11. morally loose, wanton, licentious, debauched, dissipated, dissolute, profligate, promiscuous; indecent, immoral, improper; intemperate, immoderate, incontinent.

12. munificent, generous, liberal, lavish, prodigal, charitable, unstinting, open-handed, free-handed, free-hearted, giving; profuse, immoderate, extravagant, copious, unstinted, bountiful, bounteous; handsome, considerable, ample.

13. gratuitous, gratis, *Inf.* on the house. See (*def.* **15**).

—adv. **14.** freely, openly; copiously; independently. See **freely**.

15. without cost, free of charge, gratis, gratuitously, *Inf.* on the house, *Inf.* for free, for nothing, at no cost.

—v. **16.** release, let go, set at liberty; liberate, emancipate, manumit, disenthrall, decolonize; disprison, parole, discharge, furlough; acquit, exonerate, clear, absolve, exculpate, vindicate.

17. loose, cut loose, set loose, let loose, turn loose; untie, unbind, unfetter, unshackle, unchain, unmanacle; disengage, disencumber, disentangle, extricate; deliver, ransom, redeem, rescue, save.

18. exempt, except, make an exception of, privilege, excuse; relieve, rid; (*both usu. of government restrictions*) deregulate, decontrol.

freebooter, *n.* **1.** pirate, viking, corsair, buccaneer, rapparee, privateer; highwayman, footpad, *Sl.* yegg *or* yeggman, bandit, bravo, *Sp. bandolero, Southwest U.S.* ladrone, *Australian.* bushranger, brigand, picaroon, desperado, outlaw.

2. pillager, plunderer, marauder, despoiler, depredator, vandal; predator, ransacker, sacker, looter, rifler, forager, raider, robber.

freedom, *n.* **1.** liberty, autonomy, sovereignty; independence, self-determination, self-direction, self-government.

2. liberation, emancipation, manumission, disenthrallment, decolonization; release, relief from, riddance from, deregulation, decontrol; discharge, nonconfinement, parole, furlough.

3. latitude, range, elbowroom, Lebenstraum; scope, play, swing, margin, discretion, wide berth, rope; nonintervention, noninterference, laissez faire; laxity, looseness, abandon, unrestraint, lawlessness; licentiousness, profligacy.

4. free will, volition, will, *Psychol.* conation, velleity; noncoercion, noncompulsion; choice, option, preference, alternative.

5. privilege, prerogative, right, authority; exemption, exception, immunity; license, franchise, authorization; unrestricted use, blanket permission, unconditional authority, carte blanche, *Sl.* the run of the place.

6. leisure, free time, spare time, *It. dolce far niente*; idleness, otiosity, idle hours, time on one's hands.

7. frankness, openness, sincerity, candor, candidness; informality, unceremoniousness, casualness; unrestraint, unreservedness, unconstraint; naturalness, artlessness, ingenuousness, outspokenness, downrightness, directness, bluntness.

8. overfamiliarity, disrespect, impertinence, impudence; forwardness, presumption, arrogance; impropriety, unseemliness, indecorum.

free-handed, *adj.* generous, munificent, giving, openhanded, unselfish, unsparing, unstinting, free, liberal; charitable, altruistic, philanthropic, benevolent, beneficent.

free-hearted, *adj.* light-hearted, gay, glad, blithe, happy, joyful, joyous; spontaneous, natural, automatic, instinctive; willing, freewill, free, ungrudging, unreluctant; generous, liberal, magnanimous; frank, unreserved, unreticent, straightforward.

freely, *adv.* **1.** openly, candidly, frankly; unreservedly, unconstrainedly, naturally, artlessly; casually, informally, unceremoniously.

2. lavishly, liberally, generously; munificently, unstintingly, open-handedly; like water, profusely, copiously, bountifully; immoderately, extravagantly, excessively; handsomely, considerably, amply.

3. independently, autonomously; voluntarily, of one's own accord, of one's own volition, on one's own.

free spirit, *n.* nonconformist, maverick, loner, lone wolf, solitary man, deviator; hippie, yippie, longhair, freak, Jesus freak, bohemian, beatnik; crackpot, crank, *Sl.* flake; eccentric, original, one of a kind, exception, rare bird, queer duck; curiosity, rarity, peculiarity; *All Sl.* weirdo, oddball, screwball, nut, ding-a-ling.

free-spoken, *adj.* outspoken, plain-spoken, unreserved; frank, open, candid, sincere, unequivocal, honest, ingenuous; blunt, not mincing words, calling a spade a spade; forthright, to the point, direct.

freethinker, *n.* skeptic, doubter, cynic, questioner, agnostic. See **agnostic** (*def.* **1**).

free will, *n.* free choice, volition, option, discretion, voluntariness; velleity, wish, mind; freedom, free rein, latitude, liberty, license.

freeze, *v.* **1.** ice, frost, chill, refrigerate, flash freeze, deep freeze; congeal, harden, stiffen, petrify; immobilize, anaesthetize, benumb.

2. shiver, quake, shake, tremble; get goose flesh *or* pimples, turn blue, get chilblains, go numb, get chilled to the bones *or* marrow, feel Jack Frost's fingers.

3. bite, nip, sting, pierce, whip through, lash.

4. stop, go rigid, stand still, stop dead in one's tracks.

freight, *n.* conveyance, means of transport, transportation, freightage, cartage, truckage, portage; cargo, lading, shipment, haul, load, burden, charge, weight; boatload, shipload, *Chiefly U.S.* carload, wagonload, truckload; contents, merchandise, goods, stuff, baggage, luggage.

frenetic, *adj.* frantic, frenzied, overwrought, wild, berserk, mad, demented, deranged, insane. See **frantic**.

frenzied, *adj.* frantic, frenetic, wild, hysterical, out of control. See **frantic**.

frenzy, *n.* **1.** fury, rage, ire, furor, wrath, choler, spleen; mental agitation, tantrum, *Sl.* fit; monomania, obsession, fixation; fanaticism, fanaticalness, passion, excessive zeal, overzealousness, overeagerness; transport, rapture, ecstasy, nympholepsy, wild excitement *or* enthusiasm.

2. fit, outburst, spell, attack, spasm, convulsion, *Pathol.* paroxysm; mental derangement, lunacy, insanity, craziness, craze, madness, *Both Psychiatry.* mania, dementia; aberration, disorder, unsoundness, infirmity, instability; wandering, raving, *Pathol.* delirium, distraction, mental distress, light-headedness; *Both Psychiatry.* dissociation, alienation.

—v. **3.** make frantic, drive to a frenzy, madden; derange, throw into disorder, disarrange.

4. enrage, anger, infuriate, provoke, harass, agitate; disturb, perturb, unsettle, trouble, upset; disconcert, discompose, disquiet, ruffle, fluster.

5. excite, incite, fire up, stir up, arouse, stimulate; transport, enrapture, make ecstatic.

frequent, *adj.* **1.** recurrent, repeated, persistent, continuing, iterative, reiterative; numerous, many, several, quite a few.

2. constant, habitual, regular, daily, diurnal; everyday, common, ordinary, standard, normal, usual, customary.

—v. **3.** go to often, attend regularly, visit often *or* repeatedly, haunt, *Sl.* hang out *or* around at, patronize.

frequenter, *n.* regular, habitué, daily customer *or* patron, frequent visitor, haunter.

frequently, *adv.* **1.** often, *Literary.* oft, oftentimes; a lot, many times, many a time, many a time and oft; again and again, over and over, over and over again, repeatedly, recurrently, persistently; constantly, all the time, continually.

2. habitually, as a matter of habit, regularly, time after time, time and time again; daily, diurnally, each and every day, each *or* every day; customarily, ordinarily, usually, generally, commonly.

fresh, *adj.* **1.** new, recent, latest; just out, modern, neoteric; up-to-date, brand-new, modernistic, newfangled, new-fashioned.

2. garden-fresh, straight from the garden, unwilted, unfaded.

3. novel, original, unconventional, unhackneyed; different, unusual, strange, unorthodox; unaccustomed, unfamiliar.

4. energetic, full of vim and vigor, *Sl.* full of piss and vinegar; vigorous, brisk, hearty; unwearied, fresh as a daisy, lively, vital, bouncing, bright-eyed-and-bushy-tailed; alert, keen, vibrant.

5. bright, spick-and-span, undimmed, untarnished; shiny, sparkling, glistening, gleaming, brilliant.

6. cool, breezy, clear, clean, unpolluted.

7. green, inexperienced, untried, untrained; callow, immature, wet behind the ears, raw; youthful, still in rompers, naive, unsophisticated, artless; crude, undeveloped, uncultivated.

8. youthful-looking, wholesome, fair; blooming, glowing, flourishing, well.

9. *Informal.* presumptuous, forward, brazen, bold; impudent, cheeky, sassy, smart-alecky, *Sl.* wise-ass, insolent.

freshen, *v.* **1.** refresh, revive, renew; enliven, reinvigorate, stimulate.

2. recover, liven, quicken, rouse.

3. (*of drinks*) add a dollop, strengthen, lace, refill; ice.

4. ventilate, deodorize, air out, purify.

freshet, *n.* (*all of a river, stream, etc.*) swell, surge, heave, billow; flood, flash flood.

freshman, *n.* underclassman, undergraduate, *Inf.* undergrad, *Inf.* frosh, *Inf.* freshie, (*at the U.S. Mil. and Naval academies*) plebe; initiate, trainee, fledgling, learner, recruit, raw recruit, abecedarian, catechumen; beginner, novice, novitiate, neophyte, tyro, amateur, rookie, greenhorn, tenderfoot, newcomer, new boy.

fret[1], *v.* **1.** worry, agonize, writhe, lose sleep over, stay awake nights, *Inf.* stew; pout, frown, sulk, brood over *or* on, mope; complain, fuss, gripe, grumble, croak, find fault, make a fuss about, whine, *Inf.* grouse, *Sl.* squawk, *Archaic.* pine; chafe, fume, rage, storm, rant, rave, go on, *Inf.* carry on.

2. agitate, roil, anger, enrage, infuriate, inflame, rile, pique; arouse, excite, provoke, goad, spur, prod, nag; exasperate, aggravate, exascerbate, irritate, rankle, rub the wrong way; annoy, vex, irk, peeve, gall, nettle, tease; harass, harry, plague, torture, torment, trouble; hector, pester, badger, *Archaic.* haggle; bother, disturb, shake, ruffle, fluster.

3. corrode, gnaw, eat into *or* away, consume, devour, rust, *Both Chem.* oxidize, oxidate; erode, wear down *or* away, waste away; abrade, grate, fray, *Inf.* frazzle, wear, deteriorate, degenerate, canker.

—n. **4.** worry, agitation, exasperation, aggravation; annoyance, irritation, vexation, chagrin, peevishness, harassment.

5. erosion, eroding, wearing down *or* away, washing away; wearing, wear and tear, deterioration, deteriorating, dilapidation, degeneration, degenerating; corrosion, corroding, rusting, *Both. Chem.* oxidation, oxidizing; gnawing, fretting, eating into *or* away, consumption, consuming, devouring.

6. erosion, fray, *Inf.* frazzle, rub; abrasion, scrape, graze, scratch, scuff, sore, *Both Pathol.* canker, ulcer.

fret[2], *n.* **1.** fretwork, Greek key, arabesque, anthemion, honeysuckle ornament, meanders, coquillage, tracery.

—v. **2.** ornament, decorate, embellish; diversify, variegate.

fretful, *adj.* **1.** worrisome, anxious, uneasy, apprehensive; querulous, complaining, grumbling, captious, whiny, fussy, dissatisfied, discontent.

2. irritable, petulant, irascible, choleric, peppery, splenetic, splenetical, surly, ill-natured; peevish, fractious, pettish; testy, cranky, crabby, edgy, cross, touchy, tetchy, ill-humored, grumpy, grumpish, out of sorts; impatient, snappish, waspish, short-tempered; sulky, moody, poutful, mopey, sullen, morose.

friar, *n.* **1.** mendicant, monk, monastic, almsman, beggar, brother; father, padre, priest; prior, abbot, abbé.

2. Franciscan, Gray Friar; Dominican, Black Friar; Carmelite, White Friar; Augustinian, Austin Friar.

fribble, *v.* **1.** trifle, toy, play, fool, *Sl.* monkey around; dabble, putter, potter, piddle.

2. waste away, fritter away, fool away, trifle away, dribble away, *Inf.* diddle away.

—n. **3.** trifler, dallier, dabbler, potterer, putterer, piddler.

4. trifle, bagatelle, gimcrack, gewgaw, trinket, knickknack.

5. frivolousness, frivolity, foolishness, silliness.

—adj. **6.** trivial, trifling, niggling, piddling; frivo-

lous, foolish, fatuous, silly, asinine, ridiculous; inane, empty, vacuous.

friction, *n.* **1.** rubbing against, rub, rubbing down, massaging, massage; abrasion, abrading, attrition, detrition, wearing against, chafing, fretting, gnawing, fraying; grinding, whetting, filing, sanding, pumicing; grating, rasping, scouring, scraping, excoriation, excoriating.

2. dissension, dissent, dissenting, disagreement, disagreeing, contrariety, difference of opinion; discordance, discord, conflict, conflicting, controversy, contention, dispute, disputing, disputation, debate; collision, colliding, clash, clashing, argument, arguing, quarrel, quarreling, embroilment, altercation, squabble, squabbling, wrangle, wrangling, brawl, brawling, fight, fighting, strife; antagonism, hostility, rivalry, opposition.

friend, *n.* **1.** companion, sidekick, shadow, alter ego, other self, *Scot. and North Eng.* marrow; Achates; comrade, *Obs.* copemate, chum, crony, *Fr. copain, U.S. Inf.* buddy, *Inf.* pal; playmate, schoolmate, schoolfellow, classmate; messmate, dinner companion, commensal.

2. confidant, familiar, *Inf.* bosom buddy, roommate, bunkmate, *Sl.* bunkie; intimate, lover, bedfellow, pillow partner, soul mate, *Fr. intime*; paramour, concubine, mistress, *Sl.* doxy, kept woman; sugar daddy; girl friend, girl, *Inf.* boyfriend, beau, suitor.

3. ally, compatriot, confederate; collaborator, co hort, cooperator, assistant, helper, helpmate; team mate, co-worker, fellow worker; colleague, confrere associate, consociate, compeer, peer, mate.

4. patron, supporter, backer, financier, endower, angel, benefactor, Maecenas; assister, aider, abettor; advocate, encourager.

friendless, *adj.* **1.** lonely, lonesome, alone, all alone, without a friend in the world, with no one to turn to; solitary, lone, single, isolated, lone-wolfish; estranged, alienated, apart, cut off, without ties; companionless, unfriended, by oneself, mateless, unattached.

2. rejected, outcast, castaway, abandoned, forsaken; cast off, shunned, scorned, forlorn, *Poetic.* lorn, bereft, bereaved; unwanted, unwelcomed, unpopular, unliked, disliked.

3. unsocial, unsociable, uncommunicative, untalkative; *Inf.* introverted, withdrawn, retiring; reclusive, hermitic, hermitical, eremitic.

friendliness, *n.* **1.** amicability, congeniality, *Ger. Gemütlichkeit,* neighborliness, sociability, companionability; affability, approachableness, accessibility, communicativeness; easiness, openness, unreservedness, familiarity, easygoingness; amiability, pleasantness, good-naturedness.

2. sympathy, understanding, fellow feeling, good will, warmth, warm-heartedness; kindliness, kindheartedness, benignancy; graciousness, geniality, politeness, cordiality, courteousness; agreeableness, willingness, amenableness, considerateness.

friendly, *adj.* **1.** amicable, congenial, neighborly, sociable, hospitable; fraternal, brotherly, sisterly, companionable; at home with, comfortable with, on good terms, *Inf.* chummy, *Sl.* buddy-buddy, *Sl.* palsy-walsy; affectionate, fond, loving, demonstrative, intimate.

2. affable, approachable, accessible, communicative, conversive; easy, open, unreserved, familiar, free and easy, easygoing; amiable, good-humored, good-natured, pleasant; kind, kindly, *Scot.* couthie, complaisant; sympathetic, understanding; kindhearted, warm-hearted, benignant; gracious, genial, benign; polite, cordial, courteous; agreeable, willing, well-disposed, amenable; reliable, good, *Inf.* all right, *Inf.* O.K.

3. helpful, generous, benevolent; favorable, promising, propitious, auspicious, advantageous.

friendship, *n.* **1.** amity, affinity, rapport, good o, mutual understanding, good will, good feelings, peaceful relations, cordial relations; peace, concord, harmony, accord, accordance, agreement, unity, unanimity; fraternity, brotherhood, sisterhood, fellowship, comradeship.

2. amicability, cordiality, neighborliness, friendliness. See **friendliness**.

3. familiarity, friendly relations, intimacy; affection, fondness, love, devotion, esteem, deep regard.

fright, *n.* **1.** fear, scare, alarm, terror, affright, *Archaic.* fray, *Inf.* funk, panic, horror, dread; perturbation, dismay, consternation, trepidation; apprehension, misgiving, disquiet, discomfort, uneasiness; angst, fear and trembling, anguish, anxiety; trembling, shaking, quaking, quivering; *All Sl.* the heebie-jeebies, the jitters, the willies, the creeps.

2. bugbear, bugaboo, bogy, *Inf.* boogeyman, hobgoblin, ogre, specter, phantom, scarecrow; monster, gorgon; nightmare, *Fr. bête noire*.

frighten, *v.* scare, affright, *Archaic.* fray, *Scot.* fley, *Inf.* funk, panic, throw into a panic; terrify, *Inf.* scare out of one's wits, *Inf.* make [s.o.'s] hair stand on end, *Inf.* scare stiff, *Sl.* curl [s.o.'s] hair; alarm, startle, *Inf.* make [s.o.] jump out of his skin, *Inf.* scare the living daylights out of; shock, appall, consternate, daunt, unnerve, abash, floor; terrorize, intimidate, cow, browbeat, bulldoze, threaten; disturb, distress, agitate, dismay.

frightful, *adj.* **1.** dreadful, terrible, grievous, dire, grim, baleful, dark; terrifying, alarming, threatening, hazardous, dangerous, perilous; shocking, appalling, outrageous, amazing, startling, surprising; distressing, harrowing, rending; redoubtable, fearsome, fearful, formidable, awful.

2. horrible, horrid, horrendous, monstrous, atrocious; hideous, ghastly, eerie, grisly, gruesome, unspeakable; abhorrent, revolting, disgusting, repulsive, repugnant, loathsome, abominable, detestable, odious, vile; ugly, offensive, nasty.

3. *Informal.* unpleasant, unpleasing, disagreeable. See **disagreeable** (*def.* **1**).

frigid, *adj.* **1.** cold, very cold, freezing, icy, algid, gelid, ice-cold, frosty, wintry, brumal, hibernal, snowy, rimy; arctic, glacial, polar, hyperborean, hyperboreal, Siberian; bitter, zippy, sharp, brisk, snappy.

2. unenthusiastic, unperturbable, impervious, unexcitable; stony, flinty, steely, callous, hardened, obdurate, thickskinned, stoical, stoic; unemotional, unfeeling, unperturbed, unruffled; unimpassioned, passionless, lacking ardor.

3. stiff, formal, prim, rigid, strait-laced; remote, distant, inaccessible, forbidding, austere, aloof, unapproachable, stand-offish, *Inf.* offish; reserved, reticent, uncommunicative, unfriendly, unsociable, unamicable.

4. (*sexually, of a woman*) unresponsive, unexcitable, inorgasmic; cold, cold as ice, indifferent, uninterested, passive.

5. insensitive, unsympathetic, unsolicitous, heartless, cold-hearted, uncaring; soulless, not simpatico, unimaginative, unpoetic, overly pragmatic, unromantic.

frigidity, *n.* **1.** chill, coldness, cold, gelidity, al gidity, iciness, frozenness; bitterness, rawness, sharpness.

2. indifference, apathy, inertia, lifelessness, tameness, dullness; imperturbability, imperturbation, stoniness, callousness, obdurateness, hardness, inflexibility, stoicism.

3. formality, stiffness, primness; remoteness, inaccessibility, aloofness, reserve; reticence, unfriendliness, unsociability, unamicability; standoffishness, sternness, severity, austerity, seriousness, lack of humor.

frill, *n.* **1.** fringe, border, trimming; ruff, ruffle, flounce, furbelow, galloon; valance, orphrey, purfle; decoration, ornament, flourish.

2. finery, frippery, frilliness, frills and furbelows, falderal, fuss, frou-frou, *Inf.* foofaraw, *Sl.* jazz; affectation, ostentation, meretriciousness, flamboyance, showiness, *Sl.* flash.

fringe, *n.* **1.** border, trimming; frill, ruff, ruffle, flounce, furbelow; filigree, decoration, ornament.

2. perimeter, periphery, edge, rim, verge, skirt.

3. *Slang.* fringe benefit, bonus, extra, plus; perquisite, *Inf.* perk. See **emolument** (*def.* **1**).

fringed, *adj.* trimmed, befringed, fimbriate; bordered, edged, skirted; decorated, ornamented, embellished.

frippery, *n.* **1.** finery, best clothes, best bib and tucker, *Inf.* Sunday clothes, *Inf.* Sunday best, *Inf.* Sunday-go-to-meetings, *Sl.* glad rags, *Sl.* heavy threads.

2. frilliness, frills, frills and furbelows, falderal, trumpery, gaudery, fuss, *Inf.* foofaraw, *Sl.* jazz; ostentation, meretriciousness, flamboyance, showiness, show, flashiness, *Sl.* flash; gaudiness, garishness, tawdriness.

3. decorations, ornamentation, adornments, tinsel, spangles; trifles, trinkets, baubles, knickknacks, gimcracks, gewgaws, *Inf.* doodads, *Inf.* fandangles.

frisk, *v.* frolic, cavort, gambol, caper, cut capers, curvet, skip, trip, jump about, romp.

frisky, *adj.* lively, active, animated, spirited, coltish, *Inf.* full of beans, *Inf.* full of pep; gay, exuberant, joyful; playful, sportive, frolicsome.

fritter, *v.* **1.** squander, dissipate, waste, scatter, disperse; spend, spend money like water, spend to the last penny *or* farthing, *Sl.* blow, overspend; gamble away, fool away, misuse, misspend; while away, idle away, dilly-dally, putter, dawdle.

2. shred, tear up, rip up, clip, cut up, strip, make into confetti; grate, pulverize, shiver, crumble, splinter, shatter.

3. dwindle, shrink, lessen, decrease; degenerate, deteriorate, dry up, drain away, ebb.

—*n.* **4.** shred, fragment, piece, scrap, remnant, bit, ort, morsel; snip, chip, rag, tatter, wisp.

frivolity, *n.* light-heartedness, gaiety, levity, lightness; foolishness, folly, silliness, fribble, puerility, frivolousness; clownishness, zaniness, buffoonery; triviality, superficiality, shallowness.

frivolous, *adj.* **1.** trivial, trifling, fribbling, yeasty, nugatory, niggling, *Inf.* piddling; unimportant, insignificant, inconsiderable, petty, paltry, *Sl.* small-time, *Sl.* two-bit; superficial, shallow, inane, empty, vacuous; light, airy, frothy, slight, flimsy.

2. flighty, giddy, dizzy, facetious, lightsome, flyaway; scatterbrained, featherbrained, birdbrained, *Sl.* gaga.

3. idle, silly, foolish, asinine; childish, immature, juvenile, puerile.

frizzle[1], *v.* **1.** friz, crinkle, scallop, ripple, corrugate; crisp, crimp, crape; curl, turn up, wave, flip.

—*n.* **2.** curl, twist, roll, coil, crinkle; ringlet, curlicue, lovelock.

frizzle[2], *v.* **1.** sizzle, sputter, hiss, sibilate, fizz, fizzle, effervesce, popple.

2. fry, grill, roast, bake, broil, barbecue.

frock, *n.* **1.** dress, gown, garment, tunic, sari, mantle, dolman.

2. smock, apron, jumper, overalls, pinafore, chemise.

3. robe, cloak, cassock, cope, soutane, rochet; surplice, scapular, alb, dalmatic, chasuble, amice, tunicle; canonicals, priestly garb, pontificals, *Inf.* clericals, *Judaism.* ephod.

frolic, *n.* **1.** merry play, fun, sport, play, game, *Sl.* buster; lark, antic, prank, caper, trick, monkey trick; gambol, romp, skylarking; gaiety, merriment, mirth, pleasantry, jollity, laughter.

2. merrymaking, *Brit.* holiday-making, jollification, festivity; revelry, *Inf.* whoopee, *Sl.* high jinks, fun and games; conviviality, amusement, entertainment, recreation.

—*v.* **3.** gambol, have fun, disport, play, frisk, skip about, sport; dance about, jump about, romp, rollick; cavort, caper, cut capers, curvet.

frolicsome, *adj.* playful, frisky, full of fun, coltish, prankish, sportive, *Scot.* daft; gay, joyful, exuberant, *Inf.* full of pep, animated, spirited, gamesome; jolly, jovial, festive, merry, mirthful.

from, *prep.* **1.** starting at, beginning with *or* at, originating in; out of, leaving, away from, venturing out; hailing from, forth out of, starting out at *or* of, coming from.

2. because of, as a result of, in consequence of, on account of, on the score of, by virtue of; due to, due to the fact that, owing to, by reason of, as.

front, *n.* **1.** forepart, foremost part, forefront, foreground, anterior, fore; forestage, *Theat.* apron, downstage.

2. face, façade, exterior; frontage, waterfront, oceanfront, shore, lakeshore.

3. *Military.* front line, vanguard, first line, forward line, *Fr. avant-garde*, battle line; firing line, no-man's land, outpost; sentry, vedette.

4. prow, nose, bow, bowsprit, jib, beak, figurehead.

5. bearing, demeanor, air, mien, look, countenance; presence, address, manner, appearance; port, carriage, conduct, comportment, behavior.

6. haughtiness, self-importance, arrogance, overbearance; effrontery, audacity, bumptiousness; impertinence, impudence, brass, *Inf.* cheek, nerve.

7. forehead, brow; face, visage, countenance, physiognomy, features; *All Sl.* mug, pan, kisser, phiz, map, dial.

8. coalition, bloc, cartel, syndicate, league; cabal, conspiracy, movement.

9. dicky, jabot, tucker, shirt front, chemisette; bib, napkin.

10. **out front** ahead of, in advance, in the lead, in the van, vanward.

—*adj.* **11.** frontal, headmost, foremost, at the front, at the fore; forward, fore, anterior, lead, head; obverse, heads, opposite.

12. exterior, outward, outer, external; facial, frontal.

—*v.* **13.** face, look out on, look toward; stand over, dominate.

14. confront, encounter, meet, meet face to face, breast, face up to, cross, challenge; brave, withstand, buffet, buck; oppose, oppugn, resist, repel.

15. cover, cover up, disguise, mask, conceal; camouflage, screen, cloak, shroud, veil.

16. lead, stand at the head, come to the fore, take the lead; go ahead of, go in advance of, go before, precede, forego, forerun.

frontier, *n.* borderland, march, far reaches, no man's land; boundary, border, bound; confines, limit, bourn, pale; edge, rim, extreme.

frost, *n.* **1.** freeze, rime, hoarfrost; *All Meteorol.*

ice crystals, diamond dust, frost mist, frost snow, ice needle, poudrin, snow mist.

2. coldness, coolness, iciness, glaciality, frigidity; aloofness, reserve; unfriendliness, inhospitality, cold shoulder.

—*v.* **3.** ice, freeze, chill; wither, shrivel, brown.

4. *Slang.* anger, *Sl.* burn up, annoy, vex, irk, *Sl.* bug, irritate.

frosting, *n.* icing, coating, sugar-coating; finish, topping, cap, crown, polishing.

frosty, *adj.* **1.** freezing, frigid, glacial, arctic, polar; icy, cold, chilly, cool, algid; wintry, brumal, hiemal, hibernal; nippy, bleak, raw, bitter, bone-chilling.

2. cool, aloof, reserved, stand-offish, distant; unloving, indifferent, cold-hearted.

3. white, gray-white, hoary, niveous.

froth, *n.* **1.** foam, spume, head, suds, yeast, fizz, bubbles, *Brit. Inf.* barm; saliva, spittle, spit; foaminess, frothiness, spumescence, effervescence, bubbliness.

2. emptiness, verbosity, prolixity, wordiness, running off *or* on at the mouth, empty talk, hot air, *Inf.* gab, *Sl.* gas; idle talk, jabber, patter, gabble, babble, gibberish, twaddle, blather, drivel; claptrap, trumpery, humbug, flummery, bunkum *or* bumcombe, *Sl.* bunk. See **nonsense** (*def.* **2**).

—*v.* **3.** foam, froth, cream, come to a head, fizz, fizzle, burble, bubble up *or* over, effervesce; aerate, carbonate, shake up; spume, whip, beat, suds *or* soap up, lather.

4. seethe, ferment, simmer, stew, steam, boil over, mantle, foam at the mouth; salivate, drivel, dribble, sputter, slaver; spew, spout, spit, emit, eject, ejaculate.

frothy, *adj.* **1.** foamy, foamlike, spumy, spumous, spumescent, sudsy, yeasty, barmy; foaming, frothing, bubbling, bubbly, fizzing, fizzy, effervescent, sparkling, *Fr. mousseux*.

2. shallow, unsubstantial, without substance, trivial, trifling, trite, hackneyed; nonsensical, meaningless, worthless, valueless, unimportant, insignificant; hollow, empty, void.

frown, *v.* **1.** scowl, glower, glare, lower, gloom, look sullen, look black, look daggers, *Scot.* glunch, *Sl.* give a dirty look, *Sl.* don the hate-mug.

2. frown on *or* **upon** disapprove, disfavor, view with disfavor, look askance at, not think much of, not take kindly to, *Inf.* take a dim view of, *Sl.* be turned off by.

—*n.* **3.** scowl, glower, grimace, pout, *Fr. moue*, knitted brow.

frowning, *adj.* scowling, glowering, lowering, threatening, angry, surly, dark, black, black-browed; sullen, sulky, morose, gloomy, glum, dour, long-faced, mopish; stern, solemn, sober, grave, grim, unsmiling.

frowzy, *adj.* **1.** slovenly, slatternly, sluttish, dirty, shabby; blowzy, frumpish, unkempt, untidy, draggletailed, *Inf.* sloppy.

2. ill-smelling, musty, moldy, mildewy, fusty, stale, stuffy, *Brit. Inf.* frowsty.

frozen, *adj.* **1.** glacial, ice-cold, bitterly cold, freezing, wintry, arctic, Siberian; shivering, half-frozen, frozen to death, chilled to the bone.

2. unfeeling, cold-blooded, cold-hearted, cold, frigid, icy.

fructify, *v.* **1.** fruit, bear fruit, flower, bloom, blossom.

2. fertilize, enrich; fecundate, prolificate.

frugal, *adj.* **1.** sparing, saving, thrifty, chary; abstemious, abstinent, self-denying, self-sacrificing; self-controlled, temperate, moderate, conservative; conservant, conservational, careful, unwasteful, economical, prudent, provident; scrimping, penny-pinching, parsimonious, penurious; miserly, niggardly, stingy, tight, tight-fisted, closefisted, cheap.

2. meager, scanty, skimpy, scant, scrimpy; small, puny, slight, brief, *Inf.* measly, mere; very little, paltry, poor, piddling, nominal, minute, negligible, inadequate, insufficient.

frugality, *n.* **1.** sparingness, frugalness, thrift, thriftiness; husbandry, careful management, conservation; conserving, saving, economizing, economy; moderation, temperance, self-control, self-restraint; abstemiousness, abstinence, abstention, self-denial, self-sacrifice; scrimping, penny-pinching, parsimony, parsimoniousness, penuriousness; miserliness, niggardliness, stinginess, tightness, tight-fistedness, closefistedness, cheapness.

2. meagerness, scantiness, skimpiness, scrimpiness; smallness, puniness, slightness, briefness; paltriness, poorness, minuteness, negligibleness; inadequacy, insufficiency.

frugalness, *n.* frugality, sparingness, thriftiness. See **frugality** (*defs.* **1, 2**).

fruit, *n.* **1.** product, result, effect, consequence, upshot, outcome.

2. return, yield, harvest, crop; revenue, income, profit *or* profits, earnings, pay, payment, emolument, compensation, remuneration, recompense; reward, punishment, just deserts.

fruitful, *adj.* **1.** fruit bearing, fructuous, feracious, fructiferous, frugiferous; productive, fecund, generative, potent, fructificative, progenerative.

2. prolific, bounteous, proliferous, proliferating, spawning, multiparous, pullulating; profuse, abundant, plenteous, full, copious, *Rare.* uberous; exuberant, luxurious, lush, rank, rife, rich, flush.

3. profitable, well-spent, worthwhile, effective, efficacious, successful; gainful, remunerative, yielding.

fruition, *n.* **1.** attainment, achievement, acquirement, success, realization, fulfillment, consummation; maturation, ripening, coming of age, completion, perfection.

2. satisfaction, gratification, appreciation, enjoyment, pleasure, delight, joy, happiness.

fruitless, *adj.* **1.** futile, vain, idle, unavailing, abortive, bootless, worthless, useless; ineffectual, ineffective, inefficacious; unproductive, unyielding, unprofitable, profitless, unremunerative, unrewarding, unpaying, gainless; unsuccessful, *Inf.* no-go, to no purpose, to no avail, for naught.

2. unfruitful, *Bot.* acarpous, barren, sterile, infertile, unprolific, infecund.

frumpish, *adj.* dowdy, frumpy, old-fashioned, out-of-date, *Inf.* tacky; shabby, dirty, blowzy, slatternly, sluttish, slovenly; untidy, unkempt, draggletailed, bedraggled, *Inf.* messy, *Inf.* sloppy.

frustrate, *v.* **1.** defeat, undo, disappoint, thwart, check, stop, abort, foil, balk, antagonize; spoil, mar, cripple, clip the wings of, hamstring; undermine, cut the ground from under one, take the wind out of one's sails.

2. cancel, nullify, render null and void, render invalid, neutralize; circumvent, contravene, obstruct, impede, interfere, intercept, inhibit, hamper, hinder, *Sl.* screw up, *Inf.* short-circuit; checkmate, override; baffle, confound, outwit, disconcert, stymie, *Inf.* discombobulate, confuse, puzzle, perplex.

frustrated, *adj.* disappointed, thwarted, foiled, aborted, checked; cancelled, nullified, obstructed, intercepted, inhibited; baffled, confounded, puzzled, confused, perplexed, outwitted, disconcerted, stymied, *Inf.* discombobulated.

frustration, *n.* **1.** defeat, nonsuccess, disappointment, nonfulfillment; vain attempt, miscarriage, abortion; fizzle, fiasco, washout, *Sl.* no-go.
2. thwarting, foiling, balking; circumvention, contravention, interference, hindrance, obstruction, interception, inhibition; checkmate, cancellation, nullification, preclusion; bafflement, *Inf.* discombobulation, confusion, puzzlement.

fry, *v.* pan-fry, sauté, braise, fricassee, griddle; brown, toast, frizzle, scorch, burn, burn to a crisp.

fuddle, *v.* **1.** intoxicate, inebriate, liquor up, get drunk. See **inebriate** (*def.* **1**).
2. muddle, confuse, puzzle, perplex; bewilder, nonplus, bother, addle, upset, frustrate, *Inf.* discombobulate.

fuddled, *adj.* **1.** drunk, inebriated, intoxicated, tipsy, *Sl.* crocked, *Sl.* potted, *Sl.* stewed. See **drunk** (*defs.* **1-3**).
2. muddled, confused, puzzled, perplexed; bewildered, nonplused, bothered, addled, upset, frustrated, *Inf.* discombobulated.

fudge[1], *n.* **1.** nonsense, gibberish, babble, twaddle, blather. See **nonsense** (*defs.* **2, 3**).
—*v.* **2.** talk nonsense, babble, *Inf.* talk through one's hat; twaddle, *Brit.* twattle, blather, drivel, drool; gibber, *Sl.* gibber-jabber, jargon; jabber, prate, bleat, cackle; chatter, prattle, patter, gabble.

fudge[2], *v.* evade, dodge, hedge, waffle, equivocate; shuffle, shift ground, skirt the issue, beat around the bush, hem and haw; maneuver, do an end run; qualify, doubletalk; straddle the fence, tergiversate, vacillate; back-pedal, backtrack, recant, disavow.

fuel, *n.* **1.** combustible, kindling, tinder; wood, coal, oil, petroleum, kerosene, gasoline, gas, *Brit.* petrol; peat, buffalo chips.
2. nutriment, sustenance, food, calories; incentive, stimulus, goad, incitement, provocation, prodding.
—*v.* **3.** stoke, gas up, feed, nourish.

fugitive, *n.* **1.** escapee, runaway, *Archaic.* runagate, refugee; deserter, *Sl.* AWOL, *Sl.* lamster; renegade, apostate.
—*adj.* **2.** fleeting, fugacious, transitory, transient, ephemeral; impermanent, temporary, deciduous; momentary, passing, short-lived, brief; volatile, evanescent, shadowy.
3. wandering, roving, roaming, traveling, itinerant, vagabond, nomadic, gypsyish, tent-pitching.

fulfill, *v.* **1.** accomplish, achieve, execute, carry out, effect, effectuate, bring about; consummate, attain, realize, perfect, complete.
2. obey, observe, follow, mind, heed, keep; acknowledge, respect; perform, discharge; comply with, abide by, acquiesce in, adhere to, cling to, live up to, be faithful to, keep faith with.
3. satisfy, meet, answer; fill the bill, deliver the goods.
4. end, terminate, conclude, finish, complete; close, bring to a close, wind up, clinch; crown, cap, round out, dispatch; knock off, dispose of, put the finishing touch to.

fulfillment, *n.* **1.** accomplishment, achievement, execution, effectuation, implementation, establishment; perfection, realization, consummation, attainment, completion, termination, end, conclusion, close, culmination; crowning of the edifice, finishing touch, *Archit.* finial.
2. performance, discharge, observance, adherence, fidelity, respect, acknowledgment; obedience, compliance, acquiescence, concurrence, abidance.
3. satisfaction, meeting, answering; filling the bill, making good, delivering the goods.

full, *adj.* **1.** filled, filled up, filled to the brim *or* capacity, abrim, brimful, brimming; jam-packed, cram-full, shot through, chock-a-block, *Inf.* chock-full, *Brit.* chocker; stuffed, packed, crammed, crowded, solid, *Inf.* wall-to-wall; sated, satiated, gorged, glutted, cloyed.
2. complete, entire, whole, integral, total, gross, maximum; comprehensive, thorough, all-inclusive, catholic, liberal, generous; broad, all-encompassing, extensive, vast, voluminous; intact, unabridged, unshortened, uncut.
3. ample, sufficient, adequate, enough; well-supplied, well-stocked, well-equipped, well-furnished; abundant, plentiful, plenteous, plentitudinous, *Inf.* aplenty, replete, rife; flush, bountiful, bounteous, superabundant, copious, more than enough, inexhaustible.
4. bouffant, puffed out, puffy, balloonlike; mature, fully grown *or* developed, filled out, rounded out, well-rounded; shapely, well-shaped, curvaceous, full-figured, buxom, *Inf.* busty, voluptuous, sexy; stout, chunky, chubby, plump, pleasingly plump, pudgy, *Chiefly Brit.* podgy, hippy, steatopygous, heavy, overweight, fat.
—*adv.* **5.** directly, right, straight, squarely, smack, *Inf.* smack-dab.
6. quite, very, really, extremely, exceedingly; entirely, wholly, completely, altogether, thoroughly.
—*n.* **7.** maximum, limit, utmost, full measure, as much as possible, as much as one could want; capacity, brim, top, tiptop.
8. in full completely, wholly, as a whole, entirely, in its entirety, in total, *Latin. in toto*; without abridgment, without reduction.
9. to the full up, to the top *or* brim, to the maximum *or* utmost *or* limit, to the greatest extent *or* degree.

full-grown, *adj.* mature, adult, grown-up, fully grown; of age, marriageable, nubile, womanly, manly; ripe, ripened, fully developed, full-fledged, full-blown, in full bloom, in one's prime.

fullness, *n.* **1.** satiation, satiety, the point of satisfaction; capacity, the fill, the top, the brim.
2. completeness, entirety, wholeness, totality, intactness; comprehensiveness, thoroughness, inclusiveness; broadness, extensiveness, vastness, voluminousness.
3. ampleness, sufficiency, adequacy, enough; abundance, plentifulness, plenteousness, plenty, repletion; richness, luxuriousness, profusion, copiousness.
4. maturity, matureness, ripeness; shapeliness, curvaceousness, buxomness, voluptuousness, voluptuosity; roundness, roundedness, rotundity, rotundness, puffiness, swollenness, turgescence, tumidity, tumidness; plumpness, chubbiness, pudginess, *Chiefly Brit.* podginess, chunkiness, stoutness, hippiness, steatopygia, heaviness, fatness.

fully, *adv.* **1.** completely, entirely, totally, blankly; comprehensively, in every respect, at length, from tip to toe, from head to foot, cap-a-pie, over every inch; thoroughly, inside out, heart and soul, root and branch. See **full** (*defs.* **8, 9**).
2. amply, sufficiently, adequately, enough; abundantly, plentifully, plenteously, *Inf.* aplenty; copiously, superabundantly, bountifully, generously.

fulminate, *v.* **1.** detonate, explode, blow up, *Archaic.* displode; burst, *Sl.* bust, break open, fly apart, fly to pieces; go off, discharge, pop, shoot off, bang, blast *or* blast off; report, sound, boom, roar, thunder, clap.
2. *Usu.* **fulminate against** denounce, condemn, denunciate, *Inf.* knock, *Sl.* put down; decry, discredit, minimize, depreciate, disparage, belittle, deprecate, disapprove; criticize, animadvert on *or* upon, arraign,

censure, reprobate; remonstrate, protest against, inveigh against, rail against, declaim against, attack, assail.

fulmination, *n.* **1.** violent denunciation, condemnation, criticism, *Inf.* knock, *Sl.* put-down; censure, disapproval, disapprobation, reprobation, reprehension, objection; animadversion, *Inf.* brickbat, aspersion, obloquy; tirade, philippic, diatribe.

2. violent explosion, blow-up, blast, detonation, *Archaic.* displosion; crash, eruption, bursting, breaking open, flying apart, dissiliency, dissilience; bang, shot, crack, discharge, report, boom, roar, thunder, clap, rumble, roll.

fulsome, *adj.* **1.** excessive, extravagant, immoderate, inordinate, overdone; adulatory, idolatrous, hero-worshiping, overappreciative, excessive in one's praise.

2. disgusting, sickening, nauseating, nauseous, noxious, foul, vile; repulsive, repellent, revolting, odious, hateful, loathsome, detestable.

3. gross, coarse, vulgar, raw, low, broad; uncouth, rude, crude, crass, tasteless, in bad *or* poor taste; obscene, indecent, gutter.

fumble, *v.* **1.** grope, grabble, search *or* feel about, search blindly *or* uncertainly; feel one's way, tiptoe, walk on eggs; flounder, stumble, stumble around.

2. blunder, miss, err, *Inf.* drop the ball, *Inf.* bobble; muff, bungle, botch, mismanage, boggle, spoil, *Inf.* make a mess *or* hash of, *Inf.* flub, *Inf.* foul up, *Sl.* blow.

fume, *n.* **1.** vapor, haze, gas, smoke, pollution; reek, smell, stink, effluvium, noxious odor.

2. huff, puff, fret, pet, stew, dudgeon, pique, rage; fit, storm, outburst, agitation, passion.

—*v.* **3.** emit, give out, vaporize, exhale, puff, smoke; reek, smell, stink.

4. fuss, bluster, flare up, rant, rave, rage, storm, explode; fidget, chafe, fret, champ at the bit; seethe, boil, boil over, foam at the mouth, get in a lather; *All Inf.* get steamed up, steam, get hot under the collar, blow one's top *or* gasket, flip one's lid, flip out, fly off the handle, raise the roof, loose one's cool.

fumigate, *v.* disinfect, purify, sterilize, cleanse, sanitize, sanitate.

fumy, *adj.* smoky, fuliginous, hazy, steaming, reeking; fumelike, gaseous, vaporous.

fun, *n.* **1.** pleasure, enjoyment, amusement, play, sport, entertainment, recreation, relaxation, distraction, pastime; mirth, merriment, laughter, glee, hilarity, jollity, high spirits; cheer, delight, gladness, gaiety, cheerfulness, zest, sunshine, brightness; festivity, frolic, merrymaking, celebration, exhilaration, joy, jubilance, jubilation, exultation, rejoicing.

2. playfulness, clowning, clowning around, tomfoolery, horseplay.

3. joking, jesting, banter, levity, badinage; nonsense, teasing, fooling, twitting, *Sl.* wisecracking.

4. in fun *or* **for fun** jokingly, in jest, half-seriously, facetiously, with tongue in cheek, with a gleam in one's eye, with a chuckle, laughingly, *Inf.* with a straight face, *Inf.* without cracking a smile, *Inf.* without giving away the game; as a lark, for a joke *or* gag, playfully, blithely, buoyantly, gayly, gleefully, with a poke in the ribs; humorously, amusingly, wittily, drolly, roguishly, archly, mischievously, waggishly.

5. make fun of deride, scoff at, mock, jeer, ridicule, knock; taunt, gibe, rag; rib, kid, *Inf.* roast, *Sl.* razz; lampoon, satirize, parody; make sport of, poke fun at, make a fool out of, make the butt of, *Inf.* needle *or* give [s.o.] the needle; insult, belittle, run down, disparage.

function, *n.* **1.** use, purpose, role, operation; charge, duty, task, chore, assignment, mission; job, occupation, business, profession, work, employment; vocation, calling, line, forte, métier, *Sl.* thing, *Sl.* bag.

2. affair, concern, interest, matter, *Inf.* lookout; post, position, situation, capacity, office, station; scope, sphere, province, realm, compass, bailiwick.

3. ceremony, ceremonial, formal; fete, gala, affair; formality, ritual, rite, *Anthropol.* rite of passage; service, observance, solemnity; commencement, graduation.

—*v.* **4.** act, work, operate, perform, run, go; be in action *or* operation, be in commission *or* running order, *Sl.* fly; practice, *Sl.* do one's thing *or* stuff.

5. serve, officiate, do duty; act as, perform as, function as, work as, play *or* act the role *or* part of, have the function *or* job *or* mission of.

functionary, *n.* official, office-holder, office-bearer, *Brit.* placeman, *Rare.* officiary; minister, commissioner, (*in the U.S.S.R.*) commissar; representative, *Inf.* rep, deputy; public official, public servant; bureaucrat, civil servant, red-tapist.

fund, *n.* **1.** savings, nest egg, investment; portfolio, endowment, capital, grant; stock, store, supply; stack, pile, heap, mass, accumulation, collection; pool, reservoir, reserve, well; hoard, cache, *Sl.* stash, treasure.

2. funds treasury, coffer, exchequer, fisc, bursary; money, money in hand, ready money, pin money, pocket money, *Sl.* pocket; cash, hard cash, *Sl.* shekels, *Sl.* bucks, dollars, *Sl.* lucre, *Sl.* jack, *Sl.* dough, *Sl.* loot, wampum; currency, coins, specie; means, ways and means, wherewithal; capital, assets, finances, bankroll, resources; substance, wealth, fortune, riches, pelf, property, stocks and bonds.

—*v.* **3.** endow, grant, vest in, finance, capitalize.

fundamental, *adj.* **1.** basic, basal, underlying, foundational, *Sl.* gut, bottom, base; necessary, vital, *Inf.* meat-and-potatoes, critical, essential, indispensable; inherent, intrinsic; organic, structural, constitutional, inseparable; primary, original, first, cardinal, initial, prime.

—*n.* **2.** principle, basis, foundation, groundwork, elementariness, *Sl.* nitty-gritty, *Inf.* bare bones; essence, quintessence, elixir; heart, soul, backbone, lifeblood; core, nucleus, kernel, pith, gist; keystone, essential, *Latin. sine qua non;* crux; suchness, quiddity.

funeral, *n.* **1.** obsequies, exequies, rites *or* ceremonies; *Rom. Cath. Ch.* Requiem *or* Requiem Mass, black mass, *Obs.* obit; burial, burying, entombment, sepulture, interment, inhumation, inurnment; *All Euph.* send-off, farewell, last good-by.

2. funeral procession, cortege.

funereal, *adj.* **1.** funeral, exequial, funerary, mortuary, sepulchral; defunctive.

2. mournful, dirgeful, dirgelike, lamenting, elegiac, lugubrious, woeful, sorrowful, grievous; gloomy, clouded, dark, Cimmerian, dismal, dreary, depressing, heavy, feral; somber, grave, solemn, long-faced, unhappy, sad, melancholy, *Fr. triste.*

fungus, *n.* **1.** mushroom, truffle, morel, toadstool, puffball, mold, lichen, *All Plant Pathol.* mildew, rust, smut; phycomycete, *Bot.* ascomycete, basidiomycete; saprophyte, parasitic plant.

2. fungous, fungal, fungic, funguslike.

funk, *n.* **1.** *Informal.* fear, dread, fright, fearfulness; terror, horror, panic; alarm, perturbation, dismay, consternation, trepidation; uneasiness, butterflies, faint heart; hesitation, cold feet, second thoughts; recoiling, flinching, quivering, trembling, shaking, palpitation. See **fear** (*defs.* **1, 2**).

2. depression, dejection, melancholy, low spirits, doldrums. See **dejection**.

—*v.* **3.** *Informal.* fear, dread, be afraid, be scared,

take fright, be alarmed. See **fear** (*defs.* **4, 5**).
4. frighten, scare, affright, panic; terrify, *Inf.* scare one out of one's wits; *Inf.* make [s.o.'s] hair stand on end. See **frighten**.
5. cower, cringe, shrink, flinch, wince, quail, recoil, shy, blench; shake, tremble, quiver, quake, *Inf.* shake in one's boots or shoes; turn tail, run away.
funky[1], *adj. Informal.* frightened, fearful, fearsome, scared,afraid, *Archaic.* affrighted; terrified, panic-stricken, terror-stricken; cowardly, craven, pusillanimous, white-livered, lily-livered. See **afraid** (*def.* **1**).
funky[2], *adj. Slang.* evil-smelling, ill-smelling, rancid, stinking, stinky, rank, mephitic, noisome, foul.
funky[3], *adj.* **1.** earthy, sensual; soulful, erotic.
2. blues-like, mournful, melancholy, sad.
3. *Slang.* stylish, modish, *Sl.* hip, *Inf.* in.
funnel, *n.* **1.** cone, cylinder.
2. smokestack, stack, chimney; flue, tube, shaft, ventilator; stovepipe, pipe, duct, channel, conduit.
funny, *adj.* **1.** amusing, comical, risible, humorous, *Inf.* boffo; hilarious, hysterical, riotous, side-splitting, *Sl.* a scream, *Sl.* a gas; entertaining, diverting, *Inf.* fun; jolly, mirthful, merry, jovial, jocose, jocular, waggish; teasing, joking, jesting, *Inf.* kidding, *Inf.* funning, playful, sportive, clowning; laughable, ludicrous, absurd, farcical, ridiculous, silly.
2. witty, clever, smart; facetious, droll, salty.
3. suspicious, deceitful, underhanded, sneaky, sneaking, furtive.
4. insolent, impertinent, saucy, *Inf.* sassy, smart-alecky, *Sl.* wise.
5. *Informal.* curious, strange, peculiar, odd, weird, queer, bizarre.
—*n.* **6. funnies** *U.S. Informal.* comics, comic strip, funny papers; funny books, comic books.
furbish, *v.* liven up, spruce up, brighten up, burnish, polish up, shine, clean up; fix up, touch up, brush up, paint; refurbish, renovate, redo, redecorate, repaint, refurnish.
furious, *adj.* enraged, raging, infuriated, *Rare.* infuriate, fuming, very angry, horn-mad; wrathful, wroth, irate, ireful, incensed, in high dudgeon; inflamed, flaming, flaring, flared up, heated, red-hot, white-hot, hot under the collar; distraught, overwrought, *Inf.* in a dither, *Inf.* in a tizzy; indignant, up in arms, riled; worked up, agitated, stirred up; passionate, impassioned, impassionate, overexcited; upset, feverish, hysterical, not rational; violent, fierce, savage, unrestrained, uncontrollable; ranting, raving, *Scot.* redwood, storming, foaming at the mouth, rabid, fanatical, frenzied; frantic, crazed, mad, *Pathol.* delirious, *Inf.* wild, out of one's mind, beside oneself.
furl, *v.* roll, roll up, fold up, wrap up *or* around, wind around, curl up, coil.
furlough, *n.* **1.** leave, leave of absence, congé, vacation, time off; rest and recreation, *Inf.* R & R.
2. layoff, dismissal, discharge.
furnace, *n.* forge, kiln, *Brit.* oast; blast furnace, reverberatory, smelter, calcar; incinerator, crematory, crematorium; oven, stove, cooker, range, kitchener; hearth, grate, fireplace, *Brit. Dial.* ingle, firebox; heater, boiler, radiator, hypocaust.
furnish, *v.* **1.** supply, equip, provide, purvey, render, accommodate, *Archaic.* dight, *Obs.* appoint; gird, ready, prepare, store, stock, stock up, fill up, *Chiefly Scot.* plenish; outfit, fit out, fit up, fit, accouter, rig, rig up, rig out, turn out, gear; endow, endue, invest; *All Mil.* arm, forearm, munition, *Sl.* heel, *Archaic.* harness.
2. array, deck, deck out, bedeck, caparison, trap, adorn, ornament; dress, dress out, clothe, vest, garb, attire, apparel, habit; robe, gown, drape.
furniture, *n.* **1.** home *or* house furnishings, house fittings, household goods; movables, movable articles; bric-a-brac; belongings, effects, chattels, *Sl.* stuff.
2. equipment, apparatus, gear, paraphernalia, accouterments, appurtenances, appointments, furnishings; fixtures, fittings, habiliments, *Inf.* things; tools, contrivances, machinery; implements, appliances, utensils, conveniences; outfit, out-fittings, turnout, rig; supplies, material, wherewithal; caparison, trappings, tack, tackle, harness, rigging; *All Mil.* arms, armaments, munitions, matériel.
furor, *n.* **1.** outburst, temper, tantrum, fit, convulsion, paroxysm; passion, flush, lust, intensity; transport, ecstasy, raptus, rapture; zeal, fervor, fervency, ardor, fire; verve, gusto, enthusiasm, abandon, élan.
2. mania, craze, rage, obsession, fad, *Sl.* bug; latest thing, latest word, *Fr. dernier cri*, *Sl.* the thing, *Sl.* the go.
3. fury, rage, madness, frenzy, fever; insanity, lunacy, raving, hysteria, delirium.
4. commotion, tumult, rush, turbulence, turmoil, tempest; hurly-burly, brouhaha, hubbub, ado, to-do.
furrow, *n.* **1.** groove, rut, trench, ditch, fosse; hollow, cut, track; channel, dike, gutter, trough, canal; sulcation, flute, rib, ridge; line, seam, pucker, fold; score, scratch, gash, streak.
2. wrinkle, crow's-foot, crease, contraction, rimple, rumple, crinkle.
—*v.* **3.** plow, harrow, turn up, entrench; rib, ridge, flute, corrugate; groove, channel, cut, hollow; grave, engrave, incise, chisel, etch, carve.
4. wrinkle, crinkle, rumple, rimple; crease, crumple, pucker, knit.
furrowed, *adj.* **1.** plowed, harrowed, grooved; fluted, ribbed, striated, corrugated; sulcate, channeled, rutted, vermiculate; caniculate, canaliculate, bisulcous, trisulcate.
2. wrinkled, creased, rumpled, rimpled, crinkled, knitted.
further, *adv.* **1.** farther, at a greater distance, yonder, at a far remove, farther off *or* away, far off; afar, abroad, away, far and away, beyond range, over the hills and far away, out of range.
2. to a greater extent, to a greater degree, more, any more, longer, any longer.
3. moreover, in addition, additionally, besides, what's more; furthermore, also, too, likewise, and so, to boot, withal; then, again, then again, at the same time, by the same token, yet; on top of, over and above, beyond, *Fr. au reste, Fr. en plus;* together with, along with, in conjunction with, conjointly, as well as.
—*adj.* **4.** farther, more remote, remoter, more distant; yonder, yon, thither, ulterior.
5. more extended, longer, more protracted, going beyond, to a greater length.
6. additional, more, extra, supplementary, supplemental; new, afresh, another, other; auxiliary, spare, accessory.
—*v.* **7.** promote, advance, forward, contribute to; foment, nourish, urge, push; aid, assist, abet, help lend a hand; back, support, second, patronize; favor, smile on, oblige, countenance.
furtherance, *n.* promotion, elevation, preferment; boosting, boost, lifting, lift, uplift; advancement, aggrandizement, augmentation; support, patronage, help, backing; aid, assistance, succor, hand; advocacy, championship, defense; favor, interest, countenance.
furthermore, *adv.* moreover, in addition, besides. See **further** (*def.* **3**).
furthest, *adj.* **1.** remotest, farthest, furthermost,

most distant; outmost, ultimate, uttermost, extreme.
2. last, hindermost, rear, rearmost, final; aft, aftmost, at the tail end, at the end, bringing up the rear.
3. longest, lengthiest, past all others, most extended, greatest.

furtive, *adj.* **1.** secret, secretive, surreptitious, clandestine, covert, hidden, hugger-mugger, backdoor; underhand, undercover, under-the-table, under-the-counter.
2. sly, cunning, crafty, foxy, wily, *Inf.* cagey; sneaky, sneaking, skulking, stealthy, feline.

fury, *n.* **1.** anger, rage, passion, furor, frenzy; ire, wrath, choler, rancor, dudgeon, *Inf.* dander; virulence, spleen, gall, bile; acerbity, asperity, maliciousness, malignancy; enmity, hate, spite, malice.
2. violence, fierceness, ferocity, force, brute force, severity, intensity; vehemence, turbulence, tempestuousness; excitement, hot blood, fieriness, impetuosity, precipitancy, huff; tumult, storm, bluster, squall, tempest; fit, convulsion, paroxysm, temper, tantrum.
3. shrew, virago, vixen, termagant, shedevil; scold, *Sl.* battle-ax, fishwife, *Sl.* bitch; hotspur, hothead, hellcat, hellhound, spitfire; hag, witch, beldam, crone; demon, devil, fiend, tiger, dragon.

fuse[1], *n.* match, friction match, lucifer, fuze, ignition, squib; detonator, exploder, blasting cap, percussion cap, cap.

fuse[2], *v.* **1.** melt, melt down, smelt, refine, condense; run, flux, deliquesce, dissolve, liquefy, fluidify; weld, solder, braze.
2. combine, unite, amalgamate, consolidate, incorporate; blend, compound, commix, commingle, intermingle, intermix, interfuse; merge, coalesce, converge, flow together, come together.

fusillade, *n.* **1.** volley, salvo, broadside, cannonade, burst, spray, hail of bullets; enfilade, crossfire, raking *or* sweeping fire.
2. discharge, outburst, outpouring, outpour, outflow, effluence, effusion, efflux.

fusion, *n.* **1.** liquefaction, melting, dissolving, deliquescence; smelting, refining, condensation.
2. unification, amalgamation, consolidation, incorporation; combination, conjunction, *Zool., Bot.* coadunation; blending, commixture, intermixture, interfusion; coalescence, convergence, merging.

fuss, *n.* **1.** fluster, flurry, dither, twitter, fret, bother, pother, *Inf.* stew, *Inf.* tizzy, *Archaic.* pucker; commotion, agitation, disquiet, unrest, stir, much ado about nothing, tempest in a teapot, *Inf.* foofaraw, *Inf.* to-do, *Sl.* flap, *Sl.* hoo-ha.
2. argument, altercation, dispute, falling-out, quarrel, row, squabble, dustup, *Inf.* barney, *Inf.* hassle, *Brit. Dial.* fratch.
—*v.* **3.** make a fuss, *Inf.* kick up a fuss, complain, *Inf.* gripe, *Inf.* grouse, *Sl.* bellyache; make a big thing out of nothing, make a mountain out of a molehill, *Inf.* carry on; fret, chafe, fidget, squirm, fret and fume, *Inf.* take on.
4. bustle, flutter, rush around, tear around, buzz around, whiz around.
5. annoy, irritate, bother, pester, perturb, disturb; nag, henpeck, carp at, fret at, *Inf.* pick at.

fussbudget, *n.* fusspot, *Inf.* fuddy-duddy, carper, caviler, pettifogger, faultfinder, *Inf.* nitpicker; crab, bear, curmudgeon, *Inf.* crosspatch; complainer, grumbler, *Inf.* grouch, *Inf.* grouser, *Inf.* sorehead, *Inf.* squawker, *Sl.* bellyacher.

fussy, *adj.* **1.** particular, overparticular, finicky, picky, *Inf.* choosy; dainty, *Inf.* fuddy-duddy, *Inf.* pernickety, discriminating, highly selective; fastidious, hard to please, difficult, critical, demanding, exacting, painstaking; minute, detailed, circumstantial, fine, nice, thorough, searching; scientific, mathematical, severe, rigorous, rigid, strict, close.
2. conscientious, hard-working, assiduous, industrious, operose; careful, cautious, prudent, politic, discreet, judicious, circumspect; mindful, thoughtful, regardful, heedful, attentive, solicitious.
3. overelaborate, too detailed, busy, ornate, elaborate; excessive, overdone, overworked, overwrought.
4. fidgety, fretful, restless, impatient; whiny, complaining, cranky, crotchety.
5. nervous, uneasy, worried, overanxious, apprehensive, fearful.
6. picayune, niggling, little, small, trivial, trifling, insignificant, unimportant.

fustian, *n.* **1.** bombast, rant, grandiosity, rodomontade, pomposity, magniloquence, grandiloquence; tumidity, turgidity, flatulence, *Archaic.* tympany; extravagance, high-flown language, flowery speech, exaggerated language, overstatement, sesquipedality; bravado, braggadocio, bluster, gasconade; claptrap, prose run mad, words run amuck, purple passages; euphuism, affectation, overly ornate writing; periphrasis, circumlocution, jargon, bureaucratese, newspeak.
2. short-napped twill, stout cloth, coarse cotton goods.
—*adj.* **3.** (*of language*) pompous, lofty, inflated, overstated, ostentatious, showy, pretentious; grandiose, sesquipedalian, extravagant, high-flown, exaggerated; affected, flowery, euphuistic.
4. worthless, cheap, low, unrefined, coarse, vulgar; unpolished, ill-mannered, loutish, cloddish, plebeian, inelegant, tasteless, common.

fusty, *adj.* **1.** musty, moldy, mildewed, stale, stale-smelling, sour, rancid, rank; stuffy, close, oppressive, unventilated; smelly, strong-smelling, bad-smelling, malodorous, *Rare.* mucid; fetid, gamy, noisome, mephitic, stinky.
2. old-fashioned, out of fashion, out-of-date, outdated; antiquated, archaic, obsolete, obsolescent, anachronistic, passé; moth-eaten, faded, worn-out.
3. old-school, behind the times, conservative, fogyish, old-fogyish.

futile, *adj.* **1.** useless, vain, unavailing, bootless, ineffective, inefficacious; fruitless, unproductive, barren, abortive, sterile, impotent; unprofitable, profitless, gainless; unsuccessful, *Sl.* no-go, to no purpose, for naught.
2. trivial, worthless, valueless, nugatory, good-for-nothing, not worth a straw; petty, insignificant, trifling, piddling, negligible, inconsequential, inessential; empty, hollow, idle, inane, vapid.

futility, *n.* **1.** uselessness, bootlessness, ineffectiveness, nonsuccess, nonfulfillment, failure; fruitlessness, unproductiveness, abortiveness, barrenness, sterility, impotence; unprofitableness, carrying coals to Newcastle, carrying water in a sieve, cutting a whetstone with a razor, milking the ram, running around in circles.
2. trifle, frivolity, unimportance, insignificance, worthlessness, valuelessness, nugacity; nonsense, folly, inanity; emptiness, hollowness.

future, *n.* **1.** coming time, time ahead, time to come; hereafter, afterworld, world to come; end of time, doomsday, Judgment Day; millennium, utopia; eventuality, the morrow, tomorrow, *Sp. mañana; Inf.* down the road, *Inf.* down the pike.
2. prospect, outlook, offing; expectation, anticipation, probability, presumption, likelihood.
—*adj.* **3.** prospective, in the offing, coming, to come, anticipated, expected, probable, likely, yet un-

born; pending, impending, imminent, overhanging; near at hand, close at hand, about to be, next.

fuzz, *n.* **1.** lint, fluff, fluffy stuff, loose nap, down. **2.** *U.S. Sl.* policeman, detective, *Inf.* cop, *Sl.* narc. See **policeman**.
—*v.* **3. fuzz up** confuse, obfuscate, muddle, bungle, *Sl.* screw up.

fuzzy, *n.* **1.** linty, fuzz-covered, woolly, downy, *Bot., Zool.* pubescent.
2. blurred, out of focus, not clear; dim, dark, shadowy, misty; indistinct, indefinite, ill-defined, obscure.
3. incoherent, confused, foggy; muddled, bemuddled, muddleheaded, befuddled, crapulent, crapulous.

G

gab, *v.* **1.** *Informal.* jabber, babble, buzz, gossip, blab, chatter. See **chatter** (*def. 1*).
—*n.* **2.** *Informal.* small talk, gossip, patter, jabber, babble, chatter. See **chatter** (*defs.* **2, 3**).

gabble, *v.* **1.** jabber, clack, clatter, rattle, *Sl.* run off *or* on at the mouth; chatter, chitter, prattle, cackle; prate, twaddle, twattle; talk nonsense, *Inf.* talk through one's hat, blather, blab, gush, *Inf.* spout, drivel; gibber, *Sl.* gibber-jabber, jargon; mutter, mumble, splutter, sputter; stammer, stutter.
2. cackle, cluck, chuckle, click, clack; crow, quack, honk.
—*n.* **3.** babble, babbling, babblement, prattle, prattling; gibber, gibbering, gibberish, jabber, jabbering, Jabberwocky, *Sl.* gibber-jabbering; chatter, chattering, cackle, cackling; twaddle, twaddling, *Both Brit.* twattle, twattling; blather, blathering, drivel, driveling; nonsense, moonshine, *Fr. bavardage,* gobbledegook, hocus-pocus, mumbo jumbo, abracadabra, open sesame; humbug, flummery, *Sl.* bunk, rubbish, *Inf.* rot, *Sl.* garbage, *Sl.* horsefeathers; balderdash, hogwash, stuff and nonsense, *Inf.* bosh, *Brit. Sl.* tosh, fudge, foolishness, rigmarole *or* rigamarole; poppycock, *Inf.* fiddle-faddle, *Inf.* piffle, *Inf.* kibosh, *Inf.* flapdoodle.

gabbler, *n.* jabberer, blatherskite, blabber, gossip, magpie, prattler, babbler, chatterbox. See **chatterbox.**

gabby, *adj.* talkative, loquacious, voluble, garrulous, glib; wordy, diffuse, verbose, prolix, long-winded, *Sl.* windy, *Sl.* gassy; effusive, gushing, gushy, bubbling, blabbing, pattering; chattering, clacking, babbling, blathering, prattling, jabbering; buzzing, prating, tattling, tongue-wagging, gossipy, chatty.

gad, *v.* *Usu.* **gad about** gallivant, run around, flit about; ramble, roam, rove, range, *Inf.* traipse; wander, meander, saunter, stroll, perambulate, promenade.

gadabout, *n.* **1.** rambler, rover, wanderer, nomad, gypsy; migrant, itinerant, peripatetic, globetrotter, world traveler, *Sl.* W.T.; vagrant, beachcomber, vagabond, tramp, hobo; transient, fly-by-night.
2. busybody, prier, Paul Pry, meddler, *Inf.* snoop, *Sl.* snooper, *Dial.* nibby nose.

gadget, *n.* **1.** contrivance, device, invention, creation, artifice, makeshift, hickey, widget, Rube Goldberg; mechanism, apparatus, machine, appliance; instrument, implement, tool, utensil.
2. *All Inf.* contraption, whachamacallit, thingumajig, thingamabob, doohickey, do-hinkey, dingus, doodad, gismo, fandangle, *Australian.* doover.

gaffer, *n.* old man, old fellow, *Inf.* old guy, old peasant, old rustic; countryman, yokel, country bumpkin, *Inf.* hayseed, *Inf.* hick, *Sl.* rube.

gag[1], *v.* **1.** (*all of a person's mouth*) stop up, clog, plug, block; smother, stifle, muffle, still, quiet, silence.
2. (*all of speech*) muzzle, curb, check, restrain, hold back, keep from, inhibit, suppress, repress.
3. choke, strangle, strangulate, throttle; garotte, bowstring, hang, lynch, *Inf.* string up; suffocate, asphyxiate, burke.
4. choke, retch, keck, dry-heave; gasp, convulse, struggle for air, puff, pant, blow.

gag[2], *v.* **1.** *Informal.* joke, tell a joke, jest, *Inf.* josh, tease, *Inf.* kid, *Inf.* fun; play a practical joke on, play a prank *or* trick on, *Inf.* pull a shenanigan, caper.
—*n.* **2.** *Informal.* joke, jest, quip, *Inf.* wisecrack, witticism, pun; practical joke, April fool, prank, trick, *Inf.* shenanigan, *Sl.* monkeyshine, caper.

gage, *n.* **1.** challenge, defiance, dare; glove, gauntlet.
2. pledge, pawn, token, earnest, deposit, down payment; security, surety, bond, guaranty, guarantee, warrant, warranty.

gaiety, *n.* **1.** cheer, cheerfulness, gladness, gayness, good *or* high spirits; blitheness, blithesomeness, light-heartedness, buoyancy, optimism, good nature; joy, sunshine, delight, pleasure, happiness, felicity, bliss; joyfulness, joyousness, jubilation, jubilancy, exhilaration, exultation, glee, elation; joviality, merriment, jollity, mirth, mirthfulness, hilarity, laughter.
2. *Often* **gaieties** merrymaking, festivity, convivality, jollification, rejoicing, jubilance, revelry, revels, *Brit. Inf.* mafficking; celebration, *Brit.* holiday-making, party, frolic, gala, jubilee.
3. finery, frippery, showiness, brilliance, glitter, sparkle, gaudiness, garishness.

gaily, *adv.* **1.** merrily, cheerfully, happily, blithely, joyfully, joyously, jubilantly, gleefully, exultantly.
2. showily, brilliantly, gaudily, garishly.

gain, *v.* **1.** obtain, get, acquire, procure, secure; reach, attain, achieve, arrive at, come to; win, (*of a bill or motion*) carry; earn, merit, capture, net, bag; harvest, garner, reap, gather, collect, pick up, glean; increase in, put on, add on; win over, persuade, prevail upon, enlist.
2. profit, avail, benefit, advance; net, clear, realize, make, yield, produce.
3. improve, advance, progress; recuperate, get better, rally, pick up, gain ground.
4. *Often* **gain on** close in, close in on, narrow the

gap, get nearer, catch up, catch up with, approach, overtake; widen the gap, do better, get farther ahead, draw away from.

5. **gain time** procrastinate, stall, temporize, *U.S. Congress.* filibuster; delay, dally, use dilatory tactics, maneuver; postpone, put off, hold in abeyance, put on a back burner.

—n. 6. profit, advantage, behoof, interest; benefit, good, avail, efficacy, use, usefulness.

7. **gains** profits, winnings, *Sl.* take, *Sl.* velvet; proceeds, *Sl.* clean-up, pickings; revenue, income, earnings; return, interest, yield.

8. increase, augmentation, addition, increment, accretion, accumulation; rise, elevation, enhancement, ennoblement.

9. advance, advancement, forward movement, headway; progress, step forward, breakthrough, major development, discovery, finding.

10. acquisition, acquirement, obtainment; getting, striving, achieving, achievement.

gainful, *adj.* profitable, remunerative, paying, rewarding, productive, fruitful; lucrative, money-making, rich, fat; beneficial, advantageous, worthwhile, valuable, useful, desirable.

gainsay, *v.* 1. deny, dispute, controvert, naysay, disbelieve; contradict, traverse, nullify, negate, disaffirm; disprove, confute, refute, discredit; protest, oppose, contravene; dissent, differ, challenge, impugn; object, demur, refuse assent, disagree; say no to, turn thumbs down, turn a deaf ear; prohibit, proscribe, veto.

—n. 2. denial, contradiction, disaffirmation, negation, denegation; disavowal, unsaying, repudiation, disclaimer, disclamation, gainsaying, recantation; refutation, disproof, confutation; protest, objection, contravention.

gait, *n.* 1. walk, step, stride, tread; manner of going, bearing, carriage; stalk, saunter, run.

2. (*all of horses*) rack, single-foot, amble, pace, trot, job, gallop.

gaiter, *n.* spat, spatterdash, legging, puttee, *Western U.S.* chaps, (*in Mexico*) chaparajos, gambado, galligaskin, gambado, *Armor.* greave.

gala, *adj.* 1. festive, festal, festival, holiday, in holiday spirits; merry, joyous, gleeful, mirthful, convivial; gay, sportive, uproarious; diverting, entertaining, amusing, pleasing; spirited, lively, dashing; rollicking, rompish, romping; jovial, jolly, good-time.

2. showy, colorful, glittering, flashy, flaunting, ostentatious, pompous, pretentious; spectacular, dramatic, theatrical, with flying colors, with flourish of trumpet; majestic, stately, grand; magnificent, gorgeous, splendid, sumptuous; ceremonial, ritualistic, solemn; formal, dress-up, silk-stocking, black tie, white tie.

—n. 3. holiday, religious feast day, holy day; festivity, festival, fete, field day, carnival; event, occasion, red-letter day, anniversary, jubilee; celebration, ceremony, ritual; pageant, exhibition, procession, demonstration; party, ball, dance, cotillion, extravaganza, happening, *Inf.* shindig, *Sl.* wing-ding, *Sl.* bash.

galaxy, *n.* 1. constellation, starry host, starry cope, heavens, deep space; Milky Way.

2. brilliant assemblage, eminent company, host of luminaries, illustrious group, notables.

gale, *n.* 1. windstorm, storm, tempest, blast, blow, wind, khamsini, disturbance, turbulence, hurricane, tornado, whirlwind, cyclone, twister; squall, williwaw, blizzard; mistral, monsoon, simoom, sirocco, big blow, hard blow, northeaster.

2. peal, ring, burst, shriek, shout, roar, scream, howl; outburst, explosion, eruption, ebullition, outpouring.

gall¹, *n.* 1. bitterness, rancor, malice, spite, animosity, acrimony, cynicism; malignity, venom, virulence, spleen; acerbity, asperity, mordacity, sarcasm, invective.

2. impudence, insolence, brashness, audacity, cheek, brass, face, sauciness; effrontery, front, brazenness, nerve, temerity, *Sl.* chutzpah, *Sl.* crust, *Sl.* moxie.

3. **gall and wormwood** resentment, deep resentment, umbrage, pique, dudgeon, anger; irritation, annoyance, exasperation.

gall², *n.* 1. abrasion, scrape, scratch, graze, scuff, sore, canker, ulcer, excoriation.

—v. 2. chafe, abrade, rub, fret, rasp, grate, scratch, scrape, excoriate; chap, roughen, redden.

3. vex, irritate, rankle, exasperate, aggravate, exacerbate, rub the wrong way; annoy, irk, nettle, tease; harass, harry, ride, nag, get on one's back; disturb, agitate, shake, unsettle, ruffle; pique, roil, rile, madden, anger, enrage, infuriate, inflame, *Inf.* burn [s.o.] up; arouse, excite, provoke, goad, spur; hector, pester, badger, bother, offend; provoke, incense; persecute, molest, sting.

gallant, *adj.* 1. showy, splendid, grand, *Inf.* splendiferous, magnificent, brilliant, glorious; elegant, lavish, sumptuous; majestic, imposing, august, princely, imperial, regal; dignified, lofty.

2. brave, courageous, valiant, valorous, heroic, heroical; stout-hearted, lionhearted, great-hearted; manly, manful, chivalrous, chivalric; intrepid, fearless, dauntless; unafraid, unblenching, unblenched, undaunted; bold, bold-spirited, high-spirited, daring, dashing, adventurous.

3. firm, resolute, resolved, staunch, steadfast, stalwart; indomitable, redoubtable, unyielding, unbending, unbowing, unshrinking, unfaltering, unhesitating, unswerving, unwavering, undeviating; mettlesome, plucky, gritty, game, red-blooded, spirited, *Inf.* spunky.

4. polite, courteous, deferential, considerate, thoughtful, obliging, gentle, kindly; gentlemanly, mannerly, courtly, well-bred; suave, urbane.

—n. 5. hero, champion, paladin, knight; stalwart, valiant, cavalier, chevalier, brave man, brave, man of courage *or* mettle.

6. beau, suitor, wooer, pursuer, admirer, adorer; escort, squire, date, partner; lover, swain, sweetheart, beloved, Romeo; gentleman, gentleman friend, fiancé, betrothed, young man, boy friend; man about town, man of the world.

gallantry, *n.* 1. chivalrousness, courtliness, courteousness, mannerliness, gentlemanliness; magnanimity, nobleness, liberalness, kindliness, thoughtfulness, considerateness.

2. chivalry, bravery, courage, valor, heroism, stoutheartedness, lionheartedness; manliness, manfulness; intrepidity, fearlessness, dauntlessness; boldness, bold-spiritedness, high-spiritedness, daring, derring-do, audacity.

3. fortitude, endurance, tenacity, determination; firmness, resoluteness, indomitableness, steadfastness, stalwartness, doughtiness; mettle, pluck, spirit, backbone, gumption, heart, nerve, grit, *Sl.* guts, *Sl.* moxie.

4. high-mindedness, noble-mindedness; justness, fairness, impartialness, equitableness; virtue, virtuousness, nobility, honor, uprightness, upstandingness; fidelity, dedication, devotion, reliability, reliableness, dependability.

5. courtesy, politeness, politesse, civility, good man-

ners; respect, respectfulness, deference; decorousness, propriety, formality, ceremony; correctness, tact, diplomacy; cordiality, amenity, geniality, affability, amiability, agreeability; helpfulness, complaisance, obligingness, *Fr. prevenance.*

6. gentility, gentleness, graciousness, good breeding; urbanity, suavity, social graces, manners; nicety, elegance, refinement, culture, polish, sophistication; social procedures, decorum, protocol.

7. courtship, wooing, flirtation, love-making.

gallery, *n.* **1.** corridor, hall, hallway, passageway, walk; loggia, *Archit.* arcade, *Archit.* cloister, *Chief. Brit.* piazza, *Archit.* triforium, *Archit.* ambulatory; porch, veranda, portico, *Gk. Archit.* stoa.

2. upper gallery, *Inf.* peanut gallery; seats, bleachers, grandstand.

3. audience, spectators, observers, listeners; congregation, assembly, house; general public, crowd, gathering.

4. art gallery, art museum, exhibition hall, salon.

5. tunnel, underground passage, shaft, *Mining.* crosscut, *Mining.* drift, *Mining.* adit, airway, air course.

gallimaufry, *n.* **1.** hodgepodge, mishmash, jumble, farrago; mixture, medley, mélange, olio, potpourri, *Inf.* combo; miscellany, miscellanea, salmagundi, olla-podrida.

2. stew, hotchpotch, goulash, ragout, hash.

galling, *adj.* irritating, chafing, rasping, stinging; exasperating, exacerbating, acerbating, embittering, rankling; annoying, provoking, peeving, nettling, nettlesome, *Inf.* aggravating; vexatious, vexing, irksome, irking; troublesome, thorny, fretful.

gallivant, *v.* **1.** gad about, run around, flit about; ramble, roam, rove, range, *Inf.* traipse; wander, meander, saunter, stroll, perambulate, promenade.

2. court, woo, *Inf.* spark, serenade, play the gallant; escort, squire around.

gallop, *v.* **1.** ride at full speed, rack, canter, lope; prance, frisk.

2. race, speed, zoom, rush, tear along, run, bound, sprint; hurry, hasten, post, hie, flee; dash, whisk, whiz, spank; dart, shoot, spring, bolt; scamper, scurry, scuttle, scud.

gallows, *n.* gibbet, *Archaic.* bough, scaffold, *Brit.* Tyburn tree.

galore, *adv.* in abundance, in large numbers, in large quantity, in plentiful amounts, *Inf.* aplenty; all over the place, everyplace, everywhere, everywhere one looks; more than enough, in excess, more than one could ever want, coming out one's ears, in unending supply.

galvanize, *v.* **1.** electrify, energize, dynamize, charge; treat [s.o.] with electric current.

2. shock, jolt, jar, stagger, give [s.o.] a shock *or* jolt, *Sl.* give [s.o.] a heart attack; startle, astonish, surprise, stun, take one's breath away, pull one up short, shake, fluster; overwhelm, overpower, *Inf.* bowl [s.o.] over, paralyze, petrify.

3. stimulate, excite, fire, rouse, arouse, spur [s.o.] on, prod; invigorate, vitalize, enliven, animate, exhilarate, inspirit, thrill, flush, *Inf.* give one a kick *or* charge.

gambit, *n.* stratagem, machination, finesse, maneuver, move, play; device, ruse, wile, ploy, artifice, trick, intrigue.

gamble, *v.* **1.** bet, wager, try one's luck *or* fortune, make a bet, lay a wager *or* bet, *Brit.* punt, *Inf.* shoot craps, *Inf.* play the ponies, *Brit. Inf.* birl, *Brit. Sl.* gaff.

2. speculate, venture, play the market, *Inf.* plunge, *Inf.* take a flier; risk, hazard, dare, tempt Providence, take *or* run the risk *or* hazard *or* chance, *Inf.* chance, *Inf.* stick one's neck out, *Inf.* go out on a limb; leave *or* trust to chance, take a leap *or* shot in the dark, buy a pig in a poke.

3. squander, lavish, waste, throw away, run through, *Inf.* spend money like water, *Inf.* spend money as if it grew on trees.

—n. **4.** risk, hazard, chance; speculation, venture, *Inf.* flier, *Inf.* plunge, *Brit. Inf.* birl, *Sl.* whack, *Sl.* crack; potshot, random shot, leap *or* shot in the dark, pig in a poke; potluck, blind bargain, sight-unseen transaction.

5. gambling, gaming, betting, wagering, risking; off-track betting, pari-mutuel, *Inf.* playing the ponies, playing the lottery, playing the numbers.

gambler, *n.* bettor, wagerer, gamester, speculator, adventurer; *Brit.* punter, *Inf.* sport, *Inf.* piker, *Inf.* tinhorn, *Inf.* crapshooter, *Sl.* boneshaker, *Sl.* big-timer; adventurist, risk-taker, hazarder, speculator, *Inf.* plunger; bookmaker, *Inf.* bookie, oddsmaker, blackleg, *Horse Racing Inf.* tout, *Inf.* tipster.

gambol, *v.* **1.** frolic, frisk, sport, disport, play, skip about; romp, rollick, dance *or* jump about; cavort, caper, cut capers, curvet.

—n. **2.** frolic, fun, sport, play, *Sl.* buster; lark, antic, prank, caper; romp, skylarking.

game, *n.* **1.** amusement, diversion, distraction, divertissement, pastime, entertainment; recreation, sport, play, fun, merriment, frolic; merrymaking, merriment, joviality, jollity, jollification; tomfoolery, foolery, mummery, buffoonery, clowning around, horseplay, *Sl.* monkey business; escapade, spree, prank.

2. contest, competition, match, tourney, regatta, meet, joust, duel; tournament, bout, round, encounter, engagement, athletic event; run-off, sudden death, showdown; Olympics, (*in ancient Greece*) agon, decathlon, marathon, (*in ancient Greece*) agonistics.

3. scheme, schema, design, plan, scenario, script; contrivance, stratagem, strategy, device, artifice, shift, invention, trick; machination, wirepulling, manipulation; designs, evil intentions.

4. joke, practical joke, prank, *Sl.* monkeyshines; jesting, kidding around, fooling around, *Sl.* goofing.

5. wild animal, wild fowl, prey, quarry, raven.

6. *Informal.* business, occupation, profession, trade, line; industry, enterprise, *Sl.* racket.

7. spirit, pluck, mettle, *Inf.* spunk; backbone, nerve, stamina, hardihood.

8. make game of ridicule, make fun of, deride, scoff at, mock, jeer; taunt, gibe, rag; rib, kid, *Inf.* roast, *Sl.* razz; poke fun at, make a fool out of, make the butt of, *Inf.* give [s.o.] the needle; lampoon, satirize, parody.

9. play the game *Informal.* **a.** go along with, conform, follow the crowd, do as others do, keep in step, toe the mark, stay in line; give in, defer, compromise. **b.** play fair, be a good sport, play by the rules, *Inf.* be up front. **c.** temporize, straddle the fence, be noncommittal.

—adj. **10.** plucky, spirited, courageous, gamy, valiant, heroic, stout-hearted, lionhearted; bold, intrepid, fearless, dauntless, dreadless, nervy, *Sl.* gutsy, unafraid, unblenching, unblenched, undaunted, unalarmed, undismayed; daring, dashing, high-spirited, adventurous.

11. willing, favorably inclined, disposed; eager, anxious, interested, enthusiastic, devil-may-care.

—v. **12.** gamble, bet, wager, try one's luck *or* for-

tune, make a bet, lay a wager *or* bet, *Inf.* shoot craps, *Inf.* play the ponies; speculate, venture, play the market, play the wheel, play roulette; risk, hazard, dare, tempt Providence. See **gamble** (*defs.* **1, 2**).

gamut, *n.* entire range, complete scale, complete sequence, whole series, full sweep, full compass, entire scope; *Music.* the major scale.

gamy, *adj.* **1.** slightly tainted, strong, strong tasting, high-flavored, *Inf.* high, *Inf.* hung; rank, strong smelling, pungent.

2. plucky, spirited, spunky, courageous; persistent, tenacious. See **game** (*defs.* **10, 11**).

gang, *n.* **1.** group, band, pack, company, crowd, gathering.

2. clique, social group, set, coterie, circle; club, brotherhood, fraternity, sorority; party, *Politics.* machine, *Politics.* junta, *Politics.* cabal.

3. squad, shift, team, troop, detachment, *Inf.* outfit; posse, search party.

4. criminal band, group of thieves, band of brigands, group of bandits, underworld mob, mob, *Inf.* family.

—*v.* **5. gang up on** *Informal.* combine against, conspire *or* plot against, *Inf.* get; ambush, attack, surround, *Sl.* mug.

gangling, *adj.* lanky, rangy, spindly, spindling, loosely built, awkwardly tall; slender, skinny, rawboned, stringy; gauche, ungraceful, ungainly.

gangster, *n.* **1.** mobster, racketeer, mafioso, desperado, terrorist; thug, tough, mugger, ruffian, rowdy, hoodlum, *Sl.* hood, *Inf.* goon, hooligan, *Inf.* roughneck, *Inf.* baddy, *Sl.* bad actor, *Sl.* gunsel, *Sl.* mug, *Australian Sl.* larrikin, *Brit. Hist.* Mohock, (*in Paris*) apache.

2. assassin, murderer, killer, slayer, sniper; strangler, cutthroat, garroter; liquidator, *Euph.* silencer, *Euph.* dispatcher; gunman, *All U.S. Sl.* gun, hired gun, hit man, triggerman, hatchet man, torpedo.

3. bandit, hold-up man, *Sl.* stick-up man, armed robber; robber, thief, *Inf.* crook, stealer, Fagin; criminal, felon, larcener; convict, *Sl.* jailbird, parolee, ex-convict, *Inf.* ex-con; recidivist, repeat offender, *Inf.* chronic crook.

4. extortionist, extortioner, blackmailer, usurer, loan shark, *Sl.* bleeder; smuggler, runner, bootlegger, contrabandist, white-slaver; swindler, confidence man, con artist, con man; forger, counterfeiter, *Fr. faux-monnayeur, Brit. Inf.* coiner.

5. villain, blackguard, miscreant, malefactor, evildoer, *Inf.* bad guy.

gap, *n.* **1.** opening, hole, cavity, space, aperture, orifice, mouth, foramen; breach, separation, break, fracture, rent, rift, fissure, cleft, *Archaic.* scissure; chink, crack, crevice, cranny; groove, furrow, trench; defile, pass, canyon, gorge, ravine, gully, gulch, barranca, arroyo, couloir, *Western North America.* coulee, *Brit. Dial.* clough; notch, score, scratch, cut, slit, split, gash, incision.

2. blank, emptiness, vacuum, void, vacancy, gape, lacuna; break, hiatus, interruption, disruption, *Prosody.* caesura, *Physiol.* synapse; pause, rest, recess, lull, halt, stop, stand-still, time out; cessation, abatement, discontinuance, suspension, suspense, abeyance; delay, wait, deferment, postponement; interstice, interval, interim, intermission, intermittence, intermittency.

gape, *v.* **1.** gawk, goggle, stare open-mouthed, show astonishment, *Inf.* rubberneck; regard with awe, stare at, stare curiously, ogle.

2. yawn, dehisce, open up, open wide, extend wide; part, crack, split.

garb, *n.* **1.** dress, costume, habit, outfit; livery, uniform, regalia, trappings, harness, rigging, *Inf.* rig, *Inf.* getup, *Inf.* turnout; style, cut.

2. clothing, clothes, attire, apparel, wearing apparel, wear; garments, vestments, habits, habiliments, raiment, *Inf.* gear, *Inf.* toggery, *Inf.* togs, *Inf.* duds, *Sl.* threads, *Sl.* rags; wardrobe, array, accouterment; investment, investiture, vesture.

3. guise, appearance, aspect, look, semblance; disguise, masquerade.

—*v.* **4.** dress, clothe, vest, attire, apparel, habit; array, bedizen, deck, deck out, bedeck, *Sl.* dude up, *Sl.* swank up; robe, gown, drape; outfit, fit out, fit up, fit, rig, rig up, rig out, trap, trap out, caparison, gear, turn out, accouter.

garbage, *n.* **1.** refuse, *Dial.* culch, rubbish, waste, *Brit.* wastrel, discarded matter; offal, carrion, rot, spoil; offscourings, dregs, draff, remains, leavings, leftovers; scraps, orts, hogwash, swill; remainder, residue, residuum, scum.

2. junk, worthless stuff, *Sl.* dreck, trumpery; trash, riffraff, *Brit. Dial.* raff, litter, chaff; filth, dirt, dust, sweepings; debris, detritus, rubble, wreckage; fragments, remnants, fag ends, bits and pieces, odds and ends; castoffs, rags, tatters, castaways, rejects, discards.

3. *Slang.* nonsense, twaddle, foolishness. See **nonsense** (*def.* **2**).

garble, *v.* **1.** distort, warp, twist, twist around, *Scot.* thraw; take out of context, color, slant, bend, stretch, exaggerate; varnish, embroider, embellish, dress up; pervert, corrupt, adulterate, tamper with, doctor, change around; misquote, misrender, misstate, misreport, falsify, misrepresent, belie; misinterpret, misconstrue, misunderstand, misread, *Inf.* get it wrong.

2. jumble, confuse, mix up; slur, run together, mutter, mumble.

garden, *n.* **1.** vegetable garden, truck garden, *Brit.* market garden, *Fr. potager;* vegetable plot, kitchen garden, herb garden, flower garden; formal garden, English garden, French garden, Chinese *or* Japanese garden, natural *or* wild garden.

2. arboretum, botanical garden; public garden, park, *Fr. jardin,* recreation area, *Inf.* rec area, playground.

3. gardens grounds, lawn, yard.

gardener, *n.* caretaker; horticulturist, cultivator, grower; farmer, granger, husbandman; landscaper, landscape architect.

gargantuan, *adj.* gigantic, enormous, monstrous, huge, *Sl.* humongous, Brobdingnagian, Cyclopean; vast, towering, colossal, immense, stupendous, prodigious, tremendous, herculean, mammoth; very large *or* big, great, *Inf.* strapping, *Inf.* whopping; elephantine, massive, ponderous, very heavy, bulky, hulking, clumsy, lubberly.

gargle, *v.* (*all of the mouth or throat*) wash out, rinse out, swish *or* swash water about in.

garish, *adj.* **1.** flashy, *Sl.* flash, loud, bold. See **gaudy** (*def.* **1**).

2. ornate, elaborate, baroque; flamboyant, showy, flaring. See **gaudy** (*def.* **2**).

garland, *n.* wreath, festoon, lei, loop; laurel, bay, crown, *Literary.* anadem, diadem; coronet, chaplet, coronal; fillet, headband, snood, fascia.

garment, *n.* **1.** cover, covering, outer covering; guise, appearance, look, aspect, semblance; disguise, masquerade.

2. garments clothing, clothes, attire, apparel, wearing apparel, wear; vestments, habiliments, habits, raiment, *Inf.* toggery, *Inf.* togs, *Inf.* duds, *Sl.* threads, *Sl.* rags; wardrobe, livery, array, accouterment; investment, investiture, vesture.

—*v.* **3.** dress, clothe, vest, attire, apparel, garb, habit; array, bedizen, deck, deck out, bedeck, *Sl.* dude up, *Sl.* swank up; robe, gown, drape; outfit, fit out, fit up, fit, rig, rig up, rig out, trap, trap out, caparison, gear, turn out, accouter.

4. cover, wrap, enwrap, envelop, cloak; muffle, swaddle; endow, endue *or* indue, invest.

garner, *v.* **1.** gather in, deposit, store, bank.

2. get, acquire; attain, achieve, arrive at, earn.

3. gather, collect, accumulate, heap up, pile up, stack up, amass; hoard, lay in, lay up, lay by, put away, stow away, cache; store up, stock up, set aside, put by; save for a rainy day, save, reserve, preserve, husband.

—*n.* **4.** granary, silo, barn; crib, bunker; storehouse, depository, depot, repository; vault, safe.

garnish, *v.* **1.** adorn, decorate, ornament, trim, embellish, furbish, *Archaic.* dight; festoon, embroider, set off, rubricate, elaborate; deck, deck out, bedeck, bespangle, bedizen, array; trap out, caparison, dress, dress up, attire, accouter; beautify, prettify, fix up, prink; *Inf.* spruce up, *Inf.* pretty up, *Inf.* trick up, *Inf.* doll up; grace, polish, enrich, enhance, smarten; spice, season, touch up.

—*n.* **2.** adornment, decoration, ornament, ornamentation, embellishment, furbishment; festoon, trimming, dressing, garniture, topping, frills; accouterment, appurtenance, appendage, attachment.

garret, *n.* attic, loft, cockloft, crow's nest, *Archit.* clerestory; mansard, dormer, housetop.

garrison, *n.* **1.** detachment, picket, militia, soldiery; guard, platoon, brigade, regiment, squadron, unit; division, battery, corps.

2. fort, post, command, hold, blockhouse; citadel, fortress, stronghold, fastness; barrack, bunkhouse, cassine, casern, casemate; camp, bivouac, *South African.* laager, zareba.

—*v.* **3.** man, fortify, defend, guard, protect, preserve; station, put on duty, post, send in, move in, billet.

4. occupy, command, hold; bivouac, camp, encamp, pitch camp.

garrulity, *n.* talkativeness, loquacity, loquaciousness, volubility, glibness, gift of gab, garrulousness; wordiness, diffuseness, verbosity, prolixity; effusiveness, gushiness, chattiness, gossipiness; chattering, babbling, blathering, prattling, jabbering.

garrulous, *adj.* talkative, loquacious, voluble, gabby, glib; wordy, diffuse, verbose, prolix, long-winded, *Sl.* windy, *Sl.* gassy; effusive, gushing, gushy, bubbling, blabbing, pattering; chattering, clacking, babbling, blathering, prattling, jabbering; buzzing, prating, tattling, tongue-wagging, gossipy, chatty.

gas, *n.* **1.** ether, vapor, steam; wind, fume, smoke, reek; effluvium, exhalation, eructation, miasma, exhaust, carbon monoxide; nitrous oxide, laughing gas; natural gas, methane, propane, butane, acetyline, ethine; hydrogen, nitrogen, oxygen, helium, carbon dioxide.

2. wind, flatus. See **flatulence.**

3. See **gasoline.**

—*v.* **4.** asphyxiate, suffocate, smother, choke, stifle.

gasconade, *n.* **1.** boasting, bluster, bravado, fanfaronade, rodomontade, *Sl.* hot air, *Sl.* bunk; bombast, bluff, bounce, much cry and little wool, *Latin. vox et praeterea nihil;* balderdash, rant, buncombe, *Inf.* bunkum, *Sl.* bunk, claptrap, humbug.

—*v.* **2.** boast, brag, bluster, crow, bluff, beat the drum, *Archaic.* vaunt; trumpet, toot *or* blow one's own horn, sing one's own praises; roister, puff, *Inf.* blow hard, *Sl.* talk big, *Sl.* shoot one's mouth.

gash, *n.* **1.** wound, cut, slash, tear, score, scotch; cleft, incision, slit, slice, slot; rift, split, crack, rent, fissure, scission, *Archaic.* scissure; notch, hack, nick, kerf, curf.

—*v.* **2.** cut, slash, tear into, score, scotch, wound; slit, incise, slice; cleave, rive, split, rent; jag, nick, nip, hack.

gasoline, *n.* gas, petrol, fuel, diesel fuel, *Fr. Canadian. gaz.*

gasp, *n.* **1.** short breath, pant, huff, snort, heave, gulp, wheeze.

—*v.* **2.** huff, snort, pant, huff and puff, puff; wheeze, choke, heave, gulp, suck in.

3. utter, exlaim, cry, aspirate.

gassy, *adj.* **1.** gaseous, gasiform, aeriform; steamy, vaporous, volatile, etheric, ethereal; effluvial, miasmic; aerodynamic, aerostatic, pneumatic.

2. flatulent, windy. See **flatulent.**

gastric, *adj.* **1.** stomachic, stomachal, stomachical; abdominal, *Anat.* celiac, intestinal, visceral, ventral, ventricular, splanchnic.

2. digestive, eupeptic, dyspeptic.

gastronomy, *n.* cookery, cuisine, diet; epicureanism, *Fr. bonne cuisine;* gourmandism, gulosity, gluttony.

gate, *n.* access, opening, entrance, adit, exit, ingress, egress; portal, *Scot.* port, door, doorway, fire door, gateway, wicket, postern; stile, turnstile; hatch, hatchway, trapdoor, porthole; (*both in England*) lich gate, resurrection gate.

gather, *v.* **1.** collect, accumulate, heap up, pile, pile up, stack up; amass, cumulate; glean, take in, pull in, harvest, reap; pick, pick up, rake up, bag; cull, sort out, pick out; hoard, garner, store up, stock up, lay by, lay up, lay in, *Inf.* stash away, reserve, set aside; save, save up.

2. group, cluster, bunch up *or* together; mass, crowd, congregate, agglomerate; flock together, throng, herd, swarm; bring together, rally, muster, call up, mobilize; round up, round in.

3. assemble, convene, forgather, come together, converge; meet, *Inf.* gang up, huddle, go into a huddle, get together, rendezvous; convoke, summon, call together.

4. compile, anthologize; organize, order, marshal.

5. grow, increase, build; swell, enlarge, expand, extend, wax; rise, roll up, heighten, deepen.

6. infer, draw an inference; assume, derive, understand, deduce, conclude.

7. contract, pucker, purse; crease, furrow, knit, wrinkle, rimple.

8. ruffle, shirr, pleat, plait, full.

9. attract, pull, draw, draw in, invite, pick up.

10. come to a head, fester, suppurate, rankle.

—*n.* **11.** drawing together, contraction; fold, ruffle, pucker, pleat.

gathering, *n.* **1.** collection, accumulation, amassment; assemblage, number, aggregation, aggregate, roundup; concentration, mass; cluster, clump, batch; cloud, cumulus, drift; store, stock, pile, heap, swell, mound; medley, jumble; agglomeration, conglomeration, congeries, lump.

2. assembly, meeting, meet, rally, turnout; group, body, circle, knot; crowd, throng, mob; bunch, gang, crew, company, troupe, band, troop; flock, pack, herd, drove, bevy, covey, swarm, hive, school, shoal; galaxy, multitude, host; congestion, press, crush; concourse, cumulation, confluence, convergence.

3. audience, congregation, community, flock; conclave, convocation, council, synod, consistory, conventicle; muster, mobilization, levy; association, union, combination; conference, convention, congress; caucus, bloc, *Rom. Antiq.* comitia, junta; forgathering, conjunction, coalescence.

4. party, get together, do; banquet, dinner, luncheon; ball, dance, cotillion; reception, function; tea, coffee, coffee klatch, social; soiree, levee, salon.

5. boil, abscess, carbuncle, ulcer, canker; pimple, pustule, *Sl.* zit.

gauche, *adj.* **1.** ill-bred, ill-mannered, uncouth, unrefined, unpolished, unladylike, ungentlemanly; coarse, indelicate, crude, cloddish; vulgar, ordinary, common; piggish, boorish, gross; tactless, insensitive, imperceptive, crass; dull, dense, mutton-headed; provincial, unsophisticated, *Inf.* just off the farm, *Inf.* hick.

2. awkward, gawky, clumsy, bumbling, maladroit; all-thumbs, having two left feet, unhandy, unskillful, inept, bunglesome, bungling, *Inf.* klutzy; ungraceful, ungainly, lumbering, lubberly, like a bull in a china shop.

gaucherie, *n.* **1.** blunder, *Fr. faux pas,* misbehavior, bad job; botch, botchery, bungle; crudity, vulgarity; breach of etiquette, social slip, gaffe.

2. gracelessness, uncouthness, bad taste, *Fr. mauvais goût;* unmannerliness, indecorum, impoliteness, inelegance; insensitivity, tactlessness, boorishness, rudeness, coarseness; awkwardness, clumsiness, gawkiness, ungainliness, *Inf.* klutziness.

gaudy, *adj.* **1.** garish, flashy, *Sl.* flash, loud, bold, painted, hard, *Inf.* honky-tonk; tawdry, meretricious, cheap, dime-store, tinselly, brummagem, gimcrack, trumpery, trashy, *Inf.* chintzy, *Inf.* tacky, *Sl.* rinky-dink; tasteless, in bad taste, indelicate, crude, vulgar.

2. ornate, baroque, elaborate, involved, *Music.* bravura; fancy, florid, flowery, high-wrought, high-flown; frilly, overdecorated, gingerbread, fussy, busy, *Archaic.* bedighted, conspicuous, striking, flagrant, obvious; flamboyant, showy, ostentatious, flaring, flaunting, pretentious.

gauge, *v.* **1.** appraise, evaluate, value, assess; estimate, figure, reckon, compute; judge, adjudge, rate, consider, determine.

2. measure, weigh, balance; mark out, delineate, trace, outline, limn.

—*n.* **3.** test, criterion, standard, guideline, touchstone, bench mark, yardstick; measure, rule, norm.

4. extent, degree, scope, area; reach, limit, bound, size, magnitude, depth, width, height; capacity, ability, capability.

gaunt, *adj.* **1.** thin, thin as a reed *or* rail, lean, meager, spare, lank, lanky; skinny, too skinny to throw a shadow, skin-and-bones, bony, rawboned; skeletal, emaciated, angular; stalky, spindly, spindle-shanked, spindle-legged; scrawny, scraggy, looking like a plucked chicken, weedy; pinched, starved-looking, withered, shriveled, wasted, hollow-cheeked.

2. haggard, looking like the wrath of God, worn-and-weary, looking like six o'clock, drawn; sickly-looking, peaked, looking like death warmed over, cadaverous.

3. bleak, desolate, dreary, dismal, forlorn; barren, bare, windswept, treeless, denuded; grim, stern, harsh, forbidding.

gauntlet, *n.* **1.** glove, mitten; mail, armor.

2. ordeal, trial, tribulation, suffering, punishment, adversity; affliction, misery, distress, hardship, hard times.

gauzy, *adj.* sheer, diaphanous, transparent, transpicuous, translucent, filmy, gossamer; revealing, see-through, *Clothing.* peekaboo; silky, silken, chiffon.

gavel, *n.* mallet, tapper, small hammer.

gawk, *n.* **1.** clod, clodhopper, clodpoll, boor, churl, looby, lubber, lout, *Chiefly Scot.* cuddy, *Inf.* lummox, *Inf.* goop, *Sl.* klutz, *Sl.* galoot, *Sl.* lug, *Brit. Sl.* joskin; bungler, bumbler, fumbler, botcher, blunderer, *Inf.* stumblebum, *Inf.* duffer.

—*v.* **2.** goggle, ogle, gape, stare, stand agog, *Inf.* rubberneck.

gawky, *adj.* clumsy, awkward, ungainly, maladroit, heavy-handed, blundering, bungling, gawkish, gauche, like a bull in a china shop, *Inf.* butterfingered, *Sl.* klutzy; loutish, oafish, doltish, cloddish, clodhopping, lumpish, lubberly.

gay, *adj.* **1.** merry, jolly, jovial, mirthful, light-hearted, gleeful, cheerful, frivolous, facetious; glad, happy, bright, airy, sunny, in good *or* high spirits; joyous, jubilant, cock-a-hoop; lively, sprightly, animated, spirited, chipper; buoyant, vivacious, effervescent, full of life, *Inf.* full of pep, *Inf.* full of get-up-and-go; playful, frolicsome, sportive, gamesome; festive, convivial, rollicking, hilarious.

2. bright, vivid, brilliant, bright-colored, many-colored, multicolored; showy, garish, gaudy, loud; rich, resplendent, splendid.

3. licentious, libidinous, lustful, salacious, prurient, concupiscent, rakish, *Archaic.* lickerish; wanton, dissolute, dissipated, debauched, profligate, incontinent, free-living, fast, loose.

4. *Informal.* homosexual, homoerotic, *Inf.* bent. See **homosexual** (*def.* **2**).

gaze, *v.* **1.** stare, gape, gawk, goggle, stand agog, *Inf.* rubberneck; ogle, *Inf.* eye, *Inf.* eyeball, *Inf.* give [s.o.] the glad eye, look over, scrutinize, *Inf.* give the once-over; look at *or* on *or* upon, take a look at, *Inf.* have a look-see.

—*n.* **2.** stare, steady *or* intent look, goggle, ogle, *Inf.* glad eye.

gazebo, *n.* **1.** summerhouse, parkhouse, gardenhouse; pavilion, (*in Turkey and Iran*) kiosk; pergola, arbor, bower, trellis, lattice; grotto, alcove, recess.

2. retreat, refuge, haven, shelter, hermitage; asylum, resort, sanctuary, ark, covert, hideaway, mew.

gear, **n.** **1.** mechanism, machine part, disk, *Mach.* flywheel, *Mach.* cam, wheel, cogwheel.

2. equipment, apparatus, tools, instruments, contrivances, machinery; implements, appliances, utensils, fixtures; fittings, outfit, outfitting, turnout, rig; supplies, material, wherewithal; caparison, harness, tack, tackle, rigging; *All Mil.* arms, armaments, matériel.

3. clothing, clothes, apparel, wear; garments, vestments, raiment, habit, habiliments, *Inf.* toggery, *Inf.* togs, *Inf.* duds; livery, uniform, regalia.

4. belongings, effects, chattels, possessions, *Inf.* things, *Sl.* stuff, *Sl.* junk; paraphernalia, accouterments, appurtenances, appointments, accessories, trappings; baggage, bag and baggage, impedimenta, dunnage, luggage, kit, duffel.

gelatinous, *adj.* jellylike, slimy, slippery, lubricous, mucous, mucilaginous, gelatinoid; glutinous, viscid, viscous, gummy, sticky, adhesive.

geld, *v.* asexualize, neuter, emasculate, alter, castrate. See **castrate.**

gelid, *adj.* icy, frigid, freezing, algid, ice-cold, frosty, wintry, snowy, rimy; arctic, glacial, polar, hyperborean, hyperboreal, Siberian; bitter, zippy, sharp, brisk, snappy.

gem, *n.* **1.** jewel, bijou, precious *or* semi-precious stone, solitaire, brilliant, pearl; ornament, trinket.

2. masterpiece, chef d'oeuvre, work of art; master stroke, *Fr. coup de maître;* perfection, quintessence, prize, pick, flower, cream, *Fr. crème de la crème;* marvel, wonder, prodigy, rara avis, one in a million, nonpareil.

gender, *n.* sex; *All Gram.* neuter, feminine, masculine.

genealogy, *n.* pedigree, family tree; ancestry, ancestral line, lineage, descent, parentage, birth, derivation, extraction, filiation; family, dynasty, house, tribe; race, strain, stock, breed, bloodline, stem, branch, stirps; heredity, heritage, background, past, history, roots.

general, *adj.* **1.** collective, generic, comprehensive; sweeping, extensive, widespread; inclusive, non-exclusive, not specific, blanket, across-the-board, not partial, not particular, not special; universal, pandemic, ecumenical, world-wide, catholic, public, popular.

2. common, ordinary, usual, regular, conventional, everyday, household, run-of-the-mill; frequent, prevalent, rife; current, prevailing; customary, habitual, wonted, accustomed.

3. extended, panoramic, bird's eye; heterogeneous, mixed, assorted, miscellaneous, encyclopedic; diversified, various, variegated; composite, blended, hybrid, mongrel.

4. vague, indefinite, unspecified, ill-defined, abstract; inexact, inaccurate, approximate; impersonal. —*n.* **5.** *Military.* officer, commander in chief, generalissimo, *All U.S. Army.* brigadier general, lieutenant general, major general, general, general of the army.

6. in general a. as a whole, on the whole, for the most part, in the main. **b.** as a rule, usually, most of the time.

generalist, *n.* nonspecialist, general practitioner, jack-of-all-trades; Renaissance man, universal man, universalist, polymath, encyclopedist, *Inf.* know-it-all.

generality, *n.* **1.** vague statement, loose statement, indefinite statement, general phrase, generalization.

2. general principle, general rule, general law, abstraction, universality.

3. greater part, majority, bulk, mass, main, body.

4. lack of particularity, indefiniteness, vagueness, uncertainty, inexactitude, inexactness, indeterminateness, looseness; miscellany, miscellaneousness, collectiveness, indiscriminateness, promiscuity, promiscuousness; diversification, heterogenity, variety, assortment.

5. universality, catholicity, ecumenicity, generalness, publicness; average, common run, ordinary run, mean; conventionality, regularity; custom, habit.

generalize, *v.* **1.** infer a generality *or* principle *or* law *or* rule; make inferences, draw conclusions, *Logic.* induce; form an opinion *or* notion, come to a conclusion.

2. universalize, make general, make common *or* prevalent, make well-known *or* popular, suit [s.t.] to the masses; extend, broaden, diversify, make inclusive.

3. speak *or* talk in generalities, think in loose *or* broad *or* general terms, make vague statements, be imprecise *or* inexact *or* indefinite; categorize, pigeonhole.

generally, *adv.* **1.** for the most part, in the main, on the whole, mainly, in general, by and large; principally, chiefly.

2. ordinarily, as a rule, usually, commonly, habitually, customarily; frequently, often, repeatedly; universally, extensively, always.

generalship, *n.* **1.** soldiery, military expertise *or* skill *or* know-how; tactics, science of war, military *or* troop management, castramentation; strategics, military strategy *or* planning.

2. leadership, headship, captaincy, presidency, chieftaincy, chieftainship; direction, lead, rule, regulation, management, government, guidance; mastery, command, control, power, authority, influence, sway, say-so.

generate, *v.* **1.** beget, sire, father, spawn, procreate; bring into being, bring to life, give life to, call into existence, cause to exist; produce, breed, fructify.

2. originate, invent, innovate, coin; make, fashion, fabricate, frame; design, contrive, devise, develop, construct; shape, form, mold, forge; imagine, conceive, *Inf.* dream up, *Inf.* hatch; visualize, envisage, evolve.

3. create, found, institute, establish, initiate, give rise to, occasion, break ground, sow the seeds of; generate, spread around, proliferate, propagate.

4. engender, bring about, arrange, inaugurate, start, effectuate, launch, incept; *Inf.* start the ball rolling, *Inf.* take the first step, *Inf.* make the first move.

generation, *n.* **1.** procreation, siring, fathering, breeding, giving birth, propagation, fecundation, proliferation; spontaneous generation, *Biol.* abiogenesis, *Biol.* parthenogenesis.

2. creation, origination, invention, innovation; beginning, start, inception, genesis, engenderment; embodiment, formulation; establishment, constitution, institution.

3. formation, development, production, construction, fabrication; design, contrivance, conception.

4. progeny, issue, offspring, offshoot, seed.

5. era, age, time *or* times, day *or* days, epoch; lifespan, span, lifetime.

generic, *adj.* **1.** common, general, collective; all-inclusive, all-encompassing, comprehensive, sweeping, extensive, blanket.

2. nonexclusive, not specific, unlabeled, unregistered.

generosity, *n.* **1.** bounteousness, munificence, openhandedness, lavishness, liberality, beneficence, bounty.

2. goodness, nobleness, good will, benevolence, bigheartedness; high-mindedness, unselfishness, altruism, humanitarianism; magnanimity, disinterestedness, charity, charitableness.

3. giving, gift, present, donation, grant, gratuity; good turn, good deed, benefaction, largess.

4. largeness, fullness, amplitude, abundance, plenty, full measure; plenitude, sufficiency, repletion, plethora.

generous, *adj.* **1.** bountiful, munificent, charitable, benevolent, beneficent, magnanimous, liberal, open-handed; large-hearted, big-hearted.

2. altruistic, philanthropic, humanitarian, humane, public-spirited, other-directed, unselfish, disinterested; kindhearted, kind, good, noble, honorable.

3. lavish, unrestricted, unstinted, free-handed, ungrudging, extravagant, effusive, prodigal; obliging, accommodating, considerate, cordial, hospitable.

4. abundant, bounteous, rich, copious, overflowing, plentiful, ample.

genial, *adj.* **1.** amiable, good-humored, good-natured, pleasant; cordial, cheerful, courteous, polite; agreeable, willing, well-disposed, amenable; friendly, amicable, congenial, neighborly, sociable, hospitable; kind, kindly, *Scot.* couthie, complaisant, sympathetic, understanding; gracious, benign, generous; happy, cheery, smiling, sunny, optimistic; merry, jovial, jolly, mirthful, gay, light-hearted, joyous.

2. temperate, clement, fair, mild, gentle, pleasant; good, nice, warm, sunny; balmy, soft, soothing; cool, comfortable, refreshing; calm, peaceful, tranquil, halcyon.

geniality, *n.* **1.** cheerfulness, gladness, gayness, gaiety; blitheness, blithesomeness, light-heartedness, buoyancy, optimism, sunniness; sprightliness, liveliness, vivaciousness, animation; happiness, felicity, blissfulness; joyfulness, joy, jubilance, jubilancy.

2. friendliness, amicability, congeniality, neighborliness; affability, approachableness, accessibility, communicativeness; amiability, pleasantness, good-naturedness, good nature; easiness, openness, unreservedness, familiarity, easygoingness; kindliness, kind-heartedness, benignancy; graciousness, cordiality, courteousness, politeness; agreeableness, willingness, amenableness, considerateness.

genitals, *n.* genitalia, sexual organs, sex organs, reproductive organs, organs of generation; private parts, privy parts, privates; penis, phallus, lingam, testis, scrotum; vulva, pudenda, clitoris, yoni.

genius, *n.* **1.** brilliance, aptness, cleverness, ingenuity, astuteness; intelligence, intellectualness, wit, brains, mind, *Gk. Philos.* nous; agility, quickness, smartness, acuity, sharpness; acumen, perspicacity, percipience, insight, intuition, perception; sagacity, cognition, reason, wisdom, understanding; inventiveness, imagination.

2. virtuoso, prodigy, muse, maestro, master, master hand, *Inf.* wizard, *Inf.* whiz, *U.S. Slang.* crackerjack.

3. intellectual, intellect, thinker, *Inf.* brain, *Inf.* an Einstein, mastermind, mental giant.

4. gift, talent, faculty, ability, capability, ableness; facility, flair, bent, turn, knack, forte, dowry; capacity, potential.

5. essence, complexion, gist, sense, *Latin. genius loci;* spirit, character, nature, quality, *Obs.* tenor.

6. (*all of Islamic Myth.*) jinn, djin, genie; daemon, god, goddess, deity; tutelary guardian, guardian angel, patron saint, *Latin. genius loci.*

7. genii demons, devils, spirits, *Islamic Myth.* genie.

genre, *n.* **1.** genus, species, kind, sort, style, fashion, type, brand, name, variety.

2. class, category, school.

genteel, *adj.* **1.** wellborn, gentle, aristocratic, silk-stocking, patrician, noble, blue-blooded, thoroughbred; elegant, graceful, *Scot.* genty; fine, delicate, exquisite; well-bred, refined, polite, civil, mannerly, well-mannered, courteous; decorous, proper, *Fr. comme il faut,* fitting, becoming; gracious, ladylike, ladyish, courtly, gentlemanly, gentlemanlike; debonair, chivalrous, chivalric, gallant, cavalier.

2. polished, finished, refined, cultivated; urbane, suave, sophisticated, cosmopolitan; fashionable, stylish, à la mode, modish, high-toned, *Sl.* tony, high-class, *Sl.* classy, *Inf.* swank.

3. affected, mannered, unnatural; pretentious, *Inf.* highfalutin, *Inf.* high-hat, on one's high horse; haughty, lordly, hoity-toity, arrogant, proud, snobbish, disdainful; pompous, ostentatious, showy, flashy.

gentile, *n.* **1.** non-Jew, *Often Disparaging.* goy, *Yiddish.* shiksa, *Yiddish.* shegetz; uncircumcised man, Christian.

2. heathen, pagan, unbeliever, infidel, *Turkish. giaour;* alien, stranger, foreigner, outlander, outsider.

gentility, *n.* **1.** refinement, good-breeding, mannerliness, polished behavior, savoir-faire, courtliness, gentlemanliness, gallantry, chivalry, courtesy, politeness, civility, comity, decency; affability, amenity, *Fr. prévenance,* decorum, propriety, etiquette, conventionality, punctilio, formality; elegance, polish, urbanity, suavity, cultivation, culture, presence, dignity.

2. aristocracy, patriciate, nobility, *Fr. noblesse,* (*in Britain*) peerage, elite, upper class, ruling class; rank, distinction, gentle birth, good extraction, superior descent, good family, good blood, blue blood.

gentle, *adj.* **1.** kind, kindly, tender, gracious, considerate, thoughtful; indulgent, lenient, clement, humane, merciful, compassionate, tender-hearted, gentle-hearted, *Fr. gentil;* benign, amiable, affable, sweet-tempered.

2. mild, moderate, soothing, easy, soft, zephyr-like, balmy, light, bland, slight; smooth, unruffled, motionless, waveless, undisturbed; tranquil, calm, still, quiet, untroubled; halcyon, halcyonian, peaceful, pacific, irenic, reposeful, restful.

3. genteel, well-born, high-born, *Sl.* blue-blooded, noble; artistocratic, armigerous, patrician, royal, princely, titled, thoroughbred; of gentle birth, of good family, of good extraction, of superior descent.

4. respectable, honorable, proper, correct, suitable, acceptable, seemly; fitting, *Fr. comme il faut,* becoming; graceful, *Scot.* genty, fine, delicate; polished, refined, finished, cultivated, well-educated, well-schooled, well-trained; suave, sophisticated, urbane, cosmopolitan, worldly; polite, civil, courteous, decorous, well-mannered, mannerly, courtly, gracious; chivalric, chivalrous, well-bred, gentlemanly, gentlemanlike, ladylike.

5. meek, manageable, doçile, tractable, easily handled; tame, trained, schooled, broken; restrained, controlled, curbed; harmless, unaggressive, unbelligerent.

—*v.* **6.** mollify, pacify, appease; still, smooth, quiet, tranquilize, lull; soothe, stroke, pet, pat.

7. tame, break, subdue, dominate, gain control over, master.

gentleman, *n.* **1.** aristocrat, patrician, *Sl.* gent, (*in India*) sahib, *Inf.* blue blood; prince, noble, peer, lord, duke, marquis, monseigneur, earl, count, viscount, baron; grandee, magnifico, don, hidalgo, *Fr. Hist.* chevalier, knight, caballero.

2. squire, esquire, manservant, man, valet, gentleman's gentleman, butler, attendant, aide-de-camp, orderly, footman.

3. rich man, man of means, man of substance, capitalist, *Sl.* coupon-clipper, *Sl.* silk-stocking; landowner, gentleman-farmer.

gentlemanly, *adj.* genteel, well-bred, mannerly, well-mannered, well-behaved, courteous, polite, civil; courtly, chivalrous, gallant, brave, manly; thoughtful, considerate, agreeable, obliging, accommodating, compliant; decent, decorous, discreet, dependable, punctual, punctilious; refined, elegant, polished, suave, sophisticated, urbane; civilized, cultivated, well-educated, well-trained, poised, dignified.

gentry, *n.* **1.** gentlefolk, ladies and gentlemen, quality, better sort, elite; aristocracy, patriciate, upper classes, *Fr. crème de la crème, Inf.* upper crust, upper strata, *Sl.* silk-stockings, *Inf.* bigwigs, *Sl.* biggies, *Sl.* high muck-a-mucks, the high and the mighty.

2. landowners, *Chiefly Brit.* squirearchy, *Amer. Hist.* patroon, armigers, armigerous people.

genuflect, *v.* **1.** kneel, bow down; fall on one's knees; pay homage *or* tribute, make obeisance, admire, revere; worship, pray.

2. kowtow, salaam, curtsy; knuckle under, bow and scrape, eat humble pie; yield, concede, do [s.o.'s] bidding.

genuine, *adj.* **1.** authentic, real, *Dial.* sure-enough, simon-pure, sterling; the real McCoy; bona fide, veritable, *Sl.* real live, *Inf.* honest-to-goodness, *Inf.* kosher, *Archaic.* authentical, *Australian.* dinkum; legitimate, rightful, lawful, just, legal, licit; valid, authenticated, verified, confirmed; attested, vouched for, warranted, certified, guaranteed; standard, accepted, approved, conventional, orthodox.

2. sincere, heartfelt, earnest, all wool and a yard wide; unfeigned, unpretended, unaffected, natural; ingenuous, artless, guileless, innocent, naive, unsophisticated; simple, pure, undeceitful, honest, up front, truthful, veracious; frank, open, free, candid, plain, straightforward.

3. full-blooded, pure-blooded, *Fr. pur sang,* 100 percent; thoroughbred, purebred, pedigreed; out-and-out, thoroughgoing, unqualified, complete, thorough, absolute.

genus, *n.* subdivision, subfamily; class, kind, ilk, sort, type; category, genre, nature, denomination.

germ, *n.* **1.** microbe, microorganism, bacterium, bacillus, virus, *Inf.* bug.

2. beginning, commencement, start, inception, origin, alpha; embryo, bud, seed, root; source, fount, fountainhead.

germane, *adj.* relevant, pertinent, apropos, material, applicable; related, analagous, comparable, akin, allied; apposite, appropriate, apt, fitting, suited, felicitous.

germicide, *n.* antiseptic, disinfectant, fumigant, fumigator, bactericide, microbicide.

germinate, *v.* sprout, pullulate, burgeon, shoot up, spring up, push up, grow up; grow, develop, vegetate, flourish, thrive.

gestation, *n.* incubation, pregnancy, gravidity, parturiency, *Inf.* the family way.

gesticulate, *v.* gesture, motion, wave, flail the arms, saw the air; signal, signalize, nod, *Inf.* give [s.o.] the high sign *or* nod; hold up the finger, wiggle *or* crook one's finger, wag one's finger; give thumbs-down to; *All Disparaging. Sl.* give [s.o.] the finger, *Sl.* slip [s.o.] the bird, *Sl.* give [s.o.] figs *or* the pig, thumb one's nose, cock a *or* one's snook.

gesture, *n.* **1.** motion, movement, gesticulation, gest, *Theat.* stage business; sign, signal, broad hint, nod, nudge, wink, *Inf.* high sign; pantomime, charade, dumb show; body language, *Inf.* body English.

2. flourish, *Fr. beau geste,* fine gesture; display, show, demonstration.

—*v.* **3.** gesticulate, motion. See **gesticulate.**

get, *v.* **1.** receive, come by, realize, inherit, succeed to, fall into; gain, win, achieve, attain, reach; benefit, profit, avail; (*all usu. of wages*) earn, make, *Sl.* pull down, gross, clear, net, *Inf.* take home, pocket.

2. obtain, acquire, secure, procure, purchase, buy, pick up; take in, harvest, garner, reap, gather, collect, glean.

3. capture, seize, grasp, bag; grip, grab, lay hold of, collar; catch, entrap, ensnare; take, snatch.

4. fetch, go for *or* after, go get, *Hunting.* retrieve; bring to, convey to, transport, carry; collect, take away, haul away.

5. communicate with, reach, contact, get in touch with; write, drop a line *or* note, epistolize; telephone, *Inf.* phone, call, *Chiefly Brit.* ring *or* ring up, dial *or* dial up, *Inf.* buzz.

6. sense, perceive, hear, take in; grasp, apprehend, learn, *Inf.* catch on, *Inf.* get the hang of, *Inf.* get into *or* through one's head; master, lay hold of, *Inf.* get a fix *or* handle on; absorb, digest, assimilate.

7. *Informal.* comprehend, understand, see, fathom, follow, *Inf.* make heads or tails of.

8. prevail upon, persuade, induce, talk [s.o.] into [s.t.]; influence, sway, bring [s.o.] round, enlist, win over; wheedle, cajole, coax; bribe, suborn.

9. (*all usu. of animals*) beget, procreate, generate; father, sire; spawn, breed.

10. affect, move, stir, touch, touch to the quick, *Inf.* get to; arouse, stimulate, excite, *Inf.* turn [s.o.] on; grip, hold; impress, leave a mark on, make an impression on, have an impact on; soften, melt, mollify.

11. hit, strike, smite, slap, smack, punch, *Sl.* sock, *Inf.* slug, pummel, pelt; shoot; wound, hurt, harm, injure, damage.

12. take vengeance on, get back at, get even with; pay [s.o.] back, even *or* settle a score with, *Inf.* give [s.o.] a taste of his own medicine; retaliate, revenge, avenge, return like for like, give tit for tat, demand an eye for an eye.

13. suffer from, be afflicted *or* visited with, be sick *or* ill with, have.

14. *Slang.* irritate, annoy, vex, pique, *Sl.* bug; provoke, anger, nettle, rankle, exasperate, aggravate; grate on, rub [s.o.] the wrong way; disconcert, unsettle, agitate, disquiet, perturb; ruffle, rattle, fluster; confound, confuse, nonplus, baffle, bewilder, perplex, puzzle.

15. become, come to be, turn into, change into; grow, wax.

16. begin, commence, start, set about.

17. **get across** make [s.t.] understood *or* clear, communicate, get [s.t.] over *or* through to [s.o.], reach; convey, transmit, impart.

18. **get ahead** prosper, flourish, thrive, make good, do well, succeed, be successful; rise up in the world, achieve prestige *or* status, *Sl.* go places, *Sl.* get somewhere.

19. **get around a.** circumvent, outwit, outsmart, outmaneuver. **b.** cajole, flatter, wheedle, coax. **c.** socialize, travel, get about, circulate, visit, entertain.

20. **get back a.** return, come back, arrive home; come again, revisit. **b.** recover, regain, recoup, retrieve. **c.** be avenged. See **get** (*def.* **12**).

21. **get behind** support, endorse, second, back, finance, *Inf.* angel; promote, push, plug, *Inf.* hype, talk up.

22. **get by** cope, manage; subsist, fare, survive, get along; keep body and soul together, keep the wolf from the door, make both ends meet, keep one's head above water.

23. **get on a.** progress, advance, proceed, move forward, gain ground. **b.** manage, survive. See **get** (*def.* **22**). **c.** get along with, be compatible with, be congenial with. **d.** grow older, advance in age; become senile *or* debilitated, weaken, *Rare.* senesce; age, mature, ripen.

24. **get out a.** leave, depart, go away, be off, *Sl.* split, *Inf.* vamoose; withdraw from, retire from, get out of. **b.** make public, publicize, spread, circulate, broadcast, bruit about, noise abroad; become public *or* known. **c.** eject, expel, throw out, *Sl.* bounce.

25. **get over a.** recover from, recuperate, pull through, get well, rally. **b.** forget, write [s.t.] off, think no more of, come round, be reconciled, let bygones be bygones.

26. **get together a.** accumulate, gather, assemble, amass, compile. **b.** congregate, meet, socialize, *Inf.* party, visit. **c.** agree, concur, compromise, meet halfway, come to terms, reach a settlement *or* agreement, come to an understanding.

—*n.* **27.** (*usu. of animals*) offspring, progeny, issue; litter, brood, spawn, hatch.

28. *Sports.* return, save.

getup, *n. Informal.* **1.** format, style, mode, fashion, vogue, look.

2. costume, outfit, trappings, *Inf.* rig, *Inf.* turnout; dress, garb, apparel, clothes, clothing, attire.

get up and go, *n.* energy, vigor, vim, vitality, life, bounce, *Inf.* starch, *Inf.* zip, *Inf.* pep, *Sl.* oomph; enthusiasm, desire, drive, push, initiative, ambition.

gewgaw, *n.* gimcrack, *Inf.* whim-wham, bauble, trinket, knickknack, doodad, bagatelle, trifle, kickshaw, brummagem, toy, plaything; gaud, showy ornament, spangle, sequin, tinsel, clinquant; worthless finery, frippery, *Archaic.* trumpery, junk; bric-a-brac, miscellany, odds and ends, bits and pieces.

ghastly, *adj.* **1.** frightful, dreadful, awful, terrible, horrid, horrible, horrendous, hideous, ugly, frightening, terrifying, *Inf.* scary; gruesome, grisly, gory, disgusting, repulsive, repugnant, revolting, sickening, *Sl.* gross.

2. drawn, haggard, worn, *Inf.* beat, drained, washed-out; pale, pale-faced, pallid, wan, blanched, ashen, colorless, hueless; pasty, pasty-faced, white, white as a sheet, white as a ghost, ghostly, ghost-like, spectral; cadaverous, corpse-like, deathlike, like death warmed over.

3. terrible, very bad, unforgiveable, abominable, abhorrent, apalling, shocking; odious, heinous, criminal, foul, loathesome, contemptible; mean, nasty, dirty, low, base.

ghost, *n.* **1.** spirit, soul, shade, (*all in Roman religion*) manes, lemures, larvae; specter, *Inf.* spook, revenant, wraith, (*in Irish folklore*) banshee; Doppelganger, doubleganger; apparition, phantom, eidolon, phantasm, phantasma, materialization, illusion, delusion, hallucination, mirage, image, representation.

2. demon, devil, evil spirit; goblin, hobgoblin, boogeyman.

3. shadow, trace, hint, suggestion, impression, semblance, appearance.

ghostly, *adj.* **1.** ghost-like, spectral, phantom-like; unreal, illusory, illusive, shadowy, phantasmal, phantasmic, phantasmical, phantasmatic; supernatural, preternatural, unearthly, wierd, strange, uncanny, mysterious, frightening, *Inf.* scary, *Inf.* spooky, haunted.

2. ghastly, pale, white, white as a sheet, white as a ghost. See **ghastly** (*def.* **2**).

ghoul, *n.* **1.** demon, devil, evil spirit, fiend, succubus, incubus, lamia; goblin, hobgoblin, bogy, bogyman; monster, ogre, brute, savage; cannibal, maneater, anthropophagite; vampire, werewolf.

2. grave robber, body snatcher; necrophile, necrophiliac.

ghoulish, *adj.* **1.** fiendish, diabolic, diabolical, devilish; satanic, Mephistophelian, demonian, demonic, demoniacal, cacodemonic; infernal, hellish, hellborn.

2. inhuman, barbarous, barbaric, savage, Tartarian, Hunnish, Vandalic; brutal, brutish, murderous, slaughterous, bloodthirsty, sadistic; ferocious, ruthless, vicious, feral, ferine; pitiless, merciless, heartless, cruel, cold-blooded; monstrous, hideous, abominable, horrible, horrid, horrendous, accursed, damnable.

giant, *n.* **1.** colossus, titan, man-mountain, giantess, Amazon, (*collective*) nephilim; Goliath, Pantagruel, Brobdingnagian, Antaeus, Cyclops, Briareus, Cottus, Gyges, Gog, Magog, Og, King Kong, Paul Bunyan; behemoth, leviathan, monster, mammoth, mastodon, dinosaur; elephant, jumbo, whale, hippopotamus, hippo.

2. strongman, Hercules, Samson, muscleman, powerhouse, tower of strength; bruiser, stalwart, *Inf.* big guy, Superman, Tarzan; strapper, hulk, block, *Inf.* whopper, *Inf.* thumper.

—adj. **3.** huge, enormous, colossal. See **gigantic.**

4. great, eminent, celebrated, grand, distinguished, illustrious; prominent, influential, renowned, notable, famous, famed.

gibber, *v.* **1.** babble, prate, tattle, twaddle, *Brit.* twattle; patter, gabble, blather, drivel, *Sl.* gibber-jabber, jargon; mutter, mumble, splutter, sputter, stammer.

2. chatter, jabber, prattle, cackle, speak foolishly; chit-chat, chitter-chatter, chaffer, bandy words; gossip, buzz, talk idly, *Sl.* gas, *Inf.* gab, *Sl.* bull; palaver, clack, clatter, rattle, *Sl.* run off *or* on at the mouth; gush, blab, *Inf.* spout; be talkative, ramble, maunder.

—n. **3.** gibberish, nonsense, gobbledegook. See **gibberish** (*def.* **1**).

gibberish, *n.* **1.** jabber, Jabberwocky, chatter, prattle, cackle, gibber; babble, babblement, prate, tattle, twaddle; patter, gabble, blather; jargon, gobbledegook, nonsense, hocus-pocus, mumbo-jumbo, abracadabra, open-sesame; babbling, *Fr. bavardage;* humbug, flummery, *Sl.* bunk, rubbish, *Inf.* rot, *Sl.* garbage, *Sl.* horsefeathers; balderdash, hogwash, stuff and nonsense, fudge, foolishness, rigmarole *or* rigamarole; poppycock, *Inf.* fiddle-faddle, *Inf.* piffle, drivel, *Inf.* bosh, *Inf.* kibosh, *Inf.* flapdoodle; small talk, *Sl.* bull.

2. palaver, claptrap, rodomontade, *Sl.* hot air, *Sl.* gas, pretentious talk; wordiness, verbosity, prolixity, prolixness, verbiage, verbalism; diffuseness, profuseness, effusion, effusiveness, gushing; obfuscation, padding, redundancy, superfluous words.

gibbet, *n.* gallows, *Archaic.* bough, scaffold, *Brit.* Tyburn tree.

gibe, *v.* **1.** jeer, mock, sneer at, jibe, gird; ridicule, knock, deride, scoff at; taunt, tease, twit, rag, chaff, rib, kid, *Sl.* razz; hiss, boo, heckle, hoot at, rail at, catcall.

—n. **2.** jeer, jibe, fleer, raillery, chaff; poke, dig, cut, rub, barb; taunt, quip, wisecrack, thrust, skit; boo, hiss, hoot, catcall, cry, raspberry; derision, mockery, ridicule, sarcasm.

giddy, *adj.* **1.** frivolous, light-hearted, carefree, insouciant, irresponsible; impulsive, fickle, erratic, flippant, changeable, inconstant; whimsical, capricious, crotchety, notional; flighty, airy, light-minded, birdwitted, scatterbrained, hare-brained; mercurial, volatile, flyaway, skittish.

2. dizzy, vertiginous, light-headed, faint; unsteady, reeling, *Inf.* woozy, muddled, confused.

gift, *n.* **1.** present, favor, *Scot.* propine, endowment; *Law.* acquest, *Law.* bequest, *Law.* legacy, heritage, inheritance, dowry; benefaction, bounty, largess, donation, donative, contribution, offering, *Eccles.* offertory, *Eccles.* alterage, peace offering; bonus, prize, premium, giveaway, freebie, benefit, blessing, boon; charity, alms, dole, gratuity, honorarium, tip, fee, *Fr. pourboire,* (*in India, Turkey, etc.*) baksheesh, (*in chinese ports*) cumshaw, handout; grant, aid, allowance, allotment, stipend, subsidy, subvention.

2. presentation, bestowal, conferment, conferral, benefaction, donation, contribution; endowment, endowing, granting, subsidizing; offertory, almsgiving, charity.

3. talent, faculty, endowment, genius, facility, flair, bent, turn, knack, forte, strong point, dowry; aptitude, intelligence, mother wit, ingenuity, cleverness, aptness, mind for.

4. ability, ableness, capacity, capability, potential, potentiality, potency, power; skill, skillfulness, dexterity, adroitness, address, deftness, knowhow, savoir-faire.

—v. **5.** present, give, bestow, confer, proffer, *Archaic.* propine; endow, will, leave, *Law.* bequeath, *Law.* devise, dower; largess, donate, contribute, offer; dole, tip, (*in India, Turkey, etc.*) basksheesh.

gifted, *adj.* **1.** talented, well-endowed; skillful, skilled, dexterous, adroit, deft, *Brit. Dial.* feat; expert, masterful, masterly, *Fr. au fait;* topflight, top drawer, first-rate, *Inf.* topnotch, ace, *Inf.* crack, *Sl.* crackerjack, *Sl.* on the ball, *Inf.* whiz-bang, *Brit. Sl.* whizzo; able, capable, competent, proficient, adept, good at, accomplished, finished, polished.

2. intelligent, brilliant, apt, clever, ingenious; astute, bright, agile, quick, smart, acute, sharp.

gigantic, *adj.* enormous, huge, large, immense, prodigious, herculean; cyclopean, titanic, Brobdingnagian, Atlantean; mammoth, jumbo, colossal, monumental, monstrous, gigantean; great, great big, towering, staggering, mountainous, stupendous, tremendous, *Sl.* humongous; elephantine, hippopotamic, leviathan, dinosaurian, dinotherian, megatherian; oversize, kingsize, overlarge; *All Inf.* whopping, spanking, walloping, strapping, thundering, thumping.

giggle, *v.* snicker, snigger, titter, teehee, ha-ha, *Sl.* yuk-yuk; laugh, chortle, chuckle.

gigolo, *n.* **1.** (*all hired*) escort, companion, dancing partner, *It. cicisbeo.*

2. pimp, pander, procurer.

3. paramour, lover, amorist, gallant, *Archaic.* leman.

4. playboy, ladykiller, ladies' man, man about town; cad, two-timer, *Derogatory.* male chauvinist *or* male chauvinist pig.

gild, *v.* **1.** gilt, aurify, aureate, make golden, inlay *or* outlay with gold; coat, plate, electroplate; enamel, lacquer, paint.

2. decorate, embellish, furbish, adorn, brighten up, cheer up; bedizen, bedeck, deck out, deck, array, *Archaic.* bedight; dress up, dress, caparison, *Inf.* doll up, *Inf.* pretty up, beautify, prettify; enrich, enhance, polish, smarten.

3. sugarcoat, coat, whitewash, window-dress; disguise, camouflage, conceal.

gimcrack, *n.* gewgaw, bauble, trifle, trinket. See **gewgaw.**

gimmick, *n.* contrivance, device, *Inf.* contraption, invention, apparatus, gadget, hickey; design, plan, scheme, strategy; stratagem, *Inf.* wrinkle, artifice, trick, *Inf.* flimflam, wile, ruse, ploy, trap; subterfuge, blind, *Inf.* dodge, fetch; maneuver, deception, feint, sleight, shift, shuffle; catch, snag, hitch, rub, drawback, fly in the ointment.

gimmicky, *adj.* contrived, devised, faked, false, *Sl.* hokey; commercial, plastic, *Sl.* mickey mouse, artificial; tricky, wily, shifty, deceitful, deceptive.

gin, *n.* trap, snare, ensnarement, noose, pitfall, net, toil; decoy, lure, bait, hook.

gingerly, *adv.* cautiously, charily, warily, cannily, carefully, heedfully, attentively; prudently, politicly, discreetly, judiciously, circumspectly; watchfully, vigilantly, guardedly, timidly, timorously, shyly.

gird, *v.* **1.** encircle, circle, *Archaic., Poetic.* cincture; belt, bind, truss, girdle, begird; wrap, swathe, swaddle, bandage; buckle, strap, tie, hitch, pinion, fasten, secure.

2. encompass, compass, circumscribe, circumvent, environ, ring, loop, ensphere, surround; confine, enclose, hem in, hedge, pen, coop.

3. *Usu.* **gird oneself** strengthen, fortify, brace, buttress, steel, harden, prepare.

girdle, *n.* **1.** corset, *Chiefly Brit.* stays, *Obs.* bodice, corselet; foundation garment, panty girdle, garter belt, *Sl.* undie; back brace, *Med.* truss.

2. belt, sash, obi, waistband, cummerbund, cestus, *Archaic.* zone, *Archaic., Poetic.* cincture; baldric, cord, cordon, braid, thong, strap, (*for a horse*) surcingle.

3. circumference, perimeter, edge, skirt; circuit, compass, ambit, outline, confine; bound, limit, border, boundary.

—*v.* **4.** encircle, belt, wrap, gird. See **gird** (*def.* **1**).

5. enclose, encompass, environ, gird. See **gird** (*def.* **2**).

girl, *n.* **1.** female child, lass, lassie, *Inf.* filly, maid, maiden, *Irish. Eng.* colleen; miss, mademoiselle, young lady, demoiselle, *Archaic.* damoiselle, damsel; young unmarried woman, *Ger. Fräulein,* virgin; wench, *Inf.* gal, *Inf.* petticoat, *Inf.* number, *Inf.* baggage, flapper; soubrette, nymph, nymphet, Lolita; minx, hoyden, tomboy, romp.

2. maidservant, *Fr. bonne,* handmaid, lady's maid, abigail; help, cook, domestic, scullion.

3. girlfriend, sweetheart, darling, lady love, fiancée, betrothed; inamorata, lover, mistress.

girth, *n.* **1.** circumference, perimeter, periphery, edge, rim; circuit, compass, ambit, frame, outline, confine; bound, limit, bourn, pale; border, boundary, line.

2. surcingle, strap, thong, braid, cord, cordon, baldric; band, belt, girdle, sash, waistband, cummerbund, cestus, *Archaic.* zone, *Archaic., Poetic.* cincture.

gist, *n.* substance, essence, quintessence, quiddity, suchness, elixir; heart, soul, backbone, lifeblood; core, nucleus, kernel, pith; keystone, essential, *Latin. sine qua non*, crux; sum and substance, burden, bulk, better part.

give, *v.* **1.** bestow, present, donate, contribute; turn over, hand over; confer, award; accord, grant, vouchsafe; leave, entrust.

2. allot, apportion, assign, allocate; mete out, distribute, dispense, dole, *Inf.* fork out, hand out, supply; *Inf.* shell out, *Inf.* dish out, pay.

3. offer, set forth; show, display; evidence, manifest, indicate, demonstrate.

4. consign, yield, relinquish; concede, surrender, give up, let go.

5. furnish, proffer, provide, lend, offer.

6. produce, result in, put out, afford; cause, occasion, make.

7. impart, communicate, transmit; send, purvey, convey, transfer, render.

8. deal, deliver; administer, execute; pay.

9. collapse, break down, buckle; fall apart, come apart; fail, expire.

10. **give away a.** reveal, let slip, disclose, divulge, expose, let the cat out of the bag. **b.** betray, blow the whistle on, *Sl.* rat on, *Sl.* fink on.

11. **give off** emit, send out, exude, throw out, pour out.

12. **give up a.** despair, despond, lose *or* abandon hope, lose heart, falter. **b.** stop, desist from, quit, *Inf.* call it quits, swear off, cut out; renounce, forswear, forgo, reject, *Inf.* chuck; forsake, leave, desert, abandon. **c.** concede, acquiesce, submit, give in; succumb; draw in one's horns, put one's tail between one's legs, retreat, retire; surrender, turn up one's toes, capitulate, cry *or* say uncle, throw in the towel *or* sponge.

give-and-take, *n.* **1.** cooperation, interaction, joint effort, mutual effort, collaboration; reciprocity, *Inf.* back scratching, exchange of favors, bartering, *Chiefly U.S.* logrolling; compromising, finding a happy medium *or* a middle ground.

2. banter, bantering, badinage, raillery, back-and-forth, volleying, crossfire; interchange, exchange, conversation, *Inf.* rapping, *Inf.* shooting the breeze *or* the bull.

give-away, *n.* **1.** slip, letting the cat out of the bag, betrayal; disclosure, revelation, divulgence, blurting; hint, clue, inkling, idea, intimation.

2. premium, dividend, bonus, benefit; gift, present, *Inf.* freebie.

given, *adj.* 1. stated, fixed, specified, settled, arranged, appointed, agreed upon; set, prearranged, preordained.

2. addicted, given over to, devoted, dedicated to, prone to, accustomed, attached to, habituated, in the habit of, used to; inclined toward, disposed toward, predisposed, wont.

3. conferred, bestowed, accorded, presented, awarded, delivered, handed over; donated, granted.

4. assumed, understood, taken for granted, postulated, presupposed, conceded; submitted, proposed, declared, pronounced; allowed, acknowledged, recognized.

giver, *n.* donor, donator, grantor, contributor, benefactor, supporter, backer, angel; fairy godmother, Santa Claus, Father Christmas.

glacial, *adj.* 1. icy, ice cold, bitterly cold, frigid, gelid, freezing, frozen, polar, arctic, Siberian, wintry, hiemal.

2. unfeeling, cold-blooded, cold-hearted, cold; unsympathetic, unmoved, immovable.

glad, *adj.* 1. delighted, elated, well-pleased, well-contented, thrilled, tickled, *Inf.* tickled pink, pleased as punch, *Dial.* in hog heaven, *Brit. Sl.* chuffed; pleased, contented, gratified, satisfied.

2. cheering, pleasing, gratifying, satisfying; encouraging, enheartening, inspiring; delightful, gladsome; exhilarating, invigorating, animating, enlivening.

3. gay, merry, jolly, jovial, light-hearted, gleeful, cheerful, mirthful, frivolous; happy, bright, airy, sunny; joyous, jubilant, cock-a-hoop; playful, frolicsome, sportive, gamesome; festive, convivial, rollicking.

4. willing, more than willing, ready, unreluctant, unloath, nothing loath.

gladden, *v.* cheer, animate, vivify, enliven, brighten, hearten, enhearten, embolden; delight, elate, exhilarate, fill with joy, pleasure, tickle, *Inf.* tickle pink; inspire, raise the spirits, pick up, buoy up, boost, *Inf.* give a lift.

gladly, *adv.* cheerfully, happily, smilingly, with pleasure; willingly, ungrudgingly, unreluctantly, with good grace, *Archaic.* fain; delightedly, joyfully, joyously; gaily, lightheartedly, cheerily, merrily, gleefully, mirthfully, laughingly; enthusiastically, exuberantly, animatedly, heartily, spiritedly, vivaciously, zestfully, with zest, with gusto.

gladness, *n.* cheer, cheerfulness, gayness, gaiety; good *or* high spirits, blitheness, blithesomeness, lightheartedness, buoyancy; joy, delight, pleasure, happiness, felicity; joyfulness, joyousness, jubilation, exhilaration, exultation, glee, elation; joviality, merriment, jollity, mirth, mirthfulness, hilarity.

gladsome, *adj.* 1. cheering, pleasing, gladdening, gratifying, satisfying; happy, glad, good, pleasant, encouraging, heartening, enheartening, inspiring; exhilarating, invigorating, animating, enlivening; refreshing, stimulating, quickening, stirring, exciting.

2. gay, merry, jolly, cheerful; joyous, jubilant; playful, frolicsome, sportive. See also **glad** (*def.* 3).

glamorous, *adj.* 1. charming, attractive, alluring, inviting, enticing, tempting, tantalizing, irresistible; captivating, provocative, intriguing, fascinating, entrancing, beguiling, intoxicating, bewitching, enrapturing; interesting, appealing, piquant; irresistible, magnetizing, hypnotizing, mesmerizing; enchanting, bewitching, enthralling, enravishing.

2. exciting, thrilling, spine-tingling, electrifying, hair-raising, *Inf.* far-out, *Inf.* rip-roaring; stimulating, stirring, rousing, inspiring, invigorating, excitant, excitative; moving, impelling, compelling, soul-stirring, heart-moving; overpowering, overwhelming, overcoming.

3. fantastic, fabulous, enviable, once-in-a-lifetime, stupendous, never-to-be-forgotten.

glamour, *n.* 1. excitement, adventure, commotion, *Inf.* razzle-dazzle, brouhaha, hubbub, fuss, flurry, flutter, fluster, bustle, to-do; glitter, tinsel, sparkle, pizzazz.

2. charm, attractiveness, appeal, desirability, desirableness; beauty, beautifulness, pulchritude, loveliness, prettiness, comeliness.

3. magic, spell, influence, rune, *Scot.* cantrip, enchantment, bewitchment, bedevilment; illusion, delusion, mirage; fascination, delight, entrancement, enravishment; captivation, attraction, possession, obsession; bliss, rapture, transport.

4. temptation, allurement, seduction, beguilement; voice of the Sirens, forbidden fruit.

glance, *v.* 1. look quickly *or* briefly, cast a brief look at, catch a glimpse of, snatch a glimpse, glimpse, look hurriedly, regard hastily, peek, peep, sneak a look *or* peek, squint; observe, witness, view, behold, contemplate, see; pray, watch for, be on the lookout, scan.

2. flash, gleam, glare, coruscate; glitter, glimmer, glisten, *Archaic.* glister, glint, scintillate; shimmer, shine, flicker, sparkle, twinkle, reflect.

3. bounce off, fly off, ricochet, rebound, carom; skim, touch, graze, brush, lick, kiss.

4. allude, make an allusion to, cite, refer to, advert to, point to, speak of; mention, mention in passing, touch upon; hint at, intimate, suggest, insinuate.

—*n.* 5. brief look, look, quick view, *Scot.* glisk, peek, peep, *Fr. coup d'oeil, Scot.* blink; *Inf.* once-over, *Inf.* look-see, *Sl.* gander; vision, ken.

6. flash, gleam, glitter, glimmer, glint; shimmer, flicker, sparkle, twinkle, reflection.

7. ricochet, rebound, carom; graze, brush, lick, kiss.

8. allusion, reference, intimation, suggestion, passing mention, insinuation, innuendo, hint.

glare, *n.* 1. brilliance, brightness, dazzling, splendor, resplendence; shine, luster, illumination, luminosity, effulgence, radiance; blinding flash, harsh *or* strong light, intensity, vividness; blaze, flare, flame, fulguration, coruscation, scintillation; glittering, glistening, glistering, glimmering; shimmering, sparkling, twinkling; flickering, fluttering, fluctuating, oscillation, vacillating; glint, gleam, sheen, gloss.

2. glower, scowl, lower, frown, angry *or* fierce look; black *or* dark look, dirty *or* nasty look; riveting *or* fixing gaze, scrutinization, piercing stare; long face, moping, fretting, pouting, sulking.

3. showiness, flauntiness, floridness, showy appearance; gaudiness, garishness, ostentation, extravagance; flashiness, vividness, brightness, gayness, colorfulness, distinctness; loudness, cheapness, tawdriness, meretriciousness.

—*v.* 4. light, illuminate, effulge, shine brilliantly; dazzle, blind, gleam, flash; beam, streak, coruscate, fulgurate; shimmer, flicker, twinkle, glimmer, glitter, sparkle; glint, glisten, *Archaic.* glister, flutter; flare, spark, scintillate, fluctuate, oscillate; flame, blaze, burn; radiate, incandesce, phosphoresce.

5. glower, gloat, scowl, lower, frown; stare angrily, look at darkly *or* blackly; look daggers, menace, threaten.

glaring, *adj.* 1. dazzling, brilliant, very bright, resplendent; shining, lustrous, illuminating, radiating; bedazzling, dazing, blinding, overpowering, intense, strong, harsh, vivid; blazing, flaring, flaming, flash-

ing, fulgurating, coruscating; glittering, glistening, *Archaic.* glistering, glimmering; shimmering, sparkling, twinkling; flickering, fluttering, scintillating, fluctuating, oscillating, vacillating.
2. showy, flaunting, ostentatious, flashy; garish, gaudy, tawdry, loud, cheap, meretricious, *Inf.* tacky; bright, gay, florid, distinct; gorgeous, colorific, color ful, chromatic.
3. obvious, conspicuous, evident, apparent, patent, prominent; overt, open, manifest, undisguised; flagrant, blatant, egregious, extreme, heinous, outrageous, notorious; audacious, impudent, bold, brazen; shameless, immodest.
4. staring *or* looking angrily, glowering, lowering, scowling, frowning, giving a dirty look; ogling, scrutinizing, riveting, fixing; sulking, pouting, moping.

glass, *n.* **1.** crystal, (*in prescriptions*) vitrium; silica, quartz, agate, granite, obsidian.
2. window, pane, glazing; mirror, looking glass, speculum.
3. tumbler, beaker, connikin, goblet, chalice, wine glass; glassware, crystal, vitrics.
4. lens, eyepiece, ocular, magnifying glass, microscope; spyglass, telescope, reflector.
5. barometer, mercury barometer, aneroid barometer, barograph, altimeter, altigraph, *Meteorol.* aneroid barograph.
6. glasses eyeglasses, spectacles, *Inf.* specs, bifocals, pince-nez, contact lenses, *Inf.* lenses; eyeglass, monocle; lorgnon, lorgnette, opera glasses, field glasses, binoculars.

glassy, *adj.* **1.** vitreous, vitric, vitriform, crystal, crystalline, glasslike; clear, crystal clear, transparent, transpicuous, lucid, limpid, pellucid, translucent, diaphanous; mirrorlike, reflective, reflecting, glossy, shiny, shining, gleaming, shimmering; smooth, slick, icelike, icy.
2. expressionless, blank, empty, vacuous, void; dull, poker-faced, sphinxlike, deadpan, dead; glassy-eyed, staring, gazing, in a daze, in a trance, hypnotic, hypnotized; fixed, unmoving, motionless, still.

glaze, *v.* **1.** gloss, luster, polish, shine, furbish, burnish; paint, color, enamel; candy, sugarcoat.
—*n.* **2.** gloss, polish, shine, burnish, luster, finish, patina; icing, frosting.

gleam, *n.* **1.** flash, glare, beam, ray, shaft; streak, lightning, patch, coruscation, fulguration; shimmer, flicker, twinkle, glitter, glimmer; sparkle, shine, glint, glistening; flutter, flare, spark, scintilla.
2. subdued light, glow, incandescence; luminosity, phosphorescence; luster, shine, iridescence; splendor, brilliance, radiance, refulgency, effulgence.
3. brief manifestation, trace, vestige; scintilla, glimmering, inkling; evidence, indication, impression.
—*v.* **4.** beam, glare, radiate, shine, illuminate; light, lighten, brighten, illumine, *Archaic.* illume, irradiate, gloze; glow, phosphoresce, incandesce.
5. flash, streak, glint, dart, fulgurate; shimmer, glitter, twinkle, flicker; glisten, *Archaic.* glister, glimmer, flutter; sparkle, scintillate, coruscate.

glean, *v.* **1.** (*all slowly or laboriously*) collect, gather, cull, harvest, reap, take in, pick up, pull in.
2. discover, learn, find out, hear of, catch wind of.

glee, *n.* merriment, jollity, joviality, mirth, mirthfulness, hilarity; joyfulness, joyousness, jubilation, exhilaration, exultation, elation, rapture, exuberance; joy, delight, pleasure, happiness, felicity, bliss; cheerfulness, cheer, gladness, gaiety, gayness; good *or* high spirits, blitheness, blithesomeness, light-heartedness.

gleeful, *adj.* gay, merry, jolly, jovial, light-hearted, cheerful, mirthful, frivolous, gleesome; glad, happy, bright, sunny, airy; joyous, jubilant, exultant, cock-a-hoop, overjoyed, beside oneself.

glib, *adj.* slick, smooth, smooth-tongued, smooth-talking, smooth-spoken, fast-talking; oily, unctuous, suave, fluent, fluid, easy; talkative, loquacious, garrulous, voluble, prolix, verbose, long-winded, possessed of the gift of gab.

glide, *v.* **1.** slide, move smoothly, glissade, slip; skim, graze, brush; sail, skate, float, drift along; flow, stream, coast, roll, issue.
2. elapse, lapse, pass by, steal away, proceed, roll on.
3. *Aeronautics.* volplane, plane, soar, drift.
—*v.* **4.** continuous motion, smooth movement, sliding, glissade, gliding; floating, drifting, flowing, rolling, streaming.

glimmer, *n.* **1.** gleam, glare, fulguration, coruscation; shimmer, flicker, twinkle, glitter, *Scot.* glisk, sparkle, glistening; spark, scintilla, trace.
2. inkling, dim perception, vague notion, feeling.
—*v.* **3.** gleam, glare, effulge, fulgurate, coruscate; streak, stream, beam; glitter, glister, glint; shimmer, shine, flicker, sparkle, twinkle.

glimpse, *n.* **1.** brief look, look, glance, *Fr. aperçu, Scot.* glisk, *Fr. coup d'oeil.* See **glance** (*def.* **5**).
2. inkling, vague notion, dim perception, feeling.
—*v.* **3.** catch sight of, *Sl.* get a load of, take in, look on *or* upon, set *or* lay eyes on, see with one's own eyes.
4. glance, look quickly *or* briefly, cast a brief look at, peep, peek. See **glance** (*def.* **1**).

glint, *n.* **1.** glimmer, glimmering, glinting, glistening, glistering; twinkle, twinkling, shining, sparkle, sparkling; spark, scintillation, scintilla; flicker, flickering, flutter, fluttering, quivering, shivering, ripple, rippling; shimmer, shimmering, dancing, dazzling, bedazzling, dazzle, bedazzlement; flash, flashing, flare, flaring, fulguration; gleam, gleaming, glare, glaring, coruscation.
2. luster, sheen, shine, gloss; polish, burnish, reflection, reflected light; glow, illumination, radiance, brilliance; incandescence, phosphorescence, iridescence, opalescence.
3. inkling, trace, vestige, scintilla; indication, evidence, impression; show, showing, apparition, emergence, brief manifestation *or* occurrence; happening, incident, incidence.
—*v.* **4.** glimmer, glitter, glisten, *Archaic.* glister; shine, sparkle, twinkle, light, spark, scintillate; flicker, blink, wink, flutter; quiver, shiver, ripple; shimmer, dance, dazzle, bedazzle; flash, flare, fulgurate, gleam, glare, coruscate; brighten, illuminate, illumine, make lustrous *or* radiant, glow; reflect, make iridescent, incandesce, phosphoresce.
5. dart, dartle, dash, *Inf.* scoot, scuttle, *Inf.* skedaddle; run, sprint, scud, tear; rush, hasten, hurry; fly, run like the wind, race, streak; bolt, bound, spring, leap; start quickly, *Sl.* tear off, *Inf.* take off.

glisten, *v.* **1.** glint, glimmer, glitter, *Archaic.* glister, reflect; sparkle, twinkle, flicker; blink, wink, flutter, flare *or* flare up; waver, sway, quiver, shiver, ripple; shimmer, dance, dazzle, bedazzle; light, spark, scintillate, flame; flash, fulgurate, gleam, glare, coruscate; oscillate, vacillate, fluctuate; move to and fro, undulate, vibrate; tremble, twitter, twitch, shudder.
2. glow, gleam faintly, shine; luminesce, incandesce, phosphoresce, make radiant *or* lustrous; illuminate, illumine, *Archaic.* illume, *Obs.* enlumine; brighten, light up, cast light upon, make brilliant *or* luminous; radiate, irradiate, effulge; shine forth, beam, stream.
—*n.* **3.** glint, glinting, glimmer, glimmering, glis-

tening, glister, glistering, glittering; shining, sparkling, sparkle, spark, twinkling, twinkle, scintillation, scintilla; flickering, flicker, fluttering, flutter, quivering, quiver, shivering, shiver, rippling, ripple; shimmering, shimmer, dancing, dazzling, dazzle, bedazzling; flash, flare, fulguration, gleam, gleaming, glare, coruscation; oscillating, oscillation, vacillating, vacillation, fluctuating, fluctuation; undulation, undulating, vibrating, vibration, trembling, twittering, twitching, shuddering.

4. glow, afterglow, faint gleam *or* glare, shine; luster, gloss, sheen, iridescence, incandescence, phosphorescence, radiance; brilliance, illumination; luminosity, luminance; refulgence, refulgency, refulgentness, effulgence; beam, ray, shaft, streak, patch, subdued *or* tremulous light.

glitter, *v.* **1.** glint, glimmer, glisten, *Archaic.* glister; shine, sparkle, twinkle, light, spark, scintillate; flicker, blink, wink, flutter; quiver, shiver, ripple; shimmer, dance, dazzle, bedazzle; flash, flare, fulgurate, gleam, glare, coruscate; brighten, illuminate, illumine, make lustrous *or* radiant.

2. flaunt, show off, put on a show, *Inf.* put on the dog; exhibit, disport, air, display ostentatiously; parade, swagger, strut, swashbuckle.

—n. **3.** glint, glimmer, glistening, glister, glistering, twinkling; shining, sparkling, spark, scintillation, scintilla; flickering, fluttering, quivering, shivering, rippling; shimmering, dancing, dazzling, bedazzling; flash, flare, fulguration, gleam, glare, coruscation; illumination, glow, radiance, incandescence, phosphorescence, iridescence; luster, sheen, gloss, shine, reflected light.

4. showiness, flauntiness, floridness, showy splendor, pomp, pomposity, pompousness, fanfare, *Inf.* razzle-dazzle; gaudiness, garishness, ostentation, parade, pageantry, spectacle; flashiness, flash, pizzazz, vividness, brightness, gayness, colorfulness; radiance, resplendence, splendor, resplendency, brilliant display *or* exhibition.

gloat, *v.* **1.** relish, enjoy, take great pleasure in, delight in, revel in; rejoice, triumph, glory in, exult, *Inf.* rub it in, lord it over; boast, crow about, brag, vaunt, talk up.

2. glare, look hard at, stare at, ogle, eye, leer.

global, *adj.* **1.** world-wide, universal; extensive, broad, vast, far-reaching, wide-ranging; encyclopedic, comprehensive, all-inclusive, exhaustive, complete, thorough.

2. globular, globulous, globe-shaped, globate, globoid, globose, globelike; spherical, spheroidal, orbicular, orbiculate, round, rounded, rotund, bulbous, bulb-shaped; oval, ovate, oviform, ovoid, egg-shaped; elliptical, ellipsoidal, circular, cyclindrical, cyclindroid; bell-shaped, campanulate; pear-shaped, pyriform.

globe, *n.* **1.** *Usu.* **the globe** the planet earth, the world, terrene, terra, the whole world, the universe.

2. planet, moon, star, heavenly *or* celestial body, orb.

3. terrestrial globe, celestial globe; map of the world.

4. sphere, ball, orb, round, globoid; globule, spherule, spheroid, oval.

globe-trotter, *n.* jet-setter, world traveler, *Sl.* W.T.; voyager, excursionist, tourist, sight-seer, itinerant, peripatetic, traveler, wayfarer, peregrinator; migrant, gadabout, rambler, rover, wanderer, nomad, gypsy.

globular, *adj.* global, globulous, globe-shaped, globate, globose. See **global** (*def.* **2**).

globule, *n.* spherule, spheroid, round, ball, oval, bulb, knob; bead, pellet, shot, bullet, marble, pea, pill, pilule; bubble, drop, dewdrop, pearl, tear, teardrop.

gloom, *n.* **1.** gloominess, dimness, obscurity, shade, shadow, dusk, duskiness, murkiness, murk; dark, overcast, cloud, cloud over, cloudiness, dullness, dinginess, darkness, swarthiness, blackness.

2. melancholy, sadness, sorrow, woe; moroseness, depression, despondency, dejection, desolation; heaviness, heaviness of mind, low spirits, weariness, the blues, doldrums, dumps, despond; distress, hopelessness, pessimism, despair, grief, misery, dolor; disconsolateness, cheerlessness, mopishness, sullenness.

—v. **3.** frown, glower, scowl, lower, look black, be morose; look sullen, sulk, mope, pout, be ill-tempered.

gloomy, *adj.* **1.** dark, dusky, shadowy, dim, shaded, darksome, dark as pitch, black; murky, inky, pitchy, somber, dull, swarth, swarthy; sunless, dingy, shady, unilluminated.

2. dismal, melancholy, dispirited, cheerless, glum, dour, lugubrious; grim, frowning, sullen, sulky, surly; ill-tempered, ill-humored, morose, splenetic, saturnine, moody, mopish; sad, desolate, doleful, sorrowful, atrabilious; unhappy, down in the dumps, down in the mouth, in the doldrums; downcast, crestfallen, chapfallen, discouraged, heavy-hearted, downhearted, miserable; forlorn, despondent, dejected, lowspirited, *Inf.* dead.

3. depressing, dreary, morbid, funereal; dejecting, discouraging, damping, disappointing; disheartening, dispiriting, depressive, depressant; saddening, heartbreaking, distressing, painful; dismal, hopeless, grave, *Inf.* downbeat.

glorify, *v.* **1.** exalt, dignify, ennoble, enthrone, canonize; eulogize, panegyrize; honor, adore, worship, crown, bless, idolize, pay tribute to, pay homage to; reverence, venerate, revere, consecrate, sanctify; deify, apotheosize, idealize, romanticize; value, esteem, respect, admire, look up to.

2. elevate, raise, upraise, raise up, make lofty; lift, uplift, lift up, cast up; promote, advance, boost, upgrade; improve, ameliorate, better; transfigure, transform, renew, change; enhance, intensify, magnify, heighten, strengthen; increase, enlarge, aggrandize, extend, widen; illuminate, illumine, irradiate, brighten, light up, spotlight.

3. praise, sound the praises of, sing the praises of, extol, cry up, *Inf.* crack up, *Archaic.* magnify, emblazon; encore, root for; approve enthusiastically, hail, commend, sanction, endorse; recommend, say a good word for, put in a good word for; compliment, flatter, puff, boost, swell, lionize, belaud, make much of; applaud, acclaim, cheer, celebrate, congratulate, *Archaic.* gratulate.

gloriole, *n.* halo, nimbus, aureola, glory; aura, ring, circle. See **halo.**

glorious, *adj.* **1.** delightful, charming, captivating, enchanting, delectable; wonderful, wondrous, marvelous, spectacular, fabulous, winning; ecstatic, exultant, enraptured, entranced, elated, blissful; jubilant, ebullient, overjoyed; surprising, singular, unusual, awe-inspiring; excellent, superb, splendid, consummate, *Inf.* peachy, *Brit. Sl.* ducky; enjoyable, pleasurable, pleasant, pleasing, gratifying, agreeable, congenial; halcyon, peaceful, serene, tranquil, pacific, heavenly.

2. dignified, stately, courtly, solemn, grave; majestic, noble, imposing, august, commanding, striking, towering; aristocratic, regal, royal, lordly, princely, imperial; lofty, elevated, sublime, grand, exalted, glorified; transcendent, *Inf.* out of this world, celestial; ethereal; praiseworthy, admirable, estimable, honorable, adorable; worthy, excellent, exemplary, meritorious, impressive.

3. eminent, prestigious, notable, conspicuous; famous, famed, illustrious, notorious; renowned, celebrated, popular, distinguished, distingué; noted, named, marked; peerless, unique, unrivalled; preeminent, superior, surpassing, supreme; triumphant, successful, victorious.

4. magnificent, splendid, resplendent, elegant, prosperous; radiant, refulgent, effulgent, shining, glowing; bright, brilliant, illuminating, lustrous, nitid, glossy; luminous, glittering, sparkling, shimmering, glimmering, dazzling.

glory, *n.* **1.** extolment, laudation, acclaim, acclamation, kudos, accolade, *Archaic.* magnification, citation, éclat; tribute, testimonial, credit, recognition; eulogy, eulogium, eulogization, encomium, panegyric; exaltation, glorification, honor, crown; approval, approbation, endorsement, sanction, commendation, recommendation; congratulation, *Archaic.* gratulation, celebration, paean.

2. dignity, stateliness, courtliness, solemnity, gravity; majesty, nobility, nobleness, imposingness; loftiness, sublimity, grandeur, exaltation, gloriousness; worthiness, excellence, impressiveness.

3. eminence, prestige, notability; fame, illustriousness, repute, reputation, notoriety, notoriousness; renown, distinction, note, name; celebrity, popularity, popular favor, vogue, figure, mark; object of pride, boast.

4. esteem, admiration, appreciation, respect; honor, reverence, veneration, adoration, worship; *Eccles.* benediction, blessing, *Archaic.* benison, hosanna; praise, thanksgiving, gratitude.

5. magnificence, splendor, resplendence, pomp; triumph, success, victory, flying colors; flourish, fanfare, éclat, parade, pageantry, show, display; elegance, luxury, affluence, state; prosperity, good fortune, heyday, prime; zenith, summit, acme, crest, pinnacle, height, top; culmination, consummation; maximum, optimum.

6. radiance, refulgence, effulgence, shining; brightness, brilliance, brilliancy, illumination; luminosity, glitter, sparkle, shimmer, glimmer, dazzle; luster, sheen, gloss.

7. omniscience, omnipresence, omnipotence, *Theol.* Ubiquity; infinity, infinite wisdom, infinite goodness, infinite justice, infinite truth, infinite love, infinite mercy.

8. heaven, paradise, eternity, kingdom come, Promised Land, kingdom of heaven, celestial happiness; Eden, Elysium.

—*v.* **9.** exult, rejoice, triumph, jubilate, thank one's lucky stars; luxuriate, bask, revel, delight; take pride in, be proud of, plume oneself, pride oneself; vaunt, show off, boast.

—*interj.* **10.** **glory be** Glory be to God, thank God, thanks be to God, heaven be praised; hallelujah, alleluia, hosanna, praise God, praise the Lord; my word, of all things, wow, shiver me timbers, good heavens.

gloss[1], *n.* **1.** shine, polish, luster, sheen, brightness, glitter, shimmer, glow, luminousness; glaze, varnish, veneer, lacquer, enamel, japan.

2. front, façade, camouflage, mask, disguise; pretense, masquerade, deceptive show, show, surface, semblance, false appearance; speciousness, brummagem, sham, tinsel; imitation, paste, ersatz, *Inf.* hokum, scagliola.

—*v.* **3.** polish, glaze, shine, give a shine to, varnish, lacquer, enamel, japan, gloze.

4. mask, veil, disguise; smooth over, cover up, slick over; color, falsify, alter, doctor up.

gloss[2], *n.* **1.** explanation, apology, comment, annotation, scholium, footnote; commentary, critique, exegesis, explication, elucidation; interpretation, translation, metaphrase, reading, understanding.

2. glossary, index, addendum. See **glossary.**

3. extrapolation, misleading interpretation, glib *or* slick story, contrivance, concoction, cover-up, white lie, fabrication, *Inf.* fairy tale, *Inf.* hoked-up story, *Inf.* song and dance.

—*v.* **4.** annotate, explain, interpret, analyze; explicate, read, read into, comment on; react to, respond to.

5. explain away, make plausible, excuse, paint a rosy picture, gloss over, whitewash, extenuate, palliate, gloze; apologize for, play down, downplay, soft pedal; tell a good story, talk a good game.

glossary, *n.* gloss, nomenclature, word list, listing, directory; addendum, annotation, notes; appendix, index, table of reference; catalog, concordance.

glossy, *adj.* **1.** shiny, lustrous, glowing, burnished, polished, waxed, glassy, glistening, shining, silken, smooth, sleek, satiny; velvety, elegant, finished.

2. deceptive, fraudulent, meretricious, slick, factitious; false, unreal, insincere; artificial, contrived; assumed, put-on, pseudo; specious, theatrical, pretended, feigned, simulated, make-believe, sham, mock, ersatz, synthetic, plastic, *Sl.* hokey.

3. bogus, spurious, supposititious; counterfeit, fraudulent, imitation, not genuine, brummagem, fake, *Inf.* phony.

glove, *n.* mitten, mitt, gauntlet, gage; muff.

glow, *n.* **1.** subdued light, glowing, afterglow; incandescence, luminosity, phosphorescence; luster, shine, iridescence; splendor, brilliance, radiance, refulgency, effulgence; illumination, flash, glare, beam, ray, shaft; streak, patch, coruscation, fulguration; shimmer, flicker, twinkle, glitter, glimmer, sparkle, glint, glistening; flutter, flare, spark, scintilla; flame, blaze, burning, white heat.

2. brightness, vividness, intensity, radiance; splendor, resplendence, brilliance, shine, effulgence, luster; colorfulness, richness, gayness, depth, intensity; strength, freshness, distinctness, loudness; showiness, flashiness, garishness.

3. fever, fever heat, febris; flush, blush, burning, glowing; *Both Pathol.* pyrexia, inflammation.

4. ruddiness, red, redness, rubicundity, sanguineness, floridness; crimson, scarlet, rubescence, erubescence; rose, blush, pink, coral, russet, murrey.

5. warmth, emotion, feeling; passion, ardor, fervor, fervency, zeal; gusto, eagerness, earnestness, enthusiasm, inspiration, animation; excitement, elation, ecstasy, thrill, *Inf.* rush, tingling.

—*v.* **6.** incandesce, light, illuminate, radiate; phosphoresce, shine; flash, glare, beam, streak, coruscate, fulgurate; shimmer, flicker, twinkle, glimmer, glitter; sparkle, glint, glisten, *Archaic.* glister; flutter, flare, spark, scintillate; flame, flare, blaze, burn.

7. add luster *or* brilliance, brighten, color, make luminous; make rich, make intense, strengthen, heighten, deepen; make vivid, make resplendent, shine.

8. turn red *or* scarlet, crimson, redden, rouge; blush, flush, color, grow red, become sanguine; glow, mantle, suffuse, spread; get a fever, become fevered *or* febrile; grow flush, burn, tinge, rubricate, incarnadine; flood, flow, diffuse; *Pathol.* inflame.

9. warm, move, make animated *or* inspired; arouse passion, inflame, make excited *or* elated, enthuse; thrill, tingle, arouse, awaken, enkindle, stir, stimulate; exhort, spur, quicken.

glower, *v.* **1.** glare, lower, scowl, frown, look black, look fierce, look daggers, *Scot.* glunch, *Sl.* give a dirty *or* nasty look, *Sl.* don the hate-mug.

—*n.* **2.** glare, scowl, frown, dirty *or* nasty look fierce *or* threatening look.

glowing, *adj.* **1.** incandescent, candescent, candent, aglow, in a glow.

2. (*all of coloring*) rich, warm, vibrant; (*all of complexion*) ruddy, sanguine, flushed, florid, red-faced; radiant, shining, beaming, rosy-cheeked; hot, heated, fiery, burning, feverish.

3. complimentary, highly favorable, laudatory, acclamatory, eulogistic, panegyrical, encomiastic; flattering, adulatory, hero-worshipping, excessive.

gloze[1], *v.* explain away, extenuate, gloss over, palliate. See **gloss[2]** (*def.* **5**).

gloze[2], *v.* shine, brighten, gleam, glow. See **gleam.** (*def.* **4**).

glue, *n.* **1.** paste, cement, epoxy, mucilage, gum, fixative; putty, size, lute, mortar, plaster.

—*v.* **2.** paste, agglutinate, cement, seal, gum, lute, conglutinate; adhere, stick, cling, cleave to, fix.

gluey, *adj.* sticky, viscid, gummy, adhesive, mucilaginous, cohesive; tenacious, clinging, tacky; viscous, glutinous, pasty, tacky, *Archaic.* sizy; mucous, albuminous, ropy, stringy.

glum, *adj.* gloomy, silent, morose, woebegone, dismal, sullen, dejected, dispirited, pessimistic, cynical, grumpy, glowering. See **gloomy** (*def.* **2**).

glut, *v.* **1.** sate, fill, satiate, stuff, overfeed, overfill; cloy, surfeit, pall; sicken, weary, overdo, jade.

2. flood, saturate, inundate, supersaturate, surcharge, load.

3. choke up, clog, obstruct, dam up, stop up, check, retard.

4. gorge, engorge, cram, overeat, gormandize, engulf, overindulge, *Archaic.* gluttonize; gobble up, devour, guzzle, bolt, gulp down, wolf down, raven, *Sl.* pig out; eat like a pig *or* horse *or* ox, make a beast of oneself, play a good knife and fork, eat out of house and home, worship one's belly, indulge one's appetite.

—*n.* **5.** excess, surfeit, surplus, superfluity, superabundance, superflex; redundance, plethora, overabundance, overprofusion, nimiety; load, overload, overdose, oversupply, overfill; repletion, congestion, engorgement; overspill, overflow, flood, inundation, deluge; more than enough, enough with over-measure, enough and to spare.

6. satiety, satisfaction, saturation, supersaturation; full supply, full stomach, heart's content, bellyful.

glutinous, *adj.* sticky, gummy; albuminous, ropy. See **gluey.**

glutton, *n.* gormandizer, gourmand, trencherman, big eater, *Sl.* chowhound, wolf, pig, hog, gobbler, horse, ox, cormorant; pantophagist, eater, omnivore; *Sl.* belly-god, *Sl.* belly-slave, *Sl.* greedy-guts.

gluttonous, *adj.* **1.** voracious, ravenous, ravening, devouring, gormandizing, cormorant, edacious; openmouthed, hoggish, piggish, porcine, swinish, gross.

2. greedy, insatiable, insatiate, unquenchable, omnivorous; desirous, cupidinous, avaricious, esurient; hungry, craving, grasping, acquisitive, *Sl.* grabby, predacious, rapacious.

gluttony, *n.* ravenousness, voracity, voraciousness, gormandism, edacity, open-mouthedness, hoggishness, piggishness, *Sl.* pigging in, swinishness, grossness, crapulousness; insatiability, insatiateness, omnivorousness, gulosity.

gnarl, *n.* **1.** knot, protuberance, hump, bump, lump, bunch; gibbosity, swelling, excrescence, tumescence, protrusion; knob, knur, knar, knurl, nurl; nub, node, nodule, nodosity; boss, torus, bunion, button.

—*v.* **2.** twist, screw, twine, wrest, wring; contort, distort, warp, bend; wriggle, writhe, vermiculate.

gnarled, *adj.* **1.** knotty, lumpy, bumpy, humpy, gnarly, knotty, knarry; knurled, knarred, knotted, nodular, snaggy; bent, twisted, crooked, arthritic; warped, contorted, distorted, cross-grained.

2. rugged, rough, weatherbeaten, seasoned, toughened; leathery, wrinkled, furrowed, craggy.

3. cantankerous, crotchety, crabby, cranky, grouchy, grumpy, dyspeptic; disagreeable, peevish, snappish, huffy.

gnash, *v.* (*of the teeth*) grind, strike together, grit, rasp, grate, scrape.

gnaw, *v.* **1.** nibble, peck, bite; chew, champ, masticate, munch, crunch, mumble, ruminate, (*both of cattle, deer, etc.*) browse, graze.

2. corrode, fret, eat into *or* away, consume, devour, rust, *Both Chem.* oxidize, oxidate; erode, wash away, wear down *or* away; waste away, deteriorate, degenerate.

3. exasperate, aggravate, irritate, annoy, vex, irk, peeve, gall, nettle, tease; harass, harry, plague, torture, torment, trouble; hector, pester, badger, *Archaic.* haggle; bother, disturb, shake, ruffle, fluster.

gnome[1], *n.* dwarf, troll, leprechaun, clurichaun; elf, brownie, kobold, pixie, Hobbit; goblin, hobgoblin, hob, fairy, gremlin, imp, sprite, nix, nixie.

gnome[2], *n.* aphorism, maxim, adage, apothegm, epigram; saw, proverb, saying; truth, truism, dictum, precept.

go, *v.* **1.** move, proceed, pass, advance, make way, forward; get on, make headway, gain ground; budge, stir; walk, tread, pace, stride, amble; travel, journey, tour, trek; wend, trail, hie, *Scot.* gang, gather way.

2. leave, depart, quit; move off, decamp, steal away, make off, slip away, abandon; abscond, *U.S. Sl.* vamoose, *Jocular.* absquatulate, *Sl.* scram; evacuate, emigrate, migrate; flee, fly, flit, take wing; withdraw, retreat, retire, repair, recede; sally forth, start out, set out, embark, weigh anchor.

3. function, perform, operate, work, run, act, play; *Inf.* tick, *Inf.* percolate, *Inf.* perk.

4. become, grow, grow into, come to be, wax; turn to, change to, convert to.

5. reach, extend, stretch to, spread to; give access to, open to, communicate to.

6. elapse, lapse, pass, pass by, expire; slip away, tick away, flow, glide, fly, *Inf.* zip by; drag, crawl, creep.

7. be applied, be allotted, be awarded, be assigned, be devoted to; be transferred, be granted, be ceded, be given, be conveyed; be bequeathed, be willed, be left.

8. conduce, tend, incline, lean, set, verge, gravitate, work towards; point to, show a tendency, look to; contribute to, lend itself to, serve, lead to, redound to.

9. result, turn out, end, end up, eventuate; ensue, emerge, come out.

10. belong, have a place, be there, fit in, lie, stand, rest; be located, be situated, be found.

11. harmonize, go together, blend, accord, comport, jibe, correspond; be compatible, be suited, be adapted.

12. fit, conform, suit, comply, meet, accommodate; observe, follow, fall in with.

13. vanish, disappear, cease to be, be no more, leave no trace, vanish into thin air, *Sl.* go poof; fade away, melt away, dissolve, die out, *Inf.* peter out; be consumed, be eaten up, be exhausted, be spent; be finished, be wiped out, be eradicated, be annihilated, be destroyed.

14. die, perish, decease, pass away, expire.

15. be discarded, be thrown away, be disposed of, be

dropped, be shed; be dismissed, be put aside, be cast aside, be done with, be gotten rid of; be forgotten, be shelved, *Sl.* be canned.

16. develop, progress, proceed, move along; evolve, mature, bloom, ripen; work out, unfold, unwind, unfurl.

17. pass, circulate, get abroad, go around, get out; become public, acquire currency, get afloat.

18. sound, say, translate, pronounce; be phrased, be said, be spoken, be formed; be pronounced, be voiced, be vocalized; be written, be composed, be spelled.

19. wear out, tire out, weaken, deteriorate, degenerate; decline, fade, flag, lose power; become weakened, become worn out, become ineffective, become useless.

20. break, fail, give way, collapse, burst, pop; snap, tear, crack, give; fall down, cave in, tumble; crumble, crumple, disintegrate, fall to pieces.

21. **go down** **a.** lose, suffer defeat, fall, be the loser; be beaten, be upset, *Sl.* be licked, *Sl.* be drubbed. **b.** be remembered, be recalled, be memorialized, be commemorated.

22. **go off** explode, fire, detonate, fulminate; blow up, pop, burst, erupt, blow, *Sl.* go boom.

23. **go on** **a.** happen, take place, occur, come about, arise, ensue. **b.** endure, last, continue, stay; abide, remain, run.

24. **go out** expire, fade out, die out; be extinguished, be doused, be quenched, be turned off, be unplugged.

25. **go over** review, examine, inspect, study, look over; read, scan, peruse, run over, skim, give a quick once over.

26. **go through** bear, experience, suffer, withstand, undergo; put up with, stand, take, tolerate, submit to; weather, brook, brave.

27. **go together** date, keep company, court, go with, go out with; go steady with, *Brit.* walk out with, see, woo, *Inf.* be honeys.

28. **let go** release one's hold, unarm, unhand, disengage; free, release, set free, liberate, loose, open the door to.

—*n.* **29.** energy, spirit, animation, vigor, dynamism; life, élan, dash, zest, verve, vim; get up and go, *Inf.* pep, *Inf.* zip, vim, vigor and vitality; drive, enterprise, initiative, push.

30. attempt, try, trial, essay, *Archaic.* assay; *Inf.* shot, *Inf.* fling, *Sl.* whirl, *Sl.* stab, *Sl.* crack, *Sl.* whack; venture, endeavor, effort, bid, gambit.

31. success, triumph, victory; prosperity, good fortune, run of luck, luck; winner, *Sl.* smash, *Inf.* hit.

32. **from the word "go"** since the beginning, from the very start, from the first, *Inf.* since way back when, *Latin. ab initio, Latin. ab ovo.*

33. **all the go** fashionable, chic, stylish, modish, smart, *Sl.* hip; in vogue, in fashion, à la mode.

—*interj.* **34.** start, get going, move, run, hop to it, take off; step lively, get a move on, *Sl.* get the lead out.

35. begone, be off, *Archaic.* avaunt, away, away with; get out, go away, get along, get *or* be on your way, get out of here; get out of my sight, *Inf.* make yourself scarce, *Sl.* beat it, *Sl.* vamoose, *Sl.* scram, *Sl.* get lost, *Sl.* hit the road.

goad, *n.* **1.** prod, rowel, stick, shaft, staff, shepherd's staff, quarterstaff, stave, pole, rod, crook, shepherd's crook; lance, spear, point.

2. stimulus, stimulant, incentive, fillip, provocative, motive; spur, prick, jog, jolt, poke; incitement, inducement, instigation, encouragement, abetment, provocation, egging on, putting up to; dare, taunt, gibe.

—*v.* **3.** prick, poke, stick, rowel, spur, prompt, prod, thrust; push, drive, propel, hound, whip, lash, flog.

4. incite, provoke, instigate, actuate, look for trouble, *Inf.* start something; foment, agitate, excite, arouse, rouse, whip up, work up, stir up, wind up, enflame, inflame, fire up, kindle, touch off; encourage, urge, egg on, put up to.

5. anger, incense, huff, enrage, infuriate, madden, outrage; exasperate, exacerbate, ruffle, roil, pique, chafe, vex; annoy, irritate, aggravate, hector, nettle, disturb, perturb, torment, plague, badger, pester, needle, persecute, harass, bullyrag.

go-ahead, *n.* permission, leave, *Inf.* green light, *Inf.* the nod; sanction, authorization, approval, say-so, *Inf.* okay *or* OK.

goal, *n.* **1.** aim, purpose, intent, intention, aspiration, ambition, ideal; end, end in view *or* mind, object, objective, target, mark, destination, bourne; endpoint, end of the road, end of the line, journey's end, terminus, terminal, last stop, home, *Sl.* payoff; finish, finish line, line, (*in track and field*) tape, (*in horse racing, etc.*) pole.

2. score, hit, bull's-eye, touchdown, *Inf.* pay dirt.

goat, *n.* **1.** buck, ram, billy goat, billy; nanny goat, nanny, nan, doe; kid.

2. *Informal.* scapegoat, whipping boy, *U.S. Sl.* fall guy; dupe, gull, victim, sitting duck, easy *or* soft mark, *Sl.* patsy, *Sl.* pigeon, *Sl.* soft touch; laughingstock, butt, fair game, fool, everybody's fool, *Brit. Sl.* mug.

3. lecher, satyr, whoremonger, dirty old man, old goat.

4. **get one's goat** *Informal.* annoy, irritate, vex. See **irritate** (*def.* **1**).

goatish, *adj.* **1.** goatlike, hircine, caprine, *Zool.* caprid.

2. lustful, lecherous, lascivious, licentious, libidinous, lubricous, concupiscent, *Archaic.* lickerish, *Sl.* horny, *Sl.* hot, *Sl.* hot to trot; sexual, erotic, prurient, lewd, salacious, carnal.

gobble, *v.* engorge, devour, raven, bolt, gulp down, wolf down, ingurgitate; glut, gorge, cram, stuff, *Sl.* shovel; gluttonize, gormandize, guttle, play a good knife and fork.

gobbledegook, *n.* **1.** obfuscation, confusion, complexity, buzz word; educationese, computerese, academese, bureaucratese, legalese, medicalese; wordiness, verbosity, prolixity, prolixness, verbiage, verbalism; diffuseness, profuseness, profusiveness, effusion, effusiveness, gushing; redundance, redundancy, pleonasm, padding, repetition, battology.

2. circumlocution, *Inf.* circumbendibus, ambagiousness, periphrasis, periphrase, roundabout *or* indirect expression; tautology, *Rare.* tautologism, begging the question; shifting, dodging, equivocation, deceptiveness; ambiguity, subtlety, vagueness, indirection, quibble, quibbling; digression, excursus, rambling, winding, meandering, *Archaic.* ambages.

3. jargon, gibberish, nonsense, moonshine, *Fr. bavardage;* hocus-pocus, abracadabra, mumbo jumbo; humbug, flummery, *Sl.* bunk, rubbish, tommyrot, *Inf.* rot, *Sl.* garbage, *Sl.* horsefeathers; balderdash, hogwash, stuff and nonsense, *Inf.* bosh, *Brit. Sl.* tosh, fudge, foolishness, rigmarole *or* rigamarole; poppycock, *Inf.* fiddle-faddle, *Inf.* piffle, *Inf.* kibosh, *Inf.* flapdoodle.

gobbler[1], *n.* turkey, turkey cock, turkey gobbler, tom, tom turkey, *Scot.* bubbly-jock.

gobbler[2], *n.* glutton, gormandizer, trencherman, gourmand, *Sl.* chowhound; wolf, pig, hog, horse, ox, cormorant; pantophagist, eater, omnivore; *All Sl.* belly-god, belly-slave, greedy-guts.

go-between, *n.* intermediary, interagent, internuncio, medium; middleman, broker, factor, agent, dealer, distributor, wholesaler, jobber; mediator, negotiator, peacemaker, makepeace; arbiter, referee, umpire, judge, moderator, third *or* disinterested party; ombudsman, ombudswoman, consumer advocate, *Sl.* Nader-raider; link, liaison, tie, connection, contact, friend at court; pimp, pander *or* panderer, procurer, gigolo, fancy man; procuress, *Archaic.* bawd.

goblet, *n.* wineglass, *Literary.* chalice, *Chief. Scot.* tass; glass, tumbler, rummer, cup, beaker.

goblin, *n.* hobgoblin, barghest, kobold; gnome, elf, imp, leprechaun, brownie, nix, fairy, sprite; gremlin, specter, phantom, ghost; bugbear, bogy, boogeyman, ogre; demon, devil.

God, *n.* **1.** God Almighty, the Almighty, the Godhead, Divine Being, the Deity, Providence, Holy One; God the Father, Divine Father, Our Father; Jehovah, Yahweh, Allah; the Supreme Being, Supreme Goodness, The All-Powerful, the Omnipotent, the All-Merciful, The All-Wise, the All-Knowing, the Omniscient; the Infinite, the Eternal, the Absolute; Lord, Lord of Lords, King of Kings, King of Glory; Creator, Author of all things, the Maker, the Maker of Heaven and Earth, the First Cause, the Prime Mover, the Light of the World, Ruler of Heaven and Earth, Sovereign of the Universe, Most High.

2. (*l.c.*) deity, divine being, divinity, numen, spirit, power, genius; demiurge, *Rom. Relig.* lares and penates, *Hindu.* avatar, joss, tutelary.

3. (*l.c.*) idol, icon, graven image, golden calf.

goddess, *n.* **1.** female deity; nymph, *All Class. Myth.* dryad, Fury, Muse.

2. beauty, belle, Venus, *Inf.* knockout, *Sl.* looker, *Sl.* dish, *Sl.* babe; siren, seductress, charmer, enchantress.

godless, *adj.* **1.** atheistic, agnostic, nullifidian, skeptical, freethinking.

2. unrighteous, sinful, wicked, evil; irreligious, profane, ungodly, impious, blasphemous, sacrilegious; unholy, heathen, pagan.

godlike, *adj.* **1.** divine, deiform, deified, godly; sacred, religious, holy, saintly, sainted, venerable, angelic, seraphic, blessed, blest.

2. heavenly, celestial, spiritual, ethereal, supernal; beatific, blissful, rapturous, ecstatic; supreme, exalted.

3. supernatural, preternatural, superhuman; transcendent, supermundane, hyperphysical, immaterial.

godly, *adj.* devout, pious, God-fearing, religious, spiritual; pietistic, reverent, devoted, humble; believing, inspired; righteous, moral, virtuous, good; godlike, saintly, holy, seraphic, angelic, pure.

godsend, *n.* boon, blessing, benediction, *Archaic.* benison; windfall, bonanza, stroke of fortune, piece of luck, lucky find, gravy.

goggle, *n.* **1.** **goggles** protective glasses *or* spectacles.

2. stare, gape, ogle, leer, hard look, glare.

—*v.* **3.** stare, gape, gawk, roll one's eyes, glare, look hard at; ogle, eye, leer, *Sl.* check out, *Inf.* give the once-over.

goggle-eyed, *adj.* staring, gawking, glaring, ogling, leering; agog, wide-eyed, wonderstruck, awe-struck, open-mouthed, agape; stunned, thunderstruck, *Inf.* snowed, *Inf.* hit by the thunderbolt; spellbound, dumfounded, dazed, amazed, astonished; surprised, stupefied, blank, confounded, *Inf.* discombobulated, *Inf.* flabbergasted; taken aback, pulled up short.

going-over, *n.* **1.** examination, investigation, analysis, study, research, probe; review, survey, checkout, audit; close inspection, scrutiny, scrutinization.

2. scolding, call-down, chiding, upbraiding, *Inf.* talking to, *Inf.* dressing-down, tongue-lashing; reprimand, reproof, rebuke, reproach.

3. thrashing, beating, whipping, *Dial.* whupping, flogging, lashing; spanking, strapping, belting; drubbing, trouncing, buffeting.

goings on, *n. Informal.* **1.** conduct, behavior; misconduct, misbehavior, *Inf.* hanky-panky, *Sl.* funny business, *Sl.* monkey business, mischief, prankishness, *Inf.* shenanigans.

2. happenings, events, occurrences, performances, doings; merry-making, revelry, jollification, partying, bacchanalia, festivity, celebration.

gold, *n.* **1.** precious yellow metal, *Chem.* aurum; gold dust, gold nugget, coin gold, gold pieces, bullion, gold ingot, gold bar, *Inf.* goldbrick.

2. money, wealth, fortune, treasure, riches, affluence, opulence, opulency; Midas touch.

3. gold-colored, golden, gilt. See **golden** (*def.* **1**).

goldbrick, *n. Informal.* shirker, shirk, *Sl.* goof-off, dodger, malingerer, *Inf.* boondoggler, *Sl.* sleaze; loafer, idler, do-nothing, fainéant, drone, *Inf.* bum.

golden, *adj.* **1.** gold-colored, gold, gilt, gilded, auriferous; yellow, yellowish, xanthous; bright, metallic, glittering, glittery, shining, shiny, lustrous; gleaming, brilliant, dazzling, splendrous, splendid, resplendent.

2. priceless, invaluable, very valuable, precious, highly prized, of great worth; costly, high-priced, dear, expensive.

3. fine, rich, superb, excellent, perfect; favorable, propitious, good, timely, opportune, advantageous, profitable; fortunate, lucky, providential, auspicious; optimistic, promising, rosy, roseate, sunny, smiling.

4. radiant, glowing, shining, sparkling; exuberant, alive, vigorous, vital, healthy.

5. prosperous, halcyon, flourishing, thriving, palmy, successful, glorious, good; happy, peaceful, blessed, blest, beatific, blissful, joyous, delightful, pleasant.

6. talented, gifted, exceptional, special; favored, favorite, pet, cherished, beloved, loved; acclaimed, applauded, lauded, praised, *Inf.* much-touted.

7. rich, deep, soft, low, smooth, mellow, velvety.

8. *Slang.* wealthy, rich, opulent, affluent, well-to-do, well-off, *Inf.* well-heeled; moneyed, fat, flush, *Inf.* in the money, *Sl.* in the bucks, *Sl.* in the dough.

good, *adj.* **1.** virtuous, moral, righteous, honorable, honest, high-minded, noble, lofty; wholesome, pure, chaste, virginal, lily white, innocent, unsullied, untainted; pious, saintly, angelic, godlike, godly, God-fearing, devout, religious.

2. satisfactory, acceptable, serviceable, presentable, admissible, good enough, passable, tolerable; all right, *Inf.* O.K., *Inf.* okey-dokey, *Inf.* okle-dokle, *Sl.* hunky-dory, *Sl.* hunky; superior, extraordinary, marvelous, superfine, *Inf.* super, sterling, exemplary, excellent, capital, first-class, first-rate, ace, *Inf.* topnotch.

3. right, correct, proper, decorous, seemly, permissible, allowable; fit, fitting, meet, suitable, appropriate, timely.

4. well-behaved, obedient, minding; well-mannered, mannerly, courteous.

5. beneficent, benefic, altruistic, benevolent; kind, kindhearted, kindly, benign, sympathetic, humane. See **good-hearted.**

6. honorable, upstanding, upright, respectable, respected, in good standing, well thought of; worthy, of worth, praiseworthy, laudable, commendable, admirable, creditable, deserving, meritorious, of merit.

7. reliable, dependable, trustworthy, trusty, credible, believable; safe, secure, sound, stable, solid.

8. genuine, authentic, actual, *Inf.* kosher, *Archaic.* authentical, *Australian.* dinkum; accurate, precise, strict, faithful; real, realistic, lifelike, true-to-life, *Inf.*

honest-to-goodness, *Sl.* real live.

9. valid, authenticated, verified, confirmed, true, *Obs.* veritable; legitimate, lawful, legal, licit; warrantable, sanctionable, approvable.

10. wholesome, healthful, salutary, salubrious, nutritional; beneficial, helpful, advantageous, worthwhile; favorable, fortunate; propitious, auspicious, profitable.

11. delicious, delectable, scrumptious, flavorful, appetizing, tasty, *Inf.* yummy, *Archaic.* gustable; palatable, edible, eatable, comestible, esculent, fit to eat.

12. agreeable, pleasant, pleasing, to one's liking *or* fancy, likable; genial, companionable, congenial, friendly, amiable, amicable, sociable, social, convivial, *Scot.* couthie. See **good-natured.**

13. attractive, comely, handsome. See **good-looking.**

14. close, bosom, intimate, familiar, fast, *Inf.* thick, *Scot.* pack; dear, cherished, valued.

15. large, sizeable, full, ample; considerable, substantial, healthy, goodly, *Inf.* tidy; adequate, sufficient.

16. competent, capable, accomplished, efficient, knowledgeable, qualified; skillful, adept, adroit, proficient, expert.

17. quality, select, prime, choice, grade A; best, finest, nicest, newest; fine, special, fancy, dressy, party, Sunday; elegant, luxurious, posh, *Sl.* ritzy.

18. full, entire, whole, complete; solid, straight, unbroken.

19. (*of the weather*) fair, halcyon, balmy, mild, calm, gentle; clear, cloudless, unclouded; sunshiny, sunny, bright.

20. **make good** **a.** compensate for, make recompense for, make up for, make restitution *or* amends for, pay for, atone for, expiate; repay, reimburse, refund, pay back. **b.** fulfill, accomplish, deliver, deliver the goods, fill the bill, *U.S. Sl.* come through; satisfy, answer, meet, live up to; perform, discharge, carry out. **c.** succeed, be successful, get ahead, *Inf.* make it; set the world on fire, take the world by storm, reach the top. **d.** verify, validate, authenticate, document, prove; confirm, substantiate, back up.

—n. **21.** benefit, behoof, advantage, gain, profit; interest, behalf, welfare, well-being, happiness, *Obs.* wealth, *Archaic.* weal; enjoyment, use.

22. kindness, service, benefaction, good turn *or* deed; blessing, boon, benediction, godsend, windfall, *Archaic.* benison. See **good fortune.**

23. virtue, goodness, morality, uprightness, righteousness; right, rightness, rectitude, probity.

24. **goods** **a.** possessions, belongings, property, chattels, effects, trappings, *Inf.* trap, things, stuff, *Sl.* junk; paraphernalia, appurtenances, apparatus, gear. **b.** merchandise, wares, commodities, produce, stock in trade, stock. **c.** dry goods, yard goods, material, cloth fabric, textiles.

—interj. **25.** fine, good enough, very well; all right, okay, *Inf.* O.K., *Inf.* okey-dokey.

good-by, *interj.* **1.** farewell, bye, *Inf.* bye-bye; God be with you, Godspeed, adios, adieu; see you later, be good, *Inf.* so long, *Inf.* toodle-oo, *Chiefly Brit.* tata, *It. Inf. ciao*; until we meet again, sayonara, aloha, *Fr. au revoir, It. arrivederci, Ger. auf Wiedersehen, Sp. hasta la vista, Latin. Vale, Latin. vive valeque.*

—n. **2.** farewell, aloha, sayonara, *Inf.* so long, *Latin. Vale;* swan song, valedictory, *Inf.* send-off.

good fellowship, *n.* **1.** geniality, affability, pleasantness, agreeableness; congeniality, friendliness, amicability, sociability, conviviality.

2. comradeship, colleagueship, mateship, camaraderie, comradery, esprit de corps, clubbiness, *Inf.* chumminess; companionship, fellowship, togetherness, fraternization, brotherhood, friendship, amity, good will.

good-for-nothing, *adj.* **1.** worthless, of no worth, useless, of no use, no-good, valueless, of no value; do-nothing, lazy, slothful, sluggard, idle, fainéant, indolent.

—n. **2.** ne'er-do-well, black sheep, *Fr. vaurien,* worthless person; idler, fainéant, loafer, drone, do-nothing, *Inf.* bum; sluggard, slugabed, lazybones, malingerer, shirker, *Inf.* goldbrick, *Sl.* good-off.

good-hearted, *adj.* kind, kindly, kind-hearted, benign, benignant, good, warm-hearted, big-hearted, loving; considerate, thoughtful, well-meaning, well-intended; compassionate, understanding, sympathetic, soft-hearted, tender-hearted, tender, gentle; humane, merciful, clement, lenient, forbearing; beneficent, benevolent, charitable, giving, open-handed, unselfish; generous, liberal, munificent, philanthropic, altruistic.

good humor, *n.* **1.** gaiety, jocundity, joyousness, gay spirits, high spirits, good spirits; light heart, levity, optimism, sunniness; amiability, pleasantness, likableness, good-naturedness; joviality, jocularity, jollity; exhilaration, vivacity, alacrity; cheerfulness, cheer, mirthfulness, mirth, hilarity, merriment.

2. affability, approachableness, accessibility, communicativeness; easiness, openness, geniality, amicability, friendliness; congeniality, neighborliness, sociability; benignity, good nature, generosity, goodness.

good-humored, *adj.* cheerful, gay, cheery, blithe, blithesome, jocund, jolly, merry, gleeful; smiling, sunny, optimistic, in good spirits, positive; genial, convivial, amiable, affable; free and easy, easygoing, pleasant, good-natured, mellow, *Inf.* laid-back; happy, pleased, contented, glad; enthusiastic, vivacious, animated, spirited, flushed, buoyant; sprightly, light-hearted, lively, airy; jocular, jocose, joking, jesting, waggish; playful, gamesome, frolicsome, sportive; jovial, mirthful, delightful, gladsome, hilarious; sparkling, scintillating, effervescent.

good-looking, *adj.* **1.** beautiful, comely, attractive, handsome, seemly, goodly, sightly, *Inf.* eye-filling, pulchritudinous, well-favored, fair, pretty, bright-eyed, rosy-cheeked, *Scot.* bonny, *Chiefly Literary.* beauteous; shapely, well-proportioned, glamorous, sleek, sexy, (*of a woman*) foxy; ravishing, bewitching, enchanting, alluring, enticing, captivating, intriguing, inviting, irresistible.

2. tasteful, elegant, artistic, aesthetic, picturesque; well-made, well-put-together.

good looks, *n.* beauty, loveliness, comeliness, fairness, prettiness, pulchritude; attractiveness, handsomeness, glamour, sexiness, foxiness; nice body, good figure, good build *or* physique, shapeliness.

good luck, *n.* good fortune, fortune, luck, smiles of fortune, fate on one's side; run *or* streak of good luck *or* fortune, fair weather, halcyon days; stroke of fortune, piece of luck, blessing, boon, benefaction, *Archaic.* benison; godsend, lucky find, windfall, bonanza, jackpot, gravy.

goodly, *adj.* **1.** quality, superior, high grade, choice, select; excellent, first-rate, first-class, prime, top-drawer, *Inf.* topnotch; pure, solid, sterling, 100%; splendid, *Inf.* splendiferous, magnificent, *Sl.* swell, *Sl.* cool, *Brit. Sl.* nipping.

2. good-looking, beautiful, attractive, well-favored. See **good-looking** (*def.* **1.**).

3. considerable, substantial, sizable, *Inf.* tidy; large, ample, immense, great, vast, extensive, voluminous; significant, consequential, weighty.

good-natured, *adj.* **1.** agreeable, willing, amenable, obliging, accommodating; gracious, genial, gentle, peaceful, benign; polite, cordial, courteous, mannerly.

2. benevolent, kind, good, good-hearted, warm-hearted, humane, loving; altruistic, unselfish, considerate, thoughtful; kindly, kind-hearted, beneficent, benignant, generous, charitable, bounteous; magnanimous, big, humanitarian; neighborly, friendly, amicable, amiable, understanding, sympathetic, tender-hearted, broad-minded.

3. good-humored, cheerful, optimistic, in good spirits. See **good-humored.**

goodness, *n.* **1.** virtue, virtuousness, morality, high morals, uprightness, righteousness, piety, piousness; honorableness, honesty, integrity, high-mindedness, nobility; wholesomeness, innocence, purity, chasteness, virginity; saintliness, godliness.

2. kindness, kindliness, benignity, benignancy, kind-heartedness, warm-heartedness, big-heartedness, considerateness, thoughtfulness, compassion, understanding, soft-heartedness, tender-heartedness, humanity; beneficence, benevolence, charitableness, open-handedness, unselfishness, generosity, generousness, munificence, philanthropy, altruism.

3. excellence, high quality *or* standard, perfection; superiority, extraordinariness, superlativeness.

4. quintessence, essence, cream, *Fr. crème de la crème,* cream of the crop, pick of the litter, pick, flower, pearl, jewel, prize; value, worth, merit, asset, strength, strong *or* good point, best quality *or* trait.

good will, *n.* **1.** benevolence, beneficence, kindness, goodness, graciousness; humanitarianism, humaneness, humanity, altruism, unselfishness, consideration; magnanimity, brotherly love, sympathy, empathy; love, affection, concern; friendliness, hospitality, *Archaic.* gree.

2. acquiescence, willingness, agreeableness; flexibility, compliance, geniality, cordiality; consent, assent, concurrence, accordance.

goody-goody, *adj.* **1.** self-righteous, righteous, sanctimonious, hypocritically devout, holier than the Pope, holier-than-thou; affected, overnice, overprecise, overrefined, namby-pamby; hypocritical, false, insincere, canting, Pecksniffian, mealy-mouthed.

—n. **2.** goody-two-shoes, namby-pamby, nice nelly; old maid, prude, prig; milksop, pantywaist.

goose flesh, *n.* goose skin, goose pimples, *Inf.* goose *or* duck bumps, horripilation, *Pathol.* formication; (*all sensations of fear or cold*) chills, *Inf.* shivers, *Inf.* cold shivers, *Inf.* dithers, *Sl.* creeps, *Sl.* cold creeps.

gore, *n.* **1.** blood, clot, coagulation, grume, scabbiness; carnage, slaughter, butchery, murder.

—v. **2.** horn, butt, hook; pierce, transpierce, penetrate, disembowel, gut; puncture, prick, gouge; stab, spear, lance, pink, stick, impale, spit.

gorge, *n.* **1.** cleft, chasm, canyon, abyss, gulf; crevasse, crevice, rift, fissure; defile, pass, *Fr. couloir,* gap, notch; gulch, gully, wadi, gullet, ravine, *Brit.* clough, ditch.

2. throat, gullet, esophagus.

3. stuff, cram, glut, fill, sate, saturate, surfeit; devour, bolt down, gobble, gulp, swallow whole; gluttonize, gormandize, overeat, overindulge, eat the whole thing; play a good knife and fork, wipe up one's plate, eat out of house and home.

gorgeous, *adj.* **1.** splendid, splendrous, *Inf.* splendiferous, magnificent, resplendent; exquisite, elegant, sumptuous; luxurious, rich, opulent; dazzling, glittering, brilliant, refulgent, radiant; impressive, stately, imposing; beautiful, breath-taking, *Literary.* beauteous, good-looking, attractive, pulchritudinous, lovely, charming.

2. pleasant, enjoyable, fine, *Inf.* nifty, *Sl.* swell, terrific; glorious, marvelous, *Sl.* marvy, delightful, wonderful; excellent, great, grand, *Inf.* colossal; first-rate, *Inf.* super, sensational, superb, perfect, sublime.

gormandize, *v.* gluttonize, gorge, stuff, cram, make a pig of oneself; devour, eat greedily, *Sl.* eat like there's no tomorrow, *Sl.* pig in; eat richly, dine well, *Sl.* eat high off the hog.

gory, *adj.* **1.** bloody, bleeding, bloodstained, bloodsoaked, sanguinary, sanguineous; like a slaughterhouse *or* abattoir.

2. murderous, cruel, brutal, savage; fell, fierce, destructive, dreadful, horrendous, bloodthirsty.

3. unpleasant, disagreeable, distasteful, repellent, revolting; messy, *Sl.* yucky, embarrassing; awful, terrible, grim, ghastly.

gospel, *n.* **1.** (*often cap.*) Christian doctrine, the teachings of Christ, Christianity, Christian revelation, the good news, glad tidings; Scripture, the New Testament, the writings of the evangelists. See **Scripture** (*defs.* **1, 2**).

2. truth, certainty, fact, verity, authenticity; *Inf.* the whole truth and nothing but the truth.

3. belief, creed, credo, doctrine, ethic, principle, tenet.

gossamer, *n.* **1.** cobweb, spiderweb; thistledown, feather; gauze, tissue, chiffon.

—adj. **2.** gossamery, cobwebby, feathery, silky; thin, light, fine, delicate, flimsy, frail; diaphanous, sheer, transparent, see-through, translucent; unsubstantial, airy, light as an angel's breath.

gossip, *n.* **1.** rumor, grapevine, *Inf.* scuttlebutt, hearsay, *Fr. oui-dire,* report, *Archaic.* bruit; an earful, *Sl.* dope, *Inf.* inside info, *Sl.* poop, tittle-tattle; scandal, dirt, whispering campaign, mud-slinging.

2. prattle, idle talk, *Sl.* schmooze, small talk, palaver, *Scot.* clishmaclaver; chat, chitchat, *Sl.* yackety-yak, *Sl.* yak, twaddle, blather.

3. gossipper, gossipmonger, newsmonger, rumormonger; whisperer, tattler, talebearer, tattletale; loud mouth, *Inf.* blabbermouth, *Sl.* big mouth; yenta, tabby, cat; quidnunc, busybody, Paul Pry, snoop, meddler, *Australian. Sl.* stickybeak, eavesdropper; chatterer, gabbler, chatterbox, magpie; babbling brook, blatherskite, prattler, flibbertigibbet.

—v. **4.** tattle, *Inf.* blab, rumor, circulate, bruit, *Scot.* clishmaclaver, whisper; spread stories, squeal, dish the dirt; prattle, prate, palaver; chatter, chat, chitchat, *Sl.* yak, *Sl.* schmooze; gibber, blather, gabble, run off at the mouth, *Sl.* have diarrhea of the mouth, *Sl.* jaw, shoot the breeze.

gothic, *adj.* **1.** medieval; barbaric, barbarous, uncivilized, rude.

2. (*of literary style*) gloomy, grotesque, macabre, violent; (*of novels*) mystery.

gourmand, *n.* **1.** gastronome, epicure. See **gourmet.**

2. gormandizer, trencherman. See **glutton.**

gourmet, *n.* gastronome, epicure, connoisseur, *Fr. bon vivant, Fr. bon viveur;* dainty feeder, refined feeder, good palate, Lucullus.

govern, *v.* **1.** rule, reign, exercise control over, hold sway, wield the scepter, wield the power *or* authority, wear the crown, occupy the throne, have the whip hand; command, order, dictate, call the shots, run the show; boss, lay down the law, be in the driver's seat, be in the saddle, wear the pants *or* trousers.

2. supervise, superintend, oversee, preside over; direct, manage, guide, conduct, have *or* be in charge of; take the lead, lead; hold *or* keep in line, discipline, maintain order, regulate.
3. control, restrain, check, keep in check, curb, hold *or* keep back, contain, arrest; harness, bridle, rein in, hold in, leash, constrain; subdue, get the better of, suppress.

governable, *adj.* manageable, controllable, restrainable; dutiful, obedient, submissive, amenable; docile, tractable, malleable, pliant, teachable; tame, domesticated, broken.

governess, *n.* duenna, *Fr. gouvernante,* tutoress, instructress; nurse, nursemaid, *Chief. Brit.* nanny, *Fr. bonne,* (*both in India*) amah, ayah.

government, *n.* **1.** administration, management, direction, guidance, control, regulation, conduct; supervision, superintendence, surveillance, overseeing, oversight, charge, command; jurisdiction, dominion, regime, rule, reign; directorship, leadership, rulership, headship, presidency, magistracy; statesmanship, statecraft; authority, law, *Derog.* big brother; *Both U.S.* Uncle Sam, *Sl.* the Fed.
2. council, ministry, cabinet, department, chamber; parliament, congress, (*in Israel*) Knesset, diet, duma, soviet, senate.
3. discipline, regimentation, restraint, constraint, reining in, holding in, suppression.

governor, *n.* administrator, director, manager, executive, bureaucrat, functionary, official, marshal, magistrate; minister, regent, dean, chairman, chairwoman, chairlady, chairperson; president, head, chief, principal, *Inf.* kingpin, *Inf.* number one.

gown, *n.* **1.** evening dress, evening gown, dinner dress, dinner gown; dress, frock, robe; garment, raiment.
2. mantle, cloak, cassock; garb, canonicals, cloth vestments, *Inf.* clericals; academicals.
—*v.* **3.** robe, drape, dress, clothe, vest, garb, attire, apparel, habit, *Sl.* dude up.

grab, *v.* **1.** clutch, snatch, clasp, grasp, grip, fasten upon, lay hold of, lay hands on, *Inf.* get one's fingers *or* hands on, *Inf.* latch on *or* onto; catch, catch hold of, capture, take, hook, snag, ensnare, secure, *Inf.* collar, *Sl.* nab.
2. seize, appropriate, take up, take over, assume; commandeer, expropriate, confiscate; usurp, misappropriate, arrogate.
3. grab at jump at, snatch at, *Inf.* snap up; scramble for, fall all over oneself, get all excited about.
—*n.* **4.** clutch, grasp, grip, gripe, clasp, snatch.
5. seizure, appropriation, takeover, assumption, arrogation, usurpation, commandeering.
6. up for grabs *Informal.* available, obtainable, attainable, accessible, to be had, *Inf.* anybody's *or* anybody's ballgame.

grace, *n.* **1.** elegance, tastefulness, fineness; refinement, culture, cultivation, polish, urbanity, suavity; taste, good taste, discrimination, discernment; savoir-faire, tact, finesse; propriety, decorum, mannerliness, manners.
2. charm, winsomeness, winningness, appealingness, appeal; attractiveness, comeliness, beauty, beautifulness, pulchritude, handsomeness, loveliness; gracefulness, suppleness, fluency, fluidity, smoothness, symmetry, poetry in motion; ease, facility.
3. favor, boon, benefit, benefaction, benediction, *Archaic.* benison.
4. kindness, kindliness, benevolence, beneficence, benignity; love, brotherly love, good will; graciousness, indulgence, condescension.
5. mercy, mercifulness, mildness, lenity, leniency, forgiveness, compassion, compassionateness; reprieve, quarter, respite, stay of execution.
6. virtue, moral strength, goodness, quality, merit; conscience, knowledge of right and wrong.
7. blessing, thanks, thanksgiving, grace before meals.
—*v.* **8.** adorn, decorate, embellish, ornament, garnish; beautify, prettify, *Inf.* pretty up; enhance, enrich, set off to advantage; dignify, distinguish, honor, favor, *Brit. Dial.* mense; glorify, intensify, heighten, deepen.

graceful, *adj.* **1.** elegant, tasteful, fine; refined, cultured, cultivated, polished, courtly, urbane, suave; decorous, mannered, mannerly, well-mannered; discriminating, discerning, tactful.
2. charming, winsome, winning, appealing; attractive, comely, beautiful, lovely, handsome; supple, fluent, fluid, smooth, easy, facile; agile, nimble, lightsome.

graceless, *adj.* **1.** awkward, clumsy, gawky, ungainly, ungraceful; uncouth, coarse, crude, rude, raw, gross, low; gauche, unpolished, unsophisticated, unrefined, inelegant.
2. corrupt, degenerate, depraved; incorrigible, irreformable, lost; shameless, brazen, brazen-faced, bold, unabashed; insolent, impudent, impertinent, disrespectful.

gracious, *adj.* **1.** kind, kindly, benevolent, benign, benignant; kind-hearted, warm-hearted, warm; friendly, cordial, sociable, affable, amiable, pleasant, familiar; courteous, polite, well-mannered, mannerly.
2. tasteful, comfortable, easy, luxurious; urbane, suave, refined, polished, cultured, cultivated.
3. indulgent, obliging, accommodating, compliant, complaisant; patronizing, condescending.
4. merciful, compassionate, lenient, humane; mild, gentle, clement.
—*interj.* **5.** my, my oh my, dear me, goodness, goodness gracious, goodness gracious me, my goodness, good heavens, *Sl.* for crying out loud, land of Goshen.

gradation, *n.* **1.** progression, succession, sequence, course, order, series; continuance, continuation, consecutiveness, step-by-step progress, gradual advance, regular progression.
2. stage, degree, step, level, rank, plateau, plane, place; mark, point; pitch, extent, measure, amount, rate.
3. shading, depth, intensity.

grade, *n.* **1.** degree, stage, gradation, scale; step, rung, stair, peg, notch; point, mark.
2. status, rank, standing; position, station, place, class, caste; worth, value, merit, quality; situation, condition, lot, estate.
3. mark, rating, measure, evaluation, score, average, ratio.
4. angle, slant, inclination, pitch, attitude.
5. bank, rise, hill, aclivity, declivity, slope, upgrade, incline, downgrade, decline.
6. make the grade qualify, pass, pass muster, stand the test, measure up, come up to scratch *or* standard, *Sl.* cut it, *Sl.* hack it; accomplish, finish, achieve, win, get through.
7. up to grade satisfactory, acceptable, adequate, sufficient, suitable, up to par, up to snuff.
—*v.* **8.** level, smooth, flatten, even out, roll; equalize, correct.
9. sort, assort, size; class, type, name, label, tag, ticket, brand; classify, arrange, range, order, dispose,

place, group, organize; categorize, pigeonhole, distinguish, rate, rank, graduate.
10. blend, shade, blur, intermingle, synthesize, homogenize, harmonize; mingle, amalgamate, fuse.

gradient, *n.* **1.** slope, incline, ramp, rising ground, inclined surface *or* plane.
2. grade, rate, degree, point, mark, indicator.

gradual, *adj.* regular, deliberate, steady, even; slow, moderate, leisurely, unhurried, slow-paced, snail-like, at a snail's pace, inchmeal, imperceptible, measured, paced; progressive, continuous, methodical, methodic, systematic, orderly; gradational, by degrees, graduated, step-by-step.

gradually, *adv.* slowly, inchmeal, a little at a time, little by little, bit by bit, regularly, progressively, through all the gradations, constantly, continuously, continually; drop by drop, inch by inch, at a regular pace, imperceptibly.

graduate, *n.* **1.** alumnus, alumna, bachelor, licentiate.
—*v.* **2.** grade, calibrate, mark off, measure off, divide, arrange; rate, rank, range, order, dispose, place, group; adjust, modify, adapt, accommodate, regulate.

graduation, *n.* commencement, graduation day, graduation ceremony.

graft[1], *n.* **1.** shoot, bud, scion, new growth, sprout, implantation, transplant.
—*v.* **2.** slip, ingraft, implant, insert, infix, join, transplant.

graft[2], *n.* **1.** jobbery, racket, spoils; *All Inf.* pickings, rake-off, cut, kickback; plunder, loot, booty, swag, boodle, grease, velvet, gravy, honey, payola, hush money, payoff, shake-down.
—*v.* **2.** line one's own pockets, dip into the public till, be on the take.

grain, *n.* **1.** seed, kernel, groats, grist, ground grain, grits; cereal, wheat, buckwheat, barley, corn, maize, rye, oats, rice, millet.
2. particle, piece, bit, scrap, *Scot.* curn; speck, mite, moit, mote, dot, point, dab, fleck, speck, spot; smidgen, *Inf.* smitch, iota, molecule, atom, jot, whit, tittle; granule, crumb, morsel, taste, bite. See **bit[2]** (*defs.* **1, 2**).
3. trace, touch, hint, trifle, a little bit; tinge, flavor, suggestion, suspicion, soupcon, tincture, *Archaic.* spice, shadow; spark, scintilla, gleam.
4. texture, contexture, surface; intertexture, fabric, weave, warp and woof, nap, tooth; fiber, yarn, thread, filament.

grammar, *n.* (*all of language*) system, order, organization; principles, rules, laws; rudiments, basics, essentials, accidence; linguistics, *Linguistics.* syntax, sentence structure *or* formation; *Linguistics.* structuralism, transformational grammar, *Linguistics.* generative grammar, *Linguistics.* tagmemics; prescriptive grammar.

grammarian, *n.* grammatist, *Derog.* grammaticaster, grammar specialist; linguist, philologist, philologer.

grand, *adj.* **1.** distinguished, noted, eminent, famous, well-known, celebrated, esteemed; renowned, illustrious, prominent, preeminent, notable, *Archaic.* eximious; legendary, immortal, fabled, memorable; venerable, revered, respected.
2. dignified, distingue, stately, august; imposing, majestic, magnificent, exalted, imperious; lordly, noble, kingly, imperial, princely, magisterial; aristocratic, well-bred, genteel, gentle, blue-blooded.
3. splendid, superb, marvelous; luxurious, sumptuous, glamorous, striking, gorgeous; great, large, palatial, impressive; pretentious, ostentatious, dashing, showy, glittering; lofty, sublime, *Inf.* up there.
4. ambitious, aspiring, hoping, idealistic, dreaming, wishful, yearning, longing; unrealistic, outrageous, *Inf.* out-of-this-world.
5. complete, comprehensive, all-inclusive, inclusive, blanket; exhaustive, radical, widespread, sweeping, far-reaching, expansive; universal, world-wide, catholic.
6. choice, A-1, first-rate, *Inf.* topnotch; very good, excellent, wonderful, fantastic, fabulous.

grandeur, *n.* **1.** eminence, preeminence, loftiness, majesty, exaltation, excellence, greatness; nobleness, stateliness, imperialness, augustness, nobility; magnificence, splendor, glamour.
2. impressiveness, importance, greatness; vastness, immensity, elevation.

grandfather, *n.* **1.** *Inf.* granddad, *Inf.* grandpop, *Inf.* grandpa, *Inf.* grandpapa, *Inf.* gramps, *Archaic.* grandsire.
2. forefather, father, ancestor, forebear, progenitor, *Archaic.* predecessor.
3. founder, creator, author, originator, generator, initiator; inventor, framer, designer.

grandiloquence, *n.* bombast, grandiosity, pomposity; lofty language, fustian, euphuism, Johnsonese. See **bombast.**

grandiloquent, *adj.* bombastic, pompous, orotund, fustian, pretentious, ostentatious; magniloquent, Johnsonian, Ossianic. See **bombastic** (*def.* **1**).

grandiose, *adj.* **1.** grand, impressive, imposing, majestic, magnificent. See **grand** (*defs.* **1-3**).
2. pompous, *Inf.* highfalutin, highflown, high-sounding, big-talking; bombastic, grandiloquent, fustian. See **bombastic.**

grant, *v.* **1.** bestow, confer, vouchsafe, give, accord, impart, award, present; offer, donate, contribute, dispense; provide, endow, furnish, supply.
2. agree to, accede to, assent to, consent to, allow, let, permit, approve of, go along with; admit, concede, acquiesce in, yield, cede; submit to, comply with, adhere to, conform to.
3. transfer, convey, *Both Law.* bequeath, dower; assign, *Law.* devise, transmit; will, pass on, hand down, commit, entrust; consign, lease, let, rent.
—*n.* **4.** endowment, contribution, donation; benefit, boon, benefaction, bestowal, bestowment; present, gift, *Fr. cadeau,* award, tribute, honorarium; largess, bounty; offering, favor, douceur, gratuity, tip, fee; dole, handout, alms, allotment, share, portion; pension, subsidy, subvention, subscription.
5. fellowship, scholarship, assistantship, stipend, allowance.
6. transfer, conveyance, consignment, bequeathal, *Law.* bequest, *Law.* legacy, *Law.* dower, dowry, *Law.* devise, will.

granulate, *v.* grain, powder, levigate, pulverize, triturate, comminute; crush, grind, pound, bray; crumble, crumb, fragment, disintegrate; roughen, file, rasp, scrape, abrade.

granule, *n.* grain, particle, crumb, bit, corpuscle, fragment, mite; pellet, bead, pebble, globule; seed, spore, *Biol.* sporule.

graph, *n.* grid, chart, diagram, table, map, blueprint, picture, drawing, sketch, outline.

graphic, *adj.* **1.** pictorial, picturesque, descriptive, expressive, realistic; particular, detailed; distinct, well-defined, well-delineated, well-drawn, vivid, striking, telling; cogent, effective, forcible, lively, energetic, trenchant; explicit, express, specific, definite, precise, exact, pointed; lucid, clear, crystal-clear, manifest, plain, obvious, unmistakable; unequivocal, unam-

biguous, outright, out-and-out.
2. diagrammatic, mathematical; delineative, chartable.
3. written, drafted, delineated, drawn, inscribed.

grapple, *v.* **1.** seize, take hold of, snatch, grab; grip, clinch, hold, squeeze, press; fasten, secure, make fast, hook, catch, pin.
2. *Usu.* **grapple with a.** struggle, fight, wrestle, tussle, scuffle; encounter, clash, combat, battle, brawl. **b.** tackle, contend with, deal with, try to overcome.

grasp, *v.* **1.** grip, gripe, clutch, clench; clasp, hold, grapple, clinch; take, lay hold of, nab, seize, grab, snatch, catch at, catch.
2. comprehend, understand, apprehend, realize, *Chiefly Scot.* ken; perceive, apperceive, cognize, know, *Sl.* savvy, get, get the picture, follow, *Inf.* latch on *or* onto, *Sl.* dig, *Brit. Sl.* suss out; *Inf.* make head or tail of.
—n. **3.** grip, gripe, clutch, clench; grapple, clinch; clasp, handclasp, embrace.
4. scope, extent, measure, range, breadth; compass, reach, sweep, limits, bound.
5. comprehension, understanding, apprehension, realization; awareness, sense, perception, apperception, cognition; knowledge, *Sl.* savvy, *Inf.* fix, *Brit. Sl.* suss.
6. hold, holding, possession; power, mastery, clutches.

grasping, *adj.* **1.** greedy, avaricious, acquisitive, grabbing, *Sl.* grabby, rapacious; selfish, hoarding, possessive; miserly, penurious, parsimonious, grudging; chary, sparing, *Rare.* illiberal, niggardly; stingy, mean, shabby, closefisted, tight-fisted, close, *Inf.* tight, griping, penny-pinching; sordid, exacting, extortionate, mercenary, venal, usurious.
2. eager, avid, desirous, cupidinous, anxious, breathless, impatient, longing, thirsting, athirst, ardent; agog, zealous, fervent, burning; ambitious, aspiring, hungry, craving, esurient.
3. ravenous, ravening, voracious, devouring, wolfish, gluttonous; hoggish, piggish, swinish; insatiable, insatiate, unquenchable, omnivorous.

grass, *n.* **1.** herbage, vegetation, pasturage, verdure, *Trademark.* Astroturf; fodder, hay; pasture, lawn, green; sward, greensward, turf, sod.
2. *Slang.* marijuana. See **dope** (*def.* **2**).

grassland, *n.* pasture, prairie, campo, veld, veldt; savanna, steppe, the Steppes, pampas, llano; meadow, *Archaic.* mead, meadowland, lea, downs; heath, moor, moorland, wold, plains, tundra.

grass roots, *n.* **1.** countryside, rural districts, farm country, *Inf.* sticks, *Sl.* boondocks, *Sl.* boonies; provinces, hinterlands, backwoods, back country, wilds, middle of nowhere; heartland, *U.S.* Peoria, *U.S.* Main Street, *U.S.* River City, down on the farm.
2. countrypeople, countryfolk, farmers, tillers of the soil; country cousins, hicks, rubes, yokels, rustics, hayseeds; common folk *or* people, democracy, commoners, we the people, average man; little guys, hometown folks, *U.S.* Middle America; hoi polloi, general public, *U.S.* John Q. Public, *Sl.* Joe Blow, *Sl.* Joe Doakes, the great unwashed, the masses; rank and file, workingmen, middle class, taxpayers, *Sl.* peons, ones who work for a living.

grassy, *adj.* grasslike, gramineous, turfy; green, verdant, verdurous, emerald, aquamarine.

grate[1], *v.* **1.** irritate, aggravate, exasperate, exacerbate, rub the wrong way; annoy, vex, irk, peeve, gall, nettle; wear on, weary, fatigue, fatigate, tire; tax, strain, burden.
2. rasp, grit, gride, scrape, clank, jangle; screech, creak, screak, shrill, stridulate, sound off key; squawk, caw, croak, bray; jar, clash, set one's teeth on edge.
3. shred, rasp, file, whet, sand, sandpaper, pumice; grind, mortar, levigate, triturate, comminute, pulverize, granulate, disintegrate.

grate[2], *n.* **1.** fireholder, coal holder, fireplace, *Brit. Dial.* ingle; grill, gridiron, barbecue.
2. grille, perforated screen, lattice, latticing, latticework, trellis, trelliswork; guard, cover, barrier, partition, grating.

grateful, *adj.* **1.** thankful, appreciative, mindful of, obliged, obligated, under obligation, indebted, beholden, filled with gratitude.
2. agreeable, pleasing, pleasant, satisfying, gratifying, cheering, pleasurable, refreshing; enticing, inviting, welcome, acceptable, happy, felicitous, restful, relaxing.

gratification, *n.* satisfaction, self-satisifaction, fulfillment, self-fulfillment, contentment, self-contentment, content; happiness, felicity, pleasure, joy, enjoyment, delight, fun; self-gratification, self-indulgence, hedonism.

gratify, *v.* **1.** satisfy, fulfill, content, make content, make one feel good, do one's heart good; please, give pleasure to, delight, make happy, warm the cockles of one's heart.
2. indulge, give in to, comply with; humor, pacify, appease, mollify, soothe; favor, pamper, baby, coddle, *Obs.* fondle; spoil, overindulge.

gratifying, *adj.* satisfying, fulfilling, heartwarming, rewarding; pleasing, pleasant, agreeable, delightful, fun, pleasurable, enjoyable; lovely, nice, good, great, *Sl.* swell, fine.

grating[1], *adj.* **1.** irritating, aggravating, exasperating, exacerbating; annoying, vexatious, irksome, galling, peeving, nettling; disturbing, bothersome, distressing; wearing, fatiguing, tiring, tiresome; offensive, unpleasant, unpleasing, displeasing, disagreeable.
2. harsh, jangling, jarring, strident, raucous; rasping, stertorous, gritting, grinding, scraping, scratchy, scratching, clanking; screeching, creaky, creaking, screaky, screaking, rusty; sharp, piercing, shrill, shrilling, stridulatory, stridulous, stridulant, twangy, twanging; hoarse, gravelly, croaky, croaking, squawky, squawking; discordant, dissonant, absonant, cacophonous, disharmonious, unmelodic, unmusical.

grating[2], *n.* perforated screen, latticework. See **grate[2]** (*def.* **2**).

gratis, *adv.* **1.** free of charge, *Inf.* for free, without charge, gratuitously, *Inf.* on the house, for nothing, at no cost; freely, voluntarily, of one's own volition, of one's own accord, on one's own, without being asked.
—adj. **2.** gratuitous, free, complimentary; costless, expenseless, chargeless.

gratitude, *n.* gratefulness, thankfulness, appreciation, sense of obligation; recognition, acknowledgment, thanks, thanksgiving.

gratuitous, *adj.* **1.** free, gratis, complimentary. See **gratis** (*defs.* **1, 2**).
2. groundless, ungrounded, unfounded, baseless; unjustified, unreasonable, irrational, silly; unprovoked, unnecessary, uncalled-for, needless, superfluous, without reason *or* cause.

gratuity, *n.* tip, douceur, fee, lagniappe, *Fr. pourboire, Ger. Trinkgeld, Archaic.* vail, (*in Chinese ports*) cumshaw, (*in India, Turkey, etc.*) baksheesh; present, gift, *Inf.* a little something; reward, honorarium, award, prize; perquisite, *Inf.* perk, bonus, extra, plus, dividend, fringe benefit.

grave[1], *n.* **1.** crypt, tomb, vault, sepulcher, burial chamber, burial pit, mausoleum; last home, long home, low house, wooden house, narrow house; coffin, casket, *Sl.* wooden kimono *or* overcoat.

2. death, decease, demise, expiration, end, rest, eternal rest.

3. have one foot in the grave dying, expiring, going, slipping, sinking, fading *or* fading fast; near death, at death's door, knocking on heaven's door, on one's deathbed, *Inf.* on one's last legs, *Latin. in extremis.*

grave², *adj.* **1.** sedate, staid, sober, solemn, serious, somber; thoughtful, earnest, pensive, preoccupied; grim, grim-faced, grim-visaged, stone-faced, frowning, unsmiling.

2. weighty, momentous, important, all-important, essential, of the essence, vital, *Inf.* gut; critical, crucial, pivotal, eventful, climacteric; dangerous, hazardous, perilous.

graveclothes, *n.* cerements, cerecloth, shroud, winding sheet.

gravelly, *adj.* **1.** rocky, stony, pebbly, shingly; sandy, gritty, granular, grainy, granulated.

2. guttural, throaty, thick, croaking; harsh, raspy, rasping, hoarse, gruff, raucous, roupy, grating.

graveyard, *n.* cemetery, burial ground *or* place, necropolis, city of the dead, golgotha, *Western U.S.* boot hill; churchyard, potter's field, memorial park, God's acre; charnel house, ossuary, (*of wild animals*) boneyard.

gravitate, *v.* **1.** sink, fall, drop, descend, precipitate, settle.

2. be attracted to, incline to, lean toward, head toward, have a proclivity for, feel for.

gravitation, *n.* **1.** sinking, falling, drop, descent.

2. pull, drift, move, trend; tendency, disposition, inclination, magnetism, bent; proclivity, propensity, proneness, leaning, penchant.

gravity, *n.* **1.** dignity, solemnity, soberness, dourness, grimness, gloominess; austerity, asceticism, severity.

2. seriousness, significance, importance, import, full meaning; momentousness, magnitude, enormity, weight, ponderousness.

gray, *adj.* **1.** ashen, pale, pallid, colorless, bloodless; pearly, pearl-gray, griseous, silvery, dove-gray, gun-metal gray; smoky, sooty, fuliginous, tattletale gray.

2. gloomy, dismal, dreary, somber; misty, cloudy, overcast; darkening, foreboding, threatening.

3. old, ancient, venerable, over-the-hill; gray-haired, silver-haired, with silver threads among the gold, hoary, grizzled.

graybeard, *n.* old man, old-timer, venerable, patriarch, grandfather, golden-ager; gaffer, codger, *Sl.* geezer.

2. sage, solon, Solomon, philosopher, thinker.

graze¹, *v.* **1.** feed, browse, crop, ruminate, forage, roam, range over.

2. pasture, turn out to pasture.

graze², *v.* **1.** brush, brush against, glance off, shave, rub *or* touch lightly, sweep past; skim, sweep over, run over *or* through.

2. scrape, abrade, scratch, chafe, irritate, rub, redden, grate; scuff, bark, bruise, contuse.

—*n.* **3.** scrape, abrasion, scratch, striation, bruise, contusion.

grease, *n.* **1.** lard, bacon fat, drippings, tallow, butter; oil, *Relig.* unction.

—*v.* **2.** lard, butter, dress, smear, daub; oil, lubricate.

greasy, *adj.* **1.** fatty, fat, sebaceous, adipose, pinguid, oleaginous, unguinous, lardacious, butyraceous; soapy, saponaceous, waxy; buttery, floating in grease *or* butter.

2. oily, unctuous, slippery, smooth, slithery, suave, smooth-tongued, glib, facile, mealy-mouthed, fawning, gushing, groveling, flattering.

3. slimy, dirty, grimy, begrimed, smudged, *Inf.* sloppy, *Sl.* grungy, *Sl.* yucky.

great, *adj.* **1.** prodigious, unlimited, boundless, vast, immense, grand, extensive, spacious, capacious; large, big, huge, massive, gigantic, monstrous, gargantuan, Cyclopean, titanic, Brobdingnagian; numerous, many, multitudinous, manifold, abundant, voluminous, ample, countless.

2. extreme, pronounced, excessive, exorbitant; preposterous, outrageous, unreasonable, undue, inordinate.

3. important, salient, significant, consequential, weighty, momentous, commanding, influential, dominant, paramount, critical, serious, vital; noteworthy, essential, principal, primary, main, capital.

4. illustrious, famed, prominent, noted, eminent, renowned, admirable; preeminent, distinguished, celebrated, exalted, elevated, dignified, esteemed; major, notable, leading, of high rank, supreme, signal, grand, superior, peerless, matchless, incomparable, high, top, popular, well-known.

5. high-minded, magnanimous, philanthropic, altruistic, noble, generous, unselfish, humane, beneficent; benevolent, kind-hearted, kindly, gracious; just, fair, impartial, unbiased, unprejudiced; honorable, chivalrous, heroic, lofty, princely.

6. sublime, magnificent, majestic, grand, august; glorious, imperial, towering, tall.

7. absolute, positive, utmost, uttermost, unequivocal, unconditional, unqualified, intense, profound; perfect, complete, thoroughgoing, full, consummate, thundering; stark, sheer, arrant, flagrant, downright, glaring.

—*n.* **8.** leader, prince, champion, person of distinction, legend, legend in one's own time; star, superstar, headliner; patriarch, teacher, *Inf.* guru, prophet; forerunner, pioneer, trailblazer; captain, father, founder.

greatness, *n.* **1.** magnitude, immensity, largeness, bigness, enormity; dimension, scope, mass, volume, bulk, size, vastness; depth, height, extent; measure, full measure, amplitude, fullness, quantity, deal, abundance, sufficiency.

2. high degree, intensity, potency, power, force, influence, strength; excellence, fineness, quality, distinctiveness, caliber, attainment.

3. importance, significance, influence; seriousness, gravity, import, urgency, solemnity.

4. majesty, nobility, loftiness, augustness, grandeur, stateliness; eminence, preeminence, distinction, dignity; fame, celebrity, renown, notoriety.

5. magnanimity, generosity, altruism, nobleness, high-mindedness, loftiness of purpose, liberality, disinterestedness, humanitarianism.

greed, *n.* **1.** avarice, graspingness, acquisitiveness, *Sl.* grabbiness, rapaciousness; selfishness, miserliness, penuriousness, parsimony, niggardliness; stinginess, meanness, closefistedness, tight-fistedness; mercenariness, venality.

2. ravenousness, voraciousness, gluttony, gormandism, edacity, open-mouthedness, hogginess, piggishness; insatiability, insatiateness, omnivorousness, gulosity.

3. avidity, cupidity, yearning, craving, covetousness; eagerness, keenness, itch, appetite, stomach, *U.S. Dial.* big eye, appetence; anxiousness, breathlessness, impatience, longing, ardor, fervency, passion; aspiration, hunger, ambitiousness.

greedy, *adj.* **1.** avaricious, grasping, acquisitive, *Sl.* grabby, rapacious; selfish, hoarding, possessive; miserly, penurious, parsimonious, grudging, niggardly, *Rare.* illiberal; stingy, mean, closefisted, tightfisted, close, *Inf.* tight, penny-pinching; mercenary, venal, usurious.

2. (*usu. in reference to food*) ravenous, ravening, voracious, devouring, gluttonous, gormandizing, cormorant, edacious; open-mouthed, hoggish, piggish, swinish; insatiable, insatiate, unquenchable, omnivorous.

3. eager, avid, desirous, cupidinous, *Archaic.* fain, *Archaic.* lickerish; anxious, breathless, impatient, longing, ardent; agog, zealous, fervent, burning; ambitious, aspiring, hungry, craving, covetous, esurient.

green, *adj.* **1.** greenish, viridescent, virescent, emerald, bluish-green, greenish-blue, grue, aqua, aquamarine, sea-green, grass-green, olive green, pea-green, glaucous.

2. verdant, grass-covered, plant-covered, grassy, verdurous.

3. young, vigorous, sturdy, sound, healthy; strong, active, robust, energetic; growing, developing.

4. unseasoned, not aged, undeveloped, not perfected, unfinished; fresh, recent, new, raw; supple, pliant, elastic.

5. unsophisticated, inexperienced, immature, callow; inexpert, untrained, unskilled, unversed, awkward, amateurish; gullible, naive, easily fooled, credulous, simple.

—*n.* **6.** lawn, grassy area, sward; common, village green, campus, turf; putting green, golf course.

greenhorn, *n.* **1.** rookie, newcomer, beginner, amateur, novice, tyro, neophyte; gosling, tenderfoot, kitten, cub, pup, whelp; initiate, novitiate, learner, apprentice, *Sl.* jaboney.

2. dupe, *Sl.* fall guy, *Sl.* sucker, gull, cat's-paw; pigeon, easy mark, easy victim, *Archaic.* cully; stooge, puppet, instrument; fool, tool, April fool; butt, scapegoat.

greenhouse, *n.* hothouse, conservatory, *Brit.* glasshouse; summerhouse, gazebo, pavilion; nursery, arboretum, vinery; pleasure-garden, pleasure-grove, green court, viridarium.

greenness, *n.* **1.** verdancy, viridity, verdure, *Bot.* virescence.

2. youthfulness, childishness, immaturity, unripeness, incompleteness, inexperience, callowness, awkwardness.

3. innocence, simplicity, gullibility, naiveté, credulity, credulousness, trustfulness.

greet, *v.* **1.** address, salute, accost, hail, flag, wave to, give [s.o.] the glad hand *or* eye; hello, halloo, nod to, smile at, wink at, tip the hat to, doff the cap to; shake hands, squeeze *or* pump the hand, *Sl.* press flesh.

2. welcome, receive, meet, *Archaic.* gratulate; present, introduce, usher in, call in.

greeting, *n.* **1.** salutation, address, salute, salaam, hail, welcome; hello, halloo, aloha, how do you do; bow, curtsy, genuflection, scrape; handshake, handclasp, kiss, peck; nod, bob, duck, kowtow, prostration, homage.

2. message, note, tidings, missive, letter, cable, telegram, wire.

3. greetings respects, regards, best wishes, good wishes, compliments, devoirs.

gregarious, *adj.* sociable, social, affable, companionable, folksy, neighborly, brotherly; friendly, amicable, genial, cordial, hospitable, warm-hearted, kindly; hearty, hail-fellow-well-met, convivial.

gremlin, *n.* specter, phantom, ghost; goblin, hobgoblin, barghest, kobold; gnome, elf, imp, leprechaun, brownie, nix, fairy, sprite; bugbear, bogy, bogeyman, ogre; demon, devil.

grenade, *n.* explosive, hand grenade, bomb, *Sl.* egg, Molotov cocktail, letter bomb; shell, ball, gas bomb, incendiary bomb, napalm bomb, stink bomb, time bomb.

grief, *n.* **1.** anguish, misery, *Archaic.* bale, dolor, *Archaic.* dole; sorrow, sadness, woe, ruth, heartache, heartbreak, broken heart; ache, hurt, pain, suffering, *Archaic.* teen; torture, torment, agony; lamentation, bereavement, mourning; wretchedness, heaviness of heart, desolation, despondency, dejection, despair, slough of despond, moroseness, melancholy.

2. regret, rue, remorse, repentance, contrition, penitence, compunction.

3. distress, affliction, grievance, trouble, worry, vexation, *Inf.* worriment; plight, strait, predicament, sea of troubles, difficulty, rub; burden, load, albatross, cross, onus, crown of thorns, bitter pill, millstone around one's neck; trial, travail, tribulation, curse, ordeal, infliction.

4. misfortune, adversity, loss, mischance, mishap, casualty, accident; reverse, hard luck, ill luck, bad luck, bad fortune, ill fortune, hard times, evil days; hardship, privation, austerity, pinch, extremity; disaster, calamity, catastrophe, evil; trauma, blow, shock.

5. come to grief fail, miscarry, *Inf.* come a cropper, *Inf.* come to no good, go to wrack and ruin.

grievance, *n.* **1.** wrong, unjust act, injustice, disservice, unfairness; injury, damage, hurt; outrage, atrocity, enormity, calamity; offense, affront, indignation, indignity.

2. complaint, *Law.* gravamen, charge, accusation, imputation, allegation, plaint; grudge, *U.S. Sl.* beef, *U.S. Inf.* gripe, *Inf.* ax to grind, bone to pick, *Brit.* crow to pluck.

grieve, *v.* **1.** sorrow, ache, suffer, eat one's heart out, anguish; mourn, lament, bewail, bemoan; weep, wail, cry, sob, shed tears, cry one's eyes out.

2. rue, regret, repine, deplore; take to heart, lay to heart.

3. pain, sadden, aggrieve, make one's heart bleed, break one's heart; hurt, injure, cut up, wound, scathe, cut to the quick, cut to the heart.

4. afflict, distress, disquiet, discomfort; deject, depress, oppress; torture, torment, agonize, harass, vex.

grievous, *adj.* **1.** sorrowful, mournful, sad, distressing, agonizing, crushing; painful, acute, sharp, cutting; heart-rending, moving, *Inf.* tear-jerking, pathetic, tragic, pitiful.

2. flagrant, blatant, egregious, heinous, shameful; atrocious, enormous, outrageous, flagitious, iniquitous, nefarious; shocking, appalling, glaring, gross, dire, grave; deplorable, lamentable, calamitous, dreadful.

3. burdensome, oppressive, heavy, afflictive; unbearable, torturous, impossible; unendurable, insufferable, insupportable, more than flesh and blood can bear.

grill, *n.* **1.** gridiron, grate, barbecue; griddle.

—*v.* **2.** broil, barbecue; fry, griddle.

3. persecute, torment, torture, excruciate, burn, scald.

4. *Informal.* cross-examine, cross-question, interrogate, quiz, pump, catechize.

grim, *adj.* **1.** stern, uncompromising, unyielding, unbending, inflexible, unamenable; firm, tenacious, intractable, adamant; obstinate, steadfast, obdurate, headstrong; unrelenting, relentless, inexorable, implacable; harsh, hard, severe, iron; resolute, determined, decided, set, strong-willed, dead set; indomitable, dogged, indefatigable; unflinching, unwavering, unshaken, unfaltering, unshrinking.

2. dreadful, dire, direful, dark, black, baleful, terrible; terrifying, frightful, dread, appalling; alarming, distressing, harrowing, rending; redoubtable, fearsome, formidable, awful; horrible, horrid, horrendous, monstrous, atrocious; hideous, ghastly, eerie, grotesque, macabre, grisly, gruesome, unspeakable; outrageous, shocking, enormous, flagrant; nefarious, heinous, flagitious, villainous; infamous, notorious, odious; wicked, evil, vile, iniquitous, *Archaic.* facinorous; abhorrent, revolting, repulsive, repugnant, loathsome, despicable, detestable, hateful.

3. surly, sullen, sulky, somber, sour, morose; crusty, crabby, cantankerous, churlish; cross, testy, ill-natured, ill-tempered, irascible, petulant; forbidding, threatening, menacing, sinister, lowering; gloomy, dismal, dreary, *Literary.* drear, miserable; wretched, abject, squalid, sorry, destitute.

4. fierce, savage, ferocious, vicious, fell, truculent; bestial, brutish, feral, ferine, tigerish, wolfish, lupine; brutal, violent, inhuman, barbarous, barbaric, hellish, Tartarian, Hunnish, Gothic, Vandalic; murderous, homicidal, slaughterous, bloodthirsty, sanguinary; sadistic, animalistic, cannibalistic, fiendish, ghoulish, ogreish; diabolical, demonic, devilish, satanic; pitiless, merciless, heartless, cruel, ruthless; hard-hearted, cold-hearted, stony-hearted, marble-hearted, cold-blooded.

grimace, *n.* **1.** face, wry face, *Archaic.* mow, *Sl.* mug, mouth, contortion; frown, scowl, glare; pout, *Fr. moue;* sneer, smirk, grin.

—*v.* **2.** mouth, *Sl.* mug, *Inf.* make a face, mop, *Archaic.* now, contort; frown, scowl, glower, glare; sneer, smirk, grin; pout, stick out one's lower lip, *Fr. faire la moue.*

grime, *n.* **1.** dirt, filth, squalor; smudge, stain, tarnish, rust; mud, muck, mire; slime, scum, *Sl.* crud, *Inf.* gook, *Sl.* yuk; dust, soot.

—*v.* **2.** soil, dirty, blacken, tarnish, begrime; sully, befoul, defile, contaminate; spatter, muddy, bemire, blotch, smudge, smirch, spot, stain.

grimy, *adj.* dirty, filthy, blackened, tarnished, begrimed; muddied, bedraggled, dirt-encrusted, befouled, besmeared; soiled, stained, spotted, smudged; squalid, slovenly, sleazy, *Sl.* crummy, *Sl.* grungy, *Sl.* yukky.

grin, *v.* **1.** smile, laugh; grin from ear to ear, grin like a Cheshire cat.

—*n.* **2.** smile, laugh; grimace, simper, smirk.

grind, *v.* **1.** whet, mill, kibble, stone, sand, sandpaper, pumice; grate, file, rasp, scrape, gride; smooth, polish, burnish, buff.

2. crush, bray, pound, beat, mash, smash, *Sl.* smush; pulverize, mortar, comminute, triturate, levigate, powder, granulate, shatter, crumble, disintegrate.

3. persecute, afflict, dragoon, abuse, mistreat, maltreat, ill-treat, scourge; castigate, chastise, punish; torture, molest, torment, plague, trouble, bother; harass, harry, hound, hector, pester, badger, *Archaic.* haggle; oppress, suppress, subdue, keep down.

4. grit, grate, rasp, gride, abrade, rub; scrape, scratch, clank, jangle, clash; screech, creak, screak, shrill, stridulate, set one's teeth on edge.

5. crank, wind, coil, turn, rotate, wheel, winch, windlass.

6. produce, generate, turn out, bring forth; manufacture, make, create.

7. *Often* **grind away** study, lucubrate, read, do schoolwork *or* homework, have one's nose buried in a book, burn the midnight oil, *Brit. Sl.* muzz; work, toil, labor, slave, drudge, *Inf.* sweat; keep one's nose to the grindstone *or* shoulder to the wheel *or* hand to the plow.

8. (*of dancing*) bump, swivel, rotate.

—*n.* **9.** whetting, milling, stoning, sanding, sandpapering, pumicing; grating, filing, rasping, scraping; smoothing, polishing, burnishing, buffing; crushing, braying, pounding, beating, mashing, smashing, *Sl.* smushing; pulverization, pulverizing, mortaring, comminution, comminuting, trituration, triturating, levigation, levigating, powdering, granulation, granulating, shattering, crumbling, disintegration, disintegrating.

10. grating, rasp, gride, scrape, scratching, clank, jangle, clash; screech, creak, screak, stridor, stridulation.

11. drudgery, pain, travail, toil, labor, exertion.

grip, *n.* **1.** grasp, gripe, clutch, clench; grapple, clinch; clasp, handclasp, embrace, hug, hold, arms.

2. seizure, seizing, grasping, griping, clutching; reach, reaching, snatching, snatch, grabbing, grab.

3. hold, control, clutches, possession, custody, keeping; command, government, direction, rule, authority; mastery, domination, dominion, sovereignty.

4. small suitcase, valise, Gladstone bag, traveling bag, overnight bag; satchel, bag, shoulder bag, gym bag, duffel bag, duffel; kit bag, knapsack, sack, backpack, pack.

5. mental hold *or* grasp, *Inf.* fix, *Sl.* handle; understanding, comprehension, apprehension, realization; awareness, sense, feel, perception, apperception, cognition; knowledge, ken, *Sl.* savvy, *Brit. Sl.* suss.

6. knob, lever, handle, hilt.

7. sharp pain, pang, spasm, contraction, convulsion, paroxysm, throe.

8. grippe, influenza, flu, *Pathol.* ague.

9. **come to grips with** face, deal with, cope with, handle, encounter, meet head on.

—*v.* **10.** hold fast, gripe, clutch, clench, clasp, hug, grapple, clinch; take hold of, *Inf.* latch on *or* onto, take, grasp; seize, jump at, leap at, reach for, grab, catch *or* catch at, nab; snatch, *Inf.* snitch, take away from.

11. take hold on *or* of, absorb, engross, involve, take in, engulf; hypnotize, mesmerize, rivet, spellbind, enchant, entrance, fascinate.

gripe, *v.* **1.** grasp, grip, clutch, clasp; clinch, grapple, seize, snatch, lay hold of.

2. distress, trouble, worry, disturb, oppress; hurt, ache, pain, pinch, twinge, squeeze; tighten, constrict, compress, cramp, contract.

3. *Informal.* complain, grumble, croak, *Inf.* grouse, *Sl.* kvetch, *Sl.* bitch, *Sl.* bellyache, *Sl.* beef, *Inf.* grouch; find fault, cavil, carp; whine, fret, repine.

4. *Nautical.* secure, fasten, make fast, fix, tie; anchor, harbor.

—*n.* **5.** grasp, clutch, grip, clasp; control, sway, hold.

6. claw, talon, paw, hook, clutching hand; hilt, handle, haft, lug.

7. *Informal.* complaint, grumble, objection, protest, *Sl.* beef, jeremiad, lamentation.

grisly, *adj.* **1.** gruesome, gory, ghastly, frightful, horrible, horrid, horrendous, awful, dreadful, terrible, hideous, ugly; disgusting, repulsive, repugnant, revolting, sickening; shocking, appalling, abominable, abhorrent, detestable, offensive, hateful, odious.

2. formidable, grim, threatening, ominous, foreboding, forbidding, harsh, unyielding; sinister, evil-looking, dangerous, frightening, *Inf.* scary.

grit, *n.* **1.** dust, powder, dirt, soot; airborne particles, air pollution, particulate matter.
2. mettle, mettlesomeness, spirit, pluck, pluckiness, gameness, nerve, chutzpah, backbone, gumption, heart, stout heart, blood, marrow, *Archaic.* pith, stamina, toughness, true grit, *U.S. Inf.* sand, *Inf.* starch, *Inf.* spunk, *Inf.* spunkiness, *Sl.* guts, *Sl.* gutsiness, *Sl.* moxie; courage, courageousness, bravery, valor, valorousness, valiancy, valiance, heroism, prowess; intrepidity, intrepidness, fearlessness, dauntlessness, awelessness, dreadlessness; fortitude, endurance, tenacity, determination, will, will power; firmness, resolution, resoluteness, indomitableness, indomitability, invincibleness, invincibility, unconquerableness; staunchness, stanchness, stalwartness, steadfastness, doughtiness, sturdiness, hardiness, hardihood, bulldog, courage.
3. sand, gravel, pebbles, stones, gritrock, gritstone, *Chiefly Brit.* shingle, *Rare.* attritus.
—*v.* **4.** grate, grind, gnash, rasp, scrape, rub, gride; clench, lock, lock together.

gritty, *adj.* **1.** sandy, sandlike, sabulous, arenaceous, arenose, arenulous, *Obs.* arenarious, *Obs.* arenate, *Obs.* arenated; grainy, grained, granular, granulate, granulated; gravelly, pebbly, pebbled, shingly, shingled; dusty, powdery, pulverous, pulverulent.
2. plucky, mettlesome, game, spirited, red-blooded, *Inf.* spunky; brave, courageous, valiant, valorous, heroic, hero-like, heroical, stout-hearted, lionhearted, ironhearted, great-hearted, high-hearted; intrepid, fearless, dauntless, aweless, dreadless, nervy, *Sl.* gutsy, unafraid, unblenching, unblenched, undaunted, undismayed, unalarmed, unappalled.
3. firm, resolute, determined, staunch, stanch, steadfast, stalwart, *Archaic.* stalworth, doughty, sturdy, hardy; indomitable, invincible, unconquerable, unyielding, unshrinking, unbending, unbowing, unfaltering, unhesitating, unwavering, unswerving, undeviating.

groan, *n.* **1.** sigh, moan, murmur, mutter, grumble, grunt, grouse, complaint, gripe, *Sl.* bitch; yapping, *Inf.* yammering, whine, whimper, sob, blubbering, sniveling, sniffling; cry, crying, weeping, wailing, wail, ululation, bleat; bawling, vociferation, howl, yelp; scream, yell, *Inf.* holler, shout, roar, bellow.
2. creak, squeak, screech, grating, harsh sound.
—*v.* **3.** murmur, mutter, grumble, grunt, grouse, complain, gripe, *Sl.* bitch; yap, *Inf.* yammer, whine, whimper, sob, blubber, snivel, sniffle; cry, weep, wail.
4. sigh, moan, bemoan, bewail, lament, keen, mourn, grieve; fret, worry over, tear one's hair out, beat one's head against a brick wall.
5. creak, squeak, screech, grate, resound harshly.
6. be overloaded, be overburdened, be weighed down, be bogged down.

groggy, *adj.* **1.** dazed, stunned, stupefied; staggered, overpowered, overcome, *Inf.* bowled over, knocked over, K.O.'d; benumbed, numbed, desensitized, anesthetized; drugged, narcotized, hypnotized, mesmerized, in a stupor, in a trance, deadened; doped, *Inf.* dopey, sluggish, lethargic, enervated; befuddled, muddled, addled, mystified, puzzled; confused, bewildered, confounded, perplexed, baffled.
2. tired, exhausted, sleepy, dozing, unable to keep one's eyes open. See **exhausted** (*def.* **1**).

groom, *n.* **1.** stableboy, stableman, hostler, ostler, equerry.
2. bridegroom, newly married man, man about to be married; benedict, husband, spouse, consort, partner, better half, mate.
—*v.* **3.** arrange, fix, adjust, do, dress, adorn; put in order, tend, make tidy, tidy up, freshen up, refresh, spruce up; smooth, disentangle, untangle, unsnarl, get the knots out; curry, brush, rub, rub down, clean.
4. train, coach, break in; initiate, ground, prepare; ready, prime, harden, inure; teach, instruct, tutor, school, inform, enlighten, edify.

groove, *n.* **1.** indentation, hollow, furrow, gouge, stria; flute, trench, channel, trough, canal, *Archit.* glyph.
2. routine, habit, rut, *Inf.* grind *or* daily grind; treadmill, squirrel cage, jog trot, *Inf.* rat race.
—*v.* **3.** furrow, channel, trough, flute, trench, ditch, rut.
4. **groove on** *Slang.* enjoy, like, love, rejoice in, revel in, *Sl.* dig, *Sl.* be into, *Sl.* get high on, *Sl.* get off on, *Sl.* freak out on, *Sl.* trip on, *Sl.* be turned on by, *Sl.* be blown away by.

grope, *v.* **1.** feel one's way, probe, grabble, scrabble, fumble, poke around, pick one's way, move blindly.
2. fish for, angle for, hunt for, look for, cast *or* beat around for; send out a feeler, send up a trial balloon, see how the land lies, see which way the wind is blowing.

gross, *adj.* **1.** aggregate, entire, whole, all, all-inclusive, inclusive, comprehensive.
2. unqualified, unmitigated, complete, total, absolute; rank, arrant, sheer, uttermost, outright, out-and-out, downright.
3. flagrant, blatant, glaring, egregious, obvious, manifest, plain; outrageous, reprehensible, heinous, grievous, shameful.
4. indelicate, indecent, risqué, ribald, bawdy, raffish; crude, vulgar, raw, rude, broad, earthy, low, foul-mouthed; carnal, sensual, erotic, sexual, animalistic; obscene, pornographic, gutter, gutter-level.
5. unrefined, unsophisticated, uncultured, uncultivated; crass, cloddish, boorish, oafish, loutish, lumpish, lubberly; dull, obtuse, stupid, thick, dim-witted.
6. large, big, great; bulky, hulky, ponderous, cumbersome, unwieldy; huge, colossal, tremendous, stupendous, prodigious, immense, massive.
7. obese, very fat, extremely overweight, adipose.
—*n.* **8.** take, intake, takings, receipts, profits; box office, gate, handle, *Brit. Sl.* get.

grossness, *n.* **1.**, completeness, totality, absoluteness, unqualifiedness, unmitigatedness; rankness, sheerness, arrantness, outrightness, downrightness.
2. flagrancy, blatancy, glaringness, obviousness, manifestness, plainness; outrageousness, reprehensibleness, heinousness, grievousness, shamefulness.
3. indelicateness, indecency, ribaldry, bawdiness, raffishness; crudeness, vulgarity, rawness, rudeness, earthiness, lowness; carnality, sensuality, eroticism, sexuality, animalism.
4. unsophistication, lack of refinement *or* polish, uncultivatedness, crassness; cloddishness, loutishness, oafishness, lumpishness, lubberliness.

grotesque, *adj.* **1.** strange, weird, bizarre, freakish, *Inf.* freaky, *Sl.* rum, *Sl.* far-out; odd, peculiar, curious, queer, offbeat; uncommon, unusual, deviate, aberrant, anomalous, abnormal, irregular.
2. misshapen, distorted, twisted, gnarled, deformed, misproportioned, humpbacked, hunchbacked; monstrous, frightful, hideous, horrible, horrendous; repugnant, repellent, repulsive.

grotto, *n.* **1.** cave, cavern, cove, *Chiefly Literary.* grot; subterrane, catacomb.
2. retreat, refuge, haven, shelter, burrow, hermitage; asylum, resort, sanctuary, ark, covert, hideaway, mew.
3. recess, hollow, cavity, concavity; alcove, niche,

nook, corner, cubbyhole, cubby.

grouch, *v.* **1.** *Informal.* complain, moan, *Inf.* gripe. See **grumble** (*def.* **1**).
—*n.* **2.** *Informal.* grumbler, crab, curmudgeon. See **grumbler.**

grouchy, *adj.* *Informal.* surly, cantankerous, irascible. See **grumpy.**

ground, *n.* **1.** soil, earth, mold, *Archaic.* glebe, *Archaic.* marl, land, terrain; sod, turf; loam, clay.
2. **grounds** tract, property, acres, estate, farm; surroundings, lawn, yard, common, field, park.
3. *Often* **grounds** foundation, base, basis, root; reason, rationale, argument; proof, evidence, testimony, demonstration, premise, proposition; motive, cause, why and wherefore; object, purpose, excuse.
4. **grounds** dregs, lees, grouts, sediment, deposit, precipitate, settlings.
—*v.* **5.** found, base, set, bottom; fix, settle, stabilize, secure; establish, consolidate, organize, install, institute.

groundless, *adj.* **1.** unsupported, ungrounded, unfounded, unsound, unbased, baseless, without basis; conjectural, speculative, suppositional, hypothetical, academic, academical, theoretical, imaginary, illusory; unsubstantial, tenuous, faulty, erroneous, apocryphal.
2. unjustified, unjustifiable, unwarranted, unprovoked, uncalled-for, wanton, gratuitous, without cause *or* motive *or* reason; illogical, irrational, unreasonable, senseless, preposterous, absurd, ridiculous, asinine, *Sl.* cockeyed.

groundwork, *n.* foundation, ground, base, basis; bottom, footing, underpinning; basics, ABCs, elementals, essentials; preparation, preliminaries, *Inf.* homework; preface, prologue, first things.

group, *n.* **1.** collection, assemblage, accumulation, amassment; heap, pile, mass, cumulation; agglomeration, conglomeration.
2. class, classification, family, species, genus, phylum; subdivision, variety, branch, section.
3. set, series, array, assortment; cluster, clump, *Bot.* sorus, bunch, batch; lot, pack, packet.
4. company, party, body, congregation, assembly, gathering, crowd; team, crew, band, troupe, squad, gang, detail, work party, force, corps, detachment; association, league, sisterhood, brotherhood, sorority, fraternity, sodality, guild; circle, set, clique, coterie; flock, herd, drove, bevy, covey, gaggle, swarm, shoal, school, colony; clan, tribe, sept, phyle, caste.
—*v.* **5.** classify, class, bracket; rank, size, grade, graduate; sort, sift, categorize, assign, dispose; organize, arrange, marshal, coordinate; line up, file, catalog, register, tabulate, index; align, range.
6. associate, get together, keep company with; mingle, hobnob, consort, fraternize.

grove, *n.* stand, copse, copsewood, thicket, brake, canebrake, boscage, covert, pinery, *Southwestern U.S.* chaparral, *Brit.* spinney, *Chiefly Brit.* coppice, *Archaic.* bosk; orchard, orangery, *Obs.* arbor; wood, woods, woodland, wooded area, wildwood, forest.

grovel, *v.* **1.** kowtow, bow, bow before, bow to, bow and scrape, bend, bend before, stoop, squat, crouch, slouch, hunch; cringe, cower, squirm; whine, whimper, snivel; lick [s.o.'s] shoes, lick *or* kiss [s.o.'s] feet, kiss the hem of [s.o.'s] garment, *Inf.* bootlick; court, pay court to, curry favor, keep time to, dance attendance upon, be at [s.o.'s] beck and call, agree to anything, *Inf.* be a yes man to; toady, toady to, toad-eat, fawn, fawn upon, *Sl.* fall all over, wheedle, slaver, puff, puff up, inflate, *Inf.* play up to, *Inf.* apple-polish, *Inf.* butter up; *Sl.* shine up to, *Sl.* suck up to, *Sl.* brown-nose, *Sl.* earn brownie points.
2. crawl, creep, creep before, slither, sneak, sneak along, steal, steal along, worm, worm along, worm one's way; kneel, kneel before, fall on one's knees; lie prone, lie low, prostrate oneself, throw oneself at the feet of.
3. (*all in mean or base things*) wallow, wallow in, wallow in the mire, welter; revel in, rejoice in, delight in, luxuriate in, indulge in.

groveling, *adj.* **1.** servile, slavish, obsequious, *Obs.* obsequent, subservient, menial, *Obs., Rare.* vernile; submissive, docile, deferential, acquiescent, compliant, unassertive, Tomish, Uncle Tomish, tractable, mealy-mouthed; kowtowing, bowing, bowing and scraping, bending, stooping, squatting, crouching, slouching, hunching; cringing, cowering, squirming; crawling, creeping, slithering, sneaking, stealing, worming; whining, whimpering, sniveling; sycophantic, sycophantical, sycophantish, toadyish, toadying, toad-eating, truckling, wheedling, timeserving, *Inf.* bootlicking, *Sl.* footlicking, *Inf.* apple-polishing, *Sl.* brown-nosing, *Obs.* blanding, *Obs., Rare.* blandiloquous.
2. base, base-spirited, mean, mean-spirited, low, low-spirited, vile, scurvy, despicable, contemptible, debased, abased; shabby, paltry, dirty, beggarly, beggared.

grow, *v.* **1.** increase, fill out, expand, develop, enlarge, swell, wax, become greater *or* larger; add to, augment, reinforce, supplement; double, triple, quadruple, multiply; extend, distend, stretch, spread; widen, heighten, lengthen, deepen, thicken; amplify, magnify, aggrandize.
2. issue, arise, originate, spring up, sprout, bud, germinate, pullulate, shoot up; burst forth, mushroom, burgeon, boom, develop vigorously; thrive, prosper, flourish, luxuriate; bloom, blossom, flower, bear fruit, fructify; mature, maturate, ripen.
3. advance, get ahead, go up in the world, progress, make headway; succeed, *Brit. Dial.* fadge, fare well, get *or* go along.
4. unite, coalesce, come together, become attached; combine, merge, converge, blend, amalgamate.
5. become, come to be, get to be; work up to, progress, advance.
6. raise, produce, generate, breed, propagate, cause to grow; cultivate, nurture, till, farm, garden; plant, *Hort.* bed, sow, scatter seed.
7. **grow into** **a.** become large enough for; fit into. **b.** progress, advance, work up to, become qualified for.
8. **grow on or upon** **a.** influence, affect, impress, touch, stir. **b.** become used to, get accustomed to, get in the habit of; accept, begin to like.
9. **grow out of** **a.** outgrow, develop beyond, mature beyond; leave behind, discard, abandon, put *or* lay aside. **b.** originate in, develop from, come out of, spring from, issue from, result from.
10. **grow up** **a.** become fully grown, become mature *or* of age, become an adult. **b.** come into existence, arise, appear, come into being, develop, spring *or* shoot up; burst forth, mushroom, burgeon, bloom.

growing, *adj.* **1.** increasing, expanding, crescive, crescent, accrescent, enlarging, aggrandizing, swelling, waxing; extending, distending, spreading, stretching; widening, heightening, lengthening, deepening, thickening.
2. prospering, thriving, palmy; mushrooming, burgeoning, booming, ascendant, in the ascendant, on the rise *or* upswing; flourishing, lush, luxuriant, exuberant; blooming, blossoming, flowering; developing,

maturing, maturating, ripening.

growl, *v.* **1.** snarl, murmur, gnarl, gnar, groan; bank, howl, yelp, yap; roar, bellow, rumble, thunder, boom, resound.

2. complain, grumble, crab, *Inf.* gripe, fume, clamor, *Inf.* raise a fuss, *Inf.* yammer, *Sl.* grouse, *Sl.* grouch, *Sl.* squawk, *Sl.* beef, *Sl.* bitch, *Dial.* holler; lament, moan, groan, *Sl.* kvetch, *Sl.* bellyache.

—n. **3.** snarl, murmur, groan.

grownup, *n.* adult, man, gentleman, woman, lady.

grown-up, *adj.* mature, old enough to know better; adult, of age, at the age of consent, at the age of majority; big, grown, developed, fully developed, fully grown, full-grown; (*of movies and literature*) X-rated, pornographic, obscene.

growth, *n.* **1.** augmentation, increase, proliferation, multiplication, enlargement, aggrandizement, expansion, extension; magnification, amplification, deepening, heightening; widening, thickening, broadening; inflation, distension, dilatation, dilation; waxing, swelling.

2. development, maturation, germination, evolution; burgeoning, pullulation, shooting up, springing up, upcropping, sprouting; unfolding, opening, blooming, blossoming, flowering, ripening.

3. progress, movement forward, headway; promotion, furtherance, improvement, advancement, rise, elevation.

4. *Pathology.* excrescence, excretion, *Biol.* auxesis, tumor, lump, intumescence, tumefaction; protuberance, protrusion, prominence; blister, blain, boil.

5. consequence, result, effect, event, outcome, issue, upshot; outgrowth, aftermath, turnout.

grub, *v.* **1.** dig, delve, spade, excavate, unearth, disinter; root out, uproot, deracinate, extirpate, extract, pull *or* tear out, extricate; search, seek, hunt, probe, rummage, ferret out, explore, mine.

2. study, labor over, peruse, scrutinize; inspect, examine, look into; research, survey, scan, analyze.

3. grovel, toady, cringe, truckle; skimp and scrime, work around the clock; slave, plod. See **drudge** (*def.* 2).

grubby, *adj.* **1.** dirty, unclean, unwashed, *Sl.* crummy, *Sl.* grungy, messy, *Sl.* looking like the cat's breakfast; filthy, foul, repulsive, wretched; sordid, squalid, ratty; slovenly, *Sl.* raunchy, *Inf.* scruffy, unkempt, untidy, shabby, seedy; frowzy, dowdy, frumpish, slatternly.

2. comtemptible, despicable, loathsome, abhorrent, abominable, hateful; worthless, *Sl.* cruddy, *Sl.* schmucky, mean; base, low, low-down, wormy, *Sl.* putzy, vile.

grudge, *n.* **1.** resentment, spite, umbrage, offense, pique; grievance, bone to pick, *Inf.* ax to grind, *Brit.* crow to pluck; bitterness, ill will, malice, rancor, hard feelings, discontent; hatred, enmity, animosity, hate, virulence; spleen, gall, bile, venom; malevolence, malignancy, antipathy; envy, jealousy, covetousness, cupidity.

—v. **2.** give in, give unwillingly, drag one's feet, force oneself to, do with regret; be loath, be averse, be reluctant.

3. resent, begrudge, mind, feel; envy, covet, be jealous of; take umbrage, take ill, take offense, take exception; be offended, be indignant, be piqued.

grudging, *adj.* reluctant, not in the mood, with regret, regretting, half-hearted; unwilling, averse, loath, opposed; indisposed, disinclined, unacquiescent.

grueling, *adj.* exhausting, tiring, wearying, fatiguing, uphill; severe, harsh, stern, intense, hard, fierce; arduous, laborious, strenuous, draining; relentless, inexorable, unsparing, remorseless.

gruesome, *adj.* horrible, ghastly, grisly, hideous, terrible, horrendous; repulsive, revolting, repellent, loathsome, abominable; macabre, grotesque, monstrous, sick, ugly; frightful, spine-chilling, unnerving, fearsome, shocking.

gruff, *adj.* **1.** low, harsh, hoarse, coarse, gutteral, throaty, husky, roupy; raucous, grating, cracked, strident, ragged, thick, hollow.

2. surly, sullen, sulky, ill-humored, ill-tempered; churlish, bearish, boorish, crusty; grumpy, grouchy, snarling, sour, crabbed, peevish; abrupt, curt, short, brusque, clipped; rough, crude, blunt; bluff, burly, brash, bold, brazen, barefaced, insolent, impudent, contumelious; sharp, keen, trenchant, acrimonious, caustic, stinging, cutting, biting, piercing, stringent; brutal, cruel; inconsiderate, tactless, blustering; rude, uncivil, unceremonious, ungracious, discourteous, impolite, unmannerly.

grumble, *v.* **1.** complain, moan, mutter, fuss, make a fuss, *Brit.* natter, *Inf.* kick up a fuss, *Inf.* gripe, *Inf.* grouse, *Inf.* grouch, *Sl.* bellyache, *Sl.* bitch.

2. growl, snarl, gnar.

3. rumble, roll, roar, thunder, boom, peal.

grumbler, *n.* curmudgeon, crab, bear, *Inf.* crank, *Inf.* crosspatch, *Inf.* grouch, *Inf.* grouser, *Inf.* griper, *Inf.* sorehead, *Sl.* bellyacher, *Sl.* grump, *Sl.* bitch.

grumbling, *n.* complaining, muttering, muttering under one's breath, faultfinding, carping, criticizing, *Inf.* grousing, *Sl.* bellyaching, *Sl.* grouching, *Sl.* bitching; discontent, dissatisfaction, protestation.

grumpy, *adj.* surly, cantankerous, irascible, crabbed, iracund, choleric, brusque, peppery, crusty, dyspeptic, crotchety, thorny, bearish, snarling, growling, *Inf.* grouchy; cross, feisty, huffy, irritable, peevish, cranky, bilious, out of sorts; testy, touchy, ill-tempered, bad-tempered, short-tempered; fractious, quarrelsome, caviling, disagreeable, *Inf.* ornery, *Inf.* bitchy, *Inf.* ugly; sharp, uncivil, rough, harsh; abrupt, curt, short, terse, blunt.

guarantee, *n.* **1.** warrant, warranty, guaranty, *Law.* covenant of warranty, *Law.* warranty deed, *Law.* certificate, *Law.* certification, *Obs.* vouch; insurance, indemnity, protection, *Insurance.* coverage; contract, compact, covenant, obligation, engagement, agreement; gentlemen's agreement, handshake, bargain, deal, pact, convention, treaty; certainty, *Inf.* sure thing, *Sl.* cinch.

2. pledge, promise, assurance, word, word of honor, oath, sworn statement, *Archaic.* plight; endorsement, testimonial, attestation, recommendation.

3. guarantor, warrantor, voucher, sponsor, bonder, *Law.* bondsman, *Law.* bondswoman; insurer, ensurer, indemnitor, underwriter, *Insurance.* coverer; *Law.* covenantor, obligator; endorser, attester, patron, supporter, backer.

4. insured, indemnitee, mortgagee, *Rare.* insurant.

5. collateral, surety, *Law.* security, earnest, deposit, *Law.* earnest money; pawn, gage, bail, *Insurance.* bond, *Law.* mortgage, *Law.* mortgage bond, *Law.* bail bond, *Rare.* hostage.

—v. **6.** ensure, secure, *Finance.* bond, *Law.* mortgage, *Sl.* cinch; pawn, gage, put up collateral, give earnest money, make a deposit, obligate; warrant, vouch, attest to, testify to, endorse, certify; contract, covenant, enter an agreement, make a bargain *or* deal, shake on it.

7. sponsor, countersign, underwrite, witness, answer for, stand behind, back up.

8. promise, pledge, plight, give one's solemn word *or* promise, state on one's honor, swear to, state under oath; assure, offer assurance, asseverate, avouch, aver, affirm, say for certain *or* sure.

9. insure, indemnify, protect, *Insurance.* cover.

guarantor, *n.* warrantor, voucher, sponsor, guarantee, bonder, *Law.* bondsman, *Law.* bondswoman; insurer, ensurer, indemnitor, *Insurance.* coverer; covenanter, obligator; endorser, attester, patron, supporter, backer.

guaranty, *n.* **1.** warrant, warranty, guarantee, *Obs.* vouch; contract, compact, covenant, obligation, engagement, agreement, gentlemen's agreement, handshake; pledge, promise, assurance, word, word of honor, oath, sworn statement, *Archaic.* plight.

2. collateral, surety, *Law.* security, earnest, *Law.* earnest money, deposit; pawn, gage, *Insurance.* bond, *Law.* mortgage, *Law.* mortgage bond, bail, *Law.* bail bond, *Rare.* hostage.

3. securing, ensuring, *Sl.* cinching; warranting, *Early Eng. Law.* voucher, vouching, endorsement, attestation; assurance, promising, pledging, swearing.

—*v.* **4.** ensure, secure, sponsor, assure, pledge. See **guarantee** (*defs.* **6-8**).

guard, *v.* **1.** protect, watch over, stand guard over, police, secure, defend; shield, shelter, screen, cover, cloak; preserve, save, conserve; escort, conduct, convoy, ride shotgun.

2. supervise, hold watch, keep under surveillance; control, keep under guard, govern, constrain, restrain, suppress, repress.

3. keep watch, be alert, be on the qui vive, take care, beware, *Inf.* be on one's toes, *Inf.* keep one's nose to the ground, *Inf.* keep an eye out, *Inf.* keep one's eyes peeled.

—*n.* **4.** protector, defender, guardian, guarder, guardsman; custodian, watchman, night watchman; sentinel, sentry, picket, patrol, garrison; escort, convoy, safe-conduct; jailer, warder, keeper, turnkey, *Sl.* screw, *Sl.* bull; scout, lookout, watchdog.

5. vigilance, heed, care, caution, wariness; watch, close watch, eagle eye, sharp eye.

6. safeguard, defense, protection, security, safety; bulwark, shield, fence, screen; fender, bumper, buffer, cushion, pad; safekeeping, protective custody.

7. **off one's guard** unwary, unalert, unwatchful, unvigilant; unprepared, unready; asleep, napping, *Inf.* not on the job, *Sl.* goofing off, *Sl.* looking out the window.

8. **on one's guard** wary, vigilant, watchful, on the watch, on the lookout, on the qui vive, all eyes and ears; cautious, precautious, careful, heedful, mindful.

guarded, *adj.* **1.** careful, cautious, circumspect, mindful, heedful; on guard, alert, on the alert, on the qui vive, watchful, discreet; wary, chary, leery, apprehensive, suspicious, *Inf.* cagey; reluctant, loath; reticent.

2. protected, defended, safeguarded, sheltered, shielded; watched over, under surveillance; restrained, under restraint, under control, constrained.

guardian, *n.* **1.** protector, defender, champion, paladin, *Fig.* knight in shining armor; patron, foster parent.

2. trustee, warden, keeper, custodian, caretaker, curator; steward, fiduciary, *Brit.* warder, *Scot.* factor.

guerrilla, *n.* partisan, irregular, bushfighter, bushwhacker, underground *or* resistance fighter, jayhawker.

guess, *v.* **1.** conjecture, surmise, estimate, reckon, hypothesize, postulate, *Inf.* figure, *Inf.* talk off the top of one's head, *Inf.* take a stab *or* shot, *Inf.* take a shot in the dark, *Sl.* guesstimate.

2. think, suppose, fancy, believe, imagine; feel, opine, judge, allow, deem, daresay.

—*n.* **3.** conjecture, supposition, assumption, presumption, inference, surmise, guesswork; hypothesis, postulate; random shot, pot shot, *Inf.* shot in the dark, *Inf.* shot, *Sl.* whack, *Sl.* crack, *Sl.* guesstimate.

guesswork, *n.* conjecture, guess, surmise, supposition, presupposition, assumption, presumption, *Inf.* shot in the dark, *Sl.* guesstimate; hypothesis, postulate, theory; augury, forecast, prediction, prophesy.

guest, *n.* visitor, caller, company; uninvited guest, gate crasher; roomer, boarder, *Inf.* freeloader, *Sl.* moocher *or* mooch; regular, frequenter, habitué.

guffaw, *n.* horselaugh, hearty laugh, cachinnation, heehaw, *Inf.* belly laugh, *Inf.* boffo; (*all of laughter*) bellow, roar, howl, shriek.

guidance, *n.* **1.** direction, instruction, advisement, recommendation; warning, admonition, persuasion, urging, encouragement, exhortation.

2. leadership, steerage, pilotage, navigation; control, mastership, regulation, handling, manipulation, disposal, charge, rule.

3. advice, counsel, wisdom, teaching, *Brit. Dial.* rede; suggestion, word to the wise, tip, hint, pointer, clue, cue.

guide, *v.* **1.** lead, lead the way, conduct, usher; pilot, drive, navigate, hold the reins, take the helm, be at the helm; direct, give directions to, steer [s.o. *or* s.t.] toward, head [s.o. *or* s.t.] toward, show the way, orientate, put on the right track, map out the route.

2. escort, convoy, accompany, attend, companion, chaperon; guard, watch over, keep an eye on, look after, be by one's side.

3. advise, counsel, instruct, teach, tutor, tell about, take under one's wing, *Inf.* steer; recommend, suggest, offer an opinion, give [s.o.] a tip, *Inf.* hint, tell [s.o.] what to do.

4. supervise, oversee, preside, be master over, boss, dominate, domineer; manage, superintend, handle, manipulate; regulate, govern, rule, control.

—*n.* **5.** leader, cicerone, conductor, director, coryphaeus, pilot, captain, skipper, commandant; usher, escort, chaperon, convoy, attendant; manager, fugleman.

6. adviser, counselor, mentor, guidance counselor, confidant, therapist, guru, master; coach, teacher, instructor, educator, tutor, preceptor, trainer.

7. indicator, pointer, mark, landmark, directory, direction; sign, signal, beacon, lodestar; token, symbol, key; clue, hint, tip-off, cue, suggestion.

8. guidebook, handbook, manual. See **guidebook.**

9. exemplar, example, model, original, archetype, pattern, paradigm, prototype; ideal, paragon, pink, phoenix; standard, norm, criterion, rule, rule of thumb; precedent, parallel case.

guidebook, *n.* guide, handbook, manual, vade mecum, catalogue, ABC; itinerary, tour book, travelogue, chart, roadbook; Baedeker, Fodor, Michelin, Murray, Guide Bleu.

guideline, *n.* **1.** stricture, bound, restraint, limit; margin, perimeter, confine, borderline.

2. indication, guide, key, index, marker, pointer; measure, gauge, standard, touchstone, bench mark, yardstick; instruction, direction, regulation, rule, prescription.

guild, *n.* union, society, fraternity, brotherhood, craft, order, lodge; organization, association, company, corporation, combine; federation, alliance, coalition, confederacy, axis; cartel, bloc, consortium, front; league, syndicate, trust.

guile, *n.* cunning, duplicity, fraud, deception, deceit, subtlety, gamesmanship; artfulness, wiliness, slyness, foxiness, guilefulness, craftiness, wiles; finesse, shrewdness, slickness, shiftiness, insidiousness; chicanery, jugglery, skulduggery, quackery; treachery, perfidy.

guileful, *adj.* cunning, artful, crafty, wily, sly, subtle, foxy, vulpine, feline; shrewd, canny, *Inf.* cagey, *Scot. and North Eng.* pawky, sharp; shifty, slick, smooth, slippery, stealthy; deceitful, deceptive, tricky, underhanded, crooked, double-dealing; insidious, scheming, plotting, designing, calculating; perfidious, treacherous, traitorous.

guileless, *adj.* **1.** open, open-hearted, ingenuous, sincere, genuine, undeceptive, undeceitful, undeceiving, unfeigning, undissembling, undissimulating; aboveboard, open and aboveboard, up front, up and up, on the level, no-nonsense; honorable, just, fair, straight, square, upright, upstanding, fair and square, square-dealing, plain-dealing, square-shooting, straight-shooting; honest, trustworthy, *Inf.* trusty, uncorrupt, uncorrupted, *Inf.* O.K.

2. candid, frank, forthright, foursquare, direct, straightforward, straight-from-the-shoulder; plain, plain-spoken, plain-speaking, downright, outright, explicit, unequivocal, unambiguous, undisguised, undisguising, *Inf.* straight-out, *Inf.* flatfooted, *Inf.* matter-of-fact; outspoken, free-spoken, free-speaking, free-tongued, free, unreticent, bold, unreserved, unrestrained, unconstrained, unchecked, uncurbed, unabashed, uninhibited, unsparing, unshrinking; blunt, bluff, brusque, brash, tactless.

3. artless, naive, simple, simple-minded, innocent, childlike; unsophisticated, undeveloped, unworldly, green, born yesterday, wet behind the ears; unsuspicious, trustful, trusting, unwary, unguarded.

guilt, **n.** **1.** guiltiness, culpability, *Latin. culpa,* criminality; illegality, illicitness, illegitimacy, illegitimateness, lawlessness, unlawfulness; reprehensibility, blame, blameworthiness, censurability, censurableness, reproachableness; feloniousness, wrongfulness, sinfulness.

2. remorse, regret, contrition, contriteness, compunction; sorrow, sorrowfulness, penitence, repentance; self-reproach, self-accusation, self-condemnation, self-reproof.

guiltless, *adj.* innocent, free from guilt, clear, *Sl.* clean; blameless, inculpable, unblamable, uncensurable, unimpeachable, irreproachable, above reproach, above suspicion, like Caesar's wife; sinless, stainless, spotless, immaculate, pure; uncorrupted, undefiled, untainted, unspotted, unsullied, unsoiled, unblemished, unmarred, untarnished; faultless, sterling, perfect, saintly, without fault.

guilty, *adj.* **1.** culpable, criminal, unlawful, illegal, illicit, illegitimate, lawless; reprehensible, condemnable, reproachable, blameworthy, blamable, at fault, censurable; felonious, wrong, amiss, penitentiary, transgressive; condemned, convicted, sentenced.

2. sinful, peccant, erring, errant; wicked, iniquitous, nefarious, villainous, heinous, flagitious; corrupt, unholy, demeritorious.

3. remorseful, regretful, contrite, compunctious; sorry, sorrowful, penitent, repentant, penitential; conscience-stricken, conscience-smitten, self-condemning, self-accusing, self-reproaching; hangdog, sheepish.

4. red-handed, *Latin. in flagrante delicto, Sl.* caught with one's pants down, *Inf.* caught with one's hand in the cookie jar.

guise, *n.* **1.** external appearance, aspect, look, semblance, outward form, exterior, image, likeness; figure, visage, face, countenance, features; mien, air, cast, character, presence, attitude; demeanor, bearing, carriage, deportment, conduct, behavior; cover, *Inf.* front, show, pretense, presentment.

2. disguise, costume, outfit, *Inf.* get-up, habit, dress, trappings, clothes, clothing; style, fashion, manner, wise, custom.

gulch, *n.* ravine, valley, gully, canyon, gorge, *Brit. Dial.* clough; gulf, abyss, abysm, chasm, hollow, pit, hole; gap, cleft, crevasse, fissure, crevice, crack, cut; notch, passage, pass, corridor, defile.

gulf, *n.* **1.** bay, harbor, cove, bight, basin; inlet, arm, sound, loch, fjord, *Both Chiefly Scot.* firth, frith; estuary, mouth, *Dial.* creek, outlet, *Southern U.S.* bayou, lagoon.

2. chasm, abyss, abysm, hollow, pit; hole, opening, space; rift, breach, separation, break; cleft, cut, notch, gap; crack, fissure, split, crevice, crevasse; gulch, gully, canyon, gorge, ravine, valley.

gull, *v.* **1.** cheat, rook, fleece, defraud, swindle, *Archaic.* chouse; bilk, pluck, mulct; victimize, exploit, play on *or* upon, take advantage of; overcharge, *Sl.* soak, *Inf.* gyp, *Sl.* chisel, *Sl.* gaff.

2. delude, deceive, beguile, mislead, hoodwink; pull the wool over [s.o.'s] eyes, put [s.t.] over on [s.o.]; cozen, bluff, take in, bamboozle, *Sl.* hornswoggle, cully, jockey, *Inf.* buffalo, *Inf.* finagle, *Sl.* con, *Inf.* flimflam, *Sl.* flam, *Sl.* sting; trick, fool, *Inf.* kid, spoof, put [s.o.] on; overreach, circumvent, get around.

—n. **3.** dupe, gudgeon, simpleton, *Brit. Dial.* cull, *Archaic.* cully, *Inf.* chump, *Sl.* sap, *Sl.* schnook, *Sl.* schlemiel, *Sl.* boob; greenhorn, sitting duck, easy *or* soft mark *or* target, *Inf.* sucker, *Inf.* cinch, *Sl.* patsy, *Sl.* pigeon, *U.S. Sl.* fall guy, *Sl.* softie *or* soft touch, *Sl.* pushover, *Inf.* trusting soul; butt, fair game, fool, everybody's fool, *Inf.* goat, *Brit. Sl.* mug.

4. pawn, puppet, tool, instrument, flunky, lackey, cat's paw; creature, minion, dummy, *Sl.* stooge.

gullet, *n.* **1.** esophagus, throat, pharynx, crop, craw.

2. ditch, trench, channel, drain, culvert, run; gully, gulch, ravine, gorge, flume.

gullible, *adj.* credulous, trustful, easily deceived, unsuspicious, unsuspecting; unsophisticated, naïve, innocent, innocent as a new-born babe, born yesterday, wide-eyed and innocent, wet behind the ears; ingenuous, simple, foolish; green, green as they come, inexperienced, immature.

gully, *n.* valley, ravine, gulch, canyon, gorge. See **gulch.**

gulp, *v.* **1.** swallow, quaff, swig, drain one's glass, toss down *or* off, guzzle, swill; tipple, wet one's whistle, lap up, *Inf.* chug-a-lug; engorge, ingurgitate, bolt, gobble, devour, tuck in, eat like a pig.

2. suppress, stifle, strangle, choke back, gag, gasp, smother, cut short.

—n. **3.** swallow, mouthful, draught, dose.

gumption, *n. Informal.* initiative, resourcefulness, ingenuity, enterprise, courage, *Inf.* starch; energy, get up and go, stamina, virility, forcefulness. See **gut** (*def.* 4).

gun, *n.* **1.** pistol, revolver, *Trademark.* Colt, repeater, automatic; derringer, shooting iron, six-shooter, shooter, hand gun, sidearm, *Sl.* rod, *Sl.* piece, *Sl.* Saturday night special, *Sl.* heater, *Sl.* zip gun, *Sl.* enforcer; rifle, carbine, shotgun, sawed-off shotgun; musket, breechloader, flintlock, firelock, blunderbuss, matchlock, harquebus.

2. cannon, field piece, mortar, howitzer; machine gun, Gatling gun.

gunman, *n.* **1.** assassin, murderer, killer, slayer, cutthroat, liquidator, bravo, sniper, *Euph.* silencer, *Euph.* dispatcher; *All U.S. Sl.* gun, hired gun, hit man, hatchet man, trigger-man, torpedo.

2. bandit, hold-up man, *Sl.* stick-up man, armed robber; terrorist, desperado, gangster, mobster, racketeer, mafioso; thug, hoodlum, *Sl.* hood, *Inf.* goon, hooligan, ruffian.

gurgle, *v.* **1.** bubble, ripple, murmur, babble, tinkle, guggle.

2. play, splash, plash, sputter, foam, froth, boil; roll, purl, trickle, cascade.

gush, *v.* **1.** flow, run, stream; issue, emanate, surge, swell, well *or* rush forth; effuse, spout, spurt, jet; overflow, flood, brim over, well over, run over, spill over *or* out; pour *or* burst forth, disembogue, debouch; abound, teem, cascade, fall, rush; emit, send forth, eject.

2. effervesce, bubble over, emote, be effusive *or* ebullient, overflow with enthusiasm, wax enthusiastic, make much of, be carried away over, fuss over; prattle, gabble, chatter, rattle, prate, jabber, blather, babble.

—n. **3.** flood, outpouring, tide, flow, stream, flush; overflow, spillover, torrent, freshet, flash flood, spate.

4. outburst, eruption, ebullition, bubbling over, exuberance, profusiveness, effusion.

gushing, *adj.* **1.** running, streaming, emanating, flooding *or* pouring out, spouting, spurting, spilling, overflowing; emitting, discharging.

2. enthusiastic, demonstrative, ebullient, effusive, gushy; unreserved, unrestrained, expansive, lavish, generous; exuberant, rhapsodic, hearty, ardent, fervent, zealous; warm, sentimental, overly affectionate, *Sl.* gooey.

3. glib, oily, slick, unctuous, fawning, *Inf.* sickening; pleonastic, wordy, verbose, long-winded.

gust, *n.* **1.** wind, blast, blow, flurry; draft, puff, breeze; squall, gale, storm.

2. outbreak, burst, outburst, paroxysm, eruption, explosion.

3. excitement, tumult, scene, frenzy; fever, heat, flush.

gusto, *n.* relish, zest, enthusiasm, exhilaration; enjoyment, satisfaction, delight, pleasure, appreciation, appetite, taste, liking, fondness.

gut, *n.* **1.** abdomen, belly, stomach, *Inf.* tummy, *Sl.* breadbasket, *Scot. and North Eng.* wame; midalimentary canal, intestine, bowel, colon; colonic cavity, intestinal cavity; visceral cavity, *Anat., Zool.* venter, ventral region, ventricular cavity, *Anat.* epigastrium; pouch, (*of birds*) crop, craw, maw, ingluvies, (*of birds*) proventriculus; (*both of ruminating animals*) first stomach, rumen.

2. intestinal tissue, intestinal fiber; catgut.

3. *Often* **guts** insides, inwards, *Inf.* innards; vitals, vital organs, vital parts, viscera, (*of animals*) entrails; *Inf.* gizzard, *Inf.* solar plexus, *Sl.* where one lives.

4. **guts** *Informal.* **a.** courage, bravery, backbone, grit, nerve, *Sl.* gutsiness, heart, fortitude, intestinal fortitude; gumption, spunk, spunkiness, pluck, pluckiness; game, gameness, mettle, spirit. **b.** confidence, assurance, fearlessness, dauntlessness; stout-heartedness, valor, boldness, audacity, audaciousness, daring, derring-do. **c.** willpower, tenacity, staying power, integrity; endurance, stamina, resourcefulness.

5. narrows, pass, passage, canal, channel, sound, strait, dell, neck, isthmus, *Scot.* kyle; gap, ravine, gorge, notch, flume, defile; gulch, gully, trench.

6. disembowel, embowel, bowel, eviscerate, *Rare.* viscerate, exenterate.

7. devitalize, weaken, enervate; debilitate, enfeeble, deplete, sap, exhaust.

8. rob, loot, strip, pirate, plunder, sack, ransack; pillage, forage, maraud, raid, rifle, spoil, despoil, spoliate; rape, ravage, ravish, devastate, waste, lay waste, depredate, harry.

9. consume, annihilate, demolish; raze, level, fell; ruin, destroy.

—adj. **10.** *Informal.* instinctive, intuitive, emotional, visceral.

11. relevant, key, essential, quintessential; fundamental, basic, *Inf.* meat-and-potatoes.

gutter, *n.* drain, sewer, cloaca, culvert, conduit; duct, *Civ. Eng.* aqueduct, watercourse, canal, channel, flume; trough, eaves-trough, open tube, trench, ditch, *Brit.* sough; shoot, hole, furrow, groove, race, rut, chase; spout, gargoyle, watersprout, outlet.

guttural, *adj.* throaty, thick, croaking, gravelly; harsh, raspy, rasping, hoarse, husky, gruff; raucous, roupy, grating.

guy, *n.* *Informal.* fellow, man, male, *Inf.* chap, *Inf.* dad, *U.S. Inf.* buddy, *Inf.* pal, *Sl.* joe, *Sl.* dude, *Sl.* cat, *Sl.* gazebo, *Sl.* bozo, *Fr. homme, Fr. type, Sp. hombre;* blade, young man, *Scot.* chield, boy, *Inf.* kid; old man, gaffer, *Inf.* codger, *Sl.* pops; mister, sir, *Fr. monsieur, Ger. Herr, Sp. señor, It. signore;* gentleman, *Archaic.* goodman, squire, esquire, don, hidalgo, cabellero; individual, person, *Inf.* customer, *Sl.* cookie.

guzzle, *v.* swill, toss off, drink quickly, *Sl.* chug-a-lug, *Sl.* chug; swig, drink down, quaff, *All Inf.* put it down *or* away, soak it up, take it in, pack away *or* down, tuck it in; drain, empty, finish, finish off, *Sl.* knock off, *Sl.* polish off, *Sl.* take care of, *Sl.* do a job on, *Sl.* do in; devour, consume, swallow up, gulp *or* gulp down.

gymnasium, *n.* gym, arena, rink; court, quadrangle, ring; hall, auditorium, stadium, coliseum, bowl; health spa, *Sl.* fat farm *or* camp; *Gk. Antiquity.* palestra.

gymnast, *n.* acrobat, tumbler, somersaulter, high vaulter, gymnasiast; circus performer *or* artist; athlete; equilibrist, balancer; aerialist, aerial performer *or* artist.

gymnastics, *n.* tumbling, somersaulting, high-vaulting; acrobatics, acrobatic feats; athletics; calisthenics, exercises, gymnastic exercises.

gyp, *v.* *Informal.* **1.** cheat, swindle, defraud, rob, rook. See **cheat** (*def.* **3**).

—n. **2.** swindle, fraud, cheating, *Sl.* ripoff. See **cheat** (*def.* **2**).

3. gypper, cheater, cheat, swindler. See **cheat** (*def.* **1**).

gypsy, *n.* Romany, Bohemian; nomad, Bedouin, Arab; wanderer, roamer, rover, rambler, gadabout; mover, rolling stone, migrant, *Usu. Disparaging.* Okie, migrator, bird of passage; drifter, *Inf.* floater, transient, fly-by-night; vagabond, tramp, hobo, beachcomber, *Inf.* bum, *Sl.* bindlestiff.

gyrate, *v.* rotate, revolve, circumvolve, wheel, wheel around, turn round, circulate, roll, troll; whirl, pirouette, twirl, *Archaic.* trundle, swirl, spin, swivel; bump, grind.

gyration, *n.* rotation, circumrotation, revolution, circumgyration, gyre, circular motion, spiral motion; wheeling, turning around, circulation, rolling, roll, trolling, convolution, circumvolution; whirling, whirl, pirouette, swirl, swirling, twirl, twirling, spinning, swiveling.

H

haberdasher, *n.* clothier, outfitter, hosier; costumer, costumier, modiste, couturier, couturière; furrier, cloakmaker; tailor, *Hum.* sartor; seamstress, tailoress; dressmaker; hatter; glover.

habiliments, *n.* **1.** equipment, equipage, apparatus, gear, accouterments, paraphernalia, appurtenances, appointments, furnishings, furniture; fixtures, fittings, *Inf.* things; tools, instruments, contrivances, machinery; implements, appliances, utensils, conveniences; supplies, material, materials, matériel, wherewithal.
2. dress, garb, costume, habit, cloth, outfit; array, wardrobe, accouterment; regalia, uniform, livery, trappings, harness, riggings, *Inf.* rig, *Inf.* getup, *Inf.* turnout; vestments, habits, raiment; (*all usually of a particular profession*) clothes, clothing, attire, apparel, wearing apparel.

habit, *n.* **1.** custom, practice, way, fashion, style, mode; procedure, policy, rule; convention, wont, praxis, usage, observance, habitude; consuetude, tradition, *Law.* prescription, routine, course; conventionality, matter of course, formality, form; pattern, groove, rut, one's old way.
2. bent, inclination, predisposition, aptness, tendency, conatus, propensity, proclivity, leaning, penchant, proneness; addiction, dependence, drug *or* physical *or* psychological dependence, weakness, vice, mania, appetency, insatiable desire.
3. disposition, nature, second nature, humor, temperament, temper, grain, mood, vein; outlook, mind-set, frame of mind; character, make-up, inner man, qualities, constitution, idiosyncrasy.
4. dress, garb, costume; attire, apparel, clothes, clothing; garments, vestments, raiment, habiliments, *Inf.* gear, *Inf.* toggery, *Inf.* togs, *Inf.* duds, *Sl.* threads, *Sl.* rags; investment, vesture, investiture; array, wardrobe, accouterment; livery, uniform, regalia.
—*v.* **5.** dress, clothe, garb, vest, apparel, attire, *Sl.* dude up, *Sl.* swank up; adorn, array, deck, deck out, bedeck, bedizen, dress up; trap, trap out, caparison; outfit, fit out, fit up, rig, rig up, turn out, accouter; *All Inf.* doll up, pretty up, gussy up, spruce up.

habitable, *adj.* inhabitable, occupiable, tenantable, livable, lodgeable, residential, fit for residence, fit for dwelling, fit to live in; homey, homely, homelike, homish, cozy, warm, snug, intimate, comfortable, *Inf.* comfy, lived-in.

habitat, *n.* **1.** environment, natural *or* native environment, element, natural element, natural abode, natural home, homeground, *Inf.* homefront; environs, surroundings, precincts; setting, background, medium, milieu, condition; territory, ground, zone, range, sphere, domain, realm, haunt, *Inf.* stomping *or* stamping grounds; area, vicinity, region, whereabouts, locale, locality.
2. spot, place, haunt, rendezvous, meeting place, *Inf.* hangout, *Inf.* watering hole, *Chiefly Brit.* local; nest, lair, den, cave; mew, cover, covert, sanctuary, hideout, hiding place, hideaway; refuge, retreat, shelter, hospice, hermitage, sanctum, sanctum sanctorum.
3. home, abode, domicile, domicil, residence, residency, dwelling, dwelling place, dwelling home, habitation, inhabitancy, *Scot. and North Eng.* bigging, *Scot.* howff; address, location, situation, whereabouts, place.

habitation, *n.* **1.** home, abode, domicile, domicil, residence, residency, dwelling, dwelling place, dwelling home, *Scot. and North Eng.* bigging, *Scot.* howff; lodging, lodgings, lodging place, lodgment, nest, roost, perch; quarters, living quarters, rooms, accommodations, housing, roof over one's head, *Inf.* pad, *Inf.* crash pad, *Chiefly Brit. Inf.* diggings, *Brit. Inf.* digs; apartment, flat, tenement, rent, walk-up, coldwater flat, *Brit.* chambers, *Chiefly Brit.* maisonette; penthouse, townhouse, condominium, *Inf.* condo; mobile home, motor home, camper, trailer; address, location, whereabouts, place; manor, manor house, country house, country seat, house, villa, estate, country estate; farm, farmhouse, grange, homestead, *Brit.* croft, *Brit.* home-croft, *Scot. and North Eng.* steading; ranch, rancho, rancheria, hacienda; plantation, manor farm.
2. occupancy, occupation, occupying, settlement, settling, inhabitance, inhabitancy, inhabitation, inhabiting, habitancy, moving in, tenancy, tenure, residence, residency, residing, abiding, living, dwelling, *Law.* commorancy; housing, domiciliation, domiciliating, hospitality, lodging, lodgment, billeting, quartering, locating, ensconcing; taking up residence, taking up one's abode, making one's home, establishing oneself, *Inf.* hanging up one's hat; nestling, roosting, perching, squatting.
3. colony, settlement; community, township, society, commonwealth.

habitual, *adj.* **1.** set, fixed, rooted, established; chronic, inveterate, confirmed, hardened; traditional, conventional, consuetudinary, orthodox; standard, uniform, approved, recognized, accepted; general, prevailing, prevalent, universal.
2. accustomed, customary, usual, wonted, regular, daily routine, normal, natural; ordinary, everyday, commonplace, common.
3. seasonal, cyclic, successive, frequent, periodic, periodical, recurrent; repetitious, repeating, iterative, reiterative, repetitive; persistent, constant, continual, on-

going, nonstop, perpetual, permanent.

habituate, *v.* accustom, make used to, familiarize, make familiar with, make routine; acclimate, acclimatize, adapt, naturalize, domesticate; break in, train, drill, discipline; harden, toughen, inure, season, temper, anneal.

habitude, *n.* **1.** disposition, nature, second nature, temperament, habit. See **habit** (*def.* **3**).

2. custom, practice, procedure, rule; tradition, routine, matter of course, habit. See **habit** (*def.* **1**).

habitué, *n.* frequenter, attender, constant guest, familiar face, visitor; customer, patron, client, (*collectively*) clientele; purchaser, shopper, marketer, patronizer; fan, follower, votary.

hacienda, *n.* **1.** (*in Spanish America*) estate, demesne, house and grounds, homestead, holdings, *Law.* messuage, manor; villa, chateau, mansion, country house, residence, abode, home.

2. (*in Spanish America*) farm, farmstead, grange, dairy farm, plantation, ranch.

hack[1], *v.* **1.** cut, cut down, hew, saw down, fell, chop, chop down, splinter; lop off, truncate, butcher, amputate, detach, remove; trim, clip, dock, snip, nip, snap; shear, crop, (*of the hair*) bob.

2. gash, slash, *Archaic.* carbonado, tear into, lance, slit, slice; notch, ridge; sever, abscind, split, cleave, sunder; rend, rive, tear, rip.

3. mutilate, mangle, lacerate, damage, destroy; shatter, smash, batter, break, fracture; disfigure, scar, deface; spoil, mark, spot, stain, blemish.

4. cough, *Inf.* bark, choke, gasp.

—*n.* **5.** cut, gash, slash, tear, score, scotch; notch, nick, indentation, dent, cleft, chink, serration; incision, kerf, slice, slot, slit, rift; split, crack, rent, fissure, crevice.

6. ax, hatchet, broadax, maul, mattock, pickax, pick, adz, *Archaic.* celt; cleaver, hewer, chopper, cutter; battle-ax, poleax; sickle, scythe.

7. short broken cough, smoker's cough, *Inf.* bark, rasp, gasp.

8. stammer, stutter, faltering, hesitation, speech block, speech impediment.

hack[2], *n.* **1.** work horse, hired horse, draft horse, dray horse, cart horse, plow horse, thill horse, pack horse, *Archaic.* sumpter, carriage horse, pad, hackney; jade, worn-out horse, tired old horse, padnag, crock, *Inf.* rip, nag, *Sl.* skate, *Sl.* screw, rosinante, *U.S. Sl.* plug.

2. literary drudge, word-seller, penny-a-liner, grubstreet writer, scribbler, ghost writer.

3. mercenary, hireling, free lance, adventurer.

4. drudge, plodder, toiler, *Sl.* grind, plugger; common laborer, slave, factotum; menial, flunky, fag, *Inf.* sucker.

5. *U.S.* hackney, taxicab, taxi, cab.

—*v.* **6.** let out for hire, lease, rent, lend.

7. hackney, make dull *or* trite, overuse, overdo; weaken, obtund, deaden, make less pungent.

—*adj.* **8.** hired, leased, rented, chartered, employed; subservient, servile, menial, degrading.

9. hackneyed, trite, commonplace, banal. See **hackneyed.**

hackneyed, *adj.* banal, trite, overdone, *Inf.* bromidic, platitudinous, *Inf.* corny; tired, thin, threadbare, shopworn, worn-out, played out, *Inf.* old hat, motheaten, warmed-over; unimaginative, unoriginal, stale, insipid, uninspired; prosaic, prosy, dull, tedious, matter-of-fact; conventional, humdrum, commonplace, stock, familiar, stereotyped; simple, fatuous, inane, feeble, wishy-washy.

Hades, *n.* underworld, lower world, nether world; purgatory, limbo; hell, inferno, infernal regions; Pandemonium, Tartarus, Gehenna, Abaddon, (*in Hebrew theology*) Sheol, Archeron, *Hinduism.* Naraka, Arallu. See **hell** (*defs.* **1, 5**).

hag, *n.* **1.** crone, beldam, *Sl.* old bat; fury, *Sl.* battle ax, fishwife, gorgon, harridan, ogress, old witch; hellcat, harpy, shrew, virago, vixen, nag, *Sl.* bitch, Xanthippe.

2. witch, sorceress, hex, enchantress, Circe.

haggard, *adj.* **1.** drawn, hollow-eyed, worn, weary, tired; run-down, wearied, toilworn, wayworn; drained, spent, worn-out, played out; exhausted, beaten, *Inf.* beat, *Inf.* done in, ready to drop.

2. seedy, *Inf.* under the weather, peaked, pale, pallid, wan; colorless, white, white as a sheet *or* ghost, ghostly, ghost-like, cadaverous, death-like, ghastly, like death warmed over.

3. gaunt, wasted, emaciated, emaciate; hollow-cheeked, pinched, withered, shriveled, shrunken; spindly, scrawny, scraggy, straggly, like a plucked chicken; thin, thin as a reed *or* rail, skinny, too skinny to throw a shadow, skin-and-bones, bony, skeletal.

4. wild, wild-looking, wild-eyed, delirious, distracted; hysterical, frenzied, frenetic, frantic, panicked, panicky, frightened, terrified; crazed, insane, mad, violent, furious, angry.

haggle, *v.* **1.** bargain, chaffer, higgle, palter, dicker, *Scot.* argle-bargle; drive a bargain, *Inf.* beat *or* talk down; underbid, stickle, give [s.o.] a hard time, drive a hard bargain; exchange, barter, bandy, swap, swop, traffic, deal, peddle, truck, huckster, hawk; trade, transact, negotiate, have dealings, make *or* strike a bargain.

2. wrangle, dispute, cavil, carp, complain, quibble, pettifog, pull to pieces, *Inf.* nitpick; harangue, filibuster, talk [s.o.'s] head off, *Sl.* argue the pants off of, *Inf.* argue until one is blue in the face; nag, fuss, *Inf.* hassle; jibe at, criticize, find fault, make mountains out of molehills; belittle, deprecate, disparage, impugn, decry, *Sl.* grouse, *Sl.* moan and groan; blame, chide, reproach, censure, rebuke, reprove, sneer at, discredit, animadvert.

3. hack, hack away at, chop, gash, rend, rip, rip to pieces, rive, slash, hackle, chip, dissever, mangle.

—*n.* **4.** argument, quarrel, row, squabble, dustup, spat; dispute, controversy, discord, clash, falling-out, *Inf.* hassle, *Inf.* barney; fracas, brouhaha, *Inf.* scrap, *Inf.* run-in, *Inf.* set-to, *Sl.* rhubarb; embroilment, imbroglio; dissension, variance.

hail[1], *v.* **1.** salute, greet, welcome, hello, nod to, wave to, smile at, wink at, tip one's hat to; receive, meet.

2. signal, flag down, flag, wave down; call, cry out, sing out, halloo, accost; cry, exclaim, shout, yell, *Inf.* holler; scream, roar, bellow, clamor, *Inf.* jump up and down.

3. acclaim, applaud, cheer; approve enthusiastically, congratulate, felicitate, compliment, huzzah, rejoice in; praise, sound the praises of, extol, laud, commend, *Archaic.* magnify; exalt, eulogize, glorify; pay tribute to, pay homage to, honor, crown; present, introduce, usher in, call in; name, credit, slap on the back.

—*n.* **4.** call, cry, outcry, clamor, shout, *Inf.* holler; signal, cooee, sooey; greeting, salutation, salute, salaam, welcome, address; hello, halloo, aloha, how do you do; bow, curtsy, genuflection; handshake, handclasp, kiss, peck; wave, nod, bob, duck, kowtow, prostration, homage.

5. acclamation, applause, cheer, ovation, standing ovation, bravo, plaudits, *Inf.* hand, curtain calls, encore; hosanna, hurrah, huzzah, three cheers.

hail², *n.* **1.** hailstones, hailstorm, sleet, pellets; frozen rain, soft hail, tapioca snow, graupel.

2. shower, storm, pelting, rain.

—v. **3.** shower, storm, rain, rain down on, pelt, pepper, beat, beat down on; batter, riddle, bombard, wallop, stone, thump, buffet.

hair, *n.* **1.** filament, thread, fiber, fibril, fibrilla, *Bot.* villus, bristle.

2. (*all of humans*) locks, tresses, curls, ringlets; crine, head of hair, *Sl.* mane; thatch, shock, *Sl.* mop; bangs, fringe of hair; down, fuzz, fluff, soft *or* fine hairs; whisker, mustache; eyelash, cilia; pubes, pubic hair, *Sl.* pubies.

3. (*all of animals*) mane, coat, fur, pelt, fell, skin, hide; wool, fleece; down, feathers.

4. hair's-breadth, fraction of an inch, skin of one's teeth; split second, instant, moment.

hairdo, *n.* coiffure, *Inf.* coif, *Sl.* do, haircut, cut, hairstyle; set, permanent, permanent wave, wave, marcel, cold wave, finger wave; updo, upsweep, pompadour, beehive; bob, pixie cut, shag, pageboy; bun, chignon; plait, braid, cornrows, *Archaic.* tress; afro, *Sl.* fro, natural; crew cut, crop, *U.S.* butch haircut; ducktail, *Sl.* D.A.

hairdresser, *n.* hair stylist, coiffurist, *Fr.* coiffeur; haircutter, barber, beautician.

hairiness, *n.* crinosity, furriness, downiness, pilosity, *Both Bot., Zool.* pubescence, pubescency; wooliness, shagginess, hirsuteness, *Med.* hirsutism; bristliness, *Bot., Zool.* hispidity.

hairless, *adj.* bald, baldheaded, baldpated, *Scot.* beld, calvous, *Zool., Bot.* glabrous, *Zool.* glabrate; whiskerless, beardless, clean-shaven, smooth-shaven, smooth-faced; smooth, shaven, depilated, tonsured, *Obs.* polled.

hairsplitting, *adj.* carping, caviling, quibbling, pettifogging, niggling, *Inf.* nitpicking, subtle, fine, nice, jesuitical; hypercritical, critical, captious, censorious, severe, overcritical, faultfinding.

hairy, *adj.* shaggy, hirsute, crinite, comose, comate, piliferous; downy, nappy, *Bot., Entomol.* tomentose, fuzzy, linty; woolly, lanate, fluffy, fleecy, furry, pileous, *Bot., Zool.* pubescent, *Bot.* villous; tufted, flocculent, *Bot.* awned, *Bot.* aristate, *Bot.* pappose, *Bot., Zool.* barbate; bearded, whiskered, bewhiskered, whiskery, goateed, unshaven; stubbly, bristly, setaceous, bristlelike, *Bot., Zool.* strigose, *Both Bot., Zool.* hispid, hispidulous; filamentous, *Bot., Zool.* fimbriate.

halcyon, *adj.* **1.** mild, pleasant, moderate, temperate, halcyonian, halcyonic; warm, summery, sunny; calm, peaceful, tranquil, pacific, serene, restful, reposeful, placid; still, motionless, smooth, undisturbed, unagitated, unruffled, quiet, windless, waveless, stormless.

2. prosperous, successful, thriving, flourishing, palmy; fruitful, profitable, rewarding, satisfying; rich, wealthy, well-off; promising, favorable, propitious, auspicious.

3. happy, pleased, contented; carefree, light-hearted, blithe, blithesome, animated, buoyant; joyful, joyous, elated, jubilant.

hale, *adj.* healthy, well, in good health, blooming, fresh, in fine fettle, fit, *Inf.* fit as a fiddle, *Inf.* fine, *Inf.* in the pink, *Inf.* in tip-top shape; vigorous, lusty, flourishing, full of vim and vigor, energetic, bursting with health, hearty, athletic, in excellent condition, *Inf.* in shape; sound, able-bodied, robust, strong, hardy, sturdy, mighty, forceful, spirited; rugged, strapping, stalwart, brawny, muscular, sinewy, well-knit, husky, stout, doughty, staunch, solid.

half, *n.* **1.** part, equal part, fifty percent; bisection, hemisphere, semisphere, division.

2. match, double, twin, alternate, companion, mate, one of a pair.

—adj. **3.** halved, divided, bisected; semi-, demi-, hemi-; partial, incomplete, limited, moderate, dichotomous; fractional, fragmentary, sectional.

—adv. **4.** in part, partly, incompletely; up to *or* as far as the middle, half-full, half-empty, halfway; after a fashion, within bounds, passably, tolerably, insufficiently, feebly.

half-baked, *adj.* **1.** shallow, superficial, cursory, rudimentary; premature, unformed, abortive, embryonic, embryotic, unfinished, unripe; unthought out *or* through, undeveloped, immature, crude, rough, unrefined; coarse, rude, raw, unpolished, in the rough; short-sighted, ill-judged, groundless, injudicious, precipitate; pointless, foolish, hare brained, impractical, *Sl.* half-assed.

2. indifferent, mediocre, middling, average; wanting, deficient, scanty, partial, meager, sketchy, skimpy, inadequate; inferior, below par *or* the mark; imperfect, unhatched, pretentious, *Inf.* half-cocked.

3. young, green, wet behind the ears, provincial; unseasoned, callow, unfledged, unskilled, unpracticed, unequipped, unfitted; ignorant, naive, inexperienced.

half-breed, *n.* half-caste, half-blood, crossbreed, hybrid, cross, mixed blood, mongrel; mulatto, mestizo, Ladino, sambo, Eurasian, Anglo-Indian; creole, quadroon, mustee, octaroon, *Inf.* high yellow.

half-hearted, *adj.* **1.** indifferent, uninterested, apathetic, unconcerned, uncaring, neutral, lukewarm, cool; untouched, unmoved, unexcited, unemotional, dispassionate; superficial, perfunctory, cursory.

2. phlegmatic, sluggish, listless, languid, insouciant, nonchalant, lackadaisical; careless, devil-may-care, blasé, unruffled.

3. timid, irresolute, faint, poor, lame; feeble, weak.

halfway, *adv.* **1.** to midpoint, to the middle, in the middle, in the midst, between two extremes; with the worst behind one; half-over, half-finished, half-done; at the apex, around the turn, *Inf.* over the hump, *Inf.* on the downgrade, *Inf.* home free, *U.S. Inf.* rounding second, *Inf.* in the home stretch.

2. partially, to some degree *or* extent, in moderation, moderately; almost, nearly, just about, rather, in part, partly, to a degree, in some measure; within bounds, fairly; by *or* in half measures, imperfectly, with divided effort.

3. meet halfway compromise with, come to terms with, give and take, *Inf.* go fifty-fifty; trade off, concede, adjust, modify, accommodate; arbitrate, negotiate; find a happy medium, strike a balance, find the middle ground; *Inf.* scratch one another's back.

—adj. **4.** midway, equidistant, mid, central, middlemost, midmost, axial, pivotal; intermediate, middle, medium, mean, medial, *Law.* mesne.

5. partial, part-way, moderate, mediocre, half-baked, middling; incomplete, imperfect, circumscribed, conditioned, limited.

halfwit, *n.* simpleton, dunce, dullard, moron, idiot, imbecile, mental defective, incompetent; dolt, blockhead, dunderhead, *Inf.* numbskull, *Sl.* birdbrain; fool, zany, nitwit, *Inf.* crackpot, *Inf.* nut, *Inf.* screwball.

half-witted, *adj.* **1.** feeble-minded, simple, witless, stolid, cretinous, doltish, *Inf.* weak in the upper story. See **feeble-minded**.

2. foolish, stupid, nitwitted, *Sl.* nutty, *Sl.* balmy, *Sl.* batty, *Sl.* loony.

hall, *n.* **1.** corridor, gallery, way, passageway, passage, hallway, breezeway, *Naut.* companionway.

2. lobby, foyer, vestibule, threshold, entry.

3. auditorium, lecture room, classroom, schoolroom; meetinghouse, assembly *or* convention hall; theater, amphitheater, lyceum.

hallelujah, *interj.* **1.** hosanna, praise the Lord, praise God, praise be, glory be, glory to God, glory be to God in the highest, thanks be to God.

—*n.* **2.** hosanna, paean, alleluia; cheer, hoorah, hooray, huzzah; exclamation, cry, shout, yell.

hallmark, *n.* **1.** seal, stamp, seal *or* stamp of approval, cachet; trademark; (*of gold and silver*) plate mark.

2. mark, earmark, keynote, brand, badge, device; sign, sure sign, telltale sign, index, indicator, symptom.

hallo, *n.* **1.** salutation, address, hail, call; cry, shout, exclamation.

—*v.* **2.** exclaim, cry, cry out, shout, yell; hail, accost, salute, greet, call to, call out to.

hallow, *v.* **1.** sanctify, consecrate, dedicate; immortalize, enshrine, bless, dignify; ordain, anoint, lay hands on, make holy.

2. venerate, revere, reverence, worship, adore, pay homage to, pay honor to; respect, honor, esteem, consider sacred; glorify, *Archaic.* magnify, exalt, deify, canonize, saint.

hallowed, *adj.* venerated, revered, reverenced, adored, worshiped, regarded as holy; holy, sacred, sanctified, consecrated, blessed; sacrosanct.

hallucinate, *v.* have hallucinations, fantasize, daydream, imagine, envision, *Inf.* see things; *Sl.* trip *or* trip out, *Sl.* turn on, *Sl.* freak out, *Sl.* have a bad trip.

hallucination, *n.* **1.** illusion, aberration, false conception, imagining, figment of the imagination, *Inf.* pink elephant; mirage, vision, dream, daydream, *Psychol.* fantasy, *Sl.* trip, delirium; phantom, phantasm, ghost, *Inf.* spook, apparition, specter, shade, incubus, *Spiritualism.* ectoplasm, *Ger. Doppelganger*, wraith.

2. false notion, fallacy, misbelief, misconception, misconstruction, misinterpretation; delusion, self-deception, self-deceit, distortion; misapprehension, *Psychiatry.* confusion, *Psychiatry.* disorientation, *Psychiatry.* hallucinosis.

halo, *n.* **1.** nimbus, aureole, aureola, gloriole, crown, light, crown *or* ring of light; *Both Fine Arts.* vesica piscis, mandorla; corona, luminous cloud, *Astron.* chromosphere, *Astron.* coma, *Biol.* areola, *Photography.* halation; ring, band, circle, disk, O, doughnut, annulus, annulation, *Entomology.* annulet.

2. radiance, brilliance, brilliancy, luminosity, luminousness, illumination, luster, flow, effulgence, refulgence, refulgency, fulgentness; brightness, lucency, shine, gleam, sparkle, *Rare.* lucence, *Archaic.* fulgar.

3. splendor, splendidness, resplendence, resplendency; glory, gloriousness, sublimity, grandeur, majesty, regalness; sanctity, sacredness, holiness, hallowedness, blessedness, saintliness, sainthood, godliness, spiritualness, spirituality.

4. aura, air, atmosphere, ambience; quality, complexion, tone.

halt¹, *v.* **1.** stop, come to a stop *or* a stand, cast anchor, brake, draw reign, (*of an automobile*) pull over, (*of a ship*) lie to, stop short, stop dead in one's tracks, stall *or* stall out, stand still, balk; draw *or* pull up, hold up, wait *or* wait up, stay, mark time.

2. arrest, bring to a stop *or* halt, check, stem, curb; terminate, end, bring to an end *or* close, quell, quash, crush, nip in the bud, put an end to, break up; block, blockade, obstruct, frustrate, foil, thwart, hinder, impede, clip one's wings, hold back, restrain.

3. cease, desist, cease and desist, discontinue, leave off, quit, call it a day, *Inf.* knock off, *Inf.* call it quits, hang up one's tools, shut down, close down; come to an end, finish up, conclude, draw to a close, run its course; pause, take a break *or* breather, break off, lapse.

—*n.* **4.** stop, stoppage cessation, desistance, discontinuance, stay, standstill; pause, interval, interlude, intermission, break, hiatus, *Prosody.* caesura; recess, rest, respite, breather, breathing spell *or* space, time-out.

halt², *v.* **1.** falter, hesitate, pause; stammer, stutter, sputter, splutter, speak brokenly; stumble, trip, flounder, stagger, bumble, fumble, hobble, wobble.

2. boggle, scruple, have qualms *or* misgivings, be uncertain *or* unsure, be in doubt; think twice, take another look, linger over, be indecisive, be betwixt and between, not know one's own mind, get bogged down *or* lost in, be at sea; waver, fluctuate, sway, vacillate, tergiversate, shift, swing, shuffle, shilly-shally, seesaw, straddle the fence, go back and forth, be of two minds; equivocate, skirt, hedge, evade the issue, beat around the bush, hem and haw, hem, haw, mutter, mumble, hum, *Scot. and North Eng.* haver, *Brit. Dial.* mammer; delay, play for time, *Inf.* stall.

halter, *n.* **1.** bridle, harness, headstall, headgear, hackamore; lasso, leash, checkrein, rein, line, rope, thong; governor, control, restraint, trammel, check, curb.

2. noose, hangman's noose *or* knot, bowstring, garrote, strangler; gallows, gibbet, scaffold, *Archaic.* bough, *Brit.* Tyburn tree; hanging, execution, capital punishment, death.

halve, *v.* cut in half, split in two, split, divide, bisect, dichotomize, sever *or* sunder in two, *Obs.* dimidiate; share equally, go in together, *Inf.* go Dutch.

ham, *n.* **1.** *Theater Slang.* overdramatic actor, *Archaic.* histrionic; *Inf.* show-off, exhibitionist, flaunter; *Sl.* hotshot, *Sl.* hot dog, grandstander.

—*v.* **2.** *Theater Slang.* overact, overdramatize, milk a scene, play it for all it's worth, out-Herod Herod, ham it up; make a scene, be theatrical, sentimentalize.

hamlet, *n.* village, dorp, *Archaic.* thorp, *Amer. Ind.* pueblo, crossroads; *Inf.* jerkwater town, *Sl.* hick town; town, municipality.

hammer, *n.* **1.** beetle, claw hammer, sledge, sledge hammer, fuller, kevel, maul, rammer, martel; gavel, tapper, mallet, tamper; *Firearms.* cock.

—*v.* **2.** beat, batter, pound, pommel, pummel, pelt, *Sl.* paste; cudgel, fustigate, bludgeon, baste, cane, bastinado, club, *Sl.* clobber; hit, strike, slap, *Inf.* slug, *Inf.* wallop.

3. *Often* **hammer out** shape, form, mold, forge; chisel, carve, cut, roughcast, block out; generate, create, fashion, model, manufacture, make, fabricate.

4. *Often* **hammer out** produce, cause, effect, bring about, accomplish, carry out, carry through, bring to pass; settle, finish, complete, resolve.

5. *Often* **hammer away** persevere, persist, attempt repeatedly; plod, drudge, labor, *Sl.* plug away; keep on, stay at, stick to, hold on, hold out.

hamper¹, *v.* **1.** encumber, cumber, hinder, inhibit, hold back; impede, retard, slow, handicap; obstruct, block, oppilate, cramp, choke, smother; frustrate, thwart, interfere with; control, limit, circumscribe, confine, restrict; restrain, check, curb, shackle, bridle, muzzle, trammel; bar, blockade, barricade.

2. curtail, reduce, decrease, diminish, lessen, cut, cut short, cut down, cut back.

hamper², *n.* basket, creel, pannier, dosser, punnet, *Brit.* scuttle, bucket; wicker, wickerwork, hanaper, receptacle, container, holder, box, case, vessel.

hamstring, *v.* **1.** hock, cut [s.o.'s] hamstring; cripple, becripple, lame, make lame; injure, impair, disable, incapacitate.

2. thwart, frustrate, foil, balk, prevent, stop; check, curb, clip [s.o.'s] wings.

hand, *n.* **1.** palm, open hand; fist, closed hand, *Sl.* duke, *Brit. Dial.* nieve; extremity, *Sl.* mitt, *Sl.* paw, *Sl.* fin, *Sl.* flipper; (*all of animals*) paw, foot, pad, trotter, hoof, unguis, *Zool.* forefoot, *Anat., Zool.* manus; (*all of birds of prey*) claw, talon, pounce; (*all of crustaceans*) claw, pincer, nipper.

2. worker, laborer, workman, hired hand *or* man, man, employee.

3. skill, art, workmanship, artistry, craftmanship; touch, characteristic manner, mark.

4. crewman, crew member.

5. *Often* **hands** power, possession, hold, grasp, control, clutches, disposal, authority, jurisdiction; management, guidance, supervision, watchful eye, guardianship, wardenship; custody, keeping, arms, care.

6. assistance, aid, help, relief, succor, helping hand, a leg up, boost.

7. side, direction.

8. penmanship, handwriting, writing, script. See **handwriting.**

9. signature, *Inf.* John Hancock, *Inf.* John Henry; mark, x, cross.

10. round of applause, ovation, clap.

11. bunch, cluster, bundle, sheaf.

12. at hand a. near, nearby, close, close-by, adjacent, neighboring, next to, next door to; fast by, not far, but a stone's throw, but a step. **b.** on hand, close at hand, imminent, impending, about to happen, drawing near *or* nigh, approaching; on the verge *or* brink of, at the point of. **c.** within reach, within range, within an arm's reach, handy, convenient; at one's fingertips, under one's nose, right here; available, at one's disposal, ready, set, *Sl.* all set, ready to go.

13. by hand manually, with one's hands.

14. from hand to mouth improvidently, precariously, unstably, uncertainly, insecurely; scantily, skimpily, meagerly, scrimpily.

15. hand in hand a. holding hands, with hands clasped, arm in arm. **b.** together, jointly, conjointly, closely, in close association, side by side, concurrently.

16. hands down a. effortlessly, easily, with no contest. **b.** indisputably, undeniably, incontestably, incontrovertibly, absolutely, positively, unquestionably.

17. on hand a. in one's possession, at one's disposal, with one, *Sl.* on one. **b.** at hand, imminent. See **hand** (*def.* **12b.**).

18. try one's hand try, try one's skill, try one's luck, *Sl.* take a shot, attempt, essay.

19. with a heavy hand a. severely, oppressively, tyrannically, despotically. **b.** clumsily, awkwardly.

20. with a high hand arbitrarily, arrogantly, haughtily, presumptuously, dictatorially, imperiously, overbearingly, domineeringly.

—*v.* **21.** deliver, hand-deliver, present, give; get, reach, pass, pass over; bring forward, *Sl.* come out with, produce, furnish, supply, *Sl.* come up with, *Sl.* cough up; hand over, turn over, surrender, give up, *Inf.* fork up *or* out *or* over.

22. help, aid, assist, lend a hand, give a leg up, boost; give a helping hand, help out, do a favor, do a good turn.

23. hand down a. (*of a court decision*) deliver, give, impart, communicate. **b.** transmit, transfer, pass on *or* down, hand on *or* down, bequeath, will.

24. hand out give out, distribute, pass out, deal out, *Inf.* dish out; apportion, portion out, mete out, dole out.

—*adj.* **25.** handmade, hand-done, made *or* done by hand, handcrafted, handwoven, handloomed.

26. manual, hand-run, hand-operated.

handbag, *n.* **1.** pocketbook, bag, shoulder bag; purse, evening bag; wallet, billfold, card case.

2. valise, briefcase, small suitcase; gym bag, flight bag, traveling bag, satchel.

handbill, *n.* circular, announcement, advertisement, *Sl.* advert, *U.S.* flyer, broadside, broadsheet, handout, throwaway; brochure, pamphlet, booklet, leaflet, folder; notice, bulletin, placard, poster, bill.

handbook, *n.* manual, guide, enchiridion, guidebook, vade mecum, pocket manual, booklet, catalog; primer, bible, basic text, *Inf.* ABC; instruction book, directory, book of directions, *Sl.* how-to *or* do-it-yourself book; itinerary, travel guide, tour book; road guide, atlas, map, chart, plan.

handcart, *n.* pushcart, barrow, handbarrow, wheelbarrow, small cart *or* wagon; stroller, baby carriage, go-cart, *Chiefly Brit.* perambulator, *Chiefly Brit. Inf.* pram.

handcuff, *n.* **1.** *Usu.* **handcuffs** manacles, cuffs, *Brit. Sl.* darbies, *Sl.* bracelets. See **fetter** (*def.* **1**).

—*v.* **2.** impede, hinder, thwart, frustrate, hamper, inhibit.

handful, *n.* fistful, small amount, modicum; a few, a little.

handicap, *n.* **1.** disadvantage, impediment, imposition, hindrance, check, curb, trammel, restraint, constraint, restriction; burden, weight, encumbrance, millstone; obstacle, obstruction, barrier, block, stumbling block; drawback, inconvenience, difficulty.

2. advantage, edge, odds, points; head start.

—*v.* **3.** impede, impair, hinder, hamper, disable, put at a disadvantage; check, curb, restrain, constrain, trammel, bridle, hold back; burden, encumber, weigh down, saddle.

handicraft, *n.* craft, handiwork, manual art *or* skill, industrial art *or* skill; craftsmanship, workmanship, artisanship.

handicraftsman, *n.* artisan, artificer, craftsman, master craftsman; skilled laborer, mechanic, *Obs.* artist.

handily, *adv.* **1.** dexterously, proficiently, competently, capably, efficiently; skillfully, cleverly, deftly, nimbly, adroitly; authoritatively, masterfully, expertly.

2. conveniently, advantageously, suitably; helpfully, agreeably, pleasantly.

3. easily, facilely, readily, *Inf.* with no sweat *or* strain, hands-down; effortlessly, comfortably, with one's eyes closed, with one's hands tied; like shooting fish in a barrel.

handiness, *n.* **1.** convenience, accessibility, attainability, availability; usefulness, practicality, workability.

2. cleverness, adroitness, dexterity, deftness; expertness, proficiency, efficiency; skill, ability, capability; aptitude, expertise, know-how, knack; green thumb, magic touch.

handkerchief, *n.* **1.** hanky, veronica, (*in ancient Rome*) sudarium, *Fr. mouchoir;* tissue, *Trademark.* Kleenex, *Sl.* snot rag.

2. kerchief, neckerchief, scarf.

handle, *n.* **1.** hilt, haft, helve, grip; knob, pull, shank, shaft, handlebar, bail; lug, peg, butt; hold, grasp, command.

—*v.* **2.** touch, feel, finger; carry, hold, pick up, lift, heft, heave; pat, *Yiddish.* glet, caress, stroke, fondle, pet, hug; palpate, massage, knead, rub, press.

3. manage, direct, oversee, superintend, supervise; administer, execute, transact; regulate, operate, swing, run; control, command, rule; head, govern, boss, take charge of, take the reins *or* wheel *or* helm of; steer,

pilot, guide, train, drive.
4. use, utilize, employ; wield, ply, manipulate, exercise.
5. deal in, traffic in, sell, buy and sell; trade, peddle, truck, market.

handout, *n.* **1.** alms, charity, dole.
2. press release, release, bulletin, notice; public relations release, promotional material, *Inf.* literature; leaflet, handbill, folder, *U.S.* flyer, bill, throwaway, circular, broadside.
3. free sample, *Sl.* freebie; free *or* complimentary ticket, *Inf.* comp, free pass, pass, *Inf.* twofer, *Sl.* Annie Oakley.

handsome, *adj.* **1.** attractive, good-looking, personable, comely, fair, sightly, lovely, pretty, *Chiefly Scot.* bonny, *Inf.* proper, *Sl.* easy on the eyes, *Sl.* not hard *or* easy to look at, *Sl.* long on looks.
2. elegant, graceful, tasteful, exquisite, aesthetic, fine, *Scot. and North Eng.* braw; well-made, well-constructed, well-formed, well-proportioned, *Inf.* well-put-together; symmetrical, balanced, proportioned.
3. liberal, considerable, sizable, goodly, large, big, bounteous; ample, sufficient, satisfactory, enough, more than enough.
4. gracious, princely, noble, chivalrous; magnanimous, big, big-hearted, great-hearted; generous, munificent, openhanded, free, unselfish, unsparing, unstinting, lavish.

handwriting, *n.* **1.** penmanship, script, manuscript, longhand, *Inf.* fist, *Scot.* hand of writ, chirography; calligraphy, good hand; cacography, bad hand, scribble, scrawl, scratch.
2. handwriting on the wall omen, premonition, portent, foreboding, sign, warning, warning sign, forewarning.

handy, *adj.* **1.** accessible, available, at hand, on hand, close at hand, at one's fingertips, within reach; convenient, nearby, next-door, just around the corner.
2. useful, helpful, serviceable, employable, expedient, practicable, functional, beneficial, worthwhile.
3. deft, dexterous, adept, adroit, apt, proficient, good at, strong in; expert, masterful, masterly, *Inf.* crack, *Sl.* crackerjack; versatile, adaptable, all-around *or* all-round.
4. maneuverable, manageable, governable, tractable, responsive; wieldy; easy, practical, foolproof, trouble-free.

handyman, *n.* jack-of-all-trades, man of all work, factotum, do-all, handy-andy, *Inf.* Mr. fix-it.

hang, *v.* **1.** suspend, sling, pend, set; hang up, hook up, hitch.
2. truss up, string up, gibbet, garrote, bowstring, bring to the gallows; noose, neck, *Sl.* stretch, strangle.
3. drape, curtain, deck, cover; trail, flow, descend, slope.
4. attach, annex, fasten, fix, append; paste, cement, stick, glue.
5. deadlock, stalemate, hang up, thwart; seize up, stall, freeze.
6. dangle, depend, hang down, bob, swing, sway; be pendent, be suspended.
7. lean over, overhang, overlap, overlie, imbricate; arch over, beetle, extend; jut out, project, stick out, poke out, hang out; drop, droop, nod, bow, sag, lower, swag.
8. be contingent, be dependent, be conditioned, be subject to; depend, rely, hang on, lie on, rest on; hinge on, turn upon, lean upon.
9. waver, hesitate, vacillate, shilly-shally, hem and haw, beat around the bush, toss and turn; pause, hang back, shuffle, flounder, hold back; straddle, blow hot and cold, tergiversate; doubt, have one's doubts, have qualms.
10. remain, stay, abide, attend, stand by, stick by; linger, persist, endure, continue, hold, hang upon.
11. float, glide, drift, waft; flutter, flit; hover, hang over.
12. hang around *Informal.* **a.** frequent, resort, haunt, *Sl.* hang out, hang about. **b.** linger, dally, loiter, mosey, idle, bide one's time; potter, piddle, dawdle, *Sl.* putz.
13. hang back stay back, hold back, flinch, shy; recoil, shrink, shirk, cower, crouch.
14. hang on **a.** hold fast, cling to, cleave to, stick, adhere; grip, cohere, hold to, clutch, grasp. **b.** persevere, persist, hold out, endure, perdure, hang in there; go on, carry on, hold on, hold up; fight to the end, go down fighting, stand up against. **c.** give ear, absorb, listen devotedly, be rapt, be attentive, give one's undivided attention.
15. hang over **a.** be postponed, be delayed, be prorogued, be put off, be laid over. **b.** loom, threaten, impend, menace; approach, near, come on, draw near; be imminent, be near at hand, be around the corner.
16. hang up **a.** cause delay, obstruct, block, clog, bottleneck; slow down, retard, hinder, hold up, hamper, restrict, **b.** break the connection, replace the receiver, disconnect, cut off.
—n. **17.** *Informal.* meaning, thought, significance, signification, sense; purport, import, connotation, denotation; gist, trend, tenor, bearing.
18. *Informal.* knack, way, turn, manner, procedure, system; wise, style, usage.

hangdog, *adj.* **1.** browbeaten, intimidated, defeated, crestfallen; abject, miserable, wretched, degraded, debased; cringing, cowering, cowardly, spineless, pusillanimous.
2. embarrassed, shamefaced, ashamed, abashed, guilty-looking, conscience-stricken; sneaky, sneaking, furtive, shifty, skulking.

hanger-on, *n.* dependent, vassal, minion, lackey, flunky, retainer, henchman, *U.S. Politics.* ward heeler; parasite, leech, sycophant, *Sl.* sponge; toady, *Inf.* yes man, flatterer, fawner, *Inf.* apple-polisher, *Inf.* bootlicker; follower, appendage, shadow, satellite, *Sl.* groupie, *Inf.* puppydog, *Inf.* gofer.

hanging, *n.* **1.** gibbeting, lynching, *Inf.* swinging, *Inf.* necktie party, execution.
2. suspension, pendency, pensility, pendulousness, drooping, dangling.
3. *Often* **hangings** drapery, curtain, tapestry, arras; pictures, paintings, artwork. See **drapery**.
—adj. **4.** pendent, suspended, swinging; pensile, dangling, drooping, pendulous.

hangman, *n.* public executioner, official killer, *Brit. Sl.* Jack Ketch.

hangover, *n.* aftereffects, unpleasant aftereffects, crapulousness, crapulence, crapulency, *Sl.* morning after, *Sl.* head.

hang-up, *n.* *Informal.* preoccupation, fixation, fixed idea, *Fr. idée fixe,* quirk, *Sl.* kink; psychological block, impediment.

hank, *n.* skein, roll, length, piece; twist, coil, loop, knot.

hanker, *v.* *Usu.* **hanker after** *or* **for** long for, yearn for, itch for, hunger for, thirst for, pant for, lust for, *Sl.* lech after, *Inf.* yen for, wish for; crave, desire, covet, want, want with all one's heart, set one's heart on, want in the worst way, pine for, be dying for, die for; have an eye to, be bent on, have a fancy for.

hankering, *n.* desire, *Inf.* yen, itch, hunger, thirst;

longing, yearning, craving, *Sl.* letch, lust, appetite, passion, ardor; coveting, cupidity; fancy, weakness, wish.

haphazard, *adj.* **1.** chance, coincidental, arbitrary, random, desultory; fortuitous, serendipitous, aleatory, *Inf.* fluky; accidental, unintentional, unintended, unexpected, unanticipated, unforeseen, unlooked-for, sudden; stray, incidental, occasional, sporadic, contingent, adventitious.

2. casual, nonchalant, unplanned, careless, hit-or-miss, thrown *or* slapped together, slapdash, willy-nilly, *Inf.* scratch; cursory, superficial; unarranged, unsystematic, unmethodical, disorganized, orderless, disordered, disorderly, irregular; unconsidered, uncalculated, unpremeditated, undesigned, unplanned, undirected,aimless.

hapless, *adj.* luckless, unlucky, out of luck, down on one's luck, unfortunate, fortunateless, unprosperous; ill-fated, star-crossed, cursed, ill-starred, evil-starred, born under an evil star; crossed, hoodooed, *Inf.* jinxed, Jonahesque; wretched, miserable, unblessed, unhappy, woebegone, forlorn, hopeless.

happen, *v.* **1.** take place, occur, come to pass, come about, come, *Archaic.* hap, *Inf.* come off, befall, supervene, betide, chance, *Archaic.* bechance, *Archaic.* arrive; transpire, intervene, crop up; become, come into being, appear, fall, materialize, take effect; result, eventuate, turn out, prove; ensue, issue, arise.

2. befall, be one's fortune *or* misfortune, be one's lot, be the case.

3. discover unexpectedly, chance upon, hit upon, stumble on, meet with; turn up, bring to light, dig up, uncover, unearth.

happening, *n.* occurrence, event, incident, occasion; affair, *Archaic.* hap, episode, action; incident, incidence, proceeding; case, matter, circumstance; eventuality, phenomenon, fact; accident, chance, happenstance, casualty, mishap; adventure, venture, experience.

happenstance, *n.* coincidence, fluke, accident, chance, one in a million, twist of fate, incidental occurrence, unpredictable event; fortuity, serendipity, happening, hazard.

happily, *adv.* **1.** with pleasure, gladly, delightedly, with relish, lief; with open arms, graciously, sincerely, lovingly, devotedly; freely, willingly, agreeably, contentedly, *Fr. de bonne grâce, Archaic.* fain; with zeal, zestfully, enthusiastically, heartily; with all one's heart, with heart and soul.

2. joyfully, joyously, elatedly, gleefully; blithely, buoyantly, light-heartedly; cheerfully, merrily, gaily, mirthfully.

3. luckily, fortunately, as luck would have it, providentially; auspiciously, favorably, propitiously, prosperously.

4. appropriately, opportunely, seasonably, in the nick of time; advantageously, conveniently, expediently; gracefully, skillfully, tactfully; artfully, cleverly.

happiness, *n.* **1.** cheerfulness, gladness, gaiety, gayness; good *or* high spirits, blitheness, blithesomeness, light-heartedness, buoyancy; joy, delight, pleasure, felicity, bliss; joyfulness, joyousness, jubilation, exhilaration, exultation, glee, elation; joviality, merriment, jollity, mirthfulness; jubilance, jubilancy, enjoyment; enchantment, transport, captivation, fascination.

2. paradise, heaven, seventh heaven, Eden, utopia; Elysium, Arcadia, sunshine, halcyon days; beatitude, serenity, peace, eudemonia; gratification, fulfillment, contentment.

happy, *adj.* **1.** delighted, glad, pleased, contented, gratified, satisfied; elated, well-pleased, thrilled, tickled, *Inf.* tickled pink, pleased as punch, *Dial.* in hog heaven, *Brit. Sl.* chuffed; euphoric, on cloud nine, on top of the world, walking *or* floating on air, starry-eyed.

2. cheerful, cheery, full of cheer, gay, sunny, in good *or* high spirits; blithe, blithesome, light-hearted, buoyant, optimistic, positive, *Inf.* upbeat, beamish; debonair, free and easy, carefree, easygoing, breezy, airy, happy-go-lucky, untroubled; jovial, merry, jocund, jolly, mirthful, hilarious; riant, laughing, smiling, happy as a lark; joyful, joyous, jubilant, rejoicing, gleeful; exultant, in seventh heaven, elated, overjoyed, thrilled, exhilarated.

3. lucky, fortunate, auspicious, favorable; advantageous, beneficial, helpful, convenient, opportune, seasonable, timely; valuable, profitable, gainful, lucrative; prosperous, successful, thriving, flourishing, palmy; fruitful, rewarding, satisfying, gratifying.

4. apt, appropriate, fitting, fit, befitting, seemly, expedient; proper, correct, right, good, essential; relevant, to the point, germane, applicable.

happy-go-lucky, *adj.* carefree, insouciant, free and easy, easygoing, heedless, untroubled, unconcerned, unworried, *Inf.* living the life of Riley; nonchalant, casual, indifferent, blasé, devil-may-care; animated, spirited, flushed, buoyant, frisky, skittish; rollicking, playful, gamesome, frolicksome, sportive; jocular, jocose, joking, jesting, waggish; flighty, scatterbrained, unreflecting.

hara-kiri, *n.* suicide, self-destruction, felo-de-se, *Hindu.* suttee; disembowelment, evisceration; self-immolation; drinking hemlock, falling on one's sword, bowing out, taking the gas *or* a powder, taking the long walk; asking for it, asking for punishment, death wish, going up without a safety net.

harangue, *n.* **1.** declamation, stump speech, ciceronianism; oration, speech, talk, address, recitation; hard sell, *Inf.* spiel, appeal; bombast, rodomontade, bluster, *Sl.* big stink, hot air; effusion, expatiation.

2. lecture, sermon, preachment, homily, allocution, exhortation; discourse, prelection, disquisition, dissertation, *Rhet.* peroration.

3. philippic, diatribe, rant, tirade; screed, vituperation, excoriation, denunciation.

—*v.* **4.** orate, speechify, declaim, hold forth, go on and on, perorate, drone on; expound, expatiate, prelect; spout forth, *Inf.* bark; take to the hustings, *Inf.* stump, soapbox, get up on a soapbox; preach, sermonize, lecture, pontificate; rant and rave, hoot and holler; denounce, excoriate, scold.

harass, *v.* **1.** raid, harry, beset, beleaguer, drive *or* press hard; terrorize, persecute, molest, oppress, afflict, victimize.

2. bother, pester, hector, *Sl.* bug, *Sl.* hassle, *Sl.* drive [s.o.] nuts *or* crazy *or* bananas, *Sl.* drive [s.o.] up the wall; hound, dog, nag, pick on, pick at, be *or* get on [s.o.'s] back, *Inf.* give [s.o.] a hard time, *Sl.* ride, *Sl.* put the heat on; torment, taunt, bedevil, tease, tweak, mock, heckle, *Brit.* chevy; plague, trouble, fret, worry; bait, provoke, badger.

harbinger, *n.* **1.** herald, forerunner, *Archaic.* messenger, advance man; precursor, avant-courier, pioneer, *Mil.* point man, front rider; Cassandra, warner, bearer of tidings; usher, marshal, announcer.

2. omen, sign, portent, augury; signpost, clue, indication, symptom, ground waves, feeling in one's bones, gut feeling; premonition, foreboding, warning light, handwriting on the wall; prediction, prophecy, prognostication, auspice.

harbor, *n.* **1.** port, anchorage, harborage, haven.

2. shelter, refuge, asylum, sanctuary, sanctum, safety zone, port in a storm, *Scot.* bield.

—*v.* **3.** house, shelter, give shelter to, lodge, provide lodging for, put up, take in, have as a guest *or* lodger, roof, provide with a roof; quarter, provide quarters for, billet, bed, berth, bunk, board, provide room and board.
4. conceal, hide, shield, screen, cloak, cover, cover up, *Archaic.* shroud; protect, guard, safeguard, secure, keep.
5. cherish, hold dear, hold, have, have and hold, hold onto; maintain, entertain, believe, imagine, fancy.

hard, *adj.* **1.** firm, solid, solidified, compact, condensed, close, compressed, pressed; flinty, stony, rocky, steely, concrete, hardened, petrified, stonelike, rocklike, glassy, lithoid, marblelike, granitelike; strong, substantial, stout, fixed, stable, sound, set; tight, secure, fast, not easily cut *or* separated; tough, callous, horny, leathery, coriaceous; unyielding, resistant, renitent; impervious, impenetrable, impregnable, thick, dense, repelling, unassailable; rigid, stiff, unmalleable, unpliable, rugged.
2. fatiguing, exhausting, arduous, laborious, heavy, strenuous, toilsome, uphill, full of obstacles, Herculean, *Inf.* wicked, *Inf.* rough, *Inf.* tough, *Inf.* nasty; rigorous, not easy, exacting, painstaking, tedious, unmitigating, endless, tiresome, boring.
3. perplexing, knotty, puzzling, enigmatic; baffling, bewildering, labyrinthine, inextricable; complicated, tangled, complex, involved; trying, unmanageable, unwieldy, awkward, clumsy, incomprehensible, insolvable, irresoluble, irreducible; vague, obscure, deep, profound, inscrutable; nice, delicate, ticklish, thorny.
4. oppressive, pitiless, ruthless, harsh, cruel, merciless, unrelenting; unfeeling, insensible, unsympathetic, unemotional. See **hard-boiled, hard-handed,** and **hard-hearted.**
5. bad, unendurable, unbearable, intolerable, insupportable, insufferable; afflictive, injurious, consuming; grievous, disastrous, calamitous, devastating; intense, racking, agonizing, torturous, distressing, painful, excruciating.
6. hard-working, persevering, plodding, earnest, diligent, industrious, unflagging, untiring, resolute, unfaltering; conscientious, assiduous, sedulous, determined, persistent, constant, enduring, indefatigable; keen, intent, ardent, eager, zealous, avid, energetic, vigorous, dynamic, aggressive, operose.
7. (*of a beverage*) alcoholic, strong, corned, turned, overpowering, *Sl.* pickling, *Sl.* strong enough to grow hair on one's chest *or* on a cueball.
8. (*of drugs*) addictive, habit-forming; detrimental, injurious, deleterious, noxious, harmful.
9. (*of bread*) crusty, crunchy, chewy; crisp, stale, dry, crackly.
—*adv.* **10.** strenuously, heavily, with might and main, laboriously, arduously, toilsomely, industriously, with all one's might, by the sweat of one's brow; earnestly, intently, diligently, persistently, perseveringly; conscientiously, unfalteringly, indefatigably, untiringly, energetically, actively, dynamically, vigorously, with vigor, lustily; intensely, keenly, avidly, eagerly, heartily, spiritedly, ardently, urgently, zealously; constantly, undeviatingly, incessantly, steadily, sedulously, studiously, unswervingly, ploddingly, steadfastly, determinedly, tenaciously; severely, austerely, emphatically, vehemently, relentlessly; exactingly, painstakingly, slowly.
11. harshly, severely, mercilessly, pitilessly; with a heavy hand, overbearingly, tyrannically, unbearably, insufferably, onerously, high-handedly; violently, forcibly, fiercely, ruthlessly, savagely, madly, wildly.
12. hard by *or* **upon** close, close by, near, near by, nigh, at one's fingertips, under one's nose; in sight of, not far away, but a step away, within an inch of, within call *or* hearing, within earshot; at one's door, within a stone's throw, at close quarters, at one's elbow, within reach *or* range; on the brink *or* verge, about, on every side, bordering, beside, against, around.

hard-and-fast, *adj.* binding, set, fast, hard, exacting; unremitting, uncompromising, unbending, unyielding, strict, stringent, unswerving; irrevocable, unalterable, immutable, rigorous, inflexible, inescapable, leaving no choice, compelling; incontrovertible, incontestable, indisputable, undeniable, unquestionable.

hard-bitten, *adj.* **1.** tough, hard, stubborn, strong-willed; rigid, uncompromising, hard-shell; obstinate, bullet-headed, obdurate, pertinacious, mulish; headstrong, opinionated, pig-headed.
2. casehardened, hardened, inured, thick-skinned, insensitive, immovable, unfeeling. See **hard-hearted.**
3. unsentimental, realistic, practical, shrewd. See **hard-boiled** and **hard-nosed.**

hard-boiled, *adj.* unsentimental, tough, hard-bitten, pragmatic, realistic, matter-of-fact, down to earth; direct, straight, straightforward, unceremonious, graphic, to the point; frank, outspoken, blunt, point-blank, open, candid; brash, brusque, short, gruff, harsh, brutal.

harden, *v.* **1.** solidify, set, stabilize, establish; toughen, starch; temper, bake, anneal, vulcanize, *Metall.* caseharden; densify, freeze, inspissate, *Pharm.* incrassate; press, compress, compact, make compact; cement, fix, make tight, lock in, consolidate, amalgamate.
2. indurate, ossify, petrify, fozzilize, crystallize, vitrify, *Archaic.* lapidify; congeal, coagulate, clot, cake, cake, encrust.
3. strengthen, inure, caseharden, callous; fortify, brace, stiffen, buttress, gird; toughen, discipline, train, put in trim; season, mellow, prime; accustom, acclimatize, break in; form, prepare, reinforce, restore.
4. blunt, deaden, dull, numb, benumb, paralyze, stun; sear, embitter, poison, brutalize.

hardened, *adj.* **1.** hard, steely, casehardened, tempered, annealed, indurated, dried, fossilized, ossified, crystallized, insoluble, *Pathol.* sclerosed; set, fixed, firm, concrete; compressed, condensed.
2. steeled, tough, seared, hard-boiled, seasoned; inured, untouched, deadened, benumbed, unfeeling, uncaring, callous, unsusceptible, impervious, insensible, cruel, hard-hearted, stony, cold, flinty; obtuse, obstinate, unbending, obdurate, unyielding, rigid, inflexible, adamantine; remorseless, inexorable, unmerciful, implacable, unrelenting.
3. reprobate, inveterate, incorrigible, unregenerate, irredeemable, irreclaimable, lost; habituated, accustomed, chronic, habitual; impious, impenitent, uncontrite, shameless, unashamed.

hard-handed, *adj.* oppressive, tyrannical, cruel, harsh, brutal, ruthless, heartless; bloodthirsty, savage, barbarous, bestial, brutish, pitiless, inhuman, merciless, unmerciful, hard-hearted; dictatorial, despotic, ironhanded, overbearing, coercive, inquisitorial, extortionate.

hard-headed, *adj.* **1.** practical, shrewd, cool, cool-headed, rational, level-headed; sensible, well-balanced, sound, sane, clear-headed, resourceful; sharp, sharp-witted, keen, acute, discerning, clear-thinking, alert, aware, astute, judicious, sagacious, wise.
2. obstinate, stubborn, inflexible, unyielding, strong-minded, pertinacious; headstrong, adamantine, intractable, refractory, recalcitrant, contrary, perverse, wayward, cross-grained, balky, ungovernable, unruly.

hard-hearted, *adj.* unfeeling, hard, cold, frigid, unmerciful, pitiless, implacable; callous, marble-hearted, fell, flinty, stony, indurated; aloof, distant, disdainful, stiff; insentient, impervious, indifferent, unsusceptible; untouched, unmoved, unstirred, unsympathetic, uncompassionate, uncaring, unmindful, unconcerned, hardened, thick-skinned, insensitive; soulless, passionless; hostile, adverse.

hardihood, *n.* **1.** fortitude, strength, stamina, endurance. See **hardiness** (*defs.* **1, 2**).

2. courage, bravery. See **hardiness** (*def.* **3**).

3. rashness, impetuousness, temerity, temerariousness, daredeviltry, daredevilry, foolhardiness; recklessness, wantonness, carelessness, incautiousness, imprudence.

hardiness, *n.* **1.** strength, strongness, able-bodiedness, might, mightiness, virility, power, powerfulness, potence, potency, force, forcefulness, *Literary.* puissance; toughness, ruggedness, sinew, sinewiness, wiriness, sturdiness, soundness, hardihood; brawniness, muscularity, huskiness, burliness, stoutness, heftiness; robustness, haleness, heartiness, red-bloodedness, vigorousness, vigor, vim and vigor; healthiness, fitness, fettle; resilience, resiliency, buoyancy, ability to bounce back.

2. fortitude, stamina, fiber, moral fiber, endurance, stability, steadiness, constancy, perseverance, tenacity, holding *or* lasting *or* staying power; determination, will, stalwartness, resolution, resoluteness, staunchness, stanchness, steadfastness, firmness, stubbornness, doughtiness, doggedness, bulldog courage.

3. courageousness, bravery, valor, valorousness, valiancy, valiance, heroism, prowess, stout-heartedness, lionheartedness, ironheartedness, great-heartedness, high-heartedness, chivalry, chivalrousness; courage, pluck, backbone, grit, *U.S. Inf.* sand, nerve, nerves of steel, inner strength, intestinal fortitude, *Sl.* guts; intrepidity, intrepidness, fearlessness, dauntlessness, awelessness, dreadlessness, lack of fear; adventurousness, adventuresomeness, venturousness, venturesomeness, high-spiritedness, spiritedness, spirit, mettle, game, gameness, *Inf.* spunk, *Inf.* spunkiness, *Archaic.* pith; boldness, bold-spiritedness, daring, derring-do, pluckiness.

hardly, *adv.* barely, scarcely, only, just, only just, not quite; little, not at all, almost not at all; with little likelihood, by no means, no way, in no way, in no manner; seldom, rarely, not often, infrequently, uncommonly, once in a blue moon.

hardness, *n.* **1.** firmness, solidity, compactness, density; impenetrability, imperviousness, renitency, resistency; stiffness, rigidity, rigidness, inextensibility, inelasticity, inflexibility, unmalleability, intractability, unbendingness; immutability, unchangeableness, unalterability; induration, ossification, petrification, frozenness, glaciation, insolubility.

2. rigor, tightness, strictness, stringency, severity, stoicism; harshness, acerbity, callousness, induration, obdurateness, toughness, unimpressibility; want of feeling, unfeelingness, insensibility, insensitivity; impassiveness, impassivity, indifference, coldness, iciness, sternness, grimness, sharpness; hard-heartedness, inhumanity, pitilessness, mercilessness; relentlessness, unyieldingness, inclemency, cruelty, truculence, ruthlessness; gall, rancor, asperity, bitterness, acridness, virulence.

3. difficulty, arduousness, toilsomeness, laboriousness, exhaustiveness, heaviness.

hard-nosed, *adj.* hard-headed, tough, unsentimental, practical; shrewd, prudent, sensible, efficient, calculating, politic, businesslike; uncompromising, unbending, hard-line, *Inf.* one-way.

hard-pressed, *adj.* burdened, weighed down, loaded, loaded down, overloaded, overburdened, overworked; harried, harassed, ground down, pushed; penned in, hemmed in, in a corner, in a tight spot, up against it, between a rock and a hard place; pressured, under pressure, taxed, over-taxed, strained, troubled, careworn; oppressed, abused, subjugated, encumbered, impeded, hampered, hindered, handicapped, shackled; bound, caught up, entangled; faltering, ready to give up.

hardship, *n.* **1.** affliction, adversity, hurt, harm, ruin, ruination, bane, desolation; austerity, privation, want, need, neglect; severity, rigor, stringency, deprivation, destitution, prostration; difficulty, plight, strait, predicament, trouble, peck *or* sea of troubles, stress, storm and stress; misfortune, infelicity, ill *or* bad luck, ill *or* bad fortune, ambsace, evil eye, evil wind, dark cloud *or* star, storm clouds; ordeal, trial, tribulation, cross, burden, weight, load, heavy load *or* burden, oppression; misery, wretchedness, pain, agony, torture, torment, travail; distress, suffering, *Archaic.* bale.

2. mishap, mischance, miscarriage, misadventure, *Scot. and North. Eng.* mischanter, glitch, casualty, accident, injury; shock, blow, heavy *or* nasty *or* staggering blow, buffet, stroke, stroke of bad luck *or* fortune; reverse, reversal, setback, comedown, bringdown, bitter pill, bitter cup; disaster, tragedy, calamity, catastrophe, cataclysm; infliction, visitation, scourge, blight.

hardware, *n.* **1.** metalware, hard goods, durables, appliances, *Brit.* ironmongery.

2. equipment, gear, accouterments, appurtenances, fixtures, paraphernalia, *Inf.* things; tools, contrivances, machinery, implements, utensils, conveniences; *All Mil.* arms, armaments, munitions, matériel.

hardy, *adj.* **1.** sturdy, rugged, strong, mighty, powerful, iron, Atlantean, able-bodied, able, virile; brawny, muscular, muscled, strapping, athletic, husky, burly, stout, hefty, broad-shouldered, well-developed, *Derog.* muscle-bound; sound, sinewy, wiry, thewy, leathery, cast-iron, *Inf.* hard as a rock, *Inf.* tough as nails; robust, hale, hearty, red-blooded, vigorous, healthy, fit, fit as a fiddle, in fine fettle *or* condition *or* shape.

2. strenuous, rigorous, rugged, Spartan, herculean; exacting, laborious, onerous, arduous; hard, tough, uphill, difficult; fatiguing, tiring, wearisome.

3. resolute, stalwart, *Archaic.* stalworth; staunch, dogged, determined, firm, steadfast, fixed, stubborn, strong-willed; indomitable, enduring, lasting, indefatigable; unyielding, unflinching, unshrinking, unwavering.

4. courageous, brave, valiant, valorous, heroic, stout-hearted, lion-hearted, iron-hearted, great-hearted, chivalrous, doughty, *Scot.* bardy; undaunted, dauntless, fearless, dreadless, aweless, unafraid, intrepid; bold, bold-spirited, daring, plucky, nervy, gritty, *Inf.* spunky, *Sl.* gutsy; adventurous, adventuresome, venturous, venturesome, high-spirited, spirited, game, mettlesome.

5. rash, impetuous, headstrong, temerarious, daredevil, foolhardy; reckless, careless, wanton, incautious, imprudent.

hare, *n.* jackrabbit, leveret; rabbit, cottontail, lapin, *Inf.* bunny *or* bunny rabbit.

harebrained, *adj.* **1.** foolhardy, madcap, wild, ridiculous, ludicrous; reckless, rash, headlong, precipitate, breakneck; improvident, uncautious, unwary.

2. giddy, dizzy, flighty, fanciful, whimsical, fickle, capricious, notional, unsteady, *Sl.* gaga; frivolous, facetious, silly, foolish, scatter-brained; empty-headed, brainless, witless, stupid.

harem, *n.* seraglio, (*in India*) zenana, (*in India, Pakistan, etc.*) purdah (*in ancient Greece*) gynaeceum; *Sl.* stable.

hark, *v.* **1.** listen, attend, mark, notice, pay *or* give heed, pay attention, pay mind, give ear, harken.

2. hark back revert, regress, retrovert, retrogress, go back, change back, turn back; remember, recall, recollect, think back, look back.

harken, *v.* listen, lend an ear, bend an ear, listen with both ears, keep one's ears open, strain one's ears, perk up one's ears, be all ears, hark, *Med.* auscultate; heed, take heed, attend, pay attention, notice, take notice, regard, observe, take cognizance of.

harlequin, *n.* **1.** buffoon, jester, fool, clown, zany, merry-andrew, motley fool. See **buffoon**.

—adj. **2.** checkered, variegated, varicolored, particolored, motley, multicolored, many-colored, diverscolored, many-hued.

harlequinade, *n.* **1.** farce, travesty, lampoon, caricature; pantomime, dumb show, charade.

2. buffoonery, clownery, clownishness, foolery, tomfoolery, *Inf.* shenanigans, *Sl.* monkeyshines.

harlot, *n.* **1.** whore, hussy, slut, slattern, demirep, cocotte, demimondaine, loose woman, fallen woman, wanton, tramp, vamp, white slave, *Sl.* bitch, *Sl.* broad, *Sl.* chippy; prostitute, lady of the evening, woman of the profession, Mrs. Warren, *Fr. fille de joie*, trollop, strumpet, *Archaic.* wench, trull, drab, quean, painted woman, woman of the streets, streetwalker, bar girl, *Inf.* pick-up, call girl, Cyprian, *All Sl.* cat, tart, hustler, bim, moll, hooker, floozie, working girl, *Brit. Sl.* bird, *Mexican Sl.* caliente; madam, bawd, procuress, pander.

2. paramour, courtesan, mistress, concubine, kept woman, *Sl.* doxy.

3. temptress, siren, seductress, Jezebel, Delilah, flirt, coquette, minx; adventuress, hetaera.

harlotry, *n.* prostitution, whoredom, streetwalking, Mrs. Warren's profession, the oldest profession; whoremongering, whoremastery, pimping, pandering, procuring, hustling.

harm, *n.* **1.** harmfulness, injury, perniciousness, ill, woe, trauma, hurt, pain, torment, suffering, adversity; abuse, detriment, damage, defacement, destruction, waste, ruin, bane, havoc, loss, desolation; defilement, pollution, poisoning, contamination.

2. badness, meanness, moral injury, vice, sin, sinfulness, evil, iniquity, wickedness, nefariousness, maleficence, malignancy; malefaction, wrong, wrongdoing, mischief, deviltry, foul play, perfidy; outrage, atrocity, abomination, infamy.

—v. **3.** maltreat, abuse, attack, maul, molest, misuse; injure, inflict injury on, do violence to, lay hands on, hurt; wound, maim, cripple, stab, rape, beat, beat up, batter, pummel, *Sl.* mug; *Sl.* work over, *Sl.* do a job on, *Sl.* let [s.o.] have it, *Sl.* give [s.o.] the works.

4. damage, blemish, mar, distress, impair, spoil, ruin, defile, pollute.

harmful, *adj.* **1.** dangerous, detrimental, deleterious, pernicious; injurious, hurtful, damaging, baneful; ruinous, destructive, fell, extirpative; unhealthy, insalubrious, unwholesome, noxious, poisonous, venomous, septic, toxic, virulent, corrosive.

2. bad, evil, malign, malefic, satanic; inimical, sinister, corrupting, subversive, undermining, seditious, treasonous.

harmless, *adj.* innocuous, innoxious, inoffensive, unhurtful; unoffending, innocent, blameless; mild, non-irritating, gentle, soft; unobjectionable, bland, insipid, pallid; G-rated, perfectly O.K.; impotent, powerless, ineffective, disarmed, manageable.

harmonic, *adj.* consonant, in accord, agreeable, compatible, concordant, harmonious. See **harmonious** (*defs.* **1, 2**).

harmonica, *n.* mouth organ, harmonicon, *Dial.* French harp; ocarina, sweet potato, jew's-harp.

harmonious, *adj.* **1.** agreeable, compatible, peaceable, in rapport, in harmony, attuned, in unison, at one; loving, affectionate, friendly, amicable, cordial, amiable, sociable, fraternal, neighborly; acquiescent, cooperating; united, allied, sympathetic, hand and glove, hand-in-hand, on good terms.

2. congruous, correspondent, consonant, concordant, consistent, coherent; unified, unanimous, consentaneous; symmetrical, concinnous, equal, even, balanced, proportionate; coordinated, systematized, synchronized; methodical, systematic, orderly, well-regulated; apt, suitable, fit, apposite, appropriate, becoming; related, relevant, pertinent, seasonable, timely.

3. melodious, tuneful, euphonious, symphonious, harmonizing, canorous, assonant; sweet-sounding, clear-toned, liquid, mellifluous, orphean; mellow, soft, smooth, dulcet, lyric; rhythmic.

harmonize, *v.* **1.** adapt, attune, adjust; compose, order, balance, make symmetrical, quadrate; regulate, modulate, methodize, systematize, coordinate, orchestrate, direct; reconcile, patch up, placate, accommodate, settle differences; mediate, arbitrate, conciliate, moderate, attemper, restore harmony, render accordant, heal the breach, pour balm into, pour oil on the waters, restore to friendship, negotiate a peace between.

2. *Music.* accompany, complete, score, instrumentate.

3. agree, accord, assent; think alike, be of one mind, hit it off, *Inf.* click; acquiesce, accede, consent to, comply with, abide by; correspond, coincide, conform to, tally with, comport with, *Inf.* gee with, jibe with, be in unison with, chime in with, tone in with; fit, suit, match, resemble, be appropriate, *Brit. Dial.* fadge; dovetail, mesh, square, equal, parallel; combine, blend, symphonize; work together, pull together, fall in together.

harmony, *n.* **1.** agreement, accord, accordance, concord, concordance, concurrence, assent; unanimity, consentaneity, oneness, union, unity, consensus, one voice; amity, love, friendship, brotherhood, like-mindedness, fellowship, comradeship, fraternity; congeniality, cordiality, amicableness, good feeling, good will, good understanding, affinity, rapport, sympathy; peace, rapprochement, tranquillity.

2. congruity, correspondence, consonance, compatibility, correlation; symmetry, proportion, conformation, concinnity, parallelism, balance; euphony, attunement, symphoniousness, *Music.* chord, *Music.* polyphony; synchronization, *Inf.* sync, coincidence, juxtaposition, apposition; consistency, coherence, integrality; synthesis, blending, amalgamation, coalescence, conjunction; fitness, propriety, appropriateness, suitability; aptness, appositeness, relevancy.

harness, *n.* **1.** tack, equipage, accouterment, yoke, bridle; restraint, bonds, strait jacket, framework.

2. in harness working, on the job, *Sl.* in the groove, forging ahead; in a rut, on a treadmill, tied down.

—v. **3.** control, bridle, rein; utilize, channel, turn to account, capitalize on.

harp, *n.* **1.** lyre, Kithara, jew's-harp, aeolian *or* wind harp.

2. *Slang.* harmonica, harmonicon, mouth organ, mouth harp, *Chiefly Dial.* French harp.

—v. **3. harp on** *or* **upon** dwell on, persist in, insist on, push, press, *Sl.* beat [s.o.] over the head; repeat, *Inf.* ding, reiterate, play a broken record, go on, *Sl.*

beat *or* run into the ground; go over and over, emphasize, stress, impress in *or* on [s.o.'s] mind, fix in [s.o.'s] mind, hammer into [s.o.'s] head, drill into [s.o.'s] head, pound *or* beat into [s.o.'s] head.

4. harp at nag, *Sl.* bug, pester, bother, harass, *Sl.* give [s.o.] a hard time, *Sl.* hassle.

harpy, *n.* **1.** swindler, cheater, cheat, sharper, sharpie, *Sl.* shark; mercenary, *Sl.* money-grubber.

2. shrew, virago, termagant, harridan. See **harridan**.

harridan, *n.* shrew, harpy, virago, termagant, vixen, scold, nag, *Sl.* bitch, fishwife; witch, hellcat, Xanthippe, tartar, *Sl.* battle-ax, spitfire, fury; hag, crone, gorgon, beldam, jade, *Sl.* old bat, *Sl.* old bag, *Yiddish.* macheshefeh.

harried, *adj.* **1.** besieged, pressured, hard-pressed, put upon; frantic, hectic, agitated, all worked up, overwrought, distraught; at wit's end, up a wall.

2. overworked, overtaxed, overburdened, *Inf.* swamped, *Inf.* snowed *or* snowed under; frazzled, worn out, wearied, exhausted, *Sl.* bushed, *Sl.* beat.

3. harassed, plagued, troubled, worried, distressed, disturbed; annoyed, irritated, exasperated, *Inf.* hassled, *Sl.* bugged.

harrow, *v.* **1.** rake, plow, hoe, spade, raft, dibble; till, cultivate, delve, dig, turn over, break up.

2. disturb, distress, disconcert, perturb, harry, discompose; dismay, daunt, disquiet, afflict.

3. frighten, terrify, scare, panic; startle, rattle, shake, unnerve, unman, put the fear of God into; horrify, chill, petrify, freeze, make one's blood run cold, make one's hair stand on end.

harry, *v.* **1.** harass, plague, trouble, molest, *Brit.* chevy; pressure, press [s.o.] hard, get on [s.o.'s] back, put the heat on [s.o.]; weary, exhaust, tire out, wear down, fag out; overwork, overtax, jade, overburden.

2. annoy, vex, bother, pother, worry; gall, chafe, irritate, nettle, pique, irk, roil, exasperate; distress, disturb, harrow, haunt.

3. hector, badger, fret, torment; nag, *Inf.* hassle, ride, harp at, hound, pester, keep after, *Sl.* bug; bully, intimidate, cow, browbeat, bullyrag, buffalo, push around.

4. ravage, devastate, lay waste, desolate, ruin, lay in ruins; destroy, level, raze, burn, demolish, shatter, wreck.

5. pillage, plunder, rob, despoil, *Archaic.* spoil, spoliate; maraud, rape, ravish; ransack, sack, loot, gut, fleece, strip, rifle, steal.

harsh, *adj.* **1.** abrupt, brusque, curt, blunt, short, clipped; rude, impolite, discourteous, unmannerly, uncivil, ungracious; crusty, gruff, bluff, bearish, churlish, bad-tempered, choleric, splenetic, morose, surly, sullen, sulky; petulant, peevish, shrewish, waspish, irascible, irritable, touchy, moody, grouchy, thorny, cross; bristling, quarrelsome, peppery, snarling, growling, miserable, bilious, rancorous; tart, acrimonious, bitter, sarcastic, mordant, caustic, sour, acerbic; mean, vulgar, crass, offensive, obnoxious, uncouth, ill-bred, ugly, brutish, doggish, swinish, boorish.

2. grim, severe, austere, stern; stiff, rough, Spartan, stark, stringent; unsparing, unremitting, inexorable, implacable, uncompromising, unbending, inflexible, obdurate; ruthless, merciless, pitiless, cruel, brutal, savage; hard-boiled, cold-blooded, hard-hearted, ironhanded, iron-fisted, iron-hearted; despotic, inquisitorial, tyrannical, abusive, coercive, punitive; distressing, agonizing, afflictive, torturous, tormenting, painful, racking, grinding, biting, cutting; unkind, uncompassionate, remorseless, insensitive, unfeeling, unconcerned, inhuman, soulless.

3. desolate, stark, bare, barren, rugged, rough, bleak, waste, wild, inhospitable, empty.

4. (*of sounds*) grating, jarring, strident, grinding, twanging, clashing, sour; dissonant, cacophonous, unharmonious, discordant, untuneful, unmelodious, *Music.* atonal; shrill, acute, jangling, ear-piercing; guttural, husky, hoarse, scratching, rasping, gravelly, raspy, croaking, squawking.

5. rough, jagged, coarse, coarse-grained, rough-grained; scraggy, rugged, craggy, choppy, bumpy, lumpy; wrinkled, rugose, corrugated; knotted, nodose, nodous, gnarled; uneven, irregular, broken, abrupt; unpolished, unsmooth.

6. (*of sight and color*) unrefined, crude, raw; blatant, bold, gaudy, garish, flaunting, flashy, loud, crass, brassy; inartistic, ungraceful, unaesthetic, rude, vulgar, repellent, offensive, distasteful.

harum-scarum, *adj.* **1.** rash, precipitate, hasty; reckless, careless, heedless, thoughtless, pell-mell, helter-skelter, head-over-heels; brash, incautious, injudicious, ill-advised, indiscreet, unwary, foolish; abrupt, sudden, unexpected, premature.

2. disorganized, chaotic, disorderly; haphazard, slapdash, topsy-turvy; jumbled, littered, scattered, askew, awry, slipshod, hugger-mugger.

3. uncontrolled, impetuous, impulsive, unrestrained, ungoverned, unchecked, unbridled; feverish, impatient, frantic, impasioned; madcap, madbrained, foolhardy, daredevil, breakneck, adventurous, hotheaded, harebrained, bird-witted, giddy-brained, giddy-headed, barmy-brained, empty-headed, rattlepated, crazy; volatile, flighty, frivolous, erratic, fickle, unreliable, irresponsible; wild, giddy, dashing, over-confident, rampant, quixotic, punch-drunk, death-defying, devil-may-care, dangerous, ruinous, perilous.

—adv. **4.** headlong, precipitately, hurriedly, hastily; abruptly, suddenly, unexpectedly, prematurely, inopportunely, too soon, without notice *or* warning, on the spur of the moment, like a bolt from the blue, like a thief in the night; incautiously, unadvisedly, foolishly, unwarily, impetuously, impulsively, impatiently; rashly, wildly, recklessly, carelessly, heedlessly, thoughtlessly, slapdash, at half cock, helter-skelter, head over heels.

—n. **5.** a reckless person, troublemaker, mischief-maker, devil.

harvest, *n.* **1.** crop, produce, vintage, fruit, yield, output.

2. autumn, fall, fall of the year, harvest time, harvest tide, harvest home.

3. supply, stock, store, quantity, lot, *Chiefly U.S. Dial.* grist; accumulation, amassment, hoard, cache, stockpile, collection.

4. result, outcome, effect, consequence, product, upshot.

—v. **5.** reap, gather, glean, collect, pick, pluck.

6. acquire, obtain, get, procure, secure, garner; earn, make, *Sl.* pull down; net, bag, sack.

hash, *n.* **1.** mess, muddle, jumble, scramble, mix-up, hodgepodge, mishmash; bungle, botch, foozle; fiasco, bad job, sad work, clumsy attempt.

—v. **2.** mince, chop, chop up, grind, grind up.

3. bungle, botch, muff, fumble, make a mess of, *Inf.* mess up, *Inf.* foul up, *Sl.* screw up, *Sl.* louse up, *Sl.* gum up, *Sl.* goof up; spoil, butcher, murder, make sad work of.

4. discuss, debate, bandy, talk over, *Sl.* kick *or* toss *or* throw around; review, recapitulate, go over *or* through, run over *or* through.

hassock, *n.* footstool, footrest, ottoman, taboret, cricket; cushion, squab, (*in India*) musnud.

haste, *n.* **1.** swiftness, fleetness, speed, quickness;

dispatch, rapidity, hurriedness, expedition, expeditiousness; velocity, acceleration, celerity; instantaneousness, immediateness, urgency, promptness, promptitude; briskness, abruptness, smartness; alacrity, agility, nimbleness, liveliness, tall stepping.

2. hurry, rush, hustle, bustle, dash, scurry; eagerness, zeal, fervor, avidity, enthusiasm, vehemence, intentness, ardor; impatience, uneasiness, agitation, perturbation, trepidation; restlessness, unrest, nervousness, worry, anxiety, fidgetiness, inquietude, dither, jitters, *Inf.* stew, *Inf.* sweat, *Inf.* cold sweat; scramble, furor, fuss, whirl, hurly-burly, flutter, stir, pother, *Dial.* feeze; turbulence, turmoil, commotion, pell-mell, helter-skelter, hurry-skurry, ado, hubbub.

3. undue celerity, hurriedness, hastiness, precipitance; impetuosity, rashness, recklessness, foolhardiness; prematurity, untimeliness, precocity, inopportuneness, inopportunity, inexpedience; impulsiveness, unrestraint, carelessness, heedlessness, thoughtlessness, imprudence, incautiousness; folly, gamble, leap in the dark, bungle, blunder, plunge, blind bargain; audacity, temerity, over-confidence, presumption; impatience, fretfulness, petulance, testiness.

hasten, *v.* **1.** hurry, go quickly, lose no time, rush, *Scot.* swith, *Literary.* haste; race, scurry, skip, spurt, whisk, run, sprint; press on, push on, ride hard, canter, trot, gallop, lope, clap spurs to one's horse; shoot, tear, fly, fly on the wings of the wind, outstrip the wind, wing one's way, take wing, take to flight; scour, hustle, bustle, scamper, scuttle, trip, flit; flee, hotfoot, hotfoot it, hightail, hightail it, *Inf.* skedaddle, be on the run, beat a retreat; whip off, whip away, dash off, run like mad, *Sl.* go like a bat out of hell, go *or* run wide open, go all out, go at full blast, *Inf.* go like a shot, *Sl.* go hell-bent, *Inf.* go like greased lightning; speed up, put on more speed, step on the gas, *Sl.* step on it, *Sl.* burn up the road, cover ground; bound, spring, jump, make strides, do some tall stepping, bowl along, hie one's way.

2. accelerate, quicken, push forward, advance, precipitate; stimulate, arouse, rouse, vivify, animate, bestir, instigate, motivate, inspire, exhort, excite, provoke, incite; press, prod, shove, job, move, drive on, urge on, egg on, hound on, goad, whip, flog, prick; boost, prompt, thrust, impel, propel, give an impetus to; hurry on, dispatch, send away quickly, send off summarily, lend wings to; expedite, facilitate, aid, assist, help, set on one's legs, put on one's feet.

hastily, *adv.* **1.** quickly, speedily, hurriedly; promptly, instantly, straightway, *Sl.* pronto, in a wink, in an instant, double-quick, *Inf.* like greased lightning, like a shot, like a thunderbolt, *Sl.* like mad, *Sl.* like a bat out of hell; directly, at once, without delay, in less than no time, before one can say "Jack Robinson," before the ink is dry, *Sl.* P.D.Q., *Inf.* lickety-split; swiftly, rapidly, fast, full tilt, full pelt, hotfoot, at full blast, in high gear, as fast as one's legs can carry one.

2. precipitately, hurriedly, headlong; abruptly, suddenly, unexpectedly, prematurely, inopportunely, too soon, without notice *or* warning, on the spur of the moment, like a bolt from the blue, like a thief in the night; incautiously, unadvisedly, foolishly, unwarily, impetuously, impulsively, impatiently; rashly, recklessly, carelessly, heedlessly, thoughtlessly, slapdash, at half cock, pell-mell, harum-scarum, helter-skelter, head over heels.

3. summarily, cursorily, fleetingly, perfunctorily, superficially; transitorily, momentarily, slightly, briefly, temporarily.

hasty, *adj.* **1.** quick, rapid, swift, fleet, fast, brisk; prompt, expeditious, instantaneous, immediate; rushing, hurried, running, urgent, winged, light-footed, light-legged, light of heel, eagle-winged, quick as lightning, quick as a wink, swift as an arrow; nimble, snappy, active, sprightly, lively, dynamic, bustling.

2. unduly quick, rash, precipitate, headlong; reckless, careless, heedless, thoughtless, pell-mell, helter-skelter, harum-scarum, head over heels; brash, incautious, injudicious, ill-advised, indiscreet, unwary, foolish, abrupt, sudden, unexpected, premature; impetuous, impulsive, unrestrained, ungoverned, uncontrolled, unchecked, unbridled, feverish, impatient, frantic, impassioned; madcap, madbrained, foolhardy, daredevil, breakneck, adventurous.

3. cursory, fleeting, slight, superficial; brief, perfunctory, short-lived, temporary, transitory, fugacious, impermanent; short, rapid, momentary; volatile, meteoric, flying, urgent; passing, mortal, perishable, deciduous, caducous; ephemeral, evanescent.

4. irritable, impatient, irascible; quick-tempered, hot-tempered, hot-blooded, like tinder, like touchwood, volatile, excitable, explosive, fiery, volcanic, inflammable, high-strung, high-mettled; choleric, splenetic, fretful, captious; quarrelsome, querulous, angry, simmering; fierce, quick, ungovernable, impulsive, impetuous; petulant, touchy, tetchy, contentious, peppery, snappish, waspish, shrewish; brusque, abrupt, brash, bearish, gruff, boorish, churlish, moody, hostile, resentful; acerbic, jaundiced, sour.

hat, *n.* cap, headpiece, headgear, headdress, chapeau; crown, crownpiece, mortarboard, helmet, sallet, casque, casquetel, *Sl.* tin hat, hard hat; busby, Balmoral, glengarry, topee, kepi, pill box; beanie, skullcap, yarmulke, calotte, zucchetto, *Rom. Cath. Ch.* biretta, miter; nightcap, stocking cap, tuque, *Inf.* toboggan; beret, tam, tam-o'-shanter, calpac, toque, cloche hat; fez, turban, puggree, burnoose, tarboosh, shako; fedora, panama, felt hat, crush hat; ten-gallon hat, *Sl.* Stetson, cowboy cat, tricorne; homburg, trilby, soft hat, billycock; bowler, derby, topper, top-hat, stovepipe hat, opera hat, *Inf.* kelly; straw hat, boater, skimmer, leghorn, astrakhan; coonskin cap, beaver, castor, montero; mobcap, dunce's cap.

hatch[1], *v.* **1.** bring forth, brood, incubate, sit, set, cover.

2. pip, come forth, break out, emerge.

3. devise, concoct, contrive, plan, scheme; coin, *Inf.* cook up, design; create, produce, conceive, dream up, imagine; invent, cast, forge, spin; develop, mature, evolve; formulate, fashion, make up, originate, compose.

—*n.* **4.** brood, nest, get, clutch, *Rare.* nide, *Rare.* aerie; covey, bevy, exaltation.

hatch[2], *n.* **1.** opening, porthole, peephole, outlet, escape, door; small door, trap door, wicket, *Naut.* booby hatch, *Naut.* scuttle, bulkhead, hatchway, cellarway.

2. cover, lid, top, cap.

3. bin, crib, hutch, caddy, hold; compartment, hamper, casket.

hatchet, *n.* ax, tomahawk, cleaver, machete; mattock, pickax, poleax, battle-ax, bill, billhook.

hatchway, *n.* hatch, trap door, *Naut.* scuttle, porthole.

hate, *v.* **1.** abhor, loathe, abominate, execrate, despise, detest, have an aversion to, be hostile to, feel hostility toward; not to be able to bear *or* abide, not be able to stand, shudder at, shrink from, blench from, view with horror; be sick of, be tired of, have no stomach *or* use for; feel *or* bear malice toward, hold *or* bear a grudge against; dislike, mislike, disfavor, disrelish.

2. be unwilling, be reluctant, dislike, feel disinclined to; not have the heart, shy away from, flinch from, quail from.

—*n.* **3.** hatred, abhorrence, loathing, abomination, execration, odium, rancor, detestation; animosity, hostility, enmity, malevolence, ill will, malice, malignity; aversion, dislike, antipathy, mislike, disfavor, disrelish; revulsion, repugnance.

hateful, *adj.* **1.** abhorrent, loathsome, abominable, execrable, odious, heinous, cursed, anathematic; detestable, despicable, scurvy; hostile, inimical; invidious, malevolent, malicious.
2. repulsive, repellent, offensive, revolting; obnoxious, repugnant, aversive, disgusting, rank, noisome, insufferable, disagreeable; distasteful, foul, rotten, putrid, vile, sickening; ugly, horrid, horrible, hideous, grotesque; dislikable, unlikable, unpleasant, displeasing, unendurable, unbearable.
3. malevolent, malicious, malignant, rancorous, mean; evil, sinister, wicked, devilish, infernal, hellish, spiteful.

hatred, *n.* hate, abhorrence, loathing, abomination, execration, odium, rancor; animosity, invidiousness, enmity, malevolence, malignity, malice, maliciousness, venom, bitterness; hostility, animus, inimicality, inimicalness; vindictiveness, revenge, grudge, *Archaic.* despite; aversion, antipathy; dislike, disrelish, disaffection, disfavor; revulsion, repugnance.

haughtiness, *n.* arrogance, pomposity, superciliousness, conceit, disdain. See **hauteur.**

haughty, *adj.* proud, self-important, self-satisfied, self-complacent; vain, puffed up, *Sl.* swell-headed, egotistical, know-it-all, conceited; arrogant, fastuous, overbearing, overweening, presumptuous, assuming; contemptuous, disdainful, scornful, derisive, belittling, insolent; supercilious, patronizing, condescending; snobbish, *Sl.* uppish, *Sl.* snooty, on a high horse, *Inf.* high-hat, *Inf.* nose-in-the-air, high-and-mighty, *Sl.* stuck-up, too good for the rest of us, *Sl.* sniffy, *Sl.* snotty; aloof, detached, remote, above-it-all, distant; cold, icy, indifferent; unbending, stiff-necked, unapproachable, forbidding; imperious, lordly, domineering, commanding, high-handed, magisterial; vainglorious, thrasonical, pompous; pretentious, hoity-toity, affected, *Inf.* highfalutin.

haul, *v.* **1.** drag, draw, pull, strain, heave, hale, lug; tow, take in tow, tug.
2. carry, cart, bear; convey, transport, convoy, truck, bus, van, ship, ferry, barge.
3. take *or* bring into court, drag into court, bring to trial, put on trial, call to account, bring to book, bring to justice.
—*n.* **4.** drag, draw, pull, heave, lug, tug, strain.
5. catch, yield, take; bag, net, capture.
6. *Informal.* plunder, spoils, booty, loot, prize, takings, pickings, stealings, *Sl.* swag.

haunch, *n.* hip, hindquarter, leg and loin, huckle, thigh, (*of beef*) round; rump, buttocks, fundament, breech, nates, (*of a horse*) croup, *Zool.* podex.

haunt, *v.* **1.** *Dial.* hant, *Inf.* spook.
2. obsess, possess, dwell in, prey on the mind, prey on *or* upon one, haunt the memory; recur, come back, stay with.
3. trouble, worry, oppress, burden, weigh upon; harass, harry, plague, torment, beset, disturb, disquiet.
4. frequent, resort to, *Sl.* hang around *or* about at, *Sl.* hang out at, *Sl.* make the scene.
—*n.* **5.** spot, place, rendezvous, meeting place, *Inf.* hangout, *Inf.* watering hole, *Inf.* stamping ground, *Chiefly Brit.* local; refuge, retreat, shelter, sanctuary, hide-out, hiding place, hideaway; nest, lair, den, cave, mew, covert.

hauteur, *n.* haughtiness, arrogance, self-importance, presumptuousness, overconfidence, fastuousness; pretentiousness, hoity-toity, affectedness, pomposity, pompousness; snobbery, snobbishness, airs, conceit, conceitedness, vaingloriousness, bovarism, egotism, pride, vanity; complacency, smugness, self-satisfaction, self-adulation; boastfulness, braggadocio, jactation, bluster, fanfaronade, gasconade; imperiousness, lordliness, overbearingness, high-handedness; impertinence, bumptiousness, self-assertion, *Inf.* pushiness; insolence, impudence, brazenness, effrontery, audacity; contemptuousness, disdainfulness, superciliousness, scornfulness, contumeliousness.

have, *v.* **1.** possess, own, keep, hold for use, hold, retain, preserve; get, receive, take, obtain, acquire, secure, procure; occupy, tie up, use.
2. contain, include, embrace, comprehend, comprise; embody, incorporate, take in, count, number.
3. *Usu.* **have to** be obliged to, be under obligation to, be bound to, must, *Inf.* have got to; be made to, be compelled to, be forced to, be driven to, be coerced to, be pushed into, be pressed into.
4. experience, have a taste of, encounter, meet *or* meet with, find; undergo, endure, suffer, be subjected to, go *or* pass through.
5. hold in mind, entertain, think about, keep *or* bear in mind; maintain, harbor, shelter, foster, nurse, cultivate, cherish.
6. require, make, cause, oblige; force, coerce, drive, push, press; induce, prevail upon, talk into, persuade; ask, request, bid, order, tell, command, direct, enjoin.
7. show, exhibit, display, express, demonstrate, evidence, manifest, evince.
8. engage in, carry on.
9. permit, allow, put up with, let go on; tolerate, stand, abide, endure, brook, bear, suffer, support.
10. beget, give birth to, bear, bring into the world, bring forth, deliver.
11. *Slang.* **a.** outwit, deceive, take in, dupe, fool, trick, cheat, swindle. **b.** bribe.
12. have sexual intercourse with, *Inf.* have sex with, copulate, *Sl.* get it on; have carnal knowledge of, *Biblical.* know.
13. **had better** *or* **had best** ought to, should.
14. **have on** **a.** wear, be dressed in, be clothed in. **b.** have planned, have on the agenda, have going.

haven, *n.* **1.** harbor, harborage, port, anchorage, moorage; inlet, cove, bay, gulf, bight; wharf, quay, pier, dock, landing.
2. asylum, sanctuary, sanctum, sanctum sanctorum, safety zone, port in a storm, refuge, shelter; retreat, hospice, hermitage, cloister, ashram; nest, lair, den, cave, hole, dugout, abri; mew, cover, covert, coverture, hideout, hiding place, hideaway; stronghold, fortress, fortification, citadel, bastion, keep, safehold, tower, pillar, tower *or* pillar of strength, rock, rock of ages.

haversack, *n.* knapsack, rucksack, kitbag, backpack; gunnysack, gunny-bag, duffelbag; bag, shoulder bag, pouch, sack, pack, satchel, ditty bag; saddlebag, sabretache.

havoc, *n.* **1.** devastation, destruction, ruination, rack and ruin, holocaust, demolition, wipe-out, debacle, ruin; spoliation, despoliation, ravage, pillage, plunder, sack; robbing, plundering, gutting, ransacking, vandalizing, wasting, *Sl.* trashing; rapine, ravishment, predation, depredation.
2. desolation, waste, wreckage, ravagement; extermination, extirpation, obliteration, annihilation; disaster, calamity, catastrophe, cataclysm.
—*v.* **3.** devastate, destroy, demolish, wreck, *Sl.* total, knock to pieces, wreak havoc on, play havoc with; raze, gut, fell, topple, prostrate, level; pull down, tear down, take down, bring down, break down, throw down; flood, deluge, inundate, sweep away.

4. desolate, lay waste, ravage, ruin, *Dial.* ruinate, bring to ruin, bring to naught, lay in ruins; despoil, rob, plunder, pillage, ransack; vandalize, waste, *Sl.* trash; annihilate, obliterate, extirpate, exterminate, stamp out.

hawk[1], *n.* falcon, caracara, buzzard, vulture, kite, osprey, kestrel, harrier, goshawk, eagle.

hawk[2], *v.* peddle, vend, market, sell; cry, *Inf.* bark; bargain, higgle, haggle, higgle-haggle, *Scot.* argle-bargle.

hawker, *n.* peddler, huckster, vendor, salesman; pitchman, spieler, concessionaire; traveling salesman, door-to-door salesman, Fuller Brushman, colporteur; merchant, dealer, pushcart entrepreneur, come-on artist, sutler; bargainer, higgler, haggler.

hawk-eyed, *adj.* sharp-sighted, gimlet-eyed, perceptive. See **eagle-eyed**.

hay, *n.* **1.** straw; fodder, provender, feed, forage, pasturage.

2. make hay while the sun shines seize the day, *Latin. carpe diem*, strike while the iron is hot, make the most of a situation; capitalize on, exploit.

hayseed, *n.* **1.** grass seed, grass, straw, chaff, grain; shuck, huck, shell, hull, pod, bran, wisp, bur.

2. *Slang.* rustic, peasant, provincial, country cousin, countryman, hobnail; farmer, plowman, plowboy, chuff, swain, gaffer, kern *or* kerne, son *or* tiller of the soil, *Archaic.* hind; yokel, bumpkin, country bumpkin, hawbuck, *Dial.* lumpkin, *Often Disparaging.* hillbilly, *Disparaging.* bogtrotter, *Inf.* chawbacon, *Inf.* cider squeezer, *Sl.* hick, *Sl.* woodhick, *Sl.* rube, *Sl.* hoosier, *Fr. Sl. truffe*.

haystack, *n.* haycock, cock, stack, rick, *Chiefly Brit.* hayrick.

haywire, *adj.* **1.** *Informal.* in disorder, disordered, disorganized, disarranged, deranged, discomposed, disturbed, upset; in disrepair, out of order, *Inf.* out of commission, *Inf.* out of kilter, *Inf.* out of whack, *Sl.* on the blink, *Sl.* on the fritz.

2. *Informal.* insane, crazy, mad, out of one's mind, *Inf.* out of one's head, *Inf.* psycho, *Sl.* nuts, *Sl.* loony, *Sl.* bananas, *Sl.* bonkers, *Sl.* bughouse, *Sl.* cuckoo.

hazard, *n.* **1.** danger, endangerment, risk, jeopardy, threat; peril, imperilment, insecurity, precariousness; crisis, predicament, dilemma.

2. chance, contingency, unpredictability, uncertainty, gamble, venture; accident, surprise, unintentional happening, unforeseen fortuity; occurrence, contretemps, mischance.

—*v.* **3.** venture, submit, offer, volunteer, throw out, advance.

4. endanger, imperil, peril, expose to danger, risk, put in jeopardy; stake, pawn, invest, involve, sink.

5. dare, chance, gamble, run a risk, undertake against odds, attempt, adventure.

hazardous, *adj.* **1.** dangerous, fraught with danger, perilous, jeopardous, venturesome, dire, *Archaic.* parlous, *Sl.* hairy; threatening, disquieting, menacing, minatory, ominous, inauspicious, unfavorable, boding ill; risky, insecure, precarious, unsafe, unsound, unstable, unsteady, shaky, rickety, slippery; exposed, unsheltered, vulnerable, defenseless; critical, difficult, ticklish, thorny.

2. chancy, haphazard, random, incidental, accidental, fortuitous, casual; unpredictable, dicey, *Inf.* fluky, speculative, undecided, undetermined, uncertain, unsettled, unforeseeable.

haze[1], *n.* **1.** fog, mist, cloud, fogbank, cloudbank; smog, smaze, *Inf.* pea soup, *Brit. Inf.* London special; gauze, film, vapor, frost.

2. vagueness, uncertainty, haziness, cloudiness, fogginess, nebulosity; obscurity, indistinctness, dimness; confusion, muddle, befuddlement, bewilderment.

haze[2], *v.* ridicule, mock, tease, tantalize, taunt, badger; twit, jest, rally, banter, chaff, rag; make a fool of, victimize, bait, *Sl.* razz, make a monkey out of, make a goat of, send on a fool's errand; harass, harry, hector, bully.

hazel, *adj.* nutbrown, acorn, reddish brown, umber; cinnamon, beige, khaki, buff, fawn; tawny, fuscous, foxy, tan, russet.

hazy, *adj.* **1.** cloudy, foggy, misty, steamy, smoggy, overcast, overclouded; nebulous, nubilous, shadowy, opaque.

2. vague, indefinite, obscure, ill-defined, dim, indistinct; unrecognizable, blurry, bleary, filmy, fuzzy, indistinguishable; clouded, shrouded, veiled, in a fog, *Inf.* muzzy; confused, bewildered, muddled, befuddled, mixed-up, addled.

head, *n.* **1.** skull, cranium, cephalon, brainpan, poll, pate, *Inf.* sconce, *Archaic.* mazard, *Archaic.* costard; *All Inf.* upstairs, upper story, belfry, noggin, dome; *All Sl.* bean, nut, nob, noodle, noddle, crumpet, gourd, conk.

2. intellect, mind, intelligence, wit, wisdom, genius; grain, sensorium, sensory, *Inf.* gray matter, *Latin. mens*, nous, *Fr. esprit*; understanding, wits, sense, reason, rationality, sensibility.

3. authority, command, reins, control, charge, lead; throne, place of honor, first place, top, helm, wheel; primacy, dominion, priority, precedence; captaincy, headship, directorship, leadership.

4. leader, chief, commander, chieftain, senior, captain; director, manager, superintendent, controller, supervisor, *Inf.* boss, administrator; master, principal, headmaster, dean, provost; chairman, governor, president, premier, prime minister.

5. top, summit, tip, peak, vertex, crest; pitch, acme, apex, crown, pinnacle, zenith, apogee; upper part, cap, brow, *Latin. caput*; nib, end, extremity, spike, cusp, point.

6. front, fore, forepart, forefront, forecourt, face, proscenium; vanguard, van, front line, avant-garde, point.

7. climax, culmination, issue, pitch, consummation, crescendo; crisis, critical point, cap, turning point, failsafe, juncture, crossroads.

8. froth, foam, suds, lather, puff, collar.

9. promontory, headland, foreland; cape, hook, spur, point, bill, tongue, *Scot.* mull; reef, spit, breakwater, jetty, jutty.

10. origin, provenience, rise, source, fount, font, fountainhead; well, wellspring, spring, wellhead, headwater; mainspring, springhead, riverhead.

11. *Nautical.* bow, prow, nose, jib, bowsprit, fore, stem, figurehead.

12. *Nautical.* toilet, lavatory, rest room, water closet, *Sl.* john, *Sl.* can, latrine, commode.

13. bracket, cadre, section, division, category, class, designation, heading; chapter, rubric, title, caption, headline; topic, subject, theme, text, motif, point, issue.

14. come to a head culminate, climax, crown, consummate, ripen; crest, overtop, surmount, go over the top.

15. head over heels a. intensely, passionately, ardently, perfervidly, vehemently, earnestly; completely, thoroughly, fully. **b.** impulsively, impetuously, rashly, wildly, quixotically; carelessly, heedlessly, recklessly.

16. heads up *Informal.* watch out, watch it, fore, look out, be careful; duck, look out below, gardyloo.

17. keep one's head remain calm, keep one's wits about oneself, keep cool, *Inf.* keep one's cool, *Inf.* roll with the punches.

18. lose one's head lose control, explode, blow up, *Inf.* lose one's cool, become excited; *Sl.* flip out, *Sl.* blow one's lid, *Sl.* flip one's lid, *Sl.* freak out.

—*adj.* **19.** first, chief, leading, premier, main, principal, cardinal; supreme, paramount, capital; crowning, culminating, capping, consummating; zenithal, apical, meridian, acmic; maximal, extreme, ultimate.

20. frontal, fore, anterior, front, forward; topmost, headmost, top, uppermost, overmost, foremost; cephalic, cranial, occipital, sincipital.

21. opposing, counter, contrary, impeditive; oncoming, head-on, fronting.

—*v.* **22.** lead, precede, lead the way, go first, forerun, forego, antecede; crown, top, surmount, top off, cap; lead off, *Inf.* kick off; herald, introduce, usher in.

23. outdo, excel, take the lead, beat, best, better; surpass, pass, get ahead of, come to the front; outrank, overbear, outweigh, overbalance; outrun, outride, outstrip, outpace; outdistance, distance, leave behind, leave in the lurch.

24. direct, command, rule, control, regulate, sway; govern, lead, boss, administer; supervise, superintend, oversee; guide, conduct, run, pull the strings; preside, captain, pilot.

25. turn, steer, direct, aim, point; warp, bias, jibe; head for, make for, bear for; move towards, gravitate, tend, induce, lean; verge, bend to, go, point, lead, dispose.

26. head off intercept, catch, cut off, stop on the way, step in, interpose; stay, restrain, inhibit.

headache, *n.* **1.** pain in the head, splitting *or* throbbing headache, sick headache, migraine, *Obs.* megrim, *Med.* cephalalgia, *Pathol.* hemicrania, *Pathol.* hemialgia.

2. *Informal.* bother, trouble, inconvenience, nuisance, annoyance, bane.

headdress, *n.* **1.** head covering, coiffure, headpiece, headgear; cap, hat, bonnet, capote, turban; hood, cowl, capuche. See **hat**.

2. hairdo, hairstyle, haircut, cut, coiffure, *Inf.* coif. See **hairdo**.

headfirst, *adv.* **1.** headlong, headforemost, head-on; diving, in a nose dive, *Inf.* in a header, in a dive; plunging, pitching, head over heels, ducking, on one's head.

2. rashly, hastily, hurriedly, impetuously, impulsively, on the spur of the moment, abruptly; recklessly, heedlessly, carelessly, incautiously, foolishly; helter-skelter, pell-mell, in confusion.

heading, *n.* **1.** headpiece, cap, crown, crest.

2. title, caption, rubric; headline, head, banner, banner head *or* line, superscription, streamer.

3. section, division, category, class, division.

4. course, bearing, direction, aim, way.

headland, *n.* cape, point, hook, spur, promontory, foreland, head, *Scot.* mull; peninsula, chersonese; spit, sandspit, sandbar.

headless, *adj.* **1.** acephalous, acephalic, topless, crownless; decapitated, decollated, beheaded, guillotined.

2. leaderless, undirected, unguided, ungoverned, reinless, rudderless; aimless, directionless, wayward, rambling, roving.

3. unintelligent, stupid, brainless, mindless, witless, senseless, idiotic, moronic; empty-headed, pea-brained, *Inf.* harebrained, dim-witted; foolish, *Inf.* fool, silly, fatuous.

headline, *n.* **1.** caption, title, heading, head, banner, banner head *or* line, streamer, superscription, *Journalism.* screamer, *U.S. Inf.* scarehead.

—*v.* **2.** title, caption, head.

3. feature, spotlight, star, give top billing to.

headlong, *adv.* **1.** headforemost, headfirst, head-on, diving, in a dive, plunging, in a nose dive.

2. quickly, speedily, hurriedly; promptly, instantly, straightway, *Sl.* pronto, in a wink, in a jiffy, in a trice, in an instant, double-quick, *Inf.* like greased lightning, like a shot, like a thunderbolt, *Sl.* like mad, *Sl.* like a bat out of hell; directly, at once, without delay, in less than no time, before one can say "Jack Robinson," before the ink is dry, *Sl.* P.D.Q., *Inf.* lickety-split; swiftly, rapidly, fast, full tilt, full pelt, hotfoot, at full blast, in high gear, as fast as one's legs can carry one.

3. precipitately, hurriedly, hastily; abruptly, suddenly, unexpectedly, prematurely, inopportunely, too soon, without notice *or* warning, on the spur of the moment, like a bolt from the blue, like a thief in the night; incautiously, unadvisedly, foolishly, unwarily, impetuously, impulsively, impatiently; rashly, wildly, recklessly, carelessly, heedlessly, thoughtlessly, slapdash, at half cock, pell-mell, harum-scarum, helter-skelter, head over heels.

4. unduly quick, rash, precipitate, hasty, hurried; reckless, careless, heedless, thoughtless; running, pell-mell, helter-skelter, harum-scarum, head-over-heels; brash, incautious, injudicious, ill-advised, indiscreet, unwary, foolish; abrupt, sudden, unexpected, premature.

5. impetuous, impulsive, unrestrained, ungoverned, uncontrolled, unchecked, unbridled; feverish, impatient, frantic, impassioned; madcap, madbrained, foolhardy, daredevil, breakneck, adventurous, hot-headed, harebrained, blindfolded; volatile, flighty, frivolous, erratic, fickle, unreliable, irresponsible; wild, giddy, dashing, over-confident, rampant, quixotic, punch-drunk; death-defying, devil-may-care, dangerous, ruinous, perilous.

6. headfirst, headforemost, head-on; diving, in a dive, plunging, in a nose dive.

headman, *n.* **1.** chief, leader, captain, *Inf.* boss, *Inf.* bossman, man-in-charge; *Inf.* king-pin, *Inf.* number one, *Inf.* Mr. Big, *Sl.* top dog, *Sl.* head honcho, *Sl.* big cheese, *Fr. grand fromage*, *Sl.* big wheel, *Sl.* high man on the totem pole; head, chairman, headmaster, principal, dean, director, administrator; manager, overseer, supervisor, superintendent, *Inf.* super, foreman, *Brit.* gaffer.

2. superior, commander, commanding officer, commandant, general, chieftain, (*of some tribes of American Indians*) sachem; president, premier, chief-of-state, head-of-state, captain of the ship of state, ruler, king, prince, sovereign, emperor; lord, overlord, *Hist.* suzerain, lord and master, master.

3. headsman, executioner, beheader.

headmaster, *n.* principal, head, dean, director, man-in-charge, *Inf.* boss; administrator, superintendent, *Inf.* super.

headmost, *adj.* foremost, supreme, head, first, premier, paramount, *Inf.* boss; main, chief, principal, cardinal, prime, primary, uppermost, most important; dominant, superior, surpassing, preeminent.

head-on, *adj.* straight-on, straight-ahead; head-to-head, face-to-face, eyeball-to-eyeball; frontal, forward, foremost; opposing, opposite.

headquarters, *n.* main offices, home base *or* station, center of operations, H.Q., *Mil.* base *or* post, *U.S. Army.* command post, high command.

headstone, *n.* gravestone, tombstone, stone, slab, tablet, marker; obelisk, column, shaft, pillar; monument, memorial.

headstrong, *adj.* **1.** stubborn, stubborn as a mule, mulish, obstinate, obdurate, inflexible, adamant, intransigent, intractable, unyielding, pigheaded, bullheaded, muleheaded; willful, self-willed, contrary, perverse, froward, refractory, recalcitrant, contumacious, cross-grained, *U.S. Inf.* notionate, *Archaic.* untoward; disobedient, ungovernable, unmanageable, unruly, fractious, wayward, incorrigible, difficult.

2. rash, reckless, imprudent, incautious, improvident, heedless, unwary, foolhardy; headlong, breakneck, precipitate.

heads-up, *adj.* alert, aware, on the qui vive, watchful, wide-awake, not missing a trick; quick, expeditious, ready, nimble, on one's toes; bright, sharp, keen, shrewd, perspicacious, astute; opportunist, adaptable, accommodating.

headway[1], *n.* **1.** progress, progression, advance, forward movement *or* motion; way, passage, procession, procedure.

2. improvement, betterment, advancement, furtherance, promotion.

3. make headway advance, progress, go, proceed; gain, gain ground, get ahead, come on, *Inf.* come along; roll, cover ground, make strides *or* rapid strides.

headway[2], *n.* headroom, room, room to spare, free passage, clear space, clearance.

headwork, *n.* thought, hard thought, brainwork, using one's little gray cells; beating *or* cudgeling one's brains out; cogitation, meditation, contemplation, mulling, pondering; concentration, reasoning, ratiocination, analysis, deduction, problem-solving, riddle-solving, planning; study, homework, hitting the books, burning the midnight oil, lucubration, *Inf.* pulling an all-nighter, cramming, memorizing; exercising one's brain, mental workout, mental calisthenics.

heady, *adj.* **1.** intoxicating, intoxicative, inebriating, inebriative, inebriant.

2. exciting, thrilling, galvanizing, electrifying, breathtaking; exhilarating, invigorating, stimulating, enlivening, rousing, arousing; overpowering, overwhelming.

3. rash, reckless, foolhardy, heedless, incautious, imprudent, unwary, improvident; impetuous, impulsive, precipitate, headlong, breakneck; headstrong, willful, self-willed, ungovernable, unmanageable.

4. violent, destructive, ruinous, devastating, desolating, ravaging.

5. clever, shrewd, crafty, astute, canny, sharp, knowing, *Inf.* cagey.

heal, *v.* **1.** cure, work *or* effect a cure, restore, remedy, repair, rehabilitate, make well, set on one's feet; renew, revivify, regenerate, rejuvenate, reinvigorate, resuscitate, bring round *or* around; treat, minister to, doctor, nurse, medicate, physic.

2. conciliate, reconcile, settle, patch up, make good *or* right, set *or* put straight, square, bring to terms; compose, appease, subdue, pacify; mitigate, ameliorate, meliorate, palliate, assuage, allay, modify, soften.

3. clean, cleanse, purge, purify; disinfect, sterilize, decontaminize, sanitize.

4. mend, be on the mend, recover, recuperate, get well, pull through, come through, come round *or* around, be oneself again; improve, show improvement, grow better, look up, pick up, perk up.

healing, *adj.* **1.** curing, curative, restoring, restorative, remedial, medicinal, therapeutic, corrective, analeptic, sanative, sanatory.

2. recovering, recuperating, mending, on the mend, feeling better, feeling oneself; improving, showing improvement, growing better, looking up, picking up, perking up.

health, *n.* **1.** physical condition, condition, physical fitness, fitness, well-being; good condition, good trim, good *or* fine shape, *Inf.* top *or* tip-top shape, fine fettle, *Inf.* fine whack, *Inf.* fine *or* high feather; bloom, flush, glow.

2. healthiness, healthfulness, haleness, soundness, heartiness, hardiness, robustness, vigorousness, lustiness.

3. vigor, strength, power, potency, force, birr, *Literary.* puissance; vitality, vivacity, energy, go, get up and go, liveliness, zing, *Inf.* zip, *Inf.* pep, *Inf.* bounce, *Sl.* pizzazz, *Brit. Sl.* stingo.

healthful, *adj.* **1.** salubrious, salutary, salutiferous, hygienic; wholesome, beneficial, good for one; nutritious, nourishing, health-giving; invigorating, bracing, stimulating, refreshing, tonic.

2. healthy, hale, hearty. See **healthy** (*def.* **1**).

healthy, *adj.* **1.** fit, physically-fit, sound, in sound condition, in good condition, in fine fettle, *Inf.* in shape, *Inf.* in good *or* fine shape, *Inf.* in fine *or* high feather, *Inf.* in fine whack, *Inf.* in the pink, *Brit. Dial.* bonny; well, in good health; ruddy, vigorous, full of vigor, hale, hearty, hale and hearty, robust, lusty, strong and healthy, bursting with health *or* vigor.

2. healthful, salutary, salubrious. See **healthful** (*def.* **1**).

heap, *n.* **1.** pile, stack, mass, accumulation, bulk, drift, cumulus; hoard, store, stock, stockpile, supply; lump, deposit, swell, mound, tumulus; bank, hillock, hill, mountain; bale, bundle, cock, shock, rick, mow; load, barrow, cartload, wagonload, carload, cargo.

2. collection, amassment, assemblage, aggregation; concentration, agglomeration, conglomeration, cluster, congeries; clump, bunch, batch.

3. *Informal.* abundance, bounty, volume, plenty; quantities, profusion, *Inf.* lots, *Inf.* raft, storm, shower, ocean, sea, world; multitude, throng, array, legion, crowd; numbers, scores, pack, host, swarm, mob.

4. *Informal.* hoard, store, quite a little, considerable deal, great deal; *Inf.* lots, mess, peck, *Inf.* load, *Sl.* pot, mint, *Inf.* oodles, *Inf.* tons; chunk, *Sl.* wad, lump, *Inf.* hunk, gob, *Sl.* scad, *Inf.* slew.

5. *Slang.* jalopy, rattletrap. See **jalopy**.

—*v.* **6.** *Often* **heap up** *or* **on** *or* **together** accumulate, pile, pile up, roll up, stack, pack; compile, amass, cumulate; hoard, squirrel away, load up, stow away.

7. gather, glean, take in, pull in, harvest, reap; garner, store up, stock up, lay by, lay up, lay in, *Inf.* stash away, reserve, set aside; save, save up.

8. group, cluster, bunch up *or* together, huddle; mass, crowd, congregate, agglomerate.

9. *Often* **heap on** *or* **upon** give, assign, bestow, confer; supply, provide, load, burden.

hear, *v.* **1.** have the sense of hearing, have the auditory faculty, perceive *or* receive sound, apprehend sound.

2. be told of, be informed of, be made aware of, receive information *or* knowledge of, gather; learn of, find out about, pick up, get scent *or* wind of, *Inf.* hear tell of, learn through the grapevine, *Inf.* get the lowdown *or* inside info, *Sl.* get the dope *or* scoop; overhear, listen in, get an earful, eavesdrop.

3. listen to, keep one's ears open, listen with both ears, strain one's ears, be all ears, *Med.* auscultate; hark, harken, pay attention to, be attentive, attend, heed, take heed, notice, take notice, observe, regard, take cognizance of; take in, get, catch, understand, comprehend.

4. give audience to, grant a hearing to, audition, take [s.o.'s] statement *or* testimony, *Law.* try; examine, investigate, look into, inquire into, question, interrogate; consider, think over, judge, adjudicate, pass judgment on.

5. give an ear to, lend an ear to, bend an ear, take time to listen to, hear [s.o.] out, give [s.o.] the time of day; recognize [s.o.], acknowledge [s.o.], give [s.o.] a chance to talk *or* speak, give [s.o.] a turn as speaker *or* at the podium.

6. *Often* **hear of** think of, let [s.t.] enter one's head *or* mind, entertain the idea of, consider; approve, condone, sanction, see as fit, consent *or* agree to, *Inf.* O.K.

hearing *n.* **1.** ear, audition, sense *or* faculty of hearing, aural sense *or* faculty, ability to hear, *Anat., Physiol.* auditory perception; audience, listening, hearking, harkening, auscultation.

2. audience, interview, opportunity to be heard, chance to speak *or* talk, opportunity to see *or* go before [s.o.], *Obs.* audit; fair hearing, day in court, chance to tell one's story, inquest, inquisition, appearance before a grand jury; inquiry, investigation, probe, examination, review; interrogation, questioning, question and answer session.

3. earshot, earreach, hearing distance, carrying distance, range of one's voice, sound of one's voice.

hearsay *n.* **1.** secondhand information, what other people say, what one hears, mere talk, only talk, word-of-mouth information, *Law.* hearsay evidence, *Law.* earwitness account.

2. rumor, grapevine, talk, word, common talk *or* knowledge, *Inf.* scuttlebutt, *Fr. oui-dire, Archaic.* bruit; gossip, idle talk, tittle-tattle, buzz, chatter, talk of the town, what's going around, topic of the day, *Sl.* schmooze; an earful, big news, news, story, tale, dirt, *Inf.* inside info, *Sl.* dope, *Sl.* poop.

heart *n.* **1.** *Sl.* ticker, organ of circulation; bosom, breast.

2. inner feeling, feelings, soul, spirit, *Sl.* gut; sentiment, feeling, emotion; sensibility, responsiveness, passion; nature, disposition, temperament.

3. sympathy, fellow feeling, understanding, compassion, pathos, commiseration, concern; beneficence, kindness, goodness, graciousness; humanitarianism, humaneness, humanity, love; magnanimity, good will, brotherly love.

4. courage, bravery, valor, stout-heartedness; intrepidity, fearlessness, dauntlessness, awelessness, boldness; mettle, pluck, spirit, backbone, gumption, nerve, *Sl.* guts.

5. core, center, nucleus, germ, kernel, seed, nut; marrow, pith, gist, substance, essence, sum and substance, essential part, quintessence, heart of the matter, *Inf.* nub, *Inf.* nitty-gritty; keystone, essential, *Latin. sine qua non,* crux.

6. after one's own heart much to be desired, desirable, worth having; who fits the bill.

7. at heart in reality, truly, really, fundamentally, basically; intrinsically, innately.

8. break [s.o.'s] heart cause [s.o.] pain, make [s.o.'s] heart bleed; jilt, two-time, give [s.o.] the gate.

9. by heart by memory, by rote; word for word.

10. cross one's heart swear to goodness, hope to die; promise, vow, pledge.

11. do one's heart good delight, excite, gladden, cheer; please, satisfy, gratify, fulfill.

12. eat one's heart out grieve, sorrow, mourn, pine, agonize, ache.

13. from the bottom of one's heart sincerely, heartily, heart and soul, with all one's heart.

14. have a change of heart change one's mind, change one's song *or* tune; give in, relent, come round, forgive and forget.

15. have a heart be kind, be considerate, be sympathetic, be compassionate, be merciful, be lenient.

16. have one's heart set on want, want in the worst way, be willing to do anything for, be bent upon, long for, wish for.

17. heart and soul **a.** heartily, cordially, wholeheartedly, from the bottom of one's heart; willingly, gladly, eagerly, with open arms.

b. thoroughly, through and through, root and branch, head and shoulders, from the ground up.

18. lose one's heart to fall in love with, fall head over heels in love with, fall for, take to, cotton to, take a liking *or* fancy to.

19. set one's heart against oppose, go against, resist.

20. take heart cheer up, brighten up, perk up; snap out of it, come out of it; regain one's courage, become heartened.

21. take *or* **lay to heart** **a.** consider seriously, think over. **b.** take the wrong way, take personally, take offense.

22. to one's heart's content as long *or* as much as one pleases, until one has had enough.

23. with one's heart in one's mouth fearfully, apprehensively, with fear and trembling, with bated breath.

heartache, *n.* **1.** sorrow, grief, *Archaic.* dole, sadness, woe, ruth, heartbreak; anguish, misery, *Archaic.* bale, dolor; wretchedness, heaviness of heart, desolation, despair, slough of despair, moroseness, melancholy, dejection, despondency; ache, pain, hurt, suffering, *Archaic.* teen; torment, torture, agony.

2. distress, affliction, disquiet, disquietude; regret, rue, remorse, repentance, contrition, penitence, compunction.

heartbreak, *n.* sorrow, grief, anguish. See **heartache** (*def.* **1**).

heartbreaking, *adj.* heartrending, tragic, sad, pitiful, poignant; disheartening, depressing, distressing, desolating; agonizing, tortuous, torturing, racking, painful; raw, sharp, cutting, bitter, biting, acute, severe, intense; insufferable, unbearable, unendurable; anguishing, excruciating, plaguing, harrowing, rending; tormenting, persecuting, afflictive; consuming, crushing, oppressive, heavy, cruel, harsh.

heartbroken, *adj.* downcast, dejected, disheartened, dispirited, downhearted, down; crestfallen, disappointed, broken-hearted, heartsick, dismayed, daunted, discouraged; miserable, morose, woebegone, heavy-hearted, disconsolate, sorrowful, mournful, lachrymose, funereal; depressed, weighed down, burdened, crushed, *Inf.* broken, *Sl.* bummed out; despondent, spiritless, lifeless, enervated, weakened, weary, tired, drained; unhappy, cheerless, glum, gloomy, doleful.

heartburn, *n.* **1.** *Pathology.* indigestion, dyspepsia, stomach upset, gastric distress, brash, cardialgia, pyrosis, water brash.

2. envy, jealousy, resentment, grudge, begrudging, green-eyed monster, enviousness; discontentment, malcontentedness, dissatisfaction, unhappiness, heartburning.

heartburning, *n.* **1.** envy, jealousy, resentment, heartburn, grudge. See **heartburn** (*def.* **2**).

2. animosity, ill will, hostility, invidiousness, abhorrence, aversion; antipathy, rancor, enmity, animus, loathing, hatred, detestation; anger, pique, malice, spite, antagonism.

hearten, *v.* cheer, cheer up, console, comfort, *Archaic.* recomfort; inspirit, *Inf.* pep up, buoy up, raise [s.o.'s] spirits, pluck up, give [s.o.] a lift; gladden, enhearten, embolden; fortify, strengthen, restore, revitalize, revivify, revive; animate, vivify, energize, *Sl.* give a shot in the arm to, invigorate, give new life to; exhilarate, uplift, elate.

heartfelt, *adj.* deep-felt, strongly *or* keenly felt, *Archaic.* homefelt, profound, deep; warm, hearty, cordial, friendly; glad, eager, responsive, enthusiastic; earnest, sincere, serious, genuine, *Inf.* for real; wholehearted, devoted, dedicated, committed; ardent, fervent, fervid, perfervid, zealous, passionate, impassioned, intense.

hearth, *n.* **1.** fireside, fireplace, fire, hearthside, hearthstone, chimney corner, *Brit. Dial.* ingle, *Brit. Dial.* ingleside, *Chiefly Brit.* inglenook *or* ingle nook.
2. home, home sweet home, homestead, hearth and home, hearthstead, household, family, family circle, domestic circle, bosom of one's family, seat of one's affections, *Inf.* place where one hangs his hat, home life, family life, domestic life.

heartily, *adv.* **1.** affectionately, warmly, cordially, genially, with open arms; amicably, amiably, affably, congenially; pleasantly, favorably, agreeably.
2. sincerely, feelingly, genuinely, from the bottom of one's heart, deeply, profoundly.
3. avidly, ardently, zealously, fervently, perfervidly; eagerly, earnestly, willingly, gladly; vehemently, heatedly, passionately.
4. enthusiastically, zestfully, vibrantly, fitfully; exuberantly, ebulliently, spiritedly, animatedly, with zest, with gusto; vigorously, energetically, forcefully, keenly; lustily, vivaciously, hardily.

heartless, *adj.* unfeeling, unsympathetic, unkind, insensitive, uncaring; unmoved, untouched, impervious, passionless; harsh, cruel, savage, cold-blooded; merciless, pitiless, ruthless, hard-hearted, cold-hearted; implacable, remorseless, inexorable, relentless; insensible, hardened, cold, frigid, stern.

heartrending, *adj.* distressing, heavy, heartbreaking, depressing, disheartening; agonizing, excruciating, afflictive, painful, aching; poignant, sharp, bitter, biting, burning; sad, dolorous, lamentable, grievous, tragic, rueful; affecting, tear-jerking, pathetic, pitiful.

heartsick, *adj.* dejected, depressed, disheartened, dispirited, downcast, heartbroken. See **heartbroken.**

heartwarming, *adj.* **1.** warming, moving, touching, affecting; cheering, gladdening, cheerful, glad; inspiring, encouraging, heartening, inspiriting, uplifting.
2. gratifying, satisfying, rewarding, contenting; comforting, pleasing, pleasurable, enjoyable, agreeable.

hearty, *adj.* **1.** affectionate, warm-hearted, cordial, warm, genial; jovial, amiable, amicable, affable, congenial; friendly, neighborly, folksy, hospitable, backslapping.
2. genuine, sincere, authentic, unfeigned; heartfelt, wholehearted, deep, deepest, profound, well-meant, well-meaning.
3. zealous, avid, ardent, fervent, perfervid; eager, willing, ready, glad, earnest; passionate, heated, vehement, devout.
4. exuberant, unrestrained, irrepressible; enthusiastic, zestful, lively, spirited, animated, fitful; gushing, ebullient, buoyant, bouncy.
5. vigorous, lusty, stalwart, virile, hardy, mettlesome; hale, robust, healthy, sound, in fine fettle; sturdy, rugged, tough, stout.
6. substantial, solid, abundant, ample, sizable, goodly; nourishing, filling, nutritious, gustable.

heat, *n.* **1.** hotness, calefaction, warmth, warmness, caloric, caloricity; torridity, torridness, fieriness, red heat; incandescence, white heat; tepidity, tepidness, lukewarmness, lukewarmth.
2. fever, temperature, *Inf.* temp, *Pathol.* pyrexia, febricity, feverishness, flush, redness.
3. heat wave, hot streak, sultriness, dog days; swelter, summer, oppressive *or* tropical heat.
4. warmth, intensity, vehemence, passion, ardor, fervor, fervidness, zeal, eagerness, enthusiasm; exhilaration, excitement, arousal, stimulation, agitation, furor.
—*v.* **5.** *Often* **heat up** reheat, warm up *or* over, make hot *or* warm, *Obs.* chafe, precook, parboil; cook, bake, microwave, fire, kiln; toast, broil, charbroil, grill, barbecue; sauté, braise, panfry, brown, fry, griddle, frizzle, fricassee; brew, mull; superheat, boil, bring to a boil, seethe, stew, simmer, steam, scald; parch, roast, torrefy, scorch, singe, sear, cauterize; burn, overcook, char, carbonize, cremate, incinerate, deflagrate; (*all of metals*) melt *or* melt down, fuse, smelt, cupel, scorify.
6. warm, enthuse, inspirit, enliven, animate, flush; excite, arouse, stimulate, quicken, rouse, stir, awaken, kindle, spark, set in motion; inflame, impassion, fire up, light a fire under [s.o.], set on fire, ignite.

heated, *adj.* **1.** heated up, warmed *or* warmed up, *Obs.* chafed, reheated, warmed over; baked, cooked, toasted.
2. excited, exhilarated, *Inf.* psyched *or* psyched up, enthusiastic, enlivened, inspired, animated; inflamed, fiery, vehement, passionate, impassioned, worked-up, stimulated, aroused, *Inf.* hot, *Inf.* hot under the collar; ardent, eager, fervent, fervid, perfervid, frenzied, frenetic, frantic.

heater, *n.* radiator, steam heater, electric heater, gas heater, infrared heater; furnace, incinerator, forge, fireplace; stove, range, oven, kiln, microwave oven, toaster-oven, toaster, hot plate, cooker; brazier, foot warmer, hot-water bottle, heating pad, electric blanket.

heathen, *n.* **1.** unbeliever, infidel, pagan, *Islam.* kaffir, gentile; atheist, freethinker, disbeliever, nullifidian; agnostic, skeptic, Pyrrhonist, doubter, Doubting Thomas; iconoclast, secularist; apostate, heretic, backslider, antichrist.
2. primitive, aboriginal, barbarian, philistine; savage, Caliban; idolator, sun worshipper, fire worshipper.
—*adj.* **3.** heathenish, infidel, pagan, gentile, godless; atheistic, freethinking, disbelieving, nullifidian; agnostic, skeptical, cynical, doubting, Pyrrhonistic, iconoclastic; irreligious, worldly, secularist, irreverent, scoffing; heretical, not-born-again, unsaved, unChristian, impenitent, unrepentant, living in a state of sin, bound for hell.
4. unenlightened, primitive, philistine, untamed, uncivilized; barbarous, idolatrous, savage, brutish; polytheistic, pantheistic, voodooistic.

heave, *v.* **1.** raise, hoist, lift, boost; uprear, upraise, upheave, lever.
2. fling, cast, throw, toss; hurl, sling, catapult, launch; dart, *Brit. Sl.* bung, fire, shoot, let sail *or* fly; dash, chuck, pitch, peg, send, *Inf.* put some oomph into it; *All Baseball.* throw smoke, put smoke on it, bear down, throw a high, hard one.
3. pant, gasp, puff, blow, sigh, suspire; palpitate, throb, billow, surge.
4. vomit, retch, regurgitate, disgorge, throw up, *Sl.* frow up, spit up; be sick to one's stomach, *Inf.* have the throw-ups, get the dry heaves, *Sl.* puke, *Sl.* barf, *Sl.* upchuck, *Sl.* toss one's cookies, *Sl.* return one's breakfast, *Sl.* blow lunch.
5. haul, pull, tug, yank; put one's back into it, put some muscle behind it, grunt and groan.

heaven, *n.* **1.** paradise, bliss, abode of God, infinity, life everlasting; hereafter, life to come, world to come, next world, afterworld, sweet by-and-by; our Father's house, Divine abode, home, Abraham's bosom, abode of the saints, heavenly kingdom, kingdom of God, kingdom of heaven, city of God, city of light, heavenly city, holy city, celestial city, New Jerusalem, Zion, throne of God; Valhalla, Olympus, Elysium, Elysian Fields, empyrean, *Islam.* the Seven Heavens, Avalon, the Islands *or* Isles of the Blessed, the Fortunate Isles *or* Islands, the Happy Isles; happy hunting grounds, great hangar in the sky.

2. ecstasy, transport, pleasure, supreme happiness, perfect content, *Buddhism.* Nirvana, seventh heaven; Shangri-la, utopia, Eden, heaven on earth, millennium, Jubile, kingdom come, Beulah Land; glory, rapture, delight, fairyland, dreamland, happy valley, pie in the sky.

3. *Usu.* **heavens** sky, firmament, aerosphere, ether; canopy of heaven, vault of heaven, celestial sphere, the blue, *Inf.* wild blue yonder.

heavenly, *adj.* **1.** cosmic, extraterrestrial, empyrean, unearthly, unworldly, extramundane, not of this world, superphysical, hyperphysical, spiritual; empyreal, empyrean, paradisiacal, divine, celestial, elysiac, Olympic, Elysian; holy, glorified, blessed, beatific, beatified, divine, good; cherubic, angelic, seraphic, archangelic, saintly, sainted.

2. blissful, delightful, pleasurable, ambrosial, delectable, gratifying, entrancing, enrapturing; beautiful, dazzling, bright, radiant, shining, brilliant, superb, exquisite, sublime, golden, glorious; unblemished, flawless, unsullied, pure, unalloyed, matchless, perfect, faultless; fadeless, never-fading, imperishable, immortal, deathless; utopian, Edenic, ideal, consummate.

heaviness, *n.* **1.** heft, heftiness, weight, weightiness, ponderousness, gravity; size, volume, mass, substance, bulk, bulkiness, largeness, bigness, amplitude.

2. turbulence, tempestuousness, storminess, wildness, roughness.

3. graveness, seriousness, criticalness, crucialness, importance.

4. deepness, profoundness, esotericalness, abstruseness; impenetrableness, incomprehensibleness, unfathomableness.

5. burdensomeness, onerousness, oppressiveness, hardness, harshness, severity.

6. depression, dejection, melancholy, gloominess, gloom.

7. dullness, boringness, tediousness, dryness, *Sl.* deadness; blandness, insipidness, flatness, vapidness; monotonousness, uneventfulness, humdrum.

8. soberness, somberness, staidness, sedateness, solemnity, grimness.

heavy, *adj.* **1.** hefty, weighty, bulky, substantial, dense, ample; big, large, huge, gigantic, titanic, enormous, massive, ponderous, prodigious, mammoth, mighty, colossal, immense; unwieldy, cumbrous, cumbersome, awkward, unmanageable.

2. turbulent, tempestuous, stormy, squally; raging, howling, roaring, wailing, thundering; violent, savage, wild, rough.

3. fat, overweight, obese; stout, portly, corpulent, *Scot.* fodgel; chubby, tubby, pudgy, plump; paunchy, pot-bellied, big-bellied, great-bellied, *Sl.* beer-bellied, *Obs.* gorbellied.

4. grave, serious, crucial, critical, climacteric, acute; important, all-important, essential, of the essence, vital, heartbeat, *Inf.* gut.

5. deep, profound, esoteric, recondite, abstruse, *Sl.* heavy-duty; impenetrable, incomprehensible, past *or* beyond comprehension, unfathomable.

6. intense, extreme, keen, sharp, poignant; piercing, penetrating, cutting, biting, stinging; indelible, deeply-felt, heartfelt, *Archaic.* homefelt; overpowering, overwhelming, overcoming, overmastering.

7. burdensome, onerous, oppressive, hard, harsh, severe; distressing, grievous, baneful, baleful; intolerable, unbearable, backbreaking.

8. trying, difficult, troublesome, bothersome, worrisome; irksome, vexatious, wearisome, tiresome.

9. broad, blunt, thick, coarse.

10. weighted, weighed-down, laden, heavy-laden, loaded, loaded-down, taxed; encumbered, cumbered, burdened; strained, overloaded, overburdened, overtasked, overtaxed.

11. fraught, charged; momentous, decisive, pivotal.

12. depressed, dejected, downhearted, gloomy, morose, melancholy, downcast, sad, mournful; disconsolate, inconsolable, grief-stricken, cheerless, joyless, heartsick, heavy-hearted; crestfallen, chapfallen, long-faced, *Inf.* down in the mouth.

13. dull, boring, uninteresting, tedious, dry, dry-as-dust, *Sl.* dead; tasteless, bland, insipid, jejune, flat, vapid, *Sl.* for the birds, *Sl.* blah, *Sl.* nothing; uneventful, humdrum, monotonous, run-of-the-mill, prosaic.

14. cloudy, overcast, gray; lowering, leaden, dark, darkened; dreary, dismal, bleak, *Scot. and North Eng.* dowie, *Literary.* drear.

15. clumsy, lumbering, clodhopping; stolid, bovine, lumpish; sluggish, phlegmatic, lethargic, torpid, lifeless, spiritless.

16. sober, somber, staid, sedate, solemn; grim, grim-faced, grim-visaged, stone-faced, frowning, unsmiling.

—*n.* **17.** *Theater.* villain, antagonist, *Inf.* bad guy, *Sl.* baddie.

heavy-handed, *adj.* **1.** oppressive, harsh, hard, severe; iron-fisted, iron-handed, despotic, tyrannical, autocratic, overbearing; relentless, inexorable, implacable, remorseless, merciless, unmerciful, pitiless; cruel, brutal, ruthless, inhuman.

2. clumsy, awkward, graceless, ungraceful, like a bull in a china shop; unskillful, inept, inexpert, maladroit, unhandy, blundering, bungling, *Inf.* all thumbs, *Inf.* butterfingered.

heavy-hearted, *adj.* sad, sorrowful, mournful, disconsolate, inconsolable, grief-stricken, cheerless, joyless, heartsick; forlorn, miserable, wretched, woebegone, bowed-down, crushed, broken; depressed, dejected, downhearted, gloomy, morose, melancholy; downcast, chapfallen, crestfallen, long-faced, *Inf.* down-in-the-mouth.

heavyweight, *adj.* **1.** weighty, thick, bulky, hefty; durable, longlasting.

—*n.* **2.** *Informal.* notable, dignitary, personage, *Inf.* V.I.P., *Inf.* bigwig, *Sl.* big shot, *Sl.* biggie, *Sl.* big gun, *Sl.* big wheel, *Sl.* heavy, *Sl.* high-muck-a-muck.

3. *Informal.* intellectual, scholar, theorist, thinker, savant, bibliophile, man of letters, aesthete, pundit, highbrow, *Inf.* egghead, *Inf.* longhair.

heckle, *v.* badger, annoy, provoke, taunt, bait, tease, bedevil, plague; harass, hector, harry, torment, pester, bother, *Sl.* hassle, *Sl.* bug; irritate, peeve, nettle, chafe, vex, *Inf.* aggravate, *Chiefly U.S.* rile, *Inf.* needle, *Sl.* razz; hoot, catcall, jeer, gibe, mock, boo; fluster, ruffle, discompose, discountenance, disturb, disquiet, exasperate; give trouble, make trouble for, make it hard for, give a hard time to, interrupt, disrupt, upset.

hectic, *adj.* **1.** feverish, frenetic, frenzied, fitful, furious; rabid, delirious, raging, ranting; excited, passionate, heated; confused, boisterous, rambunctious, rampageous, riotous; uproarious, wild, mad, unruly, rampant; tumultuous, turbulent, tempestuous, raging, stormy.

2. febrile, hot, burning, feverish; inflamed, flushed,

fevered, pyretic, *Pathol.* pyrexic; feverous, warm, glowing, fiery, red, flaming.

3. consumptive, degenerative, phthisic, phthisical, wasting; tuberculous, marasmic, malarial.

hector, *n.* **1.** bully, bullyboy, bucko, rowdy, ruffian, tough, *Inf.* tough guy, coercer; intimidator, browbeater; oppressor, tyrant, terror.

2. braggart, brag, braggadocio, boaster, gascon, fanfaron, *Latin. miles gloriosus*; blusterer, bluffer, blatherskite, *Sl.* blowhard, *Sl.* windbag, *Sl.* gasbag, *Sl.* big mouth; roisterer, swaggerer.

—*v.* **3.** bully, bullyrag, coerce, *Inf.* bulldoze, steamroller, *Sl.* strong-arm; threaten, menace; intimidate, cow, browbeat, huff, beat down, *U.S. Inf.* buffalo.

4. badger, bait, torment, bedevil, plague; terrorize, persecute, molest, torture; harass, harry, beset, beleaguer; hound, dog, nag, pick on, pick at, be *or* get on [s.o.'s] back, *Brit.* chevy, *Inf.* give [s.o.] a hard time, *Sl.* ride, *Sl.* put the heat on.

5. brag, boast, trumpet, blow one's own trumpet, toot one's own horn, sing one's own praises; bluster, roister, puff, *Sl.* blow hard, *Sl.* blow, *Sl.* talk big; swagger, crow, gloat, lord it over.

hedge, *n.* **1.** hedgerow, row of boxwood *or* hawthorn, row of shrubs *or* bushes, weir, *Chiefly Brit.* quickset; fence, skirt, hem, rim, wall; border, circumference, circuit, compass, perimeter; boundary, bound, limit, confine, confines, edge, edging, fringe, margin; barrier, barricade, blockade, fortification.

—*v.* **2.** *Often* **hedge in** *or* **off** enclose, surround, rim, skirt, encircle, circumvent, circumscribe, wall in; delimit, define, outline, demarcate, mark off; set off, block off, separate, divide off, section off, partition off, isolate; blockade, barricade, fortify.

3. *Often* **hedge in** *or* **about** confine, fence in, cage in *or* up, pen in, imprison, close in, cramp, crowd, hem in, inhibit; restrict, limit, restrain, hinder, straiten, constrain, repress; collar, bridle, fetter, put one in a bind, tie one's hands, tie down, put one in a straight jacket; obstruct, block, curb, get in the way.

4. compensate for, make allowances for, make *or* leave room for, counterbalance, balance off; cover oneself, shield oneself, protect oneself, insure *or* secure oneself against, safeguard against, protect *or* guard against, defend against, leave oneself a way out.

5. equivocate, prevaricate, quibble, make qualifications, be vague *or* indefinite *or* ambivalent, refrain from committing oneself, be noncommittal, *Sl.* waffle; doubletalk, palter, weasel, use weasel words, *Inf.* talk out both sides of one's mouth, *Inf.* give [s.o.] the runaround; skirt the issue, fence, hem and haw, hem, haw, hesitate, halt, beat around the bush, temporize, play for time; evade, dodge, duck, fudge, shift, shuffle, change the subject, get around [s.t.], elude; escape, get out of, wriggle out of, weasel out of, back out of, back-pedal, back-track, beg off, *Sl.* cop out.

hedonism, *n.* **1.** epicureanism, epicurism, sybaritism; Benthamism, utilitarianism, eudemonics, *Ethics.* eudemonism.

2. pleasure-seeking, pursuit of pleasure, la dolce vita; wild *or* riotous *or* free living, *Inf.* high living, *Sl.* partying, *Sl.* swinging; luxuriousness, extravagance, indulgence, self-indulgence, overindulgence, immoderation, intemperance, excessiveness, crapulence, gluttony, gulosity, edacity; self-gratification, gratification, satisfaction-seeking; sensuality, sensualism, sensualness, voluptuousness, carnality; debauchery, dissipation, dissoluteness, rakishness, profligacy, libertinism, libertinage.

hedonist, *n.* **1.** epicurean, epicure, sybarite; Benthamite, utilitarian, *Ethics.* eudemonist.

2. pleasure seeker, *Inf.* high liver, *Sl.* swinger, *Sl.* party girl, *Fr. bon vivant*; indulger, glutton, gourmand, hog, belly-god, winebibber, heavy drinker, double-fisted drinker; sensualist, voluptuary, debauchee, roué, rake, profligate, libertine.

heed, *v.* **1.** listen to, give ear to, pay attention to, give attention to; mark, observe, consider, note, take note, take notice, give heed to; regard, remark, *Archaic.* animadvert, bear in mind, take into account; mind, obey, respect, follow; abide by, hold by, adhere to, practice; keep an eye on, keep an eye out, be on guard, be alert, be cautious, watch out, look before leaping, stop, look and listen.

—*n.* **2.** attention, notice, observation, ear; consideration, thought, care, caution, solicitude, prudence; respect, regard, note; vigilance, watchfulness, guard, watch; alertness, advertence, heedfulness, regardfulness; attentiveness, carefulness, mindfulness, wariness, chariness.

heedful, *adj.* attentive, careful, mindful, regardful, advertent; prudent, circumspect, thoughtful, *Scot.* canny, provident, precautious; alert, vigilant, ready, on guard, on one's toes, on the qui vive, alive to, all ears; watchful, wary, chary, awake, wide-awake, observant, open-eyed, *Inf.* on the job.

heedless, *adj.* careless, thoughtless, unmindful, unheeding, disregardful, deaf, blind; reckless, precipitate, headlong, rash, impulsive; inattentive, inadvertent, regardless, *Fr. distrait*; unobservant, unnoticing, unremarking; improvident, imprudent, unthinking, unprepared, unready; unalert, incautious, unwatchful, unvigilant, unwary; off guard, unguarded, *Inf.* asleep on the job, *Inf.* not on the job, *Inf.* asleep at the switch, distracted.

heel, *n.* **1.** foot, hoof, kicker, *Latin. calx*; heelbone, *Anat.* calcaneus, *Anat.* os calcis; (*of some animals*) hock, *Anat.* hallux, (*of birds*) spur.

2. lift, heelpiece, heeltap, spike, wedgie.

3. conclusion, tail end, fag end, rind, crust; remnant, remainder, leftovers, stump, butt, rump.

4. *Usu. Naut. or Aeronaut.* cant, tilt, angle, slant, inclination; sheering, veering, tipping; yaw, deviation, shift.

5. **Achilles' heel** vulnerability, weakness, soft underbelly; sore spot, imperfection, defect; nemesis, undoing, downfall.

6. **down at the heels** shabby, slipshod, run-down, slovenly, seedy, dowdy; out at the elbows, impoverished, poor, destitute, down and out.

7. **take to one's heels** flee, escape, run away *or* off, take flight, *Inf.* skedaddle, *Inf.* hightail, *Inf.* show a clean pair of heels, *Sl.* fly the coop, *Sl.* split.

—*v.* **8.** follow closely, dog, bedog, hound, prowl after, pursue, chase, shadow, trail, track, trace, *Inf.* tag *or* tag after, *Inf.* tail.

9. (*all of shoes*) put heels on, mend, patch, repair, cobble.

10. (*all of gamecocks*) arm with spurs, spur, fit with gaffs; equip, accouter, furnish, ready.

11. dance, caper, leap, prance, frisk, frolic, gambol, cut a caper, cavort, antic; jump, spring, capriole, curvet; *Dressage.* caracole, *Dressage.* wheel.

12. *Naut.* incline, cant, tilt, lean, list, careen, tip; yaw, jib, shift, deviate; wear, haul off, veer, sheer, swerve, turn aside.

heeled, *adj.* wealthy, rich, affluent, prosperous, flush, well-off, well-to-do, moneyed, worth a great deal, *Inf.* made of money, *Inf.* rolling in money *or* dough, *Inf.* loaded, *Inf.* in the dough *or* money *or* chips, *Inf.* well-heeled, *Sl.* filthy-rich; comfortable, easy, fat, *Inf.* on Easy Street, *Inf.* high on the hog, *Inf.* in clover, *Inf.* on velvet, *Inf.* well-situated, *Inf.* well-fixed, *Brit. Inf.*

warm.

heft, *n.* **1.** weight, weightiness, heaviness, ponderousness, ponderosity, gravity; size, volume, mass, substance, bulk, bulkiness, largeness, bigness, amplitude, ampleness.

—*v.* **2.** weigh, weight, balance, weigh in the balance. **3.** lift, lift up, boost, boost up, raise, raise up, hike, hike up; heave, throw up, upthrow, cast up, upcast; hoist, hoist up, jerk up, *Scot. and North Eng.* heeze *or* heize.

hefty, *adj.* **1.** heavy, weighty, bulky, substantial, dense, ample; big, large, huge, gigantic, titanic, enormous, massive, ponderous, ponderable, burdensome, prodigious, mammoth, mighty, colossal, immense; unwieldy, cumbrous, cumbersome, awkward, clumsy, unmanageable, inconvenient.

2. muscular, brawny, strapping, muscled, well-muscled, full-muscled, powerfully-built, broad-shouldered, *Derog.* muscle-bound; stalwart, rugged, husky, solid, well-knit; powerful, potent, mighty.

hegemony, *n.* supremacy, primacy, preeminence, upper *or* whip hand, sway, dominion; control, rule, command, mastery, domination; reign, sovereignty, suzerainty, empery, (*in India*) raj; kingship, lordship, mastership, leadership, seignority; authority, jurisdiction, power, *Inf.* say *or* say-so.

hegira, *n.* exodus, migration; deliverance, delivery, release, freedom; escape, flight, departure, *Archaic.* scape.

height, *n.* **1.** highness, altitude, elevation, loftiness, extent *or* distance upward; stature, tallness, length.

2. *Often* **heights a.** hill, mound, elevation, eminence, mountain; overlook, plateau, scenic outlook; promontory, headland, bluff, cliff, precipice, overhang, projection, prominence. **b.** top, mountaintop, hilltop, highest part, head; apex, summit, vertex, apogee, crest, pinnacle, peak, spire, tip, tiptop.

3. maximum, ceiling, limit, utmost, uttermost, extreme, extremity; high point, acme, zenith, climax, culmination, crowning point, capper, *Latin. ne plus ultra*; meridian, sublimity, supremacy, perfection, consummation.

heighten, *v.* **1.** elevate, raise, lift up, uplift, upraise; exalt, glorify, deify, idolize, idealize, put on a pedestal. **2.** increase, augment, add to, supplement, build up, reinforce, strengthen; improve, ameliorate, meliorate, enhance, enrich, add color to, embellish, dress up, exaggerate; amplify, magnify, intensify, deepen; enlarge, make bigger *or* larger, make greater, *Chiefly Literary.* greaten, aggrandize; expand, extend, spread, spread out; widen, thicken, broaden; lengthen, prolong, protract, stretch *or* stretch out, fill out, pad.

heinous, *adj.* **1.** atrocious, grievous, nefarious, villainous, iniquitous, diabolic, profligate; sinister, forbidding, satanic, devilish, infernal, hellish, wicked; peccant, sinful, immoral, *Archaic.* felonious, *Archaic.* facinorous; infamous, opprobrious, flagitious, vicious, baleful, baneful, malefic, venomous, flagrant, black, evil, *Obs.* pernicious, bad, wrong; monstrous, horrid, horrible, ghastly, shocking, ugly.

2. abominable, abhorrent, execrable, odious, loathsome, detestable, invidious, despicable, hateful; awful, terrible, dire, ill; accursed, cursed, damned, damnable; offensive, repugnant, revolting, repulsive, fulsome; noisome, distasteful, obnoxious, nauseating, nauseous, sickening, nasty, rotten; unbearable, unendurable, insufferable, intolerable; objectionable, annoying.

3. reprehensible, culpable, censurable, blameworthy, deplorable, regrettable, lamentable; contemptible, outrageous, scandalous; shameful, disgraceful, unmentionable, uncommendable, unpraiseworthy; mean, base, low, beggarly, shabby, scurvy, *Brit. Inf.* beastly.

heir, *n.* **1.** inheritor, heritor, heir apparent, heir at law, heiress, heritress, inheritrix; coheir, coheiress, joint heir, *Law.* parcener; successor, *Inf.* next in line, follower; beneficiary, recipient, receiver, devisee, legatee, *Law.* reversioner; *Both Law.* executor, donee.

2. descendant, scion, offspring; children, progeny, brood, spawn, issue, seed, posterity, future generations.

helix, *n.* spiral, screw, thread, corkscrew, whorl, twist, volute; coil, loop, ring, circumvolution; curl, curlicue, ringlet, tendril.

hell, *n.* **1.** the lower world, abode of evil spirits, inferno, Pandemonium, perdition; abyss, bottomless pit, hellfire, fire and brimstone, eternal fires; Gehenna, *Class. Myth.* Tartarus, *Hinduism.* Naraka, *Scand. Myth.* Niflheim, *Bible.* Tophet, *Buddhism.* Avichi, Abaddon, *Class. Myth.* Erebus.

2. torment, misery, suffering, affliction, anguish, agony, dolor, passion; wretchedness, despair, woe, bale, desolation; torture, rack, pang, throe; holocaust, horror, nightmare; punishment, condemnation, punition, retribution.

3. censure, criticism, disapprobation, objection; upbraiding, scolding, castigation, reprehension; invective, vituperation, objurgation.

4. powers of evil, powers of darkness, devils, demons, fiends, fallen angels, apostate angels; evil spirits, demonkind, demoniac forces, hosts of hell.

5. abode of the dead, underworld, nether regions, grave; *Heb. Myth.* Sheol, Hades, Orcus, Dis, Avernus.

6. catch hell *Slang.* be scolded, be reprimanded, be reproached, be chided; *Inf.* get yelled at, *Inf.* catch the dickens, *Sl.* get it.

7. hell of a *Slang.* **a.** very bad, disagreeable, unpleasant, terrible, horrible, awful. **b.** extraordinary, notable, noteworthy, outstanding, exceptional, great, grand. **c.** very, extremely, excessively, exceedingly, remarkably, quite, utterly.

8. raise hell *Slang.* **a.** revel, romp, riot, carouse, party, *Inf.* raise the roof, *Sl.* raise Cain. **b.** object, protest, complain, remonstrate, expostulate, disapprove, deplore; grumble, growl, groan, grouse.

hellbent, *adj.* dogged, set on, persistent. See **determined.**

Hellenic, *adj.* Hellenistic, Grecian, Greek, Athenian, Attic; Golden-Age, Periclean, classical; elegant, exquisite, well-proportioned, balanced, ordered; cultured; refined, pure, chaste, simple, clean; tight, spare, lean.

hellish, *adj.* **1.** diabolical, fiendish, ghoulish, hellborn, infernal; demonic, demoniac, demoniacal, devilish, satanic, Mephistophelian.

2. inhuman, barbarous, barbaric, savage, Tartarian, Hunnish, Vandalic; brutal, brutish, murderous, slaughterous, bloodthirsty, sanguinary, sadistic, bestial, ogreish; terrible, harsh, fell, truculent; ferocious, ruthless, vicious, feral, ferine; pitiless, merciless, heartless, unkind, unfeeling, cruel, hard-hearted, stony-hearted, cold-blooded; unrelenting, relentless, remorseless, inexorable.

3. wicked, iniquitous, evil, sinful, odious, *Obs.* scelerous; impious, unholy, ungodly, godless; base, vile, sinister, dire, dark, dreadful, baleful, black; black-hearted, corrupt, depraved, *Archaic.* facinorous; profligate, immoral, dissolute, vitiated, perverted, perverse; pestilential, malevolent, malicious, malign, maleficent, malefic, venomous; nefarious, flagitious, unspeakable, villainous, heinous; damnable, abominable, execrable, horrible, horrid, horrendous, miserable; hideous, monstrous, atrocious, accursed; hateful, detestable, infamous, despicable, loathsome, abhorrent.

4. *Class Myth.* Hadean, Plutonian, Plutonic, Stygian, Styxian, Tartatean, Acherontal, Cocytean, Phlegethontal, Avernal; pandemoniac, chthonian, chthonic.

helm, *n.* **1.** wheel, tiller, rudder, automatic pilot, *Fig.* reins.

2. throne, seat of authority, *Inf.* saddle, *Inf.* driver's seat.

helmet, *n.* headpiece, headgear, head armor, hard hat, (*of motorcycling and car racing*) *Sl.* skid lid, head covering, headdress, crest; casque, morion, comb morion, cabasset, helm *or* great helm, heaume; *All Armor.* sallet, salade, basinet *or* great basinet, burgonet; *All Armor.* beaver, buffe, wrapper; face-guard, *Armor.* visor.

help, *v.* **1.** aid, assist, bestead, accommodate, oblige, abet, befriend; contribute, join in, *Inf.* pitch in, *Inf.* chip in, lend a hand, lend oneself to, play *or* do one's part, boost, give a boost to, give a lift to; (*all usu. negative*) lift a finger, lift a hand, raise a finger, raise a hand; (*all usually followed by* with) collaborate, cooperate, conspire, connive, coact, combine, join, unite, synergize, side, go *or* go along, team up, take part, *Inf.* hitch horses, join forces; support, back, second, uphold, maintain, sustain, endorse, smile upon, concur, *Inf.* go to bat for, *Inf.* stick up for, *Inf.* stick by, stand by.

2. save, rescue, deliver, retrieve, redeem, extricate, bring off *or* through, come to the rescue, take in tow, form a lifeline, pull back from the brink, pull out of the fire; free, release, emancipate, liberate, unshackle, unchain, unfetter, manumit, ransom, reprieve, disenthrall, disimprison, set free, let loose, let out, break out, *Inf.* bust out.

3. facilitate, ease, make easier, expedite, cut through red tape; speed, speed up, accelerate, hasten, quicken, lend wings to; intercede, pave the way, clear the way, open the way, run interference for, block for; disburden, disencumber, rid, disembarrass, deobstruct, lighten the load; subsidize, underwrite, contribute to, give a share to; bolster, elevate, prop up, enhance, tide over, put on one's feet, set up, get going; promote, further, advance, forward, advocate, cultivate, favor; persuade, incline, dispose, bend, turn, coax, ply.

4. meliorate, ameliorate, improve, better, profit, prosper, benefit, avail, advantage; subserve, stand in good stead, be useful *or* profitable to, *Inf.* come in handy.

5. (*usu. preceded by* can *or* cannot) avoid, abstain, shun, eschew, refrain from, stay away from, turn away from, turn one's back upon, keep from, get away from, escape, break loose; dodge, evade, circumvent, get around, keep clear of; resist, forbear, let alone, let pass, let slip, put off, help oneself, help out; stop, cease, halt, break the habit.

6. diversify, vary, alter, alternate, break up, variegate; change, transform, convert, metamorphose, modulate, make different; moderate, temper, modify.

7. nurse, doctor, minister, nurture, tend, nourish; remedy, restore, mend, cure, make whole, bring through *or* round; revive, rejuvenate, recondition, rehabilitate, set on one's feet; inspire, inspirit, vivify, revivify, invigorate, reinvigorate; encourage, embolden, enhearten, hearten, buck up, pluck up, bear up, build up, buoy up; meliorate, ameliorate, alleviate, mitigate, palliate, salve; comfort, soothe, solace, console, succor; reassure, assure, calm, allay, put at ease, quiet one's fears.

8. stop, halt, arrest, prevent, deny, repel, repulse, avert, thwart, balk, check, hold in check, keep within bounds, keep back, hold back, hold at bay, turn aside, ward off, fend off, stave off, stand against, hold out against, bear up against, stem *or* turn *or* breast the tide; hinder, stall, slow, slow down, deflect, curb; counteract, countervail, counterbalance, counterpoise, contravene, neutralize; correct, rectify, redress, adjust, fix, square, amend, right, set right *or* straight.

9. take, appropriate, expropriate, arrogate, impress, annex, commandeer, dispossess, usurp, take possession of, lay hold of, take for oneself, possess oneself of, *Sl.* boost, *Sl.* walk off *or* away with; steal, pirate, plagiarize, *Euph.* borrow, *Sl.* lift, *Sl.* pinch; make use of, make free with, take liberties with.

10. **so help me** (*used as a mild oath*) on my honor, on my word, on my word of honor, I swear, I swear to God, *Inf.* swear to God.

—*n.* **11.** aid, assistance, use, utility, avail, service, subvention, benefit, facilitation, helping hand, lift, boost; relief, succor, championship, protection, friendship; encouragement, abetment, abetting, collaboration, cooperation; support, patronage, backing, promotion, advocacy, countenance, care, upholding, sustenance, favor, blessing, grace, sponsorship, auspices, good offices, kind regard; fosterage, furtherance, advancement, advance, advantage, welfare; maintenance, ministry, ministration, restoration; boon, good deed, kind deed, good turn; gift, subsidy, contribution, donation; kindness, beneficence, benevolence, benefaction, humanitarianism, altruism, philanthropy, charity, almsgiving.

12. aid, aider, assistant, attendant. See **helper** (*defs.* **1-3**).

13. supporter, advocate, adviser, patron, sympathizer, patronizer, backer, champion, endorser, upholder, sanctioner, approver; follower, partisan, adherent, disciple; agent, promoter, furtherer, advancer, favorer; subsidizer, underwriter, maintainer, sustainer, benefactor, benefactress, benefiter, *Inf.* fairy godmother, friend in deed; comforter, succorer, good Samaritan, ministering angel, friend in need.

14. employee, hand, man, girl, apprentice, hired helper *or* hand, hireling, help, helping hand, worker, workman, workhand, workingman, laborer, wage worker, day laborer, (*esp. in Mexico*) peon, *Hist.* retainer; personnel, staff, force, work force, crew, *Inf.* gang, *Inf.* team.

15. servant, domestic, domestic servant, factotum, maid, maidservant, handmaid *or* handmaiden, butler, valet, (*in the British army*) batman; menial, inferior, underling, *Sl.* stooge; tenant farmer, farm laborer, migrant, migratory worker.

16. remedy, cure, relief, corrective, correction, restorative, preventive, preventer, prevention; way, means, resource, step, shift, resort, measure, working proposition; artifice, device, contrivance, expedient, stopgap, makeshift, subterfuge.

helper, *n.* **1.** aid *or* aide, assistant, attendant, subsidiary, adjutant, coadjutant, coadjutor, coadjutress *or* coadjutrix, adjunct, adjuvant, adjutator, *Obs.* adjutor; acolyte, deputy, auxiliary, ancilla, second, man Friday, gal Friday, henchman, right hand, right-hand man, *Sl.* gopher.

2. partner, comrade, ally, colleague, associate, consociate, yokefellow *or* yokemate, companion, helpmate, helpmeet, *Obs.* helpfellow, co-worker, co-aid, copartner; consort, confrere, sidekick, crony, friend, *Inf.* buddy, *Chiefly Brit.* mate.

3. cooperator, collaborator, contributor, participator, participant; confederate, conniver, conspirer, conspirator, fellow conspirator, abettor, accomplice, accessory, *or Chiefly Law.* accessary, *Law.* principal, *Law.* accessory before *or* after the fact, *Law.* particeps criminis, partner in crime, *Sl.* gun moll *or* moll.

4. worker, workingman, laborer, hand, help, helping hand, apprentice; servant, maid, handmaid *or* handmaiden, maidservant, butler, valet, (*in the British army*) batman; menial, inferior, lesser, underling.

5. supporter, advocate, adviser, patron, patronizer, backer, champion, endorser, upholder, sanctioner, approver, maintainer, sustainer; follower, disciple, partisan, disciple, devotee, sectary, votary; agent, promoter, furtherer, advancer, favorer; financer, funder, subsidizer, underwriter, angel, *Inf.* staker, *Inf.* grubstaker, *Sl.* meal ticket; benefactor, benefactress, benefiter, friend in deed, *Inf.* fairy godmother; comforter, succorer, good Samaritan, ministering angel, friend in need.

helpful, *adj.* **1.** useful, of use, practical, pragmatic, utilitarian, beneficial, advantageous, propitious, favorable, valuable, profitable, constructive, commodious, instrumental, conducive, contributory, contributive; serviceable, servicing, of service, aidful, aiding, obliging, accommodative, accommodating, helping, available, at-hand, handy, convenient, well-disposed, well-affected; auxiliary, ancillary, subsidiary, accessory, attendant, adjuvant, adjunct, subservient, *Obs.* adjutory, *Obs., Rare.* adjutorious.

2. healthful, healthy, salubrious, salutary, edifying, wholesome, *Inf.* good for.

3. friendly, neighborly, cooperative, synergetic, coalitional, collaborative, supportive; kind, sympathetic, benign, merciful, benevolent, beneficent, munificent, charitable, philanthropic.

helpless, *adj.* **1.** weak, faint, feeble, infirm, *Rare.* imbecile; dependant, invalid, disabled, lame, crippled, hobbled, prostrate, laid-up, flat on one's back, laid-out, paralyzed, palsied, incurable; exhausted, debilitated, enervated, devitalized, worn-out, effete, spent, at the end of one's rope *or* tether, *Sl.* wasted, *Sl.* blown away.

2. outcast, abandoned, forsaken, exposed, deserted, neglected, done for; alone, forlorn, naked, desolate, destitute, adrift, guideless, friendless, fatherless, defenseless, resourceless, aidless, unaided.

3. impotent, powerless, strengthless, weaponless; unmanned, unnerved, unarmed; vulnerable, on the ropes, pregnable, expugnable, vincible, conquerable, unguarded, unprotected, unsupported, unfortified, open to attack, over a barrel.

4. confused, confounded, perplexed, bewildered, befuddled, baffled, mystified, nonplused, buffaloed, uncertain, at a loss, at sea, at the end of one's wits.

5. useless, worthless, inadequate, insufficient, inapt; incapable, incompetent, inept, inefficient, unendowed, unqualified, unfit; shiftless, irresponsible, unresourceful, without initiative; spineless, without backbone, sinewless; inane, fatuous, empty, barren, sterile.

helpmate, *n.* **1.** aid *or* aide, assistant; companion. See **helper** (*def.* **1**).

2. spouse, husband *or* wife, mate, partner, consort, common-law wife *or* husband, *Inf.* better half; married man, benedict, bridegroom, groom, *Inf.* hubbie, *Sl.* old man, *Archaic.* goodman; married woman, wedded wife, bride, housewife, woman, lady, matron, *Amer. Ind.* squaw, wife of one's bosom, *Law.* feme, *Law.* feme covert, concubine, *Inf.* missis *or* missus, *Inf.* little woman, *Hum.* rib, *Sl.* old lady *or* woman, *Scot. Inf.* wifey, *Archaic.* goodwife *or* goody; *All Rhyming Slang.* storm and strife, struggle and strife, trouble and strife, worry and strife, *Rare.* war and strife, Duchess of Fife, drum and fife, *Hum. or Derog.* joy of my life, *Obs.* bit of tripe, *Obs.* carving knife; (*girl*) mother of pearl, (*missis*) cheese and kisses, (*missis*) plates and dishes.

helter-skelter, *adv.* **1.** pell-mell, hurry-scurry, harum-scarum, wildly; headlong, headfirst, head over heels; rashly, recklessly, precipitately, unwarily, carelessly, heedlessly, injudiciously, thoughtlessly; impetuously, impulsively, hastily, hurriedly.

2. confusedly, chaotically, aimlessly, unsystematically, unmethodically, erratically, haphazardly, irregularly, unevenly; topsy-turvy, higgledy-piggledy, hugger-mugger, arsy-varsy, *Inf.* willy-nilly, *Inf.* every which way; in confusion, in disorder, in disarray, in a jumble, in a tumble, in a muddle, in a mess, all over the place; here, there, and everywhere.

—n. **3.** confusion, disorder, turmoil, moil, chaos, pandemonium, bedlam, hugger-mugger.

—adj. **4.** confused, chaotic, muddled, jumbled, hugger-mugger, higgledy-piggledy, topsy-turvy, *Sl.* arsy-varsy.

5. disorderly, disordered, disarranged, deranged; unorganized, disorganized, unmethodical, unsystematic; irregular, indiscriminate, haphazard, random, aimless, pell-mell, hit-or-miss.

hem, *v.* **1.** *Usu.* **hem in** circumscribe, surround, encircle, circle, encompass, environ; gird, engird, girdle, belt; circumvent, trap; close in, shut in, hedge in, pen in, keep within bounds, demarcate.

2. fringe, befringe, trim; bind; purfle, purl.

3. border, edge, skirt, verge; frame, bound, margin, marginate.

—n. **4.** fringe, trimming, edging, bordering; ruff, ruffle, flounce, furbelow; frill, valance, orphrey, purfle.

5. border, perimeter, periphery, edge, rim, verge, skirt; circumference, circuit, compass, ambit, margin, frame, outline, confine; brink, brim, brow; bound, limit, bourn, pale, extremity.

he-man, *n.* powerhouse, brute, a real man, muscle man, *Inf.* bruiser, *Sl.* hunk, *Sl.* jock, *Brit. Sl.* bucko; Titan, Goliath, Samson; Hercules, Atlas, Tarzan, Man Mountain Dean.

hence, *adv.* therefore, thus, ergo; consequently, consequentially, inferentially, subsequently; inevitably, naturally, accordingly, logically; wherefore, whence, thence.

henceforth, *adv.* henceforward, from now on, from this day on, hereafter, hereinafter; in time to come, later on, subsequently, tomorrow and tomorrow and tomorrow.

henchman, *n.* **1.** underling, subordinate, second banana, lackey, flunky, *Sl.* gofer, *U.S.* ward heeler, tool; hanger-on, camp follower, parasite, sponger; bootlicker, lickspittle, yes-man, toady, sycophant; *Sl.* hit man, gun slinger, *Sl.* gunsel, hired killer *or* gun; trigger-man, hatchet man, torpedo, assassin; mobster, mafioso, *Sl.* mafooch; thug, hoodlum, *Sl.* hood, gangster, Ku Kluxer, Ku Klux Klanner; racketeer, goon, *Sl.* scab, bullyboy, tough, roughneck; weasel, worm.

2. attendant, aide, counselor, advisor, privy councilor, liege; confidante, member of the kitchen cabinet, right-hand man, good right arm; friend, ally, sidekick, pal, partner, *Sl.* pard, Little John, man Friday, Tonto, colleague; champion, supporter, backer; disciple, follower, votary, acolyte.

henpeck, *v.* browbeat, bully, hector; lord it over, domineer, keep on a tight rein, keep at one's beck and call; treat like dirt, cut up, emasculate, castrate; nag, *Sl.* jaw, chide, rebuke, scold; criticize, find fault, niggle, carp, cavil; complain, grouse, grumble, mumble, mutter, whine, yammer.

henpecked, *adj.* bullied, browbeaten, dominated, subjugated, led around by the nose, on a leash; spineless, acquiescent, having no mind of one's own, cringing, cowering; like Casper Milquetoast, timid, meek, Mittyish, docile; spaniel-like.

herald, *n.* **1.** messenger, envoy, runner, advanceman, avant-courier, courier, scout, *Mil.* point man, front rider.

2. precursor, predecessor, pioneer, forerunner, harbinger; sign, omen, portent, augury; indication, symptom, signal, ground waves, feeling in one's bones *or* in the air, gut feeling, intuition, anticipation; premonition, foreboding, forewarning, warning light, handwriting on the wall; prediction, prophecy, prognostication, auspice, augury.

3. crier, town crier, bearer of tidings, announcer, reporter, broadcaster, proclaimer, trumpeter, extoller.

—*v.* **4.** give tidings of, harbinger, announce, proclaim, trumpet, ballyhoo, beat the drum, promulgate, declare openly, call out, *Scot. and North Eng.* kithe; blurb, broadcast, air, make known, advertise, publish, print, publicize, bill; post, display, blazon, circularize; circulate, distribute, propagate, propagandize, spread, spread by word of mouth, disseminate.

5. tell, state, inform, notify, give notice, apprise, signal; usher in, lead, lead the way, pave the way, prepare the way for.

6. indicate, show, signify, mean, promise, bode; presage, prognosticate, portend, foreshow, foreshadow, foretoken, forebode, augur; forecast, predict, prophesy.

heraldry, *n.* **1.** blazonry, emblazonry.

2. coat of arms, *Heraldry.* arms, escutcheon, scutcheon, *Brit.* hatchment; symbol, design, emblazonment, ensign, emblem; crest, badge, insignia, regalia, regale, device.

3. pomp, circumstance, pageantry, ceremony, *Inf.* to-do; splendor, glitter, flourish, display, showing off.

herculean, *adj.* **1.** arduous, laborious, operose, onerous, toilsome, strenuous, uphill; backbreaking, grueling, punishing, killing; difficult, hard, rough, tough; formidable, *Sl.* wicked, *Sl.* hairy.

2. mighty, powerful, all-powerful, *Literary.* puissant; brawny, strapping, muscular, well-muscled.

3. huge, massive, enormous, gigantic, colossal, vast, immense, mammoth, *Sl.* whopping, *Sl.* walloping.

4. courageous, brave, valiant, valorous, heroic.

herd[1], *n.* **1.** flock, drove, pack, bunch, cluster.

2. *Disparaging.* throng, crowd, multitude, host, horde, crush, press, mass.

3. the herd the hoi polloi, the masses, the many, the commonality, the great unwashed; rabble, ruck, rout, riffraff.

—*v.* **4.** flock, assemble, congregate, gather, foregather, collect, muster, come together.

5. wrangle, round up, corral, cage.

herd[2], *n.* **1.** herder, drover, *Chiefly Brit.* herdsman. See **herder**.

—*v.* **2.** tend, guard, protect, watch, watch over, shepherd, ride herd on; drive, drove, punch cattle; spur, goad, prick, whip, lash.

herder, *n.* herd, shepherd, cowherd, *Chiefly Brit.* herdsman, drover, cattle-herder, *Chiefly Brit.* grazier, *Brit.* cowman, *Obs.* neatherd; cowboy, cowpoke, cowpuncher, cow hand, *Southwestern U.S.* vaquero, gaucho.

here, *adv.* **1.** this place, this spot, in this location, inside, herein; hither, to here, to this place.

2. now, then, there; at this point, at this juncture, at this time, at this point in time.

3. here and now immediately, without delay, quickly, at this very moment, *Fr. tout de suite,* (*in pidgin English*) chop chop, right away.

—*n.* **4.** this world, this place, the present, this life, this day and age.

hereafter, *adv.* **1.** later, subsequently, then, by and by, presently, after this, after a time *or* while, afterwards, in the course *or* process of time, in the fullness of time, in due time *or* course; ultimately, finally, eventually; hence, henceforth, from this time on.

2. in the next life, beyond the grave, in heaven, in paradise; perpetually, continually, eternally, forever.

—*n.* **3.** afterworld, afterlife, future world, future life, life after death, the beyond, the sweet by-and-by; heaven, Zion, the New Jerusalem, the heavenly city, the city of God, the celestial city; our Father's house, Abraham's bosom, the final home; Elysium, Elysian Fields, Islands of the Blessed, Valhalla, happy hunting grounds, paradise; immortality, perpetuity, deathlessness, eternity.

4. later life, the rest of life, subsequent life, ensuing years, remaining years, the future.

hereditary, *adj.* **1.** inheritable, hereditable, heritable, transmissible, passable, transferrable; genetic, genetical, genesic, in the genes *or* blood, obtained by heredity, *Biol.* genic; congenital, innate, inborn, inherent, natural, native, natural-born, connate, connatural, ingenerate, constitutional, intrinsic.

2. ancestral, lineal, geneological, geneologic, racial, tribal; family, in the family, maternal, paternal, patrimonial; inherited, passed down *or* on, transmitted, transferred; willed, bequeathed, left, obtained through inheritance, *Law.* devised; traditional, customary, age-old, ancient.

heredity, *n.* **1.** genetics, interaction of genes, transmittal *or* transference of genetic characteristics, passing on of family traits.

2. inheritance, genetic makeup, congenital traits, constitution; blood, chromosomes, *Genetics.* genes.

heresy, *n.* **1.** heterodoxy, unorthodoxy, heterodox belief; nonconformity, free thought, free thinking, iconoclasm; dissent, dissension, recusancy, infidelity, disloyalty.

2. apostasy, conversion; superstition, delusion; paganism, idolatry, idol worship; disbelief, unbelief, misbelief, skepticism; irreligion, impiety, agnosticism, atheism.

heretic, *n.* **1.** dissenter, nonconformist, seceder; renouncer, abjurer, repudiator, rejecter; deserter, renegade, apostate, recreant, defector, traitor; bolter, turncoat, retractor, recanter; tergiversator, straddler.

2. nonbeliever, disbeliever, unbeliever, denier, atheist; irreligionist, infidel, iconoclast.

3. skeptic, doubter, Pyrrhonist, nihilist, nullifidian; agnostic, freethinker, rationalist, materialist, positivist; heathen, pagan, idolater, idolist.

—*adj.* **4.** heretical, iconoclastic. See **heretical**.

heretical, *adj.* **1.** unorthodox, heterodox, heretic, iconoclastic; agnostic, freethinking, rationalistic, materialistic, positivistic; skeptical, doubting, Pyrrhonistic, nihilistic; heathen, pagan, idolatrous.

2. backsliding, renouncing, repudiating; apostatizing, tergiversating.

3. disbelieving, unbelieving, nonbelieving, incredulous, atheistic; infidel, infidelic, *Obs.* unfaithful; impious, irreligious, irreverent.

heretofore, *adv.* formerly, previously, aforetime, before this time, *Archaic.* beforetime; in times past, in past ages, in days of yore; long ago, earlier, until now, hitherto.

heritage, *n.* **1.** portion, share, birthright, lot; background, past, history; ancestry, ancestral line, dynasty; lineage, family, descent, birth, extraction, derivation, filiation; heredity, bloodline, pedigree, strain, stock, race.

2. due, deserts, measure, worth; promise, prospect, expectation; reward, compensation, recompense, remuneration; punishment, retribution, nemesis, *Inf.* what's coming to one.

3. *Law.* inheritance, legacy, bequest, endowment. See **inheritance** (*def.* **1**).

hermaphrodite, *n.* **1.** androgyne, epicene, intersex, sex-intergrade, pseudohermaphrodite, gynandroid, *Biol.* gynandromorph; transsexual, bisexual, *Sl.* bi, unisexual.

—*adj.* **2.** androgynous, epicine, hermaphroditic, pseudohermaphroditic, intersexual, *Biol.* gynandromorphic, *Bot.* gynandrous, *Bot.* monoclinous; transsexual, bisexual, unisexual.

hermit, *n.* **1.** anchorite, anchoret, eremite, recluse, solitary, *Islam.* marabout, *Islam.* santon, *Obs.* beadsman; nun, anchoress, ancress, hermitess, *Obs.* hermitress; troglodyte, cave dweller, incluse; stylite, pillarist, pillar-saint; ascetic, celibate, monk, monastic, holy man.

2. loner, isolate, isolato, solitudinarian, *Inf.* introvert, *Inf.* lone wolf.

hermitage, *n.* **1.** retreat, refuge, haven, shelter, asylum, resort, sanctuary, sanctum sanctorum, ark, covert, hideaway, mew; arbor, bower.

2. cloister, monastery, abbey, priory, friary, convent, nunnery, cenoby.

3. cabin, cottage, cot, hut, bungalow, shack, shanty; villa, lodge; den, lair, cave, grotto, hibernaculum, hibernacle.

hero, *n.* **1.** champion, paladin, knight; conqueror, conquering hero, victor, master, man of the hour *or* day; stalwart, gallant, valiant, cavalier, chevalier, a man, brave man, man of courage *or* mettle; brave, warrior, soldier, fighter, fighting man, fearless *or* dauntless soldier, intrepid warrior; lion, tiger, bulldog, gamecock, fighting cock.

2. ideal, ideal specimen, ego ideal, beau ideal, acme, apogee, apotheosis, cynosure, highest *or* perfect type, (*in Nazi doctrine*) Aryan *or* Arian; model, exemplar, shining example, paragon, phoenix.

3. luminary, notable, dignitary, great man, personage, person of note *or* consequence, figure, public figure, social lion, *Inf.* somebody, *Inf.* name *or* big name, *Inf.* bigwig, *Inf.* fat cat, *Inf.* Mr. Big, *Inf.* top dog, *Inf.* Grand Poobah, *Sl.* heavy, *Sl.* big cheese, *Fr. Sl.* *grand fromage;* celebrity, star, superstar, idol, matinée idol, popular idol, popular figure, *Sl.* popstar, *Sl.* pop hero.

4. protagonist, principal, principal character *or* role, title role, starring *or* lead *or* leading role, headliner, headline *or* feature attraction; male lead, male star, leading man, lead actor, jeune premier.

5. immortal, god, deity, divinity; demigod, inferior deity, petty deity, minor *or* lesser deity, godkin, godlet, godling, god-man, god-king, half-god; warrior-king, warrior-chieftain, warrior-chief.

heroic, *adj.* **1.** brave, courageous, valiant, valorous, heroical, hero-like, stout-hearted, lionhearted, iron-hearted, great-hearted; virile, manly, manful, gallant, chivalrous, chivalric; intrepid, fearless, dauntless, aweless, dreadless, nervy, *Sl.* gutsy, unafraid, un blenching, unblenched, undaunted, undismayed, unappalled, unawed, unalarmed; bold, bold-spirited, high-spirited, daring, dashing, adventurous, audacious, rash, reckless, foolhardy.

2. firm, resolute, resolved, determined, staunch, stanch, steadfast, stalwart, *Archaic.* stalworth, doughty, sturdy, hardy; indomitable, invincible, unconquerable, unyielding, unshrinking, unbending, unfaltering, unhesitating, unwavering, unswerving, undeviating; plucky, mettlesome, gritty, game, spirited, red-blooded, *Inf.* spunky.

3. noble, princely, handsome; altruistic, selfless, unselfish, magnanimous, liberal, generous, big-hearted.

4. drastic, desperate, extreme, *Inf.* last-ditch; furious, mad, intense, rigorous.

5. classic, classical, Homeric; mythological, legendary; fabulous, fantastic, fantastical, wonderful, wondrous, remarkable, marvelous, miraculous.

6. epical, heroical, Homeric; grandiloquent, magniloquent, grandiose, orotund, high-sounding, big-sounding; pompous, bombastic, rhetorical, turgid, inflated, pretentious.

7. (*all of style or language*) noble, grand, distinguished, majestic, august; lofty, soaring, towering, elevated, eminent, prominent, high; sublime, superb, god-like, magnificent.

8. prodigious, stupendous, huge, vast, massive, gigantic, immense, mighty, titanic, colossal, monumental, larger-than-life.

—*n.* **9. heroics** bombast, bluster, rant, grandiosity, grandiloquence, magniloquence, pomposity, orotundity, puffery, turgidity, pretension; braggadocio, bragging, boasting, rodomontade, bravado, bravura; exaggeration, excess, hyperbole, immoderacy, extravagance, exorbitance.

heroine, *n.* **1.** female hero, heroic woman, intrepid woman, fearless *or* dauntless woman, woman of courage, woman of the day *or* hour.

2. ideal, ideal specimen, ego ideal, acme, apogee, apotheosis, cynosure, highest *or* perfect type, (*in Nazi doctrine*) Aryan *or* Arian; model, exemplar, shining example, paragon, phoenix.

3. luminary, notable, dignitary, personage, person of note *or* consequence, figure, public figure, *Inf.* somebody, *Inf.* name *or* big name; celebrity, star, starlet, superstar, idol, matinée idol, popular idol, popular figure, *Sl.* pop star, *Sl.* pop heroine.

4. protagonist, principal, principal character *or* role, leading lady *or* woman, lead actress, premiere, jeune premiere; diva, prima donna, prima ballerina, premiere; danseuse.

5. immortal, goddess, deity, divinity; demigoddess, inferior deity, minor *or* lesser deity, godling, godkin, godlet; warrior-queen, Amazon, female warrior.

heroism, *n.* **1.** courage, bravery, valor, valorousness, valiancy, valiance, prowess, stout-heartedness, lionheartedness, iron-heartedness, great-heartedness, high-heartedness; virility, manliness, manfulness, manhood, gallantry, chivalry, chivalrousness; nobleness, unselfishness, selflessness, altruism; intrepidity, intrepidness, fearlessness, dauntless, awelessness, dreadlessness; boldness, bold-spiritedness, high-spiritedness, daring, derring-do, audacity, audaciousness, recklessness.

2. fortitude, endurance, tenacity, determination, will, will power, the power of the will; firmness, resolution, resoluteness, indomitableness, indomitability, invincibleness, invincibility, unconquerableness, unconquerability, staunchness, stanchness, steadfastness, stalwartness, doughtiness, sturdiness, hardiness, hardihood, bulldog courage; mettle, mettlesomeness, pluck, pluckiness, backbone, pith, marrow, spirit, gameness, nerve, *Sl.* chutzpah, gumption, heart, stout heart, stamina, toughness, grit, true grit, *U.S. Inf.* sand, *Inf.* starch, *Inf.* spunk, *Inf.* spunkiness, *Sl.* guts, *Sl.* gutsiness, *Sl.* moxie.

hero worship, *n.* **1.** adulation, worship, adoration, idolization, deification, apotheosis; exaltation, glorification, extolment.

2. reverence, veneration, awe, deep respect, high esteem; admiration, idealization, putting on a pedestal.

hesitancy, *n.* **1.** pause, break, stop, stopping, stoppage, halt, hesitation, hesitance; cessation, ceasing, inaction, inactivity; discontinuance, interruption, suspension, suspense, postponement, deferment, deferral, abeyance, prorogation; delay, wait, stall, stalling, drag, dragging, lag, lagging, procrastination, cunctation; waiting period, waiting game, holding pattern, status quo.

2. indecision, indecisiveness, irresolution, irresoluteness, indetermination, indeterminacy, uncertainty; doubt, doubtfulness, dubiousness, misgiving, qualm; unsettlement, fluctuation, vacillation, oscillation, alternation, wavering, faltering, shilly-shally; evasion, avoidance, dodging, skirting, equivocation.

3. disinclination, unwillingness, reluctance, halfheartedness; constraint, reserve, reservation; demur, demurral, scruple, boggle; timidity, shyness, demureness, diffidence.

4. stammer, sputter, splutter, stutter; mutter, hum, hem, haw, *Brit.* haver.

hesitant, *adj.* **1.** pausing, halting, stopping, hesitating, hesitative; waiting, delaying, stalling, dragging, lagging, dallying; tardy, dilatory, deferring, postponing, procrastinating, procrastinative, cunctating, cunctatious, cunctatory.

2. undecided, unresolved, unsettled; uncertain, unsure, doubtful, dubious; indecisive, indefinite, irresolute, go-slow, indeterminate; wavering, hovering, fluctuating, wobbling, faltering; alternating, vacillating, vacillant, oscillating, oscillatory; shilly-shallying, shifting, seesawing; debating, deliberating, weighing; demurring, scrupling, boggling; equivocating, equivocal, quibbling, evasive; inconstant, changeable, fickle.

3. disinclined, unwilling, reluctant, loath, half-hearted; constrained, restrained, reserved; timid, shy, bashful, fidgety, tremulous, diffident.

hesitate, *v.* **1.** pause, wait, delay, hang back; procrastinate, hold off, hold [s.t.] up, lay [s.t.] over, refrain from further action, let the matter stand; balk, recoil, shrink, swerve, shy; dally, dillydally; temporize, put off, *Inf.* drag one's feet, *Inf.* footdrag, gain time, play for time; *Inf.* stall, stave off, hold out.

2. equivocate, dissemble, evade, skirt, hedge, fence, quibble, pussyfoot, pull back, straddle the fence; waver, hover, scruple, demur, boggle, doubt; vacillate, oscillate, alternate, fluctuate, shilly-shally, shift, falter, change one's mind, blow hot and cold, seesaw, go back and forth, tergiversate; deliberate, debate, ponder, balance, linger, weigh and consider, think twice.

3. stammer, sputter, splutter, stutter; stumble, fumble, halt; mutter, hum, hem, haw, hem and haw, *Brit.* haver, *Brit. Dial.* mammer.

heterodox, *adj.* unorthodox, heretical, heretic, iconoclastic; skeptical, doubting. See **heretical**.

heterodoxy, *n.* unorthodoxy, heresy, nonconformity; dissent, dissention, recusancy. See **heresy**.

heterogeneity, *n.* **1.** disparateness, inconsistency, incongruity, unconformity, nonconformity, *Geol.* disconformity; dissimilarity, dissimilitude, variance, inharmoniousness, *Biol.* heteromorphism.

2. multiformity, polymorphism, omniformity, nonuniformity, variation; variety, diversity, multifariousness, many-sidedness, variegation, multiplex.

heterogeneous, *adj.* **1.** different, disparate, unlike, dissimilar, *Biol.* heteromorphic; incongruous, incompatible, inharmonious; unrelated, discrepant.

2. multiform, polymorphic, nonuniform, omniform; many-sided, many-headed, composite, multifold; multifarious, various, diverse, multiplex; manifold, sundry, miscellaneous, farraginous, mixed, variegated, diversified.

heterosexual, *adj.* drawn to the opposite sex, *Sl.* straight, *Sl.* hetero.

hew, *v.* **1.** chop, hack, ax; strike, smite, hit, whack.

2. cut down, fell, drop, raze, level; chop down, mow down, bring down, knock down, *Inf.* down, *Inf.* whack down.

3. carve, sculpt, sculpture, shape, fashion, form, make; whittle, cut, chip, square, incise; mold, cast, roughcast, hammer out, block out, chisel, roughhew.

4. sever, cut off, dissever, cleave, truncate, rive; trim, saw off, lop, slice; clip, prune, shear, dislimb.

heyday, *n.* prime, pink, efflorescence, fructification, flower, full flowering *or* blossoming, bloom, blossom; peak, pinnacle, summit, acme, zenith, height, top, tiptop; cap, crown, crowning point, meridian, culmination, consummation.

hiatus, *n.* **1.** gap, gape, blank, emptiness, vacuum, void, vacancy, lacuna; break, interruption, disruption, *Prosody.* caesura, *Physiol.* synapse; pause, rest, recess, lull, halt, stop, standstill, time out; cessation, abatement, discontinuance, suspension, suspense, abeyance; delay, wait, deferment, postponement; interstice, interval, interim, intermission, intermittence, intermittency.

2. opening, slot, hole, cavity, space, aperture, orifice, foramen; breach, separation, scission, rent, rift, fissure, cleft. *Archaic.* scissure; chink, crack, crevice, cranny; groove, furrow, trench, chasm, gulf, channel; notch, score, scratch, incision; slit, split, chap, cut, gash.

hibernate, *v.* **1.** lie dormant, lie idle, lie fallow, stagnate, vegetate, *Zool.* estivate; winter.

2. withdraw, retire, drop *or* keep out of sight, seclude oneself, go into hiding, hide; lie hid *or* hidden, *Dial.* lie snug *or* close, *Inf.* lie low, *Inf.* hide out, *Sl.* hole up, *Sl.* sit tight.

hick, *n.* *Informal.* yokel, bumpkin, country bumpkin. See **bumpkin**.

hidden, *adj.* concealed, veiled, masked, shrouded, enshrouded; obscure, indistinct, indefinite, unclear, shadowy, cloudy, nebulous, vague, ambiguous; secret, cryptic, arcane, perdu, private, covert, top-secret, under wraps, *Inf.* hush-hush; occult, mysterious, inexplicable, unaccountable, insoluble; impenetrable, incomprehensible, inapprehensible, past *or* beyond comprehension *or* understanding, unknowable, incognizable, unfathomable; mystic, transcendental, supernatural, preternatural.

hide[1], *v.* **1.** conceal, screen, veil, shroud, enshroud, *Inf.* cover up; dissemble, disguise, camouflage; gloss over, varnish, *Inf.* whitewash.

2. secrete, hide away, ensconce, closet, stow away, store away, file and forget, lock up, seal up.

3. obstruct, block, eclipse; cloud, becloud, obscure, darken, adumbrate, obfuscate.

4. withhold, harbor, hold in, *Sl.* hold out on; keep secret, keep mum, keep dark, *Inf.* keep under one's hat, *Inf.* keep under wraps; suppress, hush, hush up.

5. withdraw, retire, hibernate, drop *or* keep out of sight, seclude oneself, conceal oneself, go into hiding, cover one's tracks; lie hid *or* hidden, lie perdu, *Dial.* lie snug *or* close, *Inf.* lie low, *Inf.* hide out, *Sl.* hole up, *Sl.* sit tight.

hide[2], *n.* **1.** pelt, skin, coat, jacket, fleece, fell, fur, leather.

2. *Informal.* safety, welfare, well-being, behalf, interest; benefit, profit, advantage.

3. **hide nor hair** trace, vestige, spoor; sign, mark, indicator, indication; hint, suggestion, intimation; clue, cue, key, *Inf.* lead.

—*v.* **4.** *Informal.* thrash, whip, flail, whale, beat, *Inf.* lick, *Inf.* wallop, *Inf.* give [s.o.] a shellacking, *Inf.* tan [s.o.'s] hide.

hideaway, *n.* **1.** hideout, hiding place, covert, coverture, cover, mew; nest, lair, den, cave, hole, dugout, abri; retreat, hospice, hermitage, cloister, ashram; shelter, refuge, asylum, haven, sanctuary, sanctum sanctorum, safety zone.

—adj. **2.** hidden, concealed, disguised, camouflaged, covered-up.

hidebound, *adj.* **1.** narrow-minded, closed-minded, illiberal, intolerant; rigid, rigorous, stiff, firm, fixed, rooted, settled, creedbound; obstinate, obdurate, inexorable, unyielding, uncompromising, intractable.

2. ultraconservative, orthodox, fundamentalist, opposed to change; prudish, priggish, puritanical, prim, proper, stiff-necked, sanctimonious.

hideous, *adj.* very ugly, grotesque, monstrous, ogreish, gorgonian, beastly; repulsive, offensive, repellent, revolting, *Sl.* gross, disgusting, sickening, unsightly; horrible, frightful, frightening, dreadful, terrible, horrid, awful; shocking, outrageous, appalling, horrifying, gruesome, grisly, ghastly; heinous, hateful, odious, abominable, abhorrent; foul, vile, loathesome, despicable, contemptible, execrable, damnable.

hiding, *n.* **1.** concealment, secretion, hiding away; covering, screening, veiling, masking, shielding; clouding, obscuring.

2. hideaway, hiding place, hideout. See **hideaway** (*def.* **1**).

hie, *v.* hasten, hurry, go quickly *or* with haste, lose no time, speed, rush, *Scot.* swith; hustle, *Sl.* get a move on, run, scamper, scuttle, dart, dash *or* dash off; take off, shoot, *Inf.* go like a shot, tear, *Sl* rip, fly. See **hasten** (*def.* **1**).

hierarchy, *n.* **1.** system of layers *or* levels *or* strata, ranking, *Inf.* pecking *or* peck order; caste system, homogeneous grouping; separation, segregation, apartheid; *Fig.* ladder, *Fig.* totem pole.

2. ecclesiastical government, hierocracy, theocracy, episcopacy, prelacy, clericalism; (*collectively*) ecclesiastics, bishops, archbishops, cardinals, church dignitaries, prelates, primates, patriarchs.

3. officialdom, ruling body, upper class, elite, men at the top, inner circle, in-crowd, the high and the mighty, *Inf.* higher-ups, *Inf.* heavyweights, *Inf.* bigwigs.

hieratic, *adj.* priestly, sacerdotal, hieratical; clerical, ministerial, pastoral, ecclesiastical, churchly; sacred, divine, holy, consecrated.

hieroglyphic, **1.** hieroglyph, symbol, figure, ideogram, ideograph, rune, stenograph.

2. *Usu.* **hieroglyphics** hieroglyphic *or* hieratic writing, demotic writing.

3. **hieroglyphics** code, cipher, cryptograph, cryptogram, shorthand.

hierology, *n.* sacred literature, religious lore, Scripture, hagiography, hagiology; theology, divinity.

hierophant, *n.* **1.** (*in reference to sacred mysteries*) expounder, expositor, explicator, explainer, interpreter, revealer, teacher.

2. divine, theologian, hierologist; exegete, Biblical scholar, textualist, Talmudist, Talmudic scholar; canonist, decretist.

3. clergyman, ecclesiastic, minister, priest, preacher, parson.

higgle, *v.* bargain, haggle, palter, dicker. See **haggle** (*def.* **1**).

high, *adj.* **1.** lofty, tall, elevated, steep, soaring, towering.

2. intensified, intense, potent; sharp, strong, forcible, of great force, violent, vigorous; of great number, of great degree, extreme, far advanced, remote, *Music.* altissimo.

3. expensive, exorbitant, costly, dear, high-priced, of great price, *Inf.* stiff, *Inf.* steep.

4. exalted, eminent, prominent, significant, important, influential, distinguished, notable; conspicuous, preeminent, august, ranking, rank-bearing, noble, ruling, powerful.

5. chief, dominant, leading, main, major; prime, primary, principal, cardinal, first; uppermost, foremost, capital.

6. grave, serious, earnest, weighty, heavy, deep, momentous, telling, far-reaching; urgent, pressing, crucial, essential, vital, critical, crying, desperate.

7. haughty, lofty, arrogant. See **high-and-mighty**.

8. elated, ecstatic, transported, rhapsodic, enraptured, merry, jolly, gay, happy, in high spirits, exultant, gleeful, mirthful; hilarious, joyous, jovial, jocose, playful, light-hearted; happy as a king, happy as a goat in a can factory, happy as a clam at high tide, happy as a lark, happy as can be, in high feather, happy as a child on Christmas morning, overjoyed; *Inf.* intoxicated, *Inf.* drug-affected, *Sl.* turned on, *Sl.* tripping, *Sl.* grooving.

9. rich, grand, extravagant, luxurious, lavish; sybaritic, intemperate, prodigal, wasteful, marked by conspicuous consumption.

high-and-mighty, *adj.* **1.** haughty, arrogant, excessively proud, self-important, presumptuous, fastuous, proud, vainglorious, overconfident, overweening; conceited, snobbish, *Inf.* stuck-up, *Inf.* uppish, *Inf.* uppity, on one's high horse; pompous, egotistic, lofty, *Inf.* toplofty; condescending, disdainful, supercilious, cavalier, contemptuous, scornful.

2. affected, showy, flashy, ostentatious, *Inf.* hoity-toity, peacockish, foppish, dandified.

3. imperious, overbearing, domineering, high-handed; dictatorial, despotic, authoritative, dogmatic, magisterial.

4. brazen, impudent, insolent, defiant, rude, audacious, impertinent; swaggering, blustering, *Inf.* pushy, bumptious, self-assertive, self-assured, self-assuming.

5. excessive, exaggerated, immoderate, intemperate, extravagant; high-flown, *Inf.* highfalutin, preposterous, unconscionable, disproportionate; unreasonable, undue, unfounded, uncalled-for, unwarranted.

highbinder, *n.* **1.** swindler, sharper, sharpie, bilker, shark, diddler, chiseler, cheat, cheater; confidence man, *Sl.* con man, *Sl.* flimflam man; crook, bandit, desperado, outlaw, bad guy; badman, criminal, felon.

2. malfeasant, bribe-taker, *Law.* misfeasor; corruptionist, corrupt official *or* politician, abuser; malefactor, wrongdoer, offender, *Brit. Sl.* bad hat.

highborn, *adj.* aristocratic, patrician, blue-blooded, silk-stocking; noble, well-born, gentle, genteel; royal, princely, kingly, titled; (*all of animals*) thoroughbred, pedigreed, purebred, highbred.

high-class, *adj.* superior, top-flight, A-one, first-rate, tiptop, tops, *Inf.* super; above-average, upper-class, above-the-milling-throng; luxurious, deluxe, elegant, sumptuous, posh.

high-flown, *adj.* grandiloquent, grandiose, magniloquent, extravagant, lofty, vaulting, high-sounding, Johnsonian, Ossianic, sonorous, sesquipedalian; bombastic, bombastical, inflated, swollen, bloated, flatulent, turgid, plethoric; overdrawn, overdone, exaggerated, hyperbolic, *Inf.* too-too; pretentious, affected, pompous, condescending, *Inf.* highfalutin, *Inf.* la-di-da, *Inf.* high-hat; euphuistic, flowery, florid, ornate, ostentatious, showy, flashy, flamboyant.

high-handed, *adj.* arbitrary, despotic, tyrannical, autocratic, dictatorial; peremptory, imperious, lordly, ironhanded; demanding, severe, oppressive; inexorable, unbending, implacable, pitiless, not giving a whit; capricious, whimsical, unreasonable; overbearing, arrogant, haughty, disdainful, contemptuous.

highland, *n.* **1.** plateau, tableland, butte, mesa, bluff, headland, promontory; ridge, razorback, hogback, spine, crest, chine.

2. **highlands** mountains, peaks, heights, uplands, hill country.

highlight, *v.* **1.** feature, spotlight, play up, set off, give prominence to, bring to the fore, bring into relief, *Inf.* headline; emphasize, stress, lay stress *or* emphasis upon, give emphasis to, punctuate, accent, accentuate; underscore, underline, italicize, point up, call attention to, mark; intensify, strengthen, deepen, heighten.

2. light, light up, lighten, illuminate; shine light upon, shed light upon, cast *or* throw light upon; floodlight, flood *or* bathe with light.

3. *Photography.* touch up, spot, spot out.

—*n.* **4.** also, **high light** feature, outstanding feature, distinctive feature; high spot, high point, memorable part, best part, cream, cream of the crop.

5. focus, prime focus, focal point; cynosure, center of attraction, center of attention, center of interest.

6. the point, main point, cardinal point, central point, salient point, keynote, key; essence, nucleus, heart, core, pith, meat; essential, fundamental, principal, keystone, cornerstone; gist, tenor, import, purport, substance, sum and substance, *Inf.* nub.

highly, *adv.* **1.** very, very much, much, well, *Inf.* plenty, *Inf.* plenty well, quite; greatly, vastly, immensely, tremendously, hugely; exceedingly, extremely, supremely, extraordinarily; considerably, eminently, incomparably, preeminently.

2. appreciatively, approvingly, favorably, with esteem *or* praise *or* approbation, respectfully, deferentially.

high-minded, *adj.* lofty, noble, honorable, admirable; good, worthy, pure, upright, righteous, saintly, spiritual; conscientious, scrupulous, principled, ethical, moral; honest, truthful, aboveboard, square-dealing, even-handed, fair, just; generous, magnanimous, giving, open, thoughtful, kind.

high-powered, *adj.* **1.** energetic, dynamic, galvanic, electric; capable, effective, efficient, efficacious; enterprising, industrious, eager; vigorous, active, aggressive, attacking, go-ahead, hustling, pushing, persistent.

2. driving, forceful, powerful, mighty, puissant, potent; forcible, compelling, emphatic; intense, intensive, vehement, power-packed, high-tension.

high-pressure, *adj.* vigorous, active, energetic. See **high-powered** (*defs.* **1, 2**).

high-priced, *adj.* expensive, costly, dear, high, *Inf.* steep, *Inf.* stiff; exorbitant, excessive, unreasonable, extortionate.

highroad, *n.* **1.** main road, thoroughfare, main street, *Inf.* drag, *Brit. Sl.* toby; throughway, artery, avenue, boulevard, strip, concourse; route, highway, turnpike, pike, tollroad, state highway; freeway, *Brit.* clearway, expressway, parkway, causeway, *U.S. Inf.* interstate; speedway, (*in Germany*) autobahn, superhighway.

2. easy *or* certain way, beaten track *or* path, well-traveled road.

high school, *n.* secondary school, senior high school, *Inf.* senior high, *Brit.* grammar school, (*in France*) lycée; preparatory school, *Inf.* prep school, *U.S.* private school, *Brit.* public school; day school, boarding school, academy, seminary, institute, finishing school; classical school, Latin school, (*in Germany*) gymnasium; junior high school, *Inf.* junior high.

high-sounding, *adj.* grandiloquent, magniloquent, grandiose, high-flown. See **high-flown**.

high-spirited, *adj.* **1.** energetic, lively, spirited, *Sl.* go-go, full of life, animated, vibrant, vital; dynamic, vigorous, electric; active, alive, full of energy, *Inf.* full of pep, *Inf.* peppy, *Inf.* snappy, full of vim and vigor.

2. courageous, brave, bold, bold-spirited, daring, dashing, mettlesome, adventurous; intrepid, fearless, dauntless, dreadless, nervy, *Sl.* gutsy, unafraid, unblenching, unblenched, undaunted, unalarmed, undismayed, unappalled.

high-strung, *adj.* nervous, tense, all wound up, restless, feverish, febrile, excited, worked-up, wrought-up, *Sl.* jittery, skittish; hyperactive, hyper; sensitive, passionate, moody, overreacting, easily frightened, excitable; irritable, snappish, peevish, intolerant, testy, touchy, irascible; quick, impatient, on edge, agitated; neurotic, unquiet, uneasy, afraid, timid, timorous, tremulous.

high-toned, *adj.* **1.** high-principled, respectable, reputable, ethical, moral, uncorrupt; straightforward, aboveboard, disinterested, dispassionate, truthful, candid; dignified, distinguished, distingué, impressive, imposing; honorable, venerable, revered; noted, eminent, famous, well-known, celebrated, esteemed.

2. elegant, high-class, *Sl.* classy, *Sl.* tony; suave, urbane, sophisticated, cosmopolitan.

3. affected, insincere, unnatural; assumed, adopted, put on; empty, hollow, shallow; pretentious, ostentatious, high-flown, *Inf.* high-hat, *Inf.* highfalutin; mannered, studied, *Inf.* la-di-da, *Inf.* too-too.

highway, *n.* main road, highroad, thoroughfare, public road, roadway; street, terrace, circle, row; drive, avenue, boulevard, strip, *Inf.* drag; turnpike, pike, tollroad, state highway, *U.S. Inf.* interstate; freeway, *Brit.* clearway, expressway, parkway, causeway, throughway; speedway, (*in Germany*) autobahn, superhighway; artery, channel, canal, waterway, seaway.

highwayman, *n.* footpad, *U.S.* road agent, highway robber, bandit, brigand, *Inf.* hold-up man, *Sl.* stick-up man, mugger, robber, *Sp. bandolero.*

hijack, *v.* commandeer, seize, steal, skyjack; kidnap, abduct; mug, rob at gunpoint, *U.S. Inf.* hold up, *Sl.* stick up.

hijacker, *n.* skyjacker, air *or* sky pirate, *Sl.* commando, kidnaper, abductor.

hike, *v.* **1.** walk, march, *Sl.* hoof it, *Inf.* leg it, tramp, trudge, plod, trek; traipse, walk through *or* around, wander, ramble, rove, roam, range.

2. *Often* **hike up** hitch up, jerk *or* pull up, raise, move up, lift, jack up.

3. increase, raise, *Inf.* jack up, boost, augment, add to.

—*n.* **4.** walk, march, trek; stroll, ramble, turn, airing; excursion, outing, trip, jaunt.

5. increase, rise, boost, augmentation, added increase.

hilarious, *adj.* **1.** gay, cheerful, cheery, in good *or* high spirits; jovial, jocund, jolly, mirthful, laughing; buoyant, *Inf.* upbeat, optimistic, sunny, beamish; smiling, happy, happy as a lark, felicitous, joyful, joyous; jubilant, gleeful, elated, exhilarated, exuberant, thrilled, excited, enthused, animated, vivacious, sparkling, effervescent, bubbling, lively; playful, sportive, larking, frolicsome; boisterous, rowdy, rowdyish, noisy, vociferous, *Sl.* hell-raising, rabble-rousing.

2. very funny, highly amusing, humorous, entertaining, side-splitting, *Sl.* hysterical, *All Slang.* a riot, a gas, a scream.

hilarity, *n.* gaiety, gayness, mirth, mirthfulness,

good *or* high spirits; joviality, jollity, merriment, levity, buoyancy, light-heartedness, blithesomeness; cheer, cheerfulness, joyfulness, joyousness; joy, delight, pleasure, happiness, felicity; elation, exhilaration, exuberance, enthusiasm, vivacity, animation, liveliness, effervescence; exultation, glee, jubilance, jubilancy, rejoicing, celebration, jollification; fun, enjoyment, revelry, revel, conviviality, festivity, partying, playing, sport; noise, noisiness, vociferousness, boisterousness, rowdiness, *Sl.* hell-raising, rabble-rousing.

hill, *n.* **1.** elevation, eminence, promontory, mount, rise, foothill; bluff, highland, moor, down, *Archaic.* holt; *Western U.S., Canada.* butte, *South African.* kop, *Geol.* drumlin, tor.

2. incline, acclivity, slope, *Scot. and North Eng.* brae, rise; grade, gradiant, climb, ramp, hillside, upgrade.

3. heap, pile, stack, mound, drift; molehill, anthill, termite hill.

hillock, *n.* hummock, hump, swell, knoll, knob, monticle, monticule, *South African.* kopje; dune, talus, *Brit.* barrow, *Dial.* knap.

hilt, *n.* **1.** haft, handle, grip, grasp, hold, helve, shaft.

2. to the hilt completely, fully, wholly, entirely, heart and soul, root and branch, from top to toe, from first to last; totally, without reserve, *Inf.* all the way, *Inf.* no holds barred, to the bitter end, to the nth degree.

hind, *adj.* rear, back, posterior, hinder, *Rare.* posterial, *Anat.* gluteal, *Anat., Zool.* caudal, *Bot.* posticous; hindmost, last, rearmost, aftermost, *Naut.* aftmost, terminal, final.

hinder[1], *v.* **1.** hamper, impede, interfere, interrupt; frustrate, thwart, foil, balk, *Inf.* short-circuit; handicap, encumber, clog *or* scotch the wheels; retard, set back, delay, defer, postpone, slow down, forestall; filibuster, stalemate, deadlock; baffle, stymie, confuse.

2. limit, circumscribe; curb, inhibit, restrain, hold back, rein in, bridle, *Sl.* put a crimp in; shackle, fetter, bind hand and foot; smother, choke, silence, muzzle, gag; constrict, control, trap, cage, pinion, clip one's wings.

3. stop, check, arrest, abort; prevent, deter, preclude, obstruct, block, stand in the way; prohibit, forbid, taboo, bar, disallow; oppose, cross, contravene, counteract, fly in the face of, turn one's face against.

hinder[2], *adj.* See **hind.**

hindmost, *adj.* last, furthest behind, nearest the rear, rearmost, aftermost, final, terminal, *Obs.* hindermost, *Naut.* aftmost; endmost, most remote, furthest, farthest, ultimate.

hindrance, *n.* **1.** impediment, obstacle, obstruction, *Archaic.* remora, oppilation, interference, *Law.* estoppel; barrier, stop, stopper, block, stumbling block, barricade; curb, check, balk, catch, hitch, snag, difficulty; encumbrance, handicap; retardation, retardment, delay, postponement, stoppage.

2. restriction, stricture, limitation, inhibition; constraint, restraint, repression; forbiddance, prohibition, interdiction, injunction, proscription, preclusion, ban, embargo, veto, taboo.

hinge, *n.* **1.** joint, articulation, knee, elbow; condition, rule, principle, premise, basis, foundation.

—*v.* **2.** turn, center, pivot, rotate *or* revolve around; depend, hang, rest; bud from, arise from, spring from, emanate from, issue from, ensue from.

hint, *n.* **1.** clue, tip, inkling, *Sl.* tip-off, cue; suggestion, idea, *Inf.* flea *or* bug in one's ear; intimation, implication, imputation, insinuation, innuendo; omen, foreshadowing, warning; signal, sign, *Inf.* high sign, reminder, memorandum, whisper; denotation, allusion, connotation.

2. suspicion, soupcon, trace, tinge; touch, speck, sprinkling, dash; flavor, taste, sniff, scent.

—*v.* **3.** intimate, suggest, *Inf.* give to understand, imply, insinuate, *Inf.* put a bug *or* flea in one's ear; clue, *Inf.* tip off, cue, prompt; jog one's memory, signal, *Inf.* give a high sign, wink; breathe, whisper; connote, allude, advert, refer, signify, indicate.

hip[1], *n.* haunch, loin, pelvis, innominate bones, lumbar region; rump, posterior, (*of a horse*) crupper, croup, buttocks, *Sl.* butt, breech, hindquarters, *Sl.* behind, *Sl.* arse, *Sl.* ass, bottom.

hip[2], *adj.* *Slang.* informed, knowledgeable, *Sl.* savvy, knowing, *Sl.* up on, *Sl.* tuned in; smart, sharp, clever, bright, intelligent, brainy, *Inf.* having lots of gray matter, having a good head on one's shoulders; discerning, perspicacious, perceptive; astute, shrewd, sagacious, canny; aware, wide-awake, alert, on the qui vive, *Sl.* wise to, *Sl.* in on; worldly-wise, experienced, educated, having savoir-faire; sophisticated, worldly, cosmopolitan, *Inf.* knowing one's way around, *Sl.* cool, *Sl.* in, *Sl.* with it.

hire, *v.* **1.** engage, employ, retain, secure the services of, contract with; enlist, appoint, sign on, take on, *Inf.* take on board.

2. lease, sublease, let, sublet; rent, rent out, hack, charter, get, secure; (*usu. of oneself*) hire out, ship out, loan.

3. bribe, suborn, oil, graft, buy off, *Sl.* pay off, cross *or* grease [s.o.'s] palm; rig, *Inf.* fix, *Sl.* square.

—*n.* **4.** compensation, pay, salary, wage, *Brit. Sl.* get, emolument, remuneration, earnings; payment, *Hist.* scot, fee, stipend, honorarium; recompense, requital, reward, deserts.

5. cost, charge, price; quotation, estimate, amount, figure; rent, rental, dockage; fare, toll; freight, freightage, haulage, cartage, porterage, ferriage.

hireling, *n.* employee, hired hand, servant, factotum, wage slave, slave, menial, minion, hack; tool, instrument, victim, puppet; henchman, flunky, toady; mercenary, hired soldier, adventurer. See also **help** (*defs.* **14, 15**).

hirsute, *adj.* hairy, shaggy, crinite, comose; fuzzy, linty, fleecy, furry; bearded, whiskered, unshaven. See **hairy.**

hiss, *n.* **1.** hissing, sibilation, sibilance, buzz, fizzle, whiz, whistle, wheeze, whisper.

2. derision, mockery, outcry, clamor, hue and cry; catcall, jeer, hoot, *Sl.* razz, *Sl.* raspberry, *Sl.* Bronx cheer; mock, taunt, scoff, fleer, sneer, flout, twit, fling, gibe, *Inf.* zip.

—*v.* **3.** sibilate, rasp, whiz, wheeze, whistle, whiffle; fizz, fizzle, sizzle; disdain, cry down, express disapproval, laugh to scorn, hiss off the stage *or* platform; catcall, boo, hoot, fleer, scoff, snort, point the finger of scorn at, point at, *Sl.* razz, *Sl.* give the raspberry *or* Bronx cheer; flout, ridicule, jeer, gibe, twit, taunt, mock, revile, cock a snook at.

historian, *n.* antiquarian, antiquary, paleologist, historiographer, expert, authority; chronicler, annalist, archivist, researcher; compiler, reporter, recorder, scribe, chronographer; writer, storyteller, narrator; biographer, memorialist.

historic, *adj.* **1.** well-known, well-remembered, unforgettable, famous, famed, notable, noted, noteworthy, known far and wide; renowned, celebrated, eminent, illustrious, distinguished, solemn, marked, impressive, great, prominent, important; crucial, critical, significant, momentous, eventful, salient, consequential; remarkable, extraordinary, rare, special, unusual,

uncommon, signal, red-letter, particular; outstanding, conspicuous, noticeable, striking, stirring, vivid.
2. historical, memorable, treasured. See **historical.**

historical, *adj.* **1.** true, authentic, real, actual, factual, verifiable, reliable; archival, recorded, documented, chronicled, supported by facts, confirmed, storied, remembered, memorable, commemorated.
2. traditional, former, past, prior; obsolete, bygone, of another era *or* time, ancient, extinct.

history, *n.* **1.** story, account, depiction, portrayal, representation, interpretation, explanation, study, summary, recapitulation, delineation, exposition, unfolding of events; recital, narrative, narration, review, retelling, relation; report, news, information, intelligence; anecdote, incident, series of incidents, events, episodes; tale, drama, romance, legend, saga, epic, *Inf.* yarn.
2. experiences, fortunes, adventures, confessions, memoirs, biography, autobiography, life, life story, psychohistory.
3. record, public record, facts; chronicle, calendar, almanac, yearbook, annual; journal, diary, daybook, log; annals, chronology, genealogy, archives; register, registry, docket, roster, schedule, minutes, proceedings, transactions; ana, memorabilia, memories, nostalgia, tradition.
4. the past, yesterday, yesteryear, former *or* happier times, the good old days, old days, bygone days *or* eras, days *or* times of old, times gone but not forgotten; water over the dam, water under the bridge, *Inf.* ancient history, *Fr. fait accompli.*

histrionic, *adj.* **1.** dramatic, dramaturgic, dramaturgical, theatrical, theatric; thespian, Roscian, histrionical, *Sl.* ham *or* hammy; scenic, stagy; operatic.
2. affected, mannered, unnatural, ostentatious, forced, overwrought; artificial, false, insincere, bogus, sham, put-on, *Inf.* fake, *Sl.* phony; overdone, overacted; emotive, emotionalistic, overemotional, melodramatic; sensational.

histrionics, *n.* **1.** drama, dramatic representation, dramatics, dramaturgy, theatricals, theatricalism, histrionism, thespianism; acting, playacting, performing, playing, enacting, enactment; overacting, *Sl.* ham acting, *Sl.* hamming *or* hamming up.
2. affectation, pretension, show, false show, sham; posture, masquerade, façade, front, false front, display; humbug, hypocrisy, fakery, bluff, posing, feigning, pretending, making believe; veneer, gloss, lip service *or* homage.

hit, *v.* **1.** strike, smite, thwack, slap, smack, *Australian.* ding; cuff, buffet, knock, punch, box, sandbag, *Scot.* dunt, *Scot. and North Eng.* paik, *Inf.* clout, *Inf.* slug, *Inf.* whack, *Inf.* knock [s.o.'s] block off, *Inf.* wallop, *Inf.* crown, *Sl.* conk, *Dial.* hit [s.o.] upside the head, *Sl.* bash, *Sl.* plug, *U.S. Sl.* biff, *Sl.* bop; *Sl.* belt, *Sl.* sock, beat, batter, pound, lay on, pommel, pummel, pelt, *Sl.* paste, *Sl.* lay into, *Sl.* let [s.o.] have it, *Archaic.* belabor; thrash, flog, lash, switch, birch, scourge, flagellate, whip, horsewhip, curry, strap, thresh, flail, cowhide, spank, *Brit. Dial.* yerk, *Inf.* tan [s.o.'s] hide, *Inf.* trim, *Inf.* thump, *Inf.* lace, *Inf.* lambaste, *Inf.* whale, *Sl.* whomp; cudgel, fustigate, bludgeon, baste, cane, bastinado, club, hammer, sledge hammer; tap, rap, fillip.
2. collide with, impact, crash against, smash into, dash against, jolt, jar, bang into *or* against; bump, knock into, clap together, percuss, run into, meet head-on, impinge upon *or* against.
3. reach, touch, gain, attain, achieve; arrive at *or* in, land in; make, appear in; make a bull's eye, send to the mark, fell, drop, sink, bring down, shoot, *Sl.* blast, *Sl.* zap.
4. drive, bat, propel.
5. affect, have an effect on, influence, make an impact *or* impression on, impinge upon, leave a mark on.
6. *Often* **hit out** assail, attack, revile, vituperate, lash out, belabor, rail against, inveigh against, argue *or* debate against, dispute; criticize, carp, find fault with, castigate, *Inf.* knock, *Inf.* light into, *Sl.* blast; censure, disapprove of, condemn; vilify, asperse, malign, slander, defame, slur, traduce, calumniate, backbite; decry, denounce, denigrate, berate, disparage, deprecate, depreciate, run *or* put down, belittle, minimize.
7. solicit, demand, ask for, request, petition; appeal, seek, entreat, plea, beg; implore, beseech, supplicate.
8. come upon, light *or* fall upon, happen *or* chance upon, blunder upon, meet with, *Inf.* dig; find, discover, uncover, unearth, ferret out, dig up, learn of *or* about; detect, descry, notice, espy, perceive, discern, *Inf.* spot, *Sl.* pick up; pitch on *or* upon, think of, get into one's head, come up with, dream up, hatch, concoct.
9. suit, fit, befit; dovetail with, square with, tally with, meet, correspond with, coincide with; blend in with, harmonize with, jibe with, agree with; accord, please, appeal to, delight, gratify, tickle.
—n. **10.** collision, impact, crash, clash, bang, bump, thud, thump; blow, bastinado, punch, box, knockout, *Both Boxing.* left, right, *Scot.* dunt, *Scot. and North Eng.* paik, *Inf.* wallop, *Inf.* whomp, *Both Brit. Dial.* yerk, douse, *Sl.* conk, *Sl.* hash, *U.S. Sl.* biff, *Sl.* bop; buffet, cuff, strike, hit, thwack, slap, smack, *Inf.* whack, *Inf.* clout.
11. attack, assailment, abuse, vituperation, revilement, belaboring; criticism, stricture, castigation, animadversion, *Inf.* knock, *Inf.* slam; censuring, condemnation, reprehension; vilification, aspersion, traducement, calumniation, calumny, obloquy, slur, slap in the face; maligning, defamation, denigration, slander, libel, *Inf.* backbiting; scorn, derision, insult, ridicule, sneer, scoff, jeer, *Sl.* put-down; mockery, satire, lampoon, pasquinade.
12. sarcasm, gibe, taunt, wipe, dig, cut; retort, repartee, riposte, counterstroke, *Sl.* comeback.
13. success, winner, sensation, attraction, best seller, sellout, box office, *Inf.* smash; coup, triumph, victory, stroke of genius, master stroke, *Fr. coup de maître*, *Inf.* ten-strike, *Inf.* trump card; lucky stroke *or* venture, piece of good luck *or* fortune.

hitch, *v.* **1.** fasten, join, connect, unite, tie, bind, lash; chain, couple, link, concatenate; lace, string, tether; bolt, lock, pinion, clamp; secure, anchor, moor; attach, annex, tack, staple, affix, fix, hook, nail, pin, rivet; harness, moor, picket.
2. hike up, tug, jerk, jolt, raise with jerks.
3. falter, stagger, totter; stumble, shuffle, limp, hobble, hop.
4. hitchhike, thumb, *Inf.* bum a ride, get free rides.
5. catch, entangle, trip up, ensnare, snare, entrap, trap, snag, hook.
—n. **6.** fastening, connection, attachment, joining, linking, uniting, binding, yoking; connecting, conjoining, coupling; link, tie, bond, knot, yoke; coupler, coupling, connective; joint, joiner, articulation, commisure; clamp, clasp, latch, buckle, clip.
7. hindrance, impediment, obstacle, obstruction, oppilation, interference; barrier, stop, stopper, block, stumbling block, barricade; curb, check, delay, halt; catch, snag, difficulty, encumbrance, handicap.
8. jerk, pull, tug, yank, jolt.
9. stagger, shuffle, limp, hobble; spasm, twitching; staggering, faltering, tottering.

hitherto, *adv.* previously, until now, up to this time, of late, latterly, to this day, to the present day, thus far; formerly, no longer, before, before this, before *or* ere now, heretofore, already; in time past, in the past, years ago, long ago, some time ago, some time back, *Inf.* way back, in ancient times, anciently, of old, in olden times, once upon a time.

hit-or-miss, *adj.* **1.** careless, neglectful, neglective, negligent, neglecting, remiss; inattentive, heedless, unheeding, disregardful, disregardant, regardless, lackadaisical, easygoing, half-hearted, apathetic.

2. haphazard, lax, loose, perfunctory, perfunctionary, perfunctorious, cursory, offhand; irregular, uneven, random, disorganized, orderless, casual, undirected, aimless.

hive, *n.* **1.** beehive, apiary, bee tree, wasp's *or* hornet's nest, vespiary.

2. swarm, cloud, flight.

hoar, *n.* frost, hoarfrost, rime, rime frost, glaze, glaze ice, silver frost, silver thaw, verglass, Jack Frost.

hoard, *n.* **1.** store, stock, stockpile, supply, provisions, reserve; garner, harvest, gathering, gleaning; fund, quantity, reservoir, profusion, abundance, wealth, treasure, holdings, savings, *Inf.* loot.

2. collection, accumulation, heap, pile, mass, cumulation; amassment, assemblage; aggregation, concentration, agglomeration, conglomeration.

—*v.* **3.** accumulate, collect, heap up, pile, pile up, roll up, stack up; assemble, mass, aggregate, bring together, congregate; amass, cumulate, agglomerate.

4. store up, stock up, lay by, lay up, lay in, garner; cache, squirrel away, load up, stow away, *Inf.* stash away, reserve, set aside, reposit, husband; save, save up, bank; gather, harvest, get in, take in, pull in.

hoarse, *adj.* dry, scratching, cracked; harsh, rough, raucous, gruff, raspy, gravelly, grating; guttural, throaty, roupy.

hoary, *adj.* **1.** grizzled, grizzly, gray *or* white with age, gray-haired, white-haired.

2. elderly, old, grown old, old as the hills, at an advanced age, aged, ancient; venerable, time-honored, hallowed, immemorial.

hoax, *n.* **1.** trick, ruse, jest, joke, practical joke, *Inf.* spoof, *Sl.* goof.

2. deception, fraud, sham, mock, fake, imitation, imposture, humbug, *Inf.* phony; cheat, swindle, *Inf.* flam, *Inf.* rip-off; *Sl.* scam, *Sl.* gyp.

—*v.* **3.** trick, fool, deceive, delude, beguile, dupe, hoodwink, humbug, take in, put one over on [s.o.], pull a fast one, pull the wool over [s.o.'s] eyes, *Inf.* bamboozle, *Sl.* snow, *Sl.* hornswoggle; mislead, misguide, misdirect, *Sl.* give [s.o.] a bum steer; gull, cozen, defraud, cheat, swindle.

hobble, *v.* **1.** limp, hitch, walk lamely; shuffle, shamble, drag one's feet; halt, pause, hesitate; toddle, dodder, falter, move unsteadily; totter, stagger, weave, reel.

2. hopple, trammel, fetter, shackle, gyve; chain, tether, hitch, picket, stake out; tie *or* tie up, truss, hogtie, bind, strap, last, pinion.

3. hinder, hamper, impede, retard, slow up *or* down, delay, *U.S.* filibuster, hogtie; handicap, cripple, disable, hamstring, clip [s.o.'s] wings; check, curb, curtail, limit, restrict, inhibit, cramp, confine; bridle, harness, rein, restrain, keep *or* hold back.

—*n.* **4.** limp, claudication, hitch, jerk, uneven gait, toddle; shuffle, shamble, halting, pausing, hesitation; doddering, tottering, staggering, weaving, reeling.

5. strap, thong, line, leash, tether, rope, tie, bond; fetter, shackle, trammel, gyve, chain; bridle, bit, curb bit, snaffle bit.

hobby, *n.* avocation, sideline, side interest; pastime, diversion, recreation, relaxation, divertissement, entertainment; amusement, fun, play, sport, game; *Inf.* cup of tea, *Sl.* thing, *Sl.* bag.

hobgoblin, *n.* **1.** bogy, evil spirit, demon, devil, ghoul; boogeyman, bugbear, bugaboo; ghost, *Inf.* spook, specter, apparition, phantom.

2. hob, goblin, (*in German folklore*) kobold, devilkin, imp, *Irish Folklore.* leprechaun, pixy, puck, sprite, elf, brownie, bad fairy; (*in Scandinavian folklore*) troll, gnome, dwarf, pygmy.

hobnob, *v.* fraternize, mingle, mix, rub elbows with; socialize, *Sl.* club *or* party with; keep company with, consort, associate, go around with, *Inf.* pal around with, *Inf.* hang around with, *Sl.* hang out with.

hobo, *n.* **1.** tramp, vagrant, beachcomber, vagabond, derelict, *Dial.* bawky, street Arab; *Inf.* bum, *Sl.* vag, *Sl.* bo, *Sl.* stiff, *Sl.* bindle stiff, *Sl.* canvas back.

2. migrant *or* migrant worker, *Usu. Disparaging.* Okie, drifter, *Inf.* floater, transient, fly-by-night, bird of passage, *Sl.* rolling stone; rambler, rover, roamer, wanderer, gypsy, nomad.

hocus, *v.* **1.** trick, practice trickery *or* deception upon, deceive, hoodwink, jockey; dupe, gull, take in, cozen, befool, *Archaic.* chouse; humbug, *Inf.* flimflam, *Inf.* practice upon; cheat, bilk, swindle, defraud, palm off, job, victimize, diddle; hoax, betray, *Inf.* sell out, play false; mislead, bluff, beguile, delude, impose upon, mystify, bamboozle, pull the wool over [s.o.'s] eyes; fake, counterfeit, dissemble, dissimulate, sham, pretend, *Brit. Inf.* gammon; bait, lure, entice, inveigle, ensnare, snare, entangle, entrap, trap, deacon; circumvent, outwit, outmaneuver, overreach, evade.

2. drug, narcotize, *Sl.* dope *or* dope up; stupefy, deaden, dull, blunt; anesthetize, numb, benumb, paralyze, render insensible *or* incompetent; corrupt, adulterate, treat, alter, contaminate, doctor, falsify.

hocus-pocus, *n.* **1.** mumbo jumbo, abracadabra, open sesame, magic word, magic formula; incantation, chant, invocation, conjuration, conjuring, evocation.

2. juggler's trick, jugglery, sleight of hand, legerdemain, prestidigitation, *Brit.* hanky-panky; feint, deception of the eye, trompe l'oeil, *Inf.* dodge, fetch; magic, conjuring, conjuration.

3. trickery, hokey-pokey, chicane, chicanery; deception, deceit, artifice, shrewdness, hanky-panky; stratagem, wile, finesse, ruse, shift, maneuver, circumvention; trap, scheme, intrigue, plan, contrivance, complot, conspiracy; trick, hoax, humbug, sham, delusion, pretense; prank, jape, spoof; cunning, slyness, craft, craftiness, guile; cheat, cozenage, *Inf.* gyp; swindle, *Archaic.* chouse, fraud, imposture; cardsharping, double-dealing, duplicity, *Obs.* cog, confidence game, con game, the old army game.

4. obfuscation, elaboration, magnifying, amplification; padding, redundancy, superfluous words, overstatement, repetition; wordiness, verbosity, prolixity, prolixness, verbiage, verbalism; diffuseness, profuseness, effusion, effusiveness; jargon, cant, nonsense, gobbledegook.

—*v.* **5.** trick, practice trickery *or* deception upon, deceive, hoodwink, jockey; dupe, gull, take in, cozen, befool, *Archaic.* chouse; humbug, *Inf.* flimflam, *Inf.* practice upon; cheat, bilk, swindle, defraud, palm off, job, victimize, diddle; hoax, betray, *Inf.* sell out, play false; mislead, bluff, beguile, delude, impose upon, mystify, bamboozle, pull the wool over one's eyes; fake, counterfeit, dissemble, dissimulate, sham, pretend, *Brit. Inf.* gammon; bait, lure, entice, inveigle, ensnare, snare, entangle, entrap, trap; circumvent, outwit, outmaneuver, overreach, evade.

hodgepodge, *n.* mixture, jumble, melange, gallimaufry, farrago, patchwork, mosaic; potpourri, mishmash, *Brit.* hotchpotch, hash; all sorts, oddments, sundries, odds and ends, old curiosity shop, a little of this and a little of that; this, that and the other; tangle, mess, scramble, welter, clutter, litter, higgledy-piggledy; miscellany, miscellanea, olla-podrida, olio, variety, *Inf.* omnium-gatherum, *Inf.* mixed bag; conglomeration, composite, commixture, combination.

hoe, *n.* **1.** rake, trowel, spade, scuffle, scraper.
—*v.* **2.** dig, scrape, spade, rake; harrow, weed, delve, dibble; cultivate, till.

hog, *n.* **1.** pig, sow, boar, razorback; peccary, warthog, babirusa; porker, grunter, oinker, tusker; swine, barrow; shoat, shote, piglet, pigling, piggy, suckling-pig, hogling.
2. *Informal.* **a.** glutton, cormorant, gourmand, eater; trencherman, big eater, wolf. **b.** monopolist, self-server, self-pleaser, self-seeker, egotist; road hog.
—*v.* **3.** keep for oneself, take for oneself, be selfish, monopolize, corner, tie up; have it all to oneself, take it all, *Sl.* bogart.

hoggish, *adj.* **1.** porcine, piggish, swinish.
2. selfish, egotistic, self-seeking, self-pleasing, self-serving; self-indulgent, self-devoted, self-centered; possessive, greedy, acquisitive, avaricious, covetous.
3. gluttonous, ravenous, voracious, edacious, rapacious, insatiable; glutting, gorging, omnivorous, crapulous.
4. filthy, dirty, foul, unclean, unwashed, slimy, *Inf.* gloppy; sloppy, sloshy, sludgy, muddy, miry.

hogtie, *v.* hobble, tie up, truss up, tie hand and foot; manacle, enchain, handcuff, hamstring; restrain, shackle, gyve, fetter, strap; lash, leash, bind, tether, hopple, tie down; hamper, thwart, trammel, impede, hinder, frustrate, constrain, hold back.

hogwash, *n.* **1.** swill, slop, refuse, *Dial.* culch; garbage, waste, offal; dregs, remains, offscourings; leavings, sweepings, scraps, orts, leftovers; remainder, residue, residuum, scum, filth.
2. junk, worthless stuff, trumpery; trifles, trinkets, gimcrackery, baubles, gewgaws, frippery; remnants, fragments, fag ends, bit and pieces, odds and ends; cast-offs, rags, tatters, castaways, rejects, discards.
3. nonsense, falderal, gibberish, babble, babbling, babblement, *Fr. bavardage;* twaddle, twaddling, *Both Brit.* twattle, twattling; blather, blathering, drivel, driveling, drool, drooling; jargon, Greek, *Chiefly Southern U.S.* Choctaw; hocus-pocus, mumbo jumbo, abracadabra, fiddle-de-dee; moonshine, gobbledegook, humbug, foam, froth, bunkum *or* buncombe, *Sl.* bunk, *U.S. Sl.* blah; flummery, *Inf.* hokum, *Sl.* applesauce, *Sl.* eyewash; rubbish, *Sl.* tripe, refuse, *Dial.* culch, chaff, trash, *Inf.* truck, trumpery; tommyrot, *Inf.* rot, *Sl.* garbage, *Sl.* crap, *Sl.* crock, *Sl.* bull; balderdash, *Sl.* horsefeathers, stuff, stuff and nonsense, *Inf.* bosh, *Brit. Inf.* gammon, *Brit. Sl.* tosh; fudge, foolishness, folly, rigamarole *or* rigmarole, amphigory; footle, *Inf.* malarkey, *Sl.* bushwa, *Sl.* baloney, *Sl.* bilge *or* bilge water, *Sl.* meshugaas, *Scot. and North Eng.* haver; poppycock, *Inf.* fiddle-faddle, *Inf.* piffle, *Inf.* hooey, *Inf.* kibosh, *Inf.* flapdoodle; idle talk, *Inf.* gab, *Sl.* gas, palaver, palavering, palaverment; claptrap, rodomontade, fustian, bombast, rant, *Sl.* hot air; Jabberwocky, jabber, jabbering, prate, prating; patter, pattering, gabble, gabbling; clack, clacking, clatter, clattering, rattling, *Sl.* running off *or* on at the mouth; chatter, chattering, prattle, prattling, chippering, cackle, cackling; chit-chat, chitter-chatter, small talk, *Anglo-Indian.* bukh.

hoi polloi, *n.* the common people, the masses, the vulgus, *Archaic.* the vulgar; commonalty, commonage, citizenry, demos; proletariat, plebians, third estate, bourgeoisie; the multitude, the many, the populace, *Chiefly Brit.* admass, rank and file; rag, tag, and bobtail; *Latin. hoc genus omne;* grass roots, *Inf.* the silent majority, the man in the street, *Jocular.* booboisie, *U.S.* Middle America, Main Street USA; the vulgar herd, the great unwashed, the rabble, the mob, King Mob, the crowd.

hoist, *v.* **1.** raise, lift, elevate, heave, move up, set up; thrust up, raise aloft, uprear, uplift, rear, erect, escalate; boost, upheave, upcast, upthrow, upthrust; pull up, hike up, pick up, jerk up; crane, jack up, take up, winch, bear up; raise up, upraise, weigh, whip.
—*n.* **2.** crane, winch, tackle, halyard, davit; windlass, capstan, gin, pulley; elevator, lift, dumbwaiter; jack, jackscrew, booster, lifter.

hoity-toity, *adj.* disdainful, assuming, arrogant, proud; snobbish, conceited, *Inf.* uppity, self-important. See **haughty**.

hold, *v.* **1.** grasp, clutch, clasp, seize, keep fast, gripe; have, palm, retain, *Inf.* latch onto, clench, clinch; hug, embrace, *Brit. Dial.* clip; keep, have and hold, harbor; cherish, treasure, fondle, *Archaic.* bosom.
2. reserve, set aside, put aside, set by, lay aside, lay up; retain, preserve, save, put away for a rainy day.
3. bear, carry, take, shoulder; sustain, support, bolster, hold up, keep up, uphold, upbear; prop, brace, buttress, shore.
4. keep, maintain, engross, occupy, absorb, immerse, involve, engage; hold one's attention, monopolize one's attention, engage one's mind *or* thoughts; arrest, enthrall, spellbind, keep spellbound, fascinate.
5. detain, hold up, confine, impound, hold in custody; keep under constraint, lock up, coop up, put behind bars, imprison, incarcerate, *Sl.* throw in the clink.
6. engage in, carry on, join in; bring together, gather, muster; preside over, direct, administer, conduct, run, prosecute, officiate at; observe, celebrate, mark.
7. hinder, restrain, hold back, check, impede, bar; suppress, squelch, put down; curb, hold down, hold in, control; hold up, stop, retard, delay, clog, *Inf.* bottle up, bottleneck, slow down, tie up.
8. occupy, be in, *Sl.* hold down, fill, be incumbent; own, possess, have, enjoy, control, command, boast.
9. contain, accommodate, compose, comprise, bear, comprehend; have a capacity for, retain, carry, take.
10. think, believe, maintain, harbor, opine, affirm, propound; embrace, espouse, advocate, put faith in; swear by, go with, *Inf.* bank on, bet on, be sure of.
11. consider, regard, deem, esteem, judge, acknowledge; conjecture, gather, conceive, surmise; fancy, guess, estimate, allow; reckon, see, suppose, suspect, daresay.
12. defend, fend off, turn aside, stand seige, stave off; secure, cover, guard, protect, fortify, safeguard, garrison; resist, repel, repulse, hold off, keep at bay; stonewall, thwart, block, blockade, shut out.
13. point, aim, direct, train, level, peg, address, turn to.
14. bind, force, oblige, compel, coerce, expect of; bear upon, make incumbent upon, make responsible for, make answerable to.
15. remain, stay, persist, last, endure, obtain; continue, go on, carry on, go through; adhere to, stick to, uphold, follow; stay with, *Inf.* see through, follow through, keep up.
16. adhere, cling, stick, cleave, hang on, hold on; hug, embrace, hold tight, hold fast, cohere, freeze to; stick like a leech, cling like a winkle, cling like a burr, stick like wax, stick like a wet shirt.
17. be in force, remain valid, be the case, be true, prove out; hold up, hold good, square with the facts, stand up, *Inf.* wash, *Inf.* hold water, stand the test.

18. refrain, stay, forgo, spare; forbear, desist from, give up, abandon; do without, not touch, abstain, dispense with; break off, leave off, relax, loosen.

19. hold back **a.** keep back, retain possession of, not use. **b.** withhold, refuse, deny, suppress, stifle, not disclose, *Inf.* take the fifth.

20. hold forth **a.** extend, offer, hold out, proffer, tender, submit, put forth; propose, advance, broach, volunteer. **b.** harangue, lecture, sermonize, discourse, preach; orate, declaim, perorate, prelect; electioneer, soapbox, *Inf.* stump.

21. hold off defer, postpone, hold over, suspend, put off; put aside, hang up, lay over, stay over.

22. hold on keep going, continue, perpetuate, bide, abide; stay on, carry on, hold one's course, hold steady.

23. hold out last, persist, carry on, persevere, go ahead; stand firm, stick to one's guns, mean business, stand pat, hang on; fight to the end, fight to the last man, go down fighting, never say die.

24. hold up **a.** display, exhibit, show, flaunt, dangle before one's eyes; wave, brandish, unfurl, unroll; show off, *Inf.* trot out, expose, call into notice, lay open. **b.** *U.S. Informal.* rob, *Sl.* stick up, *U.S. Sl.* heist, *Sl.* jack up, *Sl.* knock over, *Sl.* hit, *Sl.* roll.

—n. **25.** grasp, grip, gripe, clasp, clutch, clench, clinch; iron grip, tight grip, firm hold; embrace, hug, bear hug; purchase, leverage, fulcrumage; footing, foothold, toehold, stand, stance, perch, *Fr. point d'appui.*

26. handle, haft, helve, grip; handstaff, crop, snath; crank, shaft, bar, shank, rounce; rail, railing, bannister, crook.

27. support, mount, mounting, setting, backing, bearing, bushing.

28. influence, power, sway, force, *Inf.* clout, effect; charm, charisma, magnetism; mastery, dominance, dominion, control, ascendancy.

29. pause, delay, respite, reprieve, remand; postponement, deferment, prorogation, demurral.

holder, *n.* owner, possessor, freeholder, proprietor, landlord; lessee, lease holder, renter, permittee, tenant; occupant, resident, resider.

holding, *n.* **1.** leasehold, rental, lease; piece of property, land, estate, demesne, tenancy; allodium, freehold, possession, asset.

2. holdings property, real property, real estate, land, tenements; assets, resources, capital, wealth, means; stocks, bonds, securities, investments, stake, equitable assets, frozen assets; liquid assets, cash, money.

holdout, *n.* **1.** milker, exploiter, moneymonger, money grubber; hard bargainer, tough customer, stubborn *or* unyielding person, *Inf.* mule; staller, delayer, *Inf.* footdragger.

2. damper, kill-joy, wet blanket, *Sl.* party pooper, *Sl.* crape-hanger.

holdover, *n.* **1.** leftover, member of the previous administration, relic, remnant; charter member, old war horse, veteran, old stager, *Inf.* old-timer.

2. carry-over, hit *or* smash production, box office attraction.

holdup, *n.* **1.** *U.S. Informal.* robbery, purse-snatching, *Inf.* mugging, *U.S. Sl.* stickup, *Sl.* hustle, *Sl.* heist, *Sl.* jumping, *Sl.* rolling; highway robbery, banditry, brigandage, piracy, buccaneering, freebooting, *Obs.* latrociny.

2. delay, hold, detention, wait, slowdown, *Sl.* hang up; interruption, halt, stop, cessation, stay.

hole, *n.* **1.** opening, vent, scupper, mouth, orifice, aperture, eye; foramen, *Anat., Zool.* fenestra, spiracle, pore, *Biol.* cell, *Anat., Zool.* alveolus, *Anat.* sinus; puncture, perforation, cut, incision, split, gash, scotch, rent, slit, slot; gap, space, hiatus, rift, breach, break; leak, fault, flaw, nick, notch.

2. impression, indentation, dent, dint; dip, depression, hollow, scoop, concavity, cavity, crater, *Anat.* fossa; fissure, cleft, crevasse, crevice, cranny, chink, crack, groove, sulcus; chasm, abyss, gorge, ravine, bergschrund; gulch, gully, rut, furrow, ditch, trench.

3. excavation, pit, shaft, mine, tunnel; cave, cavern, grotto, dugout, retreat, shelter; burrow, den, lair; niche, nook, nest, recess.

4. hut, hovel, shack, shanty, lean-to, shed; slum, *Sl.* dump, *Inf.* dive, *Sl.* joint, hole in the wall.

5. dungeon, prison, prison cell, cage, *Sl.* pen, pound, brig, keep, donjon.

6. predicament, dilemma, plight, *Inf.* pickle, *Inf.* fix, difficulty, trouble, *Inf.* hot water, scrape; corner, tight spot, *Sl.* box, bind, double bind, catch-22; strait, *Inf.* squeeze, pinch, push, quagmire; quandary, muddle, mess, botch, jumble.

7. *U.S.* cove, lagoon, inlet, bay; harbor, anchorage, moorage, basin.

—v. **8.** perforate, puncture, spike, pierce, stab, lancinate, pink, stick; cut, rent, gash, split; drill, bore, tunnel, excavate, burrow.

9. hole up **a.** hibernate, lie dormant, sleep, retire. **b.** *Slang.* hide, hide out, lie low, conceal oneself.

holiday, *n.* **1.** vacation, day off, time off, breathing space *or* spell, respite, recess; furlough, leave, leave of absence, sabbatical.

2. gala day, red-letter day, banner day, field day; occasion, event, birthday, anniversary, jubilee; carnival, fair, kermis, Mardi gras; fete, gala, *Inf.* do, *Sl.* jamboree; junket, frolic, spree, whirl, lark, treat.

3. festival, saint's day, holy day, feast day, *Rom. Cath. Ch.* holy day of obligation, (*in ancient Rome*) feria; rite, ritual, ceremony, celebration, observance, keeping; remembrance, memorialization, commemoration.

—adj. **4.** festal, festival, in holiday spirits, *Inf.* Christmassy; festive, convivial, joyous, merry, mirthful, gleeful; gay, sportive, fun-making, rollicking, good-time.

5. commemorative, memorial, in honor of.

holier-than-thou, *adj.* sanctimonious, self-righteous, pharisaic, pharisaical, tartuffian, pietistic, pietistical; unctuous, smug, self-satisfied, *Inf.* uppity, *Inf.* uppish, haughty, snobbish.

holiness, *n.* sanctity, sanctitude, saintliness, godliness; sacredness, divineness, divinity; religiosity, spirituality, devoutness, piety, religiousness, reverence; righteousness, goodness, virtue, virtuousness, purity, chastity, grace.

holler, *v.* *Informal.* shout, cry out, halloo; hurrah, huzzah, cheer, whoop; bellow, roar, thunder, bawl, howl, yowl; yell, scream, shriek, squall, yammer, clamor.

hollow, *adj.* **1.** empty, unfilled, hollowed, not solid, not dense, excavated, drained, vacant, blank; depressed, concave, dented, indented, caved in, *Inf.* stoved in; incurved, incurving, incurvate, cupped, cup-shaped, alveolate, alveolated; dipping, sunk, sunken, cavernous.

2. muffled, dull, *It. sordo*, deep, not resonant, flat, toneless, dead, sepulchral.

3. valueless, useless, inefficacious, unavailing, of no use *or* avail, bootless, fruitless; gainless, profitless, unprofitable, worthless, too dear, not worth it, Pyrrhic; meaningless, unmeaning, senseless, without sense, insignificant, unsignificative, trivial.

4. insincere, hypocritical, artful, cunning, wily, tricky, sophistic; feigned, sham, counterfeit, artificial, spurious, made-up, fabricated; false, mendacious, lying, dissembling, truthless, untruthful, uncandid, untrue; deceptive, two-faced, *Inf.* fork-tongued.

5. hungry, starved, half-starved, famished, half-famished, ravenous, perishing from hunger.

—*n.* **6.** hole, pigeonhole, cubby, cubbyhole, nook, cranny, niche, recess; cavity, concavity, concave, indentation, dent, dimple; dip, depression, hollow, sink, pothole, crater; pit, well, basin, bowl, valley, dale, dell, bottom, glen, gorge, ravine.

—*v.* **7.** scoop out, gouge out, dig out, excavate; furrow, groove, channel, dredge; dish, indent, dent, depress, dint.

holocaust, *n.* **1.** fire, firestorm, incendiarism, malicious burning; destruction, demolition, cataclysm, catastrophe, upheaval, havoc; ravage, devastation, ruin, Armageddon; extinction, extermination, elimination, eradication, annihilation; massacre, mass murder, pogrom; butchery, carnage, Saturnalia of blood.

2. burnt offering, sacrifice, immolation, incense, votive offering, sacramental offering; slaughter, hecatomb, human sacrifice, self-immolation, suttee, sutteeism.

holy, *adj.* **1.** blessed, blest, sanctified, hallowed, consecrated; sacred, religious, sainted, venerable, angelic, seraphic; divine, godlike, deiform, deified; heavenly, heaven-born, celestial, ethereal, supernal; beatific, blissful, rapturous, ecstatic; supreme, exalted.

2. godly, pious, pietistic, reverent, God-fearing, devout, devotional, faithful, believing; righteous, moral, upright, right-minded, just, good, virtuous; spiritual, unworldly, saintly, saintlike, innocent, childlike, lamblike, dovelike; perfect, pure, chaste, clean, immaculate, sinless; spotless, unspotted, unstained, undefiled, untainted, uncorrupted.

3. awesome, awe-inspiring, frightening, fearful, dreadful.

Holy Ghost, *n.* Holy Spirit, Spirit of God, the Dove, the Comforter, Paraclete, The Spirit of Truth.

Holy Writ, *n.* See **Scripture**.

homage, *n.* **1.** respect, high regard, deference, honor, esteem, estimation, admiration, awe; worship, adoration, glorification, apotheosis; veneration, adulation, reverence.

2. obeisance, courtesy, greeting, salute, salutation, presenting arms, recognition; bowing, curtsying, salaaming, kowtowing, tugging the forelock; genuflection, kneeling, bending the knee, prostration.

3. tribute, vassalage, servitude, submission, abasement, bondage, subservience, servility, bondedness.

4. faithfulness, fidelity, constancy, loyalty; allegiance, devotion, duty, adherence.

home, *n.* **1.** abode, domicile, domicil, dwelling, dwelling place, dwelling home, residence, residency, habitation, inhabitancy, *Scot. and North Eng.* bigging, *Scot.* howff; lodging, lodgings, lodging place, lodgement *or* lodgment, nest, roost, perch; quarters, living quarters, rooms, accommodations, housing, roof over one's head, *Inf.* pad, *Inf.* crash pad, *Chiefly Brit. Inf.* diggings, *Brit. Inf.* digs; apartment, flat, tenement, walk-up, cold-water flat, *Brit.* chambers, *Chiefly Brit.* maisonette; penthouse, townhouse, condominium, *Sl.* condo; mobile home, motor home, camper, trailer; address, location, situation, whereabouts, place.

2. mansion, palace, palatial *or* stately dwelling *or* residence, *Fr. hôtel, It. palazzo,* villa, château, castle, *Chiefly Brit.* hall, *Brit.* court, *Archit.* folly, *Sl.* spread; manor, manor house, manor seat, estate, country estate, country home, country seat, country house, house and grounds, house and lot, *Brit. Dial.* toft, demesne, *Law.* messuage; farm, farmstead, farmplace, *Archaic.* farmhold, *Brit.* farmery, grange, *Brit.* croft, *Brit.* homecroft, *Scot. and North Eng.* steading; ranch, rancho, rancheria, hacienda; plantation.

3. cottage, cot, bungalow, bower, cabin, log cabin, blockhouse, *Brit. Dial.* cote, *Scot.* but-and-ben; hut, hutch, shed, shack, shanty, bothy; hovel, hole, hole in the ground, dump, garbage heap, sty, pigsty, pigpen, tumbledown shack, wretched hut, mean dwelling, miserable quarters.

4. hearth, hearthstone, hearth and home, hearthside, fireside, fireplace, chimney corner, *Brit. Dial.* ingle, *Brit. Dial.* ingleside, *Chiefly Brit.* inglenook *or* ingle nook; homestead, household, family, family circle, domestic circle, bosom of one's family, seat of one's affections, home sweet home, *Inf.* place where one's heart is, *Inf.* place where one hangs his hat.

5. shelter, retreat, refuge, haven, hospice, hermitage, sanctum, sanctum sanctorum, port in a storm, *Scot.* bield; almshouse, poorhouse, charitable institution, eleemosynary institution, shelter for the homeless *or* afflicted, orphanage; hospital, state hospital, clinic, sanitorium, sanitarium, asylum, institution, lazaretto, *Fr. hôtel Dieu;* insane asylum, lunatic asylum, mental institution, mental hospital, madhouse, bedlam, *Fr. maison de santé, Derog. Sl.* nuthouse, *Derog. Sl.* crazyhouse, *Derog. Sl.* bughouse, *Derog. Sl.* booby hatch, *Derog. Sl.* funny farm, *Derog. Sl.* loony bin; rest home, retirement home, nursing home, convalescent home, old-age home.

6. habitat, natural habitat, environment, native *or* natural environment, element, natural element, homeground, *Inf.* stomping *or* stamping ground, *Inf.* home front; territory, ground, zone, range, sphere, domain, realm; area, vicinity, region, locale, locality.

7. mew, cover, covert, coverture, hideout, hiding place, hideaway, sanctuary; nest, lair, den, hole, cave, burrow; spot, place, haunt, rendezvous, meeting place *or* spot, *Inf.* hang-out, *Inf.* watering hole, *Chiefly Brit.* local.

8. birthplace, homeplace, hometown, *Obs.* homestall; village, hamlet, township, town, city; land, homeland, fatherland, motherland, native land, country, native country, native soil.

9. destination, goal, bourn; terminus, terminal point, finish, end, journey's end, end of the road, end of the line, last stop; grave, cemetery, eternal home *or* resting place; heaven, paradise, *Teutonic Myth.* Valhalla, *Buddhism.* (*often cap.*) nirvana, nibbana, *Buddhism, Hinduism, Jainism.* moksha, mutki.

10. *Baseball.* homeplate, the plate, homebase.

11. at home a. in, present, available. **b.** used to, familiar with, in one's own *or* proper element, on home territory *or* ground, in smooth water; cool, poised, composed, relaxed, easy, at ease, unexcited, unruffled, unperturbed, undisturbed, untroubled, unvexed, unplagued, unmolested; serene, sedate, placid, tranquil, quiet, peaceful, at peace, complacent, unexcitable, imperturbable. **c.** proficient, able, capable, competent, good at, qualified, endowed; skillful, skilled, dexterous, adept, adroit, deft, sure; expert, masterful, masterly; well-informed, well-versed, well-briefed, well-read, current, up on, in the know, *Inf.* in on, *Sl.* hip, *Brit. Sl.* suss.

—*adj.* **12.** domestic, domiciliary, internal, interior; native, natural, natal, vernacular, indigenous, aboriginal, autochthonous, autochthonal, autochthonic; homegrown, home-raised, homebred, homemade, home-born, native grown; familiar, acclimated, accustomed, one's own; established, rooted, fixed, ingrained.

13. direct, to the point, close, effective, piercing, penetrating, home-reaching, deep-felt, poignant, intimate; deep, profound, pregnant, highly significant; neat, clear, summary, terse, curt, acute, keen, emphatic, decided, pointed; caustic, astringent, trenchant, incisive, sharp, stinging, biting, cutting, barbed, razor-edged, knife-edged; rough, harsh, severe.

—*adv.* **14.** homeward, homewards, homeward bound, to *or* toward *or* at one's home *or* abode; indoors, within doors, in the house, inside, in.

15. deep, to the heart, to the core *or* innermost core, to the quick, to the mark, to the heart, to the vital center *or* seat, to the innermost feeling *or* sensibility, *Inf.* where it hurts, *Inf.* in the breadbasket, *Inf.* right here.

16. effectively, with telling effect, decidedly, completely, entirely; deeply, profoundly, indelibly; closely, directly, neatly, clearly; summarily, curtly, tersely, acutely, keenly, emphatically, pointedly; caustically, astringently, trenchantly, incisively, sharply, stingingly, cuttingly, bitingly, with a vengeance, with force; roughly, harshly, severely.

17. bring home to a. emphasize, lay emphasis on, give emphasis to, stress, lay stress on; feature, accent, accentuate, underscore, underline, highlight; press home, drive home, hammer away, pound away, harp on. **b.** clarify, make clear, clear up, shed light on, make manifest, manifest, illuminate, elucidate, make plain, make explicit; expose, lay open, bring to light, unfold, unmask, unveil.

18. write home about *Informal.* note, make note of, take note of, speak of, tell of, talk about, carry on about, go on about, rave *or* rave on about; mention, report, describe, tell, state, remark, remark on, comment on, pass comment on.

—*v.* **19.** live, live at, reside, reside at, abide, *Archaic.* bide, dwell, tenant, stay, stay at, remain, sojourn.

20. domicile, domicil, domiciliate, establish oneself, take up residence, take up one's abode, make one's home, inhabit, occupy, settle, locate, ensconce, *Inf.* hang up one's hat; take *or* strike root, plant oneself, anchor, come to anchor, drop anchor, moor; nest, nestle, roost, perch, squat, burrow, hive.

21. house, shelter, give shelter to, lodge, provide with lodging *or* lodgings *or* lodgement, put up, take in, roof, provide with a roof; quarter, provide quarters for, billet, bed, bunk, berth, have as a guest *or* lodger.

22. direct, guide, steer, maneuver, navigate, head, lead, pilot; fix, fix on, set, determine, sight, sight on, home in, home in on, zero in on, pinpoint, position, place, situate, locate; aim, aim at, level, level at, point, point at *or* to, train, train at, train *or* turn upon.

homebred, *adj.* **1.** domestic, domiciliary, internal, interior; native, natural, natal, indigenous, aboriginal, autochthonous, autochthonal, autochthonic; homespun, homegrown, homemade, home-born, home-raised, native-grown.

2. unpolished, unsophisticated, unrefined, uncultured, uncultivated, unworldly; coarse, rough, roughcast, rough-hewn, linsey-woolsey, indelicate, inelegant; uncouth, crude, crass, raw; loutish, oafish, doltish, stolid, lumpish, lumpen, cloddish, clodhopping, boorish.

3. rustic, rural, bucolic, bucolical; inurbane, backwoods, provincial, countrified *or* countryfied, country-bred, country-born, upcountry, from the sticks, yokelish, *Sl.* hickish, *Sl.* rube, *Sl.* hayseed; homey, homely, homelike, homish, down-home, homespun, (*usu. of thought or philosophy*) cracker-barrel, *Scot.* raploch, *Yiddish.* heimish, *Inf.* folksy; plain, simple, modest, unpretentious, unpretending, unaffected, normal, informal.

homeless, *adj.* exiled, outcast, disinherited, dispossessed; forsaken, abandoned, derelict, desolate, forlorn; vagabond, houseless, unsettled; estranged, alienated.

homelike, *adj.* homey, cozy, warm, snug, intimate; quiet, peaceful, restful, tranquil, serene, easy, easeful, relaxing; familiar, comfortable, customary, accustomed, acclimated, wonted, common, normal; domestic, homespun, downhome, homebred, plain, simple, modest, informal, unsophisticated, unaffected, unpretentious, unpretending, unassuming; friendly, congenial, genial, cordial, cheerful, hospitable, agreeable, pleasant.

homely, *adj.* **1.** plain, plain-featured, plain-looking; unshapely, unsightly; unattractive, unlovely, unpretty, unhandsome, unbeautiful, uncomely, rather ugly; ugly, ill-favored, bad-looking, *Inf.* not much to look at, *Inf.* short on looks, *Inf.* not much for looks, *Sl.* hard *or* rough on eyes.

2. unsophisticated, unpolished, unrefined, uncultured, uncultivated, uncouth, graceless, lacking in the social graces, ill-mannered, ill-bred; crude, crass, raw, loutish, oafish, doltish, boorish, churlish, clownish; rustic, rural, bucolic, bucolical, provincial; backwoods, inurbane, countrified, country-bred, country-born, upcountry, from the sticks, yokel, yokelish, *Sl.* hick, *Sl.* hickish, *Sl.* rube, *Sl.* hayseed.

3. homey, homelike, homish, down-home, homespun, homebred, domestic, *Scot.* raploch, *Yiddish.* heimish, *Inf.* folksy; plain, simple, modest, unaffected, unpretentious, unpretending, unassuming, normal, natural, informal; cozy, warm, snug, intimate, comfortable, *Inf.* comfy, lived-in; quiet, peaceful, restful, relaxing, tranquil, serene, easy, easeful.

4. common, commonplace, ordinary, usual, familiar, nothing out of the ordinary, everyday, workday, workaday, household-variety, garden-variety; nondescript, prosaic, matter-of-fact, *Inf.* no big thing.

5. friendly, amicable, amiable, genial, congenial, cordial, social, sociable; cheerful, affable, hearty, backslapping; hospitable, neighborly, welcoming, open-armed.

homemade, *adj.* **1.** home-manufactured, home-produced, home-worked, home-wrought, produced *or* manufactured locally, locally produced, locally-manufactured, made locally, locally-made; homespun, home-woven, home-loomed.

2. domestic, domiciliary, internal, interior; native, natural, natal, indigenous, vernacular, aboriginal, autochthonous, autochthonc, autochthonal; homegrown, home-raised, native-grown, native-raised, home-born.

3. self-made, hand-made, hand-crafted, hand-woven, hand-knitted, hand-stitched; coarse, rough, rough-hewn, rough cast, unsmooth, uneven, linsey-woolsey, indelicate; crude, amateurish, amateur, unskilled, unprofessional, nonprofessional, avocational.

homemaker, *n.* home economist, family manager; (*all of a home*) manager, administrator, overseer, treasurer; factotum, handywoman, housekeeper, hausfrau, cook, *Inf.* chief cook and bottle washer; housewife, matron, mistress, lady *or* woman of the house, *Chiefly Scot.* goodwife, *Scot. Inf.* wifey, *Inf.* missis.

Homeric, *adj.* heroic, epic; grand, imposing, impressive, magnificent; mighty, colossal, monumental, towering, titanic.

homespun, *adj.* **1.** home-woven, home-loomed; homemade, home-manufactured, home-produced, home-worked, home-wrought; self-made, hand-made, hand-crafted; hand-knitted, hand-woven, hand-stitched.

2. plain, simple, modest, unpretentious, unpretending, unaffected, unassuming, normal, informal; homey, homely, homelike, homish, homebred, downhome, (*usually of thought or philosophy*) cracker-barrel, *Scot.* raploch, *Yiddish.* heimish, *Inf.* folksy; rustic, rural, bucolic, bucolical; inurbane, backwoods, provincial, countrified *or* countryfied, country-bred, country-born, upcountry, from the sticks, yokelish, *Sl.* hickish, *Sl.* rube, *Sl.* hayseed.

3. unpolished, unsophisticated, unrefined. See **homebred** (*def.* **2**).

homestead, *n.* **1.** estate, country estate, manor, country manor, country seat, house and grounds, house and lot, *Brit. Dial.* toft; demesne, *Law.* messuage.

2. farm, farmstead, grange, farmplace, *Archaic.* farmhold, *Brit.* farmery, *Brit.* croft, *Brit.* homecroft, *Scot. and North Eng.* steading; ranch, rancho.

3. home, home sweet home, abode, place where one hangs his hat, *Scot. and North Eng.* bigging; hearth, hearth and home, hearthstone, fireplace, fireside, chimney corner, *Brit. Dial.* ingle, *Brit. Dial.* ingleside, *Chiefly Brit.* inglenook *or* ingle nook; domicile, dwelling place, dwelling, dwelling home, residence, residency, habitation, *Scot.* howff; retreat, refuge, hermitage, hospice, shelter, sanctum, sanctum sanctorum.

—*v.* **4.** settle, occupy, inhabit, populate, people, colonize, establish.

homesteader, *n.* settler, colonist, colonial, colonizer; squatter, nester; pioneer, sooner; frontiersman, trailblazer, trailbreaker, pathfinder; backwoodsman, woodsman, backsettler.

homeward, homewards *adv.* homewardly, homeward bound, home, to *or* toward *or* at one's home, back home, to one's family *or* native land *or* homeland.

homicidal, *adj.* murderous, death-dealing, killing, lethal, mortal, deadly; cruel, brutal, blood-thirsty, bloody-minded, sanguinary, bloody, bloodstained; ferocious, violent, wild, berserk, amuck, maniacal. See also **murderous** (*def.* **1**).

homicide, *n.* **1.** murder, manslaughter, slaying, killing, bloody *or* foul killing *or* slaying, murder most foul, assassination, (*in India*) thuggee, *Sl.* hit; patricide, matricide, parricide, fratricide, sororicide, uxoricide, infanticide, regicide, vaticide. See also **murder** (*def.* **1**).

2. murderer, killer, slayer, manslayer, man-killer, cutthroat, thug; assassin, liquidator, bravo, sniper, gunman, silencer, dispatcher; *All Sl.* gun, hired gun, hit man, triggerman, torpedo, hatchet man. See also **murderer** (*defs.* **1, 2**).

homily, *n.* **1.** sermon, preachment, lecture, harangue, screed; parable; lesson, instruction, teaching, talk.

2. discourse, address, speech, oration, declamation, *Rhet.* apostrophe, salutation, valedictory; treatise, study, thesis, dissertation, descant, essay.

homogeneity, *n.* identicalness, identity, sameness, oneness; uniformity, regularity, constancy; consistency, consonancy, accordance, agreement; similarity, similitude, likeness, resemblance, semblance; comparableness, comparability, analogousness; equivalence, parity, correspondence, correlation, parallelism.

homogeneous, *adj.* **1.** identical, the same, one and the same, all one, all alike, alike, of a piece; uniform, regular, constant, unvaried, unvarying; consistent, consonant, accordant; homogenetic.

2. similar, like, comparable, corresponding, correspondent, correlative, parallel, analogous; cognate, connatural, allied, connected, akin.

homogenize, *v.* emulsify, blend, compound, combine, coalesce, fuse, merge; standardize, equalize, stereotype, make uniform, *Fig.* boil down.

homologous, *adj.* similar, like, comparable, analogous, corresponding, correspondent, parallel; relative, cognate, connatural, allied, connected, akin; uniform, regular, constant, consistent, consonant, accordant.

homosexual, *adj.* **1.** homoerotic, homophile, sexually inverted, *Inf.* gay, *Inf.* bent; *All Sl.* kinky, fruity, left-handed; *All Derog.* queer, faggy, flitty, limp-wristed; effeminate, *Sl.* swishy, camp, campy; lesbian, tribadic, sapphic, *Sl.* butch.

—*n.* **2.** homosexualist, homophile, third sex, invert; *All Sl.* queen, limp-wrist, camp, three-dollar bill, *Brit.* ginger, *Brit.* ginger beer, *Brit.* poof, *Brit.* poofter; *All Derog.* homo, queer, faggot, fag, fruit, flit, fairy, pansy, nance, auntie; pederast, pathic, catamite, *Sl.* punk, *Sl.* chicken, *Sl.* gunsel; transvestite, drag queen; lesbian, sapphist, tribade, *Sl.* butch, *Sl.* femme, *Derog.* dyke, *Derog.* bull dyke, *Archaic.* fricatrice.

homosexuality, *n.* homosexualism, homoeroticism, sexual inversion, homosex, *Derog.* faggotry, *Derog.* faggism, *Inf.* gayness; lesbianism, sapphism, tribadism *or* tribady.

homunculus, *n.* **1.** midget, dwarf, little man, pygmy, manikin, chit, fingerling, dapperling, cock-sparrow, hop-o'-my-thumb, Tom Thumb, Lilliputian, *Chiefly Scot.* wee fellow *or* lad *or* one, *Obs.* pigwidgin, *Archaic.* dandiprat; shrimp, runt, pee-wee, squirt, pipsqueak, half-pint, *Inf.* shorty; imp, elf, fairy, sprite, goblin, (*in German Folklore*) kobold, *Irish Folklore.* leprechaun, *Chiefly Brit.* little person.

2. fetus, embryo; zygote, oospore.

hone, *n.* **1.** whetstone, grindstone, grinding wheel, emery wheel; rasp, file, nail file, razor strap, abrasive.

—*v.* **2.** whet, grind, rasp, file, abrade; sharpen, edge, put an edge on.

honest, *adj.* **1.** upright, upstanding, incorruptible, uncorrupt, uncorrupted; ethical, moral, principled, high-principled, high-minded; truthful, veracious, veridical, truth-telling, truth-speaking, truth-dealing, truth-loving; trustworthy, *Inf.* trusty, to be trusted, responsible, reliable, dependable, tried and true, to be depended *or* relied upon, to be counted on, as good as one's word, honest as the day is long; loyal, faithful, staunch, steadfast, true, truehearted, true-blue.

2. honorable, worthy, right, decent, good, *Sl.* white; just, fair, impartial, equitable, objective, balanced, disinterested, dispassionate, even, even-handed, *Inf.* level; straight, square, fair and square, square-dealing, plain-dealing, square-shooting, straight-shooting; unbiased, nonbiased, unprejudiced, nonprejudiced, nonprejudicial, unprepossessed, unjaundiced, open-minded; uninfluenced, unbought, unbribed, unswayed.

3. legitimate, valid, sound; rightful, proper, lawful, licit, legal.

4. open, open and sincere, open-hearted, ingenuous, guileless, artless, genuine, sincere, undeceptive, undeceitful, undeceiving, unfeigning, undissembling, undissimulating; aboveboard, open and aboveboard, up front, out front, up and up, on the up and up, on the level, no-nonsense; natural, uncontrived, unaffected, unassumed.

5. candid, frank, forthright, foursquare, direct, straightforward, straight-from-the-shoulder, man-to-man, heart-to-heart; plain, plain-spoken, plain-speaking, downright, outright, explicit, unequivocal, unambiguous, undisguised, undisguising, *Inf.* straight-out, *Inf.* flat-footed, *Inf.* matter-of-fact; outspoken, free-spoken, free-speaking, free-tongued, unreticent, free, bold, unreserved, unrestrained, unconstrained, unchecked, uncurbed, unabashed, uninhibited, unshrinking; blunt, bluff, brusque, brash, tactless.

6. genuine, authentic, real, true-to-claims, sterling, bona fide, *Australian.* dinkum, *Inf.* honest-to-God, *Inf.* card-carrying, *Sl.* sure-enough; inartificial, unsynthetic, unsimulated, unfeigned, undisguised, *Inf.* unfaked; unadulterated, unalloyed, undiluted, untainted, unmixed, uncut, undistorted, (*of measures*) full.

7. respectable, reputable, creditable, estimable, highly respectable, straight-arrow; law-abiding, law-loving; virtuous, righteous, uprighteous; chaste, sinless, spotless, pure, immaculate, unblemished, unstained, unspotted, unsullied, untarnished, undefiled, unsmirched.

8. believable, credible; conceivable, plausible, colorable, specious.

9. humble, modest, simple, unassuming, unpretentious, unpretending, unpresumptuous, unpresuming; plain, unadorned, undecorated, unornamented, ungarnished, unvarnished, unembellished.

honestly, *adv.* **1.** uprightly, upstandingly, incorruptibly, uncorruptly, uncorruptedly; ethically, morally, high-mindedly; truthfully, trustworthily, *Inf.* trustily, responsibly, reliably, dependably; loyally, faithfully, staunchly, steadfastly.

2. honorably, worthily, right, decently, well; justly, fairly, impartially, equitably, objectively, disinterestedly, dispassionately, even, even-handedly, squarely, fair and square.

3. legitimately, soundly, validly; rightfully, properly, lawfully, licitly, legally.

4. open-heartedly, ingenuously, guilelessly, artlessly, sincerely, genuinely; overtly, openly, aboveboard, in open sight, in the open, out in the open, in full view, in plain view, in public, in public view, publicly, for all to see; up front, out front, on the table.

5. candidly, frankly, forthrightly, straightforwardly, to one's face, man to man, heart to heart, from the heart; explicitly, unequivocally, plainly, in plain words *or* English, with no nonsense, all joking aside; outspokenly, freely, boldly, unreservedly, unrestrainedly, unabashedly; bluntly, bluffly, brusquely, brashly, tactlessly.

honesty, *n.* **1.** uprightness, rectitude, probity, honor, integrity; justice, justness, fairness, impartiality, equity, equitableness, objectivity, objectiveness, disinterestedness, evenness, evenhandedness, *Inf.* levelness; straightness, squareness, square dealing, plain dealing, square shooting, straight shooting; open-mindedness, freedom from bias *or* prejudice.

2. truthfulness, veracity, veraciousness, truth-telling, truth-speaking, truth-loving, truth-dealing; candor, candidness, frankness, forthrightness, straightforwardness, calling a spade a spade, *Inf.* calling it as one sees it, *Sl.* telling it like it is; plainness, plain-spokenness, plain-speaking, downrightness, outrightness, explicitness, unequivocalness; outspokenness, free-spokenness, free-speaking, nonreticence, freeness, boldness, unreserve, unrestraint, unconstraint, uninhibitedness, unabashedness; bluntness, bluffness, brusqueness, brashness, tactlessness.

3. openness, open-heartedness, ingenuousness, guilelessness, artlessness, sincerity, sincereness, genuineness, undeceptiveness, undeceitfulness.

honey, *n.* **1.** nectar, syrup, molasses, *Brit.* treacle, sorghum.

2. flattery, praise, compliment, music to one's ears; syrupiness, sweetness, cajolery, cajolement, flummery, puff, blarney; delight, pleasure, bliss, rapture, ecstasy.

3. (*often cap.*) sugar, sweetie, honeybunch, honeybun, dear, darling, sweetheart.

4. *Informal.* peach, gem, jewel, pearl.

honeycomb, *n.* **1.** comb, honey cells, cellular structure; labyrinth, maze; sieve, perforation, sifter, strainer.

—*v.* **2.** perforate, pit, riddle, *Fine Arts.* cribble; pierce, puncture, prick, pinprick, poke holes in, stick, shoot through.

honeycombed, *adj.* cellular, cellulate, multicelled, alveolate, *Anat., Zool.* alveolar; perforated, porous, spongy, spongelike, holey, cribriform, criblé, sievelike; pin-pricked, pitted, riddled, shot through, punctured, pierced.

honeyed, *adj.* **1.** dulcet, mellifluous, mellifluent, sweet-sounding; melodious, melisonant, sonorous, resonant, full; mellow, soothing, soft, easy-listening, pleasant, agreeable.

2. flattering, cajoling, syrupy, sickeningly sweet, sugar-coated, *Inf.* buttery; ingratiating, ingratiatory, winsome, winning, charming, enchanting; smooth-tongued, smooth, suave, unctuous.

3. sweetened, sweet, candied, nectared, nectarous, nectareous, nectarean, saccharine, sugared, sugary, honey, confectionary; rich, delicious, cloying, sickening.

honor, *n.* **1.** esteem, regard, consideration, respect; repute, reputation, note, good name, good report; distinction, notability, eminence, prestige, influence, authority; fame, bays, illustriousness, glory, exaltation.

2. honesty, integrity, probity, uprightness, truth, truthfulness, veracity; straightforwardness, forthrightness, justness, justice, fairness; righteousness, goodness, morality, decency; scrupulousness, principles, conscientiousness, moral fiber, self-respect; worth, merit, honorableness, rectitude; nobility, dignity, izzat, virtue, virtuousness; sincerity, candor, candidness, openness; trustworthiness, credibility, fidelity, faithfulness, constancy.

3. credit, pride, satisfaction, pleasure; joy, blessing, feather in the cap, ornament.

4. admiration, deference, veneration, adoration, adulation; acknowledgment, recognition, tribute, homage; approbation, approval, compliment; applause, praise, acclaim, acclamation; accolade, award, privilege, kudos; laurels, prize, trophy; laud, encomium, eulogy, eulogium.

5. chastity, virginity, purity, innocence; modesty, pudency.

—*v.* **6.** revere, reverence, respect, admire, defer to, look up to; venerate, adore, worship, idolize; esteem, value, prize; appreciate, approve.

7. celebrate, pay homage *or* tribute to, lionize; praise, commend, compliment, laud, extol; applaud, acclaim, salute, hail, toast; cheer, hurrah, huzzah, let the welkin ring; eulogize, panegyrize, sing paeans to; glorify, exalt, dignify, ennoble, aggrandize, magnify.

8. reward, pay, crown, garland, deck with garlands, laurel.

honorable, *adj.* **1.** upright, upstanding, honest, incorruptible, uncorrupt, uncorrupted; ethical, moral, principled, high-principled, high-minded, noble-minded; truthful, veracious, veridical, truth-telling, truth-speaking, truth-loving, truth-dealing; trustworthy, *Inf.* trusty, to be trusted, responsible, reliable, dependable, tried and true, to be depended *or* relied upon, to be counted on as good as one's word, honest as the day is long; loyal, faithful, constant, staunch, stanch, steadfast, true, truehearted, true-blue.

2. noble, illustrious, venerable, *Archaic.* eximious; distinguished, prestigious, eminent, preeminent, prominent; noted, notable, of note, marked, of mark; honored, revered, esteemed, held in esteem *or* high esteem, respected, held in respect, exalted, high, held in high regard; celebrated, applauded, acclaimed, widely *or* highly acclaimed, admired, much admired, highly reputed, highly regarded, in favor, in high favor, highly considered, well-thought-of.

3. respectable, reputable, creditable, estimable, meritorious, highly respectable, straight-arrow; law-abiding, law-loving; virtuous, righteous, uprighteous; chaste, sinless, spotless, pure, immaculate, unblemished, unstained, unspotted, unsullied, untarnished, undefiled, unsmirched.
4. worthy, right, decent, good, *Sl.* white; just, fair, impartial, equitable, objective, balanced, disinterested, dispassionate, even, evenhanded, *Inf.* level; straight, square, fair and square, square-dealing, plain-dealing, square-shooting, straight-shooting; unbiased, nonbiased, unprejudiced, nonprejudiced, nonprejudicial, unprepossessed, unjaundiced, open-minded; uninfluenced, unbought, unbribed, unswayed.
5. open, open and sincere, open-hearted, ingenuous, guileless, artless, genuine, sincere, undeceptive, undeceitful, undeceiving, unfeigning, undissembling, undissimulating; aboveboard, open and aboveboard, up front, out front, up and up, on the up and up, on the level, no-nonsense.

honorarium, *n.* reward, recompense, remuneration, compensation; fee, salary, pay, payment, emolument; altarage, token acknowledgment, token of appreciation, *Inf.* a little something; tip, gratuity, douceur, *Fr. pourboire, Ger. Trinkgeld*, cumshaw, (*in India and Turkey*) baksheesh; bonus, extra, gift, present.

honorary, *adj.* honorific, honorifical, *Latin. honoris causa*; titular, in name *or* title only, nominal; ex officio.

hood, *n.* cowl, capuche, mantilla, veil, coif, wimple, headcloth; scarf, head scarf, fascinator, kerchief, head covering, rain bonnet *or* hat, southwester; bonnet, capote, calash, cap, hat.

hoodoo, *n.* **1.** bad luck, evil, vexation, bane, affliction, torment, harm, misfortune, calamity, trouble.
2. voodoo, conjure, rootwork; black magic, evil eye, evil star; jinx, hex, juju, fetish; bogy, bugbear, bugaboo, hobgoblin, imp, evil spirit.
—*v.* **3.** vex, trouble, beset, annoy, harass, distress, *Inf.* jinx; curse, plague, blight, scourge, injure, harm, destroy, doom.

hoodlum, *n.* **1.** gangster, mobster, racketeer, mafioso, desperado, terrorist; murderer, killer, slayer, sniper, assassin; strangler, cutthroat, garroter; gunman, *All U.S. Sl.* gun, hired gun, hit man, triggerman, hatchet man, torpedo.
2. burglar, robber, thief, stealer; bandit, hold-up man, *Sl.* stick-up man, armed robber; shoplifter, purse-snatcher, cutpurse, pickpocket; criminal, felon, convict, *Sl.* jailbird.
3. rowdy, ruffian, tough, *Inf.* toughie, thug, mugger, *Sl.* hood, *Sl.* yap, *Inf.* plugugly, *Inf.* goon; hooligan, *Chiefly Brit.* rough, *Inf.* roughneck, *Inf.* baddy, *Sl.* bad actor, *Sl.* gunsel, *Sl.* mug, *Australian Sl.* larrikin, *Brit. Hist.* Mohock, (*in Paris*) apache.
4. brute, bully, brawler, barbarian; savage, vandal, yahoo, *Sl.* ugly customer; scoundrel, knave, wretch, *Archaic.* caitiff; blackguard, villain, hellhound, fiend; rascal, rapscallion, scamp, imp.

hoodwink, *v.* **1.** deceive, delude, bamboozle, pull the wool over [s.o.'s] eyes, throw dust in [s.o.'s] eyes, *Inf.* throw [s.o.] a curve; fool, *Inf.* fake [s.o.] out, take in, dupe, gull; trick, outwit, get the better of, pull a fast one on, *Inf.* slip *or* sneak one by, *Inf.* put one over on; mislead, *Inf.* lead [s.o.] down the garden path, lead on, *Inf.* string along, take [s.o.] for a ride; trap, *Inf.* rope [s.o.] in, entrap, ensnare; *All Inf.* fast-talk, flam, hype, jive, buffalo; *All Sl.* con, snow, suck in, sucker in, *U.S.* murphy.
2. cheat, *Inf.* gyp, *Sl.* gaff, *Sl.* take, *Inf.* flimflam, hoax, *Sl.* hornswoggle; defraud, mulct, bilk, cozen, swindle, fleece, *Sl.* pluck; rook, victimize, *U.S. Inf.* bunco, *Archaic.* chouse, exploit, impose on *or* upon, take advantage of, *Inf.* diddle, *Inf.* do.

hoof, *n.* trotter, foot, unguis, cloven hoof, *Scot. and North Eng.* cloot; paw, pad, coffin, *Zool.* forefoot, hand, extremity.

hoofed, *adj.* ungulate, ungulous; cloven-hoofed, cloven-footed.

hook, *n.* **1.** scythe, sickle; falchion, cutlass, scimitar, saber.
2. snag, trap, snare, springe, noose.
3. crook, angle, dogleg, hairpin turn, horseshoe, loop; curve, curvature, incurvature, bow, arc, turn, twist, tortuosity; bend, bending, flexion, flexure, inflection.
4. holdfast, fastening, clasp, catch, clip, snap, hook and eye, fastener; pin, buckle, agraffe; clamp, vise, brace.
5. **by hook or by crook** somehow or other, no matter how, by any means, in one way or another, somehow, someway.
6. **hook, line, and sinker** *Informal.* entirely, completely, through and through, wholly, thoroughly.
7. **off the hook** *Slang.* **a.** exonerated, cleared, let off, vindicated, acquitted. **b.** under no obligation, uncommitted, unpledged, not bound.
—*v.* **8.** ensnare, enmesh, entrap, snag, catch, catch hold of; seize, capture, nab, collar, noose; fasten, clasp, grip.
9. trick, hoodwink, bamboozle, beguile; dupe, hoax, inveigle, take in, gull; put one over, get around.
10. angle off, shoot off at an angle, bear off; meander, zigzag, wind, wind in and out, sinuate; bend, crook, flex, bow, twist, curve.
11. **hook up a.** hitch, harness, moor, picket; fasten, join, connect, unite, tie, bind, lash; chain, couple, link, concatenate; lace, string, tether; attach, annex, affix. **b.** assemble, put together, piece together, lay together.

hooked, *adj.* **1.** aquiline, falcate, falciform, *Biol.* uncinate, adunc, *Anat.* hamate, *Biol.* hamular, *Biol.* hamulate, *Biol.* hamulose, hook-shaped, hook-like; crooked, bent, flexed, bowed, arcuate, twisted, contorted; curved, incurvated, angular, curled, spiral, looped.
2. *Slang.* dependent on, devoted to, given to; drug-dependent, *Inf.* strung-out.

hookup, *n.* **1.** connection, connecting, conjunction, conjoining, coupling; combination, junction, unification, accouplement, joinder; tie-up, link, linking, joining, splicing.
2. alliance, coalition, entente, union, federation, confederation.

hooligan, *n.* ruffian, rowdy, hoodlum, *Inf.* roughneck. See **ruffian** (*def.* **1**).

hoop, *n.* **1.** ring, band, wheel, cordon, annulus; bracelet, circlet, armlet, collar; *All Basketball.* basket, *Inf.* ring, rim.
2. hoop skirt, crinoline, farthingale, hoop petticoat.
—*v.* **3.** circle, surround, encircle, ring; belt, girdle, gird, enclose, hedge in, hem in; ring round, circumnavigate, circumambulate, ensphere; encompass, compass, envelop, embrace.

hoot, *v.* **1.** bellow, bawl, caterwaul, yowl, yelp; clamor, shout, roar, chorus, *Inf.* holler.
2. deride, cry down, express disapproval, laugh to scorn, hoot off the stage *or* platform; catcall, boo, hiss, jeer, fleer, scoff, snort, hiss and boo; point the finger of scorn at, point at, *Sl.* razz, *Sl.* give the raspberry *or* Bronx cheer; flout, ridicule, gibe, twit, taunt, mock, revile.

3. ululate, shrill, pipe, screak, shriek, screech, howl, scream, squawk, whoop, wail.

—*n.* 4. shout, bellow, clangor, caterwauling; commotion, rumpus, hubbub, noise, din; outcry, clamor, hue and cry.

5. derision, mockery, catcall, jeer, hiss, *Sl.* razz, *Sl.* raspberry, *Sl.* Bronx cheer; mock, taunt, scoff, fleer, sneer, flout, twit, fling, gibe, *Inf.* zip.

hop, *v.* 1. jump, leap, jump *or* leap over, leapfrog, vault, clear; bound, buck, buckjump, frisk, skip, romp, spring.

—*n.* 2. jump, leap, vault, bound, buck, buckjump, frisk, skip, romp, spring.

3. *Informal.* trip, quick trip, jaunt, junket; flight, short flight, leg, whistle stop.

4. *Informal.* dance, dancing party, social, hoedown, *Inf.* shindig, *U.S. Inf.* prom, *U.S. Inf.* sockhop.

hope, *n.* 1. expectation, desire, longing, want, fancy, wish; eagerness, craving, yearning, hankering, longing, *Inf.* yen, *Sl.* letch; aspiration, ambition, dream, daydream, hopefulness.

2. promise, prospect, assurance, security, expectancy, confidence, anticipation, optimism, assumption; reliance, trust, faith, conviction.

—*v.* 3. expect, desire, believe, hold, doubt not; assume, deem likely, suppose, surmise, suspect.

4. anticipate, foresee, contemplate, look forward to, count upon, reckon on, aspire, watch for; be hopeful, have faith, hope against hope; rest assured, trust, believe, take heart, feel confident, be reassured, look on the bright *or* sunny side.

5. **hope for** long for, wish, have an eye to, have one's heart set on, have a fancy for; desire, be bent upon, aspire to, dream of; languish for, yearn for, hanker for, crave, pine for, hunger *or* thirst for, pant for.

hopeful, *adj.* 1. expectant, full of hope, anticipative, anticipating, looking forward to; optimistic, assured, confident, *Inf.* bullish.

2. promising, raising one's hopes, looking up, upbeat; encouraging, inspiriting, heartening, fortifying, vivifying, elating; auspicious, of good omen, favorable, propitious, assuring, reassuring; fair, pleasant, bright, rosy, roseate, gladdening.

hopeless, *adj.* 1. beyond hope, despaired of, lost, irredeemable; beyond recovery, irrecoverable, irrevocable, past cure, incurable, irremediable, remediless; beyond repair, irreparable, irretrievable, irreclaimable; serious, grave, fatal, deadly.

2. desperate, reckless, rash, precipitate, impetuous; ill-conceived, headlong, breakneck, madcap, foolhardy, harebrained; incautious, imprudent, indiscreet, injudicious; dangerous, risky, hazardous, death-defying, daring, bold; frantic, mad, violent, wild, passionate, frenzied, frenetic; last-ditch, do-or-die.

3. despairing, despondent, disconsolate, inconsolable, comfortless, suicidal; dejected, depressed, melancholy, forlorn, downcast, *Inf.* down; wretched, miserable, broken-hearted, heartbroken; grief-stricken; cheerless, sad, plaintive, woeful, woebegone, rueful, sorrowful, dolorous, doleful, mournful, lugubrious, funereal; discouraged, disheartened, daunted, intimidated; concerned, worried, anxious.

4. impossible, futile, useless, vain; worthless, pointless, empty, idle; ineffective, unavailing, unattainable, unachievable, unobtainable, unfeasible.

5. inadequate, incompetent, inferior, poor, *Sl.* no good, *Sl.* lousy; unteachable, unmanageable, untractable; unserviceable, unusuable; a lost cause.

hopple, *v.* hobble, tether, fetter. See **hobble**.

horde, *n.* 1. crowd, mob, mass, throng, large group, gathering, multitude, host; concourse, confluence, lot, entourage, caravan, procession, cavalcade.

2. nomadic group, tribe, troop, legion, company, band; moving pack, herd, swarm, flock.

horizon, *n.* skyline, *Astron.* azimuth, range of vision, field of view, field of vision, vista, view; offing, prospect, outlook.

2. scope, limit of perception, range of knowledge, realm, compass, confines.

horizontal, *adj.* flat, plane, level, *Math.* homaloidal, flush, supine, prone; flat as a pancake, flat as a flounder, flat as an ironing board, smooth as glass, flat as a millpond.

horn, *n.* 1. cornu, antler, projection; crest, tuft, plume, topknot, coxcomb; spike, spine, quill, feeler, tentacle, (*in aphids*) cornicle.

2. corn, callous, calloused *or* toughened *or* hardened skin.

3. cornucopia, horn of plenty, conch, cornet, pirou ette, cone, funnel, pyramid.

4. (*of saddles*) pommel, nubble, nub, knob, handle, protuberance.

5. *Music.* musical instrument, brass instrument, wind instrument; trumpet, cornet, bugle; French horn, English horn, hand horn, trombone, baritone, tuba, helicon, sousaphone, bass.

6. honker, klaxon, siren, alarm; buzzer, sounder, noisemaker; bullhorn, foghorn, megaphone, loudspeaker.

horny, *adj.* 1. corneous, ceratoid, hornlike, horn; callous, calloused, tough, toughened, thick-skinned, hard, hardened, indurate, indurated; bony, bonelike, ossified.

2. horned, cornute, cornuted, corniculate; antlered, bicorn, bicornuate, bicornuous, biconical, bicone.

3. horn-shaped, cornucopiate, cornual; conical, cone-shaped, funnel-shaped; crescent-shaped, crescentlike, crescentoid, crescentic.

4. *Slang.* lecherous.

horrendous, *adj.* horrible, dreadful, awful. See **horrible** (*def.* 1).

horrible, *adj.* 1. dreadful, awful, horrid, horrendous; horrifying, terrifying, terrible, frightful, frightening, *Inf.* scary, appalling, harrowing; hideous, ghastly, grisly, gruesome, ghoulish, macabre, bloodcurdling, unspeakable.

2. disgusting, sickening, nauseating, revolting, repellent, repulsive; loathsome, abominable, abhorrent, detestable, hateful, despicable; odious, obnoxious, contemptible, beneath contempt, vile, foul, reprehensible; atrocious, outrageous, heinous, villainous, monstrous.

3. deplorable, lamentable, regrettable, woeful, rueful; pitiful, piteous, pitiable, pathetic.

horrid, *adj.* horrible, horrendous, horrifying, dreadful. See **horrible** (*def.* 1).

horrify, *v.* 1. shock, startle, astound, stun, stupefy, paralyze, petrify; appall, consternate, daunt, unnerve, abash, floor; disturb, distress, harrow, agitate, dismay; outrage, scandalize, shock, *Sl.* gross out; disgust, nauseate, sicken, *Inf.* turn one's stomach; offend, repel, repulse, *Sl.* turn [s.o.] off, *Inf.* put [s.o.] off.

2. terrify, frighten, frighten out of one's wits, scare, scare to death, panic, throw into a panic, *Sl.* curl one's hair, *Inf.* make one's hair stand on end, make one's blood run cold, *Inf.* scare stiff; alarm, startle, *Inf.* make [s.o.] jump out of his skin; *Inf.* scare the living daylights out of [s.o.]; terrorize, intimidate, *Sl.* freak [s.o.] out.

horror, *n.* 1. fear, fearfulness, dread, fright, *Inf.* funk; terror, panic, alarm, perturbation, trepidation, dismay; angst, fear and trembling, anguish, anxiety; uneasiness, apprehensiveness, *Inf.* butterflies, nervousness, queasiness.

2. abhorrence, abomination, loathing, loathsomeness, execration, detestation, odiousness, rancor; aversion, hatred, hostility, antipathy, animosity, animus, ill will; repugnance, repulsion, revulsion, disgust, distaste, nausea.

3. horribleness, dreadfulness, awfulness, horridness, frightfulness; hideousness, ghastliness, gruesomeness, ghoulishness.

hors d'oeuvre, *n.* appetizer, starter, apéritif, entrée, *Sp. tapa,* smorgasbord, antipasto, relish.

horse, *n.* **1.** equine, *Sl.* hoss, pony, *Sl.* critter, mount, steed, *Literary.* courser; outlaw, *Sl.* bronc, bronco, bucking bronco, *Sl.* sunfisher; mustang, cow pony, cutting horse, range horse, *U.S.* cayuse; galloper, racer, race horse, bangtail, stake horse; entry, starter, favorite; mudder, mud lark; Thoroughbred. Arab, quarter horse; trotter, pacer, hackney, Hambletonian; hunter, saddle horse, bidet, riding horse, cob, palfrey, Shetland pony, Morgan; cavalry horse, charger, Bucephalus; dobbin, plow horse, draft horse, *Archaic.* sumpter, Clydesdale, Percheron, Belgian; roan, chestnut, bay, sorrel, pinto, piebald, skewbald; nag, *Sl.* crowbait, jade, *Sl.* plug, *Sl.* scrag, Rosinante; geld ing; stallion, stud, sire; mare, broodmare, dam; foal, colt, filly, yearling; centaur, Pegasus, Bayard.

2. mule, ass, donkey, burro, zebra, eohippus.

3. stand, trestle, frame; sawhorse, buck, sawbuck.

horseman, *n.* **1.** rider, horseback rider, equestrian; jockey, *Sl.* jock, exercise boy *or* girl; cowboy, cowgirl, *Sl.* buckeroo, broncobuster, *South American.* gaucho; postilion, cavalier; cavalryman, dragoon, *Medieval Hist.* knight, trooper, cuirassier, lancer; Cossack, hussar, buzkashi player.

2. trainer, equerry, groom, stableboy, hostler, ostler.

horseplay, *n.* clowning, buffoonery, harlequinade, fooling, tomfoolery, monkeyshines, *Sl.* shenanigans, *Sl.* cutting up; capers, pranks, trickery, monkeytricks, monkey business, antics, practical jokes.

horse sense, *Informal.* practicality, judgment, soundness. See **common sense**.

horticulture, *n.* cultivation of gardens; olericulture, floriculture, arboriculture.

hosanna, *n.* shout of praise, hallelujah, allelujah; hurrah, huzzah, cheer, whoop; song of praise, paean, laud, laudation, glorification, exaltation.

hose, *n.* **1.** sock, stocking, tights, hosiery. See **hosiery**.

2. tube, tubing, *Med.* catheter, siphon; conduit, pipe, drain, outlet, channel.

hosiery, *n.* hose, stockings, nylons, tights, pantyhose, opaques, fishnets; socks, anklets, knee socks, kneehighs, over-the-calf hose, thigh-highs; leggings, gaiters, puttees, gambados.

hospitable, *adj.* friendly, neighborly, convivial, congenial, amicable, sociable; easy, open, approachable, receptive; welcoming, warm, warmhearted, kindhearted, kindly, kind, *Scot.* couthie, benignant; polite, cordial, courteous, gracious, genial, benign; agreeable, well-disposed, amenable; helpful, generous, openhanded, benevolent.

hospital, *n.* medical center, clinic, policlinic, infirmary, sick bay, dispensary; pesthouse, lazaretto; asylum, sanatorium, sanitarium, *Fr. hôtel-Dieu*; home, old folks' home, nursing home, convalescent home; rehabilitation center, halfway house; mental institution, insane asylum, madhouse, crazyhouse, *Sl.* nuthouse, *Sl.* bughouse, *Sl.* loonybin, *Sl.* funny farm; hospice, hospitium, retreat, refuge.

hospitality, *n.* friendliness, neighborliness, amicability, congeniality, *Ger. Gemütlichkeit,* conviviality, sociability; easiness, openness, approachability, receptiveness; welcomeness, warmth, warmheartedness, kindheartedness, kindliness, benignancy; graciousness, geniality, politeness, cordiality, courteousness; generosity, open-handedness, benevolence.

host[1], **1.** hostess, party-giver, party-thrower, inviter, treater; entertainer, emcee, M.C., master *or* mistress of ceremonies.

2. innkeeper, hotelkeeper, hotelman, boniface, hosteler, *Fr. hôtelier;* landlord, landlady, manager, proprietor, proprietress, proprietrix, master, mistress.

host[2], *n.* multitude, lot, crowd, throng, crush, mess, horde, mob, rabble; drove, bevy, herd, pack, flock, swarm, gaggle, school, shoal; army, legion, tribe, band, troop, company, group, body, assemblage, assembly, congregation, aggregation, array.

hostage, *n.* pawn, gage, prisoner; security, surety, leverage.

hostel, *n.* hostelry, hospice, youth hostel, youth hotel, caravansary, khan; inn, motor lodge, motel, hotel, tourist *or* guest home, pension, boarding house, lodging, lodgment, shelter, resting place.

hostile, *adj.* **1.** antagonistic, opposed, adverse, averse, contrary, oppugnant; anti, against, *Sl.* agin, down on; inimical, unfavorable, unpropitious, inauspicious.

2. aggressive, warlike, belligerent, bellicose; combative, contentious, militant, warring, fighting; bickering, quarreling, wrangling, clashing; discordant, fractious, factious.

3. unfriendly, unkind, unsympathetic, inhospitable, cold, unsociable; malicious, mean, ugly, malevolent.

hostility, *n.* **1.** antagonism, animus, ill will, ill feeling, grudge, spite, contempt; enmity, hatred, hate, dislike, disaffection, odium; malevolence, maliciousness, malice, meanness; bitterness, anger, wrath, dudgeon, rancor; rankling, bad blood, contumely.

2. unfriendliness, unkindness, unneighborliness, inhospitableness, unsociableness; inimicality, unfavorableness, unpropitiousness.

3. opposition, contraposition, contradiction, clash, antipathy, oppugnancy; resistance, unwillingness, contrariness, contrariety, recalcitrance.

4. hostilities war, warfare, fighting, conflict, militancy; contention, strife, aggression; state of war, state of siege; battles, sieges, raids, bloodshed, struggles, action.

hot, *adj.* **1.** heated, warm, calescent; fiery, piping hot, red hot; burning, flaming, blazing, scorching, roasting, searing; toasting, baking, ovenlike; scalding, boiling, sizzling, simmering, steaming; torrid, sultry, parching, sweltry, sweltering, blistering.

2. feverish, febrile, flushed, feverous, fevered, red; pyretic, hectic, *Med.* pyrexic, malarial, *Pathol.* calentural.

3. peppery, spicy, sharp, piquant, curried; pungent, biting, tart, strong, astringent, burning.

4. ardent, fervent, fervid, zealous, enthusiastic; vehement, passionate, impetuous, spirited; excited, animated, agitated, inflamed, impassioned, kindled; angry, furious, irate, enraged, infuriated; wrathful, splenetic, choleric, hot-tempered; seething, raging, fuming.

5. eager, avid, keen, assiduous, earnest, sedulous; anxious, intent, *Sl.* gung-ho, desirous; enterprising, industrious, hustling.

6. lustful, lascivious, salacious, lecherous, libidinous, lubricious, *Archaic.* lickerish; animalistic, bestial, carnal, sensual, voluptuous, goatish; prurient, wanton, concupiscent, ruttish; priapic, randy, *Sl.*

horny, sex-crazy, sex-crazed, sex-mad, sex-hungry.
7. violent, furious, vigorous, fierce, ferocious, savage; intense, forcible, strong, strenuous; stormy, tempestuous, turbulent, tumultuous; uproarious, boisterous, rampant.
8. new, fresh, recent, late, latest; brand-new, *Inf.* spanking new, just out, just released, just issued, *Inf.* hot off the griddle, *Inf.* hot off the presses.
9. popular, in demand, sought after, in vogue, well-liked, well-loved, in high esteem; successful, marketable, commercial, salable.
10. disposed, of the mind, given to, in the mood, *Inf.* up for; eager for, keen on, *Inf.* game for, *Sl.* psyched for, *Sl.* all hopped up about, *Sl.* all worked up about.
11. charged, live, electrified, powered, high-powered, galvanic, high-tension, low-tension.

hotbed, *n.* nest, cradle, nidus, nursery, womb; breeding ground, fertile soil, seedbed.

hot-blooded, *adj.* **1.** excitable, edgy, skittish, restless, restive, fitful; impetuous, impulsive, temperamental, quixotic.
2. adventuresome, exciting, venturesome, heady; adventurous, doughty, audacious, bold.
3. ardent, passionate, fiery, heated, impassioned; virile, lusty, vigorous, spirited; sensual, carnal, voluptuous, prurient; randy, priapic, *Sl.* horny, sex-hungry, sex-crazy, itching, *Scot. and North Eng.* cadgy.

hotel, *n.* inn, motel, motor inn, motor hotel, tavern, house, *It. albergo*; the Ritz, the Plaza, Grand Hotel; lodging, pension, rooming house, boarding house; resort hotel, hunting lodge, caravansary, caravanserai, khan; hostel, hospice; *Sl.* crash pad, *Sl.* flophouse, *Sl.* fleabag, *Sl.* dump.

hotheaded, *adj.* **1.** rash, impetuous, headlong, wild, foolhardy, precipitate, reckless; unruly, unbridled, ungovernable; hellbent, temerarious, breakneck, madcap, daredevil.
2. hot-tempered, quick to anger, *Sl.* short-fused, short-tempered, hot, quick; combustible, explosive, inflammable, volcanic.

hothouse, *n.* **1.** greenhouse, *Brit.* glasshouse, conservatory.
—adj. **2.** delicate, fragile, dainty, frail; feeble, weak, strengthless, unsturdy, brittle, breakable, perishable.
3. overprotected, protected, sheltered, shielded, smothered, defended; pampered, spoon-fed, indulged, spoiled, coddled; smothering, stultifying, oppressive, suppressive.
4. artificial, unnatural, man-made; imitation, simulated.

hound, *n.* **1.** hunting dog, *Southern U.S. Dial.* hound dog, bird dog, bloodhound, bird dog, harrier, beagle, pointer, setter, retriever, greyhound, staghound, foxhound, boarhound, Russian wolfhound; spaniel, terrier, dachshund, mastiff, police dog, sheep dog, St. Bernard, Newfoundland.
2. dog, canine, pup, puppy, whelp, bitch, *Inf.* bow-wow, *Inf.* pooch, cur, mongrel, *Inf.* mutt, pariah dog; house dog, watchdog, fancy dog, lap dog.
3. *Informal.* mean fellow, scoundrel, villain, *Inf.* rat; rogue, knave, cad, blackguard, *Inf.* scalawag, black sheep, *Brit. Sl.* rotter, miscreant, *Inf.* wrong 'un, rascal, roué, rake, debauchee, *Brit. Sl.* bounder.
4. *Informal.* devotee, addict, fanatic, extreme enthusiast, fan, infatuate, faddist, *Inf.* bug, *Inf.* nut.
—v. **5.** pursue, dog, follow, stalk, chase, trail, hunt, *Inf.* tail, heel, follow on the heels of, shadow, go after, fly after.
6. pursue unremittingly, persecute, bully, *Inf.* lean on; browbeat, *Inf.* bulldoze, *Inf.* buffalo, harass; nag, pester, annoy, tag after, keep after, hang on the skirts of, hang on the coattails of.
7. urge, urge on, *Inf.* egg on, incite, move, motivate, prompt, provoke to action; push, propel, impel, spur, prick, goad, prod, lash, whip, bring pressure to bear on, force.

hour, *n.* sixty minutes; the time, the time of day, the specific time, a particular time, an appointed time, time slot, customary *or* usual time, critical time.

house, *n.* **1.** dwelling, residence, home, abode, homestead, household; domicile, dwelling house, lodgings, quarters, *Chiefly Brit. Inf.* diggings *or* digs; mansion, castle, palace, manor house; villa, chateau, chalet, country seat, hall; hacienda, plantation, farmstead, grange; townhouse, condominium, suite, apartment house, apartment, *Inf.* pad, tenement, flat, *Chiefly Brit.* maisonette; inn, hotel, motel, hostelry, hospice; cabin, cottage, bower, log house, bungalow, hut, shanty, shack, lean-to, hovel.
2. household, home, family circle, domestic establishment, ménage, home roof, homestead; hearth, chimney corner, *Brit. Dial.* ingleside, *Chiefly Brit.* inglenook; fraternity, fraternity members.
3. family, family tree, lineage, kindred, ancestors; ancestry, derivation, extraction, pedigree, descent; blood, race, strain, stock, root, people; clan, *Rom. Hist., Anthropol.* gens, *Irish., Anthropol.* sept; nation, dynasty.
4. public building, theater, concert hall, auditorium; church, temple, synagogue.
5. congregation, audience, listeners, spectators, public, gathering, assembly.
6. legislative body, advisory *or* deliberative group, congress, council assembly, legislature, (*in Anglo-Saxon England*) gemot; lower chamber, Commons; (*of a legislative body*) quorum.
7. business firm, commercial establishment, company, stock, business, corporation; partnership, copartnership; shop, store; enterprise, undertaking.
—v. **8.** lodge, quarter, furnish with housing, enclose, board, put up, billet, bed, roof; dwell, reside, abide, remain, continue, live; room, bunk, tenant.
9. shelter, harbor, take in, befriend, care for, maintain, sustain, foster.
10. accommodate, contain, have room for, have capacity for, have space for.
11. remove from exposure, safeguard, secure, make fast, preserve; guard, shield, encase, sheathe; protect, look after, tend.

housebreaker, *n.* burglar, robber, thief; *Inf.* second-story man, *Sl.* cracksman, *Brit.* picklock, Raffles; sneak thief, cat burglar, prowler; stealer, purloiner, pilferer, filcher, *Inf.* crook, *Sl.* yegg *or* yeggman; criminal, gangster, felon.

household, *n.* **1.** family, family circle, domestic establishment, ménage, home roof, homestead; hearth, chimney corner, *Brit. Dial.* ingleside, *Chiefly Brit.* inglenook.
—adj. **2.** ordinary, usual, common, everyday, average, typical; regular, routine, ritual, repeated, established, standard, conventional; plain, run-of-the-mill, garden-variety; domestic, homespun, workaday.

householder, *n.* **1.** landowner, property owner, lord of the manor, landlord, landlady, master, mistress, host, hostess; proprietor, proprietress, innkeeper, hotel keeper.
2. family head, patriarch, matriarch, father, master, paterfamilias, elder.

housekeeper, *n.* housewife, matron, mistress, home economist; maid, chief maid, female servant, cleaning lady, *Inf.* help.

housewife, *n.* homemaker, hausfrau, housekeeper, home economist, family manager, *Sl.* chief cook and bottle washer; wife, mate, consort, *Inf.* better half.

housing, *n.* **1.** shelter, protection, covering; abode, dwelling, house, home, roof; domicile, lodgment, lodging, quarters, *Chiefly Brit. Inf.* diggings *or* digs; stopping place, stopover; accommodations, residence, habitation.
2. provision of housing, quartering, boarding, billeting, harboring, accommodation.
3. container, shield, box, case, cask, capsule; enclosure, encasement, jacket, wrapper, envelope, sheath.

hovel, *n.* **1.** hole, hole in the ground, dump, sty, pigsty, pigpen, tumbledown shack, wretched hut; hut, hutch, shack, shanty, *Brit.* bothy; cottage, cot, bungalow, bower, cabin, *Brit. Dial.* cote, *Scot.* but-and-ben.
2. shed, open shed, tool shed, work shed, crib; coop, chicken coop, cattle shed; pen, corral, enclosure.

hover, *v.* **1.** hang suspended, hang over, ride in the air, hang in the air; fly, be wafted, float.
2. wait nearby, linger near, stay near, stand guard, protect; impend, threaten, menace, loom.
3. waver, fluctuate, alternate, oscillate, vary, seesaw.

how, *adv.* **1.** (*used interrogatively*) in what way, in what manner, by what means, by virtue of what, by what, whereby; to what extent, to what degree; in what state, in what condition, in what shape.
2. (*used interrogatively*) why, for what reason, *Inf.* how come, for what, wherefore, for what purpose, on what account; to what effect, with what meaning, in what context, in what light, by what standard.
3. and how *Informal.* certainly, absolutely, positively, surely, of course, *Inf.* you bet, *Inf.* you're not kidding.
—conj. **4.** the manner, the method, the way, the way in which, the means, the mode.
5. in whatever manner, in whatever way, however.

however, *adv.* **1.** nevertheless, howbeit, anyway, anyhow, regardless, in spite of the fact, despite the fact, notwithstanding; no matter what, all *or* just the same, at any rate, in any case, in any event, at all events; but, still, yet, even so; on the other hand, at the same time; although, albeit, even if, even though.
2. howsoever, to whatever extent, to whatever degree; no matter how, anywise, in any way *or* respect, in any manner, by any means.
3. (*used interrogatively*) how, in what manner, in what way, by what means, how under the circumstances.
—conj. **4.** in whatever way *or* manner, in whatever state, in whatever condition.

howl, *v.* **1.** yowl, ululate, bark, bay; cry *or* cry out, wail, bawl; caterwaul, screech, shriek, scream; yell, shout, *Inf.* holler, bellow, roar.
2. *Informal.* laugh loudly, roar with laughter.
—n. **3.** howling, yowl, yowling, ululation, bark, barking, baying; cry, crying, wail, wailing, bawling; caterwauling, screech, screeching, shriek, shrieking, scream, screaming; yell, yelling, shout, shouting, *Inf.* holler, *Inf.* hollering, bellow, bellowing, roar, roaring.

hoyden, *n.* **1.** tomboy, romp, rowdy, termagant, *Inf.* roughneck, *U.S.* tough; whippersnapper, wench, hussy.
—adj. **2.** tomboyish, boyish, rough and tumble, rompish; boisterous, rambunctious, rowdy, unruly, wild; mischievous, troublesome, ill-behaved, hoydenish; unladylike, ill-bred, ill-mannered, ungenteel, rude; impudent, pert, saucy, fresh, cheeky, smart-alec, smart-alecky, minxish.

hub, *n.* **1.** nave, pivot, axis, *Biol.* centrosome.
2. center, center of activity, focal point, focus, point of convergence, middle; core, heart, navel, nucleus, backbone.

hubbub, *n.* uproar, din, brouhaha, clamor, blare, noise; racket, clatter, shivaree, charivari, *Northeastern U.S.* callithump; commotion, chaos, confusion, pandemonium, bedlam, upheaval, disorder; tumult, turmoil, turbulence, hullaballoo, *Inf.* bobbery; disturbance, agitation, stir, unrest, disquiet; excitement, pother, bustle, fuss, ado, *Inf.* to-do, *Inf.* foofarow, *Inf.* stew, *Sl.* hoo-ha, *Sl.* flap; melee, hurly-burly, fracas, rumpus, *Inf.* ruckus, *Inf.* shindy.

huckster, *n.* **1.** hawker, peddler, cheap-jack, vendor, salesman; pitchman, barker, spieler, concessionaire; traveling salesman, door-to-door salesman, Fuller Brush man, colporteur; merchant, dealer, sutler; bargainer, higgler, haggler.
2. miser, niggard, skinflint, *Sl.* skin, *Sl.* cheapskate, *Inf.* piker, muckworm, *Sl.* screw; penny pincher, pinchpenny, lickpenny, *Inf.* tightwad; cheeseparer, hoarder, save-all, *Scot.* carl; scrooge, Harpagon, money-grubber, harpy; curmudgeon, churl, hunks.

huddle, *v.* **1.** gather, cluster, bunch up, crowd, throng, herd, pack, cram *or* jam together, squeeze up *or* in *or* together; surge, swarm, stream; converge, flock together, concentrate, mass; throw *or* toss together, heap, amass.
2. *Often* **huddle up** curl up, crouch, nestle, snuggle, cuddle.
3. meet, confer, consult, discuss.
—n. **4.** group, crowd, throng, herd, pack; cluster, clump, bunch, mass, heap, imbroglio, pile, stack.
5. confusion, disorder, topsy-turvy, muddle, hugger-mugger, disarray; mess, tangle, jumble, jungle, wilderness.
6. meeting, conference, consultation, discussion.

hue[1], *n.* color, chroma, tint, tinge, tinct, tincture; tone, shade, cast; coloring, blush, flush.

hue[2], *n.* outcry, cry, whoop, hoot, call; yell, shout, bellow, howl, yowl; clamor, yammer, uproar, hurly-burly, hullabaloo, racket, commotion, Babel.

huff, *n.* **1.** temper, bad mood, ill humor, tiff, miff, snit, pet, fume, pique, *Inf.* stew, *Archaic.* pucker; burst *or* fit of anger, rage, passion.
—v. **2.** anger, incense, raise [s.o.'s] ire *or* hackles, get [s.o.'s] back up, *Inf.* burn [s.o.] up, *Sl.* tick *or* tee [s.o.] off; enrage, madden, infuriate, make [s.o.'s] blood boil, *Inf.* make [s.o.] see red; provoke, arouse, rouse, inflame, agitate.
3. vex, pique, annoy, irk, peeve, nettle, chafe, *Chiefly U.S.* rile, *Inf.* aggravate, *Inf.* miff, *Inf.* give [s.o.] a pain, *Inf* get under [s.o.'s] skin, *Sl.* bug; exasperate, ruffle, roil, put out, get, *Sl.* get [s.o.'s] goat.
4. bully, hector, heckle, badger, torment, harass, abuse, taunt, tease, bullyrag; intimidate, browbeat, cow, daunt, dismay; bluster at, storm at, rage at; ridicule, mock, jeer, gibe, disparage, slander; insult, affront, offend; snub, look down on; humiliate, mortify.
5. exhale, blow, puff.

huffish, *adj.* **1.** irritable, out of sorts, snappish, snappy, curt, short, impatient; touchy, testy, thin-skinned, waspish, peevish, petulant; cross, irascible, choleric, ill-tempered, ill-humored, splenetic; crabby, crabbed, cranky, grouchy, grumpy, cantankerous, crotchety, crusty; bitter, sour, caustic, churlish, surly.
2. swaggering, blustering, puffed up, haughty; proud, vain, arrogant, imperious; pompous, bombastic, high-flown, lofty; bold, brazen, brash, audacious, insolent, impudent, insulting, contumelious; contemptuous, disdainful, supercilious, scornful; bullying, hectoring, harassing, intimidating, browbeating,

cowing.

huffy, *adj.* **1.** irritable, touchy, cranky, huffish. See **huffish** (*def.* **1**).

2. hurt, injured, wounded, stung, offended; sulky, moping, sullen, glum, morose.

hug, *v.* **1.** embrace, take into one's arms, squeeze, clasp, press to one's bosom, embosom, enfold; hold in one's arms, caress, cuddle, snuggle, lie together, *Inf.* smooch, *Sl.* clinch; welcome, receive warmly, receive with open arms.

2. clutch, clench, cling to, hold onto, hold tight, hang onto; grasp, grip, gripe, fasten upon; cherish, love, be attached to, *Both Sl.* be hooked on, be stuck on; have confidence in, trust in, attach weight to, swear by.

3. keep close, stay near, follow closely, hover near, keep in sight of, shadow, go near.

—*n.* **4.** embrace, bear hug, squeeze, clasp, *Sl.* clinch; hold, grasp, grip, clutch.

huge, *adj.* **1.** gigantic, gargantuan, enormous, *Archaic.* enorm, huge, hugeous, large, big, bulky, immense, great, prodigious, herculean; substantial, considerable, sizeable; vast, massive, large-scale, mammoth, jumbo, colossal, monumental, monstrous, gigantean; cyclopean, titanic, Brobdingnagian; towering, staggering, mountainous, stupendous, tremendous, *Sl.* humongous; elephantine, hippopotamic, leviathan, dinosaurian; oversize, kingsize, overlarge; *All Inf.* whopping, roaring, spanking, walloping, strapping.

2. infinite, unlimited, unbounded, unrestricted, boundless, limitless; comprehensive, inclusive, all-inclusive; complete, exhaustive, thorough.

hugger-mugger, *n.* **1.** confusion, disorder, disarray, disorganization, disarrangement, derangement, confusedness; jumble, mess, *Inf.* stew, huddle, *Scot. Inf.* guddle, mix-up, *Inf.* foul-up, *Sl.* ballup; upheaval, anarchy, chaos, turmoil, tumult, pandemonium, bedlam, commotion.

2. secrecy, concealment, obscurity, privacy; hiding, covering, sheltering, ensconcing; disguising, camouflaging, screening, veiling; dissembling, cover-up.

—*adj.* **3.** secret, private, confidential, hush-hush, dark, closed, closed-door, closet; hidden, concealed, ensconced, shrouded, disguised, veiled, in the dark; mysterious, arcane, intriguing; covert, undercover, clandestine, feline, nighttime, back-alley.

4. disorderly, in disorder, confused, in disarray, disarranged, deranged, disorganized, jumbled, higgledy-piggledy; muddled, tangled, snarled, *Inf.* fouled-up, *Inf.* balled-up, bungled.

—*v.* **5.** keep secret, keep dark, keep it all in, keep quiet about, conceal; hush up, *Inf.* cover up, *Sl.* keep the lid on; dissemble, cloud, becloud, befog, screen, mask, cloak, veil, curtain, keep in the shade *or* dark.

hulk, *n.* **1.** derelict, ruin, skeleton, shell, wreck, shipwreck; tumbledown building, eyesore, debris.

2. oaf, lout, lubber, *Sl.* clumsy ox, *Inf.* bull in a china shop, *Sl.* klutz.

hulking, *adj.* unwieldly, cumbersome, cumbrous, awkward, gross, hulky, bulky; clumsy, ungainly, ungraceful, lubberly, lumpish; unmanageable, incommodious, difficult to handle, ill-proportioned; massive, ponderous, weighty, overgrown, towering; uncouth, loutish, graceless, inelegant.

hull, *n.* **1.** shell, rind, skin, peel, *Bot.* epicarp; shuck, cornhusk, legume, peasecod, peapod; husk, pod, case, capsule, theca, pericarp, *Bot.* testa, bur; cover, coat, crust.

2. body, framework, frame, skeleton; form, structure, casing.

—*v.* **3.** shuck, shell, husk, peel, strip, slip, skin, pare, trim.

hullabaloo, *n.* **1.** uproar, roar, noise, racket, din, outcry, clamor, clang, clangor, chorus, hue and cry, alarm; commotion, tumult, pandemonium, bedlam, *Inf.* sideshow, *Inf.* circus, *Inf.* three-ring circus, hubbub, babel, ado, to-do, stir, brouhaha; brawl, donnybrook, fracas, rumpus, ruckus, turmoil, embroilment, melee, scramble, *Inf.* bobbery.

2. promotion, *Inf.* ballyhoo, *Inf.* hype.

hum, *v.* **1.** drone, murmur, thrum, vibrate, throb, buzz, purr, whir, zoom; sing, croon, whisper.

2. move, stir, bustle, move briskly, scintillate, vibrate, pulse, pulsate, quiver, *Inf.* tick, *Inf.* jump.

—*n.* **3.** murmur, droning, drone, buzzing, buzz, zooming, zoom, whirring, whir, whizzing, whiz, purring, purr; susurration, vibration, throbbing.

human, *adj.* **1.** humane, kindly, sensitive, accessible, down-to-earth, earthy; vulnerable, flesh and blood, weak, defenseless, unguarded; faulty, errant, erring. See **humane.**

2. mortal, corporeal, transient, transitory, fleeting, passing, short-lived, fugacious; earthborn, physical, natural, temporal, perishable, ephemeral; bodily, carnal, corporal.

3. anthropoid, hominine; primate, biped, manlike.

—*n.* **4.** human being, mortal, person, man, woman, individual; fellow man *or* creature, member of the human race; soul, living soul, one, someone, somebody; everyman, John *or* Jane Doe; *Inf.* guy, *Inf.* gal, *Inf.* character.

humane, *adj.* good, kind, kindly, kindhearted, human, compassionate, sympathetic; pitying, forbearing, lenient, forgiving, merciful, clement, benignant, benign, gentle, tender; helpful, benevolent, magnanimous, generous, bounteous, beneficient, charitable, unselfish, big-hearted, large-hearted; warm-hearted warm, good-natured, amiable; gracious, accommodating, obliging.

humanist, *n.* classicist, classical scholar, student of the classics, man *or* woman of letters *or* learning, philologist, bibliophile, *Inf.* bookworm; philosopher, thinker, pundit, sage, scholiast.

humanitarian, *adj.* **1.** See **humane.**

—*n.* **2.** philanthropist, altruist, benefactor, good Samaritan, friend of man, friend to man, lover of mankind, almsgiver, almoner.

humanity, *n.* **1.** human race, people, humankind, mankind, race of man; the world *or* earth, the human community, society, public, folk; the masses, proletariat; man, human species, *Latin. Homo,* Homo sapiens.

2. human nature, humanness, mortality, flesh, flesh and blood, animal nature, sensuality.

3. kindness, goodness, kindheartedness, good-heartedness, benevolence, charity, sympathy, compassion, pity, ruth; good will, fellow feeling, kindliness, mercy, forbearance, tolerance, brotherhood; altruism, love for mankind, brotherly love, milk of human kindness, Christian charity; benignity, soft-heartedness, sensibility, tenderness, clemency, lenity, beneficence; big-heartedness, generosity, magnanimity, unselfishness, consideration; amiability, grace, good nature.

4. the humanities classics, classical studies, classical literature, classical languages; liberal arts, litterae humaniores, literature, philosophy, art.

humanize, *v.* soften, temper, ease, mellow; make humane *or* human; humble, subdue, dulcify, chasten, tame; melt, disarm, touch, reach, win over, *Sl.* get to.

humble, *adj.* **1.** modest, unpretentious, unpretending, unpresuming, free from pride, without arrogance, unostentatious, reserved, restrained.

2. meek, mild, submissive, obsequious, servile, subservient, subsidiary, slavish, broken in spirit, unambitious, unresisting; manageable, docile, acquiescent, obedient, adaptable, tractable, ductile, consentient; broken, resigned, subdued, sedate, tame.

3. unassuming, plain, common, commonplace, ordinary, humdrum; simple, poor, plebian, proletariat, earth-born, of low birth, low in rank, of low rank, low-ranking, unequal, inferior, baseborn, of low *or* mean parentage; homely, homespun, unrefined, vulgar, ill-bred, underbred, lowbred, uncouth, unfit, shabby, scruffy, scrubby; mean, low, ignoble, inglorious, base, infamous, ignominious, contemptible, sordid, despicable.

4. inconsequential, of little *or* small importance, insignificant, small, minute, little, obscure, undistinguished, trivial, paltry, petty, puny, trifling, peddling, piddling, *Inf.* measly, *Sl.* small potatoes, *Inf.* small time.

5. polite, respectful, gracious; deferential, obliging, complaisant, compliant, agreeable, biddable; hesitant, diffident, timid, timorous, shy, bashful, demure, meek-spirited.

6. godly, reverential; apologetic, regretful, remorseful, rueful, penitent, penitential, contrite, compunctious, expiatory, supplicatory; content, tolerant, enduring, stoic, stoical; clement, gentle, peaceful, peaceable, placid, passive.

—*v.* **7.** humiliate, mortify, bring down, *Inf.* take *or* bring down a notch *or* peg, *Sl.* put down, make [s.o.] eat humble pie, *Inf.* make [s.o.] eat crow, *Inf.* make [s.o.] eat his words, (*of oneself*) *Inf.* swallow one's pride, pull down, bring low, chasten, subdue; disgrace, shame, dishonor, put to shame; abase, debase, degrade, vitiate, lower, demote, downgrade.

8. demean, belittle, disparage, deprecate, depreciate, decry, deflate, derogate.

9. snub, rebuke, put in one's place, scorn, spurn, slap in the face, pin [s.o.] ears back, rebuff, reprove, chide, squelch; deny, deprive, repel, reject; overlook, neglect, *Inf.* cast into the shade, set aside, *Inf.* cold shoulder, disregard, omit, slight, (*of oneself*) *Inf.* take a back seat.

10. crush, break, destroy, defeat utterly, rout, discomfit, overwhelm, obliterate, smash, conquer, vanquish, bring to one's knees, tread *or* trample underfoot.

11. confuse, abash, perplex, bewilder, confound, nonplus, dumfound; disconcert, discompose, discountenance, put out of countenance; intimidate, daunt, cow, browbeat; embarrass, put to the blush.

12. slur, asperse, impute, libel, slander, defile, scandalize, smear, smirch, besmirch, stain, tarnish, brand, stigmatize.

humbled, *adj.* **1.** crushed, broken, destroyed, routed, discomfited, overwhelmed, obliterated, smashed, conquered, vanquished.

2. belittled, disparaged, deprecated, derogated, deflated, decried; reduced, lowered, depressed, devalued, depreciated.

3. humiliated, mortified, meekened, chastened, subdued, made to eat humble pie; shamed, disgraced, dishonored, reproached; discredited, disfavored, *Sl.* in the doghouse; debased, abased, degraded, vitiated.

4. insulted, affronted, abused, ill-treated, maltreated, slighted; outraged, scandalized.

5. slurred, aspersed, libeled, slandered, denigrated, defamed; smirched, besmirched, smeared, stained, tarnished, branded, stigmatized.

humbug, *n.* **1.** hoax, fraud, wile, ruse, sham, *Archaic.* chouse; deception, delusion, imposition, imposture, artifice, pretense, humbuggery; dissemblance, misrepresentation, falsehood, lie, fabrication, fiction, dodge, blind, feint, shift, *Inf.* song and dance, *Inf.* story; swindle, cheat, trickery, trick, confidence game, *Sl.* con game, *Inf.* flimflam, *Sl.* rip-off.

2. imposter, fake, fraud, empiric, charlatan, mountebank, humbugger, *Inf.* quack, *Inf.* phony, *Australian.* bunyip; pretender, feigner, malingerer, masquerade, deceiver, dissembler, inveigler, wolf in sheep's clothing; trickster, bamboozler, swindler, cheater, chiseler, bilker, diddler, sharpie, shark, fast talker, crook, confidence man, *Sl.* con man, *Sl.* flimflam man. See **cheat** (*def.* **1**).

3. flummery, trumpery, stuff, *Inf.* hokum, *Sl.* bull, *Sl.* applesauce, *Sl.* eyewash; nonsense, bumkum *or* buncombe, baloney, *Inf.* bosh, *U.S. Sl.* blah, *Sl.* bunk, *Brit. Inf.* gammon, *Brit. Sl.* tosh; rubbish, trash, hogwash, *Inf.* truck, *Inf.* rot, *Sl.* tripe, *Sl.* garbage, *Sl.* crap, *Sl.* crock, *Dial.* culch. See **nonsense** (*def.* **2**).

—*v.* **4.** delude, mislead, bamboozle, *Sl.* hornswoggle, pull the wool over [s.o.'s] eyes, take [s.o.] in, cully, cozen, bluff, *Inf.* buffalo; trick, hoodwink, dupe, gull, fool, chouse; feign, sham, malinger, pretend, dissemble, misrepresent; cheat, swindle, defraud, fleece, rook, bilk, take advantage of, *Inf.* diddle, *Inf.* do, *Inf.* finagle, *Sl.* burn. See **cheat** (*defs.* **3, 4**).

humdinger, *n. Slang. Inf.* beaut, *Sl.* lulu, *Sl.* lollapalooza, *Inf.* dilly, *Sl.* doozy, *Inf.* rip-snorter, *Sl.* corker, *Sl.* pip; *Sl.* something, *Sl.* something else *or* something else again, *Sl.* hot stuff, *Inf.* knockout, *Sl.* winner; *Sl.* daisy, *Inf.* dandy, *Inf.* honey, *Sl.* dream.

humdrum, *adj.* uneventful, monotonous, repetitious, routine, unvaried, undiversified, unvarying, unchanging, undeviating; dull, tedious, tiresome, boring, boresome, wearisome; prosaic, prosy, matter-of-fact, uninteresting, ho-hum, *Sl.* dead, dry, dry-as-dust, unexciting, uninspiring; mediocre, second-rate, half-baked, so-so, fair, fair to middling; *Inf.* O.K., all right, *Sl.* no big deal, *Sl.* no biggie, *Sl.* nothing great, *Inf.* nothing to write home about, *Sl.* nothing *or* nothing special; ordinary, run-of-the-mill, common, commonplace, everyday, household, familiar; banal, platitudinous, hackneyed, trite, stock, set; tasteless, bland, insipid, jejune, flat, vapid, *U.S. Sl.* blah, *Sl.* for the birds.

humid, *adj.* muggy, *Inf.* close, sticky, clammy, moist, damp; sultry, sweltering, sudorific, diaphoretic; steamy, dank, soggy, watery, wettish, dewy; foggy, vaporous, vaporific, misty, drizzly, dripping, rainy.

humidity, *n.* **1.** humidness, dampness, moisture, dew, damp, wetness, wateriness, sogginess; mugginess, sultriness, steaminess, dankness, clamminess; steam, mist, fog, vapor.

2. relative humidity, absolute humidity, dew point.

humiliate, *v.* humble, mortify, bring down. See **humble** (*defs.* **7-12**).

humiliated, *adj.* **1.** mortified, humbled, meekened, made to eat humble pie; shamed, disgraced, dishonored, reproached; discredited, disfavored, *Sl.* in the doghouse; debased, degraded, abased, vitiated.

2. belittled, disparaged, deprecated, derogated, deflated, decried; reduced, lowered, depressed, devalued, depreciated.

3. insulted, affronted, abused, ill-treated, maltreated, slighted; outraged, scandalized.

4. slurred, aspersed, libeled, slandered, denigrated, defamed; smirched, besmirched, smeared, stained, tarnished, branded, stigmatized.

5. crushed, broken, destroyed, routed, discomfited, overwhelmed, obliterated, smashed, conquered, vanquished.

humiliating, *adj.* **1.** mortifying, humbling; disgraceful, shameful, dishonorable, reproachable, *Obs.* reproachful; disreputable, discreditable, disfavorable.

2. belittling, derogatory, deprecatory, disparaging, depreciatory.

3. base, vile, odious, opprobrious, infamous, ignominious, scurrilous; degrading, demoralizing, abjective.

humiliation, *n.* **1.** mortification, humble pie, humbled pride; disgrace, shame, dishonor, reproach, disrepute, disreputation, ill repute, bad repute, discredit, disfavor, obloquy, loss of face; degradation, debasement, abasement, self-abasement, vitiation, downfall, fall, depression, reduction, depreciation, devaluation; belittlement, derogation, detraction, deprecation, deflation, disparagement, *Inf.* put-down.

2. odium, opprobrium, execration, infamy, ignominy; scurrility, scurrilousness.

3. humbling, mortifying, belittling; shaming, disgracing, dishonoring, putting to shame; crushing, breaking, smashing, overwhelming, vanquishing, conquering.

4. humbleness, humility, meekness, lowliness, abjection, submission, resignation.

5. indignity, insult, affront, slight, discourtesy, contumely; abuse, outrage, ill-treatment, maltreatment.

6. impeachment, indictment, renunciation, recrimination, reproof; slur, imputation, vilification, slander, libel, smear, smirch, blot, scandal, brand, stigma.

humility, *n.* **1.** humbleness, meekness, mildness; submissiveness, servility, subservience, obsequiousness, lowliness, lowliness of spirit *or* heart *or* mind, inferiority; obedience, subjection, resignation; self-abasement, abasement, mortification.

2. modesty, unpretentiousness, unpresumptuousness, unobtrusiveness, freedom from pride *or* arrogance, reserve, restraint.

3. timidity, timorousness, diffidence, meekness of heart *or* mind *or* spirit, confusion, hesitation; shyness, bashfulness, demureness.

4. godliness, reverence; penitence, supplication, contrition; contentment, tolerance, forbearance, endurance, stoicism, clemency; gentleness, peacefulness, peaceableness, passiveness, placidity.

hummock, *n.* hammock, hillock, knoll, rise, hump, mogul, bump; mound, elevation, *Brit.* barrow. See **hillock**.

humor, *n.* **1.** comedy, funniness, facetiousness, drollery; wit, ready wit, wittiness, Attic wit, dry wit; gallows humor, black comedy; jocularity, waggishness, banter, raillery; badinage, persiflage, repartee, quip, wisecrack, sarcasm; irony, satire, burlesque, parody, caricature, travesty, ridicule; witticism, bon mot, gag, pleasantry, jest, jocosity, joke; *Sl.* chestnut, *Sl.* bromide, wheeze, Joe Millerism; pun, wordplay, play on words, spoonerism, malapropism; amphigory, nonsense, nonsense rhyme, doggerel, limerick; merriness, playfulness, good spirits, *Inf.* laughs; ridiculousness, ludicrousness; *Sl.* shenanigans, buffoonery, tomfoolery, horseplay; trick, prank, practical joke.

2. temper, mood, frame of mind; vein, spirit, heart, soul; temperament, disposition, nature, character, attitude; tendency, bent, inclination, leaning, propensity; stripe, cast, mold, set of one's jib.

3. whim, caprice, fancy, whimsy; fickleness, mercuriality, erraticism; quirk, crotchet, vagary, freak, kink; idiosyncrasy, characteristic, peculiarity, eccentricity, oddness, queerness; bee in one's bonnet, mania, monomania, obsession, fixation, *Fr. idée fixe*, fascination.

—*v.* **4.** soothe, placate, appease, mollify, satisfy, gratify; please, content, gladden, delight, amuse, tickle; indulge, pamper, spoil, cosset, coddle, mollycoddle, baby.

5. adapt, accommodate, stretch a point, make excuses for, make provision for; give in, concede, yield, acquiesce, oblige, relent; permit, tolerate, suffer, allow.

humorist, *n.* comedy writer, *Inf.* gag writer, cartoonist, caricaturist, lampoonist, parodist; jokester, joker, comic, comedian, comedienne, *Inf.* standup comic, clown, slapstick artist; harlequin, punch, punchinello, scaramouche, fool, jester; droll fellow, funny person, banterer, *Inf.* wisecracker, punster; cutup, zany, madcap, antic; *Fr. farceur*, mummer, mime, mimic.

humorous, *adj.* **1.** funny, comic, laughable, ridiculous, farcical, ludicrous, absurd; rib-tickling, side-splitting, screamingly funny; witty, clever, sharp, sarcastic, ironical, satirical.

2. droll, facetious, jocose, jocular, jovial, jolly, merry; lively, amusing, *Inf.* cute, waggish, devilish, roguish, prankish, arch, mischievous; sportive, playful.

hump, *n.* **1.** protuberance, prominence, (*of a bone*) tuberosity, projection, protrusion, bulge, convexity, hunch; nodule, node, knob, mass, lump, bump; swelling, swell, intumescence, tumefaction, dilation, enlarging.

2. hummock, hillock, knoll, monticle. See **hillock**.

3. **over the hump** out of the woods, over the worst of it, in the clear; safe, secure, on the way up, on the road to recovery.

—*v.* **4.** hunch, arch. See **hunch** (*def.* **1**).

humpback, *n.* See **hunchback**.

humpbacked, *adj.* See **hunchbacked**.

humus, *n.* soil, earth, dirt, ground, sod, clod, *Archaic.* glebe; loam, clay, marl, mold, dust, gumbo, till, adobe.

hunch, *v.* **1.** thrust out, arch, vault, curve, hump, crook; incurve, turn, curl, flex, bend, embow; bunch up, curl up, tuck, fold up.

2. shove, push, jostle, elbow, shoulder; poke, jog, press, plunge, nudge; bump, buffet, jounce; squeeze, wedge, slice, *Chiefly Dial.* scrouge; push through, drive through, bulldoze, ram, butt.

3. lunge forward, thrust, foin, pass, cut, cut and thrust; rush, charge, propel.

4. stoop, crouch, *Dial.* scrooch, *Dial.* scrouch; bend, squat, cringe; get down, hunker.

—*n.* **5.** lump, hump, protuberance, gibbosity. See **hump** (*def.* **1**).

6. push, shove, jog, jolt, jostle; thrust, blow, buffet; nudge, poke, stroke, joggle; butt, bunt, boost; propulsion, impulsion, impulse.

hunchback, *n.* **1.** humpback, crookback, camel back, *Med.* kyphosis, Quasimodo, *Fr. bossu.*

2. crooked back, bunchback, round shoulders, stoop shoulders, *Vet. Pathol.* sway-back, *Pathol.* scoliosis, gibbosity, stoop, hump; deformation, malformation, misshape.

hunchbacked, *adj.* humpbacked, bunchbacked, crookbacked, camel-back, hunchedback, crookedback, *Pathol.* scoliotic; humped, stooped, *Med.* kyphotic, gibbous, stoop-shouldered; misshapen, deformed, malformed, misbegotten.

hundred, *n.* **1.** centum, *Welsh.* centef, 100, C; century, centennial, centenary, centennium.

2. *U.S. Informal.* one hundred dollars, hundred-dollar bill, *Sl.* C-note, *Sl.* C, *Sl.* one bill, *Sl.* century.

3. *Brit. Informal.* one hundred pounds.

hunger, *n.* **1.** hungriness, appetite, appetition, appetence, stomach, taste; tapeworm, *Pathol.* bulimia, canine appetite, *Inf.* sweet tooth; ravenousness, edacity, voraciousness.

2. craving, thirst, coveting, want; yearning, longing, pining, desire, yen, *Inf.* hankering; urge, mania, cacoethes.
—*v.* **3.** be hungry, feel hunger, have a good appetite, crave food, *Inf.* starve, be ravenous, *Inf.* lick one's chops.
4. want, long for, pine for, yearn for, *Inf.* hanker for, have a yen for; itch for, ache for, be hurting for, be dying for, burn for, die for; covet, crave, thirst after, lust after, pant after, desire, gasp for.

hungry, *adj.* **1.** starving, famishing, craving, esurient, appetitive; hungering, ravening, ravenous, sharp-set; famished, starved, peckish; half-starved, half-famished, hungry as a bear, growling.
2. desirous, wishful, wistful, longing, yearning, pining; solicitous, desiderative, needing, wanting; covetous, greedy, avaricious, voracious, rapacious; devouring, gobbling, grasping; eager, hungering, *Inf.* hankering; keen on, bent on, set on, itching to, aching to, dying to, fain to, *Inf.* spoiling for; desiring, libidinous, lusting, lustful.
3. poor, barren, sterile, *Bot.* acarpous, fallow; spare, lean, thin, slight, meager, jejune; depleted, unproductive, unfertile, fruitless; underfed, undernourished, stinted, malnourished, starved; worn, wasted, emaciated, gaunt, hollow, wizened.

hunk, *n.* **1.** *Informal.* chunk, large piece, block, square; portion, serving, share, *Inf.* whack, part; cut, slice, wedge, chop, slab, rasher, *Brit. Dial.* collop; mass, lump, clump, clod; mound, *Inf.* gob, dollop, blob.
2. Adonis, god; he-man, *Inf.* bruiser, muscle-man.

hunt, *v.* **1.** chase, give chase, run down *or* after, make after, pursue, course, *Brit.* chevy, (*in India*) shikar, follow close *or* hot on one's heels; hound, dog, hawk, pigstick; stalk, still-hunt, track, trail, follow, shadow, haunt, *Inf.* tail; track down, hunt down, trace down, search out, seek out; ferret out, drive out, chase out, put to flight.
2. *Often* **hunt up** *or* **out** search *or* search for, quest for, go in search *or* quest for, treasure-hunt, look for, seek *or* seek for; dig for, dive for, fish *or* fish for, try to find, forage for, scrounge around, rummage through; ransack, go through, take apart, dismantle, turn everything upside down *or* inside out; leave no stone unturned, search thoroughly, rake, scour, look high and low, look all over *or* everywhere; explore, delve into, investigate, study, research, *Inf.* check out, examine, go over with a fine-tooth comb; ask around, query, question, inquire into, look into, pry into; search out, nose out, sniff out, find out.
—*n.* **3.** pursuit, chase, chasing, hunting, sport, sporting, course, coursing, (*in India*) shikan, *Brit.* chevy, *Archaic.* venery; hawking, falconry, *Chiefly Brit.* beagling, fox hunting; stalking, still hunt, tracking *or* tracking down, hunting down; pursuing, following, trailing, *Inf.* tailing.
4. search, forage, rummage, ransacking; quest, treasure hunt, exploration, look, *Sl.* look-see; inquiry, investigation, study, research.

hunter, *n.* **1.** huntsman, huntress, gunner, chaser, courser, *Fr. chasseur,* (*in India*) shikari, sportsman; pursuer, stalker, tracker; deer-stalker, fox hunter, hawker, falconer, pig-sticker.
2. seeker, searcher, quester, treasure hunter, explorer.
3. hunting horse, stalking-horse, hunting mount; hunting dog, hound, *Southern U.S. Dial.* hound dog; foxhound, retriever, deerhound.

hunting, *n.* pursuing, chasing, sporting, coursing. See **hunt** (*def.* **3**).

huntsman, *n.* hunter, gunner, chaser, courser. See **hunter** (*def.* **1**).

hurdle, *n.* **1.** obstacle, impediment, handicap, hindrance, obstruction, barrier, bar, check; difficulty, stumbling block, snag; interference, interruption, counteraction, setback; barricade, barricado, blockade, block, stopper, stoppage.
2. fence, picket fence, railing, rail, paling, boarding, balustrade, palisade; wall, rampart, circumvallation, lattice, latticework; hedge, hedgerow.
—*v.* **3.** leap over, jump over, clear, negotiate, vault.
4. master, overcome, surmount, prevail; weather, survive.

hurl, *v.* **1.** cast, throw, toss, dart, shy, chuck, pitch; dash, sling, let fly, send, launch; fling, flirt, heave, jerk, cant, shoot, fire; propel, project, jaculate, catapult.
2. lash out, fling out, fulminate, explode, blast, bellow, blare, thunder forth.
—*n.* **3.** throw, toss, pitch, fling, cast.

hurly-burly, *n.* commotion, tumult, turmoil, turbulence, storm and stress; pandemonium, bedlam; uproar, racket, hubbub, brouhaha; disorder, chaos, confusion, upheaval; disquiet, unrest, disturbance, distraction, excitement, furor, agitation, disruption, perturbation, *Sl.* flap; bother, pother, trouble, fuss, fuss and feathers, *Inf.* to-do, *Inf.* foofaraw, *Inf.* stew, *Inf.* tizzy, *Sl.* lather.

hurrah, *interj.* **1.** hurray, hallelujah, huzzah, rah, yippee, yippee-yi-o, hot diggetty, hot dog, hot snaps; three cheers, hip hip hooray, hip hip hurrah; boola boola, brackety-ax-co-ax-co-ax, oo-sa-sa; how to go, that's showin' 'em, way to go, hail hail, bravo; *Japanese. banzai, It. viva, Fr. vive, Ger. hoch;* hosanna, praise the Lord, glory be, glory be to God, glory to God, *Islam.* hamd'Allah.
2. interjection, exclamation, ejaculation, yell, cheer; exultance, exultation, elation, exuberance; hubbub, commotion, fanfare.

hurricane, *n.* **1.** typhoon, tropical cyclone, cyclone, extratropical cyclone, *Philippines.* baguio, *Central America.* cordonazo, *Australia.* willy-willy; tempest, storm, gale, blast, blow, big blow; tornado, twister, whirlwind, squall, williwaw, chinook, foehn; wind, heavy winds, levanter, monsoon; blizzard, northeaster, nor'easter, north wind, Arctic blasts, tramontana, mistral; duststorm, duster, sandstorm, windstorm, khamsin, harmattan, simoom, samiel, sirocco.
2. outburst, explosion, uproar, commotion, maelstrom; wild time, howl, roaring good time; violence, vehemence.

hurried, *adj.* **1.** rushed, driven, pressed for time; expeditious, urgent, pressing; hustling, bustling, fluttering, darting, scurrying, scuttling; feverish, frantic, frenetic, hectic.
2. hasty, cursory, superficial, shallow, perfunctory, passing, offhand; slapdash, lax, loose, slack; rash, reckless, careless, heedless, thoughtless; precipitate, headlong, breakneck.

hurry, *v.* **1.** move quickly, hasten, lose no time, rush, make haste, *Scot.* swith, *Scot.* whirry, *Literary.* haste; race, scurry, skip, spurt, whisk, run, sprint; press on, push on, ride hard, canter, trot, gallop, lope, clap spurs to one's horse; shoot, tear, fly, fly on the wings of the wind, outstrip the wind, wing one's way, take wing, take to flight; scour, hustle, bustle, scamper, scuttle, trip, flit; flee, hotfoot, hotfoot it, hightail, hightail it, *Inf.* skedaddle, be on the run, beat a retreat; whip off, whip away, dash off, run like mad, *Sl.* get cracking, *Sl.* get one's rear in gear, *Sl.* shake a leg, *Sl.* go like a bat out of hell, go *or* run wide open, go all out, go at full blast, *Inf.* go like a shot, *Sl.* go hellbent for leather, *Inf.* go like greased lightning; hustle, speed up, put on more speed, step on the gas, *Sl.* step on it, *Sl.* burn up the road, cover ground; bound, spring, jump, make strides, do some tall stepping, bowl along, hie one's way, *Inf.* make it snappy, look alive.

2. accelerate, quicken, hasten, push forward, advance, precipitate; stimulate, arouse, rouse, vivify, animate, bestir, instigate, motivate, inspire, exhort, excite, provoke, incite; press, prod, shove, jog, move, drive on, urge on, egg on, hound on, goad, whip, flog, prick; boost, prompt, thrust, impel, propel, give an impetus to; dispatch, send away quickly, send off summarily, lend wings to; expedite, facilitate, aid, assist, help set on one's legs, put on one's feet.

—n. **3.** haste, rush, precipitation; confusion, agitation, disquietude, perturbation, fidgetiness, dither, jitters, *Inf.* stew, *Inf.* sweat, *Inf.* cold sweat; flurry, flutter, fuss, furor, ruffle, turmoil, commotion; stir, whirl, pother, *Dial.* feeze, ferment; scurry, scampering, dash; harum-scarum, hurry-scurry, pell-mell, helter-skelter, bustle, ado, hubbub; impatience, eagerness, anxiety, urgency.

4. velocity, speed, rapidity, dispatch, celerity, quickness, expedition, promptitude, hastiness.

hurry-scurry, *n.* **1.** haste, rush, precipitation; confusion, disorder; agitation, perturbation, disquietude, fidgetiness, dither, jitters, *Inf.* stew, *Inf.* sweat, *Inf.* cold sweat; flurry, flutter, fuss, furor, ruffle, turmoil, commotion; stir, whirl, pother, *Dial.* feeze, ferment; scurry, scampering, scramble, dash; hubbub, ado, hurly-burly, *Archaic.* harum-scarum, pell-mell, helter-skelter; rumpus, racket, ruckus, melee, pandemonium.

—adv. **2.** hurriedly, hastily, precipitately; confusedly, disorderedly; headlong, harum-scarum, helter-skelter, pell-mell, head over heels, holus-bolus, *Inf.* slam-bang; rashly, carelessly, heedlessly, recklessly, riotously, tumultuously, turbulently, agitatedly.

—adj. **3.** hurried, hasty, rushed, precipitate; confused, disorderly, chaotic, bustling, scrambling; holus-bolus, hugger-mugger, hurly-burly, harum-scarum, helter-skelter, pell-mell, head over heels; rash, careless, heedless, reckless, riotous, tumultuous, turbulent, agitated.

—v. **4.** rush *or* go hurry-scurry. See **hurry** (*def.* **1**).

hurt, *v.* **1.** ache, smart, burn, sting, bite, nip, pinch, gripe; gnaw, grind, grate, rasp, chafe; throb, palpitate, tingle.

2. injure, wound; cut, scratch, prick, pierce, stab, lancinate; bruise, sprain, strain; beat, pommel, batter, pound, lay on, drub; cudgel, club, bludgeon, hammer, blackjack, baste, *Inf.* lambaste, bastinado; sandbag, buffet, box, punch; strike, smite, hit.

3. whip, thrash, *Inf.* lace, flog, flail, flagellate; strap, belt, cane, birch; spank, *Archaic.* swinge, trounce; chastise, punish.

4. abuse, maltreat, ill-treat, ill-use, misuse, do violence to; manhandle, maul, mangle, mutilate, *Sl.* lay into, maim, scar; lame, cripple, becripple, hamstring; disable, incapacitate, debilitate.

5. pain, torment, anguish, agonize, torture, rack, excruciate; aggrieve, grieve, sorrow, sadden, despond, dishearten, depress; scathe, cut to the quick, cut to the heart, wound the feelings; insult, affront, give offense, give umbrage; snap at, assail, bite the hand that feeds one.

6. harrow, distress, discommode, afflict; faze, shake, unstring, discompose.

7. spoil, harm, impair, disqualify, unfit; mar, damage, vitiate, *Law.* damnify; blemish, blight, blunt, dull, crack, craze; break, break up, break apart, fragmentize, burst; smash, smash to smithereens, shatter; devastate, lay waste, make waste, desolate; pillage, ravage, despoil.

8. corrupt, subvert, canker; debase, pervert, warp, prostitute, degrade; defile, deflower, contaminate, taint, pollute, infect; alloy, adulterate, tamper with, doctor; weaken, enfeeble, *Archaic.* extenuate, debilitate, devitalize, exhaust, sap, sap the strength of, spend.

—n. **9.** pain, soreness, ache, aching, discomfort, malaise; throb, throbbing, twinge, pinch; sting, gripe, nip, pang, shock, crick, stitch; sore, scratch, cut, laceration; malady, illness, disease; wound, trauma, blow, shock.

10. injury, harm, impairment, vitiation, damage, scathe; abuse, misuse, ill-usage, maltreatment, ill treatment; oppression, cruelty, brutality, persecution, molestation; evil, wrong, bad, badness; foul play, bad turn, ill turn, ill service, disservice.

11. torture, torment, agony; misery, woe, *Archaic.* bale, dolor, anguish, affliction; distress, trouble, bother, botherment, pother.

12. block, impediment, reversal, setback, comedown, detriment, loss; plight, strait, predicament, sea of troubles; ordeal, trial, tribulation, infliction; burden, cross, crown of thorns, load, bitter pill; cares, pressure, stress, strain; adversity, accident, mishap; bad fortune, bad luck, bad times, hard times, evil days; malediction, bane, curse, anathema.

13. destruction, breakage, breaking; devastation, laying waste, desolation, labefaction.

14. corruption, subversion, adulteration, perversion; defilement, pollution, contamination; canker, blight, cancer, blast, plague, infestation.

—adj. **15.** injured, wounded; aching, bruised, pierced, stung, griped, stabbed, pricked, chafed, galled, burnt; tortured, tormented, agonized, excruciated.

16. aggrieved, grieved, pained, suffering, sorrowful, sad, rueful, mournful; heartsick, heartbroken, brokenhearted, heart-stricken, heavy-hearted, heavy-laden; weary, careworn, dejected, cheerless, comfortless; woeful, woebegone, wretched, gloomy, dismal, morose; melancholy, unhappy, infelicitous.

17. chagrined, embarrassed, ashamed, shamed; sorry, regretful, regretting, remorseful, repentent.

18. shocked, appalled, horrified; offended, annoyed, displeased, piqued, miffed; resentful, resenting, bitter, rancorous, virulent.

19. unwell, indisposed, ailing, unsound, diseased; feeble, enfeebled, unsteady, lame, crippled; fading, declining, deteriorating, deteriorated.

20. damaged, impaired, broken, out of repair, in disrepair, *Sl.* out of whack; worn, dilapidated, ruined, wasted, *Sl.* totaled.

hurtful, *adj.* **1.** injurious, harmful, detrimental, inimical, deleterious, damaging, endamaging, mischievous; destructive, baneful, pernicious, noisome, noxious, disastrous, ruinous.

2. impairing, marring, spoiling, blighting, wounding, vitiating, undermining; bursting, breaking, shattering, cracking, defacing, scarring; laming, crippling, becrippling, maiming, mangling, mutilating.

3. corrupting, subverting, contaminating, polluting, tainting; infecting, defiling, perverting, prostituting; sapping, weakening, deteriorating, degenerating, crumbling.

hurtle, *v.* **1.** rush, rush headlong, cascade, plunge, tumble; tear, *Inf.* go hellbent for leather, *Inf.* go lickety-split, stir up a duststorm; scramble, *Inf.* make tracks, *Inf.* zip, steam, *Inf.* beat feet, scurry, hustle; hie, hasten, go in haste, hurry, accelerate, put one's foot on the floor.

2. precipitate, propel, impel; fling, hurl, heave, pitch, cast, dash; thrust, push, *Inf.* gun.

—n. **3.** clash, collision, smash-up; clatter, rattle, banging.

husband, *n.* **1.** married man, benedict, groom, bridegroom, common-law husband; spouse, mate, consort, *Inf.* the other half; *Inf.* old man, *Inf.* hubby, *Inf.* dad, *Inf.* bed warmer, *Inf.* roommate; lord and master, head of the house *or* household, ruler of the roost, breadwinner.
2. manager, overseer, conservator, custodian.
—*v.* **3.** conserve, preserve, save, put by, save for a rainy day, economize, count the pennies; retain, reserve, put aside, store, stow, garner, hoard; manage, oversee, maintain, watch over.

husbandry, *n.* **1.** farming, agriculture, agronomy, agronomics, farm management, agribusiness, geoponics; tillage, tilth, tilling; cultivation, horticulture, gardening, olericulture, viticulture, forestry, silviculture.
2. frugality, thrift, thriftiness, careful management, good housekeeping, conservation; economy, economizing, conserving, saving; sparingness, frugalness.

hush, *interj.* **1.** silence, be *or* keep quiet, quiet down, be *or* keep still, shush, sh, not another word, hold your tongue, *Inf.* shut up, *Inf.* shut your mouth, *Inf.* pipe down, *Inf.* clam up, *Sl.* shut your face, *Sl.* stow it, *Sl.* can it, *Sl.* button your lip, *Sl.* put the lid on it.
—*v.* **2.** fall silent, quiet, quiet down, *Chiefly Brit.* quieten, *Inf.* pipe down, *Archaic.* whist.
3. silence, shush, still, soft-pedal; mute, muzzle, stifle, gag, *Inf.* put the lid on, *Sl.* put the kibosh on.
4. *Usu.* **hush up** suppress, smother, squash, quash, squelch, *Fig.* kill, keep secret *or* dark, *Inf.* cover up.
5. calm, calm down, mollify, dulcify, tranquilize, lull, relax, soothe, compose; allay, assuage, placate, pacify, appease.
—*n.* **6.** quiet, quietness, silence, soundlessness, still, stillness, lull, rest, *Chiefly Irish.* whist.

hush money, *n.* bribe, boodle, sop, payoff, *Inf.* payola, *Sl.* palm oil, *Sl.* grease, *Sl.* soap; extortion, blackmail; protection.

husk, *n.* **1.** hull, shell, covering, coating, coat, tegument, integument, capsule, pod, case, pericarp; chaff, bran, scale, bract, shuck, *Bot.* glume, *Bot.* lemma, *Bot.* tegman.
2. rind, skin, peel, peeling, paring; cornhusk, husk, legume, peapod, peascod.

husky, *adj.* **1.** brawny, beefy, strapping, sturdy, well-built; burly, stout, thickset, heavyset, stocky; muscular, hefty, able-bodied, rugged, athletic, solid; hardy, manly, virile, tough, powerful, strong, big and strong.
2. hoarse, coarse, gruff, rough, roupy, dry; throaty, thick, guttural.

hussy, *n.* **1.** vamp, seductress, temptress, *Fr. femme fatale,* Jezebel, Delilah; demimondaine, loose woman, strumpet, trollop, wench, jade, baggage, *Sl.* chippy, *Sl.* broad, *Sl.* piece, *Chiefly Brit. Sl.* tart.
2. malapert, minx, queen, brazenface, boldface, *Inf.* saucebox.

hustle, *v.* **1.** hurry, rush, make time, make haste, move in double time, go like a bat out of hell, move along at a good clip; run, dash, sprint, dart, zip, bolt, make tracks; fly, whiz, whisk, breeze, go like the wind; scramble, scamper, scurry, scoot, scuttle; bustle, stir, fuss, flutter, flit, commove, *U.S. Inf.* rustle.
2. shove, buffet, push, press forward; jostle, justle, jolt, jar, jounce, jog, joggle; bump, elbow, shoulder, poke, nudge, butt, bunt.
3. prompt, urge, goad, drive, propel, egg on, induce, motivate; prod, prick, spur, whip, lash; energize, animate, actuate; accelerate, expedite, hasten, speed up, spurt, step up, *Sl.* step on it, *Sl.* pour it on, *Archaic.* dispatch.
4. pressure, compel, impel, force, coerce, give [s.o.] a hard sell, *Inf.* put the squeeze on; harass, hound, badger, pester, nag.
—*n.* **5.** activity, action, doings, busyness, stir, motion, movement; dispatch, expeditiousness, briskness, robustness, alacrity, celerity, fleetness, rapidity, swiftness, speediness, quickness; rushing, hurrying, scurry, hurry-scurry, haste; fuss, flurry, flutter, pother, ado, *Inf.* to-do, *Sometimes Facetious.* do; splutter, agitation, restlessness, commotion, tumult, hurly-burly, hubbub.
6. shoving, buffeting, pushing, pressing forward; jolting, jouncing, jarring, jostling, justling, jogging, joggling; bumping, shouldering, elbowing, poking, nudging.

hustler, *n.* **1.** *Informal.* go-getter, dynamo, demon, pusher, hard worker, man of action, doer, powerhouse, *Inf.* eager-beaver, *Inf.* live wire, *Inf.* busy bee, *Inf.* fire-ball, *Inf.* ball of fire, *Inf.* crackerjack, *Inf.* human dynamo; workaholic, workhorse.
2. *Slang.* swindler, cheat, defrauder, flimflam man, *Inf.* bilker, *Sl.* chiseler; sharp, sharper, shark, confidence man, *Inf.* con man *or* artist, *Inf.* bunco artist.
3. *Slang.* prostitute, streetwalker, call girl, *Sl.* hooker.
4. speeder, flier, racer, runner; *All Inf.* hummer, scorcher, hell-driver, speed demon, speed merchant.

hut, *n.* **1.** shed, shack, shanty, hutch, *Brit.* bothy; cottage, cot, bungalow, bower, cabin, log cabin, blockhouse, *Brit. Dial.* cote, *Scot.* but-and-ben; hole, hovel, dump, sty, pigsty, pigpen, tumbledown shack, wretched hut, mean dwelling.
—*v.* **2.** quarter, provide quarters for, bed, bunk, berth; house, shelter, give shelter to, lodge, provide lodging *or* lodgings *or* lodgment for, put up, have as a guest *or* lodger, roof, provide with a roof.
3. lodge oneself, take refuge, seek protection, take cover.

hutch, *n.* **1.** pen, animal pen, coop, enclosed coop, fold, confine, cage; compound, farmyard, barnyard, stockade, corral, paddock, pound, dog pound, kennel; sty, pigsty, pigpen, chicken yard, chicken coop, sheep fold.
2. hut, cabin, cottage, cot, hogan, wigwam, wickiup, teepee, igloo, adobe, sod house, bunkhouse; lean-to, shed, booth, stall, shack, shanty.
3. box, caddie, casket, cellaret; chest, cupboard, cabinet; crate, storage bin, depository, coffer, crypt, vault, locker, safe.

huzzah, *interj.* hurrah, hurray, rah. See **hurrah** (*defs.* **1, 2**).

hyaline, *adj.* glassy, glasslike, made of glass; clear, clear-as-glass, crystalline, crystal-clear, hyalescent; transparent, translucent, lucid, vitrious, vitreal, vitrean; diaphanous, diaphane, sheer, gauzy, gossamer, gossamery.

hybrid, *n.* **1.** crossbreed, mixed breed, mongrel; half-breed, half-blood, *Sp. mestizo,* mulatto, quadroon, quintroon, octoroon, *Inf.* high yellow, Eurasian; mule, degenerate breed, deteriorated breed.
2. mix, mixture, conglomerate, composite, compound, combination, *Inf.* combo; miscellany, *Fr. mélange,* medley, mess, *Inf.* mix; hash, hodgepodge, jumble, patchwork, potpourri, Noah's ark.
—*adj.* **3.** mutated, modified, altered, changed, metamorphosed, transmuted; varied, merged, combined, married.
4. variegated, heterogeneous, intermingled, commingled; impure, contaminated, alloyed, bastard, degenerate, derivative; mongrel, half-blooded, half-bred, half-breed, half-caste, half-and-half.

hydraulics, *n.* hydrodynamics, hydromechanics, hydrostatics, hydrokinetics, fluviology.

hydrous, *adj.* watery, containing water, aqueous, aquatic, lymphatic, balneal; wet, moist, hydrated, liquid; juicy, succulent, sappy.

hygiene, *n.* **1.** hygienics, sanitation, disinfection, sanitary measures, *Med.* regimen, regime, preventive medicine, public health.
2. cleanliness, cleansing, washing, bathing, douching; oral hygiene, tooth brushing, tooth cleaning, flossing.

hygienic, *adj.* sanitary, clean, cleanly; disinfected, sterile, germ-free, aseptic; harmless, uninjurious, innoxious, pure, unpolluted; wholesome, salubrious.

hymeneal, *adj.* **1.** nuptial, bridal, wedding, epithalmic; matrimonial, marriage, marital, married, wedded, connubial; conjugal, spousal, husbandly, wifely.
—n. **2.** wedding march *or* song, epithalmion, epithalmium.

hymn, *n.* **1.** psalm, paean, alleluia, hallelujah, gloria, doxology, spiritual, religious song, hymn tune, *Eccles.* cantus firmus; chant, plainsong, plainchant, Gregorian chant, *Eccles.* antiphon, *Eccles.* responsory, *Eccles.* offertory, *Eccles.* introit; canticle, chorale, choral, *Music.* cantata, *Music.* motet; anthem, national anthem, state song, song of praise, song, melody, tune, air, composition; ode, poem, verse, (*in ancient Greece*) chorus.
—v. **2.** psalm, doxologize, carol, sing the praises of; chant, intone, cantillate, descant, *Archaic.* deacon; praise, laud, exalt, glorify, extol, celebrate.

hyperbole, *n.* exaggeration, overstatement, magnification, maximization, enlargement, expansion, inflation, swelling; enhancement, deepening, heightening, intensification; stretch of the imagination *or* the truth, excess, instance of overkill.

hypercritical, *adj.* **1.** overcritical, overabusive, overcensorious; trenchant, defamatory, calumnious, denunciatory; cutting, maledictory, scurrilous, derogatory.
2. rigorous, exacting, pedantic, fussy; overparticular, hypercorrect, overscrupulous; severe, puritanical, overexacting, strict; overdeliberate, overdiligent, overfastidious, overrigid, overrigorous.

hypersensitive, *adj.* oversensitive, hypersusceptible, oversusceptible, *Med.* hyperalgesic, allergic; *Pathol.* hyperaphic, *Pathol.* hyperesthetic, *Pathol.* hypergeusesthetic; hyperexcitable, hyperreactional, hyperreactive, overreactive, high-strung, skittish, startlish; neurotic, hyperneurotic, volcanic, explosive, volatile, combustible; hyperirritable, hot-tempered, high-mettled, waspish.

hypnosis, *n.* **1.** trance, spell, mesmeric *or* hypnotic sleep, somnolence, somnipathy, somnolism; narcohypnosis, animal hypnosis, autohypnosis; insensibility, numbness, stupefaction, *Pathol.* catalepsy, daze; sleep, slumber, *Pathol.* sopor, coma, deep sleep, narcosis, unconsciousness; drowsiness, languor, sleepiness, lethargy.
2. mesmerism, hypnology. See **hypnotism** (*def.* **1**).

hypnotic, *adj.* **1.** mesmerizing, mesmeric, fascinating, spellbinding, gripping, arresting, enthralling, entrancing; engrossing, absorbing, engaging, holding.
2. soporific, somnific, somniferous, sleep-inducing, sleep-producing, somnifacient, soporiferous, somnolent; sedative, calmative, stupefactive, numbing.
3. hypnotized, mesmerized, stupefied, drugged, *Sl.* doped, numbed, narcotized; calmed, sedated, anesthetized; entranced, spellbound, under the magic influence, *Sl.* under.
—n. **4.** anesthetic, gas, anesthesia; sedative, tranquilizer, depressant, calmative, soother, *Sl.* downer; soporific, sleeping pill, somnifacient, sleeping draft, *Sl.* sleeper, sleep-bringer, opiate, barbituate, *Sl.* goofball; *All Sl.* knockout drops, Mickey Finn, blue, blue devil, blue angel.

hypnotism, *n.* **1.** mesmerism, hypnology, hypnotic suggestion, autosuggestion; od, odyle, magnetism.
2. hypnosis, somnipathy. See **hypnosis** (*def.* **1**).

hypnotist, *n.* hypnotizer, mesmerist, mesmerizer, Mesmer, Rasputin, Svengali; charmer, spellbinder, enchanter, enchantress.

hypnotize, *v.* **1.** stupefy, put to sleep, drug, *Sl.* dope, narcotize, benumb, put under; calm, sedate, anesthetize, *Sl.* knock out.
2. entrance, cast a spell over, captivate, fascinate, charm, spellbind; enthrall, ensorcell, bewitch, witch, enchant, enrapture, transport, carry away.
3. engage, engross, involve, rivet, hold, absorb; hold one's attention, monopolize one's attention, engage one's thoughts.

hypochondria, *n.* **1.** imagined ill-health, valetudinarianism, anxiety, neurosis, psychoneurosis.
2. depression, melancholy, *Psychiatry.* melancholia, *Psychiatry.* hypochondriasis, despondency, doldrums, dejection, low spirits, megrims, the blues, *Archaic.* hyp.

hypochondriac, *adj.* **1.** melancholy, melancholic, melancholiac, depressed, dejected, dispirited, vaporish, disconsolate, sad, gloomy; listless, mopish, spiritless, undone, cheerless; valetudinary, hypochondriacal, malingering, anxious, worried, neurotic, psychoneurotic, preoccupied, obsessed.
—n. **2.** melancholiac, mope, malingerer, *Inf.* worrywart, *Inf.* big baby.

hypocrisy, *n.* **1.** false goodness, pietism, sanctimony, sanctimoniousness, Tartuffery, pharisaism, *Relig.* formalism; cant, lip-service, mouth-honor; sophistry, speciousness; false profession, pretense, pretext; pretension, pretending, faking, feigning, shamming, malingering.
2. falseness, untruthfulness, deceptiveness, dishonesty, insincerity, mealy-mouthedness, trickiness; charlatanry, quackery, fraud; deceit, deception, dissimulation, duplicity; guile, chicanery, double-dealing, ambidexterity, two-facedness; deceitfulness, underhandedness, indirection, mendacity; affectation, false front, crocodile tears, Judas kiss; dissembling, disguising, covering up.

hypocrite, *n.* **1.** pharisee, pietist, tartuffe, religionist, Holy Willie, *Relig.* formalist; canter, lip server.
2. faker, imposter, whited sepulcher, deceiver, *Inf.* phony, saint abroad and a devil at home, mountebank, charlatan, quack, empiric, *Australian.* bunyip; feigner, pretender, dissembler, malingerer, imitator; cheat, deceiver, swindler, confidence man, *Inf.* con man; informer, traitor, Judas; wolf in sheep's clothing, ass in lion's skin.

hypocritical, *adj.* **1.** insincere, disingenuous, deceitful, deceptive, crocodilian, untruthful, hollow, lying, false, mendacious, mealy-mouthed; dishonest, underhanded, untrustworthy; perfidious, treacherous, traitorous, faithless, Punic, treasonable; double-dealing, guileful, two-faced, double-faced, Janus-faced; smooth-spoken, smooth-tongued, slippery; dissembling, dissimulating, pretending, feigning, faking; affected, pretentious, assuming, mannered, unnatural.
2. pharisaic, pharisaical, sanctimonious, pietistic, unctuous; canting, lip-serving; puritanical, self-righteous.

hypothesis, *n.* **1.** theory, theorem, thesis, axiom, proposition, postulate, postulation.

2. premise, antecedent, ground, basis, foundation, starting point.

3. assumption, supposal, supposition, presupposition, presumption, inference; conjecture, speculation, *Sl.* guesstimate, guess, rough guess, wild guess, blind guess, *Inf.* stab, *Inf.* shot, *Inf.* shot in the dark; notion, thought, idea, fancy, imagining.

hypothesize, *v.* postulate, post, predicate, theorize, hypothecate; offer, submit, put forward, extend; conjecture, guess, surmise, assume, presume, suppose, presuppose; infer, deduce, conclude, find.

hypothetical, *adj.* **1.** supposed, assumed, presumed, reputed, putative, inferred; guessed, conjectured, surmised, suspected, imagined; debatable, questionable, doubtful, problematic, uncertain, undetermined.

2. conjectural, speculative, speculatory, postulatory; suppositional, suppositive, presumptive, notional; theoretical, academic, supposititious, drawing-board.

hysteria, *n.* **1.** outburst, burst, eruption, explosion, flare-up; fit, seizure, convulsion, spasm, paroxysm, hysterics.

2. delirium, frenzy, madness, craze, furor, fury, *Sl.* screaming-meemies.

hysterical, *adj.* **1.** mad, maddened, crazed, delirious, rabid, possessed, beside oneself, carried away, foaming *or* frothing at the mouth, out of one's wits, irrational; raving, raging, seething, convulsive, in hysterics, distracted, wild-eyed; frantic, frenetic, frenzied, wild; berserk, uncontrollable, unrestrainable.

2. (*all to an extreme degree*) excitable, emotional, highly emotional, explosive, eruptive, volcanic.

3. hilarious, extremely funny, sidesplitting, screaming, *Inf.* too much, *Inf.* too much for words, *Inf.* too funny for words.

I

ice, *n.* **1.** frozen water, frost, hoarfrost, rime; sleet, hail; icicle, iceberg, floe, glacier; (*all in drinks*) ice cubes, crushed ice, *Inf.* rocks.

2. sherbet, Italian ice, ice milk, ice cream, *Trademark.* Popsicle.

3. icing, frosting, glaze.

4. stiffness, formality, reserve, reticence, distance, aloofness; constraint, restraint, coldness, unresponsiveness, uncommunicativeness.

—v. **5.** freeze, glaciate, glaze over, harden; cool, chill, refrigerate; frost, glaze.

ice-cold, *adj.* **1.** freezing, frigid, algid, gelid, chill, cold; icy, rimy, frosty, wintry, brumal; arctic, glacial, polar, hyperborean, hyperboreal, Siberian; bleak, bitter, raw, cutting, stinging, sharp, brisk, zippy, snappy.

2. passionless, unimpassioned, unemotional, unfeeling, undemonstrative, unresponsive; unenthusiastic, unexcitable, stony, flinty, steely, callous, hardened, obdurate, thickskinned; distant, aloof, reserved, formal.

icing, *n.* **1.** frosting, glaze, ice.

2. added attraction, fringe benefit, benefit, bonus, dividend, reward, extra, supplement.

icky, *adj. Slang.* **1.** repulsive, revolting, disgusting, unpleasant, uninviting; sickly sweet, syrupy, unpalatable, unsavory, unappetizing, distasteful; maudlin, mushy, *Sl.* sappy, insipid.

2. unsophisticated, naïve, corny; behind the times, old-fashioned, dated, passé, extinct.

3. sticky, gummy, gluey, viscid, viscous, glutinous.

icon, *n.* image, idol; likeness, representation, semblance; picture, painting, figure, statue.

iconoclast, *n.* **1.** attacker, assailant, image-breaker *or* destroyer, burster of bubbles; denouncer, decrier, condemner, censurer, asperser, maligner, abuser; criticizer, critic, carper, faultfinder, *Inf.* knocker; opponent, antagonist, challenger, adversary, devil's advocate.

2. antichrist, antireligionist, atheist, agnostic, impious *or* irreverent person; denier, dissenter, skeptic, questioner; heretic, nullifidian, apostate, nonbeliever, unbeliever, infidel.

iconoclastic, *adj.* **1.** image-breaking, bubble-bursting; denunciatory, condemning, censuring, aspersive, maligning; critical, carping, faultfinding; oppositional, antagonistic, adversative, challenging.

2. antichristian, antireligious, impious, irreverent, irreligious, atheistic, agnostic; heretical, heretic, dissentient, skeptical, questioning, nonbelieving.

icy, *adj.* **1.** frozen, frore, frosty, rimy, sleety, glacial, ice-bound; glazed, glassy, slippery, slick.

2. freezing, gelid, arctic, ice-cold. See **ice-cold** (*def.* **1**).

3. passionless, unemotional, distant, ice-cold. See **ice-cold** (*def.* **2**).

idea, *n.* **1.** conception, concept, conceptualization, construct; thought, abstraction.

2. understanding, perception, apprehension, awareness, notion, inkling; observation, impression, inference, assumption, surmise, guess, suspicion.

3. opinion, view, viewpoint, position, sentiment, mind, feeling; belief, credence, conviction, persuasion; creed, doctrine, philosophy, outlook; tenets, principles, teachings.

4. plan, design, scheme, dream, vision; intention, objective, object, end, aim, goal.

5. theory, hypothesis, postulate, supposition, conjecture; conceit, concoction, fantasy, daydream, fancy, fiction, flight of fancy.

ideal, *n.* **1.** model, standard of perfection, standard of excellence, beau ideal, *Latin. ne plus ultra;* acme, height, pinnacle, peak; pink, paragon, nonpareil, nonsuch, flower, phoenix.

2. prototype, archetype, model, exemplar, example, paradigm; original, pattern, type, precedent, design, copy, die, mold, matrix, mint, text.

3. aim, goal, objective; target, butt, mark; end, destination; purpose, design.

—adj. **4.** perfect, consummate, complete; exemplary, model; supreme, absolute; faultless, excellent.

5. abstract, unreal, unsubstantial, imaginary, visionary, fancied, idealistic; intellectual, mental, psychological, spiritual, metaphysical.

6. imaginative, fanciful, illusory, shadowy, fictitious, notional, fabulous, fantastic, chimerical; mythical, mythological, legendary, romantic, Utopian; whimsical, figmental, dreamy, cloud-built, fairylike; extravagant, preposterous, high-flown, not practical, impracticable, ivory-towered.

7. advantageous, excellent, best.

idealism, *n.* **1.** pursuit of noble ideals, perfectionism, ideality.

2. idealistic philosophy, transcendentalism, metaphysics; immateriality, spiritualism.

3. romanticism, utopianism, quixotism; castle-building, dreaming; rose-colored glasses.

idealist, *n.* **1.** pursuer of ideals, perfectionist; metaphysicist, philosopher, transcendentalist, spiritualist, ideologist.

2. visionary, romanticist, Don Quixote, dreamer, castle-builder, stargazer; optimist, Pollyanna, Pangloss.

idealistic, *adj.* utopian, perfectionistic, idealistical; optimistic, visionary, dreaming, starry-eyed; romantic, quixotic, castle-building; unrealistic, impractical, impracticable, infeasible.

ideality, *n.* **1.** unreality, intangibility, impalpability; illusion, vision, myth, dream, fantasy; cloudland, fairyland, dreamland; chimera, maggot, vagary, whimsy, figment, conceit.

2. idealization, invention, conception, imagination, fancy; poetic frenzy, inspiration; flight of fancy, stretch of the imagination.

idealization, *n.* exaltation, glorification, magnification, ennoblement; apotheosis, deification.

ideally, *adv.* **1.** in a perfect world, in a Utopia, if things were as they should be, in *or* under the best of circumstances; all things being equal.

2. in idea, in thought, as conceived, as originally intended; in theory, theoretically, in principle, in the abstract.

ideational, *adj.* conceptual, idealistic, cognitive; mental, of the mind, notional, abstract, intangible; theoretical, hypothetical, suppositional, conjectural.

identical, *adj.* **1.** same, identic, one and the same, undifferent, indistinguishable, consubstantial, *Eccles.* Homoousian; the very same, selfsame, one and only, one, exact; ditto, repeat, duplicate, twin.

2. congruous, matching, convertible, interchangeable; equal, congruent, tantamount, equivalent, coequal; corresponding, coincident, coinciding.

3. similar, alike, like, much the same; synonymous, close, approximate, analogous, near; conatural, cognate, agreeing, homogeneous.

identification, *n.* **1.** recognition, detection, discernment, perception, discrimination; learning, finding, sighting; pointing out, naming, selection, *Inf.* fingering; differentiation, distinguishing, specification, characterization; designation, denomination, signification, indication.

2. ascertainment, establishment, verification, proof; certification, corroboration, substantiation, authentication.

3. mark, badge, identity card, ID card, ID, ID bracelet; identification tag, hallmark, driver's license, *Mil.* dog tag; calling card, letter of introduction; credentials, passport, visa, *Fr. carte d'identité*; signature, autograph, initials, monogram, mark, calligram; cachet, seal, stamp, signet, sigil, serial number; password, shibboleth, *Fr. mot de passe, Fr. passe-parole*, keyword.

4. empathy, relating, responsiveness, involvement; sympathy, fellow feeling, sympathetic chord, vibration, *Sl.* vibes; association, transference, synthesia.

identify, *v.* **1.** recognize, perceive, discern, see, know, distinguish; point out, select, detect, pick out, *Inf.* spot, make out, descry, *Inf.* put one's finger on; specify, pinpoint, *Sl.* peg, *Sl.* button down; name, nominate, denomiate, designate; call, dub, term, label, tag.

2. verify, establish, ascertain, tell, prove, confirm; substantiate, corroborate, certify, authenticate, endorse, attest.

3. associate, relate, regard as the same; connect, ally, equate, couple, parallel, draw a parallel to; feel with, respond to, be moved, react, relate, to, *Sl.* dig; sympathize, empathize, know what it's like, walk in another's shoes, see through another's eyes.

identity, *n.* **1.** oneness, sameness, unity, selfsameness, exactness, exactitude, identicalness; indistinguishability, *Eccles.* Homoousia, consubstantiality; equivalence, correspondence, coincidence, agreement; congruence, congruency, equality, interchangeability, convertibility.

2. oneself, itself, self, selfhood, selfness, ego; individuality, person, personality, name; particularity, singularity, uniqueness, differentness.

3. resemblance, likeness, alikeness, similarity, similitude, semblance; closeness, approximation, nearness; synonymy, analogy, accordance, consimilarity.

ideogram, *n.* ideograph, hieroglyphic, hieroglyph, symbol, figure; grammalogue, stenograph.

ideology, *n.* doctrine, teachings, dogma, tenets, doxy; creed, credo, canons, articles of faith, gospel; theory, thesis, principles, postulates, axioms; beliefs, opinions, convictions.

idiocy, *n.* **1.** imbecility, moronism, moronity, retardation, *Psychiatry.* amentia; senility, anility, dotage; simple-mindedness, shallowness, feeble-mindedness, weak-mindedness; harebrainedness, giddiness, recklessness; absent-mindedness, confusedness, confusion; featherheadedness, featherbrainedness, rattleheadedness, rattlebrainedness.

2. stupidity, stupidness, *Inf.* dumbness, *Inf.* dopiness, unintelligence, fatuity; dullness, inexpressiveness. See **fatuity** (*def.* **2**).

3. craziness, *Sl.* kookiness, *Inf.* nuttiness, daftness; insanity, madness, lunacy, derangement, anoesis, *Psychiatry.* dementia; *All Sl.* balminess, bugginess, screwiness, wackiness, goofiness.

4. asininity, foolishness, silliness, *Archaic.* insipience; absurdness, absurdity, inanity, fatuousness; unreasonableness, irrationality, illogicalness, illogicality; nonsense, nonsensicalness, nonsensicality, ridiculousness, ludicrousness; childishness, puerility, immaturity.

idiom, *n.* **1.** expression, locution, phrase, set phrase; turn of phrase *or* expression, phrasing, wording.

2. language, dialect, tongue, vernacular, speech; jargon, cant, argot, slang, street language, *Obs.* flash; parlance, *Inf.* lingo, phraseology, manner *or* style of speech, *Linguistics.* idiolect; accent, brogue, patois.

3. dialectal variation, regionalism, provincialism, colloquialism, localism.

idiosyncrasy, *n.* **1.** idiocrasy, mannerism, affectation, quirk, twist, kink, eccentricity, peculiarity, singularity, speciality; characteristic, trait, quality, feature, attribute, property.

2. nature, make-up, constitution; character, disposition, temperament, habit, mettle; humor, mood, frame *or* state of mind; tendency, bias, grain, leaning, propensity, proclivity, penchant, proneness, drift, predilection, predisposition, streak; complexion, tone, aspect, cast, turn, bent, style.

3. allergy, hypersensitivity, sensitivity, intolerance; susceptibility, susceptibleness, susceptivity; vulnerability, weakness.

idiot, *n.* imbecile, mooncalf, *Inf.* moron; fool, saphead, Simple Simon, noodle, *Inf.* jay, *Sl.* jerk, goose; simpleton, ninny, nincompoop, silly, silly billy, driveler, tomfool; dimwit, nitwit, half-wit, featherbrain, pinhead; scatterbrain, rattlehead, rattlepate, rattlebrain; dope, booby, *Sl.* lamebrain, *Inf.* dummy, *Sl.* dumbbell, *Sl.* dumbhead, *Inf.* muddlehead; *Inf.* cretin, dolt, loon, *Archaic.* lurdan, clod, oaf, dunce, *Inf.* chump, *Inf.* coot; blockhead, beetlehead, bonehead, dunderhead, dunderpate; chucklehead, *Sl.* lunkhead, *Inf.* knucklehead, dullard, *Inf.* numskull, *Sl.* zombie; donkey, ass, lubber, lout; ignoramus, know-nothing, lowbrow, illiterate; crackpot, *Sl.* nut, lunatic, maniac, psychotic; sulker, *Inf.* crank, *Inf.* grouch.

idiotic, *adj.* **1.** asinine, anserine, foolish, idiotical; silly, absurd, inane, fatuous; senseless, nonsensical, crackbrained, *Scot.* doiled, *Sl.* cockeyed, *Scot. and North Eng.* glaikit; ridiculous, laughable, risible, derisible, ludicrous, *Sl.* for the birds; childish, puerile, immature.

2. stupid, *Inf.* dumb, *Inf.* dopey, *Inf.* moronic, empty-headed, unintelligent, imbecilic, oxlike; dull, inexpressive, expressionless; addlepated, addleheaded, addlebrained, muddled, muddleheaded; dull-witted, *Sl.* dimwitted, slow-witted, half-witted, witless, unwitty, fat-witted; mindless, *Rare.* insulse, brainless, fatuitous; dense, thick, bovine, obtuse, Boeotian, stolid, oafish, loutish; cloddish, lumpish, blunt; doltish, blockish, asslike, blockheaded, dunderheaded, noodleheaded; boneheaded, wooden-headed, thickheaded, thickskulled; obstinate, stubborn, intractable, mulish, obdurate, unyielding.

3. crazy, crazed, *Sl.* bughouse, *Sl.* kooky, *Inf.* potty, *Sl.* nuts, *Inf.* nutty, daft, *Inf.* daffy; insane, mad, demented, lunatic, deranged; of unsound mind, *Latin. non compos mentis*; unbalanced, touched, *Inf.* half-baked, unhinged; not all there, not quite right, not right upstairs, *Inf.* mental, *Inf.* cracked; out of one's head, out of one's mind, mad as a hatter, mad as a March hare; maniacal, wild, raving, hysterical, frenzied, delirious, berserk; *All Sl.* balmy, dippy, batty, cuckoo, buggy, screwy, wacky, goofy, loony.

4. simple-minded, simple, *Sl.* bird-brained, weak-minded, weak-headed, feeble-minded; harebrained, giddy, mercurial, reckless; absent-minded, scatter-brained, confused, bemused; featherheaded, feather-brained, rattleheaded, rattlebrained, light-minded, light-headed; empty, void, vacant, vacuous, blank, unoccupied.

5. dazed, moon-struck, possessed, infatuated; peculiar, strange, odd, eccentric, pixilated; irrational, illogical, unreasonable; unreasoning, unthinking, insensate, incogitant, thoughtless.

idle, *adj.* **1.** inactive, unoccupied, at leisure, doing nothing; unemployed, workless, out of work, not working, jobless, out of a job, *Inf.* collecting, on the dole, on welfare; vagrant, *Inf.* on the bum.

2. unfilled, vacuous, vacant, empty, not in use, unused; not in operation, not operating, not utilized, still, dormant; fallow, uncultivated, untilled.

3. lazy, listless, lethargic, languid; indolent, loitering, loafing; dawdling, laggard, slothful, sluggish, shiftless, dronish, do-nothing, inert, supine, stretched out, recumbent; torpid, heavy, leaden.

4. unimportant, trivial, trifling, shallow, depthless, superficial; worthless, insignificant, meaningless, unmeaning; senseless, nonsensical, inane, *Inf.* dumb, absurd, fatuous, fatuitous.

5. baseless, groundless, unreasonable; fallacious, illogical, *Logic.* paralogistic, unsound, inconclusive; inconsequential, a waste of time.

6. frivolous, fiddling, vain, foolish, valueless, trashy, wasteful, prodigal, superfluous, unnecessary, unneeded, purposeless; fruitless, abortive, unproductive, useless, unserviceable, unprofitable, ill-spent, gainless, profitless; useless, unavailing, of no avail, unsuccessful, ineffective, inefficacious, ineffectual, bootless.

—*v.* **7.** loaf, loll, lounge, laze, while; be inactive, vegetate, do nothing, hibernate, mark time, take it easy; fritter, *Sl.* futz, *Sl.* knock about *or* around, fool away time, *Inf.* goof off.

8. loiter, slouch, move idly, saunter, dawdle, lag, *Inf.* lollygag; putter, potter, dabble; wait, delay, procrastinate, dillydally; drowse, doze, nap, snooze.

9. work slowly, operate in low gear, coast, drift.

idleness, *n.* **1.** inoccupation, unemployment, idle hands, idle hours, time on one's hands; leisure, ease, *Chiefly Literary.* idlesse, spare time, free time, *Inf.* time to burn, *Inf.* dodge time, command time; vacation, recess, *Inf.* letup.

2. inertness, inertia, inactivity, inaction, laziness, indolence, slothfulness; hibernation, vegetation, torpor, languor, lethargy, lassitude, sluggishness.

3. loafing, loitering, shirking, malingering, *Sl.* goofing off; dawdling, *Fr. flânerie*, dillydallying, procrastination, shiftlessness.

idler, *n.* loafer, lounger, loiterer, lazybones, sluggard, slugabed, sloth, dawdler, snail, laggard, slouch, lolle, Weary Willie; dreamer, lotus-eater, castle-builder; vagrant, drifter, tramp, beggar, *Inf.* bum, *Brit.* layabout, deadbeat, pike, piker, *Inf.* goof-off, do-nothing, fainéant; good-for-nothing, no-account, ne'er-do-well, gentleman of leisure, waiter on Providence; drone, *Inf.* leech, *Inf.* moocher, *Yiddish.* schnorrer, sponger; malingerer, shirker, truant, clock-watcher, benchwarmer.

idol, *n.* **1.** icon, effigy, image, likeness, fetish, (*in China*) joss, (*in India*) Juggernaut *or* Jagannath; graven image, false god, Baal.

2. sacred cow, favorite, darling, pet, jewel, fondling, apple of one's eye; cynosure, luminary, celebrity, star, superstar, matinee idol, *Sl.* pop hero *or* star; lion, social lion; hero, heroine, folk hero.

3. vision, dream, fancy; hallucination, illusion, phantasmagoria, mirage, vapor, delusion; phantasm, phantom, shadow, specter, chimera, bubble.

4. fallacy, false notion, mistaken notion, misconception, misbelief, misapprehension, misjudgment, miscalculation.

idolater, *n.* **1.** fetishist, idolist, idolatress, iconodule, iconolater.

2. devotee, votary, follower, *Inf.* fan, *Inf.* buff; worshiper, idolizer, fanatic, groupie, *Sl.* nut, *Sl.* freak, *Sl.* bug.

idolatrous, *adj.* **1.** idol-worshiping, idolistic, icon-worshiping, fetishistic; heretical, unorthodox, pagan, heathen.

2. adulatory, adoring, worshiping, worshipful, idolizing, deifying, lionizing; fulsome, uncritical, uncensorious, unreproachful; awestruck, awed, in awe; reverent, reverential, venerative.

idolatry, *n.* **1.** idolism, idolization, idolatrism, idol-worship *or* idol-worshiping, fetishism, iconolatry, iconoduly, icon-worship *or* icon-worshiping; paganism, heathenism.

2. hero worship, adulation, adoration, breathless adoration; deification, apotheosis; glorification, exaltation, extolment, idolizing, lionizing.

idolize, *v.* adulate, adore, worship, worship the ground [s.o.] walks on, hero-worship, idolatrize; exalt, glorify, magnify, lionize, put on a pedestal; deify, apotheosize; honor, revere, reverence, venerate.

idyll, *n.* **1.** pastoral, bucolic, eclogue, georgic, Virgilian verse.

2. wonderful *or* pleasant time, honeymoon, moment of bliss *or* joy, day in the country, getting away from it all; Garden of Eden, paradise, heaven on earth, Shangri-la.

if, *conj.* provided, providing, on condition, in case, granting, supposing; though, although, yet, for all that; whether, whether or not.

iffy, *adj. Informal.* **1.** questionable, uncertain, doubtful, dubious, undecided, unsettled, up in the air, unresolved, indeterminate; problematical, arguable, indeterminable, moot.

2. tentative, unsure, provisional; dependent, contingent.

3. perplexing, confusing, thorny, knotty, involved, intricate, tricky, many-faceted.

ignite, *v.* **1.** set on fire, light, *Inf.* put the match to, illuminate, kindle, enkindle; set fire to, conflagrate, inflame, touch off; fire, burn, blow up; relight, rekindle, relume, relumine; *Both Chem.* heat intensely, roast.

2. catch fire, take fire, conflagrate, flare up, fire up, blaze, flame, glow, smolder, incandesce.

ignoble, *adj.* **1.** mean, petty, small, shabby; base, vile, low, low-down; degraded, debased, abased, disgraceful, shameful; dishonorable, ignominious, infamous; contemptible, despicable, abject, paltry, deplorable; execrable, detestable, abominable, abhorrent; scurvy, rotten, *Sl.* cruddy, *Inf.* lousy; vulgar, indecent, crude, coarse, boorish, loutish, obnoxious; depraved, gross, bad; sneaky, dastardly, weaselly, wormy.

2. inferior, substandard, below par, not measuring up; worthless, no good, *Sl.* n.g., bastardly; sleazy, *Inf.* junky, *Inf.* crummy, *Sl.* crappy.

3. lowborn, untitled, baseborn, of humble birth; proletarian, lowly, humble, plebeian; peasant, rude, uncouth, crude; common, *U.S.* rednecked, sorry, scrubby.

ignominious, *adj.* **1.** shameful, contemptible, disreputable, disgraceful, despicable, dishonorable; scandalous, outrageous, wicked, abominable, heinous, atrocious; discreditable, ignoble, inglorious; unworthy, indecorous, undignified, *Latin. infra dignitatum*, infra dig.

2. hateful, vile, scurvy, disgusting, offensive, revolting; shabby, mean, paltry, dirty, scrubby; base, low, abject, humiliating, degrading, mortifying.

ignominy, *n.* **1.** dishonor, disgrace, shame, disrepute, discredit, disfavor, ill repute; obloquy, opprobrium, infamy, disapprobation; odium, stain, blot, stigma, brand, badge of infamy; debasement, degradation, abjection.

2. wickedness, improbity, villainy, base conduct, depravity, degeneracy, turpitude, derogation; dishonesty, bad faith, fraudulence, double-dealing, deception; infidelity, betrayal, disloyalty, faithlessness, treachery, perfidy; foul play, roguery, knavery, rascality.

ignoramus, *n.* fool, blockhead, bonehead, lowbrow, dumbbell, dunce, *Inf.* numskull; simpleton, dolt, dullard, scatterbrain, featherbrain, novice, greenhorn, plebe, beginner, amateur, dabbler; bungler, blunderer, fumbler, *Inf.* duffer.

ignorance, *n.* unawareness, unenlightenment, unconsciousness, benightedness, darkness, blindness, nescience, want *or* lack of knowledge; illiteracy, illiterateness, lack of education *or* learning; innocence, simplicity, inexperience, greenness; bewilderment, perplexity, confusion; denseness, thickness, stolidness, dumbness, stupidity, empty-headedness.

ignorant, *adj.* **1.** illiterate, unlettered, uneducated, uninstructed, untaught, unschooled, untutored, unlearned; green, wide-eyed, innocent, inexperienced.

2. unaware, unacquainted, unconversant, unapprised, uninformed, uninitiated, unenlightened, unread; unconscious, blind, unwitting, unknowing; benighted, nescient, in the dark, knowing nothing, *Sl.* out of it.

3. uncultivated, rude, crude; superficial, shallow, sciolistic, unscholarly, half-baked, *Sl.* half-assed; dense, obtuse, thick, slow, empty-headed, *Inf.* dumb.

ignore, *v.* **1.** disregard, cut, pass over *or* by, *Inf.* give [s.t.] a miss *or* the go-by; snub, pay no heed to, be inattentive to, brush aside, slight, pretend not to see, look right through *or* past [s.o.], cold-shoulder, *Sl.* give [s.o.] the brush *or* brush-off, *Sl.* brush [s.o.] off; set aside, fly in the face of, shrug off *or* away, push aside, write off, turn one's back on, close *or* shut one's eyes to, blink, wink at; turn a blind eye on, be blind to, fail to notice, turn a deaf ear to, not trouble oneself with, bury *or* hide *or* have one's head in the sand, be inattentive to.

2. omit, not take into account, overlook, neglect, leave out, skip.

ilk, *n.* kind, sort, kidney, type, brand, breed; make, cast, cut, mold, form; grain, feather, tone, color, stripe, stamp; character, makeup, composition; family, class, genre, category.

ill, *adj.* **1.** sick, sickly, sickened, ailing; unhealthy, unsound, unwell, *Sl.* off one's feed, poorly; afflicted, diseased, morbid, poisoned, nauseated, strung out; in a bad way, on the sick list, *Inf.* under the weather, *Inf.* out of sorts, not up to snuff, *Inf.* on the blink; feverish, aching, sore; weak, weakly, feeble, infirm, wasting away; indisposed, laid up, bedridden, confined; disordered, out of order, out of commission; invalided, valetudinarian.

2. evil, wicked, sinful, iniquitous, nefarious; bad, low, mean; wrong, corrupt, depraved, degenerate, immoral.

3. objectionable, unsatisfactory, deficient, insufficient, unacceptable; unskillful, inexpert, faulty, poor.

4. hostile, antagonistic, belligerent, bellicose; unfriendly, unkindly, unkind; irascible, cross, fractious, snappish, snappy, irritable; cantankerous, crabby, crabbed, sullen.

5. unfavorable, adverse, unlucky, unpropitious, inauspicious, unpromising, infelicitous; pernicious, harmful, injurious, nocuous, hurtful; detrimental, deleterious, baleful, fell; destructive, ruinous, calamitous, damaging.

—n. **6.** evil, harm, mischief, injury, hurt, *Archaic.* bale, pain; trouble, misfortune, affliction, grievance, misery, suffering, woe; destruction, damage, ruin; disaster, calamity, catastrophe, debacle, cataclysm.

7. illness, sickness, ailment, malady, disease; disorder, infirmity, indisposition; infection, contagion.

—adv. **8.** wickedly, evilly, malignantly, banefully, hurtfully, harmfully, mischievously.

9. objectionably, unsatisfactorily, insufficiently, poorly, badly, faultily, improperly.

10. hostilely, antagonistically, belligerently, inimically.

11. unfortunately, adversely, unluckily, unfavorably, unpropitiously, inauspiciously.

ill-advised, *adj.* **1.** imprudent, incautious, indiscreet, inappropriate, unseemly, unsuitable, irresponsible, foolish; injudicious, ill-judged, inexpedient, unwise, ill-considered, ill-suited, impolitic, unadvised, unadvisable; misguided, miscounseled, wrong-headed, perverse.

2. impetuous, impulsive, hasty, over-hasty, shortsighted, heedless, unheeding; foolhardy, headlong, brakeneck, hazardous; rash, hot-headed, brash, unwary, unguarded; uncircumspect, thoughtless, careless, reckless, harebrained, madcap, temerarious, wild; spontaneous, unpremeditated, sudden, abrupt, precipitate.

ill-at-ease, *adj.* uncomfortable, uneasy, unquiet, disquieted, anxious, distressed, troubled; nervous, *Sl.* antsy, *Inf.* on pins and needles, on tenterhooks; fearful, afraid, distrustful, apprehensive, watchful, guarded; self-conscious, awkward, faltering, unsure, uncertain.

ill-bred, *adj.* ill-mannered, bad-mannered, unmannerly, rude, impolite, uncivil, unceremonious, discourteous, disrespectful, misbehaved; indelicate, uncourtly, ungallant, indecorous, ungracious; ungentlemanly, unladylike; brash, bold, hoydenish, *Scot.* randy; brazen, barefaced, insolent, impudent, insulting, impertinent, pert, saucy, fresh; bluff, surly, sullen, bearish, gruff; inconsiderate, insensitive, tactless, *Scot. and North Eng.* misleared; abrupt, blunt, brusque, curt, clipped, short; rough, crude, boorish, churlish, loutish, vulgar, coarse.

ill-disposed, *adj.* **1.** antagonistic, opposed, adverse, averse, contrary, oppugnant; anti, against, *Sl.* agin, down on.

2. hostile, antipathetic, unfriendly, unsympathetic, inhospitable, cold, unsociable; belligerent, bellicose, pugnacious; combative, contentious, bickering, quarreling, wrangling, clashing; discordant, fractious, factious.

illegal, *adj.* unlawful, illegitimate, *Sl.* illegit, lawless, criminal; unconstitutional, illicit, unlicensed, unauthorized, wildcat, unofficial, unsanctioned, unwarranted; contraband, black-market, under-the-counter, under the table; prohibited, banned, outlawed, proscribed, interdicted; forbidden, *Fr. défendu, Ger. verboten.*

illegible, *adj.* unreadable, indecipherable, undecipherable, unintelligible, clear as mud; hieroglyphic, hieroglyphical, hard to read; scrawled, scrawly, scribbled, *Sl.* scribbly, squiggly.

illegitimate, *adj.* **1.** illegal, unlawful, unconstitutional, illicit. See **illegal.**

2. (*all of a person*) natural, bastard, *Fr. bâtard,* unfathered, misbegotten, baseborn, born out of wedlock, adulterine.

3. irregular, nonstandard, informal, slang, slangy; dialectal, regional, colloquial, local, provincial; ungrammatical, incorrect, *Linguistics.* substandard.

ill-fated, *adj.* **1.** star-crossed, ill-starred, ill-omened, doomed, born under an evil star; unlucky, luckless, unfortunate, hapless; untoward, unfavorable, adverse, contrary, unpropitious, inauspicious; ill-boding, ominous, sinister, threatening, portentous, menacing, minatory.

2. harmful, hurtful, injurious, damaging, destructive, baneful, baleful, pernicious; ruinous, disastrous, calamitous, catastrophic.

ill-favored, *adj.* **1.** ugly, ugly-looking, unsightly, hideous, *Sl.* gross-looking; homely, plain, unpretty, unlovely, uncomely, unbeautiful, *Chiefly Literary.* unbeauteous, unattractive, undesirable.

2. offensive, objectionable, obnoxious, rude, nasty, unkind; unpleasant, disagreeable, distasteful, disgusting, *Sl.* gross, repulsive, repellent; coarse, crude, off-color, in bad taste, tasteless.

ill humor, *n.* bad mood, temper, huff, tiff, miff, pet, fume, pique, *Inf.* stew, *Archaic.* pucker; rage, passion; touchiness, testiness, thin-skinnedness, fretfulness, petulance; irritability, curtness, tartness, sharpness; ill temper, irascibility, waspishness, peevishness, spleen, bile, choler; crossness, crabbedness, crabbiness, crankiness, grouchiness, grumpiness; moodiness, sulkiness, gloominess, sullenness, moroseness; bitterness, acerbity, asperity, sourness, churlishness, surliness.

ill-humored, *adj.* **1.** irritable, out of sorts, snappish, snappy, huffish, huffy, curt, short, impatient; piqued, in a pique, in a fume, *Archaic.* in a pucker, *Inf.* in a stew; touchy, testy, thin-skinned, waspish, peevish, petulant; cross, irascible, choleric, ill-tempered, splenetic; crabby, crabbed, cranky, grouchy, grumpy, cantankerous, crotchety, crusty; bitter, acrimonious, acerbic, sour, caustic, tart, churlish, surly; moody, sulky, sullen, dour, gloomy, sullen, morose; hurt, injured, wounded, sore, offended, indignant; angry, irate, in high dudgeon, wrathful, raging, fuming, furious, worked up.

2. unkindly, unamiable, unfriendly, unaccommodating; captious, quarrelsome, querulous, fractious; hostile, antagonistic, inimical, ill-willed; spiteful, malicious, malevolent, hateful.

illicit, *adj.* backdoor, furtive, secret, secretive, sneaky, underhanded, underhand; unauthorized, unlicensed, unlawful, illegal. See **illegal.**

illimitable, *adj.* limitless, unlimited, boundless, unbounded, infinite; unending, endless, eternal, ceaseless; immeasurable, unfathomable, incalculable; immense, vast, enormous, stretching to the far horizons.

illiteracy, *n.* **1.** ignorance, unenlightenment, benightedness, nescience, lack of education, illiterateness.

2. (*all of reading or writing*) inaccuracy, incorrectness, solecism, malapropism, error, mistake; nonstandard *or* substandard usage.

illiterate, *adj.* unlettered, unalphabetic, unlearned, unschooled, uninstructed, untaught, uneducated; unenlightened, benighted, nescient, in the dark; ignorant, unversed, uninformed, unscholarly.

ill-mannered, *adj.* ill-bred, bad-mannered, unmannerly, rude, impolite, uncivil. See **ill-bred.**

ill-natured, *adj.* **1.** unkindly, unamiable, unfriendly, unaccommodating; quarrelsome, contentious, fractious, captious; hostile, antagonistic, inimical, ill-willed; spiteful, malicious, malevolent, hateful.

2. ill-tempered, ill-humored, cross, irascible, choleric, splenetic; crabby, crabbed, cranky, grouchy, grumpy, cantankerous, crotchety, crusty; irritable, touchy, testy, thin-skinned, waspish, peevish, petulant; moody, sulky, sullen, dour, gloomy, sullen, morose; bitter, acrimonious, acerbic, sour, caustic, tart, churlish, surly.

illness, *n.* sickness, ailment, malady, disorder, complaint, indisposition; affliction, disease, infection, morbidity, *Pathol.* affection; invalidism, valetudinarianism; weakness, feebleness, infirmity; pain, hurt, ache, wound; disability, handicap; mental disorder, derangement, neurosis, psychosis, insanity, madness.

illogical, *adj.* unreasoning, unreasonable, irrational; unsound, absurd, preposterous, *Sl.* far-out, *Sl.* screwy, *Sl.* wacky, *Sl.* nutty; sophistic, casuistic, fallacious, wrong, *Logic.* paralogistic; fallible, untenable, unproved; contradictory, incongruous, inconsistent.

ill-omened, *adj.* ill-starred, ill-fated, star-crossed, doomed, unlucky. See **ill-fated** (*def.* **1**).

ill-proportioned, *adj.* misproportioned, misshapen, disproportionate, *Inf.* put together all wrong, not jibing; asymmetric, unsymmetrical, askew, skewed, irregular; distorted, lopsided, wry, twisted, crooked.

ill-smelling, *adj.* smelly, stinky, stinking, reeking, fetid, mephitic; foul, malodorous, rank, rancid, rotten; putrid, miasmic, noisome; sickening, *Sl.* sick-making, nauseous; musty, moldy, fusty, sour; stale, stuffy, close.

ill-sounding, *adj.* dissonant, discordant, absonant, unmelodious, unmelodical, inharmonious; strident, stridulous, stridulant, raucous, harsh, grating, shrill, sharp, piercing; brassy, tinny, metallic; jarring, clashing, jangling; out of tune, off-tune, off-pitch, off-key, flat, *Inf.* sour.

ill-starred, *adj.* ill-omened, ill-fated, star-crossed, doomed, unlucky. See **ill-fated** (*def.* **1**).

ill temper, *n.* irascibility, waspishness, peevishness, spleen, bile, choler; crossness, crabbedness, crabbiness, crankiness, grouchiness, grumpiness; moodiness, sulkiness, gloominess, sullenness, moroseness; bitterness, acerbity, asperity, sourness, churlishness, surliness; irritability, curtness, tartness, sharpness; ill humor, touchiness, testiness, thin-skinnedness, fretfulness, petulance.

ill-tempered, *adj.* ill-humored, cross, irascible, choleric, splenetic; crabby, crabbed, cranky, grouchy, grumpy, cantankerous, crotchety, crusty; irritable, touchy, testy, thin-skinned, waspish, peevish, petulant; moody, sulky, sullen, dour, gloomy, sullen, morose; bitter, acrimonious, acerbic, sour, caustic, tart, churlish, surly; huffish, huffy, in a pique, piqued, *Archaic.* in a pucker, *Inf.* in a stew, in a fume; angry, irate, in high dudgeon, wrathful, raging, fuming, furious, worked up.

2. unkindly, unamiable, unfriendly. See **ill-humored** (*def.* **2**).

ill-timed, *adj.* inopportune, untimely, mistimed, inconvenient, inexpedient; inauspicious, unpropitious, unfavorable, unfortunate, unhappy, unlucky; ill-omened, ill-fated, ill-starred, doomed.

ill-treat, *v.* abuse, maltreat, harm. See **mistreat.**

illuminate, *v.* **1.** light up, light, lighten, brighten; illumine, *Archaic.* illume, *Obs.* enlumine; irradiate, radiate, cast light upon, shine, beam, stream; make flare *or* flame, burn, glow, incandesce, phosphoresce; shimmer, sparkle, scintillate, glitter, gleam; flash, flicker, fulgurate, coruscate; make resplendent *or* illustrious.

2. clarify, elucidate, explain, make plain, explicate, make lucid *or* clear; define, expound, make explicit; interpret, decipher, literalize, render intelligible; clear up, solve, resolve, simplify, shed *or* cast light on, throw light upon; expose, bare, lay open, bring to light, *Archaic.* enucleate; unfold, unmask, unveil, uncover; show, demonstrate, illustrate, hold the mirror up to; manifest, point out, set forth, exhibit; describe, delineate, margin, gloss, annotate.

3. enlighten, inform, make aware, disabuse, give insight to; open the eyes of, shed *or* cast light on, bring out of the wilderness, civilize; instruct, teach, indoctrinate, educate, guide; tell, acquaint, familiarize with, make known to; apprise, notify, reveal, divulge, impart; communicate, initiate, introduce, edify, inculcate; school, tutor, train, nurture, prepare, prime, counsel, advise; discipline, drill, exercise, coach, lecture, catechize; persuade, convince, prevail upon, induce; stimulate, inspire, animate, exalt, ennoble, elevate; instill, impart, fill with genius, light the torch.

4. emblazon, blazon, *Archaic.* emblaze; color, imbue with color, brighten, rubricate; (*all of manuscripts*) illustrate, miniate, elaborate; daub, paint, crayon, pigment, stain, dye; tinge, tint, gild; enamel, lacquer.

5. decorate, adorn, ornament, embellish, enrich, enhance, beautify; grace, embroider, trim, dress, trick out; bedizen, deck, bedeck, *Archaic.* bedight, array, festoon, garnish; spruce up, make smart, *Inf.* titivate.

illumination, *n.* **1.** lighting up, lighting, luminescence; luminosity, radiation, shining, beaming, gleaming; irradiation, glowing, fluorescence, incandescence, phosphorescence.

2. lightness, luminousness, radiance, shine, effulgence; reflection, glimmer, glitter, twinkle, sparkle, shimmer.

3. enlightenment, edification, awareness, insight, understanding; education, learning, wisdom, sapience; apprisal, information, knowledge.

4. light, beam, ray, shaft of light, illuminant, source of light; lamp, lamplight, chandelier, electrolier, gas light, bulb, candle, taper, candelabrum; sunshine, star, shining star, blaze, fire.

5. decoration, adornment, ornamentation, embellishment, trim, dressing, garnish, emblazonment, enhancement; design, illustration, drawing, sketch, picture.

illumine, *v.* light up, light, brighten; clarify, elucidate, shed *or* cast light on; enlighten, give insight to, open the eyes of. See **illuminate** (*defs.* **1-3**).

illusion, *n.* **1.** fantasy, hallucination, mirage, phantasmagoria, vapor, pipe dream, delusion; phantasm, shadow, specter, chimera, phantom, will-o'-the-wisp; aberration, haunt, fear, haunting fear, nightmare; whimsy, whim, caprice, figment, maggot; flight, flight of fancy, notion, vagary, conceit, imagining, crazy notion *or* idea, *Inf.* screwball *or* wacky idea.

2. fallacy, false notion, mistaken notion, misconception, misbelief, misapprehension, misjudgment, miscalculation.

illusory, *adj.* **1.** deceptive, misleading, beguiling, tricky; delusive, delusory, illusive, illusionary; false, falacious, erroneous, mistaken; untrue, unfactual, wrong, all wrong; specious, seeming.

2. unreal, imaginary, imagined, fancied, nonexistent, all in the mind, all in one's head; fanciful, notional, quixotic, idealistic; chimerical, dreamy, dreamlike, air-built, cloud-built.

illustrate, *v.* **1.** exemplify, give an example, instance, give an instance *or* case, cite a case in point, tell a story *or* anecdote about, *Rare.* example; clarify, clear up *or* make clear, illuminate, shed light on, make understandable, render intelligible; explain, explicate, describe, elucidate, footnote, comment upon; demonstrate, exhibit, present, run through, show [s.o.] how to do [s.t.].

2. decorate, adorn, embellish, ornament, trim, garnish; illuminate, emblazon, brighten up, dress up; draw, sketch, diagram, make designs *or* pictures, do artwork.

illustration, *n.* **1.** drawing, sketch, diagram, line drawing, black and white, pen and ink; design, artwork, vignette, frontispiece; depictment, depiction, representation, portrayal, portrait, photograph, figure, cartoon, caricature.

2. example, exemplification, case, typical case, case in point, instance, typical instance, *Inf.* for instance, anecdote; specimen, sample, exemplar, representative, epitome, exponent, *Archaic.* ensample; comparison, analogy, similar case.

3. explanation, explication, definition, interpretation, exegesis, commentary, note; clarification, elucidation, illumination; exposition, delineation, outline, demonstration.

illustrative, *adj.* exemplary, exemplifying, typical, sample, representative, epitomic, epitomical, model; explanatory, elucidative, explicative, expository, commentorial; descriptive, expressive, interpretive, exegetic; diagrammatic, delineative, pictorial, graphic.

illustrious, *adj.* **1.** renowned, well-known, prominent, famous, famed, popular, well-liked, *Inf.* name; eminent, preeminent, noted, notable, esteemed, respected, venerable, distinguished, *Archaic.* eximious.

2. celebrated, acclaimed, touted, much-touted, exalted, honored; glorious, lustrous, brilliant, radiant, shining; great, grand, big-time.

ill will, *n.* animosity, hostility, inimicalness, invidiousness, abhorrence, aversion; antipathy, opposition, rancor, antagonism, malevolence, malignity, malice; enmity, animus, bad blood, loathing, hatred, hate, detestation; anger, pique, umbrage, resentment, grudge; acrimony, bitterness, virulence, spleen, gall; unfriendliness, dislike; no love lost.

image, *n.* **1.** likeness, representation, resemblance, simulacrum; effigy, figure, figurine, straw man, scarecrow, doll; idol, icon, fetish, joss, graven image, false god; photograph, *Inf.* photo, picture, snapshot, *Inf.* snap; portrait, portrayal, painting; sculpture, bust, statue, statuette, bronze, clay model.

2. idea, concept, conception, notion, fancy, thought, impression, perception, apprehension, opinion; picture, vision, mental picture *or* impression, *Psychol.* recept, *Psychoanal.* imago.

3. appearance, semblance, guise, aspect; form, shape, frame, cast, mold, build, cut, stamp, turn.

4. counterpart, parallel, coordinate, correspondent, complement, pendant, mate, fellow; double, Doppelgänger, alter ego, other self; match, twin, living *or* very image, chip off the old block, *Inf.* spit and image *or* spitting image; copy, duplicate, reproduction, replica, facsimile, ectype; clone.

5. symbol, emblem, token; insignia, device, badge, banner; mark, earmark, hallmark.

6. type, archetype, representative, example, specimen; embodiment, incarnation, materialization.

imagery, *n.* **1.** visualization, envisioning, imagination, imagining, picturing, calling to the mind's eye, objectification.

2. figurative language, figurativeness, nonliteralness, word painting; metaphors, similes, allusions, figures of speech, word pictures *or* paintings.

imaginable, *adj.* conceivable, thinkable, supposable; believable, credible; possible, within the bounds of possibility, *Latin. in posse*; within reach; probable, likely, in *or* on the cards.

imaginary, *adj.* fictitious, unreal, fancied, fanciful, fantastic; illusory, dreamy, visionary, shadowy, chimerical; mythical, legendary, mythological; figmental, fictive, notional, abstract; quixotic, utopian, romantic, idealistic; extravagant, wild, high-flown, preposterous; cloud-built, air-drawn, unsubstantial; phantasmal, phantasmic, spectral, ghostly; phantasmagorial, phantasmagoric, nightmarish, Kafkaesque.

imagination, *n.* **1.** imaginative faculty, imaging power, creative power; imaginativeness; fancy, mind's eye, castle-building, dreaming, reverie, daydream; originality, creativity, resourcefulness, inventiveness.

2. mental image, concept, conception, conceptualization, idea, notion; perception, thought, impression, reflection; fancy, conceit, vagary, whim; myth, figment, legend; romance, vision, dream, illusion; shadow, chimera, phantom, delusion, bugbear; man in the moon, castle in Spain, castle in the air, Atlantis, Utopia, fairyland.

imaginative, *adj.* **1.** creative, inventive, original; fertile, productive, constructive, ingenious, clever, resourceful, innovative; intellectual, ideal, romantic, poetic; quixotic, visionary, dreamy.

2. fanciful, whimsical, notional, imaginary; legendary, mythical, mythological; fictitious, unreal, fabulous, fantastical, figmental; shadowy, chimerical.

imagine, *v.* **1.** envision, image, picture, *Inf.* feature; dream, dream up, *Inf.* see things; conjure up, conceive, idealize, visualize, envisage, indulge in reverie, rhapsodize.

2. think, believe, fancy, opine, apprehend; assume, presume, suppose, *U.S. Dial.* reckon; conclude, judge, infer, deduce; hypothesize, theorize, guess, conjecture.

imbecile, *n.* **1.** retardate, incompetent, mental defective; half-wit, simpleton, moron, dullard, *Inf.* mental midget, *Sl.* dingbat.

—adj. **2.** feeble-minded, half-witted, simple, witless, defective, deficient, mindless, vacant; dull, slow, muddleheaded.

3. silly, absurd, fatuous, foolish, giddy, asinine, senseless, inane, addlepated, flighty, crazy, stupid, *Inf.* wacky.

imbecility, *n.* **1.** feeble-mindedness, mental defectiveness, mental retardation, incompetency, dullness, *Psychiatry.* amentia; feebleness, weakness, incapability, unfitness, ineptitude, disability.

2. silliness, absurdity, fatuity, foolishness, asininity, inanity, senselessness, brainlessness, flightiness, nonsense, folly, craziness.

imbibe, *v.* **1.** drink, quaff, sip, sup, *Archaic.* bib, *Inf.* swig, *Inf.* belt, *Inf.* pull; drain, wash down, toss off; gulp, swallow, *Sl.* guzzle *or* guzzle down, *Sl.* swill *or* swill down; (*all of alcoholic beverages*) tipple, tope, bouse, *Inf.* booze, nip, *Archaic.* dram; *All Inf.* gargle, wet *or* moisten one's whistle, take a drop, *Sl.* chug, *Sl.* chug-a-lug, lap, lap up, commune with the spirits, drown one's sorrows; *All Sl.* hit the sauce *or* bottle *or* booze, tie one on, scoop a few, knock a few back, liquor up, souse, dip the beak, bend *or* crook *or* exercise *or* raise an elbow.

2. absorb, suck up, draw up *or* in, take up *or* in, osmose; sponge, sponge up, soak up, blot up, sop up; eat, ingest, ingurgitate, gulp down, gobble up *or* down.

3. learn, acquire, gain, get, pick up, digest; assimilate, get by osmosis, gain *or* glean knowledge, *Inf.* get hold of.

imbroglio, *n.* **1.** complication, complexity, perplexity, problem; difficulty, entanglement, involvement; confusion, uncertainty, quandary; muddle, mess, botch, jumble, hodgepodge; trouble, *Inf.* hot water, scrape; dilemma, predicament, plight, *Inf.* pickle, *Inf.* fix, *Inf.* stew; corner, tight spot, *Sl.* box, bind, double bind, catch-22, vicious circle, strait, *Inf.* squeeze, pinch; impasse, standstill, stalemate, deadlock, stymie.

2. disagreement, conflict, opposition, strife; controversy, contention, altercation, argument, quarrel, *Sl.* mix-up, dispute, disputation.

3. commotion, disturbance, turmoil; fracas, row, donnybrook; bedlam, chaos, babel.

4. labyrinth, maze, jungle, wilderness; network, complex, complicacy, complexity; web, webwork, tangle, tangled skein, sleave; bafflement, riddle, puzzle, knot, Gordian knot.

imbrue, *v.* **1.** drench, soak, bathe, steep, infuse, tincture, penetrate, impregnate; saturate, imbue, permeate, souse, drown, inundate; douse, wash, wet; immerse, immerge, dip, dunk, submerse, submerge.

2. stain, taint, sully, defile.

imbue, *v.* **1.** impregnate, fill with, inject with; indoctrinate, inculcate, implant; impress, instill, ingrain.

2. inspire, inflame, arouse; fire, charge, stir, stimulate; affect, infect, influence.

3. imbrue, drench, infuse, tincture, penetrate, permeate. See **imbrue** (*def.* **1**).

imitate, *v.* **1.** pattern *or* model after, do like, emulate, parallel; copy, copycat, follow as an example, take after, walk in the footsteps of, tread in the steps of, tear *or* take a page from [s.o.'s] book, follow suit, match.

2. mimic, ape, monkey, parrot, repeat, reflect, mirror, echo; impersonate, *Sl.* make like, mock, parody, take off, caricature, burlesque; simulate, assume, represent, take on, affect.

3. duplicate, reproduce, make a copy, replicate, *Trademark.* Xerox, clone.

4. counterfeit, forge, fake, sham; plagiarize, *Sl.* lift.

imitation, *n.* **1.** imitating, mimicking, mimicry, *Zool.* mimesis, apery, monkeying; impersonation, mocking, parody, take-off, caricature, burlesque, travesty.
2. simulation, representation, replica, repetition, duplication, copy, facsimile; semblance, adaptation.
3. counterfeit, forgery, fake, sham; plagiarism, paraphrase; brummagem, tinsel, fraud.
—adj. **4.** imitative, simulated, synthetic. See **imitative** (*def.* **2**).

imitative, *adj.* **1.** mimic, *Archaic.* mimical, mimetic, apish, parrot-like; derivative, secondary, unoriginal; copied, plagiarized.
2. counterfeit, forged, fraudulent, imitation, fake, *Inf.* phony; not genuine, bogus, spurious, supposititious, bastardly.
3. pretended, feigned, simulated, make-believe, sham, flash; unreal, false, insincere, mock, ersatz, synthetic; artificial, factitious, contrived, *Sl.* hokey, fictitious; assumed, put-on, pseudo; specious, meretricious, theatrical.

imitator, *n.* copier, copyist, *Inf.* copycat, follower, shadow, epigone; mimic, impersonator, monkey, ape, parrot, echo; feigner, pretender; counterfeiter, forger, plagiarist.

immaculate, *adj.* **1.** spotless, unstained, stainless, refined, unsoiled, untarnished, unsullied; white, snowy, snow-white, speckless; washed, laundered, fresh, starched; spick-and-span, neat, tidy, clean, natty, spruce.
2. virgin, untouched, untainted, unspoiled; unadulterated, pristine, uncontaminated, unpolluted; disinfected, sanitized, hygienic, aseptic, sterile.
3. pure, undefiled, unblemished, unfouled, undebased; virginal, chaste, innocent, vestal, lily-white; virtuous, holy, incorrupt, saintly, sinless, guiltless; irreproachable, irreprehensible, unimpeachable, above suspicion.
4. flawless, faultless, errorless, perfect, impeccable; consummate, ideal, infallible, indefectible, correct.

immanent, *adj.* **1.** indwelling, inborn, innate, inbred, ingenerate; inherent, intrinsic, indigenous; native, connate, connatural, natural, natural-born; hereditary, inherited, in the blood, in the family.
2. rooted, deep-rooted, inveterate; ingrained, engrained, inwrought, enwrought.

immaterial, *adj.* **1.** inconsequential, unimportant, unessential, inessential, nonessential, insignificant, irrelevant; inconsiderable, inappreciable, trifling, trivial, petty, slight, of little account, of no moment; diminutive, small, inferior, minor, light.
2. not material, incorporeal, discarnate, bodiless, disembodied, unfleshly, impalpable, intangible; metaphysical, spiritual, transcendental, supernatural, ethereal, unearthly, superphysical, hyperphysical, supersensible, extramundane; aerial, ghostly, spectral, shadowy; animistic.

immature, *adj.* unripe, undeveloped, unfinished, unformed, imperfect, incomplete; rudimental, rudimentary, embryonic, half-grown, premature, abortive; crude, raw, green, tender, fresh, new, unmellowed; callow, inexperienced, unsophisticated, gullible, unversed, *Inf.* wet behind the ears; youthful, infantile, juvenile, puerile, childish, boyish, beardless.

immaturity, *n.* **1.** imperfection, incompleteness; unripeness, greenness, crudity, crudeness, rawness; rudimentariness, abortiveness, incipiency.
2. youth, youthfulness, boyishness; nonage, minority, wardship, juniority, puerility, juvenility, juvenescence; infancy, incunabula, childhood, boyhood, pupilage, adolescence, teens, tender age; bloom, virginity.

immeasurable, *adj.* limitless, boundless, illimitable, unlimited, unbounded, uncircumscribed, shoreless; incalculable, measureless, unfathomable, fathomless, undeterminable, undetermined, indeterminate; vast, extensive, immense, great, as far as the eye can see; innumerable, countless, untold, uncounted, numberless; endless, interminable, never-ending, inexhaustible, infinite.

immediate, *adj.* **1.** instant, instantaneous, simultaneous, sudden, abrupt; prompt, swift, speedy, hasty, early, lightning-fast, like a flash.
2. present, now, current, on hand, running, up-to-the-minute; latest, actual, that be, existing, extant, existent.
3. nearest, next, closest, close, nigh; adjacent, adjoining, abutting, contiguous, neighboring; proximate, approximate, propinquitous.
4. direct, first-hand, experiential, personal, head-on, hands-on, face-to-face; on-the-job, in-the-field, on-the-scene, on-the-spot.

immediately, *adv.* **1.** instantly, at once, right away, forthwith, without delay, instanter, *Jocular.* immediately if not sooner; this instant, this very moment *or* minute, now, *Sl.* pronto; directly, *Inf.* right off the bat, straightway, straightaway, straight off, presently, *Archaic.* anon; promptly, speedily, summarily, quickly, *Inf.* lickety-split, posthaste, *Inf.* before you can say "Jack Robinson;" suddenly, abruptly, *Music.* subito, presto, on the spur of the moment, on a moment's notice; instantaneously, in the same breath, in the wink of an eye, in the twinkling of an eye, *Inf.* in a jiffy, in a tick; in a moment, at the drop of a hat, on the spot, at a blow, in double time, in double-quick time.
2. closely, nearby, nigh, in the vicinity, in the neighborhood, in the area; close to, fast by, at close range, at close quarters, in propinquity; next door, alongside, at one's door, under one's nose.

immemorial, *adj.* time-honored, ancestral, traditional, customary; ancient, age-old, dateless, *Archaic.* olden, archaic; long-standing, fixed, rooted, inveterate, habitual; established, enduring, lasting, living, permanent; unchangeable, immutable, unchanging.

immense, *adj.* **1.** vast, extensive, broad, wide, expansive, *Archaic.* vasty, *Archaic.* immane; voluminous, bulky, capacious, massive; huge, enormous, large, big, prodigious; great, towering, staggering, great big, stupendous, tremendous, *Sl.* humongous, *Sl.* hulking; titanic, cyclopean, Atlantean, Brobdingnagian; colossal, mammoth, gigantic, monstrous, monumental, jumbo; elephantine, hippopotamic, leviathan, behemoth, dinosaurian, megatherian.
2. immeasurable, boundless, illimitable, unlimited, uncircumscribed, unbounded, limitless, shoreless; endless, interminable, infinite, inexhaustible, never-ending; incalculable, measureless, fathomless, unfathomable, undeterminable, indeterminate.

immensity, *n.* **1.** vastness, immenseness, spaciousness, *Archaic.* vastitude, *Archaic.* immaneness; hugeness, enormity, enormousness, gigantism; greatness, bigness, largeness, monstrousness; fullness, bulkiness, massiveness, sizableness; voluminousness, capaciousness.
2. boundlessness, infinity, infinitude, infinite space, endlessness; abyss, abysm, maw, gulf, chasm; void, depths, stretches; immeasurability, illimitability, interminableness, never-endingness.
3. expanse, breadth, latitude, width; extent, measure, sweep, reach, compass; volume, magnitude, amplitude.

immerse, *v.* **1.** immerge, plunge, dive, dip; submerge, duck, dunk, sink; soak, steep, swash, slosh; bathe, douse, drench, souse, imbue, saturate; flood, inundate, drown.

2. baptize, christen, *Archaic.* dip; cleanse, purify, lustrate.

3. embed, bury, inhume, *Obs.* inter.

4. engage, occupy, hold, take up, involve; absorb, engross, preoccupy, monopolize, engulf, consume; enthrall, fascinate, captivate, spellbind, mesmerize; whelm, overwhelm; attract, allure, draw.

immersion, *n.* **1.** immergence, immerging, plunging, diving, dipping; submergence, submerging, ducking, dunking, sinking; soaking, steeping, swashing, sloshing; bathing, dousing, drenching, sousing, imbuement, imbuing, saturation, saturating; flooding, inundation, inundating, drowning.

2. baptism, baptizement, christening, liturgy, *Eccles.* sacrament; dunking, *Archaic.* dipping; ablution, cleansing, purification, lustration.

3. engagement, occupation, involvement; absorption, engrossment, brown study, preoccupation, monopolization, engulfment, consummation; enthrallment, fascination, captivation, mesmerization.

immigrant, *n.* **1.** nonnative, naturalized citizen, *Chiefly Brit.* incomer; foreigner, alien, outsider, outlander, tramontane, barbarian; illegal alien, *Often Disparaging.* wetback; migrant, migrator, emigrant, expatriate.

2. entrant, arrival, newcomer, new kid *or* boy *or* girl, new kid on the block *or* in town.

immigrate, *v.* migrate, change one's place of residence, move, resettle, emigrate; enter the country, come *or* pass into the country, set foot on foreign soil, cross the border; change one's citizenship, start a new life, put down new roots.

imminent, *adj.* **1.** approaching, coming, forthcoming, toward, nearing, drawing near *or* nigh; near, close, close by, nearby, nigh, proximate, close at hand, at hand, within reach *or* sight, staring [s.o.] in the face; just about *or* almost here, about to happen, going to happen soon, upon us, likely to occur at any moment, momentary, immediate.

2. impending, lying in wait, in store, in the air *or* wind; overhanging, projecting, lowering; threatening, looming, brooding.

immobile, *adj.* immovable, motionless, immotive, unmoving, stock-still; stationary, fixed, rooted, riveted, like a statue; staunch, firm, constant, steadfast; inflexible, rigid, *Inf.* standpat; quiescent, inactive, dormant, at rest. See **immovable** (*defs.* **1, 2**).

immobility, *n.* immovability, fixity, stability, firmness; inflexibility, stiffness, rigidity, rigidness, rigor mortis; inertia, inertness, quiescence, inactivity, quietus, retirement.

immoderate, *adj.* **1.** excessive, inordinate, overweening, high-flown, overblown, extreme, extravagant; exorbitant, unreasonable, unwarranted, uncalled-for, exaggerated, undue, preposterous, outrageous, unconscionable.

2. unbridled, unrestrained, unlimited, uncurbed, uncontrolled; intemperate, incontinent, wanton, free-living, Saturnalian, self-indulgent; lavish, prodigal, profligate, squandering, dissipative.

immoderation, *n.* **1.** excess, excessiveness, inordinateness, *Obs.* inordinacy; extremeness, extravagance, exorbitance, exorbitancy; lavishness, prodigality, profuseness.

2. unrestraint, abandon, self-indulgence; wantonness, profligacy, dissipation, dissoluteness; intemperance, overindulgence, drunkenness; incontinence, licentiousness, lechery.

immodest, *adj.* **1.** undignified, undecorous, indecent, indelicate; shameless, shameful, disgraceful, unblushing; wanton, unrestrained, loose; lascivious, lewd, bawdy, coarse, smutty.

2. forward, impudent, impertinent, insolent; overbearing, overweening, arrogant; fresh, *Inf.* cheeky, nervy; brazen, bold, bold as brass, brassy.

immodesty, *n.* **1.** indecorum, indecency, indelicacy, shamelessness; wantonness, coarseness, lewdness, bawdiness, lasciviousness.

2. impudence, insolence, arrogance; boldness, cheek, nerve, brass, gall.

immolate, *v.* sacrifice, offer as a sacrifice, *Obs.* mactate; (*all as sacrifice*) kill, slay, put to death.

immoral, *adj.* **1.** corrupt, depraved, unprincipled, reprobate, unscrupulous, unredeemable, unregenerate, shameless, abandoned; wicked, evil, iniquitous, heinous, nefarious, flagitious, vicious, villainous, miscreant; foul, base, vile; degenerate, demoralized, deteriorated, debauched, warped, perverted; sinful, bad, dishonorable, disreputable; peccant, evil-minded, vice-minded; lost, irreformable, irreclaimable, incorrigible, unrepentant, hardened.

2. dissolute, dissipated, profligate, licentious, wanton, libertine, lascivious, lewd, lecherous, lustful, libidinous, *Archaic.* lickerish; concupiscent, prurient, salacious, goatish, *Sl.* horny; obscene, pornographic, dirty, indecent, immodest; carnal, sensual, animal, animalistic; unchaste, impure, of easy virtue, whorish, fast.

immorality, *n.* **1.** wickedness, evilness, badness, iniquitousness, heinousness, nefariousness, flagitiousness, viciousness, villainousness, miscreancy; corruption, depravity, turpitude, moral turpitude, unscrupulousness, shamelessness; foulness, baseness, vileness; sinfulness, unrighteousness, unvirtuousness, ungodliness; dishonorableness, disreputableness, evil-mindedness, vice-mindedness.

2. dissoluteness, dissipation, profligacy, prodigality, licentiousness, wantonness, abandonedness, lasciviousness, lecherousness, libidinousness, *Archaic.* lickerishness; concupiscence, prurience, salaciousness, goatishness, *Sl.* horniness; unchastity, impurity, uncleanliness, whorishness, fastness; indecency, immodesty; carnality, sensualness, animalism.

immortal, *adj.* **1.** deathless, undying, never-dying; ever-living, eternal, *Archaic.* eterne, everlasting, *Literary.* sempiternal; imperishable, perdurable, indestructible, indissoluble, incorruptible, unfading, undecaying, amaranthine, perennial, (*of trees*) evergreen; endless, never-ending, ceaseless, interminable.

2. famous, celebrated, remembered, praised, honored, lauded, commemorated, glorified, enshrined.

3. perpetual, lasting, constant; enduring, abiding, aeonian; immutable, unchanging, changeless, unwavering, unfaltering, undiminished; invariable, fixed, durable, stable, steady, permanent, *Latin. aere perennius.*

immortality, *n.* **1.** deathlessness, athanasia; incorruptibility, indestructibility, imperishability; everlastingness, perdurability; endlessness, unceasingness, perpetuity; eternity, infinity.

2. celebrity, repute, fame, gloriousness, renown; perpetuation, commemoration, glorification, enshrinement, canonization, beatification; niche in the temple of fame.

immortalize, *v.* **1.** render deathless, eternize, deify, apotheosize; perpetuate, make everlasting, make last, protract, prolong, preserve, save, conserve, maintain, sustain, continue.

2. commemorate, memorialize, celebrate, solemnize; glorify, canonize, beatify, enthrone, ennoble; signalize, exalt, salute, extol, elevate, acclaim, compliment, laud, pay tribute, make forever famous.

immovable, *adj.* **1.** stable, set, fast, fixed, secure, riveted, moored, anchored, planted, grounded; immobile, stationary, static, frozen, stiff, rigid.

2. motionless, unmoving, at a standstill, stock-still, dead-still, still as a statue, statuelike.

3. unalterable, unchangeable, immutable, permanent; irrevocable, irreversible, irrefutable, incontrovertible, settled; constant, changeless, unchanging, invariable, unvarying.

4. emotionless, unemotional, unfeeling, impassive, unresponsive, unsympathetic; cold, cool, frigid, icy; cold-blooded, cold-hearted, hard-hearted.

5. steadfast, staunch, stanch, steady, unflinching, unbending, unbowing, unwavering, unswerving; resolute, firm, determined, stubborn, dogged, obdurate, adamant, adamantine, tenacious; inflexible, unyielding, uncompromising, irreconcilable, not to be moved, *Inf.* hard-core, *Inf.* hard-shell; inexorable, implacable, relentless.

immune, *adj.* inoculated, protected, safe, not subject to, not liable to, unsusceptible, insusceptible, invulnerable, unvulnerable, unaffected, untouched; exempt, free, freed, scot-free, released, absolved, excused, dismissed from, relieved of, *Inf.* off the hook; excepted, spared, excluded, left out, passed by *or* over.

immunity, *n.* **1.** insusceptibility, inoculation, protection, safety.

2. exemption, impunity, indemnity; freedom, release, excusal, absolution, *Rom. Cath. Ch.* dispensation, *Archaic.* franchise; exception, exclusion.

3. privilege, prerogative, right; liberty, charter, license, permission, permit; favoritism, special treatment.

immunize, *v.* **1.** inoculate, give [s.o.] his shots, *Med.* vaccinate; protect, shield, safeguard, guard, keep, preserve.

2. neutralize, offset, counteract, counterbalance, countervail; cancel out, undo, nullify, negate.

immure, *v.* enclose, inclose, wall up *or* in, board up, close up *or* in; pen *or* pen in, coop *or* coop up, cage, encage; shut up *or* in, impound, confine, put into confinement; hold captive, hold, keep in custody, detain; imprison, put in prison, jail, put in jail, put behind bars, embar, lock up, incarcerate; *Inf.* send up the river, *Sl.* throw into the jug *or* clink, *Naut.* throw into the brig, *Sl.* throw into the coop, *Sl.* throw into the can *or* cooler.

immutable, *adj.* **1.** changeless, unchangeable, invariable, unalterable, incommutable, irreversible, inflexible; undeviating, unfaltering, unwavering, steadfast, reliable, steady; firm, fast, fixed, constant, durable, solid, stable, permanent.

2. enduring, abiding, lasting, persisting; indestructible, unbreakable, infrangible, imperishable, perdurable, inextinguishable, indissoluble; perpetual, unfading, incorruptible, undecaying, amaranthine, perennial, *Bot.* (*of leaves*) indeciduous, (*of trees*) evergreen; deathless, undying, immortal, eternal, *Archaic.* eterne, everlasting.

imp, *n.* **1.** devilkin, little devil, demon, evil spirit, hobgoblin, bogy, boogeyman, *Obs.* bugbear; hob, goblin, (*in German folklore*) kobold, *Irish Folklore.* leprechaun, pixy, puck, sprite, elf, brownie, fairy, fay; (*in Scandanavian folklore*) troll, gnome, dwarf, pygmy.

2. rascal, urchin, gamin; prankster, *Inf.* cut-up, mischief-maker, troublemaker.

impact, *n.* **1.** collision, crash, clash, striking, bump; slam, bang, knock, thump, whack, thwack; blow, stroke, punch, smack, slap, *Inf.* clip, smash.

2. percussion, shock, force, full force, brunt; pressure, impetus, momentum, energy.

3. influence, bearing, effect; results, repercussions, consequences.

—*v.* **4.** pack in, ram down, force in *or* down, compress, condense; push in, press in, shove in, wedge in, cram in, stuff in, jam in, squeeze in, fit in.

5. congest, throng, fill, fill up, crowd, overcrowd, overfill, overstuff, fill to overflowing, fill to the brim.

6. collide with, bump into, run into, bang into, smash into, slam into, dash against; hit, strike, smack, knock, thump, whack, thwack, punch, *Inf.* clip, slap.

7. *Usu.* **impact on** affect, influence, alter, change; work upon, impress, act on, bear on, relate to, impinge on.

impair, *v.* weaken, lessen, enervate, water down, attenuate; vitiate, debase, adulterate, pollute, corrupt; debilitate, enfeeble, sap, undermine; wear down *or* out *or* away; cripple, disable, crush, shatter; damage, injure, harm, hurt; spoil, mar, blemish, deface, disfigure.

impale, *v.* transfix, pierce, stab, prick, stick; puncture, perforate, bore; pink, spear, spike, spit; run through, gut, disembowel, eviscerate.

impalpable, *adj.* **1.** intangible, imperceptible, imponderable; insubstantial, unreal, unworldly, dreamlike; light, airy, ethereal, shadowy, cloudy, wispy; evanescent, fleeting.

2. subtle, obscure, vague, tenuous; unclear, ambiguous, blurred, fuzzy, clouded, veiled; mysterious, esoteric, recondite, secret.

impart, *v.* **1.** tell, relate, pass on, communicate, transmit, publish, report, proclaim; apprise, make known, disclose, uncover, reveal, divulge, *Inf.* break; inform, confide, mention, hint, hint at, intimate, suggest.

2. bestow, grant, cede, confer, render; deal, apportion, allot, allocate, assign, award; dispense, distribute, give, present, contribute, donate; deliver, hand over, hand out, part with, fork over, shell out; entrust, lend, consign, relegate.

impartial, *adj.* unbiased, unprejudiced, unbigoted; uncolored, disinterested, dispassionate, detached, objective; neutral, without favoritism, uninfluenced, incorrupt, aboveboard, punctilious, legal, by the rules; equitable, even, even-handed, fair, fair-minded, just, true, *Inf.* square, unwarped.

impartiality, *n.* equity, fairness, justice, justness, fair play, even-handedness; objectivity, dispassion, disinterest, disinterestedness, neutrality.

impassable, *adj.* **1.** impenetrable, impervious, impermeable; unnavigable, untraversable, inaccessible; blocked, obstructed, barricaded; washed-out, pathless.

2. insurmountable, insuperable, unconquerable.

impasse, *n.* **1.** deadlock, stalemate, standstill; halt, stop, stoppage, full stop, dead stop, quietus, cessation; stand, stay, check, checkmate, mate; block, blockage; stand-off, tie, draw.

2. dilemma, perplexity, nonplus; predicament, hole, *Inf.* fix, corner; bind, double bind, catch-22; dead end, blind alley, cul-de-sac.

impassioned, *adj.* **1.** passionate, impassionate, ardent, vehement, zealous; overzealous, overeager, overanxious, *Inf.* gung-ho; fervent, fervid, perfervid; earnest, eager, animated, enthusiastic, *Inf.* enthused, *Inf.* psyched *or* psyched up; excited, sparkling, glowing, lively, alive, full of life, vivacious, *Inf.* bright-eyed and

bushy-tailed; enlivened, inspired, inspirited, invigorated, energized, energetic, vivified, vitalized; vigorous, forceful, dynamic, high-powered.
2. stimulated, aroused, burning, *Inf.* hot, *Inf.* turned on; inflamed, infatuated, lusting after, *Sl.* hot for, *Sl.* letching after, mad about, *Inf.* wild about; desirous, intense, amorous, sensual, sexual, erotic.
3. emotional, emotive, temperamental, high-strung; excitable, spirited, high-spirited; volatile, volcanic, fiery, hot-headed, inflammable, kindled, enkindled; agitated, nervous, tense, fretful; disturbed, perturbed, shaken, stirred up, worked up; heated, white-hot, inflamed, flaming, flared up, flaring; irate, wrathful, wroth, incensed, very angry; enraged, raging, fuming, infuriated, infuriate, furious; overwrought, distraught, upset, feverish, hysterical, not rational, violent; ranting, raving, foaming at the mouth, rabid, fanatical, frenzied; frantic, crazed, *Pathol.* delirious, mad, *Inf.* wild.

impassive, *adj.* **1.** apathetic, emotionless, unemotional, impassible, insensitive; stolid, phlegmatic, stoical, imperturbable, unexcitable; unconcerned, nonchalant, reserved, reticent, taciturn; indifferent, uncaring, *Sl.* blah, unmoved, unfeeling, dispassionate, passionless; cool, cold, frigid, *Inf.* like a cold fish, with ice water in one's veins; cold-blooded, stony-hearted, with a heart of stone, having a lump of coal for a heart.
2. calm, serene, peaceful, tranquil, halcyon, in the clouds; unruffled, composed, collected, content, drifting along.
3. unconscious, insensible, insensate; impervious, deaf and blind to, zombie-like, half-alive; hardened, indurated, callous, thick-skinned.

impassivity, *n.* **1.** apathy, indifference, unconcern, dispassion, impassibility; insensitivity, imperturbability, nonchalance, casualness, stoicism, stolidity; reserve, reticence, silence; cold shoulder, coldness, coolness, iciness, frigidity.
2. calmness, serenity, tranquility, placidity, composure, sang-froid.
3. hardness, dullness, callousness, obdurateness; thick skin, hard shell.

impatience, *n.* **1.** nervousness, agitation, *Inf.* whim-whams; anxiety, jitteriness, disquiet, restlessness, restiveness; excitability, flutter, fluster, *Sl.* flap; impetuosity, eagerness, avidity, precipitateness; itchiness, itchy feet, *Sl.* ants in one's pants, formication.
2. brusqueness, testiness, shortness, waspishness, snappishness; irascibility, hotheadedness, *Sl.* short fuse, short temper, jumpiness; intolerance, nonendurance.

impatient, *adj.* **1.** unquiet, uneasy, anxious, jumpy, nervous; restless, restive, jittery, fidgety, skittish, *Sl.* itchy; agitated, excitable, high-strung.
2. irritable, irascible, testy, querulous; fretful, peevish, waspish, snappish, short, rude; brusque, abrupt, short-tempered, *Sl.* short-fused; seething, chafing; intolerant.
3. hasty, precipitate, quick, headlong; eager, agog, avid, keen, *Sl.* hot-to-trot, *Sl.* antsy; impulsive, impetuous, reckless, rash, heedless, madcap, hotheaded; irrepressible, clamorous, straining at the bit, rampant, raging.

impeach, *v.* **1.** accuse, charge, indict, *Law.* arraign, *Law.* impute, incriminate, criminate, recriminate, *Rare.* implead; denounce, implicate, inculpate; blame, hold [s.o.] accountable *or* responsible, lay at [s.o.'s] door, point the finger at [s.o.]; (*all in reference to culpability*) allege, ascribe, attribute, assign, impute, lay.
2. challenge, question, call into question, impugn, assail, revile, attack; discredit, impair, deprecate, disparage, belittle, *Sl.* badmouth; stigmatize, brand, slur, asperse, cast aspersions on, malign, slander, defame, vilify; inveigh against, rail against, declaim against, fulminate against.

impeccable, *adj.* **1.** faultless, correct, perfect, ideal, flawless; immaculate, spotless, unspotted, stainless, unblemished, clean, clear; complete, finished, absolute.
2. irreproachable, unerring, virtuous, upright, exemplary, aboveboard, unimpeachable, above suspicion, *Fr. sans peur et sans reproche;* blameless, inculpable, impeccant, incorrupt; innocent, pure, chaste, sinless, guiltless, undefiled, pure as the driven snow.

impecunious, *adj.* penniless, out of money, cleaned out, insolvent, bankrupt, *Inf.* broke, *Inf.* flat, *Inf.* flat-broke; embarrassed, *Inf.* pinched, *Inf.* short, *Sl.* hard up, *Sl.* strapped, out of pocket, without a penny *or* a nickel to one's name, without a sou; poor, poor as a church mouse, poor as Job's turkey, impoverished, poverty-stricken, destitute, down and out, unable to make ends meet, unable to keep the wolf from the door, needy, indigent, necessitous, penurious.

impede, *v.* obstruct, block, contravene, hinder, thwart, balk, inhibit, frustrate, foil, confound, bar; undermine, sabotage, spike, *Inf.* spike [s.o.'s] guns, *Inf.* throw a spike in the wheels *or* a monkey wrench into the works; prevent, preclude, forestall, obviate, deter; stand in the way, interfere, interrupt, intervene, intercept, *Inf.* short-circuit; restrict, restrain, tie up, cramp, hamper, handicap, encumber, cumber, entangle, checkmate, stymie, tree, corner; set *or* put back, delay, stave *or* ward off, stop *or* dam up, clog, choke, hold back, *Inf.* bottleneck; turn aside, avert, counteract, offset, neutralize, countercheck; check, stay, arrest, put the breaks on, put a stop to, repress, nip in the bud.

impediment, *n.* **1.** hindrance, encumbrance, obstacle, obstruction, stumbling block, road block; knot, hitch, curb, clog, bit, tether; inhibition, restriction, determent, damper, restraint; bar, barrier, block, counteraction, embargo, stricture, blockade; opposition, objection, discouragement, difficulty, drawback, disadvantage; delay, hang-up, snag, bottleneck, red tape; interference, setback, drag; load, burden, deadweight.
2. stammer, stutter, lisp, hesitance, hesitation, falter, speech defect.

impedimenta, *n.* equipment, supplies, matériel, traps, trappings, gear; baggage, luggage, paraphernalia, accouterments, things, goods, effects, movables, excess baggage, encumbrances; equipage, tackle, harness, rigging, apparatus, appurtenances.

impel, *v.* **1.** urge *or* drive forward, press *or* urge on, exhort, impress; induce, persuade, prevail upon, insist upon, railroad, ramrod; constrain, oblige, necessitate, require, demand, force, make, exact, leave no option *or* choice; apply pressure, *Inf.* pressure *or* high-pressure, *Inf.* lean on, *Inf.* squeeze, *Inf.* put the screws on *or* to, *Inf.* twist [s.o.'s] arm; draft, conscript, commandeer.
2. move, actuate, set in motion, get going; propel, push, shove, thrust, nudge; spur, prod, prick, goad, poke; lash, whip.

impending, *adj.* **1.** imminent, about to happen, at hand, near *or* close at hand, near, close; coming, upcoming, forthcoming, to come, approaching, nearing; in store, in the wind, in the air, *Inf.* in the cards, *Inf.* on the books; in view, in prospect, in the offing, on the horizon.
2. threatening, menacing, lowering, looming, lurking; brewing, gathering, collecting.

impenetrable, *adj.* **1.** impervious, imperviable, impassable, unpassable, inaccessible, unaccessible, jungly, jungled, overgrown; trackless, pathless, wayless, untrodden, *Obs.* invious.
2. proof, resistant, tight, snug, compact, hermetic,

hermetically sealed; closed, shut, sealed, locked; solid, hard, rock-hard, adamantine; impermeable, unporous, nonporous, watertight, waterproof; punctureproof, imperforable, unperforable, imperforate, imperforated, unpierceable, unpierced, holeproof.

3. dull, dense, thick, stolid, obtuse, stupid, senseless; crass, gross, indelicate, boorish, oafish; prejudiced, prejudicial, bigoted, biased, close-minded, narrow-minded; callous, calloused, insensitive, thickskinned, hard, hardened, indurate, indurated, inured, stony, flinty, steely; inflexible, rigid, fixed, unswayable, unmovable, unpliable, uninfluenceable, unpersuadable; impassive, indifferent, insensible, unfeeling, cold, unresponsive, unapproachable, unreachable, beyond reach, out of reach.

4. unfathomable, inscrutable, incomprehensible, uncomprehensible, past *or* beyond comprehension, unknowable, beyond understanding, incognizable, indecipherable, undecipherable; profound, deep, recondite, esoteric, abstruse, abstract; mystic, mystical, occult, supernatural, preternatural, fey, otherworldly, supermundane; inexplicable, unexplainable, insolvable, insoluble, unaccountable, *Obs.* inextricable; puzzling, enigmatic, enigmatical; dark, obscure, dim, vague, nebulous; hidden, secret, mysterious.

impenitent, *adj.* unrepentant, unrepenting, irrepentant, uncontrite; remorseless, obdurate, hard, hardened, inured, indurate, callous, insensible, unfeeling; incorrigible, reprobate, miscreant, unreformed; lost, abandoned, irreclaimable.

imperative, *adj.* **1.** inescapable, unavoidable, compulsory, mandatory, obligatory, binding, prescriptive; requisite, required, called-for, in demand, needful, needed; necessary, vital, indispensable, essential, of the essence; compelling, pressing, urgent, exigent, high-priority, high-pressure.

2. commanding, mandating, instructive, prescriptive, authoritative; imperious, peremptory, overbearing, domineering, lordly, magisterial, masterful; authoritarian, dogmatic, arbitrary, despotic, dictatorial, tyrannical.

—*n.* **3.** command, commandment, order, dictate, bidding, behest, *Inf.* word, *Inf.* say-so; direction, injunction, instruction, precept, prescription, mandate.

4. obligation, duty, charge, responsibility, liability, onus, burden.

5. dire necessity, urgent need, urgency, exigency, matter of life and death.

imperceptible, *adj.* **1.** unnoticeable, unapparent, subtle, slight, gradual; inappreciable, inconsiderable, inconsequential; minute, minuscule; microscopic, infinitesimal.

2. invisible, unseeable, imperceivable, unperceptible, indiscernible, indistinguishable; ill-defined, indistinct, indefinite, obscure, vague, unclear, shadowy; faint, inaudible, muted, muffled.

imperceptive, *adj.* unperceptive, undiscerning, impercipient; blind, purblind, blind as a bat; oblivious, insensible, unconscious; uncomprehending, unapprehending, dull, dim, obtuse, slow, slow-witted, dull-witted, dim-witted, thick-witted.

imperfect, *adj.* **1.** faulty, defective, inoperative, unserviceable, out of order, out of commission, *Inf.* on the blink, *Inf.* on the fritz, *Inf.* out of kilter, *Sl.* out of whack, *Sl.* gone kerflooie, *Sl.* kaput, *Scot.* stickit, *Sl.* on the bum; broken, disfigured, injured, flawed, deformed, mutilated, decrepit, lame, crippled; weak, frail, feeble.

2. incomplete, not entire, partial, unfinished, inchoate; undeveloped, immature, premature, rudimentary, abortive.

3. deficient, insufficient, inadequate; mediocre, indifferent, middling, below par, so-so, mean, average, fair, moderate, ordinary; inferior, crude, rough, bad, inexact.

imperfection, *n.* **1.** defect, flaw, fault, blemish; snag, catch, tear, rent, run, *Chiefly Brit.* ladder; cut, scratch, crack, break; spot, taint, stain; deformity, disfigurement, malformation.

2. imperfectness, defectiveness, faultiness, weakness, infirmity, frailty; inadequacy, inferiority, unsoundness, deficiency, drawback; incompleteness, immaturity; shortcoming, foible, weak point, liability, limitation, failing; omission, transgression, misdeed, error, offense, vice, wrong, sinfulness, badness.

imperial, *adj.* **1.** sovereign, regal, royal, monarchal, imperatorial; kingly, kinglike, queenly, queenlike, princely.

2. supreme, absolute, dominant, predominant, preeminent, paramount, chief, ruling.

3. commanding, mandating, imperative, prescriptive, authoritative; imperious, peremptory, overbearing, domineering, lordly, magisterial, masterful; authoritarian, dogmatic, despotic, dictatorial, tyrannical, arbitrary.

4. majestic, magnificent, splendid, grand, lofty, imposing, stately.

imperialism, *n.* **1.** sovereignty, empire, empery, emperorship, royalty, majesty; kingship, kinghood, queenship, queenhood; the throne, the crown, the scepter, the purple.

2. monarchism, royalism; expansionism, colonialism, neocolonialism, the white man's burden.

imperil, *v.* endanger, expose to danger, jeopardize, put in jeopardy, compromise, *Sl.* put on the spot, *Sl.* lay on the line; hazard, risk, gamble, gamble with, tempt fate *or* providence, take a chance, play with fire, sail too near the wind, *Inf.* press *or* push one's luck, expose, lay open, bare.

imperious, *adj.* **1.** peremptory, overbearing, overweening, domineering, high-handed, hands-on, *Inf.* bossy; commanding, lordly, high-and-mighty, magisterial, masterful; bumptious, assertive, heavy-handed; authoritarian, dogmatic, arbitrary, despotic, dictatorial, tyrannical.

2. urgent, exigent, compelling, pressing, imperative, high-priority, high-pressure; necessary, vital, indispensable, essential, of the essence; requisite, required, called-for, in demand, needful, needed.

imperishable, *adj.* indestructible, inextinguishable, indissoluble, infrangible, unbreakable; indelible, ineradicable; immutable, unalterable, unchangeable, changeless, incommutable; unfading, undecaying, incorruptible, amaranthine, perennial, (*of leaves*) *Bot.* indeciduous, (*of trees*) *Bot.* evergreen; enduring, lasting, abiding, everlasting, eternal, *Archaic.* eterne, immortal.

impermanent, *adj.* transitory, transient, temporary, temporal, fly-by-night; momentary, short-lived, ephemeral, evanescent, volatile, passing, fleeting, fading, flitting; mortal, perishable, corruptible, unendurable, nonpermanent; mutable, changeable, changeful, alterable, variable, permutable, inconstant; unstable, unfixed, unsteady, unsettled.

impermeable, *adj.* **1.** impenetrable, impassable, impervious, imperviable, inaccessible; jungly, jungled, overgrown; trackless, pathless, wayless, untrodden, *Obs.* invious.

2. proof, resistant, tight, airtight, snug, compact, hermetic, hermetically sealed; closed, shut, sealed, locked; solid, hard, rock-hard, adamantine; unporous, nonporous, watertight, waterproof.

impersonal, *adj.* **1.** detached, disinterested, dispassionate, objective, nonsubjective, fair, even-handed, equitable; unbiased, unprejudiced, unswayed, unprepossessed, unjaundiced.

2. stiff, wooden, rigid, starch, stuffy, stilted, strait-laced, prim, formal; mechanical, machinelike, computerlike; matter-of-fact, businesslike, business-as-usual.

impersonate, *v.* imitate, pretend to be, mimic, ape, *Sl.* make like, monkey, parrot, repeat, reflect, mirror, echo; simulate, assume, represent, take on, affect; mock, parody, take off, caricature, burlesque.

impersonation, *n.* personation, mocking, imitating, imitation, parody, take-off, caricature, burlesque, travesty; mimicking, mimicry, *Zool.* mimesis, apery, monkeying.

impertinence, *n.* **1.** insolence, impudence, audacity, effrontery, presumption, presumptuousness; boldness, brazenness, freshness, brashness, pertness, sauciness, shamelessness, *Inf.* cheekiness, *Inf.* sassiness, *Inf.* brassiness; impoliteness, unmannerliness, ill-manneredness, incivility, rudeness; bumptiousness, cockiness, forwardness, chutzpah; meddlesomeness, intrusiveness, officiousness.

2. *All Inf.* brass, sass, face, cheek, back talk, guff, crust, sauce; *All Sl.* gall, nerve, mouth, lip.

3. malapert, minx, hussy, boldface, brazenface, whippersnapper, upstart, *Inf.* saucebox, *Inf.* smart aleck, *Inf.* smarty pants, *Sl.* wise guy, *Sl.* smart *or* wise ass.

4. irrelevance, immateriality, inapplicability, inappropriateness, inappositeness, inconsequence; unrelatedness, unconnectedness; absurdity, ludicrousness, ridiculousness.

impertinent, *adj.* **1.** insolent, impudent, audacious, presumptuous, out-of-line, out-of-keeping; bold, brazen, brazen-faced, fresh, brash, pert, saucy, shameless, *Inf.* flip, *Inf.* cheeky, *Inf.* sassy, *Inf.* brassy, *Sl.* wise, *Sl.* mouthy, *Sl.* smart-mouth; impolite, unmannered, unmannerly, ill-mannered, uncivil, rude, ill-bred, vulgar, coarse, crude; bumptious, cocksure, cocky, arrogant, forward; meddlesome, intrusive, officious.

2. irrelevant, inapposite, inapplicable, immaterial, inconsequent; unrelated, unconnected, beside the point, beside the question, beside the mark, nothing to do with the case, *Inf.* off base *or* way off base.

imperturbable, *adj.* inexcitable, unflappable, even-tempered, easy-going; self-controlled, steady, poised, balanced; calm, collected, composed, self-possessed, cool, *Inf.* cool as a cucumber, *Inf.* together; nonchalant, at ease, unruffled, untroubled, undismayed, unperturbed, undisturbed, unexcited, unmoved; sedate, tranquil, serene, placid, peaceful, dispassionate.

impervious, *adj.* **1.** impassable, impenetrable, impermeable, inaccessible, imperviable; jungly, jungled, overgrown; trackless, pathless, wayless, untrodden.

2. proof, resistant, tight, airtight, snug, compact, hermetic, hermetically sealed; closed, shut, locked, sealed, sealed-off; solid, hard, rock-hard, adamantine; unporous, watertight, waterproof; punctureproof, imperforable, imperforate, unpierceable, holeproof.

3. imperishable, indestructible, indissoluble, inextinguishable, infrangible, unbreakable; enduring, lasting, abiding, everlasting, eternal, immortal, deathless, undying.

4. callous, calloused, thickskinned, insensitive, unfeeling, hard, hard-hearted, hardened, inured, indurate, stony, flinty, steely; cold-hearted, cold-blooded, cold, frigid, frosty, icy, unsympathetic, unresponsive; uninfluenceable, unswayable, unmovable; unpliable, inflexible, unyielding, obdurate, unpersuadable; unreceptive, unamenable, closed to.

impetuosity, *n.* **1.** hastiness, abruptness, precipitateness, impetuousness; rashness, temerity, recklessness, boldness, brashness, foolhardiness; impulsiveness, thoughtlessness, offhandedness, heedlessness, incaution; hot-bloodedness, excitability, hotheadedness; unruliness, intractability, intractableness, obstinacy, obstinateness, willfulness, stubbornness.

2. eagerness, enthusiasm, ardor, ardency, ardentness, fervor, fervency, ferventness; spirit, élan, dash, liveliness, buckishness, spiritedness; spontaneity, abandon, unrestraint.

3. violence, force, power, might, vigor; rage, fury, frenzy; ferocity, fierceness, ferociousness, furiousness.

impetuous, *adj.* **1.** hasty, quick, abrupt, swift; precipitate, headlong, careless, slapdash; eager, energetic, dashing, buckish, spirited, lively.

2. impulsive, spontaneous, unreflective, thoughtless, unreasoned, unreflecting, offhand, spur-of-the-moment, ill-conceived; mercurial, fickle, capricious; overhasty, rash, reckless, madcap, temerarious; brash, heedless, incautious, heady, foolhardy; excitable, impatient, hot-blooded, *Inf.* quick on the trigger, *Inf.* trigger-happy; hotheaded, fiery, ardent, passionate, overzealous; burning, fervid, perfervid.

3. violent, forceful, powerful, vigorous, raging; rampant, unrestrained, uncontrolled, unbridled, wild, ungoverned; unrestrainable, ungovernable, uncontrollable, unruly; intractable, headstrong, willful, stubborn, obstinate.

impetus, *n.* **1.** instigation, actuation, moving force, spark, stimulus, stimulation, incentive, motivation, inducement, inspiration, encouragement, influence; urging, pressing, spurring, pricking, whipping, lashing, goading; spur, prick, whip, lash, goad.

2. momentum, propulsion, continuing motion, energy, thrust, impelling force, drive, push.

impiety, *n.* **1.** ungodliness, godlessness, irreligion; apostasy, recidivism, backsliding; atheism, agnosticism, paganism, heathenism.

2. irreverence, disrespect, disrespectfulness, lack of respect; insolence, impertinence, mockery, scoffing, derision; ridicule, insult, jeering, sneering, smirking.

3. sin, sinfulness, wickedness, vice, wrong, wrongdoing, malpractice; corruption, evildoing, transgression, offense, trespass; sacrilege, abomination, desecration, befoulment, defilement; cursing, swearing, foul language, blasphemy, profanity, taking the Lord's name in vain.

impinge, *v.* **1.** encroach, infringe, intrude, invade, trespass, *Inf.* horn in, usurp.

2. strike, hit, dash, run against, knock against, butt against, bump against, collide with; jolt, push, prod, shove, come into conflict with.

3. affect, impress, touch, touch upon, influence, exert influence, relate to, have a relation to, bear upon, have to do with, *Inf.* tie in with, pertain to.

impious, *adj.* **1.** irreverent, irreligious, indevout, ungodly; pharisaical, canting, pietistical, sanctimonious, hypocritical; blasphemous, sacrilegious, desecrative; unrighteous, iniquitous, sinful, wicked, satanic, diabolic; perverted, reprobate, immoral, iniquitous, impure.

impish, *adj.* mischievous, full of mischief, mischief-making, prankish; imp-like, pixyish, puckish, elfish, elfin; devilish, trouble-making, unruly, unmanageable, difficult to handle, intractable, perverse; obnoxious, annoying, *Inf.* pesky, insufferable.

implacability, *n.* mercilessness, pitilessness, lack of compassion, lack of sympathy, hard-heartedness, heartlessness; rigidity, firmness, hardness, inexorability, relentlessness; unforgiveness, grudge-holding, lack of forgiveness, revenge-seeking, vengefulness.

implacable, *adj.* unappeasable, not to be appeased,

unpacifiable, not to be pacified, unmollifiable, unreconcilable; unforgiving, grudge-holding, vengeful, revengeful; rigid, firm, adamant, unbending, hard, inexorable, relentless; merciless, unmerciful, pitiless, unpitying; uncompassionate, uncompassioned, unsympathizing, unsympathetic, hard-hearted, heartless.

implant, *v.* **1.** instill, insinuate, inject, inculcate, introduce, inoculate, indoctrinate; train, teach, imprint, impress.
2. influence, inspire, impregnate, imbue, imbrue, move.
3. imbed, root, insert, inlay, set in.

implausible, *adj.* incredible, unbelievable, hard to believe, unimaginable, inconceivable, unheard of; improbable, unlikely, doubtful, dubious; questionable, debatable, disputable, equivocal; indefinite, conjectural, unfounded, precarious, unreasonable.

implement, *n.* **1.** tool, utensil, appliance, instrument, apparatus, mechanism, contrivance, device, *Inf.* contraption, invention, gadget, hickey, *Sl.* gimmick; engine, motor, machine.
2. piece of equipment *or* gear, article of clothing.
3. agent, cause, medium, channel, means, expedient, wherewithal, resources.
—*v.* **4.** fulfill, carry out, execute, perform; accomplish, achieve, realize, put into effect, bring to pass, bring about.
5. fill out, supplement, add to, augment.

implicate, *v.* **1.** incriminate, criminate, inculpate, (*of an innocent person*) frame; inform against, *Sl.* rat on, fink, squeal.
2. accuse, charge, blame, impeach; (*all in reference to culpability*) allege, ascribe, attribute, assign, impute, lay.
3. involve, concern, affect, influence; relate to, connect with, impinge upon; draw in, entangle, enmesh, ensnare.
4. imply, import, mean, denote, connote; signify, represent, betoken, bespeak.

implication, *n.* **1.** suggestion, hint, intimation, insinuation, innuendo; inference, assumption; allusion, reference.
2. intent, purpose, purport, drift; significance, sense, import, meaning, connotation, interpretation, signification; gist, burden, essence, substance, pith, upshot; effect, outcome, result, fallout, consequence, aftermath.
3. incrimination, crimination, inculpation; involvement, connection, entanglement, enmeshment, ensnarement.

implicit, *adj.* **1.** absolute, perfect, complete, entire, whole, total; sheer, utter, unmitigated, unrestricted, unlimited; unqualified, categorical, unconditional, unconditioned, unreserved; positive, determinate, certain, veritable, unequivocal, unambiguous, explicit, express; sure, assured, cocksure, confident, unquestioning, undoubting, unquestionable.
2. implied, inferred, inferential, deduced, deducible; understood, tacit, unspoken, unexpressed.

implicitly, *adv.* absolutely, completely, wholly, fully, entirely; totally, nothing short of, unqualifiedly, utterly; categorically, unconditionally, unreservedly; purely, clearly; beyond the shadow of a doubt, positively, certainly, veritably, unquestionably, unequivocally, unambiguously, explicitly; ultimately, infinitely, infallibly.

implied, *adj.* understood, unspoken, undeclared, tacit; implicit, inferred, inferential, deduced, deducible; signified, indicated, denoted, connoted; suggested, intimated, hinted at, insinuated, inferred, between-the-lines.

implore, *v.* appeal to, beg, beseech, entreat, obsecrate, plead, *Brit. Inf.* prig, pray, crave; ask, request, seek; call upon, invoke, pray to; petition, solicit, supplicate, obtest, adjure, conjure, *Rare.* sue; urge, press, importune, insist, demand.

imply, *v.* **1.** involve, entail, presuppose, suppose, presume, assume, include, depend on, point to.
2. signify, express, mean, import, denote, connote, betoken.
3. intimate, suggest, infer, hint, *Inf.* give to understand, insinuate, *Inf.* put a bug in [s.o.'s] ear; clue, *Inf.* tip off, cue, prompt; jog one's memory, signal, *Inf.* give a high sign, wink; breathe, whisper; allude to, advert, refer, indicate.

impolite, *adj.* rude, discourteous, uncivil, unceremonious, unmannerly, bad-mannered, ill-bred, disrespectful, misbehaved; indelicate, uncourtly, ungallant, indecorous, ungracious; ungentlemanly, unladylike, brash, bold, hoydenish, *Scot.* randy; brazen, barefaced, insolent, impudent, insulting, impertinent, pert, saucy, fresh; bluff, surly, sullen, bearish, gruff; inconsiderate, tactless, *Scot. and North Eng.* misleared; abrupt, blunt, brusque, curt, clipped, short; rough, crude, boorish, churlish, loutish, vulgar, coarse.

impolitic, *adj.* **1.** inexpedient, unshrewd, disadvantageous, unprofitable, undesirable, unfavorable, detrimental, harmful; inadvisable, unadvised, unadvisable, ill-advised, unrecommendable, unrecommended, miscounseled, misguided; inappropriate, unsuitable, ill-suited, wrong.
2. injudicious, ill-judged, unwise, unsage, unsagacious; imprudent, ill-considered, inconsiderate, tactless, thoughtless, senseless; indiscreet, short-sighted, incautious, uncircumspect; careless, temerarious, rash, hasty, overhasty, reckless, hot-headed, foolhardy.

imponderable, *adj.* **1.** inconsiderable, uncontemplatable, ungraspable, hard to grasp, unapprehensible, hard to understand, unponderable; incomprehensible, inconceivable, unthinkable, unimaginable, beyond the human mind; subtle, tenuous, attenuated, rarefied; abstract, ethereal, immaterial, airy, vaporous, gaseous, pneumatic.
2. unweighable, unmeasurable, inestimable; unweighty, insubstantial, unsubstantial, light, light as a feather *or* thistle down, weightless; minute, microscopic, minuscule, minute, imperceptible.

import, *v.* **1.** introduce, bring into the country, present, carry.
2. convey, portend, mean, denote; purport, signify, symbolize, betoken, mark, indicate; connote, imply, intimate, suggest, allude, drive at.
3. carry weight, be of import *or* importance, have meaning; count, make a difference, matter, be of consequence; concern, be of concern *or* interest.
—*n.* **4.** foreign commodity, foreign-made article, goods *or* merchandise from abroad, importation, nondomestic commodity.
5. meaning, purport, denotation, sense, gist, essence, pith, core, heart, sum and substance, intent, intention; connotation, implication, inference, intimation, illation, allusion, suggestion.
3. importance, significance, signification, portent, matter, salient point, value; moment, substance, weight, weightiness, gravity, force; consequence, result, effect, issue, issuance, upshot, outcome, turnout, sequel; fallout, aftermath, aftereffect, afterclap, wake, repercussion; corollary, concomitant, attendant.

importance, *n.* **1.** significance, consequence, matter, value, account, concern, *Archaic.* concernment; moment, weight, weightiness, substance, greatness, magnitude, force; gravity, graveness, heaviness, seriousness, solemnity; priority, precedence, press, urgency, emergentness.

2. distinction, prominence, prestige, eminence, high standing, high position *or* rank; regard, esteem, notability, note, mark, merit, high caliber; influence, sway, power, powerfulness; self-importance, superiority, pomposity, grandeur.

important, *adj.* **1.** significant, portentous, of great import; consequential, of great consequence, critical, decisive, material; momentous, weighty, heavy, ponderous, pregnant, carrying great weight, of substance; serious, grave, solemn, sober; crucial, urgent, emergent, exigent, pressing, importunate, imperative, taking priority *or* precedence, requiring immediate attention.

2. *Usu.* **important to** mattering, carrying weight, meaning a lot, of import; of concern *or* interest, of account, counting; valuable, necessary, essential, vital, life-sustaining.

3. salient, prominent, outstanding, noticeable, conspicuous; notable, noteworthy, of note, signal; worthy, meritorious, of merit, remarkable.

4. major, main, principal, prime, primary, leading; large, great, big, sizeable, substantive, substantial; considerable, inestimable, immeasurable, invaluable.

5. influential, of influence, well-connected, with connections, impressive; effective, powerful, of power; mighty, formidable, imposing, commanding.

6. eminent, superior, high-ranking, high-level, top-level, of high station *or* standing, big-time; prestigious, distinguished, of distinction, highly regarded, well thought of, esteemed, respected.

7. self-important, vainglorious, egotistical, conceited, boastful, inflated, puffed up; pretentious, pompous, grandiose, grand, majestic, haughty, condescending, *Inf.* toplofty, *Inf.* highfalutin.

importunate, *adj.* **1.** pressing, urgent, instant, crying, exigent, demanding, exacting; claiming, clamorous, insistent, dunning, entreating, solicitous, suppliant; supplicatory, supplicant, imploratory, imprecatory, precatory, invocatory, on bended knee.

2. pertinacious, persistent, dogged, unremitting, continuous; adamant, undismayed, unshakable, sedulous.

3. troublesome, annoying, vexatious; bothersome, pesky, harassing, tormenting.

importune, *v.* **1.** beset, ply, dun, tax, besiege, press, push; set upon, urge, call upon, insist, *Inf.* work on; plead, appeal to, clamor for, cry for; supplicate, beseech, entreat, implore, beg, sue, petition, solicit; pray, appeal, adjure, obtest, apostrophize, imprecate, impetrate, throw oneself at the feet of.

2. coax, wheedle, cajole, inveigle; pester, vex, plague, harass, badger, hound, *Sl.* hassle, *Sl.* bug.

importunity, *n.* **1.** insistence, stress, contention, emphasis; pressing, urging, dunning, plying, taxing; coaxing, cajolery, wheedling, blandishment; entreaty, supplication, prayer, beseechment, imploration; obsecration, imprecation, adjuration, obtestation; plea, cry, call, appeal, *Eccles.* rogation; urgence, instance, persistence.

2. **importunities** solicitations, demands, requests, requisitions; petitions, suits, overtures, addresses.

impose, *v.* **1.** lay on, set, put on, place, enjoin; levy, assess, charge, burden; encumber, superpose, saddle with; prescribe, dictate, mark out, inflict, direct, command, decree, bid, call upon; demand, require, ask, exact, tax, *U.S.* doom.

2. obtrude, thrust upon, take advantage of, presume upon; interfere, intervene, interrupt, interpose, insinuate, interlope; intrude, impose upon, put out, wear out one's welcome; discommode, trouble, bother, inconvenience; put upon, foist upon, break in upon, cut in; barge in, *Sl.* butt in, *Sl.* horn in, *Sl.* crash, *Sl.* crash the gates.

3. **impose on** *or* **upon** **a.** misuse, misapply, misappropriate; take advantage, exploit, prostitute, pervert, profane. **b.** pass off, palm off, practice upon, foist off, fob off; put over, hoodwink, pull the wool over the eyes, con; cheat, defraud, bilk, gyp, *Inf.* flimflam, swindle, *Sl.* diddle, *Sl.* daddle; deceive, dupe, hoax, bamboozle, *Sl.* hornswoggle, take in, mislead; double-cross, trick, cross up, do.

imposing, *adj.* **1.** dignified, majestic, lofty, grand, august, stately. See **impressive** (*def.* **1**).

2. towering, monumental, enormous, mountainous, immense, stupendous, tremendous; huge, gigantic, titanic, monstrous, mighty.

imposition, *n.* **1.** infliction, laying on, application, superposition, charging, burdening, loading, placement; levying, assessment, prescription, enactment.

2. charge, task, burden, duty; tax, load, onus, encumbrance; requirement, injunction, ultimatum; impost, levy, toll, tithe, surtax, *U.S.* doomage, rating; assessment, tariff, cess, tribute, fine, penalty.

3. obtrusion, interloping, intrusion, interposition, interposure, insinuation; interference, intervention, interruption; presumption, undue advantage *or* liberty.

4. imposture, deception, delusion, deceit, dissimulation; fraud, fake, swindle, cheat, trick, stratagem; hoax, humbug, gammon.

5. **imposition of hands** laying on of hands, confirmation, ordination.

impossible, *adj.* **1.** illogical, self-contradictory, incompatible, absurd, preposterous, ridiculous; out of the question, not possible, hopeless, *Sl.* no go, not to be thought of.

2. unthinkable, unimaginable, unbelievable, incredible, inconceivable; beyond conception, beyond the bounds of possibility, contrary to reason, beyond the realm of reason.

3. unsolvable, unresolvable, insoluble, unworkable; unperformable, inoperable, incurable; impracticable, unrealizable, unachievable, infeasible, unviable; insurmountable, insuperable, unbridgeable, impassible, unnavigable, beyond one's power, too much for; unapproachable, inaccessible, unobtainable; unavailable, unacquirable, not to be had; unreachable, out of reach, ungettable, beyond one's grasp.

4. inadmissible, unacceptable, unsuitable, untenable, objectionable, exceptionable; unprovable, unverifiable, unconfirmable, uncertifiable, unascertainable.

impost, *n.* tax, taxation, tribute, duty, excise, toll, custom, levy, *Brit.* rates; customs duty, customs tax, tariff.

impostor, *n.* **1.** deceiver, bamboozler, hoodwinker, trickster, pettifogger; misleader, bluff, bluffer, *Inf.* fourflusher, deluder, duper; cheat, cheater, *Inf.* gyp *or* gypper, swindler, *Archaic.* chouser, chiseler, *Inf.* diddler, defrauder, bilker; exploiter, confidence man, *Sl.* con man, *Sl.* rip-off artist, *Sl.* flimflam man, smooth *or* fast talker; sharper, sharpie, shark.

2. masquerader, humbug, wolf in sheep's clothing, dissembler, hypocrite, pharisee; pretender, fake, *Inf.* faker, fraud, sham, phony; charlatan, quack, mountebank, *Inf.* shyster.

imposture, *n.* **1.** imposition, exploitation, swindle, swindling, defraudation, bunco, misrepresentation; hoax, trick, artifice, wile, ruse; deception, duplicity, double-dealing, sharping, sharking; cheating, trickery, cozenage, chicanery, knavery; confidence game, *Inf.* con game, *Inf.* flimflam game, *Inf.* ripoff, *Sl.* rip.

2. deception, humbug, pretense, delusion, fraud, sham; charlatanry, charlatanism, quackery.

impotence, *n.* **1.** powerlessness, helplessness, weak-

ness, feebleness, frailty, infirmity, impuissance; exhaustion, enfeeblement, prostration, demoralization; enervation, debilitation, disablement; decrepitude, senility, senescence, valetudinarianism, superannuation.
2. ineffectiveness, ineffectualness, inefficacy, inadequacy, inefficiency, incompetence, ineptness; uselessness, inutility, worthlessness, valuelessness, meritlessness, nugacity; futility, bootlessness, unavailingness, idleness; unprofitableness, profitlessness, nonsuccess, failure, defeat.
3. sterility, infertility, childlessness, unprolificness, infecundity, *Med.* agenesis, effeteness.

impotent, *adj.* **1.** powerless, helpless, weak, feeble, frail, infirm, impuissant; exhausted, worn out, enfeebled, spent, all in, done for; prostrate, shattered, demoralized; enervated, nerveless, debilitated; disabled, decrepit, crippled, paralytic, palsied; senile, senescent, valetudinary, superannuated.
2. ineffective, ineffectual, inefficient, incompetent, inadequate, inept, inoperative; worthless, valueless, meritless, nugatory; futile, vain, idle, bootless, useless, unavailing; unproductive, unyielding, unprofitable, profitless, gainless, unrenumerative, unpaying; unsuccessful, to no avail, to no purpose, for naught.
3. barren, sterile, *Bot.* acarpous, unprolific, infecund, infertile, *Med.* agenetic, abortive, effete, unfruitful, fruitless.

impound, *v.* **1.** (*all usu. of animals*) pen, pen in, shut up, cage, encage, coop up, rail, fence in; tie up, secure.
2. confine, enclose, contain, hold in, check, bound, limit; shut in, imprison, incarcerate, immure, wall up, hem in.
3. appropriate, take possession of, seize, commandeer, expropriate, claim, *Scot.* poind, *Law.* distrain; avail oneself of, make free with, help oneself to.

impoverish, *v.* **1.** reduce to poverty, pauperize, beggar; ruin, *Dial.* ruinate, break, bankrupt, destroy financially.
2. exhaust, use up, deplete, drain, sap, take all one's strength; wear out, tire out, fatigue, *Inf.* do in, *Sl.* do a number on, *Sl.* waste; weaken, enervate, enfeeble.

impoverished, *adj.* **1.** poverty-stricken, destitute, penurious, impecunious, beggared, pauperized; indigent, poor, needy, necessitous, bad off, badly off, *Sl.* in rough *or* tough shape; pinched, straitened, distressed, in a bad way, *Inf.* strapped, tight, in a bind, *Inf.* up against it, *Inf.* on one's uppers, *Inf.* hard up; financially embarrassed, out of cash, *Inf.* short, *Brit. Sl.* skint, *All Inf.* broke, dead broke, flat broke, stone broke; bankrupt, ruined, wiped out, *Inf.* on the rocks, insolvent, overdrawn, in the red; down and out, out at the elbows, down at the heels, seedy.
2. exhausted, depleted, drained, used up, worn out, spent, played out; weakened, weak, feeble.
3. (*all of a country or region*) barren, stripped, deprived, poor, meager, scanty, scarce, lean; bare, dry, arid, bald, naked; dead, waste, desolate, empty, forlorn.

impracticability, *n.* impracticableness, infeasibility, impossibility, infeasibleness, hopelessness; uselessness, inutility, inefficaciousness, inoperativeness, impracticality, ineffectiveness, unserviceableness.

impracticable, *adj.* **1.** unfeasible, impossible, unachievable, unattainable, unobtainable, out of the question.
2. unsuitable, useless, inutile, inefficacious, ineffective, inoperative, unserviceable, impractical.

impractical, *adj.* useless, inutile, inefficacious, ineffective, inoperative, unserviceable; theoretical, abstract, speculative; quixotic, chimerical, visionary, romantic, ideal; starry-eyed, wild, absurd, crackpot.

imprecate, *v.* execrate, anathematize, send to perdition, curse, *Sl.* put the whammy on, *Inf.* jinx; damn, denounce, denunciate, condemn; blaspheme, slander.

imprecation, *n.* curse, malediction, ban, anathema, *Archaic.* malison, execration; evil eye, *Sl.* whammy, hoodoo, jinx; denunciation, condemnation, damning, proscription; blasphemy, slander, abuse, threat.

imprecatory, *adj.* execratory, maledictory, denunciatory, damning, proscriptive; threatening, menacing, warning; blasphemous, slanderous.

imprecise, *adj.* inexact, approximate; incorrect, not right, untrue, inaccurate, wide-of-the-mark, off; ambiguous, inexplicit, indistinct, indefinite, vague, ill-defined; hazy, cloudy, wispy, fuzzy, fuzzy around the edges, *Inf.* muzzy, blurred; disorderly, inchoate, confused, careless.

impregnable, *adj.* **1.** invulnerable, indestructible, undestroyable, imperishable, nonperishable, *Obs., Rare.* imperdible; invincible, unconquerable, impenetrable, inviolable, inexpugnable; unassailable, unattackable, insuperable, insurmountable, undefeatable, unbeatable; formidable, powerful, mighty; tenable, secure, safe, safe and sound; stout, strong, sturdy, solid, stable, staunch, stanch; indomitable, redoubtable, unyielding.
2. indisputable, incontestable, irrefutable, undeniable, unquestionable, indubitable, incontrovertible, sure, certain, absolute; unimpeachable, irreproachable; perfect, flawless, unflawed, faultless.

impregnate, *v.* **1.** inseminate, make pregnant, get with child *or* young, *Sl.* knock up; fertilize, fructify, make fruitful, fecundate; beget, create, procreate, engender, generate.
2. permeate, spread throughout, overspread, fill, suffuse, imbue, imbrue; soak, steep, saturate, drench, flood, inundate; pervade, penetrate, infuse, inject; tinge, tincture, dye.

impresario, *n.* manager, director, producer, administrator; conductor, maestro, choirmaster, concert master, precentor, coryphaeus; ballet master.

impress[1], *v.* **1.** move, sway, bend, influence; persuade, win over, bring round; touch, reach, go to one's heart, *Sl.* get under one's skin; affect deeply, stir, disturb, bother, trouble; grab, galvanize, electrify, strike, overwhelm, overpower, bedazzle.
2. fix deeply, establish, ground, instill, plant, install.
3. urge, prevail upon, spur, prompt, induce; emphasize, bring home to.
4. stamp, imprint, mark, seal, engrave.
5. draw attention to oneself, show off, flaunt, swagger; make a show, cut *or* make a figure, *Sl.* cut a dash, *Inf.* cut a swath, *Sl.* cut a shine, *Sl.* cut a feather; make an impression, make a splash, *Sl.* snow; play up to, *Sl.* shine up to, work on.
—*n.* **6.** mark, imprint, print, stamp, seal, impression.
7. hallmark, earmark, keynote, characteristic; sign, sure sign, telltale sign, index, indicator.

impress[2], *v.* **1.** (*usu. in reference to military service*) draft, induct, conscript, conscribe, press, *Naut.* shanghai, crimp; recruit, enlist, *Archaic.* list, levy, muster in; activate, call up, mobilize.
2. seize, take possession of, expropriate, appropriate, arrogate, assume; requisition, confiscate, impound, *Law.* distrain; wrest from, take from, usurp, accroach; commandeer, hijack.
3. persuade, convince, induce, prevail on *or* upon; impel, oblige, constrain, compel, coerce; wheedle, cajole, coax.

impressibility, *n.* softness, yieldingness, impressionability; flexibility, pliableness, pliability, plasticity, malleability, moldability, fictileness, clayiness. See **im-**

pressionability.

impressible, *adj.* See **impressionable.**

impression, *n.* **1.** strong effect, influence, sway, hold, power, control.

2. feeling, sensation, sense; intuition, inkling, vague feeling, *Inf.* funny feeling, suspicion, *Inf.* hunch; consciousness, awareness, sentience, sensibility, perception; remembrance, recollection; sentiment, fancy, notion, idea, thought, conception, belief.

3. mark, figure, brand, indentation, impress, *Archaic.* impressure.

4. impersonation, imitation, mimicry, parody, takeoff.

impressionable, *adj.* susceptible, persuadable, yielding, receptive, susceptive; impressible, soft, pliable, plastic, malleable; flexible, fictile, moldable; young, undeveloped, unfledged, callow, inexperienced, innocent, open, tender; responsive, alive to, sensitive, sentient, sensible, feeling, intuitive, perceptive.

impressionability, *n.* susceptibility, persuadability, yieldingness; receptiveness, receptivity, susceptiveness, responsiveness; youth, callowness, inexperience, innocence, openness, tenderness; sensitivity, sensibility, feeling, intuition, perception; impressibility, softness, pliableness, pliability, plasticity, malleability, flexibility; fictileness, clayiness, moldability.

improbable, *adj.* unlikely, highly unlikely, not probable *or* likely, doubtful, dubious, questionable, *Inf.* fishy; implausible, impractical, unrealistic, incredible, unbelievable; inconceivable, unthinkable, out of the question, ridiculous, absurd, crazy, impossible.

improbity, *n.* dishonesty, fraud, falseness, disingenuousness, breach of faith, faithlessness; malpractice, misconduct, bad conduct, scandal; crookedness, *Law.* malfeasance, wrongdoing; maliciousness, scurviness, reprobacy, depravity; unrighteousness, wickedness, badness; villainy, baseness, knavery, roguery, miscreancy.

impromptu, *adj.* **1.** unprepared, unpremeditated, unrehearsed, unprompted; extemporized, extemporaneous, extemporary, extempore, ad-lib, *Sl.* off-the-cuff, offhand; improvised, makeshift, jury-rigged.

2. spontaneous, spur-of-the-moment, last-minute, impulsive, impetuous.

improper, *adj.* **1.** incorrect, false, erroneous, mistaken, wrong; inexact, inaccurate, faulty, amiss, off base, off the mark; unsound, untrue, inapplicable.

2. unseemly, unbecoming, indecorous; unladylike, ungentlemanly, ungenteel, impolite; undignified, unrefined, unpolished, inelegant, indelicate; impolitic, imprudent, indiscreet, tactless, injudicious; untoward, *Inf.* out-of-the-way, *Inf.* off-key, out-of-bounds, out-of-line, out-of-order.

3. indecent, risqué, off-color; offensive, obscene, lewd, smutty; immoral, corrupt, sinful, wicked, reprehensible; illicit, illegitimate, unlawful.

4. inappropriate, inapt, inapposite, unmeet, unfitting, unbefitting; unwarranted, uncalled-for, out of place, out of keeping; inopportune, ill-timed, unseasonable, untimely, infelicitous; unfavorable, incommodious, inconvenient, uncongenial, unlikely; unsuitable, unsuited, unfit, ill-adapted, incompatible; inexpedient, inadvisable, impractical, inapplicable, unfeasible.

5. abnormal, irregular, unusual.

impropriety, *n.* incorrectness, nonconformance, indecorum, indecorousness, bad taste; unseemliness, imprudence, immodesty; inappropriateness, incongruity, unsuitability, unsuitableness.

2. blunder, slip, mistake, error, faux pas, fault; mishap, misstep, gaucherie, absurdity.

improve, *v.* **1.** amend, better, ameliorate, meliorate, make better; straighten out, reform, rehabilitate, set right, put right, redress, redeem; humanize, civilize, cultivate, modernize, elevate, ennoble; correct, rectify, restore, cure, heal, regenerate; repair, fix up, touch up, spruce up, give a face-lift to; brush up, refurbish, furbish, embellish, rub up, vamp up; lift, uplift, upgrade; remodel, reorganize, redo, recast, remold, reconstruct, rearrange.

2. rework, revamp, redact, emendate; emend, polish, doctor; revise, rewrite, enhance, enrich; refine, purify, cleanse, clean, purge; perfect, develop, elaborate, finish, mature, mellow.

3. make good use of, put to good use, turn to account, take advantage of, avail oneself of; profit, gain, benefit.

4. become better, recuperate, convalesce, gain strength, grow better; advance, promote, further; forward; mend, gain, heal, come along, make headway; recover, rally, revive, get better; pick up, brighten up, perk up, come around, turn the corner.

improvement, *n.* **1.** amelioration, melioration, betterment, bettering; correction, rectification, restoration; reformation, reform, rehabilitation, regeneration; civilization, cultivation, humanization, modernization, elevation; reconditioning, refurbishment, renovation, refreshment; reparation, repair, overhaul, overhauling, face-lift; remodeling, reorganization, rearrangement, reconstruction.

2. revision, revise, rewriting, rewrite; redaction, emendation, revampment; enhancement, enrichment, edification; development, elaboration, perfection, maturation; refinement, purification, purgation, purge, cleansing, cleaning, polishing.

3. change, change for the better, progress, progression; mending, healing, recuperation, convalescence, restitution; upswing, *Inf.* pickup, recovery, *Inf.* up, rise, the road to recovery, *Inf.* comeback; advancement, promotion, furtherance, addition, advance.

improvidence, *n.* **1.** thoughtlessness, imprudence, unmindfulness, unthinkingness; inadvertence, unwariness, unwatchfulness, unvigilance; heedlessness, carelessness, incaution, disregardfulness, inattention, inattentiveness, oversight; neglect, negligence, dereliction; recklessness, rashness, precipitancy, temerariousness, temerity.

2. thriftlessness, unthriftiness, unprovision, uneconomy, unfrugalness; short-sightedness, indiscretion, injudiciousness; prodigality, extravagance, lavishness, profuseness, wastefulness, dissipation, squandermania; shiftlessness, fecklessness, lackadaisicalness; slackness, laxity, laxness, remissness.

improvident, *adj.* **1.** incautious, unwary, imprudent, unobservant, unwatchful, unalert, unvigilant; heedless, careless, reckless, precipitate, temerarious, rash, headlong; thoughtless, unthinking, unmindful, disregardful; inattentive, inadvertent, regardless, *Inf.* asleep on the job, *Inf.* asleep at the switch.

2. thriftless, unthrifty, spendthrift, unfrugal, uneconomical, unproviding; short-sighted, injudicious, indiscreet; wasteful, prodigal, negligent, squandering; extravagant, lavish, profuse, dissipated, penny-wise and pound-foolish; shiftless, feckless, lackadaisical, happy-go-lucky; slack, remiss, lax.

improvisation, *n.* **1.** extemporizing, ad-libbing; making do, jury-rigging, making the best of it.

2. impromptu, extemporization, extempore remark, ad lib; spontaneousnes, impulsiveness, impetuosity; impulse, flash, brainstorm.

improvise, *v.* **1.** extemporize, ad-lib, *Sl.* wing it, *Inf.* play by ear, rise to the occasion, ride with the waves, fake it.

2. devise, jury-rig, make do, come up with something; create, coin, invent.

improvised, *adj.* unprepared, unpremeditated, unrehearsed, unprompted; extemporized, extempore, ad-lib, *Sl.* off-the-cuff, offhand; makeshift, jury-rigged, strung-together.

2. spontaneous, spur-of-the-moment, last-minute, impulsive, impetuous; potluck, catch-as-catch-can.

imprudence, *n.* indiscretion, inconsiderateness, thoughtlessness, irresponsibility; inexpedience, injudiciousness, impoliticness; incaution, incautiousness, carelessness, recklessness, temerity, foolishness, folly; foolhardiness, rashness, hotheadedness, brashness, unwariness, unguardedness; impulsiveness, hastiness, short-sightedness, heedlessness.

imprudent, *adj.* **1.** indiscreet, inconsiderate, thoughtless, irresponsible, incautious, foolish; injudicious, ill-judged, inexpedient, unwise, ill-advised, unadvised, ill-considered, ill-suited, impolitic; guided, wrong-headed, perverse.

2. impetuous, impulsive, hasty, over-hasty, short-sighted, heedless, unheeding; foolhardy, headlong, breakneck, hazardous; rash, hotheaded, brash, unwary, unguarded; uncircumspect, careless, reckless, harebrained, madcap, temerarious, wild; spontaneous, unpremeditated, sudden, abrupt, precipitate.

impudence, *n.* **1.** impertinence, insolence, audacity, effrontery, presumption, presumptuousness; boldness, brazenness, pertness, brashness, freshness, sauciness, shamelessness, *Inf.* cheekiness, *Inf.* sassiness, *Inf.* brassiness; impoliteness, disrespect, unmannerliness, ill-manneredness, incivility, rudeness; bumptiousness, cockiness, self-assertiveness *or* self-assertion, chutzpah, forwardness; meddlesomeness, intrusiveness, officiousness.

2. *All Inf.* brass, sass, cheek, guff, back talk, sauce, face, crust; *All Sl.* gall, nerve, lip, mouth, *Brit.* side.

impudent, *adj.* impertinent, insolent, audacious, presumptuous, out-of-line, out-of-keeping; bold, brazen, brazen-faced, brash, fresh, pert, saucy, shameless, *Inf.* flip, *Inf.* cheeky, *Inf.* sassy, *Inf.* brassy, *Sl.* wise, *Sl.* mouthy, *Sl.* smart-mouth; impolite, disrespectful, ill-mannered, unmannerly, unmannered, uncivil, ill-bred, rude, crude, coarse, vulgar; bumptious, cocksure, cocky, arrogant, forward; meddlesome, intrusive, officious.

impugn, *v.* **1.** malign, gibbet, vilify, vituperate, vilipend, run down, defame, denigrate, scandalize, asperse, impute, insinuate, cast aspersions, speak ill of, speak evil of, backbite, *Sl.* badmouth, *Sl.* poormouth; slander, libel, calumniate, traduce, falsify, accuse falsely, misrepresent, belie; attack, assail, stab, injure, abuse, berate, upbraid, castigate, reprimand, scold, chide, admonish, rebuke; criticize, knock, carp at, cavil at, peck at; denounce, deplore, curse, rail, condemn, execrate, anathematize, *Obs.* exprobrate.

2. censure, reproach, impeach, bring to book, call to account, accuse, charge, cry down, slate, inveigh against, perstringe, animadvert upon, reprove, recriminate, reprehend, reprobate, pass strictures; disapprove, disfavor, dislike, frown upon, look askance; doubt, query, question, disbelieve, misbelieve, distrust, mistrust; challenge, dispute, argue, wrangle, haggle, hassle, altercate, oppose, object to, protest, enter a protest, conflict with, take exception to, join issue upon; deny, disprove, gainsay, rebut, contradict, contravene, controvert, pick holes in, pick to pieces.

impulse, *n.* **1.** impetus, propulsion, send-off, goad, spur, force, stimulus, stimulation, incitement; incentive, motive, inducement, encouragement, boost.

2. inclination, tendency, proclivity, bent; itch, yen, urge, desire, mania, liking, appetite, want; emotion, feeling, sense.

impulsive, *adj.* **1.** spontaneous, extemporaneous, unplanned, offhand; hasty, spur-of-the-moment, snap, right-off-the-bat, precipitate, sudden, quick; rash, impetuous, impulsive, brash; reckless, madcap, foolhardy, incautious, careless, devil-may-care, *Sl.* what-the-hell; thoughtless, heedless, shooting-from-the-hip, natural, instinctive.

2. compelling, powerful, forcible, forceful; propulsive, driving, dynamic.

impunity, *n.* exemption, immunity, indemnity; freedom, release, excusal, exception, exclusion; absolution, pardon, amnesty, reprieve, stay of execution; remission, respite, relief.

impure, *adj.* **1.** contaminated, tainted, infected, poisoned, polluted; foul, feculent, turbid, muddy, murky, clouded, cloudy, unclear; unclean, dirty, dirtied, filthy, sullied, soiled, maculate, spotted, stained.

2. adulterated, alloyed, mixed, combined, fused; hybrid, mongrel.

3. unchaste, unvirgin, unvirginal, defiled; corrupted, debased, lowered, degraded, vitiated, degenerate, base, low; perverted, depraved, evil, vile, sinful, wicked; immoral, amoral, loose, promiscuous, wanton, immodest, shameless; dissolute, licentious, libertine, profligate, incontinent, unrestrained, *Pathol.* nymphomaniacal, *Pathol.* satyrical; lascivious, prurient, passionate, sensual, sexual, *Inf.* hot, desirous, concupiscent; lewd, lustful, lecherous, libidinous, *Archaic.* lickerish, salacious.

4. obscene, dirty, vulgar, pornographic, smutty; bawdy, indecent, ribald, improper, risqué, suggestive, sexy, racy, blue, off-color; gross, crude, coarse, rough, indelicate.

impurity, *n.* **1.** contamination, befoulment, pollution, adulteration, infection; uncleanness, dirtiness, filthiness, foulness, feculence; turbidity, turbidness, muddiness, murkiness, cloudiness.

2. unchasteness, unchastity, defilement, corruption, perversion; debasement, degradation, vitiation, degeneration; baseness, vileness, evilness, evil, sinfulness, wickedness; depravity, depravedness, immorality, amorality, looseness, promiscuity, wantonness; dissoluteness, licentiousness, libertinism, profligacy, profligateness, incontinence, incontinency, *Pathol.* nymphomania, *Pathol.* satyriasis; lasciviousness, prurience, pruriency, passion, desire, concupiscence, sensuality, sexuality; lust, lustfulness, lewdness, lecherousness, libidinousness, *Archaic.* lickerishness, salaciousness, salacity.

3. obscenity, vulgarity, vulgarness, smuttiness; bawdiness, indecency, impropriety, immodesty, impudicity; grossness, crudeness, coarseness, roughness, indelicacy.

4. *Often* **impurities** dirt, filth, grime, smut; spots, stains, soil marks, marks, smudges, smutches, smirches.

imputable, *adj.* **1.** attributable, ascribable, accreditable, creditable, referable, assignable; owing to, due to; associable, connectable.

2. accusable, chargeable, challengeable, allegeable, assertable, citable; implicatory, implicative, criminative, incriminatory, accusatory, putative; indictable, impeachable; censurable, blameworthy, blamable; reproachable, imprecatory, denunciable; accursed, damnable, execrable, maledictory, comminatory, anathematic, *Obs.* exprobatory.

imputation, *n.* **1.** (*all usu. in reference to fault or wrongdoing*) attribution, ascription, arrogation, accounting, charge, challenge, accusation, assertion, allegation, citation, incrimination, crimination, implication, *Obs. Rare.* accrimination; arraignment, impeachment, indictment, censure, blame, reproach, inculpation, railing, commination, invective, denunciation, revilement, contumely, malediction, curse, animadversion, imprecation, delation, *Archaic.* exprobation.

2. defamation, denigration, vilification, vituperation, scandal, *Inf.* skeleton in the closet, yellow journalism; shame, disgrace, dishonor, odium, opprobrium, obloquy, loss of face, ill-repute, disrepute; belittlement, deprecation, disparagement, detraction, deflation, depreciation, derogation, devaluation; humiliation, humble pie, mortification.

3. slander, calumny, calumniation, libel, misrepresentation, false report, falsehood, lie, untruth, aspersion, insinuation, innuendo, *Inf.* brickbat; abuse, injury, backbiting, mud-slinging; slur, blot, blot on the escutcheon, smear, smirch, taint, attaint, stain, tarnish, spot, black spot *or* mark, blemish, smudge, brand, stigma.

impute, *v.* **1.** accuse, charge, challenge, allege, assert, cite, implicate, incriminate, criminate, *Obs., Rare.* accriminate; point to, set down to, lay at the door of, saddle with, father upon, account for, call to *or* hold in account; arraign, impeach, indict; censure, cry down, reproach, revile, execrate, denounce, fulminate, imprecate, damn, curse, anathematize, comminate, delate, *Obs.* exprobrate.

2. attribute, ascribe, accredit, credit, invest with, refer, assign, arrogate, appropriate; associate, connect with.

3. shame, disgrace, dishonor; debase, abase, vitiate, degrade, defile, corrupt, pervert; discredit, disprove, disfavor; belittle, disparage, detract, deprecate, deflate, devaluate, depreciate, derogate, decry; humiliate, humble, mortify, *Sl.* put down.

4. slander, libel, calumniate, traduce, falsify, accuse falsely, misrepresent, belie, asperse, insinuate; injure, abuse, insult, backbite, *Sl.* badmouth, engage in personalities; slur, sully, soil, smear, smirch, besmirch, stain, blacken, taint, tarnish, smudge, spot, brand, stigmatize, drag through the mud *or* mire, heap dirt upon, fling dirt, throw mud upon, spatter, bespatter, *Sl.* dump on.

5. defame, vilify, vilipend, denigrate, vituperate, scandalize, run down, berate, impugn, revile, *Obs.* avile, malign, gibbet, speak ill of, speak evil of, sneer at, muckrake.

in, *prep.* **1.** within, on the inside of, surrounded by; among, amid, in the midst of, in the thick of; during, while, in the time of, throughout; because, inasmuch as, in that.

—adv. **2.** (*of a place, position, state, relation*) into; in charge, in office, in power; in possession, in occupancy; in favor, on good terms; in season, in with.

—adj. **3.** inner, internal, located within.

4. well-liked, favored; fashionable, chic, modish, stylish, in style, voguish, in vogue, *Inf.* go-go, *Inf.* all the rage; *All Sl.* hep, hip, cool, the most, *Brit. Sl.* suss.

5. private, secret, esoteric, reserved, limited, restricted, exclusive.

6. inward, incoming, inbound.

7. plentiful, abundant, bountiful, ample; available.

—n. **8.** *Usu.* **ins** leaders, bosses, officeholders, incumbents.

9. influence, *Sl.* pull; advantage, opportunity, chance, prospect; connection, link, tie.

—v. *Dial.* **10.** harvest, round up, gather.

11. enclose, surround, encircle, circle, encompass.

inability, *n.* **1.** incapability, incapableness, incapacity, disablement, incapacitation; disability, handicap, defect, weakness, frailty, infirmity; feebleness, decrepitude, impotence, impuissance, powerlessness, helplessness.

2. inefficiency, inefficacy, incompetence, incompetency, unadeptness, unskillfulness; inaptitude, ineptness, ineptitude, inaptness, unaptness; unsuitableness, unsuitability, unfitness, unqualifiedness, ineligibility.

inaccessible, *adj.* **1.** unapproachable, ungetatable, *Inf.* un-come-at-able; unreachable, beyond reach, out of reach; out-of-the-way, godforsaken, back-of-beyond; impassable, impenetrable, impervious, imperviable, impermeable; trackless, pathless, wayless, untrodden, *Obs.* invious.

2. unattainable, unobtainable, unavailable, unacquirable, not to be had, not to be had for love or money; closed to, denied to, lost to.

inaccuracy, *n.* **1.** inexactness, inexactitude, imprecision, unpreciseness, laxness, laxity, looseness; erroneousness, fallaciousness, mistakenness, wrongness, incorrectness, faultiness.

2. error, mistake, corrigendum; blunder, botch, bungle, flub, muff; leak, slip, slip of the tongue *or* pen, *Inf.* slip-up; *All Sl.* pratfall, fool mistake, foul-up, louse-up, screw-up, boner, boo-boo, goof, blooper, clinker, clunker.

3. misunderstanding, misconception, misapprehension; misidentification; miscalculation, misestimation; misjudgment, error in judgment, misreckoning; misconstruction, misreading, misinterpretation, wrong interpretation; misstatement, misquotation, misreport.

4. fallacy, false *or* mistaken notion, misbelief; sophistry, sophism, casuistry, *Logic.* paralogism, *Latin. non sequitur.*

inaccurate, *adj.* **1.** inexact, imprecise, loose, lax; slipshod, haphazard, hit-or-miss.

2. mistaken, erroneous, amiss, incorrect, wrong, all wrong, dead wrong, *Sl.* all wet, *Sl.* full of beans *or* prunes, *Sl.* full of hot air; false, fallacious, untrue, not true, devoid of truth, not right; imperfect, faulty, flawed, unsound, illogical, *Sl.* cockeyed; in error, in the wrong; astray, wide of the mark, *Inf.* off base *or* way off base, *Inf.* cold, *Sl.* off the beam, *Sl.* at sea, *Sl.* out in left field.

inactive, *adj.* **1.** inert, lifeless, inanimate; immovable, immobile, motionless; stationary, unmoving, becalmed, still, stock-still, *Chiefly Literary.* stilly.

2. dull, sluggish, passive, sedentary, lethargic, stagnant; sleepy, somnolent, slumberous, torpid, torpescent; indolent, idle, slothful, lazy, supine, otiose; listless, languid, lackadaisical.

3. calm, quiet, reposeful, serene, placid, tranquil; unruffled, unagitated, undisturbed, untroubled; pacific, peaceful, restful; silent, hushed.

4. inoperative, nonfunctioning, nonperforming; unused, unoccupied, unbusied, unemployed, *Sl.* on the shelf; suspended, deferred, postponed, abeyant, in abeyance; pausing, stopping, breaking, waiting, hesitating, hesitant, delaying.

5. quiescent, dormant, latent; implicit, undisclosed, unexpressed; undeveloped, unrealized, potential.

inactivity, *n.* idleness, unemployment, inertia, stasis, motionlessness, immobility, inaction, inactiveness, want of action; passivity, lethargy, lassitude, listlessness, torpor, sluggishness, dullness, heaviness, languor; inertness, stagnation, vegetation, hibernation, dormancy; sloth, laziness, indolence, inexertion, donothingness, fainéance; *It. dolce far niente.*

inadequacy, *n.* **1.** insufficiency, deficiency, incompleteness; incommensurability, unsuitability; mediocrity, inferiority, unsatisfactoriness, unacceptableness; scantiness, skimpiness, scrimpiness, meagerness, *Inf.* slim pickings.

2. shortage, deficit, lack; dearth, scarcity, paucity, poverty; short supply, sellers' market, none to spare.

3. inaptness, ineptness, ineptitude, incompetence, incapability, incapacity, inability; unskillfulness, inexpertness, unproficiency, undeftness, undexterousness, maladroitness; inefficiency, inefficacy, inefficaciousness, ineffectiveness.
4. fault, flaw, failing, foible, weakness; weak link, chink in one's armor, Achilles heel.

inadequate, *adj.* **1.** insufficient, too little, not enough, found wanting; mediocre, inferior, unsatisfactory, displeasing, disappointing, no good, not good enough, incommensurate, unsuitable; imperfect, defective, flawed, faulty, incomplete, deficient, lacking, wanting, needing, missing, partial, short *or* short of, *Inf.* shy; meager, scanty, skimpy, scrimpy, bare, scant; scarce, sparse, in short supply, at a premium.
2. inapt, inept, incompetent, incapable, unable, unfit, unfitted, unqualified, unworthy, not up to; unskillful, inexpert, undeft, unapt, inadept, unproficient, undexterous, maladroit; inefficient, ineffective, ineffectual, inefficacious, feckless.

inadmissible, *adj.* unallowable, prohibitive, preclusive, exceptional; unacceptable, unsuitable, objectionable, undesirable, impossible, untenable; impracticable, unfeasible, inexpedient; impertinent, inapposite, inappropriate, inapplicable, immaterial, inconsequent; irrelevant, beside the point, beside the mark, beside the question, nothing to do with the case, not at issue.

inadvertence, *n.* **1.** inattention, inattentiveness, inconsiderateness, heedlessness, unmindfulness, disregard, thoughtlessness, want *or* lack of thought, inadvertency; carelessness, laxity, slackness, looseness; absent-mindedness, absence of mind, forgetfulness; negligence, neglect, neglectfulness, remissness, dereliction.
2. oversight, omission, slip, *Inf.* slip-up, lapse, loose thread, *Obs.* balk; mistake, error, *Inf.* mix-up, *Sl.* goof, *Sl.* boo-boo.

inadvertent, *adj.* **1.** inattentive, unmindful, heedless, unheeding, unobservant, unobserving, disregardful, regardless.
2. inconsiderate, thoughtless, unthinking, unreasoning, unreflecting, absent-minded; careless, uncircumspect, unwary; slack, lax, loose; negligent, neglectful, derelict.
3. unintentional, unpremeditated, undesigned, unplanned, unstudied, uncalculated, indeliberate, accidental, chance; unwitting, unconscious, involuntary, reflex, automatic, *Sl.* gut.

inadvertently, *adv.* **1.** inattentively, unmindfully, heedlessly, disregardfully; thoughtlessly, unthinkingly, inconsiderately; carelessly, unwarily, unguardedly, off-guard, in an unguarded moment; neglectfully, negligently, remissly, loosely, laxly, slackly.
2. accidentally, unintentionally, undesignedly, without design, by accident, by mistake; involuntarily, unwittingly, unconsciously, automatically.

inadvisable, *adj.* ill-advised, unrecommended, inexpedient, unwise, foolish, unsagacious, unreasonable, irrational, unintelligent, imprudent, injudicious, impolitic; unseemly, indiscreet, improper, uncircumspect; undesirable, objectionable, inappropriate, unfit, unsuitable, unsatisfactory, ineligible.
2. inopportune, inconvenient, discommodious, impractical, unuseful; unprofitable, unbeneficial, disadvantageous, bad.

inalienable, *adj.* unforfeitable, untransferable, not to be conveyed, unconsignable, unsalable, unnegotiable; positive, absolute, inherent; unchallengeable, *Law.* imprescriptible, inviolable, sacrosanct, indefeasible, not to be annulled, not to be made void, permanent.

inamorata, *n.* lover, ladylove, love, beloved, *Inf.* flame; sweetheart, darling, angel; fiancée, betrothed, girl friend; paramour, mistress, concubine; intimate, *Fr. intime,* friend.

inamorato, *n.* lover, swain, amorist, gallant; suitor, wooer, pursuer, admirer, adorer; beau, sweetheart, spark, *Inf.* flame, love, beloved, Romeo; fiancé, betrothed, young man, boy friend; paramour, intimate, *Fr. intime,* friend, *It. cicisbeo.*

inane, *adj.* **1.** silly, absurd, pointless, fatuous, foolish; ridiculous, ludicrous, laughable; senseless, nonsensical, *Scot. and North Eng.* glaikit, cockeyed; unreasonable, irrational, illogical; preposterous, extravagant, excessive; amphigoric, poppycockish, *Sl.* cockamamie, *Inf.* piffling; childish, puerile, immature; asinine, idiotic, *Inf.* moronic, imbecilic; crazy, crazed, *Sl.* kooky, *Scot.* doiled, mad; daft, *Inf.* daffy, crackbrained, *Inf.* nutty; *All Slang.* balmy, dippy, batty, cuckoo, buggy, screwy, wacky, goofy, loony.
2. dull, inexpressive, expressionless, stupid, witless, *Inf.* dopey, empty-headed; unthinking, unreasoning, incogitant, thoughtless; unintelligent, unintellectual; vapid, insipid, banal, bland.

inanimate, *adj.* **1.** lifeless, exanimate, inert, dead; inorganic, vegetable, mineral.
2. spiritless, soulless, vapid, apathetic; sluggish, phlegmatic; listless, torpid, torpescent; dull, flat, heavy, leaden, slow; inactive, not moving, dormant, stagnant, quiescent, abeyant; still, at rest, resting, unmoving, immobile, unstirring, stationary, statuelike, dead still, perfectly still, like stone.

inanition, *n.* **1.** starvation, extreme hunger, extreme malnutrition; fasting, *Psychiatry.* anorexia, *Psychiatry.* anorexia nervosa.
2. lack of vigor, lethargy, listlessness, languor, languidness, torpor, torpitude; emptiness, vacuity, vacuousness.

inanity, *n.* **1.** silliness, absurdity, absurdness, pointlessness, fatuousness, foolishness, *Archaic.* insipience, folly; tomfoolery, foolery, fooling, clownery; senselessness, nonsense, nonsensicalness, nonsensicality, meaninglessness; poppycock, amphigory, bosh, drivel, gibberish, balderdash; unreasonableness, irrationality, illogicalness, illogicality; inappropriateness, ineptness, ineptitude, improperness, impropriety, incongruousness, incongruity, inconsistence, inconsistency; preposterousness, extravagance, excessiveness.
2. ridiculous, ridiculosity, laughableness, ludicrousness; comicality, comicalness, funniness, humor, humorousness, drollness; asininity, idiocy, idioticalness, *Inf.* moronism, *Inf.* moronity, imbecility; craziness, *Sl.* kookiness, madness, daftness, *Inf.* nuttiness; *All Slang.* balminess, bugginess, screwiness, goofiness, wackiness, looniness.
3. dullness, inexpressiveness, stupidity, witlessness, fatuity, *Inf.* dopiness, empty-headedness; unintelligence, unintellectualness, thoughtlessness; emptiness, voidness, vacancy, vacuousness, blankness; vapidity, insipidness, banality, blandness.
4. triviality, triflingness, pettiness; unimportance, inconsequentiality, immateriality, inconsiderableness, insignificance; superficiality, shallowness, frothiness, frivolousness; paltriness, meagerness.

inappeasable, *adj.* implacable, not to be pacified, unpacifiable, unmollifiable, unreconcilable; unforgiving, grudge-holding, vengeful, revengeful; rigid, firm, adamant, unbending, hard, inexorable, relentless; merciless, unmerciful, pitiless, unpitying; uncompassionate, uncompassioned, unsympathizing, unsympathetic, hard-hearted, heartless.

inapplicable, *adj.* **1.** unsuitable, unsuited, unfitting, unfit; unapt, inapt, inappropriate.
2. irrelevant, ungermane, nongermane, inapposite,

unpertinent, impertinent, beside the point *or* question, off the mark, *Inf.* off base; nonrelated, nonrelational, unrelated, irrelative, nonrelative, unconnected; inconsequent, inconsistent, nothing to do with the case *or* matter at hand, off the subject, out of keeping; alien, foreign, extraneous, superfluous.

inapposite, *adj.* **1.** irrelevant, ungermane, nongermane, inapplicable, unpertinent, impertinent, beside the point *or* question, off the mark, *Inf.* off base. See **inapplicable**.

2. unsuitable, unsuited, unfitting, unfit; unapt, inapt, inappropriate, out of place.

inappreciable, *adj.* **1.** imperceptible, unperceptible, unperceivable, microscopic, infinitesimal, minuscule; minute, wee, slight, tiny, diminutive, *Inf.* teeny, *All Baby Talk.* teensy-weensy, teentsy-weentsy, ittybitty, itsy-bitsy.

2. insignificant, unimportant, immaterial, of little or no import; unportentous, unmomentous, inconsequential, of no matter *or* concern; negligible, nugatory, not worth worrying *or* thinking about; petty, paltry, trifling, trivial, piddling, insubstantial, unsubstantial.

inappropriate, *adj.* **1.** unsuitable, unfitting, unbefitting, unmeet, inapt, inapposite; unsuited, unfit, ill-adapted, incompatible, uncongenial, incommodious; incongruous, inconsistent, out of keeping, out of character; disproportionate, inequitable, unfair, unjust.

2. inexpedient, disadvantageous, inadvisable; impractical, inapplicable, useless, no good, unfeasible; inopportune, unseasonable, untimely, infelicitous; irrelevant, nongermane, impertinent; unwarranted, uncalled-for, out of place.

3. unseemly, unbecoming, indecorous, improper; unladylike, ungentlemanly, ungenteel, impolite; impolitic, imprudent, indiscreet, tactless, injudicious; untoward, *Inf.* out-of-the-way, *Inf.* off-key, out-of-bounds, out-of-line, out-of-order.

inapt, *adj.* **1.** unsuited, unsuitable, unfitting, unfit, inappropriate, unapt, out of place; inapposite, inapplicable, impertinent, unrelated, nonrelated; inconsistent, incongruent, incongruous, out of keeping, alien, foreign.

2. inept, incapable, incompetent, unadept; unadroit, maladroit, undexterous, undeft, unskillful, left-handed, *Inf.* all thumbs, *Inf.* butterfingered; clumsy, awkward, ungraceful, graceless, ungainly, like a bull in a china shop; oafish, cloddish, lumbering, heavy-footed, heavy-handed, *Inf.* klutzy; stiff, wooden, stodgy, stolid, unwieldy.

inaptitude, *n.* **1.** ineptness, ineptitude, unfitness, inaptness, unaptness, unsuitableness, unsuitability; unadeptness, incompetence, incompetency, incapability, incapableness, incapacity, inability, lack of ability; ineligibility, unqualifiedness, unpreparedness.

2. unskillfulness, unadroitness, maladroitness, undexterousness, left-handedness; clumsiness, awkwardness, ungainliness, ungracefulness, gracelessness; oafishness, cloddishness, heavy-footedness, heavy-handedness.

inarticulate, *adj.* **1.** mumbled, muttered, muffled, blurred, indistinct; thick, garbled, husky, throaty, guttural, harsh, growled; lisped, lisping, stammering, stuttering.

2. nonvocal, wordless, unspoken, aphonic; dumb, silent, speechless, mute, voiceless, mum, soundless; tongue-tied, reticent, taciturn.

inattention, *n.* **1.** inattentiveness, preoccupation, distraction, detachment, forgetfulness, absent-mindedness, inadvertence, oversight; daydreaming, mental wandering, woolgathering, nodding, oscitance, reverie, staring into space, inapplication, brown study, apathy.

2. carelessness, neglect, negligence, remissness, slackness; thoughtlessness, heedlessness, offhandedness, unmindfulness, disregard, unconcern, indifference, inconsideration, rudeness.

inattentive, *adj.* **1.** heedless, unmindful, neglectful, unheeding, careless, inconsiderate, negligent, remiss; unobservant, unwatchful, unaware, undiscerning.

2. wandering, daydreaming, musing, vague, dreamy, listless, supine, drowsy, sleepy, nodding, oscitant; abstracted, preoccupied, engrossed *or* lost in thought *or* reverie, rapt, lost, absent, deaf, blind, staring into space; off in a world of one's own, with one's head in the clouds, in the clouds, a million miles away; oblivious, detached, distracted, faraway, off guard, caught napping, absent-minded, forgetful; in a brown study, in a blue funk, indifferent, apathetic.

inaudible, *adj.* imperceptible, out of earshot *or* hearing, impossible to hear, not heard; indistinct, faint, muted, soft, gentle, quiet, dull, low; muffled, stifled, unclear, hard to hear, hard to make out; whispered, muttered, mumbled, murmured; mute, still, silent, noiseless.

inaugurate, *v.* **1.** initiate, begin, start, commence, *Inf.* kick off; break ground, ring up the curtain on, get the show on the road, get underway; launch, *Inf.* get off the ground, start off, forward; set out on, start out, enter into, take the first step; get going, set sail, hit the road *or* trail, be off.

2. induct, install, instate, *Rare.* auspicate; introduce, bring in, lead in, usher in, inaugurate, invest, chair, establish; crown, enthrone; frock, *Eccles.* ordain, consecrate.

inauguration, *n.* **1.** initiation, beginning, outset, start, commencement, *Inf.* kickoff; breaking ground, getting underway.

2. induction, installation, instatement; introduction, bringing in, ushering in; inauguration, investiture, chairing, establishment; coronation, crowning, enthronement; frocking, *Eccles.* ordination, *Eccles.* ordainment, consecration.

inauspicious, *adj.* unpropitious, unpromising, hostile, dark, gloomy, threatening, lowering; unfortunate, unlucky, infelicitous, untoward, untimely, unhappy; ominous, ill-boding, portentous, sinister, menacing, of bad omen, ill-starred, ill-omened, ill-fated, doomed.

inborn, *adj.* innate, inherent, *Archaic.* ingenerate, native; inbred, congenital, connate, connatural, natural; organic, constitutional, structural; inherited, hereditary, in the blood, in the family, in the genes.

incalculable, *adj.* **1.** measureless, immeasurable, fathomless, unfathomable; inestimable, incomputable, uncountable, not to be reckoned; innumerable, countless, untold, uncounted, numberless, sumless, without number; unmeasured, indeterminate, undetermined; endless, infinite, inexhaustible, no end of, without end, bottomless; multitudinous, very great, enormous, immense, vast.

2. unpredictable, undeterminable, unforeseeable, undivinable; chance, fortuitous, adventitious, accidental, haphazard; *Inf.* fluky, *Inf.* dicey, *Inf.* chancy, coincidental, epiphenomenal, noncausal, casual.

3. uncertain, unsure, unaccountable, unmotivated; unexplainable, inexplicable, puzzling, enigmatic, paradoxical.

incandescence, *n.* phosphorescence, fluorescence, illumination, irradiation, tribophosphorescence; nitidity, luminescence, luminosity, triboluminescence; sheen, glow, splendor, luster; brilliance, brightness, effulgence, radiance, iridescence, resplendence, refulgence, *Archaic.* fulgor; shine, fire, flame, blaze; flash, fulguration, beam, ray; twinkle, twinkling, sparkle.

sparkling; coruscation, scintillation, glistening, shimmer, glint, glance; gleam, glitter, glimmer, flicker, *Archaic.* glister.

incandescent, *adj.* **1.** alight, lit, lighted, illuminating, lambent, irradiant; sunny, sunshiny, shining, beaming, beamy; fulgid, glittering, rutilant; fulgent, effulgent, refulgent; luminous, luminescent, luminiferous, luciferous; sparkling, twinkling, flashing, gleaming, agleam; scintillating, scintillant, coruscating.

2. phosphorescent, glowing, aglow, white hot, candent; intensely hot, red hot, volcanic; ablaze, blazing, afire, on fire, fiery; aflame, in flames, flaming, conflagrant, flaring; burning, parching, torrid, oppressively hot, *Archaic.* calid; heated, thermal, warming, calorific.

3. bright, brilliant, splendent, resplendent, splendrous; radiant, dazzling, vivid, intense; shining, lucid, lucent, *Archaic.* relucent; lustrous, nitid, glossy, sheeny, sheenful, shiny; gleaming, glaring, glassy, polished, burnished.

4. brilliant, bright, intelligent, intellectual, cerebral, brainy; gifted, precocious, talented, apt; expert, proficient, accomplished, masterful; inventive, resourceful, ingenious; adroit, dexterous, skillful, deft, handy; lucid, perceptive, percipient, perspicacious, discerning; quick, clever, alert, keen, sharp, aware; observant, clear-eyed, farsighted, sagacious, shrewd; astute, penetrating, acute, subtle; nimble-witted, keen-witted, sharp-witted, quick-witted; enlightened, enlightening, luminous.

5. excited, exhilarated, enlivened, inspired; animated, enthusiastic, *Inf.* psyched *or* psyched up, eager; zealous, ardent, vehement, impassioned, passionate; fervent, fervid, perfervid; stimulated, aroused, *Inf.* hot, intensely desirous.

incantation, *n.* **1.** chant, chanting, invocation, conjuration, summoning; magic formula, hocus-pocus, mumbo-jumbo, magic word, abracadabra, open sesame; jinx, hex, adverse influence.

2. spell, charm, rune, *Scot.* cantrip, enchantment, bewitchment, bedevilment; trance, hypnosis, hypnotism, mesmerism; fascination, rapture.

3. magic, sorcery, witchcraft, witchery, wizardry, wonderworking; necromancy, thaumaturgy, theurgy; black magic, black art, voodoo, hoodoo, obiism *or* obeahism; deviltry *or* devilry, demonology, demonolatry, diabolism; supernaturalness, shamanism, mysticism, spiritualism, occultness, psychomancy, fetishism; ritual, rite, apotropaism, magical ceremony, voodooism, exorcism.

4. wordiness, verbosity, prolixity, prolixness, verbiage, verbalism; diffuseness, profuseness, effusion, effusiveness, gushing; obfuscation, padding, redundancy, superfluous words, repetition.

incapability, *n.* **1.** inability, incapacity, incapableness; incompetence, inefficiency, ineffectiveness, inefficacy; inadequacy, insufficiency, unproficiency; unfitness, ineptitude, ineptness, unqualification, disqualification, disability, unaptness.

2. impotence, powerlessness, forcelessness, impuissance; helplessness, defenselessness, prostration, decrepitude, weakness, feebleness.

incapable, *adj.* **1.** unable, incompetent, inefficient, ineffective, inefficacious; unproficient, inadequate, insufficient; unfit, unqualified, unfitted, unsuitable; inept, unapt, unskilled, unequal to, not up to, not up to par, not making the grade, *Inf.* not cutting the mustard, *Inf.* not up to snuff.

2. powerless, impotent, impuissant, unvirile, forceless; helpless, defenseless, prostrate, on one's back, decrepit, feeble, weak.

3. **incapable of** **a.** unable to, cannot, can't; unqualified for, disqualified for, lacking the ability to, lacking the skill *or* know-how to, not knowing how to. **b.** not open to, not admitting, resistant, ill-disposed, impervious; not susceptible, not disposed, not likely, not inclined, not liable, not prone.

incapacitate, *v.* **1.** disable, debilitate, unfit, indispose, inactivate, deactivate; neutralize, disarm, demilitarize; devitalize, enfeeble, extenuate, weaken, enervate, exhaust; cripple, paralyze, lame, maim, hamstring, *Inf.* hogtie; prostrate, cramp, hock; impair, mar, ruin, damage, break; undermine, sabotage, wreck; emasculate, unman, effeminize, geld, castrate, neuter, spay, caponize, sterilize, vasectomize.

2. disqualify, invalidate, disenable, disentitle; clip the wings of, tie the hands of, take the wind out of one's sails, draw the teeth of, break the back of, put a spoke in one's wheel; put out of action, put out of commission, put out of gear, *Sl.* put out of whack, take out of action, *Inf.* sideline, lay up, hospitalize.

incapacity, *n.* **1.** incapability, inability, unfitness, incompetence; inaptitude, unaptness, ineptitude, unqualification, unproficiency, inadequacy; disability, infirmity, handicap, decrepitude, senility, weakness, feebleness; exhaustion, enervation, enfeeblement, prostration, helplessness; impotence, impuissance, powerlessness, forcelessness; disqualification, disenablement, invalidation.

2. unintelligence, brainlessness, witlessness, ignorance; stupidity, mental deficiency, idiocy, imbecility, half-wittedness.

incarcerate, *v.* **1.** imprison, embar, confine, jail, impound, intern, hold captive, *Sl.* jug; lock up, bolt in, clap up, put under lock and key, *Archaic.* engaol.

2. enclose, hem in, hedge in, keep in, shut in; corral, pen in, rail in, fence in; coop up, immure, cage, encage, cloister; wall in, box up, mew up, shut away; constrict, restrict, trammel, check; constrain, restrain, bind, tie.

incarnate, *adj.* **1.** embodied, corporal, corporeal, bodily, fleshly, carnal, somatic, physical; earthly, material, substantial, tangible, palpable; concrete, real, true, actual.

2. personified, typified; signifying, symbolic, representative, emblematic; manifested, made manifest, revealed, demonstrated.

3. flesh-colored, incarnadine, pale pink; crimson, red.

—*v.* **4.** concretize, substantialize, substantiate, reify, actualize, embody, incorporate, corporealize, materialize.

5. typify, personify, represent, signify, symbolize.

incarnation, *n.* **1.** materiality, corporeality, substantiality, physicalness, bodiliness, concreteness, flesh and blood; earthiness, fleshliness, tangibility, palpability, actuality, realness.

2. embodiment, avatar, corporealization, materialization, substantiation, personification, concretization, reification.

incautious, *adj.* **1.** unwary, unwatchful, unvigilant, unalert; off guard, unguarded, *Inf.* asleep on the job, *Inf.* not on the job, *Inf.* asleep at the switch *or* wheel, distracted; unmindful, thoughtless, unthinking, unthoughtful, inattentive, inadvertent, nonobservant, disregardful.

2. unwise, imprudent, injudicious, indiscreet, improvident; uncircumspect, careless, heedless, unheeding; impetuous, impulsive, hasty, over-hasty; rash, hotheaded, brash, foolhardy, headlong, precipitate, breakneck; reckless, harebrained, madcap, temerarious, wild.

incendiary, *adj.* **1.** combustible, flammable, burnable, ignitable.

2. inflammatory, inflaming, infuriating, enraging, maddening, incensing, angering; aggravating, outraging, exasperating; inciting, instigating, fomenting.

3. provocative, arousing, exciting, stimulating, piquing; stirring, thrilling, electrifying; fiery, blazing, ardent, hot, smoldering.

—*n.* **4.** arsonist, building-burner, fire-setter, firebug, *Sl.* torch, pyromaniac.

5. agitator, instigator, inciter, *Fr. agent provocateur;* rebel, insurgent, mutineer, revolutionary, Tom Paine, firebrand; troublemaker, mischief-maker, rabble-rouser, organizer, ringleader.

incense[1], *n.* **1.** perfume, aroma, fragrance, bouquet, redolence, balm, odoriferosity, sweet scent.

2. homage, respect, reverence; obeisance, deference, veneration, worship; adulation, adoration, admiration; honor, tribute, acknowledgment, appreciation.

incense[2], *v.* **1.** anger, raise [s.o.'s] ire, run afoul of [s.o.], get [s.o.'s] back *or* hackles up, *Inf.* get [s.o.'s] Irish *or* dander up, *Inf.* burn [s.o.] up, *Sl.* tee [s.o.] off, *Sl.* tick [s.o.] off; enrage, madden, infuriate, make [s.o.'s] blood boil, *Inf.* make [s.o.] see red; provoke, arouse, rouse, inflame, enflame, agitate, fire up, work up, whip up, stir up, wind up; displease.

2. vex, pique, irritate, peeve, nettle, chafe, irk, annoy, *Chiefly U.S.* rile, *Inf.* aggravate, *Inf.* miff, *Inf.* give [s.o.] a pain, *Inf.* get under [s.o.'s] skin, *Inf.* get in [s.o.'s] hair, *Sl.* bug; exasperate, ruffle, roil, put out, get, *Sl.* get [s.o.'s] goat.

3. embitter, exacerbate, gall, rankle, envenom; insult, offend, affront.

incensed, *adj.* wrathful, wroth, irate, ireful, very angry; enraged, raging, fuming, infuriated, *Rare.* infuriate, furious; inflamed, flaming, flaring, flared up, heated, red-hot, white-hot; distraught, overwrought, upset, feverish, hysterical, not rational; violent, unrestrained, uncontrollable, ranting, raving, storming, foaming at the mouth, rabid, fanatical, frenzied; frantic, crazed, *Pathol.* delirious, mad, *Inf.* wild, out of one's mind, beside oneself.

incentive, *n.* inducement, impetus, incitement; stimulus, stimulant, goad, spur, impulse; provocation, exhortation, encouragement, inspiration, persuasion; motivation, carrot-and-stick *or* reward-and-punishment ploy; reason, good reason, reason why, *Inf.* what for; ground, cause, enticement, lure, bait, *Inf.* come-on; occasion, purpose, object, excuse.

inception, *n.* beginning, commencement, exordium; start, starting point, dawn, alpha, first, outset; opening, debut, onset, outbreak, conception; inauguration, initiation, installation; origin, source, derivation, root, provenance.

incertitude, *n.* **1.** uncertainty, unsureness, doubtfulness, doubt, dubitation, hesitancy, hesitation; ambivalence, indecision, indecisiveness, undecidedness, irresoluteness, inconclusiveness, lack of certainty, *Psychol.* ambitendency; unassuredness, lack of assurance *or* confidence, self-doubt.

2. insecurity, insecureness, instability, unsteadiness, shakiness, inconstancy; indefiniteness, dubiety, dubiousness, dubiosity, ambiguity, vagueness, haziness, fogginess, unknownness, open question.

incessant, *adj.* **1.** ceaseless, unceasing, nonstop, constant, uninterrupted; continual, continuous, ongoing, unbroken; unremitting, unintermitting, relentless, persistent; recurrent, repeated, frequent, habitual.

2. unending, endless, never-ending, interminable, Sisyphean; eternal, perpetual, everlasting, lasting, en during, perennial, permanent.

incestuous, *adj.* **1.** adulterous, adulterate, fornicatory, copulative; carnal, bestial, abusive; lecherous, lustful, lascivious, licentious, libidinous, concupiscent, prurient.

2. taboo, forbidden, banned, outside one's moral code, illicit, unlawful, illegal, criminal; immoral, corrupt, depraved, degenerate.

3. nepotistic, nepotistical, within the family; partisan, partial, biased.

inchoate, *adj.* **1.** incipient, beginning, just begun, commencing, *Archaic.* inchoative; inceptive, inaugural, original, initial; nascent, newborn, a-borning, embryonic, embryonical, germinal, genetic, genetical; early, primitive, primal, prime, primordial, primigenial; elementary, rudimentary, rudimental, basal, preparatory, fundamental, basic.

2. developing, undeveloped, immature, drawing-board, in the planning *or* blueprint stage; imperfect, incomplete, unfinished.

3. unorganized, disorganized, unorderly, out of order; incoherent, loose, disconnected, illogical, nonsensical; discursive, rambling, all over the place.

incidence, *n.* **1.** rate, frequency, prevalence, commonness, common occurrence, oftenness; range, scope, extent, compass, area; direction, course, line, aim; drift, tendency, trend, bearing, tenor, set.

2. realization, materialization, eventuality, coming to pass *or* be; event, occurrence, occasion, circumstance; happening, befalling, affecting; fact, phenomenon, experience.

3. relation, relationship, connection, tie, *Inf.* tie-in, hookup, bond, link, linkage; association, affiliation, union, alliance.

incident, *n.* **1.** event, occurrence, occasion, circumstance; happening, proceeding, transaction; concern, matter, phenomenon; fact; experience, adventure.

2. (*all of stories, narratives, plays, etc.*) episode, passage, chapter, piece of action; act, scene.

3. eventuality, contingency, juncture, conjuncture; minutia, small detail, minor detail, incidental; particular, item, detail, point; aspect, facet, factor; regard, respect.

4. confrontation, encounter; affair, border incident; brush, scrap, fray, flare-up; crisis, emergency.

5. *Chiefly British.* bomb run, bombing mission, bombing raid; air raid, air strike, air attack.

—*adj.* **6.** likely, probable, possible; occurring, happening, taking place, going on, on, under way; in the cards, in the air, in the wind, afloat, afoot, astir, in hand.

7. pertaining, appertaining, belonging, relating, referring; related, relevant, pertinent, germane, material, applicable, applying, apposite, apropos, to the point.

8. conjoined, attached, connected, joined, linked, coupled, tied, knotted; affiliated, associated, allied; contingent, circumstantial, conditional, provisional, dependent, accompanying; accidental, occasional; additional, supplementary, supplemental.

incidental, *adj.* **1.** chance, fortuitous, serendipitous, *Inf.* fluky; indiscriminate, random, haphazard, casual, hit or miss, careless, leaving much to chance; occasional, accidental; contingent, conditional, circumstantial, provisional, dependent, accompanying; odd, extra, spare-time, part-time; adscititious; subsidiary, subordinate, secondary, accessory.

2. negligible, unimportant, of little *or* small importance, of no great importance, inconsequential, of little consequence, insignificant, inconsiderable, inappreciable; extrinsic, extrinsical, extraneous, external, nonessential, unessential, inessential, adventitious;

parenthetical, by-the-way.

3. meager, paltry, puny; petty, trivial, trifling; little, small, minute, *Sl.* dinky; *Inf.* small-time, *Sl.* two-bit, *Sl.* small potatoes.

—*n.* **4.** incident, event, occurrence, occasion, circumstance; eventuality, contingency, juncture, conjuncture.

incidentally, *adv.* **1.** casually, randomly, haphazardly; fortuitously, by chance, perchance, as it chanced, as luck would have it, by a piece of luck, by a fluke.

2. by the way, by the by, parenthetically, by way of parenthesis; in passing, en passant; speaking of, while on the subject, apropos *or* apropos of.

incinerate, *v.* burn, parch, bake, overbake, overcook, roast, scorch, scald, char; burn up, carbonize, reduce to ashes, cremate; torrefy, smelt, melt down, scorify.

incipient, *adj.* beginning, just begun, commencing, *Archaic.* inchoative; inceptive, inaugural, original, initial; nascent, newborn, a-borning, embryonic, embryonical, germinal, genetic, genetical; early, primitive, primal, prime, primordial, primigenial; inchoate, rudimentary, rudimental, elementary, basal, preparatory, fundamental, basic.

incise, *v.* **1.** cut *or* cut into, make an incision, slit *or* slit open, gash; notch, nick, scratch, score, groove, furrow.

2. engrave, grave, *Archaic.* insculp, etch, carve, sculpt, sculpture.

incised, *adj.* **1.** cut, slit, slashed, gashed; cut into, notched, nicked, grooved, furrowed; sulcated, cleft, cloven, split.

2. engraved, graven, *Archaic.* insculpt, etched, carved, *Literary.* carven, sculpted, sculptured.

incision, *n.* deep cut, slit, slash, gash; split, crack, cleft; furrow, groove, notch, nick, scratch.

incisive, *adj.* **1.** penetrating, acid, caustic, tart, acrid, acrimonious, acerbic; cutting, sarcastic, satirical, sardonic, ironic, cynical; biting, trenchant, stinging, astringent; critical, disparaging, disapprobatory, censorious.

2. sharp, keen, alert, acute, piercing, right to the point; astute, astucious, perceptive, knowing, shrewd, canny, smart, perspicacious, judicious; clever, smart, sharp as a tack.

incisiveness, *n.* **1.** trenchancy, acidity, acridity, acrimoniousness, acerbicity, pungency; sarcasm, satire, ridicule, irony, cynicism; criticism, disparagement, disapprobation, censorship.

2. sharpness, keenness, alertness, acuity, acumen, acuteness; discernment, astuteness, perception, knowledge, shrewdness, canniness, aptness, perspicacity, judiciousness.

incite, *v.* instigate, provoke, foment, actuate, urge, goad, spur, prompt, prod, prick, poke, thrust, push, drive, hound, egg on, put up to; excite, arouse, rouse, agitate, whip, whip up, work up, stir, stir up, wind up, inflame, fire, fire up, enkindle, kindle, touch off, *Inf.* psych up, *Australian.* sool; stimulate, animate, whet, invigorate, motivate, inspire, inspirit, rally, awaken, vivify, bestir, enliven, liven up, jolt, jog; encourage, abet, embolden, nerve, build up, buck up; induce, impel, constrain, press, move, force; persuade, exhort influence, prevail upon, sway, coax, wheedle; tempt lure, inveigle, beguile.

incitement, *n.* **1.** instigation, provocation, fomentation, actuation, insistence, incitation; excitement, arousal, agitation, inflammation; stimulation, animation, invigoration, motivation, inspiration, vivification; encouragement, abetment, emboldenment; inducement, impulsion, obligation; persuasion, exhortation, influence, temptation, inveiglement, beguilement, enticement, blandishment.

2. urging, goading, spurring, prompting, prodding, pricking, poking, thrusting, pushing, driving, hounding, egging on; exciting, arousing, rousing, agitating, working up, stirring up, winding up, inflaming, enflaming, firing, firing up, enkindling; motivating, inspiring, rallying, awakening, vivifying, bestirring, enlivening, livening up; encouraging, abetting, emboldening, nerving, building up, bucking up; inducing, impelling, constraining, pressing, moving, forcing; persuading, exhorting, influencing, prevailing upon, swaying, coaxing, wheedling; tempting, luring, inveigling, beguiling.

3. stimulus, fillip, provocation, incentive, motive; press, goad, spur, prick, prod, jolt, jog, poke, thrust; impulse, urge, drive, push, itch, desire; dictate, call.

incivility, *n.* **1.** uncivil behavior, rudeness, bad manners, unmannerliness, impoliteness, indecorum, misbehavior; discourteousness, disrespect, impertinence; unbecoming conduct, ungentlemanliness, unladylike behavior, ill breeding, bad breeding; coarseness, boorishness, barbarism, vulgarity, roughness; tactlessness, bluntness, *Fr. brusquerie,* unkindness; acerbity, acrimony.

2. uncivil act, slight, cut, snub, affront, insult, provocation, *Inf.* red flag, *Inf.* slap in the face; uncomplimentary remark, left-handed compliment, aspersion, *Inf.* brickbat.

inclemency, *n.* **1.** cruelty, pitilessness, hard-heartedness, mercilessness, unmercifulness, remorselessness, unfeelingness, callousness, coldness, stoniness, implacableness; malevolence, ruthlessness, ferociousness, savagery, barbarity.

2. (*all of weather*) severity, rigor, harshness, bitterness, rawness, cold; storminess, blustering, windiness, gustiness; violence, roughness, tempestuousness.

inclement, *adj.* **1.** harsh, cruel, hard-hearted, rigorous, severe; grim, stony, cold, implacable; unmerciful, unkind, unfeeling, unpitying, merciless, pitiless, ruthless; remorseless, inexorable, unrelenting.

2. (*all of weather*) squally, windy, rainy, gusty, blustery, raw; stormy, violent, tempestuous, rough; bad, *Sl.* lousy, messy.

inclination, *n.* **1.** proclivity, propensity, leaning, bent, turn, cast, inclining, *Biol.* tropism; tendency, tending, bearing, verging, gravitation, drift; proneness, subjectability, aptness, liableness, likeliness, susceptibility, weakness, openness; disposition, mindset, *Pathol.* diathesis, idiosyncrasy, idiosyncrasis, *Archaic.* crasis, grain; temperament, temper, mind, humor, vein.

2. penchant, predisposition, predilection, partiality; prejudice, tendentiousness, bias, preference; affinity, attraction, sympathy, fancy, liking, fondness, affection, love, ardor, fervor, zeal, passion; desire, longing, wishing, hankering, craving, itch, avidity; appetite, appetency, relish, taste; voracity, pruriency, concupiscence, lust.

3. obliqueness, obliquity, angle, miter, bevel, cant, diagonal; grade, slope, pitch, slant, ramp, hill, bank, incline, inclined plane; acclivity, rise, ascent; declivity, declination, descent, fall, drop, dip, sag, downgrade; divergence, digression, swing, swerve, veer, turn, angling, fork, *Both U.S. Facetious.* zig, zag; list, listing, heel, heeling, *Naut.* careen, careening.

incline, *v.* **1.** tend, have a preference for, have a penchant for, have an affinity for, be attracted to; be disposed to, be prone to, be apt to, be liable to, be likely to, be subject to, be open to.

2. angle, bevel, cant, slope, pitch, slant, grade, bank;

ascend, rise, descend, fall, drop, dig, sag; swerve, swing, veer, turn, curve, fork, *Both U.S. Facetious.* zig, zag; list, heel, *Naut.* careen.

3. approximate, near, approach, *Archaic.* nigh; verge, gravitate, drift; (*all followed by* towards) lean, bend, bear.

4. (*of persons*) *Usu.* **incline to** dispose, predispose, prejudice, bias; influence, affect.

5. (*of the head, body, etc.*) bow, nod, lower, cast down; kneel, genuflect, curtsy; salaam, bend down, stoop.

—*n.* **6.** slope, slant, pitch, grade, ramp, hill, bank, inclined plane, inclination; acclivity, rise, ascent; declivity, declination, descent, fall, drop, dip, downgrade.

inclined, *adj.* **1.** (*usu. followed by* to) disposed, tending, *Archaic.* propense, of a mind; prone, apt, liable, likely, susceptible, open; predisposed, given, partial, prejudiced, biased; attracted, sympathetic, keen, willing, eager, *Archaic.* fain, zealous, ardent, fervent, avid.

2. leaning, bending, tilting, gravitating, verging, bearing.

3. oblique, angular, angled, mitered, beveled, cantic, diagonal; graded, sloping, sloped, shelving, aslant, slanting, slanted; pitching, pitched, banked, steep, precipitous; acclivitous, acclivous, rising, ascending; declivitous, declinational, descending, falling, dropping, dipping, sagging; swerving, turning, angling, *Both U.S. Facetious.* zigging, zagging; listing, heeling, *Naut.* careening.

include, *v.* **1.** enclose, incorporate, comprise, comprehend, embrace, embody, hold; admit, take in, cover.

2. involve, refer to, take into account, count, number, reckon *or* number among; append, subjoin, subsume.

3. categorize, classify, group, arrange, place; tabulate, index, file, list, catalog, register.

inclusive, *adj.* **1.** enclosing, embracing, incorporating, embodying, comprehending, comprising, surrounding, encircling, taking in; from start to finish, from beginning to end, up and down, without exception.

2. comprehensive, extensive, wide, full; all-embracing, all-encompassing, blanket, umbrella; sweeping, general, across-the-board; broad, compendious, catch-all.

incognito, *adj.* **1.** (*all in reference to one's identity*) concealed, undisclosed, unidentified, unrecognized; clandestine, sub rosa, under the rose, secretive, mysterious; disguised, masked, veiled, camouflaged, sailing under false colors; shielded, sheltered, protected, secreted; unrevealed, *Latin. in pectore, It. in petto.*

—*adv.* **2.** under an assumed name, under cover, on the sly, mysteriously, privately, confidentially, clandestinely; discreetly, quietly, with circumspection, without fanfare, out of the limelight, secretly, on the q.t., under wraps.

—*n.* **3.** masquerader, domino, mystery man, woman of mystery, confidential agent, secret agent, double agent; recluse, *Inf.* clam.

4. concealment, secrecy, privacy, circumspection, discretion, seclusion, obscurity, secretiveness.

5. disguise, masquerade, camouflage, mask, screen, smokescreen, false identity, cover, act, sham, blink, charade; assumed name, alias, pseudonym, nom de plume, pen name.

incognizable, *adj.* **1.** impenetrable, incomprehensible, uncomprehensible, inapprehensible, past *or* beyond comprehension, beyond understanding, unknowable, incognoscible, inscrutable, unfathomable, indecipherable, undecipherable; mystic, mystical, cabalistic, supernatural; occult, cryptic, perdu, secret, hidden, concealed; mysterious, arcane, inexplicable, unexplainable, insolvable, insoluble, unaccountable, *Obs.* inextricable; puzzling, enigmatic, enigmatical.

2. unperceivable, imperceptible, unobservable; undistinguishable, indistinguishable, unnoticeable, unrecognizable.

incognizant, *adj.* unaware, unconscious, ignorant, unknowledgeable, unenlightened, uninitiated; unknowing, unsuspecting, innocent, unprepared, off guard, napping; inattentive, unmindful, heedless, thoughtless, careless.

incoherence, *n.* **1.** unconnectedness, disjointedness, disconnectedness, brokenness, incoherency; rambling, wandering, straying, discursiveness, digression, deviation; illogicalness, irrationality, irrationalness, wildness, confusion, mix-up, muddle, scramble, jumble; unintelligibility, unintelligibleness, inarticulateness, mumbling, muttering, murmuring.

2. difference, discrepancy, inconsistency, contradiction; incongruousness, incongruity, inharmoniousness, incompatibleness, incompatibility; discord, disharmony, dissonance, discordancy, inconsonance; disagreement, difference of opinion, variance, clashing, opposition, contrariness.

incoherent, *adj.* **1.** illogical, unconnected, disjointed, disconnected, broken; rambling, aimless, wandering, straying, discursive, digressive, deviating; irrational, wild, confused, mixed-up, muddled, addled, scrambled, jumbled; unintelligible, inarticulate, mumbled, muttered, murmured.

2. loose, unattached, detached, broken off.

3. different, incompatible, inharmonious, incongruous, incongruent, inconsonant, discordant, dissonant; discrepant, disagreeing, differing, inconsistent, contradictory, clashing, variant, at odds, opposing, opposite, contrary.

incombustible, *adj.* uninflammable, flameproof, fireproof, unburnable, unignitable, asbestine, wetdown; flame retardant *or* resistant.

income, *n.* **1.** returns, revenue, incomings, receipts, gross; annuity, pension, subsidy, allowance; profits, gain, yield, interest; winnings, *Sl.* velvet, *Sl.* take, proceeds, net, *Sl.* clean-up, pickings, *Sl.* gravy.

2. wages, salary, pay, *Brit. Sl.* get; emolument, compensation, payment, hire, remuneration, consideration, competence; stipend, fee, honorarium; perquisites, *Inf.* perks, fringe benefits, benefits, *Inf.* fringes, *Inf.* extras.

3. recompense, reward, *Archaic.* meed, *Literary.* guerdon, deserts.

incommensurable, *adj.* **1.** incomparable, utterly unlike, dissimilar, like apples and oranges; inconsonant, inharmonious, discrepant.

2. unsuitable, unfit, unapt; disproportionate, incongruent, out of line, amiss, *Dial.* all skewgy; lopsided, unbalanced, ill-balanced.

incommensurate, *adj.* unequal, disproportionate, disproportional; insufficient, inadequate, not enough, too little; extreme, excessive, extravagant, inordinate.

incommode, *v.* inconvenience, discomfort, discommode, put out, trouble; unsettle, disturb, bother, *Sl.* bug, *Sl.* hassle; impose upon, encroach upon, burden.

incommodious, *adj.* **1.** inconvenient, unhandy, unsuitable, disadvantageous; bothersome, irksome.

2. cramped, restricted, *Obs.* incapacious, unroomy, boxy, cell-like; narrow, confined, tiny, *Inf.* teeny, lacking elbow-room.

incommunicable, *adj.* **1.** unrevealable, unimpartable, noncommunicable; confidential, top-secret, eyes-only, private, personal, privy.

2. inexpressible, unutterable, unmentionable, unspeakable, untranslatable; indescribable, ineffable, undefinable.

3. noninfectious, noncontagious, nontransferable, untransmissible, not catching.

incommunicative, *adj.* quiet, closed-mouthed, uncommunicative, silent, mum, mute, dumb, *Sl.* buttoned-up; noncommittal, evasive; brief, of few words, laconic, terse, curt, short; unsociable, shy, reserved, reticent, taciturn.

incomparable, *adj.* **1.** superior, superlative, beyond compare, supreme; rare, exceptional, unusual, uncommon; exquisite, singular, unique, one and only, inimitable, beyond imitation, *Inf.* the greatest.

2. unequaled, matchless, peerless, without equal, nonpareil; unparalleled, unrivaled, unapproachable, unsurpassed; transcendent, surpassing, unmatchable.

incompatibility, *n.* incongruity, disparity, dissimilitude, contrariety, variance, discordancy, inharmoniousness, disharmony, dissonance, inconsistency, discrepancy; disagreement, quarrel, wrangle, discord, dispute, dissension, conflict, dissidence; difference, misunderstanding, controversy; uncongeniality, divergency, disunion, division, diversity, irreconcilability; antagonism, antipathy, hostility, bad blood.

incompatible, *adj.* **1.** unsuitable, unsuited, mismatched, poorly matched, ill-assorted; inappropriate, out of place, unbecoming, incongruous, uncomplementary.

2. contrary, opposed, discordant, inconsonant, inharmonious, jarring, clashing, factious, dissentient, contradictory, inconsistent; opposite, antipathetic, diametrically opposed, at opposite poles, on opposite sides of the fence, like night and day; uncongenial, unamiable, unsympathetic, unaccommodating, disagreeing, like cats and dogs, irreconcilable; antagonistic, adverse, hostile.

incompetence, *n.* unfitness, weakness, feebleness, failure; incompetency, inability, incapability, unqualification, unsuitability, inadequacy, insufficiency, deficiency, incapacity, disability, impotence, uselessness; inefficiency, ineffectiveness, ineptitude; awkwardness, clumsiness, *Sl.* klutziness; ignorance, benightedness, stupidity.

incompetent, *adj.* **1.** unfit, unqualified, incapable, unable; inefficient, ineffectual, ineffective; inadequate, insufficient, deficient, unequal, unapt, unsuitable, lacking qualifications, useless.

2. inept, awkward, bungling, clumsy, maladroit, gauche; stumbling, foundering, floundering, having two left feet, *Sl.* klutzy; unskillful, inexpert, unskilled, unhandy, all thumbs; ignorant, benighted, stupid, *Sl.* out of it.

—n. **3.** simpleton, dullard, dolt, *Sl.* dimwit; idiot, imbecile, moron, retardate.

incomplete, *adj.* **1.** unfinished, unaccomplished, not completed, unexecuted; imperfect, inchoate, undeveloped, immature, abortive; inexhaustive, fragmentary, partial; crude, rough, sketchy.

2. deficient, lacking, defective; not total, not entire, failing, wanting; shortened, curtailed, abridged, expurgated, bowderlized; inaccurate, garbled, broken, mutilated, defaced, distorted; mangled, butchered, maimed, hashed; truncated, docked.

incomprehensible, *adj.* **1.** unintelligible, uncomprehensible, inapprehensible, indecipherable, undecipherable, ununderstandable, Greek to one; incoherent, incarticulate, jumbled, muddled.

2. difficult, hard, over one's head, *Inf.* tough; complex, complicated, perplexed, *Inf.* tricky; intricate, involved, tangled, knotty, crabbed.

3. impenetrable, unfathomable, unknowable, inscrutable, incognizable, past *or* beyond comprehension, beyond understanding; profound, deep, esoteric, recondite, abstruse, abstract, heavy, *Sl.* heavy-duty; mystic, mystical, transcendental, cabalistic, supernatural; occult, cryptic, perdu, secret, hidden, concealed; obscure, vague, dim, dark, nebulous; mysterious, arcane, inexplicable, unexplainable, insolvable, insoluble, unaccountable; puzzling, enigmatic, enigmatical.

4. fantastic, fabulous, wondrous, wonderful, marvelous, miraculous, phenomenal, prodigious; impossible, unbelievable, incredible; unthinkable, inconceivable, unimaginable.

5. infinite, endless, boundless, limitless, unlimited, immeasurable, unmeasurable.

incompressible, *adj.* incondensable, compact, solid, dense, firm, hard; tight, close, consolidated, solidified, unified, cohesive, as one; condensed, concentrated, thick, compacted, compressed, packed together; impermeable, impassable, impenetrable.

incomputable, *adj.* incalculable, inestimable, uncountable, not to be reckoned; innumerable, innumerous, countless, untold, uncounted, numberless, without number, sumless; unmeasured, indeterminate, undetermined, indefinite; measureless, immeasurable, fathomless, unfathomable; infinite, unlimited, limitless, without limit, illimitable, unbounded, boundless; inexhaustible, endless, unending, interminable, no end of, without end, bottomless; multitudinous, very great, enormous, prodigious, immense, vast, astronomical.

inconceivable, *adj.* unimaginable, unthinkable, incomprehensible, incredible, implausible, incogitable; impossible, not possible, out of the question, not to be thought of; unbelievable, contrary to reason, unheard-of, undreamed-of, unthought-of, hard *or* difficult to believe, passing *or* staggering belief; preposterous, absurd, ridiculous, ludicrous, outlandish; wondrous, wonderful, miraculous, fabulous, fantastic, *Sl.* mind-blowing, *Sl.* mind-boggling; strange, passing strange.

inconclusive, *adj.* indefinite, indecisive, open to doubt *or* question, still open, *Inf.* up in the air; unproved, undemonstrated, unestablished, unsettled, undetermined, unconfirmed, unsubstantiated; fallible, liable *or* open to error; unconvincing, unsubstantial, hollow, flimsy, tenuous, *Inf.* shaky, weak, feeble, lame.

incongruity, *n.* **1.** incompatibility, inconformability, discrepancy, disparity, divergence, diversity, difference, dissimilitude; inappropriateness, inaptness, inappositeness, unsuitabilty, unfitness, unfittingness, impropriety, unseemliness.

2. inconsonance, inharmoniousness, discordancy, dissonance, absonance; disproportion, inequality, incongruousness.

3. inconsistency, inconsequence; contrariety, contrast, contradiction, conflict; illogicalness, unreasonableness, reasonlessness.

incongruous, *adj.* **1.** incompatible, inconformable, discrepant, disparate, divergent, disagreeing, out of line, out of step, out of keeping; inappropriate, inapt, inapposite, inapropos, unsuitable, unfit, unfitting, improper, unseemly, unbecoming.

2. inconsonant, inharmonious, discordant, dissonant, absonant, out of tune, clashing, jarring.

3. inconsistent, inconsequent, inconsequential, not following; contrary, contradictory, conflicting; illogical, unreasonable, reasonless, contrary to reason.

inconsequent, *adj.* **1.** fragmentary, in bits and pieces, discontinuous, out of sequence; disconnected,

detached, apart.
2. inconsistent, not following, incongruous, inconsonant, incompatible, inconformable; illogical, unreasonable, reasonless, contrary to reason.
3. irrelevant, inapplicable, inapposite, inapt, impertinent, immaterial, neither here nor there; beside the point, beside the mark, beside the question, off the subject, off base *or* way off base, adrift, *Sl.* at sea, *Sl.* in left field; not at issue, nothing to do with the case.
4. inappropriate, unsuitable, unfit, unfitting, improper, unseemly, unbecoming, out of keeping, out of line, out of step.
5. inconsequential, trivial, *Sl.* small-time. See **inconsequential** (*def.* **1**).

inconsequential, *adj.* **1.** insignificant, inconsiderable, inappreciable, negligible, unimportant, of minor importance, of little *or* no account, no great shakes; trivial, trifling, petty, niggling; small, dinky, puny, piddling, *Sl.* small-time, *Sl.* two-bit.
2. inconsistent, illogical; irrelevant, inapplicable. See **inconsequent** (*defs.* **2, 3**).

inconsiderable, *adj.* inconsequential, insignificant, negligible, unimportant; trivial, petty, niggling; small, puny, *Sl.* small-time. See also **inconsequential** (*def.* **1**).

inconsiderate, *adj.* **1.** unthoughtful, incogitant; unkind, uncharitable, unbenevolent, harsh, severe.
2. thoughtless, unthinking, unmindful, heedless, inadvertent, inattentive, unobservant, regardless, undiscerning, careless, uncircumspect; tactless, insensitive, unsolicitous, rude, boorish.
3. rash, reckless, precipitate, headlong, head over heels; overhasty; unwise, injudicious, imprudent, impolitic, indiscreet; ill-considered, ill-advised, ill-gauged, ill-judged, ill-contrived, misguided.

inconsistency, *n.* **1.** inharmoniousness, inconsonance, dissonance, discordancy, absonance; incompatibility, inconformability, incongruity; discrepancy, divergence, disagreement, difference, dissimilarity, dissimilitude.
2. inconsequence, incoherence, uncohesiveness, garbledness, confusion; contrariety, contrast, contradistinction; illogicalness, unreasonableness, reasonlessness.
3. inconstancy, instability, unsteadiness, changeableness, mutability; capriciousness, fickleness, flightiness, erraticism, mercurialness.
4. contradiction, self-contradiction, paradox, oxymoron.

inconsistent, *adj.* **1.** self-contradictory, paradoxical, oxymoronic; contradictory, contrary, conflicting; illogical, unreasonable, reasonless, contrary to reason, without rhyme or reason; incoherent, uncohesive, confused, garbled.
2. inharmonious, inconsonant, discordant, dissonant, absonant, clashing, jarring; incompatible, inconformable, incongruous, out of keeping, out of line, out of step; discrepant, divergent, disagreeing, different, dissimilar; at variance, at odds, at cross-purposes, in conflict.
3. inconstant, unstable, unsteady, changeable, mutable; capricious, fickle, erratic, mercurial, volatile.

inconsolable, *adj.* disconsolate, comfortless, heartbroken, broken-hearted, heartsick, sick at heart, soulsick, sick to one's soul; forlorn, desolate, despairing, cheerless, joyless, hopeless; woebegone, wretched, miserable; overwhelmed, overcome, undone, stricken, crushed, bowed-down, prostrate with grief, *Inf.* broken-up, *Inf.* torn-up.

inconspicuous, *adj.* unnoticeable, half-visible, indistinct, indefinite; unobtrusive, unimposing, low-profile; modest, unostentatious, unassuming, low-key.

inconstant, *adj.* changeable, changeful, variable, mutable, permutable; unstable, unsteady, unsettled, unfixed; fickle, capricious, moody, volatile, mercurial, flighty, giddy; erratic, irregular, unmethodical, fitful, spasmodic, desultory, stop-and-go, come-and-go; uncertain, unsure, indecisive, irresolute, indefinite, vacillating, fluctuating, wavering, blowing hot and cold.

incontestable, *adj.* indisputable, incontrovertible, undeniable, irrefragable, irrefutable, unquestionable, beyond question, admitting no question *or* doubt, indubitable, beyond a shadow of a doubt, apodictic; *Law.* peremptory, unappealable; conclusive, decisive, definite, definitive, solid, fixed, final; impregnable, invincible, unassailable, insuperable, undefeatable, unbeatable; certain, sure, *Inf.* for-sure, absolute, positive.

incontinence, *n.* **1.** licentiousness, libertinism, debauchery, dissoluteness, dolce vita, dissipation, profligacy, profligateness; lechery, lewdness, *Pathol.* satyriasis, goatishness, *Pathol.* nymphomania; concupiscence, lust, prurience, pruriency; lustfulness, libidinousness, salacity, salaciousness; promiscuity, wantonness, abandon, lawlessness, unrestraint.
2. lack of bladder *or* bowel control; *Med.* enuresis, bed-wetting.

incontinent, *adj.* **1.** unrestrained, unbridled, unchecked, uncurbed, ungoverned, uncontrolled; uninterrupted, unceasing, incessant, unending, nonstop, constant, continual, continuous, unbroken.
2. licentious, lascivious, libertine, debauched, dissolute, dissipated, rakish, rakehell; lecherous, lubricous, satyric, satyrical, satyrlike, goatish, *Sl.* horny, *Archaic.* lickerish; concupiscent, prurient, lustful, libidinous, salacious; ruttish, beastly, bestial, swinish; obscene, lewd, Fescennne, Cyprian, indecent, dirty, foul, indelicate; loose, wanton, wild, profligate, abandoned; promiscuous, whorish, of easy virtue, unchaste, impure; coarse, crude, gross.
3. lacking bladder *or* bowel control; (*of children*) not toilet-trained; *Med.* enuretic, bed-wetting.

incontrovertible, *adj.* incontestable, indisputable, undeniable, unquestionable, indubitable, apodictic; conclusive, decisive, definitive, solid; certain, sure, absolute, positive. See also **incontestable**.

inconvenience, *n.* **1.** awkwardness, cumbersomeness, unfitness, onerousness; unhandiness, inopportuneness, inappropriateness, untimeliness, unseasonableness; disadvantageousness, troublesomeness, *Inf.* worriment.
2. trouble, bother, annoyance, pain; nuisance, *Sl.* pain in the neck, disturbance, *Sl.* drag, bore; disadvantage, discommodity, drawback; encumbrance, burden, Albatross around one's neck, millstone around one's neck, monkey on one's back; stumbling block, impediment, hindrance, roadblock.
—*v.* **3.** incommode, discommode, discomfort, discompose, put out, cumber, trouble, make [s.o.] go out of his way; unsettle, put off, disturb, bother, worry, *Sl.* bug, *Sl.* hassle; impose upon, encroach upon, interfere; impede, hinder, distract, annoy, burden, weigh on.

inconvenient, *adj.* awkward, burdensome, annoying, troublesome, *Sl.* pesky, unsettling, bothersome, distracting; disadvantageous, discommodious, inopportune; ill-timed, untimely, unseasonable, coming at the wrong time and wrong place; inexpedient, unsuited, unfit, inappropriate, out-of-place.

incorporate, *v.* **1.** file corporation papers, conglomerate, federate, confederate, organize, affiliate, associate.
2. merge, coalesce, integrate; fuse, blend, amalgamate; unite, combine, join, conjoin, link; consolidate, unify, compact.
3. embody, incarnate, personify; exemplify, express,

identify, reify; include, comprise, embrace.
—*adj.* **4.** incorporated, integrated, coalesced, united; fused, merged, blended.

incorporation, *n.* merger, integration, coalescence, fusion, amalgamation; blending, combining, joining, consolidating, unifying.

incorporeal, *adj.* insubstantial, asomatous, nonmaterial, immaterial, spiritual; unearthly, unworldly, extramundane, ultramundane; unreal, chimerical, illusory, ethereal, impalpable, intangible; psychical, spectral, ghostly, supernatural, *Inf.* spooky, occult.

incorrect, *adj.* **1.** inaccurate, inexact, imprecise, unfactual, not according to the facts; false, fallacious, untrue, not true, devoid of truth, not right, not straight; in error, mistaken, erroneous, wrong, in the wrong, all wrong, dead wrong, *Sl.* all wet, *Sl.* full of beans *or* prunes, *Sl.* full of hot air; off, way off, not even close, *Inf.* cold, *Inf.* off base, *Inf.* off the beam; wide of the mark, astray, *Inf.* off target, *Sl.* out in left field, *Sl.* at sea.
2. improper, unbecoming, unseemly, indecorous, indecent, unladylike, ungentlemanly, ungentlemanlike; unsuitable, inappropriate, amiss.
3. faulty, imperfect, defective, flawed; unsound, illogical, twisted, *Sl.* cockeyed, backwards, *Sl.* screwy.

incorrectness, *n.* **1.** inaccuracy, inaccurateness, inexactness, inexactitude, imprecision, impreciseness; falseness, falsehood, fallaciousness, untruth, untrueness; erroneousness, mistakenness, wrongness.
2. impropriety, unbecomingness, unseemliness, indecorousness, indecency; unsuitability, unsuitableness, inappropriateness.
3. faultiness, imperfection, defectiveness, flawedness; unsoundness, illogicalness, illogicality.

incorrigible, *adj.* **1.** irreformable, unreformable, unreformative, irreclaimable, irredeemable, beyond *or* past help; irrecoverable, irretrievable, unsalvageable, unsavable, lost; incurable, uncurable, irremediable, irreparable; hopeless, beyond *or* past hope, a lost cause.
2. impervious, obstinate, stubborn, unyielding, obdurate, inflexible; impenetrable, thick, unteachable; unmanageable, untractable, uncontrollable; reprobate, bad, miscreant, villainous, vicious; depraved, sinful, wicked, iniquitous; uncontrite, impenitent, unsorry, unrepentant; inveterate, hardened, hard-core.

incorruptibility, *n.* **1.** incorruptibleness, honesty, honestness, integrity, uprightness, probity; honor, honorableness, high-mindedness, nobility, nobleness; right-mindedness, virtue, virtuousness, goodness, purity; sinlessness, blamelessness, irreproachableness, irreproachability, unimpeachability, unimpeachableness; guiltlessness, inculpability, inculpableness, innocence; impeccability, immaculacy, immaculateness, cleanness, spotlessness, stainlessness; faultlessness, flawlessness, inerrancy, perfection, perfectness; infallibility, infallibleness, inerrability, inerrableness, unerringness.
2. indissolubility, indissolubleness, indestructibility, indestructibleness; imperishability, imperishableness, undyingness, deathlessness, immortality; eternity, eternalness, everlastingness, enduringness, perpetuity, perpetualness, endlessness, eternal continuity *or* continuance.

incorruptible, *adj.* **1.** unbribable, unbuyable, untemptable, untempted; honest, honorable, high-minded, right-minded, noble, virtuous, good, upright, moral, high-principled; pure, sinless, blameless, irreproachable, above suspicion, unimpeachable, guiltless, inculpable, innocent; impeccable, immaculate, clean, spotless, stainless, unstained, unspotted, unsoiled, unsullied, untarnished, unblemished; faultless, flawless, inerrant, perfect, infallible, inerrable, unerring.
2. indissoluble, undissolvable, not bio-degradable; indestructible, imperishable, undying, deathless, immortal; eternal, everlasting, amaranthine, unfading; enduring, perpetual, constant, endless, unending, continuing, on-going.

increase, *v.* **1.** enlarge, make larger, make greater, *Chiefly Literary.* greaten, aggrandize; magnify, amplify, enhance, deepen, heighten; widen, thicken, broaden; lengthen, prolong, protract; expand, extend, spread out, stretch out, branch out; inflate, distend, puff out, dilate; wax, swell.
2. augment, supplement, add to, superadd to; accrue, accumulate, cumulate, amass, pile up, heap up.
3. elevate, raise, boost, exalt; rise, ascend, mount, skyrocket; burgeon, shoot up, flourish.
4. escalate, step up, give a boost to, *U.S. Sl.* soup up, *Sl.* hop up, *Sl.* jazz up; accelerate, snowball, mushroom; intensify, concentrate; exaggerate, maximize, make much of, make the most of, overstate; exacerbate, aggravate.
5. strengthen, reinforce, build up; improve, advance, further; grow, develop, mature.
6. propagate, reproduce, produce, breed; procreate, beget, engender, generate, bring into being; fructify, be fruitful, be prolific, proliferate; germinate, sprout, pullulate.
—*n.* **7.** enlargement, aggrandizement, expansion, extension; magnification, amplification, enhancement, deepening, heightening; widening, thickening, broadening; spreading out, stretching out, branching out; lengthening, prolongation, protraction; inflation, distension, dilatation, dilation; waxing, swelling.
8. augmentation, supplement; addition, increment, accession, access; accrual, accruement, accumulation, cumulation, amassing, piling up, heaping up.
9. elevation, raise, boost, rise; mounting, ascending, skyrocketing; upsurge, upswing, shooting up, upturn, step-up; burgeoning, flourishing.
10. escalation, acceleration, intensification, concentration; exaggeration, maximization, overstatement; exacerbation, aggravation.
11. strengthening, reinforcement, build-up; improvement, advancement, upgrading, *Inf.* pickup; growth, development, maturation.
12. profit, gain, *Sl.* velvet, rake-off, *Sl.* clean-up, bonus, prize, booty, advantage, graft; product, result, harvest, return, yield, produce.
13. propagation, reproduction, breeding; procreation, begetting, engendering, generation.

incredible, *adj.* **1.** extraordinary, superhuman, fantastic, miraculous, seemingly impossible; fabulous, great, prodigious, tremendous, marvelous, wonderful, awe-inspiring; astounding, astonishing, amazing.
2. unbelievable, hard to believe, unreal, unrealistic; fictitious, mythical, legendary; highly unlikely *or* improbable, unlikely, improbable; doubtful, dubious, questionable, *Inf.* fishy, suspect, suspicious, funny, strange; inconceivable, unimaginable, unthinkable, preposterous; crazy, ridiculous, absurd, *Sl.* cockamamie.

incredulity, *n.* incredulousness, disbelief, unbelief; distrust, mistrust, suspicion, suspiciousness; skepticism, doubt, doubtfulness, dubiety, dubiousness.

incredulous, *adj.* unbelieving, disbelieving; distrustful, distrusting, mistrustful, mistrusting, suspicious; skeptical, doubtful, dubious, doubting, cynical.

increment, *n.* **1.** addition, accretion, accession, access; augmentation, supplement, annex, annexation, appendage, appendix, addendum, adjunct; accrual, accruement, accumulation, cumulation; multiplication, doubling, redoubling, trebling, tripling, quadrupling.

2. increase, enlargement, expansion, extension; widening, thickening, broadening; lengthening, prolongation, protraction; inflation, dilatation, dilation, waxing, swelling.

3. profit, benefits, bonus, interest, perquisite, rakeoff, *Sl.* cleanup, *Sl.* velvet; earnings, winnings, returns; yield, gain, outcome, result, product, produce.

4. magnification, amplification, enhancement, deepening, heightening; escalation, acceleration, intensification; strengthening, reinforcement, concentration; exaggeration, overestimation, maximization, overstatement.

5. growth, development, upgrowth, maturation; upsurge, upturn, upswing, step-up; burgeoning, shooting up, springing up, sprouting; germination, pullulation, vegetation.

incriminate, *v.* **1.** charge, accuse, indict, *Law.* arraign, *Law.* impute, criminate, recriminate, impeach, *Rare.* implead; blame, *Sl.* pin *or* stick [s.t.] on [s.o.], hold [s.o.] accountable *or* responsible, lay at [s.o.'s] door, point the finger at [s.o.]; (*all in reference to culpability*) allege, ascribe, attribute, assign, impute, lay.

2. implicate, inculpate, (*of an innocent person*) *Inf.* frame; involve, entangle, ensnare, enmesh, *Sl.* drag *or* suck [s.o.] into [s.t.]; inform against, *Sl.* rat on, *Sl.* fink, squeal.

incrust, *v.* **1.** overlay, face, veneer; tile, pave, tar, cement; cover, line, coat, paint, wallpaper, whitewash, stucco, plaster; plate, enamel, lacquer, japan, varnish, glaze.

2. inlay, set; ornament, embellish, decorate, adorn, gild, emboss.

incrustation, *n.* **1.** crust, hard coating, incrustant, scab, covering; casing, shell, hull, husk, rind, skin, bark, *Bot.* cortex.

2. inlay, inlaying, setting; ornament, ornamentation, embellishment, decoration, adornment, gilding, embossing.

incubate, *v.* **1.** (*all of eggs*) sit on *or* upon, brood, hatch; put *or* keep in an incubator.

2. give form to, raise, bring up, nurture, nurse, take care of, help develop *or* grow.

3. develop, grow, take form, mature.

incubus, *n.* **1.** demon, fiend, evil spirit, devil, cacodemon; ghoul, vampire, werewolf, lycanthrope, *Fr. loup garou*; goblin, hobgoblin, gremlin; banshee.

2. nightmare, succubus; night horror, bad dream, haunting fear, dread; chimera, phantasmagoria.

3. burden, load, care, anxiety, pressure, stress; oppression, weight, strain, tax, affliction, cross, trouble, trial, sorrow; encumbrance, dead weight, drag, impediment, handicap, millstone around one's neck, hindrance, *Archaic.* fardel.

inculcate, *v.* instill, infix, implant, ingrain, infuse, impregnate, imbue; teach, train, instruct, enlighten, guide; indoctrinate, beat *or* hammer into, drill, prime, ground; preach, propagandize, insinuate; influence, affect, bias, incline, initiate, inspire.

inculpable, *adj.* blameless, guiltless, moral, virtuous; upright, uncensurable, irreproachable, unimpeachable, above suspicion, like Caesar's wife; innocent, innocent as a newborn babe, stainless, spotless.

inculpate, *v.* charge, accuse, indict, *Law.* arraign, *Law.* impute, incriminate, criminate, recriminate, impeach, *Rare.* implead. See **incriminate** (*defs.* **1, 2**).

inculpatory, *adj.* recriminatory, imputing blame, accusative, accusatory, denunciatory; implicating, exposing, revealing, incriminating, incriminatory, damning.

incumbent, *adj.* **1.** holding office, in power, responsible, in, inside, in the driver's seat, holding the reins, holding sway, holding down the fort.

2. obligatory, binding, compelling, constrictive, commanding, demanding, necessary, inescapable, prescribed, compulsory, mandatory.

3. resting, lying, leaning, reclining, reposing, lounging, *Sl.* flopping.

—*n.* **4.** office holder, official, functionary; occupant, resident, tenant, sojourner.

incur, *v.* **1.** enter into, fall into, fall in with.

2. assume, bring on *or* upon, run up; bring down, contract, bargain for; welcome, invite, admit of, expose oneself to, lay oneself open to; be liable, be subject to, lie under.

incurable, *adj.* hopeless, past *or* beyond hope, affording no hope, beyond recall, terminal; unhealable, inoperable, immedicable, irremediable, cureless.

incurious, *adj.* uninquisitive, uninquiring; uninterested, disinterested, unconcerned, apathetic, indifferent, impassive, dispassionate, bored; nonchalant, blasé, pococurante; careless, heedless, inattentive, inadvertent, unmindful, regardless; carefree, insouciant, *Fr. sans souci.*

incursion, *n.* **1.** raid, foray, sally, sortie; attack, assault, onslaught, onset; invasion.

2. inroad, intrusion, infiltration, penetration; trespass, encroachment, infringement, irruption; transgression, overstepping; usurpation, takeover, seizure.

indebted, *adj.* **1.** obligated, obliged, beholden, owing, bound, bounden; liable, accountable, answerable, chargeable, responsible.

2. grateful, thankful, appreciative.

3. in arrears, in debt, *Sl.* in debt up to one's ears, encumbered, *Sl.* in hock, in the hole, in the red; insolvent, bankrupt, *Inf.* on the rocks.

4. outstanding, unpaid, due, liquidated.

indebtedness, *n.* **1.** debts, liabilities; *Accounting.* debit, deficit, due, score; default, arrears, arrearage; insolvency, bankruptcy, failure.

2. obligation, *Obs.* beholdenness; accountability, accountableness, chargeability, answerability, responsibility.

3. gratitude, gratefulness, thankfulness, appreciation.

indecency, *n.* **1.** impropriety, improperness, indecorum, indecorousness; gaucheness, gaucherie, uncouthness, crassness, boorishness, rudeness, ill-breeding, unmannerliness, ill-manneredness, uncivility, uncivilness, ungentlemanliness; inappropriateness, unsuitability, unsuitableness, unaptness, unseemliness, unacceptability, unacceptableness.

2. indelicacy, inelegance, immodesty; grossness, rankness, repulsiveness, repulsivity, offensiveness, suggestivity; abusiveness, scurrilousness, blackguardism.

3. vulgarity, vulgarness, vulgarism, obsceneness, obscenity, salaciousness, salacity, vileness, foulness; filthiness, nastiness, *Sl.* raunchiness; lecherousness, lubricity, lustfulness, bawdiness, libidinousness, concupiscence, carnality, carnalness, sexiness, sensuality; licentiousness, lasciviousness, wantonness, looseness, promiscuity, promiscuousness; immorality, dissoluteness, dissipation, rakishness, shamelessness.

indecent, *adj.* **1.** indelicate, inelegant, immodest, shameless, broad; gross, rank, repulsive, offensive, disgusting, distasteful, risqué, suggestive, off-color, *Inf.* blue; outrageous, sensational, lurid, scandalous, shocking; abusive, ribald, scurrilous, blackguardly, thersitical, profane, foul-mouthed, Fescennine, *Obs.* blackguard.

2. vulgar, obscene, lewd, salacious, pornographic, vile, foul, filthy, dirty, smutty, nasty, scatologic, scatological, *Sl.* raunchy; lecherous, lubricous, goatish, lustful, libidinous, concupiscent, carnal, sexy, sensual, *Archaic.* lickerish; licentious, lascivious, Cyprian, prurient, wanton, loose, libertine, promiscuous, Paphian, unchaste; immoral, degenerate, dissolute, dissipated, debauched, rakish, profligate, depraved, perverted.

3. improper, indecorous, unacceptable; inappropriate, unsuitable, unapt, unfitting, unbefitting, unseemly, tawdry, *Inf.* tacky; unbecoming, unflattering, unattractive.

indecipherable, *adj.* **1.** illegible, unreadable, undecipherable; unclear, *Inf.* clear as mud, indistinct, indistinguishable, undistinguishable, unrecognizable; blotted, blurred, smudged; (*all of writing*) cramped, squeezed, squeezed together, pinched; (*all of writing*) run-on, run together, strung together; (*all of writing*) deleted, erased, effaced, eradicated, wiped *or* rubbed out, blotted out.

2. hieroglyphic, hieroglyphical, cryptographic, cryptographical, *Obs.* steganographic *or* steganographical.

3. secret, hidden, concealed, veiled, cryptic, perdu; impenetrable, incomprehensible, uncomprehensible, unfathomable, inscrutable, unknowable, incognizable, incognoscible; abstruse, recondite, esoteric, abstract.

4. difficult, hard, *Inf.* tough; complex, complicated, perplexed, *Inf.* tricky; intricate, involved, tangled, knotty, crabbed; obscure, dim, dark, vague, nebulous, *Rare.* imperspicuous; puzzling, baffling, enigmatic, enigmatical; mysterious, arcane, inexplicable, unexplainable, insolvable, insoluble, unaccountable, *Obs.* inextricable.

indecision, *n.* irresolution, irresoluteness, indecisiveness, uncertainty, incertitude, unsettledness, infirmity of purpose, ambivalence, double-mindedness; fence-sitting, fence-straddling, mugwumpery; tergiversation, change of mind, second thoughts; hesitation, hesitancy, diffidence, faltering; vacillation, fluctuation, shilly-shally, wavering, blowing hot and cold; capriciousness, fickleness, moodiness, changeableness.

indecisive, *adj.* **1.** inconclusive, open, still open, open to doubt *or* question, up in the air; undetermined, unsettled, unestablished, unproven, undemonstrated, unsubstantiated, moot.

2. irresolute, unresolved, undecided, uncertain, ambivalent, of two minds; hesitant, faltering, diffident, wavering, fluctuating, vacillating, shilly-shallying, blowing hot and cold, sitting on *or* straddling the fence; infirm of purpose, wishy-washy, namby-pamby, weak-willed, weak, spineless; fickle, capricious, moody, changeable, mercurial, volatile.

3. indistinct, indeterminate, indefinite, undefined, formless, shapeless; vague, unclear, obscure, blurred, blurry, fuzzy, hazy, misty.

indecorous, *adj.* **1.** unbecoming, unseemly, improper; unmannerly, uncivil, impolite, unladylike, ungentlemanly; ungenteel, ill-bred, ill-mannered, unrefined, uncultured, uncultivated; uncourtly, unchivalrous, ungallant, rude, uncivil; undignified, unpolished, unsophisticated, countrified, provincial, unsophisticated, countrified, provincial, boorish; crude, coarse, vulgar, common, uncouth, crass, gross; churlish, loutish.

2. inappropriate, inapt, unmeet, unfitting, unbefitting; unwarranted, uncalled-for, out of place, out of keeping; untoward, *Inf.* out-of-the-way, *Inf.* off-key, out-of-bounds, out-of-the-line, out-of-order.

3. shameful, disgraceful, discreditable, disreputable, reprehensible; indecent, offensive, lewd, obscene, loose, ribald, risqué, suggestive.

indecorum, *n.* **1.** impropriety, improperness, incorrectness, unseemliness, unbecomingness, inappropriateness, unsuitableness, unfittingness, indecorousness; inelegance, indelicacy, tastelessness, bad taste; impoliteness, incivility, ungentlemanliness, rudeness, ill *or* bad manners, unmannerliness, ill breeding; crudeness, coarseness, grossness, crassness, vulgarity, gaucherie.

2. faux pas, gaffe, social blunder, indiscretion, slip in conduct, mistake in conduct *or* etiquette *or* propriety, breach of etiquette *or* manners; transgression, dereliction, misconduct, misdeed; false step, wrong step, misstep, trip, stumble, bad move, wrong move, false move; offense, peccadillo, oversight, omission; slip, lapse, lapsus; mistake, error, blunder, botch, bungle, *Inf.* slip-up, *Sl.* boo-boo, *Sl.* boner, *Sl.* goof.

indeed, *adv.* **1.** truly, in fact, in truth, in reality, precisely, exactly, verily, *Archaic.* forsooth, *Archaic.* pardi; surely, certainly, assuredly, *Archaic.* certes; I assure you, on my honor, by my troth, upon my word, on my oath, I swear; of course, by all means, *Brit.* Hear! Hear!, amen, naturally, as you say, as you wish; to be sure, quite, absolutely, positively, just so, *Brit.* rather; as a matter of fact, in point of fact, to tell the truth, all joking aside, in all seriousness, seriously, strictly speaking, in effect.

2. yes, aye, yea, *Inf.* yeah, *Inf.* yep; yes sir, yes ma'am, affirmative, *Inf.* yes sirree, *Inf.* yes indeedy; all right, alright, OK, *Inf.* righto, *Inf.* roger; very well, good, good enough, fine.

—*interj.* **3.** really, you don't say, you're kidding, is it so, *Fr. n'est-ce pas*; egad, gad, zounds, gad so, what, what ho, my word, *Sl.* for crying out loud; good lord, by jove, by george, by jiminy, my stars, oh my, *Archaic.* marry; holy Moses, holy Christmas, holy mackerel, holy cow, holy smoke, God bless me, heavens and earth, my stars; my goodness, good gracious, goodness gracious, well, good heavens, dear me, good night, *Sl.* heavens to Betsy; cheese and crackers, *Inf.* golly, *Inf.* gee, *Sl.* geez, *Sl.* geewhiz.

4. mercy, *Sl.* land sakes alive, *Sl.* shiver me timbers, *Sl.* well I'll be blowed, *Sl.* blow me down, *Sl.* well I'll be a monkey's uncle, *Sl.* I'll be jiggered; what on earth, what in the world, did you ever, I declare, as I live and breathe, the deuce you say, I'll be, can you beat that; imagine, fancy, fancy that, well I never, do tell; what do you know, will wonders never cease, what do you know about that, *Latin. mirabile dictu, Fr. sacré bleu.*

indefatigable, *adj.* tireless, untiring, inexhaustible; on the go, on the move, astir, bustling; unsleeping, unwearied, never-tiring, sleepless, undrooping; unflagging, unfaltering, unwavering, unswerving, persistent, pertinacious; undaunted, tenacious, firm, determined; plodding, dogged, steady, persevering, indomitable, unfailing, patient; unremitting, relentless, steadfast; studious, assiduous, sedulous, industrious, hard-working, diligent.

indefensible, *adj.* **1.** inexcusable, unjustifiable, unvindicable; unpardonable, unforgivable, irremissible, inexpiable, irredeemable.

2. defenseless, unfortified, vulnerable, vincible, pregnable, exposed; unguarded, unarmed, weaponless, unprotected, unsheltered; helpless, unresisting, nonresisting, submissive, surrendering.

3. untenable, insupportable, unarguable, unmaintainable, undefendable; weak, flawed, faulty, specious, implausible; impeachable, unacceptable, inadmissible.

indefinite, *adj.* **1.** unlimited, illimitable, limitless, immeasurable, incalculable, unfathomable; endless, infinite, inexhaustible, boundless; unspecified, indeterminate.

2. undetermined, imprecise, inexact, undefined; dim, obscure, indistinct, indistinguishable, ill-defined, ill-marked; fuzzy, blurred, out of focus, misty, hazy, cloudy, opaque, obfuscated, delitescent, veiled.

3. vague, doubtful, confused, confusing, uncertain; unfixed, unspecific, inexplicit, loose, lax, unsettled, *Inf.* iffy; ambiguous, equivocal, *Inf.* neither fish nor fowl; questionable, inconclusive, evasive; puzzling, problematic, problematical, mysterious, abstruse, recondite, enigmatic; cryptic, abstract, oracular, mystic, transcendental, occult.

4. undecided, wishy-washy, hesitant, hesitating; vacillating, wavering, inconstant, fluctuating, shilly-shallying, on the fence.

indelible, *adj.* inerasable, ineffaceable, ineradicable, unexpungeable, unobliterable, uncancelable; permanent, ingrained, indestructible, enduring, unfading; imperishable, inextinguishable, insoluble, indissoluble; firm; fresh, green, unforgotten, vivid; unforgettable, memorable, haunting, stamped on one's memory.

indelicacy, *n.* vulgarity, coarseness, roughness, loudness, rudeness, offensiveness; bad form, no manners, unmannerliness, boorishness, churlishness; inurbanity, inelegance, uncourtliness, incivility; impropriety, unseemliness, unbecomingness, indecorum, bad taste, tastelessness; unrefinement, barbarism, ungentlemanliness, loutishness; immodesty, indecency, impurity, impudicity, shamelessness; ribaldry, bawdiness, bawdry, obscenity, smuttiness, suggestiveness.

indemnification, *n.* compensation, recompense, quittance, indemnity; amends, atonement, reparation, redress, restitution, expiation; satisfaction, payment, reimbursement, restoration, return; tit for tat, measure for measure, *Latin. quid pro quo*; retribution, requital, retaliation, repayment, reckoning; revenge, reprisal, retribution, vengeance, an eye for an eye, a tooth for a tooth, *Inf.* comeuppance, just deserts, due reward, punishment.

indemnify, *v.* **1.** compensate, make good, satisfy; reimburse, remunerate, pay, repay, reward, return, pay back; expiate, requite, make restitution, make amends, atone, *Inf.* make it up to; retaliate, reckon with, take revenge on, take vengeance on, punish.

2. insure, underwrite, warrant, guarantee; countersign, set one's seal to, endorse, certify, answer for, stand behind; assure, make certain, secure, make secure, give security to, guard.

indemnity, *n.* **1.** insurance, underwriting, warrant, guarantee, endorsement, certification, assurance; protection, safekeeping, preservation, conservation, protectorship, guardianship, custody, care, auspices, charge.

2. compensation, consideration, remuneration, reimbursement, return, reward; reparation, expiation, restitution, *Latin. quid pro quo*; indemnification, redress, restoration. See **indemnification**.

3. legal exemption, diplomatic privilege, privilege, prerogative, impunity, untouchability, *Inf.* being above the law.

indent, *v.* **1.** dent, dint, make a dent in, push in *or* down, depress, bruise, dimple, pit, stave in; notch, nick, groove, furrow, scallop, pink, serrate.

2. set in, set back, begin farther in, stagger.

indentation, *n.* cut, notch, nick, cleft, gash, score, serration, scallop, *Archit.* dentil; concavity, concave, indentation, incurvature, incurvation; cavity, depression, dip, hollow, impress; sinkhole, sink, swallow, swallow hole; cup, basin, bowl, crater, pit, excavation, deep recess.

indenture, *n.* **1.** contract, compact, covenant, deal; written agreement, deed, lease, document, certificate; legal document, cartel, acknowledgment, written acknowledgment, written guarantee, written warranty, written pledge *or* promise, stipulation; bond, commitment, obligation.

2. indentation, dent, recess, depression; cut, notch, nick.

—*v.* **3.** apprentice, article, bind, tie, contract, attach, associate; employ, engage, enroll, place, position; enslave, enthrall.

independence, *n.* **1.** self-government, self-direction, self-rule, self-legislation, self-determination; freedom, liberty, autonomy, sovereignty.

2. liberation, emancipation, manumission, disenthrallment, decolonization; release, relief from, riddance from; deregulation, decontrol.

3. privilege, prerogative, right, authority; exemption, exception, immunity; license, franchise, authorization.

4. self-reliance, confidence, self-confidence, self-assurance, aplomb, boldness, *Inf.* spunk; unrestraint, unreservedness, unconstraint; naturalness, artlessness, ingenuousness, outspokenness, downrightness, directness, bluntness.

5. self-sufficiency, affluence, wealth, prosperity, competence, competency.

independent, *adj.* **1.** self-governing, self-legislating, self-ruling, self-directing, inner-directed; free, sovereign, autonomous, autonomic, allodial, unsubject, uncolonial, noncolonial; enfranchised, freeborn.

2. unfettered, untrammeled, unrestrained, unconstrained; unregulated, ungoverned, unrestricted, laissez-faire; separate, unattached, disjoined, unconnected, unrelated, distinct.

3. free-thinking, individualistic, different, unconventional, bohemian; uninhibited, unceremonious, casual, familiar, free and easy; natural, artless, ingenuous; unreserved, outspoken, free-spoken, frank, open, direct, blunt; confident, self-confident, self-assured, self-willed, headstrong, bold, *Inf.* spunky; self-reliant, on one's own, standing on one's own two feet; free-wheeling, foot-loose, unconfined, at liberty, at large.

4. nonpartisan, disinterested, neutral, *Politics.* unaffiliated; uninfluenced, unswayed, unbiased, unprejudiced, unbigoted.

5. voluntary, unforced, uncoerced, uncompelled, spontaneous, unprompted, unbidden, unasked for, unsolicited.

6. self-sufficient, affluent, moneyed, well-to-do, well-off, wealthy, rich, flush, *Sl.* on easy street.

—*n.* **7.** do-it-yourselfer; *Both Politics.* nonpartisan, unaffiliated.

indescribable, *adj.* **1.** ineffable, inexpressible, beyond words, incommunicable, undescribable; undefinable, indefinite, nondescript, unnamable, nameless, unutterable, unspeakable.

2. inconceivable, incredible, unheard of, unusual, signal; strange, marvelous, wonderful, wondrous, *Sl.* something else; singular, extraordinary, remarkable, amazing, prodigious, astonishing, stupendous, miraculous; striking, stunning, dazzling, foudroyant.

indestructible, *adj.* **1.** deathless, undying; imperishable, inextinguishable, indissoluble, infrangible, unbreakable; indelible, ineradicable; immutable, unalterable, incommutable, changeless, unchangeable; unfading, incorruptible, undecaying, amaranthine, perennial, (*of leaves*) *Bot.* indeciduous, (*of trees*) evergreen.

2. enduring, abiding, lasting; constant, firm, fixed, fast, stable, durable, steady, permanent; endless, unceasing, immortal, eternal, *Archaic.* eterne, everlasting.

indeterminate, *adj.* **1.** undetermined, unmeasured, uncounted, uncalculated, indefinite, unknown; uncertain, unsure, unsettled, undecided; unestablished, undefined, unset, unfixed; uncategorized, borderline, neither fish nor fowl.

2. undeterminable, undistinguishable, unclear, vague, nebulous, obscure; ambiguous, equivocal, imprecise, inexact, inexplicit; ill-defined, dim, hazy, clouded, cloudy, misty; fogged, foggy, blurred, blurry, confused, muddy, clear as mud.

index, *n.* **1.** catalog, directory, guide, key, *Obs.* table of contents.

2. sign, mark, token, indication, indicant, clue, hint.

3. index finger, forefinger, first finger, pointer; *Print.* fist, hand.

indicate, *v.* **1.** denote, show, bespeak, betoken, signal, mark, be a sign of; signify, connote, suggest, imply; mean, add up to.

2. point out, point to, designate; specify, particularize.

3. show, register, exhibit, display, present, demonstrate, manifest, evince, evidence; make known, reveal, disclose, tell, express, state.

indication, *n.* **1.** sign, token, symptom, signal, foreshadowing; omen, augury, portent, foretoken, forewarning; signification, denotation, showing, bespeaking, connotation, implication; hint, intimation, suggestion, allusion, mention.

2. manifestation, spark, flash, glimmer, trace, vestige; trail, track, spoor, footprint, mark, evidence.

3. sign, signpost, signboard, billboard; guidepost, marker, trail marker, blaze, cairn; milepost, mile marker, milestone, landmark.

indicative, *adj.* *Usu.* **indicative of** indicatory, indicating, pointing to, *Obs.* indicant; suggestive, suggesting, symptomatic, symptomatical, diagnostic; denotative, denoting, representative, representing, typical, characteristic; symbolic, emblematic, connotative, connotating, significative, significant, meaningful; telling, revealing, expressive, demonstrative, showing.

indict, *v.* accuse, charge, *Law.* arraign, *Law.* impute; bring to trial, bring to justice, put on trial, *Law.* prosecute; incriminate, criminate, recriminate, impeach, *Rare.* implead; denounce, implicate, (*of an innocent person*) *Inf.* frame, inculpate, inform against; cite, summon, serve with a summons *or* with papers.

indictable, *adj.* **1.** chargeable, arraignable, accusable, *Rare.* impleadable; citable, summonable, open to summons *or* subpoena; liable, accountable, answerable; incriminatory, inculpatory, blameable, blameful, blameworthy, imputable, implicatable; impeachable, triable, open to prosecution, *Law.* prosecutable.

2. unlawful, illegal, illicit, criminal, felonious; unjustifiable, unwarrantable, inexcusable, unpardonable, unforgivable.

indictment, *n.* **1.** accusation, charge, *Law.* gravamen, *Law.* true bill, *Law.* plaint, *Law.* complaint; citation, summons, *Law.* arraignment; incrimination, crimination, recrimination, denunciation; implication, inculpation, blaming, accusing; (*all in reference to wrongdoing*) imputation, attribution, ascription, assignment, allegation.

2. reproach, slur, innuendo, insinuation, animadversion, criticism; censure, rebuke, reproof, reprehension.

indifference, *n.* **1.** apathy, disinterest, disinterestedness, uninterestedness, unconcern, lack of interest *or* concern, aloofness, distantness, insouciance; nonchalance, pococurantism, lukewarmness, lukewarmth, coolness, frigidness, frigidity; impassiveness, impassibility, impassibleness, dispassion, dispassionateness, passionlessness, unemotionalness, emotionlessness; listlessness, phlegmaticness; insensibility, insensitivity, lack of sympathy *or* compassion, callousness; stoicalness, Stoicism, stoniness.

2. unimportance, immateriality, irrelevance; insignificance, inconsequence, inconsequentness, triviality, trivialness, pettiness, meanness, paltriness.

3. mediocrity, moderateness, passableness; averageness, ordinariness, commonplaceness.

indifferent, *adj.* **1.** apathetic, apathetical, unconcerned, uninterested, distant, aloof, removed, Laodicean, insouciant; impassive, impassible, dispassionate, passionless, unemotional, emotionless, unexcited, uncaring, careless, nonchalant, pococurante, perfunctory, *Archaic.* impassionate; lukewarm, cool, cold, frigid, icy; listless, phlegmatic, dull, dead; insensible, insensitive, insensate, unfeeling, unsympathetic, uncompassionate, inconsiderate, callous; unsusceptible, impenetrable, unimpressable, unreachable, stoical, stolid, Spartan, stony.

2. neutral, impartial, disinterested, unbiased, unprejudiced, nondiscriminatory, nondiscriminative, unbigoted; objective, nonsubjective, detached, not personally involved; equitable, even-handed, fair, fair-minded, just, *Inf.* square.

3. mediocre, middling, moderate, medium; fair, so-so, not bad, *Inf.* O.K., such as it is; passable, reasonable, acceptable, adequate, sufficient; average, modest, ordinary, commonplace, lightweight, *Inf.* not so hot.

4. unimportant, immaterial, irrelevant, neither here nor there; insignificant, inconsequential, inconsequent, of no consequence, minor, of no matter; trivial, trifling, inappreciable, slight, petty, mean.

5. unessential, unnecessary, unneeded, expendable; unrequired, nonobligatory, exemptible.

indigence, *n.* poverty, penury, destitution, impecuniousness, impecuniosity, beggary, pennilessness, neediness; insolvency, bankruptcy, liquidation; distress, straits, difficulties, indebtedness; pauperism, pauperage, pauperdom, mendicancy, mendicity; hand-to-mouth existence, starvation, hunger; insufficiency, scantiness, threadbareness, privation, deprivation, want, lack, need.

indigene, *n.* native, inhabitant, habitant, dweller, citizen, local; countryman, compatriot, *Yiddish.* landsman; aborigine, aboriginal, autochthon, *Australian Inf.* boong, primitive.

indigenous, *adj.* **1.** native, endemic, endemical, original, aboriginal, autochthonous, autochthonal, autochthonic; indwelling, immanent, intrinsic, inherent; inborn, inbred, connate, connatural, natural, natural-born, ingenerate; congenital, hereditary, inherited, in the blood, in the family.

2. inveterate, rooted, deep-rooted, planted, implanted, fixed, infixed, ineradicable; permanent, inseparable, built-in; ingrained, in the grain, inwrought.

indigent, *adj.* **1.** poverty-stricken, impoverished, penurious, impecunious, beggared, pauperized; destitute, poor, needy, necessitous, barefoot, ragged, bad off, badly off; beggarly, mendicant; pinched, straitened, distressed, *Inf.* strapped, *Inf.* up against it, *Inf.* on one's uppers, *Inf.* hard up; financially embarrassed, out of cash, penniless, *Inf.* short, *Brit. Sl.* skint, *Inf.* broke, *Inf.* dead broke, *Inf.* flat broke, *Inf.* stone broke; unable to make both ends meet, poor as Job's turkey, unable to keep the wolf from the door; bankrupt, ruined, wiped out, *Inf.* on the rocks, insolvent, overdrawn, in the red; down and out, out at the elbows, down at the heels, seedy.

2. lacking, wanting, in need; deprived, deficient, bereft, devoid, destitute of; without, sans; helpless, stranded, high and dry.

—*n.* **3.** pauper, poor person, have-not, ragamuffin, tatterdemalion, hobo, *Sl.* bindle stiff; beggar, cadger, *Inf.* panhandler, mendicant, beadsman, almsman, *Scot.* gaberlunzie.

indigestible, *adj.* heavy, disagreeing, hard to swallow, hard to stomach, unassimilable, undigestible, indigestive; distasteful, unpalatable, sickening, nauseating, nauseous; obnoxious, offensive, repulsive, revolting.

indigestion, *n.* upset stomach, gastric *or* stomach distress, dyspepsia, hyperacidity; queasiness, nausea, nauseousness; heartburn, brash, water brash, *Pathol.* pyrosis, *Pathol.* cardialgia.

indignant, *adj.* irate, ireful, incensed, angry, angered, wrathful, wroth, *Inf.* mad, *Inf.* sore, *Sl.* teed-off, *Sl.* ticked-off, *Sl.* hot, *Sl.* hot under the collar; uptight, in a temper, in a pet, in high dudgeon, in a huff, *Inf.* huffy, resentful; annoyed, irritated, peeved, piqued, irked, exasperated, provoked, *Chiefly U.S.* riled, *Inf.* aggravated, *Inf.* miffed.

indignation, *n.* resentment, offense, umbrage, pique, righteous anger; anger, ire, wrath, dudgeon, high dudgeon; displeasure, disapproval, disapprobation, disapprobrium, dissatisfaction, disgruntlement, unhappiness; irritation, annoyance, vexation, exasperation, *Inf.* aggravation; gall, bile, spleen, choler, rancor; virulence, acrimony, asperity, acerbity, exacerbation, bitterness.

indignity, *n.* affront, insult, *Archaic.* insultation, outrage, slap in the face; abuse, mistreatment, injury, wound, sting, blow; discourtesy, slight, snub, *Inf.* fine how-do-you-do; aspersion, cut, *Sl.* put-down.

indirect, *adj.* **1.** roundabout, out-of-the-way, oblique, ambagious, circuitous, circumambient; divergent, deviant, deviative; erratic, wandering, meandering, roving, winding, curving, tortuous, zigzag; circumlocutory, discursive, digressive, long-drawn-out.

2. incidental, accidental, circumstantial; contingent, collateral, secondary, subordinate; implied, implicit, understood, tacit, unexpressed, inferential.

3. devious, dishonest, crooked, *Inf.* shady, lefthanded, backhand, backhanded; deceitful, fraudulent, guileful, insidious, sharp, slippery, shifty, tricky; furtive, surreptitious, clandestine, covert, undercover, underhand, sneaky, back-door; secretive, evasive, unstraightforward.

indiscernable, *adj.* **1.** imperceptible, imperceivable, indistinguishable, unnoticeable, unapparent, subtle, slight, gradual; inappreciable, inconsiderable, inconsequential; minute, minuscule; microscopic, infinitesimal.

2. invisible, unseeable, unperceptible; ill-defined, indistinct, indefinite, obscure, vague, unclear, shadowy, nebulous, cloudy.

indiscreet, *adj.* **1.** imprudent, injudicious, impolitic, improvident, ill-advised, ill-considered, ill-judged, ill-gauged, ill-contrived, unwise; hasty, rash, brash, reckless, temerarious, impulsive, impetuous, audacious; headlong, head-over-heels, precipitate, breakneck, harum-scarum; foolhardy, foolish, harebrained, wild, madcap; heedless, careless, uncautious, unwary, unchary, uncircumspect; thoughtless, unthinking, unreflecting, mindless, witless, inadvertent; inconsiderate, insensitive, tactless, untactful.

2. indelicate, indecent, immodest, shameless, brazen, bold; indecorous, improper, inappropriate, unseemly, unbecoming.

indiscretion, *n.* **1.** imprudence, improvidence, injudiciousness, impolicy, inexpediency; hastiness, rashness, brashness, recklessness, temerity, impulsiveness, impetuosity, audacity; folly, foolishness, foolhardiness; heedlessness, carelessness, unwariness, uncharinesss; thoughtlessness, mindlessness, witlessness, unwittingness, unthinkingness, inadvertence; inconsiderateness, insensitivity, tactlessness.

2. indelicateness, indecency, immodesty, shamelessness, brazenness, boldness; indecorum, indecorousness, impropriety, improperness, inappropriateness, unseemliness, unbecomingness.

3. faux pas, gaffe, social blunder, slip in conduct, mistake in conduct *or* etiquette *or* propriety, breach of etiquette *or* manners; transgression, dereliction, misconduct, misdeed; false step, wrong step, misstep, stumble, trip, bad move, wrong move, false move; offense, peccadillo, slip, lapse; mistake, error, blunder, botch, bungle, *Inf.* slip-up, *Sl.* boo-boo, *Sl.* boner.

indiscriminate, *adj.* **1.** unselective, unparticular, uncritical, undifferentiating, undiscriminating, indiscriminative, promiscuous; wholesale, extensive, broad, wide, sweeping.

2. haphazard, random, casual, hit-or-miss, unmethodical, methodless, unsystematic, systemless; unordered, orderless, disordered, unorganized, unarranged; erratic, desultory, fitful, spasmodic, stop-and-go, come-and-go.

3. mixed, jumbled, scrambled, thrown-together; incoherent, confused, harum-scarum, higgledy-piggledy; motley, medley, miscellaneous, diverse, diversified, varied, manifold.

indispensable, *adj.* **1.** vital, essential, of the essence, important, of the utmost importance; imperative, urgent, exigent, instant, pressing, compelling, high-priority, high-pressure, life-and-death *or* life-or-death; necessary, needed, needful, called-for, in demand, requisite, required; fundamental, elementary, rudimentary, basic, bedrock, material, substantive, *Inf.* square-one.

2. inescapable, unavoidable, ineludible, ineluctable, inevasible; certain, for certain, sure, for sure, sure as death, sure as death and taxes, inevasible, inevitable; mandatory, compulsory, obligatory, prescriptive, binding.

—*n.* **3.** requirement, requisite, necessity, essential, must, must-item, *Inf.* must-have.

indispose, *v.* **1.** incapacitate, disable, debilitate, unfit, inactivate; disqualify, invalidate, disenable; put out of action, put out of commission, put out of gear, *Sl.* put out of whack, *Inf.* sideline, lay up, hospitalize; devitalize, enfeeble, extenuate, weaken, enervate, exhaust; cripple, paralyze, lame, maim, *Inf.* hogtie.

2. sicken, nauseate, disgust, turn one's stomach, disease.

3. disincline, be averse *or* unwilling; disenchant, damp, throw cold water on, throw a wet blanket over, put a damper on; discourage, dishearten, dispirit.

indisposed, *adj.* **1.** sick, sickly, sickened, ill, ailing, valetudinarian; unhealthy, unsound, unwell, squeamish, queasy; in a bad way, on the sick list, *Inf.* under the weather, *Inf.* out of sorts, not up to snuff, *Inf.* on the blink; laid up, bedridden, confined, hospitalized; out of order, out of commission, incapacitated, disabled.

2. adverse, unwilling, disinclined; hesitant, reluctant, resistant; renitent, recalcitrant, obdurate, restive; loath, averse, hostile, inimical, not in favor of, disliking.

indisposition, *n.* **1.** sickness, sickliness, illness, unhealthiness; invalidism, valetudinarianism; exhaustion, enervation, enfeeblement, prostration; disability, infirmity, decrepitude, weakness, feebleness; disorder, complaint, malady; nausea, indigestion, common cold, headache, migraine.

2. disinclination, unwillingness, averseness, loathness, indisposedness; reluctance, hesitance, hesitancy; opposition, recalcitrance, recalcitrancy, resistance, renitence.

indisputable, *adj.* **1.** incontestable, incontrovertible, undeniable, irrefragable, irrefutable, unquestionable, beyond question, beyond dispute, indubitable, beyond a shadow of a doubt, apodictic; conclusive, de cisive, definitive, solid, fixed, final; certain, sure, absolute, positive, definite.

2. evident, self-evident, obvious, unmistakable, patent, plain, *Inf.* plain as the nose on one's face, clear, clear-cut, crystal-clear, manifest, apparent.

indissoluble, *adj.* **1.** undissolvable, indissolvable, insoluble, infusible; indivisible, irreducible, indiscerptible; indestructible, imperishable, undying, deathless, inextinguishable, infrangible, unbreakable, irrefrangible; indelible, ineradicable; immutable, unalterable, incommutable, changeless, unchangeable; unfading, incorruptible, undecaying, amaranthine, perennial, (*of leaves*) *Bot.* indeciduous, (*of trees*) evergreen.

2. firm, fixed, fast, constant, solid, stable, durable, permanent; unwavering, unfaltering, steadfast, steady; abiding, enduring, lasting.

3. binding, obligatory, irrevocable, imperative, mandatory, compulsory, requisite, *Law.* peremptory.

indistinct, *adj.* **1.** fuzzy, filmy, misty, blurred, bleary, out of focus; inaudible, muffled, low, mumbled, muttered, unintelligible; pale, faded, undecipherable, illegible.

2. ambiguous, equivocal, dubious, ill-defined, vague, obscure, murky, *Archaic.* caliginous; muddy, incomprehensible, confused, doubtful, uncertain, indeterminate, nebulous, cloudy, undefined.

3. faint, dim, weak, feeble, imperceptible, faraway; indefinite, undistinguishable, shadowy, crepuscular.

indistinguishable, *adj.* **1.** identical, one, same, self-same, twin, joint, corresponding; balanced, equal, equivalent, comparable; kindred, similar, alike, like two peas in a pod; coinciding, coincident, synonymous, simultaneous, collateral.

2. indiscernible, imperceptible, unnoticeable, hard to make out, indefinite, obscure, unseen, shrouded, camouflaged, invisible.

indite, *v.* compose, draft, frame, couch, formulate; write, write down *or* out, pen, commit to paper; dictate, transcribe, tape, record; dash off, scrawl, scribble; type, typewrite, pound out; redo, revise, edit, redact.

individual, *adj.* **1.** single, sole, lone, separate, solitary; distinct, peculiar, defined, complete; alone, exclusive, detached, isolated, restricted.

2. particular, characteristic, personal, private, proper, custom; typical, representative, express, inherent, intrinsic, internal, specific.

3. special, especial, distinguished, select; different. distinct, singular, unique; original, unconventional, uncommon, unusual; rare, unparalleled, unequaled, unmatched; strange, outstanding, extraordinary, curious; odd, outlandish, bizarre, freakish.

—*n.* **4.** person, entity, creature, human, human being, being; personage, soul, living soul, spirit, mortal; one, someone, body, somebody; personality, character, party, head, hand.

5. free spirit, nonconformist, maverick, loner, lone wolf; deviator, eccentric, original, one of a kind, exception, rare bird, rara avis; queer duck, crackpot, crank, flake; curiosity, rarity, peculiarity, *Sl.* weirdo, *Sl.* oddball, *Sl.* screwball; bohemian, beatnik, hippy, yippie, longhair, freak.

individualistic, *adj.* **1.** individual, distinctive, distinguishing, distinct, original, uncommon, novel; separate, unallied, nonpartisan, uncommitted; personal, intrinsic, inherent, characteristic, marked, typical; private, exclusive, intimate; particular, definite, limited, specific.

2. independent, free-thinking, unconstrained, unor thodox; special, unique, rare, extraordinary, bizarre, unconventional; idiosyncratic, peculiar, eccentric, singular, strange, odd, conspicuous, *Sl.* oddball, *Sl.* weird.

individuality, *n.* **1.** distinctness, separateness, difference, definiteness, distinction, particularity, originality, uniqueness.

2. integrity, completeness, unity, entity, wholeness, vitality.

3. identity, personality, self, ego; character, makeup, essence, nature, traits; disposition, temperament, stripe, spirit, humor.

4. variation, peculiarity, singularity, characteristic, feature, trait; trick, mannerism, idiosyncrasy, quirk.

individualize, *v.* **1.** make individual, make distinctive, call by name, classify; distinguish, define, separate, characterize, differentiate, set apart, mark off.

2. mention, specify, designate, name, mention, mark, notice; indicate, point out, denote, pick out; consider, select, single out, point up.

indivisible, *adj.* undivisible, undividable, indiscerptible, inseparable, unseparable, impartible, unpartible, not divisible *or* separable; indissoluble, undissolvable, insoluble, unsoluble; unbreakable, infrangible.

indocile, *adj.* unsubmissive, intractable, stubborn, obstinate, pig-headed, mulish, obdurate, headstrong, willful, self-willed, opinionated; cross-grained, perverse, contrary, forward, resistant, opposed, restive, balking; refractory, recalcitrant, disobedient, rebellious, contumacious; unmanageable, ungovernable, uncontrollable, unruly, bad, incorrigible, unteachable; unyielding, unbending, rigid, inflexible, immovable, unpersuadable, unalterable, unchangeable, inexorable; impervious, uninfluenced, unaffected, unmoved, unpersuaded, untouched.

indoctrinate, *v.* indoctrinize, instruct, teach, school, educate, prepare, qualify; (*all of learning*) give, impart, imbue, impregnate, infect, infuse, inspire, charge, spark, fire; enlighten, initiate, introduce, give the basics, ground; familiarize with, break in, habituate, get [s.o.] used to; discipline, train, exercise, drill, beat [s.t.] into [s.o.'s] head, pound [s.t.] into [s.o.'s] head, get [s.t.] through [s.o.'s] head; inculcate, impress on *or* upon, instill, implant, ingrain; brainwash, propagandize, persuade, proselytize, convert.

indoctrination, *n.* indoctrinization, instruction, teaching, learning, book learning, schooling, education; tutelage, tutorage, guidance, preparation, qualification; enlightenment, initiation, introduction, grounding, familiarization, habituation; discipline, training, exercise, practice, drill; inculcation, instillation, instillment, infusion, implantment, ingraining; brainwashing, propaganda, propagandism, persuasion, proselytism, conversion.

indolence, *n.* laziness, idleness, otiosity, otioseness, fainéance, faineancy, shiftlessness; procrastination, dilatoriness, slothfulness, sluggardliness, laggardness; slowness, slow-motion, heaviness, loginess, sluggishness, lethargy, slackness, languidness, languor; lackadaisicalness, listlessness, dullness, apathy, indifference, impassiveness, impassivity, unresponsiveness; drowsiness, sleepiness, soporiferousness; stagnation, stagnancy, stagnance, inaction, inactivity, inactiveness, inexertion, inertia, inertness; dormancy, passivity, passiveness, supineness, torpor, torpidity, torpidness, stupor, stupefaction.

indolent, *adj.* lazy, idle, otiose, fainéant, do-nothing, shiftless; procrastinative, dilatory, dronish, slothful, sluggardly, laggard; slow, slow-moving, heavy, leaden, logy, sluggish, lethargic, slack, languid; lackadaisical, listless, dull, apathetic, indifferent, impassive, unresponsive; drowsy, sleepy, soporific, somnolent, comatose; stagnant, inactive, inert, dormant, passive, resting, supine, torpid.

indomitable, *adj.* **1.** invincible, unconquerable, invulnerable, impregnable, impenetrable, inviolable, insuperable, unassailable, insurmountable, undefeatable, unbeatable, insuppressible; stout, stout-hearted, stalwart, *Obs.* stalworth, steadfast, doughty, hardy, solid, stable, tough, staunch, stanch, cast-iron, *Inf.* hard as rock, *Inf.* tough as nails; firm, resolute, determined, resolved, intransigent, inflexible, adamant, adamantine; defiant, unyielding, unflinching, unwavering, unswerving, undeviating; persevering, unrelenting, irrepressible, indefatigable, tireless, untiring, weariless, unwearying, unflagging.

2. courageous, brave, valiant, valorous, heroic, heroical, hero-like, lionhearted, ironhearted, great-hearted, high-hearted; virile, manly, manful; intrepid, fearless, dauntless, aweless, dreadless, unafraid, undaunted, unblenching, unblenched, undismayed, unappalled, unalarmed; bold, bold-spirited, high-spirited, daring, audacious; plucky, mettlesome, nervy, gritty, spirited, red-blooded, *Inf.* spunky, *Sl.* gutsy.

indubitable, *adj.* beyond doubt, beyond a shadow of a doubt, admitting no question *or* doubt, beyond question, beyond dispute, unquestionable, undeniable, indisputable, irrefragable, irrefutable, incontestable, incontrovertible, apodictic; certain, sure, *Inf.* for-sure, absolute, positive, definite.

induce, *v.* **1.** persuade, convince, talk into, prevail on, sway, get; influence, inspire, rouse, encourage, stimulate; propel, impel, provoke, instigate, incite; prompt, actuate, move, drive, motivate, put up to; urge, goad, spur, prod, egg on, nudge; entice, inveigle, lure, seduce, win over, enlist; coax, wheedle, cajole, *Inf.* butter up.

2. cause, produce, bring on *or* about, effect; make, create, generate; occasion, develop, originate, lead to.

inducement, *n.* **1.** persuasion, influence, inspiration, encouragement; convincing, getting, urging, prodding, prompting, instigating, actuating.

2. incentive, stimulus, incitement, impetus, provocation; motive, reason, wherefore, *Sl.* what for, cause; attraction, lure, *Sl.* come-on, enticement; spur, goad.

induct, *v.* **1.** introduce, initiate, install, instate, establish; chair, invest, inaugurate; crown, enthrone; frock, *Eccles.* ordain, consecrate; bring in, lead in, usher in.

2. *U.S.* draft, levy, conscript, enlist, enroll, sign up, register, matriculate.

induction, *n.* **1.** initiation, installation, instatement, introduction; chairing, investiture, inauguration; coronation, crowning, enthronement, frocking, *Eccles.* ordination, *Eccles.* ordainment, consecration.

2. selective service, draft, levy, conscription; enlistment, enrollment, signing up, registration, matriculation.

3. presentation, bringing forward, production; revelation, disclosure, exposure; offering, showing, exhibit, exhibition; manifestation, appearance.

4. prelude, introduction, foreword, preface, preamble, prologue.

indulge, *v.* **1.** live hard, live high, be intemperate, be excessive, splurge, run riot, *Inf.* go whole hog; sow one's wild oats, *Sl.* paint the town red, *Sl.* go to town; plunge into dissipation, go on a spree, hit the booze, *Sl.* go off the wagon; carouse, regale, wine and dine; luxuriate, *Inf.* live it up, *Inf.* live high off the hog.

2. satisfy, gratify, relieve, appease, satiate, fulfill; yield to, give way to, treat oneself to.

3. oblige, humor, favor, go along with, comply with; wait on *or* upon, attend, make comfortable, attend to the convenience of, minister to, pander to; serve, do for, do service for, work for; bear with, give in to; allow, permit, suffer, tolerate, brook, endure.

4. pamper, cocker, coddle, spoil, cater to, baby; pet, fondle, cosset, caress; cajole, wheedle, coax, flatter; curry favor, *Inf.* bootlick, fawn, toady to, *Inf.* butter up, *Inf.* sweet-talk, *Inf.* soft-soap, *Sl.* suck up to.

5. indulge in give oneself up to, give loose rein to, give license to, wallow in, revel in.

indulgence, *n.* **1.** self-gratification, dissipation, intemperance, intemperateness, immoderation, immoderateness; prodigality, extravagance, profligateness, unrestraint, excess; voluptuousness, sensuality, sybaritism, epicureanism; dissoluteness, licentiousness; animalism, debauchery, crapulousness, crapulence; inebriety, drunkenness, intoxication; fast living, high living, free living, fastness; carousal, revelry, riotousness, saturnalia, spree, orgy, debauch.

2. satisfaction, gratification, appeasement, satiation, fulfillment, relief.

3. favor, courtesy, kindness, good will; allowance, permission, sufferance; toleration, tolerance, endurance, *Obs.* patience, forbearance, forgiveness, excuse; leniency, lenity, liberality; clemency, mercy, quarter; privilege, grant, license.

4. obliging, humoring, favoring, fostering; going along with, complying with; waiting on *or* upon, attending, ministering to, pandering to, serving, working for; pampering, coddling, spoiling, catering to, babying; petting, fondling, caressing.

5. considerateness, humanity, hospitality; gentleness, tenderness, fondness, mildness; compassion, empathy, sympathy, charity.

indulgent, *adj.* **1.** permissive, lenient, liberal, lax, easy; tolerant, allowing, permitting, suffering; enduring, *Archaic.* forbearing, forgiving, excusing, sparing; merciful, compassionate, clement; conciliatory, placatory, placating; amiable, amicable, complaisant, genial, agreeable, well-disposed; inclined, *Archaic.* propense, disposed, predisposed, favorably disposed; willing, *Archaic.* fain, in the mood, minded.

2. obliging, humoring, favoring, fostering; pampering, coddling, spoiling, catering; petting, fondling, caressing; considerate, humane, hospitable, courteous, kind, patient; empathetic, sympathetic, charitable, generous, unselfish; benevolent, benign, pleasing, pleasant, gracious; gentle, fond, tender, mild, easygoing, pacific, tender-hearted.

3. self-gratifying, dissipating, intemperate, immoderate; prodigal, extravagant, profligate, unrestrained, unbridled, excessive, inordinate; voluptuous, sensual, luxurious, sybaritic, epicurean, carnal; riotous, fast, wild, carousing; dissolute, dissipated, licentious, debauched, lascivious, wanton, lustful, concupiescent, libidinous, salacious, lecherous, goatish; animalistic, gluttonous, crapulous, crapulent; drunk, sottish, inebrious, intoxicated, *Inf.* boozy, winebibbing.

4. satisfying, gratifying, appeasing, satiating, fulfilling, relieving; yielding, complying, acquiescing.

indurate, *v.* **1.** harden, make hard, strengthen, stiffen, starch, thicken; temper, steel, toughen, vulcanize; ossify, petrify, fossilize, *Archaic.* lapidify; calcify, vitrify, crystallize.

2. inure, accustom, condition, season, set; habituate, caseharden, train, addict, indoctrinate, acclimate.

—adj. **3.** hardened, hard, adamantine, steely, callous, strong; stony, gritty, flinty, granitic, rocky, stony, concrete; horny, corneous, bony, cartilaginous, *Archaic.* lapidific, osseous, sclerotic; vitreous, crystalline, aphanitic, porphyritic.

4. rigid, obstinate, stubborn, obdurate, recusant; unfeeling, cold, frigid, chilled; remorseless, unrepentant, impenitent, uncontrite; incorrigible, irreclaimable, irredeemable, irremissible.

5. inflexible, unbending, inelastic, unyielding; inured, accustomed, unchangeable, casehardened, conditioned, set.

induration, *n.* **1.** hardening, petrification, ossification, fossilization; sclerosis, cornification, vitrification.

2. hardness, stiffness, rigidity, resistance, intractability; toughness, firmness, grittiness, callousness.

3. obduracy, obstinacy, stubbornness, recusancy; remorselessness, coldness, frigidity, unfeelingness, impenitence, uncontrition, unrepentance; inflexibility, unbendingness, unyieldingness, inelasticity.

industrialist, *n.* producer, manufacturer, constructor, builder; magnate, tycoon, baron, boss, capitalist, *Inf.* big wig, captain of industry, lord of industry.

industrious, *adj.* hard-working, energetic, dynamic, eager-beaver, busy as a bee; busy, bustling, hustling, on the go, on the move; at work, in harness, hard at it, astir, active, up and doing, up and coming; vigorous, aggressive, go-ahead, forceful, intense; laborious, operose, diligent, assiduous, sedulous, studious, intent; plodding, unflagging, indefatigable, tireless, undrooping, unsleeping; persistent, pertinacious, constant, earnest, patient; workmanlike, businesslike, enterprising.

industry, *n.* **1.** manufacturing, production, construction, making, fabrication; establishment, trade, manufacture, commerce.

2. business, field, line, craft, métier; trade, art, handiwork, handicraft.

3. labor, work, toil, efforts; activity, undertaking, task, chore, duty, service; employment, job, occupation, vocation, pursuit, profession, position.

4. diligence, assiduity, sedulity, painstaking; application, attention, concentration, intentness; effort, devotion, devotedness, laboriousness, industriousness; workaholism, the Protestant ethic, Stakhanovism; energy, enterprise, dynamism, vim, vigor, bustle, hustle, beehive of activity; indefatigability, tirelessness, labor, earnestness, determination, perseverance, persistence.

inebriate, *v.* **1.** intoxicate, besot, make drunk, *Inf.* light-up, *Inf.* put under the table; stupefy, addle, fuddle, befuddle, muddle; *All Sl.* plaster, pollute, souse, stew, crock, swack, pickle, stone, sozzle, booze-up, liquor-up, likker-up.

2. exhilarate, invigorate, stimulate, animate, inspirit; thrill, elate, galvanize, electrify, take one's breath away, *Inf.* give one a kick *or* thrill *or* lift; overcome, overpower, overwhelm, send one's head spinning, make one's head spin *or* reel; enrapture, enchant, bewitch, entrance; charm, infatuate, captivate, fascinate.

—n. **3.** drunk, drunkard, sot, soak, tosspot, toper, bibber, bibbler, *Obs., Rare.* biberon, barfly; alcoholic, chronic alcoholic *or* drunk, dipsomaniac; drinker, hard drinker, problem drinker, serious drinker; *All Inf.* guzzler, swiller, soaker, sponge, lovepot; *All Sl.* boozer, boozehound, lush, souse, rummy, wino, alky, juicehead, juicer, hooch hound, gin hound, swillbelly, swillpot, stew, stewbum, elbow-bender, elbow-crooker.

—adj. **4.** intoxicated, inebriated, inebrious, crapulent, crapulous, *Archaic.* intoxicate; drunk, drunken, sodden, besotted, sottish, awash, *Literary.* in one's cups. See **inebriated**.

inebriated, *adj.* **1.** intoxicated, inebriate, inebrious, crapulent, crapulous; drunk, drunken, sodden, besotted, sottish, awash, *Literary.* in one's cups; under the influence, under the weather, with a glow on, the worse for liquor; saturated, soused, full, *Scot.* fou; tipsy, grogged, *Archaic.* groggy, fuddled, befuddled, muddled, obfuscated, woozy, bleary-eyed, pie-eyed, glassy-eyed; far-gone, stupefied, staggering, staggering drunk, drunk as a lord, drunk as a piper *or* a fiddler, drunk as a skunk *or* owl; merry, happy, gay, jolly; maudlin.

2. *All Inf.* boozy, tight, lit, lit-up, lit to the gills, illuminated, liquored-up; pickled, lathered, high, high as a kite; mellow, feeling good, feeling no pain; blind, blind drunk, paralyzed, knocked-out, out, out of it, passed-out, under the table. See also **drunk** (*def.* **2**).

3. *All Sl.* loaded, lubricated, oiled, well-oiled, stewed, stewed to the gills, tanked, *Brit.* pissed, *Brit.* bevied; primed, gassed, bombed, stoned, polluted, cocked, crocked, crocked to the gills, canned, sloshed, potted, plastered; stiff, stinking, stinko, stinking drunk, plotched, spiflicated, swacked, blotto, smashed, skunk-drunk, burning with a low blue flame. See also **drunk** (*def.* **3**).

inebriety, *n.* **1.** drunkenness, intoxication, insobriety, inebriation, intemperance, sottedness, besottedness, tipsiness; alcoholism, chronic alcoholism, dipsomania, habitual drunkenness, bibulousness, bibulosity, bibacity, bibaciousness, crapulence, crapulency, crapulousness.

2. drink, drinking, heavy *or* serious *or* problem drinking; imbibing, tippling, toping, bibition, bibation, bibbing, bibbling, *Rare.* bibbery, *Inf.* boozing, *Inf.* swilling, *Sl.* hitting the bottle *or* booze *or* sauce, *Brit. Sl.* bevying.

inedible, *adj.* uneatable, unedible, unconsumable, not fit to eat, not fit for human consumption, not fit for a dog; sickening, disgusting, offensive, noisome, *Sl.* yukky; rotten, turned, spoiled, tainted, sour, putrid, fetid, bad; unwholesome, unhealthy, unhealthful, noxious, nocuous, harmful, injurious, hurtful, deleterious, detrimental to one's health, bad for you; poisonous, deadly, lethal, fatal, *Archaic.* lethiferous.

ineffable, *adj.* **1.** inexpressible, beyond words, incommunicable, indescribable, undescribable; undefinable, indefinite, nondescript, nameless.

2. unmentionable, unspeakable, not to be spoken, unutterable, unnamable.

ineffaceable, *adj.* inerasable, ineradicable, indestructible. See **indelible**.

ineffective, *adj.* **1.** inefficacious, impotent, weak. See **ineffectual**.

2. inefficient, unproficient, unskillful; incompetent, unfit, inept, unapt, not up to par *or* snuff; incapable, unable, lacking in ability; worthless, useless, inutile, unserviceable.

3. unmoving, unarousing, unthrilling, uninspiring; unstriking, untelling, dull, flat.

ineffectual, *adj.* **1.** ineffective, inefficacious, inadequate, inefficient, incompetent, unserviceable, inoperative; useless, inutile, worthless, valueless, meritless, nugatory.

2. futile, unavailing, bootless; fruitless, unproductive, abortive, barren, sterile, fallow, unprolific, infecund; unprofitable, profitless, unremunerative, unpaying, unrewarding, gainless; unsuccessful, to no purpose, to no avail, for naught.

3. weak, feeble, powerless, impotent, lame, effete, worn out, washed out.

inefficacious, *adj.* **1.** ineffective, ineffectual, incapable, inadequate, inefficient, incompetent, inept; useless, inutile, worthless, valueless, meritless, nugatory.

2. futile, vain, bootless, unavailing, idle; unproductive, unyielding, barren, abortive, sterile, infertile; unprofitable, profitless, unremunerative, unrewarding, unpaying, gainless; unsuccessful, *Inf.* no-go, to no avail, to no purpose, for naught.

3. weak, feeble, powerless, lame, effete, impotent.

inefficacy, *n.* **1.** ineffectuality, ineffectualness, inefficaciousness; incapacity, inability, inadequacy, inefficiency, incompetence, ineptitude; uselessness, inutility, worthlessness, valuelessness, meritlessness, nugacity.
2. futility, bootlessness, fruitlessness, abortiveness, barrenness, sterility; unprofitableness, profitlessness, nonsuccess, failure, defeat.
3. weakness, feebleness, powerlessness, lameness, effeteness, impotence.

inefficient, *adj.* **1.** incompetent, inept, inapt, unapt, unfit, unfitted, unqualified, unprepared, deficient; incapable, unable, lacking in ability *or* skill, not up *or* equal to; inefficacious, ineffectual, ineffective, impotent, unpowerful, weak. See **ineffectual**.
2. slack, loose, lax; careless, remiss, derelict, negligent; haphazard, slipshod, sloppy.

inelastic, *adj.* **1.** inflexible, unflexible, unbendable, unpliant, irresilient, inductile, flaccid, flabby; stiff, rigid, hard, unyielding, unretractable; firm, tense, unmalleable, unlimber, *Inf.* stiff as a poker, *Inf.* out of condition.
2. unadaptable, unadjustable, unaccommodating, unresponsive, uncompliant, intolerant, stubborn, uncompromising; callous, tough, *Inf.* hard as nails, *Inf.* stiff as a ramrod, *Inf.* set in one's ways, old-fashioned, conservative, *Inf.* old-poopish, *Inf.* fossilized.

inelegant, *adj.* **1.** unrefined, uncultivated, unpolished, uncultured, uncourtly, undignified, unfinished; barbarous, savage, common, plain, plebian; homely, homespun, homebred, down-home, countrified, unsophisticated.
2. awkward, clumsy, ungainly, graceless, ungraceful, gauche; crude, rude, coarse, vulgar, rough, uncouth, ill-bred.
3. stiff, formal, constrained, forced, labored; harsh, dry, bald, abrupt, halting.
4. turgid, tumid, inflated, bombastic, fustian; ponderous, affected, euphuistic, artificial, mannered.

ineligible, *adj.* **1.** unqualified, unworthy of choice, undesirable, unworthwhile; unacceptable, totally unacceptable, *Inf.* out of the question, *Inf.* beyond the pale, legally disqualified; improper, inappropriate, unsuitable, not meet, unseemly.
2. unmarriageable, not nubile, not a proper suitor, *Inf.* unavailable, married, wed.

inept, *adj.* **1.** unskilled, unskillful, untrained, inefficient, incompetent, ineffective, unproductive, inadequate, unfit; awkward, undextrous, maladroit, ungraceful, graceless, ungainly, bungling, oafish, unmannered.
2. inappropriate, out of place, unseemly, unsuitable, unfitting, improper, unmeet, out of keeping; inexpedient, impolitic, injudicious, unwise, imprudent, ill-advised; undesirable, unworthy, ineligible, inadmissable, unsatisfactory, objectionable, wrong.
3. absurd, foolish, silly, stupid, asinine, inane, imbecile, crazy, *Inf.* screwy; pointless, nonsensical, senseless, insensate, meaningless, amphigoric, farcical, ridiculous, ludicrous.

ineptitude, *n.* **1.** inaptness, inaptitude, unfitness, incompetence, incompetency, inadequacy; awkwardness, gracelessness, ungainliness, unmannerliness, gaucherie.
2. inappropriateness, unseemliness, unsuitability, unmeetness; inexpediency, impoliticness, injudiciousness, imprudence, imprudentness, imprudency; undesirability, unworthiness, ineligibility, inadmissibility, objectionability, wrongness.

inequality, *n.* **1.** disparity, imparity, imbalance, unevenness, incongruity, disproportion; discrepancy, inconsistency, inconformity, nonconformity; difference, dissimilarity, unlikeness, dissimilitude, contrast, confliction.
2. injustice, unfairness; partiality, bias, prejudice.
3. unevenness, roughness, irregularity.

inequitable, *adj.* unjust, unfair, partial, not equitable; biased, prejudiced, closed-minded, narrow-minded, intolerant, bigoted, one-sided, partisan; wrongful, wrong, bad, iniquitous; unlawful, illegitimate, illegal; unjustifiable, indefensible, unwarrantable, unreasonable.

inequity, *n.* **1.** unfairness, unfair *or* unjust treatment, injustice; mistreatment, maltreatment, abuse, injury, hurt; grievance, imposition, infringement *or* encroachment on one's rights; wrongdoing, foul play, dirty trick, villainy, *Law.* tort.
2. discrimination, partiality, favoritism, one-sidedness, bias, prejudice, bigotry.

inert, *adj.* **1.** inactive, lifeless, inanimate; immovable, immobile, motionless; stationary, unmoving, fixed, rooted, riveted; still, stock-still, *Chiefly Literary.* stilly, quiet, quiescent.
2. comatose, unconscious; knocked out, out cold, *Inf.* out like a light, passed out, dead to the world.
3. dull, sluggish, passive, sedentary, lethargic, phlegmatic, stagnant; sleepy, somnolent, slumberous, torpid, torpescent; indolent, idle, slothful, lazy, supine, otiose; listless, languid, lackadaisical.

inertia, *n.* **1.** inactivity, inaction, inactiveness, idleness, unemployment; stagnation, inertness, stasis, motionlessness, immobility.
2. sluggishness, dullness, heaviness, langor, lethargy, lassitude, listlessness, torpor, passivity; sloth, laziness, indolence, inexertion, do-nothingness, fainéance.

inescapable, *adj.* unavoidable, ineluctable, ineludible, inevasible; inexorable, unpreventable, unyielding, unalterable, uncontrollable; fated, destined, predestined; certain, sure, *Inf.* for sure, sure as death, sure as death and taxes, not to be avoided.

inestimable, *adj.* **1.** incalculable, incomputable, uncountable, not to be reckoned; innumerable, countless, untold, endless, infinite; immeasurable, measureless, unmeasured, fathomless, unfathomable; multitudinous, manifold, voluminous, very great; prodigious, unlimited, boundless, vast, immense.
2. priceless, precious, invaluable, costly, worth its weight in gold, worth a king's ransom; rare, peerless, matchless, unparalleled, inimitable; superlative, superfine, excellent, *Archaic.* eximious; prime, tiptop, *Inf.* crack.

inevitable, *adj.* inescapable, inexorable, irrevocable, unchangeable; automatic, mechanical, involuntary; destined, *Inf.* in the cards, bound to happen, *Inf.* in the bag, out of one's hands; authoritative, ordained, unequivocal, absolute, conclusive, infallible, undisputed; unquestionable, indisputable, undeniable, indubitable, incontestable, apodictic, irrefutable, incontrovertible. See **inescapable**.

inexact, *adj.* inaccurate, incorrect, faulty, false, wrong, erroneous, fallacious, in error; off, off-base, not right, wide of the mark; imprecise, indistinct, indefinite; loose, fuzzy, muddled, *Inf.* muzzy, *Inf.* out of line.

inexcusable, *adj.* unjustifiable, indefensible, unwarrantable, unexcusable; unpardonable, irremissible, unforgivable, unexpiable, unatonable; blameworthy, reprehensible, censurable, reproachable, reprovable, condemnable; blameful, discreditable, disreputable, ignoble, shameful, immoral, wrongful; wicked, nefarious, iniquitous, flagitious.

inexhaustible, *adj.* **1.** unlimited, limitless, illimitable, unstinted; infinite, boundless, unrestricted, endless, exhaustless; unmeasured, measureless, indeterminate, incalculable; copious, bountiful, lavish, abundant, ample.

2. indefatigable, tireless, untiring, unwearying, weariless; unfailing, unfaltering, undrooping; unwavering, unflagging, unremitting, persevering.

inexorable, *adj.* **1.** inescapable, ineluctable, unavoidable, destined, fated; unalterable, binding, irrevocable.

2. unyielding, immovable, obdurate, adamantine; intransigent, uncompromising, inflexible, unbending, stiff; implacable, unappeasable, unforgiving; strict, iron-handed, severe, exacting, stringent, harsh; rigorous, Draconian, relentless, unrelenting, unsparing; grim, dour, stern, austere; hard, hardened, hardhearted, cold-hearted, stony, unfeeling; unmerciful, merciless, unpitying, pitiless, remorseless, ruthless, cruel.

inexpedient, *adj.* **1.** impolitic, unshrewd, unprofitable, undesirable, unfavorable, disadvantageous, detrimental, harmful; inappropriate, unsuitable, ill-suited, wrong.

2. ill-advised, unadvisable, inadvisable, unadvised, unrecommendable, unrecommended, miscounseled, misguided; injudicious, ill-judged, unwise, unsage, unsagacious; imprudent, ill-considered, inconsiderate, thoughtless, senseless, nonsensical, wrong-headed, foolish, harebrained, stupid, *Inf.* dumb.

inexpensive, *adj.* low-cost, low-priced, moderately priced, reasonable, economical, cheap; reduced, slashed, lowered, bargain *or* sale priced, half-price, marked down, discounted, cut-rate, wholesale, warehouse priced, catchpenny, priced to move, *Inf.* budget, *Inf.* bargain-basement.

inexperience, *n.* callowness, immaturity, greenness, verdancy; unsophistication, naïveté, innocence; rawness, untrainedness, ignorance; unskillfulness, inexpertness, incompetence.

inexperienced, *adj.* callow, immature, green, verdant, unfledged; unsophisticated, naïve, innocent, born yesterday, wet behind the ears; new, raw, fresh, young, in one's salad days; unschooled, untrained, untutored, undrilled; uninitiated, uninformed, unconversant, unversed, ignorant; unacquainted, unfamiliar, unaccustomed, unpracticed, unseasoned.

inexpert, *adj.* unskilled, untrained, unschooled, untutored, unpracticed, unseasoned, green, inexperienced; incompetent, unskillful, left-handed, maladroit, bunglesome; unhandy, inept, clumsy, awkward, bungling, bumbling, blundering.

inexpiable, *adj.* **1.** irreparable, unrectifiable, irremediable; indefensible, inexonerable, unjustifiable; unforgiveable, inexcusable, unpardonable.

2. serious, grave, mortal, capital, criminal, felonious; reprehensible, vile, heinous; sinful, bad, evil, wicked, villainous, nefarious, black, black-hearted.

3. implacable, unappeasable, unplacatable, unpacifiable, not to be appeased *or* placated *or* pacified; merciless, unmerciful, pitiless, unpitying, unforgiving; hardhearted, stony-hearted, flinty, cold-blooded, heartless, uncompassionate, inhumane; inexorable, unrelenting, relentless, stern, strict, rigid, firm, unbending, unyielding; ruthless, cruel, harsh, grim, hard, severe.

inexplicable, *adj.* **1.** unaccountable, insoluble, insolvable, inexplainable, unexplainable, *Obs.* inextricable; puzzling, enigmatic, enigmatical, baffling, bewildering, confounding, mystifying, perplexing.

2. impenetrable, unfathomable, incomprehensible, uncomprehensible, past *or* beyond comprehension *or* understanding, undecipherable, unknowable, incognizable, incognoscible, inscrutable; abstruse, recondite, abstract, heavy, *Sl.* heavy-duty.

3. mysterious, esoteric, occult, hermetic, hermetical; mystic, mystical, cabalistic, transcendental, supernatural, preternatural, otherworldly; strange, weird, bizarre; odd, curious, peculiar, queer.

4. fantastic, fabulous, wondrous, wonderful, marvelous, miraculous, too much for words; impossible, unbelievable, incredible; inconceivable, unthinkable, unimaginable.

inexpressible, *adj.* **1.** ineffable, beyond words, incommunicable, undescribable, indescribable; unspeakable, unutterable; undefinable, nondescript, nameless, unnamable.

2. strange, marvelous, wondrous, wonderful, *Sl.* something else; amazing, astonishing, stupendous, prodigious, incredible, unheard of.

inexpressive, *adj.* **1.** expressionless, blank, dead, deadpan, poker-faced, inscrutable; emotionless, unemotional, unmoved, impassive, cold, stony; unanimated, unlively, immobile, motionless, inactive, passive, lifeless, inert.

2. dull, flat, boring, unexciting, devoid of expression; meaningless, empty, void, vacuous.

inextinguishable, *adj.* unquenchable, unsuppressible, irrepressible; imperishable, indestructible, enduring, lasting; unconquerable, ungovernable, stanchless; volcanic, fiery, burning, ardent, ever-burning.

inextricable, *adj.* knotty, entangled, tangled, raveled, *Sl.* screwed-up; intricate, involved, convoluted, complicated, complex; maze-like, labyrinthine; perplexing, baffling, *Sl.* mind-blowing, mystifying, bewildering, puzzling.

infallibility, *n.* unerringness, faultlessness, accuracy, rightness; certainty, certitude, surety; assurance, undeniability, incontestability, irrefutability, reliability; dead *or* absolute certainty, *All Sl.* sure thing, sure bet, cinch, lead-pipe cinch.

infallible, *adj.* **1.** unerring, inerrant, inerrable, unfailing; flawless, impeccable, faultless, perfect; positive, solid, sound, *Sl.* absolutely OK; believable, credible.

2. dependable, trustworthy, foolproof, *Inf.* sure-fire, reliable; certain, sure, *Inf.* sure as shooting, right, right as rain; incontestable, incontrovertible, indisputable, irrefutable; unquestionable, unequivocal, indubitable, undeniable.

infamous, *adj.* **1.** disreputable, ignominious, having a bad name, of ill repute, discreditable, dishonorable; scandalous, notorious, obloquial, disgraceful, shameful, flagrant, stigmatized.

2. detestable, loathsome, contemptible, despicable, abhorrent, abominable; reprehensible, low, low-down, base, mean, petty, vile, abject, wormy; execrable, outrageous, ignoble, wretched, paltry; nefarious, wicked, villainous, heinous, flagitious, iniquitous; corrupt, depraved, *Sl.* yutzy, *Sl.* putzy, rotten, scurvy, *Sl.* cruddy; knavish, sinister, odious, obnoxious, atrocious, bad, revolting.

infamy, *n.* **1.** ignomimy, obloquy, opprobrium, disrepute, ill repute, notoriety; shame, disgrace, dishonor, discredit; stigma, stain, blot, blot on the escutcheon, badge of infamy.

2. wickedness, improbity, villainy, baseness, meanness, pettiness; depravity, degeneracy, turpitude, corruption; knavery, roguery, rascality; dishonesty, double-dealing, deception, foul play, *Sl.* dirty tricks, *Sl.* low blow, treachery, perfidy; infidelity, disloyalty, faithlessness, back-stabbing.

infancy, *n.* **1.** babyhood, early childhood, the cradle, the nursery.

2. start, commencement, beginning, origin, onset,

outset, outbreak, dawn, conception, birth, genesis, exordium; rise, arising, beginnings, emergence, incipience, incunabula, nascence.

infant, *n.* **1.** baby, babe, newborn babe, bambino, toddler, (*Amer. Ind.*) papoose, neonate; suckling, nursling, weanling, foundling.

2. beginner, novice, novitiate, neophyte, tyro, amateur, rookie, greenhorn, tenderfoot, newcomer, new boy; student, pupil, freshman, *Inf.* frosh *or* freshie, learner, initiate, apprentice, trainee; recruit, raw recruit, abecedarian, catechumen.

3. ingénue, unsophisticate, innocent, simple soul, child, mere child, babe in the woods, lamb.

infanticide, *n.* **1.** (*all of a child*) murder, homicide, slaying, killing.

2. (*all of a child*) murderer, killer, slayer.

infantile, *adj.* **1.** babyish, childish, *Rare.* childly, puerile, infantine, infant; immature, juvenile, adolescent.

2. newborn, newfledged, unfledged, callow, unripe, green, raw, undeveloped, wet behind the ears; in the cradle, in swaddling clothes, in diapers, *Brit.* in nappies, at the breast, on the bottle.

3. beginning, initial, incipient, introductory, inchoate; formative, creative, natal, nascent, incunabular.

infantry, *n.* foot soldiers, foot, groundtroops, trymen, men-at-arms, *Sl.* grunts, *Sl.* dogfaces, *Sl.* footsloggers; rank and file, cannon fodder, (*in U.S. army*) G.I.'s *or* Yanks *or* doughboys, (*in British army*) Tommies *or* (*esp. of Scot. troops*) Jocks.

infatuate, *v.* **1.** stultify, besot, befool, make a fool of, *Sl.* make a monkey of.

2. enamor, endear, win *or* capture one's heart, take the fancy of, *Inf.* make a hit with; charm, captivate, intrigue, allure, beguile, turn one's head, *Sl.* turn on; entrance, enrapture, enravish, enthrall, hold in thrall, transport, carry away, sweep off one's feet; bewitch, ensorcell, spellbind, mesmerize, hypnotize; obsess, possess, beset, preoccupy, grip, hold, not let go.

—*n.* **3.** fanatic, zealot, devotee, enthusiast, aficionado, energumen, *Inf.* fan, *Inf.* buff, *Sl.* nut, *Sl.* bug, *Sl.* freak, *Sl.* hound, *Sl.* fiend, *Sl.* demon, *Sl.* sucker for.

infatuated, *adj.* **1.** enamored, taken with, *Inf.* smitten, *Inf.* sweet on, *Sl.* stuck on; in love, hopelessly in love, head over heels in love, *Inf.* keen about, *Inf.* mad about, *Inf.* crazy about, *Inf.* wild about, *Sl.* nuts about; charmed, fascinated, captivated, intrigued, beguiled, bewitched, spellbound, mesmerized, hypnotized; possessed, obsessed, fixated, preoccupied, gripped, held, *Sl.* hung up.

2. fond, overfond, affectionate, overaffectionate, doting, loving.

infatuation, *n.* **1.** stultification; captivation, allurement, beguilement, ensorcellment, mesmerization, hypnotization.

2. foolishness, besottedness, self-deception, self-delusion, blindness; dotage, fondness; fanaticism, overzealousness, overeagerness, overenthusiasm.

3. liking, passing fancy; *Inf.* crush; love, *Inf.* puppy love, *Inf.* calf love.

4. craze, mania, passion, furor, rage; fascination, *Sl.* bug; obsession, prepossession, fixation, complex, monomania, *Sl.* hang up.

infeasible, *adj.* impracticable, impractical, unfeasible; unworkable, inoperable, undoable, unperformable, unnegotiable; impossible, not possible, out of the question; unattainable, unachievable, beyond one; insuperable, insurmountable; improbable, unlikely, hardly possible, doubtful, dubious, questionable.

infect, *v.* **1.** contaminate, affect, poison, empoison, envenom, toxicate; ulcerate, canker; taint, spoil, blight, mar, impair.

2. corrupt, pollute, vitiate, pervert; debauch, defile, debase, degrade, deflower, ravish; foul, befoul, besmirch.

3. imbue, infuse, inform, inject; influence, impress, affect, touch, leaven; excite, inflame, enkindle, enthuse, inspire; animate, stimulate, provoke, quicken, whet.

infection, *n.* **1.** contamination, taint, poisoning, spoilage.

2. contagion, virus, bacillus, germ, bacteria; poison, miasma, venom, toxin; toxicity, virulence, septicity.

3. disease, epidemic, plague, bubonic plague, Black Death, pandemic; pestilence, pest, murrain, pox, scourge.

4. corruption, pollution, vitiation, perversion; defilement, debauchment, debasement, degradation, deflowering, ravishment; fouling, befouling, besmirchment.

5. influence, inspiration, infusion, enlivenment, afflatus; impulse, stimulation, animation, provocation, excitation, suscitation.

infectious, *adj.* **1.** communicable, contagious, catching, spreading, infective, transmissible, transferable.

2. pestilent, baneful, malign, pestiferous, morbific, morbiferous; noisome, *Dial.* plaguy, germ-laden, zymotic, inoculable; poisonous, venomous, deadly, toxic, mephitic; noxious, virulent, septic, miasmic; epidemic, endemic, pandemic, epizootic.

3. habit-forming, inducive, addictive, irresistible, compelling.

infecund, *adj.* unfruitful, barren, sterile. See **infertile**.

infecundity, *n.* fruitlessness, barrenness, sterility. See **infertility**.

infelicitous, *adj.* **1.** unhappy, woeful, miserable, sad, melancholic, woebegone, forlorn, brokenhearted; unfortunate, unlucky, wretched, pitiable, poor, gloomy; hopeless, desperate, desolate, heavy-laden, cheerless, despondent, depressed; chagrined, sorrowful, afflicted, pained, mortified, remorseful, regretful.

2. unfavorable, unpropitious, inauspicious, sinister, lowering, bleak; inopportune, untimely, premature; unblest, adverse, untoward, unprosperous, unsuccessful.

3. inapt, inappropriate, unfitting, unfit, unsuitable, inapplicable; inconsistent, incongruous, irrelevant; malapropos, ill-chosen, gauche, awkward, wrong, out of place; unadvisable, ill-advised, inexpedient, amiss.

infelicity, *n.* **1.** unhappiness, sadness, melancholy, woe, dole, wretchedness, misery, gloom; hopelessness, despair, desolation, despondency; sorrow, chagrin, affliction, pain; tribulation, mortification, remorse, regret.

2. misfortune, bad luck, adversity, no luck; suffering, hardship, ill fortune, depression, hard times, bad times; travail, trials, troubles.

3. curse, blight, misfortune, bane, scourge, infliction, cup; ill wind, cold wind, blast, draught.

4. inaptness, inappropriateness, unfitness, unsuitability; inconsistency, inapplicability, incongruity, irrelevance; unadvisableness, inexpedience, amissness, wrongness.

infer, *v.* **1.** deduce, reason, conclude, come to *or* reach *or* arrive at a conclusion, draw a conclusion, derive, obtain *or* get an answer, calculate, put two and two together, *Inf.* figure, *Sl.* dope out; gather, construe, understand, *Archaic.* collect; presume, assume, take for granted, suppose, opine, think, believe, *Inf. Chiefly Midland and Southern U.S.* reckon; speculate, surmise, suspect, imagine; conjecture, theorize, hypothesize; estimate, judge, guess, *Sl.* guesstimate, jump to a conclusion.

2. (*of facts, circumstances, statements*) indicate, point to, signify, be a sign *or* symptom of; evidence, demonstrate, show, tell, bespeak, mark, designate; foreshadow, prefigure, adumbrate, lead to, be the first step in.

3. imply, intimate, insinuate, hint at, suggest; allude to, refer to, advert to.

inference, *n.* **1.** reasoning, logic, ratiocination, deductive *or* inductive thinking, *Both Logic.* induction, deduction.

2. deduction, conclusion, illation, corollary, derivation, answer; what it all adds up to; presumption, assumption, supposition, understanding, construe, impression, belief; estimate, calculation, finding, determination, judgement, opinion, guess, suspicion, reckoning, *Sl.* guesstimate; surmise, speculation, probability, likelihood, conjecture, hypothesis, theory, *Rare.* surmisal.

3. implication, intimation, insinuation, hint, clue, suggestion; allusion, reference.

inferior, *adj.* **1. inferior to** lower than, less than, below, under, subordinate to.

2. lower, subordinate, secondary, junior, second-fiddle; subsidiary, ancillary, tributary, *Law.* puisne; second-class, small-time, one-horse, bush, bush-league, *Sl.* two bit, *Sl.* small potatoes, *Sl.* mickey mouse; minor, insignificant, unimportant, petty, puny, small, paltry; lowly, humble, subservient, servile, menial.

3. bad, awful, terrible, wretched, grubstreet, *Inf.* lousy, *Sl.* crappy; slipshod, shoddy, sleazy, miserable; poor, mean, base, low, rank; lesser, second-rate, low grade, cheap, dimestore, bargain-basement, *Inf.* junky, *U.S. Sl.* cheesy, *Brit. Sl.* humpty; lightweight, amateurish, unprofessional, incompetent, not up to par *or* snuff; mediocre, middling, moderate, so-so, indifferent, passable, tolerable, *Inf.* O.K.

inferiority, *n.* **1.** subordination, secondary *or* junior status *or* standing, second fiddle; lowliness, subservience, subserviency; pettiness, paltriness, unimportance, insignificance.

2. lowness, meanness, baseness, rankness, shoddiness, sleaziness, cheapness, lower *or* inferior quality, *Inf.* junkiness, *U.S. Sl.* cheesiness; badness, awfulness, terribleness, wretchedness, *Inf.* lousiness; amateurishness, unprofessionalness, incompetence; mediocrity, moderateness, passableness, indifference.

infernal, *adj.* **1.** *Class. Myth.* Hadean, Plutonian, Plutonic, Stygian, Styxian, Tartarean, Acherontal, Cocytean, Phlegethontal, Avernal; pandemoniac, chthonian, chthonic.

2. diabolical, fiendish, ghoulish, hellish, hellborn; demonic, demoniac, demoniacal, devilish, satanic, Mephistophelian.

3. nefarious, flagitious, heinous, infamous, unspeakable; wicked, iniquitous, evil, sinful; odious, obnoxious, villainous, *Obs.* scelerous, depraved, corrupt, *Archaic.* facinorous; ungodly, godless, impious, unholy; base, vile, sinister, dark, dire, black, dreadful, baleful; damnable, execrable, abominable, horrible, horrid, horrendous, hideous, monstrous, atrocious, accursed; pestilential, malevolent, malicious, malign, maleficent, malefic.

4. outrageous, flagrant, *Inf.* flaming; excessive, great, enormous.

infertile, *adj.* unfruitful, infecund, barren, unproductive, fallow, effete, sterile; fruitless, unfructuous, *Bot.* acarpous, arid; impotent, unprolific, childless.

infertility, *n.* unfruitfulness, infecundity, aridness, unproductiveness, fallowness, fruitlessness; impotence, barrenness, sterility, effeteness, unprolificness.

infest, *v.* overrun, take over, spread like wildfire, run through, overspread, pervade, permeate, penetrate, infiltrate; swarm, crawl, creep, throng; beset, plague, torment, drive crazy, discommode, incommode, discomfort, inconvenience; bother, annoy, pester, trouble, haunt.

infidel, *n.* unbeliever, disbeliever, heathen, heretic, irreligionist; *Turkish.* giaour, pagan, alien, gentile; doubter, skeptic, nullifidian, scoffer, agnostic, freethinker.

infidelity, *n.* **1.** breach of trust, faithlessness, bad faith, treachery, perfidy, perfidiousness; disloyalty, unfaithfulness, falseness, falseheartedness; apostasy, traitorousness, Iscariotism, treason, recreancy; deceit, double-dealing, duplicity; disaffection, breach, estrangement.

2. adultery, cuckoldry, *Law.* criminal conversation, *Sl.* fooling *or* playing around, *Sl.* skipping *or* stepping out, *Sl.* swinging, *Sl.* running around, *Sl.* getting some on the side, *Sl.* cheating; intrigue, liaison, affair, amour, *Sl.* hanky-panky; libertinism, licentiousness, unchastity, playing fast and loose.

infiltrate, *v.* **1.** pervade, permeate, interpenetrate, soak into, saturate, imbue, imbrue; percolate, filter through, seep, moisten, dampen.

2. intrude, slip *or* sneak in, creep into, invade, get behind the lines, get into the enemy camp, insinuate, penetrate.

infinite, *adj.* **1.** unlimited, limitless, without limit, illimitable, unbounded, boundless; inexhaustible, endless, unending, interminable, no end of, without end, bottomless; multitudinous, very great, enormous, prodigious, immense, vast, astronomical.

2. innumerable, innumerous, countless, untold, uncounted, numberless, myriad, without number, sumless; unmeasured, indeterminate, undetermined, indefinite; undeterminable, indeterminable, incalculable, inestimable, uncountable, measureless, immeasurable, unmeasurable, fathomless, unfathomable.

3. perfect, whole, complete, total; omnipotent, all-powerful, all-encompassing, all-embracing.

4. eternal, everlasting, enduring, perpetual, undying, immortal, deathless; permanent, perdurable, unfading, imperishable, amaranthine, perennial; constant, unceasing, ceaseless, nonstop, unremitting, continuous, continual, ongoing, unbroken, uninterrupted, incessant, never-ending.

infinitesimal, *adj.* **1.** minute, tiny, very small, minuscule, microscopic, atomic, imperceptible; wee, little, diminutive, miniature; mini, midget, Lilliputian, pygmyish, dwarfish.

2. inappreciable, insignificant, inconsiderable, negligible; slight, puny, paltry, mere, meager, scanty, exiguous; piddling, petty, trifling, *Inf.* picayune.

infinity, *n.* **1.** infinitude, infiniteness, unlimitedness, limitlessness, illimitability, illimitableness; unboundedness, boundlessness, bottomlessness, inexhaustibility, inexhaustibleness; enormousness, greatness, hugeness, prodigiousness, immensity, immenseness, vastness.

2. innumerableness, innumerability, unmeasuredness, indeterminateness, indefiniteness; undeterminableness, indeterminableness, incalculability, incalculableness, inestimability, inestimableness; measurelessness, unmeasurableness, fathomlessness.

3. perfection, perfectness, wholeness, completeness, totality, omnipotence.

4. eternity, everlastingness, enduringness, perpetuity, perpetualness, undyingness, immortality, deathlessness; permanence, permanency, perdurability, perdurableness, imperishability, imperishableness, perenniality; constancy, unceasingness, ceaselessness, endlessness, interminableness, interminability; continuality, continualness, continuity, incessancy, incessantness, uninterruptedness, unbrokenness.

infirm, *adj.* **1.** feeble, enfeebled, weak, frail, fragile, debilitated, drooping, withered, wasted, worn, worn-out, enervated, exhausted, helpless, powerless, played out, spent; decrepit, impotent, failing, senile, anile, old-womanish, puerile, childish, in one's second childhood, dotty, *Inf.* crocked, *Inf.* cracked; unhealthy, in poor health, in declining health, on the decline, reduced to skin and bones, skeleton-like; ailing, sick, sickly, *Inf.* poorly, ill, unwell, indisposed, *Inf.* under the weather, *Inf.* off one's feed, taken ill, *Inf.* laid up, *Inf.* in a bad way, in danger, *Inf.* laid low, prostrate; confined, bedridden, invalided, *Brit.* in hospital; crippled, lame, halt; hurt, injured, suffering, wounded.

2. unstable, faltering, trembling, doddering, wavering, vacillating, inconstant, fickle, unsteadfast, changeable, irresolute; undetermined, indecisive, undecided, pliable, easily led, gullible, naïve.

3. rickety, tottering, unsteady, unsubstantial, shaky, precarious, insecure, unsound; rotten, decayed, seedy, deteriorated, the worse for wear, on its last legs, tumbledown, jerry-built, flimsy.

infirmary, *n.* **1.** hospital, hospice, clinic, sick bay, school *or* college hospital; sanitarium, sanatorium, nursing home, rest home, home, asylum, *Fr. maison de santé;* pest house, lazaretto, leprosarium; health resort, spa, watering place, baths, springs, hot springs, thermae, pump room.

2. dispensary, dispensatory, pharmacy, *Brit.* chemist's shop, apothecary's shop, drugstore.

infirmity, *n.* **1.** ailment, malady, disorder, complaint, indisposition, infection, affliction, illness, loss of health; sickness, disease, contagious *or* infectious disease, epidemic, pestilence, pest, plague.

2. impairment, defect, debility, debilitation, disability; senility, anility, *Inf.* second childhood, decrepitude, decline, decay, deterioration; weakness, delicacy, delicate health, invalidism; breakdown, collapse.

3. moral weakness, moral failing, immorality, fault, foible, defect, imperfection, flaw; lapse, relapse, backsliding, recidivism, recrudescence; perversion, reversion, retrogression, deterioration; apostasy, fall, fall from grace.

infix, *v.* **1.** fix, fasten, drive in, rivet, ingrain; implant, infuse, introduce, inject, insinuate.

2. instill, inoculate, inculcate, indoctrinate; train, teach, imprint, impress.

inflame, *v.* **1.** fire, ignite, kindle, torch, deflagrate, burn, burn up *or* down, set aflame *or* alight *or* on fire, set fire to, put to the torch, *Obs.* accend, *Obs.* flagrate.

2. incite, provoke, actuate, poke, prod, prick, goad, prompt, spur; encourage, urge, abet, egg on, put up to; instigate, look for trouble, *Inf.* start something; foment, agitate, suscitate, excite, impassion, intensify, arouse, rouse, madden, craze, stir up, work up, wind up, whip up, lash into a fury, *Inf.* psych up, heat up, fire up, enflame, enkindle, touch off, ignite the spark, stir the embers, fan the fire, add fuel to the flame *or* fire, fuel.

3. stimulate, animate, reanimate, whet, invigorate, motivate, inspirit, inspire, galvanize, electrify, energize, activate, vivify, rally, revive, enliven, liven up, pep up, awaken, wake up, waken, shake up, jolt, jog; impel, induce, compel, constrain, move, press, drive, stir, fillip; elicit, evoke, call forth, summon up, sound *or* raise the alarm.

inflammability, *n.* **1.** combustibility, combustibleness, inflammableness, flammableness, flammability, deflagrability, ignitability *or* ignitibility, *Rare.* accendibility.

2. excitability, excitableness, nervousness; testiness, edginess, shortness, irascibleness, cantankerousness, hot-headedness; tempestuousness, vehemence, wrathfulness; spiritedness, passionateness, fieriness, fervidness, ferventness; impetuousness, impulsiveness, precipitateness, impatience, hastiness.

inflammable, *adj.* **1.** combustible, flammable, ignitable *or* ignitible, burnable, deflagrable, *Rare.* accendible.

2. excitable, nervous, high-strung, inflammatory, frantic, furious, frenzied; testy, edgy, short, irascible, irritable, choleric, cantankerous, temperamental, short-tempered, short-fused, hot-headed; tempestuous, vehement, wrathful; spirited, passionate, fiery, fervid, fervent; impetuous, impulsive, precipitate, precipitative, impatient, hasty.

inflammation, *n.* **1.** firing, igniting, kindling, torching, lighting, burning, burning up *or* down, setting aflame *or* alight *or* on fire, setting fire to, putting to the torch; combustion, ignition, deflagration, *Rare.* accension.

2. inciting, incitement, incitation, instigating, instigation, provoking, provocation, actuating, actuation, poking, prodding, pricking, goading, prompting, spurring; fomenting, fomentation, agitating, agitation, suscitating, suscitation, exciting, excitation, impassioning, intensifying, arousing, arousal, rousing, maddening, stirring up, working up, winding up, whipping up, lashing into a fury, *Inf.* psyching up, heating up, firing up, inflaming, enflaming, enkindling, kindling, touching off, igniting the spark, stirring the embers, fanning the fire, adding fuel to the flame *or* fire.

3. fire, blaze, heat, flame, bonfire, *Brit. Dial.* ingle; conflagration, holocaust, *Obs.* flagration, wildfire, forest fire, ring *or* sea of fire, wall *or* sheet of flames.

4. anger, ire, animosity, irritation, exacerbation, vexation, *Inf.* dander; wrath, rage, violence, hot blood; explosion, outburst, ebullition, paroxysm, tantrum, fit; pet, fume, tiff; turbulence, ferment, storm, *Archaic.* pucker, fire and fury, vials of wrath; virulence, acerbity, choler, bile, gall, bad blood.

5. *All Pathology.* redness, rash, efflorescence, eruption, disturbed function, suppuration, hyperemia, erysipelas, phlogosis, exanthema; fever, heat, calenture; swelling, pain, tenderness.

inflammatory, *adj.* **1.** passionate, spirited, fiery, fervent, fervid; incendiary, enflaming, inflaming, flaming, burning, scorching, red-hot; ebullient, explosive, volcanic; wrathful, tempestuous, vehement, violent, raging, frantic, frenzied; inciting, incitive, instigating, instigative, actuating, provoking, provocative, fomenting, rabble-rousing, demagogic, riotous; rebellious, revolutionary, insurgent, mutinous, dissentious, seditious, restive, recalcitrant, refractory; lawless, anarchic.

2. excitable, nervous, high-strung, testy, edgy, short, temperamental, short-tempered, short-fused, hot-headed; irascible, irritable, cantankerous, virulent, acerb, choleric.

inflate, *v.* **1.** dilate, distend, overdistend, *Obs.* sufflate, aerate; swell, bloat, puff out, blow up, pump up, tumefy; expand, overexpand, stretch, stretch out, outstretch; spread, spread out, outspread; grow, wax, fill out, fatten.

2. increase, enlarge, make larger, make bigger, make greater, *Chiefly Literary.* greaten; widen, thicken, broaden; extend, overextend, lengthen, prolong, prolongate, protract.

3. escalate, step up, give a boost to, *U.S. Sl.* soup up, *Sl.* hop up, *Sl.* jazz up; exaggerate, overstate, overstress, overdraw, overcolor; augment, supplement, add to, superadd to; magnify, amplify, deepen, heighten; intensify, aggravate, worsen.

4. raise, elevate, boost, advance; rise, mount, ascend, skyrocket; burgeon, shoot up, spring up, sprout.

5. give [s.o.] a swell head, turn [s.o.'s] head, go to [s.o.'s] head, puff up, make proud, elate; flatter, overpraise, lionize; *Inf.* bootlick, toady to, *Inf.* butter up.

inflated, *adj.* **1.** distended, overdistended, dilated, *Obs.* sufflated; swollen, bloated, puffed out, blown, tumefied, puffy, ballooning; expanded, overexpanded, stretched, stretched out; increased, enlarged, extended, overextended.

2. escalated, stepped-up, *Sl.* jazzed-up, accelerated; raised, elevated, advanced; exaggerated, overstated, overstressed, overdrawn; magnified, amplified, deepened, heightened; intensified, aggravated, worsened.

3. conceited, puffed-up, egotistic, proud, boastful; self-important, cocky, smug, immodest, self-satisfied; narcissistic, vain; arrogant, haughty, condescending, *Inf.* toplofty; exultant, cock-a-hoop, elated.

4. bombastic, high-flown, *Inf.* highfalutin, orotund, fustian, extravagant; pretentious, pompous, stilted, stuffy, declamatory, artificial; pedantic, highbrowed, rhetorical; turgid, flatulent, tumid, overblown; grandiloquent, magniloquent, altisonant, altiloquent.

inflation, *n.* **1.** false prosperity, overenlarged currency; runaway prices, high prices, stiff prices, steep prices; stagflation.

2. conceit, conceitedness, egotism, pride, vainglory, vaingloriousness; narcissism, self-love, self-admiration, self-esteem, egocentrism, vanity; self-glorification, self-laudation, self-praise, self-applause; arrogance, haughtiness, self-importance, self-complacency, condescension; pretension, pretentiousness, affected manner, airs, ostentation.

3. bombast, orotundity, fustian, extravagance, rant; pretentiousness, pomposity, pompousness, stuffiness; turgidity, flatulence, tumidness, tumidity; grandiloquence, magniloquence, altiloquence, altisonance; grandiosity, affectation, big talk, ostentation, showiness, flashiness; bragging, boasting, rodomontade.

4. distension, dilatation, dilation, *Obs.* sufflation; swelling, puffiness, intumescence, tumefaction, blowing up, bloatedness; expansion, stretching, spreading; growth, spread, swell.

5. increase, enlargement, aggrandizement; widening, thickening, broadening; extension, lengthening, prolongation, protraction; addition, accretion, increment, accession, access; augmentation, supplement, annexation, annex; development, enhancement, intensification, exaggeration.

inflect, *v.* **1.** curve, bend, turn, loop, round, bow, flex; hook, crook; arch, vault; reflect, reflex; incurve, incurvate; retroflex, recurve, decurve, bend back.

2. modulate, intonate, intone, vocalize, phonate; (*all of the voice*) vary, alter, diversify, change; accent, accentuate, stress, emphasize; moderate, temper, tone, tone down.

3. *Grammar.* decline, conjugate, parse, grammaticize, analyze.

inflection, *n.* **1.** modulation, phrasing, suspension; pronunciation, articulation, enunciation, utterance, vocalization, voice, voicing, phonation; elocution, diction, dialect, speech pattern, manner of speaking, mode of expression; delivery, presentation, attack, force of utterance.

2. pitch pattern, intonation pattern *or* contour; pitch, tone, frequency; timbre, tonality, tone quality, coloring; tune, melody, lilt, swing, jingle, flow, harmonious flow, rhythmic flow; resonance, sonority, sonorousness; tonelessness.

3. accent, accentuation, emphasis, stress, syllable stress; cadence, beat, rhythm, tempo, pulse, throb; pulsation, cadency, rhythmicity.

4. *Grammar.* affix, suffix, prefix; conjugation, declension; accidence, syntax, word order; paradigm; derivation, word formation, pattern of formation.

5. bend, curve, turn, turning, veer, swerve, meander, hairpin turn *or* bend, S-turn, U-turn; bow, arc; angle, crook, hook; deflection, flex, flexure, conflexure; curvature, curvation, curvity, deviation.

inflexibility, *n.* **1.** rigidity, stiffness, unbendableness, unadjustability, unyieldingness; firmness, tenseness, unmalleability, unlimberness; hardness, petrifaction, fossilization, crystallization, vitrification, flintiness.

2. immovability, unadaptability, unresponsiveness, uncompliance; stubbornness, mulishness, obstinacy, intractability, obdurateness, unbendingness, intolerance, adamantineness; implacableness, implacability, unappeasableness, unpacifiableness, unmollifiableness, unreconcilableness; vengefulness, revengefulness, inexorability, relentlessness; mercilessness, unmercifulness, pitilessness, uncompassion, hard-heartedness, heartlessness, inclemency.

3. unalterability, arbitrariness, unchangeability, unvariability; hard-and-fastness, rigor, resoluteness, steadfastness, perseverance, pertinacity, persistence, doggedness, grit, determination, resolve; tenacity, tenaciousness, *Inf.* stick-to-it-ive-ness, staying power, indefatigability; firmness, decision, *Inf.* backbone, strength of mind, strength of will, indomitableness.

inflexible, *adj.* **1.** rigid, stiff, unbendable, unadjustable, hard, unyielding, unretractable; firm, tense, unmalleable, unlimber, *Inf.* stiff as a poker, *Inf.* out of condition.

2. immovable, *Inf.* hard as nails, *Inf.* stiff as a ramrod; unadaptable, unaccommodating, unresponsive, uncompliant; stubborn, obstinate, intractable, obdurate, unbending, intolerant; adamant, relentless, implacable, unappeasable, unpacifiable, not to be pacified, unmollifiable, unreconcilable; unforgiving, grudge-holding, vengeful, revengeful; merciless, unmerciful, pitiless, unpitying; uncompassionate, uncompassioned, unsympathizing, unsympathetic, hardhearted, heartless, cruel.

3. unalterable, unchangeable, unvarying, hard and fast, ironclad; undeviating, resolute, steadfast, persevering, resolved, determined, tenacious, decided, firm, indomitable; *Inf.* set in one's ways, overly conservative, *Inf.* old-poopish, refractory, perverse.

inflict, *v.* impose on, visit upon, cause to suffer; administer, serve out, deal out, lay on; wreak, execute, perpetrate; bring to bear, put upon, force on.

infliction, *n.* **1.** imposition, perpetration, administration; punishment, castigation, chastening, chastisement; penalty, requital, retribution, nemesis.

2. trouble, worry, affliction, suffering, hurt; irritation, annoyance, vexation; torture, torment, trial, tribulation, ordeal; load, burden, curse, bitter pill, crown of thorns; scourge, plague, visitation, disaster, calamity.

influence, *n.* **1.** power, potency, force, strength, pressure; effect, impact, weight, clout; control, sway, mastery, hold; guidance, leadership, direction, reign, rule; domination, authority, ascendancy, prevalence, predominance, supremacy.

2. good offices, connections, *Sl.* pull, *Sl.* drag; importance, favor, prestige, standing, footing, *Obs.*

credit.

—*v.* **3.** affect, sway, bias, incline; change, alter, modify, transform; act on, play on, work on, impress upon, impact upon, effect; move, impel, motivate, actuate; incite, rouse, arouse, instigate, induce, persuade, *Inf.* jawbone.

4. determine, regulate, direct, govern, manage; lead, guide, control, subject, master, hold; dominate, predominate, wield, command, reign, rule.

5. carry weight, swing one's weight, throw one's weight around; *Inf.* pull rank, *Inf.* pull strings, *Inf.* pull wires.

influential, *adj.* powerful, potent, *Literary.* puissant, strong, forceful, forcible; effective, effectual, efficacious, telling, cogent; moving, arousing, instigating, persuasive; controlling, leading, guiding, directing, ruling; authoritative, dominant, predominant; weighty, carrying a lot of weight, substantial; recognized, significant, important, reputable, prestigious.

influenza, *n.* grippe, flu; Asian flu, Hong Kong flu, Russian flu, A-Victoria flu; chills and fever; *Pathol.* croup; *All Inf.* the bug, the virus, the miseries.

influx, *n.* influent; inflow, inrush, ingress; invasion, intrusion; river mouth, delta, débouché.

inform, *v.* **1.** apprise, advise, notify, let know, tell, relate; impart, acquaint; brief, *Sl.* clue in, *Brit. Sl.* give the gen, *Sl.* background; *Sl.* give the low-down, *Sl.* give the inside dope *or* story, fill [s.o.] in; caution, warn, *Sl.* put [s.o.] wise; announce, proclaim, publish, broadcast, report, communicate; instruct, teach, school, enlighten, illuminate, inculcate; disclose, divulge, let slip, leak, *Sl.* spill the beans, *Sl.* blow the lid off.

2. animate, inspire, fire, kindle, arouse; infuse, imbue, instill.

3. tell tales, *Inf.* snitch, *Inf.* tell on, tell tales out of school, *Inf.* blow the whistle on, turn in; *All Sl.* fink, peach, stool, rat, rat on, squeal, squeak; *All Sl.* put the finger on, finger, name names, sell [s.o.] down the river, sing, weasel.

informal, *adj.* **1.** irregular, unusual, out of the usual, uncustomary, nonconforming, unconventional; unofficial, unorthodox, unsystematic; original, *Latin. sui generis,* unique.

2. casual, natural, unceremonious, cavalier, homespun, down-home, shirtsleeve; unpretentious, simple, familiar, unassuming, unaffected; plain, common, everyday, workaday, humdrum, garden-variety; easygoing, *Dial.* daisyish, bohemian, lackadaisical, offhand, lax.

3. colloquial, vernacular, unliterary, slangy; off-the-cuff, ad-lib, extemporized, improvised, glib, fluent.

informality, *n.* **1.** irregularity, unusualness, eccentricity; unconventionality, unorthodoxy, nonconformism.

2. naturalness, unceremoniousness, simplicity, casualness; casual lifestyle, California lifestyle; bohemianism, *Fr. la vie bohème*; insouciance, carefreeness, relaxedness; laxity, looseness, freedom.

informant, *n.* appriser, adviser, notifier; announcer, reporter, newsmonger, instructor; mouthpiece, spokesman, spokeswoman, public relations man *or* woman, *Sl.* flak, advance man; source, *Inf.* tipster, *Inf.* horse's mouth, *Sl.* Deep Throat.

information, *n.* **1.** data, facts, *Brit. Sl.* gen, knowledge, intelligence; input, *Computer Technol.* readout, briefing, background information, background, dossier; news, tidings, report, communication, communiqué, message, account, recital; notice, tip, advice, pointer, counsel; instruction, enlightenment, wisdom; word, lowdown, *Sl.* info, *Sl.* poop, dirt, dope, inside story, *Sl.* scoop.

2. telling, advising, apprising, notification; teaching, schooling, enlightening.

informer, *n.* **1.** informant, appriser, notifier. See **informant**.

2. tattletale, whistle blower, *Inf.* snitch, *Inf.* snitcher, *All Sl.* fink, rat, ratfink, peacher, stool pigeon, stoolie, canary, nightingale, squealer, weasel.

3. spy, agent, secret agent, undercover agent, double agent, counterspy.

infraction, *n.* breach, violation, break, trespass, overstep; transgression, contravention, malfeasance, misfeasance; misdemeanor, wrongdoing, offense, lawbreaking; infringement, intrusion, encroachment, invasion, poaching, *Archaic.* extravagation.

infrangible, *adj.* **1.** unbreakable, indestructible, shatterproof, chip-proof, bulletproof, unshatterable; indivisible, undividable, indiscerptible, inseparable, impartible; insoluble, indissoluble, indissolvable, infusible; solid, dense, compact, tight, close, cohesive, thick.

2. inviolable, inalienable, inviolate; sacrosanct, sacred, holy, hallowed.

infrequency, *n.* **1.** rarity, rareness, seldomness, unwontedness, infrequence; uncommonness, unusualness, exceptionality; irregularity, intermittence, occasionalness, occasionality, sporadicity.

2. fewness, scarcity, scarceness, scantness, scantiness, meagerness, sparseness.

infrequent, *adj.* **1.** rare, seldom, seldom met, seldom seen, unfrequent, uncustomary; uncommon, unusual, exceptional, unwonted.

2. irregular, occasional, casual, incidental, every now and then, every now and again; sporadic, inconstant, intermittent.

3. few, scarce, spare, scant, sparse, meager; not many, few and far between, hardly any, not plentiful.

infringe, *v.* **1.** break, disobey, violate, infract, breach; flout, fly in the face of, disregard, take no notice of; transgress, overstep, contravene.

2. encroach, move in on, impinge, squat; trespass, poach, invade, intrude, break into, broach, step over the line, trample on.

infringement, *n.* **1.** disobedience, noncompliance, violation, infraction, breach, outrage, transgression, contravention, evasion, lawlessness.

2. encroachment, intrusion, inroad, incursion, infiltration, trespass, ingress, invasion; dispossession, seizure, usurpation, assumption, imposition; irruption, raid, foray, sally, sortie, drive.

infuriate, *v.* **1.** enrage, madden, make [s.o.'s] blood boil, *Inf.* make [s.o.] see red; incense, anger, raise [s.o.'s] ire *or* hackles, get [s.o.'s] back up, *Inf.* get [s.o.'s] Irish *or* dander up, *Inf.* burn up, *Sl.* tee off, *Sl.* tick off; provoke, arouse, rouse, inflame, enflame, agitate, fire up, work up, stir up; vex, pique, irritate, annoy, irk, peeve, nettle, chafe, *Chiefly U.S.* rile, *Inf.* aggravate, *Inf.* miff, *Inf.* give [s.o.] a pain, *Inf.* get under [s.o.'s] skin, *Inf.* get in [s.o.'s] hair, *Sl.* bug; exasperate, ruffle, roil, put out, get, *Sl.* get [s.o's] goat, *Sl.* freak [s.o.] out.

2. embitter, exacerbate, gall, rankle, envenom; affront, insult, offend, sting to the quick.

infuriated, *adj.* furious, enraged, raging, *Rare.* infuriate, fuming, very angry, horn-mad; wrathful, wroth, irate, ireful, incensed, in high dudgeon; inflamed, flaming, flaring, flared up, heated, red-hot, white-hot, hot under the collar; distraught, overwrought, *Inf.* in a dither, *Inf.* in a tizzy; indignant, up in arms, riled; worked up, agitated, stirred up; passionate, impassioned, impassionate, overexcited; upset, feverish, hysterical, not rational; violent, fierce, savage, unrestrained, uncontrollable; ranting, raving, *Scot.* redwood, storming, foaming at the mouth, rabid, fanatical, frenzied; frantic, crazed, mad, *Pathol.* delirious, *Inf.* wild, out of one's mind, beside oneself.

infuse, *v.* **1.** saturate, imbue, permeate, souse, drown, inundate, pervade; immerse, immerge, dip, dunk, submerse, submerge, drench; soak, bathe, steep, tincture, tinge, macerate, fortify, season, flavor, *Inf.* lace.

2. inculcate, instill, infix, implant, ingrain, fill, impregnate, penetrate; teach, train, instruct, enlighten, inform, guide; indoctrinate, beat *or* hammer into, drill, prime, ground; preach, propagandize, insinuate; influence, infect, affect, bias, incline; initiate, inspire, breathe into, inflame, arouse; fire, charge, stir, stimulate, animate.

infusion, *n.* **1.** saturation, permeation, immersion, submersion, submergence; soaking, steeping, infusing, macerating; bath, plunge, dip, soak.

2. coloring, tincture, tinge, shade, stain, flavor.

3. inculcation, instillation, implantation, impregnation, penetration; instruction, introduction, indoctrination; insinuation, infiltration; inoculation, injection, transfusion.

ingathering, *n.* **1.** gathering, garnering, collecting, accumulating, amassing, bringing in, taking in, scraping together.

2. collection, amassment, accumulation, garner; harvest, crop, yield, fruit, produce, production; gleanings, pickings, cleanup, aftermath, windfall, boon; return, profit, dividend, margin; winnings, takings, proceeds, receipts, *Inf.* rake-off, *Inf.* take; gain, recompense, remuneration.

ingenious, *adj.* **1.** clever, witty, shrewd, *Archaic.* parlous, canny, subtle, cunning, sly, wily, crafty, foxy, *Inf.* cute; sagacious, apt, smart; keen, acute, astute, sharp, brilliant, bright.

2. felicitous, adept, proficient, facile; skillful, skilled, dexterous, adroit, deft, handy, neat, *Brit. Dial.* feat; gifted, talented, well-endowed, topflight, top drawer, first-rate, *Inf.* topnotch, ace, *Inf.* crack, *Sl.* crackerjack, *Sl.* on the ball, *Inf.* whiz-bang, *Brit. Sl.* whizzo; expert, masterly, *Fr. au fait*, competent, efficient, good at, capable, able.

3. inventive, resourceful, Daedalian, original, originative, creative, imaginative.

ingenuity, *n.* **1.** cleverness, wittiness, shrewdness, canniness, subtleness, cunning, cunningness, slyness, wiliness, craftiness, foxiness, *Inf.* cuteness; sagaciousness, sagacity, aptness, smartness; keenness, acuteness, sharpness, brilliance, brightness.

2. felicity, adeptness, proficiency, address, facility, readiness; skillfulness, skill, dexterousness, dexterity, sleight, adroitness, deftness, handiness, neatness; gift, giftedness, endowment, genius, talent, faculty; flair, bent, turn, knack, forte, dowry.

3. inventiveness, resourcefulness, ingeniousness; imaginativeness, imagination, creativity, creativeness, originality, inspiration.

4. invention, creation, original, one-of-a-kind, inspiration, design; attainment, accomplishment, feat, trick.

ingenuous, *adj.* **1.** open, open and sincere, openhearted, sincere, genuine, undeceptive, undeceitful, undeceiving, unfeigning, undissembling, undissimulating; aboveboard, open and aboveboard, up front, up and up, on the level, no-nonsense; straight, square, upright, upstanding, just, fair, fair and square, *Inf.* square-dealing, plain-dealing, square-shooting, straight-shooting; honest, trustworthy, *Inf.* trusty, uncorrupt, uncorrupted, *Inf.* o.k. *or* OK.

2. candid, frank, forthright, foursquare, straightforward, straight-from-the-shoulder, direct; plain, plain-spoken, plain-speaking, downright, outright, explicit, unequivocal, unambiguous, undisguised, undisguising, *Inf.* straight-out, *Inf.* flat-footed, *Inf.* matter-of-fact; outspoken, free-spoken, free-speaking, free-tongued, free, unreticent, bold, unreserved, unrestrained, unconstrained, unchecked, unabashed, uninhibited, unsparing, unshrinking; blunt, bluff, brusque, brash, tactless.

3. artless, guileless, naïve, simple, simple-minded, innocent, childlike; unsophisticated, undeveloped, green, born yesterday, wet behind the ears; unsuspicious, trustful, trusting, unwary, unguarded.

ingenuousness, *n.* **1.** openness, openheartedness, sincerity, sincereness, genuineness, undeceptiveness, undeceitfulness; honorableness, justness, fairness, uprightness, straightness, squareness, square dealing, plain dealing, square shooting, straight shooting; honesty, trustworthiness, *Inf.* trustiness, uncorruptedness.

2. candor, candidness, frankness, forthrightness, straightforwardness, calling a spade a spade, *Sl.* telling it like it is; plain-speaking, plain-spokenness, downrightness, outrightness, explicitness, unequivocalness; outspokenness, free-spokenness, free-speaking, freeness, nonreticence, boldness, unreserve, unrestraint, unconstraint, uninhibitedness, unabashedness; bluntness, bluffness, brusqueness, brashness, tactlessness.

3. artlessness, guilelessness, naïveté, naïveness, simpleness, simple-mindedness, innocence, unsophisticatedness, greenness; trustfulness, unsuspiciousness, unwariness, unguardedness.

inglorious, *adj.* **1.** disgraceful, shameful, dishonorable; infamous, ignominious, odious, contemptible, despicable, opprobrious, detestable, sordid, degenerate, depraved, horrible, heinous, vicious, atrocious, flagitious; corrupt, reprehensible, unprincipled, debased, base, vile, evil, sinful, bad, wrong, low, ignoble, nefarious.

2. shocking, scandalous, notorious, arrant, flagrant, outrageous; improper, unseemly, unbecoming, *Obs.* indign, unworthy, undutiful, delinquent, objectionable.

3. disreputable, discreditable, disfavorable; uncommendable, illaudable; censurable, blameworthy, culpable, chargeable, impeachable, imputable; humiliating, mortifying.

ingloriousness, *n.* **1.** dishonor, disgrace, shame, degradation, debasement, vitiation, ill repute; ignominy, infamy, odium, opprobrium.

2. baseness, vileness, meanness, lowness, viciousness, badness; sordidness, ignobility, sinisterness, darkness; malice, maleficence, invidiousness; wickedness, iniquity, nefariousness, flagitiousness, heinousness; sinfulness, ungodliness, profanity, blasphemy; abomination, outrage, enormity, flagrancy, atrocity; criminality, feloniousness, lawlessness; perfidy, treachery, recreancy, traitorousness, disloyalty, treason.

3. offensiveness, objectionableness, obnoxiousness, disagreeableness, repulsiveness, shamefulness, contemptuousness, discreditability; unseemliness, indecorum, indecency, impropriety.

ingot, *n.* bullion, bar, cast, casting.

ingrain, *v.* **1.** fix, infix, implant, introduce, instill, inculcate, insinuate, inject; train, teach, imprint, impress, rivet, indoctrinate; influence, inspire, imbue, imbrue, move.

2. impregnate, permeate, saturate, tincture, infuse, penetrate, soak.

3. furnish, endow, endue, equip; clothe, cloak, attire, invest.

ingrained, *adj.* **1.** fixed, infixed, planted, implanted, rooted, deep-rooted, inveterate; permanent, inseparable, built-in; essential, basic, radical, organic, fundamental, substantial; characteristic, subjective, constitutional, idiosyncratic.

2. indwelling, immanent, inborn, inbred, ingenerate; inherent, intrinsic, indigenous; native, connate, connatural, natural, natural-born; hereditary, inherited, in the blood, in the family; inwrought, enwrought, engrained.

ingrate, *n.* ungrateful *or* thankless wretch, *Fig.* bad investment; self-seeker, opportunist.

ingratiate, *v.* **1.** get on the good *or* right side of, *Inf.* rub the right way, worm *or* work oneself in, *Inf.* get in with, *Inf.* get cozy *or* tight with; gain influence, win friends and influence people.

2. flatter, wheedle, cajole, blandish, *Inf.* soft soap, *Inf.* apple-polish, *Sl.* butter up, *Sl.* brown-nose; puff, puff up, inflate; fawn, toady, toady to, toadeat, truckle, *Sl.* fall all over; court, pay court to, curry favor, dance attendance upon, *Sl.* buddy up to, *Sl.* shine up to, *Sl.* play up to, *Sl.* suck up to; lickspittle, lick [s.o.'s] shoes, lick *or* kiss [s.o.'s] feet, *Sl.* bootlick; agree to anything, *Inf.* be a yes-man to.

ingratiating, *adj.* **1.** charming, winning, winsome, engaging, lovable, sweet; pleasant, cordial, friendly, affable, genial, familiar, agreeable, obliging; courteous, polite, well-mannered, well-bred; chivalrous, gallant, genteel; gracious, suave, urbane, smooth.

2. sycophantic, toadyish, toadeating, flattering, fawning, wheedling, cajoling, timeserving, *Sl.* bootlicking, *Sl.* brown-nosing, *Obs., Rare.* blandiloquous; buttery, candied, unctuous, oily, honey-mouthed, smooth-talking, smooth-tongued, sweet-talking, *Rare.* blandiloquent.

ingratitude, *n.* unthankfulness, thanklessness, ungratefulness, benefits forgot; nonacknowledgment, nonrecognition; grudging *or* halfhearted thanks.

ingredient, *n.* element, component, constituent, member, part, unit; factor, leaven, agent; feature, item; *Inf.* makings, *Inf.* fixings, contents.

ingress, *n.* **1.** entrance, entry, entryway, entrée, inlet; approach, drive, driveway, lane, adit; path, pathway, route, road, roadway, course, way, means; street, avenue, boulevard, highway; opening, aperture, hatch, door, doorway, gate, gateway, postern, portal; threshold, stile, turnstile, wicket; hall, hallway, passage, passageway, walkway, arcade, gangway, corridor, gallery, lobby, foyer, vestibule, anteroom, waiting room; anteporch, porch, portico.

2. access, admission, admittance, permission to enter, right of entry.

3. coming in, going in, entering, inflow, influx; invasion, incursion, inroad, irruption; break-in, intrusion, trespassing, infiltration, penetration.

inhabit, *v.* **1.** live, live at, abide, *Archaic.* bide, reside, dwell, tenant, stay, stay at, sojourn, remain; domicile, domiciliate, establish oneself, take up residence, take up one's abode, occupy, settle, settle down, locate, ensconce, make one's home, *Inf.* hang up one's hat; take *or* strike root, plant oneself, anchor, drop anchor, come to anchor, moor; nest, nestle, perch, roost, squat, burrow, hive; lodge, rent, room, bunk, berth, quarter *or* billet at, put up at, *Inf.* hang out, *Sl.* crash, *Brit. Sl.* doss down; camp, camp out, bivouac, pitch one's tent.

2. colonize, people, populate, denizen, settle, settle in.

3. indwell, dwell in, rest in, lie in, lie within, exist in, exist within, abide in, be present in, consist in, subsist in, repose in, be comprised in, be contained in.

inhabitant, *n.* **1.** resident, resider, residencer, residentiary, permanent resident, habitant, dweller, occupant, occupier, denizen, householder, addressee, *Archaic.* inhabiter, habitant; indweller, incumbent, inmate; tenant, lodger, boarder, roomer, paying guest, *Sl.* crasher; renter, lessee, leaseholder.

2. settler, homesteader, colonist, squatter, cottager, cottier, *Scot.* cotter *or* cottar; villager, townsman, burgher, burgess, oppidan.

3. native, aborigine, aboriginal, autochthon, indigene.

inhalation, *n.* **1.** breathing, inspiration, insufflation, inhalement; taking in, sucking in, suction, aspiration; sniff, sniffle, snuffle; gasp, gulp.

2. puff, *Inf.* drag, *Sl.* toke, (*of drug use*) *Sl.* hit, (*of drug use*) *Sl.* toot, (*of drug use*) *Sl.* snort.

inhale, *v.* **1.** breathe in, draw in, suck in, inspire, inbreathe; sniff, snuff, sniffle, snuffle; gasp, gulp.

2. take in, puff, *Inf.* drag, *Sl.* toke, (*of drug use*) *Sl.* take *or* have a toot, (*of drug use*) *Sl.* snort, (*of drug use*) *Sl.* take a hit.

inharmonious, *adj.* **1.** discordant, cacophonous, dissonant, absonant, inharmonic, unharmonious; unmelodious, unmusical, tuneless, atonal; out of tune, out of step, out of key, off beat, off key, off pitch, flat; harsh, jarring, jangling, raucous, strident.

2. disagreeable, uncongenial, incompatible, irreconcilable, negative; disputatious, quarrelsome, dissentient, factious, clashing, litigious; conflicting, contradictory, controversial, antagonistic, antipathetic.

inharmoniousness, *n.* **1.** discordance, dissonance, cacophony, disharmony, absonance, discord; unmelodiousness, unmusicality, tunelessness, atonality; cat's concert, Dutch concert, caterwauling, racket; jangling, raucousness, harshness, marrowbones and cleavers.

2. disagreeability, disagreeableness, discordancy, uncongeniality, incompatibility, irreconcilability; disagreement, argumentation, dissidence, variance, discaccord, disunion, divergence; clash, antagonism, opposition, conflict, faction, controversy.

inhere, *v.* **1.** belong intrinsically, be inherent, be immanent, be part of; belong, stay, reside; fill, inhabit, occupy; abide, live, dwell.

2. form, constitute, make, make up, compose, *Inf.* comprise; pertain, relate, connect, correspond.

inherent, *adj.* **1.** inborn, inbred, innate, ingenerate; immanent, indwelling, inherent, indigenous, intrinsic; permanent, inseparable, built-in.

2. native, natural, natural-born; congenital, hereditary, inherited, in the blood, in the family; ingrained, engrained, inwrought, enwrought, *Obs.* inhering, *Obs.* infixed.

3. characteristic, subjective, constitutional, idiosyncratic.

4. essential, basic, rooted, deep-rooted, radical, organic, fundamental, substantial.

inherit, *v.* **1.** come into, fall *or* become heir to, *Inf.* come by; acquire, get, receive, come in for; be willed, be left, be bequeathed, be transferred, *Law.* be devised; be passed on *or* down to, be turned *or* given over to, devolve on.

2. (*usu. of an office, title or position*) accede to, succeed to, enter upon; assume, take on *or* over, accept; attain, arrive at, reach; come to, rise to, be promoted to, be elevated to, graduate to.

inheritance, *n.* **1.** legacy, bequest, endowment, heirdom, heirship, *Archaic.* heritance, gift, donation; dot, dowry, *Law.* dower, *Law.* jointure; estate, patrimony, *Law.* hereditament, property, possessions; portion, share, birthright, lot.

2. (*usu. of an office, title or position*) accession, succession, assumption, taking on *or* over; entering upon, arrival at, advent to; elevation, promotion, rise, coming to, reaching, attainment; induction, installation, initiation, inauguration, investiture.

3. heritage, portion, share, birthright, lot; lineage, descent, birth, extraction, derivation, filiation; background, past, history, ancestry, ancestral line, dynasty, family; heredity, bloodline, pedigree, strain, stock, race.

inheritor, *n.* **1.** heir, heritor, heir apparent, heir at law, heiress, heritress, inheritrix; coheir, coheiress, joint heir, *Law.* parcener; successor, *Inf.* next in line, follower; beneficiary, recipient, receiver, devisee, legatee, *Law.* reversioner; *Both Law.* executor, donee.

2. descendant, scion, offspring; children, progeny, brood, spawn, issue, seed, posterity, future generations.

inhibit, *v.* **1.** restrain, repress, suppress, hold back; curb, constrain, rein in, harness, bridle, hold in leash; control, coerce, compel, govern, restrict, *Inf.* cramp one's style; impede, hinder; interfere; muzzle, smother, gag; check, arrest, abort, stop; prevent, obstruct, bar.

2. forbid, prohibit, interdict; veto, ban, proscribe, taboo, disallow.

inhibition, *n.* **1.** restraint, repression, restriction, stricture; curb, constraint, coercion, control; check, arrest, stop, preclusion; obstruction, impediment, hindrance, oppilation, blockage; encumbrance, handicap; interference, intervention, interposition, obtrusion.

2. *Psychol.* mental block, *Sl.* hang-up.

3. prohibition, forbiddance, interdiction; veto, ban, taboo, embargo; proscription, disallowance.

inhospitable, *adj.* **1.** unfriendly, cool, cold, aloof, unsocial, unsociable; reclusive, antisocial, antisocialistic, hostile, inimical; ill-disposed, unsympathetic, unsympathizing, unreceptive, closed, closed-minded, narrow, narrow-minded, intolerant; unpleasant, disagreeable, rude, incivil, uncivil, impolite, discourteous, ill-mannered; ungracious, uncongenial, unamicable, unamiable; unneighborly, unkind, unkindly, inconsiderate, unaccommodating, unobliging.

2. (*all of a region, climate, etc.*) unfavorable, uninviting, barren, bare, empty; forlorn, desolate, solitary, isolated, lonely, deserted, uninhabited, uninhabitable, wild; desert, dry, arid, droughty; poor, infertile, infecund, unfruitful, sterile.

inhospitality, *n.* inhospitableness, unfriendliness, coolness, coldness, aloofness, unsocialism, unsociability, unsociableness, antisociality; hostility, inimicalness, inimicality; ill-disposedness, unreceptiveness, close-mindedness, narrow-mindedness, intolerance; unpleasantness, disagreeableness, rudeness, incivility, uncivility, uncivilness, impoliteness, discourtesy, discourteousness, ill-manneredness; ungraciousness, uncongeniality, unamicability, unamicableness, unamiableness, unneighborliness, unkindness, unkindliness, inconsideration, inconsiderateness.

inhuman, *adj.* **1.** pitiless, merciless, heartless, unkind, inhumane; unfeeling, uncompassionate, unsympathetic; cruel, hard-hearted, stony-hearted, marblehearted, cold-blooded; cold, callous, insensitive, hardened, obdurate.

2. barbarous, barbaric, savage, hellish, Tartarian, Hunnish, Vandalic; brutal, brutish, murderous, slaughterous, bloodthirsty; sadistic, bestial, animalistic, cannibalistic, fiendish, ghoulish, ogreish; diabolical, satanic, demonic, demoniac, devilish; terrible, harsh, grim, hard, severe; ferocious, ruthless, vicious, fell, truculent; wolfish, lupine, fierce, feral, ferine; tyrannical, Draconian, inquisitorial, oppressive; unrelenting, relentless, remorseless, implacable, inexorable, grinding; rancorous, venomous, envenomed, malicious, malignant, maleficent, malign, malefic.

3. nonhuman, androidal, robotlike, automatous, machinelike.

inhumanity, *n.* cruelty, cruelness, brutality, brutishness; barbarity, barbarousness, ferocity, fierceness, savagery, savageness, truculence; atrocity, murderousness, bloodthirstiness, cold-bloodedness; viciousness, malice, maliciousness, malevolence, ill will, unkindness, spite, malignity, venom; acrimony, bitterness, sharpness, harshness, severity, severeness, grimness; ruthlessness, hard-heartedness, pitilessness, mercilessness, heartlessness; relentlessness, remorselessness, implacability, inexorability; sadism, masochism; fiendishness, deviltry, diablery.

inhume, *v.* bury, inter, *Archaic.* inearth, inurn, entomb, ensepulcher, sepulcher; lay away, *Inf.* lay to rest, *Sl.* put six feet under, consign to the grave, *Dial.* funeralize.

inimical, *adj.* **1.** harmful, dangerous, detrimental, deleterious, pernicious; injurious, hurtful, damaging, baneful; ruinous, destructive, extirpative; noxious, unhealthy, unwholesome, poisonous, venomous, septic, toxic, virulent.

2. hostile, antagonistic, opposed, adverse, averse, contrary; unfriendly, unkind, unsympathetic, inhospitable, cold, unsociable; malicious, mean, ugly, malevolent; aggressive, belligerent, bellicose.

inimitable, *adj.* faultless, perfect, consummate, ideal; superlative, preeminent, crack, prime, very best; incomparable, model, unexampled, unmatched, admirable, recherché, *Archaic.* eximious. See **incomparable.**

iniquitous, *adj.* **1.** wicked, sinful, evil, *Archaic.* facinorous, *Obs.* scelerate, *Obs.* scelerous; nefarious, villainous, flagitious, heinous, infamous, notorious, *Rare.* nefast; black-hearted, sinister, perverse, arrant, ignoble; bad, base, vile, foul, low, mean, odious, obnoxious; abominable, execrable, horrible, atrocious, grievous; damnable, damnatory, accursed, cursed; malevolent, maleficent, malefic, ill-intentioned, evil-minded; unholy, unrighteous, unblest.

2. criminal, wrong, reprehensible, felonious, lawless; unfair, unjust, inequitable; unscrupulous, unprincipled, crooked, dishonorable; blackguardly, knavish, scoundrelly, thievish; unregenerate, unrepentant, impenitent, obdurate, incorrigible; degenerate, corrupt, turpitudinous; depraved; immoral, dissolute, profligate, reprobate, abandoned, dissipated; opprobrious, disgraceful, shameful; scandalous, shocking, flagrant, outrageous.

iniquity, *n.* **1.** wickedness, evil, vice, improbity, sin, sinfulness, deviltry, ungodliness, godlessness; nefariousness, flagitiousness, heinousness; vileness, viciousness, badness, baseness, foulness, meanness; atrocity, outrage, abomination, crime, malefaction, wrongdoing, feloniousness, lawlessness; perfidy, treachery, foul play; villainy, knavery, rascality, delinquency.

2. inequity, unfairness, unjustness, partiality, bias, prejudice, closed-mindedness, narrow-mindedness, intolerance, bigotry; wrongfulness, unlawfulness, illegality.

3. crime, offense, transgression, violation, injury, *Law.* malfeasance, malefaction; atrocity, monstrosity, horror, outrage.

initial, *adj.* **1.** first, prime, primary, original, aboriginal, autochthonous; incipient, inchoate, incunabular, beginning, commencing, opening; nascent, natal, infant, infantile; inaugural, introductory, initiating, initiative; elementary, fundamental, rudimentary, foundational; creative, formative, drawing-board.

—v. **2.** sign, undersign, put one's mark *or* cross on, *Inf.* put one's John Hancock on; letter, inscribe, en-

grave, mark, *Archaic.* character.

—n. **3.** **initials** monogram; mark, mark of signature, cross, christcross, crisscross, X.

initiate, *v.* **1.** begin, commence, start, start off, start the ball rolling, *Inf.* kick off, set off, trigger, actuate, instigate, set in motion, ring up the curtain on; open, pioneer, take the first step, take the initiative, take the lead, take the plunge, make a start, break the ice, lead off, lead the way, blaze the trail; institute, inaugurate, found, establish, set up, organize, originate, break ground, lay the first stone, lay the foundation; introduce, launch, broach, usher in; create, beget, engender, father, conceive, give birth to, give rise to, sow the seeds of.

2. teach, instruct, tutor, coach, break in, prime, familiarize with; train, drill, exercise, practice; prepare, ready; indoctrinate, inculcate, infuse, imbue, instill, implant, infix, drum in, hammer *or* pound in.

3. induct, install, instate, invest, ordain; enlist, enroll, sign up, sign on.

—n. **4.** beginner, novice, novitiate, neophyte, tyro, amateur, rookie, greenhorn, tenderfoot, newcomer, new boy, pledge; student, pupil, learner, apprentice, trainee, fledgling, freshman, *Inf.* frosh *or* freshie; recruit, raw recruit, abecedarian, catechumen.

5. member, member in good standing, card-carrying member, card-carrier; associate, fellow, one of us, insider, epopt; enrollee, enlistee.

initiation, *n.* **1.** admission, admittance, acceptance, reception; enlistment, enrollment, induction; installation, inauguration, instatement, introduction; ordination, investiture; baptism.

2. ceremony, function, celebration, ritual, rite, rite of passage; service, observance, formality, solemnity; commencement, graduation.

3. actuation, instigation, creation, inception, beginning; institution, establishment, origination, organization, foundation; instruction, indoctrination, inculcation, implantation, imbuement, infixion, infusion.

4. debut, first *or* opening appearance, premiere, *Inf.* coming out.

initiative, *n.* **1.** first step, first *or* opening move, first blow; beginning, commencement, onset, outset, *Inf.* kick-off, *Inf.* jump-off, *Inf.* send-off, *Inf.* take-off, *Inf.* blast-off; new *or* fresh start, new departure.

2. enterprise, ambition, ambitiousness, hustle, aggressiveness; energy, vim, verve, fire, dash, drive, spunk, *Inf.* punch, *Inf.* snap, *Inf.* pep, *Inf.* pizzazz, *Inf.* zip, *Inf.* zing, *Inf.* get up and go.

initiatory, *adj.* initial, introductory, initiating, initiative, inaugural; elementary, fundamental, foundational, rudimentary; creative, formative, drawing-board; incipient, inchoate, incunabular, beginning, commencing, starting, opening.

inject, *v.* **1.** introduce, intromit, insinuate, insert, interject; intrude, force in, ram in, thrust in, stick in, drive in, foist in, work in, worm in, squeeze in, edge in, drag in, lug in.

2. instill, infix, implant, inspire, fire the imagination; infuse, imbue, impregnate, steep.

3. (*all of drug use*) *All Sl.* shoot, shoot up, crank, fix, mainline, pop, skin-pop.

injection, *n.* **1.** introduction, insertion, interjection, insinuation, intromission; intrusion; instillment, infixion, implantation; infusion, imbuement, impregnation; (*all of drug use*) *All Sl.* mainlining, shooting-up, cranking, fixing, popping *or* skin-popping.

2. dose, overdose, *Sl.* fix, *Sl.* hit, *Sl.* bang; shot, booster, inoculation, vaccine, vaccination.

3. cathartic, purgative; enema, *Med.* lavement, *Med.* lavage.

injudicious, *adj.* **1.** ill-judged, unwise, unsage, unsagacious; imprudent, ill-considered, inconsiderate, thoughtless; unreasonable, irrational, senseless, nonsensical, wrong-headed, foolish, silly, harebrained, stupid, *Inf.* dumb.

2. ill-advised, inadvisable, unadvised, unadvisable, unrecommendable, unrecommended, miscounseled, misguided; impolitic, unshrewd, inexpedient, unprofitable, unfavorable; undesirable, inappropriate, unsuitable, ill-suited, wrong.

injunction, *n.* requirement, requisition, exaction, demand, imposition; command, commandment, order, dictate, dictation, dictum, instruction, direction, directive, behest, *Archaic.* hest, imperative, ultimatum; precept, prescript, prescription, will, enjoinment, ordainment; admonition, charge, exhortation.

injure, *v.* **1.** damage, impair, hurt, harm, wound; ruin, spoil, scotch, break; mar, disfigure, deface; sully, stain, blemish, smirch, besmirch; maim, cripple, lame; deform, mangle, mutilate; weaken, enervate, enfeeble, wear down, waste.

2. maltreat, mistreat, ill-treat, misuse, abuse, wrong, molest, violate, *Sl.* kick around; outrage, offend, affront, insult, slight; pervert, deprave, demoralize, degenerate, debauch; oppress, persecute, harass, harry, hound; malign, vilify, denigrate, vituperate, blacken, traduce; libel, calumniate, slander, do [s.o.] dirt.

injured, *adj.* **1.** damaged, impaired, hurt, harmed, wounded; ruined, spoiled, scotched, broken; marred, disfigured, defaced; sullied, stained, smirched, besmirched, blemished; maimed, crippled, lamed; deformed, mangled, mutilated; weakened, enervated, enfeebled, worn down, wasted.

2. wronged, offended, abused, misused, mistreated, maltreated, ill-treated, molested, violated, *Sl.* kicked around; pained, grieved, aggrieved, cut, cut to the quick, stung; maligned, vilified, vituperated, denigrated, traduced, blackened; libeled, calumniated, slandered.

3. reproachful, condemnatory, censorious, denunciatory; disapproving, disapprobatory, displeased, dissatisfied, disgruntled, unhappy.

injurious, *adj.* **1.** harmful, hurtful, pernicious, baneful, deleterious, damaging; disadvantageous, detrimental, unfavorable; fell, dire, ruinous, destructive, disastrous, calamitous; vicious, malignant, malign, malevolent, maleficent; corruptive, corrupting, corrosive, corroding; virulent, noxious, noisome; unhealthful, unhealthy, insalubrious, unwholesome, unsalutary, peccant, bad for.

2. wrongful, prejudicial, unjust, unfair, inequitable, partial, partisan, interested, undispassionate; unbalanced, unequal, uneven, one-sided; biased, warped, influenced, swayed.

3. abusive, harsh, scurrilous, withering, caustic; contemptuous, insulting, offensive, sarcastic, cutting; derogatory, deprecatory, detractory, disparaging, belittling; defamatory, denigrating, vituperative, vilipenditory, scandalous; slanderous, libelous, calumnious, calumniatory, false, misrepresentative; imputative, aspersive, insinuating.

injury, *n.* **1.** hurt, harm, damage, impairment, detriment, loss; mischief, trouble, disadvantage, prejudice; misfortune, adversity, affliction, bane; ruin, ruination, havoc, destruction, perdition; defacement, disfigurement, deformation, mutilation.

2. wound, lesion, trauma, sore, *Sl.* boo-boo; cut, gash, laceration; abrasion, scrape, scuff; puncture, stab, stab wound; bruise, contusion, black-and-blue mark; black eye, *Sl.* shiner, *Sl.* mouse.

3. injustice, grievance, disservice, *Sl.* raw deal, *Sl.* bum rap; abuse, maltreatment, ill treatment, ill usage, ill handling; wrong, violation, offense, evil, ill, iniquity, foul play; misdeed, misdemeanor, misfeasance, malfeasance, malefaction, *Law.* tort; outrage, enormity, atrocity, scandal; insult, affront, indignity, humiliation, slap in the face, aspersion, imputation, *Sl.* put-down; slander, libel, calumny, misrepresentation, lie, falsehood.

injustice, *n.* **1.** inequitableness, unfairness, unjustness, unrighteousness, obliquity; inequality, disparity, unevenness; discrimination, favoritism, partiality, leaning, prepossession, one-sidedness, bias, prejudice, bigotry.
2. inequity, unfairness, unfair *or* unjust treatment; mistreatment, maltreatment, abuse, hurt, injury; grievance, imposition, infringement *or* encroachment on one's rights; oppression, persecution, tyranny; wrong, offense, violence, crime; wrongdoing, foul play, dirty trick, villainy, *Law.* tort; iniquity, evil, sin, transgression.

inkling, *n.* **1.** hint, clue, whisper; intimation, insinuation, innuendo; suggestion, inference, implication.
2. suspicion, idea, notion, vague idea *or* notion, some insight into *or* understanding of, glimmering, soupçon, trace, whiff, glimpse.

inkwell, *n.* inkhorn, inkstand, *Brit.* inkpot; ink bottle *or* jar, container of ink.

inky, *adj.* **1.** black, pitch-black, pitchy, coal-black; ebony, ebon, raven, sable; jet, jetty, nigritudinous, atramentous; dark, swarthy, swart, nigrescent.
2. inked, ink-stained, blackened, sooty, smoky, charcoaly, fuliginous; stained, dirty, dingy, soiled, sullied, grimy, begrimed; smudgy, smudged, smirched, besmirched.

inlaid, *adj.* veneered, enameled, tessellated, mosaic, checkered, enchased; ornamented; set, studded, worked; laid, tiled, lined.

inland, *adj.* **1.** interior, internal, upcountry, upriver, inshore, backwoods.
—n. **2.** inlands, upcountry, upriver, backwoods; midland, midlands, hinterland, heartland.

inlay, *v.* line, interlard, set in, work in; inset, insert, encase, enchase, implant, bed in; tile, tessellate, damascene, checker, parquet.

inlet, *n.* **1.** cove, nook, bay, fjord, arm, armlet, arm of the sea, bight; firth, frith, bayou, *Scot.* loch, *Brit.* creek, reach; strait, channel, narrow, narrows, sound, *Scot.* kyle.
2. entry, entrance, ingress, intake, access, opening; path, door, doorway, way, entranceway, vestibule, portal.

inmate, *n.* **1.** patient, valetudinary, bedlamite; case, subject.
2. prisoner, captive, convict, *U.S. Sl.* jailbird, *Brit. Sl.* gaolbird, *Sl.* con, *Sl.* bird.

inmost, *adj.* innermost, innate, intrinsic; basic, intuitive. See **innermost** (*defs.* **1-7**).

inn, *n.* **1.** lodging, hotel, motel, *Fr. auberge*, hostelry, hostel, hospice; tourist court, motor court, rooming house, pension, boardinghouse, guest house; caravansary, khan, serai; resthouse, *Sl.* flophouse, bunkhouse, *Brit. Sl.* doss-house, *Brit. Sl.* kip, *Brit.* ordinary.
2. cafe, tavern, bar, saloon, alehouse, *Inf.* pub, *Brit. Inf.* local, *Brit.* public house; cabaret, bistro, roadhouse, gin mill, grog shop, dram shop, toddy shop, honky-tonk; barroom, *Chiefly Brit.* taproom, speakeasy, beerhall, *Scot.*, *Irish Eng.* shebeen.

innate, *adj.* **1.** inborn, inbred, native, natural, natural-born, ingenerate; congenital, hereditary, inherited, in the blood, in the family; intrinsic, inherent, indigenous, indwelling, immanent; ingrained, engrained, inwrought, enwrought.
2. inmost, farthest inward, innermost, *Scot.*, *Irish.* benmost, deep within.
3. essential, quintessential, basic, organic, radical, constitutional, fundamental.
4. instinctive, intuitive, impulsive, involuntary, spontaneous; visceral, intestinal, *Sl.* gut.

inner, *adj.* **1.** inside, within, interior; inward, internal; inmost, innermost, *Scot.*, *Irish.* benmost.
2. private, privy, nonpublic, intimate, personal, confidential; restricted, reserved, privileged; secret, veiled, hidden, occult, esoteric.
3. mental, spiritual, psychic, psychological; nonphysical, metaphysical.

innermost, *adj.* **1.** inmost, farthest inward, *Scot.*, *Irish.* benmost, deep within.
2. innate, intrinsic, inherent, indigenous, indwelling, immanent; ingrained, engrained, inwrought, enwrought.
3. essential, basic, radical, organic, constitutional, fundamental; pithy, substantial, meaty, quintessential.
4. private, privy, personal, intimate, confidential; restricted, reserved, privileged; esoteric, secret, occult, veiled, hidden, enclosed, obscure.
5. instinctive, intuitive, impulsive, involuntary, spontaneous; visceral, intestinal, *Sl.* gut.
6. intense, heartfelt, moving, stirring, overpowering.
7. profound, deep, detailed, penetrating.
—n. **8.** inmost part, interior part, *Both pl.* recesses, penetralia.
9. center, middle, nucleus; gist, heart, core, marrow, pith.
10. depths, hold, womb, bowels, belly; abyss, chasm, cavity, gulf.

innkeeper, *n.* hotelkeeper, hotelman, hosteler, *Fr. aubergiste*, innholder, *Brit.* victualer; keeper, boniface, landlord, host.

innocence, *n.* **1.** sinlessness, virtue, virtuousness, decency, probity; immaculateness, faultlessness, flawlessness, impeccability; stainlessness, spotlessness, cleanness; chastity, purity, incorruption, incorruptibility, righteousness, uprightness; virginality, virginity, modesty.
2. guiltlessness, blamelessness, inculpability; clean hands, clear conscience, clear mind; unimpeachability, irreproachability, irreprehensibility.
3. simplicity, ingenuousness, artlessness, guilelessness; inexperience, greenness, unworldliness; unsophistication, unaffectedness, unartificiality, naturalness; sincerity, honesty, candor, openness, frankness; naïveté, unsuspicion, trustingness, trustfulness.
4. harmlessness, innocuousness, playfulness, safeness; uninjuriousness, inoffensiveness, hurtlessness, unhurtfulness, innoxiousness, unobjectionableness.

innocent, *adj.* **1.** pure, sinless, virtuous, unfallen; immaculate, faultless, flawless, spotless, impeccable, clean; unstained, undefiled, unblemished, unsullied; chaste, virginal, vestal, moral, decent; righteous, upright, sterling.
2. guiltless, blameless, clear, inculpable; above suspicion, clean-handed; irreproachable, unblameworthy, unimpeachable, irreprehensible.
3. harmless, innocuous, safe, playful; uninjurious, unhurtful, innoxious, hurtless, unobjectionable, inoffensive.
4. simple, ingenuous, childlike, natural, unaffected, unartificial; unsophisticated, artless, guileless, undesigning; candid, open, frank, sincere, honest; naive, unsuspicious, confiding, trusting, trustful, credu-

lous; inexperienced, unworldly, unhardened, shockable, green, wet behind the ears.

—*n.* **5.** ingenue, child, babe, infant, babe in the woods; lamb, dove, calf, pup, cub; greenhorn, beginner, novice.

innocuous, *adj.* **1.** harmless, innocent, uncorrupting, unhurtful, hurtless, safe, uninjurious; mild, moderate, soft, gentle, dovelike; domesticated, tame. See **harmless.**

2. inoffensive, unobnoxious, unobjectionable, above suspicion; unblameworthy, irreprehensible, irreproachable.

3. dull, uninspiring, uninteresting, dry, dry-as-dust; bland, insipid, jejune, flat, vapid; monotonous, humdrum, run-of-the-mill, commonplace, *Sl.* blah.

innovate, *v.* *Often* **innovate on** *or* **in** make changes, introduce new blood, modernize, revolutionize; change, alter, transform, metamorphose; remodel, recast, restyle, renovate; coin, neologize, neoterize.

innovation, *n.* novelty, new measure, *Rare.* novation, modernism, *Inf.* wrinkle, new wrinkle; change, alteration, transformation, metamorphosis; modernization, renovation, remodeling, recasting, restyling; coining, neoterism, neology, neologism.

innuendo, *n.* insinuation, intimation, implication, allusion, suggestion, hint, inkling, cue; imputation, reflection, stricture, left-handed compliment, animadversion, criticism, aspersion.

innumerable, *adj.* many, very many, myriad, untold, *Inf.* umpteen, *Sl.* skaty-eight, *Sl.* forty-'leven, *Inf.* more than one could shake a stick at, more than one can count; numberless, unnumbered, countless, infinite, incomputable, incalculable.

inoculate, *v.* **1.** immunize, give [s.o.] his shots, *Med.* vaccinate; protect, shield, safeguard.

2. indoctrinate, teach, instruct, train; (*of ideas*) instill, infix, implant, inculcate, ingrain, infuse, imbue, impregnate.

inoculation, *n.* **1.** immunization, *Med.* vaccination, injection, shot; protection, shield, safeguard.

2. indoctrination, teaching, instruction, training; (*of ideas*) inculcation, implanting, instilling, infixing, ingraining, infusion, imbuement, impregnation.

inoffensive, *adj.* harmless, innocuous, innocent; unoffending, nonprovocative, quiet, unobjectionable. See **innocuous** (*defs.* **1, 2**).

inoperative, *adj.* **1.** not operative, not in operation, not in effect, not in force.

2. ineffectual, ineffective, inefficacious, inadequate, inefficient; useless, inutile, worthless, valueless, meritless, nugatory.

3. futile, unavailing, bootless, fruitless, unproductive, abortive, barren, sterile, fallow, unprolific, infecund; unprofitable, profitless, unremunerative, unpaying, unrewarding, gainless; unsuccessful, to no purpose, to no avail, for naught.

4. unserviceable, collapsed, shattered, given way, broken, not functioning, out of order, out of commission; *Inf.* on the blink, *Inf.* on the fritz, *Inf.* out of kilter, *Sl.* out of whack, *Sl.* gone kerflooie, *Sl.* kaput, *Sl.* on the bum.

5. legally ineffectual, legally unenforceable, not binding, nonviable; invalid, null, void, null and void, annulled, nullified; set aside, quashed, vitiated, vacated, disestablished; canceled, discharged; repealed, revoked, rescinded, abolished, reversed, abrogated; renounced, repudiated, disclaimed, disavowed.

inopportune, *adj.* **1.** inconvenient, ill-timed, untimely, badly timed, unseasonable, coming at the wrong time and wrong place; unsuited, unsuitable, unfit, inappropriate, inapt, infelicitous, unseemly, out-of-place, malapropos, *Inf.* off-key, out-of-bounds, out-of-line, out-of-order.

2. ill-advised, inadvisable, disadvantageous, inexpedient; impolitic, imprudent, indiscreet, tactless, injudicious.

3. inauspicious, unfavorable, untoward, unpropitious; unlucky, ill-starred, unfortunate.

inordinate, *adj.* **1.** excessive, immoderate, extravagant, beyond all bounds; unrestrained, unlimited, intemperate; unreasonable, disproportionate, undue, uncalled-for, unwarranted, unneeded, needless, unnecessary; exorbitant, extreme, too much, unconscionable, outrageous, preposterous; superabundant, overabundant, copious, profuse, plethoric, overfull; adscititious, supplemental, additional; redundant, superfluous, oversufficient, *Inf.* too much, *Inf.* a bit much.

2. irregular, erratic, fitful, variable, unregulated; unconventional, anomalous, unusual, abnormal, aberrant.

inorganic, *adj.* **1.** inanimate, lifeless; *Farming.* chemical, man-made, artificial, hydroponic.

2. extraneous, adventitious, extrinsic; unessential, nonessential, irrelevant, alien, foreign.

inquietude, *n.* restlessness, unrest, restiveness, uneasiness, skittishness; jumpiness, nervousness, jitters, fidgets, *Sl.* antsiness, formication, edginess, irritation; impatience, dissatisfaction, anxiety, apprehension; discontent, discomposure, disquiet, disquietude, troubled soul, troubled heart; discomfort, malaise, anxiety, angst.

inquire, *v.* **1.** ask, question, query, quiz; examine, interrogate, *Inf.* grill, cross-examine, catechize.

2. study, scrutinize, scan, inspect; examine, sound, fathom; search, seek out, probe, dig out, dig, delve, unearth; research, investigate, look into, explore; track down, ferret out, *Inf.* nose out; reconnoiter, scout, spy out; test, analyze, assay.

inquiring, *adj.* asking, questioning, querying, quizzing, interrogating; scrutinizing, exploring, investigating; digging, probing, delving, unearthing; wondering, musing, pondering; skeptical, doubting. See **inquisitive** (*def.* **1**).

inquiry, *n.* **1.** investigation, inquest, exploration, probe; search, quest, research, pursuit; scrutiny, study, examination, audit, test; review, survey, inspection, analysis, autopsy.

2. interrogation, query, question; questioning, cross-examination, catechizing, inquisition.

inquisition, *n.* **1.** inquiry, inquest, assize, hearing, trial.

2. interrogation, third degree, grilling, *Sl.* rubber hose, *Sl.* beating it out.

3. investigation, examination, research. See **inquiry** (*defs.* **1, 2**).

inquisitive, *adj.* **1.** inquiring, questioning, probing, investigative; curious, eager, eager for knowledge, interested, burning with curiosity, dying to know.

2. prying, snoopy, *Inf.* nosy, meddlesome; intrusive, impertinent, persistent; spying, peeping, eavesdropping.

—*n.* **3.** questioner, interrogator, researcher; meddler, *Inf.* Nosy Parker, busybody, Paul Pry; snoop, spy.

inroad, *n.* encroachment, trespassing, *Chiefly Brit.* poaching, infringement, infiltration, interpenetration; forced entry, break-in; invasion, intrusion, irruption, incursion; raid, foray, predation, plunder, pillage; aggression, attack, assault, onset, onslaught; drive, charge, offensive, rush, sally, sortie.

insalubrious, *adj.* unsalubrious, unhealthy, unhealthful, bad for one's health; foul, dirty, unclean, not fit to eat *or* drink, unsanitary, insanitary, unhygienic, unsanitized; unwholesome, jejune, innutritious, unnutritious, unnutritive, nonnutritious, nonnutritive; harmful, hurtful, detrimental, damaging, injurious, noxious, deleterious, noisome, destructive; pestilential, pestilent, pestiferous, mephitic, infectious, septic; toxic, poisonous, virulent, venomous, envenomed; deadly, fatal, lethal, pernicious.

ins and outs, *n.* **1.** physical features, windings, turns, twists, bends, curves; nooks, crannies, recesses, corners.

2. intricacies, tricks of the trade, loopholes, rules of the game, one's way around; patterns, ways, habits, customs; features, characteristics, traits, particularities, peculiarities, idiosyncrasies; particulars, details, specifics.

insane, *adj.* **1.** crazy, crazed, mad, demented, lunatic, deranged; of unsound mind, *Latin. non compos mentis*; psychotic, schizophrenic, *Sl.* schizo; daft, *Inf.* daffy, unbalanced, touched, *Inf.* unglued, *Inf.* half-baked, *Brit. Sl.* bonkers, unhinged, distracted; eccentric, flighty, odd, idiosyncratic, offbeat, queer, bizarre, *Chiefly Brit. Inf.* potty, *Inf.* dotty, *Inf.* crackpot; brainsick, *Sl.* kooky, *Sl.* meshuga; *All Sl.* balmy, dippy, batty, bats, cuckoo, buggy, bughouse, bugs, screwy, wacky, wacko, goofy, loony, squirrelly, bananas, nuts, nutty, nutty as a fruitcake, Section Eight.

2. out of one's head, out of one's mind, *Scot.* redwood, *Sl.* loco, mad as a hatter, mad as a March hare, far-gone, stark raving mad; not all there, not quite right, not right upstairs; *Inf.* out in left field, *Sl.* in outer space, *Sl.* in orbit, *Inf.* off the wall; *Inf.* cracked, *Inf.* mental, *Sl.* off one's rocker, *Sl.* out of one's tree, *Sl.* off one's trolley, *Brit. Sl.* off one's chump; *All Sl.* have bats in one's belfry, have a few buttons missing, have a few loose screws.

3. maniacal, hysterical, madding, *Archaic.* wood, delirious; frantic, frenzied, frenetic; ranting, raving, storming, foaming at the mouth, convulsing; overwrought, distraught, upset, worked-up, wrought-up, stirred-up; exasperated, provoked; beside oneself, at one's wit's end; out of control, uncontrollable, unrestrainable, corybantic, *Inf.* haywire, berserk, rabid, wild; violent, stormy, fierce, tempestuous, tumultuous, turbulent.

4. absurd, silly, inane, fatuous, crackbrained, foolish; irrational, wild-eyed, illogical, unreasonable; senseless, nonsensical, pointless; ridiculous, laughable, risible, derisible, ludicrous, *Sl.* for the birds; asinine, anserine, idiotic, *Inf.* moronic, imbecilic; childish, puerile, immature.

5. stupid, simple-minded, bird-brained, feeble-minded, dull-witted; harebrained, light-minded, light-headed, giddy, rambling, driveling, wandering, incoherent; scatterbrained, absent-minded, confused; muddled, muddlepated, bemused.

6. impractical, injudicious, unsensible; unfounded, groundless, unsound; preposterous, extravagant, excessive; inappropriate, inept, improper, incongruous, inconsistent; imprudent, indiscreet; unwise, ill-considered, ill-suited, ill-advised; short-sighted, careless, unwary, irresponsible; reckless, rash, harum-scarum; unsafe, dangerous, perilous.

insanitary, *adj.* **1.** unhygienic, unsanitary, unsanitized, unclean; dirty, dirtied, filthy; impure, contaminated, polluted, foul, feculent; infective, infected, germy, septic, bacteria-infested, bacterial, disease-causing.

2. unhealthy, unhealthful, unwholesome; insalubrious, unsalubrious, bad for one's health; noxious, deleterious, injurious to one's health.

insanity, *n.* **1.** lunacy, derangement, madness, *Psychiatry.* dementia, dementedness, insaneness; distraction, disorientation, unbalance, unsoundness; mental illness, loss of reason, unsound mind, diseased mind; craziness, *Sl.* kookiness, *Inf.* nuttiness, daftness, brainsickness; eccentricity, oddness, queerness; *All Sl.* balminess, bugginess, screwiness, wackiness, goofiness.

2. psychosis, neurosis, psychoneurosis; schizophrenia, *Psychiatry.* dementia praecox, monomania, automania, dipsomania, pyromania, delusion of grandeur; senility, anility, dotage, *Psychiatry.* amentia; *Psychol.* kleptomania, *Psychol.* split personality; *All Psychiatry.* melancholia, hypochondria, paranoia, mania, lyssophobia, fugue, alienation, delusion.

3. frenzy, franticness, furor, delirium, phrenitis, anoesis, hysteria; *Pathol.* delirium tremens, blue devils, *Sl.* the horrors, *Sl.* jimjams; ranting, raving, storming, foaming at the mouth; storminess, fierceness, tumult, tumultuousness, turbulence, violence.

4. absurdity, absurdness, silliness, inanity, fatuousness, sottage, foolishness, folly; irrationality, illogic, illogicality, illogicalness, unreasonableness; senselessness, nonsense, nonsensicalness, nonsensicality, *Obs.* morology, pointlessness; ridiculousness, ridiculosity, ludicrousness; asininity, imbecility, idiocy, *Inf.* moronism, *Inf.* moronity; light-headedness, harebrainedness; childishness, puerility, immaturity.

5. impracticality, unsensibleness, preposterousness, unreasonableness; inappropriateness, impropriety, ineptitude, ineptness, incongruity, inconsistency; imprudence, indiscretion; irresponsibility, carelessness, unwariness, foolhardiness, recklessness.

insatiable, *adj.* **1.** insatiate, unappeasable, unquenchable, omnivorous; greedy, desirous, cupidinous, avaricious, avid, esurient; hungry, craving, grasping, exacting, extortionate, acquisitive, *Sl.* grabby, predacious, rapacious.

2. voracious, ravenous, ravening, devouring, gluttonous, gormandizing, cormorant, edacious; openmouthed, hoggish, piggish, porcine, swinish, gross; unsatisfied, unsated, famished, dry, athirst, thirsty, parched, arid.

inscribe, *v.* **1.** engrave, enscroll, imprint; impress, stamp, blaze, brand, mark, put a mark *or* seal on; write *or* print on, letter, pen, write down, put in writing, set down, *Rare.* scribe.

2. autograph, give [s.o.] one's autograph, sign, put one's John Henry *or* John Hancock on, endorse, docket; address, dedicate, make an inscription; scrawl, scribble, dash off.

3. enroll, enlist, register, poll, enter one's name on the roll, put [s.o.] on the list, sign [s.o.] up, *Archaic.* list; catalogue, inventory, record, tally, *Bookkeeping.* post.

inscription, *n.* **1.** epigraph, engraving, epitaph, legend, quotation, words; dedication, address, message, line, note, notation, entry, *Inf.* memorandum, *Inf.* memo; autograph, signature, hand, mark, John Hancock, John Henry, endorsement, stroke *or* dash of the pen.

2. engrossment, engraving, inscribing, writing, handwriting, penmanship, calligraphy.

inscrutable, *adj.* **1.** impenetrable, incomprehensible, uncomprehensible, undiscoverable; hidden, concealed, secret, cryptic, perdu, occult; poker-faced, deadpan, sphinxlike.

2. mysterious, arcane, inexplicable, unexplainable, insolvable, insoluble, unaccountable, *Obs.* inextricable; puzzling, baffling, enigmatic, enigmatical; unfathomable, unknowable, incognoscible, indecipherable, undecipherable, past *or* beyond comprehension, beyond understanding.

inscrutableness, *n.* impenetrability, impenetrableness, incomprehensibility, incomprehensibleness, inscrutability; poker face, dead pan, sphinx, Mona Lisa smile; mysteriousness, mystery, inexplicability, inexplicableness, unexplainableness, insolvability, insolubility, insolubleness; darkness, obscurity, obscureness, dimness, vagueness, nebulousness; uncertainty, ambiguity; unfathomableness, unknowableness, unknowability, indecipherability, indecipherableness; impassivity, unexpressiveness, expressionlessness.

insect, *n.* **1.** bug, mite, vermin, hexapod, arachnid, arthropod, ephemera; fly, housefly, face fly, blowfly, bluebottle fly, fruit fly, may fly, vinegar fly, tsetse fly; gnat, flea, no-see-um, earwig, water bug; mosquito, wasp, tick, bedbug, weevil, beetle, stinkbug, locust, grasshopper, termite, cockroach, silverfish; ant, pismire, *Chiefly Dial.* emmet, spider, cricket, bee, moth, butterfly, dragonfly, ladybug.
2. cur, wretch, pariah; *All Inf.* grub, creep, worm, mutt, jerk, schmuck; *All Inf.* pantywaist, jellyfish, milquetoast, Caspar Milquetoast, Walter Mitty.

insecticide, *n.* bug spray, insect powder, poison, contact poison, fumigant, chemosterilant; pesticide, miticide, acaricide, vermicide, anthelmintic; roach powder, roach paste, *Inf.* bug bomb, *Inf.* bugstrip.

insecure, *adj.* **1.** unsafe, unsound, unstable, untrustworthy, unreliable; precarious, dangerous, perilous, hazardous, ticklish, risky, chancy, slippery, hanging by a thread, *Sl.* hairy.
2. vulnerable, open, susceptible, assailable, unprotected, defenseless; exposed, unsheltered, unshielded, ill-protected, unguarded; endangered, in danger, expugnable, not out of the woods, between the devil and the deep blue sea.
3. infirm, shaky, wobbly, unsteady, decrepit, not firm, weak, frail, flimsy, unsubstantial; wobbling, tottering, teetering, rickety.
4. diffident, uncertain, doubtful, hesitant, dubious, undecided, not sure; dismayed, disconcerted, lacking confidence, not confident, unsure, timid; apprehensive, restive, shaken, unnerved, wrung; tremulous, fearful, uneasy, skittish, jumpy, nervous.

insecurity, *n.* **1.** instability, weakness, frailty, precariousness, danger, jeopardy, hazard, peril, risk, riskiness, chancefulness, chanciness.
2. vulnerability, susceptibility, assailableness, defenselessness; exposure, openness to attack, imperilment.
3. self-doubt, diffidence, timidity, timorousness, apprehension, faintheartedness; bashfulness, shyness, abashment, embarrassment, sheepishness; lack of self-confidence, reluctance, hesitancy, doubtfulness, backwardness; self-consciousness, constraint, uncertainty, incertitude, doubt, misgiving, hesitation, dubiousness, dubiety; irresolution, wariness, leeriness, fear, anxiety.

inseminate, *v.* **1.** sow seed, inject seed into, plant, implant, set, sow, seed, seed down; fertilize, spermatize, pollinate, pollinize, cross-fertilize, cross-pollinate, cross-pollinize; breed, propagate, proliferate, multiply.
2. impregnate, make pregnant, get with child *or* young, *Sl.* knock up; fructify, make fruitful, fecundate; create, procreate, generate, beget, get, engender.
3. give rise to, give being to, bring *or* call into existence, hatch; start, begin, establish, introduce, initiate, launch, originate; invent, occasion, *Inf.* sow the seeds of, found, establish, institute, lay the foundation of; inspire, provide the inspiration for, motivate, provide the motivation for, incite, kindle, *Inf.* spark, light the spark of; evoke, inculcate, indoctrinate, inoculate, infuse, instill, imbue.

insensate, *adj.* **1.** unfeeling, sensationless, numb, insensible, insentient, unperceiving, unconscious, comatose, anesthetized, *Inf.* out, *Inf.* completely out, *Inf.* zonked.
2. inanimate, lifeless, exanimate, inert, dead; inorganic, vegetable, mineral.
3. insensitive, insensible, impassive, unimpressionable, inured; callous, hardened, hard; thick-skinned, pachydermatous, casehardened; unemotional, apathetic, uninterested, uncaring, insouciant, disregardful, nonchalant, inattentive, *Inf.* tuned out, blind *or* deaf to things; dispassionate, insusceptible, frigid, cold, cold-hearted, cold-blooded.
4. senseless, nonsensical, irrational, judgmentless, illogical, unreasonable; fatuous, *Inf.* fatheaded, stupid, witless, dumb, doltish, asinine, addlebrained, *Inf.* out to lunch; unintelligent, unreasoning, mindless, brainless.

insensibility, *n.* **1.** unconsciousness, insentience, insensitiveness, insensitivity; coma, stupor, narcosis, anesthetization, hypnosis.
2. imperviousness, hardness, callousness, toughness, cold-bloodedness, ruthlessness; apathy, coolness, passionlessness, emotionlessness, impassibility, impassibleness; inattentiveness, absent-mindedness, indifference, insouciance, nonchalance; disregard, half-heartedness, indifference; dullness, lethargy, languidness, sluggishness; phlegm, phlegmaticalness, phlegmaticness; heaviness, leadenness, torpidity.

insensible, *adj.* **1.** unconscious, insentient, unperceiving; comatose, anesthetized, *Inf.* knocked out, *Inf.* out, *Inf.* completely out, *Inf.* zonked.
2. impervious, inured, hard, hardened, callous, thickskinned, pachydermatous; tough, toughened, casehardened, cold-blooded, ruthless.
3. unaware, inappreciative, incognizant, unknowing; uncultivated, uncultured, unrefined, low-brow, Philistine, unenlightened, unconversant, unsophisticated, undiscerning, undiscriminating.
4. imperceptible, incognizable, unascertainable, indiscernible, indistinguishable, incomprehensible; indistinct, unclear, unrecognizable, blurred, ill-defined, vague, mysterious, obscure, uncertain, confusing.
5. apathetic, cool, passionless, emotionless; impassible, insensitive, detached, inattentive, absent-minded, *Inf.* out to lunch; dispassionate, indifferent, uninterested, insouciant, *Fr. sans souci*, nonchalant; disregardful, half-hearted, lukewarm, indifferent; dull, lethargic, languid, sluggish, phlegmatic; heavy, leaden, torpid.

insensitive, *adj.* **1.** tough, callous, insentient, unfeeling; numb, anesthetized, dead, deadened.
2. insusceptible, immune, proof, impervious, unaffectable, unimpressionable, unreactive, nonreactive, nonallergic.
3. unkind, mean, nasty, uncaring; merciless, unmerciful, pitiless, unpitying, uncompassionate, uncompassioned, unsympathetic, unsympathizing, hard-hearted, heartless.
4. insensible, unaware, inappreciative, incognizant, unknowing; uncultivated, uncultured, unrefined, low-brow, Philistine, unenlightened, unconversant, unsophisticated, undiscerning, undiscriminating.

insentient, *adj.* inanimate, lifeless, exanimate, inert, dead; inorganic, vegetable, mineral; insensate, numb, anesthetized, deadened, unfeeling, insensible, unperceiving, unconscious, comatose, *Inf.* knocked out, *Inf.* out, *Inf.* completely out, *Inf.* under, *Inf.* zonked.

inseparable, *adj.* **1.** unseparable, inseverable, impartible, unpartible, indivisible, undivisible, undividable, indiscerptible; indissoluble, undissolvable, insoluble, unsoluble; unbreakable, infrangible.
2. *Usu.* **inseparables** concomitants, salt and pep-

per, bread and butter, horse and carriage, gin and tonic.

3. *Usu.* **inseparables** constant companions, shadows, best friends, *U.S. Inf.* bosom buddies, a pair, a couple; twins, Siamese twins, Chang and Eng; Damon and Pythias, David and Jonathan, Romulus and Remus, Laurel and Hardy, Abbott and Costello, Tweedledum and Tweedledee.

insert, *v.* **1.** put in *or* into, inset, inlay, set *or* place in; tuck in, pop in, slide in, slip in; work in *or* into, press in, push in, thrust in, force in, drive in, wedge in, sandwich in, jam in, cram *or* stuff in, ram in *or* up, stick in *or* up; (*all of words, phrases, etc.*) parenthesize, interline, interlineate, margin, add in, write in.

2. introduce, indoctrinate, inoculate, imbue, infect, impregnate; instill, infuse, insinuate, inculcate; infix, implant, imbed, ingrain.

3. inject, interject, interpolate, interpose, intercalate; intervene, intercede, interfere, come between; interrupt, intrude, break in on.

—n. **4.** inset, extra page *or* leaf; printed paper, notice, bulletin, announcement; circular, advertisement, ad.

inside, *prep.* **1.** on the inner side, on the inner part, within, inside of; prior to, before.

—adv. **2.** indoors, in the house, in the building; off the streets.

3. instinctively, intuitively, impulsively; emotionally, viscerally, intestinally; involuntarily, spontaneously; immediately.

4. naturally, basically, fundamentally, inherently, innately, intrinsically.

—n. **5.** interior, interior part; inner part, inner space, inner side, inner surface.

6. *Usu.* **insides** viscera, body organs, internal organs, internals; inwards, *Inf.* innards, *Sl.* guts; vital parts, vital organs, vitals, *Inf.* solar plexus, *Sl.* where one lives; intestine, intestines, bowel, bowels, colon, colons, (*of swine*) chitterlings, (*of animals*) entrails; alimentary canal, abdomen, belly, stomach, *Inf.* tummy, *Inf.* gizzard, *Sl.* breadbasket; pouch, (*of birds*) crop, craw, maw, ingluvies, (*of birds*) proventriculus; (*both of ruminating animals*) first stomach, rumen.

7. contents, parts, elements, components, constituents.

8. select group, select circle, exclusive group, exclusive circle, chosen group, chosen circle, *Inf.* in crowd, *Sociol.* ingroup.

9. **inside out,** **a.** reversed, backward, back in front. **b.** perfectly, completely, thoroughly, *All Inf.* backward and forward, backwards and forwards, from A to Z.

—adj. **10.** interior, inner, internal; on the inside, in the inside; indoor, intramural, *Latin. intra muros.*

11. inmost, innermost, *Scot., Irish.* benmost.

12. innate, intrinsic, indwelling, immanent, intimate, inherent, indigenous; ingrained, engrained, inwrought, enwrought.

13. fundamental, elemental, radical, basic, organic, constitutional; pithy, substantial, meaty, essential, quintessential; central, nuclear.

14. private, privy, intimate, personal, nonpublic, confidential; restricted, reserved, privileged; esoteric, secret, occult, veiled, hidden, enclosed, obscure.

insidious, *adj.* guileful, artful, arch, crafty, cunning, Machiavellian; subtle, sly, feline, wily, snaky, foxy, *Sl.* crazy like a fox, *Scot. and North Eng.* pawky; deceitful, tricky, crooked, dishonest, underhanded, *Inf.* left-handed; false, false-hearted, double-dealing, two-faced, Janus-faced; shifty, slippery, shady, smooth, slick; disingenuous, insincere, scheming, plotting, designing, calculating, contriving; perfidious, treacherous, traitorous, Punic, treasonable.

insight, *n.* **1.** intuition, perception, *Psychol.* apperception, percipience, sensitivity, flair; apprehension, understanding, *Obs.* skill, cognition, comprehension; perspicacity, keenness, acuteness, sharpness, acuity; acumen, perceptiveness, perspicaciousness, penetration; discernment, discrimination, distinguishment; cleverness, astuteness, shrewdness, ingenuity, ingeniousness.

2. intelligence, knowledge, profundity, depth; sagacity, sagaciousness, wisdom; foresightedness, farsightedness, long-headedness; divination, clairvoyance; mother wit, wit, esprit; sense, common sense, good sense, judgment, prudence, brains, smartness, brightness; clearheadedness, clear-sightedness, clear vision.

3. ascertainment, determination, observance, notice; realization, awareness, eyeopener, *Literature.* epiphany, *Fr. aperçu.*

insignia, *n.* **1.** badge, decoration, *Mil.* bar, oak leaf cluster, *U.S. Navy.* star, eagle; award, token, medal, medallion, ribbon, cockade, aiguillette, aglet; crest, emblem, button, shield, chevron, shoulder strap, brassard, stripes; ensign, sign, symbol, sigil, signet, seal, stamp, brand, marker, *Archaic.* recognizance.

2. mark of distinction, trademark, earmark, tab, identification, label; indication, signal; trait, characteristic, distinction, diagnostic.

insignificance, *n.* **1.** unimportance, inconsequence, inconsequentiality, immateriality, irrelevance; paltriness, pettiness, meanness, smallness; triviality, worthlessness, emptiness, nothingness, nullity; matter of indifference, trifling matter, no great matter, mere nothing; nothing worth mentioning, nothing worth speaking of, nothing to speak of, nothing to boast of, nothing to write home about, *Inf.* no great shakes, nothing particular.

2. cipher, nonentity, *Inf.* picayune, *Inf.* small potatoes, small fry, *Chiefly Brit. Sl.* small beer, insignificancy; flash in the pan, nine days' wonder; trumpery, trifle, bagatelle, froth, feather, farthing; drop in the bucket.

insignificant, *adj.* **1.** unimportant, of minor importance, of little *or* no import, negligible, nugatory, inconsiderable, inconsequential, of no consequence; inapplicable, irrelevant, immaterial, unessential; unportentous, unmomentous, of no matter *or* concern, of little *or* no account, of no moment, of no great weight; *Inf.* no great shakes, not worth mentioning, not worth speaking of, not worth thinking *or* worrying about, not worth a rap *or* a straw; trivial, trifling, paltry, petty, niggling; small, minor, puny, dinky, piddling, *Inf.* picayune, insubstantial, unsubstantial; trite, *Sl.* mickey-mouse.

2. (*of persons*) uninfluential, *Sl.* small potatoes, small fry; second-rate, third-rate, inferior, *Inf.* small-time, *Sl.* two-bit, *Inf.* penny ante; nondescript, nonentitive.

3. contemptible, despicable, vile, abject, base, low, mean, scurvy, sorry.

insincere, *adj.* disingenuous, uncandid, unfrank, mealy-mouthed; artificial, plastic, *Inf.* phony; dissembling, dissimulating, hypocritical, crocodilian; deceitful, dishonest, underhanded, crooked, tricky, double-tongued; faithless, disloyal, perfidious, treacherous; false, untrue, false-hearted, double-dealing, two-faced, mendacious, lying, untruthful; artful, insidious, guileful, scheming, plotting, calculating, contriving, designing; cunning, crafty, Machiavellian, sly, wily, foxy; evasive, shifty, slippery, smooth, slick.

insincerity, *n.* **1.** disingenuousness, uncandidness, unfrankness, mealy-mouthedness; artificiality, *Inf.* phoniness, dissembling, dissimulation, cant, lip service, mouth honor, *Inf.* hokum, flattery, smooth talk; deceitfulness, dishonesty, underhandedness, crookedness, trickiness; faithlessness, bad faith, betrayal, Judas kiss, disloyalty, perfidy, treachery, foul play; falseness, false-heartedness, double-dealing, duplicity, hypocrisy, mendacity, lying, untruthfulness, hollowness, emptiness; artfulness, insidiousness, guilefulness, cunning, craftiness, slyness, wiliness, foxiness; shiftiness, slipperiness, smoothness, slickness.

2. deceit, trick, stratagem, ruse, artifice, pretense; contrivance, wile, misrepresentation, distortion, exaggeration; sham, hoax, imposture, *Inf.* flimflam, *Inf.* flam.

insinuate, *v.* **1.** intimate, suggest, infer, imply, hint, *Inf.* give to understand, *Inf.* put a bug in [s.o.'s] ear; clue, *Inf.* tip off, cue, prompt; whisper, breathe; allude to, advert, refer, indicate.

2. (*all artfully*) infuse, inject, interject, instill, implant; introduce, inculcate, impress.

3. worm *or* work *or* weasel one's way into favor, curry favor with; flatter, *Inf.* soft-soap, *Inf.* butter up, fawn on, truckle to, pander to, jolly, humor.

insipid, *adj.* **1.** flat, uninteresting, unentertaining, inexpressive, unimaginative, colorless, jejune, *Sl.* blah; unanimated, spiritless, zestless, sapless, tame, lifeless, empty, *Sl.* dead, *Sl.* nothing; pointless, impotent, weak, feeble, anemic, limp, namby-pamby, *Dial.* limpsy; dry, dry-as-dust, prosaic, prosy, matter-of-fact, arid, barren, sterile; dull, boring, boresome, monotonous, humdrum, tedious, tiresome, wearisome; stale, tired, trite, hackneyed, banal, platitudinous, overworked; indistinctive, run-of-the-mill, ordinary, commonplace, average.

2. tasteless, flavorless, bland, vapid, *Fr. fade*; thin, watery, watered-down, washy, wishy-washy, milk-and-water; unsavory, unappetizing, unpalatable.

insipidity, *n.* **1.** flatness, uninterestingness, jejuneness, jejunity, colorlessness, inexpressiveness, unimaginativeness, lack of imagination *or* expression, insipidness; lifelessness, saplessness, spiritlessness, zestlessness, lack of vitality *or* animation, tameness, emptiness, *Sl.* deadness, *Sl.* nothingness; pointlessness, impotence, weakness, feebleness, anemia, limpness; dryness, prosaicness, prosiness, aridity, barrenness, sterileness, sterility; dullness, monotonousness, monotony, tediousness, tiresomeness, wearisomeness; staleness, tiredness, triteness, banality, platitude, platitudinousness; indistinctiveness, ordinariness, commonplaceness.

2. tastelessness, flavorlessness, unsavoriness, blandness, vapidity, vapidness; thinness, wateriness, washiness, wishy-washiness.

insist, *v.* **1.** be emphatic, be firm, be resolute, hold, be pertinacious; emphasize, stress, lay stress *or* emphasis on, give emphasis to; underline, underscore, point up, call attention to, mark, bring home, press home; harp on, dwell on.

2. assert, allege, vow, avow, vouch, predicate, swear, assure; maintain, uphold, contend, aver, propound; profess, pronounce, claim, testify, proclaim, declare.

3. demand, call for, require, command; request, solicit, entreat, importune, talk [s.o.] into; urge, persuade, exhort, advise, counsel, suggest, admonish, remonstrate, expostulate.

insistence, *n.* **1.** emphasis, stress, pressure, importunity; underlining, underscoring, insisting; perseverance, persistence, insistency, determination, singleness of purpose, *Inf.* stick-to-it-iveness, pertinacity, tenacity, tenaciousness, obstinacy.

2. assertion, allegation, vow, assurance, affirmation, averment; profession, pronouncement, claim, proclamation, declaration.

3. demand, requirement, command; request, solicitation, entreaty, importuning; urging, goading, prodding, spurring; persuasion, exhortation, advice, counsel; admonition, remonstration, expostulation.

4. dogmatism, imperativeness, peremptoriness, positiveness; bigotry, intolerance, close-mindedness; arrogance, imperiousness.

insistent, *adj.* **1.** persistent, tenacious, pertinacious, importunate, unfaltering; unrelenting, uncompromising, unyielding, obstinate, stubborn; iterative, repeated, repetitive, recurrent, incessant; inexorable, refusing to take "no" for an answer.

2. determined, resolute, purposeful, strong-minded, strong-willed; earnest, intense, intensive; certain, assured, sure, positive, definitive; decided, explicit, express.

3. urgent, pressing, compelling; forceful, forcible, high-pressure, pressuring, coercive.

4. emphatic, stressed, emphasized, accentuated, underlined, underscored; affirmative, assertive, assured, confident, reassuring.

5. dogmatic, doctrinaire, opinionated; peremptory, imperative, absolute; outspoken, mouthy, loudmouthed.

insobriety, *n.* **1.** drunkenness, intoxication, inebriety, inebriation, intemperance, sottedness, besottedness, tipsiness; alcoholism, chronic alcoholism, dipsomania, habitual drunkenness, bibulousness, bibulosity, bibacity, bibaciousness, crapulence, crapulency, crapulousness.

2. drink, drinking, heavy *or* serious *or* problem drinking; imbibing, tippling, toping, bibition, bibation, bibbing, bibbling, *Rare.* bibbery, *Inf.* boozing, *Inf.* swilling, *Sl.* hitting the bottle *or* sauce *or* booze, *Brit. Sl.* bevying.

insolence, *n.* **1.** impertinence, impudence, audacity, effrontery, presumption, presumptuousness; boldness, brazenness, brashness, pertness, freshness, shamelessness, *Inf.* cheekiness, *Inf.* sassiness, *Inf.* brassiness; impoliteness, disrespect, contemptuousness, unmannerliness, ill-manneredness, incivility, rudeness; bumptiousness, cockiness, cocksureness, self-assertiveness *or* self-assertion, chutzpah, forwardness; meddlesomeness, intrusiveness, officiousness.

2. *All Inf.* brass, sass, cheek, guff, back talk, sauce, face, crust; *All Sl.* gall, nerve, lip, mouth, *Brit.* side.

insolent, *adj.* **1.** impertinent, impudent, audacious, presumptuous, out-of-line, out-of-keeping; bold, bold-faced, brash, brazen, brazen-faced, pert, fresh, saucy, shameless, *Inf.* flip, *Inf.* cheeky, *Inf.* sassy, *Inf.* brassy, *Sl.* wise, *Sl.* mouthy, *Sl.* smart-mouth; impolite, ill-mannered, unmannerly, uncivil, ill-bred, crude, coarse, vulgar, rude; disrespectful, contemptuous, disdainful, scornful; bumptious, cocksure, cocky, arrogant, forward; meddlesome, intrusive, interfering, officious.

—*n.* **2.** malapert, brazenface, whippersnapper, jackanapes, upstart, minx, hussy, *Inf.* saucebox, *Inf.* smart aleck, *Inf.* smarty pants, *Sl.* wise guy, *Sl.* wise *or* smart ass.

insoluble, *adj.* **1.** indissoluble, undissoluble, indissolvable, undissolvable, unsoluble, infusible, unthawable, *Archaic.* irresoluble.

2. insolvable, unsolvable, inexplicable, unexplainable, inextricable; puzzling, enigmatic, enigmatical, baffling, bewildering, perplexing, confounding, mystifying.

3. impenetrable, incomprehensible, uncomprehensible, inapprehensible, past *or* beyond comprehension, beyond understanding, unknowable, incognizable, incognoscible, inscrutable, unfathomable, indecipherable, undecipherable, undiscoverable.

4. hard, difficult, over one's head, *Inf.* tough; complex, complicated, perplexed, *Inf.* tricky; intricate, involved, labyrinthine, Byzantine, tangled, knotty, crabbed.

5. mysterious, arcane, cryptic, perdu; oracular, sphingine, sphinxian, sphinxlike; mystic, mystical, cabalistic, transcendental, supernatural, preternatural.

insolvency, *n.* bankruptcy, inability to pay, indebtedness, liquidation, failure, default, nonpayment; pauperism, pauperage, beggary, pennilessness, mendicancy, mendicity; destitution, impecuniousness, poverty, impoverishment, penury, indigence, straits.

insolvent, *adj.* bankrupt, indebted, defaulting; beggared, ruined, wiped out, pauperized, broken, wrecked, on the shoals of despair; in arrears, in debt, behindhand, *Inf.* in the hole, *Inf.* in the red, *Inf.* on the rocks; straitened, pinched, *Inf.* strapped, stripped, reduced; destitute, impoverished, impecunious, penurious, poverty-stricken, *Inf.* hard up, *Inf.* uptight; penniless, moneyless, out of cash, *Inf.* short, *Brit. Sl.* skint, *Inf.* broke, *Inf.* flat broke, *Inf.* flat.

insomnia, *n.* sleeplessness, insomnolence, wakefulness, restlessness, *Latin. pervigilium.*

insouciance, *n.* carefreeness, nonchalance, indifference, unconcern; heedlessness, laxity, laxness, pococurantism, lackadaisicalness, casualness; happy-go-luckiness, easiness, easygoingness; light-mindedness, flightiness, airiness, volatility; frivolousness, flippancy, capriciousness, whimsicality; jauntiness, sunniness, breeziness, buoyancy, carelessness.

insouciant, *adj.* carefree, untroubled, unworried, unconcerned, heedless; happy-go-lucky, free and easy, easy, easygoing, devil-may-care, *Fr. sans souci;* indifferent, nonchalant, casual, lackadaisical, pococurante; light-minded, airy, volatile, flighty, bird-witted; frivolous, flippant, mercurial, capricious, whimsical; sunny, jaunty, buoyant, smiling, breezy.

inspect, *v.* examine, scrutinize, audit, scan; study, peruse, pore over; check out, go over, give the eye; view, survey, reconnoiter, observe, notice, *Sl.* eyeball, watch; assess, criticize, appraise, evaluate, *Inf.* give [s.o.] the once-over; look [s.o.] up and down, *Sl.* glom.

inspection, *n.* examination, scrutiny, audit, perusal, *Inf.* once-over; observation, survey, overview, reconnaissance, surveillance; investigation, inquiry, probe, research.

inspector, *n.* **1.** examiner, investigator, auditor, checker; appraiser, evaluator, assessor; viewer, observer, watchman, night watchman; efficiency engineer, efficiency expert; ticket taker, *Fr. contrôleur, Sl.* bluecoat.

2. detective, *Sl.* dick, *Sl.* gumshoe, Maigret, Gideon, Dick Tracy, *Sl.* bloodhound, *Inf.* sherlock; policeman, police officer, *Sl.* flatfoot, *Sl.* the man, *Sl.* bull, *Sl.* fuzz, *Sl.* cop, *Sl.* copper; private investigator, *Sl.* private eye, shadow, tail, *Inf.* bird dog, *Inf.* sleuth; FBI agent, G-man.

inspiration, *n.* **1.** stimulus, fillip, stimulation, arousal, incentive, provocation; revelation, Muse, afflatus; influence, encouragement, exhortation, prompting, goad, spur; whet, kindling, inflaming, igniting, *Inf.* sparking; incitement, instigation, rousing, stirring; awakening, rejuvenation, revitalization, revitalizing, revival, rally.

2. energy, spirit, élan, dash, ardor; passion, zeal, gusto, vigor; eagerness, animation, *Inf.* ginger, invigoration, exhilaration; enthusiasm, sparkle, ebullience, excitement; ecstasy, thrill, *Inf.* rush, tingling, quickening.

3. brightness, warmth, encouragement, shot in the arm, perking up; assurance, reassurance, confirmation; comfort, comforting, solace, quieting, calming; unburdening, relief, alleviation, assuagement; salve, soothing, palliation, mitigation; aid, assistance, support, sustenance, nourishment; strength, strengthening, buttressing, bracing, reinforcement; fortification, building up, restoration.

4. revelation, communication, suggestion, explanation; divulging, divulgence, impartation, impartment, disclosure; illumination, enlightenment, awareness, disabusal, insightfulness; instruction, teaching, indoctrination, indoctrinization, education, guide.

5. inhalation, breathing, respiration, *Pathol.* eupnea; indraft, sniffle, snuffle, *Sl.* snort, *Brit. Sl.* toot.

inspire, *v.* **1.** animate, invigorate, energize, vivify, vitalize, exhilarate; reanimate, revive, revivify, revitalize, rejuvenate; awaken, waken, stir, rally, rouse, arouse; stimulate, inspirit, quicken, whet; excite, thrill, enthuse, exalt.

2. produce, bring on *or* about, cause, effect; influence, affect, impress, act on; change, alter, transform, modify.

3. hearten, enhearten, take heart, cheer *or* cheer up; brighten, warm, give a lift to, uplift, encourage; *Inf.* pep up, perk up, buoy up, give a shot in the arm, boost one's spirits; assure, reassure, confirm, comfort, solace; improve, ameliorate, meliorate; aid, assist, support, sustain; strengthen, buttress, brace, reinforce; embolden, nerve, fortify; build up, nourish, restore.

4. reveal, communicate, suggest, enlighten, make aware, disabuse; give insight to, open the eyes of, shed *or* cast light on, bring out of the wilderness; make known to, tell, explain, divulge, impart; instruct, teach, indoctrinate, educate, guide; familiarize with, acquaint, interest.

5. give rise to, prompt, instigate, incite, exhort, impel, spur, goad; touch off, inflame, set on fire, ignite; kindle, enkindle, fire *or* fire up, *Inf.* light a fire under, *Inf.* spark, *Inf.* sparkplug.

6. inhale, breathe in, inbreathe, respire; draw breath, draw in, suck in, gasp; snuff, snuffle, sniff, sniffle, *Sl.* snort, *Brit. Sl.* toot.

inspired, *adj.* animated, enlivened, exhilarated, invigorated; inspirited; afflated, energized, vivified, vitalized; reanimated, revived, revivified, revitalized, rejuvenated; enthused, stimulated, aroused, excited; enkindled, kindled, *Inf.* sparked, inflamed, fired up, stirred up, aroused, awake, active, quick, bright; elated, exalted, heartened, enheartened.

inspirit, *v.* enliven, animate, quicken, vivify; excite arouse, stir, *Sl.* goose, *Sl.* give [s.o.] some get-up-and-go; stimulate, embolden, hearten, steel; brighten, sharpen; encourage, cheer, gladden; invigorate, refresh; galvanize, incite, kindle, inflame, fire.

instability, *n.* **1.** impermanence, unsteadiness, unendurability; shakiness, flimsiness, unsubstantiality, ricketiness; sleaziness, unsafeness, unsoundness; weakness, frailty, precariousness, *Sl.* chanciness, uncertainty; insecurity, vulnerability, susceptibility, defenselessness.

2. vacillation, wobble, wavering; capriciousness, inconsistency, volatility; fluctuation, flightiness, inconstancy, irresolution, indecision, tergiversation.

3. infirmity, decrepitude, feebleness; unreliability, untrustworthiness, undependability; feeble-mindedness, *Sl.* goofiness, *Sl.* wackiness.

install, *v.* **1.** put in, place, locate, situate, emplace, station; fix, set, embed, lodge, insert, plant.

2. induct, introduce, initiate; instate, establish, chair, invest, inaugurate; crown, enthrone; bring in, lead in, usher in; frock, *Eccles.* ordain, consecrate.

installation, *n.* **1.** placement, placing, lodgment, positioning, location, stationing, emplacement, fixation.

2. instatement, investiture, chairing, inauguration, solemnization; initiation, introduction, induction, bringing in, ushering in; coronation, crowning, enthronement; frocking, *Eccles.* ordination, *Eccles.* ordainment, consecration.

3. *Military.* post, base, station, camp, establishment, settlement; lodgings, quarters, accommodations.

installment, *n.* **1.** partial payment, earnest, deposit, advance payment.

2. part, portion, segment, section, chapter, act, scene.

instance, *n.* **1.** example, case, precedent; case in point, specific, *Inf.* for instance; typical situation, representative case, illustration, exemplification; quotation, citation.

2. for instance as an example, for example.

instant, *n.* **1.** moment, minute, twinkling, flash, jiffy, breath, trice, crack, burst, flick, *Inf.* whipstitch, flash of lightning, twinkling of an eye, *Fr. coup d'oeil.*

2. present time, this very minute, this very hour, specific moment, stroke of time, particular time, moment, hour, time of day.

—adj. **3.** immediate, sudden, abrupt, direct, instantaneous; prompt, quick, expeditious; rapid, swift, fast, smart, hasty, speedy, on-the-spot.

4. urgent, pressing, critical, earnest, crying, exigent, importunate, absorbing.

instantaneous, *adj.* instant, immediate, direct, on-the-spot; prompt, quick, expeditious; rapid, fast, swift, hurried, precipitate, headlong; cursory, fleeting, momentary; sudden, abrupt, hasty, speedy.

instantaneously, *adv.* immediately, instantly, at once, abruptly, suddenly; now, on the instant, on the moment, right away, forthwith; in a trice, in a jiffy, in no time, in less than no time, in a fraction of a second; directly, without delay, *Archaic.* anon, straightaway; quick as thought, quick as greased lightning, like a shot, like a thunderbolt, *Sl.* like mad, *Sl.* like a bat out of hell, in the twinkling of an eye, before you can say "Jack Robinson," before you can turn around, before the ink is dry; urgently, *Sl.* pronto, in the same breath, at one jump, posthaste, apace, fast, *Inf.* lickety-split, full-tilt, at full blast, in high gear, as fast as one's legs can carry one.

instate, *v.* install, invest, induct, initiate, *Rare.* auspicate; inaugurate, swear in, administer the oath of office; establish, chair, seat; crown, enthrone; frock, *Eccles.* ordain.

instead, *adv.* preferably, in preference to, rather than; instead of, in lieu of, *Fr. au lieu de;* as a replacement for, in the place *or* stead of, as a substitute for, as proxy for.

instep, *n.* arch, metatarsal arch, *Anat., Zool.* metatarsus.

instigate, *v.* **1.** incite, actuate, provoke, initiate, generate, start, *Inf.* start something, look for trouble; poke, prod, prick, thrust, goad, prompt, spur, egg on; stimulate, animate, whet, invigorate, motivate, inspire, inspirit, rally, awaken, vivify, bestir, enliven, liven up, jolt, jog; encourage, abet, embolden, nerve, build up, buck up; induce, impel, constrain, press, push, move, force; persuade, incline, dispose, lobby, predispose, influence, prevail upon, coax, ply, sway, talk into; tempt, inveigle, beguile, entice, wheedle, lure, allure, *Obs.* allect.

2. foment, agitate, excite, arouse, rouse, whip, whip up, work, work up, stir, stir up, wind up, inflame, enflame, fire, fire up, kindle, enkindle, touch off, *Inf.* psych up.

instigation, *n.* **1.** inciting, actuating, provoking, poking, prodding, pricking, thrusting, goading, prompting, spurring, egging on; stimulating, motivating, inspiring, rallying, awakening, vivifying, bestirring, encouraging, abetting, emboldening, inducing, impelling, constraining, pressing, pushing, moving, forcing; persuading, inclining, predisposing, influencing, lobbying, coaxing, plying, swaying; tempting, inveigling, beguiling, enticing, wheedling, luring.

2. fomenting, agitating, exciting, arousing, rousing, whipping up, working up, stirring up, winding up, inflaming, enflaming, firing up, kindling, enkindling, touching off, *Inf.* psyching up.

3. incitement, incitation, actuation, provocation, initiation; stimulation, animation, infection, invigoration, motivation, inspiration, vivification; inducement, impulsion; persuasion, inclination, predisposal, influence; temptation, inveiglement, beguilement, allurement, enticement, blandishment, *Obs.* allectation.

4. fomentation, agitation, excitement, *Rare.* suscitation, perturbation; demagoguery, sensationalism, rabble-rousing, soap-box oratory.

5. incentive, stimulus, provocative, fillip, motive; press, goad, spur, prick, prod, jolt, jog, poke, thrust; impulse, urge, drive, push, itch, desire; dictate, call.

instill, *v.* **1.** infuse, saturate, imbue, permeate, immerse, steep, familiarize with; inculcate, infix, implant, engraft, ingrain, fill, impregnate, penetrate, transfuse, inject.

2. teach, educate, school, tutor, train, instruct, enlighten, inform, guide, guide step by step; indoctrinate, drill, prime, ground, qualify, bring along, coach, exercise; preach, propagandize, insinuate, sow the seeds of, lead along the path.

3. influence, infect, affect, bias, incline; initiate, inspire, breathe into, show the way, inflame, arouse; fire, charge, stir, stimulate, animate.

instillation, *n.* **1.** infusion, transfusion, insertion; saturation, permeation, infiltration, immersion, submersion, steeping; dissemination, unfoldment, revelation, familiarization; inculcation, implantation, impregnation, penetration.

2. instruction, teaching, edification, education, tutelage, schooling; preparation, introduction, training; indoctrination, persuasion, propagandism, proselytism, insinuation.

instinct[1], *n.* **1.** impulse, inclination, tendency, leaning, propensity, proclivity, penchant, predisposition.

2. talent, gift, ability, capacity, aptitude; flair, knack, bent; trait, characteristic, faculty, habit.

3. intuition, prompting, sixth sense; sense, feel, awareness; empathy, sensitivity, feeling; heart, soul.

instinct[2], *adj.* *Usu.* **instinct with** imbued, inspired, informed, impregnated, pregnant; filled, infused; abounding in, rife, replete, alive with, *Sl.* lousy with.

instinctive, *adj.* **1.** inborn, inbred, innate, ingenerate; immanent, indwelling, inherent, indigenous, intrinsic; intuitive, intuitional, untaught, involuntary, unpremeditated, noninferential.

2. impulsive, automatic, immediate, spontaneous, direct, on-the-spot; emotional, visceral, intestinal, *Inf.* seat of the pants, *Inf.* played by ear, *Sl.* gut.

3. native, natural, natural-born; congenital, hereditary, inherited, in the blood, in the family; subjective, constitutional, idiosyncratic; ingrained, engrained, inwrought, enwrought.

institute, *v.* **1.** found, establish, start, give rise to, create, originate, bring into being, bring about; set up, organize, develop.

2. inaugurate, break ground, lay the foundation, lay the first stone; introduce, launch, broach, usher in; initiate, actuate, instigate, set in motion, start the ball rolling, take the first step, take the initiative, take the plunge, make a start, break the ice; open, pioneer, lead off; beget, engender, father, conceive, give birth to, sow the seeds of, produce, occasion, bring on.

3. begin, commence, get [s.t.] going, start [s.t.] off, get [s.t.] under way, put [s.t.] into operation.

—*n.* 4. society, association, alliance, league, union, guild, consortium; organization, affiliation.

5. academy, seminary, school, college, university, educational establishment, conservatory, polytechnic; learned association *or* institution, athenaeum, fellowship of artists *or* scientists, research center, foundation, developmental organization, *Inf.* think tank.

6. training center, preparatory school, *Inf.* prep school, private school, *Brit.* public school, boarding school, day school, finishing school; classical school, Latin school, (*in Germany*) gymnasium.

institution, *n.* 1. establishment, formation, organization, constitution; construction, erection; creation, commencement, start, origin, foundation, founding, beginning, inception, initiation; installation, appointment, ordainment; introduction, inauguration, confirmation, certification, authorization, enactment.

2. rule, custom, principle, practice, code, tradition, usage; order, canon, regulation, ordinance, bylaw, law, statute, decree, edict, prescript; fundamental, rudiment, source, grounds, purpose, motive, rationale.

3. association, society, alliance, league, coalition, union, guild, brotherhood, sodality; fellowship, fraternity, confraternity.

4. medical center, sanatarium, sanatorium, clinic, hospital, asylum, retreat; museum, library, institute, academy. See **institute** (*def.* 5).

5. business, firm, concern, company; corporation, trust, syndicate, conglomerate, banking house, savings and loan association, financial house.

institutional, *adj.* 1. organized, established, accepted, orthodox, conventional, stable, customary, formal, preordained, systematic, methodical, orderly, by the book *or* the rules, ritualistic, ceremonial, *Inf.* establishment.

2. uniform, same, monotonous, unvarying, unvaried, regimented, unchanging, set; bland, insipid, drab, dull; cold, inhuman, heartless, indifferent, forbidding, remote, inhospitable.

instruct, *v.* 1. direct, command, order; prescribe, enjoin, bid, charge; dictate, decree, mandate, ordain, appoint; demand, require, tell; urge, importune.

2. teach, tutor, school, educate, enlighten, edify; question, catechize, drill, beat into, cram; indoctrinate, inculcate, instill, infuse; train, coach, initiate, ground, prepare, ready; counsel, advise, guide, preach, lecture, moralize, sermonize; admonish, reprimand, warn.

3. notify, inform, brief; mention, point out, tell, describe, demonstrate; acquaint with, familiarize with, introduce to, apprise of; promulgate, make known, broadcast, announce, publish; propagate, disseminate, spread, propagandize.

instruction, *n.* 1. teaching, education, tuition, tutelage; grounding, training, coaching, drilling; direction, guidance, nurture, breeding, development; inculcation, indoctrination, initiation, discipline.

2. learning, knowledge, lore, information, skill; preparation, schooling, training, initiation, apprenticeship; erudition, scholarship, study; enlightenment, edification, culture, cultivation.

3. didactics, pedagogics, pedagogy. See **pedagogy** (*def.* 2).

4. *Usu.* **instructions** direction, command, mandate, briefing, order, *Law.* writ, injunction, charge, admonition; precept, directive, dictate, guideline, bidding, maxim; recommendation, suggestion, advice, counsel.

instructive, *adj.* informative, informational, instructional, how-to, propaedeutic; educational, educative, academic, school; didactic, moralistic, homiletic, homiletical, *Inf.* preachy, doctrinal; cultural, humanistic, scientific, broadening, edifying, uplifting.

instructor, *n.* 1. teacher, trainer, coach; educator, pedagogue, educationist, *Educ.* methodologist; schoolteacher, schoolmaster, *Chiefly Scot.* dominie, schoolmistress, schoolmarm, instructress; professor, doctor, master, tutor, fellow, *Brit.* don, preceptor, lector, lecturer, *Brit.* reader; schoolman, scholastic, academician, academe, gownsman.

2. mentor, counselor, advisor; guide, cicerone, docent; explainer, explicator, expositor, expounder; interpreter, (*in the Orient*) dragoman; annotator, glosser.

3. indoctrinator, inculcator, informer, informant; demonstrator; exponent, propagator, propagandist, missionary, apostle; preacher, moralizer, sermonizer; mystagogue, catechist, catechizer, *Hinduism.* guru.

instrument, *n.* 1. tool, implement, utensil, appliance, apparatus; machine, automaton, robot; device, contrivance, invention, contraption, gadget; aid, convenience, time-saver, *Archaic.* conveniency.

2. agency, mechanism, instrumentality; means, way, ways and means, wherewithal; power, moving force, principle, elements; catalyst, mover, prime mover, cause, causer, effecter, *Chem.* reagent, *Gram.* causative; producer, doer, accomplisher, actor, executor, perpetrator.

3. legal document, paper, contract, compact, pact, concordat, cartel, written agreement; charter, muniment, deed, title, warrant, grant.

4. agent, intermediary, medium, middleman, go-between, broker, *Chiefly Brit.* factor, *Sl.* ten percenter; assistant, aide, helper, girl Friday, right-hand man, *Sl.* gopher; subordinate, deputy, acolyte, auxiliary, second; pawn, puppet, creature, jackal, cat's paw; flunky, lackey, handmaid, servant, minion; dummy, dupe, *Sl.* stooge.

instrumental, *adj.* helpful, of help, assistant, of assistance, ministrant, ministerial; useful, of use, serviceable, of service, *Obs.* utile; contributory, contributive, accessory, ancillary, supportive; catalytic, causative, effective, effectual, efficacious; conducive, beneficial, advantageous, good for; valuable, important, significant, of prime importance, primary; necessary, essential, indispensable.

instrumentality, *n.* 1. helpfulness, helping hand, assistance, aid, ministry; conduciveness, contributiveness, help, support, patronage, advocacy, backing; aegis, auspices, good offices.

2. usefulness, utility, serviceability, serviceableness; service, action, intervention, mediation, good word; effectiveness, effectuality, efficacy, efficaciousness, avail; power, influence, *Sl.* pull, *Sl.* clout, *Sl.* drag; value, importance, significance, indispensibility, indispensibleness.

3. means, way, vehicle, expedient, wherewithal, resource; strategy, system, method, manner, mode, *Latin. modus operandi;* agency, instrument, device, mechanism, machine, machinery; catalyst, mover, prime mover, aide, help, stepping stone, way up the ladder; key, passkey, passport, way in, door opener, password, open sesame, magic words.

insubordinate, *adj.* 1. unsubordinate, defiant, rebellious; insurrectional, mutinous, revolting, seditious, insurgent, riotous, revolutionary; anarchistic, lawless.

2. disobedient, refractory, recalcitrant, contumacious, undutiful, uncomplying, noncomplying, uncompliant, noncompliant, noncooperative, uncooperative, nonconforming; cross-grained, perverse, contrary, froward, opposed, restive, balking, dissentient, recusant,

resistant; stubborn, obstinate, pig-headed, mulish, obdurate, headstrong, willful, wayward; intractable, unsubmissive, indocile, disorderly, unruly, bad; incorrigible, unmanageable, ungovernable, uncontrollable. —*n.* **3.** rebel, insurrectional, upriser, mutineer, insurgent, rioter, revolutionary; dissenter, recusant, resistant, nonconformist; striker, picketer, protester, protest marcher.

insubordination, *n.* **1.** defiance, defiantness, rebelliousness, mutinousness, insurrectionalism, revolutionariness, seditiousness, insurgence, riotousness.

2. rebellion, insurrection, mutiny, revolt, uprising, revolution, sedition, insurgency; riot, disorder, disturbance, disruption, outbreak; strike, picketing, protest, protest march, demonstration, sit-in; (*all of laws*) violation, breach, break *or* breaking, infraction, infringement, transgression.

3. disobedience, refractoriness, recalcitrance, contumaciousness, contumacity, contumacy; undutifulness, noncompliance, noncooperation, uncooperativeness, nonconformity; cross-grainedness, perverseness, contrariness, frowardness, opposition, restiveness, dissension, recusancy, resistance; stubbornness, obstinateness, obstinancy, pig-headedness, mulishness, obdurateness, headstrongness, willfulness, waywardness; intractability, intractableness, unsubmissiveness, insubmission, indocility, disorderliness, unruliness, badness; incorrigibility, incorrigibleness, unmanageableness, ungovernableness, ungovernability.

insubstantial, *adj.* **1.** unsubstantial, slight, flimsy, tenuous, thin, watery, watered-down; poor, weak, feeble, frail, fragile; delicate, dainty, light, fine, ethereal, gauzy, gossamer, cobwebby.

2. insignificant, unimportant, of little *or* no import, negligible, nugatory, inconsiderable, inconsequential; trivial, trifling, petty, niggling, minor, piddling, *Inf.* picayune; paltry, meager, mere, scant, small, puny, dinky.

3. unreal, illusory, illusive, false, delusive, hallucinatory, phantom, phantasmal, spectral, ghostly; intangible, impalpable, immaterial, incorporeal, spiritual; visionary, imaginary, imagined, chimerical, dreamy, fanciful; airy, vaporous, wild, idle, empty; fantastic, make-believe, made-up, fictitious.

insufferable, *adj.* intolerable, unbearable, unendurable, insupportable; impossible, more than flesh and blood can bear, not to be borne, past bearing, untakeable; enough, too much, enough to drive one mad, enough to try the patience of Job, all that one can stand; painful, excruciating, agonizing, afflictive; dreadful, harrowing, grim, grievous, torturous.

insufficiency, *n.* **1.** deficiency, inadequacy, inadequateness, insufficience, insufficientness; scarcity, dearth, exiguity, paucity, scantiness, scantness, meagerness, none to spare, stint, lack, want, short supply, need, wantage; falling short, shortcoming, shortage, deficit, short measure, short allowance; poverty, destitution, indigence, penuriousness, pennilessness, beggary, pauperism.

2. imperfection, defectiveness, incompletion, unsatisfaction; incompetence, incapability, inability, unqualification.

insufficient, *adj.* **1.** deficient, inadequate, lacking, wanting, needful, in short supply, at a premium; meager, scant, scarce, scanty, exiguous, spare, lean; too little, too small, not enough, too little too late; in want of, short of, shy of, shy, short, minus, missing, catalectic; penurious, impoverished, impecunious, poverty-stricken, penniless, destitute, poor.

2. incomplete, imperfect, unsatisfactory; incompetent, unequal to, incapable, unqualified, unable; incommensurate, unequal, uneven, unbalanced; undermanned, understaffed, underpowered.

insular, *adj.* **1.** archipelagic, isleted, circumfluous, seagirt.

2. detached, isolated, alone, separate; unattached, distinct, apart, segregated, insulated; self-sufficient, separative, free-standing.

3. exclusive, illiberal, narrow-minded, narrow, parochial, provincial; restricted, limited, circumscribed.

insulate, *v.* **1.** cover, wrap, enwrap, encase, ensheathe; wind around, bind about, enclose, envelop, shield.

2. pad, stuff, cushion, cork, plug; seal, stanch, bung, block; make soundproof, make heatproof, make fireproof.

3. segregate, isolate, separate, disengage; sequester, sequestrate, quarantine, keep apart, zone; detach, divide, disjoin, part, sever, divorce; set apart, exclude, dissociate.

insulation, *n.* **1.** stuffing, padding, cushioning, cushion, packing, wadding, cork; seal, sealant, bunging; soundproofing, heatproofing, fireproofing.

2. separation, isolation, segregation, disengagement; sequestration, quarantine, keeping apart, seclusion; detachment, disjunction, parting, division, disconnection, severance, disunion; exclusion, setting apart, dissociation.

insult, *v.* **1.** affront, slight, *Sl.* put down, *Sl.* cut up, give offense to, disoblige; call names, *Sl.* rank out, fling dirt at, slap in the face, point at; denounce, decry, disparage, discredit, vilipend, depreciate, minimize; disdain, contemn, scout, flout; scorn, spurn, deride, misprize, jeer, ridicule, mock, scoff, laugh in *or* up one's sleeve at; burlesque, lampoon, make a fool of, guy, twit, gibe at, taunt, fleer; heckle, hoot, hiss, catcall, boo; abuse, wrong, vilify, impugn, traduce, slur, calumniate; blaspheme, profane, take [s.o.'s] name in vain; malign, defame, denigrate, slander, libel, *Inf.* backbite; gibbet, drag through the mud; humiliate, belittle, put to shame, shame, chagrin, disgrace, degrade; offend, injure, hurt, hurt the feelings of, harm, ill-treat, smart, wound, damage.

2. irritate, nettle, chafe, gall, *Chiefly U.S.* rile, disturb; annoy, make [s.o.'s] blood boil, raise [s.o's] dander, anger; vex, provoke, *Inf.* kick in the pants, aggravate, incense, inflame, exasperate, tease, *Inf.* rag, distress, fret; pique, *Inf.* miff, chafe, disgruntle, *Inf.* put [s.o.] off, give umbrage to, displease.

3. embarrass, disconcert, abash, mortify, *Inf.* gross out, upset; confuse, fluster, ruffle, discountenance, distract, discompose, confound.

4. snub, turn one's back upon, give the cold shoulder to, *Inf.* cold-shoulder, look coldly upon, keep at arm's length; overlook, disregard, ignore, pass by, push aside, show the door to; exclude, keep out.

—*n.* **5.** affront, slight, slur, dig, barb, *Sl.* cut, *Sl.* put-down, slap in the face; abuse, contumely, contempt, disdain, scorn, disparagement; derision, ridicule, sarcasm, mockery, scoffing, sneering; flout, gibe, jeer, taunt, fling, quip; hoot, hiss, catcall, sibilation; vilification, impugnment, traducement, aspersion, calumniation, calumny, obloquy; maligning, defamation, denigration, slander, libel, *Inf.* backbiting; impertinence, insolence, flippancy, *Inf.* cheek, impudence, *Inf.* sauce, sauciness, *Rare.* procacity; obscenity, vulgarity, blasphemy, profanity, scurrility.

6. rudeness, disrespect, ill-treatment; offense, indignity, discourtesy, uncourteousness, incivility, dishonor, outrage; shame, disgrace, ignominy, degradation, humiliation, abasement, mortification; snub, cold shoulder, neglect, coldness, indifference; wound, blow, injury; provocation, kick in the pants, vexation, irritation, annoyance; short answer, rebuff, hard words, tartness, acerbity, acrimony.

insulting, *adj.* **1.** offensive, slighting, *Archaic.* affrontive, disobliging, outrageous; disparaging, denouncing, derogatory, denunciable, discreditable, depreciating; disdainful, contemptuous, contemning, contemnible, supercilious, contumelious, scouting, flouting; scornful, derisive, jeering, ridiculing, mocking, scoffing; twitting, gibing, taunting, fleering; hissing, booing, catcalling.

2. abusive, vilifying, vituperative, impugnable, traducing, slurring, calumnious; blasphemous, scurrilous, irreverent, sarcastic; profane, ribald, foulmouthed, obscene, vulgar; maligning, defamatory, denigrating, slanderous, libelous; injurious, harmful, damaging, invidious; vexatious, provoking, aggravating, incensed, inflammatory, exasperating, teasing, distressing; irritating, chafing, disturbing, annoying, displeasing.

3. rude, impolite, disrespectful, discourteous, uncourteous, uncivil, incivil, dishonorable; impertinent, insolent, flippant, impudent, fresh, saucy, bold, *Archaic.* malapert; ill-mannered, ill-bred, ill-behaved, ungentlemanly, unladylike, unrefined; unmannerly, ungracious, ungallant, rustic, boorish, churlish; surly, bad-tempered, ill-tempered; obnoxious, objectionable, odious.

4. snobby, cold, cool, icy, arrogant, haughty, exclusive; indifferent, aloof, neglectful; humiliating, belittling; shameful, disgraceful, opprobrious, degrading, ignominious; blunt, gruff, brusque, harsh, acrimonious; caustic, cutting, trenchant; overbearing, obtrusive.

insuperable, *adj.* **1.** insurmountable, overwhelming, overpowering, overcoming, overmastering, overmatching; oppressive, burdensome, backbreaking, crushing, demoralizing, defeating.

2. invincible, unconquerable, inviolable, inexpugnable; impenetrable, inaccessible, unaccessible, impassable; impregnable, invulnerable, indestructible, undestroyable, imperishable, nonperishable, *Obs., Rare.* imperdible; unassailable, unattackable, formidable, powerful, mighty; indomitable, redoubtable, unyielding, undefeatable, unbeatable; tenable, secure, safe, safe and sound; stout, sturdy, strong, solid, stable, staunch, stanch.

insupportable, *adj.* **1.** unbearable, intolerable. See **insufferable.**

2. indefensible, untenable, unmaintainable, unarguable, undefendable; implausible, weak, flawed, specious, disputable, doubtful.

insuppressible, *adj.* indomitable, irrepressible, unstoppable; inextinguishable, unquenchable; uncontrollable, ungovernable, unmanageable, intractable, incorrigible, refractory, recalcitrant, contumacious; obstreperous, unruly, restive, wild, fractious, out of hand, out of control.

insurance, *n.* **1.** surety, security, indemnity, guaranty, guarantee, warranty, warrant, bond, *Brit.* assurance; contract, covenant, promise, pledge, word.

2. precaution, foresight, forethought, providence, provision; safeguard, preventive measure *or* step.

insure, *v.* guarantee, guaranty, warrant, bond, underwrite; protect, guard, safeguard, secure; ensure, assure, make sure, make certain.

insurgency, *n.* insurrection, uprising, rebellion. See **insurrection.**

insurgent, *n.* **1.** rebel, revolutionary, revolter, insurrectionist, insurrectionary, seditionist; anarchist, *U.S.* Weatherman; malcontent, rioter, brawler.

—adj. **2.** rebellious, revolutionary, insurrectionary, seditious, factious; mutinous, insubordinate, disobedient; traitorous, treasonable, subversive; lawless, riotous, ungovernable, uncontrollable, out of control, unmanageable.

insurmountable, *adj.* **1.** insuperable, overwhelming, overpowering, overcoming, overmastering, overmatching; oppressive, burdensome, backbreaking, crushing, demoralizing, defeating.

2. invincible, unconquerable, impenetrable, inviolable, inexpugnable; impregnable, invulnerable, indestructible, undestroyable, imperishable, nonperishable, *Obs., Rare.* imperdible; unassailable, unattackable, undefeatable, unbeatable; formidable, powerful, mighty; tenable, secure, safe, safe and sound; stout, sturdy, strong, solid, stable, staunch, stanch; indomitable, redoubtable, unyielding.

insurrection, *n.* rebellion, revolt, revolution, insurgence, insurgency, uprising, rising, outbreak; mutiny, insubordination; sedition, subversion; riot, anarchy, civil disorder, mob-law, street-fighting, fighting in the streets; peasant revolt, jacquerie; *Ger. Putsch,* coup d'état, overthrow, takeover.

insurrectionary, *adj.* **1.** rebellious, insurgent. See **insurgent** (*def.* **2**).

—n. **2.** rebel, revolutionary. See **insurgent** (*def.* **1**).

insusceptible, *adj.* unimpressionable, unimpressible, unsusceptible, unresponsive, unsympathetic, impassive, immovable; insensate, insensible, oblivious, deaf to, dead to; unfeeling, unemotional, emotionless, cold, cool, frigid, icy, cold-hearted, cold-blooded; callous, calloused, insensitive, thickskinned, hard, indurate, inured, hardened, hard-hearted, stony, flinty, steely.

intact, *adj.* **1.** solid, unbroken, unsevered, undivided, uncut, unshorn, unshortened, unabridged, all in one; undiminished, unlessened, unreduced, unabated.

2. sound, unimpaired, undamaged, unharmed, uninjured, unscathed, unmutilated, undecayed, inviolate; unmixed, unmingled, unblended, unalloyed; faultless, flawless, defectless; unblemished, unspotted, untainted, unsullied.

3. unchanged, unaltered, unaffected; uninfluenced unswayed, unmoved, untouched.

4. complete, whole, entire, full, integral, plenary; comprehensive, universal, all-inclusive, all-embracing, inclusive.

intangible, *adj.* **1.** impalpable, untouchable, insubstantial; incorporeal, immaterial, nonmaterial, asomatous; discarnate, bodiless, disembodied; psychical, spectral, ghostly, supernatural, *Inf.* spooky, occult; unreal, unworldly, dreamlike.

2. evanescent, fading, fleeting; light, airy, ethereal, shadowy, cloudy, wispy.

3. inappreciable, imperceptible, unperceptible, unperceivable, microscopic, infinitesimal, minuscule; unnoticeable, unapparent, hardly there.

4. subtle, obscure, vague, tenuous, imponderable; unclear, ambiguous, blurred, fuzzy, clouded, veiled; mysterious, esoteric, recondite, secret.

integral, *adj.* **1.** constituent, component, integrant; inherent, intrinsic, innate; essential, necessary, indispensable, requisite; basic, fundamental, elemental.

2. entire, complete, whole, total, aggregate, comprehensive; unified, integrated, intact; uncut, unabridged, undivided, indivisible, unbroken.

integrate, *v.* **1.** concatenate, articulate, unite, combine, amalgamate, consolidate; blend, homogenize, merge with, melt into; mingle, commingle, cohere.

2. desegregate, abolish Jim Crow, end discrimination, balance racially; open up, open to all, assimilate.

integrated, *adj.* **1.** desegregated, unsegregated, mixed, racially balanced.

2. harmonious, smooth, flowing, concordant; interrelated, interconnected, interlocked, meshed; cohesive, unified.

integration, *n.* concatenation, articulation; unification, consolidation, amalgamation, commingling, *Inf.* getting it all together; assimilation, desegregation.

integrity, *n.* **1.** uprightness, honesty, probity, rectitude; truthfulness, veracity, candidness, sincerity, forthrightness; trustworthiness, faithfulness; justness, fairness, *Inf.* square shooting; honor, goodness, decency, morality, moral fiber; conscientiousness, scrupulousness, principle, virtue; courage, intestinal fortitude, *Sl.* guts, backbone.

2. unity, oneness, wholeness, entirety, completeness, totality.

3. soundness, intactness, perfection, flawlessness, mint condition.

integument, *n.* **1.** skin, crust, peeling, rind, husk, shuck, pod, *Dial.* cod, hide, shell, hull, bark; membrane, pellicle, involucre, involucrum, tegument, *Anat., Zool.* cortex, *Bot.* perigonium, *Biol.* investment.

2. cover, covering, coat, coating, case, casing, wrapping, wrapper, cloak, sheath, sheathing, envelope, *Pharm.* capsule; enclosure, container, bag, sack, pocket, *Midland U.S. and Scot.* poke.

intellect, *n.* **1.** reason, cognition, rationality, consciousness, comprehension, understanding, thought, sense, common sense; apprehension, intuition, perception, percipience, insight; brain, head, skull, headpiece, cerebrum, *Inf.* noggin.

2. aptitude, intelligence, intellectuality, mind, mentality; brains, brainpower, braininess, wit, parts, *Inf.* gray matter, *Sl.* smarts, *Gk. Philos.* nous.

3. genius, intellectual, *Inf.* brain, *Inf.* an Einstein, mastermind, mental giant, thinker.

intellection, *n.* **1.** cognition, comprehending, reasoning, thinking; understanding, learning, apprehending, perceiving, analyzing.

2. conception, concept, thought, idea.

intellectual, *adj.* **1.** mental, cognitive, cerebral; abstract, metaphysical, transcendental.

2. intelligent, brainy, profound, gifted, well-endowed, talented; cognoscitive, academic, educated, well-instructed, well-schooled; erudite, knowledgeable, learned, literate, lettered, versed, punditic, well-read.

3. rational, reasonable; logical, sensible, nonsensual; objective, judicious, prudent.

—*n.* **4.** genius, intellect, *Inf.* brain. *Inf.* an Einstein, mental giant, mastermind.

5. academician, scholar, schoolman, philosopher, philosophe, theorist, thinker, thinking man; savant, pantologist, literate, bibliophile, bibliomaniac, bluestocking, man of letters, *Archaic.* clerk; pundit, cognoscente, aesthete, connoisseur; (*all sometimes disparaging*) pedant, bookworm, highbrow, *Inf.* egghead, *Inf.* longhair, *Inf.* know-it-all, *Inf.* walking encyclopedia.

6. rationalizer, reasoner, intellectualizer, analyzer, philosophizer.

intelligence, *n.* **1.** aptitude, intellect, intellectuality, mind, mentality, brain, brains, braininess, brainpower, *Inf.* gray matter, *Sl.* smarts, reason, sense, *Gk. Philos.* nous; intellectualness, wit, sagacity, sageness, wisdom, sapience, sapiency, *Archaic.* counsel; acumen, discernment, perspicacity, penetration; perception, percipience, insight; astuteness, shrewdness, *Sl.* savvy, keenness, long-headedness, hard-headedness, common sense; ingenuity, cleverness, aptness, parts; adroitness, deftness, agility, quickness; alertness, brilliance, brightness, acuity, sharpness.

2. rationality, consciousness, comprehension, cognition, understanding.

3. information, news, tidings, word, data, facts, notification,tip, *Inf.* tip-off, knowledge, inside information, *Inf.* low-down, *Sl.* dope; notification, account, story, report, coverage; secrets, confidence; rumor, gossip, *Inf.* scuttlebutt.

4. surveillance, observation, scrutinization, investigation, spying, spy, watching.

5. (*usu. cap.*) the Omniscient, Omniscience, Mind, God, Allah, Supreme Being.

intelligent, *adj.* **1.** perspicacious, discerning, penetrating, perceptive, percipient, insightful; gifted, well-endowed, talented, intellectual, intelligential, brainy; educated, learned, instructed, well-schooled; erudite, knowledgeable, versed, well-read, aware, knowing, *Fr. au fait*; astute, shrewd, *Sl.* savvy, keen, long-headed, hard-headed, subtle; ace, topflight, top-drawer, first-rate, *Inf.* topnotch, *Inf.* crack, *Sl.* crackerjack, *Sl.* on the ball, *Inf.* whiz-bang, *Brit. Sl.* whizzo.

2. ingenious, apt, clever, adroit, deft, smart, foxy; alert, wide-awake, brilliant, luminous, bright, acute, sharp, sharp-witted, sharp as a tack; agile, quick, quick-witted, ready; sagacious, sage, wise, sapient, sapiential; rational, logical, reasonable, commonsensical, having a good head on one's shoulders; judicious, prudent, sensible; able, capable, competent.

3. rational, conscious, higher order; sane, lucid.

intelligentsia, *n.* intellectuals, literati, *Sl.* brains, philosophes, cognoscenti, savants, academes, the learned, mental giants, think tank, brain trust, masterminds; illuminati, the enlightened, aesthetes, connoisseurs, (*all sometimes disparaging*) highbrows, *Inf.* upper crust; bohemians, free spirits, free thinkers.

intelligibility, *n.* understandability, understandableness, comprehendibility, comprehendibleness, comprehensibility, comprehensibleness, penetrability; perceptibility, discernibleness, apprehensibility, decipherability, legibility; lucidity, lucidness, luminousness, luminosity, perspicuity, clarity, clearness, plainness, plain language *or* speaking; explicitness, preciseness, precision, exactness, definiteness, clear-cutness, unambiguousness, unambiguity, lack of ambiguity; apparentness, evidentness, obviousness, manifestness.

intelligible, *adj.* understandable, comprehendible, comprehensible, cognizable, cognoscible, fathomable, penetrable, knowable; perceptible, discernible, apprehensible, appreciable, legible, decipherable; clear, crystal clear, clear as day, lucid, luminous, perspicuous, pellucid, translucent; simple, plain, plain as day, plain as the nose on one's face; explicit, precise, definite, clear-cut, unambiguous, unobscure; transparent, transpicuous, apparent, obvious, evident, manifest.

intemperance, *n.* **1.** alcoholism, dipsomania, drunkenness, intoxication, inebriety, oenomania, crapulence; saturnalia, bacchanals, carousal, orgy, debauch, spree, *Inf.* bender, *Sl.* tear, *Sl.* binge.

2. self-gratification, self-indulgence, unrestraint; licentiousness, libertinism, debauchery, dissoluteness, dolce vita, dissipation, profligacy, profligateness; lechery, lewdness, *Pathol.* satyriasis, goatishness, *Pathol.* nymphomania; concupiscence, lust, prurience, pruriency; lustfulness, libidinousness, salacity, salaciousness; promiscuity, wantonness, abandon, lawlessness, incontinence, unrestraint.

3. gluttony, gormandizing, swinishness, hoggishness; voracity, voraciousness, ravenousness, omniverousness, insatiety, insatiateness, insatiability, insatiableness.

4. immoderation, excess, excessiveness, inordinateness, exaggeration; extravagance, exorbitance, exorbitantness; unreasonableness, preposterousness, outrageousness, unconscionableness.

intemperate, *adj.* **1.** drunken, sottish, *Inf.* boozy, *Sl.* pifficated, *Sl.* pie-eyed; alcoholic, dipsomaniacal,

bibulous, bibacious; intoxicated, inebriated, *Rare.* inebrious; winebibbing, oenomaniacal, *Sl.* wino; Bacchanalian. See also **drunk**.
2. licentious, libertine, loose, wanton, wild; dissolute, dissipated, profligate, abandoned, promiscuous; lascivious, debauched, lecherous, satyric; lustful, libidinous, salacious; coarse, gross, crude.
3. gluttonous, gormandizing, swinish, hoggish, piggish, porcine; voracious, ravenous, omnivorous, insatiable.
4. immoderate, excessive, inordinate, extortionate; overweening, high-flown, overblown, exaggerated, extreme, extravagant; exorbitant, unreasonable, unwarranted, uncalled-for, undue; preposterous, outrageous, unconscionable.
5. unbridled, unrestrained, unlimited, uncurbed, uncontrolled; incontinent, free-living, Saturnalian, self-indulgent; lavish, prodigal, profligate, squandering, dissipative.
6. torrid, tropical, oppressively hot, sweltering, stifling.

intend, *v.* **1.** have in mind, have at heart, have ir view; mean, purpose; contemplate, think of, talk of dream of, project, expect; have a mind to, aspire to aim at, drive at, labor for, pursue.
2. plan, propose, design, calculate, devise, scheme determine, resolve, mean business.

intended, *adj.* **1.** purposed, planned, designed, devised, contrived, calculated; deliberate, intentional, purposeful, meant, willful, volitional, voluntary; premeditated, studious, considered, weighed; preconcerted, prearranged, predesigned, preplanned, preplotted, predevised, precontrived.
2. prospective, future, expected; coming, forthcoming, approaching, at hand.

intense, *adj.* **1.** acute, strong, fierce, severe, harsh; pointed, sharp, keen, cutting, incisive, trenchant, piercing, wounding; caustic, stinging, smarting, acrimonious, acid, mordant; sarcastic, satirical, biting, piquant; tart, bitter, poignant, pungent; concentrated, profound, deep, dark, intensified, consuming; burning, flaming, blazing, flaring, flashing; brilliant, vivid, rich, exquisite.
2. grievous, distressing, harrowing, afflictive; grave, serious, critical; heartbreaking, shocking, heartrending; harmful, hurtful, injurious, invidious; painful, excruciating, agonizing, racking, crushing, torturous; violent, vehement, angry, rancorous, wrathful; malevolent, cruel, malicious, spiteful; waspish, hostile, inimical.
3. earnest, eager, animated, enthusiastic, excited; ardent, zealous, *Inf.* gung ho, impassioned, passionate; fervent, fervid, perfervid; frenzied, frantic, crazed, mad, *Inf.* wild; strenuous, energetic, vigorous, rigorous; brisk, dynamic, high-powered, forceful; strong, mighty, potent, puissant; violent, extreme, drastic, excessive; diligent, hard-working, devoted, studious; industrious, busy, active; persevering, sedulous, assiduous, resolute, determined; ambitious, aspiring, up-and-coming, enterprising, pushing, *Inf.* pushy, aggressive.
4. emotional, emotive, temperamental, high-strung; nervous, tense, excitable, touchy, testy, peppery; spirited, high-spirited, volatile, fiery, hot-headed; heated, feverish, white-hot, inflamed, volcanic; overwrought, upset, hysterical, not rational, head-strong, stubborn; impetuous, impatient, impulsive, hasty; sensitive, feeling, sentient, demonstrative, responsive; sensuous, warm, sentimental, deep-feeling; poignant, touching, moving; transported, rapt, enraptured, rapturous, ecstatic.

intensify, *v.* **1.** sharpen, heighten, deepen, thicken; strengthen, concentrate, *Inf.* beef up, reinforce; magnify, enhance, enrich; exaggerate, make much of, overstate, overstress, overcharge.
2. aggravate, exacerbate, worsen; accelerate, snowball, mushroom; inflame, add insult to injury, add fuel to the fire *or* flames, *Inf.* rub it in, pour oil on the fire.
3. escalate, step up; tone up, give a boost to, *U.S. Sl.* soup up, *Sl.* hop up, *Sl.* jazz up; stimulate, whet, pique; warm up, build up; increase, raise, augment, extend.

intensity, *n.* **1.** high degree, excess, extremity, immoderation, inordinateness, extravagance, magnitude.
2. strength, power, potency, *Literary.* puissance; vigor, force, energy, determination, vehemence; emotion, animation, *Inf.* ginger, pep; excitement, enthusiasm, eagerness, earnestness, keenness, concentration, intentness; fervor, ardor, fervency, warmth, glow, fire, heat; devotion, devotedness, zeal, feverishness, passion, fanaticism.

intent[1], *n.* purpose, goal, design, plan, meaning, intention. See **intention**.

intent[2], *adj.* **1.** steadfast, fixed, concentrating, focused; attentive, observant, observing, watchful, heedful, regardful, mindful, alert; occupied with, engrossed in, wrapped up in, absorbed in; rapt, enrapt, enraptured, taken up with; contemplative, reflective; painstaking, persevering, diligent, sedulous, assiduous, studious.
2. firm, resolute, set on, bent on, determined, *Inf.* bound and determined, decided, purposeful; ambitious, aspiring; earnest, serious, sincere, in earnest, *Inf.* for real; thoughtful, solemn, grave; devoted, dedicated, committed, wholehearted; intense, fervent, fervid, perfervid, vehement, heated, ardent, zealous, agog, passionate, impassioned; avid, enthusiastic, *Inf.* gung ho, *Inf.* rah-rah, eager, keen.

intention, *n.* **1.** purpose, goal, aim, intent; end, end in view *or* mind, object, objective, target, mark, destination, bourne; wish, aspiration, ambition, ideal.
2. design, plan, proposal, project, undertaking; contemplation, idea; decision, determination, resolve, resolution; direction, inclination, bent, set.
3. meaning, significance, purport; implication, indication, denotation; upshot, gist.

intentional, *adj.* deliberate, purposive, purposeful, meant, willful, volitional, voluntary; designed, devised, contrived, *Obs.* consulted, *Obs.* intrigued, schemed, calculated, plotted, planned, intended; premeditated, preconceived, preconceptional, aforethought, predeterminate, predetermined, prepense; meditated, studious, studied, considered, weighed; preconcerted, prearranged, predesigned, preplanned, preplotted, predevised, precontrived.

inter, *v.* bury, inhume, *Archaic.* inearth, inurn, entomb, ensepulcher, sepulcher; lay away, *Inf.* lay to rest, *Sl.* put six feet under, consign to the grave, *Dial.* funeralize.

intercede, *v.* **1.** mediate, negotiate, intermediate, arbitrate, moderate; interpose, step in, intervene; reconcile, propitiate, appease, make peace, pacify, meet halfway; act for, represent, involve with, act in one's behalf, use one's good offices; umpire, referee, judge.
2. plead for, sue for, petition for, pray for, plea for; entreat, enjoin, adjure, implore, obtest, supplicate, solicit.

intercept, *v.* **1.** stop on the way, seize in passage, cut off; expropriate, impound, confiscate, commandeer, wrest from, dispossess, possess oneself of; run away with, catch, *Football.* pick off.
2. interrupt, check passage, interfere, interpose; obstruct, block, hinder, impede; stop, put a stop to,

check, arrest, abort, prevent, preclude; detain, stay, delay, retard; restrain, inhibit, constrain, repress; frustrate, thwart, foil.

intercession, *n.* **1.** mediation, agency, good offices, mediatorship; intermediation, intervention, interposition, interjacence; negotiation, arbitration, parley; reconciliation, propitiation, pacification, appeasement.

2. entreaty, supplication, prayer, orison, imploration, obtestation, interpellation; suit, petition, plea, bid, invocation, beseechment, solicitation.

intercessor, *n.* intermediary, middleman, go-between, intermediate, intermedium, *Sl.* connection; mediator, negotiator, arbitrator, moderator, umpire, referee, judge, *Sl.* ump, *Sl.* ref; interceder, intervener, internuncio, interagent; peacemaker, reconciler, propitiator, appeaser, pacificator, marriage counselor.

interchange, *v.* **1.** substitute, counterchange, replace, supplant, supersede, transfer; transpose, change, change places, switch; permute, commute, shuffle, (*chess*) castle; convert, change money.

2. exchange, trade, trade off, swap, swop, barter, give and take, bandy, truck; reciprocate, return, return the compliment, rejoin, respond, pay back, requite.

3. alternate, vary, intermit, rotate; seesaw, take turns, come and go.

—*n.* **4.** exchange, trade, trading, swap, swop, barter, commerce; reciprocation, reciprocity, give and take, mutuality, interplay, cross fire; transposal, transposition, metathesis, change, switch, commutation, permutation, shuffle; measure for measure, an eye for an eye, tit for tat, quid pro quo, (*chess*) castling, (*tennis*) rally, battledore and shuttlecock; substitution, replacement, supplanting, transference, transferal, supersession.

5. alteration, variation, rotation; intermittence, succession, periodicity, reoccurrence, cycle, run, round.

interchangeable, *adj.* exchangeable, transposable, *Rhet.* metathetical, synonymous; correlative, comparable, equivalent, equal, even, corresponding; standard, uniform; changeable, convertible, commutable, permutable, returnable; reciprocative, reciprocal, mutual.

interchangeably, *adv.* exchangeably, mutually, reciprocally; in exchange, in return, *Fr. au pair*; vice versa, conversely, correspondently, equivalently, equally, synonymously, metathetically; by turns, in turn, turn about, turn and turn about, each in its turn.

intercourse, *n.* **1.** dealings, trade, commerce, traffic, *Inf.* truck, business, affairs; buying and selling, trading, wholesaling, trafficking, *Inf.* wheeling and dealing, jobbing.

2. interchange, reciprocity, exchange, interplay, give and take; communication, connection, liaison, contact, congress, union; correspondence, communion, intercommunion; speaking, talking, conversation, speech, discourse; interlocution, colloquy, *Sl.* rapping.

3. coitus, coition, sexual relations, sexual union *or* congress; mating, *Archaic.* venery, copulation, carnal knowledge, *Sl.* humpery; love-making, act of love, intimacy.

interdict, *n.* **1.** prohibition, proscription, interdiction, outlawry, forbiddance, *Latin. interdictum*; disallowance, injunction, restraint, restraining order, preclusion, exclusion; ban, embargo, veto, countermand, taboo; suppression, repression, censorship.

—*v.* **2.** forbid, prohibit, disallow, ban, veto, rule out; countermand, abrogate, inhibit, shut out; restrict, restrain, bar, stop, issue an injunction; outlaw, proscribe, taboo, preclude, exclude; impede, prevent, obstruct, hinder; repress, suppress, censor.

interest, *n.* **1.** engrossment, engagement, absorption, undivided attention; attentiveness, advertence, heed, concernment; concern, regard, attention, consideration, scrutiny, notice, study; curiosity, inquisitiveness, itch, interestedness.

2. concern, consequence, moment, substantiality, weight, significance, pith, import; importance, gravity, seriousness, solemnity; urgency, primacy, priority.

3. care, concern, affair, business, matter of concern *or* interest; pastime, hobby, amusement, diversion, avocation; cup of tea, *Sl.* kick, *Sl.* trip, *Sl.* bag, *Sl.* thing, *Sl.* bug.

4. share, stake, stock, equity; part, portion, piece, cut, bit, slice, half; right, title, license, claim, grant.

5. increase, increment, return, usury, dividend, premium; percentage, profit, gain, *Inf.* take; net, clean profit, neat profit.

6. partiality, partisanship, partisanism, one-sidedness, undetachment; involvement, unneutrality, undispassionateness; leaning, preference, favoritism, discrimination.

7. benefit, benison, profit, service, avail, use; advantage, value, worth, behalf, behoof, self-interest, self-gain.

8. **in the interest of** in behalf of, in the name of, by proxy for, for the sake of, on the part of, in favor of, in aid of; to the advantage of, for the benefit of, in the furtherance of, to the advancement of.

—*v.* **9.** engage, engross, grip, rivet, absorb; fascinate, captivate, hold, hold the attention of, focus the attention of; attract, magnetize, mesmerize, hypnotize, catch the eye, draw the attention.

10. excite, infect, kindle, enkindle, arouse, quicken, whet; incite, provoke, enliven, instigate, spur, goad, animate.

11. concern, involve, respect, regard, bear upon, apply to; relate to, pertain to, correspond to, answer to, have to do with; affect, touch, strike.

12. induce, influence, sway, persuade, prompt, move; enlist, engage, impress, press, urge; incline, dispose, lead, lure, tempt; prevail upon, draw over, win over, talk into, bring over.

interested, *adj.* **1.** concerned, involved, a party to, included, implicated, in on.

2. partisan, partial, one-sided, warped, swayed; participatory, undetached, nonobjective, undispassionate; prejudiced, biased, colored, influenced, jaundiced.

3. engaged, engrossed, absorbed, preoccupied, intent on; rapt, held, fixed, riveted, gripped, under the sway; attracted, excited, piqued, tickled, fascinated, captivated; curious, inquisitive, quizzical, open-eyed, wide-eyed, agog, open-mouthed, agape.

4. selfish, self-interested, self-seeking, nepotistic, egocentric, self-centered.

interesting, *adj.* engaging, engrossing, absorbing, riveting, gripping, fixing; provocative, stimulating, provoking, intriguing, thought-provoking; amusing, entertaining, diverting; exciting, tantalizing, tempting, inviting; fascinating, captivating, charming, spellbinding, enchanting; attractive, taking, catching.

interfere, *v.* **1.** *Often* **interfere with** hamper, hinder, impede, encumber, act as a drag; obstruct, block, dam up, barricade; inhibit, restrain, cramp, handicap, trammel, put a crimp in; frustrate, thwart, foil, balk, cut the ground from under one; brake, check, arrest, abort, put a stop to; cripple, clip the wings of; sabotage, throw out of gear.

2. *Often* **interfere with** *or* **in** meddle, intrude, interrupt; intercede, interpose, intervene; horn in, butt in, thrust in, put in one's oar, *Inf.* kibitz, put one's two cents in.

3. clash, collide, conflict, be at variance; oppose, be

opposed, be in opposition, contravene.

interference, *n.* **1.** impediment, obstacle, obstruction, hindrance; difficulty, block, stumbling block, hitch, snag, clog, setback; opposition, *Inf.* flak, head wind; encumbrance, handicap, dead weight, impedimenta; drag, load, burden; check, brake, damper, wet blanket; tether, trammel.
2. meddling, intrusion, interruption; intervention, intercession, interception; butting in, horning in, *Inf.* kibitzing; meddlesomeness.

interim, *n.* **1.** meantime, meanwhile, intervening time, interlude, interspace, parenthesis, interval, while; interruption, interregnum, pause, intermission, break, respite, recess.
—adj. **2.** temporary, provisional, substitutive, substitutional, substitutionary; improvised, makeshift, stopgap, emergency.

interior, *adj.* **1.** inside, internal, on the inside, in the inside; inward, further toward the center.
2. inner, inmost, innermost, *Scot., Irish.* benmost; private, privy, nonpublic, intimate, personal, confidential; restricted, reserved, privileged; secret, esoteric, veiled, hidden.
3. innate, intrinsic, indwelling, immanent, intimate, inherent, indigenous; ingrained, engrained, inwrought, enwrought.
4. instinctive, intuitive, impulsive, involuntary, spontaneous, *Sl.* gut; intense, heartfelt, moving, stirring, overpowering; intestinal, visceral, abdominal, splanchnic; gastric, stomachic, stomachal, stomachical, *Anat.* celiac, ventral, ventricular.
5. inland, landlocked, non-coastal, non-border.
6. domestic, civil, civic, local.
7. mental, spiritual, psychic, psychological; nonphysical, metaphysical.
—n. **8.** the inside, inside part, inner part, inner space, inner side, inner surface, internal part.
9. pith, substance, gist, crux, core, heart, marrow, meat, essence, quintessence; center, middle, nucleus; basis, base, foundation, constitution.
10. depths, hold, womb, recesses, penetralia; abyss, chasm, cavity, gulf.
11. vital organ, body organ; intestines, intestinal cavity, colon, colonic cavity, *Inf.* innards; abdomen, belly, stomach, *Inf.* tummy, *Sl.* breadbasket, *Scot. and North Eng.* wame.
12. inner life, nonphysical self, soul, spirit, psyche.
13. midland, hinterland, upcountry; backwoods, *U.S. Inf.* the sticks.

interject, *v.* interpolate, interpose, intercalate, introduce, insert, inject, put in; instill, infuse, insinuate, inculcate; infix, implant, imbed, ingrain; mix in, intermix, intermingle, interlard, intersperse, sprinkle *or* scatter throughout; (*all of words, phrases, etc.*) parenthesize, interline, interlineate, margin, add in, write in.

interjection, *n.* **1.** interpolation, interposition, intercalation, introduction, insertion, injection; instillment, instillation, infusion, inculcation, infixion, implantation, imbedding, ingraining; intermixture, intermingling, interlarding, interspersion, *Esp. Brit.* interspersal; (*all of words, phrases, etc.*) parenthesizing, interlining, interlineation, margining, adding in, writing in.
2. exclamation, ejaculation; utterance, remark, statement, *Gram.* parenthesis, *Gram.* appositive.

interlace, *v.* **1.** crisscross, zigzag, weave, lace; interweave, intermingle, combine, interlink, interlock, fit together; intertwist, twist together, entwist, entwine, braid, plait, pleat, fold across; intertwine, entangle, enmesh, ensnarl, ensnare; mat, tie, knot.
2. mingle, commingle, scramble, interlard; blend, mix, commix, intermix; compound, combine.
3. diversify, change, variegate, alternate, substitute, shuffle; interchange, commute, switch; alter, modify, vary; restyle, reconstruct, remodel, transfigure, transform.

interlard, *v.* **1.** diversify, vary, change; variegate, color, spice up, dress up; intermix, intermingle, interfuse, put in, mix in; intersperse, sprinkle, pepper.
2. interject, interpolate, interpose, intercalate; interweave, intertwine, intertwist, interlace.

interlink, *v.* link, join, unite, connect; mesh, interlace, interweave, intertwine; dovetail, splice.

interlocution, *n.* conversation, dialogue, colloquy; discussion, confabulation, *Inf.* confab, converse, discourse, communication; conference, parley, *Inf.* powwow, interview; chitchat, chat, talk; chatter, palaver, *Sl.* schmooze, gossip, tête-à-tête.

interlocutor, *n.* **1.** announcer, master of ceremonies, mistress of ceremonies, M.C., emcee; humorist, stand-up comic, straight man, foil.
2. converser, chatterer, questioner, interrogator, quiz master.

interloper, *n.* trespasser, encroacher, poacher, invader, marplot; meddler, *Yiddish.* cochleffel, *Sl.* buttinsky, interferer, Paul Pry.

interlude, *n.* **1.** interruption, recess, pause, pause that refreshes, respite; interval, entr'acte; truce, cease-fire; interregnum.
2. intermezzo, divertissement, divertimento; diversion, farcetta, curtain raiser; entertainment, charade, spectacle, tableau, masque, harlequinade, burlesque, vaudeville, pantomime.

intermeddle, *v.* meddle, interfere, pry, *Inf.* snoop, *Inf.* butt in, stick one's nose in, *Inf.* kibitz, mind someone else's business; interpose, intrude, obtrude, interrupt, intervene; interlope, encroach, insinuate, invade, trespass; *Inf.* horn in, *Inf.* cut in, *Inf.* muscle in, *Inf.* worm in, *Inf.* edge in.

intermediary, *adj.* **1.** intermediate, in-between, medial.
—n. **2.** mean, medium, median, median strip.
3. go-between, mediator, intermediator, intercessor, interceder, intervener; broker, agent, interagent, medium, middleman, jobber, wholesaler, dealer, distributor; connection, contact, *Inf.* front, *Inf.* front man, lobbyist; moderator, arbiter, arbitrator, negotiator, third *or* disinterested party, umpire, referee, interlocutor, peacemaker, make-peace; instrument, tool, factor, steward, proctor; spokesman, advocate, consumer advocate, *Sl.* Nader-raider, champion, patron; spokesman, *Inf.* mouthpiece, attorney, solicitor, friend at court, ombudsman, ombudswoman; diplomat, diplomatic agent, plenipotentiary, ambassador, envoy, emissary, minister, chargé d'affaires, legate, nuncio, internuncio.
4. pimp, pander *or* panderer, procurer, procuress, *Archaic.* bawd, madam.

intermediate, *adj.* **1.** in-between, intervening, intermediary, intervenient, interposed, inserted, interfering; halfway, medial, median, in the middle; transitional, temporary, interregnal.
—n. **2.** See **intermediary** (*def.* 3).
—v. **3.** intervene, mediate, arbitrate. See **intervene** (*def.* 1).

interment, *n.* burial, burying, entombment, inhumation, sepulture, inurnment; funeral, exequies, obsequies, rites *or* ceremonies.

interminable, *adj.* **1.** unending, endless, unceasing, incessant, ceaseless; constant, nonstop, unremitting, recurring; continuous, continual, uninterrupted, unbroken, without end, never-ending, everlasting, eternal.

2. monotonous, tedious, tiresome, wearisome, humdrum, boring; long-winded, prolix, wordy, verbose, rambling, loquacious.

3. unlimited, limitless, boundless, illimitable, termless, infinite; countless, numberless, untold, innumerable; unmeasured, measureless, unmeasurable, indeterminable, incalculable.

intermingle, *v.* mingle, commingle, mix, commix, intermix, blend; compound, combine, confound; unite, fuse, amalgamate, incorporate; interweave, interlace, intertwine, interfuse, intersperse.

intermission, *n.* interim, interval, interlude, entr'acte, intermittence, interregnum; rest, pause, respite, lull, recess, *Inf.* breather, time-out; break, interruption, delay, holdup; suspension, remission, letup; pendency, abeyance, quiescence, latency, dormancy; (*all temporary*) stop, halt, arrest, breaking off, stay, stand, standstill, cessation, cease, abruption, discontinuance, discontinuation, desistance.

intermit, *v.* **1.** (*all temporarily*) discontinue, suspend, end, halt, stay, arrest, terminate, put an end to, have done with.

2. pause, recess, break, take a break, take a breather, take time out, take five, rest on one's oars.

3. (*all temporarily*) cease, stop, break off, interrupt, let up, desist, *Archaic.* surcease, quit, leave off, finish, conclude.

intermittent, *adj.* fitful, spasmodic, irregular, sporadic, random, *Pathol.* arrhythmic; recurring, recurrent, remittent, on-again off-again, on-and-off, hot-and-cold, alternate, alternating; serial, periodic, cyclic, cyclical, seasonal; rhythmic, pulsating, punctuated; discontinuous, broken, interrupted, broken off, disconnected.

intern¹, *v.* **1.** restrict, confine, enclose, pen in *or* up, cage in *or* up, encage; shut in *or* up, imprison, lock up, put behind bars.

2. impound, seize, take and hold in custody, detain, keep, stay. See **imprison** (*defs.* **1, 2**).

intern², *n.* **1.** resident doctor, resident; *All Educ.* student teacher, practice teacher, pupil teacher, teaching *or* teacher's aide, teaching assistant, *Inf.* T.A., graduate assistant.

2. apprentice, journeyman, trainee, probationer; learner, pupil, student, protégé, disciple; novice, novitiate, beginner, tyro, neophyte, catechumen, tenderfoot, *Sl.* greenhorn; newcomer, new member, entrant.

internal, *adj.* **1.** interior, inside, inner, inward.

2. intrinsic, innate, natural, true, native; inborn, inherent, indwelling, immanent; inbred, ingrained, infixed, implanted.

3. domestic, civil, interior, intestine, in-house.

4. subjective, mental, psychological, in one's mind *or* head.

—*n.* **5.** *Usu.* **internals** intestines, entrails, innards, insides, guts.

international, *adj.* world-wide, cosmopolitan, global, universal; general, ecumenical, nonsectarian, nondenominational.

internecine, *adj.* (*in reference to conflict or struggle*) familial, family, domestic, civil, intestine, internal, in-house, in-group, intramural.

2. destructive, annihilative, ravaging, devastating; slaughterous, murderous, bloody, gory, sanguinary, sanguineous, bloodthirsty; deadly, mortal, extirpatory.

interplay, *n.* interaction, meshing, interweaving; reciprocal influence *or* action *or* play; reciprocity, give-and-take.

interpolate, *v.* intercalate, insert, interline; inject, stick in, throw in, work in, put in, parenthesize, add; introduce, insinuate, interlard, sandwich, jam in, interrupt, intervene; alter, doctor, revise, emend, edit, rewrite.

interpolation, *n.* intercalation, insert, insertion, interlining, injection, insinuation; prefix, marginalia, scholium, footnote, annotation; kicker, tag, tag line; addition, addendum, adjunct, supplement, appendix, rider, codicil; suffix, postscript, postfix; interruption, parenthetical remark, aside, ad lib.

interpose, *v.* **1.** interject, intercalate, interjaculate; introduce, insert, insinuate, inject, implant; interlay, sandwich; foist in, work in, drag in, lug in, worm in, squeeze in, edge in, thrust in, throw in, toss in.

2. intrude, obtrude, interfere, butt in, horn in, cut in, *Inf.* barge in, *Inf.* muscle in, *Inf.* chisel in; meddle, intermeddle, busybody, pry, stick *or* poke one's nose in, *Inf.* kibitz.

3. intervene, intercede, step in, come between; mediate, intermediate, negotiate, bring to terms; arbitrate, moderate, referee, umpire; judge, adjudicate.

interposing, *adj.* **1.** intermediate, interjacent, intercalary, intervenient, interjectional; medial, mesial.

2. intrusive, obtrusive, interfering; meddlesome, meddling, intermeddling, officious, prying, *Inf.* nosy, *Inf.* snoopy, *Inf.* kibitzing.

3. interventional, intercessory, mediating, mediatory, intermediary, intermedial; diplomatic, reconciliatory, propitiatory.

interpret, *v.* **1.** explain, explicate, expound, spell out, simplify; elucidate, clarify, clear up, make clear, illuminate, shed *or* throw light upon; demonstrate, show, illustrate; comment upon, annotate, gloss, edit.

2. construe, understand, understand by, take, take to mean, take it that, make out; read, read into, read between the lines, put two and two together, figure out; diagnose, solve, resolve, work out, *Sl.* dope out; decode, decipher, crack; untangle, disentangle, unravel, unriddle, unfold.

3. translate, transcribe, transliterate; paraphrase, rephrase, restate, reword, rehash.

4. (*all of musical or dramatic compositions, etc.*) perform, execute, render, do, play; act, enact, playact.

interpretation, *n.* **1.** explanation, explication, elucidation, clarification, illumination; demonstration, illustration, definition; decipherment, decoding, cracking; solving, resolving, working out; untangling, unriddling, unraveling, sorting out; hermeneutics, exegesis, tropology, cryptology, lexicography, diagnostics, criticism.

2. construction, construal, deduction, inference; diagnosis, reading; understanding, conception; version, rendering.

3. portrayal, depiction, presentation, performance, execution, enactment.

4. translation, transcription, transliteration; paraphrase, restatement, rewording, rehash; metaphrase, word-for-word *or* literal *or* faithful translation; gloss, glossary, key; *Inf.* crib, *Sl.* pony, *Sl.* trot.

interpreter, *n.* **1.** exponent, expounder, expositer, explainer, clarifier; exegete, exegetist, hermeneut; translator, metaphrast, paraphrast; annotator, commentator, scholiast; critic, editor; guide, cicerone, dragoman; decoder, decipherer, cryptographer.

2. spokesman, mouthpiece, front man, public relations *or* PR man, press agent, *Sl.* flak.

3. oracle, prophet, seer, soothsayer, augur.

interregnum, *n.* interval, interim, interlude; pause, recess, respite, rest, lull, *Inf.* letup; intermission, *Sports.* half time *or* half-time intermission; suspension, abeyance; interruption, discontinuance, cessation; gap, break, hiatus, lacuna.

interrogate, *v.* question, put to the question, query, ask, inquire, inquire of, make inquiry; pose a question, demand an answer; examine, investigate, probe, interpellate; catechize, quiz, test, inquisition, pick [s.o.'s] brains; *Inf.* grill, pump, third-degree, put [s.o.] through the third degree, put [s.o.] through the wringer, cross-examine, cross-question, *Inf.* roast, *Inf.* put the pressure on, *Sl.* go *or* work over, *Sl.* put the screws to.

interrogation, *n.* **1.** examination, investigation, interpellation, inquisition; cross-examination, cross-questioning, third degree, grilling, pumping, *Sl.* the grill; catechizing, quizzing, testing.

2. question, query, inquiry, *Archaic.* demand; issue, topic, problem, poser, moot point, controversial point, bone of contention; question before the house; burning question.

interrogative, *adj.* questioning, inquiring, interrogatory; inquisitorial, investigative, catechistic; inquisitive, quizzical, curious.

interrupt, *v.* **1.** suspend, intermit, discontinue, lay aside; stop, put a stop to, halt, cease, end, terminate, bring to a stand *or* standstill, abort, cancel, drop, *Inf.* scrub; break off, sever, dissever, dissolve, sunder, disjoin; desist, refrain, leave off, *Inf.* lay off.

2. interfere, intrude, obtrude, interpose; talk out of turn, cut short, cut in, break in, barge in, *Inf.* butt in, *Inf.* horn in, *Inf.* muscle in, *Inf.* chisel in; *Inf.* chip in, *Inf.* chime in, *Inf.* put in one's two cents' worth.

interruption, *n.* **1.** suspension, discontinuance, intermission, abeyance; cessation, stop, stoppage, stopping, stay, halt; cancellation, abruption, severance, sunderance, disconnection, division, disunion, dissolution.

2. intrusion, obtrusion, interference, interloping, imposition, injection, insinuation, interjection.

3. interval, interim, interlude, interregnum; pause, recess, rest, respite, lull, *Inf.* letup; truce, cease-fire, armistice; *Sports.* half time *or* half-time intermission; gap, break, breach, fissure, hiatus, lacuna.

intersect, *v.* **1.** bisect, halve, divide, divide in half, cut in two, dichotomize, *Obs.* dimidiate; split, cleave, sunder, cut down the middle.

2. intercross, cross, crisscross, crosscut, cut across, decussate; meet, join, unite, connect, converge, come together.

intersection, *n.* **1.** junction, interchange, crossroads; traffic circle, rotary, *Brit.* roundabout; cloverleaf.

2. juncture, nexus, connexus, point of union *or* contact, connection; focus, focal point, focalization; coalescence, confluence, convergence; network, web.

interspace, *n.* **1.** interstice, space, gap, lacuna, slot, mesh; crevice, crevasse, cranny, groove, sulcus, stria, *Archaic.* scissure; split, cleft, fissure, crack, chap, check, rift, breach, scission, separation, rupture, fracture; slit, gash, scotch, rent, cut; hole, cavity, opening, aperture.

2. interim, meantime, meanwhile, interval, interlude, interregnum, intervening period *or* time; intermission, entr'acte, break, hiatus, interruption, parenthesis; pause, breath, breather, breathing spell, lull, respite, rest, recess, interphase, *Biol.* interkinesis.

intersperse, *v.* **1.** sprinkle, pepper, dot, permeate; scatter among, strew among, bestrew, distribute *or* disburse among, spread among, disperse through, broadcast throughout.

2. interpose, interpolate, insert, interject, intercalate, wedge in; interspace with, alternate with, switch off, place *or* put in between *or* among, diversify, variegate, vary; interfuse, incorporate, interweave, intertwine, interwind, interwork, work in; intermingle, intermix, mix in *or* up, combine, interblend, blend in, fold in.

interstice, *n.* **1.** interspace, space, gap. See **interspace** (*def.* **1**).

2. interlude, interim, interval. See **interspace** (*def.* **2**).

intertexture, *n.* **1.** intertwining, interweaving, interlacement, interdigitation; intersection, decussation, *Anat.* anastomosis.

2. network, reticulation, transverseness, web, mesh, meshwork, net, tissue, plexus; spider's web, *Optics.* reticle; twill, twill weave, plait, wicker, wickerwork; coil, convolution, skein; lattice, latticework, trellis, *Chiefly Brit.* wattle, grill, fretwork, tracery, filigree.

intertwine, *v.* twine *or* twist together, coil, convolute, twirl, entwine, interwind, interweave, weave, wreathe, braid, plait, plat; link, join, couple, unite, connect; interlace, bind, tie together, merge, dovetail, mesh, splice.

interval, *n.* **1.** interlude, interim, interregnum, meantime, meanwhile, in-between time.

2. intermission, entr'acte, break, hiatus, interruption, parenthesis; interphase, *Biol.* interkinesis, *Both. Geol.* interstade, interstadial; pause, breath, breather, breathing spell, time-out, half time, seventh inning stretch, rest, vacation; lull, respite, *Inf.* letup, *Australian.* spell; cessation, discontinuance, stoppage, stop, halt.

3. interstice, interspace, space, some room, distance between; gap, lacuna, mesh, slot, slit, crack, some daylight; aperture, hole, opening, void, empty space.

intervene, *v.* **1.** arbitrate, mediate, negotiate, bargain, bring to terms, parlay; intercede, conciliate, placate, reconcile; interpose, step in, come into, umpire, referee, *Inf.* ref.

2. interrupt, disturb, disrupt, intrude, discommode, break into; intercept, check, hinder, arrest; arise, emerge, issue, crop up, turn up; throw off balance, frustrate, balk, foil.

3. interfere, tamper, meddle, *Inf.* kibitz, horn in, butt in, put in one's oar, *Inf.* put in one's two cents' worth, *Inf.* poke one's nose in, *Inf.* mess in *or* with.

intervening, *adj.* **1.** intermediate, interjacent, intervenient, between, interpolated, interposed, intercalary, interjectural, intercurrent, meantime.

2. intermediary, intercessory, conciliatory, pacificatory, propitiatory, reconciliatory, mediatory.

3. intrusive, interfering, encroaching, interloping, coming between; incidental, parenthetical, stray, obstrusive, betwixt and between, importunate.

intervention, *n.* **1.** mediation, intercession, negotiation, arbitration, peacemaking, ministry, good offices.

2. intrusion, obtrusion, interference, infringement, overstepping, infraction, inroad, incursion; interval, interruption, hiatus, disjuncture, break, pause, discontinuation, respite.

3. interjacence, intercurrence, insertion, interjection, interposition, interpolation, intercalation; insinuation, interpenetration, interspersion.

interview, *n.* **1.** conference, discussion, parlay, palaver, *Fr. pourparler, Inf.* powwow; consultation, audience, confabulation, *Inf.* confab, exchange; talk, discourse, meeting, dialogue, duologue, tête-à-tête; colloquy, interlocution, intercourse, commerce, communion.

2. sitting, hearing, question and answer session, *Inf.* Q. and A., *Inf.* session, press conference; confrontation, investigation, probe, inquiry, *Inf.* Woodstein.

—*v.* **3.** question, examine, sound out, consult, confer with, bombard with questions; inquire, ask, query, probe, quiz, fish for, pry into, *Inf.* pump; evaluate, look into, scrutinize, investigate, make inquiry into, subject to examination, ferret out, nose out; interrogate, *Inf.* grill, put through the third degree, cross-examine, put in the hot-seat *or* the spotlight, put through the wringer.

interweave, *v.* **1.** weave, interlace, intertwine, interdigitate; intertwist, twine, entwine, wreathe; braid, plait, plat; intersect, decussate, cross, crisscross, twill.

2. intermingle, associate, mix, combine, mesh, commingle; weave in and out, inweave, integrate, consolidate, amalgamate, splice, interlink; blend, incorporate, fuse, hide, tuck in, *Inf.* bury, *Inf.* slip in.

intestinal, *adj.* enteric, *Med. Obs.* alvine, abdominal, ventral, *Anat.* celiac, splanchnic, visceral, *Sl.* gut; colonic, duodenal, stomachic, gastric.

intestine, *n.* **1.** *Often* **intestines** alimentary canal, bowel, bowels, colon, colons, (*of swine*) chitterlings, (*of animals*) entrails, small intestine, large intestine; viscera, body organs, internal organs, internals; insides, inwards, *Inf.* innards, *Inf.* gizzard, *Sl.* guts; vital parts, vital organs, vitals.

2. domestic, civil, civic, local; native, native-born, homebred, home-grown, home-raised, homemade; internal, in-house, intramural, *Latin. intra muros.*

intimacy, *n.* **1.** warmth, feeling, caring, affection, tenderness, endearment, fondness; love, amorousness, sexual intimacy, love-making; closeness, dearness, nearness and dearness, familiarity, confidentiality; amity, chumminess, friendliness, brotherliness, sisterliness; fast friendship, friendship, comradeship, fellowship, brotherhood, fraternity, fraternization.

2. close association, deep understanding; knowledge, mastery, comprehension, grasp, handle, hold, *Sl.* fix; acquaintance, conversance, personal knowledge, firsthand knowledge, experience.

3. privacy, seclusion, isolation, solitude, retreat.

intimate[1], *adj.* **1.** close, dear, familiar, *Scot.* pack, confidential, bosom; clubby, chummy, hob-and-nob, hand and glove, *Inf.* thick, *Inf.* thick as thieves, *Sl.* buddy-buddy, *Sl.* palsy-walsy; friendly, neighborly, amicable, sociable; companionly, comradely, brotherly, fraternal.

2. warm, cozy, comfortable, *Inf.* comfy, snug, *Fr. intime*; small, numerically limited *or* restricted, tête-à-tête, person-to-person, face-to-face.

3. personal, private, privy, secret, confidential; own, exclusive, special, especial, peculiar.

4. sexual, carnal, fleshly; amorous, amatory, erotic, passionate; adulterous, fornicatory; unchaste, impure, immoral.

5. experiential, firsthand, immediate, direct, personal, first person.

6. detailed, deep, thorough, exacting, penetrating, incisive.

7. innermost, inmost, inner, internal, interior, inward; intrinsic, inherent, deep-seated.

—*n.* **8.** confidant, *Inf.* bosom buddy, roommate, bunkmate, *Sl.* bunkie; lover, bedfellow, pillow partner, soul mate, familiar, *Fr. intime.*

9. close friend, Achates, sidekick, constant companion, shadow, alter ego, other self, *Scot. and North Eng.* marrow; comrade, *Obs.* copemate, chum, crony, *Fr. copain, U.S. Inf.* buddy, *Inf.* pal; teammate, coworker, fellow worker, *Sl.* benchmate, *Sl.* benchie; colleague, confrere, associate, consociate, compeer, peer, mate.

intimate[2], *v.* imply, suggest, infer, hint, drop a hint, *Inf.* give to understand, insinuate, *Inf.* put a bug in [s.o.'s] ear; clue, give an inkling of, *Inf.* tip off, cue, prompt; jog one's memory, signal, *Inf.* give a high sign, wink; breathe, whisper; allude to, advert, refer, indicate.

intimately, *adv.* **1.** warmly, affectionately, tenderly, lovingly, fondly; closely, dearly, familiarly, confidingly, fraternally, inseparably; personally, privately, confidentially, secretly, privily.

2. sexually, carnally; amorously, amatorially, erotically, passionately.

3. thoroughly, completely, fully, through and through, in detail; fundamentally, deeply, to the core.

intimation, *n.* implication, suggestion, hint, insinuation, inference, innuendo; inkling, clue, cue; allusion, reference, indication; whisper.

intimidate, *v.* **1.** overawe, awe, cow, subdue, daunt; domineer, bully, bullyrag, browbeat, buffalo, push around; terrify, petrify, frighten, affright, scare; dismay, appall, alarm, abash.

2. tyrannize, terrorize, threaten, coerce, compel, *Inf.* (*often used jocularly*) twist [s.o.'s] arm, bulldoze; extort, pressure, *Inf.* rough up, *Inf.* lean on, *Inf.* bear down on.

3. dishearten, deter, discourage, dispirit, *Inf.* psych out, *Inf.* one-up.

intimidation, *n.* **1.** intimidating, daunting, overawing; bullying, browbeating, threatening; tyranny, terrorism, reign of terror; coercion, pressure, *Inf.* armtwisting; extortion, the badger game; mastery, one-upmanship.

2. fright, affright, terror, dread, fear, funk, abject funk; alarm, dismay, trepidation, flutter, tremor, disquietude.

into, *prep.* **1.** *Slang.* interested in, involved in, steeped in, in tune with; knowledgeable about, versed in, at home with, familiar with, conversant with, *Sl.* up on; taken by, enamored of, infatuated with, *Sl.* turned on by.

2. **be into** *Slang.* like, *Sl.* dig, *Sl.* get off on; care about, identify with, relate to, sympathize with, empathize with.

intolerable, *adj.* **1.** insufferable, unbearable, unendurable, insupportable; impossible, more than flesh and blood can bear, not to be borne; enough, too much, enough to drive one mad, enough to try the patience of Job, all that one can stand; painful, excruciating, agonizing, afflictive; dreadful, harrowing, grim, grievous, torturous.

2. excessive, immoderate, beyond all bounds; unreasonable, disproportionate, undue, inordinate, uncalled-for, unwarranted, unneeded, needless, unnecessary; extreme, outrageous, preposterous, monstrous, rank, egregious.

intolerance, *n.* bigotry, discrimination, want of forbearance; narrow-mindedness, narrowness, illiberality; prejudice, partiality, bias, one-sidedness; dogmatism, fanaticism, opinionativeness, zealotry, chauvinism, jingoism, monomania.

intolerant, *adj.* **1.** unforbearing, unsympathetic, unindulgent, untolerating; inhospitable, inconsiderate, unfriendly, disobliging; uncharitable, misanthropic, cynical.

2. bigoted, illiberal, close-minded, closed, narrow-minded, narrow; insular, parochial, provincial, confined; prejudiced, biased, warped, twisted, jaundiced, partial, one-sided; sexist, chauvinistic, jingoistic, racist, anti-Semitic; fanatical, dogmatic, opionionated, unreasonable.

—*n.* **3.** bigot, illiberal, *Inf.* little person; racist, chauvinist, sexist; fanatic.

intonation, *n.* **1.** pitch pattern, intonation pattern *or* contour; speech pattern, manner of speaking, mode of expression; pitch, tone, frequency; timbre, tonality,

tone quality, coloring; tune, melody, lilt, swing, jingle, flow, harmonious flow, rhythmic flow; overtone, monotone, undertone; tonelessness, resonance, sonority, sonorousness.
2. accent, accentuation, emphasis, stress, syllable stress; attack, delivery; cadence, beat, rhythm, tempo, pulse, throb; pulsation, cadency, rhythmicity.
3. pronunciation, articulation, enunciation, utterance; vocalization, phonation, voice; inflection, modulation, phrasing, suspension; regional *or* foreign accent, drawl, twang, brogue, burr, broad accent *or* speech.
4. chant, Gregorian chant, *Eccles.* versicle, mantra, Vedic hymn *or* chant; prayer, invocation, supplication.

intone, *v.* **1.** speak, utter, say, articulate, voice, give voice; pronounce, enunciate, mouth; accentuate; aspirate, whisper, murmur; emit, deliver.
2. chant, *Obs.* chaunt, cantillate; singsong, chime, drawl; sing, croon, carol; warble, lilt, trill; chirp, chirrup, twitter, pipe, whistle; hum.
3. intonate, modulate, inflect, vocalize, phonate.

intoxicant, *adj.* **1.** alcoholic, intoxicating, *Archaic.* intoxicative, inebriant, inebriating, inebriative.
2. exciting, breath-taking, thrilling, heady, stirring, moving; exhilarating, exuberating, invigorating, stimulating, animating, inspiring.
—*n.* **3.** alcoholic beverage *or* drink, drink, potation; liquor, alcohol, spirits, John Barleycorn, the demon rum, *Inf.* booze, *Inf.* hard stuff, *Sl.* likker, *Sl.* hooch, *Sl.* sauce, *Sl.* medicine; *Sl.* redeye, *Sl.* rotgut, *Sl.* blue ruin; *U.S. Inf.* moonshine, *Inf.* firewater, *Sl.* mountain dew, *Sl.* white lightning; mixed drink, cocktail, highball, *Inf.* chaser; stimulant, bracer, *Inf.* eye-opener; nightcap, *Brit. Inf.* sundowner; the bottle, the cup, the cup that cheers.
4. drug, narcotic, *Sl.* dope; soporific, opiate; *Sl.* Mickey Finn, *Sl.* knockout drops.

intoxicate, *v.* **1.** inebriate, besot, make drunk, *Inf.* light up, *Inf.* put under the table; stupefy, addle, fuddle, befuddle, muddle; *All Sl.* plaster, pollute, souse, stew, crock, swack, pickle, stone, sozzle, booze up, liquor- *or* likker-up.
2. exhilarate, invigorate, stimulate, animate, inspirit, enliven; rouse, arouse, inflame, enflame, kindle, fire, fire up; thrill, elate, galvanize, electrify, take one's breath away, *Inf.* give one a kick *or* thrill *or* lift; overcome, overpower, overwhelm, send one's head spinning, make one's head spin *or* reel; enrapture, enchant, bewitch, entrance; charm, infatuate, captivate, fascinate.

intoxicated, *adj.* **1.** inebriated, inebriate, inebrious, crapulent, crapulous, *Archaic.* intoxicate; drunk, drunken, sodden, besotted, sottish, awash, *Literary.* in one's cups; under the influence, under the weather, with a glow on, *Sl.* off the wagon, the worse for liquor; saturated, soused, full, *Scot.* fou; tipsy, grogged, *Archaic.* groggy, fuddled, befuddled, muddled, obfuscated, woozy, bleary-eyed, pie-eyed, glassy-eyed; far-gone, stupefied, staggering, staggering drunk, drunk as a lord, drunk as a piper *or* fiddler, drunk as a skunk *or* owl; merry, happy, gay, jolly; maudlin.
2. *All Inf.* boozy, tight, lit, lit-up, lit to the gills, illuminated, liquored-up; pickled, lathered, high, high as a kite; mellow, feeling good, feeling no pain; blind, blind drunk, dead drunk, paralyzed, knocked-out, out, out of it, under the table, passed-out. See also **drunk** (*def.* **2**).
3. *All Sl.* loaded, lubricated, oiled, stewed, stewed to the gills, tanked, *Brit.* pissed, *Brit.* bevied; primed, gassed, bombed, stoned, polluted, crocked, cocked to the gills, canned, sloshed, potted, plastered; stiff, stinko, plotched, spificated, swacked, blotto, smashed, skunk-drunk, burning with a low blue flame. See also **drunk** (*def.* **3**).
4. excited, breathless, beside oneself; exhilarated, invigorated, stimulated, animated, inspirited; ecstatic, enraptured, rapt, transported, abandoned; captivated, enchanted, charmed, fascinated; fervid, fervent, ardent, impassioned, passionate; inflamed, enflamed, fired-up, hot, red-hot, heated; flushed, feverish, delirious.

intoxication, *n.* **1.** drunkenness, insobriety, inebriety, inebriation, intemperance, sottedness, besottedness, tipsiness; alcoholism, chronic alcoholism, dipsomania, habitual drunkenness, bibulousness, bibulosity, bibacity, bibaciousness, crapulence, crapulency, crapulousness.
2. drink, drinking, heavy *or* serious *or* problem drinking; imbibing, tippling, toping, bibition, bibation, bibbing, bibbling, *Rare.* bibbery, *Inf.* boozing, *Inf.* swilling, *Sl.* hitting the bottle *or* booze *or* sauce, *Brit. Sl.* bevying.
3. exhilaration, invigoration, stimulation, animation; ecstasy, elation, excitement, excitation; madness, delirium, frenzy, raving; enchantment, enravishment, transportation; fascination, infatuation, captivation.
4. *Pathology.* poisoning, *Pathol.* autointoxication, *Pathol.* autotoxicosis, *Pathol. autotoxemia or* autotoxaemia.

intractability, *n.* **1.** intractableness, indocility, unsubmissiveness, insubmission, incompliance, incompliancy, uncooperativeness, nonconformity; stubbornness, obstinateness, obstinacy, pervicaciousness, pig-headedness, mulishness, obdurateness, hard-headedness, headstrongness, willfulness, waywardness, wrong-headedness; cross-grainedness, perverseness, perversity, contrariness, frowardness, resistance, opposition, restiveness, balkiness.
2. disobedience, refractoriness, fractiousness, recalcitrance, recalcitrancy, contumaciousness, contumacity, contumacy; rebelliousness, rebellion, insubordination, defiance, defiantness, recusancy; uncompliableness, indomitability, indomitableness, unmanageableness, ungovernability, ungovernableness; wildness, unruliness, rowdiness, rowdyishness, disorderliness; difficulty, impossibility, impossibleness, incorrigibility, incorrigibleness, badness.
3. intransigence, intransigency, uncompromisingness, irreconcilability, irreconcilableness, implacability, implacableness, inexorability, inexorableness; unyieldingness, unbendingness, rigidity, rigidness, strictness, inflexibility, inflexibleness, hard-and-fastness; immovability, immovableness, unalterableness, unchangeability; hardness, toughness, firmness, steadfastness; doggedness, tenaciousness, tenacity, persistence, persistency, insistence, pertinaciousness, pertinacity; determination, determinedness, resolvedness, resoluteness, resolution, resolve.

intractable, *adj.* **1.** indocile, unsubmissive, uncompliant, incompliant, uncooperative, unconforming, nonconforming; stubborn, obstinate, pervicacious, pig-headed, mulish, obdurate, headstrong, willful, strong-willed, wayward, wrong-headed; cross-grained, perverse, contrary, froward, resistant, opposed, restive, balky, balking.
2. disobedient, refractory, fractious, recalcitrant, rebellious, insubordinate, defiant, contumacious, recusant; uncompliable, indomitable, unconquerable, unsubduable; unmanageable, ungovernable, uncontrollable, wild, unruly, rowdy, rowdyish, disorderly; difficult, hard to handle, bad, unteachable, incorrigible, impossible.
3. intransigent, uncompromising, unyielding, unbending, hard-line, strict, rigid, inflexible. See **intransigent** (*defs.* **1, 2**).

intransigent, *adj.* **1.** uncompromising, irreconcilable, implacable, unappeasable, inexorable; unrelenting, relentless, unmerciful, pitiless, hard-hearted, unfeeling; impervious, uninfluenced, unaffected, unmoved, unpersuaded, untouched.

2. unyielding, unbending, hard-line, strict, rigid, inflexible, cast-iron, hard-and-fast; immovable, unmoveable, unpersuadable, unalterable, unchangeable; firm, hard, hard as a rock, tough, hardened, hardcore, confirmed, inveterate, die-hard; stubborn, obstinate, pervicacious, pig-headed, mulish, obdurate, hard-headed, headstrong, willful, strong-willed; dogged, tenacious, persistent, insistent, pertinacious; determined, resolved, resolute, steadfast, hard-set.

intrepid, *adj.* **1.** fearless, dauntless, unafraid, dreadless, aweless, Spartan, nervy, *Sl.* gutsy, *Sl.* ballsy, unblenching, unblenched, undaunted, undismayed, unappalled, unalarmed; bold, bold-spirited, high-spirited, daring, dashing, adventurous, audacious, rash, reckless; brave, courageous, valiant, valorous, heroic, hero-like, stout-hearted, lionhearted, iron-hearted, great-hearted; virile, manly, manful, gallant, chivalrous, chivalric, tall in the saddle.

2. firm, resolute, indomitable, unconquerable, invincible, staunch, stanch, steadfast, stalwart, *Archaic.* stalworth, doughty, sturdy, hardy; unflinching, unshrinking, unyielding, unswerving, unwavering, undeviating, unfaltering, unbending, unhesitating; mettlesome, plucky, gritty, game, tough, spirited, redblooded, *Inf.* spunky.

intrepidity, *n.* **1.** fearlessness, dauntlessness, awelessness, dreadlessness, intrepidness; boldness, boldspiritedness, high-spiritedness, daring, derring-do, audacity, audaciousness, temerity, rashness, recklessness; courage, bravery, valor, valorousness, valiancy, valiance, heroism, prowess, stout-heartedness, lionheartedness, iron-heartedness, great-heartedness, highheartedness; virility, manliness, manfulness, manhood, gallantry, chivalry, chivalrousness.

2. fortitude, endurance, tenacity, determination, will, will power; firmness, resolution, resoluteness, indomitability, indomitableness, invincibleness, invincibility, staunchness, stanchness, steadfastness, stalwartness, sang-froid, doughtiness, sturdiness, hardiness, hardihood, bulldog courage; mettle, pluck, pluckiness, spirit, backbone, gumption, blood, heart, nerve, grit, *U.S. Inf.* sand, *Inf.* starch, *Inf.* spunk, *Sl.* cojones, *Sl.* guts, *Sl.* moxie.

intricacy, *n.* intricateness, complexity, complexness, knottiness; perplexity, nonplus, puzzlement, enigma, puzzle, riddle, conundrum; labyrinth, maze, anfractuosity, tortuosity; snarl, knot, Gordian knot, tangled web, web.

intricate, *adj.* **1.** tangled, entangled, raveled, twisted, knotty, convoluted, involute, mazelike, labyrinthine; anfractuous, sinuous, tortuous; circuitous, roundabout, winding, serpentine; jumbled up, chaotic; Byzantine, rococo, ornate.

2. complex, complicated, kaleidoscopic, daedal; perplexing, mystifying, puzzling, enigmatic; arduous, difficult, thorny, trying, tough, *Inf.* tough to figure, *Inf.* nasty; crabbed, obscure, unfathomable.

intrigue, *v.* **1.** interest, attract, absorb, appeal to, fascinate, pull, draw, rivet one's attention; stimulate, arouse, pique, stir, excite, tickle, titillate; beguile, divert, charm, captivate, carry away, seduce.

2. puzzle, baffle; worry, perturb, concern, disturb, bother.

3. finagle, wangle, contrive, machinate, manipulate, finesse; scheme, plot, conspire, complot, cabal; devise, hatch up, concoct, maneuver; frame, stoop to conquer, get the better of, seize the opportunity.

4. have an affair, keep trysts, carry on, take a mistress; philander, play Lothario, *Sl.* swing, *Sl.* run *or* play *or* fool around, *Sl.* cheat.

—n. **5.** finagling, wangling, contriving; machination, manipulation, Machiavellianism; plot, conspiracy, complot, cabal; scheme, maneuver, trickery, subterfuge, guile, craftiness; dirty trick, racket, duplicity, double-dealing, deception, dodge; stratagem, ruse, wile, cunning, artifice, expedient.

6. amour, liaison, affair; adultery, lascivious carriage, lasciviousness, lewdness; cheating, *Inf.* hanky-panky; tryst, assignation.

intriguer, *n.* intrigant, finagler, wangler, manipulator, machinator; plotter, schemer, Machiavelli, conspirator; snake, snake in the grass, *Sl.* baddie, *Sl.* yutz, not nice person, trickster, someone who can't be trusted as far as you can throw him *or* throw a piano; sly boots, *Sl.* cutie, *Sl.* sharpy, charmer, charm school graduate, seducer, fast shuffler, fast dealer.

intriguing, *adj.* **1.** interesting, attractive, absorbing, appealing, fascinating; stimulating, arousing, stirring, exciting; beguiling, diverting, charming, captivating, seductive; engaging, inviting, winning.

2. sly, wily, devious, Machiavellian; crafty, tricky, cunning, foxy; subtle, *Sl.* slick, slippery; circuitous, tortuous, crooked, sinister; designing, conniving, deceptive.

intrinsic, *adj.* **1.** indwelling, immanent, inherent, indigenous; inborn, inbred, innate, connate, connatural, natural, natural-born, native, ingenerate; congenital, hereditary, inherited, in the blood, in the family.

2. inveterate, rooted, deep-rooted, planted, implanted, fixed, infixed, ineradicable; permanent, inseparable, built-in; engrained, inwrought, enwrought, in the grain.

3. true, real, genuine, authentic, actual, honest; essential, basic, organic, radical, constitutional, fundamental, substantial.

introduce, *v.* **1.** (*of persons*) acquaint, get [s.o.] acquainted, make known to each other, bring together, put on speaking terms; present formally, make introductions.

2. present, announce, present to an audience, bring in; usher in, ring in, harbinger, herald.

3. originate, start, begin, inaugurate, launch, break ground; instigate, set in motion, take the first step toward, start the ball rolling on, bring into use; create, beget, engender, father, conceive of, give birth to, bring into being, coin; institute, pioneer, found, establish, actuate, set up.

4. propose, suggest, mention, broach, bring up, bring before the public, bring to [s.o.'s] attention, bring into notice; advocate, advance, promote, speak for *or* in favor of.

5. preface, precede, prelude, premise, lead into, make introductory remarks *or* comments; open, commence, start off, begin, lead off; explain, give an explanation of, give an exposition on, give the background on, acquaint [s.o.] with the subject.

6. insert, interject, inject, interpose, interpolate, intercalate, put *or* place *or* set into, bring into; incorporate, interfuse, interweave, intertwine, interwind, interwork, work in, blend *or* fold in; insinuate, infuse, instill, implant, embed.

introduction, *n.* **1.** acquaintance, acquaintedness, acquaintanceship; knowledge, familiarity, awareness.

2. presentation, announcement, heralding, harbingering.

3. foreword, preface, preamble, prelude, prologue, prolegomenon, proem, preliminary, prelim., *Gk. pro-*

logos, Inf. intro; opening, lead, commencement, beginning, start; exposition, explanation, explication, opening *or* introductory remarks *or* comments.

4. fundamentals, groundwork, rudiments, basics; elementary course, primer, basal text; survey, overview, insight, look, glimpse.

5. insertion, interjection, injection, interposition, interpolation, intercalation; incorporation, interfusion, interspersion, interspersal, interworking; insinuation, infusion, instillment, instillation, implantation, embedment.

introductory, *adj.* **1.** prefatory, preludial, preludious, prelusive, prelusory, prologomenous, proemial; preliminary, precursory, antecedent, preceding; leading, lead off *or* in; initiatory, initiative, inaugural, beginning, initial, starting.

2. preparatory, explanatory, expositional, background; elementary, fundamental, basic, basal, rudimental; primary, first level, first grade, embryonic, incipient.

introspect, *v.* look into oneself, examine one's mind *or* conscience, search one's heart, search one's soul; think over, bethink, sleep on it, consult one's pillow; ponder, muse, meditate, contemplate; reflect, brood, ruminate, speculate, deliberate.

introspection, *n.* self-examination, self-analysis, self-observation, self-contemplation, self-judgment; soul-searching, heart-searching; self-consultation, self-communion, self-counsel; musing, meditation, contemplation, relection, speculation, rumination, brooding, deliberation.

introspective, *adj.* reflecting, musing, pondering, ruminant, meditative, deliberative; contemplative, speculative, reflective, thoughtful; engrossed, lost in thought, rapt, absorbed, concentrating, abstracted; immersed *or* plunged in thought, occupied, preoccupied.

introvert, *n.* self-inspector, self-counselor, self-scrutinizer, self-observer; brooder, muser, ponderer; shy person, bashful person, timid person, wallflower.

intrude, *v.* **1.** obtrude, break in, interfere, intervene, interrupt, interpose, insinuate; meddle, pry, *Inf.* snoop, *Inf.* kibitz, poke one's nose into; busybody, have one's finger in every pie, have one's nose in every door; impose upon, interlope, thrust upon, force upon, foist upon; storm in, burst in, *Inf.* barge in, cut in, *Sl.* butt in, *U.S. Sl.* horn in, crash, crash the gates; chime in, interject, inject, put one's two cents in; muscle in, worm in, irrupt; discommode, inconvenience, trouble, annoy, vex, dun, bother, pester, irk.

2. encroach, infiltrate, invade, poach; infringe, impinge, entrench, trench; overstep, transgress, trespass, overrun.

intruder, *n.* **1.** meddler, intermeddler, interloper, interferer; busybody, *Inf.* snoop, prier; back-seat driver, *Inf.* kibitzer, *Sl.* yenta, *Sl.* buttinsky, cuckoo.

2. invader, raider, attacker, aggressor, encroacher, infiltrator; squatter, poacher, trespasser, stowaway, gate-crasher, crasher, uninvited guest, unwelcome guest.

3. parvenu, upstart, newcomer, incomer, outsider.

intrusion, *n.* **1.** obtrusion, interloping, meddling, intermeddling; imposition, interposition, interposal, insinuation, interference, interruption.

2. encroachment, invasion, infringement, impingement, poaching; incursion, inroad, irruption, illapse, influx, ingress; overstepping, transgression, trespass, overrunning; aggression, attack, overture.

3. presumption, presumptuousness, obtrusiveness, meddlesomeness; officiousness, impertinence, forwardness.

intrusive, *adj.* **1.** intruding, interruptive, obtrusive, invasive; irruptive, ingressive, incursive, incoming; interfering, meddling, meddlesome, inquisitive, *Inf.* nosy, *Inf.* snoopy, prying; distracting, disturbing, importunate.

2. annoying, bothersome, irksome, worrisome, troublesome, irritating, vexatious; officious, presumptuous, impertinent, forward, pushing.

intuit, *v.* **1.** ,sense, feel, realize, discover, become aware of, know, feel ın one's bones, *Inf.* have a hunch, *Inf.* have a sneaking suspicion.

2. perceive, grasp, understand; see, comprehend, apprehend; ken, fathom, take in.

intuition, *n.* **1.** discernment, perception, perspicacity, percipience, sagacity; apprehension, comprehension, understanding, grasp, mental hold.

2. insight, clairvoyance, divination; instinct, prompting, sixth sense; foreknowledge, precognition, presentiment.

3. intimation, hint, clue; inkling, glimmer, glimmering, a feeling in one's bones, *Inf.* hunch, *Both pl.* vibrations, *Sl.* vibes; qualm, suspicion, misgiving; boding, foreboding, forewarning, premonition, omen, augury, portent.

4. telepathy, extrasensory perception, ESP, clairvoyance, second sight.

intuitive, *adj.* **1.** instinctive, involuntary, intuitional, untaught, unpremeditated, noninferential; impulsive, automatic, immediate, spontaneous, direct, on the spot; emotional, visceral, intestinal, *Inf.* seat-of-the-pants, *Inf.* played by ear, *Sl.* gut; inborn, inbred, innate, ingenerate; immanent, indwelling, inherent, indigenous, intrinsic.

2. perceptive, insightful, clairvoyant, presentient, knowing; discerning, percipient, discriminating.

intumesce, *v.* swell, tumefy, become tumid, *Obs.* incrassate; distend, inflate, bloat, puff out, blow up, bubble up, dome; protrude, bulge, bag, belly; fill out, fatten; expand, extend, spread, spread out, outspread, stretch, stretch out; enlarge, make larger, increase, grow, magnify, augment.

intumescence, *n.* **1.** swelling, bloating, tumefaction, turgescence, turgidness, turgidity; distention, inflation, expansion, extension, spread; enlargement, increase, amplification, widening, thickening, broadening, dilation, dilatation.

2. protuberance, protrusion, projection, growth, bulge, excrescence, tumor, tuberosity.

inundate, *v.* **1.** flood, overflow, deluge, overrun, pour over; submerge, drown, cover, engulf, bury; drench, saturate, soak; surge, swell, stream forth, pour forth, disembogue, debouch.

2. overwhelm, overpower, overspread, overburden; sate, glut, choke, fill [s.o.] up to his ears; bog down, mire down, swamp.

inundation, *n.* **1.** flood, deluge, flash flood, alluvion, freshet, *Brit.* spate; overflow, spillover; torrent, cataract; tidal wave, high tides, roller, breaker, tsunami; cloudburst, downpour, drenching rain; gullywasher, *Inf.* gullywhomper, monsoon.

2. outpouring, overflowing, flow, stream, tide, flush, wave, cascade; plenteousness, *Obs.* galore, profusion; overabundance, superabundance, plethora, excess, nimiety; superfluity, surplus, *Sl.* enough to choke a horse; *All Inf.* tons, barrels, heaps.

inurbane, *adj.* indelicate, uncourtly, ungallant, indecorous, ungracious, ungentlemanly, unladylike; ill-bred, ill-mannered, bad-mannered, unmannerly, rude, impolite, uncivil, unceremonious, discourteous, disrespectful, misbehaved; brash, bold, hoydenish, *Scot.* randy; brazen, barefaced, insolent, impudent, insulting, impertinent, pert, saucy, fresh; gruff, surly, sullen, bearish; inconsiderate, insensitive, tactless, *Brit.* misleared.

inurbanity, *n.* incivility, unmannerliness, bad manners, rudeness, impoliteness, unceremoniousness, discourtesy, discourteousness, disrespectfulness, misbehavior; indelicacy, uncourtliness, ungraciousness, ungentlemanliness, unladylikeness; roughness, crudeness, boorishness, churlishness, loutishness, vulgarness, coarseness, tactlessness; brashness, boldness, brazenness, barefacedness; insolence, impudence, impertinence, pertness, sauciness, freshness.

inure, *v.* harden, indurate, toughen, season, temper, anneal; accustom, familiarize, make used to, habituate, naturalize; adapt, acclimate, acclimatize, get used to.

inurn, *v.* bury, inter, inhume, sepulcher, lay away, *Inf.* lay to rest, consign to the grave, *Dial.* funeralize; entomb, ensepulcher.

inutile, *adj.* **1.** useless, of no use, of no service; unavailing, ineffective, ineffectual, inefficacious, bootless; valueless, worthless, meritless, good-for-nothing, not worth a straw; futile, purposeless, idle, vain, inane; to no purpose, to no avail, for naught; fruitless, unproductive, profitless, unprofitable, gainless.

2. inefficient, incompetent, inept, inadequate; sterile, impotent, barren; worn out, effete, obsolete; inoperative, unserviceable, not working, *Inf.* no-go, no good, *Sl.* on the shelf.

inutility, *n.* **1.** uselessness, ineffectuality, ineffectualness, inefficaciousness, inefficacy, bootlessness; pouring water into a sieve, carrying coals to Newcastle, casting pearls before swine, beating the air, kicking against the pricks, baying the moon; futility, inanity, purposelessness; valuelessness, worthlessness, meritlessness.

2. inoperativeness, unserviceableness, inefficiency, incompetence, ineptitude, inadequacy; fruitlessness, unproductivity, unprofitableness, profitlessness.

invade, *v.* **1.** attack, irrupt, assail, assault, strike at; begin hostilities, declare war, go to war, make war; penetrate, cross frontiers, march into, march against, thrust at, overrun, raid, storm, blitz, blitzkrieg; cross the Rubicon, cross the Alps, breach the Maginot line, cross the 38th parallel.

2. intrude, obtrude, interrupt, intervene, *Inf.* cut in; interlope, move in, take over, encroach, supercede, insinuate, *Inf.* horn in, *Inf.* muscle in, *Inf.* worm in, *Inf.* edge in; trespass, *Inf.* crash, *Inf.* crash the gate, break in.

3. overstep, infringe upon, transgress, trample upon, ride roughshod over.

4. permeate, pervade, fill; penetrate, spread into, spread over, overspread, spill over into.

invader, *n.* attacker, assailant, aggressor, assaulter, enemy, foe; frontier-violator, gate-crasher, intruder, interloper, trespasser, encroacher, infringer, overrunner, raider, vandal, Hun.

invalid[1], *n.* **1.** sickly person, infirm person, convalescent, shut-in, valetudinarian; patient, inpatient, outpatient, case; the sick, the infirm, the handicapped; sufferer, carrier, cripple, incurable, victim; hypochondriac, *Pathol.* neurasthenic, malingerer.

—adj. **2.** sick, sickly, infirm, unwell, ill, ailing, valetudinarian, valetudinary; weak, weakly, feeble, enfeebled, frail, helpless, debilitated; exhausted, prostrate; unhealthy, diseased, morbose, unsound, under doctor's care; indisposed, confined, laid up, bedridden; handicapped, crippled, disabled, lame; paralyzed, paralytic; superannuated, retired; senescent, doting, senile, decrepit; moribund, dying, flagging, drooping.
—v. **3.** weaken, enfeeble, debilitate, devitalize; incapacitate, disable, lay up, confine, hospitalize; afflict, distress, pain, upset.

invalid[2], *adj.* **1.** indefensible, unjustified, unjustifiable, unsupportable, unwarrantable, unwarranted, unsubstantiated, untenable; unfounded, ill-founded, unproved, unscientific, groundless, baseless; illogical, irrelevant, unreasonable, irrational, incoherent, absurd, preposterous; fabricated, invented, trumped-up, far-fetched; faulty, false, fallacious, untrue, spurious, wrong, incorrect, erroneous; defective, imperfect, unsound, impaired; unsatisfactory, unacceptable, inadequate, insufficient, deficient, inappropriate, unsuited; inconsistent, incongruous, incongruent, contradictory; changed, altered, distorted, corrupt.

2. weak, ineffectual, inefficacious; powerless, impotent, vulnerable; unconvincing, lame, vague, flimsy; vain, idle, futile, unavailing, useless, nugatory, worthless, good-for-nothing; insipid, uninteresting, pointless, vapid; diluted, watery, attenuated; wishy-washy, namby-pamby, milk-and-water, wavering, vacillating, hesitant, indecisive.

3. legally ineffectual, legally unenforceable, not binding, inoperative, nonviable; null, void, null and void, annulled, nullified; set aside, quashed, vitiated, vacated, disenacted, disestablished; cancelled, discharged; repealed, revoked, rescinded, abolished, reversed, abrogated; renounced, repudiated, disclaimed, disavowed.

invalidate, *v.* **1.** disprove, refute, confute, rebut; dispute, deny, oppose, controvert, counter; contradict, belie, negate; overturn, overthrow, subvert; expose, reveal, unmask; discredit, disparage, demean, debase; mar, spoil, ruin, wreck, destroy.

2. weaken, undermine, enfeeble, debilitate; enervate, exhaust, sap, devitalize; disable, cripple, paralyze.

3. void, avoid, declare null and void, render null and void, nullify, disannul, annul; quash, vitiate, vacate, disestablish; cancel, discharge; set aside, supersede; cease, *Law.* nol-pros, stop, discontinue, break off; countermand, counterorder, override, overrule; veto, negate.

4. revoke, rescind, abrogate, reverse, repeal, *Rare.* disenact, abolish; recant, retract, withdraw, take back, undo, unmake, recall; renounce, relinquish, repudiate, abjure, forswear, abnegate; disavow, disclaim, disown, deny; unsay, go back on one's word, eat one's words, back-pedal, renege.

5. terminate, dissolve, put an end to, bring to an end, do away with; discard, dismiss, get rid of, cast aside, throw out.

invalidation, *n.* **1.** refutation, disproving, disproof, confutation, rebuttal; disputation, denial, opposition; contradiction, negation; overturn, overthrow, subversion; exposé, *Latin. reductio ad absurdum,* unmasking; discredit, disparagement, debasement; marring, spoiling, ruin, wrecking, destruction, destroying.

2. weakening, undermining, enfeeblement, debilitation; enervation, exhaustion, sapping, devitalization, disablement, crippling, paralysis.

3. voidance, avoidance, disannulment, annulment, nullification, *Law.* defeasance, quashing, vitiation, *Obs.* vacatur, disestablishment, setting aside; cessation, *Law.* nolle prosequi, discontinuance, suspension; countermand, counterorder, overriding, overruling; veto, negation.

4. revocation, rescinding, rescindment, rescission, abrogation, reversal, repeal, abolishment, abolition; recantation, retraction, retractation, withdrawal, taking back, undoing, recall; renouncement, renunciation, relinquishment, repudiation, abjuration, abnegation; disavowal, disclaimer, disclamation, denial.

5. termination, dissolution, putting an end to, bringing to an end, doing away with; discarding, dismissal, getting rid of, casting aside, throwing out.

invalidism, *n.* **1.** sickness, infirmity, illness, valetudinarianism, invalidity; weakening, weakness, feebleness, enfeeblement, frailty, frailness, helplessness; debilitation, debility, devitalization, decrepitude; exhaustion, prostration; disease, morbosity.

2. indisposition, confinement, hospitalization, disablement, incapacitation; retirement, superannuation; senescence, dotage, senility, decrepitude.

invalidity, *n.* **1.** untenableness, inconclusiveness, unscientificness; illogicalness, illogicality, irrelevance, unreasonableness, senselessness, irrationality, incoherence, absurdity; falseness, falsity, fallacy, fallaciousness, erroneousness; speciousness, sophism, *Logic.* paralogism, elenchus, false refutation, perversion; inconsistency, incongruity, disparity; contradiction, antilogy.

2. weakness, weak point, ineffectualness, inefficacy; powerlessness, impotence, vulnerability; unconvincingness, lameness, vagueness, obscurity, flimsiness; futility, uselessness, nugacity, worthlessness; insipidness, pointlessness, vapidity; attenuation, dilution, indecisiveness, hesitancy, vacillation.

3. voidness, nullity, emptiness, invalidation. See **invalidation** (*defs.* **3-5**).

invaluable, *adj.* **1.** precious, valuable, incalculably valuable, inestimably valuable, priceless, beyond price; dear, expensive, costly, high, high-priced, *Inf.* worth a pretty penny, *Inf.* worth its weight in gold, *Inf.* worth a king's ransom.

2. excellent, superexcellent, superlative, *Inf.* super; rare, golden, unusual, exceptional, extraordinary, unparalleled, unequaled, inimitable, matchless, peerless, unique, one of a kind; exquisite, superfine, capital, *Inf.* first-class, first-rate, *Inf.* top-drawer.

3. useful, very useful, nonexpendable, essential, requisite, required, needful, imperative, indispensable.

invariable, *adj.* **1.** unchangeable, changeless, unchanging, constant, static, fixed, firm, fast, solid, steady, stable; permanent, abiding, enduring; immutable, unalterable, unmodifiable, untransformable, nonconvertible, incommutable, irreversible.

2. invariant, unvarying, unvaried; uniform, regular, always the same, identical, same, unbroken, all of a piece, homogeneous; even, symmetrical, smooth, level; stereotyped, cliché, undeviating, monotonous, dreary; systematic, methodical, reliable, dependable, unvacillating, unvicissitudinous, unfluctuating, unwavering, certain, sure.

3. recurrent, repeated, frequent, habitual; unremitting, relentless, persistent, perpetual, endless, never-ending, interminable, Sisyphean, ceaseless, incessant, unceasing.

invariability, *n.* **1.** unchangeability, unchangeableness, unchangingness, changelessness, immutability; firmness, fastness, fixedness, solidity, steadiness, stability; permanence, permanency, incorruptibility, irreversibility; constancy, reliability, dependability, regularity, certainty, indubitability; incontrovertibility, incontestability, irrefutability.

2. frequency, habitude, habitualness; persistence, relentlessness, endlessness, interminableness, interminability, ceaselessness; incessancy, monotony, routine; uniformity, sameness, regularity, symmetry, symmetricalness; smoothness, levelness, evenness.

invariably, *adv.* **1.** always, every time, at all times, on every occasion, without exception; constantly, regularly, repeatedly; continually, incessantly, uninterruptedly; day in, day out; inevitably, unfailingly, infallibly, surely, certainly.

2. perpetually, everlastingly, endlessly, unceasingly, ceaselessly, interminably.

invasion, *n.* **1.** hostile ingress, frontier violation, irruption, aggression, attack, foray, assault, assailment, raid, drive, offensive, blitzkrieg.

2. incursion, intrusion, infiltration, infringement, inroad, encroachment; violation, transgression, infraction, breach, trespass.

invasive, *adj.* **1.** invading, irruptive, offensive, attacking, incursive, besetting.

2. intrusive, intruding, interfering, interposing, obtrusive, *Inf.* pushy; interruptive, intervening, interloping, encroaching, insinuative; prying, *Inf.* snoopy, ferrety, meddlesome, overly curious, supercurious.

invective, *n.* **1.** diatribe, tirade, philippic, denunciation; disparagement, discrediting, depreciation, deprecation, insinuation, belittlement, minimization; objurgation, fulmination, contumely, berating, upbraiding, scolding, tongue-lashing; castigation, chastisement, reprimand, admonition, reproach, rebuke, reproval, slap in the face, *Inf.* rap on the knuckles.

2. vituperation, railing, assailment, revilement, belaboring; curse, execration, imprecation, malediction, anathematization; condemnation, censure, accusation, accusal, blame, inculpation, incrimination, crimination, implication, *Obs., Rare.* accrimination, impeachment, indictment.

3. ribaldry, scurrility, billingsgate, profanity, abuse, *Archaic.* bawdry; obscenity, vulgarism, vulgarity, salacity, filth, dirt, smut; curse word, swearword, oath, dirty word, four-letter word, *U.S. Inf.* cuss; vilification, impugnment, traducement, aspersion, calumniation, calumny, obloquy, slur, defamation, denigration, slander, libel.

—adj. **4.** vituperative, damnatory, execratory, animadversional; denunciatory, denunciative, disparaging, depreciatory, depreciating, deprecative, deprecatory, deprecating, derogatory, derogative, belittling; fulminatory, objurgatory, objurgative, contumelious.

5. abusive, insulting, affronting, offensive, injurious; calumnious, calumniatory, aspersive, slurring, maligning, defamatory, denigrating, slanderous, libelous.

inveigh, *v.* **1.** protest, remonstrate, complain about, object to; decry, denounce, censure, criticize, disparage; deprecate, depreciate, discredit, belittle, minimize, run *or* put down, *Inf.* knock.

2. rail against, vituperate, revile, oppugn; assail, attack, abuse, belabor, lash, *Inf.* sail into, *Inf.* jump down [s.o.'s] throat, *Archaic.* clapperclaw; scold, rate, slate, harangue, rant, tongue-lash, curse, execrate, imprecate, anathematize; upbraid, objurgate, excoriate, lambaste, flay, fulminate against, *Inf.* spout off at; berate, castigate, chastise, reproach, rebuke, reprove, *Inf.* dress down, *Sl.* strafe; vilify, traduce, asperse, calumniate, impugn, slur, malign, defame, denigrate, slander, libel, backbite, bespatter.

inveigle, *v.* **1.** *Usu.* **inveigle into** ensnare, enmesh, entangle, catch, *Sl.* rope in, *Sl.* suck in, bamboozle, delude; persuade, talk into, convince, induce, move; entice, lure, allure, decoy, tempt, beguile, seduce, tantalize, pique, *Archaic.* trepan; wheedle, cajole, *Inf.* sweet-talk, coax, blandish, *Sl.* soft-soap, flatter.

2. *Usu.* **inveigle from** *or* **away** win, obtain, acquire, procure, get, get one's hands on, secure.

inveigler, *n.* tempter, beguiler, seducer, persuader; bamboozler, swindler, deluder; wheedler, cajoler, coaxer, blandisher.

invent, *v.* **1.** originate, discover, create, compose, excogitate; think up, *Sl.* dope out, hit upon; devise, contrive, work up, work out, plan, plan out; design, draft, frame, coin, mint, shape, form, construct, fashion; patent, license, register.

2. imagine, conjure up, conceive, idealize, visualize, envisage, indulge in reverie, rhapsodize; envision, image, picture, *Inf.* feature; dream, *Inf.* dream up, *Inf.* see things; improvise, make up, ad-lib.

3. fabricate, concoct, spin, *Inf.* pull out of a hat, *Inf.* cook up, *Sl.* hoke up, rig, set up, trump up, hatch; prevaricate, lie, fib; misrepresent, distort, pervert, exaggerate, dress up, embroider, varnish.

invention, *n.* **1.** origination, creation, composition, discovery; fabrication, concoction, construction, production; device, contrivance, instrument, mechanism, contraption, gadget, *Inf.* thingumagig, *Inf.* thingamabob; expedient, step, measure, maneuver, stratagem, devisal, excogitation, plan, design, formulation; bright idea, coup, master stroke, *Inf.* trump card.

2. imagination, creativity, artistry, originality, ingenuity, resourcefulness, inventiveness; inspiration, verve, genius, cleverness, adeptness, adroitness, skillfulness.

3. fantasy, daydream, reverie, vision, illusion; whim, romanticism, romance, myth, ideality.

4. figment, fiction, fable, yarn, tall tale *or* story, fish story, cock-and-bull story, *Inf.* song and dance; falsehood, lie, fib, untruth, prevarication, mendacity, untruthfulness; forgery, fake, couterfeit, sham, falsification, minting, coinage.

inventive, *adj.* **1.** creative, imaginative, originative, visionary, inspired; concoctive, devising, contriving, composing, shaping, making; talented, artistic, endowed, gifted; original, fanciful, ingenious, resourceful; clever, quick, sharp, able, adept, adroit; skilled, skillful, deft, expert.

2. imaginary, fictitious, fictive, invented; fancied, dreamed up, illusory.

inventor, *n.* creator, author, originator, coiner, generator, initiator, prime mover, father; contriver, deviser, planner; discoverer, framer, maker, designer; builder, organizer, establisher, institutor; artist, craftsman, architect, producer.

inventory, *n.* **1.** list, listing, tally, enumeration, numeration, census, poll, statistics; table, index, portfolio, directory, ledger, calendar, schedule; roster, register, account, description, record, rota, roll, statement; slate, bill, menu, sheet, score, price list, checklist.

2. stock, goods, items, merchandise, wares, store, produce, provisions, dry goods; assets, effects, commodities, assortment, contents, ingredients.

inveracity, *n.* **1.** untruthfulness, mendacity, falseness, fallaciousness, dissembling; deception, deceitfulness, insincerity, dissimulation, duplicity, equivocation.

2. untruth, falsehood, lie, fib, prevarication; fabrication, fiction, invention, deceit.

inverse, *adj.* **1.** reversed, transposed, reverse, converse, counter, retroverted; palindromic, metathetical, right to left, back to front, *Rare.* ananymous; anastrophic, hyperbatic, *Rhet.* chiastic, backward; opposite, antipodal, contrary, diametrical, contraposed, antithetical.

2. inverted, upside down, wrongside up, on one's head, head over heels; topsy-turvy, *Inf.* arsy-varsy, *Fr. sens dessus dessous,* outside in, inside out, bottom up.

—*n.* **3.** opposite, contrary, antipode, antithesis, antipole, counterpole; reverse, converse, the other side, obverse, *Sl.* flip side, the other side of the coin, mirror image.

inversion, *n.* **1.** reversal, transposition, transposal, reversion, turning back, retroflexion; retroversion, palindrome, *Rare.* ananym, metathesis, tmesis; *All Rhet.* anatrophe, hyperbaton, hypallage, hysteron proteron, chiasmus.

2. opposite, antithesis, contrary, antipole, antipode; contradiction, contrariety, opposition; reverse, converse, obverse, the other side.

3. overturning, overturn, *Fr. bouleversement,* capsizing, capsizal, upset, spill, turning over; somersault, *Inf.* tumbersault, cartwheel, flip, gainer; introversion, eversion, turning in, invagination, intussusception.

invert, *v.* **1.** reverse, interchange, transpose, put the cart before the horse; back, turn back, retrovert, retroflex, turn about, turn the tables; turn around, wheel around, veer around, supinate, pronate.

2. introvert, turn inside out, evert, fold, invaginate, intussuscept; upturn, topple, tilt, flip, tip.

3. capsize, spill, turn over, turn turtle, overturn, overthrow, upset, *Fr. bouleverser,* inverse; tip over, flip over, keel over, bottom up.

invest, *v.* **1.** put money to use, put money into, sink money into; (*all of money*) advance, pay *or* lay out, risk, venture; provide money *or* capital for, fund, subsidize, back *or* support financially, patronize.

2. spend, expend, disburse, *Inf.* put out, give, offer, contribute, use, devote, donate; furnish, supply, provide, arm, gird, equip, accouter; prepare, ready, outfit, fit out, rig out, set up, fix up.

3. endow, give, entrust, vest, confer, bestow, grant; empower, enable, make possible, privilege; authorize, license, sanction.

4. install, induct, initiate, *Rare.* auspicate; instate, inaugurate, swear in, administer the oath of office; establish, chair, seat; crown, enthrone; frock, *Eccles.* ordain.

5. clothe, attire, apparel, dress, garb, vest, robe, enrobe, gown; deck out, array, *Archaic.* bedight, adorn; enwrap, envelop, muffle, enfold, swathe; overspread, cover, drape, shroud, sheathe.

6. enclose, confine, hedge, pen in, hem in, beset; circle, encircle, circumscribe, compass, encompass, environ, form a ring around, gird, girdle, engird; surround, crowd around, crowd in on, beseige, lay seige to, beleaguer.

investigate, *v.* research, probe, explore, search for *or* seek out clues, track down, ferret out, smell out, nose out, *Inf.* smoke out; ransack, rummage, rake, scour, leave no stone unturned; inquire into, canvass, see about, check into *or* on *or* up on, *Inf.* give [s.t.] the once-over, *Sl.* check out, *Brit. Sl.* suss out, *U.S. Sl.* case, *Sl.* bird-dog; inspect, examine, audit, look into, scrutinize, study, analyze, go over with a fine-tooth comb, sift through, winnow.

investigation, *n.* inquisition, inquest, research, fact-finding; exploration, probe, search, quest; inquiry, canvass, questioning, interrogation, hearing, audit; inspection, examination, scrutinization, scrutiny, *Inf.* once-over, *Sl.* casing; study, analysis, sifting, winnowing, review, dissection.

investigator, *n.* researcher, researchist, searcher, fact-finder; detective, private investigator, *Inf.* bird dog, *Inf.* sherlock, *Inf.* sleuth, *Sl.* bloodhound, *Sl.* private eye, *U.S. Sl.* dick, *U.S. Sl.* gumshoe; inspector, examiner, auditor, scrutinizer, scrutator, scrutineer; questioner, inquisitor, inquisitionist, inquirer; analyst, reviewer, fact-sifter.

investiture, *n.* **1.** installation, instatement, chairing, inauguration; coronation, crowning, enthronement; frocking, *Eccles.* ordination, *Eccles.* ordainment, consecration; induction, introduction, ushering in, bringing in, establishment.

2. vestment, robe, mantle, garment; clothing, dress, attire, habit, garb, apparel, raiment.

investment, *n.* **1.** venture, speculation, risk, *Inf.* plunge; legals.

2. investiture, vestment, endowment, empowerment, enablement. See **investiture** (*def.* **1**).

3. siege, besiegement, beleaguerment, blockade, cutting off of supply lines; encirclement, envelopment, pincers movement.

inveterate, *adj.* **1.** habitual, chronic, continuous, continual; confirmed, inured, hardened, hard-core, die-hard, dyed-in-the-wool.

2. ingrained, implanted, deep-seated, deep-rooted; fixed, rooted, riveted, set; entrenched, established, long-established, longstanding, of long standing; venerable, time-honored, immemorial, hallowed.

invidious, *adj.* **1.** antagonistic, inimical, hostile, malicious, rancorous, vexatious, spiteful; adverse, provoking, troublesome, *Sl.* bitchy, odious, hateful, unfriendly, unpopular; offensive, objectionable.

2. deleterious, injurious, harmful, hurtful; pernicious, baneful, baleful, malefic, maleficent, *Obs.* malefical, malign, malignant, mischievous; detrimental, damaging, destructive, internecine, disastrous, ruinous, prejudicial.

invigorant, *n.* bracer, tonic, cordial, stimulant, *Inf.* eyeopener, *Inf.* pick-me-up *or* pick-up; elixir, panacea, restorative, theriac, ptisan, *Med.* roborant.

invigorate, *v.* energize, fortify, strengthen; enliven, liven up, animate, pep up; stimulate, whet, motivate, inspirit, inspire, vivify, vitalize, quicken; galvanize, electrify, *Inf.* turn on, *Inf.* psych up, *Inf.* spark, *Inf.* sparkplug; jolt, jog, waken, wake up, shake up; arouse, rouse, excite, fire *or* fire up, inflame.

invigorating, *adj.* stimulating, animating, enlivening, vivifying, vitalizing, bracing, invigorative; energizing, fortifying, strengthening; restorative, restoring, remedial, *Med.* analeptic; healthful, healthy, salubrious, salutary, salutiferous, tonic, wholesome.

invincible, *adj.* **1.** unconquerable, invulnerable, impregnable, impenetrable, inviolable, indestructible, undestroyable, imperishable, undefeatable, unbeatable, unassailable; formidable, powerful, mighty, *Literary.* puissant; indomitable, insuppressible, stout, stout-hearted, stalwart, *Archaic.* stalworth, steadfast, doughty, hardy, solid, stable, tough, staunch, stanch, cast-iron, *Inf.* hard as a rock, *Inf.* tough as nails; firm, resolute, resolved, determined, intransigent, inflexible, adamant, adamantine; defiant, unyielding, unflinching, unwavering, unswerving, undeviating; persevering, unrelenting, relentless, irrepressible, indefatigable, untiring, tireless, weariless, unwearying, unflagging.

2. courageous, brave, valiant, valorous, heroic, heroical, hero-like, lionhearted, iron-hearted, great-hearted, high-hearted; virile, manly, manful; intrepid, fearless, dauntless, dreadless, aweless, unafraid, undaunted, unblenched, unblenching, undismayed, unappalled, unalarmed; bold, bold-spirited, high-spirited, daring, audacious; plucky, mettlesome, nervy, gritty, spirited, red-blooded, *Inf.* spunky, *Sl.* gutsy.

3. insuperable, insurmountable, overwhelming, overpowering, overcoming, overmastering, overmatching; oppressive, burdensome, backbreaking, crushing, demoralizing, defeating.

inviolability, *n.* **1.** inalienability, inviolacy, untouchability; sacredness, sanctity, sacrosanctness, holiness.

2. invulnerability, impregnability, impenetrability, invincibility, indomitability, unconquerability; unassailableness, unattackableness, insuperability, insurmountability.

3. incorruptibility, uncorruptness, honesty, upstandingness, righteousness, virtuousness; loyalty, faithfulness, constancy, steadfastness, trueness, true-blueness; reliability, dependability, trustworthiness, *Inf.* trustiness.

inviolable, *adj.* **1.** inalienable, inviolate, untouchable; sacred, sacrosanct, holy.

2. invulnerable, impregnable, impenetrable, invincible, indomitable, unconquerable; unassailable, unattackable, insuperable, insurmountable.

3. incorruptible, uncorrupt, honest, upstanding, righteous, virtuous; faithful, loyal, constant, steadfast, true, true-blue; reliable, dependable, trustworthy, *Inf.* trusty, tried and true, as good as one's word.

inviolate, *adj.* **1.** invulnerable, impregnable, invincible, indomitable, unconquerable, indestructible, imperishable; unassailable, unattackable, insuperable, insurmountable; inalienable, inviolable, untouchable; sacred, sacrosanct, holy; hallowed, consecrated, blessed, sanctified.

2. undisturbed, unchanged, unaltered; untouched, undamaged, unharmed, unhurt, unviolated, unscathed, unimpaired; unspoiled, unmarred, unstained, unsullied, undefiled, unprofaned.

3. intact, unbroken, whole, entire, complete.

invisibility, *n.* **1.** imperceivability, imperceptibility, indiscernibility, indistinguishableness, unseeability.

2. imperceptibility, unnoticeability, unapparentness; inappreciableness, impalpableness, imponderableness, intangibleness.

3. concealment, secretion, hiding, covering up, hushing up; subterfuge, deception, smoke screen.

invisible, *adj.* **1.** imperceivable, imperceptible, indiscernible, indistinguishable, unseeable.

2. hidden, concealed, veiled, shrouded, enshrouded, screened, cloaked; disguised, masked, camouflaged; unseen, unnoticed, unobserved, unbeheld, unperceived.

3. imperceptible, unnoticeable, unapparent; inappreciable, impalpable, imponderable, intangible; microscopic, infinitesimal.

4. unrevealed, undisclosed, undivulged, unexposed, covered-up, hushed-up; covert, undercover, *Inf.* under wraps, secret, top-secret, hush-hush.

invitation, *n.* **1.** request, *Inf.* invite; application, *Law.* motion, appeal; imploration, entreaty, plea, prayer, invocation; petition, suit, solicitation, supplication, obtestation, adjuration, *Archaic.* conjuration.

2. summons, call, challenge, dare, defiance.

3. attraction, draw, pull, magnetism; allurement, enticement, temptation, lure, bait; tantalization, teasing, flirtation, coquetry; suggestion, hint, *Sl.* come-on, proposition; overture, proposal, tender, offer, proffer.

invite, *v.* **1.** ask, request, summon, beckon, call *or* call for, bid; ask for, apply for, look for, seek, call upon, appeal to; beg, *Inf.* say please *or* pretty please, implore, beseech, entreat, plead, *Brit. Inf.* prig, pray, get down on one's knees, crave; petition, solicit, supplicate, obtest, adjure, conjure, *Rare.* sue, invoke, *Archaic.* invocate.

2. attract, draw, allure, entice, tempt, lure; tantalize, tease, *Inf.* dangle [s.t.] in front of [s.o.'s] nose, lead on; flirt with, court, leave the door open to, encourage; promote, foster, instigate, incite, provoke, start; be the cause of, cause, bring on, bring [s.t.] upon oneself, induce, make happen; push, press, ask for, beg for, look for.

inviting, *adj.* **1.** tempting, tantalizing, appetizing, mouth-watering; alluring, enticing, beckoning, beguiling, flirtatious, coquettish; seductive, stimulating, exciting, arousing; sensuous, *Inf.* sexy, beautiful.

2. attractive, magnetic, appealing, nice, charming, winsome, winning, engaging; fascinating, enchanting, entrancing, bewitching, captivating, enrapturing, ravishing, irresistible.

3. favorable, propitious, promising, bright, good,

rosy, sunny; pleasant, agreeable, nice, friendly.

invocation, *n.* entreaty, adjuration, impetration, imploration, imploringness, solicitation, soliciting; request, prayer, praying, orison, plea, pleading, intercession; supplication, beseechment, beseeching, obtestation, obsecration; petition, petitioning, suit, appeal; calling upon, summoning, summons; conjuration, evocation, calling up by incantation.

invoice, *n.* **1.** itemization, particularization, description, detailing; list, inventory, enumeration, numeration.

2. bill, statement, check, charge, tabulation, *Inf.* tab; manifest, score, tally, account.

invoke, *v.* **1.** call for, pray for, request; supplicate, implore, entreat, adjure, obtest; solicit, beseech, obsecrate, imprecate, impetrate; beg, importune, cry for, beg a boon.

2. call on, petition, address, appeal, plead, *Rhet.* apostrophize; bid, pray, sue.

3. call forth, call up, raise, conjure; evoke, summon, cite, summon forth, muster, convoke.

involuntary, *adj.* **1.** independent, automatic, spontaneous, uncontrolled, reflex, mechanical, conditioned.

2. unconscious, instinctive, impulsive, subliminal, *Sl.* gut; unthinking, unwitting, blind; unintentional, undeliberate, indeliberate, unpremeditated, unmeditated.

3. unwilling, reluctant, against one's will, against one's wishes, grudging; unconsenting, averse, loath, disinclined, indisposed; choiceless, forced, coercive, compulsive; compulsory, obligatory, imperative, binding, necessary.

involution, *n.* **1.** involvement, entanglement, tanglement, convolution; enmeshment, embarrassment, circumvolution.

2. complexity, complication, intricacy, intricateness, perplexity; tortuosity, ambagiousness, wilderness, jungle, confusion.

3. rolling up, folding up, infolding, envelopment, inversion; invagination, intussusception, retroflexion, retroversion.

involve, *v.* **1.** imply, entail, signify, insinuate, suggest, mean, admit; denote, betoken, connote, spell; represent, symbolize, typify, epitomize; indicate, refer to, allude to, designate.

2. include, contain, comprehend, comprise; embrace, hold, encompass, enclose; number among, count in, reckon in, embody, incorporate; affect, take in, subsume, presume, presuppose.

3. complicate, perplex, confound, confuse, mix up, ramify; mix, blend, combine, entangle, tangle, snarl, knot, embrangle, catch up in; embroil, embarrass.

4. implicate, incriminate, inculpate, criminate, accuse; connect, *Inf.* mix up, draw into, associate, cohort.

5. engage, engross, hold, hold the attention, focus the attention; preoccupy, absorb, rivet, grip; concern, commit, pledge, interest, bind.

6. envelop, enfold, enwrap, wrap, enclasp; surround, cover, shroud, compass, encompass, enclose.

7. engulf, swallow up, overwhelm, overcome, bury, engorge; submerse, swamp, deluge, flood, inundate.

involved, *adj.* **1.** intricate, complex, complicated, perplexing, confusing; knotty, tangled, entangled, snarled, twisted, matted; sophisticated, ramified, elaborate, involuted, convoluted; confused, confounded, mixed up, crabbed.

2. implicated, inculpated, incriminated, *Inf.* mixed up in *or* with; connected with, associated with, in on, a party to.

3. committed, engaged, pledged, concerned, dedicated, engagé; immersed, submerged, intent on, *Sl.* into; absorbed, engrossed, rapt, preoccupied, held, fixed, gripped.

involvement, *n.* **1.** entanglement, tanglement, convolution, involution, circumvolution; enmeshment, embarrassment, embranglement; complexity, intricacy, complication, perplexity; imbroglio, quandary, dilemma, embroilment; confusion, wilderness, jungle; stew, commixture, immixture, blend, intermixture; admixture, combination, hodgepodge, farrago, jumble.

2. commitment, responsibility, engagement, concernment, dedication; implication, interest, association, connection.

invulnerability, *n.* **1.** indestructibility, indestructibleness, undestroyability, undestroyableness, imperishability, imperishableness, nonperishability, nonperishableness, unwoundability, unwoundableness, *Obs., Rare.* imperdibility, *Obs., Rare.* imperdibleness.

2. invincibility, invincibleness, unconquerability, unconquerableness, impregnability, impregnableness, impenetrability, impenetrableness, inviolability, inviolableness, inexpugnability, inexpugnableness, unassailability, unassailableness, unattackability, unattackableness, insuperability, insuperableness, insurmountability, insurmountableness, incontestability, incontestableness, undefeatability, undefeatableness; formidableness, powerfulness, mightiness; tenability, tenableness, security, secureness, safety, safeness.

invulnerable, *adj.* **1.** indestructible, undestroyable, imperishable, nonperishable, unwoundable, *Obs., Rare.* imperdible.

2. invincible, unconquerable, impenetrable, inviolable, inexpugnable; unassailable, unattackable, insuperable, insurmountable, incontestable, undefeatable, unbeatable; formidable, powerful, mighty; bulletproof, bombproof, shellproof; tenable, secure, safe, safe and sound.

inward, inwards, *adv.* **1.** within, inside, toward the inside, interiorly, internally, *Chiefly Literary.* inly, inwardly.

—adj. **2.** interior, internal, inside, inner, inmost, innermost.

3. mental, psychological, spiritual, psychic.

4. private, privy, personal, intimate, confidential, special, secret, hidden.

—n. **5.** inside, interior, inner part.

6. **inwards** entrails, innards, intestines, viscera, bowels, guts, insides, internals.

inwardly, *adv.* **1.** internally, interiorly, *Chiefly Literary.* inly, inside, within, inward; mentally, psychologically, psychically, spiritually.

2. privately, privily, personally, intimately, confidentially, secretly, to oneself.

iota, *n.* bit, mite, speck, smidgen, *Inf.* smitch, molecule, atom, jot, whit, tittle; dot, point, dab, fleck, speck; particle, moit, mote; fraction, hair, shaving, paring, sliver, shive, splinter, flake, scale, fragment, shard; morsel, crumb, grain, granule; trace, touch, hint, trifle, tinge, suggestion, suspicion, soupçon, tincture, *Archaic.* spice, shadow; spark, scintilla, gleam; drop, droplet, dash.

irascibility, *n.* testiness, touchiness, thin-skinnedness, irritability, edginess, hastiness, short fuse; choler, pepperiness, spleen, gall, bile, ill temper, bad temper, ill nature, ill humor; tartness, acerbity, asperity, acrimony, bitterness, harshness; crankiness, grouchiness, crabbiness, crabbedness, gruffness, moodiness, crotchetiness; crossness, surliness, churlishness, snappishness, waspishness, petulance, peevishness, huffishness, huffiness, captiousness; cantankerousness, querulousness, quarrelsomeness, contentiousness; anger, belligerence, pugnacity, volatileness, fieriness.

irascible, *adj.* testy, touchy, thin-skinned, irritable, edgy, *Sl.* uptight, hasty; choleric, peppery, quick-tempered, short-tempered, *Inf.* short-fused, *Inf.* trigger-happy; cross, surly, churlish, snappy, snappish, waspish, petulant, peevish, huffy, huffish, captious, fractious, perverse; cranky, grouchy, crabbed, crabby, gruff, sour, moody, crotchety; splenetic, spleenful, bilious, dyspeptic, ill-tempered, *Australian.* crook, bad-tempered, ill-natured, ill-humored; cantankerous, querulous, quarrelsome, contentious; angry, belligerent, up in arms, pugnacious, bellicose; volatile, volcanic, explosive, hot-tempered, hot-headed, fiery, inflammable.

irate, *adj.* **1.** wrathful, wroth, very angry, ireful, incensed; enraged, raging, fuming, infuriated, *Rare.* infuriate, furious; inflamed, flaming, flaring, flared up, heated, red-hot, white-hot; distraught, overwrought, upset, feverish, hysterical, not rational; violent, unrestrained, uncontrollable; ranting, raving, storming, foaming at the mouth, rabid, fanatical, frenzied; frantic, crazed, *Pathol.* delirious, mad, *Inf.* wild, out of one's mind, beside oneself.

2. peeved, annoyed, vexed, irritated; piqued, chafed, galled, riled, nettled, *Inf.* fit to be tied; offended, affronted, displeased, indignant; worked up, stirred up, kindled, enkindled; passionate, impassioned, impassionate, overexcited.

3. irritable, cross, surly, snappish, petulant, peevish; testy, choleric, touchy, huffy, peppery; splenetic, spleenful, bilious, cranky, ill-tempered, bad-tempered; irascible, quick-tempered, short-tempered, *Inf.* short-fused; quarrelsome, contentious, belligerent, pugnacious, bellicose; volatile, volcanic, explosive, hot-tempered, hot-headed, fiery, inflammable.

ire, *n.* **1.** anger, dudgeon, high dudgeon, *Scot.* birse, *Inf.* Irish, *Inf.* dander; wrath, passion, hot blood, hot temper, vials of wrath; rage, fury.

2. choler, bile, spleen, gall, ill *or* bad humor, ill *or* bad temper, ill *or* bad feeling; embitterment, bitterness, resentment, bitter resentment, exacerbation, hard feelings; enmity, animosity, ill will, bad blood; virulence, acrimony, acerbity.

3. exasperation, irritation, annoyance, vexation, *Inf.* aggravation; displeasure, dissatisfaction, discontentment, disapproval, disapprobation.

ireful, *adj.* **1.** wrathful, enraged, furious, infuriated, *Rare.* infuriate, maddened; angry, irate; irritated, annoyed, vexed, peeved, *Inf.* aggravated; exasperated, fed up.

2. irritable, irascible, petulant, short-tempered, ill-tempered, bad-tempered; testy, edgy, touchy, grouchy, peevish, crabby; snappish, bearish, currish; surly, gruff, brash, brusque; acrimonious, caustic, virulent, mordant, trenchant, venomous, envenomed.

irenic, *adj.* peaceful, peaceable, peaceloving, dovish, mild, gentle; pacific, pacificatory, peacemaking, diplomatic; conciliatory, propitiatory, appeasing, mollifying, placating.

iridescence, *n.* shimmer, shimmering, glisten, glistening, glimmer, glimmering, flickering, sparkle, sparkling, glitter, shine, shininess, dazzle, dazzling, luster, lustrousness; reflection, reflectiveness, reflectivity, interplay of light and color; opalescence, pearliness, irisation; changeableness, changeability, variableness, variability, variance; variegation, variedness, polychromaticism.

iridescent, *adj.* **1.** shimmery, shimmering, glistening, glittering, glittery, flickering, sparkling, shiny, shining, dazzling, reflective, reflectional; pearly, opalescent, opaline, mother-of-pearl, nacreous, nacred; kaleidoscopic, kaleidoscopical, changeable, changeful, variable, variant, varying.

2. multicolored, multicolor, polychromatic, polychromatic, of many colors *or* shades *or* hues, prismatic, prismatical, spectral, rainbowy, rainbowlike, colorful, brilliant; shot, variegated, varied, varicolored, parti-colored, marble, marbly, marmoreal, marmorean, streaked, motley.

irk, *v.* **1.** irritate, annoy, provoke, vex, pique, peeve, nettle, chafe, get on [s.o.'s] nerves, tread on [s.o.'s] toes, go against the grain, run afoul of [s.o.], *Chiefly U.S.* rile, *Inf.* aggravate, *Inf.* miff, *Inf.* give [s.o.] a pain, *Inf.* rub [s.o.] the wrong way, *Inf.* get under [s.o.'s] skin, *Inf.* get in [s.o.'s] hair; exasperate, ruffle, roil, disturb, disquiet, discompose, discountenance, put out, put off, try [s.o.'s] patience, *Inf.* put [s.o.'s] nose out of joint, get, *Sl.* get [s.o.'s] goat; set one's teeth on edge, stick in one's craw *or* crop, *Inf.* grate on *or* grate on one's nerves.

2. bother, pester, harass, hector,, *Sl.* bug, *Sl.* hassle, *Sl.* drive [s.o.] nuts *or* crazy *or* bananas, *Sl.* drive [s.o.] up the wall; (*all from continual harassment*) tire, fatigue, exhaust, wear out, fag, fag out.

3. anger, incense, raise [s.o.'s] ire *or* hackles, get [s.o.'s] back up, *Inf.* get [s.o.'s] Irish *or* dander up, *Inf.* burn [s.o.] up, *Sl.* tick [s.o.] off, *Sl.* tee [s.o.] off.

irksome, *adj.* irritating, annoying, vexing, vexatious, *Inf.* aggravating; bothersome, pestering, *Inf.* pesky, *Inf.* pestiferous, hectoring, harassing; troubling, troublesome, distressing, painful; worrying, worrisome, *Archaic.* plaguy; tiring, tiresome, wearying, wearisome, fatiguing; trying; boring.

iron, *n.* **1.** pig iron, cast iron, wrought iron, steel.

2. flatiron, electric iron, steam iron, sadiron, mangle.

3. **irons** fetters, chains, shackles, gyves, bilboes, trammels; bonds, pinions; manacles, handcuffs, cuffs, *Sl.* bracelets, *Brit. Sl.* darbies; hampers, clog, governor, restraint, constraint.

—*adj.* **4.** ironlike, ferrous, ferruginous, *Chem.* ferric, chalybeate.

5. stern, harsh, severe, unfeeling, cruel; stark, grim, inexorable; ironclad, rigid, unbending, inflexible, adamantine, obdurate, stubborn, obstinate, tenacious.

6. hard, firm, unyielding, resolved, determined, decided; indomitable, invincible, powerful; heroic, stalwart, mighty, strong, vigorous, robust, *Literary.* puissant; stout, hardy, sturdy.

—*v.* **7.** smooth, press, hot-iron, hot-press, steam, mangle.

8. **iron out** straighten out, solve, resolve; finalize, perfect, get rid of the wrinkles *or* bugs; reconcile, harmonize, smooth over.

ironic, *adj.* **1.** figurative, nonliteral, double-edged; contradictory, paradoxical, irreconcilable, incongruous, jarring; unexpected, unforeseen, unanticipated, surprising; serendipitous, happenstantial, coincidental; bewildering, puzzling, mysterious, irrational, unexplainable.

2. mocking, ridiculing, derisive, derisory, scornful, sardonic, Rabelaisian, ironical; cynical, satirical, burlesque; contemptuous, contumelious, disparaging, sneering, disdainful, supercilious, haughty, arrogant; taunting, teasing, chaffing, quizzical, gibing, jeering, scoffing; critical, captious, carping, censorious, faultfinding.

3. caustic, sarcastic, mordant, mordacious, acrimonious, bitter, acrid, acidulous, acid, pungent; trenchant, cutting, incisive, slashing, scathing; keen, pointed, sharp, sharp-tongued; penetrating, piercing, stinging, pricking, nipping, biting; spiteful, virulent, malicious, malificent, venomous, vicious, malevolent, malignant; insulting, excoriating, denouncing, berating, abusive, scurrilous, offensive, vituperative.

ironworks, *n.* smithy, smithery, farriery, forge, stithy, blacksmith's workshop, foundry.

irony, *n.* **1.** incongruity, incongruousness, absurdity, illogicality; contrariety, contradiction, paradox, enigma; double entendre, *Rhet.* enantiosis.

2. derision, ridicule, sarcasm, scorn, mockery, cynicism, *Rhet.* asteism; satire, lampoon, burlesque, parody, travesty, farce, persiflage; skit, squib, caricature, mimicry; taunt, fleer, gibe, jeer, flout, scoff, sneer, wipe, quip, nip; raillery, banter, badinage, chaff.

3. contempt, disparagement, disdain, superciliousness; criticism, censure, hit, fling, *Inf.* flak, rub, dig; acrimony, acrimoniousness, causticity, asperity, mordancy, acridness, acridity, pungency, venomousness, venom.

irradiate, *v.* **1.** illuminate, light up, light, brighten; illumine, *Archaic.* illume; cast light upon, shine, beam; shimmer, sparkle, scintillate, glitter, gleam, coruscate; make resplendent *or* illustrious.

2. enlighten, inform, make aware, give insight to; open the eyes of; instruct, teach, indoctrinate, educate, guide; communicate, initiate, introduce, edify, inculcate; tutor, nurture, prepare, prime, counsel, advise; stimulate, inspire, animate, exalt, elevate; instill, impart, light the torch.

3. treat with radiation, x-ray, expose.

irradiation, *n.* **1.** illumination, brightness, brilliance, brilliancy, splendor, refulgence, luminousness; radiation, luminescence, phosphorescence, luminosity; glow, shimmer, coruscation.

2. enlightenment, advancement, edification, perception, insight, elucidation, refinement.

3. beam, ray, infrared *or* ultraviolet rays, radiance, radiant heat; x-ray treatment.

irrational, *adj.* **1.** illogical, meaningless, preposterous, extravagant, unreasonable; incredible, inconceivable, unimaginable, unthinkable; invalid, unsound, unscientific, groundless, fallible; implausible, untenable; doubtful, doubtable, dubitable, questionable.

2. absurd, ridiculous, silly, foolish, half-baked, childish, *Sl.* cockeyed; ludicrous, nonsensical, senseless, amphigoric, *Sl.* cockamamie; asinine, idiotic, *Inf.* moronic; pointless, inane, fatuous, stupid; crazy, mad, wild, insane, demented, daft, *Inf.* daffy, *Sl.* kooky, *Sl.* wacky, *Sl.* cuckoo; peculiar, unusual, anomalous, strange, odd; empty-headed, harebrained, unintelligent, dull-witted, *Inf.* dumb; vacuous, muddled, muddleheaded, addlebrained, half-witted, senseless, confused, bemused; addlepated, brainless; funny, laughable, risible, derisable, humorous, droll, comical, farcical.

irrationality, *n.* **1.** illogic, illogicality, meaninglessness, extravagance, preposterousness; incredibleness, inconceivableness, unimaginableness, unbelievableness, implausibility, untenableness, questionableness.

2. lack of judgment, stupidity, brainlessness, unsoundness, injudiciousness; incoherence, aberrancy, oddness, lunacy, craziness, insanity, *Psychiatry.* dementia.

3. absurdity, ridiculousness, ridiculosity, silliness, foolishness, folly, childishness, tomfoolery, absurdness; ludicrousness, nonsense, senselessness; amphigory, bosh, poppycock, drivel, gibberish, balderdash, fiddle-faddle; babble, twaddle, prattle; pointlessness, inanity, fatuity, fatuousness; asininity, idiocy, imbecility; madness, wildness, daftness, *Sl.* kookiness; peculiarity, unusualness, strangeness; empty-headedness, unintelligence, *Inf.* dumbness, dullness; humor, hilarity, hysterics.

irreclaimable, *adj.* unreclaimable, irredeemable, unredeemable, irreformable, unreformable, unreformative, incorrigible, reprobate, beyond *or* past help; irrecoverable, unregainable, unrecoverable, irretrievable, unsalvageable, unsavable, lost; incurable, immedicable, unmedicable, uncurable, cureless, terminal, unremediable, irremediable, remediless; unrestorable, irreparable, unfixable, uncorrectable, unrectifiable; irreversible, indefeasible, unreversible, irrevocable, unrevocable, unrepealable; hopeless, beyond *or* past hope, a lost cause.

irreconcilable, *adj.* **1.** unresolvable, unsolvable, irresolvable, unfixable, irreparable, unadjustable.

2. incompatible, unsuitable, unsuited, ill-suited, mismatched; incongruous, discordant, at odds *or* variance, conflicting, opposite, opposing, contrary, clashing.

3. implacable, inexorable, intransigent, uncompromising, unyielding, unbending; hardline, strict, rigid, inflexible, cast-iron, hard-and-fast.

irrecoverable, *adj.* unrecoverable, unregainable, irretrievable, irreclaimable, unreclaimable, irredeemable, unredeemable, lost; unrestorable, irreparable, unfixable, uncorrectable, unrectifiable. See **irreclaimable**.

irredeemable, *adj.* **1.** unredeemable, irreclaimable, unreclaimable. See **irreclaimable**.

2. incontrovertible, uncontrovertible, indisputable, undisputable, incontestable, uncontestable, undeniable, unquestionable.

irreducible, *adj.* **1.** not reducible, rock-bottom.

2. unchangeable, immutable, incommutable, unalterable, intransmutable.

irrefutable, *adj.* **1.** incontrovertible, incontestable, indisputable, undeniable, irrefragable, unquestionable, beyond question, admitting no question *or* doubt, indubitable, beyond a shadow of a doubt, apodictic; conclusive, decisive, definite, definitive, solid, fixed, final; impregnable, invincible, unassailable, insuperable, undefeatable, unbeatable; certain, sure, *Inf.* for-sure, absolute, positive.

2. evident, manifest, apparent, obvious, patent, palpable, express; clear, clear-cut, plain, plain as day, plain as the nose on your face, *Fr. en évidence*; proven, demonstrated.

irregular, *adj.* **1.** asymmetric, unsymmetrical, unequal; uneven, unlevel, rough, jagged, rugged, craggy, broken, hilly, knotty; lumpy, bunchy; pitted, holey; crooked, circuitous, roundabout, tortuous, devious, twisting, turning, curving, bending, swerving.

2. unmethodical, immethodical, methodless, inconsistent, desultory, unsystematic, systemless, unparliamentary, inconstant, erratic, eccentric, capricious, orderless, variable, changeable, mutable; rambling, wandering, straying, roving; disarranged, disordered, confused, unsettled; spasmodic, fitful, uncertain, aperiodic, unpunctual, disconnected, stop-and-go, come and go.

3. anomalous, anomalistic, aberrant, deviate, deviant; abnormal, unnatural, freakish, *Inf.* freaky, monstrous, heteroclite, heteroclitical, heteromorphous, heteromorphic; odd, peculiar, queer, quizzical, curious, offbeat, strange, bizarre, weird, *Inf.* quirky; singular, exceptional, unusual, uncommon, unorthodox, unconventional.

4. lawless, unruly, disorderly, wild, turbulent; improper, indecent, immoral, licentious, lascivious, lewd, promiscuous, lax, *Inf.* loose; wanton, depraved, degenerate, dissolute, dissipated; inordinate, intemperate, excessive, extravagant.

5. flawed, marked, imperfect, blemished, spotted, smudged, soiled, damaged, torn.

6. *Military.* (*all of troops*) guerrilla, partisan, underground, resistance.

—*n.* 7. (*all of merchandise*) factory, second, third. **8.** *Military.* guerrilla, partisan, maquis, *Fr. maquisard*, underground *or* resistance fighter, bush fighter, *Sl.* bushwhacker; the resistance, the underground.

irregularity, *n.* **1.** asymmetry, lack of symmetry, unequality, unequalness; unevenness, roughness, jaggedness, ruggedness, cragginess; lumpiness, bunchiness, humpiness; crookedness, circuitousness, circuity, roundaboutness, tortuousness, deviousness.

2. unmethodicalness, immethodicalness, methodlessness, inconsistency, desultoriness, unsystematicalness, systemlessness, inconstancy, erraticism, eccentricity, capriciousness, caprice, orderlessness, variableness, variation, changeableness, changeability, fickleness, mutability, mutableness; disorderliness, confusion, disarrangement, unsettledness; spasmodicalness, fitfulness, uncertainty, unpunctualness, disconnectedness.

3. oddness, strangeness, queerness, curiousness, bizarreness, freakishness; singularity, singularness, exceptionality, exceptionalness, unusualness, uncommonness, uncommonality, unconventionality.

4. anomaly, aberration, perversion, *Rare.* anomalism; abnormality, abnormity, monster, monstrosity, mutant, freak, heteroclite, malformation, miscreation, abortion, deformity; oddity, peculiarity, curiosity, rarity.

5. deviation, aberrance, aberrancy, divergence, digression; lawlessness, unruliness, disorderliness, wildness, turbulence; impropriety, indecency, immorality, licentiousness, lasciviousness, lewdness, promiscuity, promiscuousness, *Inf.* looseness, laxity; wantonness, depravity, degeneracy, dissoluteness, dissipation; inordinacy, intemperance, excessiveness, extravagance.

irregularly, *adv.* **1.** intermittently, periodically, off and on, hot and cold, by turns, at intervals, at irregular intervals.

2. unmethodically, methodlessly, unsystematically, systemlessly, desultorily, erratically; fitfully, spasmodically, unevenly, jerkily, uncertainly, disconnectedly, aperiodically, unpunctually, by fits and starts, by jerks, by snatches.

irrelevant, *adj.* inapposite, nongermane, impertinent, inapplicable, immaterial, foreign, alien, unrelated, unconnected; extraneous, gratuitous, unessential, insignificant; beside the point, neither here nor there, beside the question, beside the mark, nothing to do with it, *Inf.* off base, not to the point, *Inf.* off the beam, *Inf.* off the wall; unwarranted, out of place, uncalled-for, inappropriate, malapropos; inconsistent, illogical, inconsequent, self-contradictory, incongruous.

irreligion, *n.* **1.** atheism, godlessness, ungodliness, unholiness, disbelief, unbelief, nonbelief, unbelievingness, nonspirituality, nonspiritualness; infidelity, heathenism, heathenness, heathendom, heathenhood, paganism; agnosticism, skepticism, doubt, Pyrrhonism, nihilism.

2. impiety, impiousness, irreverence, irreligiousness; apostasy, straying, recidivism, backsliding, laxity; heresy, hereticalness, iconoclasm, antireligion, antireligiousness, antireligiosity, sacrilegiousness, sacrilege, sinfulness, wickedness, evilness, badness, blasphemousness, blasphemy, profaneness, profanity.

irreligious, *adj.* **1.** atheistic, disbelieving, unbelieving, nonbelieving, godless, ungodly, nonspiritual; infidel, infidelic, heathenish, heathen, paganistic, pagan, unenlightened; agnostic, skeptical, doubting, questioning, Pyrrhonic, nihilistic.

2. impious, irreverent; heretical, iconoclastic, antireligious, antichristian, dissentient, denunciatory, hostile *or* antagonistic toward the Church; sacrilegious, sinful, wicked, evil, bad; blasphemous, profane, cursing, swearing.

irremediable, *adj.* remediless, incurable, cureless, past cure; beyond hope, hopeless, unameliorable, immitigable, beyond redress *or* relief, over-the-hill; incorrigible, irreformable, irredeemable; ruined, irreparable, undone. See **irreparable**.

irremissible, *adj.* unpardonable, inexpiable, inatonable, unforgivable, irredeemable; inexcusable, reprehensible.

2. exigent, urgent, pressing, insistent.

irremovable, *adj.* immovable, rooted, riveted, fixed; anchored, tethered, stuck fast, glued to the spot; solid, firm, firm as the rock of Gibraltar; unchangeable, immutable, inalterable, permanent; secure, *Sl.* unfirable, tenured, *Inf.* in a rut.

irreparable, *adj.* ruined, irreclaimable, irreversible, irretrievable, undone; past mending, beyond recall, irrevocable, irrecoverable; ready to go, ready for the rag pile *or* junk yard, *Sl.* shot, *Sl.* kaput, done for, on its last legs, at the end of the line, gone, gone-gone-and-double-gone, finished.

irreplaceable, *adj.* **1.** unique, rare, one of a kind, one and only; priceless, valuable, invaluable, inestimable, precious, worth its weight in gold.

2. indispensable, unexpendable, vital, essential; necessary, requisite, needed, unforgoable.

irrepressible, *adj.* **1.** unrestrainable, uncontrollable, insuppressible, ungovernable, unmanageable, intractable; unconstrained, unrestrained, free, unbridled, unbound, loose; uninhibited, unsuppressed, unreserved, unchecked.

2. cheerful, lively, ebullient, effervescent, spirited, buoyant; animated, alive, vivacious, sprightly, spry, alacritous.

3. automatic, spontaneous, mechanical, reflex; involuntary, instinctive, impulsive, unthinking.

irreproachable, *adj.* **1.** blameless, faultless, unblamable, unblameworthy; irreprehensible, unimpeachable, inculpable, irreprovable, above suspicion; guiltless, sinless, unerring, innocent, clean-handed; honest, respectable, ethical, moral, principled, righteous.

2. impeccable, immaculate, flawless, errorless, spotless, stainless, unblemished; perfect, ideal, correct, peerless, indefectible, infallible.

irresistible, *adj.* **1.** unconquerable, invincible, in domitable; unquenchable, irrepressible, insuppressible; overpowering, overwhelming, overmastering, overriding, knockdown; strong, powerful, mighty, puissant, potent; compelling, forceful, forcible, urgent, emphatic, imperative.

2. unavoidable, inevitable, ineluctible, inevasible, inescapable, unpreventable; inexorable, unstoppable, relentless, remorseless, inflexible, certain, sure.

3. tempting, tantalizing, enticing, seductive, alluring, ravishing, inviting; intriguing, captivating, charming, fascinating.

4. loveable, adorable, endearing, enchanting; cute, lovely, huggable, squeezable, cuddly, cuddlesome, kissable.

irresolute, *adj.* **1.** doubtful, dubious, uncertain, shifting, unreliable; undecided, indecisive, undetermined, unresolved, wishy-washy, hesitant, fickle, *Sl.* candy-assed; infirm, vacillating, wavering, faltering, oscillating, shuffling, flickering, fitful, alternating; inconstant, unstable, double-minded, of two minds, inconsistent, changeable, variable; half-hearted, indifferent, lukewarm, passive, apathetic, lackadaisical; unsteadfast, unstaunch, unpersevering, unsteady.

2. squeamish, cowardly, fainthearted, yellow, pusillanimous; weak, frail, feeble, faint; spineless, weak-kneed, chicken-hearted, lily-livered; timid, timorous, shaky, tremulous, fearful; submissive, yielding, pliant, soft.

irresolution, *n.* **1.** infirmity, vacillation, indecision, indecisiveness, uncertainty, doubt, dubiety; hesitancy, hesitance, tergiversation, changeableness, irresoluteness, fickleness, wishy-washiness; inconstancy, instability, variability, unsteadiness, unsteadfastness; half-heartedness, indifference, lukewarmness, lackadaisicalness, apathy, passivity.

2. faintheartedness, squeamishness, cowardice, pusillanimity, yellow streak, poltroonery; timidity, timorousness, tremulousness, fearfulness; weakness, frailty, feebleness, faintness; submissiveness, softness, pliancy, yieldingness.

irrespective, *adj.* *Usu.* **irrespective of** without regard to, regardless of, ignoring, discounting; apart from, independent, separate, distinct; in spite of, despite, notwithstanding.

irresponsible, *adj.* **1.** untrustworthy, unreliable, devil-may-care; unaccountable, unanswerable, fly-by-night; lawless, unruly, unrestrained, reckless, rash, harum-scarum.

2. capricious, erratic, flighty, mercurial, featherbrained; light-minded, frivolous, *Inf.* no-account, trifling; inconstant, changeable, fickle, giddy, volatile; unstable, unsteady, vacillating, wavering, mutable, fluctuating, variable, irresolute, infirm of purpose; half-hearted, undecided, uncommitted, unsettled, arbitrary, foot-loose and fancy-free; thoughtless, inconsiderate, self-centered.

irresponsive, *adj.* **1.** uncommunicative, reticent, reserved, secretive, taciturn, unconversable, quiet; silent, mum, mute, close-mouthed.

2. indifferent, unconcerned, unresponsive, uninterested, incurious, uninquisitive; aloof, removed, detached, withdrawn.

3. apathetic, impassive, unemotional, unfeeling, dispassionate, insentient, insensible; cool, cold, frigid, icy; phlegmatic, lethargic, listless, languid, dull.

irretrievable, *adj.* irrecoverable, unrecoverable, unregainable, unsalvageable, unsavable, lost; irreclaimable, unreclaimable, irredeemable, inredeemable; irreformable, unreformable, incorrigible, reprobate, beyond *or* past help; irreparable, unrestorable, unfixable, uncorrectable, unrectifiable; incurable, immedicable, unmedicable, uncurable, cureless, terminal, unremediable, irremediable, remediless; hopeless, beyond *or* past hope, lost cause.

irreverence, *n.* **1.** disrespectfulness, unrespectfulness, discourtesy, discourteousness, uncourtesy, uncourteousness, impoliteness, incivility, uncivilness; rudeness, impudence, impudency, impertinence, impertinency, impertinentness, insolence.

2. impiety, impiousness, unpiety, blasphemy, blasphemousness, profanity, profaneness, sacrilege, sacrilegiousness, desecration; irreligion, undevoutness, ungodliness, unholiness.

irreverent, *adj.* **1.** disrespectful, unrespectful, discourteous, uncourteous, impolite, incivil, uncivil; rude, impudent, impertinent, insolent, insulting.

2. impious, unpious, blasphemous, profane, sacrilegious, desecrative; irreligious, unreligious, indevout, undevout, ungodly, unholy.

irreversible, *adj.* **1.** unreversible, indefeasible, unannullable, irrevocable, unrevocable, unrepealable, irrepealable, unrecallable; irrecoverable, unrecoverable, unregainable, irretrievable, irreclaimable, unreclaimable, irredeemable, unredeemable.

2. unchangeable, unalterable, untransmutable, incommutable, uncommutable, invariable; irreparable, unrestorable, unfixable, uncorrectable, unrectifiable; incurable, immedicable, unmedicable, uncurable, cureless, terminal, unremediable, irremediable, remediless.

irrevocable, *adj.* unrevocable, unrepealable, irrepealable, unrecallable; irreversible, unreversible, indefeasible, unannullable. See **irreversible**.

irrigate, *v.* water, spray, sprinkle, *Dial.* use ditchwater *or* branch water; soak, flood; dampen, moisten, wet, swash, splash, drench, douse, ret; douche, syringe.

irrigation, *n.* watering, wetting, spraying, soaking, flooding, drenching; greening.

irritability, *n.* **1.** testiness, petulance, snappishness, irascibility, touchiness, prickliness; excitability, fieriness, inflammability; peevishness, waspishness, raspiness, fretfulness, edginess, nervousness.

2. grouchiness, crankiness, grumpiness, cantankerousness, huffiness, crabbiness; churlishness, bearishness, crotchetiness, gruffness; spleen, choler, moodiness, ill nature, ill temper; crossness, crustiness, sharpness, asperity, tartness, acerbity; resentfulness, fractiousness, captiousness, querulousness, contentiousness.

irritable, *adj.* **1.** testy, touchy, snappish, petulant, irascible, prickly; excitable, fiery, inflammable, hasty, quick, trigger-happy; high-strung, hot-tempered, hot-blooded, thin-skinned, quick-tempered; peevish, huffish, waspish, raspy, peppery, fretful; huffy, edgy, on edge.

2. grumpy, cranky, grouchy, crotchety, churlish, bearish; gruff, cantankerous, impatient, crabby; splenetic, choleric, dyspeptic, moody, temperamental, out of sorts; cross, crusty, crabbed, ill-tempered, ill-humored; sharp, tart, acerbic; fractious, quarrelsome, querulous, contentious, resentful, captious; currish, shrewish, vixenish.

irritant, *adj.* **1.** bothersome, pestering; nettlesome, irritating. See **irritating**.

—*n.* **2.** nuisance, bother, pest, annoyance, bur, thorn in the side *or* flesh, pea in the shoe, salt in the wound, *Inf.* headache, *Inf.* pain, *Sl.* pain in the neck *or* rear, *Sl.* hassle; trouble, problem, affliction; trial, ordeal, tribulation; weight, load, burden, heavy load *or* burden; bore, crashing bore; peeve, pet peeve, gripe, complaint, grievance; sore spot, sore point, *Inf.* touchy subject *or* matter; mortification, humiliation, skeleton in the closet.

irritate, *v.* **1.** vex, provoke, pique, annoy, irk, peeve, nettle, chafe, get on [s.o.'s] nerves, tread on [s.o.'s] toes, go against the grain, *Chiefly U.S.* rile, *Inf.* aggravate, *Inf.* miff, *Inf.* give [s.o.] a pain, *Inf.* rub [s.o.] the wrong way, *Inf.* get under [s.o.'s] skin, *Inf.* get in [s.o.'s] hair; exasperate, ruffle, disturb, disquiet, discompose, discountenance, put out, put off, try [s.o.'s] patience, *Inf.* put [s.o.'s] nose out of joint, get, *Sl.* get [s.o.'s] goat; set one's teeth on edge, stick in one's craw *or* crop, *Inf.* grate *or* grate on one's nerves.

2. bother, pester, hector, harass, *Sl.* bug, *Sl.* hassle, *Sl.* drive [s.o.] nuts *or* crazy *or* bananas, *Sl.* drive [s.o.] up the wall; hound, dog, nag, pick on, pick at, *Sl.* ride, *Inf.* give [s.o.] a hard *or* bad time; bedevil, torment, tease, taunt, tweak, mock, *Inf.* needle; trouble, plague, fret, worry, *Scot.* thraw, *Scot.* fash.

3. anger, incense, raise [s.o.'s] ire *or* hackles, get [s.o.'s] back up, *Inf.* get [s.o.'s] Irish *or* dander up, *Inf.* burn [s.o.] up, *Sl.* tick [s.o.] off, *Sl.* tee [s.o.] off.

4. agitate, inflame, enflame, kindle, fire, fire up, stir up, work up, wind up; incite, ignite, touch off.

irritated, *adj.* **1.** annoyed, piqued, bothered, vexed nettled, riled; tormented, harassed, pestered, pained, plagued.

2. inflamed, red, chafed, smarting, burning, hurting, tingling; raw, tender, sore, sensitive, hypersensitive, *Med.* algetic.

irritating, *adj.* **1.** provoking, agitating, inflaming, inflammatory, enflaming, kindling; inciting, igniting, instigating.
2. angering, incensing, irksome, irking; maddening, infuriating, enraging; exacerbating, rankling, galling, embittering.
3. nettlesome, nettling, irritative, irritant, *Inf.* aggravating, *Inf.* in one's hair; disturbing, ruffling, disquieting.
4. annoying, bothersome, pestering, *Inf.* pesky, *Inf.* pestiferous, vexatious, vexing; troublesome, troubling, thorny, fretful, worrisome, worrying, *Archaic except Dial.* plaguy; hectoring, harassing, hounding, dogging, nagging, tormenting.

irritation, *n.* **1.** annoyance, vexation, exasperation, *Inf.* aggravation; displeasure, dissatisfaction, disapproval, disapprobation, discontent.
2. anger, ire, dudgeon, high dudgeon; offense, umbrage, indignation, huff, tiff, fume, pique, *Inf.* slow burn.
3. embitterment, bitterness, exacerbation, bitter resentment, resentment, hard feelings; spleen, choler, gall, bile, ill *or* bad humor, ill *or* bad temper, ill *or* bad feeling; virulence, acerbity, acrimony; hurt feelings, wounded pride.

irruption, *n.* incursion, invasion, intrusion, forcible entry, interjection, illapse; attack, aggression, foray, raid, sally, sortie, inroad; breaking in, bursting in, storming in, crashing in, *Inf.* barging in.

island, *n.* isle, islet, ait, *Brit. Dial.* eyot, *Brit. Dial.* holm; cay, key; atoll, reef, archipelago; iceberg, icefloe, floe, calf; oasis.

ism, *n.* doctrine, principle, tenet, precept; belief, faith, practice, dogma, conviction; view, opinion, philosophy; theory, hypothesis; system, method, procedure, scheme; affiliation, advocacy, adherence.

isolate, *v.* **1.** set apart, put by itself, segregate, insulate, cut off, *Med.* quarantine; seclude, keep in solitude, sequester, lock up, pen up; exclude, banish, outlaw, exile, expatriate, ostracize, excommunicate, blacklist.
2. separate, detach, disunite, disjoin; sever, dissever, part, disconnect, divide, divorce, dissociate, abstract.

isolated, *adj.* **1.** solitary, separate, alone, single; detached, segregated, exiled, retired, private, sequestered, insular; lonely, forsaken, godforsaken, forlorn; eremitical, troglodytic, hermitical, monastic, anchoretic, *Eccles. Hist.* stylitic.
2. secret, hidden, covert, secluded, outlying, out-of-the-way, remote, unfrequented, uninhabited, deserted, abandoned, inhospitable, desolate.

isolation, *n.* **1.** separation, dissociation, disconnection, detachment; segregation, sequestration, insulation, quarantine, insularity; (*in prison*) *Sl.* icebox.
2. loneliness, solitude, solitariness, aloneness; seclusion, retirement, privacy; concealment, obscurity, delitescence; reclusion, reclusiveness, anchoretism, hermitry, monasticism, self-exile; unsociableness, inhospitality, withdrawal, introversion, aloofness, remoteness.

issue, *n.* **1.** issuance, promulgation, publication, proclamation; distribution, propagation, dissemination, broadcasting, dispersion.
2. edition, copy, number, printing, version.
3. emergence, appearance, materialization, disclosure; exhibition, presentation.
4. crux, point in question, question *or* point at issue, moot point, bone of contention; question, problem, poser; topic, subject, matter, point; political football.
5. effect, result, consequence, upshot; outcome, outgrowth, aftermath, aftereffect; end, ending, consummation, conclusion, termination, finale, *Inf.* payoff, windup; denouement, catastrophe.
6. offspring, progeny, young, children, sons and daughters, family, heirs, scions; descendants, posterity, younger generation; brood, litter, seed, spawn.
7. outflow, effusion, effluence, efflux; discharge, debouchment, emanation.
8. egress, exit, outlet; passage, door, opening, portal.
—*v.* **9.** put out, send out, deal out, get out, distribute, dispense; propagate, disseminate, disperse, broadcast, circulate; promulgate, proclaim, utter, declare, announce, herald; print, publish, mint.
10. emit, effuse, exude, discharge; gush, spurt, flow forth, stream, pour; trickle, seep, percolate, ooze.
11. emerge, come forth, appear, loom, rise up; go forth, sally forth, remove; take off, make off, depart, leave, take leave.
12. originate, emanate, flow, spring, stem, arise; derive, proceed, bud, sprout; result, ensue.

italicize, *v.* underscore, underline, mark, point up, call attention to, bring home, press home; emphasize, stress, lay stress *or* emphasis upon, give emphasis to, punctuate, accent, accentuate; feature, highlight, spotlight, play up, give prominence to, bring to the fore, bring into relief, *Inf.* headline; intensify, strengthen, heighten, deepen.

itch, *v.* **1.** tingle, prickle, tickle, sting; crawl.
2. hanker, crave, yearn, *Inf.* yen, pine for, long for; desire, want, wish; hunger, thirst, set one's heart on, die to, pant to, lust.
3. annoy, irritate, *Sl.* give the willies *or* creeps, pester; bother, *Sl.* drive cuckoo *or* up the wall, exasperate, exacerbate, irk, harass.
—*n.* **4.** itchiness, tingling, prickling, stinging; crawling, formication, *Sl.* creepy-crawlies, *Pathol.* paresthesia; rash, mange, scabies, eczema.
5. hankering, *Inf.* yen, yearning; desire, longing, hope; appetite, hunger, thirst, passion, burning passion, *Sl.* letch, craving; urge, cacoëthes, mania; impulsion, propulsion, impulse.

itchy, *adj.* **1.** itching, scratchy, tingling, prickling, tickling, ticklish, stinging, crawling, titillated.
2. desirous, longing, hankering, yearning, thirsting, hungry, craving.
3. restless, restive, impatient, *Sl.* antsy, fidgety, breathless; eager, avid, keen, burning, fervid, *Sl.* hot to trot, *Sl.* rarin' to go; edgy, nervous, *Inf.* in a dither.
4. acquisitive, avaricious, greedy, grasping, covetous; money-hungry, having an itchy palm; *Sl.* looking out for number one, *Sl.* on the make.

item, *n.* article, detail, feature, point, consideration; particular, component, element, ingredient, member, integer; particularity, specific, aspect, circumstance; entry, note, minute, memorandum, memo, jotting, reminder; blurb, filler.

itemize, *v.* list, record, codify, alphabetize, tabulate, group, register, rank, arrange, file; detail, particularize, mention *or* list in detail, tick off, count off, point out, mention, indicate, specify, list particulars.

iterate, *v.* repeat, reiterate, restate, go over the same ground; reword, rehash, recount, retell, recapitulate; revert to, return to, refer, echo, battologize; dwell on, emphasize, stress, underscore, press one's point; harp on, hammer *or* pound away at, sound like a broken record; tautologize.

itinerancy, *n.* wandering, roaming, roving, rambling, wayfaring, drifting, gallivanting, gad, gadding, *Dial.* traipsing, *Australian.* swagging, *Australian.* waltzing matilda, *Sl.* bumming; nomadism, peripateticism, vagabondism, hoboism, vagrancy; wanderlust, *Sl.* itchy feet.

itinerant, *adj.* **1.** itinerating, traveling, journeying, wayfaring, peregrinating, peripatetic; roving, roaming, wandering, rambling; galavanting, flitting, gadding, jetting; thumbing, backpacking.

2. unsettled, nomadic, gypsy, vagrant, migratory; living in one's hat, living out of a suitcase, having itchy feet, having sand in one's shoe; travelweary, wayworn, weather-beaten.

—*n.* **3.** minister, missionary, circuit rider; judge, circuit court judge; traveling salesman, door-to-door salesman, drummer; migratory *or* migrant worker, *Inf.* dust cropper, *Inf.* Okie, *Usually Disparaging.* wetback; junketter, campaigner, *Inf.* whistle-stopper; tramp, hobo, vagrant, vagabond, beachcomber; circuit player, *Inf.* ski bum, *Inf.* tennis bum, *Inf.* gypsy pilot; nomad, kuchi, gypsy, bohemian, wanderer.

4. traveler, wayfarer, voyager, peregrinator, peripatetic; rambler, rover, roamer, adventurer, landloper, explorer, soldier of fortune; pilgrim, trekker, hiker, backpacker; tourist, globe-trotter, jetsetter, world traveler, *Sl.* W.T.; excursionist, sightseer; gadabout, bird of passage.

itinerary, *n.* **1.** travel plan, timetable, schedule, *Inf.* sked; agenda, program, docket, calendar, flight plan, *Inf.* game plan, *Inf.* battle plan, *Inf.* plan of attack; arrangements, preparations, provisions, projection, prospectus, outline, line-up.

2. route, map, course, plot, circuit, progress, passage, career, line *or* path of travel, way, track, lane, beaten path; grand tour, *Ger. Wanderjahr.*

3. log, logbook, journal, diary, record; chart, daybook.

ivory-towered, *adj.* **1.** aloof, retiring, distant, remote, removed, withdrawn, detached, in the clouds; cloistered, secluded, sequestered, retired, sheltered, far from the madding crowd.

2. impractical, unfeasible, unrealizable, academic, theoretical; quixotic, visionary, idealistic.

J

jab, *v.* **1.** poke, thrust, prod, dig, nudge, elbow, bump; tap, chuck, flick, *Sl.* goose; stab, lunge, stroke, bayonet, plunge.
2. punch, box, swipe, rap, whack, smack, hook, cuff; belt, thump, thwack, *Sl.* sock, *Sl.* bash, *Sl.* slug, *Sl.* clip; *Inf.* biff, *Inf.* bonk, *Inf.* whop, *Inf.* plunk.
—*n.* **3.** poke, prod, dig, nudge, thrust; tap, flick, chuck, *Sl.* goose; lunge, stab, stroke.
4. rabbit punch, uppercut, hook, shot; rap, punch, swipe, smack, whack, thwack; cuff, belt, *Inf.* biff, *Inf.* plunk, *Inf.* bonk, *Inf.* whop; *Sl.* sock, *Sl.* slug, *Sl.* bash.

jabber, *v.* **1.** chatter, prattle, cackle, gibber, *Sl.* gibber-jabber, jargon; babble, prate, tattle, twaddle, *Brit.* twattle; patter, gabble, blather, drivel; mutter, mumble, splutter, sputter; stammer, stutter; chit-chat, chitter-chatter, chaffer, bandy words; gossip, buzz, talk idly, *Sl.* shoot the breeze, *Sl.* gas, *Inf.* gab, *Sl.* bull; palaver, clack, clatter, rattle, *Sl.* run on *or* off at the mouth; gush, blab, *Inf.* spout; be loquacious *or* talkative, ramble, maunder.
—*n.* **2.** gibberish, chatter, Jabberwocky, prattle, cackle, gibber; babble, babblement, prate, tattle, twaddle, *Brit.* twattle; patter, gabble, blather, drivel; jargon, gobbledegook, nonsense, hocus-pocus, mumbo jumbo, abracadabra, open sesame; babbling, *Fr. bavardage;* humbug, flummery, *Sl.* bunk, rubbish, *Inf.* rot, *Sl.* garbage, *Sl.* horsefeathers; balderdash, hogwash, stuff and nonsense, *Inf.* bosh, fudge, foolishness, rigmarole *or* rigamarole; poppycock, *Inf.* fiddle-faddle, *Inf.* piffle, *Inf.* kibosh, *Inf.* flapdoodle; small talk, *Anglo-Indian.* bukh, chit-chat, chitter-chatter, gossip, idle talk, *Inf.* gab, *Sl.* bull; palaver, claptrap, *Sl.* hot air, *Sl.* gas.

Jabberwocky, *n.* nonsense, gibberish, gobbledegook. See **jabber** (*def.* **2**).

jack, *n.* **1.** lift, lifter, booster, erector, hoist, tackle; jackscrew, pneumatic jack, hydraulic jack.
2. flag, pennant, standard, banner, banneret, streamer; colors, *Latin. vexillum*, ensign, merchant flag, swallowtail, pennon.
—*v.* **3.** lift, lift up, hoist, boost, move up; heave, thrust up, rear, uprear, erect, raise; uplift, upthrust, upheave, upcast, upthrow; jerk up, hike up, pull up, pick up, haul up.
4. *Informal.* raise, escalate, up, inflate, push up, drive up; increase, accelerate, augment, extend, make higher.

jack-a-dandy, *n.* dandy, dude, fop, coxcomb, Beau Brummel, *Sl.* peacock, popinjay, fancy Dan, silk-sock Sam; prettyboy, exquisite, silk-stocking, fashion plate, clotheshorse; zoot suiter, macaroni, sharp dresser, fashionable; blade, gay blade, buck, *Chiefly Brit.* blood, spark, *Sl.* swell, *Brit. Inf.* toff; beau, boulevardier, man-about-town, gallant, ladykiller, ladies' man.

jackal, *n.* drudge, hack, slave, flunky, fag, drone, minion; lackey, toady, yes man, creature, cat's paw, votary; doormat, carpet knight, *Inf.* bootlicker, lickspittle, groveler; stooge, follower, tool, dupe, puppet, instrument, henchman; hanger-on, parasite, leech, bloodsucker, sycophant, fawner.

jackanapes, *n.* **1.** whippersnapper, malapert, pup, boldface, brazenface, swaggerer; upstart, wiseacre, weisenheimer, *Sl.* wise guy, smarty, smart-aleck, smarty-pants.
2. imp, mischief-maker, monkey, hooligan, rascal, punk, gamin; rapscallion, devil, scamp, *Inf.* bugger; bad boy, *Fr. enfant terrible*, *Inf.* holy terror, brat, spoiled brat.

jackass, *n.* **1.** ass, male donkey, donkey, jack, burro; dickey, *Sl.* neddy, *Sl.* longear, *Brit. Sl.* moke, *Chiefly Scot.* cuddy.
2. fool, dolt, blockhead, imbecile, moron; ignoramus, idiot, tomfool, tomnoddy, noddy; oaf, clod, dunce, boob, boobie, ninny, *Sl.* schmuck; bungler, boggler, lubber, clodpole, looby; simpleton, *Sl.* simp, loon, dullard, witling, *Sl.* dummy, *Sl.* dumbbell, *Sl.* numskull, ninnyhammer; *Sl.* dingbat, *Sl.* ding-a-ling, *Sl.* jerk, *Sl.* goof, *Sl.* galoot, *Sl.* goofball; sap, chump, *Sl.* klutz, *Sl.* mutt, *Sl.* schlemiel; dope, dimwit, nincompoop, lamebrain, *Sl.* juggins, *Sl.* muggins, halfwit; flibbertigibbet, stupid, *Sl.* nitwit, *Sl.* dimwit.
3. dumbhead, dullhead, jughead, *Ger. Dummkopf*; lunkhead, knucklehead, chowderhead, chucklehead; pinhead, bonehead, thickhead, fathead, muttonhead, woodenhead, bullethead; blubberhead, dunderhead, dunderpate, blunderbuss; cabbagehead, pumpkinhead, puddinghead, mushhead, *Brit. Inf.* jolterhead, *Archaic.* toddyhead; *Sl.* charley, *Sl.* tony, *Sl.* noodle, *Sl.* doughhead; scatterbrain, rattlebrain, rattlepate, harebrain, featherbrain, featherhead; goose, ass, donkey, silly goose, silly, dumb bunny, calf, cuckoo, gull.

jacket, *n.* **1.** coat, coatee, pea jacket, mackinaw jacket *or* mackinaw, *Inf.* mac, windbreaker, dreadnought, parka, anorak; cardigan, camisole, sack, jumper; sports coat *or* jacket, blazer; (*in the Renaissance*) doublet, (*in the eighteenth and nineteenth centuries*) spencer, (*in Greece and the Levant*) grego, (*formerly of sailors*) monkey jacket, *Clothing.* reefer.
2. casing, case, encasement, sheath, sheathing, envelope; cover, covering, wrap, wrapper, wrapping.

jackknife, *n.* pocket knife, penknife, clasp knife, folding knife, *Brit. Dial.* jockteleg.

jack-of-all-trades, *n.* handyman, handy-andy; factotum, do-all, general servant, man of all work.

jackpot, *n.* **1.** *Poker.* pot, pool, kitty, stakes, bank.
2. first prize, main prize, prize, award, reward.
3. hit the jackpot *Slang.* succeed, score a success, hit it, hit the mark, turn up trumps, strike it rich, *Inf.* break the bank, *Inf.* make a killing.

jackstraw, *n.* **1.** scarecrow, strawman, man of straw, effigy.
2. nonentity, nobody, nothing, cipher, insignificancy, little fellow, *Inf.* little guy, man on the street, John Doe, *Inf.* small fry, *Sl.* small fish, *Sl.* nebbish, *Sl.* Joe Blow *or* Joe Doakes.

jade[1], *n.* nephrite, jadeite, jadestone, gemstone.

jade[2], *n.* **1.** hack, nag, padnag, crock, rosinante, whistler, roarer, *Inf.* bagabones *or* rackabones, *Inf.* rip, *Sl.* skate, *Chiefly U.S. Sl.* plug, *Chiefly Brit. Sl.* screw, (*usu. a race horse*) *Sl.* stiff.
2. hag, crone, witch, beldam, quean, harridan, *Sl.* bitch, *Sl.* old bag, *Sl.* old battle-ax; hussy, vixen, shrew; wench, trull, drab, baggage, loose woman, woman of easy virtue, pickup, *Sl.* chippy, *Sl.* floozy, *Sl.* broad, tart; prostitute, whore, harlot, strumpet, trollop, cocotte, scarlet woman, *Archaic.* doxy; call girl, streetwalker, *Sl.* hustler, *Sl.* hooker.
—*v.* **3.** exhaust, enervate, wear out, wear down, do in; tire, weary, fatigue, *Inf.* tucker out; overwork, overtask, overtax; get tired, grow weary, flag, droop, wilt, burn out, *Inf.* peter out, *Sl.* poop out.
4. cloy, pall, glut, gorge; sate, satiate, slake, allay; have enough, have one's fill, have had it, have all one can stand *or* take, *Inf.* have a bellyful, *Inf.* be fed up, *Inf.* have it up to here, *Sl.* have a snootful.

jaded, *adj.* **1.** exhausted, enervated, worn-out, played-out, spent, good and tired, dead tired, dog-tired, bone-weary, weary, wearied, fatigued, done-in, *Inf.* dead, *Inf.* fagged, *Inf.* beat, *Inf.* tuckered-out, *Sl.* bushed, *Sl.* whipped, *Sl.* wiped out, *Sl.* pooped, *Sl.* too pooped to pop.
2. satiated, sated, slaked, allayed, satisfied; gorged, glutted, cloyed, surfeited; dulled, numbed, stupefied, blunted; fed-up, tired of, sick of, sick and tired of.
3. dissolute, dissipated, wanton, abandoned, profligate, debauched; corrupt, degenerate, depraved, decadent; loose, loose-moraled, of loose morals, of easy virtue, *Inf.* easy, promiscuous.

jag[1], *n.* **1.** projection, spur, snag, tooth, sawtooth; cog, sprocket, ratchet.
—*v.* **2.** notch, nick, cut, slash, gash, score, scarify; scallop, crenelate, serrate, knurl, tooth, *Coining.* mill.

jag[2], *n.* **1.** intoxication, inebriety, inebriation, insobriety, intemperance, drunkenness, sottedness, besottedness, tipsiness.
2. *Informal.* spree, carouse. See **spree** (*def.* **2**).

jagged, *adj.* **1.** notched, notchy, serrated, serrate, serriform, saw-toothed, toothed; ragged, craggy, scraggy, ridged, rugose, nicked, chipped, rugged, uneven, irregular; spinous, spiny, spiniferous, spinigerous, bristly, spiculate, pointy, snaggy, studded.
2. zigzag, zigzagged, pinked, Vandyke edged, herringbone; crotched, forked, crenelate, crenelated, *Heraldry.* indented.

jail, *n.* **1.** lockup, jailhouse, station house, police station, *Scot.* tollbooth, *Inf.* clink, *U.S. Inf.* calaboose, *Brit. Inf.* bridewell; guardhouse, guardroom, *U.S.* brig; prison, penitentiary, *Sl.* pen, house of detention, penal institution, *Sl.* big house, *Sl.* slammer, *Sl.* stir; *All Sl.* can, cooler, coop, jug, hoosegow, boobyhatch, pokey, *Brit.* choky, *Brit.* quod.
—*v.* **2.** imprison, incarcerate, embar, intern, confine, lock up, clap up, *Brit.* gaol, *Sl.* run in, *Sl.* jug, *Sl.* lag.

jailbird, *n.* prisoner, convict, *Sl.* con, trusty *or* trustee, *Inf.* lifer, *Sl.* lag, *Sl.* lagger; parolee, *Brit.* (*formerly*) ticket-of-leave man; ex-convict, *Sl.* ex-con; recidivist, repeat offender, *Inf.* chronic crook.

jailer, *n.* turnkey, warder, keeper, jailkeeper, *Sl.* screw, *Sl.* bull; warden, *Brit.* governor.

jalopy, *n.* *Informal.* wreck, rattletrap, *Facetious.* flivver, *Inf.* clunker, *Inf.* crate, *Inf.* junk, *Sl.* bomb, *Sl.* buggy, *Sl.* tin lizzie, *Sl.* bucket of bolts; car, motorcar, vehicle, automobile, auto.

jam[1], *v.* **1.** wedge, sandwich, stick in *or* into, insert; ram, thrust, shove, push, jamb, force in *or* into; press, squeeze, cram, pack; pack in, shove in, press in, pack tight as sardines; stuff, overstuff, overcrowd, overfill, fill to overflowing, stuff to the gills, fill to the brim.
2. obstruct, block, plug, clog, close up *or* off; deadlock, prevent motion, gum, *Sl.* gum up the works; hinder, stop, stall, arrest, kill; lock up, stick, freeze up, cease, halt.
—*n.* **3.** tie-up, stoppage, slowdown, halt, jamb, bottleneck.
4. crush, mob, rabble; crowd, throng, swarm, horde, herd, pack, flock, sea, mass, legion, army.
5. *Informal.* predicament, plight, fix, *Inf.* pickle, *Inf* hot *or* tight spot.

jam[2], *n.* preserves, conserves, marmalade, jelly, apple *or* peach butter, confiture, confection.

jamb, *n.* doorjamb, doorpost, doorframe, doorcase; upright, post, pillar, column, *Masonry.* jambstone.

jamboree, *n.* festival, fete, carnival, jubilee, celebration; festivity, party, merriment, merrymaking, revelry, revels, charivari, *Inf.* shivaree, *Inf.* shindig, *Inf.* do, *Sl.* bash, *Sl.* wingding; rally, roundup, get-together, gathering; meeting, convention, (*in ancient Greece and Rome*) symposium.

jangle, *v.* **1.** clank, clatter, rattle, jar; clang, clangor, clash, crash, din.
2. wrangle, altercate, quarrel, brawl, broil, feud, be at [s.o.'s] throat; bicker, squabble, spat, tiff, have words; conflict, contend, dispute, *Rare.* discept, disagree; take issue, argue, contest, contravene, spar, cross swords, lock horns.
—*n.* **3.** clank, clatter, rattle, clang, clangor, clash, crash, din, racket; cacophony, stridor, dissonance, jar, jarring, reverberation.
4. argument, wrangle, altercation, dispute, *Rare.* disception, row, *Inf.* set-to; quarrel, squabble, dustup, spat, tiff, *Brit. Dial.* fratch; discord, disagreement, imbroglio, conflict, friction, contention; encounter, engagement, meeting, confrontation, showdown; brawl, broil, feud, cross fire; struggle, fight, skirmish, *Inf.* run-in, *Inf.* scrap, brush, fray, affray.

janitor, *n.* cleaning man, superintendent, *Inf.* super, handyman, custodian, caretaker, guardian; doorman, doorkeeper, concierge, ostiary, usher, porter; gatekeeper, watchman, sentinel, sentry.

jape, *n.* jest, joke, gag, quip, *Inf.* wisecrack, *Inf.* crack; drollery, waggery, witticism, squib, pun, crank; trick, practical joke, prank, caper, antic, shenanigan, tomfoolery, monkeyshine; jeer, gibe, twit, fleer.

jar[1], *n.* vessel, urn, vase, *Gk. and Rom. Antiq.* amphora; container, receptacle, crock, cruse, pot, canister, can; jug, pitcher, ewer; carafe, decanter, flagon, bottle, demijohn, cruet, caster, flask, carboy.

jar[2], *v.* **1.** grate, rasp, scratch, squeak, screech,

screak; jangle, clank, clatter, clang, clangor, clash, din.
2. rattle, vibrate, burr, buzz, hum; shake, agitate, stir; jounce, bounce, jog, joggle, jiggle; jolt, bump, jerk.
3. See **jangle** (*def.* 2).
4. surprise, startle, shock, stun, stupefy; disconcert, take aback, *Inf.* faze, daunt, shake up; upset, unsettle, stir, disquiet, discompose, ruffle, fluster, befuddle, muddle, daze; trouble, bother, worry, disturb, perturb; chafe, nettle, irk, vex, gall, rankle, irritate, get on one's nerves, aggravate, annoy; offend, hit a sore spot, sting, cut, pierce.
—*n.* 5. cacophony, stridor, stridence, stridency, dissonance; blare, blast, bong; jangle, clank, clatter, clang, clangor, clash, crash, din, racket; grating, rasp, rasping, scratching, squeak, screech, screak.
6. rattle, agitation, vibration, reverberation, buzz, burr, hum; shaking, trembling, tremble, quaver; shake, jolt, jerk, yank, bump, jounce, bounce, jog, joggle, jiggle, quake, stir; lurch, rock, sway.
7. shock, surprise, blow, stroke, turn, trauma; thunderclap, thunderbolt, bolt out of the blue, eye-opener.
8. quarrel, tiff, *Brit. Dial.* fratch, spat, dustup, squabble; argument, wrangle, altercation, dispute, *Rare.* disception, row, *Inf.* set-to; discord, disagreement, imbroglio, conflict, friction, contention; brawl, broil, feud, cross fire.

jardiniere, *n.* flower stand, plant stand; vase, pot, flower bowl, epergne; urn, *Archaeol.* patella, *Gk. and Rom. Antiq.* amphora.

jargon, *n.* 1. cant, argot, patois, *Inf.* lingo, slang; vernacular, idiom, parlance, dialect, tongue; pidgin, creole.
2. phraseology, diction, usage, vocabulary, specialized *or* professional language; educationese, computerese, academese, bureaucratese, legalese, journalese, medicalese; buzz word.
3. gibberish, nonsense, moonshine, *Fr. bavardage,* gobbledegook, hocus-pocus, mumbo jumbo, abracadabra, open sesame; humbug, flummery, *Sl.* bunk, rubbish, tommyrot, *Inf.* rot, *Sl.* garbage, *Sl.* horsefeathers; balderdash, hogwash, stuff and nonsense, *Inf.* bosh, *Brit. Sl.* tosh, fudge, foolishness, rigmarole; poppycock, *Inf.* fiddle-faddle, *Inf.* piffle, *Inf.* kibosh, *Inf.* flapdoodle.
—*v.* 4. talk nonsense, gibber, *Sl.* gibber-jabber, *Inf.* talk through one's hat; babble, twaddle, *Brit.* twattle, blather, drivel; jabber, chatter, chipper, prattle, cackle.

jaundice, *n.* 1. *Pathol.* icterus, yellow jaundice, *Biol.* grasserie, yellowness.
2. prejudice, distorted judgment, prejudgment, preconception, preconceived judgment, prenotion; predisposition, presumption, foregone conclusion, fixed idea, *Fr. idée fixe;* bias, narrow-mindedness, pedanticism, pedantry; cynicism, pessimism, misanthropy, disapprobation, disapproval, disparagement, overcriticalness, faultfinding; suspicion, doubt, dubiousness, discredence, disbelief; skepticism, mistrust, distrust; misgiving, scruple, qualm, hesitation.
—*v.* 3. prejudice, influence, prepossess; bias, warp, twist, mold, shape, give a bias to; color, tint, tinge, shade, cloud.

jaundiced, *adj.* 1. yellow, yellowed, yellowish, yellow-faced, yellow-tinged, yellow-skinned; sallow, sickly, pale, wan.
2. prejudiced, prejudging, prejudged, preconceived, predisposed, presumptive; biased, narrow-minded, cynical, pessimistic, misanthropic; disapproving, disparaging, overly critical; suspicious, doubting, dubious, disbelieving, skeptical, mistrusting, distrustful, hesitant.

jaunt, *v.* 1. stroll, ramble, promenade, *Inf.* take a spin, take an outing, take a trip, day-trip; peregrinate, travel, journey, tour.
—*n.* 2. short journey, short haul, short trip, little trip, day trip, short excursion, outing, airing; ramble, stroll, promenade, *Inf.* spin, short drive; peregrination, trip, vacation, mini-vacation, tour, cruise; *U.S. Politics. Disparaging.* junket.

jaunty, *adj.* 1. bouncy, buoyant, brisk, sprightly, lively, frisky, pert, *Inf.* chipper, *Inf.* in fine fettle; easy, relaxed, effortless, elastic, free, free and easy; gay, cheerful, light-hearted, blithe; jolly, jovial, merry, joyful, eager.
2. smart, stylish, chic, debonair; becoming, attractive, trim, neat, *Inf.* natty, *Inf.* spruce; showy, flashy, colorful, *Inf.* splashy, *Inf.* sporty, fancy, flamboyant, gaudy, garish.

javelin, *n.* spear, shaft, bolt, harpoon, gaff, pike, half-pike, spontoon; assegai, jereed, eelspear, gig, dart, arrow.

jaw, *n.* 1. jawbone, maxilla, mandible, jowl; mouthparts, mouth, *Sl.* mug, *Sl.* trap, *Sl.* chops, (*of an animal*) maw, (*of an animal*) muzzle.
2. *Usu.* **jaws** craggy opening, entrance, ingress, entryway, orifice, aperture.

jawbone, *n.* 1. jaw, maxilla, mandible.
—*v.* 2. *Informal.* persuade, talk [s.o.] into, *Sl.* smooth talk, convince, win over; influence, manipulate, control.

jazz, *n.* 1. (*all of music*) Dixieland, ragtime, rag; swing, jive, bop, bebop, big band music, jitterbug music; blues, rhythm and blues, boogie, boogie-woogie; hot jazz, le jazz hot, cool jazz, jazz rock, fusion music; syncopation, improvisation.
2. *Slang.* liveliness, sprightliness, vivacity, spark, dash, spirit, zest, buoyancy.
3. *Slang.* nonsense, balderdash, drivel, twaddle, moonshine, poppycock, bosh, *Inf.* flimflam, *Inf.* guff, *Inf.* malarkey; *All Sl.* bull, baloney, bushwa, crap.

jazzy, *adj. Slang.* 1. (*all of music*) swinging, bopping, rocking, jumping, *Jazz.* hot, *Sl.* jive.
2. wild, spirited, animated, lively, vivacious, brisk, zestful, buoyant; flashy, fancy, stylish, *Inf.* nifty, smart, *Sl.* snazzy.

jealous, *adj.* 1. begrudging, grudging, resentful, envious, green-eyed, green with envy, yellow, envying; covetous, desirous, itching, yearning, hankering; discontent, malcontent, dissatisfied, displeased, unhappy.
2. suspicious, imagining the worst, distrustful, mistrustful, doubting; insecure, anxious, threatened, vulnerable.
3. heedful, mindful, careful, cautious, wary, chary; precautious, circumspect, prudent, discreet, politic.
4. vigilant, watchful, Argus-eyed, attentive; on the watch, on the alert, on the lookout; guarded, on guard, defensive.

jealousy, *n.* 1. resentment, ill will, spite, grudge, begrudging, heartburning, bitterness; envy, enviousness, green-eyed monster, heartburn; rivalry, cupidity.
2. suspicion, distrust, mistrust, doubt, foreboding; insecurity, anxiety, uneasiness, apprehensiveness, vulnerability, lack of confidence, paranoia; discontentment, malcontentedness, dissatisfaction, unhappiness.
3. vigilance, watchfulness, attentiveness, guardedness, defensiveness.

jeans, *n.* slacks, trousers, pants, overalls, blue jeans, *Trademark.* Levi's, bell-bottoms, *Inf.* bells, denims, dungarees, corduroys, *Inf.* cords, chinos, khakis.

jeer, *v.* 1. scoff at, mock, gibe, ridicule, knock, gird at; fleer, laugh at, guy, *Australian.* chiack; taunt, twit, rag; tease, rally, *Inf.* roast, banter, chaff, rib, kid, *Sl.*

razz; flout, scorn, sneer at, disdain, pooh-pooh; scout, contemn, flout; hiss, boo, hoot at, heckle, catcall, rail at, cry down.

—*n.* **2.** jibe, fleer, raillery, chaff; poke, dig, cut, rub, barb; taunt, quip, wisecrack, thrust, skit; boo, hiss, hoot, catcall, cry, raspberry; derision, mockery, ridicule, sarcasm.

jejune, *adj.* **1.** innutritious, meager, skimpy, thin, slight, diluted; flavorless, tasteless.

2. insipid, uninteresting, *Sl.* blah, dull, vapid; flat, empty, arid, dry; tame, lifeless, spiritless, unanimated, wishy-washy; tiresome, boring, tedious, *Sl.* draggy, *Sl.* yawn-making; prosaic, commonplace, humdrum, trite, ordinary, banal, hackneyed.

3. uninformed, inexperienced, naïve; ignorant, *Inf.* dumb, *Sl.* dopey, wet behind the ears.

4. juvenile, childish, *Sl.* kiddish, immature; puerile, silly, inane, senseless, pointless.

jell, *v.* **1.** congeal, jellify, gelatinize, gelatinate, *Physical Chem.* gel; set, solidify, harden, stiffen; coagulate, thicken, curdle, clot.

2. crystallize, materialize, take form *or* shape, shape up, come together.

jelly, *n.* **1.** jell, *Fr. gelée,* jam, preserves, conserves, marmalade, apple *or* peach butter, confiture, confection.

2. gelatin, *Trademark.* jello, aspic, gelatinoid; pudding, blancmange, *Cookery.* mousse.

jellyfish, *n.* *Informal.* namby-pamby, milquetoast, Walter Mitty, *Sl.* wimp; sissy, *Inf.* pantywaist, *Sl.* pansy; *Sl.* pushover, *Sl.* turkey, *Sl.* turk; *Sl.* schlepp, *Sl.* nebbish, *Sl.* creep, *Inf.* lightweight, featherweight.

jellylike, *adj.* gelatinous, gelatinoid, thick, viscous, viscid, glutinous, sticky.

jeopardize, *v.* put in jeopardy, endanger, imperil, peril, menace, threaten, expose *or* lay open to danger, have [s.t.] at stake; hazard, venture, risk, stake, bet, gamble; chance, take a chance, tempt fate, sail too near the wind, fly too close to the sun.

jeopardy, *n.* **1.** endangerment, imperilment, menace, threat; (*all of danger*) exposure, openness, liability, vulnerability, vulnerableness, susceptibility, susceptibleness.

2. peril, danger, hazard, risk, venture, chance, gamble; uncertainty, instability, unstableness, insecurity, unsecureness, insecureness, precariousness.

jeremiad, *n.* lamentation, lament, *Archaic.* plaint; complaint, groan, moan, wail, keening, keen, sob, cry.

jerk, *n.* **1.** yank, pull, tug; twist, tweak, twitch, pluck, twang, nip, pinch.

2. start, lurch, bolt, quick *or* sudden movement; thrust, push, shove; jolt, bump, jog, jounce, bounce, joggle, jostle.

3. **the jerks** *U.S.* spasms, convulsions, fit, *Pathol.* paroxysm; palsy, *Pathol.* chorea, *Pathol.* St. Vitus dance; tremors, the shakes, shaking, trembling.

4. *Slang.* undesirable, *Sl.* spas, *Sl.* creep, *Sl.* fruit, *Sl.* nurd, *Sl.* yoyo, *Sl.* banana, *Sl.* drip, *Sl.* schlepp, *Sl.* schlemiel, *Sl.* turkey, *Sl.* twit; fool, gull, dupe, incompetent, silly billy, *Inf.* silly, *Inf.* dummy, *Sl.* dimwit, *Sl.* stupe.

—*v.* **5.** yank, pull, tug; twist, tweak, twitch, pluck, twang, nip, pinch.

6. thrust, push, shove; jolt, jog, jounce, jar, joggle, jostle, bump, bounce around; start, jump, lurch.

jerky, *adj.* **1.** spasmodic, palsylike, palsied, uncontrolled, out of control, *Pathol.* spastic; convulsive, fitful, shaking, tremulous, tremulant.

2. jolty, jouncing, joggling, jogging, stop-and-go; shaky, bumpy, bouncy, rough.

jerry-built, *adj.* flimsy, unsubstantial, unsolid, unsound, unstable, weak, frail; defective, faulty, flawed; rickety, ramshackle, tumbledown, gimcrack, junky, cheap, shabby, sorry; slipshod, haphazard, thrown together, carelessly *or* sloppily built; improvised, do-it-yourself, Rube Goldberg, Rube Goldbergian, Goldbergian.

jest, *n.* **1.** joke, witticism, quip, one-liner, bon mot, *Sl.* funny; wisecrack, crack, sally, repartee, riposte; pun, play on words, wordplay, *Rhet.* paronomasia; practical joke, hoax, prank, leg-pull.

2. raillery, badinage, banter, persiflage, pleasantry, *Sl.* put-on, gibe.

—*v.* **3.** joke, tell jokes, crack jokes, crack wise, wisecrack, quip; fool, tease, *Inf.* josh, *Inf.* kid, *Inf.* put [s.o.] on, pull [s.o.'s] leg; make merry with, banter, chaff; jabber, *Sl.* scat talk, *Sl.* scat sing; pun.

4. deride, gibe, scoff, give [s.o.] the business, roast; poke fun at, make fun of, mock, ridicule, satirize, parody; jeer, sneer, snigger.

jester, *n.* **1.** wit, quipster, comic, prankster. See **joker** (*def.* 1).

2. fool, court clown, Feste; wearer of the motley, harlequin, Sganarelle, merry-andrew; buffoon, clown, Joey, zany, Pierrot, mime, mummer; pantaloon.

jesting, *adj.* playful, merry, laughing, frolicsome, rollicking; comic, comical, droll, funny, facetious, tongue-in-cheek, humorous; waggish, roguish, jocund, jocose; witty, fast with the quips, quick-witted, clever, facile-tongued; kidding, joking, spoofing; silly, inane, nonsensical.

Jesus, *n.* **1.** Jesus Christ, Christ, Christ Jesus, Jesus of Nazareth, the Nazarene, the Galilean, *Literary.* Jesu; the Redeemer, the Savior, Emmanuel, Immanuel, the Messiah, the Star of David, the Son of David, the Annointed, the Expected One; the King, the King of Kings, the Lord of Lords, the Prince of Peace, the Lord, Christ the Lord, God Incarnate, the Incarnation, God in Man, the Hypostatic Union, the King of Heaven, the King of Glory, the Lord of Our Righteousness, God the Son, the Godhead, the Only Begotten, the Son of God, the Son of Mary, the Son of Man; the Babe, the Holy Infant, the Infant Redeemer, the Child of Bethlehem, the Christ Child.

2. the Alpha, the Alpha and Omega, the Beginning and the End; the Ideal Man, Perfected Humanity, the Perfection, Wonderful, the Light of the World, the Morning Star, the Son of Righteousness; the Word of God, the Incarnate Word, the Word Made Flesh, Logos; the Counsellor, the Mediator, the Intercessor, the Advocate, the Judge; the Great Physician, the Healer, the Comforter, the Good Shepherd, the Man of Sorrows; the Crucified, the Lamb, the Lamb of God, the Offering of the Lord, the Risen; the Vine, the True Vine, the Servant, the Way, the Door, the Truth, the Life, the Way of Life, the Bread of Life.

jet[1], *n.* **1.** stream, gush, fountain, spring, rush, flush, spate, *Fr. jet d'eau;* gusher, geyser, well, *Inf.* spouter; spout, spurt, squirt, spray, spit, *Chiefly Dial.* spritz.

2. nozzle, spout, sprinkler, tip, sparger, nose, snout; shower head, sprinkler head, rose, rosehead.

3. jet plane, jetliner, turbojet, ramjet; SST, supersonic transport, jumbo jet, 747, 707.

—*v.* **4.** shoot, spout, gush, rush, flush; flow, stream, well, spill; surge, leap, burst forth, break forth, erupt; squirt, spray, sparge, spurtle, splutter, spit, *Chiefly Dial.* spritz.

5. fly, take wing, wing, take to the air, take flight; zoom, soar, zip, break the sound barrier, *Sl.* buzz, whoosh, zing.

jet[2], *adj.* black, pitch, pitchy, coal, ebony, ebon,

inky; tar-black, jet-black, pitch-black, jetty; dark, pitch-dark, sooty, raven, sable, sloe, atramentous; black as night, black as the ace of spades, black as a crow, black as midnight.

jettison, *n.* **1.** expulsion, ejection, discharge, throwing overboard *or* away, casting over *or* away, tossing out, defenestration; disposal, dumping, discarding, *Sl.* deep six, *Sl.* the boot, *Sl.* the old heave-ho.

2. jetsam, flotsam, flotsam and jetsam, castoff, slough, derelict, lagan.

—*v.* **3.** chuck, eject, expel, throw off, throw over *or* overboard, cast over; discharge, discard, defenestrate, toss out *or* over, dump, *Sl.* deep-six, *Sl.* give the deep six.

jetty, *n.* **1.** pier, jutty, breakwater, seawall; mole, embankment, barrier, groin, bulkhead.

2. wharf, quay, dock, dockage; marina, basin, bund, harbor, port, landing.

jewel, *n.* **1.** gem, stone, precious stone, *Sl.* rock, bijou; sparkler, brilliant, diamond, pearl, emerald, ruby, sapphire, rhinestone.

2. ornament, trinket, bauble, adornment; bangle, brooch, *Archaic.* ouch, earring, ring, nosering; badge, medal, medallion, crest; stub, pin, breast-pin, tie clasp, tie clip; fob, charm, locket, pendant, amulet; curio, gewgaw, knicknack, knack, bibelot, gimcrack, *Sl.* doodad.

3. treasure, pearl, diamond, flower, pure gold; pride, boast, talk, pride and joy, cream; prize, plum, work of art, masterpiece; *Sl.* winner, find, godsend; *Sl.* humdinger, *Sl.* crackerjack, *Sl.* ace.

4. *Informal.* gentleman, good man, prince, king, god; real man, man after one's heart, saint, one in a thousand; diamond in the rough, good egg, good Joe; lady, good woman, real woman, princess, queen, goddess; doll, *Sl.* pussycat.

jeweler, *n.* lapidary, engraver, glyptographer, gemologist; craftsman, artist, watchmaker, horologist.

jewelry, *n.* **1.** gems, jewels, bijouterie, jewel-work, finery, glass, costume jewelry, *Sl.* ice.

2. necklace, necklet, chain, beads, chaplet, rosary, wampum; bracelet, wristlet, anklet, armlet, torque; diadem, tiara, coronet, crown.

Jezebel, *n.* reprobate, loose woman, wanton, jade; whore, woman of easy virtue, easy woman, wench; drab, trull, trollop, hussy, baggage, grisette; pickup, slut, *Sl.* bitch, quean; strumpet, cocotte, scarlet woman, tart, *Sl.* floozy, *Sl.* chippy, *Sl.* broad; vamp, temptress, demimondaine, demirep; Delilah, Messalina, Lais, seductress, witch, femme fatale.

jibe, *v.* agree, concur, be in accord, be in harmony, harmonize; go together, *Sl.* jive, fit together, mesh; correspond, match, coincide, be synchronized.

jiffy, *n.* *Informal.* a little while, a short time, *Inf.* whipstitch; minute, moment, second, *Inf.* sec, split second, instant; flash, twinkling, twinkle, breath, trice; eyewink, wink of the eye, *Fr. coup d'oeil,* twinkling of an eye, *Inf.* bat of an eye, two shakes of a lamb's tail.

jig, *n.* **1.** hornpipe, fling, Highland fling, reel, rigadoon, folk dance.

—*v.* **2.** dance a jig, bob up and down, bobble, bounce, jounce, jiggle, joggle, shake; wiggle, wriggle, *Sl.* wiggle one's hips; twist, turn, jerk, flounce; hop, skip, leap, jump about.

jiggle, *v.* **1.** joggle, jog, jostle, shake, agitate, rock, vibrate, wobble, waggle, move to and fro; jerk, jolt, twitch, pluck, pull, tug, yank.

2. bob, bobble, bounce, jounce, jig; wiggle, wriggle, *Sl.* wiggle one's hips; twist, turn, flounce.

jilt, *v.* (*all of a lover or sweetheart*) reject, cast aside, discard, get rid of, drop, ditch, dump, give the gate, *Inf.* give the mitten, *Sl.* give the brush-off; throw over, leave, forsake, abandon; (*all of a relationship*) break up, break off, end, discontinue, terminate, finish, conclude.

jingle, *v.* **1.** tinkle, tink, ding, ding-dong, ring, chime, tintinnabulate; clink, chink, jangle, clang, clangor, clank; rattle, shake, vibrate.

—*n.* **2.** tinkle, tinkling, ting, tinging, ringing, ding, ding-dong, chime, chiming, tintinnabulation; clink, clinking, chink, chinking, jangle, jangling, clang, clanging, clangor, clangoring, clank, clanking.

3. ditty, carol, chorus, chant, catchy tune, tune, melody, song, ballad; rhyme, couplet, Hudibrastic, stanza, crambo; poem, verse, lyric, limerick, doggerel.

jingoism, *n.* patriotism, superpatriotism, blind patriotism, nationalism, chauvinism, flag-waving, wrapping oneself in the flag, belief in my country right or wrong, spread-eagleism.

jinx, *n.* **1.** curse, hex, spell, charm, incantation, conjuration, invocation, magic formula; black magic, voodoo, hoodoo, juju, evil eye, *It. malocchio*, *Inf.* Indian sign, *Sl.* whammy, *Sl.* double-whammy, *Archaic.* wanion; imprecation, execration, malediction.

2. bad luck, evil, misfortune, calamity, trouble; bane, affliction, scourge, plague, torment; harm, evil days *or* time; annoyance, vexation.

3. Jonah, bogy, bugbear, bugaboo, *Inf.* albatross; hobgoblin, goblin, imp, ouphe, demon, incubus, succubus, devilkin, barghest; Fury, evil genius, witch, witch doctor.

—*v.* **4.** *Informal.* bewitch, curse, hex, witch, becharm, cast a spell on, *Inf.* spook, *Sl.* put *or* slam the whammy on; demonize, bedevil, possess; plague, blight, scourge, injure, harm, destroy, doom; vex, trouble, beset, annoy, harass, distress, agonize, harrow; confuse, muddle, confound, frustrate; befuddle, rattle, raffle; throw off, put off, trip up, cause to fumble *or* stumble; mess up, cause trouble, wreck, sabotage, undermine, throw a monkey wrench in the works, *Inf.* bug, *Inf.* screw up.

jitter, *n.* **1. jitters** nervousness, uneasiness, fear, trembling, shaking, quivering, quaking, *Inf.* the shakes; fidgetiness, perturbation, tension, restlessness, skittishness, *Inf.* fantods, *Sl.* willies, *Sl.* heebie-jeebies, *Sl.* whim-whams, *Sl.* jimjams, *Inf.* screaming-meemies, *Inf.* the creeps.

—*v.* **2.** fidget, move by fits and starts, *Scot.* fidge, twitch, jerk; tremble, shake, quiver, quake; fuss, flurry, stew, pace, walk the floor, chew one's nails, look over one's shoulder, jump at every sound.

jive, *n.* **1.** (*all of music*) swing, jazz, bop, bebop, big band music, jitterbug music; boogie, boogie-woogie, rhythm and blues, blues.

2. *Slang.* nonsense, drivel, twaddle, moonshine, poppycock, bosh, *Inf.* flimflam, *Inf.* guff, *Inf.* malarkey; *All Sl.* jazz, bull, baloney, bushwa, crap.

—*v.* **3.** jitterbug, lindy, *Inf.* hop.

4. *Slang.* fool, trick, *Inf.* flimflam, bluff, take in; banter, tease, *Inf.* fun, *Inf.* kid, *Inf.* rib, *Inf.* josh, *Sl.* razz; make fun of, mock, ridicule, *Inf.* rag.

job, *n.* **1.** work, undertaking, proceeding, business, matter at hand; task, chore, activity, exercise, performance; project, affair, venture, enterprise, effort; contribution, accomplishment, achievement, role, function, part.

2. concern, charge, duty, office, capacity; assignment, commission, trust, mission, errand; place, station, billet, berth; appointment, sinecure.

3. employment, occupation, livelihood, living, pursuit, vocation, calling, profession, field, métier, area, province; trade, craft.

4. transaction, deal, dealings, *Inf.* iron in the fire.

5. drudgery, toil, hack work, grind, daily grind.

6. graft, corruption, jobbery. See **jobbery.**

—*v.* **7.** buy and sell, wholesale, distribute, dispense, consign, apportion, allocate.

8. contract, job out, subcontract, farm out, commission, consign, sublet, lease, relegate, send out; do odd jobs, hire oneself out, free-lance.

9. swindle, scheme, exploit, manipulate, maneuver, pettifog, machinate, gerrymander, gouge, line one's pockets, feather one's nest, *Sl.* pull wires *or* strings, *Sl.* porkbarrel.

jobber, *n.* **1.** wholesaler, wholesale merchant, broker, dealer, consignor, dispenser, supplier, middleman; agent, salesman, representative.

2. pieceworker, wageworker, day laborer *or* worker, laborer; hired hand, hand, help, workman; handyman, jack-of-all-trades, all-around man, man-of-all-work; migrant, *Inf.* wetback, itinerant, migratory worker; hack, drudge, hireling, freelancer, *Inf.* gypsy, *Inf.* tramp.

3. grafter, swindler, fraud; manipulator, operator, gerrymanderer, wirepuller, stringpuller, wheeler-dealer; schemer, strategist, intriguer, machinator; sharper, pettifogger, carpetbagger, graft merchant.

jobbery, *n.* graft, racket, spoils; *Inf.* pickings, rake-off, cut, kickback; plunder, loot, booty, swag, boodle, grease, velvet, gravy, honey, payola, hush money, pay-off, shake-down; pettifogging, fraudulence, gerrymandering, putting in the fix, pulling wires *or* strings.

jockey, *n.* **1.** rider, horseback rider, horseman, equestrian, trainer, exercise boy, *Inf.* jock.

—*v.* **2.** ride, race, run, mount, sit; train, exercise; guide, steer, handle, control.

3. maneuver, manage, negotiate, manipulate; adjust, set right, trim, ease, ease into position; coax, cajole, induce, wheedle, beguile; court, woo, flatter, curry favor, fawn over, dance attendance upon, *Inf.* soft-soap, ingratiate *or* insinuate oneself; *Inf.* butter up, *Inf.* shine up to, *Inf.* get on the good side of.

4. trick, deceive, cheat, bamboozle, delude, hoodwink, pull the wool over [s.o.'s] eyes, take in, *Sl.* con; fool, dupe, hoax, humbug, *Brit. Inf.* gammon; outwit, overreach, circumvent, get around, put one over on, take for a ride; victimize, exploit, play on *or* upon, take advantage of, get the better of, get the upper hand, get the inside track, dice, leave in the dust; do, diddle, fleece, rook, gouge, pluck.

jocose, *adj.* jesting, joking, teasing, *Inf.* kidding, *Inf.* funning; roguish, arch, mischievous; playful, prankish, sportive, clowning; entertaining, diverting, light, *Inf.* fun, full of fun; witty, quick-witted, nimble-witted, waggish, jocular, droll, facetious, salty; funny, comical, comic, (*of verse*) doggerel, risible, humorous, amusing, *Inf.* boffo; laughable, ludicrous, absurd, farcical, ridiculous, silly; hilarious, hysterical, riotous, side-splitting, *Sl.* a scream, *Sl.* a gas; nonsensical, whimsical.

jocosity, *n.* **1.** playfulness, prankishness, sportiveness, clownishness; jocularity, drollery, facetiousness, wit, humor; humorousness, comicalness, amusingness, drollness, delightfulness; laughableness, ludicrousness, absurdity, farcicality, ridiculousness, silliness, whimsicality; hilarity, riotousness, hysteria.

2. jesting, joking, teasing, fooling, *Inf.* kidding, *Inf.* funning; joke, jest, jape, gag, quip, *Inf.* wisecrack, *Inf.* crack; waggery, witticism, squib, pun, crank; trick, practical joke, prank, caper, antic, shenanigan, monkeyshine, foolery; entertainment, diversion, amusement, levity, fun.

jocular, *adj.* waggish, facetious, tongue-in-cheek, droll, witty, quick-witted, nimble-witted, salty; jesting, joking, entertaining, funny, jocose. See **jocose.**

jocularity, *n.* waggishness, drollery, facetiousness, wit, humor; jesting, joking, jocosity. See **jocosity.**

jocund, *adj.* cheerful, cheery, full of cheer, gay, sunny, in good *or* high spirits; blithe, blithesome, lighthearted, lightsome, buoyant, optimistic, positive, *Inf.* upbeat, beamish; debonair, free and easy, carefree, easygoing, breezy, airy, happy-go-lucky, untroubled; genial, convivial, amiable, good-natured, friendly; jovial, merry, jolly, mirthful, hilarious; riant, laughing, smiling, happy as a lark; happy, glad, blissful, beatific, pleased, delighted, *Inf.* tickled pink; joyful, joyous, jubilant, rejoicing, gleeful; exultant, in seventh heaven, elated, overjoyed, thrilled, exhilarated; animated, lively, *Inf.* chipper, jaunty, vivacious, sprightly, fresh.

jocundity, *n.* **1.** gaiety, cheer, cheerfulness, gladness, gayness, good *or* high spirits; blitheness, blithesomeness, light-heartedness, buoyancy, optimism, good nature; joy, sunshine, delight, pleasure, happiness, felicity, bliss; joyfulness, joyousness, jubilation, jubilancy, exhilaration, exultation, glee, elation; joviality, merriment, jollity, mirth, mirthfulness, hilarity, laughter.

2. animation, liveliness, vivacity, sprightliness, *Inf.* peppiness; playfulness, sportiveness, zest, enthusiasm, eagerness.

jog, *v.* **1.** jolt, jar, jerk; start, shake, dislodge.

2. nudge, bump, jostle; prod, poke, push, move; tap, flip, flick.

3. joggle, jiggle, bounce, jounce, rattle; roll, sway, bob, wag; rock, lurch, wobble, waggle, wiggle.

4. run, gallop, canter, lope, trot, dogtrot; pad, stump it, walk.

—*n.* **5.** nudge, push, poke, prod, shake; trot, lope, canter, dogtrot, run.

6. notch, nick, indentation, dent; cleft, slash, gash, cleft; projection, jut, jag, protrusion, protuberance, nub, knob.

joggle, *v.* jiggle, jog, jostle, shake, move to and fro, jerk, pull; bob, bobble, bounce, jounce. See **jiggle** (*defs.* **1, 2**).

join, *v.* **1.** *Usu.* **join together** link, couple, splice, unite, tie, bind, yoke; connect, bridge, span; fix, fasten, attach; combine, mix, converge, coalesce, commingle; associate, consolidate, amalgamate, merge, conglomerate, unify.

2. glue, glue together, agglutinate, conglutinate, paste, paste together; seal, affix, concrete; fuse, weld, solder.

3. ally, league, unionize, confederate, join forces *or* hands, team up, side with, go along with, band together, *Inf.* hitch horses; federate, federalize, centralize; affiliate, associate, consociate, throw in with, join forces with, take part; cooperate, collaborate, concur, coact, synergize.

4. enlist, enlist in, sign up, join up; enroll, enroll in, enter, enter into; throw in one's lot with, cast one's lot with.

5. participate, contribute, partake, mingle, mix, join in, *Inf.* chip in, lend a hand; (*of conversation*) *Inf.* chime in, *Inf.* put in one's two-cents worth.

6. marry, wed, mate, match, *Sl.* hitch; unite in marriage, join *or* unite in holy wedlock.

7. meet *or* engage in battle, join battle, give *or* do battle, join issue; battle, combat, contest, contend against, grapple with, close with, fight against, *Inf.* take on.

8. adjoin, conjoin, impinge; meet, coincide; butt, torch, reach, extend, kiss; juxtapose, border, meet end to end; border on *or* upon, verge upon, lean on *or* upon *or* against.

joiner, *n.* **1.** link, bond, tie, knot, nexus; coupler, coupling; miter, dovetail joint, rabbet; clamp, clasp, latch, buckle, clip; seam, stitch, suture.

2. carpenter, woodworker, cabinetmaker, window *or* door maker, artisan, *Naut. Sl.* chips.

3. playboy, social lion, man about town, *Brit. Sl.* trendy, mixer, good mixer, life of the party; excellent companion, good *or* pleasant company, *Fr. bon vivant.*

joint, *n.* **1.** junction, juncture, intersection, union, nexus, connexus, point of union *or* contact; link, tie, bond, knot, yoke; coupler, coupling; miter, dovetail joint, rabbet.

2. *Slang.* nightclub, club, *Inf.* nightspot; tavern, bar, speakeasy, *Sl.* honky-tonk. See **cabaret** (*def.* **1**).

3. *Slang.* place, location, *Inf.* spot, *Sl.* dive. See **establishment** (*def.* **6**).

4. *Slang.* reefer, *Sl.* j., *Sl.* stick. See **reefer**.

5. out of joint a. dislocated, displaced, out of the socket; unjointed, disjointed. **b.** inauspicious, unfavorable, unpromising, unpropitious; ominous, foreboding, bodeful, portentous; unfortunate, unhappy, unlucky; untimely, unseasonable, ill-timed, inopportune, ill-considered. **c.** inappropriate, unsuitable, unfit, inapt; out of place, out of line, out of keeping, out of hand; out of proportion, blown-up.

—adj. **6.** mutual, shared, common, communal, communistic, collective, commutal; cooperative, cooperating, collaborative, collaborating, coordinated, coordinate, synergetic, synergistic; concerted, coactive, hand in hand, arm in arm; coalitional, conjunctive, corporate, corporative; federal, confederate, league, union; concordant, agreeing, concurrent, consentual, consentaneous, concommitant, consentient, unanimous, like-minded.

7. joined, linked, tied, bound, coupled; conjoined, conjoint, conjunct, conjugate; merged, combined, associated, amalgamated, consolidated, incorporated; united, unified, leagued, allied, confederated, federated; in union, in league, in alliance; in common, in conjunction, in association.

—v. **8.** disjoint, dismember, dislimb, dissever; (*all at a joint*) cut, carve, hew, hack, cleave, chop, sunder, sever, detach.

jointly, *adv.* together, in combination, in common, concurrently, coactively, concertedly; mutually, communally, collectively, commutually; cooperatively, cooperatingly, in cooperation, collaboratively, in collaboration, in partnership, in collusion, *Sl.* in cahoots; in union, in league, in association, corporately; by mutual agreement *or* consent *or* assent, unanimously, consentually; side by side, arm in arm, cheek by jowl, back to back, shoulder to shoulder, hand in hand, in unison, in close harmony, in company with.

joke, *n.* **1.** witticism, wisecrack, crack, sally, quip, one-liner, jest, *Sl.* funny, bon mot, pun, play on words, wordplay; Joe Miller, bromide, chestnut; comedy, humor, facetiousness, drollery, whimsy; howl, *Sl.* rib-tickler, *Sl.* yuk, *Sl.* haha, *Sl.* gasser, *Sl.* kneeslapper; silliness, asininity, nonsense, foolishness; *Sl.* nuttiness, *Sl.* goofiness, ridiculousness; gag, prank, practical joke, jape, caper, monkeyshine, *Inf.* dido, trick; irony, satire, parody, spoof, lampoon; farce, burlesque, *Sl.* schtick; cartoon, caricature, funnies, comic strip, *Sl.* comicals.

2. laughingstock, butt, goat, *Sl.* laugh, figure of fun, game, fair game, April fool, *Fr. poisson d'avril.*

3. (*in negative constructions*) trifle, paltry matter, triviality, *Inf.* hill of beans.

4. child's play, *Sl.* picnic, *Inf.* snap, *Sl.* cinch, *Sl.* lead-pipe cinch.

—v. **5.** tell jokes, crack jokes, deadpan, crack wise, wisecrack, quip, jest, *Sl.* josh, make merry with; clown around, play the clown, make faces; horse around, fool around, *Inf.* cut up, kid around; caper, gambol, sport, frolic.

6. tease, twit, *Inf.* kid, spoof. See **jest** (*def.* **4**).

joker, *n.* **1.** humorist, comic, comedian, *Inf.* card, *Inf.* character, funnyman; jester, wag, droll; clown, Joey, mime, zany, *Archaic.* antic; buffoon, *Inf.* cutup, *Inf.* life of the party; stand-up comic, Milton Berle, Phyllis Diller; quipster, wit, punster, gagman, epigrammist, banterer, wisecracker, *Sl.* kibitzer; prankster, practical joker, *Sl.* kidder, spoofer.

2. catch, *Sl.* catch-22, *Sl.* hooker, hitch; rub, impediment, drawback, snag, hindrance; pitfall, trap, snare; hidden clause, codicil, rider, fine *or* small print, *Disparaging.* nigger in the woodpile, something rotten in the state of Denmark, curve ball.

3. trick, hoax, ruse, subterfuge, artifice, gambit; sleight-of-hand, machination, *Inf.* fast one; expedient, contrivance.

4. chap, guy, fellow, *Brit. Sl.* cove, *Sl.* bastard, *Sl.* mamzer; wiseguy, wiseacre, smart aleck, smarty.

jollity, *n.* **1.** gaiety, gayness, merriness, joy, joyfulness, joyousness, joviality, jocundity, jolliness, glee, gleefulness, mirth, mirthfulness, good *or* high spirits, *Rare.* heyday; frolicsomeness, friskiness, playfulness; jubilancy, jubilance, jubilation, buoyancy, light-heartedness, blitheness, blithesomeness, elation, good mood.

2. jollities merriment, merrymaking, rejoicing, jollification, frolic, fun, *Brit. Inf.* mafficking, *Brit.* holiday-making, gay *or* jolly time; fun and games, sport, romp, spree, escapade, *Inf.* goings-on, *Inf.* whoopee, *Sl.* high jinks, *Inf.* skylarking, revelry, revels, carousal, wassail, high old time, conviviality, party spirit; festivity, festivities, party, celebration, gala, fete, jubilee, jamboree, charivari, *Inf.* shivaree, *Inf.* shindig, *Inf.* do, *Sl.* bash, *Sl.* wing-ding, *Sl.* blowout.

jolly, *adj.* **1.** gay, joyous, joyful, jocund, riant, jubilant, cock-a-hoop; merry, mirthful, gleeful, cheerful, cheery, bright, sunny, happy, glad; buoyant, lighthearted, blithe, blithesome, elated, exuberant, in good *or* high spirits, in fine *or* high feather, in a good mood; frolicsome, frisky, sportive, playful, prankish, coltish, full of fun, *Scot.* daft; convivial, hearty, waggish, jovial, jocose, jocular, effervescent, bubbly, full of life.

2. festive, festful, party, celebrative, holiday, fun; rollicking, gregarious, hilarious, lively, spirited, animated, *Sl.* whoop-it-up.

jolt, *v.* **1.** jar, shake, jostle, jog, joggle, nudge; shove, push, elbow, butt; hit, strike, bump into, bang into, skim into, collide with.

2. astonish, astound, amaze, *Sl.* blow one's mind; surprise, startle, scare, frighten; shock, stun, dumfound, daze, stupefy, knock out, *Boxing.* k.o.

3. shake *or* shake up, discompose, disconcert, disquiet, perturb, disturb, upset, agitate.

4. interrupt, break in on, barge in on, intrude, push *or* force one's way into, push *or* stick one's nose into, pry, meddle, interfere.

5. start, jump, twitch, jerk; pluck, tug, pull, yank; jog, jostle, shake, joggle, jiggle; jounce, bounce,

bump, lurch; rock, sway, wobble, waggle.
—*n.* **6.** jar, shake, agitation; jerk, start, jump, sudden movement; pluck, tug, pull, yank; jog, jostle, joggle, jiggle; push, nudge, shove, elbow; bump, jounce, bounce, lurch; stroke, hit, bang, slam, collision.
7. shock, surprise, bombshell, knockout, *Sl.* mindblower; blow, rejection, defeat, upset; turnabout, turnaround, 360° turn.
8. dose, *Inf.* bracer, *Inf.* shot, nip, *Sl.* hit.

jostle, *v.* **1.** brush against, jog, bump; jolt, jar, shock; joggle, jiggle, jerk, shake, justle; bounce, jounce; strike against, collide, *Rare.* hurtle, clash, hit against, batter, run against, butt against, lunge against; attack, assault, assail, bombard; charge, rush at, tilt, run into, have at; bunt, butt.
2. force, push, shove, thrust, hunch; elbow, hustle, press against, shoulder; prod, poke, goad; herd, drive; rush, impel, urge, propel; boot, kick, punt.
3. disturb, stir, perturb, agitate, unsettle; ruffle, *Inf.* shake up, confound, upset, disconcert, discomfit.
4. compete, rival, strive against, vie, contend, contest; pit oneself against, play against, oppose, take on, face, challenge.
—*n.* **5.** push, shove, thrust; bump, brush; jolt, jar, shock, jerk, shake, tussle; bounce, jounce.

jot, *v.* **1.** *Usu.* **jot down** write down, mark down, note, note down, set down, put down, take down; make a note of, make a memorandum of; list, make a list; scribble, write hastily *or* carelessly; tally, register, record, chronicle.
—*n.* **2.** bit, little bit, trace, touch, hint, trifle, tinge, suggestion, suspicion, tincture, shadow; spark, scintilla, gleam; mite, speck, smidgen, *Inf.* smitch, iota, tad, molecule, atom, whit, tittle; dot, point, dab, fleck, speck, freckle; minimum, pittance, modicum, driblet; item, article, particular, detail.

jotting, *n.* note, *Inf.* memo, memorandum, message; record, list, tally; excerpt, cutting, clipping, *Inf.* clip.

jounce, *v.* **1.** bounce, bob, *Inf.* bobble; joggle, jiggle, jerk, jostle, bump; jolt, jar, shock; quake, vibrate, tremble, move up and down.
—*n.* **2.** bounce, bob, bobble; joggle, jiggle, jerk, jostle, bump; jolt, jar, shock; quake, vibration, tremor, trembling.

journal, *n.* **1.** record, chronicle, diary, memoir, *Fr. journal intime*; dossier, *Latin. adversaria*, notes, commonplace book; album, scrapbook, record book, memory book; yearbook, almanac, annals, history, chronology, narrative; registry, register, log, logbook, cartulary, catalogue, ledger, roll; schedule, calendar, datebook; notebook, minute book, daybook, Acta, transactions, minutes.
2. newspaper, gazette, daily, tabloid; circular, newsletter, extra, bulldog, *Inf.* sheet, *Inf.* rag.
3. periodical, magazine, publication, review, news magazine, slick; quarterly, weekly, fortnightly, monthly; serial, trade organ, house organ.

journalism, *n.* **1.** reporting, writing, editing, rewriting, composition; broadcasting, recording, feature-writing; coverage, correspondence, news.
2. the press, news business, newspaper world, newspaperdom, Fleet Street, fourth estate, print media, publishing industry.

journalist, *n.* newspaperman, *Brit.* pressman, newscaster, *Archaic.* gazetteer, newswriter, newsmonger, newshound; reporter, *Sl.* legman, gentleman of the press, newsman, newswoman, correspondent, contributor, stringer, paragrapher, *Brit.* paragraphist; broadcaster, anchor man, commentator; columnist, critic, reviewer, diarist, gossip-writer, sob-sister; editor, editorialist, author, scribbler, scribe, *Brit.* leader writer; reviser, rewrite man, copyman, copywriter, copy editor; publicist, PR person, press agent, flak, ghostwriter, blurb writer, hack, penny-a-liner.

journalistic, *adj.* editorial, reportorial, publishing, published, printed, press; newspaperish, magazinish.

journalize, *v.* **1.** record, make entries, keep a diary *or* record *or* log; enter, set down, jot down, note, scribble down, put down, put into writing; list, register, chronicle, take down, docket, take the minutes.
2. report, publicize, editorialize; comment, write, copy, review, correspond.

journey, *n.* **1.** travel, journeying, wayfaring, itinerancy, globe-trotting; trip, tour, excursion, jaunt, junket, outing; ride, drive, walk, *Inf.* hop, *Inf.* spin, (*of fish*) run; peregrination, wandering, roving, roaming; migration, emigration, transmigration, meander; expedition, campaign, sally, trek, voyage, cruise, safari; odyssey, quest, pilgrimage, hajj.
2. passage, progress, transition, transit, transilience; movement, way, course, route, march, career.
—*v.* **3.** travel, roam, rove, peregrinate, itinerate, wayfare, jaunt; make *or* take a trip, tour, cruise, sail, fly; range, globe-trot, go abroad, go overseas, see the world, sightsee; trek, hike, march, wend, take the road, take to the road, hit the road; proceed, pass, go hie, *Scot.* gang, process; meander, ramble, gad, gallivant; divagate, travel the open road, migrate, emigrate, transmigrate, immigrate.

journeyman, *n.* craftsman, handicraftsman, master craftsman, artisan, artificer, *Obs.* artist; mechanic, skilled laborer.

journeywork, *n.* **1.** craft, handicraft, skill; profession, trade, occupation; calling, vocation; métier, forte, *Sl.* thing, *Inf.* bag, *Sl.* trip.
2. treadmill, hack work, assembly line, *Sl.* the pits; drudgery, toil, moil, travail, hard work, slave labor, *Sl.* dollar-a-day, *Brit.* fag.

joust, *n.* **1.** tilt, tournament, tourney; contest, encounter, engagement, match, meeting; test, trial.
—*v.* **2.** tilt, tourney, break a lance with, run a tilt *or* tilt at.

jovial, *adj.* jolly, jocose, jocular, jocund, gay, boon, merry, mirthful, cheerful, light-hearted, frivolous, facetious; glad, happy, airy, bright, sunny, breezy, in good *or* high spirits; joyous, jubilant, cock-a-hoop; lively, sprightly, animated, spirited, chipper; buoyant, vivacious, effervescent, full of life, *Inf.* full of pep, *Inf.* full of get up and go; playful, frolicsome, sportive, gamesome; festive, convivial, rollicking, hilarious.

joviality, *n.* gaiety, gayness, merriness, joy, joyfulness, joyousness, jollity, jocundity, glee, gleefulness, mirth, mirthfulness, good *or* high spirits, hilarity, *Rare.* heyday; frolicsomeness, friskiness, playfulness, sportiveness, gamesomeness; jubilancy, jubilation, buoyancy, light-heartedness, blitheness, elation, sunniness, rosiness, airiness, breeziness.

jowl, *n.* jaw, chop, muzzle; cheek.

joy, *n.* **1.** delight, pleasure, enjoyment, delectation, gratification; gladness, *Archaic.* joyance, happiness, felicity, beatitude, blessedness, exaltation, rapture, bliss; seventh heaven, ecstasy, ravishment, transport.
2. peace, peacefulness, serenity, sereneness, tranquillity, tranquilness, placidity, placidness, quiet, contentment.
3. excitement, thrill, *Sl.* kick, *Sl.* charge, *Sl.* rush.
4. gaiety, gayness, sunshine, cheerfulness, gladsome-

ness, cheer, good nature, high spirits; levity, blitheness, blithesomeness, light-heartedness, buoyancy, optimism; jocundity, joviality, merriment, jollity, mirth, mirthfulness, laughter, hilarity; enthusiasm, animation, sparkle, excitement; exhilaration, exultation, glee, elation, joyfulness, joyousness, jubilation, jubilance, jubilancy; rejoicing, frolic, fun, revelry, revel, conviviality, festivity, celebration.

joyful, *adj.* **1.** glad, delighted, pleased, gratified, *Inf.* tickled *or* tickled pink; happy, blessed, contented, blissful; jubilant, exultant, gleeful, exhilarated, enthused, excited, animated, sparkling; elated, overjoyed, beside oneself with joy, thrilled, in seventh heaven, *Sl.* flying high; enraptured, *Literary.* raptured, rapturous, ravished, transported, carried away.

2. gay, joyous, full of joy, cheerful, cheery, sunny, bright, optimistic, upbeat, positive; blithe, blithesome, light-hearted, buoyant, in good *or* high spirits; jocund, jovial, merry, jolly, mirthful, laughing, riant, smiling, hilarious.

3. gladsome, good, pleasing, gratifying, rewarding; heartwarming, cheering, reassuring, comforting, heartening, encouraging, uplifting; delightful, agreeable, pleasant.

joyless, *adj.* **1.** unhappy, dejected, depressed, down, downcast, downhearted; disheartened, dispirited, discouraged, despondent, down in the mouth; sad, melancholy, plaintive, wistful; sorrowful, grief-stricken, afflicted, saddened, heavy-hearted, disconsolate; grievous, dolorous, doleful, mournful, rueful, lugubrious, funereal; morose, gloomy, saturnine, glum, cheerless, sullen; somber, solemn, grave, serious, tragic; miserable, wretched, woeful, woebegone, inconsolable; heartsick, heartsore, aching, grieving, mourning, lamenting, weeping, tearful, lachrymose.

2. gloomy, drab, dreary, dull, depressing, dismal; bleak, cold, comfortless, barren, grim, austere; forlorn, desolate, lonely, deserted, empty, abandoned, uninviting; dark, somber, sunless, lightless, murky, dingy.

jubilance, *n.* exultation, triumph; overjoyedness, elation, joy; ecstasy, rhapsody. See **jubilation** (*def.* **1**).

jubilant, *adj.* rejoicing, exultant, triumphant, triumphal, on top of the world; overjoyed, elated, exhilarated, thrilled, excited, beside oneself, jumping for joy, in high spirits, flushed, *Inf.* tickled pink; ecstatic, euphoric, transported, delirious, rhapsodic, rapturous, enraptured, *Literary.* raptured, ravished, on cloud nine, in seventh heaven, walking on air, in orbit, flying, Elysian, *Dial.* in hog heaven, *Dial.* in high cotton; joyful, joyous, blissful, delighted, pleased, happy as a lark *or* king *or* clam, happy, glad, gladsome, sunny, bright, beaming, in good spirits, in a good mood, in high *or* fine feather; gay, jocund, gleeful, cheerful, riant, merry, mirthful, blithe, blithesome, buoyant, light-hearted.

jubilate, *v.* **1.** rejoice, exult, triumph, glory, be on top of the world; crow, sing about, sing with joy *or* delight, express one's pleasure, clap one's hands over, hug oneself over, jump for joy, skip *or* dance with joy *or* delight; delight, joy, beam, be delighted *or* joyful *or* glad, be happy as a lark *or* king *or* clam; be elated, be in high spirits, be exhilarated, be in transport, be in ecstasy, be in seventh heaven, be on cloud nine, be in orbit, *Dial.* be in hog heaven, *Dial.* be in high cotton.

2. celebrate, have a celebration, throw a party, party, make merry, revel, rollick, frolic.

jubilation, *n.* **1.** exultation, triumph, jubilance, jubilancy; overjoyedness, elatedness, elation, exhilaration, excitement, high spirits; ecstasy, euphoria, delirium, rhapsody, rapturousness, rapture, transport, ravishment; joy, joyousness, joyfulness, jollity, jolliness, bliss, blissfulness, delight, delightedness, happiness, gladness, pleasure; gayness, glee, gleefulness, cheer, cheeriness, cheerfulness, merriness, mirth, mirthfulness, blitheness, blithesomeness, buoyancy, light-heartedness.

2. celebration, jubilee, festivity, festivities, fete, carnival, gala, merrymaking, merriment, rejoicing, victory party; jamboree, charivari, *Inf.* shivaree, *Inf.* shindig, *Inf.* do, *Sl.* bash, *Sl.* wing-ding, *Sl.* blowout.

jubilee, *n.* **1.** celebration, commemoration, observance; jubilation, exultation, rejoicing, merriment, merrymaking, conviviality; festival, fete, carnival, festivity, party, gala; jamboree, charivari, *Inf.* shivaree, *Inf.* shindig, *Inf.* do, *Sl.* bash, *Sl.* wing-ding, *Sl.* blowout; revelry, revels, carousal, wassail.

2. holiday, holy day, red letter day, feast day; anniversary, birthday, *Fr. anniversaire*; centennial, centenary, bicentennial, *Chiefly Brit.* bicentenary.

judge, *n.* **1.** justice, magistrate, judicator, adjudicator, *U.S.* surrogate, *Inf.* his Honor, *Islam.* mullah, cadi; justice of the peace, *Inf.* J.P., circuit judge, *Inf.* circuit rider, judge of probate, police court judge, Supreme Court judge, Chief Justice; (*collectively*) judiciary.

2. arbiter, arbitrator, mediator, moderator, censor, umpire, *Inf.* ump, referee, *Inf.* ref, linesman.

3. connoisseur, virtuoso, one of the cognoscenti; critic, reviewer, appraiser, evaluator, assessor, *Latin. arbiter elegantiae.*

—*v.* **4.** adjudge, adjudicate, referee, *Inf.* ref, umpire, *Inf.* ump; rule, find, hold, *Sports.* call; pass sentence, give a verdict, pronounce a verdict, settle, decree.

5. hear evidence, hear arguments, consider, regard, examine; investigate, appraise, diagnose, review, survey, value, assess, size up, weigh, measure, gauge; try, test, *Inf.* test-drive.

6. think, reckon, conclude, determine, deduce, believe, form an opinion; interpret, gather, figure out, ascertain, perceive, derive, glean; deem, decide, decide upon, make a judgment, resolve; referee, mediate, arbitrate, umpire.

7. estimate, make an estimate, guess, surmise, infer, conjecture, suppose, assume, suspect.

judgment, *n.* **1.** decision, judicial decision, opinion, official opinion, adjudication, ruling, finding, verdict, decree, award, call; determination, resolution, outcome, upshot, result, penalty.

2. punishment, fate, doom, misfortune; condemnation, conviction, damnation, proscription, sentence, *Inf.* rap; death sentence, death warrant.

3. judging ability, discernment, discretion, prudence; wisdom, judiciousness, sagacity, clearheadedness, perspicacity, sense, good sense, common sense, level-headedness, *Inf.* street sense; shrewdness, sharpness of mind, acumen; intelligence, brains, reasoning power, *Inf.* gray matter; understanding, penetration, perception, grasp; savoir faire, *Inf.* know-how, discrimination, taste, virtuosity, artistic taste, connoisseurship, aesthetic discernment.

4. *All Law.* monetary judgment, obligation, debt, judgment debt, damages, *Inf.* the damage, *Inf.* tariff.

judicial, *adj.* **1.** judiciary, judicatory, juridical, juridic, juristic, jurisdictive, legal, forensic.

2. judgelike, magisterial, *Rare.* magistral.

3. critical, discriminative, discriminating, differentiating, distinguishing, disjunctive, analytical; discerning, perceptive, perspicacious, percipient, keen.

4. decreed, sanctioned, ordained, ordered, commanded, dictated, pronounced, proclaimed; decided, determined, adjudicated, settled.

judicious, *adj.* **1.** discreet, prudent, politic, provident, practical, expedient; circumspect, careful, cautious, mindful, heedful, wary; sensible, commonsensical, long-headed; sagacious, sage, wise, sapient, Solomonic, rational, reasonable, logical; well-advised, well-considered, well-judged; discerning, discriminating, judicial. See **judicial** (*def.* **3**).

2. shrewd, astute, *Sl.* savvy, keen, clever, subtle, diplomatic, tactful; calculating, sharp, acute; intelligent, smart, apt, ingenious, bright; knowledgeable, versed, enlightened, aware, knowing, wide awake, far-sighted.

judo, *n.* aikido, jujitsu; martial art.

jug, *n.* **1.** container, vessel, receptacle; bottle, flask; pitcher, carafe, decanter.

2. crock, pot, urn, vase, bowl.

3. *Slang.* jail. See **jail** (*def.* **1**).

juggle, *v.* **1.** fake, alter, change, tamper with, *Inf.* doctor, *Inf.* cook; maneuver, manipulate, fix, rig; load, pack, stack, stack the deck; salt, salt the mine, *Sl.* plant.

2. delude, deceive, mislead, beguile, dupe, trick, hoax, humbug, take in, put [s.t.] over on [s.o.], pull a fast one on [s.o.], *Inf.* slip one over on [s.o.], *Inf.* bamboozle, *Sl.* snow, *Sl.* diddle, *Sl.* hornswoggle; cheat, swindle, defraud, gull, gammon, victimize, fleece, bilk.

juggler, *n.* **1.** circus artist *or* performer; magician, illusionist, conjurer, prestidigitator, legerdemainist, sleight-of-hand performer.

2. trickster, deceiver, deluder, beguiler, *Inf.* bamboozler; cheat, swindler, defrauder, double-dealer, sharp, sharper, *Inf.* flimflam man, *Sl.* con man *or* artist, *Brit. Sl.* magsman; imposter, fraud, fake, *Inf.* phony, charlatan, mountebank, quack.

jugglery, *n.* **1.** juggling; magic, prestidigitation, legerdemain, conjuration, sleight of hand, hocus-pocus, mumbo jumbo.

2. trickery, deception, subterfuge, deceit; chicanery, pettifoggery, artifice, *Inf.* skulduggery; foul play, sharp practice, underhand dealing; imposture, fraudulency, humbug, false pretense, *Chiefly Brit.* jiggery-pokery.

juice, *n.* **1.** liquid, fluid, water, secretion; sap, latex, blood, serum, *Anat.* lymph, grume, *Class. Myth.* ichor; extract, broth, soup, liquor; nectar, must, wine; drink, beverage, potable, liquid refreshment; cold drink, thirst quencher.

2. essence, strength, vitality, vigor, pith, force.

juicy, *adj.* **1.** succulent, lush, dripping, dribbling, flowing; wet, watery, serous, sappy; damp, moist, spongy.

2. colorful, vivid, picturesque, graphic, vibrant, exciting; suggestive, racy, risqué, spicy; stimulating, stirring, rousing, sensational, thrilling; alluring, inviting, enticing, tempting, tantalizing; captivating, provocative, intriguing, fascinating.

jumble, *v.* **1.** disorganize, shuffle, dishevel, make a shambles, *Inf.* turn topsy-turvy, *Inf.* muss up; clutter, litter, mess, tumble, scatter, strew about; disarrange, disorder, unsettle, discompose; bunch, heap, pile, mass, huddle, cram, throw together; mix, mingle, tangle, entangle; muddle, fuddle, confuse, mistake.

—n. **2.** heap, mass, agglomeration, bunch, mess, huddle; confused medley, hash, patchwork, olla-podrida, olio, gallimaufry, farrago, jungle, hodgepodge, hotchpotch, mishmash, salmagundi; miscellany, pot-pourri, odds and ends, motley collection, lumber; litter, clutter, trash, *Inf.* garbage.

3. chaos, confusion, disarray, mix-up, muddle, fuddle, tangle, tumble, minglement.

jump, *v.* **1.** spring, leap, hop, vault, bound, buck, pounce; skip, caper, *Inf.* hippety-hop, leapfrog; frolic, frisk, cavort, gambol, bob, bounce; high-jump, broad-jump, pole-vault; upleap, upswing, caracole, curvet, gambado.

2. rise up, start, start up, pop up, bob up, flinch, jump out of one's skin; startle, frighten, surprise; jerk, jolt, shock, jostle.

3. skip, miss, omit, neglect, leave out, cut; let pass, let slip, let dangle; pass by *or* over, bypass, overlook, gloss over, disregard, ignore.

4. parachute, sky-dive, bail out, eject, *Inf.* hit the silk, *Brit. Sl.* make a brolly hop.

5. leap over, hurdle, steeplechase, clear, negotiate; overjump, go over, sail over, overleap, overshoot; make it over, pass over, flop over, shoot over.

6. anticipate, get ahead of, steal a march on, have the edge on, get the drop on; start before, go before, forego, jump the gun, misstart, get a headstart, get a jump on.

7. increase, raise, hike, *Inf.* jack up, boost, escalate, elevate, up; advance, accelerate, appreciate, augment, enlarge, extend; surge, rise, mount, ascend.

8. *Informal.* ambush, attack, assail, blitz; fall on, pounce on, descend on, set upon, swoop down on, come down on; *Inf.* bushwhack, *Inf.* mug, *Sl.* hit.

9. **jump at** grab, grab at, snatch, swoop up, catch, reach for, jump on; get excited about, be enthusiastic about, be willing, be eager.

10. **jump into** join, enter into, get into, hop into; interrupt, burst in, *Sl.* butt in, chime in, interject, intrude, put one's two cents in.

11. **jump off** **a.** spring from, descend, detrain, alight, dismount, get down, get off; land, touch down, plop down. **b.** launch, start, open, begin; set in, embark on, undertake, venture into.

—n. **12.** leap, spring, vault, hop, skip, caper, bound, buck; leapfrog, frolic, gambol, bounce, bob; high jump, long jump, broad jump, hop, skip and jump, running jump, pole vault; upleap, caracole, curvet, capriole, gambado; leaping, saltation, dancing, *Ballet.* entrechat, *Ballet.* jeté.

13. hurdle, obstacle, fence, rail, hedge, *Gymnastics.* horse; obstruction, handicap, impediment.

14. gap, space, hole, hiatus, breach; interstice, interval, break, lacuna, interruption, caesura, elision; fissure, rift, cleft, scissure, slit, rent, rupture.

15. descent, parachuting, sky-dive, *Brit. Sl.* brolly hop.

16. rise, boost, raise, increase; escalation, inflation, elevation, mounting, upsurge, upswing; ascent, advance, appreciation, augmentation.

17. start, jolt, jar, jostle, jerk; lurch, shock, bump, blow; shake, twitch, jiggle, quiver.

jumpy, *adj.* **1.** skittish, fidgety, jittery, fluttery, nervy, edgy, on edge; shaky, quivery, itchy, scratchy, twitching; tremulous, trembling, quivering, aflutter, atremble, all of a twitter.

2. nervous, apprehensive, fretful; excited, anxious, disquieted, *Sl.* uptight, uneasy, restive; fussing, unquiet, unsteady, unrelaxed, tense; scared, frightened, afraid, panicky, alarmed, funky; shy, timorous, timid, diffident.

3. saltatory, jerky, spastic, fitful, convulsive, spasmodic, by fits and starts; choppy, bumpy, joggling, jiggly, jolting, jarring, rough.

junction, *n.* **1.** unification, accouplement, joinder; juxtaposition, collocation; joining, linking, splicing,

uniting, binding, bonding, yoking; connecting, conjoining, coupling; meeting, touching, bordering, edging, abutting.
2. union, association, conjugation, conjunction, conjuncture; congress, congregation, convergence, concentration, concourse, gathering, assemblage; cohesion, coherence, adhesion, adherence.
3. juncture, intersection, nexus, connexus, point of union *or* contact; focus, focal point, focalization; coalescence, confluence; abutment, abuttal.
4. joint, joiner, articulation, commissure; pivot, hinge, elbow, knee, dovetail joint, rabbet, rabbet joint; linkage, concatenation, coupling, coupler; seam, suture, welt.
5. connection, tie, tie-in, bond, link, *Inf.* hook-up; alliance, confederation, league; conspiracy, cabal; merger, amalgamation, consolidation, incorporation.
6. railroad station, train station, main station, terminus, terminal.
7. crossroads, interchange, crossing, *Brit.* crosspoint.

juncture, *n.* **1.** point, point in time, period, stage; time, moment, minute, hour, day, season; occasion, advent; circumstance, occurrence, event, incident; contingency, eventuality.
2. crisis, crux, crunch; crossroads, turning point, critical moment *or* point, crucial moment, critical juncture, moment of truth, zero hour; emergency, exigency; predicament, plight, dilemma, quandary, strait, extremity; pinch, rub, scrape, squeeze, push, *Inf.* hole, *Inf.* clutch.
3. junction, intersection. See **junction** (*def.* **3**).
4. unification, accouplement, joinder. See **junction** (*def.* **1**).
5. union, association. See **junction** (*def.* **2**).
6. joint, joiner, articulation. See **junction** (*def.* **4**).

jungle, *n.* **1.** forest, timberland, tropical *or* rain forest, wildwood, woods, wilderness, wilds, the bush, *Inf.* the brush.
2. jumble, heap, mass, agglomeration, bunch, mess, huddle, pile; tangle, tumble, disarray, chaos, confusion; hodgepodge, hotchpotch, mishmash, farrago, gallimaufry, hash, confused mixture *or* medley.
3. inner city, *Inf.* asphalt jungle, inner-city school, blackboard jungle.
4. law of the jungle survival of the fittest, might makes right, law of club and fang; dog-eat-dog, each man for himself, cutthroat competition; brute force, Hobbesian world.

junior, *adj.* **1.** younger, *Law.* puisne, inferior, subordinate, subaltern, lower; lesser, minor, secondary.
—*n.* **2.** subordinate, subaltern, inferior, underling.

junk, *n.* **1.** trash, litter, garbage, rubbish, riffraff, *Brit. Dial.* raff, chaff, crap, *Sl.* dreck, *Sl.* schlock, trumpery; refuse, *Dial.* culch, waste, leavings, leftovers, scraps, sweepings; fragments, remnants, fag ends, odd bits, bits and pieces, odds and ends, truck; castoffs, rags, tatters, castaways, rejects, discards; piece of junk, trifle, trinket, gimcrack, gewgaw, bauble.
—*v.* **2.** *Informal.* throw out *or* away, discard, dispose of, get rid of, *Inf.* trash, *Sl.* can, *Sl.* put in file 13 *or* 17, *Sl.* put in the round *or* circular file.
—*adj.* **3.** trashy, *Sl.* junky, *Sl.* crappy, worthless, *Inf.* no-good; cheap, shoddy, shabby, poor, inferior, second-class, second-rate.

junket, *n.* **1.** custard, blancmange, pudding, tapioca pudding.
2. excursion, picnic, frolic, spree, outing; drive, ride, airing, walk, stroll, hike, trek; expedition, journey, trip, voyage, tour, sail, cruise, pleasure cruise.
—*v.* **3.** feast, picnic, eat, drink and be merry; entertain, host, regale.
4. go on an excursion *or* outing, take a trip, go on a cruise.

junta, *n.* **1.** council, assembly, conclave, convocation, synod, consistory.
2. cabal, camarilla, junto, self-appointed committee, ring, gang, band, crew, party; faction, clique, coterie, set, *Inf.* push; union, coalition, combination, league, confederacy.

junto, *n.* self-appointed committee, cabal, camarilla, junta. See **junta** (*def.* **2**).

jurisdiction, *n.* **1.** authority, dominion, domination, administration; sovereignty, prerogative, predominance, rule, reign, hegemony; control, sway, mastery, influence, guidance, leadership; authorization, permit, power, force, sanction.
2. judicature, judicatory.
3. domain, realm, dominion, province, principality, palatinate; bailiwick, area, *Inf.* ballpark, *Inf.* lap.

jurisprudence, *n.* **1.** law, science of law, *Law.* jus, legal philosophy; law-writing, nomology, nomography; *Civil Law.* court decisions.
2. body of laws, system of law, legal code, corpus juris, *Law.* digest, *Law.* equity; common law, statute law, international law, criminal law, *Brit.* Crown law; canon law, Corpus Juris Canonici, Codex Juris Canonici.

jurist, *n.* **1.** lawyer, attorney, attorney-at-law, solicitor; counsel, counselor, legal advisor, legist; advocate, defense attorney, *Inf.* mouthpiece; prosecuting attorney, public prosecutor, district attorney, *Inf.* D.A., attorney general, publicist; criminal lawyer, *Inf.* shyster, *Inf.* ambulance chaser, *Inf.* pettifogger; notary, notary public, *Scot.* law agent, *Scot.* writer to the signet, *India.* pundit; *All Brit.* barrister, King's *or* Queen's Counsel, *Inf.* K.C., *Inf.* Q.C., silk, silk gown, junior barrister, junior counsel, sergeant at law, tubman.
2. judge, (*collectively*) judiciary, justice, judicator, magistrate, justice of the peace, *Inf.* J.P.; judge advocate, presiding judge, probate judge, police judge, circuit judge, Supreme Court judge, Chief Justice, *Inf.* his Honor; *All Brit.* Lord Justice, Lord Chancellor, Vice-Chancellor, Chief Justice, Lord Chief Justice, Master of the Rolls; his Lordship, his Worship, barmaster, judge of assizes, *Inf.* beak.
3. arbiter, arbitrator, moderator, umpire, *Inf.* ump, referee, *Inf.* ref, linesman.
4. lawwriter, nomologist, codifier; statute maker, legislator.

jury, *n.* **1.** body of jurors, *Law.* veniremen, twelve just men, *Inf.* twelve men in a box, panel of peers, *Law.* country, *Law.* tales; grand jury, petty jury, coroner's jury, inquest, panel.
2. judges, adjudgers, prize jury, awards committee.

jury-rigged, *adj.* makeshift, stop-gap, expedient, improvised, temporary, impermanent, provisional, substitute, succedaneous; alternative, emergency, *Fr. pis aller.*

just, *adj.* **1.** fair, impartial, fair-minded, equitable, even, even-handed; unbiased, objective, disinterested, dispassionate, unprejudiced, open-minded, neutral, tolerant; uninfluenced, unswayed, unbigoted, unwarped, undistorted.
2. upright, righteous, honorable, upstanding, noble; ethical, proper, moral, conscionable; principled, high-minded, right-minded, uncorrupt; good, sincere, true, earnest, conscientious, scrupulous; honest, truthful,

veracious, straight, *Inf.* square, *Inf.* fair and square; straightforward, candid, open, aboveboard.
3. rightful, right, lawful, legitimate, *Inf.* kosher, legal, licit; constitutional, statutory; valid, justified, sound, well-founded, well-grounded, substantial, solid, firm; justifiable, defensible, warrantable, vindicable, supportable, reasonable; judicious, well-advised, sensible, wise.
4. true, truthful, veracious, honest, authentic, bona fide; correct, factual, actual, literal, true-to-life, true-to-form; accurate, exact, precise, close, faithful, strict; flawless, faultless, perfect, defectless, errorless, inerrant.
5. deserved, merited, earned; rightful, proper, due; well-deserved, (*of punishment*) condign, fitting, appropriate, apt, suitable, meet.
—adv. **6.** only now, but a moment before, a moment ago; recently, lately, not long ago, a short time ago.
7. exactly, precisely.
8. barely, hardly, scarcely, *Dial.* scantly, only just; by a narrow margin, *Inf.* by the skin of one's teeth, by a hair's breadth, by a little bit, by an inch.
9. only, merely, solely, simply; but, nothing but, no more than, at most.
10. actually, in reality, really, truly; positively, absolutely, without a doubt, indubitably, certainly, definitely.

justice, *n.* **1.** fairness, fair play, impartiality, impartialness, fair-mindedness, equity, equitableness, evenness, even-handedness; unprejudicedness, objectivity, objectiveness, disinterestedness, dispassionateness, open-mindedness, neutrality, tolerance.
2. uprightness, righteousness, honorableness, upstandingness, nobility, nobleness; honor, integrity, probity, virtuousness, virtue, rectitude; ethicalness, ethicality, properness, propriety, morality, rightness, conscionableness; high-mindedness, right-mindedness, uncorruptedness; goodness, sincerity, sincereness, truth, earnestness, conscientiousness, scrupulousness; honesty, truthfulness, veracity, veraciousness; openness, *Inf.* straightforwardness, candor, frankness.
3. rightfulness, lawfulness, justness, legitimacy, legitimateness, legality, constitutionality; validity, validness, soundness, substantiality, substantialness, solidity, solidness, firmness; justifiability, justifiableness, defensibility, defensibleness, warrantableness, vindicability, supportability, supportableness; reasonableness, reasonability, judiciousness, sensibleness.
4. compensation, recompense, remuneration; requital, retribution, nemesis.
5. judgment, judicature, *Law.* equity; ruling, verdict, *Law.* adjudication, sentence, *Law.* award; ruling, decree, statement, declaration, decision, determination, finding; opinion, view, feeling.
6. judge, magistrate, judicator; arbitrator, arbiter, referee, umpire.

justifiable, *adj.* **1.** warrantable, authorizable, legitimate, lawful, just, right, rightful; reasonable, within reason, sensible, sane, acceptable; plausible, credible, believable, undeniable, unquestionable; sound, well-grounded, solidly based, defensible, supportable; sustainable, tenable, maintainable, assertible.
2. exculpable, vindicable, absolvable, forgivable, excusable, pardonable.

justification, *n.* **1.** reason, basis, grounds, just cause, authorization, sanction; plea, explanation, defense, substantiation, support; argument, assertion, allegation, *Law.* deraignment; story, rationalization, apology, apologia, excuse, extenuation, palliation, *Law.* demurrer, *Law.* rebutter, *Law.* essoin, *U.S. Inf.* alibi, *Inf.* song and dance.
2. warranting, authorizing, legitimation, legitimating, legitimatization, legitimatizing, legalization, legalizing; substantiating, defending, supporting, sustaining, bolstering, backing; maintaining, asserting, advocacy, advocating, *Obs.* advocation, *Obs.* vouch; explaining, extenuating, palliating.
3. exculpation, exculpating, proof *or* declaration of innocence, removal of guilt, freedom from blame; acquittal, acquittance, acquitting, compurgation, clearance, clearing one's name; release, dismissal, discharge, freedom, liberty, liberation, emancipation, deliverance, delivery, redemption; vindication, vindicating, exoneration, exonerating, redress, redressing, righting, setting *or* putting right; absolution, absolving, forgiveness, forgiving, excusing, pardon, pardoning, amnesty.

justificatory, *adj.* **1.** substantiative, substantiating, supportive, supporting, upholding, sustaining, justificative, justifying; apologetic, extenuatory, extenuating, mitigative, mitigating, palliative, palliating.
2. exculpatory, exculpating, acquitting, compurgatory; exonerative, exonerating, vindicatory, vindicative, vindicating; absolutory, absolvent, absolving, excusatory, excusing.

justify, *v.* **1.** warrant, authorize, legitimate, legitimatize, legalize; substantiate, give sufficient grounds for, show just cause, give reasons for; explain, tell one's story, rationalize, apologize, extenuate, palliate, make excuses, *Inf.* alibi, *Inf.* do a song and dance.
2. defend, champion, fight for, plead for, stick up for, stand up for; support, uphold, sustain, bolster up, back, maintain, assert, *Law.* deraign, advocate, vouch, second, stand by.
3. exculpate, prove *or* declare innocent, uphold innocence, pronounce *or* declare not guilty, remove guilt, free from blame; acquit, clear, clear one's name; release, set free, let go, dismiss, discharge; free, liberate, emancipate, deliver, let out of, let off, *Inf.* let off the hook, *Theol.* redeem; vindicate, exonerate, redress, right, set *or* put right, absolve, forgive, excuse, pardon.

justly, *adv.* fairly, equitably, equally, impartially, impersonally, dispassionately, disinterestedly, honestly; accurately, rightly, properly, just so, correctly, faultlessly; deservedly, fairly and squarely, rightly, rightfully, justifiably, properly, lawfully.

justness, *n.* **1.** lawfulness, justice, equity, equitableness, even-handedness; rightness, rightfulness, meetness, properness, what is right; justifiableness, justifiability.
2. correctness, exactness, accuracy, faithfulness, fidelity; niceness, nicety, exactitude, preciseness, meticulousness, faultlessness.

jut, *v.* stick out, project, protrude, protuberate; poke out, stand out, *Inf.* stick out like a sore thumb; overhang, beetle, shoot forward.

juvenile, *adj.* **1.** young, minor, underage, teenaged, in the teens, preteen; fresh, blooming, budding, unfledged, new-fledged.
2. childlike, youthful, *Inf.* like a kid; boyish, girlish; childish, *Inf.* kiddish, puerile, jejune; inexperienced, tender, green, wet behind the ears, immature, unripe, callow; baby-faced, beardless, smooth-cheeked, downy-cheeked; juvenescent, pubescent.
—n. **3.** child, young person, teenager, teen, preteen, youth, youngster, minor; kid, beginner, young hopeful, hopeful, *Inf.* cute kid, *Inf.* sweet young thing, *Dial.* young'un; girl, schoolgirl, young lady, lass, las-

sie, mademoiselle, damsel, maiden, maid, slip, sprig, sprite, mite, *Inf.* chit; tomboy, hoyden, teeny-bopper, jail bait; boy, schoolboy, young man, scion, lad, junior, cadet, cub, stripling, fledgling, sapling, whelp; whipper-snapper, juvenile delinquent, J.D.; brat, urchin, street urchin, puppy, *Inf.* snip, *Inf.* minx.

juxtapose, *v.* appose, *Rare.* juxtaposit, place *or* set *or* put side by side, place parallel, place near, bring near; compare, put alongside; pair, partner, match, collocate.

K

kaleidoscopic, *adj.* **1.** motley, variegated, many-colored, dappled, rainbow-like, many-splendored; changeable, mutable, mobile, variable, alterable; ever-changing, protean, checkered; labile, unstable, unsteady, inconstant; vacillating, wavering, fluctuating, shifting, ever-moving; capricious, erratic.

2. surrealistic, hallucinatory, psychedelic, phantasmagoric, nightmarish, Kafkaesque, *Inf.* wild, *Sl.* far-out.

3. complex, intricate, daedal, complicated, convoluted, topsy-turvy; varied, tumbled, confused, disordered, disarranged.

kaput, *adj.* *Slang.* dead, defunct, expired, passed away, extinct, no more; finished, all over, over, *Sl.* washed-up, *Sl.* done for, *Sl.* fini, *Sl.* shot, *Sl.* zapped, *Sl.* wiped out, *Sl.* had it, *Sl.* down the drain, *Sl.* S.O.L., *Sl.* eighty-sixed; demolished, ruined, destroyed, wrecked, undone, *Inf.* done in.

keel, *n.* **1.** (*all of a boat*) bottom, bottom side, underside; board, centerboard, keelson.

2. barge, raft, float; ship, boat, vessel, bark, craft, hull, hulk, packet, watercraft, *Sl.* tub, *Sl.* bucket.

—*v.* **3.** overturn, upset, capsize, overset, tip over, topple over; turn turtle, turn upside down, turn topsy-turvy.

4. **keel over** faint, swoon, fall in a faint, fall senseless, *Inf.* pass out, black out, go out like a light.

keen¹, *adj.* **1.** sharp, razor-sharp, sharpened, edged, sharp-edged, knife-edged, fine-edged, featheredged.

2. cogent, penetrating, piercing, incisive, pointed, rapier-like; trenchant, mordant, mordacious, pungent; cutting, biting, stinging, scathing, scorching, withering; satirical, sardonic, mocking, derisive, derisory, insulting; harsh, severe, stringent, rough; unkind, uncharitable, malicious, malevolent, malignant, cruel; virulent, bitter, acrimonious, acrid, acid, acerb, acerbic, rancorous, venomous, envenomed, tart.

3. acute, sensitive, discerning, discriminating, perceptive; conscious, cognizant, aware, sentient, sensible, comprehending, understanding; sympathetic, responsive, *Sl.* in tune, *Sl.* tuned-in.

4. astute, wise, sagacious, sapient; intelligent, smart, bright, *Inf.* brainy; quick, quick-witted, sharp-witted, smart as a whip, knowing, *Inf.* nobody's fool, *Inf.* no dummy, *Sl.* no dumbbell; shrewd, clever, subtle, crafty, canny, cunning, sly, slick, wily, foxy, *Sl.* crazy like a fox, *Scot. and North Eng.* pawky.

5. intent, earnest, diligent, assiduous; enterprising, aggressive, ambitious, hustling; energetic, vigorous, dynamic, kinetic; animated, lively, spirited, high-spirited, vivacious, lusty, active, *Sl.* go-go; *All Inf.* snappy, zippy, peppy, full of pep, full of get up and go.

6. eager, avid, ebullient, enthusiastic, full of enthusiasm, *Inf.* enthused, ready and willing, *Archaic.* fain, *Sl.* gung-ho, *Sl.* psyched, *Sl.* turned-on; anxious, agog, all agog, *Sl.* all hopped up; impatient, champing at the bit, bursting to, itching to, raring to; ardent, fervent, fervid, zealous; impassioned, passionate, feverish, heated, *Sl.* all fired-up.

7. intense, extreme, excruciating, heavy; poignant, heartfelt, deepfelt, *Archaic.* homefelt; deep, profound, indelible.

keen², *n.* **1.** keening, lamentation, jeremiad, complaint, *Archaic.* plaint; moan, groan, wail, ululation, howl, cry.

2. elergy, requiem, monody, threnody; dirge, epicedium, (*in Scotland and Ireland*) coronach, death song.

—*v.* **3.** lament, mourn, sorrow, grieve; wail, weep, sob, cry, ululate, howl; go into mourning; wear *or* put on mourning; moan, groan, fret, repine.

keen-eyed, *adj.* sharp-sighted, quick-sighted, eagle-eyed, hawk-eyed, lynx-eyed; all-seeing, all-observant, not missing a thing, taking it all in; perspicacious, discerning, discriminating, perceptive, percipient, clear-sighted; keen, acute, sharp, sharp as a tack, alert, bright, wide-awake, *Sl.* on the job, *Sl.* on the ball; on the watch for, watchful, vigilant, Argus-eyed; on the alert, on the qui vive, on guard, on the lookout; wary, chary, cautious, careful, circumspect, prudent, discreet.

keenness, *n.* **1.** cogency, penetration, incisiveness, pointedness; mordancy, mordaciousness, trenchancy, pungency, cuttingness, bitingness, stingingness, scorchingness; satiricalness, sardonicism, derisiveness, mockingness, insultingness; harshness, severity, stringency, roughness; unkindness, uncharitableness, maliciousness, malevolence, malignancy, cruelty; virulence, bitterness, acrimony, acrimoniousness, acridness, acidity, acerbity, rancorousness, venomousness.

2. acuteness, sharpness, sensitivity, discernment, discrimination, perception, percipience, perspicacity; consciousness, cognizance, awareness, sentience, sensibility, comprehension, understanding; sympathy, empathy, responsiveness.

3. astuteness, wisdom, sagacity, sapience; intelligence, smartness, *Sl.* smarts, brightness, *Inf.* braininess; shrewdness, cleverness, subtlety, canniness, cunning, slyness, wiliness, foxiness, *Scot. and North Eng.* pawkiness.

4. intentness, earnestness, diligence, assiduousness; enterprise, aggressiveness, ambitiousness, ambition, hustle; energy, vigorousness, vigor, dynamism; animation, liveliness, spiritedness, high-spiritedness, vivacity, vivaciousness, lustiness, activeness; *All Inf.* snappiness, snap, zippiness, zip, peppiness, pep, get up and go.

5. eagerness, avidness, ebullience, enthusiasm, readiness, willingness; anxiousness, impatience; ardor, fervidity, fervency, zeal, zealousness; passion, passionateness, feverishness, heatedness.

6. intensity, extremeness, excruciatingness, heaviness; poignancy; deepness, profundity, indelibleness.

keep, *v.* **1.** maintain, carry on, continue, stay with, proceed, persist, persevere; hold in abeyance, hold on to, put on a back burner; protract, prolong, sustain; abide, endure, last, be constant, be steadfast, stand, remain in.

2. preserve, maintain, secure, conserve, sustain, keep alive, keep fresh, hold, embrace; maintain in order, keep fixed, keep up; support, uphold, shore up, brace, bolster, prop, stay, ground.

3. restrain, keep down, keep back, hold back, check, hold in check, curb, limit, keep within bounds; arrest, hold in captivity, detain, retain; master, subjugate, control, dominate; prohibit, inhibit, keep from, forbid, interdict, withhold, disallow, restrict, deny; hinder, encumber, deter, hamstring, obstruct, stall, retard, cramp; grasp, clench, clasp, gripe, clutch, grip; tie up, shackle, chain.

4. furnish, stock, have in stock, carry, trade in, store, deal in; have, possess, accumulate, save up, husband, treasure up, amass, hoard up, lay in, garner, pile.

5. associate with, fraternize, accompany, mingle with; keep company with, date, court, go out with, take out; *Inf.* hang around with, consort with, flock together with, *Inf.* herd together, row in the same boat, chum, *Inf.* pal, *Inf.* pal up with, *Inf.* pal around with, *Inf.* buddy, *Inf.* buddy up with, *Inf.* take up with, *Inf.* gang with, *Inf.* latch on *or* onto.

6. have custody of, be responsible for, supervise, superintend, manage; tend, mind, take care of, care for, watch over, look after, keep an eye on; guard, protect, defend, safeguard, shelter, cover, shield.

7. conceal, keep dark, withhold, hide, keep hidden, keep secret, hugger-mugger; hush, hush up, stifle, suppress, muffle, silence, not breathe a word *or* syllable about; veil, screen, shroud, beshroud, curtain, mask, cloak; obscure, cloud, becloud, befog; camouflage, disguise, dissemble; bury, secrete, cache, shelter, cover, hide one's light under a bushel.

8. observe, obey, abide by, comply with, submit to, conform to, keep faith with, be regulated by; mind, heed, pay attention to; acknowledge, respect, defer to, accede; follow, fulfill, carry out, accomplish, effect, effectuate; complete, achieve, execute, consummate.

9. observe, celebrate, ceremonialize, ritualize, commemorate, memorialize; hallow, solemnize, dedicate; signalize.

10. support, maintain, foster, nurture, nourish; provide for, provision, feed, victual; afford, pay for, board, subsidize.

11. keep at a. persist, persevere, endure, hold out, hold up, keep going, be steadfast, stick, *Inf.* stick it out; finish, complete, do thoroughly; see it through, hang in there, follow to a conclusion, *Sl.* stay the distance, die in harness, die at one's post, die with one's boots on, go down trying, go down with flying colors. **b.** be resolute, be tenacious, be stubborn, be obstinate, be determined, be pertinacious, be firm, be constant, be unswerving, be aggressive. **c.** plod, peg, peg away, peg along, plug; drudge, grind, toil, moil, labor, slave, work like a dog *or* slave. **d.** keep after, follow, follow up, pursue, go after, trail, shadow, track; keep an eye on, search for, seek, hunt, look for, quest; prosecute, stay on [s.o.'s] back, run after.

—n. **12.** subsistence, maintenance, upkeep, support, livelihood, sustenance, sustainment, sustentation, necessaries, provision; board and lodging, room and board; nourishment, nurture, nutriment, aliment, rations, fare, diet, regimen, grubstake.

13. inner tower, donjon, dungeon, stronghold, fastness; castle, chateau, citadel; fort, fortress, fortification.

14. for keeps a. seriously, intently, gravely, sincerely, earnestly, soberly, grimly, determinedly, resolutely. **b.** finally, permanently, resolutely, unequivocally, ultimately, conclusively; once and for all, for good, forever.

keeper, *n.* **1.** jailer, *Sl.* screw, turnkey, sheriff; guard, warden, doorkeeper, watchman; sentry, sentinel, outpost.

2. guardian, chaperon, (*in Spain and Portugal*) duenna; escort, bodyguard, convoy; governess, nurse, wet nurse, dry nurse, nursemaid, (*in India and the Orient*) amah, *U.S.* mammy; guardian angel; lifeguard.

3. manager, proprietor, owner, entrepreneur; superintendent, director, supervisor, administrator, executive; maintenance man, janitor, custodian, caretaker, housekeeper, concierge, steward; curator, conservator; overseer, proctor, procurator.

4. (*all of animals*) gamekeeper, game warden; cowkeeper, cowboy, cowpuncher, cowgirl, drover, herder, herdsman, herdboy, cowherd; swineherd, goatherd, gooseherd, shepherd, shepherdess, sheeprancher; stockman, breeder, trainer; stableman, equerry, groom, ostler, hostler; beekeeper, apiculturist, apiarist.

keeping, *n.* **1.** agreement, congruity, harmony, conformity; correspondence, accordance, concurrence, accord, consistency; likeness, similarity, uniformity, resemblance, affinity, similitude; proportion, balance, evenness, parallelism; compliance, obedience, assent, concession, consent, acquiescence, acknowledgment, accommodation; performance, observance.

2. protection, safekeeping, safeguard; care, charge, custody; auspices, aegis, patronage; guardianship, trusteeship, *Law.* ward, tutelage, wardenship, detention, protectorship, protectorate.

3. keep, subsistence, maintenance, upkeep, support. See **keep** (*def.* **12**).

4. retaining, preserving, reserving, keeping in possession, maintaining; saving, hoarding, amassing, husbanding, storing up, putting by for a rainy day; holding, holding fast, gripping, embracing, grasping, clutching.

keepsake, *n.* remembrance, memento, relic, souvenir, favor, token, token of remembrance, token of appreciation.

keg, *n.* barrel, cask, hogshead, puncheon, butt, tierce, tun, rundlet; vat, tank, tub, firkin; container, vessel.

ken, *n.* **1.** cognizance, knowledge, familiarity, acquaintance; percipience, discernment, discrimination; perception, apprehension, comprehension, understanding, appreciation; awareness, consciousness, sentience, sensibility, sensitivity; realization, recognition, notice.

2. purview, field of vision, field of view, vision, visibility, view, range of vision, eyeshot, eyesight, sight.

kennel, *n.* **1.** doghouse, doghole; dog pound, dog shelter.

2. lair, den, cave, hole, burrow; shelter, hiding place, haunt.

kerchief, *n.* scarf, babushka, headdress, kaffiyeh; neckerchief, muffler, bandana, handkerchief, cloth.

kernel, *n.* **1.** grain, seed, stone, *Embryol.* germ, nut, nutlet, nutmeat, meat.

2. nucleus, core, center, soul, heart, vital part; marrow, pith, gist, substance, essence, sum and substance, essential part, quiddity, fundamental, *Law.* gravamen; inner core, quintessence, heart of the matter, *Inf.* nub, *Inf.* nitty-gritty, *Inf.* brass tacks.

3. bit, morsel, jot, iota, ounce; fraction, fragment, trace, touch.

ketchup, *n.* sauce, condiment, seasoning, relish.

kettle, *n.* **1.** pot, stewpot, cauldron, boiler, pan, saucepan, stewpan; vat, tub, crucible; teakettle, coffeepot.

2. kettledrum, timpani, tympanum, percussion instrument, drum.

key[1], *n.* **1.** opener, latchkey; skeleton key, passkey.

2. means, expedient, agent, device, instrument; path, way, passageway, access.

3. index, catalog, directory, guide, *Obs.* table of contents; manual, code book, answer book, solution book; legend, table, code; gloss, note, annotation, word of explanation, explication, exposition, clarification, resolution, description, illustration.

4. tone, pitch, *Music.* timbre, tonality, tone color; scale, mode; inflection, modulation; mood, humor, vein, style, character, spirit.

5. cotter, pin, linchpin, dowel, bolt, fastener, fastening; wedge, plug, quoin, cornerstone.

6. degree, intensity, magnitude, strength, shade.

7. wrest, wrench, lever, tool, contrivance.

—adj. **8.** important, essential, of the essence, fundamental, main, leading, principal, cardinal, chief, major.

key[2], *n.* cay, low island, reef.

keynote, *n.* **1.** *Music.* tonic, leading note.

2. gist, theme, main idea, salient point, cardinal point; center, heart, core, nucleus; substance, essence, quiddity, sum and substance, pith, marrow.

3. policy line, platform, stand, standing, position.

—v. **4.** announce, introduce, promulgate, proclaim; speak, declaim, harangue; set the tone, lead the bandwagon, start the proceedings, *Inf.* get the show on the road.

keystone, *n.* cornerstone, quoin, linchpin, crux; foundation, base, bed, ground, groundwork, footing, support; root, source, mainspring, spring, motive; principle, reason, basis, why.

khaki, *n.* **1.** **khakis** uniform; chinos, jeans.

—adj. **2.** yellowish-brown, brownish-yellow, mustard-colored, clay-colored, dun, grayish-brown, tan, sienna, earth-colored, mud-colored, brownish, brown, umber.

kibosh, *n.* **1.** *Informal.* nonsense, balderdash, malarkey, *Sl.* baloney, poppycock, *Inf.* flapdoodle.

2. *Informal.* **put the kibosh on** check, curb, nip in the bud, cut short *or* off, stop; squelch, quell, put down, quash, suppress, repress; contain, put the lid on, sit on *or* sit down on, crack down on, clamp down on, tighten up on.

kick, *v.* **1.** *Sl.* boot, *Obs.* foot, kick away; *Football.* punt, drop-kick, place-kick; (*all of the foot*) strike, hit, tap; propel, push, shove.

2. recoil, backlash, react; spring back, rebound, resile, bounce back, snap back; kick back, fly back, return, come back.

3. *Informal.* resist, oppose, recalcitrate, protest, remonstrate, object; complain, moan, groan, grumble, grouch, *Inf.* grouse, *Sl.* beef, *Inf.* gripe, *Sl.* bitch.

4. **kick around** *Slang.* **a.** abuse, misuse, maltreat, mistreat, treat badly, walk all over, push around. **b.** discuss, talk over, debate, moot, bandy words, *Sl.* hash over, argue the pros and cons, go over, thresh out *or* over.

5. **kick in** *Slang.* contribute, give, put in, *Inf.* chip in, *Sl.* shell out, *Inf.* fork out; produce, pay *or* pay up, *Inf.* ante up, hand over, *Sl.* cough up, come up *or* through with.

6. **kick off a.** *Slang.* die, *Sl.* kick the bucket, *Sl.* kick, pass away *or* on, give up the ghost. **b.** *Informal.* initiate, start, begin, start the ball rolling, break ground, lay the first stone.

7. **kick out** *Informal.* eject, oust, expel, remove, *Sl.* give the bum's rush; get rid of, force out, thrust out, push out, *Sl.* boot out, *Inf.* throw out *or* out on one's ear, toss out, turn out; dismiss, discharge, show the door, *Sl.* give the gate, send packing, send about one's business; fire, *Sl.* give the boot, give [s.o.] his walking papers *or* pink slip, *Inf.* give [s.o.] the ax, *Sl.* sack, *Sl.* can, *Sl.* bounce.

8. **kick up a.** kick upward, drive upward, force upward, push upward. **b.** raise *or* make a fuss, cause a scene, make a row, create a disturbance, *Inf.* raise a ruckus, kick up a storm, *Sl.* raise Cain.

—n. **9.** kick, boot; *Football.* punt, drop kick, place kick; (*all of the foot*) stroke, blow, hit, tap.

10. potency, strength, harshness, sharpness, pungency, piquancy; bite, nip, tang, spiciness, hotness, pepperiness; zip, zing, punch.

11. recoil, backlash, reaction, rebound, resilement, return.

12. *Informal.* objection, protest, protestation, remonstrance, remonstration, opposition, recalcitration; complaint, grievance, grumble, *Inf.* grouse, *Sl.* beef, *Inf.* gripe, *Sl.* bitch.

13. vigor, vim, energy, *Inf.* punch, vitality, life, bounce, *Sl.* snap; zest, enthusiasm, sparkle, vivacity, liveliness, verve, animation, *Inf.* ginger.

14. *Slang.* thrill, excitement, *Sl.* charge, *U.S. Sl.* rush, *U.S. Sl.* bang; enjoyment, pleasure, fun, amusement.

kickback, *n.* *Informal.* percentage, share, cut, commission; bribe, graft, *Inf.* payola, *Inf.* plugola, *Inf.* hush money, *Inf.* protection *or* protection money, *Sl.* boodle; reward, gift, pay, payment, payoff; remuneration, recompense, compensation.

kickoff, *n.* **1.** *Ice Hockey.* face-off, *Basketball.* jump ball.

2. *Informal.* initial stage, beginning, debut, start, outset, commencement, first step.

kicker, *n.* *Slang.* rub, hitch, snag, fly in the ointment, catch, *Inf.* fine print, trick, snare, trap, *Sl.* hooker; disadvantage, drawback, liability, handicap, weakness, weak spot, flaw, defect, fault, minus; inconvenience, trouble, problem, difficulty, pain in the neck; stumbling block, impediment, hindrance, obstacle, barrier, hurdle.

kid[1], *n.* **1.** doeling, young *or* baby goat; goat, ibex; doe, nanny goat, nanny, nan, she-goat; buck, ram, billy goat, billy, he-goat.

2. kidskin, goatskin, doeskin, leather, tanned hide *or* skin, hide skin; doeskins, kid gloves, leather gloves.

3. *Informal.* child, youngster, youth, youngling, young one, moppet, tyke, *Inf.* kiddy, *Archaic.* childe, *Usu. Offensive.* pickaninny; son, daughter, *Scot. and North Eng.* bairn; juvenile, adolescent, teenager, *Sl.* chavey, *Scot.* wain; girl, little girl, lass, lassie, *Irish Eng.* colleen, miss, *Inf.* missy, *Inf.* junior miss, *Inf.* chicken; boy, little boy, lad, stripling, sprig, junior, *Inf.* shaver, *Scot. and North Eng.* callant, *Both Irish Eng.* spaleen, gossoon; brat, imp, urchin, gamin, whippersnapper, *Sl.* punk, *Contemptible.* whelp; tomboy, gamine, hoyden; shrimp, wisp, *Inf.* small fry, *Inf.* squirt; tot, toddler, tiny tot, *U.S. Inf.* tad, preschool-

er; puppy, pup, cub, kitten, chit, chick, lambkin; baby, babe, infant, newborn, neonate, papoose, suckling, nursling, weanling, cherub, innocent, *Fr. enfant, It. bambino.*

kid[2], *v.* **1.** *Informal.* tease, badinage, chaff, pull [s.o.'s] leg, *Inf.* josh, *Inf.* rib, *Inf.* fun, *Sl.* put [s.o.] on, *Sl.* jive; ridicule, make fun of, mock, mimic, make game of, sport, *Inf.* rag; banter, jest, joke, joke *or* kid around, be facetious, be frivolous *or* flippant; trifle with, toy with, play with, make sport of, make light of.
2. *Informal.* trick, hoax, play a practical joke on; fool, befool, dupe, gull, take in, bamboozle, *Inf.* put [s.t.] over on; humbug, deceive, delude, cozen, cheat, swindle, *Inf.* flimflam, *Inf.* flam; impose upon, abuse, misuse, maltreat, use, take advantage of.

kiddish, *adj. Informal.* youthful, young, young at heart, girlish, boyish, kidlike, childlike, *Rare.* childly; juvenile, juvenescent, adolescent, puerile, jejune; childish, babyish, infantile, infantine, immature.

kidnap, *v.* **1.** (*usu. of persons*) abduct, rape, capture, seize, steal, *Sl.* snatch, hold as hostage, hold for ransom; make off with, lay hold of, lay hands on, carry off, bear away, take away, snatch, pluck; petnap, dognap; (*usu. in reference to military service*) impress, press, conscript, *Naut.* shanghai, crimp.
2. commandeer, take over by force, hijack, skyjack, pirate; expropriate, appropriate, misappropriate.

kidnapper, *n.* abductor, rapist, thief, robber, crook; petnapper, dognapper; deerjacker; skyjacker, hijacker, sky *or* air pirate.

kidnapping, *n.* **1.** abduction, capture, rape, seizure, robbery, theft; man-stealing, child-stealing; petnapping, dognapping; impressment, conscription.
2. commandeering, hijacking, air *or* sky piracy, skyjacking; expropriation, arrogation, misappropriation.

kidney, *n.* **1.** urinary organ, (*usu. pl.*) *Archaic.* reins.
2. disposition, nature, humor, spirit, temperament, temper, grain, mood; outlook, mind-set, frame of mind; character, make-up, inner man, qualities, constitution.
3. kind, sort, type, brand, name, variety; make, cast, cut, mold, form, style, manner; grain, tone, color; species, genus, breed, brood, genre.

kill, *v.* **1.** slay, murder, assassinate, poison, do to death, liquidate, erase, blot *or* wipe out, put an end to, get rid of, put away, put out of the way, silence, carry off, remove, dispatch, finish, finish off, do for, fix, settle, lay out, lay low, *Inf.* put the kibosh on, *Inf.* nip in the bud; *All Sl.* off, hit, zap, waste, croak, eighty-six, take off, rub out, bump off, snuff out, knock off, polish off, give [s.o.] the works *or* the business; *All Euph.* send west, take for a ride, put [s.o.] out of his misery.
2. shoot, shoot down, riddle, *Sl.* blow [s.o.'s] brains out, *Sl.* pump [s.o.] full of lead; club, beat, batter, pound, hammer, blackjack, brain, *Sl.* knock *or* beat [s.o.'s] brains out; choke, strangle, throttle, garrotte, stifle, *Sl.* scrag; knife *or* stab, cut [s.o.'s] throat, jugulate, cut, cut down, bayonet, pierce, lancinate, run through, put to the sword, impale, spear, lance, *Euph.* let the daylight in; smother, suffocate, asphyxiate, burke.
3. execute, put to death, behead, decapitate, guillotine, decollate; hang, gibbet, lynch, *Sl.* string up, *Sl.* stretch; stone, lapidate; burn at the stake; electrocute; drown.
4. slaughter, butcher, cut to pieces, ax, hew, hack, hack to pieces, chop, chop to pieces, dismember, draw and quarter, tear limb from limb, disembowel, mutilate, savage, maul, shed *or* spill blood; wade in blood, run amuck, go berserk, give no quarter, show no mercy.
5. immolate, sacrifice, burn; (*all of oneself*) commit suicide *or* hara-kari, *Inf.* overdose, *Sl.* O.D., *Sl.* brodie, *Sl.* take the gas, *Sl.* take a powder.
6. annihilate, exterminate, obliterate, discreate, reduce to nothing, destroy totally, eradicate, extirpate, abolish, extinguish; massacre, decimate, destroy a great number.
7. neutralize, negate, nullify, deaden, undo, depotentiate; offset, equalize, balance, counterbalance; weaken, dilute, mix, admix, alloy, (*of drugs or alcohol*) water *or* water down, (*of drugs or alcohol*) cut.
8. mar, spoil, despoil, ruin, damage, impair, hurt, harm; detract from, reduce, decrease, diminish.
9. (*all of time*) pass, while away, beguile, fill, occupy, spend, expend, exhaust, take up, employ, wait through; consume, absorb, use up, eat up, devour, swallow up, guzzle, put in; waste, dissipate, squander, fritter *or* fool away, lose, throw away, lavish, misspend, misuse, *Sl.* blow.
10. overwhelm, overpower, overcome completely, stagger, amaze, bedazzle; *Sl.* break *or* knock one dead *or* out, *Sl.* knock *or* lay them in the aisles, *Sl.* break *or* crack one up; stir, affect, move, transport, impassion, touch, influence, incite, stimulate, excite, electrify.
11. irk, gall, vex, displease, annoy, disturb, provoke, irritate, nettle, rile, pique, chafe, ruffle.
12. muffle, deaden, damp, dampen, dull, smother, mute, silence.
13. exhaust, tire, tire out, fag, fag out, *Inf.* tucker, *Inf.* tucker out, fatigue, wear out, weary, sap; debilitate, weaken, prostrate, enervate, tax, strain, overtire, overwork, overtax, overtask, overburden.
14. cancel, delete, expunge, remove, cross out, cut out, scratch, excise, withdraw, edit, amend, obliterate, strike *or* rule out, write off; erase, efface, eradicate, wipe *or* blot out.
15. veto, vote down, turn down, countermand, defeat, reject, overrule, disallow, prohibit.
16. (*all of machinery*) stop, cease, discontinue, turn off, shut off, cut off, terminate, stall, pause, brake; pull up.
17. *Informal.* (*usu. of food or drink*) consume, devour, absorb, swallow up, drink up, guzzle down, bolt down, gulp down, gobble down; drain, empty, exhaust, deplete, finish, finish off, do in, *Sl.* eighty-six.
—*n.* **18.** deathblow, killing blow, finishing stroke, final assault, *Inf.* haymaker, *Sl.* sockdolager, *Inf.* Sunday punch, *Sl.* mop-up, *Fr. coup de grâce,* dispatch, death; finish, end, conclusion, termination.
19. prey, quarry, game, raven, victim, meat, carcass.

killer, *n.* **1.** slayer, murderer, manslayer, mankiller, cutthroat, thug, poisoner, strangler, impaler; assassin, liquidator, bravo, sniper, gunman, knifer, *Euph.* silencer, *Euph.* dispatcher; *All Sl.* gun, hired gun, hit man, triggerman, torpedo, hatchet man; executioner, executionist, *Sl.* Jack Ketch, decapitator, headsman, beheader, lyncher, hangman, garrotter, burker, burkist, *Bullfighting.* matador; butcher, slaughterer, Bluebeard, ripper, mass-murderer, mass-slayer, exterminator, annihilator, destroyer; bloodspiller, bloodshedder, bloodletter.
2. homicide, suicide, patricide, matricide, parricide, fratricide, sororicide, uxoricide, infanticide, regicide, vaticide; aborticide, insecticide, fungicide, germicide.
3. *Slang.* humdinger, killer-diller, doosy, dinger, *Brit.* ripper, the cat's meow, *Brit.* the bee's knees, mindblower, mindboggler, trip, trip-and-a-half; honey, lulu, dilly, beaut, beauty; lady's man, ladykiller, playboy, rake.

killing, *n.* **1.** murder, slaying, manslaughter, thuggee, fatality, death, violent death, bloody *or* foul murder, murder most foul, foul play, assassination, shooting, strangling, strangulation, garrotting, poisoning; execution, capital punishment, judicial murder; hanging, lynching, *Euph.* necktie party; decapitation, decollation, guillotining; electrocution, gassing; martyrdom, immolation, crucifixion, impalement, lapidation, stoning, burning, burning at the stake; homicide, suicide, patricide, matricide, parricide, fratricide, sororicide, uxoricide, infanticide, regicide, vaticide; aborticide, insecticide, fungicide, germicide.

2. butchery, massacre, carnage, slaughter, bloodbath, bloodshed, fusillade of blood, effusion of blood, *Rare.* trucidation, *Rare.* internecion, wholesale *or* general slaughter; mass murder, mass slaying, mass homicide, mass execution, mass destruction, decimation, liquidation, blotting *or* wiping out, genocide, pogrom, holocaust, *Euph., Hist.* Final Solution, extermination, obliteration, organized murder, elimination.

3. coup, stroke of luck *or* fortune, piece of good luck *or* good fortune, *Inf.* smash *or* big hit, hit, fluke, run of luck, godsend, windfall, bonanza; master stroke, stroke of genuis, *Fr. coup de maître,* feat, achievement; *Inf.* cleanup, harvest, fortune, profit, take, takings, winnings, booty, prize, gain.

—adj. **4.** murderous, homicidal, cutthroat, assassinative; death-dealing, lethal, fatal, mortal, mortiferous, deadly, deathly, *Archaic.* lethiferous; slaughterous, internecine, savage, barbarous, cruel, brutal, fiendish; cannibalistic, anthropophagous, bloodthirsty, bloody-minded, sanguinary, sanguine, sanguineous, sanguinolent, bloody, gory, bloodstained, ensanguined; ferocious, violent, frenzied, wild, berserk, amuck, raging, maniacal; annihilating, exterminating, obliterating, extirpative, extirpating, extinguishing, eliminating, withering, devastating, decimating, destructive, destroying.

5. exhausting, debilitating, enervating, prostrating, overtiring, overtaxing, overtasking, overburdening; taxing, straining, hard, difficult, laborious, arduous; tiring, fatiguing, wearying, weakening, sapping, draining.

6. *Informal.* screaming, hilarious, uproarious, screamingly funny, highly amusing, too funny for words; funny, comic, comical, amusing, quizzical; ludicrous, ridiculous, absurd, nonsensical, outrageous, outlandish, foolish, laughable, risible, farcical; droll, drollish, rich.

kill-joy, *n.* spoilsport, damper, *Sl.* partypooper, wet blanket, grouch, *Inf.* sourpuss, malcontent; cynic, pessimist, gloom and doomer, *Inf.* gloomy Gus, *Sl.* crapehanger; nihilist, negativist, defeatist; worrywart, prophet of doom, Cassandra; scowler, sneerer, snarler, growler, grumbler; critic, complainer, faultfinder, detractor; scoffer, satirist, carper, caviler, *Inf.* knocker; skeptic, nullifidian, doubter.

kilt, *n.* skirt, wraparound, filibeg.

kilter, *n.* *Informal.* order, working order, condition, *Sl.* whack; shape, state, form, alignment, *Inf.* sync, *Brit. Dial.* kelter; fettle, trim, repair, fitness, feather; regularity, array, disposition, course, even tenor.

kimono, *n.* robe, gown, dressing gown, peignoir, *Fr. robe de chambre,* smoking gown, tea gown; bathrobe, housecoat, lounging robe; morning dress, negligee, deshabille, wrapper.

kin, *n.* **1.** relatives, kinsfolk, kith, kith and kin, kindred; relations, connections, distant relatives; family, folks, people, tribe, brood, clan; house, nationality, gentility.

2. kinship, relationship, relation, consanguinity, alliance, connection; blood, blood ties, flesh and blood, family ties; common ancestry, patrilineage, matrilineage, parentage; affiliation, cognation, agnation, enation; propinquity, nearness, closeness; extraction, lineage, descent, stock, breed, stirps; ilk, kind, line, sept.

—adj. **3.** akin, related, kindred, fraternal, twin; consanguineous, consanguine, cognate, agnate, enate, german, uterine; affiliated, family, allied, affined, affinal; near, close, propinquitous; of the same family, of the same blood, of the same nature.

kind[1], *adj.* **1.** good, benevolent, benign, benignant, beneficent; mild, gentle, tender, *Fr. gentil;* compassionate, loving, *Inf.* Christian, humane, decent, noble, human; gracious, generous, charitable, bounteous, giving; lionhearted, big-hearted, altruistic, magnanimous, humanitarian, philanthropic; warmhearted, kindhearted, tender-hearted, soft-hearted; clement, lenient, temperate, merciful, pitying, placable, unhardened.

2. considerate, understanding, thoughtful; indulgent, forbearing, forbearant, patient, forgiving; helpful, obliging, accommodating; chivalrous, gallant, courteous; neighborly, friendly, nice, genial, hospitable, affable; kindly, cordial, amiable, amicable, good-natured, well-disposed; well-meant, well-meaning, well-intended, well-intentioned, well-affected; sympathetic, sympathizing, warm, affectionate, commiserating; tactful, diplomatic, delicate, mindful, heedful; motherly, fatherly, maternal, paternal, grandmotherly, grandfatherly; brotherly, fraternal, sisterly, cousinly, avuncular.

kind[2], *n.* **1.** class, category, genre, order; group, set, suit, variety; genus, species, phylum, subgenus, subspecies, strain, sept; race, breed, people, folk; clan, family, tribe, brood, ilk, kin, stock, stirps.

2. nature, aspect, character, temperament, disposition, temper, humor, habit; persuasion, bent, leaning, inclination, diathesis; lot, style, manner, cast, mold, stamp, brand, kidney; grain, make, mark, cue; color, stripe, streak, feather, vein; description, designation, number, *Inf.* the like *or* likes of.

3. type, sort, exemplar, representative, case; example, specimen, instance, sample.

4. in kind in like manner, in the same way, in the same manner, similarly, correspondingly, likewise, like.

5. kind of *Informal.* a little, a bit, to a degree, *Inf.* sort of, in a way, to some extent; somewhat, rather, pretty, fairly.

kindhearted, *adj.* warm-hearted, good-natured, good-hearted; good, gentle, nice. See **kind** (*defs.* **1, 2**).

kindheartedness, *n.* goodness, compassion, warmheartedness. See **kindness** (*defs.* **1, 2**).

kindle, *v.* **1.** fire, ignite, torch, deflagrate, burn, burn up *or* down, set aflame *or* alight *or* on fire, set fire to, put to the torch, put *or* apply a match to, *Obs.* accend, *Obs.* flagrate.

2. incite, provoke, actuate, poke, prod, prick, goad, prompt, spur; encourage, urge, abet, egg on, put up to; instigate, foment, agitate, suscitate, excite, impassion, intensify, arouse, rouse, madden, craze, stir up, wind up, work up, whip up, lash into a fury, *Inf.* psych up, heat up, *Obs.* calefy, fire up, inflame, enflame, enkindle, touch off, ignite the spark, stir the embers, stoke *or* fuel *or* fan the fire, add fuel to the flames *or* fire.

3. stimulate, animate, reanimate, whet, invigorate, motivate, inspirit, inspire, galvanize, electrify, *Inf.* spark; energize, activate, vivify, rally, revive, enliven, liven up, pep up, awaken, wake up, waken, shake up, jolt, jog; push, drive, press, force, force along, propel, hound, whip, lash, flog; impel, induce, compel, constrain, move, stir, fillip; evoke, elicit, call forth, summon up, raise *or* spread the alarm.

4. illuminate, illumine, *Archaic.* illume, irradiate, light up, lighten, shine light, shed light, flood with light, floodlight, brighten, brighten up, *Archaic.* overshine.

kindliness, *n.* **1.** goodness, benevolence, compassion, warm-heartedness. See **kindness** (*defs.* **1, 2**).

2. good deed, good turn, act of kindness. See **kindness** (*def.* **3**).

kindling, *n.* **1.** firewood, *Southern U.S.* lightwood, brushwood, brush, driftwood; tinder, log, fagot, twigs, shavings, leaves; coal, charcoal; fuel, lighting *or* lighter fluid.

2. burning, firing, igniting, lighting, enflaming; enkindling, awakening, arousing, inciting, fomenting, fueling; stimulating, inspiriting, quickening, vivifying.

kindly, *adj.* **1.** kindhearted, sympathetic, warm. See **kind** (*defs.* **1, 2**).

2. pleasant, agreeable, winsome, charming, taking; felicitous, welcome, inviting; fair, nice, pleasurable, dulcet; cheerful, warm, refreshing, sweet, enjoyable.

3. favorable, suitable, fit, adaptable, usable; serviceable, beneficial, advantageous, helpful; profitable, worthwhile, edifying; fertile, fecund, productive, prolific.

—adv. **4.** considerately, thoughtfully, understandingly, sympathetically; kindheartedly, tender-heartedly, warm-heartedly, soft-heartedly; benevolently, charitably, benignly, altruistically, philanthropically; compassionately, mildly, humanely, lovingly; mercifully, clemently, ruthfully, decently, nobly.

5. cordially, hospitably, graciously; heartily, warmly, genially, good-naturedly; deeply, profoundly, from the bottom of one's heart; amiably, amicably, affably, nicely.

6. favorably, agreeably, approvingly, affirmatively, acquiescently, assentingly; with liking, well, affectionately, fondly.

7. obligingly, please, pray, *Archaic.* prithee, *Fr. s'il vous plait,* if you please; be so good as to, have the goodness to, be good enough to, for mercy's sake, for goodness sake, for heaven's sake.

kindness, *n.* **1.** goodness, benevolence, benignity, benignancy, beneficence; mildness, gentleness, tenderness, *Archaic.* gentilesse; compassion, love, lovingness, brotherly love, humanity, humaneness, decency; generosity, charity, bounty, largesse; charitableness, good will, liberality, open-handedness; graciousness, lionheartedness, big-heartedness, altruism, unselfishness; philanthropy; warm-heartedness, kindheartedness, tender-heartedness, soft-heartedness, goodheartedness, bonhomie; clemency, leniency, lenity, temperance; mercy, ruth, ruthfulness, pity, quarter, bowels of compassion.

2. consideration, thoughtfulness, understanding; indulgence, forbearance, tolerance, patience, forgiveness; helpfulness, obligingness, chivalry, gallantry, courtesy; neighborliness, friendliness, friendship, niceness, geniality, hospitality, good-naturedness; kindliness, cordiality, amiability, amicability, affability; sympathy, empathy, commiseration; affection, warmth, fondness, liking; delicacy, mindfulness, heedfulness, diplomacy, tact; motherliness, fatherliness, maternalness, paternalness, grandmotherliness, grandfatherliness; brotherhood, sisterhood, brotherliness, sisterliness, fellow feeling, fellowship.

3. good deed, good turn, kind act, act of charity, act of grace, almsgiving, favor, *Sl.* solid; service, aid, assistance, help, succor; relief, comfort, solace.

kindred, *n.* **1.** family, tribe, clan, brood, house, household, hearth, ilk, *Fr. ménage;* race, people, folks, nationality, nation.

2. kinfolk, kin, kith. See **kinfolk.**

3. kinship, relationship, affinity. See **kinship** (*defs.* **1, 2**).

—adj. **4.** allied, associated, affined, affinal, family; akin, related, consanguineous, consanguine; fraternal, twin, sib, sibling; cognate, agnate, enate, german, uterine; of the same blood, of the same family, of the same nature; patrilineal, matrilineal, patriuxorial, matriuxorial, patrivirile, matrivirile; *Biol.* patriclinous, *Biol.* matriclinous; foster, novercal, step.

5. like, similar, analogous, correlative, congeneric; near, close, propinquitous, approaching, approximating; collateral, parallel, cognate, connate, synonymous, paronymous; corresponding, correspondent, matching, resembling, paired, homologous; agreeing, accordant, concordant; germane, apposite, suitable, fitted, applicable.

kinetic, *adj.* bodily, body, physical, corporal; mobile, moving, in motion; unstatic, dynamic, intense, active, lively, animated, spirited, electric, vivacious; energetic, vigorous, brisk.

kinfolk, *n.* kinsfolk, kin, kindred, kith, kith and kin, brethren, cousinage; folks, family, people, ilk; children, offspring, progeny, issue, seed; relations, relatives, distant relatives, near relatives, connections; ancestry, ancestors, forbears, forefathers; posterity, descendants, heirs, sons, daughters; distaff side, spindle side, spear side, sword side.

king, *n.* **1.** sovereign, monarch, ruler, crowned head, majesty, royal personage, potentate, dynast, *Latin. rex;* caesar, czar, *Ger.* Kaiser; prince, prince consort, prince regent, regent; protector, governor, tetrarch; paramount, paramount lord, suzerain, overlord, overking; chief, chieftain, high chief.

2. patriarch, dean, doyen, superior, senior; personage, leading light, luminary, star, superstar; director, manager, executive, *Inf.* mogul, *Inf.* nabob, *Inf.* tycoon; chief, boss, *Inf.* kingpin, *Inf.* kingfish, *Sl.* high-muck-a-muck, *Sl.* his nibs, *Sl.* himself, *Sl.* head honcho, *Sl.* Mr. Big, *Sl.* top dog, *Sl.* big shot, *Sl.* wheel, *Sl.* big wheel.

kingdom, *n.* **1.** country, land, nation, state, sovereign nation *or* state; kingdom, empire, realm, dominion, domain, principality, empery, principate; monarchy, duchy, dukedom, earldom, palatinate, province, possession, colony.

2. division, classification, grouping, class, order, category, group, family, genus, kind.

3. sphere of influence, orbit, ambit, bailiwick; home ground *or* territory, territory, turf, stamping ground, corner.

kingliness, *n.* regality, imperiality, imperialness, augustness, stateliness; grandeur, eminence, preeminence; loftiness, majesty, excellence, greatness, nobility, nobleness; magnificence, splendor, glamour, sovereignty, supremacy, dominance, dominancy, authority, authoritativeness; dignity, honorableness, gallantry, courtliness.

kingly, *adj.* **1.** regal, royal, sovereign, imperial, basilic, of high *or* noble birth; noble, dignified; proud, proud-hearted, assured, self-assured, poised; imposing, impressive, awe-inspiring, stately, majestic, princely; powerful, authoritative, commanding; strong, mighty, important, absolute; autocratic, tyrannical, despotic, domineering, imperious.

2. grand, distinguished, eminent, celebrated, esteemed; renowned, illustrious, prominent, preeminent; honorable, venerable, revered, respected; aristocratic, blue-blooded, distingué.

3. splendid, luxurious, sumptuous, opulent, *Inf.* posh; glamorous, striking, gorgeous; large, palatial, pretentious, ostentatious.

kingship, *n.* **1.** dominion, power, rule, command, ascendancy, supremacy; sway, authority, sovereignty, regnancy; monarchy, the throne, the crown, the scepter, reign, regime; accession, succession, election.

2. dignity, royalty, augustness, loftiness, eminence, glory, honor, illustriousness; nobility, aristocracy, majesty, regality, noble bearing; honorableness, irreproachableness, high-mindedness, character; fidelity, devotion, steadfastness, staunchness.

kink, *n.* **1.** twist, curl, twirl, screw, corkscrew, coil, curlicue, whorl, spiral, helix, volute; crimp, crisp, crinkle, warp, zigzag.

2. crick, hitch, pinch, tweak, stab, stitch, stitch in the side, *Inf.* charley horse; stiffness, tightness, soreness; seizure, spasm, twinge.

3. flaw, imperfection, fault, defect, deformity, deformation; crookedness, asymmetry, lopsidedness; distortion, deviation, warp.

4. whim, caprice, whimsy, vagary; notion, fancy, crazy idea, *Inf.* fool notion; crotchet, conceit, quirk, *Archaic.* maggot, bee in one's bonnet.

—v. **5.** curl, coil, twist, bend, distort, contort, screw, wring, twine; warp, crumple, crisp, friz, frizzle, crinkle, crimp, put a crimp in; knot, knarl, whirl.

kinky, *adj.* **1.** twisted, curled, coiled, crimped, kinked, crinkled, warped; twisty, curly, frizzly, frizzy, frizzed, crispy, crisp, crisped; wavy, wiry, coiling, tangled, knotted, tortured, sigmoid.

2. whimsical, capricious, fanciful, fantastic; eccentric, erratic, idiocratic, idiosyncratic, crotchety; different, odd, peculiar, strange, bizarre, outlandish, freakish; quirky, dotty, skittish, fitful, queer, *Inf.* queer in the head, *Sl.* screwy, *Sl.* screwball, *Sl.* nutty, *Sl.* wacky, *Sl.* flaky, *Sl.* oddball.

3. unconventional, unorthodox, out of the way, way-out, far-out, *Inf.* offbeat; irregular, out of step, out of place, out of line, out of keeping, not done, not kosher, *Brit. Inf.* not cricket; inconsistent, chimerical, unsteady, wanton, vagrant, errant; vacillating, unreliable, fluctuating.

4. perverted, *Sl.* preverted, warped, unnatural, abnormal, deviative, deviant; depraved, degenerate, degenerated; licentious, lascivious, lewd, suggestive; sadistic, masochistic, *Sl.* s-m; homosexual, homoerotic, homophile, *Inf.* gay, *Inf.* bent; lesbian, sapphic, tribadistic; bisexual, bisexed, *Sl.* switch-hitting, *Inf.* AC-DC, amphierotic; heteroclite, heteromorphic; hermaphroditic; epicene, androgynous, transsexual.

kinship, *n.* **1.** relationship, kin, relation, consanguinity, filiation, apparentation; blood, blood ties, family ties, flesh and blood; common ancestry, ancestry, descent, lineage, patrilineage, matrilineage, parentage; cognation, agnation, enation; propinquity, nearness, closeness; extraction, stock, breed, strain, kind, stirps, line, sept.

2. affinity, bearing, association; correspondence, agreement, concordance, accordance; parallelism, equivalence, symmetry, congeniality, harmony.

kinsman, *n.* relative, kinswoman, relation, consanguinean; clansman, tribesman, fellow countryman, compatriot; next of kin, kissing kin, kissing cousin; cognate, enate, agnate, affine; father, mother, brother, sister, son, daughter; uncle, aunt, nephew, niece, cousin; grandfather, grandmother, grandson, granddaughter; stepfather, stepmother, stepbrother, stepsister; great-uncle, granduncle, great-aunt, grandaunt.

kiosk, *n.* **1.** (*in Turkey and Iran*) summerhouse, gardenhouse, pavilion, gazebo, pergola, trellis, lattice.

2. arbor, bower, retreat, refuge, shelter, haven, hermitage.

3. bandstand, platform, structure, stage; newsstand, bookstall, stall.

kipper, *v.* (*of all fish*) cure, smoke-cure, smoke, dry, salt, pickle, preserve, can, *Chiefly Brit.* tin.

kismet, *n.* destiny, fate, predestination, preordination, foreordination, predetermination, what is to be *or* come, *Sp. que sera sera,* what is written in the stars, stars, planets, *Class. Myth.* Moira, what bodes *or* looms; portion, fortune, wheel of fortune, handwriting on the wall, lot, one's lot in life, cup, inevitability; end, doom; God's will, Providence, will of Allah, *Islamic. insh'allah.*

kiss, *v.* **1.** salute, greet, kiss the hand of; *Inf.* buss, *Inf.* smack, osculate; *Inf.* smooch, *Inf.* canoodle, *Inf.* make out, *Inf.* fool around, *Inf.* neck, bundle, *Inf.* spoon; blow a kiss.

2. touch gently, brush, brush lightly, graze, glance over, waft over, lick, contact gently, come into contact with.

—n. **3.** accolade, salute, handkiss; *Inf.* buss, *Inf.* smack, *Inf.* smooch, osculation.

4. touch, light touch, taction, contact; glance, brush, feel, sensation.

kit, *n.* **1.** set, collection, parts; tools, equipment, apparatus, implements, utensils, gear, necessaries, tackle, rigging, trappings, appurtenances, accouterments, things, paraphernalia; supplies, fittings, provisions, furnishings.

2. uniform, livery, wardrobe, clothing, turnout, outfit, *Inf.* rig, dress.

3. case, fitted case, tool box, instrument case; knapsack, rucksack, haversack, *Australian.* tucker bag, duffel bag, sea bag, ditty bag *or* box, *Inf.* boodle bag, school bag.

kitchen, *n.* **1.** cookroom, cookhouse, cookery, bakehouse, bakery, galley, *Brit.* caboose; scullery, pantry, larder, *Brit.* stillroom.

2. culinary department, cuisine, table d'hôte, ordinary, menu, meals, board.

—adj. **3.** (*all of speech*) provincial, regional, local, colloquial, vernacular, informal, unliterary; inferior, substandard, mongrel, bastard.

kite, *n.* **1.** box kite, tetrahedral kite, dragon kite, eddy kite, Hargrave *or* cellular kite.

2. small hawk, bird of prey, black kite, swallow-tailed kite, white-tailed kite, elanet.

—v. **3.** *Informal.* ascend, mount, rise, arise, uprise, go up, get up, come up, rise up, start up; soar, sail, fly, hover, float, drift, glide, dip, swoop.

4. *Commerce.* write bad checks, counterfeit checks, *Inf.* boost checks, *Inf.* bounce checks, *Inf.* pass bad paper, *Inf.* paper, *Inf.* manufacture, forge, counterfeit securities.

kitten, *n.* **1.** young cat, young feline, kit, kitty, pussy, pussycat, puss, *Archaic.* catling.

—v. **2.** bear kittens, deliver, bear, give birth, drop, spring, throw, bring forth young.

kittenish, *adj.* **1.** playful, playsome, full of play, playful as a kitten; sportive, funloving, frolicsome, frisky, *Fr. folâtre.*

2. *All Disparaging.* cute, overly-cute, too cute, cutesy, *Brit. Sl.* twee; infantile, girlish; coquettish, coy, tricksy.

klutz, *n.* *Slang.* **1.** bungler, botcher, *Inf.* duffer, *Sl.* butcher, mismanager; fumbler, butterfingers, blunderer, stumbler, *Inf.* bull in a china shop; lubber, looby, lummox, *Sl.* galoot, lout, oaf, *Sl.* shlemiel.

2. blockhead, dunce, dolt, dullard, ignoramus, *Sl.* yoyo, simpleton; lunkhead, bonehead, knucklehead, pinhead, *Sl.* bananahead, numskull.

knack, *n.* talent, aptitude, aptness, forte, gift, genius, endowment; ability, bent, turn for, faculty, capacity, qualification, propensity, readiness, quickness; skill, skillfulness, adroitness, facility, finesse, art; proficiency, competence, dexterity, dexterousness, trick, trick of the trade, *Inf.* hang.

knapsack, *n.* backpack, *Inf.* poke, pocket, pouch, bag, saddlebag, *Inf.* housewife; kit, war bag, rucksack, haversack, *Australian.* tucker bag, duffel bag, holdall.

knave, *n.* **1.** scoundrel, blackguard, wretch, dastard, reprobate, cur, dog, *Inf.* hound, *Sl.* lowlife, *Archaic.* caitiff, *Archaic.* coistrel; villain, bad guy *or* man, snake, viper, reptile, snake in the grass, evildoer, fiend, hellhound, miscreant, devil; rogue, cad, churl, louse, bully, ruffian, brute, abuser, *Sl.* stinker, *Sl.* rat, *Sl.* creep, *Sl.* jerk, *Sl.* bastard, *Sl.* SOB, *Obs.* stinkard; good-for-nothing, ne'er-do-well, vagabond, black sheep, *Inf.* rip, *Sl.* bum, *Chiefly Brit.* wastrel, *Chiefly Brit. Sl.* rotter, *Chiefly Brit. Sl.* bounder, *Brit. Sl.* blighter; rascal, scamp, scalawag, rapscallion, scapegrace, bad *or* naughty boy, picaroon, pettifogger, mischief-maker, troublemaker.

2. traitor, renegade, betrayer, Judas, recreant, sneak, *Inf.* double-crosser, *Sl.* two-timer; hypocrite, pharisee, deceiver, pretender, dissembler, bluff, bamboozler, *Inf.* four-flusher; fake, faker, fraud, humbug, masquerader, mountebank, charlatan, imposter, wolf in sheep's clothing, *Inf.* quack, *Inf.* phony, *Australian.* bunyip; cheat, cheater, trickster, sharper, sharpie, fox, sly fox, shark, *Inf.* shyster, confidence man, *Sl.* con man, *Sl.* flim-flam man; crook, *U.S. Sl.* chiseler, swindler, bilker, diddler.

knavery, *n.* **1.** rascality, roguery, roguishness, unscrupulousness, baseness, knavishness; villainy, miscreancy, deviltry, evildoing, wrongdoing, evil ways, dark and crooked ways; mischief, mischievousness, pettifoggery, chicanery, shenanigans, hanky-panky, messing around, *Sl.* funny business, *Sl.* monkey business, *Sl.* monkeyshines.

2. treachery, treason, betrayal, recreance, recreancy, disloyalty; deception, deceit, trickery, fraudulence, fraud, dissimulation, cozenage, dupery; duplicity, double-dealing, talking out of both sides of one's mouth, dishonesty; trickery, guile, wiles, foxiness, craftiness, craft, cunning, artfulness, finesse, hocus-pocus, *Inf.* razzle-dazzle; cheating, swindling, *Inf.* dirty pool.

3. trick, stratagem, artifice, pretense, Trojan horse, *Obs.* cog; wile, subterfuge, misrepresentation, imposture, imposition, *Law.* cavin; fake, sham, hoax, fraud, humbug, feint, blind; swindle, shuck, *Inf.* flimflam, *Inf.* flam, confidence game *or* trick, *Sl.* con game.

knavish, *adj.* **1.** rascally, rascal, roguish, blackguardly, dastardly; mischievous, naughty, scampish, waggish; low, base, rotten, stinking, rank, dirty, contemptible, awful, terrible; villainous, nasty, mean, cruel, brutal.

2. unscrupulous, dishonorable, unprincipled, unethical, reprobate, immoral, depraved, corrupt; dishonest, insincere, disingenuous, untruthful, lying, mendacious, hypocritical; deceitful, deceptive, delusive, misleading, dissembling, dissimulative, beguiling, *Sl.* double-crossing, *Sl.* two-timing; treacherous, sneaky, double-dealing, underhanded, cheating, crooked, tortuous; tricky, trickish, sly, shrewd, sharp, cunning, wily, foxy, artful, insidious, subtle, *Archaic.* tricksy; conniving, collusive, designing, scheming, plotting.

knead, *v.* work, manipulate, *Brit. Dial.* ply, press, fold; form, shape, mold; massage, rub, rub down, stroke.

knee, *n.* **1.** patellar region, joint, stifle.

2. bring [s.o.] to his knees subjugate, conquer, vanquish, make [s.o.] cry uncle; make [s.o.] crawl, make [s.o.] beg; humiliate, humble, mortify, make [s.o.] eat crow.

kneecap, *n.* **1.** patella, kneepan.

2. kneepad, kneepiece, *Armor.* knee cap, *Armor.* poleyn, *Armor.* genouillère.

kneel, *v.* get down on one's knees, fall to one's knees; genuflect, bow, bow down, bow and scrape, salaam, kowtow, prostrate oneself, fall at the feet of, make obeisance; bob, curtsy.

knell, *n.* **1.** death knell, death toll, death *or* funeral *or* mourning bell; (*all of funeral bells*) toll, tolling, *Archaic.* knolling, sounding, resounding, peal, pealing, ring, ringing, chime, chiming, tintinnabulation.

—*v.* **2.** toll, *Archaic.* knoll, sound, resound, peal, ring, chime, tintinnabulate; herald, announce, proclaim; call, summon.

knickers, *n.* knickerbockers, breeches, knee breeches, knee pants, small clothes, *Brit.* plus fours, trousers; shorts, *Inf.* cut-offs, bermuda shorts *or* bermudas, pedal pushers, clam diggers, knee knockers; jodhpurs, riding breeches; culottes, gauchos.

knickknack, *n.* gewgaw, gimcrack, *Inf.* whimwham, bauble, trinket, doodad, bagatelle, trifle, kickshaw, brummagem, toy, plaything; gaud, showy ornament, spangle, sequin, tinsel, clinquant; worthless finery, frippery, *Archaic.* trumpery, junk; bric-a-brac, miscellany, odds and ends, bits and pieces.

knife, *n.* **1.** blade, (*collectively*) cutlery; jackknife, Swiss Army knife, pocketknife, penknife, switchblade, *Sl.* shiv; saber, *Japanese.* aikuchi, sword, Excalibur, cutlass; rapier, foil, épée; bayonet, scimitar, bill, billhook, cold steel, snickersnee; bowie knife, trench knife, dagger, *Malay.* creese, *Malay.* kris, dirk, poniard, *Fr. poignard;* stiletto, stylet, *Scot.* skean, scalpel, *Medieval.* misericord; cleaver, hatchet, ax, halberd, tomahawk; machete, bolo; utility knife, saw, hacksaw; spear, lance, *South Africa.* assegai, harpoon.

—*v.* **2.** cut, stab, pierce, lancinate, *Inf.* stick, cut up, slash; run through, impale, transfix; bayonet, spear, lance; cleave, slice, divide.

3. stab in the back, double-deal, betray, *Sl.* slip a Mickey, pull the rug out from under.

knight, *n.* **1.** cavalryman, equestrian, horseman; soldier, fighter, warrior; gallant, flower of chivalry, knight-errant, Sir Lancelot, Sir Galahad, *Medieval Romance.* Amadis.

2. nobleman, prince, lord, pasha, emir, sheik; chevalier, cavalier; gentleman, aristocrat, patrician, blue blood; champion, defender, guardian, protector.

knight-errantry, *n.* idealism, Quixotism, visionariness, romanticism, impracticality; rashness, impetuosity, foolhardiness, heedlessness. See **knighthood.**

knighthood, *n.* chivalry, valor, gallantry; courage, bravery, dauntlessness, intrepidity, heroism; temerity, audacity, boldness; nobility, benevolence, generosity, altruism, charity, kindliness, courtesy, gentlemanliness.

knit, *v.* **1.** purl, crochet, hook, knot; weave, interweave, interlace, interthread, intertwine.

2. wrinkle, draw in, gather, fold.

3. draw together, become whole, heal, mend, get well.

knob, *n.* **1.** handle, grip, hold, handhold.

2. protuberance, protuberancy, knop, nub, nubble, node, nodule; bunch, bulge, hump, bump, swell, lump, tumor; protrusion, projection, tuberosity, prominence, snag; tumescence, swelling; whelk, pimple, pustule, *Pathol.* papule; outgrowth, excrescence, tubercle; knot, knarl, knur, knurl, gnarl.

3. hill, hillock, hummock, (*in South Africa*) kopje, *Chiefly Brit.* barrow, knoll, mound, dune; monticule, mountain, ridge.

knobby, *adj.* bumpy, lumpy, tumorous, *Bot.* torose, bony, carunculate, knobbed; tuberous, warty, verrucose; pimpled, papular; knotty, gnarled, knurled, knarled; protuberant, nodose, nodous, nodular; uneven, rough, unsmooth, unfinished, flawed, blemished.

knock, *v.* **1.** rap, tap, hit, thump, bang, drum, pound, hammer.

2. strike, smite, thwack, smack, cuff, buffet, punch, box, *Scot.* dunt, *Inf.* slug; slap, *Inf.* whack, *Inf.* clout, *Inf.* wallop, *Inf.* crown, *Sl.* conk, *Sl.* bop, *Sl.* belt, *Sl.* sock; beat, batter, pound, lay on, pommel, pummel, pelt.

3. collide with, impact, crash against, smash into, dash against; jolt, jostle, jar, bang into *or* against; bump, run into, meet head-on, percuss.

4. *Informal.* cavil, carp, find fault, peck at, *Inf.* nitpick, pick apart, pick to pieces, *Inf.* pick holes in, *Sl.* cut up *or* to pieces, haul over the coals, criticize, judge; shoot down, run down, put down, *Inf.* pan, *Inf.* slam, attack; deprecate, minimize, *Sl.* badmouth.

5. **knock around** *or* **about** *Slang.* **a.** wander, *Inf.* traipse, range, ramble, rove, *Sl.* bat around, kick around; gad about, gallivant, run about; jaunt, stroll, saunter. **b.** loiter, loaf, idle, waste time, slack off, *Sl.* goof off; take it easy, vegetate. **c.** mistreat, maltreat, ill-treat, abuse; manhandle, maul, batter, beat up, *Archaic.* belabor; harm, damage, bruise, wound, hurt, injure.

6. **knock down** **a.** fell, level, floor, raze; wreak, destroy, break up, smash, demolish, lay in ruins, devastate; hew down, cut down, bring down, pull down, cast down, throw down, fling down. **b.** *Informal.* lower the price of, reduce, put on sale.

7. **knock off** *Slang.* **a.** stop work, call it a day, call it quits, quit, close shop, lock up, shut down. **b.** finish, terminate, conclude, draw to a close, bring to an end, dispose of. **c.** kill, slay, assassinate, get rid of, put out of the way, silence, finish off; *All Sl.* off, hit, zap, waste, bump off, polish off, rub out. **d.** die, expire, give up the ghost, *Sl.* croak, *Sl.* go west.

8. **knock out** render unconscious, *Boxing.* flatten, prostrate, floor, k.o., knock [s.o.] galley-west; defeat, trounce, overthrow.

9. **knock up** **a.** damage, mar, impair, spoil. **b.** injure, wound, hurt, bruise; beat up, pound, batter. **c.** *Slang.* impregnate, get with child *or* young.

—*n.* **10.** rap, tap, hit, thump, bang, pound, pounding, hammering.

11. blow, bastinado, punch, box, *All Boxing.* left, right, jab; *Inf.* wallop, *Inf.* whomp, douse, *Sl.* conk, *Sl.* hash, *U.S. Sl.* biff, *Sl.* buff, *Sl.* bop; buffet, cuff, strike, slap, smack, thwack, *Inf.* whack, *Inf.* clout.

12. thud, bump, clash, crash, impact, collision.

13. *Informal.* criticism, stricture, castigation, animadversion, *Inf.* slam; censuring, condemnation, reprehension; insinuation, implication, imputation; vilification, aspersion, traducement, calumniation, calumny, obloquy, slur, slap in the face.

knoll, *n.* hillock, hummock, hill, (*in South Africa*) kopje, *Chiefly Brit.* barrow, elevation, mound, eminence; dune, sandhill, swell, wave; molehill, anthill, bump, hump, knob, protuberance, protuberancy, bulge.

knot, *n.* **1.** interlacement, intertwinement, loop, twist, bend, tie, plexus; slipknot, bowline; bowtie, Windsor knot.

2. frog, bow, rosette, aiguillette, aglet, epaulet.

3. cluster, bunch, clump; gathering, throng, crowd, mob; company, crew, group, band, gang; set, circle, ring; aggregation, agglomeration, assemblage, mass, pile, heap.

4. gnarl, hump, lump, knob; knur, knar, knurl, nurl; nub, node, nodule, boss, protuberance, button.

5. perplexity, problem, dilemma, horns of a dilemma; conundrum, riddle, puzzle, jigsaw puzzle, poser, Rosetta stone; Gordian knot, tough nut to crack, tangled web; intricacy, complexity, complication; labyrinth, maze, tortuosity.

—*v.* **6.** tangle, entangle, entwine, twist, ravel, knit, screw.

7. tie, bind, secure, clinch; lash, leash, truss, tether, hogtie; noose, lasso, rope.

8. gnarl, contort, distort, warp, bend, disfigure, deform.

knotty, *adj.* **1.** gnarled, gnarly, nodose, lumpy, bumpy; knarry, knurled, knarred; warped, contorted, distorted, cross-grained; bossy, protuberant, carunculated; coarse, rough, uneven, unpolished, flawed, blemished.

2. tangled, entangled, raveled, twisted, convoluted, involute, mazelike, labyrinthine; anfractuous, sinuous, tortuous, winding; jumbled up, garbled, chaotic; complex, intricate, Byzantine, complicated, kaleidoscopic, daedal; perplexing, mystifying, baffling, puzzling, enigmatic; arduous, difficult, thorny, trying, tough; formidable, Herculean, obscure, crabbed, unfathomable, *Inf.* tough to figure, *Inf.* nasty.

know, *v.* **1.** comprehend, realize, *Inf.* get through one's head, *Inf.* have the hang of, grasp, *Inf.* lay hold of, *Inf.* catch on, *Sl.* latch onto, *Inf.* get a fix on, *Inf.* get it, *Inf.* have it; understand, fathom, penetrate, *Sl.* savvy; discern, make out, *Inf.* make heads or tails of, perceive, apprehend, receive, sense, recognize, see, see through, see the light, get the picture, read, read [s.o.] like a book, *Brit.* twig.

2. possess, have memorized, have learned by heart; have stored, have in one's head, have at one's fingertips, have at the tip of one's tongue; know inside out, know backward and forward, know backwards, know down to the ground, know from A to Z, *Brit.* know from A to Zed.

3. cognize, be cognizant of, *Chiefly Scot.* ken, be aware of, be conscious of, be enlightened, be familiar with, appreciate.

4. be intimate with, be thick with, be close to, fraternize with, be amiable with, be friends with, socialize with; be in the good graces of, be on good terms with, be on good footing with, have dealings with, be conversant with, have the ear of.

5. *Usu.* **know how to** remember, recall, recollect; have expertise in, be accomplished in, have experience in, have know-how, have savoir-faire, have the knack, be sophisticated about; be aware, be worldly, be worldly-wise, have savoir-vivre, *Sl.* be hip, *Sl.* be with it, *Sl.* be on the ball.

6. distinguish, discriminate, know which is which, know a hawk from a handsaw, *Inf.* tell day from night.

7. **know the ropes** *Inf.* have down pat, *Inf.* have down cold, *Inf.* know one's stuff, *Sl.* know one's onions.

—*n.* **8.** cognizance, awareness. See **knowledge**.

9. **in the know** privy to, *Inf.* tipped off, *Inf.* having the low-down. See **knowledgeable** (*defs.* **2, 3**).

knowable, *adj.* **1.** comprehensible, cognizable, cognoscible, conceivable, realizable, intelligible, understandable, fathomable, penetrable; ascertainable, discoverable, acquirable, learnable, memorizable.

2. discernible, perceptible, apprehensible, appreciable, legible, decipherable; recognizable, conspicuous, observable, noticeable, seeable, visible, material, sensible.

3. apparent, distinct, unambiguous, unequivocal, express, explicit; defined, clear, crystal clear, clear as day; unclouded, unobscure, unobscured, undisguised, unscreened; transparent, transpicuous, obvious, evident, manifest, unmistakable, clear cut, plain, plain as day, plain as the nose on your face; palpable, patent, ostensible; bare, naked, uncloaked, undraped, uncovered, uncurtained, unshrouded, unveiled, unmasked; exposed, revealed, disclosed, unconcealed; luminous, lucid, perspicuous, translucent, pellucid.

know-how, *n.* **1.** expertise, knowledge, expertness, savoir-faire, mastery, experience; proficiency, adeptness, capableness, capability, competence.

2. faculty, ability, ableness, talent, gift, the stuff, *Inf.* what it takes, *U.S. Inf.* the goods; skill, skillfulness, art, technique, execution, trick, hang, knack, flair; dexterity, dexterousness, adroitness, deftness, handiness.

knowing, *adj.* **1.** shrewd, smart, sagacious, *Archaic.* parlous, *Sl.* savvy; ingenious, clever, canny, subtle, *Inf.* cute; artful, crafty, cunning, wily, foxy; astute, keen, acute, sharp, sharp-witted, sharp as a tack.

2. revealing, secretive, *Obs.* abstruse; privy to, *Sl.* in the know, *Inf.* tipped off, *Inf.* having the low-down.

3. profound, deep, intelligent, intelligential, brainy; erudite, scholarly, literary, lettered, enlightened, cultured, cultivated; learned, knowledgeable, versed, well-read, well-informed, well-posted, well-educated, well-schooled, well-instructed, well-taught; discerning, perspicacious, perceptive, percipient, apperceptive; sage, wise, sapient, sapiential, Solomonic, gash; rational, logical, reasonable; judicious, circumspect, prudent, politic, discreet, sensible, sound.

4. aware, sophisticated, worldly, worldly wise, *Sl.* wise, *Fr. au courant, Sl.* hip, *Sl.* with it, *Sl.* on the ball.

5. intentional, intended, deliberate, willful, purposeful, on purpose, by design; conscious, cognizant, witting, sensible, meaning.

knowingly, *adv.* intentionally, with intent, deliberately, willfully, purposefully, on purpose; designedly, by design, determinedly, calculatedly, studiously, studiedly; wittingly, mindfully, consciously, with one's eyes wide open, meaningfully.

know-it-all, *n.* **1.** fountain of knowledge, mine of information, storehouse, *Inf.* walking encyclopedia, Sir Oracle, aphorist, *Inf.* know-all; egotist, egoist, egomaniac; *Sl.* blow-hard, blusterer, swaggerer, braggart, boaster, ranter, *Sl.* mouth, *Sl.* windbag.

—adj. **2.** pretentious, arrogant, inflated, egotistical, egomaniacal, conceited; oracular, sententious; blustery, blusterous, swaggering, bragging, boastful, ranting, mouthy, talkative.

knowledge, *n.* **1.** erudition, scholarship, education, schooling, instruction, tuition, learning, letters, book learning; sciolism, smattering.

2. acquaintance, familiarity, conversance, intimacy; intelligence, sense, understanding, *Sl.* savvy, appreciation, appreciativeness; sophistication, expertise, expertness, proficiency, adeptness; experience, know-how, savoir-faire.

3. awareness, consciousness, *Obs.* conscience, cognizance, ken; knowingness, certainty, determination, assuredness, positiveness; conviction, avowal, affirmation, belief, opinion, judgment; instinct, second sense, foreknowledge, foresight, prescience.

4. cognition, comprehension, discernment, conception, grasp, *Inf.* fix; perception, apprehension, intuition, sixth sense, impression; recognition, notice, detection, discovery, lesson; insight, realization, enlightenment, revelation; admission, acknowledgment.

5. information, facts, data, news, tidings, word; sidelight, gossip, hearsay, rumor, *Inf.* scuttlebutt, talk; intelligence, privity, inside information, *Inf.* low-down, *Sl.* dope, tip, *Inf.* tip-off.

6. pantology, truths, verities, realities, principles, laws; literature, letters, lore, legend; sciences, humanities.

knowledgeable, *adj.* **1.** erudite, punditic, scholarly, academic, educated, well-educated; cultured, learned, *Archaic.* studied, literate, lettered, versed, well-read, well-informed; intelligent, brainy, sharp, understanding.

2. aware, appreciative, appreciatory, appreciating, conscious, cognizant, sensible; enlightened, knowing, *Sl.* wise, *Sl.* in the know, sophisticated, worldly, worldly-wise, *Sl.* hip, *Sl.* with it, *Fr. au courant, Sl.* on the ball; acquainted, familiar, up, conversant, intimate.

3. expert, proficient, adept, skilled, skillful; experienced, practiced, accomplished, *Inf.* knowing the ropes, *Sl.* savvy, *Fr. au fait;* capable, able, competent.

4. perceptive, percipient, discerning, penetrating, perspicacious, insightful; sage, sagacious, sapient, Solomonic, wise, gash; rational, reasonable, logical; judicious, prudent, politic, discreet, sensible; commonsensical, having a good head on one's shoulders.

known, *adj.* **1.** comprehended, cognized, conceived, realized, grasped, *Chiefly Scot.* kenned; understood, fathomed, penetrated, appreciated; discerned, perceived, apprehended, sensed, received, recognized, seen; possessed, memorized, learned; determined, ascertained, computed, figured, reckoned, estimated.

2. recognized, familiar, household, famous, well-known, celebrated, noted; prominent, on the map, public, popular, exoteric, prevalent, proverbial; notorious, infamous, ill-famed; commonplace, hackneyed, trite, banal, stale.

3. acknowledged, avowed, confessed, admitted, declared, proclaimed, blazoned, heralded; published, aired, vented, publicized, advertised; exposed, revealed, disclosed, unconcealed, discovered, come to light; uncloaked, undraped, uncovered, uncurtained, unshrouded, unveiled, unmasked; unclouded, unobscure, unobscured, undisguised, unscreened; clear, crystal clear, clear as day; clear cut, plain, plain as day, plain as the nose on your face; obvious, evident, manifest, transparent, transpicuous; palpable, patent, ostensible.

know-nothing, *n.* **1.** ignoramus, dunce, dolt, fool, thickhead, blockhead, Mortimer Snerd; idiot, moron, imbecile; dupe, gull, greenhorn; *All Inf.* stupid, knucklehead, muttonhead, woodenhead, chump; *All Sl.* sap, jerk, stupe, numskull, fathead, clodpate, hammerhead, bonehead, dumbbell, dummy, dum-dum, boob, one numb from the neck up *or* with nothing upstairs.

2. agnostic, doubter, skeptic, disbeliever, unbeliever, nullifidian; questioner, cynic, doubting Thomas, Pyrrhonist; atheist, free-thinker.

knuckle, *n.* **1.** finger joint, knucklebone; joint, articulation, geniculation; angle, bend, crook, hook.

2. joint of meat, cut of meat.

—v. **3. knuckle down** *Informal.* apply oneself, exert oneself, lay oneself out, put oneself out; buckle down, get down to, put one's nose to the grindstone, go at; take the bull by the horns, put one's shoulder to the wheel; launch into, launch upon, fire away; get going, get busy, get into.

4. knuckle under defer to, be regulated by, be governed by, be subject to; stoop, bend to, bow to, truckle to, humble oneself to, bend the knee to, knuckle to, do [s.o.'s] bidding; yield, surrender, give in, give way to; capitulate, succumb to, fall, raise the white flag, cry *or* say uncle; resign oneself, acquiesce, throw in the towel, give up the ship, cease the struggle, grin and bear it.

knurled, *adj.* **1.** ridged, notched, corrugated, milled, serrated.

2. knurly, gnarled, gnarly, knotty, knarred, knarry, nodose; lumpy, bumpy, humpy, nodulous; warty, papillose, tuberous; bossed, embossed, chased, caruncular.

kosher, *adj.* **1.** *Informal.* genuine, real, *Dial.* sure-enough, simon-pure, pure, sterling; the real McCoy; bonafide, veritable, *Inf.* honest-to-goodness, *Archaic.* authentical, *Australian.* dinkum.

2. *Informal.* legitimate, rightful, lawful, just, legal, licit; standard, accepted, approved, conventional, orthodox, according to Hoyle; proper, acceptable, fitting, fit; permitted, allowed, OK'd.

kowtow, *v.* **1.** bow, kneel before, salaam, genuflect; prostrate oneself, fall on one's knees, lie prone, throw oneself at the feet of; humble oneself to, defer to, stoop, get down.

2. bow and scrape, grovel, truckle to, fawn; lickspittle, lick [s.o.'s] shoes, lick *or* kiss [s.o.'s] feet, kiss the hem of [s.o.'s] garment, *Sl.* bootlick; court, pay court to, curry favor, keep time to, dance attendance upon, be at [s.o.'s] beck and call, Uncle Tom, Tom, agree to anything; toady, toady to, *Sl.* fall all over; *Sl.* shine up to, play up to, *Sl.* suck up to, *Inf.* apple-polish, butter-up, *Sl.* brown-nose.

kudos, *n.* **1.** praise, extolment, laudation, acclaim, acclamation, *Archaic.* magnification; approval, approbation, endorsement, sanction, commendation; tribute, credit, recognition, citation; congratulation, *Archaic.* gratulation, compliment, flattery, puffery, bouquet; applause, cheering, clapping, plaudits, salvo, accolade.

2. glory, honor, dignity; fame, renown, distinction, popularity, popular favor; prestige, notability.

L

label, *n.* **1.** tag, ticket, *Brit.* docket, tab, sticker, identification, ID, earmark; stamp, brand, mark, hallmark, plate mark, imprint.
2. epithet, nickname, sobriquet, *Inf.* pet name; name, denomination, designation, appellation, style, title; description, portrayal, characterization.
3. motto, catch phrase, catchword, slogan.
4. brand, trademark, logo; symbol, sign, badge, representation, seal, emblem, crest.
—*v.* **5.** tag, ticket, put a label on, put a sticker on; mark, stamp, brand, hallmark, imprint.
6. indentify, call, name, denominate, title, entitle, designate, term, style, dub, nickname; describe, portray, characterize.
7. classify, class, group, categorize, pigeonhole, *Sl.* peg.

labor, *n.* **1.** work, employment, job, occupation, living, livelihood, means of support.
2. toil, travail, sweat of one's brow, moil, drudgery, grind, menial work; hard work *or* toil, hard labor, slavery; exertion, effort, strain, struggle, laboriousness, plodding, *Inf.* plugging, pegging; industry, industriousness, operoseness, diligence.
3. workers, laborers, workmen, hands, working men and women, employees; working class, proletariat. See **laborer.**
4. job, commission, task, chore, odd job, errand; duty, charge, assignment, mission; function, role, activity, business, affair; undertaking, enterprise, business venture.
5. travail, labor pains *or* pangs, contractions, throes; parturition, delivery, childbirth, birth.
—*v.* **6.** work *or* work hard, toil, moil, drudge, grub, grind; work one's fingers to the bone, slave *or* slave away, work like a slave, work like a Trojan, *Sl.* kill oneself; work day and night, burn the midnight oil, burn the candle at both ends, overdo, overwork, overexert oneself; sweat, struggle, *Sl.* beat one's brains out; peg away at, *Inf.* plug away at, keep trying, plod along; force oneself, push oneself, make oneself, strain oneself, exert oneself, make an effort, work at, apply oneself to; ply one's trade, work away at, be busy with, be employed at, occupy oneself with.
7. **labor for** strive for *or* towards, work for *or* towards; endeavor to, attempt to, try to, make an *or* every effort, do all that is humanly possible, do one's best, do one's utmost, do all one can.
8. be in labor, be in travail, undergo pain, suffer; give birth to, bear, deliver.
9. roll, pitch, heave, toss, turn.
10. belabor, dwell on, *Inf.* beat into the ground, overdo; elaborate, develop, expound on, expand on.
11. burden, load *or* load down, overload, overburden; tire, fatigue, fag, weary, exhaust, *Sl.* do in, wear out, *U.S. Inf.* tucker out, take all one's strength, *Sl.* zap.

laboratory, *n.* lab, proving *or* testing ground; language lab, photography lab, *Inf.* photo lab, darkroom; studio, atelier, workshop, workroom, practice room, study.

labored, *adj.* **1.** heavy, difficult, strained, forced, laborious.
2. elaborate, involved, intricate, complicated, complex; excessive, overdone, overworked, overwrought, ornate; formal, affected, stiff, unnatural, artificial.

laborer, *n.* worker, hand, workman, toiler, moiler, drudge, unskilled laborer, manual laborer, blue-collar worker, *Inf.* hardhat, (*in the Southern U.S.*) *Disparaging.* redneck; employee, help, hired hand, hireling, servant; working man *or* woman, wage earner, skilled laborer, white-collar worker, professional.

laborious, *adj.* **1.** toilsome, toilful, difficult, uphill, tough, hard; heavy, burdensome, hefty, weighty; arduous, strenuous, straining, exertive, vigorous; tiring, tiresome, fatiguing, wearying, wearisome, tedious, weariful, wearing.
2. careful, painstaking, precise, exact, detailed, particular, scrupulous, thorough; hard-working, industrious, diligent, operose, earnest, zealous, energetic; unflagging, unfailing, untiring, tireless, indefatigable; persistent, persevering, pertinacious, dogged, tenacious, unrelenting, relentless; assiduous, sedulous, constant, unremitting, steady; unswerving, undeviating, steadfast, plodding, *Inf.* plugging.
3. labored, heavy, difficult, strained, forced.

laboriously, *adv.* **1.** toilsomely, toilfully, by the sweat of one's brow; with difficulty, toughly, heavily, burdensomely, heftily; arduously, vigorously, strainingly; wearingly, wearisomely, tediously, wearifully.
2. carefully, painstakingly, precisely, exactly, particularly, in detail, scrupulously, thoroughly; industriously, diligently, operosely, earnestly, zealously, energetically; unflaggingly, unfailingly, untiringly, tirelessly, indefatigably; persistently, ploddingly, perseveringly, unswervingly, undeviatingly, steadfastly; pertinaciously, doggedly, tenaciously, unrelentingly, relentlessly; assiduously, sedulously, constantly, unremittingly, steadily.

labyrinth, *n.* **1.** maze, garden maze, winding path, winding course, circuitous course, webwork, complicated arrangement; convolution, circumvolution, winding, windings and turnings, meander, meanderings and turnings; *Anat.* inner ear.

2. mystery, enigma, riddle, puzzle, Gordian knot, knotty problem; intricacy, intricate state, confused situation, difficulty, complication, complexity, tangle, tangled skein.

labyrinthian, *adj.* **1.** labyrinthine, labyrinthlike, mazelike, mazy; meandering, wandering, circuitous; circumlocutory, *Inf.* roundabout, daedal, Daedalian, Daedalic.

2. intricate, complicated, complex, involved, Byzantine; involute, involuted, convolute, convoluted; tortuous, twisted, gnarled, tangled, tangly, entangled, knotty, Gordian, raveled, snarled.

3. confusing, puzzling, perplexing, mystifying, enigmatic; confounding, bewildering, baffling, unsoluble, unsolvable.

lace, *n.* **1.** tatting, lacework, crochet, needlework, fancywork; openwork, network, net, netting, meshwork, mesh, filigree, web, cobweb, *Zool.* webbing; arabesque, ornamentation, decoration, embellishment, adornment; ribbon, braid, braiding, cordon, trim, trimming.

2. cord, tie, string, lacing; shoestring, shoelace, thong, *Archaic.* latchet; lanyard, twine, cording, yarn, cable.

—*v.* **3.** thread, string, lace up; tie, truss, sew *or* stitch together; hitch, fasten, bind, clinch, secure.

4. trim, edge, rim, ribbon; adorn, decorate, ornament, embellish.

5. infuse, mix in, pour in, blend in, fold in, add to, streak *or* intermix *or* intermingle with, interweave, shoot through with, dope, *Inf.* spike, strengthen, stiffen, fortify.

6. *Often* **lace into** assail, vituperate, revile, rail against, inveigh against, belabor, *Inf.* sail into, *Inf.* jump on, *Inf.* jump down [s.o.'s] throat, *Sl.* jump all over, *Sl.* strafe; scold, tongue-lash, rate, slate, lay into, harangue, rant at, rave at, *Archaic.* clapperclaw; upbraid, objurgate, excoriate, fulminate against, flay, *Inf.* dress down, *Inf.* slam.

7. *Often* **lace into** whip, horsewhip, flail, lash, thrash, thresh, flagellate, spank, beat; strap, belt, switch, birch, *Inf.* whale, *Inf.* welt; attack, assault, abuse, set upon, pounce upon, fall on, light into, *Inf.* rip into, *Inf.* tear into, *Sl.* let [s.o.] have it, *Sl.* zap.

lacerate, *v.* tear, rend, gash, slash, cut, slice, stab; mangle, deface, mutilate; hurt, wound, pain.

lacerated, *adj.* **1.** torn, rent, cut, slit, slashed, gashed, split, jagged, ragged, jaggy, erose; mangled, mutilated, damaged, impaired.

2. wounded, bruised, hurt, injured, harmed; pained, aching, tortured, tormented, agonized.

laceration, *n.* **1.** tearing, ripping, rending; slashing, gashing, cutting, wounding.

2. tear, rent, rip; gash, slash, cut, scratch; mutilation, wound, gouge, lancination.

lachrymation, *n.* weeping, crying, shedding *or* dropping tears; watering, tearing, moistening, overflowing, running; fit of weeping, *Inf.* a good cry, flood of tears.

lachrymose, *adj.* **1.** tearful, teary, *Inf.* weepy; close to tears, ready to cry *or* break down, with tears in the eyes, on the verge of tears, with brimming *or* overflowing eyes; melting, giving way, ready to burst into tears, breaking down; weeping, crying, sobbing, blubbering, sniveling; lachrymal, lachrymatory.

2. mournful, woeful, distressing, dismaying, dolorous, lugubrious; lamentable, pitiable, piteous, pathetic; touching, moving, affecting, poignant, saddening.

lacing, *n.* **1.** lace, string, cord, tie; shoelace, shoestring, thong, lanyard, *Archaic.* latchet; twine, cording, cable, yarn.

2. lacework, tatting, filigree; braiding, braid, cordon. See **lace** (*def.* **1**).

3. whipping, horsewhipping, flailing, lashing, flagellation; thrashing, threshing, spanking, strapping, belting, switching, birching, beating, *Inf.* whaling, *Inf.* welting.

lack, *n.* **1.** want, deficiency, deprivation, need; absence, nonexistence, emptiness, void, vacancy; something missing, missing ingredient *or* link; omission, gap, hole, break, discontinuity, interval, deletion, hiatus, lacuna.

2. shortcoming, inadequacy, imperfection, inferiority, deficit, insufficiency, short measure; defectiveness, impairment, incompleteness, unevenness, patchiness, sketchiness; shortage, scarcity, scarceness, dearth, meagerness, sparsity, scantiness, paucity; poverty, impoverishment, destitution, famine, malnutrition, hunger, starvation, drought; wantage, underage, defalcation, arrearage, outage, ullage.

3. fault, defect, kink, flaw, crack, rift, weakness, frailty, failing, foible, weak point, chink in one's armor, weak link, Achilles' heel; mediocrity, underdevelopment, immaturity, inferiority, second-ratedness; decline, slump, failure.

—*v.* **4.** need, require, find necessary; want, fall short of, miss, feel the want of, stand in need of.

5. fall short, not measure up, not reach, not make it, be found wanting, not pass muster, not bear inspection; fall flat, fall down, come to nothing *or* naught, fizzle out, go up in smoke, be tried and found wanting, not be sufficient, not fill the bill, not answer; come short, run short, not reach the mark, not come up to par *or* to the mark, *Sl.* not cut *or* hack it, *Inf.* not make the grade, *Inf.* not come up to scratch; decline, collapse, lag, slump; lose ground, stop short, fail.

lackadaisical, *adj.* **1.** listless, languid, languorous, spiritless, enervated; lethargic, sluggish, soporific, hebetudinous, lentitudinous; somnolent, oscitant, dopey, dull, heavy, leaden.

2. lazy, idle, idlish, loafing, laggard, indolent, otiose, slothful; inactive, torpid, supine, do-nothing, fainéant, inert, passive; shiftless, unambitious, unaspiring, unenterprising, dronish.

3. carefree, easygoing, insouciant, devil-may-care; nonchalant, blasé, indifferent, neuter, neutral, lukewarm, unimpressed, uninterested, unconcerned, unsolicitous, pococurante; careless, thoughtless, disregardful, disregardant, regardless, respectless.

4. apathetic, impassive, insensible, phlegmatic, lymphatic; unexcited, unexcitable, unemotional, unfeeling, uninspired, unaffected, unanimated, unstirred, untouched, unmoved, unruffled, imperturbable; soulless, numb, numbed, cold, frigid, icy, heartless, passionless.

5. dreamy, woolgathering, pensive, soulful, preoccupied, abstracted, distracted.

lackey, *n.* **1.** footman, steward, house steward, seneschal, factotum, butler, major-domo, waiter, *Fr. garçon*; servant, liveried servant, footboy, page, *Brit.* boots, *Brit.* buttons; valet, man, gentleman, manservant, *Archaic.* varlet, *Fr. valet du chambre, Fr. valet de pied;* help, domestic, domestic servant, household servant *or* help, *Brit. Inf.* slavey, *Fr. bonne à tout faire*; kitchenman, scullion; hired man, man of all work, menial; groom, equerry, livery, hostler, ostler, groomsman, stableman, stableboy; flunky, servitor, yeoman, retainer, pensionary, pensioner, pursuivant, follower; squire, courtier, *Scot.* gillie, helot, acolyte, thrall, vassal, leigeman, cupbearer, trainbearer, bearer, usher; attendant, escort, accompanier, companion, shadow, *Sl.* gofer; assistant, ancilla, helper, apprentice, boy, office boy; bellboy, bellhop, bootblack, caddie, hireling, mercenary, bondsman, bondman, bond slave.

2. underling, inferior; tool, puppet, instrument, creature, pawn, cat's paw, rubber stamp, doormat, footstool, *Sl.* stooge, dupe, gull, patsy; toady, toadeater, sycophant, fawner, flatterer, truckler, tufthunter, wheedler, puffer, backslapper, backscratcher, timeserver, *Inf.* apple-polisher, *Sl.* brown-nose, *Sl.* brownnoser, *Sl.* brownie, *Obs., Rare.* blander, *Archaic.* pickthank; parasite, leech, *Inf.* sponge *or* sponger, hanger-on; yes-man, jackal, spaniel, bootlick, bootlicker, footlicker, lickspit, lickspittle, kowtower, Uncle Tom, *Sl.* oreo; cringer, groveler, sniveler.

lacking, *prep.* **1.** without, wanting, in want of, sans; destitute of, short of; for want of.

—*adj.* **2.** deficient, needing, missing, shy; imperfect, defective, flawed, impaired, incomplete, unfinished; inadequate, insufficient, unsatisfactory, mediocre, inferior, unsuitable, incommensurate, incapable, incompetent, not up to par, not up to snuff, unable to measure up, unequal to, unqualified.

lackluster, *adj.* **1.** tasteless, bland, insipid, jejune, flat, dull, vapid, *Sl.* nothing, *Sl.* blah; uneventful, humdrum, monotonous, ordinary, run-of-the-mill, commonplace, prosaic, matter-of-fact; tedious, tiresome, boring, boresome, wearisome, uninteresting, *Sl.* dead, dry, dry-as-dust.

2. dingy, dark, dim, dun, dusky; drab, dismal, dreary, cheerless; colorless, tarnished, faded, washed-out; deadened, dulled, muted, muffled; shadowy, gloomy, tenebrous, obscure; murky, hazy; smutchy, dirty, grimy, soiled, muddy; shabby, seedy, worn, run-down, sloppy, crummy.

3. unresponsive, passionless, indifferent, uncaring; sluggish, phlegmatic, lethargic, torpid, heavy, lifeless; languid, listless, spiritless, apathetic; inactive, inert, stagnant; lazy, oscitant, drowsy.

4. unimaginative, undiscerning, unintelligent, witless, slow-witted, dull-witted; dense, thick-headed, *Inf.* thick, slow, stupid; backward, doltish, simple; empty-headed, vacuous.

laconic, *adj.* concise, brief, terse, succinct; summary, short, short and sweet, neat; pithy, to the point, pointed, blunt, crisp; elliptical, economical; incisive, trenchant, keen, sharp, biting; unloquacious, untalkative, of few words, ungarrulous; silent, quiet, unspeaking, mum, close-mouthed, mute; reticent, reserved, secretive, taciturn, uncommunicative.

laconism, *n.* **1.** conciseness, brevity, terseness, succinctness, brachylogy; shortness, pithiness, pointedness, incisiveness; silence, taciturnity, reticence.

2. aphorism, gnome, apothegm, maxim, motto, catch phrase; mot, witticism, quip, epigram; saw, saying.

lacquer, *n.* **1.** Chinese lacquer, varnish, japan, shellac; enamel, glaze, coating, finish, veneer; lac, resin, rosin, colophony, oleoresin.

—*v.* **2.** lacker, japan, varnish, shellac; enamel, glaze, luster; coat, cover, veneer, paint, finish.

3. gloss, gloze, smooth; explain away, excuse; extenuate, soften, palliate, mitigate; color, whitewash.

lacuna, *n.* gap, hiatus, opening, hole, cavity, gulf, *Prosody.* caesura, omission; break, rift, crack, fissure; space, interstice, interval, interspace, interruption, intermission, interim.

lacy, *adj.* lacelike, filigree, filigreed, tatted, crocheted; meshy, meshed, netlike, webby, weblike, cobwebby, open; delicate, fine, sheer, thin, light, lightweight, gossamer, gossamery, gauzy, gauzelike; diaphanous, transparent, translucent, see-through.

lad, *n.* **1.** boy, youth, young man, *Irish Eng.* gossoon, *Fr. garçon, Scot.* laddie, *Inf.* laddo; young fellow, son, *Inf.* sonny, *Inf.* sonnyboy, *Inf.* tad, master, *Inf.* shaver, *Inf.* little shaver; hobbledehoy, schoolboy, stripling; urchin, street urchin, gamin; cub, whelp, pup, puppy; young one, *Dial.* young'un, youngster, *Inf.* kid, *Inf.* sprout, *Inf.* young sprout, *Inf.* sprig; whippersnapper, brat; chip off the old block, junior.

2. *Informal.* chap, guy, fellow, *Dial.* feller, *Brit.* cove, pal, chum, joker.

ladder, *n.* **1.** stairs, stairway, stepladder, library steps, folding ladder; companionway, rigging, scaling ladder, fire escape; *All Naut.* jack ladder, pilot ladder, Jacob's ladder.

2. ascent, upward mobility; hierarchy, scale, stratification, social order *or* organization, pecking order.

lade, *v.* **1.** load, laden, stevedore, freight, pack, stow; fill *or* fill up, cram, pack in, pile in.

2. burden, encumber, charge, weigh down, overburden, overload.

3. ladle, dip, scoop up, draw up, lift up. See **ladle** (*def.* **2**).

laden, *adj.* burdened, loaded, weighted, encumbered, charged, weighed down, heavy-laden; full, filled, *Archaic.* fraught, replete; saturated, filled to the gills *or* brim, topful, brimful, brimming, filled to overflowing; chockfull, cram-full, stuffed, jammed, packed.

la-di-da, *adj. Informal.* **1.** affected, mannered, unnatural, artificial, foppish, excessively refined; pretentious, show-offish, conceited, snobbish, snobby, *Inf.* snooty, *Inf.* snotty.

—*n.* **2.** affected behavior, unnaturalness, artificialness, artificiality, foppishness; pretentiousness, show-offishness, conceitedness, snobbishness, snobbiness, snobbery, *Inf.* snootiness, *Inf.* snottiness.

3. dandy, jack-a-dandy, fop, coxcomb, exquisite, *Sl.* swell.

lading, *n.* cargo, freight, freightage, haul, load, burden, charge, weight; shipment, shipload, boatload, wagonload, cartload, truckload, *Chiefly U.S.* carload; contents, merchandise, goods, stuff, baggage, bags, luggage, boxes.

ladle, *n.* **1.** dipper, scoop, spoon; bail, bailer, bucket, vessel, container, receptacle.

—*v.* **2.** dip, scoop *or* scoop up, draw up, lift up, raise up; spoon out, dish up *or* out, shovel out, bail out, bail, bucket up *or* out; (*all with a ladle*) transfer, convey, carry.

lady, *n.* **1.** gentlewoman, noblewoman, milady, dona, donna, (*in India*) begum; countess, duchess, marchioness, margravine, archduchess, viscountess, peeress, baroness; princess, maharanee, (*in India*) ranee, queen, empress, czarina, czarevna, first lady.

2. woman, female, matron, *Sl.* dame; madame, madam, Mrs., Ms., mistress, *Chiefly Scot.* goodwife, senora, senhora, *Ger. Frau*, signora, (*in India*) memsahib; young lady, mademoiselle, miss, senhorita, senorita, signorina; young woman, *Sl.* chick, girl, little miss, *Inf.* filly.

3. wife, woman, *Inf.* little woman, *Sl.* better half; helpmate, spouse, mate, partner.

—*adj.* **4.** female, feminine, woman.

ladylike, *adj.* **1.** womanlike, womanly, womanish, feminine, female.

2. gentlewomanly, noble, genteel, aristocratic, high-class, wellborn; refined, cultured, cultivated, polished, finished; dignified, courtly, stately, elegant, queenly; respectable, matronly, matronal, proper, correct, formal, decorous; well-bred, well brought up, well-behaved, well-mannered, mannerly; mild-mannered, gentle, nice, considerate, gracious, well-spoken, polite, courteous, civil, kind.

ladylove, *n.* sweetheart, heartthrob, truelove, love of one's life, love, *Inf.* flame, *Fr. amour;* darling, beloved, angel, idol, apple of one's eye, pet, sweet, precious, jewel, dear one, honey; girlfriend, girl, best girl, steady, *Sl.* baby, woman, *Sl.* old lady; lover, paramour, *Fr. amante*, inamorata, *Fr. intime*; mistress, *Archaic.* doxy, concubine, *Fr. covivante*, kept-woman.

lag, *v.* **1.** loiter, linger, dally, dillydally, waste time, trifle, idle, dawdle, *Sl.* mess around, tarry, delay, procrastinate, put off; hang back, drag one's feet, shuffle, move slowly, inch along, poke, move at a snail's pace; saunter, stroll, *U.S. Inf.* mosey, take one's time, go leisurely; fall back, fall behind, trail, *Inf.* bring up the rear.

2. flag, wane, ebb, fall off, diminish, decrease; ease *or* let up, abate, slacken, slow up *or* down, decelerate; lose strength, fail, go downhill, falter, faint.

laggard, *n.* **1.** lagger, lingerer, loiterer, lounger, loller, dallier, trifler, dawdler; *Inf.* slowpoke, *Sl.* poke, snail, sluggard; do-nothing, fainéant, idler, drone, *Inf.* bum, *Inf.* lazybones, *Sl.* slugabed.

—adj. **2.** slow, *Inf.* poky, sluggish, backward; slow-moving, *Sl.* draggy, torpid, lethargic; indolent, otiose, slothful, fainéant, idle, lazy.

lagniappe, *n.* bonus, extra, plus, dividend, fringe benefit, perquisite, *Inf.* perk; gratuity, tip, douceur, fee, *Fr. pourboire, Ger. Trinkgeld, Archaic.* vail, (*in Chinese ports*) cumshaw, (*in India, Turkey, etc.*) baksheesh; present, gift, *Inf.* a little something; reward, honorarium, award, prize.

lagoon, *n.* shoal, shallows, *Southern U.S.* bayou, marsh, *Brit.* fen, bog, swamp; pool, pond, lake, tarn, *Chiefly Brit. Dial.* mere; estuary, *Dial.* creek, inlet, arm, sound, loch, *Irish Eng.* lough, fjord, *Both Chiefly Scot.* firth, frith; harbor, cove, bight, basin, gulf.

laic, *adj.* **1.** laical, lay, secular, secularistic, civil, temporal, worldly, profane; nonreligious, unreligious, nonecclesiastic, nonecclesiastical, nonministerial, nonpastoral.

—n. **2.** layman, secular, secularish, nonecclesiastic.

laid-back, *adj. Informal.* relaxed, unhurried, unhasty, easy, leisurely; informal, unceremonious, casual, easygoing, offhand, free and easy; nonchalant, blasé, unexcitable, unflappable, imperturbable, indifferent, unconcerned; lackadaisical, lazy, indolent.

lair, *n.* **1.** den, cave, hollow, dugout, hole, burrow, cavern, tunnel, covert, grotto; niche, nook, cranny, nest, recess; aerie, roost; territory, haunt, purlieu, homeground, preserve.

2. hideaway, hideout, hiding place, retreat, asylum, sanctuary, haven, safehold, stronghold; sanctum, sanctum sanctorum, holy of holies, ivory tower; home, lodge, anchorage, snug harbor, harbor, couch; hermitage, cubicle, cell, cloister, mew; study, library, quiet room, place of one's own.

laissez faire, *n.* free enterprise, free-enterprise system, private enterprise, laissez-faireism; individualism, rugged individualism, free trade, *Inf.* no holds barred; noninterference, nonintervention, nonrestriction, *Fr. laisser-aller, Inf.* hands-off policy; decontrol, deregulation; go-slow policy, wait-and-see policy, live-and-let-live policy, do-nothing policy; do-nothingness, noninvolvement, indifference.

laissez-faire, *adj.* permissive, noninterfering, nonrestrictive, lax, relaxed, loose, *Inf.* hands-off; uninvolved, *Fr. dégagé, Inf.* no strings, *Inf.* do-nothing, *Inf.* live-and-let-live.

laity, *n.* **1.** congregation, parish, worshipers, church members, flock, fold, people.

2. laymen, seculars, secularists, nonecclesiastics.

lake, *n.* pond, pool, lagoon, tarn, basin, reservoir; oxbow lake, bayou lake, glacial lake, volcanic lake, mountain lake, lakelet, pondlet; water hole, fish pond, mill pond, tidal pond *or* pool; *Scot.* loch, *Irish.* lough, *Africa.* nyanza, *Chiefly Brit. Dial.* mere.

lam¹, *v. Slang. Usu.* **lam out** *or* **into** beat, strike, thrash, batter, pound, lay on, pummel, pelt, *Sl.* paste; flog, lash, switch, birch, scourge; strap, thresh, flail, spank, *Inf.* tan [s.o.'s] hide, *Inf.* trim, *Inf.* thump, *Inf.* lace, *Inf.* lambaste, *Inf.* whale, *Sl.* whomp; hit, smite, thwack, slap, smack; punch, knock, cuff, buffet, box, sandbag, *Inf.* clout, *Inf.* slug, *Inf.* whack, crown, *Sl.* conk, *Sl.* bash, *Sl.* belt, *Sl.* sock, *U.S. Sl.* biff, *Sl.* bop; maul, manhandle, rough up, *Inf.* give it to, *Sl.* knock around *or* about, *Sl.* give [s.o.] the business, *Sl.* give [s.o.] the works, *Sl.* give [s.o.] what for, *Sl.* work over, *Sl.* let [s.o.] have it, *Sl.* lay into; cudgel, fustigate, bludgeon, baste, cane, bastinado, club, hammer, sledge hammer; trounce, drub, *Inf.* wallop, *Inf.* whale, *Sl.* clobber, *Sl.* pin [s.o.'s] ears back.

lam², *n. Slang.* **1.** escape, flight, running away, bolting, decampment, *Inf.* making oneself scarce, *Sl.* getting the hell out; *Sl.* disappearing act, *Sl.* hasty retreat, *Sl.* scramming, *Sl.* skedaddle, *Sl.* skedaddling, absquatulation; French leave, absence without leave, AWOL; break, breakout, jailbreak, prisonbreak, *Inf.* getaway.

2. on the lam escaping, fleeing, running for cover, on the run, at liberty; escaped, on the loose, fled, flown, at large, scot-free; hiding, going to earth *or* ground, *Inf.* holing up, in hiding, hidden out, lying hid, *Inf.* lying low.

3. take it on the lam escape, flee, get away, make good one's escape, gain one's liberty, slip away, run off *or* away, run for one's life, take to one's heels, *Inf.* make tracks, *Inf.* make a getaway, *Inf.* cut out *or* cut and run, *Inf.* hightail it; get out, break loose, *Inf.* bail out, *Inf.* leap over the wall, *Inf.* jump, *Inf.* skip, *Sl.* bust loose, *Sl.* fly the coop; break out, break jail, escape from prison.

lamb, *n.* **1.** lambkin, cosset, ewe lamb, yearling, weanling.

2. innocent, ingénue, unsophisticate, simple soul, dove; infant, babe, newborn babe, babe in the woods, child, mere child.

3. dupe, gull, gudgeon, *Brit. Dial.* cull, *Archaic.* cully, *Inf.* chump, *Sl.* sap, *Sl.* schnook, *Sl.* schlemiel, *Sl.* boob; greenhorn, sitting duck, easy *or* soft mark *or* target, *Inf.* sucker, *Inf.* cinch, *Sl.* patsy, *Sl.* pigeon, *U.S. Sl.* fall guy, *Sl.* softie *or* soft touch, *Sl.* pushover; fool, everybody's fool, fair game, *Inf.* goat, *Brit. Sl.* mug.

lambaste, *v.* **1.** *Informal.* beat, thrash, drub, maul, beat black and blue, *Dial.* larrup, *Inf.* lather, *Sl.* shellac; whip, horsewhip, lash, flog, flail, whale, *Inf.* hide, *Inf.* tan, *Inf.* tan [s.o.'s] hide; cane, birch, switch; strike, thump, thwack, bang, *Inf.* clout, *Inf.* wallop, *Inf.* paste, *Inf.* biff, *Sl.* whump, *Sl.* cream; club, cudgel, bludgeon, pummel, buffet, batter, hammer, pulverize, *Archaic.* belabor; punish, chastise, castigate, fustigate.

2. *Informal.* censure, excoriate, scarify, scathe, flay, *Inf.* skin alive, *Inf.* roast; rail at, tongue-lash, *Sl.* jaw; reprove, rebuke, reprimand, scold, chide, admonish, upbraid; *All Inf.* call down, dress down, jump on, jump all over, jump down [s.o.'s] throat, get on [s.o.'s] back, rake *or* haul [s.o.] over the coals; *All Sl.* bawl out, chew out, give what-for.

lambent, *adj.* **1.** lightly touching, barely touching, hardly touching, playing lightly over *or* upon; flitting, dancing, skipping, playing; flickering, licking, fluttering, wavering, quivering.

2. glowing, aglow, incandescent, candescent, luminous, luminant, suffused.

lamblike, *adj.* **1.** meek, mild, gentle, gentle as a lamb, peaceable, pacific, dovelike; passive, submissive, compliant, acquiescent, unresisting; subdued, chastened, tame, broken; resigned, reconciled, long-suffering, longanamous.

2. innocent, ingenuous, artless, guileless, simple; naive, unworldly, unsophisticated; trustful, trusting, unwary, unsuspicious, gullible; childlike, childish, infant, infantile, born yesterday, *Inf.* wet behind the ears.

lame, *adj.* 1. hamstrung, hobbled, hobbling, limping, halt, *Inf.* game, (*of horses*) *Vet. Pathol.* spavined *or Chiefly Scot.* spaviet; crippled, maimed, disabled, incapacitated, injured, impaired, damaged, hurt.

2. weak, feeble, thin, wishy-washy, flimsy, unconvincing; inadequate, insufficient, deficient, wanting, lacking; unsatisfactory, unsatisfying, inferior, mediocre, displeasing, disappointing, no good, not good enough; poor, clumsy, ineffective, ineffectual, inefficacious, of no effect, half-baked, *Sl.* half-assed.

—*v.* 3. hamstring, hobble, wing; disable, incapacitate, maim, cripple; injure, hurt, damage.

lament, *v.* 1. mourn, mourn for, sorrow, grieve, grieve for, feel for, be *or* feel sorry for, weep for, pity; condole, commiserate, compassionate, sympathize; deplore, bewail, bemoan, moan, groan, *Inf.* sing *or* cry the blues; regret, repine, rue, rue the day, *Archaic.* pine; fret, reproach oneself, *Sl.* kick oneself, cry over spilt milk.

2. weep, cry, sob, *Scot. and North Eng.* greet; keen, ululate, wail, howl; beat one's breast, flagellate oneself, tear one's hair, gnash one's teeth; go into mourning, wear *or* put on mourning.

—*n.* 3. lamentation, complaint, *Archaic.* plaint; moan, groan; keen, wail, ululation, howl; cry, outcry, bawl, jeremiad; sob, whine, whimper.

4. elegy, requiem, monody, threnody; dirge, epicedium, (*in Scotland and Ireland*) coronach, (*in the Scottish Highlands*) pibroch, death song; death *or* dead march, funeral march.

lamentable, *adj.* 1. regrettable, deplorable, rueful, woeful, woebegone, unfortunate; pitiful, pitiable, piteous, to be pitied; sad, doleful, dolorous, sorrowful, distressing, depressing, mournful, grievous, plaintive; sore, sharp, bitter, painful; comfortless, discomforting, uncomfortable; dreary, cheerless, joyless, dismal, lugubrious; miserable, wretched, abject, squalid, stark.

2. *Figurative.* insufficient, inadequate, unsatisfactory, unsatisfying; poor, meager, scanty, skimpy, scrimpy, beggarly, niggardly, sorry, slight; paltry, puny, petty, piddling, poky, *Inf.* measly, *Sl.* crummy, *Sl.* lousy, *Sl.* rotten.

lamentation, *n.* 1. mourning, grieving, lamenting, groaning, moaning, bemoaning, bewailing; wailing, howling, keening; crying, weeping, sobbing, bawling; commiseration, commiserating, condolence, condoling, consolation, consoling, sympathy, sympathizing.

2. repentance, remorse, contrition, compunction; regret, self-reproach, self-condemnation.

3. lament, complaint. See **lament** (*defs.* 3, 4).

lamina, *n.* 1. cover, covering, covering layer; coat, coating, veneer, overlay, lamella; facing, sheathing, weatherboard, clapboard, shingle, outside paneling, stuccowork, adobe; skin, integument, membrane, *Anat., Zool.* cortex, pellicle, peel, rind, bark; plate, plating, protective covering, mail, coat of mail, chain mail; crust, incrustation, scab; shell, carapace, marine shell, nutshell, pastry shell, wingcover, elytron.

2. cut, slice, rasher, shave, shaving, curl; leaf, leaflet, sheet, foil, petal, scale, flake.

laminate, *v.* 1. separate, split, *Med.* desquamate, peel off, exfoliate, flake, flake off.

2. veneer, coat, cover, crust, incrust, overlay, lay over, superimpose, overspread, plate, foliate; face, sheathe, shingle, panel, stucco; stratify, layer.

—*n.* 3. lamination, plastic coating, *Trademark.* Formica, *Trademark.* Marlite; plywood, plywood paneling.

4. stratification, delamination, *Med.* desquamation, scaliness, squamousness.

laminated, *adj.* 1. lamellate, lamelliform, lamellose, laminiferous, lamellar; stratified, stratiform, layered; scaly, flaky, scabby, scurfy, squamous, squamoid, squamate, crusty.

2. membranous, covered, overlaid, coated, plated; carapaced, carapacial, incrusted; veneered, faced, sheathed, shingled, paneled, stuccoed.

lamp, *n.* 1. illuminant, luminary, luminant, illumination; light, light vessel, lampad; lamplet, gas lamp, oil lamp, Carcel lamp, Argand lamp, petane lamp, Hefner lamp; table lamp, floor lamp, bridge lamp, music lamp, piano lamp, night light, picture light, wall-washer; lantern, railroad lantern, magic lantern, Chinese lantern, Japanese lantern, paper lantern, jack-o'-lantern.

2. electric light, incandescent light, fluorescent light, neon light, infra-red light, ultra-violet light; carbon light, vacuum tube, tungsten light, tantalum lamp, vapor lamp, mercury lamp, mercury-arc lamp, arc lamp; flashlight, battery lamp, *Brit.* electric torch, *Brit. Inf.* torch, freon tube; spotlight, baby spotlight, *Inf.* spot, *Brit.* limelight, *Films.* pickle, *Films.* rifle; floodlight, floodlamp, *Inf.* flood, *Films.* klieg light, searchlight.

3. signal light, beacon, flare, lighthouse, pilot light, buoy light; traffic light, *Inf.* stop-and-go, red light, green light; airport landing light, radio-range beacon, navigation light, course light, approach light, obstruction light, fixed light.

4. (*all of vehicles*) headlight, headlamp, fog light, sidelight, taillight, brake light, directional light, *Inf.* directional, turn indicator, *Inf.* signal, emergency light, *Inf.* flasher.

5. candle, taper, tallow, wax, bayberry candle, rush candle, rushlight; corpse candle, death light.

6. chandelier, globe, light globe, light fixture, candelabra, gas fixture, gasolier; bulb, electric bulb, filament, carbon filament, tungsten filament; tube, vacuum tube, Braun tube, Crookes tube, Geissler tube; burner, gas burner, Argand burner, Bunsen burner; mantle, gas mantle, Welsbach mantle; jet, gas jet.

7. inspiration, inspirer, *Hinduism.* guru; teacher, mentor, good influence; stimulus, galvanizer, animator, awakener, rouser.

—*v.* 8. *Slang.* look at, ogle, eye, give [s.o.] the eye.

lampoon, *n.* 1. satire, squib, pasquil, pasquinade, burlesque, travesty, skit, parody; satirical cartoon, political cartoon, caricature, distorted portrait; malicious attack, virulent attack, near-slander, near-libel; derision, ridicule, mockery, invective, defamation, fulmination.

—*v.* 2. mock, ridicule, hold up to ridicule, make fun of; pasquinade, burlesque, satirize, parody, do a take-off on; belittle, *Inf.* run down, *Inf.* put down; asperse, disparage, hold up to scorn; vilify, malign, *Inf.* cut [s.o.] up, revile; engage in personalities, fulminate, stigmatize, defame, give a bad name, drag through the mud, heap dirt on, sully, stain, blot, taint, bespatter.

lance, *n.* 1. spear, spontoon, pike, half-pike, harpoon; javelin, jerred, assegai, shaft.

2. lancet, surgical knife, knife, scalpel.

—*v.* 3. cut, cut open, open, slit, incise; puncture, penetrate, spear, lancinate, stab, stick, prick.

lance-shaped, *adj.* spear-shaped, lanceolate, lanciform.

land, *n.* 1. earth, ground, terra firma, terra, dry land, solid ground; shore, seashore, coast, seacoast, coastland, beach, waterside, foreshore; continent, subcontinent, mainland, main, island, islet, isthmus, neck, peninsula, cape, foreland; reef, jetty, sandbank, sand bar, shoal, bar, key.

2. soil, dirt, turf, sod, clod, topsoil, subsoil; loam, mold, sand, humus, clay, till, gumbo, mud.

3. field, expanse, stretch, open space *or* area, champaign; common, green, park, mall, veld, veldt, wold, *U.S.* campus, *Anglo-Indian.* maidan.

4. terrain, earth's surface, topography; plain, flats, tundra, moor, heath, *Chiefly Brit.* moorland; meadow, grassland, pasture, pasturage, savanna, lea, campo, pampas, *Archaic.* mead; glade, glen, grove, dell, weald, copse, copsewood, brake, cannebrake, thicket, covert, boscage, pinery, *Southwestern U. S.* chaparral, *Brit.* spinney, *Chiefly Brit.* coppice, *Archaic.* bosk, wood, woods, woodland, wildwood, forestland, forest, jungle; plateau, table, tableland, steppe, butte, ledge, shelf, bluff, promontory, precipice, cliff, jetty, headland, palisade; incline, slope, rise, grade, climb, hillside; hill, hillock, mound, bank, embankment, hump, dune, sand dune, knoll, downs, *Archaic.* down, *U.S.* horseback; mountain, mount, alp, height, steep, summit, peak, pinnacle; spine, ridge, crest, *Dial.* knap, *Geol.* hogback, mountain range, range, chain; bottoms, bottomland, lowland, *Brit. Dial.* holm, *Geog.* basin; marsh, marshland, saltmarsh, swamp, swampland, bog, mire, quagmire, wetlands, fenland, *Brit.* fen; declivity, decline, descent, downgrade, drop; valley, vale, gorge, ravine, canyon, gulch, chasm, abyss, crevasse; gap, pass, defile.

5. real property *or* estate, property, acreage, acres; tract, lot, parcel, plot, plat, site, spot, patch, piece of property *or* land, *Brit. Dial.* toft; property, place, grounds, yard, lawn, *Inf.* spread; estate, demesne, plantation, manor, manor farm, country manor *or* estate, *Chiefly Western U.S.* ranch, rancho, hacienda, *Law.* messuage, *Law.* hereditament, *Law.* freehold, allodium, allod.

6. farm, farmstead, farmplace, grange, *Archaic.* farmhold, *Brit.* farmery, *Brit.* croft, *Brit.* homecroft, *Brit.* glebe land, *Scot. and North. Eng.* steading; countryside, provinces, rural districts, *U.S.Inf.* the sticks, *Sl.* the boondocks, *Sl.* the boonies; backwoods, hinterlands, backcountry, wilds, wilderness, brush, bush, *Sl.* the bushes, *Australian.* outback; wasteland, waste, barrens, desert.

7. country, nation, homeland, mother country, native land, fatherland, *Latin. patria*; state, republic, dominion, commonwealth, city-state; ward, precinct, canton, county, shire, parish, township, hundred, wapentake, tithing, riding, political division; citizenry, citizens, polity, public, population, people, society, community.

8. area, region, district, zone, quarter, section, parts; neighborhood, vicinity, vicinage, environs, *Inf.* neck of the woods, *U.S.* block; territory, realm, sphere, hemisphere, domain, province; diocese, bailiwick, domain, province; principality, palatinate, duchy, dukedom, chiefdom, kingdom, empire, *Archaic.* empery.

—v. **9.** alight, light, hit ground, settle upon, plant oneself upon; touch down, splash down, make a landing, come in for a landing, fall, descend, pancake, belly flop, *Aeron.* belly land; set down, bring in *or* down, take in *or* down, bring in for a landing; anchor, drop anchor, come into port, arrive, reach one's destination, come to a stop, come to rest; debark, disembark, dismount, get off *or* down, deplane, unship, go ashore.

10. *Sometimes* **land up** end up, wind up, get into, find oneself; put, get, take.

11. *Informal.* catch, capture, apprehend, arrest, take captive *or* prisoner, take into custody, lasso, *Inf.* nab, *Inf.* collar, *Inf.* pinch, *Inf.* nail, *Inf.* corral, *Inf.* bag, *Inf.* lay by the heels, tackle; seize, lay hold of, grasp, grab, wrest, snatch, fasten onto; get, obtain, acquire, procure, secure; earn, merit, gain, reap, harvest, win, be given *or* awarded, (*of a bill or motion*) carry, carry off, *Inf.* cop.

landing, *n.* **1.** debarkation, disembarkment, disembarkation, dismounting, deplaning, going ashore, arrival; alighting, lighting, touchdown, splashdown, pancake, belly flop, belly whop, belly whopper, *Aeron.* three-point landing, *Aeron.* belly-landing.

2. dock, wharf, pier, quay, jetty, landing, stage, anchorage, mooring, moorings, *U.S.* slip, embankment, (*in India, China, Japan, etc.*) bund, port, seaport, harbor; runway, airfield, landing field, *Aeron.* airstrip, airport, airdrome, *Chiefly Brit.* aerodrome, *Inf.* port.

3. *Architecture.* head *or* top of the stairs, platform, estrade.

landlady, *n.* **1.** proprietress, proprietrix, lady of the house, the lady *or* woman in charge, mistress, *Chiefly Brit.* manageress; concierge. See **landlord** (*defs.* **1, 5**).

landlord, *n.* **1.** proprietor, proprietary, owner of the building, lessor, *Chiefly Brit.* letter; absentee landlord, slumlord; manager, resident manager, the man in charge, master; superintendent, *Inf.* super.

2. innkeeper, innholder, hotelkeeper, keeper, boniface, hosteler, host, *Fr. hôtelier, Fr. aubergiste,* restaurateur, *Brit.* victualer, *Brit. Inf.* publican, *Archaic.* taverner.

3. landowner, property owner, owner, property holder, householder, man of the house, holder, freeholder; squire, member of the landed gentry, *Scot.* laird.

landmark, *n.* **1.** guidepost, guide, cairn, milepost, distinctive feature, historic structure, *Archaeology.* menhir; seamark, beacon, lighthouse, buoy.

2. milestone, turning, critical point, crisis; Rubicon, decisive point; historic *or* significant event.

3. stake, pale, post, picket, peg, pike, demarcator, marker; boundary line, boundary, border, fence, edging.

—adj. **4.** precedent-setting, historic, history-making; significant, monumental, momentous, important.

landscape, *n.* **1.** scene, scenic view, aspect, outlook, prospect, *Chiefly Brit.* lookout, perspective, vista; rural *or* country scene, natural scene, countryside, *Fr. paysage, It. paesaggio.*

2. painting, sketch, picture, depiction, representation; tableau, scenograph, panorama, cyclorama.

lane, *n.* **1.** way, passage, avenue, channel, passageway, alley, alleyway; by-path, byway, throughway, crosscut, short cut; path, pathway, footpath, *Brit.* footway, towpath, bike path, bikeway; trail, track, walk, walkway, crosswalk.

2. access, approach, ramp, runway, adit, entrance; entry, entryway, driveway, entrée, inlet, ingress; byroad, by-street, side road *or* street; drive, terrace, circle, row; street, main road, *Inf.* drag, strip, pavement; thoroughfare, artery, highroad, roadway; highway, turnpike, pike, tollroad, state highway; freeway, expressway, parkway, causeway, throughway, *U.S. Inf.* interstate; speedway, autobahn, superhighway.

language, *n.* **1.** speech, tongue, dialect, parlance, idiolect; vernacular, common speech, vulgate, vulgar tongue; mother tongue, native tongue, parent language, linguistic stock; slang, idiom, vulgarism, colloquialism, vernacularism, archaism; patois, pidgin, pidgin English, trade language, lingua franca, Spanglish; provincialism, regionalism, localism, barbarism; brogue, twang, cockney, isogloss; Americanism, Yankeeism; Englishism, Anglicism, Britishism, Frenchism, Gallicism, *Fr. Franglais,* Canadianism, Scotticism, Irishism, Hibernicism, Yiddishism; artificial language, auxiliary language, Esperanto, Interlingua, interlanguage, idioglossia.

2. communication, intercourse, verbal intercourse, discourse, words; speaking, telling, talking; conversation, interlocution, colloquy, converse, interchange.

3. jargon, *Inf.* lingo, argot, cant; bureaucratese, journalese, newspaperese, businessese, shoptalk, Washingtonese, Pentagonese, officialese, newspeak, educationese, cinemaese, legalese, medicalese; thieves' Latin, peddler's French, St. Giles Greek, pig Latin; jabber, gibberish, gibber, gobbledygook, empty talk; prattle, mumbo jumbo, palaver, patter, rhyming slang.

4. diction, talk, accent, tone, expression, utterance, word of mouth; rhetoric, style, elocution, grandiloquence; manner, manner of speaking, vein, mode, strain, phrasing, wording, terminology, phraseology, vocabulary, locution.

languid, *adj.* **1.** faint, weak, feeble, poor, unhealthy, frail, anemic, *Pathol.* atonic; declining, on the decline, fading, sickly, valetudinarian; powerless, strengthless, invalid; flagging, drooping, languishing, weary, tired, exhausted, debilitated; spent, fatigued, wearied, worn out, *Sl.* pooped out, enervated; strained, worn, used, deflated, weather-beaten.

2. slack, listless, lackadaisical, lethargic, languorous; otiose, indolent, idle, lazy, slothful; inactive, inert, inanimate, exanimate, lifeless; torpid, lentitudinous, slow, dronish; yawning, nodding, sleepy, somnolent, half-awake, half-asleep, drowsy, dozy; asleep, out, dead to the world, *Sl.* zonked out, *Sl.* buzzed out; unconscious, comatose, supine.

3. indifferent, apathetic, spiritless, lukewarm, uninterested; incurious, inexcitable, unenthusiastic, bored, blasé; unfeeling, unemotional, insensitive, passionless, passive, half-hearted; dull, leaden, hebetudinous, phlegmatic, lymphatic, heavy.

languidness, *n.* sluggishness, torpor, lethargy. See **languor** (*defs.* **2, 3**).

languish, *v.* **1.** droop, fade, fail, flag, wilt; weaken, decline, soften, give, sag, yield; go downhill, come apart at the seams, *Sl.* poop out, *Sl.* fizzle out, *Sl.* peter out, devitalize, enfeeble, debilitate, enervate, sap; fag, weary, tire, exhaust, fatigue, wind.

2. drop, sink, stagger, swoon, fall; yawn, nod, sleep, succumb, collapse, *Inf.* cave in.

3. waste away, wither away, decay, die away, rot, collect dust; ebb, abate, dwindle, diminish, drop off, fall off; be abandoned, be neglected, be disregarded.

4. pine for, yearn for, long for, hunger for *or* after, thirst for *or* after, *Inf.* hanker for *or* after; die for, cry for, want with all one's heart, want in the worst way, have one's heart set upon; pant for, rave for, gasp for, have a yen for, wish, covet.

5. grieve, mourn, lament, repine, pine, bewail, bemoan; despond, despair, lose heart, give up, admit defeat, *Sl.* throw in the towel, *Sl.* hang one's hat on the rack; mope, sigh, brood, sulk, eat one's heart out.

languishing, *adj.* **1.** fading, flagging, drooping, declining, failing, on the decline, *Sl.* on the skids; weak, faint, feeble, poor, anemic; deteriorating, waning, slipping, sliding, ebbing, going to pieces.

2. melancholic, despairing, despondent, dejected, depressed, woebegone, in the doldrums, in low spirits, in a blue funk; lovesick, heartbroken, lovelorn, heavy-hearted; pining, longing, yearning, wistful, *Dial.* honing, desirous, nostalgic, homesick.

3. lingering, slow, drawn-out, lasting, long, prolonged, protracted, long-drawn.

languor, *n.* **1.** weakness, faintness, feebleness, frailty, enfeeblement; debility, *Pathol.* asthenia, *Pathol.* adynemia, *Pathol.* atony; decrepitude, infirmness, infirmity, sickliness, invalidism; strain, eyestrain, fatigue, tiredness, enervation, exhaustion; lassitude, strengthlessness, powerlessness, anemia, *Inf.* the blahs.

2. sluggishness, languidness, laggardness, *Archaic.* languishment; torpidity, torpor, *Archaic.* lenitude, slowness, lethargy, (*in the Middle East*) kef; indolence, sloth, slothfulness, lotus-eating; inactivity, inertia, inertness, inaction, inanimateness, inanimation, lifelessness; sleepiness, drowsiness, doziness, somnolence.

3. spiritlessness, listlessness, lackadaisicalness; apathy, indifference, uninterestedness, inexcitability, incuriousness, enthusiasm; boredom, ennui, dullness, hebetude, phlegm; passionlessness, passivity, half-heartedness; unfeelingness, unemotionalness, insensitivity, insensibility, stolidity.

4. stillness, tranquillity, quiescence, calm, lull, windlessness, calm before the storm; silence, din of silence, dead calm, deathlike calm, flat calm.

languorous, *adj.* languishing, lethargic, spiritless, listless. See **languid** (*defs.* **1-3**).

lank, *adj.* **1.** long, slender, lean, thin, skinny, attenuate; gaunt, haggard, emaciated, meager, spare, scrawny; scraggy, spindly, spindle-shanked, skeletal, bare-boned, raw-boned, skin-and-bones, twiggy; bony, lanky, gangling, gangly, gawky, *Inf.* weedy; tall, long-legged, rangy, long-necked, giraffelike, leggy.

2. awkward, ungraceful, ungainly, oafish, lubberly, clumsy.

lantern, *n.* lamp, light, dark lantern, *Sl.* glim, bull's-eye; oil lamp, lampion, hurricane lamp, tornado lamp, safety lamp, miner's lamp; jack-o'-lantern, magic lantern, Japanese lantern, Chinese lantern; barn lantern, kerosene lamp, Coleman lantern, carriage lamp, side light, riding light; gas lamp, gaslight, filament lamp, carbon lamp; police lantern, railroad lantern, search lamp, pilot light, navigation light, signal lamp.

lap[1], *n.* **1.** seat, knees.

2. security, secureness, safeness, comfort, protection, refuge.

3. responsibility, obligation, charge, job, task; bailiwick, turf, neighborhood, territory.

lap[2], *v.* **1.** wrap, wrap up, wind around, dress; fold up, case, enclothe, clothe; cover, sheathe, circumvest, swathe, swaddle, garb; envelop, enfold, enwrap, encase, surround, invest.

2. overlap, fringe, margin, marginate, edge, border, hem, skirt; bound, rim, list, marge, line, verge, side. —*n.* **3.** circuit, compass, ambit, circuition, orbit, circle, loop; tour, full circle, round trip, trip, revolution.

lap[3], *v.* **1.** wash against, beat upon, slap, splash against; slosh, swash, wash, swish, ripple, purl, trill; trickle, drip, dribble; babble, burble, bubble, murmur, gurgle, guggle.

2. lick up, tongue, drink up, mouth; sip, nip, sup, bib; swill, swig, tipple, tope; drink off, imbibe, quaff. —*n.* **3.** plash, swash, wash, backwash, swish, splash; ripple, trill, purl, trickle, *Naut.* cat's-paw, dribble; babble, burble, bubbling.

lapse, *n.* **1.** decline, fall, descent, *Fr. chute*; falling, slipping, backslide, subsidence; drop, sinkage, slump, collapse, *Meteorol.* katabasis; deterioration, degeneration, worsening, declension; downturn, weakening, turn for the worse; downfall, decline and fall, debacle.

2. slip, error, mistake, *Inf.* slip-up, blunder, fluff; failure, failing, breach, flaw, sin, wrong; negligence, laxity, dereliction, omission, oversight, inadvertence, *Law.* nonfeasance; relapse, recidivism, reversion, regression.

3. interval, passage, elapse, course of time, sweep of time; intermission, hitch, recess, *Sports.* half-time, *Sports.* time-out, *Baseball.* seventh-inning stretch; interim, interregnum, respite, remission, interlude; lull, pause, stay, cease-fire; hiatus, *Prosody.* caesura, break, interruption.

4. discontinuance, cancellation, invalidation, nullification, abrogation, revocation; termination, cessation, end, expiration, expiry.

—*v.* **5.** fall, decline, lower, drop; slip, give way, slide, slump, glide; sink, submerge, subside; ebb, abate, fall back, recede, wane; retrograde, retrogress, regress, backslide, recidivate; deteriorate, fail, worsen, weaken, fade, languish; go downhill, degenerate, go from bad to worse, get no better; go to seed, *Sl.* go to pot; decay, fall into disuse.

6. terminate, end, expire, cease; discontinue, stop, cancel, invalidate, nullify, abrogate, revoke.

7. pass away, elapse, pass, flow, fly; roll, advance, proceed, run its course; go by, go on, glide, flit, flutter.

lapsed, *adj.* past, lost, gone, bygone, no more, ago, elapsed, by-past, over; irrecoverable, dead and buried, forgotten, extinct; passé, late, passed; antiquated, out of date, outdated, outworn, obsolete; old, former, archaic, of other times, pre-war; superannuated, superseded, disused, on the shelf; expired, run out, discontinued, terminated, invalidated, abrogated.

lard, *n.* **1.** fat, fatty tissue, animal fat, adipose, adipocere, blubber, tallow; grease, suet, oil, dripping, *Physiol.* sebum; butter, ghee, margarine, oleomargarine, oleo; porpoise oil, whale oil, sperm oil, spermaceti, cetaceum, tuna oil, goose grease.

—*v.* **2.** grease, oil, oleaginize, glycerate, smear; baste, butter, lubricate, dress.

larder, *n.* pantry, chamber, scullery, cuddy; store, storage, storage room, storeroom, supply room; buttery, stillroom, cannery, *Brit. Dial.* spence, food room, cooler, refrigerator room.

lardy, *adj.* oily, greasy, unctuous, oleaginous, buttery, slippery, butyraceous; tallowy, suety, *Physiol.* sebaceous; fat, fatty, pinguid, blubbery, adipose, lardaceous.

large, *adj.* **1.** big, great, huge, enormous, colossal, herculean, mighty; prodigious, gigantic, giant, gigantean, monstrous, monumental; stupendous, tremendous, towering, staggering, imposing, mountainous; tall, high, grand, grandiose, great big, *Sl.* humongous, *Sl.* gigando; sizable, considerable, goodly, substantial, excessive; titanic, cyclopean, Atlantean, Brobdingnagian; mammoth, jumbo, ponderous, massive, massy, gargantuan, elephantine; leviathan, whalelike, dinosaurian, dinotherian, megatherian; oversize, king-size, man-size, giant-size, overlarge, *Archaic.* mickle; *All Inf.* whopping, spanking, walloping, thumping, thundering, whacking, banging.

2. extensive, broad, expansive, wide, large-scale; immense, vast, sweeping, panoramic, far-reaching, far-flung, wide-reaching, wide-ranging; unlimited, limitless, illimitable, unbounded, boundless, measureless, interminable, endless, infinite; spacious, capacious, roomy, ample, generous, copious, commodious, voluminous.

3. burly, stout, heavy, thickset, heavyset, stocky, chunky; beefy, brawny, husky, sturdy, strapping, well-built; hulky, hulking, bulky, gross; muscular, hefty, stalwart, rugged, solid, strong, powerful; fat, fatty, weighty, obese, corpulent, adipose, rotund, portly; hypertrophic, swollen, tumid, pot-bellied, *Archaic.* gorbellied, bloated, pregnant, puffy; beamy, hippy, spread out, outspread, splay, thick, hippopotamic; bosomy, *Inf.* busty, top-heavy, fleshy.

4. comprehensive, encyclopedic, compendious, of great scope; inclusive, all-inclusive, exhaustive, all-embracing; general, universal, worldwide, widespread, ecumenical.

5. at large a. at liberty, free, unconfined, unconstrained, unrestrained, uncaught; escaped, missing, wanted; truant, fugitive, runaway. **b.** at length, to a large extent, to a great degree, greatly, considerably, much. **c.** as a whole, generally, in the main, for the most part, mainly, chiefly, principally, on the whole, as a rule, by and large, in general.

large-hearted, *adj.* **1.** generous, kindhearted, charitable, bountiful, bounteous, giving, liberal; big-hearted, humanitarian, philanthropic, munificent; benevolent, benificent, benign, benignant, magnanimous, open-handed; altruistic, public-spirited, unselfish, disinterested, other-directed; kind, good, noble, humane, decent, honorable; merciful, pitying, placable, unhardened, lenient, temperate, clement, ruthful.

2. compassionate, gentle, soft, tender, mild, *Inf.* Christian, loving; gracious, lionhearted, good-hearted, gallant, chivalrous; understanding, indulgent, forbearing, forbearant, forgiving, sympathetic; neighborly, friendly, nice, hospitable, genial.

largely, *adv.* **1.** chiefly, generally, mainly, mostly, principally, in general, by and large; above all, eminently, essentially, particularly; in great part, in the main, as a whole, for the most part, on the whole, as a rule.

2. much, pretty much, very much, muchly, so, ever so; greatly, highly, considerably, abundantly; to a large extent, to a great degree, at length, on a large scale, in the large, in a big way, in great measure; a lot, a great deal, no end of, galore, *Fr. beaucoup*, in abundance; freely, without stint, *Inf.* to the skies.

largeness, *n.* **1.** bigness, greatness, enormity, enormousness, hugeness, grandiosity, grandness, grandeur; magnitude, size, dimension, measure, muchness; mass, bulk, proportion, caliber; sizableness, substantiality, largishness, biggishness, considerableness; tallness, highness, height; tremendousness, stupendousness, excessiveness; gigantism, giganticness, colossality, monumentality, prodigiousness; mountainousness, monstrousness, monstrosity, massiveness, mightiness, ponderosity.

2. vastness, immensity, broadness, wideness, extensiveness, expansiveness; extent, expanse, extension, scope, range, area, reach, spread, width, breadth; boundlessness, unboundedness, unlimitedness, illimitability, limitlessness, measurelessness; interminableness, interminability, endlessness, infinity, infinitude.

3. comprehensiveness, compendiousness, inclusiveness, all-inclusiveness, exhaustiveness; ampleness, amplitude, plenitude, fullness; volume, voluminousness, capacity, capaciousness; room, content, accommodation, space; roominess, spaciousness, commodiousness, generousness, copiousness.

4. bulkiness, hulkiness, hulkingness, burliness, stoutness, heaviness, stockiness, chunkiness; beefiness, brawniness, huskiness, sturdiness, grossness; overlargeness, overbigness, overheaviness, overstoutness; heftiness, muscularity, solidity, ruggedness, strength, power, might; weightiness, corpulence, obesity, fatness, fattiness, adiposity, girth, rotundity, portliness; hypertrophy, swollenness, tumescence, tumidity, bloatedness, puffiness; bosominess, *Inf.* bustiness, top-heaviness, fleshiness; beaminess, hippiness, thickness.

large-scale, *adj.* **1.** extensive, expansive, wide, broad, diffuse; sweeping, far-flung, vast, far-reaching, wide-reaching, wide-ranging, far-flying, wide-stretching; of great scope, large, sizable, substantial, in large; all-out, wholesale, indiscriminate, liberal.

2. blown-up, enlarged, increased, magnified, inflated;

expanded, widened, extended, broadened.

largess, *n.* **1.** charity, alms-giving, philanthropy, altruism; beneficence, munificence, generosity, bounty, open-handedness, liberality.

2. gift, present, *Scot.* propine, benefaction, bestowal, donation, donative, contribution, endowment; offering, *Eccles.* offertory, *Eccles.* altarage, oblation; grant, aid, allowance, allotment, stipend, scholarship, fellowship, subsidy, subvention; inheritance, heritage, *Law.* dower, *Obs.* dowry, *Law.* acquest, *Law.* bequest, *Law.* bequeathment, *Law.* legacy, *Law.* devise; reward, prize, bonus, extra, plus, dividend, perquisite, *Inf.* perk, fringe benefit; honorarium, fee, pay, gratuity, tip, lagniappe, douceur.

lariat, *n.* lasso, riata; rope, thong, tether, leash, line.

lark[1], *n.* bird, songbird, songster, warbler; skylark, meadowlark, titlark.

lark[2], *n.* **1.** frolic, spree, fling, *Sl.* buster, romp, gambol, *Inf.* skylarking, fun, sport, play, game; antic, caper, prank, trick, *Sl.* monkeybusiness, *Inf.* shenanigans, mischief, *Sl.* horsing around.

—*v.* **2.** frolic, romp, rollick, have fun, gambol, disport, play, sport, *Inf.* skylark; frisk, leap, curvet, cavort, skip about, dance about, jump about; caper, cut capers, play pranks, pull tricks, *Inf.* pull shenanigans, make mischief, *Sl.* horse around.

lascivious, *adj.* **1.** lewd, lecherous, lubricous, *Archaic.* lickerish, satyric, satyrical, satyrlike, hircine, goatish, ruttish, *Sl.* horny; lustful, randy, *Sl.* hot *or* hot for; concupiscent, prurient, libidinous, salacious; fleshly, carnal, sensual, voluptuous, erotic; licentious, loose, Cyprian, wanton, abandoned, incontinent; debauched, rakish, rakehell, dissolute, dissipated, profligate; promiscuous, whorish, of easy virtue, *Sl.* cheap, shameless; depraved, degenerate, perverted, incestuous, masochistic, sadistic, pederastic, coprophilic; immodest, impure, unchaste, unvirtuous.

2. obscene, lurid, blue, pornographic, *Inf.* porno, *Inf.* porn, smutty, *Sl.* raunchy; indecent, offensive, suggestive, vulgar, coarse, gross, crude; dirty, unclean, foul, filthy, vile; foul-mouthed, dirty-minded; ribald, scurrilous, irreverent; bawdy, Fescennine.

lasciviousness, *n.* **1.** lewdness, lechery, lecherousness, lubricity, goatishness, ruttishness; lust, lustfulness, concupiscence, prurience, pruriency, libidinousness, salacity, salaciousness; carnality, carnalness, carnalism, sensuality, voluptuousness, promiscuity, eroticism, erotism; immodesty, impudicity, impurity, unchasteness, unchastity, unvirtuousness.

2. debauchery, dissoluteness, rakishness, dissipation, profligacy; licentiousness, wantonness, unrestraint, abandon, incontinence, self-indulgence; aphrodisia, sexual desire *or* passion, *Pathol.* satyriasis, *Pathol.* nymphomania; unnatural desire, perversion, incest, incestuousness, pederasty, sodomy, buggery, sadism, masochism; *Psychiatry.* coprophilia.

3. obscenity, obsceneness, luridness; pornography, *Inf.* porno, *Inf.* porn, smut, smuttiness; bawdiness, bawdry, scurrility, ribaldry; vulgarity, vulgarism, vulgarness, coarseness, crudity, crudeness.

lash[1], *n.* **1.** whip, knout, scourge, flagellum, bullwhip, cat-o'-nine-tails, cat, cowhide, rawhide, quirt, *U.S.* blacksnake.

2. blow, stroke, bang, hit, smack, rap; knock, buffet, cuff, *Inf.* wallop, slam, swat, slap, whack, thwack, *Inf.* bat, *Inf.* sock, *Inf.* whop, *Inf.* lick, *Sl.* smackeroo, *Sl.* zinger; strike, thump, tap, pat, poke, swipe, dab, jab.

3. goad, prod, whip, sting, prick, spur.

—*v.* **4.** thrash, flog, switch, swat, birch, scourge, whip, horsewhip, thresh, flail; *Inf.* lambaste, *Inf.* whale, *Inf.* whomp; smite, thwack, slap, smack.

5. drive, push, propel, hound, whip, flog; prick, poke, stick, rowel, spur, prompt, prod; provoke, instigate, incite, actuate; foment, agitate, excite, arouse, rouse, whip up, work up, stir up, wind up, enflame, fire up, kindle, touch off; encourage, urge, egg on, put up to.

6. berate, scold, chide, tongue-lash, rate, harangue, rant, curse, execrate, imprecate, anathematize; upbraid, objurgate, excoriate, *Inf.* lambaste, flay, fulminate against; castigate, chastise, berate, censure, criticize, reproach, rebuke, reprove, *Inf.* jump on, *Inf.* dress down, *Inf.* slam, *Sl.* jump all over, *Sl.* chew out, *Inf.* bawl out, *Sl.* strafe.

7. *Often* **lash out** vilify, traduce, asperse, calumniate, impugn, slur, malign; denounce, decry, disparage, discredit, belittle, minimize, run *or* put down, *Inf.* knock.

8. flick, flicker, bat, flutter, flap, wag, waggle, whip, switch.

lash[2], *v.* fasten, attach, affix, fix; tie, bind, tether, make fast, hitch, rope, string, belay, strap, lace, leash; secure, join connect.

lass, *n.* **1.** girl, female child, lassie, *Inf.* filly, maid, maiden, *Irish Eng.* colleen; miss, mademoiselle, young lady, demoiselle, *Archaic.* damoiselle, damsel; young unmarried woman, *Ger. Fraülein,* virgin; soubrette, nymph, nymphet, Lolita; minx, hoyden, tomboy, romp.

2. girlfriend, sweetheart, darling, lady love, fiancée, betrothed; inamorata, lover, mistress.

lassitude, *n.* **1.** languor, languidness, lethargy, sluggishness, loginess, heaviness, slow-motion, slowness; drowsiness, sleepiness, soporiferousness, oscitance, oscitancy; stagnation, stagnancy, stagnance, inaction, inactivity, inactiveness, inexertion, inertia, inertness; dormancy, passivity, passiveness, supineness, torpor, torpidity, torpidness, stupor, stupefaction.

2. indolence, laziness, idleness, otiosity, otioseness, fainéance, fainéancy, shiftlessness; procrastination, dilatoriness, slothfulness, sluggardliness, laggardness.

lasso, *n.* lariat, riata. See **lariat**.

last[1], *adj.* **1.** hindmost, rearmost, aftermost, *Naut.* aftmost, *Anat.* caudal, behind; posterior, subsequent, after.

2. latest, most recent, proximate; current, up-to-the-minute, up-to-date.

3. final, end, ending, concluding, ultimate, terminal, terminating, eventual.

4. conclusive, definitive, settling, determinative, determinating; deciding, resolving, inarguable.

5. utmost, extreme, ultra; farthest, outside, topping.

6. at last a. finally, *Fr. enfin*, ultimately, in conclusion; at length, after a while. **b.** high time, about time, finito, eureka; amen, Q.E.D.; hurrah, yippee.

—*adv.* **7.** after, behind, in the rear, astern, aft, *Naut.* abaft; hindward, rearward; finally, concludingly, in the end, ultimately.

—*n.* **8.** conclusion, end, ending, finish, termination, completion, upshot, windup; tail end, tag end, tag, rear end, bitter end, fag end; discontinuance, cessation, stopping, quitting; denouement, *Sl.* curtains, *Sl.* payoff; rear guard, also-ran.

last[2], *v.* continue, persist, keep on, endure, perdure; subsist, exist, live, outlive, survive; abide, *Archaic.* bide, stay, remain; maintain, keep, hold good, stand, stand up, wear, wear well, outwear; be permanent, be constant, be steadfast.

last[3], *n.* mold, pattern, form, model, matrix; prototype, original, example; standard, paradigm.

lasting, *adj.* enduring, standing the test of time, going on and on, long-lived, life-long, long-standing; abiding, continuing, persisting; permanent, perdurable, eternal, *Literary.* sempiternal, immortal, undying, deathless, imperishable, indestructible, indissoluble, unfading, everlasting, amaranthine, perennial; perpetual, unending, endless, never-ending, ceaseless, unceasing, incessant, unremitting; constant, durable, steady, stable, solid, like the Rock of Gibraltar, fixed, firm, steadfast; immutable, unchangeable, changeless, unalterable, invariable; established, deep-rooted, strong, entrenched; interminable, prolonged, protracted, long-drawn-out, lasting for a year and a day, long, lengthy, day-in-day-out, ongoing; surviving, surviving through thick and thin *or* for better or worse; extended, boundless, illimitable; dateless, ageless, unaging, evergreen, ever-young, ever-new.

last-ditch, *adj.* desperate, frantic, frenzied, wild; gasping, straining, struggling, struggling mightily, fighting; do-or-die, *Sl.* all-out, down-to-the-wire, *Sl.* down-and-dirty, dug-in, with one's back against the wall; last, last-chance, final; heroic, epic, stout-hearted, lionhearted; reckless, rash, heedless.

lastly, *adv.* finally, concludingly, in conclusion; at last, in the end, after all, on the whole, in fine, all things considered; in last place, bringing up the rear, hindmost, rearmost.

latch, *n.* **1.** clasp, hasp, bolt, bar, buckle, lock, padlock, fastening, fastener.
—*v.* **2.** fasten, secure, close, slam; lock, padlock, bolt.

late, *adj.* **1.** tardy, behind, behind time *or* schedule, not on time, unpunctual; overdue, past due; slow, procrastinative, procrastinatory, dilatory, delaying, cunctation, cunctatory, *Rare.* cunctative.
2. prolonged, protracted, extended, drawn-out, lengthened; delayed, stayed, put-off, postponed, belated.
3. recent, new, fresh, up-to-the-minute, up-to-date, current.
4. previous, preceding, prior, antecedent; former, *Inf.* ex, old, one-time.
5. deceased, dead; defunct, nonextant.
6. of late lately, recently. See **lately** (*def.* **1**).
—*adv.* **7.** tardily, unpunctually, slowly, procrastinatively, dilatorily.
8. at the eleventh hour, at the last minute *or* moment, at the tail *or* tag end.
9. late into the night, until *or* at all hours, until *or* at the wee *or* small hours, until the early hours of the morning, until *or* at dawn, until *or* at daybreak, until *or* at cockcrow.
10. lately, recently, formerly, previously. See **lately** (*def.* **2**).

latecomer, *n.* **1.** Johnny-come-lately, late arrival, *Inf.* ten o'clock scholar; procrastinator, cunctator, postponer, delayer; dallier, dawdler, idler, trifler, lingerer, loiterer; laggard, *Inf.* slow-poke, *Inf.* poke, snail.
2. newcomer, arriviste, parvenu, *Fr. nouveau riche*, the newly rich, upstart.

lately, *adv.* **1.** of late, recently, in the past few days, in the last couple of weeks, in the past month; not long ago, a little while back, a short time ago; not long since, just last week, just the other day, yesterday.
2. late, formerly, previously, before this time, heretofore.

latency, *n.* **1.** potentiality, possibility; indication, suggestion, implication, hint, insinuation, intimation, undercurrent.
2. dormancy, quiescence, inertness, inertia, inactivity, inaction, passivity, idleness; lifelessness, motionlessness, immovability, immobility, stillness; slumber, somnolence, sleep, hibernation, estivation; lethargy, torpor, languidness, languor, sluggishness, dullness, stagnancy.
3. abeyance, postponement, deferment, deferral; suspension, halt, stop, pause, recess, break; interstice, interim, interval, intermission, intermittence, intermittency; delay, wait, waiting period, *Psychoanal.* latency period, *Pathol.* latent period.
4. secrecy, tacitness, covertness, concealment.

lateness, *n.* **1.** tardiness, unpunctuality, unpunctualness; slowness, laggardness, lagging, loitering, lingering, tarrying, dallying, dilly-dallying, dawdling, hanging back.
2. delay, cunctation, procrastination, dilatoriness, procrastinativeness; postponement, putting off, deferment, deferral, prorogation, suspension, holdup, stay; prolongation, protraction, extension, lengthening.

latent, *adj.* **1.** dormant, dormient, quiescent; veiled, hidden, *Obs.* latitant, *Inf.* closet, delitescent; potential, undeveloped, unrealized, possible; unsuspected, unseen, invisible, unapparent, indiscernible, undiscernable, imperceptible, inconspicuous, unsuggested, unindicated, unintimated, unintended.
2. secret, cryptic, enigmatic, mysterious, occult, arcane, esoteric, recondite; mystic, mystical, cabalistic, cabalistical; anagogic, anagogical; cryptographic, cryptographical; symbolic, figurative, emblematic, emblematical, metaphorical.
3. implied, implicit, implicated, implicative, implicatory, implicational, indicated, indicative, meant, hinted at, suggested, suggestive, adumbrative; insinuated, insinuatory, insinuative, insinuating, intimated; inferred, inferential, derived, derivative, concluded, conclusional, construed, constructive; unexpressed, unmentioned, unsaid, unstated, undeclared, unuttered, unarticulated, unproclaimed; unacknowledged, undisclosed, unexposed.
4. idle, inactive, passive, unstirring; inert, lifeless, motionless, immovable, immobile, unmoving, stationary; still, stock-still, *Chiefly Literary.* stilly, becalmed; resting, slumbering, slumberous, somnolent, sleeping, sleepy, hibernating, estivating, (*of land*) fallow; dull, sluggish, sedentary, stagnant, lethargic, listless, languid.
5. inoperative, nonfunctioning, nonperforming, unused; suspended, deferred, postponed, in abeyance; pausing, stopping, breaking, waiting, hesitating, hesitant, delaying, abeyant.
6. tacit, covert, concealed, confidential, covered up, undercover, underground, underhand, underhanded, devious, clandestine; indirect, deceptive, subversive, surreptitious; illicit, crooked, dishonest, fraudulent, *Inf.* shady; indefinite, undefined, dim, vague, unclear, hazy, cloudy, nebulous, indistinct.

later, *adj.* **1.** subsequent, next, following, coming; succeeding, successive, sequent, sequential.
—*adv.* **2.** subsequently, next, successively, sequentially, in sequel.
3. later on, at a later date, at a future time *or* date, at some point in the future, at a later time, *Inf.* farther down the road; by and by, in the future, hereafter, in time to come, in days to come; in *or* after a while, in *or* after a bit, before too long.

lateral, *adj.* sidewise, sideways, sidelong, sideward, sidewards; edgewise, edgeways; sideling, indirect, oblique, sloping, slanting; askance, askant, asquint; bordering, marginal, edging, verging, flanking, fringing, skirting; sided, flanked; abreast, collateral.

laterally, *adv.* sideways, sidewise, sideway, sidewards, sideward, sideling, sidelong; obliquely, slopingly, aslant, slantwise, slantways; edgeways, edgewise, broadside; abreast, alongside, to one side, beside, by the side of; neck and neck, side by side, cheek to cheek; askant, askance, asquint, askew, awry; transversely, crosswise, crossways, athwart, *Naut.* athwartships, across.

latest, *adj.* **1.** last, final, ultimate.
2. most recent, newest, *Inf.* in, current, up-to-date,

up-to-the-minute.

—*n.* **3. the latest** most recent news, most recent advance *or* development.

4. the latest thing *Inf.* the in thing, the last word, *Fr. dernier cri,* the ultimate, the end-all, *Sl.* the living end.

lath, *n.* slat, spline, splat, batten, panel, wood panel, plank, rail, *Naut.* strake.

lather, *n.* **1.** foam, froth; suds, soapsuds.

2. swelter, sweat.

3. *Informal.* dither, twitter, flutter, fluster, fret, fuss, flap, pother, *Inf.* tizzy, *Inf.* foofaraw, *Archaic.* pucker.

—*v.* **4.** foam, froth; suds *or* suds up, soap *or* soap up.

5. *Informal.* beat, thrash, drub, maul, beat black and blue, *Dial.* larrup, *Sl.* shellac; whip, horsewhip, flog, flail, whale, lash, *Inf.* hide, *Inf.* tan, *Inf.* tan [s.o.'s] hide; cane, birch, switch; strike, thump, thwack, whack, bang, *Inf.* clout, *Inf.* wallop, *Inf.* paste, *Inf.* biff, *Sl.* whump, *Sl.* cream; club, cudgel, bludgeon, pummel, buffet, batter, hammer, *Archaic.* belabor; punish, chastise, castigate, fustigate, *Inf.* lambaste.

lathery, *adj.* foamy, frothy; soapy, sudsy, soap-sudsy, bubbly.

latitude, *n.* **1.** parallel, meridian, grid line.

2. extent, range, scope, reach, compass, space, measure, stretch; breadth, width, span, spread, expanse; amplitude, fullness, wideness, broadness.

3. freedom, liberty, license, indulgence; free *or* unrestricted use, carte blanche, blank check; field, play, free play, free scope, free swing, full swing, swing; clearance, leeway, room, elbow room, margin, wide berth, spare room, room to spare; rope, enough rope, long rope *or* tether.

latitudinarian, *adj.* **1.** broad-minded, open-minded, liberal-minded, liberal, progressive, tolerant, unbigoted, unprepossessed; catholic, ecumenical; freethinking, unprejudiced, unbiased, unjaundiced, unwarped, unswayed, unaffected, uninfluenced; just, fair, impartial, equitable, even-handed, balanced, disinterested, dispassionate, straight, straight-shooting, square-dealing, fair and square; indulgent, lenient, permissive, nonrestrictive, easy, forbearing, amenable.

—*n.* **2.** liberal, progressive; free thinker, ecumenist, (*in religious matters*) libertine; independent, free lance, free spirit, nonpartisan, neutral.

latrine, *n.* toilet, bathroom, *Naut.* head, *Chiefly Dial.* jakes, *Sl.* john, *Sl.* can; *Chiefly Brit.* water closet *or* w.c., *Chiefly Brit.* convenience, *Brit. Inf.* loo; lavatory, rest room, wash room, comfort station, men's room, boys' *or* little boys' room, women's *or* ladies' room, girls' *or* little girls's room, powder room, lounge; privy, outhouse, backhouse, stool, closet, cloaca, necessary, *Brit. Sl.* bogs.

latter, *adj.* **1.** second-mentioned, (*of two*) last-mentioned.

2. later, following, succeeding, successive, after, consequent, ensuing.

3. posterior, rear, rearward, back, backward, hind, hinder, hindmost, aftermost, tail.

latter-day, *adj.* **1.** latter, successive. See **latter** (*def.* 2).

2. modern, recent, present-day, present-age, present-time, twentieth-century, contemporary, contemporaneous.

latterly, *adv.* recently, not long ago, a short time ago, a little while ago, just the other day, only yesterday; now, just now, *Inf.* right now; lately, of late, any more.

lattice, *n.* trellis, fretwork, grate, grating, grille; network, reticulation.

laud, *v.* **1.** praise, sound the praises of, sing the praises of, extol, cry up, *Inf.* crack up, *Archaic.* magnify, emblazon; encore, root for; approve enthusiastically, hail, commend, sanction, endorse; recommend, promote, say a good word for, put in a good word for; compliment, flatter, puff, boost, swell, lionize, belaud, make much of; applaud, acclaim, cheer, celebrate, congratulate, *Archaic.* gratulate.

2. eulogize, panegyrize, glorify, bless, exalt, elevate; pay tribute to, pay homage to, honor, crown, worship, adore; reverence, venerate, revere; appreciate, value, esteem, respect, admire.

—*n.* **3.** paean, hymn, song of praise, canticle, psalm; chant, plainsong; panegyric, encomium.

laudable, *adj.* praiseworthy, commendable, meritorious, estimable, admirable, *Brit. Dial.* gradely; reputable, creditable, respectable, deserving, worthy; sterling, exemplary, excellent, good, noble; honorable, virtuous, righteous, upright, just, right-minded, principled; unimpeachable, irreproachable, blameless.

laudation, *n.* **1.** praise, acclaim, acclamation, extolment, kudos, accolade, *Archaic.* magnification, citation; approval, approbation, endorsement, sanction, commendation, recommendation, advocacy, espousal; celebration, paean, congratulation, *Archaic.* gratulation; exultation, triumph, jubilation.

2. tribute, testimonial, credit, recognition; eulogy, eulogium, eulogization, exaltation, glorification, encomium, panegyric; honoring, crowning; homage, reverence, devotion, veneration; blessing, *Eccles.* benediction, *Archaic.* benison; honor, glory, repute, celebrity, fame, notoriety; esteem, favor, admiration, adulation; compliment, flattery; appreciation, estimation, respect, regard, affection, love.

laudatory, *adj.* praising, praiseful, acclamatory; panegyrical, eulogizing, eulogistic, eulogistical, encomiastical; approving, approbatory, approbative, commendatory; complimentary, flattering, uncritical, uncensorious; celebrative, celebratory, favorable, positive; glorifying, benedictory.

laugh, *v.* **1.** giggle, snicker, snigger, titter, tee-hee, ha-ha, haw-haw, *Sl.* yuk-yuk; *Inf.* break up, *Inf.* crack up, burst out laughing; shake with laughter, be convulsed, split one's sides, *Inf.* roll on the floor, *Inf.* be in stitches, *Inf.* double up *or* over, *Inf.* die; guffaw, *Sl.* yuk it up, *Sl.* yuk; chortle, chuckle, cackle; cachinnate, roar, shriek.

2. laugh off laugh away *or* down, ridicule, dismiss, ignore, pay no attention *or* mind to, overlook, shrug off.

3. laugh at a. deride, scoff at, mock, jeer, ridicule, knock, gird at; fleer, guy, horselaugh, *Australian.* chiack; make fun of, lampoon, satirize, parody, pasquinade; make sport of, poke fun at, make a fool out of, make the butt of, *Sl.* make an ass of; tease, rally, *Inf.* roast, banter, chaff, rib, kid, *Sl.* razz; flout, scorn, sneer at, disdain, pooh-pooh; hiss, boo, hoot at, heckle, catcall; harass, *Sl.* put down, abuse. **b.** reject, spurn, discount, rule out; disbelieve, refuse to accept, ignore, close one's eyes to.

4. laugh on the other side of one's face *or* mouth be dejected, be disheartened, be dispirited, be downcast, be down in the dumps, *Sl.* be bummed out; be discouraged, be dismayed; get one's comeuppance, get a taste of one's own medicine.

—*n.* **5.** giggle, snicker, snigger, titter, tee-hee, hee-hee, haw-haw, hee-haw; guffaw, *Sl.* yuk, *Sl.* yuks, horselaugh, *Inf.* belly laugh; chortle, chuckle, cackle; cachinnation, roar, shriek, scream, screech; laughter, risibility; fit of laughter, peal of laughter, burst of laughter; *Both Inf.* boff, boffo.

laughable, *adj.* **1.** funny, amusing, comical, risible, humorous, *Inf.* boffo; hilarious, hysterical, riotous, uproarious, too funny for words, side-splitting, *Sl.* a scream, *Sl.* a gas; entertaining, diverting, *Inf.* fun; jolly, mirthful, merry, jovial, jocose, jocular, waggish; teasing, joking, jesting, *Inf.* kidding, *Inf.* funning, playful, sportive, clownish, clowning.

2. ludicrous, absurd, ridiculous, nonsensical, foolish, *Sl.* cockeyed; poppycockish, *Sl.* cockamamie, amphigoric; crazy, crazed, *Sl.* kooky, *Scot.* doiled; daft, *Inf.* daffy, crackbrained, *Inf.* nutty.

laughing *n.* **1.** laughter, laugh, risibility; giggle, snicker, snigger, titter. See **laugh** (*def.* **5**).

—adj. **2.** happy, cheerful, cheery, full of cheer, gay, sunny; jovial, merry, jocund, jolly, mirthful; riant, smiling, happy as a lark; joyful, joyous, jubilant, rejoicing, gleeful; exultant, in seventh heaven, elated, overjoyed.

3. giggling, snickering, sniggering, tittering; guffawing, *Sl.* yukking, chortling, chuckling, cackling; cachinnating, roaring, shrieking.

4. funny, amusing, comical, laughable. See **laughable** (*def.* **1**).

laughingstock, *n.* butt, fool, everybody's fool, ass, joke, fair game, *Inf.* goat, *Brit. Sl.* mug; dupe, gudgeon, *Brit. Dial.* cull, *Archaic.* cully, *Inf.* chump, *Sl.* sap, *Sl.* schnook, *Sl.* schlemiel, *Sl.* boob; greenhorn, sitting duck, easy *or* soft mark, easy *or* soft target, *Inf.* sucker, *Inf.* cinch, *Sl.* patsy, *Sl.* pigeon, *U.S. Sl.* fall guy, *Sl.* softie, *Sl.* soft touch, *Sl.* pushover; pawn, puppet, tool, instrument, cat's paw, creature, minion, dummy, *Sl.* stooge.

laughter *n.* **1.** laugh, risibility; giggle, snicker, titter. See **laugh** (*def.* **5**).

2. laughing, giggling, snickering. See **laughing** (*def.* **3**).

3. amusement, entertainment, exhilaration; joviality, gaiety, gayness, merriness, joy, joyfulness, joyousness, jollity, jocundity, glee, mirth, mirthfulness, good *or* high spirits, hilarity, *Rare.* heyday; elation, sunniness, rosiness, airiness, blitheness, light-heartedness.

launch, *v.* **1.** set afloat, float; send off *or* forth, send, push off; move, actuate, set in motion, set going; propel, impel, push, shove, thrust; spur, prod, prick, goad, poke, urge *or* drive forward.

2. begin, commence, start, go ahead; embark, set sail, set to *or* about, turn to, *Inf.* take off, *Inf.* kick off; take steps, get going, get a move on, get on the stick, start off, start out, move out, get the show on the road; start in, plunge in, *Inf.* dive in, *Inf.* get one's feet wet, *Inf.* get down to it, *Inf.* get to it.

3. initiate, instigate, start the ball rolling, take the first step, take the initiative, take the plunge, make a start, break the ice; institute, inaugurate, found, establish, set up, organize, originate, break ground, lay the foundation; introduce, broach, usher in; create, beget, engender, give birth to, give rise to, sow the seeds of.

4. hurl, cast, throw, toss, dart, shy, chuck, pitch; dash, sling, let fly, send; fling, flirt, heave, jerk, cant, shoot, fire; propel, project, jaculate, catapult.

launder, *v.* wash, wash up *or* out, scrub, soap; wash and iron, press, do up; clean, clean up, *Sl.* crumb up, cleanse, purify, delouse; rinse, soak, ret, bleach, blue; bathe, lave, tub; scour, polish; dry clean.

launderer, *n.* washer, washerman, washerwoman, washman, washwoman, laundress, wash lady, wash maid, *Fr. blanchisseur, Fr. blanchisseuse,* laundry man *or* woman; cleaning man *or* woman, cleaning lady, domestic; maid, servant, downstairs maid, chambermaid, valet, manservant; mother's helper, au pair girl.

laundry, *n.* **1.** wash, washing, dirty clothes, *Sl.* socks and jocks, *Sl.* skivies; clothes for the cleaner.

2. laundromat, launderette, *Fr. blanchissage*; tub room, laundry room, lavatory; dry cleaner, cleaner and presser; Chinese laundry.

laureate, *adj.* honored, recognized, lauded, praised, acclaimed, noted; notable, distinguished, renowned, illustrious, famous, famed, well-known.

laurel, *n.* **1.** evergreen tree; mountain laurel, rhododendron.

2. (*all of honor*) emblem, badge, mark, sign, token.

3. (*all of laurel foliage*) branch, stem, twig, wreath, garland.

4. *Usu.* **laurels** honors, awards, commendations, citations, tributes, honorable mentions; gifts, prizes, trophies, blue ribbons; praises, praise, kudos, extolment, laudation, acclaim, acclamation, *Archaic.* magnification; glory, honor, distinction, prestige, notability; fame, renown, illustriousness, celebrity, popularity.

lava, *n.* **1.** molten *or* fluid rock, *Geol.* magma, panhoehoe; scoria, *Geol.* ash, *Geol.* cinders.

2. igneous rock; granite, rhyolite, obsidian, pumice, andesite, basalt.

lavation, *n.* wash, washing, cleaning, cleansing, lavage, *Archaic.* laving, bath, bathing, *Both Brit. Inf.* tub, tubbing. See **wash** (*def.* **9**).

lavatory, *n.* **1.** bathroom, washroom, wash-up, *Inf.* lav; restroom, *Sl.* donnicker, comfort station, powder room, women's *or* ladies' room, girls' *or* little girls' room, men's room, boys' *or* little boys' room; *All Chiefly Brit.* water closet, w.c., convenience; toilet, *Sl.* john, *Sl.* can, *Chiefly Dial.* jakes, *Naut.* head, potty, *Brit. Inf.* loo; latrine, privy, cloaca, outhouse, backhouse, stool, *Chiefly New England.* necessary, *Brit. Sl.* bog.

2. washbowl, washbasin, sink, washstand; washtub, bathtub, tub.

lave, *v.* **1.** bathe, bath, wash, wash up, clean, clean up, scrub up, cleanse, lather, soap, *Brit. Inf.* tub, *Chiefly Scot.* dight; deterge, (*of clothes*) launder, shampoo, *Brit. Dial.* buck; shower, rinse, flush, douse, douche; foment, sponge, swab, wipe, mop, rub; immerse, submerge, dunk, dip; soak, steep, wet, irrigate, drench, imbue, saturate.

2. (*all of a river, sea, etc.*) splash, dash, wash against, break against, beat against, thrash against; roll, lap, undulate, surge, swell, wave, ripple; rush, flow, run, sweep.

lavish, *adj.* **1.** generous, unstinting, open-handed, bountiful, liberal, big-hearted, great-hearted, unselfish, princely; extravagant, excessive, wasteful, profligate, squandering, improvident, prodigal, thriftless, intemperate; epicurean, sybaritic, unrestrained, wild.

2. profuse, excessive, fulsome, immoderate, exaggerated; in excess, overmuch, superfluous, redundant, *Fr. de trop,* unnecessary, surplus, unwarranted, inordinate; effusive, overly emotional, grandiloquent, overdone, *Inf.* a bit much, overwhelming.

3. limitless, unlimited, myriad, unmeasured, plenty, plenteous, plentiful, abundant, superabundant, copious, ample, abounding, unstinted, wholesale; luxuriant, opulent, ornate, Byzantine, sumptuous, gorgeous, rich, costly, dear; ostentatious, pretentious, showy, *Inf.* ritzy, *Inf.* fancy, *Inf.* high-falutin; imposing, splendid, *Inf.* splashy, *Inf.* swanky, *Inf.* swank, *Inf.* spiff, *Inf.* jazzy, *Inf.* toney.

—v. **4.** heap, pour, shower, spill, be generous with, bestow, give freely, thrust upon; waste, squander, dissipate, drain, exhaust; *Inf.* fling away, *Inf.* throw away, *Inf.* run through, spend recklessly, *Inf.* scatter to the winds.

lavishness, *n.* **1.** generosity, bounty, largess, openhandedness, liberality, munificence; hospitality, unselfishness, big-heartedness, great-heartedness.

2. extravagance, profligacy, improvidence, prodigality, thriftlessness, immoderation, intemperance, wastefulness, Sybaritism, Epicureanism, self-indulgence.

3. superfluity, excess, overabundance, surplus, superfluity; showiness, ostentation, display, show, parade; splendor, shine, dash, *Inf.* splash.

4. plenty, plenitude, abundance, amplitude, sumptuousness, luxury, opulence, richness.

law, *n.* **1.** principle, regulation, rule, ordinance, bylaw, statute; enactment, act, measure, bill; control, restriction, ban, embargo, prohibition.

2. command, mandate, commandment, directive, order, court order, injunction, decree, edict, dictate, dictum; canon, *Both Rom. Cath. Ch.* bull, encyclical; pronouncement, pronunciamento, proclamation, declaration, statement, manifesto.

3. constitution, body of laws, set of principles, rules and regulations, bylaws, code, charter.

4. system of law, legal code, corpus juris, *Law.* digest, *Law.* equity; common law, statute law, international law, criminal law, *Brit.* crown law; canon law, Corpus Juris Canonici, Codex Juris Canonici.

5. jurisprudence, science of law, *Law.* jus, legal philosophy; law-writing, nomology, nomography; *Civil Law.* court decisions.

6. bar, legal profession.

7. litigation, legal action, *Law.* action, proceeding *or* legal proceeding; *Law.* prosecution, action *or* suit at law, lawsuit, *Law.* cause, *Law.* case.

8. lawmen, officers *or* agents of the law, police, *Inf.* cops, *Sl.* bulls, *Sl.* pigs, *Sl.* the man.

9. moral law, golden rule, rule of conduct, rubric, precept; directive, direction, instruction, guideline, rule of thumb, basic rule; formula, formulary, recipe, method, way; model, canon, standard, criterion, convention, custom, practice; natural law, general truth, universal truth, maxim, axiom, truism, truth *or* self-evident truth; principle, tenet, doctrine, dogma, belief, opinion, theory; mathematical rule, *Math.* proposition, *Math.* corollary.

10. the law Law of Moses, Ten Commandments, Decalogue.

law-abiding, *adj.* lawful, obedient, obeying, compliant, complying, dutiful, duteous; good, principled, upright, honorable, upstanding.

lawbreaker, *n.* **1.** criminal, felon, misdemeanant; convict, *Sl.* jailbird, parolee, ex-convict, *Inf.* ex-con, recidivist, repeat offender, *Inf.* chronic crook; transgressor, trespasser, offender, culprit, miscreant; malefactor, evildoer, wrongdoer, sinner; malfeasant, misfeasor; perjurer; *Inf.* scofflaw.

2. gangster, mobster, racketeer, mafioso, desperado, terrorist; thug, tough, *Inf.* toughie, mugger, ruffian, *Inf.* plugugly, rowdy, hoodlum, *Sl.* hood, *Inf.* goon, hooligan, *Inf.* roughneck, *Inf.* baddy, *Sl.* bad actor, *Sl.* gunsel, *Sl.* mug, *Australian Sl.* larrikin, *Brit. Hist.* Mohock, (*in Paris*) apache.

3. assassin, murderer, killer, slayer, sniper; strangler, cutthroat, garroter; liquidator, *Euph.* silencer, *Euph.* dispatcher; gunman, *All U.S. Sl.* gun, hired gun, hit man, trigger-man, hatchet man, torpedo.

4. bandit, hold-up man, *Sl.* stick-up man, armed robber; robber, burglar, thief, stealer, *Inf.* crook, *Law.* larcener *or* larcenist; shoplifter, pickpocket, purse-snatcher, cutpurse; embezzler, peculator, *Law.* defalcator.

5. extortionist, blackmailer; smuggler, runner; forger, counterfeiter; kidnapper, abductor; arsonist, incendiary; rioter, bomb-planter.

lawbreaking, *n.* offense, violation, contravention, infraction, breach, infringement; misdemeanor, *Law.* delict, transgression, fault, misdeed, wrongdoing, *Law.* malfeasance, *Law.* misfeasance; *Law.* felony, capital crime, outrage; moral offense, error, sin, wrong, trespass, *Both Rom. Cath. Ch.* venial sin, mortal sin; slip, lapse, backsliding; failure, neglect, negligence, delinquency, dereliction, omission, *Law.* nonfeasance.

lawful, *adj.* **1.** legal, jural, according to law, de jure, licit, constitutional, permitted *or* allowed by law permissible, allowable.

2. legitimate, *Sl.* legit, vested, entitled, rightful, right, just, valid, legally sound; sanctioned, authorized, empowered, chartered, licensed, legalized, warranted, commissioned; statutory, statutable, legislative, legislated; enacted, prescribed, ordained, ordered, decreed, edicted, mandated; appointed, constituted, designated, named, selected, chosen; approved, recognized, acknowledged, accepted, canonical.

3. judicial, judiciary, judicatory, juridical, jurisprudential, juristic, jurisdictive, forensic.

4. law-abiding, obedient, obeying, compliant, complying. See **law-abiding.**

lawfulness, *n.* **1.** legality, constitutionality; permissibility, permissibleness, allowableness.

2. legitimacy, legitimateness, accordance with the law; right, rightfulness, validness, validity, legal soundness.

3. permission, liberty, license, formal consent, sanction; authority, authorization, legalization, warrant, commission; appointment, ordination, decreeing, designation, naming, selection; approval, recognition, acknowledgment, acceptance.

lawless, *adj.* **1.** rebellious, mutinous, insurrectionary, insurgent, seditious, seditionary, revolutionary, secessionist, riotous, terrorist; defiant, unsubmissive, insubordinate, disobedient, wayward; ungovernable, intractable, uncontrollable, unconformable, noncompliant; refractory, recalcitrant, contumacious; nonconformist, unconventional, nonconforming, eccentric, deviatory, deviative, divergent.

2. unbridled, unrestrained, unchecked, ungoverned; chaotic, rampageous, unruly, lax, loose, disorderly, disorganized; nihilistic, anarchic, anarchical, anarchistic; intemperate, immoderate, incontinent, self-indulgent; dissipated, licentious, wanton; wild, rampant.

3. illegal, unlawful, illicit, law-breaking; criminal, felonious, larcenous, malfeasant, misfeasant, transgressive, offending, violating, violational, violative.

4. dishonest, unprincipled, unscrupulous, *Inf.* crooked, villainous, piratical; nefarious, wicked, iniquitous, flagitious; vile, foul, corrupt, venal, miscreant; reprobate, miscreant, depraved, degenerate, dissolute; knavish, roguish, rascally, scampish.

lawlessness, *n.* **1.** anarchy, anarchism, chaos; terrorism, nihilism, violence, destructiveness; reign of terror, ochlocracy, mobocracy, mob rule; rebellion, mutiny, insurrection, sedition, insurgency, revolt, uprising, revolution, riot.

2. crime, criminality, felonious *or* larcenous conduct, malfeasance, misfeasance, racketeering, piracy; dishonesty, unscrupulousness, unscrupulosity, unprincipledness, *Inf.* crookedness; illegality, unlawfulness, illicitness.

3. unrestraint, abandon, license, unruliness, laxity, looseness; disorder, confusion, disarray, disorganization.

4. licentiousness, wantonness, dissipation, profligacy; self-indulgence, intemperance, immoderation, incontinence.

5. disobedience, insubordination, waywardness, in-

tractability, uncontrollability; noncompliance, nonconformity, recalcitrance, contumaciousness.

6. wickedness, iniquity, corruption, venality, bribery; depravity, degeneracy, dissoluteness; roguery, knavery, rascality.

lawmaker, *n.* **1.** legislator, lawgiver, solon, elder statesman, statesman, politician, politico.

2. Member of Congress, M.C., Member of Parliament, M.P.; senator, congressman *or* congresswoman, legislatrix, *U.S.* congressman-at-large, representative, *Sl.* rep, *Amer. Hist.* burgess, conscript fathers; state legislator, state senator, state representative, *U.S.* assemblyman; councilman, (*in most New England states*) selectman.

lawn[1], *n.* greensward, grassplot, patch of grass, green, grassy land; grass, turf, sod, sward, artificial grass, *Trademark.* Astroturf; grounds, gardens, grassland, field, meadow, *Archaic.* mead; greenery, verdure, green vegetation, herbage, pasturage.

lawn[2], *n.* linen, cotton cloth; cloth, fabric, material, textile, woven fabric.

lawsuit, *n.* litigation, contention, dispute, argument, legal argument, disputation; suit at law, legal action *or* proceedings, legal remedy; action, proceedings, case, cause, bringing of charges, laying of charges, bringing to book; prosecution, arraignment, indictment, allegation, charge, bill of particulars.

lawyer, *n.* **1.** attorney, attorney-at-law, legal advisor, *Law.* counsel, counselor, courselor-at-law, advocate; officer of the court, member of the bar, legal practitioner, legalist; legist, jurist, jurisprudent, *Civil Law.* jurisconsult, civilian; pleader, friend of the court, amicus curiae; patent attorney, conveyancer, criminal lawyer, public defender, defense counsel, attorney for the defense; prosecutor, prosecuting attorney, district attorney, *Inf.* D. A., public prosecutor, attorney general; *Sl.* shyster, *Sl.* ambulance chaser, *Sl.* jailhouse lawyer, *Sl.* latrine lawyer, *Sl.* mouthpiece, *Inf.* pettifogger, *Inf.* Philadelphia lawyer.

2. agent, factor, deputy, proctor, proxy, substitute, procurator, attorney-in-fact; mediator, intermediator, intercessor, ombudsman, go-between, spokesman, negotiant, arbitrator.

3. judge, justice, judicator, moderator, justice-of-the-peace, J.P., magistrate, jurat, notary, scrivener.

4. *British.* barrister, solicitor, bencher, gownsman, king's *or* queen's Counsel, K. C. *or* Q. C., *Old. Eng. Law.* tubman, *Old Eng. Law.* postman.

lax, *adj.* **1.** loose, slack, negligent, neglectful, remiss; careless, inattentive, inadvertent, unmindful, unthoughtful, unthinking, nonobservant, disregardful; imprudent, injudicious, indiscreet, uncircumspect; unwary, incautious, off-guard, unguarded, asleep at the switch, unheeding, heedless; unreliable, undependable, insecure, unsound, infirm, unsolid, unstable, unsubstantial, unsteady, desultory.

2. inexact, inaccurate, unprecise, unmeticulous, unrigorous, unconscientious, unfussy, unpunctilious; nonspecific, broad, general, shapeless, amorphous, *Sl.* blobby; vague, indefinite, indecisive, random, inchoate, disordered, chaotic, hit-or-miss, *Inf.* chancy.

3. unstrict, undemanding, nonrestrictive; gentle, lenient, permissive, overpermissive, overindulgent, easy, easygoing, *Inf.* wishy-washy, weak, relaxed, complaisant, mild, moderate, mellow, tender, unexacting, tolerant, indulgent, forbearing; malleable, elastic, pliable, pliant, tractable, flexile, flexible.

4. disorderly, sloppy, untidy, *Inf.* messy; slovenly, slatternly, *Sl.* raunchy; unorganized, *Inf.* harum-scarum; casual, indifferent; perfunctory, blasé, devil-may-care, thoughtless, forgetful, absent-minded; lackadaisical, listless, apathetic; lazy, indolent, improvident, free and easy, untroubled, unconcerned, unworried, happy-go-lucky, insouciant.

5. dissolute, licentious, libertine, lascivious, debauched, wasted; wanton, wild, unbridled, profligate, abandoned, promiscuous, of easy virtue *or* morals; coarse, gross, crude; degenerate, depraved, corrupt, perverted; wicked, immoral, sinful, peccant, vice-ridden; unregenerate, unredeemable, unprincipled; shameful, disgraceful.

6. hanging, drooping, droopy, bagging, baggy, sagging, saggy, flapping, *Inf.* floppy; limp, flabby, soft, flaccid, rubbery.

laxative, *n.* cathartic, purgative, aperient, physic, ipecac, castor oil, ricinus oil, salts, dose of salts; purgation, purge, dose, *Med.* catharsis.

laxity, *n.* **1.** looseness, slackness, laxness, carelessness, heedlessness, mindlessness, inattention, unmindfulness, absent-mindedness; neglect, negligence, dereliction, remissness; unrigorousness, noninterference, laissez faire, nonrestriction; nonobservance, unwariness, obliviousness, disregard, turning one's head; oversight, overlooking, lapse, failure, default, omission, nonfeasance, *Law.* laches.

2. inexactness, inaccuracy, inexactitude, unpreciseness, imprecision; slovenliness, *Inf.* sloppiness; vagueness, indefiniteness, broadness, generality, amorphousness, shapelessness, *Sl.* blobbiness; inchoateness, disorder.

3. relaxedness, nonchalance, casualness, ataraxia; listlessnesss, lack of concern, sloth, acedia, indolence, laziness, lethargy, languidness, languor; indifference, perfunctoriness, insipidity, vapidity; unconcern, disinterest, disregard, insolicitude, unanxiousness, pococurantism.

4. gentleness, easiness, lenience, leniency, mildness; unstrictness, permissiveness, overpermissiveness, overindulgence, softness, weakness; relaxation, flexibility, pliancy, tolerance, allowance; humoring, pampering, coddling, giving in, catering to.

5. freedom, release, letting go, license, indulgence, unrestraint, abandon; loose morals, easy virtue, immorality, promiscuity, improbity, indecency.

6. flaccidity, flaccidness, flabbiness, limpness, rubberiness, floppiness, laxation, yield, *Inf.* give, plasticity, nonrigidity.

lay[1], *v.* **1.** put, place, set, rest, *Inf.* stick, leave, park, plant; set down, seat, settle; incline, lean.

2. drop, floor, lay low, prostrate; fell, knock *or* cut *or* strike down, sink.

3. lodge, submit, present, prefer, bring forward.

4. repose, impute, lay to; attribute, assign, ascribe, designate, insinuate.

5. bet, wager, give odds, gamble; chance, hazard, risk; plunge, play; deposit, put down, stake.

6. impose, apply, inflict; enjoin, prescribe; demand, exact, order.

7. posit, station, locate, site, situate; pitch, camp; establish, set up.

8. cover, spread, overspread, overlay; finish, veneer, varnish.

9. devise, arrange, plan, contrive, make; prepare, work up, plot, schematize.

10 level, flatten, smooth, even, plane.

11. allay, relieve, assuage, ease; alleviate, mitigate, palliate, soften, soothe, salve; calm, still, quiet.

12. aim, direct, train, point, sight, angle.

13. *Slang.* copulate, couple, mate, have sex, have sexual relations, have intercourse; sleep with, lie with, go to bed with, *Sl.* get in the hay with, *Sl.* shack up with, *Euph.* go all the way with.

14. **lay about one** **a.** lay into, *Sl.* light into, strike out, flail, *Inf.* slug, sock, *Sl.* give the one-two, *Sl.* windmill; take the offensive, attack, assault, assail; attack tooth and nail, harry, harass; set upon, beset, beleaguer, besiege, storm. **b.** proceed, set out, *Inf.* get a move on, stir, scramble, bestir oneself; move, *Inf.* mogate, start, push on *or* ahead; go at it, plug away, carry on, keep the ball rolling, keep going, keep busy, fall to with a will.

15. lay aside a. abandon, reject, *Inf.* leave out in the cold, discard, wash one's hands of; disregard, repudiate, renounce, drop, drop the subject; brush off, shrug off. **b.** put aside, push aside, cast aside, shunt, dismiss; put out of mind, *Inf.* pay no mind, forget, ignore; put off, *Inf.* put on the back burner, *Inf.* sweep under the rug; postpone, sleep on, delay, defer; shelve, table, pigeonhole, file away, do it mañana.

16. lay away a. lay in, store, stockpile, hoard, accumulate, amass; garner, collect, treasure; pile, stack, stow away, *Inf.* stash, heap; reserve, save, put away, put *or* lay aside, set by, preserve, retain; deposit, reposit, shelve; build up a nest egg, save for a rainy day, husband, economize. **b.** bury, inter, inhume, entomb, consign to the grave; lay to rest, put to rest, *Inf.* plant, *Sl.* put six feet under, *Sl.* deep-six.

17. lay bare expose, uncover, divest, lay open; unmask, unveil, undrape, unclothe, uncloak, undress, remove the mask *or* veil *or* chadri; lift the curtain, bring to light, let into the sunshine; peel, shuck, bare, show, strip; unearth, exhume, exhibit, disinter; disclose, divulge, reveal; broadcast, publish, air, make known, relate, tell, utter, unfold, narrate, breathe; make a clean breast, unburden, open; confess, acknowledge, admit, own, allow; blurt out, blab, let slip, leak, let the cat out of the bag.

18. lay down give, give up, drop, quit, relinquish; yield, cede, turn over, surrender, submit.

19. lay down the law command, dictate, order, mandate; direct, govern, regulate, control, call the shots; crack down, put one's foot down, read the riot act, brook no denial, not take no for an answer, insist, demand; dogmatize, assert, proclaim, maintain; dominate, take the upper hand, rule the roost, show who's boss; domineer, intimidate, *Inf.* bulldoze, ride roughshod over, rule with an iron fist, lord it over.

20. lay for *Slang.* lie in wait for, ambush, ambuscade, lurk, skulk, prowl; *Sl.* set up, *Sl.* set up for a fall; entrap, set a trap for, ensnare, waylay, await, sneak up on.

21. lay hold of grab, nab, seize, snatch; catch, get hold of, get, stop, snag; clutch, grip, clasp, grasp; clinch, grapple; wrest, pull, jerk, twist.

22. lay it on *Informal.* **a.** exaggerate, embroider, hyperbolize, stretch a point, stretch the truth, talk big, boast, blow one's own horn. **b.** flatter, *Inf.* soft-soap, jolly, butter up, slaver, fawn, drool; blarney, wheedle, cajole; praise, overpraise, praise to the skies, overlaud, pile it on, lay it on with a trowel, slather; give fulsome praise, overdo it.

23. lay off a. dismiss, discharge, let go, fire, cashier, strike off the rolls, give [s.o.] the pink slip; sack, kick out, can, give the ax, ax, bounce, chuck. **b.** *Slang.* (*usu. imperative*) quit, quit it, stay, stop; withhold, desist, *Naut.* avast, cease, belay, hold off, let up, get off my back; enough, aw c'mon, *Sl.* alright already; knock it off, cut it out, can it; come off it; psst, hush, shh, shush.

24. lay out a. arrange, lay in order, prepare, set up *or* forth; design, plan, map, chart; outline, put down, sketch. **b.** spend, expend, pay, disburse; shell out, fork out, ante up; contribute, give. **c.** *Slang.* knock out, K.O. *or* kayo, knock galley-west, put out of action; flatten, strike down, topple, fell; demolish, annihilate, destroy, blitz, kill.

25. lay out in lavender *Slang.* tell off, bawl out, yell at, tell a thing or two, tell where to go, give a piece of one's mind, call on the carpet; upbraid, reprove, rebuke, reprimand; scold, admonish, chide, berate, take to task, *Inf.* give what for, put the fear of God into; tear the hide off, scorch, wither, demolish.

26. lay over a. postpone, put over, defer, let hang fire, table, lay aside. **b.** stop, stop over, rest, break, overnight.

27. lay up ail, fall ill, disable; get the miseries, catch a bug; droop, languish, fail, wilt, weaken, lose strength; take to one's bed.

—n. **28.** form, order, posture, attitude, stance; plan, design, appearance; terrain, course.

lay[2], *adj.* **1.** laic, nonclerical, nonordained, nonministerial; profane, nonreligious, nonecclesiastical; mundane, temporal, earthly, worldly, common, ordinary.

2. nonprofessional, dilettante, dilettantish, proletarian, plebian; unschooled, untaught, amateur.

lay[3], *n.* poem, lyric, epode, canzone, canzona, ballade, ballata, rhyme, rime, canto; song, strain, air, descant, refrain, canzonet, roundelay; ballad, lied, cantata, canticle, *Music.* cantus firmus, carol; art song, ditty, madrigal, recitative.

layer, *n.* **1.** skin, shell, rind, peel; membrane, *Anat., Zool.* cortex, lamella, pellicle; integument, tegument, tegmen; scale, flake, lamina; lamination, laminate.

2. sliver, splinter, shive, shaving; slice, rasher, cutting, cut, slab, piece; plate, wafer, disc; pane, panel, plank, board.

3. cover, covering, blanket, mantle, cloak, curtain, mask; sheet, carpet, coat, coating, film, gloss, veneer, finish; overcoat, overcoating, overlay; wrapping, envelope, lining, casing; course, coping, cap; flap, fold.

4. story, tier, floor, level, stratum, stratification, substratum; band, belt, zone; ridge, *Geol.* esker.

5. *Horiculture.* shoot, sprout, runner, tendril, graft; branch, spray, switch, twig, stem, limb, bough.

lay figure, *n.* **1.** artist's model, model, figure, figurine, puppet, doll; image, effigy.

2. mannequin, manikin, dummy, dressmaker's model.

3. nonentity, nobody, nothing, cipher, insignificancy, jackstraw, little fellow, *Inf.* little guy, man on the street, John Doe, *Inf.* small fry, *Sl.* small fish, *Sl.* nebbish, *Sl.* Joe Blow *or* Joe Doakes.

layman, *n.* laic, parishioner, one of the flock *or* assembly; nonprofessional, catechumen, dilettante, amateur.

layoff, *n.* dismissal, discharge, firing, sacking; unemployment, hard times, lean times, depression.

layout, *n.* **1.** arrangement, disposal, spread; plan, design, outline; chart, blueprint, map, sketch, display.

2. collection, set, group, aggregation, *Inf.* bunch, *Inf.* bundle; *Inf.* setup.

layover, *n.* stopover, stop, stay, stayover, overnight stop *or* stay; rest, pause, break, interruption, delay.

laze, *v.* **1.** idle, loaf, lounge, do nothing, *Inf.* lallygag; lie around, lounge around, loll around, stand around, hang around *or* about, loiter around *or* about, *Brit. Dial.* lollop around, *Sl.* goof off, *Sl.* sit on one's butt *or* duff.

2. pass time, while away the hours, waste time, kill time, consume time; trifle, fritter, fool away, waste precious hours.

laziness, *n.* **1.** idleness, indolence, slothfulness, sloth, fainéance, do-nothingness, otiosity; unindustriousness, unenterprisingness, unambitiousness, want *or* lack of ambition *or* enterprise, nonaggressiveness; listlessness, *Dial.* limpsiness, lackadaisicalness, insouciance, pococurantism; shiftlessness, worthlessness, good-for-nothingness; slackness, laxity, remissness, negligence, neglectfulness, carelessness.

2. inertia, inactivity, stagnation, torpor, supineness; sluggishness, lumpishness, lethargy, phlegm, heaviness, dullness, languidness, languor, hebetudinousness, lentitudinousness; somnolence, sleepiness, drowsiness.

lazy, *adj.* **1.** idle, indolent, slothful, fainéant, do-nothing, otiose; unindustrious, unenterprising, unambitious, nonaggressive; listless, *Dial.* limpsy, lackadaisical, insouciant, pococurante, easy-going, free-and-easy, carefree; shiftless, worthless, good-for-nothing, ne'er-do-well; slack, lax, remiss, negligent, neglectful, careless.

2. slow-moving, slow-going, creeping, crawling, *Inf.* poky; lingering, loitering, lagging, dillydallying, dallying, laggard, foot-dragging; inert, inactive, stagnant, torpid, supine; sluggish, lumpish, lethargic, phlegmatic, heavy, dull, languid, languorous, hebetudinous, lentitudinous; sleepy, drowsy, somnolent, yawny.

lazybones, *n.* *Informal.* lie-abed, slugabed, *Inf.* lazyboots; *Inf.* lazylegs; idler, loafer, lounger, loller, fainéant, do-nothing, slouch, sluggard, *Inf.* goldbricker, *Sl.* goof-off, *Brit. Sl.* skiver; laggard, loiterer, lingerer; dallier, dillydallier, dawdler, moper.

lea, *n.* **1.** meadow, meadowland, *Archaic.* mead; pasture, pasturage, pastureland, *Scot.* shieling; plain, prairie, range; grassland, savanna, steppe, pampas, veld, (*in South America*) campo, (*in Spanish America*) llano.

—*adj.* **2.** fallow, untilled, uncultivated, unsown.

leach, *v.* percolate, lixiviate; filter, filtrate, strain, extract, drain.

lead[1], *v.* **1.** guide, conduct, marshal, usher, escort, convoy; take the lead, lead the way. See **lead**[1] (*def.* **8**).

2. precede, antecede, come *or* go before, come first, go ahead of, go in advance; rate, rank, outrank, have precedence, have priority.

3. influence, affect, weigh with; cause, induce, prompt, move, incline, dispose, predispose; persuade, convince, sway, bring round, prevail upon, win over, talk into, wear down, soften up, *Inf.* con, *Inf.* sell [s.o.] on; bend, bend to one's will, *Inf.* lead by the nose, *Sl.* twist [s.o.'s] arm; counsel, advise, admonish, point out; call forth, bring on, elicit, evoke, provoke, instigate.

4. command, order, prescribe, lay down the law; rule, reign, dominate, predominate, have the ascendancy, have the upper *or* whip hand, crack the whip, call the shots, *Inf.* rule the roost, *Inf.* wear the pants; head, *Inf.* head up, preside over, hold the reins, be in the driver's seat, take the helm, pilot, captain, *Inf.* skipper, quarterback, call the signals; supervise, superintend, oversee, *Inf.* boss; direct, govern, manage, regulate, handle, carry on, drive, *Inf.* run.

5. excel, exceed, surpass, transcend, outstrip, outrun, outdistance, distance, leave behind, steal a march on; eclipse, outshine, overshadow, throw into the shade; outdo, outplay, outperform, outrival, outpoint, outstep, overleap, overcome, best, better, *Inf.* go one better; cap, top, overtop, tower above, put to shame, *Inf.* show up, *Inf.* run rings *or* circles around.

6. **lead off** begin, commence, start, go ahead, *Inf.* jump off, *Inf.* kick off; take steps, get going, get a move on, get on the stick, start off, start out, move out, get the show on the road; start in, plunge in, *Inf.* pitch in, *Inf.* steam in, *Inf.* dive in, *Inf.* get one's feet wet, *Inf.* get down to it, *Inf.* get to it.

7. **lead on** mislead, delude, deceive, trick, hoax, dupe, hoodwink, *Inf.* bamboozle, *Inf.* put one over on [s.o.]; beckon, invite, draw on, bait, bait the hook; tempt, lure, allure, seduce, beguile, inveigle, entice, charm, tantalize; entrap, trap, ensnare, snare, net, bag; court, pay court to, woo; wheedle, cajole, blandish, blarney, *Inf.* soft-soap.

8. **lead the way** **a.** guide, conduct. See **lead**[1] (*def.* **1**). **b.** initiate, instigate, actuate, set off, set in motion, trigger, start the ball rolling, ring up the curtain on; open, pioneer, take the first step, take the initiative, take the lead, take the plunge, make a start, break the ice, lead off, blaze the trail; institute, inaugurate, found, establish, set up, organize, originate, break ground, lay the first stone, lay the foundation; introduce, launch, broach, usher in.

9. **lead up to** **a.** prepare the way, pave the way, clear the way, open the way; do the groundwork *or* spadework, smooth the path *or* road. **b.** approach, make advances, overture, make an overture *or* overtures; intimate, insinuate, imply, hint at.

—*n.* **10.** head, lead *or* front *or* advance position, first place, *Inf.* top spot; van, vanguard, cutting edge, spearhead; primacy, preeminence, priority, primacy, supremacy.

11. guide, conductor, cicerone, (*in the Orient*) dragoman; pointer, index, arrow, direction, signpost, guidepost, milepost *or* milestone; clue, cue, key, *Inf.* hot lead, *Inf.* tip-off; trace, vestige, spoor; hint, intimation, suggestion.

12. example, model, pattern, standard, criterion, precedent.

13. leash, tether. See **leash** (*def.* **1**).

14. *Theater.* **a.** lead role, starring role, title role, principal part, fat part. **b.** star, headliner, featured player *or* attraction, feature *or* headline attraction, drawing card; hero, heroine, protagonist, principal, principal character; male lead, male star, leading man, lead actor, jeune premier; female lead, female star, leading lady *or* woman, lead actress, première, jeune première; diva, prima donna, prima ballerina, première danseuse.

—*adj.* **15.** main, principal, cardinal, prime, primary, uppermost, most important; supreme, head, first, foremost, headmost, chief, premier, paramount, *Inf.* boss; ruling, reigning, commanding, controlling, directing, governing, leading.

lead[2], *n.* **1.** graphite, black lead, plumbago, *Chem.* plumbum; white lead ore, *Mineral.* cerussite.

2. weight, sinker, bob, plumb, plummet, plumb bob, plumb line, sounding line, sounding rod, sounding head, sounding, bottle, fathomer.

3. shot, ammunition, *Inf.* ammo.

leaden, *adj.* **1.** heavy, hefty, weighty, bulky, substantial, dense, ample; ponderous, unwieldy, cumbrous, cumbersome, awkward, unmanageable.

2. stodgy, stiff, stuffy, wooden, stilted, labored, turgid; lumbering, plodding, elephantine; dull, boring, uninteresting, tedious, dry, dry-as-dust, *Sl.* dead; tasteless, bland, insipid, jejune, flat, vapid, *Sl.* for the birds, *Sl.* blah, *Sl.* nothing, *Sl.* ho-hum; uneventful, humdrum, monotonous, run-of-the-mill, prosaic.

3. gray, grayish, gray-colored; flat, mat, lusterless, lackluster, dingy, muddy; pale, ashen, anemic, bloodless.

4. gloomy, oppressive, dreary, dismal, bleak, *Literary.* drear, *Scot. and North Eng.* dowie; cloudy, overcast, hazy, foggy; lowering, dark, darkened.

5. inanimate, lifeless, spiritless; inert, inactive, stagnant, static, dormant; sluggish, listless, lethargic, torpid, languid, languorous, phlegmatic, hebetudinous, lentitudinous; groggy, *Sl.* dopey.

6. lead, leady, plumbeous, plumbiferous, *Chem.* plumbous, *Chem.* plumbic, *Rare.* plumbaginous.

leader, *n.* **1.** chief, head, doyen, principal, *Inf.* boss, *Inf.* bossman, *Inf.* kingpin, *Inf.* number one, *Inf.* Mr. Big, *Sl.* big cheese, *Sl.* biggest fish *or* frog in the pond; director, superior, dean, chairman; manager, overseer, supervisor, superintendent, *Inf.* super, foreman, headman, *Brit.* gaffer.

2. sachem, chieftain, warlord, war chief, commander, commandant; ruler, overlord, lord, master, lord and master, paramount, suzerain.

3. pacesetter, pacemaker, trend-setter; mover, prompter, actuator, motivator, encourager, inspirer, firer, spark, *Inf.* sparkplug; ringleader, bellwether, *Sl.* the brains.

4. conductor, orchestra conductor, orchestra leader, band leader, bandmaster, concertmaster, Konzertmeister; choirmaster, chorister, precentor, Kapellmeister, *Eccles.* cantor; coryphaeus; band major, drum major.

5. forerunner, antecedent, precursor, predecessor, foregoer; front *or* lead runner, outrider, vaunt-courier, avant-courier; advance guard, vanguard, spearhead, cutting edge; point, point man, decoy; pioneer, frontiersman, pathfinder, trail blazer, explorer, scout; innovator, groundbreaker, avant-gardist.

6. loss leader, lead item, *Sl.* hot item, special, feature.

leadership, *n.* **1.** headship, managership, proctorship, governorship, directorship, superintendency; mastership, lordship, seigniory; captaincy, chieftainship, kingship, premiership, presidency, dictatorship.

2. supremacy, superiority, primacy, hegemony, dominance, domination, mastery; dominion, reign, sovereignty, suzerainty; rule, command, control; influence, sway, power, potency, *Literary.* puissance, *Inf.* say *or* say-so, *Inf.* clout, *Sl.* muscle.

3. direction, guidance, instruction, advice, counsel, suggestion, recommendation; management, administration, supervision, superintendence, regulation, governance, lead, leading, handling, *Inf.* running.

leading, *adj.* **1.** chief, cardinal, prime, primary, main, most important, uppermost, topmost, headmost, foremost; supreme, paramount, preeminent, supereminent, toprank, of the first rank, crowning, highest, maximum, sovereign, suzerain; dominant, predominant, prevailing, preponderant, hegemonic; best, greatest, second to none; inimitable, incomparable, beyond compare, in a class by itself, peerless, matchless; unrivaled, unequaled, unapproached, unsurpassed, unexcelled.

2. first, front, frontal, advance, antecedent, anterior; fore, forward, foregoing, heading, precessional; prior, preceding, precedent.

3. ruling, governing, commanding, reigning; directing, directive, guiding, managing, managerial, supervising, supervisory, superintendent, in charge; controlling, regulating, handling, *Inf.* running.

leadoff, *n.* start, beginning, commencement, onset, outset, outbreak, dawn; initiation, actuation, instigation, creation, inception; institution, inauguration, introduction, constitution, establishment, origination, organization, foundation; *All Inf.* kickoff, jump-off, send-off, takeoff, blast-off.

leaf, *n.* **1.** frond, leaflet, foliole, blade, *All Bot.* bract, bractlet, bracteole; flag, needle, pine needle, pad, lily pad; petal, seed leaf, *Bot.* cotyledon, *Bot.* calyx, *Bot.* sepal.

2. foliage, foliation, foliature; verdure, *Bot.* vernation, frondescence, flora, vegetation.

3. page, sheet, folio, insert, flyleaf, *Print.* recto, *Print.* verso; title page, imprint, table of contents, list of illustrations, index, errata.

4. cover, covering, covering layer, scale, coat, coating; veneer, overlay, lamination, lamella, lamina; layer, cut, slice, rasher, shaving, curl; sheet, foil, petal, flake.

5. turn over a new leaf reform, begin anew, begin again, become a new man *or* woman, turn away from sinning, regenerate, convert, amend; *Inf.* go back to go, *Inf.* go back to square one, get a new start, be reborn, be born again; change, change completely, metamorphose, *Inf.* shape up, alter, modify, revamp, *Inf.* come around; rally, take a turn for the better, *Inf.* turn the corner; improve, get better, advance, make progress, make up for lost time, mature, *Inf.* come into one's own, *Inf.* finish with sowing one's wild oats.

—v. **6.** bud, put out leaves, burst into leaves, foliate.

7. thumb, thumb through, turn, turn over, *Inf.* flip over pages, peruse casually, riffle.

leafage, *n.* foliage, foliature, greenery, verdure, *Bot.* vernation, leafery, leafy growth, frondescence, vegetation.

leaflet, *n.* **1.** handbill, bill, brochure, pamphlet, throwaway, flyer, folder; broadside, tract, booklet, advertisement, *Inf.* ad, circular.

2. small leaf, young leaf, leaf bud, seed leaf, needle.

leafy, *adj.* **1.** leafed, leaved, *Archaic.* leavy; green, verdant, arborescent, arboreal, *U.S. Inf.* woodsy, *U.S. Inf.* woody, wooded; bosky, *Brit.* copsy, bucolic.

2. leaflike, foliaceous, laminate, in strips, in sheets, flaky, scaling, sliced.

league, *n.* **1.** covenant, compact, pact, mutual assistance pact, entente, accord; treaty, concordat, contract, formal agreement, settlement, arrangement, understanding, cordial understanding, agreement, gentleman's agreement.

2. alliance, confederation, confederacy, coalition, combination; union, trade union, labor union; bloc, Bund, association, society, guild, grange; fraternity, sorority, fellowship, clan; partnership, copartnership, affiliation, corporation, incorporation, conglomerate, trust, syndicate, cartel, consortium, combine, machine, *Sl.* plunderbund; pool, cooperative, co-op, group; council, junta, conclave, assembly, meeting, convention, diet; faction, party, splinter group, clique, ring, *Inf.* push, *Inf.* crew, *Inf.* gang, (*in China*) tong.

3. group of teams, group of athletic teams; class, category, level of ability, ability group, group of equals, group of peers, equals, coequals, matches, well-matched opponents.

4. in league with leagued, *Inf.* in cahoots, allied, amalgamated, *Inf.* hooked up with, *Inf.* linked up with, *Inf.* in bed with; cooperating, coactive, collaborative; *Inf.* hand in glove with, *Inf.* shoulder to shoulder with, as one, as one man, *Inf.* of the same stripe.

leak, *n.* **1.** hole, opening, vent, scupper, drain, mouth, orifice, aperture, egress; puncture, perforation, cut, incision, split, gash, scotch, rent, slit, slot; gap, space, rift, break; fault, flaw, nick, notch; fissure, cleft, crevasse, crevice, cranny, chink, crack, groove.

2. leakage, leaking, seepage, seeping, oozing, outflowing, effusion, effluence, *Pathol.* defluxion.

—v. **3.** escape, exude, ooze, ooze out. drip, dribble, drain, seep; discharge, gush, disembogue, cast forth; emanate, issue forth, emit, pour forth, send forth, send out, eject; void, teem, empty, stream, gush, spurt, flood.

4. divulge, disclose, reveal, make known, tell, impart, inform, relate, utter, declare, break the news;

blurt out, give away, *Inf.* let on; release, break, report, publish, communicate, broadcast, *Archaic.* divulgate; come out with, let slip, let the cat out of the bag, spill the beans, blow the lid off, *Inf.* let it all hang out, *Sl.* sing, *Sl.* spill one's guts; expose, uncover, unmask, unveil, bring out, *Inf.* plant, bring out into the open, lay open, bring to light.

leakproof, *adj.* waterproof, wetproof, rainproof, moistureproof, floodproof, weatherproof, weathertight, stormproof; airtight, watertight, sealed, hermetic; impervious, impenetrable, nonporous, imperforate.

leaky, *adj.* **1.** porous, perforated, holey, percolative; pervious, permeable, penetrable.
2. damaged, injured, imperfect, defective.
3. effusive, gushing, outpouring, overflowing.

lean¹, *v.* **1.** incline, bend, angle, bevel, cant, slope, slant, pitch, grade, bank; slouch, slump, bow over; descend, fall, drop, dip, sag; swerve, swing, veer, turn, curve, fork; sway, totter, falter; careen, list, heel, tip.
2. tend, have a tendency, have a propensity, have a proclivity; have a preference for, prefer, show preference for, have as lief, would as lief; see fit, think best, had rather *or* sooner; have a penchant for, have an affinity for, like, have a liking for, gravitate toward, be attracted to; be disposed to, be prone to, be apt to, be liable to, be likely to, be subject to, be open to.
3. rest against *or* on, recline on, repose on; be supported by, be sustained by.
4. depend on, rely on, count on, trust in, have faith in, believe in, give credence to; swear by, pin one's faith on, have full confidence in, set store by.
5. **lean over backwards** bend over backwards, go to great pains, go to great lengths, go to the trouble, go out of one's way, put oneself out, make a special effort; sacrifice, make a sacrifice.

lean², *adj.* **1.** (*of persons or animals*) slender, lank, thin, skinny, attenuate; gaunt, haggard, emaciated, meager, spare, scrawny; scraggy, spindly, spindle-shanked, skeletal, bare-boned, rawboned, skin and bones, twiggy; bony, lanky, gangling, gangly, *Inf.* weedy; hollow-cheeked, pinched, withered, shriveled, shrunken, wasted; underfed, undernourished, hungry, half-famished, half-starved, hungry as a bear.
2. barren, unproductive, unyielding, unfructuous, unfruitful, fruitless; exhausted, depleted, worn-out, impoverished; meager, scanty, scarce, sparse, empty, forlorn; poor, bare, dry, arid, bald, wasted, desolate, dead, naked.

leaning, *n.* **1.** proclivity, propensity, inclination, bent, turn, cast; tendency, tending, bearing, gravitation, drift; proneness, subjectability, aptness, liableness, likeliness, susceptibility, weakness, openness; disposition, mind-set, idiosyncrasy, idiosyncrasis, *Archaic.* crasis.
2. penchant, predisposition, predilection, partiality; prejudice, tendentiousness, bias, preference; affinity, attraction, sympathy, fancy, liking, fondness, affection, love, ardor, fervor, zeal, passion; desire, longing, wishing, hankering, craving, itch, avidity; appetite, appetency, relish, taste; voracity, pruriency, prurience, lust.

lean-to, *n.* shack, shed, shanty, hut, hutch; hovel, sty, pen; booth, stall; shelter, building, structure; annex, addition.

leap, *v.* **1.** jump, bound, spring, upspring, run and jump, take off, leave the ground *or* one's feet; high jump, broad jump, pole vault, steeplechase; (*of horses*) prance, rear up, buck, buckjump; leapfrog, overleap, jump over, overjump, vault, hurdle, cross over, sail over, shoot over, go *or* pass over, take it over, clear, negotiate.
2. hop, skip, bounce, bob, *Inf.* hippety-hop; caper, frolic, frisk, cavort, romp, gambol, curvet, capriole, dance around *or* about.
3. *Often* **leap to** rush *or* hurry to, hurtle, form hastily *or* quickly, jump to; come to, arrive at, reach; conclude, decide, make up one's mind.
4. surge, increase by leaps and bounds, shoot up, skyrocket, rocket, soar; increase, rise, progress, climb, mount, ascend, appreciate, go up; advance, accelerate, escalate, grow.
—*n.* **5.** jump, bound, spring, vault, running jump, high jump, broad *or* long jump, pole vault, *Ballet.* entrechat, *Ballet.* jeté; (*of horses*) curvet, capriole, gambado, gambade, buck; hop, skip, bounce, bob; a hop, skip and a jump; caper, frolic, gambol, dance, prance.
6. hurdle, bar, *Gymnastics.* buck, *Gymastics.* horse; obstacle, obstruction, fence, rail, hedge.
7. saltation, abrupt transition, quick change; advance, movement, progression.
8. upsurge, upswing, surge, skyrocketing, rocketing, soaring; increase, rise, elevation, mounting, climbing, ascent; appreciation, augmentation, acceleration, escalation, growth.

leapfrog, *v.* **1.** jump, jump over, overjump, overleap; vault, hurdle, cross over, sail over, shoot over, go *or* pass over, make it over, clear, negotiate.
2. advance, forward, promote, move [s.t.] *or* [s.o.] forward, move [s.t.] *or* [s.o.] to the front of the line *or* the head of the class, get [s.t.] *or* [s.o.] up front; push, shove, press [s.t.] *or* [s.o.] forward, overtake, surpass, outdistance.

learn, *v.* **1.** comprehend, realize, *Inf.* get into *or* through one's head; master, grasp, *Inf.* lay hold of, *Inf.* catch on to, *Inf.* latch on to, *Inf.* get the idea, *Inf.* get a fix on, *Inf.* get *or* have it; cognize, perceive, apprehend, see, see the light, get the picture, *Inf.* make heads or tails of, *Brit.* twig.
2. ascertain, determine, detect, trace, hunt down; discover, find out, stumble upon, fall on *or* upon, hit upon, chance upon, light upon; uncover, bring to light, *Sl.* get wise to; disinter, exhume, unearth, dig up, root up, worm out, ferret out, fish out.
3. memorize, possess, con, commit to memory, learn by heart, have in one's head, have at one's fingertips.
4. glean, acquire, receive, absorb, assimilate, digest, take in, pick up, drink in, imbibe.
5. *Usu.* **learn of** hear, hear of, get word, get wind of, *Sl.* get the low-down, *Sl.* be tipped off; understand, gather.

learned, *adj.* **1.** erudite, punditic, wise, sage, scholarly, knowledgeable, *Archaic.* intelligent of; cultured, literate, lettered, versed, well-read, well-informed, (*usu. disparagingly*) know-it-all, *Archaic.* studied; educated, well-educated, well-schooled, well-instructed, well-tutored, well-trained, well-posted, well-grounded.
2. academic, scholastic, literary; intellectual, studious, profound, deep; bibliophilistic, bibliophilic, bibliophagous, bibliophagic; (*all sometimes disparaging*) highbrowed, *Inf.* long-haired, pedantic, bookish.
3. sophisticated, worldly, worldly-wise, *Sl.* wise, *Sl.* savvy, knowing, *Sl.* in the know; enlightened, aware, cognizant, conscious, alive to; acquainted, familiar, conversant, intimate; expert, masterful, masterly, *Fr. au fait;* proficient, adept, skillful, skilled; experienced, practiced, accomplished, *Inf.* knowing the ropes.

learner, *n.* **1.** scholar, academician, student, studier, pupil, educatee; schoolchild, schoolgirl, schoolboy, collegian, college girl *or* woman, coed, college boy *or* man, sophister; apprentice, *Inf.* prentice, trainee; disciple, follower, protégé; proselyte, catechumen.

2. novice, novitiate, neophyte, tyro, abecedarian, tenderfoot, greenhorn, *Inf.* greenie; beginner, newcomer, initiate; matriculate, matriculater, entrant, freshman; recruit, rookie, enlistee, draftee, probationer.

learning, *n.* **1.** erudition, scholarship, wisdom, sapience, education, schooling, instruction, tuition; letters, culture, *Archaic.* literature, book learning, pedantry; knowledge, information, facts, data, lore.

2. study, studying, research, researching, investigation, investigating, inquiry, inquiring, query, questioning; search, searching, quest, questing, exploration, exploring, hunt, hunting; enlightenment, cultivation, cultivating, edification, edifying, acquisition.

lease, *n.* **1.** rental agreement, sublease, sublet; contract, subcontract, agreement.

—*v.* **2.** rent out, hire out, farm out, let, let out, sublet, sublease, underlet, *Law.* demise; lend out, loan out, grant temporary use of.

3. rent, pay rent on *or* for, live in, occupy temporarily; charter, hire, farm, take.

leash, *n.* **1.** lead, tether, rein, harness, bridle, halter, yoke, collar; thong, line, strap, rope, cord, chain, tie, binding.

2. check, curb, restraint, hold, constraint; control, order, discipline, line.

—*v.* **3.** tether, hitch, harness, bridle, collar, rein; lash, string, strap, chain, tie up, secure.

4. control, keep under control, be in control of, exercise control over, govern, rule, be the master of, be in the driver's seat, manage, channel, direct, guide, employ *or* use judiciously *or* prudently; restrict, check, curb, restrain, hold, constrain; confine, lock up, pen up, hold in, bind, pinion.

5. bind *or* tie together, hook up, fasten, yoke, couple; connect, link, associate, join, unite.

leather, *n.* **1.** tanned hide *or* skin, chamois, kid, suede, cordovan, mocha, glove leather; doeskin, deerskin, goatskin, capeskin, lambskin, sheepskin, pigskin, sealskin, shark's skin; snakeskin, alligator, crocodile, lizard; horsehide, buffalo hide, cowhide, shoe leather; rawhide, shagreen; imitation *or* fake leather, *Trademark.* Leatherette, *Trademark.* Leatheroid.

—*adj.* **2.** leathern, made of leather, like leather, leatherlike, coriaceous, leathery.

—*v.* **3.** *Informal.* strap, belt, beat, flog, whip, lash, flagellate, scourge, horsewhip; flail, thrash, *Inf.* wallop, thresh, *Inf.* hide, *Inf.* tan [s.o.'s] hide.

leathery, *adj.* leathern, leatherlike. coriaceous; coarse, rough, rugged, strong, tough, resistant, inflexible, rigid; durable, long-lasting, long-lived, long-wearing.

leave[1], *v.* **1.** quit, depart, go away, go along, take one's leave, take leave; part, part company, separate from, go, go out, be off, get off, exit, make an exit, make off, be gone; push off, shove off, *Inf.* hightail it, *Inf.* buzz along, *Inf.* (*both usu. imperative*) buzz off, *Sl.* go fly a kite; *Sl.* blast off, *Sl.* breeze off *or* out, *Sl.* cut *or* cut out, *Sl.* split, *Sl.* vamoose, *Brit. Sl.* beetle off, *Brit. Sl.* bugger off; evacuate, vacate, pull up stakes, break camp; fly, flee, *Inf.* skip, flit, *Brit. Sl.* do a moonlight flit; say good-by, bid farewell, bid adieu, bid Godspeed; withdraw, remove, retreat, take oneself away.

2. embark, entrain, enplane, embus; sail forth, set sail, weigh anchor, hoist anchor, ship out.

3. abandon, quit, desert, forsake; surrender, yield, relinquish; drop, *Inf.* drop like a hot potato, turn one's back on, wash one's hands of; leave behind, leave in the lurch, take leave of; discard, jettison, cast away.

4. cease, desist, give up, intermit, abandon, drop; *Inf.* shut up shop, *Inf.* call it a day, call it quits; surrender, resign, abdicate, *Chiefly Scot.* demit, renounce, throw up; let go, release.

5. bequeath, bequest, endow, endow with, leave behind, hand down; dower, assign dower; devise, will, will to, give by will, bless with; commit, consign, refer.

6. **leave out in the cold** snub, slight, shun, reject, rebuff, *Inf.* high-hat; neglect, overlook, ignore, gloss over; let slip, let slide, forget; put aside, *Inf.* give the go-by, refuse to acknowledge, turn from, turn away from, turn one's back on, disregard; dodge, pass by, by-pass, pass up.

7. **leave in the lurch** desert, abandon, quit, reject, *Inf.* cop out on, jilt, forsake, run away from; leave stranded, leave high and dry.

8. **leave off** stop, desist, cease, halt, discontinue; stay, refrain, restrain, pause, rest; hang fire, hold off, hold back.

9. **leave out** omit, eliminate, exclude, bar, count out; reject, repudiate, throw out, cut, cut out, cast aside, set aside; pass over, slide over, gloss over, slough over.

leave[2], *n.* **1.** permission, liberty, allowance, sanction, license, warrant, authorization; exemption, concession, special favor, *Rom. Cath. Ch.* dispensation, sufferance, vouchsafement; tolerance, toleration, indulgence, indulgency, grace.

2. furlough, rest and recuperation, R & R; respite, rest, recess, break, time off; sabbatical, leave of absence; vacation, *Brit.* holiday; excursion, trip.

3. departure, leaving, going, exit, egress; leave-taking, parting, farewell, adieu, valediction, congé; retirement, retreat, removal, withdrawal, evacuation.

leaven, *n.* **1.** leavening, ferment, barm, pepsin, soda; baking soda, baking powder, yeast, zyme, enzyme, zymogen; maltase, diastase, invertase, zymase.

2. catalyst, catalytic agent, agent, factor, element, determinant; transformer, modifier, alterer, alterative, alterant; modificator, adapter, changer, converter.

—*v.* **3.** raise, ferment, lighten, work, expand; effervesce, pepsinate.

4. permeate, infuse, pervade, imbue; diffuse, suffuse, transfuse, penetrate, instill; enliven, lift, elevate, inspirit, stimulate, enhearten, quicken, inspire.

5. infect, tinge, season, temper, soften, affect; lighten, mitigate, palliate, assuage, reduce, abate; moderate, alter, adjust, transform, make; qualify, restrict, modify, limit; make into, turn into, reduce to, render.

leave-taking, *n.* **1.** leave, parting, farewell, good-by, adieu, valediction, congé; departure, leaving, going, exit, egress; embarkation, sailing, takeoff, outset, start.

2. abandonment, retreat, withdrawal, removal, evacuation, decampment, decamping.

leaving, *Usu.* **leavings** *n.* **1.** waste, wastage, remains, refuse, spoils; offscourings, scourings, sweepings, scum; sawdust, shavings, parings, filings, scrapings, raspings; chaff, stubbles; slag, sprue, dross, sordes; (*all of skin*) shreddings, sloughings, scurf, furfur, dandruff.

2. residue, residuum, remainder, rest, balance; remnants, leftover, (*both usu. of food*) leftovers, orts; oddments, rummage, odds and ends, truck, junk, *Inf.* crap; rejectamenta.

3. ruins, rubble, detritus, debris, litter; cinders, ashes, embers, coals, soot, carbon, smut, *Chem.* precipitate; lava, *Geol.* clinker.

4. rubbish, trash, garbage, offal, refuse, swill, slop, riffraff, *Brit. Dial.* raff; carrion.

5. deposit, alluvium, alluvion, *Geol.* diluvium *or*

diluvion; moraine, silt, loess, sinter; dregs, draff, sediment, settlings, lees, heeltap, grounds.

6. droppings, guano, ordure, manure, fertilizer; dung, muck, excrement, feculence, feces, stool.

lecher, *n.* libertine, wanton, profligate, debauchee, debaucher, dissipator; rake, roué, rakehell, playboy, *Inf.* rip, *Sl.* swinger, fast man; adulterer, fornicator, seducer, *Inf.* wolf; womanizer, lady-killer, bedhopper, chaser, lover; whoremonger, whoremaster, pimp, gigolo; Don Juan, Lothario, Casanova; rapist, raper, violator, ravisher; satyr, goat, old goat, *Sl.* dirty old man, pervert, *Sl.* flasher, *Sl.* letch.

lecherous, *adj.* **1.** wanton, profligate, abandoned, incontinent, intemperate; dissolute, dissipated, rakehell, degenerate, depraved, decadent, dirty-minded; lewd, lascivious, lubricous, *Archaic.* lickerish, licentious; prurient, libidinous, salacious, carnal, sensual; swinish, hoggish, piggish, bestial, beastly, brutish; satyric, stayrical, goatish, hircine, ruttish, *Sl.* horny; priapic, lustful, randy, *Sl.* hot.

2. suggestive, erotic, lurid, indecent, offensive; vulgar, gross, crude, coarse, dirty, filthy; obscene, blue, pornograhic, *Sl.* porno, smutty, *Sl.* raunchy; ribald, bawdy, Fescennine, scurrilous, irreverent.

lechery, *n.* indulgence, intemperance, incontinence, immoderation, self-indulgence, overindulgence; profligacy, dissipation, dissolution, dissoluteness, libertinism, gallantry, debauchery, rakishness; wantonness, unrestraint, abandon, *Pathol.* satyriasis; whoring, wenching, womanizing, *Sl.* leching, sex indulgence; lewdness, lasciviousness, lecherousness, lubricity; goatishness, satyrism, ruttishness, randiness, *Sl.* horniness; lust, lustfulness, libidinousness, salacity, prurience, pruriency; carnality, carnalism, sensualism, priapism, venery.

lectern *n.* podium, pulpit, rostrum, bench, dais, stage, platform, soapbox, stump; desk, reading desk *or* table, (*both in an early Christian church*) ambo, ambon, *Rare.* pulpitum; stand, table, holder, tripod, support.

lecture, *n.* **1.** speech, talk, address, discourse, prelection, sermon, homily; commentary, comment, descant, exposition, exposé, elucidation, explanation, exegesis, explication; dissertation, treatise, tract, tractate, thesis, essay, paper; oration, declamation, salutation, valedictory, *Rhet.* apostrophe; diatribe, tirade, philippic, screed, harangue, *Inf.* spiel, *Rhet.* peroration.

2. reprimand, reproof, reproval, rebuke, reproach, remonstration, scolding, chiding; correction, disciplining, criticism, admonition, admonishment, warning; upbraiding, berating, excoriation, fustigation, objurgation, fulmination, tongue-lashing, *Inf.* dressing down, *Sl.* strafing, *Sl.* chewing out, *Sl.* jawing.

—*v.* **3.** speak, talk, make *or* read a speech, give a talk, read *or* deliver an address, platform, take the floor; comment, descant, elucidate, explain, talk *or* speak on *or* about, explicate, spell out; discourse, prelect, sermonize, preach, pontificate, moralize; declaim, orate, mouth, hold forth, soapbox, *Inf.* stump, harangue, expound, propound, go on, *Inf.* perorate, *Inf.* spout off, *Inf.* spiel.

4. instruct, teach, tutor, educate, school, give *or* present a lesson to; edify, enlighten, inform, present information to, impart knowledge to, apprise; indoctrinate, inculcate, instill, infuse; counsel, advise, guide.

5. reprimand, scold, rebuke, reproach, chide, take [s.o.] to task; correct, criticize, discipline, admonish, warn; upbraid, berate, excoriate, fustigate, objurgate, flay, fulminate against, tongue-lash, lash, rail at, call down, *Inf.* dress down, *Inf.* call on the carpet, take to task, *Inf.* haul over the coals, *Sl.* strafe, *Sl.* chew out, *Sl.* lay out in lavender, *Sl.* jump all over, *Sl.* jump down [s.o.'s] throat, *Sl.* jaw, *Archaic.* clapperclaw.

lecturer, *n.* **1.** speaker, talker, addresser, discourser, prelector, lector, reciter, reader; orator, speechmaker, public speaker, spokesman, spokeswoman, rhetorician, speechifier, *Inf.* stumper; declaimer, perorator, expounder, exponent, descanter; expositor, explicator, explainer, commentator, commenter, annotator; sermonizer, preacher, moralizer, haranguer.

2. instructor, graduate assistant, laboratory *or* lab assistant, teaching assistant, tutor, preceptor, *Educ.* fellow; educator, educationist, pedagogue, teacher, schoolteacher, schoolmaster, schoolmistress, schoolmarm, faculty member, *Chiefly Brit.* master, *Brit.* don, *Chiefly Scot* dominie; professor, schoolman, scholastic, academician, academe, gownsman; indoctrinator, inculcator, propagandist.

ledge, *n.* **1.** shelf, slab of wood, sill, raised edge, mantel, mantelpiece, hob, *Eccles.* gradin; shelf of rock, projection, protrusion, overhang.

2. reef, coral reef, ridge, line of rocks, bar, sand bar, sandbank.

ledger, *n.* account book, expense account book, register, registry, record book, file, log; journal, diary.

lee¹, *n.* **1.** shelter, protection, cover, refuge.

2. leeward. See **leeward** (*def.* **2**).

lee², *n.* *Usu.* **lees** dregs, grounds, sediment, deposit, settlings, draff, dunder, *Chem.* sublimate, crystals, *Chem.* precipitate; residue, residuum, remainder, remains, dross, scoria.

leech, *n.* **1.** bloodsucker, *Sl.* bleeder, extortioner, extortionist, usurer, Shylock.

2. parasite, *Inf.* sponge *or* sponger, *Sl.* mooch *or* moocher, *Inf.* freeloader, hanger-on, barnacle, bur, appendage; courtier, minion, follower, attendant, satellite; flunky, lackey, yes-man, jackal, spaniel, bootlick, bootlicker, footlicker, lickspit, lickspittle; kowtower, *Contemptuous.* Uncle Tom, *Sl.* oreo, cringer, groveler, sniveler; sycophant, toady, toadeater, tufthunter, fawner, fawning flatterer, truckler; flatterer, wheedler, puffer, backslapper, timeserver, *Inf.* applepolisher, *Sl.* brown-nose, *Sl.* brown-noser,*Sl.* brownie, *Obs., Rare.* blander, *Archaic.* pickthank.

leer, *v.* **1.** glance at sideways, look askance at, look at slyly *or* out of the corner of one's eye; look at, eye, watch, follow with the eyes; stare at, ogle, *Inf.* give the once-over, *Sl.* check [s.o.] out, undress with the eyes; glare at, glower at, give a dirty look, give a look to kill, give the evil eye.

—*n.* **2.** sly look, sidelong glance; lascivious look, lecherous look, stare, ogle, *Inf.* the once-over; malicious look, the evil eye, killing look, deadly glance; cockatrice, basilisk.

leery, *adj.* wary, suspicious, shy, distrustful, distrusting, mistrustful, mistrusting, untrustful, untrusting; hesitant, hesitating, undecided, unsure, uncertain; cautious, careful, chary, circumspect, guarded; on one's guard, watchful, heedful, attentive, observant, mindful, aware, awake, alert.

leeward, *adj.* **1.** *Chiefly Naut.* lee.

—*n.* **2.** lee, lee side, sheltered side, protected side.

—*adv.* **3.** toward the lee, to leeward, *Naut.* under the lee, alee, away from the wind.

leeway, *n.* **1.** drift, deviation.

2. extra time *or* space, margin, margin for error; extra room, elbowroom, room to move around, room to maneuver, room to operate; slack, play, freedom, latitude. See **latitude** (*def.* **3**).

left, *adj.* **1.** sinister, sinistral, sinistrous; left hand, *Naut.* port, *Naut.* larboard; *Bot.* sinistrorsal.

2. (*all of politics*) leftwing, liberal, progressive; socialistic, communistic, communalistic, Bolshevistic; radical, anarchistic.

—*n.* 3. left side, *Print.* verso, *Naut.* port, *Naut.* portside, *Inf.* wrong hand.

4. **the Left** leftists, left wing, liberals, progressives; socialists, Communists, social reformers; anarchists, Maoists, radicals, P.L.O. members, terrorists, Weathermen.

left-handed, *adj.* 1. sinistral, sinistromanual, sinistrodextral, dextrosinistral; sinistrocerebral, sinistrocular, sinistrogyrate, sinistrogyric.

2. ambiguous, double-meaning, paradoxical, doubtful, dubious, equivocal, questionable; enigmatic, ironic, sardonic, indefinite, indistinct, veiled, cryptic; insulting, disparaging, derisive, mocking, disrespectful; clumsy, backhanded, tactless, graceless, crude, maladroit, gauche.

leftist, *n.* member of the Left, liberal, radical, socialist, progressive, Bolshevist, Maoist, anarchist, Communist, *Inf.* pinko, P.L.O. member, terrorist, Weatherman; Left sympathizer, fellow traveler.

leftover, *n.* *Usu.* **leftovers** 1. residue, residuum, rest, remainder, balance, carry-over; remnants, fragments, scraps, shards; (*of food*) orts, leavings; oddments, rummage, odds and ends, truck, junk, *Inf.* crap; rejectamenta.

2. waste, wastage, remains, refuse, spoils; offscourings, scourings, sweepings, scum; sawdust, shavings, parings, filings, scrapings, raspings; chaff, stubbles; slag, sprue, dross, sordes.

3. excess, superfluity, extra, surplus, surplusage, *Commerce.* overage.

4. ruins, rubble, detritus; rubbish, trash. See **leaving** (*defs.* 3, 4).

leg, *n.* 1. limb, lower limb, member; *Anat.* tibia, *Anat.* fibula, shinbone, shin, shank, *Sl.* gam, *Inf.* peg, *Inf.* pin, (*usu. pl.*) *Inf.* stumps; calf, thigh, (*usu. pl.*) hams.

2. support, underpinning, standard, prop, brace, framework; post, column, pillar, upright; trestle, horse.

3. portion, segment, part, stretch; section, sector, piece, fraction.

4. **give a leg up** give assistance, give an assist, give a hand, lend a helping hand, set up, put on one's feet, give new life to, see [s.o.] through; boost, advance, stand behind; aid, come to the aid of, assist, help, support, take care of, succor.

5. **not have a leg to stand on** lack support *or* a valid basis, be full of holes, be undermined; be impotent, be ineffective, be defenseless, be vulnerable.

6. **on one's** *or* **its last legs** about to break down, about to die, about to collapse, about to fail; failing, fading fast, dying, at death's door.

7. **pull [s.o.'s] leg** a. tease, put [s.o.] on, banter, chaff, rib, kid, *Sl.* razz; deride, *Inf.* roast, scoff at, mock, jeer, knock; fleer, laugh at, make fun of, guy, taunt, gibe, twit, rag. b. deceive, mislead, misinform, misguide; trick, delude, fool, take in, throw dust in [s.o.'s] eyes, pull the wool over [s.o.'s] eyes.

8. **shake a leg** a. *Slang.* hurry, move quickly, hasten, lose no time, rush, make haste; run like mad, *Sl.* get cracking, *Sl.* get one's rear in gear, *Sl.* go like a bat out of hell, *Sl.* go like greased lightning. b. *Slang.* dance, *Sl.* shake your booties, *Sl.* hoof *or* hoof it, *Sl.* boogie, trip the light fantastic, *Sl.* cut a rug.

9. **stretch one's legs** take a walk, go for a walk, promenade, go for a stroll; get some exercise, stretch out the kinks.

—*v.* 10. **leg it** run *or* walk quickly, hotfoot, hotfoot it, hightail, hightail it, *Inf.* skedaddle, *Inf.* vamoose.

legacy, *n.* 1. bequest, inheritance, patrimony, bequeathal, *Law.* dower, *Law.* will, *Law.* devise, *Civil Law.* fideicommissum, *Law.* reversion, *Law.* hereditament, *Obs.* dowry, *Archaic.* heritance; endowment, bestowal, dotation, disposition, gift, present, donation; heirloom, hand-me-down.

2. heritage, bequeathment, ancestry; history, past, background.

legal *adj.* 1. lawful, licit; constitutional, statutory, by the book; permissible, allowable, admissible; sanctionable, approvable, acceptable; warrantable, authorizable.

2. legitmate, *Sl.* legit, vested, rightful, right, valid, sound, well-founded, *Inf.* kosher, *Inf.* O.K.; permitted, licensed, authorized, warranted, commissioned; enacted, statutable, ordained, prescribed, ordered, decreed, edicted, mandated.

3. judicial, judiciary, judicatory, juridical, jurisprudential, juristic, jurisdictive, forensic.

legality, *n.* 1. lawfulness, constitutionality, permissibleness, permissibility, admissibleness.

2. legitimacy, legalism, accordance with the law; rightfulness, validity, soundness.

legalize, *v.* 1. legitimize, legitimatize, codify, conform to the law, make acceptable; constitute, institute, formalize, establish, set up; enact, ordain, legislate, pass as law, enter into the books; confirm, ratify, bind.

2. authorize, warrant, license, certify, accredit, validate; invest, empower, enable, entitle, commission, depute; permit, allow, consent *or* subscribe to, agree to, vouchsafe; sanction, approve, give one's nod of approval, countenance, accept, *Inf.* O.K., *Chiefly U.S.* approbate.

legate, *n.* emissary, agent, envoy, attaché, diplomat, ambassador, plenipotentiary; representative, commissioner, delegate, nuncio, internuncio, *Rom. Cath. Ch.* vicar; deputy, proxy, substitute; intermediary, go-between, middleman, mediator; messenger, courier, herald.

legatee, *n.* beneficiary, recipient, receiver, devisee, *Law.* reversioner; *Both Law.* executor, donee; heir, inheritor, heritor, heir apparent, heir at law, heiress, heritress, inheritrix; coheir, coheiress, joint heir, *Law.* parcener; successor, *Inf.* next in line, follower.

legation, *n.* 1. embassy, delegation, deputation, representation, staff; ambassadors, envoys, emissaries, delegates, deputies; committee, subcommittee.

2. mission, commission, diplomatic establishment abroad.

legend, *n.* 1. tale, drama, romance, saga, epic, *Inf.* yarn, myth, tradition, old wives' tale; history, story, adventure, account, depiction, portrayal, representation, interpretation; recital, narrative, narration; fable, apologue, allegory, parable, moral, bestiary; nursery rhyme, fairy tale, ballad, rhyme, song.

2. inscription, dedication, motto, slogan, device; imprint, impression.

3. key, code, cipher, table of symbols.

legendary, *adj.* 1. fabled, storied, traditional, mythical, mythic; chimerical, figmental, fanciful, imaginary, fantastic, fantastical, fabulous; heroic, superhuman, supernatural, marvelous, strange; visionary, dreamy, quixotic, extravagant, eidetic; romantic, idealistic, storybook, Cinderellaesque; fictitious, fictional, made-up, make-believe, invented.

2. celebrated, immortal, historical, famous, famed, renowned, well-known, prominent, *Inf.* big-name; illustrious, great, glorious, radiant, lustrous; honored, exalted, acclaimed, much-touted, popular, well-liked.

legerdemain, *n.* **1.** sleight of hand, jugglery, juggling, prestidigitation, conjuring, hocus-pocus; magic, trickery, thaumaturgy.

2. deception, deceit, dissimulation, duplicity, dark and crooked ways, evil ways; fraud, cheating, chicane; trumpery, dupery, fraudulence, shenanigan; craft, wiles, finesse, *Inf.* razzle-dazzle, cozenage, double-dealing; chicanery, knavery, *Inf.* hanky-panky, *Sl.* funny business, *Sl.* monkey business.

3. trick, stratagem, ruse, Trojan horse, artifice, pretense, *Obs.* cog; contrivance, subterfuge, misrepresentation; fake, sham, hoax, swindle, shuck, feint; imposture, imposition, humbug, *Inf.* flimflam, *Inf.* flam; falsehood, fib, untruth, prevarication.

legerdemainist, *n.* prestidigitator, sleight of hand artist, juggler; magician, trickster, wizard, conjurer; theater artist, theatrical performer, artiste, artist.

legerity, *n.* **1.** agility, nimbleness, deftness, dexterousness, light-footedness, spryness, *Dial.* gainliness; grace, coordination, suppleness, litheness; alacrity, celerity, quickness, fleetness, fleet-footedness, swiftness, rapidity; liveliness, sprightliness, aliveness, briskness, dapperness.

2. alertness, smartness, cleverness, quick-wittedness, wittiness; originality, brilliance.

leggings, *n.* **1.** chaps, (*in Mexico*) chaparajos, gambados, galligaskins, leg harness; gaiter, spats, spatterdashes, puttee, putty, puttie; leg wrap, bandage, covering, protection; *All Armor.* greaves, jambos, jambart, jambear, cuisse, poleyn.

2. snow pants, overalls, heavy *or* warm pants, woolens; trousers, pants, slacks, breeches; tights, pantyhose, hose, stockings.

legibility, *n.* **1.** readability, readableness, decipherability, ease of reading, easiness on the eyes, legibleness; neatness, cleanness, tidiness, evenness, regularity, severity; clearness, clarity, lucidity, lucidness, perspicuity, plainness, simplicity; explicitness, preciseness, precision, exactness, definiteness, distinctness, clear-cutness; discernibleness, perceptibility, apprehensibility; coherence, cogency, comprehensibility, intelligibility, intelligibleness, understandability, understandableness, penetrability.

2. vividness, graphicness, boldness, visibility, visibleness, obviousness, apparentness, evidence, manifestness, palpability, patentability.

legible, *adj.* **1.** readable, easy to read, easily read, decipherable, capable of being made out; neat, clean, tidy, even, regular, well-written, sure-handed, carefully printed, painstakingly inscribed, typed; clear, clear as day, plain, plain as day, simple, perspicuous, lucid; distinct, definite, precise, explicit, express, certain.

2. discernible, perceptible, apprehensible, ascertainable, distinguishable, recognizable; coherent, cogent, intelligible, comprehensible, comprehendible, understandable, salient.

legion, *n.* **1.** army, brigade, regiment, battalion, company, squadron; troop, corps, phalanx, squad, tribe, band; division, unit, detachment.

2. host, throng, crowd, horde, drove, *Inf.* caboodle, *Inf.* kit and caboodle; mass, pack, gang, mob, rabble; group, bevy, flock, gaggle, swarm, herd, school, shoal; lot, multitude, abundance, plenitude, profusion, myriad, array.

legionary, *n.* soldier, military man, cavalryman, infantryman, foot soldier; fighting man, warrior, *Inf.* cannon fodder.

legislate, *v.* **1.** make laws, enact laws, pass laws, formulate laws, establish laws; ordain, put in force, constitute, constitutionalize; authorize, prescribe, fix, set, establish, charter, formulate, formalize, regulate, codify.

2. compel legally, decree, order, make mandatory; necessitate, require, oblige, force, *Inf.* strong-arm, dragoon; coerce, force upon, cram *or* force down [s.o.'s] throat.

legislation, *n.* **1.** lawmaking, law enacting, law formulation; codification, regulation, prescription.

2. body of law, law, statutes; corpus juris, code, constitution, canon, ordinances, pandects; act, enactment, rule, ruling; prescript, dictate, bylaw.

legislative, *adj.* lawmaking, lawgiving, judicial, legislatorial, congressional, senatorial, synodical, parliamentary, jurisdictive.

legislator, *n.* **1.** lawmaker, lawgiver, solon, elder statesman, statesman, politician, politico, *Inf.* pol.

2. Member of Congress, M.C., Member of Parliament, M.P.; senator, congressman *or* congresswoman, legislatrix, *U.S.* congressman-at-large, representative, *Sl.* rep, *Amer. Hist.* burgess, conscript fathers; state legislator, state senator, state representative, *U.S.* assemblyman, councilman, (*in most New England states*) selectman.

legislature, *n.* **1.** congress, senate, diet, upper house, lower house; caucus, convention, session, convocation, council, governing body, *Inf.* graybeards.

2. Congress of the United States, U.S. Senate, U.S. House of Representatives; General Assembly, State Senate, State House; (*in Russia*) Duma, (*in the U.S.S.R.*) Soviet, (*in France*) Chamber of Deputies, (*in Germany*) Reichstag, (*in West Germany*) Bundestag, (*in Sweden*) Riksdag, (*in Norway*) Storthing, (*in Austria, Swtizerland*) Bundesversammlung, (*in Denmark*) Rigsdag, (*in Eire*) Oirechtas, (*in Spain*) Cortes, (*in Portugal*) Cortes Geraes, (*in the Netherlands*) States-General, (*all in Great Britain*) Parliament, House of Lords, House of Commons.

legitimate, *adj.* **1.** legal, licit, lawful, *Sl.* legit; within the law, by law, de jure, legally sound; statutory, legislated, enfranchised; constitutional, decreed, ordained, prescribed, mandated; licensed, chartered, empowered, indefeasible.

2. proper, right, rightful, *Inf.* O.K., *Inf.* A-O.K.; going by the rules, according to Hoyle, *Inf.* kosher; permitted, permissible, within bounds, allowable; sanctioned, warranted, approved; equitable, just, fair, *Inf.* straight-arrow, on the level, on the up and up, aboveboard; accurate, authoritative, unerring, unerrant, on the straight and narrow; honest, honest as the day is long, true-blue; all wool and a yard wide.

3. logical, reasonable, rational, inferable; coherent, holding together; admissible, sound, valid; plausible, credible, believable, reliable.

4. genuine, unspurious, real, *Inf.* for-real, *Inf.* the real McCoy; true, authentic, *Inf.* eighteen-carat; sincere, heartfelt, trustworthy; pure, natural, unsynthetic, unfaked, unadulterated, raw; sound as a dollar.

—*v.* **5.** legalize, pronounce lawful, justify. See **legitimize.**

legitimize, *v.* legalize, pronounce lawful, legitimatize, legitimate; justify, vindicate, authorize, sanction, warrant, give the stamp of approval; validate, certify, entitle; legislate, decree, ordain, mandate; license, charter; launder.

legume, *n.* **1** seed vessel, seedcase, pod, seed pod, capsule, hull, pericarp.

2. lentil, bean, green bean, *Fr. haricot vert*, soybean, pea, pulse, vetch.

leisure, *n.* **1.** freedom, liberty, disengagement, unrestraint; inactivity, *It. dolce far niente*, inoccupation, unemployment, retirement; free *or* vacant *or* spare time, time to burn *or* spare *or* kill, idle hours; breathing spell, breather, pause, respite, *Inf.* letup, relief, breathing space; day off, holiday, vacation, recess, rest.

2. ease, comfort, *It. dolce vita,* good life; restfulness, relaxation, repose, quiet, tranquillity, peace; slowness, unhurriedness, one's own sweet time, snail's pace; loafing, *Inf.* knocking about, *Sl.* flopping around.

—adj. 3. leisured, free, spare, unoccupied, idle; discretionary, unclaimed, unrestricted, unencumbered, clear; casual, carefree, nonchalant, *Inf.* at-home.

leisurely, *adj.* 1. leisured, slow, slow-moving, unhurried, deliberate; lingering, *Inf.* poky, tortoiselike, snaillike; easy, gentle, comfortable, restful, easygoing; peaceful, tranquil, halcyon, serene, pleasant; carefree, relaxed, laid-back, loose, loose as a goose, slack, lax; unconstrained, *Fr. dégagé,* unfettered.

2. dilatory, laggard, dillydallying, loitering, tardy; droopy, languid, indolent, otiose, slow-acting, slower than molasses in January; lazy, idle, loafing; motionless, quiescent, inactive; torpid, sluggish, inert, lethargic, listless, phlegmatic.

—adv. 3. slowly, without haste, unhurriedly, deliberately, at a snail's pace; in one's own sweet time, in time, eventually, at one's leisure, at one's convenience, when one feels like it, mañana; easily, comfortably, *Sl.* with no sweat.

leitmotif, *n.* (*all recurrent*) motif, theme; subject, idea, notion, concept; strain, melody, air; element, phrase; convention, device.

lemon, *n.* 1. citrus fruit, citron.

2. light yellow, pale yellow, lemon yellow, yellow.

3. *Inf. Sl.* dog, *Inf.* dud, bad *or* rotten apple, *Sl.* clunker, piece *or* hunk of junk.

—adj. 4. lemonish, lemonlike, lemony; tangy, tart, sour, acid; lemon-colored, pale-yellow, citrine, light-yellow, lemon-yellow, greenish-yellow, citreous, yellow, yellowish, xanthous.

lend, *v.* 1. loan, make a loan of, let [s.o.] use, *Fr. prêter;* lend money, accommodate, advance, give on credit.

2. furnish, provide, impart, give.

3. give freely, contribute, *Inf.* pitch in, donate, *Inf.* chip in, put in *or* out, spend, expend.

4. **lend a hand** give a hand *or* helping hand, help *or* help out, assist, aid, give a leg up.

lender, *n.* loaner, moneylender, pawnbroker, creditor, credit union; usurer, Shylock, *Inf.* loan shark.

length, *n.* 1. linear extent, reach, span, measure, distance lengthwise, *Geog.* longitude; measurement, dimension, proportion, size, magnitude.

2. duration, length of time.

3. (*all of a certain extent*) piece, portion, section, measure.

4. longness, lengthiness, extensiveness, elongation, protractedness; wordiness, verbosity, verboseness, prolixity, prolixness, tediousness, long-windedness.

5. **at length** a. completely, in *or* to the fullest extent, in full, without abridgment, in depth, thoroughly, to the full, to the greatest extent. b. for a long time, for ages *or* hours, interminably, endlessly, for what seemed like forever. c. after a time, after a long while, finally, at last, at long last.

lengthen, *v.* make longer, elongate, let down *or* out; draw out, stretch, extend, prolong, protract, continue; pad, add to, fill out, flesh out, develop, expand, make more complete.

lengthwise, *adj.* 1. longitudinal, vertical, horizontal.

—adv. 2. lengthways, endways, endwise, longitudinally, vertically, horizontally; along the length, from end to end, from one end to the other, from stem to stern, from head to foot *or* toe.

lengthy, *adj.* 1. very long, extensive, (*of words or expressions*) sesquipedalian; extended, drawn out, dragged out, protracted, long-drawn, long-drawn-out; prolonged, lengthened, elongated, elongate.

2. verbose, wordy, prolix, long-winded, tedious, boring; discursive, digressive, rambling, wandering; diffuse, garrulous, talkative, loquacious, voluble.

lenience, *n.* indulgence, permissiveness, tolerance, easiness, easygoingness, condonation; liberality, liberalness, moderation, temperance, temperateness; patience, forbearance, longanimity, long-suffering; magnanimity, forgivingness, charitableness, charity, bigness, big-heartedness, generousness; lenity, mildness, gentleness, clemency, mercy, mercifulness, ruth, ruthfulness, benevolence, humaneness, humanity, kindness, kindheartedness, softness, soft-heartedness, tenderness, tender-heartedness; compassion, considerateness, consideration, sympathy, commiseration, understanding, pity, fellow feeling.

lenient, *adj.* indulgent, permissive, tolerant, easy, easygoing, condoning; liberal, moderate, temperate; patient, forbearing, longanamous, long-suffering; forgiving, magnanimous, big, big-hearted, charitable, exorable, placable; mild, clement, merciful, ruthful, benevolent, humane, kind, kindhearted, soft, soft-hearted, tender, tender-hearted; compassionate, considerate, sympathetic, commiserative, understanding, pitying.

lenitive, *adj.* 1. palliative, mitigative, mitigating, alleviative, alleviating, relieving, easing; soothing, softening, assuasive, assuaging, mollifying, demulcent, emollient, balmy, balsamic, *Archaic.* lenient; calmative, sedative, relaxing; lubricative, lubricant, lubricating.

—n. 2. palliative, emollient, anodyne; cream, ointment, salve, liniment, embrocation, balm, lotion, nard, unguent, *Pharm.* cerate.

lenity, *n.* mildness, gentleness, clemency, mercy, mercifulness, ruth, ruthfulness, benevolence, humaneness, humanity; kindness, kindheartedness, softness, soft-heartedness, tender, tender-heartedness; compassion, compassionateness, consideration, considerateness, sympathy, commiseration, understanding, pity, fellow feeling; maganimity, charitableness, bigness, big-heartedness, large-heartedness, great-heartedness, generousness; patience, forbearance, longanimity, long-suffering; liberality, liberalness, moderation, temperance, temperateness; lenience, indulgence, permissiveness, tolerance, easiness, easygoingness, condonation.

lens, *n.* 1. eyepiece, *Optics.* ocular, *Optics.* objective, *Optics.* object glass *or* lens; telescope, field glass, spy glass; magnifier, magnifying glass, glass, hand lens, loupe; monocle, eyeglass.

2. **lenses** binoculars, opera glasses, lorgnette; eyeglasses, glasses, spectacles, *Inf.* specs, reading glasses, pince-nez, bifocals, trifocals, *Brit. Dial.* barnacles, *Sl.* eyes, *Sl.* cheaters; contact lenses, *Inf.* contacts, soft *or* hard lenses; sunglasses, dark *or* colored glasses, *Inf.* sun-specs, *Sl.* shades.

lenticular, *adj.* 1. lens-shaped, lenslike.

2. biconvex, convexo-convex, lentoid, bowed, excurved, excurvate; bulging, swelling, protuberant, (*usu. of the moon*) *Astron.* gibbous.

leonine, *adj.* lionlike; mighty, powerful, strong; kingly, lordly, imperial; aweless, fearless, courageous, lionhearted.

leper, *n.* lazar, untouchable; pariah, outcast, social outcast, castaway.

leprechaun, *n.* elf, gremlin, imp, kobold; fairy, fay, sprite, brownie; gnome, dwarf; (*all collectively*) little people, wee folk, fairy folk, elfin folk.

leprous, *adj.* scaly, scabby, scabrous, leprose, *Bot.*

lepidote; morbid, mortified, decayed, diseased.

lesbian, *adj.* **1.** (*all of women*) homosexual, homoerotic, homophile, sexually inverted, *Inf.* gay, *Inf.* bent, *Sl.* kinky; tribadistic, sapphic; mannish, *Sl.* butch.

2. erotic, sexual, sensual, carnal; amorous, amatory.

—n. **3.** sapphist, tribade, *Sl.* butch, *Sl.* femme, *Derog.* dyke *or* bull dyke, *Archaic.* fricatrice.

lese majesty, *n.* treason, high treason, petty treason, misprision; insurrection, sedition; iconoclasm.

lesion, *n.* **1.** injury, wound, trauma, hurt, harm, impairment, sore *or* tender spot; disfigurement, disfiguration, defacement, mutilation; abrasion, scratch, scrape, scuff, chafe, gall, excoriation; cut, gash, slash, laceration, tear, rip, rent, run; stab, stab wound, puncture, incision; bruise, contusion, black-and-blue mark; black eye, *Sl.* shiner, *Sl.* mouse; break, fracture, rupture; burn, first- *or* second- *or* third-degree burn, scald, scorch.

2. disorder, abnormality, derangement; growth, tumor, swelling, tumescence, neoplasm.

3. ulcer, ulceration, abscess, noma, fester, festering, gathering, tubercle, *Obs.* apostem, *Obs.* apostemation, *Archaic.* impostume; gumboil, parulis, whitlow, agnail; canker, chancre, chancroid, soft chancre, simple chancre; boil, blain, furuncle, furunculus, carbuncle, pustule, pimple, papule, papilla, inflammation, pock, wen, whelk, *Rare.* bleb, *Archaic.* botch; sore, open *or* running sore.

4. *Plant Pathology.* blister, vesicle, bulla; blemish, mark, spot; scab.

less, *adv.* **1.** to a smaller extent *or* amount *or* degree, not very, not so much; other, in any way different.

2. **less than** hardly, by no means, in no way, in no manner, not at all, not in the least, far short of.

—adj. **3.** not so great, smaller, slighter, shorter, narrower, lower; fewer, not as much, not many, hardly any, little; lessened, abated, reduced, limited, deficient.

4. inferior, below par, imperfect, ignoble, lesser; commonplace, mediocre, second-rate; junior, secondary, minor; small, insignificant, of no consequence, of no account, unimportant, immaterial, unessential.

—n. **5.** not so much, smaller amount, minimum.

—prep. **6.** minus, subtracting, without, excepting.

lessee, *n.* tenant, holder, renter; lodger, boarder, roomer; occupant, occupier, dweller.

lessen, *v.* **1.** abate, decrease, diminish, lower, mitigate, bate; subside, ebb, let up, moderate, tail off, intermit, relax, slacken, remit; approach an end, come to a close, wind down, slow down, die down.

2. decline, fall off, taper off, wane, fade away; melt away, deliquesce; dwindle, run low, grow less; weaken, attenuate; fail, languish, waste away, shrivel, wither; decay, crumble, erode.

3. reduce, retrench, cut back, minify; shrink, constrict, contract, narrow; pare, cut, prune, truncate, crop, lop, dock, clip; condense, cut down, compress, epitomize, shorten, abridge, boil down; abbreviate, curtail, cut short.

4. allay, assuage, alleviate, *Rare.* lenify, palliate, appease, soothe, *Archaic.* attemper, relieve, ease, soften, cushion, mollify, lighten; quell, slake, deaden, dull, blunt, take the edge off of; modify, moderate, temper, qualify; minimize, extenuate, make light of, soft-pedal, play down, downplay, underestimate, underrate.

5. deduct, subtract, take away, take from; deplete, thin out, decimate.

lesser, *adj.* smaller, slighter, shorter, narrower, lower; inferior, below par, imperfect; commonplace, mediocre, second-rate, less; subordinate, subaltern, junior, secondary, minor.

lesson, *n.* **1.** assignment, homework, exercise, practice, *Inf.* day's ration; instruction, teaching, studies; lecture, reading, recitation; example, theorem, axiom, truth, proof, dogma; portion, stint, job, duty, obligation, charge, responsibility.

2. didacticism, didactive narrative, preachings, preachment; parable, apologue, essay, moral fable, allegory; sermon, prelection, discourse; precept, maxim, advice, saying, wise saying, proverb, adage, aphorism, epigram, profound saying, pithy saying.

3. correction, lecture, curtain lecture; warning, a word to the wise, a flea in the ear, notification; hint, sharp hint, caution, caveat, admonition, threat; rap on the knuckles, reproof, chiding, reproval, reproach, rebuke, reprimand, remonstrance, expostulation; scolding, taking to task, talking-to, *Sl.* call-down; piece of one's mind, tongue-lashing, castigation, *Inf.* bawling out, upbraiding, *Inf.* raking over coals, *Inf.* trimming, *Inf.* roasting, *Inf.* slam, *Inf.* slap; denunciation, censure, chastisement, punishment.

4. *All Ecclesiastical.* lection, pericope, reading, daily reading, text, *Rom. Cath. Ch.* epistle.

lessor, *n.* landlord, landlady, *Brit.* letter, property owner; mortgagee, lender, moneylender, loaner; creditor, credit man, creditress.

lest, *conj.* for fear that, in order to avoid *or* prevent, if, perchance.

let, *v.* **1.** allow, permit, give permission *or* leave to, grant; authorize, sanction, warrant, entitle, empower, enable, license, commission; vouchsafe, favor, privilege; affranchise, give one his head, give carte blanche, give the green light, give the go-ahead, give [s.o.] enough rope; approve of, go along with, submit to, yield, accede to; assent to, agree to, consign, consent to, acquiesce in; admit of, be compatible with, tolerate, countenance, put up with, hear of, *Inf.* stand for, bear, support; suffer, stand, brook, abide, endure.

2. allow to pass *or* come *or* go. See **let** (*def.* **5**).

3. rent, lease, sublease, sublet, underlet; hire *or* hire out, farm, job *or* job out, contract, charter; lend, loan.

4. **let down** **a.** disappoint, fail, dissatisfy, disillusion, disenchant. **b.** betray, play [s.o.] false, *Inf.* sell out, *Inf.* double-cross; desert, abandon, forsake, quit, jilt, leave in the lurch, turn one's back on. **c.** slacken, abate, mitigate, diminish, lessen, reduce, ease up; loosen, relax.

5. **let in** admit, open the door to, allow to enter, give access to, give right of entry to, yield passage to, grant *or* afford entrance to; take in, receive, welcome, greet: accept, include, embrace, incorporate; induct, install, initiate, inaugurate, invest, vest.

6. **let off** excuse, pardon, forgive, acquit, clear, vindicate, exonerate, absolve; discharge, release, reprieve; disregard, ignore, pass over, gloss over, let pass, let slide; overlook, wink at, shut one's eyes to; neglect, pay no heed *or* mind, brush aside, push aside, slight.

7. **let on** *Informal.* **a.** See **let** (*def.* **8**). **b.** pretend, feign, affect, put on, assume, make a show of; make believe, seem, act, simulate, fake; disguise, conceal, mask, wrap, hide, dissimulate.

8. **let out** **a.** divulge, make known, disclose, reveal, expose. **b.** release, discharge, liberate, set free. **c.** terminate, stop, end, finish, close.

9. **let up** *Informal.* **a.** slacken, abate, mitigate, ease up, diminish, lessen, decrease. **b.** cease, stop, halt, end, quit, terminate, leave off.

10. **let up on** *Informal.* ease up on, *Inf.* go easier on, be more lenient with, be temperate *or* moderate with, be kind *or* charitable to; slacken, loosen, relax.

letch, *n. Slang.* **1.** craving, hankering, longing, yearning, *Inf.* yen, appetite; hunger, covetousness, greed, inordinate desire, rapacity, cupidity, avarice.

2. liking, strong liking, predilection, weakness for; preference, choosing, bias, inclination, leaning toward, predisposition.

3. lecher, roué, debauchee, degenerate, pervert, *Inf.* dirty old man; rake, rakehell, *Inf.* rip.

letdown, *n.* **1.** decrease, decline, declension, gradual loss; wane, ebb, reflux, fall, falling off, slowdown, depreciation, shrinkage; reduction, cutback, cutting down, retrenchment; curtailment, abridgment, shortening, dwindling; abatement, lessening, letup, mitigation, diminishing, diminution, subsidence, easing off.

2. disillusionment, disappointment, disenchantment; dissatisfaction, discontent; mortification, chagrin, frustration, balk, bafflement; regret, rue, sorrow, pain; bitter pill, setback, blow, blow to one's pride, *Inf.* comeuppance; humbling, *Inf.* comedown, humiliation, disgrace, shame, shaming.

3. failure, *Inf.* flop, defeat, collapse; nonfulfillment, nonsuccess; fiasco, *Inf.* washout, fizzle, flash in the pan, *Inf.* no-go, shipwreck; miscarriage, abortion.

4. depression, deflation, discouragement, dejection; despondency, blues, unhappiness, *Psychiatry.* melancholia, disconsolation, disconsolateness; dispiritedness, low-spiritedness, doldrums, *Inf.* dumps, disheartenment, downheartedness; dolefulness, gloominess, dolor, sorrow, grief; misery, despair, desolation, hopelessness, bleakness, dreariness, darkness, sadness.

lethal, *adj.* deadly, fatal, mortal, mortiferous, deathful, *Archaic.* lethiferous; killing, suicidal, slaughtering, slaughterous, murderous, death-dealing, internecine, internecive; destructive, ruinous, annihilative, calamitous, disastrous; pernicious, dangerous, hazardous, deleterious, detrimental; harmful, injurious, nocuous, hurtful, nocent, baleful, noisome; noxious, malicious, malign, malignant, menacing; venomous, virulent, toxic, morbific; fell, baneful, mephitic, viperous, poisonous, *Archaic.* venenose; pestilential, pestiferous, infective, infectious, pestilent, contaminative, contagious, leprous, septic.

lethargic, *adj.* **1.** sluggish, phlegmatic, dull, slow, heavy, hebetudinous, lethargical; lazy, supine, indolent, slothful, fainéant, idle; languid, languorous, listless, lackadaisical, apathetic, indifferent, impassive; spiritless, lifeless, passive, inactive, inanimate; inert, insensible, torpid, dormant, stupefied, stuporous, narcose, comatose.

2. drowsy, sleepy, slumberous, slumbery, dozy, somnolent, oscitant; sleeping, dozing, drowsing; weary, tired, exhausted, fagged out, fatigued, *Sl.* beat, *Sl.* bushed, *Sl.* pooped; enervated, weak, weakened, anemic.

3. soporific, somniferous, somnific, somnifacient, sleep-inducing; narcotic, sedative, opiate, stupefacient; hypnotic, mesmeric.

lethargy, *n.* **1.** sluggishness, dullness, hebetude, slowness, heaviness, phlegm; stupefaction, stupor, torpor, torpidity, torpidness, numbness; inertia, inactivity, lifelessness, inertness, spiritlessness, inanition, comatoseness, comatosity.

2. languor, languidness, listlessness, *Inf.* the blahs; apathy, indifference, impassiveness, impassivity; insensibility, passivity, passiveness, dormancy, coma; laziness, supineness, indolence, sloth, idleness.

3. weariness, lassitude, exhaustion, fatigue, tiredness; drowsiness, sleepiness, narcosis, slumberousness, doziness, somnolence, oscitancy, oscitance; drowse, doze; *Pathol.* sopor; rest, repose, ease, contentment, euphoria, (*both usu. drug induced*) (*in the Middle East*) kef, *Med.* narcoma.

letter, *n.* **1.** missive, dispatch, written message; epistle, *Obs.* billet, note, line, bulletin; answer, reply, acknowledgement, bread-and-butter note, thank-you note; business letter, form letter, drop letter; love letter, billet-doux, *Inf.* mash note, fan letter; card, Christmas card, postcard, picture postcard; *Rom. Cath. Ch.* encyclical.

2. alphabetic character, written character, sign, symbol, phonetic character; initial, majuscule, uncial, ideogram, rune, hieroglyphic character, hieroglyph, cuneiform character, hierogram; letter of the alphabet, ABC.

3. type, piece of type, impressed form, stamp, print; linotype, monotype, stereotype, electrotype, autotype, albertype, ambrotype, chromotype, zinctotype, stenotype, lithotype; logotype, ligature; lower case, minuscule, upper case, majuscule, capital, *Inf.* cap, small capital; strike, matrix, jet, sprue, body, type body, face, typeface.

4. (*all type styles*) Old English, Gothic, German text, antique, clarendon, French, Elzevir, Caslon, Caslon old style, Ionic, Chapel text, typewriter; black letter, roman, italic, cursive, script; standard, lightface, boldface, fullface, extrabold face, extrabold; Braille.

5. letters a. literature, belles-lettres, the humanities, *Latin. litterae humaniores*, the classics, philosophy; the world of letters, the field of letters, writing, play-writing, journalism; book publishing, bibliogony, bibliography, librarianship, bibliopoly; linguistics, science of language, philology, lexicography, glossology, semantics, etymology, lexicology, grammar, diction. **b.** learning, booklore; culture, liberal education, higher education, scholarship, study, studies, erudition.

6. to the letter literally, *Latin. literatim*, literal, according to the letter, verbatim, word for word, *Fr. mot à mot*, in the same words, *Latin. sic*, thus; strictly speaking, chapter and verse, by the rules, *Inf.* according to Hoyle, *Inf.* kosher, orthodox, authentic, faithful, conforming, canonical, scriptural, textual; exactly, precisely, accurately.

—*v.* **7.** inscribe, write, mark, character, initial, sign, stencil.

letter carrier, *n.* postman, mail carrier, mailman, post boy, postal clerk; carrier, bearer, carrier pigeon, messenger; courier, dispatch bearer, post rider, runner; go-between, intermediary, connection.

lettered, *adj.* educated, well-educated, erudite; learned, literate, informed, well-informed, enlightened; well-versed, well-posted, well-grounded; literary, well-read, widely read, *Inf.* highbrow; cultivated, cultured, accomplished, polished, refined.

letter-perfect, *adj.* well-rehearsed, well-prepared, perfectly drilled; memorized, *Inf.* learned by heart, learned by rote, committed to memory; precise, exact, accurate, perfect, authentic, faithful; literatim, letter for letter, verbatim, word for word, *Fr. mot à mot*, to the letter, literal, in the same words, *Latin. sic*, thus.

letup, *n.* **1.** abatement, reduction, lessening, slackening, moderation, tempering; decrease, fall-off, diminution, remission; retardation, retarding, slowing down; alleviation, mitigation, assuagement, relief, palliation, mollification, softening, easing up; waning, fading, decline; weakening, attenuation.

2. cessation, termination, ending, completion, finish, conclusion, close, desinence; discontinuance, breaking off, abruption; ceasing, ending, quitting, desisting, desistance; arrest, halt, stand, standstill, stoppage.

3. intermission, pause, interlude, interim, pause,

cease, rest, break, *Inf.* breather, lull, respite, recess, time out, leaving off; suspension, interruption, discontinuation, abeyance, remission.

levee[1], *n.* **1.** embankment, bank, mound, elevation of earth; dike, dam, breakwater, mole.

2. ridge, mound, hill, hillock.

levee[2], *n.* party, soiree, social gathering, gathering, get-together; reception, ceremonious party, celebration, fete, gala.

level, *adj.* **1.** even, plane, smooth, complanate, *Math.* homaloidal; flat, flat as a pancake, smooth as glass; flush, straight, true; balanced, right, equalized; symmetrical, proportionate, proportional, proportioned, commensurate, correlative.

2. equal, coequal, equipotent, equipollent; on equal *or* even terms, on the same footing, on a par with; neither more nor less, *Inf.* six of one, half dozen of another; much the same.

3. equable, uniform, identical, regular, consistent; unvarying, unchanging, unfluctuating, invariable; steady, stable, constant.

4. even-tempered, imperturbable, calm, cool, collected, composed, unruffled, smooth; serene, tranquil, peaceful; neutral, uninvolved, dispassionate. See **level-headed** (*defs.* **1, 2**).

—*n.* **5.** flat surface, plane; expanse, open *or* free space, extent of land, field.

6. height, highness, altitude, elevation, loftiness, extent *or* distance upward.

7. degree, stage, grade, gradation, scale; status, rank, standing, standard; position, station, class, caste; condition, lot, estate.

8. extent, measure, magnitude, quantity, amount, fullness; shade, strength, intensity; breadth, width, depth, broadness, wideness, height, length; capacity, volume, size, gauge.

9. find one's *or* **one's own level** find one's niche, find one's groove, fit in.

10. on the level *Slang.* honest, straight, square, on the up-and-up, up front; open, aboveboard.

—*v.* **11.** flatten, make flat, flat, even out *or* off, smooth, smooth out, level off *or* out, plane.

12. raze, tear down, pull down, take down, bring down, break down, throw down, beat down, batter down; cast down, knock down, fling down, hurl down; fell, prostrate, bulldoze; cut down, chop down, hew down, mow down; demolish, destroy, wreck, devastate, desolate, lay waste.

13. equalize, equate, even up, square, *Archaic.* equal; regularize, symmetrize, harmonize.

14. aim, point, direct, draw *or* get a bead on, sight, focus, zero in on; position, mark, peg, train.

15. *Slang.* put one's cards on the table, tell the truth, hide nothing, be up front, tell the whole truth and nothing but the truth, call a spade a spade.

level-headed, *adj.* **1.** reasonable, sensible, commonsense, commonsensical; prudent, cautious, careful, circumspect; wise, sagacious, shrewd, calculating.

2. composed, calm, collected, self-possessed, *Inf.* together; cool, cool-headed, passionless, impassive, dispassionate; nonchalant, at ease, unruffled, untroubled, unperturbed, undisturbed, unexcited, undismayed; sedate, tranquil, serene, placid; self-controlled, poised, balanced, steady; imperturbable, inexcitable, unflappable, even-tempered, easy-going, relaxed; undemonstrative, unemotional, stoical, philosophical.

lever, *n.* **1.** bar, handspike, crow *or* crowbar, jimmy, *Brit.* jemmy, pry, purchase; handle, door handle.

—*v.* **2.** pry, purchase, raise, lift, hoist, boost; move, force, jam, jimmy, *Brit.* jemmy.

leverage, *n.* **1.** pry, lifting power, force, strength; advantage, vantage, edge, upper hand; backing, support, financial backing.

2. influence, weight, *Sl.* pull, *Sl.* drag, *Inf.* clout, purchasing power; authority, say *or* say-so, control.

leviathan, *n.* **1.** whale, Moby Dick, white whale, beluga, blue whale, sulphur-bottom.

2. sea monster, sea serpent, dragon, *Class. Myth.* hydra, *U.S. Inf.* behemoth.

3. enormity, colossus, titan, giant; mammoth, mastodon, jumbo, dinosaur, hippopotamus, *Inf.* hippo.

levitate, *v.* (*all in space*) lift *or* lift up, rise, elevate; float, hover, hang, be suspended; plane, glide, fly.

levity, *n.* **1.** lightness, light-heartedness, airiness; frivolity, frivolousness, flippancy, giddiness, trifling, triviality; folly, foolishness, silliness, fatuity, foolery; tomfoolery, asininity, ridiculousness, waggery; jollity, jocularity, jocundity, glee, hilarity, fun.

2. fickleness, variability, inconsistency, inconstancy, changeableness, coquettishness; unreliability, undependability, irresponsibility; flightiness, volatility, mercuriality, skittishness; inattentiveness, unmindfulness, inadvertence.

3. unsubstantiality, lightness, thinness, lack of weight; weightlessness, unheaviness.

levy, *n.* **1.** raising, collecting, collection, gathering; enrollment, induction, call-up, summons; conscription, draft, enlistment, impressment; recruitment, mobilization, muster, assemblage, call to arms, call to colors, rally, round-up, war measures.

2. tax, tariff, toll, custom, excise, surcharge, tribute; impost, assessment, *Brit.* cess, exaction, taxation; duty, dues, rate, payment; poll tax, property tax, tithe, Peter's pence.

3. troops, forces, militia, army, armed forces; recruits, reserves, reinforcements, guard.

—*v.* **4.** collect, raise, put together, gather; convoke, convene, shepherd, round up, corral; muster, mobilize, call up, activate, rally, assemble; enlist, conscript, draft, press, *Archaic.* impress, *Archaic.* list; enroll, induct, sign up *or* on; compel, coerce, force, dragoon.

5. impose, lay on, put on, set, fix, inflict; assess, rate, charge, toll, tax, excise, subject to duty.

6. (*all in reference to war*) start, begin, launch, instigate; open fire, strike the first blow, go on the warpath, take the field, rise up in arms; make war, wage war, declare war, throw down the gauntlet, draw the sword; attack, assault, assail, fall upon; raid, besiege, invade, march on.

lewd, *adj.* **1.** lecherous, lubricous, *Archaic.* lickerish, satyric, satyrical, satyrlike, goatish, hircine, ruttish, *Sl.* horny; lustful, randy, *Sl.* hot *or* hot for, concupiscent, prurient, libidinous, salacious; fleshly, carnal, sensual, voluptuous, erotic; licentious, loose, Cyprian, wanton, abandoned, incontinent; debauched, rakish, rakehell, dissolute, dissipated, profligate; promiscuous, whorish, of easy virtue, *Sl.* cheap, shameless; immodest, impure, unchaste, unvirtuous.

2. obscene, lurid, blue, pornographic, *Inf.* porno, *Inf.* porn, smutty; indecent, offensive, suggestive, vulgar, coarse, gross, crude; dirty, unclean, foul, filthy, vile; foulmouthed; ribald, scurrilous, irreverent; bawdy, Fescennine.

lewdness, *n.* **1.** lechery, lecherousness, lubricity, goatishness, ruttishness; lust, lustfulness, concupiscence, prurience, pruriency, libidinousness, salacity, salaciousness; carnality, carnalness, carnalism, sensuality, voluptuousness, promiscuity, eroticism, erotism; immodesty, impudicity, impurity, unchasteness, unchastity, unvirtuousness.

2. debauchery, dissoluteness, rakishness, dissipation, profligacy; licentiousness, wantonness, unrestraint, abandon, incontinence, self-indulgence; aphrodisia, sexual passion *or* desire, *Pathol.* satyriasis, *Pathol.* nymphomania; unnatural desire, incest, incestuousness, pederasty, sodomy, buggery, sadism, masochism; *Psychiatry.* coprophilia.

3. obscenity, obsceneness, luridness; pornography, *Inf.* porno, *Inf.* porn, smut, smuttiness; bawdiness, bawdry, scurrility, ribaldry; vulgarity, vulgarism, vulgarness, coarseness, crudity, crudeness.

lexicographer, *n.* dictionary writer, dictionary maker, dictionarist, dictionarian, compiler; definer, explainer, explicator; etymologist, philologist, philologer, lexicologist, onomatologist; glossarist, glossator, glossologist, glossographer.

lexicography, *n.* dictionary making, dictionary compiling, glossography, *Archaic.* glossology; etymology, philology, lexicology, lexigraphy, onomatology, onomastics.

lexicon, *n.* dictionary, wordbook, glossary, gloss, Webster's; wordstock, wordlist, vocabulary, onomasticon; thesaurus, gradus, synonymy, Roget's compilation, concordance; rhyming dictionary, polyglot dictionary, unabridged dictionary, college dictionary, desk-top dictionary, bilingual dictionary.

liability, *n.* **1.** indebtedness, debt, obligation, *Accounting.* debit; duty, indebtment, due, score, pledge.

2. responsibility, accountability, chargeability, amenability, amenableness.

3. drawback, disadvantage, hindrance, hamper; nuisance, holdback, drag, clog, inconvenience; impediment, undesirability, discommodity, incommodity, difficulty; encumbrance, cumbrance, onus, burden, load, weight, millstone, cross; obstacle, barrier, obstruction, bar, block, hitch, snag, stumbling block; fetter, shackle, catch.

4. liableness, susceptibility, susceptivity; exposure, vulnerability, pregnability, assailability.

liable, *adj.* **1.** exposed, open, subject; susceptible, vulnerable, pregnable, obnoxious, assailable, in danger.

2. likely, probable; apt, prone, tending, disposed, predisposed, inclined, incident to.

3. responsible, chargeable, answerable, accountable, amenable; guilty, culpable, reprehensible, censurable, *Obs.* obnoxious, blameworthy, blamable, at fault, *Law.* actionable.

liaison, *n.* **1.** contact, connection, bond, tie, vinculum, link, nexus, linkage; connective, copula, hyphen, tie-up, hook-up; joint, juncture, conjunction, jointure; mediary, intermediary, medium, intermedium, go-between; alliance, affiliation, filiation, association, relationship, relation, kinship.

2. affair, amour, amourette, romance, tryst, intrigue, entanglement, assignation; flirtation, *Sl.* thing, *Inf.* hanky-panky.

liar, *n.* prevaricator, fibber, fibster, perjurer, false witness; falsifier, deluder, fraud, duper, cheater, cheat, libeler; equivocator, hedger, misleader; dissembler, *Sl.* leg-puller, circumventor, deceiver, Ananias; hypocrite, false friend, shammer, actor; fabulist, romancer, pseudologist, yarner, spinner of yarns, storyteller, Baron von Münchhausen.

libation, *n.* **1.** *Often Facetious.* drink, beverage, liquid, liquid refreshment, draught, dram, drinkable, potable; intoxicant, potation, imbibition, potion, decoction, infusion; mixed drink, cocktail, highball, martini, Manhattan, apéritif, *Inf.* chaser, *Sl.* snifter; nightcap, *Brit. Inf.* sundowner, bracer, pickup, one for the road, *Scot.* doch-an-dorrach, parting cup; toast, health.

2. offering, oblation, tribute, offertory, propitiation; offering, sacrifice, incense, burnt offering, votive offering, peace offering.

libel, *n.* **1.** defamation, denigration, vilification, vituperation, scandal, yellow journalism, *Inf.* skeleton in the closet; censure, reproach, denunciation, curse, malediction, railing, invective, commination, *Archaic.* exprobration; shame, disgrace, dishonor, ill-repute, obloquy, loss of face; belittlement, disparagement, deprecation, detraction, deflation, depreciation, derogation, devaluation; humiliation, humble pie, mortification; mockery, lampoon, pasquinade, squib.

2. calumny, slander, false report, misrepresentation, falsehood, lie, untruth, traducement; aspersion, imputation, insinuation, *Inf.* brickbat, innuendo; abuse, injury, backbiting, *Archaic.* malison; slur, blot, blot on the escutcheon, smear, smirch, stain, taint, tarnish, spot, black spot *or* mark; blemish, smudge, brand, stigma.

—*v.* **3.** defame, vilify, vilipend, denigrate, vituperate, scandalize, run down, berate, malign, revile, gibbet, impugn, criticize, pull to pieces, *Sl.* do a hatchet job on, give a bad name, speak ill of, speak evil of, hold up to scorn, sneer at, muckrake; denounce, curse, rail, execrate, damn, imprecate, *Obs.* exprobate, anathematize, censure, cry down, reproach; disgrace, shame, dishonor, debase, vitiate, degrade, discredit, disprove, disfavor; belittle, disparage, detract, decry, deprecate, deflate, depreciate, devaluate, derogate; humiliate, humble, mortify, *Sl.* put down; lampoon, mock, ridicule, satirize, pasquinade.

4. calumniate, slander, traduce, falsify, accuse falsely, misrepresent, belie, impute, asperse, insinuate; injure, abuse, insult, backbite, *Sl.* badmouth, engage in personalities; slur, sully, defile, smear, smirch, besmirch, soil, stain, blacken, taint, attaint, tarnish, smudge, spot, brand, stigmatize, drag through the mud *or* mire, heap dirt upon, fling dirt, throw mud on, spatter, bespatter, *Sl.* dump on.

libelous, *adj.* **1.** defamatory, denigrating, vituperative, vilifying, vilipenditory; critical, denunciable, imprecatory, condemnatory, disapproving, disapprobatory, maledictory; scandalous, notorious, flagrant, outrageous; censurable, blameworthy, culpable, chargeable, accusable, impeachable, imputable; shameful, disgraceful, reproachable, dishonorable, discreditable, disfavorable, disreputable; debased, abased, vitiated, depraved, degenerate, corrupt; humbling, humiliating, mortifying; belittling, disparaging, deprecatory, derogatory, detracting, deflating, depreciating, devaluating; satirical, sarcastic, caustic, acrimonious, vitriolic, scathing.

2. slanderous, calumnious, calumniatory, traducent, false, untrue, maliciously false *or* untrue, misrepresentative, aspersive, imputative, insinuating, gossiping; abusive, thersitical, hurtful, scurrilous, *Archaic.* scurrile, injurious, contumelious, insulting, backbiting; defiling, sullying, soiling, staining, smearing, smirching, tainting, tarnishing, blemishing, smudging, stigmatizing.

liberal, *adj.* **1.** progressive, forward-looking, progressivist, reformist; radical, left-wing, leftist; libertarian, latitudinarian, libertine, free-thinking, liberal-minded, independent; humanistic, enlightened, up-to-date, modern.

2. tolerant, indulgent, unbigoted, unprejudiced, unbiased, unjaundiced, unwarped; open-minded, broad-minded, large-minded, broad, unhidebound, broad-gauged; unprovincial, unparochial, catholic, ecumenical, cosmopolitan; dispassionate, disinterested, impartial, unopinionated.

3. generous, beneficient, charitable, bounteous; munificent, philanthropic, humanitarian, magnanimous, big, big-hearted; unselfish, altruistic, benevolent, benign, benignant; open-handed, unstinting, giving, ungrudging, unsparing; kind, kindhearted, sympathetic, compassionate, gracious; handsome, princely, lordly, royal, regal.

4. lavish, profuse, rich, ample, copious, abundant; bountiful, plenteous, plentiful, rife, luxuriant; extensive, broad, wide, far-reaching, wide-reaching, wide-ranging; wholesale, full, sweeping, large-scale.

5. free, casual, unrestricted, nonrestrictive, not close, not literal, extended; deviating, unstrict, inexact, imprecise.

—n. **6.** progressivist, progressive, libertarian, latitudinarian; left-winger, leftist, radical, independent, freethinker, free spirit; reformist, humanist, ecumenicist; nonpartisan, individual, neutral, mugwump.

liberalism, *n.* libertarianism, latitudinarianism, libertinism; progressivism, left wing, left; freedom of choice, independence, unilaterality, noninterference, laissez faire; unprovincialism, unparochialism, ecumenism, ecumenicalism, catholicity, universality, cosmopolitanism.

liberality, *n.* **1.** generosity, charitableness, bounty, largess, charity, benefaction, beneficence; bounteousness, liberalness, bountifulness, open-handedness; philanthropy, humanitarianism, magnanimity, munificence, big-heartedness, bigness; altruism, unselfishness, large heart, free hand; kindness, kindheartedness, graciousness, compassion.

2. lavishness, prodigality, profuseness, profusion, ampleness, plenty, abundance, luxuriance; extensiveness, fullness, wideness, width, sweep.

3. broadness, broad-mindedness, wide-mindedness, large-mindedness, libertarianism, latitudinarianism; broad gauge, breadth, latitude, toleration, indulgence; unprejudicedness, unbigotedness, unbiasedness, equitability, objectivity; dispassion, detachment, impartiality, neutrality, dispassionateness, disinterestedness.

4. progressivism, freethinking. See **liberalism**.

liberalize, *v.* **1.** expand, extend, widen, broaden; grow, develop, increase, enlarge, lengthen, project, elongate.

2. loosen, loose, relax, soften, ease, slacken; free, liberate, release.

liberate, *v.* **1.** free, enfranchise, affranchise, franchise, manumit, emancipate; deliver, rescue, ransom, redeem, *Theol.* save; release, loose, let loose, turn loose, set loose, set free, unpen, unmew, disimprison; disenthrall, unfetter, unbind, untie, unbridle, unyoke, unshackle, unchain, unhandcuff, unmuzzle, *Archaic.* untruss; acquit, dismiss, discharge, let go, let out of, let off, *Inf.* let off the hook.

2. disengage, disunite, disjoin, disconnect, dissociate; separate, part, divide, sunder, sever, disintegrate, dissolve, break apart *or* up; loosen, detach, unfix, undo, unfasten, unhook; extricate, take out, extract, pull out; distill, volatize, vaporize, gasify, aerify, *Both Chem.* sublimate, sublime.

liberation, *n.* **1.** freedom, freeing, liberty, liberating, enfranchisement, enfranchising, affranchisement, franchisement, franchising, manumitting, emancipation, emancipating; deliverance, delivery, delivering, rescue, rescuing, ransom, ransoming, redemption, redeeming, *Both Theol.* salvation, saving; release, releasing, loosing, disenthrallment, disenthralling, unfettering, unbinding, untying, unbridling, unyoking, unshackling, unchaining; acquittal, acquittance, acquitting, dismissal, dismissing, discharge, discharging.

2. disengagement, disengaging, disuniting, disjoining, disconnection, disconnecting, dissociation, dissociating; separation, separating, parting, division, dividing, sundering, severance, severing; loosening, detachment, detaching, undoing, unfastening; extrication, extricating, extraction, extracting; distillation, distilling, *Both Chem.* sublimation, sublimating.

liberator, *n.* rescuer, savior, emancipator, freer, deliverer, redeemer, manumitter.

libertine, *n.* **1.** profligate, wanton, lecher, debauchee, debaucher, dissipator; sensualist, sybarite, voluptuary, prodigal, hedonist, epicurean; rake, rakehell, roué, gallant; playboy, fast man, fancy man, *Inf.* rip, *Sl.* swinger, free-lover, philanderer, loose liver; adulterer, fornicator, seducer, *Inf.* wolf; womanizer, lady killer, flirt, bedhopper, chaser, lover; Don Juan, Lothario, Cassanova; whoremonger, whoremaster, pimp, gigolo; rapist, raper, violator, ravisher; satyr, goat, old goat, *Sl.* dirty old man, pervert, *Sl.* flasher, *Sl.* letch.

2. freethinker, liberal, free spirit, libertarian, latitudinarian; independent, individualist, humanist, ecumenicist.

—adj. **3.** dissolute, dissipated, rakehell, degenerate; decadent, debauched, depraved, amoral; profligate, wanton, abandoned, incontinent, intemperate, Paphic; immoral, unchaste, shameless, unvirtuous, impure, sinful; licentious, lewd, lecherous, lascivious, lubricous, *Archaic.* lickerish; prurient, libidinous, salacious, concupiscent, ruttish; goatish, hircine, satyric, priapic, randy, *Sl.* horny; carnal, sensual, animal, bestial, brutish.

4. freethinking, libertarian, latitudinarian, liberal, liberal-minded, independent; catholic, humanistic, ecumenical, unprovincial, unparochial; open-minded, broad-minded, broad, large-minded, tolerant; unbigoted, unprejudiced, unbiased.

libertinism, *n.* **1.** freethinking, libertarianism, latitudinarianism, free thought; liberality, liberalism, humanism, catholicity, ecumenism, ecumenicalism, unparochialism, unprovincialism; open-mindedness, broad-mindedness, broadness, latitude, large-mindedness, toleration; unbigotedness, unprejudicedness, unbiasedness, impartiality.

2. profligacy, debauchery, dissipation, dissolution, dissoluteness, prodigality; sensualism, sybaritism, hedonism; degeneracy, decadence, immorality, amorality, unchastity, unvirtuousness, shamelessness, impudicity; wantonness, abandon, unrestraint, incontinence, intemperance; immoderation, indulgence, overindulgence, self-indulgence; licentiousness, license, lechery, lasciviousness; rakishness, gallantry, satyrism, goatishness; wildness, looseness, laxity, fastness, *Inf.* swinging, wild living, free living, *It. dolce vita*; whoring, wenching, womanizing, *Sl.* letching.

liberty, *n.* **1.** freedom, autonomy, sovereignty; independence, self-determination, self-direction, self-government, self-rule.

2. liberation, emancipation, manumission, disenthrallment, decolonization; release, relief from, riddance from, deregulation, decontrol; discharge, nonconformist, parole, furlough.

3. latitude, range, elbowroom, *Ger. Lebensraum*; scope, play, swing, margin, discretion, wide berth, rope; nonintervention, noninterference, laissez faire; laxity, looseness, abandon, unrestraint, lawlessness.

4. free will, volition, will, *Psychol.* conation, velleity; noncoercion, noncompulsion; choice, option, preference, alternative.

5. privilege, prerogative, right, authority; exemption, exception, immunity; license, franchise, authorization; sanction, vouchsafement, permission, unconditional authority, carte blanche, *Sl.* the run of the place.

6. overfamiliarity, disrespect, impertinence, sauciness, *Inf.* sauce, impudence, insolence, *Inf.* brass, *Inf.*

cheek; boldness, temerity, audacity, effrontery, gall, *Sl.* crust, *Inf.* nerve; forwardness, presumption, presumptuousness, arrogance; impropriety, unseemliness, indecorum.

libidinous, *adj.* libidinal, lubricious, hormic, lustful, randy, *Sl.* horny, *Sl.* hot; lecheropus, lewd, *Archaic.* lickerish, goatish, hircine, satyric, priapic; carnal, sensual, bestial, animal, brutish; salacious, prurient, concupiscent, ruttish; passionate, hot-blooded, steamy, *Sl.* all fired up; wanton, profligate, abandoned, intemperate, incontinent, Paphic; dissolute, debauched, dissipated; degenerate, decadent, shameless, immoral, unchaste, unvirtuous.

libido, *n.* sexual appetite, biological urge, Eros, sexual longing, lust; sexual desire, aphrodisia, sex drive, sex energy, hot blood; sexuality, sexiness, fleshliness, voluptuousness, eroticism; rut, heat, oestrus, berry, (*in female animals*) *Dial.* pride; lustfulness, lubricity, randiness, *Sl.* horniness, *Sl.* hot pants; carnality, sensuality, animality, bestiality; concupiscence, prurience, salaciousness, salacity, lasciviousness.

librarian, *n.* bibliothec, bibliothecary; bibliognost.

library, *n.* **1.** bibliotheca, *Obs.* bibliothecary, *Fr. bibliothèque*, athenaeum; public library, lending library, rental library; stacks, reference room, reading room, study hall; book room, study, den.

2. book collection, manuscripts, publications.

librettist, *n.* lyricist, writer, versemaker; dramatist, dramatizer, playwright, scriptwriter.

libretto, *n.* opera text, text, book, script, words; narrative, story, story line, plot.

license, *n.* **1.** permission, allowance, consent, vouchsafement, *Inf.* O.K.; admission, access, entrance, passage, passport, safeguard, safe-conduct.

2. authorization, authority, warrant, warranty, certification, accreditation; franchise, charter, commission, entitlement, empowerment; patent, copyright, imprimatur, *Law.* title; grant, bestowal, bestowment, conferment; sanction, approval, countenance, acceptance.

3. permit, pass, certificate, credential; document, paper, instrument.

4. deviation, divergence, departure, straying; aberration, irregularity, nonconformity, noncompliance; disregard, inattention, indifference, insouciance.

5. liberty, freedom, latitude, free will *or* choice, free course, self-determination, independence; privilege, right, prerogative, carte blanche; exemption, exception, excuse, excusal, release, leave; indulgence, indulgency, favor, immunity, impunity, indemnity, protection; presumption, presumptuousness, impertinence, insolence, effrontery, rudeness, sauciness, *Inf.* sauce, *Inf.* cheek, *Inf.* brass, *Sl.* crust; audacity, brazenness, forwardness, boldness, gall, *Inf.* nerve.

6. licentiousness, libertinism, profligateness, profligacy, epicureanism; excessiveness, immoderation, intemperance, gluttony; abandon, unrestraint, incontinence, lack of restraint *or* constraint, lack of control; lawlessness, disobedience, unmanageability, unruliness, disorderliness; immorality, laxity, looseness, wantonness, debauchery, dissoluteness, dissipation.

—*v.* **7.** warrant, authorize, allow, permit, consent *or* subscribe to, vouchsafe; sanction, approve, give one's nod of approval, *Inf.* O.K., *Chiefly U.S.* approbate.

8. certify, accredit, validate, legalize, document; franchise, charter, commission, depute, invest, empower, entitle, enable.

9. privilege, enfranchise, grant rights to; exempt, except, make an exception, excuse, release, grant leave to.

licentious, *adj.* **1.** lascivious, libertine, debauched, dissolute, dissipated, rakish, rakehell; lecherous, lubricous, satyric, satyrical, satyrlike, goatish, *Sl.* horny, *Archaic.* lickerish; concupiscent, prurient, lustful, libidinous, salacious; ruttish, beastly, bestial, swinish; obscene, lewd, Fescennine, Cyprian, indecent, dirty, foul, indelicate; loose, wanton, wild, profligate, abandoned; promiscuous, whorish, of easy virtue, unchaste, impure; bawdy, ribald, pornographic, smutty, filthy; coarse, gross, crude.

2. lawless, unrestrained, unbridled, unchecked, ungoverned; chaotic, disorderly, disorganized, anarchic, anarchical, nihilist; immoral, dishonest, unprincipled, unscrupulous, *Inf.* crooked, villainous; nonconforming, deviative, divergent, aberrant, irregular, eccentric, anomalous, unorthodox.

licentiousness, *n.* libertinism, debauchery, dissoluteness, *It. dolce vita*, dissipation, profligacy, profligateness; lechery, lewdness, *Pathol.* satyriasis, goatishness, *Pathol.* nymphomania; concupiscence, lust, prurience, pruriency; lustfulness, libidinousness, salacity, salaciousness; promiscuity, wantonness, abandon, lawlessness, incontinence, unrestraint.

licit, *adj.* **1.** lawful, legal, constitutional, statutory, by the book; permissible, allowable, admissible; sanctionable, approvable, acceptable; warrantable, authorizable.

2. legitimate, *Sl.* legit, vested, rightful, right, valid, sound, well-founded, *Inf.* kosher, *Inf.* O.K.; permitted, licensed, authorized, warranted, commissioned; enacted, statuable, ordained, prescribed, ordered, decreed, edicted, mandated, judicial.

lick, *v.* **1.** tongue, (*all with the tongue*) touch lightly, kiss, brush, graze, pass over, lap.

2. lick off, wash, clean, preen, lick clean.

3. lick up, lap up, drink *or* drink up, suck in *or* up, take in *or* up, imbibe.

4. *Informal.* hit, beat, drub, thrash, *Inf.* wallop, *Inf.* whale; flog, lash, switch, birch, whip, strap, belt, spank, *Inf.* tan [s.o.'s] hide; thwack, *Inf.* whack, strike, slap, smack, knock *or* knock around; batter, pound, pummel; beat up, *Sl.* beat to a pulp, *Sl.* pulverize, *Sl.* beat *or* pound into the ground, *Sl.* beat the stuffing out of [s.o.], *Sl.* clobber, *Sl.* shellac, *Sl.* cream. See **beat** (*def.* **1**).

5. *Informal.* defeat, win over, triumph over, conquer, overpower, overwhelm, overthrow, upset; beat, trounce, rout, vanquish, worst, *Sl.* shellac; crush, trample, *Sl.* do in, do for; quash, put down, quell, subdue, break, master.

6. *Informal.* outdo, surpass, exceed, excel, do *or* go [s.o.] one better, top, best; win out over, place first, *Sl.* beat out, outstrip; transcend, overcome, surmount, prevail over, get the better of.

—*n.* **7.** (*all of the tongue*) stroke, brush, light touch, graze, lap.

8. *Informal.* blow, stroke, box, thump, rap, cuff, buffet, *Sl.* bop, *Inf.* bat; hit, knock, thwack, *Inf.* whack, swat, slam, slap, smack. See **bat** (*def.* **2**).

9. *Informal.* speed, *Inf.* clip, pace, rate, rate of speed.

10. *Informal.* small amount, bit, dab, spot, trace, speck; mite, smidgen, *Inf.* smitch, iota, jot, whit, tittle, particle; snatch, scrap, shred, fragment, piece, morsel, crumb, grain, granule.

lickety-split, *adv.* rapidly, quickly, double-quick, speedily, with great speed, on the wings of the wind; hurriedly, hastily, posthaste; like a shot *or* bullet, like lightning *or* a streak of lightning, like a house afire, like blazes, like the devil was after one; at full tilt, at full speed, full speed ahead, in high gear, at a gallop *or* run, as fast as one's legs can carry one.

licking, *n.* **1.** *Informal.* beating, drubbing, sound thrashing, shellacking, *Inf.* tanning; whipping, *Dial.* whuppin', flogging, lashing, strapping, switching, spanking.

2. reversal, upset, setback, disappointment.

lickspittle, *n.* toady, sycophant, toadeater, tuft-hunter, fawning flatterer, truckler; flatterer, backslapper, backscratcher, timeserver, *Inf.* apple polisher, *Sl.* brown-nose, *Sl.* brown-noser, *Sl.* brownie, *Obs., Rare.* blander, *Archaic.* pickthank; parasite, leech, *Inf.* sponge *or* sponger, hanger-on; courtier, attendant, flunky, lackey, yes man; jackal, spaniel, bootlick, bootlicker, footlicker, lickspit; kowtower, *Contemptuous.* Uncle Tom, *Sl.* oreo, cringer, groveler, sniveler.

lid, *n.* **1.** cover, top, cap; cork, stop, stopper, stopple, plug.

2. ceiling, maximum, max., limit, *Inf.* tops.

3. blow the lid off *Slang.* expose, reveal, show up, take the wraps off, bring out, bring out into the open, bring to light, make known; release, break, leak, report, publish, print.

4. flip one's lid *Slang.* **a.** lose control, *Inf.* fly off the handle, lose one's cool, *Sl.* lose it, *Sl.* flip out, *Sl.* freak out, become hysterical. **b.** go insane, go mad, go crazy, *Inf.* go haywire, go berserk, go out of one's mind *or* head, go nuts, go off the deep end, go off *or* over the edge.

lie[1], *n.* **1.** falsehood, untruth, prevarication, fib, white lie, little white lie, quibble, *Inf.* taradiddle; equivocation, evasion, fencing, *Euph.* departure from the truth; falsity, fiction, falsification, invention, concoction, fabrication, half-truth, stretching of the truth; *Inf.* story, *Inf.* trumped-up story, *Inf.* tale, *Inf.* fairy tale; exaggeration, overstatement, coloring, magnification, enlargement, yarn, *Inf.* tall tale *or* story, *Inf.* cock-and-bull story, *Inf.* shaggy dog story, *Inf.* fish story, *Sl.* garbage, *Sl.* moonshine, *Sl.* hogwash, *Sl.* bull, *Sl.* crap, *Sl.* baloney.

2. misrepresentation, perversion, distortion, corruption; inaccuracy, misconstruction, slanting, straining, torturing; canard, rumor, hoax, forgery; monstrous lie, the big lie, mendacity, *Sl.* whopper, *Sl.* barefaced lie, *Sl.* dirty lie, *Sl.* shameless lie; defamation, scandal, traducement, calumny, calumniation.

3. give the lie to contradict, deny, disaffirm, gainsay, impute, controvert, dispute; oppose, counter; dissent, differ, challenge, impugn; rebut, refute; disprove, overthrow, negate, confute, belie.

—v. **4.** tell a lie *or* falsehood, prevaricate, stretch the truth; fib, mince the truth, tell a white lie; equivocate, euphemize, evade, sidestep; fabricate, invent, manufacture, make up, trump up, cook up, *Inf.* make out of whole cloth; fake, dissemble, feign, pretend, let on, put on.

5. falsify, belie, misrepresent; pervert, twist, distort, strain, warp, slant, color; gild, varnish, gloss, doctor, dress up, embellish, embroider, exaggerate, inflate, blow up, puff up, magnify, enlarge on, *Inf.* pile *or* lay it on, *Inf.* lay it on thick, carry too far; boast, brag, *Inf.* talk through one's hat.

6. mislead, deceive, lead up the garden path, throw off the scent, put [s.o.] on a false scent, drag *or* draw a red herring across the trail; misinform, give [s.o.] a bum steer, pull the wool over [s.o.'s] eyes.

7. lie in one's throat lie grossly *or* maliciously, slander, defame, libel, calumniate, traduce; perjure oneself, swear falsely, bear false witness; lie through one's teeth, lie like a trooper, lie like a rug; speak with forked tongue, *Inf.* tell the big lie.

lie[2], *v.* **1.** recline, be prostrate, be recumbent, be supine; rest, repose, relax; sprawl, loll, laze, lounge, slouch, slump.

2. rest horizontally, be level, be plane, be flat.

3. remain quiet, be immobile, be inactive; continue, abide, wait.

4. *Usu.* **lie on** *or* **upon** rest, press, weigh; burden, strain, oppress, encumber, handicap, overwhelm.

5. be situated, be placed, be located, be found, be positioned; be buried, be interred.

6. *Usu.* **lie in** consist, inhere, be present, exist.

lie-abed, *n.* slugabed, *Inf.* lazybones, *Inf.* lazyboots, *Inf.* lazylegs; idler, loafer, lounger, loller, do-nothing, slouch, sluggard; shirker, *Inf.* goldbricker, *Sl.* goof-off, *Brit. Sl.* skiver, *Brit. Sl.* scrimshanker; laggard, loiterer, lingerer, sleepy-head; dallier, dillydallier, dawdler, moper.

liege, *n.* **1.** feudal lord, liege lord, master, overlord, paramount, lord paramount, suzerain, overking, chieftain, chief; seigneur, master of the house, *Archaic.* goodman, paterfamilias, patriarch; chief, leader, superior.

2. feudal vassal, liegeman, servant, indentured servant, bondsman, bondman, yeoman, thrall, serf, helot, villein, churl; inferior, subordinate, underling, man, henchman, lackey, flunky; attendant, aide.

—adj. **3.** subject, dependent, subservient, subordinate, inferior, servile, feudal, feudatory; under command *or* orders *or* direction, at [s.o.'s] beck and call, owing allegiance, in service to.

4. loyal, allegiant, true, *Scot.* leal, true-hearted; devoted, dedicated, steadfast, staunch, true-blue, yeomanly, unwavering, unswerving, supportive; faithful, reliable, trusted, dependable, trusty, tried and true; true to one's word *or* pledge, upright, high-principled.

lien, *n.* security, security agreement, mortgage, deed of trust, chattel mortgage, *Roman and Civil Law.* pignus, tax lien, *Marine Law.* bottomry; attachment, garnish, garnishment, entailment.

lieutenant, *n.* **1.** assistant, aide, helper; deputy, proxy, representative, alter ego, second, second in command, *Inf.* backup *or* backup man; right hand, right-hand man, man Friday, gal Friday, henchman, underling, stooge, subordinate, *Sl.* second banana; lackey, flunky, tool, hanger-on, camp follower, yes man, toady, sycophant; bodyguard, *Sl.* triggerman, *Sl.* hatchet man, *Sl.* torpedo, *Sl.* goon; bullyboy, tough, roughneck.

2. attendant, counselor, advisor, *Inf.* sideman, privy councilor; confidant, member of the kitchen cabinet; good right arm, sidekick, buddy, Little John, Tonto; satellite, subordinate, subaltern, coadjutant, coadjutor, executive officer; surrogate, secondary, stand-in, understudy; follower, disciple, adherent, partisan.

3. army officer, naval officer, first lieutenant, second lieutenant, lieutenant junior grade, *Sl.* j.g., *Sl.* looie, *Brit.* sublieutenant, *India.* jemadar.

life, *n.* **1.** existence, being, animateness, viability, flesh and blood, substantiality; lifetime, days, generation, life span; duration of life, life expectancy, longevity.

2. the human condition, vicissitudes, ups and downs; trials and tribulations, the ills that flesh is heir to, man's inhumanity to man; the world, the times, state of affairs, course *or* tide of events.

3. nature, creation, wild life, flora and fauna; man and bird and beast, the fish of the sea, the denizens of the deep, the beasts of the field, the fowls *or* birds of the air; mankind, womankind.

4. human being, human, person, individual, mortal; man, woman, child.

5. animation, liveliness, vivacity, spirit; dash, élan, zest, verve, flair, zing; fire, warmth, glow, fervency, ardor; dazzle, brilliance; sprightliness, airiness, breeziness, buoyancy, cheer; ebullience, sparkle, efferves-

cence; vigor, vim, *It. brio, Inf.* pep, vitality, energy; exuberance, enthusiasm, zeal, fervor, passion, intensity.
6. soul, animating principle, vital spirit, pneuma, breath of life, anima; universal life force, world spirit, life force, *élan vital, Yoga.* kundalini; moving force, dynamic force, lifeblood, *Inf.* sparkplug.
7. pungency, flavor, spark, *Inf.* punch, *Inf.* kick; freshness, vigor, vigorousness, dynamism; invigoration, enlivenment, vivification, exhilaration.
8. lifestyle, way of life, *Sl.* thing, *Sl.* bag; walk of life, field, province, sphere, position, situation; occupation, business, line, career.
9. passion, obsession, preoccupation, *Sl.* hang-up, infatuation; loved one, beloved, favorite, idol.
10. resilience, elasticity, spring, springiness, bounce; plasticity, ductility, malleability.
11. biography, autobiography; diary, journal, confessions, letters.
life-and-death, *adj.* vital, of vital importance, life-or-death; crucial, critical, momentous, important, significant, top-priority; conclusive, decisive, final, determinate; all-out, down-to-the-wire; essential, necessary, indispensable; fundamental, basic, focal, central, pivotal.
lifeblood, *n.* inspiration, stimulus, incitement; animating forces *or* power, inspiriting force *or* power, vital energy, vital spark; vivifier, animus, raison d'être; heart, guts, life; moving *or* driving force, *Inf.* sparkplug, inspirer; essence, *Latin. sine qua non*, fundamental, basic; blood, ichor.
life-giving, *adj.* vitalizing, vivifying, animating, enlivening, energizing; invigorating, exhilarating, stimulating, quickening; encouraging, inspiriting, heartening, exciting; generative, productive, creative.
lifeless, *adj.* **1.** inanimate, abiotic, inorganic, mineral, synthetic.
2. barren, bare, denuded, treeless; arid, desert, Saharan, parched, sterile; desolate, waste, wild, bleak, stark, dreary; empty, uninhabited, unoccupied, abandoned, deserted; uncultivated, unproductive, unfructuous, unprofitable.
3. dead, deceased, defunct, departed, demised; gone, dead and gone, late, done for, *Both Euph.* sleeping, reposing; *All Sl.* stone dead, stone cold dead in the market, dead as a doornail, dead as mutton.
4. examinate, spiritless, torpid, sluggish, *Inf.* dopey, lethargic, phlegmatic; drained, enervated, exhausted, debilitated, worn out, effete, like a ragdoll, like a dishrag; inactive, passive, unanimated, inert, unmoving, immobile, deadpan, expressionless, wooden, inflexible, rigid.
5. disheartened, discouraged, dejected, sad, down-in-the-mouth, blue, *Inf.* in a funk, *Inf.* in a blue funk, *Inf.* suffering the mulligrubs, out-of-sorts; grim, stiff, humorless, unsmiling.
6. tiresome, boring, uninspiring, tedious, dull, meaningless, uninteresting, *Sl.* blah, vapid; mopey, mopish, listless, droopy, glum; flat, stale, hollow; colorless, wishy-washy, wan, pallid, pale, ashen; insipid, jejune.
7. insensate, insensible, impassive, in a faint, in a swoon; comatose, corpse-like; dead to the world, far away; knocked out, blacked out, *Inf.* out like a light, *Inf.* hearing the birdies sing, in dreamland.
lifelike, *adj.* true-to-life, animated, realistic, speaking, like the real thing; true, faithful, natural; graphic, vivid, detailed.
lifework, *n.* career, calling, profession, vocation, line; job, employment, occupation, work, business, livelihood; pursuit, activity, interest.
lift, *v.* **1.** hoist, heave, upheave, boost, pull up, pry up, lever; elevate, raise, raise up, upraise, uplift, set up, put up, place up, pick up, set upright, upright, set on its feet, stand [s.t.] up; cast up, thrust up, hold up, uphold, raise high, loft, bear aloft; display on high, manifest, show, show off, exhibit, wave, flaunt, brandish, blazon.
2. remove, withdraw, eliminate, take away, do away with; rescind, cancel, void, annul, take back; stop, end, terminate, cease, desist, put an end *or* a stop to.
3. exalt, extol, dignify, ennoble, enshrine, enthrone, place on a pedestal, deify, immortalize; aggrandize, inflate, puff up; enhance, improve, better, meliorate, ameliorate, avail, upgrade, promote, advance; moralize, purify, chasten, sublimate.
4. amplify, louden, magnify, enlarge, make louder *or* greater; trumpet, blast, blare, scream, shout, call.
5. plagiarize, copy, imitate, get from someone *or* somewhere else, abstract, *Inf.* crib, *Euph.* borrow; take, appropriate, expropriate, steal, pirate, purloin, filch.
6. rise, mount, climb, go up, wind upward; take off, lift off, leave the ground, levitate, buoy, float, fly, soar.
7. heft, pull, tug; strain, struggle, strive, labor, exert oneself.
8. ascend, arise, come up, come over the horizon, peep out *or* up from, peek out *or* up from; emerge, break, appear, materialize, show up, pop up, come into view *or* sight.
—*n.* **9.** raising, upheaval, escalation; ascent, ascension, mounting, climbing, rising, rise, levitation; soaring, flying, shooting *or* springing up, jump.
10. elevation, altitude, height, climb, distance.
11. buoyancy, lifting power *or* force; acceleration, *Auto.* pickup.
12. hoist, push, shove, heave, thrust, heave ho, a hand, a helping hand; help, assistance, aid, abettal, support.
13. ride, drive, way, means of transportation *or* transport, conveyance; piggy-back ride, ride on one's shoulders, carriage.
14. uplift, upliftment, uplifting sensation, upraiser, emotional *or* psychological boost, encouragement, inspiration, hope; *Inf.* pick-me-up, *Inf.* pickup, *Inf.* picker-upper, *Inf.* shot in the arm, *Pharm.* booster; exaltation, loftiness, bliss, rapture.
15. pulley, crane, winch, windlass, block and tackle, tackle, *Mach.* block, *Mach.* derrick. See also **lifter**.
16. incline, inclination, acclivity, grade, gradient, slope, upslope, uprising; hill, hillock, knoll, dune, mound, mount, mountain.
lifter, *n.* pulley, crane, winch, windlass, block and tackle, tackle, *Mach.* block, *Mach.* derrick; ski lift, chair lift, escalator, *U.S.* dumbwaiter, *Chiefly Brit.* elevator; dredge, steam shovel, shovel; jack, jackscrew, crowbar, jimmy, jemmy, *Mach.* lever; heaver, hoister, erector, erecter, raiser, lifter, uplifter.
ligature, *n.* **1.** binding, tying up, bandaging, wrapping; ligation, bandage, dressing, compress, *Surg.* tourniquet; tie, bond, ligament, link, vinculum, connection, nexus, *Anat.* funiculus; cord, cordon, braid, thong, band, strap, belt; strand, string, line, cable, rope.
—*v.* **2.** tie, tie up, bind, colligate, truss, ligate; bandage, tape, dress, wrap, swathe; strap, cinch, hitch, lash, hobble, fetter, pinion, shackle; secure, fasten, fix; join, unite, connect, couple.
light[1], *n.* **1.** illumination, luminescence, luminosity, radiation, shining, beaming, gleaming; luminousness, brilliance, radiance, lambency, luster, shine, effulgence; irradiation, glow, glowing, fluorescence, in-

candescence, phosphorescence; brightness, blare, glare; glimmer, gleam, sparkle, twinkle.
2. beam, ray, shaft of light; lamplight, gaslight, firelight; lamp, chandelier, electrolier, beacon, illuminant, bulb, candle, taper, candelabrum; star, shining star, blaze, fire.
3. daylight, dayshine, sunshine, sunbeam, sun; daylight hours, daytime, day, *Poetic.* daytide; dawn, Aurora, crack of dawn, daybreak, *Archaic.* dayspring; sunrise, sunup, morning.
4. enlightenment, edification, awareness, insight, understanding.
5. luminary, beau ideal, model, paragon, exemplar, example, guide.
6. **bring to light** reveal, expose, disclose; uncover, unmask, unveil, show; unearth, dig up, discover.
7. **in light of** considering, taking into account, paying attention to, keeping in mind.
8. **shed** *or* **throw light on** elucidate, clarify, clear up, explain, simplify.
—adj. **9.** illuminated, lit, well-lit, floodlit, alight, well-lighted; sunny, bright, shining, vivid, glaring; gleaming, radiant, effulgent, fulgid, lambent, luciferous; resplendent, brilliant, beaming, beamy, beamish; sparkling, scintillating, scintillant, blazing, conflagrant, afire; glowing, rutilant, luminous, lucid, incandescent, phosphorescent; clear, transparent, translucent.
10. pale, bleached, whitened, whitish; creamy, ivory, pearly, blond, fair; faded, dull, drab, colorless, washed out.
—v. **11.** set burning, set fire to, fire, set a match to, ignite, inflame, kindle.
12. *Often* **light up** illuminate, brighten, lighten; illumine, *Archaic.* illume, *Obs.* enlumine; irradiate, radiate, shine, beam, cast light upon; blaze, burn, glow, luminesce, incandesce, phosphoresce; shimmer, sparkle, scintillate, glitter, gleam; flash, flicker, fulgurate, coruscate.
13. conduct with a light, direct, guide, pilot, usher, escort.

light², *adj.* **1.** unheavy, weightless, levitative; floaty, ethereal, gossamer, feathery, delicate; slender, thin, skinny, slight, small, minute, tiny.
2. faint, obscure, dim, pale, faded, dull; unclear, indistinct, imperceptible.
3. easy, facile, simple, *Sl.* cushy, soft, slight, manageable.
4. amusing, entertaining, pleasing, pleasurable; humorous, witty, comical; diverting, distracting, recreative, sportive; trivial, inconsiderable, unimportant, inconsequential, trifling, petty, superficial.
5. digestible, peptic; (*all of a meal*) skimpy, scanty, modest, moderate.
6. airy, buoyant, flitting, winged, tripping, *Brit. Inf.* nippy, spry, lightsome, light-footed; deft, dexterous; agile, nimble, supple, sprightly, *Dial.* gainly, lithe, quick, yare.
7. cheerful, cheery, gay, sunny, in good *or* high spirits; blithe, blithesome, optimistic, positive, *Inf.* upbeat, beamish; debonair, free and easy, easygoing, breezy, happy-go-lucky, untroubled; jovial, merry, jocund, jolly, mirthful, riant, laughing, smiling, happy, happy as a lark, glad; joyful, jubilant, gleeful, elated, delighted.
8. frivolous, light-hearted, carefree, insouciant, irresponsible; impulsive, fickle, erratic, changeable, inconstant; mercurial, volatile, flyaway, skittish; whimsical, capricious, flighty, bird-witted, scatterbrained, *Sl.* out to lunch, *Sl.* out in left field.
9. giddy, dizzy, faint, light-headed; unsteady, reeling, *Inf.* woozy, muddled.

light³, *v.* **1.** get down, drop down, descend, dismount, unmount, unhorse; detrain, disembark.
2. settle, sit down; perch, land, alight.
3. **light on** *or* **upon** discover, find, come across, meet up with, encounter; happen upon, stumble upon, hit upon; make out, distinguish, detect, *Inf.* spot.
4. **light into** *Informal.* pounce upon, *Inf.* lace into, barrage, assail, lash, lambaste, attack. See **attack** (*defs.* **1, 2**).

lighten¹, *v.* **1.** illuminate, brighten, light up; illumine, *Archaic.* illume, *Obs.* enlumine; irradiate, radiate, shine, beam, cast light upon; blaze, burn, glow, luminesce, incandesce, phosphoresce; shimmer, sparkle, scintillate, glitter, gleam; flash, flicker, fulgurate, coruscate.
2. whiten, bleach, blanch, blench, pale.

lighten², *v.* **1.** disencumber, disburden, unburden, unload, lessen the load; mitigate, ease, ease up, lessen, reduce, mollify, temper; alleviate, allay, relieve, assuage; facilitate, help.
2. cheer, gladden, brighten, perk up; uplift, buoy up, hearten, encourage, comfort, reassure, warm; refresh, restore, revivify, revive; invigorate, inspirit, animate, exhilarate, enliven, quicken.

lighter¹, *n.* **1.** igniter, ignition, sparker, spark, spark coil, flint, two sticks, match, friction match, fusee, lucifer, fuze, squib, vesuvian, *Trademark.* Bic; fuse, detonator, exploder, blasting cap, percussion cap, cap; kindler, firer, fire-setter, burner, incendiary, pyromaniac, arsonist, *Inf.* firebug, *Sl.* torch.
2. flare, torch, spill, flame, candle, taper; switch, bulb, light bulb, light, lamp, flashlight, illuminator, illuminant.

lighter², *n.* barge, boat, vessel, raft, float, dinghy, tender, ship's boat, rowboat, *Naut.* hoy, *Naut.* catamaran; lightener, hauler, carrier.

light-fingered, *adj.* **1.** pilfering, filching, thievish, thieving, stealing; slick, foxy, cunning, wily, crafty, sly, shifty, furtive, underhanded, dishonest, *Inf.* crooked.
2. dexterous, nimble, agile, deft, adroit, facile, neat, *Brit. Dial.* feat; prestidigitatory, fleet, quick, rapid, fast.

light-footed, *adj.* spry, sprightly, tripping, flitting, winged, buoyant, airy, bouncy, light on one's feet, light of foot, lightsome, *Brit. Inf.* nippy; nimble, agile, supply, lithe, yare, *Dial.* gainly; fleet-footed, fleet of foot, fleet, swift, quick, speedy, mercurial.

light-headed, *adj.* **1.** frivolous, flyaway, fanciful, trifling, trivial, petty; scatterbrained, featherheaded, featherbrained, rattlebrained, harebrained, birdbrained; inane, silly, foolish, kiddish, childish, immature, irresponsible; shallow, superficial, light-minded, empty-headed, vacuous, thoughtless.
2. flighty, mercurial, volatile, capricious, whimsical, impulsive; fickle, skittish, moonish, faddish, variable, changeable, changeful, vacillating, erratic, fitful, inconstant, irregular, unsteady, unstable, undependable, unreliable.
3. dizzy, vertiginous, *Inf.* woozy, *Pathol.* giddy; foggy, hazy, dazed, befuddled, muddled, bewildered, confused, distraught; delirious, phrenetic, raving, wild, babbling, incoherent, *Inf.* out of it, mad, crazy, *Inf.* out of one's mind.

light-hearted, *adj.* cheerful, cheery, gay, sunny, bright, in good *or* high spirits, *Chiefly U.S. Inf.* chipper, lightsome; blithe, blithesome, buoyant, optimistic, positive, *Inf.* upbeat, beamish; debonair, free and easy, carefree, *Fr. sans souci*, insouciant, devil-may-care, breezy, happy-go-lucky, untroubled; jovial, merry, jocund, jolly, mirthful, riant, laughing, smiling; happy, happy as a lark, glad, gladsome; joyful, jubilant, gleeful, elated, delighted.

lighthouse, *n.* light tower, Pharos, lightship, beacon boat, sailor's landmark; watchtower, lookout, observation post; beacon, signal, warning light, guiding light, guide, *Naut.* beaconage.

lighting, *n.* setting fire to, setting a match to, igniting, kindling; illuminating, brightening; illumination, radiation, irradiation.

lightless, *adj.* dark, pitch-dark, dark as night, nightly, nightlike, unlighted, unlit, unilluminated, aphotic, tenebrous, obscure, *Literary.* darkling; black, black as ink, inky, pitchy, jetblack, nigrescent; ill-lighted, poorly lit, dim, dull, faint, dusky, gloomy, Stygian, shady, shadowy, penumbral, penumbrous, *Archaic.* caliginous.

lightly, *adv.* **1.** slightly, a little bit, (*in prescriptions*) leviter; gently, kissingly, softly; gingerly, carefully, timidly.

2. cheerfully, gaily, sunnily, brightly, blithely, optimistically, positively; buoyantly, breezily, carefreely, debonairly; merrily, mirthfully, laughingly, smilingly; happily, gladly, joyfully, jubilantly, gleefully.

3. easily, airily, buoyantly, flittingly, spryly, quickly; nimbly, agilely, supplely.

4. frivolously, flippantly, saucily, impertinently; thoughtlessly, carelessly, heedlessly; indifferently, uncaringly, slightingly, *Inf.* with a grain of salt.

light-minded, *adj.* fanciful, frivolous, flyaway, unserious, unsolemn, given to levity; trivial, trifling, light-headed, petty, small-minded; thoughtless, shallow, empty-headed, vacuous, superficial; featherheaded, featherbrained, harebrained, birdbrained, scatterbrained, rattlebrained.

lightness[1], *n.* **1.** brightness, illumination, luminescence, luminosity, radiation; luminousness, brilliance, radiance, lambency, luster, shine, effulgence, irradiation, glow, florescence, incandescence, phosphorescence; blare, glare.

2. paleness, whitishness, colorlessness; dimness, indistinctness, obscureness, faintness.

lightness[2], *n.* **1.** weightlessness, unheaviness, levitativeness; floatiness, ethereality, etherealness, featheriness, delicateness, delicacy; slightness, thinness, slenderness, skinniness.

2. airiness, bouyancy, flittingness, wingedness, spryness, quickness, lightsomeness, light-footedness; deftness, dexterousness; agility, nimbleness, suppleness, sprightliness, *Dial.* gainliness, litheness, grace, gracefulness.

3. cheerfulness, cheeriness, gaiety, sunniness, brightness; blitheness, blithesomeness, optimism, positiveness, beamishness; easygoingness, breeziness, insouciance, carefreeness; joviality, merriness, jocundity, jollity, mirth, mirthfulness; happiness, gladness, joy, joyfulness, glee, gleefulness, elation.

4. levity, frivolity, foolishness, folly, irresponsibility; impulsiveness, fickleness, changeability, inconstancy; flightiness, giddiness, capriciousness.

lightning, *n.* **1.** thunderbolt, bolt, thunderbolt of Jove, flash *or* stroke *or* heat lightning, sheet lightning, chain lightning, fork *or* forked lightning, fireball; northern lights, polar lights, aurora borealis, aurora polaris.

—adj. **2.** fulgurant, flashing, cracking, rippling, streaking; swift, speedy, split-second; instantaneous, precipitate; electrifying, dazzling.

lightsome[1], *adj.* **1.** airy, immaterial, incorporeal, bodiless, light, weightless, vaporous, vapory; visionary, phantasmal, chimeral, ethereal, otherworldly, dreamlike; feathery, fluffy, gossamery, gossamer, light as a feather; Ariel-like; buoyant, resilient, floating, bouncy, bubbly.

2. agile, nimble, light-footed, nimble-footed, spry, graceful, with winged feet; lithe, lissome, supple, flexible, pliant; skipping, springing, like a mountain goat.

3. cheery, cheerful, glad, gladsome, gleeful; happy, happy as a lark, happy as a clam at high tide, euphoric; merry, blithe, joyful, joyous, jubilant, jolly, jovial, jocund, laughing, smiling; gay, light-hearted, debonair, breezy, carefree; in high spirits, spirited, expansive, lively, animated, jaunty, perky, sprightly; frisky, coltish, playful, frolicsome, sportive, rollicking, rompish, capering; exuberant, effervescent, ebullient, vivacious; chipper, full of life, peppy, zestful.

4. frivolous, flippant, trifling, silly, foolish, giddy, flighty; changeable, mercurial, volatile, capricious, fickle; wavering, vacillatory, vacillating, irresolute, fluctuating, swaying, swaying with the wind, constant as the inconstant moon, like the shifting sands.

lightsome[2], *adj.* **1.** luminous, glowing, lambent, radiant, lustrous, gleaming, shining.

2. well-lighted, well-lit, illuminated, bright, glaring, blazing, bright as the noonday sun.

lightweight, *adj.* **1.** trivial, trifling, insignificant, unimportant, inconsequential, insubstantial; nugatory, worthless, without merit, valueless, not worth a tinker's dam; frivolous, petty, paltry, slight, lean, skimpy.

—n. **2.** *Informal.* nonentity, nobody, *Sl.* schlepp, nothing, a big nothing, cipher, zero; insignificancy, jackstraw, milquetoast, *Sl.* nebbish; bonehead, blockhead, dummy, *Inf.* poor sap; no great shakes, no great catch, *Sl.* small beer, *Sl.* small potatoes; weakling, weak sister, tower of jello, *Sl.* deadhead, *Sl.* poop, second fiddle, second banana, (*Collectively*) small fry.

likable, *adj.* pleasing, pleasant, nice, agreeable; amiable, friendly, neighborly, genial, kind, congenial, good-natured; sweet, charming, winning, winsome, engaging; attractive, cute, adorable, lovable, desirable.

like[1], *adj.* **1.** similar, homologous, much the same, pretty much the same, more or less the same, something like, not unlike; comparable, analogous, parallel, correspondent, corresponding, resembling, following; near, close, approximating, same but different; equivalent, matching, of a kind, of a piece, cast in the same mold; brothers under the skin.

—prep. **2.** similarly to, in like manner with, after the manner of, after the fashion of, on the order of, along the lines of; according to, *Fr. d'après.*

3. typical of, characteristic of, in character with; common to, peculiar to, distinctive to.

4. indicative of, illustrative of, representative of, symbolic of.

5. disposed to, inclined to, likely to, prone to, given to; in the mood to, happy to, willing to, eager to, anxious to, *Inf.* itching to, *Sl.* dying to, *Sl.* psyched to; equal to, up to, able to, ready to.

6. similar to, comparable to, analogous with, parallel to, corresponding to; in a class with, equivalent with *or* to; near to, close to.

7. *Nonstandard.* as, such as.

8. like anything *Informal.* extremely, in the extreme, very much; intensely, acutely, *Inf.* awfully, *Inf.* terribly, *Inf.* terrifically, *Inf.* something fierce, in the worst way.

9. like mad *Informal.* vehemently, furiously, fiercely, violently; madly, wildly, frantically, frenetically, fanatically, like one possessed; like a shot, like a flash, *Inf.* like greased lightning, *Inf.* like a house afire, *Inf.* like sixty, *Inf.* to beat the band, *Sl.* like a bat out of hell.

10. *Nonstandard.* **a.** as it were, in a way; somehow, in some way, in some such way, in some way or another, somehow or other. **b.** to a degree, more or less, give or take a little, for all practical purposes, *Inf.* practically.

—conj. **11.** *Nonstandard.* as, just as, in the same way as; as if.

—n. **12.** match, mate, fellow, twin; equal, coequal, peer, compeer; equivalent, opposite number, counterpart, parallel.

13. kind, sort, ilk, type, such; stamp, brand, grain, strain, cast, mold, color, stripe, kidney.

like², *v.* **1.** enjoy, take pleasure in, delight in, rejoice in, revel in, bask in; love, *Inf.* adore, relish, savor, appreciate; be partial to, be fond of, have a soft spot for, have a weakness *or* fondness for; *All Sl.* go for, dig, get into, groove on, get off on, get high on, get a kick *or* bang *or* charge *or* rise out of.

2. prize, esteem, hold dear; think well of, think highly of, regard with favor; take to, take kindly to, fancy, take a fancy to, *Inf.* cotton to, *Sl.* shine to.

3. feel inclined, have a mind to, have half a mind to, choose to, care to, please; prefer, had sooner *or* rather; will, see fit, think fit, think good; wish, desire, desiderate, want.

—n. **4.** *Usu.* **likes** preference, personal choice, *Inf.* cup of tea, *Sl.* bag, *Sl.* thing, *Sl.* trip; inclination, penchant, partiality, predilection, propensity.

likelihood *n.* probability, liability, likeliness, verisimilitude, distinct possibility; good chance, favorable chance, odds-on chance, good prospect, favorable prospect, well-grounded hope.

likely, *adj.* **1.** probable, apt, liable, to be expected, odds-on, in the cards; promising, hopeful, fair, in a fair way.

2. believable, credible, plausible, tenable, verisimilar; conceivable, imaginable, reasonable, colorable.

3. appropriate, apposite, suitable, acceptable; proper, meet, right, befitting, fitting, becoming, seemly, congruous; applicable, relevant, seasonable, opportune.

—adv. **4.** probably, in all probability, most likely, *Inf.* like enough, *Inf.* like as not; no doubt, doubtlessly.

like-minded, *adj.* agreeing, in agreement, accordant, in accord *or* accordance, in harmony, in rapport; concordant, consonant, correspondent, corresponding, complying, conforming; concurrent, concurring, consentient, consentaneous; unanimous, in unison, as one, at one, of one mind, of the same mind, single-minded; in step, *Inf.* in sync, hand-in-hand, hand-in-glove.

liken, *v.* compare, represent as like, equate, identify with; analogize, parallelize, associate, link, correlate, relate.

likeness, *n.* **1.** image, icon, representation, simulacrum; portrait, portrayal, painting, oil painting, canvas, watercolor; sketch, delineation, rough draft, drawing, charcoal drawing, study; picture, illustration, photograph, *Inf.* photo, snapshot, *Inf.* snap; effigy, straw man, scarecrow, doll, figure, figurine, sculpture, statue, statuette, bust, bronze, clay model.

2. replica, copy, duplicate, facsimile, faithful copy, reproduction, ectype, print; twin, identical twin, living *or* very image, double, look-alike, clone, exact match; perfect likeness, *Inf.* spit and image *or* spitting image, chip off the old block, *Sl.* ringer, *Sl.* dead ringer.

3. guise, semblance, resemblance, appearance, look; exterior, outward form, shape, figure, lines, features; style, ways, manners *or* mannerisms, characteristics, traits; mien, air, cast, character, presence, bearing, carriage.

4. resemblance, similarity, similitude, identicalness, identity; analogy, analogousness, agreement, parallelism, correspondence, alikeness, closeness; sameness, uniformity, homogeneity.

likewise, *adv.* **1.** moreover, futhermore, additionally, in addition, above and beyond, over and above; also, too, to boot, into the bargain, besides.

2. in like manner, in the same way, similarly.

liking, *n.* preference, favor, favoritism, partiality, bias; fondness, love, attraction, affinity, soft spot, weakness; taste, penchant, eye, appreciation; fancy, inclination, bent, leaning, tendency; predilection, propensity, proclivity, predisposal, disposition, mind.

Lilliputian, *adj.* **1.** diminutive, tiny, wee, *Inf.* teeny, *All Baby Talk.* itty-bitty, eensy-weensy, teensy, teeny-weeny, teensy-weensy; miniscule, microscopic, atomic, animalculine, animalculous; miniature, small-scale, pocket-sized, bantam, short, abridged; small, little, elfin, mini, pint-sized, *Inf.* baby; petite, delicate, dainty, minikin; homuncular, midget, dwarfish, *Med.* nanoid, pygmy, pygmoid, pygmish; undersized, underweight, lightweight, featherweight, flyweight, bantamweight; puny, runty, thin, slight, skinny.

—n. **2.** midget, homunculus, little man, minikin, pygmy, dwarf; chit, fingerling, dapperling, cocksparrow, hop-o'-my-thumb, Tom Thumb, *Chiefly Scot.* wee fellow *or* lad *or* one, *Obs.* pigwidgin, *Archaic.* dandiprat; shrimp, runt, little runt, pee-wee, squirt, pipsqueak, *Inf.* half-pint, small fry, *Inf.* shorty; gnome, (*in Scandanavian folklore*) troll, goblin, hobgoblin, (*in German folklore*) kobold, *Irish Folklore.* leprechaun, *Chiefly Brit.* little person; elf, puck, imp, fairy, fay, sprite, sylph.

lilt, *n.* **1.** swing, upswing, rhythm, cadence, measure; beat, pulsation; wave, sway, dip, dance.

2. cheerful song, pleasant song, tune, air, melody, lyric; *Music.* scherzo, *Music.* allegretto, *Music.* allegro.

lily-livered, *adj.* cowardly, coward, pusillanimous, *Sl.* yellow-bellied; uncourageous, unvaliant, unvalorous, unheroic, ungallant; unintrepid, undaring, *Inf.* spunkless; timid, timorous, unable to say "boo" to a goose, afraid, afraid of one's own shadow, fearful, *Sl.* fraidy-cat; fainthearted, chickenhearted, yellow, with a yellow strip a mile wide down one's back; unmanly, spineless, unaggressive, ineffectual, effete.

lily-white, *adj.* **1.** white, pure white, white as snow, pale, white-skinned, untannned, milk-white, ivory, ivory-skinned, porcelain; palid, wan, sallow, sickly looking, pale as death, pale as ashes, pale as a ghost, white as a sheet, bleached out; anemic, bloodless, ghastly, ghostly, haggard, ashen, chalky.

2. uncorrupted, uncorrupt, unsinful, uniniquitous, undissolute, undebauched, undepraved, undegenerate; innocent, pure, chaste, pure-hearted, modest; virgin, virginal, spotless, undefiled; stainless, unstained, unsoiled, unsullied, taintless, untainted, uninfected; clean, clean as a whistle, clean as snow, clean as a fresh sheet.

3. racist, racially prejudiced, biased, bigoted; discriminating, discriminative, discriminatory; segregated, segregative, segregational; all-white, (*of neighborhoods*) exclusive, unmixed, unintegrated.

—n. **4.** racist, segregationist, discriminator; Nazi, Ku Klux Klanner, member of the Klan; *Inf.* redneck.

limb, *n.* **1.** part, member, appendage, extension, extremity; wing, arm, leg, *Inf.* gam, *Inf.* pin, *Brit. Dial.* lith; artifical leg *or* arm, prosthesis; branch, projection, spur.

2. offshoot, shoot, scion, descendant, heir, offspring, child, *Inf.* chip off the old block.

3. *Informal.* limb of Satan, imp, devil, scamp, rascal, bad boy, Peck's bad boy.

4. **out on a limb** *Informal.* vulnerable, overextended, in a precarious situation, too close to the wind, with all one's eggs in one basket, with one's head in the lion's mouth.

limber, *adj.* flexible, flexile, flexuous, pliant, pliable, plastic; ductile, fictile, tractile, tractable, malleable, moldable, bendable; elastic, springy, resilient, stretchable; supple, lithe, lithesome, lissome, limber, graceful; extensile, extensible.

—*v.* **2.** *Usu.* **limber up** loosen up, warm up, exercise, stretch; prepare, get ready.

limbo, *n.* **1.** limbus, abode of the dead, limbo of infants, limbo of unbaptized infants, abode of the righteous dead, limbo of the fathers, limbo of the patriarchs; Lethe, land of the lotus-eaters, place of oblivion, nirvana.

2. confinement, imprisonment, incarceration, internment; committal, commitment, detention, duress, durance; captivity, slavery, bondage, thrall, enthrallment.

3. exclusion, segregation, separation, isolation, sequestration, quarantine; eviction, expulsion, ouster, displacement, dislocation, expatriation, exile; banishment, deportation, relegation, excommunication; proscription, outlawry, prohibition, banning, barring, disbarment.

4. **in limbo** in abeyance, suspended, in a holding pattern, on hold, on a back burner, on the shelf; treading water, hanging fire, hanging, up in the air, awaiting action.

limelight, *n.* **1.** fame, renown, celebrity, stardom; public notice, notoriety, publicity, *Inf.* the spotlight; illustriousness, greatness, eminence, eminency, preeminence, supremacy; notability, note, distinction, mark; prominence, rank, standing, prestige, weight, influence, significance, importance, account.

2. honor, laurels, glory, praise, kudos, éclat, acclamation, acclaim; popularity, vogue, favor, esteem, high regard, admiration, respect.

3. *Theater.* spotlight, baby spotlight, *Inf.* spot, floodlight, searchlight.

limit, *n.* **1.** boundary, frontier, frontier line, boundary line, bounding line, border line, partition line, line of demarcation, line.

2. border, perimeter, periphery, edge, rim, fringe, verge, skirt; circumference, compass, ambit, margin, frame, outline, confine, confines; brink, brim, brow, hem.

3. *Usu.* **limits** premises, confines, territory; land, ground, terrain; precinct, section, quarter, district.

4. **the limit** *Informal.* **a.** the last straw, the straw that broke the camel's back; enough, more than enough, *Inf.* it, all one can take. **b.** an outrage, a joke.

—*v.* **5.** bound, confine, shut in, fence in, pen in, hem in, keep within bounds; restrict, curb, proscribe, prohibit, bar, forbid; restrain, check, bridle, trammel, bind, stay, hold in check; cut down, cut back, *Inf.* watch; impede, hinder, hamper, tie one's hands; frustrate, thwart, clip one's wings.

6. demarcate, define, delimit, deliminate, mark off, rope off, stake out; determine, specify, fix, draw *or* mark boundaries; circumscribe, encircle, encompass, gird, begird, girdle, belt.

limitation, *n.* **1.** limit, bound, boundary, border. See **limit** (*defs.* **1, 2**).

2. impediment, hindrance, encumbrance, obstacle, obstruction, stumbling block, roadblock; restriction, bar, barrier, block, counteraction, embargo, stricture, blockade; deterrent, catch, snag, hitch, rub, fly in the ointment, drawback, liability; curb, clog, bit, tether.

3. inability, incapability, incapacity; weak point, weakness, defect, handicap, frailty.

limited, *adj.* **1.** confined, restricted, hemmed in, hedged in; tied down, checked, curbed; constrained, bound, restrained, hampered, cramped; fixed, delimited, delimitated, demarcated; circumscribed, encircled, encompassed, girded.

2. unimaginative, undiscerning, unperceptive; unintelligent, witless, slow-witted, dull-witted, dull; stolid, obtuse, crass, Boeotian, bovine, blockish, lumpish; dense, thick-headed, *Inf.* thick, slow, stupid, *Brit., Australian Inf.* dill, *Scot. and North Eng.* dowf; backward, doltish. *Sl.* birdbrained, simple; empty-headed, vacuous.

limiting, *adj.* confining, restricting, restrictive, checking, curbing, limitative; constraining, binding, bounding, restraining, hampering, cramping; delimiting, delimitative, delimitating, fixing, circumscribing; provisional, provisory, modifying, qualifying, qualificatory, qualificative.

limitless, *adj.* boundless, unbounded, unlimited, uncircumscribed, unrestricted, illimitable, shoreless; immense, vast, great, extensive; incalculable, undetermined, indeterminate, indefinite, undefined; immeasurable, measureless, beyond measure, innumberable, numberless, myriad, countless, untold, uncounted; infinite, endless, without end, unending, never-ending, interminable, inexhaustible; unceasing, constant, uninterrupted, perpetual, eternal; enduring, everlasting, permanent.

limp[1], *v.* **1.** hobble, hitch, walk lamely; totter, dodder, toddle, stagger, seesaw, move unsteadily, teeter; falter, halt, pause, hesitate; shuffle, shamble, drag one's feet.

2. crawl, creep, inch, drag, move slowly.

—*n.* **3.** hobble, hitch, jerk, claudication, uneven gait, *Sl.* gimp, tottering, staggering, doddering, shamble, halting, shuffle; lameness, infirmity, crippled leg, talipes, clubfoot.

limp[2], *adj.* **1.** flaccid, flabby, soft, quaggy, unfirm, unfit, *Inf.* out of shape; slack, lax, unstiff, unstiffened, unstarched, starchless, *All Dial.* limpsy, limpsey, limsy.

2. tired, fatigued, lethargic, weary, boneweary, worn, worn-out, exhausted, wasted, sapless, unenergetic, spent, played out, effete; weak, feeble, enfeebled, frail, puny, infirm, debilitated, shaky, sickly, anemic, failing, decrepit, lame, unsteady, unstable.

3. flimsy, supple, flexile, flexible, pliable, pliant, malleable, tractable, ductile, plastic; yielding, submissive, giving in, unresisting, irresolute, unsteadfast, unstaunch, half-hearted, lukewarm; characterless, spineless, nerveless, marrowless, sinewless, pithless, namby-pamby, *Sl.* gutless; weak-kneed, wishy-washy, chicken-hearted, lily-livered, timid, timorous, *Sl.* chicken, *Sl.* candy-assed; impotent, powerless, ineffective, strengthless, insipid, jejune, senile, anile, old-womanish.

limpid, *adj.* **1.** clear, transparent, transpicuous, crystal-clear, crystalline, crystal, glassy, glass-like, hyaline, vitreous, see-through; (*of air*) pure, unpolluted, sunny, sunshiny, shiny, bright; pellucid, translucent, lucent, diaphanous, sheer, thin.

2. lucid, perspicuous, clear as day, plain, plain as day, plain as the nose on your face, plain-spoken, simple, straightforward, exoteric; intelligible, understandable, comprehensible, comprehendible, apprehensible, ascertainable, perceptible, discernible; coherent, rational, logical, reasonable, pervious; clear-cut, distinct, explicit, precise, exact, sharp, express, articulate, well-defined, well-spoken, well-written, graphic; obvious, evident, self-evident, apparent, manifest, salient, palpable, patent; unambiguous, unconfused, unquestionable.

3. serene, placid, tranquil, pacific, calm, still, peaceful, halcyon, quiet, quiescent, irenic, composed, sedate; undisturbed, unperturbed, unruffled, unagitated, unshaken, undistressed, unworried, untroubled.

line[1], *n.* **1.** rule, bar, score, underline, underscore, hairline; mark, stroke, streak, dash, hyphen, virgule, diagonal; marking, inscription, inscript, engraving, incision; scratch, notch, slash, etch, hatching.

2. band, stripe, strip, belt, zone, layer, ring; seam, stitch, joint, weld, commissure; furrow, groove, rut, slit, slot; gutter, ditch, trench, foxhole; wrinkle, crow's foot, crease; scar, cicatrix, cut, gash.

3. row, series, sequence, run, succession, progression; concatenation, catenation, chain, catena, continuum; queue, string, thread, swath, procession, train, Indian file, single file; file, rank, column, tier, bank; parade, motorcade, review, formation, array; caravan, cavalcade, cortege, coffle.

4. verse, stave, strophe, bar, stich, versicle; measure, meter, foot; refrain, note, tune, melody.

5. limit, demarcation, border, edge, rim, curb; periphery, perimeter, compass, margin, circumference, bourn, threshhold, *Psychol.* limen; fringe, skirt, verge, brink, hem, brim; boundary, frontier, border line, boundary line, line of demarcation.

6. course, procedure, policy, course of action, *Latin. modus operandi;* practice, technique, routine; scheme, method, system, order, style; manner, way, mode, means; approach, attack, address.

7. direction, course, route, road, lane, avenue, channel; beat, tack, drift, set, path; way, aim, trend, track, bend, range; orientation, collimation, bearing, tenor, tendency, lay, lie.

8. **lines** outline, contour, figure, features, figuration, configuration; delineation, lineation, lineament, silhouette, profile, cameo.

9. department, office, province, discipline, domain, realm, walk; activity, business, field, specialty, forte, specialization; trade, profession, *Inf.* racket, *Inf.* game; line of work, line of business, walk of life; occupation, job, work; vocation, calling, pursuit, venture, career, lifework.

10. descent, parentage. See **lineage.**

11. thread, string, twine, yarn; wire, fiber, strand, filament, tendril; cord, rope, cable, cordage; strap, strop, thong, chain; ribbon, tape, tape measure, inkle; towline, lanyard, mooring, hawser, painter; clothesline, fishline, ripcord.

12. track, railway line, rail line, railroad line; tramline, tramroad, trolley line, streetcar line, subway line, metro line, *Brit. Inf.* tube line, elevated railway line; main line, trunk line, feeder line, sidetrack.

13. assortment, stock, merchandise, goods; kind, brand, stamp, sort, type; variety, number, description; color, stripe, grain, make.

14. wire, telegraph line, telephone line; party line, trunk line, private line, WATS line (wide area telecommunications service).

15. **draw the line** restrict, limit, check, bar, fix, determine; proscribe, confine, constrain, put on the brake, halt, stop, lay down the law, put one's foot down; cut off, interrupt, step in, break off, part company, depart.

16. **in line** **a.** straight, in a row, in column, in file; in alignment, right, direct, plumb, true. **b.** in conformity, in agreement, in accord, in step, in harmony, in rapport, in consonancy. **c.** under *or* in control, within bounds, in balance, in moderation, in *or* within reason.

—*v.* **17.** *Usu.* **line up** range, align, straighten, bring into line, string out, bank; arrange, array, order, right, put *or* set in order; list, group, place, fix, dispose, distribute; space, regiment, marshal, rally.

18. *Usu.* **line up** secure, get, obtain, procure, acquire; get hold of, come up with, dig up, uncover; sign up, enlist, enroll, contract with; employ, engage, hire.

19. delineate, draw, trace, mark, mark out, *Archaic.* limn; define, depict, describe, demarcate, delimit; portray, figure, silhouette.

20. rule, score, hatch, underline, underscore; wrinkle, furrow, crease, rut, groove; scratch, scrape, chisel, engrave, cut, inscribe, etch; streak, striate.

21. *Usu.* **line out** outline, sketch, rough in, block in; draw up, lay out, draft, trace, chart; devise, plot, frame, make up, project.

22. skirt, hem, embroider, edge, border, rim, form a line along; bound, fringe, margin, marginate, marge; verge, side, adjoin.

line[2], *v.* **1.** interline, interlineate, panel, face, back, back up, wainscot, ceil; coat, sheathe, wrap; interlard, inlay, incrust, bush; upholster, paper, wallpaper.

2. cover, drape, curtain, blanket, mantle, cloak; lay over, overlay, spread over, overspread.

lineage, *n.* **1.** ancestry, family tree, extraction, parentage, pedigree, bloodline, strain; descent, genealogy.

2. dynasty, house, family, race, people, tribe, clan; stirps, descendants, heritage, succession, progeny.

lineal, *adj.* in a direct line, linear; hereditary, family, racial; parental, patriarchal, matriarchal, ancestral.

lineament, *n.* line, feature, configuration, mark, distinguishing mark; form, contour, profile, cut; physiognomy, *Sl.* phiz, visage; particularity, singularity, idiosyncrasy; aspect, delineation.

linear, *adj.* **1.** aligned, alined, lineal; straight, direct, undeviating, unbent; one-dimensional, lengthwise, longitudinal.

2. lined, scored, etched, sketched; penned, calligraphic, inked, outlined.

linen, *n.* **1.** cloth, fabric, material, textile, woven fabric, damask.

2. *Often* **linens** bedding, bed linens, bedclothes; sheets, pillowcases, pillowslips, pillow shams; towels, washcloths, facecloths, washrags; table linen, tablecloths, napkins.

liner[1], *n.* **1.** ocean liner, ship, steamship, steamer, passenger vessel, boat, hydroplane; airplane, plane, aircraft, *Aeronaut.* airliner.

2. eyeliner, eye pencil, mascara, eye shadow.

liner[2], *n.* **1.** lining, facing, inner lining, interlining. See **lining** (*def.* **1**).

2. cover, album cover, cardboard cover, jacket.

linesman, *n.* sports official, umpire, *Inf.* ump, referee, *Inf.* ref, field judge, lineman.

line-up, *n.* **1.** line, queue, row; list, schedule.

2. *Sports.* roster, list of players, batting order.

linger, *v.* **1.** loiter, tarry, stay, wait, remain, *Sl.* hang around, *Sl.* stick around; continue, persist, stay on, endure, abide, persevere, hang on.

2. dawdle, delay, lag, procrastinate, put off, dally, shirk, *Sl.* goof off.

3. loll, idle, *Inf.* lallygag, lounge, poke, *Inf.* diddle, dilly-dally; slouch, loaf, vegetate, waste time, fritter time away; mill around, trifle, potter, putter, play.

4. saunter, stroll, perambulate; amble, ramble, mosey; traipse, wander, meander, inch; shuffle, shamble, slouch; toddle, totter.

lingerie, *n.* underwear, undergarments, underclothing, underclothes, *Inf.* undies; *All Euph.* dainties, things, unmentionables, nice things, finery, linen;

Facetious., Sl. skivvies; underpants, pants, panties, bikinis, G-string, drawers, bloomers; brassiere, bra, see-through bra, strapless bra, training bra, tops; camisole, vest, undervest, undershirt, shirt; slip, petticoat, half-slip, hoopskirt, chemise, shift, shimmy; hosiery, hose, pantyhose, stockings, nylons; corset, girdle, corselette, garter belt, panty girdle, *Brit.* stays; nightwear, sleepwear, nightgown, bedgown, nightie, pajamas, *Inf.* P.J.s; kimono, dressing gown, wrapper, bathrobe, bedjacket.

lingo, *n.* *Informal.* argot, cant, jargon, parlance; slang, idiom, terminology, phraseology, vocabulary; patois, pidgin, pidgin English, trade language, lingua franca; vernacular, dialect, tongue, talk, speech, language, shoptalk; journalese, officialese, Washingtonese, bureaucratese, newspeak, medicalese, legalese; thieves' Latin, pig Latin, peddler's French, St. Giles Greek; gobbledygook, patter, mumbo jumbo, gibberish, gibber.

linguist, *n.* **1.** polyglot, bilinguist, bilingual, multilingual; interpreter, translator; one with an ear for languages, one with sprachgefühl.

2. semanticist, semasiologicist, lexicologist, *Archaic.* glossologist, *Brit.* philologist, *Brit.* philologer, *Rare.* linguistician, etymologist, *Obs.* glottologist; phonetician, phonologist, grammarian, dialectologist, morphologist.

linguistic, *adj.* lingual, semantic, semasiological, lexicological, *Brit.* philological, etymological, *Archaic.* glossological, *Obs.* glottologic, dialectologic, phonologic; syntactic, grammatical.

linguistics, *n.* semantics, semasiology, lexicology; etymology, phonology, phonemics, phonetics, morphology, syntax, grammar; speechlore, paleography.

liniment, *n.* ointment, embrocation, balm, salve; lotion, wash, soothing liquid, abirritant, demulcent; cream, oil, balsam, unguent; anodyne, alleviative, alleviatory, palliative, lenitive, *Med.* emollient, *Pharm.* cerate.

lining, *n.* inlayer, inlay, interlining; wainscot, wainscoting, brattice, reinforcement; backing, doublure, doubling; *Elect.* bush, *Chiefly Brit.* bushing; insole; packing, padding, filling, stuffing, wadding.

link, *n.* **1.** connection, connective, copula, coupler, coupling; bond, tie, knot, yoke; joint, joiner, articulation, commissure; pivot, hinge, elbow, knee, dovetail joint, rabbet, rabbet joint; concatenation, chain, linkage; clamp, clasp, clip, latch, buckle.

2. association, affiliation, relationship, relatedness, tie-in, hook-up, mutual interest, joint interest; attachment, dependence, mutual dependence.

—*v.* **3.** chain, couple, concatenate; connect, join, unite, tie, bond, splice, fasten; conjoin, subjoin, affix, fix, annex, attach; bridge, bridge over, span; (*of transportation*) connect up, continue, run, go on.

4. relate, identify, ally, bracket, equate, parallel, draw a parallel; attribute, attribute to, assign, assign to, ascribe, ascribe to, impugn, impute to, charge to, credit *or* accredit with; saddle on *or* upon, father upon, blame for, fix on *or* upon, pin on, *Inf.* pinpoint, *Sl.* hang on.

5. link together league, confederate, unionize, band together, join forces *or* hands, team up, *Inf.* hitch horses.

linsey-woolsey, *n.* jumble, scramble, hodgepodge, mishmash, mash, hash, mess, mingle-mangle, mix-up, muddle, tangle, gallimaufry.

lint, *n.* **1.** down, thistledown, flue, floss, fluff, fuzz; mote, wisp, dust; fuzzball, furball, dustball, *Inf.* bellybutton lint.

2. cotton, gauze, sponge.

lion, *n.* **1.** cat, lioness, lionet; *Heraldry.* lioncel; *Astron.* Leo.

2. lionheart, stalwart, valiant, a man, brave man, man of courage *or* mettle, cavalier, chevalier; hero, champion, paladin, knight; conqueror, conquering hero, victor, master, man of the hour *or* day; brave, warrior, soldier, fighter, fighting man, fearless *or* dauntless soldier, intrepid warrior; tiger, bulldog, wildcat, gamecock, fighting cock.

3. personage, person *or* figure of note *or* consequence, public figure, social lion, luminary, notable, dignitary, great man, great; *Inf.* somebody, *Inf.* name *or* big name, *Inf.* bigwig, *Inf.* Mr. Big, *Inf.* big gun, *Inf.* VIP; *Sl.* heavy, *Sl.* big cheese, *Sl.* high-muck-a-muck, *Sl.* big shot, *Sl.* his nibs, *Sl.* BMOC *or* big man on campus; celebrity, star, superstar, *Sl.* megastar, idol, popular idol *or* figure, *Sl.* pop star, *Sl.* pop-hero.

4. beard the lion in his den tempt Providence, defy danger, court destruction, go in harm's way, play with fire, skate on thin ice, dance on the razor's edge, put one' head in the lion's mouth, march up to the cannon's mouth; confront, face, brave, *Inf.* meet eyeball to eyeball, face up to, stand up to; brazen, brazen out *or* through, take the bull by the horns, bell the cat.

lionhearted, *adj.* **1.** brave, courageous, valiant, valorous, heroic, hero-like; stout-hearted, ironhearted, great-hearted; virile, manly, manful, gallant, chivalrous; intrepid, fearless, dauntless, aweless, dreadless, unafraid; bold, bold-spirited, high-spirited, audacious.

2. firm, resolute, staunch, steadfast, stalwart, *Archaic.* stalworth, doughty, sturdy; indomitable, invincible, unconquerable, unyielding, unshrinking, unbending; plucky, mettlesome, gritty, game, spirited, redblooded, nervy, *Inf.* spunky, *Sl.* gutsy.

lionize, *v.* **1.** glorify, magnify, make much of; extol, exalt, panegyrize, eulogize, celebrate, acclaim, laud, tribute, praise, sound *or* ring the praises of; elevate, uplift, raise, ennoble, aggrandize, put on a pedestal; adulate, idolize, hero-worship, deify, apotheosize.

2. (*all in reference to celebrities*) pursue, follow, chase after, run after; hang on, tag along; court, pay court to, woo, dance attendance upon, curry favor, *Sl.* play up to, *Sl.* shine up to, *Sl.* suck up to.

3. *British.* sightsee, see the sights, take in the sights, *Inf.* see the lions, *Sl.* rubberneck, *Sl.* hit the hot spots.

lion's share, *n.* largest *or* biggest portion, largest *or* biggest part, major part, better part, bigger *or* greater half; majority; bulk, mass.

lip, *n.* **1.** *Usu.* **lips** labia, mouth.

2. *Slang.* impudence, insolence, sauciness, *Inf.* sauce, *Inf.* sassiness, *Inf.* back talk, *Dial.* sass, *Inf.* cheek, *Sl.* mouth, *Sl.* mouthing off, *Sl.* smarting off; discourtesy, rudeness, incivility, impertinence, flippancy, brashness, disrespect, disdain, contempt, derision, *Sl.* freshness, *Sl.* fresh talk; impudent talk, audacity, effrontery, boldness, presumption, brazenness.

3. edge, rim, brim, verge, brink, ledge; border, margin, *Archaic.* marge, skirt, fringe; hem, brow, flange.

4. *Music.* (*all of brass or wind instruments*) control, touch, intonation; mastery, command, virtuosity, proficiency; prowess, technique, adeptness, competence; grace, style, finesse.

5. bite one's lip hold back, refrain, forbear, hold *or* stay one's hand, repress.

6. button one's lip keep quiet *or* mum *or* still, shut *or* close one's mouth, *Inf.* shut up, *Inf.* save one's breath; hold one's tongue, keep one's tongue between one's teeth, bite one's tongue, hold one's peace, not utter a word, *Inf.* play dumb; *Sl.* keep one's trap *or* yap shut, *Sl.* keep one's bazoo shut, *Sl.* dummy up, *Sl.*

clam up, *Sl.* make like a clam; let pass, say nothing, seal one's lips, not breath a word, *Inf.* not let out a peep, *Inf.* not say "boo," *Inf.* let ride *or* let it ride, *Inf.* let the chips fall where they may, let alone, leave well enough alone, not make waves, let sleeping dogs lie, not get involved, *Sl.* leave be; be mute, stand mute, fall silent, *Inf.* cool it, *Inf.* button up; keep one's thoughts to oneself, be like the wise old owl.

7. **smack one's lips** enjoy, show pleasure, take delight in, savor, relish, anticipate, look forward to; feast on, roll over the tongue, devour, eat up; gloat over, covet, *Inf.* slobber *or* drool over.

8. **keep a stiff upper lip** keep up one's courage, bear up, *Inf.* keep one's chin up, hold one's head up, *Inf.* hang in, *Inf.* hang in there, *Inf.* hang on for dear life, *Inf.* hang tough; steel oneself, keep one's nerve, pluck up heart *or* courage, face up to, not flinch *or* shrink from, face the music, bite the bullet; fight back the tears, face adversity, keep one's feelings to oneself, turn the other cheek, go down with all colors flying, stand fast.

—*v.* **9.** mouth, whisper, breathe, utter softly; give voice, give tongue, articulate, enunciate, pronounce, phonate, voice, sound.

lip service, *n.* **1.** insincerity, artificiality, disingenuousness, uncandidness, mealy-mouthedness; flattery, smooth talk, mouth honor, *Inf.* hokum, *Inf.* phoniness; hypocrisy, falseheartedness, falseness, two-facedness, duplicity; dissemblance, dissimulation; simulation, show, false show, false air *or* front; pose, posing, posture; guile, wiliness, mockery, hollow mockery; crossed fingers, tongue in cheek, tokenism, token gesture, empty gesture, crocodile tears, *Inf.* sweet talk, *Inf.* soft soap, *Inf.* put-on, *Inf.* moonshine, *Inf.* eyewash, *Inf.* hogwash.

2. sanctimony, sanctimoniousness, false piety, pietism, piousness; self-righteousness, cant, mummery, drivel, snivel, snuffle; unctuousness, oiliness.

liquefy, *v.* dissolve, liquidize; suspend, put into solution, condense; fluidize, smelt; thaw, melt, melt down; soak, souse, saturate, permeate; run, flux, stream.

liqueur, *n.* stimulant, appetizer, aperitif; cordial, after-dinner drink, *Inf.* pick-me-up, *Inf.* pickup, *Inf.* nightcap.

liquid, *adj.* **1.** fluid, flowing, running, streaming, sappy, freely flowing; watery, runny, liquidy; liquefied, melted, molten, liquescent; dissolved, solvent, thin; muddy, slushy, sloshy, splashy, sloppy, squishy, oozy, miry, sloughy, plashy; viscous, viscid, syrupy, juicy, succulent; damp, wet, hydrous.

2. clear, smooth, lucid, pure, fluent; agreeable, pleasant, clear-toned, euphonious, euphonic, sweet, dulcet, honeyed, lyric, tripping, harmonious, melodious, melodic, mellow, mellifluent, mellifluous, ariose; celestial, seraphic.

3. transparent, clear, limpid, unclouded, crystalline, crystal-clear, bright, glowing, gleaming.

4. *Finance.* convertible, negotiable.

—*n.* **5.** fluid, liquor, drink, beverage, potation; liquid *or* fluid extract, semiliquid, juice, sap, syrup, *Inf.* goo, *Inf.* goop, *Inf.* gook, *Inf.* gunk.

liquidate, *v.* **1.** pay in full, pay off, discharge, settle, retire; square, clear, honor, satisfy, *Finance.* amortize; redeem, redeem one's pledge *or* pledges, make good, *Inf.* pay up, *Inf.* pay the piper.

2. cash, convert, convert to cash, sell off, *Inf.* get out, *Inf.* clear the decks, *Inf.* cash in one's chips, *Inf.* cash out, *Inf.* take the money and run; sell stock, throw on the market, dump, unload, close out, sell out, terminate.

3. (*of a partnership or business*) break up, part company, split up, disband, go separate ways; abolish, dissolve.

4. kill, slay, assassinate, poison, do to death, blot *or* wipe out, put an end to, get rid of, put away, put out of the way, silence; dispatch, finish, finish off, settle, *Inf.* put the kibosh on; *All Sl.* hit, zap, snuff out, rub out, bump off, polish off, give [s.o.] the works *or* the business; *All Euph.* let the daylight in, send west, take for a ride, put [s.o.] out of his misery.

5. cut down, run through, put to the sword; smother, suffocate, asphyxiate, burke; execute, put to death, garrotte, behead, decapitate, guillotine, hang, gibbet, lynch, *Sl.* string up.

6. annihilate, exterminate, obliterate, discreate, reduce to nothing, destroy totally, eradicate, erase, extirpate, extinguish; massacre, decimate, destroy, wipe off the face of the earth.

liquor, *n.* **1.** spirits, intoxicant, inebriant, alcohol, John Barleycorn, the demon rum, whiskey, schnapps, grog, brandy; drink, bouse, strong drink, *Inf.* booze, *Inf.* hard stuff, *Sl.* likker, *Sl.* hooch, *Sl.* sauce, *Sl.* juice, *Sl.* medicine; moonshine, home brew, *Sl.* sneaky pete; firewater, *Sl.* red-eye, *Sl.* rot-gut, *Sl.* blue-ruin, *Sl.* mountain dew, *Sl.* white lightning; the bottle, the cup, the cup that cheers; potation, beverage, liquid refreshment; bracer, refresher, *Inf.* pick-me-up, *Inf.* pickup.

2. broth, bouillon, stock, juice, *Fr. jus;* extract, essence, distillate, concentrate.

lisp, *n.* **1.** sibilation, sibilance, assibilation, indistinct speech, *Inf.* baby talk; hiss, hissing, siss, sissing, shush, shushing, hush, hushing, sizzle, sizzling, fizz, fizzing; speech impediment *or* defect, *Pathol.* dyslexia, lisping.

—*v.* **2.** sibilate, assibilate, hiss, siss, hush, shush, mispronounce, speak indistinctly, *Inf.* talk like a baby *or* talk baby talk.

lissome, *adj.* lithe, lithesome, pliant, bendable, flexible, flexile; plastic, moldable, adaptable, compliant, tractable, malleable, ductile, fictile; limber, supple, *Archaic.* lithy, loose-limbed, loose; nimble, agile, quick, light.

list[1], *n.* **1.** list of names, roll, attendance, muster *or* muster roll, roster, *Sports.* line-up, beadroll, slate, docket; listing, enumeration, shopping list, inventory, catalog; *Library Science.* card *or* union catalog, file, index, table of contents, directory, telephone book, yellow pages; register, social register, Who's Who, record, chartulary; schedule, social calendar, program, reading list, syllabus.

—*v.* **2.** record, write down, chronicle, *Law.* docket; catalog, file, alphabetize, tabulate; arrange, classify, codify, group.

3. enroll, enter, register, sign up *or* sign up for, enlist, join.

list[2], *n.* **1.** border, bordering strip, panel.

2. selvage, edge, finished edge.

3. band, strip, stripe, streak, striation; stroke, line, dash, bar, tape, tag, label; fillet, fascia, ribbon, headband, frontlet; wristband, *Eccles.* maniple; belt, baldric, cord, cordon, braid, thong; sash, cummerbund, girdle, waistband.

list[3], *v.* (*all of a vessel*) incline, slant, slope, lean, heel *or* heel over, careen, cant, tilt, tip.

listen, *v.* **1.** harken, hark, *Archaic.* list; *Med.* auscultate, listen to [s.o.'s] heartbeat; pay attention, *Inf.* listen up, attend to, give heed, listen hard *or* good, prick up one's ears, listen carefully, keep one's ears open; listen to, give an ear to, lend an ear to, bend an ear to, be attentive to, give [s.o.] one's full attention, be all ears, hang on [s.o.'s] every word.

2. heed [s.o.'s] words, mind, obey, do as one is told.
3. **listen in** eavesdrop, listen in on, wiretap, *Sl.* bug; overhear, *Inf.* pick up, catch, hear.

listless, *adj.* 1. languid, languorous, sluggish, phlegmatic, lethargic, torpid, weary, fatigued, enervated, enervate; heavy, leaden, hebetudinous, drowsy, dozy, sleepy, slumberous, soporific, somnolent, comatose, narcose, oscitant, supine; lackadaisical, indolent, lazy, slothful, fainéant, recumbent, idle; spiritless, unenergetic, vigorless, zestless, lifeless, passive, inactive, dormant, inert, dull, dead.
2. apathetic, apathetical, indifferent, Laodicean, unconcerned, disinterested, uninterested, nonchalant, pococurante, insouciant, lukewarm, cool, half-hearted, impartial, neutral; impassive, dispassionate, impassible, passionless, unexcited, unemotional, emotionless, *Archaic.* impassionate; uncaring, careless, unsympathetic, uncompassionate, unfeeling, insensible, insensitive, insensate; aloof, distant, removed, withdrawn, abstracted, absent, absent-minded, in another world, oblivious, inattentive, heedless.

listlessness, *n.* 1. languor, languidness, lassitude, ennui, *Inf.* the blahs; phlegmaticness, lethargy, sluggishness, fatigue, weariness, enervation; hebetude, heaviness, phlegm, leadenness, drowsiness, sleepiness, (*in the Middle East*) kef; lackadaisicalness, indolence, laziness, slothfulness, fainéance, fainéancy, idleness, recumbence, recumbency; spiritlessness, vigorlessness, zestlessness, lifelessness, dullness, passivity, inactivity, dormancy, inertia, deadness.
2. apathy, indifference, disinterest, disinterestedness, uninterestedness, unconcern; insouciance, nonchalance, pococurantism, lukewarmness, lukewarmth, coolness, half-heartedness; impassiveness, impassibility, impassibleness, dispassion, dispassionateness, passionlessness, unemotionalness, emotionlessness, insensitivity, lack of sympathy *or* compassion, carelessness; aloofness, distantness, abstraction, absentness, absent-mindedness, obliviousness, inattentiveness, heedlessness.

lit, *adj.* 1. lighted, lighted up, alight, burning, on; luminous, illuminated, illumined; agleam, gleaming, glowing, aglow, glaring.
2. *Sl.* drunk, intoxicated, inebriated, sottish, *Sl.* soused. See **drunk.**

litany, *n.* 1. prayer, petition, supplication, invocation, importunity.
2. recitation, recital, account, narration, summary, recapitulation.
3. catalogue, list, listing, compilation, enumeration, beadroll, roll, slate, muster, directory; index, table, file; inventory, record, roster.

literacy, *n.* articulateness, intelligence, erudition, learning, learnedness, scholarship; culture, enlightenment, edification.

literal, *adj.* 1. word-for-word, verbatim, *Fr. mot à mot,* line-for-line, letter-for-letter, literatim, *Latin. verbatim et literatim;* accurate, exact, precise, close, faithful, true, honest, strict, undeviating; explicit, express, unambiguous, clear, unequivocal; factual, actual, true-to-life, realistic, credible, believable, natural.
2. objective, direct, straight, unbiased, unprejudiced, undistorted, unwarped; plain, simple, unvarnished, pure, *Inf.* honest-to-goodness, gospel; unexaggerated, unembellished, unadulterated.
3. (*all of persons*) literal-minded, matter-of-fact, prosaic, prosy, unimaginative, dull, boring, colorless; vapid, humdrum, tedious, tiresome, wearisome, uninteresting; slow, simple-minded, obtuse, blunt, heavy, ponderous.
4. veritable, real, true, unimaginary, unfictitious; genuine, authentic, *Inf.* sure-enough, bona fide, legitimate.

literally, *adv.* 1. word for word, verbatim, *Fr. mot à mot,* line for line, letter for letter, literatim, *Latin. verbatim et literatim;* exactly, precisely, accurately, closely, faithfully, honestly, strictly, to a hair, to the letter; in the strict sense of the word, strictly speaking, in plain English, simply, plainly.
2. actually, really, truly; apparently, evidently, obviously; surely, certainly, definitely; positively, absolutely, undeniably, indubitably, unquestionably, indisputably.

literalness, *n.* 1. literality, accuracy, exactness, exactitude, precision, preciseness, closeness, faithfulness, trueness, truth, authenticity, honesty, explicitness; unambiguousness, unambiguity, clearness, unequivocality; factualness, factuality, actuality, actualness, realism, reality, credibility, credibleness, believableness, naturalness.
2. objectivity, directness, straightness, plainness, simpleness, simplicity, pureness.
3. literal-mindedness, prosaicness, prosiness, unimaginativeness, unimagination, dullness, boringness, boredom; vapidity, tediousness, tiresomeness, wearisomeness; slowness, simple-mindedness, obtuseness, bluntness, heaviness.
4. narrowness, hideboundness, inflexibleness, inflexibility, rigidness, rigidity.

literary, *adj.* 1. written, of writing, of books, of literature, of letters, of belles-lettres; published, printed, in print, in black and white, of the printed word.
2. versed, well-versed, conversant, well-read, book-learned, lettered, cultured, cultivated, refined; highbrow, highbrowed, *Inf.* long-haired *or* longhair, *Inf.* arty, *Sl.* artsy; knowledgeable, educated, well-educated, well-schooled, well-instructed, well-tutored, well-trained, well-posted, well-grounded, well-informed, *Archaic.* studied, erudite, punditic, scholarly, scholastic, academic, professorial, pedagoguish, donnish; pedantic, pedantical, pedantesque, pompous, know-it-all; stilted, stiff, stuffy, formal.
3. bookish, bibliophilistic, bibliophilic, bibliophagous, bibliophagic, like a bookworm; studious, always with one's nose in a book, intellectual, cerebral, brainy.

literate, *adj.* 1. educated, book-learned, schooled, instructed, tutored, trained, able to read and write; well-educated, well-schooled, well-instructed, well-tutored, well-informed, *Archaic.* studied; knowledgeable, erudite, punditic, scholarly.
2. literary, lettered, of letters, of literature, of belles-lettres; versed, well-versed, well-read, cultured, cultivated, refined. See also **literary** (*def.* **2**).
3. well-written, grammatical, correct, stylish, polished, skillful; lucid, perspicuous, clear, articulate, express, explicit, sharp, legible; coherent, intelligible, understandable, comprehensible, comprehendible.

literati, *n.* intellectuals, intelligentsia, cognoscenti, philosophes, *Sl.* brains, savants, learned men *or* women, academes, the learned, mental giants, masterminds; pundits, sages, wise men *or* women; illuminati, the enlightened, aesthetes, connoisseurs, (*all sometimes disparaging*) highbrows, *Inf.* eggheads, *Inf.* longhairs; elite, *Inf.* upper-crust; bohemians, free spirits, free thinkers.

literatim, *adv.* letter for letter, exactly, precisely, word for word. See also **literally** (*def.* **1**).

literature, *n.* 1. letters, belles-lettres, literary works, writings, republic of letters; prose, poetry, writing, creative writing, written art; classics, publications, books, the printed word; body of knowledge *or* information, knowledge, pantology, lore.

2. printed matter, reading material, food for thought; brochure, pamphlet, leaflet, circular, handbill, handout; exposition, treatise, tract, tractate, thesis, dissertation, paper; information, explanation, facts, publicity, propaganda.

lithe, *adj.* lithesome, pliant, bendable, flexible, flexile; plastic, moldable, adaptable, compliant, tractable, malleable, ductile, fictile; limber, supple, lissome, *Archaic.* lithy, loose-limbed, loose; nimble, agile, quick, light.

lithoid, *adj.* lithoidal, stonelike, stony, lithic; hard, adamantine, adamant, granite, marble, rock-hard, hard as rock; petrified, ossified, hardened; craggy, harsh, rough, rugged; impervious, impenetrable, unpenetrable.

litigant, *n.* **1.** litigator, *Law.* party, opponent, disputant, contestant, contender; *Law.* plaintiff, *Law.* suitor, complainant, suer, petitioner, claimant, *Law.* appellant, accuser, accusant, *Law.* prosecutor; *Law.* defendant, *Law.* appellee, accused.

—adj. **2.** litigating, contesting, disputing, contending; accusing, *Law.* prosecuting, defending.

litigate, *v.* **1.** contest at law, dispute in court; contend; charge, accuse, claim, maintain, hold.

2. carry on a lawsuit, go to court, file *or* bring suit, institute legal proceedings, bring legal action against, press charges, sue, prosecute.

litigation, *n.* lawsuit, contention, dispute, contest, controversy, legal argument, disputation; suit at law, legal action *or* proceedings, legal remedy; action, proceedings, case, cause, bringing of charges, laying *or* filing of charges, bringing to book; prosecution, arraignment, indictment, allegation, accusation, charge, bill of particulars.

litigious, *adj.* **1.** litigable, controvertible, contestable, disputable, actionable; controversial, polemic, polemical, eristic.

2. argumentative, argumentatious, disputatious, quarrelsome, contentious, dissentious, dissentient, exceptive; battlesome, combative, pugnacious, bellicose, belligerent, aggressive.

litter, *n.* **1.** rubbish, scattered rubbish, refuse, debris, junk, trash, motley collection; tumble, tangle, shreds, odds and ends, hodgepodge, hash, mishmash, muddle, rummage; ollapodrida, *Inf.* stew, *Inf.* Duke's mixture, accumulation.

2. disorder, untidiness, clutter, confusion, disarray, chaos; irregularity, lack of system, disorganization; muss, mess, jumble, disarrangement, dishevelment, scramble.

3. issue, offspring, young; multiple birth, brood, hatch, spawn, progeny.

4. stretcher, pallet, swing, hammock, sling; bier, sedan chair, palanquin, portable couch, horse litter, camel litter; (*in Ceylon*) tonjon, (*in India*) jampan, (*in India*) muncheel, (*in the East Indies*) dooly, (*in Japan*), norimon.

5. bedding, animal bedding, stable floorcover, straw; mulch, leaf cover, plant protection, winter cover.

—v. **6.** strew, mess, mess up, misarrange, displace, put out of place; throw into disorder, disarray, make a shambles of, disarrange, clutter, scatter *or* strew objects about.

7. cover, cradle, bed down, cover with straw.

8. give birth, produce, bring forth, bring forth young, *Inf.* come due, *Inf.* come in, drop, spring, throw, pup, whelp, cub, kitten, foal, calve, lamb, spawn.

litterbug, *n.* strewer, scatterer, broadcaster, litterer; polluter, defiler, desecrator; barbarian, vulgarian, boor, sloven, slattern; *Inf.* pig, *Sl.* slob.

littery, *adj.* messy, disorderly, helter-skelter, bestrewn, littered; dirty, grubby, sloppy, filthy; untidy, disarranged, disorganized; unkempt, uncared for, untended, *Inf.* not picked up.

little, *adj.* **1.** small, tiny, teeny, pint-size, wee, mini, short, snub; *All Baby Talk.* teeny-weeny, itty-bitty, itsy-bitsy, itty, teensy-weensy; Lilliputian, elfin, like Tom Thumb, pygmy, *Inf.* peewee, baby, child's toy, bantam; undersized, underweight, lightweight; diminutive, petite, minikin, dainty, slender, slim, thin, slight, skinny; midget, miniature, miniscule, minute, atomic, infinitesimal, microscopic; puny, runty, stunted, scrubby, dwarfish, homuncular, shrunken.

2. brief, limited, abbreviated; fleeting, transitory, fugacious, fugitive, momentary, passing, transient, volatile; ephemeral, over in a wink, soon over with, short-lived, unenduring.

3. skimpy, sparse, scant, exiguous, meager; insufficient, thinly scattered, stinted, piddling.

4. paltry, trifling, trivial, halfpenny, nugatory, inconsiderable, *Inf.* dinky; frivolous, unimportant, insignificant, inappreciable, imperceptible, inconspicuous; not vital, immaterial, inconsequential, worthless, inadequate, useless; unknown, obscure, nameless, unnoticed.

5. weak, powerless, unforceful, feeble, poor; faint, frail, delicate, fragile, flimsy; soft, quiet, low, hushed, subdued; indistinct, inaudible, muffled, muted, stifled; mediocre, imperfect, inferior, second-rate, third-rate, below par.

6. mean, petty, picayune; illiberal, intolerant, narrow, narrow-minded; shallow, insular, parochial, provincial, blinded, unimaginative, purblind; biased, bigoted, opinionated, unreasonable, arbitrary, uncompromising, stiff-necked, inflexible; niggardly, penurious, close, close-fisted, tight, scrimpy, miserly, stingy.

7. contemptible, despicable, despised, nasty, rotten, low-down, base, vile, dastardly, *Sl.* schmucky, *Sl.* yutzy; sordid, *Sl.* yucky.

—adv. **8.** not at all, by no means; not much, only just, barely, imperceptibly, inappreciably, hardly, not quite, limitedly; vaguely, slightly, in some degree, faintly, rather.

9. rarely, seldom, infrequently, uncommonly; once in a while, once in a great while; from time to time, once in a blue moon, scarcely, hardly ever.

—n. **10.** hardly any, practically nothing, next to nothing, *Sp. un poco*; *Inf.* smidgen, few, scantling, modicum, trifle; jot, whit, spot, bit, tittle, pennyworth; dash, dab, dollop, crumb, driplet, drop, thimbleful; particle, speck, sprinkling, grain; germ, molecule, atom; snippet, snip, scrap, shred, hair, splinter, sliver, fraction; touch, suggestion, soupçon, hint, suspicion.

11. short distance, a hoot and a holler, a piece, down the road a piece, stone's throw, bit, few steps, spitting distance.

12. short time, *Sl.* a mo, *Sl.* a sec, second, trice, less than no time, two shakes of a lamb's tail, before you can say Constantinople, a wink.

little people, *n.* **1.** elves, fairies, leprechauns, imps, brownies, dwarfs, gnomes, trolls, fays, pixies, nymphs, dryads, sprites, sylphs.

2. midgets, shrimps, runts, pee-wees, squirts, pipsqueaks, half-pints, small-fries, *Inf.* shorties, Lilliputians, *Chiefly Scot.* wee fellows *or* laddies.

3. commonalty, the great unnumbered, the general public, the public, the many; the masses, the humbler classes, rank and file; populace, citizenry, proletariat, hoi polloi, bourgeoisie; commoners, peasantry, salt-of-the-earth; the lower classes, low life, underlings, *Inf.* the great unwashed; mob, rabble, hoard, herd, rout.

littoral, *adj.* **1.** coastal, seaboard, coastwise, shore, seaside, beachfront, waterside, riparian.

—*n.* **2.** seacoast, seashore, shore, seaside, seaboard, strand, coast, water's edge; shoreline, coastline, strand line; beach, sands, sand, foreshore, inning, *Fr. plage, Chiefly Brit.* shingle.

liturgical, *adj.* ritual, ceremonial, formal, solemn; sacerdotal, hieratical, liturgic; sacramental, eucharistic, baptismal, chrismal, paschal; ceremonious, ritualistic, formular, sabbatarian, sacramentarian; liturgiological, euchological.

liturgy, *n.* ritual, worship, service, ceremony; rite, rite of passage; observance, practice, celebration; function, office, exercise, duty; solemnity, formality, formulary, formula; mystery, sacrament, ordinance; liturgics, litany, liturology.

livable, *adj.* **1.** habitable, inhabitable, occupiable, fit, lodgeable; comfortable, decent, respectable, convenient; adequate, acceptable, admissible, satisfactory, usable; unobjectionable, unexceptionable, passable, sufficient; all right, OK, better than nothing, fair, not bad, not all that bad, pretty good.

2. companionable, conversable, compatible, harmonious, easy, easy to live with; affable, friendly, sociable, amicable; gregarious, congenial, genial; civil, gracious, courteous, urbane.

3. endurable, bearable, supportable, tolerable, sufferable, worth living, worthwhile.

live[1], *v.* **1.** be alive, have life, be, exist, have being, walk the earth; breathe, respire; arise, rise, originate, quicken, come forth, appear, see light, come into existence.

2. subsist, remain alive, cling to life, survive, outlive; keep a hold on, hold on, stick out, stick to; persevere, persist, endure, last, continue, remain, stand, abide, obtain, prevail; be permanent, be steadfast, be constant.

3. *Usu.* **live on** *or* **by** subsist, maintain life, rely for maintenance; feed, be nourished, be supported; thrive, increase, wax, augment, multiply, flourish, grow, fare; support [s.o.], earn a living, follow an occupation, make one's living, earn money, get ahead; keep, maintain, nourish, support, foster, nurture; provide for, provision, victual, afford, board, subsidize.

4. *Often* **live in** *or* **at** dwell, reside, tarry, sojourn, occupy, inhabit, people, populate; tenant, room, billet, lodge, take up one's quarters, take up residence; anchor, moor, take *or* strike root, establish oneself.

5. behave, act, acquit oneself, comport oneself, demean oneself, conduct oneself.

6. flourish, thrive, prosper, luxuriate; enjoy life, be happy, live it up, live high, live high off the hog, *Latin. carpe diem*; make the most of life, take the earth's bounty, make every moment count, bask in the sunshine, find one's place in the sun, live a charmed life, live in clover, sail before the wind, make *or* cut a figure, swim with the tide, get along swimmingly.

live[2], *adj.* **1.** alive, living, vital, breathing, viable, sensible, subsistent, existent, extant, animate, quick, vivified, *Biol.* motile; real, palpable, in the flesh, fleshly, bodily, substantial, embodied, incarnate, corporeal, material, physical, tangible; under the sun, this side of the grave, on the face of the earth.

2. lively, energetic, vigorous, spirited, dynamic, *Inf.* peppy, *Inf.* snappy, active, brisk, frisky; breezy, effervescent, vivacious, stirring, sparkling, glowing, bright, brilliant; ardent, eager, enthusiastic, intense, keen; alert, wide-awake; industrious, enterprising.

3. teeming, swarming, abounding, overflowing, thronged; fraught, full, rife, replete; restless, bustling, busy.

4. glowing, burning, smoldering; alight, aflame, flaming, inflamed, ignited, igneous, fiery, blazing, ablaze, afire; aglow, incandescent, candent, white-hot, red-hot.

5. vivid, bright, bright-colored, colorful, chromatic; gay, deep, gorgeous, rich; florid, showy, garish, flashy.

6. resilient, elastic, rebounding, recoiling; buoyant, bouncy, springy; tensile, ductile; yielding, rubbery.

7. loaded, combustible, explodable, explosive, explosible, unexploded, fulminant.

8. still in use, current, latest, up-to-date, active, in the air, at hand, at issue; happening, going on, in the wind; prevailing, prevalent, in question; controversial, debatable, doubtful, moot, unsettled, lively, touchy, *Sl.* hot, *Sl.* hairy.

livelihood, *n.* **1.** maintenance, living, subsistence, keep, upkeep, support, sustenance, sustainment, sustentation, necessaries, provision; board and lodging, room and board; nourishment, nurture, nutriment, aliment, rations, fare, diet, regimen, grubstake.

2. occupation, profession, career, vocation, métier, line of work, employment, job, trade, craft, business; capacity, office, function, position, walk of life, incumbency; venture, undertaking, activity, enterprise; specialty, specialization, forte, *Inf.* racket.

liveliness, *n.* **1.** vivacity, sprightliness, animation; dynamism, energy; briskness, vitality, alacrity, nimbleness, agility, quickness, pertness; spark, fire, warmth, dash, élan, spirit, spiritedness; fervor, ardor, zeal, intensity, eagerness, enthusiasm, sanguineness; speed, celerity, promptitude; airiness, buoyancy, effervescence; sparkle, brilliance, glow.

2. gaiety, merriment, jollity; exultation, exhilaration, ecstasy; glee, mirth, joviality; pleasantry, felicity, blithesomeness; fun, sport, sportiveness, playfulness; amusement, celebration, jollification, merrymaking, festivity, jubilee; boisterousness, revelry, heyday.

livelong, *adj.* (*of time*) whole, entire, total, full, lifelong; solid, complete; undivided, unbroken; dragged-out, drawn-out, long-drawn, long-drawn-out.

lively, *adj.* **1.** alive, full of life, active, vigorous; brisk, frisky, sprightly, spry, nimble, agile, quick, pert, *Dial.* peart, yare, *Scot. and North Eng.* crouse; dynamic, animated, spirited, go-go, mettlesome; vivacious, gay, jocund, breezy, buoyant, sanguine, effervescent; *Inf.* peppy, *Inf.* chipper, *Inf.* snappy, *Inf.* up-to-date, *Sl.* jazzy, swinging; fervent, ardent, eager, intense, enthusiastic; excited, heated, hearty, zealous.

2. eventful, memorable, notable, noteworthy, remarkable, consequential; stirring, stimulating, exciting, interesting, captivating, fascinating, entertaining, curious; striking, effective, powerful, distinctive, momentous, weighty, important, critical, salient.

3. strong, keen, sharp, powerful; distinct, distinctive, clear, manifest, well-defined, palpable, recognizable; explicit, pointed, graphic, visible, trenchant, forcible.

4. vivid, bright, bright-colored, colorful, chromatic; gay, deep, gorgeous, glowing brilliant, rich; florid, showy, garish, flashy.

5. fresh, invigorating, energizing, animating, bracing; restorative, *Med.* analeptic, healthful, salubrious, wholesome.

6. resilient, elastic. See **live** (*def.* **6**).

7. astir, bustling, busy, restless; teeming, swarming, abounding, overflowing, thronged; fraught, full, rife, replete.

liven, *v.* **1.** *Often* **liven up** put life into, animate, activate, motivate, move, rouse, waken; incite, stimulate, arouse, rouse up; fire, fire up, kindle, enkindle, stir, stir up, goad, spur on, prod; boost, promote, prompt, *Inf.* spark, *Inf.* sparkplug, instigate, foment, excite, work up.

2. enliven, invigorate, energize, fortify, strengthen; encourage, inspire, inspirit, buoy, hearten, enhearten, embolden; elate, gladden, cheer, brighten, perk up, lighten, *Inf.* pep up, *Inf.* buck up; delight, exhilarate.

liver, *n.* resident, inhabitant, dweller, resider, *Law.* commorant; abider, sojourner; habitant, denizen, occupier, occupant, incumbent, tenant; lodger, renter, boarder, roomer, paying guest; householder, homesteader, lessee; villager, citizen, townsman, oppidan, burgher, burgess; indigene, native, compatriot, autochthon.

liverish, *adj.* **1.** jaundiced, yellow, yellowed, yellowish, yellow-faced, yellow-tinged, yellow-skinned; sallow, sickly, pale, wan.

2. bilious, atrabilious, spleeny, spleenful; bitter, sour, soured, *Inf.* sour as a crab apple; disagreeable, crabbed, crabby, cranky, grumpy, grouchy; surly, nasty, rude, testy, touchy, thin-skinned, irritable, choleric, irascible; sullen, sulky, morose, moody, saturnine; gloomy, melancholy, depressed, despondent, dismal, doleful, glum, dispirited.

livery, *n.* uniform, regalia, regimentals, costume, suit, habit, dress; garb, clothing, clothes, attire, apparel; raiment, garments, vestments, *Inf.* gear, *Inf.* togs, *Sl.* rags, *Sl.* threads; ensemble, outfit, *Inf.* get-up.

livestock, *n.* domestic animals, farm animals, stock; herds, droves, flocks; cattle, cows, neat, *Archaic.* kine; horses, sheep, goats, pigs.

live wire, *Slang.* *n.* dynamo, hustler, pusher, demon, hard-worker, go-getter, *Inf.* eager beaver; man of action, powerhouse, *Inf.* fireball, *Inf.* ball of fire, *Sl.* hot one, *Sl.* hot ticket; *Inf.* busy bee, doer, Stakhanovite, overdoer, workaholic, workhorse.

livid, *adj.* **1.** discolored, bruised, black and blue, purplish, bluish, *Pathol.* cyanopathic; dull blue, grayish-blue.

2. enraged, infuriated, furious, furibund, fuming, inflamed, ireful, wrathful.

3. pale, blanched, ashen, ashy, white; bloodless, drained, ghastly.

living, *adj.* **1.** alive, live, vital, breathing, viable. See **live**[2] (*def.* **1**).

2. still in use, current, latest, up-to-date; in the air, at hand, at issue; active, happening, going on, in the wind; prevailing, prevalent, in question.

3. active, strong, lively, vigorous; energetic, dynamic, spirited.

4. glowing, burning, smoldering; alight, aflame, flaming, inflamed, ignited, igneous, fiery, blazing, ablaze, afire; aglow, incandescent, candent, white-hot, red-hot.

5. (*usu. of water*) moving, flowing, fluent, profluent; streaming, coursing, rushing, swirling, circulating, revolving, fluctuating.

6. natural, native, indigenous, original.

—n. **7.** being, existing, existence, subsisting, subsistence; animation, vitality, activity, breathing, respiring, walking the earth.

8. livelihood, maintenance, subsistence; occupation, profession, career. See **livelihood** (*defs.* **1, 2**).

living room, *n.* parlor, sitting room, front room, drawing room, salon; family room, *Inf.* rec room, rumpus room, game room.

lizard, *n.* saurian, reptile, iguanid, iguana, gecko, skink, chameleon; crocodile, alligator, Gila monster, dinosaur.

load, *n.* **1.** contents, merchandise, goods, stuff; burden, charge, weight; boatload, shipload, *Chiefly U.S.* carload, wagonload, truckload; lading, *U.S. and Canada.* freight, freightage, haul.

2. burden, weight, onus, cross, millstone, albatross; duty, charge, obligation, responsibility, tax; strain, encumbrance, impediment, hindrance, handicap; trouble, care, anxiety, worry; hardship, difficulty, affliction, oppression; trial, tribulation, ordeal.

3. assignment, schedule, stint, routine; chore, job, task.

4. **loads** *Informal.* lots, numbers, scores, hordes; numerous, multitudinous, countless, quite a few, immeasurable, measureless, numberless.

5. **get a load of** *Slang.* **a.** glance, look quickly *or* briefly, cast a brief look at, glimpse, peek, peep, sneak a look *or* peek; observe, witness, view, behold, contemplate, see; pry, watch for, be on the lookout, scan; ogle, *Inf.* eye, *Inf.* eyeball, *Inf.* give [s.o.] the glad eye, look over, scrutinize, *Inf.* give the once-over; take a look at, *Inf.* have a look-see. **b.** listen, listen to, heed, prick up one's ears, give an ear to, lend an ear to, bend an ear to, be all ears, give [s.o.] one's full attention.

—v. **6.** fill, fill up, fill to the brim, fill to overflowing, overfill, stuff, overstuff, crowd, congest; lade, burden, overburden; cram, force in, ram down, pack in, push in, shove in, press in, jam, squeeze.

7. heap on *or* upon, give, assign, bestow, confer; supply, provide, burden.

8. weigh down, weight, burden, saddle with, charge, tax; encumber, cumber, impede, hamper, handicap; strain, overload, overburden, overtask, overtax, overwhelm.

9. (*all usu. of a word, statement, etc.*) overcharge, overcolor, embellish; color, tinge, imbue, impregnate.

10. **load the dice** stack the deck, fix, rig; prearrange, precontrive, predesign; put in the hole, put behind the eight ball.

—adv. **11.** **loads** a lot, much, very much, a great deal, a whole lot.

loaded, *adj.* **1.** full, filled, filled up, filled to the brim *or* to capacity, abrim, brimful, brimming; jam-packed, cram-full, shot through, chock-a-block, *Inf.* chock-full, *Brit.* chocker; stuffed, packed, crammed, crowded, solid, *Inf.* wall-to-wall; sated, satiated, gorged, glutted, cloyed.

2. containing ammunition, ready to shoot, ready to fire.

3. charged, overcharged, full of meaning.

4. *Slang.* drunk, intoxicated, inebriated, sottish, *Sl.* soused.

5. *Slang.* rich, well-to-do, wealthy, full of money, moneyed, well-off, rolling in riches, affluent, on easy street, flush, *Sl.* stinking.

loadstone, *n.* **1.** magnetite, magnetic ore; magnet, magnetic stone; attraction, pull.

2. lodestar, guide, beacon.

loaf[1], *n.* block, brick, cake, slab; lump, *Inf.* hunk, *Inf.* chunk.

loaf[2]. *v.* **1.** laze, lounge, idle, do nothing, vegetate, watch the river flow, let the grass grow under one's feet, twiddle one's thumbs, *Inf.* lallygag; lie around, lounge around, loll around, stand around, hang around, loiter around *or* about, not lift a finger, not move a muscle, take it easy, *Brit. Dial.* lollop around *or* about, *Sl.* sit on one's butt *or* duff; *Sl.* knock around *or* about, *Sl.* screw around, *Sl.* futz around; shirk, malinger, slack off, sleep at one's post, *Inf.* lie down on the job, *Inf.* goldbrick, *Sl.* featherbed, *Sl.*

goof off, *Brit. Sl.* skive, *Brit. Sl.* scrimshank.
2. pass time, wile away the hours, waste time, kill time, consume time; triffle, fritter, fool away, waste precious hours.

loafer, *n.* idler, do-nothing, slouch, sluggard, lounger, loller, fainéant, *Fr. flâneur, Brit.* layabout, *Sl.* drugstore cowboy; malinger, shirker, clock watcher, *Inf.* goldbricker, *Sl.* goof-off, *Sl.* featherbedder, *Both Brit. Sl.* skiver, scrimshanker; nonworker, drone, good-for-nothing, wastrel, ne'er-do-well, *Inf.* dead beat *Sl.* bum, *Sl.* lounge lizard; beachcomber, *Inf.* ski bum, *Inf.* surf bum, *Inf.* tennis bum; *Inf.* lazybones, lie-abed, slugabed, *Inf.* lazylegs, *Inf.* lazyboots.

loaferish, *adj.* **1.** lazy, idle, indolent, slothful, fainéant, do-nothing, otiose; unindustrious, unenterprising, unambitious, nonaggressive; shiftless, worthless, good-for-nothing, ne'er-do-well; lackadaisical, listless, *Dial.* limpsy; insouciant, carefree, easy-going, pococurante.
2. slow-moving, slow-going, creeping, crawling, *Inf.* poky; loitering, lagging, dillydallying, foot-dragging; stagnant, inert, torpid, supine, inactive; sluggish, lethargic, phlegmatic, dull, logy.

loam, *n.* clay, sand, clay loam, sandy loam, silt loam; mud, silt, earth, ground, soil, fertile *or* rich soil.

loan, *n.* **1.** lending, advancing, loaning, moneylending; usury, *Sl.* loan-sharking, *Sl.* shylocking.
2. advance, allowance, accomodation; credit; (*in World War II*) lend-lease.
—*v.* **3.** lend, advance, allow, credit, accommodate, *Sl.* push; (*in World War II*) lend-lease.

loan shark, *n. Informal.* usurer, Shylock, moneylender, moneymonger; extortionist, extortioner, shakedown artist, blood-sucker, *Sl.* bleeder, leech; exacter, wrester.

loath, *adj.* reluctant, unwilling, disinclined, indisposed, averse, not in the mood, *Sl.* not into, *Sl.* not psyched.

loathe, *v.* **1.** abhor, abominate, execrate, detest, despise; hate, feel an aversion to, feel hostile toward, not be able to bear *or* abide, shudder at, shrink from, recoil from, blench from; contempt, scorn, anathematize, misprize; dislike, disrelish.
2. feel repugnance toward, feel disgust toward, feel distaste for, have no stomach *or* use *or* taste for, be unable to stomach, sicken at.

loathing, *n.* **1.** abhorrence, execration, hate, hatred, abomination, odium, detestation, rancor, hostility, inimicalness, aversion, antipathy; enmity, contumely, virulence, rankling, ill will, bad blood, grudge, bitterness.
2. repugnance, revulsion, repulsion; disgust, distaste.

loathly, *adv.* reluctantly, unwillingly, aversely, resistingly, resistantly; hesitantly, hesitatingly, shyly, haltingly, slowly, laggardly, sluggishly, unhurriedly, unhurryingly.

loathsome, *adj.* **1.** abhorrent, abominable, execrable, odious, heinous, anathematic, detestable, despicable, invidious, atrocious, hateful, *Rare.* loathful; dislikable, unlikable, insufferable, unendurable, unbearable, intolerable.
2. repulsive, repellent, noisome, offensive, annoying, revolting, atrocious, obnoxious, deplorable, repugnant, disgusting, rank, disagreeable; distasteful, unpalatable, sickening, nauseating, nauseous; vile, rank, reprehensible, contemptible, scornful; ugly, horrid, horrible, base.

lob, *v.* loft, hit *or* throw aloft, lift; throw, toss, chuck, fling; flip, shy, skip, skim; pitch, heave, hurl, hurtle.

lobby, *n.* **1.** corridor, passage, passageway, hall, hallway, entrance, entranceway, entry, entrée, entryway, entrance hall, foyer; vestibule, antechamber, anteroom, waiting room, reception room.
2. pressure group, interest group, lobbyists, solicitors, representatives, agents.
—*v.* **3.** influence, affect, pull strings *or* wires, throw one's weight around; sway, persuade, move, talk into; urge, press, push *or* push for, promote.

lobe, *n.* lobule, *Anat.* lobus, *Anat.* lobulus, division; projection, protuberance, tubercle, knob, node, nodule; knot, lump, bump.

lobed, *adj.* lobate, lobulate, lobulated, nodulous, nodulose; tubercular, nodular, rounded, knoblike, knobby.

local, *adj.* **1.** positional, locational, spatial, situational.
2. provincial, parochial, municipal, regional, sectional, divisional, territorial; county, district, town, city; neighborhood, small-town, red-brick.
3. home, homemade, homespun; native, indigenous, autochthonous, aboriginal; domestic, popular, vernacular, topical.
4. near, close, nigh, proximate, approximate; nearby, adjacent, close by, neighboring; adjoining, surrounding, circumjacent, contiguous; in the area, at hand, accessible.
5. limited, circumscribed, confined, restricted, delimited; particular, fixed, specific, special, definite, exact.
—*n.* **6.** local person, local inhabitant, towner, *Sl.* townie, city man; *Inf.* local yokel, cockney, resident, townsman, oppidan, parishioner; native, aborigine, autochthone.

locale, *n.* **1.** place, spot, site; quarter, zone, neighborhood. See **locality.**
2. scene, setting, stage, set; background, backdrop, ground; theater, arena.

localism, *n.* **1.** (*all of a particular area*) dialect, patois, idiom, folk dialect, subdialect; provincialism, regionalism, colloquialism, slang; accent, twang, brogue, drawl, burr.
2. (*all of a particular area*) habit, tradition, institution, law, usage; custom, observance, practice, fashion, way.

locality, *n.* **1.** place, locale, site, situs, stead, *Latin. locus, Fr. lieu*; sport, point, position, *Law.* venue, scene of the crime, scene, setting; quarter, zone, pale, area, division; region, territory, realm, province, shire, county; neighborhood, district, bailiwick, section, precinct, township; diocese, parish, ward, bishopric; neck of the woods, backyard, home; ground, terrain, soil, *Sl.* turf; habitat, environment, climate, clime, domain, abode, range.
2. vicinity, vicinage, environs, purlieus, whereabouts, hereabouts; field, demesne, station, circuit, beat, orbit.

localize, *v.* **1.** restrict, confine, contain, restrain, constrain, fix in; surround, bound, limit, compass, encompass, encircle, circumscribe; cut off, hem in, pen in, delimit, quarantine.
2. specify, pinpoint, narrow down, zero in on; particularize, differentiate, identify, individualize.

locally, *adv.* around here, in these parts, hereabouts, in this spot, in *or* around town, in the neighborhood, in the vicinity; nearby, around the corner, close, close-by, close at hand, within walking distance.

locate, *v.* **1.** discover, find, uncover, unearth; come across, run across, stumble upon, stub one's toe on, lay *or* put one's finger *or* hands on; meet with, bump into, light upon, alight upon, happen upon, chance upon, hit upon; track down, worm out, hunt down, ferret out, fish out, sniff out, smell out; reveal, expose, disclose, bring to light, root up *or* out, turn up; detect, discern, descry, spot, espy; get at, reach, determine.

2. establish, fix, set, base, ensconce; settle, place, situate, position, pinpoint, seat, collocate, assign; set down, lay down, park; quarter, house, reposit, deposit; consign, localize, post, station.

3. reside, occupy, move in, settle, take up one's quarters *or* abode; take root, cast anchor, anchor, pitch camp, camp, bivouac, pitch one's tent; put up at, set up housekeeping, keep house, take up residence; squat, plant, moor, dock; perch, roost, nest, *Inf.* hang up one's hat, make one's house; set up shop, *Inf.* hang up one's shingle, set up in business.

location, *n.* **1.** residence, settlement, base, colony; quarter, zone, pale, area, division; region, territory, realm, province, shire, county, bailiwick; neighborhood, district, section, precinct, township; diocese, parish, ward, bishopric; neck of the woods, backyard, home; ground, terrain, soil, *Sl.* turf; habitat, environment, climate, clime, domain, abode, range; vicinity, vicinage, environs, purlieus, whereabouts, hereabouts.

2. place, situation, position, emplacement, site, seat, stead; spot, point, bearings, latitude and longitude; scene, *Law.* venue, *Latin. locus, Fr. lieu.*

3. placement, localization, emplacement, placing, positioning; disposition, assignment, collocation, deposition, reposition; locating, pinpointing, centering; establishment, situation, settling, colonization; installation, lodgment, fixation, investiture.

4. discovery, finding, uncovery, unearthing; exposure, disclosure, revelation; detection, descrial, discernment, recognition, determination, espial, spotting.

lock[1], *n.* **1.** bolt, latch, hook, holdfast, padlock; hasp, pin, peg, bar; fastener, clasp, securer, clincher.

2. catch, ratchet, pawl, brake; safety, safety catch, safety lock, cutoff; (*in a firearm*) gunlock, discharger, exploder.

3. sluice, sluice gate, gate, penstock, water gate, valve, *Civ. Eng.* floodgate.

—*v.* **4.** *Sometimes* **lock up** bolt, latch, hook, padlock; hasp, bar, throw the pin; fasten, clasp, secure, seal.

5. *Often* **lock up** confine, shut in *or* up *or* off, close off, seal off, clap up, cage, coop up, pen in, wall in, fence in, rail in, pale, picket, corral, enclose, trap; imprison, jail, incarcerate, impound, embar, immure, bolt up, place *or* keep under lock and key, put behind bars, *Sl.* run in, *Sl.* jug, *Sl.* lag; shackle, manacle, handcuff, put in irons.

6. interlock, interlink, intertwine, entwine, entangle, bear, *Mech.* engage; join, conjoin, unite, league, attach, connect, link, yoke, brace, couple, marry, bind, lash, tie together, cinch, truss, girdle, gird, pin, pinion, hogtie, *Naut.* seize; bond, seal, graft, weld, glue, cement, solder, mortise, *Metallurgy.* braze; fuse, set, immobilize, freeze up, lock up, jam.

7. clasp, clutch, grip, grasp, shake hands; hug, embrace, hold, grapple, wrestle, gripe, squeeze, *Both Boxing.* clinch, clench.

8. **lock out** bar, debar, shut out, close out; exclude, keep out, ostracize, exile, banish, excommunicate.

lock[2], *n.* **1.** tress, curl, ringlet, curlicue, lovelock, elflock; plait, braid, shock.

2. **locks** curls, ringlets, tresses; hair, bangs, crime, *Sl.* mane, *Sl.* mop.

3. flock, tuft, bunch *or* piece of wool *or* fur.

lockbox, *n.* **1.** strongbox, safe, vault, coffer, money box, treasure chest, treasury, repository; trunk, chest, case, casket, crate, coffret, locker.

2. mailbox, post box, box, postal *or* post office box, bin, hold, receptacle, *Chiefly Brit.* letter box; cubicle, compartment, pigeonhole, cubbyhole, cubby, niche, nook.

locker, *n.* **1.** trunk, footlocker, chest, storage chest, case, casket, crate, coffret, *Brit. Inf.* lockup; closet, cabinet, carrel, carol, cage, cell, booth, stall, bay, cubicle, compartment; lockbox, strongbox, safe, vault, coffer, money box, treasure chest, treasury, repository.

2. freezer, cooler, refrigerator, ice box, *Inf.* fridge, *Trademark.* Frigidaire; storeroom, storage room, cellar, cellerage, buttery, larder.

lockup, *n.* jail, jailhouse, station house, police station, *Inf.* clink, *Inf.* calaboose, *Scot.* tollbooth, *Brit. Inf.* bridewell, *All Sl.* can, cooler, coop, jug, hoosegow, drunk tank, booby hatch, poky, *Brit.* choky, *Brit.* quod; guardhouse, guardroom, brig; prison, penitentiary, penal institution, house of correction, house of detention, reformatory, *Sl.* big house, *Sl.* slammer, *Sl.* stir; patrol wagon, police wagon, *Sl.* paddy wagon.

locomotion, *n.* movement, motion, action, progression; traveling, moving, stepping, striding, walking, jogging, running, run.

locution, *n.* expression, phrase, idiom, metaphor, simile, *Rhet.* trope; word, term, saying, turn of speech; wording, phrasing, phraseology, choice of words; language, dialect, *Linguistics.* idiolect, accent, patois, brogue; diction, style.

lodestar, *n.* **1.** polestar, North Star, *Astron.* Polaris.

2. guide, beacon, signal, sign; direction, directory, mark, landmark, indicator, pointer.

lodge, *n.* **1.** shelter, habitation; cabin, hut; hunting house; summer cottage; resort hotel.

2. (*all of American Indians*) wigwam, tent, tepee, wickiup, *Navaho.* hogan, *Eskimo.* igloo.

3. (*all of animals*) den, lair, cave, excavation, dugout, hole, furrow; nest, aerie, nidus, rookery; haunt, retreat, refuge, mew, shelter.

—*v.* **4.** reside, live, abide, *Archaic.* bide, dwell; sojourn, stay, tarry, remain; room, bunk, tenant; quarter, take up quarters, settle, be settled, keep house, establish oneself, plant oneself, put down stakes, anchor; pitch tent, encamp, bivouac; nestle, roost, perch, burrow, tabernacle, put up at, *Sl.* hole up.

5. quarter, house, furnish with lodgings, board, put up, billet, bed down, roof, take in; shelter, harbor, shield, protect, guard.

6. deposit, place, put, reposit, bank; file, set, lay, cache, park, station, stow; transmit, entrust, vest, consign, transfer, deliver over.

7. house, contain, encase, enclose; shield, sheathe.

lodger, *n.* roomer, tenant, occupant, renter, lessee; guest, paying guest, boarder; inmate, incumbent.

lodgment, *n.* **1.** boarding, lodging, quartering, housing, sheltering.

2. accumulation, collection, aggregation, compilation, assemblage, accretion, profusion, conglomeration; amassing, gathering, hoarding; pile, stock, stockpile, heap, bulk, fund; harvest, garner, store, reserve, supply, quantity, accruement.

3. lodgings, lodging place, diggings, *Inf.* digs, rooms, quarters, chambers, *Inf.* pad; abode, home, domicile, address, apartment, dwelling, residence.

loft, *n.* upper level, attic, garret, mansard, cockloft; gallery, balcony; hayloft.

lofty, *adj.* **1.** towering, skyscraping, elevated,

high, soaring, sky-high, aerial, aloft; distant, remote, faraway, far-reaching; skyward, heavenly, celestial, empyreal, supernal.

2. grand, distinguished, noted, eminent, famous, well-known, celebrated, esteemed; renowned, illustrious, prominent, predominant, leading, preeminent, notable, *Archaic.* eximious; legendary, immortal, fabled, memorable; honorable, venerable, revered, respected; dignified, distinguished, stately, august; sublime, exalted, magnificent, majestic, imposing, imperious; lordly, noble, kingly, queenly, imperial, princely, magisterial; aristocratic, patrician, well-bred, genteel, gentle, blue-blooded, thoroughbred.

3. arrogant, haughty, proud, self-important, vainglorious, peacockish; overconfident, overweening, conceited, high-and-mighty, snobbish, *Inf.* snotty, *Inf.* snooty, *Inf.* stuck up, *Inf.* uppish, *Inf.* uppity, on one's high horse; pompous, inflated, puffed up, egotistic, condescending, *Inf.* toplofty; disdainful, supercilious, cavalier, contemptuous, scornful, insulting, contumelious.

log, *n.* **1.** (*all of wood*) trunk, limb, branch; stump, block, chunk, piece; pole, beam, puncheon.

2. record, account, register, chart, tally, logbook; journal, diary, daybook.

—*v.* **3.** (*all of trees*) cut down, chop down, bring down, hew, fell, drop; raze, level.

4. record, register, report, set down, chart; book, note, keep an account, keep a journal; jot down, make a note of; tally, tabulate, compile, amass, catalog.

5. travel, go, traverse, cover.

loggerhead, *n.* **1.** blockhead, dunce, lunkhead, bonehead, knucklehead; fool, tomfool, dope, nincompoop, lightweight. See **blockhead.**

2. at loggerheads quarreling, wrangling, bickering, squabbling; contending, feuding, estranged, on the outs; on the warpath, at each other's throats, at swords' points; opposed, at odds, at variance.

logging, *n.* lumbering, lumberjacking, woodcutting, woodchopping.

logic, *n.* **1.** science of reasoning, dialectics, symbolic logic, logistic; polemics, art of disputation *or* controversy.

2. reasoning, argumentation, ratiocination, process of reasoning; *Logic.* inference, *Logic.* deduction, *Logic.* induction, syllogization, syllogistic reasoning, synthesis, method of reasoning; chain *or* course *or* line of reasoning, argument, rationale, rationalization, explanation.

3. reason, sound judgment, good sense, presence of mind, foresight, wisdom; sense, *Inf.* brains, *Sl.* smarts, common sense, *Inf.* horse sense.

logical, *adj.* **1.** logistic, logistical; deductive, inductive, inferential; syllogistic, syllogistical, ratiocinative.

2. reasonable, rational, sound, sensible; smart, intelligent, wise, judicious, equitable.

logician, *n.* reasoner, dialectician, ratiocinator, logistician, syllogizer, casuist, *Gk. Hist.* sophist.

logistics, *n.* strategy, stratagems, plan *or* plans, tactics, strategics, maneuvers, moves; engineering, orchestration, coordination, masterminding; management, conducting, direction, *Inf.* quarterbacking, superintendence, supervision, oversight, handling, running, execution.

logjam, *n.* jam, bottleneck, tie-up, traffic jam, *Fr. embouteillage*, conjestion, clog, blockage, stoppage, *C.B. Radio.* parking lot.

logo, *n.* logotype, trademark, design, figure; trade name, manufacturer's *or* company name; *Journalism.* nameplate, masthead; letterhead, seal, stamp, mark, symbol.

logy, *adj.* sluggish, phlegmatic, lethargic, lethargical, dull, sleepy, sleeping, drowsy, hebetudinous; laggard, slow, slow-moving, thick, heavy; indolent, supine, slothful, lazy, laid-back, fainéant, idle; languid, languorous, listless, lackadaisical, apathetic, indifferent, impassive; spiritless, lifeless, passive, inactive, inanimate, inert; insensible, torpid, dormant, stupefied, stuporous, narcose, drugged, comatose.

loin, *n.* **1.** flank, (*of mutton, venison, etc.*) saddle.

2. *Chiefly Literary.* **loins** sexual *or* physical prowess, strength, potency, virility, manliness, power, courage, hardiness, stamina, thews; reproductive organs, genitalia, private parts.

3. gird one's loins prepare, arm, ready, make ready; (*all of oneself*) brace, steel, fortify.

loiter, *v.* **1.** linger, tarry, stay, wait, remain, *Sl.* hang around, *Sl.* stick around; continue, persist, stay on, endure, abide, persevere, hang on.

2. loll, idle, *Inf.* lallygag, lounge, poke, dally, dillydally; slouch, loaf, vegetate, waste time, *Inf.* diddle, procrastinate, fritter time away; dawdle, take one's time *or* one's own sweet time, kill time; mill around, trifle, potter, putter, play.

3. saunter, stroll, perambulate; amble, ramble, mosey; traipse, wander, *Sl.* mooch, meander, inch; shuffle, shamble, slouch.

loll, *v.* **1.** lounge, *Brit. Dial.* lollop, rest, lie on, lie around, recline on, lean on, repose on; sprawl, slump, flop, slouch; languish, vegetate, doze; loaf, loiter, take it easy, relax, not worry about anything.

2. dangle, hang, hang down, depend, droop, sag; drag, draggle, trail; swing, sway, oscillate, vibrate.

lone, *adj.* **1.** alone, solitary, by oneself, *Scot.* waff; unaccompanied, unattended, companionless; sole, single, individual; apart, cut off, separated, separate, isolated.

2. lonesome, lonely, friendless, unfriended, forlorn, bereft, forsaken; abandoned, deserted, derelict, desolate.

3. mateless, wifeless, husbandless; unmarried, widowed, divorced, separated; unattached.

lonely, *adj.* **1.** lone, sole, single, individual; apart, cut off, separate, separated, isolated; solitary, unaccompanied, companionless, unattended, *Scot.* waff.

2. alone, lonesome, friendless, unfriended, unsocial, unsociable; retiring, reclusive, withdrawn, *Inf.* introverted, hermitlike, hermetical, monastic, monachal, eremitical, eremitic, anchoritic, stylitic, troglodytic.

3. estranged, alienated, outcast, forlorn, forsaken, bereft, abandoned, deserted, homeless; unwanted, unwelcomed, rejected, unpopular, unliked, disliked.

4. unfrequented, unvisited, unpopulated, unpeopled, uninhabited, desolate, barren; out of the way, obscure, insular, in a backwater; remote, set apart, secluded, solitudinous, recluse, sequestered, cloistered, hidden, concealed, private.

loner, *n.* **1.** isolate, isolato, solitary, solitudinarian, *Inf.* introvert, *Inf.* lone wolf; stay-at-home, homebody; recluse, hermit, anchorite, eremite, *Islam.* marabout, *Islam.* santon; nun, anchoress, hermitess, *Obs.* hermitress; troglodyte, cave dweller, incluse; stylite, pillarist.

2. nonconformist, individualist, outsider, alien, *Sl.* freak; outcast, pariah, Ishmael.

lonesome, *adj.* **1.** lonely, friendless, unfriended, companionless, by oneself; alone, all alone, without a friend in the world, with no one to turn to; alienated, apart, cut off, without ties; unwanted, unwelcomed, rejected, unpopular, unliked, disliked; estranged, outcast, forlorn, forsaken, bereft, abandoned, deserted, homeless.

2. (*all for want of companionship*) sad, depressed, melancholy, maudlin, *Inf.* down, *Inf.* down in the dumps, *Inf.* blue, *Inf.* low. See **sad.**

3. remote, desolate, barren; unfrequented, unvisited, unpopulated, untraveled, unpeopled, uninhabited; out of the way, obscure, insular, in a backwater; set apart, secluded, recluse, solitudinous, sequestered, hidden, concealed; eerie, ghostly, *Inf.* scary.

long[1], *adj.* **1.** extensive, extended, expanded, expansive; broad, wide, widespread, spread out, outspread, stretched out, outstretched.

2. lengthy, protracted, prolonged, elongated, elongate, sustained; longish, overlong, long-drawn, long-drawn-out, marathon; drawn out, dragged out, spun out, strung out; interminable, without end.

3. verbose, wordy, prolix, long-winded, tedious, boring; discursive, digressive, rambling, wandering; diffuse, diffusive, garrulous, loquacious, voluble.

4. **before long** soon, before you know it, any minute now, in a minute, presently, shortly, in a short time *or* while.

5. **the long and short of** sum and substance, better part, gist, crux; core, nucleus, kernel, pith.

long[2], *v.* desire, wish for, long for, desiderate, want; yearn for, hope for, care for, pine for, sigh for; hanker after, have a yen for, covet, fancy, have a fancy for; have an eye to, be attracted to, have a mind to, have at heart, be bent upon; be inclined towards, be prone to, be predisposed towards, prefer; aspire to, set one's sights on, set one's heart on, dream of; crave, hunger, thirst, relish; lust after, burn for, *Inf.* be wild *or* mad about, *Sl.* have the hots for, *Inf.* letch after, lust after.

long-drawn, *adj.* **1.** prolonged, protracted, lengthy, long, longsome, overlong. See **long[1]** (*def.* **2**).

2. long-winded, windy, long-spun, copious; repetitious, redundant, battological, pleonastic, tautologic; meandering, roundabout, circumlocutory, ambagious; verbose, wordy, prolix, tedious, long. See **long[1]** (*def.* **3**).

longevity, *n.* **1.** long life; life span, lifetime, length *or* duration of life.

2. seniority, tenure, length of service.

longhair, *n.* **1.** *Informal.* intellectual, academician, scholar, schoolman, philosopher, philosophe, theorist, thinker, thinking man *or* woman; one of the cognoscenti, one of the intelligentsia, aesthete, connoisseur; pundit, expert, authority; (*all sometimes disparaging*) pedant, bookworm, highbrow, *Inf.* egghead, *Inf.* know-it-all, *Inf.* walking encyclopedia.

2. *Informal.* hippie, *Sl.* freak, yippie, flower child; nonconformist, original, dissenter, protester, dropout; Bohemian, beatnik.

long-headed, *adj.* far-sighted, foresighted, far-seeing, prescient, anticipatory; wise, sagacious, shrewd, acute, discerning; astute, perceptive, clear-eyed, penetrating; keen, sharp, acute, quick; knowing, aware, sensitive; alert, quick-witted, bright, smart, clever, subtle; sensible, thoughtful, provident, prudent, discreet, judicious, cautious, watchful.

longing, *n.* wish, wishing, desire, desideration, want, wanting; yearning, hope, hoping, pining, sighing; hankering, *Inf.* yen, *Sl.* itch, fondness, liking, attraction; aspiration, ambition; inclination, predilection, preference, propensity, proclivity; predisposal, predisposedness, bent, leaning; fancy, fancying, coveting, covetousness, eagerness, ardor, craving; appetency, appetite, hunger, thirst, ravenousness; relish, rapaciousness, voracity, voraciousness; avidity, greed, greediness, cupidity, avarice.

long-lived, *adj.* **1.** longevous, macrobiotic; old, old as Methuselah, elderly, centenarian, nonagenarian, octogenarian.

2. long-lasting, durable, lasting, enduring.

longstanding, *adj.* long-established, established, fixed, ingrained, rooted, inveterate; venerable, hallowed, hoary, time-honored, immemorial; durable, lasting, enduring, abiding; long-lasting, of long duration.

long-suffering, *adj.* **1.** longanimous, forbearing, suffering, patient, patient as Job; uncomplaining, stoical; lenient, indulgent, permissive, tolerant, condoning; magnanimous, forgiving, charitable, exorable, placable.

—*n.* **2.** longanimity, forbearance, sufferance, patience; stoicism, fortitude, self-control; lenience, indulgence, permissiveness, tolerance, condonation; magnanimity, forgivingness, charitableness; lenity, mildness, gentleness, clemency, mercifulness, ruthfulness, humaneness, humanity.

long-winded, *adj.* **1.** verbose, prolix, garrulous, wordy, longiloquent, *Inf.* windy; diffuse, discursive, digressive, maundering, rambling, wandering, roving, aimless; circumlocutory, roundabout, ambagious.

2. extended, protracted, prolonged, lengthened, drawn-out, long-drawn-out, spun-out, dragged-out, stretched-out; long, lengthy, overlong, too long, interminable, unending, never-ending, endless, everlasting, unrelenting; redundant, repetitious, repetitive, battological, pleonastic, tautological, *Inf.* broken-record.

look, *v.* **1.** see, visualize, behold, notice, take in; bend the eye, cock the eye, fix the eye, fix one's gaze, focus, rivet one's eyes; regard, study, inspect, take stock of; examine, contemplate, pore over, *Rare.* perlustrate; review, check out, overlook, monitor; peruse, read, scan, run the eyes over, scrutinize, *Inf.* give the once-over; view, survey, scout, sweep, reconnoiter; watch, observe, witness.

2. glance, glimpse, take a look at, have a look-see, give a look; gaze, peer, ogle, leer, stare, goggle; *Obs.* squinny, gape, gawk, *Archaic.* gloat; squint, blink, wink, *Sl.* take a gander; spy, peep, peek, steal a glance at; glare, glower, look down at, look daggers, scowl, stare down.

3. appear, seem, seem to be, look to be, have the look of; sound, strike one as, have every appearance of; have every indication of; look like, seem like, sound like, appear like, resemble, have the earmarks of.

4. face, overlook, look out on, look towards; front, front on, look over; give out on, open out on.

5. **look after** **a.** pay attention to, heed, mark, mind, reck, watch one's step; concern oneself with, see to, take pains to. **b.** take care of, care for, take charge of, mind, baby-sit, sit with; chaperon, keep tabs on, *Brit.* play gooseberry, keep under observation, spy on, keep an eye on; minister to, nurse, succor, attend to, tend to, serve.

6. **look back** review, recall, bring to mind, recollect; reflect, muse, brood, ponder, ruminate, mull over; return in thought, reminisce, be retrospective; conjure up, summon up, call to mind, hark back to, dredge up.

7. **look down on** *or* **upon** disdain, contemn, hold in contempt, misprize; despise, loathe, scorn, turn one's nose up at, disparage; look askance, look asquint, look down one's nose, turn one's back on, *Inf.* pooh-pooh.

8. **look for** **a.** seek, search, pursue, hunt for, go for; look around for, cast around for, poke around for, forage. **b.** anticipate, expect, look to, watch for, keep in view; reckon upon, count on, calculate on, pin hope on, prepare oneself for, be in readiness for.

9. **look forward to** anticipate, await, wait for, be unable to wait for; envisage, envision, look ahead, foresee, see ahead.

10. **look into** investigate, explore, poke into, dig into,

delve into; examine, probe, fathom, plumb; inquire into, ask about, search into, go into, *Archaic.* indagate, research.

11. look on *or* **upon** **a.** watch, *Obs.* spectate, witness, observe, eye, view, take in. **b.** consider, deem, regard, reckon, judge, opine; hold, think, reason, speculate, see, take.

12. look out be on guard, be alert, be wary, be vigilant; watch out, keep one's eyes peeled, keep an eye out, keep one's eyes open.

13. look over examine, inspect, check, monitor, proctor; run through, dash through, zip through, flip through; peruse, scan, speed-read.

14. look to **a.** see to, not forget, attend to, do, make sure to do; give mind to, pay attention to, advert to, give thought to, devote oneself to. **b.** turn to, refer to, resort to, have recourse to, betake oneself to; revert to, fall back on, avail oneself of, make use of.

15. look up **a.** search for, run down, seek out, hunt up, track down; ransack, rummage, ferret through. **b.** visit, pay a visit to, call upon, drop in on, go to see, look in on. **c.** improve, ameliorate, shape up, progress, gain; perk up, pick up, show improvement, make headway; come along, get better, grow better, make strides.

16. look up to esteem, admire, regard highly, think highly of, think well of; hold in admiration, have a high opinion of, revere, defer to; honor, extol, exalt, venerate, put on a pedestal; idolize, worship, adore, lionize.

—n. **17.** glance, glimpse, side glance, regard; squint, glint, blink, wink, *Fr. coup d'oeil*; ogle, leer, stare, gaze, come-hither look; dirty look, scowl, glower, glare, evil eye, *It. malocchio*; peek, peep, flash.

18. sight, espial, first sight; inspection, search, examination, *Inf.* once-over, *Inf.* look-see, *Sl.* the eye, *Sl.* gander; scrutiny, contemplation, inquiry, autopsy; survey, sweep, reconnaisance, observation, observance, watch; review, overlook, oversight, bird's-eye view; preview, view, prospect, pre-examination.

19. aspect, appearance, expression, looks, air, hang; guise, front, facade, impression, effect; demeanor, mien, stance, posture, bearing; set, figure, cut, trim, build, frame; side, profile, shape, outline; complexion, visage, physiognomy, countenance, color, feature; semblance, resemblance, seeming, likeness, similarity, similitude, hint, fashion.

look-alike, *n.* double, twin, identical twin, clone, living *or* very image, exact match; perfect likeness, *Sl.* ringer, *Sl.* dead ringer, *Inf.* spit and image *or* spitting image, chip off the old block; replica, copy, duplicate, facsimile, reproduction, ectype.

looker, *n.* **1.** seer, observer, spectator, onlooker, looker-on; witness, eyewitness, passerby; watcher, gazer, ogler, goggler, gaper, beholder, girl-watcher.

2. *Slang.* belle, good-looking woman, beauty, raving beauty, picture, vision, sight for sore eyes; *Sl.* doll, *Sl.* dish, *Inf.* knockout, peach, dazzler, charmer.

lookout, *n.* **1.** watch, guard, vigil, wake.

2. sentinel, sentry, guard, watchman; ranger, forest ranger.

3. lookout station, lookout tower, ranger's station, firetower, watchtower, guard tower.

loom, *v.* **1.** emerge, appear, become visible, come into view *or* notice, uprise,come to light, come to the fore; materialize, surface, reveal itself, show itself.

2. tower, rise, mount, soar, ascend; hover, bulk.

3. impend, threaten, menace, hang over.

loony, *adj.* **1.** *Slang.* lunatic, insane, crazy, crazed, *Sl.* kooky, *Scot.* doiled, mad, demented; daft, *Inf.* daffy, crackbrained, *Inf.* nutty; peculiar, *Inf.* dotty, strange, odd; *All Sl.* barmy, dippy, batty, cuckoo, buggy, screwy, wacky, goofy; weak-minded, simple, simple-minded, birdbrained; featherheaded, feebleminded, dim-witted, half-witted.

—n. **2.** *Slang.* lunatic, crackpot, *Sl.* nut, *Sl.* kook, maniac, madman, psychotic; dimwit, nitwit, half-wit, featherbrain, pinhead, simpleton.

loop, *n.* **1.** noose, bow, circle, ring, hoop; spiral, helix, convolution, whorl, coil, curl, twirl; arc, arch, curve, bend.

—v. **2.** roll, furl, coil, wind; spiral, twirl, curl, curlicue, twist, kink; arc, arch, curve, bend, round, turn.

3. circle, encircle, ring, hoop, wreathe, enwreathe; surround, encompass, gird, girdle; embrace, span, belt.

loose, *adj.* **1.** unbound, untied, unchained, unshackled, unfettered, untrammeled; unlocked, unlatched, unfastened; unclasped, unhooked, unattached, untied; unpinned, unbuttoned; unconnected, disconnected, detached, floating; insecure, infirm, unsteady.

2. inaccurate, inexact, roundabout, imprecise, unprecise, unmeticulous, unrigorous; unconscientious, unfussy, unpunctilious; nonspecific, broad, general, amorphous, vague, indefinite, indecisive; random, inchoate, disordered, chaotic, hit-or-miss, desultory.

3. lax, dissolute, licentious, libertine, lascivious, debauched, dissipated, wasted, rakish, rakehell; lecherous, lubricous, goatish; concupiscent, prurient, lustful, libidinous, salacious; indecent, dirty, foul, indelicate; wanton, wild, profligate, abandoned, unrestrained, uncurbed; promiscuous, whorish, of easy virtue, unchaste, impure; coarse, gross, crude; degenerate, corrupt, perverted; wicked, nefarious, flagitious; immoral, sinful, peccant, vice-ridden; unregenerate, unprincipled, shameless, unscrupulous; reprobate, shameful, disgraceful, worthless; notorious, infamous, scandalous, disreputable.

4. slack, hanging, drooping, droopy, bagging, baggy, sagging, saggy, flapping, *Inf.* floppy; limp, *Dial.* limpsy, flabby, flaccid; shaky, rickety; dangling, streaming.

5. free, unconfined, at liberty, at large, on the loose; freed, liberated, released, let out, let go.

6. remiss, neglectful, negligent; disorderly, sloppy, untiddy, *Inf.* messy; unorganized, casual, slapdash, slipshod, offhand, *Inf.* harum-scarum; casual, indifferent, perfunctory, devil-may-care; lackadaisical, listless; free and easy, untroubled, unconcerned, unworried, happy-go-lucky, *Inf.* loose as a goose.

7. moderate, mellow, undemanding, lenient, tolerant, indulgent, forbearing; careless, easy, unexacting, offhand, *Inf.* wishy-washy.

8. unregulated, ungoverned, unrestricted, unimpeded, unhampered, laissez-faire, no-holds-barred, catch-as-catch-can; unqualified, unconditioned, unconditional, no-strings-attached.

9. uninhibited, relaxed, informal, unceremonious, unreserved, unconstrained; open, candid, frank, sincere, outspoken, free-spoken; bold, brash, audacious; indecent, improper, intemperate, immoderate, incontinent.

10. on the loose free, unconfined, on the run, at liberty; fled, flown, at large, scot-free; running for cover, escaping, fleeing, on the lam, escaped, runaway.

11. break loose escape, run off, flee, get away, make good one's escape, gain one's liberty, run for one's life, take to one's heels, *Inf.* make tracks, *Inf.* make a getaway; get out, *Inf.* bail out, *Sl.* bust loose; *Sl.* fly the coop, break out, break jail, escape from confinement *or* prison.

12. cast loose loosen, unloosen, unfasten, undo, unhitch, detach, disengage, unattach, set adrift, cast off, weigh anchor.

13. **cut loose** a. leave, quit, depart, become free *or* independent, cut the knot *or* apron strings, *Sl.* split. b. celebrate, carry on, blow *or* let off steam, abandon restraint, let go, let one's hair down, *Inf.* cut up, *Inf.* fool *or* horse around, *Inf.* raise Cain, *Inf.* have a good time, *Inf.* raise the dead, *Inf.* cut capers, *Sl.* go hog-wild.

14. **let loose** emit, break out, burst out with, give out with, shout, yell, give a whoop, *Inf.* hoot and holler; sing, bellow, explode.

—*v.* 15. free, release, let go, set at liberty; liberate, emancipate, manumit; let loose, set loose, turn loose.

16. loosen, untie, unbind, unfetter, unshackle, unchain; disengage, disencumber, disentangle, extricate; undo, unpin, let fall; unhook, unclasp, unbuckle, unbutton, unsnap; unlace, unstrap, unscrew, unstick, unglue; unfasten, unfix.

17. relax, moderate, mellow, make less strict, slacken, ease, soften; mitigate, extenuate, ameliorate, attenuate, weaken; reduce, diminish, lessen.

18. shoot, discharge, fire off, eject; catapult, hurl, throw out, project.

loosen, *v.* 1. slacken, slack, untighten, relieve tension, *Obs.* slake; relax, ease up *or* off.

2. remit, mitigate, assuage, allay, relieve, alleviate, palliate; mollify, moderate, modify, temper, subdue, chasten, soften, weaken, tone down; abate, reduce, diminish, lessen, lighten, attenuate, wane; decrease, decline, subside, recede, ebb, lull; yield, submit, give in.

3. unfasten, unhook, undo, unfix, detach; disengage, disunite, disjoin, disconnect, unpin, unstick, unglue; separate, part, divide, sunder, sever, break apart.

4. unbind, untie, unfetter, unshackle, unchain, unhandcuff, unbridle, unyoke, unmuzzle, *Archaic.* untruss; release, loose, disenthrall, extricate, free, liberate; set free, set loose, let loose, turn loose, let go, unpen, unmew, disimprison; emancipate, manumit, enfranchise, affranchise, franchise; deliver, rescue, ransom, redeem, *Theol.* save.

5. disperse, scatter, dispel, dissipate, break up, disintegrate, disseminate, spread out.

looseness, *n.* 1. slackness, laxity, laxness, carelessness, heedlessness, mindlessness, inattention; relaxation, loosening, offhandedness, casualness, easiness, indifference, nonconcern, insouciance; neglect, negligence, remissness, dereliction, unrigorousness, noninterference, laissez faire, nonrestriction; nonobservance, unwariness, disregard, unmindfulness.

2. inaccuracy, inexactness, inexactitude, unpreciseness, imprecision; vagueness, indefiniteness, broadness, generality, amorphousness, *Sl.* blobbiness, inchoateness; disorder, chaos, anarchy; informality, informalness, relaxedness, nonchalance, casualness, ataraxia; indifference, perfunctoriness; slovenliness, *Inf.* sloppiness, *Inf.* messiness, *Inf.* haphazardness; shakiness, ricketiness.

3. tolerance, allowance, lenity, leniency, indulgence, permissiveness, detachment, disinterestedness, unstrictness, unrestraint, weakness.

4. license, wildness, fastness, dissoluteness, abandon, licentiousness, libertinism, dissipation, debauchery, unchasteness, indecency, incontinence, intemperance; wantonness, promiscuity, waywardness, loose morals, easy virtue, whorishness, *Inf.* sleeping around, *Inf.* swinging.

5. flaccidity, flaccidness, laxation, flabbiness, *Sl.* blubberiness; give, suppleness, litheness, limberness, floppiness.

loot, *n.* 1. booty, *Archaic.* boot, spoil, spoils, plunder, pillage, *Archaic.* prey, *Scot. Obs.* reif; stolen goods, *Inf.* steal, *Sl.* hot goods, *Sl.* boodle, *Sl.* the take, *Sl.* the goods, *Sl.* swag.

2. *Informal.* valuables, treasures, prizes, gifts, possessions, purchases, goods; riches, hoardings, savings, stock, cache.

3. *Slang.* money, wealth, riches. See **money**.

4. plundering, pillaging, sacking, *Rare.* sackage, despoliation, foraging; ravishment, seizure, grab, rape.

—*v.* 5. abduct, kidnap, *Sl.* snatch, rape, capture, seize, make off with, carry off, steal; commandeer, expropriate.

6. despoil, spoliate, plunder, pillage, sack, ransack, forage; ravage, harry, maraud, depredate.

7. rob, burglarize, burgle, steal from, embezzle from; fleece, raid; swindle, defraud.

lop[1], *v.* 1. cut off, chop off, sever, truncate, obtruncate, detruncate; trim off, detach, amputate, prune, dock, crop, shorten, clip, top, shear, mow, cut short, bob, pare, shave, snip; gash, slice off, abscind, split, carve, cleave, sunder; rend, rive, divide; section, apportion, dissect, cut apart, disjoint, disjoin, disunite; dismember, mutilate, commit mayhem.

2. edit, abridge, abbreviate, condense; contract, epitomize, summarize, abstract; curtail, cut back, reduce, diminish, cut down on; dilute, water down, water, thin out; adulterate, weaken, *Inf.* doctor; eliminate, expurgate, bowdlerize.

lop[2], *v.* droop, hang limply, sag, hang down; bend, bow, (*of trees, flowers, etc.*) nod; dip, lean, curve; sink, slump, settle, drop; hang loosely, depend from, dangle, loll.

lope, *v.* bound, leap, spring, gambol, frolic, frisk, caper, romp, prance, dance along, buck; jump, hop, bob, curvet, skip; *Inf.* move right along, canter, gallop; hurry, hasten, hie, dart, scamper.

lopsided, *adj.* unsymmetrical, asymmetrical, unbalanced, unequalized, uneven, unequal, disproportioned, disproportionate, irregular; out of line, askew, awry, *Sl.* cockeyed, crooked, warped, out of shape.

loquacious, *adj.* 1. talkative, garrulous, voluble, multiloquous, long-tongued, *Inf.* big-mouthed, *Sl.* all jaw, *Sl.* gassy, *Sl.* windy; chattering, chatty, gabby, gibbering, babbling, blabbering, blathering, jabbering, gossipy, *Inf.* blessed with *or* possessed of the gift of gab.

2. long-winded, wordy; diffuse, discursive, digressive, maundering, wandering, rambling, roving, aimless; circumlocutory, roundabout, ambagious.

loquacity, *n.* 1. talkativeness, garrulity, verbosity, prolixity, long-windedness, longiloquence, multiloquence, *Inf.* gabbiness, *Inf.* windiness, *Inf.* gassiness, *Inf.* gift of gab; overtalkativeness, loose tongue, *Inf.* big mouth.

2. chatter, jabber, babble, prating, prattle, palaver, gabble, blabber, blather; chitter-chatter, prittle-prattle, tittle-tattle, mere talk, idle talk, idle gossip; *All Sl.* yakkety-yak, blah-blah, guff, gas, hot air.

lord, *n.* 1. lord and master, overlord, master, chief, ruler, tyrant, dictator; king, sovereign, monarch, majesty, crowned head, potentate, dynast; prince, emperor, rajah, maharajah, czar, caeser, kaiser, *Fr. roi, Latin. rex,* sheik, khan, governor, tetrarch; president, *Inf.* prez, premier, chief-of-state, head-of-state, chief executive, captain of the ship of state; superior, commander, commandant, general, chieftain, high chief, (*of some tribes of American Indians*) sachem.

2. headman, head, captain, *Inf.* boss, *Inf.* bossman, *Inf.* big boss, man-in-charge; chairman, headmaster, principal, dean, director, administrator; executive, manager, overseer, supervisor, superintendent, *Inf.* super, foreman, *Brit.* gaffer; *Inf.* kingpin, *Inf.* king-

fish, *Inf.* number one, *Inf.* Mr. Big. *Sl.* top dog, *Sl.* head honcho, *Sl.* big cheese, *Fr. grand fromage, Sl.* big wheel *or* wheel, *Sl.* high man on the totem pole.

3. landlord, proprietor, owner, landowner, landholder; feudal lord *or* superior, feudal overlord, *Hist.* suzerain; seigneur, *Japanese Hist.* daimyo, signor; squire, *Scot.* laird, *Russian Hist.* boyar, (*in medieval Germany*) landgrave.

4. nobleman, noble, peer; grand duke, archduke, duke, marquis, margrave, earl, count, viscount, baron; grandee, magnifico, don, hidalgo.

5. Lord God, God Almighty, the Almighty, the Godhead, Divine Being, The Deity, Providence, Holy One; God the Father, Divine Father, Our Father; Jehovah, Yahweh, Allah; the Supreme Being, Supreme Goodness, the All-Powerful, the Omnipotent, the All-Merciful, the All-Wise, the All-Knowing, the Omniscient; the Infinite, the Eternal, the Absolute; Lord of Lords, King of Kings, King of Glory; Creator, Author of all things, the Maker, the Maker of Heaven and Earth, the First Cause, the Prime Mover, the Light of the World, Ruler of Heaven and Earth, Sovereign of the Universe, Most High.

6. Lord Jesus, Jesus Christ, Christ, Christ Jesus, Christ the Lord; Jesus of Nazareth, the Nazarene, the Galilean, *Literary.* Jesu; the Redeemer, the Savior, Emmanuel, Immanuel, the Messiah, the Star of David, the Son of David, the Anointed, the Expected One; the Son of God, the Son of Man, the Prince of Peace, God Incarnate, the Incarnation, God in Man.

—*v.* **7. lord it over** play the lord, boss *or* boss around, command, dictate to, order around, tell [s.o.] what to do, direct, control; domineer, rule with an iron *or* heavy hand, be overbearing, rule dictatorially; tyrannize, oppress, repress, keep down, suppress.

lordly, *adj.* **1.** lordlike, kinglike, kingly, regal, royal, imperial, noble, princely; formal, dignified, stately, splendid, impressive, imposing, grandiose; grand, magnificent, glorious, majestic, august; high, lofty, exalted, sublime; elegant, lavish, sumptuous, luxurious, *Inf.* swank, *Inf.* swanky, *Inf.* posh, *Sl.* ritzy, *Sl.* classy, high-class.

2. imperious, magisterial, high and mighty, overbearing, overweening, domineering; high-handed, arbitrary, presumptuous, peremptory, arrogant, haughty, insolent; cocky, overconfident, conceited, proud, condescending, patronizing, *Inf.* uppity, *Inf.* uppish, snobbish, snobby, *Inf.* snotty, *Inf.* snooty; self-assertive, aggressive, pushing, *Inf.* pushy, willful, forceful, imperative, commanding; masterful, authoritarian, authoritative, *Inf.* bossy, dictatorial; despotic, autocratic, tyrannical, iron-handed, oppressive.

—*adv.* **3.** imperiously, magisterially, overbearingly, overweeningly, domineeringly; high-handedly, arbitrarily, presumptuously, peremptorily, arrogantly, haughtily, insolently; cockily, overconfidently, conceitedly, proudly, condescendingly, patronizingly, *Inf.* uppishly, snobbishly, snobbily, *Inf.* snottily, *Inf.* snootily.

lore, *n.* **1.** folklore, traditional knowledge *or* teachings.

2. knowledge, know-how, learning, erudition, letters, scholarship; book learning, education, schooling, instruction, tuition.

lose, *v.* **1.** misplace, mislay; forget, *Inf.* clean forget, not remember, disremember, have no remembrance *or* recollection of, *Inf.* draw a blank; lose sight of, lose in the crowd.

2. outstrip, overtake, overhaul, pass, lap, leave behind, leave in the dust, leave flatfooted.

3. elude, evade, escape, duck, dodge, give]s.o.] the slip, *Sl.* duck and run, *Sl.* dog it, *Sl.* ditch [s.o.] *Sl.* throw [s.o.] off the scent, *Sl.* shake [s.o.] off.

4. forfeit, default, give up, *Inf.* give in, have enough, admit defeat, yield, yield the palm, *Inf.* say uncle, *Inf.* throw in the towel; succumb, bow to, *Inf.* tip the hat to, *Sl.* hand it to; bite *or* lick the dust, *Sl.* take the count; let slip through one's fingers, *Sl.* drop, *Sl.* kiss good-bye.

5. be defeated, get *or* have the worst of, come to grief, meet one's Waterloo, come off second best, *Inf.* lose out; fall, fall flat, *Inf.* fall on one's face, *Sl.* fall down; fail, *Sl.* blow it, *Inf.* not work out, *Inf.* not make it, *Inf.* not come off, *Inf.* flunk *or* flunk out, *Sl.* not hack it.

6. waste, squander, lavish, dissipate, deplete, consume, drain, pour down the drain, use up, exhaust; spend, expend, spend money like water, spend money as if it grew on trees, spend money like a drunken sailor, throw money around, run through money; fool away, fritter away, trifle away, fribble away.

7. depreciate, deteriorate, go to waste, come to nothing, come to naught, *Inf.* go up in smoke, *Inf.* go down the drain.

8. lose face be shamed, incur disgrace, fall into disrepute, earn a bad name, lose one's good name *or* reputation; disgrace oneself, demean oneself, degrade oneself, debase oneself, lower oneself, stoop.

9. lose ground fall behind, fall back, slip back, lag behind, get behind.

10. lose heart despond, despair, give oneself up *or* over to despair, fall *or* sink into despair, lose hope, abandon hope, give up all hope; reach *or* plumb the depths, hit rock bottom, touch bottom, *Sl.* hit the pits.

11. lose one's head lose control, take leave of one's senses, *Inf.* go haywire; rage, explode, *Sl.* blow up, *Sl.* blow one's cool, *Sl.* blow a gasket *or* fuse, *Sl.* blow one's top *or* stack, *Sl.* flip, *Sl.* flip one's wig *or* lid, *Sl.* flip out, *Sl.* freak *or* freak out; fly into a passion, *Inf.* fly off the handle, go into hysterics, have a tantrum, have a fit, *Inf.* have a conniption *or* conniption fit, *Inf.* have a cat fit, *Inf.* hit the ceiling *or* roof, *Sl.* have a hemorrhage.

loser, *n.* **1.** also-ran, runner-up, *Inf.* defeatee; the vanquished, the defeated; good loser, *Inf.* sport, good sport.

2. *Informal.* failure, lead balloon, *Sl.* flop, *Sl.* washout, *Inf.* dud, *Sl.* bomb, *Inf.* clunker, *Inf.* lemon, *Sl.* clinker, *Inf.* bummer, *Sl.* bust; two-time loser, three-time loser.

3. *Slang.* unfortunate, *Inf.* born loser, fortune's fool, *Inf.* Charlie Brown, *Sl.* sad sack, *Sl.* hard case *or* hard-luck case, *Sl.* schlemiel, *Sl.* schlimazel, *Sl.* dog.

loss, *n.* **1.** detriment, disadvantage, prejudice; impairment, injury, damage, hurt, harm, disablement, incapacitation; step backward, regression, retrogression, lapse.

2. privation, deprivation, bereavement; sacrifice, denial, forfeiture; nonrestoration.

3. waste, wastage, depletion, dissolution, exhaustion, consumption, impoverishment; corrosion, erosion, ablation, wear and tear, wear, weathering.

4. destruction, ruin, undoing, perdition, total *or* complete *or* dead loss; breakdown, collapse; disrepair, dilapidation; wreckage.

5. at a loss a. at less than cost, at a financial loss, unprofitably, *Inf.* to the bad. **b.** perplexed, confounded, confused, bewildered, baffled, puzzled, mystified, nonplussed, *Inf.* beat, *Inf.* stuck, *Inf.* stumped; at an impasse, at a standstill, at one's wit's end; in a dilemma, on the horns of a dilemma, in a quandary, between a rock and a hard place, between the devil and the deep blue sea, between Scylla and Charybdis.

lost, *adj.* **1.** forfeited, gone, no more, by the board, out the window, down the drain, long-lost; missing, vanished, disappeared, lost to sight *or* view, out of sight.

2. forgotten, unrecalled, unremembered, unrecollected, unretained, out-of-sight-out-of-mind; consigned to oblivion, buried *or* sunk in oblivion.

3. irreclaimable, irretrievable, irrecoverable, irrevocable, irreversible, unsalvageable, past hope, hopeless, past praying for, beyond recall.

4. wasted, squandered, misspent; consumed, used up, exhausted, expended, spent.

5. astray, adrift, at sea, off the track, out of one's bearings, disoriented, going around in circles; (*all as to place, direction, etc.*) confused, perplexed, baffled, bewildered, confounded, puzzled, mystified, nonplussed, at a loss.

6. destroyed, ruined, wrecked; undone, done in, finished, ended, *Sl.* eighty-sixed; obliterated, effaced, eradicated, extirpated, wiped *or* blotted out.

7. preoccupied, bemused, abstracted, engrossed, rapt, taken up, lost in thought; absent, far away, somewhere else, not there.

8. distraught, desperate, hopeless; distracted, wild, frenzied, frantic, crazy, mad, maddened, beside oneself, carried away.

lot, *n.* **1.** straw, pebble, counter, check, chip, number; die, *Inf.* bone.

2. lottery, drawing, pulling, drawing straws, casting lots; sweepstakes, raffle.

3. luck, chance, hazard, gamble, *Archaic.* hap; random shot, tossup, pot luck; fortuity, serendipity, fluke, stroke, happenstance, lucky pick, lucky number.

4. fortune, fate, destiny, kismet; circumstances, estate, state, condition, situation, status, station; portion, cup, plight, end, final lot, doom; *Inf.* the way the cookie crumbles *or* the ball bounces.

5. part, share, interest, alloted share *or* portion, apportionment, allotment, measure; allowance, proportion, ration, dole, pittance, *Archaic.* meed; commission, percentage, *Inf.* cut, *Sl.* rake-off, *Sl.* whack, *Sl.* piece of the pie.

6. plot, tract, patch, plat; division, field, piece of ground, property, house lot, building lot; block, square, section.

7. parcel, packet, package, set, bundle, pack, batch, load, shipment; collection, clutter, *Inf.* mess, *Sl.* slew.

8. group, party, band, crew, outfit, pack, cohort; flock, company, body, complement, contingent, *Inf.* crowd, *Inf.* team, *Inf.* string, *Inf.* stable; troop, gang, army, multitude, host, *Sl.* mob.

9. *Informal.* kind, sort, ilk, type; variety, species, family, class, order; tribe, clan, race, strain, blood, breed, caste.

10. a lot, lots *Informal.* deal, good *or* great deal, a great quantity, quantity, much, much of a muchness; volume, mass, mountain, load, tons, barrels, worlds, acres, oceans, heap, heaps, pile, piles, stack, stacks, loads, slews; mint, peck, oodles, gobs, scads; considerable, considerable number, many, numerous; *Sl.* boodle, *Sl.* caboodle, *Dial.* aplenty.

11. throw one's lot in with join fortunes with, make common cause with, ally *or* align oneself with, link up with; wed, marry, bind, league, affiliate, combine with, join, *Inf.* throw in with, *Sl.* hook up with; support, stand with *or* by, stand up with, go with, run with, join forces with, make a commitment to, pledge one's support to, *Inf.* jump on the bandwagon, *Inf.* join the parade.

—*v.* **12.** allot, allocate, share *or* parcel out, divide, *Inf.* cut up the pie; assign, earmark, tag, mark *or* portion off, assign to.

lotion, *n.* ointment, balm, salve, unguent, (*in prescriptions*) unguentum, inunction, *Pharm.* cerate; unction, balsam, oil, demulcent, emollient, spikenard, nard, pomade, pomatum; liniment, embrocation, vulnerary, *Med.* collyrium, eyewash; lubricant, moisturizer, cream, face cream, cold *or* cleansing cream, lanolin, skin *or* body lotion, hand lotion, after-shave lotion.

lottery, *n.* **1.** drawing, sweepstakes, raffle; lotto, bingo, keno, *Brit.* tombola; numbers *or* interest lottery, pool, numbers game, numbers pool; tontine.

2. gamble, risk, hazard, venture; uncertainty, incertitude, unforseeableness; chance, chanciness, tossup, touch and go.

loud, *adj.* **1.** loud-sounding, deafening, earsplitting; stentorian, stentorious, rumbling, roaring, rolling, crashing; full, sonorous, full-throated; thunderous, booming, thundering, fulminating, growling; resounding, ringing, plangent, pealing, forte, fortissimo, loudish; window-rattling, earthshaking, enough to wake the dead; intense, head-splitting, ear-piercing, piercing, penetrating, harsh, harsh-sounding, grating, jarring, grinding.

2. resonant, vibrant, vibrating, pulsing, pulsating, throbbing; resounding, reverberating, reverberant, rebounding, repercussive, sounding, echoing, reechoing, reboant; deep, deep-toned, heavy, bass, baritone.

3. howling, yowling, wailing, whining, bawling; ululant; noisy, clamorous, shouting, yelling, crying, screaming, yelping, yapping, yammering, *Inf.* hollering; blaring, blatting, rackety, clattery, clangorous, clanging.

4. vociferous, vociferant, obstreperous, strepitous, strepitant; brawling, boisterous, loud-mouthed, loud-voiced, big-voiced, clarion-voiced, bombastic, *Rare.* boanergean; uproarious, tumultuous, raucous, blustering, rip-roaring, rowdy, *Brit.* mafficking; swaggering, roisterous, roistering, rollicking

5. emphatic, asserting, pressing, insistent, demanding, clamant, urgent, importunate, nagging.

6. garish, gaudy, flashy, tasteless, lurid, glaring, flaring, flashy, blinding; conspicuous, striking, flagrant, outstanding, outlandish, pronounced, obtrusive, extravagant, spectacular, out-of-place; ostentatious, showy, flaunting, snazzy, *Inf.* splashy, *Sl.* jazzy; tawdry, garish, meretricious.

7. bold, brassy, brazen, vulgar, gross, crass, rough, earthy, ribald; uncouth, uncivilized, unrefined, illbred; wild-and-woolly, rough-and-ready, hooliganish; coarse, rude, gruff, crude, raw, boorish, loutish, rowdyish, *Sl.* roughneck.

loud-mouth, *n.* **1.** braggart, braggadocio, brag, boaster, *Sl.* bullshooter, Thraso, Rodomonte; blusterer, swaggerer, gascon, fanfaron, trumpeter, tooter; blowhard, windbag, blatherskite, *Sl.* gas bag, *Sl.* bigmouth; bluffer, humbug, fourflusher.

2. gossip, chatterbox, chatterer, palaverer, magpie, popinjay, *Inf.* jay; gabbler, prattler, blabber, blabbermouth, tattler, tattletale, telltale, tale-bearer.

loudspeaker, *n.* speaker, speaker unit, speaker system, public address system, PA *or* PA system, intercommunication system, *Inf.* intercom, *Inf.* squawk *or* bitch box; megaphone, bullhorn, horn, hailer, loudhailer; microphone, *Inf.* mike, lapel mike.

lounge, *v.* **1.** idle, pass time idly, trifle, potter, fiddle, piddle, *Inf.* fiddle-faddle; dally, dilly-dally, *Inf.* lallygag; daydream, shilly-shally, procrastinate.

2. loll, *Brit. Dial.* lollop, rest, lie on; lie around, recline on, lean on, repose on; sprawl, slump, flop, slouch; languish, vegetate, doze; loaf, loiter, take it easy, relax, not worry.

3. saunter, stroll, perambulate; amble, ramble, mosey; traipse, wander, *Sl.* mooch, meander, inch; shuffle, shamble.

4. dawdle, waste time, *Inf.* diddle, take one's time *or* one's own sweet time, kill time, fritter time away.

—*n.* **5.** sofa, couch, divan, ottoman, *U.S.* davenport; love seat, settee, causeuse; studio couch, sleep sofa, day bed, *Trademark.* Castro convertible; chaise longue, glider, hammock.

6. lobby, waiting room, reception room, terminal; vestibule, antechamber, anteroom; entrance hall, foyer.

7. cocktail lounge, bar, barroom, taproom; bistro, cabaret, nightclub, disco.

8. bathroom, restroom, washroom, lavatory, *Euph.* facilities; ladies' room, powder room, men's room; toilet, *Sl.* john, *Sl.* can, *Sl.* head.

lousy, *adj.* **1.** lice-infested, lice-ridden, lice-infected; pedicular.

2. *Informal.* **a.** contemptible, despicable, detestable, loathsome; mean, vile, base, low, low-down, wretched, scurvy, *Sl.* no-good. **b.** poor, miserable, shoddy, sloppy, slipshod, slovenly, careless, *Sl.* half-assed; inferior, sleazy, unsatisfactory, inadequate.

3. lousy with *Slang.* well-supplied with, rolling in, up to one's neck in, covered with, coming out one's ears.

lout, *n.* dolt, oaf, clod, clodhopper, clodpoll, clodpate, gawk, looby, lubber, ox, clown, slouch, *Chiefly Scot.* cuddy, *Inf.* lummox, *Sl.* klutz, *Sl.* galoot, *Sl.* lug, *Chiefly Brit. Sl.* joskin; bungler, bumbler, fumbler, botcher, blunderer, boggler, *Inf.* butterfingers, *Inf.* stumblebum, *Inf.* duffer, *Sl.* slob; churl, curmudgeon, brute, barbarian, yahoo, *Chiefly Scot.* tyke, *Brit. Sl.* mucker; Philistine, vulgarian, vulgarist, ribald, low *or* vulgar *or* ill-bred fellow.

loutish, *adj.* obtuse, stolid, dull, dense, *Inf.* thick, oafish, doltish, cloddish, clodhopping, lumpish, lumpen, clownish, lubberly; rude, uncouth, coarse, vulgar, boorish, churlish, unmannerly, ill-mannered, ill-bred; awkward, clumsy, inept, maladroit, heavy-handed, blundering, bungling, gawky *or* gawkish, like a bull in a china shop, *Inf.* butterfingered, *Sl.* klutzy.

lovable, *adj.* adorable, dear, endearing, cherishable; likeable, estimable, amiable; engaging, winsome, winning, captivating, taking, pleasing; enchanting, alluring, attractive, charming; sweet, good, warm, warm-hearted; tender, affectionate, cuddly.

love, *n.* **1.** affection, fondness, warmth; cherishing, adoration, devotion; like, liking, adulation, esteem, regard; attachment, attraction, mutual attraction, friendship, Platonic love; closeness, intimacy.

2. passion, tender passion, amativeness, true love, free love; infatuation, fancy, puppy love, calf love, *Sl.* crush, *Sl.* case; lust, aphrodisia, desire, libidinousness, *Sl.* hot pants, *Sl.* hots; hankering, longing, wanting, pining, craving, yearning; emotion, heart, heat, ardor, fervor, flame, rapture.

3. sweetheart, sweet, sweetie, *Sl.* sweet patootie, *Fr. petit chou, Fr. chou-chou, Fr. poulet*; honey, darling, beloved, dear, dear one, dearest; heartthrob, heart's desire, true love, love of one's life, one's all; lover, paramour, *Fr. intime,* sex partner, bed mate; admirer, boyfriend, girlfriend; young man, suitor, beau, swain, inamorato, wooer; betrothed, intended, fiancé, fiancée; mistress, courtesan, best girl, ladylove, inamorata; mate, spouse, helpmate, better half, husband, wife, old man, old lady, bride; turtledove, angel.

4. amour, affair, meaningful relation, relationship, liaison, intrigue, romance; assignation, tryst, rendezvous.

5. concern, sympathy, caring, care, solicitude; tenderness, feeling, good feeling; rapport, affinity, amity, concord, accord, harmony, brotherhood, friendliness.

6. Eros, Cupid, Amor; Venus, Aphrodite; *Teutonic Myth.* Freya, *Hindu Myth.* Kama; amorino, amoretto.

7. predilection, partiality, disposition, inclination, bent, penchant, proclivity; weakness, relish, taste, delight, soft spot in one's heart; mania, *Sl.* thing.

8. beneficence, charity, *Latin.* caritas, Christian charity, agape, brotherly love; benevolence, kindliness, kindness, goodness, grace, grace of God; veneration, idolizing, reverence.

—*v.* **9.** like, have a liking, care for, care a lot for, be fond of, hold dear, cherish; treasure, admire, esteem, prize, think the world of, be attracted to.

10. be in love with, be smitten, love to distraction, lose one's heart to; adore, adulate, worship, idolize; desire, want, yearn for, pine for, long for, pant for, burn; lust for, *Sl.* letch after, *Sl.* have the hots; have a crush on, be infatuated.

11. delight in, appreciate, relish, savor, enjoy, *Sl.* eat up; get a bang *or* kick out of, approve, applaud.

12. need, require, have to have, benefit from, dote on, find good, find helpful.

13. embrace, hug, cuddle, *Sl.* smooch, neck, pet, *Sl.* make out, *Inf.* romance, fondle, *Inf.* canoodle, caress, have foreplay; make love, have sex, have intercourse, go to bed, lie with, bed down; have a romp in the hay.

love affair, *n.* **1.** affair, amour, romance, liaison, intrigue, relationship, meaningful relationship; tryst, assignation, rendezvous, secret rendezvous; engagement, betrothal.

2. enthusiasm, passion, mania, love, relish, appreciation, real liking; eagerness, ardor, zeal, fervor, devotion, *Sl.* nuttiness.

loveless, *adj.* **1.** lovelorn, unloved, unlamented, uncherished, unbeloved, unwanted, unappreciated; disliked, abhorred, disrelished, detested, hated, despised, loathed.

2. unloving, unfriendly, disaffecting; cold, cool, frigid, heartless, cold-hearted, icy; sterile, neutral, emotionless, passionless, with ice in one's bloodstream; like a cold fish.

lovely, *adj.* **1.** beautiful, comely, attractive, handsome, seemly, becoming, sightly, *Inf.* eye-filling, good-looking, pulchritudinous, *Chiefly Literary.* beauteous; fair, pretty, *Chiefly Scot.* bonny, shapely, well-proportioned, glamorous, sexy; charming, *Inf.* fetching, engaging, captivating, enthralling, enchanting, alluring, fascinating, winsome, winning, bewitching, enticing, tempting, seductive, ravishing.

2. personable, pleasant, *Inf.* divine; graceful, elegant, artistic, aesthetic; delicate, dainty, sweet.

3. *Informal.* delightful, pleasing, agreeable, congenial.

love-making, *n.* **1.** courting, courtship, wooing; caressing, embracing, kissing, *Sl.* making out, *Inf.* necking, *Inf.* petting, *Inf.* spooning.

2. act of love, intimacy, sexual intercourse, intercourse, sex, coitus, coition, sexual relations, sexual union *or* congress; mating, *Archaic.* venery, copulation, carnal knowledge, *Sl.* humpery.

lover, *n.* **1.** infatuate, beau, swain, courter, Romeo, wooer; suitor, gallant, amorist; ladies' man, playboy, *Sl.* sheik, *Sl.* stud; philanderer, paramour, *Fr. bon ami*, adulterer; Lothario, rake, libertine, Casanova, Don Juan; gigolo, *It. cicisbeo*, escort, cavalier; ladylove, coquette, flirt. See also **love** (*def.* **3**).

2. aficionado, enthusiast, fan, devotee, buff, *Sl.* nut, *Sl.* bug, *Sl.* hound, *Sl.* freak; champion, supporter, *Inf.* booster.

loving, *adj.* affectionate, fond, devoted, amatory, amorous; caressing, caring, tender, gentle, kind, cordial, thoughtful; warm-hearted, warm, benign, sympathetic, friendly, amiable; desirous, smoldering, flaming, ardent, passionate, earnest, lovesick.

low[1], *adj.* **1.** ground-level, low-lying, low-hanging, unelevated; coastal, sea-level; flat, depressed, concave, sunken; nether, under, underground, buried, submerged, underwater, submarine, undersea, deep.

2. short, small, little, stumpy, truncated, squat, knee-high, ankle-high; scrubby, stunted, stubby; crouching, crouched, stooping, bent.

3. shallow, dried up, (*both of tides*) neap, ebb; reduced, diminished, decreased, lessened, attenuated, abated; drained, expended, consumed, used up, depleted, exhausted, spent, impoverished.

4. feeble, weak, frail, fragile, delicate, weakly, sickly, not strong, unhealthy, *Scot.* shilpit, ailing; unsteady, infirm, *Inf.* dotty, shaky, trembling; impotent, powerless, impuissant, helpless; decrepit, invalid, unsound, weakened, enfeebled, debilitated; exhausted, enervated, enervate, languid, languishing, drooping, fading, declining, failing, sinking, expiring, dying.

5. inferior, below par, wanting, unacceptable, inadequate, insufficient; incompetent, not up to par *or* snuff, unprofessional, amateurish, lightweight; second-rate, mediocre, middling, moderate, so-so.

6. depressed, dejected, disheartened, dispirited, downhearted, downcast, down, *Inf.* down in the dumps, low-spirited; discouraged, daunted, dismayed, distressed, disappointed, crestfallen, broken-hearted, heartsick, *Inf.* broken up; unhappy, cheerless, glum, gloomy, under a cloud, doleful, *Archaic.* wan; saddened, sad, blue, forlorn, melancholy, mopey, mopish, long-faced, chapfallen, *Inf.* down in the mouth, *Sl.* off one's feed; woebegone, heavy-hearted, disconsolate, sorrowful, mournful, lachrymose, funereal; weighed down, crushed, *Inf.* broken, *Sl.* bummed out, despondent, spiritless.

7. humble, poor, plebian, proletarian, earth-born, of low birth, lowborn, low ranking, lowly. See **lowly** (*def.* **1**).

8. wretched, sorry, abject, squalid, destitute, miserable, dismal, abysmal, dreary, *Literary.* drear; beggarly, scrubby, seedy, sleazy, abased.

9. mean, base, vile, sordid, bad, foul, wrong; depraved, debased, wicked, evil, iniquitous, sinful; corrupt, black-hearted, ignoble, sinister, miscreant, evil-minded; nefarious, flagitious, villainous, heinous, scandalous; disloyal, unfaithful, traitorous, treacherous, perfidious, unprincipled; reprehensible, blameworthy, culpable; scoundrelly, knavish, thievish, roguish, nasty, snide; vicious, invidious, malicious, maleficent; contemptible, mean-spirited, currish, despicable, insufferable, opprobrious, obnoxious.

10. course, vulgar, obscene, rude, crude, gross; lewd, lurid, scurrilous, Fescennine; ribald, bawdy, pornographic, smutty, *Sl.* raunchy; foul, foul-mouthed, rank, filthy, dirty; indelicate, indecent, unseemly, improper, offensive, disgusting, revolting.

11. soft, subdued, quiet, whispered, murmured, gentle, dulcet; muted, stifled, hushed, inaudible, imperceptible, indistinct, unclear.

12. dead, near death, prostrate, downthrown.

low[2], *v.* moo, bellow, blare; bleat, blat, baa, bray, bawl.

lowborn, *adj.* humble, poor, simple, plebian; insignificant, obscure, untitled, low. See **low** (*def.* **7**).

lowbred, *adj.* coarse, uncivil, uncouth, rude, crude, crass, unpolished; rough-hewn, homespun, homely, earthy, common; rustic, countrified, loutish, churlish, boorish, ignorant, unsophisticated; ill-mannered, ill-bred, impolite; unmannerly, ungentlemanly, unladylike, unwomanly; unseemly, unbecoming, indecorous; gruff, bearish, boisterous, *Inf.* loud, brazen, brassy.

low-down, *n.* **1.** *Informal.* dope, inside information, inside story, intelligence, dirt, *Sl.* info, *Sl.* poop, *Sl.* scoop; the facts, the real story, the unadorned facts, the truth.

—adj. **2.** mean, base, contemptible; reprehensible, knavish. See **low** (*def.* **9**).

lower[1], *v.* **1.** let down, drop, depress; thrust down, detrude, plunge, immerse, engulf, souse, douse; let sink, vail, dip, submerge, submerse; bury, sink, put down; raze, level, bring down, fell, demolish; bend down, couch, duck.

2. reduce, decrease, diminish, lessen, abate, bate; mitigate, alleviate, allay, assuage, *Rare.* lenify, palliate; appease, sooth, *Sl.* simmer down, relieve, ease, soften, cushion, mollify; quell, slake, dull, blunt, take the edge off of; modify, temper; minimize, extenuate, make light of, soft-pedal, play down, downplay.

3. modulate, soften, quiet, hush, subdue, *Music.* flatten; turn down, tone down, soft-pedal, muffle, damp, deaden, dull, mute; stifle, throttle, suppress, repress.

4. degrade, debase, abase, defame, vitiate; discredit, devalue, detract; shame, disgrace, dishonor, humble, humiliate, mortify; belittle, demean, deprecate, disparage, deflate, derogate; discredit, tarnish, taint, vilify; (*all of oneself*) stoop, condescend, deign.

5. depreciate, devaluate, downgrade; demote, declass, disrate, cashier, disbar, defrock, depose; discount, mark down, mark off, deduct, subtract, take off.

6. subside, let up, moderate, dwindle, run low; intermit, cease, decline, fall off; wane, taper off, drop off, tail off, fade away, ebb, slacken; weaken, fail, languish.

7. descend, come down, sink, go down; recede, retrocede, fall away, fall back; droop, flop, sag, flag, swag; slope, dip, slant, lean, list, cant, tilt, incline; stoop, slump, dive, plunge, nosedive; founder, go under.

lower[2], *v.* **1.** darken, grow dark, darkle, dusk, blacken, black; gloom, cloud up *or* over, becloud, overshadow, shadow, dim, grow dim; loom, overhang, impend, threaten, be brewing, be in the works.

2. frown, look sullen, lour, pull *or* make a long face, stick out one's lower lip, turn down the corners of one's mouth, pout, sulk, mope, *Scot.* glunch; scowl, glower, glare, look black, look daggers, knit one's brow, *Sl.* give [s.o.] a dirty look, *Sl.* don the hate-mug.

lowering, *adj.* **1.** overcast, cloudy, clouded over, overclouded; gloomy, dismal, dreary, bleak, tenebrous, murky, *Archaic.* caliginous; shadowy, dim, gray, dusky, darkish, dark, pitch-dark, black, pitch-black, *Literary.* darkling; ominous, menacing, minatory, sinister, threatening, overhanging, looming, brewing, in the works, in the wings, impending, approaching, nearing, coming, on its *or* the way, coming this way.

2. frowning, louring, gloomy, glum, long-faced, chapfallen, crestfallen, unsmiling, sulky, pouting, mopish; melancholy, depressed, dejected, blue, sad, sorrowful, doleful, dolorous, *Inf.* down in the dumps, *Inf.* down in the mouth; dour, sullen, brooding, grim, solemn, sober, grave, morose, funereal, lugubrious; scowling, glowering, black-browed; surly, angry, mad; saturnine, stern, severe, taciturn.

low-key, *adj.* restrained, understated, played down, low-keyed; modulated, toned down, softened; soft-sell, subtle, indirect, quiet; mellow, laid-back, relaxed, loose.

lowland, *n.* flat, flat *or* open country, plain, steppe, tundra, champaign; prairie, grassland, meadow, savannah, *Brit.* heath, *Chiefly Brit.* moor, (*both in*

South America) pampas, campo; plateau, tableland, mesa; marsh, morass, bog, swamp, swampland, marshland, wetlands.

lowly, *adj.* **1.** humble, poor, plebian, proletarian, earth-born, of low birth, lowborn, low; unequal, inferior, baseborn, of low *or* mean parentage, untitled; simple, plain, homespun, homely, rustic, countrified; common, commonplace, ordinary, average, humdrum; inconsequential, of little *or* small importance, insignificant, *Archaic.* inglorious, unknown, obscure, undistinguished; subordinate, mean, low-ranking, second-rate; trivial, paltry, petty, puny, trifling, peddling, piddling, niggling, *Inf.* measly, *Sl.* small potatoes, *Inf.* small time.

2. wretched, sorry, abject, squalid, destitute, miserable, dismal, abysmal, dreary, *Literary.* drear.

3. modest, unpretentious, unpretending, unpresuming, unassuming, unaspiring; free from pride, without arrogance, unostentatious, reserved, restrained, unobtrusive; meek, mild, docile, submissive, passive, placid, peaceable, peaceful, lamblike; dutiful, obedient, servile, menial, slavish, subservient, bowed-down.

low-minded, *adj.* coarse, vulgar, obscene, rude, crude, uncouth, crass, gross; lewd, lurid, scurrilous, Fescennine; ribald, bawdy, smutty, *Sl.* raunchy; foul, foul-mouthed, sordid, rank, filthy, dirty; indelicate, indecent, unseemly, improper, offensive, disgusting, revolting; corrupt, ignoble, base, degraded, debauched, degenerate, depraved, immoral, dissolute.

loyal, *adj.* **1.** faithful, allegiant, true, *Scot.* leal, true-hearted; devoted, pledged, patriotic, dedicated; steadfast, fast, steady-going, unchanging, constant, incorruptible; staunch, true-blue, yeomanly, unwavering, unswerving, firm, stable, solid; supportive, dutiful, obedient.

2. reliable, trusted, dependable, good, trustworthy, trusty, tried and true; honest, sincere, earnest, conscientious, scrupulous; truthful, veracious, straight, true to one's word, as good as one's word; unbought, unbribed, uncorrupted.

loyalist, *n.* patriot, true supporter, adherent, sustainer, upholder, maintainer, faithful person, devotee; follower, admirer, votary, partisan; die-hard, *Inf.* stand-patter, conservative, reactionary, reactionist, member of the old guard, right-winger; *U.S. Hist.* Tory, *Sp. Civil War.* Republican, *Brit. Hist.* Stuart supporter; Bourbonist.

loyalty, *n.* **1.** loyalness, faithfulness, fidelity, fealty, trueness, true-heartedness; allegiance, patriotism, devotion, dedication, single-heartedness; steadfastness, steadiness, unchangingness, constancy, abidingness, lastingness, enduringness, permanence; staunchness, unswervingness, firmness, resoluteness; stability, stableness, solidity, solidness, strength, incorruptibility, incorruptibleness.

2. trustworthiness, trustiness, reliability, reliableness, dependability, dependableness, responsibleness, responsibility; honesty, honestness, credibility, credibleness; truthfulness, veracity, veraciousness; sincerity, sincereness, earnestness, conscientiousness, scrupulousness; uprightness, integrity, probity, righteousness, honorableness, upstandingness.

lozenge, *n.* tablet, pill, pastille, drop, cough drop, *Pharm.* troche, *Both Pharm., Vet. Med.* bolus, electuary; comfit, bonbon, sweet, sweetmeat, sugarplum, jujube.

lubber, *n.* **1.** lout, dolt, oaf, clod, clodhopper, clodpoll *or* clodpate, gawk, looby, ox, clown, slouch, *Chiefly Scot.* cuddy, *Inf.* lummox, *Sl.* klutz, *Sl.* galoot, *Sl.* lug, *Chiefly Brit. Sl.* joskin; bungler, bumbler, fumbler, botcher, blunderer, boggler, *Inf.* butterfingers, *Inf.* stumblebum, *Sl.* slob; *Naut.* landlubber.

2. fool, dunce, boob, boobie, ninny, nincompoop, simpleton, ignoramus, dullard, dope, dimwit, nitwit, lamebrain, know-nothing; fathead, blockhead, meathead, knucklehead, muttonhead, bonehead, dunderhead, peabrain, numbskull; *All Sl.* dingbat, dumbbell, dumb cluck, dumb bunny, retread.

3. loafer, idler, worthless idler, bum, do-nothing, good-for-nothing, *Inf.* goldbrick *or* goldbricker, *Sl.* goofball, *Sl.* goof-off, *Sl.* stiff, *Brit. Sl.* skiver; sponger, freeloader, cadger, parasite, non-worker, drone, *Inf.* lounge-lizard.

—adj. **4.** loutish, cloddish; awkward, clumsy. See **lubberly**.

lubberly, *adj.* awkward, clumsy, inept, maladroit, heavy-handed, blundering, bungling, gawky *or* gawkish, ungainly, like a bull in a china shop, *Inf.* butterfingered, *Sl.* klutzy; loutish, oafish, doltish, lumpish, lumpen, cloddish, clodhopping, clownish; dull, dense, stupid, duncical, duncish, stolid, obtuse, *Inf.* thick; rude, vulgar, uncouth, crass, unrefined, coarse, boorish, churlish, unmannerly, ill-mannered, ill-bred, low-bred.

lubricant, *n.* **1.** lubricator, emollient, oil, mineral oil, vegetable oil, olive oil, petroleum; grease, fat, lard, butter, glycerin; unguent, ointment, (*in prescription*) unguentum, *Relig.* unction, lotion; graphite, plumbago, black lead. See also **lotion**.

—adj. **2.** moisturizing, lubricating, lubricous, lubricative; lentive, emollient, oily, unctuous, greasy; fatty, adipose, sebaceous; buttery, slippery, smooth, slick, sleek.

lubricate, *v.* oil, grease, smear with grease; lard, butter, dress, smear, daub; soap, wax, pomade, smooth, slick, make slippery, make smooth; oil the wheels, smooth the way, soap the way.

lubricity, *n.* **1.** oiliness, slipperiness, greasiness, slitheriness; smoothness, sleekness, glassiness, glossiness, skiddiness, iciness; soapiness, waxiness, butteriness, unctuousness, oleaginousness, mucosity.

2. instability, unsteadiness, inconstancy, infirmity; uncertainty, doubtfulness, irresolution; shiftiness, vacillation, wavering; capriciousness, whimsicality, fickleness, flightiness, volatility; changeableness, changefulness, variableness, variability; tergiversation, unreliability, undependability; fleetingness, transitoriness, transience, momentariness.

3. lewdness, lecherousness, lechery, licentiousness; lasciviousness, lustfulness, lust, passion; wantonness, libertinism, abandon, debauchery, dissipation; dissolution, incontinence, intemperance, intemperateness, immoderation; degeneracy, degradation, decadence, immorality, unchastity, unvirtuousness, shamelessness, impurity; salacity, prurience, concupiscence; carnality, sensualism, priapism, venery; satyrism, goatishness, ruttishness, randiness, *Sl.* horniness.

4. pornography, obscenity, smut, filth, dirt; bawdry, bawdiness, ribaldry, Fescennity; coarseness, vulgarity, grossness, crudity, *Sl.* raunchiness; scurrility, indelicacy, impurity, indecency, suggestiveness. offensiveness.

lubricous, *adj.* **1.** oily, slippery, slithery, greasy, greased, lubricated, oiled; buttery, oleaginous, unctuous, slick, *Physiol.* synovial; sleek, glassy, skiddy, icy, glossy, polished, varnished; soapy, waxy, lathered.

2. unstable, unsteady, unsteadfast, inconstant; mercurial, fickle, flighty, volatile, wishy-washy; uncertain, doubtful, irresolute, skittish, changeable, changeful, variable; shifty, wavering, vacillating, fitful, capricious; undependable, unreliable, tergiversating; fleeting, transitory, transient, passing, momentary, fugitive; here-today-gone-tomorrow.

3. lewd, lecherous, libidinous, libidinal, *Archaic.* lickerish; salacious, concupiscent, prurient, ruttish;

carnal, sensual, bestial, animal; priapic, satyric, goatish, hircine, randy, *Sl.* horny, *Sl.* hot; wanton, abandoned, dissolute, debauched, dissipated, incontinent, intemperate, Paphian; shameless, impure, unchaste, unvirtuous, immoral, degenerate.

4. obscene, pornographic, *Sl.* porno, blue, smutty, *Sl.* raunchy; ribald, bawdy, Fescennine, scurrilous, irreverent; lurid, indecent, off-color, offensive, suggestive, risqué; vulgar, gross, filthy, coarse, dirty, crude.

lucid, *adj.* **1.** clear, limpid, pellucid, translucent, transparent, crystalline, hyaline, vitreous, glassy, clear as glass.

2. easily understood, understandable, intelligible, comprehensible, perspicuous, perceptive, acute, penetrating; plain, distinct, straightforward, evident, self-evident, obvious, apparent, easy to see; graphic, explicit, unequivocal, unmistakable, unambiguous; manifest, crystal-clear, clear to see, easy to grasp; undisguised, uncloaked, clearly discernible, unhidden, revealed, disclosed, overt, bare, naked, unconcealed; well-marked, clear-cut, clearly delineated, sharply defined, sharply outlined; simple, direct, pointed, to the point, concise, cogent; specific, absolute, conclusive, unqualified, categorical.

3. sane, rational, able to reason, *Inf.* sound, sound of mind, of sound mind, mentally capable, *Latin. compos, Latin. compos mentis,* mentally competent, *Inf.* competent, competent to stand trial; *Inf.* normal, *Inf.* balanced, *Inf.* all there, *Inf.* with everything there, *Inf.* with all one's marbles, possessing all one's faculties; right, all right, in one's right mind.

4. shining, bright, bright as day, bright as a star, starry; gleaming, radiant, luminous, luminiferous, luminative, lucent; lightsome, luciferous, shiny, beamy, beaming, lustrous.

luck, *n.* **1.** chance, mere chance, happy chance, happenstance, fortuity, serendipity; fortune *or* Fortune, Lady *or* Dame Fortune, *Irish Eng. Inf.* cess; Lady Luck, wheel of fortune *or* chance, heads or tails, roll *or* cast *or* toss *or* throw of the dice; accident, coincidence, contingency, contingence; vicissitudes, ups and downs, fickle finger of fate, way things fall, *Inf.* the breaks, *Inf.* how the cookie crumbles, *Inf.* how the ball bounces.

2. destiny, fate, lot, draw, cup, portion, die, doom, *Chiefly Scot.* weird; predestination, kismet, God's will; stars, planets.

3. success, successfulness, prosperity, prosperousness; felicity, good luck, good fortune, happy fortune; advantage; fortunateness, luckiness.

4. fluke, lucky stroke, stroke of luck *or* fortune, stroke of good luck *or* fortune; windfall, godsend, blessing, accidental advantage, piece of good luck *or* fortune; *Inf.* pennies from heaven; lucky chance, *Inf.* big chance, *Sl.* break, *Sl.* lucky *or* good *or* big break.

5. charm, amulet, talisman, periapt, phylactery; lucky charm, lucky piece, good-luck piece, rabbit's foot; fetish, voodoo.

6. in luck fortunate, lucky, fortuitous, happy, felicitous, *Scot. and North Eng., Irish Eng.* sonsy; favored, blessed, blessed with luck, born under a lucky star, born with a silver spoon in one's mouth; successful, crowned with success, well-off, out in front, ahead of the game, on top, *Sl.* on top of the heap.

7. out of luck unfortunate, unlucky, luckless, sad, unhappy, infelicitous, *Scot.* donsie; short of luck; thwarted, crossed, scotched.

luckily, *adv.* **1.** fortunately, happily, providentially; favorably, promisingly, auspiciously, propitiously.

2. fortuitously, by chance, by mere chance, as it chanced, by a fluke, by luck *or* fortune; by good luck, by good fortune, by a piece of luck, by a piece of good luck *or* fortune.

luckless, *adj.* **1.** unlucky, unfortunate, fortuneless, unblessed, hapless, down on one's luck, out of luck, unsuccessful, unprosperous, having a streak *or* run of bad luck; unhappy, woebegone, woeful, forlorn, miserable, wretched, pitiful, pitiable, sorry.

2. ill-fated, ill-starred, star-crossed, born under an evil star, jinxed, hoodooed, hexed, voodooed, Jonahesque; ill-omened, doomed, foredoomed, cursed, accursed, curse-laden, damned, *Brit. Dial.* fey; unpropitious, inauspicious, unfavorable, untoward, adverse, contrary, cross; disastrous, calamitous, catastrophic, ruinous.

lucky, *adj.* **1.** fortunate, fortuitous, happy, felicitous, *Scot. and North Eng., Irish Eng.* sonsy; favored, blessed, blessed with luck, in luck, charmed, born under a lucky star, born with a silver spoon in one's mouth; successful, crowned with success, prosperous, halcyon, rich, well-off, *Sl.* in a good way; flourishing, thriving, booming, succeeding, out in front, ahead of the game, on top, *Sl.* on top of the heap.

2. auspicious, propitious, providential, favorable, advantageous, ripe, expedient; opportune, seasonable, timely, well-timed, just in time, convenient; encouraging, promising, full of promise, of promise; rosy, bright, fair, golden, benign, benignant.

3. *Informal.* hot, red-hot, *Inf.* cooking, *Inf.* smoking, going strong, *Sl.* on.

lucrative, *adj.* profitable, profit-making, gainful, moneymaking, remunerative, paying, well-paying, high-paying, fat; productive, fruitful, feracious, fructuous, generative, yielding, fecund, fertile, rich; well-rewarding, rewarding, worthwhile, worth one's while *or* time *or* effort, well-spent; prosperous, valuable, beneficial, advantageous, propitious, favorable, desirable.

lucre, *n.* profit, profits, gain, proceeds, winnings, *Sl.* take, *Sl.* velvet, *Sl.* clean-up; return, fruit, yield, harvest, interest, dividend; remuneration, recompensation, recompense, emolument, pay, payment, paycheck, earnings, income, revenue; money, cash, *Sl.* coin, *Sl.* bucks, *Sl.* green stuff, *Sl.* cabbage, *Sl.* lettuce, *Sl.* spinach, *Sl.* dough, *Sl.* bread, *Sl.* loot, *Sl.* scratch, *Sl.* gravy, *Sl.* moola, *Sl.* do-re-mi, *Sl.* wampum, *Disparaging.* filthy lucre. See **money**.

lucubrate, *v.* **1.** study, apply oneself, excogitate, cerebrate, con, cogitate, burn the midnight oil; dig, grind, *Brit. Inf.* swot, *Brit. Inf.* vet, *Inf.* cram, *Sl.* hit the books, *Sl.* crack the books; toil, fag, moil, slave; pore over, concentrate, deliberate, weigh, intellectualize; bury oneself in, plunge into, rack one's brains, cudgel one's brains, hammer away at, think hard.

2. discourse, dissertate, *Archaic.* dissert; expound, exposit, expatiate, descant, explain, explicate; criticize, *Sl.* critique, review, comment on, discuss.

lucubration, *n.* **1.** studiousness, application, diligence, assiduity, concentration; study, deliberation, rumination, contemplation; deep thought, headwork, brainwork, *Sl.* grind.

2. dissertation, treatise, thesis, treatment, discussion; exposition, essay, descant, disquisition, screed, pandect; critique, commentary, tract, excursus, *Archaic.* inditement; explication, explanation, exegesis; manuscript, composition, monograph, opus; work, writing, paper, term paper, research paper.

luculent, *adj.* **1.** clear, lucid, crystal clear, clear-cut, graphic, perspicuous; explicit, express, manifest, plain, direct, to the point; understandable, intelligible, comprehensible.

2. cogent, logical, sound, rational, reasonable; credible, plausible, well-founded, well-grounded; convincing, persuasive, inducive, compelling, forcible; unquestionable, irrefutable, incontrovertible, indisputable.

ludicrous, *adj.* **1.** comical, farcical, burlesque; satirical, ironical, sarcastic, cynical; laughable, good for a laugh, derisible, risible, ridiculous, *Sl.* for the birds; humorous, funny, too funny for words, droll; waggish, witty, roguish, jocular, jocose, facetious, sportive; diverting, entertaining, mirthful, amusing; sidesplitting, screaming, hilarious, uproarious.

2. absurd, inane, pointless, fatuous; nonsensical, senseless, *Inf.* damfool, *Inf.* damfoolish, tomfoolish, foolish, *Scot. and North Eng.* glaikit, *Sl.* cockeyed; poppycockish, *Sl.* cockamamie, amphigoric; asinine, anserine, idiotic, *Inf.* moronic, imbecilic; stupid, unintelligent, mindless, fatuous, slow, brainless; emptyheaded, blank, vacant, vacuous; childish, puerile, green, immature; crazy, crazed, *Sl.* kooky, *Scot.* doiled, mad, wild, insane, demented; daft, *Inf.* daffy, crackbrained, *Inf.* nutty; *All Slang.* balmy, dippy, batty, cuckoo, buggy, screwy, wacky, goofy, loony.

3. unreasonable, irrational, illogical, without rhyme or reason, meaningless; preposterous, extravagant, outrageous, monstrous, outlandish, bombastic, highflown; eccentric, odd, *Archaic.* antic, out-of-the-way, strange, peculiar, quaint; queer, quizzical, grotesque, bizarre; imaginary, fantastic, fabulous, illusory, illusive, chimerical; incredible, inconceivable, unimaginable, unthinkable; unbelievable, hard to believe, beyond belief, implausible, untenable, unheard of; doubtful, doubtable, dubitable, questionable.

4. untrue, fallacious, impossible, sophistic, sophistical, incorrect, erroneous; self-contradictory, paradoxical, inconsistent.

5. inappropriate, incongruous, improper, unbecoming, impractical, *Fr. outré*, unwise, ill-considered, ill-suited, ill-advised; egregious, glaring, flagrant, gross, arrant.

lug, *v.* **1.** pull along, drag, trawl, trail, troll; pull, tug, tow, heave, *Inf.* yank; haul, hale, draw, snake.

2. tote, carry, bear, shift; convey, move, bring, transport, portage.

—*n.* **3.** haul, pull, heave, heave-ho, *Inf.* yank; tug, drag, draw, strain, draft.

luggage, *n.* baggage, effects, goods, things, belongings; gear, tackle, kit, bag and baggage, dunnage; accouterments, paraphernalia, appurtenances, movables, impediments; suitcases, valises, trunks, packs, grips, cases, bags, carry-ons; portmanteaus, garment bags, briefcases, attaché cases, Gladstones, carpetbags; flight bags, duffel bags, satchels, carryalls; backpacks, knapsacks, tote sacks.

lugubrious, *adj.* mournful, funereal, black, dark, dirgelike, somber, elegiac; dismal, gloomy, saturnine, dreary, *Literary.* drear, bleak; melancholy, sorrowful, rueful, joyless, cheerless; sad, doleful, morose, miserable, disconsolate; forlorn, depressing, lowering, dispiriting, disheartening.

lukewarm, *adj.* **1.** warm, tepid, blood-warm, room-temperature, skin-temperature; mild, temperate, balmy, summery, estival.

2. indifferent, uninterested, impassive, disinterested; half-hearted, dispassionate, zealless, perfunctory; nonchalant, insouciant, lackadaisical, listless, Laodicean, negligent, devil-may-care; unresponsive, apathetic, spiritless, sluggish, phlegmatic; uninspiring, unimpassioned, untouched, unmoved, unstirred.

3. half and half, middle-of-the-road, uncommitted, noncommittal, moderate; blowing hot and cold, neither one thing nor the other, neither hot nor cold; choiceless, neutral, *Inf.* on the fence, undecided, irresolute.

lull, *v.* **1.** put to sleep, rock, rock to sleep, cradle, gentle, lullaby; hypnotic, mesmerize, drug, narcotize, sedate, anesthetize, put under, *Sl.* dope.

2. soothe, quiet, hush, still, silence; calm, compose, smooth, becalm, dulcify, subdue, quell; assuage, allay, ease, relieve, alleviate; pacify, tranquilize, mollify, mitigate.

3. let up, subside, slacken, decline, diminish; abate, ebb, recede, sink, shrink, fall off; decrease, lessen, dwindle, wane, die down.

—*n.* **4.** quiet, stillness, hush, silence, soundlessness, not a sound; calm, repose, restfulness, composure; tranquility, quiescence, placidness, serenity, peace.

5. respite, recess, interlude, intermission, interim; interval, time-out, *Sports.* halftime, pause; cessation, break, lapse, caesura, hiatus; truce, cease-fire, armistice, moratorium; suspension, abeyance, suspense, mid-air; standstill, discontinuance, stop, halt.

6. abatement, letup, subsidence, decline; lessening, decrease, diminution, slackening; slack season, slow time, off-season.

7. murmur, whisper, rush, rustle, sigh, sough, susurration, murmuration; hum, purr, whir, buzz, drone, thrumb; patter, gurgle, babble, plash, lapping, purl.

lullaby, *n.* cradlesong, song, *Music.* berceuse, ditty; soft music, lulling tune.

lumber[1], *n.* **1.** timber, logs, boards, planks; wood, hardwood, softwood; siding, wallboard, clapboard; beam, post; lath, strip of wood.

2. jumble, heap, mass, agglomeration, bunch, mess, huddle; medley, hash, patchwork, olla-podrida, olio, gallimaufry, farrago, jungle, hodgepodge, *Brit.* hotchpotch, mishmash, salmagundi; miscellany, potpourri, odds and ends, motley collection; litter, clutter, trash, *Inf.* garbage, rubbish, riffraff, *Brit. Dial.* raff, litter, chaff; castoffs, rags, tatters, castaways, rejects, discards.

—*v.* **3.** cut timber, fell trees, log, prepare logs.

4. heap, pile, bunch, mass, huddle, cram, throw together; jumble, mix, mingle, tangle, entangle; clutter, litter, mess, tumble, scatter, strew about; disarrange, disorder, unsettle, discompose; disorganize, shuffle, dishevel, make a shambles, *Inf.* turn topsy-turvy, *Inf.* muss up.

5. fill, fill up, fill to the brim, fill to overflowing, overfill, stuff, overstuff, crowd, overcrowd, congest; force in, pack in, push in, jam, squeeze, pack like sardines; encumber, make impassable, block, bar, blockade.

lumber[2], *v.* move clumsily, gangle, clump, stump, stamp; plod, trudge, drag, shuffle, *Sl.* schlepp, shamble, drag one's feet, drag one's freight; stumble, fumble, toddle, dodder, falter, move unsteadily, waddle, flounder; hobble, limp, hitch, walk lamely.

lumbering, *adj.* **1.** clumsy, awkward, ungraceful, ungainly; oafish, doltish, cloddish, heavy-footed, lubberly, bearish, bovine, lumpish, hulking; stodgy, stolid, heavy, unwieldy, ponderous; stiff, uneasy, wooden, gawky, constrained.

2. bungling, blundering, bumbling, bunglesome, heavy-handed; left-handed, all thumbs, maladroit; unhandy, inefficient, inept, incapable.

lumberman, *n.* lumberjack, logger, woodsman, wood chopper, wood cutter.

luminary, *n.* **1.** celestial *or* heavenly body, sun, moon, star, shining star.

2. light, lighter, illuminant, illuminator, source of light; ray, beam, shaft of light; lightbulb, lamp, chandelier, electrolier, flashlight, flood lamp, search light, lantern, beacon; candle, taper, candelabrum, match, torch, flare, flame, blaze, fire.

3. star, superstar, bright light, guiding light, leading light, leader, standout, lion, *Inf.* big name; celebrity, *Sl.* celeb, notable, dignitary, toast of the town, somebody, famous *or* well-known person, name, household name, *Inf.* V.I.P., *Inf.* bigwig, *Inf.* big shot, *Sl.* biggie, *Sl.* big gun, *Sl.* big wheel, *Sl.* big cheese, *Sl.* high-muck-a-muck; genius, bright mind, intellect, mental giant, sage, wise man, savant, *Inf.* brain, *Inf.* Einstein.

luminesce, *v.* shine, radiate, irradiate, glare, effulge; glow, phosphoresce, fluoresce, incandesce; glitter, twinkle, sparkle, flicker, flutter, scintillate, coruscate; gleam, glisten, glimmer, shimmer, *Archaic.* glister; flash, streak, glint, blink, dart, fulgurate.

luminescence, *n.* **1.** illumination, luminosity, luminance, shining, beaming, glaring, incandescence, effulgence, refulgence, refulgency; radiation, irradiation, fluorescence, phosphorescence, bioluminescence, glowing, ultraviolet, *Physics.* photoluminescence, *Meteorol.* noctilucence.

2. light, daylight, sunshine, dayshine, sunlight, sun, starlight, moonlight; beam, sunbeam, shine, ray, shaft of light, glare, flash, glint; lamplight, *All Elect.* corposant, corona discharge, electric glow, St. Elmo's fire, brush discharge; gaslight, firelight, blaze; glow, radiance, radiancy, black light, luster, lambency; ignis fatuus, friar's lantern, will-o'-the-wisp, jack-o'-lantern; aurora, aureole, aureola, corona, gleam, sparkle, twinkle, glitter, glimmer; *All Meteorol.* aurora borealis, aurora polaris, northern lights, aurora australis, southern lights.

luminescent, *adj.* luminous, luminiferous, luciferous, lucent, lambent, effulgent, refulgent, fulgent; shining, sunshiny, sunny, beaming, beamy, beamish, bright, resplendent, radiant, glaring. See also **luminous** (*def.* **1**).

luminosity, *n.* **1.** luminance, luminescence, effulgence, refulgence, refulgency, refulgentness, fulgentness; incandescence, fluorescence, phosphorescence, bioluminescence, *Physics.* photoluminescence, *Meteorol.* noctilucence; radiance, radiancy, brilliance, brightness, shininess, lucency, splendor, resplendence, *Rare.* lucence, *Archaic.* fulgor.

2. genius, braininess, intelligence, intellect, wit, sharpness, keenness, quickness, mental acuity, intellectual *or* mental ability, *Brit. Dial.* wittiness; perspicacity, discernment, penetration, perceptivity, insight, sagacity, sagaciousness, cleverness, shrewdness; enlightenment, awareness, irradiation, erudition, knowledge, wiseness, sageness, savoir-vivre, worldliness.

3. bright spot, shining light *or* star, luminary, star, standout.

luminous, *adj.* **1.** shining, bright, sunny, lighted, lit, alight, illuminated, well-lighted; radiant, lambent, resplendent, brilliant, dazzling, ablaze, aflame, afire; fulgent, effulgent, refulgent; lustrous, lucid, lucent, *Rare.* relucent; glowing, aglow, luminescent, luminiferous, incandescent, phosphorescent; shiny, glossy, gleaming, glaring, sheenful, sheeny, nitid, polished, burnished; sparkling, glittering, twinkling, shimmering; glimmering, glistening, *Archaic.* glistering, rutilant, fulgid.

2. intelligent, bright, gifted, brilliant, intellectual, cerebral; quick, clever, alert, clear-headed; perceptive, percipient, discerning, nimble-witted, sharp-witted, keen-witted; understanding, apprehending, comprehending, knowing, cognitive; sage, sapient, wise, judicious; profound, deep, penetrating, philosophical; scholarly, erudite, educated, learned, well-read, enlightened; acute, subtle, perspicacious; sagacious, shrewd, long-headed, hard-headed.

3. clear, concise, intelligible, straightforward, lucid, luculent; understandable, comprehensible, perceptible, perspicuous; explicit, express, plain, well-marked; prominent, conspicuous, salient; evident, self-evident, axiomatic; obvious, palpable, patent, apparent, manifest; strong, distinct, vivid, graphic; clear-cut, unquestionable, decided, unmistakable; overt, open, disclosed, revealed; undisguised, unhidden, unveiled, uncloaked.

lump[1], *n.* **1.** mass, clot, gob, gobbet, pat, dab, spot; piece, chunk, *Inf.* hunk, hunch; wad, ball; clump, clod, cluster, bunch; heap, mound, pile, stack; agglomeration, group, aggregation, aggregate, assemblage, collection, amassment, accumulation.

2. protuberance, projection, tuberosity, *Anat.* condyle, protrusion, prominence, *Bot.* apophysis; node, nodule, *Anat.* nodulus, bulb, knob, knot, gnarl, knurl; growth, excrescence, excretion, *Biol.* auxesis, tubercle; swelling, tumescence, intumescence, enlargement; bump, *Inf.* goose egg, hump, buckle, bulge; *Pathol.* tumor, *Pathol.* neoplasm, *Pathol.* cyst, *Pathol.* wen, *Pathol.* blain, corn, wart, boil, *Pathol.* carbuncle, inflammation, blister, *Pathol.* callus.

3. majority, plurality, bulk, the greater part, the greatest number, multitude, mass.

—adj. **4.** total, combined, aggregate.

—v. **5.** *Often* **lump together** unite, consolidate, join, combine, put *or* throw together, pool; blend, mix *or* mix together, commix, fuse, merge; bring together, conglomerate, collect, cluster, aggregate, mass, assemble, gather, congregate, group, bunch up *or* together; accumulate, heap up, pile, pile up, stack up; compile, amass, cumulate.

6. clot, form lumps, swell, bulge, buckle.

lump[2], *v.* *Informal.* put up with, take, suffer with, bear with; stand, tolerate, brook, endure.

lumpish, *adj.* **1.** lumpy, knobby, cloddy, clodlike; heavy, ponderous, elephantine, lumbering; clumsy, *Sl.* klutzy, lubberly, loutish, oafish; bungling, awkward, ungainly, maladroit, gawky; unpolished, rough, boorish, churlish, peasantlike, rustic; coarse, crude, rude, vulgar, gross.

2. dull, dull-witted, slow, slow-witted, backward, ignorant, unintelligent; doltish, cloddish, stolid, obtuse, crass, Boeotian, bovine, blockish; dense, thick-headed, *Inf.* thick, stupid, *Inf.* dumb, *Inf.* dopey, sluggish; laggard, torpid, lethargic, slow-moving, inactive, inert, passive; hebitudinous, listless, apathetic, phlegmatic, indifferent.

lumpy, *adj.* **1.** full of lumps, chunky, knobby, nodulous, nodous, knotty, gnarled, knurled, knurly; bumpy, uneven, bulging, protuberant.

2. heavy, clumsy, lubberly, loutish, crude. See **lumpish** (*def.* **1**).

3. (*both of water*) rough, choppy.

lunacy, *n.* **1.** insanity, insaneness, madness, derangement, *Psychiatry.* dementia, dementedness; distraction, disorientation, unbalance, unsoundness; mental illness, loss of reason, unsound mind, diseased mind; craziness, *Sl.* kookiness, *Inf.* nuttiness, daftness, brainsickness; possession, infatuation; eccentricity, oddness, queerness; *All Sl.* balminess, bugginess, screwiness, wackiness, goofiness.

2. psychosis, neurosis, psychoneurosis; schizophrenia, *Psychiatry.* dementia praecox, monomania, automania, dipsomania, pyromania, delusion of grandeur; senility, anility, dotage, *Psychiatry.* amentia; *Psychol.* kleptomania, *Psychol.* split personality; *All Psychiatry.* melancholia, hypochondria, paranoia, mania, lyssophobia, fugue, alienation, delusion.

3. frenzy, franticness, furor, delirium, phrenitis, anoesis, hysteria; *Pathol.* delirium tremens, blue devils, *Sl.* the horrors, *Sl.* jimjams; ranting, raving, storming, foaming at the mouth; storminess, fierceness, tumult, tumultuousness, turbulence, violence.

4. foolishness, folly, absurdity, absurdness, silliness, inanity, fatuousness, dotage; irrationality, illogic, illogicality, illogicalness, unreasonableness; senselessness, nonsense, nonsensicality, nonsensicalness, *Obs.* morology, pointlessness; ridiculousness, ridiculosity, ludicrousness; asininity, imbecility, idiocy, *Inf.* moronism, *Inf.* moronity; stupidity, fatuity; lightheadedness, harebrainedness; childishness, puerility, immaturity.

5. preposterousness, unsensibleness, impracticality, unreasonableness; inappropriateness, impropriety, ineptitude, ineptness, incongruity, inconsistency; imprudence, indiscretion; irresponsibility, carelessness, unwariness, rashness, foolhardiness, recklessness.

lunate, *adj.* lunated, crescent, crescent-shaped, semilunar, semicircular; crescentlike, crescentoid, crescentic, moon-shaped.

lunatic, *n.* **1.** madman, *Sl.* loony, maniac, bedlamite, *Inf.* crackpot, *Sl.* kook, *Sl.* nut, *Sl.* screwball; psychotic, *Sl.* sickie, psychopath, schizophrenic, *Sl.* schizo; paranoiac, *Psychiatry.* manic-depressive; *Psychiatry.* megalomaniac, pyromaniac, *Psychol.* kleptomaniac, dipsomaniac, automaniac.

2. eccentric, nonconformist, Bohemian; dreamer, Don Quixote, highflier, rhapsodist; enthusiast, fanatic, crank, zealot, phrenetic; energumen, demoniac.

3. imbecile, idiot, mooncalf, *Inf.* moron; dimwit, nitwit, half-wit, featherbrain, pinhead; fool, crackbrain, *Sl.* lamebrain, saphead, Simple Simon, noodle, *Inf.* jay, *Sl.* jerk, goose; simpleton, ninny, nincompoop, silly, silly billy, driveler, tomfool; sulker, *Inf.* grouch, *Inf.* crank.

—adj. **4.** insane, crazy, crazed, mad, lunatical, demented, deranged; of unsound mind, *Latin. non compos mentis*, mentally ill; daft, *Inf.* daffy, unbalanced, touched, *Inf.* unglued, *Inf.* half-baked, *Brit. Sl.* bonkers, *Brit. Sl.* barmy, unhinged, distracted; dazed, moon-struck, possessed, infatuated; odd, peculiar, queer, bizarre, *Chiefly Brit. Inf.* potty, *Inf.* dotty, *Inf.* crackpot; brainsick, *Sl.* kooky, *Sl.* meshuga; *All Sl.* balmy, dippy, batty, bats, cuckoo, buggy, bughouse, bugs, screwy, wacky, wacko, goofy, loony, squirrelly, bananas, nuts, nutty, nutty as a fruitcake.

5. out of one's head *or* mind *or* senses *or* wits, *Scot.* redwood, *Sl.* loco, mad as a hatter, mad as a March hare, far-gone, stark raving mad; not all there, not quite right, not right upstairs; *Inf.* out in left field, *Sl.* in outer space, *Sl.* in orbit, *Inf.* off the wall; *Inf.* cracked, *Inf.* mental, *Sl.* off one's rocker, *Sl.* out of one's tree, *Sl.* out of one's kugel, *Sl.* off one's trolley, *Brit. Sl.* off one's chump; *All Sl.* have bats in one's belfry, have a few buttons missing, have a few loose screws.

6. maniacal, hysterical, madding, *Archaic.* wood, delirious; frantic, frenzied, frenetic; ranting, raving, storming, foaming at the mouth, convulsing; overwrought, distraught, upset, worked-up, wrought-up, stirred-up; exasperated, provoked; beside oneself, at one's wit's end; out of control, uncontrollable, unrestrainable, corybantic, *Inf.* haywire, berserk, rabid, wild; violent, stormy, fierce, tempestuous, tumultuous, turbulent.

7. absurd, silly, inane, fatuous, crackbrained, foolish; irrational, wild-eyed, illogical, unreasonable; senseless, nonsensical, pointless; ridiculous, laughable, risible, derisible, ludicrous; asinine, anserine, idiotic, *Inf.* moronic, imbecilic; childish, puerile, immature.

8. stupid, simple-minded, bird-brained, feeble-minded, dull-witted; harebrained, light-minded, light-headed, giddy; rambling, driveling, wandering, incoherent; scatterbrained, absent-minded; confused, muddled, muddlepated, bemused.

9. featherheaded, light-hearted, giddy, carefree, *Inf.* dizzy; frivolous, superficial, frothy; eccentric, idiosyncratic; flighty, whimsical, capricious.

10. impractical, injudicious, unsensible; unfounded, groundless, unsound; preposterous, extravagant, excessive; inappropriate, inept, improper, incongruous, inconsistent; imprudent, indiscreet; unwise, ill-considered, ill-suited, ill-advised; short-sighted, careless, unwary, irresponsible; reckless, rash, harum-scarum; unsafe, dangerous, perilous.

lunch, *n.* **1.** luncheon, *Brit.* tiffin, *Fr. déjeuner*; brunch, *Brit.* elevenses.

2. light meal, light repast, collation, *Inf.* snack, *Inf.* bite, *Inf.* nosh; refreshments.

3. luncheonette, lunchroom, lunch counter, lunch bar, bar, bar and grill, grill, grill room, diner; cafeteria, canteen, automat; café, restaurant; snack bar.

lunge, *n.* **1.** stab, thrust, jab, poke, pass, cut, swing, feint.

2. plunge, leap, jump, spring, pounce.

—v. **3.** dash, dive, pitch, pitch into, leap, pounce, jump; lay at, have at, lash out at, swing at, take a swing *or* crack *or* swipe *or* poke at, make a thrust *or* pass at, deal *or* aim a blow at.

4. thrust, cut, cut and thrust, poke, jab, feint.

lupine, *adj.* **1.** wolfish, wolflike.

2. savage, ferocious, fierce, bloodthirsty; predatory, predacious, raptorial; ravenous, ravening, rapacious.

lurch, *n.* **1.** list, roll, reel, pitch, toss, tumble; swing, sway, veer, swerve, skew; stagger, totter.

—v. **2.** (*all of a ship*) roll, reel, pitch, toss, pitch and toss, toss and tumble, tumble, flounder, welter, wallow, make heavy weather, be the sport of wind and waves; slant, keel, list, tilt, sway, rock.

3. stagger, totter.

lure, *n.* **1.** attraction, attractant, inducement, incitement, *Sl.* come-on, allurement; magnet, captivator, bewitchment, blandishment, siren song; temptation, charm, drawing card, forbidden fruit, intrigue, stratagem.

2. decoy, stool pigeon, shill; hook, bated hook, bait, flytrap, flypaper, deadfall, trap, pitfall, snare, springe.

—v. **3.** attract, entice, captivate, induce, allure; fascinate, enchant, bewitch, tempt, charm, enrapture; inveigle, decoy, tantalize, titillate, whet the appetite; seduce, lead down the primrose path; draw in, lead in, magnetize; beguile, persuade, blandish, cajole; ensnare, hook, rope in, entrap, snare.

lurid, *adj.* **1.** fiery, burning, flaming, glowing, aglow, glaring; ruddy, flame-red, orange-red, scarlet, crimson, cherry-red; blood-red, blood-colored, bloody, gory, sanguine; overbright, brilliant, dazzling.

2. sensational, melodramatic, vivid, stimulating, *Both Journalism. Inf.* scare, *Inf.* yellow; agitating, perturbing, exaggerated, extravagant, extreme; startling, shocking, tantalizing.

3. gruesome, grisly, grim, macabre; terrible, awful, frightful, appalling; dire, horrible, horrid, repugnant, disgusting, revolting; coarse, vulgar.

4. intense, fierce, furious, passionate; vehement, vigorous, turbulent, tumultuous; ardent, bursting out, raging, stormy, frenzied; wild, hot, savage, unrestrained; explosive, volatile, volcanic.

5. sallow, wan, pallid, pale, colorless, ashen, ashy, ghastly; murky, cloudy, overcast, crepuscular, lowering, leaden, dusky; dismal, gloomy, dull, drab, dreary, somber; baleful, menacing.

lurk, *v.* skulk, sneak, slink, prowl, steal, tiptoe, move with stealth; lie in wait, lie low; hide, hide out, conceal oneself, play peek-a-boo; melt into the shadows, darkle; ambush, waylay.

luscious, *adj.* **1.** delectable, delicious, *Inf.* scrumptious, tasty, dainty, appetizing, tempting; mouthwatering, flavorful, saporous, savory, tangy, spicy, piquant, epicurian; succulent, juicy, rich, creamy; ambrosial, ambrosian, nectarous, nectarean, mellifluous, sweet, tender; palatable, sapid, toothsome, *Scot.* gustable.
2. delightful, enjoyable, pleasing, pleasurable, pleasant, agreeable; dulcet, melodious; fragrant, aromatic, perfumed, scented.
3. luxurious, grand, splendid, magnificent, sumptuous, superb; refined, fine, elegant.
4. voluptuous, sensuous, sexy, gorgeous, beautiful, attractive.

lush[1], *adj.* **1.** fresh, succulent, juicy, sappy, moist, watery; pulpy, fleshy, soft, spongy.
2. luxuriant, luxurious, dense, thick, overgrown, overrun; jungly, jungled, tropical; flourishing, verdured, verdurous, verdant, green; superabundant, exuberant, rank, excessive, prolific.

lush[2], *n. Slang.* alcoholic, dipsomaniac, drinker, hard *or* problem drinker; drunkard, drunk, inebriate, sot, soak, tosspot, toper, bibber, bibbler, barfly; *All Inf.* guzzler, swiller, soaker, sponge; *All Sl.* boozer, boozehound, souse, rummy, alky, dipso, juicehound, juicer. See also **drunkard**.

lust, *n.* **1.** sexual appetite, libido, Eros, biological urge, sexual longing; sexual desire, aphrodisia, sex drive, sex energy, hot blood; sexuality, voluptuousness, sexiness, fleshliness, eroticism; rut, heat, *Zool.* estrus, (*in female animals*) *Dial.* pride.
2. lecherousness, salaciousness, salacity, prurience, pruriency, concupiscence; lasciviousness, lewdness, lubricity, lustfulness; randiness, *Sl.* horniness, *Sl.* hots, *Sl.* hot pants; goatishness, ruttishness, satyrism, priapism, venery, lechery; carnality, bestiality, animality, sensuality; *Pathol.* nymphomania, andromania, *Pathol.* satyriasis, gynecomania, clitoromania, eroticomania; libertinism, wantonness, immorality, unchastity; profligacy, dissipation, debauchery, dissolution, dissoluteness, incontinence, intemperance.
3. desire, greed, greediness, cupidity, avarice, avariciousness; voracity, rapacity, ravenousness, wolfishness, avidness, avidity, covetousness, acquisitiveness; ambition, status-seeking, power-hunger, careerism, climbing.
4. enthusiasm, relish, gusto, zest, zestfulness, élan; animation, liveliness, spirit, life, spiritedness, perkiness; glow, ardor, robustness, vivacity.
—*v.* **5.** crave, hunger for *or* after, thirst for *or* after, *Inf.* hanker for *or* after; pant after, gasp after, covet, run mad after; long for, pine for, hurt for, ache for, itch for, be consumed with desire for, *Sl.* letch after.

luster, *n.* sheen, burnish, shine, gloss, glow; gleam, glimmer, glint, glitter, sparkle, twinkle, shimmer.
2. polish, wax, oil, rosin, coating.
3. brilliance, dazzle, radiance, luminousness, lambency, refulgence, effulgence; irradiation, glowing, fluorescence, incandescence, phosphorescence, iridescence, opalescence; luminescence, luminosity, radiation.
4. merit, credit, glory, honor, distinction, fame, notability, illustriousness.

lusterless, *adj.* dull, flat, matte, unpolished, unburnished; dingy, dark, dim, dun, dusky; drab, colorless, tarnished, faded, washed out; shadowy, gloomy, tenebrous, obscure; murky, hazy; smutchy, dirty, grimy, soiled, muddy.

lustful, *adj.* **1.** craving, desiring, desirous, wanting; greedy, avaricious, avid, covetous, cupidinous, acquisitive; wolfish, hoggish, piggish, gluttonous; rapacious, voracious, ravenous, ravening; insatiable, unsated, unappeasable, unsatisfied; power-hungry, ambitious, careerist, self-advancing, aspiring.
2. lewd, lecherous, libidinous, libidinal, lubricous, *Archaic.* lickerish; randy, *Sl.* horny, goatish, hircine, satyric, priapic; carnal, sensual, bestial, brutish, animal; prurient, salacious, concupiscent, ruttish; passionate, hot-blooded, *Sl.* hot, steamy; wanton, profligate, abandoned, intemperate, incontinent, Paphian, dissolute, debauched, dissipated; degenerate, decadent, shameless, immoral, unchaste, unvirtuous.

lustrous, *adj.* **1.** shiny, shining, glossy, gleaming, agleam, bright; sheenful, sheeny, nitid, polished, burnished, rutilant; radiant, irradiant, lambent, resplendent, beaming, beamy; dazzling, vivid, intense, ablaze, aflame, afire; fulgent, effulgent, refulgent; aglow, glowing, luminous, luminescent, luminiferous, incandescent, phosphorescent; iridescent, (*both usu. of gems*) orient, oriental; sparkling, scintillating, scintillant, coruscating, twinkling, shimmering, glimmering, glittering, aglitter, fulgid.
2. brilliant, magnificent, superb, rich, gorgeous; splendid, splendrous; glorious, illustrious, distinguished; renowned, famous, celebrated, eminent, prominent; august, admirable, majestic, honorable, noble, revered.

lusty, *adj.* **1.** vigorous, full of vigor, robust, robustious, hardy, hale, hale and hearty, strong and healthy, bursting with health *or* vigor, *Sl.* gutsy; energetic, full of energy, lively, full of life, youthful, blooming, (*of a woman*) buxom; sound, healthy, in good health, in good condition, fit, physically fit, in fine fettle, *Inf.* in good shape, *Inf.* in shape, *Inf.* the picture of health.
2. stout, staunch, stanch, firm, sturdy, tough, iron, inured, hardened, enduring, staminal, resilient, *Inf.* tough as nails, *Inf.* hard as rock; stalwart, rugged, hefty, husky, burly, solid, well-knit; able-bodied, able, athletic, sinewy, wiry; muscular, brawny, strapping, powerfully built, broad-shouldered, *Derog.* musclebound; powerful, potent, mighty.
3. hearty, heavy, substantial, ample, plenty, filling, satisfying, satiating, sating.

luxuriant, *adj.* **1.** prolific, proliferous, teeming, profuse, bounteous; pullulating, alive with; abundant, plenteous, full, *Rare.* uberous; exuberant, luxurious, lush, rank, rife, rich, fat, flush; jungly, jungled, dense, wild, overrun.
2. copious, ample, abounding, overflowing, overspilling, spilling over, running over; lavish, thriving, superabundant; fruitful, fertile, fecund, productive.
3. florid, flowery, frilly, busy, ornate, baroque, elaborate, involved, *Music.* bravura; adorned, decorated, embellished, embroidered, festooned; overdone, overwrought, rococo, arabesque, *Fine Arts.* rocaille; ostentatious, flamboyant, showy, *Sl.* flashy, gaudy, garish, tawdry; (*all of writing*) high-flown, bombastic, rhetorical, figurative, tropical, euphuistic.

luxuriate, *v.* **1.** enjoy, bask in, indulge in, swim in, wallow in; feast on, savor, appreciate, gloat over, *Inf.* smack one's lips over, eat up; like, love, fancy, take to, *Sl.* dig; take pleasure in, be pleased with, take satisfaction in, derive pleasure from; delight in, relish in, rejoice in, revel in, riot in, *Sl.* groove on; *Sl.* get a bang *or* kick *or* boot out of, *Sl.* get a charge *or* lift out of, *Sl.* get high off, *Sl.* get off on.
2. thrive, prosper, flourish; grow, bloom, blossom, flower, bear fruit, fructify; mature, maturate, ripen; burst forth, mushroom, burgeon, boom, develop vigorously; issue, arise, originate, spring up, sprout, bud, germinate, pullulate, shoot up.
3. live in luxury, live in comfort, live off the fat of

the land, live high off the hog, be in clover; have a good time, have a time of it, *Inf.* have the time of one's life, *Inf.* have a ball; take it easy, live the life of Riley.

4. overindulge, overdo, go too far, carry to excess, be intemperate.

luxurious, *adj.* **1.** rich, costly, dear; extravagant, grand, opulent, sumptuous, gorgeous; plush, posh, *Inf.* swank, *Inf.* swanky; ostentatious, pretentious, showy, *Inf.* ritzy, *Inf.* fancy.

2. comfortable, agreeable, easy, easeful; enjoyable, pleasurable, gratifying; exciting, titillative, titillating, tantalizing, appealing.

3. epicurean, sybaritic, sensual, carnal, voluptuous; self-indulgent, intemperate, free-living, Saturnalian; excessive, inordinate, immoderate; wild, unrestrained, orgiastic.

4. copious, ample, abounding, overflowing, overspil ling, luxuriant. See **luxuriant** (*defs.* **1, 2**).

5. florid, flowery, frilly, busy, ornate; adorned, decorated, embellished; (*of writing*) bombastic, figurative. See **luxuriant** (*def.* **3**).

luxury, *n.* **1.** luxuriousness, luxe, sumptuousness, lavishness, opulence, splendor, purple and fine linen; abundance, profuseness,excessiveness, exorbitance.

2. indulgence, ease, *Inf.* easy street, *Inf.* velvet; *Inf.* clover; comfort, well-being, sufficiency, bed of roses, rose garden; wealth, affluence, richness.

3. self-indulgence, epicureanism, sybaritism, hedonism, voluptuousness, sensuality, *It. dolce vita, Sl.* high living; unrestraint, immoderation, intemperance, intemperateness; pleasure, enjoyment, delight.

4. extravagance, nonessential, treat, rarity, prodigality, lavishment; accessory, frill, extra, dainty; delicacy, elegance, refinement, nicety.

lyceum, *n.* **1.** *U.S.* academy, institute, seminar, chautauqua.

2. lecture hall *or* room, assembly room, hall, convention hall, exhibition hall; gallery, theater, amphitheater, auditorium.

3. secondary school, high school, senior high school, *Inf.* senior high, (*primarily in France*) lycée, *Brit.* grammar school; preparatory school, *Inf.* prep school, *Brit.* public school, (*in continental Europe, esp. Germany*) gymnasium.

lydian, *adj.* (*all of music*) voluptuous, sensual, sensuous, luxurious, luxuriant; soothing, relaxing, mellow, dulcet.

lying, *n.* **1.** untruthfulness, truthlessness, unveracity, unveraciousness, mendacity, mendaciousness; dishonesty, crookedness, deceit, deceitfulness, falseness, falsity, hypocrisy, double-dealing; guile, guilefulness, disingenuity, disingenuousness, uncandidness, unfrankness; fibbing, *Psychiatry.* mythomania.

—*adj.* **2.** untruthful, unveracious, mendacious, forked-tongued; dissembling, disingenuous, insincere, hypocritical, uncandid, unfrank, guileful, mealy-mouthed; deceitful, dishonest, crooked, double-dealing, two-faced, Janus-faced; deceptive, misleading, false, fraudulent, untrue.

lymphatic, *adj.* **1.** serous, rheumy, phlegmy, humeral, ichorous.

2. languid, languorous, lethargic, listless, lifeless, inanimate, spiritless, zestless, *Inf.* pepless; dull, heavy, sluggish, lumpish, torpid, supine, hebetudinous, *Sl.* dopey.

lynch, *v.* hang, gibbet, *Sl.* string up, *Sl.* scrag, *Sl.* stretch; execute, put to death, kill, murder, slay; stone, lapidate, burn at the stake.

lynching, *n.* murder by mob, mob-murder; hanging, *Sl.* stringing up, *Sl.* scragging, *Sl.* stretching, *Sl.* necktie party; execution; lapidation, stoning, burning, burning at the stake; martyrdom, crucifixion, impalement.

lynx-eyed, *adj.* sharp-sighted, eagle-eyed, quick-sighted, keen-sighted, hawk-eyed; all-seeing, far-seeing, all-observant, not missing a thing; clear-sighted, perspicacious, discerning, discriminating, perceptive; insightful, intuitive, keen, acute, wide awake, sharp, sharp as a tack, alert, bright; Argus-eyed, watchful, vigilant, on the watch, on the alert, on the qui vive, on guard, on the lookout; wary, prudent, discreet; sleepless, never sleeping, wide awake, with both eyes open, alive, clear-headed, canny, shrewd, *Inf.* on top of things, *Inf.* nobody's fool.

lyric, *adj.* **1.** (*all of poetry*) songlike, singing, musical, melodic, melodious, lyrical; subjective, personal, expressive, deep-felt, direct, earnest, ardent, warm, deep; passionate, impassioned, fervid, moving; rhapsodic, elegiac.

2. (*all of a voice*) light, of modest range, limited, small; graceful, flowing, lilting; silvery, clear, dulcet, sweet, mellifluous, mellifluent, mellisonant; pure, tempered, refined; concordant, harmonious, euphonious, mellow.

3. (*all of style*) rapturous, rhapsodic, effuse, effusive, spontaneous; undisciplined, ungoverned, uncontrolled, self-indulgent; impulsive, burning, exciting.

—*n.* **4.** poem, lied, rondeau, roundel, roundelay; triolet, villanelle, ballade, madrigal; elegy, ode, sonnet.

5. **lyrics** words to a song, libretto, book, text.

lyricism, *n.* **1.** lyric style, musicality, musicalness, song-like quality; subjectivity, expressiveness, directness, earnestness; warmness, passion, fervidness, rhapsody.

2. enthusiasm, over-enthusiasm, gushiness, effusiveness, emotionalism, lack of restraint, demonstrativeness, lack of reserve; eagerness, keenness, intentness, intensity, excitement; fervor, ardor, fervency, warmth, glow, fire; spirit, abandon, liveliness, vivacity; emotion, animation, exuberance, ebullience; vitality, life, buoyancy, *It. brio*, zest, verve; vigor, force, energy, vehemence; elation, rapture, ecstasy.

M

macabre, *adj.* **1.** grotesque, gruesome, gory, hideous, grisly, grim, morbid, monstrous, monsterlike; sadistic, brutal, savage, violent, fierce, fell, cruel, inhuman, fiendish, ghoulish, ogreish; horrid, horrible, horrifying, horrendous, horrific, terrifying, frightful, fearsome, eerie, frightening, scary; ghastly, dread, dreadful, dire, direful, terrible, awful, atrocious; shocking, appalling, alarming, abhorrent, odious, heinous, loathsome, outrageous, unspeakable, repugnant, repulsive, foul, revolting, sickening, *Sl.* gross.
2. deathly, deathlike, deathful, deadly; cadaverous, corpse-like, skeletal, gaunt, emaciated, wasted, withered, shriveled, drawn, hollow-eyed, haggard; ghostly, ghostlike, ashen, wan, pallid, pale, livid, bloodless, anemic, white, white as a sheet *or* ghost.

macaroni, *n.* **1.** pasta, paste, dough.
2. dandy, fop, jack-a-dandy, Beau Brummel, fancy Dan, coxcomb, popinjay, *Sl.* peacock, *Sl.* swell, *Fr. petit maitre*; fashion plate, fashionable, clothes horse, pretty-boy, sharp dresser, Zoot suiter, the glass of fashion and the mold of form, exquisite, silk-stocking, *Brit. Inf.* toff; dude, man about town, boulevardier, blade, gay blade; buck, spark, ladies' man, gallant, *Chiefly Brit.* blood.

mace[1], *n.* **1.** club, cudgel, bludgeon, bastinado, blackjack, *Chiefly Irish Eng.* shillelagh, *Obs.* truncheon; bat, flail, billy, billy club.
2. scepter, staff of office, rod of authority, verge, fasces, warder, *Class. Myth.* caduceus; staff, rod, baton, wand; cane, crosier, crook, stick.

mace[2], *n.* tear gas, tear bomb, tear shell, tear grenade; gas, mist, vapor, chemical, irritant; spray, atomizer, *Trademark.* Chemical Mace.

macerate, *v.* **1.** pulp, mash, squash, soften up; liquefy, soak, steep, soften.
2. waste away, become thin *or* emaciated, lose weight, shrivel up, shrink away, wither.

maceration, *n.* **1.** soaking, steeping, saturation; pulping, mashing.
2. emaciation, wasting away, shrinking, shriveling, withering, drying up.

machete, *n.* **1.** knife, bolo, cutlass, cane-cutter, cleaver, broadsword, *Scot.* claymore.
2. tarpon, game fish.

machiavellian, *adj.* cunning, devious, crafty, guileful, artful; deceptive, deceitful, dishonest, crooked, unscrupulous; wily, sly, foxy, slippery, stealthy; tricky, scheming, designing, intriguing, conniving, shrewd, astute; circuitous, tortuous, roundabout, subtle, insidious; shifty, perfidious, treacherous, two-faced, double-dealing, false-hearted; expedient, opportunistic, seizing the moment, furtive, clandestine, underhanded, sub rosa.

machiavellianism, *n.* cunning, deception, deceit, dishonesty, duplicity, *Inf.* hanky-panky; treachery, perfidy, double-dealing; slyness, foxiness, stealth, craftiness, surreptitiousness; trickery, sharp tricks, artifice, guile, roguery, knavery; machination, intrigue, subterfuge, *Inf.* finagling.

machinate, *v.* scheme, plot, conspire, intrigue, complot; maneuver, *Sl.* wheel and deal, manipulate, pull strings, *Inf.* finagle, *Inf.* wangle, manage, *Sl.* pull off; contrive, devise, make up, trump up, fabricate, *Sl.* hoke up; brew, concoct, hatch, invent, come up with, design, plan, work out a strategy.

machination, *n.* **1.** *Usu.* **machinations** schemes, plots, intrigues, conspiracies, complots; dirty tricks, *Inf.* hanky-panky, *Sl.* monkey business, *Inf.* shenanigans; designs, plans, expedients, contrivances, artifices, devices, ruses, tricks, wiles; stratagems, strategy *or* strategies, tactics, ploys, moves; maneuvers, logistics.
2. contriving, devising, scheming, plotting, planning; maneuvering, manipulation, *Inf.* finagling, *Inf.* wangling, *Sl.* wheeling and dealing.

machinator, *n.* schemer, plotter, conspirator, intriguer, contriver; deviser, planner, strategist; manipulator, *Sl.* wheeler-dealer, *Inf.* finagler, *Inf.* wangler.

machine, *n.* **1.** engine, motor, mechanism, generator, apparatus, contrivance, device; contraption, gadget, *Inf.* gismo; appliance, utensil, tool, implement, instrument; lever, wheel and axle, pulley, inclined plane, wedge, screw.
2. vehicle, automobile, auto, car, motorcar, *Inf.* flivver; airplane, plane, flying machine; helicopter, *Inf.* whirlybird, *Inf.* eggbeater.
3. agency, organization, party, ring, gang; faction, junta, council; cabal, clique, coterie, set, circle.
4. robot, automaton, puppet; drudge, menial.

machinery, *n.* **1.** equipment, matériel, paraphernalia, apparatus, gadgetry, contrivances; tackle, gear, outfit, equipage; mechanism, works.
2. instrument, instrumentality, vehicle, channels; organization, system, setup, workings; brass tacks, *Sl.* nitty-gritty, nuts and bolts.

machinist, *n.* technician, engineer, mechanic, *Sl.* grease monkey; operator, operative, mechanician, repairman; craftsman, artisan, skilled worker; tinker, *Inf.* tinkerer, inventor, contriver, concocter; electrician, *Sl.* sparks, *Inf.* troubleshooter.

machismo, *n.* virility, masculinity, manliness; he-manliness, two-fistedness, *Sl.* the cult of balls; male chauvinism, sexism, air of a super stud; toughness, brawn, grit, courage; arrogance, scorn, indifference; unsentimentality, insensitivity; *All Fig.* muscle-flexing, chest-beating, hairiness.

macrocosm, *n.* **1.** universe, cosmos, globe, world, wide world, *Inf.* the whole wide world, all of creation, nature; heavens, firmament, sky, canopy, the blue, empyrean, vault of heaven, *Chiefly Literary.* welkin; heavenly bodies, celestial bodies *or* spheres, stars, planets, orbs; solar system, galaxy, nebula, extragalactic nebula.

2. total structure, totality, entirety.

3. enlargement, *Photog.* blow-up.

macula, *n.* **1.** macule, mark, spot, speck, freckle; blemish, pimple, whitehead, *Pathol.* milium, blackhead, *Med.* comedo, *Sl.* zit, *Sl.* woogit; pock, pockmark, pit, cicatrix, scar; imperfection, disfigurement, defect, flaw, mar; bruise, *Sl.* hickey; blotch, patch, discoloration, birthmark, *Med.* nevus, mole, wart.

2. maculation, stain, taint, spot, mark; soil, dirty mark, smudge, smutch, smear, smirch, blur.

maculate, *v.* **1.** mark, spot, speckle, bedaub, bespatter, spatter, splash; stain, smudge, smutch, smirch, smear; soil, dirty, sully, besmirch, muck *or* muck up, bemire; tarnish, blacken, discolor, mar, spoil.

2. pollute, infect, poison, contaminate, befoul *or* foul up, corrupt, defile, spoil, taint.

—adj. **3.** spotted, stained, marked, speckled, bespattered; stained, soiled, dirtied, sullied, besmirched; smudged, smutched, smirched, smeared, blurred; tarnished, blackened, discolored, marred, spoiled, mucked up.

mad, *adj.* **1.** insane, crazy, crazed, demented, lunatic, deranged; of unsound mind, *Latin. non compos mentis*; daft, *Inf.* daffy, unbalanced, touched, *Inf.* unglued, *Inf.* half-baked, *Brit. Sl.* bunkers, unhinged, distracted; eccentric, flighty, odd, idiosyncratic, offbeat, queer, bizarre, *Chiefly Brit. Inf.* potty, *Inf.* dotty, *Inf.* crackpot; brainsick, *Sl.* kooky, *Sl.* meshuga; *All Sl.* balmy, dippy, batty, bats, cuckoo, buggy, bughouse, bugs, screwy, wacky, wacko, goofy, loony, squirrelly, bananas, nuts, nutty, nutty as a fruitcake.

2. out of one's head, out of one's mind, *Scot.* redwood, *Sl.* loco, mad as a hatter, mad as a March hare, stark raving mad; not all there, not quite right, not right upstairs; *Inf.* out in left field, *Sl.* in outer space, *Sl.* in orbit, *Inf.* off the wall; *Inf.* cracked, *Inf.* mental, *Sl.* schizo, *Sl.* off one's rocker, *Sl.* out of one's tree, *Sl.* off one's trolley, *Brit. Sl.* off one's chump; *All Sl.* have bats in one's belfry, have a few buttons missing, have a few loose screws.

3. enraged, raging, fuming, infuriated, *Rare.* infuriate, furious; angry, irate, ireful, incensed, wrathful, wroth; in a huff, up in arms, in high dudgeon; at the end of one's rope, *Inf.* fed up, ready to burst; inflamed, flaming, flaring, fiery, flared up, flushed with anger, red-hot, white-hot.

4. irritated, annoyed, peeved, vexed; piqued, chafed, galled, riled, nettled; displeased, indignant.

5. maniacal, hysterical, madding, *Archaic.* wood, delirious; frantic, frenzied, frenetic; ranting, raving, storming, foaming at the mouth, convulsing; overwrought, distraught, upset, worked-up, wrought-up, stirred-up; exasperated, provoked; beside oneself, at one's wit's end; out of control, uncontrollable, unrestrainable, corybantic, *Inf.* haywire, berserk, wild; violent, stormy, fierce, tempestuous, tumultuous, turbulent.

6. impractical, injudicious, unsensible; unfounded, groundless, unsound; preposterous, extravagant, excessive; inappropriate, inept, improper, incongruous, inconsistent; imprudent, indiscreet; unwise, ill-considered, ill-suited, ill-advised; short-sighted, careless, unwary, irresponsible; reckless, rash, harum-scarum; unsafe, dangerous, perilous.

7. absurd, silly, inane, fatuous, crackbrained, foolish; irrational, wild-eyed, illogical, unreasonable; senseless, nonsensical, pointless; ridiculous, laughable, risible, derisible, ludicrous, *Sl.* for the birds; asinine, anserine, idiotic, *Inf.* moronic, imbecilic; childish, puerile, immature.

8. stupid, simple-minded, bird-brained, feeble-minded, dull-witted; harebrained, light-minded, light-headed, giddy; wandering, rambling, driveling, incoherent; scatterbrained, absent-minded, confused; muddled, muddlepated, bemused.

9. enthusiastic, excited, avid, eager, zealous; ardent, fervid, fervent, passionate, impassioned; fanatical, *Inf.* wild, dithyrambic; intense, rabid, vehement.

10. infatuated, moon-struck, possessed; enamored by *or* with, *U.S. Sl.* ape over *or* for, keen on *or* about, wild about, mad about *or* after, fond of, *Inf.* gone on; desirous, covetous, avid for *or* of; *All Sl.* all hopped-up about, hepped up *or* over, hot about *or* for *or* on, steamed up about, nuts about *or* on.

11. like mad *Slang.* ardently, fervently, passionately, intensely, like crazy; devotedly, devoutly; enthusiastically, madly, furiously, excitedly. See **madly** (*def.* **1**).

madam, *n.* **1.** madame, *Inf.* ma'am, Mrs., Ms., mistress, dame, lady, *Chiefly Scot.* goodwife; senhora, signora, senora, *Ger. Frau, Dutch. vrouw, Archaic.* madonna, (*in India*) memsahib.

2. bawd, procuress, pander *or* panderer.

madcap, *adj.* **1.** impulsive, wild, reckless, rash, daring, adventurous; hasty, imprudent, heedless, careless, incautious, foolhardy; foolish, crazy, senseless, impractical.

—n. **2.** adventurer, adventuress, daredevil, devil, hothead, fire-eater; prankster, *Inf.* cutup, joker, clown, merry-andrew, buffoon.

madden, *v.* **1.** derange, dement, unhinge, unbalance; craze, frenzy, distract, make *or* send [s.o.] mad, drive [s.o.] mad *or* insane *or* crazy, *Archaic.* mad.

2. enrage, infuriate, lash into a fury, whip into a frenzy, make [s.o.'s] blood boil, *Inf.* make [s.o.] see red; anger, incense, irk, raise [s.o.'s] ire *or* hackles, get [s.o.'s] back up, *Inf.* burn [s.o.] up, *Sl.* tee [s.o.] off, *Sl.* tick [s.o.] off, *Brit. Sl.* put [s.o.'s] monkey up; provoke, agitate, inflame, enflame, fire up; exacerbate, acerbate, envenom, embitter.

3. irritate, annoy, vex, pique, get on [s.o.'s] nerves, *Chiefly U.S.* rile, *Inf.* aggravate; exasperate, ruffle, roil, try [s.o.'s] patience; bother, pester, harass, hector, *Sl.* bug, *Sl.* hassle, *Sl.* drive [s.o.] nuts *or* bananas, *Sl.* drive [s.o.] up the wall; provoke, bait, badger, torment, bedevil, plague.

4. rage, rant, rave, rant and rave, fulminate, roar, bellow; seethe, sizzle, smolder, boil, stew, simmer, fume, stir, *Inf.* do a slow burn, *Inf.* steam *or* steam up, *Inf.* get all steamed up, *Sl.* work oneself into a lather *or* sweat *or* stew.

maddening, *adj.* **1.** aggravating, provoking, irritating, exasperating, disturbing; infuriating, enraging, vexatious, riling, galling; agitating, unsettling, perturbing, discomposing, disturbing, disquieting; upsetting, annoying, troubling, troublesome, nagging, bothersome, *Inf.* pestiferous.

2. outrageous, excessive, flagrant, notorious, offensive; unrestrained, unmitigated, immoderate.

3. furious, raging, fuming, raving; turbulent, tumultuous, stormy; wild, fierce, violent, ferocious; intense, passionate, vehement.

made, *adj.* **1.** handmade, ready-made.

2. machine made, artificially made.

3. invented, made-up, concocted, devised, contrived, fabricated; make-believe, imagined, fictional, unreal, untrue, false; pretended, feigned, fake, sham, spurious, simulated, bogus; synthetic, artificial, ungenuine, counterfeit.

made-up, *adj.* **1.** invented, concocted, made, devised, contrived, fabricated. See **made** (*def.* **3**).

2. painted, powdered, rouged.

3. put together, finished, ready, prepared, fixed.

madhouse, *n.* **1.** insane asylum, lunatic asylum, mental institution, state hospital, psychiatric hospital, *Fr. maison de santé, Obs.* bedlam; *Sl.* nuthouse, *Sl.* crazy house, *Sl.* bughouse, *Sl.* loonybin, *Sl.* funny farm, *Sl.* laughing academy, *Sl.* booby hatch.

2. bedlam, chaos, wild confusion, jungle, jumble, mess, disorder, disarray, disarrangement; three-ring circus.

madly, *adv.* **1.** insanely, distractedly, deliriously, hysterically; enthusiastically, excitedly, frenziedly, frantically; ardently, fervently, heatedly, glowingly, feverishly, passionately, intensely; devotedly, devoutly, fanatically, till one is black *or* blue in the face; *All Sl.* like mad, like crazy, *Inf.* in the worst way, *Inf.* something awful.

2. fiercely, furiously, wildly, violently, vehemently, rabidly; desperately, with a vengeance, exceedingly, severely; turbulently, tumultuously, uproariously; impetuously, hastily, hurriedly; carelessly, recklessly, wantonly.

3. absurdly, inanely, fatuously, foolishly; crazily, daftly, ridiculously, ludicrously, humorously, funnily; asininely, idiotically, stupidly.

madman, *n.* **1.** lunatic, *Sl.* loony, maniac, bedlamite, *Inf.* crackpot, *Sl.* kook, *Sl.* nut, *Sl.* screwball; psychopath, *Sl.* sickie; schizophrenic, *Sl.* schizo, paranoiac, manic-depressive, psychotic; megalomaniac, pyromaniac, kleptomaniac, dipsomaniac, automaniac.

2. eccentric, *Inf.* crackpot, nonconformist, bohemian; dreamer, Don Quixote, highflier, rhapsodist; enthusiast, fanatic, crank, zealot, phrenetic; energumen, demoniac.

3. imbecile, idiot, mooncalf, *Inf.* moron; dimwit, nitwit, half-wit, featherbrain, pinhead; fool, crackbrain, *Sl.* lamebrain, saphead, Simple Simon, noodle, *Inf.* jay, *Sl.* jerk, goose; simpleton, ninny, nincompoop, silly, silly billy, driveler, tomfool; sulker, *Inf.* grouch, *Inf.* crank.

madness, *n.* **1.** insanity, insaneness, lunacy, derangement, *Psychiatry.* dementia, dementedness; distraction, disorientation, unbalance, unsoundness; unsound mind, diseased mind; craziness, *Sl.* kookiness, *Inf.* nuttiness, daftness, brainsickness; *All Sl.* balminess, bugginess, screwiness, wackiness, goofiness.

2. psychosis, neurosis, psychoneurosis; schizophrenia, *Psychiatry.* dementia praecox, monomania, automania, dipsomania, pyromania, delusion of grandeur; senility, anility, dotage, *Psychiatry.* amentia; *Psychol.* kleptomania, *Psychol.* split personality; *All Psychiatry.* melancholia, hypochondria, mania, lyssophobia, fugue.

3. rabies, *Pathol.* hydrophobia.

4. absurdity, absurdness, silliness, inanity, fatuousness, foolishness, folly; irrationality, illogic, illogicality, illogicalness, unreasonableness; senselessness, nonsense, nonsensicalness, nonsensicality, pointlessness; ridiculousness, ridiculosity, ludicrousness; asininity, imbecility, idiocy, *Inf.* moronism, *Inf.* moronity; childishness, puerility, immaturity.

5. impracticality, unsensibleness, preposterousness, unreasonableness; inappropriateness, impropriety, ineptitude, ineptness, incongruity, inconsistency; imprudence, indiscretion; irresponsibility, carelessness, unwariness, recklessness.

6. frenzy, franticness, furor, delirium, *Pathol.* delirium tremens, phrenitis, anoesis, hysteria; ranting, raving, storming, foaming at the mouth; violence, storminess, fierceness, tumult, tumultuousness, turbulence.

7. rage, enragement, fury, infuriation; anger, wrath, wrathfulness, ire, irateness, choler, irascibility, irascibleness; indignation, resentment, exasperation.

8. enthusiasm, excitement, eagerness, zealousness, fanaticism; passion, ardentness, keenness, ferventness.

9. infatuation, fascination, possession, entrancement, intoxication; ecstasy, rapture, bliss, thrill.

maelstrom, *n.* **1.** whirlpool, vortex, gurge, Charybdis, indraft, eddy, swirl, whirl.

2. confusion, chaos, tumult, commotion, uproar, turbulence; disorder, disarray, disarrangement, jumble, mess.

magazine, *n.* **1.** periodical, publication, journal; weekly, biweekly, monthly, quarterly; pulp, *Inf.* slick, *Derog., Inf.* rag, scandal sheet.

2. arsenal, armory, *Mil.* depot, *Mil.* ammunition *or* munitions dump; storehouse, warehouse, entrepôt, depository, repository.

magenta, *n.* **1.** fuchsin, basic magenta.

2. fuchsia, reddish purple, purplish red, crimson, carmine.

maggot, *n.* **1.** larva, insect larva, flyblow, worm, grub.

2. odd fancy, whim, whimsy, caprice, *Archaic.* megrim, vagary, humor, crotchet, kink.

maggoty, *adj.* **1.** flyblown, wormy, grubby, maggot-infested, maggot-ridden.

2. fanciful, whimsical, crotchety, capricious, flighty, unpredictable, erratic, irregular; odd, eccentric, strange, bizarre, queer, outlandish, freaky, freakish, kinky.

magic, *n.* **1.** sorcery, witchcraft, witchery, wizardry, incantation, wonderworking; necromancy, thaumaturgy, theurgy; black magic, black art, voodoo, hoodoo, obiism *or* obeahism; deviltry *or* devilry, demonology, demonaltry, diabolism; supernaturalness, shamanism, mysticism, spiritualism, occultness, psychomancy, fetishism; ritual, rite, apotropaism, magical ceremony, voodooism, exorcism.

2. fortunetelling, soothsaying, horoscopy, astrology; foreboding, presage, presentiment; omen, augury, portent, indication; forecast, prediction, prognostication; thought-reading, clairvoyance, telepathy.

3. spell, jinx, hex, negative influence, charm, rune, *Scot.* cantrip, enchantment, bewitchment, bedevilment; trance, hypnosis, hypnotism, mesmerism, fascination, rapture; captivation, obsession, possession; entrancement, allurement, seduction.

4. conjuration, conjury, conjure, *U.S. Dial.* root work; invocation, summoning; magic formula, hocus-pocus, mumbo jumbo; magic word, abracadabra, open sesame; legerdemain, sleight of hand, artful trickery, skillful deception.

—adj. **5.** enchanting, charming, fascinating; bewitching, spellbinding, spell-weaving; entrancing, mesmeric, hypnotic, obsessive; magnetic, alluring, captivating; irresistible, seductive, glamorous.

6. magical, wonder-working, miracle-working; incantatory, incantational; alchemical, alchemistic; thaumaturgic, theurgical, necromantic; cabalistic, mystic, occult, spiritualistic, shamanistic.

magician, *n.* **1.** conjurer, sorcerer, sorceress, black magician, voodoo; wizard, Wizard of Oz, Merlin, magus, necromancer, warlock, witch, hex, hexer, Hecate; exorcist, witch doctor, medicine man, shaman; theurgist, miracle-worker, wonder-worker, thaumaturge, thaumaturgist, fairy godmother; charmer, incantator, evocator, enchanter, enchantress, Circe, bewitcher, mesmerist, hypnotist; medium, telepathist, mind reader, psychic, psychic medium, clairvoyant, dowser; fortuneteller, soothsayer, diviner, prophet, prophetess, seer, seeress, astrologer.

2. conjurer, illusionist, sleight-of-hand artist, legerdemainist; juggler, trickster, archimage, *Archaic.* mage, Houdini, escape artist; snake charmer.

magisterial, *adj.* **1.** authoritative, *Rare.* magistral, important, consequential, significant, of great weight *or* importance, weighty, momentous.

2. imperious, high and mighty, lordly, domineering, overbearing, overweening; high-handed, arbitrary, presumptuous, cocky, overconfident; arrogant, haughty, insolent, contemptuous, disdainful, supercilious; proud, lofty, condescending, patronizing, *Inf.* uppity, *Inf.* uppish, snobbish, snobby, *Inf.* snotty, *Inf.* snooty; assertive, self-assertive, forward, aggressive, pushing, *Inf.* pushy; self-willed, willful, forceful, imperative, commanding, masterful, authoritative, authoritarian, *Inf.* bossy; peremptory, dictatorial, despotic, autocratic, tyrannical, ironhanded; heavy-handed, oppressive, harsh, hard, tough, strict.

3. formal, grave, serious, dignified, stately.

magistrate, *n.* **1.** civil magistrate, syndic; chief magistrate, mayor, governor, prefect, consul, doge, burgomaster, *Ger. Bürgermeister*, corregidor, (*in England*) bencher, atchon, ephor; municipal officer, (*in Britain*) bailiff, (*both in Scotland*) bailie, provost, (*in England*) alderman, (*in Spain and Southwestern U.S.*) alcalde.

2. judicial official, constable, justice of the peace, *Inf.* J.P., circuit judge, *Inf.* circuit rider, judge of probate, police court judge; judge, justice, *Chiefly Brit. Sl.* beak, *U.S.* surrogate, *Inf.* his honor, *Islam.* mullah, cadi.

magnanimity, *n.* **1.** magnanimousness, big-heartedness, large-heartedness, great-heartedness, bigness, largeness; tolerance, toleration, liberalness, open-heartedness; leniency, lenience, condonation, forbearance, long-suffering, easiness, permissiveness; unspitefulness, forgivingness, forgiveness, patience, kindness, benevolence.

2. high-mindedness, noble-mindedness, nobleness, nobility of mind, loftiness of spirit, greatness of heart *or* soul; princeliness, chivalry, chivalrousness.

3. unselfishness, selflessness, self-sacrifice, sacrifice, disinterest, impartiality, fairness, justness; charitableness, charity, altruism, generosity, generousness; munificence, largess, bounty, bountifulness, bounteousness, open-heartedness, free-heartedness.

magnanimous, *adj.* **1.** forgiving, merciful, big, unspiteful, unresentful, unrevengeful; liberal, broad-minded, unbigoted, unbiased, big-hearted, large-hearted, great-hearted; tolerant, indulgent, lenient, patient, forbearing, long-suffering; impartial, fair, just, disinterested.

2. charitable, kind, kindly, benign, benignant, benevolent, humanitarian; brotherly, fraternal, human, humane, *Inf.* Christian; generous, generous to a fault, altruistic, philanthropic; unselfish, unsparing of self, giving, self-sacrificing, ungrudging, unstinting.

3. high-minded, noble-minded, noble, great of heart *or* spirit, idealistic; lordly, princely, dignified, august, stately; elevated, lofty, sublime, exalted; magnificent, majestic, grand.

magnate, *n.* **1.** tycoon, big businessman, businessman, enterpriser, financier, entrepreneur; industrialist, captain of industry, baron, *Inf.* robber baron, *Inf.* wheeler-dealer; top executive, business leader, director, manager; *Sl.* honcho, *Sl.* top dog, *Sl.* Mr. Big.

2. personage, person of importance, person of influence *or* consequence, man of distinction *or* eminence, person to be reckoned with; giant, leading figure, mastodon; power, power elite, *Chiefly Brit.* notability, leading light, luminary, worthy, pillar of society, dignitary, distinguished person; personality, name, big name, star, super-star, celebrity, person of eminence; elder, elder statesman, panjandrum, sachem; *All Inf.* somebody, Very Important Person, V.I.P., big shot, big gun, bigwig, big brass; *All Inf.* lion, wheel, big wheel, big cheese, big-timer, big-time operator; *Sl.* top banana, *Sl.* high-muck-a-muck.

3. aristocratic, lord, peer, nobleman, noble, partrician.

magnet, *n.* **1.** lodestone, magnetite, paramagnet; attractor, attractant; field magnet, bar magnet, horseshoe magnet, electromagnet, solenoid.

2. focus, focal point, prime focus, point of convergence; center of attraction *or* interest, center *or* focus of attention, cynosure, lodestar, polestar.

3. lure, charm, fascination, captivation, attraction, interest, appeal, drawing card, draw card, bait; temptation, tantalization, allure, allurement, enticement, invitation.

magnetic, *adj.* **1.** attracting, drawing, attrahent, pulling, dragging, tugging; magnetized; attractive, interesting, appealing, engaging, alluring, fascinating, enthralling, captivating, enchanting; hypnotic, mesmerizing, mesmeric, entrancing, irresistible, taking, winning, winsome; inviting, tempting, enticing, seductive, provocative, siren, tantalizing, *Inf.* come-hither; charming, glamorous, witching, bewitching, beguiling.

2. gripping, holding, arresting, engrossing, binding, absorbing, intriguing, grabbing, catching; electric, electrical, dynamic, exciting, kinetic, charged; powerful, potent, forceful, vital, effective, authoritative, overwhelming, overpowering, spellbinding, persuasive, compelling, charismatic.

magnetism, *n.* **1.** magnetic force *or* intensity, *Elect.* gauss, *Elect.* oersted; magnetomotive force, magnetomotivity, magnetic flux density, magnetic field, electromagnetic field, electroaffinity, electromagnetic attraction, electromagnetic repulsion.

2. gravity, gravitation; capillarity, capillary attraction; affinity, sympathy, inclination, tendency.

3. attraction, interest, charm, glamour, appeal, enchantment, attractiveness, seductiveness, winsomeness, winning ways, likability, lovability; charisma, *Sp. duende*, personal magnetism, animal magnetism, sex appeal, *Sl.* SA; power of attraction, force, power, personality, energy, potency, vitality, dynamism, authority, hold, sway, dominance, influence; pulling *or* drawing power, drag, pull, tug, traction, electrification.

4. allurement, irresistibility, fascination, captivation, enchantment; desirability, lure, witchery, bewitchment, spell, magic; temptation, enticement, seduction, provocativeness; sorcery, mesmerism, hypnotic influence, siren song, invitation; come-hither quality, flame to a moth, that certain something, *Sl.* come-on.

magnetize, *v.* **1.** magnify, electromagnetize, electrify, charge, energize.

2. attract, pull, draw, drag, tug; lure, charm, entice, tempt, seduce, lead on, ensnare, *Archaic.* entoil, draw in, *Inf.* suck *or* rope in; inveigle, entangle, get a hold on; compel, galvanize, rivet, electrify, carry away, sway, move, spellbind, interest, appeal, engage; influence, act on, work on, take hold of, *Inf.* get at, *Inf.* get the ear of; intrigue, hold the attention of.

magnification, *n.* increase, enlargement, extension.

expansion; intensification, enhancement, heightening, deepening, strengthening; exaggeration, hyperbole, overstatement, overemphasis; glorification, ennoblement, elevation, aggrandizement; exaltation, lionization, deification, apotheosis.

magnificence, *n.* **1.** splendor, resplendence, grandeur, glory, majesty, nobility; grandiosity, sublimity, imposingness, impressiveness; exquisiteness, superbness, splendidness, *Inf.* splendiferousness; state, stateliness, pomp, circumstance, pomp and circumstance, solemnity.

2. luxury, luxuriousness, sumptuousness, lavishness, gorgeousness; brilliance, radiance; grace, elegance; *All Inf.* ritziness, plushness, poshness, swankness.

magnificent, *adj.* **1.** splendid, *Inf.* splendiferous, resplendent, superb, glorious, brilliant, radiant; luxurious, lavish, sumptuous, gorgeous, *Sl.* out of this world; *All Inf.* posh, plush, swank, ritzy.

2. noble, sublime, majestic, august, stately; imposing, impressive, commanding, awe-inspiring, *Archaic.* magnific; grand, distinguished, royal, regal, kingly, princely; elegant, graceful, handsome.

magnifico, *n.* **1.** grandee, hidalgo, seignior, don; nobleman, patrician, lord, peer, Brahman, silk-stocking, blue blood, *Sl.* swell.

2. personage, great man, person of consequence, man of mark *or* note, somebody, name, nabob, mogul, magnate, *Inf.* big name, *Inf.* bigwig, *Inf.* VIP, *Inf.* bashaw; *All Sl.* big shot, big gun, big wheel, high-muck-a-muck.

magnify, *v.* **1.** increase, enlarge, expand, aggrandize, greaten, amplify; augment, add to, build up; widen, broaden, distend, develop.

2. exaggerate, hyperbolize, overstate, overemphasize; color, embroider, enlarge upon; overreact, blow up, blow out of proportion, *Inf.* make a mountain out of a molehill, *Inf.* make a big thing out of nothing, make much ado about nothing.

3. intensify, dramatize, deepen, heighten; enhance, strengthen, *Inf.* beef up; concentrate, condense, consolidate; aggravate, worsen, make worse, exacerbate, rub salt in the wound, add insult to injury, pour oil on the fire.

magniloquence, *n.* bombast, fustian, pomposity, orotundity; grandiloquence, high-soundingness, pretentiousness, grandiosity, *Archaic.* magnisonance; turgidity, tumidity, tumescence; boastfulness, braggadocio, fanfaronade, gasconade; (*all of speech*) vanity, pride, vaingloriousness, vainglory, arrogance, haughtiness.

magniloquent, *adj.* pompous, bombastic, fustian, orotund; grandiloquent, high-sounding, high-flown, *Inf.* highfalutin, pretentious, stilted, grandiose, *Archaic.* magnisonant; turgid, tumid, inflated, puffed-up; boastful, thrasonical, bragging, braggart, crowing, vaunting, fanfaronading; (*all of speech*) proud, vain, vainglorious, arrogant, haughty, *Inf.* high-hat.

magnitude, *n.* **1.** size, extent, measure, proportions, dimensions; amplitude, volume, mass, bulk.

2. greatness, largeness, bigness; immensity, vastness, enormousness, tremendousness; expanse, boundlessness, infinity.

3. abundance, superabundance, plenitude, plenty, profusion, much, copiousness; quantity, good *or* great deal, *Inf.* heap, *Inf.* pile, *Inf.* mess; quantities, bags, barrels, tons.

4. importance, consequence, note, mark, distinction; eminence, loftiness, sublimity; fame, glory, renown.

5. of the first magnitude of the utmost importance, of the utmost significance; important, significant, major, consequential, momentous, world-shaking, earth-shattering; notable, noteworthy, celebrated, prominent, eminent, outstanding, distinguished, esteemed, prestigious; of importance, of significance, of consequence, of moment, of note, of weight.

magpie, *n.* chatterbox, chatterer, jabberer, gabbler, babbler, prattler, prater, twaddler, *Brit.* twattler, driveler; palaverer, popinjay, *Inf.* jay; gossip, blabber, blabbermouth, gusher; blatherskite, *Sl.* windbag, *Sl.* windjammer, *Inf.* hot-air artist.

maid, *n.* **1.** girl, lass. See **maiden** (*def.* **1**).

2. maidservant, domestic, girl, au pair *or* au pair girl, upstairs girl, *Fr. bonne*, chambermaid, *Brit.* betweenmaid, *Brit. Inf.* tweeny; maid-of-all-work, *Brit. Inf.* slavey; handmaid *or* handmaiden, *Archaic.* ancilla, lady's maid, waiting maid, abigail, soubrette.

maiden, *n.* **1.** girl, young girl, lass, lassie, maid, miss, missy, little missy, school girl, *Irish Eng.* colleen, *Chiefly Scot.* burd, *Fr. jeune fille, Ger. Fräulein*, damsel, *Archaic.* demoiselle *or* damozel; nymph, nymphet, young thing, slip, wench, flapper, *Inf.* baggage, *Australian Inf.* girl-o; tomboy, hoyden, romp; malapert, minx, insolent; virgin, vestal, vestal virgin, celibate; single, single girl, bachelor girl, *Law.* femme sole; *All Sl.* jailbait, chick, *Brit.* bird, piece, gall, doll, dame, tomato, babe, cutie, skirt, jill, filly.

—*adj.* **2.** unmarried, unwed, unwedded, single, spouseless, husbandless.

3. first, initial, inaugural; new, fresh, untried, untested, untapped.

4. virgin, virginal, chaste, pure, undefiled, intact.

maidenhood, *n.* virginity, maidenhead, maidhood, intactness; celibacy, singleness, *Euph.* single blessedness.

maidenly, *adj.* **1.** feminine, womanly, womanlike, womanish, ladylike; girlish, little-girlish, maiden, kittenish.

2. modest, decent, decorous, proper, seemly, becoming.

3. virgin, virginal, vestal, intact; unsullied, unsoiled, undefiled, undebauched, undissipated, undissolute, unwanton; chaste, virtuous, immaculate, spotless, pure.

maidservant, *n.* maid, handmaiden, lady's maid. See **maid** (*def.* **2**).

mail[1], *n.* **1.** letters, packages, messages, missives; post, correspondence, communication; air mail, sea mail, parcel post, special delivery, certified mail, registered mail.

2. mails postal system, post office, postal service, *Chiefly Brit.* post.

—*v.* **3.** send, post, dispatch, air-mail; transmit, remit, consign; direct, address, forward, drop a letter; freight, ship, express, air freight.

mail[2], *n.* armor, panoply, harness, armature, chain mail, coat of mail, plate armor; hauberk, byrnie, habergeon, plastron; cuirass, corselet, lorica, breastplate, backplate.

mailman, *n.* postman, carrier, mail carrier, letter carrier, delivery man *or* boy; courier, messenger, runner, dispatcher, bearer.

maim, *v.* **1.** cripple, lame, hobble; mangle, mutilate, tear, rip, rend, hack, maul, savage; lacerate, wound, skin, flay; scotch, cut, gash, slash, slit, score, scarify; stab, stick, plunge, puncture, pierce; break, rupture, fracture, sprain, wrench, dislocate; amputate, truncate, obtruncate, detruncate, cut off; castrate, geld, emasculate, effeminate, unman, neuter, spay, caponize.

2. impair, injure, hurt, harm; disable, hamstring, unfit, incapacitate, wing, put out of action *or* commission; deface, mar, despoil, disfigure.

main, *adj.* **1.** chief, principal, cardinal, prime,

primary, capital; paramount, preeminent, premier, supreme, first, foremost, head, headmost, top, topmost; leading, crowning, ruling, overruling, prevailing; uppermost, important, most important, predominant, dominant; great, star, arch, banner, ranking, sovereign; most, utmost, major, maximum, maximal; substantial, sizable, considerable, large, big; powerful, strong, mighty, forceful, puissant; total, full, comprehensive, plenary.

2. essential, requisite, vital, necessary, indispensable, unexpendable; critical, crucial, consequential, pivotal; exigent, instant, pressing, urgent, imperative, high-priority; marked, signal, salient, notable, memorable; outstanding, remarkable, special, especial, particular.

3. sheer, brute, pure, dead, downright, consummate; utmost, utter, total, absolute, complete, out-and-out; direct, plain, bare, stark.

4. wide, vast, immense, broad; extensive, expansive, widespread, spacious, roomy, spread out, outspread.

—*n.* **5.** conduit, pipe, pipeline, duct, aqueduct, channel, canal; gutter, runnel, sewer, trough, shoot, chute; sluice, lock, floodgate, watergate, weir.

6. majority, bulk, mass, gross; substance, preponderance, meat, marrow; kernel, core, heart, nucleus, key, gist.

7. strength, power, force, might, potency, puissance; energy, vitality, vim, vigor; forcefulness, powerfulness, vehemence, virility, virulence.

8. *Literary.* sea, ocean, ocean blue, high seas, the open ocean, the deep, the seven seas, the bounding main; the deep blue sea, the vasty deep, the briny deep, the briny, *Sl.* the drink, the watery waste.

9. **in the main** chiefly, principally. See **mainly**.

mainland, *n.* main, principal land, continent, continental land.

mainly, *adv.* chiefly, principally, particularly, especially, primarily; mostly, for the most part, in the main, on the whole, by and large; overall, all in all, all things considered, on balance, in the long run, to all intents and purposes; substantially, effectually, effectively, essentially, for all practical purposes; generally, usually, predominantly, in general, as a rule; commonly, broadly, routinely, as a matter of course; to the greatest extent, above all, to a large degree.

mainspring, *n.* **1.** principal spring, wheelwork, inner spring, essential part.

2. chief motive, impelling cause, impulse, prime motivation; source, origin, wellspring, fountainhead; ground, basis, key, keystone, root; prime mover, chief agent, most essential worker, author, generator, dynamo, *Inf.* sparkplug.

mainstay, *n.* chief support, principal support, main strength; chief reliance, anchor, sheet anchor, *Inf.* anchor to windward, anchorman; prop, staff, refuge, security; foundation, base, substructure; rock, *Inf.* rock of Gibraltar, reliable person, Atlas.

maintain, *v.* **1.** continue, keep going, retain, prolong, keep alive, keep living, keep in existence; cherish, nurture, nurse, nourish, sustain, feed; support, support financially, *Inf.* keep, *Inf.* stake, *Inf.* grubstake, *Inf.* carry; hold up, uphold, support, bolster up, brace, shore up, truss, buttress, prop, prop up, stay.

2. keep intact, preserve, keep up, save from decay, keep in good condition; care for, take good care of, groom, conserve.

3. affirm, testify, attest, vouch, avouch, asseverate, witness, warrant; insist, hold, contend, profess; acknowledge, admit, give credence to, give currency to, certify; say, assert, aver, allege, claim; declare, state, set forth, annunciate, announce; publish, publish abroad, air, vent, ventilate, blow; propagate, circulate, spread, spread abroad, diffuse; put forward, put forth, issue, broach, utter; broadcast, shout from the rooftops, herald, blazon abroad, publicize.

4. defend, advocate, plead for, argue for, represent, speak for, champion, back up, back, second, stand by, go to bat for, rationalize for, give reasons for, make excuses for; vindicate, justify, make a case for; shield, screen, aid, help, succor, assist, fight for, take up the cudgels for.

5. persist, persevere, bear up, adhere, *Inf.* stick things out, keep one's course, go the course, be resolute; keep on, carry on, continue; stand fast, be steadfast, stand one's ground, hold out.

maintenance, *n.* **1.** preservation, upkeep, seasonal upkeep, annual upkeep, keeping up; care, grooming, painting, yard work.

2. continuance, continuity, extension, prolongation; perpetuation, persistence, perseveration, repetition.

3. means of support, subsistence, livelihood, living; allowance, (*of marital settlements*) alimony *or* child support, stipend, remittance; income, revenue, salary, wages; assets, resources, funds, moneys, finances; nourishment, sustainment, food, room and board, keep.

majestic, *adj.* regal, kingly, princely, royal, lordly, noble, monarchal, monarchial, monarchical, imperial, magisterial, *Rare.* magistral; august, stately, dignified, distingué, distinguished, proud; grand, magnificent, pompous, palatial, splendid, resplendent, marvelous, superb; sublime, elevated, high, lofty, exalted, glorious; awesome, imposing, impressive, striking.

majesty, *n.* **1.** regalness, kingliness, princeliness, royalty, lordliness, nobility, nobleness, imperialness; augustness, stateliness, dignity, distinction; loftiness, sublimity, exaltedness; grandeur, magnificence, pomp, splendor, palatialness, resplendence, glory, marvelousness; awesomeness, imposingness, impressiveness, strikingness.

2. sovereignty, supremacy, supremeness, regality, monarchy, dominion, paramountcy; authority, power, divine right.

3. *Usu.* **Majesty** Highness, Royal Highness, His *or* Her Majesty, Eminence.

major, *adj.* **1.** greater, larger, large, higher; extreme, highest, supreme, greatest, utmost, uttermost.

2. important, *Sl.* big-time; capital, principal, chief, foremost, predominant; prime, primary, paramount, preeminant, superior, great, first-rate.

major-domo, *n.* chamberlain, steward, seneschal, butler, factotum; purveyor, manciple.

majority, *n.* **1.** greater part *or* number, more than half, plurality, bulk, mass, preponderance, lion's share.

2. commonality, the public, the general public, the many, the great unnumbered; populace, citizenry, proletariat, hoi polloi, bourgeoisie, the masses, rank and file.

3. legal age, drinking age, adulthood.

make, *v.* **1.** fabricate, manufacture, produce, mint; construct, build, assemble, set up; erect, elevate, raise, rear, put up; mold, form, fashion, model, shape, frame; create, invent, originate, devise, contrive, compose, write, put together; cast, block, hammer, forge, sculpture; draw, trace, figure, stamp, imprint.

2. effect, cause, bring about, accomplish; execute, carry out, render, do, perform, practice.

3. appoint, name, designate, nominate, tab; assign, select, *Mil.* detail; elect, vote in, place in office, install, invest, *Obs.* ordain.

4. organize, develop, embody, beget, engender; lay down, enact, establish, institute, found, originate, base; settle, determine, decide, conclude, seal; define,

limit, delimit; stabilize, ground, plant, implant, install.
5. fix, prepare, concoct, *Inf.* whip up, *Inf.* throw together, cook up, cook.
6. convert, transform, metamorphose, transfigure, transmute, transubstantiate, transmogrify; change, alter, modify, permute, modulate, inflect, mutate.
7. compel, coerce, force, press, drive, constrain, pressure, oblige, hustle, railroad; impel, urge, impress, provoke, exhort, cause, require, exact, necessitate; draft, conscript, commandeer; persuade, induce, prevail upon, insist upon; apply pressure, *Sl.* lean on *or* against, armtwist, twist [s.o.'s] arm, put the screws on *or* to, *Inf.* strong-arm, put the heat on, squeeze.
8. gain, acquire, obtain, secure, get; procure, gather, garner, glean, reap; (*all usu. of wages*) earn, clear, *Sl.* pull down, pocket, bag; gross, net, *Inf.* take home.
9. *Often* **make of** account for, explain, interpret, understand, construe; consider, deem, think, adjudge; look upon, view, regard, contemplate; spell out, decipher, unravel, decode, elucidate.
10. estimate, reckon, judge, gage, gauge, compute, calculate.
11. serve as, do the part of, answer for.
12. deliver, utter, pronounce, declare, put forth, recite.
13. reach, arrive at, get to, land at *or* on, attain.
14. *Informal.* go, leave, move, proceed, travel, journey.
15. **make as if** *or* **as though** *Informal.* pretend, act as if, feign, affect, seem, pass off as.
16. **make away with a.** steal, filch, rob, pilfer, purloin, finger, pick, *Inf.* snitch, cabbage, abstract, *Chiefly Brit.* prig, *Euph.* borrow; shoplift, palm, *Sl.* boost, walk off *or* away with, *Euph.* remove; *All Sl.* heist, pinch, hook, swipe, hustle, rip off, frisk, crook, cop, lift. **b.** destroy, kill, slay, slaughter, end, put an end to; murder, dispose of, *Sl.* do in, *Sl.* tap; assassinate, get rid of, mow down, do away with, *Inf.* wipe out, remove. **c.** consume, devour, eat up, swallow up, gulp down; finish, finish off, *Sl.* polish off, *Inf.* pack away *or* in, *Inf.* put away *or* down.
17. **make believe** pretend, act as if, imagine, fancy, dream, envision, picture, *Inf.* feature; fabricate, invent, concoct, romance; conjure up, conceive, idealize, visualize, envisage; simulate, personate, affect, assume, suppose.
18. **make bold** *or* **so bold** presume, take the liberty, dare, venture, be so rash.
19. **make do** get along *or* by, scrape along *or* by, manage, *Inf.* make out, survive, eke out.
20. **make for a.** go toward, head for, aim for, steer for, be bound for, steer a course for; approach, near, move closer to, draw nigh to, edge closer to. **b.** attack, lunge at, charge, rush, storm, raid, assault; set upon, pounce upon, descend upon, fall on. **c.** facilitate, favor, promote, subserve, forward, advance, contribute to, conduce to.
21. **make good a.** make up for, compensate for, offset, make restitution for, make amends, recompense, repay, requite, remunerate, recoup; square, settle, set right, rectify, remedy, correct; restore, reintegrate, make whole, repair, mend, renew, rejuvenate, reconstruct, recondition. **b.** succeed, do well, prosper, flourish, win, triumph. **c.** fulfill, realize, accomplish, carry out, be as good as one's word, deliver the goods.
22. **make known** reveal, disclose, divulge, let out; tell, relate, impart, mention, let fall, let on, communicate; inform, *Inf.* tip off, bring to the ears of, acquaint with; announce, proclaim, declare, publish, report, send word.
23. **make like** *Slang.* pretend to be, try to be, imitate, simulate, personate, impersonate, act like.
24. **make merry** celebrate, feast, banquet, junket, carouse, revel; *Inf.* party, *Inf.* live it up, *Sl.* paint the town red, do the town, have one's fling, sow one's wild oats; sport, disport, amuse oneself, play pranks; gambol, frolic, caper, romp, frisk.
25. **make much of a.** amplify, magnify, exaggerate, hyperbolize, overstate, make the most of; embroider, heighten, color; accentuate, emphasize, stress; make a stir about, make a big deal out of, make much ado about, make a mountain out of a molehill. **b.** cherish, dote on, pamper, cocker, coddle, cosset, indulge, pet, humor; flatter, blandish, cajole, *Inf.* soft-soap, *Inf.* butter up.
26. **make off** run away *or* off, flee, take to one's heels, make a quick exit, *Inf.* take off, *Inf.* clear out, *Inf.* make tracks, *Inf.* cut out, *Inf.* cut and run, *Inf.* fly the coup, *Sl.* split, *Sl.* scram, *Sl.* hightail it; make a getaway, beat a retreat *or* a hasty retreat, *Inf.* beat it, *Inf.* skip out, *Inf.* skip town, *Inf.* skedaddle, *Sl.* skidoodle, *Sl.* skido, *Sl.* vamoose.
27. **make off with** carry off, steal, filch, rob, pilfer, make away with. See **make** (*def.* **16**).
28. **make out a.** write out, complete, fill out. **b.** establish, prove, show to be true, substantiate, evidence, support, back up; authenticate, validate, certify, confirm, verify; attest to, affirm, corroborate, aver. **c.** discern, see, behold, perceive, cognize; observe, notice, catch a glimpse of, espy, descry, detect, discover; decipher, figure out, ascertain, determine; distinguish, pick out, recognize. **d.** imply, suggest, insinuate, hint, intimate, indicate, impute. **e.** *Informal.* manage, get along *or* by, scrape along *or* by, survive, fare, eke out, make do; fare well, succeed, prosper, thrive, come through with flying colors. **f.** *Slang.* kiss, neck, pet, fondle; romance, *Inf.* spoon.
29. **make over a.** alter, remodel, redo, redecorate; amend, improve, better, ameliorate; touch up, brush up, brighten up, polish; correct, emend, rectify, restore, repair **b.** transfer, convey, *Law.* alienate, transmit, assign; sign over, turn over, bequeath, leave, pass down, hand down.
30. **make sport of** make light of, laugh at, scoff at, ridicule, guy, *Inf.* roast, make a fool of, jeer at, gibe at, mock, fleer, deride, parody, travesty, burlesque, make game of; play with, toy with, trifle with, make fun of, poke fun at; tease, *Inf.* kid, badinage, chaff, pull [s.o.'s] leg, *Inf.* josh, *Inf.* rib, *Inf.* rag, *Inf.* fun, *Sl.* put [s.o.] on, *Sl.* jive.
31. **make up a.** constitute, form, compose, weave, fabricate, construct, frame; put together, compile. **b.** concoct, brew, invent, hatch, coin, forge; devise, contrive, project. **c.** *Also* **make up for** compensate for, offset, recompense, make good. See **make** (*def.* **21a**). **d.** complete, finish; conclude, settle, decide. **e.** settle differences, reconcile, come to terms, come to an understanding, bury the hatchet. **f.** powder, rouge, use mascara, use eyeshadow, put on lipstick.
32. **make up to a.** *Informal.* fawn on, *Sl.* fall all over, truckle to, toady to, *Sl.* play up to, *Sl.* shine up to, *Inf.* be a yes man to, *Inf.* apple-polish, *Inf.* butter up. **b.** make advances, flirt with, make eyes at, cast sheep's eyes at, make calf eyes at.
33. **make water** urinate, *Sl.* pee.
34. **make way** allow to pass; clear the way, make a space for, make room for.
—n. **35.** form, build, construction, structure, shape, configuration; composition, make-up, fabric, texture.
36. kind, brand, sort, type; mark, stamp, label, trademark; quality, grade, class.
37. character, nature, disposition, temper, tempera-

ment, humor; manner, style.

38. on the make a. *Informal.* increasing, adding to; advancing, rising, on the rise, up and coming. **b.** *Slang.* on the prowl, *Sl.* mashing, *Sl.* tomcatting, hustling.

make-believe, *n.* **1.** fantasy, fabrication, concoction, invention, creation; figment, fiction, fable; pretense, masquerade, disguise, feigning, pretending; sham, counterfeit, fake, simulation, falsification.

—adj. **2.** fictitious, imaginary, made-up, unreal, fantastic, illusory; pretended, feigned, assumed; fabricated, trumped up, invented, created; sham, mock, pseudo, pinchbeck, fake, false, spurious, simulated, counterfeited.

maker, *n.* **1.** author, composer; artist, architect, builder, constructor, former, forger, framer; manufacturer, producer, cause, agent, doer.

2. Maker God, Father, Creator, Author of all things, Maker of Heaven and Earth, Prime Mover, First Cause. See **God** (*def.* **1**).

makeshift, *n.* **1.** stopgap, temporary, expedient, make-do, arrangement; improvisation, contrivance; jury rig; substitute, succedaneum; last resort, *Fr. pis-aller.*

—adj. **2.** emergency, on-the-spot, unplanned, undesigned, unarranged, unconsidered; haphazard, *Inf.* sloppy, slapdash, thrown-together; temporary, provisional, tentative, stand-by, impermanent; jury, improvised, contrived; ersatz, artificial, synthetic.

make-up, *n.* **1.** cosmetics; rouge, blusher, highlighter, powder, pancake, *Inf.* gunk, *Theat.* grease paint; eyeshadow, eyeliner, mascara, eyebrow pencil; lipstick, lip gloss.

2. constitution, composition, arrangement, formation; form, build, construction, structure, configuration; fabric, texture.

making, *n.* **1.** building, construction, formation, fabrication, manufacture, production; invention, creation, composition.

2. constitution, structure, make-up. See **make-up** (*def.* **2**).

3. *Usu.* **makings** capacity, potential, potentiality, potency, possibility; ability, faculty.

maladjusted, *adj.* **1.** unadjusted, unconformed, maladapted, unadapted, unhabituated; unsuited, unfitted.

2. mixed-up, confused, muddled, messed up, *Sl.* screwed up, *Sl.* untogether, *Sl.* not straight.

maladministration, *n.* mismanagement, misgovernment, misdirection, misrule, misconduct, *Chiefly Law.* malversation; misapplication, mistake, bungling, blunder; impolicy, bad policy, inexpediency; incompetence, incompetency, inefficiency, ineffectiveness, ineffectuality, inefectualness.

maladroit, *adj.* **1.** unskillful, unskilled, inexpert, *Fr. inhabile,* inept, unhandy; unapt, unfit, unsuited, unqualified; incompetent, uncompetent, inefficient, *Inf.* no-good.

2. awkward, clumsy, like a bull in a china shop, *Sl.* klutzy, bumbling, bungling, left-handed, ambisinister, all thumbs, butterfingered; ungraceful, ungainly, inelegant, graceless; oafish, doltish, cloddish, lumbering, heavy-footed, lubberly, loutish; boorish, churlish, uncouth, ill-mannered, rustic, rough, unpolished, coarse, crude, rude, gross, crass; thoughtless, insensitive, inconsiderate, tactless, gauche, untoward, inappropriate, unfitting.

malady, *n.* disease, disorder, distemper, *Pathol.* affection, affliction; illness, sickness, ailment, complaint, indisposition; weakness, malaise, feebleness, infirmity, invalidism, valetudinarianism; disability, handicap; pain, hurt, ache, wound; infection, *Inf.* virus, *Inf.* bug, fever, temperature, *Inf.* temp; contagion, plague, pestilence; mental disorder, derangement, neurosis, psychosis, insanity, madness.

malaise, *n.* weakness, feebleness, infirmity, illness, sickness, suffering, aching, pain; discomfort, uneasiness, anxiety, disquiet, unquiet, inquietude, worry; despondency, depression, downheartedness, discouragement, dejection, *Sl.* the blahs.

malapropos, *adj.* unsuitable, unfitting, unbefitting, unmeet, inapt, inapposite; unsuited, irrelevant, nongermane, impertinent, unwarranted, uncalled for, out of place; unseemly, unbecoming, indecorous, improper; impolite, discourteous, rude, indiscreet, tactless, gauche, untoward; *Inf.* out-of-the-way, *Inf.* off-key, out-of-bounds, out-of-line, out-of-order.

malaria, *n.* yellow fever, yellow jack, swamp fever, ague, calenture, delirium, paroxysm, quartan, tertian; fever, feverishness, febricity, (*in prescriptions*) febris, chills, cold sweat, hot flashes, *Pathol.* pyrexia; *Both Pathol.* jaundice, icterus; disease, sickness, illness, infection, *Inf.* bug.

malarial, *adj.* **1.** malarian, malarious, aguelike; feverish, febrile, fevered, feverous, fever-ridden, flushed, hot, burning, *All Pathol.* pyretic, pyrexic, pyrexical; *Both Pathol.* jaundiced, icteric; stricken, infected, diseased, sick, ill.

2. malaria-carrying, disease-carrying, infectious, infective, mephitic, miasmal, pestilential, pestilent, pestiferous, *Pathol.* septic, *Med.* virulent; deadly, mortal, fatal, lethal, pernicious, morbific, morbifical, deleterious; noxious, nocuous, harmful, injurious, insalubrious, unsalubrious, unhealthy.

malarkey, *n.* *Informal.* twaddle, rot, nonsense, stuff and nonsense, blather, blatherskite, *Inf.* bosh, poppycock; baloney, foolishness, *Sl.* meshugaas, balderdash, piffle, kibosh, tommyrot, *Inf.* fiddle-faddle; bunkum, *Sl.* bunk, hogwash, *Sl.* bushwah, *Sl.* hokum, *Sl.* bull; applesauce, flummery; claptrap, rodomontade, humbug; garbage, pack of lies, rubbish, *Sl.* crap; silliness, inanity, idiocy, drivel; phoniness, *Sl.* phony baloney; gobbledegook, jargon, gibberish.

malcontent, *adj.* **1.** discontent, discontented, dissatisfied, disgruntled, unhappy, displeased, unsatisfied; uneasy, unquiet, restless, nervous, restive, irritated, agitated; concerned, worried, perturbed, disturbed; gloomy, morose, sad, blue, down in the dumps, down in the mouth, downcast; sulky, pouting, complaining, fault-finding, grumpy, edgy, hard to get along with, with a chip on one's shoulder.

2. factious, dissentious, rebellious, *Inf.* loaded for bear; contumacious, contrary, perverse, pigheaded, defiant, refractory, ungovernable.

—n. **3.** discontent, fault-finder, *Inf.* sorehead; churl, grouch, grumbler, complainer, *Sl.* beefer, *Sl.* bellyacher; mumbler, mutterer, murmurer.

4. negativist, nihilist, obstructionist; agitator, fomenter, insurrectionist, rebel, revolutionary.

male, *adj.* **1.** masculine, manly, manlike; virile; paternal.

—n. **2.** man, boy, lad, youth, *Irish. Eng.* bucko; fellow, chap, guy; gentleman, sir, mister; husband, father, brother, son, uncle, nephew.

3. stallion, buck, stag, hart, bull; boar, ram, billy goat; tom, tomcat; cock, gander, drake, rooster.

malediction, *n.* **1.** curse, imprecation, damning, damnation, execration, *Archaic.* malison, anathema; incantation, *Sl.* whammy, voodoo, hoodoo; commination, threat; giving the finger, thumbing one's nose.

2. slander, libel, defamation, traducement, calumny, obloquy; reproach, aspersion, vilification, derogation, vituperation, revilement, invective; denunciation, diatribe, insult, contumely, fulmination, condemnation, proscription, criticism.

malefaction, *n.* crime, wrongdoing, offense, transgression, breach, contravention; violation, trespass, encroachment, infringement; wrong, malfeasance, felony, *Law.* tort, *Law.* malversation, foul play; misdeed, misfeasance, hurt, harm, dirty trick, foul; atrocity, enormity, monstrosity, outrage, horror, abomination.

malefact, *n.* **1.** criminal, felon, larcener, larcenist, misdemeanant, lawbreaker; convict, *Sl.* jailbird, parolee, exconvict, *Inf.* ex-con, recidivist, repeat offender, *Inf.* chronic crook; transgressor, trespasser, offender, culprit, miscreant; wrongdoer, evildoer, sinner; malfeasant, misfeasor; perjurer; *Inf.* scofflaw.

2. gangster, mobster, racketeer, mafioso, desperado, terrorist; thug, *U.S.* tough, *Inf.* toughie, mugger, ruffian, *Inf.* plugugly, rowdy, hoodlum, *Sl.* hood, *Inf.* goon, hooligan, *Chiefly Brit.* rough, *Inf.* roughneck, *Inf.* baddy, *Sl.* bad actor, *Sl.* gunsel, *Sl.* mug, *Australian Sl.* larrikin, *Brit. Hist.* Mohock, (*in Paris*) apache.

3. assassin, murderer, killer, slayer, sniper; strangler, cutthroat, garroter; liquidator, *Euph.* silencer, *Euph.* dispatcher; gunman, *All U.S. Sl.* gun, hired gun, hit man, triggerman, hatchet man, torpedo.

4. bandit, hold-up man, *Sl.* stick-up man, armed robber; robber, burglar, thief, stealer, purloiner, *Inf.* crook; cracksman, Raffles, second-story man, cat thief; shoplifter, pickpocket, purse-snatcher, cutpurse; embezzler, peculator, *Law.* defalcator.

5. highwayman, footpad, *Sl.* yegg *or* yeggman, outlaw, *Sp. bandolero, Southwest U.S.* ladrone, *Australian.* bushranger, bravo, brigand; picaroon, rogue, (*in India and Burma*) dacoit.

6. extortionist, blackmailer, usurer, loan shark, *Sl.* bleeder; smuggler, runner, bootlegger, contrabandist, white-slaver; swindler, trickster, sharper, confidence man, con artist, con man; forger, counterfeiter, *Fr. faux-monnayeur, Brit. Inf.* coiner.

7. kidnapper, abductor, rapist; sodomist, pervert, degenerate, child molester, *Sl.* short eyes.

8. arsonist, incendiary; rioter, revolutionary, insurgent; bomb-thrower, bomb-planter.

9. villain, blackguard, reprobate, miscreant, knave, wretch, *Archaic.* caitiff; scapegrace, scoundrel, rogue, *Archaic.* varlet, scamp, *Inf.* scalawag, rapscallion; monster, demon, devil, hellhound, fiend; imp, rascal, mischief-maker.

maleficent, *adj.* **1.** pernicious, perilous, inimical, hurtful, harmful, baleful, baneful, deleterious, injurious, pestilential, pestiferous, noxious, detrimental, destructive; deadly, lethal, *Obs.* lethiferous, fatal, poisonous, toxic.

2. malign, malignant, malevolent, malicious, malefic, evil-intentioned, evil-disposed; hostile, antagonistic, unfriendly, obnoxious, ill-natured, churlish, surly; depraved, degenerate, debased, evil, villainous, base, vile, foul, heinous, atrocious; inhuman, *Archaic.* immane, unnatural, pitiless, merciless, unfeeling; implacable, relentless, grim, black-hearted, hard-hearted, cold-blooded, vicious, harsh, oppressive, cruel; ruthless, brutal, truculent, ferocious, savage, bloodthirsty, murderous, homicidal, feral, ferine; fiendish, demoniac, diabolic, evil-minded, fell, devilish, satanic, hellish, infernal.

malevolence, *n.* **1.** malice, maliciousness, malignity, malignance, animosity, antagonism, hostility, hate, hatred, enmity, wrath, violence, ferocity, anger, dudgeon, bad blood; venom, rancor, ill will, spite, spitefulness, grudge, pique, ire, acrimony, acerbity, bitterness; gall, bile, spleen, virulence, invidiousness, envy, resentment.

2. inhumanity, *Archaic.* immaneness, *Obs.* immanity, unnaturalness; pitilessness, mercilessness, uncharitableness, unkindliness, implacability, heart of stone, hard-heartedness; cold-bloodedness, viciousness, harshness, cruelty, brutality, truculence, savagery, barbarity, bloodthirstiness, ferity, fiendishness.

malevolent, *adj.* **1.** malign, malignant, malicious, maleficent, malefic, evil-intentioned, evil-disposed, evil-minded, unfriendly, obnoxious, ill-natured, churlish, surly, disobliging, ungracious; spiteful, hateful, invidious, ill-willed, ill-disposed, revengeful, vindictive, rancorous, bitter, embittered, acrimonious, sardonic, venomous, envenomed, acerb, virulent; sullen, resentful, envious; perfidious, treacherous, traitorous, disloyal, unfaithful; inhuman, *Archaic.* immane, unnatural, pitiless, merciless, unfeeling; implacable, grim, black-hearted, hard-hearted; cold-blooded, vicious, harsh, cruel, fierce, fell; brutal, truculent, ferocious, savage, bloodthirsty, feral, ferine; fiendish, demonic, demoniac, diabolic, devilish, satanic, hellish, infernal.

2. pernicious, perilous, inimical, hurtful, harmful, baleful, baneful, deleterious, injurious; pestilential, pestiferous, noxious, detrimental, destructive; deadly, lethal, fatal, poisonous, toxic.

3. ominous, portentous, sinister, ill-omened, ill-starred, boding ill, unpropitious, inauspicious; minatory, menacing, threatening, unpromising, unfortunate, unfavorable, untoward, unlucky; extremely bad, calamitous, disastrous, catastrophic.

malformation, *n.* faulty formation, deformity, disfigurement, distortion, misproportion, assymetry; monstrosity, abortion; contortion, crookedness, twist, *Pathol.* kyphosis, screw, warp, knottiness; ugliness, eyesore, blemish, imperfection.

malformed, *adj.* misshapen, distorted, deformed, anamorphous; unsymmetric, irregular, not straight, ill-proportioned, misproportioned; misbegotten, ill-made, grotesque, awry, crooked, askew; round-shouldered, hunchbacked, humpbacked, bowlegged, bandy-legged, knock-kneed, clubfooted, splay-footed, taliped, snub-nosed; stumpy, stunted, dwarfed.

malice, *n.* **1.** malevolence, maliciousness, malignity, malignance, animosity, antagonism, hostility, evil eye, hate, hatred, detestation, abhorrence, enmity; wrath, anger, dudgeon, bad blood, unfriendliness; venom, rancor, ill will, spite, spitefulness, evil intent, grudge, choler, pique, ire, acerbity, acrimony, bitterness, gall, bile, spleen, virulence, invidiousness, envy, resentment, ill feeling.

2. inhumanity, *Archaic.* immaneness, *Obs.* immanity, unnaturalness; pitilessness, mercilessness, implacability, obduracy, callousness, heart of stone, hard-heartedness, cold-heartedness, evil disposition; viciousness, harshness, cruelty, brutality, violence, ferocity, truculence, savagery, barbarity, bloodthirstiness, murderousness, ferity, fiendishness.

malicious, *adj.* **1.** malevolent, malign, malignant, maleficent, malefic, wanton, *Archaic.* despiteous, evil-intentioned, evil-disposed. See **malevolent** (*defs.* **1, 2**).

2. defamatory, denigrating, vituperative, vilifying, vilipenditory; slanderous, libelous, calumnious, calumniatory, traducent, false, untrue, false-spoken, misrepresentative; abusive, scurrilous, *Archaic.* scurrile, aspersive, imputative, insinuating, gossiping.

maliciously, *adv.* cruelly, viciously, brutally, harshly, meanly, malignantly; spitefully, resentfully, nastily, hatefully, wickedly; deliberately, with evil intent, with malice aforethought, with malice prepense, *Sl.* accidentally-on-purpose.

malign, *v.* **1.** slander, libel, calumniate, traduce, falsify, accuse falsely; misrepresent, belie, asperse, impute, insinuate; injure, abuse, assail, stab, insult, backbite, *Sl.* badmouth, engage in personalities; slur, sully, defile, smear, smirch, besmirch, soil, blacken, tarnish, stain, taint, smudge, blemish, spot, brand, stigmatize, drag through the mud, *Sl.* dump on.

2. defame, vilify, vilipend, denigrate, vituperate, scandalize, run down, berate, impugn, revile, gibbet, criticize, pull to pieces, cut up, shred, *Sl.* do a hatchet job on; give a bad name, speak ill of, speak evil of, sneer at, lampoon, pasquinade, muckrake; denounce, rail, curse, execrate, damn, imprecate, *Obs.* exprobate, anathematize, censure, cry down, reproach; belittle, disparage, deprecate, minimize, derogate, detract, decry, depreciate, devaluate, deflate, damn with faint praise; humiliate, humble, mortify, *Sl.* put down.

—adj. **3.** pernicious, perilous, inimical, hurtful, baleful, baneful, harmful, deleterious, injurious, pestilential, pestiferous, noxious, detrimental, destructive; ominous, portentous, sinister, ill-omened, ill-starred, boding ill, unpropitious, inauspicious, minatory, menacing, threatening; unpromising, unfortunate, unfavorable, untoward, unlucky; extremely bad, calamitous, disastrous, catastrophic.

4. malevolent, malicious, wanton, malignant, maleficent, malefic, antagonistic, unfriendly, hostile, unkindly, obnoxious; spiteful, hateful, invidious, revengeful, vindictive, ill-disposed, rancorous, bitter, embittered, acrimonious, sardonic, venomous, envenomed, acerb; fiendish, demoniac, diabolic, evil-minded, fell, devilish, satanic, hellish, infernal; vicious, harsh, severe, cold-blooded, cold-hearted, inhuman, unnatural.

malignant, *adj.* **1.** malevolent, malicious, wanton, malign, antagonistic, unfriendly, hostile, maleficent, malefic, unkindly, obnoxious. See **malign** (*defs.* **3, 4**).

2. *Pathology.* deadly, lethal, virulent, fatal, poisonous, toxic.

maligner, *n.* **1.** defamer, vilifier, vilipender, vituperator, denigrator, scandalizer, asperser, impugner, backbiter, evil-speaker, carper, caviler, *Inf.* knocker; censor, reviler, castigator, inveigher, reprover, disapprover, denouncer, railer, curser, execrator, imprecator, anathematizer, critic; lampooner, satirist, muckraker, hack; belittler, disparager, deprecator, detractor, derogator, depreciator.

2. slanderer, libeler, calumniator, traducer, falsifier, liar; mud-slinger, dirt-flinger.

malignity, *n.* **1.** malevolence, malice, malignancy, animosity, maliciousness, enmity, hate, hatred, wrath, hostility, violence, ferocity, anger, dudgeon; venom, rancor, ill will, irascibility, spite, grudge, choler, pique, ire, acrimony, acerbity, bitterness, gall, bile, spleen, virulence, invidiousness, envy, resentment.

2. rage, towering rage, fury, frenzy; fit, spasm, convulsion, paroxysm.

3. harmfulness, hurtfulness, destructiveness, perniciousness, balefulness, banefulness, deleteriousness, deadliness, fatalness.

malinger, *v.* shirk, slack, lie down on the job, procrastinate, loaf, *Inf.* boondoggle; fail, default, abandon, leave undone, neglect; *Inf.* goldbrick, *Sl.* goof off, *Brit.* skulk, soldier, slink, *Sl.* dog; call in sick, get out of, slip out of, slide out of, sneak out of; evade, avoid, dodge, duck; play truant, skip, *Sl.* cut, *Sl.* bag, overstay leave.

malingerer, *n.* shirker, shirk, *Brit.* skulker, soldier, *Inf.* goldbricker, clock watcher, *Sl.* goof-off, *Inf.* boondoggler; slacker, procrastinator, idler, loafer, fainéant, trifler, Micawber; avoider, evader, deserter, absconder; truant, absentee, dodger, defaulter, neglector.

mall, *n.* **1.** promenade, walk, gallery, avenue, arcade; path, garden path, close, alley, passage, lane, street, road; parade, esplanade, boardwalk, public walk, boulevard.

2. median, median strip, medial strip, middle, middle of the road.

3. shopping center, shopping plaza, plaza, shopping complex.

malleable, *adj.* **1.** extensile, extensible, ductile, tractile, plastic, stretchable; bendable, flexible, flexile, flexuous, pliant, pliable, whippy; elastic, supple, lithe, limber, willowy, lissom; yielding, bending, shapable, moldable, fictile.

2. adaptable, adjustable, resilient, movable, mobile; tractable, manageable, governable, corrigible, domitable; impressible, impressionable, susceptible, persuasible, suasible; responsive, receptive, sensitive, amenable, influenceable; formable, teachable, educable, trainable, docile, tamable, domesticable.

mallet, *n.* **1.** beetle, hammer, gavel; tapper, tamper, pounder, rammer.

2. club, stick, croquet mallet, *Golf.* wood, *Golf.* driver.

malnutrition, *n.* undernourishment, poor diet, unbalanced diet, starvation, *Psychiatry.* anorexia; emaciation, gauntness, haggardness, witheredness, shrunkenness, boniness, scrawniness, skinniness, wasting away; weakening, enfeeblement, impairment, enervation, inanition, exhaustion, prostration, *Psychiatry.* anorexia nervosa.

malodorous, *adj.* fetid, reeky, reeking, smelly, stinky, stinking, stenchful, foul-smelling, ill-smelling, strong-smelling, odorous; noisome, mephitic, foul, rank, offensive, disgusting, nauseating, sickening, unpleasant, disagreeable; putrid, rancid, rank, rotten, tainted, spoiled, strong, game, putrescent, miasmal, miasmatic, miasmatical, miasmic; dirty, unwashed, unclean; stuffy, moldy, musty, fusty, frowzy, stale, unfresh, close.

malpractice, *n.* **1.** misdeed, offense, violation, transgression, fault, *Law.* tort, *Both Law.* malfeasance, misfeasance, *Chiefly Law.* malversation; negligence, dereliction, laxity; corruption, graft, jobbery, wrongdoing.

2. abuse, misuse, misemployment, misapplication, misappropriation; misconduct, misbehavior, behavior unbefitting [s.o.], unethical practice, impropriety, indecorum, *Obs.* misdoing.

maltreat, *v.* abuse, mistreat, injure. See **mistreat**.

maltreatment, *n.* abuse, mistreatment, battery. See **mistreatment**.

mama's boy, *n.* milksop, sop, mollycoddle, sissy, weakling, *Inf.* pantywaist, *Sl.* pansy, *Sl.* wimp; namby-pamby, *Inf.* jellyfish, Walter Mitty; *Sl.* schlepp, *Sl.* schlemiel, *Sl.* nebbish, *Sl.* schnook, *Sl.* twirp, *Sl.* twit, *Sl.* nerd; *Inf.* lightweight, featherweight, *Sl.* pushover, *Sl.* patsy, *Sl.* sap; loser, *Sl.* sad sack.

mammon, *n.* riches, means, wealth, opulence, affluence, fortune, money, *U.S. Sl.* bucks, *Sl.* dough, lucre, *Disparaging.* pelf.

mammonist, *n.* mammonite, materialist, bourgeois; rich man, man of means, plutocrat, millionaire, billionaire, nabob.

mammoth, *n.* **1.** elephant.

—adj. **2.** huge, enormous, gigantic, titanic, gargantuan, very large *or* big, monstrous, *Sl.* humongous, Brobdingnagian, Cyclopean; vast, colossal, monumental, gigantean, immense, prodigious, stupendous, tremendous, herculean; great, great big, towering, staggering, astronomical, mountainous; elephantine, massive, ponderous, very heavy, bulky, hulking; hippopotamic, leviathan, dinosaurian, dinotherian, megatherian; jumbo, oversize, kingsize, overlarge; *All Inf.*

whopping, spanking, walloping, strapping, thundering, thumping.

man, *n.* **1.** adult male, husband, *Inf.* common-law husband, *Inf.* lover; chap, fellow, *Sl.* gazabo; beau, blade, sir, squire, sahib, hidalgo, don; Mister, Mr., *Sp.* Señor, *Fr.* Monsieur, *Port.* Senhor, *Ger.* Herr.

2. Homo sapiens, human beings, the human race, mankind, mortals, humankind.

3. human, human being, individual, someone, anyone, anybody.

4. follower, employee, enlisted soldier; manservant, gentleman's gentleman, valet, house boy, houseman, butler, attendant; subject, liege, vassal, subordinate, dependent; bachelor-at-arms; cup-bearer, page, equerry, groom, orderly, aide-de-camp; boots, flunky, footman, waiter; hireling, satellite, puppet, mercenary, bondsman; thrall, drudge, churl, workman, handyman, man-of-all-work, hired man, cleaning man, day laborer, hack; factotum, henchman, *Inf.* right hand, *Inf.* right-hand man.

5. exemplary man, man of honor, gentleman, *Yiddish.* mensch; brave man, valorous man, Galahad; hero, warrior, soldier, paladin, knight, knight-errant, chevalier; *Inf.* trump, *Inf.* brick, *Inf.* square shooter; *Inf.* jewel, paragon, model, standard, good person, man among men.

6. as one man unanimously, in complete accord, with one voice, concordantly, in concert; all together, by common consent, one and all, without contradiction, without one dissentient, without one "nay" vote, without a blackball.

7. to a man with no exception, everyone, each and every one, the whole team, *Fr. tout ensemble*; all hands, all hands and the cook, every mother's son, the whole batch of them, the whole tribe.

8. man and boy since childhood, all one's life, all one's born days, all one's natural life; always, forever, *Inf.* since Hector was a pup.

9. one's own man independent, unconstrained, unrestrained, unchecked, unhampered, unhindered; unobstructed, unrestricted, unconfined, uncontrolled, untrammeled; unsubject, ungoverned, unenslaved, unenthralled, unvanquished; unmarried, bachelor, unattached, free, foot-loose, foot-loose and fancy-free.

—*v.* **10.** staff, people, garrison, station, equip, arm, outfit, gird, fit out.

11. fortify, strengthen, restrengthen; brace, reinforce, buttress, prop up; prime, stiffen, give strength to, shore up.

man about town, *n.* playboy, buck, ladies' man, *Sl.* lover boy, philanderer, Casanova; dandy, fop, beau, dude, *Sl.* swell; sophisticate, roué, rake, debauchee; rich young man, eligible bachelor, *Inf.* hot prospect.

manacle, *n.* **1.** *Usu.* **manacles** handcuffs, hand shackles, cuffs, *Brit. Sl.* darbies, *Sl.* bracelets, *Sl.* nippers; restraints, checks.

—*v.* **2.** handcuff, *Sl.* cuff, restrain, tie up; put in irons, put in chains, curb, check, control, keep within bounds, fasten; impede, thwart, frustrate, inhibit, hamper.

manage, *v.* **1.** arrange, contrive, engineer, maneuver; effect, bring about, cause.

2. take charge of, run, direct, command, govern, rule, order, dictate; oversee, regulate, supervise, head, superintend; conduct, take the helm, watch over, take care of.

3. dominate, impress, sway, master, hold the reins; influence, control, treat, guide, steer, lead, mastermind, quarterback, pilot; train, teach, instruct.

4. wield, use, operate, manipulate; ply, swing, work, handle; brandish, flourish.

5. function, make out, make do, survive, get along, cope; eke out a living, work it out, keep one's head above water, weather the storm.

manageable, *adj.* governable, tractable, controllable; corrigible, impressionable, susceptible, persuasible; receptive, amenable, teachable, trainable, educable, tamable; flexible, pliant, compliant; namby-pamby, weak, insipid, wishy-washy; pusillanimous, timid, meek, without a mind of one's own; docile, gentle, yielding, submissive, willing.

management, *n.* **1.** regulation, administration, superintendence, supervision; direction, control, government, command, leadership, oversight; stewardship, care, charge, conduct, guidance, treatment.

2. skill, executive ability, finesse, address, dispatch; adroitness, deftness, capability, mother wit.

3. executives, bosses, owners, controllers, directors, *Sl.* high muckety-mucks *or* high muck-a-mucks; top men, *Sl.* top dogs, *Sl.* top bananas.

manager, *n.* **1.** helmsman, pilot, fugleman, gerent, leader; organizer, master, governor; mayor, *Brit.* bailiff, town *or* city manager, town planner; adviser, mastermind, Rasputin, power behind the throne; guide, cicerone, dragoman; proctor.

2. administrator, executive, superintendent, supervisor; boss, chief, overseer, foreman, director, straw boss; skipper, kingpin, *Inf.* old man.

3. controller, comptroller, treasurer, husband; steward, major-domo, seneschal; housekeeper; factor, agent.

mandate, *n.* **1.** fiat, decree, edict, ukase, bull, firman; order, dictate, precept, command, charge, injunction, writ, ruling; instruction, prescript; authorization, authority, commission, warrant; behest, bidding, ultimatum; ordinance, statute, act, regulation, requirement.

2. colony, protectorate, dependency, mandated territory, occupied territory; province, state.

mandatory, *n.* obligatory, required, requisite, essential, necessary, needed; compulsory, imperative, binding, preceptive; ordered, demanded, commanded, bidden, compelled, coerced; exigent, urgent, pressing.

man-eater, *n.* **1.** cannibal, anthropophagite; ogre, ogress, monster, fiend, brute, ghoul, barbarian; Polyphemus, Thyestes; vampire, bloodsucker, Count Dracula.

2. tiger, lion, shark, great white shark.

man-eating, *adj.* cannibalistic, flesh-eating, anthropophagical, Thyestian, polyphagian; bestial, fiendish, monstrous, ghoulish, ogreish, barbarous; bloodsucking, vampirish, bloodthirsty; non-vegetarian, carnivorous.

manes, *n. Roman Religion.* shades, souls of the dead, spirits, ghosts, phantoms, specters, shadows; *All Rom. Religion.* lemures, lares, penates.

maneuver, *n.* **1.** move, gambit, stroke, coup, step, measure, proceeding; tactic, intrigue, machination, contrivance, manipulation; stratagem, ruse, artifice, device, wile, subterfuge, shift, red herring; ploy, dodge, sleight, feint, game; procedure, scheme, plot, plan, design.

2. maneuvers exercises, operations, war games, actions, movements; logistics, war plans, tactics, strategy, kriegspiel.

—*v.* **3.** manipulate, handle, manage, finesse; conduct, work, operate, run, engineer; steer, drive, be in the driver's seat, be at the reins, take the wheel; pilot, direct, lead, turn, jockey; navigate, guide, captain, cox, take the helm.

4. scheme, intrigue, plot, plan, contrive, engineer, *Inf.* angle, pull the strings, have [s.o.] on the string;

circumvent, overreach, trick, outsmart, outwit, outdo, go one better, get the better of; *Inf.* finagle, *Inf.* wangle, gerrymander.

maneuverer, *n.* logistician, planner, strategist, tactician, plotter, politician; intriguer, wire-puller, *Sl.* wheeler-dealer, Machiavelli, machinator; slyboots, snake, artful dodger, schemer, fox; mastermind, promoter, jobber.

manful, *adj.* masculine, virile; brave, courageous, bold. See **manly** (*defs.* **1-3**).

mange, *n.* rot, *Pathol.* scabies, itch, rash, *Pathol.* psoriasis, *Pathol.* psora, *Sl.* creeping crud; eruption, breaking out, *Pathol.* exanthema.

manger, *n.* trough, feeding-trough, box, rack, crib, hutch, tray.

mangy, *adj.* **1.** scabby, itchy, scaly, diseased; psoriatic, exanthematic, erupted, broken out.

2. contemptible, base, odious, *Archaic.* caitiff; disgraceful, disreputable, ignominious; mean, nasty, hateful, spiteful, *Inf.* ornery, vicious; low, despicable, vile, scurvy, repulsive.

3. squalid, wretched, miserable, abject, dire; shabby, seedy, poor, sorry, trashy, sordid, sleazy, scrubby; slovenly, unkempt, unclean, foul, dirty, filthy, dingy, mucky; ramshackle, run-down, deteriorated, dilapidated.

manhandle, *v.* maul, rough up, *Sl.* knock around *or* about, *Sl.* give one the works; batter, beat, beat up, pound, pommel, pummel, thrash, trounce, pelt, *Sl.* clobber, *Archaic.* belabor; hit, strike, smite, slap, smack, cuff, buffet, *Inf.* slug, *Inf.* whack, *Inf.* wallop, *Sl.* belt; harm, damage, bruise, hurt, pain, injure; mishandle, mistreat, maltreat, ill-treat, abuse, ill-use, *Sl.* kick around; *Inf.* paw; bully, trample upon, bullyrag, hector.

man-hater, *n.* misanthrope, misanthropist, hater of mankind, cynic; recluse, hermit, anchorite, loner, solitary; eremite, ascetic, monk.

manhole, *n.* hole, opening, hatch, hatchway, scuttle, trap door.

manhood, *n.* **1.** virility, manliness, mannishness, masculinity, masculineness, maleness, (*in Hispanic cultures*) machismo.

2. manfulness, spirit, pluck, firmness, grit; hardihood, fortitude, strength, force, resolution, determination, will; indomitableness, indomitability, courage, mettle, stamina, endurance, *Sl.* guts, intestinal fortitude; boldness, daring, audacity, bravery, valor, heroism.

mania, *n.* **1.** craze, rage, urge, compulsion, desire, craving, cacoëthes; yen, yearning, *Sl.* letch, infatuation, passion, obsession, fixation, fascination, preoccupation; fanaticism, monomania.

2. enthusiasm, excitement, furor; commotion, uproar, hullabaloo, *Inf.* to-do.

3. *Psychiatry.* frenzy, franticness, furor, delirium, phrenitis, anoesis, hysteria; ranting, raving, storming, foaming at the mouth, wildness, violence.

maniac, *n.* **1.** madman, lunatic, *Sl.* loony, *Inf.* crackpot, *Sl.* kook, *Sl.* nut, *Sl.* screwball, bedlamite; psychotic, *Sl.* sickie, psychopath, schizophrenic, *Sl.* schizo; paranoiac, *Psychiatry.* manic-depressive, *Psychiatry.* megalomaniac, pyromaniac, *Psychol.* kleptomaniac, dipsomaniac, automaniac.

2. fanatic, monomaniac, enthusiast, zealot, crank, phrenetic; energumen, demoniac; eccentric, nonconformist.

—adj. **3.** maniacal, hysterical, madding, *Archaic.* wood, delirious; frantic, frenzied, frenetic; raving, ranting, foaming at the mouth. See **maniacal.**

maniacal, *adj.* **1.** crazy, crazed, lunatic, lunatical, insane, mad, maddened, demented, deranged; of unsound mind, *Latin. non compos mentis*, mentally ill; psychotic, schizophrenic, *Sl.* schizo, paranoiac; daft, *Inf.* daffy, unbalanced, touched, *Inf.* unglued, *Inf.* half-baked, *Brit. Sl.* bonkers, unhinged, distracted; dazed, moon-struck, possessed, infatuated; odd, peculiar, queer, bizarre, *Chiefly Brit. Inf.* potty, *Inf.* dotty, *Inf.* crackpot; brainsick, *Sl.* kooky, *Sl.* meshuga; *All Sl.* balmy, dippy, batty, bats, cuckoo, buggy, bughouse, bugs, screwy, wacky, wacko, goofy, loony, squirrelly, bananas, nuts, nutty, nutty as a fruitcake.

2. out of one's head *or* mind *or* senses *or* wits, *Scot.* redwood, *Sl.* loco, mad as a hatter, mad as a March hare, far-gone, stark raving mad; not all there, not quite right, not right upstairs; *Inf.* out in left field, *Sl.* in outer space, *Sl.* in orbit, *Inf.* off the wall; *Inf.* cracked, *Inf.* mental, *Sl.* off one's rocker, *Sl.* out of one's tree, *Sl.* off one's trolley, *Brit. Sl.* off one's chump; *All Sl.* have bats in one's belfry, have a few buttons missing, have a few loose screws.

3. hysterical, madding, maniac, *Archaic.* wood, delirious; frantic, frenzied, frenetic; ranting, raving, storming, foaming at the mouth, convulsing; overwrought, distraught, upset, worked-up, wrought-up, stirred-up; exasperated, provoked; beside oneself, at one's wit's end; out of control, uncontrollable, unrestrainable, corybantic, *Inf.* haywire, berserk, rabid, wild; violent, stormy, fierce, tempestuous, tumultuous, turbulent.

4. impractical, injudicious, unsensible; unfounded, groundless, unsound; preposterous, extravagant, excessive; inappropriate, inept, improper, incongruous, inconsistent; imprudent, indiscreet; unwise, ill-considered, ill-suited, ill-advised; short-sighted, careless, unwary, irresponsible; reckless, rash, harum-scarum; unsafe, dangerous, perilous.

manic, *adj.* excited, agitated, perturbed; hyperactive, *Inf.* hyper, *Sl.* hyped up, *Inf.* high, *Inf.* up; frenzied, frantic, worked-up, stirred-up, wrought-up; hysterical, *Sl.* freaked-out, out of control.

manifest, *adj.* **1.** apparent, evident, self-evident, manifestative, *Fr. en évidence*; visible, seeable, in full view, open, public, exposed, showing, naked, bald, unhidden, uncovered, unveiled, unshrouded, uncurtained; obvious, patent, palpable, conspicuous, prominent, striking, blatant, flagrant, egregious; overt, displayed, shown, presented, professed, avowed, ostensible; surface, on the surface, superficial, *Psychoanal.* conscious.

2. lucid, perspicuous, clear, clear-cut, plain, plain as day, plain as the nose on your face, transparent, translucent; distinct, express, explicit, definite, unmistakable, unambiguous, indubitable, indisputable, unquestionable; discernible, perceivable, perceptible, recognizable, ascertainable, salient, apprehensible, comprehensible, comprehendible, cognizable, intelligible, understandable; frank, candid, straightforward, straight, downright, up front.

—v. **3.** exhibit, show, display, present, demonstrate, exemplify, illustrate, describe, *Scot. and North Eng.* kithe; declare, express, make known, set forth, avow, profess, advertise, publicize, announce, broadcast; blazon, flaunt, vaunt, flourish, parade, show off [s.t.]; expose, air, reveal, lay open, bring to light, disclose, unveil; uncover; divulge, betray, give away.

4. prove, substantiate, corroborate, evidence, evince, certify, *Inf.* go to show; establish, determine, settle, set at rest, conclude.

5. record, register, enter, put down; list, enumerate, tally.

—n. **6.** inventory, checklist, bill of lading, bill of entry, cargo *or* freight list; list, listing, enumeration,

numeration, tally, record; roster, register, roll, directory, passenger list.

manifestation, *n.* **1.** display, showing, show, exhibit, exhibition, presentation, exposition, demonstration, exemplification, example, illustration, description; declaration, expression, profession, avowal; announcement, publication, airing, broadcasting, advertisement, public statement; exposure, exposé, revelation, revealment, epiphany; disclosure, uncovering, unveiling, divulgence.

2. evidence, sign, symbol, token, mark; indication, symptom, syndrome; proof, substantiation, testimony, corroboration, certification.

manifesto, *n.* proclamation, pronouncement, pronunciamento, promulgation; statement, declaration, announcement, annunciation, broadcast, publication, issuance, airing; notice, formal notice, notification, circular, handbill, bill, broadside, placard, poster, *Fr. affiche, Both Rom. Cath. Ch.* encyclical, bull.

manifold, *adj.* **1.** multifold, multiplex, multiple, numerous, many, several; multifarious, of many kinds, varied, miscellaneous, various, diverse, divers, sundry; diversified, eclectic, many-faceted, many-sided, many-faced, complex, multitudinous.

2. copy, photographic copy, photocopy, duplicate, *Inf.* ditto, *Trademark.* Mimeograph, *Inf.* mimeo, *Trademark.* Xerox, facsimile, reproduction, print, ectype.

manikin, *n.* **1.** dwarf, midget, homunculus, little man, pygmy, atomy, Lilliputian; chit, fingerling, dapperling, cock-sparrow, hop-o'-my-thumb, Tom Thumb, Thumbelina, *Chiefly Scot.* wee fellow *or* lad *or* one, *Obs.* pigwidgin, *Archaic.* dandiprat; shrimp, runt, peewee, squirt, pip-squeak, *Inf.* half-pint, small-fry, *Inf.* shorty; imp, elf, fairy, fay, sprite, nymph, *Obs.* urchin; goblin, hobgoblin, (*in German folklore*) kobold, (*in Irish Folklore*) leprechaun, *Chiefly Brit.* little person, gnome, (*in Scandinavian folklore*) troll, Hobbit.

2. mannequin, dummy. See **mannequin**.

manipulate, *v.* **1.** handle, manage, work, operate, control; use, wield, ply, exercise, practice, exert, brandish, flourish; apply, adhibit, utilize, employ, make use of.

2. influence, work on, move, motivate; play on, exploit, take advantage of, *Inf.* stroke; contrive, plot, scheme, intrigue, machinate, pull the strings, have one on the string; engineer, wheel and deal, maneuver, *Inf.* angle, jockey; circumvent, overreach, trick, outsmart, outwit, outdo, go one better, get the better of; *Inf.* finagle, *Inf.* wangle, gerrymander.

3. juggle, falsify, fake, rig, trump up, pack, stack; tamper with, doctor, fiddle with, twiddle with, play with, fix.

4. direct, lead, head, regulate, orientate; turn, finesse, conduct, guide, steer; drive, take the wheel, be in the driver's seat, take the reins; captain, *Inf.* cox, navigate, pilot, be at the helm.

manipulation, *n.* **1.** management, direction, guidance, operation, administration; agency, conduct, regulation, control, governance, charge, order; maneuvering, handling, treatment, working, exploitation.

2. appliance, use, adhibition, application, praxis, employment, utilization; execution, exercise, practice, performance, play.

3. influence, machination, maneuvering, maneuvers, wire-pulling, scheming; engineering, plotting, juggling, *Inf.* finagling, rigging, *Inf.* frame-up.

manipulator, *n.* **1.** handler, operator, performer, agent; engineer, conductor, pilot, driver, steersman, navigator.

2. exploiter, machinator, maneuverer, intriguer; conspirator, coconspirator, schemer, plotter; conniver, *Inf.* finagler, *Inf.* wangler, wire-puller.

mankind, *n.* **1.** the human race, flesh, the human species, Homo sapiens; humanity, humankind, the world *or* earth; people, folks, the human community, society, the public; the masses, the multitude, proletariat.

2. men, menfolk, males.

manlike, *adj.* **1.** male, masculine; bold, courageous, valiant. See **manly** (*defs.* **1-3**).

2. unfeminine, Amazonian. See **mannish** (*def.* **1**).

manliness, *n.* **1.** masculinity, manlihood, maleness, manhood, manfulness; virility, machismo, potency; strength, power, powerfulness, puissance, might, main, force, thews.

2. vigor, vitality, hardiness, robustness, lustiness, red-bloodedness; brawn, muscularity, huskiness, burliness, heftiness, sturdiness, ruggedness.

3. courage, bravery, valor, intrepidity; heroism, gallantry, chivalry; fearlessness, dauntlessness, daring, audacity, boldness; firmness, resolution, confidence, stability, steadfastness; fortitude, hardihood, pluck, gameness, spunk, mettle, backbone, *Sl.* balls; nerve, doughtiness, grit, stamina, *Sl.* guts, intestinal fortitude.

manly, *adj.* **1.** masculine, male, manful, manlike; *Inf.* he, virile, potent, macho, *Inf.* two-fisted, *Inf.* he-mannish, *Inf.* hairy-chested.

2. strong, powerful, sturdy, mighty, puissant, forceful; able-bodied, athletic, well-built, well-knit; brawny, muscular, sinewy, wiry; husky, strapping, broad-shouldered, burly, thickset, hefty; virile, hale, hearty, robust, vigorous; lusty, red-blooded, hardy, stout, rugged.

3. bold, courageous, brave, valiant, valorous, intrepid; audacious, daring, venturesome; fearless, dauntless, indomitable, tough; plucky, game, spunky, doughty, nervy, *Sl.* ballsy; mettlesome, high-spirited, spirited, lionhearted, stout-hearted; resolute, firm, confident, stable; unflinching, unshrinking, steadfast, ready for anything; heroic, gallant, chivalrous; noble, honorable, decent, sterling.

manna, *n.* **1.** (*all of a spiritual nature*) food, nutriment, nourishment, refreshment, sustenance, provender; divine providence.

2. godsend, boon, blessing, manna from heaven, *Inf.* [s.t.] out of the blue; gift, favor, benefit, benefaction, benevolence, grace, comfort, ease, remedy; windfall, bonus, premium, surprise, *Inf.* surprise package, *Brit. Inf.* perk, *Sl.* gravy.

3. aid, help, assistance, succor; assist, helping hand, boost, help in time of need; support, maintenance, sustainment, subsistence, provision, keep, economic support, subsidization, patronage, subsidy, lift, bounty.

mannequin, *n.* manikin, dummy, lay figure; model, high-fashion model.

manner, *n.* **1.** way, means, wise, method, mode, fashion, style; habit, custom, pattern, habit, wont, characteristic *or* customary way; system, approach, technique, procedure, course, practice, order, line, lines, attack, tack; methodology, process, proceeding, line of action, routine, *Brit.* the drill, *Latin. modus operandi*, mode of operation, *Inf.* MO, manner of working; procedure, standard operating procedure, *Inf.* SOP.

2. aspect, air, deportment, style, bearing, demeanor, mien, cast, turn, form, shape; complexion, tenor, tone, color; carriage, posture, stance, guise, garb, address, traits, *Inf.* cut of one's jib; presence, seeming, outward appearance, appearance, outwardness, exteriority.

3. sort, kind, strain, denomination, stripe, line, grain, make, mark; form, mold, ilk, type, variety, description, stamp, brand, feather, kidney, category, species; genre, nature, class, order.

4. manners a. behavior, *Archaic.* havior, conduct, comportment, social behavior, life style, way of life, modus vivandi, ways, system of values, ethos, common practice, folkways, customs, mores, goings on, doings. **b.** etiquette, social code, rules of conduct, formalities, social procedures *or* conduct, good manners, politeness, politesse, comity, civility; social graces, proprieties, decorum, good form, courtliness; formality, formalness, ceremony, ritual, formalization; fashionableness, prevalence, currency, normality, routineness; propriety, decorousness, correctness, *Fr. convenance, Fr. bienséance*; decency, seemliness, civilized behavior, dictates of society *or* of Mrs. Grundy, p's and q's; amenities, decencies, civilities, proper thing, what is done, social convention, *Fr. bon ton,* protocol, diplomatic code. **c.** pattern, behavior pattern, cultural pattern, behavioral norm, rule, procedure, form, run of things, matter of course; convention, custom, habit, established way, social usage, time-honored practice, tradition, folkway, practice, standing custom *or* practice, observance, ritual, praxis, consuetude.

5. to the manner born aristocratic, patrician, blueblooded, silk-stocking, noble, gentle, genteel, wellborn, highborn; royal, princely, kingly, titled; thoroughbred, pedigreed, of noble blood; elegant, graceful, fine; well-bred, polite, civil, mannerly, well-mannered, courteous; decorous, proper, *Fr. comme il faut*; gracious, ladylike, courtly, gentlemanly; debonair, chivalrous, chivalric, gallant, cavalier; polished, finished, refined, cultivated; urbane, suave, sophisticated, cosmopolitan, worldly; fashionable, hightoned, *Sl.* tony, high-class *Sl.* classy, *Inf.* swank.

mannered, *adj.* affected, unnatural, artificial, insincere, *Sl.* phony; pretentious, on one's high horse, *Inf.* highfalutin, *Inf.* high-hat, *Inf.* stuck-up, *Inf.* la-di-da; theatrical, stagy, posed, overdone, histrionic, overacted, *Inf.* too-much, *Inf.* fake *or* faked; haughty, lordly, hoity-toity, arrogant, proud, snobbish, disdainful, sneering, with one's nose in the air.

mannerism, **1.** affectation, pretension, exaggeration, pretense, insincerity, airs, (*esp. in Victorian England*) prunes and prisms; artificiality, unnaturalness, manneredness, artifice, overelegance, overelaboration, overniceness, overnicety, overrefinement; formality, stiffness, frill, *Inf.* put-on, *Inf.* putting on the dog.

2. habit, trick, quirk, peculiarity, peculiar trait, idiosyncrasy, characteristic gesture, body language; tic, twist, kink; eccentricity, erraticism, oddity, differentness, unconventionality, outlandishness; characteristic, singularity, particularity, feature; distinctive feature, stamp, mark, trademark, earmark, hallmark, individualism, specialty; style, mode, manner, fashion, way.

mannerly, *adj.* **1.** courteous, well-mannered, polite, civil, respectful, deferential, deferent; decorous, proper, formal, *Fr. comme il faut*, ceremonious; tactful, diplomatic, politic; cordial, genial, affable, amiable, good-humored, pleasant, sociable, considerate, thoughtful, nice, *Inf.* nice as pie; pleasing, winning, charming, ingratiating, complaisant, agreeable, obliging, attentive; mild, bland, fair-spoken, kindly, self-effacing.

2. well-behaved, well-bred, refined, polished, poised, cultivated, smooth, *Inf.* smooth as silk, civilized; genteel, gentle, ladylike, gracious, kind; gentlemanly, gentlemanlike, courtly, gallant, chivalrous, chivalric; urbane, suave, debonair, sophisticated, elegant.

—adv. **3.** courteously, politely, civilly, respectfully, deferentially, attentively, obligingly, accommodatingly, complaisantly; graciously, gracefully, with good grace, like a lady; courtly, gallantly, chivalrously, like a gentleman; urbanely, suavely, smoothly, with polish.

mannish, *adj.* **1.** (*all of women, usu. derogatory*) mannified, unfeminine, unwomanly, unladylike, Amazonian; *Sl.* butch; hoidenish, tomboyish, rompish.

2. masculine, manly, manful, manlike, male; virile, potent, *Inf.* he-mannish, *Inf.* two-fisted.

3. brave, courageous, valiant, valorous; intrepid, fearless, dauntless, aweless; bold, bold-spirited, high-spirited, nervy, plucky, mettlesome; resolute, firm, stalwart, *Archaic.* stalworth, stout, doughty; stout-hearted, lionhearted, great-hearted.

man of means, *n.* rich man, wealthy man, moneyed man, man of wealth, man of substance, nabob, nawab, moneybags, *Brit. Inf.* warm man, *Sl.* fat cat; millionaire, multimillionaire, billionaire; sugar daddy; plutocrat, capitalist.

man of war, *n.* warship, ship of war, war vessel; ship of the line, line-of-battle ship, corvette; battleship, *Inf.* battlewagon, cruiser, destroyer, gunboat; aircraft carrier, carrier, *U.S. Navy Inf.* flattop.

manor, *n.* estate, country estate, country seat, manor seat, house and grounds, house and lot, *Sl.* spread, *Brit. Dial.* toft; demesne, *Law.* messuage; manor house, country house, country home; mansion, palace, palatial *or* stately dwelling *or* residence, house on the hill.

manse, *n.* parsonage, vicarage, deanery, rectory, *Rom. Cath. Ch.* presbytery, *Brit. Archaic.* glebe house.

manservant, *n.* male servant, servant, *Fr. garçon, Archaic.* groom; man, valet, gentleman's gentleman, *Mil.* orderly, (*in the British army*) batman; attendant, servitor, squire, *Scot.* gillie, *Chiefly Brit.* buttons, *Archaic.* yeoman; lackey, footman, *Contemptuous.* flunkey; steward, head servant, major-domo, butler, chamberlain; factotum, man-of-all-work, do-all, *Brit.* general servant.

mansion, *n.* **1.** palace, palatial *or* stately residence, *Fr. hotel, It. palazzo,* villa, chateau, castle, *Chiefly Brit.* hall, *Brit.* court, *Archit.* folly, *Sl.* spread.

2. manor, manor house, manor seat, estate, country estate, country home, country house, country seat, hacienda.

3. *Often* **mansions** *British.* apartment house, apartment building, apartment block, apartment complex, tenements, high rise, high riser, high-rise apartments.

manslaughter, *n.* murder, slaying, killing, (*in India*) thuggee; assassination, dispatch, *Sl.* hit; lynching, murder by mob, mob-murder, *Sl.* necktie party; homicide, patricide, matricide, parricide, fratricide, sororicide, uxoricide, infanticide, regicide, vaticide.

manslayer, *n.* **1.** murderer, killer, slayer, man-killer, cutthroat, thug; assassin, liquidator, bravo, sniper, gunman, silencer, dispatcher, *Sl.* gun, *Sl.* hired gun, *Sl.* hit man, *Sl.* triggerman, *Sl.* torpedo, *Sl.* hatchet man; executioner, *Sl.* Jack Ketch, lyncher, garotter, burker; butcher, Bluebeard, ripper; bloodspiller, bloodshedder, bloodletter.

2. homicide, patricide, matricide, parricide, fratricide, sororicide, uxoricide, infanticide, regicide, tyrannicide, vaticide.

mantilla, *n.* **1.** head scarf, scarf, fascinator, shawl, wrap, head covering, kerchief; veil, coif, wimple, headcloth; hood, cowl, capuche.

2. mantle, cape, cloak, pelisse, covering.

mantle, *n.* **1.** cape, shawl, cloak, pelisse, pelerine, cope, drape, burnoose, sari; tunic, toga, *Gk. Antiq.* chiton, *Gk. Antiq.* chlamys, (*in ancient Greece and Rome*) pallium; mantilla, mantua, mantellet, (*in Spain*

and Spanish America) manta, dolman.
2. cover, covering, envelope, sheath, sheathing; pall, cloud, shade, film; mask, disguise, guise.
—*v.* **3.** cover, envelop, cloak, clothe, invest, swathe, enwrap, enshroud, shroud, drape; veil, blanket, curtain; cloud, obscure, shade, shadow; conceal, hide, disguise, mask.
4. flush, blush, color, color up, turn *or* change color, turn red, redden, get *or* become red in the face, crimson.
5. foam, froth, form a head; sparkle, effervesce, fizz, fizzle; bubble, burble.

manual, *n.* handbook, enchiridion, vade mecum, guidebook, *Inf.* how-to book; primer, gradus, workbook, abecedary; textbook, text, schoolbook.

manufacture, *n.* **1.** production, construction, building, making, fabrication, formation, creation; assembling, putting together; handiwork, workmanship, craft, craftmanship.
—*v.* **2.** produce, construct, build; make, work up, assemble, contrive, fashion, shape; create, frame, chisel, develop, carve, turn out, forge, form.
3. fabricate, concoct, elaborate, invent, make up; weave, tell a tall tale, fictionalize, romance; lie, lie like a rug, lie through one's teeth; prevaricate, misstate, equivocate; speak with forked tongue, spin it out, embroider, embellish, make up out of whole cloth; cook up, gloss over; draw the long bow; trifle with the truth, color, hyperbolize.

manumission, *n.* emancipation, emancipating, liberation, liberating, freeing, affranchisement, affranchising, enfranchisement, enfranchising, franchisement, franchising, manumitting; release, releasing, loosing, loosening, letting loose, setting loose, turning loose, discharge; disimprisonment, disimprisoning, disenthrallment, disenthralling, unfettering, unbinding, untying, unbridling, unyoking, unshackling, unchaining; deliverance, delivery, rescue, rescuing, ransom, ransoming, redemption, redeeming, *Both Theol.* salvation, saving.

manumit, *v.* emancipate, liberate, free, set free, set at liberty, give [s.o.] his liberty, affranchise, enfranchise, franchise; release, release from bondage, let loose, turn loose, set loose, loose, loosen, let go, discharge, dismiss; disimprison, unmew, disenthrall, unfetter, unbind, untie, unbridle, unyoke, unshackle, unmanacle, unchain, unharness, unhandcuff, unmuzzle, *Archaic.* untruss; deliver, rescue, ransom, redeem, *Theol.* save.

manure, *n.* **1.** fertilizer, organic fertilizer, plant food; compost, dressing, side-dressing; marl, bone meal, *Inf.* yesterday's gardenias.
2. excrement, excreta, egesta; fecal matter, waste matter, stools, *Sl.* do, waste, feculence; dung, muck, ordure, guano, animal droppings, night soil, cow *or* buffalo chips, *U.S. West* cow pies, coprolites, coproliths, *Sl.* flops, stable refuse.
—*v.* **3.** fertilize, spread manure over, enrich.

manuscript, *n.* **1.** handwritten script, written document, instrument, deed, holograph, folio, scripture, scroll, codex.
2. original, author's copy, draft, rough draft, prototype, typescript, MS, source document.
3. script, playbook, book, promptbook, libretto, score; text, dialogue, lines, actor's lines.
4. handwriting, hand, penscript, chirography, penmanship, pencraft; inkslinging, pencil pushing, scrivenery; autograph, signature.

many, *adj.* **1.** multitudinous, myriad, sundry, divers, several; various, manifold, multifarious; innumerable, countless, numerous, numerous as the grains of sand on the seashore, numerous as the stars in the Milky Way; multifold, multiple, multiplied, *Inf.* umpteen; abundant, profuse, teeming, prevalent, plentiful, copious; great, considerable, large.
—*n.* **2.** lots, a lot, *Sl.* scads, *Sl.* a scad, piles, a pile, *Inf.* heaps, *Inf.* a heap; bags of, *Inf.* gobs of, bags, barrels, tons, a bunch, a bushel and a peck; mass, shipload, passel; array, aggregation, assemblage, accumulation, amassment, assortment; myriad, legion, army, host; crowd, throng, multitude, horde, *Inf.* scillions, *Inf.* zillions, a thousand and one, scores, numbers, a number; multiplicity, multitudinousness, plenty, abundance, profusion, galaxy, Milky Way; school, shoal, bevy, covey, hive, flock, swarm, brood, drove; endless stream, river, torrent, flood, ocean, sea, world.

many-colored, *adj.* multicolored, polychrome, polychromatic, many-hued, variegated, rainbowlike, rainbowy; iridescent, irisated, opalescent; versicolor, particolored, kaleidoscopic; spectral, prismatic; gawdy, flashy, garish; like the aurora borealis; piebald, skewbald, pied, dappled; motley, harlequin, plaid, spotted, flecked, checkered, mosaic.

many-sided, *adj.* **1.** multilateral, trilateral, quadrilateral, triquetrous, polyhedral, tetrahedral, tetragonal.
2. multifaceted, hydraheaded, complex, compound; intricate, involved, difficult.
3. versatile, well-rounded, all-around, all-round; protean, changeable, adaptable; handy, talented, able, capable, deft, dexterous, gifted; Renaissance, cultured, interested, broad-minded; curious, deep, profound.

map, *n.* **1.** chart, plan, *U.S.* plat, graph, cartogram, Rand-McNally; table, outline, diagram, plot; road map, relief map, topographical map; projection, grid; guide, street guide; atlas, gazetteer.
2. representation, description, designation; reproduction, mirror; delineation, design.
—*v.* **3.** chart, delineate, represent; outline, trace, diagram, picture, depict.
4. map out, plot, plan, project, prepare; chalk out, sketch, draw up, lay out, lay down, set out, prognosticate, predetermine; devise, scheme, contrive; organize, arrange.

mar, *v.* **1.** impair, spoil, wreck, ruin; vitiate, debase, degrade, subvert, corrupt, pervert, adulterate, contaminate; sully, stain, taint, infect; blight, pollute, *Inf.* foul up, befoul, dirty; scathe, crack, break, *Inf.* bust, smash; despoil, devastate.
2. injure, harm, hurt, damage; disfigure, deface, scar, blemish; deform, distort, warp; cripple, lame, mangle, mutilate, wound.

maraud, *v.* **1.** pirate, freeboot, buccaneer, privateer, filibuster; seize, capture, steal, thieve, carry off, rape.
2. plunder, despoil, *Archaic.* spoil, spoliate, pillage; ravage, harry, devastate, depredate; ransack, sack, loot, gut, fleece, strip, rifle; raid, foray, forage, prey on *or* upon; lay waste, desolate, wreak havoc upon.

marauder, *n.* **1.** pirate, rover, viking, corsair, buccaneer, privateer, freebooter, rapparee, (*in the Scottish Highlands*) cateran.
2. pillager, plunderer, despoiler; ransacker, sacker, depredator, rifler, looter, forager, raider; ravager, destroyer.
3. kidnapper, abductor, rustler; hijacker, skyjacker, air *or* sky pirate.
4. robber, burglar, thief, stealer, *Inf.* crook, housebreaker; highwayman, footpad, *Sl.* yegg or yeggman, bandit, *Sp. bandolero, Southwest U.S.* ladrone, *Australian.* bushranger, brigand, picaroon, outlaw, des-

perado.

marauding, *adj.* roving, raiding, plundering, pillaging, ravaging; buccaneering, privateering, piratical, piratic; preying, predatory, predacious, rapacious; thievish.

marble, *n.* **1.** chalcedony, limestone, quartz; agate, *Sl.* aggie, *Sl.* glassy, shooter.
—adj. **2.** hard, polished, smooth, vitreous, glossy, shiny, lustrous.
3. marble-hearted, cold-hearted, hard-hearted; cold, austere, harsh, flinty, steely; unsympathetic, unfeeling, uncompassionate, uncaring, indifferent; merciless, relentless, unforgiving; rigid, stiff, stiff-necked; unkind, cruel, icy.
—v. **4.** variegate, mottle, stipple, fleck, striate; spot, spatter, sprinkle, spangle, dapple.

march, *v.* **1.** walk, step, pace, tread, goose-step, stride; file, parade, defile; shuffle, plod, tramp, mush; hike, trudge, foot, hoof, stump; stamp, amble, stroll, perambulate, saunter; strut, traipse, stalk, prance, swagger, flounce.
2. advance, proceed, go forward, forge ahead, get ahead, pass along; make headway, make progress, make strides, gain ground; go on, continue on, roll on, flow on, cover ground; develop, evolve, rise, further, prefer.
—n. **3.** column, file, train, retinue; parade, procession, cortege, caravan, cavalcade, coffle.
4. pace, stride, step, gait, walk; stamp, tread, parade, promenade; stalk, strut, traipse, flounce, prance; trudge, shuffle, saunter, stroll; trek, hike, excursion, trip, perambulation, peregrination; quick step, quick march, double march, double time, slow march, half step, goose step.
5. route, career, course, passage, itinerary; way, track, tack, direction, beat, path.
6. advance, move, forward movement; progression, progress, headway, gain; development, evolution, furtherance, advancement, preferment, rise.
7. dirge, threnody, monody, toll, knell, dead march, funeral march; wedding march, processional march, recessional march, martial music.

mare, *n.* broodmare, dam, female *or* mother horse, filly; horse, equine, mount, steed, *Sl.* hoss, *Sl.* critter, *Literary.* courser; doe, jenny, jennet, gen.

mare's nest, *n.* **1.** delusion, hoax, deception, fraud; sham, mock, fake, imitation, imposture, humbug, *Inf.* phony.
2. jumble, mess, *Inf.* stew, huddle, *Scot. Inf.* guddle, mix-up, snafu, *Inf.* foul-up, *Sl.* ball-up, *Brit. Sl.* balls-up; confusion, chaos, disorder, disarray, disorganization, disarrangement, derangement, confusedness.

margin, *n.* **1.** border, edge, perimeter, periphery, rim, lip, fringe, skirt; extremity, verge, brink, brim, brow, hem; circumference, circuit, compass, ambit, frame, outline.
2. frontier, frontier line, boundary, boundary line, bounding line, border line, partition line, line of demarcation, line.
3. limit, limits, outer limits, city *or* town limits; confine, confines, bound, bounds, bourn, pale.
4. leeway, latitude, free play, freedom, scope, range, room, elbow room, room to move *or* operate in, space.

marginal, *adj.* **1.** borderline, peripheral, peripheric; unessential, nonessential, unnecessary, dispensable, expendable.
2. minimal, minimum, least possible; barely adequate, passable, tolerable, indifferent, so-so.

marine, *adj.* **1.** sea, aquatic, saltwater, oceanic, pelagic, thalassic.
2. maritime, nautical, naval; seagoing, seafaring, (*of a vessel*) ocean-going.
—n. **3.** soldier, sailor, *Inf.* devil dog, *Sl.* leatherneck, *Mil. Sl.* grunt.
4. shipping, tonnage, merchant vessels, merchant marine; navy, armada, warships, fleet, flotilla, squadron.
5. seascape, marine painting.

mariner, *n.* **1.** sailor, seaman, seafarer, *Inf.* tar, bluejacket, Jack, *Inf.* gob, *Sl.* limey, *Brit. Sl.* matelot; sea dog, *Inf.* salt, shellback; *Fr. matelot, Ger. Matrose, Sp. marinero, Sp. marino, It. marinaio.*
2. skipper, captain; first mate, chief mate, first *or* chief officer, *Naut.* mate; helmsman, steersman, pilot, navigator; petty officer, boatswain, coxswain; crewman, *Naut.* deck hand, hand; midshipman, *Inf.* middy.
3. skin-diver, scuba diver, deep-sea diver, underseas explorer, aquanaut, hydronaut.

marionette, *n.* puppet, Punch and Judy, Polichinelle, *It. fantoccio*, dummy, doll.

marital, *adj.* conjugal, connubial, matrimonial, concubinary; nuptial, bridal, hymeneal, epithalamial, wedded, married; spousal, wifely, husbandly, uxorial, virile.

maritime, *adj.* **1.** sea, oceanic, Neptunian, aquatic; marine, thalassic, pelagic; bathyal, deep-sea, bathypelagic, benthic; hydrographic, oceanographic, bathymetrical.
2. nautical, naval, seamanlike, seamanly, sailorly, *Inf.* salty; seafaring, seagoing, oceangoing; navigational, sailing, coasting.
3. littoral, coastal, tidal, shore, seashore, seaside, grallatorial; riverine, riverside, riparian, estuarine.

mark, *n.* **1.** trace, line, score, rule, underline, underscore, streak, stroke; cut, gash, scratch, slash, scar, cicatrix, pock; tick, notch, chip, nick, pit, hachure; dent, impression, bruise; stain, blemish, blot, pimple; spot, dot, speck, blotch, splotch, smudge.
2. sign, symbol, indication, watermark; brand, identification, marking, trademark, hallmark; badge, emblem, token, evidence, proof; symptom, clue, hint, scent, omen; device, motto, monogram, signet, cachet, seal, signum; signature, autograph, cipher, figure, cross, X, hand, imprint, countermark, initials; fingerprint, thumbprint, footprint.
3. trace, vestige, remains, relic; track, tread, footprint, footmark, hoofmark; trail, wash, wake; scent, spoor, slot, smell, whiff.
4. landmark, waymark, direction post, marker, pointer; signpost, milestone, seamark, leader, cynosure.
5. punctuation, point, period, stop, dot, elipsis; comma, colon, semicolon, virgule, slash; quotation marks, apostrophe, exclamation mark, question mark; parenthesis, brackets, crotchets, braces; hyphen, dash, caret; asterisk, star, dagger, obelisk, squiggle, section; bullet, index, leader, paragraph; accent, grave accent, acute accent, circumflex, wedge; diaeresis, umlaut, tilde, macron, cedilla, breve.
6. norm, standard, criterion, measure; scale, yardstick, gauge, rule; model, type, pattern, prototype.
7. distinction, importance, consequence, prominence, greatness; repute, note, notability, report, fame; eminence, preeminence, prestige, glory, dignity, honor, celebrity, popularity; standing, rank, account, regard, name.
8. trait, characteristic, feature, peculiarity, lineament, attribute, quality; stamp, print, earmark, stigma, tattoo.
9. goal, objective, quarry, purpose, aim, end, intent, intention; point, destination, terminus, object; target,

bull's-eye, butt.
10. **wide of the mark a.** inaccurate, erroneous, off-target, out of order, amiss; inexact, faulty, fallacious, illogical. **b.** irrelevant, pointless, beside the mark, inapplicable, beside the point, inapposite; inconsequential, academic, parenthetic, neither here nor there.
—*v.* **11.** distinguish, brand, imprint, impress, stamp, earmark, seal, punch, emboss; sign, countersign, autograph, endorse, X, initial, paraph; score, rule, underline, underscore, annotate.
12. scratch, cut, scar, gash, slash, *Scot.* scart; notch, tick, nick, chip, pock, pit, chalk, dent, bruise; spot, dot, blotch, splotch; stain, streak, blot, smudge; deface, mar, disfigure, deform.
13. indicate, designate, signify, betoken, specify, point out; define, determine, set, fix, stipulate, assign, pin down, name, denominate; identify, label, tag, ticket, docket, tab.
14. heed, pay attention to, mind, note, pay heed to, obey, respect; bear in mind, take into consideration, give a thought to, hold in view; consider, give attention to, regard, hearken.
15. notice, observe, take note, *Sl.* get a load of; see, discern, make out, descry, recognize; spot, watch, witness, eye.
16. **mark down** reduce, decrease, cheapen, lower the price, depreciate, devaluate; cut, slash, go for a song, give away; undersell, undercut, undercharge.
17. **mark out a.** trace, form, outline, figure, represent, *Archaic.* limn; profile, delineate, sketch, depict, portray, shape, picture. **b.** single out, point out, distinguish, set apart, *Inf.* keynote; exclude, except, select; stigmatize, discriminate, differentiate. **c.** delimit, demarcate, bound, mark off, separate; restrict, restrain, circumscribe. **d.** destine, intend, reserve, purpose.
18. **mark up** raise, hike, boost, jack up; escalate, up, increase, inflate, appreciate, make higher, double.

marked, *adj.* **1.** noticeable, conspicuous, showing, salient, pointed, prominent, pronounced; striking, glaring, telling, flagrant, egregious; singular, peculiar, unique, uncommon, special, particular; distinguishable, unmistakable, identifiable, recognizable; manifest, apparent, evident, obvious, patent, self-evident, written all over one.
2. celebrated, eminent, notable, outstanding, memorable, unforgettable; remarkable, extraordinary, exceptional, signal, noteworthy; estimable, reputable, prestigious, noble, honorable; noted, renowned, distinguished, famed, famous, acclaimed, heralded.
3. doomed, fated, destined, condemned, foredoomed, *Brit. Dial.* fey.
4. striped, streaked, painted; lined, engraved, graven, inscribed, cut; enchased, tooled, carved, chiseled, sculptured; impressed, stamped, imprinted, printed.

marker, *n.* **1.** indication, mark, sign, symbol, token, identification, marking; indicator, arrow, index, paragraph; needle, finger, hand, hour-hand; bookmark, locater, place marker, pagemarker; weathercock, wind sock, weathervane, vane, straw in the wind; beacon, lighthouse, Pharos, lightship; lodestar, pole star, north star; landmark, waymark, pointer, direction post, post; signpost, guidepost, milestone, seamark, buoy, leader.
2. monument, memorial, plaque, cross; tombstone, gravestone, headstone, footstone; cairn, barrow, mound.
3. counter, chip, token, slug; coupon, check, tag, ticket, slip.
4. timekeeper, scorekeeper, scorer, recorder.

market, *n.* **1.** marketplace, markethouse, mart, open market, exchange, trading center; shopping center, commercial resort, place of traffic, forum, market town, *Hist.* staple; fair, exposition, emporium, rialto.
2. grocery, grocery store, food store, food mart, delicatessan, *Inf.* dely *or* deli, *Brit.* cash and carry, supermarket, *Brit.* hypermarket; meat market, butchery, butcher shop, butcher, *Obs.* butcher-row; vegetable *or* produce stand *or* mart, fruit and vegetable stand.
3. trade, traffic, sale, commerce, transaction, interchange, commercial enterprise, marketing, nundination; buying and selling, business, mercantry, mercantilism, commercialism, jobbing, brokerage, speculation; *Inf.* truck, dealing, barter, bargaining, negotiation, swap; hucksterism, haggling, hassling, hustling, chaffer, mongering.
4. demand, call, call for, request, appeal; need, want, desire.
5. price, current price, market price, exchange rate, rate, cost, amount, charge, expense; quotation, estimation, appraisal, appraisement, assessment, valuation; value, worth, monetary worth, equivalent, money's worth, par.
6. **in the market for** in need of, wanting, lacking, without; ready *or* looking *or* seeking to buy.
7. **on the market** for sale, up for sale, available, obtainable, at hand, purchasable, accessible, attainable.
—*v.* **8.** deal, traffic, trade, transact, exchange, interchange, buy and sell, job, speculate, *Inf.* truck, nundinate, handle, negotiate; bargain, barter, higgle, haggle, chaffer, *Scot.* argle-bargle.
9. transport, ship, send, dispatch, convey, freight, post, express, consign, send off; truck, move, cart, run, deliver, haul, carry, bring, transmit.
10. sell, sell off, retail, dispense, dispose of, regrate, auction, furnish, offer, offer for sale, put up for sale, vend, peddle, hawk, hustle; undersell, undercharge, undercut, sell at a loss, unload, dump.

marketable, *adj.* **1.** salable, vendible, merchantable, *Obs., Rare.* merchandisable, commerceable, exchangeable, interchangeable, staple; readily-sold, of ready sale, disposable; in demand, sought-after, desirable, desired, wanted, needed, requested, called-for; in vogue, fashionable, popular, *Sl.* hot.
2. commercial, mercantile, *Rare.* mercatorial; retail, wholesale; for sale, up for sale, on the market, available, obtainable, purchasable, at hand, accessible, attainable.

marksman, *n.* sharpshooter, rifleman, bersagliere; good shot, crack shot, dead shot, *Sl.* deadeye.

maroon, *v.* abandon, forsake, cast off, leave behind, turn one's back upon; isolate, seclude, cut off.

marriage, *n.* **1.** matrimony, holy matrimony, wedlock, holy wedlock; bond of matrimony, conjugal bond *or* tie *or* knot, wedding knot; match.
2. wedding, nuptials, espousals, spousals, espousement, bridal, hymeneal rites; wedding song, nuptial song, hymeneal, prothalamium, epithalamium.
3. alliance, union, affiliation, association, merger, liaison, *Inf.* hook-up, *Sl.* tie-up; unification, incorporation, amalgamation, consolidation, integration.

marriageable, *adj.* nubile, marriable, ripe, in full bloom; of age, at the age of consent.

married, *adj.* **1.** wedded, united in wedlock, joined in holy matrimony, one, one body and one flesh; mated, matched, coupled, spliced, yoked.
2. marital, matrimonial, connubial, spousal, conjugal, bridal, nuptial, epithalamial, hymeneal; wifely, husbandly.

marrow, *n.* **1.** core, pith, kernel, nucleus, *Anat.* medulla; center, focus, focal point, *Inf.* nub; sap, spirit, heart, soul, heart and soul; gist, sum and substance; matter substance, stuff, meat, nuts and bolts, *Inf.* nitty-gritty.

2. strength, power, potency, force, might, *Literary.* puissance; energy, vigor, vitality, vim, verve, fire, starch, *Inf.* moxie, *Inf.* punch, *Inf.* pizzazz.

marry, *v.* **1.** wed, wive, espouse, tie the knot, take the plunge, say one's vows, say "I do", walk down the aisle, become man and wife, *Sp.* splice, *Sl.* hitch up with, *Archaic.* husband; lead [s.o.] to the altar, walk [s.o.] down the aisle, give away; hook up, join in holy wedlock *or* matrimony, *Sl.* hitch.

2. mate, couple, partner, twin, pair *or* match up; unite, join, bond, fuse, weld, glue, cohere, stick together, put together; yoke, bind, tie together; connect, link, chain; unify, bring *or* draw together, make close; associate, affiliate, ally; coalesce, league, club; team, band, herd, pool, merge.

marsh, *n.* swamp, swampland, fen, fenland, marshland, quagmire, quag, bog, slough, morass, mud, mud flat, *Brit.* holm, *Brit.* sough, *Brit. Dial.* sump, *Chiefly Scot. and North Eng.* moss.

marshal, *n.* **1.** commander in chief, generalissimo, general of the army, five-star general, field marshal.

2. sheriff, peace officer, law enforcement agent, arm of the law, *Sl.* long arm of the law, *Sl.* John Law; officer, executive officer, sergeant-at-arms.

3. master of ceremonies, *Inf.* MC, *Inf.* emcee.

—*v.* **4.** order, put *or* set in order, organize; gather, arrange, dispose, deploy, distribute.

5. array, draw up, line up, draw up *or* line up for battle.

6. usher, escort, shepherd, guide, conduct, lead.

marshy, *adj.* swampy, muddy, boggy, fenny, quaggy, moory, miry, poachy, paludal.

mart, *n.* market, market place, open air market, flea market, trade *or* trading center, rialto, emporium, entrepôt; shopping center, shopping plaza, plaza, shopping mall, *Inf.* mall, shopping *or* commercial complex.

martial, *adj.* **1.** militant, warlike, aggressive; bellicose, belligerent, combative, pugnacious, truculent, full of fight, *Sl.* scrappy; hostile, antagonistic, inimical, enemy.

2. military, military-minded, soldierly, soldierlike; brave, courageous, valiant, valorous; stout, stalwart, staunch, doughty; stout-hearted, lionhearted, greathearted.

3. (*all of music*) patriotic, flag-waving; stirring, moving; brassy, blaring; marching, drum-beating, rhythmic, measured.

martial arts, *n.* savate; judo, jujitsu, aikido, karate; kung fu, wu-su, t'ai chi chu'an *or Inf.* t'ai chi; taekwan-do.

martinet, *n.* strict *or* severe disciplinarian, rigid formalist, stickler; hard master, taskmaster, drillmaster, drill sergeant, drill instructor, DI; slave-driver, oppressor, Simon Legree.

martyr, *n.* **1.** sufferer, victim; breast-beater, self-flagellator, *Fig.* masochist.

—*v.* **2.** martyrize, make a martyr of; throw to the lions, burn at the stake, immolate, stone, lapidate, nail to the cross, crucify, impale.

3. torture, persecute, harrow, agonize, excruciate, rack, break on the rack, stretch on the wheel; prolong the agony, kill [s.o.] by inches, let [s.o.] twist slowly in the wind.

martyrdom, *n.* **1.** martyrization; crucifixion, impalement, immolation, lapidation, stoning.

2. torture, torment, agony, anguish, suffering, persecution, excruciation; bitter cup, crown of thorns, vale of tears; purgatory, hell, hell on earth.

marvel, *n.* **1.** wonder, wonderful thing, amazing thing, quite a thing, really something; prodigy, miracle, phenomenon; sight, spectacle, sensation, eye opener, *Sl.* stunner, *Sl.* mind-boggler, *Sl.* mind-blower; curiosity, rarity, nonesuch, one in a thousand; *All Inf.* one for the book, something to brag about, something to write home about, something to shout about, something else.

—*v.* **2.** wonder *or* wonder at, stare, gape, gawk, goggle, look *or* stand aghast *or* agog, rub one's eyes, not believe one's eyes *or* ears.

marvelous, *adj.* **1.** wondrous, extraordinary, remarkable, phenomenal; surprising, unheard-of, unprecedented, unparalleled, unexampled; fabulous, fantastic, *Sl.* far-out; amazing, astounding, astonishing, miraculous, surpassing belief; staggering, breathtaking, *Sl.* stunning; indescribable, ineffable, mind-boggling, *Sl.* mind-blowing.

2. superb, splendid, glorious, divine, terrific, *Sl.* terrif, sensational, exceptional, *Sl.* marvy, *Sl.* out-of-this-world; wonderful, smashing, superfine, superexcellent, *Sl.* super, *Inf.* super-duper, *Australian.* bonzer; excellent, great, first-class, superior, *Inf.* A-1 *or* A-one *or* A-number-one, *Brit. Sl.* spot on, *Brit. Sl.* bang on.

3. improbable, unlikely, hard *or* difficult to believe, unbelievable, implausible, inconceivable, incredible.

marvelously, *adv.* **1.** wondrously, extraordinarily, remarkably, phenomenally; surprisingly, amazingly, astoundingly, astonishingly, miraculously; fabulously, fantastically, staggeringly, breathtakingly, *Sl.* stunningly; indescribably, ineffably, mind-bogglingly, *Sl.* mind-blowingly.

2. superbly, splendidly, gloriously, divinely, terrifically, sensationally, exceptionally; wonderfully, smashingly.

3. improbably, implausibly, unbelievably, inconceivably, incredibly.

mascot, *n.* charm, good luck charm, talisman, amulet, lucky piece; lucky charm, horseshoe, rabbit's foot, wishbone, *Brit.* merrythought; periapt, abraxas, scarab, phylactery, fetish; protector, preservative, safeguard.

masculine, *adj.* **1.** manly, virile, manful, macho; robust, muscular, athletic, brawny, sinewy, wiry, strapping, husky, stalwart, sturdy, hardy; strong, vigorous, lusty, energetic, powerful, mighty, forceful, forcible, potent, puissant, dynamic; brave, courageous, bold, bold-spirited, daring, valiant, valorous, heroic, gallant; stout, stout-hearted, lionhearted, ironhearted, intrepid, fearless, unafraid, dauntless, dreadless, nervy, *Sl.* gutsy.

2. male, men's, man's, of *or* for men; androcentric, male-dominated, male-oriented, patriarchal.

3. (*of a woman*) mannish, manlike, *Sl.* butch; unfeminine, unwomanly; Amazonian; hairy, hirsute.

masculinity, *n.* manliness, virility, manfulness, maleness, manhood, masculineness, machismo, macho; robustness, muscularity, muscle, brawn, brawniness, sinew, sinewiness; strength, stongness, vigor, vigorousness, lustiness, power, powerfulness, mightiness, forcefulness, potency, *Literary.* puissance; bravery, courage, boldness, valiance, valiancy, valor, valorousness, prowess, heroism, gallantry, gallantness, *Usu. Disparaging.* bravado; stout-heartedness, lionheartedness, ironheartedness, intrepidity, intrepidness, fearlessness, dauntlessness, awelessness, dreadlessness, nerve, pluck, grit, *Sl.* guts.

mash, *n.* **1.** mass, mush, cooked cereal, *Inf.* glop, *Inf.* goop; squash, ooze, slush, pulp, paste, pap, dough, beer wort, livestock feed.

2. *Slang.* **a.** crush, infatuation, flirtation, *Inf.* case;

puppy love, calf love, enchantment, obsession, fixation. **b.** sweetheart, sweetie, flame, spark; inamorata, true love, ladylove, light of one's life, *Inf.* girl; inamorato, best beau, favorite, boy friend. **c.** flirt, coquette, *U.S. Inf.* vamp; Casanova, philanderer, *Sl.* lounge lizard; *Sl.* masher, *Inf.* dirty old man.

—*v.* **3.** crush, pulp, pulpify, smash, squash, masticate, jellify; beat, pound, thresh; bruise, contuse, crunch, *Inf.* smush, *Inf.* scrunch.

4. mix, combine, unite, unify, incorporate, consolidate, inosculate; alloy, amalgamate, syncretize; blend, merge, coalesce, put together.

5. *Slang.* flirt with, court, pay court to; woo, make love to, *Inf.* spark, set one's cap for, address, sue, press one's suit; attempt to beguile, make overtures to, attempt to seduce, proposition.

mask, *n.* **1.** masque, false face, vizard, visor, domino, grotesque face, Halloween mask.

2. swim mask, snorkel mask, diving helmet.

3. theatrical mask, tragic mask, comic mask, witch-doctor's mask; death mask, life mask.

4. disguise, guise, cover, camouflage, incognito, veil; mummery, shield, deflection, false front, false colors, pretense, obscuration; false identity, *Inf.* cover, pseudonym, alias.

5. masker, mask wearer, masquer, mummer, mime, domino; disguiser, incognito, Zorro; secret agent, undercover man, spy, double agent, government agent, *U.S.* narcotics agent, *U.S. Inf.* narc, *U.S.* F.B.I. agent, *U.S.* C.I.A. agent, vice-squad member, plainclothes policeman *or* policewoman; imposter, wolf in sheep's clothing, pretender, poseur, fraud, charlatan, *Inf.* fake, *Inf.* faker, bluffer, *Inf.* bluff; milk masquerading as cream.

6. protective mask, surgeon's mask, industrial mask, shop mask, safety goggles, gas mask; hockey goalie's mask, catcher's mask, fencer's mask, skier's mask, football facemask.

7. masquerade, masque. See **masquerade** (*def.* **1**).

—*v.* **8.** disguise, conceal, hide, obscure; screen, cloak, shroud, cover; dissimulate, feign, put on, pretend, fake, put on an act, posture, sail under false colors, put on a false front, *Inf.* four-flush; *Inf.* dish bull, deceive, beguile, *Inf.* pull the wool over [s.o.'s] eyes, hood-wink, flim-flam; conceal the real facts, act hypocritical, be deceptive, make pretensions; lie, be mendacious, be untruthful, deceive; be Machiavellian, be two-faced.

9. masquerade, put on a mask, veil, masque, adopt a disguise, disguise oneself; go incognito, *Inf.* go underground, *Inf.* fade into the woodwork, affect a pseudonym.

masked, *adj.* **1.** disguised, mask-wearing, concealed, hidden, camouflaged; veiled, obscured, covered, shrouded, screened.

2. incognito, under a pseudonym, masquerading, flying under false colors, parading as something else, pretending; posturing, affected, bluffing, fake, false, fraudulent; hypocritical, deceptive, dissembling, prevaricative, prevaricatory, evasive, shifty; lying.

mason, *n.* bricklayer, brickmason, stonemason, tiler, *Scot.* cowan, *Brit. Dial.* diker.

masonry, *n.* **1.** bricklaying, brickmasonry, stonemasonry, tiling.

2. stonework, brickwork, rubblework, rubble.

masquerade, *n.* **1.** masked ball, mask, masque, masquerade ball, costume party, *Fr. bal masqué, Fr. bal paré, Fr. bal costumé*; mummery, revel, harlequinade, carnival, Mardi gras, Halloween party.

2. costume, disguise, mummery, theatrical costume; mask, visor, domino; camouflage, cloak

3. pretense, subterfuge, guise, feint, trick, artifice; ruse, pretext, excuse, expedient, plea.

4. false colors, imposture, pose, pretense, *Inf.* front, dissimulation, faking, bluff, *Inf.* an act, deception, lie.

—*v.* **5.** go incognito, disguise oneself. See **mask** (*def.* **9**).

masquerader, *n.* masker, domino, mummer, guiser; pretender, poseur, impostor, imitator; incognito, plainclothesman, *Inf.* undercover cop; bluffer, flimflammer, deceiver, liar, hypocrite, faker, *Inf.* fake.

mass, *n.* **1.** pile, heap, stack, accumulation, bulk, drift, cumulus; hoard, store, stock, stockpile, supply; lump, deposit, swell, mound, tumulus; bank, hillock, hummock, hill, mountain; bale, bundle, cock, shock, rick, mow; load, barrow, cartload, wagonload, carload, cargo; cake, nugget, block, chunk, hunk; clot, coagulum, curd.

2. collection, amassment, assemblage, aggregation; concentration, agglomeration, conglomeration, cluster, congeries; assortment, variety, medley, miscellany, jumble, hodgepodge; clutter, *Inf.* mess.

3. abundance, bounty, volume, plenty; quantity, profusion, *Inf.* lots, *Inf.* raft, storm, shower, ocean, sea, world; hoard, store, considerable amount, deal, great deal; *Inf.* lots, peck, *Inf.* oodles, *Inf.* tons; *Sl.* gobs, *Sl.* scads, *Inf.* slews.

4. whole, totality, entirety, aggregate; total, sum, sum total, everything; concretion, gross amount, *Sl.* whole bit, *Sl.* whole schmear.

5. clump, tuft, tussock, thicket, grove, truss, *Bot.* raceme, *Bot.* panicle; bouquet, posy, bunch, batch; shock, sheaf; fagot, fascicle.

6. group, knot, band, company; body, congregation, assembly, gathering; crowd, number, mob, throng; bevy, covey, gaggle, flock, swarm, hive, school, pack, drove, herd; lot, parcel; multitude, galaxy, constellation; throng, array, legion, score.

7. majority, main body, greater part, almost all, lion's share, preponderance.

8. size, dimension, magnitude, capacity; bigness, massiveness, immensity; greatness, ampleness, bulkiness, hugeness, ponderosity.

9. **the masses** the common people, the working class, the lower class, huddled masses; the common man, the man in the street; peasants, proletariat, plebeians, the hoi polloi; rabble, *Both Disparaging.* the great unwashed, the undeserving poor.

—*v.* **10.** assemble, accumulate, amass; group together, draw together, lump together; compile, collate, collocate, colligate, unite, join together; anthologize, collect, garner, glean, marshal; organize, order, codify, methodize, systematize.

11. convene, forgather, come together; meet, *Inf.* gang up, huddle, go into a huddle, get together, rendezvous.

12. group, cluster, concentrate, bunch up *or* together; crowd, congregate, agglomerate; flock together, throng, herd, swarm, surge; rally, muster, mobilize, levy; round up, round in.

massacre, *n.* **1.** carnage, slaughter, butchery; wholesale slaughter, random *or* indiscriminate slaughter, general slaughter, wholesale killing, mass murder, mass homicide, mass slaying, mass execution, mass destruction; blood bath, effusion of blood, fusillade of blood, noyade, *Rare.* internecion, *Rare.* trucidation; decimation, annihilation, extermination, liquidation, pogrom, genocide.

—*v.* **2.** decimate, destroy a great number, kill off; annihilate, exterminate, eliminate, liquidate, obliterate, eradicate, *Brit. Mil. Sl.* scupper; erase, blot out; butcher, slaughter, cut to pieces, maul, savage, hew, hack, hack to pieces, chop, chop to pieces, mow down, mutilate, tear limb from limb, dismember, disembowel; wade in blood, give no quarter, show no mercy, run amuck, go berserk; kill, murder, slay, cut down, do to death, execute, put to death, put to the sword, destroy, shed *or* spill blood, assassinate.

massage, *n.* **1.** rub, rubdown, rubbing, friction, attrition; kneading, handling, stroking, palming, palpation, manipulation, osteopathic alignment; Rolfing, *Japanese.* Shiatsu, reflexology.

—v. **2.** rub, rub down, knead, make supple; handle, stroke, palm, palpate; manipulate, align, Rolf.

massive, *adj.* **1.** bulky, big, large, hulking, huge, hugeous, massy; immense, prodigious, enormous, *Archaic.* enorm, gigantic, gargantuan; vast, large-scale, mammoth, jumbo, colossal, monumental, monstrous, gigantean; cyclopean, titanic, Brobdingnagian; towering, staggering, mountainous, stupendous, tremendous, *Sl.* humongous; elephantine, hippopotamic, leviathan, dinosaurian; oversize, kingsize, overlarge; *All Inf.* whopping, roaring, spanking, walloping; cumbersome, cumbrous, unwieldy, burdensome.

2. obese, fat, corpulent, stout, portly, fleshy; thickset, brawny, burly, *Inf.* strapping, *Inf.* bouncing.

3. great, imposing, mighty; solid, substantial, considerable; heavy, weighty, ponderous.

mast, *n.* **1.** *Nautical.* spar, yard, boom, gaff; foremast, mainmast, topmast, mizzen, mizzenmast.

2. pole, flagpole, flagstaff, post, support.

master, *n.* **1.** lord, lord and master, overlord, ruler, tyrant, dictator, despot; king, sovereign, monarch, majesty, crowned head, potentate, dynast; prince, emperor, rajah, maharajah, sultan, czar, Caesar, kaiser, *Fr. roi, Latin. rex,* sheik, khan, governor, tetrarch; president, Chief Executive, commander in chief, *Inf.* pres, premier, chief of state, head of state, captain of the ship of state.

2. leader, chief, chieftain, head, headman, captain; superior, commander, commanding officer, senior officer, commandant, general, chief of staff, high chief, (*of some tribes of American Indians*) sachem; employer, *Inf.* boss, *It. padrone, Fr. patron*; *Inf.* bossman, *Inf.* big boss, man-in-charge, chairman, director, administrator; headmaster, schoolmaster, principal, dean; executive, manager, overseer, taskmaster, slave driver, supervisor, superintendent, *Inf.* super, foreman, *Brit.* gaffer; *Inf.* kingpin, *Inf.* kingfish, *Inf.* number one, *Inf.* Mr. Big, *Sl.* top dog, *Sl.* head honcho, *Sl.* big cheese, *Fr. grand fromage, Sl.* wheel *or* big wheel, *Sl.* high man on the totem pole, cock of the walk.

3. owner, possessor, holder, keeper, slaveholder, slave owner; landlord, proprietor, landowner, landholder; feudal lord *or* superior, liege, lord, *Hist.* suzerain; seigneur, *Japanese Hist.* daimyo, signior, signor; squire, *Scot.* laird, *Russian Hist.* baoyar, (*in medieval Germany*) landgrave.

4. nobleman, noble, peer; grand duke, archduke, duke, marquis, *Hist.* margrave, earl, count, viscount, baron; grandee, magnifico, don, hidalgo.

5. captain, skipper, commander.

6. patriarch, master *or* man of the house, *Irish Eng.* himself; *Inf.* boss, father, papa, *Inf.* pa, *Inf.* dad, daddy, *Inf.* pop, *Chiefly Midland and Southern U.S.* pappy.

7. teacher, guide, leader *or* spiritual leader, guru, rabbi, *Japanese. roshi.*

8. **the Master** Jesus Christ, Jesus, Christ, the Nazarene, the Galilean; the Redeemer, the Savior, Emmanuel, the Messiah, the Son of God.

9. victor, conqueror, triumpher, champion, winner, hero; conquistador, subjugator, subduer, defeater, vanquisher.

10. master hand, expert, proficient. See **master hand**.

11. boy, young man *or* fellow, *Scot.* chield, youth, adolescent, teenager, teen *or* teener, minor, hobbledehoy; male child, *Inf.* kid, youngster, stripling, lad, cub, sprig, schoolboy, whippersnapper; son, sonny, cadet, scion.

—adj. **12.** chief, principal, main, predominant, cardinal, prime; leading, most important, dominating, commanding, controlling, ruling, directing.

13. masterful, masterly, skillful, skilled. See **masterly** (*def.* **1**).

—v. **14.** conquer, vanquish, triumph over, defeat, beat, *Inf.* whip; overmaster, overpower, overwhelm, overthrow, take over; prostrate, break, smash, crush, flatten, bring [s.o.] to his knees; subdue, subjugate, subject, subordinate, enslave, enthrall; beat down, put down, quash, quell, stamp out; repress, suppress, keep down.

15. (*all of animals*) break, break in, tame, domesticate.

16. dominate, rule, control, govern; command, order around, dictate to, boss around, tell [s.o.] what to do; direct, manage, call the shots *or* plays, run the show, rule the roost, lay down the law; lord it over, domineer, be overbearing, rule with a high *or* iron hand, tyrannize; ride herd on, ride roughshod over, intimidate, browbeat, bully.

17. learn thoroughly, acquire skill in, become proficient in, make oneself a master of, know inside out *or* backwards and forwards.

masterful, *adj.* **1.** commanding, controlling, dominating, ruling, bossy; authoritative, powerful, domineering, oppressive; overbearing, arrogant, haughty, lordly; peremptory, imperative, demanding; imperious, dictatorial, tyrannical, despotic, despotical, autocratic, autocratical, arbitrary, high-handed, self-willed.

2. preeminent, expert, skillful. See **masterly** (*def.* **1**).

master hand, *n.* **1.** expert, master, ace, proficient, adept, mavin, *Chiefly Brit. Inf.* dab hand, *Brit. Dial.* dabster; maestro, virtuoso, talent, genius, prodigy, standout; *Inf.* wizard, *Inf.* whiz, *U.S. Sl.* crackerjack, *Chiefly Brit.* crack, *Sl.* sharp, *Sl.* shark; professional *Inf.* pro, journeyman, veteran, past master *or* mistress, old hand, old stager; specialist, authority, pundit, scholar; connoisseur, critic; (*both of martial arts*) black belt, dan.

2. expertness, expertise, mastery, skill, excellence; masterfulness, masterliness, skillfulness, proficiency, adeptness; knack, touch, finesse, address, ingenuity, genius, subtlety; dexterity, adroitness, facility, ease, felicity, deftness, handiness, ambidexterity.

masterly, *adj.* **1.** supreme, consummate, matchless, peerless, expert, virtuosic; excellent, superior, preeminent, distinguished, top-flight, top-drawer, first-rate, ace, *Inf.* topnotch, *Inf.* crack, *Sl.* crackerjack, *Inf.* whiz-bang, *Brit. Sl.* whizzo; finished, polished, admirable, accomplished, *Fr. au fait*; proficient, adept, apt; adroit, deft, dexterous, gifted, talented; skillful, skilled, artistic, workmanlike.

—adv. **2.** expertly, masterfully, excellently, preeminently; proficiently, adeptly, aptly, admirably; skillfully, dexterously, adroitly, deftly.

mastermind, *v.* **1.** conceive, contrive, think up, come up with, have the bright idea, *Inf.* hatch, *Inf.* dream up; devise, frame, forge, plan, design, shape, form, mold, develop, work up; originate, innovate, initiate, found, establish, start, instigate, inaugurate, launch; create, author, invent, produce, generate, make; execute, carry [s.t.] out, move [s.t.] forward, engineer, manage, direct, guide, lead.

—*n.* **2.** conceiver, contriver, mind, intellect, genius, *Sl.* brains, *Inf.* think tank; deviser, framer, forger, planner, designer, architect; instigator, instigant, inciter, provoker; originator, initiator, founder, father, founding father, institutor, establisher; creator, author, producer, maker, generator, builder; executor, prime mover, pusher, engineer, orchestrator, manager, executive, director, guide, leader, master.

masterpiece, *n.* masterwork, chef-d'oeuvre, magnum opus, work of art, creation.

master stroke, *n.* stroke of genius, tour de force, *Fr. coup de maître*, coup; (*all of a highly successful nature*) stroke, move, maneuver, act, action, deed, feat, exploit, stunt; triumph, victory, complete success, *Inf.* ten-strike, hit, *Inf.* smash.

mastery, *n.* **1.** control, domination, upper hand, whip hand; government, order, rule, sway; jurisdiction, authority, power, influence; sovereignty, hegemony, preeminence, leadership, headship, mastership.
2. command, management, handling, direction; grasp, hold, comprehension, understanding, knowledge, cognizance; discernment, perception, apprehension; acquisition, acquirement, achievement, attainment, accomplishment.
3. conquest, ascendency, supremacy, superiority, victory over, victoriousness, triumphancy, triumph, win, success, *Chiefly Scot.* gree; vanquishment, defeat of, subjugation.
4. expertise, expertness, masterliness, masterfulness, master hand, virtuosity; proficiency, adeptness, address, finesse, finish, polish; facility, felicity; skillfulness, skill, dexterity, dexterousness, adroitness, deftness.

masticate, *v.* **1.** chew, crunch, craunch, munch, champ, mumble, gnaw, nibble, bite, *Dial.* chaw, *Archaic.* manducate; chew well, Fletcherize; ruminate, remasticate, rechew, chew the cud.
2. pulverize, comminute, triturate, levigate, powder, granulate, break down, liquefy; grind, bray, pestle, kibble, mill; crush, knead, mash, smash, *Sl.* smush, pound, beat; crumble, disintegrate, shatter.

mastication, *n.* **1.** chewing, crunching, craunching, munching, champing, mumbling, Fletcherism, Fletcherizing, gnawing, nibbling, biting, *Dial.* chawing, *Both Archaic.* manducation, manducating; rumination, remastication.
2. pulverization, pulverizing, comminution, comminuting, trituration, triturating, levigation, levigating, powdering, granulating, granulation; grinding, braying, pestling, kibbling, milling; crushing, mashing, kneading, smashing, *Sl.* smushing, pounding, beating; crumbling, disintegration, disintegrating, shattering.

masturbation, *n.* self-gratification, self-manipulation, autoeroticism, manustupration, onanism; self-abuse, self-defilement, *Sl.* playing with oneself.

mat[1], *n.* **1.** throw-rug, rug, floor-cover, drugget, doormat, welcome mat; dropcloth, oilcloth, matting.
2. canvas, pad, floor, ground; ring, wrestling ring.
3. mass, tangle, knot, mesh; thatch, crop, mop, shag, mane, shock.
—*v.* **4.** interweave, intertwine, entwine, entangle, ravel, dishevel; interlace, lace, enlace, net; plait, braid, plat, twill, felt; interknit, knit, wreathe, twist, loop, pleach.

mat[2], *adj.* **1.** lusterless, dull, drab, flat, dead; lackluster, cloudy, gray, leaden; dingy, faded, discolored, washed out, dimmed.
—*n.* **2.** dullness, flatness, drabness, deadness; lusterlessness, lackluster, cloudiness, grayness.

matador, *n.* bullfighter, toreador, torero, tauromachian, *Sp. tauromaquista*; bandillero, picador.

match[1], *n.* **1.** mate, twin, double, look-alike, counterpart, one of a pair, bird of a feather, *Astron.* comes; duplicate, copy, facsimile, replica, replication, reproduction, same thing, *Inf.* spit and image, *Inf.* spitting image, *Sl.* ringer.
2. parallel, pendant, correspondence, reciprocal, equivalent; equal, peer, compeer, colleague, fellow; confrere, brother, sister, kin, congener.
3. competition, competitor, rival, vier, challenger.
4. contest, game, competition, meet, bout, tournament, tourney, trial, duel, spar, race, *Curling.* bonspiel, *Scot.* spiel, *Football.* scrimmage, *Sports.* event; contention, rivalry, *Obs.* emulation.
5. prospect, candidate, potential partner, *Inf.* Mr. Right; spouse, consort, helpmate, helpmeet, husband, wife; betrothed, fiancé, fiancée.
6. engagement, betrothal, betrothment, compact, contract, promise; marriage, union, alliance, association, affiliation.
—*v.* **7.** equal, measure up to, tie, keep pace with, keep up with; duplicate, reproduce, copy; parallel, compare to *or* with, analogize, be in the same category; resemble, look like, take after, *Inf.* favor.
8. adapt, accommodate, adjust, suit; fit, proportion, shape *or* mold; correspond, tally, accord, agree, go together; complement, harmonize, blend, coordinate.
9. rival, vie, compete, emulate; contend, meet, challenge, oppose, go up against.
10. marry, give away, hook up, join in holy wedlock *or* matrimony, *Sl.* hitch; mate, couple, partner, pair off *or* up; unite, join, conjoin, bond, link, put together; ally, associate, affiliate, play matchmaker, find a husband *or* wife for.

match[2], *n.* **1.** light, lighter, igniter, *Fr. allumette*; fusee, vesuvian, vesta, Congreve; friction match, lucifer, locofoco, safety match.
2. wick, taper, cord; fuse, squib.

matchable, *adj.* analogous, synonymous, equivalent, comparable. See **matching** (*def.* **1**).

matched, *adj.* **1.** identical, twin, double, same, equal. See **matching** (*def.* **1**).
2. mated, coupled, paired, yoked, geminate, bigeminate, bijugate; married, wedded, one, partnered.

matching, *adj.* **1.** parallel, comparable, analogous, equivalent, homologous; corresponding, correspondent, complemental, corresponsive; duplicate, replicate, identical, twin, double; like, same, of a kind, of a piece, in kind, of a set; synonymous, correlative, cognate, collateral; akin, related, kindred, allied, alike.
—*n.* **2.** analogy, comparison, parallelism, likening, similitude, similarity; correlation, correspondence, cognation.

matchless, *adj.* **1.** peerless, unequaled, unparalleled, unmatched, unrivaled, without equal, *Fr. sans pareil*; incomparable, inimitable, unmatchable; unsurpassed, unapproachable, beyond compare; consummate, perfect, transcendent, quintessential, superlative, impeccable; sterling, gilt-edged, precious, golden; rare, priceless, invaluable, unique, irreplaceable, one of a kind.
2. supreme, greatest, chief, foremost, first, great; best, best ever, champion, *Australian.* bonzer, top, A1; top-notch, topflight, tip-top, first-rate, first-class, front-rank; elite, choice, select, elect, handpicked, prize; paramount, sovereign, second to none, *Latin. nulli secundum*, dominant; prime, cardinal, preeminent.

matchmaker, *n.* **1.** marriage arranger, marriage broker, matrimonial agent, go-between, *Yiddish. schatchen*.

2. promoter, organizer, developer, enterpriser, planner, setter-up, *Inf.* booster.

mate, *n.* **1.** twin, fellow, other half, one of a pair, *Astron.* comes; counterpart, parallel, correspondence, peer, equal, equivalent; match, double, bird of a feather, duplicate, copy, facsimile; complement, completer, accessory, concomitant, concurrent.

2. spouse, consort, helpmate, helpmeet, *Sl. Facetious.* better half; husband, bridegroom, groom, man, *Facetious.* lord and master, *Inf.* old man, *Inf.* hubby; wife, bride, woman, rib, squaw, *Inf.* old lady.

3. companion, crony, copain, sidekick, shadow, alter ego, *Inf.* pal, *U.S. Inf.* buddy, *Sl.* cully, *Sl.* Siamese twin, *Obs.* consort; associate, colleague, compeer, coworker, yoke-fellow, yoke-mate, *Scot. and North. Eng.* marrow, *Archaic.* peer; fellow, confrere, brother, sister; comrade, chum, ally, affiliate, friend, acquaintance, amigo, *Fr. ami*; teammate, playmate, classmate, shipmate, messmate, housemate, roommate, *Inf.* roomie.

—v. **4.** couple, partner, twin, double, pair *or* match up; unite, join, bond, fuse, weld, glue, cohere, stick together, hold together; yoke, bind, tie together, bracket; connect, attach, link, chain, shackle; associate, affiliate, ally.

5. marry, lead [s.o.] to the altar, walk [s.o.] down the aisle, give away, hook up, join in holy wedlock *or* matrimony, *Sl.* hitch; wed, wive, espouse, tie the knot, take the plunge, say one's vows, say "I do," walk down the aisle, become man and wife, *Sl.* splice, *Sl.* hitch up with, *Archaic.* husband.

6. compare, analogize, consider together, see *or* look at together, put in the same category.

7. (*all of animals*) copulate, breed.

8. (*all of a gear, rack, worm*) interlock, meet, fit, synchronize, coordinate, *Mach.* mesh, *Mech.* engage.

material, *n.* **1.** substance, matter, stuff, something, materiality, medium; meat, marrow, sum and substance; raw material, stock, staple, store, goods; building blocks, bricks and mortar, sticks and stones, lath and plaster; earth, clay, cement, concrete; lumber, timber, wood.

2. element, component, constituent, unit, ingredient; feature, part, parcel, factor, piece, portion, item.

3. fabric, cloth, textile, texture, weave, tissue; napery, rag, weft, woof.

4. data, facts, information, figures; notes, notabilia, documents, papers.

5. **materials** apparatus, articles, supplies, resources, means; tools, utensils, instruments, implements, equipment, plant; gear, tackle, outfit, rigging.

—adj. **6.** corporeal, corporal, physical, bodily, somatic, hylic; real, solid, concrete, substantial, substantive; palpable, tangible, sensible, touchable, ponderable, appreciable.

7. unspiritual, materialistic, *Philos.* hylozoistic, nonspiritual, nonpastoral; worldly, mundane, temporal, earthly, earthy, external; secular, lay, worldly-minded, earthly-minded, carnal-minded, carnal.

8. important, consequential, momentous, weighty, considerable, significant; great, grave, serious, big; of importance, of interest, of concern, of note; vital, essential, indispensable; evidential, indicative, attestative, convincing, telling, pointing.

9. **material to** pertinent, relevant, applicable, apropos; appertaining, pertaining, apposite, germane; applying, involving, belonging, in point.

materialize, *v.* **1.** realize, bring about, produce, effectuate; create, form, shape, take form; effect, achieve, attain, accomplish; institute, set up, inaugurate.

2. appear, become visible, come into view *or* sight, turn up, show oneself, present oneself; come to light, reveal oneself, *Motion Pictures.* fade in; emerge, rise, arise, issue, come forth, burst forth.

3. incorporate, embody, reify, personify; corporealize, substantialize, substantiate, transubstantiate; incarnate, reincarnate.

materially, *adj.* **1.** considerably, greatly, to a great extent, much, largely, in great measure; enormously, immensely, vastly, momentously; significantly, importantly, tellingly, memorably, emphatically.

2. substantially, essentially, in essence, in substance, at the core, at the heart, in the main; fundamentally, basically, primarily, at bottom, *Fr. au fond, Latin. per se.*

3. physically, corporeally, substantially, somatically; palpably, tangibly, sensibly, ponderably.

matériel, *n.* **1.** equipment, apparatus, gear, accouterments, furnishings, furniture, appurtenances, appointments; tools, contrivances, machinery; implements, appliances, utensils, office supplies, conveniences; fixtures, fittings, paraphernalia, habiliments, *Inf.* things; outfit, outfitting, turnout, rig; supplies, material, wherewithal; caparison, harness, trappings, tack, tackle, rigging.

2. *Military.* arms, armaments, weapons, guns, munitions, ammunition.

maternal, *adj.* motherly, parental; nurturing, nourishing, fostering; vigilant, guarding, guardian, protecting, protective, sheltering, shielding; sympathetic, understanding, caring, warm, warm-hearted, kind, tender, gentle; affectionate, fond, devoted, doting.

maternity, *n.* motherhood, parenthood; motherliness, maternalism, protectiveness; tenderness, gentleness, kindness, warmth, warm-heartedness.

mathematical, *adj.* **1.** arithmetical, numerative, numerical, statistical; algebraic, equational, geometrical, trigonometrical, logarithmic, differential; fractional, divisional, multiplicational, additive, subtractive; analytic, holomorphic.

2. precise, exact, definite, well-defined; strict, rigid, rigorous, unerring; particular, careful, correct, punctilious, scrupulous, meticulous, finical.

matin, *n.* **1.** **matins** *Ecclesiastical.* first canonical hour; Morning Prayer, public prayer service, daybreak service.

2. morning song, *Music.* aubade.

matriarch, *n.* head of household, head of the family; mother, materfamilias, *Brit. Inf.* mater; dame, matron, elderly woman, grandma, grandmother, ancestress; dowager, duchess, grand duchess, empress, queen, monarch, sovereign, wearer of the crown, ruler, ruler of the roost, mistress.

matriculate, *v.* enroll, enter, *Brit.* go up, sign up, enlist, *Mil. Inf.* re-up; admit, register, record, catalogue, book, inscribe; certify, validate, attest.

matrimonial, *adj.* marital, nuptial, connubial, conjugal, wedded, married, spousal; hymeneal, epithalamic; bridal, affianced, plighted.

matrimony, *n.* **1.** marriage ceremony *or* sacrament, wedding, nuptials, spousals, espousal, *Anc. Rom.* confarreation, *Inf.* saying the I-do's, *Inf.* tying the knot; *All Fig.* Hymen, orange blossoms, the march down the aisle.

2. marriage, wedlock, match, union, legal union, nuptial knot, spousehood; cohabitation, living together, living as husband and wife, common-law marriage.

matrix, *n.* mold, die, last, stamp, cast, mint, form, format, frame; punch, seal, intaglio, lithographic stone; prototype, pattern, model, example, exemplar, original.

matron, *n.* **1.** dame, matriarch, *Inf.* old lady, dowager, lady, grandmother.

2. warden, housemother, head mistress; governess, housekeeper, stewardess; supervisor, overseer, directress; head nurse, principal.

matronly, *adj.* maternal, matriarchal, motherly, grandmotherly, wifely; mature, middle-aged, mellow, venerable; respected, admired; sedate, proper, decorous, dignified; serious, grave, sober; plump, rounded, settled, portly.

matted, *adj.* **1.** tangled, snarled, snaggy, tangly, knotted, raveled; tousled, disheveled, bedraggled, *Inf.* mussed up; raddled, rumpled, tumbled.

2. plaited, woven, braided, twilled; interlaced, intertwined, interwoven.

3. shaggy, hairy, hirsute, hispid, crinose; woolly, fleecy, furry, curly, fuzzy; uncombed, unshorn, mopheaded.

matter, *n.* **1.** substance, material, stuff, materiality, medium, something, body; protoplasm, plasma, element; flesh, meat, marrow, sum and substance.

2. pus, suppuration, purulence, discharge; ooze, juice, sap, latex, milk; mucus, phlegm, grume, gore; *All Pathol.* gleet, sanies, ichor, leukorrhea.

3. situation, affair, state; business, proceeding, transaction, doing; thing, concern, concernment; event, circumstance, happening, happenstance, occasion; episode, incident, adventure, experience; particular, phenomenon, fact, article, case, instance.

4. subject, topic, focus, text, content; essence, gist, purport; point, issue, question, case, concern; thesis, motif, theme.

5. amount, extent, measure, quantity, sum; magnitude, mass, bulk, size.

6. consequence, significance, importance, moment, weight, pith; import, implication, signification, intention; meaning, tenor, drift, purport, sense.

7. difficulty, trouble, distress, ailment, worry; embarrassment, predicament, plight, pass, strait, pinch, mess; quandary, dilemma, problem, puzzle, perplexity, enigma.

8. ground, cause, basis, reason, rationale, *Sl.* what for; explanation, excuse, pretext, pretense; the why, the wherefore, the why and wherefore, *Inf.* the idea, *Sl.* the big idea.

9. **as a matter of fact** actually, in reality, really, truly, veritably; truthfully, in truth, to tell the truth; in point of fact, in fact, in effect, *Fr. au fait.*

10. **no matter** it makes no difference, it is unimportant, it doesn't count; pay it no mind, don't give it another thought, don't bother with it; don't worry about it, never mind, forget it, *Inf.* drop it.

—*v.* **11.** signify, import, be of importance, purport, bespeak; indicate, imply, mean, connote, denote, express; weigh, carry weight, count, make a difference, make no difference, tell, amount to.

matter-of-fact, *adj.* **1.** factual, strict, literal, word-for-word, line-for-line, verbatim, exact, precise, close; faithful, accurate, true, honest, straight, unexaggerated, unvarnished, undistorted, unadulterated, unwarped; prosaic, prosy, unpoetic, plain, plainspoken, uncreative, unimaginative, unembellished; uninteresting, unexciting, unentertaining, tame, dull, flat, insipid, jejune, dry, arid; ordinary, commonplace, pedestrian, everyday, workaday, usual, average, *Inf.* run-of-the-mill; unoriginal, stale, banal, hackneyed, trite; boring, humdrum, plodding, monotonous, tedious, tiresome, wearisome, *Inf.* ho-hum.

2. practical, pragmatic, pragmatical, realistic, down-to-earth, *Inf.* meat and potatoes, *Inf.* nuts and bolts; earthy, unaffected, genuine, real, authentic, *Sl.* out-front; direct, straightforward, straight-shooting, frank, candid, open, outspoken, downright, blunt, *U.S. Inf.* straight-out.

mattress, *n.* pallet, feather bed, water bed, pad, cushion, *Inf.* tick, *Chiefly Brit.* paillasse; bedding, litter, shakedown, sleeping bag, *Sl.* hay; bed, bunk, recliner, *Brit.* lair, *U.S. Sl.* sack, *Brit. Sl.* kip.

maturate, *v.* mature, ripen, mellow; grow up, reach adulthood. See **mature** (*def.* **8**).

mature, *adj.* **1.** full-grown, grown, grown up, adult, full-fledged, of age; marriageable, nubile, pubescent; womanly, manly, in the prime of life, in one's prime, middle-aged, older; experienced, practised, knowledgeable, sophisticated, worldly.

2. ripe, ripened, mellow, soft; full-blown, in full bloom *or* flower, florescent, in bloom, blooming, out; seasoned, well-aged, fully-aged, aged, old.

3. settled, on one's own, out of the nest, independent, self-sufficient; responsible, dependable, reliable; sensible, prudent, judicious, wise, sage.

4. complete, fully developed, refined, polished, perfected; operational, ready to go, prepared.

5. *Finance.* due, payable, cashable, at the end of the term, worth the face value.

—*v.* **6.** season, age, bring to maturity; nurture, parent, bring up.

7. develop, work up, work on, refine, polish, elaborate; complete, finish, perfect, bring to perfection, put the finishing touches on, crown, consummate; get [s.t.] ready, make [s.t.] operational, put [s.t.] in working order.

8. grow, grow up, come of age, reach adulthood, become an adult, earn *or* have one's wings; ripen, maturate, mellow, soften; bloom, blossom, flower.

9. *Finance.* become due *or* payable, reach the end of the term, reach full value.

maturity, *n.* **1.** ripeness, mellowness, softness, plumpness, roundness; full bloom *or* flower, florescence.

2. adulthood, grown-upness, full growth, matureness; womanhood, manhood, voting age, drinking age, prime of life, heyday, middle age, old age; pubescence, puberty, nubility, marriageability, marriageableness, age of consent.

3. responsibleness, responsibility, dependability, dependableness, reliableness, reliability; sensibleness, prudence, judiciousness, wiseness, sagacity.

4. full development, fullness, completion; refinement, consummation, perfection; readiness, preparedness, state of readiness *or* preparedness, operational status.

maudlin, *adj.* **1.** sentimental, mawkish, emotional; soupy, romantic, having the soul of a shopgirl, mushy, slushy, *Inf.* gloppy, cow-eyed, calf-eyed; teary, lachrymose, weepy, *Inf.* drippy, soppy; babyish, tender, soft, tender-hearted, susceptible, thin-skinned; weak, feeble, simple; unsophisticated, unworldly, unrealistic, unrestrained; loose, lax, *Inf.* letting it all hang out, uncontrolled.

2. mawkishly drunk, *Sl.* sloppy drunk, sloppy, mellow, in a crying jag, blubbering, sniveling, feeling sorry for oneself; muddled, fuddled, befuddled, addled; dull-witted, foggy, hazy; besotted, *All Sl.* sozzled, smashed, plastered, crocked, under the table, three sheets to the wind; zonkered, out of it, blotto.

maul, *n.* **1.** sledge hammer, sledge; mace, club, cudgel, bludgeon, *Inf.* billy *or* billy club, mallet.

—*v.* **2.** manhandle, rough up, bully, bullyrag, *Sl.* knock around *or* about, *Sl.* give one the works; batter, beat, beat up, pound, lay on, pommel, pummel, thrash, trounce, pelt, *Inf.* whale, *Sl.* clobber, *Archaic.* belabor; hit, strike, smite, slap, smack, cuff, buffet, *Inf.* slug, *Inf.* whack, *Inf.* wallop, *Sl.* belt; club, flog, drub, cudgel, fustigate, baste, bludgeon, hammer, sledge hammer; mistreat, maltreat, ill-treat, abuse, ill-use, mishandle, *Sl.* kick around.

3. injure, hurt, pain, harm, bruise, wound, damage, impair.

4. *All U.S.* ax, split, chop, cut.

mauling, *n.* **1.** mishandling, mistreatment, manhandling, ill-treatment, misusage; punishment, injury, damage, harm.

2. beating, cudgeling, drubbing, clubbing, pounding, thumping, battering, punching; shoving, pushing, bulldozing, knocking around; fustigation, bastinado, licking, trouncing; bruising, rain of blows, trampling.

maunder, *v.* **1.** gibber, blather, ramble on, chatter, babble, prattle, gabble; mumble, stammer, hem and haw; run off at the mouth, run on, rattle on, twaddle.

2. wander, meander, ramble, traipse; straggle, *Sl.* schlepp, stray, mosey, shuffle, saunter; stumble *or* limp *or* hobble along, founder, flounder; drift, float, follow the wild goose; skip around, wander from pillar to post, go off in all directions; putter, loiter, dawdle, dillydally, loaf; flub, blunder, bungle, bobble.

mausoleum, *n.* tomb, sepulcher, shrine, tholos, crypt, house of death, charnel house; Taj Mahal, Pyramid of Cheops *or* Khufu.

mauve, *adj.* pale bluish purple, lilac, lavender, violet.

maverick, *n.* **1.** *Southwestern U.S.* unbranded cow *or* steer, unbranded calf, motherless calf.

2. dissenter, dissident, objector, protester, protestant; malcontent, agitator, rabble-rouser, instigator, inciter, troublemaker; rebel, recusant, revolutionary, radical, extremist; separatist, sectarian, schismatic, apostate, heretic.

3. nonconformist, individualist, bohemian, eccentric, *Inf.* character, *Archaic.* original, rara avis; explorer, pioneer, trailblazer, pathfinder, forerunner, leader, vanguard; trend-setter, style-setter.

maw, *n.* **1.** mouth, jaw, jaws, chops, chaps, throat, gullet; orifice, opening, gape, chasm, cavity, hole, cavern.

2. craw, crop, gizzard, ventriculus; stomach, *Anat., Zool.* venter.

mawkish, *adj.* **1.** sickening, nauseating, nauseous, vomitory; repellent, sour, gone bad, putrid, foul, fetid, smelly; unsavory, tongue-puckering; unpleasant, flat, stale, tasteless; insipid, namby-pamby, vapid, jejune, *Sl.* blah.

2. sentimental, *Sl.* gooey, soppy, mushy, slushy, crybabyish. See **maudlin** (*def.* **1**).

mawkishness, *n.* unpleasantness, insipidity, flatness, staleness, sourness; sentimentality, *Sl.* drip, romanticism; mush, *Sl.* glop, slushiness, gushiness, soppiness, drivel, slather.

maxim, *n.* **1.** aphorism, proverb, apothegm, gnome, mot, adage, *Archaic.* word, *Archaic.* sentence; saw, pithy statement, sententious saying, saying; axiom, precept, prescript, dictum; epigram, witticism, *Fr. jeu d'esprit*, quip, Atticism; cliché, hackneyed phrase, platitude, truism, *Inf.* bromide, commonplace.

2. standard, code, principle, canon, rule, golden rule, motto, moral, byword.

maximize, *v.* **1.** increase, enlarge, expand, aggrandize, greaten, amplify, magnify; augment, add to, build up, develop; widen, broaden, distend, inflate, fill out; elongate, protract, draw out, lengthen, stretch.

2. emphasize, overemphasize, play up, overplay, overdo; exaggerate, hyperbolize, overstate; color, embroider, enlarge upon; extol, overpraise, overrate; intensify, dramatize, deepen, heighten; enhance, strengthen, *Inf.* beef up.

3. exploit, milk, make the most of, strike while the iron is hot, make hay while the sun shines.

maximum, *n.* **1.** most, utmost, uttermost, max., *Math.* extremum; extremity, extreme, outer limit, limit, bound, boundary, border, frontier.

2. height, top, tip, tiptop; pinnacle, peak, crest, heights; summit, apex, vertex, apogee, *Latin. ne plus ultra*; acme, zenith, meridian, high noon; climax, pitch, high point, culmination; crown, cap, head.

—adj. **3.** supreme, superlative, paramount, maximal, greatest; most, utmost, uttermost, extreme.

4. highest, uppermost, upper, topmost, top, tiptop; summital, apical, apogeal, apogean; meridian, meridional, climactic, climactical, culminating, culminant, crowning.

maybe, *adv.* perhaps, possibly, mayhap, *Chiefly Dial.* mayhappen, *Literary.* perchance, *Archaic.* peradventure; haply, as the case may be, it may be, for all *or* aught one knows; if possible, if at all *or* humanly possible, God willing, wind and weather permitting.

mayor, *n.* city manager, burgomaster, syndic, (*in Britain*) Lord Mayor, (*in Scotland*) provost *or* Lord Provost.

maze, *n.* **1.** labyrinth, Chinese puzzle; complex, tangle, snarl, knot, *Inf.* mess, *Sl.* snafu.

2. confusion, bewilderment, bafflement, befuddlement, perplexity, disorientation.

mazy, *adj.* **1.** labyrinthine, labyrinthian, daedal, meandering, sinuous, tortuous, serpentine, snaky, anfractuous, convolutional, winding, twisting, twisting and turning.

2. confusing, perplexing, bewildering, baffling, confounding, puzzling, mystifying.

meadow, *n.* lea, meadowland, *Archaic.* mead; pasture, pasturage, pastureland, *Scot.* shieling.

meager, *adj.* **1.** scarce, scanty, scant, sparse, exiguous, in short supply, at a premium, not to be had, *Inf.* scarce as hen's teeth; poor, inadequate, insufficient, lacking, wanting, short, short of, not enough, too little; bare, slight, skimpy, scrimpy; puny, paltry, petty, piddling, poky, picayune, pathetic, *Inf.* chintzy, *Inf.* measly; shabby, *Sl.* crummy, *Sl.* lousy, *Sl.* rotten; beggarly, miserly, niggardly, stingy, stinted.

2. lean, thin, skinny, thin *or* skinny as a rail, lank, lanky; gaunt, scraggy, scrawny, emaciated, underfed, undernourished, starved, half-starved; bony, spindly, rawboned, mere flesh and bones.

meagerness, *n.* **1.** scarceness, scantiness, scantness, exiguity, shortness; want, lack, need, stint, scarcity, poverty, paucity; poorness, inadequacy, insufficiency; bareness, slightness, skimpiness, scrimpiness; puniness, paltriness, pettiness, piddlingness, pokiness, *Inf.* chintziness; shabbiness, *Sl.* crumminess, *Sl.* lousiness, *Sl.* rottenness; beggarliness, miserliness, niggardliness, stinginess.

2. leanness, thinnesss, skinniness, lankness, lankiness; gauntness, scragginess, scrawniness; boniness, spindliness.

meal[1], *n.* **1.** repast, collation, refection, banquet, feast, *Inf.* feed; breakfast, brunch, lunch, luncheon, *Fr. déjeuner, Fr. déjeuner à la fourchette, Brit.* tiffin, supper, dinner; tea, snack, bite; picnic, barbecue, cookout, clambake, *Fr. fête champêtre, Brit.* bump-supper, *Chiefly Brit. Sl.* beanfeast *or* beanfest.

2. fare, menu, board, table, diet, regimen, bill of fare, table d'hôte, *Inf.* spread; food, foodstuffs, edibles, aliment, viands, bread, *Inf.* grub, *Sl.* eats, *Sl.* chow, *Sl.* chuck, *Sl.* munchies; *Chiefly Brit. Sl.* scoff;

nourishment, nutriment, sustenance, subsistence, pabulum, manna, staff of life; victuals, provisions, provender, rations, dietary, commons, comestibles, cheer, *Western U.S. Sl.* chuck, *Brit. Sl.* prog; mess, swill, *Inf.* glop, *Sl.* slop.

meal[2], grain, cereal, grits, groats, grist, farina, *Trademark.* Pablum; oatmeal, corn meal, pearl barley, hominy, pearlhominy, rye hominy, pinole; oats, buckwheat, corn, maize, barley, rye, rice, millet, whole wheat; bran, flour, powder.

mealy, *adj.* **1.** crumbly, friable, granular, granulated, powdered, ground; flaky, floculent, scaly, scurfy.

2. farinaceous, oatlike, branny, branlike, furfuraceous.

mealy-mouthed, *adj.* **1.** mincing, overnice, nice, overdelicate, delicate, overdainty, dainty, euphemistic, euphemistical, euphemious, affected; priggish, prim, proper, *Sl.* uptight; tartuffian, pious, moral, self-righteous, sanctimonious, holier-than-thou, pharisaic, pharisaical; oversubtle, casuistic, sophistic, sophistical, *Both Offensive.* jesuitic, jesuitical.

2. circumlocutory, periphrastic, circuitous, roundabout, indirect, uncandid, unfrank, prevaricating, hedging, shifty, equivocating, equivocal, vague, ambiguous; hypocritical, double-tongued, two-faced, Janus-faced, crocodilian; specious, insincere, disingenuous, deceitful, misleading, lying, mendacious, dishonest, untruthful; honeyed, smooth, smooth-tongued, smooth-spoken, unctuous, oily, artful, slick.

3. fawning, flattering, blandishing, sycophantic, ingratiating; obsequious, groveling, servile, slavish; cringing, sniveling, fearful, scared, lily-livered, chicken-hearted, *Inf.* yellow.

mean[1], *v.* **1.** intend, have in mind, have in heart, have in view; contemplate, think of, talk of, dream of; purpose, plan, have plans *or* intentions, expect; aspire to, hope to, aim to, drive at, strive for, work for, labor for, pursue.

2. meant for made for, destined for, predestined for, preordained for, predetermined for, fated for; well-suited, suited, well-matched, perfect, perfectly matched.

3. denote, designate, denominate, indicate, betoken, show; signify, stand for, symbolize, represent, typify; prefigure, foreshadow, portend, presage, omen, augur; connote, imply, import, purport, propose, suggest, allude to, drive at, get at, intimate, hint at, insinuate.

4. mean well have good intentions, have one's heart in the right place.

mean[2], *adj.* **1.** inferior, low-grade, cheap, catchpenny, bargain-basement, *U.S. Sl.* cheesy, *Brit. Sl.* humpty, flimsy, jerry-built; second-rate, second-class, third-class, third-rate; mediocre, unprofessional, amateurish, not up to par *or* snuff; half-baked, *Sl.* half-assed, sloppy, shoddy, slipshod, sleazy; poor, grubstreet, *Inf.* no-good, *Inf.* junky, trashy, rubbishy, worthless, useless, valueless; bad, *Inf.* lousy, *Sl.* crummy, *Sl.* crappy, miserable; awful, terrible, wretched, horrible, disgusting.

2. plebeian, proletarian, humble, modest, low, lowly; of low birth, lowborn, baseborn, earthborn; simple, plain, homespun, homely, rustic; common, commonplace, ordinary, average, mediocre; undistinguished, *Inf.* inglorious, unknown, obscure.

3. small-time, one-horse, bush, bush-league, minor-league; *Sl.* two-bit, *Inf.* penny-ante, lightweight, *Sl.* small potatoes, small fry, *Sl.* mickey mouse; insignificant, unimportant, of little *or* no import, negligible, nugatory, inconsiderable, inconsequential; trivial, trifling, paltry, beggarly, petty, niggling; small, minor, puny, dinky, piddling, *Inf.* picayune, insubstantial, unsubstantial.

4. unimposing, shabby, scruffy, seedy, broken-down, run-down, worn-down; poor, squalid, mangy, wretched, sorry, abject, miserable; dismal, abysmal, dreary, *Literary.* drear.

5. small-minded, narrow-minded, selfish; meanspirited, petty, ungenerous, unaccommodating, unforgiving; ignoble, base, low, low-down, dishonorable, disreputable, discreditable, disgraceful, shabby, shameful, scandalous, opprobrious; corrupt, depraved, perverted, debased, miscreant; vile, sordid, bad, foul, rotten, nasty, ugly, black; scurvy, contemptible, despicable, execrable, abominable; cruel, brutal, brutish, inhuman, bestial, beastly; terrible, awful, *Inf.* godawful, horrible, horrendous, horrid; nefarious, heinous, infamous, atrocious, flagitious, villainous, criminal, hateful, odious; wicked, evil, iniquitous, sinful, *Archaic.* facinorous, peccant; black-hearted, malevolent, sinister, diabolic, diabolical, satanic, evil-minded; malicious, vicious, spiteful, invidious, maleficent; dishonest, unscrupulous, crooked, obliquitous, fraudulent, tricky, deceitful, insidious; rascally, scoundrelly, knavish, thievish, roguish; untrustworthy, disloyal, false, unfaithful, perfidious, traitorous, treacherous, reptilian.

6. stingy, niggardly, miserly, parsimonious, carking, skinflinty; penurious, tight, tight-fisted, closefisted; cheap, *Rare.* illiberal, penny-pinching, grudging, begrudging, stinting.

7. scanty, meager, skimpy, scrimpy, scant; meanly small, beggarly, paltry, poor, piddling, *Inf.* measly, mere; slight, slender, narrow, puny, very little; insufficient, inadequate, short, shy; insubstantial, nominal, minute, negligible.

8. offensive, disagreeable, unpleasant, rude, obnoxious; currish, snarling, nasty, curmudgeonly, churlish, irascible; cross, surly, ill-natured, bad-tempered, sour; crabbed, grouchy, grumpy, cantankerous, cranky, crotchety.

9. *Slang.* skillful, impressive, very good, great, excellent.

mean[3], *n.* **1.** *Usu.* **means** agency, factor, medium, vehicle; method, mode, manner, way, course, route, road, alternative, option; process, measures, actions, procedures; instrument, device, contrivance, appliance, convenience, machine, apparatus; aid, auxiliary, expedient, resort, resource, reserve.

2. means a. resources, capital, finances, income, revenue, profit, gain, lucre, *Sl.* velvet; wherewithal, funds, money, cash, ready cash, *U.S.* bankroll, cold *or* hard cash, *Inf.* pocket; paper money, bills, greenbacks, dollars, *Sl.* wad; *Sl.* dough, *U.S. Sl.* bucks, *Sl.* shekels, *Sl.* bread. **b.** substance, wealth, capital, riches, *Disparaging.* pelf; mammon, affluence, opulence, fortune, millions, billions; possessions, property, estate.

3. median, midpoint, middle *or* middle point, center *or* center point; medium, middle state, average, norm, normal; golden mean, happy medium, middle road *or* way, compromise, moderation, moderateness; mediocrity.

4. by all means a. at any cost, no matter what, without fail, **b.** certainly, of course, surely, definitely, absolutely, positively.

5. by no means in no way, not at all, *Inf.* no way.

6. not by any means not in any way, absolutely not, positively not, most definitely not.

—*adj.* **7.** middling, average, mediocre, fair-to-middling, so-so, *Inf.* O.K., *Inf.* all right, acceptable, passable, tolerable; *Inf.* nothing great, no great shakes, *Inf.* no big deal, *Inf.* nothing to write home about, *Inf.* nothing to get excited *or* worked up about.

meander, *v.* **1.** wind, zigzag, be circuitous, be roundabout, change direction; curve, bend, turn.
2. circumambulate, stroll, amble, *Inf.* mosey *or* mosey along; wander, ramble, rove, roam, drift; deviate, digress, stray, go off the track; peregrinate, tramp, nomadize, *Sl.* bum around.
—*n.* **3.** *Usu.* **meanders** turnings, windings, curvings, tortuosities, zigzags; winding path, anfractuosity, *Archaic.* ambages; maze, labyrinth; indirect course, circuitous journey, detour.

meandering, *adj.* **1.** circuitous, indirect, devious; anfractuous, winding, turning, sinuous, serpentine, snaky, tortuous, vermicular, vermiculate; roundabout, ambagious, flexuous, curvy, curved, wavy, undulating; spiraling, circling, convoluted, volute, coiled; twisted, tortile, crooked, bent; mazy, labyrinthine.
2. excursive, circumlocutory, periphrastic, digressive, desultory, deviating, rambling, meandrous; diffuse, prolix, protracted, episodic, rhapsodic.

meaning, *n.* **1.** intent, purport, tenor, tone, vein, drift; implication, connotation, signification, denotation, acceptation; sense, import, spirit, gist, upshot, sum and substance, effect, essence, core, pith, content; message, point.
2. intention, purpose, purport, significance; design, plan, aim, goal, end, object.

meaningful, *adj.* **1.** significant, consequential, momentous, portentous, prognostic; ominous, boding, foreboding; important, of great import, critical, decisive, material; weighty, heavy, pregnant, carrying great weight, of substance, pithy; serious, grave, solemn, sober; crucial, urgent, emergent, exigent, pressing, importunate.
2. expressive, eloquent, emphatic, meaning; suggestive, indicative, allusive.

meaningless, *adj.* **1.** purposeless, hollow, empty, vain, useless; inane, pointless, worthless; senseless, without rhyme or reason, unreasonable, irrational, nonsensical, preposterous; foolish, fatuous, silly, asinine, absurd, farcical, stupid; inexpressive, unintelligible, incomprehensible, undecipherable.
2. insignificant, inconsequential, of no consequence, unimportant, of minor importance, of little *or* no import, negligible, nugatory, inconsiderable; inapplicable, irrelevant, immaterial, unessential; unportentous, unmomentous, of no moment, of no great weight, of no matter *or* concern, of little *or* no account; *Inf.* no great shakes, not worth mentioning, not worth speaking of, not worth thinking *or* worrying about, not worth a rap *or* a straw; trivial, twaddling, trifling, frivolous, paltry, petty, niggling; small, minor, puny, dinky, piddling, *Inf.* picayune, insubstantial, unsubstantial; trite, *Sl.* mickey-mouse.

meaningly, *adv.* **1.** significantly, importantly, critically, consequentially, momentously, portentously, prognostically; ominously, forebodingly, bodingly, threateningly, minatorily, minaciously; heavily, weightily, substantially, pithily; seriously, gravely, solemnly, soberly.
2. expressively, eloquently, emphatically; suggestively, indicatively, meaningfully; knowingly, tellingly, warningly, admonishingly, monitorially.

meanly, *adv.* **1.** poorly, lowly, humbly, modestly; commonly, ordinarily, averagely, typically.
2. basely, ignobly, dishonorably, shamefully, disgracefully; contemptibly, despicably, vilely, abjectly; shabbily, ungenerously, unfairly, badly, miserably.
3. stingily, niggardly, parsimoniously, skinflinty, penuriously, tightly, cheaply, grudgingly, stintingly.

meanness, *n.* **1.** baseness, lowness, ignobility, ignobleness; dishonorableness, disreputability, disreputableness, disgracefulness; shabbiness, unfairness, injustice; contemptibility, contemptibleness, despicableness, scurviness, vileness, abjectness; sordidness, badness, foulness, rottenness, nastiness, ugliness.
2. small-mindedness, narrow-mindedness, meanspiritedness, selfishness, ungenerosity, pettiness; spitefulness, viciousness, maliciousness, invidiousness, maleficence; wickedness, evil, evilness, sinfulness, iniquity, iniquitousness; black-heartedness, malevolence, sinisterness, fiendishness; ill will, hatred, malice, spite, malignity.
3. stinginess, niggardliness, miserliness, parsimony, parsimoniousness, skinflintiness, penuriousness, tightness, cheapness.

meanspirited, *adj.* small-minded, narrow-minded, petty, ungenerous, unforgiving. See **mean**[2] (*def.* **5**).

meantime, *adv.* meanwhile, in the intervening time, *Chiefly Brit.* whilst, *Scot.* whiles, while; in the interim, in the meanwhile, in the interval, in the interregnum, in the hiatus; for the time being, for now, for then, for a time *or* season, for the duration; at the same time, simultaneously, during, throughout, all along, synchronously, coincidentally.

measurable, *adj.* gaugeable, determinable, appraisable, estimable, reckonable; mensurable, surveyable, assessable, appreciable, computable, fathomable.

measure, *n.* **1.** measurement, mensuration, metage. See **measurement** (*def.* **1**).
2. size, dimensions, proportions, expanse, extent, scope, range, spread, area; magnitude, amplitude, mass, bulk, volume; weight, quantity, capacity; bounds, duration, sum, aggregate; amplitude, magnitude.
3. rule, graduated rod, gauge, meter, scale; level, plummet, plumb line, compass, calipers, square, T-square, tape, line, ell, yardstick; quadrant, vernier, balance; weighing machine, calorie counter; calculator, computer.
4. linear measure, cubic measure, liquid measure, dry measure, square measure, chain measure, apothecaries' fluid measure, surveyor's area measure, metric measure.
5. share, allotment, portion, division, piece, part; quota, dole, pittance, allowance, driblet, dose, cupful, handful; dividend, *Inf.* divvy, percentage, commission, *Inf.* rake-off, contingent, fee, *Inf.* pay-off.
6. standard, criterion, norm, test, rule; pattern, type, model, prototype, original, paradigm, archetype; touchstone, canon, principle, precedent, example; sample, dressmaker's model, die, mold, matrix, cast; mint, seal, stamp, punch, intaglio, negative; outline, sketch, drawing, diagram, design, pattern, plans, blueprint, layout, roughdraft, proof.
7. limit, limitation, bound, extent, extreme, terminus, terminal, end; pale, march, bound, confine, fence, bourn; boundary line, high-water mark, line of demarcation.
8. statute, public act, bill, law.
9. *Usu.* **measures** step, direction, course, course of action, action, plan; deterrent action, intimidation, stifling action, *Inf.* strong-arm tactics, *Inf.* the arm.
10. rhythm, meter, cadence, beat; phrase, bar, motif, theme.
11. **beyond measure** immeasurably, limitlessly, boundlessly, infinitely, fathomlessly; endlessly, interminably, extremely, immensely, vastly, inexhaustibly; incalculably, beyond all measure, out of measure; excessively, redundantly, beyond need, needlessly.
12. **for good measure** as an extra, in addition, additionally; as a bonus, as a dividend, as a premium, as bounty, as a gift, as a tip; freely, for free, gratis, gratu-

itously, without charge, without extra charge.

—*v.* **13.** gauge, meter, rule, *Archaic.* mete; space, divide, delimit, mark off, mark out; inch, step, step off, survey; graph, plot, plot out, lay out, map, pattern; weigh, weigh out, balance, plumb, probe, sound, fathom.

14. *Usu.* **measure out** mete out, ration, ration out, allot; apportion, portion, parcel out, partition, divide, *Inf.* divvy *or* divvy up; carve, split, split into shares; distribute, disperse, dispense, assign, allocate.

15. show, indicate, give indication of; show the extent of; make clear, reveal, make manifest, bring forward, show in bas-relief; denote, betoken, argue, tell, bespeak, connote; testify to, attest, evidence, confirm, affirm; bear out, substantiate, verify, bring home.

16. **measure up** **a.** equal, equate, match, correspond, keep pace *or* step with, be on a level with, parallel. **b.** qualify, *Inf.* come up to scratch, *Inf.* be up to snuff, *Inf.* make the grade; be adequate, be competent, be up to the job, be capable, be able, be efficient; be fitted for *or* fit the task, be equal to the task, *Inf.* be able to cut the mustard.

measured, *adj.* **1.** regulated, modulated, proportioned; like clockwork, precise, exact, determined.

2. steady, regular, constant, uniform, even; unchanging, unvarying, unvaried, rhythmical, singsong, monotonous, with a steady beat, at a steady pace, metronomic, like the beat-beat-beat of the tom-toms.

3. deliberate, intentional, studied, considered, weighed; premeditated, prepared, planned; thought-out, calculated, mulled, pondered, reasoned, unimpulsive; leisurely, unhurried, slow, careful, cautious; restrained, judicious, prudent.

measureless, *adj.* boundless, unbounded, without bounds, unlimited, limitless, illimitable; endless, interminable, unending, infinite; immeasurable, incalculable, innumerable, numberless, countless, unfathomable; immense, vast, enormous, prodigious, gargantuan, gigantic, colossal, huge; bottomless, inexhaustible; indescribable.

measurement, *n.* **1.** mensuration, metage, measuring; reckoning, calculation, computation; survey, valuation, evaluation, appreciation; assessment, appraisal, assize, assizement; estimation, estimate, gauging.

2. latitude, longitude, altitude, azimuth; dimensions, size. See **measure** (*def.* 2).

meat, *n.* **1.** animal flesh, flesh, cut of meat; beef, veal, pork, lamb, mutton.

2. food, nutriment, aliment, nourishment, sustenance, nurture; viand *or* viands, victuals, vittles; feed, fare, rations, *Sl.* grub, provisions; edibles, combustibles; meal, dinner, supper.

3. gist, crux, fundamentals, essentials, basics; import, meaning, sense, essence, signification; pith, substance, heart, kernel, marrow.

meaty, *adj.* pithy, meaningful, substantive; rich, full, loaded; profound, involved, wide-ranging, copious; expansive, extensive, comprehensive.

mechanic, *n.* technician, engineer, machinist, *Sl.* grease monkey; operator, operative, mechanician, repairman; craftsman, artisan, smith, forger, wright, skilled worker, skilled laborer; tinker, *Inf.* tinkerer, inventor, contriver, concocter; electrician, *Sl.* sparks, *Inf.* troubleshooter.

mechanical, *adj.* **1.** motor-driven, engineered, power-driven; handy, clever with one's hands, deft, dextrous.

2. unspontaneous, unimpulsive, perfunctory, businesslike, indifferent; spiritless, lifeless, dead, unanimated; uninspired, colorless, vapid; superficial, heedless, thoughtless, negligent, casual, careless, uncaring.

3. habitual, routine, standard, usual, accustomed; automatic, computerized, robotistic, robotlike; instinctive, unthinking, unconscious, involuntary, reflexive.

4. utilitarian, materialistic, banausic, practical; mundane, earthly, worldly, mercenary, unspiritual, temporal.

mechanically, *adv.* **1.** indifferently, flatly, lifelessly, dully, drably, woodenly; perfunctorily, heedlessly, unthinkingly, uncaringly.

2. routinely, habitually, automatically; instinctively, involuntarily, unconsciously, reflexively; blindly, by heart, by rote, willy-nilly.

mechanics, *n.* **1.** kinematics, statics, kinetics, dynamics, technology, technical science.

2. routines, techniques, procedures, methods, logistics; details, nitty-gritty, nuts and bolts; machinery.

mechanism, *n.* **1.** motor, engine, linkage, generator; apparatus, device, machine.

2. equipment, matériel, paraphernalia, machinery, apparatus, mechanical appliances, gadgetry; tackle, gear, outfit, works.

3. instrument, instrumentality, vehicle, means, agency; organization, system, setup, workings; procedure, method, routine.

4. execution, technique, technology, performance, carrying out.

mechanize, *v.* industrialize, motorize, automate, computerize.

medal, *n.* medallion, decoration, badge of honor; cross, star, ribbon, blue ribbon; emblem, insignia; award, reward, recognition, honor, commemoration, testimonial, citation, trophy, prize.

meddle, *v.* interfere, intermeddle, *Brit. Dial.* mell, interlope; intrude, butt in, horn in, obtrude; impose, interpose, intervene; nose into, stick one's nose in, stick one's nose where it doesn't belong, mind other people's business, put one's two cents in, put in one's oar, *Inf.* kibitz; tamper with, pry, snoop, peep.

meddler, *n.* interferer, interloper, busybody, *Yiddish.* cochleffel, *Inf.* buttinsky, *Inf.* kibitzer, intruder, obtruder; *Australian.* stickybeak, quidnunc, *Inf.* nosey Parker, gossip, snooper, peeper.

meddlesome, *adj.* officious, impertinent, forward, presumptuous, pushing, *Inf.* pushy, importunate; intrusive, meddling, interfering, ultracrepidarian, obtrusive; overbusy, busy, busybody, overcurious; prying, snooping, inquisitive, *Inf.* kibitzing, *Inf.* nosy, *Inf.* snoopy.

medial, *adj.* **1.** median, middle, intermediate, mediate, *Law.* mesne; midmost, middlemost, mid, middling; central, halfway, between, intervenient; interjacent, equidistant, mediterranean, intercurrent, equatorial.

2. mean, average, medium, mesial; ordinary, fair, commonplace, common, usual, routine; passable, so-so, half and half, moderate, mezzo; normal, standard, middle of the road.

mediate, *v.* **1.** arbitrate, negotiate, bargain, arrange; umpire, judge, referee, moderate; intercede, interpose, step in, intervene, intermeddle, go between.

2. settle, reconcile, compromise; bring together, be instrumental, use one's good offices; pacify, propitiate, placate, appease; make peace, restore harmony, bring to terms, bring to an understanding, bring to an agreement.

mediation, *n.* **1.** arbitration, negotiation, parley; arbitrage, umpirage, refereeship; good offices, ministry, mediatorship, intermediation, instrumentality, agency; intervention, intercession, interjacence, interposition, interference, stepping in, involvement.

2. reconciliation, reconcilement, conciliation; pacification, peacemaking, appeasement, placation; compromise, settlement, terms, understanding.

mediative, *adj.* **1.** mediatory, mediating, intermediary, intermedial, arbitrative, arbitrational; intercessional, intercessory, interfering, interlocutory, interventional.

2. propitiatory, pacificatory, reconciliatory, conciliatory; irenic, pacific, peacemaking, diplomatic.

mediator, *n.* **1.** middleman, liaison, go-between, common friend, agent, *Archaic.* daysman; arbitrator, negotiator, intermediary, moderator; referee, arbiter, umpire, *Inf.* ump, *Inf.* ref, third party; intervener, interventionist, interceder, intercessor; internuncio, intermediate, interagent.

2. pacifier, peacemaker, fence-mender, smoother-over, make-peace; reconciler, conciliator, appeaser, marriage counselor.

medicable, *adj.* curable, healable, treatable, remediable, reparable; recoverable, retrievable, reclaimable; reversible, mendable, restorable.

medical, *adj.* healing, curative, therapeutic, therapeutical, sanative, sanatory, remedial; medicinal, medicative, restorative, *Med.* analeptic, salutiferous, health-bringing, salutary, corrective, tonic, febrifugal, palliative, *Med. Obs.* alterative, *Archaic.* corroborant.

medicament, *n.* medicine, remedy, *Med.* specific, *Med. Obs.* alterative; panacea, palliative, catholicon, cure-all, patent medicine, nostrum, elixir, potion, snake-oil; home remedy, home cure, ptisan, barley water, chicken soup, camomile tea, sulphur and molasses; curative substance, corrective; antidote, theriac; antiseptic, prophylactic, febrifuge, antipyretic; anticatarrhal, terpin hydrate and codeine, expectorant, cough syrup, cough drops, horehound; diaphoretic, mustard plaster; eye drops, collyrium, eyewash; nose drops, nasal spray; emetic, nauseant; physic, cathartic, purgative, carminative, laxative, lenitive, aloes, bran, castor oil, epsom salts, dose of salts; tonic, stimulant, restorative, analeptic, roborant, cordial; sedative, soporific, narcotic, anodyne, drug, opiate; depressant, *Sl.* downer; calmative, tranquilizer, soothing syrup, pacifier; analgesic, paregoric, *Inf.* pain killer, *Inf.* pain pill; sleeping draught *or* pill, *Sl.* goofball, sleeper; barbiturate, *Sl.* barb, *Inf.* dope; balm, salve, *Pharm.* cerate, ointment, balsam, oil, lotion, liniment, embrocation, witch hazel, *Med.* cataplasm, poultice, plaster, traumatic, healing application. See also **medicine** (*def.* **1**).

medicate, *v.* treat, doctor, attend, care for, give care to, nurse; drug, dose, *Sl.* dope up, cure, remedy, heal; minister, administer, relieve, restore, palliate; dress, poultice, plaster; salve, bathe, anoint, oil, embrocate.

medicinal, *adj.* **1.** remedial, curative, therapeutic, *Med.* analeptic, adjuvant; stimulating, bracing, invigorating, reviving, refreshing, *Med.* roborant; alleviative, assuasive, lenitive, sedative, calmative, tranquilizing, narcotic, soothing, balmy, emollient, demulcent; analgesic, anodyne, paregoric; antidotal, antitoxic, antibiotic; prophylactic, preventive, protective, *Med.* alexipharmic; aseptic, antiseptic, disinfectant, depurative; purgative, laxative, *Med.* aperient, cathartic, carminative, diuretic. See **medical**.

2. (*of flavor or odor*) unpleasant, disagreeable, distasteful, unpalatable, nasty, offensive, noxious, repellent, rebarbative; sickening, nauseating, poisonous, *Inf.* icky, *Sl.* puky, *Sl.* yukky; bitter, sour, sharp, biting, caustic, astringent, pungent, strong-tasting *or* -smelling, foul-tasting *or* -smelling.

medicine, *n.* **1.** medication, medicament, drug, pharmaceutical, prescription drug, officinal, prescription, preparation; over the counter drug *or* medicine, nonprescription medication, proprietory medicine; miracle *or* wonder drug, antitoxin, vaccine; antibiotic, antibody, materia medica. See also **medicament**.

2. dose, draft, potion; shot, injection, booster; tablet, pill, capsule, *Pharm.* troche, lozenge, *Both Pharm., Vet. Med.* bolus, electuary.

3. medical treatment *or* attention, therapeutics, allopathy, pharmacognosy; surgery, acupuncture; dosing, doctoring.

4. medical science, healing art, folk medicine, preventive medicine, *Archaic.* physic; medical practice *or* profession, practice of medicine.

5. **give [s.o.] a dose *or* taste of his own medicine** repay, repay in kind, pay back, pay back in full measure, requite, revenge oneself, retaliate in kind, give in return, get even, even the score, settle the score, turn the tables on, get one's own back, *Inf.* get back at, make [s.o.] eat crow *or* his hat, give [s.o.] his deserts *or* just deserts, *Inf.* give [s.o.] what is coming to him, *Inf.* give [s.o.] his comeuppance, *Inf.* settle *or* square accounts.

6. **take one's medicine** take the consequences, pay the piper, swallow a bitter pill, take it on the chin, take the blame, answer for, take *or* accept responsibility, *Inf.* face the music, *Inf.* get what is coming to one, *Sl.* take the rap.

medieval, *adj.* **1.** Middle-Age, Dark-Age, post-Classical, pre-Renaissance; Gothic, barbarous, rude.

2. antiquated, archaic, superannuated, antique, obsolete; old-fashioned, behind the times, antediluvian, outmoded, passé; backwards, undeveloped, underdeveloped, unprogressive, unsophisticated, rustic; uncultured, unintelligent, unenlightened.

mediocre, *adj.* **1.** ordinary, average, middling, moderate, medium, mean; commonplace, run-of-the-mill, garden-variety, everyday.

2. indifferent, so-so, fair, fair to middling, betwixt and between, *Inf.* no great shakes, *Inf.* nothing to write home *or* brag about; undistinguished, unexceptional, unnotable, modest, of sorts, of a sort; neutral, bland, *Sl.* ho-hum, *Sl.* blah.

3. adequate, passable, acceptable, tolerable, respectable, presentable, admissible, fairly good, *Inf.* not that good, not bad, not too bad; poor, inferior, second-rate, bush-league, minor league, amateurish; unimportant, insignificant, slight, trifling, inconsiderable, inappreciable, negligible, limited, lesser, paltry, meager, scant.

mediocrity, *n.* **1.** moderateness, indifference, neutrality, mediocreness; ordinariness, commonplaceness, average standard, normality; passableness, tolerableness, adequateness, satisfactoriness, acceptability; lower quality, inferiority; inconsiderableness, immaterialness, unimportance, insignificance, paltriness, triviality.

2. insignificancy, nonentity, obscurity, a nobody; little fellow, lightweight, small fry; man in the street; Tom, Dick and Harry.

meditate, *v.* **1.** devise, contrive, machinate, cabal, plan, scheme, plot, design, *Obs.* intrigue, *Obs.* consult; frame, concoct, invent, brew, hatch; purpose, aim, project, destine, intend, mean, have in view; conceive, think up, imagine, fancy, have ideas about, *Inf.* dream up.

2. contemplate, muse, ponder, brood, mull over, dwell on, be in a brown study; reflect, cogitate, rack one's brains, cudgel one's brains, ruminate, chew over, chew one's cud; think about *or* over, cerebrate, put on one's thinking cap, be abstracted, be lost in thought; concentrate on, focus on, put one's mind to, have one's mind on, wonder about; consider, speculate, surmise, suppose, conjecture, theorize, hypothesize; deliberate, excogitate, take to heart, *Archaic.* perpend; revolve, review, turn over, weigh, evaluate, study, examine, con.

meditation, *n.* **1.** contemplating, musing, pondering, brooding, mulling over, dwelling on; reflecting, cogitating, ruminating, chewing over, chewing one's cud; thinking about *or* over, cerebrating, being lost in thought; concentrating on, focusing on, having one's mind on, wondering about; considering, speculation, speculating, surmising, supposing, conjecture, conjecturing, theorizing, hypothesizing; deliberation, deliberating, excogitation, excogitating, revolving, weighing, evaluation, evaluating, studying, examination, examining, conning.

2. contemplation, reflection, cogitation, rumination, brown study; thought, cerebration, concentration, lucubration, brain work, headwork.

meditative, *adj.* contemplative, contemplating, musing, pondering, brooding, mulling over; reflective, reflecting, cogitative, cogitating, ruminant, ruminative, ruminating, chewing, chewing one's cud; pensive, thoughtful, concentrating, intent, abstracted, rapt in thought, lost in thought, bemused, *Archaic.* museful; deliberative, excogitative, lucubrative.

medium, *n.* **1.** mean, median, midpoint, middle *or* middle point, center *or* center point; middle state, average, norm, normal; golden mean, middle way *or* road *or* path, compromise, balance, measure, moderation, moderateness, temperateness, happy medium; mediocrity.

2. environment, habitat, element; surroundings, milieu, conditions, influences, circumstances, *Fr. mise en scène*; entourage, ambience, atmosphere, mood, aura; setting, scene, background.

3. agency, means, instrumentality, factor, vehicle, intermediary; method, mode, manner, way, course, channel, route, road, alternative, option; process, measures, action, actions, procedures; instrument, tool, device, contrivance, mechanism, apparatus, convenience; aid, auxiliary, expedient, resort, resource, reserve.

4. telepathist, mind reader, psychic, clairvoyant, dowser, automatist; fortuneteller, soothsayer, diviner, prophet, prophetess, seer, seeress, crystal-gazer, astrologer; hypnotist, mesmerist, enchanter, enchantress, charmer, incantator, evocator.

—adj. **5.** average, mean, medial, median, middle, mezzo, intermediate, intermediary, moderate; normal, standard, on a par; typical, common, ordinary, usual, everyday, commonplace, garden-variety; fair, not bad, mediocre, middling, so-so, indifferent; passable, tolerable, decent, run-of-the-mill, *Sl.* no great shakes, *Sl.* no big deal, *Sl.* nothing to write home about, *Sl.* not so hot.

medley, *n.* collection, batch, group, grouping, cluster, set, series, array; assortment, mixture, mélange, miscellany, omnium-gatherum, potpourri, olio, olla-podrida, motley; salmagundi, stew, ragout, goulash, hash; conglomeration, mishmash, hodgepodge, *Brit.* hotchpotch, pastiche, pasticcio, jumble, farrago, gallimaufry, Chinese menu.

meek, *adj.* **1.** humble, lowly, modest, unpretentious, unpretending, unpresuming, unassuming, free from pride, without arrogance, unostentatious.

2. deferential, obliging, complaisant, compliant, conformable, agreeable, biddable, willing; submissive, yielding, docile, acquiescent, adaptable, tractable, ductile, consentient, unresisting; manageable, governable, obedient; broken, resigned, subdued, spiritless, sedate, tame; apologetic, obsequious, servile, subservient, subsidiary, slavish, unambitious.

3. patient, forbearing, tolerant, enduring, long-suffering; mild, lamblike, gentle, pacific, peaceable, clement, placid, passive; shy, retiring, reserved, restrained.

meekness, *n.* **1.** humility, humbleness, modesty, unpretentiousness, unassumingness, unpresumptuousness, unobtrusiveness, freedom from pride *or* arrogance, reserve, restraint.

2. submissiveness, deference, compliance, complaisance, willingness, acquiescence; adaptability, tractability, obedience, subjection, resignation, spiritlessness, tameness; servility, subservience, obsequiousness, lowliness, lowliness of spirit *or* heart *or* mind; self-abasement, abasement, mortification.

3. patience, forbearance, tolerance, endurance; mildness, gentleness, peacefulness, peaceableness, clemency, placidity, passiveness.

meet[1], *v.* **1.** encounter, come upon, accost, face, come into contact, meet with, come across; fall across, run across, *Inf.* run into, *Inf.* bump into; happen upon, chance upon, stumble upon, light upon, hit upon.

2. make acquaintance with, be introduced to, be presented to; welcome, greet, speak with.

3. tackle, come to grips with, cope with; brave, meet head on, face up to; meet face to face, come face to face with, front, stand in front of, stand facing.

4. contend, confront, clash, conflict with, skirmish, struggle; engage, join, face, battle; grapple, wrestle, spar, box, fight.

5. assemble, collect, gather, come together, ingather, forgather, muster, rally, round up *or* in, group *or* herd together; congregate, convene, convoke; cluster, huddle, crowd, concentrate; parley, confer, hold a session.

6. oppose, thwart, cross, counter, contradict; dispute, challenge, oppugn; defy, stand up to, face in defiance.

7. handle, dispatch, discharge, dispose of, take care of, deal with, do with; carry out, execute, perform; pay, defray, settle, liquidate, recompense; respect, observe, heed, acknowledge.

8. keep pace with, live up to, come up to, act up to; adhere to, be faithful to, keep faith with; satisfy, fulfill, gratify; equal, match, conform with, tie, parallel.

9. concur, agree, correspond, accord; cohere, harmonize, be of like *or* one *or* the same mind, see eye to eye.

10. meet halfway make a deal, give and take, *Inf.* go fifty-fifty, bridge over; agree on *or* upon, come to an agreement *or* understanding, arrive at an agreement, come to terms, strike a bargain, *Inf.* get together, make the best of; reciprocate, exchange, trade, trade off; concede, yield, adjust, modify, accommodate.

11. meet with a. encounter, come upon, come across. See **meet** (*def.* **1**). **b.** experience, undergo, go through, endure, live through, suffer, bear, receive.

—n. **12.** assembly, congregation, meeting. See **meeting** (*def.* **4**).

13. contest, competition, match, tourney, game, regatta, joust, duel; tournament, bout, round, encounter, engagement, *Fr. concours*; race, run, sprint; trial, heat, scrimmage; run-off, sudden death, showdown.

meet[2], *adj.* suitable, fit, fitting, befitting, appropriate, congruous, expedient; right, rightful, proper, seemly, decorous, becoming; apposite, apt, suited, opportune, pertinent, relevant, applicable; condign, well-deserved, adequate, commensurate, consistent, compatible, harmonious.

meeting, *n.* **1.** rendezvous, tryst, assignation; confrontation, coming together, encounter, congress.

2. presentation, introduction, reception, greeting, welcome, salutation.

3. combat, battle, skirmish, conflict; fight, contest, duel, bout, feud, *Sl.* scrap, joust, tilt; clash, contention, struggle; scuffle, tussle, brawl, fray, affray; colli-

sion, engagement, rencounter.
4. assembly, congregation, gathering, get-together; convention, congress, conclave, conference, parley, discussion; council, committee, synod, *U.S.* caucus.
5. assemblage, group, body, company, flock, bevy; concourse, throng, crowd, mob.
6. junction, union, association, conjugation, conjunction, conjuncture, confluence; convergence, concentration; intersection, connection; cohesion, coherence, adhesion, adherence.

meeting house, *n.* **1.** church, place of worship, house of prayer, house of God, the Lord's house, (*usu. in reference to Nonconformists*) conventicle; basilica, cathedral, minster; chapel, oratory, sacellum, chantry, shrine, vestry, bethel; sanctuary, tabernacle; pantheon, mosque, temple, synagogue; nave, *Archaic.* auditory.
2. auditorium, hall, durbar, assembly hall, assembly room.

melancholy, *n.* **1.** despondency, dejection, depression, mopishness, *Psychiatry.* hypochondria; gloominess, *Psychiatry.* melancholia, misery, miserableness, wretchedness, distress, broken-heartedness; grief, sadness, *Fr. tristesse*, sorrow, dolor, anguish; doldrums, dumps, blues; hopelessness, disheartenment, dismay, discouragement; defeatism, pessimism; disconsolateness, unconsolability.
2. thoughtfulness, earnestness, pensiveness, preoccupation, wistfulness; sedateness, gravity, staidness, soberness, sobriety, seriousness, somberness.
—adj. **3.** depressed, dejected, disheartened, dispirited, low-spirited, downhearted, downcast, *Inf.* down, *Inf.* down in the dumps, *Inf.* low; discouraged, daunted, dismayed, distressed, disappointed, crestfallen, broken-hearted, heartsick, *Inf.* broken up; unhappy, cheerless, glum, gloomy, under a cloud, doleful, *Archaic.* wan; dismal, dull, *Scot. and North Eng.* dowie; saddened, sad, blue, forlorn, mopey, mopish, long-faced, chapfallen, *Inf.* down in the mouth, *Sl.* off one's feed; miserable, morose, heartbroken, woebegone, heavy-hearted, disconsolate, sorrowful, mournful, lachrymose, funereal; burdened, weighed down, crushed, prostrate, *Inf.* broken, *Sl.* bummed out, despondent, hypochondriac, hypochondriacal, *Brit.* hipped, spiritless, lifeless, *Scot.* ourie, exanimate, enervated, weakened, weary, languid, tired.
4. bilious, liverish, crabbed; disagreeable; petulant, sulky, sullen, morose; ill-humored, ill-natured, peevish, splenetic, crotchety, crusty, out of sorts.
5. thoughtful, earnest, pensive, dreamy, wistful, quiet, preoccupied; grave, sedate, staid, sober, solemn, serious, somber; grim, stone-faced, frowning, unsmiling.

mélange, *n.* medley, olio, potpourri, olla-podrida, combination, *Inf.* combo; miscellany, miscellanea, omnium-gatherum, menagerie, motley; hash, stew, goulash, salmagundi, *Fr. Cookery.* ragout, (*in China, India, etc.*) chow-chow, Chinese menu; jumble, mishmash, hodgepodge, gallimaufry, farrago, mess; assortment, collection, set, series, array; group, grouping, assemblage, cluster, aggregation, aggregate; mosaic, patchwork, pastiche, pasticcio; mixture, blend, intermixture, admixture, compound, composite.

meld, *v.* **1.** merge, combine, consolidate, amalgamate; incorporate, syndicate, federate, confederate; join, marry, wed, unite, coalesce, associate, ally, link; intertwine, interweave, put together, lump together, pool, throw together, jumble, scramble.
2. blend, mix, commix, admix, intermix, mingle, intermingle, commingle, interlard, *Brit. Dial.* mell; compound, alloy, *Chem.* levigate, synthesize, homogenize, hybridize, mongrelize; fuse, inosculate, bond, weld.

melee, *n.* **1.** fracas, free-for-all, donnybrook, brawl, *Sl.* rumble, *Scot.* collieshangie; fight, scuffle, tussle, fray, wrangle, row, *Inf.* set-to; fisticuffs, bout, spar, boxing match, scrimmage, skirmish, battle, heated battle, battle royal, hand-to-hand combat, brush, encounter.
2. commotion, pandemonium, hubbub, clamor, racket, rumpus, *Inf.* ruckus, *Inf.* shindy; confusion, chaos, upheaval, jumble, mess; turmoil, tumult, turbulence, storm, outbreak, riot, *Fr. émeute*; agitation, excitement, disorder, disturbance, disquiet, unrest; uproar, imbroglio, broil, brouhaha, hullaballoo, hurly-burly; fuss, squabble, scrap, quarrel, affray, altercation, dispute, heated debate, *Sl.* flap.

meliorate, *v.* improve, mend, better, recover. See **ameliorate.**

melioration, *n.* improvement, betterment, recovery. See **amelioration.**

mellifluence, *n.* euphony, melodiousness, sweetness, musicality, mellowness, tunefulness; smoothness, concinnity, softness, dulcetness; harmony, tune, concord, accord; eloquence, facundity, flow, fluency, orotundity.

mellifluous, *adj.* **1.** smooth, flowing, euphonic, euphonious, musical, rhythmical, harmonious, mellisonant; sweet-sounding, silver-toned, dulcet, melodious, melodic; graceful, easy, soft, golden, silvery, mellifluent, fluent, liquid, tripping; eloquent, silver-tongued, golden-tongued, orotund; canorous, sonorous, resonant, clear, clear as a bell.
2. honeyed, nectared, nectarous, ambrosial; treacly, sugary, sweet.

mellow, *adj.* **1.** soft, ripe, tender, mature; luscious, full-flavored, sweet, delicious.
2. softened, aged, improved, toned down; seasoned, tempered, ripened.
3. rich, full, creamy, pearly, nacreous, *Archaic.* mellowy; mild, quiet, soft, light, pale, eggshell; pastel, subtle, pure, subdued, delicate, patinated, hushed, muted.
4. resonant, resonating, ringing, rolling, full, full-toned, vibrant; musical, rhythmical, euphonious, songlike, ariose.
5. gentle, easy, easy-going, pacific, untroubled; tranquil, serene, placid, quiet, calm; still, halcyon, zephyrlike.
6. genial, good-natured, cordial, gracious, affable, amiable, amicable; jovial, cheerful, felicitous, pleasant, agreeable.
—v. **7.** age, develop, grow, wax, mature, improve, steep; ripen, soften, season, temper.

melodion, *n.* **1.** harmonium, parlor organ, reed organ, melodica, organophone, symphonion.
2. accordion, concertina, mellophone, seraphina, *Inf.* squeeze box.

melodious, *adj.* **1.** tuneful, melodic, harmonious, concordant, accordant; lyrical, lyric, melic, orchestral, symphonic; ariose, *Music.* cantabile, songlike, songful, singable, catchy; pleasant, agreeable, appealing; singing, ringing, resonant, canorous, sonorous, clear.
2. musical, euphonic, euphonious, flowing, rhythmical, mellisonant; sweet-sounding, mellifluous, silver-toned, golden-toned; dulcet, silvery, golden, tripping.

melodrama, *n.* **1.** sentimental drama, *Inf.* soap opera, *Inf.* tear-jerker, *Inf.* corn; suspense drama; thriller, *Inf.* chiller, *Sl.* cliffhanger.
2. theatrics, histrionics, sensationalism, emotionalism; theatricality, melodramatics, blood and thunder.

melodramatic, *adj.* **1.** sentimental, emotionalistic, mawkish, maudlin, treacly, bathetic, oversentimentalized; *All Inf.* mushy, gushy, tear-jerking, gushing; *All Sl.* hokey, schmaltzy, sappy.

2. exaggerated, theatrical, histrionic, buskined, stagey, *Inf.* hammy; overwrought, spectacular, sensational; frantic, hysterical, high-wrought, overacted.

melody, *n.* **1.** harmony, concinnity, concord, accord; euphony, musicality, mellowness, melodiousness; rhythm, tunefulness, smoothness, fluency, flow; sweetness, mellifluence, dulcetness.

2. tune, song, descant, aria, aretta; chant, plainsong, canticle; lyric, cantilena, chanson, carol, ballad, ditty; theme, measure, air, strain, cantabile.

melt, *v.* **1.** liquefy, dissolve, deliquesce, liquidize, fluidize; thaw, unfreeze, defrost, de-ice, flux, colliquate; fuse, liquate, ablate, smelt, scorify.

2. dwindle, sink, shrink, decrease, drop, decline, descend; pass, fade, disappear, dematerialize, waste away; evanesce, vanish, disperse, dissipate, evaporate, disintegrate.

3. blend, shade, mix, coalesce, incorporate, compound; change into, merge into, grow into, assimilate.

4. mollify, soften, assuage, subdue, disarm; relax, gentle, mellow, lenify, dulcify; move, touch, affect, penetrate, pierce; touch to the core *or* quick, come home to, touch one's heart, touch a chord; propitiate, appease, conciliate, mediate, placate.

member, *n.* **1.** adherent, inhabitant, one who belongs, one who is in, in person; dues payer, card-carrying member; initiate, trial member.

2. organ, limb, appendage; leg, arm, wing; foot, hand, paw; nose, tongue, ear.

3. element, constituent, component; portion, part, segment; detail, fragment, fraction, section, division.

membership, *n.* **1.** admission, matriculation, belonging; adherence, allegiance.

2. body, company, society, club, association, group; fraternity, fellowship, sodality, sorority; roster, rolls, personnel.

membrane, *n.* tissue, integument, skin, film, sheet, layer, drumhead; pellicle, meninx, tympanic membrane, pericarp, chorion.

memento, *n.* **1.** remembrance, remembrancer, souvenir, memorial, keepsake; record, relic, vestige; trophy, token; (*pl.*) memorabilia.

2. reminder, warning, caution, caveat; memento mori, skull and crossbones, Jolly Roger, death's-head, skeleton at the feast; Banquo's ghost, the ghost of Christmas past.

memoir, *n.* **1. memoirs a.** history, chronicle, account, record, annals, chronology. **b.** memories, recollections, reminiscences, experiences, adventures, fortunes; confessions, journal, diary, letters.

2. biography, autobiography, *Inf.* bio, personal narrative *or* history, life story, life, life history.

memorable, *adj.* **1.** unforgettable, not to be forgotten, not soon forgotten; signal, red-letter, illustrious, famous, historic, important, great, eventful, momentous, significant, consequential, crucial, critical; notable, noteworthy, remarkable, outstanding, extraordinary, out of the ordinary, uncommon, unusual, special, rare, unique, one of a kind, once in a lifetime; excellent, fantastic, marvelous, top notch, first-rate, *Inf.* A-1; striking, vivid, forceful, powerful, formidable, dramatic, eloquent, telling; sensational, thrilling, exciting, electrifying, *Sl.* socko; moving, inspiring, soul-stirring, heart-rending.

2. memorizable, learnable, commitable; retainable, holdable, keepable; recallable, recollectable, retrievable.

memorandum, *n.* note, reminder, *Chiefly Brit.* chit, *Inf.* memo, message; record, written statement, minute.

memorial, *n.* **1.** monument, statue, herm, hermes, herma; shrine, reliquary, mausoleum, pyramid, cenotaph; inscription, plaque, marker, grave marker, tombstone, headstone, stone, slab, *Chiefly Brit.* hatchment, (*in Polynesia*) ahu, *All Archaeol.* dolmen, cromlech, menhir.

2. commemoration, commemorative, remembrance, reminiscence, reminder, memento, memory; observance, celebration, memorial service *or* ceremony, wake, funeral, obsequy, eulogy, eulogium, *Obs.* observation.

3. memorandum, remonstrance, expostulation, protest, grievance, *Law.* petition; bill of particulars, itemization, listing.

memorialize, *v.* commemorate, remember, observe, honor, pay homage *or* tribute to, celebrate, eulogize; monument, mark, build [s.t.] in honor of, make an inscription for; enshrine, immortalize, preserve, keep for perpetuity.

memorize, *v.* commit to memory, con, learn by heart *or* rote, imprint on the memory *or* brain, learn word for word, make [s.t.] one's own; keep in mind, hold in remembrance, have at one's fingertips; retain, get, concentrate on.

memory, *n.* **1.** retention, retentive memory, recall, total recall, *Psychol.* mneme; photographic memory, camera eye; mind, *Inf.* rememberer, storehouse of the mind, intelligence, wit, awareness; calling to mind, retrospection, recollecting, remembering, minding, looking back, reviewing the past, summoning up the past.

2. remembrance, recollection, reminiscence, retrospect; thought, glimmering from the past, whisper from the past, something from the dim recesses of the mind, reminder, prompting.

3. posthumous glory, reputation, fame; renown, honor, respect, regard, esteem, repute.

4. commemoration, memorial, memento, testimonial; token, souvenir, keepsake; memory jogger, hint, suggestion.

menace, *n.* **1.** danger, peril, risk, hazard; deathtrap, quicksand, sleeping volcano, time bomb, bomb; specter, terror, dread, fright, apprehension, sword of Damocles, impending danger *or* doom.

2. intimidation, threat, warning, commination; Cassandra, bird of ill-omen, handwriting on the wall, gathering clouds, clouds on the horizon, brewing storm.

—*v.* **3.** threaten, frighten, scare, terrify, alarm; intimidate, daunt, terrorize, cow; browbeat, bully, thunder at, yell at, fulminate; snarl, growl, rattle one's sabers, bark; lower, glower, scowl.

4. tower over, hang over, beetle; impend, loom; portend, forebode, forewarn; be in the air, be in the offing.

menacing, *adj.* threatening, frightening, terrifying, intimidating, minacious; dangerous, perilous, hazardous, risky, chancy; formidable, horrible, making one's hair stand on end; looming, pending, impending, portending, hanging over, hanging heavy, over one's head.

ménage, *n.* **1.** household, family, kin, those near and dear; nuclear family, extended family, commune.

2. housekeeping, housecleaning, stewardship, household management.

menagerie, *n.* **1.** zoo denizens, circus animals; trained animals, Gunther Gebel-Williams animals.

2. zoo, zoological park *or* garden, animal farm, *Ger. Tiergarten,* vivarium, Bronx zoo.

mend, *v.* **1.** repair, remedy, fix, fix up, doctor *or* doctor up, patch up, patch; put back together, put back in one piece, restore, rehabilitate, make good as new; sew *or* sew up, stitch, darn, strengthen, reinforce; cure, heal, restore to health, make well *or* whole, *Inf.* bring around, put back on one's feet; reclaim, save, bring back from the dead, give a new lease on life.

2. correct, amend, emend, rectify, set right *or* straight; adjust, arrange, straighten, put in order; better, make better, ameliorate, meliorate, improve, reform; revise, update, redo, do over, redecorate, touch up, retouch, rework; remake, make over, renovate, revamp, recondition, remodel, rebuild, reconstruct, refashion; renew, freshen, spruce up, liven up, add color to.

3. recover, convalesce, get better, improve in health.

4. on the mend recovering, recuperating, convalescing, convalescent, getting better, improving, on the improve, on the upswing.

mendacious, *adj.* **1.** false, untrue, fraudulent, deceptive, prevaricative, perjured, misleading; fictitious, falsified, distorted, fabricated, invented, made up, trumped up; spurious, sham, bogus, mock, feigned, pretended, make-believe; exaggerated, hyperbolical, colored, misrepresented, misstated; counterfeit, fake, forged, meretricious, ungenuine.

2. lying, untruthful, dishonest, unveracious; dissembling, disingenuous, insincere, hypocritical, guileful, forked-tongue; deceitful, crooked, double-dealing, two-faced, Janus-faced.

mendacity, *n.* **1.** untruthfulness, inveracity, prevarication, equivocation, evasion, truthlessness; falsity, falseness, mendaciousness, deceit, duplicity, deception, dissimulation, crookedness; hypocrisy, disingenuousness, guilefulness, double-dealing.

2. falsehood, lie, untruth, perjury, prevarication, fib, white lie; falsification, fiction, invention, concoction, fabrication, half-truth; *Inf.* story, *Inf.* tale, *Inf.* fairy tale, canard, yarn; *Inf.* cock and bull story, *Inf.* fish story, *Inf.* tall tale; inaccuracy, distortion, corruption, perversion; misrepresentation, misstatement, exaggeration, coloring, overstatement, *Sl.* barefaced lie, big lie, *Sl.* whopper, *Sl.* dirty lie.

mendicancy, *n.* beggary, mendicity, pauperism, pauperage; alms-begging, *Inf.* panhandling, scrounging, *Inf.* bumming; poverty, indigence, penury, destitution, pennilessness, impecuniosity, neediness; *Inf.* hardupness, Queer Street, skid row; insolvency, bankruptcy, indebtedness, broken fortune, impoverishment; straits, distress, hardship, needy circumstances, hand to mouth existence, bare sustenance; beggarliness, raggedness, seediness, shreds and tatters.

mendicant, *adj.* **1.** begging, scrounging, cadging, supplicant, petitionary, on bended knee, on one's hands and knees.

—n. **2.** beggar, almsman, beggarman, alms-hunter, cadger, *Inf.* panhandler, *Scot.* gaberlunzie, *Brit.* mumper; moocher, scrounger, *Inf.* sponger, *Inf.* bummer, *Sl.* schnorrer, palmer, parasite, borrower; *U.S. Inf.* bum, tramp, hobo, vagrant, vagabond, drifter, gypsy; beachcomber, garbage picker, ragpicker, *Chiefly Brit.* mudlark; pauper, poor man, ragamuffin, tatterdemalion, charity case, hardcase, welfare client.

menial, *adj.* **1.** attendant, attending, serving, servitial; helping, waiting, ministering.

2. servile, slavish, subservient; fawning, obsequious, flattering, sycophantic, parasitical, *Sl.* bootlicking; groveling, truckling, cringing, sniveling, crouching, crawling; prostrate, timeserving, obeisant; degrading, abject, lowly, beggarly, humble, low; ignominious, base, mean, vile, ignoble.

—n. **3.** servant, hireling, domestic, orderly, peon, creature, hand; attendant, underling, helper, subordinate, assistant, understrapper, subaltern; lackey, flunky, fag, *Sl.* erk, toiler, moiler; valet, footman, gentleman, gentleman's gentleman, manservant, factotum; butler, steward, majordomo, buttons, houseman, cupbearer; yeoman, retainer, squire, chamberlain; jockey, groom, equerry, stableman, hostler; page, boy, boots, kitchen boy, turnspit; maid, maid-of-all-work, handmaiden, maidservant, abigail, stewardess, *Fr. bonne;* cook, scullion, *Brit.* slavey, *Brit.* skivvy, *Brit.* tweeny, *Brit.* betweenmaid; governess, babysitter, tutor, nurse, wetnurse, nanny, (*in India*) amah, (*in India*) ayah; laundress, housekeeper, cleaning woman, washer woman, chambermaid, charwoman.

4. toady, yes man, *Sl.* bootlicker, lickspittle, follower, timeserver; sycophant, flatterer, fawner, parasite, leech, hanger-on, minion; stooge, henchman, tool, puppet, pawn.

menstruation, *n.* bleeding, *Physiol.* menses, *Physiol.* catamenia, period, discharge, courses, *Archaic.* flowers; *Inf.* that time of the month, *Inf.* my friend, *Inf.* monthlies, *Sl.* the curse, *Sl.* the curse of Eve, *Sl.* holy week.

mental, *adj.* **1.** psychical, cerebral, rational, intellectual, psychological; conceptual, theoretical, abstract, noetic, noological, ideative; inward, metaphysical, subliminal, subconscious; thinking, reasoning, knowing, phrenic, perceptual, cognitive, prehensive.

2. pensive, thoughtful, wistful, reflective, cogitative; contemplative, deliberative, introspective, ruminative, speculative; penetrative, perspicacious, keen, shrewd, clever, percipient, discerning; intelligent, wise, scholarly, bright, learned, erudite, well-informed; brainy, smart, gifted, talented, knowledgeable.

3. *Informal.* insane, deranged, mad, lunatic, demented, *Latin. non compos mentis;* paranoiac, psychopathic, psychotic, neurotic, neurasthenic, mentally ill, abnormal.

4. *Informal.* pixillated, unhinged, bedeviled, deluded, *Sl.* off one's rocker, disturbed; queer, odd, eccentric, peculiar, funny; strange, weird, daft, not right, maladjusted; *All. Sl.* loony, crazy, loopy, screwy, nuts, wacky; loco, balmy, bats, nutty, batty; bananas, bonkers, crackers.

mentality, *n.* **1.** mind, intellect, brains, intelligence, cognition, reason, rationality, *Gk. Philos.* nous; intellectuality, intellectualism, noology, ideation; perception, percipience, discernment, perspicacity; understanding, comprehension, judgment, cognizance, noesis; wit, sense, wisdom, sagacity, intuition, insight; faculty, capacity, endowment, parts, *Sl.* smarts; power, acumen, acuity, reach, IQ, intelligence quotient.

2. disposition, temperament, frame of mind, mind-set, mental state; attitude, view, outlook, opinion, feeling.

mentally, *adv.* **1.** intellectually, rationally, cognitively, prehensively, psychologically, psychically; theoretically, noetically, abstractly, metaphysically; temperamentally, dispositionally, spiritually, emotionally.

2. thoughtfully, reflectively, pensively, introspectively, cogitatively; contemplatively, deliberatively, ruminatively.

mention, *v.* **1.** refer to, speak of, allude to, invoke, bring up; make mention of, touch on, comment upon, animadvert upon, make note of, point out; name, specify, indicate, direct attention to, call attention to, bring to one's notice, call to mind.

2. tell, say, utter, speak, remark; state, declare, announce; apprise, advise, inform, enlighten, serve notice; notify, communicate, let know, give one to understand; suggest, hint, imply, insinuate, lead one to believe; intimate, disclose, divulge, confide, whisper, breathe.

3. cite, quote, adduce, publish, broadcast; remember, trot out, recount, report, post.

4. not to mention without mentioning, not counting, in addition to, over and above, besides, aside from, as well as; together with, along with, in conjunction with, to boot, also, too.

—n. **5.** reference, mentioning, referral, referment;

allusion, notice, citation, quotation, indication, specification; notification, apprising, advisement; hint, suggestion, inkling, innuendo, implication, insinuation; word, account, statement, declaration, communication, announcement, report.

6. recognition, honorable mention, citation, acknowledgment, kudos, tribute.

mentor, *n.* counselor, advisor, guide, guidance counselor, therapist, confidant; master, guru, spiritual leader, oracle; coach, teacher, pedagogue, instructor, preceptor, educator, tutor, trainer; sage, wise man, pundit, expert, authority, luminary.

menu, *n.* bill of fare, *Fr. carte,* card; dessert menu, wine list; fare, board, table, diet, regimen, table d'hôte, *Inf.* spread, meal.

mephitic, *adj.* **1.** noisome, smelly, stinking, stenchful, foul-smelling, ill-smelling, strong-smelling, odorous, odoriferous, malodorous, fetid, reeky, reeking; putrid, rancid, rank, rotten, tainted, spoiled, strong, game, putrescent; foul, offensive, disgusting, nauseating, sickening, unpleasant, disagreeable.

2. poisonous, noxious, venomous, morbific, *Pathol.* septic, infective, infectious; pestilential; miasmal, miasmatic, miasmatical, miasmic, baneful, deadly, mortal, lethal.

mercantile, *adj.* commercial, of business, of trade, of buying and selling; trading, bartering, dealing; merchantable, marketable, saleable, vendible.

mercenary, *adj.* **1.** hireling, hired, paid, auxiliary; purchased, bought, venal, *Sl.* on the take.

2. avaricious, greedy, covetous, eager for gain; acquisitive, grasping, *Sl.* grabby, rapacious, ravenous, ravening, predatory, predacious; mean, usurious, sordid, selfish, hoarding, possessive.

—n. **3.** hired soldier, auxiliary, soldier of fortune, condottiere, myrmidon, legionary, legionnaire, Hessian, campaigner; hireling, hired hand *or* man *or* girl, wage slave, menial, minion, factotum; flunky, toady; hack.

merchandise, *n.* goods, commodities, vendibles, wares, produce, stock in trade, stock, staples, supplies; dry goods, yard goods, food stuffs, hardware; cargo, freight, shipment.

merchant, *n.* **1.** trader, tradesman, salesman, traveling salesman, *U.S.* drummer, dealer, businessman; seller, wholesaler, jobber, *Chiefly Brit.* monger; vendor, chandler, sutler, packman, peddler, colporteur, *Brit.* chapman, hawker, huckster, *Chiefly Brit.* costermonger; trafficker, middleman, (*in stolen goods*) *Sl.* fence, *Sl.* duffer.

2. retailer, storekeeper, shopkeeper, shopman.

3. merchant prince, magnate, mogul, tycoon, *U.S.* baron; industrialist, financier.

merchantable, *adj.* marketable, saleable, vendible; popular, in demand.

merchantman, *n.* trading vessel, cargo boat, freighter, coaster, steamship, argosy, galleon.

merciful, *adj.* compassionate, full of mercy, forgiving, pardoning, placable, exorable; humanitarian, humane, tender, tender-hearted, soft-hearted, sympathetic; patient, forbearing, tolerant, understanding; pitying, commiserative, commiserable, condolent, condolatory, ruthful, *Archaic.* piteous, *Rare.* pitiful; clement, lenient, sparing, mild, soft, easy; gentle, benign, benignant, benevolent, charitable, beneficent; kind, kindly, kindhearted, considerate, thoughtful; big, big-hearted, large-hearted, magnanimous, generous, bountiful, liberal, indulgent, giving.

merciless, *adj.* pitiless, unforgiving, uncompassionate, unpitying; cruel, heartless, hard-hearted, flinty, stony-hearted, cold-blooded, unfeeling; insensitive, unsensitive, indifferent, uncaring, unconcerned, unsympathetic, callous, hardened; hard, harsh, tough, stern, strict, severe; rigid, inflexible, unyielding, inexorable; unappeasable, implacable, relentless, remorseless, ruthless; inhuman, brutal, brutish, vicious, savage, barbarous.

mercurial, *adj.* **1.** active, lively, sprightly, vivacious, high-spirited, energetic, electric, charged; dynamic, animated, enthused, enthusiastic, ebullient, irrepressible, spirited.

2. changeable, variable, flightly, inconstant, volatile, quicksilver; fickle, capricious, erratic, spasmodic, irregular; irresolute, undecided, blowing hot and cold, wavering, fluctuating, vacillating, unsteady, unstable; impulsive, impetuous, hasty, quick, rash.

mercury, *n.* **1.** quicksilver.

2. messenger, herald, envoy, runner, courier.

mercy, *n.* forgiveness, clemency, quarter, indulgence, pardon, grace; mercifulness; big-heartedness, large-heartedness, magnanimity, magnanimousness, generosity, generousness, liberality, liberalness; compassion, compassionateness, *Latin. misericordia,* pity, sympathy; patience, forbearance, tolerance, understanding; commiseration, condolence, condolement, ruthfulness; humaneness, tenderness, tender-heartedness, soft-heartedness; leniency, lenity, sparingness, gentleness, mildness, softness, easiness; benignancy, benevolence, humanity, humanitarianism, charitableness, charity, beneficence; benignity, kindness, kindliness, kindheartedness; consideration, considerateness, thoughtfulness, thought, concern, care.

mere *adj.* **1.** only, utter, complete, absolute; bare.

2. ordinary, common, commonplace, insignificant, nugatory; slight, inappreciable, petty, trifling, niggling, piddling, paltry.

merely, *adv.* simply, just, only, solely; purely, utterly, completely, entirely, absolutely; but, nothing but, no more than, at most; barely, hardly, scarcely, *Dial.* scantly, only just.

meretricious, *adj.* **1.** gaudy, garish, flashy, *Sl.* flash, showy, bedizened, flaunting; loud, bold, painted, hard, *Inf.* honky-tonk; tawdry, cheap, dime-store, tinselly, brummagem, gimcrack, trumpery, trashy, *Inf.* chintzy, *Inf.* tacky, *Sl.* rinky-dink; tasteless, in bad taste, indelicate, crude, vulgar.

2. specious, bogus, sham, counterfeit, spurious, pseudo, mock, artificial; false, fraudulent, deceitful, deceptive, hollow, insincere; deceiving, misleading, evasive, elusive, dodgy, shifty, slippery.

3. whorish, trollopy, licentious, dissolute, lewd, indecent, unchaste.

merge, *v.* **1.** unite, unify, join, combine, amalgamate, consolidate; incorporate, syndicate, confederate, federate, centralize, concentrate; associate, coalesce, league, club, team up; pool, group *or* mass together, put *or* lump together, band *or* herd together, draw *or* pull together, join forces.

2. *Often* **merge in** *or* **into** blend, combine, mix, commix, admix, intermix, conglomerate; commingle, mingle, intermingle, interlard, interwine, interweave; homogenize, hybridize, meld, *Brit. Dial.* mell; bond, fuse, weld, glue, inosculate, cement, cohere, agglutinate, stick together.

3. *Often* **merge in** *or* **into** run into, melt into, become absorbed by, become a part of, become assimilated by, be swallowed up by; become lost in, be buried in, become embedded *or* enveloped in, become immersed *or* immerged *or* submerged in, disappear; grow together, ankylose, become one with, lose one's indentity *or* individuality.

merger *n.* **1.** incorporation, conglomeration, consolidation, syndication, mergence, *Commerce.* amalgamation; union, coalition, association, combination, joining.

2. conglomerate, combine, syndicate; alignment, bloc, pool, cartel, monopoly, trust company, *Commerce.* trust.

meridian, *n.* **1.** acme, zenith, noon, noontide, apogee, climax, culmination, pitch, crowning point, high point, orgasm, supreme moment; prime, heyday, maturity, fruition, bloom, full flower; height, extremity, extreme, utmost, uttermost, *U.S. Sl.* the tops; sublimity, supremacy, consummation, perfection; summit, apex, vertex, tip, top, tiptop; pinnacle, peak, crest, spire, heights; crown, cap, headpiece, head.

—adj. **2.** culminating, culminant, climactic, climactical, crowning, meridional; summital, apical, highest, uppermost, topmost, top, tiptop, apogeal, apogean; sublime, supreme, consummate, perfect; peerless, incomparable, unequalled, second to none, *Fr. sans pareil;* superlative, superior, best, finest, prime, choicest, greatest, maximal, utmost, uttermost.

merit, *n.* **1.** excellence, worth, worthiness, quality, value, virtue, integrity, good, goodness; asset, strong point, plus; credit, desert, due, reward, recompense, *Archaic.* meed.

—v. **2.** deserve, be worthy of, be qualified for; earn, be entitled to, have a right to, have a claim to; have [s.t.] coming to one.

merited, *adj.* deserved, earned; just, rightful, right, due equitable, fair; fitting, (*of punishment*) condign, suitable, appropriate, meet; reasonable, justified, justifiable.

meritorious, *adj.* praiseworthy, laudable, commendable, *Brit.* gradely, estimable, admirable; reputable, creditable, deserving, worthy; sterling, exemplary, excellent, good, noble; honorable, virtuous, righteous, upright, just, right-minded, principled; heroic, manly, chivalrous; generous, unselfish, charitable; unimpeachable, irreproachable, blameless.

mermaid, *n.* **1.** sea-maid, sea nymph, nymph, *Class. Myth.* siren; water spirit, undine.

2. swimmer, natator, naiad, *Sl.* fish.

merriment, *n.* gaiety, gayness, mirth, mirthfulness, hilarity, good *or* high spirits, jocundity; joviality, jollity, levity, buoyancy, light-heartedness, blithesomeness; cheer, cheerfulness, joyfulness, joyousness; joy, delight, pleasure, happiness, felicity; elation, exhilaration, exuberance, enthusiasm, vivacity, animation, liveliness, effervescence; exultation, glee, jubilance, jubilancy, rejoicing, celebration, jollification; fun, enjoyment, cakes and ale, revelry, revel, conviviality, festivity, partying, playing, sport; noise, noisiness, vociferousness, boisterousness, laughter, rowdiness, *Sl.* hell-raising, rabble-rousing.

merry, *adj.* **1.** cheerful, cheery, full of cheer, gay, sunny, in good *or* high spirits; blithe, blithesome, lighthearted, lightsome, buoyant, optimistic, positive, *Inf.* upbeat, beamish; debonair, free and easy, carefree, easygoing, breezy, airy, happy-go-lucky, untroubled; genial, convivial, amiable, good-natured, friendly; jovial, jocund, jolly, mirthful, hilarious; riant, laughing, smiling, happy as a lark; happy, glad, blissful, beatific, pleased, delighted, *Inf.* tickled pink; joyful, joyous, jubilant, rejoicing, gleeful; exultant, in seventh heaven, elated, over-joyed, thrilled, exhilarated; animated, lively, *Chiefly U.S. Inf.* chipper, jaunty, vivacious, sprightly.

2. make merry a. celebrate, feast, banquet, carouse, revel. See **make** (*def.* **25**). **b.** make fun of, make light of, deride, scoff at, mock, jeer, ridicule, knock; taunt, gibe, rag; rib, kid, *Inf.* roast, *Sl.* razz; make sport of, poke fun at, make a fool out of, make the butt of, *Inf.* needle *or* give [s.o.] the needle; lampoon, satirize, parody.

merry-andrew, *n.* buffoon, clown, jester, fool, *Archaic.* antic, zany, droll, jokester, *Inf.* stooge, wiseacre; comedian, funnyman, wit, wag, mime, mimic, pantomimist, mummer; goliard, gracioso, pantaloon; scaramouch, punchinello, pierrot, harlequin, punch; acrobat, contortioner, juggler.

merry-go-round, *n.* **1.** carrousel, *Chiefly Brit.* roundabout, whirligig.

2. whirl, reel, spin, turn, swirl, twirl; tizzy, *Inf.* dither, confusion, fluster, flurry.

merrymaking, *n.* **1.** festivity, festival, celebration, wing-ding; gaiety, merriment, convivality, revelry, revels, jollification, hilarity, mirth, glee, jollity, sport; fun, fun-making, *Inf.* whoopee, *Inf.* whoop-de-doo, *Inf.* hoopla; antics, capers, *Sl.* high jinks.

2. carousal, bacchanal, bacchanalia; debauch, debauchery, saturnalia.

—adj. **3.** festive, convivial, joyous, merry, mirthful, gleeful; gay, sportive, fun-making, uproarious, jovial, jolly, good-time; festal, festival, holiday.

mesa, *n.* butte, plateau, tableland, upland, hillock; mount, peak, alp, mountain.

mesh, *n.* **1.** net, netting, network, fishnet; web, webbing, weaving, lace, lacework; tracery, latticework, trellis, screen, screening; sieve, strainer, grater.

2. **meshes** snare, springe, trap, noose, grip, teeth.

—v. **3.** entangle, ensnare, snare, net; trap, entrap, nab, grab, clinch.

4. interlock, enmesh, hook together, interweave; match, coordinate, come together.

mesmeric, *adj.* **1.** mesmerized, hypnotized; mesmerizing, hypnotic, spellbinding, stupefying.

2. compelling, fascinating, entrancing, enthralling, enchanting, bewitching; attractive, alluring; arresting, gripping, stunning; engrossing, absorbing, engaging.

mesmerism, *n.* **1.** hypnosis, hypnotism, trance, spell, mesmeric trance; insensibility, *Pathol.* catalepsy, numbness, unconsciousness, stupefaction.

2. fascination, attraction, enchantment, absorption; compulsion, obsession, involvement, mania.

mesmerize, **1.** hypnotize, put to sleep, put under, stupefy, benumb, narcotize, *Sl.* knock out.

2. spellbind, captivate, cast a spell over, entrance, enthrall, enchant, enrapture; charm, delight, transport, bewitch, ensorcell.

3. compel, overpower, overwhelm; induce, prevail, persuade, oblige; constrain, coerce, pull, stay, force.

mess, *n.* **1.** untidiness, slovenliness, slatternliness, dirtiness, filthiness, *Sl.* crumminess; disgustingness, offensiveness; rathole, dump, garbage pile *or* heap, pig pen, pigsty, *Brit.* piggery, Augean stables, snake pit, mare's nest.

2. disorder, disarray, disorganization, displacement, disarrangement; clutter, litter, Fibber McGee's closet; hodgepodge, mishmash, jumble, scramble, tangle; conglomeration, medley, farrago, miscellany, mixture, olio, potpourri, mélange; salmagundi, gallimaufry, hash, olla-podrida.

3. confusion, imbroglio, muddle, perplexity; quandary, incertainty, dilemma, the horns of a dilemma; tumult, turmoil, chaos, bedlam, pandemonium; uproar, hubbub, hullabaloo, ado,fuss.

4. plight, predicament, *Inf.* pickle, jam; mix-up, *Inf.* foul-up, *Sl.* screw-up, *Sl.* ball-up, snafu; *Inf.* can of worms, botch, stew, fix, pretty fix, fine kettle of fish; difficulty, trouble, pinch, *Inf.* bad scene.

5. meal, sitting, table; dish, food, victuals, vittles.

—v. **6.** clutter, litter, turn upside-down; dirty, make a shambles of, track up; disarray, dishevel, tou-

sle, muss *or* muss up.

7. confuse, muddle, mix up, *Inf.* foul up, *Sl.* screw up, *Sl.* ball up, *Sl.* bollix up; disturb, disrupt, scramble, jumble, snarl, tangle, upset the apple cart, throw a monkey wrench into the works.

message, *n.* **1.** communication, communiqué, missive, dispatch, transmittal, transmission, transmittance; letter, epistle, *Inf.* memorandum, *Inf.* memo, note, line, few words, card, postcard; telegram, cablegram, cable, wire, wireless, radiogram, *Rare.* marconigram, *Brit.* express; reply, response, rejoinder, answer.

2. news, tidings, good news, word; information, intelligence, report; content, what [s.o.] says *or* writes.

3. announcement, notice, bulletin, brief word, *Both Rom. Cath. Ch.* encyclical, bull; statement, speech, declaration, manifesto, address.

4. meaning, point, idea, hidden *or* underlying meaning, intimation; intent, aim.

messenger, *n.* **1.** courier, carrier, bearer, bringer, intelligencer, carrier pigeon; postman, mailman, mail carrier, letter carrier, postrider, post boy, pony express rider, dispatch rider, rider, estafette; Pheidipides, Hermes, Mercury, Iris, Ariel.

2. envoy, emissary, legate, go-between, intermediary, (*in Turkey*) chiaus; runner, errand-runner, bellhop, *U.S.* bellboy, porter, office boy, page, *Sl.* gopher; lackey, servant, slave.

messiah, *n.* **1.** deliverer, savior, redeemer, emancipator, liberator, manumitter; lifesaver, rescuer, preserver, saver, *Euph.* life-preserver.

2. zealot, firebrand, leader, charismatic leader, helmsman, *German. Fuehrer.*

3. Messiah a. expected Deliverer, Savior; *Hebrew. Meshiach*; spiritual leader, prophet, forerunner, messenger, harbinger. **b.** Jesus Christ, King of Kings, Lord of Lords. See **Jesus.**

messmate, *n.* commensal, table-mate, bench-mate, eating partner; buddy, comrade, comrade-in-arms, mate, fellow, pal, chum, *Inf.* side kick; shipmate, roommate, *Inf.* roomie; partner, companion, confrere, friend, fast friend, colleague, crony.

messy, *adj.* **1.** dirty, grubby, sloppy, filthy, *Sl.* grungy; slovenly, slatternly, frowzy, piggy, dowdy, bedraggled, frumpy; unkempt, slipshod, untidy, disheveled; disorderly, disarranged, disorganized, at sixes and sevens; confused, muddled, macaronic, jumbled, topsy-turvy, every whichway; turbid, chaotic, entangled, snarled up, *Sl.* fouled up, *Sl.* bollixed up, at cross-purposes.

2. embarrassing, awkward, inconvenient, disconcerting, frustrating, discombobulating, ticklish; difficult, inextricable, uncontrollable; thorny, hard, tough, bad; unpleasant, disturbing, perturbing; bothersome, worrisome, rotten, nasty.

metal, *n.* **1.** element, mineral, ore, bullion, *Metall.* pig; alloy.

2. spirit, temper, mettle, pluck, resoluteness, strength of mind, *Inf.* toughness, *Inf.* backbone.

metallic, *adj.* **1.** metalline, iron, leaden, steely; hard, solid, firm, hard as nails; tempered, heat-treated, hardened, toughened.

2. shiny, glossy, gleaming, lustrous, argentine, polished, burnished, reflective; smooth, slick, sleek.

3. (*all of sound*) raucous, dissonant, grating, harsh, shrill, tinny; clashing, jangling, jangly, jarring.

metamorphic, *adj.* changeable, alterable, mutable, protean, proteiform; unstable, unfixed, mobile, plastic, changing, transitory; ever-changing, changeful, variable, chameleonlike.

metamorphose, *v.* **1.** transform, transfigure, transmute, transubstantiate, metabolize, mutate, transmogrify; change into, alter into, develop *or* evolve into, convert, change over, become; undergo a change, go through a change, turn into, alter; be renewed, turn the corner, take a turn; come about, adapt, adjust, modulate, modify, shift, swerve.

2. change, switch, redo, make over, remake, recast, reshape, refashion, *Inf.* revamp.

metamorphosis, *n.* **1.** transformation, transubstantiation, translation, transfiguration; mutation, transmutation, metastasis, transmogrification, metaplasia.

2. change, alteration, permutation, modification; change of heart, change of allegiance *or* conviction, reversal, about face, volte-face, *Inf.* switch, *Inf.* turnabout, *Inf.* 180-degree turn.

3. rebirth, renewal, regeneration, recreation; conversion, changeover, passage; reformation, reclamation, recrudescence.

metaphor, *n.* figure of speech, image, symbol, trope, figure; transference, *Obs., Rare.* tralation, analogy, parallelism, likening, comparison; simile, similitude, correlation, likeness; symbolism, imagery, personification, figurativeness, metonymy; allegory, allegorization, apologue, anagoge, parable, fable.

metaphorical, *adj.* symbolic, figurative, metonymous, tropological, tropical; typical, allegorical, emblematical, tralatitious, parabolical, apologal, anagogic; analogous, allusive, referential, comparative, similitudinous; hyperbolic, exaggerated, euphemistic, euphuistic; descriptive, pictorial, depictive, illustrative.

metaphysical, *adj.* abstract, immaterial, unsubstantial, intangible, impalpable, incorporeal; spiritual, psychical, ideal, intellectual, visionary, speculative, hyperphysical, supersensible; abstruse, incomprehensible; ontological, Platonistic, epistemological, philosophical, cosmological.

metaphysics, *n.* ontology, epistemology, science of existence, speculative philosophy, cosmology.

mete[1], *v.* *Usu.* **mete out** apportion, admeasure, measure out *or* off; allot, allocate, assign; portion out, parcel out, deal out, dole out, ration out, *Inf.* dish out; pass out, hand out, give out, distribute, dispense.

mete[2], *n.* limit, boundary, frontier, frontier line, boundary line, bounding line, border line, partition line, line of demarcation, line, fence.

metempsychosis, *n.* transmigration, reincarnation; reembodiment, rebirth, regeneration, metamorphosis, transmogrification.

meteor, *n.* meteoroid, meteorite, aerolite, shooting star, falling star, *Astron.* bolide, fireball; fiery streak, *Astron.* tail, comet.

meteoric, *adj.* **1.** transient, transitory, ephemeral, short-lived, brief, momentary, fleeting, flitting, evanescent; unlasting, unpermanent, impermanent, nonpermanent.

2. sudden, unexpected, instantaneous, swift, mushroom, meteorlike, meteor; quick, fast, rapid, speedy.

3. meteorological, meteorologic, atmospheric, atmospherical.

meteorology, *n.* **1.** science of weather, science of climate, climatology, aerography, *Obs.* aerology.

2. weather, atmospheric conditions; climate, clime.

method, *n.* **1.** way, manner, mode, process, procedure, *Latin. modus operandi*; means, technique, formula, principle, practice.

2. order, system, plan, design, discipline; course, routine, program, line; standard, precept, code, guide, pattern; methodology, rule, attack, approach, line, wise.

3. arrangement, sequence, systematization, methodization; disposition, array, distribution, assignment, disposal; categorization, classification, organization.

methodical, *adj.* **1.** systematic, orderly, ordered, regular, exact, uniform, constant; methodic, businesslike, regulated, routine, tidy, neat, step by step.

2. painstaking, laborious, slow; exact, meticulous, precise, punctilious.

methodize, *v.* systematize, regulate, organize, classify, schematize; straighten out, put to rights, reduce to order, lay out; regularize, standardize, centralize, normalize, routinize; arrange, order, coordinate, alphabetize, grade, rank.

métier, *n.* **1.** trade, craft, skill, job, livelihood, living, work; occupation, vocation, calling, profession, career, pursuit, lifework.

2. forte, field, line, sphere, speciality, major, concentration.

meticulous, *adj.* exact, precise, accurate, correct; punctilious, scrupulous, conscientious, careful; particular, finical, finicky, picky, fussy, hard to please; critical, exacting, demanding, painstaking, fastidious; minute, detailed, fine, nice, thorough, searching; scientific, mathematical, severe, rigorous, strict, close.

metropolis, *n.* capital, capital city; city, metropolitan area, municipality, town, *Inf.* burg; megalopolis, urban sprawl; center, downtown, business district *or* section; inner city, core city, asphalt jungle.

mettle, *n.* **1.** disposition, temperament, character, nature, makeup, complexion, stripe, stamp, type, mold, *Archaic.* constitution; temper, humor, habit, vein, tenor, frame of mind; inclination, bent, bias, turn, turn of mind.

2. vigor, vigorousness, energy, spirit, vim, go, animation, vivacity, life, liveliness, zest, zestfulness, gusto, robustness, lustiness, *Inf.* zip, *Inf.* pep, *Inf.* snap, *Inf.* bounce, *Inf.* punch, *Sl.* pizzazz, *Sl.* oomph, *Brit. Sl.* stingo; zeal, ardor, fervor, fervidness, vehemence, intensity; enthusiasm, eagerness, keenness, ebullience; élan, dash, fire, panache.

3. pluck, pluckiness, backbone, pith, marrow, sap, blood, heart, nerve, gumption, gameness, mettlesomeness, grit, *U.S. Inf.* sand, *Inf.* starch, *Inf.* spunk, *Sl.* guts, *Sl.* moxie; courage, bravery, valor, valorousness, valiancy, valiance, heroism, prowess, stoutheartedness, lionheartedness, great-heartedness, high-heartedness; intrepidity, intrepidness, fearlessness, dauntlessness, awelessness, dreadlessness; boldness, boldspiritedness, high-spiritedness, daring, derring-do, audacity, audaciousness, rashness, recklessness.

4. fortitude, endurance, tenacity, determination, will power, will; firmness, resolution, resoluteness, indomitableness, indomitability, invincibleness, invincibility, unconquerableness, staunchness, stanchness, steadfastness, stalwartness, doughtiness, sturdiness, hardiness, hardihood, bulldog courage.

mettlesome, *adj.* **1.** plucky, gritty, game, spirited, red-blooded, *Inf.* spunky; brave, courageous, valiant, valorous, heroic, hero-like, stout-hearted, lionhearted, ironhearted, great-hearted, high-hearted; intrepid, fearless, dauntless, unafraid, dreadless, aweless, nervy, *Sl.* gutsy, unblenching, unblenched, undaunted, undismayed, unappalled, unalarmed; bold, bold-spirited, high-spirited, daring, dashing, adventurous, audacious, rash, reckless.

2. vigorous, full of vigor, energetic, full of energy, active, spirited, animated, vivacious, gay, lively, full of life, brisk, zesty, zestful, full of zest, robust, lusty, *Inf.* zippy, *Inf.* peppy, *Inf.* snappy, *Inf.* bouncing; zealous, ardent, fervid, fervent, vehement, intense; enthusiastic, eager, keen, ebullient.

mew[1], *n.* **1.** meow, miaow, purr, cat's cry, whine, whimper; caterwaul, howl, screech, squall.

—*v.* **2.** meow, miaow, purr, *Fr. miauler*, cry, mewl, whine, whimper, pule; caterwaul, howl, screech, squall.

mew[2], *n.* **1.** cage, pen, coop, hutch, kennel, run, enclosure, corral; shed, barn, stable, *Brit.* byre.

—*v.* **2.** pen up *or* in, coop *or* coop up, cage, encage; confine, corral, enclose, shut up *or* in, impound, immure, imprison, embar.

mew[3], *v.* shed, shed the skin, molt, exuviate, cast off, slough; come off, peel off, peel, exfoliate, *Pathol.* desquamate.

mewl, *v.* cry, whimper, whine, pule, snivel; bawl, blubber, sob, boohoo, weep.

mezzanine, *n.* entresol.

miasma, *n.* mephitis, mofette, *Archaic.* malaria; fetor, reek, stench, effluvium, exhalation; *Mining.* chokedamp *or* blackdamp.

miasmal, *adj.* mephitic, miasmic, miasmatic, miasmatical; fetid, noxious, noisome, fulsome, virulent, vile, foul, putrid, bad; malodorous, odorous, stinking, reeking; poisonous, toxic; unhealthful, unwholesome, insalubrious, unsalutary, deleterious, morbific.

microbe, *n.* microorganism, schizomycete, microzoon, microparasite, *Bacteriol.* micrococcus, *Bacteriol.* vibrio; germ, germ cell, bacillus, bacterium, pathogen, coccus, *Bacteriol.* spirillum, *Bacteriol.* spirochete, *Inf.* bug.

microphone, *n.* *Inf.* mike, *Inf.* local mike, *Inf.* lapel mike, radiomicrophone, *Inf.* radio mike; dictaphone; hidden microphone, tap, wire-tap, wire-tapping device, pick-up, *Sl.* bug; loudspeaker, bullhorn, hailer.

microscope, *n.* magnifier, (*loosely*) magnifying glass; magnifying lens, meniscus.

microscopic, *adj.* **1.** infinitesimal, minute, atomic, microbic, microorganic; invisible, imperceptible, indiscernible, unseeable.

2. tiny, wee, minuscule, diminutive, pocket-sized, vest-pocket, *Inf.* teeny, *Baby Talk.* teeny-weeny *or* teensy-weensy, *Baby Talk.* itty-bitty *or* itsy-bitsy.

3. exact, precise, pinpoint; strict, severe, rigorous, rigid.

mid, *adj.* middle, mean, medial, mesial, median, medium. See also **middle** (*def.* **2**).

midday, *n.* noon, noontime, noontide, noonday, high noon, midnoon, *Chiefly Dial.* nooning, twelve o'clock, eight bells.

middle, *adj.* **1.** central, centric, focal; equidistant, midway, halfway; midmost, middlemost, centermost.

2. intervening, intervenient, intermediary, intermediate, intermedial, interjacent, *Law.* mesne; mean, mediate, medial, mesial, medium, mid, mezzo; moderate, middle-of-the-road, MOR.

—*n.* **3.** center, midpoint, *Archaic.* mid; epicenter, dead center, bull's eye; midst, thick, thick of things, thick of it.

4. midriff, *Inf.* midsection, waist, waistline; abdomen, stomach, belly, *Sl.* gut, *Sl.* breadbasket; diaphragm, *Anat.* solar plexus, *Anat.* celiac plexus.

5. mean, median, medium, happy medium, golden mean; middle of the road, middle ground, middle course, *Latin. via media*; average, norm, normal, par, par for the course, rule, run, generality.

middle age, *n.* **1.** the middle years, middle life, meridian of life, wrong side of forty; dangerous age, midlife crisis.

2. maturity, adulthood, prime of life, peak *or* pinnacle of one's powers.

middle-aged, *adj.* **1.** mid-life, *Fr. entre deux ages;*

graying, fortyish; balding, pot-bellied; dowdy, frumpy, stocky.

2. complacent, satisfied, settled, comfortable, content.

middle class, *n.* **1.** bourgeoisie, bourgeoise, petite bourgeoisie; middle orders, shopkeepers, small tradesmen.

2. the common people, the masses, the hoi polloi, *Jocular.* the booboisie; Middle America, the silent majority, the grass roots; commonalty, the public, the general public, citizenry.

middle-class, *adj.* bourgeois, suburban, *Sl.* plastic; conventional, middlebrow, middle-of-the-road, MOR; common, commonplace, ordinary, average, run-of-the-mill, *Inf.* garden-variety.

middleman, *n.* **1.** broker, agent, interagent, medium, jobber, wholesaler, distributor, dealer.

2. intermediary, intermediator, mediator, intercessor, interceder, intervener, go-between; moderator, arbiter, arbitrator, negotiator, third *or* disinterested party, umpire, referee, interlocutor, peacemaker, makepeace.

3. connection, contact, *Inf.* front, *Inf.* front man, *U.S. Politics.* lobbyist; advocate, consumer advocate, *Sl.* Nader-raider, champion, patron; spokesman, *Inf.* mouthpiece, solicitor, friend-at-court, ombudsman, ombudswoman.

4. diplomat, plenipotentiary, ambassador, envoy, emissary, minister, chargé d'affaires, legate, nuncio, internuncio.

middle of the road, *n.* center, middle ground, neutral position, moderate position, *Inf.* fence; mean, golden mean, *Fr. juste-milieu*, middle, median; medium, happy medium, compromise; middle course, middle way, *Latin. via media*.

middle-of-the-road, *adj.* **1.** (*all in reference to politics*) moderate, centrist, *Inf.* on the fence, *Inf.* fence-sitting; noncommittal, mugwumpish, mugwumpian.

2. average, ordinary, common, commonplace, *Inf.* run-of-the-mill; conventional, conformist, middlebrow, commercial, MOR, *Inf.* square, *Inf.* straight; middle-class, bourgeois, *Sl.* plastic.

middling, *adj.* **1.** average, moderate, medium, mean; ordinary, commonplace, everyday, run-of-the-mill; mediocre, indifferent, so-so, fair, fair to middling, betwixt and between, *Inf.* no great shakes, *Inf.* nothing to write home *or* brag about; undistinguished, unexceptional, unnotable, modest, of sorts, of a sort; adequate, passable, acceptable, tolerable; respectable, presentable, fairly good, *Inf.* not that good, not too bad.

—adv. **2.** moderately, fairly, slightly, rather, somewhat, *Inf.* pretty; sufficiently, adequately, satisfactorily, tolerably, passably.

midget, *n.* little man, manikin, dwarf, homunculus, chit, fingerling, dapperling, midge, cock-sparrow, hop-o'-my-thumb, Tom Thumb, Lilliputian, *Chiefly Scot.* wee fellow *or* laddie *or* one, *Obs.* pigwidgin, *Archaic.* dandiprat; shrimp, runt, pee-wee, squirt, pipsqueak, half-pint, small-fry, *Inf.* shorty.

midmost, *adj.* **1.** middlemost, centermost; central, centric, focal.

—adv. **2.** in the midst of, in the thick of.

midnight, *n.* **1.** dead of night, hush of night, witching hour, 12 at night.

—adj. **2.** nocturnal, night, nighttime, nightly.

3. dark, black, pitch-black, pitch-dark, black *or* dark as pitch, black *or* dark as night.

4. burn the midnight oil lucubrate, *Obs.* elucubrate, study, *Inf.* cram, *Inf.* grind, *Sl.* bone, *Brit. Sl.* swot; work overtime, work day and night, work late; stay late, stay up late, stay up into the small hours, keep late hours.

midst, *n.* thick, thick of things, thick of it; heart, core, kernel, nucleus, hub; center, middle, midpoint, *Archaic.* mid; epicenter, dead center, bull's eye.

midway, *adj.* **1.** equidistant, halfway; mean, medial, mesial, medium, mezzo, mid, middle.

—adv. **2.** halfway, in the middle, betwixt and between, *Inf.* plumb *or* smack *or* smack-dab in the middle; half and half, neither here nor there, *It. mezzo-mezzo.*

midwife, *n.* deliverer, obstetrician, baby doctor, Lucina, *Fr. accoucheuse.*

midwifery, *n.* obstetrics, tocology; delivery, parturition.

mien, *n.* air, aura, presence, demeanor, attitude, feel, climate; manner, mode, mood, style, way; poise, composure, easy way, self-confidence, self-possession, self-assuredness; deportment, conduct, behavior, actions; bearing, carriage, port, posture, stance, stand, pose, position, aspect, appearance, semblance, complexion, cast, guise, form, feature; countenance, look, visage, expression.

miff, *n.* **1.** *Informal.* pique, pet, huff, dudgeon, bile, gall, sulk, rancor, *Archaic.* pucker; bad mood, peevishness, petulance, *Rare.* petulancy, indignation, resentment, grudge, bitterness, acerbity; annoyance, irritation, displeasure, disgruntled state; choler, ill temper, temper, ire, fume, state, *Inf.* dander, *Inf.* stew.

2. tiff, spat, squabble, dustup, *Inf.* hassle, *Brit. Dial.* fratch; disagreement, difference of opinion, falling-out; quarrel, argument, altercation, row, *Inf.* barney.

—v. **3.** offend, give offense to, hurt, hurt [s.o.'s] feelings, chagrin, insult, injure, smart, wound, damage, harm; wrong, grieve, aggrieve, abuse, mistreat, ill-treat; pique, huff, give umbrage to, embitter, put [s.o.] in a bad mood, make [s.o.] sore, *Inf.* put [s.o.] off, *Sl.* tee [s.o.] off; displease, disgruntle, upset, irritate, annoy, vex, chafe, nettle, provoke, anger, rile, raise [s.o.'s] dander.

might, *n.* **1.** force, power, strength, mightiness, brute force *or* strength, toughness, powerfulness, forcefulness, sturdiness, stalwartness; brawn, beef, muscle, physique, *Inf.* beefiness, *Inf.* huskiness, *Inf.* heftiness; stability, solidity, staunchness, hardness, thew, thews, sinew, sinews, musculature, *Literary.* puissance; robustness, potency, vigor, energy, intensity, vehemence, fortitude, staying *or* sticking power, grit, stamina, *Sl.* guts, *Sl.* gutsiness; ruggedness, heartiness, lustiness, stoutness, main, muscularity, brawniness.

2. authoritativeness, influence, ability, *Sl.* clout; authority, weight, superiority, stature, consequence, eminence, rank, seniority; importance, prominence, dominion, domination, sway; ascendance, prerogative.

3. prowess, competence, capability; durability, endurance; invincibility, indomitability, invulnerability, impregnability, impenetrability, unassailability, insuperability.

4. with might and main mightily, powerfully, forcefully, with all one's strength; vigorously, strongly, stoutly, stalwartly, robustly, soundly, staunchly, with utmost effort, with everything at one's command, full force, full blast; lustily, heartily, energetically, giving one's all, with everything one has got, intensely.

mightily, *adv.* **1.** strongly, powerfully, by main force, forcibly, with a strong hand, by brute strength *or* force, soundly, firmly; in a mighty manner, manfully, potently, forcefully, strenuously, with Herculean effort, with all one's might, with everything that is in one, sturdily, ruggedly; vigorously, hammer and tongs, tooth and nail, heart and soul, *Latin. vi et armis*, with might and main, with a vengeance; to the best of one's ability, so far as one can, as best one can, as lies in one's power *or* scope; dynamically, strikingly, tellingly, to good account *or* purpose. See **might** (*def.* **4**).

2. intensely, loudly, deafeningly.

3. very, very much, exceedingly, to a great extent, in large degree, greatly, largely; *Inf.* awfully, *Inf.* terribly, *Inf.* terrifically, *Inf.* mighty, *Dial.* almighty; decidedly, clearly, obviously, noticeably, truly, undeniably.

mighty, *adj.* **1.** powerful, influential, prestigious, *Literary.* puissant; ascendant, predominant, hegemonic, prepotent, potent; strong, great, capable, equal to, up to; authoritative, commanding, consequential, weighty, authoritarian, absolute, autocratic, *Sl.* take-charge.

2. eminent, high, exalted, elevated, lofty, held in awe, awesome, high and mighty; glorified, ennobled, illustrious, majestic, imposing.

3. sturdy, stalwart, rugged, steely; hale, hardy, stout; robust, vigorous, hearty, lusty, strapping, doughty, full-blooded, red-blooded, having the strength of ten; sturdy as an ox, strong as a bull *or* a horse *or* a lion, *Inf.* husky, *Inf.* hefty, *Inf.* beefy; able-bodied, well-set, well-knit, well-built, muscular, burly, brawny, musclebound; firm, solid, solid as a rock, made of iron.

4. impregnable, unassailable, invulnerable, unconquerable, indomitable, having the strength of Gibraltar, unyielding, impenetrable, inviolable, inexpugnable; forceful, irresistible, omnipotent, incontestable, unbeatable, more than a match for, armed to the teeth, invincible, unsubduable; overwhelming, overpowering; resistant, proof, tight.

5. huge, giant, gigantic, enormous, tremendous, stupendous, massive, bulky; larger than life, titanic, colossal, Herculean, monster, monstrous, Gargantuan, Brobdingnagian, mammoth, elephantine, mastodonic; substantial, prodigious, monumental, towering, mountainous; oversized, outsized, full-blown, king-size, *Sl.* whopping, *Sl.* whacking, *Sl.* walloping, *Sl.* thwacking, *Sl.* thundering.

6. grand, immense, vast, great, big; infinite, boundless, cosmic, galactic; profound, abysmal, deep, grave, serious, heavy, intense; astronomical, consequential, considerable, comprehensive, extensive, exhaustive, voluminous, immeasureable; great, superior, uncommon, consequential, important, preponderant; heroic, epic, Homeric.

migrant, *adj.* **1.** roving, wandering, migrating, migratory. See **migratory** (*defs.* **1, 2**).

—*n.* **2.** migrator, journeyer, wanderer, traveler, wayfarer, viator, trekker; passerby, peregrinator, bird of passage, landloper; globetrotter, world-traveler.

3. migrant *or* migratory worker, itinerant, *Inf.* dust cropper, *Inf.* Okie, *Inf.* wetback; day laborer, roustabout, floater, drifter, rounder, *Sl.* stiff, *Sl.* bindlestiff; tramp, knight *or* king of the road, *Sl.* hobo, *Sl.* bo, *Sl.* haut beau; *All Australian. Inf.* sundowner, swagman, swagsman.

4. commuter, transient, shuttler, passenger, fare, *Inf.* straphanger; voyager, sailor, mariner; beachcomber, beach bum, surf bum, tennis bum, ski bum; troubadour, wandering minstrel, strolling player.

5. gypsy, bohemian, kuchi, Romany, *Sp. gitano*, tzigane; nomad, Bedouin, Arab.

6. immigrant, *Fr. émigré*, emigrant, expatriate; evacuee, displaced person, DP, stateless person, Wandering Jew, Ancient Mariner, Ishmael, Flying Dutchman; peripatetic, rolling stone, peregrine.

7. waif, homeless waif, ragamuffin, gamin, gamine, urchin, street urchin, street Arab, mudlark, *Inf.* guttersnipe; beggar, tatterdemalion, street person, street dweller, ragman, rag and bones man, ragpicker, bag lady, junk *or* trash picker; vagabond, vagrant, *Inf.* bum.

migrate, *v.* **1.** emigrate, expatriate, decamp, take leave, go forth, sally *or* fare forth, take passage; immigrate, transmigrate, move, resettle, relocate, transfer, make a change, get a change of scenery, move out, get out, *Inf.* up and move; pilgrimage, colonize, go overseas, pull up stakes, *Inf.* take off, *Inf.* look for greener pastures, *Inf.* follow the rainbow; travel, trek, journey, fare, go; voyage, ply, sail, push off, set sail, ship out; wing one's way, take flight *or* wing, jaunt, peregrinate; take to the road, go on the road, *Inf.* hit the trail, *Inf.* ride the rods *or* rails, *Inf.* ride the shoe-leather *or* hobnail express; hike, hie oneself to, make one's way, tramp, *Dial.* traipse, backpack, *Sl.* schlepp.

2. commute, shuttle, ferry, pass, drift; move on, move along, go along, wend one's way, direct one's course, bend one's step *or* course, transit, pass through; wander, roam, nomadize, range, *All Inf.* knock about *or* around, hitchhike, hitch, make the rounds, *Sl.* catch a ride, *Sl.* thumb *or* bum a ride.

migratory, *adj.* **1.** migrating, migrational, transmigratory, going, moving, trekking, passing, peregrine, peregrinative; immigrant, emigrant, transient, transitory, unsettled, displaced, uprooted, dislocated, deracinated; moving, transferring; outgoing, incoming.

2. itinerant, itinerating, traveling, journeying, wayfaring, peregrinating, peripatetic; commuting, shuttling, circuit-riding, strolling, floating, drifting, wandering, roving, roaming, rambling; nomad, nomadic, gypsy, gypsy-like; vagrant, vagabond, footloose, footloose and fancy free, touring, gadding, *Dial.* traipsing, flitting; living in one's hat, living out of a suitcase, having itchy feet, having sand in one's shoe; on the move, on the go, on the trail, making the rounds.

mild, *adj.* **1.** tender, gentle, soft, soft-hearted, tender-hearted, sensitive, sympathetic, empathetic, compassionate, humane, forbearing, gracious, considerate, tactful, kind, civil; conciliatory, nonviolent, mollifying, pacific, peaceable, peaceful, pacifistic; merciful, lenient, clement, easy, easy-going, forgiving; easy-natured, gentle as a lamb, placid, serene, good-natured, good-tempered, amiable, affable, genial, bonhomous, easy to get along with, calm, tranquil, docile, tame, mild as milk *or* mother's milk; uncomplaining, unassertive, passive, nonopposing, submissive; unassuming, meek, quiet, subdued, tractable, yielding, indulgent, melting; mellow, temperate, pleasant.

2. (*all of weather*) sunny, fair, balmy, halcyon, sunshiny, summery, estival; pretty, lovely.

3. average, moderate, neutral; weak, tepid, lukewarm; bland, insipid, tasteless, spiceless, unflavored, wishy-washy, vapid, inane, jejune, flat, *Sl.* blah.

mildew, *n.* fungus, mold, blight, rust, blast; discoloration, stain, smut, dry-rot, rot, *Inf.* crud; must, mustiness, fustiness, fetidness, *Sl.* funkiness.

mildness, *n.* **1.** gentleness, tenderness, softness; amiability, affability, geniality, cordiality, graciousness, kindheartedness, benignity, benignancy, mansuetude, kindliness, warmth, milk of human kindness, sweetness; forbearance, patience, toleration, leniency, lenity, clemency, humaneness, compassion; indulgence, humoring, compliance, complaisance, obligingness, agreeableness; moderation, moderateness, steadiness, evenness, unexcessiveness; meekness, tameness,

peaceableness, quietness, calmness, serenity, tranquillity, calm; docility, tractability, yieldingness, flexibility.
2. blandness, insipidness, flatness, vapidity, inanity, jejuneness, tastelessness, flavorlessness, weakness, wishy-washiness.

mileage, *n.* **1.** wear, use, usage, usefulness, service, serviceability; advantage, profit, benefit, gain, good; coverage, promotion, publicity.
2. viaticum, allowance, reimbursement, compensation, payment, recompense; ration, allotment, amount, percentage.
3. charge, fee, price, exaction; levy, tax, toll, rate; truckage, wharfage, towage, freightage, tollage.
4. (*all in miles*) length, extent, distance; gap, space, span, reach, range.

milestone, *n.* **1.** milepost, marker, millary column, waymark; signpost, direction post, post, mark, pointer.
2. climax, point, degree, stage, junctures, climacteric.

milieu, *n.* environment, sphere, medium, element, condition; ambience, atmosphere, air, aura, climate, tone, feeling, spirit; background, setting, backdrop, scene, stage; arena, locale, field, ground, theatre; surroundings, environs, vicinity, precincts, circle, purlieus, neighborhood.

militancy, *n.* aggressiveness, aggression, combativeness, activism, activity; belligerency, bellicosity, pugnacity, war fever; contentiousness, fierceness, ferocity, truculence; warmongering, saber rattling, jingoism, chauvinism; hawkishness, martialism, militarism.

militant, *adj.* **1.** aggressive, combative, truculent, offensive, activist; belligerent, bellicose, pugnacious, martial, warlike; hawkish, warmongering, flag-waving, saber-rattling, chauvinistic, jingoistic; war-loving, bloodthirsty, sanguinary, fierce, ferocious; hostile, contentious, antagonistic, unfriendly, enemy.
2. warring, contending, campaigning, attacking, up in arms; at war, on the warpath, on the offensive, at grips; embattled, arrayed, engaged, mobilized.
—*n.* **3.** combatant, contender, battler, fighter, struggler, scuffler; soldier, serviceman, warrior, brave; assailer, assaulter, attacker, aggressor, fighting man.

militarism, *n.* military spirit, war fever, jingoism, chauvinism, Prussianism. See **militancy**.

militarist, *n.* warlord, warmonger, hawk, jingoist, chauvinist; mercenary, condottiere, soldier of fortune, adventurer, crusader, ghazi.

military, *adj.* **1.** army, martial, militant, naval, service, fighting.
2. soldierly, soldierlike, military-minded; combative, contentious, militarist, aggressive. See **militant** (*def.* **1**).
—*n.* **3.** armed forces, army, service, forces, regular army, standing army, the military establishment; soldiery, troops, contingents, janissaries, legions, ranks, cannon fodder; recruits, reinforcements, the line, storm troops.

militate, *v.* *Usu.* **militate against** operate against, go against, side against, war against, contend against; contradict, belie, counter, work against, traverse, cross, not conduce to; rebuff, spurn, foil, counteract; countervail, counterpoise, cancel out, conflict with; antagonize, oppose, counterattack, oppugn, resist.

militia, *n.* national guard, guard, reserves, minutemen, home reserves, home guard; yeomanry, volunteers, *Eng. Hist.* trainband, posse, posse commitatus.

milk, *n.* **1.** cream, cow's milk, goat's milk, beestings, breast milk, mother's milk, kumiss; whey, curds, junket, buttermilk, skim milk; bonnyclabber, posset, *Fine Arts.* casein.
2. latex, sap, juice, fluid.
—*v.* **3.** extract, remove, draw out, draw off, siphon off, pump out; decant, empty, tap, let out, squeeze out; phlebotomize, bleed.
4. drain, bleed, suck dry, sap; misuse, abuse, exploit, use, take advantage of.

milk-livered, *adj.* cowardly, pusillanimous, poltroon, caitiff; weak-kneed, *Sl.* chicken, *Sl.* gutless, skittish; faint-hearted, chicken-hearted, lily-livered, chicken-livered, *Inf.* mousy; sniveling, cringing, skulking, quailing, cowering; timid, timorous, shy, meek, tame, mild; weak, frail, effeminate, soft, womanish; unmanly, sissy, sissified, milksoppy, candy-assed; afraid, frightened, fearful, intimidated, cowed.

milksop, *n.* coward, poltroon, *Archaic.* caitiff, dastard; milquetoast, sop, mama's boy, namby-pamby, *Inf.* jellyfish; weakling, chicken, baby, crybaby, sissy, mouse, *Sl.* fraidy-cat, *Sl.* scaredy-cat; effeminate, *Inf.* pantywaist, *Sl.* pansy, *Sl.* wimp, eakling, mollycoddle, softy; weak sister, goody-goody, mother's darling, nancy, Lord Fauntleroy.

milky, *adj.* **1.** lacteal, lactic, milk, milch; lactescent, lactiferous, emulsive.
2. white, creamy, pearly, nacreous, chalky, cretaceous; cloudy, opaque, fumé, frosted, semipellucid, mat; whitish, albescent, adularescent, canescent; snowy, niveous, hoar, hoary; milk-white, snow-white, swan-white; ivory, alabaster, eburnean, eggshell, glaucous, off-white.
3. meek, tame, mild, gentle, pacific; timid, timorous, shy. See **milk-livered**.

Milky Way, *n.* *Astronomy.* Galaxy, *Latin.* Via Lactea.

mill, *n.* **1.** factory, manufactory, plant, foundry, works, industrial center; workshop, shop; windmill, *Fr. moulin*; gin, roller, crusher, grinder, grater, quern.
—*v.* **2.** grind, granulate, pulverize, comminute, triturate, powder; grate, bray, pound, crush, crunch.
3. stir, beat, whip, whisk, froth.
4. *Slang.* beat, pummel, punch, *Inf.* slug, hit, strike; fight, box, spar; overcome, defeat, trounce.
5. *Often* **mill about** *or* **around** move around, wander, amble, meander; jostle, bump into, shoulder.

millennium, *n.* **1.** a thousand years, chiliad, millenary.
2. **the millennium** the Second Coming, the Second Advent, the Parousia.
3. golden age, utopia, halcyon days, heaven on earth.

milliner, *n.* hatter, modiste.

million, *n.* **1.** great number, lot, heap, *Inf.* slew, jillion, *Inf.* tons, *Inf.* loads, *Inf.* gobs; reams, slathers, *Sl.* scads, *Sl.* wad.
2. **the million** the general public, the public; the multitude, the masses, the common people, the working class, the lower class, the common herd, huddled masses; the common man, the man in the street; proletariat, plebians, the hoi polloi, the rank and file.

millionaire, *n.* man *or* woman of means, rich man, wealthy man, moneyed man, man of wealth, man of substance, coupon clipper, nabob, nawab, *Inf.* moneybags, *Brit. Inf.* warm man, *Sl.* fat cat; Midas, Croesus, Dives; multimillionare, billionaire; sugar daddy; plutocrat, capitalist.

millstone, *n.* **1.** grindstone, muller; mill, quern, grinder, mortar and pestle, crusher, chopper, grater.
2. load, burden, tax, *Archaic.* fardel, weight, dead weight, onus; duty, obligation, responsibility, charge, task; affliction, trouble, misfortune, cross.

milquetoast, *n.* namby-pamby, mama's boy, milksop, sop, mollycoddle, Walter Mitty, *Inf.* jellyfish; sissy, eakling, *Inf.* pantywaist, *Sl.* pansy, *Sl.* wimp; *Sl.* schlepp, *Sl.* schlemiel, *Sl.* nebbish, *Sl.* schnook, *Sl.* twirp, *Sl.* twit, *Sl.* nerd; *Inf.* lightweight, featherweight, *Sl.* pushover, *Sl.* patsy, *Sl.* sap; loser, *Sl.* sad sack.

mime, *n.* **1.** pantomime, impersonation, personation, harlequinade, farce: parody, caricature, burlesque, burletta, travesty, satire, *Inf.* take-off, lampoon; comedy, slapstick comedy, tragedy, drama, play; entertainment, amusement, diversion, divertissement.

2. mimer, pantomimist, mimist, mummer, Marcel Marceau, impersonator; satirist, *Fr. farceur*, performer, actor, actress, entertainer, player, strolling player, *Fr. comédien ambulant*; jester, fool, clown, merry-andrew, zany, harlequin, buffoon; pantaloon, straight man, foil, *U.S. Sl.* fall guy; comedian, comedienne, comic, stand-up comic.

3. mimic, imitator, copyist. See **mimic** (*def.* **3**).

—*v.* **4.** mimic, impersonate, copy. See **mimic** (*def.* **1**).

mimic, *v.* **1.** imitate, copy, *Inf.* copycat, ape, monkey; impersonate, personate, represent, mirror, simulate, make like, affect *or* put on [s.o.'s] mannerisms; satirize, *Inf.* do a take-off on, mock, ridicule, make fun of; parrot, echo, repeat, cuckoo.

2. resemble, look like, be similar to.

—*n.* **3.** mimicker, imitator, copyist, *Inf.* copycat; ape, monkey, echo, parrot, mockingbird; impersonator, personator, mime, mimer, pantomimist, mimist. See **mime** (*def.* **2**).

—*adj.* **4.** mimetic, *Archaic.* mimical, imitational, mock, simulated, fake, pseudo; ungenuine, unreal, false, counterfeit, sham, feigned, pretended, pretend, make-believe.

5. imitating, imitative, copying, me-too, parroting, echoing, repeating.

mimicry, *n.* imitation, copying, reproduction, apery, *Rhet.* mimesis; impersonation, personation, representation, simulation, affectation; mimicking, parroting, echoing, repeating; mockery, pretense, ridicule, derision, raillery; *Inf.* take-off, satire, satirization, burlesque, burletta, travesty, lampoon, parody, caricature; mime, harlequinade, farce.

minacious, *adj.* minatory, minatorial, menacing, threatening, ominous; portentous, unpropitious, unfavorable, bad, dangerous; dark, cloudy, clouded, overcast, like rain.

mince, *v.* **1.** dice, hash, cube, chop up, chop, cut up, slice; splinter, sliver, crumble, crumb, fragment, break up; subdivide, divide up, *Inf.* divvy, apportion, partition.

2. euphemize, speak in euphemisms, use nice *or* mild *or* delicate language, use delicate speech, soften one's speech, curb one's speech, hold one's tongue.

3. attitudinize, strike a pose, pose, put on airs, be affected, put on a show; act *or* be dainty *or* delicate, effeminate, *Inf.* extend one's pinkie; simper, lisp; pussyfoot, take baby steps, putter, walk like a girl *or* woman, *Sl.* swish.

mincing, *adj.* **1.** (*of gait, speech, behavior, etc.*) dainty, overdainty, precious, sweet, effeminate, feminine, womanish, girlish, sissyish, sissy, pussyfooting, namby-pamby, niminy-piminy, *Sl.* cutesy; dandified, dandyish, foppish, coxcombic, coxcombical; mealy-mouthed, overnice, nice, overdelicate, delicate, euphemistic, euphemistical, euphemious; proper, prim, prudish, priggish, finicky, finical, fastidious, *Sl.* uptight.

2. affected, assumed, mannered, studied, pretentious, put on, *Inf.* la-di-da, *Inf.* too-too.

mind, *n.* **1.** intellect, intellectual *or* mental faculty *or* powers, cognitive function; psyche, ego, subconscious, *Psychoanal.* the conscious, *Metaphys.* I, *Philos.* self; soul, spirit, inner being, inner man, psychic *or* spiritual being.

2. genius, intellectual, mental giant, thinker, *Inf.* brain, *Inf.* Einstein, *All Inf.* wizard, wiz, whiz.

3. intelligence, intellectuality, mentality, mental aptitude *or* capacity *or* capability *or* ability; cognitive ability, ability to comprehend *or* understand, percipience, insight, apperception, perception; brainpower, braininess, brains, brain, cerebrum, wit, parts, *Inf.* gray matter, *Sl.* smarts, *Gk. Philos.* nous; head, good head on one's shoulders, *Inf.* noggin, *Inf.* noodle; cleverness, wittiness, quickness, esprit.

4. sanity, saneness, soundness of mind, presence of mind, senses, wits, *Sl.* marbles; rationality, reason, sense of reason, logical *or* ratiocinative powers, judgment, common sense.

5. disposition, temperament, temper, nature, humor, grain, vein, cast; inclination, tendency, turn, bent, leaning, proneness, proclivity, propensity.

6. sentiment, feeling, affection, partiality, partialness, bias, liking; belief, credence, conviction, persuasion, thought, faith; opinion, view, viewpoint, position, attitude, impression.

7. notion, idea, whim, fancy, temptation; urge, itch, desire, willingness, will; intention, intent, aim, purpose, design.

8. **bear** *or* **keep in mind** remember, retain, don't forget, hold; be mindful of, take cognizance of.

9. **cross one's mind** occur to one, enter one's head, come to one; enter one's thoughts, come into one's consciousness.

10. **know one's own mind** be resolute *or* resolved, be decisive, be decided, be certain, be definite *or* absolute, be absolutely certain, be firm *or* fixed; be self-assured, understand *or* be in touch with oneself, have assurance *or* confidence, be self-confident, be poised.

11. **make up one's mind** decide, come to *or* reach a decision, resolve, conclude; draw a conclusion, settle on, form an opinion; *Inf.* fish *or* cut bait, choose, pick *or* pick out, select.

12. **meeting of minds** agreement, mutual understanding, concurrence; accord, accordance, concord, concordance, harmony; consensus, unanimity, unison.

13. **presence of mind** rationality, rationalness, sanity, saneness; intelligence, wits about oneself, control, quickness.

14. **put in mind** remind, recall, call up, take one back to [s.t.]; suggest, connote, bring up, allude to.

15. **to one's mind** in one's opinion, according to one's way of thinking, the way one looks at [s.t.], to one's view *or* viewpoint, to one's thinking, in one's judgment, in one's estimation.

16. thoughts, thinking, consciousness, whole being; attention, eye, ear.

—*v.* **17.** attend to, pay attention to, give one's attention to, turn one's attention to, advert to, pay a mind to, fix *or* set one's mind on; notice, take notice of, note, take note of, mark; watch, see, observe, regard, perceive; heed, pay heed to, listen to, hear, give ear to; obey, follow, abide by, practice, hold by, adhere to, respect.

18. attend, tend to, watch, watch over, look after, keep an eye on *or* out for; take care of, care for, sit, babysit.

19. guard, be on guard, be alert, be careful *or* cautious about, be wary *or* guarded, watch out, stop, look and listen; think about *or* over, think twice about, consider, weigh, censor.

20. care, care about [s.t.], care one way or the other, feel concern about; object to, disapprove of, look askance at, condemn; have any objection to, feel inconvenienced *or* annoyed by, get disturbed by, be offended by; dislike, disrelish, have no taste for, disdain, turn up one's nose at, have an aversion to, detest, loathe, abhor, despise, hate; eschew, avoid, steer clear of, refuse to touch with a 10-foot pole; shun, shy away from, recoil from, shrink from, shudder at.

21. **never mind** disregard [s.t.], pay no attention to [s.t.], strike *or* cancel [s.t.] from one's mind, forget it; don't give [s.t.] a thought *or* think twice about it, don't bother.

minded, *adj.* disposed, inclined, tending toward, leaning toward, of a mind, in the mood; desirous, willing, ready, enthusiastic, eager, keen; determined, resolved, bent upon, intending, aiming, designing, planning.

mindful, *adj.* **1.** *Usu.* **mindful of** attentive, observant, regardful, noticing, open-eyed, alert, wide-awake, sharp, alive to, *Inf.* on the job; listening, all ears, advertent, *Archaic.* attent; heedful, obedient, compliant, respectful.

2. *Usu.* **mindful of** careful, cautious, wary, chary, guarded, on guard, watchful, aware, on the lookout, on the qui vive, vigilant; prudent, circumspect, thoughtful, considerate, astute, shrewd, wise, *Scot.* canny; prepared, ready, on one's toes, provident, precautious.

mindless, *adj.* **1.** senseless, nonsensical, insensate, brainless, witless, empty-headed, *Brit. Inf.* gormless, *Rare.* insulse; unintelligent, dull, dull-witted, dim-witted, slow, slow-witted, half-witted, weak-minded, weak-headed, feeble-minded, retarded, imbecilic, *Inf.* dopey, *Inf.* dill, *Inf.* moronic, *Inf.* dumb, *Inf.* cretinous, *Sl.* lamebrained; bird-brained, harebrained, simple-minded, simple, featherbrained, featherheaded, light-headed, foolish, silly, absurd, half-baked, inane, asinine, anserine, fatuous, fatuitous, idiotic, idiotical, *Inf.* damfool; scatterbrained, rattleheaded, rattlebrained, addleheaded, addlebrained, addlepated, muddleheaded; irrational, illogical, unreasonable, unreasoning; mentally unsound *or* unstable, demented, insane, out of one's mind, crackbrained, mad, crazy, *Sl.* cockeyed, *Sl.* cuckoo, *Sl.* nuts.

2. inattentive, heedless, unheeding, unobservant, unnoticing, regardless, inadvertent, blind, deaf; musing, wandering, distracted, daydreaming, engrossed *or* lost in thought *or* reverie, off in a world of one's own, a million miles away, faraway, *Fr. distrait.*

3. careless, unmindful, unwary, unwatchful, unvigilant, unguarded, off guard, caught napping, *Inf.* asleep on the job, *Inf.* not on the job, *Inf.* asleep at the switch *or* wheel; improvident, unprepared, unready, short-sighted, negligent, neglectful, remiss; imprudent, indescreet, ill-considered, unwise, ill-advised, inconsiderate, thoughtless, unthinking; precipitate, rash, impulsive, headlong, reckless, foolhardy, irresponsible.

mine, *n.* **1.** colliery, excavation, well, pit; open pit, strip mine, quarry; lode, vein, deposit, *U.S.* bonanza.

2. wealth, abundance, gold mine, fund; source, store, storehouse, treasury, reservoir, repository.

3. explosive, *Inf.* ashcan, depth charge; land mine, booby trap, infernal machine, time bomb.

4. sap, trench, ha-ha, tunnel, burrow, shaft, adit.

—*v.* **5.** excavate, dig, delve; core, burrow, tunnel; extract, scoop out, remove.

6. undermine, sap, subvert, wear down, erode; beleaguer, besiege.

mingle, *v.* **1.** associate, hobnob, pal around, get together, fraternize, band together, hang out; socialize, keep open house, keep the latchstring out, *Sl.* party, rub elbows, rub shoulders, mill.

2. participate, take part, join in, enter in, get in the swim.

3. mix, commingle, intermingle, intermix; consolidate, amalgamate, jumble; combine, blend, merge; intertwine, interweave.

4. unite, join, conjoin, connect, marry; unify, coalesce; fuse, agglutinate.

miniature, *adj.* small-scale, mini, midget, bantam, toy, Lilliputian, vest-pocket; reduced, diminished, abridged, shrunk; diminutive, wee, little, tiny, minute, microscopic; small, teeny, weeny.

minikin, *adj.* dainty, exquisite, lovely, fastidious, finicky; delicate, fragile, frail, slight, wispy, doll-like; mincing, affected, precious, précieuse; simpering, coy, cute, *Sl.* cutesy, nice, *Sl.* nicy-nice.

minimize, *v.* **1.** lessen, attenuate, decrease, cut down, prune, pare, minify; reduce, diminish, condense, abridge, curtail, abbreviate, shorten.

2. slight, underestimate, underrate, undervalue, beggar, extenuate, underreckon, misprize, think nothing of, set no store by, fail to count on; de-emphasize, underplay, make light of, make little of, downplay, *Inf.* play down, *Inf.* soft-pedal; decry, detract, disparage, demean, deprecate, belittle, deflate, depreciate, devaluate, downgrade, damn with faint praise, *Inf.* talk down; criticize, dispraise, cut up, shred, pull to pieces, *Sl.* do a number on, *Sl.* do a hatchet job on, carp at, cavil at, peck at, *Inf.* knock, *Inf.* rap; lampoon, pasquinade, caricature, satirize; ridicule, mock, poke fun at, laugh at.

minimum, *n.* **1.** least *or* lowest amount, minimal amount, least quantity; lowest limit, bottom line; least, limit, margin.

2. cover charge, service charge, fee, admission.

minion, *n.* **1.** flunky, lackey, yes man, jackal, spaniel, bootlick, bootlicker, footlicker, lickspit, lickspittle, kowtower, Uncle Tom, Tom, *Sl.* oreo; sycophant, fawner, toady, toadeater, truckler, tufthunter, courtier, wheedler, puffer, backslapper, backscratcher, timeserver, *Inf.* apple-polisher, *Sl.* brownnose, *Sl.* brown-noser, *Sl.* brownie; parasite, leech, sponge, sponger, *Sl.* mooch, *Sl.* moocher, hanger-on.

2. favorite, idol; darling, jewel, apple of one's eye, beloved.

3. minor official, subordinate, deputy, assistant; hireling, underling, inferior.

minister, *n.* **1.** clergyman, cleric, ecclesiastic; pastor, shepherd, parson, *Dial.* dominie, man of the cloth, servant of God, reverend; father, padre, priest; liturgist, *Obs., Rare.* liturge; preacher, evangelist, missionary, revivalist, *Usu. Disparaging.* pulpiteer; rector, vicar, dean, *Brit.* incumbent; curate, curé, abbé, chaplain, *U.S. Mil. Sl.* sky pilot, *U.S. Mil. Sl.* Holy Joe; divine, canonist, exegete, hierophant.

2. department chief, department head, superintendent; cabinet member, secretary, commissioner, chancellor, provost; official, dignitary; premier, prime minister.

3. ambassador, diplomat, plenipotentiary, *Brit.* diplomatist; emissary, envoy, consul, agent, legate, representative, delegate; chargé d'affaires.

4. servant, underling, subordinate, lieutenant, surrogate, proxy, deputy, agent, substitute, *Brit.* locum tenens.

—*v.* **5.** (*of religious functions*) officiate, execute, perform, carry out; preside, direct, administer, lead; serve, do duty.

6. *Usu.* **minister to** serve, care for, attend to, wait on pander to; accommodate, oblige, befriend, favor; help, aid, assist, abet, succor, relieve, comfort, console, give solace; doctor, nurse, heal, cure, remedy.

7. *Usu.* **minister to** give to, contribute to, supply, furnish, favor with; lavish, indulge, shower upon, dote upon; offer, present, dole out.

ministerial, *adj.* **1.** clerical, priestly, sacerdotal, pastoral; ecclesiastical, hierarchical, prelatic, canonical, capitular.

2. ambassadorial, diplomatic, consular, emissary, representative, plenipotentiary, official, *Inf.* cabinet.

3. ministering, serving, comforting, assuaging, nursing, doctoring, solacing; aiding, assisting, helping, ministrant.

4. instrumental, contributory, subsidiary, attendant, assistant, subservient, clerkly, auxiliary, ancillary.

ministration, *n.* **1.** supervision, stewardship, care, administration, superintendence, protectorship; direction, regulation, management, government, conduct, execution.

2. aid, aidance, help, assistance, cooperation, coadjuvancy, *Obs.* opitulation; support, succor, relief, subvention; promotion, advance, furtherance, patronage, auspices; countenance, favor, advocacy, championship; solace, comfort, consolation, care, alleviation.

3. religious service, liturgy, rite, ritual, ceremony, ceremonial; preaching, counseling, ministering; sacrament, extreme unction, last rites, visitation of the sick, viaticum.

ministry, *n.* **1.** holy orders, sacred calling, religious vocation, religion, priesthood, the pulpit, the desk; prelacy, pastorate, rectorship, vicarage.

2. clergymen, clergy, clericals, the cloth; presbytery, elders.

3. department, agency, administration.

4. instrumentality, agency, service, *Inf.* good graces, auspices, intervention, interposition.

5. See **ministration** (*def.* **2**).

minor, *adj.* **1.** lesser, smaller, secondary, subordinate, lower, second-fiddle; subsidiary, ancillary, tributary, *Law.* puisne; second-class, small-time, one-horse, bush, bush-league, *Sl.* two bit, *Sl.* small potatoes, small-fry; unimportant, insignificant, inconsequential, inconsiderable, not worth mentioning, slight, little; petty, trite, *Sl.* mickey mouse, trivial, trifling, niggling, piddling, paltry, *Inf.* picayune.

2. mediocre, middling, moderate, so-so, indifferent, passable, tolerable, *Inf.* O.K.; inferior, second-rate, low grade, lightweight, amateurish, unprofessional, incompetent, not up to par *or* snuff.

3. under-age, adolescent, junior, infant.

—n. **4.** child, infant, *U.S. Inf.* tad, youngster, youth, stripling, adolescent, teenager; lad, lass, lassie, maiden, girl, schoolgirl, schoolboy, boy, whippersnapper, cub, small fry.

5. subordinate, inferior, underling, subject, menial; deputy, assistant, subsidiary, hireling; nonentity, cipher, nobody, *Inf.* whiffet.

minority, *n.* **1.** smaller part *or* number, less than half, handful.

2. splinter group, faction, contingent, sector, section, side; ethnic group.

3. nonage, juniority, pupilage; infancy, childhood, girlhood, boyhood, youth, adolescence, puberty, juvenility, juvenescence.

minstrel, *n.* **1.** wandering minstrel, troubadour, bard, (*in medieval France and Norman England*) jongleur; skald, minnesinger, meistersinger *or* mastersinger, (*in ancient Greece*) rhapsodist; musician, singer, balladeer, poet; lyric poet, lyrist, poet laureate, laureate, epic poet, epicist.

2. *Theat.* blackface, *U.S.* interlocutor, end man; vaudevillian, song-and-dance man, comedian, comic, actor, performer, player, entertainer.

minstrelsy, *n.* song, ballad, recitative, lyric poem, poem, epic poem, rhapsody.

mint[1], *n.* **1.** spearmint, peppermint, horsemint; crème de menthe.

—adj. **2.** mint-flavored.

mint[2], *n.* **1.** *Informal.* fortune, small fortune, millions, billions; money, *U.S. Sl.* bucks, *Sl.* bread; (*all of money*) *Sl.* wad, pile, stack, heap, *Inf.* stash.

—adj. **2.** unused, uncancelled, unstamped, new, brand-new, perfect, excellent.

—v. **3.** (*all of coins or money*) stamp *or* stamp out, die, coin, monetize, print.

4. make, make up, compose, fabricate, invent, create, come up with, coin, neologize, neoterize; devise, concoct, brew, contrive, frame, hatch; formulate, design, conceive, germinate, think of, dream up; manufacture, fashion, form, construct, produce; forge, counterfeit, copy.

minus, *prep.* **1.** from, less, take away, subtract; decreased by, diminished by.

2. lacking, missing, short, without.

—n. **3.** deficit, loss; lack, insufficiency, deficiency; weakness, weak spot, liability, disadvantage, drawback.

minute[1], *n.* **1.** a short time, a little while, bit, *Inf.* jiffy, *Inf.* whipstitch; moment, second, *Inf.* sec, split second, instant; flash, twinkling, twinkle, breath, trice; eyewink, wink of an eye, *Fr. coup d'oeil*, twinkling of an eye, *Inf.* bat of an eye, two shakes of a lamb's tail.

2. rough draft, sketch, outline, summary, resumé; memorandum, *Inf.* memo, note.

3. **minutes** (*all of a meeting*) record, notes, log, transcript.

4. **up to the minute** modern, up-to-date, trendy, fashionable, smart, modish, stylish, in style, chic, in vogue, all the rage; *Inf.* in, *Sl.* with it, *Sl.* hip, *Sl.* cool.

minute[2], *adj.* **1.** minuscule, infinitesimal, microscopic, atomic, animalculine, animalculous, imperceptible; diminutive, Lilliputian, tiny, wee, *Inf.* teeny, bitty, itty-bitty, eensy-weensy, teensy, *Baby Talk.* teeny-weeny, *Baby Talk.* teensy-weensy; miniature, small-scale, pocket-sized, bantam, short; small, little, mini, pint-sized, *Inf.* baby; petite, delicate, dainty, minikin; homuncular, midget, dwarfish, *Med.* nanoid, pygmy, pygmoid, pygmyish.

2. insignificant, unimportant, inconsequential, minor, small, little; trivial, trifling, petty, *Inf.* picayune, niggling; meager, mere, paltry, puny, slight, slender, thin, dinky, piddling; insubstantial, unsubstantial, negligible, nugatory, inconsiderable, inappreciable.

3. detailed, exact, precise, punctilious, scrupulous, strict, close; particular, meticulous, careful, painstaking.

minutiae, *n.* details, particulars, fine points; trivia, trivialities, trifles, inessentials, nonessentials, unessentials.

minx, *n.* impudent lass, pert girl, *Inf.* baggage; hussy, shrew, quean; jade, harridan, hag, *Sl.* bitch; malapert, *Inf.* saucebox; flirt, coquette, vamp, belle, gold digger; jilt, wanton, tart, demirep; prostitute, harlot, strumpet, drab, trollop, *Archaic.* wench, trull, slut.

miracle, *n.* marvel, wonder, wonderwork, prodigy; sign, portent, omen; supernatural event, phenomenon; curiosity, spectacle, rarity.

miraculous, *adj.* **1.** supernatural, preternatural, preternormal, superhuman, preterhuman, thaumaturgic, thaumaturgical; divine, almighty, omnipotent, godly, godlike; otherworldly, unearthly, supermundane, supramundane, extramundane; incomprehensible, impenetrable, beyond comprehension *or* understanding, unfathomable; unaccountable, inexplicable, unexplainable; freakish, curious, unusual, mysterious, awesome.

2. marvelous, wondrous, extraordinary, remarkable, phenomenal; surprising, unheard-of, unprecedented, unparalleled, unexampled; fabulous, fantastic, *Sl.* far-out; amazing, astounding, astonishing; staggering, breathtaking, mind-boggling, *Sl.* mind-blowing, *Sl.* out of this world.

mirage, *n.* optical illusion, looming, hallucination, vision, phantasmagoria; phantasm, shadow, specter, apparition, phantom, will-o'-the-wisp, ignis fatuus.

mire, *n.* **1.** marsh, swamp, swampland, fen, fenland, marshland, quagmire, quag, bog, slough, morass, *Brit. Dial.* lair, mud, mud flat, *Brit.* holm, *Brit.* sough, *Brit. Dial.* sump.

—*v.* **2.** soil, dirty, begrime, blacken, tarnish; sully, befoul, defile; smear, tar, grease; draggle, bemire, *Archaic.* daggle, spatter, muddy, blotch; smudge, smutch, smirch, bedaub.

3. sink, sink down, bog, bog down, stick in the mud; become entangled, become tangled up, become enmeshed, become involved.

mirror, *n.* **1.** reflecting surface, reflector; looking glass, cheval glass.

2. reflection, twin, counterpart; imitation, reproduction, copy, replica, replication; representation, semblance, likeness.

3. exemplar, paragon, ideal, beau ideal, *Latin. ne plus ultra*; model, pattern, paradigm; archetype, prototype, original.

—*v.* **4.** reflect, return, give back; echo, reecho, repeat.

5. imitate, emulate, do like, simulate, copy, follow suit, parallel, model after, copycat; ape, monkey, parrot; impersonate, mock, parody, take off, caricature.

6. reproduce, represent, show, exhibit, manifest, display; disclose, bring to view, put before one's eyes.

mirth, *n.* **1.** gaiety, gayness, mirthfulness, merriment, hilarity, good *or* high spirits, glee, jocundity; joviality, jollity, levity, buoyancy, light-heartedness, blithesomeness; fun, enjoyment, cakes and ale, revelry, revel, conviviality, festivity, partying, playing, sport; noise, noisiness, vociferousness, boisterousness, laughter, rowdiness, *Sl.* hell-raising, rabble-rousing.

2. cheer, cheerfulness, joyfulness, joyousness; joy, delight, pleasure, happiness, felicity; elation, exhilaration, exuberance, enthusiasm, vivacity, animation, liveliness, effervescence; exultation, jubilance, jubilancy, rejoicing, celebration, jollification.

mirthful, *adj.* **1.** cheerful, cheery, full of cheer, merry, gay, sunny, in good *or* high spirits; blithe, blithesome, light-hearted, lightsome, buoyant, optimistic, positive, *Inf.* upbeat, beamish; debonair, free and easy, carefree, easygoing, breezy, airy, happy-go-lucky, untroubled; genial, convivial, amiable, good-natured, friendly; jovial, jocund, jolly, hilarious; riant, laughing, smiling, happy as a lark; happy, glad, blissful, beatific, pleased, delighted, *Inf.* tickled pink; joyful, joyous, jubilant, rejoicing, gleeful; exultant, in seventh heaven, elated, overjoyed, thrilled, exhilarated; animated, lively, *Chiefly U.S. Inf.* chipper, jaunty, vivacious, sprightly.

2. amusing, laughable, funny, comical, witty, humorous, jolly; hilarious, sidesplitting, ludicrous, ridiculous, farcical; facetious, droll, salty, waggish.

miry, *adj.* dirty, unclean, soiled, grimy, grubby, stained, spotted, smudged; filthy, muddy, muddied, slimy, oozy; bedraggled, dirt-encrusted; foul, begrimed, besmeared, smirchy, befouled; *Inf.* sloppy, *Inf.* scruffy, *Sl.* crummy, *Sl.* grungy, *Sl.* yucky.

misadventure, *n.* **1.** misfortune, mishap, mischance, miscarriage, *Scot. and North Eng.* mishanter, glitch, casualty, accident; shock, blow, nasty *or* staggering blow, buffet, stroke, stroke of bad luck *or* fortune; tragedy, disaster, calamity, catastrophe, cataclysm.

2. mistake, blunder, *Inf.* slip-up, *Sl.* boner, *Sl.* boo-boo; slip, leak; failure, fiasco, *Inf.* flop, *Inf.* fizzle, *Inf.* dud, *Inf.* washout, *Sl.* bomb, *Sl.* turkey.

3. adversity, affliction, hurt, harm, evil, woe, *Archaic.* ruin, ruination, bale; infelicity, ill *or* bad luck, ill *or* bad fortune, evil wind, dark cloud *or* star, storm clouds; trouble, the devil to pay; reverse, reversal, reverse of fortune, setback, comedown, bitter pill; cross, check, checkmate.

misanthrope, *n.* hater of mankind, man-hater, woman-hater, misogynist, misogamist; loner, hermit, recluse, lone wolf; egoist, narcissist, cynic.

misanthropic, *adj.* man-hating, woman-hating, misogynic; egoistic, narcissistic, egocentric, cynical, wrapped up in oneself; antisocial, unsociable, hard to get along with; surly, discourteous, short, rude, impolite; uncaring, unsympathetic, inhumane.

misanthropy, *n.* hatred *or* distrust of mankind, misogyny, misogamy; egoism, narcissism, egocentricity, selfishness, going one's own way, looking out for number one, cynicism; surliness, cruelty, inhumanity, malevolence.

misapply, *v.* misuse, misemploy, misappropriate.

misapprehend, *v.* misunderstand, mistake, be mistaken, misread, misconstrue, misconceive, misinterpret; misjudge, miscalculate, miscount, misreckon; get the wrong idea, get a false impression; slip up, *Sl.* goof, err, blunder.

misapprehension, *n.* misunderstanding, misconstruction, misreading, mistaking, misconception, misinterpretation; misjudgment, miscalculation; warped *or* mistaken notion, wrong idea, false belief *or* impression; fallacy, error, delusion, distortion.

misappropriate, *v.* **1.** steal, peculate, embezzle, *Law.* defalcate; swindle, pocket, mulct, shark.

2. misuse, misemploy, misapply; abuse, profane, desecrate, prostitute, pervert; misspend, squander, waste, dissipate, *Sl.* blow.

misappropriation, *n.* **1.** stealing, theft, thievery, robbery; peculation, embezzlement, *Law.* defalcation; swindling, pocketing, mulcting, sharking.

2. misuse, misapplication; abuse, profanation, desecration, prostitution, perversion.

misbegotten, *adj.* **1.** illegitimate, misbegot, bastard, spurious, base; natural, unfathered, baseborn, hedgeborn, adulterine.

2. ill-gotten, illicit, unlawful, contraband, black-market.

3. deformed, miscreated, misshapen, ill-made, ugly, grotesque; hunchbacked, humpbacked, malformed, twisted, crippled, crooked.

misbehave, *v.* misconduct oneself, show poor manners, be bad, disobey, not listen, *Brit.* kick over the traces; carry on, act up, *Inf.* fool around, *Inf.* cut up, *Inf.* horse around; *Inf.* raise the devil, *Inf.* raise heck, *Inf.* raise hob, *Inf.* raise red, *Sl.* raise hell; forget oneself, err, transgress, trespass; fail, slip, trip, commit a faux pas, offend.

misbehaved, *adj.* naughty, bad, impish, mischievous, disobedient, misbehaving; disorderly, rowdy, boisterous, noisy; unmannerly, rude, ill-mannered, ill-behaved, discourteous; ungentlemanly, unladylike, ungracious, uncivil, indecorous.

misbehavior, *n.* misconduct, badness, naughtiness, misdemeanor, delinquency; disorderly conduct, bad manners, indiscipline, disobedience, insubordination; disorder, disorderliness, *Inf.* goings on; roughhouse, horseplay, mayhem, rowdyism, rowdiness, boisterousness; indiscretion, faux pas, trip, slip, blunder, error.

misbelief, *n.* **1.** miscreance, heresy, heterodoxy, heresiarchy, superstition, false creed; skepticism, doubt, Pyrrhonism; fallacy, error, mistake.

2. delusion, illusion, false impression, wrong impression; misconception, misapprehension, misunderstanding, misinterpretation, misconstruction.

miscalculate, *v.* misjudge, misreckon, miscount, miscompute; misestimate, misdeem, misread, misevaluate, misappreciate, misvalue; underestimate, overestimate, undervalue, overvalue, underreckon, overreckon, underrate, overrate; rush to conclusions, jump to a conclusion; err, blunder, go wrong, mistake, miss, slip up.

miscarriage, *n.* **1.** failure, nonsuccess, nonfulfillment, defeat, frustration; failing, abortion, no-go, vain attempt, flash in the pan, disappointment; accident, casualty, mishap, misfortune, mischance; miss, botch, muff, slip, blunder; washout; collapse, fizzle, fiasco, wild-goose chase; deathblow, checkmate, rebuff, repulse; overthrow, rout; wreck, shipwreck, crash, debacle, ruination.

2. abortus, spontaneous abortion, premature birth *or* delivery, untimely birth, unnatural birth.

miscarry, *v.* fail, go wrong, abort, be unsuccessful; flounder, slip, stumble, blunder; shipwreck, run aground, come to grief, meet with disaster; miss the mark, miss the boat, fall short of, fall through, fall flat, come to nothing, fizzle; be defected, lick the dust, bite the dust, lose the day, end *or* go up in smoke, go to wrack and ruin.

miscellaneous, *adj.* **1.** diverse, varied, mixed, various, selected, assorted; variform, multiplex, multiform, many-sided, multiphase; multifarious, manifold, omnifarious.

2. heterogeneous, diversified, farraginous; indiscriminate, promiscuous; motley, variegated, patched, patchwork; commingled, commixed, composite, compound, blended.

miscellany, *n.* **1.** assortment, diversity, mixture, mélange, medley; gallimaufry, farrago, salmagundi, potpourri, hodgepodge, *Brit.* hotchpotch; hash, stew, jumble, tangle, mess; oddments, all sorts, *Inf.* mixed bag, odds and ends, sundries, old curiosity shop; variegation, patchwork, mosaic, motley; a little of this and a little of that; this, that, and the other; olla-podrida, olio, variety; commixture, conglomeration, combination, *Inf.* omnium-gatherum, *Inf.* mingle-mangle, Noah's ark.

2. miscellanea, collectanea, anthology, ana, compendium, collection; florilegium, flowers, spicilegium.

3. miscellanies, marginalia, jottings, notes, selections, pieces, thoughts; extracts, excerpta, analecta, analects.

mischance, *n.* **1.** accident, misfortune, mishap, miscarriage, misadventure, *Scot. and North Eng.* mishanter *or* mischanter, glitch, casualty, contretemps; blow, nasty *or* staggering blow, buffet, stroke, stroke of bad luck *or* fortune; disaster, tragedy, calamity, catastrophe, cataclysm.

2. mistake, blunder, *Inf.* slip-up, *Sl.* boner, *Sl.* booboo; slip, leak; oversight.

3. fluke, freak accident, one in a million, twist of fate; shock.

4. adversity, affliction, hurt, harm, evil, woe, *Archaic.* ruin, ruination, bale; infelicity, ill *or* bad luck, ill *or* bad fortune, evil wind, dark cloud, storm clouds; trouble, the devil to pay; reverse, reversal, reverse of fortune, setback, comedown, bitter pill; cross, check, checkmate; failure, fiasco, *Inf.* flop, *Inf.* fizzle, *Inf.* washout, *Inf.* dud, *Sl.* bomb, *Sl.* turkey.

mischief, *n.* **1.** harm, trouble, hurt, ill, wrong; destruction, unmaking, undoing, disruption, demolition, sabotage; vexation, annoyance, nuisance, agitation, pique.

2. injury, impairment, damage, disablement, incapacitation, weakening; ravage, scathe, detriment.

3. misconduct, misbehavior, misdemeanor, delinquency; badness, naughtiness, bad manners, disobedience; roguery, impishness, rascality, elfishness; *Inf.* goings-on, *Inf.* hanky-panky, *Sl.* monkey business.

mischief-maker, *n.* **1.** troublemaker, imp, bad boy, little devil, *Inf.* bugger, *Inf.* booger; elf, puck, pixie, little rascal, little monkey; rascal, rogue, rapscallion, knave, scamp; rowdy, hoodlum, juvenile delinquent, hooligan, hell-raiser, thug, ruffian, vandal.

2. talebearer, rumormonger, storyteller, gossip, busybody; tattler, tattletale, wag; quidnunc, meddler, *Sl.* stickybeak.

3. agitator, firebrand, rabble-rouser, instigator; provoker, inciter, fomenter, rouser, *Fr. provocateur.*

mischievous, *adj.* **1.** harmful, injurious, hurtful, damaging, scatheful; pernicious, detrimental, baleful, deleterious, baneful; noxious, venomous, poisonous, malign, malignant.

2. impish, waggish, prankish, elfish, puckish; naughty, roguish, scampish, arch, *Scot.* hempy; playful, sportive, full of mischief, fond of mischief, frolicsome; annoying, vexatious, exasperating, teasing.

misconceive, *v.* misunderstand, misapprehend, misconstrue, misread, misinterpret; misjudge, miscalculate; form the wrong notion, get the wrong idea; get off on the wrong foot, get a false start, jump the gun, go off half-cocked.

misconception, *n.* misunderstanding, misapprehension, misconstruction, misreading, misinterpretation, miscalculation, misjudgment; delusion, distorted idea *or* notion, false belief *or* impression; fallacy, failure to understand.

misconduct, *n.* **1.** bad conduct, wrong behavior, misbehavior, wrongdoing, malefaction, malfeasance; misdeed, wickedness, sinfulness, delinquency; turpitude, transgression, misstep.

2. mismanagement, misgovernment, miscarriage; venality, malpractice, misfeasance; nonfeasance, dereliction, negligence.

—*v.* **3.** mismanage, misdirect, *Sl.* screw up, mess up, *Sl.* bollix up, foul up; bungle, boggle, muff, fumble; botch, make a mess *or* hash of, *Sl.* blow; take a wrong turn, put the cart before the horse.

4. misbehave, transgress, backslide, sin, slip, trip; err, stray, go astray, stray from the straight and narrow; sow wild oats, *Inf.* go to the dogs, *Sl.* go to hell in a handbasket; act up, make mischief.

misconstruction, *n.* misinterpretation, misunderstanding, misreading, misconception, miscalculation, misjudgment; warped *or* mistaken notion, wrong idea, false belief *or* impression, fallacy, delusion, distortion, coloring of the facts.

misconstrue, *v.* misinterpret, misunderstand, misapprehend, misread, misconceive; misjudge, miscalculate, misreckon; put the wrong meaning on, garble, change the sense of, get the wrong idea, get a false impression; *Sl.* goof, *Sl.* screw up, mix up, misrepresent.

miscount, *v.* **1.** misjudge, misreckon, miscompute. See **miscalculate**.

—*n.* **2.** miscalculation, misjudgment, miscomputation, misreckoning, misestimation, misreading; underestimation, overestimation, underrating, overrating, overvaluation, undervaluation; mistake, error, blunder, *Inf.* slip-up.

miscreant, *adj.* **1.** depraved, debased, corrupt, degenerate; villainous, criminal, unprincipled, unscrupulous, scoundrelly, knavish, roguish, rascally; base, evil, wicked, nefarious, iniquitous; vile, foul, reprehensible.

2. misbelieving, idolatrous, pagan, heathen, unbelieving; unorthodox, unsound, heretical, schismatic; infidel, faithless.

—*n.* **3.** villain, blackguard, reprobate, knave, wretch, *Archaic.* caitiff; scapegrace, scoundrel, rogue, rascal, *Archaic.* varlet, scamp, *Inf.* scalawag, rapscallion; ne'er-do-well, good-for-nothing, vagabond, tramp.

4. monster, demon, devil, hellhound, fiend; imp, rascal, mischief-maker.

5. profligate, reprobate, degenerate; rake, roué, libertine, debauchee.

6. traitor, conspirator, *Inf.* snake in the grass, *Inf.* back-stabber, squealer, *Sl.* fink.

7. gangster, mobster, racketeer, mafioso, desperado, terrorist; thug, *U.S.* tough, *Inf.* toughie, mugger; ruffian, rowdy, hoodlum, *Sl.* hood, hooligan, *Chiefly Brit.* rough, *Inf.* roughneck, *Inf.* baddy, *Sl.* bad actor, *Sl.* gunsel, *Sl.* mug, *Australian Sl.* larrikin.

8. criminal, felon, larcener, larcenist, misdemeanant, lawbreaker; convict, *Sl.* jailbird, parolee, ex-convict, *Inf.* ex-con; recidivist, repeat offender, *Inf.* chronic crook; transgressor, trespasser, offender, culprit; wrongdoer, evildoer, malefactor, sinner; malfeasant, misfeasor; *Inf.* scofflaw.

9. heretic, schismatic, dissident, sectarian; apostate, recreant, renegade, deserter; unbeliever, atheist, agnostic; heathen, pagan, infidel.

miscreated, *adj.* misshapen, unshaped, deformed, malformed, ill-proportioned, misproportioned; defected, distorted, contorted, curved, awry, askew, crooked, gnarled, crippled, lame; stooped, roundshouldered, bent, humpbacked, hunchbacked, *Pathol.* kyphotic; bowlegged, bandy-legged, knock-kneed, clubfooted, splayfooted, taliped, pigeon-toed, harelipped; stumpy, stunted, dwarfed; abnormal, aberrant, irregular, unnatural, grotesque, gross, monstrous, hideous, ugly, unsightly; loathsome, repulsive, revolting, offensive; warped, twisted, perverted.

misdate, *v.* date incorrectly, antedate, predate, postdate.

misdeed, *n.* malefaction, malfeasance, offense, crime, wrongdoing, wrong, trespass, transgression, sin; delinquency, dereliction, violation, infringement; injury, hurt, harm; felony, *Law.* misdemeanor, *Law.* tort; atrocity, monstrosity, enormity, horror, outrage; disgrace, abomination, scandal, shame; blunder, error, peccadillo, faux pas.

misdemeanor, *n.* **1.** misbehavior, ill behavior, ill conduct, misconduct, badness, naughtiness, delinquency; disorderly conduct, bad manners, indiscipline, disobedience, insubordination; disorder, horseplay, mayhem, rowdyism, rowdiness, boisterousness.

2. *Law.* delict, *Law.* tort, violation, offense, crime, malefaction, malfeasance; wrong, trespass, transgression, infringement; indiscretion, faux pas, trip, slip, blunder, error.

misdoing, *n.* **1.** wrongdoing, evildoing, wickedness, sinfulness, iniquity, vice; knavery, dishonesty, villainy.

2. malefaction, malfeasance, crime, offense, misdeed. See **misdeed**.

misemploy, *v.* misuse, misapply, misappropriate.

miser, *n.* niggard, skinflint, *Sl.* skin, *Sl.* cheapskate, *Inf.* piker, muckworm, *Sl.* screw; penny pincher, pinchpenny, lickpenny, *Inf.* tightwad; cheeseparer, hoarder, save-all, *Scot.* carl; scrooge, Harpagon, money-grubber, harpy; curmudgeon, churl, hunks.

miserable, *adj.* **1.** forlorn, woeful *or* woful, woebegone, *Archaic.* woesome, *Obs.* baleful, heartsick, downhearted, broken-hearted, heartbroken, crushed, broken, desolate, despairing; worried, anxious, afflicted, stricken, heavy-laden; down, disconsolate, dejected, depressed, despondent, melancholic, gloomy, dismal, dreary, *Literary.* drear, lugubrious, funereal; somber, glum, low-spirited, disheartened, discouraged, *Inf.* broken-up, *Inf.* cut-up, *Sl.* bummed-out *or* bummed; sad, unhappy, infelicitous, sorrowful, doleful, dolorous, dolorific, grieved, mournful, lachrymose, lachrymal, lachrymatory, comfortless, joyless, cheerless, inconsolable.

2. destitute, indigent, poverty-stricken, abject, needy, in need, wanting, lacking, in want, beggared, beggarly; poor, underprivileged, disadvantaged, deprived, bereft, ill-off, badly *or* poorly off, *Inf.* hard-up; impoverished, pauperized, ruined, failed, down and out, down at the heels, out at the elbows, *Sl.* busted, *Sl.* broke.

3. contemptible, beneath contempt, worthy of contempt, despicable, detestable, base, base-spirited, mean, mean-spirited, low, vile, paltry, *Archaic.* caitiff.

4. wretched, sorry, pitiful, pitiable, piteous, *Inf.* lousy, *Sl.* rotten; adverse, difficult, troublesome, hard, trying; star-crossed, ill-starred, evil-starred, unlucky, luckless, unfortunate, hapless; tragic, ruinous, fatal, dire, black, grievous, joyless, grim, stark, bleak; abject, sordid, slummy, slum-like.

5. pitiful, pathetic, pathetical; sad, distressing, plaintive; lamentable, regrettable, deplorable, rueful; touching, moving, affecting, affective, affectional, melting, heartrending, heart-moving, heart-breaking.

miserliness, *n.* **1.** stinginess, niggardliness, parsimony, penuriousness, churlishness, nearness; meanness, selfishness, tightness, tight-fistedness, closefistedness, cheapness, *Sl.* chintziness; graspingness, avidity, avarice, avariciousness, greed, cupidity, rapacity, rapaciousness, covetousness; mercenariness, venality, usuriousness, sordidness.

2. scrimpiness, shabbiness, grudgingness, begrudgingness, reluctance *or* unwillingness to give; thrift, thriftiness, frugality, spareness, chariness, economy.

miserly, *adj.* **1.** stingy, niggardly, *Rare.* illiberal, parsimonious, carking, skinflinty; penurious, mean, tight, tight-fisted, closefisted, cheap, *Sl.* chintzy; moneygrubbing, grasping, avaricious, greedy, rapacious, covetous; self-seeking, mercenary, venal, usurious, churlish, sordid.

2. scrimping, cheeseparing, penny-pinching, grudging, begrudging, ungenerous, stinting, reluctant *or* unwilling to give; thrifty, frugal, sparing, chary; economical, prudent, saving, penny-wise.

misery, *n.* **1.** trial, tribulation, trial and tribulation, test, ordeal; load, burden, heavy load *or* burden; trouble, adversity, misfortune, affliction, suffering, distress, oppression, mortification; blow, shock, stab, pain, throe.

2. destitution, indigence, poverty, penury, privation, need, want; mendicancy, beggary.

3. woe, wretchedness, grief, heartgrief, heartfelt grief, anguish, agony of mind *or* spirit, bitterness, *Archaic.* bale; sorrow, sadness, infelicity, unhappiness, dolor, heartache, aching heart, heartbreak, broken heart, broken-heartedness, heartsickness, heartsoreness, bleeding heart, heavy heart; desolation, bereavement, prostration, extremity, depths of misery; despair, disconsolateness, despondency, depression, gloom, melancholy, melancholia; anxiety, angst, worry, fret, solicitude, concern, carking, care; agony, torture, torment, pain.

misfit, *n.* maverick, dropout, loner, lone wolf, solitary, solitary man, fish out of water, *Inf.* square peg in a round hole; nonconformist, individual, deviator, radical, *Sl.* punk; crazy, flake, freak, three-dollar bill, crackpot, rare bird, queer fellow, queer duck, *Inf.* fruitcake; *All Sl.* weirdo *or* weirdy, oddball, screwball, nut, loony, case, kook, squirrel, creep.

misfortune, *n.* **1.** affliction, adversity, hurt, harm, woe, ruin, ruination, *Archaic.* bale; infelicity; ill *or* bad luck, ill *or* bad fortune, ambsace, evil eye, evil wind, dark cloud *or* star, storm clouds; trouble, the devil to pay; trial, tribulation, burden, weight; reverse, reversal, reverse of fortune, setback, comedown, bringdown, bitter pill; cross, check, checkmate.

2. mischance, mishap, miscarriage, misadventure, *Scot. and North Eng.* mishanter *or* mischanter, glitch, casualty, accident; shock, blow, nasty *or* staggering blow, buffet, stroke, stroke of bad luck *or* fortune; calamity, catastrophe, cataclysm, disaster, tragedy.

3. fluke, freak accident, one in a million, twist of fate; fortuity, happening, hap, hazard.

misgiving, *n.* doubt, question, hesitation, uncertainty, qualm, scruple; suspicion, mistrust, distrust, *Sl.* bad vibes; uneasiness, apprehensiveness, *Inf.* butterflies, nervousness, queasiness, *Sl.* heebie-jeebies, the jitters, *Sl.* the willies, *Sl.* the creeps; apprehension, fear, foreboding, presentiment, premonition, prescience, presage, feeling, odd feeling, bad feeling, *Inf.* funny feeling, anxiety, dread, worry, alarm, disquiet, solicitude, care, concern.

misguided, *adj.* misled, misdirected, misadvised, misinstructed, misinformed, deceived, led astray; unwise, injudicious, imprudent, impolitic, ill-advised, ill-considered, ill-contrived, ill-devised, ill-judged; mistaken, erroneous, fallacious, wrong, dead wrong, all wrong, at sea, wide of the mark, *Inf.* off, *Inf.* way-off, *Inf.* off by a mile, *Inf.* off base; on a false scent, on the wrong scent, on the wrong trail, *Inf.* barking up the wrong tree.

mishandle, *v.* **1.** mistreat, abuse, maltreat. See **mistreat.**

2. mismanage, misconduct, misgovern; bungle, fumble, blunder, botch, muddle, hash, make a mess of, mess up, misdo, *Inf.* muff, *Inf.* make a hash of, *Sl.* screw up; misuse, misemploy, misapply, misappropriate.

mishap, *n.* **1.** accident, misfortune, misadventure, mischance, miscarriage, casualty, glitch, *Scot. and North Eng.* mishanter *or* mischanter; blow, nasty *or* staggering blow, buffet, stroke, stroke of bad luck *or* fortune; calamity, catastrophe, cataclysm, disaster, tragedy.

2. wreck, crash, car crash, collision, smash-up, crack-up, pile-up; flat, puncture, blowout; breakdown.

3. mistake, blunder, contretemps, *Inf.* slip-up, *Sl.* boo-boo, *Sl.* boner; slip, leak; oversight.

4. fluke, freak accident, one in a million, twist of fate; shock; fortuity, happening, hap, hazard.

5. adversity, infelicity, ill *or* bad luck, ill *or* bad fortune, affliction, hurt; ruin, collapse, downfall; reverse, reversal, reverse of fortune, setback, comedown, bitter pill; cross, check, checkmate; failure, fiasco, *Inf.* flop, *Inf.* fizzle, *Inf.* washout, *Sl.* bomb, *Sl.* turkey; muddle, mess, scrape.

mishmash, *n.* hodgepodge, *Brit.* hotchpotch, jumble, scramble, tangle, confused mess, mess; conglomeration, pastiche, pasticcio, farrago, gallimaufry, Chinese menu, mélange, miscellany, omnium-gatherum, potpourri, olio, olla-podrida, motley; salmagundi, stew, ragout, goulash, hash; clutter, litter, Fibber McGee's closet; heap, mass, bunch, huddle.

misinterpret, *n.* misunderstand, misconstrue, misapprehend, misread, misconceive; misjudge, miscalculate, misreckon; put the wrong meaning on, garble, get it all wrong, hear it wrong, get the wrong idea; misrepresent, misteach, mix up, *Sl.* screw up, change the sense of.

misinterpretation, *n.* misconstruction, misreading, misapprehension, misunderstanding, mistake, error; misrendering, mistranslation, misquotation, garbled quotation, misstatement; misexplanation, misexplication, misexposition; distortion, perversion, corruption, falsification, misrepresentation, false coloring.

misjudge, *v.* miscalculate, misreckon, miscount, miscompute, *Inf.* bet on the wrong horse; misapprehend, misunderstand, misconstrue, misinterpret; misestimate, misdeem, misread, misevaluate, misappreciate, misvalue; underestimate, overestimate, undervalue, overvalue, underreckon, overreckon, underrate, overrate; rush to conclusions, jump to a conclusion; err, blunder, go wrong, mistake, miss, slip up.

misjudgment, *n.* miscalculation, misreckoning, miscount, miscomputation, misestimation, misreading; misapprehension, misconstruction, misinterpretation, misunderstanding; underestimation, overestimation, underrating, overrating, overvaluation, undervaluation; mistake, error, blunder, *Inf.* slip-up.

mislay, *v.* misplace, displace, dislocate, mislocate, lose; forget, *Inf.* clean forget, not remember, disremember, have no remembrance *or* recollection of, *Inf.* draw a blank; lose sight of, lose in a crowd.

mislead, *v.* lead astray, misguide, misdirect, misinform, *Sl.* give [s.o.] a bum steer, throw [s.o.] off the scent; delude, deceive, fool, take in, throw dust in the eyes of, pull the wool over the eyes of, slip *or* pass one over on; cozen, dupe, gull, defraud, cheat; rook, victimize, *Archaic.* chouse, defraud, bilk, swindle; steal a march on, cog, *Sl.* take, *Sl.* snooker; pass off, palm off, impose upon, pull a fast one on, *Inf.* throw a curve; humbug, gammon, bluff, juggle, have [s.t.] up one's sleeve, *Inf.* flimflam; hoodwink, trick, outwit, bamboozle, overreach; entrap, ensnare, enmesh, trip up; beguile, seduce, bait, decoy; lead on, take for a ride, *Inf.* fake [s.o.] out, *Inf.* rope [s.o.] in, *Inf.* string along, *Inf.* lead up the garden path; *Inf.* fast-talk, *Inf.* flam, *Inf.* hype, *Sl.* jive, *Sl.* mau-mau, *Inf.* buffalo, *Inf.* bulldoze; *All Sl.* con, snow, suck in, sucker in, murphy; betray, sell down the river, play false, double-cross, two-time, *Sl.* shaft, *Sl.* cross [s.o.] up.

misleading, *adj.* deceiving, deceptive, evasive, elusive, dodgy, shifty, slippery; fraudulent, false, deceitful, hollow; catchy, tricky, subtle, sophistical, casuistic; fallacious, illusory, illusive, spurious, factitious.

mislike, *v.* dislike, disrelish, disfavor, disesteem; find disagreeable, feel repugnance toward, not be able to bear *or* abide *or* stand, *Sl.* get turned off by, be disinclined toward, shrink from, recoil from; turn up one's nose at, object to, mind; have no stomach *or* use *or* taste for, not be able to stomach; shun, eschew, steer clear of; abhor, detest, loathe, despise, hate.

mismanage, *v.* maladminister, misgovern, misdirect, misrule, misconduct, mishandle; misspend, squander, waste, dissipate; be incompetent, be inefficient; bungle, botch, *Inf.* muff, *Inf.* flub, spoil, *Inf.* foul up, *Sl.* blow; hash, muddle, mangle, *Sl.* screw up, *Sl.* mess up, *Sl.* louse up, *Inf.* bollix; gum up the works, make a hash of, make a mess of, make sad work of, *U.S. Inf.* throw a monkey wrench into.

mismatched, *adj.* unsuited, poorly matched, unfit,

ill-adapted, incompatible, uncongenial, incommodious, uncomplementary, unsympathetic; inappropriate, unsuitable, unfitting, unbefitting, unmeet, inapt, inapposite; incongruous, inconsistent, ill-assorted, out of keeping, out of order, out of character; displeasing, inharmonious, discordant.

misname, *v.* miscall, misterm, mistitle, label incorrectly.

misnomer, *n.* misnaming, malapropism, wrong name *or* title *or* designation.

misogynist, *n.* woman-hater, misogamist; loner, *Inf.* lone wolf, hermit, recluse, *Inf.* confirmed bachelor; male chauvinist, male supremacist, sexist, bigot; egoist, narcissist, self-centered man.

misplace, *v.* **1.** lose, lose sight of, mislay, let slip, let slip through one's fingers; displace, misfile, put in the wrong place, dislocate.

2. misapply, misdirect, give wrongly, give unwisely; invest unwisely, invest illegally, employ improperly, use wrongly.

misprint, *n.* printing error *or* mistake, erratum, corrigendum; typographical error, editorial oversight, *Inf.* slip of the pen; oversight, blunder, *Inf.* boner, fault; miss, slip, flaw, *Inf.* boo-boo; inaccuracy, inexactitude, false information, erroneous facts, perverted *or* distorted information.

misprize, *v.* **1.** undervalue, hold cheap, underestimate, underrate, hold for naught; disprize, hold in disrespect, look down on, set no store by; sneeze at, spit upon, *Inf.* look down one's nose at; despise, scorn, condemn, be contemptuous of, disdain; feel contempt for, hold in contempt, revile, deprecate, disparage, *Inf.* put down, ridicule, poke fun at; belittle, minimize, *Inf.* run down.

2. slight, disregard, overlook, push aside, spurn reject; snub, *Inf.* cut, rebuff, *Inf.* put [s.o.] in his place, *Inf.* high-hat, *Inf.* cold-shoulder; turn one's back on, *Inf.* cut dead, *Inf.* leave out in the cold, steer clear of.

mispronounce, *v.* articulate incorrectly, mangle words, slur, speak thickly, speak indistinctly, stutter, falter; commit cacology, speak cacophonously; murder the King's English, distort vowels, drop final consonants.

mispronunciation, *n.* inarticulate speech, distorted vowels, dropped consonants, incorrectly accented words; mangled *or* slurred words, thick speech, indistinct speech, stuttering, stammering, faltering speech, cacophonous speech.

misquote, *v.* **1.** quote incorrectly, quote *or* take out of context, miscite, misreport, misstate, misrepeat; falsify, distort, twist, pervert, garble; varnish, dress up, embroider, elaborate on, exaggerate, stretch, overstate, understate; misrepresent, whitewash, clean up.

—n. **2.** erroneous quotation, misreport, *Inf.* putting words in [s.o.'s] mouth, misrepresentation; perversion, distortion, exaggeration, overstatement, *Inf.* wash job.

misread, *v.* misinterpret, misunderstand, mistranslate, lose something in the translation; misconstrue, put a false construction on, get a false impression, not understand, miss the meaning, miss the point.

misreckon, *v.* miscalculate, miscount, miscompute; underestimate, overestimate, misjudge, not take everything into account; make a mistake, err, *Inf.* get off the track.

misreport, *v.* **1.** report incorrectly, misstate, misquote, miscite; garble, *Inf.* beat around the bush; trim, embroider, dress up, varnish, whitewash; report falsely, falsify, state falsely; misrepresent, distort, dissemble; prevaricate, lie.

—n. **2.** incorrect report, misstatement, wrong citation, circumlocution; false report, slander, misrepresentation, distortion, perversion, prevarication, lie, libel.

misrepresent, *v.* **1.** falsify, deliberately mislead, belie, distort, misstate; understate, minimize, overstate, exaggerate, overdraw, stretch the truth; embroider, dress up, doctor, color, disguise.

2. represent poorly, embarrass, be a poor ambassador for, be a poor example of; parody, caricature, mock, ridicule.

misrepresentation, *n.* **1.** falsification, misstatement, overstatement, understatement, exaggeration, coloration, *Inf.* whitewash job; distortion, anamorphosis, bad likeness, poor likeness, inexact copy, distorted image; invention, fabrication, perversion; equivocation, prevarication, perjury, *Sl.* the big lie, slander, deceit, deception, *Inf.* con job.

2. parody, spoof, take-off, travesty, caricature, burlesque, mockery.

misrule, *n.* **1.** misgovernment, mismanagement, misdirection, misguidance, maladministration.

2. disorder, chaos, commotion; tumult, turmoil, turbulence, rioting; lawlessness, anarchy, frontier justice, lynch law, mob rule, mobocracy.

—v. **3.** misgovern, mishandle, mismanage, misdirect, misguide; maladminister, *Sl.* screw up, mess up, *Sl.* foul up, *Sl.* bollix, botch.

miss[1], *v.* **1.** fail to catch *or* get, miscalculate, mistime, ill-time; bobble, bungle, goof, muff, slip; let slip through one's fingers, misplace, lose; fail to attain *or* accomplish, come up short, *Sl.* blow the chance, *Sl.* blow, be left at the starting gate, slip up; fail to see *or* hear, overlook, disregard, give no heed, pass over, let pass by, let come in one ear and go out the other.

2. fail to perform *or* attend, bow out, take a walk, *Inf.* turn up missing; absent oneself, skip, forego, stay away, take a raincheck; take French leave, *Sl.* vamoose, *Sl.* split.

3. feel nostalgia for, long for, pine for, yearn for, ache for, desiderate; regret, bemoan, lament.

4. escape, flee, evade, avoid; steer clear of, get out of, dodge, sidestep, ward off.

5. fail to perceive, misunderstand, misapprehend, misconstrue, misinterpret, misconceive, get the wrong idea, garble; let one's attention wander, forget, let slip, not enter one's head; fail to grasp.

6. fail, be unsuccessful, lose out, not hack it; *Inf.* flop, *Inf.* flunk, *Inf.* flunk out, *Sl.* screw up, foul up; fall on one's face, *Sl.* fall on one's ass, *Sl.* take a pratfall, come a cropper; *Sl.* lay an egg, *Sl.* bomb, go over like a lead balloon; come to nothing *or* naught, come to grief, fall through, fall flat, fall short; go up in smoke, fizzle out, miscarry, misfire, abort; run aground, go on the rocks, break down.

—n. **7.** failure, fiasco, flop, *Inf.* ground-out, fizzle; slip, error, mistake, blunder, *Sl.* goof-up, *Sl.* screw-up; omission, oversight, loss, deletion.

miss[2], *n.* young unmarried woman, maiden, virgin; young lady, girl, *Sl.* girly, schoolgirl; lass, lassie, damsel, demoiselle, *Irish Eng.* colleen; nymph, nymphet, *Sl.* teeny-bopper, *Sl.* bobby-soxer; *Inf.* gal, coed, *Sl.* chick, *Sl.* mouse, *Sl.* popsy, *Brit. Sl.* bird.

missal, *n.* mass book, service book, Book of Common Prayer, *Eastern Ch.* euchologion *or* euchology; formulary, ordinal, lectionary, pontifical; breviary; prayer book; Gospel book, evangelistary, evangeliary.

misshapen, *adj.* deformed, malformed, miscreated, unshapen; unshapely, ill-proportioned, misproportioned; distorted, contorted, warped, twisted, curved, crooked, gnarled, awry, askew; round-shouldered, stooped, bent, hunchbacked, humpbacked, *Pathol.* kyphotic; bowlegged, bandy-legged, knock-kneed, clubfooted, splayfoot *or* splayfooted, flatfooted, taliped, harelipped; stumpy, stunted, dwarfish, dwarfed, pygmy, pygmoid, pygmyish, homuncular, midget; unnatural, abnormal, aberrant, irregular; crippled, lame, paralyzed, paralytic, *Pathol.* paraplegic; grotesque, gross, monstrous, hideous, ugly, unsightly.

missile, *n.* **1.** projectile, shot, ball, cannonball, bullet, shell, grenade, hand grenade; explosive, bomb, atom *or* atomic bomb, A-bomb, fission bomb, neutron bomb, napalm bomb, fire bomb, hydrogen bomb, rocket bomb, aerial bomb; torpedo, hydrobomb; guided missile, aerial missile, rocket, *Rocketry.* ballistic missile, ICBM.

2. weapon, tomahawk, hatchet, ax; dart, *Mil.* flechette, arrow, *Fr. flèche*, boomerang; lance, spear, harpoon, javelin, pike, assegai.

missing, *adj.* lacking, minus, wanting, absent, not here; lost, gone, nowhere to be found; misplaced, mislaid, mislocated, displaced, dislocated.

mission, *n.* **1.** business errand, assignment, commission; aim, goal, purpose, objective, object; charge, trust, duty, task; job, chore, work, stint; office, appointment.

2. vocation, calling, profession, occupation, employment, position; métier, trade, line; pursuit, venture, undertaking, activity; concern, affair, interest.

3. embassy, legation; delegation, deputation; (*all collectively*) ambassadors, diplomats, envoys, legates, agents, commissioners, deputies, delegates, emissaries.

missionary, *n.* **1.** evangelist, proselytizer, propagandist, spreader of the faith *or* the Word, minister of the Gospel, preacher, padre, missioner; revivalist, faith healer; apostle, pioneer; colporteur; clergyman, cleric, priest, minister.

2. crusader, campaigner, promoter, *Inf.* pusher, advocate, supporter, champion, defender, apologist.

missish, *adj.* prim, proper, prudish, modest, demure, decorous, sedate; strait-laced, *Sl.* straight, puritanical, austere, strict, rigid, priggish, stiff, formal; unnatural, affected, mannered, *Fr. maniéré;* fastidious, difficult, hard to please, overparticular, particular, fussy, finical, finicky, picky.

missive, *n.* letter, dispatch, telegram, written message, communication; epistle, *Obs.* billet, note, line, bulletin; answer, reply, acknowledgment, bread-and-butter note, thank-you note; business letter, form letter, drop letter; love letter, billet-doux, *Inf.* mash note, fan letter; card, Christmas card, postcard, picture postcard; open letter, *Rom. Cath. Ch.* encyclical; (*all collectively*) mail, post, correspondence.

misspend, *v.* squander, waste, dissipate, throw away, throw good money after bad, pour down the drain; lavish, hang the expense, *Sl.* blow; throw money around, play the profligate *or* prodigal, spend money like water, spend like a drunken sailor, spend money as if it grew on the trees, spend money as if it were going out of style.

misstate, *v.* misquote, quote out of context, miscite, misreport, misrelate; misrepresent, belie, falsify, put in a false light; garble, distort, pervert, twist, warp, slant, color, miscolor, give a false coloring to.

misstatement, *n.* misquotation, miscitation, misreport, misrendering, mistranslation, misinterpretation; misconstruction, misrepresentation, coloring, false coloring, perversion, distortion; lie, untruth, falsehood, falsification; mistake, error, faux pas, gaffe, solecism, blunder, slip of the tongue, *Latin. lapsus linguae, Sl.* boner, *Sl.* blooper, *Sl.* howler.

misstep, *n.* trip, stumble, false step, wrong step, bad move, wrong move, false move; faux pas, gaffe, social blunder *or* indiscretion, indiscretion, slip in conduct, mistake in conduct *or* etiquette *or* propriety, breach of etiquette *or* manners; transgression, dereliction, misconduct, misdeed; offense, peccadillo, oversight, omission, miss; leak, slip, lapse, lapsus; mistake, error, blunder, botch, bungle, *Inf.* slip-up; *All Sl.* boner, boo-boo, goof, boot, bobble, blooper, dumb trick, fool mistake, screw-up, foul-up, louse-up.

mist, *n.* **1.** cloud, vapor, haze, gauze, film; fog, brume, *Inf.* pea soup; smog.

2. drizzle, *Dial.* mizzle, fine rain, light rain, misty rain.

—*v.* **3.** cloud, becloud, cloud up, cloud over; fog, befog; blur, dim, film, pale, soften, defocus, go soft around the edges.

4. drizzle, *Dial.* mizzle, rain lightly.

mistake, *n.* **1.** error, inaccuracy, fallacy, erratum, corrigendum, *Sports.* miscue; fault, flaw, human error; oversight, omission.

2. blunder, botch, bungle, fumble, flub, muff, *Inf.* bobble; leak, slip, slip of the tongue *or* pen, *Inf.* slip-up; *All Sl.* pratfall, fool mistake, dumb trick, foul-up, louse-up, screw-up, boner, boo-boo, boot, goof, blooper, clinker, clunker.

3. misunderstanding, misconception, misapprehension; misidentification; miscalculation, misestimation; misjudgment, error in judgment, misreckoning; misconstruction, misreading, misinterpretation, wrong impression.

4. faux pas, gaffe, social blunder *or* indiscretion, indiscretion, slip in conduct, mistake in conduct *or* etiquette *or* propriety, breach of etiquette *or* manners; misdeed, transgression, dereliction, misconduct, contretemps; false step, wrong step, misstep, false move, wrong move, bad move, trip, stumble; offense, peccadillo.

—*v.* **5.** confound, confuse, confuse with one another, take for, take for another, mix up, mischoose.

6. misunderstand, misconceive, misapprehend; misinterpret, misread; misjudge, misdeem; miscalculate, miscount, misreckon; misconstrue, take wrong *or* the wrong way, get wrong.

7. err, slip, *Inf.* slip up, make a mistake, fly in the face of, miscue, sin; blunder, botch, bungle, fumble, flub, muff, *Inf.* drop the ball, *Inf.* put one's foot in one's mouth; *All Sl.* goof, boot, bobble, screw up, foul up, louse up, gum up, make *or* pull a boner, make a boo-boo.

8. be in the wrong, be at fault; be wide of *or* off the mark, *Sl.* bark up the wrong tree, *Sl.* be way off base; deceive *or* delude *or* trick oneself.

mistaken, *adj.* **1.** inaccurate, inexact, imprecise, unprecise; faulty, flawed, unsound, illogical, *Sl.* cockeyed; misinterpreted, misread, misunderstood, misapprehended, misconstrued.

2. erroneous, incorrect, amiss, wrong, all wrong, *Sl.* all wet, *Sl.* full of beans *or* prunes, *Sl.* full of hot air; false, fallacious, untrue, not true, not right; groundless, unfounded.

3. in error, erring, in the wrong; astray, wide of the mark, *Inf.* off base, *Sl.* off the beam, *Sl.* at sea, *Sl.* out in left field; deceived, deluded.

mister, *n.* **1.** Mr., Esquire, Esq., Master, *Fr. monsieur, It. signore, It. signorino, Sp. don, Sp. señor, Ger. Herr, Swahili. bwana, Hindustani. sahib.*

2. *Informal.* (*used in direct address*) sir, sire, sirrah, you, you there; *All Sl.* buster, buddy, bud, mack, pal, son, brother, man, fellah, guy, big boy, sport, *U.S.* Joe, *U.S.* Jack, *Chiefly Scot.* Jimmy.

3. *Informal.* husband, spouse, mate, *Archaic.* goodman; lord and master, head of the house *or* household, ruler of the roost, breadwinner; *All Inf.* the other half, old man, hubby, pop, dad, bed warmer, roommate.

mistimed, *adj.* **1.** ill-timed, inopportune, inconvenient, untimely, badly timed, unseasonable, coming at the wrong time and wrong place; unsynchronized, unsynchronous, *Inf.* out of sync; too late, too early, ahead of time, behind time; unsuited, unsuitable, unfit, inappropriate, inapt, inaposite, infelicitous, unseemly, out-of-place, malapropos.

2. inauspicious, unpropitious, unfavorable, untoward; unhappy, unfortunate, unlucky, ill-starred.

mistiness, *n.* cloudiness, haziness, fogginess; dimness, blurriness, obscurity, paleness.

mistreat, *v.* abuse, maltreat, mishandle, ill-use, ill-treat; wrong, aggrieve, do an injustice to, disrespect, walk all over [s.o.], *Inf.* shaft, *Inf.* give [s.o.] the shaft, *Sl.* do one dirty, *Sl.* kick around; bully, trample upon, bullyrag, hector, harass, grind, harry; persecute, torment, agonize, afflict, torture, rack, *Sl.* give one the works; manhandle, maul, batter, *Sl.* knock around *or* about, beat, beat up, pound, thrash, hit, strike, *Archaic.* belabor; harm, damage, bruise, hurt, pain, injure.

mistreatment, *n.* abuse, maltreatment, ill-treatment, mishandling, ill-use, ill-usage; persecution, tormenting, torturing; manhandling, mauling, battery, beating, thrashing; harming, damage, hurting, injury.

mistress, *n.* **1.** female sovereign, headwoman, maharanee; matron, madam, *Archaic.* dame; housekeeper, homemaker; landlady, female proprietor, female owner, hostess.

2. *British.* schoolmistress, instructress, governess.

3. paramour, courtesan, concubine, kept woman, *Sl.* doxy, odalisque.

4. *Archaic.* sweetheart, ladylove, flame, inamorata; beloved, darling, sweetie.

mistrust, *n.* **1.** distrust, distrustfulness, mistrustfulness, wariness, chariness, leeriness; doubt, skepticism, uncertainty, scruple, discredit; suspicion, qualm, misgiving, misdoubt, diffidence.

—*v.* **2.** distrust, half-believe, misdoubt; doubt, question, have reservations, greet with skepticism.

3. suspect, misbelieve, disbelieve, misgive; *Sl.* smell a rat, have doubts, scent a fallacy, discredit.

mistrustful, *adj.* suspicious, distrustful, untrustful, skeptical, cynical, incredulous; dubious, doubtful, uncertain, agnostic; apprehensive, anxious, leery, wary, chary.

misty, *adj.* **1.** cloudy, foggy, hazy, vaporous, brumous, smoggy, *Archaic.* caliginous; drizzly, moistful, spraylike; frosted, opaque, filmy, semipellucid, semitransparent.

2. obscure, vague, indistinct, obfuscated, indistinguishable; nebulous, shadowy, fuzzy, blurry, bleary, dusky; shapeless, formless, amorphous, undefined; unclear, dim, gray, mat; smoky, fuliginous, sooty, murky.

misunderstand, *v.* misapprehend, misread, misconstrue, misconceive, misinterpret; misjudge, miscalculate, miscount, misreckon; read it wrong, get it all wrong, get the wrong idea, get a false impression, miss the point, see through a glass darkly.

misunderstanding, *n.* **1.** disagreement, variance, difference, clash, imbroglio, no meeting of the minds; dissension, dispute, controversy, discord; spat, tiff, quarrel, set-to, bicker; rift, falling out, split, rupture.

2. misapprehension, misconstruction, misreading, misconception, misinterpretation, miscalculation, misjudgment; false impression, wrong idea, failure to get the drift.

misusage, *n.* **1.** misapplication, misemployment, misappropriation, misuse; impropriety, malapropism, solecism, catachresis, corruption, barbarism, bad grammar.

2. abuse, ill-use, ill-usage, mishandling, mistreatment, maltreatment, ill-treatment; manhandling, mauling, battery, beating, thrashing; harming, damage, hurting, injury; persecution, tormenting, torturing.

misuse, *n.* **1.** misapplication, misemployment, misappropriation, misusage.

—*v.* **2.** misapply, misemploy, misappropriate; wrong, aggrieve, profane, disrespect, pervert, prostitute; exploit, impose upon, take advantage of.

3. abuse, mistreat, maltreat, mishandle, ill-use, ill-treat, bullyrag; manhandle, maul, batter, beat, thrash, hit, strike, *Sl.* belabor; harm, damage, bruise, hurt, pain, injure; persecute, torment, agonize, torture, rack, *Sl.* give one the works.

mite, *n.* **1.** small contribution, one's fair share, small sum of money.

2. small child, little one, little fellow, tot, *Inf.* kid, *U.S. Inf.* tad.

3. bit, smidgen, speck, *Inf.* smitch, iota, molecule, atom, jot, whit, tittle; dot, point, dab, fleck, speck; trace, touch, hint, trifle, tinge, suggestion, suspicion, tincture, *Archaic.* spice, shadow; minimum, pittance, modicum, driblet.

—*adv.* **4. a mite** to an extent, to some extent, to some degree, in some measure; somewhat, some, *Inf.* kind of, *Inf.* sort of.

mitigate, *v.* alleviate, reduce, diminish, lessen, weaken; abate, let up, slacken, remit, relax; allay, assuage, *Rare.* lenify, palliate; appease, soothe, *Archaic.* attemper, relieve, ease, soften, cushion, mollify, lighten; smooth over, calm, compose, tranquilize, still, quiet, hush, lull; solace, console, succor, remedy; quell, slake, deaden, dull, obtund, blunt, take the edge off of; smother, check, curb, tame, subdue; moderate, temper, make allowances, modify, qualify.

mitigating, *adj.* extenuating, extenuative, extenuatory, palliative, mitigative, mitigatory; exculpatory, exonerative, justifying, justificatory, justificative, excusatory, vindicating, vindicatory, vindicative; qualifying, modifying, tempering.

mitigation, *n.* alleviation, assuagement, palliation, appeasement; soothing, relief, easing, easement; softening, cushioning, mollification, lightening; smoothing over, calming, composing, tranquilizing, sedation, lulling; abatement, remission, reduction, diminution, lessening; slackening, weakening, relaxation; subduing, subdual, quelling, slaking, deadening, dulling, numbing, blunting; tempering, moderating, moderation, qualifying; bettering, improvement, amelioration.

mix, *v.* **1.** commix, admix, intermix, immix; combine, mingle, intermingle, commingle, put together, blend, *Brit. Dial.* mell, homogenize; compound, alloy, *Chem.* levigate, *Chem.* synthesize, adulterate; interweave, intertwine, interlard, intersperse, interpolate, infiltrate; amalgamate, unite, inosculate, join, conjoin, fuse, interfuse, coalesce, merge, incorporate; mass, agglomerate, conglomerate.

2. *Often* **mix up** jumble, scramble, tangle, entangle, snarl; mess, muss, clutter, disarrange, disorder, throw together; confuse, confound, muddle, mistake.

3. cross, crossbreed, interbreed, hybridize, cross-fertilize, cross-pollinate.

4. associate, socialize, fraternize, hobnob, consort, keep company, get together, hang out, *Sl.* party.

—*n.* **5.** commixture, minglement, compound, union, mixture. See **mixture** (*def.* **1**).

6. *Informal.* mess, muddle, jumble, scramble, tangle,

confusion.

mixed, *adj.* **1.** commixed, admixed, intermixed, immixed; combined, mingled, intermingled, commingled, blended, homogenized; compounded, alloyed, adulterated; interwoven, intertwined, interlarded, interspersed; amalgamated, united, inosculated, joined, fused, interfused, coalesced, merged, incorporated; massed, agglomerated, conglomerated.

2. assorted, miscellaneous, varied, various, diverse, of different kinds; heterogeneous, motley, diversified, variegated; multifarious, manifold, omnifarious.

3. hybrid, crossbred, interbred, half-and-half, mongrel.

4. mixed up confused, confounded, muddled, mistaken; jumbled, scrambled, messed up, mussed up, disarranged, disordered, disorderly, cluttered; tangled, entangled, snarled.

mixer, *n.* **1.** *Informal.* socializer, mingler, outgoing person, extrovert, everybody's buddy *or* friend; hail-fellow, hail-fellow well met, *Inf.* glad hander, *Inf.* backslapper; party-goer, life of the party, social butterfly, *Sl.* party girl.

2. electric beater, electric blender, food processor; rotary beater, eggbeater, whisk.

mixture, *n.* **1.** mixing, commixture, admixture, intermixture, blend, blending; minglement, mingling, intermingling, commingling; intertwining, interweaving, interlarding; composite, compound, compounding, alloy, alloying, adulteration, *Chem.* levigation, merging, coalescence, uniting; junction, union, fusion, fusing, interfusion, synthesis; combination, amalgamation, assimilation, incorporation.

2. assortment, mélange, miscellany, medley, omnium-gatherum, potpourri, olio, olla-podrida, motley; salmagundi, stew, ragout, goulash, hash; conglomeration, mish-mash, hodgepodge, *Brit.* hotchpotch, pastiche, pasticcio, jumble, farrago, gallimaufry, Chinese menu; collection, batch, group, grouping, cluster, set, series, array.

3. hybrid, cross, crossbreed, mongrel, half-breed, half-blood, half-caste.

mix-up, *n.* **1.** clutter, tangle, jumble, mishmash, hodgepodge, scramble; muddle, mess, *Sl.* screw-up, *Sl.* ballup, *Inf.* foul-up, snafu; disorder, disarrangement, disorganization; complication, Gordian knot, complexity, imbroglio, perplexity, quandary, dilemma; confusion, misunderstanding, predicament, plight; maze, labyrinth, puzzle, poser, jigsaw puzzle, tangled skein, tangled web.

2. *Informal.* fight, battle, strife; tussle, skirmish, fray, fracas; row, *Inf.* shindy, rumpus; brawl, mêlée, donnybrook, free-for-all, riot, uproar, *Sl.* knock-down-drag-out; struggle, scrimmage, roughhouse; confrontation, commotion, breach of peace, troubles.

moan, *n.* **1.** groan, sough, sigh, hum; murmur, whimper, breathing; rumble, ruffle, ripple; susurration, susurrus, whisper, rustle; wail, ululation, keen.

—*v.* **2.** groan, wail, sigh; keen, ululate, weep, sob, cry; yawp, bawl; whine, whimper, mewl, pule, snivel.

3. sough, murmur, breathe, whisper.

4. bewail, lament, bemoan, mourn, sorrow, grieve; deplore, regret, rue.

moaning, *n.* groaning, sighing, sough; keening, ululating, weeping, chanting, wailing; grieving, sorrowing, mourning; lamentation, plaint, wail of woe; donning sackcloth and ashes, tearing one's hair.

moat, *n.* ditch, dike, fosse, trench, canal, channel, gully, trough; bulwark, entrenchment, barricade.

mob, *n.* **1.** rabble, rout, surge; horde, Huns, barbarians, *Inf.* mob scene.

2. crowd, throng, multitude, force, host, legion, mass; herd, pack, swarm, flock, drove, bevy, shoal, school, gaggle; jam, press, crush; tribe, crew, band, troop, group, company, party, body, gathering; assemblage, collection, accumulation, amassment, array; agglomeration, conglomeration, clump; lot, pack, bunch, batch, *Inf.* raft; assortment, variety, medley; ocean, sea, world.

3. populace, commonalty, vulgar masses, public, general public; hoi polloi, rank and file, great unwashed, citizenry; every Tom, Dick and Harry; proletariat, the four million, commoners, peasantry, peons; bourgeoisie, middle class; lower class, riffraff, dregs of society, ragtag and bobtail, canaille, doggery.

4. gang, syndicate, organized crime, Cosa Nostra; Mafia, hoodlums, bandits, hitmen, gangsters.

—*adj.* **5.** lawless, disorderly, anarchic, ungovernable, unmanageable, unruly, unbridled; riotous, violent, ferocious, frenzied, turbulent; boisterous, obstreperous, tumultuous; manic, crazy, excitable; irrational, insane, *Sl.* nutty, *Sl.* screwy, unbalanced; barbarous, ravening, wild, headstrong, intemperate.

6. vulgar, uncivilized, unpolished, ill-bred; unintelligent, uninformed; common, base, crass, proletarian, plebian; loutish, boorish, doltish, cloddish, hick.

—*v.* **7.** crowd around, clamor, raise a hullabaloo, brawl; attack, assail, assault; descend on, swoop down on, march on *or* against; charge, rush at, raid; go at, strike at.

mobile, *adj.* **1.** movable, *Biol.* motile, portable, transportable, unstationary, unfixed; moving, motive, motional, kinetic, in motion, unquiet; traveling, itinerant, peripatetic, migratory, migrant, unsettled, roving, roaming, nomadic, vagrant; active, on the move, on the go, busy, on the wing, volitant, *Inf.* hyper, *Sl.* go-go.

2. fluid, flowing, running, runny, oozy; syrupy, watery, liquidy, liquescent, liquid, molten.

3. changeable, transformable, transmutable, flexible, malleable, plastic, (*of the face*) animated, expressive, sensitive; adaptive, vicissitudinary, vicissitudinous; changing, changeful, varying, variable, protean; vacillatory, vacillant, vacillating, fluctuating, fluctuant, mutable, chameleonlike, chameleonic, inconstant, unstable; mercurial, capricious, fickle, faddish, whimsical, flighty.

4. responsive, reactive, agile, nimble, quick, prompt, ready, alert; impulsive, impetuous, rash, hasty; volatile, excitable, temperamental, moody.

mobility, *n.* **1.** movability, fluidity, power of movement; locomotion, ambulation; *Biol.* motility.

2. upward mobility *Sociology.* advancement, advancing, betterment, upgrading; progress, progression, progressiveness, promotion, success.

mobilize, *v.* **1.** summon, call up, call to arms, raise troops, draft, enlist, conscript, levy, *Both Mil.* activate, put on active duty *or* alert; muster, assemble, gather together, collect, round up *or* in, amass, accumulate, group *or* mass together; marshal, arrange, organize, systematize, put in order, set up, line up, array.

2. adapt, adjust, modify, alter, change, permute, make suitable; convert, transform, metamorphose, transmute, transshape, remodel, restyle, recast; reorganize, reorder, permutate, shift; prepare, *Inf.* prep, ready, get [s.t.] ready, put in a state of readiness, outfit, arm.

mob rule, *n.* mobocracy, ochlocracy, vigilante rule, vigilantism, lynch law, Ku Kluxism, Ku Kluxery, taking the law into one's own hands; terrorism, Reign of Terror, violence, brute force; lawlessness, riot, turmoil, tumult, chaos, pandemonium, mayhem, bedlam, confusion, mess, disorderliness, disorder; anarchy, Hobbesian universe, Bakuninism, absence of government, nihilism.

mock, *v.* **1.** ridicule, jeer, make fun of, fleer, laugh at, guy, make [s.o.] the butt of a joke, *Australian.* chiack; tease, kid, rib, rally, taunt, rag, gibe, twit, banter, poke fun at, make sport of, spoof, *Inf.* roast, *Sl.* razz; sneer at, deride, scout, flout, knock, put down, make snide remarks about, cry down, *Scot. and North Eng.* geck; defy, challenge, spurn, flout, scoff at, laugh in the face of, pooh-pooh, *Inf.* thumb one's nose at, *U.S.* give the Bronx cheer *or* raspberry to; scorn, curl one's lips at, disdain, contemn, insult, run down, assail, abuse.

2. mimic, ape, monkey, parrot, echo, imitate, impersonate, mime, *Sl.* make like; lampoon, satirize, parody, pasquinade, burlesque, caricature, travesty, do a take-off on.

3. simulate, copy, copy-cat, duplicate, clone; counterfeit, forge, fabricate, fake; sham, feign, pretend, make believe, playact, act like, personate, play the role, assume, put on, take on, affect; dissemble, mislead, play a hoax on, fake out, do a number on, deceive, delude, dupe, fool, make a fool of.

—adj. **4.** fake, sham, flash, counterfeit, forged, faked, fraudulent, spurious, meretricious, pinchbeck, bastardly, *Inf.* phony, bogus, *Australian.* bunyip; mimic, mimical, mimetic, imitation, imitative, near, simulated, synthetic, artificial, plastic, ersatz, pseudo, so-called, *Sl.* hokey; pretend, make-believe, play, (*of money*) paper.

mocker, *n.* **1.** ridiculer, jeerer, giber, taunter; teaser, banterer, spoofer, *Sl.* kidder; sneerer, derider, flouter, scoffer, spurner; scorner, contemner, insulter, assailer, abuser.

2. mimic, ape, monkey, parrot, echo, imitator, mime, impersonator; lampooner, lampoonist, pasquinader, burlesquer, caricaturist, satirist, parodist.

3. copier, copyist, simulator, epigone, *Inf.* copycat; counterfeiter, forger, fabricator, faker; fake, mountebank, charlatan, quack, empiric, *Inf.* phony, *Australian.* bunyip; impostor, deceiver, feigner, pretender.

mockery, *n.* **1.** ridicule, jeering, taunting; spoofery, funning, kidding, teasing, banter, badinage, persiflage; derision, scoffing, scorn, disdain, contempt, disrespect.

2. jeer, gibe, fleer, gaunt, raillery, contumely, nasty remark, sarcasm, *Inf.* roast; poke, dig, cut, rub, chaff, barb, thrust, quip, wisecrack, skit; boo, hiss, hoot, catcall, cry, *U.S.* raspberry, *U.S.* Bronx cheer, *Sl.* razz, *Sl.* bird.

3. mimicry, mimicking, apery, monkeying, imitation, impersonation, *Rhet.* mimesis; spoof, take-off, burlesque, lampoon, parody, pasquinade, pasquil, satire, caricature; travesty, sham, farce, mummery, insult, misrepresentation, bastardization, corruption, abuse, miscarriage.

4. joke, laugh, ridiculosity, the most ridiculous *or* ludicrous thing one has ever seen; absurdity, inanity, preposterous idea, dumb *or* stupid thing.

mocking, *adj.* ridiculing, jeering, fleering, taunting, gibing; spoofing, teasing, kidding, ribbing, bantering, *Sl.* razzing; derisive, derisory, sneering, flouting, scoffing, pooh-poohing, thumbing one's nose, disrespectful, irreverent, impudent; scornful, disdainful, contemptuous, sarcastic, sardonic, cynical; snide, cutting, biting, nasty, ugly, insulting, contumelious, assailing, abusive, scurrilous.

mode[1], *n.* **1.** manner, method, way, wise; system, approach, technique, procedure; process, methodology, standard operating procedure, *Inf.* SOP, *Latin. modus operandi.*

2. form, disposition, tenor, appearance, guise, aspect; type, kind, sort; form, mold, shape, configuration.

mode[2], *n.* style, fashion, vogue, look, trend, rage, *Fr. dernier cri*, latest thing, last word, fad, craze; habit, wont, usage, pattern, routine; custom, convention, practice.

model, *n.* **1.** prototype, archetype, type; mold, original, protoplast, example, pattern, design, paradigm, sample; standard, criterion, gauge, norm, test, rule, precedent, touchstone, canon, principle.

2. epitome, ideal, exemplar, paragon, beau idéal, *Middle Eng.* parfit gentil knight; nonsuch, nonpareil, *Latin. ne plus ultra*, acme; gem, jewel, pearl, flower, cream, *Fr. la crème de la crème.*

3. outline, sketch, drawing, diagram, plans, blueprint, layout, roughdraft.

4. die, mold, matrix, last; mint, seal, stamp, punch, intaglio, negative, proof; architect's model, scale model, shipbuilder's model, half-lift model.

5. dressmaker's model, *Inf.* dummy, clotheshorse, figure, puppet, artist's model, manikin, lay figure; couturier's model, mannequin, fashion model, photographic model, face model, hand model, *Inf.* cheesecake model.

—adj. **6.** exemplary, exemplifying, illustrative, representative; unequaled, unparalleled, inimitable, consummate, *Fr. par excellence.*

—v. **7.** fashion, mold, shape, sculpt, carve, carve out; draw, cast, build, erect, construct.

8. (*all of clothes*) wear, display, show, parade, put on, dress oneself in.

moderate, *adj.* **1.** reasonable, within reason, judicious, just, sober, rational, sensible; temperate, controlled, restrained, regulated, limited; continent, disciplined, abstinent, sparing, frugal; light, occasional, sporadic; self-controlled, steady, calm, composed, even-tempered, level-headed.

2. average, modest, unpretentious, unassuming; medium, middle, mean; mediocre, fair, so-so, passable, ordinary, middling; (*all usu. of politics or religion*) middle-of-the-road, nonliberal, nonradical, nonconservative, nonreactionary.

—n. **3.** (*all in reference to politics or religion*) middle-of-the-roader, nonliberal, nonradical, nonconservative, nonreactionary; member of the silent majority; middle-American.

—v. **4.** mitigate, alleviate, reduce, diminish, lessen, weaken; abate, let up, slacken, remit, relax; allay, assuage, *Rare.* lenify, palliate; appease, soothe, *Archaic.* attemper, relieve, ease, soften, cushion, mollify, lighten; slake, deaden, dull, blunt, take the edge off of; smother, curb, check; muffle, mute, still, quiet, soft-pedal, lower, turn down, tone down, *Both Music, Acoustics.* damp, dampen.

5. preside over, chair, facilitate, lead; govern, direct, control, regulate, manage; oversee, supervise, co-ordinate, order, organize; emcee.

moderation, *n.* **1.** temperance, temperateness, moderateness, avoidance of extremes; restraint, self-restraint, self-control; refrainment, forbearance, desistance; abstention, nonindulgence, abstemiousness, continence.

2. happy medium, golden mean, *Latin. aurea mediocritas;* middle way, *Latin. via media*, middle road, middle ground; moderate amount, measure.

3. discretion, prudence, sophrosyne, providence, care, caution, deliberateness; composure, self-assurance, self-possession, poise; coolness, cool-headedness, level-headedness; calmness, equanimity, equilibrium, imperturbability, imperturbableness; tranquillity, peace, repose, ease, contentment; quiet, quietness, quietude, serenity.

4. mitigation, palliation, alleviation, diminution, lessening, let-up; remission, abatement, relaxation; assuagement, soothingness, allaying, calming, quieting.

moderator, *n.* chairman, chairwoman, chairlady, chairperson, chair; presiding officer, speaker, leader, facilitator; toastmaster, master of ceremonies, *Inf.* emcee, *Inf.* M.C.; mediator, arbitrator, umpire, referee; anchor man, co-ordinator; interviewer, discussion leader.

modern, *adj.* **1.** contemporary, present-day, new, immediate, present, current; existing, existant, topical, contemporaneous, twentieth-century, present-time *or* -age, abreast of the times, *Sl.* now, *Sl.* today, *Sl.* with it; recent, newly-come, late.

2. up-to-date, the latest thing, up-to-the-minute, new-fashioned, new-minted, new-coined, late-model, fresh from the factory, just out, hot off the press *or* fire; fashionable, in fashion, in style *or* vogue, all the rage, modish; newest, latest, last, most recent, newest of the new, *Sl.* trendy, *Sl.* in, *Sl.* in thing, *Sl.* the latest, *Sl.* hip, *Sl.* hep, *Sl.* mod; prevalent, prevailing, popular, reigning, ruling, regnant, usual, routine, ordinary, standard.

3. advanced, progressive, forward-looking, avant-garde, neoteric, newfledged; modernistic, modernized, ultra-modern, ultra-ultra, ahead of its *or* one's time, streamlined, *Inf.* far-out, *Inf.* way-out; novel, newfangled, unfamiliar, unknown, uncommon, unheard-of, unestablished, untried, never-before-seen.

modernist, *n.* **1.** modern, person of today, *Inf.* now person, *Inf.* with-it person, *Inf.* swinger.

2. avant-gardist, trend-setter, pacesetter, innovator; neologist, neoterist; precursor, bannerman, forerunner, pioneer, trailblazer, pathfinder.

3. modernizer, reformer, transformer, innovationist; schismatic, apostate, maverick, *Inf.* young Turk.

modernistic, *adj.* **1.** modern, contemporary, up-to-date, avant-garde. See **modern** (*defs.* **1, 2**).

2. original, novel, unique, new, fresh; advanced, progressive, forward-looking; inventive, creative, visionary, seminal, germinal.

modernity, *n.* modernness, innovation, departure, new departure, neoterism, neologism; novelty, newness, novel idea, *Inf.* newfangled device *or* contraption *or* idea, *Inf.* new *or* latest wrinkle, *Inf.* new slant *or* twist, *Sl.* new handle, *Fr. dernier cri*; vogue, fashion, modishness, fashionableness, latest fashion *or* fad, *Inf.* the latest thing, *Inf.* the rage, *Inf.* the go, *Inf.* the last word, *Inf.* what's happening, *Inf.* the in thing; new look, newest trend, new trend, *Inf.* trendiness, modernism.

modernize, *v.* **1.** update, make modern, redesign, do over, reshape, reform; renovate, revamp, redo, streamline; refurbish, refresh, rejuvenate, regenerate, bring up to date, *Inf.* slick up; automate, computerize, mechanize.

2. get up to date, get in the swim *or* the mainstream, move with the times, *Inf.* get on the ball, *Inf.* get with it, *Inf.* join the twentieth-century, *Inf.* join the parade.

modest, *adj.* **1.** self-effacing, unassuming, unpresuming, diffident, free from vanity *or* from pride; shy, hesitant, reluctant, reticent, reserved, retiring, bashful, demurring, *Archaic.* verecund, unwilling, timorous, timid, blushing; self-abasing, self-abnegating, self-deprecating.

2. humble, unpretentious, plain, simple, homely, lowly, neat, small, *Inf.* homey, *Inf.* tidy; presentable, good enough, adequate, satisfactory, all right, *Sl.* OK; better than nothing, acceptable, *Inf.* not bad, *Inf.* not half bad; moderate, medium, respectable, passable, tolerable, fair, middling, *Inf.* fair to middling; so-so, *Fr. comme ci comme ça*, nothing to brag about, *Inf.* nothing to write home about.

3. decent, decorous, delicate, proper, becoming, seemly; demure, undemonstrative, quiet, constrained; innocent, chaste, virtuous, continent.

modesty, *n.* **1.** self-effacement, humbleness, humility, unobtrusiveness, unpretentiousness, unostentatiousness, unassumingness, unboastfulness, unambitiousness; reticence, reticency, constraint, subduedness; reserve, retirement, retiring disposition, meekness.

2. diffidence, shyness, bashfulness, demureness; timidity, timidness, shamefacedness, prudency, coyness; prudishness, *Inf.* nice-nellyism.

3. decency, seemliness, propriety, decorum, decorousness, delicacy.

4. artlessness, ingenuousness, guilelessness, simpleheartedness; moderation, prudence, discretion, control, steadiness, evenness, self-restraint, self-control; simpleness, ordinariness, homeliness, matter-of-factness.

modicum, *n.* trifle, little, little *or* tiny *or* teeny bit, bit, granule, grain, speck, jot, iota, particle, atom, whit, molecule, tittle, *Inf.* mite, *Inf.* smithereen; fragment, scrap, snatch, shred, slip, snip, snippet, peeling, paring, shaving; fraction, chip, splinter, sliver, shard, *Brit. Dial.* collop, minimum; nip, bite, morsel, crumb; thimbleful, ounce, dram, dollop, drop, dot, minim, driblet, *Inf.* dab, spot, flyspeck, fleck; dash, sprinkle, sprinkling, pinch, *Inf.* smidgen, *Inf.* smitch, tinge, hint, eyedropperful.

modification, *n.* **1.** alteration, slight change, modulation, inflection; change, conversion, reduction; innovation, transposition, substitution, revision; mutation, permutation, deviation; transition, transfiguration, transformation, metamorphosis, transmutation, transubstantiation.

2. qualification, limitation, restriction, condition, proviso, provision, stipulation, arrangement; exception, exemption, *Inf.* escape clause; amendment, codicil, rider, supplement, appendix.

modify, *v.* **1.** change slightly, vary, inflect; adjust, readjust, adapt; square up, even up, balance, trim; accommodate, *Inf.* make do, make fit; change, alter, reshape, remold, recast; reconstruct, revamp, remodel, make changes, innovate, make innovations, make modifications, redo; reform, give new shape to, reorganize, regroup, *Inf.* shuffle the deck, shift things around; mutate, transform, transfigure, metamorphose, transmute, translate; revise, edit, amend, redact.

2. diminish, abate, reduce, decrease, lower, tone down, dulcify; deaden, dull, blunt, subdue; water down, thin out, moderate, temper, modulate, soften, mitigate; qualify, restrict, limit, narrow, restrain.

modish, *adj.* in vogue, *Inf.* in, *Inf.* voguish, a la mode, of-the-moment, up-to-the-minute, up-to-date, the latest thing, of the latest style, *Inf.* fresh from Paris; trendy, current, *Sl.* now, a-go-go; popular, with-it, all the rage, modern, *Inf.* mod, new; *Sl.* cool, *Inf.* nifty, *Sl.* neat, *Sl.* hip, *Sl.* hep; the cat's meow, the cat's pajamas, the bee's knees, *Inf.* hot stuff; chic, smart, fashionable, high-style, *Inf.* citified, urbane, sophisticated, cosmopolitan, chi-chi; tony, *Sl.* ritzy, *Sl.* snazzy, *Sl.* sharp, *Sl.* sharp as a tack.

modiste, *n.* dressmaker, seamstress, designer, couturier, couturiere, costumier; milliner, hat maker, hatter, bonnet maker.

modulate, *v.* **1.** regulate, adjust, moderate, temper, season; soften, lower, tune *or* turn down, cut down; mitigate, alleviate, assuage, subdue, palliate.

2. inflect, intonate, intone, vocalize, voice, phonate; (*all of the voice*) adapt, accommodate, accord, fit, qualify; vary, alter, diversify, change, modify; accent, accentuate, stress, emphasize.

3. *Music.* attune, tune, *Sl.* tune in, pitch, harmonize, chime, symphonize.

modulation, *n.* **1.** alteration, change, variation, modification; transition, shift, qualification; adjustment, adaptation, accommodation, *Radio.* amplitude modulation *or* AM, *Radio.* frequency modulation *or* FM; tempering, softening, tuning *or* turning down, lowering; reduction, mitigation, abatement; alleviation, palliation, relaxation, easing, *Inf.* easing up.

2. inflection, phrasing, suspension; pronunciation, articulation, enunciation, utterance, vocalization, voice, voicing, phonation.

3. pitch pattern, intonation pattern *or* contour; pitch, tone, frequency; timbre, tonality, tone quality, coloring.

4. accent, accentuation, emphasis, stress, syllable stress; cadence, beat, rhythm, tempo, pulse, throb; pulsation, cadency, rhythmicity.

mogul, *n.* magnate, personage, important person, notable, celebrity; official, *Inf.* bigwig, *Inf.* bashaw, *Sl.* big shot, *Sl.* big wheel; tycoon, *U.S.* baron.

moiety, *n.* **1.** half, fifty percent, equal part; bisection, hemisphere, semisphere.

2. fraction, piece, segment, part, portion, division, subdivision, slice; fragment, bit, particle, mite, trifle; morsel, crumb, chip, chunk, scrap, snip, snippet, shaving; ration, allotment, measure, dole, dose; chunk, hunk.

moil, *v.* **1.** drudge, work hard, toil, labor, *Brit.* fag; slave, plod, grub, *Inf.* plug *or* plug along, *Inf.* grind, wade through; exert oneself, tax one's energies; keep one's nose to the grindstone, work in a sweatshop, work in the salt mines, work like a horse; sweat and strain, get rock-pile duty, scrub, pound away.

—*n.* **2.** drudgery, hard work, toil, travail, *Brit.* fag, slave labor; sweatshop work, sweat of one's brow; treadmill, hack work, assembly line, *Sl.* the pits.

3. disorder, upheaval, turmoil, tumult, *Brit. Dial.* stour; anarchy, chaos, pandemonium, bedlam, babel, hugger-mugger, topsy-turvydom; commotion, turbulence, brouhaha, uproar, pother, hurly-burly, convulsion; disturbance, trouble, to-do, row, riot, mêlée, fracas, rumpus, brawl.

moist, *adj.* **1.** damp, dewy, wet, wettish, watery, aqueous; dank, steamy, clammy, muggy, humid; foggy, vaporous, misty, drizzly, dripping, rainy; swampy, marshy, boggy, fenny, miry.

2. (*all of the eyes*) tearful, lachrymose, misty.

moisten, *v.* dampen, moisturize, bedew, humidify. vaporize, damp; lick, tongue, pass the tongue over; wet, sodden, soak, saturate; irrigate, water, wash, sponge.

moisture, *n.* dampness, moistness, dew, damp, wet, wetness, water, wateriness, sogginess; humidity, steaminess, dankness, mugginess, clamminess; fog, mist, vapor; sweat, perspiration; teardrops, tears.

mold[1], *n.* **1.** hollow form, *Print.* matrix, intaglio, die, block, stamp.

2. shape, figure, form, turn, cast; contour, outline, lines; fit, set; frame, structure, formation, arrangement, organization, format, construction, build; cut, style, model, pattern; type, kind, brand, make.

3. prototype, archetype, original, model, example, exemplar, pattern, paradigm, mirror; ideal, pink, paragon, phoenix; precursor, forerunner, predecessor, ancestor.

4. nature, character, cast, form; manner, way, style, fashion; type, kind, sort, ilk, kidney.

—*v.* **5.** cast, die, mint, coin, stamp, print, impress, imprint.

6. shape, form, work into, knead; fashion, model, pattern; construct, build, frame, make, design; sculpture, carve, chisel, cut, hew.

7. influence, affect, form, make.

mold[2], *n.* fungus, blight, rust, blast; discoloration, stain, smut, dry-rot, rot, *Inf.* crud; must, mustiness, fustiness, fetidness, stench, stink.

moldy, *adj.* **1.** mildewed, blighted, decayed, carious; decomposed, decomposing, decaying, rotting, rotten, putrefactive, putrescent, putrid; bad, spoiled, tainted, gamy; rancid, rank, malodorous, foul, foul-smelling, fetid; stinking, stinky, smelling, smelly.

2. musty, stale, unfresh, smoky, stuffy, fusty.

mole[1], *n.* spot, blemish, speck, freckle, mark, macula; blotch, patch, discoloration, birthmark, *Med.* nevus, wart; pustule, pimple, whitehead, *Pathol.* milium, blackhead, *Med.* comedo, *Sl.* zit, *Sl.* woogit; pock, pockmark, pit, cicatrix, scar; imperfection, disfigurement, defect, flaw, mar.

mole[2], *n.* breakwater, sea wall, jetty, jutty, groin, barrier, embankment, dike; pier, wharf, dock, landing, *Fr. quai*; harbor, haven, port.

molecular, *adj.* atomic, subatomic; microscopic, infinitesimal, minute; imperceptible, indiscernible, invisible, unseeable; impalpable, imponderable, intangible.

molecule, *n.* **1.** *Physics, Chem.* ion, *Physics.* atom, quark; *Physics, Chem.* electron *or* magneton, *Physics, Chem.* proton, *Physics.* magneton, *Physics.* neutrino, *Physics.* meson *or* mesotron, *Chem.* monad.

2. particle, iota, speck, fleck, dot, jot, mote, *Inf.* mite, fraction, *Inf.* smidgen.

molest, *v.* **1.** torment, afflict, plague, beleaguer, beset, besiege; harrow, worry, trouble, bait, *Scot.* fash; harass, harry, hector, badger, hound, heckle, pester, bother, disturb, *Brit.* chevy, *Scot.* sturt; exasperate, aggravate, annoy, vex, irk; irritate, gall, rub, chafe, roil, *Chiefly U.S.* rile, *Inf.* drive up the wall; provoke, needle, nettle, bullyrag, tease, *Brit.* rag; perturb, upset, derange, agitate, convulse, toss, rattle, shake up, stir up; discompose, unnerve, ruffle, fluster, disconcert, discomfit, disquiet, *Inf.* faze, *Inf.* drive crazy.

2. accost, solicit, approach, make a pass at, make an advance toward, be familiar with; mistreat, maltreat, mishandle, ill-use, ill-treat, aggrieve, wrong, *Inf.* paw; manhandle, maul, batter, beat up, *Sl.* knock around *or* about, *Archaic.* belabor; harm, damage, injure, bruise, wound, hurt, pain; assault, attack, persecute, torture, agonize, *Archaic.* insult; violate, outrage, ravish, rape, deflower, *Obs.* devirginate, *Obs.* constuprate, *Obs.* stuprate.

mollification, *n.* **1.** softening, softness, mellowing, relaxing, relaxation, loosening, loosening up, easing up; meekening, subdual, taming; pacification, appeasement, dulcification, tranquilization, composing.

2. mitigation, abatement, weakening, alleviation, palliation; assuagement, tempering, moderating, moderation.

mollify, *v.* **1.** soften, mellow, gentle, meeken; relax, loosen, ease up, let up on; subdue, tame, smooth down, tone down; pacify, calm, compose, tranquilize, lull, soothe, still, quiet, hush; appease, *Archaic.* attemper, placate, dulcify; solace, console, comfort.

2. mitigate, abate, reduce, diminish, lessen, weaken; alleviate, palliate, allay, assuage, *Rare.* lenify; ease, relieve, cushion, lighten, temper, moderate.

mollifying, *adj.* soothing, calming, *Med.* calmative, assuasive, demulcent; softening, soft, gentle, bland, mild, cool, cooling; healing, remedial, lenitive, alleviative, alleviatory, mitigative, mitigatory, *Med.* abirritant; relaxing, numbing, dulling, quieting, lulling.

mollycoddle, *n.* **1.** milquetoast, milksop, sop, mama's boy, namby-pamby, *Inf.* jellyfish; weakling, chicken, baby, crybaby, sissy, mouse, *Sl.* fraidy-cat, *Sl.* scaredy-cat; effeminate, *Inf.* pantywaist, *Sl.* pansy, *Sl.* wimp, weakling, softy; weak sister, goody-goody, mother's darling *or* mother's little darling, nancy, Lord Fauntleroy *or* Little Lord Fauntleroy.

—*v.* **2.** coddle, pamper, cocker, cosset, dandle,

Obs. fondle; pet, spoil, baby, indulge, dote on, cater to, wait on hand and foot.

molt, *v.* mew, shed, shed the skin, exuviate, cast off, slough; come off, peel *or* peel off, exfoliate, *Pathol.* desquamate.

molten, *adj.* melted, fused, smelted, liquefied, liquidized, fluidized, dissolved; igneous, volcanic; heated, red-hot, white-hot.

moment, *n.* **1.** instant, second, *Inf.* sec, minute, short time, little while; no time, less than no time, twinkling, twinkling *or* twinkle of an eye, wink, wink of an eye, trice, flash, *Inf.* jiffy *or* jiff, *Inf.* whipstitch, *Inf.* two shakes, *Inf.* two shakes of a lamb's tail, *Inf.* a brace of shakes.

2. period, point, point in time, time; juncture, hour, day, season, stage.

3. importance, import, significance, consequence, first order, first rank; weight, gravity; prominence, eminence, mark, note; concern, *Archaic.* concernment, consideration, interest.

momentarily, *adv.* **1.** for a moment, for a second, for a minute, for a little *or* short while, for a short time, shortly, briefly.

2. every moment, all the time, from moment to moment, from minute to minute.

3. at any moment, any moment now, any time now, any second now, any minute, now.

momentary, *adj.* **1.** instantaneous, instant, immediate, quick, quick as a flash, quick as thought *or* lightning; abrupt, sudden.

2. brief, short, short-lived, temporary, impermanent, transient, transitory, here today and gone tomorrow, fly-by-night; ephemeral, evanescent, fleeting, flitting, passing, fading.

momentous, *adj.* crucial, critical, climacteric, eventful, pivotal, decisive; heavy, portentous, fraught, charged, laden; serious, grave, weighty, consequential, significant; major, considerable, landmark, vital, of vital interest, all important, of the utmost importance, high-priority, earthshaking; important, of importance, of significance, of consequence, of weight, of moment, of concern, of interest, not to be overlooked, *Inf.* not to be sneezed at.

momentum, *n.* impetus, impulse, driving power, drive, thrust, push, force, energy; speed.

monachism, *n.* See **monasticism**.

monarch, *n.* **1.** sovereign, ruler, rex, crowned head, potentate, dynast, majesty, royal personage, king, queen, Pharaoh; emperor, empress, king of kings, czar, kaiser, Great Mogul, (*in ancient Rome*) imperator, (*in Incan empire*) Inca, (*in medieval China*) khan, (*in Japan*) mikado, (*in Ethiopia*) Negus.

2. autocrat, monocrat, autarch, overlord; dictator, tyrant, despot; absolute monarch, absolute ruler, supreme master.

monarchal, *adj.* royal, regal, monarchical, monarchic, kingly, queenly, lordly, princely.

monarchism, *n.* royalism, imperialism, divine right of kings *or* divine right; conservatism, rightism, (*in Great Britain*) Toryism, (*in France*) Bourbonism.

monarchy, *n.* **1.** kingdom, sovereign nation *or* state, realm, domain, dominion, principate, principality, empire, empery; duchy, dukedom, earldom, palatinate, caliphate.

2. autocracy, absolutism, despotism, totalitarianism, authoritarianism, monocracy, one-man rule, one-party rule, Caesarism, Stalinism; tyranny, uncontrolled *or* unlimited authority, complete control, absolute power *or* control, iron hand, iron fist, iron rule.

monastery, *n.* **1.** cloister, abbey, priory, friary, charterhouse, cenoby, (*usu. contemptuous*) monkery; hospice; *Tibetan Buddhism.* lamasery, *Buddhism.* vihara, *Hinduism.* ashram.

2. convent, nunnery. See **convent**.

3. novitiate, seminary. See **seminary** (*def.* **1**).

monastic, *adj.* **1.** cenobitic, conventual, communal, monachal, canonical, *Eccles.* regular, capitular, cloistral, abbatial, monastical, *Rare.* monkly, (*usu. derogatory*) monkish; clerical, priestly, ecclesiastical.

2. ascetic, celibate, disciplined, self-disciplined, friarlike; austere, severe, stern, harsh, rigid; unadorned, stark, plain.

3. holy, saintly, pious, dedicated, reverent, devout; prayerful, meditative, contemplative, spiritual.

4. secluded, isolated, cloistered, sheltered, sequestered; solitary, recluse, reclusive, eremitic, eremitical, eremitish, anchoritic.

—*n.* **5.** See **monk** and **nun**.

monasticism, *n.* **1.** monkhood, monachism, cenobitism, monkism, friarhood, brotherhood, monkdom, (*usu. contemptuous*) monkery; the cloister, the contemplative life, life of prayer, the better part; sisterhood, nunhood, nunship.

2. asceticism, self-denial, self-discipline, celibacy; mysticism, contemplation, spirituality, self-negation, *via negativa*.

3. anchoritism, eremiticism, solitude, reclusion, reclusiveness, seclusion, self-exile, remoteness, separation.

monetary, *adj.* financial, pecuniary, money, pocketbook, *Inf.* bread and butter; capital, sterling; fiscal; numismatic, nummary, nummular.

money, *n.* **1.** medium of exchange, circulating medium, standard of value; note, government certificate, bond, government bond, savings bond; currency, cash, cold *or* hard cash, legal tender, greenbacks; coin, specie, change, pocket *or* small change, coppers, pennies, nickles and dimes, *Sl.* chickenfeed, *Sl.* peanuts, *Sl.* small potatoes; paper money, bills, banknotes, *Inf.* folding money; almighty dollar, lucre, *Disparaging.* filthy lucre, *Disparaging.* pelf; *All Sl.* dough, bread, moolah, mazuma, jack, long green, shekels, spondulicks, cabbage, lettuce, spinach, scratch, dibs, do-re-mi, loot, gravy, simoleons, wampum, *U.S.* bucks, *U.S.* kale.

2. mint, pile, heap, wad, *Inf.* boodle, *Sl.* bundle, *Sl.* big bucks.

3. wealth, affluence, opulence, prosperity; riches, treasure; property, means, wherewithal, pocket; capital, funds, assets, finances; nest egg, *Sl.* cushion, *Sl.* tidy bundle.

4. profit, gain, *Inf.* percentage, take, *Sl.* rake-off, *Brit. Dial.* get.

5. **in the money** *Slang.* rich, well-off. See **moneyed**.

6. **make money** gain, profit, make *or* realize *or* draw *or* reap a profit; succeed, score a success, hit it, hit the mark, turn up trumps, strike it rich, coin money, *Inf.* break the bank, *Inf.* make a killing, *Inf.* clean up, *Sl.* hit the jackpot.

moneybag, *n.* **1.** purse, pocketbook, wallet, *Fr.* *porte-monnaie*; handbag, bag, pouch, sack, pocket, *Midland U.S. and Scot.* poke.

2. **moneybags** rich man, wealthy man, moneyed man, man of means, man of wealth, man of substance, nabob, nawab, *Brit. Inf.* warm man, *Sl.* fat cat; millionaire, multimillionaire, billionaire; plutocrat, capitalist.

moneyed, *adj.* wealthy, rich, affluent, prosperous, flush, well-off, well-to-do, worth a great deal, heeled, *Inf.* well-heeled, *Inf.* made of money, *Inf.* rolling in money *or* dough, *Inf.* loaded, *Sl.* stinking, *Sl.* in the money *or* dough *or* chips, *Sl.* filthy rich, *Sl.* disgustingly rich; comfortable, easy, fat, *Inf.* on Easy Street, *Inf.*

high on the hog, *Inf.* in clover, *Inf.* on velvet, *Inf.* well-situated, *Inf.* well-fixed, *Brit. Inf.* warm.

moneyless, *adj.* **1.** penniless, without a cent, *Fr. sans sou,* poor as a churchmouse, poor as Job's turkey, unable to keep the wolf from the door; busted, *Inf.* broke *or* flat broke, *Inf.* hard up, *Sl.* stony *or* stone-broke; bankrupt, out of pocket, without funds, impecunious, penurious; short of cash, depleted, drained, strapped, pinched, straitened, pressed; tight, stinted, restricted, limited; deprived, bereft, empty-handed.

2. impoverished, needy, in need, distressed, indigent, necessitous; poverty-stricken, destitute, extremely poor; out at the elbows, down at the heels, shabby, shoddy, seedy, in rags; reduced, pauperized, ruined, bad *or* badly off, *Inf.* on the rocks.

moneymaking, *adj.* profitable, gainful, remunerative, lucrative; fat, paying, well-paying; advantageous, worthwhile, worth one's while, worth one's time and effort.

mongrel, *n.* **1.** half-breed, cross, hybrid, half-blood, bigener, crossbreed; half-caste, mulatto, mestizo, quadroon, *Fr. métis.*

2. cur, *Sl.* mutt, lurcher.

monition, *n.* **1.** admonition, warning, reprehension, remonstrance, dissuasion; caution, word to the wise, caveat, hint, tip, pointer, one's two cents' worth; instruction, exhortation, expostulation; recommendation, advice, counsel, directive, direction, suggestion.

2. notice, notification, advice; subpoena, summons, writ, citation, warrant; mandate, precept, process, injunction.

monitor, *n.* **1.** admonisher, admonitor, reprimander, remembrancer, reminder; warner, cautioner, dissuader.

2. adviser, counselor, confidant, consultant; prompter, recommender, mover, urger; mentor, guide, Nestor, instructor, teacher, tutor; preceptist, proctor, prefect; overseer, director, superintendent, supervisor.

3. detector, recorder, scanner, observer, noter, counter, examiner.

—*v.* **4.** dissuade, admonish, warn, caution, advise against; counsel, advise, recommend, prescribe, give fair warning, forewarn; urge, prompt, expostulate, exhort, move, encourage.

5. observe, record, scan, examine, *Brit.* vet; detect, check; scrutinize, audit, review, check out, study; oversee, overlook, supervise, superintend.

monitory, *adj.* admonitory, monitive, warning, cautionary, dehortative; dissuasive, deterrent, discouraging; recommendatory, hortative, prescriptive, consultative, advisory; instructive, informative, directive, exemplary; deprecatory, expostulative, exhortative; didactic, moral, moralizing, sententious.

monk, *n.* **1.** cenobite, conventual, monastic, celibate, religious, contemplative, *Archaic.* cloisterer; abbot, abbé, prior, brother, lay brother, *Tibetan Buddhism.* lama, *Islam.* fakir, *Islam.* marabout, *Eastern Ch.* caloyer, *Hinduism.* ashramite, *Hinduism.* sanyasi.

2. friar, mendicant, beadsman, pilgrim, palmer; hospitaler.

3. solitary, recluse, eremite, hermit, anchorite, stylite.

4. ecclesiastic, churchman, priest, father.

5. abbess, prioress, canoness; anchoress; *Hinduism.* sannyasini.

monkey, *n.* **1.** simian, *Inf.* monk, chimpanzee, *Inf.* chimp, ape, *Archaic.* jackanapes; capuchin, langur, guenon, macaque, spider monkey, rhesus monkey, jacko; marmoset, grivet, hoolock, tota, chacma, tamarin; sapajou, marikina, mangabey, sagoin, guariba, lar, entellus, teetee.

2. imp, puck, little rascal, little devil, *Inf.* bugger, *Inf.* booger; mischief-maker, troublemaker, rascal, scamp, rapscallion.

3. mime, mimic, pantomimist, copyist, copier, ape; imitator, *Inf.* copycat, echo, shadow, parrot; actor, feigner, pretender, affecter.

4. laughingstock, butt, gazingstock, target, victim, dupe; fool, sucker, game, fair game, jest, joke, April fool, *Inf.* goat, *Brit. Sl.* mug.

5. **make a monkey out of a.** make a fool of, ridicule, make fun of, make a laughingstock of; *Inf.* ride, *Sl.* roast, *Sl.* razz, *Sl.* rag. **b.** humiliate, mortify, embarrass, humble, put to shame, disgrace, take the wind out of one's sails, *Inf.* put one's nose out of joint.

—*v.* **6.** *Informal.* fool, play, trifle, fribble, dabble; amuse oneself, kill time, pass time; toy, fiddle, *Inf.* mess around, *Inf.* screw around; tinker, potter, putter, *Sl.* putz.

7. imitate, ape, mimic, mime, *Sl.* make like; do like, follow suit, affect, take the appearance of; copy, simulate, duplicate, replicate, parallel, reproduce; impersonate, *Inf.* take-off on, mirror, parrot, reflect; parody, mock, burlesque, caricature.

monkey business, *n.* **1.** *Slang.* misconduct, misbehavior, misdemeanor, *Chiefly Law.* malversation; skulduggery, chicanery, trickery, dupery, connivery, pettifoggery.

2. mischief, elfishness, rascality, impishness, puckishness, prankishness, naughtiness, badness; *Inf.* goings-on, *Inf.* hanky-panky, *Inf.* hokey-pokey, *Inf.* shenanigans, *Inf.* antics, *Scot. and North Eng.* daffing; horseplay, foolery, tomfoolery, foolishness, fooling around, silliness; buffoonery, clownery, clowning, harlequinade, playing, fun.

monkeyshine, *n.* *U.S. Slang.* prank, trick, joke, practical joke, antic, *Inf.* dido, *Fr. espièglerie*; escapade, caper, adventure, lark, gambado.

monocracy, *n.* autocracy, dictatorship, despotism, czarism, kaiserism, tyranny, absolutism; monarchy, sovereignty.

monologue, *n.* monodrama, one-man show, tour de force; soliloquy, *Rhet.* apostrophe, lengthy aside; reading, recitation, speech, address, oration, allocution, lecture, sermon, philippic.

monomania, *n.* fixation, fixed, idea, *Fr. idée fixe*, obsession, bee in one's bonnet, compulsion; fetish, fetishism, craze, mania; psychosis, insanity, delusion, illusion; fanaticism, zealotry, zeal, fervor, furor; infatuation, passion.

monopolize, *v.* **1.** gain exclusive control of, corner the market of; appropriate, take control of, own; control, dominate, rule over, reign over, exercise control over; keep all to oneself, *Sl.* hog, *Sl.* bogart.

2. (*all of a person's time*) absorb, occupy, fill, fill up, take up, use up; corner, tie up.

monopoly, *n.* **1.** exclusive possession, corner, edge, margin; control, domination, power, ascendancy; charge, direction, jurisdiction, lead.

2. trust, bloc, cartel; merger, alignment, combine, amalgamation, corporation, joint concern, company, firm.

monotone, *n.* drone, uniformity of tone, sameness of intonation *or* style; singsong, cant, chant; buzz, whirr, hum.

monotonous, *adj.* **1.** unvarying, unchanging, undeviating, repetitious; uneventful, humdrum, routine, unvaried, undiversified, all the same, uniform; banaustic, mechanical, practical; dull, tedious, tiresome, boring, boresome, wearisome; prosaic, prosy, matter-of-fact, uninteresting, ho-hum, *Sl.* dead, dry, dry-as-dust, unexciting, uninspiring, dreary, heavy; ordinary, run-of-the-mill, common, commonplace, everyday, familiar, household; tasteless, bland, flat, vapid, *Sl.* blah.

2. droning, chanting, drumming; singsong, canting; buzzing, whirring, humming.

monotony, *n.* **1.** lack of variety, changelessness, tedium, tediousness, routine, fixed routine, rut, groove, fixed schedule; uniformity, sameness, self-sameness; lack of excitement, dullness, humdrum, deadness, flatness; wearisomeness, dreariness, stuffiness; boredom, ennui; iteration, reiteration, repetition, recurrence, redundancy, tautology.

2. droning, chanting, drumming; singsong, canting; buzzing, whirring, humming.

monsoon, *n.* **1.** typhoon, hurricane, cyclone, *Philippines.* baguio, *Central America.* cordanazo, *Australia.* willy-willy; tempest, storm, gale, blast, blow, big blow; tornado, twister, whirlwind, squall, williwaw, chinook; wind, heavy winds, levanter.

2. rainy season, rains.

monster, *n.* **1.** centaur, chimera, dragon, cockatrice, basilisk, gargoyle; griffin, hippocapus, hircocervus, hippogriff, manticore, mermaid, merman, Loch Ness monster, *Chiefly Brit. Inf.* Nessie, roc, satyr, sea serpent, sea monster, unicorn, wivern, *Arabian Myth.* afreet *or* afrit; Gorgon, Harpy, Hydra, Kraken, Leviathan, Minotaur, Phoenix, Sagittary, Sphinx.

2. monstrosity, miscreation, malformation, abortion, deformity, mutant, freak, freak of nature, teratogeny, two-headed calf, *Biol.* teratism; ogre, ogress, nightmare, terror, horror, incubus, succubus, vampire, Dracula *or* Count Dracula, bloodsucker; ghoul, cannibal, maneater, anthropophagite; werewolf, apeman, Godzilla, Frankenstein *or* Frankenstein's monster; ghost, phantom, spectre, apparition, wraith, spirit, shade, *Irish Folklore.* banshee.

3. deviate, deviant, deviator, deviation, aberration, anomaly, abnormality, abnormity; oddity, peculiarity, curiosity, curio, rarity, nonesuch, funny *or* strange thing, queer *or* peculiar thing; wonder, marvel, phenomenon, miracle, prodigy; spectacle, spectacular, sight, eyeopener, eyesore, *Sl.* mind-boggler, *Sl.* mind-blower.

4. fiend, brute, demon, devil, mad dog; miscreant, villain, terrorist; killer, murderer, slayer, cutthroat, man-killer, man-slayer, mad-dog killer, barbarian, butcher, savage, mauler, ripper, slaughterer, Bluebeard, bloodspiller, bloodletter, bloodshedder; destroyer, exterminator, liquidator, annihilator, mass-killer, mass-murderer, mass-slayer.

5. giant, behemoth, enormity, colossus, titan; Alcides, Anteus, Briareus, Brobdingnagian, Paul Bunyan, Gargantua, Gog and Magog, Goliath, Hercules, Polyphemus; ape, gorilla, elephant, mammoth, mastodon, jumbo, dinosaur, hippopotamus, *Inf.* hippo, whale.

—adj. **6.** huge, enormous, gigantic. See **monstrous** (*def.* **3**).

monstrosity, *n.* **1.** monstrousness, freakishness, nightmarishness, horribleness; ghoulishness, fiendishness, brutishness, demoniac, devilishness; miscreancy, villainy; murderousness, barbarousness, barbarity, butchery, savageness, savagery, slaughterousness.

2. miscreation, malformation, abortion, deformity, mutant, freak, freak of nature, teratogeny, two-headed calf, *Biol.* teratism; ogre, ogress, nightmare, horror, terror.

3. deviate, deviant, deviator, deviation, aberration, anomaly, abnormality, abnormity; spectacle, spectator, sight, eyeopener, eyesore, *Sl.* mind-boggler, *Sl.* mind-blower.

4. giant, enormity, colossus, titan; ape, gorilla, elephant, mammoth, mastadon, jumbo, dinosaur, hippopotamus, *Inf.* hippo, whale, sea serpent, sea monster.

monstrous, *adj.* **1.** frightful, terrifying, horrific, harrowing, hellish, awful, dreadful, *Inf.* scary; hideous, horrible, grotesque, horrendous, extremely ugly, repugnant, repellent, repulsive, disgusting, beastly; grisly, gruesome, ghastly, sickening, bloodcurdling, spinechilling, lurid; cadaverous, macabre, creepy.

2. shocking, scandalous, notorious, flagrant, shameless, outrageous; loathsome, revolting, gross, foul, base, debased, vile, evil, nefarious, *Obs.* scelerous; horrid, terrible, nasty; infamous, ignominious, odious, contemptible, despicable, opprobrious, detestable, sordid, degenerate, depraved, heinous, vicious, atrocious, flagitious, corrupt, reprehensible, unprincipled.

3. huge, enormous, titanic, gigantic, immense, prodigious, colossal, vast, stupendous, mammoth, tremendous, gargantuan, behemothian, elephantine, *Sl.* humongous, giant, towering, mighty, strapping, hulking.

4. deviate, deviant, deviating, aberrant, irregular; abnormal, anomalous, anomalistic; unnatural, freakish, weird, strange, bizarre, *Inf.* freaky; miscreated, malformed, deformed, misshaped, misshapen, heteroclite, heteroclitical, heteromorphic, heteromorphous, teratological, teratoid, teratogenetic.

month, *n.* four weeks, thirty days, lunation, lunar month, solar month, calendar month, synodic month, sidereal month, anomalistic month, nodical month, draconic month.

monument, *n.* **1.** memorial, shrine, reliquary; gravestone, marker, tombstone, headstone; tomb, sepulcher, mastaba, mausoleum; vault, crypt.

2. pillar, column, obelisk, shaft, slab; *All Archaeol.* cromlech, dolmen, megalith.

3. relic, remains, vestige, trace, token; enduring evidence, reminder, remembrance, reminiscence, memento, commemoration, commemorative; eulogy, eulogium, obsequy, *Obs.* observation.

4. exemplar, model, paragon; pattern, standard, ideal.

monumental, *adj.* **1.** massive, immense, prodigious, enormous, *Archaic.* enorm, gigantic, gargantuan; vast, large-scale, mammoth, jumbo, colossal, monstrous, gigantean; bulky, big, large, hulking, huge, hugeous; towering, staggering, mountainous, stupendous, tremendous, *Sl.* humongous; elephantine, hippopotamic, leviathan, dinosaurian; oversize, king-size, overlarge; *All Inf.* whopping, roaring, spanking, walloping.

2. impressive, imposing, conspicuous, striking; majestic, grand, august, stately, dignified; grandiose, magnificent, overwhelming, awesome, awe-inspiring, lofty, wondrous, marvelous, prodigious; distinguished, eminent, illustrious, glorious, brilliant, radiant, lustrous.

mood, *n.* **1.** temper, humor, spirit, vein, vibrations, *Inf.* vibes; temperament, disposition, nature, attitude; tendency, bent, inclination, leaning, propensity; stripe, cast, mould, set of one's jib; prejudice, tendentiousness, bias, preference: desire, longing, wishing, hankering, craving; appetite, taste.

2. feeling, consciousness, awareness, sentience, sensibility, perception, sensitivity; opinion, outlook, mind, frame of mind, mind-set, viewpoint, point of view; attitude, stance, position, posture, way of thinking.

3. moods depression, dejection, despondency, funk, mopes; pessimism, fits of uncertainty, heaviness, sadness; doldrums, blues, mopes, low spirits.

moody, *adj.* **1.** gloomy, unhappy, down in the dumps, down in the mouth, in the doldrums; out of sorts, *Both Inf.* off feed, off one's feed; downcast, crestfallen, chapfallen, discouraged, heavy-hearted, down-hearted, miserable; cheerless, glum, dour, lugubrious; grim, frowning, sullen, sulky; morose, splenetic, saturnine, mopish, dismal, melancholy, dispirited, sad, desolate; disheartened, comfortless, disconsolate, doleful, atrabilious.

2. temperamental, irritable, ill-humored, snappish, snappy, huffish, huffy, curt, short, impatient; piqued, in a pique, in a fume, *Inf.* in a stew; touchy, testy, thin-skinned, waspish, peevish, petulant; irascible, choleric, ill-tempered; crabby, crabbed, cranky, grouchy, grumpy, cantankerous, crotchety, crusty; hurt, wounded, injured, sore, offended, indignant; angry, irate, in high dudgeon, worked up.

3. capricious, impulsive, fickle, skittish, inconstant, moonish, changeable, changeful, variable, faddish; flighty, mercurial, volatile, unsteady, unstable; fitful, erratic, irregular, spasmodic, uneven; irresolute, uncertain, indecisive, undecided, vacillating, wavering, infirm of purpose.

moon *n.* **1.** satellite, secondary planet, celestial body, *Archaic.* lamp.

2. new moon, increscent moon, waxing moon, decrescent moon, waning moon, old moon; crescent, lune, meniscus, half-moon, demilune; full moon, hunter's moon, harvest moon; disk, orb, sphere, globe, ball.

3. month, lunation, lunar month.

4. once in a blue moon rarely, seldom, not very often, hardly ever.

—*v.* **5.** *Informal.* daydream, dream, fantasize, imagine, indulge in reverie, gaze *or* look out the window, stargaze, go off into one's own world; mope, pine, languish, brook; fret, sulk, pout.

6. *Informal.* (*all of time*) waste, squander, fritter, spend idly, pass, *Sl.* blow.

moonlight, *n.* **1.** moonshine, *Fr. clair de lune,* moonbeams, *Fr. rayons de lune.*

—*v.* **2.** *Informal.* work two jobs, work nights.

moon-shaped, *adj.* crescent, crescentic, crescent-shaped, demilune, half-moon, meniscoid; lunate, lunar, lunular, lunulate, luniform; sickle-shaped, falcate, falciform, bicorn; semiglobular, hemispheric; curved, bow-shaped, convexo-concave, semicircular.

moonshine, *n.* **1.** *U.S. Informal. U.S.* bootleg, *Sl.* hootch, smuggled *or* contraband whiskey, *Fr. alcool de contraband*; homemade whiskey, corn whiskey.

2. moonlight, *Fr. clair de lune*, moonbeams, *Fr. rayons de lune.*

3. nonsense, *Sl.* hot air, humbug, claptrap, rodomontade, fustian, bombast, rant; idle *or* foolish talk, *Inf.* gab, *Sl.* gas, palaver, chatter, chit-chat, jabber, prate; jargon, gobbledegook, Jabberwocky, gibberish, babble, *Fr. bavardage*, twaddle, *Brit.* twattle, blather, drivel; foam, froth, bunkum, *Sl.* bunk, *U.S. Sl.* blah; flummery, *Inf.* hokum, *Sl.* applesauce, *Sl.* eyewash; rubbish, *Sl.* tripe, refuse, *Dial.* culch, chaff, trash, *Inf.* garbage, *Sl.* crap, *Sl.* crock, *Sl.* bull; balderdash, *Sl.* horsefeathers, hogwash, stuff, stuff and nonsense, *Inf.* bosh, *Brit. Inf.* gammon, *Brit. Sl.* tosh; fudge, foolishness, folly, rigmarole, amphigory; footle, *Inf.* malarkey, *Sl.* bushwa, *Sl.* baloney, *Sl.* bilge *or* bilge water, *Sl.* meshugaas, *Scot. and North Eng.* haver; poppycock, *Inf.* fiddle-faddle, *Inf.* piffle, *Inf.* hooey, *Inf.* kibosh, *Inf.* flapdoodle.

moon-struck *adj.* **1.** crazed, crazy, mad, maddened, lunatic, lunatical, insane, demented, deranged; dazed, moon-stricken, possessed, infatuated; of unsound mind, *Latin. non compos mentis*, mentally ill; daft, *Inf.* daffy, unbalanced, touched, *Inf.* unglued, *Inf.* half-baked, *Brit. Sl.* bonkers, *Brit. Sl.* barmy, unhinged, distracted; brainsick, *Sl.* kooky, *Sl.* meshuga; *U.S. Sl.* balmy, dippy, batty, bats, cuckoo, buggy, bughouse, bugs, screwy, wacky, wacko, goofy, loony, squirrelly, bananas, nuts, nutty, nutty as a fruitcake.

2. out of one's head *or* mind *or* senses *or* wits, *Scot.* redwood, *Sl.* loco, mad as a hatter, mad as a March hare, far-gone, stark raving mad; not all there, not quite right, not right upstairs; *Inf.* out in left field, *Sl.* in outer space, *Sl.* in orbit, *Inf.* off the wall; *Inf.* cracked, *Inf.* mental, *Sl.* off one's rocker, *Sl.* out of one's tree, *Sl.* off one's trolley, *Brit. Sl.* off one's chump.

3. hysterical, delirious, maniacal, madding, *Archaic.* wood; frantic, frenzied, frenetic; ranting, raving, storming, foaming at the mouth; beside oneself, at one's wit's end; out of control, uncontrollable, corybantic, *Inf.* haywire, berserk, rabid, wild.

4. absurd, silly, inane, fatuous, crackbrained, foolish; irrational, wild-eyed, illogical, unreasonable; senseless, nonsensical, ridiculous, ludicrous; asinine, anserine, idiotic, *Inf.* moronic, imbecilic; childish, puerile, immature.

5. stupid, simple-minded, bird-brained, feebleminded, dull-witted; harebrained, light-minded, light-headed, giddy; rambling, driveling, wandering, incoherent; scatterbrained, absent-minded; confused, bewildered, hazy, muddled, bemused.

6. odd, peculiar, queer, bizarre, strange, anomalous, *Chiefly Brit. Inf.* potty, *Inf.* dotty, *Inf.* crackpot; abnormal, aberrant, irregular, deviant, perverse.

moor¹, *n.* heath, wasteland, moorland, *Scot. and North Eng.* fell; upland, plateau, tableland, mesa, wold; open country, prairie, grassland, veld, meadow, meadowland, pasture, pasturage, grazing land; (used esp. in Southern England) downs, savannah, (*both in South America*) pampas, campo; plain, flat, steppe, tundra, champaign; bush, scrub, scrubland; marsh, bog, swamp, *Brit.* fen.

moor², *v.* secure, fix firmly, anchor; fasten, tie up, bind, hitch, tether, picket.

moory, *adj.* scrubby, barren, bare, waste; open, campestral, champaign, flat, level; low, marshy, swampy, boggy, fenny, quaggy, muddy, miry, poachy, paludal.

moot, *adj.* **1.** debatable, disputable, arguable, confutable, refutable; questionable, doubtful, dubious, controvertible, contestable; open to discussion *or* question, in question, at issue, controversial; undetermined, unestablished, unresolved, unsettled, undecided; doubted, contested, questioned, under a cloud, under suspicion, suspect, suspicious.

2. theoretical, hypothetical, conjectural, speculative; problematical, notional, postulatory, suppositional; ideal, impractical, academic, armchair.

—*v.* **3.** introduce, bring up, put before, proffer; present, set forth, pose, propose, propound, postulate, posit; broach, advance, submit, put forward, make a motion.

4. dispute, discuss, debate, argue, polemicize; contend, plead, litigate, *Rare.* discept, ventilate, reason about.

mop, *n.* **1.** swab, swabber, sponge mop; duster, dust mop, dry mop.

2. *Slang.* crop, mass, mat, thatch; head of hair, shock, shag, mane, crine.

—*v.* **3.** swab, scrub, wash, sponge, wipe, clean; dust, whisk, sweep.

mope, *v.* **1.** brood, pout, sulk, pine, fret, grump; moue, *Brit.* mump, grimace, mow, grouch; ache,

agonize, grieve, complain; languish, despond, droop, sink; despair, lose heart, lose the will to live, give up.
—*n.* **2.** brooder, melancholic, sobersides, croaker, moper; pessimist, *Sl.* gloomy Gus, damper, wet blanket; sourpuss, sorehead, grouch, crosspatch, complainer, hypochondriac.
3. dillydallier, dallier, slouch, goldbricker, sluggard, loafer, idler, *Inf.* stick-in-the-mud; laggard, dawdler, clock watcher, time killer, putterer, potterer.
4. mopes blues, low spirits, *Inf.* dumps, doldrums; sulks, *Sl.* mulligrubs, *Inf.* blahs, megrims, mumps.

mopish, *adj.* dejected, despondent, depressed, melancholy, atrabilious; sullen, glum, blue, sulky, dark, beetle-browed; funky, mopey, low, down, sad, dispirited, out of sorts; spiritless, lackadaisical, listless, sluggish, heavy; doleful, moody, grim, dumpish, mumpish; long-faced, dreary, crestfallen, brooding, moping; jaundiced, disconsolate, gloomy, woebegone.

moppet, *n.* child, tyke, cherub, innocent; dear, love, darling, mignon, doll, jewel, honey, apple of one's eye; pet, favorite, cosset, lamb, dumpling, duck; young girl, kitten, chick, baby, nymph, nymphet.

moral, *adj.* **1.** ethical, righteous, just, good, fair, square; upright, honest, honorable, moralistic, decent, noble; open, straightforward, veracious; high-minded, principled, responsible; proper, meet, right, correct, fit; fitting, seemly, decorous, appropriate, becoming, befitting.
2. moralizing, didactic, instructive, sententious, platitudinous; monitory, recommendatory, hortative, prescriptive, directive.
3. virtuous, chaste, pure, innocent, platonic; saintly, clean, spotless, immaculate, vestal, virginal; continent, temperate.
—*n.* **4.** teaching, lesson, commandment, rule, golden rule, canon, formula, formulary; platitude, dictum, precept, proverb, phylactery, saw; maxim, aphorism, gnome, epigram, adage, apothegm.
5. morals mores, ethos, customs, habits, manners; ethics, principles, standards, ideals; integrity, morality, probity, rectitude.

morale, *n.* state, mood, temper, humor, condition, attitude, emotion, feelings; spirit, confidence, hope, hopefulness, zeal; firmness, resolve, grit, mettle, will, backbone, stiff upper lip; heart, spunk, pluck, gameness, nerve, resolution.

morality, *n.* **1.** uprightness, goodness, probity, rectitude, righteousness; honesty, integrity, honor, character, decency, respectability; responsibility, fidelity, faithfulness, trustworthiness, constancy, loyalty; equity, justice, principle, fair play, fairness, scrupulousness, justness; propriety, meetness, fittingness, decorum, seemliness, fitness, correctness, appropriateness.
2. chastity, virtue, piety, purity, innocence, pudicity; stainlessness, immaculateness, cleanness, spotlessness, virginality; continence, temperance.
3. ethics, morals, principles, standards, ideals; conscience, moral sense, inner monitor, scruples, sense of duty, good faith.

moralize, *v.* teach, instruct, tutor, point a moral, enlighten, inculcate, exhort; sermonize, preach, lecture, homilize, evangelize.

morass, *n.* slough, wash, wallow, squash, *Brit.* sough, *Brit. Dial.* sump, *Scot.* moss; marsh, fen, bog, swamp, quagmire; mire, quicksand, ooze, mud; moor, peat bog, flat, mud flat; everglade, forest swamp, taiga; swampland, marshland, fenland, bottomland, slobland, moorland.

morbid, *adj.* **1.** somber, morose, pessimistic, blue, melancholic, atrabilious, hypochondriacal; depressed, despondent, dejected, out of sorts, *Inf.* in the dumps; gloomy, lugubrious, dreary, dull, glum.
2. unwholesome, unhealthy, sick, unsound; sickly, diseased, weak, weakly; tainted, corrupted, vitiated, contaminated, infected, polluted; pathogenic, pathological, distempered, disordered; degenerative, tubercular, *Pathol.* phthisical, consumptive; arthritic, rheumatic, palsied, paralytic, rickety; anemic, diabetic, leukemic, hemophilic; ulcerous, gangrenous, cankerous, leprous, *Pathol.* scabietic, *Pathol.* leukodermatous; cancerous, *Pathol.* carcinomatous; syphilitic, venereal; febrile, feverish, pyretic, aguish, flushed, hectic.
3. gruesome, grisly, ghoulish, grim, hideous; macabre, grotesque, ghastly, monstrous; horrible, terrible, horrid, horrendous, horrifying, dreadful, fell.

morbific, *adj.* pestiferous, pestilential, noxious, poisonous, toxic, venomous, *Archaic.* venenose; pernicious, deleterious, harmful, hurtful, insalubrious, unhealthy, unwholesome; morbiferous, baneful, nocuous, destructive, deadly, lethal; noisome, mephitic, septic, foul, miasmal; contaminated, infected, polluted, tainted; virulent, malign, malignant, infectious, contagious, epidemic, zymotic.

mordacious, *adj.* mordant, caustic, acrimonious, bitter, acrid, acidulous, acid, pungent; penetrating, piercing, stinging, nipping, biting. See **mordant.**

mordant, *adj.* **1.** caustic, acrimonious, bitter, acrid, acidulous, acid, mordacious, pungent; trenchant, cutting, incisive, slashing, scathing; keen, pointed, sharp, sharp-tongued; penetrating, piercing, stinging, pricking, nipping, biting; astringent, severe, acerb, acerbic, stern, austere, harsh, stringent; spiteful, virulent, malicious, malificent, venomous, vicious, malevolent, malignant; invidious, hateful.
2. sarcastic, satirical, ironic, ironical, cynical; double-edged, edged; contemptuous, contumelious, taunting, teasing; scornful, mocking, derisive, derisory, disdainful, sardonic.
3. insulting, excoriating, denouncing, berating, lashing; abusive, scurrilous, offensive, vituperative; corrosive, corroding, erosive, withering; cruel, mean, brutal; unkind, uncharitable, unbenevolent, uncordial, unamiable, unfriendly.
4. peevish, petulant, pettish, crabbed, testy, touchy, waspish, irascible, edgy; ill-tempered, ill-humored, ill-natured, short-tempered; hostile, resentful, indignant, piqued, angry; morose, surly, sour, moody.
5. rude, churlish, boorish, bearish, graceless, unceremonious, rough; unmannerly, uncivil, ill-bred, ungracious, impolite, discourteous; abrupt, brusque, blunt, curt, snappish, short, gruff, crusty.

more, *adj.* **1.** greater amount of, additional, supplementary, supplemental, additory, additamentary; extra, spare, fresh, new; further, other, over and above, superadditional, added.
—*n.* **2.** additional amount *or* number, greater quantity; addition, supplement, supplementation, increase, increment; appendage, adjunct.
—*adv.* **3.** to a greater extent, further, longer, again, some more.
4. besides, in addition, furthermore, moreover. See **moreover.**

moreover, *adv.* in addition, additionally, too, also, besides, as well, to boot, ditto, yet; and, plus, as well as; furthermore, further, over and above, more than that; together with that, therewithal, *Archaic.* thereto; including, along with, together with; in conjunction with, conjointly.

morgue, *n.* charnel house, dead house; mortuary, funeral home *or* parlor; crematory, crematorium.

moribund, *adj.* **1.** dying, near death, *Latin. in extremis,* on one's deathbed, at death's door; comatose, gravely ill, on one's last legs, with one foot in the grave, breathing one's last, *Latin. in articulo mortis*; fading, wasting away, failing, waning, ebbing.
2. stagnant, static, at a standstill, not progressing, not advancing.

morning, *n.* **1.** dawn, daybreak, daylight, *Archaic.* dayspring, cockcrow, sunrise, sunup; *Chiefly Literary.* morn, ante meridiem, a.m., forenoon, *Fr. matin,* early part of the day, *Archaic.* morrow.
—*adj.* **2.** matin, matinal, matutinal, antemeridian, forenoon.

morning star *n.* daystar, bright planet; Venus, Lucifer, Phosphor, Phosphorus.

moron, *n.* **1.** retardate, *Sl.* retard, slow learner, *Euph.* special *or* exceptional student; (*all collectively*) the mentally handicapped, the educable mentally retarded, EMR, the trainable mentally handicapped, TMR.
2. *Informal.* idiot, imbecile, mooncalf, *Sl.* zombie; simpleton, Simple Simon, saphead, noodle, cuckoo, *Inf.* jay; lamebrain, dimwit, nitwit, half-wit; dullard, dolt, dunce, *Inf.* deadhead, *Sl.* dummkopf, *Inf.* dummy, *Sl.* dodo, *Sl.* dope, *Sl.* dumbbell, *Sl.* dumbhead, *Sl.* meatball *or* meathead, ignoramus, know-nothing; *Sl.* blubberhead, oaf, clod, *Sl.* klutz, lubber, lout; blockhead, woodenhead, loggerhead, thickhead, *Inf.* chump, coot; mutton-head, fathead, numskull, beetlehead, bonehead, dunderhead, dunderpate, chucklehead, *Inf.* knucklehead, *Sl.* lunkhead, *Inf.* lardhead, *Sl.* stupidhead, *Sl.* goon; ass, donkey, fool, tomfool, goose, ninny, nincompoop, ninnyhammer, *Sl.* yo-yo; pinhead, *Sl.* birdbrain, featherbrain, scatterbrain, addle-brain, addle-head, rattlebrain, harebrain, *Sl.* ding-a-ling, *Sl.* ding-bat, *Sl.* flake; *All Sl.* jerk, retread, schmuck, boob, booby, nudnik.

morose, *adj.* sullen, saturnine, somber, sober, austere, severe, stern, taciturn, silent; glum, gloomy, grum, grim, frowning, scowling, dark, black, bleak, dismal, long-faced; lugubrious, atrabilious, atrabiliar, funereal, morbid, mournful, melancholy, sorrowful, doleful, dolorous, sad, unhappy, cheerless; sulky, poutful, pouting, mopish, in the doldrums, chapfallen, crestfallen, down in the mouth, down in the dumps, down, depressed, dejected, dispirited, hypochondriacal, hypochondriac; surly, cross, grouchy, crabbed, gruff, churlish, sour, vinegary, in a bad mood; moody, ill-humored, ill-natured, bad-tempered, cranky, crusty, crotchety, cantankerous, petulant, splenetic, spleenful, spleenish.

moroseness, *n.* sullenness, saturnineness, saturnity, morosity, somberness, soberness, austerity, severity, acerbity, taciturnity, silence; glumness, gloominess, grumness, grimness, bleakness, darkness, black looks; lugubriousness, atrabiliousness, morbidity, sorrowfulness, dolefulness, dolorousness, sadness, unhappiness, cheerlessness; sulkiness, mopishness, depression, dejection; sourness, surliness, crossness, grouchiness, gruffness, churlishness, crabbedness, bad mood; moodiness, ill humor, spleen, crankiness, crotchetiness, cantankerousness, petulance.

morrow, *n.* tomorrow, the next day, *Fr. demain, It. domani, Ger. morgen, Sp. mañana;* morning, dawn, daybreak; future, time ahead, time to come, eventuality, *Inf.* down the road, *Inf.* down the pike.

morsel, *n.* **1.** bite, mouthful, spoonful, chew, *Dial.* chaw; sip, sup, nip, drink, draught, shot, *Inf.* swig, *Sl.* hit, *Sl.* slug; taste, flavor, soupçon, sample, sampling, hint, suggestion, idea.
2. bit, crumb, grain, granule, chip, piece, fragment, particle; chunk, hunk, lump, gob; section, segment, portion, part, ration, dose, share, rasher, *Brit. Dial.* collop, *Australian.* sherrick; slice, cut, cutting, snip, snippet, shard, splinter, shive, paring, shaving, shred; scrap, snatch, remnant, fritter; pinch, smidgen, speck, moiety, moit, mote, fraction, hair.
—*v.* **3.** *Often* **morsel out** mete out, measure out, admeasure, portion out, ration out, parcel out, dole out, deal out, dispense, distribute, hand out, pass out, give out; allow, allocate, apportion, divide, subdivide, *Inf.* divvy.

mortal, *adj.* **1.** temporal, transitory, fleeting, flitting, transient, passing; ephemeral, short-lived, temporary, impermanent, *Med.* monohemerous; evanescent, momentary, fugitive, fugacious; perishable, caducous.
2. human, earthborn, earthly; terrestrial, tellurian, telluric, worldly, terrine, mundane; corporeal, fleshly, corporal, bodily, hominine.
3. fatal, deadly, lethal, mortiferous, deathful, *Archaic.* lethiferous; destructive, ruinous, calamitous, disastrous, tragic; murderous, homicidal, slaughterous, slaughtering, death-dealing, killing; suicidal, internecine, internecive, bloodthirsty, sanguinary, bloody.
4. long, wearisome, fatiguing, tiresome; tedious, *Scot.* dree, humdrum, boring, *Fr. ennuyant,* dull, uninteresting; heavy, ponderous, irksome.
5. extreme, grave, intense; excessive, great, inordinate, enormous, terrible, awful.
—*n.* **6.** human being, human, man, earthling; person, individual, soul, creature, *Inf.* body; *Rare.* deathling.

mortality, *n.* **1.** mortalness, temporalness, temporality; impermanence, transientness, transitoriness, temporariness; ephemeralness, fugaciousness, fugacity; evanescence, momentariness, perishability, caducity, volatility, volatileness; humanness, vulnerability, fallibility, susceptibility, corruptibility, weakness.
2. humanity, earthlings, tellurians, terrene dwellers; mortals, all flesh, the human race, Homo sapiens, man, mankind; people, folk, persons, society; all individuals, all souls, all human creatures, *Rare.* deathlings.
3. death rate, number of deaths, death frequency, *Inf.* body count.
4. death, destruction, genocide, mass murder; holocaust, massacre, saturnalia of blood; epidemic, pandemia, pestilence, pest, plague.

mortar[1], *n.* **1.** pulverizer, muller, apothecary's vessel.
2. cannon, field gun, siege gun, *Inf.* big gun; trench mortar, howitzer, *Inf.* Big Bertha; carronade, falconet, ten-pounder, *Fr. bouche à feu.*

mortar[2], *n.* plaster, grout, chinking, daubing; adobe, clay, composition, cement, concrete.

mortgage, *n.* **1.** *Law.* pledge, guaranty, warranty security, collateral security.
2. bond, debenture, debenture bond, mortgage debenture, lien, mortgage instrument.
—*v.* **3.** obligate, pledge, hypothecate, put up for security, place under lien, *Inf.* hock.

mortification, *n.* **1.** humiliation, humble pie, humbled pride; shame, disgrace, dishonor, reproach, disrepute, disreputation, ill repute, bad repute, disfavor, disapproval, disapprobation, discountenance, obloquy, loss of face; degradation, debasement, abasement, vitiation, depreciation, devaluation; belittlement, derogation, detraction, deprecation, deflation, disparagement.
2. displeasure, dissatisfaction, vexation, discontent, discomfort, dislike, disappointment, chagrin, pique;

trouble, annoyance, grievance, irritation, nuisance, bother, worry, pest, plague, *Inf.* sore subject; confusion, perplexity, abashment, bewilderment; embarrassment, disconcertment, discomposure; intimidation, perturbation, consternation, trepidation, browbeating.

3. asceticism, austerity, self-denial, sacrifice, abstinence, fasting, penance, maceration, flagellation, anchoritism, self-abasement, purgation, lustration; sackcloth and ashes.

4. *Pathology.* gangrene, necrosis, cancer, carcinoma, sphacelus, canker, corruption, decay, rot.

mortified, *adj.* **1.** humiliated, humbled, meekened, made to die a thousand deaths, made to eat humble pie; shamed, disgraced, dishonored, reproached; discredited, disfavored, *Sl.* in the doghouse; debased, degraded, abased, vitiated.

2. belittled, disparaged, deprecated, derogated, deflated, decried; reduced, lowered, depressed, devalued, depreciated.

3. confused, abashed, perplexed, bewildered, confounded, dumfounded; intimidated, daunted, cowed, perturbed, browbeaten; embarrassed, put to the blush, made to blush, made to change color; dissatisfied, chagrined, discontented, vexed, disappointed, put out, displeased; harassed, irritated, bothered, provoked, harried, hectored, plagued, worried, annoyed, troubled.

4. crushed, broken, routed, discomfited, destroyed, overwhelmed, obliterated, smashed, conquered, vanquished.

5. *Pathology.* gangrenous, necrotic, rotted, suppurative, corrupted, decayed, decomposed, putrified, putrid, cankerous.

mortify, *v.* **1.** humiliate, humble, bring down, *Inf.* take *or* bring down a notch *or* peg, *Sl.* put down, make [s.o.] eat humble pie, pull down, make lowly, bring low, teach [s.o.] his place, *Inf.* make [s.o.] sing small, meeken, chasten, subdue; disgrace, shame, dishonor, put to shame, fill with shame; degrade, debase, abase, vitiate, lower, depress, reduce, demote, downgrade.

2. demean, belittle, disparage, deprecate, depreciate, decry, deflate, derogate.

3. confuse, abash, perplex, bewilder, confound, nonplus, dumfound; intimidate, daunt, cow, perturb, browbeat; embarrass, put to the blush, make [s.o.] blush, make [s.o.] change color; dissatisfy, chagrin, cause discontent, vex, disappoint, put out, displease; harass, irritate, disquiet, bother, provoke, harry, hector, plague, pester, worry, annoy, trouble.

4. crush, break, destroy, defeat utterly, rout, discomfit, overwhelm, obliterate, smash, conquer, vanquish, bring to one's knees, tread *or* trample underfoot.

5. (*all of the body*) subjugate by asceticism, practice rigorous austerities, discipline, deny, sacrifice, fast, abstain, do penance, flagellate, wear a hair shirt, sit in sackcloth and ashes; purify, cleanse, purge, macerate, lustrate.

6. *Pathology.* gangrene, necrose, rot, sphacelate, suppurate, corrupt, decay, decompose, putrify, putresce, fester, canker.

mortifying, *adj.* **1.** humiliating, humbling; shameful, disgraceful, *Obs.* reproachful; disreputable, disfavorable, discreditable.

2. belittling, derogatory, deprecatory, disparaging, depreciatory, demeaning, deflating.

3. confusing, perplexing, bewildering, confounding; intimidating, daunting, disconcerting, perturbing; embarrassing; dissatisfying, vexing, disappointing, displeasing; irritating, bothersome, disquieting, provoking, harrying, hectoring, plaguing, pestering, worrying, annoying, troubling.

4. crushing, overwhelming, obliterating, smashing.

5. (*all of the body*) disciplining, denying, sacrificing, fasting, abstaining, doing penance, flagellating, wearing a hair shirt, sitting in sackcloth and ashes; purifying, cleansing, purging, macerating, lustrating.

6. *Pathology.* rotting, suppurating, corrupting, decaying, decomposing, putrescent, putrifying, festering.

mortuary, *n.* funeral home, funeral parlor, funeral residence, funeral church, funeral chapel, undertaker's establishment.

mosaic, *n.* **1.** marquetry, parquetry, buhl, buhlwork, inlaid work.

2. conglomeration, pastiche, pasticcio, farrago, gallimaufry, mélange, miscellany, omnium-gatherum, potpourri, olio, olla-podrida, motley; mishmash, hodgepodge, jumble, scramble, tangle; salmagundi, stew, heap, mass, bunch.

—adj. **3.** tessellated, inlaid, checkered; diverse, diversified, varied; variegated, multicolored, many-colored; checked, plaid, tartan.

Moslem, *adj.* Muslem, Muslim, Mohammedan, Islamic, Islamite, Saracen, Saracenic, dervish, Turk.

moss, *n.* lichen, liverwort, locopod, lycopodium.

mossback, *n. Informal.* **1.** old fogy, square-toes, *Inf.* stick-in-the-mud, *Inf.* fud *or* fuddy-duddy *or* old fuddy-duddy, *Inf.* fossil, *Inf.* antique, *Inf.* relic, *Inf.* back number, *Inf.* dodo.

2. conservative, ultraconservative, diehard, reactionary, old-liner, *Inf.* standpatter.

3. rustic, peasant, provincial, country cousin, countryman, hobnail; yokel, bumpkin, country bumpkin, hawbuck, *Dial.* lumpkin, *Often Disparaging.* hillbilly, *Disparaging.* bogtrodder, *Inf.* chawbacon, *Inf.* cider squeezer, *Sl.* hick, *Sl.* woodhick, *Sl.* rube, *Sl.* hayseed, *Sl.* hoosier.

4. backwoodsman, woodsman, woodslander; frontiersman, mountain man; backsettler, hinterlander, *Australian.* bushman.

most, *adj.* **1.** greatest, largest; utmost, ultra, extreme, maximum; farthest, furthest; nearly all.

—n. **2.** utmost, outer limit, peak; majority, greater part, almost all, nearly all; greatest number.

—adv. **3.** extremely, very, to the greatest degree *or* extent.

mostly, *adv.* **1.** for the most part, on the whole, by and large, all in all, largely.

2. chiefly, mainly, primarily, especially, principally, predominantly.

3. generally, usually, customarily, ordinarily, commonly, normally.

mot, *n.* witticism, bon mot, quip, pleasantry; pun, catchword, byword; repartee, retort, riposte; epigram, apothegm, motto, gnome, aphorism; maxim, saw, saying, proverb, adage.

mote, *n.* particle, speck, flyspeck, grain; drop, dab, dollop; atom, *Archaic.* atomy, mite; snip, snippet, spot, dot, bit, trifle; scintilla, crumb, modicum, iota, jot, whit, tittle; moit, burr, seed.

mother, *n.* **1.** genetrix, female parent, parent, materfamilias; dam, broody, laying hen; matriarch, matron, earth mother, housewife, the hand that rocks the cradle; mother-in-law, stepmother, foster mother, adoptive mother; *All Inf.* mater, old lady, mom, mommy, ma, maw, mamma, mammy, mam, mum, mummy, mumsy, motherkins.

2. maternal affection, nurturing instinct, love for children, quality of mercy.

—v. **3.** give birth to, spawn, bear, beget, procreate; engender, originate, create, issue, bring forth; produce, author, design, mastermind.

4. nurture, nourish, rear, raise, bring up, parent; care for, protect, shelter, watch over, keep in tow, tie to one's apron strings; overprotect, smother.

motherhood, *n.* maternity, motherliness, maternalness, parenthood.

motherly, *adj.* maternal, parental; nurturing, protective, shielding, sheltering; solicitous, considerate, caring, interested; affectionate, fond, loving, devoted; gentle, tender, kind.

mother wit, *n.* **1.** native intelligence, brains, *Sl.* smarts, *Inf.* gray matter, *Fr. matière grise,* intellect; power, ability, capacity, capability, aptitude, potential, talent, genius; cleverness, resourcefulness, inventiveness, ingenuity, skillfulness, skill, knack.

2. common sense, *Inf.* horse sense, good *or* plain sense, practicality, practicalness, sound judgment; wisdom, worldly wisdom, *Inf.* the voice of experience; prudence, discernment, foresight, longheadedness, shrewdness; intuition, feel, gut feeling, understanding; presence *or* coolness of mind, level-headedness, reasonableness, perspective, balance, ballast; composure, calmness, sang-froid.

motif, *n.* (*all recurrent*) leitmotif, theme, subject, idea, notion, concept; strain, melody, tune, air; form, shape, figure, pattern; element, phrase; convention, device.

motion, *n.* **1.** movement, moving, changing place, changing position, driftage, travel, traveling, going; activity, action, activeness, stir, flux; flow, stream, passage, progress, transit; trend, drift, course, current, run, swing; roving, roaming, swaying, wandering.

2. mobility, power of movement, movability, fluidity.

3. gait, stride, step, walk, tread; bearing, carriage.

4. gesture, gesticulation, gest; sign, signal, broad hint, hint, cue, nod, nudge, shrug, wink, *Inf.* high sign; pantomime, charade, dumb show; display, show, demonstration.

5. proposal, suggestion, recommendation, submission, offering.

6. tendency, inclination, predilection, preference; liking, desire, fancy, free will.

7. in motion moving, stirring; in operation, in progress, under way; working, *Inf.* on.

—v. **8.** gesticulate, gesture, wave, flail the arms, saw the air; signal, signalize, nod, *Inf.* give [s.o.] the high sign; wiggle *or* crook one's finger, wag one's finger; give thumbs-down *or* thumbs-up to.

9. go through the motions make as if *or* as though, make out like, let on, put on an act, put up a front, bluff, pretend, fake, feign, counterfeit, simulate, make believe, make a show of; give short shrift, do *or* perform perfunctorily.

motionless, *adj.* **1.** unmoving, still, stock-still, *Chiefly Literary.* stilly; stationary, fixed, immobile, immovable, static; inert, inanimate, lifeless, dead.

2. calm, quiet, quiescent, tranquil, silent, reposeful; inactive, idle, passive, dormant, dormient, latent, stable; slumbering, sleeping, resting; unstirring, stagnant, becalmed.

motion picture, *n.* movie, moving picture, picture show, film, cine, *Inf.* flick, show, *Chiefly Brit.* cinema, motion pictures, silver screen, movies, pictures, *Inf.* pix, films; screenplay, photoplay; silent movie, talking picture, *Sl.* talkie; G-rated film, Disney movie; adult film, X-rated movie, blue movie, *Sl.* porno *or* porno film, *Sl.* skin flick, *Sl.* nudie; rerun, *Inf.* oldie *or* golden oldie; feature *or* feature film, short, short subject, documentary, travelogue; cartoon, animated cartoon; filmstrip, videotape, slide show.

motivate, *v.* move, prompt, actuate, incite, provoke, prick; rouse, arouse, stir up, excite, *Inf.* turn on, set on fire, kindle, enkindle, inflame, fire up, light a fire under [s.o.], get [s.o.] going *or* moving; instigate, start, trigger, bring [s.t.] on, cause; cause [s.o.] to do [s.t.], make [s.o.] do [s.t.], impel, drive, force, railroad; propel, push, shove, give [s.o.] a kick *or* boot; spur, prod, goad, egg on, urge *or* urge on, encourage; coax, wheedle, cajole, twist around one's little finger, manipulate, influence; persuade, talk [s.o.] into [s.t.], convince, bring around, make [s.o.] see it one's way.

motive, *n.* **1.** motivation, incentive, inducement, *Inf.* what turns [s.o.] on, *Inf.* what makes [s.o.] tick; incitement, stimulus, spur, goad, urge, prod; persuasion, encouragement, inspiration; power, pressure, thrust, push, impulse, reason, ground, cause, basis, what's behind something; occasion, angle, consideration; enticement, lure, attraction.

2. intent, intention, purpose, object, objective; goal, aim, end, target; ambition, wish, desire, plan.

—adj. **3.** kinetic, mobile, moveable, operative; moving, driving, impelling, stimulating, dynamic, active.

motley, *adj.* **1.** heterogeneous, diverse, diversified, assorted, miscellaneous, pluralistic; dissimilar, unlike, divergent; incongruous, discordant, clashing; raggletaggle, patchwork, ragged; jumbled, macaronic, mixed, mixed-up, scrambled, mingled, commingled; irregular, haphazard, promiscuous.

2. many-colored, multicolored, polychrome, polychromatic, many-hued, variegated, rainbowy, rainbowlike; harlequin, plaid, spotted, flecked, dappled, mosaic; iridescent, irisated, opalescent; versicolor, parti-colored, kaleidoscopic; spectral, prismatic, like an artist's palette *or* smock.

—n. **3.** kaleidoscope, mosaic, variegation, rainbow, flower garden, jigsaw puzzle.

4. medley, mix, mixture, mélange, miscellany, omnium-gatherum; conglomeration, mishmash, hodgepodge, jumble, scramble, mess, farrago, pastiche, pasticcio; combination, commingling, mingling, assortment, variety, array, batch; gallimaufry, salmagundi, olla-podrida, olio, potpourri.

motor, *n.* **1.** engine, internal-combustion engine, gasoline engine, gas engine; aeromotor, air motor *or* engine; inboard-outboard engine, outboard motor; power plant, power source, innards.

2. electric motor, dynamo, dynamotor, generator, turbine, transformer, transducer, universal motor.

3. automobile, car, auto, vehicle, machine, motorized vehicle, motorcar, autocar, voiture, *Inf.* wheels, *Inf.* bus, *Inf.* buggy, *Inf.* bug, *Inf.* jalopy, *Inf.* wreck, *Inf.* rattletrap, *Inf.* clunker, *Sl.* bomb, *Sl.* crate, *Sl.* tub, *Sl.* boat, *Sl.* heap, *Sl.* bucket of bolts; coupe, landau, limousine, *Inf.* limo, convertible, roadster, touring car, runabout, two-seater, phaeton, *Auto. Obs.* brougham, *Auto. Obs.* cabriolet, electric car, electromobile, locomobile, steamer, *Inf.* flivver, *Inf.* tin Lizzie, classic, antique car, antique; compact car, hardtop, sedan, sports car; station wagon, country *or* beach wagon, camper, van, jeep, land rover, beach *or* dune buggy, swamp buggy; race car, racer, racing car, stock car, Indy car, midget racer, funny car, *Sl.* dragster, *Sl.* hotrod.

4. police car, patrol car, *Inf.* prowl car, *Inf.* black and white, cruiser; truck, trailer truck, trailer, pickup truck, pickup, tractor trailer, semi-trailer, *Inf.* semi, *Inf.* rig, *Brit.* lorry; bus, motorbus, autobus, motor coach, coach, omnibus, *Inf.* jitney, *Inf.* double-decker; cab, taxicab, taxi; rental car, hired car, *Inf.* rent-a-car; motorcycle, motorbike, bike, road bike, *Inf.* chopper; trailbike, minibike, pedicab *or* pedibike, *Inf.* roadrunner.

—adj. **5.** impelling, propelling, propellant, driving.

—v. **6.** drive, ride, go for a ride *or* drive, tour, travel, take *or* make a trip, taxi, bus; *Inf.* cruise, *Inf.* cruise along, *Inf.* tool, *Inf.* tool along; go by road,

take to the road, travel the highways and byways, take the back roads.

mottle, *v.* **1.** dapple, dot, spot, bespot, speckle, bespeckle, stipple, fleck, bedaub, maculate, freckle, sprinkle, spangle, pepper; water, damascene *or* damaskeen, variegate, motley, polychrome; striate, stripe, streak, marbelize, marble.

—*n.* **2.** dapple, dot, spot, point, fleck, patch, watermark; speck, speckle, shot, tittle, jot; stipple, stripe, strip, streak, dash, wave, squiggle.

3. mottledness, dappledness, dapple, stipple, stippling, pointillism, pointillage, spottiness, maculation, speckledness, dottedness; striation, striature, stripe, striping, streaking, marbelizing; variegation, multicolor, pleochroism, irisation, polychrome, opalescence, iridescence, *Philately.* burelé *or* burelage.

mottled, *adj.* **1.** motley, blotched, blotchy, piebald, pied, skewbald, tabby, brindled, splotched, splotchy, pepper and salt; dotty, patchy, spotted, dappled, pointillé, pointillistic; speckled, specked, *Inf.* speckly; flecked, dotted, freckled, spangled, sprinkled, peppered, studded; striated, striped, veined, marbled, marmoreal; shot, watered, clouded.

2. variegated, parti-colored, multicolor, varicolored, many-hued, many-colored; opalescent, polychromatic, pleochroitic, iridescent, pavonine; versicolor, kaleidoscopic, prismatic, swirling, nacreous, nacred, pearly, tortoise-shell; diversified, daedal, confused.

motto, *n.* **1.** maxim, aphorism, apothegm, adage, saying, saw, gnome; catchword, byword, word, dictum, axiom, truism, precept, sutra; words of wisdom, words to live by, guide, formula, teaching, wisdom; principle, standard, rule, law, canon, model, prescript; moral, proverb, recipe, rule of thumb, epigram, mot, reflection, thought, ana; platitude, commonplace, cliché, bromide, banality, *Inf.* chestnut.

2. legend, inscription, epigraph, slogan, watchword; device, imprint, impression.

mound, *n.* **1.** hillock, hill, hummock, hump, swell, knoll, butte, ridge, knob, monticule, *South African.* kopje; dune, talus, tumulus, mole; elevation, rise, foothill, *Geol.* drumlin, tor, *Brit.* barrow, *Dial.* knap; moor, down, highland; incline, acclivity, slope.

2. heap, pile, stack, drift; bank, embankment; haystack, hayrick; molehill, anthill, termite hill.

—*v.* **3.** pile up, heap up, stack up, build up, bank, bank up.

mount[1], *v.* **1.** ascend, rise up, go up, climb up, climb; shoot up, spring up, leap up, fly *or* pop *or* vault up, rocket, skyrocket; rise, soar, fly, fly aloft, zoom, spire, curl upward, spiral; fountain, gush, jet, spurt, surge; take off, take to the air, leave the ground *or* get off the ground, leave the earth behind, gain altitude, become airborne, *Aeron.* chandelle; arise, levitate, go onward and upward, scale, escalade.

2. climb up on, scramble up on, clamber, clamber up, scramble up, work *or* inch one's way up, struggle, claw one's way up, scrabble up, *Inf.* shin *or* shinny up; board, go on board, get on board, go aboard, get *or* jump in *or* on, *Inf.* pile in *or* on, *Inf.* hop in *or* on; climb onto, surmount, get on, climb on, bestride, bestraddle, take horse.

3. elevate, raise, lift into place, lift, hoist *or* hoist up, hang up, nail up; enshrine, put on a pedestal.

4. install, put in place, set *or* set up, put *or* stick up; place, put, set, arrange, position, locate, situate, fix, relegate *or* assign to a place, set *or* put out, line up, organize, harmonize; posit, coordinate, settle in place, set forth, collocate, compose, dispose.

5. display, show, exhibit, expose to view, put on display, illuminate, highlight, spotlight, make a show of, dramatize; parade, bring out, roll out, *Inf.* trot out; present, state, produce, put on, showcase.

6. mount up collect, accrue, appreciate, pile up, multiply, go up, increase, grow, balloon, rise, run *or* shoot up, proliferate, boom; intensify, gain strength, wax, swell, snowball, accumulate.

—*n.* **7.** climb, ascent, rise; climbing, spiraling, gyring up, shooting up. See **mounting** (*def.* **1**).

8. horse, saddle horse, riding horse, hunter, steed, charger, palfrey, cavalry horse, courser, war-horse; race horse, racer, steeplechaser, *Inf.* bangtail, *Inf.* pony; posting horse, stalking horse, polo pony; bronco, bronc, range horse, *Western U.S.* cayuse, mustang, cow pony, bucking bronco, sunfisher, *Dial.* hoss, *Dial.* critter, *Inf.* nag, *Inf.* dobbin; mare, stallion, equine.

9. mounting, arrangement, setting, structure, frame, box, case. See **mounting** (*defs.* **2, 4**).

mount[2], *n.* **1.** hill, mountain. See **hill** (*defs.* **1, 2**). See **mountain** (*def.* **1**).

2. *Poetical.* Olympus, Olympian height, lofty mountain, wooded mountain, towering alp, lofty peak, cloud-capped *or* snow-clad peak, vast eminence, templed hill, dizzy height.

mountain, *n.* **1.** peak, alp, pinnacle, point, spur, tor, height, *Chiefly Brit.* pike, mountaintop, summit; precipice, crag, butte, promontory, cliff, bluff, headland, plateau, hump; monticule, escarpment, upland, steep, mound.

2. mountains mountain range, range, chain, sierra, ridge, highlands, crest.

mountainous, *adj.* **1.** rocky, hilly, alpine, rolling, knobby, upland, elevated; lofty, high, high-reaching, sky-high, soaring, towering, beetling, overtopping; heaven-kissing, cloud-capped, cloud-touching, supernal; precipitous, sheer, steep, rising, Olympian.

2. large, bulky, formidable, huge, enormous, mighty; prodigious, gigantic, giant, monumental; stupendous, staggering, awe-inspiring; tall, grand, grandiose, big, *Sl.* humongous; sizable, mammoth, ponderous, massive, *Inf.* whopping, *Inf.* thumping, *Inf.* thundering; immense, large-scale, far-reaching; limitless, boundless; hulking, rugged, solid, strong, powerful.

mountebank, *n.* charlatan, quack, quack doctor, quacksalver, *Archaic.* empiric; pretender, imposter, impersonator, *Sl.* ringer; sham, shammer, bluff, bluffer, *Inf.* phony; huckster, pitchman, snake oil man, medicine man, fast-talker, *Sl.* spieler, *Sl.* hot-air artist; fraud, fake, *Inf.* faker, thimblerigger, carpetbagger, crimp, *Inf.* bunko steerer, *Inf.* bunko artist; cheat, deceiver, swindler, confidence man, *Inf.* con man; *Sl.* shill, *Sl.* decoy, *Sl.* come-on man, *Sl.* plant, *Sl.* capper; trickster, chiseler, hoaxer, fourflusher, defrauder, cozener, beguiler, allurer; adventurer, knave, rogue, rascal, Cagliostro.

mounting, *n.* **1.** rise, rising, ascent, ascending, ascension, climb, clamber; climbing, spiraling, soaring, zooming, gaining altitude, taking off, shooting *or* rocketing up, surge, upsurge, upswing, upsweep, upturn, uptrend; increase, gain, growth, development, buildup, intensification, heightening, strengthening, augmentation, enlargement, greatening, amplification, widening, broadening, extension; advance, accrual, appreciation, accumulation, increment, accretion; inflation, swelling, booming, waxing, snowballing, raise, *Sl.* hike, *Inf.* step up, *Sl.* upping, *Sl.* up; levitation, elevation, leap, jump; fountain, spout, spurt, jet.

2. arrangement, plan, scheme, design, blueprint, master plan, prearrangement, schema; setup, format, layout, line-up, make-up; working plan, ground plan, spadework, groundwork, plot, chart; program, conception, projection, outline, delineation, scenario, procedure, plan of action, *Inf.* game plan; prepara-

tion, fixing, readying, making ready, forming, shaping.
3. display, demonstration, exhibition, configuration, coverage, incorporation, encompassment; distribution, disposition, deployment, formation, routine, *Brit. Inf.* the drill; form, array, order, organization, grouping, placement, coordination, collation; production, staging, presentation, packaging, design, style, styling, creation; orchestration, scoring, instrumentation, adaptation, transcription.
4. setting, background, stage setting, stage set, set, scene, backdrop, scenery; ground, field, site, locale, environment, surroundings; arena, stage, theatre, platform, mount, dais, estrade; support, underframe, base, rigging, scaffolding; framework, structure, skeleton, bones; window dressing, illumination, lighting; motif, pattern, theme, ornamental theme; ornamentation, decor, embellishment, trimming, emblazonment; fitting, casing, display case *or* cabinet, case, box, shadow box, frame, edging, backing, matting, foil.
—adj. **5.** ascending, ascensive, ascendant, ascensional; rising, leaping, springing, skyrocketing, spiraling, upward spiraling, soaring, climbing, surging; increasing, gaining; inflationary, swelling, ballooning; appreciating, advancing, booming, ever-increasing.

mourn, *v.* **1.** grieve, sorrow, lament, ache, suffer, eat one's heart out, be sad, be anguished, bewail, bemoan; weep for, be sorry for, deplore, regret, repine, rue, rue the day; yearn, languish, despair; break down, give way, melt into tears, cry one's eyes out.
2. weep, cry, sob, *Scot. and North Eng.* greet; keen, ululate, wail, howl, *Yiddish.* kvitch, *Yiddish.* geshrie; beat one's breast, flagellate oneself, tear one's hair, gnash one's teeth, rend one's clothes, put on sackcloth and ashes, wear mourning, wear widow's weeds; be dumb with grief, elegize, give sorrow words, *Inf.* sing the blues.

mourner, *n.* sorrower, griever, lamenter, weeper, wailer, bewailer, bemoaner, elegizer, repiner, groaner, whimperer; survivor, widow *or* widower, bereaved person, orphan, *Sl.* relict; commiserator, condoler, pallbearer, bearer, undertaker, *Brit. Obs.* mute, professional mourner, *Inf.* crepe hanger.

mournful, *adj.* **1.** sad, sorrowful, doleful, dolorous, downcast, downhearted, heavy-hearted, low-spirited, discouraged; woeful, cheerless, joyless, forlorn, woebegone; sorrowing, attended with sorrow, *Fr. triste*, unhappy, afflicted, disheartened, bowed-down, wan, blue, pensive, grim-visaged, long-faced; in mourning, in sackcloth and ashes; grief-stricken, prostrate, overcome, overcome with grief, dashed, broken-hearted, despairing, heartsick, disconsolate, despondent, melancholy, desolate, cut up; lugubrious, lachrymose, tearful, shedding tears, bathed in tears, crying; moaning, groaning, wailing, keening, *Yiddish.* kvitching.
2. sad, grievous, lamentable, painful, regrettable, distressing, afflictive, deplorable; pitiable, piteous, pathetic, touching, affecting, heartbreaking, heartrending, tragic; dismal, disheartening, depressing, dreary, somber, dark, gloomy; solemn, wailful, sepulchral, funereal, melancholic, plaintive; threnodic, dirgelike, dirgeful, epicedial, elegiac.

mourning, *n.* **1.** sorrowing, lamentation, grieving, lamenting, groaning, moaning, bemoaning, bewailing; wailing, howling, keening, *Yiddish.* kvitching; crying, weeping, sobbing, bawling; complaint, *Archaic.* plaint, moan, groan; keen, wail, ululation, howl; cry, outcry, bawl, jeremiad; fit of crying, flood of tears, tears, lachrymation; pulling one's hair, rending one's clothes *or* garments, beating one's chest, crying out in sorrow, *Inf.* singing the blues; murmuring, whimpering, sighing, suspirating.
2. bereavement, heaviness of heart, desolation, despondency, despair, slough of despair, moroseness, melancholy; anguish, misery, sorrow, sadness, woe, ruth, heartache, heartbreak; ache, hurt, pain, suffering.
3. funeral trappings, black garments, black veil, weeds, widow's weeds, mourning band, black armband, sackcloth and ashes.

mouse, *n.* **1.** vole, murine, rodent, vermin; meadow mouse *or* vole, field mouse, harvest mouse, wood mouse, white-footed mouse, deer mouse, vesper mouse, pocket mouse; rat, pack rat, kangaroo rat, water rat.
2. *Slang.* black eye, *Sl.* shiner.
—v. **3.** hunt out *or* down, track down, ferret out, search out, search around, hunt around; prowl about, lurk about, sneak about, slink about, skulk about.

mousy, *adj.* **1.** drab, dull, lackluster, colorless, neutral; gray, grayish, mouse-colored, mouse-dun, brownish-gray.
2. quiet, soft, light, silent, inaudible, noiseless, soundless.
3. timid, timorous, fearful, shy, withdrawn; unaggressive, unassertive, docile, tractable, compliant, obedient.

mouth, *n.* **1.** orifice, oral opening *or* cavity, muzzle, *Sl.* kisser, *Sl.* yap, *Sl.* trap, *Sl.* bazoo, chops, jaw *or* jaws; jawbone, maxilla, mandible.
2. utterance, expression, ventilation, airing, voice, vocalization.
3. idle *or* empty talk, boasting, bragging, vaunting, braggadocio, *Sl.* hot air; claptrap, rodomontade, fustian, bombast.
4. *Slang.* impudence, insolence, impertinence, sauciness, smartness, pertness, flippancy, *Inf.* freshness, *Sl.* fresh *or* smart talk, back talk, *Inf.* sass; rudeness, incivility, discourtesy, disrespect; *Inf.* cheek, brashness, audacity, effrontery, boldness, forwardness, presumptuousness.
5. grimace, face, wry face, *Archaic.* mow, *Sl.* mug, contortion; frown, scowl, glare; pout, *Fr. moue*; sneer, smirk, grin.
6. opening, aperture, hatch, *Naut.* booby hatch, trap door; door, doorway, gate, gateway, postern, portal; entrance, entry, entryway, entrée; passage, passageway, passage in *or* out, way in *or* out; exit, outlet, vent, window, porthole, loophole.
7. mouth of a river, embouchure, estuary, outlet, outfall.
8. down in the mouth *Informal.* depressed, disheartened, dejected, downcast, dispirited, daunted, low-spirited, downhearted, down, *Inf.* down in the dumps; discouraged, disappointed, crestfallen, broken-hearted, heartsick, *Inf.* broken up.
—v. **9.** lip, murmur, read *or* utter softly; articulate, pronounce, enunciate, voice, sound, sound out, phonate; vocalize, say aloud, read *or* speak aloud, deliver, give, go through the motions.
10. put *or* take into the mouth, ingest, imbibe, eat, drink, sip, sup, lap up, suck in *or* up; nibble at, peck at, bite, chew on, munch on, chump on, *Dial.* chomp on; chew, masticate.
11. grimace, *Inf.* make a face, *Sl.* mug, mop, *Archaic.* mow, contort; frown, scowl, glower, glare; sneer, smirk, grin; pout, stick out one's lower lip, *Fr. faire la moue.*
12. mouth off *Slang.* spout off, *Sl.* shoot *or* go off at the mouth, forget oneself *or* one's place, dare, presume, take liberties; talk back, *Inf.* sauce, *Inf.* answer back, *Inf.* give [s.o.] lip, *Inf.* sass *or* sass back, be insolent *Sl.* get smart *or* fresh.

mouthful, *n.* bite, sip, sup, spoonful, forkful, morsel, swallow, taste, sample, small piece; chunk, lump, hunk, gob, slice; sliver, fragment, shred, scrap, crumb, grain, granule; spot, drop, dab, jot, bit.

mouthpiece, *n.* **1.** spokesman, spokeswoman, negotiator, negotiant; mediator, intermediator, intermediary, representative, *Inf.* rep, agent.

2. *Slang.* lawyer, attorney, attorney-at-law, *U.S. Inf.* barrister.

3. puppet, cat's paw, tool, instrument; operative, front, mercenary, servant, hireling, henchman.

mouthy, *adj.* loud-mouthed, vociferous, vociferant, strepitous, strepitant, boisterous, clamorous, noisy; loud, loud-voiced, big-voiced, clarion-voiced; ranting, bombastic, fustian, high-sounding, high-flown, lofty; inflated, pretentious, pompous, turgid, tumid, overblown; grandiose, grandiloquent, rhetorical, declamatory, stilted, formal, pedantic; ornate, flowery, elaborate, euphuistic, euphuistical, periphrastic, circumlocutory, roundabout.

movable, *adj.* mobile, portable, portative, transportable, transferable; unstationary, unfixed, changeable, rearrangeable.

move, *v.* **1.** budge, stir, change place *or* position; shift, yield, give way, move over.

2. flit, fly, hie, hop, dart; zoom, vroom, whoosh, sweep, skim, skim along, *Sl.* breeze in *or* out *or* along; wend, meander, gad, gad about.

3. advance, progress, go, go ahead, move forward, get along, make headway, make strides *or* rapid strides, cover ground, roll; walk, march, hike, tread, step, pace, tramp, *Dial.* traipse, jaunt, stride, trek; stroll, perambulate, saunter, *Inf.* mosey *or* mosey about; strut, parade, mince, *Inf.* sashay; plod, trudge, shuffle, drag one's feet.

4. remove, move out, move away, change residence, relocate; decamp, break camp, *Inf.* pull up stakes; leave home, emigrate, migrate, expatriate; depart, leave, quit, vacate, repair, go away, go off, make off, exit, pull out, check out, *Inf.* bow out, *Inf.* take off, *Sl.* split.

5. turn, revolve, spin, rotate, gyrate, whirl, circle; operate, perform, run.

6. (*all of the bowels*) evacuate, excrete, egest, eject, expel, discharge, void, eliminate; defecate, stool, have a bowel movement.

7. proceed, set forth, sally forth, set out *or* off, *Inf.* be on one's way, strike out, issue, issue forth.

8. submit, propose, pose, put forward, put forth, make a motion; propound, recommend, advocate, suggest; urge, counsel, advise, admonish, exhort; enjoin, charge, call upon.

9. transfer, transmit, send, dispatch; carry, convey, cart, bear, freight, lug, *Dial.* tote; take away, carry away, cart off *or* away, conduct, lead off *or* away.

10. agitate, shake, jiggle, (*of water, wine, etc.*) roil; twirl; push, propel, drive, thrust, shove.

11. actuate, set in motion, set going; spur, prompt, prod, prick, poke, goad; lash, whip; incite, instigate, provoke, foment, egg on; arouse, rouse, fire, fire up, impassion, excite; quicken, sharpen, whet, pique, stimulate, motivate; electrify, galvanize, exhilarate, inspire, inspirit.

12. impel, urge *or* drive forward, urge *or* press on; induce, persuade, prevail upon, insist upon, railroad, ramrod, *Inf.* shove *or* ram down [s.o.'s] throat; constrain, oblige, necessitate, require, demand, force, make, exact, leave no option *or* choice; apply pressure, *Inf.* lean on, *Inf.* squeeze, *Inf.* put the screws on *or* to, *Inf.* twist [s.o.'s] arm.

13. touch, touch a chord *or* familiar chord, affect, have an effect, tell; impress, make an impression, make a dent, have an impact, *Inf.* sink in; strike, smite, hit, hit hard, *Inf.* hit where it hurts, rock, jolt, stagger, shock, *Inf.* give [s.o.] a turn, *Sl.* throw [s.o.] for a loop; upset, disturb, disquiet, ruffle; pierce, penetrate, touch to the quick, come home to; melt, soften, play on, tug *or* play on the heartstrings.

—*n.* **14.** movement, motion, activity. See **movement** (*def.* **1**).

15. change of abode *or* residence, relocation, transfer.

16. step, measure, action; attempt, effort, endeavor, essay, undertaking, *Inf.* try, *Inf.* go, *Inf.* bout, *Inf.* fling, *Sl.* whack, *Sl.* crack, *Sl.* lick, *Sl.* stab; doing, deed, turn, feat, exploit, tour de force, *Inf.* stunt; stroke, coup.

17. expedient, means, means to an end; makeshift, improvisation, stopgap, temporary expedient, ad hoc measure; resort, recourse, last resort *or* recourse, *Fr. pis-aller.*

18. maneuver, stratagem, shift, dodge; tactic, device, contrivance, artifice, design, wile, craft; ploy, ruse, trick, cute trick, red herring, *Inf.* gimmick.

19. **get a move on** *Informal.* **a.** start, begin, commence; take steps, get going, get started, get on the stick, start off, start out, move out, get the show on the road, start the ball rolling. **b.** hurry, hasten, make haste, *Literary.* haste, rush, move quickly, lose no time, *Scot.* swith, *Scot.* swirry; hustle, speed up, put on more speed, step on the gas, *Sl.* step on it, *Inf.* make it snappy, *Sl.* get cracking, *Sl.* get the lead out, *Sl.* get one's rear in gear, *Sl.* shake a leg.

20. **on the move** *Informal.* **a.** active, engaged, occupied, employed, working, at work, on the job, at it, hard at it, busy, *Inf.* busy as a beaver *or* bee. **b.** on the go, on the run, on the wing *or* fly; on the road, in transit, en route. **c.** advancing, progressing, proceeding; moving, in motion, stirring.

movement, *n.* **1.** motion, action, activity, stir, move; acts, actions, proceedings, doings, goings on, comings and goings.

2. progress, progression, advance, advancement, forward motion *or* movement; flow, flux, passage, career.

3. gesture, gesticulation, gest, *Theat.* stage business; sign, signal, broad hint, nod, nudge, wink, *Inf.* high sign; pantomime, charade, dumb show; body language, *Inf.* body English.

4. course, main course, current, main current, stream, mainstream; tone, set, bearing, swing, line, direction; tendency, drift, general tendency *or* drift, course of events, way things go, way the wind blows; trend, trend of the times; spirit of the age, *Ger. Zeitgeist.*

5. drive, crusade, fund-raiser, undertaking; party, faction, wing, group; coalition, front, political front, popular *or* people's front, grass-roots movement.

6. bowel movement, *Inf.* BM, defecation, evacuation, voidance, *Med., Physiol.* dejection; excrement, excreta, feces, ordure, stool.

7. works, workings, working parts, mechanism, machinery; wheels, wheelworks, wheels within wheels, gears; innards, inner workings, what makes [s.t.] tick.

8. *Music.* **a.** division, section, part; passage, strain, phrase, musical phrase. **b.** rhythm, beat, cadence, meter, measure, lilt, swing; time, tempo.

movie, *U.S. n.* **1.** film, motion picture, moving picture. See **motion picture**.

2. motion picture theater, theater, *Brit.* theatre, *Inf.* movie house, movie palace, cine, showcase theater, (*formerly*) nickelodeon.

3. **movies** **a.** motion picture industry, Hollywood, silver screen. **b.** pictures, *Inf.* pix, films.

moving, *adj.* **1.** in motion, running, going, operating, active; mobile, motor, motive, *Biol.* motile.

2. impulsive, propelling, driving, thrusting; instigative, instigating, incitive, inciting, provocative, provoking, fomenting; motivational, motivating, animating, stimulating, stimulative; exciting, rousing, electrifying, galvanizing.

3. impressive, striking, telling, effective; stirring, soul-stirring, breath-taking, thrilling; inspiring, inspirational, heart-swelling; affecting, touching, emotive, tender, poignant; pathetic, pitiful, pitiable, heartbreaking, heartrending, heart-moving.

mow, *v.* **1.** cut, clip, shear, prune, shave, trim; mow the lawn, cut the grass.

2. *Usu.* **mow down** butcher, maul, savage, hew, hack, hack to pieces, cut to pieces, chop to pieces, mutilate, tear limb from limb; wade in blood, run amuck, go berserk, give no quarter, show no mercy; slaughter, massacre, decimate, kill a great number; kill off, annihilate, exterminate, eradicate, eliminate, liquidate.

much, *adj.* **1.** abundant, plenteous, plentiful, plenty, replete; ample, sufficient, large, considerable, *Archaic.* mickle; saturated, full, brimming, chock-full, brimful, overflowing, fulsome; liberal, generous, luxuriant, extravagant, riotous, bountiful; profuse, numerous, countless, multitudinous, inexhaustible, bottomless; swarming, teeming, rife, rampant, flush, fraught.

—n. **2.** a lot, a great deal, abundance, plenty, plenitude, repletion, galore, *Archaic.* muchness; amplitude, exuberance, myriad, lavishness, profusion, extravagance; wealth, fullness, opulence, riot, bonanza; shower, gush, stream, cascade, deluge, avalanche, volley, plethora; superfluity, superabundance, spate, satiety; fill, surfeit, copiousness, cornucopia; lots, quantities, *Sl.* scads, *Sl.* gobs, *Sl.* wads, *Inf.* oodles; tons, barrels, pecks, bushels, *Brit. Inf.* bags, *Chiefly Brit. Inf.* lashings; loads, piles, heaps, lumps, mounds, masses, stacks; raft, *Inf.* slew, mess, batch, mint, pot, stock, store; volumes, reams, pages, numbers, scores; acres, mountains, worlds, oceans, seas; host, legion, swarm, multitude, drove, flock; crowd, litter, shoal, hive, flight, pack, herd, school.

3. make much of a. amplify, overstate, heighten, emphasize, stress. **b.** pamper, flatter, coddle, indulge. See **make** (*def.* **26**).

—adv. **4.** greatly, well, largely, abundantly, highly; to a great extent, to a large degree, considerably, muchly, so, ever so; a lot, a great deal, *Inf.* no end of, galore, *Fr. beaucoup*, in abundance; in the large, in a big way, on a large scale, in great measure, at length, wholesale; freely, without stint, *Inf.* to the skies, to one's heart's content; copiously, bountifully, liberally, generously, exuberantly; riotously, profusely, plentifully, *Inf.* aplenty; vastly, immensely, enormously, hugely.

5. nearly, approximately, close, closely; about, nigh, well-nigh, almost, around, towards; just about, all but, not quite, *Inf.* pretty much; roughly, *Inf.* practically, more or less, give *or* take a little, for all practical purposes, for the most part; generally, roundly, in round numbers.

6. frequently, often, oftentimes, over and over, again and again, repeatedly; recurrently, time and again, time after time, many times, a number of times; habitually, persistently, repetitively, chronically.

mucilage, *n.* gum, putty, fixative, adhesive, resin, *Inf.* gunk, *Inf.* goo, *Inf.* glop; glue, paste, cement, epoxy, size, lute; syrup, molasses, treacle; mucus, *Physiol.* synovia, *Vulgar.* snot.

mucilaginous, *adj.* gluey, gummy, pasty, doughy, tacky, *Archaic.* sizy; sticky, adhesive, cohesive, clinging, tenacious; viscous, glutinous, gumbo, syrupy, treacly; mucous, albuminous, ropy, stringy, *Physiol.* synovial, *Vulgar.* snotty; soft, moist, slimy, clammy, slithery, *Sl.* icky, *Sl.* yechy; viscid, gelatinous, *Inf.* gooey, *Sl.* ishy.

muck, *n.* **1.** dung, manure, ordure, compost, night soil; excrement, feces, leavings, droppings, guano, *Chiefly Midwestern.* flops.

2. slop, wash, hogwash, swill, wallow, sough; sewage, matter, draff, bilge; scum, smudge, feculence, dross, gumbo; filth, dirt, grime, sludge, mire, mud, ooze; slush, squash, slime, mess, sordes, *Irish.* slob, *Inf.* glop, *Inf.* gunk, *Inf.* goo.

mucky, *adj.* **1.** muddy, oozy, miry, quagmiry; sloshy, slushy, sloppy, sludgy, squelchy; squashy, squishy, soft, splashy, plashy; feculent, foul, turbid, fetid, reeky; fecal, excrementitious, *Physiol.* stercoraceous.

2. filthy, dirty, grimy, smudgy, soiled, smeared, stained, begrimed, sooty; unwashed, piggish, sleazy, squalid, wretched, dingy, miserable, *Sl.* slummy.

mud, *n.* ooze, muck, mire, silt, clay, slush, sludge, gumbo; slime, squash, *Irish.* slob, swill, slop, slosh; quagmire, fen, bog, swamp, marsh, morass; quicksand, wallow, slough, *Brit.* sough, *Brit. Dial.* sump.

muddle, *v.* **1.** mix, mix up, jumble, jumble together, throw together, tumble; scramble, tangle, ensnarl; clutter, litter, turn upside-down, mess, mess up, make a mess of; disarrange, derange, disorder, disarray, disorganize.

2. botch, bungle, blunder, bobble, fumble, *Inf.* flub, mismanage, mishandle; spoil, mar, butcher, murder; make a hash of, mix up, *Sl.* screw up, *Sl.* louse up, *Sl.* ball up, *Sl.* bollix up, *Sl.* gum up, *Sl.* gum up the works, *Sl.* foul up.

3. confuse, confound, perplex, bewilder, puzzle, nonplus, mystify, baffle, pose, obfuscate, befog, buffalo, *Sl.* snow.

4. (*all with intoxicants*) stupefy, addle, fuddle, befuddle; intoxicate, inebriate, besot, make drunk, *Inf.* light up, *Inf.* put under the table; *All Sl.* plaster, pollute, souse, stew, crock, swack, pickle, stone, sozzle, booze up, liquor up, likker up.

5. muddle through manage, contrive, make out, *Inf.* get on *or* along, scrape along, manage somehow; make one's way, work one's way, press on.

—n. **6.** confusion, perplexity, bewilderment, bafflement, mystification, *Brit. Dial.* swither; stupefaction, uncertainty, demoralization, sixes and sevens; distraction, daze, haze, fog, *Psychiatry.* disorientation.

7. disorder, disarray, disorganization, disarrangement, derangement, hugger-mugger, confusedness; jumble, mess, tangle, *Inf.* stew, mix-up, snafu, *Inf.* foul-up, *Sl.* screw-up, *Sl.* louse-up, *Sl.* ballup, *Brit. Sl.* balls-up; clutter, litter, Fibber McGee's closet; hodgepodge, *Brit.* hotchpotch, mishmash, conglomeration.

muddled, *adj.* **1.** jumbled, tangled, snarled, ensnarled, mixed-up, all mixed-up, jumbled together, thrown together; disorganized, disorderly, in disorder, in disarray, disarranged, deranged, at sixes and sevens, hugger-mugger, helter-skelter, higgledy-piggledy, topsy-turvy, *Sl.* arsy-varsy.

2. botched, bungled, blundered, bobbled, fumbled, *Inf.* flubbed, mishandled, mismanaged; spoiled, spoilt, ruined, marred, butchered, murdered; *All Sl.* screwed-up, loused-up, fouled-up, balled-up, bollixed-up, mucked-up, gummed-up.

3. confused, confounded, mystified, perplexed, baffled, bewildered, nonplused, buffaloed; uncertain, unsure, at sea, adrift, at a loss; discomposed, flustered, aflutter, *Inf.* discombobulated, dazed, *Archaic.* bemazed; disoriented, fuzzy, in a fog, in a daze, in a stupor, *Inf.* muzzy, *Inf.* spaced *or* spaced out, *Inf.* out of it, *Sl.* in the ozone, *Sl.* in another zone.

4. tipsy, grogged, *Archaic.* groggy, obfuscated, woozy, bleary-eyed, pie-eyed, glassy-eyed; intoxicated, inebriated, drunk, sodden, besotted, sottish, awash, *Literary.* in one's cups; under the influence, under the weather, having a glow on, the worse for liquor; *All Inf.* boozy, lit, lit-up, tight, illuminated, high, mellow, feeling good, feeling no pain; *All Sl.* loaded, tanked, lubricated, oiled, stewed, bombed, plotched. See also **drunk** (*defs.* **2, 3**).

muddy, *adj.* **1.** miry, mucky, oozy, sludgy, slushy, sloshy, sloppy, squashy, squishy, squelchy, slimy, feculent; dirty, grimy, grubby, *Sl.* grungy; boggy, marshy, swampy, fenny, quaggy, sloughy, turbid.

2. dingy, sooty, smoky, smudgy, fulginous, murky; colorless, hueless, dull, mat, flat, dead, leaden, lackluster, lusterless; washed-out, faded.

3. confused, confounded, mystified, muddled, bemuddled; at a loss, at sea, adrift, uncertain, unsure; fuzzy, in a daze, *Inf.* muzzy, *Sl.* out of it, *Sl.* in the ozone.

4. (*all of expression, thought, etc.*) obscure, vague, indistinct, opaque, fuzzy, unclear, *Inf.* clear as mud.

—*v.* **5.** dirty, soil, besoil, begrime, mire, bemire, muck, smudge, smear, besmear.

6. confuse, confound, perplex, bewilder, puzzle, nonplus, mystify, baffle, pose, obfuscate, befog, buffalo, muddle, bemuddle, *Sl.* snow.

muff, *n.* **1.** failure, bungle, botch, botchery, blunder; slip, trip, stumble, bumble, fumble, clumsy performance, gaucherie; bad job, sad performance, hash, mess; careless *or* hasty work, slovenly performance, slapdash work, *Inf.* a lick and a promise, *Inf.* a once-over job.

—*v.* **2.** *Informal.* bungle, fumble, *Inf.* flub, handle clumsily; botch, spoil, make a mess of, *Sl.* blow; bosh, hash, mess up, bugger, *Inf.* gum up the works; mismanage, manage improperly, misapply, misdirect, misadminister, *Inf.* drop the ball; flounder, stumble, trip, slip up.

muffin, *n.* English muffin, bran muffin, corn muffin, blueberry muffin; bun, roll, scone, cupcake; biscuit, beaten biscuit, brioche, croissant.

muffle, *v.* **1.** *Often* **muffle up** wrap, envelop, swaddle, swathe; cloak, cover, hood; conceal, veil, shroud, mask, hide, disguise.

2. pad, damp, damper, mute, soft-pedal, tone down; hush, quiet, still, muzzle, silence; quell, suppress, stifle, gag, choke, stop.

muffled, *adj.* dampened, muted, padded; soft, softened, subdued, toned down, suppressed; faint, indistinct, unclear, dim, barely audible; nonresonant, dead, dead-sounding; *It. sordo*, flat, dull, toneless.

muffler, *n.* neck scarf, boa, neckerchief; tippet, ascot, stock, cravat; chemisette, guimpe.

mug, *n.* **1.** tankard, toby, beaker, chalice, schooner, pot.

2. *Slang.* **a.** face, visage, countenance, features, lineaments; *Sl.* pan, *Sl.* phiz, *Sl.* puss; mouth, *Sl.* kisser. **b.** grimace, sneer, frown, pout, black look, *Fr. moue*; smile, grin, smirk, sardonic expression; look, mein, aspect, expression.

—*v.* **3.** assault, attack, knock down; strong-arm, throttle, garrote, choke; rob, steal from, pursesnatch.

4. *Slang.* grimace, *Inf.* make a face, *Fr. faire la moue,* screw up one's face; frown, pout, sneer; grin, smirk, smile.

muggy, *adj.* humid, *Inf.* close, sticky, mucky, clammy, moist, damp; sultry, sweltering, sudorific, diaphoretic; steamy, steaming, dank, soggy, watery, wettish; dewy, foggy, vaporous, vaporific, misty, drizzly, dripping, rainy; tropical, hot, oppressive.

mulct, *n.* **1.** fine, penalty, amercement, (*at English universities*) sconce, settlement, *Law.* damages; forfeiture, forfeit, *Eng. Law.* praemunire, confiscation, *Law.* escheat, *Law.* sequestration; fixed fee, fee, charge, cost, *Hist.* scot.

—*v.* **2.** fine, amerce, impose a fine on, (*at English universities*) sconce; confiscate, *Law.* sequestrate, *Law.* escheat; penalize, punish, exact punishment.

3. defraud, *Law.* extort, fleece, swindle, cheat, bilk.

mule, *n.* **1.** hinny, jackass, ass, donkey, burro, jenny; hybrid, crossbreed, mixed breed, mongrel.

2. *Informal.* stubborn person, recalcitrant, irreconcilable, diehard, *Inf.* bitter-ender, stickler.

mulish, *adj.* **1.** stubborn, obstinate, pervicacious, pig-headed, obdurate, headstrong, willful, strong-willed, self-willed; intransigent, uncompromising, irreconcilable, unyielding, unbending; hard-line, determined, rigid, inflexible, dogged, pertinacious, inexorable; cross-grained, wrong-headed, perverse, contrary, froward, resistant, opposed, restive, balky, balking; intractable, indocile, unsubmissive, uncompliant, immovable, uncooperative, wayward, unconforming, nonconforming.

2. disobedient, refractory, stiff-necked, fractious, recalcitrant, rebellious, insubordinate, defiant, contumacious, recusant; uncompliable, indomitable, unconquerable, unsubduable; difficult, hard to handle, unmanageable, ungovernable, unteachable.

mull, *v.* **1.** study, examine, con, evaluate, weigh, turn over, review, revolve; ruminate, cogitate, chew, chew one's cud, reflect on, think over, rack one's brains, cudgel one's brain, trouble one's head; brood, dwell on, be in a brown study; ponder, muse, think about, wonder about, consider, speculate, dream about; concentrate, focus, put one's mind to, have one's mind on; meditate, contemplate, cerebrate, think, put on one's thinking cap, be abstracted, be lost in thought.

2. muddle, fuddle, jumble, mix up, mess up, make a mess, make a hash, confuse; bungle, botch, make sad work of, *Inf.* muff, *Sl.* blow, blunder, boggle, make a mistake, mistake, err, slip, trip, fumble, stumble, slip up, trip up, *Sl.* screw up.

multicolored, *adj.* polychromatic, polychromic, of many colors *or* shades *or* hues, versicolor, multicolor; prismatic, prismatical, spectral, rainbowy, rainbow-like, colorful, brilliant, pavonine; iridescent, pearly, opalescent, opaline, nacreous, nacred, *Crystall.* pleochroic; shot, variegated, varied, varicolored, kaleidoscopic; parti-colored, marble, marbly, marmoreal, marmorean, motley, streaked, striated, striped; piebald, pied, (*esp. of horses*) skewbald, dappled, brindled, spotted, mottled, speckled, flecked; checked, checkered, plaid, tartan.

multifaceted, *adj.* **1.** many-sided, many-faced; manifold, multifold, multiplex, multifarious, multitudinous; multitalented, diversified, variegated, eclectic.

2. intricate, complicated, complex, involved; knotty, tortuous, convoluted, difficult.

multifarious, *adj.* multitudinous, manifold, multifold, multiplex, multiple, numerous, many, several; of many kinds, varied, miscellaneous, various, diverse, divers, sundry; heterogeneous, motley, mixed; many-sided, many-faceted, diversified, variegated, eclectic; multiform, polymorphous, polymorphic, diversiform, variform, omnifarious, *Elect.* multiphase.

multiform, *n.* polymorphous, polymorphic, diversiform, variform, omnifarious, *Elect.* multiphase; multifarious, manifold, multifold, multiplex.

multiplication, *n.* **1.** increase, augmentation, addition, superaddition; enlargement, magnification, greatening, expansion, build-up, heightening, aggrandizement; doubling, duplication, redoubling, tripling, triplication, quadrupling, quadruplication, quintuplication, quintupling, sextupling, septupling, septuplication, octupling, decupling, *Bridge.* redouble; growth, accretion, acceleration, speed-up, intensification, rise, mushrooming, burgeoning.

2. propagation, breeding, generation, production; reproduction, procreation, engenderment; fructification, pullulation, proliferation, fecundation, multiparity.

multiplicity, *n.* **1.** multitude, host, array, large *or* great number, *Sl.* slew; quantity, lot, whole lot, bunch, whole bunch, batch, abundance, a great deal, large *or* great amount; volume, mass, mountain, ton, tons, barrel, barrels, acres, oceans, heaps, piles, stacks, oodles, gobs, scads.

2. multiplexity, manifoldness, multifariousness, many-sidedness, variety, diversity, diverseness, multiformity; complexity, intricacy, involvement, complicatedness, complication, complicacy, convolutedness.

multiply, *v.* **1.** double, duplicate, make twofold, redouble, triple, triplicate, quadruple, quadruplicate, quintuple, quintuplicate, sextuple, septuple, septuplicate, octuple, decuple, make tenfold, make numerous *or* multitudinous; increase, augment, add to, superadd to, enlarge, make larger, make greater, *Chiefly Literary.* greaten, build up, boost, raise, heighten, aggrandize, magnify; grow, accrete, get bigger, accelerate, speed up, intensify, snowball, mushroom, burgeon.

2. propagate, produce, generate, make fruitful *or* prolific *or* fecund, fecundate; reproduce, breed, procreate, bring forth *or* bear offspring, *Obs.* teem; engender, (*esp. of a male parent*) beget, sire, father; hatch, (*of animals*) drop, (*of swine*) farrow, (*of dogs*) pup, (*of cats*) kitten, (*of dogs, lions, etc.*) whelp, (*of sheep or goats*) yean, (*of fish*) spawn; fructify, be fruitful, bear fruit, pullulate, proliferate, be prolific, be fertile, breed like a rabbit.

multitude, *n.* **1.** host, mass, crowd, throng, crush, *Sl.* mess, horde; drove, bevy, herd, pack, flock, swarm, gaggle, school, shoal; army, legion, tribe, band, team, troop, squad, company, group, party, body; assemblage, congregation, aggregation, array, accumulation, assortment; bunch, gang, crew, *Inf.* caboodle; concentration, concourse, confluence, conflux, convergence.

2. lots, a lot, *Inf.* raft, *Sl.* scads, *Sl.* a scad, piles, a pile, *Inf.* heaps, *Inf.* a heap, lashings; bags of, *Inf.* gobs of, bags, barrels, tons, a bunch, a bushel and a peck; shipload, passel; myriad, a thousand and one, scores, numbers, a number, *Inf.* scillions, *Inf.* zillions, *Inf.* oodles, *Inf.* slew; multiplicity, multitudinousness, plenty, abundance, profusion, galaxy; congestion, jam, press, rush, *Inf.* mob scene, endless stream, river, torrent, flood, deluge, ocean, sea, world.

3. the multitude commonalty, the public, the general public, the masses; populace, citizenry, proletariat, hoi polloi, bourgeoisie, *Sl.* booboisie, rank and file; commoners, peasantry; the lower classes, low life, dregs, riffraff, mob, rabble, rout, *Inf.* the great unwashed.

multitudinous, *adj.* numerous, multiple, multiplied, multifold, *Inf.* umpteen, multifarious, manifold, various; myriad, sundry, divers, several, many; profuse, prevalent, plentiful, abundant, copious, rife; teeming, swarming, brimming, overflowing, abounding, crowded; great, considerable, large; innumerable, countless, numerous as the stars in the Milky Way, numerous as the grains of sand on the seashore, illimitable, limitless, unlimited, boundless, unbounded; immeasurable, unfathomable, incalculable.

mum, *adj.* **1.** silent, speechless, mute, dumb, noiseless, soundless, aphonic; voiceless, nonvocal, wordless, pantomimic; reticent, taciturn, quiet, uncommunicative, reserved; tight-lipped, closed-mouthed, tongue-tied, buttoned up; evasive, secretive, noncommital.

2. mum's the word keep silent, don't tell anyone, cross your heart and hope to die, keep secret, keep to oneself, keep under one's hat, play dumb.

mumble, *v.* speak inarticulately, talk incoherently, swallow one's words, utter indistinctly, mince one's words; mutter, murmur, grumble, mump, *Obs.* mussitate; splutter, hem and haw, sputter; ramble, maunder, gibber, jabber, gabble, babble, patter.

mumbo jumbo, *n.* **1.** incantation, chant, magic formula, magic word, invocation, conjuration, ritual; hocus-pocus, open sesame, abracadabra; charm, spell, rune, *Scot.* cantrip.

2. claptrap, rodomontade, fustian, bombast, rant, *Sl.* hot air; nonsense, fiddle-de-dee, gobbledegook, jargon, gibberish, Jabberwocky; moonshine, blather, drivel, foam, froth, humbug, bunkum, *Sl.* bunk, *U.S. Sl.* blah; flummery, *Inf.* hokum, *Sl.* applesauce, *Sl.* eyewash; rubbish, *Sl.* tripe, refuse, chaff, trash, *Inf.* truck, trumpery; tommyrot, *Inf.* rot, *Sl.* garbage, *Sl.* crap, *Sl.* crock, *Sl.* bull; balderdash, *Sl.* horsefeathers, hogwash, stuff, stuff and nonsense, *Inf.* bosh, *Brit. Inf.* gammon, *Brit. Sl.* tosh; fudge, foolishness, rigmarole, amphigory; footle, *Inf.* malarkey, *Sl.* bushwa, *Sl.* baloney, *Sl.* bilge *or* bilge water, *Sl.* meshugaas, *Scot. and North Eng.* haver; poppycock, *Inf.* fiddle-faddle, *Inf.* piffle, *Inf.* hooey, *Inf.* kibosh, *Inf.* flapdoodle.

mummer, *n.* masquerader, masker; actor, performer, entertainer, player, strolling player, *Fr. comédien ambulant;* pantomimist, mimist, mimer, mime, Marcel Marceau, impersonator, satirist, *Fr. farceur;* comedian, comic, jester, fool, clown, merry-andrew, zany, harlequin, buffoon, pantaloon, straight man, foil.

mummery, *n.* **1.** masquerade, harlequinade, farce; impersonation, personation, pantomime, mime; parody, caricature, burlesque, burletta, travesty, satire, *Inf.* take-off, lampoon; buffoonery, comedy, slapstick comedy; entertainment, amusement, diversion, divertissement.

2. pageantry, pomp, ostentation, display; show, spectacle, performance, ceremony, celebration, fête, gala.

munch, *v.* **1.** chump, *Dial.* chomp, champ, crunch, craunch, chew, *Dial.* chaw, eat *or* masticate noisily; bite, gnaw, nibble.

2. *Slang.* **munch out** *Sl.* pig out, *Sl.* make a pig of oneself, *Sl.* stuff one's face, glut oneself, gorge oneself.

mundane, *adj.* **1.** worldly, earthly, terrestrial, terrene, subcelestial, subastral, sublunary; secular, temporal, material, physical, corporeal, bodily, fleshly, carnal, sensual.

2. common, ordinary, everyday, usual, prosaic, household; routine, customary, regular, normal, typical; commonplace, banal, hackneyed, trite, stale, platitudinous.

municipal, *adj.* civic, civil, city, metropolitan, urban, oppidan; local, community, communal, town, burghal, village, neighborhood; public, social.

municipality, *n.* city, metropolis, capital *or* capital city, metropolitan area; megalopolis, environs, suburbs *or* suburb, *Fr. banlieue*, bedroom community; borough, township, town, (*in Scotland*) burgh, *Inf.* burg, county seat, *Esp. Brit.* county town, village, hamlet, *Archaic.* thorp, kraal; district, precinct, constituency, bailiwick, *Chiefly Brit.* parish.

munificence, *n.* **1.** bounty, bounteousness, liberality, free-handedness, open-handedness, generosity; ungrudgingness, unsparingness, lack of stint; big-heartedness, hospitality, beneficence; charity, charitableness, magnanimity; altruism, unselfishness, phi-

lanthropy, humanitarianism, benevolence, good will.
2. amplitude, abundance, full measure, more than enough, repletion; plenty, plenteousness, plenitude; sumptuousness, lavishness, prodigality, extravagance, plethora.
3. gift, present, charitable bequest; donation, grant, gratuity; largess, good turn, benefaction.

munificent, 1. bountiful, bounteous, liberal, free, free-handed, open-handed, generous, free with one's money; ungrudging, unsparing, unstinting; big-hearted, hospitable, beneficent; charitable, altruistic, unselfish; almsgiving, public-spirited, philanthropic, humanitarian.
2. plentiful, plenteous, ample, abundant; abounding, copious, rich, prodigal, extravagant, luxuriant; more than generous, more than enough, more than adequate; royal, princely, kingly; sumptuous, lavish, profuse.

munition, *n.* **1.** *Usu.* **munitions** weapons, armaments, arms, firearms; guns, ordnance, artillery, cannon, battery, siege artillery, field artillery, anti-aircraft guns; ammunition, bullets, gunpowder, powder and shot, shot, shrapnel, dum-dums; explosives, bombs, rockets, screaming-meemies, V-2 rockets; rockets, missiles; torpedoes, depth charges, mines, land mines, floating mines; hand grenades, rifle grenades; TNT, poison gas, napalm, atomic bombs, hydrogen bombs, neutron bombs.
2. material, matériel, military stores, supplies; equipment, equipage, gear, kit, outfit, apparatus, tackle, rig; trappings, fittings, appointments, accouterments, appurtenances, things; impedimenta, paraphernalia, furnishings, provisions; implements, tools, instruments.

murder, *n.* **1.** manslaughter, slaying, killing, (*in India*) thuggee, bloody *or* foul killing *or* slaying, assassination, *Sl.* hit, dispatch, shooting; strangulation, strangling, choking, garotte, garotting, throttling; lynching, hanging, *Euph.* necktie party; asphyxiation, suffocation, smothering, burking; stabbing, knifing, running through, impalement; decapitation, decollation, beheading; lapidation, stoning; drowning, burning, poisoning; homicide, patricide, matricide, parricide, fratricide, sororicide, uxoricide, infanticide, regicide, vaticide.
2. butchery, massacre, carnage, slaughter, blood bath, bloodshed, effusion of blood, fusillade of blood; wholesale *or* general slaughter, mass-killing, mass-slaying, mass-homicide, mass-execution, mass-destruction; decimation, liquidation, blotting *or* wiping out, genocide, pogrom, holocaust, *Euph., Hist.* Final Solution, extermination, obliteration, organized murder, elimination.
3. murder will out exposure, exposé, exposition, revelation, disclosure, divulgence, divulgation, unfolding, unmasking, laying open, laying bare, muckraking, publication; discovery, detection.
—*v.* **4.** kill, slay, assassinate, poison, do to death, liquidate, blot *or* wipe out, put an end to, get rid of, put away, put out of the way, silence; carry off, remove, dispatch, finish, finish off, do for, fix, settle, lay out, lay low, *Inf.* put the kibosh on; *All Sl.* off, hit, zap, waste, croak, eighty six, snuff out, take off, rub out, bump off, knock off, polish off, give [s.o.] the works *or* the business; *All Euph.* send west, take for a ride, put [s.o.] out of his misery.
5. shoot, shoot down, riddle, *Inf.* blow [s.o.'s] brains out, *Inf.* pump [s.o.] full of lead; club, beat, batter, pound, hammer, brain, blackjack, *Inf.* knock *or* beat [s.o.'s] brains out; choke, strangle, throttle, stifle, garotte, *Sl.* scrag; knife, stab, cut [s.o.'s] throat, jugulate, cut, cut down, bayonet, pierce, run through, put to the sword, impale, spear, lance, *Euph.* let the daylight in; smother, suffocate, asphyxiate, burke; execute, put to death, behead, decapitate, guillotine, decollate, hang, gibbet, lynch, *Sl.* string up, *Sl.* stretch, stone, lapidate, burn, burn at the stake, drown.
6. slaughter, butcher, cut to pieces, hew, hack, hack to pieces, chop, chop to pieces, dismember, draw and quarter, tear limb from limb, disembowel, mutilate, savage, maul, shed *or* spill blood; wade in blood, run amuck, go berserk, give no quarter, show no mercy.
7. annihilate, exterminate, obliterate, discreate, reduce to nothing, destroy totally, eradicate, extirpate, extinguish; massacre, decimate, destroy a great number.
8. *All Fig.* abuse, mangle, butcher, slaughter, mutilate, maul; mispronounce, misuse, *Rare or Obs.* solecize; mar, spoil, ruin, damage, impair, hurt, harm.

murderer, *n.* **1.** killer, slayer, manslayer, man-killer, cutthroat, thug, poisoner, strangler, impaler; assassin, liquidator, bravo, sniper, gunman, knifer, *Euph.* silencer, *Euph.* dispatcher; *All Sl.* gun, hired gun, hit man, triggerman, torpedo, hatchet man; executioner, excutionist, *Sl.* Jack Ketch, decapitator, headsman, beheader, lyncher, hangman, garotter, burker, burkist; butcher, slaughterer, Bluebeard, ripper, mass-killer, mass-slayer, exterminator, annihilator, destroyer; bloodspiller, bloodshedder, bloodletter.
2. homicide, patricide, matricide, paricide, fratricide, sororicide, uxoricide, infanticide, regicide, tyrannicide, vaticide.

murderous, *adj.* **1.** killing, homicidal, cutthroat, assassinative, death-dealing, lethal, fatal, mortal, mortiferous, deadly, deathly, *Archaic.* lethiferous; slaughterous, internecine, savage, barbarous, cruel, brutal, fiendish, cannibalistic, anthropophagous, bloodthirsty, bloody-minded, sanguinary, sanguine, sanguineous, sanguinolent, bloody, gory, bloodstained, ensanguined; ferocious, violent, frenzied, wild, berserk, amuck, raging, maniacal; annihilating, exterminating, obliterating, extirpative, extirpating, extinguishing, eliminating, withering, devastating, decimating, destructive, destroying.
2. (*all in the extreme*) difficult, arduous, strenuous, rigorous, herculean, tremendous, gargantuan, huge, prodigious; dangerous, perilous, *Archaic.* parlous, hazardous, formidable, harrowing, precarious, risky, unsafe, treacherous; trying, unendurable, intolerable, unbearable, insufferable.

murky, *adj.* **1.** dark, dusky, gloomy, dismal, dreary, bleak, grim; funereal, somber, solemn, grave, heavy; cheerless, joyless, desolate; discouraging, disheartening, dispiriting, depressing, hopeless.
2. foggy, rainy, misty, *Archaic.* caliginous, hazy, overcast, umbrageous, shadowy, shady, grey; opaque, tenebrous, *Literary.* darkling, smoggy, smoky, *Sl.* soupy, lowering; dull, dim, faint, pale, feeble, weak.
3. obscure, vague, nebulous; ambiguous, mysterious, arcane, inexplicable; enigmatic, puzzling, baffling, perplexing, confounding, bewildering; veiled, secret, cryptic, hidden, occult.
4. clandestine, illegitimate, *Inf.* shady, illicit, unethical, *Inf.* dirty.

murmur, *n.* **1.** undertone, whisper, sigh, babble, murmuration, *Inf.* whoosh; grumble, mussitation, mutter, whine, *Inf.* grouse, complaint, carping, caviling.
—*v.* **2.** mumble, mutter, whisper, speak in an undertone, babble; grumble, *Inf.* grouse, *Inf.* carp; complain softly, sigh, whine, snuffle; keen, moan, softly lament.

murmurer, *n.* sigher, whisperer, babbler; mumbler,

mutterer, grumbler, *Inf.* grouse; complainer, whiner, snuffler, carper, caviler, malcontent; faultfinder, objector, censurer.

murmurous, *adj.* **1.** sighing, whispering, babbling; mumbling, muttering, grumbling, whining, *Inf.* grousing, complaining, *Inf.* carping; malcontent, faultfinding, objecting, censorial; moaning, lamenting, sobbing.

2. soft, subdued, quiet, gentle, dulcet; muted, stifled, hushed, inaudible, imperceptible, indistinct, unclear.

muscle, *n.* **1.** sinew, sinews, thew, thews, tendon, tendons.

2. brawn, muscles, *Inf.* beef, muscularity; musculature, muscular development, physique; brawniness, huskiness, heftiness, *Inf.* beefiness.

3. power, potency, might, strength, force, muscular strength, *Literary.* puissance; mightiness, powerfulness, forcefulness; energy, effort, exertion, *Inf.* elbow grease; *All Inf.* pull, leverage, weight, clout, influence.

4. substance, essence, gist, thrust, core, meat, pith, *Inf.* nuts and bolts, *Inf.* nitty-gritty; essential, principle, fundamental; crux, crucial *or* critical point, major part, best part, point, main point, salient point, important thing, main thing, chief thing, essential matter, *Inf.* bottom line.

—v. **5.** *Informal.* push, force, drive, shove, ram, shoulder, butt, bully, strong-arm; elbow, jostle, joggle, hustle; squeeze, wedge, cram.

6. strengthen, toughen, harden, indurate, fortify, build up; renew, restore.

muscular, *adj.* **1.** sinewy, thewy, fibrous, *Rare.* muscly, *Obs.* musculous.

2. brawny, strapping, muscled, well-muscled, full-muscled, broad-shouldered, powerfully built, *Derog.* musclebound; stalwart, rugged, hefty, husky, burly, solid, well-knit; able-bodied, able, athletic, strong, wiry; stout, staunch, stanch, firm, sturdy, tough, iron, *Inf.* tough as nails, *Inf.* hard as rock; powerful, potent, mighty, all-powerful, herculean, *Literary.* puissant.

3. broad, wide, sweeping, extensive, inclusive, all-inclusive, comprehensive, widescale, general, all-embracing; wholesale, indiscriminate, unqualified.

4. active, busy, industrious, bustling, untiring, unremitting, indefatigable; diligent, earnest, hard-working; alive, energetic, dynamic, high-powered; aggressive, pushing, emphatic; ambitious, determined, resolute.

muse, *v.* **1.** meditate, contemplate, reflect, ponder, brood, mull over, dwell on; cogitate, ruminate, be in a brown study, chew, chew one's cud; deliberate, excogitate, consider, take to heart, *Archaic.* perpend; weigh, revolve, turn over, review, study, evaluate, con; think about *or* over, cerebrate, be abstracted, be lost in thought, have one's mind on; put one's mind to, concentrate, focus.

2. wonder about, question, query, examine; speculate, surmise, suppose, conjecture, theorize, hypothesize; conceive, imagine, fancy, form a notion of, guess, *Inf.* figure, *Inf. Chiefly Midland and Southern U.S.* reckon; daydream, dream, be in a reverie, gaze out the window, be in a trance.

Muse, *n.* **1.** *Classical Mythology.* goddess of the arts, deity, presider, ruler; tutelary, guardian, protectress, caretaker; Aoede, Melete, Mneme; Calliope, Clio, Erato, Euterpe, Melpomene, Polyhymnia, Terpsichore, Thalia, Urania, *Class. Myth.* Sacred Nine; *Rom. Religion.* Camenae, Carmenta, Egeria, Antevorta, Postvorta.

2. *Sometimes* **muse** inspiration, afflatus, influence, thought-provoker, idea-giver, stimulus, stimulation.

3. **muse** genius, creativity, creative powers, originality; poetic genius, expressivity, writing ability *or* talent, way with words; gift, endowment.

museum, *n.* art gallery, gallery, exhibit *or* exhibition hall, salon, *Fr. musée, It. museo*; repository, reliquary, *Obs.* conservatory.

mushroom, *n.* **1.** toadstool, puffball, coral fungus; champignon, chanterelle, morel, truffle, meadow mushroom, field mushroom.

—adj. **2.** mushroomlike, mushroomy.

3. provisional, temporary, occasional; short-lived, ephemeral, transitory, fugacious, transient, fleeting, fugitive, temporal, flitting, evanescent; brief, momentary, passing; quick, meteoric, cometary.

—v. **4.** burgeon, spring up, burst forth, develop vigorously, sprout, shoot up, rise; boom, progress, prosper, thrive, flourish, luxuriate; grow, wax, increase, gain, add to.

music, *n.* **1.** sounds, tones, rhythm; singing, instrumentation, orchestration; harmonization, harmony, euphony; cacophony, dissonance; counterpoint, polyphony.

2. melody, tune, cavatina, song, lay, descant, aria, arietta, strain; theme, passage, chorus, refrain, *Music.* burden; madrigal, round, glee, catch; lullaby, cradle song, berceuse; chanson, ballad, lied, ditty, canzonet; morning song, aubade; nocturne, serenade; carol, hymn, chorale, canticle, chant, antiphon, drone; dirge, (*in Scotland and England*) coronach; opera, operetta, oratorio, cantata, serenata.

3. opus, composition, concert piece, symphony, sonata, concerto, chamber music; prelude, overture, voluntary; adagio, andante, largo, pastorale; fugue, rondo, toccata, improvisation; capriccio, caprice, fantasia, scherzo; minuet, pavane, waltz; gavotte, galop, cotillion, mazurka, polka, bolero; hornpipe, jig, reel; foxtrot, two-step, tango; gagaku.

4. jazz, Dixieland, ragtime, swing, jive, bebop, bop, boogie-woogie; blues, rhythm and blues, R & B, country and western, C & W, bluegrass; soul, reggae, pop; salsa, bosa nova, rumba, samba; folk, folk-rock, rock, rock'n'roll, acid rock, punk rock.

5. tone, tonality, intonation, pitch, timbre, cadence; modulation, resonance; overtones, harmonics.

musical, *adj.* **1.** tuneful, melodic, melodious, harmonious, concordant, accordant; lyrical, lyric, melic, choral, operatic, vocal; instrumental, orchestral, symphonic; ariose, *Music.* cantabile, songlike, songful, singable, catchy; pleasant, agreeable, appealing; singing, ringing, resonant, canorous, sonorous, clear, orotund.

2. euphonic, euphonious, flowing, rhythmical, rhythmic; mellisonant, sweet-sounding, mellifluous, silver-toned, golden-toned; dulcet, silvery, golden, tripping.

—n. **3.** musical comedy; operetta.

musician, *n.* performer, player, instrumentalist, accompanist, virtuoso; singer, vocalist, bard, minstrel; composer, songwriter, contrapuntist, harmonist; conductor, concert master, maestro.

musing, *adj.* **1.** meditative, thoughtful, pensive, *Archaic.* museful, in a brown study; reflective, pondering, ruminative, introspective, deliberative, cogitative; speculative, philosophical, metaphysical.

2. daydreaming, absent-minded, lost in thought, dreamy, wistful; preoccupied, absorbed, distracted, abstracted, engrossed, rapt.

—n. **3.** contemplation, reflection, meditation, rumination; pensiveness, thought, deep thought, brown study; speculation, deliberation, cogitation; cerebration, pondering, thinking, study, lucubration.

4. reverie, daydreaming, woolgathering; preoccupation, engrossment, absorption; introspection, self-consultation, self-communing.

musket, *n.* breechloader, flintlock, firelock, blunderbluss, matchlock, wheel lock, harquebus, muzzleloader, petronel; rifle, Winchester rifle, carbine, shotgun.

musketeer, *n.* rifleman, dragoon, sharpshooter, carabineer, carbineer, fusileer, yagar, jaeger, grenadier, chasseur, hussar.

muss, *n.* **1.** *Informal.* disorder, disorderliness, disarray, disarrangement, disorganization; dishevelment, untidiness, clutter, mess, heap, huddle; hash, hodgepodge, mishmash, jumble, scramble, tangle; confusion, muddle, *Inf.* guddle, imbroglio; unsettledness, discomposure, disconcertment, agitation, upset; turmoil, tumult, turbulence, disruption, disturbance.

—*v.* **2.** *Usu.* **muss up** *Informal.* misarrange, put out of place, misplace, displace, dislocate, move out of place; throw into disorder, disarray, dishevel, tumble, tousle, *Chiefly Scot. Dial.* touse; mess *or* mess up, ruffle *or* ruffle up, rumple *or* rumple up; turn upside down, *Inf.* turn topsy-turvy, make a shambles of; confuse, mix *or* mix up, shuffle, jumble, scramble; muddle, snafu, fuddle; derange, incapacitate, throw out of gear.

mussy, *adj.* *Informal.* disordered, disorderly, out of order, out of place, disarranged, in disarray, deranged; untidy, cluttered, messy, disheveled, messed up, ruffled up, *Inf.* mussed up, rumpled, tousled, *Chiefly Scot. Dial.* toused; unkempt, slovenly, sloppy, shoddy, careless, slipshod; confused, chaotic, all mixed-up, upside down, *Inf.* topsy-turvy; at sixes and sevens, muddled, jumbled, hugger-mugger, scrambled, tangled.

must¹, *v.* should, have to, ought to; be obligated *or* compelled *or* forced, have no choice *or* alternative.

must², *n.* **1.** mold, moldiness, mustiness, fustiness, mildew; fungus, decay, rot, dry rot; fermentation, mother.

2. new wine, unfermented juice.

mustache, *n.* mustachio, *Sl.* tickler, whiskers, lip hair, *Sl.* soupstrainer; handlebar mustache, toothbrush mustache, *Sl.* brush, *Inf.* fuzz.

mustang, *n.* range horse, plains horse, wild horse, *U.S.* cayuse, *U.S.* bronco, *U.S.* bronc.

muster, *v.* **1.** assemble, convoke, call *or* summon together; bring together, rally, mobilize, round up *or* in.

2. *Often* **muster up** gather, collect, marshal, summon *or* summon up, call up.

3. assemble, group, convene, forgather, meet, come together, collect, gather, congregate; crowd together, huddle, cluster, bunch up *or* together, agglomerate, mass; flock together, throng, herd, swarm, stream.

—*n.* **4.** assemblage, congregation, collection, aggregation, aggregate, agglomeration, conglomeration; gathering, forgathering, assembly, meeting, meet, rally, turnout; group, body, circle, knot, cluster, bunch; crowd, throng, mob, mass, confluence, concourse; gang, crew, company, troupe, band, troop; flock, pack, herd, drove, bevy, covey, swarm, hive, school, shoal.

5. meeting, conference, *Inf.* powwow, talk, parley, palaver; conclave, convocation, council, synod, consistory, conventicle; assembly, convention, congress; *U.S.* caucus, bloc, coalition, junta, *Rom. Antiq.* comitia.

musty, *adj.* **1.** moldy, stuffy, fusty, close, stale; sour, rancid, turned; ill-smelling, foul, stagnant, frowzy; rotten, rotting, decaying, spoiled, gone bad, putrid, corrupt, tainted; fetid, stinking, malodorous, noisome, reeky, rank.

2. antiquated, aged, ancient, old, hoary, mossgrown, antediluvian; obsolete, gone by, out-of-date, old-fashioned, oldfangled; behind the times, old-school, passé, moth-eaten, threadbare.

3. apathetic, indifferent, unresponsive, impassive, emotionless; dull, vapid, insipid, banal; listless, spiritless, sluggish.

mutability, *n.* **1.** mutableness, changeability, changeableness, variability, variableness; alterability, alterableness, modifiability, modifiableness, permutability, permutableness, transmutability, transmutableness; commutability, commutableness, transposability, exchangeability, interchangeability, interchangeableness, convertibility, convertibleness, invertibility, reversibility, reversibleness.

2. inconstancy, unstableness, instability, unsettledness, unsteadiness; unevenness, irregularity, erraticism, unreliability, unreliableness, undependability, undependableness; vacillation, fluctuation, oscillation, alternation, viscissitudes, ups and downs; uncertainness, uncertainty, unsureness, indecision, irresoluteness, irresolution; fickleness, capriciousness, flightiness, mercurialness, mercuriality, lightsomeness.

mutable, *adj.* **1.** changeable, variable, alterable, modifiable, permutable, transformable, transformative, transmutable, transmutative, transmutational; commutable, substitutive, substitutable, substitutional, substitutionary, transposable, exchangeable, interchangeable, convertible, invertible, reversible.

2. changing, ever-changing, inconstant, instable, unstable, unsettled, unsteady; uneven, irregular, erratic, unreliable, undependable; vacillating, vacillatory, vacillant, oscillating, oscillatory, vicissitudinary, vicissitudinous, fluctuating, fluctuant, varying, alternating, blowing hot and cold; wavering, uncertain, unsure, indecisive, irresolute; fickle, capricious, flighty, mercurial, lightsome.

mutation, *n.* change, variation, alteration, modification, permutation, modulation, inflection; conversion, translation, transformation, metamorphosis, evolution, transfiguration, transmutation, transubstantiation, transmogrification; transposition, metathesis, commutation, interchange, exchange, inversion; reversal, about-face, turnaround, turnabout, 360° turn; transition, revolution, innovation, new thing *or* idea; shift, transfer, transference, move, divergence, deviation, digression.

mute, *adj.* **1.** silent, speechless, wordless, mum; tight-lipped, taciturn, reserved, uncommunicative, reticent, close-mouthed; still, noiseless, quiet, *Archaic.* hush.

2. dumb, speechless, voiceless, *Pathol.* aphonic; deaf-and-dumb.

3. (*all of letters*) silent, unpronounced, unarticulated, unsounded.

—*n.* **4.** *Pathol.* aphonic; deaf-mute, *Inf.* dummy.

—*v.* **5.** (*all of sound*) deaden, dull, dampen, muffle; damp, stifle, smother, suffocate, suppress; still, hush, silence, quiet, *or* quiet down, tone down.

muted, *adj.* deadened, dull, dulled, dampened, muffled; damped, stifled, smothered, suffocated, suppressed; hushed, quieted, quiet, soft, softened, toned down; silenced, silent, still, stilled.

mutilate, *v.* **1.** dismember, disjoint, dislimb, tear limb from limb; detruncate, amputate, remove a limb; hack off, chop off, lop off, cut off, tear *or* rip *or* pull off, (*of a tail*) dock, bob, trim; dissect, anatomize, vivisect, skeletonize, disembowel.

2. mangle, butcher, slaughter, hack up, chop up *or* to pieces, lacerate, cut up, knife, stab, dilacerate, tear *or* rip to pieces; cripple, maim, lame, disable, hamstring, hock, *Scot.* hough, *Law.* commit mayhem; inflict bodily damage *or* injury, damage, injure, harm, hurt; disfigure, deface, deform, disfeature, mar, spoil, blemish, flaw, scar, blotch, mark up; ruin, destroy, vandalize, tear up, *Sl.* trash.

3. (*all of language*) distort, alter, modify, change, make unrecognizable, garble, mix up, confuse, render unintelligible; bowdlerize, expurgate, purge, overedit; excise, expunge, delete, edit out, blue-pencil.

mutilated, *adj.* **1.** dismembered, disjointed, torn limb from limb; dislimbed, amputated, cut *or* chopped *or* hacked *or* lopped off, removed; detruncated, (*of a tail*) docked, bobbed, trimmed; dissected, anatomized, vivisected, skeletonized, cut up.

2. mangled, butchered, slaughtered, lacerated, cut to ribbons *or* shreds *or* pieces *or* bits, hacked up, chopped up, dilacerated, ripped *or* torn *or* pulled apart, ripped to shreds, made into mincemeat; crippled, maimed, lame, disabled, injured, hurt, harmed, damaged; disfigured, defaced, deformed, disfeatured, marred, blemished, flawed, scarred, marked; ruined, spoiled, destroyed, vandalized, torn up, *Sl.* trashed.

3. (*all of language*) distorted, altered, modified, changed, unrecognizable, bearing no resemblance to the original; garbled, incomprehensible; bowdlerized, expurgated, purged, overedited, heavily edited; excised, expunged, deleted, blue-penciled.

mutineer, *n.* insurrectionary, insurrectionist, insurgent, rebel, revolter, rioter; subversive, revolutionary, revolutionist, anarchist, member of the underground, *U.S.* Weatherman, treasonist, traitor; seditionist, agitator, demagogue, trouble-maker, firebrand, rabble-rouser, malcontent; rioter, protestor, demonstrator, striker, resister, defier.

mutinous, *adj.* **1.** insurrectionary, insurgent, rebellious, revolutionary, anarchistic, subversive, underground, treasonable, traitorous; seditious, factious, agitative, rocking the boat; malcontent, discontent, discontented, dissatisfied, disaffected.

2. insubordinate, out of line, disobedient, disrespectful, disregardful; resistant, defiant, contemptuous, contumacious, antagonistic, hostile; riotous, unruly, restive, disorderly, out of control, uncontrollable, hard to control, unmanageable, ungovernable, unsubmissive, recusant, refractory.

mutiny, *n.* **1.** insurrection, insurgence, insurgency, revolt, rebellion, uprising, rising, riot, outbreak, anarchism, act of treason, *Archaic.* sedition; revolution, subversion, overthrow, coup d'état, takeover, *Ger. Putsch.*

2. resistance, open resistance, confrontation, opposition, defiance, insubordination, disobedience; civil disobedience, protest, march, demonstration, strike, sitdown, passive resistance, non-cooperation, boycott.

—*v.* **3.** revolt, rebel, rise up against, throw down the gauntlet, declare war against, open hostilities; revolutionize, insurrectionize, incite to riot, agitate, rock the boat, make trouble among; overthrow, subvert, take over, take the law into one's own hands; defy *or* resist *or* oppose authority, be insubordinate *or* disobedient, protest.

mutter, *v.* **1.** mumble, murmur, *Obs.* mussitate, *Dial.* mump, talk sotto voce, talk under one's breath; swallow one's words, talk to oneself, slur one's words, whisper; grumble, grunt, *Inf.* grouse, complain, *Yiddish.* kvetch, *Inf.* gripe, *Inf.* bitch, whine.

2. rumble, groan, growl, gnar, snarl.

—*n.* **3.** mumble, mussitation, murmur, low utterance; groan, grunt, grumble; complaint, *Inf.* gripe, *Inf.* bitch.

mutual, *adj.* **1.** reciprocal, give-and-take; interactive, interchangeable, correspondent, complementary.

2. common, joint, shared; connected, related, associated; similar, like, identical, analogous, equivalent.

mutuality, *n.* reciprocity, mutual dependence, give-and-take, *Latin. quid pro quo,* tit for tat, interchange; one for all and all for one; likeness, similarity, equivalence; community, correspondence, correlation, agreement.

muzzle, *n.* **1.** jaws, mouth; restraint, gag, hackamore, bit.

—*v.* **2.** gag, bridle; mute, silence, quiet, muffle, stifle, choke off, throttle.

3. restrain, repress, restrict, confine; fetter, leash, snub, check, harness; inhibit, hinder, stop, arrest.

myopia, *n.* **1.** *Ophthalmology.* near-sightedness, short-sightedness.

2. narrow-mindedness, narrowness, parochialism, provincialism, insularity, hideboundness, illiberality; prejudice, partiality, bias, one-sidedness; dogmatism, fanaticism, opinionatedness, zealotry, chauvinism, jingoism.

myopic, *adj.* **1.** *Ophthalmology.* near-sighted, short-sighted.

2. narrow-minded, narrow, closed-minded, closed, bigoted, illiberal; insular, parochial, provincial, limited, confined; prejudiced, biased, warped, twisted, jaundiced, partial, one-sided; sexist, chauvinistic, jingoistic, racist, anti-Semitic; fanatical, dogmatic, opinionated, unreasonable; intolerant, unforbearing, cynical; hidebound, rooted, settled, fixed, rigid.

myriad, *n.* **1.** thousands, a thousand and one, scores, numbers, a number, *Inf.* scillions, *Inf.* zillions, *Inf.* oodles, *Inf.* slew; lots, a lot, passel, *Inf.* raft, *Sl.* scads, *Sl.* a scad, piles, a pile, *Inf.* heaps, *Inf.* heap, lashings; bags of, *Inf.* gobs of, barrels, tons, a bunch, a bushel and a peck; shipload, carload; multiplicity, multitudinousness, plenty, abundance, profusion, galaxy; endless stream, river, torrent, flood, deluge, ocean, sea, world.

2. host, mass, crowd, throng, crush, horde; drove, bevy, herd, pack, flock, swarm, gaggle, school, shoal; army, legion, tribe, band, team, troop, squad, company, group, party, body; assemblage, congregation, aggregation, array, accumulation, assortment; bunch, gang, crew, *Inf.* caboodle; concentration, concourse, confluence, conflux, convergence.

—*adj.* **3.** innumerable, numerous, untold, multiple, multitudinous, multiplied, multifold, *Inf.* umpteen, multifarious, manifold, various; sundry, divers, several, many; countless, numerous as the stars in the Milky Way, numerous as the grains of sand on the seashore, illimitable, limitless, unlimited, boundless, unbounded; immeasurable, unfathomable, incalculable, endless, infinite, without measure, interminable.

4. versatile, (*of an actor*) protean, proteiform; kaleidoscopic, complex, varied, changing, multifaceted.

mysterious, *adj.* **1.** cryptic, esoteric, arcane, occult, perdu, hermetic, hermetical; secret, veiled, hidden, masked, screened, disguised, top secret, *Inf.* hush-hush; obscure, indistinct, indefinite, unclear, shadowy, cloudy, nebulous, nubilous, nubiferous, vague; inscrutable, oracular, sphingine, sphinxian, sphinxlike; mystic, mystical, transcendental, cabalistic, supernatural, preternatural; undisclosable, unrevealable, irrevealable, undivulgeable, unspeakable, unutterable, ineffable, inviolable.

2. inexplicable, unexplainable, insolvable, insoluble, unaccountable, *Obs.* inextricable; puzzling, baffling, bewildering, confounding, perplexing, enigmatic, enigmatical, mystifying; strange, weird, bizarre.

3. impenetrable, unfathomable, unknowable, incomprehensible, uncomprehensible, incognizable, incognoscible, undefinable, past *or* beyond comprehension *or* understanding; profound, deep, recondite, abstruse, abstract, heavy, *Sl.* heavy duty.

4. ambiguous, equivocal, discreet, noncommittal; reticent, taciturn, silent, mum, close-mouthed, tight-lipped, *Inf.* buttoned-up; evasive, shifty, circuitous; secretive; covert, clandestine, under-the-table, under-the-counter; furtive, surreptitious, insidious, underhanded; stealthy, skulking.

mystery, *n.* **1.** enigma, puzzle, riddle, conundrum, question, question mark; problem, dilemma, quandary, plight, predicament, skeleton in the closet, *Inf.* pickle, *Inf.* fix, *Inf.* jam, *Inf.* stew; fog, haze, mist, murk, dark; maze, labyrinth, tangle, knot; secret, arcanum, hidden meaning, closed book; unknown, unknowable, unexplored ground, *Latin. terra incognita*; deep *or* profound secret, mystery of mysteries.

2. seer, prophet, oracle, sphynx; puzzler, poser, *Inf.* hard nut to crack, *Inf.* brain-teaser, *Inf.* mind-boggler, *Inf.* stumper, *Inf.* floorer; mystery story, detective story, *Inf.* whodunit.

3. obscurity, ambiguity, ambiguousness, vagueness, nebulousness, equivocalness; enigmaticalness, mysteriousness, inscrutability, inscrutableness; inexplicability, unexplainableness, unaccountableness, imperceptibility; mysticism, occultness, cabal, cabalism, symbolism; occultism, esotericism, esoterics, esotery; supernaturalism, preternaturalism, otherworldliness; secrecy, secretiveness, concealment, obscurantism, obscuration, mumbo jumbo, hocus-pocus; abstruseness, reconditeness, profundity, profoundness.

4. (*all of Roman Catholic doctrine*) sacramental rite, transubstantiation, Eucharistic rite, mass, sacrifice; Eucharist, Holy Communion, Communion, Holy Sacrament, Sacrament, body and blood of Christ, Host, wafer.

5. miracle, sign, revelation, divine revelation, divine truth; wonder, marvel, prodigy, *Scot.* ferly.

6. mystery play, miracle play, morality play, morality, passion play.

mystic, *adj.* **1.** symbolic, symbolical, representative, representational, figurative; allegoric, allegorical, metaphoric, metaphorical; anagogical, emblematical; significant, significative, significatory.

2. secret, undisclosed, unrevealed, unspoken, unuttered; hidden, concealed, veiled, shrouded, enshrouded; cryptic, perdu; private, privy, confidential, closed, inviolate; secretive, clandestine, covert.

3. occult, esoteric, cabalistic, cabalistical, mystical, hermetical; supernatural, preternatural, fey, otherworldly, transcendental.

4. obscure, dark, dim, indistinct, indefinite, unclear; shadowy, cloudy, nebulous, vague.

5. mysterious, arcane, inexplicable, unexplainable, unaccountable, insoluble, insolvable, *Obs.* inextricable; puzzling, enigmatic, baffling, bewildering, perplexing, confounding, mystifying, enigmatical.

6. impenetrable, incomprehensible, inapprehensible, past *or* beyond comprehension *or* understanding, unknowable, incognizable, incognoscible, undefinable, undecipherable.

mysticism, *n.* occultism, cabalism, esotericism, esotery, esoterics; hermeticism, hermetics; supernaturalism, transcendentalism; theosophy; quietism, Molinism.

mystification, *n.* perplexity, bewilderment, confoundment, bafflement, puzzlement, puzzledness, *Brit. Dial.* swither; obfuscation, obscuration; stupefaction, uncertainty, incertitude, sixes and sevens; distraction, daze, fog, haze, unhingement; disconcertment, discomfiture, discomposure, consternation, chagrin, abashment.

mystify, *v.* confuse, confound, bewilder, perplex, nonplus, baffle, puzzle, *Inf.* bamboozle, *Inf.* buffalo, *Inf.* stump; disconcert, stagger, stun, daze, astonish, astound, dumfound, boggle; fuddle, befuddle, muddle, bemuddle, fog, befog, mix up, fool, delude, trick, outwit, hoodwink, bluff, distract.

mystique, *n.* **1.** aura, atmosphere, air, feeling, *Inf.* feel, vibrations, *Inf.* vibes; quality, character, mood, ambience, tone.

2. magic, spell, charm, charisma, influence; attractiveness, appeal, desirability, desirableness; fascination, delight.

3. enigmaticalness, mysteriousness, inscrutability, inscrutableness, inexplicability, unexplainableness; supernaturalism, preternaturalism, otherworldliness; mysticism, spiritualism, occultness.

myth, *n.* **1.** legend, tale, tradition, old wives' tale, *Inf.* yarn, romance, saga, epic; history, story, adventure, account, depiction, portrayal, representation, interpretation; fable, apologue, allegory, parable, moral, bestiary; fairy tale, ballad, nursery rhyme.

2. absurdity, nonsense, farce, wild story, tall tale, whopper, folk story; lie, fib, prevarication, *Inf.* taradiddle; untruth, falsehood; fabrication, cock-and-bull story; moonshine, bosh, claptrap; invention, forgery.

3. fantasy, fancy, whimsy, whim, vagary, conceit; crazy notion *or* idea, peculiar notion, *Inf.* screwball *or* wacky idea; implausibility, unlikelihood; illusion, delusion, daydream.

mythical, *adj.* **1.** legendary, fabled, storied, traditional, mythological, mythic; chimerical, figmental, fanciful, imaginary, imagined, fantastic, fabulous, fantastical; visionary, dreamy, quixotic, extravagant, eidetic; romantic, idealistic, storybook, Cinderellaesque.

2. fictitious, fictional, make-up, make-believe, *Inf.* just pretend, pretended, feigned; invented, contrived, concocted, coined, fabricated; preposterous, trumped up, unfounded, untrue, false; unreal, suppositional, superstitious, hypothetical, supposititious.

3. celebrated, immortal, historical, famous, famed, renowned, well-known, great, glorious.

mythology, *n.* body of myths, myths collectively; folklore, lore, tradition.

N

nab, *v. Informal.* **1.** seize, grab, pounce on, snatch, clutch, lay hold of; grip, grasp, hang on to.

2. capture, arrest, catch, take into captivity *or* custody, apprehend, place under arrest; pick up, *Inf.* collar, *Sl.* nail, *Sl.* haul in, *Sl.* cop.

nadir, *n.* rock bottom, *Sl.* the pits, zero point, lowest point, lowest ebb, ebb tide, low tide; the depths, the bottom, the depths of despond.

nag[1], *v.* **1.** complain, cavil, *Yiddish.* kvetch, carp, criticize, scold; crab, grumble, *Inf.* grouse, grouch; whine, snivel, henpeck; bicker, wrangle; pester, *Inf.* drive up the wall, badger, fret, vex, irritate; harp at, pick on, harass, ride, hector.

2. distress, torment, torture, pain; perturb, disturb, worry, bother, upset.

—n. **3.** complainer, whiner, *Yiddish.* kvetch, grumbler, faultfinder; grouch, scold; shrew, harpy, termagant, fishwife; pest, *Sl.* pain in the neck.

nag[2], *n.* **1.** jade, *Sl.* crowbait, *Sl.* plug, *Sl.* scrag, Rosinante, *Sl.* bag of bones.

2. *Slang.* racehorse, Thoroughbred, Arab, *Inf.* bangtail.

3. riding horse, pony, cow pony. See **horse** (*def.* **1**).

nagging, *adj.* complaining, whining, critical, picky; shrewish, pestering, irritating; distressing, painful, aching, worrisome.

nail, *n.* **1.** spike, brad, pin, peg, skewer, rivet, staple, tack, point; common nail, finishing nail, cut nail, roofing nail, drive nail, boat nail.

2. fingernail, toenail, (*all of animals*) claw, clutch, talon, unguis, nipper, pincher, hook.

3. hit the nail on the head be accurate, be correct, say truly, put things succinctly, be concise; be right to the point, *Inf.* say it the way it is, address oneself to the issues alone.

—v. **4.** fasten, make fast, attach, fix, hold, clinch, secure, join.

5. *Informal.* catch, capture, seize, apprehend, *Inf.* catch redhanded. *Inf.* catch with the goods, find in flagrante delicto, catch in the act; *Inf.* collar, *Inf.* pinch, nab, *Inf.* run in, *Inf.* pick up, arrest, take into custody.

6. *Slang.* hit, strike, smack, *Inf.* bop; punch, thwack, bang, crack, whack, whop, thump, *Sl.* paste.

7. nail down *Informal.* make final, make definite, settle, resolve; *Inf.* firm up, *Inf.* pin down, make [s.o.] commit himself, get things in writing, *Inf.* get things in the bag, have things assured.

naïve, *adj.* **1.** artless, simple, simple-minded, simple-hearted, innocent, childlike; unaffected, unspoiled, unsophisticated, undeveloped, unworldly; unsuspecting, unsuspicious, void of suspicion, trustful, trusting, *Archaic.* trusty, confiding; overtrustful, overtrusting, overconfiding; credulous, gullible, *Obs.* cullible, foolable, befoolable, deceivable, deludable, dupable, exploitable, *Inf.* easy, *Inf.* soft.

2. raw, green, immature, unripe, unseasoned, callow, born yesterday, wet *or* dry behind the ears; inexperienced, uninitiated, uninitiate, unwise, *Inf.* unhip; uninformed, unenlightened, unacquainted, unconversant, unversed in, unused to.

3. open, open and sincere, open-hearted, ingenuous, guileless, genuine, sincere, undeceptive, undeceitful, undeceiving, unfeigning, undissembling, undissimulating; candid, frank, forthright, foursquare, straightforward, straight-from-the-shoulder; plain, plain-spoken, plain-speaking, downright, outright, explicit, unequivocal, unambiguous, undisguised, *Inf.* straight-out; aboveboard, open and aboveboard, up front, out front.

naïveté, *n.* **1.** artlessness, simplicity, simpleness, simple-mindedness, simple-heartedness, innocence; trustfulness, unsuspiciousness, overtrustfulness; credulity, credulousness, gullibility, gullibleness, *Obs.* cullibility, foolability, exploitability, exploitableness.

2. rawness, greenness, immaturity, callowness; inexperience, inexperiencedness, lack of experience, *Inf.* unhipness; uninformedness, unenlightenedness, unacquaintedness.

3. openness, open-heartedness, ingenuousness, guilelessness, genuineness, sincerity, sincereness, naïveness, naivety, undeceptiveness, undeceitfulness; candor, candidness, frankness, forthrightness, straightforwardness; honesty, trustworthiness, *Inf.* trustiness, uncorruptedness.

naked, *adj.* **1.** nude, undressed, disrobed, unclothed, ungarmented, unappareled, undraped; divested of clothes, *Inf.* without a stitch on, *Inf.* not decent, *Inf.* indecent, bared; *Fr. au naturel, Inf.* in a state of nature, *Inf.* in the raw, *Inf.* in one's birthday suit, mother-naked; *Inf.* in the altogether, *Inf.* in the buff, stark-naked, *Brit.* starkers.

2. (*all of landscapes*) treeless, grassless, bald, barren, uncovered, stripped, unsheltered; stark, bleak, destitute, forbidding, depressing.

3. bare, spare, austere, ascetic, Spartan-looking, plain, simple, unfurnished, uncurtained, undecorated, unornamented, untrimmed, ungarnished, unenriched.

4. defenseless, unguarded, unprotected, unfortified; open, wide open, vulnerable, insecure, pregnable, penetrable, invadable; open to attack, assaultable, assailable; unarmed, weaponless, impotent, helpless, weak, powerless; exposed, uncovered, unsheathed, unwrapped.

5. clear, obvious, apparent, perceptible, perceivable; plainly revealed, plain to see, plain; evident, self-evident, manifest, palpable, patent, visible, in plain view, in plain sight, seeable, observable, unveiled, uncloaked, conspicuous; definite, certain, unmistakable, ostensible, undeniable, unqualified, unmitigated; sheer, glaring, flagrant, arrant, blatant, baldfaced.

6. simple, basic, essential, fundamental, basal, elementary, primary, *Inf.* gut; underlying, intrinsic, innate, inherent; nitty-gritty, vital, *Inf.* bare-bones, out-and-out.

7. uncorrupted, undefiled, natural, pure, simon-pure; unadorned, unembellished, uncolored, *Inf.* flying its true colors, true-blue; unalloyed, unmixed, unadulterated, unexaggerated.

8. blunt, outspoken, plain-spoken, direct, overt, candid, frank; straightforward, forthright, downright, matter-of-fact.

nakedness, *n.* **1.** nudity, *Inf.* the altogether, *Inf.* the raw, *Inf.* the buff, *Inf.* a state of nature, *Inf.* birthday suit.

2. bareness, baldness, barrenness; starkness, austerity, plainness, simplicity, Spartanism.

namby-pamby, *adj.* **1.** weak, insipid, watery, colorless, anemic, vapid, wishy-washy, indecisive; effete, prissy, prim, effeminate, candy-assed; affected, mincing, *Brit.* prinking; simpering, mawkish, mushy, sentimental, gushy, *Inf.* goopy.

—*n.* **2.** doggerel verse, greeting card verse, hack writing; macaronics, macaronic verse, lame verse, *Inf.* rot; amphigory; bathos, sentimentality, *Inf.* mush, *Inf.* schmaltz.

3. sissy, mama's boy, weakling. *Inf.* weak sister; *Inf.* lily-liver, coward, milk-toast, milksop, mollycoddle, *Brit. Inf.* rabbit; *Sl.* chicken, *Inf.* jellyfish, baby, big baby, *Inf.* softy; *Sl.* pushover, *Inf.* doormat, prig, *Inf.* priss.

name, *n.* **1.** appellation, designation, title, honorific, style; epithet, appellative, byword, label, tag, *Sl.* handle, *Sl.* moniker; surname, family name, last name, first name, forename, Christian name, middle name, signature; nickname, sobriquet, cognomen, agnomen, by-name, pet name, diminutive; pseudonym, anonym, allonym, alias, assumed name, pen name, nom de plume, *Fr. nom de guerre*, stage name, *Fr. nom de théâtre;* place name, toponym; trade name, trademark.

2. character, reputation, repute, reputability, respect, admiration, honor, esteem, high regard, favor, popularity; credit, merit.

3. fame, renown, bays, stardom, illustriousness, greatness, preeminence, superiority, supremacy; eminence, notability, note, distinction, mark; prominence, rank, standing, prestige, weight, importance, account.

4. celebrity, personage, notable, dignitary, *Inf.* V.I.P., *Inf.* bigwig, *Sl.* big shot, *Sl.* biggie, *Sl.* big wheel, magnate; *Sl.* big cheese, *Sl.* fat cat, *Sl.* heavy, *Sl.* high-muck-a-muck; luminary, somebody, *Sl.* celeb, lion, *Inf.* big name; star, hero, superstar, toast of the town.

—*v.* **5.** denominate, call, term, style, nickname, dub, *Archaic.* clepe; title, entitle, address; christen, baptize; identify, label, tag.

6. designate, appoint, delegate, nominate; select choose, pick; elect, vote in, place in office, induct, or dain; employ, engage, hire; authorize, empower, entrust, charge; assign, appropriate, consign, relegate, allot.

7. specify, mention, suggest, throw out; express, speak of, note, denote, indicate, point out.

nameless, *adj.* **1.** obscure, unheard of, unknown, undistinguished, unnoted, unrenowned, renownless, *Archaic.* inglorious, unsung; insignificant, unimportant, inconsequential; humble, ignoble.

2. anonymous, anonymal, innominate, unnamed; undesignated, unspecified, unidentified, unlabeled, untagged; pseudonymous, allonymous, cryptonymous, ananymous.

3. unspeakable, unutterable, inexpressible, ineffable, unnamable; indescribable, abominable, horrible, repulsive.

namely, *adv.* that is to say, that is, *Latin. id est, i.e., Latin. videlicit, viz.;* specifically, explicitly, to wit, scilicet; for example, for instance, as a case in point, as an illustration.

nap[1], *v.* **1.** doze, doze off, drift off, drop off, drowse, catnap, take a nap; sleep, slumber, *Inf.* snooze, *Inf.* catch forty winks, *Inf.* catch some shut-eye, *Sl.* log a few z's, *Sl.* zizz, *Brit. Sl.* doss; lie down, recline, repose, rest.

—*n.* **2.** doze, *Chiefly Brit.* lie-down, siesta, *Inf.* snooze, *Inf.* forty winks, slumber, catnap; rest, repose.

nap[2], *n.* fuzz, down, fluff; texture, surface, weave, fabric, fiber.

nape, *n.* scruff, poll; *Anat.* occiput.

napkin, *n.* serviette, cloth, *Archaic.* doily, (*collectively*) linen; towel, hand towel.

nappy, *adj.* fuzzy, downy, shaggy, fluffy, velvety, velutinous; hairy, villous, woolly, fleecy, furry, peachy; soft, thick.

narcissistic, *adj.* egocentric, self-centered, egomaniacal, egoistic, egotistic; conceited, *Inf.* puffed up, swelled-headed, vain, smug, blinded by one's own glory; selfish, self-serving, looking out for oneself *or* for number one; wrapped up in oneself, in love with oneself, *Inf.* stuck on oneself, self-absorbed, self-admiring, self-satisfied.

narcotic, *adj.* **1.** soporific, opiate, Lethean, sedative, sleep-inducing, hypnotic, anesthetic; *Med.* analgesic, pain-killing, lenitive, anodyne; palliative, assuasive, calming, balsamic, soothing, pleasing.

—*n.* **2.** opium, morphine, belladonna, alcohol; aspirin, barbiturate, *Med.* analgesic, *Inf.* painkiller; sleeping pill, sedative, antidepressant, tranquilizer, *Inf.* downer; amphetamine, stimulant, *Inf.* upper, *Sl.* junk; hallucinogen.

3. drug, opiate, soother, relaxant; anodyne, nepenthe; balm, solace, comfort, consolation. See **drug** (*defs.* **1, 2**).

narcotize, *v.* **1.** stupefy, stun, anesthetize, drug, dope up; feed lotus flowers, put under, knock out, *Sl.* give knock-out drops.

2. dull, deaden, desensitize, blunt, numb, benumb; palliate, alleviate, mitigate, lessen, ease.

narrate, *v.* **1.** tell, relate, recount, rehearse, give a report *or* an account of, set forth, chronicle, report; romance, novelize.

2. repeat, review, run over, recapitulate, sum up.

3. describe, portray, sketch out; detail, circumstantiate, expatiate, dilate; mention, state, relay; disclose, reveal.

narration, *n.* **1.** account, story, tale, sketch; description, portrayal; record, report, summary.

2. fable, myth, legend, saga, epic; history, chronicle, annals, journal; diary, memoir, biography, autobiography, life; adventures, confessions, letters.

3. telling, recounting, relation, rehearsal, recitation, reading; script, background text, (*in film*) voice-over.

4. novel, romance, tall tale. See **narrative** (*defs.* **1, 2**).

narrative, *n.* **1.** story, narration, tale, account; recital, chronicle, history; fable, myth, fairy tale, epic, saga; scripture, parable, allegory; anecdote, *Inf.* yarn, tall tale *or* story, *Sl.* fish *or* war story, fiction.

2. novel, romance, novella, short story; drama, play, teleplay, script, episode; adventure story, mystery story, *Inf.* mystery, detective story, *Inf.* whodunit, thriller, suspense novel; science fiction, *Sl.* sci-fi, speculative fiction; horse opera, *Inf.* Western, soap opera, dime novel.

3. story line, plot, plot development; events, episodes, series of incidents.

4. book, volume, publication; opus, work; writing, piece of writing, composition, theme, paper.

narrator, *n.* relator, recounter, reporter; describer, delineator, outliner; storyteller, taleteller, teller of tales, *Inf.* yarn spinner *or* spinner of yarns; anecdotist, raconteur; *Film and TV.* voice-over.

narrow, *adj.* **1.** slender, thin, slim, spare, slight, gracile, narrow as an arrow, thin as six o'clock, slender as a thread; tapered, drawn out, fine-drawn, attenuated; narrowish, isthmian, narrow-gauged.

2. meager, scant, scanty, sparse, scrimpy, exiguous; pinched, cramped, confining, confined, crowded, incommodious, not roomy, *Obs.* incapacious, poor; close, near, tight, strait, straitened, close-fitting; diminished, reduced, squeezed.

3. conditioned, qualified, restricted, limited, constricted; exact, precise, nice, delicate, subtle, fine.

4. narrow-minded, prejudiced, illiberal. See **narrow-minded.**

5. exclusive, exclusory, proscriptive, select, selective; limiting, restricting, defining, restrictive, definitive.

6. meticulous, exacting, scrupulous, conscientious; punctilious, particular, fussy, finicky, strict, rigid, demanding; searching, critical, attentive, scrutinizing.

—*v.* **7.** attenuate, make thin, taper, hone down, pare *or* pare down; diminish, grow *or* become smaller *or* tighter, dwindle, thin, thin down; lessen, reduce, decrease, curtail, contract, constrict, draw in, go in; compress, squeeze, squeeze together; condense, concentrate, consolidate, draw together, pull in.

8. narrow down, qualify, condition, set limits on, *Inf.* box in; localize, pin down, fix, pinpoint, zero in on, put one's finger on, keep within bounds, keep from spreading, set the limits, limit; confine, hem, hem in, bound, pinch, constrain, tighten, straiten, circumscribe, mark off, stake out; define, determine, specify, simplify, reduce to essentials.

—*n.* **9.** inlet, cove, arm of the sea, reach, creek, estuary, firth, fjord, strait *or* straits, narrows, euripus, sound; channel, way, passage, passageway, conduit, trough, ditch, trench; ingress, egress; waterway, water gate, watercourse, culvert, gully, gulch, canal, sluice, spillway, irrigation ditch; bottleneck, isthmus, pass, defile, ravine, gorge, arroyo, draw, passage.

narrowing, *n.* **1.** attenuation, thinning, tapering, emaciation; constriction, contraction, compression, shrinkage, shrinking, reduction, curtailment; diminishing, diminishment, dwindling.

2. limitation, limiting, pinpointing, pinning down, qualifying, zeroing in on, specifying.

narrow-minded, *adj.* **1.** narrow, prejudiced, biased, bigoted; warped, twisted, jaundiced, partial, arbitrary, one-sided, opinionated, prepossessed; sexist, racist, anti-Semitic, discriminative, discriminatory; close-minded, closed, intolerant, illiberal, unreasonable; insular, parochial, provincial, *Sociol.* ethnocentric; limited, confined, constricted, unliberal, uncatholic; little-minded, small-minded, meanminded; blind, myopic, near-sighted, short-sighted, purblind, wearing blinders *or* blinkers, not able to see beyond the end of one's nose; deaf, unhearing, deaf to reason *or* new ideas; uncharitable, ungenerous, uncondoning, unforbearing, unsympathetic, unindulgent, inhospitable, inconsiderate, disobliging, undetached, undispassionate; snobbish, unfriendly, xenophobic, misanthropic, cynical.

2. conservative, opposed to change, dogmatic, fanatical, authoritarian, doctrinaire; die-hard, reactionary, know-nothing, ultra-conservative; rigorous, stiff, stiff-backed, stiff-necked, rigid, hidebound, creedbound, locked-in, non-objective; obstinate, obdurate, intransigent, unyielding, uncompromising, immovable, intractable; firm, fixed, rooted, settled, unchanging, set in one's ways, traditional, conventional, orthodox, fundamentalist; unprogressive, oldfashioned, strait-laced, *Inf.* stuffy, *Sl.* square, *Sl.* straight; prudish, priggish, puritanical, prim, proper; middle-American, middle-class, bourgeois, *Inf.* rednecked, self-righteous, smug, complacent, sanctimonious; petty, mean, small, petty-minded, mean-minded, mean-spirited.

3. ultranationalist, superpatriotic, isolationist, chauvinistic, jingoistic, partisan; (*all of politics*) right-wing, rightist, Birchist, Birchite, Bourbonian, Hunkerous, Tory, Toryish.

narrow-mindedness, *n.* **1.** narrowness, prejudice, bias, prejudgment, preconception; bigotry, warp, bent, leaning, twist, jaundice, jaundiced eye *or* view, colored *or* slanted view; partiality, arbitrariness, one-sidedness, prepossession, made-up mind; sexism, racism, anti-Semitism, male chauvinism, discrimination, racial prejudice, *Sociol.* ethnocentrism, class consciousness; closed-mindedness, intolerance, illiberality, small-mindedness, pettiness, meanness, lack of scope; blindness, myopia, near-sightedness, short-sightedness, purblindness, tunnel vision, blind side *or* spot, blinders *or* blinkers, narrow view *or* views; uncharitability, ungenerosity, disobligingness; snobbishness, xenophobia, misanthropy, cynicism.

2. conservatism, dogmatism, fanaticism; ultra-conservatism, stiffness, rigidness, hideboundness, creedboundness, monomania; stubbornness, obstinance, intransigence, immovability, intractability; fixed *or* rooted ideas; conventionality, orthodoxy, fundamentalism, unprogressive *or* old-fashioned ideas; pedantry, pedagoguery, *Inf.* stuffiness; prudishness, priggishness, puritanism, middle-class outlook, middle-class morality; self-righteousness, smugness, sanctimoniousness, holier-than-thou attitude, positivism; insularity, parochialism, provincialism, uncatholicity; chauvinism, jingoism, partisanship.

narrowness, *n.* **1.** closeness, nearness, tightness, tight squeeze, confinement; crowdedness, incommodiousness, *Obs.* incapaciousness; straitness, restriction, restrictedness, attenuation, reduction, curtailment, constriction, limitation, circumscription; thinness, slenderness, slightness, slimness; meagerness, exiguity, exiguousness, scantiness.

2. exclusiveness, insularity, snobbishness, narrow-mindedness. See **narrow-mindedness** (*defs.* **1, 2**).

nascent, *adj.* beginning, young, budding, developing, incipient, embryonic; growing, rising, advancing, evolving.

nasty, *adj.* **1.** unclean, dirty, dirtied, sullied, soiled, stained; discolored, tarnished, smirched, besmirched, smutched, smutchy, smudged, smeared, besmeared, bedaubed; spotted, spotty, maculate, maculated, blemished, blotched, splotched, splotchy, blotted; muddied, muddy, bemired, slimy, begrimed, grimy, dirt-encrusted, filthy, filthy dirty, sooty, smutty, black; impure, polluted, befouled, contaminated, tainted, spoiled, poisoned, ruined.

2. disagreeable, unpleasant, ugly, bad, distasteful, unpalatable, unsavory, unappetizing; offensive, objectionable, obnoxious, noisome, foul; malodorous, mephitic, rank, foul-smelling, rancid, sour; fetid, stinking, stinky, smelling, smelly; disgusting, nauseating, nauseous, sickening, revolting; repulsive, loathsome, repellent, odious, abhorrent; unbearable, unendurable, intolerable, insufferable.

3. obscene, profane, irreverent, blasphemous, foul-mouthed, vulgar, indecent, lewd, dirty, filthy, *Sl.* raunchy, smutty; ribald, gross, coarse, crude, rough, rude, indelicate, fulsome; suggestive, off-color, bawdy, risqué, pornographic, *Inf.* blue.

4. ill-tempered, ugly, surly, ill-humored, ill-natured, unpleasant, disagreeable; mean, vicious, spiteful, malicious; malevolent, black-hearted, evil-minded, wicked, evil, sinister, dark, *Archaic.* facinorous; sinful, peccant, iniquitous, nefarious; villainous, criminal, flagitious, heinous, hateful, odious; despicable, contemptible, vile, sordid, base, low, reprehensible, disgraceful, shameful.

5. bad, severe, critical, serious, dangerous.

nation, *n.* **1.** nationality, race, tribe, clan, ethnic group; dynasty, family, house; (*all of a nation*) people, public, population, inhabitants, natives, residents, dwellers; members, membership, subjects, citizens, citizenry; society, community.

2. country, land, republic, polity, state, commonwealth, city-state, principality; kingdom, empire, empery, realm, royal domain *or* territory; union, federation, confederation, confederacy.

national, *adj.* **1.** federal, state, tribal; civil, civic, domestic, internal, intestinal; nationwide, countrywide.

2. patriotic, nationalist, nationalistic, chauvinistic, jingoistic.

—n. **3.** (*all of a nation*) citizen, subject, member, native, inhabitant, resident.

nationalism, *n.* national spirit *or* pride, nationality, love of one's country, *Latin. amor patriae,* patriotism, chauvinism, jingoism, my country right or wrong; isolationism, isolation.

nationalist, *n.* **1.** patriot, loyal citizen, chauvinist, jingo, jingoist; isolationist.

—adj. **2.** nationalistic, national, patriotic, chauvinistic, jingoistic.

nationality, *n.* **1.** (*both of a nation*) membership, citizenship.

2. nationalism, patriotism, national spirit. See **nationalism.**

3. nation, race, tribe, clan, ethnic group; dynasty, family house; ancestry, ancestral line, lineage, descent, parentage, birth, derivation, extraction, filiation; strain, stock, breed, bloodline, pedigree, stem, branch, stirps; heredity, genealogy, family tree; heritage, background, past, history, roots.

nationwide, *adj.* country-wide, national, federal, interstate, cross-country; general, overall, broad, widespread, far-reaching, extensive.

native, *adj.* **1.** inborn, innate, inbred, connate, connatural, natural, natural-born, ingenerate; inherent, immanent, indwelling, intrinsic; congenital, hereditary, inherited, in the blood, in the family.

2. local, domestic, homemade, homegrown, indigenous; natal, aboriginal, original, vernacular; endemic, endemical, autochthonous, autocthonal, autochthonic.

3. genuine, real, authentic, legitimate, honest, actual; simple, plain, unadorned; unchanged, untouched, unaffected, unaltered, unmodified; uncombined, free, pure; unrefined, crude; untamed, wild.

4. inveterate, rooted, deep-rooted, planted, implanted, fixed, infixed, ineradicable; permanent, inseparable, built-in; ingrained, engrained, inwrought, enwrought, in the grain.

5. essential, elemental, elementary, basic, basal, primary, fundamental, underlying, radical.

6. intuitive, intuitional, involuntary, noninferential; impulsive, automatic, immediate, spontaneous, on-the-spot.

—n. **7.** inhabitant, habitant, dweller, citizen; aborigine, primitive, indigene, autochthon; countryman, compatriot, *Yiddish.* landsman.

nativity, *n.* **1.** birth, blessed event, childbirth, delivery; parturition, childbearing, giving birth, bringing *or* coming into the world, (*all of animals*) dropping, hatching, laying, casting, *Obs.* geniture.

2. background, heritage, origins, extraction, derivation, beginnings; parentage, ancestry, lineage, descent, blood, stock, breed; nationality, national origin, citizenship.

3. **Nativity** birth of Jesus Christ, coming of the son of God *or* the Savior; Christmas, celebration of the birth of Christ; manger scene, crèche.

natty, *adj.* spruce, smart, dapper, *All Sl.* spiffy, sharp, nifty, nobby, swell; sleek, trim, neat, well-groomed; chic, stylish, fashionable, well-dressed, well-turned-out, out of a band box, *Both Sl.* classy, snazzy; elegant, fancy, dressed to the teeth, dressed to kill, dressed to the nines, *Inf.* dressy, *Inf.* posh, *Inf.* ritzy, *Inf.* swanky, *Inf.* swank, *Inf.* all gussied-up, *Sl.* all dressed-up, *Sl.* all duded-up.

natural *adj.* **1.** genuine, real, authentic, honest, actual, unartificial, inartificial; unaltered, unmodified, unchanged, untouched, unaffected; pure, unmixed, uncombined; crude, raw, unrefined; wild, untamed, uncultivated.

2. native, inborn, inbred, innate, connate, connatural, natural-born, ingenerate. See **native** (*def.* **1**).

3. inveterate, rooted, deep-rooted, planted, implanted, fixed. See **native** (*def.* **4**).

4. free, unfettered, unconstrained; spontaneous, immediate, automatic, impulsive, on-the-spot, involuntary; unpremeditated, noninferential, intuitive, intuitional; unintended, unintentional, unconscious, unwitting.

5. physical, material, corporeal, substantial; tangible, palpable; simple, plain, unadorned.

6. ordinary, unexceptional, homely, commonplace, common; normal, routine, habitual, regular, standard, typical; accepted, established, usual, current, customary.

7. innocent, naïve, ingenuous, artless, guileless, simple-minded, undissembling, undesigning, childlike, unsophisticated, inexperienced; unenlightened, untaught, unstudied, untutored, uneducated.

8. open, open-hearted, plain-spoken; candid, blunt, frank, direct, straight, straightforward, unreserved; informal, unpretentious, unpretending, unassuming.

9. illegitimate, bastard, baseborn; adulterous, adulterine.

10. unreformed, unregenerate, unconverted, unredeemed.

11. logical, reasonable; subsequent, consequent.

12. elemental, elementary, essential, basic, primary, fundamental, underlying, radical.

13. subjective, constitutional, idiosyncratic.

—n. **14.** *Informal.* talent, genius, whiz.

15. idiot, imbecile, half-wit, moron, simpleton, *Sl.* dimwit; dunce, dolt, dullard, numskull, blockhead, dunderhead, dunderpate; ignoramus, ninny, nincompoop, nitwit.

naturalize, *v.* **1.** confer citizenship upon, endow

with rights of citizenship, swear in *or* admit as a citizen; enfranchise, franchise, grant suffrage to.

2. introduce, adopt, accept, assimilate, absorb, take into, incorporate, homogenize, blend together.

3. adapt, acclimate, acclimatize, become accustomed to, get used to, become familiar with, *Inf.* learn the ropes, *Sl.* get the hang of, become acquainted with; accustom, domesticate, familiarize, make used to, habituate; inure, harden, toughen, season, temper, anneal.

nature, *n.* **1.** character, personality, individuality, ego, identity; essence, essential quality, *Hinduism, Buddhism.* dharma; make-up, qualities, constitution, formation, construction, composition; peculiarity, singularity, idiosyncrasy, genius, particularity.

2. disposition, temperament, temper, complexion, grain, mood, humor, spirit; persuasion, bent, leaning, inclination, proclivity, propensity.

3. kind, class, type, sort; category, genre, order; lot, style, cast, mold, stamp, brand, kidney; grain, make, mark, hue; color, stripe, streak, feather, vein.

4. cosmos, world, universe, creation, wide world, *Inf.* the whole wide world; natural forces, natural system.

5. primitiveness, wildness, uncultivatedness, roughness, simplicity, naturalness, organicity.

6. by nature innately, naturally, congenitally, hereditarily; intrinsically, inherently, indigenously, natively; essentially, basically, organically, radically, consitutionally, fundamentally.

7. in a state of nature nude, naked, unclothed, undressed, bare, uncovered, exposed.

naught, *n.* **1.** zero, nothing, nothing at all, no such thing, nil, *Sl.* zip, *Sl.* goose egg; none, none whatever, no part, no degree, no quantity; nullity, nothingness.

2. failure, lack of success, defeat, frustration; destruction, collapse, disaster, ruin, ruination.

3. set at naught belittle, pooh-pooh, look down upon, *Sl.* put down; disregard, slight, snub, shun, cut, *Inf.* high-hat, upstage, give a cold shoulder to, turn up one's nose at, ostracize, rebuff; ignore, cut off, disavow.

—adj. **4.** lost, ruined, destroyed, wrecked; undone, done in, finished, ended, *Sl.* eighty-sixed.

naughty, *adj.* **1.** impish, waggish, prankish, elfish, *Inf.* full of the devil, puckish; roguish, scampish, arch, *Scot.* hempy; playful, sportive, full of mischief, mischievous, fond of mischief, frolicsome; annoying, vexatious, exasperating, teasing.

2. disobedient, insubordinate, noncompliant, nonobservant, defiant, disregardful; undutiful, remiss, derelict, delinquent, negligent; unruly, wayward, fractious, restive, unmanageable, ungovernable, uncomplying, indisciplined.

3. improper, indecent, risqué, off-color; offensive, obscene, lewd, smutty; immoral, corrupt, sinful, wicked, reprehensible.

nausea, *n.* **1.** sickness, upset stomach, *Inf.* throw-ups, *Inf.* collywobbles; vomiting, throwing up, *Inf.* upchucking, queasiness; seasickness, *Fr. mal de mer,* motion sickness, air sickness, car sickness.

2. disgust, loathing, abhorrence, repulsion, revulsion, repugnance; aversion, hatred, detestation; distaste, dislike.

nauseate, *v.* **1.** sicken, turn one's stomach, make one's gorge rise; disgust, repel, revolt, *Sl.* gross out; offend, outrage, appall.

2. be sick to one's stomach, vomit, disgorge, throw up, *Inf.* upchuck, *Sl.* toss one's cookies, *Sl.* barf.

nauseated, *adj.* **1.** sick to one's stomach, unwell, unsteady, under the weather, *Inf.* blue *or* green around the gills, queasy; nauseous, *Sl.* barfy, qualmish, squeamish; seasick, carsick, airsick.

2. disgusted, revolted, repelled, with a bitter taste in one's mouth, appalled, offended.

nauseating, *adj.* contemptible, disgusting, loathsome, abhorrent, revolting, funny as a crutch; nauseous, sickening, odious, abominable, despicable, execrable; offensive, distasteful, unsavory; obnoxious, foul, vile.

nautical, *adj.* maritime, naval, marine; seagoing, seafaring, ocean-going; boating, yachting, sailing; navigational.

navel, *n.* umbilicus, omphalos, *Inf.* bellybutton; dimple, depression, pit; hub, nave, middle, center, centrum.

navigable, *adj.* **1.** passable, negotiable, traversable, travelable, unobstructed.

2. steerable, sailable, boatable; seaworthy, watertight, tight, yar.

navigate, *v.* **1.** pilot, steer, skipper, *Naut.* con; drive, guide, direct, manage, plot the course.

2. cruise, sail, yacht, coast, go down to the sea, ship out; plow the waves, ride the waves, ride the bounding main, circumnavigate; fly, aviate, go by plane.

3. traverse, voyage, journey, cross.

navigation, *n.* **1.** piloting, pilotage, aviation, seamanship, helmsmanship.

2. cruising, sailing, boating, yachting; flying, aviating.

navigator, *n.* **1.** pilot, aviator, flyer; helmsman, steersman; skipper, chief, *Sl.* old man.

2. seaman, seafarer, sailor, mariner, salt, sea dog, tar, bluejacket, *Sl.* gob; boatman, yachtsman, submariner.

navy, *n.* **1.** naval forces, merchant marine, fleet, flotilla, armada, argosy; mosquito fleet, submarines, destroyers, battleships, aircraft carriers.

2. dark blue, midnight blue, ink blue, lazuline.

nay, *adv.* **1.** no, no indeed, *Inf.* nope, *Sl.* naw, *Inf.* no siree, *Inf.* no siree bob, *Sl.* uh-uh, *Sl.* forget it; never, absolutely not, not on your life, on no account; negative, in the negative,

2. indeed, even, in truth, truly, in reality, actually, to be sure.

near, *adv.* **1.** close, close by, nearby, nigh; within earshot *or* hearing, within view *or* sight, within close range; around, hereabout, about, not far off *or* away.

2. approximately, roughly, generally, about, circa, ca., more or less, or so, all but; nearly, in the neighborhood *or* vicinity, close to, next to; virtually, almost, *Inf.* most, just about, well-nigh, nearing, bordering on, approaching.

—adj. **3.** neighboring, next-door, vicinal, adjacent, juxtapositional, juxtaposed, next, proximate; close, closer, close by, nearby, nigh, at close range, a stone's throw away; accessible, within reach, close at hand, at hand, handy, at one's fingertips, *Inf.* warm, *Sl.* hot; contiguous, bordering, adjoining, conjoining, connecting, abutting, tangential, tangent, touching, contactual.

4. direct, noncircuitous, straight, short, quick, fast, speedy.

5. imminent, momentary, forthcoming, coming, approaching, toward; impending, looming, overhanging, threatening.

6. approximate, rough; quasi, imitation, imitative, mock, mimic, simulative, simulated, artificial; similar, like, analogous, corresponding, resemblant, resembling, connected, related; intimate, familiar, dear, devoted, kissing, hand in *or* and glove, hand in hand, cheek by jowl, *Inf.* thick.

7. parsimonious, penurious, niggardly, skinflinty,

hoarding, stingy, miserly; selfish, ungenerous, close, tight-fisted, close-fisted, narrow-fisted, cheap, mean; frugal, economical, thrifty, saving, scrimping, penny-saving, penny-pinching, sharing, skimping; avaricious, greedy, covetous, mercenary.

—prep. **8.** close to, close by, nigh, in the neighborhood *or* vicinity of, not far away from, a stone's throw away from, within reach of, handy to; toward, around, about, upon; next to, adjacent to, contiguous to, tangential to.

9. bordering on, neighboring on, on the brink of, on the verge of, approaching, nearing.

—v. **10.** draw nigh, draw near, come close, close with, come together, converge; approximate, border on, approach, impend, verge, lean toward, move toward, *Archaic.* nigh.

nearing, *adj.* approaching, approximating; converging, convergent; coming, coming closer, imminent, impending, drawing nigh.

nearly, *adv.* **1.** almost, *Inf.* most, all but, as good as, virtually; not quite, barely, hardly, scarcely; next to, close to, near, well-nigh, nigh, nigh upon *or* onto; nearing, approaching, toward, bordering on, verging on.

2. approximately, just about, about, roughly, generally, estimatingly, in round numbers, more or less, or so; around, circa, ca.

3. similarly, analogously, comparably, comparatively, relatively.

4. intimately, dearly, familiarly, confidentially, personally.

nearness, *n.* **1.** closeness, proximity, propinquity, proximation, proximateness; contiguity, contiguousness, adjacence, adjacency; vicinity, vicinage, neighborhood.

2. intimacy, close association, deep understanding, tenderness, warmth, affection, fondness, endearment, dearness, nearness and dearness; familiarity, friendship, comradeship, fellowship, chumminess, clubbiness, *Inf.* thickness, *Inf.* tightness.

near-sighted, *adj.* **1.** myopic, short-sighted, purblind, mope-eyed.

2. narrow-minded, narrow, closed-minded, parochial, provincial, insular, hidebound, illiberal; prejudiced, bigoted, biased, partial, one-sided, unobjective; dogmatic, fanatic, opinionated, zealous, chauvinistic, jingoistic; rooted, settled, fixed, rigid.

near-sightedness, *n.* **1.** myopia, short-sightedness, near-sight, *Rare.* mope-eye.

2. narrow-mindedness, narrowness, parochialism, provincialism, insularity, hideboundness, illiberality; prejudice, partiality, bias, one-sidedness; dogmatism, fanaticism, opinionativeness, zealotry, chauvinism, jingoism.

neat, *adj.* **1.** tidy, trim, orderly, well-ordered, in good order, shipshape, *Naut.* Bristol fashion, *Naut.* shipshape and Bristol fashion, *Chiefly Dial.* tight, *Chiefly Brit.* trig, *Inf.* apple-pie, *Inf.* neat as a pin; clean, clean-cut, well-groomed; spruce, smart, sleek, natty, smug, *Inf.* slick, *Brit. Inf.* dinky, *Archaic.* tricksy.

2. simple, plain, unadorned, unvarnished, unornamented; homey, homely, homespun, unpretentious, unassuming.

3. epigrammatic, pithy, witty, attic; felicitous, happy, apt, well-put, well-expressed, well-said.

4. well-planned, well-designed, well-devised, well-contrived, well-laid, well-worked-out.

5. *Slang.* great, wonderful, marvelous, splendid, fine, excellent, grand, capital; *All Sl.* neato, swell, dandy, Jimdandy, keen, peachy-keen, nifty, spiffy, out-of-sight, out-of-this-world, gear, something else, far-out, boss, tough, heavy, bad, groovy, cool, marvy fab, A-OK.

6. clever, ingenious, resourceful, daedal; deft, adept, adroit, apt, dexterous, handy, skillful.

7. (*all of liquor*) straight, straight-up, unmixed, undiluted, unwatered, unblended, uncut, unadulterated, pure.

—adv. **8.** smartly, sprucely, nattily, trimly, sleekly, neatly, *Inf.* slickly.

9. skillfully, expertly, adroitly, adeptly, dexterously, deftly, handily, aptly; cleverly, ingeniously, resourcefully.

neaten, *v.* tidy, tidy up, straighten up *or* out, pick up, clean, clean up, *Inf.* fix up, *Inf.* police; spruce up, groom, trim, put in trim, *Brit. Dial.* trig up *or* out; arrange, order, put in order.

nebulous *adj.* **1.** obscure, indistinct, indeterminate, hazy, fuzzy, shapeless, amorphous; faint, pale, dim; murky, opaque; muddled, confused, muddy, *Inf.* clear as mud; vague, abstract, general, generalized, nonspecific, unspecific, undifferentiated.

2. cloudy, clouded, overclouded, overcast; foggy, hazy, misty; cloudlike, nebulose, nubilous.

3. celestial, heavenly, empyrean; astral, starry, stellar, sphery, nebular.

necessarily, *adv.* **1.** of necessity, perforce, by force of circumstance, needfully, needs must, without choice; willy-nilly, willing or unwilling, whether willing or not, whether or no, like it or not; *Fr. bon gré, mal gré; Latin. nolens volens.*

2. as a result, consequently, as a consequence, in consequence; naturally, of course, as a matter of course, and so, it follows that; inevitably, unavoidably, inescapably, ineluctably; certainly, surely, without doubt.

necessary, *adj.* **1.** needed, needful, called-for, occasioned, in demand, requisite, required; indispensable, vital, essential, of the essence, important, of the utmost importance; fundamental, elementary, rudimentary, basic, bedrock, material, substantive, *Inf.* square-one; imperative, urgent, exigent, instant, pressing, compelling, high-priority, high-pressure, life-and-death *or* life-or-death.

2. compulsive, involuntary, coercive, choiceless, forced; compulsory, obligatory, binding, mandatory, prescriptive; inescapable, unavoidable, ineludible, ineluctable, inevasible, irresistible; certain, for certain, sure, for sure, sure as death, sure as death and taxes, inevitable, necessitous.

—n. **3.** necessity, requisite, requirement. See **necessity** (*def.* **1**).

4. *Chiefly New England.* privy, outhouse, backhouse, stool, closet, cloaca, *Brit. Sl.* bog.

necessitate, *v.* oblige, require, demand, exact, call for, dictate, insist upon; compel, impel, force, make, cause, cause to, have; constrain, bind, tie [s.o.'s] hands, leave no option *or* choice; drive, railroad, ramrod; bring to bear upon, bear down upon, put the pressure on, press, apply pressure, *Inf.* pressure *or* high-pressure, *Inf.* lean on, *Inf.* squeeze, *Inf.* put the screws on *or* to, *Inf.* twist [s.o.'s] arm; coerce, dragoon, bully, intimidate, *Inf.* steamroller, *Inf.* bulldoze, *Sl.* strong-arm.

necessitous, *adj.* **1.** needy, indigent, impoverished, impecunious, penurious, distressed, in reduced circumstances, reduced, straitened, in straitened circumstances, in narrow straits, in dire straits; poor, badly off, *Inf.* hard up, unable to make ends meet, unable to keep the wolf from the door; disadvantaged, underprivileged, in want, in need, mendicant, beggared, beggarly, pauperized; destitute, poverty-stricken, penniless, without a penny, without a sou, down-and-out; *All Sl.* broke, flat broke, stone broke, stony, busted,

Brit. skint.

2. unavoidable, inescapable; compulsory. See **necessary** (*def.* 2).

3. urgent, exigent, pressing. See **necessary** (*def.* 1).

necessity, *n.* 1. requirement, requisite, prerequisite, necessary; makings, what it takes; necessaries, necessities, essentials, bare essentials *or* necessities; *Latin. sine qua non.*

2. indispensability, essentiality, needfulness, *Archaic.* necessitude; compulsoriness, obligatoriness, mandatoriness.

3. need, want, desire, demand, call for; essential, indispensable, must, must-have, must item, imperative, exigency, urgency, urgent need, dire necessity, matter of life and death *or* matter of life or death; matter of necessity, case of need.

4. inevitability, inescapability, ineluctability, unavoidability, inevasibility; certainty, certitude, *Inf.* sure thing, *Inf.* sure bet; choicelessness, no choice, no alternative, Hobson's choice.

5. compulsion, obligation, obligement, necessitation, constraint; pressure, high pressure, high-pressure tactics *or* methods, duress; force, coercion, *Inf.* the strong arm, *Inf.* strong-arm tactics.

6. indigence, penury, impecuniousness, impoverishment, neediness, necessitousness; poverty, destitution, privation, beggary, pauperism, pennilessness, hand-to-mouth existence; straits, narrow straits, straitened *or* narrow *or* reduced *or* embarrassed circumstances; poor house, poor farm, wolf at the door, bare cupboard.

7. **of necessity** necessarily, perforce, by force of circumstances; willy-nilly, like it or not; consequently, as a result. See also **necessarily** (*defs.* 1, 2).

neck, *n.* 1. nape, scruff, *Anat.* cervix.

2. isthmus, tongue, cape, peninsula.

3. strait, narrows, arm, channel, canal, creek, *U.S. Dial.* kill.

4. **neck and neck** even, equal, level; abreast, side by side, nose to nose, alongside, parallel, running level, on a par.

—*v.* 5. *Informal.* kiss, *Sl.* make out, buss, *Sl.* smooch, smack, *Inf.* lollygag, osculate; fondle, pet, caress, stroke, pat; nuzzle, nestle, carry on, snuggle; bill and coo, make love, slap and tickle.

neckband, *n.* collar, ruff, dog-collar, collarband, rabato; neckerchief, kerchief, clerical collar, stole, tippet; bandanna, scarf, muffler, boa; chemisette, tucker, guimpe, fichu.

necklace, *n.* necklet, chain, string, albert, torque, riviere, *Archaic.* carcanet; choker, love beads, beads, chaplet, wampum; locket, pendant, lavaliere, amulet, medallion, gorget.

necktie, *n.* tie, cravat, bow tie, stock, four-in-hand, old school tie; ascot, neckerchief, jabot, neckpiece, *Obs.* neckcloth.

necrology, *n.* 1. obituary, obit, death notice.

2. death register, death record, death roll, casualty list; martyrology.

necromancer, *n.* magician, black magician, wizard, warlock, witch; magus, sorcerer, sorceress, spiritualist, exorcist, *Archaic.* mage; theurgist, thaumaturgist, miracle-worker, hexer, voodooist, hoodooist, root doctor; incantator, enchanter, enchantress, charmer, occultist; diviner, prophet, seer, soothsayer, astrologer, dowser.

necromancy, *n.* magic, black magic, witchery, witchcraft, wizardry; voodoo, hoodoo, voodooism, hoodooism, obi, obiism, conjure, root work; sorcery, gramarye; shamanism, demonology, diabolism, deviltry, mysticism, spiritualism; conjuration, soothsaying, horoscopy, astrology; exorcism, exsufflation; divination, black art, thaumaturgy, theurgy.

necromantic, *adj.* magical, incantatory, alchemistic, runic, voodooistic, hoodooistic, shamanistic, thaumaturgic, theurgic; occult, cabalistic, mystic, spiritualistic, magian; sorcerous, goetic, sortilegious, Circean, Chaldean.

necropolis, *n.* cemetery, graveyard, churchyard, memorial park; catacomb, columbarium; burial ground, burial place, golgotha, garden of sleep, God's acre, potter's field; ossuary, charnel house, (*of animals*) boneyard.

nectarous, *adj.* sweet, delicious, ambrosial, delectable, fit for a king, fit for the gods; luscious, succulent, juicy, *Inf.* scrumptious, *Inf.* yummy, toothsome, mouth-watering; honeyed, sugary, candied, mellifluent, melliferous, sugar-sweet, honey-sweet.

nee, *adj.* born, formerly, previously, heretofore.

need, *n.* 1. requirement, demand, requisite, prerequisite; obligation, duty, charge; necessity, essential, *Latin. sine qua non;* necessitude, essentiality, indispensability.

2. want, lack, desideratum; default, dearth, insufficiency, shortness, paucity, shortcoming.

3. exigency, emergency, crisis, pinch, urgency, stress, matter of life and death.

4. destitution, poverty, neediness, indigence, penury, privation; impecuniosity, straits, extremity, difficulty; pauperism, beggary, mendicancy.

—*v.* 5. require, demand, necessitate; want, call for, have occasion for, have need of; lack, not suffice, stand in need of, be without, miss; crave for, pine for, yearn for, desire, desiderate, hope for.

needle, *n.* 1. darner, bodkin, pin, tag, nib, neb, tip; hypodermic needle, *Brit. Sl.* jag, probe, *Surg.* trocar.

2. stylus, style, point, graver, engraver, scauper; die, tool, punch, stamp; perforator, piercer, puncturer; bit, auger, drill, borer.

3. pine needle, thorn, *Bot., Zool.* mucro, prickle, sticker; bramble, brier, bristle, spicule, spiculum.

4. arrow, pointer, compass needle, indicator; index finger, hour hand, minute hand.

—*v.* 5. *Informal.* **a.** goad, spur, prod, provoke; sting, prick, urge, press, nag, whip lash. **b.** annoy, irk, vex, nettle, aggravate, rile; pester, tease, devil, *Sl.* bug, pick on, pluck the beard of, *Sl.* razz; ruffle, disturb, exasperate, *Inf.* miff, *Inf.* peeve, pique.

needle-shaped, *adj.* pointed, needlelike, acicular, aciform, acuminate, aculeate, mucronate; spiked, spiculate, spicular, toothed, tined, pronged, barbed; sharp, long, slender, keen, thin.

needless, *adj.* 1. unnecessary, uncalled for, gratuitous, unneeded, unwanted; unessential, nonessential, useless, dispensable, expendable; superfluous, redundant, supererogatory, *Fr. de trop,* excess, in excess, spare; tautological, pleonastic, expletive, excessive, over and above; wordy, prolix, verbose, circumlocutory.

2. **needless to say** it goes without saying, obviously, of course, naturally, necessarily, as a matter of course.

needlewoman, *n.* needleworker, needlepointer, embroiderer, crewelworker, lace maker, tatter; stitcher, sewer, knitter, crocheter.

needlework, *n.* needlecraft, needlepoint, crewelwork, embroidery, petit point, gros point, point lace, lacework, tatting, tapestry; sewing, stitching, knitting, crocheting; fancywork, ornamentation, trimming.

needy, *adj.* destitute, poor, indigent, impecunious; wanting, lacking, strapped, pinched, squeezed; *Inf.* hard up, *Sl.* broke, *Sl.* flat, *Sl.* busted; mendicant, beggared, beggarly, pauperized, impoverished, poor as a church mouse, out of pocket, out of cash, short of cash; penniless, moneyless, necessitous, reduced; without a penny to one's name, without a sou, without a dollar to rub against another; disadvantaged, underprivileged, deprived, on welfare, on relief, in rags, in the poorhouse, *Brit.* on the dole; in dire straits, in reduced circumstances, poverty-stricken, down and out, bankrupt, insolvent.

ne'er-do-well, *n.* **1.** good-for-nothing, *Chiefly Brit.* wastrel, *Inf.* no-account, black sheep, *Fr. vaurien,* worthless person; unfortunate, *Sl.* loser, *Sl.* schlemiel, *Sl.* schlimazel, *Sl.* sad sack; idler, fainéant, loafer, drone, do-nothing, *Inf.* bum; sluggard, slugabed, layabout, lazybones, malingerer, shirker, *Inf.* goldbrick, *Sl.* goof-off; scamp, *Inf.* scalawag, rascal, rogue, knave, scapegrace, blackguard, reprobate.

—adj. **2.** worthless, of no worth, good-for-nothing, useless, no-good, valueless; do-nothing, lazy, slothful, sluggard, idle, fainéant, indolent.

nefarious, *adj.* **1.** wicked, evil, sinful, iniquitous, *Archaic.* facinorous, *Obs.* scelerous; villainous, flagitious, heinous, infamous, notorious, *Rare.* nefast; black-hearted, sinister, arrant, ignoble; bad, base, vile, foul, low, mean, odious, obnoxious; abominable, execrable, horrible, horrid, atrocious, grievous; ghastly, grim, dire, black, dreadful; hideous, grisly, gruesome, unspeakable; damnable, damnatory, accursed, cursed; maleficent, malefic, malevolent, ill-intentioned, evil-minded; demonic, demoniac, diabolic, devilish, fiendish, satanic, hellish, infernal; unholy, unrighteous, unblest, unsanctified, unhallowed, unconsecrated.

2. perfidious, treacherous, insidious, traitorous; unscrupulous, unprincipled, crooked, dishonorable; blackguardly, scoundrelly, thievish, ruffianly; criminal, wrong, reprehensible, felonious, lawless; unregenerate, unrepentant, impenitent, obdurate, incorrigible; unpardonable, unforgivable; degenerate, corrupt, *Rare.* turpid, depraved; immoral, dissolute, profligate, reprobate, abandoned, dissipated; opprobrious, disgraceful, shameful; scandalous, shocking, outrageous; contemptible, scurvy, abhorrent, loathsome, hateful, detestable, despicable.

negate, *v.* **1.** nullify, render null and void, declare null and void, void, disannul, annul, cancel; repeal, revoke, retract, rescind, abrogate; quash, invalidate, vitiate, vacate, disenact, disestablish; set aside, call off, supersede, discharge; cease, *Law.* nol-pros, stop, discontinue, break off; countermand, counterorder, override, overrule, veto; refuse, reject, turn down, decline, disallow, repudiate; forbid, prohibit, proscribe, disapprove, negative; abolish, eliminate, destroy, squelch, suppress, silence.

2. deny, dispute, gainsay, controvert, naysay, disbelieve; contradict, traverse, disaffirm, disprove, confute, refute, discredit; disavow, forswear, disclaim; retract, unsay, recant, take back, back-pedal; protest, oppose, contravene; object, demur, refuse assent, disagree.

negation, *n.* **1.** denial, contradiction, gainsay, disaffirmation, denegation; disavowal, unsaying, repudiation, disclaimer, disclamation, *Rhet.* apophasis; retraction, recantation, (*usu. under oath*) abjuration.

2. refusal, rejection, turndown, declination; rebuff, repulse; forbiddance, veto, disallowance, prohibition, proscription, disapproval, *Inf.* no-go; thumbs down, deaf ear.

3. refutation, answer, disproof, confutation; protest, objection, contravention; disagreement, dissent, demur, demurral.

4. renunciation, renouncement, disowning; disinheriting, disinheritance, disheriting.

5. nonentity, nullity, nothing, phantom, illusion, dream; void, blank, vacuity, vacuum.

6. opposite, reverse, antithesis, contrary; absence, want, lack, deficiency.

negative, *adj.* **1.** nullifying, voiding, disannulling, annulling, canceling, revocatory; quashing, invalidating, vitiating, vacating, disenacting; forbidding, prohibiting, proscribing, disapproving; denying, contradicting, gainsaying, traversing.

2. opposed, opposing, oppositive, oppositional; opponent, adversary, adversative, conflicting, against; counter, counteractive, counteracting, contrary, contradictory, contrapositive, adverse; antipathetic, antipathetical, repugnant, irreconcilable.

3. opposite, other; reverse, obverse, inverse, converse, contrasting.

4. pessimistic, cynical, faultfinding, complaining; gloomy, glum, mopey, mopish, morose; averse, unfriendly, uncongenial; unhelpful, uncooperative, recusant, uncompliant.

5. unrewarding, ineffective, gainless, profitless, fruitless, vain, futile.

—v. **6.** deny, gainsay, contradict, refute, disprove, negate. See **negate** (*def.* **2**).

7. nullify, veto, forbid, negate. See **negate** (*def.* **1**).

8. neutralize, counteract, offset, balance, equalize.

neglect, *v.* **1.** disregard, take no note *or* notice of, pass over, pretermit; ignore, overlook, look the other way, blink at, wink at, connive at; let [s.t.] ride, gloss over, make light of, shake off; pass by, *Inf.* give [s.t.] a miss.

2. omit, forget, lose sight of, not attend to, leave undone; scamp, skimp, shirk, *Sl.* goof off, *Inf.* lie down on the job; be remiss, be derelict, be heedless.

3. abandon, fail to care *or* provide for, *Inf.* let [s.t.] go; shun, leave alone; spurn, slight, *Inf.* cold-shoulder, scorn, contemn.

4. forbear, abstain from, do without, forgo, renounce, dispense with.

—n. **5.** disregard, omission, oversight, inattention, default, *Law.* laches; disregardfulness, inattentiveness, forgetfulness, neglectfulness; incaution, incautiousness, heedlessness, carelessness, inadvertence, inadvertency.

6. noninterference, laissez faire, passiveness, passivity; inactivity, inaction, stasis; dormancy, stagnation.

7. negligence, negligency, dereliction, delinquency, remissness, *Obs.* indiligence; laxity, slackness, looseness, *Fr. laissez-aller;* slovenliness, sloppiness, shoddiness; carelessness, inaccuracy, inexactitude, inexactness.

8. languor, languidness, inexertion, indolence, otiosity, otioseness, laziness, idleness, sloth; dilatoriness, procrastination, delay, cunctation; nonchalance, insouciance, improvidence, imprudence, imprudency, indiscretion.

neglectful, *adj.* **1.** disregardful, disregarding, disregardant, inattentive, careless, heedless, unheeding; unobservant, unwatchful, inadvertent, unguarded; thoughtless, unthinking, unmindful, forgetful, oblivious, unaware; improvident, imprudent, injudicious; reckless, rash, temerarious, *Obs.* respectless.

2. negligent, remiss, delinquent, derelict, *Inf.* asleep at the wheel *or* at the switch *or* on the job; indolent, lazy, slothful, laggard, shiftless, do-nothing, fainéant; slack, loose, lax, sloppy, slipshod; dilatory, delaying, procrastinative, cunctatious, cunctatory.

negligee, *n.* nightgown, gown, décolletage, *Inf.* nightie; dressing gown, peignoir, kimono, caftan, lounging robe, house coat, robe, bathrobe, bed jacket, wrapper, *Fr. robe de chambre.*

negligence, *n.* dereliction, remissness, laxity. See

neglect (*defs.* 5-8).

negligent, *adj.* **1.** disregardful, remiss, derelict. See **neglectful** (*defs.* **1, 2**).

2. offhand, casual, carefree; nonchalant, insoucient, devil-may-care, happy-go-lucky, lackadaisical; indifferent, unconcerned, unsolicitous, uncaring, perfunctory, cursory; unstudied, unplanned, unpremeditated.

negligible, *adj.* trifling, piddling, inconsequential, niggling, unworthy of note *or* notice; inappreciable, imperceptible, insignificant, unimportant, small, worthless, paltry, nugatory, petty; inferior, second-rate, of no account, *Inf.* no-account, small-time, *Sl.* two-bit, small potatoes.

negotiate, *v.* **1.** bargain, drive a bargain, make a deal, deal; dicker, haggle, palter, higgle, chaffer, *Scot.* argle-bargle, *Inf.* talk down, *Inf.* beat down, *Offensive.* jew *or* jew down; make a bid *or* an offer, make a counteroffer, counter, come back with, go back and forth, bandy, volley.

2. arrange, work out, confer, parley, debate, discuss, talk over, work with [s.o.] on; mediate, intermediate, arbitrate, adjudicate, umpire, referee, intercede, interpose, *Law.* intervene; give and take, compromise, reach an agreement *or* settlement *or* compromise, meet halfway, agree on, settle differences, settle, come to terms, strike a bargain, contract, conclude, complete, finish, consummate.

3. transact, conduct, carry on *or* out, perform, execute, do; manage, orchestrate, engineer, handle, deal with; bring off, carry off, *Sl.* pull off, *Sl.* swing, succeed, accomplish, fulfill, discharge; bring about, make happen, cause, effect, effectuate, produce, get.

4. clear, pass over, hurdle, vault over, leap over, jump over, spring over, bound over, bounce over, hop over, skip over, make it over, *Inf.* make; travel over, get through.

5. commute, exchange, trade, swap, swop, *Finance.* convert; spend, pass, use; transfer, pass over, hand over, deliver, consign, make over, sign over, endorse, give title to, *Law.* assign, *Law.* convey; sell, vend, peddle, take money for, give to [s.o.] for a price, dispose of, get rid of.

negotiation, *n.* **1.** discussion, parley, debate, collective bargaining, working out, give and take; mediation, intermediation, arbitration, arbitrament, adjudication, diplomacy, interposition, refereeing, umpiring.

2. bargaining, dickering, haggling, higgling, *Offensive.* jewing; bidding, offering, counteroffering, countering, *Inf.* back and forth, bandying.

3. transaction, deal, bargain, sale; trade, exchange, swap, swop, dicker; transfer, consignment, signing over, delivery, *Law.* assignment, *Law.* conveyance.

4. agreement, arrangement, understanding, meeting of the minds, compromise, settlement, mutual settlement, determination, decision; contract, collective agreement, compact, concordat, convention, covenant, treaty. bond.

negotiator, *n.* **1.** mediator, mediatress, mediatrix, arbitrator, adjudicator, judge, determiner, decider; interposer, interceder, intercessor, intervener, referee, umpire, negotiant, intermediary, intermediator, middleman, go-between; diplomat, diplomatist, ambassador, envoy, plenipotentiary, proxy, nuncio, internuncio, delegate, representative, agent.

2. bargainer, dickerer, haggler, palterer, quibbler, tough customer, shrewd buyer *or* consumer.

3. transactor, conductor of business, businessman, businesswoman, *Sl.* wheeler-dealer; salesperson, salesman, saleswoman, saleslady, dealer, trader, merchant, retailer, wholesaler; seller, vendor, peddler, haggler.

Negro, *n.* **1.** Negroid, Black, black person, dark-skinned person; Negrito, Papuan, Melanesian, Australian aborigine; Ethiopian, Moor, Bantu, Sudanese, Hottentot; Senegambian, Mandingo, Krooman, Pygmy, Zulu, Ibo, Nubian; Afro-American, Afro-European, Afro-Asiatic; colored man, man of color, *Inf.* gentleman of color, *Inf.* colored; negress, colored woman.

—adj. **2.** Negroid, black, black *or* brown-skinned.

neigh, *v.* whinny, bray; bleat, blat, baa; cry, wail, call.

neighbor, *n.* **1.** person next door, borderer, abutter, adjoining property owner, nearby dweller; fellow villager, fellow townsperson, fellow citizen, fellow man; acquaintance, associate, friend.

—v. **2.** impinge, touch, meet, verge upon, abut, adjoin, join up to, back up to, border on, border, connect.

neighborhood, *n.* **1.** vicinity, environs, precinct, quarter, part, parts, locale; district, locality, confines, area, region, community, environment, suburbs, outskirts, surrounding parts; *Inf.* neck of the woods, *Inf.* haunts, *Inf.* stamping grounds.

2. nearness, closeness, proximity, approximation, propinquity; approach, near approach, convergence.

3. in the neighborhood of approximately, nearly, around, about, almost; bordering on, nigh on to, close to, just about, a figure close to.

neighboring, *adj.* abutting, adjoining, adjacent, contiguous, touching, juxtapositional; bordering, bordering on, verging on, connecting, next, backing up to; close, near, nearest, very near, at hand, close at hand, near at hand; proximal, proximate, verging on, around, surrounding, circumjacent; nigh, nigh to, nearby, in proximity to; vicinal, in the general vicinity, not far away.

neighborly, *adj.* **1.** friendly, *Inf.* chummy, amiable, affable, agreeable, cordial, amicable; sociable, gregarious, convivial, companionable; familiar, accessible, intimate, close, near, *Inf.* cozy, homey, informal.

2. warm-hearted, generous, sharing, hospitable; kind, kindly, well-disposed, kindly-disposed, considerate, helpful; brotherly, sisterly, thoughtful, obliging, solicitous, attentive; gracious, courteous, polite, civil; peaceful, harmonious, unhostile, easy to get along with.

neither, *conj.* **1.** not either, neither one, not either one.

2. nor, nor yet, no more.

—adj. **3.** not either, not the one or the other.

—pron. **4.** not either, not one person or the other, not one thing or the other.

nemesis, *n.* **1.** requital, just deserts, just due, retribution, punishment; retaliation, vindication, revenge, vengeance.

2. downfall, ruin, destruction, undoing, Waterloo, defeat, vanquishment.

neologism, *n.* **1.** neology, neoterism, new word, new term, new phrase, new expression, coinage; made-up word, fabricated word, invented word; blend, portmanteau word; nonce word.

2. new doctrine, new interpretation, new version, new translation.

neology, *n.* neologism, neoterism, new word. See **neologism** (*defs.* **1, 2**).

neophyte, *n.* **1.** convert, proselyte.

2. beginner, abecedarian, tyro, novice, novitiate, amateur, catechumen, tenderfoot, *Sl.* greenhorn, fledgling, cub; recruit, raw recruit, rookie, freshman, pledge, initiate; newcomer, new member, entrant; learner, student, pupil, protégé, disciple; intern, student teacher, apprentice, journeyman, trainee, probationer.

nepotism, *n.* favoritism, patronage, partisanship, partisanism, partiality, bias, prejudice; injustice, inequity, inequitableness, unfairness.

nerve, *n.* **1.** strength, sinew, stamina; power, puissance, might, robustness; virility, muscle, brawn; vigor, vitality, vim, *Inf.* piss and vinegar, vim and vigor, *Inf.* starch; energy, get up and go, *Inf.* pep, verve, *Sl.* moxie; animation, zing, liveliness, vivacity; esprit, spirit, sprightliness; dash, élan, ardor, fervor, fire, zeal.

2. courage, valor, bravery, intrepidity, prowess, chivalry; fearlessness, dauntlessness, daring, derring-do; mettle, pluck, spunk, *Inf.* guts, gumption, grit, *Inf.* sand, backbone, heart; fortitude, endurance, tenacity, determination, will; firmness, staunchness, stout-heartedness, steadfastness; indomitability, invincibility, resoluteness, doughtiness, sturdiness.

3. *Informal.* impertinence, chutzpah, gall, brass, *Sl.* cheek, *Sl.* crust; effrontery, impudence, sauciness, rudeness, insolence; audacity, boldness, presumption, brazenness, brashness.

—*v.* **4.** encourage, hearten, inspire, inspirit; embolden, invigorate, animate, enliven; strengthen, steel, brace; rally, fortify, arm, bolster.

nerveless, *adj.* **1.** cool, cool-headed, calm, unruffled, unperturbed, undisturbed, untroubled, placid, tranquil, serene; composed, collected, controlled, self-controlled, self-possessed, steady, steady-handed; dispassionate, impassionate, unemotional, impassive, undemonstrative; unexcitable, imperturbable, undisturbable.

2. feeble, weak, weakly, forceless, impotent, powerless, impuissant, helpless; weakened, enfeebled, debilitated, enervated, enervate, languid, drooping.

3. spiritless, meek, tame, submissive; spineless, having no backbone, unmanly, cowardly; timid, timorous, afraid, afraid of one's shadow, frightened, *Inf.* scary; fainthearted, lily-livered, white-livered, *Inf.* chicken-hearted, *Inf.* chicken-livered, *Inf.* pantywaist, *Inf.* yellow, *Sl.* yellow-bellied, *Sl.* candy-assed.

nerve-racking, *adj.* trying, difficult, thorny, hard, tough, rough, rugged; troublesome, vexatious, vexing, irritating, annoying, chafing, bothersome, irksome; provoking, galling, harassing, aggravating, exasperating, frustrating, maddening, infuriating; perplexing, confusing, disturbing, distressing, disquieting, worrisome.

nervous, *adj.* **1.** excitable, perturbable, agitable, *Sl.* flappable; *Inf.* hyper, high-strung, tense, strained, *Sl.* uptight, keyed up; excited, worked up, wrought up, *Sl.* in a sweat; agitated, *Inf.* in a stew, *Inf.* in a dither, *Inf.* in a tizzy, *Sl.* in a flap; flustered, ruffled, disturbed, upset, bothered, perturbed; distressed, troubled, worried, concerned, disquieted, *Archaic.* disquiet; unquiet, fretful, restless, impatient, fidgety, itchy, itching, *Sl.* antsy; jumpy, jittery, edgy, on edge, *Inf.* on pins and needles, on tenterhooks; on a tightrope, on a cliff edge, waiting for the other shoe to drop, waiting for the ax to fall, waiting for the bomb to go off; uneasy, apprehensive, alarmed, anxious, with one's heart in one's mouth, fearful; frightened, scared, *Inf.* scary, afraid, afraid of one's shadow; skittish, shy, timid, timorous; tremulous, trembling, shaky, shaking, quaking.

2. neural, nerve, neurophysiological, neuroanatomical. See **neural.**

3. sinewy, firm, hard, strong, forceful, powerful; tough, rough, rugged, hardy, sturdy; robust, vigorous, nervy, active, energetic.

nervousness, *n.* excitability, excitableness, perturbability, nervosity; hypertension, tension, tenseness, strain; excitement, fluster, confusion, *Inf.* stew, *Inf.* dither, *Inf.* tizzy, *Sl.* flap; perturbation, agitation, upset, disquiet, distress, worry, trouble, concern; fretfulness, unquiet, unrest, restlessness, impatience, itchiness, *Sl.* ants in one's pants; jitters, *Inf.* butterflies, *Inf.* butterflies in one's stomach, *Sl.* heebie-jeebies, *Sl.* habdabs, *Inf.* whim-whams, *Sl.* willies, *Sl.* creeps, *Inf.* screaming meemies; uneasiness, inquietude, apprehension, alarm, anxiety, anxiousness; dread, angst, fear, fearfulness, fright; skittishness, shyness, timidity, timidness; timorousness, tremulousness, shaking, shakiness, trembling, the shakes.

nervy, *adj. Informal.* **1.** insolent, impertinent, impudent; brassy, *Inf.* cheeky, brazen, bold, brash, audacious; pushy, forward, presumptuous; saucy, *Inf.* sassy, fresh, flip, flippant; smart-alecky, *Sl.* smart-assed, wise, *Sl.* wise-assed, cocky, cocksure; contemptuous, contumelious, insulting, rude, disrespectful; ill-behaved, unceremonious, blunt, brusque, abrupt, short.

2. courageous, brave, valorous, intrepid; valiant, gallant, chivalrous, heroic; fearless, undaunted, unflinching, unshrinking, self-confident; daring, mettlesome, plucky, spunky, *Inf.* gutsy, *Sl.* ballsy, doughty; indomitable, invincible, resolute, staunch, steadfast, stout-hearted; determined, tenacious.

3. strong, sinewy, powerful, mighty, puissant, forceful, vigorous; peppy, energetic, vivacious, spirited, lively; robust, stout, stalwart, muscular, brawny, lusty; ardent, fervent, zealous, impetuous.

4. nervous, excitable, unquiet, anxious; fidgety, jittery, skittish, agitated, *Sl.* antsy; mercurial, volatile, changeable; restless, on edge, waiting for the other shoe to drop, waiting for the bomb to go off, on a tightrope, on a cliff edge.

nescience, *n.* **1.** ignorance, blissful ignorance, unawareness, unenlightenment, unconsciousness, benightedness, darkness, blindness; want *or* lack of knowledge, lack of book learning, lack of schooling, unerudition, illiteracy, illiterateness; inexperience, greenness; innocence, simplicity, insensibility, imperception; bewilderment, confusion, perplexity; stolidness, *Inf.* thickness, denseness; dumbness, stupidity, empty-headedness, brainlessness, imbecility, idiocy.

2. agnosticism, skepticism, unbelief, Pyrrhonism, doubt, disbelief, minimifidianism; cynicism, incredulity, incredulousness; atheism, freethinking, heresy, paganism, unanointed state, excommunicant.

nest, *n.* **1.** aerie, eyrie, roost, perch; incubator, hutch, coop, pen.

2. brood, covey, flock, bevy, clutch, swarm; litter, farrow, fry.

3. retreat, hermitage, asylum, refuge, cloister; lair, den, nookery, nook, *Brit.* snuggery; resting place, arbor, bower, pavilion, gazebo; home, house, habitation, dwelling, tumble-down shack; hangout, haunt, resort, purlieu; hide-out, hiding place, covert, shelter.

4. assemblage, set, series, aggregation; heap, congeries, cluster, bunch, batch, grouping.

5. hotbed, breeding place; den of iniquity, bordello, brothel, house of ill repute, a house that is not a home, good-time parlor; smoke-filled room, back room.

nestle, *v.* **1.** snuggle, cuddle, nuzzle, snug; curl up, scrunch up, squeeze together.

2. settle, nest, lodge; enfold, ensconce.

nestling, *n.* chick, fledgling; baby, babe, babe in arms, suckling, nursing baby, nursling, weanling, wee tad.

net[1], *n.* **1.** mesh, meshwork, web, webbing, lace, lacing, lacework, bobbinet; lattice, latticework, trellis, wicker, wickerwork, wattle, mat, matting; network, plexus, reticulum, tissue, *Optics.* reticle; grate, grating, grille, grillwork, grid, gridiron; fret, fretwork, meander, filigree; tracery, intertexture, interlacing, intertwining, interweaving; sieve, sifter, riddle, screen, screening; seine, *U.S.* fyke, netting, mosquito netting, veiling; cobweb, spider web; woven fabric, cheesecloth, muslin, textile, cloth.

2. catch, trap, booby trap, snare, pitfall, web, artifice, strategy, stratagem, gimmick, ploy.

—v. **3.** entrap, ensnare, snare, mesh, bag, sack, seine, gin, trap, *Archaic.* entoil, *Archaic.* trepan; capture, catch, take captive, take prisoner, *Inf.* nab, *Inf.* corral; lay hold of, *Inf.* lay by the heels, *Inf.* collar, *Inf.* nail, seize, get hold of.

net², *adj.* **1.** take-home, after taxes, bottom-line.

2. final, conclusive, concluding, closing, last, ending, terminal, terminative, *Rare.* conclusory, finishing, completing.

—n. **3.** gain, profit, take, take-in; earnings, winnings, returns.

—v. **4.** earn, make, gain, bring in, clear; win, acquire, secure, obtain, get; bag, sack, pocket; gather, collect, take in, pick up; come into, come by, realize, receive.

nether, *adj.* **1.** infernal, Hadean, Plutonian, Plutonic, Stygian, Styxian, Tartarean, Acherontal, Cocytean, Phlegethontal, Avernal; pandemoniac, chthonian, chthonic.

2. low, lower, ground-level, low-lying, lowhanging, unelevated; under, underground, buried, submerged; subordinate, inferior; bottom, base, basal; lowest point, nadir, nadiral.

netlike, *adj.* meshlike, webbed, weblike, webby, lacelike, netted; retiary, reticulate, reticulated, reticular, retiform; cancellate, cancellated, plexal, plexiform; grated, latticed; grilled; woven, interwoven, intertwined, interlaced, fretted, filigreed.

netted, *adj.* **1.** entrapped, trapped, ensnared, snared, enmeshed, bagged, seined, trawled, entangled; captured, caught, *Inf.* nabbed, *Inf.* collared, *Inf.* nailed; taken hold of, laid by the heels, apprehended, seized; clutched, clasped, grasped.

2. netlike, webbed, weblike, webby, lacelike, meshlike. See **netlike.**

netting, *n.* woven fabric, cheesecloth, muslin, lace; webwork, web, meshwork, net. See **net¹** (*def.* **1**).

nettle, *v.* **1.** irritate, irk, pique, vex, provoke, peeve, chafe, get on [s.o.'s] nerves, *Chiefly U.S.* rife, *Inf.* aggravate, *Inf.* miff, *Inf.* give [s.o.] a pain, *Inf.* rub [s.o.] the wrong way, *Inf.* get under [s.o.'s] skin, *Inf.* get in [s.o.'s] hair; exasperate, ruffle, roil, disturb, perturb, disquiet, discompose, discountenance, put out, put off, try [s.o.'s] patience, *Inf.* get, *Sl.* get [s.o.'s] goat.

2. annoy, bother, pester, hector, harass, *Sl.* bug, *Sl.* hassle, *Sl.* drive [s.o.] up the wall; hound, dog, nag, pick on, pick at, *Sl.* ride, *Inf.* give [s.o.] a bad *or* hard time; bedevil, torment, tease, taunt, tweak, mock, *Inf.* needle.

3. anger, incense, raise [s.o.'s] ire *or* hackles, get [s.o.'s] Irish *or* dander up, *Inf.* burn [s.o.] up, *Sl.* tick [s.o.] off, *Sl.* tee [s.o.] off; enrage, madden, infuriate, make [s.o.'s] blood boil, *Inf.* make [s.o.] see red; exacerbate, rankle, gall.

4. sting, prick, stab, nip, bite, burn.

nettled, *adj.* **1.** annoyed, peeved, put out, vexed, irritated; piqued, chafed, galled, riled; offended, affronted, displeased, on the outs with, indignant; worked up, *Inf.* hot under the collar, stirred up, *Inf.* sore, *Sl.* ticked off, *Sl.* teed off; kindled, enkindled; passionate, impassioned, impassionate, overexcited.

2. angry, wrathful, wroth, irate, ireful, incensed, horn-mad; enraged, raging, fuming, smoking, infuriated, *Rare.* infuriate, furious, livid, *Inf.* mad as a hornet, mad as hops, *Inf.* mad as a wet hen; inflamed, flaming, flaring, red-hot, white-hot; distraught, overwrought, *Inf.* fit to be tied; upset, feverish, hysterical, *Inf.* blue in the face, not rational.

3. irritable, cross, surly, snappish, petulant, peevish; testy, *Sl.* uptight, choleric, touchy, huffy, peppery; splenetic, spleenful, bilious, cranky, ill-tempered, bad-tempered; irascible, quick-tempered, short-tempered, *Inf.* short-fused; quarrelsome, contentious, belligerent, up in arms, bellicose.

nettlesome, *adj.* **1.** nettling, irritating, *Inf.* aggravating, *Inf.* in one's hair; disturbing, perturbing, ruffling, disquieting, vexing.

2. annoying, bothersome, pestering, *Inf.* pesky, *Inf.* pestiferous, vexatious; troublesome, troubling, thorny, fretful, worrisome, worrying; hectoring, harassing, hounding, dogging, nagging, tormenting.

3. angering, incensing, irksome, irking; maddening, infuriating, enraging; exacerbating, rankling, galling, embittering.

network, *n.* **1.** organization, order, system, method, methodology; arrangement, formulation, systemization, coordination; structure, classification, tabulation, plan; bureaucracy, red tape, regulations, interconnection, complex.

2. maze, jungle, labyrinth, jungle, tangle; wilderness, snarl, knot.

3. net, mesh, meshwork, web, webbing, lace, lacing, lacework, bobbinet; lattice, latticework, trellis, wicker, wickerwork, wattle, mat, matting; plexus, reticulum, tissue, *Optics.* reticle; fret, fretwork, meander, filigree; grate, grating, grille, grillwork, grid, gridiron. See **net¹** (*def.* **1**).

neural, *adj.* nerve, nervous, neurophysiological, neurophysiologic, neuroanatomical, neuroanatomic, *Anat.* neuronic, *Anat.* axonal, *Anat.* dendric, *Both Anat.* ganglial, gangliar, *Physiol.* sensory, neuropathic, *Pathol.* neurotic, *Med.* neurogenic; of the nervous system *or* central nervous system *or* CNS, spinal, brain, *Anat., Physiol.* cerebrospinal, *Anat., Zool.* cerebral, *Anat., Zool.* cerebellar, medullary.

neurosis, *n.* psychoneurosis, mental illness, psychological *or* emotional disorder, mental disturbance, emotional instability, mental derangement, psychopathy; sickness, ailment, malady, affliction, disease; abnormality, abnormal condition, irregularity, aberration, deviation, psychological maladjustment; phobia, *Psychiatry.* anxiety, *Psychol.* compulsion, obsession, *Psychoanal.* fixation, *Psychiatry.* fetishism, nervous breakdown, *Psychiatry.* depression, *Pathol.* neurasthenia, *Pathol.* nervous prostration, *Psychiatry.* hypochondria, hysteria.

neurotic, *adj.* **1.** psychoneurotic, emotionally disturbed *or* unstable, mentally ill, mentally deranged, disturbed, deranged, irrational, confused, *Sl.* messed up, *Sl.* screwed up; maladjusted, abnormal, aberrant, deviant, psychopathic, *Sl.* twisted, *Sl.* warped, *Sl.* psycho; phobic, anxious, obsessive, *Psychol.* compulsive, *Psychoanal.* fixated, *Psychiatry.* fetishistic, hypochondriac, hypochondriacal, *Pathol.* neurasthenic, depressed, *Psychiatry.* manic-depressive, hysterical, manic.

—n. **2.** psychoneurotic, *Psychol.* compulsive, fetishist, hypochondriac, *Pathol.* neurasthenic, *Psychiatry.* manic-depressive, hysterical personality; psychopath, psychopathic personality, deviant, *Sl.* sicko, *Sl.* psycho.

neuter, *adj.* **1.** asexual, sexless, unsexed, castrated, *Inf.* fixed, *Vet. Med.* spayed, emasculated, *All Surgi-*

cal. ovariectomized, oophorectomized, hysterectomized; barren, sterile, (*esp. of a male*) impotent.
2. impartial, unbiased, disinterested. See **neutral** (*def.* **1**).
—n. **3.** steer, gelding, eunuch.
4. nonpartisan, impartial party. See **neutral** (*def.* **6**).
—v. **5.** castrate, asexualize, emasculate, alter, (*of horses*) geld, *Inf.* fix, *Inf.* cut, (*of female animals*) spay, (*of fowl*) capon; eunuchize, unman, effeminize, womanize.

neutral, *adj.* **1.** (*of a person or government*) nonparticipating, uninvolved, disengaged, noninterventional; nonfighting, noncombatant, noncombative, pacifistic, peaceable, peaceful.
2. impartial, nonpartisan, nonparty, unbiased, unprejudiced, without favoritism, open-minded; unaligned, nonaligned, unallied, unsided, uncommitted, independent, (*of voters*) unaffiliated, free; disinterested, dispassionate, indifferent, unaffected, unimplicated; objective, detached, withdrawn, removed, remote, aloof.
3. indefinite, indeterminate, indistinguishable, unremarkable, ordinary, commonplace, average, run of the mill, everyday; flat, bland, dull, uninteresting, insipid, jejeune, *Sl.* blah.
4. (*of a color or shade*) colorless, uncolored, hueless, toneless, achromatic, achromic, achromous; pale, washed-out, drab, *Scot. and North. Eng.* blae; white, gray, black.
—n. **5.** nonparticipant, noninterventionist; unaligned state, isolationist; pacifist, nonfighter.
6. nonpartisan, independent, free thinker; impartial *or* disinterested party, detached *or* objective party, neutralist.

neutrality, *n.* **1.** impartiality, indifferentism, unprejudicedness, lack of bias *or* favoritism, neutralism, open-mindedness; nonpartisanship, nonalignment, independence, disinterestedness, disinterest, dispassionateness, dispassion, objectivity, objectiveness, detachment, disengagement, remoteness, aloofness.
2. noninterventionism, nonparticipation, noninvolvement, isolationism; noncombatance, pacifism, peaceableness.

neutralization, *n.* **1.** counteraction, offsetting, countervailing, counterpoising, counterbalancing, neutralizing, normalization; nullification, cancellation, annulment, undoing.
2. balance, equipoise, equilibrium; neutrality, normality, normalness, normalcy.

neutralize, *v.* **1.** counteract, offset, countervail, counterbalance, counterpoise, make up for, compensate for; nullify, negate, negative, cancel out, annul, void, undo, overcome *or* destroy the effect of.
2. balance out, equal out, come out even; normalize, return to normal, recover.

never, *adj.* not ever, not at all, at no time, not at any time, ne'er; absolutely not, *Inf.* not on your life, on no account, under no circumstances, under no conditions, *Inf.* not in a million years, *Sl.* when hell freezes over, *Sl.* on a cold day in hell.

never-ending, *adj.* perpetual, eternal, everlasting, timeless, interminable, Sisyphean, endless, unending; ceaseless, incessant, unceasing, nonstop, uninterrupted, continual, continuous, unbroken; unremitting, unintermitting, relentless, unrelenting, persistent; recurrent, recurring, repeated, repetitious.
2. infinite, boundless, illimitable, limitless; immeasurable, measureless, unfathomable, vast.
3. enduring, lasting, abiding, *Literary.* sempiternal, aeonian, amaranthine, perennial; immutable, constant, unwavering, unfaltering, undiminished; invariable, fixed, durable, stable, permanent, perdurable; steady, steadfast, sustained, regular.

nevertheless, *adv.* nonetheless, *Archaic.* natheless, however, howbeit, anyway, anyhow; regardless, be that as it may, for all that, after all is said and done, in spite of the fact, despite the fact, *Archaic.* withal, notwithstanding; all *or* just the same, at any rate, in any case, in any event; but, still, still and all, yet even so, after all; on the other hand, at the same time.

never-tiring, *adj.* tireless, untiring, indefatigable, inexhaustible; on the go, on the move, astir, bustling, energetic; unsleeping, sleepless, wakeful, attentive, unwearied, unwearying, undrooping, unflagging, unfaltering, unwavering, unswerving, persistent, pertinacious; undaunted, tenacious, firm, determined; plodding, dogged, persevering, indomitable, unfailing, steady, patient; unremitting, assiduous, intent, relentless, unrelenting, steadfast; studious, assiduous, sedulous, industrious, hard-working, diligent.

new, *adj.* **1.** modern, late, recent, advanced; contemporary, topical, twentieth-century, present-day, of recent make, of recent period, latter-day, of yesterday; latest, later, newest, last; hot, just out, hot off the press, hot off the griddle *or* fire; abreast of the times, up-to-the-minute, up-to-date; spanking, brand-new, in mint condition, factory-new, late-model; newly issued, newly arrived, newly come; modernistic, futuristic, ultramodern, revolutionary, modernized; avant-garde, *Sl.* far out, *Sl.* way out, ahead of its time, newfangled.
2. pristine, raw, fresh, mint, fresh as a daisy, fresh as the morning dew; callow, green, newfledged, newborn, budding, virgin, youthful, vernal, young, fledgling; immature, unripe, unfledged, undeveloped; first, maiden, initial, natal, starting, beginning.
3. smart, popular, current, *Sl.* hip, *Sl.* mod; à la mode, fashionable, chic, stylish; modish, in style, in vogue, all the rage, the latest thing, *Inf.* trendy.
4. novel, neoteric, newfashioned; original, imaginative, creative, unhackneyed; unique, authentic, unexampled.
5. unfamiliar, strange, unusual, unheard of, bizarre, extraordinary; different, peculiar, curious, odd.
6. fresh, unused, unhandled, unhandseled, untouched; unexplored, uncharted, unventured, untrodden, unbeaten; unaccustomed, unseasoned, not used to, unbroken; untested, untried, unknown, experimental.
7. further, farther, additional, additory, supplemental, supplementary, adscititious; extra, more, plus, other, another, ulterior.
8. refreshed, renewed, restored, reinvigorated, revivified; reborn, renascent, regenerated, changed; rebuilt, recreated, reconstructed, remodeled, modernized.
—adv. **9.** recently, lately, of late, just now, now; latterly, not long ago, the other day, only yesterday.
10. freshly, anew, afresh, like new, as new; once more, again, once again, *Latin. de novo, Inf.* from scratch, encore; from the ground up, *Latin. ab ovo,* from the beginning.

newborn, *adj.* **1.** just born, newfledged, neonatal; infantile, infant, babyish, baby; unlicked, still wet behind the ears, unweaned; in the cradle *or* crib, in swaddling clothes, at the breast, in diapers, *Brit.* in nappies.
2. reborn, regenerate, regenerated, renascent, recreated; reformed, changed, transformed, converted, born again.
—n. **3.** newborn infant, neonate, baby, infant, babe, papoose, *It. bambino;* weanling, nursling, suckling, fosterling, yearling; fledgling, nestling, duckling, chick, gosling, cygnet; piglet, pigling, shoat, kid, yeanling, lamb, ewelamb, lambkin; polliwog, tadpole; puppy, pup, whelp, kit, kitten, cub; calf, colt, foal, filly, fawn.

newcomer, *n.* **1.** new arrival, arrival, immigrant, emigrant, comer, incomer, naturalized citizen, alien; entrant, settler, colonist; outsider, intruder, interloper, ultramontane, barbarian, stranger, (*in India and the East*) griffin.
2. novice, beginner, amateur, tyro, neophyte; apprentice, learner, trainer, probationer, initiate, novitiate, catechumen; *Inf.* greenhorn, *Sl.* greenie, fledgling, freshman, *Sl.* jaboney, debutant, *Sl.* deb; recruit, raw recuit, inductee, *Sl.* boot.
3. parvenu, nouveau riche, upstart, arriviste, *Latin. novus homo; Inf.* Johnny-come-lately, new boy, new boy in town, new face.

newfangled, *adj.* modern, contemporary, recent; novel, imaginative, different. See **new** (*defs.* **1, 4-6**).

newfashioned, *adj.* fashionable, smart, chic. See **new** (*def.* **3**).

newly, *adv.* **1.** recently, lately, of late. See **new** (*def.* **9**).
2. anew, afresh, freshly. See **new** (*def.* **10**).
3. modernistically, modernly, futuristically; modishly, fashionably, stylishly, smartly, chicly.

newlywed, *n.* **1.** bride, blushing bride, plighted bride; groom, bridegroom.
2. newlyweds honeymooners, bridal pair, wedded pair, married couple; man and wife, bride and groom, *Latin. vir et uxor.*

newness, *n.* **1.** recency, recentness, lateness, presentness, nowness; novelty, neoterism, neology, innovation, neonomianism, newfangledness; unusualness, uncommonness, peculiarity, singularity, unfamiliarity, strangeness; uniqueness, originality, inventiveness, creativity.
2. modernization, modernity, modernism, contemporaneity; ultramodernity, ultramodernness, futurism.
3. freshness, pristineness, greenness, callowness, rawness, youthfulness; immaturity, undevelopment, virginity, maidenhood, intactness; mint condition, brand-newness; restoration, renovation, reformation, renaissance.
4. fashionableness, smartness, chicness, stylishness, modishness, *Sl.* hipness, *Sl.* modness; vogue, style, *Inf.* rage, trend, fashion, mode, *Sl.* the go, *Fr. le dernier cri, Sl.* the thing.

news, *n.* **1.** report, account, statement, publication, announcement, release, press release, news release; message, dispatch, communication, communiqué, bulletin, *Journalism.* flash *or* news flash.
2. information, *Inf.* info, intelligence, data, facts, inside facts *or* information, *Inf.* lowdown, *Inf.* scoop, *Sl.* dope; talk, rumor, buzz, whisper, *Inf.* scuttlebutt, *Inf.* hearsay, *Archaic.* bruit; gossip, idle talk, tittle-tattle, scandal, dirt.
3. word, notification, advice; tidings, glad tidings, good news; bad news.
4. newscast, broadcast, radiobroadcast, radio program; telecast, television program.
5. copy, good copy, story, news item, hot item, big news, front-page news.
6. newspaper, paper, gazette. See **newspaper.**

newscast, *n.* **1.** broadcast, radiobroadcast, radio program; telecast, television program; nightly *or* evening news; *Inf.* news roundup *or* roundup, *Inf.* news wrap-up *or* wrap-up.
2. report, account, release; dispatch, bulletin. See also **news** (*def.* **1**).

newsman, *n.* journalist, newspaperman, *Brit.* pressman, *Archaic.* gazetteer, gentleman *or* representative of the press, member of the fourth estate; reporter, *Journalism.* leg man, district man, newshound, newshen, *Inf.* newshawk, newsmonger; correspondent, contributor, stringer, paragrapher, *Brit.* paragraphist; columnist, sob sister, gossip columnist, scandalmonger, dirt-dealer; critic, reviewer; editor, editorialist, *Brit.* leader writer; newswriter; flack, hack, blurb writer, penny-a-liner; copyeditor, slot man, copyreader, rim man, copywriter, rewrite man, rewriter; newscaster, broadcaster, *Brit.* newsreader, anchorman, commentator.

newsmonger, *n.* gossip, gossipmonger, rumormonger, scandalmonger, dirt-dealer, *Inf.* hatchet man; busybody, quidnunc, *Sl.* yenta; talebearer, telltale, tattler, tattletale, tittle-tattler.

newspaper, *n.* tabloid, *Inf.* tab, paper, news, gazette, sheet, yellow sheet, scandal sheet, *Inf., Derog.* rag; journal, periodical, publication, organ, house organ; daily, weekly, bi-weekly, monthly, quarterly; extra, extra edition, special, special edition.

next, *adj.* **1.** following, ensuing, succeeding, successive, sequential, subsequent, later, after; consequent, attendant, resulting, latter.
2. adjacent, neighboring, bordering, contiguous, adjoining; closest, nearest, nearby, proximate.
—adv. **3.** subsequently, at a subsequent time, later, at a later time, afterward, after, following, successively, sequentially; thereafter, after that time, whereafter, from that time, hereon, since.
—prep. **4.** *Usu.* **next to** beside, by *or* at the side of, *Dial.* aside of, by, at one's elbow; alongside, side by side, abreast, cheek by jowl, adjacent to, in juxtaposition with, next door to; near to, close to, *Brit. Dial.* near-hand, close at hand, nearby, close by; but a step from, on the edge of, bordering upon.

nib, *n.* **1.** bill, beak, pecker, neb.
2. tip, point, end; penpoint; peak, apex, vertex, summit, top, tiptop, extremity.

nibble, *v.* pick at, pick over, peck at, take small bites, eat; snack, nosh, munch, eat between meals, *Sl.* cheat.

nice, *adj.* **1.** agreeable, pleasant, winning, winsome, taking, delightful, attractive, likable; cheering, cheerful, amusing, humorous; amiable, friendly, cordial, genial, congenial; charming, gracious, generous, warm-hearted, sympathetic, understanding, compassionate; good, kind, kindly, kindly-disposed, benignant, benevolent, charitable.
2. gratifying, pleasing, pleasurable, to one's taste, satisfying, satisfactory, good, enjoyable, pleasure-giving; smooth, rich, tender, soft, comfortable, comforting, cozy, warm, homey; piquant, sweet, appetizing, delectable, savory, toothsome, succulent, mouth-watering, *Inf.* scrumptious, *Inf.* tasty.
3. refined, of good taste, elegant, proper, right, correct; appropriate, suitable, seemly, fitting, right and proper, as it should be; in the best taste, tasteful, in good taste; cultured, civilized, cultivated, polished, sophisticated, finished; elegant, genteel, decent, decorous, respectable; virtuous, chaste.
4. precise, accurate, exact, strict, close, detailed; subtle, fine, minute; specific, clear-cut, clean-cut, well-defined; true, direct, unerring, definite, positive, sure, express, faithful, *Inf.* sure-enough, *Inf.* dead on, *Inf.* straight-up-and-down; mathematically exact, pinpoint; faultless, flawless, perfect, letter-perfect.
5. scrupulous, meticulous, careful, painstaking, methodical; particular, discriminating, choosy, perfectionistic; distinguishing, differential, selective, perceptive, perspicacious, astute, wise, judicious, sage, sapient; penetrating, acute, critical, ticklish; attentive, heedful, assiduous, discriminative, discriminatory, discretionary, discretional, discreet, keen, discerning, percipient, differentiating.
6. fastidious, delicate, fine, excellent, exquisite, dain-

ty, graceful; overrefined, overfastidious, overparticular, overscrupulous, punctilious, oversubtle, overnice, oversensitive, squeamish, queasy; hairsplitting, *Inf.* persnickety, *Inf.* pernickety; niggling, exacting, demanding, difficult, finicky, finical, overcritical, hypercritical, difficult, hard to please, fussy, *Inf.* picayune, *Inf.* fussbudgety; prudish, priggish, puritanical.

7. *All Inf.* great, dandy, jim-dandy, crackerjack, swell, rum, keen, tops, wonderful, O.K., bully.

nice nelly, *n.* prude, prig, puritan, bluenose, précieuse, *Inf.* goody-goody, *Inf.* goody two-shoes, *Inf.* Miss Prim and Proper, *Inf.* Miss Prissy *or* Miss Priss; la-di-da, Victorian.

nice-nelly, *adj.* **1.** prudish, prim, prissy, *Inf.* stuffy, *Inf.* old-maidish; narrow, censorious, puritanical, Victorian, *Inf.* goody-goody, nice, *Inf.* too nice for words. See **nice** (*def.* **6**).

2. euphemistic, overnice, overdelicate, precious, précieuse, formalistic; pretentious, affected, la-di-da, mannered, mincing, simpering; namby-pamby, mealy-mouthed.

nice-nellyism, *n.* primness, excessive propriety, prissiness, prudery, prudishness, priggishness, priggery, overniceness, *Inf.* goodiness; pretentiousness, sanctimoniousness, equivocation. (*esp. in Victorian England*) prunes and prisms; preciosity, preciousness, precisianism; euphemism, mealymouthedness, euphuism.

niceness, *n.* **1.** preciseness, precision, exactitude, mathematical exactitude, exactness; meticulousness, attention to detail, accuracy, criticalness, methodicalness; skill, skillfulness, control, technique; conscientiousness, care, infinite care, carefulness, discrimination; simplicity, clarity, clearness, definitiveness.

2. fineness, delicacy, subtlety, distinction; exquisiteness, flawlessness, handsomeness, quality, choiceness.

3. fastidiousness, scrupulousness, particularness, particularity, punctilio, punctiliousness, minuteness, strictness, exactingness, daintiness, nicety; choosiness, finickiness, finicalness, fussiness, *Inf.* pickiness; squeamishness, queasiness.

4. good taste, propriety, appropriateness, seemliness, felicity, comeliness; refinement, elegance, culture, polish, finish, finesse, grace, gracefulness; discretion, tact, circumspection, prudence; deliberateness, deliberation, formality, properness, correctness, fitness, meetness; genteelness, gentility, civility, cultivation; affectation, airs, mannerism, artificiality, foppery, frills, mincingness; euphemism, overdelicacy, overrefinement, prudishness, peculiarity, nice-nellyism.

5. sensitivity, sensibility, keenness, acuity, acuteness, appreciation, astuteness, perception, perceptiveness, perspicaciousness, perspicacity, differentiation, discernment, percipience, percipiency, scrupulosity; overcriticalness, hypercriticalness, oversubtlety, overniceness, oversensitiveness.

6. agreeability, agreeableness, likeability, cheerfulness, pleasantness, amiability, friendliness, geniality, congeniality; graciousness, generosity, warm-heartedness, solicitude, understanding, sympathy, compassion, fellow feeling, humaneness, fairness, kindness, kindliness, charity, charitableness, benevolence; goodness, sweetness, delightfulness, attractiveness, winsomeness, charm.

7. gratification, pleasurability, enjoyability; flavor, savor, deliciousness, delectableness, piquancy; richness, tenderness, softness.

nicety, *n.* **1.** punctilio, fine point, point, detail, minor detail; instance, item, particular, element, factor, facet, incidental; aspect, feature, respect, attribute; triviality, minutia, minuteness, particularity, circumstantiality.

2. shade of difference, distinction, differentiation, point of difference, nuance, subtlety, refinement, hairline.

3. **niceties** refinements, graces, amenities, comforts, creature comforts; luxuries, the good things in life, gratifications, pleasures, the little pleasures that make life worth living.

4. **to a nicety** precisely, exactly, meticulously; to the letter, to a turn, to a hair.

niche, *n.* recess, alcove, cove, nook, cranny, hole, pigeonhole, cubby, cubbyhole, corner, *Fr. coin,* private spot *or* place.

nick, *n.* **1.** notch, groove, hole, gouge; cut, incision, slit, split, score, gash, slash; indentation, indent, dent, dint, hollow, depression; scrape, scratch, scarification, chip, flaw, defect, mark, spot, blemish, defacement.

2. **in the nick of time** just in time, not a moment too soon.

—*v.* **3.** notch, groove, gouge, cut a hole in, make a cut in, chip; cut into, incise, slit, split, score, gash, slash; dent, dint, put a dent in, push *or* press in; scrape, scratch, scarify, mark, flaw, spot, blemish, mar, deface.

4. hit, bump, bruise, damage slightly; injure, hurt, wound.

5. defraud, cheat, rook, victimize, *Archaic.* chouse, skin, fleece, bilk, swindle, *Inf.* take; fool, cozen, dupe, delude, take in, throw dust in the eyes of, pull the wool over the eyes of, *Inf.* slip *or* sneak [s.t.] by, *Inf.* pull a fast one on; hoodwink, trick, bamboozle, outwit, overreach; humbug, gammon, bluff, juggle, *Inf.* flimflam; impose upon, use, take for a ride, *Inf.* rope [s.o.] in, *Inf.* throw a curve, mislead, lead [s.o.] down the garden path; *Inf.* fast-talk, *Inf.* flam, *Inf.* hype, *Inf.* jive, *Sl.* con, *Sl.* sucker in.

nickel, *n.* coin, five-cent piece, five cents, *Sl.* blip.

nickname, *n.* **1.** sobriquet, agnomen, cognomen, byname, moniker, handle; familiar name, pet name, diminutive, epithet, *Chiefly Scot.* to-name.

—*v.* **2.** give a nickname to, call by a nickname.

3. miscall, misname, call by a wrong name.

nictitate, *v.* wink, blink, *Inf.* bat *or* bat one's eyes, flutter one's eyelashes.

niggard, *n.* miser, skinflint, *Sl.* skin, *Sl.* cheapskate, *Inf.* piker, muckworm, *Sl.* screw; penny pincher, pinchpenny, lickpenny, *Inf.* tightwad; cheeseparer, hoarder, save-all, *Scot.* carl; scrooge, Harpagon, money-grubber, harpy; curmudgeon, churl, hunks.

niggardliness, *n.* **1.** parsimony, miserliness, penuriousness, meanness, churlishness, nearness; stinginess, tightness, tight-fistedness, closefistedness, closeness, closehandedness, cheapness, *Sl.* chintziness.

2. scrimpiness, shabbiness, grudgingness, begrudgingness, skimpiness, unwillingness to part with a nickel, ungenerousness, ungenerosity; frugality, spareness, chariness.

3. graspingness, avidity, avarice, avariciousness, greed, cupidity, rapacity, rapaciousness, tenacity, covetousness; mercenariness, venality, usuriousness, usury, extortion, sordidness; selfishness, hard-heartedness, unyieldingness, misanthropy.

niggardly, *adj.* **1.** stingy, parsimonious, miserly, carking, skinflinty; mean, tight, tight-fisted, closefisted; cheap, *Sl.* chintzy, moneygrubbing, grasping; penurious, *Rare.* illiberal, cheeseparing; scrimping, penny-pinching, grudging, begrudging, ungenerous, stinting, reluctant *or* unwilling to give; thrifty, frugal, sparing, chary; economical, prudent, saving, penny-wise.

2. scanty, meager, skimpy, scrimpy, scant; meanly small, beggarly, paltry, poor, piddling, *Inf.* measly, mere; slight, slender, narrow, puny, very little; insufficient, inadequate, short, shy; insubstantial, nominal, minute, negligible.

niggle, *v.* **1.** trifle, *Inf.* frivol, *Inf.* fiddle-faddle, fribble, putter, *Brit.* potter, poke, fritter one's time away, diddle, piddle, dawdle, finick, idle, fool around.

2. criticize, gripe, complain, cavil, carp, *Yiddish.* kvetch, nag; object, find fault, poke holes in; mutter in one's beard, whine, *Sl.* grouse, fret.

niggling, *adj.* **1.** petty, minor, picayune, trivial, puny; inconsequential, unimportant, insignificant, nugatory, worthless, useless; piddling, trifling, fiddling, frivolous, fribble; inane, silly, foolish, pointless, *Inf.* dumb, idiotic.

2. fussy, overelaborate, intricate, complicated, convoluted; detailed, labored, ornate.

nigh, *adv.* **1.** near, close; presently, soon, anon; nearly, almost, about, approximately, closely, roughly, generally; in general, thereabouts, somewhere about.

—adj. **2.** near, nearby, approaching, at hand; close, close by, close-at-hand, convenient, in the neighborhood; proximate, forthcoming, imminent, momentary, impending, looming.

3. short, direct, straight, quick.

—prep. **4.** close to, near, alongside of. See **near** (*defs.* **8, 9**).

night, *n.* **1.** nighttime, *Poetic.* nighttide; midnight, wee hours, dead of night; time to prowl, witching time, the time when the worms come out, killing time, the other side of the day; bedtime, slumber time.

2. evening, twilight, dying of the light, sunset. See **nightfall.**

3. darkness, dark, Cimmerian darkness, Stygian gloom; tenebrousness, gloom, shades *or* curtains of night.

4. night and day unceasingly, ceaselessly, incessantly, around the clock; continually, continuously, endlessly, nonstop; tirelessly, untiringly, indefatigably.

night clothes, *n.* bed garments, sleeping clothes, nightgown, *Inf.* nightie, nightdress, nightrobe, *Fr. robe de nuit;* pajamas, *Sl.* p.j.'s, nightshirt; bunting, sleeper, Dr. Denton, *Inf.* footsie pajamas; nightcap.

nightclub, *n.* cabaret, *Inf.* nightspot, *Inf.* nitery, *Inf.* nightery; roadhouse, dance hall, discotheque, *Inf.* disco; supper club, club, cafe; *All Inf.* hot spot, watering hole, watering place; *Inf.* pub, bar, singles bar.

nightfall, *n.* sunset, sundown, day's end, moonrise, edge of night, beginning of night, *Inf.* shank of the night, night; dusk, twilight, crepuscule, *Literary.* gloaming; late afternoon, evening, *Archaic.* vespers, eventide, evenfall, eve, *Archaic.* even, *Archaic.* evensong.

nightingale, *n. Poetic.* philomel, thrush, wood thrush; singing bird, singer, songbird, songster, warbler.

nightly, *adj.* **1.** nocturnal, night-time, noctivagant, noctivagous; night-clad, night-cloaked, night-enshrouded, night-hid.

2. recurrent, repetitious, incessant, never-failing, happening every night, performed every night.

—adv. **3.** nocturnally, by night, at night, in the night, nights; through the night, in the dark, in dark of night, nights only.

nightmare, *n.* **1.** bad dream, horrid dream; phantasmagoria.

2. horrible experience, trial, tribulation, *Sl.* bad trip, ordeal, trial by fire, duress; torture, immense suffering, mental suffering.

3. (*formerly*) monster, evil spirit, dream being, incubus, succubus; night hag, horror, demon, cacodemon, phantasm.

nightmarish, *adj.* **1.** disquieting, disturbing, frightening, frightful, fear-inspiring, *Inf.* scary; alarming, startling, dismaying, astounding, appalling; kafkaesque, terrifying, terror-inspiring, terror-fraught, horrible, horrid, horrific, awful; dire, fell, dreadful, ghastly, grim, appalling, shocking, creepy; petrifying, harrowing, rending, racking; excruciating, agonizing; odious, execrable, repulsive, forbidding, abhorrent, enough to drive one mad.

2. exasperating, annoying, irritating, provoking, mortifying, galling; plaguing, bothering, bothersome, harassing; worrying, worrisome, tormenting, haunting.

nighttime, *n.* night, dead of night, wee hours. See **night** (*def.* **1**).

nightwalker, *n.* **1.** noctambulist, noctambule, sleepwalker, somnambulist, somnambulator.

2. thief, burglar, housebreaker, robber; *Inf.* second-story man, cat burglar, sneak thief, prowler; *Sl.* cracksman, safecracker, picklock, Raffles.

3. prostitute, whore, harlot, lady of the evening; woman of the profession, woman of ill-repute, woman of the streets, streetwalker, bar girl, call girl, Cyprian; hussy, slut, demimondaine, loose woman, wanton, tramp; *Sl.* chippy, *Fr. fille de joie,* trollop, strumpet; *All Sl.* cat, tart, hustler, bim, bimbo, hooker, floozie, working girl.

nihilism, *n.* **1.** total rejection, renunciation, abnegation, denial; skepticism, nullifidianism, floccinaucinihilipilification; agnosticism, disbelief, atheism, nonbelief; cynicism, pessimism, negativism, malism.

2. nonexistence, nothingness, nihility, nullity, negativeness, existencelessness; unreality, unactuality, nonreality, nonlife, nonoccurence, *Fr. néant,* nullibicity, inexistence, nonsubsistence, incorporeity, incorporeality, inessentiality; nonentity, nonbeing, unbeing; oblivion, negation, blank, void, vacuity, vacuum, emptiness, abeyance, nothing.

3. terrorism, anarchy, lawlessness, antinomianism, syndicalism, anarcho-syndicalism; Bakuninism, Chartism, subversion, kulakism; sedition, mutiny, insubordination; traitorousness, treason, disloyalty, perfidy; destructiveness, violence, revolutionism; disorder, misrule, unruliness, chaos, turmoil; mob rule, mobocracy, ochlocracy, lynch law, license.

nihilist, *n.* **1.** anarchist, reactionary, extremist, absurdist, syndicalist, antinomian, Bakuninist; terrorist, revolutionary, counter-revolutionary, insurrectionist, insurgent, agitator; seditionist, traitor, insubordinate, mutineer, rebel, revolter, secessionist; iconoclast, wrecker, destroyer, sansculotte; factionary, protestor, marcher, demonstrator; troublemaker, rabble-rouser, tub-thumper, demagogue, firebrand, mob-orator.

2. skeptic, agnostic, doubter, doubting Thomas, nullifidian; cynic, pessimist, malist, *Sl.* gloomy Gus.

nihilistic, *adj.* **1.** anarchistic, anarchic, lawless, antinomian, syndicalistic; rebellious, mutinous, riotous, insurrectionary, incendiary, sansculottic; treasonous, traitorous, insubordinate, subversive; revolutionary, revolutionist, counter-revolutionary, reactionary; unruly, disorderly, chaotic, disorganized; destructive, demolitionary, ravaging, vandalic.

2. cynical, pessimistic, negative, negativistic, defeatist, gloomy.

nihility, *n.* nothingness, nonexistence, nullity. See **nihilism** (*def.* **2**).

nil, *n.* **1.** nothing, naught, zero, none; cipher, aught, *Sl.* goose egg, *Sl.* zip, *Sl.* zilch, *Sl.* the big O, *Cricket Sl.* duck, *Tennis.* love.

2. no quantity, no degree, no amount, none whatever, none whatsoever, nothing at all, nothing on earth, nothing under the sun; no such thing, *Sl.* nix, *Latin. nihil, Fr. rien, Span. nada; Sl.* scratch, *Sl.* squat, *Sl.* diddly, *Sl.* diddly-squat.

—adj. **3.** valueless, worthless, inconsequential, useless, nugatory; vain, meritless, empty, idle; piddling, mere, slight, niggling, picayune, miserable, paltry, petty; unavailing, unprofitable, gainless, unserviceable, good for nothing; inadequate, ineffectual, inefficacious.

nimble, *adj.* **1.** agile, lithe, sprightly, light and quick; spry, active, lively, full of life, animated, vivacious, energetic, *Inf.* chipper, *Inf.* snappy, *Inf.* full of pep, *Inf.* full of get up and go; brisk, rapid, quick, fleet, speedy, expeditious. See also **nimble-footed.**

2. alert, prompt, ready, on one's toes, awake, wide-awake; intelligent, smart, smart as a whip. See also **nimble-witted.**

nimble-fingered, *adj.* skillfull, expert, proficient, good, good at, *Inf.* no mean; adept, adroit, deft, dexterous, coordinated, handy, neat-handed, sure-handed, neat; clever, resourceful, ingenious, daedal.

nimble-footed, *adj.* fast, rapid, fleet, fleet-footed, light-legged, light of heel; speedy, brisk, quick, quick as lightning, quick as thought, quick-moving, swift as an arrow, arrowy, winged, eagle-winged; light, light on one's feet, light-footed, sure-footed, graceful; agile, spry, sprightly, *Dial.* peart.

nimbleness, *n.* **1.** agility, sprightliness, spryness, featliness, lightness, gracefulness, grace; nimble-footedness, fleet-footedness, light-footedness, light-leggedness; legerity, alacrity, celerity, activity, dispatch, expedition, expeditiousness, address; speed, speediness, swiftness, fleetness, quickness; briskness, smartness, spiritedness, energy, *Inf.* peppiness.

2. skill, skillfulness, adroitness, dexterity, deftness, finesse, nimble-fingeredness, neat-fingeredness, neat-handedness; cleverness, resourcefulness, ingenuity.

3. alertness, attentiveness, readiness, sharpness, keenness, acuteness; intelligence, smartness, *Inf.* braininess, brightness, *Sl.* smarts, *Sl.* savvy; sharp-wittedness, quick-wittedness, nimble-wittedness, clear *or* quick thinking; esprit, ready wit, quick wit, sharp wit, nimble wit.

nimble-witted, *adj.* witty, spirituel, attic; brilliant, scintillating, sparkling; acute, keen, sharp, *Sl.* sharp as a tack; intelligent, smart, *Inf.* smart as a whip, *Inf.* brainy, bright, *Inf.* nobody's fool, *Inf.* not born yesterday, *Sl.* no dumbbell *or* dummy; sharp-witted, keen-witted, ready-witted, quick-witted, *Inf.* quick on the uptake; alert, awake, wide-awake, clearheaded, clear-witted, *Scot. and North Eng.* gleg, *Sl.* on the ball.

nimbly, *adj.* **1.** agilely, spryly, featly, trippingly, gracefully, lithesomely; nimble-footedly, light-footedly, light-leggedly; fast, speedily, swiftly, fleetly, quickly, rapidly, mercurially; briskly, smartly, spiritedly, animatedly, *Inf.* snappily; readily, promptly, expeditiously, with dispatch.

2. skillfully, adroitly, dexterously, deftly, expertly, easily, nimble-fingeredly, neat-fingeredly, neat-handedly; cleverly, resourcefully, ingeniously.

3. alertly, attentively, keenly, acutely, sharply; intelligently; nimble-wittedly, quick-wittedly, ready-wittedly, sharp-wittedly; clearheadedly, clear-wittedly.

nimbus, *n.* **1.** cloud, aura, atmosphere, ambience, mood; character, air, quality, tone, feel, feeling, vibrations, *Inf.* vibes.

2. halo, aureole, aureola, gloriole, ring of light, crown of light, circle of radiance, corona, luminous cloud; effulgence, radiance, luster, luminosity, irradiation, light, glow, glowing, luminescence, shine, shining.

nimiety, *n.* excess, overabundance, superabundance, overplus, extra, spare, surplus, surplusage, superflux; flood, deluge, inundation, profusion, abundance, cornucopia, horn of plenty; surfeit, glut, plethora, overflow, overload, oversupply, more than enough, enough and to spare, enough and then some, too much; superfluity, superfluousness, redundancy, supererogation, oversufficiency, overkill, overdose, too much of a good thing, saturation, supersaturation; (*all of words*) verbiage, wordiness, verbosity, verboseness, prolixity, prolixness.

nincompoop, *n.* fool, ninny, ninnyhammer, silly, goose, silly billy, *Sl.* yo-yo, tomfool; simpleton, Simple Simon, saphead, noodle, cuckoo, *Inf.* jay, idiot, imbecile, mooncalf, *Inf.* moron, *Sl.* zombie; dimwit, nitwit, half-wit, scatterbrain, *Sl.* birdbrain, *Sl.* flake; rattlehead, rattlebrain, rattlepate, harebrain, *Sl.* dingbat, *Sl.* ding-a-ling, featherbrain, addle-brain, addle-head, addle-pate, pinhead; dolt, clod, oaf, dunce, *Inf.* chump, *Sl.* jerk, *Inf.* coot, dullard, *Inf.* numskull; dope, booby, *Inf.* dummy, *Sl.* dumbbell, *Sl.* meatball, *Sl.* meathead; blockhead, beetlehead, bonehead, dunderhead, dunderpate, chucklehead, *Sl.* dumbhead, *Sl.* lunkhead, *Inf.* knucklehead, *Sl.* stupid-head; donkey, ass, lubber, lout; ignoramus, know-nothing, lowbrow, illiterate.

nip¹, *v.* **1.** pinch, bite, bite in, tweak, vellicate, chomp, incise.

2. snip, cut, cut off, lop, sunder; crop, truncate, dock, take off, snap, crack off, shave off, shear, clip.

3. retard, check, shorten, cut short, abbreviate; blight, supress, stunt, slow down, delay, drag down; impede, hinder, inhibit, obstruct, cramp, constrain, hold back, discommode, inconvenience.

4. *Informal.* snatch, seize, clutch, snare; snag, snatch, grab, get one's fingers *or* hands on, finger, clasp, grip, grasp; bag, sack, pocket; steal, thieve, purloin, take, palm, make off with, *Inf.* borrow; annex, snitch, swipe, mooch, nick, *Inf.* cop; appropriate, usurp, help oneself to, make free with, pirate, *Inf.* lift, plagiarize.

5. nip in the bud See **bud** (*def.* **3**).

—n. **6.** pinch, tweak, vellication, bite, chomp, incision.

7. nasty remark, sharp remark, *Inf.* dig, sharp rejoinder, caustic remark, *Inf.* zinger; gibe, scoff, jeer, taunt, *Inf.* jab, *Inf.* cut, *Sl.* comeback, insult.

8. tang, tartness, zest, sharpness, piquance, piquancy; savor, high seasoning, strong seasoning, high flavor, high relish, strong taste; *Inf.* zip, *Inf.* punch, *Inf.* snack, *Inf.* twang; poignancy, pungency, pungence.

9. morsel, nibble, taste, *Inf.* sniggie, *Inf.* sample.

nip², *n.* **1.** shot, *Sl.* snort, sip, *Inf.* swig, jiggerful; gulp, portion, draft, draught, swill; dram, peg, *Brit.* half pint.

—v. **2.** tipple, drink constantly, drink on the job; *Inf.* closet-drink, drink on the sly, *Inf.* booze; *Inf.* bend the elbow, *Inf.* drink like a fish, *Inf.* lean on the stuff.

nippers, *n.* pinchers, tweezers, pliers, forceps; grippers, grip, vise, clincher, holder.

nipping, *adj.* **1.** pinching, gripping, biting, vellicative.

2. sharp, keen, stinging, smarting, raw, nippy; bitter, severe, piercing, cutting, blasting; chilling, chilly, bone-chilling; numbing, freezing, cold, icy-cold, ice-cold, wintry, hibernal.

3. sarcastic, caustic, bitter, sour, crabby; astringent, acid, acetic, acerbic, tart, vinegary; nasty, digging, gibing, scoffing, jeering; taunting, jabbing, cutting, *Inf.*

snippy, insulting.

nipple, *n.* teat, tit, titty, *Chiefly Dial.* pap, dug, *Anat.* mamilla, papilla; pacifier, sugar-tit.

nitid, *adj.* bright, shining, lucid, lucent, relucent; radiant, irradiant, effulgent, refulgent, lambent, beamy, beamish; shiny, glossy, glassy, lustrous, sheenful, sheeny, burnished, polished; glittering, glinting, fulgid, sparkling, twinkling, flashing, fulgurant; glaring, flary, brilliant, splendid, splendorous, resplendent, fulgent, dazzling; illuminated, alight, light, lit, glowing, aglow, rutilant, luminous, luminescent; incandescent, phosphorescent, iridescent, opalescent, opaline.

nit-pick, *v.* *Informal.* pettifog, split hairs, chop logic; carp, cavil, quibble, find fault, criticize, pick *or* tear apart, take apart in detail.

nitty-gritty, *n.* crux, gist, *Inf.* nub, meat, substance, essence, quintessence, sum and substance, essential part, marrow, pith, heart of the matter; core, inner core, heart, center, nucleus, kernel; base, bottom, root.

nitwit, *n.* fool, ninny, nincompoop, goose; dimwit, half-wit, simpleton, Simple Simon, *Inf.* jay, *Sl.* birdbrain, *Sl.* pinhead. See **nincompoop**.

nix[1], *n.* *Slang.* **1.** nothing, none, naught, no quantity, no amount, no degree; none whatever, none whatsoever, nothing at all, nothing on earth, nothing under the sun; no such thing, nil, *Sl.* zip, aught; *Sl.* zilch, *Sl.* scratch, *Sl.* diddly, *Sl.* squat; *Latin. nihil, Fr. rien, Sp. nada;* not one, not a one, nary a one, no one, not a thing, *Inf.* not a blessed thing.

—adv. **2.** no, nay, never. See **no** (*def.* **2**).

—interj. **3.** watch it, attention, on guard, heads up, hark; *Sl.* cheese it, *Sl.* cool it, *Sl.* keep cool.

—v. **4.** veto, override, overrule, counterorder, countermand; prohibit, disallow, proscribe, disapprove, forbid, negative; turn down, reject, refuse, repudiate, negate; quash, nullify, void, annul, invalidate, disestablish; silence, squelch, suppress, abolish.

nix[2], *n.* nixie, water sprite, fairy, siren, nymph, naiad, kelpie, undine, rusalka; sea maid, sea maiden, sea nymph, Oceanid, Nereid, mermaid.

no, *adv.* **1.** not at all, to no extent, not, in no respect, not so, *Fr. pas du tout;* far from being, far from, anything but, by no means, God forbid; noway, noways, nowise, not in the least, *Inf.* no how, nothing of the kind *or* sort; not nearly, nowhere near, not by a long shot, by no stretch of the imagination; on no account, in no case; in no way, shape or form; under no circumstances, not in a million years.

2. nay, no indeed, no sir, no ma'am, *Inf.* no siree, *Inf.* no siree bob; *Sl.* uh-uh, *Inf.* nope, *Sl.* naw, *Sl.* nah, *Sl.* forget it, *Inf.* nothing doing, no way, no, no, a thousand times no; never, not on your life, absolutely not, certainly not, not really, are you kidding; on no account, to *or* on the contrary, *Fr. au contraire;* negative, *Citizens' Band Radio Sl.* negatory, *Pig Latin.* ixnay; *Ger. nein, Fr. non, It. no, Russ. nyet;* count me out, over my dead body, *Sl.* like hell I will, out of the question, far be it from me; I won't, I will not, I refuse.

—n. **3.** denial, refusal, rejection, turndown, disapproval; rebuff, repulse, declination; repudiation, disclaimer, *Rhet.* apophasis, recantation, retraction; forbiddance, proscription, prohibition, disapproval, *Inf.* no-go.

4. negative vote, nay, thumbs down, *U.S.* Bronx cheer; veto, objection, contravention, protest, refutation, answer; disagreement, dissent, demur, demurral.

—adj. **5.** not any, no more, none, not one, not a one, nary.

no-account, *Informal.* *adj.* **1.** worthless, of no worth, valueless, of no value, useless, of no use, inutile, no-good; trifling, trivial, insignificant, unimportant, inconsequential, petty, small, minor.

—n. **2.** no-count, good-for-nothing, *Fr. vaurien,* worthless person, ne'er-do-well; idler, fainéant, loafer, drone, do-nothing, *Inf.* bum; sluggard, slugabed, lazybones, malingerer, shirker, *Inf.* goldbrick, *Sl.* goof-off.

nob[1], *Slang.* *n.* head, pate, poll, skull. See **head** (*def.* **1**).

nob[2], *Slang.* *n.* man of means, man of substance, nabob, plutocrat; personage, *Inf.* V.I.P., *Inf.* bigwig, *Sl.* big shot, *Sl.* big wheel, *Sl.* fat cat, *Sl.* heavy, *Sl.* high-muck-a-muck; celebrity, somebody, name, *Inf.* big name.

nobility, *n.* **1.** aristocracy, patriciate, royalty, baronage, peerage; high rank, high birth, high breeding, blue blood; upper classes, *Inf.* upper crust, ruling classes, the Four Hundred, (*often cap.*) establishment, high society, elite, gentry; First Families of Virginia, F.F.V.; the House of Rothschild.

2. dignity, distinction, illustriousness, glory, exaltation; notability, eminence, preeminence, prestige, loftiness; influence, authority, leadership; importance, significance, consequence; primacy, supremacy.

3. honor, izzat, virtue; moral rectitude, scrupulousness, ethics; decency, goodness, righteousness, magnanimity, high-mindedness; honesty, integrity, uprightness, probity, veracity, justness.

4. grandeur, grandness, impressiveness, sumptuousness, gorgeousness; magnificence, splendor, majesty, resplendence.

noble, *adj.* **1.** titled, aristocratic, patrician; blueblooded, highborn, high-ranking, thoroughbred, to the manner born, born with a silver spoon in one's mouth; royal, regal, princely, kingly, queenly, gentlemanly.

2. illustrious, distinguished, eminent, preeminent, prestigious; renowned, famous, famed, noted; honored, revered, esteemed, venerated; acclaimed, celebrated.

3. noble-minded, honorable, virtuous, moral, scrupulous, principled, ethical, high-minded, magnanimous; admirable, reputable, decent, good, righteous, fine, worthy; just, fair, impartial, straight, square, square-shooting; honest, honest as the day is long, truthful, truth-loving, veracious; forthright, upright, incorruptible; faithful, loyal, staunch, steadfast, true, true-blue; dependable, reliable, trustworthy, responsible.

4. sublime, lofty, elevated; excellent, sterling; well-considered, measured, well-proportioned; exquisite, lovely, pleasing.

5. stately, lordly, magnificent, grand, grandiose; august, imposing, impressive, stunning, striking, awesome; majestic, glorious, splendid, superb, resplendent; gorgeous, sumptuous, rich, elegant.

6. superior, best, very best, top-notch, first-rate; prime, choice, prize, champion; of the highest type *or* quality, of the first water, as good as they come; wonderful, *Sl.* super, great; unsurpassed, nonpareil, unequaled, unmatched, peerless, unique.

—n. **7.** noblewoman, lady, milady, gentlewoman, dame, begum, margravine, shahzadi; duchess, archduchess, grand duchess, countess, viscountess, baroness, marchioness, peeress; queen, sovereign queen, princess, czarina, empress, maharanee, maharani, rani. See **nobleman** (*defs.* **1, 2**).

nobleman, *n.* **1.** noble, aristocrat, patrician, silk-stocking, *Inf.* blue blood, gentleman.

2. king, prince, czar, emperor, sheik, khan, rajah maharajah; grand duke, archduke, lord, milord, peer, duke, marquis, *Hist.* margrave, earl, count, viscount, baron; grandee, magnifico, don, hidalgo; baronet, lordling, *Scot. Hist.* thane, princeling, princekin, princelet; seigneur, feudal lord, *Japanese Hist.* daimyo, signior, signor; squire, *Scot.* laird, *Russian Hist.* boyar, (*in medieval Germany*) landgrave; knight, cavalier, *Fr. Hist.* chevalier, *Hist.* banneret, armiger.

noble-minded, *adj.* honorable, righteous, worthy, high-minded, magnanimous, generous, decent. See **noble** (*def.* **3**).

nobleness, *n.* aristocracy, distinction, honor. See **nobility** (*defs.* **1-4**).

nobly, *adv.* **1.** honorably, virtuously, scrupulously, conscientiously, with a clear conscience; magnanimously, generously, open-handedly, open-heartedly, freely; high-mindedly, admirably, righteously, decently; honestly, truthfully, aboveboard, in good faith; candidly, frankly, openly, straight from the shoulder, in all honesty; faithfully, loyally, staunchly, steadfastly, unerringly, unfailingly; dependably, responsibly, come what may, come hell or high water, no matter what, if it kills one; vigorously, spiritedly, with might and main; justly, fairly, impartially, even-handedly, correctly.

2. courageously, bravely, valiantly, gallantly; stoutheartedly, manfully, like a man, like a lion, like a tiger, like a soldier; fearlessly, dauntlessly, boldly, daringly, audaciously; firmly, resolutely, determinedly; unshrinkingly, unhesitatingly, without a qualm; assuredly, with aplomb, with a shrug of the shoulders.

3. splendidly, superbly, magnificently, sublimely; awesomely, impressively, majestically, regally, augustly; gloriously, grandly, in grand style, handsomely, beautifully, gorgeously; wonderfully, terrifically, excellently, perfectly, outstandingly, like a house afire, *Inf.* famously, marvelously; dashingly, with flair, with panache, with style, with flying colors, in championship form, classically; well, supremely, supremely well, to perfection, to a T *or* tee.

nobody, *n.* **1.** no one, not a one, not anyone, not a blessed one, never a one, *Archaic.* ne'er a one, *Dial.* nary one; not a person, not a single solitary person, not a soul, not a blessed soul, no man, no woman; nobody on earth, nobody under the sun.

2. *Informal.* nonentity, unimportant person, *Sl.* schlepp, nothing, a big nothing, cipher, zero, lay figure; insignificancy, jackstraw, milquetoast, *Sl.* nebbish; bonehead, blockhead, dummy, *Inf.* poor sap; no great shakes, no great catch, *Sl.* small beer, *Sl.* small potatoes; second fiddle, second banana, small fry.

nocent, *adj.* harmful, hurtful, nocuous, noxious, noisome; injurious, pernicious, baneful, deleterious, baleful, menacing. See **nocuous.**

noctambulism, *n.* noctambulation, sleepwalking, somnambulism, somnambulation, somnambulance.

noctambulist, *n.* sleepwalker, noctambule, somnambulist, somnambulator, somnambulant. See also **nightwalker.**

nocturnal, *adj.* night, nighttime, nightly, noctivagant, noctivagous.

nocturne, *n. Music.* musical piece, composition, night music, *Ger. Nachtmusik;* night piece; evening song, *Ger. Abendmusik.*

nocuous, *adj.* harmful, hurtful, noxious, nocent, noisome; deleterious, pernicious, injurious, baneful, mischievous; baleful, menacing, malignant, malign; unwholesome, unhealthy, unhealthful, insalubrious; poisonous, venomous, virulent, toxic, mephitic, pestilential, pestiferous, morbific, morbifical; detrimental, disastrous, disadvantageous, disserviceable, prejudicial, damaging, corrupting, destructive, ruinous; malicious, maleficent, vicious, wicked, bad, evil, malevolent, malefic; deadly, fell, fatal, mortal, lethal, killing; murderous, internecine.

nod, *v.* **1.** motion, make a sign, signal, signify, signalize, indicate; incline the head, acknowledge, recognize, greet, give salutation, salute, say hello, hail.

2. acquiesce, show agreement, agree, concur, consent, assent.

3. doze off, drop off, drowse, be sleepy, fall asleep, go to sleep, nap.

4. be indifferent, be lax, be listless, become careless, become inattentive, become neglectful; bungle, botch, blunder, slip up, trip up, falter; be mistaken, be wrong, make a mistake, err.

5. (*of trees, flowers, etc.*) droop, bend, bow, hang down; give way, sag, sink, slump; dip, lean, curve, incline.

—*n.* **6.** motion, gesture, sign, signal, cue, indication; beckoning, command.

7. acknowledgement, sign of recognition, greeting, salutation, salute, hello, hail; obeisance, sign of reverence; sign of acquiescence, show of agreement, sign of approval.

node, *n.* **1.** protuberance, protuberancy, *Bot.* boss, knob, knop, nub, nubble, *Bot.* caruncle, *Bot.* bud, nodule, *Anat.* nodulus; knot, knur, gnarl, burl; protrusion, projection, *Anat.* apophysis, tuberosity, prominence, bulb; growth, excrescence, excretion, *Biol.* auxesis, tubercle; swelling, gibbosity, tumescence, intumescence, enlargement; lump, bump, *Inf.* goose egg, hump, buckle, bulge; *Pathol.* tumor, *Pathol.* neoplasm, *Pathol.* cyst, *Pathol.* wen, *Pathol.* blain, corn, wart, boil, *Pathol.* carbuncle, inflammation; whelk, pimple, pustule, *Pathol.* papule.

2. joint, juncture, junction, connection, link, *Bot.* articulation, *Anat.* condyle; splice, seam, *Anat.* raphe.

nodular, *adj.* knobby, knobbed, *Bot.* bossed, *Bot.* caruncular, nubby, nodose, nodous; knotted, knotty, knaggy, gnarled, gnarly, knurled, knurly, knarled; protuberant, protruding, protrusive, bulging, embossed, raised, excurved, excurvative, projecting; bumpy, lumpy, tumorous, *Bot.* torose; tuberous, warty, verrucose; pimpled, papular; uneven, rough, unsmooth, unfinished, flawed, blemished.

nodule, *n.* **1.** small node, protuberance, *Bot.* boss, knot, gibbosity, *Pathol.* cyst. See **node** (*def.* **1**).

2. lump, mass, clot, gob, gobbet; clump, clod, cluster, bunch.

noise, *n.* **1.** sound, clamor, din, hubbub, babel, racket; ballyhoo, outcry, bawl, hue and cry, vociferation; cacophony, dissonance, discord; uproar, hullabaloo, clangor, fracas, bedlam, tumult, pandemonium, turmoil, commotion, bluster, rumpus, *Inf.* ruckus; clapping, applause.

2. talk, talking, chatter, chattering, jabber, jabbering, babble, babbling. *Fr. bavardage,* prate, prattle.

3. cry, sob, wail, moan, groan, keen, ululation, whimper, whine, mewl; shout, whoop, *Inf.* holler, squall, yell, roar, bellow; scream, shriek, shrill, screech, *Scot. and North Eng.* skirl, catcall, whistle, wolf whistle, hiss.

4. (*all of animals*) bark, yap, yelp, bowwow, woof; meow, miaow, mew, purr, caterwaul; yowl, howl, bay; whinny, neigh, bray, moo, low; baa, bleat, blat, oink, squeal, grunt; cluck, cackle, gabble, quack, squawk, gobble, honk; chirp, cheep, peep, coo, bill, cuckoo; hoot, caw, crow, cock-a-doodle-doo; croak, ribbit.

5. blare, blast, bang, boom, growl, rumble, thunder; clatter, brattle, rattle, jingle, jangle; ring, ting, cling, tinkle, tintinnabulation; ding, ding-dong, chime, peal, knell, toll, sounding, resounding, reverberation; clink, chink, clank, *Inf.* clunk, click, clack, clang, twang; whistle, whir, buzz, hum, drone; hiss, whoosh, whiz, zing, *Inf.* zip; creak, grate, grind, scraping, scratching, rasp, stridulation.

6. static, interference, feedback.
—*v.* 7. spread rumors, gossip, circulate, rumor, report, *Archaic.* bruit.

noiseless, *adj.* 1. silent, mum, still, still as death, quiet, *Chiefly Literary.* stilly, *Archaic.* hush, soundless; inaudible, soft, hushed, muted, muffled, stifled, smothered, deadened.
2. mute, *Pathol.* aphonic, voiceless, speechless, tongue-tied; uncommunicative, taciturn, reserved, reticent, close-mouthed, tight-lipped; (*all of letters*) silent, mute, unarticulated, unsounded.

noisome, *adj.* 1. disgusting, repugnant, aversive, obnoxious, fulsome; nauseating, nauseous, *Med.* nauseant, sickening, distasteful, unpalatable, unsavory, unappetizing, insipid; fetid, rancid, sour, putrid, putrescent, putrified, graveolent, rotten, stinking, rank, foul, mephitic; odorous, odoriferous, olid, *Obs.* olidous, stenchful, strong, whiffy; offensive, repulsive, revolting, repellent, objectionable, off-putting; nasty, unpleasant, displeasing, disagreeable; abominable, abhorrent, odious, loathsome, detestable, *Brit. Inf.* beastly.
2. invidious, deleterious, harmful, injurious, nocent, hurtful, crippling, impairing, scatheful, noxious, nocuous; poisonous, venomous, *Pathol.* septic, virulent, morbific, morbifical, morbiferous; unhealthy, unhealthful, unwholesome, insalubrious; pernicious, baneful, baleful, malefic, maleficent, *Obs.* malefical, malign, malignant, mischievous; detrimental, damaging, destructive, internecine, disastrous, ruinous, prejudicial.

noisy, *adj.* rackety, clamorous, clamoring, boisterous, obstreperous, blustery, blusterous, brassy; riotous, uproarious, tumultuous, turbulent, pandemoniac, pandemonic; cacophonous, dissonant, discordant, harsh-sounding, harsh, grating, jarring, creaking, strident, stridulous, stridulant, stridulatory; loud, blaring, blasting, resounding, stentorian, stentorious; deafening, earsplitting, sharp, shrill, piercing, clarion; loud-mouthed, vociferous, vocal; chattering, jabbering, babbling, *Inf.* gabbing, *Sl.* gassing, talking; shouting, whooping, hooting, *Inf.* hollering, yelling, roaring, bellowing; crying, bawling, squalling, screaming, shrieking, wailing, shrilling, screeching.

nomad, *n.* Bedouin, nomadic Arab, Kuchi; gypsy, Romany, Bohemian; wanderer, roamer, rover, rambler, strayer, straggler, gadabout; mover, ambulator, traveler, peregrinator, journeyer, pilgrim; migrator, bird of passage, *Sl.* rolling stone; migrant *or* migrant worker, itinerant, *Usu. Disparaging.* Okie, drifter, *Inf.* floater, transient, fly-by-night; vagabond, tramp, vagrant, hobo, beachcomber, derelict, street Arab; *Inf.* bum, *Sl.* vag, *Sl.* bo, *Sl.* stiff, *Sl.* bindlestiff, *Sl.* canvas back.

nomadic, *adj.* vagrant, vagabond, gypsy, bohemian; wandering, roaming, roving, rambling, straying, straggling; moving, ambulant, traveling, peregrinating, journeying; migrating, migrant, migratory, itinerant, peripatetic, drifting, floating, *Sl.* rolling; transient, transitory, temporary, fly-by-night.

nomenclature, *n.* terminology, taxonomy, classification, *Biol.* trinomialism, *Zool., Bot.* binomialism, *Zool., Bot.* binomial nomenclature, Linnean method.

nominal, *adj.* in name only, titular, formal, (*of governments*) puppet; so-called, supposed, pretended, purported, represented; would-be, quasi pseudo, self-called, self-styled, self-christened; (*of a price, consideration, etc.*) token.

nominate, *v.* 1. (*all for appointment or election to an office*) propose, name, *Inf.* put up; submit, present, offer.
2. appoint, assign, place, designate, select, name, *Inf.* tab; elect, vote in, place in office; induct, invest, install, instate, inaugurate, ordain.

nomination, *n.* proposal, submission, presentation; appointment, assignment, placement, designation, selection; induction, investment, installation, instatement, inauguration, ordainment, ordination.

nominee, *n.* candidate, office-seeker, runner, bidder, aspirant; assignee, appointee, selectee.

nonacceptance, *n.* 1. rejection, refusal, denial, turndown, declination, declinature; forbiddance, veto, disallowance, interdiction, proscription, negation; renunciation, disclamation, disclaimer, disclaiming, disavowal, retraction, recantation, abnegation; disowning, disinheriting, disinheritance.
2. refutation, disproof, confutation; disagreement, dissent, objection, demur, demurral.
3. disapproval, disapprobation, disparagement, discountenance; censure, animadversion, criticism; condemnation, denunciation, objurgation, berating; remonstration, expostulation, admonition; protest, demonstration, sit-in, boycott.

nonage, *n.* 1. legal minority, *Law.* infancy, juvenility, juniority.
2. immaturity, youth, adolescence, childhood, boyhood, girlhood.

nonappearance, *n.* absence, absentation, *Inf.* failure to show, *Inf.* no-show, *Law.* default; nonattendance, truancy, truantry, cut, hooky.

nonbeliever, *n.* atheist, freethinker, minimifidian, agnostic, skeptic, nullifidian, unbeliever; doubter, disbeliever, questioner, cynic, doubting Thomas, Pyrrhonist; empiricist, materialist, phenomenalist; heretic, schismatic, backslider; infidel, pagan, heathen.

nonce, *n.* **for the nonce** for the present, for today, for the moment, for the present moment, for the present juncture, for the present hour, for the present time, for the time being, for right now, for now; at this occasion, for the particular occasion, for the present occasion, for the occasion at hand, for the immediate occasion, for the present purpose.

nonchalance, *n.* unconcern, unsolicitude, pococurantism, indifference, apathy, neutrality, lukewarmness; coolness, calmness, self-possession, collectedness, composedness; imperturbability, inexcitability, dispassionateness, unflappability, even-temperedness, mild-temperedness; carefreeness, insouciance, carelessness, easiness, easygoingness, casualness; placidity, serenity, tranquillity, sedateness; self-control, poise, balance, steadiness.

nonchalant, *adj.* unconcerned, unsolicitous, pococurante, blasé, indifferent, apathetic, uninterested, disinterested, lukewarm, cool, calm, composed, collected, self-possessed, *Inf.* together, imperturbable, unexcitable, dispassionate, unflappable, even-tempered, mild-tempered; unruffled, untroubled, unperturbed, undisturbed, unexcited; carefree, insouciant, careless, without a care in the world, happy-go-lucky, free and easy, devil-may-care, *Fr. sans souci;* easygoing, easy, at ease, relaxed, laid-back, casual; placid, serene, tranquil, sedate; self-controlled, poised, balanced, steady.

noncommittal, *adj.* 1. cautious, careful, gingerly, safe, on the safe side, playing it safe; cool, playing it cool, *Inf.* playing it close to the vest; wary, watchful, vigilant, alert, on guard, precautious, precautionary, cautionary; reserved, guarded, circumspect, discreet, politic, prudent; wise, smart, canny, *Inf.* cagey.
2. laconic, taciturn, reticent, of few words; mum, mute, unspeaking, silent; expressing no opinion, neutral, mugwumpish, mugwumpian.

noncompletion, *n.* unfulfillment, nonfulfillment, abortion, miscarriage; nonexecution, nonperformance; immaturity, incompleteness, imperfection, imperfectness, faultiness; deficiency, *Inf.* fizzle, *Inf.* dud, failure; remissness, shortcoming, neglect, negligence, omission, default.

noncompliance, *n.* **1.** nonconformity, nonconformance, nonconventionality, unconventionality; originality, uniqueness; informality, Bohemianism, *Inf.* hippiness; unorthodoxy, sectarianism, secularism, heresy, misbelief, iconoclasm, atheism.
2. dissent, dissidence, nonassent, nonconcurrence, noncooperation; nonagreement, disagreement, difference, difference of opinion; refusal of assent, recusancy, disaffection, dissension, discordance; protest, protestation, civil disobedience; objection, remonstrance, challenge, rejection.
3. nonobservance, unobservance, nonperformance; disregard, disregarding, failure, omission, default, evasion, avoidance; elusion, shunning, *Inf.* runaround, dodge.
4. refusal, refusing, declining, declination, declension; rejection, denial, negation; abnegation, disclamation, disclaimer.
5. disobedience, unruliness, insubordination, contumacy, obstinacy; infraction, infringement, violation, breach; trespass, transgression; resistance, revolt, insurgence, insurrection, rebellion, mutiny, mutinousness; outbreak, uprising, sedition, treason.

noncompliant, *adj.* **1.** nonconforming, unconventional, original, unique; informal, *Inf.* hippie, Bohemian; unorthodox, sectarian, secular, heretic, heretical, misbelieving, iconoclastic, atheistic.
2. disobediant, insubordinate, nonsubmissive; unruly, wanton, ungovernable, obstinate; resistive, revolting, insurgent, rebellious; mutinous, seditious, treasonous.
3. dissenting, dissident, nonassenting, nonconcurring, noncooperating, nonagreeing, disagreeing, differing; disaffected, protesting, objecting, remonstrating, challenging, rejective.
4. nonobservant, unobservant, disregardful; defaulting, evasive, elusive, nonproducing.

noncomformist, *n.* **1.** misfit, maverick, dropout, loner, lone wolf, solitary, solitary man, fish out of water, square peg in a round hole; deviator, radical, *Chiefly Brit.* punk; deviate, deviant, anomaly, abnormality; freak, hippie, yippie, longhair, flower child, Jesus freak, Bohemian, beatnik; crackpot, crank, flake; *All Sl.* weirdo, weirdy, oddball, screwball, nut, loony, looner, dingbat, ding-a-ling; eccentric, character, card, case, pip, sport, original, one of a kind, exception, individual, rare bird, queer duck, queer potato; curiosity, rarity, peculiarity; party pooper, wallflower, dud, *Inf.* stick-in-the-mud, *Sl.* pill, *Sl.* drag, *Sl.* bummer.
2. protestant, protester, sectary, recusant; dissenter, dissentient, nonjuror, mugwump, malcontent, noncontent; reversion, reversionist, recidivist, heretic, heterodox; schismatist, schismatic, seceder, secessionist, seditionist, separatist; apostate, recreant, backslider, renegade, lost soul, lost sheep, fallen angel; atheist, agnostic, unbeliever, nonbeliever, antichrist, antichristian, infidel.

nonconformity, *n.* **1.** nonconformance, disconformity, discord, discordance, disagreement, nonagreement; dissent, dissension, nonassent, dissidence, dissentience, recusance, recusancy, protest, opposition.
2. noncompliance, incompliance, nonobservance, nonfulfillment, Bohemianism; declination, declension, renunciation, renouncement, abnegation, disclamation, nonconsent, negation, rejection, denial, nonacceptance, disapproval, disapprobation, objection, exception, veto; disobediance, insubordination, contumacy, heresy, heterodoxy; intractability, recalcitrance, waywardness, refractiousness, contumaciousness, unruliness, mutinousness, lawlessness, transgressiveness; deviation, aberration, violation, infraction; unconventionality, nonconventionality, originality, uncommonness, uncommonality, unorthodoxy, uniqueness; oddness, queerness, curiousness, strangeness, bizarreness.

nondescript, *adj.* **1.** indefinite, amorphous, unclassifiable; indes ıbable, hard to describe, protectively colored, *Inf.* blending into the woodwork, low-profile.
2. dull, unremarkable, colorless, achromatic, gray, *U.S. Sl.* blah; bland, uninteresting, insipid, *Inf.* dull as dishwater; prosaic, common, commonplace, mediocre, average, average-looking, *Inf.* garden-variety, unexceptional.

nondrinker, *n.* teetotaler, nephalist, abstainer, water-drinker, hydropot; temperance advocate, W.C.T.U. member, prohibitionist, *Inf.* dry, blue-ribboner, blue-ribbonist, blue-ribbonite; puritan, ascetic; Rechabite, Encratite.

none, *pron.* **1.** no one, not one, not a one, nary a one, never a one, not a soul, nobody on earth.
2. not any, not a bit, not a thing, *Inf.* not a blessed thing; not a hint, not a trace, not a whit, not a speck, not an iota, not a jot, not an ounce, *Inf.* not a lick; not a whiff, not a smell, neither hide nor hair.
3. no part, nothing, none, none whatever, nothing at all. See **nothing** (*def.* **1**).
—adv. **4.** not at all, in no way, to no extent, no. See **nothing** (*def.* **9**).

nonentity, *n.* **1.** nobody, no one, nothing, unimportant person, *Inf.* nobody much, obscurity; mediocrity, common man, lightweight, insignificancy, man on the street, man from Peoria; little man, little guy, jackstraw, man of straw, dummy; a big nothing, cipher, zero, naught, an 0 without a figure, *Sl.* nebbish, *Sl.* schlepp; squirt, whippersnapper, punk, pipsqueak, runt, scrub; small fry, no great shakes, no great catch, *Sl.* small potatoes, second fiddle, second banana; John Doe, Jane Doe, Richard Roe, Mary Roe, Mr. and Mrs. Nobody; John Q. Public, (*in England*) John Bull, John K. Spelvin, (*in Russia*) Ivan Ivanovich Ivanov; Joe Doakes, Joe Blow, Joe Zilch; Tom, Dick, and Harry; Brown, Jones, and Robinson.
2. illusion, fantasy, hallucination, delusion, maya; trick, chimera, dream, daydream, bubble, *Inf.* trip; shadow, air, thin air, smoke, mist, vapor; phantom, spirit, specter, ghost, shade, will-o'-the-wisp; vision, apparition, eidolon, optical illusion, mirage, Fata Morgana; castle in the air, wildest dream, phantasmagoria.
3. nonexistence, nothingness, nihility, nihilism, nullity, existencelessness, *Fr. néant,* nullibicity; unreality, unactuality, nonreality, negativeness, nonlife, nonoccurrence; inexistence, nonsubsistence, insubstantiality, incorporeality, incorporeity; inessentiality, nonbeing, unbeing, not-being; abstraction, immateriality, imponderability, nothing, nirvana; impalpability, intangibility, imperceptibility; oblivion, blank, void, vacuity, vacuum, empty space; negation, emptiness, abeyance; absence, nonpresence, nowhereness, nonoccupancy, vacancy.

nonessential, *adj.* **1.** unnecessary, unneeded, needless, superfluous, redundant, expendable, dispensable, unrequired, uncalled-for, gratuitous; unimportant, of little *or* small importance, of no *or* no great importance, inconsequential, of little *or* no consequence, insignificant, of no significance, inconsiderable, inappreciable, of no concern, of no matter, of no account; irrelevant, immaterial, inapplicable, inapt, unconnected, inapposite, inconsequent, beside the point *or* mark, beside the question, off the subject, nothing to do with it; little, small, minute, bush-league, *Inf.* small-time, *Inf.* one-horse, *Sl.* dinky, *Sl.* two-bit, *Sl.* small potatoes.

2. extrinsic, extrinsical, extraneous, external, incidental, accidental, adventitious, inessential, unessential; extra, additional, supplementary, supplemental, adscititious; subsidiary, subordinate, secondary, accessory, collateral; circumstantial, contingent, conditional, provisional, dependent.

—n. **3.** nonentity, a nobody, *Sl.* nebbish, a nothing, cipher; little fellow, *Inf.* little guy, man on the street, John *or* Jane Doe, small fry, *Sl.* small fish, *Sl.* small potato; insignificancy, nullity, zero, thing of naught.

nonesuch, *n.* paragon, nonpareil, phoenix, one in a thousand, one of a kind, rarity, exception; best, choice, flower, pink, pearl, gem, jewel, prize, *Inf.* peach, pick of the litter, cream of the crop, *Fr. crème de la crème*, elite, first water, first class, *Commerce.* first; acme, zenith, pinnacle, height, peak, tops, *Latin. ne plus ultra;* exemplar, ideal, beau ideal, standard of perfection *or* excellence, model, pattern, prototype, archetype, original; wonder, marvel, prodigy, miracle, phenomenon, sensation, spectacle, sight, once-in-a-lifetime experience.

nonexistence, *n.* nothingness, nihility, nihilism, nullity, existencelessness, nullibicity, *Fr. néant;* inexistence, nonsubsistence, insubstantiality, incorporeality, incorporeity; unreality, unactuality, nonreality, negativeness, nonlife, nonoccurrence; inessentiality, nonentity, nonbeing, unbeing, not-being; abstraction, immateriality, imponderability, nothing, nirvana; impalpability, intangibility, imperceptibility; oblivion, blank, void, vacuity, vacuum, empty space, emptiness, negation, abeyance; absence, nonpresence, nowhereness, nonoccupancy, vacancy.

nonexistent, *adj.* null, absent, nil, void, blank; inexistent, minus, missing, lacking, left out, omitted; unreal, unsubstantial, unactual, immaterial; hypothetical, suppositional, unrealized, potential; fictional, fictive, imagined, fancied, fanciful, quixotic; mythical, legendary, fabulous; phantasmagorical, illusory, delusive; imaginary, visionary, illusionary, chimerical, notional; erroneous, unfounded, baseless, groundless, unrealistic.

nonfulfillment, *n.* **1.** nonachievement, nonaccomplishment, noncompletion, nonexecution, nonperformance; miscarriage, abortion; miss, botch, muff, slip, blunder; fiasco, fizzle, washout, *Inf.* flop, misfire, *Inf.* dud, vain attempt, flash in the pan; disappointment, failure, frustration, nonsuccess.

2. nonobservance, noncompliance, disobedience; evasion, avoidance; omission, default, oversight; neglect, negligence, laxity, laxness; nonchalance, casualness.

nonhuman, *adj.* **1.** inhumane, inhumanistic, bloodless, cold-blooded, cold-hearted, hard-hearted, stonyhearted, marble-hearted, heartless, unfeeling, unsympathetic, uncompassionate; android, automatous, mechanical, machinelike, robotistic, robotlike; unnatural, abnormal, foreign, alien, strange, not our kind; not of this world, otherworldly, unearthly, extraterrestrial, from outer space, moon, Martian.

2. inhuman, animalistic, animalian, zooid, zooidal; wolfish, lupine, feral, ferine, bestial, beastly; brutal, brutish, mean, harsh, cruel, sadistic; savage, barbarous, barbaric, bloodthirsty, cannibalistic, wild, fierce, ferocious, vicious, fell, truculent, Tartarean, Hunnish, Vandalic.

noninterference, *n.* laissez faire, nonparticipation, nonparticipance, do-nothingness; neutrality, nonintervention, nonresistance; inaction, inactiveness, want of action, inactivity, passiveness, passivity, immobility; apathy, indifference, disinterest, disinterestedness, uninterestedness, aloofness, distantness, quiescence.

nonintervention, *n.* laissez faire, nonparticipation, nonparticipance, noninterference; neutrality, nonresistance. See **noninterference.**

nonobjective, *adj.* (*of art*) nonrepresentational, abstract, abstracted; theoretical, pure, unapplied; conceptual, ideational, notional, metaphysical; immaterial, imaginary, visionary, ideal, transcendental, spiritual; impractical, intellectual; enigmatical, mysterious, dark, hidden, remote; abstruse, obscure, recondite, profound, difficult.

nonobservance, *n.* **1.** inattention, inattentiveness, heedlessness; thoughtlessness, inconsiderateness, lack of consideration; inadvertence, distraction, detachment, absent-mindedness; bemusement, absorption, self-absorption, engrossment, preoccupation, woolgathering, daydreaming, *Inf.* castle-building.

2. disobedience, unruliness, insubordination, contumacy, obstinacy; infraction, infringement, violation, breach; trespass, transgression; resistance, revolt, insurgence, insurrection, rebellion, mutiny, mutinousness; outbreak, uprising, sedition, treason.

3. nonconformity, nonconformance, nonconventionality, unconventionality, Bohemianism, *Inf.* hippiness, originality, uniqueness; unorthodoxy, sectarianism, secularism, heresy, misbelief, iconoclasm, atheism.

4. nonfulfillment, nonperformance, noncompliance, disregard, failure, omission, oversight; negligence, neglect, neglectfulness; carelessness, laxity, laxness, laziness; remissness, dereliction, dereliction of duty.

5. nonpayment, default, delinquency, welshing; insolvency, bankruptcy, failure to pay up, *Sl.* failure to cough *or* ante up.

6. evasion, *Inf.* the run-around, avoidance; elusion, shunning, dodge, side-step, shirking, retreat; nonattendance, truancy, hooky, French leave, cut, absence without leave, *Mil.* A.W.O.L.

7. faithlessness, infidelity, inconstancy; falsity, disloyalty, Punic faith, violation of vows, breach of promise.

nonpareil, *adj.* **1.** peerless, unparallelled, incomparable, without equal, unequalled, unmatched, unmatchable, unrivaled, unrivalable, unbeatable; best, choicest, supreme, highest, top, first-class, ace, excellent, prize-winning, *Inf.* champion.

—n. **2.** nonesuch, paragon, phoenix, one in a thousand, one of a kind; acme, zenith, pinnacle, height, peak, tops, *Latin. ne plus ultra;* best, choice, flower, pink, pearl, gem, jewel, prize, *Inf.* peach; pick, pick of the litter, cream of the crop, *Fr. crème de la crème,* elite, first water, first class, *Commerce.* first.

3. sprinkles, sprinklies, jimmies, shots, sugar pellets, decorative candies.

4. chocolate, candy, *Trademark.* Snow Cap.

nonpartisan, *adj.* **1.** impartial, objective, disinterested, dispassionate; just, even-handed, equitable, fair, fair and square, straight, straight-shooting, square-shooting, square-dealing; unbiased, unprejudiced, unprepossessed, unbigoted, unwarped, unjaundiced; uninfluenced; unswayed, unbought.

2. independent, free-lance; nonaligned, unaffiliated, unassociated, unconnected; neutral, even, half-and-half, *Inf.* fifty-fifty; noncommitted, on the fence, mugwumpian, mugwumpish.

—n. **3.** independent, free-lance, freethinker; neutral, unaffiliated voter; mugwump, fence-sitter, undecided *or* noncommitted voter.

nonpayment, *n.* default, nonremittal, delinquency, *Commerce.* dishonor, failure to pay, *Sl.* welshing,

Brit. Sl. the moonlight flit; evasion, *Sl.* the runaround; tax-evasion, tax-dodging.

nonplus, *v.* **1.** perplex, puzzle, confound, confuse, *Inf.* flummox, baffle, bewilder, mystify, stump; disconcert, abash, embarrass, discountenance, disturb, bother, dismay; upset, fluster, rattle, *Inf.* faze, muddle, addle, befuddle.
2. take aback, stun, stupefy, floor, dumfound, *Inf.* flabbergast, astound, astonish, amaze; check, thwart, frustrate, stop, halt, bring to a standstill, *Inf.* catch up short, gravel.
—*n.* **3.** perplexity, confusion, bewilderment, puzzlement, bafflement, abashment, embarrassment, disconcertion.
4. standstill, impasse, stalemate, deadlock, baffle; halt, stop, check; blind alley, dead end, cul-de-sac.
5. quandary, predicament, plight, pass, straits; dilemma, bind, double bind, catch-22; slough, quagmire, bog, corner, hole, tangle; trouble, difficulty, bother, vexation, *Inf.* mess, *Inf.* kettle of fish, *Inf.* how-do-you-do *or* how-de-do, *Sl.* pickle.

nonplused, *adj.* **1.** perplexed, puzzled, confounded, confused, baffled, bewildered, mystified, stumped, up a stump, *Inf.* buffaloed; at a loss, at sea, in a bind, on the horns of a dilemma.
2. disconcerted, abashed, embarrassed, out of countenance, disturbed, bothered, dismayed, discomfited, chagrined, distressed, shamefaced, self-conscious.
3. upset, discomposed, unhinged, ruffled, ill-at-ease, uncomfortable, disquieted, *Inf.* shaken; flustered, rattled, muddled, addled, befuddled, disoriented.
4. taken aback, stunned, floored, staggered, dazed, dumfounded, struck dumb, *Inf.* flabbergasted, astounded, astonished, amazed; shocked, speechless, frozen, paralyzed, incapacited, *Inf.* thrown off balance; checked, frustrated, stopped, stopped short *or* halted in one's tracks, caught up short, disarmed.

nonproductive, *adj.* **1.** sterile, unfruitful, unfertile, unfecund, unprolific, barren, unproductive, *Bot.* acarpous.
2. ineffective, ineffèctual, of no effect; futile, vain, pointless, otiose, unavailing, bootless, of no avail; useless, of no use, worthless, nugatory, nugacious; time-wasting, time-killing, time-consuming.

nonprofit, *adj.* **1.** public-service, funded, sponsored, supported, subsidized, financed, not for profit.
2. charitable, philanthropic, altruistic, eleemosynary; benevolent, beneficent, almsgiving.

nonresistance, *n.* passivity, passiveness, nonopposition, quietism; pacifism, nonviolence, *Hinduism.* ahimsa; acquiescence, yielding, submission, compliance; resignation, acceptance, complaisance; longanimity, forbearance, tolerance, sufferance, long-suffering, long-sufferingness.

nonresistant, *adj.* passive, supine, unresisting, nonresisting, nonresistive, nonviolent; acquiescent, yielding, submissive, compliant, complying, complaisant, obedient; resigned, accepting, uncomplaining, stoic, stoical; longanamous, long-suffering, forbearing, tolerant, patient, patient as Job, enduring.

nonsense, *n.* **1.** absurdity, absurdness, nonsensicalness, nonsensicality; ridiculousness, ridiculosity, ludicrousness; asininity, stupidity, fatuity, fatuousness; meaninglessness, self-contradiction, contradiction, invalidity; incongruity, incongruousness, illogic, illogicality, illogicalness; irrationality, irrationalness, senselessness, insensateness, craziness, *Sl.* screwiness; impracticality, impracticalness, foolhardiness, *Sl.* foolheadedness, unreasonableness.
2. unintelligibility, unintelligibleness, incomprehensibility, incomprehensibleness; indistinctness, confusion, cobwebs, Greek, *Chiefly Southern U.S.* Choctaw; gibberish, babble, babbling, babblement, *Fr. bavardage*; twaddle, twaddling, *Both Brit.* twattle, twattling; blather, blathering, drivel, driveling, drool, drooling; jargon, hocus-pocus, mumbo-jumbo, abracadabra, open-sesame, fiddle-de-dee; moonshine, gobbledegook, humbug, foam, froth, bunkum *or* buncombe, *Sl.* bunk, *U.S. Sl.* blah; flummery, *Inf.* hokum, *Sl.* applesauce, *Sl.* eyewash; rubbish, *Sl.* tripe, refuse, *Dial.* culch, chaff, trash, *Inf.* truck, trumpery; tommyrot, *Inf.* rot, *Sl.* garbage, *Sl.* crap, *Sl.* crock, *Sl.* bull; balderdash, *Sl.* horsefeathers, hogwash, stuff, stuff and nonsense, *Inf.* bosh, *Brit. Inf.* gammon, *Brit. Sl.* tosh; fudge, foolishness, folly, rigmarole *or* rigamarole, amphigory; footle, *Inf.* malarkey, *Sl.* bushwa, *Sl.* baloney, *Sl.* bilge, *or* bilge water, *Sl.* meshugaas, *Scot. and North Eng.* haver; poppycock, *Inf.* fiddle-faddle, *Inf.* piffle, *Inf.* hooey, *Inf.* kibosh, *Inf.* flapdoodle.
3. claptrap, rodomontade, fustian, bombast, rant, *Sl.* hot air, idle talk, *Inf.* gab, *Sl.* gas; palaver, palavering, palaverment; jabber, jabbering, Jabberwocky, prate, prating; patter, pattering, gabble, gabbling; clack, clacking, clatter, clattering, rattling, *Sl.* running off *or* on at the mouth; chatter, chattering, prattle, prattling, chippering, cackle, cackling; chit-chat, chitter-chatter, small talk, *Anglo-Indian.* bukh.
4. antic, antics, caper, *Inf.* shenanigans, *Sl.* monkeyshines, *Sl.* monkeybusiness; prankishness, mischief, *Sl.* hanky-panky, *Scot. and North Eng.* daffing; prank, trick, practical joke; fooling, foolery, tomfoolery, horseplay; clowning, clownery, clownishness; buffoonery, buffoonism, buffoonishness, harlequinade; joking, jesting, jocosity, jocoseness, jocularity, waggishness, waggery, drollery; levity, frivolity, facetiousness; silliness, inanity, childishness, puerility, juvenility, *Inf.* sappiness.
5. triviality, nugacity, frivolity, futility; stuff, trifle, trinket, gimcrackery, bauble, gewgaw, frippery.

nonsensical, *adj.* **1.** senseless, meaningless, amphigoric, skimble-scamble, incomprehensible, unintelligible; paradoxical, contradictory, self-contradictory, incongruous.
2. absurd, ludicrous, ridiculous, preposterous, harebrained; laughable, silly, frivolous, facetious; foolish, *Inf.* fool, *Inf.* foolheaded, *Inf.* tomfool, fatuous; stupid, *Sl.* dumb, asinine, idiotic, moronic, imbecilic, mad, daft, insane, crazy; *All Inf.* dizzy, cockamamie, poppycockish; *All Sl.* screwball, screwy, nutty, wacky, daffy, goofy, kooky, loony, flaky, sappy, cockeyed.

nonsentient, *adj.* **1.** unfeeling, insensible, insensitive, insensate, unresponsive; numb, benumbed, dead, deadened; unconscious, uncognizant, unaware, imperceptive, nonperceptive; drugged, *Sl.* doped, *Sl.* doped up, *Sl.* doped to the eyeballs, *Sl.* out of it, *Sl.* spaced, *Sl.* spaced out.
2. apathetic, indifferent, unconcerned, uncaring; cool, cold, frigid, frosty, icy; callous, hard, hardened, inured, indurate, thickskinned, pachydermatous.

nonspiritual, *adj.* **1.** corporeal, corporal, bodily, fleshly, incarnate, somatic, physical, material; palpable, tangible, sensible, touchable, ponderable, appreciable.
2. wordly, unspiritual, mundane, temporal, earthy, earthly, external; secular, lay, worldly-minded, earthly-minded, carnal, materialistic.
3. irreligious, unbelieving, faithless; irreverent, impious, blasphemous, sacrilegious.

nonstop, *adj.* **1.** ceaseless, unceasing, incessant, constant, uninterrupted, continual, continuous, unbroken, ongoing; unremitting, unintermitting, relentless, persistent; recurrent, repeated, frequent, habitual, regular; around-the-clock, day-in and day-out, dawn-to-dusk, at every turn.

2. unending, endless, never-ending, interminable, Sisyphean; eternal, perpetual, everlasting, lasting, enduring, perennial, permanent.
3. untiring, indefatigable, unwearied, never-failing, unwavering, unfaltering, undiminished; invariable, fixed, stable, steady.
nonsubjective, *adj.* **1.** objective, external, tangible, palpable, sensible, perceptible; physical, corporal, corporeal, bodily, substantial, material; actual, real, true, verifiable, scientific, confirmed.
2. disinterested, unbiased, impartial, impersonal, neutral; unprejudiced, dispassionate, open-minded, fair, equitable, just.
noodle, *n.* **1.** *Slang.* head, skull, cranium, *Zool.* cephalon, brainpan, poll, pate, *Inf.* sconce, *Archaic.* mazard, *Archaic.* costard; think tank, thinker; *All Inf.* upstairs, upper story, belfry, noggin, dome; *All Sl.* bean, nut, nob, noddle, crumpet, gourd, conk.
2. fool, ninny, nincompoop, silly, silly billy, *Sl.* yoyo, tomfool; simpleton, Simple Simon, saphead, cuckoo, idiot, *Inf.* jay, *Sl.* jerk, imbecile, noodlehead, mooncalf, *Inf.* moron; dimwit, nitwit, half-wit, *Sl.* zombie, goose; scatterbrain, *Sl.* birdbrain, *Sl.* flake, rattlehead, rattlebrain, rattlepate, harebrain, *Sl.* dingbat, *Sl.* ding-a-ling; featherbrain, addle-brain, addlehead, addle-pate, pinhead; dolt, clod, oaf, dunce, *Inf.* chump, dullard, *Inf.* coot, *Inf.* numskull; dope, dummy. See **fool** (*def.* **1**).
nook, *n.* niche, recess, alcove, cove, cranny, hole, pigeonhole, cubby, cubbyhole, corner, private spot *or* place; burrow, den, lair, nest; cave, cavern, grotto, dugout, depression, cavity, retreat, shelter.
noon, *n.* **1.** midday, twelve m., noonday, noontide, noontime, *Chiefly Dial.* nooning.
2. highpoint, top, apex, acme, pinnacle, summit, zenith, culmination, meridian; prime, flower, bloom.
no one, *pron.* no person, not anyone, *Dial.* nary a one, not a one, not one; nobody, not a soul, not a blessed soul, nobody under the sun, nobody on earth.
noose, *n.* **1.** hangman's halter, hangman's knot; lasso, lariat, loop, hitch.
2. tie, bond, rope, cord, line, fastening, ligature.
3. snare, springe, trap, gin.
norm, *n.* **1.** standard, criterion, canon; measure, gauge, *Survey.* bench mark, yardstick, scale; test, check.
2. general level, average, usual, rule, run, normal rate; mean, arithmetical mean, medium, normal.
normal, *adj.* **1.** usual, ordinary, conventional; widespread, general, universal, world-wide, common; prevailing, current, popular; customary, wonted, accustomed, habitual, regular, routine, repeated, recurrent; established, acknowledged, accepted; ritual, traditional, orthodox, consuetudinary, *Inf.* according to Hoyle, *Inf.* S.O.P.; received, approved, understood; familiar, known, everyday, daily, standard, *Inf.* G.I.
2. average, middle, middling, midmost, medium, mean, center; standardized, invariable, unvarying, unchanging, unchanged, steady, steadfast, even; illustrative, emblematic, symbolic, representative, typical, model.
3. *Psychology.* adjusted, well-adjusted, *Inf.* in good shape, healthy; natural, reasonable, sane, *Inf.* all there.
north, *n.* **1.** the north wind, norther, northerly; northerliness.
—*adj.* **2.** northerly, northern, northward *or* northwards, toward the north, northernmost, boreal, arctic, septentrional.
—*adv.* **3.** northward *or* northwards, northerly, northwardly, toward the north.
northerly, *adj.* north, northern, northward *or* northwards, toward the north, northernmost; boreal, arctic, septentrional.
North Star, *n.* *Astronomy.* Polaris, polestar, lodestar, brightest star in Ursa Minor *or* the Little Dipper, *Astron. Obs.* Cynosure; luminary, shining light, guiding light, guide cynosure, point of reference.
nose, *n.* **1.** neb, nib, bill, pecker, *All Sl.* beak, snoot, schnozz, schnozzle, schnozzola; snout, muzzle, *Sl.* nozzle, *Facetious.* proboscis, trunk, *Entomol.* antlia; nostrils, nasal passage *or* cavity, breather, air hole, spiracle, blow hole; sniffer, olfactory organ, olfactories, *Sl.* smeller; sense of smell, olfactory sense.
2. percipience, perception, keen sense, insight, eye; instinct, sixth sense, feel, gift *or* aptitude for discovering *or* detecting.
3. prow, *Naut., Aeron.* bow, stem, ram, rostrum; forward end, fore, front, point, tip, extremity; projection, protrusion, promontory, *Geol.* bill.
4. bouquet, aroma, essence, fragrance, perfume; smell, scent, odor, odoriferousness, redolence, savor.
5. by a nose *Slang.* by a narrow *or* slim margin, narrowly, by a hair's breadth, by the skin of one's teeth, by a whisker; barely, just, only.
6. on the nose *Slang.* **a.** precisely, exactly, perfectly, just right, just so, to a hair, to the letter, to a T *or* tee. **b.** on the dot, on the button, on the money, on target, *Inf.* on the mark; promptly, on time.
—*v.* **7.** smell, sniff, get *or* catch a whiff of, perceive, detect; smell out *or* around, sniff out *or* around, follow a scent, search for, seek out.
8. (*all with the nose*) push, shove, move forward *or* along; nuzzle, rub, snuggle, touch.
9. *Often* **nose out** beat *or* defeat by a narrow margin, just beat, win by a nose *or* a hair's breadth *or* the skin of one's teeth; edge out, squeak by.
10. *Often* **nose into** *or* **about** pry, snoop, prowl, peek, peep, peer, look, stare, gape, gaze; inquire, ask, break in, interrupt, horn in, butt in, *Inf.* kibitz; meddle, interfere, intervene, intrude.
nose dive, *n.* plunge, dive, swoop; lurch, pitch, spill, tumble, stumble, trip; sudden drop *or* decline; drop-off, downward turn, turn for the worse, tailspin, downfall.
nose-dive, *v.* plunge, dive, swoop, jackknife, jump headlong *or* headfirst; pitch, lurch, fall headfirst, take a spill *or* a fall, tumble, stumble; drop, decline, descend, fall, go down; fall off, worsen, get worse, look bad, go into a tailspin.
nosegay, *n.* bouquet, bunch of flowers, flowers, blossoms, blooms, spray, flower arrangement, *Brit. Dial.* boughpot; corsage, boutonniere, *Chiefly Brit.* buttonhole, flower; garland, wreath, festoon, chaplet.
nosh, *v.* **1.** snack, eat between meals, pop [s.t.] into one's mouth, sneak [s.t.] to eat, eat on the sly; nibble, gnaw, take small bites, pick, pick at *or* over one's food, peck at one's food, eat like a bird.
—*n.* **2.** snack, between-meal snack, bite to eat, *Sl.* munchy; tidbit, morsel, bite, taste, mouthful.
nostalgia, *n.* (*all in reference to the past*) longing, yearning, pining, languishing, aching; moping, brooding, musing, remembering, reminiscing; remembrance, memory, recollection, reminiscence; regret, regretfulness, remorse, sorrow, sadness; lamentation, lamenting, grieving, mourning, bemoaning, bewailing; homesickness, loneliness, lonesomeness.
nostalgic, *adj.* (*all in reference to the past*) longing, yearning, pining, languishing; regretful, remorseful, sorrowful, sad; homesick, lonely, lonesome; maudlin, sentimental, emotional, romantic, soupy;

teary, weepy, choked up.

nostril, *n. Anat.* naris, spiracle, blowhole.

nostrum, *n.* **1.** patent medicine, proprietary; medication, drug, potion, *Pharm.* tincture, *Pharm., Vet. Med.* electuary; pill, *Pharm., Vet. Med.* bolus, capsule; liniment, lotion, embrocation, balm, balsam, ointment.

2. quack medicine, *Inf.* pink pill, placebo; panacea, cure-all, cure, remedy, treatment, solution; elixir, alembic, arcanum, magic solution, magic answer; magic words, magic formula, prescription, recipe for success, abracadabra, open sesame; pet scheme, contrivance, invention.

nosy, *adj. Informal.* **1.** prying, snoopy, snooping, *Dial.* nibby; spying, peeping, peeking, staring, gaping, gazing; eavesdropping, overhearing, all ears; meddlesome, meddling, tending to other people's business, busy, officious; interfering, intervening, interloping, breaking, in, butting in, horning in, intrusive.

2. inquisitive, inquiring, questioning, querying, interrogating, grilling, quizzing, quizzical; sniffing *or* smelling around *or* out, probing, nosing around *or* out, searching, investigative; overcurious, supercurious, curious, burning with curiosity, dying *or* itching to know, agog, eager to know, interested.

notability, *n.* **1.** prominence, primacy, eminence, preeminence, fame, repute, reputation; illustriousness, celebrity, stardom, place in the spotlight, notoriety; conspicuousness, salience, attention-getting ability; distinction, uncommonness, rareness; singularity, peculiarity, strangeness, oddness, uniqueness; halo, glory, honor, luster; impressiveness, stature, stateliness, majesty, grandeur, dignity.

2. noteworthiness, newsworthiness, news value, good copy, banner news, headline news; interest, value, superiority, excellence; importance, significance, moment, note, consequence; momentousness, meaningfulness, memorability.

notable, *adj.* **1.** noteworthy, remarkable, signal, outstanding, noticeable, marked; memorable, unforgettable, *Sl.* hell of a, special, particular, especial; important, on the map, significant, momentous, meaningful, worthy of notice.

2. extraordinary, unusual, different, uncommon, rare, singular, exceptional, out-of-the-ordinary, *Inf.* one for the books; unique, distinct, peculiar, odd, strange, curious.

3. striking, impressive, imposing, majestic, grand, august, stately, dignified; large, big, substantial, considerable; awesome, awe-inspiring, lofty, wondrous, marvelous, prodigious; stupendous, amazing, astounding, astonishing, surprising, shocking; incredible, *Sl.* unreal, unbelievable, inconceivable, unimaginable, unthinkable, unheard of; overwhelming, overpowering, indescribable, inexpressible, ineffable, unspeakable, unutterable; fantastic, miraculous, fabulous, *Inf.* great, *Inf.* super, superb, splendid, magnificent, wonderful.

4. distinguished, eminent, famous, famed, well-known, renowned; illustrious, great, glorious, brilliant, radiant, lustrous; celebrated, honored, exalted, acclaimed, much-touted; peerless, unequalled, matchless, unmatched, unparalleled, nonpareil, *Fr. sans pareil;* unsurpassed, unexcelled, second to none, *Latin. nulli secundus.*

5. conspicuous, obvious, evident, manifest, patent, apparent, ostensible; blatant, bold, overt, obtrusive, flagrant, glaring, egregious; showy, flaunting, ostentatious.

6. visible, seeable, showing, discernible, perceptible, perceivable; unconcealed, unhidden, unveiled, uncurtained, unshrouded, uncloaked, unscreened; exposed, open, revealed, disclosed, uncovered, naked, bare; prominent, in bold relief, salient, pronounced, definite, marked; plain, clear, unmistakable, lucid, plain as day, plain as the nose on one's face, distinct, clear-cut, explicit.

—n. **7.** personage, dignitary, *Inf.* V.I.P., *Inf.* bigwig, *Sl.* big shot, *Sl.* biggie, *Sl.* big gun, *Sl.* big wheel; *Sl.* big cheese, *Fr. Sl. grand fromage, Sl.* fat cat, *Sl.* heavy, *Sl.* high-much-a-muck; celebrity, *Sl.* celeb, luminary, somebody, name, *Inf.* big name; star, superstar, toast of the town.

notably, *adv.* **1.** conspicuously, noticeably, markedly, signally, remarkably, saliently; distinctly, clearly, obviously, manifestly; glaringly, flagrantly, egregiously, notoriously, flauntingly, brazenly, boldly; prominently, eminently, preeminently, famously, illustriously, supremely, grandly; brilliantly, oustandingly, greatly, significantly, importantly.

2. surprisingly, unexpectedly, like a bolt out of the blue, stunningly, strikingly, *Inf.* with a real wallop, like a thunderbolt; strangely, curiously, oddly, extraordinarily, unusually; peculiarly, particularly, differently, in a different way, uniquely; interestingly, oddly enough, strangely enough.

notary, *n.* notary public, certifier, official, functionary, clerk, registrar, official recorder.

notation, *n.* **1.** system of symbols, code, cipher, hieroglyphics, cryptograph, crytogram, shorthand; alphabet, letters, symbols, signs, characters, figures; musical notation; numerical notation, *Arith.* decimal scale.

2. note, memorandum, *Inf.* memo, reminder, note to oneself, jotting, record, minutes.

notch, *n.* **1.** nick, groove, nock, hole, gouge; cut, incision, slit, score, gash, slash; crenation, crenelation, crenature, crenel; indentation, indent, dent, dint, dimple, hollow, depression; scrape, scratch, scarification, chip, flaw, defect, mark, spot, blemish, defacement.

2. defile, pass, mountain pass, passage, channel.

3. *Informal.* step, rung, peg, cut; degree, gradation, stage, grade, rank.

—n. **4.** nick, groove, nock, gouge, cut a hole in, make a cut in, chip; cut into, incise, slit, split, score, gash, slash; dent, dint, put a dent in, press *or* push in; scrape, scratch, scarify, mark, flaw, spot, blemish, mar, deface.

5. serrate, scallop, pink; jag, tooth, crenelate, crenel; crimp, corrugate, crease, crinkle, wrinkle, furrow, ridge, fold.

notched, *adj.* saw-toothed, serrated, serrate, serrulate, serriform, crenate, crenelated, crenelate, scalloped, pinked; crimped, corrugated, wrinkled, furrowed, ridged, creased, folded, crinkled; jagged, jaggy, zigzag, zigzagged, uneven, rough, bumpy, unfinished.

note, *n.* **1.** memorandum, reminder, *Brit.* chit, brief record, chronicle, minutes; dedication, inscription; notation, jotting, item, entry, register.

2. notes outline, rough account, rough draft, sketchy report, thumbnail sketch; synopsis, brief, skeleton.

3. commentary, annotation, footnote, scholia, scholium, gloss, marginalia; comment, remark, explanation, explication, exegesis, illustration, exposition; criticism, critique.

4. short letter, missive, dispatch, written message, epistle, *Obs.* billet; answer, reply, acknowledgement, line, work, card, postcard; love letter, billet-doux, *Inf.* mash note, fan letter; thank-you note, bread-and-butter letter; news, information, bulletin; communication, correspondence, communiqué.

5. bill, treasury note, currency, money, paper money, legal tender, tender, greenback, check; banknote, promissory note; draft, bank draft, bill of exchange; voucher, receipt, letter of credit, *U.S.* certificate, *U.S.* gold *or* silver certificate; I.O.U., I owe you.

6. distinction, prominence, prestige, eminence, high standing, high rank; regard, esteem, notability, mark, merit; influence, sway, power; fame, renown, celebrity, esteem, popularity.

7. importance, significance, consequence, matter value; account, concern, *Archaic.* concernment, interest; moment, weight, substance, greatness, magnitude, force.

8. attention, attentiveness, notice, observation, ear; consideration, thought, care, solicitude, caution; respect, regard, mindfulness, *Inf.* mind; vigilance, watchfulness, guard, devotion.

9. hint, clue, tip, inkling, *Sl.* tip-off, cue; suggestion, idea; intimation, implication, imputation, insinuation, innuendo; suspicion, soupcon, trace, tinge; touch, speck, sprinkling, dash.

10. tone, intonation, tonation, inflection, timbre, pitch, key.

11. compare notes exchange observations *or* views, share impressions, compare ideas; discuss, parley, powwow.

—v. **12.** register, catalogue, chronicle, commit to writing, put on record; record, mark down, put down, make a note of, jot down, set down; write, scribble, scrawl, pencil; make an entry, enter, insert, write in, docket, post.

13. mention, mention in passing, allude, touch upon; cite, refer to, advert to, point to, *Dial.* signify; hint, suggest, adumbrate; imply, implicate, intimate, insinuate, infer; indicate, point out, point to, designate; make known, reveal, disclose, tell, express, state.

14. annotate, gloss, footnote, interline, interlineate; comment, commentate, remark upon; explain, illustrate, expound.

15. notice, behold, see, detect, take in, look visualize; regard, study, inspect, take stock of; examine, contemplate, pore over, perlustrate; review, check out, overlook, monitor; scan, run the eyes over, *Inf.* give the once-over; watch, observe, witness; take a look at, have a look-see, give a look, glimpse, glance.

16. pay attention to, lend an ear to, be aware of, be conscious of, give thought to, appreciate; tend to, apply oneself to.

notebook, *n.* record, chronicle, diary, memoir, journal, *Fr. journal intime;* album, scrapbook, record book, memory book; dossier, *Latin. adversaria,* commonplace book; yearbook, almanac, annals; registry, register, log, logbook, catalog, ledger, roll, cartulary; schedule, calendar, datebook, engagement book, birthday book, address book; minute book, daybook, Acta; *Both Theat.* promptbook, playbook.

noted, *adj.* **1.** famous, famed, renowned, celebrated, well-known, prominent, *Inf.* name, *Inf.* bigname; notable, eminent, preeminent, esteemed, respected, venerable, distinguished, *Archaic.* eximous; illustrious, great, grand, glorious, radiant, brilliant, lustrous; honored, exalted, acclaimed, much-touted, big-time, on the map, popular, well-liked; immortal, fabled, legendary, historical, memorable.

2. registered, catalogued, chronicled; recorded marked down, put down, jotted down, set down; written, scribbled, scrawled, penciled; posted, entered written in.

3. mentioned, alluded, touched upon; cited, indicated, designated, revealed, disclosed, expressed, stated.

4. noticed, detected, seen, visualized; regarded, studied, examined, reviewed, checked out; watched, observed, witnessed.

noteworthy, *adj.* **1.** notable, remarkable, signal, outstanding. See **notable** (*def.* **1**).

2. extraordinary, unusual, exceptional, out-of-the-ordinary. See **notable** (*def.* **2**).

nothing, *n.* **1.** naught, none, none whatsoever, nothing at all, nothing under the sun, nothing on earth; no such thing, nil, *Sl.* nix, *Sl.* zilch, *Sl.* scratch, *Sl.* squat, *Sl.* diddly, *Sl.* diddly-squat; *Latin. nihil, Fr. rien, Sp. nada, Ger. nichts, Russ. nichevo.*

2. no trace, no sign, no mark, no trail; no hint, no clue, no scent, no whiff, no smell; no part, no share, not any, not a bit, not a scrap, *Inf.* not a lick, all gone, the last drop; not a speck, not an ounce, not a thing, *Inf.* not a blessed thing, not a particle.

3. nothingness, nullity, nihility, nonexistence. See **nothingness** (*def.* **1**).

4. unimportance, insignificance, inconsequentiality, triviality, frivolity; worthlessness, nugacity, emptiness, pointlessness, superficiality; uselessness, ineffectuality, ineffectiveness, valuelessness; immateriality, inconsiderableness, inappreciableness; trifling, dalliance, inessential, no great matter, no big thing, mere nothing, technicality; trivia, details, fiddle-faddle, red tape, air, hot air; bagatelle, trinket, trumpery, gimcrack, gewgaw, whimwham, knickknack, bauble.

5. nobody, unimportant person, obscurity, mediocrity, *Inf.* nobody much; insignificancy, common man, man on the street, little man, little guy; jackstraw, dummy, lay figure, *Sl.* nebbish, *Sl.* schlepp, squirt, pip-squeak; second fiddle, no great shakes, small fry, *Sl.* small potatoes, little fish in a big pond; John Doe, Richard Roe, John Q. Public, (*in England*) John Bull, Joe Blow.

6. cipher, zero, aught, naught, no runs, no score, no tally; *Sl.* zip, *Sl.* goose egg, *Sl.* the big 0, *Cricket Sl.* duck, *Tennis.* love.

7. for nothing a. free, gratis, no charge, without charge; gratuitously, for free, for the love of it. **b.** for no reason, unthinkingly, reasonlessly, unreasoningly; impulsively, rashly, quickly, impetuously. **c.** futilely, vainly, needlessly, unnecessarily, uselessly, purposelessly; to no avail, to no purpose, to little purpose.

8. make nothing of a. treat lightly, think nothing of, think no more of, overlook, dismiss, forget; take it easy, don't bother about it, don't give it a second thought, don't give it another thought, put out of mind. **b.** not comprehend, not understand, find hard to understand, find hard to grasp; not get the idea, *Sl.* not dig, not know what to make of, not get it through one's head; not be able to make heads or tails of, not see the forest for the trees.

—adv. **9.** not at all, in no degree, not in the least, never; noway, noways, nowise, by no means, *Inf.* no how; not nearly, nowhere near, not by a long shot, by no stretch of the imagnination; on no account, in no respect, under no circumstances, in no case.

10. nothing but only, solely, simply, merely; plainly, just, barely, purely.

nothingness, *n.* **1.** nihility, nullity, nonexistence, *Fr. néant,* existencelessness; nonreality, nonlife, unreality, unactuality; incorporeality, insubstantiality, nonsubsistence, inexistence; nonentity, inessentiality, nonbeing, immateriality, imponderability, impalpability, intangibility, imperceptibility; oblivion, void, blank, space, vacuum, empty space, outer space, infinity, emptiness; absence, nonpresence, nowhereness, nonoccupancy, vacancy.

2. unconsciousness, insensibility, insentience, senselessness, imperception, impercipience, obtuseness; numbness, unfeeling, narcosis, anesthesia, pins and needles; death, deadness, dullness; coma, catalepsy, catatony, sleep, lipothymy.

3. insignificance, triviality, frivolity, unimportance, valuelessness; worthlessness, emptiness, nugacity, pointlessness, superficiality; ineffectuality, uselessness, inconsequentiality; immateriality, inconsiderableness, inappreciableness, infinitesimalness; minuteness, smallness, meagerness, paltriness, diminutiveness, microdimension.

notice, *n.* **1.** information, data, facts, knowledge, intelligence; news, tiding, report, message, account, recital; word, lowdown, *Sl.* info, *Sl.* poop, dirt, dope, inside story, *Sl.* scoop.

2. notification, apprising, advisement; statement, declaration, communication, announcement, publication, publicity, airing; reference, mention, mentioning, referral, referment; allusion, citation, indication, specification; hint, suggestion, inkling, innuendo, implication, insinuation.

3. poster, bill, handbill, circular, bulletin, broadside, pamphlet, leaflet; advertisement, broadcast; encyclical, manifesto, edict, decree, pronouncement.

4. caution, caveat, cautioning, warning, admonition, monition, forewarning; tip, tipoff, pointer.

5. critique, criticism, critical review; review, article, piece, column, editorial, comment, commentary.

6. attention, attentiveness, note, observation, ear, *Dial.* nevermind; consideration, thought, care, solicitude; respect, regard, mindfulness, *Inf.* mind; vigilance, watchfulness.

—*v.* **7.** pay attention to, give attention to, heed, listen to, give ear to; mark, observe, consider, note, take note, take heed of, give heed to; regard, remark, *Archaic.* animadvert, bear in mind, take into account; keep an eye on, keep an eye out, be on guard, be alert, be cautious, watch out, look before leaping; stop, look, and listen.

8. discern, see, behold, perceive, cognize; descry, detect, discover, light on *or* upon, espy; make out, decipher, figure out, ascertain, determine; distinguish, pick out, recognize; differentiate, discriminate.

9. mention, mention in passing, allude, touch upon; cite, refer to, note, advert to, point to, *Dial.* signify; hint, suggest, adumbrate. See **note** (*def.* **13**).

noticeable, *adj.* **1.** conspicuous, observable, recognizable, discernible, perceptible, appreciable, distinguishable; defined, distinct, well-defined, well-marked; visible, vivid, graphic; unhidden, undisguised, unconcealed, unmistakable; unveiled, uncurtained, unshrouded, unscreened; evident, plain, plain as day, plain as the nose on one's face, under one's nose, obvious, palpable, manifest, apparent; explicit, clear-cut, patent, express; pronounced, prominent, marked.

2. notable, noteworthy, remarkable, signal, outstanding; memorable, unforgettable, *Sl.* hell of a, special, particular, especial; important, on the map, significant, momentous, meaningful, worthy of notice; extraordinary, unusual, different, uncommon, rare, singular, exceptional, out-of-the-ordinary, *Inf.* one for the books; unique, distinct, peculiar, odd, strange, curious.

notification, *n.* **1.** making known, revealing, notifying, disclosing.

2. notice, message, letter, cable, report, dispatch, aviso, communication, word; statement, publication, broadcast, announcement, pronouncement; information, *Brit.* gen, intelligence, light; caution, advice, caveat, admonition, tip-off, *Sl.* high sign; tip, hint, word to the wise, clue, suggestion.

notify, *v.* **1.** inform, give notice to, tell, advise, apprise, remind, call, telephone, phone, cable, wire, write, send word to; warn, alert, caution, tip, tip off; give the lowdown to, let know, give a clue.

2. bruit about, broadcast, air, put on the air, publish, report, communicate; disclose, reveal, divulge, let drop, let slip; announce, proclaim, herald; declare, relate, voice, mention; send up smoke signals, get the word across, get the message through, peddle the news.

notion, *n.* **1.** idea, concept, conception, conceptualization, thought, abstraction, principle; belief, view, opinion, conviction, assumption, presumption, supposition, persuasion; surmise, conjecture, hypothesis, theory, postulate, rough guess; consideration, observation, reflection, conclusion, inference, apprehension; image, eidolon, mental picture, vague idea.

2. whim, kink, quirk, quip, caprice, conceit; fancy, fit, humor, vagary, whimsy, whimsicality; prank, trick, escapade; bee in the bonnet.

3. merchandise, trifle, knickknack, bauble.

notional, *adj.* **1.** abstract, theoretical, speculative, conceptual, ideational, hypothetical, reflective.

2. unreal, imaginary, ideal, idealistic, Utopian; visionary, envisioned, dreamed, fabled, fabulous, illusory, fancied, fanciful, romantic; unsubstantiated, groundless, baseless, unfounded, figmentary.

3. whimsical, maggoty, capricious, faddish, fadmongering; fanciful, fitful, changeable, erratic, variable, quixotic, fickle, tergiversating; volatile, mercurial, uncontrolled, unrestrained; frivolous, unstable, undependable, irresponsible; frolicsome, flirtatious, coquettish, sportive, playful, skittish.

notoriety, *n.* **1.** infamy, obloquy, opprobrium, disrepute, ill repute, *Inf.* black eye; shame, disgrace, dishonor, discredit; stigma, stain, blot, blot on the escutcheon, badge of infamy.

2. publicity, public notice, spotlight, limelight; fame, renown, bays, celebrity, stardom, illustriousness, greatness, preëminence, superiority, supremacy; eminence, notability, note, distinction, mark, significance; prominence, rank, standing, prestige, weight, importance, account; reputation, repute, *Sl.* rep.

3. honor, laurels, glory, praise, kudos, éclat, acclamation, acclaim; popularity, vogue, favor, esteem, high regard, admiration, respect.

notorious, *adj.* **1.** infamous, ill-famed, disreputable, ignominious, having a bad name, of ill repute, discreditable, dishonorable; scandalous, obloquial, disgraceful, shameful, flagrant, stigmatized.

2. famous, famed, renowned, celebrated, well-known, known, prominent, *Inf.* name, *Inf.* big-name; noted, notable, eminent, preeminent, esteemed, respected, venerable, distinguished, *Archaic.* eximous; illustrious, great, grand, glorious; honored, exalted, acclaimed, much-touted; big-time, on the map, popular, well-liked; immortal, fabled, legendary, historical, memorable.

notwithstanding, *prep.* **1.** despite, in spite of, regardless of; in defiance of, in contempt of, in the face of, in the teeth of, against.

—*conj.* **2.** despite the fact that, in spite of the fact that, although, albeit, even if, even so, for all of that, even though, though.

—*adv.* **3.** nevertheless, *Archaic.* withal, however, however that may be, howbeit; anyway, anyhow, regardless, be that as it may; no matter what, at any rate, in any case, in any event, at all events; all *or* just the same, after all, after all is said and done; but, still, yet, on the other hand, at the same time.

nourish, *v.* **1.** feed, nurture, provide for, care for, take care of, cherish; foster, bring up, rear, raise, cultivate, breed; nurse, harbor, keep, hold, sustain, maintain.

2. strengthen, promote, foster, further, encourage, stimulate; boost, advance, forward, push *or* push for, advocate; support, back, contribute to, conduce to,

patronize; help, aid, abet, assist, lend a hand, give a leg up.

nourishing, *adj.* **1.** nutritious, nutritive, alimentative, alimentary, alible; life-giving, life-sustaining, health-giving, healthy, healthful, wholesome, salutary, beneficial, good for you.

2. nurturing, cherishing, fostering; strengthening, furthering, encouraging, promoting, supporting, supportive; contributive, contributing, contributary, conducive, helpful.

nourishment, *n.* food, nutriment, nutrition, nurture, pabulum, sustenance, sustentation, subsistence; aliment, viands, meat, alimentation, bread *or* daily bread, groceries, foodstuffs, solids, edibles, *Inf.* grub, *Sl.* eats, *Sl.* chow, *Chiefly Brit. Sl.* scoff; snack, between-meal snack, bite, nosh, *Sl.* munchies; victuals, provisions, cheer, provender, rations, commons, comestibles, *Western U.S. Sl.* chuck, *Brit. Sl.* prog; board, fare, meals, mess, menu, table, diet, regimen; (*all of livestock*) feed, fodder, hay, oats, barley, corn, grain, bran, meal, mash; swill, *Inf.* glop, *Sl.* slop.

nouveau riche, *n.* new-rich, parvenu, upstart, arriviste, arrivé, *Chiefly Brit. Sl.* bounder.

novel[1], *n.* **1.** narrative, story, tale, account, history, chronicle, saga, yarn; fiction, romance, *Fr. roman;* drama, adventure, mystery, detective novel *or* fiction, *Inf.* whodunit, thriller, suspense novel, spy novel, intrigue, science fiction, *Sl.* sci-fi novel, speculative fiction, cowboy story, *Inf.* Western, historical novel, war novel, Gothic novel, love story, problem novel, psychological novel, novel of manners, comic novel, picaresque novel, *Fr. roman à clef,* fictionalized account; serialized novel, dime novel, penny dreadful; light reading, bedtime reading, summer reading; latest novel, best seller.

2. book, volume, edition, tome, publication; paperback, pocket book, soft-cover, hard-cover, title, offering, trade book, juvenile, *Inf.* pot boiler; writing, work, brainchild, opus, magnum opus, great work, classic, standard work; piece of writing, composition, opuscule, production, literary production, literature.

novel[2], *adj.* **1.** new, newfashioned, neoteric, unprecedented, original, imaginative, creative, unhackneyed; advanced, recent, late, modern; latest, newest, last, hot, just out, hot off the press, hot off the griddle *or* fire, up-to-the-minute, spanking, brand-new, late-model, modernistic, futuristic, ultramodern, revolutionary, avant-garde, *Sl.* far out, *Sl.* way out, newfangled, new as tomorrow.

2. fresh, fresh as a daisy, new as a new day; first, first of its kind, bright, clever; initial, natal, pristine, raw, new-fledged, newborn, the latest thing, trendsetting, breakthrough; unused, unhandled, unhandseled, untouched, unexplored, uncharted, unventured, untrodden, unbeaten; untested, untried, unknown, experimental, still on the drawing board, worth exploring, worth looking into.

3. refreshed, renewed, restored, reinvigorated, revivified, reborn, renascent, regenerated; changed, rebuilt, recreated, reconstructed, remodeled, modernized.

4. unfamiliar, outside of one's previous experience, hitherto unknown, unheard of, something else, another story, a horse of a different color; distinctive, noteworthy, singular, exceptional, extraordinary, uncommon, not something you see every day; rare, unique, out of the ordinary, off the beaten path *or* track; different, strange, unusual, curious, foreign, alien, exotic, from another world; quaint, droll, bizarre, odd, arresting, boggling, surprising, astonishing, startling, amazing, remarkable, *Inf.* wild, *Inf.* crazy; outlandish, far-fetched, peculiar, unconventional, fanciful, freakish, unaccustomed, unwonted.

novelist, *n.* author, writer, novel writer, writer of fiction, creative writer, fictioneer, fictionist, prose writer; scribbler, logographer, penman, *Inf.* scribe; literary artist *or* craftsman, word painter, wordsmith, belletrist, littérateur, man of letters; story teller, narrator, yarn spinner, spinner of yarns, anecdotalist, teller of tales, relater, raconteur, anecdotalist, romancer, historian, chronicler; best seller, popular author *or* novelist, free lance, free-lance writer; grind, hack, literary hack, *Inf.* schlock writer.

novelty, *n.* **1.** uniqueness, difference, unusualness, uncommonness; rarity, rareness, specialty, specialness; distinctive feature, variation, variance, variety; oddity, peculiarity, strangeness, unfamiliarity, outlandishness, unorthodoxy; originality, freshness, newness, novelness, newfangledness.

2. innovation, change, alteration, transformation, new measure, *Rare.* novation, modernism, *Inf.* new *or* latest wrinkle, *Inf.* newfangled idea *or* contraption, *Inf.* latest thing, *Fr. dernier cri, Inf.* the last word, *Inf.* what's in, *Inf.* the in thing; fad, craze, rage; new notion, restyling, recasting, remodeling, renovation, modernization; coining, neoterism, neology, neologism; *Inf.* something else, *Inf.* something else again, *Inf.* another kettle of fish.

3. gimmick, doodad, gimcrack, latest fad, flash-in-the-pan, overnight sensation; whim-wham, trinket, knickknack, trifle, kickshaw, brummagen, toy, plaything; gadget, contrivance, device, invention, creation; *All Inf.* contraption, whachamacallit, thingumajig, thingumabob, doohickey, do-hinkey, gismo, crackerjack prize.

novice, *n.* **1.** beginner, abecedarian, tyro, neophyte; learner, student, pupil, protégé, disciple; intern, student teacher, apprentice, journeyman, trainee, probationer; newcomer, *Dial.* newie, kid, new kid, youngling, tenderfoot, *Sl.* greenhorn; fledgling, cub, recruit, raw recruit, rookie, freshman, pledge, new member.

2. entrant, initiate, novitiate, catechumen; (*in religious orders*) postulant, canonical, unprofessed.

novitiate, *n.* **1.** test period, trial, probation; training period, initiation, indoctrination, apprenticeship, *Archaic. or Dial.* prenticeship; guidance, tutelage, instruction, teaching.

2. (*usu. restricted quarters within*) convent, nunnery, friary, priory, abbey, seminary.

3. novice, beginner, tyro, probationer, neophyte. See **novice** (*defs.* **1, 2**).

now, *adv.* **1.** at present, at this time, at this moment, right now, just now; today, in these days, in these times, in this day and age, nowadays; for the nonce, for the time being.

2. immediately, at once, on the instant, right away, in jig time, this minute, straightaway, without delay; soon, presently, anon.

3. now and then now and again, on occasion, occasionally, once in a while, *Dial.* once and a while, every once in a while, from time to time; intermittently, sporadically, randomly, at various times, at times, sometimes, on divers occasions, at intervals; infrequently, once in a great while, rarely, once in a blue moon, when the spirit moves.

—adj. **4.** *Slang.* current, up-to-date, modern, *Sl.* with it, contemporary; in vogue, trendy, stylish, *Sl.* in, modish, fashionable, faddish.

noway, *adv.* nowise, *Sl.* noways, in no wise *or* respect *or* manner, not at all, not a bit, not in the least, by no means; in no way, shape or manner; not by a long shot, not by a long sight, not by a damn sight, absolutely not.

noxious, *adj.* harmful, hurtful, nocuous, nocent, noisome; deleterious, pernicious, injurious, baneful, mischievous; baleful, menacing, malignant, malign; unwholesome, unhealthy, unhealthful, insalubrious; poisonous, venomous, virulent, toxic, mephitic, pestilential, pestiferous, morbific, morbifical; detrimental, disastrous, disadvantageous, disserviceable, prejudicial, damaging, corrupting, destructive, ruinous; malicious, maleficent, vicious, wicked, bad, evil, malevolent, malefic; deadly, fell, fatal, mortal, lethal, killing; murderous, internecine.

nozzle, *n.* **1.** spout, sprinkler, rose, nib, neb, socket.

2. *Slang.* nose, *All Sl.* beak, snoot, schnozz, schnozzle, schnozzola; snout, muzzle.

nuance, *n.* shade, shading, gradation; nicety, subtlety, distinction, fine point, particular, refinement, delicacy; suggestion, hint, trace, tinge, touch, dash; suspicion, soupçon.

nub, *n.* **1.** knob, knop, pommel, nubbin, nubble; bump, hump, node, nodule; protuberance, protrusion, gall, growth, excrescence, tubercle, tuberculum, *Bot.* tubercule, tuberosity, tumor; bulge, swelling, tumescence, gibbosity, *Bot., Zool.* boss; knot, bunch, gnarl, knurl, burl; mound, hillock, hummock, monticule, knop, (*in South Africa*) kopje, *Chiefly Brit.* barrow, *Brit. Dial.* tump.

2. lump, clump, chunk, mass, hunk; block, square, wad, squab, *Inf.* hunch; nugget, clod; piece, fragment, bit, butt.

3. *Informal.* core, pith, kernel, nucleus, center, focus, *Law.* gravamen; meat, heart, heart and soul, soul, marrow, sap; gist, sum and substance; material, matter, fiber, fabric, *Inf.* nitty-gritty, *Inf.* nuts and bolts; essence, quiddity, haecceity; point, main point, essential point, cardinal point, *Inf.* bottom line; issue, real issue, matter at hand, *Inf.* name of the game.

nucleus, *n.* core, pith, kernel, center, focus, *Inf.* nub, *Law.* gravamen; meat, heart, heart and soul, soul, marrow, sap, See also **nub** (*def.* **3**).

nude, *adj.* **1.** naked, stark-naked, *Brit.* starkers, naked as the day one was born, *Fr. tout nu;* bare, *Sl.* bare-ass, exposed, *Inf.* in the buff, *Inf.* in the altogether, *Inf.* in one's birthday suit, *Sl.* in the raw, *Sl.* raw; unclothed, undraped, undressed, unappareled, unclad, uncovered, unattired, disrobed, divested, without a stitch, with nothing on, *Fr. au naturel.*

2. plain, unadorned, undecorated, unornamented, unembellished, unarrayed, undecked.

—*n.* **3. the nude** state of nature, *Inf.* the buff, *Inf.* the altogether, *Inf.* birthday suit, *Sl.* the raw.

nudge, *v.* **1.** elbow, poke, jog, jab, dig, prod; bump, push, jostle; touch, kick, prompt.

—*n.* **2.** elbow, elbow in the ribs, prod, poke, jab, dig; push, bump, jostle; kick, prompt.

nudist, *n.* sunworshipper; *Dial.* bankwalker, *Inf.* skinnydipper; (*in ancient India*) gymnosophist, *Rare.* nudifier.

nudity, *n.* nakedness, bareness, undress, the state of undress, state of nature, the natural state, nature's state, nature's garb, natural garb, bare skin; the nude, *Inf.* the buff, *Inf.* the altogether, *Inf.* birthday suit, *Sl.* the raw.

nugatory, *adj.* **1.** worthless, valueless, meritless, inutile, inadequate, unserviceable, impracticable, inefficient, inoperative; frivolous, trivial, trifling, piddling, picayune, niggling, finicking; inessential, insignificant, inconsequential, unimportant, superfluous, petty, superficial, shallow; baseless, groundless, insubstantial, fragile, frail; empty, idle, inane, paltry, *Dial.* footy; trashy, shabby, *Inf.* cheesy, sleazy, flimsy, jerry-built, *U.S. Sl.* cottonpicking, not worth a straw; showy, gaudy, glittering, tinsel.

2. vain, bootless, futile, unavailing, useless, Sisyphean, ineffective, inefficacious; fruitless, unproductive, abortive, barren, sterile, impotent, effete; unprofitable, profitless, unsuccessful, to no purpose, to no avail, for naught.

3. fatuous, foolish, silly, brainless, irrational; senseless, feckless, infatuated.

nugget, *n.* chunk, lump, mass, *Inf.* hunk, clump, wad, squab, *Inf.* hunch.

nuisance, *n.* **1.** pest, bother, *Inf.* headache, *Inf.* pain, *Sl.* pain in the neck *or* rear, *Sl.* hassle, vexation, annoyance; irritant, bur, thorn in the side *or* flesh, pea in the shoe.

2. gadfly, buttonholer; bore, crashing bore, frightful bore, proser, twaddler, dryasdust; wet blanket, *Sl.* drip, *Sl.* pill, *Sl.* deadhead, *Sl.* flat tire, *Sl.* retread.

3. inconvenience, disadvantage, handicap; trouble, problem, worry, affliction, difficulty; trial, tribulation, ordeal; load, burden, weight, heavy load *or* burden.

null, *adj.* **1.** ineffectual, inoperative, valueless, worthless, no-good, good-for-nothing, *Inf.* no-account, inconsequential; insignificant, trifling, trivial, piddling, immaterial; purposeless, baseless, groundless; insubstantial, unsubstantial, jejune; unavailing, futile, vain, nugatory, useless, inutile, bootless; impotent, barren, sterile, powerless, unproductive, inefficacious, unsuccessful, abortive.

2. nonexistent, inexistent, nonsubsistent; negative, minus, omitted; unprofitable, unremunerative; blank, empty, clear, bare, hollow, vacuous; senseless, inane, foolish.

3. null and void annulled, nullified, repealed, abolished, revoked, rescinded; invalid, disestablished, cancelled, discharged; renounced, repudiated, disclaimed, disavowed.

4. annihilated, obliterated, destroyed, extinguished, eradicated, exterminated, expunged, extirpated; terminated, dissolved, eliminated, effaced.

nullification, *n.* **1.** annulment, annulling, disannulment, voidance, avoidance, *Law.* defeasance; quashing, invalidation, vitiation, *Obs.* vacatur, disenactment, disestablishment, setting aside; cancellation, discharge; repeal, revoking, revocation, rescinding, rescission, reversal, abrogation, abolishment, abolition; suspension, *Law.* nolle prosequi, stopping, discontinuance, cessation.

2. recantation, retraction, retractation, abjuration, withdrawal, recall; renouncement, renunciation, repudiation, relinquishment, abnegation; denial, negation, disclaimer, disclamation, disavowal; taking back, undoing, *Cards.* renege; countermand, countermanding, counterorder, overruling, overriding, veto.

3. neutralization, frustration; counterpoise, offsetting, counterbalance, counteraction, contravention, contradiction.

4. termination, dissolution, putting an end to, doing away with, bringing to an end; elimination, destruction, extinguishment, effacement, wiping out; obliteration, annihilation, eradication, expunging, extirpation, extermination; blotting out, stamping out, crushing out, sweeping away.

nullify, *v.* **1.** annul, disannul, declare null and void, render null and void, void, avoid; quash, invalidate, vitiate, vacate, disenact, disestablish; cancel, discharge; supersede, set aside; repeal, revoke, rescind, reverse, abrogate, abolish; suspend, *Law.* nol-pros, stop, discontinue, break off.

2. recant, retract, abjure, unsay, withdraw, recall; renounce, repudiate, relinquish, abnegate, deny, disclaim, disavow, disown; take back, undo, renege; countermand, counterorder, overrule, override; veto, negate.

3. neutralize, frustrate, counterpoise, counterbalance, counteract, contravene, contradict; overbalance, outweigh.

4. terminate, dissolve, cast aside, cast behind, put an end to, do away with, bring to an end; eliminate, destroy, extinguish, efface, x out, wipe out; obliterate, reduce to nothing, annihilate, eradicate, expunge, extirpate, exterminate; blot out, stamp out, crush out, sweep away.

nullity, *n.* **1.** nothingness, nihility, existencelessness, *Fr. néant;* unreality, nonreality, unactuality, inexistence, insubstantiality, incorporeality, incorporeity; immateriality, imponderability, nothing, impalpability, intangibility; void, vacuity, vacuum, blank, space, emptiness, infinity; absence, nowhereness, nonpresence, vacancy, nonoccupancy; abeyance, voidance, invalidity, neutrality.

2. insignificance, triviality, frivolity, unimportance, valuelessness, inconsequentiality; worthlessness, emptiness, nugacity, superficiality, pointlessness; futility, aimlessness, purposelessness; inconsiderableness, inappreciableness, smallness, meagerness, diminutiveness, infinitesimalness; meaninglessness, insignificancy, senselessness, inanity, nonsensicality; trivia, details, fiddle-faddle, red tape, air; trifling, dalliance, inessential, no great matter, mere nothing, technicality, no great shakes, no big thing.

numb, *adj.* **1.** sensationless, feelingness, insensate; senseless, insentient, unperceiving; dazed, in shock, anesthetized, drugged, paralyzed.

2. callous, insensitive, thickskinned; unimpressionable, inured, hardened, hard, casehardened; unemotional, apathetic, uninterested, uncaring, insouciant; inattentive, *Inf.* tuned out, blind *or* deaf to things, dispassionate; insusceptible, lethargic, spiritless, imperturbable.

3. dull, obtuse, witless, dumb, unreasoning, mindless, addlebrained, *Inf.* out to lunch; slow-witted, *Inf.* slow on the uptake, slow to comprehend; insensible, unaware, inappreciative.

—*v.* **4.** deaden, obtund, hebetate, dull; drug, anesthetize, chloroform, *Inf.* give a shot, paralyze, stun; torpify, *Inf.* put to sleep, *Inf.* put under, hypnotize, mesmerize, stupefy; chill, freeze, glaciate.

number, *n.* **1.** sum, summation, total, aggregate, count; tally, score, tale, reckoning, gross, gross amount, whole bill; amount, quantity, product; power, exponent, progression; subtrahend, quotient, difference.

2. numeral, digit. See **numeral.**

3. edition, issue, single issue, impression, imprint, print; printing, volume, copy, folio, first edition, later edition, incunabulum.

4. numbers plurality, multitude, quantities; preponderancy, infinite number; *Inf.* raft, *Inf.* slew, *Inf.* thousand and one, *Inf.* oodles, *Inf.* scads, scores; array, bevy, galaxy, troop, legion, host, army, mob, crowd, party; *Inf.* loads, bags, tons, barrels, flocks, bunches, no end of; a tidy sum, *Inf.* a passel; swarm, herd, drove, litter.

5. numbers pool *or* **game** lottery, state lottery, racing lottery, gambling, *U.S.* policy.

6. do a number on *Slang.* gull, deceive, take in, put on an act for, *Inf.* put on; sail under false colors, pull the wool over the eyes of, put one over on; defraud, cheat, rook, bilk, swindle, *Inf.* flimflam; *Inf.* fast-talk, *Sl.* snow, seduce, beguile; betray, double-cross, *Sl.* shaft.

7. without number innumerable, many, very many, myriad, untold. See **numberless.**

—*v.* **8.** enumerate, count, count off, numerate, paginate; tally, tell, tell off, tick off; figure, cipher, figure up, tot, reckon; compute, calculate, score, sum, sum up, add, subtract, multiply, divide; estimate, make an estimate, assess; account, make an accounting, make a count, audit, balance, prove; call the roll, roll-call, take attendance; take stock, inventory, count up.

numberless, *adj.* innumerable, countless, numerous, numerous as the grains of sand on the seashore, numerous as the stars in the Milky Way; many, myriad, untold, multitudinous; multifold, multiple, multiplied, *Inf.* umpteen, *Sl.* skaty-eight, *Sl.* forty-'leven, *Inf.* more than one could shake a stick at, more than one can count; unnumbered, unnumerated, uncounted, uncountable, infinite, incomputable, incalculable, immeasurable, measureless, indeterminate, indefinite; abundant, profuse, teeming, prevalent, plentiful, plenteous, bountiful, copious.

numbing, *adj.* deadening, hebetative, dulling; narcotic, drugging, anesthetic, anesthetizing, stunning, shocking, paralyzing; hypnotic, Lethean, mesmerizing, stupefactive; chilly, freezing, frigid, glacial.

numbness, *n.* **1.** unconsciousness, insentience, insensibility, insensitiveness, insensitivity; stupor, narcosis, anesthetization, hypnosis, paralysis; shock, dazedness, confusion.

2. inattentiveness, absent-mindedness, indifference, insouciance, nonchalance; disregard, half-heartedness, dullness, lethargy, sluggishness.

3. imperviousness, hardness, callousness, toughness; apathy, coolness, passionlessness, emotionlessness, impassibility, impassibleness.

numeral, *n.* number, *Sp. numero;* cipher, digit, figure, integer, round number, whole number, fraction; cardinal number, ordinal number, Arabic number, Roman number, digital number.

numerate, *v.* **1.** number, paginate, page, foliate; mark, stamp, print.

2. count, compute, calculate, reckon, figure; tally, add, sum up, total, tot up.

3. enumerate, list, specify, name, cite, recite, estimate, check, check off, go over, run over, take account of; catalogue, detail, mark, take stock of.

numerical, *adj.* numerary, numerative, arithmetic, arithmetical, mathematical, algebraic, statistical; submultiple, reciprocal, prime, fractional, decimal, exponential, logarithmic, logometric; differential, integral, real, imaginary; rational, irrational, positive, negative.

numerous, *adj.* many, very many, ever so many, myriad, sundry, divers, several, quite a few; various, manifold, multifarious; multitudinous, innumerable, numberless, countless, untold, *Inf.* umpteen, *Sl.* skaty-eight, *Sl.* forty-'leven, *Inf.* more than one could shake a stick at, more than one can count; multifold, multiple, multiplied; unnumbered, uncounted, uncountable, infinite, incomputable, incalculable; abundant, profuse, prevalent, plentiful, plenteous, rife, bountiful; great, considerable, large.

numskull, *n. Informal.* dope, booby, fool, *Inf.* dummy, *Sl.* dumbbell, *Sl.* meatball, *Sl.* meathead, blockhead, beetlehead, bonehead, dunderhead, dunderpate, chucklehead, *Sl.* dumbhead, *Sl.* lunkhead, *Inf.* knucklehead, *Sl.* stupidhead. See **fool** (*def.* **1**).

nun, *n.* **1.** sister, religious, conventual; virgin, maiden, bride of Christ; recluse, contemplative, anchoress.

2. aspirant, postulant, novice, canonical, professed.

3. abbess, prioress, canoness, mother superior, reverend mother, mother general, reverend mother vicar.

nunnery, *n.* **1.** convent, motherhouse, novitiate; religious community, abbey, priory, cloister, cenoby; *All Obs.* religious life, sisterhood, nunhood, nunship.

2. brothel, bordello, house of ill repute. See **brothel.**

nuptial, *adj.* **1.** wedding, bridal, hymeneal, spousal, matrimonial, marital, connubial, conjugal, wedded.

—*n.* **2.** *Usu.* **nuptials** wedding *or* wedding ceremony, marriage *or* marriage ceremony, matrimony, bridal, *Class. Myth.* Nymphaea, spousals, espousals, (*among the ancient Romans*) confarreation, *Sl.* altar; wedlock, marital union *or* bond, nuptial tie *or* knot.

nurse, *n.* **1.** registered nurse, R.N., practical nurse, licensed practical nurse, L.P.N., private nurse, head nurse, *Brit.* sister; male nurse, orderly, hospital attendant; nurse's aide, *Sl.* candystriper.

2. dry nurse, governess, nursemaid, nurserymaid, *Chiefly Brit.* nanny, (*in the southern U.S.*) mammy, wet nurse.

—*v.* **3.** care for, take care of, tend to, attend to, minister to, wait on, wait on hand and foot; treat, doctor.

4. (*all of an infant*) suckle, wet-nurse, breast-feed; nurture, cradle, feed, take care of, care for; dry-nurse, parent, mother, cherish; coddle, pamper, baby, indulge, pet, mollycoddle; foster, bring up, rear, raise, train.

5. harbor, keep, hold, sustain, maintain.

nursery, *n.* **1.** baby's room, children's room, playroom, rumpus room.

2. nursery school, day nursery, day-care center, crèche, child care center, playschool, preschool kindergarten.

3. conservatory, greenhouse, hothouse, forcing house, indoor garden, cold frame.

nursling, *n.* infant, baby, newborn, neonate, *It. bambino, Fr. bébé,* papoose, suckling, weanling; foundling, changeling; young child, *Fr. enfant, Scot. and North Eng.* bairn, toddler, tot, tiny tot, *U.S. Inf.* tad, pre-schooler, nursery schooler; (*all of animals*) cub, kitten, kitty, pup, puppy, foal.

nurture, *v.* **1.** feed, nourish, sustain, maintain; provide for, care for, take care of, tend; cherish, parent, mother, dry-nurse; foster, nurse, bring up, rear, raise; form, mold, shape, build, prepare, guide, take in hand; train, discipline, teach, tutor, instruct in, *Nonstandard.* learn, educate, school.

2. cultivate, breed, develop, promote, foster, further, encourage, stimulate; boost, strengthen, advance, forward, push *or* push for, advocate; support, back, contribute to, conduce to, patronize; help, aid, abet, assist, lend a hand, give a leg up.

—*n.* **3.** upbringing, rearing, fosterage, care; training, breeding, guidance, development, cultivation, preparation; education, tutelage, tuition, teaching, instruction, schooling, learning.

4. nourishment, nutriment, nutrition, food, pabulum, sustenance, subsistence. See **nourishment.**

nurturing, *adj.* **1.** cherishing, nursing, mothering, parenting; parental, maternal, motherly; coddling, pampering, babying, indulging, petting, mollycoddling.

2. nourishing, fostering, strengthening, furthering, encouraging, promoting, supporting, supportive; contributive, contributing, contributary, conducive, helpful.

nut, *n.* **1.** kernel, nutlet, nutmeat; grain, pip, seed, meat, pith.

2. *Slang.* fan, *Inf.* buff, aficionado; devotee, enthusiast, energumen, *Inf.* fiend, *Sl.* freak, *Sl.* bug, *Inf.* demon; follower, disciple, champion, adherent; fanatic, zealot, booster.

3. *Slang.* eccentric, queer one, odd one, *Sl.* weirdo, *Sl.* screwball; fool, *Yiddish.* schmendrik, simpleton, nincompoop. See **fool** (*defs.* **1, 2**).

4. *Slang.* psychotic, psychopath, lunatic, madman, maniac, demented one, hysteric; *Inf.* crackpot, *Sl.* crazy, *Sl.* loony, *Sl.* dingaling, *Sl.* yo-yo.

nutbrown, *adj.* brown, tan, beige, ecru, puce; walnut, hazel, chocolate, coffee, cinnamon.

nutriment, *n.* nourishment, food, nutrition, pabulum, nurture, sustenance, subsistence. See **nourishment.**

nutrition, *n.* **1.** good eating habits, balanced diet.

2. nourishment, nutriment, food, pabulum, nurture, sustenance, subsistence. See **nourishment.**

nutritious, *adj.* nutritive, nourishing, alimentative, alimentary, alible, full of nutrients; life-giving, life-sustaining, health-giving, healthy, healthful, wholesome, salutary, beneficial, good for you.

nutty, *adj.* **1.** lively, zestful, zesty, animated; vital, ebullient, *Sl.* zingy; stimulating, exciting, rousing; tantalizing, fascinating; meaty, pithy, juicy, rich, interesting; flavorful, piquant, spicy, tangy.

2. *Informal.* inane, silly, fatuous, addled, addlepated, foolish, senseless, pointless, nonsensical; zany, ridiculous, laughable, absurd; *All Sl.* goofy, wacky, batty, sappy, screwy.

3. *Slang.* insane, psychotic, lunatic, crazy, crazed, psychopathic; mad, manic, hysterical; maniac, demented, deranged, irrational; manic-depressive, paranoid, schizophrenic; of unsound mind, *Latin. non compos mentis,* unbalanced, touched, *Inf.* daffy, daft; unhinged, *Inf.* unglued, *Sl.* bonkers, *Inf.* dotty, *Sl.* meshuga, mad as a hatter, *Inf.* cracked, *Inf.* mental; *All Sl.* balmy, dippy, cuckoo, buggy, bughouse, wacko, loony, squirrelly, bananas, nuts, nutty as a fruitcake; off one's rocker, off the wall, off one's trolley, out of one's gourd, off one's chump, out of one's tree; have bats in one's belfry, have a few buttons missing, have a few loose screws, not have all one's marbles.

nuzzle, *v.* **1.** burrow, root up, nose out, nose; scrounge, forage, dig up.

2. cuddle, snuggle, nestle, snug, lie closely, curl up; fondle, cosset, coddle.

—*n.* **3.** embrace, hug, caress, pet, pat; kiss, *Inf.* buss, smooch, smack.

nymph, *n.* **1.** sylph, sylphid, nymphet, wood *or* mountain nymph; water nymph, water sprite, undine, ondine, sea-maid, sea-maiden, mermaid; *All Class. Myth.* dryad, hamadryad, oread, naiad, Oceanid, Nereid, Siren, *Rom. Legend.* Napaea, *Roman Religion.* Camena, Carmenta, Egeria, Antevorta, Postvorta, (*in Scottish legend*) kelpie; fairy, fay, sprite, pixy, nix, peri, elf, brownie, *Irish Folklore.* leprechaun.

2. damsel, maiden, maid, lass, lassie, *Irish Eng.* colleen; miss, young lady *or* woman, mademoiselle, demoiselle, *Archaic.* damoiselle; girl, schoolgirl, child.

3. larva, caterpillar, worm, grub, maggot, flyblow; pupa, chrysalia, cocoon.

O

oaf, *n.* **1.** dunce, dolt, dullard, blockhead, dunderhead, dunderpate, clodpate, loggerhead, thickhead, fathead, numskull, bonehead, *Inf.* knucklehead, *Inf.* deadhead, *Sl.* lunkhead, *Sl.* meathead, *Sl.* meatball, *Sl.* lardhead, *Sl.* dummkopf, *Sl.* stupidhead, *Sl.* zombie. See **dullard.**

2. simpleton, Simple Simon, ninny, nincompoop, ninnyhammer, fool, tomfool, nitwit, chucklehead, saphead, ass, donkey, *Inf.* coot, *Inf.* chump, *Inf.* jay, *Sl.* yo-yo, *Sl.* goon, *Sl.* flake, *Sl.* ding-a-ling, *Sl.* birdbrain; *All Sl.* boob, booby, noodle, nudnik, jerk, schmuck.

3. lout, clod, clodhopper, clodpoll, looby, gawk, ox, bull in a china shop, lubber, *Inf.* lummox, *Inf.* goop, *Inf.* duffer, *Sl.* clunker, *Sl.* lug, *Sl.* palooka, *Sl.* galoot, *Sl.* schlepp, *Sl.* schlemiel, *Brit. Sl.* joskin; bumbler, fumbler, boggler, bungler, botcher, blunderer, *Inf.* butterfingers, *Inf.* duffer, *Sl.* klutz, *Sl.* stumblebum; churl, boor, yokel, bumpkin, hawbuck, *Dial.* lumpkin, *Often Disparaging.* hillbilly, *Disparaging.* bogtrotter, *Inf.* chawbacon, *Sl.* hick, *Sl.* rube, *Sl.* hayseed, *Sl.* hoosier.

4. deformed child, freak, monster; slow learner, special *or* exceptional child *or* student, retardate, moron, imbecile, idiot, half-wit, *Sl.* dimwit, *Sl.* retard, *Sl.* retread.

5. changeling, waif, orphan, foster child, stray.

oar, *n.* **1.** paddle, scull, lever; steerer, *Both Naut.* rudder, tiller.

2. rower, paddler, See **oarsman.**

—*v.* **3.** row, paddle, scull, canoe, kayak, ply the oars; propel, drive, move forward; pole, *Chiefly Brit.* punt, push.

oarsman, *n.* rower, paddler, sculler, bencher, oar; canoeist, kayakist, crewman, gondolier; boatman, boater, sailor.

oasis, *n.* **1.** watering hole, springs, green spot, fertile patch.

2. haven, refuge, sanctuary, retreat, resort, asylum, sanctum.

oat, **1.** grain, cereal.

2. oats, feed, fodder, scratch, silage, meal, millet.

oath, *n.* **1.** promise, pledge, vow, avowal, guarantee, warrant, assurance; troth, word, word of honor, faith, *Archaic.* plight; statement, declaration, attestation, adjuration; averment, asseveration, pronouncement, avouchment, *Inf.* say-so, *Latin. ipse dixit*; affirmation, assertion, proclamation.

2. curse, swearword, *Inf.* cuss, *Inf.* cussword, expletive; four-letter word, dirty word, damn, *Inf.* no-no, naughty word; dirty name, name, epithet; obscenity, profanity.

3. swearing, blasphemy, ribaldry, scurrility; malediction, imprecation, invective, bad language, Billingsgate, unparliamentary language, badmouth.

oatmeal, *n.* porridge, mush, farina, cereal, hot cereal; gruel, *Scot.* brose, *Dial.* loblolly.

obdurate, *n.* **1.** unyielding, unbending, inflexible, unmalleable; hard, obstinate, stubborn, willful, pervicacious; recalcitrant, intractable, immovable; bullheaded, pigheaded, mulish; callous, hardened, unimpressible, uninfluenced, case-hardened; opinionated, headstrong, bigoted.

2. cruel, fell, grim, ruthless, merciless, pitiless, hardhearted; steely, adamantine, flinty, harsh, coldblooded; relentless, remorseless, implacable, inexorable, unrelenting, tough, dogged; inhuman, heartless, untouched, impervious, uncaring; unresponsive, unforgiving, unsparing, uncompassionate, unsympathetic, supercilious, unconcerned; insensible, coldhearted, cold, unfeeling, indurate, insensitive.

3. impenitent, unregenerate, reprobate, uncontrite; shameless, unrepenting, profligate; atheistic, godless, infidel, sinful.

obedience, *n.* **1.** compliance, conformity, acquiescence, abidance, acceptance; yielding, submission, subjection, morigeration, allegiance, observance; reverence, deference, respect, respectfulness; submissiveness, adapability, malleability, tractability, ductility, pliancy; dutifulness, faithfulness; meekness, timidity, gentleness, passiveness, docility.

2. subservience, obsequiousness; servility, ingratiation, prostration, obeisance, abasement; truckling, bowing, scraping, fawning, cowering, cringing, crawling, toadying, *Inf.* bootlicking; self-effacement, self-surrender, self-abasement.

obedient, *adj.* **1.** compliant, acquiescent, submissive, yielding, deferential, *Rare.* morigerate, morigerous; dutiful, duteous, law-abiding, rule-abiding, loyal, faithful; conforming, cooperative, responsive, agreeable; supple, malleable, ductile, pliant; docile, meek, timid, gentle, passive; governable, tractable, biddable, under [s.o.'s] thumb.

2. subservient, servile, obsequious, ingratiating, obeisant, prostrate, *Archaic.* sequacious; truckling, bowing, scraping, fawning, cowering, cringing, crawling, toadying, toadyish, *Inf.* bootlicking; self-effacing, self-surrendering, self-abasing.

obeisance, *n.* **1.** deference, homage, worship, adoration; respect, honor, regard; reverence, veneration, estimation, esteem.

2. obsequiousness, servility, sycophancy, fawning, toadying; submissiveness, subservience, slavishness; supineness, passivity, complaisance, resignation.

3. bow, curtsy, genuflection, kneeling; salaam, kowtow, congé, stoop; salutation, salute, nod, capping, doffing.

obelisk, *n.* monolith, shaft, needle, column, pillar, monument.

obese, *adj.* **1.** fat, corpulent, overweight, *Scot.* fodgel; chubby, tubby, pudgy, plump; round, rounded out, rotund, portly; paunchy, potbellied, round-bellied, big-bellied, *Sl.* beerbellied, large-bellied, great-bellied, *Obs.* gorbellied; *Inf.* bay-windowed, *Inf.* corporational, abdominous; fleshy, well-fed.

2. full, bulging, protuberant, bloated, distended; swollen, turgid, tumid; puffy.

3. stout, thickset, full-figured.

4. big, large, great; bulky, gross, lumpish.

obesity, *n.* fatness, overweight, corpulence, corpulency, *Fr. embonpoint, Pathol.* adiposis, obeseness; chubbiness, tubbiness, paunchiness, pudginess, plumpness, roundedness, rotundity; portliness, stoutness, burliness; hulk, bulk.

obey, *v.* **1.** observe, comply with, acknowledge, respect; adhere to, abide by, conform to; acquiesce in, consent to, agree to, grant, concur, accept; accommodate, adapt, adjust, suit, fit, (*usu. of things*) respond, react; mind, heed, follow, defer to, be regulated by, be governed by.

2. surrender, relent, give in, give way to, succumb; stoop, bend to, bow to, truckle to, humble oneself to, bend the knee to, knuckle under, do [s.o.'s] bidding, *Inf.* jump through hoops; resign oneself to, get into line, toe *or* mark the line, keep in step, walk the chalk mark *or* line.

3. perform, discharge, execute, carry out, carry into effect; meet, satisfy, fulfill, complete.

obfuscate, *v.* **1.** confuse, bewilder, muddle, perplex; puzzle, baffle, confound, fluster, *Inf.* rattle; stupefy, mystify, disconcert, daze, befuddle, dazzle; jumble, mess up, complicate, scramble, garble.

2. obscure, cloud, fog, smoke, nubilate, blur, overshadow; overcloud, obnubilate, dim, bedim, becloud, befog, murk, blear; hide, conceal, cover, blind, camouflage; curtain, drape, veil, shroud, blanket.

3. darken, shadow, shade, darkle, blacken, benight; eclipse, occult, occultate, blot out, brown out, black out; adumbrate, odumbrate, obtenebrate.

obfuscation, *n.* **1.** obscurity, blurriness, fuzziness, unclairty, unclearness, vagueness; haziness, fogginess, mistiness, murkiness; clouding, overclouding, dimming, obnubilation, shadowing, overshadowing; obscurement, darkening, blackening, obscuration, obumbration, adumbration.

2. perplexity, bafflement, puzzle, jumble, scramble, complication; mystification, obscurantism, *Inf.* mumbo jumbo, confusion; bewilderment, muddle, daze, befuddlement.

3. screen, smokescreen, cloud, dust, pall; curtain, shadow, fog, mist, frost, smoke, film; cover, camouflage, blanket, drape.

obituary, *n.* obit, necrology, death notice.

object, *n.* **1.** thing, something, anything, it, body, particular, stuff; substantiality, materiality, individuality; phenomenon, article, device, contrivance; substance, element, solid, entity; gadget, item, *Fr. quelque chose,* bird in hand; creature, being, person, somebody, anybody, individual, *Inf.* what's-his-name; widget, *All Inf.* thingumajig, thingumabob, doodad, dohickey, dojigger, jigger, gizmo.

2. subject, matter, issue, thought, subject matter; study, concern, affair, argument.

3. end, goal, purpose, objective, aim, destination; target, mark, butt, bull's-eye; pursuit, prize, quarry, chase, prey, game, quintain; intent, intention, motive, desire, view; point, import, purport, implication, meaning; design, plan, scheme, plot, idea; end purpose, end in view, be-all, end-all, utlimate aim.

—*v.* **4.** argue against, plead, defend, answer, cite, attest, instance.

5. protest, disapprove, take exception to, demur, disfavor; remonstrate, expostulate, deprecate, animadvert upon; oppose, contravene, controvert, counter, dissent, differ; dislike, eschew, spurn; cavil, squabble, scruple, boggle, beg to differ.

6. refuse, deny, reject, disallow; repudiate, negate, rebut; say no, defy, shake one's head, turn thumbs down on.

objectify, *v.* **1.** externalize, actualize, materialize, hypostatize, corporealize, realize, body; embody, substantiate, incarnate, personify.

2. imagine, ideate, create, make up, concoct, think up, coin; visualize, envisage, conjure up, paint.

objection, *n.* **1.** disapproval, disapprobation, dissatisfaction; dislike, disrelish, antipathy, disaffection, resentment; disagreement, difference, variance, issue.

2. objecting, protesting, protestation; opposition, contravention, contradiction, controversion; dissent, dissidence, dissension.

3. counterstatement, defense, plea, answer, reply; denial, exception, demurrer, rebuttal; repudiation, refutation, rejection, negation; no, nay.

4. complaint, protest, veto, challenge; demur, hesitation, scruple, qualm, boggle; *Sl.* beef, *Sl.* kick, *Sl.* squawk, grievance, exception; remonstrance, expostulation, reproof, rebuke, reprimand, reproach, reprehension; stricture, blame, censure.

objectionable, *adj.* **1.** improper, indecorous, unseemly, unbecoming, unbefitting, out of place; discourteous, disrespectful, uncivil, insolent, contumelious; undesirable, unfit, unsuitable, inappropriate; unallowable, ineligible, unadvisable, uncommendable, unpraiseworthy, unsatisfactory, disagreeable; inadmissible, exceptionable, unacceptable, untenable, unfeasible, indefensible, unjustifiable.

2. offensive, ignoble, base, deplorable, disgusting; insufferable, intolerable, unbearable, unendurable; unpleasant, unpalatable, unsavory, unappetizing, displeasing; repulsive, repellent, repugnant, revolting, nauseating; rank, beastly, sickening, stinking; gross, noisome, rotten, fetid, filthy, noxious; execrable, abominable, obnoxious; despicable, detestable, contemptible, odious, loathsome, abhorrent, hateful; vile, bad, opprobrious, foul, horrid.

objective, *n.* **1.** purpose, intent, intention, animus, motive, desire, view; hope, ambition, aspiration, vision; import, purport, implication, meaning; design, plan, idea, scheme, plot; end, purpose, end in view, ultimate aim, be-all, end-all; goal, end, object, aim, destination; target, mark, point, butt, bull's-eye; quarry, prize, prey, game, pursuit, chase, quintain.

2. lens, glass, ocular, optic, optical.

—*adj.* **3.** ultimate, desired, purposed, intended; projected, planned, hoped for; final, end, terminal, eventual, destined.

4. unbiased, unprejudiced, unbigoted, impartial, impersonal; detached, neutral, judicial, sober, nonsubjective, third-person; uncolored, unwarped, unswayed, uninfluenced, unjaundiced; disinterested, dispassionate, just, fair, equitable, open-minded, even-handed.

objectivity, *n.* **1.** dispassion, disinterest, disinterestedness, indifference, detachment; equitability, fairness, justice, justness, evenhandedness, squareness; impartiality, neutrality, unprejudiceness, unbiasedness, unbigotedness, broad-mindedness.

2. reality, substantiality, essentiality; substantivity, corporeality, corporeity, materiality, ponderability, tangibility.

3. externality, outwardness, extrinsicality, nonsubjectivity, objectiveness; extraneousness, exteriority, externalization, objectification; extraversion, otherness, projection, extrapolation.

objurgate, *v.* reproach, reprimand, reprove, reprehend, rebuke; upbraid, scold, dress down, castigate, chide, admonish; berate, rail at, fulminate against, thunder against; denounce, denunciate, damn, curse, execrate, anathematize, desecrate; roast, lash, trounce, accuse, traduce, impugn; revile, vilipend, vituperate, assail, attack; throw stones at, haul over the coals.

oblation, *n.* **1.** offering, offertory, consecration, votive offering, peace offering; libation, incense, burnt offering, sacrifice; vow, dedication, collection.

2. gift, donation, contribution, present, presentation, widow's mite; alms, charity, benefaction, dole, *Brit.* box, handsel.

obligate, *v.* **1.** oblige, bind, pledge, commit; require, necessitate, command, exact, demand; elicit, call for, cry for; compel, impel, force, press, constrain; coerce, *Inf.* strong-arm, dragoon.

—adj. **2.** obliged, bound, pledged, committed; compelled, forced, pressed, constrained, coerced.

3. obligatory, required, necessary, requisite; essential, indispensable; fundamental, basic, cardinal, primary.

obligation, *n.* **1.** necessity, necessariness, necessitude; requirement, prerequisite; command, demand, must, compulsion, compulsiveness; constraint, enforcement, duress, pressure.

2. duty, function, business; responsibility, trust, charge, care; burden, onus, devoir; assignment, commission, chore, task; province, area, bailiwick, beat; accountability, liability.

3. contract, compact, covenant, deed; agreement, arrangement, understanding, treaty, bond, indenture; deal, pact, acknowledgment, transaction, warranty, stipulation; commitment, pledge, promise, guaranty; word, oath.

4. debt, indebtedness, liability, due, dues, debit; gratitude, gratefulness, thankfulness, thanks, thanksgiving, appreciation.

obligatory, *adj.* **1.** binding, obligating; commanding, exacting, demanding; compelling, impelling, forcing, forcible, pressing, constraining, coercing; unconditional, unqualified, categorical.

2. required, necessary, requisite, obligate; mandatory, compulsory, prescriptive, enforced; exigent, urgent, pressing; imperative, imperious, importunate, peremptory; involuntary, compulsive; essential, indispensable; fundamental, basic, cardinal, primary; unalterable, unchangeable, hard-and-fast.

oblige, *v.* **1.** necessitate, require, obligate, bind exact, demand, command, call for, cry for, clamor for; compel, impel, force, press, constrain; make, use force upon, force [s.o.'s] hand; pressure, high-pressure, put pressure on, put the screws on, bear down upon or against, twist [s.o.'s] arm; coerce, *Inf.* strong-arm, dragoon.

2. accommodate, favor, indulge, patronize, put oneself out for; aid, assist, help, abet, meet the wants of; befriend, lend a hand, do a favor for, show a kindness to, do right by; serve, do for, do a service for, cater to, make comfortable, attend to the convenience of; provide, supply, furnish.

obliging, *adj.* willing, accommodating, agreeable, amenable, gracious; eager, ready, fain, earnest; helpful, kind, friendly, neighborly; serving, helping, benevolent, benign; assistant, aidful, well-disposed, sympathetic.

oblique, *adj.* **1.** slanting, sloping, slated, inclined, tilted, atilt, listing, canting; diagonal, abaxial, plagihedral, rhomboidal, cater-cornered; *All Geol.* synclinal, anticlinal, anaclinal, cataclinal.

2. askew, skew, aslant, awry, wry, askant, askance, asquint; knock-kneed, *Inf.* cockeyed, *Brit.* wonky, *Brit.* skew-whiff; athwart, transverse; leaning, stooping, clinal, battered, bevel; biased, warped, shelving, shelvy, tipsy, slantways; acclivous, uphill, declivous, downhill.

3. indirect, crooked, zigzag, divergent, deviant, devious, deflectional; divagational, digressive, circuitous, ambagious, backhanded, roundabout; discursive, excursive, deviating, tangential, errant; rambling, meandering, maundering, circumlocutory, periphrastic.

4. sly, sinister, disingenuous, surreptitious; covert, hugger-mugger, masked, behind one's back, under one's breath; arcane, underground, obreptitious; cloaked, veiled, sneaking, clandestine, furtive; insidious, false-hearted, false, deceptive, deceitful, *Inf.* shady, dark, *Inf.* fishy, *Inf.* not kosher.

5. perverse, underhand, underhanded, wrong; decadent, vitiated, profligate, reprobate; immoral, corrupt, unchaste, unvirtuous; prodigal, wayward, recidivistic, wanton, carnal.

—n. **6.** slant, slash, diagonal, virgule, transverse, rhomboid.

obliquity, *n.* **1.** obliqueness, wryness, deflection, deviousness; divergence, deviation, divagation; indirection, circumlocution, meandering, maundering, swerve, zigzag, *Chess.* knight's move; digression, excursion, discursion, tangent; *Statistics.* skewness.

2. inclination, incline, slant, slope, leaning, lean; angularity, bias, bevel, bezel; tilt, pitch, sway, tip, cant, rake; grade, ramp, bank, side, scarp; *All Geol.* syncline, anticline, anacline, catacline.

3. dishonesty, underhandedness, deceit, falseness, deception; false-heartedness, insidiousness, treacherousness, perfidiousness, duplicity; cunning, *Inf.* skulduggery, sneakiness, guile, guilefulness, artfulness.

4. perversity, immorality, turpitude, decadence, corruptness; unvirtuousness, moral delinquency, ungoodness, criminality, sinfulness; prodigality, waywardness, recidivism, carnality.

5. obscurity, obfuscation, unclearness, opacity; babble, jumble, garble, scramble, blur; riddle, puzzle, enigma, perplexity, confusion.

obliterate, *v.* **1.** exterminate, annihilate, discreate, reduce to nothing, wipe out, sweep away, dissolve, eliminate, extirpate, destroy totally, decimate, liquidate; raze, ravage, level, tear down, tear to the ground, topple, gut, blast, devastate, ruin, despoil, desolate, demolish, wreck, smash, dismantle, lay in ruins, beat down, blow down; quash, quell, squash, suppress, put an end to, snuff out, stamp out, *Sl.* rub out, finish, dispel, break up; uproot, root out, deracinate, *Obs.* overruncate.

2. erase, efface, eradicate, wipe *or* blot out, sponge out, render imperceptible *or* illegible *or* undeciperable; delete, cancel, kill, expunge, blue-pencil; omit, strike out, write off, rule out.

obliteration, *n.* **1.** extermination, annihilation, discreation, dissolution, elimination, extirpation, total *or* utter destruction, decimation, liquidation, undoing, end, *Sl.* curtains, abolition, extinguishment; razing, gutting, leveling, blasting, smashing, dismantling; ravagement, devastation, ruination, desolation, demolition, wreckage.

2. erasure, effacement, eradication, wiping *or* blotting *or* sponging out, ruling out, deletion, cancellation, omission, expunction, striking out, writing off.

oblivion, *n.* **1.** obscurity, darkness, blankness; extinction, obsolescence, nowhereness, never-never land; nothingness, nothing, *Fr. néant,* nihility; nonexistence, inexistence, immateriality, nonsubsistence; abeyance, *Inf.* shelf, suspension, dormancy.

2. forgetfulness, obliviousness, Lethe, nirvana, blankness, thoughtlessness, quietism; amnesia, blackout, fugue, unconsciousness; absence, insensibility, senselessness, stupor, coma.

3. unmindfulness, absent-mindedness, unthinkingness; heedlessness, unawareness, carelessness, inconsideration, regardlessness, disregardfulness, unsolicitude.

oblivious, *adj.* **1.** forgetful, absent-minded, Lethean, amnesic, amnestic; thoughtless, thoughtfree, nirvanic, quietistic; sublimated, suppressed, repressed, blocked out; faraway, elsewhere, in nowhere land, somewhere else; unconscious, insensible, out, dead, asleep, dead to the world; absorbed, abstracted, rapt, lost, engrossed, pensive, meditative; preoccupied, mused, daydreaming, dreaming, napping; stargazing, wool gathering, in the clouds, on cloud nine, castle-building.

2. unmindful, unaware, heedless, blind, unobservant, careless; inattentive, inadvertent, disregardful, regardless, distracted.

oblong, *adj.* elongated, ellipitical, ellipsoidal; oval, ovate, ovoid. egg-shaped; rectangular.

obloquy, *n.* **1.** discredit, disrepute, disfavor, disesteem, loss of face, downfall, fall; detraction, derogation, degradation, devaluation, depreciation, disparagement, belittlement, deprecation; shame, disgrace, dishonor, scandal, ignominy, infamy, odium, opprobrium, debasement, vitiation, turpitude, ill repute, bad repute; humiliation, humble pie, mortification.

2. (*all usu. public*) censure, disapproval, disapprobation, reprobation, reprehension, objection; criticism, animadversion, *Inf.* brickbat; fulmination, denunciation, condemnation; execration, curse, malediction, imprecation, railing, invective, commination, *Archaic.* exprobation; tirade, philippic, diatribe; aspersion, defamation, denigration, vilification, revilement, traducement; slander, libel, calumny, calumniation, abuse, injury.

3. (*all usu. public*) reproof, reproach, rebuke, reprimand, stricture; upbraiding, castigation, objurgation, vituperation; scolding, dressing down, tongue-lashing, *Sl.* hell.

4. (*all usu. public*) blame, accusation, accusal, charge; imputation, incrimination, crimination, inculpation.

obnoxious, *adj.* **1.** offensive, disgusting, noisome, revolting, obscene, deplorable, objectionable; noxious, rank, foul, vile, fulsome, noisome; distasteful, nauseating, nauseous, unpalatable, unsavory, gross, unpleasant, disagreeable; odious, abhorrent, abominable, execrable, detestable, heinous, loathsome, hateful; despicable, scurvy, base.

2. annoying, unbearable, intolerable, unendurable, insufferable, *Scot.* randy.

3. subject, exposed, vulnerable, susceptible, pregnable, open, liable.

obscene, *adj.* **1.** indecent, broad, immodest, shameless, indelicate, indecorous, inelegant; vulgar, gross, risqué, suggestive, off-color, *Inf.* blue; outrageous, sensational, lurid, scandalous, shocking; abusive, ribald, scurrilous, blackguardly, thersitical, profane, foulmouthed, Fescennine, *Obs.* blackguard, *Archaic.* scurrile.

2. lewd, salacious, pornographic, vile, foul, filthy, dirty, smutty, nasty, scatologic, scatological, *Sl.* raunchy; lecherous, lubricous, goatish, lustful, ruttish, libidinous, concupiscent, sexy, erotic, carnal, sensual, *Archaic.* lickerish; licentious, lascivious, prurient, Cyprian, wanton, loose, libertine, promiscuous, Paphian, unchaste; immoral, degenerate, dissolute, dissipated, debauched, rakish, profligate, depraved, perverted.

3. abominable, atrocious, aversive, repugnant, repulsive, revolting, repellent, off-putting; obnoxious, noisome, fulsome, offensive, disgusting, rank, objectionable, insufferable, intolerable; nauseating, nauseous, sickening, distasteful, unpalatable, unsavory, unappetizing, insipid; disagreeable, unpleasant, unlikable, *Brit. Inf.* beastly.

obscenity, *n.* **1.** indecency, vulgarity, vulgarness, salaciousness, vileness, foulness, obsceneness; filthiness, nastiness, *Sl.* raunchiness; lecherousness, lubricity, lustfulness, bawdiness, libidinousness, concupiscence, carnality, carnalness; licentiousness, lasciviousness, wantonness, looseness, promiscuousness; immorality, dissoluteness, dissipation, rakishness, shamelessness.

2. indelicacy, immodesty, impropriety, improperness, inappropriateness, unsuitability, unsuitableness, unacceptability, unseemliness, tawdriness; grossness, rankness, repulsiveness, repulsivity, offensiveness, suggestivity; abusiveness, scurrilousness, blackguardism, profaneness.

3. salacity, pornography, vulgarism, filth, dirt, smut; scurrility, ribaldry, billingsgate, profanity, double entendre, *Archaic.* bawdry; curse word, swearword, oath, dirty word, four-letter word, *U.S. Inf.* cuss.

obscurantism, *n.* mystification, evasion of clarity, confusion, complication, *Inf.* mumbo jumbo; vagueness, unclearness, unclarity, fuzziness, blurriness, obfuscation, obscurity; ambiguity, ambiguousness, equivocalness, amphibology, indefiniteness, incertitude; abstruseness, reconditeness, obscureness.

obscure, *adj.* **1.** vague, unclear, indefinite, uncertain, doubtful, dubious; abstruse, recondite, arcane; ambiguous, equivocal, cryptic, enigmatic; unfathomable, impenetrable, incomprehensible, mysterious, perplexing, puzzling, confusing, confused.

2. inconspicuous, unnoticeable, insignificant, undistinguished; unknown, unheard of, unhonored, unsung, inglorious, nameless, unnoted, unrenowned; hidden, remote, retired, secluded, unnoticed, out-of-the-way.

3. faint, vague, imperceptible, indiscernible; undefined, indistinct, hazy, blurred, fuzzy, bleared, veiled.

4. dark, black, overcast, lightless, gloomy; murky, shadowy, somber, cloudy, dim, dusky, *Literary.* darkling, lowering, funereal; misty, foggy, smoky, filmy, starless, moonless, sunless, unilluminated, unlighted; tenebrous, *Archaic.* caliginous.

—*v.* **5.** obfuscate, muddy, conceal, hide, disguise, veil, make abstruse; confuse, baffle, mystify, perplex, bewilder.

6. make dim, bedim, cloud, becloud, begloom, benight, fog, befog; darken, blacken, blur, dull, dim; overcast, overcloud, overshadow, shadow, mask, curtain, cloak, shroud; eclipse, adumbrate.

obscurity, *n.* **1.** vagueness, indefiniteness, uncertainty, doubtfulness, dubiousness; abstruseness, reconditeness, profoundness; ambiguity, equivocation, obfuscation; incomprehensibility, impenetrableness, confusion.

2. inconspicuousness, unobtrusiveness, nonrecognition, namelessness, ingloriousness; insignificance, unimportance, nullity, paltriness, pettiness, worthlessness.

3. darkness, dimness, lightlessness; gloominess,

murkiness, somberness, cloudiness, mistiness, fogginess, smokiness, filminess; starlessness, moonlessness, sunlessness; indistinctness, nebulousness, faintness, vagueness; haziness, blurredness, fuzziness.

obsequious, *adj.* **1.** submissive, docile, unassertive, compliant, deferential, tractable, mealy-mouthed, *Obs.* obsequent; servile, subservient, menial, slavish, toadyish, *Obs., Rare.* vernile; prostrate, obeisant, on one's knees.

2. groveling, crawling, crouching, slithering; squirming, cringing, cowering; whining, whimpering, sniveling.

3. sycophantic *or* sycophantical *or* sycophantish, fawning, flattering, toadying, truckling, ingratiating, honey-mouthed, unctuous, *Sl.* bootlicking, *Sl.* footlicking, *Sl.* brown-nosing.

obsequy, *n.* *Usu.* **obsequies** funeral rites, funeral ceremony *or* service, last offices *or* honors, funeral oration, eulogy, final tribute; wake, deathwatch, vigil; burial, burial service, entombment, graveside service; exequies, funeral procession, dead march, cortege, *Brit.* last post; requiem, requiem mass, memorial service, month's mind mass.

observable, *adj.* **1.** noticeable, evident, obvious, apparent, manifest, patent, visible, seeable; plain, revealed, in plain view *or* sight, unhidden, unconcealed, disclosed; distinct, perceivable, clear, well-defined, well-marked, tangible, explicit, unmistakable, easy to see, plain to see, recognizable.

2. memorable, notable, noteworthy, worthy of note *or* recognition *or* celebration, special, significant, of weight *or* moment, never to be forgotten, red-letter.

observance, *n.* **1.** observation, looking, viewing, witnessing; examination, taking note, scrutiny, inspection, searching; apprehension, perception, discernment, descrying, espying, espial, reconnaissance, spying, lookout.

2. observing, seeing, watching, regarding; keeping, obedience, adherence, compliance, conformity, accordance; remarking, commending, celebrating; noticing, note, respect, regard, giving the devil his due; attention, heed, ear, consideration, thought, care; execution, discharge, fulfillment, carrying out *or* through, acquittal, performance, prosecution, enforcement.

3. orthodoxy, strictness, accordance, accord, correspondence, agreement; devoutness, devotion, devotedness, faithfulness, dutifulness, conformity, reverence.

4. rite, ritual, ceremonial, ceremony, solemnity; celebration, jubilee, holiday, festivity; anniversary, dedication, solemnization; commemoration, memorialization, memorial service; exercise, exercises, function, service, office, performance, duty; vigilance, watchfulness, vigil, watch.

5. custom, practice, habit, manner, form, formality, convention, usage, wont, consuetude; institution, tradition, ordinance, way, prevalence, customary course, fixed procedure, established way, time-honored practice, the custom of the country, folkway, common practice; proper thing, what is done, *Brit.* the drill; style, use, mode, fashion.

observant, *adj.* **1.** aware, regardful, mindful, interested, curious, intent, on the lookout, on the qui vive, on guard, wide-awake, alert, keen, sharp, *Inf.* heads-up, *Inf.* eyes-front, *Inf.* with one's eyes peeled, conscious, not missing a thing, *Inf.* on the ball *or* stick; attentive, heedful, advertent, paying attention, all eyes, quick on the trigger *or* the uptake; sensitive.

2. dutiful, duteous, meticulous, conscientious; scrupulous, nice, finicky, niggling; moral, ethical, obedient, compliant, conforming, law-abiding; orthodox, devout, devoted, loyal; practicing, active.

observation, *n.* **1.** observing, noticing, seeing, looking, watching, viewing, witnessing, eyeing; notice, note, consideration, heed, cognition, attentiveness, attention; inspection, regard, *Sl.* once-over; perceiving, perception, advertence, cognizance, awareness; espial, reconnaissance, espionage, spying, surveillance, *Inf.* stake-out; examination, visual examination, study, scrutiny, perusal, review, survey, overview, exploration; absorption, intentness, interest, concentration; staring, ogling.

2. observance, keeping, adherence, compliance, conformance.

3. comment, assertion, declaration, affirmation; commentary, description, account, illustration, depiction, sketch, report, statement; concept, sentiment, feeling, impression, reaction; expression of opinion *or* point of view, judgment, mind, opinion, say, thought, view, averment, position; consideration, reflection, idea, notion, conception; speculation, explanation, light, revelation, discovery, finding; detail, particular, note, mention; pronouncement, announcement, thinking, way of thinking, profession, declaration, *Inf.* one's two cents' worth; criticism, hint, animadversion, aspersion, derogation, *Inf.* crack, *Inf.* wisecrack; saying, word, utterance, expression, phrase, witticism, bright remark, sage comment, happy thought.

observatory, *n.* **1.** astronomical observatory, Orbiting Astronomical Observatory, OAO.

2. tower, watchtower, observation post, lookout *Naut.* crow's nest.

observe, *v.* **1.** see, look, eye, have in sight, set *or* lay eyes on, look on *or* upon, view, behold; witness, be a spectator, see with one's own eyes; sight, catch sight of, descry, get *or* catch a glimpse of, glimpse, pick out, spy, espy, *Inf.* spot, *Inf.* get a load of, *Inf.* clap eyes on; glance at, peek at, take a sidelong look; perceive, discover, detect, discern, find, cognize, take in, make out, distinguish; notice, note, mark, be aware of, be conscious of, take notice of, remark, pay attention to, heed, attend, mind.

2. regard, contemplate, consider, review, study, examine, investigate, inspect; scrutinize, pore over, peruse, explore, take a close *or* careful look; make *or* take an observation of, take note *or* cognizance of, *Inf.* take the measure of, *Inf.* take a long, hard look at, *Inf.* check, *Inf.* check out; take a look at, glance *or* look over, scan, cast an eye over, size up, take stock of, survey, see at a glance; stare at, gaze at, peer at, ogle, *Inf.* get an eyeful of, *Inf.* eyeball, *Inf.* give the once-over, *Brit. Sl.* deak, *Brit. Sl.* twig.

3. watch, keep an eye on, keep in sight *or* view, reconnoiter, keep under observation, spy upon, follow, monitor, *Inf.* keep tabs on; keep watch, be vigilant, see to, look sharp, be alert, pay attention, be watchful, be observant, keep one's eyes open, *Inf.* keep one's eyes peeled.

4. remark, utter, voice, state, say, put into words, comment, speak to, address, make mention of, refer to, make reference to, allude to; verbalize, articulate, enunciate, phrase, breathe; give tongue *or* voice to, vocalize, give utterance to; offer, suggest, present, come out with, exclaim, let fall *or* drop, break in with, interrupt, speak up, chime in with, interject; make known, announce, pronounce, aver, allege, assert, declare, proclaim; tell, impart, convey, put *or* set forth, express, give expression to, couch in terms, recite; muse, reflect, *Dial.* opine, express one's opinion, make a remark, fling off, *Inf.* get off a shot, *Sl.* get in a good one.

5. maintain, hold, hold with, respect, acknowledge, bow before *or* to, defer to, be resigned *or* submissive to; obey, follow, live up to, cling to, hold on to, be faithful to, adhere to, submit to, be guided *or* regulated by, go by; comply with, abide by, accede, acquiesce, *Inf.* toe the mark; conform to, fulfill, satisfy, meet; discharge, execute, perform, carry out, perform duly, *All Inf.* follow the beaten path, follow the rules, play the game, go by the book, stay in line, keep in step, not make waves.

6. celebrate, keep, honor, keep holy, dignify, recognize, respect, do honor to, commemorate, mark, remember, memorialize; solemnize, formalize, sanctify, hallow, consecrate; *Brit. Inf.* maffick, *Inf.* make a big deal over.

observer, *n.* spectator, onlooker, looker-on; witness, eyewitness, passerby, bystander, beholder, watcher, viewer, looker, seer, *Inf.* rubberneck, *Inf.* sidewalk superintendent; inspector, scrutinizer, examiner, perceiver, detector; reporter, auditor, commentator, evaluator; lookout, forward observer, fireguard, fire warden, forest ranger; spy, reconnoiter, *Inf.* inside man; sightseer, visitor, tourist, *Inf.* visiting fireman; gaper, goggler, ogler, *Inf.* drugstore cowboy.

obsess, *v.* (*all in reference to the mind, one's thoughts, etc.*) dominate, control, rule, monopolize; possess, grip, hold; preoccupy, occupy, be on one's mind, be uppermost in one's thoughts; haunt, haunt one's thoughts, run in the head, recur, weigh *or* prey on the mind; beset, bedevil, plague, trouble, worry, harass, harry, distress, hound, nag, vex, torment, torture; craze, madden, derange, dement, unbalance, unhinge, distract, drive one insane *or* crazy *or* mad; infatuate, bewitch, ensorcell, besot.

obsessed, *adj.* (*all in reference to the mind, one's thoughts, etc.*) dominated, controlled, ruled, monopolized; possessed, gripped, held, fixated, one-track, *Sl.* hung-up; preoccupied, prepossessed, caught up in, wrapped up in, absorbed in, lost in, immersed in; haunted, beset, bedeviled, plagued, troubled, worried, harassed, harried, distressed, hounded, nagged, vexed, tormented, tortured; crazed, maddened, deranged, demented, unbalanced, unhinged, distracted; infatuated, bewitched, besotted.

obsession, *n.* **1.** (*all in reference to the mind, one's thoughts, etc.*) domination, control, mastery; monopolization, possession, preoccupation, prepossession; bedevilment, bewitchment, enchantment, ensorcellment, spirit control.

2. fixation, fixed conviction, fixed idea, *Fr. idée fixe,* monomania, ruling passion, one-track mind, bee in one's bonnet; complex, phobia, tic, quirk, ax to grind, chip on one's shoulder, *Sl.* craze, mania, passion; compulsion, irresistible impulse, morbid drive; infatuation, fancy, crotchet, *Archaic.* maggot; phantom, illusion, delusion, halluncination.

obsolescent, *adj.* on the way out, passing out of use, disappearing, fading, waning, on the wane, dying.

obsolete, *adj.* **1.** disused, abandoned, discontinued, discarded, cast aside; dead, defunct, expired, extinct, wound up; retired, pensioned off, put away, laid on the shelf, neglected, gone to seed.

2. outmoded, antiquated, superannuated, outdated; passé, dated, out-of-date, *Inf.* has-been, *Inf.* old hat, *Inf.* back number; out, out of fashion, old-fashioned, unfashionable, out of style, behind the times; old, antique, archaic, ancient, primitive, aged; timeworn, moss-grown, outworn, worn-out, worn, past use, past one's prime, having seen better days.

—*v.* **3.** antiquate, superannuate, make redundant.

obstacle, *n.* barrier, barricade, obstruction, blockade; stop, stay, impediment, hindrance, check, deterrent, hurdle, stumbling block, block; snag, catch, drawback, liability, hitch, rub, small *or* little problem, fly in the ointment; dead end, stone wall, brick wall, impasse; blind alley, cul-de-sac; congestion, jam, blockage, stoppage.

obstetrics, *n.* tocology; midwifery.

obstinacy, *n.* **1.** inflexibility, immovability, stiffneckedness, *Inf.* hard-coreness; inexorableness, implacability, intransigence, intractability, unyieldingness; unmalleability, unpersuadability, uninfluenceability, unswayability, unpliability.

2. stubbornness, mulishness, muleheadedness, pigheadedness, bullheadedness, bullishness, headstrongness; willfulness, contrariness, perverseness, wrongheadedness, balkiness, uncooperativeness, frowardness, refractoriness, recalcitrance, contumacy, contumaciousness, *U.S. Inf.* notionateness, *Inf.* cussedness, *Archaic.* untowardness; ungovernability, unmanageability, uncontrollability, difficultness, restiveness, unruliness, waywardness, fractiousness, incorrigibleness.

3. persistence, perseverance, pertinacity, tenacity, tenaciousness, bulldog tenacity, bulldoggedness, doggedness, unrelentingness, single-mindedness, singleness of purpose; staying power, *Inf.* stick-to-it-iveness.

obstinate, *adj.* **1.** inflexible, immovable, not to be moved, adamant, adamantine, stiff-necked, set, set in one's ways, *Inf.* hard-core, *Inf.* hard-shell; inexorable, implacable, intransigent, intractable, uncompromising, unbending, unwavering, unyielding; unmalleable, unpersuadable, uninfluenceable, unswayable, unpliable; persistent, persevering, pertinacious, tenacious, dogged, bulldogged, relentless, unrelenting, singleminded.

2. stubborn, stubborn as a mule, mulish, muleheaded, pigheaded, bullheaded, bullish, headstrong; willful, self-willed, contrary, perverse, wrong-headed, cross-grained, balky, uncooperative, froward, refractory, recalcitrant, contumacious, *U.S. Inf.* notionate, *Inf.* cussed, *Archaic.* untoward; ungovernable, unmanageable, uncontrollable, difficult, restive, unruly, wayward, fractious, incorrigible.

obstreperous, *adj.* **1.** restive, unruly, disorderly, out of order, out of hand, rowdy, brawly; rambunctious, rampageous, roisterous, rip-roaring, wild, tumultuous, *Brit. Inf.* mafficking; uncontrolled, unrestrained, ungoverned, unbridled; refractory, recalcitrant, defiant, contumacious, fractious, *Inf.* ornery.

2. noisy, loud, rackety; clamorous, clamant, blatant, clangorous, vociferous, boisterous, riotous, uproarious, tempestuous; deafening, ear-splitting, ear-piercing, ear-rending.

obstruct, *v.* **1.** block, barricade, plug up, dam up, clog, oppiliate; choke off, shut off, foreclose, ban, debar; stop, prohibit, forbid, preclude, prevent; arrest, check, halt, abort, bring to a standstill.

2. hinder, hamper, impede, interfere, interrupt, intervene; frustrate, thwart, balk, deter; limit, circumscribe; suppress, inhibit, restrain, cramp, slow, retard; delay, stay, stall, suspend; curb, brake, rein, harness, bridle, control; throttle, muzzle, gag, smother; hamstring, bind, shackle, trammel, fetter, encumber, tie hand an foot.

obstruction, *n.* obstacle, impediment, hindrance, oppilation, *Archaic.* remora; barrier, stop, stopper, block, *Med.* obstruent, stumbling block, roadblock, barricade; curb, check, balk, catch, hitch, snag, difficulty, bottleneck; restriction, limitation, constraint; trammel, bridle; forbiddance, prohibition, interdiction, injunction, proscription, preclusion, ban, embargo, veto, taboo.

obtain, *v.* **1.** get, acquire, procure, secure, gain, come by, *Sl.* cop; take possession of, get one's hands on, get a hold of; capture, seize, grasp, net, bag; reap, harvest, garner, gather, glean; buy, purchase, pick up, *Scot. Archaic.* coff; reach, attain, achieve, win.

2. prevail, be prevalent; exist, be, stand, be in force;

reign. rule, have sway; be customary, be in vogue.

obtrude, *v.* **1.** impose upon, push oneself on [s.o.], push [s.t.] on [s.o.], thrust [s.t.] forward; thrust forth, push out, stick out.

2. intrude, walk in *or* into, burst in *or* into, *Inf.* barge in *or* into, break in *or* into, interrupt, *Sl.* butt in, *U.S. Sl.* horn in, force *or* push one's way in; pry, poke *or* stick one's nose into, nose into, meddle; interfere, get in the way, interfere, interpose, intercede.

obtrusive, *adj.* **1.** prominent, conspicuous, obvious, unmistakable, evident, clear, apparent, patent; overt, open, manifest, undisguised, bald, bald-faced; sheer, utter, unqualified, outright, out-and-out, absolute, unmitigated; blatant, flagrant, extreme, gross, outrageous, egregious, notorious; bold, audacious, impudent, brazen, flaunting, shameless; arrant, downright, thorough, hard-core.

2. protruding, protuberant, protrusive, projecting, beetle, beetling, overhanging; jutting out, sticking out, hanging out *or* down, showing.

obtund, *v.* blunt, dull, take the edge off; moderate, modulate, soften, tone down, muffle, mute; deaden, numb, benumb, stupefy, anesthetize.

obtuse, *adj.* **1.** blunt, rounded, smooth, unpointed, unedged.

2. phlegmatic, sluggish, slow, torpid; dormant, stagnant, inactive, inert, passive; hebetudinous, lethargic, languid, listless; torporific, droopy, spiritless, leaden, heavy, vapid.

3. insensitive, insentient, imperceptive, impercipient, insensible, undiscerning; unfeeling, cold, cool, withdrawn; thick-skinned, callous, uncaring, unsympathetic; passionless, heartless, unemotional; stolid, impassive, unmoved, numb, apathetic; unobservant, inattentive, unconscious, unaware, blind, unseeing; uninterested, heedless, indifferent, unresponsive.

4. stupid, insensate, witless, irrational, *Inf.* dumb, dull, dull-witted; unintelligent, thick, dense, thickheaded, fatheaded, blockheaded, *Sl.* pinheaded, *Sl.* birdbrained, *Sl.* peabrained; vacuous, empty-headed, inane, brainless, foolish, *Inf.* dopey, not having the brains one was born with; slow-witted, dim-witted, backward, retarded, mentally retarded, simple-minded, simple; bovine, cloddish, doltish, boorish, oafish, lumpish, lubberly, loutish; ignorant, crass, Boeotian, gross; not having much upstairs, mutton-headed, *Sl.* goony, *Sl.* schmucky; out of it, out in left field, in the ozone, in orbit; moronic, boneheaded, dunderheaded, thick-skulled, wooden-headed.

obverse, *n.* principal surface, face, top, head, front, façade; counterpart, complement, supplement.

obviate, *v.* preclude, forestall, prevent, hinder, avert, *Archaic.* forfend; intercept, obstruct; avoid, ward off, stave off, fend off, divert; rid, *Sl.* ditch.

obvious, *adj.* understandable, recognizable, discernible, palpable; clear, clear-cut, clear as crystal; plain, visible, distinct, patent, bald-faced, bald, as plain as the nose on one's face; open, overt, unconcealed; standing to reason, apparent, ostensible, evident, manifest; conspicuous, sticking out like a sore thumb, notable, pronounced, glaring, like a red flag, prominent; explicit, spelled-out.

occasion, *n.* **1.** time, instance, case; juncture, point, place, spot, position, setting; circumstance, condition, situation; conjuncture, set of circumstances *or* affairs.

2. occurrence, incident, episode, experience, adventure, event; affair, function, happening, *Archaic.* hap; observance, commemoration, service; celebration, party, get-together; gala, show, big *or* major production, big *or* major deal *or* thing.

3. opportunity, opportune *or* suitable time *or* place, season, stage, right set of circumstances, contingency; chance, opening, golden opportunity, once-in-a-lifetime chance, turn, *Inf.* shot, *Sl.* crack.

4. reason, reason why, why and wherefore, the why, the wherefore, *Inf.* the what for, rationale, explanation, excuse, basis, ground, justification, warrant; motive, motivation, inspiration, inducement, incentive, incitement, stimulus, impulse, provocation; cause, determinant, determining factor, origin, source, root, fountainhead, mainspring, derivation.

5. on occasion, now and then, once in a while, sometimes. See **occasionally.**

—*v.* **6.** give an opportunity *or* chance *or* opening for, call for, demand, raise a need for, make necessary; motivate, prompt, bring about, bring on, induce, bring forth *or* out, bring to pass, elicit, give rise to, effect, cause, provoke; generate, breed, engender, beget, give birth to, produce, make, create; start, originate, begin, set up, establish, build.

occasional, *adj.* **1.** chance, irregular, intermittent, periodic; random, sporadic, fitful, erratic; infrequent, unfrequent, unhabitual, uncustomary, uncommon, unusual, unwonted, exceptional; rare, seldom seen *or* met, seldom, scarce.

2. supplementary, supplemental, auxiliary, accessory, additional, added, annexed, multipurpose; extra, spare, surplus, nonessential, extraneous; provisional, part-time, temporary, non-permanent; incidental, odd, casual, scattered *or* sprinkled here and there *or* about, spread around.

3. purposive, special, prepared for the occasion *or* event; commissioned, solicited, requested, asked for; commemorative, memorial, in honor of [s.o.]; holiday, ceremonial, festive, celebratory; inspirational, inspired, extemporaneous, extemporary, extempore, impromptu, *Sl.* made, off the cuff.

4. causative, causal, effecting, effectuating, eliciting; motivating, influential, prompting, provocative, impelling, impulsive, propulsive, driving; germinal, seminal, beginning, starting.

occasionally, *adv.* at time, from time to time, now and then, every now and then, every now and again, now and again, on occasion, here and there, once in a while, sometimes, *Rare.* sometime; when one has a chance, when one feels like it, when one is up to it *or* gets to it; periodically, at intervals, intermittently, off and on, sporadically, irregularly, by *or* in snatches *or* fits and starts; infrequently, rarely, seldom, once in a blue moon *or* a coon's age, hardly ever.

occlude, *v.* close, shut, seal; shut off, close off, stop; stop up, plug up, cork, oppilate, dam up; fill, choke, clog, block, obstruct, *Mach.* throttle; bar, barricade, impede, trammel, *Law.* estop; shut in, enclose, hedge in, hem in; prohibit, prevent, foreclose, shut out, debar.

occult, *adj.* **1.** mysterious, arcane, inexplicable, unexplainable, inexplainable, unaccountable, insoluble, insolvable, unsolvable, *Obs.* inextricable; puzzling, enigmatic, baffling, bewildering, confounding, perplexing, mystifying; impenetrable, incomprehensible, inapprehensible, past *or* beyond comprehension *or* understanding, unknowable, incognizable, incognoscible, inscrutable, unfathomable, indecipherable, undecipherable, undiscoverable; transcendental, mystical, mystic, supernatural, preternatural.

2. secret, cryptic, perdu, private; concealed, hidden, veiled, shrouded, enshrouded; obscure, obscured, dim, vague, shadowy, cloudy, nebulous.

—*n.* **3.** occultism, cabalism, mysticism, esoterism, esotericism, esotery, hermetics, hermeticism; supernaturalism, transcendentalism.

4. the supernatural, the supersensible; mystery, puzzle, enigma, question, question mark; secret, cabala, esoterica, arcanum, closed *or* sealed book; unknowable, deep *or* profound mystery, mystery of mysteries.

--v. **5.** cover, cover up, conceal, hide, veil, mask, screen; eclipse, block; cloud, obscure; shroud, enshroud.

occultism, *n.* cabalism, mysticism, esotericism, esoterism, esotery, hermeticism, hermetics; supernaturalism, transcendentalism; theosophy; spiritualism, mediumism; magic, black magic, sorcery, witchcraft, diabolism.

occupancy, *n.* **1.** tenancy, tenure, residence, residency, residing, abiding, living, dwelling, *Law.* commorancy, occupation, occupying; settlement, settling, inhabitance, inhabitancy, inhabitation, habitation, habitancy, moving in; domiciliation, lodging, lodgment, billeting, quartering, locating; taking up residence, taking up one's abode, making one's home, establishing oneself, *Inf.* hanging up one's hat.

2. possession, possessorship, proprietorship, ownership; retention, holding.

occupant, *n.* **1.** tenant, renter, lessee, leaseholder; resident, permanent resident, resider, residencer, residentiary; inhabitant, *Archaic.* inhabiter, habitant, dweller, denizen, householder, addressee, occupier; indweller, incumbent, inmate; lodger, boarder, roomer, paying guest, *Sl.* crasher.

2. settler, homesteader, colonist, squatter, cottager, cottier, *Scot.* cotter; villager, townsman, burgher, burgess, oppidan, citizen.

occupation, *n.* **1.** business, employment, employ, job, work, living, livelihood; profession, career, lifework, vocation, calling; métier, trade, craft, skill; field, line, province, area, walk of life, station, situation, post, position; appointment, berth, billet, assignment, commission, charge, mission, duty, task, undertaking; stint, errand, chore, drudgery.

2. activity, enterprise, pursuit, avocation, hobby, *Sl.* bag, *Sl.* thing; pastime, amusement, diversion, preoccupation.

3. tenancy, residency, habitation, possession, occupancy. See **occupancy** (*def.* **1**).

4. foreign rule, colonial rule, imperial rule; (*all of foreign territory*) seizure, takeover, conquest, overthrow, defeat; possession, control, subjection, subordination, subjugation, oppression, bondage.

occupational, *adj.* professional, vocational, career, workday, workaday, industrial; official, business.

occupy, *v.* **1.** fill, fill up, permeate, pervade, cover, take up.

2. engage, employ, use, busy; interest, beguile, arrest, absorb, engross, preoccupy, concern, be on one's mind, absorb one's thoughts; entertain, divert, amuse; hold, secure, tie up, tie down, take up one's time, monopolize.

3. (*all of military invasions*) capture, seize, take by force, take over, overthrow, conquer, defeat; rule, control, dominate, subjugate, subject, oppress, hold in thrall, hold in bondage.

4. dwell in, reside, inhabit, tenant, live in; establish oneself, move into, take up residence, take up one's abode, settle, settle down, locate, ensconce, make one's home, *Inf.* hang up one's hat.

occur, *v.* **1.** happen, take place, transpire, come to pass, come about, come, *Archaic.* hap, *Inf.* come off, befall, supervene, betide, chance, *Archaic.* bechance, *Archaic.* arrive; result, ensue, follow, eventuate, turn out.

2. intervene, come up, present itself, show itself, show up, turn up, be found; arise, spring up, come into being, issue, proceed, come forth, emerge; appear, materialize, become manifest, become visible.

3. suggest itself to, come to, strike, hit; come to mind, come into one's head, enter one's head, cross one's mind.

occurrence, *n.* happening, event, episode, incident, occasion; incidence, circumstance, fact, phenomenon; affair, case, matter; action, proceeding, doing, deed; accident, *Archaic.* hap, chance, happenstance; casualty, mishap; adventure, venture, experience.

ocean, *n.* **1.** sea, Neptune, Poseidon, deep blue sea, brine, *Inf.* briny, *Inf.* the drink, *Archaic.* flood, *Chiefly Literary.* the deep; hydrospace, Davy Jones's locker; open ocean, high sea, *Literary.* the bounding main.

2. multitude, abundance, profusion, flood, *Inf.* a lot, *Inf.* raft; ton, mountain, pile, heap, stack, load, slew, mint, million, trillion, *Inf.* zillion; *Inf.* lots, *Inf.* oodles, *Sl.* scads, *Inf.* gobs.

oceanic, *adj.* **1.** pelagic, thalassic, marine, maritime, aquatic, saltwater, sea, Neptunian; bathyal, bathypelagic.

2. large, huge, big, vast, enormous, extensive, expansive; unlimited, limitless, unbounded, boundless, infinite, interminable, unending, endless.

ocular, *adj.* visual, optical, ophthalmic.

oculist, *n.* ophthalmologist, eye doctor, eye specialist; (*loosely*) optometrist.

odd, *adj.* **1.** unconventional, uncommon, unusual, unique, unorthodox, uncustomary, unwonted, rare, out of the ordinary; atypical, singular, original, exceptional, individual, lone, sole, solitary; unexampled, unparalleled, unprecedented, unfamiliar, uncomfortable; extraordinary, egregious, astonishing; deviant, deviate, aberrant, anomalous, anomalistic, abnormal, irregular.

2. peculiar, curious, queer, offbeat, oddish, quizzical, cranky, *Inf.* funny, *Inf.* kinky, *Inf.* off-center, incongruous; quaint, eccentric, idiosyncratic, droll, comical, laughable, *Inf.* quirky, flaky, *Sl.* wacky, *Sl.* squirrely, *Sl.* buggy, *Sl.* balmy *Sl.* off the wall, *Chiefly Brit.* barmy; strange, weird, bizarre, erratic, freakish, grotesque, *Sl.* rum, *Sl.* far out; fanciful, whimsical, notional, crotchety, maggoty, capricious, fickle, waggish.

3. fantastic, incredible, inconceivable; exotic, fey, supernatural, preternatural, out of this world; ridiculous, ludicrous, absurd, preposterous, outlandish, extravagant; nondescript, amorphous, indescribable, unclassifiable.

4. remote, removed, secluded, withdrawn, reclusive, private, sequestered, out-of-the-way, hidden, covert, closed, way out, shut away; isolated, solitary, solitudinous, lonely, lonesome, unfrequented; backwoods, *Sl.* out in the sticks, *Sl.* out in the boondocks *or* boonies.

5. (*all of a pair*) lone, single, sole, solitary, remaining one, without a mate, mateless; (*all of a pair*) unlike, unalike, disparate, different, divergent, diverse, irregular, unequal, unmatched, ill-matched, not matching, *Obs.* disquiparant.

6. remaining, remanent, surplus, superfluous, spare, left, leftover, left-behind, unused, unemployed; unneeded, unrequired; (*all of food*) uneaten, unconsumed.

7. casual, occasional, temporary, part-time; substitute, auxiliary, additional, supplementary, supplemental, subsidiary, fill-in, stand-in.

8. random, offhand, haphazard, indeterminate, indiscriminate, chance, fortuitous, orderless, sporadic; stray, straggling, irregular.

oddball, *n.* *Slang.* **1.** character, eccentric, card, original, pip, sport, exception, individual. See **oddity** (*def.* **1**).

—*adj.* **2.** eccentric, unconventional, uncommon, unusual, unorthordox, uncustomary, out of the ordinary; atypical, original, singular; peculiar, curious, queer, odd. See **eccentric** (*defs.* **1-3**).

oddity, *n.* **1.** curiosity, rarity; card, character, case, sport, original, pip, eccentric, exception, individual; flake, freak, crackpot, rare bird, queer duck, queer potato; *All Sl.* weirdo, weirdy, creep, oddball, nut, loony, looner, screwball; nonconformist, deviator, *Chiefly Brit.* punk; misfit, maverick, dropout, loner, lone wolf, solitary, fish out of water, square peg in a round hole.

2. oddness, strangeness, queerness, bizarreness, curiousness, quirkiness, incongruousness; uncommonness, uncommonality, unconventionality, unusualness, uniqueness, exception, singularity, singularness, individuality, individualness, distinctiveness; monstrousness, unnaturalness, freakishness; whimsicality, capriciousness, fancifulness, waggishness.

3. peculiarity, idiosyncrasy, idiocrasy, eccentricity, mannerism, quirk, twist, kink, twitch, tic, idiasm, hobby-horse; quip, crotchet, whim, caprice, flight of fancy; aberration, aberrance, aberrancy, deviation, anomaly, *Rare.* anomalism.

oddment, *n.* **1.** knickknack, notion, sundry, curio, gewgaw, bric-a-brac, novelty; keepsake, souvenir, memento, remembrance, reminder, relic, memorabilia, token.

2. scrap, remnant, leaving, paring, chip, snip, discard, sliver, chunk, shred, crumb, leftover; piece, tag, snatch, snippet, bit, fragment, gobbet, patch, modicum.

3. *All Print.* frontispiece, title page, table of contents, list of acknowledgements, list of abbreviations, pronounciation table *or* key *or* guide, glossary, notes, bibliography, addendum, addenda, appendix, appendices.

odds, *n.* **1.** probability, likelihood, chances.

2. advantage, lead, edge, handicap; superiority, supremacy, preeminence, ascendancy, predominance; inferiority, disadvantage, deficiency, inadequacy.

3. difference, disparity, unevenness, inequality; variation, discrepancy, irregularity.

4. at odds at variance, at sixes and sevens, at loggerheads, at cross purposes; in disagreement, not in keeping with, out of line with, in opposition to, different from, counter to; differing, diverging, deviating, unharmonious; disagreeing, clashing, conflicting, colliding.

5. by all odds in every respect, undoubtedly, anyway you look at it, by far, by a long shot, by any stretch of the imagination; unquestionably, indubitably, definitely, unequivocally.

odds and ends, *n.* bits, particles, fragments, gobbets, modicums, specks, morsels, flakes, crumbs, chunks; tags, patches, snatches, scantlings; remnants, leftovers, scraps; cuttings, shavings, slivers, chips, parings, pieces, snips, snippets, shreds, splinters.

ode, *n.* poem, lyric poem, lyric, lay, *Archaic.* fit; ecologue, pastoral poem; ballad, song, folk song, broadside, ditty, carol; serenade, love song, blues song; epicedium, funeral song, dirge; elegy, encomium, panegyric.

odious, *adj.* **1.** abhorrent, abominable, execrable, loathsome, detestable, heinous; scornful, contemptible, disdainful, despicable, ignominious; invidious, hateful, antipathetical: dislikable, unlikable.

2. repugnant, disgusting, aversive, rank, putrid, putrescent, foul; distasteful, nauseating, nauseous, sickening, unpalatable, obnoxious; revolting, repellent, offensive, objectionable, annoying; unendurable, unbearable, intolerable, insufferable: horrible, hideous, ugly; ignoble, abject, low; unpleasant, *Brit. Inf.* beastly.

3. reproachful, opprobrious; infamous, disreputable, dishonorable; disgraceful, obloquial, inglorious, shameful; degraded, debased, defiled.

odium, *n.* **1.** abhorrence, abomination, execration, loathing, detestation; misanthropy, misogyny; scorn, contempt, disdain, despite; acrimony, virulence, rancor, bitterness, resentment, spleen, grudge, bile; aversion, hostility, anitpathy, enmity, inimicalness; animosity, animus, malignity, malevolence, ill will; repugnance, revulsion, repulsion, disgust, distaste; hatred, hate, dislike, disrelish, disfavor, disesteem, displeasure, disaffection.

2. reproach, opprobrium; infamy, disrepute, dishonor, disgrace, ignominy, obloquy; ingloriousness, humiliation, shame; degradation, debasement, defilement.

odor, *n.* **1.** smell, scent; aroma, fragrance, perfume, redolence, odoriferousness; bouquet, savor, trail, trace, breath; stink, stench, fetor.

2. character, quality, air, atmosphere, aura, exhalation, emanation, essence, spirit; flavor, complexion, tone.

odoriferous, *adj.* aromatic, fragrant, sweet-smelling, sweet-scented, scented, essenced, perfumed, balmy, redolent, odorous; spicy, savory, pungent, piquant, ambrosial.

of, *prep.* from, belonging to, coming from, hailing from; by, produced by; about, in reference to, in respect to, concerning; made of, consisting of, formed of; on the part of.

off, *adv.* **1.** away, out, aside, at a distance, distantly.

—*prep.* **2.** from, away from, out of, out.

—*adj.* **3.** wrong, incorrect, inaccurate, mistaken, in error; misguided, misled; barking up the wrong tree, off base.

4. abnormal, *Sl.* dotty, *Inf.* nutty, *Sl.* flaky, *Sl.* dippy, *Sl.* oddball; offbeat, unconventional, peculiar, eccentric, strange.

5. substandard, subnormal, inferior, not up to par *or* snuff, irregular.

6. (*of time*) leisure, non-working, idle, vacation, free, open, unscheduled, discretionary.

7. more distant, farther, further; outlying, faraway, far.

8. get off on enjoy, take pleasure in, take satisfaction in; rejoice in, revel in, *Sl.* groove on; feast on, savor, appreciate, *Inf.* smack one's lips over, eat up; have a good time, *Inf.* have a ball, *Inf.* get a bang *or* kick *or* boot out of.

offal, *n.* **1.** guts, innards, liver and lights, entrails, gizzards; carrion, putrefying flesh, remains, carcasses.

2. refuse, rubbish, trash, junk, chaff, *Yiddish.* chozzerai; garbage, waste, dross, mess, *Sl.* crap, *Sl.* dreck, slush; junk, litter, riffraff, flotsam and jetsam, odds and ends, remnants, scraps; leftovers, lees, sediment, dregs; sweepings, scourings, castoffs, castaways, rejects, discards; debris, detritus.

off-color, *adj.* **1.** risqué, indelicate, indecorous, inelegant; unseemly, improper, inappropriate, indiscreet; racy, salty, spicy, suggestive, broad, not fit for mixed company, unprintable, not for a family newspaper; earthy, *Sl.* raunchy, smutty, dirty, blue, offensive; obscene, indecent, pornographic, X-rated, scabrous.

2. unwell, out of sorts, washed-out, *Sl.* punk, peaked, run-down; poorly, draggy, aching, full of aches and pains, droopy, languid.

offend, *v.* **1.** affront, chagrin, insult, humiliate,

slight; pique, *Inf.* miff, disgruntle, *Inf.* put [s.o.] off, displease; vex, annoy, provoke, incense, exasperate, distress; fret, irk, rankle, roil, *Chiefly U.S.* rile, rattle, ruffle; irritate, aggravate, nettle, chafe, gall, disturb.
2. disgust, repel, repulse, *Sl.* gross [s.o.] out, *Sl.* turn [s.o.] off; nauseate, sicken.
3. violate, transgress, trespass, infringe upon, encroach upon, intrude upon, step on the toes of; sin, desecrate, profane, defile, debase.
4. injure, hurt, harm, smart, wound, damage; wrong, malign.
5. *All Biblical.* tempt, seduce, lead astray, entice, allure, sway.
6. sin, go astray, fall from grace, go to the devil; transgress, trespass; break the law, fault, commit a crime; err, make a mistake, go wrong, blunder, go to the dogs, slip up, lapse, trip; misbehave, *Rare.* misdemean.

offense, *n.* **1.** violation, infraction, breach, transgression, trespass, infringement; misdeed, wrongdoing, dereliction, slip, lapse, shortcoming, peccadillo; malefaction, sin, desecration, profaneness, blasphemy, sacrilege, peccancy.
2. crime, delinquency, breaking of the law, fault, *Law.* misdemeanor, *Law.* delict, *Law.* malfeasance.
3. atrocity, enormity, abhorrence, abomination, odium, outrage.
4. umbrage, resentment, pique, huff, *Inf.* miff; petulance, indignation, annoyance, tiff, displeasure; repugnance, disgust, repulsion, revulsion; aversion, disapprobation, opposition, alienation; antipathy, animosity, animus, enmity, hostility, hatred, detestation.
5. attack, assault, onslaught, bombardment, storming, (*of troops*) dragonnade, aggression, assailment, encounter; offensive, onset, push, thrust, charge, lunge, (*both of troops*) sortie, sally; invasion, incursion, raid, escalade.
6. attackers, aggressors, assailers, assailants, besiegers, raiders, invaders; opposition, enemy, foe.

offensive, *adj.* **1.** affronting, insulting, insolent, disrespectful, *Archaic.* affrontive; rude, discourteous, unmannerly, unmannered, uncivil, ungallant; irritating, aggravating, nettling, chafing, galling; unbearable, unendurable, intolerable, insufferable; off-putting, *Brit. Inf.* beastly, unpleasant, disagreeable; vexatious, annoying, provoking, provocative, incensing, exasperating, distressing, disturbing; irksome, fretting, rattling, ruffling, rankling.
2. noisome, nauseating, nauseous, *Med.* nauseant, sickening; fetid, rancid, sour, putrid, putrescent, graveolent, rotten, stinking, rank, four, mephitic; odorous, olid, *Obs.* olidous, stenchful, strong, whiffy; distasteful, unpalatable, unsavory.
3. repugnant, disgusting, obnoxious, shocking, nasty; repulsive, repelling, repellent, revolting, objectionable; fulsome, bilious, gross; abominable, odious, heinous, detestable.
4. attacking, on the attack, on the offense, on the move; assaulting, assailing, invading, invasive.
5. aggressive, combative, incursive, martial, warlike, *Archaic.* assailant, bellicose; truculent, belligerent, pugnacious, pushing; contentious, quarrelsome, antagonistic, hostile.
—n. **6.** aggressiveness, combativeness, bellicosity, bellicoseness; belligerence, pugnacity, pugnaciousness, pushiness; contentiousness, quarrelsomeness, antagonism, animus, enmity, hostility.
7. attack, assault, onslaught, aggression, assailment, offense, encounter; charge, onset, push, thrust; invasion, incursion, raid.

offer, *v.* **1.** tender, proffer, present, hold out, extend, put *or* place at [s.o's] disposal.
2. propose, pose, put forward, suggest, recommend, advance, propound; submit, set before, put to choice; move, make a motion.
3. volunteer, come *or* step forward, present *or* proffer oneself, offer one's services, be at [s.o.'s] service *or* disposal, not wait to be asked, need no invitation.
4. sacrifice, offer sacrifice, make sacrifice to, offer up, offer up an oblation.
5. put up for sale, put up, put on the market, put on the block, ask bids for, offer for sale, offer at a bargain.
6. bid, bid for, make a bid, make an offer, offer to buy.
—n. **7.** proposal, proposition, motion; advance, approach, overture; suggestion, submission; bid, offering; presentation, proffer.

offering, *n.* **1.** sacrifice, sacrificial lamb, oblation, immolation.
2. contribution, subscription, donation, donative; gift, present; alms, charity, dole, pittance, *Sl.* handout.

offertory, *n.* hymn, hymn-tune, psalm, chorale, motet, oratorio, canticle, anthem, doxology.

offhand, *adv.* **1.** impromptu, extemporaneously, extempore, improvisationally; without notes, without preparation, at the drop of a hat, on the spur of the moment.
2. informally, unceremoniously, without ceremony; nonchalantly, casually, easily, offhandedly; cursorily, perfunctorily, once over lightly, as a matter of form, for the sake of form.
3. curtly, abruptly, tersely, shortly, gruffly, brusquely, bluffly, bluntly, sharply, pointedly, *Inf.* snippily; cavalierly, haughtily, condescendingly, patronizingly.
—adj. **4.** impromptu, extemporaneous, extempore, improvised, unrehearsed, unprepared, spontaneous, ad-lib, *Inf.* off-the-cuff.
5. informal, unceremonious, casual; nonchalant, easy, easygoing, offhanded; blasé, indifferent, apathetic, unconcerned, uninterested; cursory, perfunctory, careless, hit-or-miss.

office, *n.* **1.** base, residence, location; region, province, territory, district, precinct; building, place, seat, spot, room.
2. position, post, appointment, commission, *Brit.* berth.
3. duty, function, obligation, business; responsibility, trust, charge, care.
4. assignment, chore, task, routine, job, work; requirement, burden, onus, devoir; mission, calling; part, role, bit.
5. **offices** word, referral, advocacy, backup; auspices, aegis; intercession, intermediation.

officer, *n.* **1.** military officer, naval *or* Navy *or* Army *or* Air Force *or* Marine Corps officer, commissioned officer, non-commissioned officer, NCO; general, admiral, flag officer, colonel, commander, commandant, major, captain, *Inf.* brass.
2. policeman, police officer, officer of the peace *or* law, lawman, law enforcer, deputy, authority, gendarme, *Chiefly Brit.* constable, *Inf.* cop, *Sl.* copper, *U.S. Sl.* gumshoe, *Sl.* flatfoot, *Sl.* bull; detective, FBI agent, G-man, *U.S. Sl.* dick, *U.S. Sl.* fuzz, *Sl.* narc; military policeman, MP.
3. skipper, ship's captain, master, *Inf.* old man; mate, first mate, ship's mate, helmsman, pilot, steersman.
4. officeholder, officerbearer, official, *Brit.* placeman, *Rare.* officiary, pooh bah; functionary, government *or* public official, bureaucrat, public *or* civil serv-

ant; minister, commissioner, secretary, commissary, (*in the U.S.S.R.*) commissar, governor, regent, dean; executive, administrator, corporate officer, VIP, big man, big shot, heavy, power broker, *Sl.* big cheese, *Sl.* big gun; leader, chief, head, principal, *Inf.* kingpin, *Inf.* number one, *Inf.* Mr. Big, *Sl.* top dog, *Sl.* top banana; director, manager, superintendent, overman, overseer, overlooker, boss, *Inf.* bossman, *Sl.* the man, *Sl.* head honcho, *Brit.* gaffer.

—v. **5.** command, direct, run the show, quarterback, *Inf.* call the plays *or* shots; rule, rule the roost, govern, control, be in control *or* charge of, have the upper hand; administer, manage, superintend, conduct, run, operate, engineer, orchestrate, carry out, regulate; steer, drive, pilot, navigate, hold the reins, be at the helm, be in the driver's seat *or* saddle.

official, *n.* **1.** officer. See **officer** (*def.* **4**).

—adj. **2.** authorized, duly authorized, rightful, lawful, legitimate, legal, licit, warranted, sanctioned, approved, allowed; certified, licensed, accredited, validated, authenticated; authentic, valid, genuine, real, bona fide, verified, documented, *Inf.* kosher; elected, duly elected *or* appointed *or* invested, ordained; recognized, accepted, established, canonical, orthodox.

3. authoritative, from the top, *Latin. ex cathedra, Sl.* from the horse's mouth; imperative, commanding, directive, ordered, prescribed.

4. (*of an activity or event*) formal, functional, observant, ceremonial, solemn, serious; routine, standard, regular, customary, conventional, ritual, ritualistic, set, fixed, exact, stiff, *Latin. pro forma;* stuffy, decorous, proper, seemly; ceremonious, pompous, elaborate, ornate.

officiate, *v.* **1.** perform *or* carry out the duties *or* functions, fulfill *or* discharge the responsibilities, exercise one's role, do the job; handle *or* transact business, look after *or* maintain affairs, carry on *or* forward; fill *or* serve in an office *or* a position, serve the government, work for the government; do one's duty, do duty, serve time.

2. preside over, moderate, emcee, head, head up, rule, occupy the throne, wear the crown; direct, conduct, run, be in charge of, lead, quarterback, *Inf.* call the plays *or* shots, make the decisions; manage, administrate, govern, control, regulate, supervise, superintend, oversee, boss; (*of a sports contest or game*) referee, umpire, judge, adjudicate, mediate; keep score *or* time.

officious, *adj.* **1.** meddlesome, meddling, intermeddling, interfering, intrusive, intruding, pragmatic; prying, inquisitive, busybody, *Inf.* nosy; obtrusive, forward, overbold, *Inf.* pushy; overkind, overzealous, overly solicitous; importunate, persistent, troublesome, annoying.

2. gratuitous, unwarranted, unwanted, unasked for, unnecessary.

offing, *n.* **1.** distance, background, horizon, skyline.

2. in the offing in the wings, near, close at hand; in the near future, in the foreseeable future.

offscouring, *n.* *Often* **offscourings** filth, dirt, dust, sweepings; refuse, *Dial.* culch, garbage, rubbish, waste, *Brit.* wastrel; dregs, grounds, sediment, settlings, lees, draff; remains, leavings, leftovers, scraps, orts, hogwash, swill; remainder, residue, residuum, scum.

offset, *n.* **1.** compensation, *Latin. quid pro quo,* recompense, repayment, reimbursement; satisfaction, damages, *Law.* solatium, indemnification, indemnity, recoupment; restitution, penalty, fine; requital, quittance, return, redress; atonement, amends, expiation, reparation, retribution.

2. antidote, counterbalance, counterweight, counterpoise, balance, check, countercheck; weight, stabilizer, equalizer, neutralizer, makeweight, ballast.

3. start, beginning, commencement, outset, onset, outbreak, dawn, conception, birth, genesis, exordium; opening, inauguration, *Inf.* ribbon-cutting, *Inf.* kick-off, *Inf.* jump-off, *Inf.* send-off, *Inf.* take-off, *Inf.* blast-off; rise, arising, beginnings, emergence, incipience, nascence, infancy.

4. offshoot, branch, stem, twig, shoot. See **offshoot** (*def.* **1**).

—adj. **5.** off-center, out of balance, out of alignment, to one side, out of line; at an angle, crooked, slanted, slanting, *Sl.* cockeyed, askew, awry.

—v. **6.** juxtapose, compare, collate, contrast, set side by side, oppose, set against, *Sl.* stack up.

7. compensate for, make up for, *Inf.* even things out, countervail, counterbalance, counterweigh, counterpoise; counteract, anitdote, neutralize, nullify, cancel *or* cancel out; balance, equalize, handicap, even, square, equate; adjust, adapt, accommodate, *Naut.* (*of sails*) trim.

8. recompense, repay, reimburse, indemnify, refund; make restitution, make amends, requite, satisfy, make up for, redress, atone, expiate, make good.

9. project, protrude, stick out, jut out; branch, diverge, divide, fork.

offshoot, *n.* **1.** branch, bough, limb, twig, stem; sucker, spur, shoot, switch; runner, tendril; sprout, sprig; leafstalk, *Bot.* petiole.

2. descendant, offspring, scion, heir, son, daughter, child; relation, relative, kin, cousin; kindred, offset.

3. outgrowth, upshot, outcome, ramification, result, consequence; issue, product, effect, fruit, by-product; aftermath, trail, wake, backwash, aftereffect, fallout; addition, adjunct, annex, amendment, supplement.

offspring, *n.* **1.** children, young, brood, spawn, litter, fry.

2. child, son, junior, daughter, scion, heir, heir apparent, chip off the old block; kid, calf, lamb, whelp, foal, cub, pup, puppy, chick, chicken.

3. descendants, successors, issue, seed, progeny, offshoots, offset; posterity, lineage, succession, progeniture, younger *or* rising generation.

4. result, product, end product, effect, offshoot, consequence; upshot, outcome, ougrowth, ramification; fruit, creation, invention, design; idea, thought, brainstorm.

often, *adv.* frequently, repeatedly, *Poetic.* oft; generally, usually, habitually, regularly, as a common thing, commonly, in many cases; periodically, ever and anon, now and again; time and again, time and time again, time after time, over and over, day-in-day-out; quite a bit, a lot.

ogle, *v.* **1.** leer, *Inf.* make goo-goo eyes at, look at with sheep's eyes, look at with calf's eyes; wink, give the glad eye, roll the eyes, lock eyes; look up and down, check out, undress with one's eyes, *Inf.* give the once-over, follow with one's eyes; look shyly, squint, look out of the corner of one's eyes, give a side glance, look askance at; flirt, coquet, make up to, trifle, simper.

2. eye, stare, gawk, gape, goggle, gaze; look at, peer, scrutinize, glance, scan; glare, glower, stare down.

—n. **3.** leer, glad eye, wink, *Inf.* once-over, sly look, sidelong glance; lascivious look, lecherous look; stare, glance; fleer, sneer, smirk, a look that could kill, the look of a cockatrice.

ogre, *n.* **1.** monster, ogress, giant, Cyclops, Minotaur, Gorgon; cockatrice, basilisk; chimera, incubus, succubus; vampire, Count Dracula; barghest, hobgoblin, goblin, bogy, boogeyman, bugbear, bugaboo, specter.

2. fiend, sadist, brute, demon, devil, hellhound; miscreant, malefactor, badman, *Brit.* bad hat, *Sl.* bad news, *Sl.* bad actor; villain, scoundrel, Iago, *Sl.* rat, blackguard, cad, *Inf.* heel, *Sl.* no-goodnik, *Sl.* bastard; beast, mad dog, shark, hyena; killer, mad-dog killer, murderer, slayer, cutthroat, manslayer, butcher, slaughterer, Bluebeard; ripper, mauler, Jack the Ripper, bloodspiller, strangler, garoter, thrill killer, homicidal maniac; hatchet man, hit man, bravo, hired gun, gun-slinger, gunman, *Sl.* torpedo, executioner, *Sl.* trigger man, *Sl.* gunsel; exterminator, liquidator, annihilator, mass-killer, mass-murderer, mass-slayer, Hitler, Genghis Khan, Attila the Hun.

3. ruffian, rowdy, ugly customer, *Inf.* plug-ugly, *Sl.* creep, *Sl.* rotter, *Sl.* mug, thug, desperado, *Sl.* tough; bandit, gangster, hoodlum, *Sl.* hood, outlaw, holdup man, highwayman, robber, thief, *Sl.* gonef, *Inf.* crook, racketeer, *Inf.* mobster; *Sl.* strong-arm man, *Sl.* muscle man, *Sl.* goon; torturer, rapist, mugger; cannibal, anthrpophagite, ghoul, barbarian, savage; scum, scum of the earth, bad person, low person, *Sl.* putz; hag, harpy, beldam, witch, harridan, hellhag; werewolf, apeman, Frankenstein's monster, gargoyle, Caliban, gorilla.

oil, *n.* **1.** lubricant, lubricator, *Inf.* lube, *Pharm.* oleum, petrolatum, petroleum jelly, *Trademark.* Vaseline, baby oil; *Chem.* glycerol, *Chem.* glycerin; graphite, plumago, black lead; mineral oil, vegetable oil, olive oil, corn oil, cod-liver oil; grease, drippings, fat, lard, shortening; butter, margarine, oleomargarine, oleo, oleo oil; unguent, ointment, liniment, balm, salve, lotion, cream. See **ointment.**

2. crude oil, unrefined oil, petroleum, fuel oil, motor oil.

3. **pour oil on troubled waters,** calm, smooth, quiet, pacifly, soothe, allay.

—v. **4.** lubricate, *Inf.* lube, grease, smear with oil; anoint, embrocate, dress, pomade, smear, daub; soap, wax; slick, smooth, make slippery *or* smooth; smooth the way, soap the way, oil *or* grease the wheels.

5. bribe, *Sl.* grease [s.o.'s] palm, pay off, buy, buy off, suborn, corrupt.

—adj. **6.** oily, oleaginous. See **oily** (*defs.* **1, 2**).

oilstone, *n.* whetstone, rubstone, hone, sharpener, grinder, grindstone.

oily, *adj.* **1.** oil, oillike, oleaginous, oleoresinous.

2. greasy, greased, lubricated, lubricous, unctuous, unguinous, slippery, slithery, smooth; buttery, butyraceous; fat, fatty, adipose, lardaceous, lardlike, lardy, pinguid, *Physiol.* sebaceous; soapy, saponaceous, waxy.

3. (*all of speech*) smooth, unctuous, suave, urbane; glib, fluent, smooth-talking, honey-tongued.

ointment, *n.* unguent, *Pharm.* inunction, (*in prescriptions*) unguentum, balm, balsam, salve, vulnerary, *Pharm.* cerate; liniment, embrocation, emollient, demulcent, *Med.* abirritant, palliative; collyrium, eyewash; nard, spikenard, pomade, pomatum; lubricant, oil, baby oil, petrolatum, petroleum jelly, *Trademark.* Vaseline; lotion, liquid cosmetic, moisturizer, skin softener, cream, face *or* hand cream, cold *or* cleansing cream, lanolin, skin *or* body lotion, after-shave lotion, skin bracer.

old, *adj.* **1.** older, aging, elderly, aged, vintage, on *or* up in years, along *or* advanced in years, past one's prime, *Inf.* over the hill, *Derog.* long in the teeth; gray, gray-haired, gray-headed, grizzly, grizzled; hoary, *Rare.* hoar, venerable, patriarchal; senile, (*of women*) anile, decrepit, senescent; superannuated, immemorial, olds as the hills, remote.

2. of age, in existence, elapsed, lapsed.

3. past, bygone, *Archaic.* olden.

4. obsolete, extinct, passé, outdated, out-of-date, outworn, outmoded, out of style, out; superseded, disused, out of use, replaced, retired; obsolescent, dated, on the way out.

5. ancient, antique, antiquated, archaic. archaistic, fossil, fossilized, fossillike; autochthonal, autochthonous, aboriginal, orginal; prehistoric, preglacial, preadamic, Noachian, Noachiac, Noachical, antediluvian, before the Flood *or* Deluge.

6. early, earliest, pristine, primeval; primitive, primordial, primigenial; elementary, basic, fundamental, rudimentary.

7. experienced, knowledgeable, versed; veteran, accomplished, practiced, proficient, adept, *Fr. au fait.*

8. enduring, lasting, long-lived, longevous; age-old, longstanding, long established, time-honored, traditional, old-line.

9. time-worn, dilapidated, worn, worn out; dull, faded, paled, dusty, subdued; deteriorated, crumbling, ramshackle, tumble-down, broken-down, run-down; decayed, disintegrated, stale; weathered, weatherbeaten, battered.

10. wise, sage, sagacious; sedate, sensible, reasonable, rational.

11. dear, beloved, loved, precious, esteemed; familiar, well-known, intimate.

12. former, erstwhile, quondam, previous, foregoing, precedent, preceding; anterior, antecedent, prior, earlier, fore.

—n. **13. the old,** elderly, aged, oldsters, senior citizens, *Inf.* old-timers, *Euph.* golden-agers; retired, retirees, pensioned, pensioners.

14. past, long ago, early ages, ancient times, olden days, *Chiefly Literary.* yore, *Archaic.* eld.

old age, *n.* declining years, winter of one's life; agedness, oldness, elderliness, senescence, antiquity, ancientness, superannuation; senility, anility, dotage, second childhood; caducity, decrepitude, infirmity, feebleness, weakness.

older, *adj.* elder, senior, of greater years, more advanced in age; aging, elderly, aged, along *or* advanced in years, up *or* on in years; former, previous, foregoing, precedent, preceding; anterior, antecedent, prior, earlier, fore.

oldest, *adj.* eldest, first born, primogenital, primogenitary, senior; original, primordial, *Obs.* primigenial; earliest, pristine, primeval, initial, first.

old-fashioned, *adj.* **1.** outmoded, unfashionable, out of fashion, out of style, outworn, moss-grown; outdated, out-of-date, out, oldfangled, unmodern, dated, *Inf.* old hat, behind the times; obsolete, extinct, dead, passé, gone by; out of use, disused, superseded, replaced; obsolescent, on the way out.

2. old-time, bygone, past, *Archaic.* olden, atavistic, quondam, erstwhile; quaint, horse-and-buggy, oldworld; antiquated, antique, ancient, archaic, archaistic; prehistoric, fossil, fossillike, antediluvian.

3. traditional, old-line, conventional, of the old school, clinging to old ways, formal; conservative, diehard, right-wing, *Sl.* square, *Sl.* straight, *Inf.* standpat; nonprogressive, unprogressive, unchanging, backward, rinky-dink; old-fogyish, stodgy, *Inf.* corny.

old man, *n.* *Informal.* **1.** graybeard, old-timer, old boy, elderly man, grandfather, venerable, patriarch, Methuselah; centenarian, nonagenarian, octogenarian, sexagenarian; senior citizen, golden-ager, *Inf.* oldster; gaffer, codger, *Sl.* geezer; fogey, *Sl.* fossil.

2. father, papa, *Inf.* pa, *Inf.* paw, *Inf.* pop, *Sl.* pops,

Inf. dad, *Inf.* daddy, *Brit. Inf.* pater.

3. husband, man, spouse, mate, partner; lover, cohabitant, *Fr. covivant, Fr. intime;* boyfriend, *Inf.* steady, sweetheart.

4. *Sometimes* **Old Man** employer, boss, *Inf.* bossman, *Sl.* the Man, manager, foreman, superintendent, supervisor, *Inf.* super; commanding officer, superior, commander.

5. (*all used in direct address*) old friend, old boy, *Chiefly Brit.* old chap, *Inf.* old pal, *U.S. Inf.* old buddy.

6. old stager, old hand, past master, veteran, *Inf.* old pro, trouper.

old-time, *adj.* old-fashioned, bygone, past. See **old-fashioned** (*defs.* **1-3**).

old-womanish, *adj.* finical, finicky, hard *or* difficult *or* impossible to please, fussy, *Inf.* fuss-budgety, *Inf.* persnickety; overparticular, overfastidious, overmeticulous; prim, priggish, prudish, overmodest; strait-laced, hidebound, fuddy-duddy, stiff-necked; spinsterish, old-maidish.

old-world, *adj.* old, aged, antique, antiquarian, archaic, ancient; conservative, traditional, old-fashioned, outmoded, outdated; European, continental; gallant, chivalrous, courtly; formal, ceremonious, rigid, strict, hidebound.

oleaginous, *adj.* oil, oillike, oily, greasy, unctuous. See **oily** (*defs.* **1-3**).

oligarchy, *n.* diarchy, duarchy, duumvirate; triarchy, triumvirate; theocracy.

olio, *n.* **1.** stew, ragout, salmi, salmagundi, goulash, hash, mash, fricasse, paella, bouillabaisse, *U.S.* chowder, olla-podrida, *Sp. olla,* (*in China, India, etc.*) chow-chow, *U.S. Sl.* mulligan.

2. mishmash, hodgepodge, *Brit.* hotchpotch, jumble, tumble, scramble, tangle, mess, confused mess, confusion; conglomeration, pastiche, pasticcio, patchwork, farrago, gallimaufry, Chinese menu; clutter, litter, heap, mass, bunch, huddle.

3. medley, mélange, potpourri, variety, mixture, *Sl.* mixed bag, *Inf.* grab bag; miscellany, omnium-gatherum.

omen, *n.* **1.** portent, sign, token, foretoken, harbinger; premonition, preindication, forewarning, foreshadowing, handwriting on the wall.

2. prognostic, prognostication, prediction, forecast, prophecy, prefigurement, augury, auspice, vaticination, divination.

3. presage, presentiment, foreknowledge; feeling, vague feeling, *Inf.* funny feeling, *Inf.* feeling in one's bones, intuition, suspicion, *Inf.* sneaking suspicion; anxiety, misgiving, apprehension, boding; dread, fear, ill feeling, bad feeling, chill along the spine, *Sl.* bad vibes.

—v. **4.** portend, forebode, foretoken, foreshadow, foreshow, augur, presage, presignify, preindicate; betoken, signify, mean, indicate, point to.

5. foretell, forecast, forewarn, divine, *Rare.* premonish, *Obs.* auspicate; prognosticate, prophesy, predict, soothsay, vaticinate.

ominous, *adj.* **1.** portentous, foreboding, bodeful, ill-boding, boding evil, ill-omened, of evil portent; inauspicious, unpropitious, unfavorable, unpromising, unfortunate, unlucky, ill-fated, ill-starred, star-crossed, doomed from the start; threatening, menacing, lowering, looming, dark, black, sinister, heavy gloomy; bad, evil, malign, malignant.

2. oracular, augural, divinatory, vaticinal, mantic, sibyllic; prophetic, predictive, prognostic, foretelling, forecasting, forewarning; premonitory, significant, meaningful; preindicative, foretokening, foreshowing, foreshadowing.

omission, *n.* **1.** exception, exclusion, noninclusion, preclusion, nonadmission; (*all of a written text*) deletion, cancellation, erasure; expurgation, bowdlerization, censorship.

2. disregard, ignoring, overlooking, passing over, preterition; failure, dereliction, delinquency, default, nonfulfillment, neglect, negligence, *Law.* nonfeasance eschewal, avoidance.

3. oversight, miss, *Inf.* go-by; inadvertence, loose thread, (*pl.*) paralipomena; gap, break, hiatus, lacuna, interval; mistake, error, fault, flaw, slip, *Inf.* slip-up, *Inf.* miscue, *Obs.* balk.

omit, *v.* **1.** except, exclude, leave out; miss, give a miss, fail to mention; overlook, pass over, skip, jump; ignore, disregard, pay no attention to; (*all of a written text*) delete, cancel, erase, expunge, eradicate, rub *or* blot out; edit, edit out, blue-pencil, strike, cross out, rule out, kill, cut.

2. neglect, forget, forget about, not think of, let slip, let slide, let go, *Sl.* let ride, leave undone, not trouble oneself with; eschew, avoid, shun, shirk, abstain from, steer clear of.

omnibus, *n.* **1.** bus, motorbus, autobus, coach, motor coach, double-decker, jitney, *Trademark.* Greyhound.

2. anthology, reader, collection, treasury; compilation, collectanea, chrestomathy, analects; miscellany, garland, ana; corpus, collected works, complete works, *Fr. oeuvre.*

—adj. **3.** inclusive, comprehensive, sweeping, overall, across-the-board; encyclopedic, compendious, far-ranging, wide-ranging.

omnifarious, *adj.* omniform, omnigenous; multiform, multifold, manifold, multifarious, multitudinous, multiplex, multiphase, multiple; various, divers, of all shapes and sizes.

omnipotence, *n.* **1.** almightiness, all-powerfulness.

2. supremacy, supreme *or* unlimited power, undisputed sway, divine right.

omnipotent, *adj.* **1.** almighty, all-powerful, *Rare.* cunctipotent.

2. supreme, absolute, unlimited, plenipotent; sovereign, ruling, preeminent.

—n. **3. the Omnipotent** God, Lord, Jehovah, the Almighty, the All Powerful, the Supreme Being, the Omniscient, God Almighty, Almighty God, the Eternal Being, the Creator, the Deity, the King of Kings.

omnipresent, *adj.* all-present; infinite, boundless, limitless; ubiquitous, universal, pervasive.

omniscient, *adj.* **1.** all-knowing, all-wise, all-seeing, all-perceiving; wise, sagacious, pansophic.

—n. **2. the Omniscient** God, the Omnipotent. See **omnipotent** (*def.* **3**).

omnium-gatherum, *n.* miscellany, medley, mishmash, hodgepodge. See **olio** (*defs.* **2, 3**).

omnivorous, *adj.* pantophagous, *Rare.* pamphagous, all-devouring; greedy, rapacious, voracius, edacious, ravenous.

on, *prep.* **1.** upon, in contract with, attached to, suspended from, hung from; around, about.

2. by, near, proximate to, next to, beside, in the direction of.

—adv. **3.** fast, firmly, securely, tightly, for dear life, close, onto.

4. onward, forward, ahead, before one, along, toward, beyond.

5. steadily, without ceasing, unceasingly, without interruption, continually, continuously; perseveringly, doggedly.

6. **on and off** intermittently, discontinuously, interruptedly, brokenly; remittently, fitfully, spasmodically.
7. **on and on** at great length, unceasingly, continuously, endlessly, interminably.
—adj. 8. in use, operating, running, going.
9. taking place, occurring, happening, in existence; scheduled, planned, organized.
10. performing, broadcasting, on the air.

once, *adv.* 1. formerly, previously, aforetime, at one time, before now, *Archaic.* erenow, heretofore; some time back, some time ago, awhile ago; long ago, in the old days, in the good old days, years ago, ages ago, before you were born, once upon a time.
2. single time, one time, on one occasion.
3. ever, at any time, at a single time; possibly, by chance, by a fluke.
4. **once and for all** decisively, positively, decidedly, finally, conclusively, determinately.
5. **once in a while** at intervals, periodically, occasionally, sometimes, at times, from time to time, now and then, every now and then.
6. **once or twice** very few times, very little, infrequently, hardly ever, rarely, sporadically.
—n. 7. single occasion, single time, one time only.
8. **at once** a. together, simultaneously, at the same time, at one and the same time, in the same instant, in the same breath. b. immediately, right away, straightway, straightaway, directly, forthwith; promptly, posthaste, without delay, instantly, on the spot; in no time, in less than no time, *Inf.* before you can say Jack Robinson, in the twinkling of an eye, quick as a bunny, in a second, in a moment, in a minute.

once-over, *n. Informal.* quick look, quick appraisal, check, inspection; superficial job, hasty going-over.

oncoming, *adj.* approaching, nearing, close, looming, bearing down, onrushing.

one, *adj.* 1. single, individual, *Zool., Bot.* azygous; a, an; only, sole, solitary, lone, odd; (*of a day*) some, any.
2. complete, whole, entire; joined, unified, united, allied; wedded, married, bound, bonded, cemented, inseparable; agreeing, agreeable, like-minded, of one mind, in accord, accordant, harmonious, concordant, congenial, compatible.
3. alike, the same, one and the same, of a single kind; identical, equal.

oneness, *n.* 1. singleness, individuality, isolation, separation, distinctness; unity, undividedness, integrality, completeness, wholeness, unification, coalescence, solidarity; consistency, sameness, identity, identicalness.
2. agreement, consensus, concord, concordance, accord, accordance, consentaneity, chime, harmony; amity, friendship, congeniality, sympathy, understanding, compatibility; sisterliness, sisterhood, brotherliness, brotherhood, fellowship, comradeship; union, unanimity, conformance; rapport, connection.

onerous, *adj.* burdensome, oppressive, grievous, heavy, crushing, hard to bear, unbearable, unendurable, intolerable; laborious, arduous, strenuous, herculean, toilsome, difficult, operose, hard, hard to deal with, trying; irksome, galling, thorny, harassing, harrowing, troublesome; exhausting, taxing, tiring, wearying, wearisome, fatiguing, wearing, corrosive, corroding; destructive, deleterious, deterimental; distressing, afflictive, hurtful, painful, cruel, severe, harsh; harmful, injurious, noisome, malefic, baneful.

oneself, *pron.* 1. Number One, Numero Uno; the I, the self, ego.
2. **by oneself** a. alone, solitary, single; unaccompanied, unattended; isolated, separate; lonely, lonesome, companionless, friendless. b. unaided, unassisted, without help; independently, on one's own.

one-sided, *adj.* 1. lopsided, unsymmetrical, asymmetrical, unbalanced, unequalized, uneven, unequal, disproportioned, disproportionate, irregular.
2. partial, inequitable, unjust, unfair; biased, prejudiced, close-minded, narrow-minded, intolerant, bigoted, partisan, illiberal; insular, parochial, provincial, limited, myopic, near-sighted, short-sighted, fanatical, dogmatic, opinionated, unreasonable.

one-time, *adj.* 1. prior, earlier, former, previous, foregone; preceding, precedent, last, foregoing, antecedent, anterior; erstwhile, whilom; preexistent, preliminary; quondam, *Archaic.* sometime.
2. past, bygone, long-ago, ancient; old, gone, long gone, over and done with, late, departed.

ongoing, *adj.* 1. uninterrupted, continual, continuous, unbroken, constant, incessant, ceaseless, unceasing, nonstop; unremitting, unintermitting, relentless, persistent; recurrent, repeated, frequent, habitual, regular; around-the-clock, day-in and day-out, dawn-to-dusk.
2. unending, endless, never-ending, interminable, Sisyphean; eternal, perpetual, everlasting, lasting, enduring, perennial, permanent.

onlooker, *n.* bystander, observer, witness, eyewitness; spectator, watcher, viewer, beholder, gazer, gawker, *Sl.* rubberneck; passer-by, looker-on; inspector, scrutinizer, examiner.

only, *adv.* 1. solitarily, solely, singly, alone, exclusively; separately, individually, distinctively, apart.
2. just, merely, simply, purely; but, nothing but, not more than, at most.
3. **only too** very, extremely, exceedingly, excessively, inordinately, exorbitantly, drastically, radically.
—adj. 4. lone, alone, solitary; sole, exclusive, single, singular; individual, unique, one and only.
—conj. 5. but, on the contrary, on the other hand, nevertheless, yet; except, save, notwithstanding, however; unless, if not, except that, but for the fact that.

onrush, *n.* stampede, charge, sally, push, drive; rush, zoom, dash, race, run, flight, course, career; torrent, avalanche, landslide, niagara, cascade, cataract, falls; rapids, millrace, swift current, tidal wave, flood, deluge; surge, swell, wave, gush, spurt, spout, jet, spring, geyser, fountain; outrush, outflow, outpour, outpouring, effusion, flow, flowing, stream, current, tide, afflux, flux, efflux, effluence, issuance.

onset, *n.* 1. beginning, start, staring point, inception, early days, very first, first, top, rise of the curtain; opening, dawn, threshold, conception, birth, genesis, origin, embryo, inchoation, exordium; commencement, inauguration, first step, outset, embarkation, *Inf.* kick-off, *Inf.* jump-off, *Inf.* take-off, *Inf.* blast-off; first appearance, debut, outbreak, outburst.
2. onslaught, attack, assault. See **onslaught**.

onshore, *adv.* 1. landward, landwards, coastward, coastwards, shoreward, toward the land *or* coast *or* shore, inland; off *or* away from the water *or* sea *or* lake; with the waves.
2. coastwise, along the coast, following the coast, hugging the shore, *Archaic.* coastways.
3. ashore, into *or* at a port *or* harbor *or* dock *or* pier; tied up, on land.
—adj. 4. landward, shoreward, coastward, inland.
5. littoral, shore, shoreline, coastal; on shore, on land, on the beach, on terra firma; docked, in port, landed, *Naut.* beached, aground, grounded, shoaled, stranded, marooned, high and dry.

onslaught, *n.* rush, charge, blitz, blitzkrieg, storming, raid, foray, sortie, sally, invasion, *Fr. coup de main, Obs.* brunt; bombardment, strafing, air raid, peppering, salvo, fusillade, *Both Mil.* barrage, enfilade, *Navy.* broadside; attack, assault, besetment, onset, hit, strike.

onus, *n.* burden, weight, load, cross, millstone, albatross; obligation, debt, liability, responsibility, duty, charge, demand, tax; encumbrance, hindrance, obstruction, stumbling block, impediment, handicap, disadvantage; trouble, care, anxiety, worry; hardship, difficulty, affliction, oppression; trial, tribulation, ordeal; woe, grief, misery, sorrow, suffering, *Archaic.* bale.

onward, *adv.* **1.** onwards, forward, frontward *or* frontwards, in advance, ahead, along, on; toward the front, toward the bow, toward the fore, toward the forefront, toward the head.

2. up *or* out in front, in front, ahead, up ahead, in the fore, in the forefront, in the van, in the vanguard.

—adj. **3.** forward, advancing, progressing, ongoing, moving ahead; progressive, forward-looking, forward-moving.

ooze[1], *v.* **1.** transude, flow *or* flow out, exude, bleed, seep, filter, filtrate, leach, percolate; escape, leak, drain, strain, trickle, drizzle, dribble, drip, drop, weep.

2. sweat, perspire, secrete, discharge; send out, give off, emit, transpire, send forth; emanate, come from, issue, well out *or* forth; pour out *or* forth, effuse, disseminate, shed, release, loose *or* let loose.

—n. **3.** transudation, exudation, exudate, secretion, discharge, sweat, perspiration.

ooze[2], *n.* **1.** mud, clay, muck, mire, sludge, silt, sediment, alluvium, deposit; slime, *Inf.* glop, *Inf.* gunk, *Sl.* guck, *Inf.* goo, *Sl.* goop; slush, slosh, mush, squash, mess, slop, swill, *Irish.* slob.

2. marsh, bog, morass, swamp, wash, *Brit.* fen, quagmire; quicksand, wallow, slough, *Brit.* sough, *Brit. Dial.* sump.

oozy[1], *adj.* oozing, seepy, seeping, exuding moisture; weepy, weeping, leaking, leaky, dripping, drippy; sweating, sweaty, perspiring, perspiry; damp, moist, dewy, wet.

oozy[2], *adj.* muddy, clayey, mucky, miry, sludgy, silty, sedimentous, alluvial; slimy, *Inf.* gloppy, *Inf.* gunky, *Sl.* gucky, *Inf.* gooey, *Sl.* goopy; messy, sloppy, slushy, sloshy, mushy, soft, spongy, squashy, squishy, splashy, plashy; marshy, marshlike, boggy, boggish, swampy swampish, *Brit.* fenny, quaggy, quagmiry, sloughy.

opacity, *n.* **1.** opaqueness, nontransparency, cloudiness, filminess; muddiness, murkiness, fuliginosity, smokiness, darkness; obfuscation, obscurity, blurriness, fuzziness, unclarity, unclearness, vagueness; haziness, fogginess, mistiness; overclouding, dimming, obnubilation, shadowing, overshadowing; obscurement, darkening, blackening, obscuration, obumbration.

2. smokescreen, cloud, dust, pall; shadow, fog, mist, frost, smoke, film; cover, camouflage, drape, curtain.

3. vagueness, indefiniteness, uncertainty; abstruseness, reconditeness, profoundness; ambiguity, equivocation; confusion, perplexity, bafflement, puzzle, jumble; mystification, *Inf.* mumbo jumbo, muddle, befuddlement.

4. unintelligence, dullness, obtuseness, slowness, stupidity; backwardness, doltishness, simpleness, simplicity; empty-headedness, unimaginativeness; unperceptiveness.

opalescent, *adj.* multicolored, multicolor, polychromatic, polychromic, of many colors *or* shades *or* hues, prismatic, prismatical, spectral, rainbowy, rainbowlike, colorful, brilliant; iridescent, opaline, milky, pearly, nacreous, nacred; kaleidoscopic, kaleidoscopical, changeable, changeful, variable, variant, varying; shot, variegated, varicolored, marble, marbly, marmoreal, glittering, shimmering, streaked, motley, mottled.

opaque, *adj.* **1.** nontransparent, untransparent, nontranslucent, impervious to light; clouded, cloudy, nubilous, filmy; turbid, dense, murky; shady, hazy, foggy, misty, blurred, frosty; dirty, dingy, muddy, sooty, smoky, fuliginous; dark, black, overcast, gloomy.

2. dull, lusterless, dim, tarnished, not bright *or* shining, unglazed, mat.

3. obscure, vague, unclear, indefinite, uncertain, doubtful, dubious; abstruse, recondite, arcane; ambiguous, equivocal, cryptic, enigmatic; unfathomable, impenetrable, mysterious, perplexing, puzzling, confusing, confused.

4. unintelligent, witless, slow-witted, dull-witted, dull; stolid, obtuse, crass, Boeotian, bovine, blockish, lumpish; dense, thickheaded, *Inf.* thick, slow, stupid, *Australian Inf.* dill, *Scot. and North Eng.* dowf; backward, doltish, *Sl.* birdbrained, simple; empty-headed, vacuous; unimaginative, undiscerning.

open, *adj.* **1.** unclosed, unshut, wide open, agape, gaping, yawning, patulous, ringent, dehiscent; (*of a door*) unlocked, unbolted, unlatched, ajar, sprung, jimmied; (*of a window*) raised, up; (*of a drawer*) pulled out, sticking out, protruding; (*of a box*) unlidded, lidless, topless, coverless, unsealed; (*of a tap*) uncorked, unplugged, tapped, broached, abroach, on.

2. unenclosed, unscreened, unfenced, unbarred, unbounded; uncovered, unsheltered, roofless, unprotected, unfortified; unveiled, exposed, bare, naked, open to view, on display *or* exhibit.

3. wide, extensive, broad, wide-open, spacious, roomy, uncrowded, uncluttered, unconfining; free, unobstructed, clear, unblocked, passable, navigable; developed, unbuilt, not built up.

4. holey, full of holes *or* spaces, airy, (*of military ranks*) loose, sloppy; porous, honeycombed, lacy, spongy, spongelike, sievelike, cribiform, crible, alveolate, faveolate, faveolus; perforated, punctured, pinpricked, pierced, riddled, pitted.

5. unfolded, unfurled, unbent, straightened out, unrolled; extended, stretched out, drawn out, spread out, sprawled out.

6. public, open to the public, open to outsiders; general, inclusive, non-exclusive, nondiscriminatory, free *or* open to all.

7. accessible, enterable, reachable, within reach, obtainable, at hand; available, on hand, on call, on tap, at one's beck and call; for sale, buyable, purchasable, rentable, there for the asking *or* taking, stealable.

8. vacant, empty, void, unfilled, unoccupied, untenanted, tenantless, uninhabited; untaken, unclaimed, *Inf.* up for grabs; usable, at one's disposal *or* command.

9. unbooked, unscheduled, uncommitted, unpromised, free.

10. unrestricted, unqualified, unconditional, unregulated, no strings attached; ungoverned, laissez-faire, no-holds-barred, free-wheeling.

11. (*of weather or water*) unfrozen, ice-free, frostless, frost-free, thawed; mild, moderate, temperate, even.

12. undecided, unsettled, undetermined, indeterminate, unfixed, yet to be decided, up in the air; debatable, controvertible, contestable, arguable, disputable, disputed, questionable, problematic, moot, doubtful, dubious; experimental, indefinite, uncertain, undemonstrated, unproven, unconfirmed.

13. open-minded, receptive, amenable; broad-minded, unprejudiced. See **open-minded** (*defs.* **1, 2**).

14. *Usu.* **open to** liable, prone, disposed, predisposed, tending, leaning, inclined; subject, susceptible, pregnable, defenseless against, vulnerable.

15. manifest, overt, evident, obvious, apparent, visible, in plain view *or* sight, noticeable, conspicuous, out in the open, unhidden, unconcealed, undisguised; express, avowed, advertised, published, broadcast; palpable, patent, clear, plain, transparent, sheer, outright, downright, out-and-out, unmitigated; blatant, flagrant, glaring, egregious, barefaced, baldfaced, flaunting, brazen, shameless, arrant.

16. unreserved, heart-to-heart; candid, sincere. See **open-hearted** (*defs.* **1, 2**).

17. generous, liberal, charitable. See **open-handed**.

—*v.* **18.** (*of a door*) unlock, unbolt, unlatch, throw open, spring, jimmy; (*of a window*) raise, lift, throw up; (*of a drawer*) pull out; (*of a box*) take off the top, uncase, unseal; (*of a package*) unwrap, undo; (*of a tap*) uncork, unstop, tap, broach, turn on; break into, blast through, cut into *or* through, lance, incise, cut open, cleave; dilate, distend, become open, dehisce, burst forth, come apart, split, crack.

19. unblock, unobstruct, unstop, unclog, flush out, rout out, clear out; purge, clean out, cleanse, defecate; make clear, free up, let flow.

20. give access to, open to access *or* passage, make accessible *or* available; reopen, unclose; reexamine, reinspect, take another look at.

21. uncover, unveil, unshroud, uncurtain, unmask, expose, bare, lay bare; present, expose to view, exhibit, display, show; disclose, reveal, bring to light, bring out, show up, make manifest *or* evident; divulge, unbosom, spill, come out with, let drop *or* fall, blurt *or* let pour out, communicate *or* tell about; make known, let [s.t.] be known, release, announce, advertise, publish, air, broadcast, proclaim, *Archaic.* divulgate.

22. enlighten, broaden [s.o.'s] horizons, open [s.o.'s] eyes, make [s.o.] see the light; edify, acquaint with, familiarize with, apprise *or* inform of, introduce to; explain, expound upon, interpret, describe, illustrate; clarify, elucidate, make plain, spell out, decipher, decode.

23. unfold, unbend, unwind, unfurl, unroll, uncoil, (*both of hands*) unclutch, unclench, (*all of flowers*) blossom, bloom, flower; extend, spread out, (*of a book*) turn to a page.

24. expand, widen, enlarge, broaden, move out *or* apart; separate, set at intervals, space out, put space between, part, split up.

25. open for business, begin business, set up shop, receive business, hang out one's shingle; establish, institute, set up, organize; found, lay the first stone *or* foundation for, originate, bring into being, create, be a charter member of; pioneer, make the way for, blaze a trail for, break ground for.

26. *Sometimes* **open for** begin, start, initiate, ring in, inaugurate, launch, get [s.t.] off the ground, set [s.t.] in operation; commence, enter upon, embark upon, get going in; lead off, take the first step, take the initiative, go first, break the ice, take the plunge, get the ball rolling.

27. **open onto** border on, abut on, adjoin, connect with, be connected *or* joined with; lead *or* take [s.o.] to give access to, be a passage *or* way to, afford entrance to, be an opening *or* door *or* portal to.

28. **open up** *Slang.* **a.** open fire, being *or* start firing *or* shooting. **b.** reveal oneself, let down one's defenses; speak out, vent one's emotions, get [s.t.] off one's chest, pour out one's heart to. **c.** (*of a vehicle*) give it gas, *Inf.* gun *or* rev the engine; accelerate, speed up, speed.

open-ended, *adj.* unlimited, undefined, unconstricted, unrestricted, *Inf.* wide-open; broad, general, liberal; up in the air, indefinite, undetermined, unsettled, vague, fuzzy, indistinct.

opener, *n.* **1.** start, starter, beginning, onset; introduction, inauguration, initiation.

2. can opener, *Brit.* tin opener, *Fr. boite-ouvrir,* corkscrew, bottle screw, bottle opener, *Inf.* church key; gadget, device.

3. preliminary, preliminary bout, *Sl.* prelim; top of the inning, top of the first, starting game, kickoff; curtain raiser *or* lifter, overture, prologue, first act, preamble, first installment, preface; maiden speech, inaugural address; ice-breaker, introduction; appetizer, taster, first course.

open-eyed, *adj.* **1.** wide-eyed, goggle-eyed, agog, agape; astonished, astounded, surprised, amazed; awed, impressed.

2. watchful, alert, vigilant, on the qui vive; attentive, observant, awake, with one's ear to the ground, heedful; all-eyes, hawk-eyed, eagle-eyed, sharp-eyed, Argus-eyed; wary, leery.

3. intentional, willful, deliberate, calculated; knowing, aware, conscious, witting, cognizant.

open-handed, *adj.* generous, liberal, free-handed, bounteous, bountiful, munificent, prodigal, giving, unstinting, unselfish; charitable, eleemosynary, humanitarian, philanthropic, altruistic; benevolent, beneficent, free-hearted, magnanimous, big-hearted, large-hearted.

open-hearted, *adj.* **1.** candid, frank, forthright, straightforward, man-to-man, heart-to-heart; honest, sincere, ingenuous, guileless, naive, simple, innocent, genuine, natural; unreserved, unrestrained, unconstrained, unreticent, demonstrative, emotional, free and easy; free-spoken, free-speaking, outspoken, bold, blunt, abrupt, unchecked, bluff, tactless, brusque.

2. kindhearted, kind, kindly, goodhearted, good, benevolent; benign, benignant, soft-hearted, tender-hearted, tender, gentle, *Fr. gentil,* humane; warm-hearted, compassionate, loving, warm sympathetic, *Inf.* Christian. See **kind** (*defs.* **1, 2**).

opening¹, *adj.* initial, starting, beginning, commencing, introductory, prefatory, first.

opening², *n.* **1.** hiatus, lacuna, gap, slit, slot; hole, hollow, cavity, aperture, orifice, ostiole; interstice, areola, pore, *Anat.* sinus; peephole, buttonhole, pinhole, eye, eyelet; mouth, embochure, mouthhole, mouthpiece; breach, break, space, rift, rent; cleft, chasm, *Archaic.* scissure; crack, cranny, chink, crevice, fissure, notch, nick; cavern, cave, grotto, den; excavation, pit, well, shaft; hatch, gate, door, portal, window, scupper, vent.

2. beginning, start, commencement, inception, kickoff; birth, genesis, origin; dawn, dawning, threshold, outset, exordium; send-off, start-off, jump-off; overture, prologue, prelude, preliminary, proem, introduction, preface; debut, first step.

3. opportunity, chance, good chance, *Inf.* foot in the door, *Sl.* break, *Sl.* the breaks; *Sl.* lucky shot, Lady Luck; fortuitousness, serendipity; sure bet, good thing, inside track.

4. vacancy, job opportunity, position *or* place available.

open-minded, *adj.* **1.** receptive, open to suggestions, amenable, acquiescent, compliant; tolerant, forbearant, catholic, latitudinarian, understanding, sympathetic; broad-minded, liberal, good-hearted, good, kind, fair, reasonable, just, equitable, square, even-handed; thoughtful, thinking, enlightened, open.

2. unprejudiced, unbiased, unwarped, unbigoted, unjaundiced, unswayed; dispassionate, broad, impersonal, impartial, disinterested.

open-mouthed, *adj.* **1.** gaping, agape, wonderstruck, thunderstruck, dumfounded, stupefied; astounded, *Inf.* flabbergasted, astonished, surprised, amazed, startled, shocked; awestruck, spellbound.

2. greedy, rapacious, voracious, edacious; ravenous, famished, starving.

3. clamorous, uproarious, clamant, blustering, noisy; vociferous, loud, vocal; brassy, bold, brash, mouthy, loud-mouthed; unruly, boisterous, obstreperous.

operable, *adj.* in working condition, usable, serviceable, functional, operational; practicable, workable, feasible; possible, achievable, attainable.

operate, *v.* **1.** work, perform, act, go, *Sl.* fly; function, serve, *Sl.* do one's thing *or* stuff.

2. run, manage, handle, manipulate, conduct, maneuver, make go; use, utilize, employ, practice, ply.

3. effect, effectuate, engineer, bring about, produce; induce, elicit, evoke, call forth, summon up.

operation, *n.* **1.** employment, utilization, effectuation, manipulation, handling; performance, execution, discharge, dispatch, enactment; doing, exercise, practice; action, activity, *Rare.* operance, *Rare.* operancy.

2. agency, influence, power, potency; effect, result, consequence.

3. business transaction, commercial transaction, *Inf.* deal, *Inf.* business deal, *Stock Exchange.* turn, bargain, agreement; undertaking, venture, project, enterprise, task.

operative, *n.* **1.** workman, workingman, worker, laborer, *Sl.* working stiff; industrial *or* factory worker, factory hand, blue-collar worker, proletarian; artisan, artificer, craftsman, handicraftsman; skilled laborer, mechanic.

2. detective, private detective, investigator, private investigator, sleuth, plainclothesman; *All Sl.* dick, gumshoe, flatfoot, eye, private eye, fly ball, fly bull.

3. secret agent, undercover agent, undercover man, espionage agent, intelligence agent; spy, counterspy, double agent.

—adj. **4.** active, functional, operational, *Inf.* go; functioning, performing, operating, acting, working, running, going; engaged, in operation, in action, in play.

5. influential, instrumental, forcible, forceful, potent, powerful; employed, utilized, in force, in effect.

6. effective, effectual, efficacious, efficient; serviceable, adequate, sufficient, *Inf.* good enough; useful, advantageous, beneficial, helpful.

operator, *n.* **1.** doer, performer, actor, executor, operative, operant; worker, handler, manipulator, practitioner.

2. telephone operator, switchboard operator, PBX operator, *Obs.* central.

3. *Slang.* maneuverer, machinator, *Inf.* finagler, *Inf.* wire-puller, *Sl.* wheeler-dealer, *Sl.* big-time operator; *Sl.* slicker, *Sl.* smoothie, *Sl.* smooth-talker, *Sl.* fast-talker.

operose, *adj.* **1.** industrious, hard-working, diligent, assiduous, sedulous, studious, intent; plodding, unflagging, indefatigable, tireless, undrooping, unsleeping; persistent, pertinacious, constant, earnest, patient, painstaking, exacting; workmanlike, businesslike, enterprising, hustling, on the go, on the move; at work, in harness, hard at it, astir, active, up and doing, up and coming.

2. laborious, arduous, toilsome, heavy, strenuous; troublesome, trying, hard, difficult, burdensome, onerous; uphill, full of obstacles, herculean, *Inf.* wicked, *Inf.* rough, *Inf.* tough, *Inf.* nasty; tiring, wearying, wearisome, fatiguing, exhausting, taxing; rigorous, not easy, tedious, unmitigating, endless, tiresome, boring.

ophthalmologist, *n.* oculist, eye doctor, eye specialist, (*loosely*) optometrist.

opiate, *n.* **1.** *Informal.* drug, narcotic, depressant, sedative, tranquilizer, soporific, somnifacient, hypnotic, stupefacient; painkiller, analgesic, *Pharm.* hyoscyamine, *Pharm.* belladonna; morphine, opium, laudanum; barbiturate, *Sl.* barbs, *Inf.* down *or* downer, quaalude, *Sl.* lude, *Sl.* red; heroin, *Sl.* H. *Sl.* horse, *Sl.* smack, *Sl.* junk, *Sl.* scag, *Sl.* crank; *Sl.* dope, marijuana, *U.S. Sl.* Mary-Jane *or* MJ, *Sl.* pot, *Sl.* grass, *Sl.* weed, *Sl.* reefer; hashish, *Sl.* hash.

2. anodyne, lenitive, palliative, assuager, nepenthe, *Med.* calmative.

opine, *v.* reckon, fancy, deem, conceive, imagine; feel, think, view, see, regard; hold, consider, maintain, esteem, count; suppose, assume, surmise, *Dial.* allow, conclude, conjecture; presume, guess, suspect, *Inf.* expect, *Inf.* have a hunch, have an inkling; look upon, take for, be under the impression, have the impression.

opinion, *n.* **1.** belief, judgment, idea, thought; impression, notion, fancy, assumption; conception, concept, conceit; conviction, mind, persuasion, thinking, way of thinking; tenet, doctrine, dogma, principle, doxy, creed, precept.

2. view, sentiment, feeling, apprehension; observation, perception, image; attitude, viewpoint, point of view, slant; stand, stance, position, angle, posture.

3. appraisal, judgment, appreciation, valuation; estimate, estimation, consideration, assessment; verdict, diagnosis, prognosis, decision, finding; determination, deduction, inference, conclusion; supposition, theory, speculation, guess, two cents' worth; surmise, conjecture, premise.

opinionated, *adj.* **1.** prejudiced, biased, bigoted, jaundiced, colored, one-sided, partisan, prepossessed; stubborn, obstinate, bullheaded, pigheaded, mulish; willful, headstrong, pertinacious, self-willed, dogged.

2. dogmatic, pontifical, oracular, dictatorial, doctrinaire; positive, confident, assured, convinced; overconfident, overweening, overbearing, hubristic; arrogant, inflated, lofty, pompous, lordly, cocky; conceited, self-important, egotistic, vain.

opinionative, *adj.* **1.** credal, doctrinal, canonical, dogmatic, taught; authoritative, orthodox, recognized, standard, accepted, held.

2. obstinate, willful, headstrong; self-important, conceited. See **opinionated** (*defs.* **1, 2**).

opponent, *n.* **1.** antagonist, adversary, foe, enemy, assailant; rival, competitor, contender, contestant, vier; opposer, opposition, oppositionist, objector, protestor, dissident.

—adj. **2.** opposing, antagonistic; contentious. See **opposing** (*defs.* **1, 2**).

opportune, *adj.* appropriate, apt, suitable, expedient, fitting, fit, becoming, proper, correct, right; applicable, relevant, pertinent, germane, apropos; propitious, auspicious, favorable, advantageous, convenient, good; fortunate, seasonable, timely, lucky, providential; profitable, valuable, *Archaic.* available, efficacious; conducive, beneficial, helpful, constructive, worthwhile; useful, usable, acccessible, handy, serviceable.

opportunism, *n.* (*all of opportunities*) exploitation, taking advantage; expediency, striking while the iron is hot, *Sl.* getting while the getting is good, making hay while the sun shines.

opportunity, *n.* favorable time, good moment, perfect occasion, right season, right set of circumstances; chance, contingency, possibility; opening, golden opportunity, once-in-a-lifetime chance, *Inf.* shot, *Sl.* break, stroke of luck, turn *or* turn of events, *Sl.* twist of fate.

oppose, *v.* **1.** confront, face, encounter; resist, defy, withstand, repulse, repel, *Archaic.* reluct, recalcitrate; counteract, contravene, neutralize, cancel, militate against, countervail.

2. attack, assault, assail, collide with, clash with, combat, contest, strive against, contend with *or* against, cope with, struggle with *or* against, antagonize; battle, joust, tilt, enter the lists, tourney, cross swords; box, spar, wrestle, fence, duel, thrust and parry, come to blows, bandy blows; skirmish, jostle, scuffle, grapple *or* close with; fight, war on, make war, march against.

3. hinder, obstruct, impede, block, check, curb, restrain, restrict, inhibit, interfere, barricade, debar; thwart, foil, frustrate, cross, traverse, *Scot.* thraw; prevent, forbid, prohibit, proscribe, veto, interdict, embargo, blockade, bar, preclude.

4. contradict, dispute, refute, controvert, repugn, oppugn; protest, take issue with, take exception to, take a stand against; side against, join issue.

5. compare, contrast, offset, balance, counterbalance, set against, pit against; equate with, parallel, match, correspond; set off, foil.

opposing, *adj.* **1.** contradictory, countering, conflicting, adverse, contrary, opponent, antipathetical, oppositional, oppugnant; jarring, clashing, incompatible, discordant, discrepant, dissident, antagonistic.

2. combating, fighting, militant, battling, dueling, contending, enemy, factious, contentious, dissentious, disputatious; bickering, quarreling, feuding, broiling, wrangling, disputing, disagreeing, unfriendly.

opposite, *adj.* **1.** face to face, facing, vis-à-vis, eyeball-to-eyeball, *Dial.* fornent.

2. contrary, reverse, contrasting, opposing, contradictory, counter, antagonistic, conflicting, oppugnant; opposed, diametricaly opposed, antithetical, antipodal, antonymous; oppositional, *Logic.* contrapositive.

—n. **3.** reverse, contrary, inverse, converse, *Inf.* the other side of the coin; opposite number, counterpart, vis-à-vis; pole, antipode, antithesis; antonym.

—prep. **4.** across from, facing; parallel to, complementary to, as partner to, with.

opposition, *n.* **1.** resistance, counteraction, contravention, flak, *Inf.* a hard time; impediment, hindrance, obstruction, debarment, preclusion, barricade, blockade, frustration, inhibition, prohibition.

2. disagreement, confrontation, conflict, combat, contrariety, contradiction, antagonism, hostility, defiance, oppugnancy, *Fig.* oppugnation; contraposition, antithesis, contrast.

3. opponent, adversary, rival, competitor, opposer; antagonist, enemy, foe, oppugner, *Rare.* oppugnant; *Brit. Parl.* oppositionist.

oppress, *v.* **1.** burden, trouble, encumber, cumber, charge, weigh; strain, break, grind, press; handicap, hamper, tax; work, drive, overwork, overdrive, fag, task; exhaust, wear, wear down, weary; overload, overcharge, load, surcharge, overwhelm.

2. tyrannize, despotize, repress, overbear, overmaster; persecute, harry, harass, hound, beset; compel, coerce, subjugate, rule with an iron hand, weigh down, press down, put down, saddle, bridle; suppress, smother, keep down, *Inf.* clamp down, stamp down, ride roughshod over.

3. depress, grieve, aggrieve, lie heavily upon, drag down, weigh heavy on; afflict, pain, anguish, break one's heart, pierce one's heart; torment, desolate, crush, embitter; sadden, deject, dishearten, discourage, dispirit, dash, take the heart out of.

oppression, *n.* **1.** persecution, despotism, tyranny, fascism; iron hand, iron fist, heavy hand, high hand; compulsion, coercion, subjugation, enslavement; harassment, dogging, hounding, tormenting; cruelty, severity, harshness, hardness; ruthlessness, mercilessness, pitilessness, hard-heartedness.

2. charge, pressure, strain, drag, drain, tax; burden, *Archaic.* burthen, cross, encumbrance, cumbrance, trouble, vexation; load, weight, millstone, albatross.

3. hardship, misery, suffering, unhappiness, infelicity, wretchedness; bitterness, anguish, agony, melancholy, sadness; dejection, downheartedness, dejectedness, discouragement, disheartening; depression, affliction, sorrow, grief, woe.

4. heartache, desolation, despair, distress, grievance; torture, rack, torment, passion, dolor, ache, throe, pang; trial, tribulation, bitter pill, thorn in the side, crown of thorns.

oppressive, *adj.* **1.** burdensome, onerous, cumbersome; laborious, toilsome, arduous, operose, wearisome; grinding, wearing, exhausting, racking, trying; unbearable, unsufferable, unendurable, intolerable.

2. tyrannical, despotic, draconian, inquisitorial; overbearing, overpowering, overwhelming, domineering, high-handed, iron-fisted; harsh, cruel, crushing, heavy, brutal; ruthless, merciless, pitiless; relentless, remorseless, unrelenting, implacable, inexorable; hard, severe, stiff, rigid, rough.

3. discomforting, uncomfortable, stuffy, suffocating; close, stifling, airless, breathless, unventilated, windowless; breezeless, windless, sultry, sweltering, hot.

4. distressing, grievous, painful, afflictive, baleful; depressing, dispiriting, disheartening, discouraging; sorrowful, dolorous, miserable, mournful, sad, lugubrious; wretched, woeful, dire, grim, harrowing.

opprobrious, *adj.* **1.** disgraceful, dishonorable, shameful, degraded, inglorious; infamous, ignominious, odious, contemptible, despicable, detestable, sordid, degenerate, depraved, horrible, heinous, vicious, atrocious, flagitious; corrupt, reprehensible, unprincipled, debased, base, vile, evil, sinful, bad, wrong, low, arrant, nefarious, *Obs.* scelerous; mean, villainous, ignoble.

2. derogatory, discrediting, disapproving, disfavorable, unfavorable, disapprobatory, disapprobative; censuring, reproachful, impeaching, inveighing, reproving, recriminating, reprehensive, reprobative, reprobating; defamatory, denigrating, vituperative, vilifying, vilipenditory; slanderous, libelous, calumnious, calumniatory.

opprobrium, *n.* **1.** disgrace, dishonor, shame, degradation, debasement, vitiation, ill repute, ingloriousness; ignominy, infamy, odium, obloquy, disrepute, notoriety.

2. discredit, disfavor, disapproval, disapprobation, disesteem, loss of face; belittlement, disparagement, deprecation, deflation, derogation, depreciation, devaluation.

oppugn, *v.* **1.** criticize, attack, assail, impugn, flay, light into, *Inf.* lace into, *Sl.* rip *or* tear into; *Inf.* pan, put down, *Inf.* knock, shoot down, *Sl.* blast, *Sl.* let [s.o.] have it; haul *or* rake over the coals, *Sl.* cut up *or* to pieces, pick apart, pick to pieces, *Inf.* pick holes in, nit-pick, find fault, carp, cavil.

2. call into question, bring into question, question, contest, dispute, debate, argue; take exception, demur, object, protest, disagree, dissent, differ.

opt, *v.* *Usu.* **opt for** make a choice, choose, pick, select, single out, go for, lean toward; determine, de cide *or* decide on, make up one's mind.

optic, *adj.* **1.** optical, visual, ocular, ophthalmic. —*n.* **2.** lens, eyepiece, *Optics.* ocular.

3. *Informal.* eye, orb, *Sl.* glim, *Sl.* peepers.

optimism, *n.* cheerful *or* bright *or* rosy outlook, Pollyannaism, looking on the bright side; cheerfulness, buoyancy, enthusiasm, radiance, sanguineness, sunniness, keeping one's sunny side up; high hopes, bright hopes, fond hopes, great expectations, happy expectancy, anticipation; hopefulness, hope, faith, trust, reliance; fool's paradise, *Inf.* pipe dream, looking for pie in the sky; assurance, confidence, certainty, conviction.

optimist, *n.* hoper, hopeful dreamer, daydreamer, romancer, romantic, Pollyanna, cockeyed optimist; castlebuilder, visionary, utopian, idealist, Candide, Pangloss; enthusiast, ball of fire.

optimistic, *adj.* **1.** hopeful, expectant, full of hope, anticipative, looking forward to; assured, confident, bullish, assuring, reassuring; auspicious, favorable, propitious; promising, upbeat, looking up; encouraging, heartening, fortifying, vivifying.

2. idealistic, utopian, visionary; dreaming, dreamy, romantic, starry-eyed, castle-building, quixotic; unrealistic, impractical, impracticable, infeasible.

3. cheerful, cheery, full of cheer, sunny; blithe, blithesome, light-hearted, lightsome, buoyant, positive, upbeat, beamish; carefree, free and easy, breezy, airy, untroubled, happy-go-lucky; elated, jubilant, exhilarated, energetic, energized.

optimum, *n.* **1.** finest, first, leading, top, foremost; strongest, most powerful, healthiest; acme, height, pinnacle, peak; paragon, nonpareil, flower, phoenix; ideal, model, exemplar.

2. prize, best, prime, choice, rarest, treasure, tidbit, elect, elite, pick, select, best part; gem, jewel, pearl, flower, cream of the crop, one in a thousand.

—*adj.* **3.** optimal, best, most favorable; first-rate, first-class, prime, A-1, capital; *Inf.* champion, tiptop; consummate, perfect, excellent, ideal, sterling; prize, exceptional, singular; preferred, preferable, preferential; select, elect, singled out, chosen, hand-picked, elite, cream; superior, superlative, supreme, paramount; unique, extraordinary, unusual; unsurpassed, peerless, unexcelled.

option, *n.* **1.** choice, alternative, *Dial.* druthers, possibility; answer, way out, solution; replacement, substitute, equivalent, surrogate, Plan B.

2. choosing, selection, adoption, acceptance, embracement, espousal, choice; election, co-option, cooptation; nomination, vote, voice; appointment, assignment, determination, commitment; judgment, opinion, discretion, volition, will, conclusion; discrimination, selectivity, differentiation.

3. pleasure, taste, preference, wish, desire; propensity, inclination, partiality, predisposition, predilection, prepossession.

optional, *adj.* voluntary, unforced, uncoerced, uncompelled, spontaneous, unprompted, unbidden, unasked for, unsolicited; discretionary, elective, open, *Inf.* up to you, volitional, volitionary, free, independent, not required.

opulence, *n.* **1.** affluence, wealth, riches; fortune, plenty, bounty; prosperity, *Sl.* easy street, wealthiness; money, gold, capital, substance, property, resources, wherewithal.

2. abundance, plenitude, amplitude, fullness, richness; excessiveness, luxuriance, profusion, copiousness, plethora; surfeit, repletion, nimiety, excess, exuberance; superabundance, superfluity, cornucopia, horn of plenty.

opulent, *adj.* **1.** wealthy, rich, affluent, prosperous, moneyed, flush, well-off, well-to-do, worth a great deal, heeled, *Inf.* well-heeled, *Inf.* made of money, *Inf.* rolling in money *or* dough, *Inf.* loaded, *Sl.* in the money *or* dough *or* chips, *Sl.* filthy rich; comfortable, easy, *Inf.* on Easy Street, *Inf.* high on the hog, *Inf.* in clover, *Inf.* well-situated, *Inf.* on velvet, wallowing in wealth.

2. abundant, profuse, rife, brimming, teeming, full; plenteous, plentiful, bouteous, abounding, bountiful; copious, lavish, exuberant, luxuriant; superabundant, excessive, plethoric, overfull.

opus, *n.* **1.** work, composition, piece, production; book, volume, tome, publication, title, literary work *or* composition, *Fr. oeuvre;* opera, musical piece *or* composition; brainchild, lucubration.

2. *Informal.* motion picture, moving picture, picture, film, cinema, *Inf.* movie, flick; screenplay, photoplay, photodrama; teleplay, television drama *or* play, TV drama *or* play; radio drama *or* play, broadcast drama.

or, *conj.* otherwise, else, conversely, alternatively, optionally; in other words, on the other hand, contrarily, by way of contrast.

oracle, *n.* **1.** wiseman, sage, prophet, sibyl; augur, seer, soothsayer, prognosticator, fortuneteller, foreteller, predictor, forecaster, foreseer; diviner, divinator, necromancer, magus, sorcerer, sorceress, spiritualist; theurgist, astrologer, horoscoper, astromancer, *Obs.* astrolog, star diviner, stargazer; dowser.

2. revelation, divine communication, answer, truth, advice, judgment, injunction; augury, prognostication, prophecy, prediction, prefigurement; vaticination, soothsaying, fortune, foretelling, divination; clairvoyance, second sight; omen, sign, portent, token, prognostic, presage, bodement; premonition, forewarning, foretoken.

oracular, *adj.* **1.** prophetic, prophetical, sibylic, sibylline, vatic, vatical, vatinical, pythonic, fatidic, fatidical; augural, divinatory, haruspical, mantic, Delphic, Delphian; foretelling, presaging, foreshadowing, presentient; prognostic, predictive, predictory.

2. authoritative, absolute, positive, official, official-sounding, *Latin. ex cathedra;* commanding, judicious, judicial, philosophical, apocalyptical, apocalyptic; arbitrary, dictatorial, prescriptive, imperious, dogmatic, opinionated, self-assured; pontifical, peremptory, doctrinaire.

3. grave, solemn, magisterial, imposing, profound, weighty, heavy; pointed, aphoristic, gnomic, sententious.

4. metaphorical, symbolic, figurative, allegorical, latent, between the lines, under the surface; obscure, enigmatic, not easily understood, obfuscated, vague, nebulous, ambiguous, cryptic, arcane; mystic, orphic, occult, mysterious, dark, hidden, shrouded, clouded, impenetrable, unfathomable; confusing, unclear, indefinite, unspecific, equivocal, perplexing, puzzling, undefinable.

5. portentous, fateful, indicative, significant, boding, suggestive, allusive, allusory, pregnant; ominous, sinister, frightening, disquieting, disturbing; premonitory, foreboding, direful, alarming, fear-inspiring; threatening, menacing, minatory, making one's flesh crawl *or* creep, making one's hair stand on end, *Inf.* creepy.

oral, *adj.* **1.** spoken, uttered, said, vocalized, voiced, sounded, pronounced, enunciated, intoned;

vocal, expressed, articulated, verbal, conversational.
2. unwritten, word-of-mouth, parol, nuncupative, viva voce.
3. mouthlike, orificial, mandibular, maxillary, *Anat.* buccal.
—*n.* **4.** oral examination, examination, quiz, quizzing, questioning, trial, test, doctor's oral, master's oral, viva voce examination, *Inf.* viva; audition, hearing.

orate, *v.* declaim, speak, perorate, proclaim, hold forth; make a speech, soapbox, make an address, prelect, lecture; sermonize, preach, eulogize; soliloquize, apostrophize; speechify, harangue, rant, rail, spout, *Inf.* sound off; mouth, talk big, rodomontade.

oration, *n.* formal speech, allocution, address, valedictory, lecture, prelection; recitation, monologue, soliloquy, apostrophe; sermon, preachment, homily, eulogy, panegyric; declamation, discourse, disquisition, dissertation, treatise; tirade, harangue, *Inf.* stump speech, *Inf.* spiel.

orator, *n.* public speaker, speechmaker, declaimer; lecturer, prelector, speaker, reader, reciter; rhetor, rhetorician, *Speech.* elocutionist; sermonizer, preacher; demagogue, spellbinder.

oratorical, *adj.* **1.** rhetorical, *Speech.* elocutionary, declamatory; eloquent, articulate, well-spoken, silver-tongued, *Archaic.* facund, *Obs.* facundious, Ciceronian; (*all of speech*) poetic, graceful, easy, facile, flowing, fluent, glib, slick, smooth, smooth-tongued.
2. (*all of speech*) expressive, cogent, telling; forceful, emphatic, spirited, vigorous, impassioned, trenchant, vehement, burning; effective, persuasive, impressive.
3. mouthy, ranting, railing, spouting; bombastic, pompous, orotund, fustian, pretentious; grandiose, magniloquent, grandiloquent, Johnsonian, Ossianic, sonorous, sesquipedalian.

oratory, *n.* rhetoric, art of public speaking, declamation; eloquence, power of speech, forcefulness, expressiveness, cogency; elocution, diction, address, articulation, enunciation; gift of gab, command of words, way with words, *Archaic.* facundity; (*all of speech*) fluency, facility, ease, glibness, slickness, smoothness.

orb, *n.* **1.** heavenly *or* celestial body, sun, star, planet, moon.
2. sphere, globe, orbit, ball, round, globoid; globule, spherule, spheroid, oval.
3. eye, *Anat.* orbit, eyeball, *Sl.* glim, *Sl.* peepers.

orbicular, *adj.* orbiculate, orblike, round, rounded, rotund, bulbous, bulb-shaped; spherical, spheric, spheral, spheroidal, spheroidic, spherelike, spherular; global, globular, globulous, globe-shaped, globate, globoid, globose, globelike; oval, ovate, oviform, ovoid, egg-shaped; elliptical, ellipsoidal, circular, cycloid, cycloidal, ringlike, annular, ring-shaped; cylindrical, cylindroid; bell-shaped, campanulate; pear-shaped, pyriform.

orbit, *n.* **1.** revolution, circumgyration, circle, circuit, cycle, round; turn, circumvolution, rotation, circumrotation; path, course, track, trajectory.
2. course, pattern, routine.
3. orb, sphere, ball. See **orb** (*def.* **2**).
—*v.* **4.** revolve, circle, encircle; rotate, turn, circumrotate, circumvolve.

orchestra, *n.* **1.** symphony orchestra, symphony, philharmonic, string orchestra, *Music.* string ensemble; chamber orchestra, quartet; symphonic band, band, combo.
2. orchestra pit, pit; *U.S.* main floor, parquet, parquet circle, orchestra circle, parterre.

ordain, *v.* **1.** frock; induct, install, inaugurate, swear in, administer the oath of office, instate, *Rare.* auspicate; invest, chair, establish in office; crown, enthrone; consecrate, anoint.
2. enact, make into law, legislate, pass into law, establish, set *or* set up, arrange *or* arrange for; decree, rule, adjudge, determine; order, command, dictate, pronounce, proclaim, declare; give orders for, authorize, warrant, sanction; charge, bid, enjoin, direct, prescribe, instruct; exact, demand, require, tax with.
3. destine, fate, doom, predestine, predetermine, foreordain, foredoom.

ordeal, *n.* trial, test, trying experience, tribulation, trouble, affliction; hardship, suffering, deprivation, privation, infliction, oppression, persecution; pain, agony, torture, hell; distress, anguish, misery, grief, woe, sorrow, sadness; adversity, misfortune, tragedy, calamity, disaster; *All Sl.* drag, bummer, bad trip.

order, *n.* **1.** command, commandment, mandate, dictate, dictum, direction, directive, instruction, behest, *Archaic.* hest, imperative, ultimatum; prescript, prescription, enjoinment; rule, regulation, act, law, ordinance, statute, edict, decree, fiat, ukase, proclamation, pronunciamento, manifesto; exaction, imposition, requirement, demand, assignment; admonition, charge, injunction, exhortation; bidding, summons, call, request, notification; *All Law.* writ, subpoena, mandamus, mittimus, habeas corpus.
2. arrangement, grouping, dispersement, disposition; organization, systemization, systematization, method; classification, codification, categorization; structure, framework, form.
3. uniformity, regularity, symmetry, system; harmony, accord, apple-pie order; tidiness, neatness, trimness, orderliness, fitness.
4. condition, shape, state, health; status, situation.
5. class, sort, ilk, genre, type, kind; nature, kidney, temper, humor, disposition, spirit, constitution, character; manner, style; mold, grain, cast, stamp, brand, cut; species, breed, genus, category, variety.
6. rank, degree, grade, estate, caste, station, position; stock, stirps, lineage, descent, ancestry.
7. lodge, knighthood, Knights of Columbus, Masons, guild; club, society, sodality, secret society, Skull and Bones; fraternity, brotherhood, fellowship; sorority, sisterhood; commune, community, coterie, clique, cabal, circle, school; party, organization, machine, company, band, team, body; confederacy, alliance, junta, council.
8. denomination, sect, faction, cult; church, parishioners; persuasion, belief, ism, religion, affiliation.
9. lawfulness, law and order, quiet, peace, peace and quiet; calm, silence, serenity, tranquillity, concord.
10. regime, regimen, government, reign, management, control.
11. usage, mores, customs, manners, the way it is.
12. **out of order** **a.** inappropriate, unsuitable, out of place; unseemly, indecorous, unfit, *Sl.* not kosher, improper. **b.** inoperative, nonfunctioning, broken, out of commission, in disrepair, *Sl.* busted; gone haywire, *Sl.* out of whack, *Inf.* out of kilter, *Sl.* on the fritz, *Inf.* on the blink, *Sl.* kaput, *Sl.* shot, *Sl.* gone kerflooie.
—*v.* **13.** command, direct, adjure, charge, instruct; bid, tell, require, stipulate, demand, exact; compel, force, coerce, make; prescribe, enjoin, lay down the law, give the word, determine; decree, ordain, assign.
14. regulate, conduct, manage, run, operate; supervise, oversee, administer, steer; maintain, handle, discharge, discipline; fix, plan, plot, adjust.
15. organize, marshal, put to rights, set to rights; systemize, systematize, methodize, classify, codify,

categorize, catalogue; assort, arrange, lay out, sort out, tidy, neaten, line up, line, align.

orderly, *adj.* **1.** neat, tidy, uncluttered, trim, *Brit.* trig, neat as a pin, neat as a bandbox; shipshape, snug, spick-and-span, picked up, *Inf.* in apple-pie order, in good shape, with a place for everything and everything in its place; spruce, smart, well-groomed; balanced, well-balanced, apollonian, well-proportioned, well-arranged, harmonious, symmetrical, well-designed; regular, uniform, constant, even; steady, on an even keel, unchanging, undeviating, alike.

2. methodical, systematic, scientific; precise, sharp, keen, exact, meticulous, discriminating; efficient, businesslike, correct, careful, attentive, alert, clear-headed, clear-witted, level-headed; thorough, straightforward, direct, conventional, formal.

3. law-abiding, peaceable, well-behaved, well-mannered, mannerly, civil, courteous, polite; disciplined, obedient, dutiful, self-controlled, restrained; nonviolent, peaceful, pacific, irenic; quiet, gentle, mild, placid, serene, tranquil; civilized, considerate, thoughtful, neighborly; nonresisting, yielding, submissive.

—n. **4.** attendant, assistant, adjutant; nurse's aide, tender, steward; messenger, runner, *Sl.* gofer, errand boy; underling, factotum, menial, servant, *Brit. Mil.* batman.

ordinance, *n.* **1.** decree, edict, *Law.* writ, rescript, assize; dictate, dictum, order, command, injunction, fiat, sanction, prescript, prescription, mandate, firman; commandment, behest, dictation; word, word of command, direct order, *Inf.* the word; charge, commission, directive, direction, instruction; ruling, proclamation, pronouncement, declaration, ukase, bull; precept, canon, rubric; guideline, working principle, guiding principle.

2. law, regulation, rule, bylaw, statute; enactment, act, measure, bill; control, prohibition, ban, restriction.

3. *Eccles.* rite, ceremony, institution, form, prescribed form, mode of worship; sacrament, communion.

ordinarily, *adv.* **1.** generally, in general, in ordinary cases, under usual circumstances, usually, in the usual course of things, customarily; habitually, from habit, as a rule, from day to day, regularly, routinely, daily, *Inf.* like clockwork; frequently, for the most part, by and large, most often, often enough, *Inf.* right along.

2. plainly, simply, modestly, without fuss, quietly, unpretentiously, matter-of-factly; in an ordinary way, commonly, commonplacely, prosaically, without distinction.

3. reasonably, to the usual *or* expected extent, in most cases *or* instances, mostly, chiefly, mainly, all things considered, on balance, all in all; in the ordinary way, familiarly, normally, as a matter of course, as a rule, conventionally, *Inf.* by the book.

ordinary, *adj.* **1.** usual, conventional, regular, natural, normal, average; typical, general, prevalent, prevailing, common, current, popular; understood, approved, accepted, recognized; customary, wonted, accustomed, habitual, routine, repeated, recurrent; established, acknowledged, ritual, traditional, orthodox, consuetudinary; familiar, known, everyday, standard, *Inf.* G. I.; known, well-known, set, fixed, cut and dried, predetermined.

2. plain, simple, native, domestic, homespun, garden-variety, run-of-the-mill *or* -mine, household, commonplace, salt-of-the-earth; middle-class, stereotypical, homely, workday, workaday, vernacular, colloquial, informal, prosaic, pedestrian, plebian, bourgeois, unrefined, provincial, *Inf.* down-home; unexceptional, undistinguished, insignificant, somewhat inferior, second-rate, indifferent, unimpressive; medium, humdrum, so-so, passable, tolerable, fair; inferior, of no value, worthless, low-bred, low-brow, ill-bred; nameless, ignominious, inglorious, ignoble, *Sl.* cotton pickin', *Sl.* no great shakes, *Inf.* dime-a-dozen.

3. hackneyed, overdone, dull, stale, tired, stock, cliché; dry, trite, unimaginative, insipid, wishy-washy, tame, banal, tedious, uninspired, *Inf.* old hat, *Inf.* pat; oft-repeated, oft met with, expected, predictable, overused, worn-out, well-trodden, in the beaten path.

4. humble, modest, unpretentious, unpretending, unassuming, unostentatious.

5. inconsequential, of little *or* small *or* no importance, insignificant, small, minute, trivial, paltry, petty, puny, trifling, piddling, *Inf.* measly, *Sl.* small potatoes, *Sl.* small-time, *Inf.* bush *or* minor league, *Sl.* two-bit.

6. mean, low, vile, cheap, base; coarse, vulgar, poor, shabby, drab, ignoble; uncouth, uncultured.

—n. **7.** average, standard, norm, par; ordinary condition, the common way, the way things are, status quo, the normal order of things; convention, conventional usage, fixed practice, *Brit. Inf.* the drill; formality, habit, settled way, fashion; usual rut, groove, expected routine, beaten track *or* path, usual run, wont, standard round.

8. out of the ordinary unusual, strange, different, singular, curious, quaint, eccentric, outlandish, bizarre, weird, *Inf.* oddball, *Inf.* kooky; out of the way, uncommon, unwonted, unfamiliar, unheard of, undreamed of, off the beaten path *or* track, unexpected, offbeat, stray, rare, unique, *Fr. recherché;* extraordinary, exceptional, remarkable, wonderful.

ordination, *n.* **1.** *Eccles.* ordainment, holy orders, orders, consecration, ecclesiastical office.

2. investiture, empowering, accrediting, conferment, instatement, charging, presentation; installation, induction, nomination, designation, election, appointment, admission, acceptance, initiation, *Inf.* tapping, *Inf.* tabbing; dedication, commitment, enlistment, enrollment.

3. decreeing, ordaining, ordering; commandment, instruction; exaction, prescription, requirement; declaration, lawgiving, ruling, *Inf.* laying down the law; dictation, enjoinment, bidding, behest.

4. arranging, planning, organization, methodization, systematization; disposition, distribution, settlement, disposal; classification, codification, categorization, tabulation, alphabetization, collocation, allocation, coordination, graduation, gradation, construction, composition.

5. arrangement, order, system, routine, method; structure, form, plan, scheme, line-up, setup, layout.

ordnance, *n.* **1.** cannon, artillery, field artillery, heavy *or* light artillery, mortars, mounted guns, *Mil.* field pieces. See **artillery.**

2. weapons, arms, armament, munitions, equipment; provisions, materials of war, army *or* military supplies, stores; ammunition, *Inf.* ammo, missilery; musketry, powder and shot.

3. quartermaster corps; supply, army supply.

ordure, *n.* manure, dung, muck, fertilizer, compost, dressing; excrement, guano, night soil, droppings, cow *or* buffalo chips, *U.S. West.* cow pies, coprolites, coproliths, *Sl.* flops; feces, stools, fecula, fecal matter, feculence; refuse, filth, offal, garbage, rubbish, waste.

ore, *n.* metal, element, mineral, bullion, *Metall.* pig.

organ, *n.* **1.** pipe organ, reed organ, melodeon, harmonium, electronic organ; barrel organ, hand organ, hurdy-gurdy; accordion, piano accordion.

2. (*all of a plant or animal*) part, member, element, ingredient, component, constituent, integrant.

3. means, agency, factor, medium, vehicle; method, mode, manner, way, course, route, road, alternative, option; process, measures, steps, actions, procedures; instrument, tool, implement, device, contrivance, appliance, convenience, machine, apparatus, mechanical aid; aid, auxiliary, expedient, resort, resource, reserve.

4. (*all representing a special group*) mouthpiece, forum, publication, newspaper, paper, journal, magazine, periodical, *Inf.* sheet; *Inf.* rag; daily, weekly, bi-monthly, monthly, quarterly.

organic, *adj.* **1.** natural, nonchemical.

2. living, alive, animate, *Archaic.* quick, breathing, moving; biotic, biotical; zooid, zooidal.

3. organized, systematic, methodical, orderly, regular, consistent; formal, symmetrical, designed, planned, patterned, laid out; methodized, systemized, ordered, classified, filed, arranged in order, tabular, alphabetical, alphabetized; in order, in sequence, in place, neat, tidy, trim, shipshape.

4. anatomical, constitutional, structural; inherent, innate, intrinsic, natural, true; native, indigenous, instinctive, rooted, ingrained; essential, indispensable, vital; primary, fundamental, radical, basic, basal, rudimentary, elementary, elemental.

organism, *n.* **1.** being, body, entity, living thing, something; creature, living creature, beast, animal; plant, vegetable; *Biol.* cell, microscopic plant *or* animal; individual, human, human being, man, person, fellow, earthling.

2. organization, company, corporation, association, alliance, league, union. See **organization** (*def.* **4**).

organization, *n.* **1.** systematization, methodization, standardization; arrangement, order, ordering, ordination, disposition, disposal; coordination, grouping, group, collection, array, selection, assortment, collocation, set, series, line-up; class, classification, category, categorization, placement, place, pigeonhole, bracket; file, index, catalog, codification, tabulation; sizing, ranking, rating, grade, grading, graduation, denomination, division.

2. system, scheme, method, plan; design, pattern, format, outline, frame, framework; construction, structure, formation, conformation, configuration; composition, make-up, chemistry, constitution; form, shape, figure, build, physique, body.

3. unionization, unification, unity, combination, affiliation, association; incorporation, consolidation, blend, amalgamation, coalescence.

4. association, consortium, league, coalition, alliance, federation, confederation, confederacy; union, labor union, guild, syndication, conspiracy, collusion, cabal; organism, company, business operation, partnership, joint concern; conglomerate, *Law.* consolidation, amalgamation, combine, merger; monopoly, trust, alignment, bloc, cartel; political party, party, camorra; congregation, assemblage, society, group; band, gang, corps, team, brigade, troop, unit, *Inf.* outfit; community, circle, set, clique, faction, clan, social set, club, country club; lodge, fraternity, brotherhood, sorority.

organize, *v.* **1.** form, make, make up, create, devise, formulate, develop; originate, start, begin, initiate, spawn, give birth to, give rise to, produce; set up, found, institute, establish; build, erect, construct; frame, shape, mold, arrange, dispose, adjust, regulate.

2. systematize, methodize, standardize; coordinate, arrange in order, marshal, *Inf.* line up, array; order, put in order, put in place, collocate, *Brit. Sl.* buff down, square off; line, range, align, aline, straighten, trim; group, sort, sort out, separate, assort, class, classify, categorize, pigeonhole, bracket; file, index, catalog, codify, tabulate; size, rank, rate, grade, graduate, assign a place.

3. form a union, organize a union, unionize; unify, unite, combine, associate, incorporate, consolidate; merge, fuse, blend, amalgamate, coalesce; group together, brigade, band together, ally, join together, team up, league, federate, conferederate.

4. *Informal.* organize oneself, collect one's thoughts, *Sl.* get it together, *Sl.* get one's head together, *Sl.* get one's stuff together.

orgasm, *n.* (*usu. in reference to sexual pleasure*) climax, culmination, peak, acme, zenith, high *or* crowning point, supreme moment, consummation, fruition, *Inf.* payoff, *Sl.* come; height, epitome, extremity, maximum, *U.S. Sl.* the most, *U.S. Sl.* the greatest.

orgasmic, *adj.* orgastic; ecstatic, exalted, exhilarated, excited, enthusiastic, thrilled, elated, overjoyed, transported, ravished, overcome; rapturous, rhapsodic, blissful, in heaven, in seventh heaven, on cloud nine, happy as a clam at high tide; beside oneself, bouncing with joy, delirious, in orbit, flying, floating, walking on air; very happy, delighted, joyful, glad, felicitious, beaming.

orgiastic, *adj.* **1.** bacchanalian, saturnalian, bacchanal, bacchic, drunken, dissolute, debauched, dissipated; riotous, wild, frenzied, frenetic, mad; abandoned, wanton, licentious, intemperate, Dionysian, uninhibited, unrestrained, undisciplined; festive, gay, merry, jocund, sportive.

2. arousing, exciting, stimulating, provoking.

orgy, *n.* **1.** bacchanalia, carousal, carouse, *Archaic.* rouse, carousing, saturnalia, Dionysia, bacchanal; *Sl.* group grope, *Sl.* love-in; *Sl.* Wesson oil party, debauch, spree, *Inf.* binge, fling, drinking bout, lost weekend, *Inf.* jag, *Inf.* toot, *Sl.* tear, *Sl.* bust, *U.S. Sl.* bender; compotation, wassail.

2. revelry, reveling, revels, frolic, merry-making, *Sl.* goings-on, partying, party, celebration, *Sl.* wing-ding, *Sl.* hot time, *Sl.* ball, *Sl.* blast, *Sl.* bash; carnival, festival, festivity, jollification, conviviality.

orient, *n.* **1. the Orient** the East, Levant, Eastern Hemisphere, Asia, Far East, the China coast, east of Suez, East Indies, the Pacific, land of the sunrise.

—*adj.* **2.** lustrous, opalescent, pearly, nacred, oriental; iridescent, glossy, glowing.

—*v.* **3.** orientate, adjust, adapt, accommodate, conform, compromise; familiarize, habituate, make used to, get used to, break in, condition, season, train; reconcile, acclimatize, acclimate, regulate.

4. face, turn, turn toward, direct; front, front on, place, situate, locate, set, settle, square, collimate, fix; relate, arrange, line up, straighten out, tailor, true, true up, synchronize, *Inf.* sync.

5. take *or* get one's bearing *or* bearings, get the lay of the land, see which way the wind blows *or* the land lies; assess, reassess, feel one's way.

oriental, *adj.* *Usu.* **Oriental** eastern, far eastern, Asian, Asiatic, Levantine.

orientate, *v.* See **orient** (*defs.* **3-5**).

orientation, *n.* **1.** bearings, placement, placing, orientating; attunement, setting up, coordination, squaring, straightening out, fixing; alignment, collimation, truing, synchronization.

2. adjusting, getting one's bearings, acclimatization, acclimation, assimilation, fitting in; domestication, habituation, naturalization; adjustment, adaptation, accommodation, settlement, conformity, compromise, bending, yielding.

3. introduction, initiation, reception, receiving, welcome, welcoming, briefing; preparation, preliminaries, initial instructions *or* directions, propaedeutics; familiarization, training, accustoming, breaking in, *Inf.* showing [s.o.] around *or* the ropes.

orifice, *n.* opening, hole, vent, outlet, venthole; window, hatch, hatchway, scuttle, *Naut.* booby hatch, gate, door, portal, *Naut.* scupper; drain, exhaust, spout, tap; gap, space, breach, break, check, leak, cleft, slot, slit, sissure, cranny, fissure, gash, rime, rift, crevice; mine, tunnel, cave, shaft, pit, hollow, cavity, cavern; entrance, inlet, passage, gat; aperture, ostiole, foraman, *Anat., Zool.* fenestra, spiracle, blowhole, *Zool.* alveolus; interstice, areola, pore, stoma, *Anat.* sinus; puncture, perforation, peephole, buttonhole, pinhole, eye, eyelet; bore, caliber; gape, yawn, lacuna, mouth, oral opening *or* cavity, embouchure, mouthhole, *Sl.* yap, *Sl.* trap, *Sl.* bazoo.

origin, *n.* **1.** source, provenience, provenance; root, taproot, *Bot.* radicle, *Bot.* radix, etiology, derivation, etymon; fountainhead, fount, fountain, head, wellspring, well, spring, rise; base, basis, foundation, fundamental, rudiment, ground.

2. beginning, genesis, alpha, prime, dawn, dawning; incipience, inception, commencement, start, outset, the word "go"; germ, seed, conception, germination, embryo; budding, sprouting, emergence, first flowering, *Both Embryol.* primordium, aulage; matrix, womb, cradle, hotbed.

3. birth, nativity, parentage; ancestry, extraction, stock, stem, stirps, lineage, line, descent, pedigree, genealogy; family, house; breed, race.

original, *adj.* **1.** primary, primordial, primigenial, incipient, prime, initial, first, firsthand; primeval, primal, primitive, pristine, earliest; aboriginal, autochthonal, autochthonous, indigenous, endemic, endemical, native; radical, basic, fundamental, elemental, underlying, underived; intrinsic, inherent, inborn, innate, connate, congenital.

2. novel, new, newfangled, unprecedented, unknown, unheard-of; fresh, young, maiden, virgin, untried; unique, singular, special; rare, peculiar, uncommon, signal, extraordinary, different, unusual, out of the ordinary, *Latin. sui generis.*

3. creative, seminal, imaginative, ingenious, inventive, resourceful, originative, initiative, institutive; individualistic, independent, self-reliant, self-sufficient, self-contained, autonomous; diverse, divergent, unorthodox, unconventional, nonconforming, unimitative, unimitating, unimitated, borrowed, unborrowing.

4. prototypal, prototypic, prototypical, protoplastic; archetypal, archetypic, archetypical, exemplary; genuine, authentic, *Archaic.* authentical, actual, real, true.

—*n.* **5.** prototype, pattern, archetype, model, exemplar, type, form, mold; ideal, paragon, standard; example, specimen, sample; ancestor, precursor, precedent.

6. creation, ingenuity, breath of fresh air; protoplast, first copy.

7. source, origin, genesis, root, *Both Bot.* radix, radicle; subject, referent, actuality, the genuine article, the real thing, *Sl.* the real McCoy.

8. creator, neoteric; originator, mastermind; individualist, independent, eccentric, oddity, *Inf.* character; freethinker, bohemian, noncomformist, nonpartisan, dissenter, heretic.

originality, *n.* **1.** creativity, creativeness, imagination, imaginativeness, ingenuity, ingeniousness, inventiveness, resourcefulness, initiative; individuality, independence, self-reliance, self-sufficience, autonomy; divergence, nonimitativeness, unorthodoxy, unconventionality, nonconformity, break with tradition.

2. novelty, newness, innovativeness, newfangledness, unprecedentedness, unknownness; freshness, virginity; uniqueness, singularity, specialness, rareness, unusualness, unusuality, uncommonness, extraordinariness; peculiarity, unexpectedness.

originally, *adv.* **1.** by birth, by origin.

2. at first, initially, in the beginning, at the start; from the beginning, from the start, *Inf.* from the word go, *Inf.* from day one, *Latin. ab ovo, Latin. ab initio, Latin. ab origine.*

3. in the first place, primarily, principally, mainly, chiefly; essentially, fundamentally, basically; in essence, in substance, in the main; at core, at heart, at bottom, *Fr. au fond.*

4. personally, individually, distinctively, singularly, characteristically; uniquely, uncommonly, unusually, peculiarly.

originate, *v.* **1.** emanate, emerge, issue, come; rise, arise, spring, flow; root, stem, grow, sprout, bud, break out, shoot, burst forth; derive, descend, follow, result, be based *or* grounded on.

2. begin, start, commence, initiate, inaugurate; conceive, germinate, breed, beget, give birth to; create, devise, invent, patent, coin, design, fashion, draft, draw up; compose, contrive, plan, mastermind, concoct; construct, formulate, form, fabricate, make; generate, produce, evolve, develop; introduce, launch, institute, establish, set up, found, occasion, bring about; discover, find.

originative, *adj.* creative, imaginative. See **original** (*def.* 3).

originator, *n.* initiator, actuator, instigator, agent, starter, mover, prime mover, catalyst, *Inf.* spark *or* spark plug; founder, inaugurator, inventor, deviser, organizer; author, architect, conceiver, shaper, designer, idea man, *Sl.* the brains; creator, maker, producer, begetter, engenderer, parent, mother, father, sire.

ornament, *n.* **1.** decoration, frill, filigree, flourish, flounce, furbelow; tinsel, spangle; bauble, trinket, knickknack, gimcrack, gewgaw, *Inf.* doodad, *Inf.* fandangle; accessory, attachment.

2. finery, frippery, frills, frills and furbelows, folderol, trumpery, gaudery, fuss, *Inf.* foofaraw, *Sl.* jazz.

3. luminary, leading light, star, superstar, *Sl.* pop star; celebrity, idol, favorite; notable, personage, important person, VIP, great man, somebody, *Inf.* lion.

4. adornment, decoration, embellishment, trimming, garnish, garnishment, garniture, *Archaic.* ouch; embroidery, elaboration, trappings, festoons; array, bedizenment, enrichment, beautification, prettification; emblazonment, emblazonry, illumination; luster, flourish, veneer, gloss, gilt, gilding.

5. sham, pretense, pinchbeck; affectation, pretension, pretentiousness; ostentation, meretriciousness, flamboyance, showiness, show, flashiness, *Sl.* flash; gaudiness, garishness, tawdriness.

—*v.* **6.** adorn, decorate, embellish, trim, garnish, furbish, *Archaic.* dight, *Archaic.* ouch; embroider, elaborate, festoon, rubricate; array, bedizen, deck, deck out, bedeck, trap, trap out, caparison; dress, dress up, attire, accouter; spangle, bespangle, stud, bestud, beset; emblazon, blazon, illuminate, paint, color, bedaub; gild, varnish, trick out, emboss, enchase.

7. beautify, prettify, fix up, prink, *Inf.* spruce up, *Inf.* pretty up, *Inf.* trick up.

8. enhance, enrich; intensify, deepen, heighten,

brighten; set off, set off to advantage; glorify; grace, dignify, bring honor, *Brit. Dial.* mense.

ornamental, *adj.* **1.** decorative, decorating, embellishing, adorning, garnishing, ornamenting; sightly, fair, attractive, graceful, enhancing, becoming, agreeable.

2. ornate, fancy, elaborate, busy; baroque, rococo, arabesque; florid, flowery.

3. ostentatious, meretricious, flamboyant, showy, flashy, *Sl.* flash; gawdy, garish, tawdry; grandiose, high-flown, *Inf.* highfalutin.

ornamentation, *n.* **1.** adornment, embellishment. See **ornament** (*def.* **4**).

2. finery, frippery, frilliness, frills, frills and furbelows, folderol, trumpery, gaudery, fuss, *Inf.* foofaraw, *Sl.* jazz; ostentation, meretriciousness, flamboyance, showiness, show, flashiness, *Sl.* flash; gaudiness, garishness, tawdriness.

3. ornateness, fanciness, elaborateness, business; baroqueness, baroque, rococo, arabesque; richness, luxuriance; brilliance, splendor, magnificence.

4. decoration, frill, ornament. See **ornament** (*def.* **1**).

ornate, *adj.* **1.** elaborate, involved, busy; fussy, frilly; baroque, rococo, arabesque.

2. elegant, fine, fancy; rich, lush, luxurious, luxuriant, sumptuous; brilliant, dazzling, glittering; gilt, begilt.

3. labored, richly-wrought, highly-wrought; overdone, overwrought, overworked, overlabored; overelegant.

4. (*all to a sumptuous degree*) adorned, decorated, embellished, embroidered, elaborated, festooned.

5. ostentatious, meretricious, flamboyant, showy, flashy, *Sl.* flash; gawdy, garish, tawdry.

6. (*all usu. of speech or writing*) affected, pretentious, stilted, lofty, fulsome, high-flown, high-flying, *Inf.* high-falutin; pompous, orotund, grandiloquent; florid, flowery, euphuistic; grandiose, high-sounding, big-sounding.

ornery, *adj. Informal.* **1.** cantankerous, surly, irascible, iracund, crabbed, crabby; ill-natured, unfriendly, obnoxious, choleric; ill-tempered, bad-tempered, short-tempered, quick-tempered; brusque, peppery, crusty, grumpy, grouchy, dyspeptic, bearish, snappish, snarling; cross, feisty, huffy, irritable, cranky, peevish, bilious, testy, touchy, tetchy; argumentative, quarrelsome, fractious, contentious, disagreeable, *Inf.* bitchy, *Inf.* ugly; uncivil, sharp, abrupt, curt, short, terse, blunt, rough.

2. stubborn, stubborn as a mule, mulish, muleheaded, pigheaded, bullheaded, bullish, headstrong, obstinate; willful, self-willed, contrary, perverse, wrongheaded, cross-grained, balky, uncooperative, *U.S. Inf.* notionate, *Inf.* cussed, *Archaic.* untoward; froward, refractory, recalcitrant, contumacious; ungovernable, unmanageable, uncontrollable, difficult, restive, unruly, incorrigible.

3. base, low, vile, mean, bad, mean-spirited, base-spirited, *Inf.* low-down, *Sl.* low-down-dirty-rotten.

orotund, *adj.* **1.** (*all of the voice*) strong, powerful, mighty; full, rich, mellifluous; deep, sonorous; resonant, resounding, reverberating, rolling, ringing; big, booming, thundering.

2. (*all of a style of speaking*) pompous, bombastic, fustian, grandiloquent, grandiose, lofty, stilted; turgid, swollen, inflated, overblown, puffed-up, *Inf.* windy, *Inf.* gassy; magniloquent, high-flown, high-sounding, *Inf.* high-falutin, big-sounding, lexiphanic, *Rare.* grandisonant; overdrawn, strained, affected, put-on; sesquipedalian, polysyllabic, *Inf.* jawbreaking.

orthodox, *adj.* **1.** (*all of theological or religious doctrine*) sound, correct, accurate, faithful, true, right, proper; of the faith, of the true faith, doctrinal, *Latin. ex cathedra;* authoritative, official, approved, accepted, recognized, acknowledged, admitted, kosher.

2. conventional, customary, accustomed, according to custom *or* use, usual, regular, standard, prevailing; conformist, traditionalist, in line, in step, in keeping, in accord; middle-class, bourgeois, middlebrow, middle-of-the-road, *Inf.* square, *Inf.* straight; fixed, established, set, cut-and-dried.

3. conservative, ultraconservative, right-wing, fundamentalist; purist, hidebound, creedbound, rigid, rigorous, strict, dogmatic; straitlaced, puritanical; obdurate, inflexible, unbending, unyielding, uncompromising.

orthodoxy, *n.* **1.** religious belief, belief, faith, creed, credo; faith, true faith, truth, gospel truth, word of God; authoritativeness, authenticity, canonicalness, doctrinalness; soundness, correctness, accurateness, faithfulness, rightness, properness, trueness.

2. conformity, conformance, compliance, observance, obedience; conventionality, traditionalism; custom, tradition; line, keeping, step, accordance, agreement.

3. conservatism, ultraconservatism, fundamentalism, puritanism; purism, literalism, precisionism; straitlacedness, stiff-neckedness, hideboundness, creedboundness; firmness, strictness, rigidness, rigidity, rigorousness, stiffness; obduracy, inflexibility, uncompromisingness, unbendingness, unyieldingness.

oscillate, *v.* **1.** vibrate, move to and fro, swing, move backward and forward, come and go, librate, move from side to side, ebb and flow, seesaw, wigwag.

2. fluctuate, vacillate, waver, vary, yo-yo, teeter-totter; about-face, change, change one's mind, *Brit. Dial.* chop, *U.S. Inf.* back and fill; shift, swerve, veer; hesitate, scruple, falter; be uncertain, be unsure, be doubtful, be undecided, be undetermined, not know one's own mind, not know where one stands, hang in the balance, hang; equivocate, shilly-shally, hem and haw, blow hot and cold, tergiversate, straddle the fence, be on the fence, be of two minds, debate.

oscillation, *n.* **1.** vibration, vibrating, swing, swinging, *Astron.* libration, seesawing, wigwagging, coming and going, moving to and fro, moving backward and forward; ebb and flow, rise and fall, flux and reflux.

2. single swing, sway, wave, stroke, beat.

3. fluctuation, vacillation, wavering, instability, unsteadiness; change, variation, alternation; hesitation, ambivalence, irresolution, indecision, undecisiveness, uncertainty, infirmity of purpose; fickleness, changeableness; equivocation, shilly-shallying, blowing hot and cold, tergiversation, straddling the fence.

oscitant, *adj.* **1.** drowsy, groggy, dozy, nodding, dozing, heavy-eyed, yawning; sleepy, sleeping, asleep, half-asleep, somnolent, slumberous, slumbery; off in a world of one's own, with one's head in the clouds, in the clouds, a million miles away; oblivious, detached, distracted, faraway, off guard, caught napping, inattentive.

2. sluggish, torpid, lethargic, lentitudinous, hebetudinous, phlegmatic, lymphatic; otiose, lazy, slow, lackadaisical, indolent; dull, drugged, dazed, *Inf.* dopey; lifeless, dormant, inactive, weary, listless.

osculate, *v.* **1.** kiss, *Inf.* buss, *Inf.* smack, *Inf.* smooch, *Inf.* canoodle, *Inf.* make out, *Inf.* fool around, neck, *Inf.* park, bundle, *Inf.* spoon.

2. come into contact, be contiguous, touch, graze, skim, brush, rub; clasp, hug, embrace; meet, merge, blend, combine, inosculate; connect, join, adjoin, conjoin.

osculation, *n.* **1.** kiss, *Inf.* buss, *Inf.* smack, *Inf.* smooch, *Inf.* peck; kissing, *Inf.* smooching, *Inf.* making out, *Inf.* fooling around, necking, *Inf.* spooning.
2. close contact, touch, taction, tangency, contiguity; clasp, grip, hug, embrace; connection, link, bond, inosculation; meeting, merging, adjoining, blend, blending, combination, conjunction, junction.

osseous, *adj.* bony, skeletal; ossified, indurated, indurate, callous, hard, hardened, rigidified, rigid; stiff, inflexible, unbending, impliable; ossiferous.

ossification, *n.* bone formation, *Physiol.* ostosis, induration, hardening; fossilization, petrification.

ossified, *adj.* hardened, hard, indurated, indurate, bony, callous, rigidified, rigid, stiffened, stiff; fossilized, petrified.

ossify, *v.* **1.** convert into bone, become bone, harden, stiffen, indurate, callous; fossilize, petrify.
2. become rigid, become inflexible, become unyielding, become obdurate, become resistant, become unreceptive.

ostensible, *adj.* **1.** external, outward, superficial, pretended, feigned, assumed, put-on; supposed, presumed, reputed, inferred; professed, claimed, purported, avowed, alleged, so-called, nominal, in name only.
2. apparent, plain, clear, obvious, evident, *Fr. en évidence,* manifest, patent, ostensive; distinct, in focus, lucid, plain as day, conspicuous, noticeable, prominent, unmistakable.

ostentation, *n.* display, ritz, *Inf.* swank, splash, flourish, flashiness, frills; blazon, tinsel, trappings, spectacle, show, parade, pageantry, pomp; gilding, conspicuous consumption, window dressing, *Inf.* front, veneer, *Inf.* dog, *Inf.* keeping up with the Joneses, tasteless show, vulgar show; pomposity, pompousness, inflation, peacockery, foppery; vaunting, flaunting, affectation; semblance, pretension, pretense.

ostentatious, *adj.* **1.** pretentious, affected, overwrought, overdone, extreme; artificial, surface, specious, doggy; high-toned, high-flown, grandiose, elaborate, spectacular, fancy; orotund, conspicuous, showy, flashy, flamboyant, glittering, theatrical, *Sl.* grandstand; raw, crude, vulgar, untasteful, tasteless, *Fr. nouveau riche.*
2. pompous, bombastic, vain, vainglorious; egotistical, fustian, fastuous, boastful, bragging, flaunting; dandified, foppish, mannered.

ostracism, *n.* **1.** banishment, exile, relegation, proscription, expatriation, deportation, transportation; expulsion, ejection, ouster, ousting; excommunication, disfellowship.
2. exclusion, removal, separation, segregation, (*of races*) apartheid; repudiation, rejection, abandonment.

ostracize, *v.* **1.** exclude, shut out, bar, debar, segregate, blacklist; repudiate, disinherit, disown, cast aside; reject, discard, blackball; isolate, maroon, keep at arm's length, leave out in the cold; snub, *Inf.* cut, *Inf.* cold-shoulder, give [s.o.] the cold shoulder, *Inf.* high-hat; shun, spurn, turn one's back on, set one's face against; neglect, disregard, ignore, refuse to associate with, send to Coventry.
2. banish, exile, proscribe, relegate, expatriate, outlaw, deport, transport; excommunicate, disfellowship, disenfranchise; oust, eject, throw out, expel; discharge, drum out, cashier, *Sl.* bounce.

other, *adj.* **1.** additional, additory, additamentary; further, extra, supplementary, supplemental, second, spare; added, appended, attached, annexed; augmented, increased, raised.
2. different, distinct, separate; unidentical, dissimilar, variant, unlike; disparate, contrary, contrastive, contradistinct; diverse, divergent, discrepant, differing; incongruous, incompatible, inharmonious, inconsonant.
3. former, earlier, previous, anterior, antecedent, preexistent, prior, preceding; bygone, gone, past, old-time, ancient; aforementioned, aforesaid, before-mentioned.

otherwise, *adv.* **1.** elsewise, if not, on the other hand, under other circumstances, if this were not the situation, if it were possible.
2. differently, in another way, contrarily, inversely, in reverse, conversely; in defiance, in contempt, in disagreement, in opposition, regardless.
3. excluding, excepting, in other respects, besides, save, without, apart from this.

otherworldly, *adj.* **1.** unearthly, supermundane, supramundane, extramundane; transmundane, transcendent; metaphysical, spiritual; supernatural, supranatural, preternatural; fabulous, remarkable, extraordinary, out of the ordinary, out of this world.
2. spectral, astral, ethereal, ghostly, phantom, phantomlike, wraithlike; incorporeal, *Obs.* incorporal, unsubstantial, impalpable, intangible, bodiless, disembodied; magical, fey, unreal, insubstantial, fantastic, illusory, visionary, chimeric, chimerical.
3. occult, cabalistic, mystic, mystical, transcendental; mysterious, arcane, esoteric, unknown; eerie, weird, strange, bizarre, uncanny.

otiose, *adj.* **1.** leisured, idle, inactive, unoccupied, doing nothing; unemployed, workless, not working, out of a job, *Inf.* collecting, on the dole, on welfare; vagrant, *Inf.* on the bum; indolent, lazy, listless, lethargic, insouciant, languid; loitering, loafing, laggard, slothful, sluggish, shiftless, dronish, do-nothing.
2. ineffective, inefficacious, effete, impotent, lame; worn out, washed out *or* up, null and void; weak, feeble, powerless, inadequate, inefficient, incompetent; unserviceable, inoperative; unrewarding, unremunerative, unpaying; profitless, unprofitable, gainless, for naught, flat, stale and unprofitable; abortive, fruitless, barren, sterile, unproductive; fallow, still, dormant, not in operation.
3. superfluous, redundant, extra, not needed; pointless, to no purpose, to no avail, unsuccessful; futile, unavailing, bootless, vain; useless, inutile, worthless, valueless, meritless, nugatory, *Inf.* throwaway.

ottoman, *n.* divan, backless sofa, beanbag chair, cushiony seat; footstool, footrest, hassock, taboret.

oust, *v.* **1.** expel, drive out, force out, thrust out; extrude, eject, run [s.o.] off *or* out; suspend, *Sl.* kick out, dismiss, fire, show the door, cashier, drum out; *Inf.* give [s.o.] his walking papers, *All Sl.* sack, can, give [s.o.] the boot, bag, bump, bounce, give [s.o.] the heave-ho; disown, repudiate, reject, discard; exile, expatriate, banish, proscribe, outlaw, relegate, deport; excommunicate, unchurch, ostracize, blackball, exclude, isolate, maroon.
2. *Law.* dispossess, evict, put out, *Inf.* put on the street, make homeless.

ouster, *n.* **1.** expulsion, discharge, evacuation, dislodgement; rejection, repudiation, dismissal, removal; *All Sl.* the boot, the old heave-ho, sacking, bouncing; firing, cashiering, disbarment, drumming out; exile, banishment, expatriation, deportation, transportation; banning, ostracization, excommunication, proscription, marooning, isolation, segregation, outlawing.
2. *Law.* eviction, ejection, dispossession; wrongful exclusion.

out, *adv.* **1.** absent, abroad, away, elsewhere, gone, not at home, forth; flown, missing, not present.

2. outside, out of doors, without, beyond.
3. passé, antiquated, out of date, fallen into disuse, disused; obsolete, archaic, extinct; antique, ancient, primitive, antediluvian; timeworn, discarded, expired, bygone, forgotten; unfashionable, not in vogue, finished.
4. revealed, disclosed, unfolded, brought to light, in the open, out of the closet; apparent, evident, obvious, overt, manifest; published, broadcast, bared, exposed, made known.
5. thoroughly, completely, entirely, effectively.
—adj. **6.** exposed. See **out** (*def.* **4**).
7. incorrect, inaccurate, erring, faulty, wrong, false, off, at odds, erroneous; wide of the mark, short of the mark, off the mark, missing the mark; aberrant, distorted, perverted.
8. finished, ended, concluded, terminated, over.
9. at variance, at odds, in conflict; unfriendly, hostile, uncordial, unneighborly, unresponsive, unsociable, uncommunicative.
10. inoperative, extinguished, unserviceable, broken, not functioning, out of order, out of commission; *Inf.* on the blink, *Inf.* on the fritz, *Inf.* out of kilter, *Sl.* out of whack, *Sl.* gone kerflooie, *Sl.* kaput, *Sl.* on the bum.
—prep. **11.** through, across, over.
—n. **12.** excuse, alibi, pretext; evasion, escape, loophole; shelter, harbor, isle of safety.
13. misfit, unperson, nonperson; outcast, pariah, castaway, derelict.
14. on the outs *or* **at outs** *Inf.* alienated, estranged, unfriendly, on bad terms, in conflict.
—v. **15.** go out, come out, proceed, move out, go forth, advance, progress, pass on, pass forward.
16. become public, become evident, be revealed, be disclosed, be made known, be published, be broadcast, be brought to light, be made open.
17. *Usu.* **out with** tell, utter, make known, reveal, disclose, publish, broadcast, make manifest.

out-and-out, *adj.* thorough, throughgoing, exhaustive, in-depth, A to Z, *Brit.* A to Zed, *Brit. Dial.* gradely, comprehensive, sweeping, all-encompassing; complete, total, utter, absolute, sheer, radical, rank, gross; full-fledged, dyed-in-the-wool, hard-core, inveterate, confirmed, hardened; unqualified, unmodified, uncompromised, unconditional, unconditioned, unreserved, unmitigated; unrestricted, unlimited, unhampered, unimpeded, unbounded; unequivocal, clear, unambiguous, explicit, express.

outbalance, *v.* overbalance, outweigh, overweigh, preponderate; exceed in value, transcend, surpass, overmatch; outrank, be superior to, overtop, override, take precedence over; have the edge on, hold the advantage, tip the scales, turn the tables.

outbreak, *n.* **1.** outburst, eruption, explosion, burst, flare-up. See **outburst** (*defs.* **1-3**).
2. manifestation, appearance, materialization, emergence, rise, outcrop.
3. public disturbance, riot, disorder, disruption; strike, picketing, protest, protest march, demonstration, sit-in; civil disorder, anarchy, mob law, street-fighting, fighting in the streets, violence; insurrection, rebellion, revolt, revolution, insurgence, insurgency, uprising, rising, peasant revolt, jacquerie; mutiny, insubordination, sedition, subversion; coup d'état, coup, overthrow, takeover, *Ger. putsch.*
4. clash, argument, controversy, combat, contention, disagreement, discord; altercation, dispute, row, quarrel, squabble, dustup, spat, tiff, *Brit. Dial.* fratch; encounter, meeting, engagement, embroilment, confrontation, showdown, duel, contest; fight, gunfight, battle, struggle, strife, conflict; tussle, bout, *Scot.* sturt, *Inf.* scrap, *Inf.* run-in, *Inf.* set-to, brush; skirmish, action, fray, affray; brawl, donnybrook, free-for-all, melee, hand-to-hand fight; fracas, uproar, tumult, turbulence, excitement, perturbation, agitation, unrest, turmoil, disquiet, confusion, jumble, imbroglio; stir, fuss, commotion, *Inf.* ruckus, *Inf.* rumpus, hubbub, noise, racket, clatter.

outburst, *n.* **1.** outbreak, eruption, burst, flare-up; fit, tantrum, convulsion, spasm, seizure, attack, paroxysm; explosion, blow-up, blast, discharge, detonation, fulmination, bang, boom; dissilience, dissiliency, bursting *or* flying apart, splitting open, rupture; earthquake, quake, tremor, *Chiefly U.S.* temblor, upheaval, *Phys. Geog.* cataclysm.
2. outpouring, outpour, effusion, volley, barrage, battery, gush, stream, rush; outflow, outflowing, effluence, efflux, outflux; outwell, outstream, outgush, outrush, overflow.
3. burst, spurt, spree, *Sl.* tear.

outcast, *n.* **1.** pariah, castaway, Ishmael, unperson, nonperson; exile, expatriate, political refugee; fugitive, runaway, outlaw; excommunicate; waif, stray, foundling; untouchable, leper, rejectee; evictee, expellee, evacuee.
2. wanderer, vagabond, rover, itinerant, nomad, bird of passage, knight-of-the-road; beachcomber, vagrant, hobo, tramp; beggar, panhandler, scavenger; derelict, down-and-outer, *U.S. Inf.* bum.
—adj. **3.** abandoned, forsaken, forlorn, deserted, neglected, shunned, scorned; hopeless, wretched, friendless; ostracized, blackballed, blacklisted.
4. ousted, expelled, ejected, driven out *or* forth; deported, transported, expatriated, exiled, banished; disowned, disinherited, disenfranchised, excommunicated.
5. rejected, discarded, thrown out *or* away, unwanted, sloughed off.

outclass, *v.* exceed, outreach, excel, surpass, overtop, go beyond, outsoar, transcend; outrank, outrate, come first, be superior to, take precedence over, override, overrule; outweigh, overweigh, outbalance, tip the scales, preponderate; be a cut above, be head and shoulders above, outmatch, overmatch, outrival; outdo, outplay, *Inf.* run rings *or* circles around, *Inf.* do [s.o.] one better, one-up, get the better of, top, cap, trump, beat, win over *or* win out over, prevail over, overcome, defeat. See also **outdo** (*defs.* **1, 2**).

outcome, *n.* consequence, sequel, result, end, end result, upshot, *Inf.* payoff; effect, issue, product, crop, yield, harvest, fruit, flower, blossom; offshoot, development, outgrowth; aftereffect, aftermath, wake.

outcry, *n.* **1.** exclamation, ejaculation, outburst, burst, blurt; cry, call, shout, yell, bay, bray, bellow, howl, yelp, yap; cheer, hurrah, huzzah, whoop, *Inf.* holler, *Inf.* whoop and holler; scream, screech, squeal; war cry, war whoop, battle cry, rallying cry; hunting cry, *Chiefly Brit.* tallyho, *Fox Hunting.* huic, *Fox Hunting, Rare.* yoicks.
2. lament, plaint, moan, groan, sob, wail, wail of woe; keen, bawl, ululation; gibe, scoff, jeer, hoot, boo, catcall, *Sl.* raspberry, *Sl.* Bronx cheer.
3. clamor, racket, din, noise, clangor, clap, clatter, rattle, jangle; hue and cry, vociferation, flap, uproar, hullaballoo, hubbub, ballyhoo.
4. auction, auction sale, public auction, vendue.
—v. **5.** vociferate, cry out, call out, yell out, bellow out, shout out, sing out, *Inf.* holler out; cry aloud, shout *or* cry at the top of one's lungs *or* voice, rend the air, awake the dead.

outdistance, *v.* outgo, outrun, outstrip, *Inf.* leave in the dust, outpace, outmarch, outwalk, outswim, outrow, outride, outsail; *Inf.* get the jump on, have the edge on, hold the advantage over; outdo, *Inf.* run rings *or* circles around, *Inf.* do [s.o.] one better, one-up, get the better of, top, cap, trump, beat, win over *or* win out over, prevail over, overcome, defeat. See also **outdo** (*defs.* **1**, **2**).

outdo, *v.* **1.** surpass, exceed, outreach, excel, overtop, out-Herod, go beyond, outsoar, transcend; outclass, outrank, outrate, come first, be superior to, take precedence over, override, overrule; outweigh, overweigh, outbalance, overbalance, tip the scales, preponderate; be a cut above, be head and shoulders above, outmatch, overmatch, outrival; outplay, *Inf.* run rings *or* circles around, *Inf.* do [s.o.] one better, one-up, go [s.o.] one up; get the better of, top, cap, trump, overtrump, beat, *Inf.* beat out, win out *or* win out over, prevail over, overcome, defeat; outflank, outjockey, outmaneuver, outgeneral; outsmart, outwit, outfox, outthink, overreach.

2. outdistance, outgo, outrun, outstrip, *Inf.* leave in the dust; outstep, outpace, outmarch, outwalk, outswim, outrow, outride, outsail, outhrow, outleap, outshoot; outspeak, outpreach, outtell, outtalk, talk down, talk circles around; outstare, stare down, outgaze, outglare; outwear, outlast, outlive; outstay, outsit, outwait, outwatch; outring, outlaugh, outweep, outcry, outroar, outscream, outshriek; outshine, outdazzle, outglitter, outperform, outsing, outdance, upstage; overshadow, tower above, overstride, predominate, dominate, eclipse, dwarf.

outdoor, *adj.* open-air, alfresco, out-of-doors *or* out-of-door, outside, outdoors; outdoorsy.

outdoors, *adv.* **1.** in the open air, in the open, alfresco, out of doors, outside.

—*n.* **2.** the open air, the open, the out of doors, the great outdoors, the wide open spaces, the outside.

outer, *adj.* external, exterior, extrinsic; outlying, outward, peripheral, fringe; out, outside.

outermost, *adj.* outmost, furthest, furthest-off, farthermost, ultimate, extreme, remotest; remote, distant, far-off, faraway, far-flung, removed; ulterior, thither, yonder, yon, farther, further, more distant.

outface, *v.* **1.** outstare, stare down, stare out of countenance, outface, face down, face out, outlook; outdare, outbrave, brazen out *or* through; withstand, stand, endure, hold up, hold out, brave, not flinch *or* shrink from, *Inf.* bite the bullet.

2. defy, bid defiance, set at defiance, thumb one's nose at, cock a snoot at, snap one's fingers at, flout, slight, set at naught; beard, pluck by the beard, put one's head in the lion's mouth, march up to the cannon's mouth, bell the cat, take the bull by the horns.

3. challenge, dare, double-dare, *Sl.* double-do-dare, fling down the gauntlet, knock the chip off [s.o.'s] shoulder, slap in the face; confront, front, meet, meet face to face, meet head-on, *Inf.* meet eyeball to eyeball, square off; face, face up to, stand up to, look full in the face, look straight in the eyes.

outfit, *n.* **1.** kit, set; rig, turnout, outfitting.

2. equipment, equipage, apparatus, gear, accouterments, paraphernalia, appurtenances, appointments, furnishings, furniture; fixtures, fittings, habiliments, *Inf.* things; tools, instruments, contrivances, machinery; implements, appliances, utensils, conveniences; supplies, material, wherewithal; caparison, trappings, tack, tackle, harness, rigging.

3. belongings, effects, chattels, possessions, properties, *Sl.* stuff, *Sl.* junk; baggage, bag and baggage, duffel, luggage, dunnage, impedimenta.

4. dress, garb, apparel, attire, clothes, wardrobe, livery, *Archaic.* vesture, *Inf.* togs, *Inf.* duds, (*for a newborn*) layette; investiture, adornment, ornamentation.

5. ensemble, costume, *Inf.* getup; best clothes, best bib and tucker, *Inf.* Sunday clothes, *Inf.* Sunday best, *Inf.* Sunday-go-to-meetings, *Sl.* glad rags, *Sl.* heavy threads.

6. provision, providing, supply, supplying, accouterment, furnishing, furnishment, equipping; outfitting, fitting out; preparation, preparing, readying.

7. *Informal.* clique, coterie, set, circle. See **clique.**

8. ability, capability, makings, *Sl.* the stuff, *Sl.* the goods, *Sl.* what it takes; knowledge, expertise, technique, *Inf.* know-how, *Sl.* savvy; experience, background, qualifications.

—*v.* **9.** fit out, fit up, fit, rig, rig up, rig out, turn out, gear; array, deck, deck out, bedeck, caparison, trap, adorn, ornament; dress, dress out, clothe, vest, garb, attire, apparel, habit, *Sl.* dude up; robe, gown, drape.

10. equip, furnish, supply, provide, purvey, render, accommodate, *Archaic.* dight, *Obs.* appoint; gird, ready, prepare, *Inf.* prep *or* prep up, store, stock, stock up, fill up, *Chiefly Scot.* plenish; endow, endue *or* indue, invest; *All Mil.* arm, forearm, munition, *Sl.* heel, *Archaic.* harness.

outfitter, *n.* clothier, haberdasher, hosier; costumer, costumier; modiste, couturier, couturière; furrier, cloakmaker; tailor, *Humorous.* sartor; seamstress, tailoress; dressmaker.

outflank, *v.* bypass, avoid, give [s.o.] or [s.t.] the go-by; circumvent, get around, *Inf.* do an end run, *Inf.* short-circuit; elude, evade, go over [s.o.'s] head, overreach; outthink, outwit, outfox, outsmart, get the better of [s.o.], pull the wool over [s.o.'s] eyes, put [s.t.] over on [s.o.]; outjockey, outmaneuver, outdo, outgeneral.

outflow, *n.* outflux, efflux, effluence, outflowing, flow; outwell, outstream, outpour, outpouring, effusion, outgush, outrush, overflow; outgo, *Geol.* extravasation; issue, emanation, drainage, leakage, discharge; spout, spurt, burst, jet, gush, rush.

outgoing, *adj.* **1.** departing, leaving, withdrawing, taking off; outbound, outward bound, going out.

2. open, unreserved, familiar, easy, free and easy, easygoing; friendly, amicable, congenial, neighborly, sociable, hospitable; affable, approachable, accessible, communicative, conversive; extrovert, extroverted, other-directed, gregarious; at home, comfortable, *Inf.* chummy, *Sl.* buddy-buddy, *Sl.* palsy-walsy; demonstrative, affectionate, loving, warm.

outgrow, *v.* grow too large for, grow beyond, leave behind, shed, discard; give up, relinquish, lay aside; abandon, turn one's back on, renounce, repudiate, disclaim, disown, reject.

outgrowth, *n.* **1.** product, consequence, result, outcome, *Inf.* payoff; effect, aftereffect, aftermath; conclusion, upshot, final issue, eventuation, yield.

2. addition, supplement, postscript, sequel.

3. excrescence, offshoot, shoot, sprout, bud, burgeon, blossom, flower, fruit; projection, protuberance, bulge, knob, node, nodule, *Anat.*, *Biol.* process, *Bot.* caruncle.

outhouse, *n.* **1.** outbuilding, backhouse, shed, toolshed, toolhouse, lean-to, shack; coop, stable, barn.

2. privy, *Chiefly Dial.* jakes, stool, closet, cloaca, *Chiefly New Eng.* necessary, *Brit. Sl.* bogs, latrine.

outing, *n.* excursion, pleasure trip, airing, drive, ride, spin, tour; picnic, junket; promenade, turn, stroll, jaunt, ramble; walk, hike, trek, tramp, peregrination, pilgrimage.

outlander, *n.* **1.** foreigner, alien, stranger, unwelcome visitor, intruder, interloper, barbarian, invader, tramontane, ultramontane; visitor, tourist, *Inf.* visiting fireman; exile, refugee, émigré, displaced person, D. P.; transmigrant, migrant, sojourner, passing stranger, pilgrim, traveler, wanderer; *Disparaging.* gringo, *Disparaging.* wetback.

2. immigrant, arrival, new arrival, greenhorn, incomer, entrant; colonial, uitlander, colonizer, settler, pioneer, homesteader, squatter, nester, sooner, encroacher; bushman, backwoodsman, mountainman, mountaineer, *Inf.* hillbilly; newcomer, upstart, arriviste, parvenu, *Inf.* gate-crasher, *Inf.* crasher; tenderfoot, *Inf.* new guy in town, *Inf.* Johnny-come-lately, *Inf.* new kid on the block *or* in school, *Brit. Inf.* new boy.

outlandish, *adj.* **1.** strange, unfamiliar, unknown, foreign, exotic, alien, bohemian, unconventional, unorthodox, different, foreign looking; rare, fanciful, original, exceptional, striking, unique, wonderful, wondrous, marvelous, remarkable, fascinating.

2. bizarre, odd, unusual, uncommon; queer, peculiar, curious, singular, off-beat, *Inf.* funny, quaint, eccentric; ludicrous, ridiculous, comical, droll; weird, *Inf.* freaky, *Inf.* campy, *Inf.* kinky; unbelievable, incredible, unheard-of, extraordinary, unthought-of, undreamed-of, unexampled, unimagined, unprecedented, *Inf.* out-of-this-world; inconceivable, preposterous, indescribable, nondescript, unparalleled.

3. monstrous, abnormal, freakish, unnatural, *Biol.* teratogenic, *Biol.* teratological, grotesque, fantastic; erratic, irregular, aberrant, deviative, divergent.

4. barbarous, barbaric, barbarian, uncivilized, wild; rustic, rude, uncouth, boorish, coarse, raw, savage; rural, provincial, cloddish, *Inf.* from the sticks *or* hills, hick, backwoods, backwoodsy, wild-and-woolly, rough-and-ready.

5. out-of-the-way, remote, distant, faraway, far-off, unfrequented; isolated, inaccessible, secluded, insular, forsaken, lonely, Godforsaken, in a backwater, forgotten by the world; off the beaten path, removed, separate, apart; uncharted, unexplored, unplumbed, undiscovered; back-country, up-country, *Australian.* outback, wild, wilderness, back of beyond, over the mountain *or* hills, tramontane, ultramontane, across the sea, over the water, extraterritorial; unearthly, extraterrestrial.

outlast, *adj.* **1.** outlive, *Archaic.* overlive, live on, survive, remain after; stand, prevail, endure, endure beyond, perdure, defy *or* defeat time, last; last out, come through, live *or* last through, weather, weather the storm, live to fight another day, rally, resurge; recuperate, get over, rise from the ashes, recover from; continue, run on, go on, subsist, dwell on, bide, linger on, carry on, keep on, persist; wear well, hold up, hold on, *Inf.* hang in there, *Inf.* stay in the game, *Inf.* stay on one's feet, *Inf.* make it to the last round *or* last bell, *Inf.* drink everyone under the table.

2. outwear, wear down. See **outwear** (*def.* **1**).

3. outtalk, outspeak, talk down, filibuster, stonewall, talk [s.o.'s] ear off.

outlaw, *n.* **1.** fugitive, escapee, runaway, deserter, *Sl.* AWOL, *Sl.* lamster, *Archaic.* runagate; renegade, undesirable, *Latin. persona non grata;* reprobate; exile, outcast, social outcast, outcast of society, pariah, man without a country, expellee; convict, *Inf.* jailbird; known offender, wanted criminal, wanted man, desperate criminal, cutthroat, mad dog, desperado, public enemy.

2. bandit, brigand, highwayman, Zorro, Scarlet Pimpernel, footpad, road agent, *Sl.* yegg *or* yeggman, *Sp. bandolero, Southwest U.S.* ladrone, *Sl.* bandito, Robin Hood, *Australian.* bushranger, picaroon; gangster, criminal, mafioso, mobster, racketeer; thug, ruffian, rogue, tough, *Inf.* toughie, *Inf.* hired gun, *Inf.* plugugly, hoodlum.

3. pirate, rover, viking, corsair, buccaneer, privateer, freebooter, rapparee, (*in the Scottish Highlands*) cateran; rustler, hijacker, skyjacker, air *or* sky pirate, terrorist, Fenian; smuggler, contrabandist, runner, bootlegger.

4. pillager, plunderer, marauder, despoiler, ransacker, sacker, looter, vandal, rifler, raider.

5. robber, felon, thief, *Inf.* crook, *Inf.* hold-up man, *Sl.* stick-up man, armed robber; safecracker, Jimmy Valentine; housebreaker, *Sl.* cracksman, *Brit.* picklock, Raffles, sneak thief, cat burglar, *Inf.* second-story man.

—*v.* **6.** disallow, rule out, bar, exclude, shut out, shut the door on; ban, proscribe, prohibit, forbid, interdict, issue an injunction against, lay under interdiction, put under ban, taboo, embargo, boycott; repress, suppress, smother; limit, disallow, keep under, keep within bounds, hold back, check; withhold, stop, preclude, circumscribe, deny; segregate, cordon, cordon off, cut out, cut off, strike out *or* off, eradicate, purge, not allow; isolate, quarantine, set *or* keep apart, put beyond the pale.

7. ostracize, banish, expel, cast out, blackball, blacklist, repudiate, exile, deport, transport, send away, *Brit.* rusticate, *Inf.* ship out of town, *Inf.* run out of town; put a price on [s.o.'s] head, put on the wanted list.

outlawed, *adj.* illegal, unlawful, illegitmate, *Sl.* illegit; lawless, criminal, felonious; illicit, nonlicit, nonlegal, unallowed, impermissible, irregular, chargeable, wrongful, against the law; unlicensed, unauthorized, wildcat, unofficial, unsanctioned, unwarranted, anarchic, anarchistic; contraband, bootleg, black-market, under-the-counter, under-the-table; prohibited, banned, under the ban, taboo, tabooed, barred, unallowed; excluded, ruled out, off limits, out of bounds; proscribed, interdicted, forbidden, *Fr. défendu, Ger. verboten.*

outlay, *n.* expenditure, disbursement, expense, cost, charge, price, fee; payment, compensation, recompense, settlement; amount, rate, fare, figure, amount expended; remuneration, reward, pay; payment, investment, spending, expenses, allowance, per diem, expense account, *Inf.* swindle sheet.

outlet, *n.* **1.** exit, way of escape, escape, way out, loophole; passageway, passage, egress; door, backdoor, postern, fire door, escape hatch, trap door; *Naut.* booby hatch, porthole, portal, hatch, port; debouch.

2. vent, vent hole, valve, safety valve, duct, blowhole, spiracle; cock, stopcock, spout, spigot, faucet; opening, mouth, aperture, gate, floodgate, trap, weir, chute, sluice, race; avenue, artery, channel, watercourse, trough, trench, ditch, canal, waterway, aqueduct; gorge, ravine, gully, culvert, cut, chasm, flume; cylinder, tube, pipe, conduit, main, drain, *Naut.* scupper, sewer, cloaca, gutter, *Brit.* sough.

3. electrical outlet, socket, wall socket, *Inf.* plug; terminal, connection.

4. market, marketplace, open market, mart, farmers' market, street market, flea market; concession, trading post, retail market, wholesale market, distribution center, salesroom, show room, auction room; store, shop, cooperative, emporium, bazaar, shopping center *or* plaza *or* mall, supermarket, department store, chain store; fast food outlet, vending machine.

5. means of expression, release, escape, escape mechanism, safety valve; catharsis, purgation, emotional release.

outline, *n.* **1.** contour, boundary, limit, silhouette, profile; lineaments, delineation, configuration, conformation; horizon, coast, brim, perimeter, circumference, periphery.

2. sketch, draft, plan, lines, skeleton; framework, scenario, layout, diagram, map, study, design; tracing, suggestion, cast, rough draft, delineation, penciling.

3. summary, epitome, synopsis, compendium, symposium, compilation, digest, conspectus; condensation, abridgment, reduction, compression, abbreviation; analysis, recapitulation; résumé, abstract, brief, précis; aperçu, sketch, review, syllabus, prospectus; docket, bulletin, minute; extracts, fragments, cuttings, analects, clippings, citations; skeleton, thumbnail sketch; schedule, roster, agenda, slate.

—*v.* **4.** draw, design, frame, project, plan out; rough out, map, chart, sketch, draft; define, delineate, silhouette, profile, skeletonize; pencil, trace; diagram, block, shape, fashion.

5. summarize, epitomize, abridge; sum up, highlight, recapitulate.

outlive, *v.* **1.** survive, endure beyond, remain after.

2. outlast, survive, abide, persist, persevere, come through, pull through, recuperate, rally, resurge.

outlook, *n.* **1.** view, vista, exposure, aspect, scene, landscape, picture, spectacle, panorama.

2. expectation, expectancy, anticipation, prospect, future prospect, contingency; promise, hope, probability, likelihood, chance; possibility, susceptibility, liableness, liability; assumption, presumption, speculation, reckoning, calculation; apprehension, anxiety.

3. perspective, mental viewpoint, attitude, point of view, frame of mind, disposition, emotional tone, temper, vein, grain, mood, humor, cast, spirit; position, standpoint, interpretation, side, slant, angle, light.

4. lookout, watchtower, *Naut.* crow's nest, observatory, observaton post, lookout point, gazebo, belvedere.

outlying, *adj.* remote, distant, faraway, a long way off, *Inf.* a good ways off, far-off; detached, isolated, inaccessible, out-of-the-way, secluded, insular, lonely, forsaken, Godforsaken, in a backwater, forgotten by the world; unfrequented, off the beaten path, removed, separate, apart; peripheral, bordering, rimming, skirting, bounding, marginal, borderline; shoreline, coastal, littoral; out, outermost, ulterior, yonder, yon, farther, further, remoter, most distant; frontier, provincial, rustic, rural, country, hinterland, backcountry, upcountry, *Australian.* outback, wild, wilderness, backwood, backwoods, *Sl.* in the boondocks *or* boonies; back of beyond, up in the hills, over the mountain *or* hills, tramontane, ultramontane, extraterritorial, exterior, external; extreme, terminal, last, farthest.

outmode, *v.* **1.** displace, replace, supplant, succeed, supersede; discontinue, cut out, withdraw, terminate, cancel, *Inf.* scrub; abandon, suspend, give up, cease to use, disuse, put away, lay *or* set aside, push aside; put a stop to, put an end to, bring to an end, *Inf.* kibosh, *Inf.* put the kibosh on, *Inf.* kill, *Sl.* zap, *Sl.* wipe out, *Sl.* shoot down, *Sl.* KO, *Sl.* scrag; replace, trade in, have done with, give over, put behind one, dispense with.

2. obsolete, antiquate, superannuate, let fall into disuse, retire, shelve, put on the shelf, put in mothballs, *Inf.* sideline.

3. discard, jettison, throw away *or* out, cast off *or* aside, get rid of, abandon, say goodby to, bid farewell to, *Inf.* chuck *Inf.* scrap, *Inf.* junk, *Inf.* trash, *Inf.* dump, *Inf.* toss in the trash *or* on the junkheap, *Inf.* put on the scrap heap *or* pile, *Inf.* give [s.t.] the old heave-ho.

4. go out of style, become obsolete, obsolesce, come to an end, lapse, become extinct, run its course, lose favor *or* popularity, be all over; fall by the wayside, fall into disuse; expire, die, be no more, *Inf.* come to the end of the line.

outmoded, *adj.* **1.** old-fashioned, out-of-style, unfashionable, out-of-fashion, outdated, out-of-date, out, oldfangled, unmodern, dated, behind the times, *Inf.* old hat, *Inf.* back-number, out-of-season, secondhand, used, *Inf.* hand-me-down, *Sl.* early-Salvation-Army.

2. former, older, previous, foregoing, oldtime, sometime, onetime; stale, fusty, musty, worn, timeworn, moth-eaten, moss-grown, old, hoary, tired, *Inf.* rinky-dink, *Inf.* square, *Inf.* old-fogyish, *Inf.* old-ladyish, *Inf.* corny, *Inf.* fuddy-duddy, stodgy, conservative.

3. neglected, forgotten, abandoned, forsaken, old as the hills, remote, vintage, past its prime, *Inf.* over the hill; prior, earlier, long-forgotten.

4. discredited, refuted, repudiated, renounced, dismissed, spurned, scorned, abjured, discarded, rejected, cast-off, done with, on the shelf, all over with, *Inf.* has-been, *Inf.* washed-up, *Inf.* down the drain, *Inf.* kaput, *Inf.* dead, *Inf.* dead as a doornail, *Inf.* dead as yesterday's news.

5. retired, lapsed, elapsed, expired, run out, defunct; superseded, replaced, outworn.

6. obsolete, obsolescent, passé, past, gone by, fallen into disuse, out of use, disused, derelict; quaint, old-world, by-gone, horse-and-buggy, vanished, never to return, *Inf.* fini, *Inf.* done for.

7. prehistoric, antiquated, antique, ancient, fossil, fossilized, petrified; anachronistic, anachronous, antediluvian, before the Flood; archaic, archaistic, extinct, *Archaic.* olden, primitive, atavistic; quondam, erstwhile.

8. traditional, old-line, old-school, conventional, die-hard, nonprogressive, unchanging, backward.

out-of-the-way, *adj.* **1.** distant, remote, secluded, outlying. See **outlying.**

2. unusual, uncommon, exceptional, extraordinary, singular, strange, curious, odd; eccentric, irregular, erratic, capricious, flighty, *Inf.* odd-ball, idiosyncratic, unconventional, original; unheard-of, exotic, rare, rarely seen, once-in-a-lifetime; unparalleled, unexampled, unprecedented, unaccepted, peculiar, abnormal, outlandish, queer, weird.

3. improper, incorrect, false, erroneous, mistaken, wrong, way off the mark, off the mark, on the wrong track, faulty, amiss, remiss, off base, unsound; inappropriate, inapt, unmeet, unfitting, unbefitting; unwarranted, uncalled-for, out of place, out of keeping, inopportune, ill-timed, untimely, infelicitous; unfavorable, incommodious, inconvenient, uncongenial, unlikely; unsuitable, unsuited, unfit, ill-adapted; inexpedient, inadvisable, impractical, inapplicable, unfeasable.

4. unseemly, unbecoming, indecorous; unladylike, ungentlemanly, ungenteel, impolite; undignified, unrefined, inelegant, indelicate; impolitic, imprudent, indiscreet, tactless, injudicious, insensitive, unwise; untoward, off-key, out-of-bounds, out-of-line, out-of-order; vulgar, gauche, uncouth, crude, crass, rude, uncivil, discourteous, in bad taste; coarse, rough, base, tatty, *Inf.* tacky; ignoble, raffish, low.

5. indecent, immodest, shameless, indelicate; unsuitable, tawdry; gross, rank, repulsive, offensive, disgusting, distasteful, risqué, suggestive, off-color, *Inf.* blue; outrageous, lurid, sensational, scandalous; shocking, surprising, unexpected, *Sl.* sick; abusive, ribald, scurrilous, profane, foulmouthed; racy, salty, spicy, not fit for mixed company, unprintable, not for a family newspaper; smutty, dirty, obscene, indecent, *Sl.* raunchy; filthy, foul, nasty, scatologic, scatological; loose, prurient, unchaste.

6. embarrassing, disconcerting, discomforting, humiliating, mortifying; disturbing, upsetting, bothersome, distracting.

outplay, *v.* outdo, outstrip, top, overtop, cap, excel, surpass, transcend, tower above, trump, overtrump, outdistance, outgo; outshine, eclipse, overshadow, put to shame, *Inf.* show [s.o.] up; outmaneuver, outflank, outjockey, outsmart, outthink, outwit, outfox, outgeneral, overreach, get the better of, *Inf.* run rings *or* circles around; outpoint, outscore, lead, best, get the better of, outrival, outmatch, overmatch, *Inf.* go one up on; predominate; preponderate, prevail over, be superior to; defeat, beat, win over, upset, upend, whip, outfight, *Inf.* lick; crush, trounce, drub, floor, clobber, smash, *Inf.* leave in the dust, *Inf.* whomp, *Sl.* do in, *U.S. Sl.* skunk, *Sl.* cream, *Sl.* shellac, *Sl.* pulverize, *Sl.* skim.

outpost, *n.* **1.** outstation, outquarters, *U.S. Army Inf.* field; lookout, outlook, guardhouse, watchtower, lighthouse; outparish, outoffice, outbranch, field *or* branch office; frontier, march, outskirt, outfield, outdistrict, no man's land.

2. outrider, scout, vanguard, forward line, first line of defense, flank, flanker, detachment; sentinel, sentry, guard, watchman, *Mil.* picket, *Mil.* outguard, *Archaic.* outsentry.

outpouring, *n.* outflow, efflux, effluence, effusion, outpour, outgo, *Geol.* extravasation; flow, flowing, flux, afflux, issue, emanation; onrush, stream, current, tide, millrace; outrush, outgush, gushing, spurting, spouting, jet, spring, geyser, fountain; wave, surge, swell, torrent, niagara, cascade, cataract; overflow, flood, deluge; discharge, drainage, emission, ejection, ejaculation; (*of people*) egress, emigration, debouchment, exodus.

output, *n.* **1.** production, produce, quantity *or* amount *or* number produced, outturn; yield, harvest, garner, gathering, reaping, cutting, crop, season's growth; product, manufacture, final *or* end product, result *or* fruit of one's efforts, work, accomplishment, achievement.

2. productivity, rate of production, efficiency, expeditiousness, dispatch.

3. (*of electricity*) current, wattage, *All Elect.* voltage, amperage, current density; power, energy, force.

4. *Computer Technology.* print-out, readout; information, *Inf.* info, data, facts, figures, statistics, *Sl.* dope; report, message, communication.

outrage, *n.* **1.** atrocity, crime, act of violence, injury, hurt, foul play, harm, wrong, grievance, evil; enormity, monstrosity, abhorrence, abomination, horror, odium; disgrace, shame, scandal, perversion, prostitution; offense, violation, infraction, breach, transgression, trespass, infringement, felony; misdeed, wrongdoing, dereliction; malefaction, desecration, blasphemy, profanity, profanation, sacrilege, peccancy.

2. indignity, affront, insult, *Archaic.* insultation, slap in the face; injury, wound, sting; discourtesy, slight, *Sl.* put-down.

3. mistreatment, abuse, maltreatment, ill-treatment, mishandling, ill-use; persecution, tormeting, torturing; cruelty, barbarity, savagery, brutality, murderousness, malignity; manhandling, mauling, battery, assault, beating, thrashing.

—*v.* **4.** offend, affront, chagrin, insult, humiliate, slight, slap in the face; pique, *Inf.* miff, disgruntle, *Inf.* put [s.o.] off, displease, hurt [s.o.'s] feelings; vex, annoy, provoke, incense, exasperate, distress; irk, rankle, roll, *Chiefly U.S.* rile, rattle, ruffle; irritate, aggravate, nettle, chafe, gall, disturb; anger, enrage, infuriate, madden; add insult to injury, add fuel to the flames, make one's blood boil.

5. disgust, repel, repulse, *Sl.* gross [s.o.] out, *Sl.* turn [s.o.] off; nauseate, sicken, turn [s.o.'s] stomach; horrify, shock, traumatize; numb, paralyze, immobilize; overwhelm, astound, *Inf.* flabbergast.

6. violate, transgress, trespass, infringe upon, encroach upon, intrude upon, step on the toes of; sin, desecrate, profane, defile, debase; (*all in reference to sexual relations*) rape, ravage, ravish, deflower.

7. injure, hurt, harm, wound, damage, pain; wrong, malign, aggrieve, do an injustice to, disrespect, walk all over [s.o.]; mistreat, maltreat, abuse, mishandle, ill-use, ill-treat; manhandle, maul, batter, *Sl.* knock around.

outrageous, *adj.* **1.** intolerable, insufferable, unbearable, unendurable, insupportable; impossible, enough, too much, all that one can stand; vexatious, exasperating, provoking, provocative, aggravating, maddening, disturbing, distressing; infuriating, enraging, riling, galling.

2. offensive, scandalous, shocking, disgraceful, shameless; notorious, arrant; flagrant, egregious, grievous; infamous, flagitious, heinous, nefarious, villainous; atrocious, abominable, execrable, monstrous, horrible, horrid, horrendous; hideous, grisly, gruesome, ghastly, unspeakable, unthinkable; vile, foul, base, mean, low, bad; wicked, dark, black, grim, dreadful, dire.

3. glaring, conspicuous, flaming, crying, blatant; ostentatious, flaunted, paraded, displayed; mannered, affected, theatrical, *Both Sl.* camp, campy.

4. immoderate, excessive, inordinate, overweening, high-flown, overblown, extreme, extravagant; exorbitant, unreasonable, unwarranted, uncalled-for, exaggerated, preposterous, unconscionable; unbridled, unrestrained, unlimited, uncurbed, uncontrolled.

5. obnoxious, nasty, disgusting, repugnant; repulsive, repelling, repellent, revolting, objectionable; fulsome, bilious, gross, rank; abominable, odious, heinous, detestable.

6. indecent, indelicate, inelegant, immodest, shameless; abusive, ribald, scurrilous, blackguardly, thersitical, profane, foulmouthed, Fescennine; immoral, degenerate, dissolute, dissipated, debauched, rakish, profligate, depraved, perverted; vulgar, obscene, lewd, salacious, foul, filthy, dirty, smutty, *Sl.* raunchy, scatologic, scatalogical.

7. improper, indecorous, unacceptable; inappropriate, unsuitable, unseemly, tawdry, *Inf.* tacky.

outrank, *v.* precede, take precedence over, dominate, command, control, lead, hold the whip hand; rank, be superior to, top, overtop, preponderate, transcend, outclass.

outreach, *v.* **1.** exceed, reach beyond, extend beyond; outdistance, outstrip, overshadow, eclipse, tower above.

—*n.* **2.** extension, stretch, reach; groping, search, exploration.

3. altruism, selflessness, friendliness, other-directedness, charity, good works.

outrider, *n.* **1.** attendant, mounted attendant, escort, accompanier, companion; squire, aide, guard, bodyguard, armed guard, guardian, protector; *Navy.*

escort carrier, *Mil.* escort fighter.

2. leader, director, pacesetter, *Inf.* path beater, pilot, guide, torchbearer; herald, harbinger, advance man, usher, announcer, crier; advance guard, courier, pathfinder, explorer; vanguard, apostle, missionary, man from Cook's.

3. cowboy, ranchhand, scout, patroler; explorer, investigator, examiner, inspector.

outright, *adj.* **1.** complete, total, out-and-out, dead, categorical, unequivocal, unconditional, incontestable, flat; thorough, thoroughgoing, wholesale, comprehensive, full, exhaustive, sweeping, radical, all-out, *Inf.* flat-out; absolute, utter, sheer, stark, arrant, rank; perfect, positive, veritable, consummate, *Inf.* regular, *Inf.* plumb, *Brit. Inf.* proper.

2. downright, unqualified, unmitigated; clear, manifest, distinct, palpable, evident, self-evident, conspicuous, definite, unmistakable, undeniable.

—adv. **3.** completely, totally, categorically, dead, unequivocally, unconditionally, incontestably; thoroughly, comprehensively, fully, exhaustively, to the utmost, to the full; absolutely, utterly, sheerly, starkly, arrantly, rankly; perfectly, positively, veritably, consummately.

4. overtly, openly, up front, heart to heart; candidly, frankly, forthright, forthrightly, directly, straightforward, straightforwardly; explicitly, unequivocally, undisguisedly, plainly, in plain words *or* English, with no nonsense, all joking aside; freely, boldly, unreservedly, unrestrainedly, without restraint, unconstrainedly, uninhibitedly, unabashedly, unshrinkingly.

5. guilelessly, ingenuously, sincerely, artlessly, naively, simply, undeceptively, undeceitfully, undeceivingly, without artifice; truly, truthfully, veraciously.

6. immediately, instantly, instanter, in a moment, at once, straightaway, straightway, then and there, right away, right off, *Inf.* right off the bat; in a glance, in a moment's notice.

outset, *n.* beginning, start, starting point, inception, early days, very first, first, top, rise of the curtain; opening, dawn, threshold, conception, birth, genesis, origin, embryo, inchoation, exordium; commencement, inauguration, first step, embarkation, *Inf.* kick-off, *Inf.* jump-off, *Inf.* take-off, *Inf.* blast-off; first appearance, debut, outbreak, outburst.

outshine, *v.* **1.** outdazzle, outluster, put in the shade, make pale by comparison; overshadow, eclipse, bedim, becloud.

2. surpass, excel, outtop, outclass, outrank, outrate, come first; be superior to, take precedence over, override, overrule; outweigh, outbalance, preponderate; be a cut above, be head and shoulders above, outmatch, overmatch, outrival; look better than, upstage, dwarf.

outside, *n.* **1.** exterior, external, outer side; periphery, rim, edge, border, fringe; surface, overlayer, sheath, case, skin, shell, integument.

2. appearance, aspect, demeanor, mien, face; sham, superficiality, guise, façade, false front, *Inf.* front, veneer, coating, protective cover *or* manner; mask, image, pretense, feigning, smokescreen; window dressing, show, *Inf.* cover-up.

3. outside world, secular world, civilian world; elsewhere.

4. at the outside at the most, at the maximum, at the top, no more than, not in excess of.

—adj. **5.** exterior, outer, external, extrinsic, outward, outdoor, outlying, peripheral; superficial, surface, false, fake.

6. independent, not affiliated, nonaligned, unassociated, unconnected, uncommitted, free; extraneous, irrelevant, not bearing on; foreign, alien, not connected, having nothing to do with.

—adv. **7.** outdoors, out of the house, in the yard.

8. outside of *Informal.* aside from, besides, excepting, with the exception of, other than, exclusive of.

outsider, *n.* **1.** odd man out, third person *or* wheel, extra person; outcast, reject, castoff.

2. stranger, foreigner, alien, outlander, tramontane, non-native, unnaturalized citizen; extraterrestrial being, martian, man from Mars *or* outer space, little green man; visitor, guest, tourist, sightseer, *Inf.* visiting fireman; immigrant, emigrant, émigré, refugee, *Fr. déraciné,* displaced person, D.P. *Disparaging.* wetback, *Disparaging.* gringo; arrival, new arrival, newcomer, incomer, entrant, *Inf.* new guy in town, *Inf.* Johnny-come-lately, *Inf.* new kid on the block *or* in school, *Brit. Inf.* new boy; upstart, arriviste, parvenu, nouveau riche, new-rich; colonial, uitlander, colonizer, settler, pioneer, homesteader; squatter, nester, sooner, encroacher, trespasser; unwelcome visitor, *Inf.* gatecrasher, *Inf.* crasher, intruder, interloper, barbarian, invader.

outskirt, *n.* *Usu.* **outskirts** suburbs, edges, outlying districts, fringes; periphery, borders, confines, perimeter; bounds, boundary, verges; surrounding area, area, environs, general neighborhood, vicinage.

outsmart, *v.* **1.** get the better of, get the best of, *Inf.* euchre out; trick, hoax, take in, *Inf.* slip one over on [s.o.], *Sl.* pull a fast one on [s.o.], *Sl.* snow, *Sl.* hornswoggle; dupe, deceive, beguile, gull, pigeon, humbug, bamboozle, fool, befool, make a fool of, *Sl.* make a monkey of.

2. outwit, outthink, overreach, outmaneuver, outdo, outperform, outplay, outgeneral, outflank, outguess; finesse, circumvent, get *or* work around, elude, evade, frustrate, steal a march on, *Sl.* give [s.o.] the slip *or* runaround.

outspoken, *adj.* candid, frank, forthright, direct, straightforward, straight-from-the-shoulder, foursquare; plain, plain-spoken, plain-speaking, downright, outright, *Inf.* straight out, explicit, unequivocal, unequivocating, unambiguous, undisguised, undisguising, *Inf.* flat-footed, *Inf.* matter-of-fact; free-spoken, free-speaking, free-tongued, free, unreticent, bold, unreserved, unrestrained, unconstrained, unchecked, unabashed, uninhibited, unsparing, unshrinking; blunt, bluff, brusque, brash, tactless.

outspread, *v.* **1.** open, open up, open wide, unfold, fan out; expand, widen, broaden, spread, sprawl; extend, reach, range, sweep, stretch, outstretch, *Archaic.* outreach; develop, grow, wax, balloon, swell.

—adj. **2.** spread-out, stretched-out, outstretched, open, wide-open, opened-up, unfolded; extended, expanded; fanned-out, fanlike, fan-shaped.

3. extensive, widespread, expansive, broad, sweeping; diffuse, wide-ranging, far-reaching, far-flung.

—n. **4.** expansion, extension, broadening, widening; growth, development, waxing.

5. expanse, spread, space; area, tract.

outstanding, *adj.* **1.** prominent, conspicuous, unmistakable, noticeable, salient, bold, in bold *or* high *or* strong relief, in relief, in the foreground, pronounced, *Sl.* sticking *or* hanging out; striking, impressive, memorable, unforgettable, never to be forgotten, *Sl.* stunning; eminent, notable, noteworthy, celebrated, famed, famous, renowned; remarkable, extraordinary, out of the ordinary, signal, marked, of mark.

2. excellent, great, superb, splendid, terrific, *Sl.* terif, sensational, marvelous, *Sl.* marvy, *Sl.* out-of-this-world, smashing, superfine, superexcellent, *Sl.* super, *Inf.* super-duper, *Australian.* bonzer; first-class, superior, standout, exceptional, cut *or* stroke above,

Inf. A-1 *or* A-one *or* A-number-one, *Sl.* bang-up, *Brit. Sl.* bang-on, *Brit. Sl.* spot-on; rare, special, distinguished, choice, of choice.

3. (*all of debts, financial obligations, etc.*) unpaid, unsettled, undissolved, owed, in arrears; surviving, remaining, owing, uncollected, ungathered; due, mature, receivable, payable.

4. standing out, projecting, jutting, extruding, protrusive, protuberant; overhanging, beetle.

outstretch, *v.* **1.** extend, offer, hold out, put forward, stretch out, reach out, *Archaic.* outreach.

2. stretch beyond, overextend, overpass, pass al bounds, know no bounds, go overboard; tax, strain, overdo, overdraw, overstrain.

3. expand, stretch, stretch out, sweep, reach, spread, sprawl; open, open up, open wide, outspread, widen, broaden.

outstrip, *v.* **1.** outdo, outvie, outrival, outclass, outshine, outperform, outplay, *Inf.* run rings *or* circles around; excel, exceed, surpass, trump, transcend, overcome, better, *Inf.* go one better, cap, top, overtop; beat, best, worst; overshadow, throw into the shade, eclipse, put to shame, *Inf.* show [s.o.] up.

2. outrun, outpace, outdistance, distance; lap, pass, overpass, overtake, overhaul, get ahead of, shoot ahead of, leave behind, leave in the dust, leave standing flatfooted.

outward, *adj.* **1.** superficial, surface, exterior, exoteric; visible, seeable, observable, showing, shown, manifest, apparent, evident; ostensible, seeming, appearing, supposed, assumed, presumed, reputed, inferred; alleged, avowed, professed, claimed, purported, pretended, so-called, nominal, in name only; asserted, asseverated, averred, stated, declared, predicated.

2. physical, bodily, body, corporeal, carnal, fleshly; mundane, worldly, terrestrial, temporal, secular.

3. extrinsic, extraneous, adventitious, foreign, alien; impersonal, objective; public, civil.

4. emanent, emanating, effluent, exudative; spreading, fanning, radial, divergent, diverging, centrifugal; dispersive, dispersing.

5. outer, outermost, outside, external; outlying, remote, out-of-the-way; perimetric, peripheral.

—*adv.* *Also* **outwards** **6.** out, without, toward the outside.

7. superficially, externally, outwardly; openly, visibly, manifestly, apparently, evidently; ostensibly, seemingly, supposedly, allegedly, avowedly, nominally.

outwear, *v.* **1.** outlast, wear down, tire out, exhaust, weary, fatigue, weaken, fag, fag out, poop out; waste, dissipate, deplete, erode, destroy; protract, prolong, draw out, drag *or* spin out.

2. See **outlast** (*defs.* **1, 3**).

outweigh, *v.* overweigh, outbalance, overbalance, preponderate; exceed in value, transcend, surpass, overmatch, outmatch; outrank, be superior to, overtop, override, take precedence over; have the edge on, hold the advantage, tip the scales, turn the tables.

outwit, *v.* **1.** outsmart, outthink, overreach, get the better of, get the best of, *Inf.* euchre out; outmaneuver, outflank, outjockey; outdo, outperform, outplay, outgeneral, outguess; finesse, work *or* get around, circumvent, evade, elude, frustrate, steal a march on, *Sl.* give [s.o.] the slip *or* runaround.

2. trick, hoax, take in, *Inf.* slip one over on [s.o.], *Sl.* pull a fast one on [s.o.], *Sl.* snow, *Sl.* hornswoggle; dupe, deceive, beguile, gull, pigeon, humbug, bamboozle, fool, befool, make a fool of, *Sl.* make a monkey of.

outworn, *adj.* **1.** obsolete, disused, lapsed, abandoned, discontinued, discarded, cast aside, rejected; dead, defunct, expired, extinct, wound up, prehistoric, antediluvian; retired, pensioned off, put away, laid on the shelf, neglected, gone to seed; bygone, gone by, past, forgotten.

2. outmoded, antiquated, superannuated, outdated; passé, dated, out-of-date, horse-and-buggy, *Inf.* has-been, *Inf.* old hat, *Inf.* back number; out, out of fashion, old-fashioned, unfashionable, out of style, behind the times; old, antique, archaic, ancient, primitive, aged, moss-grown.

3. worn out, worn, shopworn, second-hand; threadbare, past use, frayed, ragged, shabby, faded, washed-out; decrepit, the worse for wear, deteriorated.

4. tired, weary, fatigued, exhausted, effete; fagged out, played out, spent, *Inf.* beat, *Inf.* bushed, *U.S. Inf.* all tuckered out, *Sl.* pooped, *Inf.* dog-tired, dead-tired; ready to drop, on one's last legs, more dead than alive, faint, drooping, enfeebled.

oval, *adj.* **1.** egg-shaped, oviform, ovate, ovoid, rounded, curved; obovoid, obovate; elliptical, ellipsoidal.

—*n.* **2.** ellipse, ellipsoid; ovoid.

ovation, *n.* applause, *Inf.* hand, handclapping, cheers, cheering, salvo, rooting, whistling, stomping; encore, plaudits, curtain calls, standing ovation; hosanna, huzzah, hurrah, bravo; éclat, outcry, outburst, fanfare; acclaim, acclamation, praise, extolment, laudation, kudos, accolade, *Archaic.* magnification, citation.

oven, *n.* stove, rotisserie, broiler; toaster oven, microwave oven, Dutch oven, baker; kiln, brickkiln, limekiln.

over, *prep.* **1.** above, on top of, atop of; higher than, in *or* to *or* at a higher place than, aloft of; over the top of, on, upon.

2. across, on *or* to the other *or* opposite side of, from one side to the other of; through, by way *or* means of.

3. superior to, higher in authority than, more elevated than, loftier than, mightier than, more powerful than; in charge *or* control *or* command of, as boss *or* supervisor of *or* to.

4. all over, all through, throughout, through the extent of, everywhere in, in all places of; around, here and there in.

5. more than, greater than, larger than; beyond, upward of, surpassing, overpassing, exceeding, transcending; in excess of, exceeding, in surplus of, over and above, over and beyond.

6. in comparison to, compared to, relative to, in relation to, in respect to; about, on, on the subject of, concerning, regarding, as regards, in reference to, apropos of, touching, on, in connection with.

7. in preference to, rather than, instead of; before, before taking, ahead of, sooner than.

8. during, for the duration of, for the extent of, for the period *or* course of, until the end of, pending the outcome of; while doing *or* engaged in *or* occupied with *or* busy with, in the thick of, in the middle *or* midst of, midway through *or* in, halfway through.

9. **over and above** in addition to, on top of, as well as, along *or* together with, plus; also, besides, further, furthermore, not to mention, let alone.

—*adv.* **10.** above, overhead, over one's head, aloft, on *or* at *or* in a high place, at a height; out, over, beyond, out from, projecting *or* protruding from, sticking out of, overhanging from.

11. all over, everywhere, over the entire surface; on top of, so as to cover.

12. over there, in that direction; down by, up by,

over by, around, near, close to; across the way, way over there, at some distance.

13. across, on the other side, to the other *or* opposite side, from one side to the other.

14. through, all the way through, from beginning to end, from cover to cover, from one end to the other, from end to end, from stem to stern, from top to bottom, from head to foot; throughout, all over, thoroughly, entirely, completely.

15. from one to another, from hand to hand; to another, to someone else, to [s.o.].

16. down, off its feet, to the ground, upside down, topsy-turvy, head over heels; inversely, in reverse, to the other *or* opposite side, wrong side up, flip side up.

17. again, once again, once more, one more time, *Fr. encore;* afresh, anew, from the top *or* beginning; in succession, in repetition, one after the other.

18. in excess, too much, extra; left over, as a remainder, remaining; as well, too, else, plus, to boot, in addition; beyond, on the side, in the bargain *or* deal, as a tip, to grow on, for good luck.

19. all over *or* all over with, finished, concluded, through, done; ended, terminated, stopped, *Inf.* done for, *Sl.* kaput.

20. **over and over** repeatedly, often, many times, several times, again and again, time and time again, time and again.

—adj. 21. uppermost, topmost, highest; top, high, lofty.

22. superior, higher up, higher, greater, better; foremost, outranking, ranking, head, leading; supervisory, managerial, administrative; controlling, commanding, dominant.

23. outer, outside, external, exterior, top, upper; protective, covering, warm, heavy, waterproof; outdoor, cold-weather, winter, snow.

24. leftover, left, residual, remaining, outstanding, still to go; extra, additional, in addition, in excess, spare, reserve; surplus, superfluous, accessory, ancillary, supplementary, odd, unused, unneeded.

25. finished, concluded, done, completed, through; ended, at an end, stopped, terminated; on the way out, run out, *Inf.* all up, *Inf.* done for, *Sl.* kaput; past, gone, bygone, all gone, gone by; out of existence, no more, extinct, dead, departed, no longer with us.

overabound, *v.* 1. superabound, overrun, run riot, run rampant, overgrow, overspread, spread over, be all over, meet one at every turn; infest, plague, beset; swam, swarm with, teem, teem with, crawl, crawl with, creep, creep with, bristle, bristle with, pullulate, be alive with, *Sl.* be lousy with; overflow, flow over, overspill, spill over, run over, well over, know no bounds.

2. overwhelm, overpower, overcome; choke, smother, suffocate; mount, mount up, pile up; flood, deluge, inundate, drench, engulf, swamp, submerge, whelm, sweep; sate, surfeit, gorge, glut, stuff.

overabundance, *n.* 1. superabundance, overfullness, overprofusion, overplentifulness, overplenteousness, overplenty, superflux; superfluity, superfluousness, oversufficiency, supererogation, redundance, redundancy; repletion, engorgement, congestion, surcharge; profusion, more than enough, enough and to spare, enough and then some.

2. surplus, surfeit, satiety, glut, plethora, excess, overflow, overspill; flood, deluge, inundation, spate, avalanche, landslide, riot, drug on *or* in the market, supersaturation; oversupply, overmeasure, overload, overburden; overdose, too much of a good thing.

overabundant, *adj.* 1. superabundant, plethoric, overfull, overprofuse, overplentiful, overplenteous, overplenty, oversufficient, overmuch; overflowing, flowing over, overspilling, spilling over, running over, welling over, brimming over; rampant, bristling, thick, thick with, teeming, teeming with, swarming, swarming with, crawling with, creeping with, alive with, *Sl.* lousy with, pullulating.

2. lavish, extravagant, excessive, profuse, profusive, exorbitant, inordinate, immoderate, beyond all bounds; uncalled-for, unwarranted, unneeded, needless, unnecessary; overgenerous, overliberal, overbounteous, overbountiful, overlavish; too much, too many.

3. wasteful, prodigal, profligate, wanton, dissipative; intemperate, incontinent, improvident.

overact, *v.* *Theat. Sl.* ham *or* ham up; affect, put on, counterfeit, sham, make a show of; overdo, overstress, overcharge, overcolor, overstate, make a mountain out of a molehill, make much ado about nothing, make much of; color, paint, paint in glowing terms, oversell, *Inf.* play up, exaggerate, *Inf.* build up *or* on; *Inf.* pile it on, *Inf.* lay it on, *Inf.* lay *or* spread it on thick, *Sl.* bull; embellish, overdevelop, magnify; romance, embroider, stretch, stretch the point.

overall, *adj.* entire, extensive, extended, long-term, long-range; complete, total, whole, wholesale; comprehensive, universal, all-embracing, inclusive, all-inclusive, blanket, umbrella; panoramic, sweeping, general; unbroken, undivided, all in one.

overawe, *v.* intimidate, cow, awe, daunt, dismay, abash, disconcert, *Inf.* faze, frighten, appall; domineer, browbeat, bully, threaten, hector, buffalo out of *or* into, bluster, bulldoze, coerce, compel, dragoon; dominate, lord it over, subdue, bend to one's will, keep under one's thumb, lead by the nose, make a puppet of; oppress, terrorize, override, ride roughshod over, rule with an iron rod.

overawed, *adj.* intimidated, daunted, cowed, dismayed, abashed, disconcerted, disheartened, discouraged, unnerved, unmanned; restrained, subdued, submissive, docile, cowering, cringing; fearful, frightened, timid, timorous, apprehensive; taken aback, nonplused, bewildered, stunned, stupefied, amazed, overcome, astonished, dazed, dumfounded, *Inf.* bowled over, *Inf.* shaken.

overbalance, *v.* 1. outweigh, overweigh, outbalance, preponderate; overshadow, throw into the shade, eclipse, put to shame, *Inf.* show up. See **outweigh.**

2. push over, tip over, tilt, knock over, knock down, topple, turn turtle, upend; overturn, overset, capsize, upset.

overbear, *v.* 1. bear down *or* down on, press down, weigh down, push down, force down.

2. overcome, conquer, triumph over, defeat, win out over, get the better of, beat, *Inf.* beat out, *Inf.* whip; overpower, overwhelm, destroy, crush, trounce, *Inf.* stomp, trample, ruin.

3. dominate, domineer, lord it over, play the lord, master, control, rule, govern; command, order, lay down the law, call the shots *or* plays, *Inf.* wear the pants, run the show, rule the roost, wear the crown, occupy the throne, have the whip hand; have the upper hand, be master of the situation, be on top of, have [s.o.] under one's thumb; wield the sceptor, wield the power, sway, bend to one's will, force, coerce.

4. tyrannize, rule with a rod of iron, rule with an iron *or* high hand, boss *or* boss around, tell [s.o.] what to do; browbeat, intimidate, threaten, bully, ride roughshod over, ride herd on; oppress, suppress, repress, keep down *or* under; step on, walk all over, use [s.o.] for a doormat; break, humble, subdue, subjugate, subject, subordinate, enthrall, enslave, reduce to slavery, hold captive, hold in bondage.

overbearing, *adj.* domineering, imperious, high-and-mighty, lordly, magisterial; high-handed, arbitrary, presumptuous, overweening, cocky, cocksure, overconfident; arrogant, haughty, insolent, contemptuous, cavalier, disdainful, supercilious; proud, prideful, overproud, vain, stuck on oneself, swellheaded, *Inf.* bigheaded, egotistical, egotistic; pompous, pretentious, lofty, *Inf.* highfalutin, hoity-toity, self-important, stuffy; conceited, *Inf.* stuck-up, condescending, patronizing, *Inf.* uppity, *Inf.* uppish, snobbish, snobby, *Inf.* snotty, *Inf.* snooty; assertive, self-assertive, pushing, *Inf.* pushy, aggressive; self-willed, willful, forceful, imperative, commanding, masterful, authoritative, authoritarian, *Inf.* bossy; peremptory, dictatorial, despotic, autocratic, tyrannical, iron-handed; heavy-handed, oppressive, harsh, strict, hard, tough.

overblown, *adj.* **1.** overdone, excessive, extravagant, lavish, profuse, copious. See **overdone** (*def.* **2**).

2. oversize, outsize, overlarge, overbig.

3. elaborate, overelaborate, overdetailed, overworked, overwrought; exaggerated, blown *or* blown up, blown up out of proportion, magnified, enlarged; inflated, overinflated, swollen, bloated, distended, tumid; plethoric, flatulent, turgid, bombastic, bombastical, fustian, orotund, pompous, pretentious, ostentatious; flamboyant, flashy, showy, flowery, florid, ornate, ornamental, fancy; high-sounding, high-flown, lofty, *Inf.* highfalutin, *Inf.* high-hat; impressive, grandiose, magniloquent, grandiloquent, Johnsonian, Ossianic, sonorous, sesquipedalian; euphuistic, euphuistical, periphrastic, circumlocutory, roundabout.

overboard, *adj.* **1.** (*all of a boat, ship, etc.*) over the side, off the deck, over the edge; in the water, *Inf.* in the drink.

2. go overboard go to extremes, go too far, go off the deep end; overreact, carry on, overdo.

overcast, *adj.* **1.** cloudy, overclouded, clouded over, overshadowed, shadowy, gray; dreary, dismal, gloomy, somber, lowering, heavy, leaden, oppressive, promising rain; darkened, dark, sunless, starless, moonless; hazy, nubilous, foggy, fogged, misty, misted, *Archaic.* caliginous, vaporous, murky, murk.

—*v.* **2.** cloud, overcloud, overshadow, overspread, adumbrate, becloud, befog; lower, darken, smoke, dim, bedim, dusk, blind, blacken; grow cloudy, gloom, darkle, promise rain; nebulize, fog, pale, mist, haze, shade, shadow; eclipse, hide, conceal, occult; dull, blur, blear; shroud, cover, cloak, veil, screen, curtain.

overcharge, *v.* **1.** charge too much, *Sl.* soak, *Sl.* sting, cheat, *Inf.* gyp, rook, short-change, *Sl.* rip off; *Sl.* take, take advantage of, *Inf.* diddle, *Inf.* do, *Sl.* burn.

2. overload, overlade, fill too full, fill to the brim *or* gills, fill to overflowing, overfill, overstuff, overcrowd; overburden, overtask, overtax, strain.

3. exaggerate, overstate, overdo, make much of, overstress, make a mountain out of a molehill, make much ado about nothing; hyperbolize, overdraw; romance, embroider, stretch, stretch the truth *or* the point, strain the imagination; overcolor, color, paint, paint in glowing terms, oversell, *Inf.* play up, *Inf.* build up *or* on; *Inf.* pile it on, *Inf.* lay it on, *Inf.* lay it on thick, *Inf.* spread it on thick, *Sl.* bull; embellish, overdevelop, enlarge on, elaborate, add to, augment; magnify, enhance, enrich, deepen, heighten.

overcoat, *n.* topcoat, outer coat, surcoat, *Chiefly Brit.* greatcoat, winter coat, heavy coat, fearnought, dreadnought; ulster, paletot, raglan; surtout, frock coat; fur, fur coat, parka; coat, wrap, cloak, mantle, *Obs.* manteau, cape, inverness.

overcome, *v.* **1.** conquer, vanquish, defeat; best, checkmate, outmaneuver; win over, prevail over, *Inf.* gain the day; subdue, quell, squash, beat, worst, trample in the dust, floor; rout, whip, drub, get the better *or* best of, put down; master, subjugate, break the back of [s.t.], subject, break.

2. surmount, rise above, triumph over; put aside *or* away, get rid of, resist successfully, *Inf.* kick.

3. overpower, whelm, overwhelm, sweep off the feet; sweep over *or* through, pervade, dominate.

—*adj.* **4.** oppressed, defeated, depleted; *Inf.* defused, exhausted, enervated; worn out, tired, jaded, *Inf.* tuckered out, *Inf.* done in; debilitated, expended, drained, spent, played out; weakened, fagged, drooping, ready to drop; haggard, wayworn, footsore, sick, unsteady, groggy.

overconfident, *adj.* **1.** cocksure, dead certain, too certain; arrogant, brazen, audacious, impertinent; swaggering, blustering, *Inf.* pushy; bumptious, self-assertive, self-assured, self-assuming; imperious, overbearing, egotistic; lofty, *Inf.* toplofty, condescending, vainglorious, conceited, high-and-mighty, pompous, self-important, riding for a fall.

2. brash, hasty, precipitate, pell-mell; impetuous, impulsive, unrestrained, ungoverned, head-over-heels; reckless, risky, incautious, careless, unwary.

3. foolhardy, harebrained, thoughtless, regardless, careless; shortsighted, daring, spontaneous, unpremeditated; injudicious, unwise; ill-considered, ill-advised, impolitic, indiscreet.

overcritical, *adj.* **1.** hypercritical, particular, overparticular, fussy, finicky, picky, hairsplitting, *Inf.* choosy, fastidious; dainty, *Inf.* fuddy-duddy, *Inf.* pernickety, discriminating, painstaking.

2. complaining, carping, censorious, querulous; difficult, disapprobatory, condemnatory, disparaging, faultfinding, caviling; harsh, sharp, severe, mean; small, picayune, niggling, demanding, exacting, hard to please.

overcrowd, *v.* jam, congest, pack, lump together, stuff, squeeze, fill, *Naut.* fill to the gunnels; choke, compress, overload, overburden, supersaturate, serry, *Inf.* pack as tight as sardines; throng, swarm, huddle, bunch up *or* together; mass, congregate, agglomerate.

overdo, *v.* **1.** do to excess, carry too far, go overboard, not know when to stop, carry *or* go to extremes; be intemperate, overindulge, overeat; run riot, be uncontrolled, be unrestrained.

2. overact, overplay, be histrionic, *Sl.* ham it up, rant, spout, carry on; overstate, hyperbolize, exaggerate, overdraw; heighten, expand, amplify, magnify, enlarge, embroider, color; stretch *or* strain a point, dwell on, belabor, harp on, run into the ground, make a production of, make a big deal of; *Inf.* lay it on thick, fall all over oneself, kill with kindness, outdo oneself, out-Herod Herod.

3. overwork, work to death, push oneself too hard, overexert, do too much, burn the candle at both ends, overtax, overburden, strain; tire, weary, exhaust, wear out, fag, jade, *U.S. Inf.* tucker out.

4. overcook, overbake, overroast, overbroil, overbrown; char, scorch, singe; burn, burn to a crisp, carbonize.

overdone, *adj.* **1.** (*all of food*) overcooked, overbaked, overroasted, overbroiled, overbrowned; charred, scorched, singed, scalded; burn, burn to a crisp, carbonized.

2. excessive, immoderate, extravagant, lavish, beyond all bounds; profuse, copious, plenteous, plentiful, abundant, prolific; superabundant, overabundant, oversufficient, *Inf.* too much, *Inf.* a bit much; exorbitant, extreme, extortionate, *Inf.* criminal, unconscionable, outrageous, monstrous, preposterous, ridiculous; unreasonable, unrealistic, disproportionate, undue, inordinate, uncalled-for, unwarranted; unneeded, needless, unnecessary, redundant, superfluous, surplus, extra; overacted, *Inf.* hammy.

3. exaggerated, overblown, elaborate, overelaborate, inflated, turgid, bombastic. See **overblown** (*def.* 3).

4. overtaxed, exhausted, prostrate, prostrated, spent, drained, worn, worn out, effete; tired, fatigued, weary, wearied, drooping, weak, faint; fagged out, played out, *Inf.* beat, beaten, *Inf.* bushed, *U.S. Inf.* tuckered out, *Sl.* pooped, *Inf.* dog-tired, dead tired; ready to drop, on one's last legs, more dead than alive.

overdue, *adj.* **1.** past due, late, tardy, behind, behindhand, behind time *or* schedule, not on time, unpunctual, slow; delayed, belated.

2. unpaid, payable, owed, outstanding, unsettled; in arrears, back.

overeat, *v.* eat too much, overindulge, surfeit; feast, banquet, gormandize, fress, gorge, engorge, glut, *Archaic.* gluttonize, *Sl.* pig out, *Sl.* stuff one's face, eat like a horse, raven; devour, tuck in, wolf, *Inf.* pack away *or* in, *Chiefly Brit. Sl.* scoff *or* scoff up, *Sl.* scarf down, *Sl.* garbage *or* garbage down.

overestimate, *v.* **1.** overrate, overvalue, overesteem, overprize, exaggerate [s.t.'s] worth, make too much of, attach too much importance to, think too much of, expect too much of.

2. overcalculate, overreckon, overcount, overmeasure, overassess, overpraise.

3. overreact, make a big thing out of nothing, make much ado about nothing, make a mountain out of a molehill, *Inf.* blow out of proportion.

—n. **4.** overestimation, overcalculation, overreckoning, overrating, overvaluation, overappraisal, overassessment.

overexcite, *v.* overstimulate, add fuel to the flame, pour oil on the fire; instigate, provoke, incite, foment, *Sl.* psych, egg on; infuriate, madden, exasperate; aggravate, exacerbate; stimulate, animate, invigorate, rally, jolt, jog; agitate, commove, impassion, *Brit. Dial.* kittle; arouse, rouse, whip, whip up, work up, stir up, inflame, enflame, fire up, enkindle, kindle, touch off.

overexert, *v.* strain, overtax, do too much, overdo, burn the candle at both ends, overwork, work to death, push oneself too hard, drive oneself; tire, weary, fatigue, exhaust, wear out, fag, jade, *U.S. Inf.* tucker out; do to excess, carry too far, not know when to stop, go overboard, go off the deep end, go to extremes.

overfeed, *v.* **1.** gorge, stuff, cram, glut, cloy, choke, fill, overfill, sate, satiate, surfeit, feed to excess.

2. overeat, devour, overindulge. See **overeat.**

overfill, *v.* **1.** fill up, fill to the brim, fill to overflowing, stuff, stuff to the gills, overstuff, crowd, congest; lade, overlade, burden, overburden; cram, force in, ram down, pack in, push in, shove in, press in, jam, squeeze; strain, overload, overburden, weigh down, oversupply.

2. fatten, distend, inflate, dilate, bloat; stretch, bulge, spread, widen, broaden, thicken.

3. overfeed, overeat, overdrink, overindulge; glut, gorge, cloy, cram, satiate. See **cram** (*def.* 3).

overflow, *v.* **1.** flow over, run over, overrun, spill over, overspill, slop over, brim over, teem, teem over, well over, swarm, swam over; overspread, spread over, overgrow, grow over, know no bounds.

2. surge, swell, stream forth, pour forth, disembogue, debouch, discharge.

3. abound, superabound, exuberate; abound with, burst with, be alive with, bristle with, throng with, be rich in.

4. inundate, flood, deluge, pour over; submerge, drown, cover, engulf, bury; drench, saturate, soak.

—n. **5.** overflowing, inundation, flood, flash flood, freshet, deluge, debacle, washout.

6. superabundance, overabundance, overfullness, overprofusion, overplentifulness, overplenteousness, overplenty, nimiety, superflux; superfluity, superfluousness, oversufficiency, supererogation, redundance, redundancy; repletion, engorgement, congestion, surcharge; profusion, more than enough, enough and to spare, enough and then some; surplus, surfeit, satiety, glut, plethora, excess; oversupply, overmeasure, overload, overburden.

overgrow, *v.* **1.** cover, grow over, swarm over, teem over, overrun, overspread, spread over, spread out, spread like wildfire, run riot; superabound, overabound, teem, pullulate.

2. outgrow; overdevelop, *Pathol., Bot.* hypertrophy.

overgrowth, *n.* **1.** luxuriance, superabundance, overabundance; jungle, denseness; overspreading, overrunning, wild *or* uncontrolled growth.

2. overdevelopment, *Pathol., Bot.* hypertrophy, gigantism, giantism, *Pathol.* elephantiasis.

overhang, *v.* **1.** hang over, suspend over, *Rare.* impend; bridge, span, arch over, overarch, vault, bestride, bestraddle.

2. jut, beetle, project, protrude, extend, stick out, hang out.

3. impend, loom, hover, lower; menace, threaten, hang over one's head.

4. permeate, pervade, suffuse, imbue, fill, extend throughout.

—n. **5.** eave, overhanging; salient, projection, protuberance, beetling, jutting.

overhaul, *v.* **1.** investigate, look into; inspect, examine, scrutinize; check, check out, check over *or* through, double-check; inventory, take inventory, take stock, take account of; audit, balance, balance the books.

2. service, repair, mend, patch up, fix, *Inf.* fix up, *Inf.* doctor, put in shape, put in commission; restore, recondition, revamp, renovate.

3. gain upon, catch up, catch up with, come up with; lap, pass, overpass, overtake, overhaul, get ahead of, shoot ahead of, leave behind, leave in the dust, leave standing flatfooted; outstrip, outrun, outpace, outdistance, distance.

—n. **4.** general examination and repair, examination, repair, reparation, overhauling, fixing, mending; inspection, check-up.

overhead, *adv.* **1.** over one's head, above, on a higher place, at a higher place, in a higher place; atop, at *or* on the top; aloft, high up, up in the air *or* sky, far above ground; skyward *or* skywards, toward the sky; in *or* to heaven, on high, in the firmament, in the celestial heights.

2. completely submerged, immersed, plunged; deep in, buried, lost in, swallowed up, consumed; engrossed, absorbed, entirely occupied *or* engaged, deeply involved; intent, preoccupied, fascinated, spellbound, rapt, mesmerized, hypnotized.

—adj. **3.** over one's head, above, aloft. See **overhead** (*def.* **1**).

—n. **4.** operating cost, expense; outlay, disbursement.

overhear, *v.* hear, take in, *Sl.* get an earful; hear of, *Dial.* hear tell of, *Inf.* catch, *Inf.* get, *Inf.* catch *or* get wind of; learn, discover, descry, become conscious *or* aware of, come to one's knowledge, get the facts.

overindulge, *v.* **1.** do to excess, carry too far, not know when to stop, go overboard, go off the deep end, go to extremes.

2. be intemperate, run riot; overdrink, guzzle, overimbibe; eat too much, surfeit, feast, banquet, gormandize, fress; gorge, engorge, glut, *Archaic.* gluttonize, *Sl.* pig out, *Sl.* stuff one's face, eat like a horse, raven.

3. spoil, baby, coddle, pet, wait on hand and foot, cater to, dote on, humor, favor; pamper, cocker, cosset, dandle, mollycoddle, *Obs.* fondle.

overlap, *v.* **1.** imbricate, overlie, lie over, overlay, lay over, lap over, reach over, extend over; overspread, spread over, overstretch, stretch over; shingle, cover.

2. coincide, intersect; correspond, parallel.

—n. **3.** imbrication, overlapping, lap, overlay, overlayer; flap, tent fly, fly.

4. coincidence, intersection; correspondence, parallel, equivalence.

overlay, *v.* **1.** superimpose, superpose, lay over; overlap, lap over, imbricate, lie over; overspread, spread over, overstretch, stretch over; shingle, cover.

2. finish, inlay; decorate, ornament, adorn, embellish, embroider, enrich; festoon; gild, varnish, trick out.

—n. **3.** covering, overlayer, appliqué; imbrication, overlap, overlapping, lap.

4. decoration, ornament, ornamentation, adornment, embellishment, embroidery.

overleap, *v.* **1.** leap over *or* across, jump over *or* across, spring over *or* across, hop over *or* across, bound over *or* across, vault, vault over, leapfrog.

2. overreach, overstep, overstretch, stretch beyond, overpass, pass all bounds, know no bounds, go overboard, go too far, carry too far, carry to an extreme.

3. omit, except, leave out; miss, give a miss, fail to mention; overlook, pass over, skip, jump; ignore, disregard, pretermit, pay no attention to; neglect, forget, forget about, not think of, let slip, let slide, let go, *Sl.* let ride, leave undone, not trouble oneself with; eschew, avoid, shun, shirk.

overload, *v.* **1.** overburden, overweight, overtax, overlade, overcharge, surcharge; weight, weigh down, load, load with, saddle with, burden, burden with, charge, tax; strain, encumber, cumber, impede, hamper, handicap, tie a millstone around [s.o.'s] neck.

—n. **2.** overburden, overcharge, surcharge; burden, *Archaic.* burthen, weight, dead weight, heavy load, oppression; strain, encumbrance, impediment, hindrance, handicap, drag, millstone.

overlook, *v.* **1.** ignore, neglect, not take into account; miss, omit, slip up on, slight, lose sight of, leave out, forget, skip; pass up, set aside, give the go-by.

2. disregard, pretermit, overpass, drop; look the other way, let [s.t.] ride, let [s.t.] go, gloss over, extenuate; wink at, blink at, close *or* shut one's eyes to, connive at; choose not to see, be blind to, fail to notice.

3. excuse, forgive, pardon, condone, make allowances, spare; forget about [s.t.], forgive and forget, let bygones be bygones.

4. overtower, tower above, crown; rise above, overtop, top, cap; look over, jut out, jut over, beetle over, project.

5. inspect, examine, peruse, scan, survey; scrutinize, study, contemplate, review; take stock of, take a glance at, give [s.t.] the once-over.

6. oversee, supervise, superintend, *Sl.* boss; manage, direct, administer, monitor, keep tabs on; conduct, pilot, steer, guide, be at the helm.

overmaster, *v.* overpower, vanquish, subjugate, conquer, subdue. See **overpower** (*def.* **2**).

overmuch, *adj., adv.* **1.** too much, excessive, fulsome, unnecessary, needless, uncalled-for, lavish, disproportionate; out of all proportion, *Inf.* a bit much, *Inf.* a bit hard to take.

—n. **2.** excess, surplus, overplus. See **overplus.**

overpass, *n.* **1.** bridge, railway bridge, trestle, highway, *Brit.* flyover; cloverleaf; arch, archway, viaduct, aquaduct; walkway, skywalk; underpass.

—v. **2.** pass over, traverse, cross, cut across; span, bridge, arch, ford; stretch *or* reach across.

3. overstep, overstep one's bounds, go too far, not know one's limits; infringe, trespass, cross the line, transgress.

4. surmount, overcome. See **overcome** (*def.* **2**).

5. exceed, surpass, overtake, catch up with, leave behind; gain on, gain ground on, gain the ascendancy.

6. overlook, disregard. See **overlook** (*def.* **2**).

overplus, *n.* excess, nimiety, superfluity, redundancy, supererogation; surplus, surplusage, superflux, overflow, overload; overabundance, superabundance, profusion, plethora, oversupply; repletion, surfeit, glut, oversufficiency, more than enough, enough and to spare, enough and then some, overkill.

overpower, *v.* **1.** overcome, overwhelm, floor, dumfound, daze, stagger, stupefy, stun, nonplus, take aback; *Inf.* knock off one's feet, *Inf.* bowl over, *Sl.* knock for a loop, *Inf.* blow one's mind; move, stir, affect, touch, touch to the quick; reach, *Inf.* get *or* get to, come home to, strike, impress strongly, melt, soften, tug at the heartstrings.

2. overmaster, surmount, master, subdue, get the upper hand, prevail; discomfit, rout, vanquish, conquer; subjugate, subject, defeat, beat, put down; smash, crush, squash, *Inf.* mop *or* wipe the floor with, trounce, drub, thrash; worst, checkmate, outmaneuver, outwit.

overpowering, *adj.* overwhelming, uncontrollable, irresistible, unbearable, unendurable; onerous, oppressive, burdensome, weighty; ponderous, prodigious, monstrous; moving, mind-blowing. See **overwhelming** (*defs.* **1, 2**).

overrate, *v.* overestimate, overvalue, overesteem, overprize, exaggerate [s.t.'s *or* s.o.'s] worth, make too much of, attach too much importance to, think too much of, expect too much of.

overreach, *v.* **1.** overshoot, overextend, extend beyond, exceed; outstretch, outreach; overdo, overexert.

2. overleap, be hoisted by one's own petard, be caught in one's own trap, defeat one's own purpose, cut one's own throat; have one's plans backfire *or* boomerang, bite off more than one can chew, overestimate one's ability.

3. outwit, outsmart, outfox, outjockey, outflank, outmaneuver, outplay; get the better of, best, worst, make a fool of, *Sl.* make a sucker of; cheat, cozen, *Sl.* con, trick, gull, hoodwink; swindle, defraud, *Sl.* beat, bilk, gyp, *Sl.* sucker, *Sl.* take, *Sl.* do; deceive, fool, delude, beguile, humbug, *Sl.* rope in; victimize, *Inf.* diddle, dupe, *Inf.* flimflam; betray, *Inf.* double-cross.

overreact, *v.* **1.** exaggerate, make a mountain out of a molehill, make much ado about nothing, make a big thing out of nothing; enlarge, *Inf.* blow up, blow out of all proportion; overplay, overact, carry on; stretch out, overstretch, overcolor.

2. get excited, *Inf.* get in a tizzy *or* dither, *Inf.* get all excited, get overexcited, *Sl.* get all hyper, *Sl.* go bonkers *or* bananas *or* ape, jump out of one's skin; panic, push the panic button, jump the gun, act irrationally, lose one's sense of balance, lose all sense of proportion, lose one's sense of humor, forget which end is up, lose sight of reality.

override, *v.* **1.** crush, trample, stamp, *Inf.* stomp, *Sl.* tromp; subdue, put down, overwhelm, overpower; defeat, beat, ruin, annihilate, destroy, raze.

2. defy, flout, rebel against, fly in the face of, snap one's fingers at, close one's mind to, turn a deaf ear to; snub, ignore, disregard, pay no heed, *Inf.* cold-shoulder; follow one's own advice, assert oneself, hold one's own, be one's own man, have a mind of one's own.

3. predominate, win out, overrule, prevail over, overcome, surmount; outweigh, preponderate, take precedence over; annul, reverse, nullify, set aside, abrogate, cancel, void, overturn, supersede.

overriding, *adj.* taking precedence, overruling, prevailing, leading, dominant, predominant, preponderant, outweighing; primary, prime, first, number one, *Sl.* numero uno; cardinal, capital, crowning; principal, paramount, chief, main, foremost, top; most important, uppermost, central, focal, pivotal.

overrule, *v.* **1.** disallow, rule against, reject, veto; say [s.o.] nay, put down, deny, gainsay, forbid, prohibit; restrain, restrict, exclude, refuse, withhold.

2. override, prevail over, predominate, overcome; reverse, annul, nullify, set aside, abrogate, cancel, void, overturn, supersede; prevent, thwart, stop; rescind, revoke, recall, repudiate, abolish.

3. rule, lead, head, direct, steer, guide, pilot; command, domineer, dominate, master; manage, oversee, supervise; influence, sway, bend to one's will.

overrun, *v.* **1.** invade, attack, irrupt, assail, assault, strike at; penetrate, cross frontiers, march into, march against, thrust at, storm, blitz, blitzkrieg; besiege, beset, ravage, terrorize, vandalize, maraud; spoil, despoil, scour, scourge; plunder, loot, strip, sack, rob, raid, pillage, devastate, lay waste.

2. spread through, overspread, grow over, cover, mantle; fill, glut, engulf, infest, saturate, supersaturate, inundate; load, choke, clog, flourish, grow wild, *Inf.* run amuck, *Inf.* run riot, overwhelm, spread like wildfire.

3. overwhelm, crush, suppress, subdue, quell, quash, put down, squelch, scotch; vanquish, overcome, overpower, ride roughshod over, *Inf.* crush under the heel, trample, conquer; oppress, harass, persecute, plague.

4. exceed, transcend, surmount, surpass, go beyond, run beyond, overshoot; overpass, overreach, extend past, overextend.

5. overflow, slop over, run over, spill, spill over.

overseas, *adv.* **1.** abroad, over *or* across the sea, in foreign parts, in foreign service.

—adj. **2.** foreign, alien, barbarian, exotic; external, colonial; ultramarine, *U.S.* European.

oversee, *v.* **1.** administer, orchestrate, quarterback, *Inf.* call the plays, run the show, mastermind; make decisions, dispose, direct; manage, superintend, run, operate, carry out, handle, manipulate; supervise, preside, counsel, advise; boss, be master over, *Sl.* honcho, dominate, domineer, ride herd on, *Inf.* keep tabs on; command, take charge, wield one's power *or* authority; control, have control over, regulate, rule, govern, be on top of, be master of; be in command, be in the dirver's seat *or* saddle, wear the pants *or* trousers, *Inf.* be where the buck stops.

2. pilot, navigate, steer, drive, hold the reins, be at the helm; guide, lead, conduct, point, aim, steer [s.o. *or* s.t.] toward, show the way, point out the way.

3. glimpse, witness, view, attend, note, notice, see by chance, observe inadvertently.

overseer, *n.* supervisor, director, manager, line manager, superintendent, *Inf.* super, foreman, fugleman; overlooker, overman, headman, boss, *Inf.* bossman, *U.S. Inf.* straw boss, gang boss, *Sl.* the man, *Inf.* honcho, *Inf.* head honcho, *Brit.* gaffer; master, commander, overlord, taskmaster; administrator, executive, bureaucrat, functionary, official, marshal; president, head, headmaster, chief, principal; governor, regent, dean, chairman, chairwoman, chairperson; provost, monitor, proctor, captain; matron, guard, forest ranger; keeper, nursemaid, babysitter; tutor, teacher, governess; watchdog, bodyguard, protector, guardian angel.

overshadow, *v.* **1.** dominate, dwarf, overtop, rise above, tower over *or* above, stand head and shoulders above, bestride; outshine, minimize, reduce, detract from, steal the spotlight from, put in the shade, *Inf.* run circles *or* rings around.

2. dim, bedim, obumbrate; cloud, becloud, overcloud; blear, fog, darken; conceal, shroud, veil, eclipse, obscure, screen.

3. spoil, sour, blight, impair, take the edge off of, chase the bloom from, take all the pleasure from.

overshoe, *n.* *Usu.* **overshoes** galoshes, rubbers, rubber boots, waterproof boots, hip boots, waders; arctics, snowboots, gumshoes, mukluks, *Brit.* Wellington boots, *Brit. Inf.* wellies.

overshoot, *v.* **1.** miss, miss aim, fly wide, fall short *or* wide of the mark.

2. pass, overreach, outreach, go too far; exceed, transcend, surpass, go beyond, run beyond; overpass, overextend, extend past, exceed the limit.

oversight, *n.* **1.** neglect, neglectfulness, negligence, inattention, lack of attention, inconsideration, inadvertence, inadvertency; disregard, indifference, nonconcern, carelessness, thoughtlessness, heedlessness, unheedfulness; oblivion, forgetfulness, unmindfulness; laxity, laxness, slackness, remissness; failure, lapse, default, dereliction, delinquency, nonfulfillment, nonperformance; fault, slight, omission.

2. mistake, error, inaccuracy, erratum, corrigendum; blunder, botch, bungle, flub, muff; leak, slip of the tongue *or* pen, *Inf.* slip-up; *All Sl.* pratfall, fool mistake, dumb trick, foul-up, louse-up, screw-up, boner, boo-boo, goof, blooper, clinker, clunker.

3. supervision, superintendence, surveillance, watchful care; management, ministration, ministry, administration, government, governance; dominion, jurisdiction; direction, guidance, tutelage, command, control; care, custody, charge, keeping, ward, hands; auspices, protection, protectorship, guardianship, stewardship, patronage.

overspread, *v.* spread over *or* through, grow over, cover, mantle; film, wrap, overlay, coat; fill, glut, engulf, infest, saturate, supersaturate, inundate; load, choke, clog; flourish, grow wild, *Inf.* run amuck, *Inf.* run riot, *Inf.* run wild, spread like wildfire, overwhelm.

overstate, *v.* exaggerate, overdo, make much of, overstress; hyperbolize, overdraw, color, overcolor, stretch the point, heighten, draw larger than life; enhance, *Inf.* touch up, expand, magnify, *Inf.* blow up, inflate, stretch, *Inf.* draw the longbow; amplify, swell, bloat, dilate, distend; increase, enlarge, make larger, intensify, maximize; embroider, make much ado about nothing, make a mountain out of a molehill, paint in glowing colors, oversell, *Inf.* play up; *Inf.* pile it on, *Inf.* lay it on, *Inf.* lay *or* spread it on thick.

overstep, *v.* exceed, go beyond, transcend, surpass; push in, encroach, infringe, trespass, intrude, invade, impinge, obtrude.

overstock, *n.* **1.** oversupply, excess, surfeit, surplus, superfluity, superabundance, superflux, glut; redundance, plethora, overabundance, overprofusion, nimiety; overload, overfill; repletion, more than enough, enough with overmeasure, enough and to spare.

—*v.* **2.** oversupply, glut, load, overload, overfill; cram, stuff, fill to overflowing; saturate, supersaturate.

overstrung, *adj.* **1.** high-strung, tense, emotional, excitable, easily excited; susceptible, easily hurt, quick to tears; hot-tempered, inflammable, volatile.

2. neurotic, nervous, *Inf.* uptight, temperamental, unpredictable; apprehensive, anxious, phobic, suggestible, obsessive, *Psychol.* compulsive; hysterical, emotionally disturbed, irrational, *Psychiatry.* paranoiac.

overt, *adj.* plain, plain to see, manifest, apparent, clearly apparent, unconcealed; clear, clear-cut, plain as day; explicit, definite, unmistakable; public, exposed, in full view; open, visible, naked, bald, unhidden; unveiled, unshrouded, uncurtained, unobscured; obvious, patent, palpable, conspicuous, prominent, blatant, flagrant, egregious, impossible to miss; professed, avowed, conscious, deliberate, willful, premeditated.

overtake, *v.* **1.** catch up with *or* up to, gain upon, reach, overhaul; go by, run by, pass; chase, run down, catch.

2. happen to, befall, fall on *or* upon, engulf, overwhelm; come up on *or* upon, strike, hit; surprise, take by surprise, catch off guard *or* unprepared.

overtax, *v.* **1.** surcharge, overcharge; fleece, gouge, screw, extort, bleed white, make pay through the nose; *All. Sl.* rob, rip off, hold up, soak, stick, clip.

2. overtask, overwork, overlabor, overexert, overextend, overexercise, overstrain, overdrive; fag *or* fag out, exhaust, enervate, debilitate, jade, tire out, wear out, prostrate, run into the ground; oppress, overload, overlade, overburden, overweigh.

overthrow, *v.* **1.** vanquish, conquer, subjugate, *Sl.* shellac; defeat, beat, rout, discomfit, worst, thrash; overpower, overmaster, be victorious over, *Inf.* whip; subvert, overturn, overcome, overwhelm, prevail over, surmount; quash, quell, squash, squelch; suppress, crush, humble, master, subdue, put down.

2. depose, oust, dethrone, unseat, remove from office, uncrown, discrown, unfrock; disestablish, disenact.

3. overturn, turn over, upset, overset, throw over, knock over, knock down; upend, tip over, capsize, turn topsy-turvy, turn upside down, reverse, invert; topple, tumble, precipitate, *Inf.* spill.

4. revolutionize, revolt, rise, rise up, rebel; disrupt, interrupt, break up, displace, disorganize, disarrange; agitate, convulse, disturb.

5. nullify, abolish, quash; cancel, discharge, set aside, render unnecessary, obviate; countermand, counterorder, overrule, override; veto, reverse; invalidate, disprove, refute, confute, rebut; dispute, deny, oppose, controvert; contradict, belie, negate.

6. annihilate, discreate, exterminate, extirpate, extinguish, abolish; erase, efface, eradicate, expunge, cancel, obliterate; excise, cut, cut out, cut off; blot out, strike out, stamp out, crush out, wipe out, rub out; kill, kill off, slay, slaughter, murder, finish, finish off, *Sl.* do in, *Sl.* zap; purge, get rid of, leave no vestige *or* trace of, liquidate, remove, dispose of; terminate, dissolve, bring to an end, put an end to, do away with.

7. devastate, desolate, demolish, lay waste; ravage, work havoc upon, destroy, ruin, *Dial.* ruinate, bring to ruin, lay in ruins; wreck, *Sl.* total, knock to pieces, dash to pieces, smash, waste, *Sl.* trash, reduce to nothing.

8. pulverize, crush, squelch, mash; crash, shatter, batter, break; fracture, splinter, tear, crack, split, rend, tear apart, wrench apart; mutilate, mangle, maim, make mincemeat of.

9. raze, tear down, pull down, break down, throw down, beat down, batter down; cast down, knock down, hurl down; fell, lay level, prostrate, level, bulldoze, flatten; cut down, chop down, hew down, mow down.

—*n.* **10.** vanquishment, conquest, subjugation, mastery, victory, triumph; defeat, rout, discomfiture; subversion, overturn, suppression, subdual; ruin, fall, downfall, labefaction, collapse, undoing.

11. quashing, quelling, squashing, squelching; overcoming, overwhelming, mastering, crushing, putting down.

12. deposition, deposal, ouster, unseating, dethronement, discrownment, unfrocking, dispossession; disestablishment, disenactment; dismissal, expulsion, discharge, removal.

13. throwing over, oversetting, knocking over, knocking down; upending, tipping over, capsizing, capsize, reversing, reversal, inverting, inversion.

14. revolution, insurrection, insurgence, uprising, mutiny, revolt, coup d'état, rebellion; overturn, upset, breakup, debacle, cataclysm, catastrophe; disruption, eruption, interruption, displacement, disorganization, breakdown, disarrangement, derangement; agitation, upheaval, confusion, convulsion, disturbance.

15. nullification, abolition, abolishment; cancellation, discharge, setting aside; countermand, counterorder, overruling, overriding; veto, reversal; invalidation, *Rare.* disproval, refutation, confutation; disputation, denial, opposition, contradiction.

16. annihilation, discreation, extermination, extirpation, extinguishment, extinction; erasure, erasion, effacement, eradication, expunction, obliteration; excision, cutting out, cutting off; blotting out, striking out, stamping out, crushing out, wiping out, rubbing out; killing, slaying, slaughter, murdering, finishing off, *Sl.* doing in; purgation, leaving no vestige *or* trace of, liquidation, removal; termination, dissolution, putting an end to, doing away with, bringing to an end.

17. devastation, desolation, demolition, havoc, laying waste; ravagement, destruction, perdition, ruin, ruination, wreckage.

overtone, *n.* hidden meaning, secondary meaning, connotation, implication, *Inf.* inference, intimation, innuendo, hint, suggestion, insinuation; drift, intent, purport, import, point, purpose; sense, significance, signification, value, force; tenor, tone, vein, spirit; coloring, slant, bias, direction, bent, leaning.

overture, *n.* **1.** offer, proposal, proposition, proffer, tender; invitation, suggestion, advance, motion, move; appeal, request, solicitation, petition, suit.

2. exordium, preface, prologue, introduction, proem, preamble, foreword, prolegomenon, voluntary.

overturn, *v.* **1.** overthrow, subvert, vanquish, conquer, triumph over, win out *or* out over, *Inf.* beat out, be victorious over, get the better of; overbear, overcome, overwhelm, overpower, overmaster, prevail over, surmount, rise above, transcend, master, control; defeat, beat, rout, discomfit, worst, thrash, *Inf.* whip, *Sl.* cream, *Sl.* shellac; destroy, crush, trounce, *Inf.* stomp, trample ruin, demolish; quash, quell, squash, squelch, suppress, put down, stamp out, extinguish; repress, keep down *or* under, break, humble, subdue, subjugate, subject, subordinate.

2. annul, nullfiy, abolish, cancel *or* cancel out, invalidate, void, negate; countermand, counterorder, overrule, override; veto, nix, *Inf.* put *or* turn thumbs down; reverse, repeal, rescind, retract, recall, take back.

3. upset, overset, throw over, push over, knock over *or* down, turn over; upend, tip over, capsize, keel *or* keel over, turn topsy-turvy, turn upside down, invert, reverse; topple, tumble, precipitate, *Inf.* spill.

overvalue, *v.* overestimate, overrate, overesteem, overprize, exaggerate [s.t.'s *or* s.o.'s] worth, make too much of, attach too much importance to, think too much of, expect too much of.

overweening, *adj.* **1.** (*all of persons*) presumptuous, assuming, cocky, cocksure, overconfident, riding for a fall; bold, forward, impertinent, audacious, *Inf.* fresh, impudent, brash, brazen, brassy; arrogant, haughty, insolent, contemptuous, cavalier, disdainful, supercilious; proud, prideful, overproud, vainglorious, vain, stuck on oneself, swellheaded, *Inf.* bigheaded, egotistical, egotistic; peacockish, strutting, flaunting, show-offish; pompous, pretentious, lofty, *Inf.* highfalutin, hoity-toity, self-important, stuffy; conceited, *Inf.* stuck-up, condescending, patronizing, *Inf.* uppity, *Inf.* uppish, snobbish, snobby, *Inf.* snotty, *Inf.* snooty; magisterial, lordly, high and mighty, imperious, domineering, overbearing, high-handed, arbitrary; assertive, self-assertive, pushing, *Inf.* pushy, aggressive; self-willed, willful, forceful, imperative, commanding, masterful, authoritative, authoritarian, *Inf.* bossy; peremptory, dictatorial, despotic, autocratic, tyrannical.

2. (*all of opinions, characteristics, etc.*) exaggerated, excessive, extravagant, overdone; elaborate, overelaborate, overdetailed, overworked, overwrought; blown *or* blown up, overblown, blown up out of proportion, magnified, enlarged; inflated, overinflated, swollen, bloated, distended, tumid; plethoric, flatulent, turgid, bombastic, bombastical, fustian, orotund; ostentatious, flamboyant, flashy, showy, flowery, florid, ornate, ornamental, fancy; impressive, grandiose, magniloquent, grandiloquent, sonorous; affected, high-sounding, high-flown, lofty, *Inf.* highhat.

overweigh, *v.* **1.** outweigh, overbalance, outbalance, preponderate; overshadow, throw into the shade, eclipse, put to shame, *Inf.* show up; exceed, transcend, surpass, overmatch, outmatch; outrank, be superior to, overtop, override, overpower, take precedence over; have the edge on, hold the advantage, tip the scales, turn the tables.

2. oppress, burden, trouble, tax, encumber, cumber, charge, crush, weigh down; exhaust, wear, wear down, weary; overload, overcharge, load, overwhelm; strain, work, drive, overwork, overdrive.

overweight, *n.* **1.** overbalance, excess baggage, excess, *Commerce.* overage.

2. obesity, fatness, excess weight, *Euph.* weight problem, overheaviness, overponderousness; heaviness, heftiness, weightiness, ponderousness, ponderosity; rotundity, portliness, stoutness, chubbiness, tubbiness, pudginess, plumpness.

—adj. **3.** overheavy, too heavy, overponderous, in excess of *or* above the allowance, over; weighty, bulky, overloaded, loaded down, heavy-laden, laden, loaded, weighed down.

4. obese, fat, corpulent, pursy, flabby, fleshy, *Scot.* fodgel, tipping the scales; heavy, hefty, portly, stout, rotund; paunchy, potbellied, big-bellied, roundbellied, large-bellied, great-bellied, abdominous, *Inf.* bay-windowed, *Inf.* corporational, *Sl.* beerbellied, *Obs.* gorbellied; chubby, tubby, pudgy, plump, rounded.

overwhelm, *v.* **1.** overpower, destroy, crush, route, discomfit, overthrow, overbear, worst, ruin, extirpate, annihilate; override, subdue, suppress, quash, quell, subjugate, master, overmaster, vanquish, conquer, triumph over, defeat, beat, overburden, overweigh, weigh down, oppress, burden, overtax, bow down, prostrate, encumber, hamper, saddle.

2. overcome, whelm, engulf, swallow, submerge, immerse, flood, swamp, deluge, inundate, bury, suffocate, glut, choke, overrun, infest, *Inf.* snow, *Inf.* snow under, *Inf.* blitz; overlay, cover, spread over, overspread.

3. daze, stagger, stupefy, dumfound, astound, confound, bewilder, stun, nonplus, take aback, astonish, amaze, *Inf.* bowl over, *Inf.* knock off one's feet, *Sl.* knock for a loop, *Inf.* blow one's mind.

overwhelming, *adj.* **1.** overpowering, uncontrollable, irresistible, knockdown; unbearable, unendurable, unyielding, inexorable; onerous, oppressive, burdensome, weighty, crushing, arduous, exhausting, wearing, wasting, devastating, despoiling; decisive, irrefutable, formidable, inevitable, inescapable.

2. prodigious, monstrous, stupendous, cataclysmic, stupefying, mind-blowing, mind-shattering, mindboggling, breathtaking, awesome, awe-striking, aweinspiring, awful; engulfing, profuse, inordinate.

overwork, *v.* **1.** overtax, overtask, overexert, overextend, overexercise, overstrain, overdrive; fag *or* fag out, enervate, exhaust, jade, wear out, prostrate, run *or* drive into the ground; oppress, overload, overlade, overburden, overweight, overcharge, surcharge.

2. work hard, work like a horse, work like a slave *or* galley slave, slave, *Inf.* sweat and slave, *Inf.* work one's head *or* tail off, work one's fingers to the bone; do double duty, work overtime, work double hours, work day and night; work late, burn the midnight oil, lucubrate.

3. foment, agitate, suscitate, excite, overexcite, impassion, inflame, stir up, work up, wind up, whip up, fire up; madden, infuriate, lash into a fury, whip into a frenzy.

4. overdo, overlabor, overuse, overemploy, overplay, *Inf.* overplay one's hand; overstress, overemphasize, play up.

5. decorate, ornament, adorn, embellish, overlay.

—n. **6.** overexertion, overexercise, overexpenditure, overstrain, strain, overtaxing, overtasking.

overwrought, *adj.* **1.** all worked-up, all wrought-up, beside oneself, not oneself, in a state, in a dither, in a titter, atwitter, *Inf.* in a tizzy; overexcited, overly excited, all wound up, all keyed up, *Sl.* choked up; aroused, all stirred up, all whipped up, all fired up, inflamed, impassioned, carried away; frenzied, in a frenzy, frantic, corybantic, hysterical, in hysterics, feverish, delerious, maddened, crazed, wild, *Inf.* out of one's head, *Inf.* off the deep end, *Sl.* out of one's skull *or* gourd, *Sl.* bananas, *Sl.* zonkers; perturbed, vexed, annoyed, exasperated, exacerbated; incensed, furious, enraged, angry, mad, hopping mad, *Inf.* in a lather, *Inf.* steamed up, *Sl.* hot under the collar, *U.S. Sl.* hopped up; agitated, shaken, ruffled, flustered, fluttered, aquiver, disturbed, unsettled; disconcerted, disquieted, discomposed, addled, muddled, confused.

2. high-strung, highly excitable *or* emotional, jumpy, twitchy, jittery, fidgety, shaky; nervous, tense, on edge, touchy, irritable, oversensitive.

3. overworked, overdone, overdrawn, strained, forced, contrived; exaggerated, hyperbolic, stretching it, excessive, *Inf.* too much, *Inf.* a bit much; pretentious, chichi, affected, mannered, self-conscious, overrefined, overnice, euphemistic, *Inf.* too-too, *Inf.* la-di-da; overelegant, high-flown, extravagant, gradiloquent, grandiose, magniloquent, pompous, ostentatious, *Inf.* highfalutin; gaudy, garish, overelaborate, overembellished, flowery, florid, ornate, baroque, rococo, busy.

ovoid, *adj.* **1.** egg-shaped, ellipsoidal, ellipsoid, oviform, ovular, obovoid; oval, elliptical, ovate, obovate.

—n. **2.** egg, *Biol.* ovule, *Archit.* ovum, *Geom.* ellipsoid; oval, *Geom.* ellipse.

owe, *v.* **1.** *Usu.* **owe to** be indebted to, be beholden to.

2. be under obligation to, be obligated to, *Scot.* aught; be in arrears, have debts, have unpaid bills; be in debt to, have a loan from.

owing, *adj.* **1.** due, unpaid, in arrears, owed; payable, immediately payable, mature, outstanding, receivable.

2. owing to due to, because of, thanks to; attributable to, assignable to, ascribable to, imputable to, chargeable to, accountable to; derivable from, deriving from, resulting from, through.

own, *v.* **1.** have, possess, *Scot.* aught; keep, hold for use, hold, retain, preserve, maintain; occupy, tie up, use.

2. recognize, see, allow as valid, concede, grant; assent to, accede to, yield to, submit to; accept, go along with, agree, concur with.

3. *Often* **own up** admit, acknowledge, confess, *Sl.* fess up, *Inf.* make no bones about; avow, profess, express, utter, declare, tell; make known, *Inf.* let on, divulge, let out, disclose, reveal, expose.

4. one one's own *Informal.* alone, by oneself, single, independent, autonomous, self-reliant, inner-directed, standing on one's own two feet; free-wheeling, foot-loose, unconfined, at liberty, at large.

owner, *n.* proprietor, proprietress, holder, possessor; landlord, landlady, householder, landowner; lord, lady, master, mistress.

ox, *n.* **1.** bullock, steer; longhorn, shorthorn, zebu, bison, buffalo, water buffalo.

2. lout, dolt, oaf, clod, clodhopper, clodpoll *or* clodpole *or* clodpate; gawk, looby, lubber, clown, slouch, *Chiefly Scot.* cuddy, *Inf.* lummox, *Sl.* klutz, *Sl.* galoot, *Sl.* lug, *Chiefly Brit. Sl.* joskin; bungler, bumbler, fumbler, botcher, blunderer, boggler, *Inf.* butterfingers, *Inf.* stumblebum, *Inf.* duffer, *Sl.* slob.

P

pabulum, *n.* food, nourishment, nutriment, nutrition, nurture, sustenance, sustentation, subsistence, alimentation, aliment; meat, viands, bread, daily bread, groceries, foodstuffs, solids, edibles, *Inf.* grub, *Sl.* eats, chow, *Chiefly Brit. Sl.* scoff; pap, baby food; snack, between-meal snack, bite, nosh, *Sl.* munchies; victuals, provisions, cheer, provender, rations, commons, comestibles, *Western U.S. Sl.* chuck, *Brit. Sl.* prog; board, fare, meals, mess, menu, diet, table, regimen; (*all of livestock*) feed, fodder, hay, oats, barley, corn, grain, bran, meal, mash; swill, *Inf.* glop, *Sl.* slop.

pace, *n.* **1.** rate of speed, velocity, *Inf.* clip, stride, career; tempo, time, meter, measure; progress, movement, motion.

2. celerity, swiftness, rapidity, quickness, *Inf.* lick; slowness, creep.

3. gait, walk, step, stride, tread; manner of going, bearing, carriage; stalk, saunter, run; (*all of horses*) rack, single-foot, amble, trot, jog, canter, gallop.

—*v.* **4.** walk, foot, tread; roam, rove, range, traverse, trek, travel; go for a walk, take a walk, stretch one's legs.

5. walk the floor, walk back and forth nervously; run, jog, trot; hit the road, pound the pavement.

paced, *adj.* counted out, measured, metered, regulated, modulated, proportioned; like clockwork, precise, exact, determined; steady, regular, constant, uniform, even; with a steady beat, at a steady pace, rhythmical.

pacer, *n.* **1.** pacemaker, pacesetter; standard-bearer, leader; trend-setter, forerunner.

2. harness horse, trotter, racehorse; five-gaited saddle horse, three-gaited saddle horse, hackney; equine, *Australian.* prad, steed, mount, charger, *Literary.* courser.

pachydermatous, *adj.* **1.** elephantine, hippopotamic, rhinocerotic.

2. thickskinned, callous, tough, obdurate, hardened, hard, hard-boiled, steeled; inured, case-hardened, insensitive, insensate, numb, unfeeling, insentient, insensible.

pacifiable, *adj.* placable, forgiving, appeasable, conciliable, propitiable, able to be won over; mollifiable, able to be soothed, able to be calmed down, able to be comforted.

pacific, *adj.* **1.** conciliatory, propitiatory, propitiative, appeasing, mollifying, placating; pacificatory, peacemaking, accommodative, mediatory, diplomatic; soothing, calming.

2. peaceable, peace-loving, irenic, dovish; pacifistic, nonviolent, unwarlike, noncombative, unbelligerent, unbellicose, unpugnacious, uncontentious; mild, tender, gentle, soft, soft-hearted, tender-hearted, sensitive; merciful, lenient, clement, easy, easy-going, forgiving, tolerant; easy-natured, gentle as a lamb, good-natured, good-tempered, amiable, affable, genial; docile, tame; uncomplaining, unassertive, passive, nonopposing, submissive; unassuming, meek, quiet, subdued, tractable.

3. at peace, peaceful; calm, still, motionless, smooth, undisturbed, unperturbed, unagitated, unruffled; windless, waveless, stormless; stationary, becalmed; tranquil, serene, restful, reposeful, placid, halcyon.

pacification, *n.* **1.** tranquilization, quieting, calming, lulling, soothing, comforting, consoling, solacing; assuagement, allaying, alleviation, palliation, relieving; mitigation, abatement, remission, relief; reduction, lessening, diminution, moderation, modulation; tempering, softening, mollifying, mollification.

2. appeasement, placation, propitiation, conciliation; atonement, reconciliation, reconciling, reconcilement, reunion; sacrifice, compromise, accommodation, adjustment; peace-making, mediation, arbitration, negotiation, intervention; settlement, terms, truce, treaty, armistice; suspension of hostilities, moratorium, relaxation of tensions, détente, peace.

3. subdual, suppression, quelling, quashing; satisfaction, satisfying, slaking, quenching; dulling, blunting, stifling, smothering.

4. peacefulness, rest, repose, tranquillity, calm, serenity; relief, comfort, consolation, solace.

pacificatory, *adj.* **1.** pacifying, appeasing, conciliatory, propitiatory, propitiating, propitiative, placatory, placative; peace-making, mediative, mediatorial, intermediatory, intercessory, intervening, interventional; negotiable, reconcilable; compromising, accommodative.

2. peaceable, agreeable, agreeing, accordant; harmonious, concordant, compatible; peaceful, pacific, peace-loving, congenial, amicable, amiable, friendly.

pacifier, *n.* **1.** teething ring, rubber nipple, sugar-tit; mollifier, appeaser, placater, *Med., Pharm.* placebo; sweetener.

2. bribe, sop; inducement, lure, reward.

pacify, *v.* **1.** quiet, calm, tranquilize, lull, soothe, compose, comfort; alleviate, relieve, palliate, allay, assuage; mitigate, abate, moderate, temper, lessen.

2. appease, placate, pacificate, *Archaic.* attemper; humor, dulcify, mollify, soften; reconcile, *Archaic.* accord, bring to terms, make peace, settle differences, defuse, pour oil on troubled waters; propitiate, conciliate, accommodate, adjust, harmonize; reunite, mediate, arbitrate, bridge the gap, negotiate, intervene; mend, patch, patch up, repair the breach, smooth over.

3. subdue, suppress, put down, quell, quash; take the edge off, deaden, dull, blunt; stifle, still, silence, hush, smother; quench, slake, satisfy, *Sl.* shut [s.o.] up, keep [s.o.] quiet, give a sop to.

pack, *n.* **1.** bundle, package, bale, parcel, packet; sack, load, gear; rucksack, knapsack, backpack, haversack, packsack, *Sl.* bindle, *Australian Sl.* swag, kit, kit bag; bag, duffel bag, suitcase, overnighter, valise, grip.

2. collection, assemblage, accumulation, congeries, amassment, agglomeration, conglomeration; heap, pile, mass, mess, barrel, ton, lot, lots, great deal, bunch, batch; peck, bushel and a peck, *Inf.* caboodle, *Inf.* kit and caboodle, *Sl.* boodle, *Sl.* scads, *Sl.* zillions, *Inf.* slew, *Inf.* raft; multiplicity, myriad, multitudinousness; multitude, crowd, throng, horde, crush, host; group, party, company, body, gang, crew, mob, band; flock, herd, drove, swarm, bevy; congregation, assembly, gathering; circle, set, clique, coterie.

—*v.* **3.** cram, fill, jam, stuff, choke, crowd, press, ram, tamp; compact, compress, constrict.

4. load, lade, stow, store, pile, charge, burden, weigh down.

5. carry, wear, tote, lug, *Sl.* shlep, haul, *Australian Sl.* hump, bear, shoulder.

6. leave, depart, go, *Inf.* take off, make oneself scarce; leave posthaste, *Inf.* scram, take French leave, scamper, *Sl.* beat it, go off like a shot, scoot, *Inf.* make time; dash off, hasten away, fly, beat a retreat, take to one's heels, whip off, *Inf.* tear off.

package, *n.* **1.** parcel, bundle, pack, bale, packet; box, case, carton, receptacle, container, crate.

2. entity, unit, package deal, combine, amalgamation.

packed, *adj.* crammed, filled, jammed, stuffed, choked, gorged; bursting, overloaded, swollen, plethoric; crowded, swarming, dense, like a beehive, like an anthill; full, filled to capacity, S.R.O., standing room only, filled wall-to-wall; filled to the brim, filled to the gunnels *or* gunwales; brimful, replete, chock-full; compact, compressed, tamped, constricted.

packet, *n.* **1.** pack, package, parcel, sheaf, pouch, *Obs.* budget, bag.

2. mailboat, *Brit.* post-boat, *Archaic.* mailer; ferry, ferryboat, ocean liner, cruise ship.

3. vessel, boat, ship; transport, freighter, tanker, oiler, troopship; steamship, steamer, steamboat; tug boat, tug, pilot, pilot boat; sternwheeler, sidewinder; sailing ship, *Inf.* windjammer, schooner.

packhorse, *n.* beast of burden, pack animal; workhorse, dobbin, plow horse, draft horse, *Archaic.* sumpter, Clydesdale, Percheron, Belgian; donkey, mule, ass, jackass, burro; nag, *Sl.* crowbait, jade, *Sl.* plug, *Sl.* scrag.

packing, *n.* **1.** packaging, package, wrapping, boxing, crating, encasement, bottling.

2. cushioning, stuffing, wadding, filling, fiber fill, filler, pad, padding, *Obs.* bombast, lining; wrapping, wrapper, wrapping paper; shredded newspaper, tissue paper, *Trademark.* Styrofoam, *Chem.* polystyrene, plastic bubbles.

pack rat, *n.* collector, saver, hoarder, storer; gatherer, accumulator, amasser; scrounger, forager, garbage picker, dump picker, salvager.

pact, *n.* agreement, covenant, concordat, compact, *Rare.* paction, contract, bond; treaty, cartel, entente, understanding, meeting of minds; league, alliance, confederation; settlement, arrangement, deal, bargain; temporary settlement, truce, cease-fire; transaction, business agreement; conspiracy, collusion, secret agreement; promise, pledge, word *or* word of honor, unwritten agreement, gentleman's agreement; assurance, guarantee, written guarantee, warranty.

pad[1], *n.* **1.** cushion, *Inf.* sit-upon, pillow, bolster; padding, filling, stuffing, wadding. See **padding** (*def.* 1).

2. pad of paper, tablet, writing pad, note pad, memo pad.

3. (*all of animals*) foot, *Zool.* forefoot, paw, forepaw.

4. gauze pad, *Med.* compress, dressing, pledget, bandage, *Trademark.* Band-Aid, *Surg.* fascia.

5. *Slang.* **a.** apartment, flat, room *or* rooms, studio *or* studio apartment, efficiency *or* efficiency apartment; home, place, residence, dwelling, abode. **b.** bed, pallet, mattress.

—*v.* **6.** fill up *or* out, stuff, wad; pack, wrap, cushion.

7. expand, fill out, flesh out, add to, augment; enlarge, increase, make larger, aggrandize; inflate, dilate, puff out, swell, distend; stretch out, stretch, extend, lengthen, widen, broaden.

pad[2], *n.* **1.** road horse, riding horse, palfrey, saddle horse, bidet.

—*v.* **2.** travel on foot, walk, peregrinate, journey on foot; traverse, walk through, pass *or* travel through, perambulate; range, roam, stray, rove; migrate, move *or* move on, *Sl.* roll, wander, ramble, meander; step, stride, stroll, promenade, saunter, amble, shamble, shuffle; go on foot, *Sl.* hoof it, foot it; hike, trek, tramp, traipse, trudge, plod.

padded, *adj.* **1.** fiber-filled, filled, stuffed.

2. expanded, filled out, fleshed out; enlarged, inflated, swollen, distended; extended, stretched, lengthened.

padding, *n.* **1.** pad, stuffing, wadding, filling, fiber fill, filler, lining, *Obs.* bombast; wrapping, wrapper, wrapping paper; packing, packing material, shredded newspaper, tissue paper, *Trademark.* Styrofoam, *Chem.* polystyrene, plastic bubbles.

2. verbiage, wordiness, verbosity, verboseness, prolixity, prolixness, redundancy, redundance; surplusage, superfluity, superfluousness, superabundance, exuberance, extravagance; overflow, extra, surplus, excess, surfeit, glut.

paddle[1], *n.* **1.** oar, scull, lever, sweep, steerer.

—*v.* **2.** row, oar, scull, canoe, kayak, ply with the oars; propel, drive, move forward; pole, *Chiefly Brit.* punt, push.

3. beat, whip, flog, *Inf.* tan, spank, chastise.

paddle[2], *v.* **1.** splash, plash, dabble, slop, stir.

2. toddle, wobble, walk unsteadily, bowl along, stagger, hobble, shuffle.

paddock, *n.* enclosure, confine, pen, yard, stockyard, fold, corral, pound, barnyard.

padlock, *n.* **1.** lock, latch, holdfast, fastener, fastening, securer, clincher, closure.

—*v.* **2.** fasten, lock, clasp, secure, seal, latch.

padre, *n.* **1.** priest, father, reverend, parson, minister, divine, rabbi; clergyman, cleric, ecclesiastic, man of God, man of the cloth, *Brit.* blackcoat; pastor, rector, vicar, curate, *Brit.* incumbent; chaplain, *U.S. Mil. Sl.* sky pilot.

2. preacher, sermonizer, sermonist, *Derog.* revivalist, *Both Usu. Derog.* pulpiteer, gospel-monger.

3. monastic, monk, friar, brother, mendicant, man of prayer.

padrone, *n.* **1.** master, overlord, lord, lord and

master, ruler, tyrant, despot, dictator; employer, *Inf.* boss, *Inf.* bossman, *Inf.* big boss, man-in-charge; leader, head, headman, captain, sachem, chief, chieftain; superior, commander, commandant; manager, overseer, taskmaster, slave driver, supervisor, superintendent, *Inf.* super, *Brit.* gaffer; *Inf.* kingpin, *Inf.* kingfish, *Inf.* number one, *Inf.* Mr. Big, *Sl.* top dog, *Sl.* head honcho, *Sl.* big cheese, *Sl.* big wheel.

2. innkeeper, innholder, proprietor, host, restaurateur, hotelkeeper, hotelman, operator, owner, landlord.

paean, *n.* psalm, hymn, alleluia, hallelujah, gloria, doxology, spiritual, religious song, hymn tune, *Eccles.* cantus firmus; anthem, national anthem, state song, song of praise, song, melody, tune, air, composition; ode, encomium, panegyric, eulogy; celebration, laudation, glorification, exaltation, magnification; canticle, chorale, choral, *Music.* cantata, *Music.* motet.

pagan, *n.* **1.** heathen, unbeliever, nonbeliever, infidel, *Archaic.* paynim, *Islam.* kafir, *Turkish.* giaour, gentile; idolater, idolizer, idolatrizer, sun worshiper, heliolater, star worshiper, fetishist, zoolater, animal worshiper, fire worshiper, devil worshiper, demon worshiper; pantheist, animist, primitive, aboriginal, barbarian, philistine; savage, Caliban; irreligionist, hedonist, earthling, worldling.

2. atheist, freethinker, disbeliever, nullifidian, nihilist, agnostic, skeptic, Pyrrhonist, minimifidian; doubter, Doubting Thomas; iconoclast, secularist; apostate, heretic, backslider, antichrist.

—adj. **3.** idolatrous, idol-worshiping, idolistic, icon-worshiping, fetishistic; heathen, heathenish, infidel, paganish, paganistic, gentile, godless; pantheistic, pantheistical, polytheistic, animist, animistic, voodooistic, demonolatrous; barbarous, primitive, uncivilized, savage; irreligious, worldly, secularist, irreverent, hedonistic; heretical, not-born-again, unsaved, impenitent, unrepentant, living in a state of sin, bound for hell; unchristian, antichristian.

4. atheist, freethinking, disbelieving, nihilistic; agnostic, skeptical, cynical, doubting, minimifidian, Pyrrhonistic, iconoclastic.

paganism, *n.* **1.** idolatry, idolism, idolization, idolatrism, idol worship, fetishism, iconolatry, iconoduly, icon worship, gentilism, heathenism; henotheism, ditheism; pantheism, animism, animal worship, zoolatry, sun worship, heliolatry, fire worship, demonism, demon worship, devil worship, demonolatry; hedonism, worldliness, materialism.

2. heresy, heterodoxy, unorthodoxy, non-belief, nihilism, disbelief, atheism; doubt, skepticism, agnosticism; nonconformity, free thought, free thinking, iconoclasm; irreligion, impiety.

page[1], *n.* **1.** leaf, flyleaf, endpaper, endleaf, endsheet; recto, verso; printed page, typescript; sheet, folio, signature, gathering.

2. (*of history*) event, incident, episode, occurrence, particular, affair, matter, series of events, related happenings; point, stage, period, era, age, time, decade, turning point, chapter.

—v. **3.** paginate, number, mark, give a number to, foliate; leaf, leaf through, leaf over, turn, turn over, thumb through, riffle.

page[2], *n.* **1.** page boy, servant, servant boy, serving boy, attendant, tender; bellboy, bellhop, cabin boy, chore boy, house boy.

2. squire, *Fr. garçon*, footboy, cupbearer, trainbearer; flunky, lackey, slavey, menial, servitor.

3. messenger, errand boy *or* girl, runner, congressional page, *Inf.* gofer; office boy, copy runner, call boy, printer's devil; usher.

—v. **4.** summon, call, call for, send after, preconize; summon forth, bid come.

pageant, *n.* **1.** spectacle, display, show, parade, pomp, ceremony; procession, masque, gala; tableau vivant, view, scene, representation, miracle play.

2. exhibit, exhibition, presentation, exposition; extravaganza, panorama, ostentation, ostentatious display.

3. light show, sound and light show, *son et lumière*, psychedelic show; spectacular, *Inf.* spec, *Inf.* special, production, review, blackouts, stage show, *Inf.* circus, *Inf.* three-ring circus, *Inf.* sideshow; road show, rock opera, *Inf.* freak show, *Inf.* horror show.

4. platform, stage, wagon, float; diorama.

pageantry, *n.* pageant, display, grand display, array, grand array; blazon, magnificence, grandeur, splendor, flair, flourish, ritual; revel, revelry, festivity, glitter and tinsel, glitter, splurge, *Inf.* splash, ritz; showiness, showy staging, window dressing, pretension, pretentiousnous, ostentatiousness, fuss, showing off. See **pageant** (*defs.* **1-3**).

pail, *n.* bucket, bail, bailer, dipper; cream pail, *Dial.* piggin; beer pail, *Inf.* growler; tub, pot, basin, tin, pan, can, pitcher; receptacle, vessel, container, holder.

pain, *n.* **1.** hurt, ache, aching, smart, smarting, soreness, discomfort; twinge, pinch, gripe, nip, pang, shock, crick, stitch, stabbing pain, sharp pain; throb, throbbing, gnawing pain, burning pain.

2. torture, torment, rack, agony; anguish, grief, woe, sorrow; dolor, suffering, travail; misery, heartache, broken-heartedness, *Archaic.* bale; wretchedness, desolation, depths of despair, despondency, unhappiness, infelicity.

3. mental suffering, uneasiness, disquiet, disquietude, distress, discomposure; anxiety, worry, care, cark, trouble; tribulation, trial, trials and tribulation, ordeal; burden, load, cross, curse, crown of thorns.

4. bother, nuisance, pest, *Inf.* worriment, fret; aggravation, annoyance, vexation, thorn in one's side; bitterness, gall, wormwood, gall and wormwood.

5. **pains a.** effort, care, carefulness, special attention *or* consideration; labor, laboriousness, diligence, trouble, troublesomeness, labored attention *or* study. **b.** labor pangs, labor, childbirth, childbed, parturition.

—v. **6.** hurt, wound, harm, injure; cut, cut up, sting, bite, smite, gripe, gnaw, chafe, burn, stab, pierce, lancinate; abuse, maltreat, disable, impair, cripple; torture, torment, rack, agonize, excruciate.

7. aggrieve, grieve, sorrow; sadden, despond, dishearten, depress; scathe, cut to the quick, cut to the heart.

8. harrow, disturb, distress, discommode, trouble, disquiet, afflict; harry, heckle, harass, tease, pester, plague, bait, bullyrag; pique, vex, gall, rile, roil, agitate, exasperate, try one's patience; worry, pother, bother, fret; annoy, grate, grate on one's nerves, grate on one's feelings, bore.

pained, *adj.* **1.** hurt, hurting, injured, wounded; pierced, stung, stabbed, pricked, chafed, burnt; tortured, tormented, agonized, excruciated, burning.

2. aggrieved, grieving, suffering, sorrowful, sad, mournful, heartsick, heartbroken, broken-hearted; heavy-hearted, heavy-laden, weary, careworn, dejected, cheerless, comfortless; woebegone, wretched, gloomy, dismal, morose; melancholy, unhappy, infelicitous.

3. uncomfortable, uneasy, ill-at-ease, disquieted; discontented, disappointed, disturbed, perturbed, galled, nettled; aroused, excited, agitated, displeased, angered.

4. chagrined, embarrassed, ashamed, shamed; sorry,

regretful, regretting, repentant, remorseful.

painful, *adj.* **1.** achy, aching, hurtful, sore, *Med.* algetic; throbbing, palpitating, tingling; biting, raw, piercing, sharp, bitter; burning, stinging, smarting.
2. tormenting, distressing, distressful, disquieting, disturbing, worrying, worrisome, perturbing, harrowing, afflictive; pestering, harassing, irritating, annoying, irksome, troublesome, *Archaic.* troublous, wearisome; vexatious, vexing, aggravating, exasperating, galling.
3. unpleasant, unpleasing, disagreeable, distasteful, uninviting; undesirable, unacceptable, unsatisfactory, unwelcome; insufferable, hateful, execrable, loathsome, horrible; disgusting, odious, revolting, nauseating, repellent, repulsive, nasty, hideous.
4. grievous, sad, dolorous, tragic, tragical; dismal, disheartening, dreary; melancholy, unhappy, unfelicitous, infelicitous; piteous, pitiful, deplorable, lamentable, rueful; affecting, moving, touching, poignant.
5. laborious, toilsome, operose, exacting, demanding; difficult, hard, tough, strenuous, rigorous, arduous, uphill; hard-earned, hard-fought, hard-won; burdensome, onerous, heavy, cumbrous, hefty, weighty, ponderous; oppressive, insupportable, unbearable, unendurable; destructive, ruinous, calamitous, disastrous.

painkiller, *n.* **1.** analgesic, aspirin, acetylsalicylic acid, sodium salicylate, buffered aspirin, headache powder; anodyne, paregoric, *Inf.* pain pill; soporific, hypnotic, barbiturate, *Sl.* barb, phenobarbital, *Pharm.* hyoscyamine, belladonna; narcotic, opiate, opium, laudanum, morphine.
2. palliative, alleviative, lenitive, assuasive, assuager, sedative; depressant, drug, remedy, cure-all.
3. balm, soothing balm, liniment, embrocation; lotion, salve, ointment; labdanum, ladanum.
4. cocaine, laughing gas, novocaine, tetracaine.
5. *Informal.* alcohol, whiskey, *Inf.* booze, *Sl.* hooch. See **alcohol**.

painless, *adj.* **1.** unpainful, without pain, unpaining, causing no pain, *Inf.* ouchless; dulling, deadening, numbing, anesthetizing.
2. fast, quick, expeditious; all over before you know it, over in the blink of an eye.
3. *Informal.* effortless, easy, facile, simple, downhill, *All Inf.* easy as 1, 2, 3 *or* ABC, easy as pie, easy as rolling off a log; a piece of cake, a pushover, a snap, a cinch, smooth *or* clear sailing; *All Sl.* no sweat, child's play, a breeze, duck soup.

painstaking, *adj.* **1.** careful, meticulous, punctilious, scrupulous, conscientious; exact, precise, accurate, correct; particular, finical, finicky, picky, fussy, fastidious; thorough, searching, strict, close, attentive, attentive to detail, sparing no pains.
2. thorough, thoroughgoing; persistent, pertinacious, dogged, plodding, slogging, plugging, industrious, operose, energetic; persevering, unremitting, unrelaxing, unfaltering, untiring, tireless, never-tiring.
3. diligent, assiduous, sedulous, hard-working; intense, intent, concentrating, steady, earnest, zealous; occupied with, engrossed in, wrapped up in, absorbed in; rapt, enrapt, enraptured, studious.

paint, *n.* **1.** pigment, dye, stain; color, colorant, coloring, tint, tincture; oils, pastels, water colors.
2. coat, coating; primer, undercoat, flat coat, ground, dead-color; calcimine, whitewash, flat wash, wash, *Brit.* distemper; enamel, varnish, lacquer.
3. make-up, facial cosmetic, cosmetics, *Inf.* war paint; greasepaint, clown white, pancake *or* pancake make-up *or* cake make-up; foundation, base; rouge, blush; lip rouge, lipstick; mascara, eye shadow, eye liner, liner.
—*v.* **4.** color, dye, stain, pigment; shade, tint, tincture, temper; illuminate, brighten, blazon, emblazon; coat, cover; whitewash, wash, calcimine; prime, undercoat, *Art.* distemper; enamel, varnish, shellac, lacquer, glaze, veneer.
5. depict, portray, picture, picturize, represent, render, delineate, set forth, *Archaic.* limn; draw, sketch, catch a likeness; draft, pencil, chalk, charcoal, crayon.
6. paint the town red *Slang.* carouse, revel, roister, wassail, bouse, make merry, cut loose, let loose, go out on the town, *Inf.* live it up, *Inf.* step out, *Sl.* make whoopee, whoop it up, raise Cain; go on a spree, make the rounds *or* the dizzy rounds, *Sl.* tie one on, *Sl.* booze it up, *Sl.* go on a drunk *or* binge *or* bender *or* toot *or* jag *or* tear *or* bat, *Sl.* bar-hop *or* bar-crawl, *Brit. Sl.* pub-crawl.

painted, *adj.* **1.** unreal, artificial, ersatz, sham, mock, fake, *Inf.* phony; unnatural, assumed, put-on, affected; fictitious, feigned, simulated, faked, counterfeited.
2. exaggerated, overstated, overdone, overworked, overlabored; overdrawn, played-up, hyperbolized; colored, embroidered, embellished, enhanced, enriched, intensified, maximized; dressed-up, deodorized.
3. misrepresented, falsified, distorted, twisted, perverted, slanted, warped, garbled, slurred; misconstrued, misstated, misquoted, misreported, misrendered; disguised, camouflaged, masked, whitewashed, glossed over, varnished.
4. colorful, high-colored, deep-colored, bright-hued, full-toned, intense, luxuriant, lustrous, brilliant, rich; multicolored, many-colored, variegated, kaleidoscopic, psychedelic.

painter, *n.* artist, portrait artist, limner; drawer, sketcher, delineator, depictor, portrayer, picturist; colorist, watercolorist, oil painter; monochromist, polychromist; illustrator, commercial artist; dabbler, dauber, dilettante.

painting, *n.* **1.** picture, picturization, depiction, delineation, representation, portrayal, illustration; sketch, drawing, image, likeness; work, study, design, composition; work of art, object of art, *Fr. objet d'art,* masterpiece, masterwork, *Archaic.* master, chef-d'oeuvre, classic; portrait, portraiture, head, profile; canvas, oil painting, oil; water color, fresco, *Fr. aquarelle*; scene, view, scape, tableau, diorama, cyclorama, panorama, montage; landscape, seascape, waterscape; still life; miniature; mural, wall painting.
2. classicism, neoclassicism; romanticism; impressionism, post-impressionism, neo-impressionism; pointillism; symbolism; realism, surrealism; cubism; Dadaism; modernism; op art, optical art, pop art; photo realism; daubery, dabbling.
3. coloring, coloration, pigmentation, dyeing, staining; tinting, tincture; illumination, emblazonry; enameling, glazing, glossing; varnishing, shellacking, lacquering; priming, undercoating; *Art.* distemper, whitewashing, calcimining; fresco, fresco secco, dry fresco, secco, buon *or* true fresco.

pair, *n.* **1.** twosome, couplet, doublet, duo, dyad, binary, matched set, two of a kind; twins, Siamese twins, *Astron.* Gemini.
2. couple, lovers, man and wife, husband and wife, married *or* wedded partners *or* pair, conjoints; (*all inseparable*) partners, sidekicks, companions, friends, comrades, cronies, *Inf.* pals, *Inf.* bosom buddies, *U.S. Inf.* buddies.
3. brace, span, yoke, tandem, team; two, both, *Archaic.* twain.
4. *Chiefly Dialect.* set, suit, suite, group, grouping, collection, combination, *Clothing.* coordinates.

—*v.* **5.** pair up, match up, put together, accompany, *Archaic.* company; couple, partner, twin, double, geminate; marry off, wed, join in holy matrimony *or* wedlock, hook up, *Sl.* hitch, *Sl.* splice, *Obs.* conjugate; conjoin, join, unite, yoke, bind *or* tie together, chain, shackle; coalesce, associate, affiliate, ally, bring *or* draw together, make close, connect, bracket, attach, link.

6. pair off hook up, become affiliated with, partner, form a partnership, go in together, team up, be a team, join forces, cooperate; go around together, fraternize, associate, keep company, consort, *Inf.* pal around together, *Inf.* hang around together, *Inf.* knock around together, *Sl.* hang out together; be seen together, go out together, go steady, stick together, stick like glue; marry, get married, intermarry, interwed, wive, espouse, become man and wife, say "I do," say one's vows, walk down the aisle, take the plunge, become one, *Sl.* hitch up with, *Archaic.* husband.

7. match, suit, fit, go with, correspond, agree with, coordinate *or* harmonize *or* blend with, complement, complete; resemble, look like, take after, *Inf.* favor.

8. (*of animals*) mate, breed, copulate.

pal, *n. Informal.* **1.** comrade, chum, crony, copain, companion, sidekick, shadow, alter ego, *Inf.* bosom buddy, *U.S. Inf.* buddy, *Sl.* cully, *Sl.* Siamese twin; friend, amigo, *Fr. ami*, playmate, classmate, schoolmate, acquaintance; schoolfellow, escort, date, beau, suitor, boy friend, guy, girl friend, steady; intimate, lover, bedfellow, pillow partner, soul mate, *Fr. intime.*

2. partner, copartner, counterpart, mate, helpmate, consort, *Inf.* other half, *Sl. Facetious.* better half, *Obs.* copemate; messmate, commensal, housemate, roommate, *Inf.* roomie, bunkmate, *Sl.* bunkie; associate, ally, affiliate, teammate, colleague, compeer, co-worker, yokefellow, yokemate, fellow, confrere, brother, sister, *Scot. and North Eng.* marrow, *Archaic.* peer; assistant, assister, aide, aider, helper, ancilla, auxiliary, coadjutor, coadjutress, attendant, best man, squire; accomplice, confederate, compatriot, abettor, collaborator, cohort, cooperator.

—*v.* **3.** *Usu.* **pal around** go around together, *Inf.* hang around together, *Inf.* knock around together, *Sl.* hang out together; keep company, associate, fraternize, consort, be on intimate terms; be seen together, go out together, go together, date, court, *Inf.* go steady.

palace, *n.* **1.** royal residence, royal house, royal mansion, *Fr. palais.*

2. mansion, palatial residence, palatial house, stately residence, kingly residence, kingly house, great house, villa, chateau, castle, *Fr. hôtel, It. palazzo, Chiefly Brit.* hall, *Brit.* court, *Archit.* folly; manor, manor house, manor seat, estate, country estate, country home, country house, country seat, hacienda, rural mansion, *Sl.* spread.

paladin, *n.* advocate, defender, vindicator, protector, champion, Prince Valiant; knight in shining armor, knight on a white horse, white knight; hero, knight-errant, Sir Lancelot, Sir Galahad, chevalier, cavalier; stout-hearted man, brave man.

palatable, *adj.* **1.** tasty, good-tasting, savory, savorous, toothsome, sapid; flavorful, flavorsome, flavorous, appetizing, relishable; delicious, *Sl.* yummy, mouth-watering, luscious, scrumptious, delectable, *Sl.* more-ish, good enough to eat, finger-lickin' good; ambrosial, ambrosian, like nectar of the gods, *Archaic.* gustable, *Fr. délicieux*; epicurean, gourmet; piquant, pungent, spicy, sweet.

2. agreeable, pleasing, pleasurable, pleasant, enjoyable, satisfying; delightful, nice, attractive, acceptable.

palate, *n.* **1.** roof of the mouth, soft palate, hard palate, pharynx, epiglottis.

2. taste, *Fr. goût*, appetite, tongue, stomach, taste buds.

3. appreciation, liking, enjoyment; zest, gusto, enthusiasm, relish, delight.

palatial, *adj.* magnificent, luxurious, sumptuous, posh; stately, majestic, grand, imposing, massive; huge, large, commodious, roomy; ornate, elegant, fancy; pretentious, ostentatious, showy, *Sl.* ritzy, *Inf.* swanky, hoity-toity, *Inf.* high-toned.

palaver, *n.* **1.** parley, *Inf.* powwow, conference, round table, colloquy; session, meeting, gathering, consultation, brainstorming, deliberation; interview, audience, hearing; talk, dialogue, discussion, confabulation, *Inf.* confab; conversation, causerie, coze, chat, *Inf.* rap, *Inf.* rap session, *Inf.* bull session.

2. chatter, chitchat, *Sl.* yakety-yak, *Sl.* yak, twaddle, blather, prattle, idle talk, *Sl.* shmooze, small talk, *Scot.* clishmaclaver, gossip, *Sl.* chinning, *Sl.* chin session; buzzing, *Inf.* gab, babble, *Brit.* natter.

3. flattery, cajolery, wheedling, honeyed words, sweet talk, soft soap, blarney; balderdash, hogwash, eyewash, nonsense, stuff and nonsense, *Inf.* bosh; flummery, *Sl.* bunk, rubbish, *Sl.* horsefeathers, tommyrot, foolishness.

—*v.* **4.** parley, *Inf.* powwow, confer, meet, sit down together; converse, discuss, talk, talk over, chat; deliberate, get in a huddle, put heads together, brainstorm; consult, exchange views *or* opinions, compare notes; negotiate.

5. chatter, chitchat, *Sl.* yak, *Sl.* shmooze; gibber, jabber, *Sl.* gibber-jabber, blather, gabble, run off at the mouth, *Sl.* have diarrhea of the mouth, *Sl.* jaw, *Sl.* chin; shoot the breeze, pass the time of day, make conversation; prattle, prate, cackle, babble, *Inf.* beat one's gums; chew the fat *or* the rag, tittle-tattle, tattle, *Scot.* clishmaclaver, gossip.

pale[1], *adj.* **1.** colorless, hueless, toneless, uncolored, achromic, achromous, achromatic; drab, dreary, flat, mat, lusterless, lackluster; bleached, blanched, washed-out, etiolated; wan, pallid, *Obs.* blate, pale-faced, anemic, sickly; waxen, sallow, pasty, ashen, ashy, livid, ghostly, ghastly, deathlike, cadaverous, lurid; bloodless, white, drained; whey-faced, sallow-faced, unhealthy looking, unwholesome looking, peaked looking; deathly pale, drained of color, like death, pale as a ghost.

2. dim, imperceptible, hardly noticeable, indiscernible; ill-defined, unclear, indistinct, blurred, blurry, clouded, obscured; obfuscated, muffled, bleared.

3. feeble, weak, impotent, powerless; enfeebled, debilitated, enervated; ineffective, incompetent, poor, unsatisfactory, half-baked; lame, insufficient, inadequate, unconvincing; faint, flimsy, thin, watery, meager.

—*v.* **4.** blanch, whiten, go white, grow pale; become pallid, *Archaic.* wan; droop, flag, sag, faint.

5. bleach, gray, wash out; etiolate, achromatize, dim, fade, cloud, grow dull, lose luster *or* brightness.

6. take alarm, fear, grow afraid, be afraid, dread; start, shy away, stand aghast; wince, flinch, hesitate, falter, lose heart.

7. lessen, abate, diminish, decrease, slacken; subside, let up, intermit, cease; taper off, drop off, die out; fade away, melt away, dissolve; evanesce, vanish.

pale[2], *n.* **1.** picket, paling, slat; post, upright, member, palisade.

2. enclosure, fenced area, pen, sty, fold, corral, paddock, pound; ring, arena, precincts; (*in South Africa*) kraal, yard, prison yard; compound, stockade, con-

centration camp; court, close, cloister, schoolyard, enceinte.
3. fence, railing, balustrade, stone wall, chain link fence, wire fence, hedge, hedgerow; barrier, barricade, wall, circumvallation.
4. realm, dominion, kingdom; nation, state, county; district, voting district, ward; quarter, section, part, division, compartment, precinct, province, (*in Great Britain*) marches; circuit, ambit, territory, demesne.
5. limits, bounds, purview; compass, sphere, range, orbit; jurisdiction, bailiwick, area, *Inf.* ball park, *Inf.* lap.
6. **beyond the pale** out of bounds, unacceptable, improper, forbidden, unthinkable; unseemly, impolitic, imprudent, indiscreet, injudicious; out-of-bounds, out-of-line, out-of-order; unsuitable, abnormal, irregular, unusual, bizarre, weird.

paleness, *n.* **1.** pallor, pallidness, sallowness, whiteness, wanness, ashenness, pastiness; lividness, ghostliness, bloodlessness, anemia; achromatism, colorlessness, etiolation.
2. dullness, dunness, dimness; faintness, weakness, imperceptibility; obscurity, vagueness, fuzziness, nebulousness; unclearness, obfuscation, bleariness.

palfrey, *n.* mount, riding horse, steed, horse, saddle horse; charger, cavalry horse, remount; cowpony, range horse, race horse, *Brit.* hack, cob; Thoroughbred, Arab, quarter horse, hunter, child's pony.

palimpset, *n.* re-inscription, *Latin. codex rescriptus*, overwriting, re-used parchment *or* scroll.

paling, *n.* **1.** fence, picket fence, log fence, balustrade; pen, fold, palisade.
2. picket, slat, upright, member.

palinode, *n.* recantation, retraction, recall, disavowal, disaffirmation, denial; contradiction, gainsay; withdrawal, revocation, rescindment; disclaimer, disclamation.

palisade, *n.* **1.** stockade, fenced area, enclosure, pen, pound, paddock, corral; (*in South Africa*) kraal, yard, prison yard, concentration camp.
2. **palisades** cliffs, bluff, incline, precipice; rocky eminence, palisado, scarp, escarpment; rocky headland, tor, promontory, ridge; Cliffs of Dover, New Jersey Palisades.
—*v.* **3.** fortify, barricade, fence, enfence, enclose, pen up, impound, corral.

pall[1], *n.* **1.** shroud, winding sheet, graveclothes, cerements, cerecloth, covering, concealment.
2. coffin, casket, sarcophagus.
3. damper, damp, check; disheartener, wet blanket, cold water.
4. somberness, seriousness, gravity; gloom, heaviness, melancholy; disheartenment, discouragement, dismay.

pall[2], *v.* **1.** glut, sate, fill, satiate, stuff, overfeed, overfill, cloy, surfeit; gorge, engorge, cram.
2. make dull, bore; make impatient, irk, annoy; weary, sicken, tire, overdo, jade.

palladium, *n.* safeguard, defense, protection, protector, guard; shelter, refuge, haven, asylum, security; shield, buckler, aegis, screen, armor, mail, cover, *Rare.* muniment; fortification, fortress, stronghold, garrison, fort, tower of strength; bulwark, bastion, rampart, parapet, redoubt; wall, barricade, buttress, palisade.

pallet, *n.* straw mattress, *Chiefly Brit.* paillasse, pad, cushion, *Inf.* tick; bedding, litter, shakedown, sleeping bag, blanket roll, *Sl.* hay; bed, cot, bunk, berth, recliner, *Brit.* lair, *U.S. Sl.* sack, *Brit. Sl.* kip, *Brit. Sl.* doss.

palliate, *v.* **1.** extenuate, minimize, make light of, soft-pedal, tone down, play down, downplay; justify, excuse, rationalize, apologize for, make allowances for; whitewash, cover up, gild, color, varnish, gloss over, smooth over, veneer; lighten, soften, lessen, diminish, moderate, temper, qualify, (*of words*) mince; sweeten, sugar-coat, candy-coat, dulcify.
2. mitigate, alleviate, reduce, weaken, abate; allay, assuage, *Rare.* lenify, appease, soothe, *Archaic.* attemper; relieve, ease, cushion, mollify; calm, compose, tranquilize, still, quiet, hush, lull; solace, console, succor, remedy; quell, slake, deaden, dull, obtund, blunt, take the edge off of; smother, check, curb, tame, subdue.

palliation, *n.* **1.** extenuation, minimizing, minimization, playing down; justification, vindication, exculpation, exoneration; excuse, rationalization, apology; whitewash, cover-up, varnish, gloss, veneer; sugarcoating, candy-coating; softening, lightening, lessening, diminution; moderation, tempering, qualifying, (*of words*) mincing.
2. mitigation, alleviation, reduction, weakening, abatement; assuagement, appeasement, soothing; relief, relieving, ease, easement, respite, letup, deliverance; consolation, solace, remedy, comfort.

palliative, *adj.* **1.** alleviative, alleviatory, mitigative, mitigatory, lenitive, *Med.* abirritant; mollifying, soothing, calming, *Med.* calmative, assuasive, demulcent; relaxing, numbing, dulling, anesthetic; painkilling, anodyne, *Med.* analgesic, deadening.
—*n.* **2.** sedative, sedation, *Med.* calmative, tranquilizer, narcotic, opiate, drug, anesthetic; painkiller, anodyne, *Med.* analgesic; softener, sweetener, demulcent, lenitive, *Med.* emollient, *Med.* abirritant; balm, salve, unguent, ointment, liniment.

pallid, *adj.* **1.** pale, wan, pale-faced, anemic, sickly, *Obs.* blate; waxen, sallow, pasty, ashen, ashy, livid; ghostly, ghastly, deathlike, cadaverous, lurid; bloodless, white, drained; wheyfaced, sallow-faced, unhealthy looking, unwholesome looking, peaked looking; deathly pale, drained of color, pale as a ghost, like death.
2. insipid, uninteresting, unentertaining, inexpressive, unimaginative, colorless, jejune, *Sl.* blah; unanimated, spiritless, zestless, sapless, tame, lifeless, empty, *Sl.* dead, *Sl.* nothing; pointless, weak, feeble, anemic, sterile, *Inf.* washed out; dull, boring, monotonous, humdrum, tedious, tiresome; stale, tired, trite, banal, platitudinous; indistinctive, run-of-the-mill, ordinary, commonplace, average; bland, vapid, thin, watered-down.

pallor, *n.* wanness, unnatural paleness, ashenness, lividness, bloodlessness, anemia; ghostliness, deathliness, sickliness, ghastliness.

palm[1], *n.* **1.** hand, open hand; extremity, *Sl.* mitt, *Sl.* paw, *Sl.* fin, *Sl.* flipper; (*all of animals*) paw, foot, pad, *Zool.* forefoot, *Anat., Zool.* manus.
2. **cross** *or* **grease someone's palm** give money to, bribe, pay off, buy, buy off, suborn, corrupt; fix, *Inf.* rig, *Inf.* square; induce, tempt, lure, entice; coax, influence.
—*v.* **3.** conceal, hide in the hand; take surreptitiously, take away, snatch, *Inf.* snitch, *Sl.* lift, filch, purloin, *Sl.* pinch, pilfer, cabbage, *Sl.* mooch, *Sl.* cop, steal.
4. *Usu.* **palm on** *or* **upon** foist on, force upon, impose upon, thrust upon, lay on *or* upon, unload upon, take advantage of.
5. touch, brush lightly, caress; pat, stroke, rub gently, massage.
6. shake hands, give a grip, *Sl.* slap [s.o.] five, *Sl.* give [s.o.] some skin.
7. **palm off** pass off, fob off, foist off.

palm², *n.* victory, triumph, success; laurels, honor, glory, fame, distinction; crown, wreath, garland, chaplet; prize, trophy, award, decoration, badge.

palmate, *adj.* radial, spoked, arranged around a hub *or* nave; hand-like, palm-like, palmy, *Bot.* digitate; star-shaped, starlike, starry, stelliform, stellar, stellular; fan-shaped, fan-like; fingered, leafed, branched, antlered, *Bot.* fronded.

palmist, *n.* palm reader, chiromancer, fortuneteller; clairvoyant, seer, soothsayer, foreseer, foreteller, presager, prognosticator, predictor, forecaster; diviner, augur, prophet, prophetess, vaticinator, sibyl.

palmistry, *n.* palm reading, chiromancy, fortunetelling; soothsaying, foretelling, prognostication, prediction, forecasting; divination, augury, prophecy, vaticination.

palmy, *adj.* prosperous, thriving, golden, flourishing, halcyon; wonderful, wondrous, marvelous, spectacular, fabulous, winning; delightful, charming, captivating, enchanting, delectable; excellent, superb, splendid, consummate, *Inf.* peachy, *Brit. Sl.* ducky; enjoyable, pleasurable, pleasant, pleasing, gratifying, agreeable, congenial; peaceful, serene, pacific, heavenly; promising, sunny, roseate, rosy, balmy.

palpable, *adj.* **1.** evident, manifest, apparent, self-evident, manifestative, *Fr. en évidence*; visible, seeable, in full view, open, public, exposed, showing, naked, bald, unhidden, uncovered, unveiled, unshrouded, uncurtained; obvious, patent, conspicuous, prominent, striking, blatant, flagrant, egregious; overt, displayed, shown, presented, professed, avowed, ostensible; plain, clear, clear-cut, plain as day, plain as the nose on your face; distinct, definite, unmistakable, unambiguous, indubitable, unquestionable; discernible, perceivable, perceptible, recognizable, ascertainable, salient.

2. tangible, tactile, tactual, touchable, sensible, ponderable, appreciable, nonabstract; incarnate, embodied, corporal, corporeal, physical, material, bodily, somatic; concrete, real, solid, substantial, substantive.

palpate, *v.* handle, touch, contact; examine, feel, probe; massage, stroke, knead, manipulate, rub, caress; finger, thumb.

palpation, *n.* handling, touching, feeling; examination, probe, physical; massage, stroking, kneading, manipulating, manipulation; rubbing, caressing; contact, touch; stereognosis.

palpitant, *adj.* pulsating, pulsative, pulsatory, pulsing, beating, throbbing; trembling, tremulous, tremulant, shaking, shaky, quivering; vibrant, vibrating, vibrative, vibratory; fluttering, twittering, twittery, flickering; agitated, disquieted, discomposed, excited; turbulent, tumultuous.

palpitate, *v.* pulsate, pulse, beat, throb; tremble, shake, quiver, quaver, quake, shiver, vibrate; flutter, twitter, flicker, patter; pound, pump, drum.

palpitation, *n.* palpitating, pulsating, pulsing, pulsation, beating, beat, throbbing, throb; trembling, tremble, shaking, quivering, quiver, quavering, quaking, shivering, vibrating, vibration, tremor, trepidation; fluttering, flutter, flittering, flitter, twittering, twitter, flickering, flicker, pattering, patter, pitter-patter; pounding, drumming, pumping; turbulency, turbulence, tumult.

palpus, *n.* palp, *Zool.* antenna, *Zool.* feeler, *Zool.* tentacle, sensory appendage, organ of touch.

palsied, *adj.* paralyzed, paralytic, crippled, spastic; shaking, shaky, trembling, tremulous, tremulant, trembly, quaking, quaky, shuddering, shuddery; shivering, shivery, quivering, quivery, quavering, quavery, quaverous.

palsy, *n.* paralysis, *Pathol.* cerebral palsy, *Pathol.* spastic paralysis; *Pathol.* shaking palsy, *Pathol.* paralysis agitans, *Pathol.* Parkinson's disease, *Pathol.* Parkinsonism.

palter, *v.* **1.** lie, stretch the truth, prevaricate, fib, *Inf.* talk through one's hat, *Inf.* tell the big lie, *Inf.* speak with forked tongue; mince words, not tell the whole truth *or* story; equivocate, quibble, *Sl.* waffle, fudge, beat around *or* about the bush, hedge, qualify; avoid, evade, dodge, sidestep; doubletalk, backtrack, back-pedal, sidetrack; tergiversate, vacillate, oscillate, shilly-shally, waver, alternate, fluctuate, go back and forth *or* up and down.

2. deceive, trick, fool, hoodwink, bamboozle, pull the wool over [s.o.'s] eyes; throw dust in [s.o.'s] eyes, throw [s.o.] for a loop; mislead, lead up the garden path, *Sl.* take for a ride; misinform, misdirect, *Inf.* give [s.o.] a bum steer; throw off the scent *or* trail, put on a false scent, drag *or* draw a red herring across the trail.

paltriness, *n.* **1.** pettiness, triviality, trivialism, *Brit.* pottiness, inconsiderableness, unappreciableness, inconsequentiality, insignificance, unimportance, irrelevance, irrelevancy, nonessentiality; littleness, smallness, minuteness, slightness, slenderness, slimness, shallowness, measliness, meagerness.

2. worthlessness, *Chiefly Dial.* footiness; averageness, commonness, ordinariness, unobjectionableness, unexceptionalness, passableness, fairness, indifference; trashiness, dirtiness, scabbiness, shabbiness, scrubbiness, scruffiness, scurviness; abjectness, miserableness, wretchedness, sorriness, poorness, beggarliness, pitifulness, pitiableness, patheticalness.

3. meanness, ignobility, ignobleness, rascality, villainy, villainousness; baseness, vileness, lowness, depravity, degradation, unprincipledness, immorality, profligacy, profligateness; evilness, badness, wrongness, arrantness; contemptibility, contemptibleness, despicability, despicableness, detestability, detestableness, sordidness, foulness, infamy, infamousness, ignominy, ignominiousness, odium, odiousness, opprobrium, opprobriousness, obnoxiousness, rankness, execrableness, degeneracy, corruptedness, corruptness, corruption, viciousness, reprehensibility, reprehensibleness, unmentionableness, heinousness, atrociousness, flagitiousness, nefariousness, iniquity, iniquitousness, *Archaic.* facinorousness.

paltry, *adj.* **1.** petty, trifling, trivial, piddling, minor, trumpery, fribbling, *Brit.* potty, *Archaic.* pelting, inconsiderable, unappreciable, inconsequential, insignificant, unimportant, irrelevant, nonessential, penny-ante, small-time, *Inf.* no great shakes; little, small, minute, slight, slender, slim, shallow, *Inf.* measly, meager.

2. worthless, *Chiefly Dial.* footy, not worth mentioning, not worth a rap *or* straw, not worth a nickel *or* dime; mediocre, secondary, second-best, second-rate, third-rate, fourth-rate; average, common, commonplace, ordinary, unobjectionable, unexceptional, *Inf.* nothing to brag about, passable, fair, *Inf.* fair-to-middling, just-so, so-so, indifferent; trashy, rubbishy, dirty, scabby, shabby, scrubby, scruffy, scurvy; abject, miserable, wretched, sorry, sad, poor, beggarly, pitiful, pitiable, pathetic, pathetical.

3. mean, ignoble, rascally, villainous; base, base-spirited, base-minded, vile, low, low-minded, debased, depraved, degraded, unprincipled, immoral, profligate, dissolute; evil, bad, wrong, arrant; contemptible, despicable, detestable, reptilian, sordid, foul, infamous, ignominious, odious, opprobrious, obnoxious, rank, execrable, degenerate, corrupt, vicious, reprehensible, unmentionable, heinous, atrocious, flagitious, nefarious, iniquitous, *Archaic.* facinorous.

pampas, *n.* plain, (*in South America*) campo, prairie, grassland, savanna, veld, meadow *or* meadowland, pasture *or* pasture land; steppe, tundra, champaign, *Brit.* heath, *Chiefly Brit.* moors *or* moorland; wold, plateau, tableland, mesa.

pamper, *v.* coddle, mollycoddle, cocker, cosher, cosset, pet, dandle; indulge, caress, favor, baby, *Obs.* fondle, humor; dote on, cater to, wait on hand and foot, overindulge, spoil, *Sl.* spoil rotten.

pamphlet, *n.* brochure, booklet, leaflet, folder, chapbook; treatise, monograph, tractate, tract, essay; bill, playbill, program; bulletin, notice, advertisement, *Inf.* ad, circular; handbill, *U.S.* flyer, broadside, broadsheet, handout, throwaway.

pamphleteer, *n.* (*all of pamphlets*) writer, author, essayist.

pan, *n.* **1.** frying pan, griddle, skillet, spider; bread pan, cake pan, pie plate *or* pan, baking dish, ramekin, patty pan, omelet pan, pizza pan; saucepan, stewpan, *Chiefly Brit.* casserole, small kettle *or* pot, *Chiefly Brit.* pannikin; chafing dish, pressure cooker, steamer, roaster, broiler *or* broiler pan.

2. bedpan, metal pot, potty, chamber pot.

3. *Slang.* face, visage, *Sl.* mug, *Sl.* phiz, *Sl.* puss, *Sl.* kisser.

4. depression, indentation, dent, dint, dip; hollow, crater, concavity, cavity, pit, hole, excavation.

—*v.* **5.** (*all of gold, etc.*) pan for, sift for, search for, look for.

6. *Informal.* criticize, find fault, pick apart, take apart, pick to pieces; *Inf.* knock, *Sl.* put down, shoot down, *Inf.* slam.

7. pan out *Informal.* turn out, work out, come out *or* along.

panacea, *n.* cure-all, elixir, cure for all ills, cure for what ails you, universal cure *or* remedy, nostrum; alembic, philosopher's stone, magic wand, magic potion, magic ingredient; magic solution *or* answer, magic *or* secret formula, abracadabra, open sesame.

panache, *n.* **1.** plume, feathers, tuft, crest; embellishment, ornament, decoration.

2. brilliance, glitter, splendor, magnificence, grandness, grand manner; flamboyance, razzle-dazzle, ostentation, éclat, pretentiousness, boldness, self-assurance; verve, spirit, animation, zest, dash, gusto, enthusiasm, élan; style, elegance, smartness, chic, discrimination; sophistication, worldliness, savoir-faire, savoir-vivre, flair, taste, good taste, cultivation; lordly air, class, distinction, nobility, that certain something, that je ne sais quoi; *Sl.* it, *Sl.* oomph, *Sl.* pizzazz.

pancake, *n.* **1.** flapjack, griddlecake, hotcake, battercake, flapcake, flannel cake, buckwheat cake, potato pancake, *Jewish Cookery.* latke; crepe, blini, blintz, tortilla, (*in India*) chapati; fritter, fried cake, fried mush.

2. pancake make-up, make-up, cake make-up, powder; greasepaint, clown white; wrinkle eraser, skin softener, beautifier.

pandemic, *adj.* **1.** (*all of diseases*) epidemic, pestilential, pestilent, pestiferous, (*of animals*) *Vet. Med.* epizootic, (*of plants*) epiphytotic; infectious, contagious, communicable, catching, zymotic.

2. general, widespread, extensive, broad, wide, far-reaching; universal, global, world-wide; rife, rampant; wholesale, indiscriminate.

—*n.* **3.** epidemic, zymosis, pestilence, plague, pandemia, scourge, (*of animals*) *Pathol.* epizootic, (*of animals*) epizooty, (*of animals*) murrain, (*of plants*) epiphytotic; bubonic plague, black plague, black death; white plague, tuberculosis, TB, consumption, phthisis, pulmonary phthisis.

pandemonium, *n.* **1.** chaos, bedlam, confusion, "confusion worse confounded" (Milton), riot, anarchy, disorder, turmoil, tumult, turbulence, frenzy, fury, rage, furor; *Inf.* hell broken loose; cacophony, noise, din, racket, static; uproar, hubbub, hue and cry, outcry.

2. commotion, hullaballoo, row, fracas, rumpus, *Inf.* ruckus, free-for-all, brawl, donnybrook, brouhaha, three-ring circus, *Inf.* shindy, *Brit. Inf.* dustup, *Sl.* rumble, *Sl.* rhubarb.

3. hell, perdition, inferno, the pit, the bottomless pit, the abyss; Hades, netherworld, underworld, infernal regions, abode of the damned.

pander, *n.* **1.** panderer, pimp, procurer, whoremonger, *Sl.* flesh-peddler, *Sl.* hustler, *U.S. Sl.* sweetman, *Fr. maquereau;* white slaver, smuggler, runner; go-between, intermediary, middleman, agent, solicitor; purveyor, supplier, provider, furnisher; procuress, *Archaic.* bawd, madam.

2. manipulator, exploiter; toady, toadeater, sycophant, fawner, flatterer, puffer, *Inf.* apple-polisher, *Sl.* brown-nose; parasite, leech, scrounger, scrounge, *Inf.* sponger *or* sponge, *Sl.* moocher *or* mooch, freeloader, scavenger, *Sl.* bum, hanger-on.

—*v.* **3.** procure, pimp, solicit, *Sl.* hustle; purvey, supply, provide, furnish.

4. *Usu.* **pander to** gratify, indulge, satisfy, please, humor; cater, pamper, attend, wait upon; toady, fawn, *Sl.* fall all over, truckle, *Sl.* suck up to, *Sl.* play up to, *Inf.* apple-polish, *Sl.* brown-nose; lickspittle, lick [s.o.'s] shoes, lick *or* kiss [s.o.'s] feet, *Sl.* bootlick; kowtow, bow, bow and scrape, stoop, kneel, grovel, crawl, creep, crouch, slither.

pane, *n.* plate of glass, glass, window glass, window pane; panel, sheet, partition, part.

panegyric, *n.* **1.** eulogy, eulogium, eulogization, encomium, citation; testimonial, declaration, discourse, oration, announcement.

2. tribute, credit, recognition; exaltation, glorification; homage, reverence, devotion, veneration; blessing, *Eccles.* benediction, *Archaic.* benison; honor, crown, glory.

3. praise, extolment, kudos, *Archaic.* magnification; approval, approbation, endorsement, sanction, commendation, recommendation, advocacy, espousal; acclaim, acclamation, applause, plaudits, salvo, accolade; celebration, paean, congratulation, *Archaic.* gratulation; compliment, flattery, adulation; hosanna, huzzah, hurrah.

panegyrical, *adj.* eulogizing, eulogistic, eulogistical, encomiastic, encomiastical; laudatory, praising, praiseful, acclamatory; approving, approbatory, approbative, commendatory; complimentary, flattering, uncritical, uncensorious; celebrative, celebratory, favorable, positive; glorifying, benedictory.

panel, *n.* **1.** wainscoting, woodwork; wood, plank, board, sheet, lamina, lamination; portion, section, segment, division, part, partition; wall, divider, *Naut.* bulkhead.

2. pane, window pane, window glass, plate of glass.

3. inset, insert, gore, godet.

4. jury, review board, council, cabinet, committee, advisory group; board, advisors, directors, trustees; *All Law.* coroner's jury, inquest, grand jury, petty jury.

pang, *n.* **1.** spasm, twitch, kink, stitch, crick, kink, tic; twinge, pinch, smart, ache; stabbing pain, sharp pain, shooting pain.

2. misgiving, qualm, scruple, mental pain, mental suffering; hesitation, hesitancy, recoil, shrinking; uneasiness, discomfort, malaise.

panhandle, *v.* *Informal.* beg, scrounge, *Inf.* bum,

Sl. hit, *Sl.* hit up, *Sl.* touch, *Sl.* put the touch on, *Sl.* schnorren; borrow, cadge, sponge, *Sl.* mooch.

panhandler, *n.* *Informal.* beggar, mendicant, *Inf.* bum, *Inf.* bummer, *Sl.* schnorrer; cadger, sponger, scrounger, parasite; loafer, idler, wastrel, good-for-nothing, ne'er-do-well.

panic, *n.* **1.** alarm, terror, horror, fear, fright, dread, trepidation; stark horror, abject fear, scare of one's life; hysteria, mental turmoil, confusion, consternation, nervousness, jitters, *Inf.* whim-whams, *Sl.* jimjams, agitation; dismay, perturbation, inquietude; cold sweats, shakes.

2. *Slang.* hilarious person, joker, *Inf.* card, *Inf.* howl, laugh a minute, clown, wit.

—*v.* **3.** be alarmed, be stricken with terror, feel sudden dread *or* fright; overreact, *Sl.* push the panic button, throw up one's hands, break out in a cold sweat, run around like a chicken with its head cut off, *Sl.* go into a tizzy *or* dither.

panic-stricken, *adj.* alarmed, aghast, terrified, horrified, frightened, terror-stricken, horror-stricken; appalled, petrified, stupefied, stunned, knocked out, floored, overwhelmed; startled, fearful, overcome with fear; nervous, panicky, agitated, perturbed, dismayed; frozen, frozen with terror, numb, pale as a ghost, white as a sheet, shaken, shaking, shaking like an aspen, goose-pimply.

pannier, *n.* basket, bushel basket, fruit basket, wicker basket, wicker; dosser, backpack, pack, carrier, container, bag, saddlebag.

panoply, *n.* suit of mail *or* armor, coat of mail *or* armor, covering, envelopment; attire, garb, dress, array; ornamentation, decoration, adornment; display, parade, show.

panorama, *n.* **1.** view, overall view, full view, uncluttered view, bird's-eye view, air view; vista, sight, scene, spectacle, vision.

2. cyclorama, *Trademark.* Cinerama, landscape, seascape, cityscape, tableau.

3. survey, overview, comprehensive view, big picture, whole picture; range, gamut, sweep, stretch, extent, full extent.

panoramic, *adj.* extensive, extended, far-reaching, far-ranging, wide, sweeping; all-encompassing, universal, general, all-embracing, all-inclusive; overall, bird's-eye.

pansy, *n.* **1.** violet, viola.

2. *Slang.* **a.** *Derogatory.* homosexual, homosexualist, homophile, sexual invert; *All Sl.* queen, limpwrist, camp, three-dollar bill, *Brit.* ginger *or* ginger beer, *Brit.* poof *or* poofter; *All Derog.* homo, queer, faggot, fag, fruit, flit, fairy, nance, auntie. **b.** effeminate, *Inf.* pantywaist, sissy, *Sl.* wimp; mollycoddle, milquetoast, milksop, mama's boy, namby-pamby, weak sister, nancy.

pant, *v.* **1.** huff, puff, huff and puff, blow, breathe hard, suck wind; wheeze; gasp, gasp for breath, gulp; (*of a locomotive*) chug.

2. yearn for, long for, pine for, languish for, sigh for, wish for, ache for, *Inf.* have a yen for; thirst for, hunger for, burn for, lust for, be dying for, *Inf.* hanker after; desire, desiderate, want, crave, covet, want with all one's heart, want in the worst way, set one's heart on, *Sl.* give one's right arm *or* eyeteeth for.

3. throb, beat, pulse, pulsate, palpitate, go pitapat, beat a tattoo; heave.

—*n.* **4.** huff, puff, breath, wind; wheeze; gasp, gulp.

5. throb, beat, pulse, pulsation, palpitation, tattoo; heave.

pantaloon, *n.* **1.** *Usu.* **pantaloons** pants, trousers, (*among Scottish Highlanders*) trews; breeches, knee breeches, *Inf.* britches, knickers, knickerbockers, plus fours, *Scot. and North Eng.* breeks; pantalets, bloomers.

2. (*all in the modern pantomime*) dupe, butt, fair game, laughingstock, everybody's fool, *Inf.* goat, *U.S. Sl.* fall guy, *Brit. Sl.* mug; straight man, foil.

pantheism, *n.* *Rare.* cosmotheism; nature worship; animism; paganism, heathenism, idolatry.

panther, *n.* **1.** cougar, puma, wild cat, black panther, painter; mountain lion, catamount, catamountain.

2. leopard, *Archaic.* pard, jaguar, cheetah, jungle cat.

3. *Informal.* wild man, savage, brute, beast, wild beast, animal, tiger, *Inf.* fire-eater, *Inf.* ugly customer, *Sl.* bad dude.

—*adj.* **4.** fierce, ferocious, savage, violent, sanguinary, *Sl.* kill-crazy.

panting, *n.* **1.** breathlessness, shortness of breath, windedness, short-windedness; huffing, puffing, huffing and puffing, gasping, heavy breathing; wheezing, labored breathing, *Pathol.* dyspnea, (*usu. of horses*) broken-windedness.

2. pulse, pulsation, palpitation, pitapat, pitter-patter, beating, throb, throbbing; heaving.

3. lust, desire, longing, yearning, wanting, craving, hunger, *Sl.* salivating.

—*adj.* **4.** breathless, out of breath, short of breath, winded; huffing, puffing, gasping, heaving; wheezing, short-winded, (*usu. of horses*) broken-winded, *Pathol.* dyspneal.

5. eager, anxious, agog, all agog; impatient, champing at the bit, *Inf.* rarin' to go.

pantomime, *n.* **1.** charade, dumb show, *Brit.* panto.

2. mime, miming, pantomiming, pantomimicry; mimicry, impersonation.

3. pantomimist. See **pantomimist.**

pantomimist, *n.* mime, *Rare.* mimester, pantomime, pantomimic, mummer, mute, mimic; actor, performer.

pantry, *n.* cupboard, cuddy, stillroom, *Brit. Dial.* spence; larder, buttery, food room, cold room.

pants, *n.* **1.** trousers, drawers, slacks, ducks, *Brit. Inf.* strides, *Brit. Sl.* bags; breeches, knee breeches, *Inf.* britches, knickers, knickerbockers, plus fours, (*among Scottish Highlanders*) trews, *Scot. and North Eng.* breeks; pantalets, pantaloons, bloomers; overalls, chaps, chaparajos; palazzo pants, (*in the Orient*) pajamas, harem pants; pegtops, *Sl.* drainpipes, straightlegs; bell-bottoms, hip-huggers, flares; jeans, bluejeans, dungarees, *Trademark.* Levi's, denims; chinos, khakis, fatigues, whites, tweeds, flannels, corduroys, *Inf.* cords, *Sl.* whistle britches; clam diggers, pedal pushers; shorts, bermuda shorts, bermudas, walking shorts, (*in Bavaria*) lederhosen, *Inf.* cut-offs; short-shorts, hot pants.

2. underpants, underdrawers, underwear, underclothes, *Brit.* smallclothes, briefs, trunks, *Sl.* skivvies, *Sl.* undies, *Trademark.* BVDs, *Trademark.* Fruit of the Looms, *Brit.* Y-fronts; boxing shorts *or* trunks; panties, *Brit.* knickers, panty girdle, panty hose, *Trademark.* Underalls; long underwear, long drawers, *Sl.* long johns, thermals.

3. wear the pants dominate, rule, control, *Inf.* rule the roost; determine, decide, dispose, *Inf.* call the shots, be in the driver's seat *or* the saddle.

pap[1]**,** *n.* **1.** baby food, *Trademark.* Pablum, *Trademark.* Beechnut's, *Trademark.* Gerber's; mash, mush, *Sl.* smush, paste, goo, *Inf.* goop, *Sl.* glop; cereal, farina, *Chiefly Brit.* porridge, oatmeal, *Scot.* corn meal, *Brit.* hasty pudding, grits, hominy grits; *Trademark.* Cream of Rice, *Trademark.* Cream of Wheat, *Trademark.* Wheatina, *Trademark.* Maypo.

2. *Slang.* (*all gained through political patronage*) favors of office, *U.S. Sl.* pork, *U.S. Sl.* pork barrel;

profits, gains, takings, dividends, rake-off; favors, special favors, privileges, dispensations, indulgences, loop holes; appropriations; appointments.

pap[2], *n.* *Chiefly Dialect.* teat, tit, titty, nipple, *Anat.* mammilla, (*of animals*) dug, (*of cows*) udder.

papa, *n.* **1.** father, sire, parent; *All Inf.* dad, daddy, pop, pops, pap, pappy, the old man, the old gent; *Brit. Inf.* pater, *Brit. Inf.* governor; *Babytalk.* dada, daddums.

2. *Rare. Rom. Cath. Ch.* the Bishop of Rome. See **pope** and **pontiff** (*def.* **2**).

papacy, *n.* primacy, pontificate, the See of Rome, the Holy See, the See of Peter, the primacy of Peter, the papal crown, the shoes of the fisherman; papality, papalism, *Derog.* papism; popedom, the Vatican, Vatican City, the Papal States.

papal, *adj.* **1.** pontifical, *Archaic.* pontific, apostolic.

2. *All Usu. Disparaging.* papistical, papistic, papist, popish.

paper, *n.* **1.** writing *or* letter paper, notepaper, stationery, vellum, parchment, papyrus; typing paper, bond paper, bond, foolscap, letterhead; tissue paper, tracing paper, onionskin, India paper, Bible paper; newsprint, Manila paper, Manila, construction paper, drawing paper, watercolor paper; kraft, wrapping paper, giftwrap; poster board, pasteboard, cardboard, corrugated paper.

2. document, official *or* legal paper, instrument, authorization, order, *Law.* writ; charter, title, *Law.* deed; will, holograph, *Law.* testament; certificate, warrant, license, credential, diploma; receipt, voucher, bill of exchange, bill of sale.

3. bill, banknote, note, greenback; legal tender, currency, money. See **paper money**.

4. papers memoirs, annals, chronicle, records, log; letters, messages, notes, memorandums, memos.

5. essay, theme, article, composition; manuscript, MS, typescript, script, work, opus; report, white paper, white book, blue book; thesis, dissertation, monograph, treatise, disquisition, exposition, discourse, commentary, discussion.

6. newspaper, journal, gazette, publication, *Inf.* rag; tabloid, newsletter, circular, bulletin, house *or* trade organ, *Inf.* sheet; periodical, serial, quarterly, monthly, fortnightly, weekly, daily.

—v. **7.** wallpaper, line, interline, interlineate, face; overlay, overspread, cover, wrap, blanket, mantle, carpet.

—adj. **8.** papery, paperlike, chartaceous. See **papery**.

paper money, *n.* bill, banknote, note, *U.S.* silver *or* gold certificate, greenback, yellowback, *Inf.* folding money, scrip, *U.S.* shinplaster, *All Sl.* long green, green stuff, lettuce, cabbage, spinach, *U.S. Sl.* kale; legal tender, tender, medium of exchange, currency, money, cash, *All Sl.* dough, bread, moolah, jack, shekels, spondulicks, scratch, dibs, do-re-mi, wampum, *U.S. Sl.* bucks.

papery, *adj.* paperlike, chartaceous, papyrine, papyral, papyrian, papyritious; paper-thin, paper-shelled, tissuey, tissual, onionskin; thin, flimsy, lightweight, light; sheer, diaphanous, gossamer, translucent, transparent, see-through; fragile, breakable, frail, delicate, unsturdy, unsound, insubstantial; pasteboard, pasteboardy, jerry-built, shoddy, cheap, *U.S. Sl.* cheesy.

papism, *n.* **1.** *Disparaging.* papalism. See **papacy** and **pontificate** (*def.* **1**).

2. *Disparaging.* Roman Catholicism. See **papistry**.

papist, *n.* *Disparaging.* See **Catholic**.

papistry, *n.* *Disparaging.* Roman Catholicism, the Catholic Church, papalism, papality, popedom; *All Derogatory.* Romanism, popery, papism, Mariolatry.

pappy, *adj.* **1.** mushy, squashy, *Inf.* squishy, soft, pulpy, pulpous; flabby, doughy, spongy.

2. insipid, wishy-washy, namby-pamby, watery, milk and water.

papule, *n.* pimple, pustule, papilla, boil, blain, furuncle, furunculus, carbuncle, wen, pock, whelk, *Rare.* bleb, *Archaic.* botch; eruption, inflammation, swelling, rising, lump, bump, wheal; blemish, mark, spot, pockmark, whitehead, *Pathol.* milium, blackhead, *Med.* comedo, *Sl.* zit, *Sl.* woogit, *Sl.* hickey.

par, *n.* **1.** parity, equality, coequality, equivalence, equipollence, parallelism; identity, oneness, synonymity, sameness, interchangeability, unity; correspondence, agreement, accordance, concurrence, coincidence, conformity; similarity, similitude, analogy, likeness, resemblance, semblance; comparison, comparability, analogousness; symmetry, proportion, balance, equilibrium.

2. average, norm, normal, mean, medium; standard, rule, constant, *Inf.* usual ration.

3. above par a. superior, excellent, first rate, of the first water; exceptional, standout, outstanding, striking; superlative, perfect, first-class; choice, prime, select, very good; fine, admirable, noteworthy; capital, *Inf.* tiptop, *Inf.* A-1, *Sl.* bang-up, *Inf.* smashing, *Brit. Sl.* ripping, *Inf.* great; marvelous, wonderful, more than one could expect. **b.** healthy, feeling good, in fine fettle, *Inf.* in fine *or* high feather, *Inf.* in the pink, full of vigor. **c.** happy, on top of the world, cheerful, full of cheer, in good *or* high spirits.

4. below par a. inferior, substandard, below standard, lesser; low grade, *Inf.* not up to snuff *or* scratch, below the mark; unsuitable, wanting, lacking, found lacking, inadequate, deficient; imperfect, faulty, flawed, second, not up to specification, *Inf.* not up to spec, below scale, unacceptable. **b.** discounted, marked down, *Sl.* knocked off, cheap. **c.** unhealthy, sickly, *Inf.* off one's feed, *Inf.* poorly, not one's usual self. **d.** sad, depressed, *Inf.* down in the dumps, unhappy; blue, melancholy, in low spirits, dispirited.

5. par for the course standard, average, typical, ordinary, usual, commonplace; unremarkable, mediocre, garden-variety; expected, predictable, not surprising.

6. on a par equal, the same, much the same; well-matched, on equal *or* even terms, having the same handicap; running abreast, keeping pace with one another, *Inf.* neck and neck.

7. up to par acceptable, up to standard *or* grade, up to the mark; adequate, satisfactory, respectable, passable, all right, presentable, admissible, enough, good enough, sufficient.

parable, *n.* **1.** allegory, allegorical story, morality tale *or* play; moral bestiary, fable; tale, apologue, lesson, sermon, homily; legend, myth, chronicle, history, narrative, Bible story.

2. proverb, maxim, axiom, aphorism, saying, old saying, adage, dictum, apothegm, wise saying, didactic saying, *Inf.* grandmother's wisdom; truism, obvious truth, self-evident statement; cliché, platitude, *Inf.* old saw.

parabolic[1], *adj.* hyperbolic, hyperbola-shaped, curved, elliptical.

parabolic[2], *adj.* allegorical, figurative, representative, symbolic, metaphoric, metaphorical; aphoristic, proverbial, axiomatic; typical, allusive, referential, comparative.

paraclete, *n.* **1.** advocate, defender, champion, vindicator; pleader, apologist, friend at court; promoter, endorser, sponsor, protagonist, propagator, propagandist, proponent, favorer, countenancer, exponent; maintainer, sustainer, upholder, supporter; backer, second, abettor, bulwark; intercessor, interceder, mediator, intermediator, intermediary, medium, intermedium, middleman, go-between, interagent; arbitrator, peacemaker, make-peace, pacificator, propitiator, conciliator, appeaser.

2. **Paraclete** Holy Spirit, God the Spirit, the Spirit, Spirit of God, Spirit of Truth; Holy Ghost, the Dove, the Inspiration, the Intercessor, the Comforter, the Consoler, the Counselor.

parade, *n.* 1. procession, promenade, progression, succession; train, file, string, straggle; caravan, troop, review, file, column, rank and file, march, march-past; cortege, funeral procession, autocade, motorcade; demonstration, field day, turnout, pageantry, fete.

2. ostentation, pretension, splash, blazon, spectacle; pomp, magnificence, grandeur, glitter, flourish; vaunting, showing off, boasting, *Inf.* sporting; *Inf.* putting on airs, cutting *or* making a figure, cutting a swath; swaggering, strutting, prinking, *U.S. Sl.* putting on the dog; parvenu behavior, blatant affluence, conspicuous consumption.

3. public walk, promenade, passageway, footpath, esplanade; seawall, boardwalk, sidewalk, ambulatory.

—*v.* 4. march, hike, file, file by, go in column; march in review, march by, ride in review, *Mil.* troop the colors.

5. flaunt, display, *Inf.* sport, exhibit, air, point out, flash; put forth *or* forward, emphasize, spotlight, draw attention to, show off; make a show, strut, peacock; put on airs, put up a front, *U.S. Sl.* put on the dog; wave, dangle in front of [s.o.], flourish.

paradigm, *n.* example, pattern, design, sample, specimen; prototype, archetype; typemold, original, protoplast; standard, criterion, gauge, norm, test, rule, precedent, touchstone, canon, principle.

paradise, *n.* 1. heaven, abode of God, our Father's house, Divine abode, home, Abraham's bosom, abode of the saints, heavenly kingdom, kingdom of God, kingdom of heaven, city of God, city of light, heavenly city, holy city, celestial city, New Jerusalem, Zion, throne of God; Annfwn, Valhalla, Olympus, Elysium, Elysian Fields, Empyrean, *Mohammedanism.* the Seven Heavens, Avalon, the Islands *or* Isles of the Blessed, the Fortunate Isles *or* Islands, the Happy Isles; infinity, life everlasting, hereafter, life to come, world to come, next world, afterworld, sweet by-and-by; the final home, beyond the grave, afterlife, eternity, immortality, perpetuity, deathlessness.

2. utopia, Eden, heaven on earth, Shangri-la; millennium, Jubile, kingdom come, Xanadu, Beulah Land; fairyland, happy valley, pie in the sky.

3. bliss, glory, rapture, delight; ecstasy, honeymoon, transport, gratification, joy, supreme happiness; blessedness, third heaven, seventh heaven, beatitude, beatification, perfect content, *Buddhism.* Nirvana, dreamland, Land of the Lotus-eaters.

paradisiacal, *adj.* 1. heavenly, out of this world, unearthly, divine, celestial, Elysian; holy, glorified, blessed, beatific, good; cherubic, angelic, seraphic, archangelic, saintly, sainted.

2. delightful, blissful, pleasurable, felicitous; ambrosial, delectable, gratifying, entrancing, enrapturing; thrilling, exciting, enchanting, ravishing, transporting; joyous, cheering, enjoyable.

3. beautiful, dazzling, bright, radiant, shining, brilliant; superb, exquisite, sublime, golden, glorious; perfect, faultless, never-fading, imperishable, immortal, deathless; utopian, Edenic, ideal, consummate.

paradox, *n.* 1. puzzle, maze, quandary, dilemma, horns of a dilemma; problem, nonplus, brain-teaser; knot, Gordian knot, stickler, Irish bull, *Geom.* asses' bridge; enigma, perplexity, riddle, intricacy; puzzlement, bafflement, uncertainty.

2. contradiction, self-contradiction, antilogy, incongruity, inconsistency, *Logic.* antilogism; oxymoron, antinomy, equivocation, reversal; ambiguity, ambivalence.

3. absurdity, nonsense, *Latin. reductio ad absurdum*; impossibility, improbability, inconceivability, unthinkability.

paradoxical, *adj.* 1. puzzling, bewildering, baffling, confounding, riddling; perplexing, enigmatic, knotty; complicated, intricate, labyrinthine; arcane, difficult, unsolvable, unresolvable; curious, ironic, strange.

2. contradictory, self-contradictory, incongruous, inconsistent, discrepant, conflicting; ambiguous, problematic, equivocal; antilogistic, oxymoronic, antinomic.

3. absurd, nonsensical, impossible, improbable; unintelligible, inscrutable, incomprehensible, inexplicable, unfathomable; inconceivable, unthinkable, inapprehensible.

paragon, *n.* model, pattern, ideal, standard, norm; paradigm, prototype, exemplar; nonesuch, nonpareil, good example, beau ideal; flower, beauty, pearl, cynosure; ace, acme, quintessence; classic, exceller, prince, queen, mirror, masterpiece, masterwork, chef d'oeuvre; prize, cream, cream of the crop, *Fr. crème de la crème,* elite, elect, select, pick; prodigy, one in a thousand, superman, superwoman, wonderman, god, goddess, hero, heroine.

paragraph, *n.* 1. passage, excerpt, column; portion, segment, subdivision, section, part.

2. note, item, article, piece, *Fr. morceau.*

paragrapher, *n.* journalist, reporter, newsman, newspaperman, writer; correspondent, editorialist, columnist.

parallel, *adj.* 1. coextensive, aligned, equidistant, collateral, equispaced, concurrent; parallelogrammatical, parallelepipedonal; alongside, side by side, even, besides, neck and neck, abreast, *U.S. Inf.* nip and tuck.

2. corresponding, equal, matched; similar, analogous, like, alike, synonymous, homonymous; allied, equivalent, twin, same, duplicate; coequal, coordinate, proportional, uniform, regular; connatural, connate, congeneric.

—*n.* 3. parallel line, parallel bar, equal sign, parallel column, parallel dash, parallel vector; parallelogram, parallelepiped, parallelograph.

4. match, counterpart, analogue, equivalent; correspondent, complement, brother, sister, twin, companion; coequal, peer, compeer, fellow, *Fr. semblable;* ally, associate, cognate; correlative, synonym, homonym, coordinate.

5. correspondence, analogy, similitude, similarity, likeness, resemblance; connaturality, connateness, affinity, kinship; coextension, correlation, equalization, parallelization; equality, coequality, parity, par; balance, equipoise, symmetry, proportion.

—*v.* 6. coextend, be parallel, parallelize; run abreast *or* alongside, run side by side *or* besides; keep pace with; equal, tie, balance, even off.

7. match, correspond, conform, *Inf.* jibe, check; agree, resemble, contrast; double, imitate, copy, duplicate, repeat; echo, reecho, ditto, follow, take after; compare, compare to *or* with, relate; measure up to, *Inf.* stack up against, vie with.

parallelism, *n.* 1. coextension, coequality, correspondence, collineation, collaterality; nonconvergence, nondivergence, concentricity; parallelization, equidistance, concurrence; balance, equipoise, equilibrium; equality, parity, equivalence, par.

2. agreement, congruity, congruency, consistency,

keeping; equivalence, symmetry, accord, concord, harmony; rapport, consonance, cooperation; conformity, synchronism, *Inf.* sync, uniformity, regularity.

3. comparison, contrast, opposition, distinction, juxtaposition; connection, correlation, relation, likeness, affinity, kinship; likening, analogy, simile, metaphor, similitude, similarity, resemblance.

parallelize, *v.* **1.** coextend, be parallel; align, collineate, match, correspond. See **parallel** (*def.* **6**).

2. draw a parallel, make a comparison, compare to *or* with, collate; connect, relate, contrast, oppose, differentiate; juxtapose, place alongside, set side by side; balance, weigh, measure; liken to, make an analogy, equate, associate, correlate.

paralysis, *n.* **1.** numbness, insentience, insensibility, insensibleness, dullness, deadness, loss of sensation, stupefaction; inactivity, immobility, inaction, motionlessness.

2. paralyzation, stoppage, suspension, arrest, standstill, halt, stop, cessation, full stop, dead stop, grinding halt; strike, work stoppage; breakdown, slowdown, blockage, shut-down, checkmate, stalemate, deadlock, *Inf.* standoff; suspended animation, stagnation, dormancy, vegetation, inertia, idleness.

3. impotence, powerlessness, disability, feebleness, lameness, inability, incapability, incapacity, incapacitation, crippling, infirmity, debility, debilitation.

4. physical disability, neural disability, motor paralysis, palsy, stroke, paralytic stroke, apoplexy; *All Pathol.* paresis, diplegia, paraplegia, hemiplegia, Parkinson's disease, paralysis agitans, St. Vitus's dance, chorea, general paralysis, infantile paralysis, poliomyelitis, *Inf.* polio.

paralytic, *n.* **1.** paralysis victim, paralyzed person, cripple, handicapped person, palsy victim.

—adj. **2.** paralyzed, numb, insentient, insensible, dull, dead, stupefied; immobile, immobilized, inert, static, stationary, motionless, dormant, inactive, idle.

3. impotent, powerless, disabled, feebled, enfeebled, incapacitated, crippled, lame, debilitated, halt, handicapped, laid up; physically disabled, palsied; *All Pathol.* diplegic, paraplegic, hemiplegic, paretic, quadraplegic.

paralyze, *v.* **1.** numb, benumb, dull, deaden, anesthetize, freeze, drug, obtund; immobilize, disable, incapacitate, make powerless, prostrate, weaken, enfeeble, debilitate, cripple, lame, becripple.

2. shock, stagger, astound, astonish, stupefy, confound, stun, take away one's breath, jolt, strike with wonder *or* awe, *Inf.* flabbergast, *Inf.* scare the life out of; unman, unnerve, devitalize, sap, sap the strength of, lay low.

3. halt, arrest, check, stop, stay, impede, block; call a halt, put a stop to, put an end to; stop cold, stop dead, bring up, bring up short, pull up, stop short, bring to a grinding *or* screeching halt, bring to a standstill; put out of order, *Inf.* put out of commission, throw out of gear, sabotage, wreck, *Inf.* throw a wrench *or* monkeywrench into the works *or* machinery, *Inf.* kibosh, *Inf.* put the kibosh on, *Inf.* spike, *Inf.* spike the guns, *Inf.* put a staff in the wheels, *All Sl.* queer, queer the works, screw up, crab, foul up, louse up, bollix *or* bollox, snafu, gum, gum up the works, put a crimp in.

4. thwart, frustrate, foil, checkmate, contravene; dam, prevent, bar, deter, obstruct, slow down; stymie, hobble, hamstring, clip the wings of, put out of action; delay, retard, drag, hold up, hinder, bog down, hogtie, tie up, tie the hands of, tie up with red tape; put aside, table, pigeonhole, shelve, *Inf.* put on ice; stand in the way of, disrupt, confound, *Sl.* flummox, *Inf.* stonewall; undermine, castrate, emasculate, break, take the wind out of [s.o.'s] sails.

5. throttle, strangle, choke off; shut up shop, close shop, lock up, shut down, lock out, close down; strike, walk out; stalemate, deadlock.

6. drag *or* stretch out, hang fire, protract, prolong, extend, hang back, hang fire, stall, stall off, stall for time, *Inf.* drag one's feet, *Sl.* choke up.

paramount, *adj.* **1.** dominant, predominant, superior, highest; supreme, preeminent, sovereign, governing, ruling, leading; top-rank, ranking, chief, principal, prime, foremost, primary, main; premier, first, top, topmost, *Inf.* number-one, *Inf.* numero uno, in the front rank; important, significant, cardinal, uppermost.

2. superlative, greatest, outstanding; unapproachable, inimitable, unparalleled, matchless, unmatched, peerless; unequaled, unrivaled, unexcelled, unsurpassed, incomparable, beyond compare; champion, prize, very best, of the first rank; sterling, splendid, *Inf.* splendiferous, *Sl.* super, *Sl.* terrific; best, optimum, model, superb, choice.

—n. **3.** overlord, master, ruler, sovereign, monarch, crowned head, potentate; superior, commander, chieftain, high chief; head, captain, *Inf.* head man, *Inf.* bossman, *Sl.* top dog, *Sl.* head honcho, *Sl.* big cheese, *Sl.* top man on the totem pole.

paramountcy, *n.* **1.** dominion, ascendancy, predominance, control, power, sovereignty, suzerainty, hegemony; supremacy, primacy, preeminence, upper *or* whip hand, sway; control, rule, command, mastery, domination; reign, empery, lordship, mastership, leadership, authority, jurisdiction, power, *Inf.* say *or* say-so.

2. importance, significance, consequence, matter, value, account, concern, moment, weight, weightiness, substance; greatness, mark, notability, fame, renown, illustriousness, glory; superiority, eminence, note, distinction, prominence, rank, standing, prestige, *Inf.* top billing; reputation, repute, name, estimation, regard, *Inf.* first place.

3. matchlessness, peerlessness, unrivaledness, superlativeness, unsurpassability.

paramour, *n.* **1.** mistress, fancy woman, inamorata; courtesan, concubine, kept woman, *Sl.* doxy, odalisque.

2. lover, fancy man, inamorato; gallant, suitor, amorist; infatuate, swain, spark, sparker, wooer, courter, Romeo; ladies' man, playboy, *Inf.* wolf, *Sl.* sheik, *Sl.* stud; philanderer, *Fr. bon ami*, adulterer; Lothario, rake, libertine, Casanova, Don Juan; gigolo, *It. cicisbeo*, escort, cavalier.

3. beloved, darling, honey, sweetheart, sweetie, ladylove, flame; girlfriend, boyfriend, young man, beau, admirer.

paranoia, *n.* **1.** madness, insanity, psychosis, mental illness, mental disease, *Psychiatry.* dementia, psychopathy, derangement, lunacy; delusion, mania, monomania, obsession; persecution complex.

2. *Informal.* suspicion, mistrust, distrust; apprehension, uneasiness, apprehensiveness, *Inf.* butterflies, nervousness, queasiness; angst, fear and trembling, anguish, anxiety; fear, dread, fright, *Inf.* funk, fearfulness; terror, horror, panic, alarm, perturbation, trepidation; *Sl.* heebie-jeebies, the jitters, *Sl.* the willies, *Sl.* the creeps.

paranoid, *adj.* **1.** mad, insane, lunatic, lunatical, crazy, crazed, demented, deranged; of unsound mind, *Latin. non compos mentis*, mentally ill; unbalanced, unhinged, distracted, possessed.

2. *Informal.* suspicious, mistrustful, distrustful; uneasy, apprehensive, nervous, anxious, worried, queasy; scared, fearful, frightened, afraid; terrified, horrified, panic-stricken, alarmed, perturbed.

—*n.* **3.** madman, lunatic, *Sl.* loon, maniac, bedlamite, *Inf.* crackpot, psychotic, *Sl.* sickie, psychopath; nervous wreck, *Inf.* mess, *Inf.* case, neurotic.

parapet, *n.* fortification, breastwork, outwork, barbican; elevation, wall, fence, palisade, barricade, barrier; bastion, bulwark, rampart, redoubt, demilune, redan, ravelin; abutment, embankment, bank, buffer, buttress; defense, protection.

paraphernalia, *n.* **1.** belongings, personal belongings, effects, personal effects, chattels, possessions, properties, *Sl.* stuff, *Sl.* junk; baggage, bag and baggage, kit, duffel, luggage, dunnage, impedimenta.

2. equipment, equipage, gear, apparatus, accouterments, appurtenances, appointments, furnishings, furniture; fixtures, fittings, habiliments, *Inf.* things; tools, instruments, contrivances, machinery; implements, appliances, utensils, conveniences; outfit, outfitting, turnout, rig; supplies, material, materials, matériel, wherewithal; caparison, trappings, tack, tackle, harness, rigging.

paraphrase, *n.* **1.** restatement, rewording, rephrasing, rehash, paraphrasis; summary, recapitulation, explanation, elucidation, gloss; indirect discourse, indirect quotation; translation, metaphrase, rendition, version, interpretation, reading.

—*v.* **2.** reword, rephrase, restate, rehash; summarize, recapitulate, explain, elucidate, gloss; translate, metaphrase, interpret, read.

parasite, *n.* **1.** bloodsucker, *Sl.* bleeder, *Biol.* entozoon, cestode, louse, plant louse; barnacle, bur, appendage.

2. leech, *Inf.* sponge *or* sponger, *Sl.* mooch *or* moocher, *Inf.* freeloader, hanger-on, *Inf.* panhandler; courtier, minion, follower, attendant, satellite; flunky, lackey, yes man, jackal, spaniel, bootlick, bootlicker, footlicker, lickspit, lickspittle; kowtower, *Sl.* oreo, cringer, groveler, sniveler; sycophant, toady, toadeater, tufthunter, fawner, fawning flatterer, truckler; flatterer, wheedler, puffer, backslapper, timeserver, *Inf.* apple-polisher, *Sl.* brown-nose, *Sl.* brown-noser, *Sl.* brownie, *Obs. Rare.* blander, *Archaic.* pickthank.

parasitical, *adj.* **1.** blood-sucking, sucking, draining, depleting, exhausting; absorbing, grasping, taking; leechlike, *Sl.* sponging, *Sl.* mooching, *Inf.* freeloading, *Inf.* panhandling, dependent.

2. sycophantic, sycophantish, toadying; flattering, truckling, wheedling, ingratiating, timeserving, *Sl.* bootlicking, *Sl.* footlicking, *Inf.* apple-polishing, *Sl.* brown-nosing, *Obs.* blanding; groveling, crawling, kowtowing, crouching, fawning, obsequious.

parasitism, *n.* **1.** bloodsucking, dependency, dependence; *Sl.* sponging, *Sl.* mooching, *Inf.* freeloading, *Inf.* panhandling.

2. sycophancy, sycophantism, toadyism, tufthunting, fawningness, flattery; truckling, *Sl.* falling all over, *Inf.* honeying, *Inf.* buttering, *Inf.* apple-polishing; *All Sl.* shining up to, playing up to, brown-nosing, buttering up; courting, paying court to, currying favor, dancing attendance upon, licking [s.o.'s] shoes, kissing [s.o.'s] feet, *Sl.* bootlicking; groveling, crawling, kowtowing, crouching.

parasol, *n.* sunshade, umbrella, beach umbrella, *Fr. parapluie, Brit. Sl.* brolly, *Brit. Facetious.* gamp, *Inf.* bumbershoot.

parboil, *v.* precook, blanch, scald, simmer; cook, boil, roast, stew, steam.

parcel, *n.* **1.** package, bundle, bale, packet; pack, *Sl.* bindle, *Australian Sl.* swag; box, carton, case, container, receptacle, crate.

2. lot, division, plot, plat, tract, patch, cantle, corner.

3. batch, bunch, heap, pile, conglomeration; collection, assortment, group, assemblage, congeries, aggregation.

4. part, portion, piece, moiety; fragment, fraction, detail, section, segment, share, shred.

—*v.* **5.** mete, apportion, dole, allot; deal out, distribute, hand out, divide, *Inf.* divvy, share.

6. bag, bale, bundle; package, wrap, gift-wrap, envelop; tie up, do up, bind, tape.

parceling, *n.* allotting, apportioning, meting, doling; assorting, dividing, *Inf.* divvying; distributing, giving out.

parch, *v.* **1.** dry, sun-dry, sun, dry out, dry up; evaporate, dehydrate, exsiccate, desiccate; sear, wither, wilt, shrivel, shrink.

2. make dry, make hot, make thirsty.

3. heat *or* heat up, warm *or* warm up, roast, toast, brown, bake.

parched, *adj.* **1.** dry, dried, sun-dried, dried up, dried out; evaporated, dehydrated, exsiccated, desiccated, *Chem.* anhydrous; sear, sere, withered, wilted, shriveled *or* shriveled up; heated *or* heated up, warmed *or* warmed up, roasted, toasted, browned, baked; burned, scorched, adust.

2. juiceless, sapless, undampened, unmoistened, thirsty, unwatered, waterless; arid, rainless, droughty; bare, barren, fruitless, sterile, unproductive.

parching, *adj.* **1.** drying, evaporating, dehydrating, exsiccating, desiccating; searing, withering, wilting, shriveling.

2. hot, heating, warm, warming; roasting, toasting, browning, baking.

parchment, *n.* **1.** paper, papyrus, vellum, bond *or* bond paper, writing paper, stationery.

2. scroll, manuscript, palimpsest; legal document, instrument, title, deed, grant, contract; official *or* public document, charter, constitution.

3. diploma, graduation certificate, *Inf.* sheepskin, degree, academic title.

pardon, *n.* **1.** clemency, indulgence, indulgency, indulging, lenience, leniency, lenity; forbearance, tolerance, allowance, permissiveness; mercifulness, mercy, grace, humanity, compassion; condonation, condoning, overlooking, disregarding.

2. amnesty, reprieval, reprieving, remission, remitting; forgiveness, forgiving, excusal, excusing, pardoning, absolution, absolving, shriving; acquittal, acquittance, acquitting, exculpation, exculpating, clearance, clearing, exoneration, exonerating, vindication, vindicating.

—*v.* **3.** remit, reprieve, amnesty, respite; forgive, absolve, shrive.

4. release, free, set free, let go, liberate, emancipate, deliver; dismiss, let off, *Inf.* let off the hook, *Inf.* let out of, *Law.* discharge; acquit, exculpate, clear, clear one's name, prove *or* declare innocent, uphold innocence, pronounce *or* declare not guilty, remove guilt, free from blame; exonerate, vindicate, right.

5. excuse, make allowances for, overlook, pass over, wink at; disregard, dispense with, forget, ignore, look the other way, pay no attention to.

pardonable, *adj.* **1.** forgivable, excusable, absolvable, remittable; justifiable, warrantable, defensible, supportable.

2. venial, minor, unimportant, insignificant, inconsequential, trivial, trifling, nugatory; condonable, sanctionable, allowable, permissible; tolerable, bearable, endurable; unobjectionable, inoffensive, harmless.

3. unblamable, inculpable, irreproachable, unreproachable, unreprovable, unreprehensible; uncondemnable, uncensurable.

pare, *v.* **1.** peel, skin, decorticate, excoriate, bark, cut *or* strip the skin from; shell, husk, shuck.

2. prune, crop, top, cut back, reduce, cut down to size; trim, clip, shear, shave, mow, cut short, dock; cut off *or* away, lop, remove, retrench.

3. cut down, cut back, retrench, curtail, limit; reduce, diminish, decrease, cut, slash, lower, lessen.

parent, *n.* **1.** genitor, father, *Inf.* old man, *Brit. Inf.* pater, paterfamilias; mother, *Inf.* old lady, *Brit. Inf.* mater, materfamilias; parents, *Sl.* fossils; (*both of animals*) dam, sire; foster parent, foster mother, foster father, guardian; stepparent, stepmother, stepfather; mother-in-law, father-in-law, in-law; godparent, godmother, godfather.

2. ancestor, antecedent, forefather, forbear, *Archaic.* sire, patriarch, matriarch; progenitor, primogenitor, *Archaic.* predecessor; procreator, begetter.

3. cause, source, root, origin, fountainhead, mainspring; agent, mover, prime mover; author, creator, producer, originator.

4. precursor, predecessor, forerunner; prototype, model, exemplar.

5. protector, protectress, guardian, guardian angel, watchdog, defender, preserver.

—*v.* **6.** foster, raise, bring up, rear; mother, care for, take care of, cherish, nurture, nourish.

parentage, *n.* ancestry, ancestral line, lineage, descent, birth, origin, derivation, extraction, filiation; family, dynasty, tribe, clan; race, strain, stock, breed, bloodline, pedigree, stem, branch, stirps; heredity, genealogy, family tree; heritage, patrimony, background, past, history, roots.

parental, *adj.* paternal, fatherly, fatherlike; maternal, motherly, motherlike.

parenthetic, *adj.* parenthetical, incidental, by-the-way; subordinate, secondary, inconsequential; extrinsic, extrinsical, extraneous, external, nonessential, unessential, inessential, adventitious; inserted, interposed, interjacent, intermediate, intermediary, intervening, interfering; explanatory, descriptive, justificatory, explicative; elucidative, commentarial, illustrative, expressive; qualifying, limiting.

pariah, *n.* **1.** outcast, castaway, Ishmael, unperson, nonperson; exile, expatriate, political refugee; fugitive, runaway, outlaw; excommunicate, rejectee, leper, untouchable.

2. wanderer, vagabond, rover, itinerant, nomad, bird of passage; beachcomber, vagrant, hobo, knight-of-the-road, tramp; beggar, panhandler, scavenger; derelict, degenerate, down-and-outer, *U.S. Inf.* bum, *U.S. Inf.* stumblebum; *Sl.* scum, *Sl.* dregs.

paring, *n.* peel, peeling, skin, rind, bark, shell, husk; slice, sliver, shive, shaving, piece, bit; scrap, remnant, shred, snip, snippet, cutting; splinter, flake, scale, fragment, shard.

parish, *n.* **1.** (*all usu. ecclesiastical*) district, vicariate, bishopric, precinct, prefecture, constituency, arrondissement, ward, province, borough, canton, quarter, region, territory, demesne, *Brit.* glebe.

2. parishioners, congregation, flock, fold, laity, laymen, brethren.

parity, *n.* **1.** equality, coequality, equivalence, equipollence, equipollency, parallelism, evenness, levelness, (*of rights*) isonomy; identity, par, oneness, sameness, unity; symmetry, proportion, balance; homogeneity, monotony, uniformity, consistency; equilibrium, equation; equal terms, quits.

2. correspondence, correspondency, agreement, accordance, concurrence, conformity, conformance, compatibility; consonance, consonancy, coherence, congruence, congruency, congruity; coincidence, connection; concert, harmony, unison; similarity, similitude, analogy, likeness, resemblance, semblance; closeness, approximation, affinity; comparison, comparability, comparableness, analogousness.

park, *n.* **1.** village green, green, greens, common, commons, square, greensward, quadrangle, quad, plaza; parkland, woodland, woods, forest, grove; grassland, field, meadow; grounds, lawn, yard; garden, pleasure garden, pleasance, formal garden.

2. *British.* reservation, reserve, preserve, sanctuary, *Chiefly Brit.* chase.

3. *U.S.* valley, dale, vale, dell.

4. parking lot, car park, parking garage, car port, driveway, lot, parking space.

5. enclosure, stadium, ballpark, bowl, arena, coliseum.

—*v.* **6.** (*all usu. of cars, bicycles, etc.*) pull over, pull up, pull in, garage, curb it.

7. *Informal.* place, put, set, seat, station, leave.

parkway, *n.* **1.** highway, main road, highroad, thoroughfare, public road, roadway; drive, avenue, boulevard, strip, *Inf.* drag; turnpike, pike, tollroad, state highway, *U.S. Inf.* interstate; freeway, *Brit.* clearway, expressway, causeway, throughway; speedway, (*in Germany*) autobahn, superhighway.

2. sidewalk, pedestrian way, footpath, promenade, esplanade, walkway.

parlance, *n.* **1.** idiom, vernacular, tongue, dialect, speech, talk, language; phraseology, phrasing, wording, manner *or* style of speech, diction, *Linguistics.* idiolect; patois, brogue, twang, accent; jargon, *Inf.* lingo, cant, argot; slang, street language, *Obs.* flash; colloquialism, provincialism, regionalism, localism.

2. discourse, discussion, parley. See **parley** (*defs.* **1, 2**).

parley, *n.* **1.** discussion, palaver, dialogue, interchange, discourse, consultation, debate, deliberation, negotiation, *Archaic.* parle; conference, huddle, meeting, summit, colloquy, colloquium, forum, round table; convention, conclave, congress, caucus, session, council, parliament, assembly.

2. conversation, exchange, talk, word, tête-à-tête; chat, confabulation, *Inf.* confab, *Sl.* rap *or* rap session, *Sl.* bull session.

—*v.* **3.** confer, hold a conference, palaver, consult together, deliberate, negotiate, *Inf.* powwow, *Inf.* put heads together, *Inf.* talk turkey; discuss, talk over, exchange views, compare notes, have a dialogue *or* interchange; meet, convene, sit down together, *Inf.* huddle, *Inf.* go into a huddle.

4. converse, talk, have a word with; chat, confabulate, *Inf.* confab, *Sl.* jaw, *Sl.* rap, *Sl.* shoot the breeze *or* bull, *Sl.* schmooze, *Archaic.* chin.

parliament, *n.* **1.** *Usu.* **Parliament** British legislature, House of Lords, Lords Spiritual, Lords Temporal, House of Commons.

2. legislature, congress, senate, diet, assembly, upper and lower house *or* chamber, *Both Early Eng. Hist.* witangemot, witan; lawmakers, *Inf.* grey beards; council, board, panel, lawmaking *or* governing body; Congress of the United States, U.S. Senate, U.S. House of Representatives; General Assembly, House of Delegates, (*in the U.S.S.R.*) Soviet, (*in Russia*) Duma, (*in France*) Chamber of Deputies, *Austrian and German Hist.* Reichstag, (*both in West Germany*) Bundesrat, Bundestag, (*in Sweden*) Riksdag, (*all in Denmark*) Folketing, Rigsdag, Landsding, (*in Eire*) Oireachtas, (*in Spain*) Cortes, (*in Portugal*) Cortes Geraes, (*in the Netherlands*) States-General, (*in Japan*) House of Councilors *or* (formerly) Peers.

3. meeting, convention, convocation, conclave, summit, caucus, session; colloquy, colloquium, forum, round table; conference, parley, palaver, consultation, huddle, *Archaic.* parle.

parliamentary, *adj.* **1.** legislative, legislatorial, congressional, senatorial, Senate, House, synodical; lawmaking, law-giving, governmental.

2. democratic, representative, republican; orderly, by the rules, by the book, by *Roberts Rules of Order.*

parlor, *n.* **1.** living room, sitting room, front room, drawing room, salon; lounge, smoking room, reading room, study, den; reception *or* visiting *or* visitors' room *or* area, locutorium, waiting room, anteroom, antechamber, lobby, vestibule, foyer.

2. shop, store, establishment, business, place of business, office.

parochial, *adj.* **1.** provincial, regional, microcultural, small-town, local; regionalistic, *Sociol.* ethnocentric, insular; limited, confined, constricted, illiberal, uncatholic, noneclectic; small-minded, little-minded, narrow-minded, mean-minded; short-sighted, myopic, near-sighted, wearing blinders *or* blinkers, not able to see beyond the end of one's nose; deaf, unhearing, deaf to reason *or* new ideas; narrow, restricted, circumscribed, hidebound; intolerant, bigoted, prejudiced, biased, unable to walk in the other person's shoes *or* moccasins, unsympathetic, unempathetic; opinionated, dogmatic, one-sided, partial, close-minded; stiff, rigid, set, set in one's ways, stiff-necked, stiff-backed; petty, small, little.

2. unsophisticated, uncultivated, uncultured, gauche, backward, countryish; traditional, conventional, unprogressive, old-fashioned, backward-looking, strait-laced, *Inf.* grannyish; rooted, settled, unchanging, unchangeable, immovable, intractable, uncompromising; smug, complacent, self-righteous, sanctimonious; *Inf.* stick-in-the-mud, fogyish, conservative, opposed to change; *Inf.* stuffy, *Sl.* square, *Sl.* straight; uninteresting, dull, vapid, *Sl.* no pizzazz.

parodist, *n.* satirist, ironist, lampooner, pasquinader, caricaturist, burlesquer, mocker; mimic, mime, pantomime, impersonator; comic, wit; writer, author, essayist, critic.

parody, *n.* take-off, spoof, *Sl.* put-on, *Brit.* send-up, amphigory; satire, lampoon, pasquinade, burlesque, caricature, exaggeration, mockery, travesty; imitation, apery, mimicry.

parole, *n.* **1.** *Penology.* conditional release, probation, trial period, furlough, leave, leave of absence.

2. word of honor, promise, solemn promise; pledge, vow, avowal, *Archaic.* plight, oath, word, solemn word; assurance, undertaking, guarantee, warrant; gentlemen's agreement, handshake; covenant, compact, agreement.

paroxysm, *n.* **1.** fit, convulsion, *Pathol.* eclampsia, spasm, *Pathol.* tetanus, throe, qualm, *Pathol.* jactation; attack, seizure, epilepsy, spell, stroke, *Pathol.* ictus, tantrum; tremor, shakes, quavering, twitching; cramp, charley horse, contraction, orgasm; outbreak, outburst, storm, explosion, eruption, upheaval, explosion, flare-up.

2. agitation, excitement, frenzy, furor, *Pathol.* phrenitis, *Inf.* dither, *Inf.* tizzy, *Inf.* stew, ferment; tempestuousness, turbulence, boisterousness, rage, fume, fury, *Inf.* conniption, *Inf.* cat fit; violent emotion, emotional upheaval, pique, huff, dudgeon; raving, hysterics, delirium, delirium tremens, *Pathol.* calenture, tarantism.

parquet, *n.* **1.** inlaid flooring, patterned floor, tile floor, tesselated floor.

2. front seats, orchestra; (*esp. in U.S.*) theater seats seating, audience.

parquetry, *n.* marquetry, mosaic work, tiling, tesselation, patterned inlay, floor inlay, checkering; ornamentation, decoration.

parricide, *n.* patricide, father-killer, matricide, mother-killer, kin-killer, fratricide, sororicide; regicide, assassinator; homicide, murderer, slaughterer, killer; traitor, criminal, sinner.

parrot, *n.* **1.** cockatoo, lory, mackaw, parakeet, myna.

2. mimic, mimicker, imitator, copyist, *Inf.* copycat; ape, monkey, echo, mockingbird.

—*v.* **3.** repeat, echo, cuckoo; mimic, imitate, copy, *Inf.* copycat, ape, monkey; mirror, simulate.

parry, *v.* **1.** ward off, fend off, divert, deflect, turn aside; shield from, defend against, stave off, *Archaic.* forfend; repulse, repel, drive back, keep off, keep at a distance, hold off; avert, prevent, obviate, preclude, forestall, debar, hinder, inhibit.

2. avoid, dodge, evade, elude; shun, stay clear of, get around, circumvent, sidestep, whiffle; fence, hedge, beat around the bush, qualify, prevaricate, quibble, equivocate, *Inf.* waffle, fudge, sidetrack; tergiversate, vacillate, blow hot and cold, shilly-shally.

parsimonious, *adj.* stingy, miserly, carking, skinflinty, mean, tight, tight-fisted, closefisted, cheap, *Sl.* chintzy, moneygrubbing, grasping; niggardly, *Rare.* illiberal, cheeseparing, penurious; scrimping, penny-pinching, grudging, begrudging, ungenerous, stinting; thrifty, frugal, sparing, chary; economical, prudent, saving, penny-wise.

parsimony, *n.* **1.** miserliness, niggardliness, penuriousness, meanness, churlishness, nearness; stinginess, tightness, tight-fistedness, closefistedness, cheapness, *Sl.* chintziness; graspingness, avidity, avarice, avariciousness, greed, cupidity, rapacity, rapaciousness, tenacity, covetousness; mercenariness, venality, usuriousness, usury, extortion, sordidness; selfishness, hard-heartedness, unyieldingness, misanthropy.

2. scrimpiness, shabbiness, grudgingness, begrudgingness, skimpiness, ungenerousness, ungenerosity; thrift, thriftiness, frugality, spareness, chariness, economy.

parson, *n.* **1.** clergyman, cleric, clerk, ecclesiastic, churchman, reverend, cassock, man of God, man of the cloth, shepherd of souls, *Brit.* blackcoat; minister, divine, padre, priest, father, confessor; theologian, hierophant.

2. preacher, minister of the Gospel, sermonizer, sermonist, *Obs. Rare.* sermoneer, *All Usu. Disparaging.* pulpiteer, pulpitarian, gospel-monger.

3. dean, pastor, rector, vicar, canon, prebendary, chaplain, *U.S. Mil. Sl.* sky pilot, curate, curé, abbé.

parsonage, *n.* **1.** parish house, church house, rectory, *Rom. Cath. Ch.* presbytery, vicarage, deanery, pastorate, *Southern U.S.* pastorium, *Brit. Archaic.* glebe house.

2. *English Eccles. Law.* benefice, pastorate, episcopate, bishopric, diocese, see, deanery, chaplaincy, curacy.

part, *n.* **1.** portion, division, majority, proportion; department, compartment, branch, group, subgroup, species, family; piece, parcel, fragment, fraction, cantle; section, sector, segment, subdivision, detail, detachment; constituent, component, ingredient, complement; factor, element, part and parcel; appurtenance, leaven, accouterment.

2. particular, item, particle, bit, scrap, shred, crumb, morsel; snippet, cutting, wisp, rag, remnant, hank; slice, wedge, rasher, sliver, finger; hunk, lump, stump, butt, chunk; fraction, half, third, quarter, fifth, *etc.*

3. attribute, feature, mark, characteristic, trait; quality, property, character, nature; grade, kind, tone, color; stamp, caliber, grain, aspect, type.

4. chapter, column, phrase, clause, subclause, sentence; stanza, verse, verselet, strophe; meter, measure, stich, stave, line; excerpt, extract, quotation; paragraph, passage, article; serial, fascicle, number, issue, installment; book, volume, edition.

5. member, limb, organ, appendage, arm, leg, extremity; joint, wing, shank, shin; torso, trunk, thorax; branch, bough, ramification, adjunct; twig, sprig, spray, switch; offshoot, spur, scion, heir, chip off the old block.

6. share, allotment, lot, apportionment, assignment; dividend, commission, stock, stake, consignment, *Sl.* cut, *Sl.* rake-off, *Sl.* whack; dose, measure, quantum, meed, contingent, modicum; quota, proportion, percentage; pittance, dole, deal, allowance, moiety, ration, budget, *Sl.* chunk, *Sl.* slice of the pie.

7. **parts** region, territory, area, place; zone, ground, terrain, *Sl.* turf; quarter, district, ward, bailiwick, precinct; neighborhood, vicinity, purlieus, environs, confines, neck of the woods.

8. participation, say, responsibility; interest, concern, care, regard, business, affair.

9. duty, function, line, office, capacity; realm, province, sphere, scope.

10. character, person, role, cast, lead; cue, lines, side.

11. **for the most part** in the main, on the whole, by and large, all in all; mostly, mainly, chiefly, principally; for all practical purposes, essentially, to all intents and purposes.

12. **in part** in some measure, to some degree, to some extent; partially, partly, comparatively, moderately, tolerably, relatively.

13. **on the part of** on behalf of, in the name of, for the sake of, for, by proxy for, acting for, under orders from.

14. **take part** participate, engage in, play a part in, be a party to, join, join in; partake, associate, have a hand in; contribute, chip in, enter into, sit in on, have a voice in, vote.

—v. **15.** divide, break, cleave, split; dissect, anatomize, dismantle, take apart, break up; subdivide, sectionalize, segment, fragment; divaricate, splay, deploy, fan out, spread; diverge, deviate, radiate, fork, bifurcate; ramify, branch out, swerve off.

16. keep apart, put apart, separate; dissolve, decompose, disintegrate, disorganize; sunder, dissever, sever, abscind; disconnect, disjoin, detach, dissociate; disunite, divorce, isolate, segregate; cut apart, cut adrift, hive off, split off.

17. come apart, break away, separate; loose, get loose, disengage, unclinch, ungear, unyoke; unmoor, cast off.

18. distribute, apportion, allot, allocate, dole, deal, parcel; divide, *Sl.* divvy up, halve, carve up; administer, assign, dispense, mete, partition.

19. depart, part company, go separate ways, split up, break up; quit, vacate, go away, go off; get up and go, be gone, take leave, withdraw, retire, make an exit; disband, disperse, scatter, dispel; break away, push off, *Sl.* hit the road.

20. **part with** give up, relinquish, abandon, renounce; forgo, have done with, be rid of, forsake; surrender, yield, cede, release; discard, get rid of, dismiss, lay aside, throw away, jettison.

—adj. **21.** half, partial, partly; bi-, semi-, hemi-, demi-; a bit, a little, a wee bit.

partake, *v.* **1.** share *or* share in, participate *or* participate in, have a part in, take part in, have a share in, have a finger in the pie.

2. *Usu.* **partake of** share, break bread, take, receive.

partaker, *n.* participator, participant, communicant; sharer, shareholder, partner, copartner, associate, colleague; joint owner, coparcener, joint heir, joint heiress, coheiress, coheir; joint tenant, roommate, housemate.

partaking, *n.* sharing *or* sharing in, participating, participation, communion; association, partnership, copartnership; joint ownership, coparcenary, joint heirship, coheirship; joint tenancy, joint occupancy.

parted, *adj.* **1.** cleft, cloven, rift, cut, riven; split, rent, slit, divided.

2. separated, set apart, isolated, segregated; detached, divorced, disjoined, disunited.

parterre, *n.* (*all of a theater, opera house, etc*). parquet circle, parquet, orchestra pit, pit, main floor.

partial, *adj.* **1.** fractional, segmental, segmentary, segmentate; local, sectional, regional; a fraction of a, half *or* a quarter of a, a part of a, a piece of a, a slice of a.

2. incomplete, fragmentary, fragmental, limited, inexhaustive, not total, not entire, not absolute; inchoate, crude, rough, sketchy, scanty; deficient, lacking, undeveloped, immature, unfinished, imperfect; inadequate, insufficient, slight, meager.

3. component, composing, constituent, constituting, forming; elemental, factorial, integral, integrant.

4. biased, prejudiced, one-sided, partisan; influenced, persuaded, affected, jaundiced, colored; unfair, inequitable, unjust, unbalanced, uneven, discriminatory.

5. **partial to** in favor of, fond of, taken with, attracted to; care for, have a liking *or* taste for, like, have an affinity for, have a weakness *or* soft spot for.

partiality, *n.* **1.** favoritism, partialness, partisanship, partisanry, partisanism, one-sidedness, unilateralism, unilaterality; discrimination, inequity, unfairness, unjustness, injustice.

2. bias, prejudice, predilection, prepossession, predisposition *or* predisposal for; leaning *or* bent *or* inclination toward, proclivity *or* propensity *or* mind for; disposition, temperament, humor, nature.

3. preference, favor, fancy, eye, taste, appreciation; attraction, affinity, weakness, soft spot; liking, relish, fondness, love, special feeling *or* spot, attachment.

partible, *adj.* divisible, dividable, *Archaic.* dividual; separable, splittable, scissile, discerptible, portionable; reducible, capable of being broken down, *Math.* factorable.

participant, *n.* **1.** participator, partaker, communicant; member, part, sharer, shareholder, partner, copartner, associate, colleague; cooperator, worker, helper, contributor; joint owner, coparcener, joint heir, coheir; joint heiress, coheiress; joint tenant, roommate, housemate.

—adj. **2.** participating, sharing, partaking.

participate, *v.* **1.** *Usu.* **participate in** partake, partake in, share, share in, have a share in, have a part in, be a part of; play a part in, have something to do with, have a finger in the pie, have a say in.

2. take part in, join in, enter in *or* into, engage in; contribute, *Inf.* pitch in, give *or* lend a hand, pull an oar, help *or* help out; cooperate, do one's share *or* part, pull one's weight, work; audit, sit in on.

participation, *n.* **1.** participating, taking part, contributing, contribution, helping, help, cooperation, cooperating.

2. sharing *or* sharing in, partaking, communion; association, partnership, copartnership; joint ownership, *Law.* coparcenary, joint heirship, coheirship; joint tenancy, joint occupancy.

participator, *n.* participant, partaker, sharer. See **participant** (*def.* 1).

particle, *n.* **1.** bit, mote, *Scot.* hate *or* haet; mite, speck, smidgen, *Inf.* smitch, iota, molecule, atom, jot, whit, tittle; spot, dot, point, dab; hair, shaving, paring, moit, sliver, shive, splinter; morsel, crumb, grain, granule; minimum, pittance, modicum, driblet; trace, touch, hint, trifle, tinge, suggestion, suspicion, tincture, *Archaic.* spice, shadow; spark, scintilla, gleam.

2. (*of a document*) clause, article, provision, condition, stipulation.

parti-colored, *adj.* variegated, varicolored, varied, shot; multicolored, multicolor, polychromatic, polychromic, of many colors *or* shades *or* hues, versicolor, kaleidoscopic; prismatic, prismatical, spectral, rainbowy, colorful, brilliant, pavonine; marble, marbly, marmoreal, marmorean, motley, streaked, striated, striped; piebald, pied, (*esp. of horses*) skewbald, dappled, brindled, spotted, mottled, speckled, flecked; checked, checkered, plaid, tartan.

particular, *adj.* **1.** specific, single, certain, special, unique, sole, peculiar, individual; separate, distinct, discrete; exact, precise, explicit, definite, express; pointed, strict, absolute, unconditional.

2. noteworthy, notable, marked, special, unusual, remarkable; exceptional, especial, outstanding, momentous.

3. detailed, minute, circumstantial, fine, nice, thorough, searching; scientific, mathematical, severe, rigorous, rigid, strict, close.

4. fussy, finicky, particular, overparticular, finical, meticulous; picky, *Inf.* choosy, dainty, *Inf.* fuddy-duddy, *Inf.* pernickety; discriminating, highly selective, careful; fastidious, hard to please, critical, difficult; overcritical, hypercritical, overdemanding, overexacting.

—*n.* **5.** item, feature, particularity.

particularism, *n.* partisanship; denominationalism, cultism; nationalism.

particularity, *n.* **1.** individuality, distinctness, separateness, difference, definiteness, distinction, originality, uniqueness.

2. carefulness, attention to details, criticalness; fastidiousness, fussiness, finickiness, finicalness, meticulousness; pickiness, *Inf.* choosiness, daintiness, *Inf.* persnicketiness.

3. brand, trademark, hallmark, stamp, print, earmark; singularity, peculiarity, characteristic feature, trait; idiosyncrasy, quirk, mannerism.

particularize, *v.* **1.** individualize, make distinct, make unique, make original; separate, differentiate.

2. specify, spell out, delineate; relate, recount, narrate, set forth; describe, depict, portray, mention; cite, note, mark, point out, designate, indicate; detail, mention *or* list in detail, give full account, *Sl.* give *or* cite chapter and verse; tick off, count off, itemize, list, record, enumerate, tabulate.

3. treat in detail, dot one's i's and cross one's t's, be meticulous, be fastidious, be fussy, be critical; be finicky *or* finical.

particularly, *adv.* **1.** especially, specially, in particular; singularly, peculiarly, exceptionally, extraordinarily, strikingly, uncommonly, unusually, excessively, surprisingly.

2. specifically, individually, markedly, distinctly, uniquely, explicitly; mainly, principally, above all; only, solely.

3. in detail, minutely, critically, scrupulously, meticulously; fastidiously, finically, fussily.

parting, *n.* **1.** division, schism, partition, separation, scission, cleavage; rift, divorce, split, severance, disunion, disjunction, disruption; disengagement, disassociation, disconnection; fissure, rupture, fracture, break; cutting, breaking, splitting, rending, sundering; separating, divorcing, disengaging, disconnecting.

2. departure, leave-taking, farewell, going, going away, leaving; saying good-by *or* God-speed, making one's adieus *or* farewells, valediction; slamming the door behind one, walking out, *Inf.* scramming, taking off; removal, release, withdrawal, retirement.

3. death, decease, demise, expiration, passing, passing away; end, cessation, termination, exit; going to sleep, going west, crossing the Great Divide; *All Sl.* kicking the bucket, croaking, conking out.

4. branching off, fork, crossroads, breach; divergence, deviation, detachment, divarication, bifurcation; juncture, crisis, crisis point.

—*adj.* **5.** farewell, *Inf.* send-off, departing, valedictory.

6. dying, deathbed, last, final, ending, closing, finishing, concluding; sinking, dropping, crumbling, tottering, toppling; passing, failing, nodding, sleepy; waning, ebbing, fading, withering, flickering, spent.

partisan, *n.* **1.** adherent, devotee, follower, supporter, upholder, backer; champion, rooter, booster, fan, enthusiast, well-wisher; disciple, votary, sectary, believer; party man, party faithful; sympathizer, ally; henchman, hanger-on, heeler.

—*adj.* **2.** partial, one-sided, taking sides, ex parte; biased, bigoted, prejudiced, seeing only one side of the picture; narrow, limited, parochial, close-minded, narrow-minded; myopic, short-sighted, near-sighted, wearing blinders *or* blinkers, unable to see beyond the end of one's nose; restricted, circumscribed, constricted, confined; dogmatic, arbitrary, opinionated, (*of politics*) hewing to the party line; stiff-necked, stiff, rigid, unbending, dogged.

3. faithful, dedicated, supportive, devoted, sympathetic; true, true-blue, trusty, trusted, trustworthy.

partition, *n.* **1.** division, dividing, *Inf.* divvying up, subdivision, subdividing; apportionment, admeasurement, measuring off *or* out; allotment, allocation, assignment; meting out, portioning out, parceling out, dealing out, doling out, rationing out, *Inf.* dishing out; passing out, handing out, giving out, distribution, distributing, dispensation, dispensing.

2. separation, partitionment, segmentation; disconnection, detachment, disjunction, splitting, scissure; severance, parting, disunion, split, breach, break, rupture.

3. separator, divider, room divider, screen; dividing wall, wall, barrier, fence; brattice, *Civ. Eng.* bulkhead.

4. part, division, subdivision, section, subsection; portion, area, sector, segment, piece, square; compartment, booth, stall, cell; pigeonhole, cubby, cubbyhole, niche, cranny, nook, recess, corner.

5. (*all of a plant or animal structure*) dissepiment, *Biol.* septum, *Anat.* mediastinum, dividing wall, membrane, *Anat.* diaphragm.

—*v.* **6.** divide into parts, divide up, *Inf.* divvy up, subdivide, cut up, cut into equal shares, split *or* split up, separate, segment; apportion, admeasure, measure out *or* off; allot, allocate, assign; mete out, portion out, parcel out, deal out, dole out, ration out, *Inf.* dish out; pass out, hand out, give out, distribute, dispense.

partly, *adv.* in part, partially, partway, somewhat, to some extent, to some degree, to *or* in some measure; after a fashion, in a way, comparatively, relatively, comparatively *or* relatively speaking; to a degree, to a point, up to a point *or* certain point, up to a limit, to a limited extent, within limits; not wholly, not entirely, not completely, incompletely, half, mostly.

partner, *n.* **1.** associate, consociate, colleague, co-worker, co-partner, co-aid, *Sl.* pard, *U.S. Dial* pardner; counterpart, special *or* limited *or* general partner, silent *or* secret partner, *Obs.* copemate *or* copesmate,

Scot. and North Eng. marrow, *Australian.* cobber, yokefellow *or* yokemate, helpmate, helpmeet, *Obs.* helpfellow, right hand, right-hand man; ally, comrade, consort, confrere, sidekick, friend, *Inf.* pal, *Inf.* buddy, *Chiefly Brit.* mate.

2. accomplice, *Law.* accessory, *Law.* accessory before *or* after the fact, *Law.* principal, partner in crime, *Sl.* gun moll *or* moll, *Law.* particeps criminis, socius criminis; confederate, abettor, aider, collaborator, cooperator, contributor, cohort, conspirator, fellow conspirator, conspirer, conniver, participant, participator; helper, aide, attendant, acolyte, deputy, subsidiary, auxiliary, ancilla, second, henchman.

3. spouse, husband *or* wife, common-law husband *or* wife, *Inf.* better half; married man, benedict, bridegroom, groom, *Inf.* hubbie, *Sl.* old man, *Archaic.* goodman; married woman, wedded wife, bride, housewife, woman, lady, matron, *Amer. Ind.* squaw, wife of one's bosom, *Law.* feme, *Law.* feme covert, concubine, *Inf.* missis, *Inf.* little woman, *Hum.* rib, *Sl.* old lady *or* woman, *Scot. Inf.* wifey, *Archaic.* goodwife *or* goody; *All Rhyming Slang.* storm and strife, struggle and strife, trouble and strife, worry and strife, *Rare.* war and strife, Dutchess of Fife, drum and fife, *Hum. or Derog.* joy of my life; (*in reference to one's girl friend*) mother of pearl, (*both in reference to one's wife*) cheese and kisses, plates and dishes.

partnership, *n.* **1.** association, consociation, affiliation, participation, fraternization, interest, joint interest, connection, combination, co-partnership; collaboration, cooperation, sharing, concurrence; fellowship, friendship, companionship, comradeship, brotherhood, brotherliness, comradery, camaraderie, amity, geniality, good feeling, good-fellowship, mutual trust; connivance, complicity, collusion, abetment, intrigue.

2. company, corporation, incorporation, conglomerate, trust, syndicate, cartel, combine, machine; junction, fusion, merger, merging; society, guild; pool, cooperative, cooperation, co-op; conspiracy, cabal, plot, complot, junto, camarilla, secret group; alliance, coalition, entente, union, league, bloc, bund, federation, federacy, confederation, confederacy.

3. contract, pact, compact, formal agreement; settlement, arrangement, understanding, cordial understanding, agreement, gentlemen's agreement, deal, bargain, transaction.

parturition, *n.* childbirth, parturiency, labor, travail, *Fr. accouchement*; bearing, childbearing, delivery, childbed, confinement, lying-in, *Med.* eutocia, *Med.* dystocia; nativity, birth, genesis.

party, *n.* **1.** social gathering, social, gathering, get-together, *U.S. Dial.* gam, *Chiefly U.S.* bee; dinner party, luncheon, brunch, après-ski, soiree, levee, reception, at-home, drop-in; dance, ball, *Inf.* hop; *Inf.* shindig, *Inf.* do, *Inf.* bust-up, *Sl.* shivaree, *Sl.* jamboree, *All Sl.* wing-ding, blast, bash, blow out, bust; saturnalia, carousal, debauch, orgy, bacchanalia; celebration, fete, festivities, doing, fun and games, frolic, high old time, spree, lark, *Inf.* highjinks.

2. assemblage, assembly, congregation, company; group, band, gang; troop, troupe, team, crew, squad, corps, body; detail, detachment, squadron, regiment, brigade, battalion, platoon.

3. contingent, sector, section, sect, denomination, division, side, interest, special interest group, faction, splinter party; coterie, coalition, caucus, bloc, camorra, cabal, camarilla, junto, *Inf.* push, (*in French and Belgian politics*) cartel; set, clique, circle, ring, knot, *Inf.* crowd, clan; league, alliance, association, affiliation, federation, union, guild, *Inf.* outfit; fraternity, brotherhood, sorority, sisterhood, sodality, club, lodge.

4. partisanship, partisanry, partisanism, party politics, sectarianism, factionalism; partiality, bias, prejudice, one-sidedness, unilaterality, unilateralism.

5. participant, participator, part, member, associate, partner, co-partner, partaker, sharer; *Law.* litigant, *Law.* plaintiff, *Law.* defendant, *Law.* signatory; confederate, conspirator, co-conspirator, contributor, helper, aide, cooperator, abettor.

6. person, individual, one, creature, human, human being, being, soul; man, fellow, guy, boy; woman, lady, girl.

—adj. **7.** partisan, coalitional, sectarian, factional, divisional, ex-parte, special interest, *Both U.S. Government.* Democratic, Republican; partial, taking sides, prejudiced, biased, one-sided, unilateral; parochial, doctrinaire, dogmatic, rigid, unbending; narrow-minded, limited, unable to see beyond the end of one's nose, short-sighted, myopic, near-sighted.

8. party-going, partying, dancing; cocktail, dance, ball, evening; special, good, dressy, fancy, frilly.

—v. **9.** *Informal.* enjoy oneself, have a good *or* merry *or* high old time, *Sl.* laugh *or* yuk it up, have a ball *or* blast, *Sl.* party hearty; go out *or* have a night out on the town, have a spree *or* a lark, *Sl.* paint the town red, night-club, barhop, pub-crawl, go out dancing *or* drinking, trip the light fantastic, dance the night away, *Sl.* boogie, *Inf.* booze it up.

parvenu, *n.* **1.** arrivé, arriviste, nouveau riche, newly rich, social climber, status seeker, snob; *Sl.* pig in clover, *Inf.* codfish aristocrat; upstart, nobody, impostor, intruder, pretender, adventurer, *Inf.* would-be.

—adj. **2.** nouveau riche, newly-rich, upstart, risen from the ranks; common, plebeian, baseborn, earthborn; pretentious, precocious, presumptuous, *Sl.* cocky, obtrusive; bluffing, pretending, feigning; forward, brash, brazen, *Sl.* brassy, *Sl.* cheeky, audacious, arrogant, impudent, insolent, impertinent.

pass, *v.* **1.** go by, move past, flow, roll, run, stream, course; glide, slide, sweep, drift; proceed, progress, advance, gain ground; move onward, work one's way, wend one's way; run along, hie, hasten, make haste, hurry along, jog along, rush, zip, fly, swoosh, whoosh.

2. disregard, overlook, pass over, omit; skip, miss, let go, let slip, waive; slight, snub, brush off, blink at; slur over, gloss over, skip over; ignore, not heed, pay no attention to, turn a deaf ear to, close one's eyes to, be blind to; put aside, push aside, forget, drop, shelve; *Inf.* pass the buck, shift, *Inf.* buck; avoid, evade, shun, elude, dodge.

3. traverse, go over, go across, cross, ford; cut across, get through, make it over; overpass, overleap, overjump.

4. qualify, satisfy, succeed, graduate; accomplish, achieve, finish, reach, *Sl.* connect, *Sl.* click, *Sl.* make a hit; come through, get through, pass with flying colors, *Sl.* ace; *Sl.* hook, *Inf.* get by, pass by the skin of one's teeth, *Sl.* cut it, *Sl.* hack it; stand the test, meet the requirements, come up to scratch; hold up, stand up, endure, live through.

5. transcend, surmount, exceed, surpass, excel, go further, go one better; outgo, override, outstrip, overtake, take the lead; overrun, overstep, overshoot, overreach; outdistance, distance, get ahead of, get in front of, lap, overlap, leave in the lurch.

6. spend, occupy, employ, use, take up, fill; while, bide, beguile; squander, fritter away, dissipate, kill.

7. spread, circulate, disseminate, propagate, pass out; vent, air, promulgate, report, make known, tell; publicize, make public, broadcast; herald, blazon, trumpet, bruit, hawk; divulge, put forth, bring into the

open, bring to the public eye; advance, promote.
8. gain currency, be current, go about, circulate, get afloat, go down; be the rage, have a run, be on everybody's lips, be the talk of the town; go the rounds, go from mouth to mouth, spread like wildfire.
9. convey, transfer, transmit, consign, grant; deliver, render, put in the hands of, hand over, give over; forward, send, post; give, confer, present.
10. discharge, void, expel, eliminate, empty; eject, egest, emit, evacuate, defecate; excrete, stool, go to stool, ease oneself, move one's bowels, empty one's bowels.
11. sanction, accept, approve, ratify, legislate, adopt; legalize, legitimate, clear, validate; charter, license, empower, warrant, authorize; decree, ordain, prescribe, enforce; enact, formulate, set up, institute, establish, constitute.
12. express, pronounce, offer, deliver, announce, annunciate, aver; impart, utter, declare, state, speak, make known, declaim; voice, communicate, articulate, enunciate, enounce.
13. depart, go away, leave, go out, exit; go forth, go off, be off, set out, set forth; withdraw, retire, recede, abscond, retreat; decamp, abandon, take off, *Jocular.* absquatulate.
14. die, perish, pass away, pass on, expire, succumb; come to an end, end, cease, terminate, go; be gone, be all over, come to naught, be all up with; run out, come to a close, draw to a close, blow over; run its course, elapse, lapse, become void; dissolve, melt; sink, recede, ebb, *Inf.* peter out; vanish, disappear, fade away, die out, become extinct; evanesce, evaporate, go up in smoke.
15. elapse, pass away, flow, lapse; crawl, drag, linger; slip by, glide, flit, fleet, drift; endure, last, continue, go on.
16. interchange, exchange, alternate, reciprocate, change; go to and fro, go back and forth, come and go; trade, bandy, traffic, counterchange; dicker, swap, barter.
17. convert, change, alter, vary; transmute, transform, metamorphose, transfigure, metabolize; transubstantiate, transmogrify, translate; become, turn, turn into, grow, mellow, ripen.
18. go unheeded, go unnoticed, escape notice, not enter one's head; slip by, sneak by, get by, get around; go unchallenged, go uncensored, let it pass, *Inf.* let it go, *Inf.* let one off, turn the other way.
19. **come to pass** occur, happen, take place, come off, go on; befall, betide, present itself, bechance; appear, arise, come up, issue, ensue, come about.
20. **pass for** be accepted as, be taken for, be mistaken for, be regarded as; act the part of, pretend to be, assume the air of, sail under false colors; serve as, go for, go as, answer for; impersonate, pose as, masquerade as, make like, act like, play.
21. **pass out** *Informal.* faint, lose consciousness, black out, swoon; *Inf.* keel over, drop, fall, go out.
22. **pass up** *Informal.* reject, dismiss, waive, refuse, forswear, decline; neglect, miss, ignore, let go; brush aside, spurn, put aside, discount; throw out, discard, turn out, brush off, *Inf.* chuck out; forgo, give a miss, draw a bye, not bid, fold.
—n. **23.** road, way, path, trail, course; channel, passage, canal, conduit, passageway; corridor, hall, alley, lane; defile, tunnel, ingress, way through; neck, bottleneck, isthmus; ravine, gulch, gully, crevasse, canyon, narrows; *Phys. Geog.* col, vale, valley, cwm, cirque.
24. permission, authorization, warrant, grant, fiat; license. authority, privilege, allowance, certification; approval, approbation, OK, blessing; release, waiver, liberty, freedom, leave, special permission; passport, visa, password, ticket, safe-conduct; green light, go-ahead, all clear, clearance, clean bill of health, *Rom. Cath. Ch.* nihil obstat, *Rom. Cath. Ch.* imprimatur; free hand, carte blanche, blank check.
25. free ticket, free admission, key, key to the city; permit, free pass, complimentary ticket, *Inf.* twofer; press card, courtesy card, *Sl.* Annie Oakley.
26. *Informal.* move, overture, advance, offer, invitation, proposition; wink, look, sly look, come-hither look.
27. state of affairs, state of things, situation, condition, circumstance, position; predicament, plight, *Sl.* fix, pinch, push, rub, straits; dilemma, quandary, perplexity, intricacy; *Inf.* clutch, *Sl.* jam, *Sl.* hole, *Inf.* mess; hot water, stew, kettle of fish, *Sl.* pickle, imbroglio, *Brit.* sticky wicket, cleft stick; emergency, exigency, crisis, urgency, extremity, juncture, closure; impasse, standstill, cul de sac, blind alley, tight corner, checkmate, stalemate; embarrassment, nonplus.
28. sleight, sleight of hand, prestidigitation, legerdemain; jugglery, juggle, trick, trickery, illusion, magic.
29. thrust, lunge, *Archaic.* foin, stab, jab; cut, cut and thrust, swipe, feint.
30. *Sports.* throw, hurl, heave, cast; fling, lob, sling, toss, flip, pitch, shot, *Inf.* peg; *Track and Field.* put, shot put, *Football.* lateral pass, forward pass, pitchout, *Tennis.* serve.

passable, *adj.* **1.** traversable, crossable, penetrable, navigable, fordable; unblocked, unimpeded, unobstructed; open, free, clear.
2. respectable, tolerable, acceptable, adequate; satisfactory, all right, unexceptional; presentable, admissible, allowable, fairly good, *Inf.* not that good, not bad, not too bad; fair, *Inf.* no great shakes, mediocre, middling, average, indifferent, so-so, *Inf.* nothing to write home *or* brag about; ordinary, common, commonplace, usual, moderate; inferior, second-rate, of sorts, paltry, scant, meager.
3. sound, valid, authentic, orthodox; current, prevailing, recognized.

passably, *adv.* fairly, moderately, tolerably, mildly; rather, somewhat, pretty much, appreciably; relatively, partly, partially, comparatively; to a certain degree *or* extent, to some degree, to a degree; in a way, in a manner of speaking, after a fashion; at best, at most, at any rate, at least, at worst.

passage, *n.* **1.** portion, section, part, bit, article; selection, excerpt, extract, (*pl.*) analects; paragraph, verse, line, sentence, clause, quotation, citation; chapter, column; fascicle, installment, serial, number.
2. phrase, measure, strain, bar; verse, stanza, division; refrain, response, chorus; ornament, cadence, flourish; theme, melody, air, coda.
3. passing, transition, transit, traverse, crossing; movement, progress, growth, motion, going, transportation; conversion, change, becoming, turning into; switch, shift, changeover; assimilation, assumption, naturalization, acclimatization; migration, transmigration, emigration, immigration, deportation.
4. permission, allowance, vouchsafement, authorization; right, privilege, authority, grant, warrant, license; passport, ticket, visa, safe-conduct; freedom, liberty, unconstraint, leave; entry, access, entrée, admission.
5. route, course, set, career; trail, path, track, road; channel, canal, conduit, duct, artery, capillary; ditch, furrow, trough, trench, gutter, anfractuosity, *Mining.* adit; defile, tunnel, channel, ingress, way through; ravine, pass, gully, gulch, crevasse, canyon, narrows; *Phys. Geog.* col, vale, valley, cwm, cirque; neck, bot-

tleneck, isthmus, spit.
6. hall, corridor, alleyway, alley. See **passageway**.
7. opening, aperture, hole, orifice; vent, porthole, mouth, spiracle, blowhole; eyelet, eye of a needle, pore; entrance, entry, entrée, access, approach; inlet, ingress, intake, way in, *Inf.* in; exit, outlet, egress, way out, *Inf.* out, gangplank.
8. voyage, trip, journey; crossing, cruise, sail, steam, run.
9. lapse, passing, expiration; flow, course, current, stream; drift, career, sweep, flux, tide, flight; progress, progression, march, step, advance; continuity, continuance, extension; period, space, stage, spell, duration.
10. enactment, ratification, legislation, establishment, constitutionalization; legalization, validation, legitimation; sanction, approval, approbation, acceptance, adoption, endorsement; ordainment, fixing, prescription.
11. interchange, exchange, give and take, intercourse, interplay, reciprocity; transaction, trading, traffic, trafficking, commerce; correspondence, communication, connection, liaison, union, congress; discussion, negotiation, interlocution, dialogue, colloquy, *Sl.* rapping.
12. transmission, transfer, transmittal, transference, *Pathol.* metastasis; transposition, transposal, transplantation, translocation, metathesis.

passageway, *n.* hall, corridor, hallway, gallery; arcade, gangway, ambulatory, mall; alleyway, aisle, passage, areaway, breezeway; portico, colonnade, covered way, cloister, pergola, loggia, peristyle; portal, port, entrance, exit, entryway, doorway, threshold, sill; sidewalk, walk, walkway, garden path; stairwell, stairs, steps, *Naut.* companionway.

passé, *adj.* **1.** out-of-date, outmoded, antiquated, outworn; obsolete, obsolescent, dated, on the way out, past its prime, out of style; superseded, out of use, disused, fallen into disuse, shelved, on the shelf, stale, gone to seed, discarded; rejected, discredited, forgotten; bygone, past, *Archaic.* olden; old-fashioned, old hat, old-time, old-fogyish; unmodern, of the old school, old-world, horse-and-buggy.
2. aged, ancient, old, elderly, archaic, fossil, antique; old as the hills, over the hill, timeworn, moss-grown; venerable, gray, hoary, patriarchal, retired.

passel, *n.* group, collection, bunch, some, lot, a lot; quantity, heap, mass, mess; array, assortment, spectrum; assemblage, agglomeration, conglomeration; multitude, host, company; party, body, congregation; gathering, crowd, drove, herd, gaggle, swarm.

passenger, *n.* **1.** rider, fare; equestrian, horseman; train patron, airplane passenger; sailor, boatman; hitch-hiker.
2. wayfarer, journeyer, voyager, trekker; tourist, sightseer, commuter, cruiser, traveler, globetrotter, jet-setter, *Inf.* bird of passage, world traveler; walker, hiker, wanderer, explorer, roamer, rover; peregrinator, itinerant, nomad, drifter, *Inf.* bum, vagabond.

passer-by, *n.* bystander, witness, spectator, passer; pedestrian, passing motorist, onlooker, watcher; dispassionate person, uninvolved bystander; good Samaritan.

passing, *adj.* **1.** elapsing, lapsing, expiring, departing, dying; dwindling, disappearing, fading, evaporating, fading away; slipping away, flitting, streaming, gliding by, going by, running its course, becoming a thing of the past, running out; proceeding, progressing, ongoing, mobile; sliding, slipping, *Inf.* slipsliding away.
2. transient, fleeting, transitory, caducous, fugacious; not lasting, mortal, vanishing, transitional, transitive; temporal, short-lived, perishable, here today and gone tomorrow; momentary, impermanent, ephemeral, temporary, nonpermanent, meteoric, cometary, flashing, flash-in-the-pan; flickering, unstable, precarious, fragile, unsubstantial; changeable, ever-changing, capricious, fickle, impulsive, impetuous, fly-by-night, wayward, vagrant; provisional, intermediate, short-term, short-termed; moving, shifting, inconstant, fugitive.
3. cursory, hasty, superficial, shallow, slight, surface; casual, off-hand, extemporaneous, extempore; brief, quick, glancing, short; fleet, speedy, breezy, brisk, sudden, rapid, swift; abrupt, brusque, summary, impatient, unthinking.
4. qualifying, admissible, worthy; acceptable, satisfactory, sufficient, sufficing, adequate, commensurate; unobjectionable, tolerable, average, par, *Inf.* par for the course, *Inf.* OK *or* okay, *Inf.* all right *or* alright; bordering, just over the line, safe, marginal, fair, fair to middling, middling, undistinguished.
—*n.* **5.** going by, disappearance, disappearing, vanishing, dissipation, dissipating, dissolving, evaporation, eclipse, end; passing away, dying, death, demise, expiration, parting, cessation, exit. See **parting** (*def.* **3**).
6. passage, adoption, yes vote, acceptance; promotion, selection, election; preferment, appointment.
7. **in passing** by the way, incidentally, parenthetically, *Fr. en passant*, by the by.

passion, *n.* **1.** rage, blind rage, fit, fit of anger *or* temper, paroxysm, convulsion, spasm, seizure; storm, eruption, explosion, outburst, rampage, tornado, whirlwind, tempest, towering rage, frenzy, blaze, blaze of temper *or* anger, *Inf.* conniption *or* conniption fit, *Inf.* dither, *Inf.* tizzy, *Inf.* tantrum *or* temper tantrum, *Inf.* huff, *Sl.* swivet, *Inf.* lather; pother, furor, ferment, bluster, dudgeon, high dudgeon, pique, pet; anger, wrath, fury, hot blood, hot temper, fire, wrathfulness, vehemence, agitation, *Inf.* stew; fierceness, temper, spleen, bile, choler, ire, irefulness; resentment, seething, indignation, *Inf.* dander.
2. ardor, zeal, fervor, fervency, emotion, excitement; strong feeling, intensity, intentness, fervidness, spirit, vitality; exhilaration, eagerness, earnestness, avidity, zest, zestfulness, vivacity, animation, verve, gusto; rush, rush *or* surge of emotion, impetuosity, abandon, vehemence, overzealousness, overeagerness, overenthusiasm, fanaticism, zealotry; excitability, explosiveness, tempestuousness, passionateness, impassionedness; theatricality, sensationalism, emotionalism, emotiveness.
3. desire, hunger, thirst, appetite, appetence *or* appentency, craving; lust, aphrodisia, carnal *or* sexual passion, coveting, concupiscence, estrous *or* oestrous, rut, goatishness, horniness, *Sl.* hot pants; flaming desire, frenzy of desire, desideration; urge, irresistible urge, drive, itch, ache, pang; arousal, distress, impatience, panting, heaving; heat, fire, fever, aching, urgency, yearning, need, longing, *Inf.* yen, *Inf.* hankering; ardor, amorousness, ecstasy, ravishment, transport, rapture, delirium, intoxication; palpitation, throb, throbbing, quiver, shiver, tremor; warmth of feeling, warmth, flush, thrill.
4. love, strong affection, predilection, partiality, *Inf.* weakness, *Inf.* crush; enthusiasm, keen interest, seriousness, application, preoccupation, fascination, dedication, compulsion; idolatry, idolization, *Inf.* hero worship, adoration; involvement, immersion, rapt attention, absorbed attention *or* interest, lust for learning, thirst for knowledge; prepossession.
5. loved one, beloved, object of one's affections; idol, hero, favorite, *Inf.* heartthrob, *Inf.* dreamgirl *or*

dreamboy, *Inf.* dreamboat; heart's desire, dearest wish, fondest dream *or* hope, craze, obsession, mania; interest, intense curiosity, matter of interest, *Inf.* hobby-horse; fancy, desideratum; aspiration, ambition; magnet, temptation, object of passion, fixation, *Psychoanal.* cathexis, *Psychoanal.* hypercathexis; ruling passion, fixed idea, *Fr. idée fixe*, possession.

passionate, *adj.* **1.** impassioned, impassionate, ardent, vehement, zealous; overzealous, overeager, overanxious, *Inf.* gung-ho; fervent, fervid, perfervid; earnest, eager, animated, enthusiastic, enthused, *Inf.* psyched *or* psyched up; excited, sparkling, glowing, lively, alive, full of life, vivacious, *Inf.* bright-eyed and bushy-tailed; enlivened, inspired, inspirited, invigorated, energized, energetic, vivified, vitalized; vigorous, forceful, dynamic, high-powered.

2. heated, white-hot, inflamed, flaming, flared up, flaring; irate, wrathful, wroth, incensed, very angry; enraged, raging, fuming, infuriated, infuriate, furious; overwrought, distraught, upset, feverish, hysterical, not rational; violent, unrestrained, uncontrollable; ranting, raving, foaming at the mouth, rabid, fanatical, frenzied; frantic, crazed, *Pathol.* delirious, mad, *Inf.* wild.

3. intense, acute, strong, fierce, severe; grievous, distressing, poignant, harrowing, afflictive; grave, critical, serious; profound, deep, intensified, consuming.

4. sexually stimulated, aroused, burning, blazing, *Inf.* hot, *Inf.* turned on; inflamed, infatuated, lusting after, *Sl.* hot for, *Sl.* letching after, mad about, *Inf.* wild about; desirous, intense, amorous, sensual, sexual, erotic.

5. testy, choleric, touchy, huffy, peppery; irritable, cross, snappish, petulant, peevish; splenetic, spleenful, bilious, cranky; irascible, quick-tempered, short-tempered, *Inf.* short-fused; quarrelsome, contentious, belligerent, pugnacious, bellicose; volatile, volcanic, explosive, hot-tempered, hot-headed; fiery, inflammable, kindled, enkindled; excitable, temperamental, emotional, emotive, high-strung; head-strong, stubborn, impatient, impetuous, impulsive, hasty; agitated, nervous, tense, fretful; unquiet, disturbed, shaken, perturbed, worked up; stirred up, stormy, tempestuous, turbulent, tumultuous.

passionless, *adj.* **1.** cold, unemotional, frigid, frozen, icy, cold-hearted; emotionless, emotionally dead *or* numb, unresponsive, unaffectionate, unloving, immovable, untouchable; undesirous, desireless, inappetent, unenthusiastic, uneager, bored, uninterested; half-hearted, perfunctory, lukewarm, *Inf.* turned off; inaccessible, unapproachable, aloof, distant, remote, withdrawn, cool, chilly, frosty; indifferent, unconcerned, uncaring, oblivious, unimpressed, unmoved, apathetic.

2. cold-blooded, hard, callous, calloused, insensitive, thickskinned, hardhearted, hardened, impervious, steeled against, steely, stony, *Inf.* hard as nails; unfeeling, insensible, unconscious, blind to, deaf to; soulless, heartless, cold as charity; unsympathetic, untouched, unstirred, unmoved, indurate, inured; unruffled, unperturbed.

3. uninviting, forbidding, inhospitable, standoffish; uninteresting, uncompelling, uninspiring, unimaginative; lifeless, dull, vapid, vacuous, vacant, blank, fatuous, inane, jejune; insipid, prosaic, flat, listless, spiritless, zestless, drab, lackluster; tame, mediocre, bloodless; humdrum, commonplace, matter-of-fact, tedious, tiresome, wearisome, uninspired, boring.

4. supine, lethargic, phlegmatic, sluggish, torpid, languid; dispassionate, impassive, stolid, bovine, hopeless, numb, benumbed, stupefied, *Inf.* dull as dishwater, *Sl.* blah; sophisticated, jaded, blasé, insouciant, nonchalant, unanxious, pococurante, lackadaisical.

5. inexcitable, imperturbable, equanimous, self-possessed, self-controlled, self-restrained, restrained, controlled, in control; stable, untroubled, collected, coolheaded, poised, *Inf.* cool as a cucumber; *Inf.* calm, cool, and collected; *Inf.* unflappable, nerveless; unruffled, even-tempered, calm, composed, placid, tranquil, serene, sedate, staid, sober, sober-minded, stoic, stoical, philosophical; at peace, at peace with oneself, at peace with the world, resigned.

6. detached, unprejudiced, unopinionated, undogmatic, open-minded, reasonable; impartial, impersonal, disinterested, unbiased, neutral, noncommitted, uncommitted, noninvolved, uninvolved, neither hot nor cold, nonpartisan.

passive, *adj.* **1.** unresponsive, undemonstrative, unemotional, dispassionate, stoic, philosophic, philosophical; impassive, unmoved, stolid, bovine; imperturbable, unprovokable; unperturbed, unagitated, unaffected, untouched, cool.

2. nonparticipating, uninvolved, uninterested, indifferent, unconcerned, apathetic, neutral; lazy, indolent, otiose, dronish, parasitic, fainéant; languid, languorous, listless, feeble, weak, faint; sluggish, lymphatic, phlegmatic, torpid, torpescent, comatose; lethargic, hebetudinous, heavy, leaden, dull.

3. inactive, lifeless, zestless, insipid, bland; quiet, still, idle, recumbent, supine, inert; quiescent, peaceful, pacific, calm, tranquil, serene, placid, reposeful, restful; motionless, unmoving, static, suspended, abeyant, stagnating, stagnant.

4. nonresisting, nonresistant, unresisting, unopposing, submissive; yielding, acquiescent, compliant, pliant; obedient, docile, tractable, conformable, biddable; malleable, pliable, influenceable, flexible, irresolute; unassertive, unasserting, obliging, agreeable, amenable, complaisant; subdued, meek, humble, lamblike, gentle, tame; deferential, servile, obsequious, toadyish.

5. tolerant, tolerating, forbearing, patient; accepting, receptive, resigned; long-suffering, enduring, endurant.

6. dormant, latent, dormient, sleeping; unexpressed, undisclosed, unrevealed, undemonstrated, implicit; potential, unrealized; internal, interior.

passiveness, passivity, *n.* **1.** unresponsiveness, undemonstrativeness, dispassion, stoicism, philosophicalness; impassiveness, impassivity, stolidity, stolidness, bovinity; imperturbability, unprovokability; cool, coolness, composure.

2. inactivity, nonparticipation, indifference, apathy; unconcern, uninterestedness; disinterest, dispassionateness, objectivity, neutrality; inaction, nonintervention, noninterference, laissez faire.

3. nonresistance, acceptance, submission; yielding, acquiescence, compliance, resignation, resignedness; tolerance, toleration, forbearance, patience; endurance, sufferance, long-suffering, longanimity.

4. submissiveness, docility, unassertiveness, meekness, humbleness, humility, gentleness, tameness; deference, servility, servileness, obsequiousness, toadyism.

5. obedience, tractability, tractableness, conformability, conformableness, biddability, biddableness; malleability, malleableness, pliability, pliableness, flexibility; obligingness, agreeability, agreeableness, amenability, amenableness, complaisance.

6. languor, lassitude, listlessness, feebleness, weakness, faintness; laziness, indolence, idleness, otioseness, otiosity, supineness; sluggishness, phlegm, lethargy, hebetude, heaviness, dullness, torpor, inertia.

7. quiet, quietness, quietude, stillness; peace, peacefulness, calmness, calm, tranquillity, tranquilness; serenity, sereneness, placidness, placidity.

8. motionlessness, immobility, inertness, stasis, stagnation; suspension, abeyance, quiescence, latency, dormancy; sleep, slumber, rest, repose.

9. repression, suppression, containment, withholding; hiddenness, concealment; potentiality, potency.

10. lifelessness, zestlessness, blandness, insipidness, insipidity, dullness, boringness.

passport, *n.* **1.** travel authorization, travel permit, travel document *or* papers, visa, permission, warrant, sanction, *Fr. carte de visite, Fr. carte d'identité.*

2. credentials, identification, identity card, ID card, ID, letter of introduction, certification, permit, license.

3. clearance, clearance papers, bill of health, clean bill of health, *Commerce.* pratique, release, waiver; safe-conduct pass, *Inf.* green light, *Inf.* OK, *Inf.* go-ahead.

4. access, admission, admittance, permission to enter, right of entry, entry, entrée, *Fr. carte d'entrée*; pass, press card *or* pass, police card, passe-partout, carte blanche, *Inf.* blank check, *Inf.* ticket; open sesame, *Inf.* the secret word, key to the city, *Inf.* the run of the place; entrance, channel, avenue, means of access, influence, *Sl.* pull.

password, *n.* **1.** watchword, shibboleth, *Fr. mot de passe, Fr. passe-parole*, word of identification; keyword, open sesame.

2. countersign, secret grip, secret handshake.

past, *adj.* **1.** gone, gone by, bygone, by, ago, long-ago, long gone; over, over and done with, forgotten, long forgotten, dead and buried, blown over; elapsed, lapsed, expired, run out, gone by; finished, finished up, defunct, no more, wound up, ended, deceased, departed, passed, passed away, dead and gone, late lamented; vanished, extinct, never to return; gone to seed, past its prime; passé, obsolete, dated, antique, antiquated, archaic, over the hill, has-been, dated, gone out, out, out of style *or* use, out of fashion, unfashionable, out-of-date; outworn, old, olden, early, ancient, immemorial; primeval, prehistoric, precultural, premundane, antediluvian, primitive, pristine.

2. recent, late, former, previous, prior, just gone by, preceding, antecedent, anterior, precedent, precurrent; ex-, onetime, sometime, erstwhile, whilom, quondam, foregoing, aforegoing, pre-existent, preliminary, fore, last, once, then, latter, earlier, foregone; older, elder, senior, retired.

—n. **3.** recent past, yesterday, yesteryear, foretime; the past, former times, times past, old *or* olden days, bygone days; horse and buggy days, the good old days, way back when, *Scot. and North Eng.* auld lang syne, long-ago days, days long gone, nostalgic memories; the dim *or* faded past, time immemorial, the dead past, days of old, days *or* times of yore, early times *or* days, once upon a time, days beyond recall, when Hector was a pup, ancient times, antiquity, ancient history, long ago.

4. previous life, youth, childhood, one's early *or* formative years, one's school *or* salad days, the springtime of one's life, memories, fond memories, recollection, reminiscence, remembrance, retrospection; experience, one's life story, memoir, biography, life, life history, review; shady past, purple past, misspent youth.

—adv. **5.** by, beyond, over, across, the other *or* far side of; near, close, hard by, nigh; nearby, close by, not far beyond, near *or* close at hand, at no great distance, only a step away, within reach *or* range, within earshot *or* call, within a stone's throw, *Inf.* in spitting distance *or* range, at one's side, within one's reach *or* grasp; farther, further.

—prep. **6.** after, later than, subsequent to, beyond, over; in excess of, over and beyond, above and beyond.

pasta, *n.* noodles, macaroni, elbow macaroni, spaghetti, spaghettini, fettucini, fusilli, vermicelli, tagliarini, gnocchi; shells, conchiglie, ravioli, tortellini; tubes, ziti, manicotti, cannelloni, rigati, rigatoni, calzone; linguini, lasagna; pastina, alphabets, macaroni wheels, rotelle, farfalle, ditali, cappelletti, little hats.

paste, *n.* **1.** adhesive, adherent, binding, binder; cement, gum, library paste, lime, luting, lute, mastic, mucilage, putty, rubber cement, glue, plaster, adhesive plaster, *Sl.* stickum, *Sl.* gunk; parget, plaster of Paris.

2. compound, blend, concoction, combination, magma; emulsion, emulsoid, colloid.

3. dough, batter, fritter *or* pancake batter, *Cookery.* sponge; sourdough, starter, biscuit dough, beancurd, curd, pastry.

4. pâté, spread, *Inf.* dip, *Inf.* dunk; purée; gruel, porridge, pabulum, pap, *Dial.* loblolly; gluten, starch paste, corn starch paste, soda paste, *Trademark.* Play-doh, *Trademark.* Silly Putty.

5. pulp, mush, mash, poultice, *Med.* cataplasm, plaster, pastille, pith, paper pulp, wood pulp, white lead; sticky mess, sludge, slime, clay, *Inf.* mishmash, *Inf.* stickey pie, *Inf.* soupy mess, *All Sl.* yuk, ick, ook, goop, goo, glop.

6. (*all of jewelry*) fake, sham, imitation, counterfeit, simulation, *Sl.* phony, *Inf.* junk.

—v. **7.** stick, affix, attach, secure, cement, set, make fast, stick on, glue, gum; stick together, bind, join, bond, unite, paste together, fix together, mend, piece together, knit.

8. spread, spread on *or* over, coat, cover, plaster, parget; smear, smear on, besmear, dab, daub, bedaub, slather.

9. *Slang.* hit, punch, *Inf.* biff, *Inf.* bash, *Inf.* clip, *Inf.* slug.

pasteboard, *n.* **1.** cardboard, strawboard, paperboard, pulpboard, *Bookbinding.* millboard, binder's board.

2. *Slang.* card, calling card, visiting card; (*plural*) playing cards, pack, deck, *Inf.* fifty-two.

3. *Slang.* ticket, ticket of admission, stub, receipt, *Inf.* chit; script, pass, coupon, *Inf.* Annie Oakley.

—adj. **4.** unsubstantial, nonsubstantial, insubstantial, unsolid, hollow; flimsy, thin, fragile, frail, weak, jerry-built, jerry, unsound, infirm, unstable, breakable, frangible; shaky, unreliable, precarious, hazardous, not to be depended *or* relied upon.

5. trumped-up, made-up, make-believe, faked, feigned, unreal, brummagem, tinsel; mock, pseudo, sham, fake, imitation, false, synthetic, counterfeit, unreal, bogus; deceptive, misleading, paste, spurious, ungenuine, *Inf.* phony; bastardly, supposititious.

pastel, *n.* **1.** shade, tint, hint, tinge, suggestion, tincture, *Literary.* tinct; softness, soft color, subtle color, tone, cast.

2. sketch, drawing.

3. crayon, chalk, pastille, drawing pencil.

4. prose study, sketch, vignette, light piece.

—adj. **5.** shaded, soft, pale, faint, subdued, delicate; soft-colored, soft-hued, softened, muted.

pastiche, *n.* (*all of a literary, musical or artistic piece*) mélange, medley, pasticcio, mosaic, collage, patchwork; potpourri, olla-podrida, combination, *Inf.* combo; mixture, blend, intermixture, admixture, compound, composite, conglomeration; miscellany, miscellanea, omnium-gatherum, menagerie, motley; mishmash, hodgepodge, *Brit.* hotchpotch, gallimaufry, farrago, jumble, scramble, tangle.

pastille, *n.* **1.** lozenge, tablet, pill, *Pharm.* troche, jujube, drop, cough drop, *Pharm., Vet. Med.* bolus; hard candy, candy, confection, bonbon, sugarplum, sweetmeat, comfit.

2. deodorizer, room deodorizer *or* deodorant, air freshener, *Trademark.* Airwick Solid.

pastime, *n.* diversion, recreation, relaxation, divertissement, entertainment, distraction; amusement, fun, play, sport, game; hobby, avocation, sideline, side interest; *Inf.* cup of tea, *Sl.* thing, *Sl.* bag.

pastor, *n.* rector, vicar, shepherd, (*in France*) curé; dean, canon, prebendary, capitular; abbot, prior, abbé; chaplain; minister, priest, reverend, father, parson, divine, *Dial.* dominie; ecclesiastic, churchman, clergyman, cleric.

pastoral, *adj.* **1.** bucolic, simple, idyllic, paradisiacal, Edenic; serene, tranquil, halcyon, quiet, restful, peaceful, placid, pacific, irenic; modest, uncomplicated, uncomplex, unsophisticated, innocent, untainted, unblemished; sweet, lovely, gentle, harmonious; quiet, slow, unrushed, easy, lazy, carefree; charming, gracious, happy.

2. rural, country, countrified, rustic, Arcadian; outdoorsy, back-country, provincial; common, humble, lowly; georgic, agrarian, agricultural.

3. ministerial, clerical, churchly, ecclesiastical.

—*n.* **4.** idyll, eclogue, bucolic, georgic; *Music.* pastorale; pastoral poem, pastoral painting.

pastorate, *n.* pastorship, rectorship, vicarship, canonship, deanship, presbyterate, deaconry, chaplaincy, abbacy, prelacy; pastorage, vicarage, parish, church, flock; episcopate, bishopric, canonry, presbytery; see, diocese, chapter, province, jurisdiction, charge; benefice, living, *Brit.* incumbency.

pastry, *n.* pie, tart, *Brit.* tartlet, puff, cream puff, éclair, French pastry, *Fr. pâtisserie*; meat pie, *Brit.* pasty, vol-au-vent, patty shell; Danish pastry, *Inf.* Danish, coffeecake, coffeebread, doughnut, donut, cake, cupcake, petit four, ladyfinger.

pasturage, *n.* **1.** feed, fodder, provender; forage, eatage, herbage, pasture, grass.

2. range, grazing ground. See **pasture** (*def.* 1).

pasture, *n.* **1.** range, grazing ground, grass, grassland, pastureland, *Scot.* shieling; meadow, meadowland, lea, *Archaic.* mead.

2. feed; pasturage. See **pasturage** (*def.* 1).

—*v.* **3.** fodder, grass, put *or* turn out to pasture.

4. (*all of livestock*) forage, graze, browse, crop; feed on *or* upon, fatten on *or* upon.

pasty, *adj.* **1.** doughy; sticky, gluey, gluelike, glutinous; gummy, gumbo, mucilaginous; viscous, viscid.

2. pale, pallid, wan, sallow, tallow, waxen; anemic, sickly, pale-faced, tallow-faced, whey-faced.

pat[1], *v.* **1.** rap, tap, slap, box, cuff; dab; caress.

2. pat on the back *Informal.* encourage, embolden, hearten, nerve, *Inf.* buck up, bolster, assure, reassure; congratulate, *Archaic.* gratulate, praise, commend, shake [s.o.'s] hand, *Inf.* stroke.

—*n.* **3.** light blow, rap, tap, slap, box, cuff; dab; endearment, caress.

4. small piece, lump, chunk, *Inf.* hunk.

pat[2], *adj.* **1.** apt, apposite, relevant, to the point, germane, pertinent, apropos, applicable; appropriate, fit, fitting, suitable, well-chosen; perfect, right, just right, *Inf.* just what the doctor ordered, *Inf.* on the money, *Inf.* on the button, *Inf.* on the spot, *Brit. Sl.* spot on; opportune, seasonable, timely, well-timed, auspicious, fortunate; convenient, expedient, advantageous; felicitous, happy.

2. (*all excessively*) glib, facile, easy, slick, smooth.

3. mastered, perfected, *Inf.* down, *Inf.* down cold *or* pat; memorized, ingrained, infixed.

—*adv.* **4.** exactly, precisely, perfectly, flawlessly, faultlessly, just right, just so, dead, *Inf.* right on target, *Inf.* right on the button, *Inf.* right on the money.

5. aptly, relevantly, exactly to the point, germanely, pertinently, applicably; appropriately, fittingly, suitably; opportunely, seasonably, auspiciously, fortunately, favorably, right on time, just in time; conveniently, expediently, advantageously; happily, felicitously.

6. stand pat cling, hold firm, hold fast, not let go; stand fast, not budge, stand *or* hold one's ground, stick to one's guns, *Inf.* stay put.

patch, *n.* **1.** piece of material, piece, *Archaic.* clout.

2. snip, snippet, tag, tatter, scrap, shred, tag, stitch.

3. tract, plot, plot of land *or* ground, plat, lot, parcel of land, field, *Brit.* croft.

—*v.* **4.** mend, sew, sew up, stitch; darn, *Archaic.* clout; strengthen, reinforce; cover.

5. (*all usu. in a hasty or makeshift manner*) fix, *Inf.* fix up, repair, restore, recondition, *Inf.* doctor *or* doctor up; jury-rig, toss *or* throw together, slap together, knock together, *Brit.* knock up.

6. settle, settle differences, set straight *or* right, bring to terms; ameliorate, meliorate, appease, pacify, propitiate, placate, conciliate, pour oil on troubled waters.

patchwork, *n.* hodgepodge, *Brit.* hotchpotch, mishmash, jumble, tumble, scramble, tangle, mess, confused mess, confusion; conglomeration, pastiche, pasticcio, farrago, gallimaufry, Chinese menu, crazy quilt; medley, mélange, potpourri, mixture, *Sl.* mixed bag, *Inf.* grab bag; miscellany, omnium-gatherum.

patent, *n.* **1.** copyright, right, certificate of invention, *Law.* letters patent; trademark, registered trademark, trade name; license, permit, grant, charter, franchise.

2. invention, creation, brainchild; work, production, contrivance; process, procedure, method.

—*adj.* **3.** patented, copyrighted, copyright, trademarked, with all rights reserved; licensed, chartered, franchised.

4. apparent, evident, ostensible, perspicuous, palpable, tangible; obvious, self-evident, plain, plain as day, plain as can be, plain as a pikestaff; clear, clear-cut, crystal-clear, clear as the nose on one's face, manifest; definite, decided, pronounced, explicit, express, unmistakable, not to be mistaken; undoubted, undeniable, indisputable, indubitable, *Inf.* open-and-shut; conspicuous, prominent, recognizable, noticeable, visible, perceptible, perceivable, observable, for all to see; overt, open, exposed, unhidden, unconcealed, unscreened, unveiled, undisguised, unmasked, uncamouflaged; bald, bald-faced, blatant, flagrant, glaring.

—*v.* **5.** copyright, trademark; register, certify; originate, create, invent, discover.

paternal, *adj.* **1.** fatherly, fatherlike; patriarchal, patriarchic, paterfamiliar; kind, kindly, kindhearted; fond, loving, devoted; indulgent, solicitous; concerned, regardful.

2. patrilineal, patrimonial; patrilateral.

paternalism, *n.* benevolent depotism; (*all of an indulgent or benevolently overbearing nature*) direction, management, administration; supervision, superintendence, surveillance, oversight, *Inf.* bossing.

paternity, *n.* **1.** fatherhood, fathership, *Archaic.* sirehood *or* sireship.

2. lineage, line, bloodline, descent, parentage, patrilineage; blood, strain, stock, extraction.

3. origin, origination, creation, production; authorship, composition, inditement; formation, fabrication, fashioning, forming, shaping, molding.

path, *n.* **1.** footpath, *Brit.* footway, towpath, bike path, bikeway; pathway, trail, track; walk, walkway, sidewalk; median, centerstrip, mall, island; passage, passageway, alley, by-path, byway, crosscut, short cut; by-road, by-street, side road *or* street; lane, road, roadway, pavement; street, avenue, strip, boulevard; route, highway, turnpike; entrance, runway, ramp, access, approach, adit, inlet, ingress.

2. route, course, run, track; circuit, circle, sphere; orbit, trajectory, revolution, turn, loop; cycle, compass, lap, round, beat, ambit.

3. course, procedure, process, method, manner, mode, form, fashion, system; approach, way, means, channel, avenue; plan, project, scheme, strategy, stratagem, design, arrangement; idea, conception, device, contrivance.

4. cross one's path encounter, come upon *or* on, run into, come across, meet unexpectedly.

pathetic, *adj.* **1.** pitiable, pitiful, piteous, to be pitied, wretched; sad, doleful, dolorous, dolorific, sorrowful, mournful, grievous, plaintive; lamentable, regrettable, deplorable, rueful, woeful, woebegone.

2. touching, moving, affecting, affective, affectional, melting, heartrending, heart-moving, heartbreaking; tender, poignant, emotional, emotive.

3. paltry, puny, petty, piddling, poky, picayune, beggarly, *Inf.* measly, *Sl.* crummy, *Sl.* lousy, *Sl.* rotten; slight, skimpy, scrimpy, meager; (*all to an extreme degree*) insufficient, inadequate, unsatisfactory, dissatisfactory, unsatisfying, ungratifying.

pathfinder, *n.* trailblazer, trailbreaker, explorer; paver of the way; scout, guide, point; pioneer, frontiersman; forerunner, precursor, front *or* lead runner.

pathless, *adj.* trackless, wayless, untracked, unpathed, unexplored, uncharted, unpenetrated, untrodden, unopened; closed, impassable, impenetrable, inaccessible, impervious, imperviable, impermeable; dense, overgrown, jungled, jungly; waste, wild.

pathological, *adj.* morbid, diseased, bad, infected, contaminated; mortified, gangrened, gangrenous, sphacelated; poisoned, septic.

pathology, *n.* **1.** pathobiology; diagnostics, pathognomy, symptomatology, *Pathol.* etiology; nosology, nosography, nosogeography.

2. pathogenesis, nosogenesis.

pathos, *n.* pity, commiseration, condolence; sympathy, sympathetic response, fellow feeling, feeling, responsiveness; care, concern.

patience, *n.* **1.** composure, containment, aplomb, sang-froid, poise, self-possession; self-control, self-command, equanimity, equilibrium, dispassion, *Inf.* cool; quiescence, quiet, repose, stillness, calmness, peacefulness, peace; tranquillity, serenity, imperturbability, inexcitability, unflappability, even-temperedness, even temper.

2. forbearance, tolerance, toleration, endurance, sufferance, restraint; leniency, brooking, bearing with [s.o.]; long-suffering, stoicism, resignation; docility, tractability, pliancy, amenability; agreeableness, acquiescence, willingness to go along.

3. stamina, indefatigability, perseverance, singleness of purpose; persistence, staying power, tenacity, *Inf.* stick-to-it-iveness; assiduity, assiduousness, diligence, constancy.

patient, *n.* **1.** sick *or* ill person, infirm person, hospital case, case; asylum inmate, convalescent, outpatient, shut-in, valetudinarian; sufferer, victim, disease victim, accident victim, surgical case.

—adj. **2.** uncomplaining, long-suffering, enduring, unmurmuring, stoical; resigned, passive, accepting, unresistant; amenable, compliant, complying, cooperative, accommodating, agreeable; forbearing, forgiving, tolerant, clement; willing, disposed, assenting; acquiescent, capitulating, submissive, yielding, lamblike.

3. calm, quiet, reposeful, serene, unruffled, unexcited, unexcitable, imperturbable, unflappable; philosophical, tranquil, placid, peaceful, pacific; poised, balanced, steady; self-controlled, self-possessed, composed, collected, contained, *Inf.* together; nonchalant, at ease, dispassionate, *Inf.* cool; even-tempered, easygoing, relaxed, easy to get along with.

4. assiduous, sedulous, persistent, pertinacious; hardy, indefatigable, indomitable; persevering, plodding, tenacious, unremitting, *Inf.* stick-to-it-ive; resolute, resolved, inexorable, uncompromising; plucky, *Inf.* spunky, *Sl.* gutsy; unflinching, staunch, steadfast, unshakeable; unswerving, undeviating, unfaltering, firm, fixed; unwearied, untiring, unflagging.

patio, *n.* terrace, brick *or* flagstone terrace, porch, piazza; yard, compound, court, courtyard, quadrangle, *Inf.* quad; *Archit.* peristyle, *Archit.* cloister.

patois, *n.* **1.** regional *or* provincial speech, vernacular, vulgar tongue, peasant dialect, native *or* mother tongue; idiom, parlance, dialect, *Inf.* lingo, colloquial speech.

2. trade language, lingua franca, peddler's French, St. Giles Greek, pidgin, pidgin English.

3. jargon, cant, argot; educationese, computerese, academese, legalese, journalese, medicalese, newspaperese; shoptalk, newspeak, officialese, bureaucratese, Washingtonese; gobbledygook, patter, mumbo jumbo, gibberish, gibber; nonsense, humbug, flummery, *Sl.* bunk, rubbish, tommyrot, *Inf.* rot, *Sl.* garbage, *Sl.* horsefeathers; balderdash, hogwash, stuff and nonsense, *Inf.* bosh.

patriarch, *n.* **1.** antediluvian patriarch, early Biblical leader, leader of the early Israelites; *Gk. Orthodox and Eastern Churches.* ecumenical patriarch *or* archbishop; *Rom. Cath. Ch.* Pope *or* Pontiff; *Mormon Ch.* highest dignitary *or* Evangelist; hierarch, prelate, reverence, eminence, high *or* chief priest.

2. elder, senior, old man, wise man, dean, statesman, councilman, master, advisor, generarch; chief leader, pillar, pillar of the community, *Inf.* plankowner; veteran, retired statesman, graybeard, emeritus, grand old man; teacher, mentor, prototype; senior citizen, sexagenarian, septuagenarian, octogenarian, nonagenerian, centenarian.

3. progenitor, primogenitor, *Archaic.* predecessor, precursor; founder, source, forerunner; ancestor, forefather, forebear; paterfamilias, *Archaic.* sire, procreator, begetter, originator, generator, initiator; prime mover, architect, framer, designer.

patrician, *n.* **1.** aristocrat, nobleman, noble, silk-stocking, *Inf.* blue blood, gentleman; peer, lord, duke, marquis, earl, viscount, baron; grandee, magnifico, don, hidalgo, *Fr. Hist.* chevalier.

—adj. **2.** aristocratic, blue-blooded, silk-stocking, noble, gentle, genteel, wellborn, highborn; royal, princely, kingly, titled.

3. elegant, stately, grand, majestic, queenly; graceful, *Scot.* genty, thoroughbred, fine, delicate, exquisite; well-bred, polite, civil, mannerly, well-mannered, courteous; decorous, formal, proper, *Fr. comme il faut*, fitting, becoming, seemly; gracious, ladylike, ladyish, courtly, gentlemanly, gentlemanlike; debonair, charming, chivalrous, chivalric, gallant, cavalier; honorable, upright, virtuous, estimable, admirable, worthy, respectable.

4. polished, finished, refined, cultivated; urbane, suave, sophisticated, cosmopolitan, worldly; fashionable, stylish, à la mode, modish, high-toned, *Sl.* tony, high-class, *Sl.* classy, *Inf.* swank.

5. affected, mannered, unnatural; pretentious, *Inf.* highfalutin, *Inf.* high-hat, on one's high horse; haughty, lordly, hoity-toity, arrogant, proud, snobbish, disdainful.

patrimony, *n.* **1.** estate, inheritance, portion, share, lot; legacy, bequest, endowment, heirship, *Archaic.* heritance, gift; dot, dowry, *Law.* dower, *Law.* jointure, *Law.* hereditament; property, possessions, family real estate, family estate, family chattels *or* goods, holdings, belongings.

2. heritage, birthright; background, past, history; lineage, ancestry, anestral line, dynasty; family, heredity, inherited traits, genetic legacy; bloodline, pedigree, strain, stock, race.

patriot, *n.* nationalist, loyalist, jingo, jingoist, chauvinist, flag waver, hundred-percenter, *U.S.* spread-eagleist, lover of one's country.

patriotic, *adj.* nationalist, nationalistic, loyal, allegiant, jingoist, jingoistic, jingoish, chauvinistic, flag-waving, public-spirited, *U.S.* spread-eagle.

patriotism, *n.* nationalism, national loyalty, allegiance, jingoism, chauvinism, *U.S.* spread-eagleism, love of country.

patrol, *v.* **1.** make the rounds, walk a beat, keep vigil *or* guard, perform sentry duty, police; keep watch, hold watch, *Inf.* keep an eye out, *Inf.* keep one's eyes peeled, *Inf.* be on one's toes; guard, protect, watch over, monitor; stand guard over, secure, defend, safeguard; escort, conduct, convoy, ride shotgun.

—*n.* **2.** sentinel, sentry, guard, garrison; scout, lookout, watchdog; protector, defender, guardian, guarder, guardsman, lifeguard, bodyguard; policeman, officer, patrolman, constable; ranger, forest ranger; jailer, warder, warden, keeper, turnkey, *Sl.* screw, *Sl.* bull; custodian, watch, watchman, night watchman.

3. defense, defending, protection, protecting, safekeeping, vigilance; guarding, making rounds, walking the beat, policing, patrolling.

patrolman, *n.* policeman, police officer, state trooper, trooper, officer, constable; sentry, guard, patrol. See **patrol** (*def.* **2**).

patron, *n.* **1.** customer, client, subscriber, prospect; regular, habitué, frequenter, patronizer; shopper, purchaser, buyer, *Chiefly Law.* vendee, marketer; spectator, audience, theatergoer, goer; attender, attendant, visitor.

2. patroness, sponsor, promoter, backer, booster, financer, angel; benefactor, benefactress, Maecenas, philanthropist, Rockefeller; helper, abettor, succorer; advocate, seconder, favorer, upholder, exponent, supporter, partisan; maintainer, sustainer, mainstay; well-wisher, encourager, sympathizer, friend, befriender; guardian, guardian angel, good fairy; friend at court, connection, in; employer, boss, master, *Brit. Inf.* governor, lord and master, patriarch, keeper; founder, saint.

patronage, *n.* **1.** business, trade, custom, commerce; shopping, purchasing, buying, dealing, marketing; subscribing, subscription; attendance, attending, visits, visiting, participating, participation.

2. sponsorship, sponsoring, auspices, support, supporting; advocacy, advocating, defense, defending, seconding, championship, favoring, upholding; ministration, help, helping, abettal, abetting, aid, assistance; succor, succoring, encouraging, encouragement, sympathizing, sympathy; promotion, promoting, backing, boosting, financing; cultivation, fosterage; maintenance, maintaining, sustenance, sustaining; approval, countenance; guardianship, wardship, influence, protection, preservation, guidance, keeping; interest, charge; friendship, association.

3. *Chiefly U.S.* spoils, political patronage, sinecures, *Sl.* plums, *Sl.* pap; jobs, positions, offices, appointments; connections, backing, influence, *Sl.* drag, *Inf.* pull, in, advantage, interest, favor, *Inf.* inside track.

4. condescension, condescendence, snobbery, underestimation, patronizing; scorn, disdain, contempt, disrespect; disparagement, discredit, slur, detraction; humiliation, dishonor, offense, insult, *Sl.* put-down; abuse, contumely.

5. condescending, deigning, stooping; indulgingness, indulgence, humoring, favoring; toleration, tolerance, allowance, sufferance, permission, endurance.

6. audacity, insolence, brazenness, impudence, impertinence, sauciness, effrontery, gall, flippancy, *Rare.* procacity; assurance, conceit, overbearingness, airs; presumption, arrogation.

patronize, *v.* **1.** trade with, deal with, do *or* transact business with, traffic with, open an account with, have an account with, buy *or* purchase from, frequent.

2. treat condescendingly, look down on, look down one's nose at; underestimate, talk down to; scorn, disdain, contemn, despise; disparage, discredit, slur, detract from, derogate from; humiliate, dishonor, offend, insult, *Sl.* put down, set down.

3. condescend, deign, vouchsafe; indulge, humor; tolerate, allow, suffer, permit, endure; acquiesce, concede, accede; yield, give in, back down, comply with; unbend, lower oneself, stoop, descend; see fit to, be so good as to, so forget oneself as to; presume, arrogate.

4. sponsor, support, uphold, second, advocate, espouse, favor, subscribe to, take up; defend, champion, stand by, stand behind *or* in back of, take the part of; help, abet, aid, assist, succor, minister to; maintain, sustain; cultivate, foster, promote, encourage, sympathize; back, lend one's name to, boost, finance, provide capital *or* money for, put up the money, pay for, subsidize; favor, approve, countenance, endorse, smile upon; befriend, associate with; guard, protect, preserve, keep, look after, take under one's wing.

patronizing, *adj.* condescending, scornful, disdainful, contemptuous, supercilious, despising; imperious, overbearing, high-handed; snobbish, snobby, priggish, *All Inf.* snippy, snooty, snotty, high-hat, high-hatted; presumptuous, arrogant, haughty, lofty; inconsiderate, self-centered, tactless, uncharitable; offensive, humiliating, insulting, insolent.

patronymic, *n.* family name, surname, last name, cognomen, father's name, ancestral name, *Dial.* birth name.

patsy, *n. Slang.* **1.** scapegoat, *Inf.* goat, *Sl.* fall guy, whipping boy; loser, born loser, *Yiddish.* nebech, *Sl.* nebbish; one who takes it on the chin, hard-luck guy, bearer of bad tidings.

2. gull, dupe, *Sl.* pigeon, *Inf.* sucker, *Sl.* sap, *Sl.* schlemiel; victim, mark, easy mark, target; cat's-paw, tool; pushover, doormat, one who can be led around by the nose, spineless one, Caspar Milquetoast, pantywaist.

3. laughingstock, *Sl.* sad sack, fool, chump, dolt, *Sl.* boob, *Sl.* schlimazel, joke.

patter[1], *v.* **1.** tiptoe, walk lightly; scurry, scuttle, trip along, skip, hie.

2. tap, pitter-patter, drum, pound, beat; thrum, palpitate, pulsate.

3. spatter, sprinkle, splash, plash; fleck, dapple, stipple.

—*n.* **4.** pitter-patter, tapping, rat-a-tat, drumming, thrum, tattoo, pounding, pulsation.

patter[2], *n.* **1.** spiel, pitch, *Sl.* flackery, harangue, address, glib talk; scat talk, scat singing.

2. chatter, gabble, *Sl.* yak, *Sl.* yakety-yak, jabber, prattle, gibber, babble, blab, blabbing; small talk, idle talk, jaw, *Sl.* chinfest, *Inf.* gab, *Inf.* gabfest, chitchat, chitter-chatter, buzzing, gossip, *Scot.* clishmaclaver; palaver, *Sl.* hot air, *Sl.* gas, *Sl.* bull; nonsense, gibberish, hogwash, poppycock; rambling, maundering, *Sl.* running off at the mouth; chattering, gabbing, jabbering, babbling, prattling, prating, twaddling.

3. jargon, cant, argot, vernacular; lingo, patois, idiom, slang, dialect; language, diction.

—*v.* 4. spiel, hold forth, spout forth, spout, harangue, *Sl.* yak, *Sl.* yak at, *Sl.* give a lot of flak; chatter, jabber, prattle, cackle, gibber, *Sl.* jibber-jabber; babble, babble like a brook, prate, tattle, twaddle, *Brit.* twattle, gabble, blather, drivel; splutter, sputter, chitter-chatter, chitchat, chaffer; bandy words about, *Sl.* shoot the breeze, *Sl.* shoot the bull, *Sl.* chew the rag, *Sl.* shmooze, pass the time of day, *Inf.* gab; gossip, buzz, *Sl.* gas, whisper; palaver, clack, clatter, rattle; run off at the mouth, *Sl.* have diarrhea of the mouth; gush, blab, carry on, talk nonstop, let the words roll out, be carried away by the sound of one's voice.

pattern, *n.* 1. design, patterning, figure, motif, device; marking, etching, engraving, chasing; decoration, decorative scheme, ornamentation; configuration, figuration, delineation, outline, conformation, formation, composition, layout.

2. type, stripe, variety, classification, class, genre; sort, cast, kind, ilk, genus; form, manner, style, brand, make, build; shape, format, cut; feather, color, kidney, strain, grain.

3. method, plan, arrangement, order, orderliness, system; consistency, repetition, congruence, sameness.

4. original, archetype, matrix, prototype; exemplar, paragon, mirror, model, ideal, beau ideal; standard, criterion, yardstick, touchstone, measure, gauge, test; example, paradigm.

5. guide, blueprint, draft, sketch; mold, die, templet, template, stamp, seal, frame, stencil.

6. flight path, skylane, airlane; landing procedure, landing direction, flight direction.

—*v.* 7. copy, duplicate, follow, stencil; imitate, echo, match, twin, clone, parallel, reflect; emulate, simulate, ape, mimic; take after, resemble, mirror.

paucity, *n.* scarcity, sparseness, sparsity, scantiness; exiguousness, slenderness, thinness, leanness, meagerness; shortage, small number, small amount, paltriness, poverty, poorness; lack, dearth, want, need, crying need; insufficiency, inadequacy, deprivation, deficiency; famine, drought; nothing to spare, next to nothing.

paunch, *n.* belly, abdomen, stomach, *Inf.* tummy, gut, (*both of ruminating animals*) first stomach, rumen, *Scot. and North Eng.* wame, *Sl.* breadbasket; potbelly, *Inf.* bay window, *Inf.* corporation, *Sl.* pot, *Sl.* beerbelly, *Sl.* spare tire, *Obs.* gorbelly.

paunchy, *adj.* 1. potbellied, round-bellied, big-bellied, *Sl.* beerbellied, large-bellied, great-bellied, *Obs.* gorbellied; *Inf.* bay-windowed, *Inf.* corporational, abdominous.

2. full, bulging, protuberant, bloated, distended; swollen, turgid, tumid; puffy.

3. chubby, tubby, pudgy, plump, round, rounded out, rotund; fat, obese, corpulent, overweight, *Scot.* fodgel; portly, fleshly, well-fed.

4. stout, thickset, full-figured.

pauper, *n.* poor person, have-not, beggar, down-and-outer; insolvent, bankrupt, debtor; cadger, *Inf.* panhandler, mendicant, beadsman, almsman, *Scot.* gaberlunzie; ragamuffin, tatterdemalion, hobo, *Sl.* bindle stiff; tramp, vagrant, bum; moocher, *Inf.* sponger, *Sl.* schnorrer, parasite, leech, hanger-on.

pauperism, *n.* poverty, destitution, penury, indigence, impecuniousness, impecuniosity, pennilessness, neediness, reduced circumstances; beggary, mendicancy, mendicity, pauperage, pauperdom; insolvency, bankruptcy, liquidation; distress, difficulties, straits, indebtedness; lack, need, necessity, want, privation; paucity, dearth, shortage, deficiency, insufficiency, scarcity, default, absence.

pauperize, *v.* impoverish, beggar, bankrupt; drain, deplete, exhaust; *Inf.* break, *Sl.* bust, ruin, *Sl.* wipe out, break [s.o.'s] back, cripple financially.

pause, *n.* 1. stop, stay, halt, rest; rest period, respite, break, time-out, recess, breather, breathing spell, vacation, *Brit.* holiday; relief, *Inf.* letup, slackening, abatement.

2. cessation, discontinuation, discontinuance; suspension, abeyance, inactivity, moratorium, lull, lapse, hold; discontinuity, disconnection, interruption, hiatus, lacuna, gap, *Prosody.* caesura, *Music.* fermata.

3. delay, wait, holdup; stoppage, deadlock, standstill, impasse.

4. hesitancy, hesitation, doubt; play for time, waiting game, *Inf.* stall, pretext, ruse.

5. **give pause** startle, take aback, dismay, disconcert, bewilder; concern, worry, frighten; be cause for concern, make one reconsider, make one stop and think.

—*v.* 6. stop, stay, rest, desist, discontinue, cut, interrupt; break, take a break, relax, unwind, catch one's breath, take a breather, *Inf.* take five.

7. delay, wait, hold back, mark time, tread water, be at a standstill; hesitate, waver, demur, *Inf.* stall, falter.

8. *Usu.* **pause upon** dwell, linger, tarry, loiter; (*all of speech or writing*) develop, expand upon, elaborate on, expatiate on, harp on.

pave, *v.* 1. macadamize, asphalt, concrete, tar, pitch, revet; cobble, flag, brick, lay stones, slab; tile, floor; surface, face, level, smooth.

2. **pave the way for** *or* **to** prepare the way for, smooth the way for, clear the way for, open the door for, make way for; make ready *or* easy, ready, facilitate; lead up to, contribute to, conduce to.

pavement, *n.* 1. paved road, highway, thoroughfare, causeway; sidewalk, pavé.

2. macadam, asphalt, concrete, cement; tar, pitch; cobblestones, flagstones, flagging, brick, stonework.

pavilion, *n.* 1. summerhouse, parkhouse, gardenhouse, gazebo, (*in Turkey and Iran*) kiosk, open-air shelter; pergola, arbor, bower; bandshell, music shell, orchestra shell, bandstand; arcade, gallery.

2. tent, canopy, canvas, *Chiefly Brit.* marquee, awning.

paw, *n.* 1. (*all of animals*) foot, pad, forepaw, *Zool.* forefoot, *Anat., Zool.* manus, hind foot; trotter, hoof, unguis; (*all of birds of prey*) claw, talon, pounce.

2. *Informal.* hand, *Sl.* mitt, *Sl.* fin, *Sl.* flipper.

—*v.* 3. (*all with the paws or feet*) strike, hit, scrape, scratch.

4. *Informal.* maul, handle roughly, manhandle; molest, attack, seize, grab.

pawn[1], *v.* 1. *Informal.* hock, put in pawn, *Rare.* impawn; deposit, put up *or* give as security, impignorate, pledge, plight, commit, obligate, bind, mortgage, hypothecate; stake, lay, wager, bet, *Poker.* ante, *Archaic.* gage, gamble, speculate; risk, venture, chance, hazard, jeopardize, endanger, imperil.

—*n.* 2. security, collateral, gage, pledge, *Archaic.* plight, impignoration; assurance, guaranty, guarantee, surety, warrant, bond, bail; deposit, down payment, partial *or* initial payment, handsel; *Law.* mortgage, *Marine Law.* bottomry; stake, wager, bet.

3. hostage, *Obs.* pledge, prisoner, *Fr. détenu.*

4. pawnage, pawning.

pawn², *n.* instrument, tool, cat's paw, puppet, creature; jackal, flunky, lackey, attendant, (*in India and Ceylon*) peon, servant, handmaid, menial; minion, follower, toady, sycophant, yes man; hireling, underling, employee, subordinate, assistant, accomplice, henchman, *Sl.* stooge; dummy, dupe, *Sl.* pigeon, gull, gudgeon, *Inf.* sucker.

pawnbroker, *n.* *Sl.* uncle, lender, loaner, moneylender, usurer, *Inf.* loan shark, Shylock.

pawnshop, *n.* pawnbrokerage, pawnbrokery, *Fr. mont-de-piété, Inf.* hock shop, *Inf.* sign of the three balls, *Sl.* my uncle's, *Brit. Sl.* pop-shop, *Brit. Sl.* spout.

pay, *v.* **1.** compensate, remunerate, reward, recompense; reimburse, indemnify, refund; (*usu. of debts, etc.*) settle, satisfy, liquidate, discharge, clear off, square, honor, meet.

2. spend, expend, disburse, pay out; give, render, hand over, *Sl.* shell out, *Sl.* dish out, *Sl.* lay out, *Sl.* cough up; *Inf.* come across with, *Inf.* fork up *or* out *or* over; defray, contribute, ante up, *Inf.* chip in, *Inf.* go Dutch, *Inf.* pick up the tab, *Inf.* foot the bill; advance, prepay, pay up front, retain.

3. yield, return, produce; profit, avail, benefit, be worthwhile, be advantageous; help, aid, be useful, stand one in good stead.

4. retaliate, requite, pay back, get back, get even, even *or* settle the score; repay, reciprocate, return like for like, give tit for tat, *Inf.* give [s.o.] a taste of his own medicine, *Euph.* return the compliment; punish, chasten, *Inf.* get [s.o.] for [s.t.].

5. suffer, atone, answer for; get one's deserts, reap what one has sown, get one's comeuppance, get what's coming to one; pay the piper, face the music, take one's medicine.

6. pay off a. settle, discharge, liquidate, satisfy. **b.** *Slang.* bribe, suborn, oil, graft, cross *or* grease [s.o.'s] palm, *Sl.* square. **c.** retaliate, get even. See **pay** (*def.* **4**).

—n. **7.** wages, salary, *Brit. Sl.* get, emolument, remuneration, compensation, consideration, earnings; payment, hire, stipend, fee, honorarium; perquisites, *Inf.* perks, fringe benefits, *Inf.* fringes, *Inf.* extras; reward, bonus, tip, gratuity, douceur, *Fr. pourboire,* (*in India and Turkey*) baksheesh; commission, percentage, brokerage, share, cut, slice, (*both usu. illicit*) *Inf.* rake-off, *Inf.* kickback.

8. payment, remittance, reimbursement. See **payment**.

—adj. **9.** profitable, remunerative, lucrative, moneymaking.

10. coin-operated, public.

payable, *adj.* **1.** to be paid, due, immediately payable, mature, receivable; outstanding, owed, unpaid, in arrears.

2. profitable, lucrative, paying, remunerative; rewarding, worthwhile, fruitful, productive, producing; valuable, beneficial, good, advantageous.

payer, *n.* paymaster, teller, defrayer, almoner; debtor. See **paymaster**.

paymaster, *n.* treasurer, cashier, bursar, holder of the purse strings, budget director *or* manager, purser.

payment, *n.* **1.** remuneration, compensation, reimbursement; remittance, installment, handsel, *Insurance.* premium; settlement, liquidation, quittance, discharge, reckoning; refund, rebate.

2. expenditure, outlay, disbursement, expense; defrayal, contribution, share, ante, stake; advance, deposit, discount, *Inf.* up front, retainer, *Law.* earnest *or* earnest money; fee, charge, *Hist.* scot, tribute, rent, fine, penalty.

3. allowance, maintenance, alimony; subsidy, grant, subvention; pension, annuity; relief, alms, dole, handout, *U.S.* welfare.

4. requital, redress, repayment; satisfaction, amends, retribution, expiation; indemnification, indemnity, damages, *Law.* solatium; reward, deserts, due.

5. retaliation, reprisal, vengeance; punishment, chastening, *Inf.* comeuppance, due, what's coming to one.

6. money, cash, cold cash, *Sl.* the green stuff, *Sl.* spondulicks, *Sl.* shekels.

7. wages, salary, pay. See **pay** (*def.* **7**).

payoff, *n.* **1.** (*all of a debt, wager, etc.*) payment, paying off, settlement, liquidation, discharge, fulfillment; remuneration, compensation, reimbursement, refund, rebate, return; remittance, installment, partial payment, initial payment, handsel, deposit, down payment, *Insurance.* premium.

2. *Informal.* bribe, *Inf.* kickback, *Inf.* payola, *Inf.* plugola, *Inf.* hush money, *Inf.* protection *or* protection money, *Sl.* boodle; ransom *or* ransom money, price.

3. settlement, reckoning, day of reckoning, judgment day, final judgment *or* reckoning; justice, retribution, reward, punishment, due, just deserts.

4. *Informal.* consequence, outcome, sequel, result, end result, upshot; conclusion, resolution, denouement, solution; final sequence *or* scene, concluding episode, finale, grand finale; end, termination, close, windup, finish; consummation, fulfillment, completion, perfection, final touch *or* stroke; summing up, summary, wrap-up, epilogue.

5. *Informal.* climax, culmination, capper, punch line, *Journ. Sl.* kicker; acme, zenith, peak, pinnacle, height, high point, crowning point, supreme moment, moment of glory, orgasm; extremity, extreme, maximum, max., utmost, uttermost, *U.S. Sl.* the most, *U.S. Sl.* the greatest, *U.S. Sl.* the tops.

pea, *n.* **1.** chickpea, garbanzo, black-eyed pea, cowpea, snow pea.

2. bead, globule, spherule, spheroid, ball, shot, marble, pearl; pill, tablet, pellet, capsule, oval; drop, dewdrop, tear.

peace, *n.* **1.** peacefulness, warlessness, nonwar, lack of warfare, absence of conflict *or* hostilities.

2. pacification, appeasement, reconciliation, settlement; truce, armistice, treaty, cease-fire, cessation *or* suspension of hostilities, end of war; abeyance, lull, interlude, respite, breathing spell, *Inf.* letup.

3. harmony, harmoniousness, symphony, consonance, concordance, concord, accord; compatability, cooperativeness, cooperation, rapport, entente cordiale, détente; amity, amicableness, amiability, friendliness, friendship, cordiality, good will, brotherhood, comradeship, fellowship, unity, oneness.

4. public order, law and order, orderliness.

5. tranquillity, tranquilness, serenity, sereneness, calmness, calm, placidness, placidity; peace of mind, ataraxia, contentment, contentedness, satisfaction, wellbeing; ease, comfort, rest, repose, complacence, resignation.

6. quiet, quietude, quietness, silence, hush; quiescence, quiescency, stillness, still, motionlessness, inactivity; restfulness, peace and quiet, peaceableness.

—interj. **7.** silence, quiet, quiet down, keep it down, keep still, shh, hush, *Inf.* shut up, *Inf.* shut your mouth.

peaceable, *adj.* **1.** pacific, pacifist, pacifistic, peaceloving, dovish, irenic; nonargumentative, nonquarrelsome, nonquarreling, uncontentious, unbelligerent, nonbelligerent, unpugnacious, nonviolent, noncombative, unbellicose, unwarlike, nonwarring, neutral; gentle, gentle as a lamb *or* kitten, mild-mannered, mild, easy-going, good-natured, imperturbable, even tempered, temperate; compatible, agreeable, cooperative, easy to get along with, congenial, genial, affable, amiable, amicable, friendly, pleasant, nice, cordial, civil; patient, forbearing, clement, merciful, lenient, forgiving, giving in; acquiescent, compliant, consentient, consentaneous, passive, meek, lamblike, nonresistant, obedient, docile, tame.

2. pacificatory, peacemaking, conciliatory; propitiatory, propitiative, appeasing, mollifying, placating, soothing, calming; mediatory, negotiating, arbitrating, diplomatic.

3. tranquil, serene, calm; still, becalmed, restful. See **peaceful** (*def.* **1**).

peaceful, *adj.* **1.** tranquil, calm, serene, placid, quiescent, halcyon, restful, at rest, reposeful, at peace; still, quiet, becalmed, inactive, motionless, stationary; unagitated, undisturbed, unruffled, stormless, waveless, windless.

2. peacetime, warless, untroubled, normal; during a cease-fire *or* truce *or* armistice.

3. pacific, peace-loving, nonviolent; gentle, mild-mannered, easy-going; compatible, agreeable, amicable. See **peaceable** (*def.* **1**).

peacefulness, *n.* **1.** tranquillity, tranquilness, calmness, calm; peace of mind, ataraxia, contentment; quiet, silence, quiescence, stillness. See **peace** (*defs.* **4, 5**).

2. peacetime, peace, nonwar, warlessness, time of normality; truce, armistice, cease-fire, suspension *or* cessation of hostilities, end of war.

3. peaceableness, pacificism, dovishness, nonviolence, opposition to war; neutrality, nonbelligerent status, conscientious objector status.

peacemaker, *n.* pacificator, pacifier, makepeace, reconciler, conciliator, propitiator, appeaser, placater; negotiator, diplomat, ambassador; interposer, interceder, intercessor, intervener, referee, umpire; arbiter, arbitrator, adjudicator, mediator, mediatress, mediatrix, intermediary, intermediator, middleman, go-between.

peace offering, *n.* **1.** sacrifice, sacrificial offering, burnt offering, offering, holocaust, immolation, propitiation; homage, tribute, oblation, libation, *Eccles.* offertory.

2. peace pipe, calumet, olive branch, white flag, *Mil.* flag of truce; inducement, bribe, sop, lure, reward.

peacock, *n.* **1.** egoist, egotist, *Inf.* swellhead; braggart, braggadocio, boaster, *Inf.* brag, *Inf.* bullshooter, *Sl.* blowhard, *Sl.* loud mouth, *Sl.* big mouth; strutter, swaggerer, poseur.

2. fop, dandy, beau, jack-a-dandy, coxcomb; spark, dude, *Sl.* swell, *Brit.* toff; Beau Brummel, fancy Dan, *Sl.* bantam cock, *Sl.* glamour puss; exquisite, *Hist.* macaroni, silk-stocking, clothes horse; popinjay, la-di-da; pompous ass, cock of the walk; prig, prinker, pretty-boy, *Archaic.* carpet knight; blade, sophisticate, gallant, cavalier; ladies' man, lady killer, *Sl.* lounge lizard; zoot suiter, sharp dresser.

peak[1], *n.* **1.** pinnacle, summit, tor, crest, ridge, needle, mountaintop; alp, promontory, headland, cliff, precipice, crag, bluff; mountain, elevation, eminence, hill.

2. apex, vertex, apogee, tip, tiptop; spire, steeple, cupola; top, head, headpiece, cap, crown, cusp, cuspid.

3. acme, zenith, meridian, maximum, climax, culmination, crowning point, *Latin. ne plus ultra*; sublimity, supremacy, perfection, consummation, best, finest, extreme, utmost, uttermost, *U.S. Sl.* the most, *U.S. Sl.* the greatest; prime, heyday, bloom, full flower, blossom. efflorescence.

4. horn, beak, nib, neb; bill, brim, visor; jut, projection, protrusion, protuberance, protuberancy, prominence.

—*v.* **5.** crest, rise, spire, tower; culminate, climax; jut, beetle, overhang, project, protrude, protuberate, bulge.

peak[2], *v.* waste away, wither away, decay, die away, rot; languish, droop, fade, fail, flag, wilt; weaken, decline, soften, sag, yield; go downhill, come apart at the seams, *Sl.* poop out, *Sl.* fizzle out, *Sl.* peter out; fag, weary, tire, exhaust, fatigue, wind down.

peaked[1], *adj.* **1.** pinnacled, crested, crowned, capped; cusped, cuspate, cuspated, cusplike, cuspidal, cuspidate, cuspidated, niblike, *Brit.* nibbed.

2. sharp, pointed, pointy, acute, tipped, *Both Bot., Zool.* mucronate, mucronated; tapered, awl-shaped, subulate; spiculate, spicular, needlelike, spiky, spikelike, spiny, spinelike.

peaked[2], *adj.* **1.** pale, wan, pallid, *Obs.* blate, pale-faced, anemic, sickly; waxen, sallow, pasty, ashen, ashy, livid; ghostly, pale as a ghost, ghastly, deathlike, cadaverous; bloodless, white, drained; whey-faced, tallow-faced, unhealthy looking, unwholesome looking; washed-out, etiolated, bleached, blanched.

2. emaciated, gaunt, drawn, haggard, pinched, hollow-eyed, withered, shriveled, shrunken, dried up, wizened, *Brit. Dial.* wizen; scrawny, scraggy, spare, skinny, thin, lean, lanky, lank, slim, attenuate, attenuated, tenuous; frail, weak, feeble, enfeebled, enervated, infirm; starved, underfed, undernourished.

peal, *n.* **1.** clang, clash, clank, clatter, clangor; ringing, sounding, tintinnabulation; bang, boom, clap, chorus, rumble, thunder, thundering, roar, racket, din; burst, detonation, percussion, explosion, fulmination, crash; discharge, report, cannonade, shot.

2. carillon, chimes, glockenspiel.

—*v.* **3.** ring, clang, bong, toll, knell, chime, tintinnabulate; blare, trumpet, blast, bang, buzz; honk, toot; bugle, blat, bray; screech, shriek, wail, whine; roar, bellow, boom, thunder; resound, resonate, trill, vibrate, reverberate, echo.

pearl, *n.* **1.** drop, droplet, dewdrop, tear; bead, globule, glob, capsule, spherule, oval; tooth, pellet.

2. jewel, bijou, precious stone, solitaire, brilliant; ornament, trinket.

3. prize, treasure, gem, pick, flower, cream, *Fr. crème de la crème,* quintessence, perfection; wonder, marvel, prodigy, one in a million, one in a thousand, apple of one's eye, *Sl.* pip; ace, find, *Inf.* trump.

—*adj.* **4.** nacreous, off-white, pearly. See **pearly** (*def.* **1**).

pearly, *adj.* **1.** nacreous, creamy, milky, white, whitish, chalky, cretaceous; cloudy, opaque, fumé, frosted; albescent, adularescent, canescent; snowy, niveous, hoar, hoary; milk-white, snow-white, swan-white; ivory, gray-white, alabaster, eggshell, off-white.

2. opalescent, opaline, iridescent, rainbowy.

peasant, *n.* rustic, provincial, country cousin, countryman, hobnail; farmer, plowman, plowboy, chuff, gaffer, swain, kerne *or* kern, son *or* tiller of the soil, (*in Egypt*) fellah, (*in Russia*) muszhik *or* mujick, (*in Spanish America and Southwestern U.S.*) peon, *Archaic.* hind; yokel, bumpkin, country bumpkin, *Archaic.* bucolic, hawbuck, *Dial.* lumpkin, *Often Disparaging.* hillbilly, *Disparaging.* bogtrotter, *Inf.* chawbacon, *Inf.* cider squeezer, *Sl.* hick, *Sl.* woodhick, *Sl.* rube, *Sl.* hayseed, *Sl.* hoosier, *Fr. Sl. truffe*; laborer, commoner, worker.

peasantry, *n.* **1.** salt of the earth, tillers of the soil, peasants; commonalty, the common people, commoners, lower classes, humbler classes, laboring class, proletariat, rank and file; the common herd, hoi polloi, the masses, the many, the multitude, the great unnumbered; low life, dregs, underlings, riffraff, *Inf.* the great unwashed; mob, rabble, hoard, herd, rout, ruck, canaille.

2. simplicity, plainness, ordinariness, insignificance; rusticity, unrefinement, inurbanity, unsophistication, inelegance; boorishness, gaucherie, crudeness, coarseness, lowness, meanness; doltishness, awkwardness, clumsiness, tactlessness.

pebble, *n.* small stone, small rock, (*collectively*) gravel, pellet; jackstone.

peccable, *adj.* liable to sin, weak, frail, unstable, infirm; wayward, *Obs.* arrant, errant, prodigal, profligate, abandoned, immoral; peccant, reprobate, recreant, sinning, sinful, iniquitous, unvirtuous, unrighteous, ungodly, unholy, unsaintly; wanton, remiss, slack, lax, unmindful, negligent, reckless, heedless, careless.

peccadillo, *n.* petty offense, violation, infraction, breach, trespass, infringement; fault, *Law.* misdemeanor, *Law.* delict, *Law.* malfeasance, delinquency; petty sin, transgression, dereliction, misconduct, misdeed, wrongdoing, slip, lapse, shortcoming; false step, wrong step, misstep, stumble, trip, false move, bad move, wrong move; mistake, error, blunder, botch, bungle, *Inf.* slip-up, *Sl.* boo-boo, *Sl.* boner; faux pas, gaffe, social blunder, slip in conduct, mistake in conduct *or* etiquette *or* manners.

peccant, *adj.* **1.** sinning, transgressing, transgressive, offending, peccable; criminal, lawless, reprehensible, objectionable, censurable, blameworthy, culpable, guilty, delinquent; bad, wicked, damned, sinful, iniquitous, nefarious, felonious; shameless, corrupt, reprobate, recreant, profligate, abandoned, immoral; wanton, dissolute, debauched, depraved, degenerate.

2. at fault, faulty, wrong, in error, erring, incorrect, inaccurate, erroneous; wayward, deviant, erratic, aberrant; inexpedient, inadvisable, unwise, injudicious, imprudent; unsuitable, unfit, unbefitting, unmeet, undue, improper, untoward, inappropriate, indiscreet; unbecoming, unseemly, indecorous.

peck[1], *n.* *Usu.* **peck of** load, loads, bushel, bushels, ton, tons, barrel, barrels, bag, bags, acres, ocean, oceans, sea, world, worlds, galaxy; bunch, heap, heaps, pile, piles, stack, stacks, mountain, mountains, mass; army, legion, bevy, flock, host, array, multitude; whole lot, lot, lots, plenty, a great *or* good deal, quite a little, sight, as much as *or* more than one can handle *or* manage; whole slew, slew, mess, gob, gobs, oodle, oodles, *Sl.* scad *or* scads, *Sl.* boodle, *Sl.* caboodle, *Chiefly Brit.* lashing *or* lashings; galore, *Dial.* aplenty; abundance, plenitude, bounty, cornucopia, endless supply, *Scot. and North Eng.* routh, *Scot.* scouth, a great *or* considerable quantity *or* amount *or* number, one thousand and one, scores; volume, quantity, quantities, fund, mine, store, mint, quite a few.

peck[2], *v.* **1.** tap, rap, dab, pat, stroke, kiss; strike, hit, knock, blow; poke, jab, dig.

2. indent, dent, dint, depress; prick, scratch, scrape, score, dot, mark, flaw; chip, notch, nick; puncture, poke a hole, pinprick, pit.

3. (*of food*) nibble, gnaw, take small bites, nosh; pick, pick at *or* over one's food, eat like a bird.

4. *Usu.* **peck at** nag, pick, henpeck, pull to pieces, carp, criticize, harp, find fault with, *Yiddish.* kvetch; ride, harass, harry, heckle, hector, bullyrag, goad, egg, tease, bait, torment, torture, plague, persecute; pester, badger, hound, fret, vex, chafe, nettle, irritate, disturb, grate on, *Inf.* drive up the wall.

—*n.* **5.** tap, rap, pat, kiss; stroke, hit, strike, knock, thump, blow; poke, jab, dig.

6. indentation, dent, dint, dimple, concavity, depression, impression; scratch, scrape, mark, spot, speckle, speck, flaw, fault; chip, nick, chink, notch, groove, crevice, furrow, rut; hole, pit, hollow, cavity, crater, excavation.

pectoral, *adj.* **1.** thoracic, chest, breast, bosom, bust; ventral, front.

2. heartfelt, deep-felt, poignant, *Archaic.* homefelt; intense, wholehearted, enthusiastic, fervent, fervid, perfervid, ardent, zealous, passionate, impassioned; genuine, *Inf.* for real, earnest, sincere, serious, sober, profound; innermost, inmost, deep-seated, deep-rooted, *Scot., Irish.* benmost, most private *or* privy, personal, intimate, confidential; near and dear, cherished, precious, close, beloved.

3. *Speech.* (*of a vocal quality*) resonant, sonorous, full-toned, full, rich; deep, low, bass, basso, baritone, low-pitched, in the low register; resounding, booming, big, strong, heavy.

4. pulmonary, lung, lobar, respiratory.

peculate, *v.* embezzle, misappropriate, *Law.* defalcate, misapply, misuse; steal, rob, purloin, abstract; dip into the public purse, *Inf.* rob the till, *Inf.* have one's hand in the till; defraud, swindle, thieve, filch, cheat; pluck, fleece, rook, bilk.

peculiar, *adj.* **1.** odd, curious, queer, offbeat, quizzical, cranky, *Inf.* funny; deviate, deviant, aberrant, anomalous, anomalistic, abnormal, irregular, incongruous, erratic; strange, weird, bizarre, grotesque, *Sl.* freaky, freakish, *Sl.* rum, *Sl.* far out; monstrous, heteroclite, heteroclitical, unnatural; quaint, eccentric, droll, comical, laughable, *Inf.* quirky, *Sl.* squirrely, *Sl.* buggy; fanciful, whimsical, capricious, waggish, notional, maggoty, crotchety, *Sl.* balmy, *Chiefly Brit.* barmy; fantastic, incredible, inconceivable, ridiculous, ludicrous, absurd, preposterous, outlandish, extravagant; nondescript, amorphous, indescribable, unclassifiable.

2. unconventional, uncommon, unusual, unique, unorthodox, uncustomary, unwonted, rare, out of the ordinary, out of the way; atypical, original, singular, exceptional, individual, lone, sole, solitary, select; unexampled, unparalleled, unprecedented, unfamiliar, uncomfortable; extraordinary, egregious, astonishing; exotic, unreal, fey, supernatural, preternatural.

3. distinct, distinctive, distinguished, diacritical, striking, marked, conspicuous, remarkable, notable, signal, outstanding, especial.

4. (*usu. followed by* of) characteristic, indicative, representative, typical, denotative, designative, connotative, suggestive, symptomatic, symptomatologic, symptomatological, diagnostic, *Med.* pathognomic, *Med.* pathognomical; (*usu. followed by* to) indigenous, intrinsic, innate, endemic, significant, significative, meaningful; idiocratic, idiosyncratic, idiomatic; indicatory, implicative, exhibitive, expressive, evidential, discriminative; distinguishing, identifying, defining, signifying, signalizing, denominative, differential, quintessential.

5. exclusive, unique, special, particular, limited, proper, specific, individual, personal; private, secret, confidential, intimate, inner, esoteric.

peculiarity, *n.* **1.** idiosyncrasy, idiocrasy, eccentricity, mannerism, quirk, twist, kink, hobby-horse; quip, crotchet, whim, caprice, flight of fancy; aberration, aberrance, aberrancy, deviation, anomaly, *Rare.* anomalism.

2. oddity, curiosity, rarity; irregularity, incongruity, variation, abnormality, discrepancy, difference, variance, dissimilitude, disparity, inconsistency; exception, singularity, particularity.

3. oddness, strangeness, queerness, bizarreness, curiousness, quirkiness, incongruousness; uncommonness, uncommonality, unconventionality, unusualness, uniqueness, exception, singularity, singularness, individuality, individualness, distinctiveness; monstrousness, unnaturalness, freakishness; whimsicality, capriciousness, fancifulness, waggishness; outlandishness, preposterousness, extravagance.

4. characteristic, trait, quality, property, attribute, part; feature, distinction, mark, earmark, hallmark, specialty, stamp, lineament; badge, indicator, indication, erraticism, mannerism, affectation, idiasm, twitch, tic; style, form, idiom, mode, cast, vein; habit, propensity, tendency, predisposition, inclination, proclivity, proneness, leaning, twist, bent, warp, set, turn; disposition, attitude, mettle, temper, temperament.

pecuniary, *adj.* monetary, money, fiscal, financial, nummary, nummular, bread-and-butter.

pedagogic, *adj.* **1.** educational, educatory, instructional, teaching, preceptorial, tutorial; academic, academical, scholastic; professorial, instructorial, schoolteacherish; methodological, disciplinary.

2. pedantic, pedagoguish. See **pedantic** (*defs.* **1-6**).

pedagogism, *n.* pedantry, pedagogery. See **pedantry** (*defs.* **1-3**).

pedagogue, *n.* **1.** educator, educationist, *Educ.* methodologist, teacher, schoolteacher; professor, doctor, master, tutor, fellow, *Brit.* don, instructor, preceptor, lector, lecturer, docent; schoolman, scholastic, academician, academe, gownsman.

2. pedant, *Inf.* know-it-all; precisionist, perfectionist. See **pedant** (*defs.* **1, 2**).

pedagogy, *n.* **1.** teaching, instruction, education, tutelage, tuition; guidance, direction, training, discipline; coaching, preparation, preparing; indoctrination, inculcation, instillment.

2. instructional methods, teaching methods, didactics, pedagogics; educational psychology, science of learning.

pedant, *n.* **1.** intellectual, pedagogue, *Inf.* know-it-all; bibliophile, bookworm, scholar, highbrow, *Inf.* egghead, *Inf.* walking encyclopedia; aesthete, *Inf.* longhair, bluestocking; platitudinizer, *Inf.* bromide, bore, stuffed shirt; attitudinarian, attitudinizer, philosophaster, philosophe, moralizer.

2. precisionist, perfectionist; pettifogger, hairsplitter, quibbler, *Inf.* nitpicker; casuist, *Logic.* parologist, sophist, scholastic, subtilizer; caviler, faultfinder, prig; formalist, literalist, precisian, dogmatist, conformist, conventionalist, philistine.

3. doctrinaire, impractical theorist, ivory-tower dreamer, ideologist, visionary.

pedantic, *adj.* **1.** (*all in reference to one's learning*) pretentious, show-offish, ostentatious, pompous, haughty, vain, conceited; pedagoguish, scholastic, pedantical; professorial, didactic, preachy; dogmatic, pragmatic, opinionated, bigoted.

2. punctilious, precise, exact; overscrupulous, scrupulous, perfectionist, overconscientious, conscientious, meticulous; fastidious, fussy, finicky, finical, overparticular, particular; overcritical, hypercritical, priggish, schoolmarmish, faultfinding, caviling, quibbling, hairsplitting, pettifogging, *Inf.* nitpicking.

3. formal, stilted, stiff; bookish, donnish, stuffy, dry; rigid, narrow, hidebound; platitudinous, unimaginative, unoriginal, uninteresting; boring, dull, tedious, tiresome.

4. unrealistic, impractical, ivory-towered, ivory-towerish; utopian, visionary, starry-eyed, quixotic, chimerical; irrelevant, nongermane, immaterial, useless.

5. sonorous, rhetorical, bombastic, euphuistic, grandiloquent, high-flown; wordy, verbose, turgid, prolix.

6. studious, scholarly, erudite, learned, academic.

pedantry, *n.* **1.** (*all in reference to one's learning*) pretension, affectation, pomposity, pompousness, haughtiness, conceit, attitudinarianism; pedagogism, pedagogery, didacticism, preachiness, pedantism, pedanticism, pedanticalness; bookishness, stuffiness, dryness, tediousness, tiresomeness, dullness.

2. precisionism, perfectionism, meticulousness, particularity, fastidiousness, finicalness, finicality; punctiliousness, scrupulosity, scrupulousness, exactness, exactitude, precision, preciseness, minuteness; sophistry, casuistry, quibbling, hairsplitting, *Inf.* nitpicking, pettifoggery.

3. formalism, literalism, rigidity, conformity, conventionality; unimaginativeness, uncreativity, uncreativeness, unoriginality; narrow-mindedness, bigotry, dogmatism, positivism, hideboundness.

4. fine point, subtlety, punctilio, particular; nicety, delicacy, refinement.

peddle, *v.* **1.** hawk, vend, sell, *Sl.* push, retail, market; go door-to-door, sell on commission; *Inf.* try to make a buck *or* dollar; tout one's goods, show one's wares.

2. deal out, pass out, dole out, dispose of, distribute, dispense, disseminate; sprinkle, scatter, strew, broadcast.

3. trifle, niggle, fribble, fiddle, fiddle around, fritter, fritter one's time away, idle, frivol, laze, waste time, loaf, daydream; piddle, dawdle, dillydally; procrastinate, put off.

peddler, *n.* hawker, cheap-jack, vendor, huckster, monger, seller, *Sl.* pusher, salesman, money changer, pedlar, pedler; packman, *Inf.* faker, *Sl.* duffer, rag-and-bone man, junk dealer, butter-and-egg man, costermonger, coster, *Sl.* shmatah salesman, rag dealer, Armenian rug peddler, medicine man, snake-oil salesman; higgler, itinerant, tinker; traveling salesman, door-to-door salesman, colporteur, Bible salesman, Fuller Brushman, Avon lady; merchant, dealer, pushcart entrepreneur, shopman.

pedestal, *n.* **1.** base, support, foundation, rest, platform, understructure, bottom, foot; stand, pillar, column.

2. set *or* **put on a pedestal** idealize, glorify, exalt; extol, praise, praise to the skies, sing paeans to; treat like a Dresden doll, show great respect for; dematerialize, spiritualize, put a halo on; bow down to, worship, idolize, revere, adore, adulate, honor, ennoble.

pedestrian, *n.* **1.** walker, nonrider, hiker, tramper, foot-traveler; perambulator, stroller, itinerant, peregrinator, peripatetic, wanderer, roamer.

—*adj.* **2.** walking, ambulatory, wandering; peripatetic, afoot, on foot.

3. spiritless, lifeless, without a spark of life, robotlike, unanimated; tiresome, boring, tedious, prosy, wearisome, *Sl.* yawn-making, *Sl.* draggy, plodding, uninteresting, like a cold *or* dead fish; unimaginative, uninspired, uncreative, without an idea in one's head, empty-headed, doltish; insipid, jejune, vapid, *Sl.* blah, stale, flat, as flat as stale beer *or* stale ginger ale; undistinguished, unimpressive, without merit, inferior, lacking distinction; colorless, wan, pale, gray, dim, dreary, fitting into the background; dull, prosaic, stodgy, commonplace, common as dirt, humdrum, trite, platitudinous, ordinary, banal, hackneyed, dull as dishwater; tepid, lukewarm, indifferent, *Fr. comme ci comme ça*, so-so, average, middling, mediocre; unexcited, unexciting, unadventuresome, afraid of one's own shadow, *Sl.* creepy; trivial, frivolous, piddling, unimportant, insignificant; everyday, matter-of-fact, oft-repeated, monotonous, stock, unvaried, unchanging, without a surprise in a carload, totally predictable.

pedigree, *n.* **1.** ancestry, ancestral line, lineage, descent, parentage, birth, derivation, extraction, filiation; family, dynasty, house, tribe; race, strain, stock, breed, bloodline, stem, branch, stirps; heredity, heritage, past, roots.
2. genealogy, family tree, family record, list of ancestors.
3. nobility, noble *or* high birth, aristocracy, blue blood; purebred, pure blood, pure ancestry.
4. derivation, origin, origination, source; history, background.

pedigreed, *adj.* purebred, pure-blooded, full-blooded, thoroughbred; royal, aristocratic, high-born, noble, blue-blooded, patrician, genteel.

peek, *v.* **1.** peep, peer, squint at, sneak a look *or* peek; glance, look quickly *or* briefly, cast a brief look at, glimpse, catch a glimpse of, snatch a glimpse, look hurriedly, regard hastily; take a look at, *Inf.* give the once-over, *Inf.* have a looksee; observe, witness, view, behold, contemplate, see.
—*n.* **2.** peep, glimpse, brief look, look, glance, furtive glance, *Archaic.* eyeshot, quick view, *Scot.* glisk, *Fr. coup d'oeil, Scot.* blink; *Inf.* once-over, *Inf.* looksee, *Sl.* gander.

peel, *v.* **1.** skin, pare, decorticate, excorticate, flay, scale, hull, bark; shell, husk, shuck; strip, denude, excoriate.
2. (*of skin, bark, etc.*) come off, detach, separate, split; exfoliate, *Pathol.* desquamate, shed, slough, molt, exuviate, flake.
3. *Informal.* undress, disrobe, take off one's clothes, doff, remove, cast off, strip, strip down, *Euph.* do a strip tease, *Sl.* drop one's drawers, *Sl.* drop trow.
4. keep one's eyes peeled *Slang.* watch closely, be on watch, be on the lookout, look out for; be on guard; be alert, *Sl.* be on the ball.
—*n.* **5.** skin, integument, rind, *Bot.* epicarp, hull, bark, shell, husk; pellicle, membrane, coating, coat, cover, covering.

peep[1], *v.* **1.** peer, sneak a look at, glimpse, peek. See **peek** (*def.* **1**).
2. begin to appear, show, become visible, become manifest; come forth, break through, see the light, emerge, rise, arise, issue, spring up, pop up.
—*n.* **3.** quick look, furtive glance, glimpse, peek. See **peek** (*def.* **2**).
4. first appearance, manifestation, materializing; emergence, rise, rising, issuance, springing; beginning, dawning, breaking forth, unfolding; revelation, exposure.
5. aperture, opening, eye, *Photog.* viewfinder, peephole. See **peephole.**

peep[2], *n.* **1.** cheep, chirp, chirrup, chip; tweet, twitter, tweedle; chitter, squeak.
—*v.* **2.** cheep, chirp, chirrup, chip, pip; tweet, twitter, tweedle, trill, sing; chitter, chatter, squeak.

peephole, *n.* aperture, opening, hole, eye, eyelet, eyehole, keyhole, peep; pinhole, puncture, perforation, interstice, pore, bore, airhole, spiracle; slit, crack, vent, slot; chink, cleft, cranny, rift, crevice, fissure, *Archaic.* scissure; mousehole; porthole.

peer[1], *n.* **1.** equal, coequal, match, like, compeer; partner, confrere, colleague, associate; mate, fellow, pendant, companion; twin, double, counterpart, equivalent, equipollent, other half, alter ego; rival.
2. nobleman, noble, aristocrat, patrician, silk-stocking, *Inf.* blue blood, gentleman; grand duke, archduke, lord, milord, duke, marquis, *Hist.* margrave, earl, viscount, baron; grandee, magnifico, don, hidalgo; baronet, lordling, *Scot. Hist.* thane, princeling; seigneur, feudal lord, *Japanese Hist.* daimyo, signior, signor; squire, *Scot.* laird, *Russian Hist.* boyar, (*in medieval Germany*) landgrave.

peer[2], *v.* **1.** squint at, try to see, try to discern, look narrowly; glimpse, glance, peep, peek. See **peek** (*def.* **1**).
2. come forth, become visible, break through, emerge, peep. See **peep**[1] (*def.* **2**).

peerage, *n.* nobility, aristocracy, patriciate, royalty, baronage; upper classes, *Inf.* upper crust, ruling classes, privileged class, dominant class; upper strata, *Inf.* upper crust, *Fr. crème de la crème, Sl.* silk-stockings, *Inf.* bigwigs, *Sl.* biggies, *Sl.* high muck-a-mucks, the high and the mighty; the Four Hundred, (*often cap.*) establishment, high society, elite, gentry; First Families of Virginia, F.F.V.; the House of Rothschild.

peerless, *adj.* unequalled, matchless, unmatched, unparalleled, nonpareil, *Fr. sans pareil*; unsurpassed, unexcelled, second to none, *Latin. nulli secundus,* unprecedented; a first; unrivaled, incomparable, inimitable; superlative, best, finest, greatest, highest, prime, select, choicest; supreme, *Latin. ne plus ultra,* paramount, preeminent, superior, sovereign, transcendent; sublime, consummate, perfect, *Sl.* the living end; excellent, first-rate, of the first order, capital, *Inf.* tiptop, *Inf.* A-1, *Inf.* A number 1, first-class, classic.

peeve, *v.* **1.** annoy, irritate, vex, provoke, pique, irk, nettle, chafe, get on [s.o.'s] nerves, tread on [s.o.'s] toes, go against the grain, *Chiefly U.S.* rile, *Inf.* aggravate, *Inf.* miff, *Inf.* give [s.o.] a pain, *Inf.* rub [s.o.] the wrong way, *Inf.* get under [s.o.'s] skin, *Inf.* get in [s.o.'s] hair; exasperate, ruffle, disturb, disquiet, discompose, discountenance, put out, put off, try [s.o.'s] patience, *Inf.* put [s.o.'s] nose out of joint, get, *Sl.* get [s.o.'s] goat; stick in one's craw *or* crop, *Inf.* grate on *or* grate on one's nerves.
2. bother, pester, hector, harass, *Sl.* bug, *Sl.* hassle, *Sl.* drive [s.o.] nuts *or* crazy *or* bananas, *Sl.* drive [s.o.] up the wall; trouble, plague, worry, *Scot.* thraw, *Scot.* fash.
—*n.* **3.** nuisance, bother, pest, annoyance, irritant, bur, thorn in the side *or* flesh, pea in the shoe, salt in the wound, *Inf.* headache, *Inf.* pain, *Sl.* pain in the neck *or* rear, *Sl.* hassle; trouble, problem, affliction; trial, ordeal, tribulation; gripe, complaint, grievance, pet peeve; sore spot, sore point, *Inf.* touchy subject *or* matter, skeleton in the closet.

peeved, *adj.* **1.** annoyed, irritated, vexed, provoked, piqued, irked, nettled, aggravated, miffed; exasperated, ruffled, disturbed, disquieted, discomposed, discountenanced, put out, put off.
2. bothered, harassed, *Sl.* bugged, *Sl.* hassled, troubled, plagued; offended, affronted, displeased, on the outs with, indignant; worked up, *Inf.* hot under the collar, *Inf.* sore, *Sl.* ticked off, *Sl.* teed off; stirred up, kindled, enkindled, passionate, impassionate, over-excited.

peevish, *adj.* **1.** ill-humored, touchy, testy, thin-skinned, waspish, petulant; cross, irascible, choleric, ill-tempered, splenetic; crabby, cranky, grouchy, grumpy, cantankerous, crotchety, crusty; irritable, out of sorts, snappish, snappy, huffish, huffy, curt, short, impatient; piqued, in a pique, in a fume, *Archaic.* in a pucker, *Inf.* in a stew.
2. moody, sulky, dour, gloomy, dyspeptic, sullen, morose; injured, wounded, sore, offended, indignant; angry, irate, in high dudgeon, wrathful, worked up.
3. captious, disputatious, quarrelsome, contentious, fractious; complaining, caviling, querulous; antagonistic, ill-willed, hostile; contrary, perverse, *Scot.* thrawn; unaccommodating, unkindly, unamiable, unfriendly; bitter, acrimonious, acerbic, sour, caustic, tart, churlish, surly; spiteful, malicious, malevolent, hateful.

peg, *n.* **1.** pin, *Carpentry.* dowel pin, thole *or* tholepin; nail, spike, brad, skewer, rivet, staple, tack, point; screw, bolt, toggle bolt, anchor bolt; hook, hanger; marker, post, stake, stick, pale, picket; stop, stopper, stopple, plug, cork, bung, tampion; spill, spile, spigot.
2. *Informal.* wooden leg, peg leg, prosthesis; leg, *Inf.* pin, *Sl.* gam.
3. occasion, reason, motive, ground, basis, cause, call, provocation; justification, explanation, rationale, rationalization; excuse, pretext, plea, ostensible reason, pretense.
4. *Informal.* notch, step, rung, cut, point; degree, gradation, grade, rank.
5. news peg, newsworthy event, *Sl.* man bites dog; feature story, headline story, top story of the day, *Journ.* banner story, lead story, *Journ.* outside story.
—v. **6. take down a peg** *Informal.* humble, *Inf.* take down a peg or two, take down a notch, put [s.o.] in his place; lower *or* reduce in rank, downgrade, demote, *Inf.* kick upstairs, declass, disrate, break *or* strip of rank, *Mil. Sl.* bust.
7. (*all of a peg*) drive, insert, stick in, ram in, push in; inset, infix, imbed; fasten, make fast, attach, join, pin, secure, clinch, nail *or* nail down; pierce, stick, stab, jab, poke, strike, hit.
8. (*all of prices, wages, etc.*) freeze, fix, set; control, limit.
9. *Sl.* class, classify, categorize, pigeonhole, *Sl.* button down, *Inf.* put [s.o. *or* s.t.] down as, *Sl.* have [s.o.'s] number; identify, label, stereotype, type, typecast; designate, denominate, style, tag, term, name, call, dub; brand, mark, stigmatize.
10. work at, make an effort, apply oneself to, work away at, *Inf.* go at *or* to it, *Inf.* plug away at, *Inf.* hack away at, hammer away at, *Inf.* bang away at; *Inf.* chip away at, *Inf.* peck away at, *Inf.* go at *or* attack bit by bit *or* one piece at a time; plod along, go slowly but surely, carry on, continue, keep trying; persevere, stick to *or* at *or* with it, persist, hang *or* hold on, *Sl.* hang in there, keep at it, keep doggedly at it; force oneself, push oneself, make oneself, exert oneself, strain oneself; do what has to be done, see [s.t.] through, see [s.t] through to the finish, not give up, never say die.

peignoir, *n.* dressing gown, kimono, caftan, lounging robe, robe, housecoat, bathrobe, bed jacket, wrapper, *Fr. robe de chambre;* nightgown, gown, *Inf.* nightie, negligee, undress, *Archaic.* dishabille.

pejorative, *adj.* disparaging, deprecatory, depreciatory, depreciative, belittling; demeaning, debasing, downgrading, lowering, lessening, cheapening, derogatory, derogative; humiliating, mortifying, humbling, degrading; derisive, derisory, ridiculing, mocking; disdainful, contemptuous, scornful, disapproving, condemnatory; rude, irreverent, disrespectful, insulting, insolent.

pelage, *n.* (*all of mammals*) hair, fur, fleece, wool, pile; coat, pelt, fell, hide, skin.

pelf, *n. Disparaging.* money, mammon, riches; means, wherewithal, wealth, property, opulence, affluence, fortune; capital, funds, assets, finances; lucre, *Disparaging.* filthy lucre, almighty dollar; *All Sl.* dough, bread, moolah, mazuma, jack, long green, shekels, spondulicks, greenstuff, cabbage, lettuce, spinach, scratch, dibs, do-re-mi, loot, gravy, simoleons, wampum, *U.S.* bucks, *U.S.* kale.

pellet, *n.* globule, spherule, spheroid, oval; pill, tablet, capsule; pea, bead, pearl, marble; stone, pebble; seed, grain, ball, bullet, shot; wad of paper, spitball.

pellicle, *n.* skin, membrane, integument, cuticle, caul, *Biol.* epithelium, peel, *Bot.* epidermis; film, scum, foam, froth; slick, oil slick, spill; thin coating *or* coat, crust, covering, cover, layer, blanket, dusting; sheet, foil, lamina, thin plate, flake, scale; veneer, facing, finish, varnish, enamel.

pell-mell, *adv.* **1.** hurry-scurry, abruptly, precipitately, slapdash, slapbang; recklessly, impetuously, rashly; carelessly, summarily, without due reflection, on the spur of the moment, spontaneously, impulsively, at short notice, extemporaneously; prematurely, too soon, out of the blue, without proper preparation, *Inf.* at half cock; heedlessly, without due caution, thoughtlessly, cursorily; feverishly, foolishly, imprudently, incautiously, unadvisedly.
2. hastily, in great haste; helter-skelter, speedily, hurriedly, breathlessly, double-quick, too quickly; in a wink, *Inf.* like greased lightning, like one possessed; like a shot, like mad, *Inf.* like a bat out of hell, full tilt, in high gear.
—adj. **3.** indiscriminate, haphazard, random; casual, hit-or-miss, unmethodical, methodless, unsystematic, systemless; unordered, orderless, disordered, disorderly, disorganized, unorganized, unarranged, irregular; scrambled, tangled, disarranged, in disarray; confused, chaotic, all mixed-up, upside down, *Inf.* topsy-turvy, at sixes and sevens, muddled, jumbled, hugger-mugger.
—n. **4.** mob, unruly group, rabble, horde; rout, surge, *Inf.* mob scene, brawlers, rioters.
5. confusion, disorder, upheaval, turmoil, tumult; agitation, stir, ferment, bustle, hurry-scurry, hubbub; commotion, turbulence, brouhaha; uproar, pother, disturbance; trouble, to-do, row, melee, fracas, rumpus, brawl, riot; anarchy, chaos, pandemonium, bedlam, babel, three-ring circus.

pellucid, *adj.* **1.** translucent, glassy, crystalline, vitreous, vitric, vitriform, hyaline; clear, transparent, transpicuous, crystal, crystal clear, diaphanous, see-through, limpid.
2. understandable, comprehensible, apprehensible; intelligible, coherent, articulate, cogent, lucid; rational, simple, plainly-worded, exoteric, unhidden, undisguised; straightforward, written for the layman, popular, *Inf.* in words of one syllable; unambiguous, perspicuous, unconfusing, with no room for confusion, clear, clear-cut, graphic, vivid, explicit, express, salient, downright, to the point, direct, not mincing words; apparent, revealed, disclosed, unconcealed; prominent, plain, pronounced, palpable, visible; unquestionable, unmistakable, unequivocal; obvious, overt, bare, naked, bald, blunt.

pelt[1], *v.* **1.** attack, assail, stone, lapidate; riddle, shower, bombard, pepper, *Brit. Sl.* prang; strafe, shell, torpedo, cannonade, *Mil.* barrage, fusillade, blitz; batter, beat, beat up, *Archaic.* belabor; pound, *Inf.* wallop, lay on, pommel, pummel, thrash, trounce, *Sl.* paste, *Sl.* clobber; maul, manhandle, rough up, *Sl.* knock around *or* about; *Sl.* work over, *Sl.* give one the works; smite, hit, strike, slap, smack, cuff, buffer; punch, *Inf.* slug, whack, *Sl.* belt.
2. throw, heave, fling, cast, throw, propel; toss, hurl, sling, catapult, launch; dart, *Brit. Sl.* bung, fire, shoot, let sail *or* fly; dash, chuck, peg, send, pitch, put, lance, bowl.
3. revile, vituperate, abuse, lash, lash out at, rail against, inveigh against; light into, *Inf.* sail into, *Inf.* tear into, *Inf.* rip into, *Inf.* lace into, *Inf.* jump down [s.o.'s] throat, *Archaic.* clapperclaw; scold, tongue-lash, rate, harangue, rant; curse, execrate, imprecate, anathematize; upbraid, objurgate, excoriate, lambaste, flay, fulminate against; castigate, chastise, berate, censure, criticize, reproach, rebuke, reprove, *Inf.* jump on, *Inf.* dress down, *Inf.* slam, *Sl.* jump all

over, *Sl.* strafe.

—*n.* **4.** whack, hard hit, bang, bump, thump; blow, bastinado, punch, box; *Inf.* wallop, *Inf.* whomp, cuff, thwack, slap, smack, *Inf.* clout; beating, battering, pounding, *Sl.* pasting; thrashing, flogging, lashing, switching; scourging, flagellation, whipping.

pelt², *n.* animal skin, animal hide, skin, hide; fleece, wool, fur, fell, coat.

pen¹, *n.* **1.** writing instrument, quill, feather, plume; style, stylus, stylograph; ballpoint *or* ballpoint pen, *Trademark.* Bic; fountain pen, cartridge pen; felt-tip *or* felt-tip pen, *Trademark.* Magic Marker, *Trademark.* Flair, *Trademark.* Pentel, *Trademark.* Bic Banana.

2. nib, penpoint.

3. writer, penman, penner, *Sl.* pen-pusher, *Sl.* pencil-pusher, *Sl.* inkslinger, *Sl.* ink spiller; *Sl.* quill driver; scribe, scrivener, amanuensis, secretary, clerk; copier, transcriber, *Judaism.* sopher; author, composer, creative writer, wordsmith, word painter; hack, scribbler, *Inf.* word-slinger, *Inf.* potboiler, *Chiefly Brit. Archaic.* penny-a-liner.

—*v.* **4.** write, commit to paper, put pen to paper, jot down, *Rare.* scribe; draft, draw up, write up *or* out; scrawl, scribble, scratch; author, compose, indite.

pen², *n.* **1.** enclosure, close, confine, pound; stall, crib; fold, corral, sty, pigsty; coop.

—*v.* **2.** enclose, confine, corral, crib, mew, *Archaic.* pound; coop in *or* up, shut in *or* up, close in, box up; contain, bound, fence in, wall in, rail in.

penal, *adj.* punitive, disciplinary, penalizing, retributive, castigatory; corrective, correctional.

penalize, *v.* **1.** punish, amerce, mulct, chasten; discipline, correct, inflict a penalty on; castigate, chastise, make [s.o.] pay the piper, *Inf.* throw the book at, make [s.o.] take his medicine; distrain, constrain; sentence, pass sentence on, impose a fine *or* sentence, fine, judge, imprison, send up the river.

2. handicap, disadvantage, put at a disadvantage, put behind the eightball, disable; distress, bother, disturb, perturb; hinder, hamper, impede, impair; check, curb, restrain, hold back; burden, encumber, weigh down, saddle.

penalty, *n.* **1.** punishment, penalization, amercement, penance; sentence, condemnation; chastening, castigation, chastisement; deserved reward, just deserts, what one asked for, *Inf.* comeuppance; pay, payment, wages; discipline, punitive action, correction; retribution, nemesis, requital, retaliation, revenge.

2. forfeiture, forfeit, fine, mulct, damages; loss, deprivation, suffering, distress, pain.

3. disadvantage, handicap, price one pays; problem, difficulty, snag, catch, *Sl.* hooker; impediment, obstacle, hindrance.

penance, *n.* punishment, penalty; atonement, reparation, amends; propitiation, lustration, placation, offering; repentance, penitence, contrition; mea culpa, humiliation, mortification, hairshirt, sackcloth and ashes, self-flagellation, sacrifice, rending of garments.

penchant, *n.* inclination, proneness, propensity, proclivity, tendency; leaning, bent, bias, prejudice, predisposition; predilection, preference, partiality, liking, desire, craving; fondness, soft spot in one's heart, fancy, whim, notion; attachment, attraction, affinity, weakness, *Sl.* thing, *Sl.* real thing; mind, turn of mind, willingness, aptitude, ear, eye, disposition, temper; taste, palate, relish, appreciation, gusto, zest, appetite; rage, passion, zeal.

pencil, *n.* **1.** lead pencil, lead, automatic pencil, writing instrument; crayon, chalk, pastel, felt-tipped pen, *Trademark.* Magic Marker, *Trademark.* Flair.

2. ray, beam, shaft, stream; finger, stem, bar, rod, stick.

—*v.* **3.** (*all with pencil*) sketch, draw, trace, outline; delineate, diagram, depict, portray, mark out, *Archaic.* limn; write, pen, scrawl, scribble, scratch; draft, compose, indite; transcribe, copy, inscribe.

pend, *v.* **1.** be undecided, be unsettled, be up in the air; be pending, be awaiting action, be in abeyance, be on a back burner, be in a holding pattern; hang in the balance, hang fire.

2. hang, hang down, dangle, depend; bob, swing, hinge, turn upon, revolve around.

pendant, *n.* **1.** necklace, lavaliere, locket, medallion, gorget, torque, riviere, *Archaic.* carcanet, chain, string; eardrop, dangling earring; necklet, scarf, tippet, furpiece; tassle.

2. chandelier, luster, corona, light fixture; gasolier, electrolier.

3. match, equivalent, counterpart, companion piece; complement, correspondent, alternate, companion, mate, fellow; parallel, analogue.

pendent, *adj.* **1.** hanging, suspended, pendulous; dangling, drooping, sagging, *Bot.* nutant, nodding, bowing, lowering; swinging, swaying.

2. overhanging, jutting out, sticking out, salient, projecting, beetling, protruding, protuberant; extending, overlying, overlapping.

3. impending, imminent, pending. See **pending** (*def.* **3**).

4. undecided, undetermined, pending. See **pending** (*def.* **2**).

pending, *prep.* **1.** until, until such time as, awaiting, while awaiting, waiting for *or* on; during.

—*adj.* **2.** undecided, unsettled, undetermined, unresolved, unfinished; indefinite, in *or* up in the air, in abeyance, abeyant, awaiting action, on a back burner, in *or* on the fire, hanging fire, in a holding pattern; quiescent, latent, dormant.

3. impending, imminent, approaching, coming, nearing, on the way, close at hand, momentary; in the air *or* wind, in the cards; inevitable, certain, inescapable.

pendulous, *adj.* **1.** hanging, suspended, pendent, dangling. See **pendent** (*def.* **1**).

2. swinging, swaying, oscillating, vibrating; rocking, moving back and forth *or* to and fro, wigwagging; undulating.

3. vacillating, fluctuating, wavering, fickle, capricious; on-again-off-again, inconstant, unsteady, erratic, spasmodic, fitful.

penetrable, *adj.* pervious, permeable, porous; open, passable, accessible; intelligible, apprehensible, comprehensible, fathomable; vulnerable, pregnable, open to attack.

penetralia, *n.* innermost *or* deepest recesses *or* parts, secret place *or* places, depths, bowels, insides; bosom, heart, heart of hearts; core, pith, marrow, kernel, nucleus, center.

penetrate, *v.* **1.** pierce, transpierce, pass through; stab, gore, gouge, spear, lance, spike, run through, *Sl.* let the daylight in; bore, drill, ream, ream out, auger; perforate, puncture, prick, punch, riddle, *Sl.* fill full of holes; impale, transfix, fix, spit, skewer, *Sl.* shish kebab.

2. permeate, pervade, saturate, honeycomb, inosculate, interosculate, interpenetrate; fill, extend throughout, leave no void; percolate, filter through, seep through, soak through; imbue, infuse, suffuse, transfuse, infiltrate, impregnate, leaven.

3. affect, touch, touch a sympathetic chord, strike a familiar chord, strike, hit; touch to the quick, go deep,

Sl. get under one's skin; stir, move, melt, soften, touch the heart, tug at the heart strings, get [s.o.] right here; impress, make an impression, have an impact, come over, come across, register, sink in, come home to, get through to.

4. understand, comprehend, apprehend, fathom, discern, see, perceive, make out, realize, *Sl.* savvy, *Sl.* dig, *Brit. Sl.* suss; follow, read, take in, *Scot.* ken, *Inf.* get the picture, *Inf.* get the message, *Inf.* get the idea, *Inf.* get it, *Inf.* catch the drift; seize, get a hold of, get a grip on; see through, see [s.t.] as it really is, see [s.t.] in its true colors, *Inf.* have [s.o.'s] number, *Sl.* be wise to, *Sl.* be on to, *Sl.* have dead to rights; solve, resolve, decode, decipher, crack, work out, figure out, untangle, unriddle, unravel.

penetrating, *adj.* **1.** sharp, pointed, piercing, incisive, penetrative; shrill, ear-splitting, ear-piercing; cutting, biting, stinging, scathing, scorching, withering; trenchant, mordant, mordacious, pungent.

2. acute, keen, sensitive, discerning, discriminating, perceptive, *Scot. and North Eng.* gleg; conscious, cognizant, aware, sentient, sensible, comprehending, understanding, *Sl.* in tune, *Sl.* tuned-in; intelligent, smart, *Inf.* smart as a whip, bright, *Inf.* brainy, sharp, keen, nimble, quick.

penetration, *n.* **1.** incision, cutting, piercing; puncture, perforation; impalement, transfixion, skewering; ingress, entrance, entry, ingoing, incoming, influx, inflow; permeation, pervasion, saturation, inosculation, interosculation, interpenetration; imbuement, instillment, infusion, suffusion, transfusion, infiltration, impregnation.

2. cogency, incisiveness, pointedness; mordancy, trenchancy, mordaciousness, pungency, cuttingness, bitingness, stingingness.

3. keenness, acuteness, sharpness, sensitivity, discernment, discrimination, perception, percipience, perspicacity, insight; consciousness, cognizance, awareness, sentience, sensibility, comprehension, apprehension, understanding.

4. intelligence, smartness, brightness, *Inf.* braininess, *Inf.* brains, *Sl.* smarts, *Sl.* savvy; sharp-wittedness, keen-wittedness, ready-wittedness, quick-wittedness, nimble-wittedness, clear *or* quick thinking.

peninsula, *n.* chersonese; cape, hook, spur, neck, tongue; point, promontory, foreland, headland, head, *Scot.* mull.

penitence, *n.* contrition, *Theol.* imperfect contrition, attrition, repentance, acknowledgment; compunction, regret, regretfulness, regrets, remorse, remorsefulness, sorrow, sorrowfulness, sadness, grief, sorriness; sackcloth and ashes, breast-beating; self-reproach, self-reproof, self-accusation, self-condemnation, self-punishment, shame, shamefacedness.

penitent, *adj.* **1.** repentant, contrite, compunctious, abject, humble, humbled, apologetic, sheepish; sorrowful, sad, sorry, sorry for one's sins, remorseful, regretful, rueful, conscience-stricken, in sackcloth and ashes; self-reproaching, self-accusing, self-condemning.

—n. **2.** confessor, penitential; sinner, prodigal son.

penitentiary, *n.* **1.** prison, state prison, maximum-security prison, minimum-security prison, penal institution, house of correction *or* detention, *Sl.* pen, *Sl.* big house, *Sl.* slammer, *Sl.* stir; reformatory, reform school, (*in England*) borstal institution.

2. jail, jailhouse, lockup, *Scot.* tollbooth, *Inf.* clink, *U.S. Inf.* calaboose, *Brit. Inf.* bridewell; guardhouse, guardroom, *U.S.* brig; *All Sl.* can, cooler, coop, hoosegow, jug, booby-hatch, pokey, *Brit.* choky, *Brit.* quod.

—adj. **3.** penal, punitive.

4. penitent. See **penitent** (*def.* **1**).

penman, *n.* **1.** scribe, scrivener, amanuensis, secretary, clerk, recorder; copier, copyist, engrosser, transcriber, *Judaism.* sopher.

2. handwriting expert, writing expert, graphologist, graphometrist, (*pertaining to ancient scripts*) paleographer; calligrapher, calligraphist, chirographer, engrossist.

3. writer, penner, pen, *Sl.* pen-pusher, *Sl.* pencil-pusher, *Sl.* inkslinger, *Sl.* ink spiller, *Sl.* quill driver; author, composer, creative writer, wordsmith, word painter; hack, scribbler, *Inf.* word-slinger, *Inf.* potboiler, *Chiefly Brit. Archaic.* penny-a-liner.

penmanship, *n.* handwriting, script, manuscript, longhand, *Inf.* fist, *Scot.* hand of writ, chirography; calligraphy, good hand, Palmer method; cacography, bad hand, scribble, scrawl, scratch.

pen name, *n.* nom de plume, pseudonym, anonym, allonym, alias; assumed name, *Fr. nom de guerre,* stage name, *Fr. nom de théâtre.*

pennant, *n.* **1.** banner, banderole, bannerol, pennon, streamer, burgee, bunting, jack; flag, colors, standard, gonfalon, vexillum, labarum, eagle; ensign, insignia, oriflamme, tricolor.

2. *Baseball.* championship, title, crown.

penniless, *adj.* **1.** without a cent, *Fr. sans sou,* poor as a churchmouse, poor as Job's turkey, unable to keep the wolf from the door; moneyless, *Inf.* broke *or* flat broke, busted, *Inf.* hard up, *Sl.* stony *or* stone broke; bankrupt, out of pocket, without funds, impecunious, penurious; short of cash, depleted, drained, strapped, pinched, straitened, pressed; tight, stinted, restricted, limited; deprived, bereft, empty-handed.

2. impoverished, needy, in need, distressed, indigent, necessitous; poverty-stricken, destitute, extremely poor; out at the elbows, down at the heels, shabby, shoddy, seedy, in rags; reduced, pauperized, ruined, bad *or* badly off, *Inf.* on the rocks.

pennon, *n.* pennant. See **pennant** (*def.* **1.**).

penny, *n.* **1.** copper, cent, *U.S. Inf.* red cent, *Brit.* pence *or* p.

2. a bad penny undesirable, *Latin. persona non grata,* bad person, bad man *or* woman *or* child, *Inf.* bad news, *Inf.* bad egg; rascal, scoundrel, knave, rogue, *Sl.* bad actor; worthless fellow, good-for-nothing, good-for-naught, ne'er-do-well.

3. a pretty penny *Informal.* considerable sum of money, mint, pile, heap, wad, *Inf.* boodle, *Sl.* bundle, *Sl.* big bucks.

penny pincher, *n.* pinchpenny, lickpenny, *Inf.* tightwad; niggard, miser, skinflint, *Sl.* skin, *Sl.* cheapskate, *Inf.* piker, muckworm, *Sl.* screw; cheeseparer, hoarder, save-all, *Scot.* carl; scrooge, Harpagon, money-grubber, harpy; curmudgeon, churl, hunks.

pension, *n.* **1.** retirement income, old age income *or* benefits, survivor's income *or* benefits, disability income *or* benefits, *U.S.* Social Security *or* veteran's benefits, fixed income; annuity, annuity certain, tontine.

2. allowance, subsistence allowance *or* payment, allotment, pittance, *Law.* alimony, child support; subsidy, subvention, grant, stipend, fellowship, scholarship; relief, aid, help, support, maintenance, dole, handout, alms, welfare, public assistance, *U.S.* unemployment compensation, workmen's compensation; check, money, payment.

3. (*in Europe*) boarding house, boarding school; room and board, bed and board; lodging, guest house, inn, hotel, motel.

pensioner, *n.* pensionary, annuitant; beneficiary, recipient, grantee, dependent.

pensive, *adj.* dreaming, dreamy, dreamful, in a reverie, daydreaming, gazing out the window, in a trance, absent-minded; thoughtful, thinking, cerebrational, absorbed, immersed, engrossed, lost in thought, bemused, *Archaic.* museful; cogitative, cogitating, contemplative, contemplating, meditative, meditating, musing, pondering, reflective; ruminative, ruminant, ruminating, chewing, chewing one's cud, mulling over, brooding, in a brown study; sulking, sulky, moody, gloomy, glum, somber, sullen, morose; dispirited, cheerless, joyless, wistful, yearning, melancholy, sad; heavy-hearted, heartbroken, woeful, woebegone, forlorn, sorrowful, dreary, doleful, rueful, mournful, lamenting, bemoaning, bewailing, grieving.

pent, *adj.* cooped in *or* up, encaged, caged, cribbed, mewed, boxed in *or* up, shut in *or* up, closed in, confined; fenced in, walled in, railed in, corralled, hemmed in, hedged in, bound, enclosed; interned, impounded, immured, cloistered, entombed, imprisoned, incarcerated.

pent-up, *adj.* bottled up, corked up, shut up *or* in, closed up *or* in, confined; held in, sealed off, kept inside *or* within *or* secret, hidden; held back, restrained, constrained, checked, curbed, bridled, repressed, suppressed.

penurious, *adj.* **1.** stingy, parsimonious, miserly, carking, skinflinty; mean, tight, tight-fisted, close-fisted; cheap, *Sl.* chintzy, moneygrubbing, grasping; niggardly, *Rare.* illiberal, cheeseparing; scrimping, penny-pinching, grudging, begrudging, ungenerous, stinting; thrifty, frugal, sparing, chary; economical, prudent, saving, penny-wise.

2. poverty-stricken, destitute, extremely poor; indigent, necessitous, in need, needy, distressed, impoverished; out at the elbows, shabby, shoddy, in rags, bad *or* badly off; pauperized, reduced, ruined, *Inf.* on the rocks.

3. penniless, *Inf.* broke *or* flat broke, busted, *Inf.* hard up, *Sl.* stony *or* stone-broke; bankrupt, out of pocket, without funds, moneyless, impecunious; depleted, drained, strapped, pinched, straitened, pressed; tight, stinted, restricted, limited; deprived, bereft, empty-handed.

4. lacking, wanting, shy, deficient; insufficient, inadequate, beggarly; skimpy, scanty, meager, scrimpy, scant; very little, paltry, poor, piddling, insubstantial, *Inf.* measly, mere.

penury, *n.* **1.** poverty, extreme poverty, destitution, need, want; straits, straitened circumstances, beggary, pauperism, pauperage; mendicancy, mendicity; impecuniousness, insolvency, bankruptcy, inability to pay, liquidation, failure, default; privation, deprivation.

2. dearth, absence, scarcity, scarceness; inadequacy, insufficiency, lack, deficiency, shortage, shortness, stint, not enough to go around; scantiness, paucity, exiguity; meagerness, rareness, sparseness, seldomness, fewness, poorness, barrenness; depletion, exhaustion, emptiness, vacuity.

people, *n.* **1.** humans, human beings, human race, members of the human race, humankind, mankind, race of man, *Latin. Homo*, Homo sapiens; mortals, persons, souls, living souls; men, women, children, individuals; everybody, *Fr. tout le monde*, the whole world.

2. race, tribe, clan, community; nation, country, state; society, public, populace, population; members, fellows, membership, voters, constituency, residents, clientele.

3. relations, relatives, kin, kinfolk, kinsmen, next of kin, kith and kin; family, *Inf.* folk, parents, father, mother, spouse, children, grandparents, aunts, uncles, cousins, *Inf.* kissing cousins, extended family, old friends; ancestors, strain, house, line, dynasty.

4. common people, masses, hoi polloi; the vulgus, *Archaic.* the vulgar, commonalty, *Inf.* common run, commonage, demos; proletariat, plebeians, *Inf.* plebs; bourgeoisie, third estate, the multitude, the many, the millions, *Derogatory.* booboisie, *Chiefly Brit.* admass, rank and file, *Contemptuous.* ragtag and bobtail; grass roots, *Inf.* the silent majority, the man in the street, Archie Bunker; *U.S.* Middle America, Main Street USA; the vulgar herd, the great unwashed, the rabble, the mob, King Mob, the crowd, the huddled masses; general public.

—*v.* **5.** populate, settle, colonize, inhabit, live in, habitate, fill; supply, stock, sow.

pep, *n. Informal.* **1.** spirit, animation, liveliness, vivacity, dash, élan, zest, verve, *Sl.* moxie, zing; fire, sprightliness, breeziness, buoyancy, cheer, vitality, life; ebullience, *Inf.* zip, sparkle, effervescence; vigor, vim, *It. brio,* energy; exuberance, enthusiasm, passion, fervor, intensity.

2. stamina, force, power, might, potency, virility; drive, push, *Inf.* get up and go, initiative, ambition, enterprise.

—*v.* **3. pep up** animate, vivify, quicken, vitalize, enliven, breathe life into, invigorate, energize, fortify, strengthen; encourage, hearten, enhearten, give heart to, embolden; elate, gladden, cheer, *Inf.* buck up, cheer up; actuate, activate, *Inf.* get going, rouse, waken; incite, stimulate, arouse, fire, *Inf.* fire up, *Inf.* light a fire under; prompt, *Inf.* spark, excite, work up, *Inf.* wind up.

pepper, *n.* **1.** condiment, spice, black pepper, white pepper; red pepper, cayenne; green *or* bell pepper; hot pepper, sweet pepper.

—*v.* **2.** season, spice, spice up, flavor, *Inf.* give some zip.

3. sprinkle, speckle, mottle, stipple, dapple; dot, stud, daub, fleck, speck, maculate.

4. pelt, shower, bombard, fire upon *or* at, shoot at, blitz; stone, lapidate, hurl things at, shell, barrage, strafe; riddle, *Brit. Sl.* prang.

peppery, *adj.* **1.** hot, burning, *Sl.* burny, spicy; racy, nippy, keen, sharp, pungent, highly seasoned, piquant, stimulating.

2. (*all of speech*) sharp, stinging, sarcastic, biting, incisive, cutting; piercing, acid, astringent, caustic, acrimonious, acerbic; trenchant, harsh, severe, mordacious, mean.

3. hot-tempered, hot-headed, testy, choleric; irritable, touchy, snappish, petulant; irascible, excitable, fiery, inflammable; hasty, quick, trigger-happy; high-strung, quick-tempered; huffish, waspish, raspy, huffy, edgy.

4. grumpy, cranky, grouchy, crotchety, churlish, gruff; cantankerous, impatient, crabby; splenetic, dyspeptic, temperamental; crusty, crabby, ill-tempered; sharp, tart, acerbic; fractious, quarrelsome, querulous, contentious, resentful, captious; mean-tempered, shrewish, vixenish, hard-to-handle.

peppy, *adj. Informal.* **1.** energetic, energetical, vigorous, dynamic, electric; active, alive, full of energy, *Inf.* full of pep, full of vim and vigor, *Inf.* snappy, *Inf.* zippy, *Inf.* full of oomph; eager, ready to go, bright-eyed and bushy-tailed; lively, spirited, *Sl.* go-go, full of life, animated, vibrant, vital; sprightly, spry, *Chiefly U.S. Inf.* chipper; brisk, exertive, physically fit and active.

2. ebullient, irrepressible, bubbling over, *Inf.* bubbly, effervescent; demonstrative, emotive, expressive, effusive.

3. jumping, hopping, cracking, busy, on the go *or*

move; industrious, hard-working, enterprising, forceful, strong, high-powered.

peptalk, *n.* encouragement, buoying up, stimulation, motivation, inspiration; rallying lecture, *Inf.* half-time talk, *Inf.* one for the Gipper, inflammatory talk, firing *or* stirring up, *Inf.* psyching up.

peptic, *adj.* digestive, *Physiol.* assimilative, enzymatic, gastric, stomachic, stomachical.

per, *prep.* a, the, each, for each, every; through, by.

peradventure, *n.* **1.** uncertainty, hesitation, indecision, undecidedness, irresolution; question, faltering, vacillation, lack of conviction, indefiniteness, indetermination, insecurity; doubt, incertitude, dubiety, dubiousness.

2. guess, conjecture, surmise, supposition, assumption, presumption, guesswork; chance, random shot, pot shot, *Inf.* shot in the dark, *Inf.* shot, *Sl.* crack, *Sl.* guesstimate.

3. fortune, luck, stroke; accident, fortuity, fluke, inadvertence; cast of the dice, flip of the coin.

perambulate, *v.* **1.** traverse, trek, travel, travel over *or* through *or* around, peregrinate; roam, rove, range, tour; walk, foot, tread, pace; make rounds, walk a beat, patrol, *Sl.* case.

2. stroll, ambulate, go for a walk, take a walk, stretch one's legs; promenade, saunter, amble, ramble, roll, roll along; meander, circumambulate, straggle, gad about, gallivant, traipse.

perceivable, *adj.* **1.** perceptible, appreciable, recognizable, noticeable, discernible, distinguishable, detectable; cognizable, knowable, intelligible, comprehensible, understandable.

2. apparent, seeable, visible; open, in full view, revealed, unconcealed, exposed, showing, unhidden, uncovered, unveiled, naked, bare; conspicuous, observable, well-marked, distinct; plain, clear, evident, obvious, manifest, patent, palpable; plain as day, plain as the nose on one's face, lucid, in focus; prominent, notable, salient, bold.

perceive, *v.* **1.** intuit, sense, feel, find, be conscious of, be aware of; hear, smell, taste; see, see through, see the light, make out, note, spot, sight, catch sight of, catch, glimpse, discern, read, *Brit.* twig, make heads *or* tails of; appreciate, *Sl.* dig, *Sl.* savvy, *Inf.* catch on, get the picture, *Inf.* get through one's head, *Inf.* get it, *Inf.* have it; observe, behold, notice, espy, descry, remark, detect, mark, discover, witness, identify; fathom, penetrate, realize, *Inf.* lay hold of, gain insight into.

2. apprehend, comprehend, understand, grasp, *Archaic.* hent; take in, receive, *Chiefly Scot.* ken; decipher, figure out, ascertain, determine; differentiate, make a distinction, discriminate, judge, distinguish, pick out; apperceive, cognize, recognize, be cognizant of, know; conclude, gather, deduce, derive, infer.

percentage, *n.* **1.** percent, rate per hundred.

2. proportion, ratio, quota, part, share, portion, allotment, dividend.

3. royalty, duty, allowance, commission, factorage, discount, deduction.

4. *Informal. Sl.* rake-off, *Inf.* cut, *Sl.* slice, gain, gains, profit, profits, *Inf.* take.

perceptible, *adj.* perceivable, appreciable, recognizable, discernible. See **perceivable** (*defs.* **1, 2**).

perception, *n.* **1.** understanding, comprehension, apprehension, grasp, mental hold; awareness, consciousness, *Obs.* conscience, ken, perspicacity, percipience, sagacity, wisdom, knowing, knowledge, intelligence; cognition, discernment, cognizance, enlightenment.

2. sensation, sense, feeling, intuition, impression; realization, revelation, insight; instinct, prompting, second sense, divination, clairvoyance, prompting, foreknowledge, foresight, prescience.

3. percept, concept, idea, notion; image, view.

perceptive, *adj.* sensitive, responsive, responding, open, open-pored, impressionable, impressible; aware, cognizant, discerning, discriminating; insightful, penetrating, piercing, understanding, knowing; conscious, sensient, sensible, alive; percipient, perspicacious, clear-sighted, alert; intelligent, smart, quick-witted, quick, sharp, keen, *Sl.* on the ball; wise, sagacious, sage, sapient; shrewd, astute.

perch, *n.* **1.** pole, rod, bar, branch, twig; roost, rest, seat, nest, aerie, eyrie; position, spot, site, location, habitation, domicile, quarters; role, situation, station; vantage point, distance, angle of viewing, perspective.

—*v.* **2.** alight, land; sit, rest upon, roost, nest; settle, plop down; set, place, put, lay, deposit, position, situate.

percipience, *n.* discernment, insight, intuition, comprehension, understanding, perception; shrewdness, long-headedness, astuteness, judgment; awareness, cognizance, alertness, acuteness, keenness, acumen, sharpness; intelligence, smartness, *Sl.* smarts, sense, good *or* common sense; clear *or* unclouded vision, perspicacity, perspicuity; sagacity, sageness, wisdom; cleverness, ingenuity.

percipient, *adj.* discerning, perspicacious, discriminating, selective; sapient, knowing, perceiving, comprehending; intelligent, smart, sharp, quick-witted, quick, bright, alert, aware, open-eyed, undeceived, not easily fooled *or* taken in; wide-awake, alive, astute, sharp-sighted, far-sighted; prudent, discreet, provident, politic, tactful, judicious, shrewd, long-headed; acute, keen, penetrating, piercing, perceptive, sensitive, feeling; sagacious, wise, sage, sensible, clear-headed, clear-eyed, rational.

percolate, *v.* **1.** filter, strain, filtrate; permeate, leech, ooze, seep, exude, transude, drip *or* pass through, leach; (*usu. of coffee*) brew, *Inf.* perk, bubble.

2. pep up, liven up, grow lively, come alive, become active, start moving, start jumping *or* hopping; bubble, enthuse.

percussion, *n.* impact, appulse, collision, crash, clash, striking, beating, drumming, sounding; bump, slam, bang, knock, thump, whack, thwack; blow, stroke, punch, smack, slap, *Inf.* clip, smash; buffet, concussion, shock, force, full force, brunt.

perdition, *n.* **1.** damnation, loss of soul, spiritual ruin, reprobacy; destruction, ruination, undoing, downfall, fall, comedown; abasement, degradation, wretchedness, desolation.

2. hell, hellfire, fire and brimstone, bottomless pit, abyss.

perdurable, *adj.* permanent, eternal, *Literary.* sempiternal, immortal, undying, deathless, imperishable, indestructible, indissoluble, unfading, everlasting, amaranthine, perennial; enduring, standing the test of time, going on and on, long-lived, life-long, long-standing; abiding, continuing, persisting; perpetual, unending, endless, never-ending, ceaseless, unceasing, incessant, unremitting; constant, durable, steady, stable, solid, like the Rock of Gibraltar, fixed, firm, steadfast; immutable, unchangeable, changeless, unalterable, invariable; established, deep-rooted, strong, entrenched; surviving through thick and thin *or* for better or for worse.

perdure, *v.* endure, last, stand the test of time, go on and on, continue, live on; subsist, survive, exist, remain; be permanent, be eternal, be immortal, be imperishable, be indestructible, be everlasting; be perpetual, be endless, be constant, be durable.

peregrinate, *v.* **1.** travel, journey, roam, rove, itinerate, wayfare, jaunt; range, globe-trot, go abroad, go overseas, see the world, sight-see; walk, ambulate, trek, hike, march, wend, take the road, take to the road, hit the road; proceed, pass, go, hie, *Scot.* gang, progress; meander, ramble, gad, gallivant; divagate, travel the open road.
2. traverse, perambulate, travel over, cross, ford, cut across.

peregrination, *n.* **1.** journeying, wayfaring, roaming, roving, walking, hiking, trekking, rambling; traversing, traveling over, crossing, fording, cutting across.
2. journey, travel, itinerancy, globe-trotting; trip, tour, excursion, jaunt, junket, outing; walk, trek, hike, sally, expedition.

peregrine, *adj.* foreign, alien, unindigenous, heterochthonous; tramontane, ultramontane, transalpine; ultramarine, transmarine, transatlantic, transpacific; unfamiliar, strange, peculiar, exotic, outlandish.

peremptory, *adj.* **1.** imperative, commanding, compelling, obliging, jussive; directive, preceptive, prescriptive, decretory, decretal; hard and fast, binding, incumbent, mandatory, obligatory, *Fr. de rigueur.*
2. imperious, arbitrary, dictatorial, despotic, tyrannical, high-handed; dogmatic, pontifical, opinionated, oracular; overbearing, oppressive, autocratic, overconfident, overweening; arrogant, supercilious, pompous; assertive, positive, emphatic, insistent.
3. absolute, categorical, incontrovertible, indisputable; unconditional, unequivocal, out and out, downright, flat; unmitigated, unqualified, unrestricted, uncircumscribed, unlimited, unreserved, implicit; certain, sure, assured, cocksure, definite.
4. decisive, conclusive, definitive; *the,* ultimate, final; irrevocable, irreversible, inappealable, unwaivable.

perennial, *adj.* **1.** enduring, constant, incessant, continual, perdurable; lasting, unfailing, stable, chronic, abiding; durable, unchanging, evergreen; immutable, undeviating; continuing, recurrent, uninterrupted, continuous, everflowing.
2. perpetual, everlasting, eternal, permanent, *Literary.* sempiternal; immortal, unending, undying, interminable, ceaseless, endless, timeless; imperishable, undecaying, indestructible, hardy, hearty; longevous, long-lived, macrobiotic.

perfect, *adj.* **1.** ideal, exemplary, admirable, model; inimitable, incomparable, paragonless, paramount, preeminent; superlative, supreme, transcendent, crowning, sublime, august, infinite; excellent, superb, capital, exquisite, extraordinary, fine, (*of a gem or pearl*) orient, second to none; invaluable, priceless, inestimable; unsurpassed, unequaled, unrivaled, unexcelled, matchless, peerless; utmost, uppermost, topmost, top; best, highest, champion, good, commendable, laudable.
2. complete, entire, comprehensive, intensive, full, fully realized; total, whole, consummate, plenary, absolute; thorough, thoroughgoing, exhaustive; utter, sheer, sweeping.
3. faultless, flawless, defectless; pure, precious, innocent, virgin, chaste; immaculate, clean, snowy, spick-and-span; unblemished, spotless, unspotted, stainless, taintless, untainted, unsullied, unsoiled; untarnished, undefiled, unscathed, undefaced, unimpaired, uninjured, undamaged, unmarred, inviolate; unmixed, unaltered, unmingled, unblended, undiluted, unalloyed; plain, simple, blank, stark, regular; impeccable, irreproachable.
4. unqualified, unlimited, unconditional, unconditioned, unreserved, unmitigated; unquestioning, implicit, undoubting, unhesitating; unrestricted, unhampered, unimpeded, unbounded; unequivocal, clear, unambiguous, explicit, express, unmistakable; pronounced, official, confirmed, authoritative, settled, fixed.
5. categorical, flat, clear-cut; downright, out-and-out, outright, straight-out, all-out, through and through; sure, certain, confident, infallible; conclusive, unquestionable, positive, indubitable, undoubted; undeniable, indisputable, undisputed; fundamental, radical, essential, real, genuine; demonstrable, demonstrated, apodictic; peremptory, imperative, imperious.
6. appropriate, fitting, fit, just right, dead right; proper, suitable, seemly, meet, apt; tailor-made, custom-made, made-to-order, made-to-measure; germane, relevant, legitimate.
7. accurate, correct, right, just, letter-perfect, unerring; exact, precise, right on, on the mark, on target; all right, A-O.K., okay; actual, factual, literal, true, veritable; authentic, lifelike; verifiable, unmistaken, reliable.
8. accomplished, practiced, experienced, efficient; skilled, skillful, polished, finished, seasoned; ripe, mature, mellow; able, capable, adroit, deft, dexterous, adept; qualified, disciplined, well-equipped, well-grounded; masterful, expert, proficient; gifted, well-endowed, talented.
—*v.* **9.** bring *or* carry to completion, bring to an end, finish, finish up, realize; complete, finalize, end, close, terminate, carry through *or* out, follow through; accomplish, compass, achieve, fulfill; bring about, effect, effectuate; culminate, consummate, cap, crown; discharge, perform, execute, enact; get through, get done, get done with; conclude, establish, clinch, fix; develop, generate, evolve, make; mature, ripen, mellow, round out.
10. make faultless, rectify, right, better, amend, ameliorate, improve; purge, cleanse, purify; correct, emend, edit, revise, clarify, mend; reform, regenerate, rehabilitate, repair; enrich, enhance, refine, retouch, remodel; elaborate, embellish, adorn; cultivate, develop; polish, shine, brighten, burnish, buff; restore, reclaim, revive, resuscitate, redo.
11. develop, train, teach, educate, form, prime, prepare; drill, exercise, discipline, practice; nurture, foster, rear; cultivate, breed; habituate, acclimatize, adapt, accustom, inure.

perfection, *n.* **1.** ideal, ideality, inimitability, inimitableness, incomparability, incomparableness; superiority, extraordinariness, preeminence, supereminence, transcendence, sublimity, infinity; goodness, holiness, virtue.
2. completeness, entirety, entireness, fullness, fulfillment; totality, wholeness, thoroughness, utterness; soundness, intactness, integrity; faultlessness, flawlessness, pureness, innocence, chasteness; spotlessness, stainlessness, taintlessness, immaculateness; impeccability, irreproachability.
3. actuality, factuality, literalness, truth, verity, veritableness, essence, authenticity; definiteness, positiveness, absoluteness; exactness, exactitude, precision, preciseness; accuracy, correctness, rightness, justness.
4. mastery, expertness, efficiency, proficiency; ripeness, maturity; ability, capability, adroitness, deftness, adeptness.
5. paragon, model, pink, pattern, mirror, standard, ideal, idealization, beau ideal; excellence, worth, merit, quality, prime; acme, quintessence, ultimate, crown; pinnacle, summit, lead, peak, height.
6. completion, consummation, realization, termination; accomplishment, attainment, achievement, effectuation; culmination, capping, crowning; maturation, ripening.
7. rectification, amelioration, improvement; correc-

tion, emendation, editing, revision, clarification; regeneration, rehabilitation, repairing; restoration, reclaiming, reviving, resuscitating, redoing; enrichment, refinement, elaboration, embellishing, adorning; expansion, development.

8. training, teaching, educating, education, preparing, preparation; drilling, exercising, disciplining, practicing; nurturing, fostering, rearing; cultivating, cultivation, breeding, habituating, acclimatizing, adapting, inuring.

perfectionism, *n.* fastidiousness, criticalness, overcriticalness, hypercriticalness, overdemandingness, demandingness, exactingness; fussiness, particularity, overparticularness, daintiness, finicalness, finicality, *Inf.* pernicketiness, meticulousness, meticulosity; minuteness, detailedness, fineness, niceness, thoroughness, completeness; painstakingness, care, carefulness, conscientiousness, scrupulosity, scrupulousness, punctiliousness; exactness, preciseness, precision, accuracy, accurateness, correctness; rigidness, rigidity, strictness, severeness, severity, rigorousness, rigorism.

perfectionist, *n.* **1.** precisionist, pedant, formalist, academic, purist.

2. stickler, *Inf.* fuddy-duddy, fussbudget, *Sl.* grind.
—adj. **3.** scrupulous, meticulous, conscientious, exacting, precise, punctilious; discriminating, discriminative, selective, picky, *Inf.* choosy; fastidious, particular.

perfectly, *adv.* **1.** ideally, admirably, inimitably, incomparably, preeminently; superlatively, supremely, sublimely, infinitely; superbly, exquisitely, extraordinarily; faultlessly, flawlessly, spotlessly.

2. completely, entirely, purely, fully, plenarily; throughout, altogether, to the nth degree; totally, wholly, consummately, absolutely, thoroughly, utterly, quite; positively, unconditionally, implicitly, undoubtedly, indubitably; unequivocally, unambiguously, clearly, explicitly, unmistakably, officially; categorically, surely, certainly, infallibly, conclusively; actually, really, truly, verily, assuredly; essentially, fundamentally, radically.

perfervid, *adj.* intense, fervid, impassioned, keen, ardent, zealous, *Inf.* gung ho; heated, fervent, feverish, inflamed, white-hot; fiery, raging, blazing, burning, flaming; seething, simmering, boiling; earnest, eager, animated, excited, passionate; high-spirited, wrought-up, overwrought, enthusiastic.

perfidious, *adj.* treacherous, traitorous, treasonous; faithless, false, disloyal, dutiless, untrue, unfaithful; deceitful, dishonest, insidious, false-hearted, knavish; double-dealing, dissembling, Janus-faced, two-faced, hypocritical; conniving, sneaking, scheming, designing, shifty, sneaky; unscrupulous, dishonorable, unconscienced, corrupt.

perfidy, *n.* **1.** treachery, traitorousness, Iscariotism, quislingism; faithlessness, unfaithfulness, disloyalty, perfidiousness, infidelity; false-heartedness, duplicity, falseness, guile, deceit; dutilessness, recreancy, defection, desertion, apostasy, resilement.

2. treason, betrayal, Judas kiss, *Sl.* stab in the back, *Sl.* sellout; double-dealing, *Sl.* double-crossing, *Sl.* double-cross; breach, breach of faith, bad faith, Punic faith, *Latin. mala fides;* foul play, dirty trick, dirty work.

perforate, *v.* **1.** make a hole in, hole, honeycomb, bore, drill, punch, pink, puncture; pierce, stab, lancinate, prick, stick; cut, slit, slot, split, gash, slash.

2. penetrate, pass into, enter, permeate, pervade, overspread.
—adj. **3.** perforated, bored, drilled, holed, holey, honeycombed, punched, pinked; punctured, pierced, stabbed, lancinated, pricked, stuck; cut, slit, slotted, split, gashed, slashed.

perforation, *n.* hole, bore, drill *or* punch hole; puncture, mark, prick; cut, slit, split, gash, slash; opening, gap, space, slot, aperture, eyelet.

perforce, *adv.* necessarily, of necessity, by necessity, by force of circumstances; needfully, requisitely, needs must; as a matter of course, without choice, compulsively, compellingly.

perform, *v.* **1.** carry out, execute, do, discharge, meet; transact, conduct, carry on; succeed in, manage, bring off, *Sl.* pull off, *Inf.* put over, *U.S. Sl.* swing, *U.S. Sl.* cut; complete, conclude, finish, carry through; dispose of, *Sl.* knock off, *Sl.* polish off, expedite, dispatch.

2. fulfill, make good, redeem; realize, carry into effect, carry out, go through, follow through; observe, keep, celebrate, commemorate; ceremonialize, solemnize, ritualize; be faithful to, obey, comply with, adhere to, stick by *or* to.

3. act, portray, play, personate; sing, dance, mimic, imitate, reproduce; represent, enact, act out, put on, produce, stage, give a show; overact, *Theat. Sl.* ham, strut one's stuff, show off.

performance, *n.* **1.** entertainment, show, production, presentation; première, matinée; engagement, appearance, stand, *Music.* gig; exhibition, exhibit, showing, public display, audition, tryout; representation, act, staging, putting on, acting out.

2. composition, piece, play, drama; spectacle, happening, pageant, extravaganza, variety show, vaudeville; comedy, tragedy, curtain raiser, entr'acte; musicale, opera, operetta, concert, recital, ballet.

3. execution, doing; accomplishment, attainment, consummation, completion, conclusion, finishing; fulfillment, realization, making good, discharge, redemption.

4. achievement, accomplishment, work; deed, feat, act, exploit, *Archaic.* gest; enterprise, endeavor, undertaking, task; procedure, production, operation, transaction, *Inf.* deal; proceeding, affair, function; action, maneuver, move, stroke, blow, coup; stroke of genius, tour de force.

performer, *n.* **1.** entertainer, actor, actress, player, stage player, stage performer, playactor, role player; trouper, *Sl.* ham, theatrician, thespian, Roscian, histrio, histrion, *Archaic.* histrionic; personator, impersonator, mime, pantomimist, mimist, mummer; satirist, *Fr. farceur;* comedian, comedienne, comic, stand-up comic; jester, fool, clown, *Circus Sl.* kinker, merry-andrew, zany, harlequin, buffoon; pantaloon, straight man, foil, *U.S. Sl.* fall guy.

2. doer, executor, executant, executrix; worker, operator, operative, operant; architect, author, maker, creator, fabricator; agent, medium; promoter, mover, prime mover; participant, participator; practitioner.

perfume, *n.* **1.** cologne, eau de Cologne, toilet water, *Ger. Kölnisch Wasser, Fr. parfum;* fragrance, scent, essence, extract; attar, scented oil.

2. scent, aroma, fragrance, fragrancy, incense, redolence, redolency, balm, balminess, bouquet; odor, smell.
—v. **3.** aromatize, make fragrant, scent, incense, cense.

perfunctory, *adj.* **1.** cursory, superficial, shallow, unthorough, incomplete, sketchy, scanty, skimming, scanning; hasty, hurried, brief, fleeting, rapid, quick, fast, rush-through; mechanical, simply going through the motions *or* steps, inattentive, with one's mind on something else, desultory, immethodical, haphazard, slapdash, slipshod, slovenly, loose; routine, usual, just enough to get through *or* by, only as required *or* necessary, no more than required *or* necessary, barely sufficient, barely adequate, barely acceptable, passable; middling, mediocre, fair, average, so-so, *Inf.* O.K., *Sl.* half-assed; poor, inferior, lame, inadequate, insufficient, unacceptable, *Inf.* not so hot.

2. indifferent, half-hearted, offhand, offhanded, devil-may-care, nonchalant, pococurante, lackadaisical; apathetic, apathetical, unconcerned, uninterested, unenthusiastic, uninspired, passionless; negligent, careless, incautious, heedless, thoughtless, unmindful.

perfuse, *v.* **1.** overspread, bespread, overlay, coat, film, cover; color, tint, tinge; paint, stain, lacquer, enamel, varnish, shellac, oil, polish; saturate, supersaturate, permeate, imbue, soak, drench, wet, dampen, moisten.

2. (*of a liquid, color, etc.*) spread, diffuse, disperse, circumfuse; pour, splash, drip, drop, slosh, slop.

pergola, *n.* **1.** arbor, leafy shelter, bower, trellis, lattice; pavilion, gazebo; (*in Turkey and Iran*) kiosk; summerhouse, gardenhouse.

2. retreat, refuge, haven, shelter, hermitage; asylum, resort, sanctuary, covert, mew.

perhaps, *adv.* maybe, it may be, as the case may be, mayhap, *Chiefly Dial.* mayhappen, *Literary.* perchance, *Archaic.* peradventure; possibly, for all one knows, it could be that, there is a chance *or* possibility that, who knows but that; if possible, if one has a chance *or* opportunity, if one can *or* gets to, if at all *or* humanly possible, God willing, wind and weather permitting.

periapt, *n.* amulet, charm, good luck charm, lucky piece, talisman, horse shoe, rabbit's foot, wishbone, *Brit.* merrythought; abraxas, phylactery, *Judaism.* tefillin, protector, preservative, safeguard; scarab, apotropaic, swastika, triskelion.

peril, *n.* **1.** risk, jeopardy, danger, hazard; menace, threat, minacity, gathering storm, handwriting on the wall, foreboding; endangerment, imperilment, liability, vulnerability, susceptibility, subjection, exposure, openness; precariousness, insecurity, unsafety, unpredictability, uncertainty, weak link, weak link in the chain.

—*v.* **2.** endanger, expose to danger, hazard, risk, imperil, jeopardize, jeopard, put in jeopardy; menace, threaten, scare; put in a tight spot, put in a canoe without a paddle.

perilous, *adj.* dangerous, fraught with danger, hazardous, chancy, jeopardous, *Archaic.* parlous, risky, venturesome; treacherous, deceptive, unreliable, untrustworthy, sneaky; threatening, menacing, minatory, minacious; building up, impending, looming, ominous, inauspicious, unfavorable, boding ill; scary, *Sl.* hairy, dire, frightening, disquieting, *Inf.* spooky, eerie; desperate, urgent, with no escape, without a parachute, past the point of no return, in no-man's land, caught in the crossfire; exposed, unsheltered, out in the open, vulnerable, defenseless, with no place to hide; precarious, shaky, tottery, rickety, about to go, on its last legs, unstable, unsteady, unsound, unsafe, unhealthy; delicate, ticklish, touchy, thorny, difficult, critical.

perimeter, *n.* circumference, boundary, bound, bourn, frontier, limits, outer limits; periphery, edge, rim, fringe, verge, skirt, brink; margin, border, frame; line, delineation; length, depth, extent, range.

period, *n.* **1.** eon, era, epoch, age, time, days, years; space, term, spell, stretch, interval, span, stage, duration.

2. generation, season, teens, middle age, middle years, twilight years, golden years, sunset years; spring, summer, autumn, fall, winter; millennium, century, decade, decennium, quinquennium; year, twelvemonth, calendar year, fiscal year; month, week, day, date, hour, minute, second, split-second, point in time, moment; round, half, quarter, inning; sentence, session, semester.

3. end, ending, limit, finis, finale, omega; close, closing, closure, termination, terminus; cessation, discontinuance, halt, stop, *Sl.* thirty, windup, wrap-up, final curtain, end of the line, end of the road; death, expiration, wipe-out.

4. *Physiology.* menstrual period, menses, *Inf.* flow, *Inf.* flows, *Inf.* falling off the roof. See **menstruation.**

5. full stop, full point, *Fr. point,* dot.

periodic, *adj.* periodical, intermittent, alternating, alternate, remittent, recurrent, recurring, cyclic, cyclical; episodic, on-again-off-again, spasmodic, sporadic; occasional, infrequent, rare, every-once-in-a-while, predictable, foreseeable; pulsating, systematic, ebb-and-flow; regular, regulated, rhythmic, isochronal, isochronous, clocklike; centennial, annual, biennial, monthly, bimonthly, semimonthly, weekly, hebdomadal, biweekly, semiweekly, daily, diurnal, hourly, minute-by-minute.

periodical, *n.* **1.** publication, magazine, *Inf.* book, serial, review, digest, comic book, funny book, house organ, employee publication; newsmagazine, newsletter, daily, weekly, monthly, quarterly, almanac, yearbook; *All Sl.* girlie magazine, skin magazine, nudie book, cheesecake *or* beefcake magazine.

2. newspaper, paper, newspaper of record, journal, bulletin, gazette; tabloid, *Sl.* tab, *Sl.* sheet, *Sl.* yellow journal, *Sl.* rag, scandal sheet, *Sl.* Daily Blat, *Sl.* Daily Bugle; throwaway, giveaway, *Dial.* shopper, flier, handbill, circular.

periodically, *adv.* intermittently, alternately, remittently, recurrently, cyclically; episodically, spasmodically, sporadically; occasionally, infrequently, frequently, rarely, from time to time, now and then, once in a while, now and again, off and on; regularly, repeatedly, repetitiously, redundantly; systematically, rhythmically, isochronally; annually, biannually, monthly, weekly, daily, nightly; night after night, day after day, week after week, month after month, year after year, down through the centuries, down through the years.

peripatetic, *adj.* **1.** itinerant, itinerating, traveling, journeying, wayfaring, peregrinating; walking, ambulating, ambulatory, pedestrian; roving, roaming, wandering, rambling; perambulating, perambulatory, traversing, traveling over; galavanting, flitting, gadding, jetting; thumbing, backpacking; living in one's hat, living out of a suitcase, having itchy feet, having sand in one's shoe, unsettled, nomadic, migratory.

—*n.* **2.** itinerant, traveler, wayfarer, voyager, peregrinator; walker, pedestrian, ambulator; rambler, rover, roamer, adventurer, landloper, explorer, soldier of fortune, *U.S. Inf.* boomer; trekker, hiker, backpacker; excursionist, sight-seer.

peripheral, *adj.* **1.** peripheric, perimetric, circumferential, outlinear, outlying, outer, on the edge, on the rim, marginal; surrounding, circumjacent, circumscribing, circumspective, encircling; ambient, circumambient, environing, circumfluent.

2. superficial, unimportant, minor, not worth mentioning, beside the point, unessential, unnecessary, dispensible.

periphery, *n.* **1.** circumference, perimeter, edge, rim, fringe, verge, skirt; circuit, compass, ambit, margin, frame, outline, confine, confines; brink, brow, brim, hem; bound, limit, bourn, pale, extremity, termination; limits, circumspection, boundary, boundary line, bounding line, border line, border, partition line.

2. surface, superficiality, superficies, façade, outside, external aspect.

3. lunatic fringe.

periphrasis, *n.* **1.** circumlocution, pleonasm, tautology, redundancy, *Inf.* circumbendibus; verbiage, verbosity, wordiness, prolixity, profuseness, diffuseness, long-windedness, longiloquence; repetition, repetitiveness, tediousness, battology; digressiveness, discursiveness, maundering, convolution, circuitousness, wandering, rambling, meandering, roundaboutness, indirection, *Archaic.* ambages; ambiguousness, vagueness, beating around the bush; newspeak, bureaucratese, gobbledegook.
2. digression, excursus, cloud *or* smokescreen of words, *Rare.* tautologism.

periphrastic, *adj.* circumlocutory, pleonastic, tautological, redundant; verbose, wordy, prolix, profuse, diffuse, long-winded, longiloquent; repetitive, tedious, battological; digressive, discursive, excursive, circuitous, roundabout, ambagious, indirect, maundering, wandering, rambling; ambiguous, vague, obscure.

perish, *v.* **1.** lose one's life, be killed, *Inf.* be wiped out, lay down one's life; die, expire, decease, meet death, *Sl.* bite the dust, *Sl.* kick the bucket, *Sl.* kick it; give up the ghost, breathe one's last, draw one's last breath, *Sl.* croak; pass away, pass on, be no more, go the way of all flesh, *Sl.* cash in, *Sl.* cash in one's chips, be numbered with the dead, *Euph.* go west.
2. end, come to an end, come to nothing, die away; degenerate, fall off, *Chiefly Biol.* retrograde, deteriorate, go to pot, break down; molder, crumble, fall to pieces, disintegrate, wear away, corrode; decay, wither, shrivel, sear, go to seed, go bad, go to waste, rot; decline, fail, atrophy, waste away, ebb, wane, fade away; melt away, dissolve.
3. vanish, disappear, be gone, be heard of no more, leave no trace, be lost to view; be destroyed, be ruined, be burned up, be demolished, be eradicated.

perishable, *adj.* destructible, decayable, decomposable, biodegradable; undurable, fragile, frail, weak, delicate; impermanent, transitory, caducous, fugacious, transient, temporary, temporal; momentary, short-lived, ephemeral, evanescent, volatile, passing, fleeting, fading, flitting; mortal, corruptible, unendurable, nonpermanent; mutable, changeable, changeful, alterable, variable, permutable, inconstant; unstable, unfixed, unsteady, unsettled.

peristyle, *Architecture.* **1.** colonnade, columniation, pilaster, row *or* file of columns *or* pillars; columns, pillars, pillarets, posts, piers, poles, shafts, uprights, verticles, supports.
2. courtyard, court, quadrangle, *Inf.* quad, *Archit.* cloister; square, plaza, yard, mall, park, open space; patio, portico, porch, veranda, gallery, arcade, *Chiefly Brit.* piazza.

periwig, *n.* peruke, powdered wig, Georgian wig, wig; toupee, hairpiece, scratch, scratch wig, *Sl.* rug.

perjure, *v.* lie under oath, give false testimony, bear false witness, forswear; lie, tell a lie *or* falsehood, be untruthful, prevaricate, fib.

perjurer, *n.* forswearer, false witness; liar, prevaricator, falsifier, fibber.

perjury, *n. Law.* (*all under oath*) lying, giving false testimony, bearing false witness, forswearing; telling a lie *or* falsehood, falsehood, mendacity, prevarication; falsification, misstatement, untruthfulness, dishonesty.

perk[1], *v.* **1.** be jaunty, be lively, *Chiefly U.S. Inf.* be chipper, act alive, *Inf.* be peppy *or* full of pep.
2. *Usu.* **perk up** cheer up, liven up, *Inf.* pep up, show signs of life, brighten up; take heart *or* courage, *Inf.* buck up, *U.S. Inf.* chirk; recover, *Inf.* snap out of it, *Inf.* come around, recuperate, regain strength, get back on one's feet; rally, *Inf.* come back, *Inf.* make a comeback.
3. (*all of oneself*) flaunt, display, *Inf.* sport, exhibit; air, hold up, flash; put forth *or* forward, emphasize, spotlight, draw attention to, show off; splash, make a splash, splurge, make a splurge; make a show, cut *or* make a figure, *Sl.* cut a dash, *Sl.* cut a shine, *Sl.* cut a feather; swagger, swank, swashbuckle, strut, *Sl.* strut one's stuff, peacock; boast, blow one's own horn, brag, vaunt, talk up; put on airs, put up a front, *U.S. Sl.* put on the dog, *Sl.* put on, *Sl.* put on the ritz.
4. *Often* **perk up** *or* **out** raise, lift up, upturn, turn upward; show sudden interest, prick up one's ears, listen attentively, be all ears.
5. dress up, *Sl.* jazz up, liven up, brighten up; spruce up, smarten up, make smart, *Sl.* spiff up; trim, decorate, adorn, add to, fix up.
—adj. **6.** perky, jaunty. See **perky** (*def.* **1**).

perk[2], *n.* *Informal.* perquisite, emolument, fringe benefit, bonus, extra. See **perquisite.**

perky, *adj.* **1.** perk, jaunty, pert, lively, full of life, alive, sprightly, *Chiefly U.S. Inf.* chipper, *Inf.* in fine fettle; active, energetic, dynamic, spirited, brisk, vigorous, fresh; frisky, playful, frolicsome, sportive, zestful; enthusiastic, enthused, excited, eager, *Inf.* gung ho; animated, bouncy, vivacious, *Inf.* full of pep, *Inf.* peppy, full of vim and vigor, bright-eyed and bushy-tailed; aglow, glowing, alight, lit up, bright, enlivened, shining, shiny; sparkling, ebullient, bubbling, bubbly, effervescent; cheery, cheerful, full of cheer, gay, sunny, in good *or* high spirits; blithe, blithesome, lighthearted, lightsome, buoyant, optimistic, *Inf.* upbeat, beamish; debonair, free and easy, carefree, easygoing, breezy, airy, happy-go-lucky, untroubled.
2. smart, dapper, spruce, *Sl.* spiffy, trim, *Chiefly Brit.* trig, neat, *Inf.* natty, well-groomed, sleek; attractive, becoming, good; fine, smartly dressed, elegant, well-dressed, stylish, chic, fashionable, *Sl.* classy.

permanence, *n.* **1.** perpetuity, everlastingness, immortality, deathlessness, athanasia; imperishability, indestructibility, indissolubility, incorruptibility; lastingness, longevity, long-livedness, endurance, abidingness, constancy; duration, durability, continuance, continuity; persistence, maintenance, sustentation, sustenance, prolongation, perpetuation, preservation.
2. immutability, unchangeableness, changelessness, unalterableness, incommutability, invariability; permanency, stability, stabilization, fixity, fixedness, soundness, substance, solidity; dependability, reliability.

permanent, *adj.* **1.** eternal, *Archaic.* eterne, infinite, everlasting, *Literary.* sempiternal; immortal, undying, deathless; imperishable, indestructible, indissoluble, incorruptible, undecaying, unfading; long-lived, longevous, amaranthine, perennial, *Bot.* (*of leaves*) indeciduous, (*of trees*) evergreen.
2. perpetual, unending, endless, never-ending, ceaseless, unceasing, incessant; unintermitting, uninterrupted, continuous, continual, unbroken; enduring, abiding, lasting, continuing, constant, durable; maintained, sustained, prolonged, protracted, perpetuated, preserved, conserved, surviving.
3. immutable, unchangeable, changeless, unalterable, incommutable, invariable; stable, stationary, firm, fixed, sound, solid, balanced; dependable, reliable, steady, steadfast; established, confirmed, inveterate, strong, deep-rooted, entrenched, ingrained; fastened, attached, rooted, anchored, moored, grounded.
—n. **4.** permanent wave, *Inf.* perm; marcel, marcel waves; home permanent, *Trademark.* Toni.

permanently, *adv.* once and for all, for good and all, for all time, for ever and ever; forevermore, for ever hereafter, till the end of time, till hell freezes over, till the cows come home, till Niagara Falls; forever, always, evermore, *Poetic.* ay, *Latin. in saecula saeculorum;* for ever and a day, eternally, everlastingly, perpetually, undyingly; constantly, continually, continuously, nonstop, incessantly, unremittingly; unceasingly, ceaselessly, endlessly, unendingly, interminably.

permeability, *n.* permeableness, perviousness, porosity, porousness, penetrability, penetrableness, passableness, openness, accessibility; vulnerability, vulnerableness, pregnability, openness to attack.

permeable, *adj.* pervious, porous, penetrable, perforable, pierceable, enterable; open, passable, accessible, reachable; vulnerable, pregnable, open to attack.

permeate, *v.* pass through, go through, walk through, cut through, slice through; penetrate, shoot through, perforate, pass into, enter; osmose, blend, fuse, inosculate, interosculate; pervade, interpenetrate, overspread, overrun, take over; infiltrate, filter into, invade, spread over *or* into, spread throughout, honeycomb, diffuse; saturate, fill, extend throughout, leave no void; percolate, filter through, seep through, leak through, come through, show through, soak through; imbue, infuse, interfuse, suffuse, transfuse, impregnate, leaven.

permeation, *n.* penetration, perforation, entrance, entry, passing through; osmosis, blending, fusing, inosculation, interosculation; spreading, diffusion, overspreading, pervasion, interpenetration, infiltration, invasion, overrunning, saturation; imbuement, infusion, interfusion, suffusion, transfusion, impregnation.

permissible, *adj.* **1.** allowable, lawful, legal, licit, legalized, legitimate, *Sl.* legit, within bounds, *Inf.* kosher; proper, fitting, right, appropriate, apt, suitable, *Inf.* O.K.; admissible, acceptable, all right, sayable, printable; acknowledgeable, concessible, grantable; authorizable, warrantable, approvable, sanctionable.

2. tolerable, permitted, tolerated, allowed; unforbidden, unprohibited, unproscribed; justifiable, vindicable, venial, excusable, pardonable.

permission, *n.* **1.** allowance, consent, assent; acquiescence, accedence, concession, *Law.* connivance; agreement, concurrence, accord, accordance, concordance; tolerance, toleration, sufferance, brooking, endurance.

2. liberty, license, leave, right, prerogative; authorization, sanctioning, warrant, warranty, franchise, affranchisement, enfranchisement; approval, assurance, countenance, approbation, going along with; support, abidance, compliance, cooperation, aid; granting, enabling, empowerment, entitlement; authority, sanction, say-so, power, grant.

3. privilege, vouchsafement, special favor, indulgence; dispensation, exemption, exception, immunity; blank check, carte blanche, free hand, go-ahead, *Inf.* green light; access, admittance, admission, right of entry; pass, congé, passport, visa, card, safe-conduct; order, declaration, decree, command; rule, law, ordinance, edict, charter, official document.

permissive, *adj.* **1.** approving, assenting, acquiescent, agreeing; affirmative, accordant, consenting, favorable; sanctioning, ratifying, ordaining, endorsing.

2. indulgent, lenient, tolerant, lax; admissive, unprohibitive, unproscriptive, permitting, allowing; easy, soft, unstrict, overindulgent, forbearing; liberal, libertine, latitudinarian, open-minded; kindly, benevolent, obliging, accommodating, agreeable.

permit, *v.* **1.** allow, give permission *or* leave to, grant, let; authorize, sanction, warrant, entitle, empower, enable, license, franchise, commission; vouchsafe, favor, privilege; affranchise, give one his head, give carte blanche, give the green light, give the go-ahead, give [s.o.] enough rope; approve of, go along with, submit to, yield, accede to; assent to, agree to, consign, consent to, acquiesce in, admit of, be compatible with; tolerate, countenance, put up with, hear of, *Inf.* stand for, bear, support; suffer, stand, brook, abide, endure.

—*n.* **2.** license, authorization, warrant, authority, sanction; card, passport, visa, safe-conduct; patent, copyright; charter, edict, order, declaration, official document.

3. permission, leave, license, franchise, consent. See **permission** (*def.* **2**).

permitted, *adj.* allowed, lawful, admissible. See **permissible.**

permutability, *n.* alterability, changeability, variability; mutability, changeableness, convertibility, modifiability, adaptability; interchangeability, commutability, exchangeability.

permutable, *adj.* changeable, alterable, mutable, modifiable, alterative, convertible; adjustable, adaptable; interchangeable, commutable, exchangeable, returnable.

permutation, *n.* alteration, transformation, transposition, translocation, *Physiol.* metastasis, metathesis; mutation, metabolism, metamorphosis, translation; transubstantiation, consubstantiation, transanimation, transmogrification.

permute, *v.* alter, change, mutate, turn into; translate, metamorphose, convert, transform, modify; transfigure, metabolize, transubstantiate, consubstantiate, transmogrify.

pernicious, *adj.* **1.** ruinous, destructive, damaging, fell, baleful; injurious, hurtful, harmful, baneful, dangerous, bad; deleterious, detrimental, unwholesome, insalubrious, nocuous.

2. lethal, deadly, fatal, mortal, deathly, killing; toxic, poisonous, venomous, virulent, septic; noxious, malicious, malign, malignant; noisome, mephitic, pestilent, pestiferous.

perorate, *v.* **1.** speak at length, discourse, expatiate, descant; orate, lecture, preach, sermonize; elocutionize, *Inf.* elocute, harangue, rant; *Inf.* spout, *Sl.* run off at the mouth, drool, *Inf.* spiel; flourish, go on and on, out-herod Herod; speechify, hold forth, declaim, tub-thump, rodomontade; take to the hustings, take the floor, climb on the soapbox.

2. summarize, sum up, conclude, bring to a conclusion, close, end, *Inf.* wind up; recapitulate, recap, recount, regurgitate.

peroration, *n.* **1.** recapitulation, recapping, recount; summation, summary, conclusion, close, closing; closing words, closing *or* concluding remarks, last words, parting shot.

2. address, talk, speech, discourse, disquisition; oration, elocution, monologue; sermon, lecture, preachment, homily; harangue, declamation; exhortation, tirade, jeremiad, diatribe, philippic, *Inf.* pep talk.

peroxide, *n.* **1.** hydrogen peroxide, bleach, oxidizing agent, bleaching agent, blanching agent.

—*v.* **2.** (*all in reference to the hair*) bleach, blanch, *Sl.* blond; whiten, yellow, silver, frost, *Inf.* streak; decolor, achromatize; (*loosely*) dye.

perpendicular, *adj.* **1.** vertical, on end, upright, at right angles to, right-angular, *Geom.* at 90 degrees to; plumb, straight, straight-up-and-down, up-and-down; bolt-upright, standing, standing upright.

2. steep, sharp, sheer, precipitous; abrupt, bold, craggy, high.

—*n.* **3.** upright, vertical, plumb, plumb line, perpendicular line *or* plane; straight angle.

4. rectitude, morality, moral uprightness, virtue, integrity, uncorruptibility; equity, fairness, honesty, trustworthiness; righteousness, uprightness, goodness, purity, impeccability; veracity, probity, truthfulness; conscientiousness, scrupulousness, honor, fidelity, faithfulness.

5. cliff, precipice, crag, bluff, rocky eminence; scarp, escarpment, incline, tor, spine, ridge, headland.

perpetrate, *v.* **1.** (*all of crime or wrong*) commit, perform, execute, *Inf.* pull off; effect, effectuate, succeed in, mastermind, make happen; accomplish, carry through, *Sl.* knock off, *Sl.* polish, expedite.

2. (*all of pranks or deception*) carry out, act, enact, actuate, practice, transact, bring about; pursue, exercise, produce, work out, discharge, *Inf.* put over.

perpetration, *n.* (*all of wrongdoing*) execution, performance, enactment, carrying out, exercise, practice; action, proceeding, doing; undertaking, enterprise, job, commission, production.

perpetual, *adj.* **1.** everlasting, eternal, *Literary.* sempiternal, never-ending; permanent, perdurable, long-lived, longevous; immortal, deathless, undying, preserved; timeless, ageless, dateless, infinite; lasting, indestructible, imperishable, perennial; unchanging, durable, unvarying, evergreen; immutable, undeviating, abiding, enduring, lasting, inviolate; inveterate, chronic, confirmed, habitual, longstanding.

2. incessant, constant, unending, ever-flowing, persistent, longlasting; continuous, uninterrupted, unintermitting, never-stopping, unbroken, marathon, around the clock; rhythmic, recurrent, nonstop, repeated; ceaseless, endless, unending, unceasing, interminable, nonterminable; unfailing, sustained, unstopped.

perpetually, *adv.* **1.** everlastingly, eternally, sempiternally, never-endingly; immortally, undyingly, deathlessly, timelessly, agelessly, infinitely, datelessly; permanently, perdurably, indelibly; in perpetuity, always, *Latin. in saecula saeculorum;* lastingly, enduringly, abidingly, immutably; ever, evermore, ever and anon, *Poetic.* ay, *Poetic.* for ay; for good, for good and all, for always, for ever and a day, till the end of time, world without end, time without end; *Inf.* till the cows come home, *Sl.* till hell freezes over, *Latin. ad infinitum;* all the time, all along, perennially, invariably; unfadingly, indestructibly, imperishably; forever, forever and forever, forever and a day, to the end of time, till doomsday, till the end of recorded time.

2. constantly, continuously, incessantly, unremittingly, longlastingly; unceasingly, ceaselessly, without cease, uninterruptedly, unvaryingly, without break, without letup; unendingly, interminably, without end, without stop; steadily, regularly, unfailingly, unbrokenly; rhythmically, recurrently, repeatedly, persistently; day in and day out, year in and year out; morning, noon, and night; night and day, day and night, at all hours, every minute, every hour, at every minute of the day, around the clock.

perpetuate, *v.* memorialize, immortalize, eternalize, eternize, put down in history; preserve, sustain, maintain, keep, keep up, save, conserve; continue, extend, protract.

perpetuation, *n.* memorialization, immortalization, eternalization, eternization; preservation, maintenance, sustenance, conservation, keeping, saving; continuance, continuation, protraction, extension, prolongation, lengthening.

perpetuity, *n.* endlessness, forever, all time, eternity, sempiternity; constancy, durability, perdurability; permanence, everlastingness, ceaselessness, never-endingness; timelessness, coeternity, endless duration; continuity, continuance, perennialness; successiveness, consecutiveness, repetitiveness.

perplex, *v.* **1.** mystify, confound, bewilder, nonplus, baffle, puzzle, make uncertain, put to it, *Inf.* bamboozle, *Inf.* buffalo, *Inf.* stump; disconcert, *Inf.* discombobulate, stagger; abash, embarrass, put [s.o.] at a disadvantage *or* loss; stun, stupefy, daze, amaze, astonish, astound, flabbergast, dumfound, boggle; fuddle, befuddle, muddle, bemuddle, fog, befog, keep [s.o.] guessing; fool, delude, trick, outwit, hoodwink, *Sl.* hornswoggle, bluff.

2. confuse, tangle, entangle, involve, snarl, mix up, jumble; mess up, clutter up, disorganize, turn topsy-turvy, put into turmoil, *Inf.* foul up; imbroil, complicate, put at sixes and sevens; distract, put in a fog, put in a haze, unhinge, *Psychiatry.* disorient.

perplexed, *adj.* **1.** bewildered, puzzled, mystified, confounded; baffled, *Inf.* bamboozled, *Inf.* buffaloed, *Inf.* stumped; disconcerted, *Inf.* discombobulated, staggered; abashed, embarrassed, at a disadvantage *or* loss; stunned, stupefied, dazed, amazed, astonished, astounded, flabbergasted, dumfounded, boggled; fuddled, befuddled, muddled, bemuddled, befogged; deluded, *Sl.* hornswoggled; distracted, in a fog, in a haze, unhinged, *Psychiatry.* disoriented.

2. involved, complicated, entangled, involuted; snarled, mixed up, jumbled; messed up, disorganized, topsy-turvy; in a turmoil, *Inf.* fouled up, *Inf.* balled up, at sixes and sevens.

perplexing, *adj.* **1.** confusing, enigmatic, enigmatical; paradoxical, paradoxal, puzzling, baffling, bewildering, confounding, mystifying; inexplicable, unexplainable, insoluble, insolvable, unaccountable, *Obs.* inextricable; strange, weird, bizarre, mysterious; hidden, veiled, masked, screened; obscure, indistinct, indefinite, unclear, shadowy, nebulous, vague; inscrutable, sphingine, sphinxlike, riddling, oracular, abstruse, recondite, abstract, heavy; impenetrable, unfathomable, incomprehensible, uncomprehensible, past *or* beyond comprehension *or* understanding; ambiguous, equivocal; noncommittal, secretive, arcane.

2. involved, labyrinthine, knotty, Gordian, intricate, complicated, complex; spiny, thorny, troublesome, vexing, vexatious; taxing, trying, bothersome, annoying, *Inf.* aggravating; nagging, *Inf.* pesky, bedeviling, teasing; disquieting, distracting, awkward, embarrassing, *Inf.* discombobulating; problematic, problematical, hard, difficult.

perplexity, *n.* **1.** bewilderment, bafflement, astonishment; mystification, confoundment, puzzlement, puzzledness, incomprehension; stupefaction, distraction, unhingement, disconcertment, discomfiture, discomposure, embarrassment, chagrin, abashment, consternation, worry.

2. uncertainty, incertitude, confusion, fluster, dazzlement, amazement, doubt; hesitation, dubiety, skepticism, mistrust, distrust, suspicion.

3. enigma, paradox, mystery, puzzle; dilemma, intricacy, *Inf.* complicated plot; knot, knotty problem, Gordian knot; maze, labyrinth, net, network, confusion; tangle, entanglement, snarl, jumble; quandary, predicament, plight, *Inf.* pickle, *Inf.* fix, difficulty, trouble, *Inf.* hot water; emergency, *Inf.* sticky business, *Chiefly Brit.* sticky wicket, inexplicable difficulty; corner, tight spot, *Sl.* box, bind, double bind, catch-22, vicious circle; strait, *Inf.* squeeze, pinch, push; difficult choice, *Fr. embarras de choix,* tough question, tough nut, poser; obfuscation, obscuration, mist, haze; jungle, muddle, disorder.

perquisite, *n.* **1.** emolument, profit, gain, advantage; *Inf.* perk, benefit, fringe benefit, *Inf.* fringe; bonus, extra, dividend, plus; fee, salary, stipend, pay, payment, compensation, recompense, remuneration, repayment; reward, gift, present, honorarium, altarage, token acknowledgement, token of appreciation,

Inf. a little something; tip, gratuity, douceur, lagniappe, *Fr. pourboire, Ger. Trinkgeld, Archaic.* vail, (*in Chinese ports*) cumshaw, (*in India and Turkey*) baksheesh.

2. due, privilege, right.

per se, in itself, by its very nature, by definition, intrinsically, inherently, innately, immanently, *Archaic.* ingenerately; alone, taken alone, solitarily, solely; separately, individually, apart, apart from anything else, taken out of context.

persecute, *v.* **1.** torture, agonize, excruciate, martyr, rack, crucify, dragoon; pain, hurt, scathe, wring, put someone through the wringer; punish, castigate, abuse, beat, beat up, *Sl.* work over, *Sl.* give one the works, *Archaic.* belabor; molest, mistreat, maltreat, ill-treat, ill-use; oppress, tyrannize, subjugate, grind, trample, burden, weigh down; aggrieve, outrage, wrong, discriminate against, *Sl.* kick around, *Sl.* do [s.o.] dirty.

2. afflict, torment, plague, hector, bully; vex, annoy, harass, harry, badger, hound, importune, bother, pester, *Brit.* chevy; exasperate, aggravate, irritate, gall, rub, chafe, roil, *Chiefly U.S.* rile; provoke, needle, nettle, bullyrag, tease, *Brit.* rag; anguish, distress, harrow, worry, trouble, disturb, *Scot.* fash; perturb, upset, disconcert, disquiet, *Inf.* faze.

persecution, *n.* **1.** torture, torturing, excruciation, agony, misery, martyrdom, suffering, infliction, crucifixion, crucifying; punishment, punishing, castigation, abuse, beating, flagellation, flogging, lashing, whipping; molestation, mistreatment, maltreatment, ill-treatment; anguish, distress, affliction, torment, plague, harrowment; atrocity, aggrievement, outrage, wronging, discrimination.

2. oppression, suppression, subjugation, tyranny, grinding down, trampling; extermination, annihilation, eradication, elimination, abolition, stamping out.

perseverance, *n.* **1.** steadfastness, persistence; continuance, endurance, abidingness, patience; stamina, indefatigableness, backbone, courage, grit, *Inf.* sand, pluck, *Sl.* guts, hardiness of spirit; application, zeal, ambition, devotion, diligence, pursuance, sedulity, sedulousness, tenacity, *Inf.* stick-to-itiveness.

2. resolve, determination, purposiveness, purposefulness, decision, decisiveness, firmness of mind, toughness of mind, pertinacity; stubbornness, mulishness, doggedness, *Inf.* cussedness, inflexibility, insistence, insistency, intransigence, intransigency, obstinacy, obstinateness, obdurateness, contumacy, contumaciousness.

persevere, *v.* **1.** continue, keep on *or* at, keep going, be steadfast, endure, abide; strive, labor, struggle, toil, moil, grub, grind, drudge, work unflaggingly, work day and night, stick to the job, *Inf.* stick it out, plug away, hammer away, do thoroughly, not do by halves, *Sl.* do it up brown, do to a frazzle; pursue, pursue relentlessly, chase, follow up, see through, leave no stone unturned, go to any lengths, go the limit, *Inf.* go the whole hog, go all the way, move heaven and earth, stop at nothing.

2. insist, stand firm, stand fast, stick to one's guns, hold one's ground; be unyielding, be obstinate, be resolute, not take "no" for an answer, brook no denial, have one's own way, have a mind of one's own; cling, cling to, adhere, be tenacious, hold fast, *Inf.* keep the faith, not give up the ship, go down fighting, die trying, die in harness, die with one's boots on.

3. bolster, sustain, maintain, uphold, support; prop, brace, buttress, underpin; shoulder, hold up, shore up, bear up.

persevering, *adj.* **1.** persistent, assiduous, constant, tenacious; patient, enduring, abiding; diligent, zealous, ambitious, industrious, sedulous, careful, attentive, painstaking, plodding; indefatigable, indomitable, untiring, unwearied, undrooping, unflagging, never-sleeping, never-wearying, never-tiring; frequent, chronic, repetitious, incessant, unceasing, unstopping, unrelenting, relentless, unremitting, continuous, continual, interminable.

2. resolute, determined, sturdy, firm, stalwart, grim, decided, decisive, undistracted, purposive, purposeful; uncompromising, unshakable, unfaltering, unswervable, unswerving, unwavering, steadfast, unshrinking, undeviating, See **persistent** (def. **2**).

persiflage, *n.* banter, badinage, repartee, word play, verbal wit, wittiness; pleasantry, frivolity, fun and games, clowning *or* fooling around, buffoonery; jesting, joking, levity, humor, drollery, jocularity, jocosity, waggery; teasing, twitting, taunting, *Inf.* joshing, *Inf.* funning, *Inf.* kidding, *Inf.* ribbing, *Sl.* jiving; (*all in jest*) raillery, ridicule, derision, mockery, *Inf.* ragging, *Brit.* quizzing.

persist, *v.* **1.** continue, persevere, keep on, keep going, be steadfast, endure; strive, labor, struggle, toil, moil, grub, grind, drudge. See **persevere** (*def.* **1**).

2. remain, last, endure, perdure, subsist, survive; abide, linger, carry on, stay, *Inf.* hang in there, *Inf.* never say die; be constant, be steadfast, be permanent; hold good, remain valid, remain unchanged.

3. insist, stand firm, stand fast, stick to one's guns, hold one's ground, be unyielding, be obstinate, be resolute. See **persevere** (*def.* **2**).

persistence, *n.* **1.** steadfastness, perseverance, continuance, endurance, abidingness, patience; stamina, indefatigableness, backbone, courage, grit, pluck. See **perseverance** (*def.* **1**).

2. resolve, determination, purposiveness, purposefulness, decision, decisiveness, firmness of mind, toughness of mind, pertinacity. See **perseverance** (*def.* **2**).

persistent, *adj.* **1.** persevering, assiduous, tenacious; diligent, zealous, ambitious, industrious, sedulous, careful, attentive, painstaking, plodding; indefatigable, indomitable, untiring, unwearied, undrooping, unflagging, never-sleeping, never-wearying, never-tiring.

2. resolute, determined, sturdy, firm, stalwart, grim, decided, decisive, undistracted, purposive, purposeful; uncompromising, steadfast, unshakable, unfaltering, unswervable, unswerving, unwavering, unshrinking, undeviating; dogged, stubborn, mulish, *Inf.* cussed, obstinate, adamant, obdurate, pertinacious, inflexible, intransigent, intractable, contumacious.

3. enduring, lasting, abiding; constant, fixed, permanent; immovable, immutable, indelible, indestructible; deep-rooted, deep-seated, ingrained.

4. frequent, chronic, repetitious, incessant, unceasing, unstopping, unrelenting, relentless, unremitting, continuous, continual, interminable.

persnickety, *adj. Informal.* **1.** fastidious, fussy, finical, finicky, *Inf.* nitpicking; particular, discriminating, discriminative, highly selective, *Inf.* choosy; picayune, hairsplitting, trifling, petty, *Inf.* fuddy-duddy; punctilious, precise, exact, attentive to detail; overscrupulous, scrupulous, meticulous, methodical, thorough, thoroughgoing, searching, careful, attentive, conscientious; overcritical, hypercritical, critical, hard *or* difficult to please; overdemanding, demanding, overexacting, exacting, strict, rigid, severe, sparing no pains.

2. painstaking, tedious, detailed, fine, minute; rigorous, arduous, difficult, hard; backbreaking, exhausting, fatiguing, tiring, tiresome, wearisome.

person, *n.* **1.** human being, human, being, creature, mortal, life, member of the human race, earthling, Adamite; individual, entity, personage, personality, persona; soul, living soul, spirit; one, someone, body, somebody; *Fig.* head, *Fig.* hand, *Fig.* nose; *All Inf.* character, customer, party, fellow, chap, lad, actor, guy, scout; *All Sl.* cat, gent, joker, warm body, joe; *Brit. Sl.* bloke, *Brit. Sl.* skate.

2. body, physical body, material body, flesh and blood, flesh, clay, mortal coil; figure, form, frame, physique, build, bulk, *Dial.* built, torso; appearance, shape, mold, cast, *Inf.* anatomy, *Inf.* corpus, *Inf.* carcass, *Sl.* bones, *Sl.* bod.

3. in person personally, bodily, in one's person, *Latin. in propria persona, Inf.* in the flesh.

persona, *n.* **1.** person. See **person** (*def.* **1**).

2. personae cast of characters, characters, dramatis personae, cast, players, troupe, company, stage people, persons of the drama, creatures of the author, people in the story.

3. exponent, speaker, voice, relator, narrator, storyteller.

4. personality, public face, public image; mask, façade, exterior, shell, surface; role, assumed role, part, capacity, relation, status, position; portrayal, representation, show, display.

personable, *adj.* **1.** attractive, handsome, good-looking, shapely, well-formed, well-built, well-made, well-proportioned; good to look at, comely, pleasing to the eye, pleasant to see, *Sl.* easy on the eyes, *Sl.* not hard to look at.

2. agreeable, friendly, easygoing, outgoing, sociable, gregarious; amiable, companionable, easy to get on *or* along with; likable, pleasant, good-natured, cordial, warm; amicable, affable, neighborly.

personage, *n.* **1.** dignitary, notable, very important person, *Inf.* V.I.P., *Archaic.* dignity; person of note *or* consequence, well-known figure, public figure, celebrity, *Sl.* celeb, somebody, something, famous *or* well-known person, household name, *Inf.* big name, *Inf.* name; luminary, worthy, high official, leader, pillar of society *or* of the community *or* of the church, patriarch; immortal, one of the greats, leading light; person to be reckoned with, politico; *Inf.* the people's choice, man at the top; standout, heavyweight, *Sl.* heavy, biggest frog in the pond, *Inf.* honcho, lion, social lion, toast of the town; hero, heroine, popular hero, *Sl.* pop hero, folk hero, star, superstar, headliner, idol, matinée idol, screen idol; magnate, captain of industry, *Inf.* tycoon, *Inf.* baron, *Inf.* power, *Inf.* top brass, *Inf.* brass hat, mogul, nabob, pooh bah, panjandrum, *Sl.* high-muck-a-muck, *Inf.* sachem, *Inf.* bigwig, *Sl.* fat cat; *All Sl.* big noise, big-time operator, BTO, big shot, biggie, big gun, big wheel, big cheese, *Fr. grand fromage,* hotshot.

2. person. See **person** (*def.* **1.**).

3. role, part, piece, *Inf.* bit, portrayal, characterization; actor, actress, character, principal, lead, hero, heroine, protagonist, villain, antagonist, *Inf.* heavy, supporting player *or* role.

personal, *adj.* **1.** individual, own; inner, internal, inward, inwardly felt, innermost, close to one's heart; private, secret, unrevealed, confidential, *Inf.* nobody else's business *or* affair; particular, especial, inherent, exclusive, intrinsic, essential; special, peculiar, idiosyncratic, subjective.

2. intimate, familiar, thick, *Inf.* chummy; one to one, *Inf.* one-on-one, face-to-face, tête-à-tête.

3. insulting, offensive, slighting, disparaging, derogatory, depreciating, deprecating; derisive, ridiculing, mocking, belittling, *Inf.* nasty.

personality, **1.** identity, self, ego, character, make-up, psyche, essence, nature, traits; mind, disposition, temperament, stripe, spirit, humor, affection.

2. individuality, distinctness, separateness, difference, definiteness, distinction, particularity, originality, uniqueness; personal identity, particularism, specialness.

3. person. See **person** (*def.* **1**).

4. charisma, charm, magnetism; attraction, personal force *or* power, drawing power, winning ways, taking ways; likability, pleasantness.

5. celebrity, *Sl.* celeb, star, superstar, headliner. See **personage** (*def.* **1**).

personalize, *v.* **1.** take personally, be subjective, define *or* explain in terms of oneself; take upon oneself, take the weight of the world on one's shoulders.

2. personify, embody, typify, represent; name, denote, designate; individualize, particularize, individuate, make special *or* unique, distingush; define, differentiate, separate, characterize, set apart *or* set off, mark off, make individual, make distinctive.

3. earmark, hallmark, give one's personal touch; initial, monogram, brand, stamp with one's own brand, mark *or* have marked as one's own, label, tag, sign, *Sl.* tag with one's moniker.

personally, *adv.* **1.** as a person, for oneself, for one's part, from one's own viewpoint, in one's own view, as far as one is concerned, from where one stands *or* sits, in one's own consideration, as one sees it.

2. privately, individually, particularly, specially, especially, specifically, expressly, individualistically, idiosyncratically, in one's own way *or* style, characteristically.

3. in person, on one's own, *Inf.* in the flesh; without anyone else, by oneself, alone, independently, under one's own power, *Inf.* all by one's lonesome, *Inf.* on one's own say-so.

personate, *v.* **1.** act, portray, play, playact, perform; represent, depict, play *or* perform a role, take a part, create a role *or* character; make believe, act out, enact; interpret, characterize, read, delineate, draw, paint, sketch, render; project, realize *or* develop a character, throw oneself into a part *or* role.

2. impersonate, assume the guise of, appear as, pretend to be, take the part *or* place of, assume the role *or* character of, do a study *or* characterization of, masquerade as, mask oneself as, take on the coloration of, represent oneself as; pass for, be taken as, pass, go as; imitate, mirror, reflect, represent, ape, take off, do a takeoff of *or* on, *Inf.* do a number on, do an impression of; mimic, mock, parody, caricature, burlesque; monkey, parrot, echo, simulate, *Sl.* make like.

3. personify, embody, exemplify, incarnate; bring to life, breathe life into.

personation, *n.* **1.** role, part, portrayal, performance, representation, characterization, interpretation, reading; delineation, sketching, rendering; acting, playacting, playing, performing, taking a role *or* part, *Inf.* doing a turn *or* bit; (*all of a role*) projection, realization, development, immersion.

2. impersonation, disguise, pretense, posing, masquerade, misrepresentation; imitation, mime, mimicry, pantomime, parody, simulation, caricature, burlesque; copying, mocking, making fun of, parroting, mimicking, aping.

3. personification, embodiment, incarnation.

personator, *n.* **1.** actor, performer, player, trouper, stage player, playactor, role player, thespian, Roscian, histrio, histrion, mime, pantomime, pantomimist, personifier; mimic.

2. impersonator, pretender, imitator, masquerader,

master of disguise, man of a thousand faces; poseur, fake, fraud, sham, charlatan, *Inf.* phony; deceiver, bamboozler, trickster, deceiver, deluder, misrepresenter; impostor, *Inf.* ringer, wolf in sheep's clothing

personification, *n.* **1.** figure of speech, figure, image, *Rhet.* prosopopoeia, pathetic fallacy; metaphor, conceit.

2. embodiment, incarnation, materialization; manifestation, appearance, likeness, semblance; reproduction, duplication, recreation, reincarnation.

3. representation, delineation, portrayal, depiction, rendition; characterization, picturization, figuration, presentation, presentment; drawing, rendering, realization, projection.

4. impersonation, personation, imitation, *Rhet.* mimesis; mimicking, miming, simulation, pantomime.

personify, *v.* **1.** embody, incarnate, personate, illustrate, demonstrate, exemplify, image, mirror, reflect, simulate; make corporeal, give human qualities to, make human, imbue with character; breathe life into, give life to.

2. (*all as a person*) represent, depict, characterize, portray; picture, paint, draw, delineate.

3. typify, signify, symbolize, be a living example of, be a good example of, stand for, be regarded as, be the equivalent of.

personnel, *n.* employees, staff, help, hired help, the help; force, work force, labor force, office force; workers, laborers, labor supply, manpower; members, associates, assemblage, group, crew, gang, troupe, company, *Inf.* bunch; troops, units, firepower, fighting force; forces, reserves, backup, spares.

perspective, *n.* **1.** view, vista, sweep, scape; exposure, aspect, scene, landscape, prospect, picture, spectacle, panorama; distance, space, reach, stretch, range, compass, command, sight, span; horizon, line of horizon, where the earth meets the sky, vanishing point.

2. viewpoint, point of view, standpoint, vantage point; mental outlook, outlook, overview; position, stand, place, bias, as one sees it, where one sits *or* stands; respect, regard, angle, slant, leaning, inclination; mind, tendency, turn of mind, *Inf.* where one is coming from, frame of reference; attitude, frame of mind, disposition, emotional tone, temper, vein, grain, mood, humor, cast, spirit.

3. sense of proportion, sense of values, posture, stance, way of looking at things, way of thinking, feelings, sentiment.

perspicacious, *adj.* discerning, astute, perceptive, clear-eyed, penetrating, piercing; keen, sharp, acute, quick; sharp-witted, keen-witted, quick-witted, *Inf.* quick on the uptake, *Sl.* sharp as a tack; bright, brainy, *Inf.* nobody's fool. *Sl.* in tune, *Sl.* tuned-in, *Inf.* not born yesterday; percipient, appercipient, discriminating, critical; sagacious, judicious, wise, sapient, knowing, comprehending, understanding, aware, sensitive; discreet, politic, prudent, Argus-eyed, mindful; clearheaded, thoughtful, sensible, intelligent, sound; alert, clever, shrewd, subtle; long-sighted, farsighted, farseeing, long-headed.

perspicacity, *n.* **1.** keenness, acuteness, sharpness, acuity; discernment, discrimination, distinguishment; acumen, perceptiveness, insight, perspicaciousness, penetration, awareness; cleverness, astuteness, shrewdness, ingenuity, ingeniousness; perception, *Psychol.* apperception, percipience, sensitivity, flair; ascertainment, determination, observance, notice.

2. apprehension, understanding, *Obs.* skill, comprehension; intelligence, knowledge, profundity, depth; sagacity, sagaciousness, wisdom; intuition, divination, clairvoyance; foresightedness, farsightedness, longheadedness; mother wit, wit, esprit; sense, common sense, good sense, judgment, prudence, brains, smartness, brightness; clearheadedness, clear-sightedness, clear vision.

perspicuity, *n.* **1.** lucidity, lucidness, clarity, clearness, plainness, unambiguousness, unambiguity, unmistakability; explicitness, preciseness, precision, exactness, definiteness, distinctness, clear-cutness; comprehensibility, comprehensibleness, understandability, understandableness, intelligibility, intelligibleness, penetrability; perceptibility, discernibleness, apprehensibility, decipherability, legibility; obviousness, apparentness, evidentness, manifestness, palpability, patentability.

2. perspicacity, perspicaciousness, sharpness, acuteness. See **perspicacity** (*def.* **1**).

perspicuous, *adj.* **1.** clear, lucid, intelligible, understandable, easily understood, comprehensible, penetrating; plain, distinct, plain as day, plain as the nose on one's face, evident, apparent, manifest, obvious, patent, palpable, tangible, evident, self-evident; clear-cut, crystal-clear, well-defined, vivid, graphic; explicit, unequivocal, unmistakable, unambiguous; discernible, undisguised, uncloaked, unhidden, revealed, disclosed, overt, bare, naked; simple, direct, pointed, to the point, concise, cogent; specific, absolute, unqualified, loud and clear, certain.

2. perspicacious, discerning, astute, perceptive, clear-eyed, penetrating. See **perspicacious.**

perspiration, *n.* sweat, sweating, *Obs.* sudation, sudoresis, *Med.* diaphoresis; excretion, transudation, exudation, exudate, emanation, effluence; *Both Euph.* wetness, dampness; body odor, b.o.

perspire, *v.* sweat, *Obs.* sudate, glow; excrete, transude, exude, emanate; be damp, be wet, drip, be dripping wet, swelter, pour sweat, be drenched with sweat; reek, have body odor, have b.o.

persuadable, *adj.* **1.** receptive, susceptive, open-minded, open to suggestions, amenable, acquiescent, compliant, agreeable; broad-minded, liberal, just, equitable, reasonable, thoughtful, thinking, open; unopinionated, dispassionate, broad, impersonal, impartial, disinterested.

2. persuasible, inducible, convincible; yielding, deferential, submissive, unresistant, unresisting, obeisant; influenceable, susceptible, impressionable, impressible, pliable, malleable, bendable, flexible, moldable; young, undeveloped, inexperienced, immature, eager.

persuade, *v.* **1.** induce, prevail upon, affect, influence, sway, bend, incline, dispose; bribe, suborn, pay off; tempt, allure, lure, entice, inveigle, vamp, seduce; move, prompt, motivate, stimulate, rouse, inspire, inspirit; urge, exhort, admonish, importune; impel, compel, force, make, cause, cause to, have; constrain, bind, tie [s.o.'s] hands, leave no option *or* choice; drive, railroad, ramrod; bring to bear upon, bear down upon, put the pressure on, press, apply pressure, *Inf.* pressure *or* high-pressure, *Inf.* lean on, *Inf.* squeeze, *Inf.* put the screws on *or* to, *Inf.* twist [s.o.'s] arm; coerce, dragoon, bully, intimidate, *Inf.* steamroller, *Inf.* bulldoze, *Sl.* strong-arm.

2. convince, convert, wean, win *or* win over, bring round *or* around, enlist, draw over, bring to reason, make [s.o.] see the light; talk into, talk over, sell, sell [s.o.] on, wangle, *Inf.* jawbone, *Inf.* rope in *or* into, *Sl.* hook, *Sl.* con; overcome, surmount, wear down; wheedle, cajole, coax, sweet-talk, soften up; assure, satisfy, lead [s.o.] to believe, put [s.o.'s] mind at ease *or* rest, rest [s.o.'s] fears, settle [s.o.'s] doubts.

persuasion, *n.* **1.** inducement, suasion, advice, exhortation, admonition; conversion, proselytization, enlistment; bribery, subornment; temptation, allurement, enticement, inveiglement, seduction; coercion,

intimidation, *Sl.* strong-arm; cajolery, blandishment, soft soap; salesmanship, sales talk, hard sell.
2. power, force, potency, *Inf.* clout, *Sl.* muscle; effect, moment, consequence, importance, weight, say; influence, pull.
3. creed, credo, belief, firm belief, fixed opinion, unshakable faith, faith; opinion, conviction, idea, convincement.
4. sect, cult, denomination, ism, communion, order, school, school of thought; group, body, organization, association, affiliation, fellowship, fraternity, brotherhood, society; faction, wing, caucus; party, interest, camp, side.

persuasive, *adj.* **1.** convincing, impressive, satisfactory, satisfying; cogent, telling, effective, effectual, efficacious; weighty, authoritative; absolute, decisive, conclusive, determinative.
2. suasive, inducive, compelling, impelling; exhortative, admonitory, advisory; cajoling, wheedling.
—n. **3.** incentive, inducement, provocation, incitement, fillip, stimulus, stimulation, whet, *Fig.* carrot; encouragement, invitation; interest, percentage, *Inf.* cut, personal advantage *or* benefit, *Inf.* sweetener.

persuasiveness, *n.* **1.** invitingness, temptingness, seductiveness, alluringness, attractiveness.
2. plausibility, tenability, credibility, believability; logicality, soundness, validity; cogency, tellingness, effectiveness, efficacy, efficaciousness; convincingness, impressiveness, compellingness; weightiness, authoritativeness.

pert, *adj.* **1.** impertinent, impudent, flippant, saucy, fresh, smart-alecky, smart-aleck, smart, smart-mouthed, malapert, *Inf.* cheeky, *Inf.* flip; audacious, out-of-line, disrespectful, rude, impolite, unmannerly, uncivil; forward, presumptuous, brazen, brazen-faced, bold, brash, outspoken, loud-mouthed, shameless, *Inf.* brassy, *Sl.* mouthy.
2. perky, perk, jaunty, bouncy, brisk, breezy, *Inf.* peppy, *Inf.* full of pep, *Inf.* chipper, *Both Dial.* peart, yare, *Scot. and North Eng.* crouse; lively, full of life, alive, vigorous, sprightly, frisky, spirited, animated, full of vim and vigor, bright-eyed and bushy-tailed, energetic, zestful; vivacious, sparkling, bubbly, ebullient, effervescent; cheery, cheerful, gay, sunny, sanguine, in good *or* high spirits; healthy, in good health, fit as a fiddle, in fine fettle *or* shape, in A-1 condition, well, good, fine.

pertain, *v.* **1.** relate to, have reference to, bear upon, be pertinent to, enter into, appertain; fit in *or* with, be appropriate to *or* for, be suited to *or* for.
2. belong to *or* with, go with, go along with, be an adjunct *or* accessory to, be a concomitant of; be a part of, be included in, fall under, come under; be the property of, be owned by, by held by.

pertinacious, *adj.* **1.** stubborn, *Inf.* ornery, pigheaded, mulish, stubborn as a mule; unyielding, intractable, obdurate, obstinate; inflexible, unbending, adamant, adamantine, rigid, stony, fixed, stiff, stiff-necked; unswerving, undeviating, uncompromising, relentless, unrelenting, unshrinking, stern; perverse, opinionated, headstrong, self-willed, willful, pervicacious; refractory, contrary, intransigent; unmanageable, ungovernable, immovable, unshakable.
2. persistent, insistent, tenacious, bulldog, dogged, determined; persevering, steadfast, staunch, stalwart; resolute, purposeful, purposive, firm; tough, tough-minded, plucky, stout, sturdy, sturdy as the Rock of Gibraltar, strong; enduring, patient, with the patience of Job, lasting, game, game to the last; assiduous, sedulous, diligent, industrious; constant, unremitting, unwavering, continuous, continuing; tireless, untiring, unsleeping, unwearying, indefatigable; unflagging, undrooping, unflinching, unfaltering.

pertinacity, *n.* **1.** stubbornness, pigheadedness, bullheadedness, mulishness, *Inf.* orneriness; obstinacy, *Inf.* cussedness, pervicaciousness; obdurateness, intractability, inflexibility, intransigence, intransigency; rigidity, will of iron, sternness, stiffness; perverseness, contumacy, contrariness, willfulness; mind of one's own, sticking up for one's ideas.
2. persistence, insistence, tenacity, holding fast, holding one's course, doggedness, determination, perseverance; constancy, the constancy of Penelope, devotion, steadfastness, steadiness; resolution, resoluteness, resolve, purposefulness, purposiveness, *Inf.* plugging away; firmness, *Inf.* stick-to-it-iveness, *Inf.* stick-at-it-iveness, seeing it through, riding it out, never giving up, never saying die; assiduity, assiduousness, diligence, sedulity, sedulousness, industriousness, hard work, hustle, knocking on every door, going back for more; toughness, *Sl.* hanging tough, *Sl.* hanging in there, *Sl.* hanging on through hell or high water; sturdiness, strength, stamina, indefatigability; endurance, weathering the storm, putting up with anything, patience, patience of Job, patience of a saint; grit, *Inf.* spunk, *Inf.* sand, pluck, mettle, backbone, courage.

pertinence, *n.* pertinency, relevance, relevancy, germaneness, relatedness; aptness, suitability, suitableness, appropriateness, appositeness, felicity, felicitousness; fitness, concordance, consonance, harmony, harmoniousness, congruousness.

pertinent, *adj.* **1.** relevant, germane, related, to the point, to the purpose, short and sweet, *Latin. ad rem,* applicable, at issue; apt, appropriate, apropos, apposite, pat, bearing on, felicitous.
2. fit, suitable, well-suited, well-adapted, fitted, useful, convenient; proper, due, meet, seemly, decorous, right, correct, fitting, befitting; correspondent, corresponding, analogous, coherent; concerning, regarding, appurtenant, pertaining to; conforming, consonant, congruous, harmonious, consistent, compatible.

pertness, *n.* sauciness, freshness, boldness, brazenness, brashness, shamelessness, *Inf.* cheekiness, *Inf.* sassiness, *Inf.* brassiness; insolence, impertinence, impudence, audacity, effrontery, presumption, presumptuousness; bumptiousness, cockiness, self-assertiveness, chutzpah, forwardness; impoliteness, disrespect, contemptuousness, unmannerliness, ill-manneredness, incivility, rudeness; meddlesomeness, intrusiveness, officiousness.

perturb, *v.* **1.** disturb, disquiet, discompose, shake, shake up, agitate, discountenance, ruffle, fluster, flutter, distract, disconcert, unsettle, put out; alarm, trouble, upset; shock, jolt, jar, stagger, rock, rattle, pull one up short; arouse, excite, suscitate, foment, impassion, stir up, work up, wind up, whip up, fire up.
2. anger, nettle, gall, chafe, vex, madden, infuriate; provoke, pique, irritate.
3. confuse, addle, muddle, unbalance, unsettle, confound, perplex, bewilder, baffle, mix up; derange, disarrange, disorder, throw into disorder, disorganize, turn topsy-turvy.

perturbation, *n.* **1.** disturbing, discomposing, ruffling, *Inf.* shaking up, bothering, pestering, harassing, *Sl.* bugging, *Sl.* hassling, *Sl.* driving [s.o.] nuts *or* crazy *or* bananas; irritating, annoying, vexing, provoking, aggravating; getting on [s.o.'s] nerves, *Chiefly U.S.* riling, *Inf.* giving [s.o.] a pain, *Inf.* getting in [s.o.'s] hair.
2. perturbment, disquiet, disquietude, unquietness, uneasiness, unease, inquietude, restlessness, unrest;

fretfulness, distress, worry, concern, alarm; anxiety, anguish, angst, fear, dread, trepidation, foreboding, consternation; nervousness, *Sl.* ants, *Inf.* butterflies, *Inf.* butterflies in one's stomach, *Sl.* heebie-jeebies, *Sl.* habdabs, *Sl.* creeps.

3. confusion, perplexity, bewilderment, bafflement, mystification, *Brit. Dial.* swither; uncertainty, stupefaction, disorientation; disconcertion, discomposure, agitation, upset, unsettlement, turmoil, storm; frenzy, shock, delirium, hysteria; madness, derangement.

4. nuisance, annoyance, vexation, interruption, pain, *Sl.* pain in the neck, *Inf.* headache, *Sl.* hassle, *Sl.* drag, *Sl.* bitch; inconvenience, imposition, irritant, bur, thorn in the side *or* flesh, pea in the shoe.

perturbed, *adj.* **1.** disturbed, disquieted, discomposed, agitated, discountenanced, ruffled, flustered, flurried, distracted, disconcerted, unsettled, upset; anxious, distressed, worried, troubled, fretful, alarmed; shocked, jolted, jarred, staggered, rocked, rattled; nervous, *Sl.* antsy, *Inf.* on pins and needles, on edge; fearful, horrified, horror-struck, overwrought; aroused, excited, suscitated, impassioned, stirred up, worked up, fired up.

2. angry, angered, nettled, galled, chafed, vexed, mad, maddened; annoyed, irritated, *Chiefly U.S.* riled, offended, affronted, put out; infuriated, enraged, furious, irate.

3. confused, addled, muddled, unbalanced, unsettled, confounded, perplexed, bewildered, baffled, taken aback, nonplused; uncomfortable, ill at ease, uneasy, queasy, *Inf.* fazed; unhinged, disorganized, ruffled, *Sl.* shook up, *Sl.* shook, *Inf.* discombobulated, flustered, *Inf.* in a dither, *Inf.* in a tizzy.

perturbing, *adj.* **1.** disturbing, *Rare.* perturbative, disquieting, discomposing, agitating, ruffling, distracting, disconcerting, nerve-racking, unsettling, upsetting, distressing, troubling, *Inf.* discombobulating, shocking, jolting, jarring, staggering, *U.S.* dumfounding; rattling; fearful, fearsome, horrifying; arousing, exciting, suscitating, fomenting.

2. annoying, irritating, *Chiefly U.S.* riling, offending, offensive, affronting; nettling, galling, chafing, vexing, maddening; infuriating, enraging.

3. confusing, addling, muddling, unbalancing, unhinging, confounding, perplexing, bewildering, baffling.

peruke, *n.* periwig, powdered wig, Georgian wig, wig; toupee, hairpiece, scratch, scratch wig, *Sl.* rug.

perusal, *n.* examination, inspection, survey, scrutiny, review, study, *Inf.* look-through, *Inf.* run-through; reading, scanning, conning.

peruse, *v.* **1.** read through, read cover to cover, read thoroughly, scrutinize; plunge into, wade through.

2. read, study, scan, look over, go over, run over, run through, run the eye over, pore *or* pore over, *Brit.* vet.

pervade, *v.* permeate, saturate, diffuse, disseminate, honeycomb, spread throughout, extend throughout, fill, leave no void; penetrate, interpenetrate, inosculate, interosculate; osmose, blend, fuse, merge; percolate, filter through, seep through, soak through; imbue, infuse, suffuse, transfuse, infiltrate, impregnate, leaven.

pervasion, *n.* permeation, saturation, diffusion, dissemination; penetration, interpenetration, inosculation, interosculation; imbuement, instillment, infusion, suffusion, transfusion, infiltration, impregnation; osmosis.

pervasive, *adj.* pervading, suffusive, transfusive; ubiquitous, omnipresent, all-present; general, widespread, extensive, broad, wide, far-reaching; universal, global, world-wide; epidemic, pandemic, rife, rampant.

perverse, *adj.* **1.** contrary, contradictory, *Archaic.* contrarious, froward, contumacious, cross-grained, seditious, refractory, querulous; wayward, disobedient, intransigent, wrong-headed; troublesome, vexatious, difficult; wild, unruly, unmanageable, uncontrollable, ungovernable; inconvenient, awkward.

2. aberrant, deviate, deviant, irregular, variable; abnormal, anomalous, anomalistic; strange, odd, peculiar, queer, incongruous; monstrous, freakish, unnatural; distorted, twisted, warped, garbled.

3. cantankerous, quarrelsome, irascible, contentious, obstreperous, ill-tempered, bad-tempered, short-tempered, hot-tempered, hot-headed, touchy, testy, churlish, crusty, edgy, *Inf.* grouchy, *Inf.* crabby, crabbed; peevish, cross, captious, petulant, piqued, vexed, petty, huffy; surly, snarling, growling, bearish, currish, snappish, waspish, *Sl.* bitchy; sullen, sour, moody, splenetic, fractious, atrabilious, bilious, virulent, acerb, acerbic; spiteful, hateful, invidious, ill-willed, ill-disposed.

4. persistent, pertinacious, tenacious, persevering, indomitable, indefatigable, constant, assiduous, unremitting, unyielding, unbending, unrelenting, untiring, unwearying, unwearied, unflagging, unswerving, undeviating, unfaltering, unflinching, sedulous, diligent, zealous; obstinate, intractable, adamant, obdurate, resolute, inflexible, pervicacious, stubborn, dogged, mulish, headstrong, hard-headed, pigheaded; willful, wanton, deliberate, intentional.

5. perverted, corrupt, corrupted, vice-ridden, immoral, unprincipled, unscrupulous, dissolute, abandoned, profligate, depraved, degenerate, degenerated, deteriorated, *Inf.* gone to the dogs, *Inf.* gone downhill; malevolent, malignant, malign, malicious, maleficent, malefic, evil-intentioned, evil-disposed, evil-minded; evil, iniquitous, base, foul, low, bad, sinful.

perversion, *n.* **1.** deviation, aberration, anomaly, abnormality, irregularity, variability, misguidance, misdirection, misadvisement; misinformation, misexplanation, misexplication; misinstruction, miseducation, miscorrection; delusion, beguilement, deceit, deception, trickery.

2. misuse, misapplication, prostitution, exploitation, misemployment, misappropriation, mismanagement, maladministration, (*all deliberately*) misconstruction, misinterpretation, mistranslation; misquotation, miscoloration, falsification, misrepresentation, subreption, eisegesis; distortion, *Fig.* butchery, *Fig.* mutilation; bias, coloration; exaggeration; evasion; embroidery, embellishment, adornment, decoration, garnish, titivation.

3. strangeness, oddness, incongruousness, peculiarity, curiousness, queerness; unconventionality, uncommonness, uncommonality, unusualness, exception, singularity, singularness, individuality, individualness; waywardness, deviousness, unacceptableness; corruption, wantonness, decadence, depravity, wickedness; licentiousness, lewdness, erotomania; (*all with reference to sexual relations*) fiendishness, psychopathy, pathology, criminality; monstrousness, unnaturalness, freakishness, *Inf.* kinkiness.

4. sadism, masochism, sadomasochism, *Sl.* s-m, algolagnia, algolagny; fetishism, voyeurism, scotophilia, narcissism, exhibitionism; sodomy, buggery; pederasty, pedophilia, child-molesting; coprophilia; necrophilia; zoophilia; incest, incestuousness.

5. deterioration, degeneration, declination, declension, downfall, labefaction, detriment; degradation, depredation, vitiation, debasement, abasement, impairment, reduction, lowering; pollution, contamination, adulteration, infection; defilement, desecration, debauchery, profanity; violation, abuse, injury, harm, ruination.

perversity, *n.* **1.** contrariness, contradictoriness, contradictiousness, *Archaic.* contrariousness, contrariety, contumaciousness, contumacity, contumacy, frowardness, seditiousness, refractoriness, querulousness; waywardness, disobedience, intransigence, intransigency, wrong-headedness.

2. aberration, aberrance, aberrancy, deviation, irregularity, variation; abnormality, anomaly; oddity, peculiarity, incongruity; monstrosity, freak, mutant, heteroclite; strangeness, oddness, incongruousness, queerness.

3. cantankerousness, quarrelsomeness, irascibility, irascibleness, contentiousness, obstreperousness, touchiness, testiness, churlishness, crustiness, edginess, *Inf.* grouchiness, *Inf.* crabbiness; peevishness, crossness, captiousness, petulance, *Rare.* petulancy, pique, vexation, pettiness, huffiness; surliness, bearishness, currishness, *Sl.* bitchiness; sullenness, sourness, moodiness, spleen, fractiousness, atrabiliousness, biliousness, virulence, acerbity; spitefulness, hatefulness, invidiousness.

4. persistence, persistency, tenacity, tenaciousness, perseverance, indomitability, indomitableness, constancy, assiduousness, sedulousness, diligence, zeal, zealousness, zealotry; obstinance, obstinacy, intractability, intractableness, obdurateness, resolution, inflexibility, inflexibleness, stubbornness, doggedness, mulishness, hard-headedness, pigheadedness; willfulness, wantonness, deliberation, intent.

5. perversion, pervertedness, corruption, corruptedness, immorality, unprincipledness, unscrupulousness, dissolution, profligateness, depravity, degeneracy, degeneration, deterioration; malevolence, malignancy, maliciousness, maleficence, evil-mindedness; evil, evilness, iniquity, iniquitousness, baseness, foulness, lowness, sinfulness.

perversive, *adj.* **1.** perverting, corrupting, corruptive, deteriorating, degenerating, degenerative, corroding, corrosive; vitiating, debasing, degrading, lowering, reducing; defiling, demoralizing, seducing, subverting, leading astray, desecrating, debauching, deflowering, profaning, violating, abusing, ruining; polluting, contaminating, adulterating, diluting, alloying, infecting, poisoning, tainting, spoiling, marring, fouling, befouling, soiling, sullying; weakening, debilitating, enervating.

2. distorting, twisting, warping, garbling, *Fig.* butchering, *Fig.* mutilating; prejudicial, biased, unfavorable, disadvantageous.

3. harmful, hurtful, nocent, pernicious, deleterious, injurious, detrimental, insalubrious, noxious, virulent, ruinous, destructive; crippling, damaging, scathing, impairing; dangerous, hazardous, unsafe; deadly, mortal, lethal.

pervert, *v.* **1.** divert, deflect, turn, turn away, turn aside, avert, sidetrack, switch, *Obs.* prevaricate; wrench, wrest, wring, skew, shunt.

2. seduce, corrupt, subvert, demoralize, lead astray, lead away; tempt, allure, entice, inveigle; trap, entrap, snare, ensnare.

3. mislead, misguide, misdirect, misadvise, sophisticate; misinform, misexplain, misexpound, misexplicate; misinstruct, misteach, miseducate, miscorrect; delude, beguile, deceive, trick, hoax, dupe, take in.

4. misuse, prostitute, exploit, misapply, misemploy, misappropriate, mishandle, mismanage, maladminister; squander, waste, throw away.

5. (*all deliberately*) misconstrue, misconstruct, misinterpret, mistranslate, misdeem, misread, misrender, misreport, miscite; misquote, misstate, lie, miscolor, belie, misrepresent, falsify; distort, warp, twist, *Scot.* thraw, *Fig.* mutilate, *Fig.* butcher, garble; torture, contort, bend, squeeze, stretch, strain; bias, color, slant; exaggerate, blow out of proportion, play up; varnish, gild, gloss, gloss over, whitewash, evade, dodge, *Inf.* fudge; embroider, embellish, adorn, decorate, garnish, titivate, dress up.

6. vitiate, debase, abase, impair, reduce, lower; pollute, contaminate, adulterate, infect, poison, taint, spoil, mar, alloy, foul, befoul, soil, sully, make impure; defile, desecrate, debauch, deflower, profane; violate, abuse, ruin.

—n. **7.** (*all with reference to sexual relations*) deviate, deviant, degenerate, fiend, maniac, psychopath, criminal; sadist, masochist, fetishist, lecher, voyeur, scotophiliac, erotomaniac, narcissist, nymphomaniac; sodomist, sodomite, bugger; pederast, pedophiliac, child-molester, catamite, *Sl.* gunsel, *Sl.* punk, *Sl.* chicken; coprophiliac; necrophiliac; zoophiliac.

8. apostate, backslider, recidivist, reversionist, schismatist, schismatic, dissenter, sectary, lost soul, lost sheep, fallen angel; heretic, unbeliever, nonbeliever, infidel, antichrist, antichristian; secessionist, seceder, seditionist, separatist; renegade, recreant, traitor, turncoat; deserter, turntail.

perverted, *adj.* **1.** *Pathology.* abnormal, anomalous, anomalistic, aberrant, deviate, deviant, irregular, variable; strange, odd, incongruous, peculiar, queer; monstrous, freakish, unnatural, heteroclite, heteroclitic, heteroclitical.

2. misguided, misled, misdirected, misadvised; deluded, beguiled, deceived, tricked, hoaxed, duped, taken in; seduced, subverted, led astray, debauched, demoralized; violated, abused, ruined, deflowered, defiled, profaned.

3. distorted, twisted, warped, garbled, *Scot.* thrawn, *Fig.* mutilated, *Fig.* butchered.

4. false, fallacious, untrue, mendacious, baseless, unfounded, groundless, unsupported, unsupportable, preposterous, ridiculous, ludicrous; unsound, invalid, erroneous, mistaken, wrong, peccant, faulty, at fault, in error, errant, heretical, heterodox; unauthentic, ungenuine, imperfect, defective, abortive.

5. licentious, lascivious, lewd; sadistic, masochistic, *Sl.* s-m, *Sl.* kinky.

6. perverse, corrupt, corrupted, vice-ridden, immoral, unprincipled, dissolute, abandoned, profligate, wanton, depraved, degenerate, degenerated, deteriorated; *Inf.* gone to the dogs, evil, wicked, iniquitous, base, foul, low, sinful; wayward, devious, untrustworthy, unreliable; vitiated, debilitated; polluted, adulterated, contaminated, fouled, befouled, rotten, tainted, infected, poisoned.

pervious, *adj.* permeable, porous, penetrable, perforable, pierceable, enterable; open, passable, accessible; reachable; vulnerable, pregnable, open to attack.

pesky, *adj.* *Informal.* annoying, irksome, irritating, nettlesome, vexatious, vexing, galling, chafing, harassing; troublesome, worrisome, worrying, provoking, gnawing, nagging, dogging, hounding, tormenting, bothersome; aggravating, exacerbating, maddening, infuriating, *Sl.* driving up the wall, driving crazy; ruffling, disturbing, perturbing, *Inf.* getting under one's skin, *Inf.* getting in one's hair, disquieting; disagreeable, distasteful, obnoxious, offensive, objectionable, unwelcome, unwanted; intolerable, unbearable, *Inf.* a bit much, too much.

pessimism, *n.* **1.** cynicism, doubt, suspicion, distrust, disbelief, expecting the worst, Murphy's Law; hopelessness, seeing things in black, seeing the shadows instead of the sun, discouragement, dejection; depression, *Ger. Weltschmerz, Latin. taedium vitae,* despair, desperation, heaviness of heart, *Sl.* blues, sadness, unhappiness, gloom, gloomy outlook, gloominess, glumness; despondency, *Psychiatry.* hypochondria, melancholy, *Psychol.* melancholia, black dog melancholy; self-flagellation, joylessness, *Psychol.* anhedonia, emotional sclerosis; trepidation, waiting for the sky to fall in; eosophobia, fear of the new day; borrowing *or* buying trouble.

2. seeing the hole instead of the doughnut, seeing a glass half empty instead of half full, carrying an umbrella on a sunny day, wearing pants with suspenders and a belt.

pessimist, *n.* cynic, doubter, doubting Thomas; prophet of doom, Cassandra, alarmist, Gloomy Gus, *Inf.* gloom and doomer, *Sl.* crapehanger; defeatist, *Sl.* cop-out, underachiever, dropout; hypochondriac, *Inf.* worrywart, Chicken Little, *Inf.* scaredy-cat; grumbler, complainer, *Inf.* nitpicker, faultfinder, caviler, carper, critic; disparager, detractor, *Inf.* knocker; spoilsport, *Inf.* wet blanket, *Inf.* grouch, *Inf.* sad sack, *Sl.* sourpuss, *Dial.* night crawler, kill-joy, depressor, malcontent; weeper, Niobe, mourner, moper.

pessimistic, *adj.* cynical, doubting, distrustful, untrusting; leery, wary, suspicious; gloomy, *Inf.* downbeat, glum, morose, dreary, dismal, bleak; hopeless, depressed, despondent, despairing, *Inf.* down, downhearted, *Sl.* in the pits, desperate; forlorn, desolate, unable to see the end of the tunnel, without a shred of hope; blue, sad, unhappy, *Inf.* in a funk, *Inf.* in a blue funk, melancholy, seized by the black dog melancholy; oppressed, weighed down; anxious, worried, at the end of one's rope, *Inf.* in a state; grumpy, *Inf.* grouchy, discontent, grumbling, muttering, misanthropic, misogynic; unpromising, inauspicious, bearish.

pest, *n.* **1.** gadfly, buttonholer, *Inf.* pain, *Sl.* pain in the neck *or* rear, *Sl.* nudnik; nag, pesterer, annoyer, harasser, heckler, badgerer; tease, teaser, tormentor, persecutor, *Sl.* itch.

2. nuisance, bother, annoyance, vexation, *Inf.* headache, *Sl.* hassle; irritant, bur, thorn, thorn in the side *or* flesh, pea in the shoe; bore, crashing *or* frightful bore, proser, twaddler, dryasdust.

3. inconvenience, handicap; trouble, problem, difficulty, affliction; trial, tribulation, worry; load, burden, weight.

4. pestilence, scourge, blight; curse, bane, visitation; epidemic, pandemic, pandemia.

pester, *v.* **1.** bother, hector, harass, heckle, *Sl.* bug, *Sl.* hassle, *Sl.* drive [s.o.] nuts *or* crazy *or* bananas, *Sl.* drive [s.o.] up the wall; hound, dog, nag, pick on, pick at, be on [s.o.'s] back, *Inf.* give [s.o.] a bad *or* hard time, *Sl.* ride; torment, taunt, bedevil, tease, tweak, mock, *Inf.* needle; trouble, plague, fret, worry, *Scot.* thraw, *Scot.* fash.

2. irritate, irk, vex, pique, provoke, peeve, nettle, chafe, get on [s.o.'s] nerves, tread on [s.o.'s] toes, *Chiefly U.S.* rile, *Inf.* aggravate, *Inf.* miff, *Inf.* give [s.o.] a pain, *Inf.* get in [s.o.'s] hair, *Inf.* get under [s.o.'s] skin; exasperate, ruffle, try [s.o.'s] patience, *Inf.* grate on [s.o.'s] nerves.

pestiferous, *adj.* See **pestilent.**

pestilence, *n.* **1.** epidemic, pandemic, pandemia, plague, zymosis, (*of animals*) *Pathol.* epizootic, (*of animals*) epizooty, (*of animals*) murrain, (*of plants*) epiphytotic; bubonic plague, black plague, black death; white plague, tuberculosis, TB, consumption, phthisis, pulmonary phthisis.

2. curse, bane, scourge, affliction, infliction, visitation, torment, calamity; canker, cancer, blight, rot.

pestilent, *adj.* **1.** pestilential, pestiferous, infective, infectious, contaminative; infested, pest-ridden, diseased, disease-ridden, infected, septic, leprous; contagious, communicable, catching; epidemic, pandemic, endemic, epizootic.

2. pernicious, dangerous, hazardous, deleterious, detrimental, destructive, ruinous; deadly, lethal, fatal, mortal, mortiferous, *Archaic.* lethiferous; harmful, injurious, nocuous, hurtful, nocent, baleful, noisome; noxious, malicious, malign, malignant, menacing; venomous, poisonous, virulent, toxic, morbific, morbid, *Rare.* morbiferous; fell, baneful, mephitic, viperous, *Rare.* virose, (*in prescriptions*) venenosus, *Archaic.* venenose; insalubrious, unhealthful, unhygienic, insanitary, unhealthy.

3. evil, wicked, iniquitous, black-hearted, sinister, vicious; base, vile, foul, mean, low, bad, odious; dire, dark, black, dreadful, grim; damnable, damnatory, accursed, cursed; maleficent, malefic, malevolent, evil-minded, demonic, diabolic, devilish; criminal, felonious, wrong, reprehensible; immoral, corrupting, polluting, debauched, debased, depraved.

4. mischievous, impish, elfish, prankish; vexatious, troublesome, naughty, annoying, irritating.

pestilential, *adj.* See **pestilent** (*defs.* **1-3**).

pestle, *n.* **1.** pulverizer, grounder, muller, brayer, pounder, masher.

—*v.* **2.** pulverize, triturate, comminute, bray, powder, reduce *or* grind to powder.

pet¹, *n.* **1.** favorite, minion, jewel, apple of one's eye, *Inf.* number-one son, *Inf.* the fair-haired boy; cosset, fondling, darling, spoiled child; teacher's pet; loved one, dear, *Inf.* dearie, sweetheart, *Inf.* sweetie, honey, honey pie *or* bunch, baby, doll, baby doll, angel, lamb, lambkin, *Inf.* snookums.

—*adj.* **2.** domesticated, tamed, tame, housebroken.

3. prized, cherished, loved, beloved, adored, treasured, held dear, dear to one's heart, precious; favorite, favored, dear, dearest, darling.

4. affectionate, fond, tender, loving, adoring.

—*v.* **5.** coddle, mollycoddle, pamper, cocker, cosset, dandle, *Obs.* fondle; baby, spoil, indulge, dote on; cater to, wait on hand and foot, be at [s.o.'s] beck and call.

6. *Informal.* fondle, caress, stroke, pat; nuzzle, nestle, snuggle, carry on, *Sl.* canoodle; make love, bill and coo, smooch, slap and tickle, *Inf.* neck, *Inf.* make out, *Inf.* park, *Sl.* fool around.

pet², *n.* **1.** pique, huff, tiff, miff, fume, temper, ill temper, bad mood, ugly mood, *Inf.* stew, *Archaic.* pucker; sulk, sulks, petulance, *Inf.* slow burn.

—*v.* **2.** sulk, mope, look sullen, look black, pull *or* make a long face, pout, frown, scowl; grumble, grump.

petard, *n.* **1.** firecracker, squib, cherry bomb, ashcan.

2. hoist by *or* **with one's own petard** caught in one's own trap, tangled in one's own web; defeated by one's own plot; outsmarted *or* outwitted by oneself.

peter, *v. Informal.* **1.** weaken, decline, fade, pine, fail, flag, wilt, droop; languish, dwindle, wither on the vine; tire, get *or* grow tired, grow weary, run out *or* down, *Inf.* run out of steam, burn out, *Inf.* give out, *Inf.* conk out, *Inf.* peg out, *Inf.* poop out.

2. *Usu.* **peter out** dissolve, melt, melt away, pass away, fade out of the picture; wane, die out *or* away, cease to be *or* exist, cease; go downhill, *Sl.* hit the skids; come to nothing, come to naught, hang fire, flash in the pan; fall through, fall flat, get bogged down, go up in smoke.

petite bourgeoisie, *n.* **1.** lower middle class; middle class, bourgeoisie, bourgeois; middle orders, shopkeepers, small tradesmen.

2. the common people, the masses, the hoi polloi, *Jocular.* the booboisie; Middle America, the silent majority, the grass roots; commonalty, the public, the general public, citizenry.

petition, *n.* **1.** suit, request, requisition, application, address.

2. supplication, obsecration, obtestation, impetration, solicitation, invocation, adjuration, imploration, beseechment, *Eccles.* rogation; plea, prayer, orison, appeal, entreaty, humble request.

—v. **3.** request, apply to, appeal to, call on *or* upon, adjure; solicit, sue, address, bid.

4. beg for, pray for, plead for; supplicate, implore, entreat, adjure, obtest; solicit, beseech, obsecrate, imprecate, impetrate, importune.

petitioner, *n.* solicitor, suitor, suppliant, supplicant, beseecher, petitionist; applicant, bidder, solicitant; candidate, aspirant, postulant, seeker; claimant, complainant, plaintiff, appellant, party.

pet name, *n.* diminutive, hypocorism; nickname, sobriquet, cognomen, agnomen, appellation.

petrifaction, *n.* **1.** ossification, fossilization, *Archaic.* lapidification, mineralization, petrification; calcification, crystallization; induration, hardening, solidification, stiffening.

2. numbing, benumbing, dulling, blunting; drugging, anesthetization, stunning, paralysation, incapacitation, insensitization; stupefying, shocking, dazing, electrifying.

3. scaring, frightening, terrifying, shocking, appalling, unnerving; terrorizing, intimidation, intimidating, disturbing, distressing.

4. hardness, firmness, solidity, compactness, density; frozenness, stiffness, stoniness, bonelikeness, rigidity, rigidness.

5. fear, dread, fright, *Inf.* funk, fearfulness; terror, horror, panic; alarm, perturbation, consternation, trepidation; apprehension, worry, disquietude, concern.

petrified, *adj.* **1.** ossified, osseous, fossilized, turned to stone, *Both Archaic.* lapidified, lapidific; mineralized, horny, corneous, bony, sclerotic; calcified, vitrified, vitreous, crystallized, crystalline; indurate, indurated, hard, hardened, hard as a rock, hard as stone, stony, stonelike, lithoid, lithoidal, rocky, rock-like, aphanitic, porphyritic; solid, solidified, dense, densified; concrete, granitic, flinty; adamantine, steely, callous, strong.

2. stupefied, paralyzed, benumbed, numbed, dumb, incapacitated, insensitized; anesthetized, stunned, frozen; staggered, taken aback, floored, shocked, jarred, jolted, *Inf.* bowled over; dumfounded, speechless, struck dumb, *Inf.* flabbergasted; shocked, electrified, dazed.

3. panic-stricken, terrified, horrified, terror-stricken, horror-stricken, scared out of one's wits; startled, overcome with fear, overwhelmed, afraid, frightened; frozen with terror, pale as a ghost, white as a sheet; shaken, shaking, shaking like an aspen, quivering, quavering.

petrify, *v.* **1.** ossify, fossilize, turn to stone, *Archaic.* lapidify, mineralize; calcify, vitrify, crystallize; indurate, harden, make hard, become hard, strengthen, stiffen, starch; solidify, densify, inspissate, *Pharm.* incrassate, thicken; steel, toughen, vulcanize.

2. numb, benumb, deaden, obtund, hebetate, dull, blunt; drug, anesthetize, stun, paralyze; chill, freeze.

3. scare, terrify, frighten, fright, horrify, strike terror into, make fearful, scare out of one's wits; stupefy, paralyze, benumb, numb, incapacitate, insensitize; stun, stagger, take aback, astound, astonish, amaze, dumfound; startle, surprise, disconcert, take unawares, alarm; shock, electrify, daze, *Inf.* take one's breath away.

petrol, *n.* *British.* gasoline, gas, fuel, diesel fuel, *Fr. Canadian.* *gaz.*

petroleum, *n.* rock oil, fossil oil, crude oil, *Archaic.* petrol.

petticoat, *n.* **1.** half-slip, slip, shift, underskirt, skirt, hoop skirt, farthingale, crinoline; undergarment, underwear, lingerie.

2. *Informal.* woman, lady, female, young lady, girl, mademoiselle, miss, young woman, *Inf.* filly, *Sl.* chick.

—adj. **3.** feminine, female, delicate, gentle, tender.

pettifog, *v.* **1.** quibble, cavil, *Inf.* nitpick, belabor a point, split hairs, chop logic, trifle, beg the question; bicker, bandy words, moot, sift, *Inf.* kick around, *Sl.* hash over; wrangle, altercate, jangle, quarrel, squabble, haggle, *Sl.* hassle, *Scot.* argle-bargle.

2. chicane, hoodwink, trick, delude, deceive, fool, bamboozle, overreach; *All Inf.* jive, fast-talk, flam, hype, buffalo, bulldoze; *All Sl.* con, snow, suck *or* sucker in, murphy.

pettifogger, *n.* dishonest lawyer, *Sl.* mouthpiece, ambulance chaser, shyster, *Brit. Sl.* greenbag; *Inf.* nitpicker, quibbler.

pettifoggery, *n.* jobbery, underhand practice *or* dealing, corruption, dishonesty, falseness, humbuggery, artifice, subterfuge; bamboozling, cheating, cozenage, swindling, fleecing; fraud, fraudulency, deceit, deception, chicane, duplicity, guile, double-dealing, *Sl.* monkey-business, *Sl.* dipsy-doodle; trickery, gulling, knavery, rascality, hoodwinking, duping, hoaxing, befooling; wiles, sophistry, *Inf.* nitpicking, artfulness, craftiness, treachery.

pettifogging, *adj.* **1.** trifling, niggling, frivolous, *Inf.* nitpicking, paltry, insubstantial, insignificant; circumlocutory, fencing, equivocating, sophistical, sophistic, casuistic, casuistical; hairsplitting, caviling, captious; finespun, over-refined, subtle.

2. deceptive, misleading, tricky, slippery; prevaricating, sneaking, sneaky, crafty, deceitful, questionable, dubious; shifty, shifting, evasive, evading, elusive.

3. dishonorable, on the take, contemptible, immoral, unlawful, illegal, criminal; untrustworthy, faithless, false-hearted, treacherous, perfidious; corrupt, corruptible, venal, knavish, roguish, recreant; unscrupulous, unprincipled, intriguing, conniving, unconscionable, conscienceless.

pettish, *adj.* **1.** peevish, ill-humored, touchy, testy, thin-skinned, waspish, petulant; cross, irascible, choleric, ill-tempered, splenetic; crabby, crabbed, cranky, grouchy, grumpy, cantankerous, crotchety, crusty; irritable, out of sorts, snappish, snappy, huffish, huffy, curt, short, impatient; piqued, in a pique, in a fume, *Archaic.* in a pucker, *Inf.* in a stew.

2. moody, sulky, dour, gloomy, dyspeptic, sullen, morose; grumpy, moping, mopish, mopey; injured, wounded, sore, offended, indignant; angry, in high dudgeon, worked up.

3. captious, quarrelsome, fractious; complaining, querulous, caviling, carping; antagonistic, inimical, ill-willed, hostile; argumentative, short-tempered, quarrelsome, disputatious; contrary, perverse, *Scot.* thrawn; unaccommodating, unkindly, unamiable, unfriendly; sour, caustic, tart, churlish, surly, spiteful.

petty, *adj.* **1.** trivial, paltry, *Archaic.* pelting, *Brit.* potty, puny, picayune, niggling, minor; trifling, piddling, fiddling, frivolous, fribble; inconsequential, unimportant, insignificant, inconsiderable, negligible, nugatory, worthless, useless; inane, silly, foolish, pointless, *Inf.* dumb, idiotic; small, dinky, *Sl.* small-time, *Sl.* two-bit; of minor importance, of little *or* no account, nothing great, no great shakes, *Inf.* no big deal, nothing to write home about, *Inf.* nothing to get excited *or* worked up about.

2. secondary, subordinate, junior, second-fiddle, lower, inferior; subsidiary, ancillary; second-class, one-horse, bush, bush-league, *Sl.* small potatoes, *Sl.* mickey mouse.

3. narrow-minded, narrow, prejudiced, biased, bigoted; little-minded, small-minded, mean-minded; warped, twisted, jaundiced, partial, one-sided, closed-minded, closed, intolerant, illiberal, unreasonable; insular, parochial, provincial, *Sociol.* ethnocentric, limited, confined, constricted, unliberal, uncatholic; blind, myopic, near-sighted, short-sighted, purblind.

4. stingy, niggardly, miserly, parsimonious, carking, skinflinty; tight, tight-fisted, closefisted; cheap, *Rare.* illiberal, penny-pinching, grudging, begrudging, stinting.

petulance, *n.* **1.** peevishness, pettishness, *Rare.* petulancy; ill-humoredness, ill humor, touchiness, testiness, waspishness, querulousness, carpingness; irascibleness, irascibility, cholericness, ill-temperedness, bad temper, spleen, spleenishness; crabbiness, crabbedness, crankiness, grouchiness, grumpiness, cantankerousness, crotchetiness; irritableness, irritability, snappiness, snappishness, huffiness, huffishness, curtness, shortness, impatience.

2. moodiness, changeableness, sulkiness, sullenness, dourness, gloominess, moroseness; cynicalness, cynicism.

3. captiousness, quarrelsomeness, fractiousness, crossness; antagonism, hostility, contrariness, perverseness, perversity; unkindliness, unamiableness, unfriendliness; sourness, causticity, tartness, churlishness, surliness, spitefulness.

petulant, *adj.* peevish, pettish, ill-humored, touchy, testy, thin-skinned. See **pettish** (*defs.* **1-3**).

pew, *n.* **1.** bench; mourner's bench; anxious seat *or* bench, amen corner.

2. box, stall, booth, compartment.

phaeton, *n.* **1.** carriage, coach, stagecoach, chariot, hansom, landau, brougham, surrey, cabriolet, coupé, victoria, barouche, four-wheeler, hackney, rockaway, *U.S.* buggy, *Chiefly Brit.* tally-ho; sulky, gig, calash, curricle, chaise, tilbury, (*in Japan, the Philippines, etc.*) jinrikisha, *Chiefly Brit.* trap.

2. sedan, roadster, limousine, *Inf.* limo, runabout, touring car; vehicle, car, motorcar, motor, automobile, auto, *Inf.* bus, *Sl.* wheels.

phalanx, *n.* **1.** legion, cohort; division, regiment, battalion, battery, brigade; detachment, contingent, body, company; platoon, squadron, squad, escadrille, wing; force, armed force, fighting force, fighting machine.

2. assemblage, assembly, group, circle; gathering, meeting, audience; concourse, rally, throng, number; entourage, cavalcade, caravan, drove; conclave, convocation, council, synod, consistory, conventicle; levy, muster, mobilization.

3. association, affiliation, society, fellowship, fraternity, brotherhood; guild, union, league; faction, splinter group, pressure group; confederation, alliance, coalition, Bund.

phantasm, *n.* **1.** apparition, vision, specter, shade, shadow, spirit, soul, revenant, wraith, eidolon, phantasma, materialization; ghost, phantom, (*in Irish Folklore*) banshee, *Inf.* spook; demon, devil, evil spirit, nightmare, incubus, succubus.

2. chimera, figment, figment of the imagination, phantom of the mind, illusion, delusion; fancy, idle fancy, fantasy, crotchet, bubble, vapor, dream, daydream, *Sl.* trip; mirage, illusion, hallucination, Fata Morgana, trick of the eyesight, optical illusion.

3. visualization, conceptualization, mental image, mental picture.

phantasmagoric, *adj.* illusory, delusory, unreal, phantasmal, chimerical, imaginary, visionary; spectral, apparitional, ghostly; dreamy, dreamlike; nightmarish; hallucinatory, phantasmagorical; surreal, surrealistic, Kafkaesque; psychedelic, kaleidoscopic.

phantasmal, *adj.* unreal, illusory, delusory, imaginary, imagined, phantasmagoric, phantasmagorical; chimerical, fanciful, fancy-bred, fancied, figmental, figmentary; aerial, unsubstantial, incorporeal, airy, vaporous, ethereal, cloud-built, air-built; spiritual, apparitional, spectral, specterlike, ghostly, ghostlike, phantomlike, wraithlike, shadowy.

phantom, *n.* **1.** incubus, succubus, evil spirit, nightmare, bad dream, *Sl.* bad trip; chimera, figment, figment of the imagination, trick of the imagination, phantom of the mind, illusion, delusion. See also **phantasm** (*def.* **2**).

2. apparition, specter, shade, shadow, spirit. See **phantasm** (*def.* **1**).

—*adj.* **3.** unreal, illusory; phantasmal. See **phantasmal**.

pharisaic, *adj.* sanctimonious, self-righteous, holier-than-thou, simon-pure, *Inf.* goody-goody; pietistic, pious, over-pious; hypocritical, Tartuffian, canting; mealy-mouthed, unctuous, oily.

pharisaism, *n.* hypocrisy, insincerity, falseness, Tartuffery, Pecksniffery; formalism, mere show, solemn mockery; sanctimony, sanctimoniousness, self-righteousness, religiosity, false piety, over-piety, pietism, piousness; cant, mummery, mouthing, lip service, mouth honor, *Archaic.* snuffling; mealy-mouthedness, unctuousness, oiliness.

pharisee, *n.* hypocrite, humbug, *Inf.* phony, whited sepulcher, Tartuffe, Pecksniff; pietist, pious fraud, "a saint abroad and a devil at home" (Bunyan); canter, mummer, dissembler, dissimulator, lip server, lip worshipper.

pharmacist, *n.* druggist, *Brit.* chemist, apothecary, pharmaceutist, posologist; pharmacologist, *Pharm.* pharmacopoeist.

pharmacy, *n.* **1.** pharmaceutics, pharmacology, pharmacodynamics, pharmacognosy, posology, dosology, materia medica.

2. drugstore, apothecary, *Brit.* chemist, *Brit. Trademark.* Boots; dispensary, dispensatory; pharmacopoeia.

phase, *n.* **1.** form, shape, figure, configuration; aspect, phasis, look, appearance, feature; posture, pose, stance, bearing, mien, demeanor; circumstance, status, situation, position, place.

2. facet, side, angle, *Inf.* slant, *Inf.* twist; view, viewpoint, point of view.

3. stage, period, point, point in time, juncture; time, moment, minute, hour, day, season; advent, occasion; occurrence, event, incident.

—*v.* **4.** order, put *or* set in order, arrange, organize; schedule, plan, set up, work out.

5. synchronize, *Inf.* sync, *Inf.* put in sync, put in phase, coordinate, harmonize; adjust, set, regulate.

6. **phase in** incorporate, include; introduce, insert, insinuate, inject, interject, put in, stick in; ease in, slip in, work in.

7. **phase out** withdraw, remove, pull out.

phenomenal, *adj.* 1. extraordinary, prodigious, remarkable, wondrous, marvelous; amazing, astounding, astonishing, miraculous, surpassing belief; fabulous, fantastic, *Sl.* far-out; indescribable, ineffable, mind-boggling, *Sl.* mind-blowing; staggering, breathtaking, *Sl.* stunning.

2. peerless, matchless, unmatched, nonpareil; unusual, uncommon, unconventional, unorthodox, uncustomary, unwonted, rare; atypical, original, singular, exceptional, individual; unexampled, unprecedented, unparalleled, unfamiliar, unheard-of, unseen, surprising; curious, odd, peculiar, queer; strange, weird, bizarre, freakish.

phenomenon, *n.* 1. event, occurrence, incident, happening, episode, experience, occasion; fact, matter of fact, particular, circumstance.

2. marvel, wonder, wonderful thing, amazing thing, quite a thing, really something; prodigy, miracle, sensation, overnight sensation, *Sl.* phenom; sight, spectacle, eyeopener, *Sl.* stunner, *Sl.* mind-boggler, *Sl.* mind-blower, *Sl.* trip; curiosity, rarity, nonesuch, nonpareil, one of a kind, one in a thousand; marvelment, wonderment, gazingstock, *Brit. Dial.* gapeseed; *All Inf.* one for the book, something to write home about, something else.

philander, *v.* 1. trifle, dally, toy, toy *or* trifle with [s.o.'s] affections, play at courtship; flirt, coquet, *Sl.* hustle, *Sl.* put *or* slap the make on.

2. debauch, wanton, rake, cruise, gallivant, womanize, chase women, *Inf.* chase around, *Sl.* chase skirts; have a woman in every port, *Inf.* play the field, *Inf.* fool around, *Inf.* run around, *Inf.* sleep around, *Inf.* love 'em and leave 'em, *Inf.* find 'em and forget 'em; *Sl.* wham-bam thank you ma'am.

philanderer, *n.* trifler, dallier, gay dog, gay deceiver, gallant, flirt, *Obs.* coquet, *Inf.* two-timer; womanizer, ladies' man, man about town, woman-chaser, *Sl.* skirt-chaser, *Sl.* wolf, *Sl.* lover boy, *Sl.* tomcat, *Sl.* masher, *Sl.* make-out artist, *Sl.* man on the make; debauchee, rake, rakehell, roué, profligate, wanton, libertine, playboy, *Inf.* rip, *Sl.* swinger; Don Juan, Casanova, Lothario, Romeo, charmer, *Inf.* lady-killer, *Sl.* stud, *Sl.* sheik.

philanthropic, *adj.* 1. benevolent, beneficent, aiding, aidful, helping, helpful, ministrant, gracious; charitable, eleemosynary, almsgiving, philanthropical, philanthropistic, caritative; munificent, generous, bountiful, bounteous, liberal, open-handed, free-handed, giving; lavish, ungrudging, unsparing, unstinting.

2. altruistic, humanitarian, humane, human, public-spirited, socially aware *or* concerned, solicitous, officious, well-meaning, well-intentioned; unselfish, selfless, other-directed, *Psychol.* extroverted; kind, kindly, kindhearted, benign, benignant; big-hearted, big, large-hearted, magnanimous, warm-hearted, loving, affectionate, friendly, well-disposed; thoughtful, considerate, compassionate, sympathetic, feeling, *Disparaging.* bleeding-heart, ruthful, pitying, *Rare.* pitiful.

philanthropist, *n.* 1. benefactor, benefactress, donor, donator, giver, contributor, grantor, almsgiver, Lady Bountiful, *Both Archaic.* almsman, almswoman; patron, patroness, sponsor, fairy godmother, good fairy, angel; Maecenas, Rockefeller, Carnegie, Mellon; supporter, backer, booster, financier, maintainer, sustainer, mainstay; helper, aider, abettor, succorer, Good Samaritan.

2. altruist, humanitarian, public servant, do-gooder; friend, well-wisher, sympathizer, pitier, *Disparaging.* bleeding heart.

philanthropy, *n.* 1. benevolence, beneficence, helpfulness, ministration, ministry, public *or* social service, do-goodism; charity, *Latin.* *caritas*, almsgiving, charitableness, munificence, generosity, bounty, bountifulness, liberality, liberalness, open-handedness, free-handedness.

2. altruism, humanitarianism, humanity, humaneness, love of mankind, Christian love, agape; public spirit, public spiritedness, other-directedness, other-direction, *Psychol.* extroversion; unselfishness, selflessness, self-sacrifice; kindness, kindliness, kindheartedness, benignacy, benignity, goodness, good will; openheartedness, big-heartedness, magnanimity; thoughtfulness, consideration, compassion, compassionateness, sympathy, pity.

3. contribution, donation, alms, offering, offertory, oblation, largesse, benefaction; good, service, ministration, favor, courtesy; aid, assistance, help, succor.

philippic, *n.* diatribe, invective, tirade, screed, jeremiad, stream of abuse, bitter harangue, verbal onslaught; vituperation, revilement, curse, execration, imprecation, malediction, anathematization, denunciation, commination, condemnation, censure; vilification, impugnment, traducement, aspersion, calumniation, calumny, obloquy, slur, defamation, denigration; disparagement, discrediting, depreciation, deprecation, belittlement; objurgation, fulmination, contumely, berating, upbraiding, scolding, *Inf.* tongue-lashing, *Sl.* dressing-down, *Sl.* bawling out, *Sl.* chewing out; reproof, rebuke, reprimand, admonition, reproval, slap in the face, *Inf.* rap on the knuckles.

philistine, *n.* 1. middlebrow, *Inf.* lowbrow, Boeotian, conventionalist, conformist; bourgeois, materialist, capitalist; traditionalist, formalist, precisian; boor, lout, Goth, barbarian, yahoo.

—*adj.* 2. *Inf.* lowbrow, uncultured, uncultivated, unrefined, rude; uneducated, untutored, untaught, unlearned, unlettered, unread, unenlightened; commonplace, common, conventional, ordinary, prosaic, dull, unimaginative, uninteresting, plain; conformist, middlebrow, conservative, *Sl.* uptight, *Sl.* button-down, *Sl.* square, *Sl.* straight; bourgeois, materialistic, capitalistic.

philistinism, *n.* middlebrowism, *Inf.* lowbrowism, conventionalism, conventionality, conformism, conformance, conformity; traditionalism, formalism, precisianism; obtuseness, dullness, boorishness, yahooism.

philologist, *n.* archivist; (*all of linguistics*) linguist, *Rare.* linguistician, phonologist, phonemicist, phonetician, morphologist, dialectologist, philologian; semanticist, semasiologist, etymologist, historical linguist, lexicologist, lexicographer; grammarian, scholar.

philology, *n.* (*all of linguistics*) linguistics, linguistic science, *Obs.* glottology, dialectology, phonetics, phonology, phonemics, morphology, morphophonemics, syntax, tagmemics; semantics, semasiology, etymology, historical linguistics, glottogony, lexicology, lexicography.

philosopher, *n.* philosophizer, philosophe, *Derog.* philosophaster; thinker, reasoner, ratiocinator, rationalist; theorist, theorizer, metaphysician, metaphysicist, logician, aesthetician; seeker *or* student of truth, scholar, sage, wise man, pundit, guru.

philosophical, *adj.* 1. philosophic, *Philos.* metaphysical, metaphysic; abstract, abstruse, recondite, esoteric.

2. thoughtful, thinking, pensive, reflective, reflecting, meditative, meditating, contemplative, contemplating, cogitative; grave, serious, sober, deep, deep-

thinking, profound; discerning, discriminating, discriminative, discriminatory, percipient, critical, judicial; judicious, wise, sage, sapient, sagacious; learned, erudite, scholarly, knowing, knowledgeable, well-informed, enlightened; understanding, aware, perceptive, acute, penetrating, piercing; shrewd, astute, perspicacious, perspicuous, farseeing, long-headed; alert, clearheaded, sharp, keen.

3. rational, reasonable, sensible, logical, practical, down-to-earth, realistic, pragmatic; composed, collected, poised, self-possessed, self-controlled, self-contained; level-headed, cool-headed, cool, equable, steady, balanced, equilibratory, equilibrious; even-tempered, equanimous, moderate, temperate; imperturbable, unperturbable, *Sl.* unflappable, unexcitable; unexcited, unruffled, unflustered, undisturbed, unperturbed; calm, reposed, quiet, quiescent, still, placid, peaceful, tranquil, serene; untouched, unaffected, unimpassioned, dispassionate, unemotional.

philosophy, *n.* **1.** study of truth, natural philosophy, moral philosophy, metaphysical philosophy; metaphysics, *Philos.* aesthetics, epistemology, logic, logistic, symbolic logic, Aristotelian logic.

2. philosophical system, philosophical doctrine *or* teaching, school of philosophy, school of thought.

3. critical study, analysis, investigation, examination, probe, research, exploration.

4. ethics, system of moral principles, moral code *or* philosophy, moral standard.

5. stoicism, composure, aplomb, sang-froid, poise, self-possession, self-control, self-command; presence of mind, level-headedness, cool-headedness, coolness, equability, equableness, equanimity.

6. opinion, attitude, viewpoint, view, point of view, feeling, sentiment, idea.

philter, *n.* love potion, aphrodisiac, cantharides, blister beetle, cantharis, Spanish fly, ginseng; magic potion *or* drug, wonder drug, elixir, panacea, cure-all.

phlegm, *n.* **1.** mucus, *Inf.* snot.

2. dullness, lethargy, hebetude, listlessness; sluggishness, slowness, languor, lassitude, indolence, torpidity, torpidness, torpor; inactivity, inactiveness, inertness, passiveness, passivity; apathy, indifference, unconcern, nonchalance, uninterestedness, disinterest; coolness, coldness, frigidity; unresponsiveness, dispassion, dispassionateness, lack of feeling *or* emotion, insentience, insensibility, insensitiveness, insensibility, unfeelingness, numbness.

3. self-possession, self-control, composure, aplomb, sang-froid, poise; presence of mind, level-headedness, cool-headedness, coolness, *Inf.* cool, collectedness; philosophicalness, even-temperedness, equability, equableness, equanimity, equilibrium; calm, calmness, repose, quiet, quiescence, quiescency, stillness; peace, peacefulness, placidity, placidness, tranquillity, tranquilness, serenity, sereneness; impassiveness, impassivity, imperturbability, imperturbableness, *Sl.* unflappability, unexcitability, unruffledness.

phlegmatic, *adj.* **1.** phlegmatical, lethargic, lethargical, hebetudinous, listless; sluggish, lymphatic, slow, slow-moving, languid, indolent, torpid; inactive, inert, passive, supine, dormant, unmoving, inanimate, lifeless; apathetic, indifferent, unconcerned, nonchalant, uninterested, disinterested, unimpassioned; unresponsive, cool, cold, frigid, frosty, icy; impassive, dispassionate, unemotional, emotionless, passionless, stolid, stoical, stoic; unfeeling, insentient, insensible, unsensitive, insensitive, numb, dull.

2. self-possessed, self-controlled, composed, poised, collected, *Sl.* together; level-headed, cool-headed, cool, equable, steady, balanced, equilibratory, equilibrious; even-tempered, equanimous, philosophical, moderate, temperate; imperturbable, unperturbable, *Sl.* unflappable, unexcitable; unexcited, unruffled, unflustered, undisturbed, unperturbed; calm, reposed, quiet, quiescent, still, placid, peaceful, tranquil, serene; untouched, unaffected, unmoved.

phobia, *n.* **1.** fear, irrational fear, abnormal fear, obsessive fear; dread, horror, panic, terror, angst, fear and trembling, anguish, anxiety; apprehensiveness, apprehension, misgiving, suspicion, distrust, qualm; worry, disquiet, disquietude.

2. aversion, hatred, dislike, distaste, peeve, pet peeve; disgust, odium, detestation, abhorrence, antipathy, repugnance; abomination, loathing, execration, detestation; disrelish, displeasure, repulsion, revulsion, nausea; craze, obsession, neurosis, mania, monomania, paranoia.

3. agoraphobia, claustrophobia, acrophobia; androphobia, gynephobia, pedophobia, anthrophobia, xenophobia; theophobia, demonophobia, phasomophobia; ailurophobia, cynophobia, musophobia, ophiciophobia, ornithophobia, arachnephobia; koniophobia *or* amathophobia, mysophobia, necrophobia, hydrophobia; chromatophobia, chaetophobia *or* trichophobia *or* pogonophobia; astraphobia, brontophobia, keraunophobia, pyrophobia, eosophobia, achluophobia; peniaphobia, tachophobia, triskaidekaphobia, autophobia, karorraphiaphobia; gephyrophobia, hodophobia, ergophobia, phagophobia, thaasophobia, katagelophobia, pnigophobia.

phoenix, *n.* paragon, perfection, consummation, nonpareil, shining example, crowning glory; culmination, pinnacle, height, top, acme, summit, peak; the last word, ultimate, pride and glory; example, standard, pattern, model, ideal, beau ideal, exemplar, classic, apotheosis, cynosure, very model, quintessence, archetype, prototype.

phone, *n.* **1.** *Informal.* telephone, telephone set, receiver, mouthpiece; extension, extension phone, wall *or* desk phone, *Inf.* intercom; headphone, headset, earphone, radiophone, ship to shore phone; *Inf.* line, *Sl.* horn, *Sl.* Ameche.

—*v.* **2.** telephone, call, *Inf.* call on the phone, *Inf.* call *or* ring *or* dial up, *Inf.* give [s.o.] a ring *or* a buzz, *Inf.* buzz, put in *or* make a call, *Sl.* get [s.o.] on the horn.

phonetic, *adj.* **1.** spoken, vocalized, vocal, uttered, intonated, pitched; sounded, voiced, said, noised, phonic; sounded out, enunciated, articulated, pronounced.

2. oral, verbal, unwritten, parole; as pronounced, as heard, by ear, said as written.

—*n.* **3.** symbol, character, sign; logographic symbol, pictograph, idiograph, hieroglyphic, hieroglyph, rune; kana, katakana, hiragana; shorthand symbol.

phonetics, *n.* study of speech sounds, speechcraft, phonemics. See **phonology**.

phonograph, *n.* record player, recording machine, stereo, phono, *Trademark.* Gramophone, *Trademark.* Graphophone, *Trademark.* Victrola; graphonola, phonogram, phonautograph, audiophile; hi-fi, high-fidelity system, jukebox, nickelodeon; tape recorder, recorder, tape deck, tape player, cassette player.

phonography, *n.* sound transcription, phonetic spelling, spelling, orthography, phonetics; stenotypy, stenography, tachygraphy.

phonology, *n.* phonetics, phonemics, speechcraft; acoustics, phonics, diaphonics, acoustic phonetics, articulatory phonetics, auditory phonetics; morphophonemics, morphology, etymology, orthoepy, study of word sounds; linguistics, *Obs.* glottology, dialectology.

phony, *adj.* **1.** *Informal.* spurious, counterfeit, bogus, imitation, not genuine; fraudulent, fake, false, forged; supposititious, bastardly, pinchbeck, *Australian.* bunyip; meretricious, feigned, simulated, make-believe; left-handed, sham, flash, *Sl.* jive, *Sl.* hokey, *Sl.* phony-baloney; unreal, mock, ersatz, synthetic, plastic, jerry-built; artificial, factitious, contrived, fictitious; assumed, pseudo, *Inf.* put-on.

—*n.* **2.** *Informal.* counterfeit, fake, forgery, two-dollar bill, wooden nickel, slug, funny money; cheat, swindle, *Inf.* put-on, *Sl.* ripoff; fraud, imposture, hoax, imposition; artifice, ruse, delusion, game.

3. faker, quack, charlatan, deceiver, mountebank, imposter, empiric, *Australian.* bunyip; feigner, poseur, pretender, imitator; counterfeiter, falsifier, copier, plagiarist.

phosphorescent, *adj.* luminous, radiant, bright, luculent, fulgent; luminescent, triboluminescent, electroluminescent, chemicoluminescent; shining, lustrous, luminiferous, rutilant, *Biol.* photogenic; fluorescent, luminal, tinseled, star-spangled, irradiate; sparkling, coruscating, scintillating, shimmery, shimmering, glimmering; twinkling, glistening, blinking, glittering.

photograph, *n.* **1.** picture, image, *Inf.* photo, snapshot, *Inf.* shot, *Inf.* snap, *Inf.* candid; color print, photoprint, print, *Trademark.* Kodak, *Trademark.* Heliocrome; *Trademark.* Polaroid; slide, transparency, lantern slide, diapositive, frame, exposure, negative, positive; daguerrotype, tintype, collotype, calotype, talbotype, photocollotype, plate; photogravure, *Obs.* heliogravure, rotogravure; portrait, glossy, matte, blowup, enlargement, reduction, *Inf.* pin-up, *Sl.* mug shot, *Inf.* close-up; copy, photostat, photocopy, facsimile, *Trademark.* Xerox *or* Xerox copy.

—*v.* **2.** take a picture, snap, kodak, shoot, film, capture on film.

photographer, *n.* photographist, cinematographer, camera man, photog; snapshotter, daguerrotypist, calotypist, talbotypist; camera bug, *Sl.* shutterbug, *Inf.* lensman, *Sl.* shooter, *It. paparazzo.*

photographic, *adj.* **1.** pictorial, representing, representative, descriptive; photo, photosensitive, telephotographic, telephoto, photogenic.

2. detailed, realistic, lifelike, graphic; minute, exact, precise, typical; true to life, true to type, faithful, natural, close in all particulars.

phrase, *n.* **1.** word group, unit, construction, term; clause, sentence, verse; portion, part, passage, excerpt; noun phrase, verb phrase, adverbial phrase, adjectival phrase.

2. phraseology, way of speaking, phrasing, manner of expression, mode of speaking; style, mode, manner, strain, mannerism, peculiarity; language, locution, words, wordage, verbiage, usage, choice of words; vocabulary, parlance, idiom, dialect; diction, speech, *Inf.* talk; colloquialism, regionalism, argot, slang, patois, jargon.

3. expression, saying, proverb, maxim, aphorism, gnome; epithet, saw, mot, prosaism, witticism, axiom, words of wisdom, sentence, stock saying; platitude, trite expression, cliché, banality, *Inf.* bromide, *Sl.* chestnut; commonplace, triviality, hackneyed saying.

4. utterance, remark, saying; statement, comment, communication, pronouncement, declaration; mention, note, thought; *Inf.* two cents' worth, *Sl.* crack, *Sl.* shot; assertion, allegation, averment, asseveration, affirmation.

—*v.* **5.** express, word, term, style, put, couch; frame, formulate, cast, put in words, clothe in words; pronounce, enunciate, accentuate.

6. remark, say, utter, mouth, voice, verbalize; relate, recite, tell, speak, make known, quote; deliver, present, impart, set out; mention, observe, note; convey, communicate, comment, parley, come out with; aver, asseverate, assert, state, declare, allege; pronounce, announce, sound, enounce.

phraseology, *n.* **1.** speech pattern, phrasing, wording, word order, syntax; verbiage, verbalism, manner of expression, usage, *Linguistics.* idiolect; delivery, style, writing, locution, elocution, speaking, oratory, rhetoric, declamation; diction, word choice, intonation, inflection, pronunciation, accent, stress, articulation, enunciation, *Linguistics.* prosody; dialect, patois, cant, argot, parlance, tongue, speech, language, *Inf.* lingo, *Inf.* talk; jargon, vocabulary, terminology.

2. phrases, idioms, verbality; colloquialism, regionalism; expressions, sayings. See **phrase** (*def.* **3**).

phylactery, *n.* amulet, talisman, periapt, abraxas, fetish, obi, obeah, voodoo, *Judaism.* tefillin; apotropaic, scarab, swastika, triskelion; safeguard, protector, preservative; charm, good luck charm, lucky piece, horseshoe, rabbit's foot, *Brit.* merrythought.

physic, *n.* **1.** laxative, cathartic, purgative, aperient, ipecac, carminative; purifier, depurative, cleanser; castor oil, ricinus oil, mineral oil, salts, Epsom salts, mineral water.

2. medicine, medication, medicament, drug, pharmaceutical; corrective, antidote, restorative, specific; remedy, cure, cure-all, elixir, panacea, wonder drug; preparation, potion, solution, concoction, home remedy; dose, draft, drink, spoonful of medicine, pill, tablet, lozenge, capsule, *Pharm.* troche, *Both Pharm., Vet. Med.* bolus, electuary.

—*v.* **3.** purge, depurate, purify, cleanse, clean out, wash out. See **purge**.

4. medicate, drug, dope, dose, administer medication *or* medicine, prescribe medicine; treat, minister, doctor, nurse; remedy, cure, heal, correct, relieve, take care of [s.o.], fix [s.o.] up.

physical, *adj.* bodily, corporeal, corporal, fleshly, incarnate, carnal, somatic; earthly, unspiritual; external, surface, visible; material, substantial, tangible, palpable, solid, concrete, real, true, actual, existent; alive, living, vital.

physician, *n.* doctor, medical practitioner, M.D., medical doctor, medical man, healer, *Sl.* pill peddler, *Sl.* doc, *Sl.* medic, *Sl.* medico, *Sl.* croaker; allopath, osteopath, homeopath; general practitioner, G.P., specialist, gynecologist, internist, ophthalmologist; ear, nose, and throat doctor; dermatologist, neurologist, psychiatrist; resident, intern; paramedic.

physicist, *n.* scientist, physical scientist, natural philosopher, applied mathematician; nuclear physicist, astrophysicist, applied physicist, theoretical physicist.

physics, *n.* science, natural philosophy, applied mathematics; theoretical physics, applied physics, astrophysics, aerophysics, nuclear physics; thermodynamics, aerothermodynamics, aerodynamics, aeromechanics, pneumatics, mechanics, kinetics, kinematics, statics, gyrostatics, aerostatics; acoustics; electrothermics, electrokinetics, electromagnetics; hydraulics, hydrodynamics, hydromagnetics, hydrostatics, hydrokinetics.

physiognomy, *n.* **1.** face, *Archaic.* mazard, countenance, visage, *All Sl.* mug, map, pan, phiz, puss, kisser.

2. features, lineaments, configuration, conformation; silhouette, profile, outline, contour; appearance, outside, façade; expression, look, mien, brow, aspect, air, demeanor.

physique, *n.* figure, body, *Sl.* bod, *Sl.* chassis; shape, frame, build, form, structure, configuration, organization.

pianist, *n.* piano virtuoso, piano player, keyboard artist, *Sl.* ivory tickler *or* thumper, accompanist; *Fr. pianiste, It. pianista;* musician, artist, concert artist, virtuoso.

piano, *n.* pianoforte, grand piano, grand, baby grand, concert grand; *Trademark.* Steinway; spinet, square piano, upright, *Sl.* box, player piano, *Trademark.* Pianola; harpsichord, clavicembalo, cembalo, clavichord, virginal, clavicylinder, clavicytherium, celesta, dulcimer, hammered dulcimer, kalimba, clavier, *Sl.* eighty-eight *or* 88, ivories, *Inf.* keyboard.

piazza, *n.* **1.** square, open square, plaza, place, mall, circle; marketplace, arcade, rialto, forum, agora.

2. veranda, porch, patio, breezeway, areaway, pergola, arbor; loggia, gallery, colonnade, peristyle, portico.

picaresque, *adj.* roguish, rascally, scampish, rakish, raffish, arch; roistering, roisterous, romping, waggish, prankish, sportive, *Inf.* full of the devil *or* Old Nick; madcap, mischief-loving; swashbuckling, adventurous, adventuresome, venturesome, bold, enterprising, foolhardy, audacious, daring, daredevil, game, *Inf.* game for anything.

picaroon, *n.* **1.** rogue, rascal, rapscallion, devil, mischief-maker, scamp, *Inf.* scalawag; scoundrel, villain, knave, blackguard, miscreant, reprobate, black sheep, good-for-nothing, prodigal, *Inf.* rip; caitiff, rotter, felon, ruffian, riffraff, recreant, snake in the grass, criminal, sharper, cheat, shyster; adventurer, soldier of fortune, renegade, ne'er-do-well.

2. thief, bandit, brigand, highwayman, Zorro, Scarlet Pimpernel, footpad, road agent, *Sl.* yegg *or* yeggman, *Sp. bandolero, Southwest U.S.* ladrone, *Sl.* banditto, Robin Hood, *Australian.* bushranger; pillager, plunderer, marauder, despoiler, looter, raider, robber; outlaw, mafioso, thug, hoodlum, *Sl.* hood, *Australian Sl.* larrikin, desperado.

3. pirate, sea dog, sea wolf, corsair, buccaneer, privateer, freebooter, sea rover, sea robber; Captain Kidd, Blackbeard, Long John Silver.

picayune, *adj.* **1.** trivial, trifling, paltry, beggarly, petty, niggling; small, minor, puny, dinky, piddling, *Inf.* rinky-dink; small-time, one-horse, bush, *Sl.* two-bit, *Inf.* penny-ante, lightweight, *Sl.* small-potatoes, small fry, *Sl.* mickey-mouse; insignificant, unimportant, of little *or* no import, negligible, nugatory, inconsiderable, inconsequential, insubstantial, unsubstantial; inane, silly, foolish, pointless, *Inf.* dumb, idiotic; of minor importance, nothing great, no great shakes, *Inf.* no big deal, nothing to write home about, *Inf.* nothing to get excited *or* worked up about, of no account.

2. mean, inferior, scarce, scanty, scant, sparse, exiguous; poor, inadequate, insufficient, not enough, too little; bare, slight, skimpy, scrimpy, poky, pathetic, *Inf.* measly, *Inf.* chintzy, low, ordinary, average, mediocre, undistinguished, nominal, minute, negligible; short, shy, meanly small, mere, very little, slender, narrow.

pick[1], *v.* **1.** choose, select, handpick, pick out, single out; decide upon, determine upon, settle upon, fix upon; make up one's mind, make one's choice, make a selection, opt, opt for; sift, sift out, sieve out, screen, screen out, sort, sort out, separate the sheep from the goats, separate the wheat from the chaff; show preference, prefer, favor; discriminate, distinguish, differentiate; choose sides, accept, embrace, espouse, affiliate, *Inf.* make one's bed; elect, vote in, place in office; adopt, approve, ratify, nominate, name, designate.

2. gather, harvest, collect, garner, reap, mow, cut; pluck, take in, bring in, hay; cull, glean, winnow.

3. pry open, prize open, crack, break into, jimmy, force; break open, open, tap, broach.

4. *Usu.* **pick at a.** nibble, *Inf.* peck at, eat like a bird, push one's food around the plate, show no appetite; eat lightly, *Inf.* snack, *Inf.* nosh. **b.** nag, nag at, hassle, bother, pester, harass.

5. pick on *Informal.* criticize, blame, find fault; ride, needle, tease, badger, hector.

6. pick off *Informal.* shoot, shoot down, fire on *or* at; strike, hit, *Sl.* plug, *Sl.* drill; gun down, fell, drop.

7. pick out a. choose, select. See pick (*def.* **1**). **b.** distinguish, perceive, notice, recognize, sight; discern, discriminate, make a distinction, distinguish between; tell apart, tell one thing from another, know which is which. **c.** excise, exclude, except, eliminate, get rid of, dispose of, remove.

8. pick up a. lift, take up, raise, raise up, elevate, hoist, heft, heave. **b.** recover, recoup, get better, improve, mend, perk up, *Inf.* shape up; advance, progress, make progress, make headway, gain, gain ground; recover, rally, make a comeback. **c.** *Slang.* find, purchase, obtain, buy; locate by chance, come across, stumble over, dig up. **d.** obtain casually, earn, make, *Inf.* pull down, win, net, bag, come by, *Inf.* glom. **e.** accelerate, speed up, liven up, move along. **f.** take [s.o.] along, give [s.o.] a ride *or* lift; get, go to get, go for *or* after, call for. **g.** strike up an acquaintance with, introduce oneself to, meet casually; encounter, run across, fall in with, take up with. **h.** *Slang.* take into custody, arrest, apprehend, nab, *Inf.* collar, *Inf.* net, *Sl.* bust, *Sl.* pinch. **i.** tidy, tidy up, clean up, neaten, straighten up *or* out, put in order, *Inf.* spruce up.

—*n.* **9.** choice, selection; option, preference, pleasure, *Dial.* druthers, dibs.

10. best, choice, prize, nonpareil, nonesuch, pick of the crop *or* litter, cream of the crop; the best, the cream, *Fr. crème de la crème;* prime, flower; *Inf.* humdinger, *Inf.* jimdandy, *Inf.* dilly; elect, chosen, winner, champion, *Inf.* the tops.

pick[2], *n.* **1.** pickax, mattock, grub ax, adz, hewer, chopper, cutter, cutting tool, chopping tool, entrenching tool; trowel.

2. icepick, toothpick.

3. plectrum.

picket, *n.* **1.** stake, pale, paling, post; upright, stanchion, pile; peg, tether.

2. picketer, demonstrator, protestor, protestant, resister, objector, rebel, agitator, dissenter, dissident, marcher, *Inf.* sit-in.

3. forward observer, lookout, spotter, scout; sentinel, guard, sentry, vedette, watch, watchkeeper; patrol, patroller, patrolman; warder, watchman, nightwatchman.

—*v.* **4.** enclose, fence, fence in, pen *or* rail in, palisade, pale, hedge *or* wall in, bound, hem in, corral, box in.

5. tie, tie up, tether, secure, fasten, make fast, leash, string, attach, moor, anchor.

6. demonstrate, protest, do *or* go on picket duty, man the picket line, sit in, sit down, strike for *or* against, strike, walk out, go out; rebel, dissent, object, *Inf.* beef, *Inf.* kick, *Inf.* squawk; challenge, remonstrate, rally, march, demonstrate for *or* against, take a stand on, make a stand, stand up and be counted, mount the barricades *or* ramparts, don one's cockade hat; importune, pressure, bring pressure to bear upon, *Inf.* put up a squawk, cry out against, *Inf.* buck, *Inf.* buck the establishment, make waves.

picking, *n.* **1.** intake, harvest, gleaning, crop, fruit; gathering, winnowing, winnows, fall, drops, windfall.

2. pickings scraps, remains, leavings, leftovers, dregs; orts, remainder, residue, residuum; sweepings, debris, fragments; remnants, fag ends, bits and pieces, odds and ends; castoffs, castaways, rejects, discards.

3. pickings spoils, booty, loot, plunder, stealings, steal, ill-gotten gains, pilferage, *Inf.* grab, *Inf.* take, *Inf.* haul, *Inf.* swag; stolen goods, *Sl.* hot goods, *Sl.* boodle.

4. profits, earnings, emolument, perquisites, *Inf.* perks; return, returns, profits, receipts, proceeds, gains, gain, income.

pickle, *n.* **1.** cucumber pickle, cornichon, gherkin, dill pickle, dill, sweet pickle, sour pickle, bread-and-butter pickle, pickled watermelon rind; relish, piccalilli, chili, chili sauce, chowchow, chutney.

2. brine, steep, marinade, sauce, soy sauce, vinegar.

3. *Informal.* predicament, *Inf.* jam, *Inf.* fix, scrape, *Sl.* bind; tight *or* tough spot, *Inf.* box, corner, cul-de-sac, hole; mess, pretty kettle of fish, fine how-do-you-do, *Sl.* screw-up, pretty pass; dilemma, quandary, *Archaic.* hobble, straits, pinch; crisis, exigency, emergency; problem, trouble, plight, distress, difficulty.

4. in a pickle between Scylla and Charybdis, between a rock and a hard place, up the creek, on the horns of a dilemma, all at sea, up against the wall, with one's back to the wall, in the middle, up to one's armpits *or* neck.

—*v.* **5.** marinade, steep, brine, corn; devil, curry, spice; preserve, conserve, can, put up; cure, kipper.

pickled, *adj.* **1.** preserved, brined, marinaded, corned, cured, steeped *or* soaked in vinegar, salted, salted down, spiced, deviled, kippered, preserved, conserved; canned, put up.

2. *Slang.* drunk, inebriated, sodden, besotted, sotted, soused, *Sl.* crocked, *Sl.* crocked to the eyeballs, *Sl.* potted, *Sl.* stewed, *Sl.* stewed to the gills, *Sl.* canned, *Sl.* ossified. See **drunk** (*defs.* **1-3**).

pick-me-up, *n.* *Informal.* **1.** pick-up, refreshment, stimulation, enlivenment, invigoration, vivification, revival, *Inf.* shot in the arm, *Inf.* boost, *Inf.* lifesaver; stimulant, stimulus, stimulator, energizer, restorative, restorer, bracer, tonic, roborant, cordial; *Inf.* just what the doctor ordered.

2. alcohol, libation, drink, potation, spirits, *Inf.* eye-opener, *Inf.* hair of the dog that bit one; *Inf.* a quick one, nightcap, cocktail, highball, parting cup, *Inf.* one for the road; draft, quaff, bumper, nip, spot, tot, shot, *Inf.* a finger or two; sip, sup, *Inf.* swig, *Inf.* snort, *Inf.* jolt; swallow, *Inf.* slug, *Inf.* guzzle, *Inf.* gargle; dram, drop, a wee drop *or* nip, peg, tipple, cheering cup, the cup that cheers; *All Euph.* medicine, something to keep the chill off *or* keep the wind out, something good for what ails one; bull's milk, grape juice, the recipe; old faithful *or* old reliable, mother's milk.

pickpocket, *n.* thief, Fagin, Artful Dodger, petty criminal, *Sl.* dip, *Sl.* light-fingered Louie; purse snatcher, cutpurse.

pickup, *n.* **1.** rapid acceleration, speed-up, increase in speed *or* velocity, speed, power, response.

2. small truck, open truck, delivery truck, farm truck, quarter-ton truck, carrier.

3. *Informal.* chance meeting *or* encounter, casual date, flirtation, impromptu friendship, spur-of-the-moment alliance, informal introduction, *Sl.* one-night stand.

4. *Informal.* improvement, change for the better, getting on the road to recovery, recovery, rally, *Inf.* comeback; mending, healing, perking up; advance, progress, making progress, making headway, gaining ground.

5. freight, load, shipment, cargo, haul, burden, charge, goods, stuff, truckload; passenger, rider, customer, fare; hitchhiker.

6. See **pick-me-up**.

picnic, *n.* **1.** outdoor meal, cookout, alfresco meal; barbecue, steak fry, clambake, fish fry, *Inf.* hotdog *or* wienie roast, *Fr. déjeuner sur l'herbe;* feast, *Inf.* spread, *Sl.* feed; outdoor party, garden party, *Fr. fête champêtre;* outing, excursion.

2. *Informal.* **a.** celebration, revel, spree, wing-ding, carnival, *Inf.* hoopla; fun, funmaking, fun and games, good *or* pleasant time, *Inf.* high old time, time of one's life, *Inf.* action, *Sl.* laughs, *Sl.* ball, *Sl.* blast. **b.** child's play, *All Inf.* cinch, snap, pushover, setup, breeze, a piece of cake, duck soup.

—*v.* **3.** eat outdoors, eat in the open air, dine alfresco, cook out, bring sandwiches, bring a lunch.

pictorial, *adj.* **1.** illustrated, pictured, sketched, photographed, painted; diagrammatic, charted, delineative, delineated.

2. vivid, striking, telling, picturesque, expressive, cogent; lucid, clear, crystal-clear, manifest, plain, obvious, unmistakable.

3. graphic, illustrative, representative; realistic, particular, detailed, distinct, well-defined, well-delineated, well-drawn, effective; realistic, explicit, express, specific, definite, precise.

—*n.* **4.** illustrated magazine, photojournalistic publication, picture supplement, Sunday supplement, rotogravure; school annual, yearbook, *Inf.* rogues' gallery.

pictorialize, *v.* illustrate, depict, portray, show in pictures. See **picture** (*def.* **8**).

picture, *n.* **1.** likeness, semblance, similitude, icon, representation, simulacrum, portrait, depictment, depiction; artwork, painting, drawing, line drawing, black and white, pen and ink, oil painting, pastel, watercolor, gouache, wash drawing, engraving, etching; realistic painting, impressionistic painting, surrealistic painting, cubist painting; illustration, sketch; photograph, *Inf.* photo, snapshot, *Inf.* snap, *Inf.* candid, *Inf.* pin-up; tableau, *Inf.* black-out, *Inf.* still.

2. image, reflection, reflected image, shadow, silhouette.

3. description, portrayal, report, detail, recountal, recreation, reenactment, recital, recitation, *Inf.* rehash; narrative, relation, account; story, tale, history, chronicle, record, memoir, vignette.

4. film, movie, motion picture, moving picture, *Dial.* picture show. See **motion picture**.

5. counterpart, replica, copy, duplicate, facsimile, faithful copy, reproduction; twin, living *or* very image; double, look-alike, carbon copy, match, exact match, perfect likeness, *Inf.* spit and image *or* spitting image, chip off the old block, *Sl.* ringer, *Sl.* dead ringer.

6. epitome, typification, archetype, prototype, model, example, perfect example; embodiment, living embodiment, living example, incarnation, corporealization, incorporation, personification.

7. *Usu.* **the picture** situation, state, the state of things, state of affairs, circumstances, the way things are; conditions, status quo, the times; background, reasons, causes, motives; factors, details, pros and cons, pluses and minuses, risks, contingencies, possibilities, options, predictions, possible outcome, *Inf.* war map; turn of events, course of events, explanation, commentary, version; plight, predicament, difficulty, dilemma.

—*v.* **8.** draw, paint, sketch, depict, delineate, pictorialize; portray, illustrate, *Archaic.* limn, trace, reproduce; represent, show, exhibit, manifest, display; disclose, bring to view, put before [s.o.'s] eyes.

9. imagine, conceive of, envision, *Inf.* feature; visualize, hypothesize, theorize, conjecture, *Inf.* dream up, fancy, call to mind, remember, summon up, *Inf.* dredge up; fantasize, romanticize, give free rein to one's imagination, see in the mind's eye.

10. describe, narrate, relate, recount, give an account of; tell, recite, express; report, set out, chronicle, paint a verbal picture, *Inf.* paint with words, outline verbally; explain, account for, answer to, clear up; define, elucidate, specify, detail, flesh out, annotate, fill in the details; indicate, denote, connote, characterize, label.

11. reflect, mirror, duplicate, represent; imitate, emulate, simulate, parallel.

picturesque, *adj.* **1.** charming, delightful, exquisite, beguiling, intriguing, fascinating; quaint, eccentric, strange, uncommon, unfamiliar, out of the ordinary, out of the pale, incongruous; odd, unique, bizarre, exotic, droll, whimsical, singular, curious, *Inf.* kooky, *Sl.* freaky.

2. (*of writing, speech, etc.*) colorful, pictorial, graphic, vivid, realistic; glowing, romantic, poignant; sparkling, vivacious, vital, telling, penetrating, compelling, stirring, spellbinding; passionate, impassioned, ardent; pungent, piquant, trenchant, incisive.

3. pleasing, attractive, seemly, comely, tasteful, beautiful; interesting, inviting, prepossessing, *Inf.* fetching, irresistible; striking, exciting, stimulating, enchanting, glamorous, provocative, unexpected, *Inf.* rich, *Inf.* priceless; impressive, effective, engaging, captivating, aesthetic, artistic, *Inf.* arty, elegant, graceful, well-composed, well-arranged, well-grouped, well-disposed.

piddle, *v.* **1.** dawdle, dally, dillydally, procrastinate, shilly-shally, vacillate, *Inf.* diddle; take one's time *or* one's own sweet time, fill time, fritter time away *or* fritter away the hours; idle, trifle, finick, potter, fiddle.

2. waste time, loiter, poke, loll, hang around, mill around; slouch, loaf, daydream, *Inf.* lallygag, lounge, vegetate; shirk, *Sl.* goof off, lie down on the job; fool around, mess around, *Sl.* screw around, do nothing, do little; lag behind, move at a snail's pace.

piddling, *adj.* trifling, peddling, fribbling, niggling; paltry, petty, small, slight, puny, picayune; minor, meager, flimsy; lightweight, shallow, frothy, frivolous, superficial; of no consequence, unimportant, insignificant, insubstantial; silly, inane, absurd, fatuous, senseless, foolish, ridiculous, *Sl.* dopey, *Sl.* wacky, dumb; worthless, meaningless, useless, trashy, not worth the paper it's printed on, as valuable as a wooden nickel, not worth a hill of beans, not worth a hoot in hell, not worth a continental.

pie, *n.* **1.** tart, turnover, *U.S.* pandowdy, *French Cookery.* quiche, pastry, *Fr. pâtisserie;* cream pie, fruit pie, meat pie, Boston cream pie.

2. pie in the sky illusions, false hopes, delusions, unrealistic aspirations *or* goals; self-deceit, self-deception, vague dreams of the future; false promises, *Inf.* campaign promises, *Inf.* courting talk; utopia, daydreams, *Inf.* pipe dreams, *Inf.* castles in the air, romanticized plans.

piebald, *adj.* pied, parti-colored, black and white, brown and white, (*esp. of horses*) skewbald; dappled, brindled, spotted, mottled, speckled, flecked, checked, checkered; varicolored, variegated, multicolored, multicolor, polychromatic, polychromic, versicolor, kaleidoscopic; rainbowy, colorful, brilliant, pavonine; marble, marbly, motley, streaked, striated, striped.

piece, *n.* **1.** part, segment, section, division, subdivision; constituent, component, ingredient, element, factor; parcel, fragment, fraction, shred, shard; particle, bit, scrap, crumb, morsel; snippet, cutting, clipping, wisp, remnant; slice, helping, serving, rasher, sliver; hunk, lump, chunk.

2. artistic production *or* product, creation, masterpiece, chef-d'oeuvre, masterwork, art object, *Fr. objet d'art;* novel, story, essay, article, report; poem, verse, rhyme; drama, play, sketch, pageant; painting, portrait, sculpture, statue, bust; dance, ballet; composition, symphony, opera, oratorio; performance, number, routine, *Sl.* bit, *Sl.* shtik.

3. portion, share, percentage, *Sl.* cut, *Sl.* slice of the pie; commission, dividend; measure, dole, allotment, allocation, allowance; quota, proportion, ration.

4. token, charm, amulet, talisman, fetish; lucky piece, rabbit's foot, wishbone, horseshoe.

5. example, specimen, instance, case, sample, sampling, illustration.

6. in pieces a. broken, smashed, shattered, pulverized, in smithereens, in shards; fallen to ruin, disintegrated, crumbling, crumbled, dilapidated. **b.** fragmented, partial, incomplete; not unified, incoherent, disjointed, choppy, disorganized, disordered.

—*v.* **7.** mend, patch, patch up, sew, darn; repair, fix, make serviceable; strengthen, reinforce, cover.

8. piece out complete, enlarge, extend, augment, add to, supplement, expand, enhance, complement.

9. piece together join, fit, attach; assemble, put together, compose; connect, unite, relate.

piecemeal, *adv.* piece by piece, part by part, bit by bit, little by little, in installments; gradually, by degrees, slowly, inch by inch, inchmeal; at intervals, irregularly, fitfully, intermittently, sporadically, in fits and starts.

pied, *adj.* See **piebald.**

pier, *n.* **1.** quay, wharf, landing, landing place, anchorage; jetty, jutty, dock; breakwater, embankment.

2. pillar, post, pile, piling, upright, column, foundation; support, buttress, brace.

pierce, *v.* **1.** penetrate, puncture, pass through *or* into, transpierce; enter, tunnel, bore, drill; perforate, make a hole *or* holes in, punch, honeycomb, riddle; run through, stab, lancinate, prick, stick, pink, gore; cut, gash, slit, gride. See also **penetrate** (*def.* **1**).

2. comprehend, grasp, fathom, get to the bottom of; understand, apprehend, seize, *Inf.* lay hold of, *Sl.* psych out; discern, read, see. See also **penetrate** (*def.* **4**).

3. affect, move, touch, cut to the quick, *Inf.* hit home, *Inf.* hit [s.o.] where it hurts, *Inf.* get *or* get to [s.o.]; make an impression, make a dent, *Inf.* sink in; melt, soften, mellow, play on, tug at the heartstrings; strike, thrill, excite, stir. See also **penetrate** (*def.* **3**).

pierced, *adj.* (*usu. for decorative purposes*) perforated, punctured, riddled, honeycombed; pitted, pocked, dented, indented; hammered, distressed, marred, blemished.

piercer, *n.* needle, stiletto, awl, *Carpentry.* bradawl, bodkin; gimlet, broach, auger, borer, trepan, *Surg.* trephine, drill, punch, dibble, corkscrew; chisel, gouge, probe, *Surg.* trocar; poignard, dagger, stylet, lance, sword, rapier, épée, spear, assegai; javelin, pike, harpoon, shaft, gaff, arrow; knife, scalpel, lancet, blade, cutter.

piercing, *adj.* **1.** (*usu. of sound*) loud, blaring, shrill, high-pitched, high; earsplitting, ear-shattering, eardrum-puncturing, air-rending; strident, grating, harsh, cacophonous; screeching, squealing, squeaking, shrieking.

2. (*usu. of eyes*) penetrating, probing, searching, analyzing; mesmerizing, mesmeric, hypnotizing, hypnotic, basilisk; spellbinding, arresting, gripping, engaging, holding; enthralling, entrancing, fascinating.

3. (*usu. of weather*) cold, freezing, arctic, frigid, wintry, numbing, raw; bitter, biting, keen, nipping, nippy.

4. perceptive, percipient, perspicacious, discerning; quick-witted, quick, alert, ready; aware, informed, shrewd, astute; subtle, keen, sharp-witted, sharp, smart, *Sl.* brainy.

5. sarcastic, caustic, mordant, acerbic, acrid, cutting, stinging, mordacious, incisive; cruel, painful, hurtful, agonizing, excruciating; intense, fierce.

pietism, *n.* **1.** sanctimony, sanctimoniousness, Tartuffery, formalism, hypocrisy, pharisaism, phariseeism; self-righteousness, *Inf.* goody-goodiness, *Inf.* goodiness; false piety, excessive piety, religiosity; dissimulation, feigning, dissembling; Machiavellism, Machiavellianism, double-dealing; cant, lip service, mouth honor, mealy-mouthedness; affectation, pretense, false pretense, bluff.

2. piety, piousness, religiousness, devotedness, devoutness. See **piety** (*def.* **1**).

piety, *n.* **1.** devoutness, godliness, saintliness, spirituality, holiness, sanctity, religiousness, devotion, faithfulness, religiosity, pietism, religious zeal.

2. respect, veneration, reverence, awe, regard, deference, obeisance, dedication.

3. dutifulness, rectitude, goodness, righteousness, virtuousness, purity, chastity, humility, grace.

pig, *n.* **1.** hog, sow, boar, razorback; peccary, wart-hog, babirusa; porker, grunter, oinker, tusker; swine, barrow; shoat, shote, piglet, pigling, piggy, suckling-pig, hogling.

2. pork, pork chops, ham, bacon, pigs' feet, pigs' knuckles.

3. *Informal.* **a.** glutton, cormorant, gormand, eater; trencherman, big eater, wolf, *Inf.* hog. **b.** vulgarian, barbarian, boor; sloven, slattern, frump.

pigeon, *n.* **1.** bird, dove, squab, homing pigeon, carrier pigeon.

2. *Slang.* dupe, gull, gudgeon, *Brit. Dial.* cull, *Archaic.* cully, *Inf.* chump, *Sl.* sap, *Sl.* schnook, *Sl.* schlemiel, *Sl.* boob; greenhorn, sitting duck, easy *or* soft mark, easy *or* soft target, *Inf.* sucker, *Inf.* cinch, *Sl.* patsy, *U.S. Sl.* fall guy, *Sl.* softie *or* soft touch, *Sl.* pushover.

pigeonhole, *n.* **1.** compartment, partition, section, part, department; area, sphere, space, place.

2. cubbyhole, cubby, niche, nook; drawer, tray, box, bin, hold, receptacle, bunker; booth, stall, cubicle, carrel, slot, alcove; closet, locker, storage space.

—*v.* **3.** file, interfile, insert, put in place, replace.

4. postpone, put off, table, shelve; sleep on it, let the matter stand.

5. catalog, categorize, classify, codify, alphabetize; rank, group, sort, assort, order, arrange; slot, peg.

piggish, *adj.* **1.** hoggish, porcine, swinish, piglike, hoglike; coarse, boorish, animal, animalistic, beastly.

2. greedy, gluttonous, ravenous, voracious, devouring, edacious, cormorant, rapacious; insatiable, insatiate, unquenchable, open-mouthed; glutting, gorging, omnivorous, crapulous.

3. filthy, dirty, foul, slimy, *Inf.* gloppy, *Sl.* cruddy, mucky, muddy; sloppy, sloshy, sludgy, miry; musty, smelly, rotten.

4. unwashed, unhygienic, unclean, bedraggled, slovenly, unkempt, sloppy, sleazy; squalid, wretched, shabby, deteriorated, ramshackle; miserable, uncared-for, dingy, *Sl.* slummy.

pigheaded, *adj.* **1.** stubborn, stubborn as a mule, mulish, muleheaded, bullheaded, bullish, headstrong; willful, self-willed, contrary, perverse, wrongheaded, cross-grained, balky, uncooperative, froward, refractory, recalcitrant, contumacious; stupid, dense, blunt, crass, undiscerning, uncomprehending; moronic, idiotic, imbecilic, mindless, witless, brainless; slow-witted, numskulled, thick-skulled, cloddish.

2. obstinate, inflexible, immovable, not to be moved, adamant, adamantine, stiff-necked, set, set in one's ways, *Inf.* hard-core, *Inf.* hard-shell; inexorable, implacable, intransigent, intractable, uncompromising, unbending, unwavering, unyielding; unmalleable, unpersuadable, uninfluenceable, unswayable, unpliable; persistent, persevering, pertinacious, tenacious, dogged, bulldogged, relentless, unrelenting, single-minded.

3. narrow-minded, narrow, prejudiced, biased, bigoted; closed-minded, closed, intolerant, illiberal, unreasonable; little-minded, small-minded, mean-minded; insular, parochial, provincial, *Sociol.* ethnocentric, confined.

pigment, *n.* **1.** dye, dyestuff, stain, paint, tempera, *Obs.* tincture, colorant, colorer, coloring agent.

2. color, coloring, tone, shade, hue, tint, tinge, tincture, *Literary.* tinct.

—*v.* **3.** color, add pigment *or* color to, tinge, tint, tincture, *Obs.* tinct, shade, paint, dye, stain.

pigpen, *n.* **1.** pigsty, *Chiefly Brit.* piggery, hogsty, hogpen; enclosure, stockyard, compound.

2. hovel, shack, *Both Sl.* dump, hole; rathole, hell-hole, garbage pile *or* heap, *Inf.* snake pit, mare's nest, mess.

pigtail, *n.* braid, plait, plat, queue, cue, ponytail.

pike[1], *n.* spear, lance, spontoon, half-pike, harpoon; shafted weapon, halberd, bill, poleax; javelin, jereed, assegai, shaft.

pike[2], *n.* **1.** turnpike, toll road, highway *or* state highway, *U.S. Inf.* interstate, freeway, *Brit.* clearway, expressway, parkway, causeway, throughway; speedway, autobahn, superhighway.

2. tollgate, toll bar, tollbooth, tollhouse; toll, payment, fee.

pile[1], *n.* **1.** heap, stack, mass, accumulation, bulk, drift, cumulus; hoard, store, stock, stockpile, supply, lump, deposit, swell, mound, tumulus; bank, hillock, hummock, hill, mountain; bale, bundle, cock, shock, rick, mow; load, barrow, cartload, wagonload, carload, cargo.

2. collection, amassment, assemblage, aggregation; concentration, agglomeration, conglomeration, cluster, congeries; clump, bunch, batch; assortment, variety, medley, miscellany, jumble, hodgepodge; clutter, *Inf.* mess.

3. *Informal.* abundance, bounty, volume, plenty; quantity, profusion, *Inf.* lots, *Inf.* raft, storm, shower, ocean, sea, world; multitude, throng, array, legion, crowd; numbers, scores, pack, host, swarm, mob.

4. *Informal.* hoard, store, quite a little, considerable, deal, great deal; *Inf.* lots, mess, peck, *Inf.* load, *Inf.* oodles, *Inf.* tons; chunk, lump, *Inf.* hunk, gob, *Sl.* scad, *Inf.* slew.

5. *Informal.* money, wealth, fortune, treasure; fund, holdings, savings, *Inf.* loot; *Inf.* bundle, money to burn, barrel of money, *Sl.* wad, *Sl.* pot, mint, sockfull, cool million, goodly sum.

—*v.* **6.** *Often* **pile up** accumulate, heap, roll up, pyramid, stack, pack; compile, amass, cumulate; hoard, squirrel away, load up, stow away.

7. gather, glean, take in, pull in, harvest, reap; garner, store up, stock up, lay by, lay up, lay in, salt away, *Inf.* stash away, reserve, set aside; save, save up.

8. group, cluster, bunch up *or* together, huddle; mass, crowd, congregate, agglomerate.

pile[2], *n.* post, pillar, column, pier, beam, I-beam, bar, rib; upright, stanchion, standard; support, foundation, piling.

pile[3], *n.* **1.** hair, down, silk, fuzz, fluff, fleece, plush; wool, fur, bristles, *Zool.* seta, pelage.

2. cord, corduroy, Turkish toweling, velvet, velveteen, rep, shag; nap, tooth; loop, fiber, strand.

pileup, *n.* **1.** accumulation, congeries, amassment,

cumulation; heap, mound, hill, mountain; pile, stack, bunch, pack, wad, lot, fistful, mass, *Sl.* gob.

2. collision, crash, chain accidents, accident, wreck, *Inf.* smash-up, *Inf.* smash, *Inf.* crack-up, *Inf.* demolition derby.

pilfer, *v.* **1.** steal, thieve, rob, filch, purloin, finger, pick, *Inf.* snitch, cabbage, abstract, *Chiefly Brit.* prig, *Brit. Sl.* snaffle, *Euph.* borrow, *Archaic.* nim; peculate, embezzle, *Law.* defalcate, misappropriate, convert; shoplift, palm, *Sl.* boost, walk off *or* away with, *Euph.* remove; *All Sl.* heist, pinch, hook, swipe, hustle, rip off, frisk, crook, cop, lift.

2. pirate, plagiarize, copy, *Inf.* lift, *Inf.* crib; forge, counterfeit, imitate, reproduce; appropriate, expropriate, arrogate, usurp.

3. mooch, scrounge, freeload, sponge, scavenge, *Sl.* bum.

4. swindle, defraud, mulct, shark, cheat, fleece, *Inf.* flimflam, rook, bilk, *Inf.* welsh, *Inf.* do [s.o.] out of, *Inf.* gyp, *Sl.* pluck, *Sl.* chisel, *Sl.* clip.

pilfering, *n.* **1.** petty thievery, theft, filching, pilferage, *Sl.* swiping, *Sl.* hustling, *Sl.* copping, *Psychol.* kleptomania; peculation, embezzlement, *Law.* defalcation, misappropriation; shoplifting, palming, *Sl.* boosting; smuggling, bootlegging; purse-snatching, *Inf.* mugging, *Sl.* jumping.

2. plagiarism, copying, *Inf.* cribbing, *Inf.* lifting.

3. expropriation, appropriation, arrogation, usurpation, accroachment, assumption.

pilgrim, *n.* **1.** palmer, *Fr. pèlerin, Islam.* hadji, crusader; worshipper, devotee.

2. tourist, sightseer, world traveler, *Sl.* W.T., excursionist, *Brit. Inf.* tripper, junketeer, globetrotter, Nelly Bly, Phineas Fogg, traveler, wanderer, journeyer, wayfarer; rambler, roamer, rover, peregrinator, peripatetic.

3. refugee, displaced person, D.P., exile, émigré, evacuee, expatriate, alien, Wandering Jew; nomad, Kuchi, Bedouin, *Sl.* wetback; transient, sojourner, migrant, bird of passage; itinerant, *U.S. Inf.* boomer, floater, drifter, hobo, tramp, vagrant.

4. settler, pioneer, homesteader, sooner; new arrival, newcomer, greenhorn, immigrant, emigrant.

pilgrimage, *n.* holy *or* sacred expedition, *Fr. pardon, Islam.* hadj; special trip, side trip, detour; excursion, expedition, trip, voyage, journey, trek; cruise, crossing, passage; peregrination, safari; tour, grand tour, world tour, *Ger. Wanderschaft.*

pill, *n.* **1.** tablet, capsule, pellet, vitamin pill, diet pill, *Med., Pharm.* placebo, *Pharm., Vet. Med.* bolus; pastille, troche, lozenge, drop, cough drop; medicine, remedy, cure, medicament, medication, physic, drug, pharmaceutical.

2. dose, bitter cup, bitter draft, bitter pill.

3. the pill birth-control pill, oral contraceptive.

4. *Slang.* disagreeable person, *Inf.* pain in the neck, *Sl.* pain, *Inf.* crank, *Inf.* grouch, *Sl.* grump.

pillage, *v.* **1.** plunder, rob, despoil, *Archaic.* spoil, spoliate, *Chiefly Scot.* reive; ravage, harry, rape, maraud, devastate, lay waste, depredate; ransack, sack, loot, gut, fleece, strip, rifle, steal; desecrate, defile, outrage, violate.

2. desolate, wreak havoc upon, destroy, damage, ruin, vandalize; burn, level, raze, demolish.

3. pirate, freeboot, buccaneer, privateer, filibuster; burglarize, burgle.

—n. **4.** plunder, plundering, plunderage, rapine, depredation, spoliation, despoliation, despoilment, *Obs.* direption, raven *or* ravin; ravaging, harrying, marauding, *Archaic.* maraud, sack, sacking, *Rare.* sackage; raid, razzia, foray; foraging, looting, ravishment, seizure, grab, rape.

5. devastation, laying waste, desolation; destruction, ruin, burning, razing, leveling, vandalism; desecration, defilement, outrage, violation.

6. brigandage, piracy, buccaneering, freebooting, banditry, highway robbery, *Obs.* latrociny, privateering, filibustering; robbery, theft, thievery, stealing, *Law.* larceny.

7. spoils, loot, plunder, booty, *Archaic.* boot, *Archaic.* prey, *Scot. Obs.* reif; prize, profits, pickings, gain, grab, *Inf.* haul; *All Sl.* the take, the goods, boodle, swag.

pillar, *n.* **1.** column, upright support, caryatid, atlas, telamon; *Archit.* columna caelata, pilaster, colonnade, peristyle; post, shaft, pier, pole, pylon; standard, stalagmite, spine, cylinder; *Naut.* mast, spar.

2. chief supporter, mainstay, backbone, pillar of the church *or* community *or* society, tower of strength; strength, support, rock, foundation.

pillow, *n.* cushion, bolster; headrest, head restraint; study pillow, prop, support; pad, *Inf.* sit-upon.

pilot, *n.* **1.** airplane pilot, aviator, *Inf.* birdman, airman, flier, avigator, aeronaut, co-pilot; steersman, helmsman, wheelman, coxswain, navigator; driver, back-seat driver.

2. guide, tour guide, cicerone; leader, chief, head, boss, *Inf.* bossman, superior; captain, conductor, director, engineer, trainmaster; man-in-charge, manager, overseer, supervisor, superintendent, *Inf.* super, foreman, headman, *Brit.* gaffer.

—v. **3.** steer, drive, fly, guide, navigate; run, operate, work, handle; conduct, lead, direct, control, manage, boss; be in charge of, have direction of, be in control of, be in the driver's seat, be at the wheel.

—adj. **4.** experimental, tentative, trial, test.

pimp, *n.* **1.** procurer, pander, panderer, whoremonger, *Sl.* flesh-peddler, *Sl.* hustler, *U.S. Sl.* sweetman, *Fr. maquereau;* white slaver, smuggler, runner; go-between, intermediary, middleman, agent, solicitor; purveyor, supplier, provider, furnisher; procuress, *Archaic.* bawd, madam.

—v. **2.** procure, pander, solicit, *Sl.* hustle; purvey, supply, provide, furnish.

pimple, *n.* **1.** pustule, papule, papilla, boil, blain, furuncle, furunculus, carbuncle, pock, wen, whelk, *Ophthalm.* sty *or* stye, *Rare.* bleb, *Archaic.* botch; eruption, inflammation, rising, lump, bump, wheal, hive, blind pimple, ingrown hair; blemish, mark, spot, pockmark, pit, whitehead, *Pathol.* milium, blackhead, *Med.* comedo, *Sl.* zit, *Sl.* woogit, *Sl.* hickey.

2. *Usu.* **pimples** goose flesh, goose skin, goose pimples, hives, horripilation, *Inf.* goose bumps, *Inf.* duck bumps.

pin, *n.* **1.** bolt, peg, dowel, thole, tholepin; nail, spike; screw, rivet; tack.

2. brooch, clip, stickpin, breastpin, chatelaine, *Archaic.* ouch; tieclasp, tie clip, tie tack; jewel, gem; ornament, decoration, adornment.

3. trifle, gewgaw, gimcrack, bauble, trinket; hair, button, straw, molehill, *Inf.* beans, *Inf.* hill of beans, *Inf.* row of pins.

—v. **4.** fasten, secure, fix, affix, attach; nail, bolt, screw, rivet, tack, staple, peg; transfix, skewer, freeze, immobilize, stabilize.

5. pin down a. bind, hold, constrain, tie, tie down, tie [s.o.'s] hands, leave [s.o.] no option *or* choice. **b.** force, make, have, cause *or* cause to, compel, press, *Inf.* pressure *or* high-pressure, *Inf.* lean on, *Inf.* squeeze, *Inf.* put the screws on *or* to, *Inf.* twist [s.o.'s] arm. **c.** determine, specify, name, designate, indicate, put *or* lay one's finger on, pinpoint, zero in on, home in on.

6. pin something on someone *Slang.* blame for, lay *or* place the blame on, fix the responsibility for, charge to, lay at [s.o.'s] doorstep, bring home to; attribute to, ascribe to, impute to, assign to, lay to, pin on, fix on, saddle on *or* upon, father upon, *Sl.* hang on; *Sl.* frame.

pinch, *v.* **1.** squeeze, compress, constrict, tighten, contract, twist, wring; grip, grasp, grab, hold; tweak, pull, jerk.
2. bite, nip, vellicate; prick, stab, pierce; gall, chafe, rasp; sting, smart, pain, hurt, ache, discomfort, distress.
3. cramp, restrict, limit, restrain, straiten; check, hamper, curb, inconvenience; hinder, impede, inhibit, block, rein, fetter.
4. scrimp, skimp, save, pinch pennies, economize, make both ends meet, make ends meet, keep within one's means; hold back, be stingy, be parsimonious.
5. *Slang.* steal, rob, thieve, pilfer. See **steal** (*def.* **1**).
6. *Informal.* arrest, apprehend, take into custody. See **arrest** (*def.* **1**).
—n. **7.** squeeze, nip, twinge, pang, stab, gripe, prick; twitch, stitch, kink, spasm; ache, pain, hurt, suffering, discomfort, distress.
8. bit, *Inf.* smidgin, *Inf.* tad; soupçon, trace, shade, touch, suggestion; small quantity, piece, morsel, scrap.
9. emergency, exigency, matter of life and death, extremity, urgency, pressure, stress; strait, pickle, scrape, jam; predicament, dilemma, difficulty, complication, trouble, rub; adversity, hardship, misery, affliction; pretty pass, pretty state of affairs, ticklish situation, delicate situation.

pinchbeck, *n.* **1.** sham, mock, fake, counterfeit, imitation, *Inf.* phony; paste, glitter, tinsel, junk, brummagem; hoax, cheat, fraud, swindle, *Sl.* rip-off.
—adj. **2.** counterfeit, spurious, bogus, fake, ungenuine, unauthentic, supposititious, bastard, pseudo, quasi, apocryphal, sham, mock, make-believe, *Inf.* phony; artificial, imitation, unreal, synthetic, ersatz; shoddy, junky, plastic, brummagem.

pinch-hit, *v.* substitute for, *Inf.* sub for, subrogate, act for, double for, fill in for, fill *or* take the place of, cover for, stand in lieu of, *Sl.* step into [s.o.'s] shoes, *Inf.* fill [s.o.'s] shoes; replace, succeed, supplant, supply, supersede; fill a vacancy *or* space *or* hole.

pine, *v.* **1.** yearn for, long for, languish for, ache for, sigh for, wish for, carry the torch for, *Inf.* have a yen for; thirst for, hunger for, burn for, be dying for, *Inf.* hanker after; desire, desiderate, want, crave, covet, want with all one's heart, want in the worst way, *Sl.* give one's eyeteeth *or* right arm for.
2. weaken, decline, fade, wane, ebb, fail, flag, droop, wilt, waste, waste away, wither on the vine; pass away, fade away, fade out of the picture, die out *or* away, cease to exist *or* be, give way; go downhill, *Sl.* hit the skids; burn out, run out *or* down, *Inf.* run out of steam, *Inf.* give out, *Inf.* conk out, *Inf.* peg out, *Inf.* poop out, *Inf.* peter out.

pinion, *v.* shackle, fetter, manacle, handcuff, put in irons, gyve, *Sl.* slap the cuffs *or* bracelets on; chain, enchain, truss, bind, bind hand and foot, tie, tie up, tie down, hogtie; trammel, entrammel, hobble, hamper, clog.

pink[1], *n.* **1.** acme, height, culmination, peak, pinnacle, summit, ultimate, quintessence, peak *or* acme of perfection.
—adj. **2.** pinkish; rose, rosy, rose-colored, rose-hued; flesh-pink, flesh-color, flesh-colored; salmon, salmon-pink, salmon-colored.

pink[2], *v.* **1.** pierce, penetrate, stab, stick, run through, *Sl.* let the daylight in; impale, skewer, spit, fix, transfix; gore, spear, lance, spike; punch, perforate; punch full of holes, honeycomb, riddle.
2. scallop, notch, knurl, mill; cut, serrate, crenellate; incise, gash, crimp, scotch, score.

pinnacle, *n.* **1.** summit, apex, vertex, apogee, crest, peak, spire, tip; tiptop, top, cap, crown, headpiece, head; steeple, loft, aerie, tower, belfry.
2. acme, zenith, meridian, maximum, climax, culmination, crowning point, *Latin. ne plus ultra;* sublimity, supremacy, best, finest, perfection, consummation, extreme, utmost, uttermost, *U.S. Sl.* the most, *U.S. Sl.* the greatest; prime, heyday, bloom, full flower, blossom, efflorescence.
3. cone, gable, pyramid, obelisk, taper; needle, spicule, tor, nib, neb, cusp, cuspid, canine.
—v. **4.** pedestal, set *or* put on a pedestal; idealize, glorify, worship.
5. crown, cap, top, tip, *Brit.* nib.

pioneer, *n.* **1.** frontiersman, backwoodsman, settler, homesteader; pathfinder, trailbreaker, trailblazer, explorer, paver of the way; scout, guide, point; forerunner, antecedent, precursor, predecessor, foregoer; outrider, front *or* lead runner, vaunt-courier, avant-courier.
2. innovator, groundbreaker, avant-gardist; pacesetter, pacemaker, trend-setter, leader.
3. combat engineer, engineer, *U.S. Navy.* Seabee, *Brit.* sapper.
—v. **4.** initiate, instigate, actuate, set off, set in motion, trigger, start the ball rolling, ring up the curtain on; open, take the first step, take the initiative, take the lead, take the plunge, make a start, break the ice, lead off, lead the way, blaze the trail; institute, inaugurate, found, establish, set up, organize, originate, break ground, lay the first stone, lay the foundation; introduce, launch, broach, usher in.
5. guide, conduct, lead, marshal, usher, escort, convoy.
—adj. **6.** initiatory, initial, initiating, initiative, introductory, inaugural; creative, formative, drawing-board.

pious, *adj.* **1.** devout, devoted, godly, God-fearing, God-loving, religious, spiritual; humble, worshipful, reverent, reverential, venerative; righteous, moral, virtuous, good, right-minded, clean-minded, clean of mind, clean of spirit, clean-spirited, pure-spirited, pure in spirit, pure in heart; holy, saintly seraphic, angelic, Christly, Christlike.
2. sanctimonious, self-righteous, holier-than-thou, simon-pure, *Inf.* goody-goody, *Inf.* too good to be true; pharisaic, pietistic, over-pious, falsely pious; hypocritical, Tartuffian, canting; mealy-mouthed, unctuous, oily.

pipe, *n.* **1.** tube, cylinder, conduit, duct, conveyor, reed, straw, stem; pipette, catheter, funnel, tubule, fistula, nipple; passage, capillary, artery, vein; hose, garden hose, rubber hose; flue, chimney, smokestack; gas pipe, gasline, pipeline, steampipe, fuel pipe, oil pipe, oil line, siphon.
2. tobacco pipe, corncob pipe, corncob, briar pipe, briar, clay pipe, clay, meerschaum; hookah, hubble-bubble, bong, water pipe, narghile, chibouk, *Sl.* carburetor, *Sl.* power-hitter; peace pipe, calumet.
3. wind instrument, woodwind instrument, wind, horn, tooter; flute, recorder, flageolet, panpipe, piccolo, fife, whistle, penny-whistle; clarinet, cormourne, krumhorn, ocarina, bassoon, contrabassoon, oboe, *Archaic.* hautboy, shawm, English horn, syrinx, saxophone, *Inf.* sax.
4. pipes *Informal.* windpipe, trachea, *Archaic.* weasand; pharnyx, epiglottis, bronchial tube, bronchus, *Brit. Dial.* wizen.
—v. **5.** tweet, squeak, cheep, chirp, peep; tweet, whistle, tweetle, tootle, skirl; shriek, squawk, screech,

squeal, shrill; sing, warble, twit, chant; ululate, wail, keen, whine, yammer, caterwaul.

6. channel, tube, flush, funnel, flume, hose; drain, siphon, tap.

7. pipe down *Slang.* be quiet, quiet down, silence, hush, shush; shut up, button one's lips, hold one's tongue, keep still, not breathe a sound, shut one's mouth.

pipe dream, *n.* *Informal.* fantasy, illusion, mirage, chimera, castle in the air; notion, vague notion, whimsy, vagary, figment of the imagination, romance; dream, daydream, reverie, vision, delusion.

piper, *n.* **1.** horn-player, fifer, flutist, flautist, tooter, horner; bugler, oboist, clarinetist, piccoloist; trumpeter, saxophonist, bassoonist, cornettist.

2. pay the piper pay the cost, foot the bill, reckon with, account for, pay in full; bear the consequences, face the music, reap what one has sown, *Sl.* take the rap, take the responsibility, take one's medicine.

piquancy, *n.* **1.** spiciness, pungency, poignancy, sharpness; zest, spice, relish, tang, *Inf.* twang; bite, sting, edge, race, zip, *Sl.* kick, *Sl.* punch, *Inf.* ginger; acidity, keenness, hotness, pepperiness, snappiness; sourness, harshness, roughness, cuttingness; mordancy, astringency, acerbity, asperity.

2. provocativeness, invitingness, bewitchery, winning ways; fascination, stimulation, provocation, attraction; appeal, interest, charm, glamor, witchery.

3. liveliness, spiritedness, spirit, vigor, vim, vehemence, pep, vitality; briskness, raciness, nippiness, crispness.

piquant, *adj.* **1.** pungent, sharp, biting, poignant, tart, spicy; zesty, zestful, tangy, well-seasoned, snappy, with a kick; hot, acid, peppery, curried, spiced, burning; sour, harsh, rough, gamy, caustic; strong, astringent, mordant, piercing, stinging, acerb, cutting, acrid.

2. stimulating, interesting, intriguing, fascinating, captivating; attractive, appealing, alluring, winning, catching, fetching; electric, exciting, challenging, galvanizing; scintillating, tantalizing, sparkling, titillating, inviting, tempting.

3. lively, spirited, vigorous, peppy, full of pep, vehement; brisk, crisp, hearty, buoyant, mettlesome, enthusiastic; sharp, clever, smart, keen, quick-witted, fast, quick.

pique, *v.* **1.** irritate, annoy, irk, vex, peeve, nettle, chafe, *Chiefly U.S.* rile, *Inf.* aggravate, *Inf.* miff, *Inf.* give [s.o.] a pain, *Inf.* get under [s.o.'s] skin, *Inf.* get in [s.o.'s] hair, *Sl.* bug; exasperate, ruffle, roil, disturb, perturb, disquiet, discompose, discountenance, put out, try [s.o.'s] patience, get, *Sl.* get [s.o.'s] goat; bother, pester, harass, fret, trouble, plague, beset; torment, tease, taunt, mock, tweak, bully, bullyrag.

3. offend, affront, insult; humiliate, mortify; (*all of the feelings, pride, etc.*) hurt, molest, wound, sting, pain.

4. (*all of the interest or curiosity*) excite, arouse, rouse, stimulate, whet, stir, goad, spur, prick; interest, tantalize, titillate, tickle, attract, fascinate, *Sl.* turn on.

5. provoke, agitate, foment, inflame, kindle, enkindle, fire, fire up, whip up, work up, stir up, wind up; incite, instigate, ignite, touch off.

—*n.* **6.** irritation, annoyance, vexation, exasperation, *Inf.* aggravation; displeasure, dissatisfaction, discontent, disapproval, disapprobation.

7. anger, ire, dudgeon, high dudgeon; offense, umbrage, indignation, huff, tiff, fume, *Inf.* slow burn.

8. embitterment, bitterness, exacerbation, bitter resentment, resentment, hard feelings; spleen, choler, gall, bile, ill *or* bad humor, ill *or* bad temper, ill *or* bad feeling; virulence, acerbity, acrimony; hurt feelings, wounded pride.

piqued, *adj.* **1.** irritated, annoyed, vexed, peeved, nettled, chafed, *Chiefly U.S.* riled, *Inf.* aggravated, *Inf.* miffed, *Sl.* bugged; ruffled, roiled, disturbed, perturbed, disquieted, discomposed, put out; bothered, pestered, harassed, fretful, troubled, plagued, beset; tormented, teased, taunted, tweaked, bullied; exasperated, fed up, sick and tired.

2. angry, angered, irate, incensed, *Inf.* mad, *Inf.* sore, *Sl.* hot, *Sl.* hot under the collar, *Sl.* ticked-off, *Sl.* teed-off; furious, infuriated, enraged, maddened, livid, hopping mad, *Inf.* boiling mad, *Sl.* mad as a wet hen, *Sl.* madder than hell; galled, embittered, exacerbated, acerbate, envenomed, rankled.

3. offended, affronted, insulted; humiliated, mortified; (*all of feelings, pride, etc.*) hurt, molested, wounded, stung, pained.

4. (*all of the interest, curiosity, etc.*) excited, aroused, roused, stimulated, stirred, pricked.

5. provoked, agitated, inflamed, enflamed, fired-up, worked-up, stirred-up, whipped-up, wound-up.

piracy, *n.* **1.** robbery at sea, brigandage, buccaneering, freebooting, banditry, highway robbery, *Obs.* latrociny, privateering, filibustering, *U.S. Inf.* (*usu. of cattle*) rustling.

2. commandeering, hijacking, skyjacking, air *or* sky piracy; (*usu. of persons*) abduction, kidnapping, *Sl.* snatch, capture, impressment, conscription, man-stealing, child-stealing; (*all of animals*) poaching, deerjacking, petnapping, dognapping.

3. plunder, plunderage, rapine, pillage, depredation, spoliation, despoliation, despoilment, *Obs.* direption, raven; ravaging, harrying, marauding, sacking, *Rare.* sackage, laying waste, devastation, desolation; raid, razzia, foray; foraging, looting, ravishment, seizure, grab, rape, predation.

4. plagiarism, literary theft, copying, *Inf.* cribbing, *Inf.* lifting, pirating; forgery, counterfeiting; expropriation, appropriation, arrogation, usurpation, accroachment, assumption.

pirate, *n.* **1.** sea robber, sea rover, sea dog, sea wolf; Blackbeard, Captain Kidd, Long John Silver.

2. viking, corsair, buccaneer, privateer; freebooter, rapparee, (*in the Scottish Highlands*) cateran; kidnapper, abductor, (*usu. of cattle*) rustler, hijacker, skyjacker, air *or* sky pirate; predator.

3. highwayman, footpad, *Sl.* yegg *or* yeggman, bandit, bravo, *Sp.* bandolero, *Southwest U.S.* ladrone, *Australian.* bushranger, brigand, picaroon, desperado; outlaw, gangster, criminal, mafioso; thug, ruffian, hoodlum, *Sl.* hood, *Australian Sl.* larrikin; rogue, picaro, (*in India and Burma*) dacoit.

4. pillager, plunderer, marauder, despoiler, depredator, vandal; predator, ransacker, sacker, looter, rifler, forager, raider.

5. *Inf.* poacher, deerjacker; smuggler, contrabandist, runner, bootlegger.

6. plagiarist, plagiarizer, *Inf.* cribber, *Inf.* copier, *Inf.* cheater; (*of copyrights or patents*) infringer; forger, counterfeiter, *Brit. Inf.* coiner.

—*v.* **7.** buccaneer, privateer, freeboot, filibuster, waylay; commandeer, hijack, skyjack, *Sl.* heist.

8. plunder, despoil, *Archaic.* spoil, spoliate, pillage, *Chiefly Scot.* reive; ravage, harry, rape, maraud, devastate, depredate; ransack, sack, loot, gut, fleece, strip, rifle; raid, foray, forage, prey on *or* upon; lay waste, desolate, wreak havoc upon.

9. plagiarize, copy, infringe, *Inf.* lift, *Inf.* crib, *Euph.* borrow; forge, counterfeit; appropriate, expropriate, arrogate, usurp.

10. steal, thieve, rob; pilfer, purloin, finger, filch, *Inf.*

snitch, cabbage; peculate, embezzle, misappropriate, pocket, shark; shoplift, *Sl.* boost, walk off *or* away with, help oneself to, make free with, *Euph.* remove.

piratical, *adj.* **1.** plundering, pillaging, marauding, buccaneering, privateering, piratic, piratelike; preying, predatory, predacious, rapacious; thievish.
2. criminal, felonious, lawless, unprincipled, unscrupulous, crooked, corrupt; dishonest, fraudulent, underhand, underhanded.

pirouette, *n.* **1.** spin, twirl, whirl; pivot, turn, revolution.
—*v.* **2.** spin, twirl, whirl; pivot, turn, revolve, wheel around.

pistol, *n.* handgun, revolver, *Trademark.* Colt, derringer, six-shooter, automatic pistol, repeater, *Mil.* side arm, zip gun, short firearm; *All Sl.* rod, piece, gat, Saturday night special, heater, iron *or* shooting iron.

pit[1], *n.* **1.** hole, cavity, excavation, quarry, diggings, workings; shaft, mine, tunnel, bank, coal mine, gold mine, silver mine; ditch, grave, burial site; dip, sink, gully, gulch, furrow, burrow, trough; foxhole, bunker, entrenchment, trench; well, abyss, chasm, deep, crevasse; crater, pocket, cup, bowl; pothole, chuckhole, mudhole.
2. trap, trapfall, deadfall, pitfall; snare, gin, meshes.
3. abode of evil spirits, hell, the lower world, the infernal regions, nether world; inferno, underworld, pandemonium, everlasting fire, hellfire; abyss, bottomless pit, maw.
4. hollow, dent, indentation, depression; dint, cleft, dimple, *Biol.* alveolus; gouge, honeycomb, imprint, stamp; sinus, socket, *Anat.* lacuna, *Anat.* antrum.
5. pock, pockmark, scar, cicatrix, mark, crater, blemish.
6. ring, arena, bowl, floor, ground; cockpit, bear garden, bull ring.
—*v.* **7.** indent, dent, dint, press in; depress, punch, dimple, tweak, hollow; notch, nick, stamp; dig, scoop, gouge; pock, pockmark, scar.
8. set against, match, oppose, set at odds, put in opposition; juxtapose, contrapose, polarize, contrast.

pit[2], *n.* stone, nut, kernel, seed, pip, core.

pitapat, *adv.* **1.** flutteringly, in a flutter, atremble, with palpitations, tremulously, twitteringly, in a twitter, pitter-patter.
—*n.* **2.** patter, pitter-patter, flutter, palpitation; drumming, pounding, beating, throbbing, pulsing, pulsation, tattoo.

pitch[1], *v.* **1.** erect, set up, raise, rear; encamp, station, locate, situate.
2. establish, fix, determine, decide upon, settle, set, stabilize; plant, put, place.
3. fling, cast, throw, toss; heave, hurl, sling, catapult, launch; dart, *Brit. Sl.* bung, fire, shoot, let sail *or* fly; dash, chuck, send, *Inf.* put some oomph into it; *All Baseball.* peg, throw smoke, put smoke on it, bear down, throw a high, hard one.
4. pave, revet, cobble, face, tar.
5. fall down, take a spill, tumble; go head over heels, plunge, plummet, dive, take a nosedive; fall over, keel over, collapse, slump, crumple, fall into a heap.
6. (*usu. of a ship*) lurch, roll, reel, flounder, welter, wallow, make heavy weather, be the sport of wind and waves; keel, list, sway, rock.
7. dip, decline, slope, incline, slant, tilt, tip, cant, go downhill.
8. pitch in contribute, add to, bear a part; join in, help, assist, lend a hand, be of service.
9. pitch into *Informal.* assail, attack, assault, set upon, *Sl.* jump; beset, besiege, importune, harass, harry; revile, vituperate, abuse, belabor, lash, rail against, light into, *Inf.* sail into, *Inf.* tear into *Inf.* rip into, *Inf.* lace into, *Inf.* jump down [s.o.'s] throat.
10. pitch on *or* **upon** choose, pick, light on, single out, decide on, determine, elect, opt for.
—*n.* **11.** position, level, grade, rung, place, station; degree, extent, reach, compass, range, measure, rate; point.
12. angle, inclination, slope, slant, tilt, cant; declivity, downgrade, decline, dip, drop, descent.
13. highest point, height, summit, top, crown, peak, apex, zenith.
14. (*all of music, speech, etc.*) tone, tonality, timbre, key; color, modulation, intensity, depth, gravity.
15. throw, toss, *Chiefly Brit.* chuck, *Chiefly Baseball Sl.* peg, cast, heave, hurl, fling, serve, jaculation.
16. forward plunge, jerk; lurch, list, roll, reel, toss, tumble; swing, sway, veer, swerve, skew; stagger, totter.
17. *Slang.* sales talk, approach, *Inf.* spiel, fast talk, hard sell, *Sl.* line, *Inf.* song and dance, *Sl.* bill of goods.

pitch[2], *n.* bitumen, asphalt, maltha, gilsonite, tar; colophony, rosin, resin, mastic; sap, turpentine.

pitcher[1], *n.* container, ewer, jar, bottle, cruse, crock, jug; urn, samovar; tankard, stein, toby, mug.

pitcher[2], *n.* thrower, flinger, hurler, shot-putter, *Chiefly Class. Antiq.* discobolus.

pitchy, *adj.* **1.** tarry, bituminous, resinous, sappy; gummy, tacky, sticky.
2. black, coal-black, jet, jetty, pitch-black; ebony, ebon, raven, sable; inky, nigritudinous, atramentous; blackish, nigrescent; dark, unilluminated, lightless, unlighted, moonless.

piteous, *adj.* pathetic, pathetical, pitiful, pitiable, to be pitied; sad, doleful, dolorous, dolorific, sorrowful, distressing, mournful, grievous, plaintive; lamentable, regrettable, deplorable, rueful, woeful, woebegone; touching, moving, affecting, affective, affectional, melting, heartrending, heart-moving, heartbreaking; tender, poignant, emotional, emotive.

pitfall, *n.* **1.** trap, snare, trap door, pit, *Obs.* toil; springe, gin, deadfall.
2. hazard, peril, danger, real danger, danger point, where one could go wrong, thing to look out *or* keep an eye out for, *Sl.* killer; catch, catch-22, trick, trip, *Sl.* hooker.

pith, *n.* **1.** essence, quintessence, quiddity, haecceity, elixir, spirit, soul, heart and soul, sap, essential part; main idea *or* point, what it's all about, the real meaning, nuts and bolts, *Inf.* nub, *Inf.* nitty-gritty, fundamental, basic point *or* idea; heart, heart of the matter, gist, meat, core, nucleus, kernel, crux, salient point; marrow, important *or* vital part, *Law.* gravamen; center, midst, focus, focal point; sum and substance, meaning, general idea, what [s.t.] boils down to.
2. weight, weightiness, gravity, graveness, heaviness, character; strength, power, potency, force, might, *Literary.* puissance, *Inf.* punch, *Inf.* pizzazz; substance, import, importance, depth, significance, moment, consequence, matter, value; soundness, solidity, firmness; basis, base, grounding, groundwork, foundation, support, backbone.

pithy, *adj.* succinct, concise, compact, tight, tight-knit, finely honed, sharply focused; epigrammatic, laconic, aphoristic, apothegmatic, gnomic, short and sweet, sententious; capsule, condensed, summary, synoptic, in a nutshell, compendious; pointed, to the point, straightforward, direct; powerful, forceful, forcible, effective, telling, potent, *Literary.* puissant; meaningful, heavy, weighty, meaty, deep, profound;

substantial, sound, solid, firm; pregnant, full, chock-full, jam-packed; significant, important, momentous, consequential, vital, essential, necessary, valuable.

pitiable, *adj.* pathetic, pitiful; sad, doleful. See **pitiful** (*defs.* **1, 2**).

pitiful, *adj.* **1.** pathetic, pitiable, piteous, sad, doleful, dolorous. See **piteous.**

2. miserable, wretched, abject, squalid, stark, dismal; poor, meager, scanty, skimpy, scrimpy, beggarly, sorry, cheap, niggardly, worthless; shabby, shoddy, scrubby, scruffy, dirty, scurvy; mean, low, base, vile, contemptible, despicable.

pitiless, *adj.* merciless, unmerciful, unpitying, unsparing, unsympathetic, unfeeling, unkind, impervious, insentient, inexorable; cold, frigid, heartless, soulless, passionless, cold-hearted, hard-hearted, marble-hearted, iron-hearted; callous, thickskinned, stony, hard, hardened, indurate, untouched, unstirred, unmoved; implacable, relentless, unyielding, obdurate, obstinate, stiff, flinty, adamant, adamantine; aloof, distant, unresponsive, apathetic, indifferent, supine, unconcerned, uninterested, unimpressible, uncaring; cruel, ruthless, brutal, savage, barbarous, inhuman, cold-blooded.

pittance, *n.* **1.** allowance, subsistence allowance, subsidy, maintenance, living expenses; pin *or* pocket money, expenses, expense account, per diem, viaticum; allotment, ration, quota, stint; stipend, grant, fellowship, scholarship, subvention; annuity, pension, *Law.* alimony, child support.

2. small change, nickles and dimes, pennies, scratch, *Sl.* peanuts, *Sl.* chickenfeed, *Sl.* small potatoes; slave wages, meager earnings, barely enough to scrape *or* get by on, not enough to live on; mite, modicum, barely anything.

pitted, *adj.* pocked, pocky, pockmarked, punctate, varioloid, variolous, variolar, *Pathol.* variolate, *Petrogeny.* variolitic, *All Biol.* foveat, foveated, foveal, foveolate, foveolar; scarred, marked, spotted, blemished, marred, defaced; craterous, cavitied, eaten away, eroded; dented, indented, depressed, hammered, pounded, beaten, distressed; riddled, shot through, pierced, pin-pricked, perforated, porous, holey, full of holes, honeycombed, lacunose, cribriform, criblé.

pitter-patter, *n.* pattering, tapping, rapping, beating, drumming; palpitating, pulsating; scurrying, scuttling, skipping.

pity, *n.* **1.** commiseration, sympathy, ruth, condolence, condolement, consolation, comfort, solace; compassion, tenderness, kindliness, heart, soft-heartedness, benevolence; lenience, lenity, mercy, mercifulness, humaneness, humanity; favor, grace, forbearance, forgivingness, liberality, magnanimity, placability, clemency, charity.

2. shame, regret; disgrace, dishonor; atrocity, desecration, sacrilege, violation, profanation, abomination.

—*v.* **3.** commiserate, condole, sympathize, express sympathy, lament with; compassionate, be *or* feel sorry for, feel grief *or* sorrow for, feel for, grieve for, bleed for, weep for; relent, forbear, melt, thaw, show mercy, have mercy upon, *Inf.* have a heart; relax, spare, give quarter, *Inf.* go easy on, *Inf.* let up on, *Inf.* give [s.o.] a break; reprieve, pardon, forgive, absolve; put out of one's misery, *Inf.* pull the plug.

pitying, *adj.* sympathetic, sympathizing, ruthful, commiserative, commiserable, commiserating, condolent, condolatory, condoling, comforting; compassionate, tender, kind, kindly, soft, gentle, mild, mild-hearted, soft-hearted, exorable, charitable, benevolent, beneficent, benignant; lenient, merciful, clement, placable, humane, forgiving, pardoning; magnanimous, gracious, liberal, forbearing.

pivot, *n.* **1.** swivel, spindle, reel, spool, bobbin, gimbal; fulcrum, axis, axle; thole, tholepin, pin, pintle.

2. hub, nave, *Inf.* nub, focal point, center, heart; crucial *or* critical point, turning point; support, prop, brace, stay, foundation; peg, raison d'être, occasion, cause, basis.

—*v.* **3.** rotate, revolve, pirouette, twist, somersault, flip-flop; spin, spin like a top, whirl, whirl like a dervish, gyrate, reel; swivel, wheel, twist, circle; hinge, swing, turn.

pivotal, *adj.* central, focal, axial; critical, crucial, vital, decisive; momentous, of great moment, significant, important, urgent, pressing, exigent; paramount, principal, chief, supreme, main, capital, cardinal, primary, prime; basic, underlying, fundamental, radical.

pixilated, *adj.* pixyish, eccentric, *Sl.* oddball, odd, uncommon, atypical, out of the ordinary; daft, *Sl.* wacky, *Inf.* daffy, *Sl.* far out, *Sl.* goofy, *Sl.* nutty, freakish, freaky, funny, *Sl.* funny-haha, *Sl.* funny-odd; prankish, playful, mischievous, elfin, impish; whimiscal, fanciful, capricious, unpredictable; kittenish, merry, mirthful; free-spirited, high-spirited, fey; light-hearted, giddy, sprightly, blithe, frivolous, bubbly, ebullient; amusing, delightful.

pixy, *n.* sprite, imp, devilkin, nix, nixie, elf, ouphe, gremlin; pixie, fay, peri, fairy; goblin, hobgoblin, brownie, bogy, boogeyman, puck, Robin Goodfellow; gnome, *Irish Folklore.* leprechaun; kobold, poltergeist, ghost, *Southern U.S.* haunt, *Dial.* hant, spirit.

placable, *adj.* appeasable, pacifiable, conciliatory, reconcilable; forgiving, forgiving and forgetting, relenting, unresentful, unrevengeful, forbearing, longanamous; magnanimous, unspiteful, generous, noble; indulgent, nonexacting, soft-hearted, tender-hearted, big-hearted; merciful, compassionate, ruthful, pitying, understanding, charitable.

placard, *n.* **1.** poster, bill, public notice, *Fr. affiche,* broadside, broadsheet; billboard, sign, notice; manifesto, bull.

—*v.* **2.** post, plaster, plaster the barns; advertise, publicize, *Sl.* plug, *Sl.* ballyhoo; circularize, publish, broadcast, promulgate, spotlight, make known, *Circus.* arrow the route *or* way.

placate, *v.* appease, mollify, propitiate, conciliate, satisfy, please; pacify, calm, quiet, still, lull, soothe; assuage, relieve, alleviate, temper, moderate, ease; subdue, win over, reconcile.

placatory, *adj.* placative, appeasing, conciliatory; designed to please, aimed to please; calming, noninflammatory, soothing, inoffensive, soft; temperate, moderate, mediatory.

place, *n.* **1.** location, locality, locale, whereabouts, hereabouts; spot, scene, scene of the crime, setting, *Law.* venue; bearings, latitude and longitude, coordinates.

2. position, situation, circumstance, condition, state, state of affairs; standing, rank, grade, means, class, estate, status; footing, station, elevation, step, *Inf.* notch; niche, slot, berth, billet.

3. job, employment, occupation, work, livelihood, living, pursuit; vocation, calling, profession, field, métier, line, forte, *Sl.* thing, *Sl.* bag; capacity, office.

4. function, use, purpose, role, operation; charge, responsibility, duty, task, chore, assignment, mission; affair, concern, interest, matter, *Inf.* lookout; scope, sphere, compass, bailiwick.

5. region, area, sector, section, quarter, zone, pale,

division; territory, realm, province, shire; district, precinct, neighborhood.

6. court, lane, way, drive, circle; alley, *Chiefly Brit.* mews, *Chiefly Brit.* terrace; road, avenue, street.

7. house, home, abode, dwelling, domicile, residence, habitation, *Scot.* howf; lodgings, quarters, living quarters, rooms, accommodations, housing, roof over one's head, *Inf.* pad, *Brit. Inf.* digs; apartment, flat, tenement, walk-up, *Brit.* chambers.

8. lieu, stead, substitution, exchange.

9. **go places** *Slang.* progress, make progress, advance, gain, proceed, get along, come on, come along, make steps, make headway, make strides *or* rapid strides; succeed, make it, make it big, *Sl.* go far.

10. **in place** in position, in trim, in order, set in order, set up, ordered, arranged, *Inf.* to rights.

11. **out of place** **a.** out of order, in disorder, disorderly, disorganized, disarranged, deranged, in a mess, helter-skelter, higgledy-piggledy, skimble-skamble, topsy-turvy, *Sl.* arsy-varsy. **b.** inapposite, out-of-line, out-of-bounds, out-of-step, out-of-keeping; unseemly, unbecoming, improper, off-color.

12. **put someone in his place** humble, humiliate, mortify, bring down, *Inf.* take *or* bring down a notch *or* peg, *Sl.* put down, make [s.o.] eat humble pie, *Inf.* make [s.o.] eat crow, *Inf.* make [s.o.] eat his words, *Inf.* make [s.o.] swallow his pride.

13. **take place** happen, *Archaic.* hap, occur, come to pass, come to be, come about, come, *Inf.* come off; befall, supervene, betide, chance, *Archaic.* bechance, *Archaic.* arrive; transpire, intervene, crop up.

—*v.* **14.** arrange, order, dispose, array, assort, collocate; group, sort, classify, class, categorize, bracket; size, grade, graduate, rank.

15. lay, set, put, seat, posit; locate, situate, position, pinpoint; quarter, house, reposit, deposit; consign, localize, post, station.

16. hire, engage, employ, retain, secure the services of, contract with; enlist, sign on, take on, *Inf.* take on board.

17. appoint, commission, charge, entrust, commit, depute, delegate; invest, install, induct, ordain; specify, fix, determine, prescribe.

18. identify, recognize, know, make out, *Inf.* spot, *Inf.* nail, *Inf.* peg.

placement, *n.* **1.** arrangement, disposition, disposal, deployment, ordering, arraying; emplacement, situation, positioning, locating, stationing; categorization, classification, stratification, ranking, grouping, pigeonholing; assortment, sorting, sorting out; attribution, ascription, imputation.

2. employment, engagement, hiring, *Inf.* taking on; appointment, assignment, instatement, installment, ordination, investiture; commission, delegation, deputation.

placid, *adj.* **1.** quiet, quiescent, calm, tranquil, serene, undisturbed, halcyon, *Brit. Dial.* (*of places*) bonny; still, stock-still, *Chiefly Literary.* stilly; unmoving, unmoved, immovable, immobile; motionless, stationary, becalmed.

2. peaceful, peaceable, pacific, restful, reposeful; sleepy, sleeping, slumbering, slumberous, slumbery, dozing, dozy, drowsing, drowsy, somnolent; inactive, latent, dormant, dormient.

3. composed, collected, self-possessed; steady, equable, level, level-headed; even-tempered, temperate, moderate, cool, cool-headed; unexcited, inexcitable, unruffled, unagitated, unperturbed, imperturbable; unemotional, unimpassioned, unimpassionate, impassive, dispassionate; stoical, philosophical.

4. reserved, reticent, taciturn, uncommunicative; sedate, meek, mild, gentle.

plagiarism, *n.* **1.** (*all chiefly in reference to literary material*) piracy, theft, thievery, robbery, stealing, pilferage; appropriation, usurpation, assumption, arrogation; deception, imposture; plagiary.

2. (*all chiefly in reference to literary material*) copy, imitation, reproduction; counterfeit, sham, fraud; pirated manuscript; *Inf.* ripoff.

plagiarist, *n.* (*all chiefly in reference to literary material*) pirate, vandal, robber, thief, pilferer, stealer, *Inf.* ripoff; imitator, forger, copier.

plagiarize, *v.* (*all chiefly in reference to literary material*) pirate, thieve, rob, steal, pilfer, purloin, *Inf.* crib, *Inf.* lift, *Inf.* rip off, *Euph.* borrow; appropriate, assume, arrogate, usurp, make use of, help oneself to, pass off as one's own; forge, counterfeit, imitate, copy.

plague, *n.* **1.** pestilence, epidemic, pandemic, pandemia, zymosis, (*of animals*) *Pathol.* epizootic, (*of animals*) *Pathol.* epizooty, (*of animals*) murrain, (*of plants*) epiphytotic; bubonic plague, black plague, black death; white plague, tuberculosis, TB, consumption, phthisis, pulmonary phthisis.

2. curse, scourge, bane, evil, affliction, infliction, visitation, torment, calamity; adversity, trial, tribulation, trouble, burden.

3. catastrophe, cataclysm, disaster, tragedy; shock, blow, heavy *or* nasty *or* staggering blow, buffet, stroke of ill *or* bad luck, stroke of ill *or* bad fortune.

4. nuisance, annoyance, aggravation, vexation, *Inf.* headache, *Sl.* hassle, *Sl.* drag, *Sl.* bitch; bother, pest, pain in the neck, canker, problem, thorn, thorn in the flesh, thorn in one's side, pea in the shoe.

—*v.* **5.** torment, torture, persecute, agonize, excruciate, rack, crucify, pain, hurt, lacerate; anguish, distress, harrow, worry, weigh *or* prey on the mind, trouble, *Scot.* fash, disturb; afflict, harass, harry, hector, beleaguer, badger, hound.

6. perturb, upset, derange, agitate, convulse, rattle, haunt, shake up, stir up; confuse, addle, muddle, *Inf.* drive crazy, unnerve, discompose, ruffle, fluster, disconcert, discomfit, disquiet, *Inf.* faze.

7. annoy, bother, vex, pester, *Brit.* chevy, irk, pique, peeve, nettle, chafe; exasperate, aggravate, irritate, gall, rub, roil, *Chiefly U.S.* rile, *Inf.* drive up the wall, provoke; tease, taunt, gibe, twit.

8. smite, afflict, visit evil *or* harm upon; scourge, punish, castigate.

plain, *adj.* **1.** clear, clear-cut, clear as crystal, crystal-clear, well-defined, vivid, graphic; distinct, visible, patent, bald-faced, bald, plain as the nose on one's face, plain as day; apparent, ostensible, evident, self-evident, manifest, standing to reason, obvious, manifestative, *Fr. en évidence;* conspicuous, sticking out like a sore thumb, notable, pronounced, glaring, prominent, striking, blatant, palpable, tangible; overt, open, unconcealed, exposed, displayed, shown, professed, avowed.

2. discernible, perceivable, perceptible, recognizable, ascertainable, salient, apprehensible, comprehensible, comprehendible, cognizable, intelligible, understandable; unmistakable, definite, pointed, loud and clear, point-blank; lucid, perspicuous, transparent, translucent.

3. downright, complete, total, outright, out-and-out, categorical, dead, flat, unqualified, unconditional, incontestable; thorough, thoroughgoing, wholesale, all-out, *Inf.* flat-out; absolute, utter, profound, sheer, stark, arrant, rank; perfect, positive, consummate, *Inf.* regular, *Inf.* plumb, *Brit.* proper.

4. candid, frank, forthright, direct, straightforward;

open, open and sincere, open-hearted, genuine, guileless. See **plain-spoken** (*def.* 2).

5. homely, plain-featured, plain-looking, unattractive, unlovely, unpretty, unhandsome, unbeautiful, uncomely; ill-favored, *Inf.* not much to look at, *Inf.* short on looks, *Inf.* not much for looks.

6. ordinary, common, commonplace, usual, familiar, nothing out of the ordinary, everyday, workday, workaday, household-variety, garden-variety; nondescript, prosaic, matter-of-fact, *Inf.* no big thing; simple, modest, humble, unaffected, unpretentious, unpretending, unassuming; normal, natural, conventional, informal, regular, average, typical, general; homey, homelike, homish, down-home, homespun, homebred, *Inf.* folksy.

7. unadorned, unembellished, unornamented, unvarnished, inelegant, unostentatious; basic, bare, pure, severe, stark, austere; lean, spare, laconic, Spartan; uncolored, colorless, monotonous, uninteresting, dull; unfinished, raw, unrefined, rough, unpainted.

8. flat, level, smooth, even; unbroken, uninterrupted, unobstructed, clear, open.

—*adv.* **9.** clearly, distinctly, starkly, patently, palpably; noticeably, visibly, conspicuously, discernibly, apparently, recognizably, perceptibly, observably; manifestly, overtly, markedly, pronouncedly, prominently; transparently, openly, plainly.

10. positively, determinately, certainly, veritably, unequivocally, unambiguously, *Inf.* flat-out, explicitly, expressly; surely, confidently, assuredly, unquestionably, beyond question, conclusively, incontestably, uncontrovertibly, undeniably.

—*n.* **11.** lowland, flat, flat *or* open country, steppe, tundra, champaign; prairie, grassland, meadow, savannah, *Brit.* heath, *Chiefly Brit.* moor, (*both in South America*) pampas, campo; plateau, tableland, mesa.

plainsong, *n.* plainchant, Gregorian chant, chant; liturgical music; hymn.

plain-spoken, *adj.* **1.** plain, plain-speaking, point-blank, blunt, to the point; abrupt, bluff, brusque, tactless, rude, downright, outright, out-and-out, explicit, unequivocal, *Inf.* flatfooted; outspoken, free, free-spoken, free-speaking, unreticent, bold, unreserved, unrestrained, unconstrained, unchecked, unabashed, uninhibited, unshrinking.

2. candid, frank, forthright, direct, straightforward, straight-from-the-shoulder, man-to-man, heart-to-heart; open, open and sincere, open-hearted, genuine; guileless, ingenuous, sincere, artless, naïve, simple, undeceptive, undeceiving, undeceitful, undissembling; aboveboard, open and aboveboard, up front, on the level, honest, truthful, on the up and up, no-nonsense.

plaint, *n.* complaint, grumble, grievance, objection, demur, *Inf.* kick, *Inf.* gripe, *Inf.* grouse; *All Sl.* bitch, squawk, bellyache, beef.

plaintive, *adj.* melancholy, wistful, sad, saddened, sorrowful, doleful, mournful, heavy-hearted, grieving, grievous, dolorous; unhappy, heartsick, *Inf.* broken up, miserable, wretched, woeful, woebegone, disconsolate, inconsolable; heart-stricken, grief-stricken, heartbroken, broken-hearted, crushed, *Inf.* broken; lachrymose, tearful, teary, weeping, crying, sobbing, wailing; funereal, gloomy, morose, dismal, dreary, dull, *Scot. and North Eng.* dowie, cheerless, glum, under a cloud, *Archaic.* wan; disappointed, discouraged, despondent.

plait, *n.* **1.** braid, plat, pigtail, twist, queue, cue.

2. pleat, fold, plication, plicature, ruck; crease, line, wrinkle, ridge, groove, furrow, corrugation, crimp, flute, ruffle; gather, shirr, pucker, tuck, dart.

—*v.* **3.** braid, plat, pleat, weave, twill; interweave, interthread, interlace, intertwine, interknit, *Brit. Dial.* raddle, *Brit. Dial.* wattle; entwine, knot, mat, interwind, interlock, interdigitate; twist, ravel, twine, tangle, entangle; wind, intort, coil, convolve, roll, cornrow; twirl, fold, enfold, curl, wreathe, loop, knit, purl, thread.

4. pleat, crease, put a crease in, fold, ruck, wrinkle; furrow, groove, ridge, corrugate, crimp, flute, ruffle; gather, shirr, pucker, tuck.

plan, *n.* **1.** scheme, design, arrangement, disposition, layout, blueprint; order, array, distribution, grouping, organization, classification; configuration, formation, pattern, construction, constitution.

2. procedure, plan of action, tactics, strategy; plot, formula, program, policy, course, order; system, method, way, means, rhyme or reason; itinerary, schedule, roster, agenda, bill, syllabus.

3. project, purpose, proposal, idea, conception, cogitation; prospect, view, intent, intention, ambition, hope, aspiration.

4. representation, diagram, map, scale drawing, chart, ground plan, floor plan; pattern, model; drawing, sketch, draft, copy; cast, skeleton, delineation, depiction.

—*v.* **5.** arrange, line up, schedule; map out, block out, work out, strategize; devise, design, develop, form, formulate, fashion, shape, mold, contrive; frame, purpose, intend; fabricate, construct, build, erect; concoct, conceive, envision, see, plot.

6. project, look ahead, predesign, prearrange; make plans, mark out a course, shape a course, draw up a plan, mastermind; think, contemplate, premeditate.

7. outline, draw, scratch, draft, chart, trace, sketch, mark out; diagram, represent, figure, *Archaic.* limn; delineate, depict, measure, line, strike out.

plane[1], *n.* **1.** level surface, level, flat surface, flat; horizon, skyline, *Astron., Navig.* azimuth; sea level, water level; table, homaloid; plain, flatland, champaign, plateau, steppe, prairie; bowling alley, bowling green, pool *or* billiard table, tennis court; ice, glass, marble, alabaster, mahogany.

2. level, position, station, status, rank, rung, stage; height, measure, remove; stratum, degree, point, mark, notch, peg; echelon, class, rate, caste, footing.

3. airplane, aircraft, *Brit.* aeroplane, flying machine, propeller plane, airliner, ship, *Sl.* bird; hydroplane, seaplane, waterplane, amphibian, floatplane; glider, sailplane, air train; jet, jet plane, jetliner, turbo jet, SST, supersonic transport, ramjet.

—*adj.* **4.** flat, planate, smooth, glabrous; regular, uniform, unwrinkled, unbroken; level, horizontal, even, flush.

—*v.* **5.** glide, sail, wing, waft, float, soar, drift, volplane; skim, slide, slip, brush, skate.

plane[2], *n.* **1.** jack plane, router, trowel, smoother, jointer.

—*v.* **2.** smooth, level, flatten, even, true, face; dress, finish, planish, mill, burnish.

3. remove, pare, shave, grade, shear.

planetary, *adj.* **1.** wandering, traveling, moving, journeying, roaming, rambling, roving, ranging; erratic, unfixed, unanchored, unsettled, restless, shifting, straying, wayward; vagrant, bohemian, gypsyish, gypseian, nomadic, migratory, transient, vagabond, itinerant, peripatetic.

2. terrestrial, earthly, terrene, subterrestrial, sublunary; global, world-wide, universal.

plant, *n.* **1.** vegetable, wort, herb, flower, shrub, tree; (*all collectively*) flora, vegetation, herbage.

2. seedling, young plant, slip, scion, cutting.

3. factory, shop, workshop, laboratory, lab, sweat-

shop; manufactory, mill, foundry, metal works, works; business, establishment, institution; buildings, equipment, machines, apparatus.
—*v.* **4.** (*all of seeds, young plants, etc.*) sow, seed, scatter; put in, set in, place in, inset, inlay, bury; transplant, replant, reset.
5. establish, implant, fix, infix, lodge, imbed, ingrain, root; instill, infuse, interfuse, insinuate, inculcate; train, teach, imprint, impress; impregnate, infect, imbue, tincture, contaminate; inoculate, indoctrinate, introduce, insert, interject, inject; bring in, import, innovate; inspire, breed, engender, foster, cultivate, encourage, promote; propagate, disseminate, sow the seeds of.
6. insert, put in *or* into, inset, inlay, set *or* place in; tuck in, pop in, slide in, slip in; work in *or* into, press in, push in, thrust in, force in, drive in, wedge in, jam in, cram *or* stuff in, ram in *or* up, stick in *or* up.
7. station, post, assign; locate, situate, place, put; *Inf.* park, put down, set down.
8. (*all of a colony, city, etc.*) establish, set up, found, institute, make, build, erect, construct; colonize, settle, people, populate.

plantation, *n.* manor, manor farm, *Inf.* spread; grange, homestead, farm, farmstead, farmplace, *Archaic.* farmhold, *Brit.* farmery, *Brit.* croft, *Scot. and North Eng.* steading; ranch, rancho, rancheria, hacienda.

planter, *n.* **1.** farmer, agriculturalist, agronomist, granger, yeoman, landsman, husbandman; plowman, plowboy, sodbuster, chuff, gaffer, swain, *Archaic.* kern, son *or* tiller of the soil; horticulturalist, gardener, nurseryman.
2. landowner, landholder, landed person, man of property, property owner; squire, lord, *Scot.* laird.
3. container, pot, urn, vessel, holder, plant-holder.
4. *Hist.* settler, colonist, colonizer, pioneer, homesteader, squatter.

plaque, *n.* **1.** plate, tablet, slab, panel, plaquette.
2. badge, medal, medallion, brooch, cameo, pin, ornament.
3. award, trophy, honor, prize.

plash, *n.* **1.** splash, lap, slosh, swash, dash, splat, wash, spatter, patter; ripple, gurgle, babble, bubble, burble, trickle, drip; murmur, purl, whisper, susurrus, susurration.
2. pool, puddle, mudhole, wallow, water hole; pond, swimming hole, fishing hole, millpond, *Scot.* linn; slosh, slush; bog, fen, marsh.
—*v.* **3.** splash, splatter, spatter, slosh, swash, dash; murmur, purl, whisper; trickle, ripple, drip, babble, bubble, burble, gurgle; sprinkle, patter; soak, wet.

plaster, *n.* **1.** stucco, albarium, mortar, grout; powdered gypsum, clay, adobe, cement; parget, roughcast, pebble dash, depeter, plaster of paris, *Trademark.* Spackle, scagliola.
2. poultice, cataplasm, dressing, compress, pack; mustard plaster, sinapism; court plaster, plaster cast, bandage.
—*v.* **3.** daub, mortar, parget, stucco, cement, roughcast; spackle, patch, fill.
4. bandage, dress, poultice, put in a cast.
5. cover, superimpose, overspread, overlay, lay over, smear; shroud, sheathe, mantle, encrust.

plastic, *adj.* **1.** moldable, easily molded, fictile, soft, clayey, claylike, ductile, shapeable.
2. creative, artistic, imaginative, inventive, inspired, original; expressionistic, clever, innovative; perceptive, feeling, intuitive.
3. impressionable, impressible, malleable, pliable, pliant, flexible; yielding, compliant, waxy, persuadable, tractable, manageable, governable, docile; susceptible, receptive, responsive, sensitive, open, unformed, undeveloped, inexperienced; amenable, agreeable, easy, easy to lead, without a mind of one's own, spineless, wishy-washy.

plasticity, *n.* malleability, flexibility, pliability, suppleness, adaptability, versatility; tractability, manageability, docility, trainability; susceptibility, receptiveness, responsiveness, openness.

plat[1], *n.* **1.** plot, lot, tract, patch, parcel, piece; yard, enclosure, close; quadrant, field, quarter, square.
2. map, chart, plan, diagram, outline; figure, delineation, drawing, tracing, sketch.

plat[2], *v.* plait, braid, weave, wreathe, twist, pleach, plash; intertwine, entwine, interweave, interlace, interknit; fold, enfold, gather, double over, tuck.

plate, *n.* **1.** dish, platter, dinner plate, *Archaic.* trencher, *Archaic.* charger; saucer, paten, disk; plaque.
2. course, dish, service; portion, serving, helping, second helping.
3. sheet, panel, pane, slab; ply, flap, slat, table; layer, leaf, lamina, plating; covering, coating, coat, foil, peel, patina.
4. shield, armor, shell, *Zool.* lorica, carapace, *Entomol.* scutum, *Bot.* epicarp, *Anat., Zool.* theca.
5. illustration, frontispiece, print, lithograph, zincograph; impression, intaglio, engraving, etching, imprint.
—*v.* **6.** coat, cover, overlay, face, back, enamel, veneer; gild, silver, nickel, platinize, electroplate, anodize.

plateau, *n.* **1.** highland, tableland, table, mesa, upland; elevated plain, bench, berm.
2. lull, relief, respite, letup, resting point, quiet spell, break, interim.
3. level, grade, plane, rung, degree, stair, step; interval, period, space, measure.

platform, *n.* **1.** stand, stage, dais, estrade; scaffold, emplacement, *Archit.* perron; catafalque; rostrum, pulpit, podium, bema, tribune, floor; soapbox, stump, hustings.
2. landing, deck, landing stage.
3. program, plank, principles, creed; plan, plan of action, policy, course, position, line; position paper, campaign promises.

platitude, *n.* **1.** cliché, truism, commonplace, saying, phrase; *Inf.* bromide, *Sl.* chestnut, banality; *Inf.* drugstore philosophy, old story, twice-told tale, old saw, old song, familiar tune; hackneyed expression, triviality, prosaicism, stereotyped expression.
2. triteness, banality, insipidity, vapidity, inanity; dullness, plainness, flatness, monotony, uninventiveness; unimaginativeness, matter-of-factness, prosaicness; unoriginality, staleness, *Sl.* corniness, *Sl.* squareness.

platitudinous, *adj.* **1.** sententious, proverbial, aphoristic, axiomatic, gnomic; formulistic, epigrammatic, pithy, terse.
2. hackneyed, cliché, stereotyped, overworked, commonplace, common; trite, banal, truistic, *Sl.* old hat, *Inf.* bromidic, set, stock, familiar; stale, dull, flat, dry, warmed-over, vapid, insipid, jejune; moldy, musty, moth-eaten, threadbare, timeworn, worn-out; unimaginative, uninventive, cut and dried, matter-of-fact, *Sl.* square, *Sl.* corny.

platonic, *adj.* (*all of love*) nonphysical, spiritual, unfleshy, incorporeal; ideal, idealistic, transcendent; philosophical, contemplative; rational, objective, intellectual; cool, dispassionate, tranquil, serene, calm.

platoon, *n.* **1.** squadron, squad, battery, team, combat team, patrol, outfit.
2. company, group, body, band, gang, crew.

platter, *n.* plate, dish, *Archaic.* trencher, *Archaic.* charger; tray, salver, palette, mortarboard.

plaudit, *n.* *Usu.* **plaudits** acclaim, acclamation, éclat; cheer, hurrah, huzzah; applause, round of applause, burst of applause, peal *or* thunder of applause, hand, big hand, ovation, standing ovation.

plausible, *adj.* credible, believable, tenable, colorable, reasonable, likely, probable; conceivable, imaginable, thinkable; cogent, logical, rational, sound, admissible, sensible; specious, meretricious, ostensible, apparent, seeming; overrefined, oversubtle, casuistic, jesuitic, sophistical; illusive, deceptive, misleading, hollow, empty.

play, *n.* **1.** drama, dramatic play, stage play; stage show, show; theatrical piece, theatricals, piece, work, vehicle; screenplay, photoplay, photodrama, *Inf.* opus; teleplay, television drama *or* play, TV drama *or* play; radio drama *or* play, broadcast drama; spectacle, extravaganza, pageant; comedy, farce, burlesque; tragedy; melodrama.
2. amusement, pastime, entertainment, recreation, cheer, good fun, *Brit.* beer and skittles, *Inf.* fun and games, *Sl.* jollies; pleasure, enjoyment, delight, gaiety; diversion, distraction, sport; merrymaking, merriment, revelry, jollification, joviality, *Inf.* whoopee; tomfoolery, skylarking, *Sl.* monkey business, *Sl.* high jinks.
3. fun, jest, joke, gag, lark; toying, trifling, fooling, make-believe.
4. pun, wordplay, play on words, double entendre.
5. manner, style, way, wise, method, fashion; habit, custom, pattern, wont, customary *or* characteristic way; system, approach, technique, practice, tack; routine, process, *Latin. modus operandi, Inf.* MO, *Brit.* the drill.
6. gambling, gaming, betting, wagering, hazarding, risking, staking, *Brit.* punting, *Inf.* plunging, speculation.
7. conduct, behavior, *Archaic.* havior, deportment, demeanor, comportment, actions, ways, manners, *Archaic.* gest; bearing, carriage, posture, port, guise, gait, air, address; lifestyle, way of life, *Latin. modus vivendi.*
8. action, activity, movement, motion; agency, operation, *Rare.* operance *or* operancy, function; performance, execution, enactment, discharge, dispatch; exercise, practice.
9. latitude, liberty, license, freedom, indulgence; free *or* unrestricted use, carte blanche, blank check; field, free play, free scope, free swing, full swing, swing; margin, room, spare room, elbow room, room to spare, wide berth; rope, enough rope, long rope *or* tether.
10. (*all by or in reference to the news media*) press, coverage, time, space, mention.
11. **make a play for** *Slang.* woo, court, pay court to, make love to, serenade, *Inf.* spark, *Inf.* court and spark, *Sl.* hustle, *Sl.* put *or* slap the make on, *Sl.* put a move on; pursue, chase, chase after, pant after.
—*v.* **12.** portray, represent, depict, personate, impersonate; act, enact, act out, give a show, tread the boards; perform, *Jazz.* jam, *Music Sl.* riff.
13. engage in, take part, become involved, be occupied, occupy oneself; undertake, take up, embark on, set *or* go about; throw oneself into, launch into, plunge *or* dive into, tackle; try, make an effort, have a go, *Sl.* take a crack at, *Sl.* take a whack at.
14. contend, compete, vie, rival, contest; oppose, challenge, pit oneself against, play against, take on, face, confront, meet; *All Fig.* battle, join battle with, set to, engage, encounter, struggle, tussle, scuffle, clash.
15. employ, use, make use of, utilize, apply; wield, ply, operate, work; handle, manipulate, put to use *or* good use.
16. gamble, bet, wager, stake, try one's luck *or* fortune, make a bet, lay a wager *or* bet, *Brit.* punt, *Inf.* shoot craps, *Inf.* play the ponies, *Brit. Inf.* birl, *Brit. Sl.* gaff; speculate, venture, play the market, *Inf.* plunge, *Inf.* take a flier, *Inf.* take a leap *or* shot in the dark.
17. do, perform, execute, carry out, accomplish, discharge, fulfill, consummate; cause, effect, effectuate, bring about, make happen.
18. sport, disport, frolic, frisk, gambol, have fun *or* a good time *or* a good old time; dance about, jump about, romp, rollick; cavort, caper, cut capers, curvet; revel, carouse, wassail, roister, whoop it up, *Inf.* make whoopee.
19. clown, clown around, play the clown; horse around, fool around, kid around, *Inf.* cut up; joke, jest, fool, tease, *Inf.* josh, *Inf.* kid, *Inf.* put [s.o.] on, *Inf.* pull [s.o.'s] leg; banter, chaff, make merry with.
20. dally, trifle, toy, make light with; potter, putter, smatter, tinker, fiddle, *Inf.* fool with.
21. **play at** pretend, feign, make believe; affect, simulate, fake, sham, give the appearance of, *Sl.* make like; assume, put on, *Inf.* do for effect.
22. **play down** belittle, disparage, decry, deprecate, demean, detract, derogate, *Inf.* talk *or* cry down; minimize, slight, underrate, undervalue, beggar, misprize, extenuate, underestimate, underreckon, think little *or* nothing of, set no store by, fail to count on; deemphasize, underplay, make light of.
23. **played out a.** weary, tired, tired out, *Inf.* dog-tired, dead-tired, *Sl.* dead, dead on one's feet; overtired, done in, all in, ready to drop; weary, fatigued, worn out, fagged, fagged out. **b.** hackneyed, trite, overused, overemployed, overworked; banal, set, stock, familiar, *Inf.* bromidic, *Sl.* old hat; stale, dull, flat, vapid, insipid, jejune, warmed-over; moldy, musty, moth-eaten, timeworn, shopworn. **c.** expended, used up, finished, finished up, gone, all gone, no more, *Sl.* eighty-sixed.
24. **play for time** stall, stall for time; temporize, make *or* gain time, *Inf.* drag one's feet; procrastinate, hesitate, hang, hang back *or* fire; filibuster.
25. **play it by ear** improvise, extemporize, ad lib, *Inf.* fake it, *Sl.* wing it; rise to the occasion, ride with the waves, roll with the punches.
26. **play on** *or* **upon** exploit, take advantage *or* unfair advantage of, abuse, misuse, walk all over [s.o.], take [s.o.] for all he's worth; impose on, trade on.
27. **play out a.** finish, complete, carry through, go *or* follow through with; settle, resolve, terminate, end, bring to an end; conclude, close, wind up, clinch, seal, *Inf.* wrap up. **b.** exhaust, consume, use up; expend, spend, dissipate, *Sl.* blow; waste, squander, fritter away, fool away, run through.
28. **play the game** *Informal.* **a.** go along with, conform, follow the crowd, do as others do; keep in step, toe the mark, stay in line, follow the rules, keep one's nose clean; yield, acquiesce, defer, compromise, give in; toady, *Inf.* bootlick, truckle. **b.** play fair, be a good sport, play by the rules, *Inf.* be up front.
29. **play up a.** emphasize, stress, lay stress *or* emphasis on, accent, punctuate; underline, underscore, italicize, point up, call attention to, mark, bring home, press home; feature, highlight, spotlight, give prominence to, bring to the fore. **b.** dramatize, overempha-

size, overstress, overaccentuate, make a mountain out of a molehill, make a big thing out of nothing, make much ado about nothing, make a federal case of, blow out of proportion; exaggerate, hyperbolize, overstate. **c.** magnify, amplify, aggrandize, build up, puff up.

30. play up to *Informal.* **a.** ingratiate oneself, get on the good *or* right side of, *Inf.* rub the right way, worm *or* work oneself in, *Inf.* get in with, *Inf.* get cozy *or* tight with. **b.** flatter, wheedle, cajole, blandish, *Inf.* soft-soap, *Inf.* apple-polish, *Sl.* butter up, *Sl.* brown-nose; puff, puff up, inflate; fawn, toady, toadeat, truckle, *Sl.* fall all over; court, pay court to, curry favor, dance attendance upon, *Sl.* buddy up to, *Sl.* shine up to, *Sl.* suck up to; lick [s.o.'s] shoes, lick *or* kiss [s.o.'s] feet, *Inf.* bootlick; agree to anything, *Inf.* be a yes man to.

31. play with fire a. tempt Providence, defy danger, court destruction, go in harm's way, ask for trouble, skate on thin ice, dance on the razor's edge, put one's head in the lion's mouth, beard the lion in his den, march up to the cannon's mouth, play Russian roulette. **b.** get hurt, hurt oneself, burn one's fingers; *Sl.* stick one's nose where it doesn't belong.

playbill, *n.* (*all of a play*) program, slate, bill, card; notice, announcement, advertisement, poster, placard; flier, leaflet, handout.

playboy, *n.* womanizer, ladies' man, man about town, woman-chaser, *Sl.* skirt-chaser, *Sl.* wolf, *Sl.* lover boy, *Sl.* tomcat, *Sl.* masher, *Sl.* make-out artist, *Sl.* man on the make; rake, rakehell, roué, profligate, wanton, debauchee, libertine, *Inf.* rip, *Sl.* swinger; philanderer, trifler, dallier, gay dog, gay deceiver, gallant, flirt, *Obs.* coquet, *Inf.* two-timer; Don Juan, Casanova, Lothario, Romeo, charmer, *Inf.* lady-killer, *Sl.* stud, *Sl.* sheik.

player, *n.* **1.** funmaker, frolicker, sport; reveler, carouser, wassailer, merrymaker, *Sl.* cutup; hedonist, pleasure-seeker, pleasure-lover.

2. athlete, sportsman, sporter, *Inf.* jock; ballplayer, baseballer, footballer, basketballer; competitor, contestant, contender, vier, participant.

3. actor, actress, performer, entertainer, stage player, stage performer, playactor, role player; trouper, *Sl.* ham, theatrician, thespian, Roscian, histrio, histrion, *Archaic.* histrionic; personator, impersonator, mimic, mummer, mime, *Rare.* mimester, pantomimist.

4. musician, music maker, music man, minstrel, *Inf.* tunester; virtuoso, master; classical musician, *Inf.* longhair; jazz musician, jazzman; rock and roller, rocker, hard rocker, punk; folk singer, *Inf.* folkie.

5. gambler, bettor, wagerer, gamester, *Brit.* punter, *Inf.* piker, *Inf.* tinhorn, *Inf.* crapshooter, *Sl.* boneshaker, *Sl.* big-timer; speculator, adventurer, adventurist, risk-taker, hazarder, *Inf.* plunger.

playful, *adj.* **1.** sportive, gamesome, frolicsome, full of fun, fun-loving; high-spirited, frisky, coltish, skittish, *Inf.* full of beans, *Inf.* feeling one's oats; mischievous, full of mischief, scampish, devilish, impish, elfish; waggish, prankish, tricksy.

2. humorous, amusing, funny, witty; joking, jesting, *Inf.* joshing, facetious, half-serious, tongue-in-cheek.

playground, *n.* park, recreation area *or* field, field, playing field, sand lot, tot lot.

playhouse, *n.* theater, amphitheater, theater in the round; odeum, hall, music hall, concert hall, opera house, auditorium.

plaything, *n.* **1.** toy; bauble, knickknack, gimcrack, gewgaw; doll, *Baby Talk.* dolly; hobbyhorse, rocking horse; top, whirligig; ball; jack-in-the-box.

2. dupe, fool, pigeon, *Sl.* fall guy; tool, instrument, puppet, minion, pawn, dummy, creature, cat's paw, *Sl.* stooge.

playtime, *n.* recess, time out; recreation, leisure time; vacation, *Brit.* holiday; liberty, shore leave; red letter day, festival day, fete day; legal holiday, *Brit.* bank holiday.

playwright, *n.* dramatist, dramaturge, dramaturgist; scriptwriter, screenwriter, scenario writer; tragedian, comedian, *Fr. farceur*; melodramatist; monodramatist; dramatic poet; *Theat.* play doctor.

plaza, *n.* public square, town square, common, town common; green, town green, rialto, piazza, forum, (*in ancient Greece*) agora; quadrangle, *Inf.* quad.

plea, *n.* **1.** defense, vindication, argument, apologia, justification.

2. excuse, pretext, reason; apology, extenuation, palliation.

3. appeal, entreaty, request, petition, suppliance, supplication, solicitation, suit; imploration, invocation, prayer.

4. cop a plea *Slang.* plead guilty, *Inf.* cop one, plea bargain; dodge the issue, evade the real issue, *Inf.* beat around the bush; get around the results, avoid the penalty, *Inf.* go out the side door.

plead, *v.* **1.** appeal, entreat, beg, beseech; supplicate, ask, apply for; seek, request, call for; appeal to, implore, *Brit. Inf.* prig; pray, petition, solicit, supplicate, obtest; adjure, conjure, *Rare.* sue; press, importune, demand.

2. argue against, reason with, debate, enjoin; counsel, exhort, urge, recommend, try to influence; suggest, persuade, push, *Inf.* lean on, coerce, use pressure.

3. argue, use as an excuse, put forward, present; assert, declare, proclaim, allege, aver, attest, asseverate; maintain, hold, profess, avow, affirm, acknowledge, admit, own.

pleasant, *adj.* **1.** pleasing, agreeable, enjoyable, delightful, pleasurable, gratifying, satisfying; delectable, delicious, palatable, tasty, toothsome, savory; lovely, nice, good, *Sl.* swell, *Sl.* fine; comfortable, easeful, *Sl.* cushy, luxurious, voluptuous.

2. (*of persons, manners, disposition, etc.*) adept, adroit, suave, polished, finished, smooth; courteous, polite, courtly; deferential, well-behaved, well-bred, genteel; cultivated, urbane, gallant, chivalrous, diplomatic, tactful, decorous, compliant, gentlemanly, ladylike; gracious, hospitable, sociable; affable, approachable, communicative, conversive; outgoing, open, easy, unreserved; gregarious, *Inf.* chummy, amiable, congenial, simpatico, sympathetic; friendly, cheerful, *Ger. gemütlich,* cheery; neighborly, *Inf.* comfortable as an old shoe, homely, *Inf.* homey; companionable, fun to be with, good company.

3. fair, balmy, sunny, warm; bright, cloudless, clear, rainless, dry; fine, calm, halcyon.

pleasantry, *n.* **1.** banter, teasing, *Inf.* kidding, *Inf.* ribbing, *Inf.* joshing; raillery, repartee, wordplay, badinage; joking, jesting, drollery, jocularity, waggery; ridicule, mockery, *Inf.* ragging, *Brit.* quizzing.

2. joke, quip, gag, wisecrack, funny remark; bon mot, mot, witticism, crack, pun, *Rhet.* paronomasia, *Fr. jeu d'esprit.*

3. prank, trick, farce, game; revel, merriment, hilarity, tomfoolery, jocularity, clowning, nonsense, antics, horseplay.

please, *v.* **1.** satisfy, content, gratify; gladden, charm, cheer, delight, *Inf.* tickle pink; do one's heart good, *Inf.* hit the spot, delectate; entertain, interest, amuse, divert; placate, appease, humor, pacify, pacificate; soothe, mollify, dulcify.

2. like, want, desire; wish, choose, prefer, elect, opt, select.

pleased, *adj.* happy, glad, contented, gratified, satisfied, well-pleased; delighted, elated, thrilled, tickled, *Inf.* tickled pink, *Inf.* pleased as punch, *Dial.* in hog heaven; euphoric, on cloud nine, on top of the world, walking *or* floating on air, starry-eyed; cheerful, full of cheer, in good *or* high spirits; complacent, *Brit. Sl.* chuffed, self-satisfied.

pleasing, *adj.* **1.** agreeable, nice, harmonious; delightful, *Inf.* scrumptious, inviting, palatable; gratifying, felicitous, welcome, refreshing.

2. (*of persons, manners, disposition, etc.*) civilized, gentle, well-mannered, polite; amiable, congenial, simpatico; cheerful, neighborly, comfortable. See **pleasant** (*def.* **2**).

3. charming, likable, engaging, winning, winsome, taking, *Inf.* fetching; tempting, enchanting, enticing, captivating, alluring, fascinating, seductive, bewitching; sweet, nice, toothsome, delectable; handsome, good-looking, shapely, attractive, lovely, fair, beautiful; prepossessing, elegant.

pleasure, *n.* **1.** enjoyment, satisfaction, gratification, fulfillment, contentment; happiness, gladness, good *or* high spirits; blitheness, blithesomeness, lightheartedness, buoyancy; jubilation, rejoicing, exhilaration, exultation, glee, elation; joy, joyfulness, joyousness; delight, bliss, jubilance, jubilancy, enchantment, transport, seventh heaven, Eden; fun, recreation, *U.S. Sl.* bang, *Sl.* a gas; joviality, merriment, jollity, mirthfulness, zest; festivity, celebration, jubilee.

2. hedonism, sensual gratification, physical pleasure, carnal pleasure; bodily enjoyment, animal gratification, the garden of earthly delights; sensuality, sensuosity, sensuousness; dissipation, *Inf.* wild oats, *Inf.* the rogue's progress; luxury, voluptuousness, comfort, ease, *Inf.* creature comforts; cakes and ale, wine and roses.

3. will, choice, option, election; wish, desire, inclination, preference, fancy.

4. gem, jewel, treasure; treat, delight, thing of beauty, sight for sore eyes; prize, charm, find, flower, one in a million.

—*v.* **5.** gratify, give pleasure, satisfy; content, make content, make one feel good, do one's heart good; delight, make happy, warm the cockles of one's heart.

6. delight in, take pleasure in, enjoy, be pleased with; relish in, rejoice in, revel in, *Sl.* groove on.

pleat, *n.* **1.** plait, box pleat *or* plait, accordion pleat, kilt pleat; fold, crease, plication, plicature, ruck, *Chiefly Scot.* wimple, *Zool., Anat.* plica; plaiting, kilting, goffer, fluting; gather, shirring, tuck, dart, pucker, corrugation, flute, crimp.

—*v.* **2.** plait, kilt, tuck, ruck, *Surgery.* plicate; fold, crease, double, double over, turn under, enfold; crimp, flute, goffer, pucker, purse, corrugate; gather, shirr, ruffle, *Sewing.* full.

plebeian, *adj.* **1.** lower-class, low-class, proletarian, working class, blue-collar; lowly, low, lowborn, baseborn; untitled, inglorious, insignificant, obscure; base, inferior, humble, ignoble, mean, raffish; poor, shabby, tawdry; simple, plain, homespun, homely, peasantlike, provincial, rustic, countrified, earthy, salt-of-the-earth, down to earth.

2. common, ordinary, average, commonplace, undistinguished; mass, of the masses, popular, prevailing, current, of the streets.

3. coarse, raw, rough-hewn, unrefined, unpolished, unsophisticated, low-brow; crude, crass, uncouth, gauche, rude, ill-bred, low-bred, unbred, ill-mannered, unmannerly, unladylike, ungentlemanly, indecorous; churlish, boorish, loutish, brutish; indelicate, immodest, shameless.

—*n.* **4.** pleb, plebe, proletarian, peasant, commoner, common person, ordinary citizen, the common man, one of the people, average guy, *Inf.* John Doe, *Inf.* John Q. Public, *Inf.* John Smith, *Inf.* one of the crowd *or* mob, *Inf.* man in the street, *Sl.* Joe Blow, *Sl.* Joe Doakes.

plebiscite, *n.* election, referendum, public *or* popular vote, vox populi; direct vote, vote, poll, ballot.

pledge, *n.* **1.** promise, assurance, word, word of honor, *Archaic.* troth, vow, oath, sworn statement, *Archaic.* plight; endorsement, testimonial, attestation; contract, compact, covenant, obligation, engagement, agreement; guarantee, guaranty, warrant, warranty, *Law.* covenant of warranty, *Law.* warranty deed, *Obs.* vouch.

2. collateral, surety, *Law.* security, earnest, deposit, *Law.* earnest money; pawn, gage, bail, *Insurance.* bond, *Law.* mortgage, *Law.* mortgage bond, *Law.* bail bond, *Rare.* hostage.

3. tentative member, newcomer, initiate, neophyte, beginner, catechumen.

4. toast, salute, cheer.

—*v.* **5.** engage, bind, adjure, draft; press, compel, oblige, require, charge, command, enjoin.

6. plight, affiance, betroth; promise, give one's solemn word *or* promise, vow, state on one's honor, swear to, state under oath; assure, offer assurance, asseverate, avouch, aver, affirm.

7. guarantee, ensure, secure, *Finance.* bond, *Law.* mortgage; pawn, *Rare.* impawn, gage, put up collateral, give earnest money, make a deposit, obligate; warrant, vouch, attest to, testify to, endorse; contract, covenant, enter an agreement, make a bargain *or* deal, shake on it.

8. toast, drink to, drink to the health of, salute, give three cheers, cheer.

plenary, *adj.* full, entire, whole, complete, thorough; absolute, unqualified, out-and-out, unconditional; unlimited, limitless, stintless, unrestricted, unbounded, large, ample, great.

plenitude, *n.* **1.** abundance, profusion, bounty, cornucopia, horn of plenty, endless supply, *Scot.* scouth *or* skouth, *Scot. and North Eng.* routh; quantity, quantities, volume, mass, fund, mine, store; full supply, good supply, full measure, good *or* great deal, quite a little.

2. fullness, amplitude, repletion, completeness, wholeness, totality, entirety, entireness, *Rare.* impletion; completion, fulfillment, culmination, consummation, realization.

plenteous, *adj.* abundant, plentiful, copious. See **plentiful**.

plentiful, *adj.* **1.** abundant, plenteous, plenitudinous, *Inf.* plenty, fat, bountiful, bounteous, copious; ample, enough and to spare, enough and then some, more than enough, more than adequate; big, large, great, huge, bumper; immeasurable, unmeasured, unstinted, inexhaustible, bottomless, infinite, innumerable; much, many, numerous, multifarious, *Inf.* dime a dozen; in quantity *or* quantities, in plenty, *Inf.* aplenty, *Inf.* galore.

2. profuse, abounding, exuberant, superabundant; bursting, overflowing, overspilling, spilling over, running over; rampant, bristling, thick, thick with, teeming, teeming with, swarming, swarming with, crawling, crawling with, alive with, *Sl.* lousy with.

3. rife, replete, well-supplied, well-provided, well-stocked, well-furnished; full, filled, abrim, chock-a-block, *Brit. Inf.* chocker, *Inf.* chock-full, jammed, packed, *Inf.* jam-packed, *Archaic.* fraught.

4. rich, lavish, luxuriant, luxurious, rank, thriving; fruitful, fertile, fecund, yielding, productive, prolific, proliferous.

plenty, *n.* **1.** quantity, quantities, volume, mass, fund, mine, store; multitude, number, numbers, scores, host, hoard, legion; sea, ocean, oceans, world, worlds, galaxy, great quantity *or* quantities; lot, lots, heap, heaps, mountain, mountains, stack, stacks, pile, piles, load, loads, mess, slew, slews, whole slew, full supply, full measure, good supply, good *or* great deal, quite a little, *Sl.* scads *or* scad, *U.S. Sl.* boodle; *All Inf.* ton, tons, bag, bags, barrel, barrels, gob, gobs, oodles, *Chiefly Brit.* lashings *or* lashing.
2. plenteousness, plentifulness, bountifulness, bounteousness, copiousness; amplitude, ampleness, fullness; numerousness; richness, exuberance, luxuriance, luxuriousness, lavishness, lavishment; teemingness, rankness, prodigality.
3. abundance, profusion, plenitude, bounty, cornucopia, horn of plenty, endless supply.
4. excess, surplus, surfeit, satiety, oversupply, overflow, nimiety, superfluity; glut, plethora, flood, deluge, overabundance, superabundance, supersaturation; riot, landslide, bonanza.
5. affluence, wealth, wealthiness, prosperity, prosperousness; opulence, opulency, comfort; money, riches, fortune, treasure; means, resources, wherewithal.

pleonasm, *n.* **1.** redundancy, tautology, periphrasis, periphrase, circumlocution, *Inf.* circumbendibus; verbiage, verbosity, wordiness, prolixity, profuseness, diffuseness, long-windedness, longiloquence; repetition, repetitiveness, tediousness, battology; digressiveness, discursiveness, maundering, convolution, circuitousness, wandering, rambling, meandering, roundaboutness, indirection, *Archaic.* ambages; ambiguousness, vagueness, beating around the bush; newspeak, bureaucratese, gobbledegook.
2. digression, excursus, cloud *or* smokescreen of words, *Rare.* tautologism.

pleonastic, *adj.* redundant, tautological, periphrastic, circumlocutory; verbose, wordy, prolix, profuse, diffuse, long-winded, longiloquent; repetitive, tedious, battological; digressive, discursive, circuitous, ambagious, roundabout, indirect, maundering, meandering, wandering, rambling; ambiguous, vague, obscure.

plethora, *n.* **1.** overfullness, superabundance, overabundance, overprofusion, overplentifulness, overplenteousness, overplenty, superflux; supererogation, oversufficiency, superfluity, superfluousness, redundancy; repletion, engorgement, congestion, surcharge; profusion, more than enough, enough and to spare, enough and then some.
2. surplus, surfeit, satiety, glut, excess, overflow, overspill; flood, deluge, inundation, spate, avalanche, landslide, riot, drug on *or* in the market, supersaturation; oversupply, overmeasure, overload, overburden; overdose, too much of a good thing.

plethoric, *adj.* **1.** overfill, overabundant, superabundant, exuberant, overflowing, overspilling, spilling over, running over, bursting; bloated, swollen, bulbous, bulging, tumorous, tumescent, *Pathol.* edematous; bulging, swelling, turgescent, *Obs.* turgent; gorged, satiated, jaded, replete, cloyed, stuffed, saturated, supersaturated.
2. (*all of speech or writing*) turgid, tumid, pompous, bombastic, inflated, puffed-up, puffy, overblown, overcharged; (*all of speech or writing*) overrun, extended, distended, dilated, redundant.

plexus, *n.* network, reticulum, tissue, *Optics.* reticle; net, mesh, meshwork, web, webbing, lace, lacework, lacing, bobbinet; tracery, intertexture, interlacing, intertwining, interweaving, weave, tapestry; maze, jungle, labyrinth, jungle, tangle; wilderness, snarl, knot.

pliability, *n.* **1.** flexibility, flexility, bendability, pliancy; suppleness, litheness, softness, limberness, lissomeness; malleability, plasticity, tractility, ductility, flaccidity; elasticity, stretch, stretchability; give, spring, springiness, resilience.
2. persuasibility, persuadableness, susceptibility, impressionability, impressibility; yieldingness, willingness, readiness, amenability, agreeability; adaptability, conformability, adjustability, adjustableness, tractability, tractableness, compliancy, compliance; passiveness, passivity, docility, obedience, deference, submissiveness, manageability.

pliable, *adj.* **1.** flexible, flexile, flexuous, bendable, pliant; elastic, supple, lithe, limber, willowy, lissome; malleable, extensile, extensible, ductile, tractile, plastic, stretchable; bending, shapable, moldable, fictile.
2. persuasible, persuadable, suasible, susceptible, impressionable, impressible; responsive, receptive, sensitive, influenceable; yielding, willing, amenable, agreeable; adaptable, adjustable, resilient, movable, mobile; compliant, tractable, manageable, governable, corrigible, domitable; formable, teachable, educable, trainable, tamable, domesticable; passive, submissive, deferential, docile, obedient.

pliers, *n.* long-nosed pliers, snub-nosed pliers, extractor; pincers, pinchers, nippers, tweezers, forceps, tongs.

plight[1], *n.* condition, state, shape, situation, position, circumstances; predicament, dilemma, quandary, strait; juncture, crisis, emergency, extremity, exigency, pinch, *Inf.* squeeze; *Inf.* pickle, hole, bind, double-bind, tight spot, box, corner, embarrassing situation; scrape, *Inf.* jam, *Inf.* fix, trouble, *Sl.* hot water, hornet's nest; problem, difficulty, stumbling block, complication; fine kettle of fish, pretty pass, pretty state of affairs, fine mess, *Inf.* fine how-do-you-do, awkward situation, ticklish *or* delicate situation; muddle, jumble, tangle, mix-up, confusion; catch-22, vicious circle; cul-de-sac, deadend, impasse, standstill, stalemate, deadlock.

plight[2], *v.* affiance, betroth, promise to marry, become engaged to; pledge, promise, give one's solemn word *or* promise, give one's word of honor, vow; engage, bind, oblige, obligate; state on one's honor, swear to, state under oath; assure, offer assurance, asseverate, avouch, aver, affirm.

plod, *v.* **1.** trudge, pace, tramp, walk heavily, lumber, *Inf.* galumph; drag oneself along, move laboriously, shuffle, shamble, drag one's feet; walk on *or* over, tread, step on, stamp, *Inf.* stomp, crush, trample.
2. drudge, work *or* work hard, toil, moil, labor, *Brit.* fag; grub, grind, work one's fingers to the bone, slave *or* slave away, work like a slave, work like a Trojan, *Sl.* kill oneself; work day and night, burn the midnight oil, burn the candle at both ends, overdo, overwork, overexert oneself; sweat, struggle, *Sl.* beat one's brains out; work at, make an effort, apply oneself to, work away at, *Inf.* go at *or* to it; peg away at, *Inf.* plug away at, *Inf.* hack away at, hammer away at, *Inf.* bang away at, pound away at; *Inf.* chip away at, *Inf.* peck away at, *Inf.* go at *or* attack bit by bit *or* one piece at a time; go slowly but surely, carry on, continue, keep trying, keep one's nose to the grindstone, keep one's shoulder to the wheel; persevere, stick to *or* at *or* with it, persist, hang *or* hold on, *Sl.* hang in there, keep at it, keep doggedly at it; force oneself, push oneself, make oneself, exert oneself, strain oneself; do what has to be done, see [s.t.] through, see [s.t.] through to the finish, not give up, never say die.

plop, *v.* **1.** drop, fall, plump, *Inf.* plunk, throw, toss; thud, thump, bump, slap, smack, hit, strike.

—*n.* **2.** drop, fall, plump, *Inf.* plunk; thud, thump, bump, slap, smack, blow.

plot, *n.* **1.** secret plan, scheme, intrigue, counterplot, machination; procedure, plan of action, tactics, maneuvers, stratagems, strategy; complot, conspiracy, confederacy, cabal.

2. main story, story line, action, intrigue; chain of events *or* incidents; plan, scheme, design, layout, blueprint; outline, skeleton.

—*v.* **3.** plan secretly, conspire, complot, cabal, scheme, intrigue, counterplot, make plans, draw up a plan; premeditate, preplan, prearrange, set up, organize, mastermind, machinate; devise, design, develop, make, form, formulate, fashion, shape, mold; fabricate, construct, build, erect; contrive, bring about, concoct, brew, frame, compose, hatch; dream up, think up, come up with, conceive, imagine, envision, envisage, visualize, see in one's mind's eye.

4. mark on a map, chart, lay out, mark out a course, map out *or* shape a course.

5. map, graph, diagram, draw to scale; blueprint, outline, draw in, block in; depict, represent, picture.

plow, *n.* **1.** harrow, breaker, cultivator, lister; rake, scooter, windrower; corn plow, drill plow, snow plow.

—*v.* **2.** till, work, farm, cultivate, prepare, dress; spade, dig, delve, turn up, hoe, rake, harrow; ridge, furrow, groove, rib.

3. plunge, lunge, drive, bulldoze, hurtle, dive; elbow, shove, jostle, push; score, cut, sweep, furrow.

plowman, *n.* **1.** tiller, tiller of the soil, plower, plowboy, farmer, farm laborer, cultivator, harrower.

2. rustic, rube, churl, hick, bumpkin, yokel, *Sl.* hillbilly, *Sl.* hayseed; countryman, swain, peasant.

ploy, *n.* stratagem, maneuver, gambit, move; ruse, wile, artifice, dodge, artful dodge, *Sl.* gimmick; subterfuge, design, scheme, craft, game; trick, decoy, red herring, feint, blind.

pluck, *v.* **1.** pull, pull off, pull out, draw, draw out, withdraw, remove, extract, take out; collect, gather, gather *or* get in, cull, glean; harvest, reap, crop, pick, cut.

2. tug, tug at, pull, pull at, hitch, hitch up, hike, hike up; twitch, vellicate, tweak, twinge.

3. yank, yank out *or* away, jerk, jerk out *or* away, snatch, snatch away, snake, wrest, wrest out *or* away, grab, grab away, grasp, grasp away, catch, clutch, *Inf.* nip; rip, rip out, rip away, tear, tear out *or* away.

4. deplume, displume, denude, denudate, fleece, remove, divest, skin, strip bare *or* clean; cut, crop, sheer, trim.

5. *Slang.* rob, steal, thieve, pilfer, purloin, finger, filch; *All Sl.* pinch, hook, swipe, cop, crook, rip off, lift, hustle; plunder, despoil, spoliate, pillage, *Chiefly Scot.* reive; ransack, sack, loot, gut, fleece, strip, rifle; swindle, defraud, mulct, shark, cheat, *Inf.* flimflam, rook, bilk, *Inf.* welsh, *Inf.* gyp, *Inf.* bunko, *Inf.* diddle, *Inf.* take [s.o.] for a ride, *Inf.* take [s.o.] to the cleaners, chisel, clip.

6. plunk, twang, thrum, strum, pick, fingerpick, finger.

7. *British Slang.* fail, flunk, flunk out, reject, *Sl.* wash out, *Brit. Sl.* bust, *Brit. Sl.* plough.

8. pluck up a. exterminate, obliterate, annihilate, erase, eradicate, sweep away, wipe *or* blot out, *Sl.* mop up, efface, dissolve, eliminate, abolish, extirpate, destroy totally; ravage, raze, raze to the ground, level, tear to the ground, gut, devastate, ruin, demolish, desolate, wreck, smash, blast, blow up, lay in ruins; uproot, root up, root out, pull up *or* out by the roots, deracinate. **b.** summon, summon up, muster, *Inf.* screw up; encourage, embolden, hearten, enhearten, cheer, reassure, buoy, buoy up; arouse, rouse, stimulate, animate, inspirit, inspire, galvanize, electrify, vivify, rally, revive, awaken, shake up, jolt, jog.

—*n.* **9.** tug, pull, hike, hitch; tweak, twinge, twitch; yank, jerk, snatch, grasp, wrest, clutch, catch, quick *or* sudden pull.

10. (*all of animals; used for food*) heart, liver, lungs.

11. mettle, mettlesomeness, spirit, pluckiness, gameness, nerve, chutzpah, backbone, gumption, heart, stout heart, blood, marrow, *Archaic.* pith, stamina, *Inf.* toughness, grit, true grit, *U.S. Inf.* sand, *Inf.* starch, *Inf.* spunk, *Inf.* spunkiness, *Sl.* guts, *Sl.* gutsiness, *Sl.* moxie; courage, bravery, valor, valorousness, valiancy, valiance, heroism, prowess, stout-heartedness, lionheartedness, iron-heartedness, great-heartedness, high-heartedness; intrepidity, intrepidness, fearlessness, dauntlessness, awelessness, dreadlessness; boldness, bold-spiritedness, high-spiritedness, daring, derring-do, bravado, élan, dash, panache; audacity, audaciousness, rashness, recklessness, foolhardiness.

12. fortitude, endurance, tenacity, determination, will, will power; firmness, resolution, resoluteness, indomitableness, indomitability, invincibleness, invincibility, unconquerableness; staunchness, stalwartness, steadfastness, doughtiness, sturdiness, hardiness, hardihood, bulldog courage.

plucky, *adj.* **1.** mettlesome, gritty, game, spirited, red-blooded, *Inf.* spunky; brave, courageous, valiant, valorous, heroic, hero-like, stout-hearted, lionhearted, iron-hearted, great-hearted, high-hearted; intrepid, fearless, dauntless, unafraid, dreadless, aweless, nervy, *Sl.* gutsy, unblenching, unblenched, undaunted, undismayed, unappalled, unalarmed; bold, bold-spirited, high-spirited, daring, dashing, adventurous, audacious.

2. firm, resolute, determined, staunch, stanch, steadfast, stalwart, *Archaic.* stalworth, doughty, sturdy, hardy; indomitable, invincible, unconquerable, unyielding, unshrinking, unbending, unfaltering, unhesitating, unwavering, unswerving, undeviating.

3. vigorous, full of vigor, energetic, full of energy, active, spirited, animated, vivacious, gay, cheerful, lively, full of life, brisk, zesty, zestful, full of zest, robust, lusty, *Inf.* zippy, *Inf.* peppy, *Inf.* snappy, *Inf.* bouncing.

plug, *n.* **1.** wedge, peg, pin, spike; stopper, stop, cork, stopple, bung; spill, spile, *Dentistry.* dowel; pledget, wadding, stuffing, packing, tampon, tampion; tap, spigot, cock, stopcock, petcock, faucet, valve; obstruction, block, occlusion, clog.

2. chew, cake, twist, quid, cud; pigtail, *Dial.* chaw, cavendish.

3. *Informal.* publicity, promotion, mention, *Sl.* boost, puff, *Sl.* buildup; commendation, recognition, good word, honorable mention; *Sl.* hype, *Sl.* blurb, word, PR, *Sl.* promo; exposure, report, *Sl.* ballyhoo, advertising.

—*v.* **4.** stop, stop up, stuff, block, occlude, bar, clog, obstruct; choke, fill, jam, pack; close, shut up, stay, cover; bung, cork, stopple, spile, stanch, caulk, seal; dam, dam up, constipate, bind.

5. *Informal.* promote, advertise, mention, publicize, sell; *Sl.* boost, build up, *Inf.* puff up, *Sl.* ballyhoo; commend, put in a good word about, make a pitch for, beat the drum for; write up, put on the map, make a household word.

6. *Informal.* plod, stuggle, toil, drudge, labor, peg away, grind, hammer away; persist, persevere, see it through, hold on, keep on *or* at; *Inf.* stick to it, never say die, *Sl.* hang in there, give it all one's got, *Sl.* give it hell, *Sl.* break a leg.

7. **plug in** connect, loop in, charge, put in, stick in.

plumage, *n.* feathers, feathering, plumosity, down, *Ornithol.* mantle, (*of a hawk*) mail; panache, hackle, tuft, crest, tussock, topknot.

plumb, *n.* **1.** lead, weight, plummet, plumb bob, bob, sinker.

—adj. **2.** true, right, perpendicular, vertical, straight, square; level, erect, straight up and down, flush.

3. *Informal.* absolute, utter, unmitigated, outright, perfect, consummate; downright, thorough, pure, total, complete.

—adv. **4.** perpendicularly, vertically, up and down, straight up and down; square, squarely, at right angles.

5. *Informal.* absolutely, completely, totally, utterly, fully; stark, sheer, plain, clean, quite, wholly.

—v. **6.** sound, fathom, measure, mark, gauge; take soundings, plumb-line, plumb the depths.

7. examine, inspect, scrutinize, probe, search out, investigate; delve into, dig into, poke into, go into, explore; ferret out, root out, get to the bottom of.

plume, *n.* **1.** feather, quill, pinion, egret, aigrette; *All Ornithol.* plumule, penna, covert, tectrix, remex, scapular.

2. feather, aglet, aiguillette, bow, ribbon, knot; panache.

—v. **3.** *Usu.* **plume oneself on** pride oneself, congratulate oneself, pat oneself on the back, hug oneself; puff, crow, boast, flourish; gloat, brag, vaunt; exult, glory, revel, delight, rejoice.

plummet, *v.* dive, nosedive, dip, go down; fall, drop, collapse. See **plunge** (*def.* **2**).

plump[1], *adj.* **1.** fleshy, fattish, fat, portly, stout, round, rotund; well-rounded, filled out, well-fed, rounded, ample, *Scot.* fodgel; moonish, chubby, tubby, podgy, pudgy; paunchy, *Inf.* chunky, dumpy, squat, squatty, pursy; round-faced, moon-faced, roly-poly; well-proportioned, full-bodied, lusty, zaftig; top-heavy, bosomy, *Inf.* busty; hippy, beamy, *Inf.* broad in the beam, steatopygous.

—v. **2.** fatten, fat, puff up, blow up, distend, fluff up, shake up.

plump[2], *v.* **1.** drop, fall, plummet, plunge, nosedive; sink, collapse, descend, fall headlong, pitch; thump, slap, clump, crump.

2. deposit, set down, plop, plunk, plank; swoop, swoop down, pounce, stoop, lunge, sprawl.

3. *Often* **plump out** blurt, utter, let fall, spill; announce, declare, come out with, proclaim; divulge, give away, speak out, *Sl.* spill the beans, *Sl.* let the cat out of the bag.

—n. **4.** fall, dive, dip, slip, plop, plunk; thump, crump, clump, clunk, thud; drop, collapse, descent, nosedive, crash dive, skydive, plunge.

—adv. **5.** precipitously, unexpectedly, suddenly, all of a sudden, of a sudden, all at once; pop, bang, plunk, plop, bing, zap; surprisingly, without warning, out of the blue, like a thunderbolt, on short notice.

6. directly, bluntly, forthright, abruptly, point-blank; to the point, not beating around the bush, not pulling any punches, straight from the shoulder.

7. squarely, plumb, full, right, straight; smack, smack-dab, plunk, kerplunk; exactly, directly, precisely.

—adj. **8.** blunt, forthright, abrupt, plain, downright; direct, straight, straightforward, forward, matter-of-fact.

plumpness, *n.* portliness, stoutness, fatness, fleshiness, rotundity, *Fr. embonpoint*; chubbiness, tubbiness, pudginess, podginess, beefiness; paunchiness, dumpiness, squatness, pursiness, *Inf.* chunkiness; squattiness, stockiness, roly-poliness, blowziness, bloatedness, puffiness; bosominess, buxomness, top-heaviness, *Inf.* bustiness; hippiness, beaminess, steatopygia.

plunder, *v.* **1.** rob, despoil, *Archaic.* spoil, spoliate, pillage, *Chiefly Scot.* reive; ravage, harry, rape, maraud, devastate, depredate; ransack, sack, loot, gut, fleece, strip, rifle; raid, foray, forage, prey on *or* upon; lay waste, desolate, wreak havoc upon.

2. pirate, freeboot, buccaneer, privateer, filibuster; seize, capture, steal, thieve, carry off.

—n. **3.** rapine, pillage, depredation, spoliation, despoliation, despoilment, *Obs.* direption, raven *or* ravin, plundering, plunderage; ravaging, harrying, marauding, sacking, *Rare.* sackage, laying waste, devastation, desolation; raid, inroad, *Archaic.* maraud, razzia, foray; foraging, looting, ravishment, seizure, grab, rape; kidnapping, hijacking, skyjacking, air *or* sky piracy, commandeering.

4. brigandage, piracy, buccaneering, freebooting, banditry, highway robbery, *Obs.* latrociny, privateering, filibustering, *U.S. Inf.* (*usu. of cattle*) rustling; robbery, theft, thievery, *Law.* larceny.

5. spoils, loot, pillage, booty, *Archaic.* boot, *Archaic.* prey, *Scot. Obs.* reif; stolen goods, *Inf.* steal, *Sl.* hot goods, *Sl.* boodle, *Sl.* the take, *Sl.* the goods, *Sl.* swag; prize, profits, pickings, gain, grab, *Inf.* haul.

plunge, *v.* **1.** immerse, submerge, baptize; sink, put under, dip, douse, duck, dunk; inundate, drown, bury, engulf, overwhelm.

2. dive, plummet, go down, go to the bottom, descend; nosedive, fall, skydive, crash dive; plop, plunk, plump; drop, collapse, have the bottom fall out; pitch, jump, fall headlong, lurch; throw oneself, leap, spring, dart; swoop, swoop down, pounce, stoop, hurl, lunge.

3. rush, dash, hasten, hurry, scurry, hie, speed; hustle, scramble, scuttle, precipitate; bustle, race, run, tear.

—n. **4.** dive, leap, fall, jump, *Inf.* header; dash, lunge, spring; plop, plunk, plump.

5. immersion, submergence, submersion, baptism; dip, dipping, duck, ducking, dunk; inundation, drowning, burial, engulfment.

6. drop, fall, decline, descent, decline and fall, collapse, denouement; dip, declivity, declination, downgrade.

plurality, *n.* **1.** most, greatest *or* greater amount *or* number, greater *or* greatest percentage *or* part; more than anyone else *or* the others, lion's share, bulk, mass; decisive *or* winning number, enough to win.

2. majority, more than half, over fifty percent; preponderance, overwhelming number, nearly all.

3. many, a number, quite a few, several; quantity, lot, whole lot, bunch, whole bunch, *Inf.* oodles, *Inf.* slew, *Inf.* raft, *Sl.* scad; a thousand and one, scores, numbers, large *or* great number *or* amount, *Inf.* scillions, *Inf.* zillions.

4. multiplicity, multitudinousness, plenty, abundance, profusion; multitude, host, array, army, legion; herd, drove, bevy, flock, swarm; mass, crowd, throng, crush, horde, pack, *Sl.* mess; river, torrent, flood, deluge, ocean, sea, world, galaxy.

plus, *prep.* **1.** and, increased by, with an increment of; and also, and [s.t.] to boot; added to, put together with, joined with, coupled with, in conjunction with.

—adj. **2.** addition, adding, summation, summing, summational, totalling; *All Math.* positive, greater than zero, in the positive domain.

—n. **3.** bonus, added bonus, fringe benefit, perqui-

site, *Inf.* perk; extra, extra added feature *or* attraction, something additional, gravy, icing on the cake; gain, profit, return, *Sl.* take, *Sl.* velvet.
4. remainder, leftover, *Bookkeeping.* carry-over, carry-forward; surplus, surplusage, overplus; excess, more than enough, enough and to spare, enough and then some; overage, too much, overabundance, superabundance.

plush, *adj.* luxurious, luxury, deluxe, custom, special, sumptuous, elegant, posh, *Sl.* classy, *Sl.* snazzy, *Sl.* ritzy, *Inf.* swank, *Inf.* swanky; ornamental, decorative, decorated, adorned, embellished, embroidered; extravagant, grand, gorgeous; opulent, costly, dear, rich; elaborate, lavish, ornate, baroque, rococo, gingerbread; florid, showy, flowery, frilly, busy; ostentatious, pretentious, overdone.

plutocrat, *n.* rich man, man of means, moneybags, capitalist, millionaire, multimillionaire, billionaire; nabob, *Sl.* fat cat, *Sl.* big fish; silk-stocking, aristocrat; Midas, Croesus, Dives, *Class. Myth.* Plutus.

Plutonian, *adj.* **1.** Plutonic, *Class. Myth.* Hadean, Stygian, Styxian, Tartarean, Acherontal, Cocytean, Phlegethontal, Avernal; pandemoniac, chthonian, chthonic.
2. infernal, diabolical, fiendish, ghoulish, hellish, hellborn; demonic, demoniac, demoniacal, devilish, satanic, Mephistophelian.

ply[1], *v.* **1.** utilize, use, make use of, employ busily, put to use, work with, apply; wield, manipulate, handle, bend; exploit, press *or* enlist into service.
2. carry on, practice, pursue, lay one's hand to, bend one's efforts to; follow, undertake, exercise; devote oneself to, persevere at, work at, occupy oneself with, exert oneself in, busy oneself with, attend to; engage in, be absorbed in, be about; hold to, persist in; set to, fall to, buckle down to.
3. provide, furnish, supply, replenish; feed, stuff, fill, glut, surfeit, satiate; load, heap, stock, store; nurture, nourish, provision, sustain; shower, lavish, treat.
4. attack, assault, raid, storm, charge; assail, besiege, beset, overwhelm, press, bombard, torture, torment.
5. thrash, flog, whip, beat, batter, lash, scourge, flagellate, flail; hit, strike, smite, pommel, trounce; pelt, pepper, strafe, open fire upon; spank, bastinado.
6. importune, beset, dun, tax, press, push; set upon, urge, call upon, insist, *Inf.* work on; plead, appeal to, clamor for, cry for; supplicate, beseech, entreat, implore, beg, sue, petition, solicit; coax, wheedle, cajole, inveigle; pester, vex, plague, harass, badger, hound, *Sl.* hassle, *Sl.* bug.
7. pass over *or* along, traverse, go over, go across, cross, go back and forth; travel, navigate.

ply[2], *n.* **1.** layer, thickness, sheet, leaf.
2. bent, inclination, disposition, predisposition, temperament, mind, turn, affection, aptness; tendency, propensity, proclivity, leaning, penchant, proneness; predilection, partiality, prejudice, bias, twist, feeling; prepossession, fondness, attraction.

poach, *v.* **1.** hunt illegally, deerjack, steal game, fish illegally; *Chiefly Brit.* trespass.
2. (*of land*) become trampled, become broken up, become slushy, become muddy.

pock, *n.* **1.** pimple, pustule, papule, papilla, boil, blain, furuncle, furunculus, carbuncle, wen, whelk, *Rare.* bleb, *Archaic.* botch; eruption, inflammation, rising, lump, bump, wheal; whitehead, *Pathol.* milium, blackhead, *Med.* comedo, *Sl.* zit, *Sl.* woogit, *Sl.* hickey.
2. blemish, mark, spot, pockmark, scar, blotch, macula, macule; pit, crater, hole; scab.

pocket, *n.* **1.** bag, pouch, sack, *Midland U.S. and Scot.* poke, *Southwestern U.S.* alforja, *Obs.* budget; saddle bag, sabretache; mail bag, mail pouch; pack, packet, satchel, container, receptacle, reticule, compartment, envelope.
2. budget, purse, pocketbook; resources, means, assets, capital, funds, finances, moneys.
3. cavity, hole, hollow, cave, cavern, crater, cup, scoop, concavity; pit, shaft, chamber, mine, bore, tunnel, excavation; abyss, crevasse; opening, aperture, orifice, fissure, crack, cleft, chink, notch, gap.
4. vein, lode, ore body.
5. cul-de-sac, impasse, bottleneck, blind, *Inf.* blind alley, *Inf.* deadend; trap, snag, quandary, predicament.
—*adj.* **6.** small, bantam, diminutive, tiny, miniature; portable, compact, (*of books*) paperback; (*all of books*) condensed, abbreviated, encapsulated, compendious, abridged.
—*v.* **7.** appropriate, take, assume; swindle, mulct, shark; peculate, embezzle, *Law.* defalcate, misappropriate; steal, rob, thieve, pilfer, purloin, finger, filch, *Inf.* snitch, cabbage, abstract, *Chiefly Brit.* prig; *Euph.* borrow, *Archaic.* nim; shoplift, palm, *Sl.* boost, walk off *or* away with, *Euph.* remove; *All Sl.* heist, pinch, hook, swipe, hustle, rip off, crook, cap, lift.
8. suffer, endure, bear, tolerate, brook, brave, take patiently, abide, stand, submit to, put up with; let pass, overlook, disregard, swallow, digest, stomach; face the music, take one's medicine, take it; accept, accommodate oneself to, reconcile oneself to, resign oneself to.
9. conceal, cover, hide, shroud, cloak, veil; screen, mask, disguise, camouflage; withhold, keep to oneself, suppress, bury, bottle up, stifle, smother, muffle; seal up, lock up.
10. confine, enclose, shut in, hem in, surround, bound; set, seclude.

pocketbook, *n.* **1.** handbag, shoulder bag, purse, clutch, evening bag, disco bag; change purse, (*in Scottish Highland costume*) sporran, wallet, money bag; bag, tote bag, sack, case, pouch, pocket; grip, valise, carpetbag; ditty bag.
2. budget, resources, means, pocket. See **pocket** (*def.* 2).

pocketknife, *n.* jackknife, clasp knife, penknife, folding knife, Swiss Army knife; switchblade.

pococurante, *adj.* caring little, indifferent, blasé, apathetic, uninterested, incurious, uninquisitive; unconcerned, nonchalant, careless, insouciant; distant, aloof, removed, Laodicean; neutral, unaffected, untouched, unstirred, unmoved, impassive, impassible, dispassionate; spiritless, passionless, unemotional, emotionless, unexcited, uncaring, perfunctory, half-hearted, *Archaic.* impassionate; lukewarm, cool, chilly, cold; languid, listless, phlegmatic, lethargic, dull; insensible, insensitive, insensate, unfeeling, unsympathetic, uncompassionate.

poem, *n.* verse composition, lyric, sonnet, villanelle, ode, *Class. Prosody.* epode, palinode, anacreontic, dithyramb, elegy; rhapsody, epic; rondelet, *Prosody.* rondeau, *Prosody.* rondel; pastoral, idyll, eclogue, bucolic, georgic; nuptial song, epithalamion; rhyme, limerick, jingle, doggerel; ditty, song, lay, ballad.

poet, *n.* poetess, versifier, versemaker, rhymer; imagist, vers-librist, lyrist, lyricist, idyllist, sonneteer, elegist; balladmonger, bard, minstrel, scop, skald; poetaster, rhymster.

poetic, *adj.* **1.** lyric, lyrical, sonnetlike, idyllic, pastoral, bucolic, georgic, elegiac; rhapsodic, epic; dithyrambic; metrical, metered, rhythmical, rhythmic, rhyming, sing-song.
2. songlike, singing, musical, melodic, tuneful, melodious; aesthetic, artistic, beautiful, graceful, flowing.

3. (*usu. of language*) figurative, symbolic, imagerial; flowery, overwrought, euphuistic; sensuous; concise, compact, compressed.

poetry, *n.* verse, versification, *Archaic.* poesy; rhythmical composition, metrical composition; light verse, free verse.

pogrom, *n.* massacre, carnage, wholesale *or* general slaughter, mass slaying, mass murder, mass killing, mass execution, mass homicide, noyade; bloodbath, bloodshed, effusion *or* fusillade of blood, *Rare.* internecion, *Rare.* trucidation; slaughter, slaying, butchery, homicide, murder, killing, execution; genocide, organized murder, extermination, obliteration, eradication, elimination, annihilation, extinction, liquidation, blotting *or* wiping out, *Euph., Hist.* Final Solution; holocaust, decimation, devastation, total destruction, laying waste, wasting; purge, purification, depuration, scouring.

poignancy, *n.* **1.** pathos, evocativeness, emotivity, emotiveness, emotion, emotionalism; sensitivity, tenderness, feeling, affectionateness, sentiment; intentness, earnestness, sincerity; keenness, intensity, acuteness, profoundness, deepness, extremeness.

2. patheticalness, pitiableness, piteousness, pitifulness; plaintiveness, wistfulness, forlornness, woefulness, woebegoneness.

3. pungency, piquancy, piquantness, tartness, sharpness; flavorfulness, tastiness, spiciness, hotness; bitterness, sourness, acidity, vinegariness, harshness; acerbity, mordancy, trenchancy, astringency.

poignant, *adj.* **1.** sorrowful, doleful, mournful, grievous, tearful, woeful, woebegone, wretched, miserable, *Archaic.* woesome; heartbreaking, heart-rending, crushing, distressing, upsetting; agonizing, tormenting, tortuous, excruciating, unbearable; lamentable, regrettable, deplorable, rueful; tragic, dreadful, disastrous, calamitous, terrible, awful; pathetic, pathetical, pitiable, piteous, pitiful; plaintive, wistful, blue, melancholy, sad.

2. keen, acute, deep, profound, intense, stimulating, interesting, extreme, compelling, intent, earnest, sincere; magnetic, appealing, attractive, tantalizing, provocative; impressive, striking, vivid, telling, effective, breath-taking, electric, galvanic, scintillating.

3. heartfelt, heart-moving, heart-swelling, stirring, soul-stirring, deep felt, *Archaic.* homefelt; moving, touching, affecting, melting, sensitive, tender, affectionate; emotional, emotive, affective, affectional, dramatic.

4. pungent, piquant, tart, sharp, nippy; tangy, spicy, highly seasoned, peppery, hot.

point, *n.* **1.** tip, nib, tapered end, sharp end, extremity; tine, prong, spike, pike; pinnacle, needle, peak, pointed top; *Naut.* bill, *Naut.* pea.

2. projection, promontory, head, foreland, headland, bluff, *Archaic.* ness; spit, tongue, cape, isthmus, peninsula, chersonese; strip, reach, stretch.

3. mark of punctuation, period.

4. place, area, locality, locale; position, location, *C.B. Radio.* twenty, site, spot.

5. direction, compass direction, compass point.

6. degree, extent; stage, condition, circumstances, position.

7. point in time, time, second, instant, moment, minute, hour; stage, stage of the game, phase, period.

8. verge, brink, edge.

9. feature, central *or* main idea, subject, keynote, focus, focal point; essential *or* important part, substance, meat, essence, quiddity, quintessence, sum and substance; marrow, pith, heart of the matter, crux, nitty-gritty, gist, *Inf.* nub; core, inner core, heart, center, nucleus, kernel; base, bottom, root.

10. meaning, significance, signification; underlying meaning, connotation, implication, import, purport, drift; spirit, tenor, tone, vein.

11. aim, end, purpose, object, objective, goal, intention, intent, motive; reason, reason behind [s.t.], cause, motivation, motivating force *or* factor.

12. subject under discussion, issue, matter, question, point in question.

13. pointer, piece of advice, hint, helpful hint, tip, suggestion.

14. consideration, thought, idea, point to remember *or* keep in mind.

15. item, particular, specific, detail, fine point, nicety, punctilio.

16. part, element, constituent, component, ingredient, essential *or* fundamental part.

17. **points** (*all of animals*) extremities, limbs, legs, feet, paws, pads, hooves, trotters.

18. unit of measure, mark, score, notch.

19. **in point of** as regards, in reference to.

20. **to the point** pertinent, relevant, apropos, fitting, appropriate, suitable, germane, applicable.

—*v.* **21.** point to, point at, point *or* direct one's finger to *or* at.

22. *Usu.* **point out** indicate, show, direct *or* call attention to; specify, list, name, designate.

23. sharpen, edge, whet, grind, strop.

24. aim, direct, level.

25. signify, indicate, denote, bespeak; promise, look like, bode, presage, omen, augur, portend; foretoken, foreshadow, forebode.

point-blank, *adj.* **1.** direct, true, sure, accurate, on target, on the mark; right, straight, undeviating, unswerving.

2. downright, outright, out-and-out, explicit, unequivocal, *Inf.* flat-footed; plain, plain-spoken, blunt, to the point, abrupt, bluff, brusque, tactless; candid, frank, forthright, straightforward, straight-from-the-shoulder; aboveboard, open and aboveboard, up front, on the level, honest, truthful, on the up and up, no-nonsense.

—*adv.* **3.** directly, straightly, in a straight line, right, undeviatingly, unswervingly.

4. bluntly, plainly, explicitly, unequivocally; frankly, candidly, forthrightly, straightforwardly; openly, sincerely, genuinely, honestly, truly, truthfully.

pointed, *adj.* **1.** barbed, peaked, cuspidate, cuspidal, *Bot.* apiculate, *Bot., Zool.* acuminate; needle-shaped, aciform, acicular; toothed, dentiform, serrate, serrated; spiculate, thorny, spinous; craggy, jagged, angular; spear-shaped, sword-shaped, *Biol.* ensiform, *Anat., Zool.* xiphoid, sagittate; tapering, *Bot., Zool.* subulate.

2. sharp, piercing, incisive, trenchant, cutting, biting; penetrating, keen, acute; forceful, powerful, potent, striking, effective; telling, impressive, significant, cogent; vivid, graphic, unmistakable, conspicuous, salient; marked, stressed, emphasized.

3. epigrammatic, terse, tight, succinct, concise; brief, short, to the point, pithy; exact, precise, neat; ingenious, witty.

4. directed, aimed, targeted, focused, sighted, trained on.

pointer, *n.* **1.** indicator, index, sign, indicant; clue, key, reference, reference mark, landmark; arrow, director, guide; guiding star, polestar, lodestar, compass, needle.

2. advice, useful information, tip, recommendation, suggestion, word to the wise, hint; rule, law, doctrine, tenet; motto, proverb, wise saying, adage, maxim; direction, command, charge, order, injunction; admonition, monition, caution, warning.

pointless, *adj.* **1.** blunt, dull, unsharp, unsharpened; unedged, edgeless, rounded, worn down, obtuse, unpointed, *Naut.* bluff.

2. meaningless, purposeless, hollow, empty, vain; inane, worthless, senseless, without rhyme or reason; unreasonable, irrational, nonsensical, preposterous; foolish, fatuous, silly, asinine, absurd, stupid; irrelevant, nongermane, inapposite, impertinent; inapplicable, immaterial, foreign, alien, unrelated, unconnected; extraneous, gratuitous, unessential, insignificant; beside the point, neither here nor there, beside the question, beside the mark, nothing to do with it; *Inf.* off base, not to the point, *Inf.* off the beam, *Inf.* off the wall; inconsistent, illogical, inconsequent, self-contradictory, incongruous.

3. weak, forceless, impotent; ineffectual, inadequate, worthless, valueless, meritless, nugatory; futile, vain, idle, bootless, useless, unavailing; unproductive, unyielding, unprofitable, profitless, gainless, unremunerative, unpaying; unsuccessful, to no avail, to no purpose, for naught, all for naught.

poise, *n.* **1.** balance, equilibrium, equipoise, equipollence, equipollency, equiponderance, equiponderancy; equivalence, equality, parity, par; correspondence, evenness, levelness; equalization, uniformity, symmetry, parallelism.

2. composure, aplomb, assurance, confidence, self-assurance, self-confidence, self-possession, self-command, self-control, collectedness; equanimity, calmness, cool, coolness, sang-froid, imperturbability; sedateness, staidness, reserve; polish, grace, refinement, urbanity, suaveness, savoir-faire.

3. steadiness, stability, stableness, stasis; suspension, wavering, hovering.

4. posture, carriage, pose, attitude.

—*v.* **5.** balance, equilibrate, counterbalance, counterpoise; level, even, square; stabilize, steady.

6. hover, hang suspended, hang in midair; float, ride, fly.

poised, *adj.* composed, calm, cool, *Inf.* together; self-assured, self-possessed, self-confident; dignified, mannered, decorous, polished, urbane, suave; nonchalant, unruffled, imperturbable, unflappable.

poisonous, *adj.* **1.** venomous, virulent, (*in prescriptions*) venenosus, toxic, morbific; fell, baneful, mephitic, viperous, *Rare.* virose, *Archaic.* venenose; pestilential, pestiferous, infective, infectious, pestilent, contaminative, contagious, leprous, septic.

2. pernicious, dangerous, hazardous, deleterious, detrimental, destructive, ruinous; deadly, lethal, fatal, mortal, mortiferous, *Archaic.* lethiferous; harmful, injurious, nocuous, hurtful, nocent, baleful, noisome; noxious, malicious, malign, malignant, menacing; insalubrious, unhealthful, unhygienic, unsanitary.

3. malevolent, maleficent, malefic, devilish, demonic, diabolic; vicious, rancorous, invidious; vindictive, revengeful, vengeful, spiteful; slanderous, libelous, calumnious, defamatory; acrimonious, caustic, bitter, envenomed, vitriolic.

poke, *v.* **1.** push, butt, jab, dig, nudge, jog, punch; thrust, force, drive, stir, impel, goad, prod; jolt, jostle, elbow, shove.

2. *Usu.* **poke out** extend, project, protrude, overhang, beetle; stick out, shoot out, hang out.

3. *Usu.* **poke into** intrude, meddle, *Inf.* kibbitz, *Inf.* butt in, *Inf.* horn in, stick one's nose where it doesn't belong; muscle in, worm in, interlope.

4. *Usu.* **poke about** *or* **around** ransack, rummage, forage, rake, scour; look around, sift through; examine, investigate.

5. *Usu.* **poke along** dawdle, dally, loiter, loll, *Inf.* lallygag, lag behind, take one's time *or* one's own sweet time; idle, loaf, potter, fiddle, piddle, dillydally, *Inf.* diddle; meander, saunter, shuffle, roam aimlessly; window-shop.

6. **poke fun at** mock, ridicule, jeer, make fun of, fleer, guy; tease, kid, rib, rally, chaff, taunt, twit, needle, make sport of, *Inf.* roast; deride, flout, put down, insult, run down, abuse, disdain.

—*n.* **7.** thrust, dig, push, shove, jab, nudge, jog, punch, jolt; finger in the ribs.

8. *Informal.* slowpoke, snail, tortoise; dawdler, laggard, lingerer, loiterer; lazybones, slugabed; procrastinator, dillydallier.

poky, *adj.* *Informal.* **1.** dawdling, dillydallying, lingering, lagging, puttering; crawling, snail-like, tortoise-like; slow, unhurried, leisurely, relaxed, easy.

2. indecisive, hesitant, uncertain, hanging back, tentative; faltering, hesitating, wavering, fluctuating.

3. tardy, late, unpunctual, behind time, behindhand.

4. small, cramped, incommodious, unroomy, cell-like, boxy; narrow, confined, tiny.

5. dowdy, frumpy, dumpy, frowzy, tacky; sloppy, slatternly, messy, unkempt.

—*n.* **6.** *Slang.* jail, jailhouse, lockup, police station, station house. See **jail** (*def.* **1**).

polar, *adj.* **1.** opposite, contrasting, contradictory, contrary, different, radically different; antagonistic, repugnant, conflicting, hostile, inimical, opposed, diametrically opposed; antithetic, antithetical, antipodal.

2. central, pivotal, key, crucial, cardinal; chief, principal, fundamental.

3. guiding, leading, directing, beacon-like.

polarity, *n.* **1.** opposition, repugnance, contrariety, antithesis; antagonism, conflict, antipathy, hostility.

2. duality, *Inf.* twoness, doubleness, dualism; ambiguity, ambivalence, paradox, self-contradiction.

pole[1], *n.* shaft, rod, post; flag pole, flagstaff; mast, spar, timber, tree; beam, stanchion; pillar, column, upright.

pole[2], *n.* **1.** extremity, extreme, limit; end of the earth, end of the rainbow, ultima Thule *or* Thule.

2. cynosure, polestar, lodestar, magnet; focus, focal point, center of attention, center of attraction, center of interest.

3. **poles apart** at opposite extremes, at opposite ends, worlds apart, widely apart *or* separated; (*all in the extreme*) different, dissimilar, distinct, discrete, separate, like night and day, like black and white; incompatible, incongruous, irreconcilable, unconformable; disagreeing, in disagreement, at odds, at variance.

polemic, *n.* **1.** debate, dispute, argument, controversy, altercation, verbal engagement, war of words, logomachy, pilpul.

2. debater, polemist. See **polemist.**

—*adj.* **3.** controversial, polemical, argumentative, argumental, dialectic, logomachic, eristic, pilpulistic; quarrelsome, contentious, disputatious, litigious; pugnacious, belligerent, bellicose, aggressive.

polemics, *n.* argumentation, argument, disputation, dispute, contention, controversy, litigation, wrangling, bickering, *Rare.* disceptation.

polemist, *n.* controversialist, debater, arguer, mooter, disputer, disputant, wrangler, *Rare.* disceptator; dialectician, polemic, polemicist, pilpulist, logomacher; logician, ratiocinator; casuist, Jesuit, Philadelphia lawyer.

police, *n.* **1.** constabulary, police force, law enforcement agency, *Inf.* the cops, *Inf.* the law, *Sl.* the long arm of the law, *Sl.* the fuzz, *Sl.* the heat, *Sl.* New York's finest; highway patrol, *Mil.* shore patrol, military police; Royal Canadian Mounted Police *or* RCMP, *Inf.* Mounties, (*in Great Britain*) Scotland Yard.

—*v.* **2.** regulate, control, maintain order, keep the peace; patrol, go on one's beat.

3. *Military.* clean, clean up, tidy, tidy up, pick up, trim up, put in trim, straighten up *or* out.

policeman, *n.* constable, officer, officer of the law, peace officer, keeper of the peace, law enforcement agent, bluecoat, *Fr. gendarme, It. carabiniere;* patrolman, roundsman; traffic cop, *Brit.* pointsman; sherriff, marshal; military policeman, MP; *All Inf.* cop, copper, *Brit.* bobby; *All Sl.* the man, John Law, bull, fuzz, shamus, beetle-crusher, *U.S. Offensive,* pig, *Brit. Obs.* peeler, *Fr. flic.*

policy, *n.* **1.** course *or* line of action, strategy, design, plan, game, scheme; mode of management, line of conduct, rule of action; system, way, custom, habit; program, platform, schedule, organization; means, means to an end, ways and means, tactics; protocol, rules, behavior, manner.

2. expediency, suitability, suitableness, seemliness, appropriateness; properness, correctness, rightness, goodness; sensibleness, reasonableness, rationality, intelligence, prudence, advisability, desirability, desirableness, practicality, usefulness, utility.

3. cleverness, astuteness, shrewdness, ingenuity, ingeniousness; sagacity, sagaciousness, wisdom; acumen, discernment, insight, perception, percipience, flair; foresightedness, farsightedness, long-headedness.

polish, *v.* **1.** wax, buff, burnish, rub down, smooth; shine, gloss, luster, brighten, glaze, *Scot. and North. Eng.* sheen; abrade, grind, pumice, scour, scrub, clean.

2. sparkle, glitter, gleam, glisten, shimmer, glow, beam, radiate.

3. perfect, consummate, finish; improve, meliorate, ameliorate, better, work out the kinks; refine, cultivate.

—*n.* **4.** wax, lemon oil; abrasive, abradant, emery, pumice, rouge, cleanser, rubbing compound.

5. waxing, buffing, burnishment, burnishing, rubbing down, smoothing; shining, lustering, brightening, glazing; abrasion, abrading, grinding, pumicing, scouring, scrubbing, cleaning.

6. smoothness, glaze; shine, gloss, luster, sheen, shimmer, shimmering; sparkle, sparkling, glitter, glittering, glistening, gleam, gleaming, glow, glowing, beam, beaming, brightness, brilliance, radiation, radiating.

7. perfection, consummation, finish, excellence, outstandingness, superiority; expertness, masterliness, masterfulness, adeptness, proficiency.

8. refinement, good breeding, cultivation, culture, elegance, elegancy; suavity, urbanity, urbaneness, sophistication, savoir-faire.

polished, *adj.* **1.** buffed, burnished, rubbed down; smooth, velvety, silky, slick, slippery, glassy, glasslike, glacé, glazed; waxed, glossy, lustrous, satiny, sheeny, glowing; shiny, shining, glistening, sparkling, shimmering, bright, brilliant, radiant, blinding.

2. refined, cultured, cultivated, well-bred, well-mannered, to the manner born, courtly, genteel; well-educated, well-spoken, intelligent, academic, lettered, erudite; suave, sleek, civilized, urbane, sophisticated, worldly; elegant, graceful, debonair, top-hat.

3. finished, perfected, perfect, flawless, faultless, impeccable, unmarred, unblemished; expert, skillful, masterly, masterful, proficient, adept, accomplished, well executed *or* performed *or* done; excellent, great, extraordinary, outstanding, remarkable, noteworthy, *Inf.* super; exquisite, superlative, consummate, supreme, superior, transcendent.

polite, *adj.* **1.** courteous, mannerly, well-mannered, civil, respectful, deferential, deferent; decorous, proper, formal, *Fr. comme il faut,* ceremonious; tactful, diplomatic, politic; cordial, genial, affable, good-humored, pleasant, sociable; pleasing, winning, charming, ingratiating, complaisant, agreeable, obliging, attentive.

2. well-behaved, well-bred, refined, polished, civilized; genteel, gentle, ladylike, gracious, kind; gentlemanly, gentlemanlike, courtly, gallant, chivalrous, chivalric; urbane, suave, debonair, sophisticated, elegant; discriminating, refined.

politic, *adj.* **1.** sagacious, judicious, wise, sapient; discreet, prudent, wary, chary, cautious; watchful, vigilant, Argus-eyed, mindful; clear-headed, thoughtful, sensible, intelligent, reasonable, sound; astute, discerning, perceptive, penetrating, piercing; keen, sharp, acute, quick; eagle-eyed, hawk-eyed, lynx-eyed, sharp-eyed; perspicacious, percipient, discriminating, appercipient; alert, quick-witted, nimble, bright, smart; long-sighted, farsighted, far-seeing, long-headed.

2. clever, cunning, wily, tricky, crafty, arch; artful, ingenious, Machiavellian, *Rare.* subdolous; shrewd, canny, *Inf.* cagey, shifty; sly, subtle, foxy, vulpine; conniving, contriving, intriguing, designing.

3. expedient, advisable, recommendable, desirable, practical, useful; to one's best interest, to one's good, all to the good, all for the best; suitable, seemly, appropriate, befitting, fitting, fit, meet; proper, correct, right, good, essential; sensible, reasonable, rational, intelligent.

political, *adj.* civil, civic, public, politic; official, bureaucratic, administrative; state, governmental, national, federal; partisan, bipartisan, factional.

politician, *n.* **1.** politico, *Inf.* pol, public servant, civil servant; office-holder, incumbent, lame duck; campaigner, office-seeker, aspirant, favorite son, dark horse, *Inf.* stumper, *Sl.* baby kisser; old campaigner, war-horse; kingpin, *Inf.* boss; hack, party hack.

2. statesman, elder statesman; diplomat; administrator, bureaucrat; congressman, senator, representative, lawmaker, legislator, (*in Great Britain*) Member of Parliament *or* MP.

3. Machiavellian, political realist; manipulator, machinator, maneuverer, wirepuller, kingmaker, power behind the throne; strategist, tactician; logroller, pork barrel politician, *Inf.* influence peddler, *Inf.* power broker; (*pl.*) boys in the back room.

politics, *n.* **1.** political science, *Inf.* poli sci; government, civics; policy, polity, party line, party position, party philosophy.

2. Machiavellianism, realpolitik, political realism; machination, manipulation, maneuvering, wire-pulling, *Inf.* influence-peddling, *Inf.* back-room politics.

3. statesmanship, statecraft, diplomacy.

poll, *n.* **1.** count, nose *or* head *or* body count, tally, tabulation, enumeration; statistics, figures, census, demography; opinion sampling.

2. voting list, list, roster, panel; muster roll, tax rolls.

3. head, skull, cranium, *Zool.* cephalon, brainpan, pate, *Inf.* sconce, *Inf.* dome, *Sl.* bean, *Sl.* gourd; nape, scruff, *Anat.* occiput.

—*v.* **4.** register as a voter, register, enroll; vote, cast one's ballot, exercise one's franchise.

5. (*all in reference to opinion sampling*) question,

query, inquire; collect, gather, assemble, amass, accumulate; analyze, examine, infer, conclude.

6. cut, clip, crop, shear, shave, snip; prune, lop off, pollard, truncate, dock, bob.

pollute, *v.* **1.** dirty, soil, sully, maculate; foul, befoul, make unclean, grime, begrime; poison, adulterate, blight, canker; spoil, mar, scar, *Inf.* muck up, *Inf.* mess up; litter, strew, *Inf.* junk up.

2. defile, contaminate, vitiate, debase, devalue, deprave, corrupt; desecrate, profane, unhallow, violate, destroy, ravage, play havoc with; despoil, abuse, misuse, ill-use.

polluted, *adj.* **1.** dirty, unclean, fouled, befouled, soiled, sooty, grimy, smoky, sullied, maculated; impure, tainted, infected, cankerous, poisoned, adulterated, *Inf.* mucky, *Inf.* mucked up, littered, litterstrewn, *Inf.* junked up.

2. defiled, contaminated, vitiated, spoiled, corrupted; malodorous, mephitic, rank, fetid, putrid, odious, noxious, noisome; slimy, *Inf.* scrummy, sludgy, *Inf.* gloppy, *Inf.* gunky; unhygienic, unsanitary, insanitary, morbific, pathogenic, pestiferous, feculent, ordurous; unhealthy, unhealthful, unwholesome.

3. debased, devalued, worsened, made worse; undermined, weakened, downgraded, endangered; harmed, injured, damaged, blighted, destroyed; desolate, wasted, laid waste; violated, ravaged, despoiled, misused, abused, mismanaged, desecrated, profaned.

poltroon, *n.* coward, dastard, craven, recreant, *Archaic.* caitiff, *Archaic.* niddering, man with the white feather, lily-livered *or* white-livered coward, craven coward; yellowbelly, mouse, baby, big baby, wheyface, invertebrate, *Inf.* jellyfish, backbone of banana; *Inf.* fraidy-cat, *Inf.* scaredy-cat, *Inf.* nervous nellie, *Sl.* chicken, *Sl.* weak sister; sissy, weakling, milksop, milquetoast, mollycoddle, *Inf.* pantywaist.

polychromatic, *adj.* **1.** polychrome, many-colored, many-hued, parti-colored, versicolored, multicolored, decorated *or* executed in many colors, *Archaic.* motley, harlequin; colorful, diversified, rich, gorgeous, gay, of all manner of colors, of all the colors of the rainbow *or* the spectrum; prismatic, kaleidoscopic, spectral, rainbow, technicolored; crazy, psychedelic.

2. variegated, nacreous, opalescent, opaline, iridescent, peacocklike, pavonine; chameleonlike, chameleonic.

polyglot, *adj.* **1.** multilingual, learned in languages, bilingual, diglot, diglottic.

—n. **2.** linguist, multilinguist, bilinguist, person of many tongues.

polymorphous, *adj.* polymorphic, multiform, manifold, variable, multiphase, multiplex; multifarious, diversified, varied; protean, everchanging, changeful, changeable, mutable, metamorphic.

pommel, *n.* **1.** knob, protuberance, protrusion, extrusion, bump, boss, button; handle, horn, hold, grip.

—v. **2.** pummel, punch, thwack, bang, bang away at, buffet, wallop, cuff, baste, *Inf.* lambaste, *Sl.* belt; pound, *Sl.* pound on, thump, box; trounce, drub, *Sl.* whump, thrash, pulverize; bruise, belabor, thresh, beat, *Sl.* beat up.

pomp, *n.* **1.** grandeur, splendor, brilliance, glory; dignity, gravity, weight, ponderousness, state, solemnity, ceremoniousness, ritual, rituality; magnificence, array, flourish, style, parade, procession, cavalcade; display, show, pageantry, ceremony, spectacle; stiffness, stiltedness, rigidness, starchiness.

2. ostentation, grandiosity, pomposity, pompousness; vainglory, fanfaronade, exhibition. See **pomposity** (*defs.* **1-3**).

pompon, *n.* **1.** fluffy tuft *or* ball, puff, bit of fluff; shakers, ball of streamers.

2. panache, plume, feather, crest, topknot; rosette, cockade, tassel.

pomposity, *n.* **1.** pompousness, haughtiness, hauteur, arrogance, self-importance, pontification, *Inf.* stuffiness; pretension, pretentiousness, affectation, airs, attitudinizing, posing, *Inf.* highfalutin' ways; vainglory, vanity, pride, foppery, dandyism, coxcombry, peacockery; flaunting, trumpeting, *Inf.* putting on the dog *or* the ritz; swaggering, bluster, strutting, bravado; boasting, boastfulness, exaggeration, bragging, self-advertising, *Inf.* blowing one's own horn, self-applause.

2. magniloquence, rodomontade, grandiloquence, orotundity, fustian, tumidity, bombast, rant.

3. vainglorious display, glitter, lofty affectation, loftiness, exhibitionism, theatrics, histrionics, dramatics, staginess, *Inf.* phoniness, *Inf.* grandstanding; ostentation, grandiosity, fanfaronade, pomp, show, parade; extravaganza, splash, splurge, gaudery, gaudiness; exhibition, display, elaborateness, *Inf.* splendiferousness.

pompous, *adj.* **1.** self-important, pretentious, vainglorious, vain; arrogant, haughty, proud, conceited, egotistic, egotistical; puffed up, *Inf.* uppity, *Inf.* toplofty, snobbish, *Sl.* snooty; pontifical, magisterial, imperious, authoritative, *Inf.* high-handed; patronizing, condescending, supercilious, disdainful, *Inf.* high-hat; affected, mannered, showy, ostentatious, grandiose.

2. inflated, bombastic, turgid, high-sounding, highflown, embellished, ornate, flowery, euphuistic, embroidered; overblown, swollen, tumid, stilted, pedantic, *Inf.* stuffy; declamatory, grandiloquent, magniloquent, orotund, fustian; theatrical, histrionic, *Inf.* stagey.

3. splendid, magnificent, lofty, solemn, moving, impressive, imposing; stately, dignified, lordly, majestic, august, illustrious; ceremonial, ritual, ritualistic.

pond, *n.* pool, water hole, still water, water pocket, puddle; small lake, fishpond, millpond, millpool, tidal pond *or* pool; lagoon, reservoir.

ponder, *v.* **1.** cogitate, think over, rack one's brains, cudgel one's brain, trouble one's head; ruminate, chew, chew one's cud, brood, mull over, dwell on, be in a brown study; reflect, speculate, wonder about, dream about, muse; meditate, contemplate, think about, cerebrate, put on one's thinking cap, be abstracted, be lost in thought; concentrate, focus, have one's mind on, put one's mind to.

2. deliberate, excogitate, consider, take to heart, *Archaic.* perpend; weigh, evaluate, revolve, review, study, scrutinize, examine, inspect, con.

ponderable, *adj.* **1.** considerable, weighty, solid; substantial, pithy, meaty, rich; profound, deep, serious, grave, momentous, important, significant.

2. heavy, hefty, ponderous; massive, bulky, gross, huge, large, big; palpable, tangible, material, physical, corporeal, bodily, incarnate, fleshly.

ponderous, *adj.* **1.** heavy, massive, weighty, hefty, bulky; prodigious, mighty, immense, gigantic, huge, large, big; awkward, unwieldy, cumbersome, unmanageable, clumsy.

2. labored, forced, dull, tedious, boring, uninteresting, monotonous, dreary, tiresome; droning, dry, dry-as-dust, pedantic, stilted; abstruse, recondite, learned, academic, profound, esoteric, *Sl.* heavy.

poniard, *n.* **1.** dagger, dirk, misericord, stiletto, stylet, *Obs.* bodkin; knife, jackknife, pocketknife, switchblade; short sword, blade, steel, rapier, *Fencing.* foil; saber, yataghan, falchion, creese *or* kris, katár, anelace, kukri; machete, bolo, butcher knife, barong.

—*v.* **2.** stab, dirk, stick, pierce, wound, puncture; scratch, prick, pink.

pontiff, *n.* **1.** prelate, primate, archbishop, bishop, diocesan, suffragan, metropolitan, chief priest, high priest, (*in ancient Rome*) pontifex.

2. *Rom. Cath. Ch.* Bishop of Rome, Supreme Pontiff, pope, Holy Father, successor to Peter, his Holiness, vicar of Christ, the Servant of the Servants of God, *Rare.* papa.

pontifical, *adj.* **1.** papal, prelatic, episcopal, sacerdotal, priestly, ecclesiastical, clerical, *Archaic.* pontific; *All Disparaging.* papistical, papist, popish.

—*n.* **2.** formulary, ordinal, lectionary, breviary, rubric, missal, mass book, service book, manual.

3. **pontificals** (*all of a pontiff*) vestments, *Archaic.* vesture, canonicals, robes, garments, attire; cope, alb, surplice, stole, maniple, cassock; insignia, miter, crosier, staff, crook.

pontificate, *n.* **1.** papacy, papalism, *Disparaging.* papism, popedom, *Disparaging.* popery, papality, primacy, Holy See, See of Peter, shoes of the fisherman, papal crown; prelacy, prelature, prelateship, episcopate, episcopacy, bishopric, see, diocese, miter.

—*v.* **2.** orate, declaim, hold forth, harangue, perorate, pronounce, expound; dogmatize, preach, lecture, sermonize.

pony, *n.* small horse, Shetland pony, Shetland, Iceland pony, Welch pony; polo pony, cow pony.

pooh, *interj.* nonsense, bosh, fiddlesticks, poppycock, balderdash, rubbish, humbug, applesauce, fiddle-faddle, fiddle-de-dee, oh fudge; anyways haha, so what?, so?, who cares?, pshaw, pah, pooh-pooh, tut, tut-tut, tisk-tisk, pish, pish-tish, bah, phoo, phooey; come-come, come now, now really, really, *Sl.* baloney, *Sl.* crap, *Sl.* crapola, c'mon now, aw c'mon.

pooh-pooh, *v.* **1.** disdain, scorn, slight, dismiss lightly, make little of, turn one's back on, fleer, curl one's lip, turn one's nose up at, *Inf.* give [s.o.] the cold shoulder *or* the fish eye; reject, dismiss, dismiss out of hand, dismiss with a sneer, dismiss as unworthy of consideration, point the finger of scorn at, point at, hold up to scorn, make light of, sneer at, scoff at.

2. disparage, twit, taunt, scout, flout, deride; grin at, mock, revile, laugh in [s.o.'s] face, jeer, jape, make fun of; ridicule, *Sl.* pan, *Sl.* razz; gibe, poke fun at, laugh at, hoot, hiss, rail at, banter, chaff, *Sl.* dump on, *Sl.* rank out.

pool¹, *n.* **1.** pond, tarn, small lake, tidal pool, lagoon, inlet, bayou, *Brit. Dial.* sump; water hole, standing water, still water, water pocket; puddle, mud hole, mud puddle, stagnant water, swamp pool, plash; quarry, reservoir.

2. swimming hole; swimming pool, natatorium, plunge, wading pool, splash pool; birdbath.

—*v.* **3.** collect, accumulate, flow together, converge, seethe, mill, stream, run together; back up, well up, bubble up.

pool², *n.* **1.** funds, fund, purse, reserves, reserve; stakes, *All Inf.* pot, jackpot, bank, kitty, ante.

2. trust, syndicate, cartel, combine, consortium, *Sl.* plunderbund; combination, stock company, shareholders, speculators, gamblers, stake players, plungers.

—*v.* **3.** combine, join forces, associate, unite, unify, ally; merge, consolidate, amalgamate, league, collaborate, band together; go into, come *or* get into, sign up *or* on, team up with, share, *Inf.* share the wealth.

poor, *adj.* **1.** destitute, poverty-stricken, impoverished, penurious, impecunious, beggared, pauperized; penniless, indigent, poor as Job's turkey, needy, necessitous, bad off, badly off; pinched, straitened, distressed, *Inf.* strapped, *Inf.* up against it, *Inf.* on one's uppers, *Inf.* hard up; financially embarrassed, out of cash, out-of-pocket, *Inf.* short, *Brit. Sl.* skint, *All Inf.* broke, dead broke, flat broke, stone broke; bankrupt, ruined, wiped out, *Inf.* on the rocks, insolvent, overdrawn, in the red; down and out, out at the elbows, down at the heels, seedy.

2. meager, scarce, scanty, scant, sparse, exiguous, in short supply, at a premium, not to be had, *Inf.* scarce as hen's teeth; lacking, wanting, short, short of, not enough, too little; slight, skimpy, scrimpy, stinted; shabby, beggarly, miserly, niggardly, stingy, puny, little, dinky, paltry, petty, piddling, *Inf.* picayune, pathetic, *Inf.* chintzy, *Inf.* measly; insignificant, unimportant, *Archaic.* seely, negligible, nugatory, inconsiderable, inconsequential.

3. barren, unproductive, unyielding, unfructuous, unfruitful, fruitless, infecund, unfecund, *Bot.* acarpous, sterile, effete; uncultivable, uncultivatable, fallow, uncultivated, unused, neglected; exhausted, depleted, drained, worn-out, impoverished; lean, empty, forlorn, bare, dry, arid, bald, waste, desolate, dead, naked.

4. unsatisfactory, inadequate, unacceptable, below standard, under *or* below par; inferior, low-grade, cheap, catchpenny, bargain-basement, *U.S. Sl.* cheesy, *Brit. Sl.* humpety, flimsy, jerry-built; weak, feeble, thin, defective, faulty, imperfect; second-rate, second-class, third-class, third-rate; mediocre, unprofessional, amateurish, not up to par *or* snuff; sorry, half-baked, *Sl.* half-assed, sloppy, haphazard, careless, shoddy, slipshod, sleazy; mean, grubstreet, *Inf.* no good, *Inf.* junky, trashy, rubbishy, *Chiefly Dial.* footy, worthless, useless, valueless; bad, *Inf.* lousy, *Sl.* crummy, *Sl.* crappy, *Sl.* rotten, miserable.

5. lean, thin, thin *or* skinny as a rail, skinny, lank, lanky; gaunt, scraggy, scrawny, emaciated, underfed, undernourished, starved, half-starved; bony, spindly, rawboned, skin and bones, mere flesh and bones.

6. cowardly, abject, mean, low, low-down, base, base-spirited, ignoble; dishonorable, disreputable, discreditable, disgraceful, shameful; contemptible, despicable, execrable, abominable; corrupt, wicked, depraved, perverted, debased, miscreant.

7. humble, modest, plain, simple, homespun, homely, rustic; plebian, common, commonplace, ordinary, everyday, average.

8. unfortunate, unlucky, luckless, out of luck, down on one's luck, hapless; unhappy, miserable, wretched, pitiable, pitiful, sorry; unsuccessful, unprosperous, fortuneless; unblest, star-crossed, ill-starred, ill-fated, ill-omened, doomed, born under an evil star, jinxed.

poorhouse, *n.* eleemosynary institution, house for paupers, *Chiefly Brit.* almshouse, beadhouse, *Brit.* workhouse; asylum, retreat, shelter, haven.

pop, *v.* **1.** explode lightly, detonate, go off, fulminate, burst, bang, boom, report, shoot, shoot off *or* out.

2. *Usu.* **pop in** *or* **off** come *or* go suddenly, drop by, stop by, come by; leave quickly, depart, *Sl.* split, rush out *or* off, take off.

3. insert, put in *or* into, set *or* place in, tuck in, slide in, slip in, push in, thrust in, stick in; put out, thrust out, stick out.

—*n.* **4.** light explosion, detonation, fulmination, boom, bang, report, shot, discharge.

5. soda, soda pop, soft drink, *Inf.* tonic, carbonated drink; cola, *Trademark.* Coca-Cola *or* Coke, *Trademark.* Pepsi-Cola *or* Pepsi.

pope, *n.* *Rom. Cath. Ch.* Bishop of Rome, Supreme Pontiff, Holy Father, his Holiness, the Vicar of Christ, the successor of Peter, the Servant of the Servants of God, *Rare.* papa; *Eastern Ch.* patriarch of Alexandria.

popedom, *n.* **1.** papal government, papality, papalism, *Derog.* papism; the papal see, the See of Rome, the Holy See, the See of Peter, the Vatican, Vatican City, the States of the Church, the Papal States.

2. Roman Catholicism, the Roman Catholic Church, *Derog.* papistry, *Derog.* popery.

popinjay, *n.* coxcomb, dandy, jack-a-dandy, fop, dude, beau, spark; blade, *Chiefly Brit.* blood, buck, jackanapes, whippersnapper; *Fr. petit maître,* Beau Brummel, macaroni, *Archaic.* princox; exquisite, *Sl.* peacock, prinker, preener, show-off; fashion plate, male clotheshorse, silk-stocking, *Brit. Inf.* toff.

poppycock, *n.* **1.** nonsense, falderal, gibberish, Jabberwocky; babble, babbling, babblement, *Fr. bavardage;* twaddle, twaddling, *Both Brit.* twattle, twattling; blather, blathering, drivel, driveling, drool, drooling; jargon, *Sl.* jive, Greek, *Chiefly Southern U.S.* Choctaw; hocus-pocus, mumbo jumbo, abracadabra, fiddle-de-dee; moonshine, gobbledegook, foolish humbug, foam, froth, bunkum *or* buncombe, *Sl.* bunk, *U.S. Sl.* blah; flummery, *Inf.* hokum, *Sl.* applesauce, *Sl.* eyewash.

2. rubbish, *Sl.* tripe, refuse, *Dial.* culch, chaff, trash, *Inf.* truck, trumpery; tommyrot, *Inf.* rot, *Sl.* garbage, *Sl.* crap, *Sl.* crock, *Sl.* bull; balderdash, hogwash, swill, *Sl.* horsefeathers; stuff, stuff and nonsense, *Inf.* bosh, *Brit. Inf.* gammon, *Brit. Sl.* tosh; fudge, foolishness, folly, rigmarole *or* rigamarole, amphigory; footle, *Inf.* malarkey, *Sl.* bushwa, *Sl.* baloney, *Sl.* bilge *or* bilge water, *Sl.* meshugaas, *Scot. and North Eng.* haver; *All Inf.* fiddle-faddle, piffle, hooey, kibosh, flapdoodle.

3. idle talk, *Inf.* gab, *Sl.* gas, palaver, palaverment; claptrap, rodomontade, fustian, bombast, rant, *Sl.* hot air; jabber, prate, patter, gabble; clack, clatter, rattling, *Sl.* running off *or* on at the mouth; chatter, prattle, chippering, cackling; chitchat, chitter-chatter, small talk, *Anglo-Indian.* bukh.

populace, *n.* **1.** general public, commonalty, common people, common folk, commoners, the people, hoi polloi; the masses, the multitude, the Four Million, the great unwashed, the great unnumbered; lower classes, proletariat, the working class, salt of the earth, peasantry; ruck, canaille, riffraff, rabble, ragtag and bobtail, mob, *Archaic.* varletry, rout; rank and file, little people, little guys, grass roots, *U.S.* Middle America, middle class, bourgeoisie.

2. inhabitants, residents, citizenry. See **population.**

popular, *adj.* **1.** in demand, wanted, desired, called-for; in favor, favored, received, accepted, approved; in vogue, in fashion, in style, *Inf.* in, fashionable, stylish, all the rage, *Inf.* all the thing, *Fr. au courant;* liked, well-liked, loved, beloved, well-loved; successful, big, *Inf.* boffo, *Inf.* box-office; famous, renowned, acclaimed, celebrated, notorious, talked-of, on everybody's lips.

2. public, civic, civil, social, societal; vernacular, vulgar, proletarian, working-class, plebian; secular, lay, laic.

3. common, commonplace, conventional, usual, standard, stock; familiar, accustomed, customary, habitual, wonted, well-known, garden-variety, household; normal, normative, average, everyday, workaday, routine; current, prevalent, prevailing, predominant, predominating; general, widespread, extensive; universal, catholic, ecumenical; rife, rampant, epidemic, pandemic.

4. middlebrow, middle-of-the-road, MOR, middle-class, bourgeois, *Inf.* straight, *Inf.* square, *Inf.* plastic.

5. lowbrow, exoteric, simple, simplified, popularized, geared-down, *Inf.* pop; commercial, accessible, direct, straightforward, understandable, easily understood, easy to understand.

6. inexpensive, cheap, low-priced, popularly-priced, priced to fit the pocketbook; reasonable, moderate, modest, manageable, within means.

popularity, *n.* **1.** repute, reputation, fame, renown, note, notoriety, name, mark, distinction; glory, kudos, plaudits, éclat, acclaim, public acclaim, acclamation.

2. acceptance, recognition, a place in the sun; favor, approval, approbation, sanction; esteem, regard; adulation, idolization, idolatry, adoration, lionization, worship, hero worship.

3. prevalence, currency, fashionableness, stylishness, modishness; fashion, vogue, style.

popularize, *v.* **1.** simplify, gear down, water down, gild the pill, make palatable, put in plain words *or* English, *Inf.* spell out; vulgarize, coarsen, bring down, prostitute.

2. generalize, universalize, broadcast, spread, make available to all, produce in quantity; give currency to.

populate, *v.* **1.** inhabit, reside in, dwell in, live in, *Archaic.* bide, tenant, stay, stay at; domicile, domiciliate, take up residence, occupy, settle down, locate, *Inf.* hang up one's hat.

2. people, *Obs.* empeople, denizen, colonize, settle, settle in; take *or* strike root, plant oneself, anchor, moor.

population, *n.* habitancy, body of inhabitants, populace, inhabitants, residents, citizens, citizenry; people, folk, commonalty; census, *Inf.* head-count; population profile, demography, statistics.

populous, *adj.* **1.** heavily populated; peopled, *Obs.* empeopled, settled, inhabited, occupied.

2. teeming, swarming, crawling, bristling, alive with, thick with; close, dense, solid, serried; jammed, packed, *Inf.* jam-packed, crammed, crowded.

porch, *n.* veranda, stoop; portico, gallery, galilee, vestibule, loggia; solarium, sun porch, sleeping porch.

pore[1], *v.* **1.** ponder, brood, dwell, muse, meditate, ruminate, *Inf.* chew the cud, dwell on; contemplate, consider, reflect, weigh, deliberate; think over, mull over, revolve in the mind, turn over in the mind.

2. gaze upon, view, inspect, survey, eye, look over; examine, scrutinize, take a close *or* careful look, take a long, hard look, *Brit. Inf.* vet.

3. study, peruse, con, go over; read, delve into, dig into, wade through; make a close study of, go over step by step, go deep into, examine thoroughly, examine point by point.

pore[2], *n.* orifice, opening, outlet.

pornographic, *adj.* obscene, prurient, salacious, indecent, lewd, smutty, *Sl.* raunchy; filthy, dirty, foul, vile, nasty, fulsome; offensive, off-color, blue; bawdy, ribald, vulgar, coarse, gross; (*all usu. in reference to books or films*) nudie, skin, porny *or* porno.

pornography, *n.* bawdry, ribaldry, indecency, obscenity; erotica; smut, filth, dirt, hard-core *or* soft-core pornography; pornographic literature, girlie books, sexploitation, *Sl.* leg art, *Sl.* cheesecake; blue movies, stag films, x-rated films, peep shows, skin flicks; *Sl.* nudie, *Sl.* porn *or* porno.

porous, *adj.* **1.** spongy, spongelike, absorbent, bibulous; sievelike, cribrose, cribriform; riddled, perforated, honeycombed, like Swiss cheese.

2. permeable, pervious, penetrable, passable.

port[1], *n.* harbor, haven, seaport; harborage, anchorage.

port[2], *n.* manner, demeanor, air, attitude, temperament; carriage, gait, bearing, posture, pose; comportment, behavior, conduct, deportment; front, mien, aspect; appearance, look, cast, presence.

portable, *adj.* **1.** movable, conveyable, transferable, transportable, transmittable, portative.

2. compact, small, bantam, pocket, pocket-sized, vest-pocket; handy, convenient, manageable.

portage, *n.* **1.** carriage, conveyance, cartage, haulage, porterage, waftage, waft; transport, transportation, transference; shipment, freight, freightage, truckage.

2. fee, toll, charge, charges, demand, fare, exaction; towage.

portal, *n.* entrance, entry, entryway, entrée, inlet, ingress; access, opening, adit; door, doorway, gate, gateway, wicket, postern, *Scot.* post; threshold, stile, turnstile.

portend, *v.* forebode, foretoken, foreshadow, foreshow, omen, augur, presage, presignify, preindicate, promise; warn, forewarn, warn in advance; foretell, forecast, predict, prophesy, prognosticate, vaticinate, *Obs.* auspicate, *Rare.* premonish.

portent, *n.* **1.** omen, sign, indication, token, foretoken, harbinger; premonition, preindication, forewarning, foreshadowing, handwriting on the wall; augury, prognostic, prognostication, prediction, prophesy, prefigurement.

2. (*all of an ominous nature*) import, importance, moment, significance, first order, first rank, weight, gravity; concern, *Archaic.* concernment, consideration, interest; urgency, exigency.

3. phenomenon, *Sl.* phenom, marvel, wonder; prodigy, miracle, sensation; sight, spectacle, eyeopener, *Sl.* stunner, *Sl.* mind-boggler, *Sl.* mind-blower, *Sl.* trip; rarity, nonpareil, nonesuch, one in a thousand, one of a kind, *Inf.* one for the books; marvelment, wonderment, *Inf.* gazingstock.

portentous, *adj.* **1.** momentous, fraught, charged, heavy, laden; serious, grave, weighty, consequential, significant; crucial, critical, climacteric, eventful, pivotal, decisive; major, landmark, considerable, vital, of vital interst, all-important, of the utmost importance, high-priority, earthshaking; important, of importance, of significance, of consequence, of weight, of moment, of concern, of interest, not to be overlooked, *Inf.* not to be sneezed at.

2. ominous, foreboding, bodeful, ill-boding, boding evil, ill-omened, of evil portent; inauspicious, unpropitious, unfavorable, unpromising, unfortunate, unlucky, ill-starred, ill-fated, star-crossed, doomed from the start; menacing, threatening, lowering, looming, dark, black, sinister, heavy, gloomy; bad, evil, malign, malignant.

3. phenomenal, extraordinary, out-of-the-ordinary, prodigious, remarkable, wondrous, marvelous; amazing, astounding, astonishing, miraculous, surpassing belief, fabulous, fantastic, *Sl.* far-out; indescribable, mind-boggling, *Sl.* mind-blowing, *Sl.* trippy; staggering, breath-taking, *Sl.* stunning.

porter¹, *n.* **1.** skycap, redcap, baggageman, retainer; carrier, conveyor, transporter, carter, bearer; cupbearer, shield bearer, stretcher-bearer, water-bearer, waterboy, caddie, busboy.

2. janitor, concierge, maintenance man, cleaning man, cleaning woman, sexton.

porter², *n.* doorkeeper, gatekeeper, doorman, portress; sentry, Cerberus, watchman, turnkey, jailer; ostiary, durwaun, receptionist.

portfolio, *n.* **1.** case, folder, folio.

2. account, scrips, investments, shares, debentures; stocks, bonds, stocks and bonds.

3. office, bureau, post, position, function, jurisdiction.

4. dossier, documents, papers, credentials.

porthole, *n.* opening, aperture, orifice; *Naut.* port, window, *Archit.* fenestra, deadlight; slot, peephole, keyhole, vent; squint, hagioscope; casement, embrasure, crenel, loophole, grill, lattice, wicket; bull's-eye, oxeye, *Fr. oeil-de-boeuf.*

portico, *n.* porch, veranda, stoop; gallery, galilee, vestibule, loggia.

portion, *n.* **1.** part, section, segment, division, proportion, majority, minority; piece, parcel, fragment, cantle, batch; sector, subdivision, detail, detachment; particle, scrap, morsel, bit, handful, cupful; slice, wedge, sliver, finger, rasher; cutting, sample, specimen, some; hunk, chunk, lump, stump, butt, corner; fraction, percentile, half, third, quarter, fifth, etc.

2. share, allotment, lot, dividend, quota, apportionment, assignment; commission, consignment, *Sl.* cut, *Sl.* whack; stake, stock, *Sl.* rake-off, percentage; measure, dose, amount, quantity, meed, modicum; pittance, dole, deal, stint; allowance, moiety, ration, *Sl.* chunk, *Sl.* slice of the pie.

3. plate, platter, serving, helping, help, course, dish; second helping, seconds, *Inf.* taste, ration.

4. dowry, dotation, *Civil Law.* dot, dower; inheritance, heritage, legacy, endowment; disposition, settlement, bequeathal, bequest, enfeoffment.

5. lot, fortune, fate, destiny, kismet, luck; cup, God's will, will of Heaven.

—*v.* **6.** distribute, disperse, allot, apportion, allocate, dole, deal, parcel; assign, consign, administer, mete, dispense; partition, quarter, break up, cut up, segment, sector, canton; divide, *Sl.* divvy up, halve, carve up, split.

7. endow, *Law.* devise, vest, invest, enfeoff; bequeath, leave, will to, pass on, hand down; bless with, favor with, grace with, give a dowry.

portly, *adj.* fat, corpulent, obese, plump, fatty; stout, stocky, well-built, large, ample, *Scot.* fodgel; strapping, burly, brawny, beefy, meaty, thickset; paunchy, potbellied, *Obs.* gorbellied, well-fed; squat, pursy, dumpy, lumpish; *Inf.* chunky, chubby, tubby, roly-poly, podgy, pudgy.

portrait, *n.* **1.** representation, likeness, facsimile, image, semblance; resemblance, depictment, illustration; simulacrum, icon, copy; painting, canvas, study; profile, cameo, silhouette, effigy, head, miniature; drawing, sketch, line drawing, pen and ink, caricature, cartoon; photograph, *Inf.* photo, snapshot, *Inf.* shot, *Inf.* candid, *Inf.* pin-up; close-up, *Inf.* still, tableau.

2. description, depiction, picturization, rendering, rendition; account, graphic account, report, detail; vignette, thumbnail sketch, characterization; narrative, relation, recounting, recreation, telling, retelling; reenactment, recital, recitation, *Inf.* rehash; story, tale, record, history, chronicle.

portraiture, *n.* **1.** representation, picturization, portrait-painting; painting, drawing, sketching, coloring, photography.

2. drawing, representation, delineation, figuration; depiction, rendition, rendering, characterization.

3. description, account, sketch, vignette. See **portrait** (*def.* **2**).

portray, *v.* **1.** represent, picture, paint, sketch, draw, cartoon, caricature, illustrate, *Archaic.* character; delineate, *Archaic.* limn, trace, figure, contour, rub; diagram, map, chart, draft, block out.

2. play, pose as, characterize, personify, assume, play or act the part of; reproduce, impersonate, personate, enact, *Inf.* take off.

3. describe, depict, figure, characterize, render; picture, paint a mental picture, paint in words, set forth, put in words; define, detail, outline, specify, elucidate, flesh out, fill in the details; recreate, revivify, evoke, bring to life; narrate, relate, recite, give an account of, recount, retell, tell, romance; record, chronicle.

portrayal, *n.* **1.** portraying, drawing, representation, figuration. See **portraiture** (*defs.* **1, 2**).

2. portrait, study, painting, sketch. See **portrait** (*defs.* **1, 2**).

pose[1], *v.* **1.** affect, attitudinize, act, play to, make a show of; assume, put on airs, *Sl.* put on the dog, profess; feign, pretend, fake, sham, go through the motions; bluff, deceive, dissemble, posture; show off, swank, be vain, talk big, boast.

2. model, sit, sit for, serve as a model *or* example.

3. place, arrange, put, position, locate; situate, seat, assign, allocate, dispose; set, lay, park, fix, establish, base; group, order, array, range, distribute; line up, align, file, space.

4. assert, propound, allege, postulate, predicate, posit; state, declare, say, pronounce; present, submit, broach, advance; aver, asseverate, affirm, avouch.

—n. **5.** posture, stance, set, position, stand; bearing, poise, presence, carriage, demeanor, port; mien, look, face, visage, countenance; cast, attitude, air.

6. affectation, pretense, airs, airs and graces, *Sl.* dog, mannerism, artifice; hypocrisy, crocodile tears, playacting; theatricality, histrionics, melodramatics; pretentiousness, artificiality, affectedness, tushery, magniloquence, preciosity, euphuism; ostentation, display, parade, pomp, pomposity, fanfaronade, exaggeration, *Inf.* front; foppery, peacockery, coxcombry, dandyism; modesty, mock modesty, prudery, sanctimony, demureness; quackery, charlatanism, humbug.

pose[2], *v.* baffle, stump, puzzle, confound, perplex, mystify; embarrass, nonplus, put out, bother, disconcert, discombobulate; confuse, dumfound, stagger; bewilder, muddle, addle the wits, *Inf.* flummox.

poser, *n.* **1.** model, sitter, subject, live model, nude model.

2. problem, question, vexed question, knotty point, knot, stickler, stumper; teaser, hard nut to crack, *Inf.* brainteaser, *Inf.* braintwister; dilemma, enigma, perplexity, intricacy; puzzle, riddle, riddle-me-ree, conundrum, mystery, Chinese puzzle.

3. affecter, actor, pretender, mannerist. See **poseur**.

poseur, *n.* affecter, poser, mannerist, attitudinizer, actor, posturer, performer, artist; hypocrite, flatterer, deceiver, bluffer, boaster; pretender, impostor, claimant, false claimant, empiric, masquerader; dandy, fop, coxcomb, peacock; quack, charlatan, mountebank, confidence man, *Sl.* con man, *Sl.* con artist.

posh, *adj.* luxurious, deluxe, luxury, sumptuous, elegant, custom, special; grand, gorgeous, opulent, rich, lavish, elaborate; ornate, baroque, gingerbread, rococo, flowery, showy, florid; *Sl.* classy, *Sl.* snazzy, *Sl.* ritzy, *Inf.* swank, *Inf.* swanky; ostentatious, decorative, pretentious, overdone, embellished.

posit, *v.* **1.** place, put, set, position, dispose. See **pose** (*def.* **3**).

2. postulate, assert, propound, predicate. See **pose** (*def.* **4**).

—n. **3.** assumption, postulate, predication; hypothesis, thesis, contention, assertion, allegation; conception, notion, thought, mind, belief, opinion.

position, *n.* **1.** location, situation, placement, disposition, arrangement, order, array, assignment, collocation; placing, emplacement, localization, positioning, deposition; localizing, pinpointing, centering; establishment, settling, settlement; fixation, lodgment, installation, investiture, insertion.

2. site, place, situation, spot, locality; seat, stand, emplacement, point, bearings, latitude and longitude; scene, *Law.* venue, *Latin.* locus, *Fr. lieu.*

3. state, situation, condition, status, mode; way, circumstance, light; lot, portion; predicament, plight, pinch, pass, *Sl.* hole, *Sl.* jam, *Sl.* fix, impasse, imbroglio.

4. upperhand, edge, odds, leverage; hold, whip hand, purchase, grasp; advantage, influence, primacy, sway; domination, dominion, mastery, supremacy, superiority.

5. status, standing, rank, step, rung, footing; degree, grade, gradation, class, caste; stage, level, ground, plane.

6. consequence, circumstance, condition, means; prominence, elevation, eminence, importance, distinction, estimation, esteem; repute, reputation, name, character, prestige, dignity, honor, izzat.

7. post, job, situation, function, office; duty, role, place, berth, billet, slot; appointment, assignment, commission, sinecure; occupation, livelihood, business.

8. posture, stance, pose, attitude, air; set, stand, bearing, poise, port, pressure; mien, face, cast.

9. stand, attitude, point of view, viewpoint, disposition, way of looking at things; bent, leaning, inclination, proclivity; angle, slant, respect, outlook; feeling, sentiment, way of thinking, opinion.

10. proposition, postulate, hypothesis, thesis; predication, contention, assertion, dictum; doctrine, principle, belief; conception, idea, estimation, notion, mind, thought.

—v. **11.** place, put, arrange, pose, set, dispose, form; order, distribute, array, organize; range, line up, align, file, space, put into shape; *Inf.* skidshoot, *Inf.* cantdog; size, group, marshal, collocate; center, localize, put one's finger on, hit, pinpoint.

12. locate, situate, establish, set, base, ensconce; settle, place, seat, assign, collocate; set down, lay down, park; consign, localize, post, station.

positive, *adj.* **1.** definite, categorical, unequivocal, precise; clear, sure, certain, sound; stipulated, expressed, stated.

2. incontrovertible, indisputable, incontestable, unquestionable; inappealable, undeniable, unanswerable; unmistakable, indubitable, unambiguous; conclusive, undisputed, unquestioned, unqualified; inescapable, irrefutable, irrefragable; reliable, unerring, authoritative.

3. emphatic, definitive, forceful; explicit, peremptory, decided, stressed; accented, underlined, underscored, italicized, in red letters; express, plain, evident, graphic.

4. confident, sure, assured, certain; secure, decided, fixed, undoubting, believing, credulous; questionless, convinced, satisfied, *Sl.* sold, persuaded.

5. overconfident, self-assured, *Inf.* cocksure, overbearing, overweening; dogmatic, pontifical, doctrinaire; arbitrary, dictatorial, despotic; opinionated, arrogant, assertive; imperious, unchangeable, obdurate, immovable; unfaltering, unwavering, determined.

6. absoute, real, veritable; actual, factual, de facto; genuine, true, authentic, *Sl.* for real; substantial, solid, touchable.

7. practical, pragmatical, matter-of-fact, realistic; utilitarian, serviceable, functional, operative; untheoretical, unspeculative.

8. optimistic, hopeful, promising, sunny, inspiriting, heartening; cheering, comforting, looking up, encouraging.

9. auspicious, favorable, propitious, promising; progressive, constructive, conducive; beneficial, contributory, salutary, profitable, good.

10. affirmative, affirmatory, assenting, assertory, agreeing, concurring; concordant, accordant, yes.

positively, *adv.* **1.** absolutely, with certainty, emphatically, categorically, unqualifiedly, dogmatically, confidently, surely; undeniably, incontrovertibly, unmistakably, unquestionably, undoubtedly, indubitably, decidedly, definitely; beyond question, beyond a doubt, beyond the shadow of a doubt.

2. really, in reality, actually, in actuality, in fact, de facto, truly, in truth, truthfully; indeed.

posse, *n.* posse comitatus, vigilantes, lynch mob, mob, throng, search party; squadron, platoon, detachment, squad; cohort, phalanx, contingent, party; constabulary, police, state police, highway patrol, troopers, mounted police, mounties.

possess, *v.* **1.** own, be the owner of, have *or* hold title to, hold, be the proud possessor of, count *or* number among one's possessions *or* belongings, *Scot.* aught; receive, acquire, gain, inherit, come into, come into possession of, win; obtain, get, secure, procure, take possession of, take.

2. have, be instilled *or* invested with, be gifted with, be born with; embody, contain, include, embrace, comprise, incorporate, take in; show, exhibit, display, demonstrate, evidence, manifest.

3. know, comprehend, understand, fathom, grasp, *Inf.* get through one's head, *Inf.* have the hang of, *Inf.* lay hold of, *Inf.* have it, *Inf.* get it, *Sl.* savvy; know inside out, know backward and forward, know backwards, know to the ground, know from A to Z, *Brit.* know from A to Zed; have memorized, have learned by heart, have stored, have in one's head, have at one's fingertips *or* at the tip of one's tongue; retain, remember, hold *or* keep *or* bear in mind.

4. *Often* **possess of** *or* **with** inform, apprise, advise, acquaint, familiarize, let [s.o.] know, notify, send word to, communicate [s.t.] to; brief, fill [s.o.] in, *Sl.* clue [s.o.] in, *Brit. Sl.* give [s.o.] the gen, *Sl.* background; enlighten, illuminate, make [s.o.] aware, *Sl.* give [s.o.] the low-down, *Sl.* give [s.o.] the inside story *or* dope, *Sl.* put [s.o.] wise; instruct, teach, school, inculcate, impart knowledge to; arm, forearm, forewarn, warn.

5. control, exercise control over, govern, be master of, (*of oneself*) keep under control; contain, hold in, constrain, restrain, keep in check, leash, curb, hold *or* keep back.

6. (*of an evil spirit or feeling*) engross, absorb, enwrap, consume, devour, preoccupy, obsess, take up all one's time, prey on one's mind; fascinate, entrance, put into a trance, captivate, hold one's attention; enchant, cast a spell over, charm, bedevil; bewitch, witch, ensorcell, voodoo, diabolize, demonize; occupy, dwell in, live in, inhabit, invade, haunt; take over, assume control, use, employ, put to work for oneself, take advantage of, abuse; dominate, rule, master, command, domineer, make [s.o.] into a slave, enslave, hold in bondage *or* thrall, enthrall, subject, hold captive *or* prisoner.

possessed, *adj.* **1.** driven, ridden, pushed, pressed, spurred, moved, forced, compelled, impelled, constrained; obsessed, preoccupied, monomaniacal, engrossed, absorbed, consumed, devoured, taken; fascinated, entranced, captivated, held, riveted; enchanted, under a spell, bewitched, witched, bedeviled, voodooed, demonized, haunted; occupied, inhabited, taken over; controlled, under the control of, dominated, ruled, commanded, under the command of, domineered; enslaved, held in bondage, held captive *or* prisoner, enthralled, subjected; used, abused, taken advantage of.

2. poised, self-possessed, in control of oneself, master of one's emotions, under control; comfortable *or* at ease with oneself, self-assured, self-confident, sure of oneself, confident, secure; calm, cool, composed, collected, at ease, *Inf.* together; steady, balanced, on an even keel, in equilibrium; unflappable, inexcitable, even-tempered, imperturbable.

3. **possessed of** possessing, possess, having, have. See **possess** (*defs.* **1, 2**).

possession, *n.* **1.** ownership, proprietorship, title, vested interest, possessorship, possessoriness, demesne, *Law.* domain, *Archaic.* aught; tenure, holding, hold, retention; occupancy, occupation, tenancy, residence, residency, inhabitance, inhabitation, habitation, habitancy, *Law.* commorancy; custody, keeping, care, guardianship, protection.

2. **possessions** belongings, holdings, effects, personal effects, chattels; paraphernalia, accouterments, appointments, appurtenances, appendages, accessories, trappings, *Inf.* things, *Sl.* stuff, *Sl.* junk; goods, movables, baggage, luggage, furniture; fixtures, machinery, inventories, stock, *Commerce.* good will; property, properties, estate, appanage, freehold, real property *or* estate, land, realm, *Law.* personalty, *Law.* choses; inheritance, legacy, heritge, patrimony, *Law.* hereditament, *Law.* reversion; dowry, dower, dot, *Law.* jointure; wealth, worth, all one's worldly goods, assets, resources, riches, fortune, money, capital, wherewithal, *Disparaging.* pelf.

possessive, *adj.* **1.** acquisitive, greedy, eager to own *or* have, covetous, desirous, envious, *Sl.* grabby; materialistic, possession-oriented, money-minded, capitalistic; hoarding, nonsharing, selfish, self-interested; stingy, niggardly, ungenerous, illiberal; petty, small, mean, little.

2. tenacious, holding, grasping, clinging; jealous, distrustful, mistrustful, suspicious; domineering, controlling, overprotective; insecure, anxious, threatened.

possibility, *n.* chance, prospect, potentiality, realm of possibility, conceivability, conceivableness; feasibility, workability, practicability; risk, hazard, gamble, off chance, outside chance, rare chance; good chance, favorable chance, odds-on chance, distinct possibility; probability, probableness, likelihood, likeliness, liability; good prospect, favorable prospect, well-grounded hope.

possible, *adj.* **1.** likely, probable, liable to be, with good odds, *Inf.* odds-on; potential, among the possibilities, *Inf.* in the running, promising, hopeful.

2. feasible, reasonable, practicable, workable; doable, performable, achievable, attainable, obtainable, within reach, affordable; realizable, procurable, compassable, accomplishable, completable.

3. conceivable, imaginable, thinkable, credible; admissible, supposable, picturable, visualizable; believable, tenable, knowable, understandable, comprehensible, apprehensible, perceivable, cognoscible.

possibly, *adv.* perhaps, maybe, mayhap, *Chiefly Dial.* mayhappen, *Literary.* perchance, *Archaic.* peradventure; haply, it may be, as the chance may be, as luck will have it, for all *or* aught one knows; if possible, if at all *or* humanly possible, God willing, if God will, *Latin. Deo volente*; wind and weather permitting, time and tide permitting, schedule permitting, in all likelihood, contingently.

post[1], *n.* **1.** shaft, pier, *Naut.* bollard, pole, pylon; picket, stake, pale, palisade, pile; prop, brace, stay, strut, shore; pillar, column, newel, stock, support, standard, stanchion, mullion, caryatid, atlas, telamon, *Archit.* columna caelata, upright, baluster, banister, leg.

—*v.* **2.** affix, tack up, hang up; placard, publicize, advertise, announce, broadcast, make known, publish, *Archaic.* divulgate, report; circulate, propagate, dis-

seminate; blaze abroad, noise abroad, trumpet, herald.
3. denounce, defame, stigmatize, brand, gibbet, asperse, cast aspersions on, malign, slander, vilify; blacklist, blackball, ostracize; disgrace, dishonor, denigrate, blacken.
4. register, record, chronicle, set down, note; enter, slate, book, enroll, list; catalogue, file.

post[2], *n.* **1.** assignment, mission, duty, chore, task, errand; appointment, situation, position, station, place, seat; office, incumbency; employment, living, job, work; calling, vocation, profession, line, métier, trade; function, role, part.
—*v.* **2.** assign, appoint, position, place, situate, put; establish, fix, settle, set; locate, camp, bivouac, house, bunk.

post[3], *n.* **1.** mailman, letter carrier, postman; messenger, runner, courier, *Brit.* express.
—*v.* **2.** hurry, hasten, lose no time, make haste; press on, push on, ride hard, canter, trot, gallop, lope, clap spurs to one's horse; shoot, tear, fly, outstrip the wind, wing one's way, take wing, take flight; scour, hustle, bustle, scamper, scuttle, trip, flit.

postdate, *v.* **1.** overdate, misdate, date after.
2. follow in time, come after, succeed.

poster, *n.* placard, bill, handbill, public notice, bulletin, *Fr. affiche*, broadside, broadsheet; circular, flier; billboard, sign, sticker, notice, advertisement; manifesto, bull.

posterior, *adj.* **1.** hind, hinder, hindmost, back, rear, rearward, backward, aftermost, tail; *Anat.* dorsal, *Anat.* caudal, *Zool.* tergal, *Bot.* abaxial, *Bot.* posticous.
2. later, following, succeeding, successive, sequent, after, consequent, subsequent, sequential; latter, second-mentioned; postprandial, after-dinner; proximate, next after, next.
—*n.* **3.** buttocks, rump, breech, *Fr. derrière*, seat, bottom, *Inf.* rear, *Inf.* behind, *Inf.* backside, *Inf.* tail; (*all of animals*) hindquarters, haunches, loins, croup. See **rump** (*defs.* **1, 2**).

posterity, *n.* **1.** future generations, succeeding generations.
2. progeny, offspring, offshoots, issue, seed; descendants, successors, heirs; children, family, brood, sons and daughters, flesh and blood.

postern, *n.* back door, rear door, rear portal, wicket, gate, gateway; private entrance, secret entry, trap door, hatchway.

posthaste, *adv.* quickly, speedily, hurriedly, hastily; promptly, instantly, straightway, *Sl.* pronto, in a wink, in an instant, double-quick, *Inf.* like greased lightning, like a shot, like a thunderbolt, *Sl.* like mad, *Sl.* like a bat out of hell; directly, at once, without delay, in less than no time, before one can say "Jack Robinson," before the ink is dry, *Sl.* P.D.Q., *Inf.* lickety-split; swiftly, rapidly, fast, full tilt, full pelt, hotfoot, at full blast, in high gear, as fast as one's legs can carry one; in seven-league boots, by leaps and bounds.

posthumous, *adj.* post-obit, *Latin. post obitum*, after-death, post-mortem.

postman, *n.* mailman, carrier, mail carrier, letter carrier, delivery man *or* boy; courier, messenger, runner, dispatcher, bearer; *Fr. facteur, It. postino.*

post-mortem, *adj.* **1.** posthumous, post-obit, subsequent to death, after-death.
2. later, next, subsequent, succeeding, following, ensuing, consequent, next-day.
—*n.* **3.** autopsy, necropsy, post-death examination; embalmment, preparation of burial.
4. review, retrospect, rehash, *Inf.* regurgitation; reconsideration, *Inf.* rerun, *Inf.* replay, survey; ex post facto analysis, next-day thinking, Monday-morning quarterbacking, parking-lot ideas.

postpone, *v.* **1.** defer, delay, suspend, table, shelve, *Sl.* put on the shelf, pigeonhole, prorogue; waive, dispense with, put aside for the time; hold off, hold up, lay over, refrain from further action, hold in abeyance, put in cold storage, put on ice, put on a back burner, hang fire, put in a holding pattern; procrastinate, wait, put off, temporize, dally, gain time, *Inf.* drag one's feet, *Inf.* footdrag; *Inf.* stall, stave off, *U.S.* filibuster.
2. adjourn, recess, discontinue, interrupt, intermit, break off; pause, break, breathe, *All Inf.* take a break, take a breath, take a breather, catch one's breath, take five; respite, stay, reprieve.
3. subordinate, place in order of importance, rank; subject, make secondary, make subservient, downgrade.

postponement, *n.* **1.** deferment, deferral, delay, putting off; tabling, shelving; suspension, interruption, adjournment, break, recess, prorogation; reprieve, stay, respite; abeyance, cessation, waiver, moratorium, wait, waiting period.
2. dilatory tactic, *Inf.* stall, *U.S.* filibuster, temporization, forestallment, avoidance, evasion.

postscript, *n.* P.S., afterthought, subscript; addition, supplement, addendum, appendix, codicil; postfix, suffix; appendage, attachment, tag.

postulate, *v.* **1.** assume, suppose, presuppose, presume, take for granted; posit, predicate, theorize, hypothesize, hypothecate, speculate; infer, gather, conjecture; guess, surmise, judge, deem, conclude, deduce.
2. ask, solicit, beg, plead, supplicate, beseech, pray for; entreat, impetrate, implore, adjure, obtest.
—*n.* **3.** axiom, self-evident truth, truth, truism; principle, rule, theorem; premise, antecedent, ground, foundation, fundamental, basis; assumption, supposal, supposition, presupposition, presumption, inference; conjecture, speculation, guesstimate, guess, rough guess, wild guess, blind guess, *Inf.* stab, *Inf.* shot, *Inf.* shot in the dark.
4. prerequisite, prerequirement, requirement; condition, necessary condition, imperative, need; stipulation, qualification, essential, necessary, necessity, desideratum.

posture, *n.* **1.** pose, stance, attitude, set, position, *Med.* decubitus; carriage, bearing, way of standing *or* walking; poise, presence, demeanor, body language; appearance, guise, aspect, cast; manner, mode, air, mien.
2. arrangement, position, location, station, footing, standing, place, post; bearings, drift, direction.
3. affectation, pretension, affectedness; unnaturalness, studiedness, artificiality, artificial manner; pose, posing, posturing; peacockery, strutting, airs, mannerisms, *Inf.* put-on ways, *Inf.* fancy ways.
4. attitude, feeling, mood; view, opinion, thought, idea; frame of mind, set, mind-set, mental state; view, outlook, orientation; tendency, inclination, leaning, bent, turn, twist, *Inf.* kink, bias, prejudice.
5. state of affairs, conditions, situation, status quo; pass, case, predicament, circumstances, things as they are.
—*v.* **6.** arrange, order, array, line, align; (*all of one's body*) contort, twist, bend, bend out of shape, warp, deform, distort.
7. attitudinize, pose, affect, show off, try to attract attention; mince, prink, strut, peacock; put on airs, assume airs, do for effect, make a show.

posy, *n.* bouquet, nosegay, bunch of flowers, blossoms, blooms, flowers, spray, flower arrangement,

Brit. Dial. boughpot; corsage, boutonniere, *Chiefly Brit.* buttonhole, flower; garland, wreath, festoon, chaplet.

pot, *n.* **1.** round deep container, receptacle, vessel; kettle, cauldron; pan, saucepan, *Chiefly Brit.* skillet; decanter, cruse, pitcher, ewer, bottle, carafe, demijohn, flask; jug, jar, crock, amphora; bowl, jorum, saucer, porringer, boat, tureen, flagon; urn, samovar; tankard, mug, cup, stein, toby, rummer, noggin, *Chiefly Scot.* tass, *Scot. and North Eng.* stoup, *Chiefly Brit.* panniken; goblet, glass, tumbler, beaker, *Literary.* chalice; alembic, *Metall.* retort, crucible, *Metall.* melting pot.

2. *Slang.* kitty, jackpot, bundle, bank, draw pile.

3. *Slang.* marijuana, dope, reefer; *All Sl.* joint, jay, jay bar, jay smoke, j..

potation, *n.* **1.** drink, intoxicant, alcoholic beverage; draft, quaff, bumper, libation, *Brit. Sl.* bevy; nip, spot, tot, jigger, *Inf.* finger or two.

2. drinking, imbibing, sipping, supping, *Archaic.* bibbing, *Inf.* swigging, *Inf.* wetting one's whistle; draining, washing down, tossing off; gulping, swallowing, *Sl.* guzzling, *Sl.* swilling.

potbellied, *adj.* paunchy, round-bellied, big-bellied, *Sl.* beerbellied, large-bellied, great-bellied, *Obs.* gorbellied, full-bellied, *Dial.* swagbellied, *Inf.* baywindowed, *Inf.* corporational, abdominous; obese, fat, corpulent, overweight, *Scot.* fodgel; chubby, tubby, pudgy, plump; round, rounded out, rotund, portly; fleshy, well-fed; bloated, distended, bulging.

potbelly, *n.* paunch, *Inf.* bay window, *Inf.* corporation, *Sl.* pot, *Sl.* beerbelly, *Sl.* spare tire, *Dial.* swagbelly; distended *or* protuberant belly, fat stomach.

potency, *n.* **1.** potentness, powerfulness, power, strength, force; energy, vigor, *Inf.* punch, *Inf.* kick, *Inf.* zip. See **power** (*defs.* **2, 3**).

2. power, authority, control, command, rule, mastery, domination, dominion, sovereignty; influence, *Inf.* clout, weight, sway, *Sl.* pull. See **power** (*def.* **4**).

3. efficacy, efficaciousness, effectiveness, forcibleness, forcibility, effectualness, effectuality, operativeness, operativity, efficiency.

4. potentiality, potential, capacity, capability, ability. See **power** (*def.* **1**).

5. power, potentate, ruler, sovereign, monarch, king, emperor. See **potentate**.

potent, *adj.* **1.** powerful, mighty, strong, *Literary.* puissant, *Archaic.* potential; forceful, *Sl.* packing a punch *or* wallop, vehement, intense, great, formidable, overwhelming, overpowering; impregnable, unassailable, invulnerable, unvulnerable, unconquerable, indomitable, unsubduable, invincible, unbeatable. See **powerful** (*defs.* **1, 2**).

2. cogent, persuasive, suasive, convincing; moving, rhetorical, eloquent, impressive, winning. See **powerful** (*def.* **4**).

3. effective, forcible, effectual, efficacious, operative, efficient.

4. influential, weighty, carrying a lot of weight, *Inf.* carrying clout; eminent, prestigious, recognized, important. See **powerful** (*def.* **5**).

potentate, *n.* **1.** sovereign, monarch, king, majesty, crowned head, dynast, prince, emperor, power, potent; lord, master, tyrant, dictator; president, premier, chief executive, head of state; superior, commander, commandant, general, chief, chieftain, captain; head, headman, *Inf.* boss, *Inf.* bossman, man-in-charge.

2. mogul, magnate, tycoon, *U.S.* baron; personage, dignitary, notable, official, *Inf.* V.I.P., *Inf.* bigwig, *Sl.* big shot, *Sl.* biggie, *Sl.* big gun, *Sl.* big wheel, *Fr. grand fromage*, *Sl.* fat cat, *Sl.* heavy, *Sl.* high-muck-a-muck; celebrity, *Sl.* celeb, luminary, somebody, name, *Inf.* big name.

potential, *adj.* **1.** possible, probable, prospective, likely, *Latin. in posse*; conceivable, imaginable, unrealized, undeveloped; latent, dormant, quiescent, abeyant, passive, inactive; covert, hidden, concealed, unapparent, undisclosed, implicit, unexpressed.

—*n.* **2.** capacity, capability, the stuff, *Inf.* what it takes, *U.S. Inf.* the goods; potentiality, potency, possibility; probability, prospect, likelihood, likeliness.

3. promise, hope, expectation; ability, aptitude, talent, gift, endowment.

potentiality, *n.* **1.** capableness, potency, likeliness; conceivableness, hopefulness, expectancy.

2. possibility, probability, conceivability, prospect, likelihood.

potentially, *adv.* possibly, probably, prospectively, likely; conceivably, imaginably, hopefully, expectantly, implicitly.

pother, *n.* **1.** commotion, turmoil, tumult, turbulence, storm, storm and stress, squall, tempest, hurlyburly; uproar, pandemonium, noise, hubbub, *Inf.* ruckus, rumpus; fracas, melee, hullaballoo, brouhaha, affray, brawl, broil, embroilment, imbroglio.

2. disorder, chaos, confusion, upheaval; disquiet, unrest, disturbance, distraction, excitement, furor, agitation, disruption, perturbation; bother, trouble, fuss, fuss and feathers, *Inf.* to-do, much ado about nothing, tempest in a teapot; fluster, *Inf.* foofaraw, *Inf.* stew, *Inf.* tizzy, *Inf.* dither, *Sl.* lather, *Sl.* flap, *Sl.* hoo-ha; flurry, ado, bustle, stir, activity, motion, movement.

—*v.* **3.** worry, bother, fret, trouble, plague; vex, irritate, annoy, pique, rile, gall, chafe, nettle, provoke; pester, disturb, hector, harass, harry, *Sl.* bug, get on [s.o.'s] nerves, *Sl.* drive [s.o.] up a wall; hound, dog, nag, pick on *or* at, get on [s.o.'s] back, *Inf.* give [s.o.] a hard time, *Sl.* jump *or* get on [s.o.'s] case, *Sl.* ride; torment, taunt, bedevil, tease, tweak, mock, make *or* poke fun of, heckle, *Inf.* needle.

potion, *n.* drink, beverage, quaff, draft, potation, libation, *Brit. Sl.* bevy; tonic, stimulant, *Pharm.* elixir; mixture, cóncoction, brew; philter, love potion.

potpourri, *n.* medley, olio, grab bag, *Inf.* mixed bag, combination, *Inf.* combo; mélange, pastiche, pasticcio, mosaic, collage, patchwork; mixture, blend, intermixture, admixture, compound, composite, conglomeration; olla-podrida, miscellany, miscellanea, omnium-gatherum, menagerie, motley, collection; mishmash, hodgepodge, *Brit.* hotchpotch, gallimaufry, farrago; hash, stew, goulash, salmagundi, *Fr. Cookery.* ragout, (*in China, India, etc.*) chow-chow, Chinese menu; jumble, scramble, tangle, mess.

pottery, *n.* ceramics, crockery, earthenware, stoneware, terra cotta, *Ceramics.* biscuit *or* bisque; porcelain, china, delft, Wedgewood *or* Wedgewood ware.

pouch, *n.* **1.** bag, sack, *Midland U.S. and Scot.* poke, *Southwestern U.S.* alforja, *Chiefly Scot.* pocket, *Obs.* budget; pack, packet, satchel, container, receptacle, reticule.

2. purse, (*in Scottish Highland costume*) sporran, change purse, money bag; pocketbook, handbag; grip, valise, carpetbag; ditty bag.

3. backpack, knapsack, kitbag, haversack, rucksack; gunnysack, gunny-bag, duffel bag.

4. saddle bag, sabretache; mail bag, mail pouch.

5. feed bag, nose bag; doggie bag.

6. paunch, belly, abdomen, stomach, *Inf.* tummy, gut, (*both of ruminating animals*) first stomach, rumen, *Scot. and North Eng.* wame, *Sl.* breadbasket; potbelly, *Inf.* bay window, *Inf.* corporation, *Sl.* pot,

Sl. beerbelly, *Sl.* spare tire, *Obs.* gorbelly; (*all of birds*) gizzard, crop, craw, maw, ingluvies, proventriculus.

7. cyst, *Both Anat., Zool.* sac, bursa; *All Bot.* sporangium, spore case, theca.

8. blister, bubble, bleb, bladder; *Anat.* saccule, sacculus, utricle; venter, ventricle; udder, teat, mammary gland; marsupium.

—*v.* **9.** put into, pocket, bag, enclose.

poultice, *n.* **1.** plaster, mustard plaster, cataplasm, sinapism, embrocation, fomentation; compress, dressing, application, pledget; bandage, bandaging.

—*v.* **2.** plaster, embrocate, foment, stupe, *Obs.* stive; bandage, dress [s.o.'s] wounds.

poultry, *n.* fowl, domestic fowl, barnyard fowl; chickens, turkeys, ducks, geese, guinea fowl.

pounce, *v.* **1.** swoop down, descend, fall upon, come down on *or* upon; drop down from the clouds, come out of nowhere, come out of the blue; surprise, take by surprise, catch *or* take unawares.

2. lunge at, leap at, spring upon, jump at; dash at, go at, have at, come at, make a move towards, make a grab at; pitch into, light into.

pound[1], *v.* **1.** beat, batter, pommel, pelt, lay on, *Sl.* paste, *Archaic.* belabor; cudgel, bludgeon, baste, bastinado, cane, club, hammer, fustigate; maul, manhandle, rough up, *Inf.* give it to, *Sl.* knock around *or* about, *Sl.* give [s.o.] the business, *Sl.* give [s.o.] the works, *Sl.* work [s.o.] over, *Sl.* let [s.o.] have it, *Sl.* lay into [s.o.].

2. pulverize, triturate, comminute, levigate, bray, grind *or* reduce to powder *or* dust; smash, mash, crush, smash *or* crush to bits, *Sl.* smash *or* crush into smithereens.

3. beat, throb, palpitate, pulse, go pitapat; drum, thrum, beat a tattoo.

—*n.* **4.** stroke, blow, bastinado, *Scot.* dunt, *Scot. and North Eng.* paik, punch, *Inf.* whomp, *Inf.* wallop, *U.S. Sl.* biff, *Sl.* bop; buffet, hit, strike, cuff, thwack, smack, *Inf.* whack, *Inf.* clout, *Sl.* conk, *Sl.* bash.

pound[2], *n.* **1.** pound avoirdupois, lb., lb. av.; pound troy, lb. t.

2. pound sterling, *Brit. Sl.* quid; pound Scots; Irish pound.

pound[3], *n.* **1.** kennel, doghouse, dog pound; confine, pen, yard, corral, kraal.

2. jail, lockup, *Inf.* clink, *U.S. Inf.* calaboose, *Brit. Inf.* bridewell; guardhouse, guardroom, *U.S.* brig; *All Sl.* can, cooler, coop, jug, hoosegow, boobyhatch, pokey, *Brit.* choky, *Brit.* quod.

pour, *v.* **1.** rain, rain hard, *Inf.* rain cats and dogs, *Inf.* rain buckets, *Inf.* rain pitchforks, *Inf.* come down in buckets, *Inf.* come down in sheets.

2. emit, let out, give vent to, discharge; expel, disgorge, spit out; open the sluices.

3. (*all in great numbers*) move, proceed, go, go forth; issue, issue forth, emerge, come forth, come out, sally, sally forth.

4. flow, stream, course, run; rush, gush, gush out, spout, spurt, spew out, jet, outpour, outflow; cascade, cataract.

—*n.* **5.** rainstorm, torrent, torrent of rain, downpour, downfall, *Scot.* brash, *Scot.* spate; flood, deluge, heavy rain, driving rain.

pout, *v.* **1.** sulk, mope, brood, make *or* pull a long face, hang the lip, look sullen, be out of sorts *or* humor; grimace, make a wry face; frown, scowl, glower, knit the brows, look black, look daggers.

—*n.* **2.** frown, scowl; grimace, wry face, *Archaic.* mow, *Fr. moue;* long face, hangdog look.

poverty, *n.* **1.** indigence, impoverishment, penury, impecuniousness, neediness, necessitousness; privation, destitution, pennilessness, hand-to-mouth existence; beggary, pauperism, mendicity; distress, difficulties, straits, narrow straits, straitened *or* narrow circumstances, reduced *or* embarrassed circumstances; starvation, hunger, bare cupboard, wolf at the door; poor house, poor farm; *Sl.* poor mouth.

2. lack, want, absence, default, dearth, paucity; stint, scarcity, short supply, shortage, insufficiency, inadequacy; depletion, exhaustion, emptiness, vacuity.

3. meagerness, scarceness, scantiness, scantness, exiguity, shortness; bareness, slightness, skimpiness, scrimpiness.

poverty-stricken, *adj.* indigent, impoverished, penurious. See indigent (*def.* **1**).

powder, *n.* **1.** dust, pounce, fine grains, loose particles, flour, meal, grain, farina, bran; sawdust, filings, grounds, crumbs; grit, soot, dirt.

2. gunpowder, ammunition, explosive, black powder, dynamite, cordite, *All Chem.* TNT, trinitrotoluene, trinitroluol, methyltrinitrobenzene, melinite, lyddite.

3. face powder, make-up, cosmetic; bath powder, dusting powder, talcum powder, talc, foot powder, baby powder, *Trademark.* Johnson's.

—*v.* **4.** granulate, pulverize, mortar, comminute, triturate, levigate, grind, crush, bray; mill, grate, scrape, kibble, stone, abrade, rub; mash, smash, pound, beat, *Sl.* smush.

5. dust, sprinkle, besprinkle, pounce, *Both Cookery.* dredge, flour, spray, shower, dot, fleck, hail, splash, spatter, speckle, dapple, mottle, sit, dabble, dribble; spread, strew, diffuse, bestrew, scatter, asperse, distribute, broadcast; top, cover, coat, screen, overlay, overspread, perfuse, suffuse.

6. disintegrate, crumble, shatter, fall apart, fall into pieces *or* bits; return to dust *or* ashes, dry rot, decay, rot.

powdery, *adj.* **1.** granulated, pulverulent, ground, fine; dusty, ashy, gritty, sandlike, sandy, arenose, arenaceous, sootlike, sooty; pulverized, crushed, mortared, comminuted, triturated, levigated, smashed, mashed, *Sl.* smushed; grated, stoned, milled, mealy, floury, granular, grainy, farinaceous, oatlike, branny, branlike, furfuraceous; flaky, flocculent, scaly, scurfy.

2. pulverizable, pulverable, frangible, breakable; crumbly, friable, loose; disintegrating, rotting, decayed, falling apart.

3. powdered, dusted, sprinkled, besprinkled, pounced, *Both Cookery.* dredged, floured; sprayed, showered, hailed, dotted, flecked, splashed, spattered, speckled, dappled, mottled, *Bot., Zool.* lentiginous; covered, topped, coated, screened, overspread.

power, *n.* **1.** ability, capacity, capability, potential, potentiality, the stuff, *Inf.* what it takes, *U.S. Inf.* the goods; intelligence, brains, *Sl.* smarts, mother wit, native ability, mind for; aptitude, talent, faculty, gift, genius, skill, flair, bent, turn, knack.

2. powerfulness, potency, potentness, strength, might, main, mightiness, brute force *or* strength, force, forcefulness, *Literary.* puissance, vehemence, intensity, formidableness, formidability, overwhelmingness, overpoweringness; impregnability, impregnableness, unassailableness, invulnerability, invulnerableness, unyieldingness, invincibility, invincibleness.

3. energy, vigor, vitality, *Inf.* pep, *Inf.* punch, *Inf.* kick, *Inf.* zip, *Sl.* pizzazz; fortitude, intestinal fortitude, inner strength, grit, *Sl.* guts, *Sl.* gutsiness, stamina, staying *or* sticking power, *Inf.* stick-to-it-iveness; red-bloodedness, full-bloodedness, doughtiness, lustiness, heartiness; activeness, athleticism, manliness, virility, vigorousness, robustness, haleness, fitness, able-bodiedness; sturdiness, stalwartness, ruggedness, toughness, steeliness; hardness, firmness, solidness, solidity, stoutness, thickness, soundness, staunchness, substantiality, substantialness; physical strength, thews, sinews, brawn, beef, muscle, physique, musculature, build, size, bigness; *Inf.* huskiness, *Inf.* heftiness, *Inf.* beefiness, burliness, brawniness, muscularity, sinewiness.

4. control, command, rule, mastery, domination, dominion, sovereignty; omnipotence, almightiness, unlimited power, unconditional authority, carte blanche; authoritativeness, authority, influence, *Inf.* clout, weight, sway, *Sl.* pull; ascendancy, political ascendancy, supremacy, primacy, predominance; superiority, stature, seniority, rank, importance, significance, consequence; eminence, preeminence, prominence, prestige, distinction, reputation.

5. potentate, sovereign, monarch, ruler, king, chief, lord, master. See **potentate.**

6. superpower, world power, world leader, powerful nation *or* state, leading *or* dominant country.

7. military force, military strength, army, navy, air force, marines.

8. *Often* **powers** deity, divinity, god, goddess; extraterrestrial *or* supernatural power.

9. horsepower, *Sl.* soup; energy, electricity, hydroelectric power, solar energy, water power, nuclear energy, thermodynamic energy.

10. energy, *Inf.* steam, force, momentum, impetus.

—*v.* **11.** supply with energy, energize, make [s.t.] run *or* go, run, make [s.t.] tick.

powerful, *adj.* **1.** potent, mighty, strong, *Literary.* puissant, *Archaic.* potential; forceful, vehement, intense, great, formidable, overwhelming, overpowering, *Sl.* packing a punch *or* wallop; impregnable, unassailable, unvulnerable, unconquerable, indomitable, unyielding, impenetrable, inviolable, inexpugnable; irresistible, almighty, omnipotent, all-powerful, incontestable, unbeatable, more than a match for; armed to the teeth, invincible, unsubduable.

2. sturdy, stalwart, rugged, tough, sinewy, steely; firm, solid, solid as a rock *or* oak, made of iron; stout, thick, sound, staunch, stanch, substantial; having the strength of ten, strong as a bull *or* horse *or* lion, sturdy as an ox, *Inf.* husky, big, *Inf.* hefty, *Inf.* beefy; able-bodied, well-set, well-knit, well-built, muscular, burly, brawny, musclebound; hale, hardy, robustious, robust, dynamic, dynamical, energetic, energetical, vigorous, virile, manly, athletic, active; hearty, lusty, strapping, doughty, full-blooded, red-blooded.

3. effective, forcible, effectual, efficacious, operative, efficient.

4. cogent, persuasive, suasive, convincing, believable; logical, rational, factual, valid, sound; moving, rhetorical, eloquent, impressive, winning; conclusive, decisive, definitive.

5. influential, weighty, carrying a lot of weight, *Inf.* carrying clout; eminent, prestigious, recognized, reputable, significant, important; ascendant, dominant, predominant, hegemonic, leading, prepotent, preeminent, supreme; dominating, authoritative, authoritarian, commanding, *Sl.* take-charge.

powerless, *adj.* **1.** impotent, impuissant, strengthless, harmless, ineffectual, ineffective, inefficacious, nugatory, null and void, inoperative; incompetent, inept, inapt, unfit, inefficient, inadequate, insufficient, incapable; useless, inutile, worthless, valueless, no good, vain, futile.

2. helpless, unable to do anything, dependent, unable to help oneself; weak, feeble, frail, infirm, *Pathol.* asthenic, *Rare.* imbecile; disabled, incapacitated, *Fr. hors de combat,* sidelined, debilitated, decrepit, invalid, crippled, lame, hobbled, paralyzed, paralytic, *Pathol.* paraplegic; enervated, devitalized, enfeebled, effete, sapless, emasculated, faint, washed-out, *Sl.* wasted, *Pathol.* adynamic; exhausted, spent, worn-out, all in, done in *or* for, laid up, flat on one's back, prostrate.

3. defenseless, unarmed, weaponless; unguarded, unprotected, unfortified, open to attack, wide open, exposed, naked, uncovered; vulnerable, pregnable, penetrable, invadable, attackable, assaultable, expugnable, vincible, conquerable; insecure, unsafe, dangerous, perilous, precarious; assailable, without defense, resourceless, with nowhere to turn; without recourse, over a barrel, on the ropes.

powwow, *n.* **1.** (*among North American Indians*) ceremony, ceremonial, rite, ritual, formality, service; celebration, festival, fete, carnival, feast; party, festivity, dance, happening, extravaganza, *Inf.* shindig, *Sl.* wing-ding.

2. conference, parley, *Archaic.* parle, palaver, consultation, huddle, tête-à-tête, *Sl.* rap *or* rap session; dialogue, interchange, discourse, discussion, talk; colloquy, colloquium, forum, round table; meeting, summit, congress, caucus, council, conclave, assembly, parliament; deliberation, negotiation.

—*v.* **3.** confer, hold a conference, parley, palaver, consult, *Inf.* put heads together, *Inf.* huddle, *Inf.* go into a huddle; discuss, talk over, exchange views, compare notes, have a dialogue *or* interchange; deliberate, negotiate, *Inf.* talk turkey; convene, meet, caucus, sit down together.

pox, *n.* **1.** *Pathology.* smallpox, *Pathol.* variola; chicken pox, *Pathol.* varicella.

2. *Informal.* venereal disease, VD, social disease, *Sl.* Cupid's itch; syphilis, *Inf.* syph, French pox.

practicability, *n.* **1.** feasibility, possibility, workability, attainability, doability, achievability.

2. usefulness, practicality, efficaciousness, effectiveness; use, handiness, value, advantageousness, advantage, expediency.

practicable, *adj.* **1.** feasible, possible, within the realm of possibility, within one's powers; workable, doable, accomplishable, performable, achievable, attainable, effectible; likely, suitable.

2. useful, utilitarian, banausic. See **practical** (*def.* **2**).

practical, *adj.* **1.** commonplace, matter-of-fact, *Sl.* nuts-and-bolts, workaday, everyday, day-to-day; mundane, ordinary, customary, usual, undistinguished.

2. utilitarian, useful, *Obs.* utile, banausic; pragmatic, applicatory, efficient, workable, serviceable; efficacious, effective, working; handy, profitable, worthwhile, valuable, advantageous.

3. experienced, knowing, versed, practiced, skilled, trained; proficient, qualified, competent, capable, able, skillful.

4. sensible, down-to-earth, realistic, wise, sagacious; businesslike, all-business, hard-nosed, hard-headed, tough, unsentimental, unromantic; judicious, prudent, politic, expedient, shrewd, canny, sharp, astute, clever; cunning, crafty, subtle.

5. humdrum, prosaic, dull, vapid, flat, insipid, unanimated; tedious, tiresome, boring, uninteresting; banal, trite, hackneyed, platitudinous, bromidic.

practically, *adv.* **1.** virtually, in effect, substantially, morally, for all intents and purposes; actually, essentially, fundamentally, basically.

2. realistically, matter-of-factly, clearly, unsentimentally; sensibly, with common sense, prudently, judiciously; getting down to business, getting down to brass tacks, to the point, pointedly; simply, with no frills, ordinarily.

3. almost, *Inf.* most, nearly, very nearly, all but, well-nigh, nigh, close to, tantamount to; about, just about, not quite.

practice, *n.* **1.** habit, custom, consuetude, wont; manner of operating, *Latin. modus operandi, Inf.* M.O., common practice, usual run of things, general *or* usual procedure; rule, routine, convention, the way it is, the way it's done, the way it's done around here; method, system, procedure, way, manner, observance, use, usage, mode, fashion; bent, inclination, disposition, penchant.

2. exercise, drill, training, preparation, study, discipline, application; workout, warm-up, run-through, rehearsal, try-out.

3. action, performance, doings; deed, act, accomplishment, achievement, work, move.

4. (*of a profession*) pursuit, conduct; business, trade, patronage, clientele.

—*v.* **5.** do as a rule, follow *or* observe habitually *or* customarily; be wont to, be accustomed to, accustom oneself to; be habituated to, be wound up in, be addicted to, be hooked on; get in rut *or* groove.

6. train, drill, exercise, study; prepare, try and try again, repeat, try out, go over and over; work out, warm up, run through, go through, rehearse, *Inf.* lick into shape, *Music.* noodle.

practiced, *adj.* **1.** experienced, versed, skilled, skillful; knowledgeable, practical, seasoned, prepared, primed, ready; expert, masterful, masterly, *Sl.* crackerjack, crack, cracking good; proficient, able, capable, competent, adept, deft, good at, dexterous; accomplished, qualified, talented, gifted; adroit, ingenious, clever; consummate, excellent, superior, superb, perfect.

2. cultivated, finished, developed, perfected; schooled, trained, educated.

pragmatic, *adj.* **1.** practical, utilitarian, practicable, efficient, effective; matter-of-fact, sensible, down-to-earth, realistic, wise; businesslike, hard-nosed, hard-headed, unsentimental, unromantic; concrete, non-abstract, basic, fundamental.

2. busy, busy as a bee, busy as a one-armed paperhanger, hard-working, occupied, industrious; diligent, assiduous, persistent; active, energetic, on the move, alert, alive, animated, vigorous.

3. officious, meddlesome, meddling, *Sl.* cochleffel, interfering, intrusive; obtrusive, *Inf.* nosy, *Inf.* pushy, forward, bold.

4. dogmatic, doctrinaire, positive, opinionated; arbitrary, dictatorial, authoritarian; partisan, one-sided, narrow-minded, prejudiced; assertive, self-assured, sure of oneself, self-confident.

prairie, *n.* grassland, pasture, campo, veld, veldt; savanna, steppe, The Steppes, pampas, llano; meadow, *Archaic.* mead, meadowland, lea, downs; heath, moor, moorland, wold, plains, tundra; open country, champaign, campagna.

praise, *n.* **1.** extolment, laudation, acclaim, acclamation, kudos, *Archaic.* magnification; approval, approbation, endorsement, reference, sanction, commendation; tribute, testimonial, credit, recognition, citation; eulogy, eulogium, eulogization, encomium, panegyric; congratulation, *Archaic.* gratulation, compliment, flattery, puffery, bouquet; recommendation, good word, glowing terms, honeyed words; applause, cheering, clapping, plaudits, salvo, accolade.

2. exaltation, glorification, honor, crown; homage, devotion, worship, reverence, veneration, adulation; thanksgiving, gratitude; blessing, *Eccles.* benediction, *Archaic.* benison; esteem, admiration, appreciation, respect; hosanna, huzzah, hurrah; Te Deum, Gloria in Excelsis Deo, Gloria, *Latin.* laus Deo, alleluia; celebration, doxology, paean, hymn, song of praise, canticle, psalm, chant, plainsong.

3. glory, honor, dignity; fame, renown, distinction, popularity, popular favor, vogue; celebrity, eminence, prestige, notability.

—*v.* **4.** laud, extol, cry up, *Inf.* crack up, boost, *Archaic.* magnify, emblazon; encore, root for; approve enthusiastically, hail, commend, endorse, back, sanction; approbate, preconize; recommend, promote, say a good word for, put in a good word for, stand up for, *Inf.* stick up for, uphold; acclaim, cheer, celebrate, congratulate, *Archaic.* gratulate; applaud, clap; compliment, flatter, *Inf.* pat on the back, hand it to [s.o.], give [s.o.] credit; puff, swell, lionize, belaud, make much of.

5. glorify, give glory to, dignify, ennoble, enthrone, canonize; eulogize, panegyrize; honor, adore, worship, crown, bless; pay tribute to, pay homage to; reverence, venerate, revere, consecrate, sanctify, hallow; deify, apotheosize, idolize, idolatrize; give thanks, say grace; appreciate, value, esteem, respect, admire, look up to, think highly of, set *or* lay store by; bow down before, salaam; hymn, chant, celebrate in song.

praiser, *n.* lauder, laudator, encomiast, eulogizer, eulogist, panegyrist, adulator, trumpeter; extoller, exalter, celebrator, glorifier; applauder, claquer; complimenter, saluter, flatterer, booster, puffer.

praiseworthy, *adj.* laudable, commendable, *Brit. Dial.* gradely, meritorious, estimable, admirable; reputable, creditable, deserving, worthy; sterling, exemplary, excellent, good, noble; honorable, virtuous, righteous, upright, just, right-minded, principled; unimpeachable, irreproachable, blameless.

prance, *v.* cavort, caper, frolic, frisk, romp, gambol; skip, hop, dance about; leap, jump, spring, bounce, bound; vault, gambado, *Dressage.* curvet; hop, bob, trip, whirl, turn, caracole; strut, swagger, parade, peacock.

prank[1], *n.* trick, caper, stunt, *Scot.* brogue; mischief, practical joke, *Fr. boutade*, spoof; antics, *Inf.* shenanigans, tomfoolery, *Sl.* monkeyshines, buffoonery, gambado, frolic, *Inf.* dido, horseplay; fun, sport, jest, game, play; escapade, lark, spree, reckless *or* wild *or* madcap adventure; romp, gambol, skylarking.

prank[2], *v.* bedeck, deck out, bedaub, bedizen, overdecorate, decorate gaudily *or* excessively; dress ostentatiously, *Inf.* dress up, trick out, *Inf.* fig out, deck out, prink, *Archaic.* bedight; adorn, *Archaic.* dight, embellish, preen, spruce up, gild, bespangle, spangle.

prankish, *adj.* **1.** mischievous, full of mischief, impish, waggish, elfish, puckish, pixilated, *Inf.* full of the devil; naughty, roguish, scampish, arch, *Scot.* hempy; annoying, vexatious, exasperating, teasing.

2. playful, sportive, frolicsome, gamesome, full of fun, fun-loving; high-spirited, frisky, coltish, skittish, *Inf.* feeling one's oats; lively, jocose, mirthful, gleeful, rollicking.

prate, *v.* **1.** palaver, blab, bleat, *Inf.* gab; gush, *Inf.* spout, *Sl.* run off *or* on at the mouth; gossip, buzz, tell tales, repeat everything one hears; be loquacious *or* talkative, ramble, maunder.

2. babble, twaddle, *Brit.* twattle, blather, drivel; talk nonsense, *Inf.* talk through one's hat; jabber, gibber, *Sl.* gibber-jabber, jargon; chatter, chipper, prattle, cackle; chitchat, chitter-chatter, chaffer, bandy words; talk idly, *Sl.* shoot the breeze, *Sl.* gas, *Sl.* bull.

—*n.* **3.** palaver, palaverment, blabbing, bleating,

Inf. gabbing; gushing, *Inf.* spouting, *Sl.* running off *or* on at the mouth; gossiping, buzzing, repeating everything one hears; loquacity, talkativeness, rambling, maundering.

4. babble, babbling, babblement, prattle, prattling; gibber, gibbering, gibberish, jabber, jabbering, Jabberwocky, *Sl.* gibber-jabbering; chatter, chattering, cackle, cackling; twaddle, twaddling, *Brit.* twattle, *Brit.* twattling; blather, blathering, drivel, driveling; nonsense, moonshine, *Fr. bavardage*, gobbledegook, hocus-pocus, mumbo jumbo, abracadabra; humbug, flummery, *Sl.* bunk, rubbish, tommyrot, *Inf.* rot, *Sl.* garbage, *Sl.* horsefeathers; balderdash, hogwash, stuff and nonsense, *Inf.* bosh, *Brit. Sl.* tosh, fudge, foolishness, rigmarole *or* rigamarole; poppycock, *Inf.* fiddle-faddle, *Inf.* piffle, *Inf.* kibosh, *Inf.* flapdoodle; small talk, *Anglo-Indian* bukh, chitchat, chitchatting, chitter-chatter, chitter-chattering; gossip, *Inf.* scuttlebutt, buzz, idle talk, *Inf.* gab, *Sl.* bull; palaver, claptrap, *Sl.* hot air, *Sl.* gas.

prattle, *v.* **1.** chatter, jabber, cackle, gibber, *Sl.* gibber-jabber, jargon; babble, prate, tattle, twaddle, *Brit.* twattle; patter, gabble, blather, drivel. See **prate** (*defs.* **1, 2**).

—*n.* **2.** chatter, chattering, cackle, cackling, gibber, gibbering; babble, babbling, babblement, *Fr. bavardage*, blather, blathering; twaddle, twaddling, *Both Brit.* twattle, twattling, drivel, driveling; prate, prating, tattle, tattling, excessive talk; jabber, jabbering, Jabberwocky, gabble, gabbling, patter, pattering; blab, blabbling, gossip, buzzing, *Inf.* gab, gushing, *Inf.* spouting, *Sl.* running off *or* on at the mouth; rambling, maundering; small talk, *Anglo-Indian.* bukh.

3. murmur, murmuring, murmuration; whisper, whispering, buzz, buzzing; hum, humming, drone, droning, purr, purring; purl, purling, sough, soughing, rustle, rustling.

prattler, *n.* babbler, prater, twaddler, *Brit.* twattler, driveler; patterer, patterist, rattlebrain, rattlepate; chatterbox, noisy chatterer, palaverer, magpie, popinjay, *Inf.* jay; excessive talker, jabberer, gabbler, blatherskite, *Sl.* windbag, *Sl.* windjammer, *Inf.* hot-air artist; blabber, blabbermouth, gusher, gossip; tattler, tattletale, telltale, talebearer.

pray, *v.* **1.** appeal to, call on *or* upon, invoke, cry to, *Rhet.* apostrophize; plead, clamor for, cry for, beg for, request; supplicate, beseech, entreat, implore, sue, solicit, obsecrate, impetrate; importune, entreat, adjure, obtest, throw oneself at the feet of; urge, press, besiege.

2. offer a prayer, say one's prayers; commune with God, meditate, contemplate; recite the rosary, *Sl.* beat the beads.

prayer, *n.* **1.** invocation, entreaty, adjuration, impetration, imploration, imploringness, solicitation, soliciting; request, praying, orison, plea, pleading, intercession; supplication, beseechment, beseeching, obtestation, obsecration; petition, petitioning, suit, appeal; calling upon, summoning, summons.

2. doxology, praise, adoration, glorification, magnification, thanksgiving.

prayer book, *n.* Book of Common Prayer, service book, *Eastern Ch.* euchologion *or* euchology, missal, mass book; formulary, ordinal, lectionary, pontifical; breviary, office book; litany, beadroll; Gospel book, evangelistary, evangeliary.

prayerful, *adj.* devout, devoted, pious, God-fearing, God-loving, religious, spiritual; godly, saintly, holy, humble; worshipful, devotional, reverent, reverential, venerative; angelic, seraphic, heavenly-minded; moral, virtuous, righteous, good, right-minded, clean-minded, clean of mind, clean of spirit; pure-spirited, pure in spirit, pure in heart.

preach, *v.* **1.** sermonize, homilize, evangelize, predicate, pulpit; spread the Word, spread the Gospel, propagate, disseminate; (*usu. disparaging*) preachify, *Scot. and North Eng.* sough.

2. proclaim, profess, make known, promulgate, hold forth, expound, pronounce, declare.

3. advocate, press, urge, exhort; discourse, prelect; indoctrinate, inculcate, imbue, instill, catechize.

4. advise, counsel, enlighten; lecture, moralize, admonish, reprimand, chastise.

preacher, *n.* **1.** evangelist, minister of the Gospel, homilist, sermonizer, sermonist, *Obs. Rare.* sermoneer, predicant, *Rare.* predicator; catechist, missionary, spreader of the Word; *Sometimes Disparaging.* revivalist; *All Usu. Disparaging.* pulpiteer, pulpitarian, pulpit drone, pulpit-thumper, gospel-monger.

2. ecclesiastic, churchman, clergyman, cleric, clerk, reverend, priest, minister, rabbi, parson, divine; pastor, shepherd, dean, rector, vicar, canon, prebendary, curate, chaplain, *U.S. Mil. Sl.* sky pilot.

3. liturgiologist, liturgist, ritualist.

4. exhorter, discourser, lecturer, moralizer, prelector.

preaching, *n.* **1.** sermon, homily, *Obs.* predication; lesson, explanation, interpretation, exegesis; discourse, disquisition, exhortation, prelection; epistle, treatise, pastoral, encyclical; homilectics.

2. sermonizing, pulpitry, religious harangue, moralizing, preachment.

3. evangelization, evangelism, propagation, promulgation, dissemination, indoctrination, inculcation.

preamble, *v.* opening statement *or* remarks, opening, beginning, exordium; introduction, proem, preface, prelude, prelusion, prologue, forward, prolegomenon; front matter, prolegomena, *Print.* preliminaries.

precarious, *adj.* **1.** uncertain, unsure, unpredictable, erratic, fickle, capricious, changeable; unsafe, unsound, unstable, unsecure, infirm, unsteady, shaky, rickety, tottery; touch-and-go, trembling in the balance, hanging by a thread.

2. doubtful, dubious, unconvincing, questionable, problematical, open to doubt *or* suspicion; suspicious, suspect, in doubt, in question, in dispute; debatable, disputable, arguable, contestable, controvertible, controversial, moot; unreliable, undependable, not to be relied *or* depended on, untrustworthy, treacherous.

3. dangerous, full of danger, fraught with danger, perilous, *Sl.* hairy, *Archaic.* parlous; hazardous, risky, riskful, full of risk, chancy, *Brit. Inf.* dicy; ticklish, tricky, delicate, *Dial.* kittle; on thin ice, on slippery ground, walking a tightrope; exposed, open, vulnerable.

4. groundless, ungrounded, baseless, without basis, unfounded, ill-founded, without foundation, unsupported; unsupportable, untenable; unwarranted, uncalled-for, idle, vain, empty.

precatory, *adj.* supplicatory, suppliant, petitionary; prayerful, imploring, beseeching, pleading, appealing; imprecatory, obtestatory, invocatory, adjuratory, rogatory; mendicant, begging, on bended knee *or* knees, on one's knees, prone, prostrate.

precaution, *n.* **1.** advance measure *or* step, preventative measure, pains; safeguard, safety valve; insurance, ace in the hole; escape, out, way out.

2. foresight, foresightedness, farsightedness, longsightedness, prevision; providence, prudence, discretion, sagacity; provision, anticipation, readiness, preparation, forethought, forethoughtedness; circumspection, caution, care, solicitude; cautiousness, carefulness, heedfulness, mindfulness; attention, attentiveness, watchfulness, alertness, vigilance; chariness, wariness, leeriness, apprehension, suspiciousness, *Inf.* caginess.

—*v.* **3.** forewarn, prewarn, *Rare.* premonish; alert, warn, give fair warning, put on guard, put on the qui vive, *Sl.* give the high sign to; caution, admonish, advise, say a word to the wise; clue in, tip off, *Inf.* put a bug in [s.o.'s] ear.

precautionary, *adj.* provident, prudent, wise, sagacious; provisional, preventative; careful, cautious, precautious, circumspect, heedful, mindful; foresighted, foreseeing, forethoughtful, forehanded; premonitory, forewarning.

precede, *v.* **1.** antecede, come *or* go before, come first, go ahead of, go in advance; lead, lead the way, head, *Inf.* head up, front; predate, antedate; presage, anticipate; usher in, herald, introduce.

2. preface, prefix, prelude, premise, prologize.

precedence, *n.* **1.** rank, seniority; preeminence, superiority, supremacy, primacy, transcendence, ascendancy, predominance; preference, priority, urgency, importance; prerogative, privilege, right, right-of-way.

2. precession, anteposition, front position, the lead.

3. antecedence, anteriority, preexistence, previousness, earliness.

precedent[1], *n.* prior instance, previous case; model, pattern, criterion, rule, measure, yardstick, barometer; type, archetype, prototype, paradigm, classic example; lead, example, exemplar.

precedent[2], *adj.* preceding. See **preceding.**

preceding, *adj.* antecedent, precedent, previous, prevenient, preliminary, forerunning, foregoing; prior, earlier, former, preexistent; aforesaid, aforementioned, above-mentioned, above-named, above-stated, stated above; anterior, advanced, forward, placed in advance *or* at the front *or* forward, ranged at the front, set in the van *or* vanguard.

precept, *n.* **1.** canon, rubric, guideline, working principle, guiding principle; unwritten law, common law, lex non scripta; ethical code, code of honor, corpus juris, code; ordinance, decree, edict, *Law.* writ, rescript, assize; dictate, dictum, order, command, injunction, fiat, sanction, prescription, mandate, firman; commandment, behest, bidding, dictation; word, word of command, direct order, *Inf.* the word; charge, commission, directive, direction, instruction; ruling, proclamation, pronouncement, declaration, ukase, bull; law, regulation, rule; control, prohibition, ban, restriction, caveat.

2. motto, moral, byword, lesson, convention; maxim, aphorism, proverb, apothegm, gnome, mot, adage; saw, pithy statement, sententious saying, saying; axiom, prescript, epigram; cliché, hackneyed phrase, platitude, truism, *Inf.* bromide, commonplace.

preceptor, *n.* instructor, teacher, tutor; educator, pedagogue, *Educ.* methodologist; schoolteacher, schoolmaster, professor; schoolman, scholastic, academician; mentor, counselor, advisor, explainer, expositor, interpreter.

precinct, *n.* **1.** district, ward, voting district; division, section, hundred; constituency, prefecture, arrondissement, bailiwick, department, ward; *U.S.* borough, province, state, canton, county, shire; city, town, community, commune; parish, diocese.

2. region, area, sphere; zone, pale, demesne, territory; locale, parts, locality, *Inf.* neck of the woods, *Inf.* stamping grounds.

3. *Usu.* **precincts** environs, surrounding area, surroundings, milieu, habitat, *Fr. mise en scène.*

4. compound, court, courtyard, quadrangle, *Inf.* quad; square, enclosure, ring; camp, concentration camp, P.O.W. camp, prison camp, prison yard, prison.

preciosity, *n.* (*all of language, style, or taste*) over-refinement, excessive refinement, fastidiousness, finickiness; preciousness, meticulosity, meticulousness; *Sl.* cutesiness, daintiness, effeminacy, effeteness; primness, prudishness, prudery, *Inf.* tightness; overniceness, floweriness, pretension, pretentiousness; affectedness, affectation, unnaturalness, studiedness, artificiality, conceit.

precious, *adj.* **1.** valuable, costly, high-priced, of high price; expensive, rich, sumptuous, beyond price, priceless; premium, fine, superfine, exquisite, dainty; rare, select, elite, superior, superlative, supreme, prize; extraordinary, special, uncommon, scarce.

2. estimable, highly esteemed, time-honored, venerable, worshipped; admirable, commendable, worthy of respect; revered, venerated, idolized; held dear, guarded, kept, *Inf.* keepsake, preserved, memorable, nurtured, *Inf.* hugged to one's bosom; dear, beloved, cherished, darling; valued, prized, favorite, favored, pet.

3. flagrant, gross, blatant, arrant, sheer, perfect; utter, downright, consummate, complete, pure, unadulterated; unqualified, clear, unquestioned; absolute, positive, utmost, unequivocal, unconditional; thundering, full-scale, glaring, screaming.

4. *Informal.* beautiful, wonderful, great; terrific, perfect, handsome, pretty.

5. (*of style, manner, etc.*) overrefined, overwrought, *Sl.* cutesy, *Brit. Sl.* twee; overnice, flowery, pretentious, affected, unnatural, studied, artificial; finicky, meticulous, dainty, effeminate, effete, prim, prudish, *Inf.* tight, *Inf.* uptight.

6. important, irreplaceable, irretrievable; necessary, requisite, required, essential; wanted, needed, in demand, vital, indispensable.

—*n.* **7.** darling, dearly beloved, sweetheart, lover, mistress; *Inf.* heart's desire, truelove, ladylove; sweet, honey, jewel, favorite, apple of one's eye.

—*adv.* **8.** *Informal.* extremely, very, exceptionally, extraordinarily, unusually, uncommonly, abnormally; remarkably, notably, damned, danged, *U.S. Inf.* darned, *Sl.* hell of a, exceedingly, excessively, inordinately, disproportionately.

precipice, *n.* cliff, bluff, crag, steep, *Chiefly Scot.* linn; incline, rocky eminence, palisades, palisado, scarp, escarpment, rocky headland, tor; promontory, ridge, edge of a canyon *or* crevasse.

precipitancy, *n.* **1.** swiftness, fleetness, speed, quickness; dispatch, rapidity, hurriedness, expedition, expeditiousness; velocity, acceleration, celerity; instantaneousness, immediateness, urgency, promptness, promptitude; briskness, abruptness, smartness, suddenness.

2. hurry, rush, hustle, bustle, dash, scurry, scramble, helter-skelter, hurry-scurry, pell-mell, *Archaic.* harum-scarum; hastiness, impetuosity, rashness, recklessness, foolhardiness; prematurity, untimeliness, precocity, inopportuneness, inopportunity, inexpedience; impulsiveness, unrestraint, carelessness, heedlessness, thoughtfulness, imprudence, incautiousness; folly, gamble, leap in the dark, bungle, blunder, plunge, blind bargain; audacity, temerity, overconfidence, presumption.

precipitate, *v.* **1.** accelerate, quicken, push forward, advance, hasten; stimulate, arouse, trigger, rouse, animate, vivify, bestir; instigate, motivate, inspire, exhort, excite, provoke, incite; press, prod, shove, jog, move, drive on, urge on, egg on, hound on, goad, whip, flog, prick; boost, prompt, thrust, impel, give an impetus to; hurry on, dispatch, expedite, facilitate; aid, assist, help.

2. throw, hurl headlong, cast headlong, fling; heave, project, jaculate, propel; chuck, pitch, shy; discharge, shoot, launch, let fly, send forth.

3. snow, rain, drizzle, sleet, pour, *Chiefly Dial.* mizzle, mist.

—adj. **4.** headlong, hurried, rushed, hasty; rapid, meteoric, quick, expeditious, speedy, swift, fleet; pressing, pushing, urgent.

5. abrupt, sudden, unexpected, at the spur of the moment, without warning, unannounced, unforeseen, unanticipated; prompt, instant, instantaneous, immediate.

6. unduly quick, rash, hasty; reckless, careless, heedless, thoughtless, pell-mell, helter-skelter, harum-scarum, head over heels; brash, incautious, injudicious, ill-advised, indiscreet, unwary, foolish; impetuous, impulsive, unrestrained, ungoverned, uncontrolled, unchecked, unbridled; feverish, impatient, frantic, impassioned; madcap, madbrained, foolhardy, daredevil, breakneck, adventurous, hot-headed, harebrained, blindfolded; volatile, flighty, frivolous, erratic, fickle, unreliable, irresponsible; wild, giddy, dashing, ever-confident, rampant, quixotic, punch-drunk; death-defying, devil-may-care, dangerous, ruinous, perilous.

—n. **7.** snow, rain, drizzle, sleet, downpour, cloudburst, deluge, ice storm, blizzard.

precipitately, *adv.* hastily, quickly, speedily, hurriedly, headlong; abruptly, suddenly, unexpectedly; prematurely, inopportunely, too soon, without notice *or* warning, on the spur of the moment, like a bolt from the blue, like a thief in the night; incautiously, unadvisedly, foolishly, unwarily, impetuously, impulsively, impatiently; rashly, recklessly, carelessly, heedlessly, thoughtlessly; slapdash, at half cock, pell-mell, harum-scarum, helter-skelter, head over heels; posthaste, *Archaic.* amain, at full speed, at full gallop, tantivy, in double-quick time, by leaps and bounds, full tilt, full pelt, *Inf.* lickety-split.

precipitation, *n.* **1.** headlong fall, plunge, nosedive, dive, fall; casting headlong, projection, thrust, pitch, fling, heave, discharge.

2. acceleration, quickening, pushing, advancing, hastening; stimulation, arousing, triggering, rousing, animation, vivification; instigation, motivation, inspiration, exhortation, excitation, provocation, inciting; pressing, prodding, shoving, jogging, moving, driving on, urging on, egging on, goading, whipping, flogging; boosting, prompting, thrusting, impelling; expedition, facilitation.

3. abruptness, suddenness, haste, rush, hurry; hustle, bustle, dash, scurry, scramble, helter-skelter, hurry-scurry, pell-mell, harum-scarum.

4. impetuosity, rashness, recklessness, foolhardiness; prematurity, untimeliness, precocity, inopportuneness, inopportunity, inexpedience; impulsiveness, unrestraint, carelessness, heedlessness, thoughtlessness, imprudence, incautiousness; folly, gamble, leap in the dark, bungle, blunder, plunge, blind bargain; audacity, temerity, overconfidence, presumption.

5. *Metereol.* condensation, rainfall, rain, dewfall, dew, hail, snow, sleet, shower, drizzle; fog, mist, mizzle; downpour, cloudburst, deluge, blizzard, ice storm.

precipitous, *adj.* **1.** steep, sheer, abrupt, perpendicular, bluff; acclivitous, ascending, uphill, rising; declivitous, downhill, descending, declining, falling away; cliffy, craggy.

2. hasty, hurried, rash. See **precipitate** (*defs.* **4-6**).

précis, *n.* **1.** summary, epitome, synopsis, abstract, compendium, digest, conspectus; condensation, abridgment, reduction, compression, abbreviation; analysis, recapitulation; résumé, brief; outline, *Fr. aperçu,* sketch, review, syllabus, prospectus; docket, bulletin, minute; extracts, fragments, cuttings, analects, clippings, citations.

—v. **2.** summarize, outline, sketch, review; abbreviate, condense, abridge, shorten, curtail, compress.

precise, *adj.* **1.** explicit, definite, fixed, distinct, express; clear, plain, obvious, unmistakable, unambiguous, unequivocal; specific, pointed, strict, absolute, unconditional.

2. exact, accurate, close, faithful; correct, unerring, *Inf.* on the mark, on target, on the money, *Inf.* right on, *Sl.* spot on, on the button, on the dot, *Inf.* on the nose; right, just, true, truthful, veracious; factual, actual, strict, literal, true to life; authentic, real, sound, valid; flawless, faultless, perfect, defectless, errorless.

3. particular, finical, finicky, fussy; meticulous, careful, punctilious, scrupulous, conscientious; minute, detailed, thorough, nice, scientific, methodical, mathematical; critical, demanding, fastidious; strict, rigorous, severe, rigid, unbending, unyielding, ungiving.

precision, *n* **1.** exactness, exactitude, closeness, preciseness, *Math.* degree of error; accuracy, accurateness, correctness, rightness, rectitude, unerringness, flawlessness, faultlessness, perfection; literalism, textualism, adherence to the letter *or* text, faithfulness, fidelity, accordance, agreement; punctuality, punctualness, promptness, dependability, regularity, reliability; conformity, propriety, decorum, niceness, preciosity, preciousness; formalness, formality, protocol, form, ceremony.

2. punctiliousness, punctilio, attention to detail, pickiness, particularity, fastidiousness, fussiness, *Inf.* persnicketiness, *Inf.* pernicketiness; meticulousness, painstakingness, methodicalness, rigorousness, thoroughness, exhaustiveness; fineness, detailedness, minuteness, tediousness; care, carefulness, scrupulousness, conscientiousness; strictness, rigidity, rigidness, severity, severeness, inflexibility, stiffness; demandingness, criticalness, exactingness, hypercriticalness, overexactingness.

preclude, *v.* **1.** prevent, hinder, hamper, impede; stop, put a stop to, check, arrest, abort; curb, inhibit, restrain, constrain, repress; obstruct, block, bar, choke, clog, dam up; interfere, interrupt, intervene, interpose; detain, delay, slacken, slow, retard, forestall; avert, avoid, draw off, stave off, nip in the bud; oppose, cross, contravene, counter; defeat, override; frustrate, thwart, foil, balk.

2. debar, exclude, omit, rule out, shut out, eliminate; forbid, prohibit, proscribe, interdict, veto, ban, taboo.

precocious, *adj.* **1.** advanced, forward, far ahead, fast, ahead of one's peers; bright, brilliant, brainy, gifted; intelligent, smart, clever, quick; progressive, ahead of one's time, born before one's time, in the vanguard *or* van, in the forefront, avant-garde, ultramodern.

2. premature, early, early-bird, *Inf.* previous; overforward, too far along, untimely, undeveloped; overmature, maturing early, blooming early; prevenient, anticipatory, precipitate, eager.

preconception, *n.* prejudgment, forejudgment, predetermination, preconceived idea *or* notion, presentiment, predisposition; conjecture, inference, guesswork, hypothesis, premise; anticipation, presumption, prematurity of opinion, premature judgment, *Inf.* jumping the gun, *Inf.* going off half-cocked; presupposition, presupposal, presurmise, prejudice, bias, prepossession; fixed idea, *Fr. idèe fixe,* locked-in idea, fixed *or* settled belief, certitude; apprehension, foreboding, anxiety.

precursor, *n.* **1.** predecessor, foregoer, forerunner, antecedent; ancestor, forebear, progenitor, forefather, father; author, creator, originator, founder, innovator, groundbreaker.

2. pathfinder, advance man, pioneer, trailblazer, explorer; harbinger, herald, messenger, usher, avant-courier; vanguard, apostle, missionary, man from Cook's; pioneer, *Mil.* point man, front rider, outrider; leader, bellwether, Judas goat.

precursory, *adj.* precursive, precedent, antecedent, prior, anterior, previous, prevenient; forerunning, foregoing, anticipatory, preparatory; preliminary, introductory, inaugural, prelusive *or* prelusory, initiatory; prognostic, prognosticative, *Pathol.* prodromal, premonitory, indicative, warning, presageful.

predate, *v.* **1.** antedate, occur earlier, precede in time, happen earlier in time, belong to an earlier time, come from an earlier time.

2. record in advance, date beforetimes; date back, set back in time.

predatory, *adj.* **1.** rapacious, predacious, preying, vulturine, raptorial; wolfish, lupine; ravenous, ravening, voracious, devouring, omnivorous, insatiable, cormorant, savage, bestial, fierce, bloodthirsty, hungry.

2. marauding, plundering, pillaging, looting, piratical, robbing; pilfering, thieving, light-fingered, larcenous; extortionate, usurious; greedy, avaricious, grasping, acquisitive, covetous.

predecessor, *n.* precursor, antecessor, antecedent, foregoer, forerunner, former job *or* office holder.

predestinate, *v.* **1.** *Theology.* (*all by divine decree or purpose*) fate, ordain, doom, *Rare.* destinate; predetermine, predestine, preordain, foreordain, foreordinate, foredoom, predecide, preelect, *Inf.* have in store for.

—adj. **2.** ordained, doomed, destined, fated, fatal, fateful, *Rare.* destinated, *Obs.* destinal, *Obs.* destinable; written, in the cards, on the books; predestined, predestinated, predetermined, preordained, foreordained, foredoomed, predecided, preelected.

predestination, *n.* **1.** predetermination, preordination, predeliberation, preelection, foreordination, foreordainment, foredoom; predetermining, preordaining, preordinating, predeliberating.

2. fate, fortune, lot, cup, portion, die, doom, *Archaic.* foredoom, *Chiefly Scot.* weird, writing on the wall, *Brit. Inf.* cup of tea; destiny, kismet, karma, *Obs.* destine. See also **destiny** (*def.* **3**).

3. *Theology.* election, appointment; double predestination.

predetermined, *adj.* **1.** prearranged, set-up, predecided, decided *or* settled in advance, predesigned, preplanned; foregone, cut-and-dried, already settled *or* decided *or* resolved.

2. deliberate, intentional, intended, meant; planned, calculated, studied, thought-out, meditated, premeditated.

3. ordained, doomed, fated, fatal, fateful, destined, *Rare.* destinated, *Obs.* destinal, *Obs.* destinable; written, in the cards, on the books; predestined, predestinate, predestinated, predeterminate, preordained, foreordained, foredoomed, preelected.

predicament, *n.* **1.** trying situation, trial, embarrassment, *Sl.* hot seat, hot spot, hot water, stew, *Inf.* dead end; crisis, conjuncture, fix, impasse, deadlock, crux, hitch, rub, bind; *All Inf.* clutch, jam, fix, scrape, corner, hole, box, mess, pretty kettle of fish, fine how-do-you-do *or* how-de-do, pretty state of affairs, pretty pass, *Sl.* screw-up.

2. dilemma, quandary, perplexity, knot, puzzle, poser, paradox, knotty place, vexed question; imbroglio, intricacy, entanglement, maze; slough, muddle, quagmire; dangerous condition, plight, extremity, hornet's nest, *Archaic.* hobble, straits, pinch, exigency, emergency, problem, trouble, distress, difficulty.

predicate, *v.* **1.** assert, affirm, maintain, advance, set forth, broach, declare, proclaim, profess, put forth, propose, propound, contend, allege, protest; state, set down, express; aver, asseverate, *Archaic.* assever, depose, avow, avouch, vouch, warrant, certify, attest.

2. signify, represent, connote, imply, suggest, indicate, intimate, implicate; import, purport, betoken, bespeak, speak to.

predict, *v.* **1.** prophesy, prognosticate, forecast, vaticinate, *Med.* prognose; foretell, forespeak, augur, divine, *Obs.* auspicate, soothsay, foresee; read *or* interpret signs and omens, read palms *or* tea leaves, tell fortunes, see in the stars; forewarn, *Rare.* premonish; project, envision, see in the future, see in one's crystal ball, speculate, guess, theorize, hypothesize, play one's hunch.

2. foreshadow, presage, portend, forebode, bode, prefigure, foretoken, point to, omen; herald, harbinger, signify, indicate, promise, hint at, tell of, announce, proclaim.

predictable, *adj.* probable, likely, liable, expected, foreseeable, calculable, determinate, secure, *Inf.* in the cards, *Inf.* odds-on, *Inf.* sure-thing, *Dial.* sure 'nuff, *Sl.* nailed down, *Sl.* in the bag; reliable, reasonable, dependable, sure.

prediction, *n.* prophecy, prognostication, forecast, vaticination; augury, divination, soothsaying; projection, prognosis, supposition, surmise, speculation, conjecture, guess, *Inf.* hunch. See also **prophecy**.

predictor, *n.* **1.** prognosticator, forecaster, prophet, seer, augur, diviner, soothsayer. See **prophet** (*def.* **1**).

2. omen, sign, portent, token, foretoken, harbinger; premonition, preindication, forewarning, foreshadowing, handwriting on the wall.

predilection, *n.* **1.** tendency, bias, inclination, bent, warp, ply, cast; proclivity, propensity, proneness, predisposition, penchant, *Path.* diathesis; mind, aptness, affection, temperament; idiosyncrasy, grain, vein, mettle, humor, drift, set.

2. partiality, preference, liking, taste, fancy, favor; weakness, fondness, attraction, prepossession, affinity; infatuation, fascination, passion; personal choice, *Dial.* druthers, *Inf.* cup of tea, *Sl.* bag, *Sl.* thing.

3. prejudice, partisanship, favoritism, one-sidedness, jaundiced eye; bigotry, blindness, blind side; preconception, prenotion, forejudgment, preconceived notion.

predispose, *v.* **1.** prearrange, prepare, ready, make ready; make preparations, lay the groundwork, lay the first stone, lay the foundations, prime, set up.

2. bias, influence, dispose, affect, move; sway, bend, warp, prejudice; persuade, induce, prompt, urge, spur.

predisposed, *adj.* inclined, partial, bent, prone, minded; fain, not loath, amenable, agreeable, willing; liable, susceptible, subject, given to, *Archaic.* propense.

predisposition, *n.* **1.** tendency, inclination, propensity; partiality, preference, attraction. See **predilection** (*defs.* **1,2**).

2. susceptibility, liability, aptitude, aptness, proneness; vulnerability, susceptivity, openness, exposure; possibility, likelihood, potentiality.

predominance, *n.* preponderance, *Obs.* prepollence, ascendancy, dominance, dominion, transcendence; prevalence, mastery, sway, hold, weight, control, rule; supremacy, sovereignty, prepotency, power, potency, *Literary.* puissance, authority, hegemony, superiority; preeminence, primacy, priority; upper hand, whip hand, edge.

predominant, *adj.* dominant, ruling, regnant, sovereign; controlling, overruling, reigning, ranking, in the ascendancy, *Inf.* in the driver's seat; paramount, preeminent, top, top-priority; imperative, peremptory, absolute; weighty, forceful, forcible, mighty; powerful, potent, *Literary.* puissant; royal, kingly, monarchic, imperial; presidential, gubernatorial, administrative, executive, official, authoritative; prevailing, prevalent, chief, primary; prominent, telling, recognized, important.

predominate, *v.* preponderate, prevail, obtain; outweigh, overshadow, override, exceed, surpass; carry weight, tell, hold, carry the day; overrule, dominate, rule, reign; have the upper hand, domineer, control; overmaster, dictate, rule the roost; get the upper hand, make one's voice heard, make one's influence felt.

preeminence, *n.* **1.** superiority, dominance, predominance, control, power, dominion, domination; pull, sway, hold, prevalence; preponderancy, paramountcy, precedence, primacy, *Obs.* prepollence; ascendancy, supremacy, sovereignty, mastery; priority, seniority, command, hegemony.

2. peerlessness, matchlessness, superexcellence, magnificence; incomparability, inimitability, virtuosity; height, maximum, optimum, zenith, acme, apex; excellence, eminence, importance, top billing; greatness, prominence, mark, note; sublimity, regard, renown, respect, prestige, grandeur, glory.

preeminent, *adj.* **1.** superior, distinguished, peerless, matchless, supreme, sublime, transcendent; incomparable, inimitable, unrivaled, unsurpassed, unmatched, unequaled, unparalleled; highest, maximal, maximum, optimal, ultimate; utmost, topmost, top, foremost, crowning; paramount, surpassing, reigning, ruling, regnant, sovereign.

2. dominant, predominant, most important, most influential, strongest; main, chief, leading, commanding, head; prevailing, prevalent, most widespread.

preeminently, *adv.* supremely, eminently, superlatively; remarkably, signally, emphatically, powerfully, mightily; prominently, conspicuously, notably, strikingly, pointedly, glaringly, manifestly; unusually, extraordinarily, singularly, uncommonly, indescribably; surprisingly, incredibly, amazingly, wondrously, astonishingly; largely, greatly, richly; incomparably, inimitably, *Fr. par excellence*, unbeatably, peerlessly, matchlessly; intensely, extremely, the most; exceedingly, surpassingly, exceptionally, above all, second to none, *Latin. nulli secundus*; chiefly, mainly, principally, particularly.

preempt, *v.* occupy, squat on, stake a claim, claim; adopt, assume, appropriate, arrogate, usurp; take over, take possession of, make free with, help oneself to; prepossess, preoccupy.

preen, *v.* **1.** (*all of animals, esp. birds*) plume, trim; groom, dress.

2. (*all of oneself*) primp, beautify, prettify, fix up, *Inf.* titivate, *Inf.* spruce up, *Inf.* doll up, *Inf.* gussy up, *Sl.* trick up, *Sl.* dude up, *Sl.* swank up, *Sl.* fig out; array, bedizen, deck, deck out, bedeck, trap.

3. (*all of oneself*) pride, take pride, be proud; glory in, exult in, bask in; congratulate oneself, hug oneself, pat oneself on the back.

preface, *n.* **1.** introduction, foreword, prologue, proem, prolegomenon, prelude, prelusion, preliminary; preamble, opening statement *or* remarks, opening, beginning, exordium; front matter, prolegomena, *Print.* preliminaries.

—*v.* **2.** introduce, prefix, premise, prelude, prologize.

prefatory, *adj.* preliminary, preparatory, precursory, prelusive, proemial; introductory, opening, exordial; preceding, precedent, previous, prevenient, foregoing, anterior, antecedent.

prefer, *v.* **1.** favor, like better, think [s.t.] best, incline *or* lean toward, be partial to; select, choose, endorse, elect, opt; fancy, take a fancy to, desire, espouse, embrace, adopt; pick, cull, single out; would rather, would sooner, had sooner.

2. put forward, proffer, present, offer, propose, tender; suggest, give, volunteer, render; lodge, charge, place, file.

3. advance, promote, move up, elevate, raise, exalt.

preferable, *adj.* favored, chosen, selected, favorite; better, best, superior, worthier, more desirable *or* pleasing; choice, select, fine, superb.

preferably, *adv.* by preference, by choice, rather, sooner, just as soon, lief, gladly, willingly.

preference, *n.* **1.** choice, first choice, favorite, top of the list, *Dial.* druthers; desire, apple of one's eye, want; selection, pick; partiality, inclination, bent, leaning, bias, predisposition, prejudice, proclivity; fancy, liking, predilection.

2. advantage, leg up, plus, edge, upper *or* whip hand, vantage, superiority.

preferment, *n.* **1.** choice, selection, favorite. See **preference** (*def.* **1**).

2. promotion, advancement, elevation, raise; furtherance, betterment, improvement.

prefigure, *v.* **1.** foreshadow, foreshow, foretoken, forecast, adumbrate; omen, portend, augur; presage, preindicate, presignify, pretypify.

2. imagine, picture, fancy, consider; presuppose, presurmise.

prefix, *n.* **1.** *Grammar.* affix.

2. name, denomination, designation, title, appellation, epithet, cognomen.

—*v.* **3.** place before; introduce, preface, prelude, prologize.

pregnancy, *n.* gestation, incubation, gravidity, parturiency, *Inf.* the family way.

pregnant, *adj.* **1.** gravid, parturient, gestational; superfetate; with child, heavy *or* big with child, childing, in a delicate condition, *Inf.* expecting, *Inf.* in the family way, *U.S. Sl.* knocked-up.

2. fraught, full, filled, replete.

3. fertile, fruitful, fecund, fructiferous; seminal, rich in, abundant, abounding in, teeming, swarming; productive, prolific.

4. meaningful, significant, suggestive, loaded, charged, charged with meaning *or* significance.

5. momentous, eventful, pivotal, decisive, consequential, weighty; critical, crucial, climacteric, important; potential, full of possibilities.

6. imaginative, inventive, clever, ingenious, original, creative.

prehistoric, *adj.* **1.** primeval, primal, prehistorical, preglacial, Noachial, Noachic, Noachical, preadamic, antediluvian; eolithic, Paleolithic, Mesolithic, Neolithic.

2. ancient, archaic, fossilized, fossillike, antiquated, antique, superannuated, oldest; immemorial, old, old as the hills, timeworn, aged.

3. primitive, primordial, primigenial; autochthonal, autochthonous, aboriginal.

prejudge, *v.* forejudge, judge beforehand *or* prematurely, *Obs.* prejudicate, jump to a conclusion, *Inf.* go off half-cocked, *Sl.* jump the gun; predecide, predetermine, preconclude, have a bias, be biased, entertain a prejudice; preconceive, presuppose, presume.

prejudice, *n.* **1.** bias, warp, twist, slant, bend, turn, blind side; preconception, preconceived notion *or* idea, jaundice, jaundiced eye; prepossession, predisposition, presupposition, predetermination, prejudgement, forejudgement, premature judgment.

2. partiality, predilection; partisanship, cronyism, favoritism, *Inf.* back scratching; unfairness, one-sidedness, unevenness.

3. intolerance, bigotry, narrow-mindedness, closed-mindedness, small-mindedness; racism, segregation, Jim Crowism, apartheid, white supremacy *or* power; color line, color barrier; discrimination, sexism, male chauvinism; superpatriotism, jingoism, chauvinism; class consciousness, class hatred, social barrier; xenophobia; anti-Semitism; misogyny; misanthropy.

4. disadvantage, detriment, drawback, liability, handicap; impairment, loss, damage, injury, hurt, harm, ill, mischief.

—v. **5.** bias, sway, bend, turn, warp, twist, slant, incline; influence, dispose, predispose, prepossess, jaundice.

6. impede, hinder, block, obstruct; damage, injure, impair, hurt, harm.

prejudiced, *adj.* **1.** biased, warped, twisted, slanted, bent, turned, influenced; predisposed, prepossessed, jaundiced; partial, partisan, unfair, uneven, one-sided; nonobjective, interested, undetached.

2. intolerant, illiberal, bigoted, closed-minded, narrow-minded, small-minded; myopic, purblind, short-sighted; insular, provincial, parochial; unreasonable, dogmatic, doctrinaire, opinionated; fanatical, chauvinistic, jingoistic, superpatriotic, ultranationalist; racist, anti-Semitic; sexist, misogynistic, misanthropic.

prejudicial, *adj.* disadvantageous, detrimental, unfavorable, counterproductive, disserviceable; hurtful, harmful, injurious, deleterious, baneful, damaging, impairing, pernicious, mischievous.

prelacy, *n.* **1.** prelatism, episcopacy, hierarchy, hierocracy, hierarchism, clericalism, theocracy.

2. prelature, prelateship, episcopate, bishopric, archbishopric, cardinalship, pontificate, papacy, primacy; canonry, prebendary.

prelate, *n.* **1.** cardinal, archbishop, metropolitan, bishop, diocesan, coadjutor, auxiliary, suffragen; primate, hierarch, high priest, archpriest, *Ethiopian Ch.* abuna, *Eastern Ch.* exarch; patriarch, pontiff, pope.

2. archdeacon, canon, prebendary, capitular; dean, pastor, rector, vicar, presbyter; abbot, prior, *Eastern Ch.* archimandrite.

preliminary, *adj.* **1.** preparatory, prefatory, precursory, prelusive, proemial; introductory, inaugural; beginning, opening, initiatory, exordial; preceding, precedent, previous, prevenient, prior, foregoing, anterior, antecedent.

—n. **2.** introductory step *or* measure, prefatory step *or* measure, groundwork, spadework, *Inf.* homework; foundation, stepping stone, building block; preparation, *Inf.* prep, readying, *Inf.* clearing the deck; rehearsal, tuning up; familiarization, briefing, basic training, *Mil. Inf.* basic.

3. curtain raiser, *Inf.* opener, *Sl.* prelim.

4. preliminaries front matter, prolegomena; preamble, opening statement, opening, beginning, exordium; introduction, proem, preface, prelude, prelusion, prologue, forward, prolegomenon.

prelude, *n.* **1.** preliminary, introductory step *or* measure, groundwork, spadework. See **preliminary** (*def.* 2).

2. overture, voluntary, vorspiel; curtain raiser, *Inf.* opener, *Sl.* prelim.

—v. **3.** preface, introduce, prefix, premise, prologize.

premature, *adj.* **1.** too soon, too early, overhasty, precipitate, advanced, anticipatory; ill-timed, untimely, unseasonable.

2. immature, incomplete, imperfect, undeveloped, unprepared; unripe, green, raw, crude; inchoate, embryonic, unhatched, unfledged, vestigial, rudimental, rudimentary, abortive.

prematurely, *adv.* too early, too soon, too hastily, precipitately; abortively, untimely, inopportunely, unseasonably; precociously.

premeditate, *v.* prearrange, precontrive, predevise, predesign, preconcert, preplan; predeliberate, precalculate, predetermine, preresolve, preconsider; plot, scheme, plan, calculate, plan *or* work out in advance.

premeditated, *adj.* prearranged, precontrived, predesigned, preplanned, planned in advance, prepense, aforethought; planned, plotted, schemed, worked-out, contrived, arranged, set-up; intentional, intended, willful, deliberate, voluntary, conscious, knowing; studied, deliberated, calculated.

premier, *n.* **1.** prime minister, first minister, head *or* chief of state, president *or* chief executive.

—adj. **2.** chief, principal, cardinal, main, primary, prime, head, headmost, topmost, foremost; highest, uppermost, of the first rank, ranking, top-rank; supreme, paramount, preeminent.

3. earliest, oldest; first, original.

premiere, *n.* **1.** debut, opening performance, opening night, *Inf.* opening.

2. female lead, female star, leading lady, lead actress, jeune première; diva, prima donna, prima ballerina, première danseuse.

—v. **3.** (*all for the first time*) present, stage, put on, perform, produce.

—adj. **4.** main, chief, principal; first, initial, original, earliest.

premise, *n.* **1.** postulate, postulation, axiom; proposition, proposal, hypothesis, thesis, lemma, theorem; presupposition, assumption, *Rhet.* prolepsis; inference, surmise, conjecture; basis, foundation, ground, starting point.

2. premises building, establishment; property, grounds.

3. proof, evidence, grounds, reason; facts, data.

—v. **4.** preface, prefix, prelude, prologize, introduce.

5. postulate, theorize, hypothesize, hypothecate; posit, predicate, lay down, set forth, assert.

premium, *n.* **1.** discount, deduction, cut, price reduction, *Inf.* rollback; refund, rebate, agio, (*all on the London stock exchange*) contango, continuation, backwardation.

2. prize, award, reward, *Literary.* guerdon, bounty, *Archaic.* meed; extra, something extra, bonus, added incentive, *Inf.* a little on the side, *Sl.* gravy, *Sl.* grease, *Sl.* salve, *Sl.* palm oil; gift, present, lagniappe, *Sl.* handout; percentage, kickback; consideration, tip, gratuity, commission, douceur, benefit, fringe benefit, perquisite, *Inf.* perk.

3. at a premium a. expensive, costly, dear, high-priced, high, beyond one's means, *Inf.* fancy, *Inf.* stiff, *Inf.* steep; overpriced, exorbitant, inordinate, excessive, immoderate, unreasonable. **b.** in short supply, scarce, scant, scanty, sparse, rare, uncommon, *Inf.* scarcer than hen's teeth; not to be had, not to be had for love or money, unavailable at any price.

premonition, *n.* **1.** preindication, forewarning, foreshadowing, handwriting on the wall; omen, sign, portent, token, foretoken, harbinger; prognostic, prognostication, bodement, forecast, augury.

2. presentiment, presage, foreboding, feeling, vague feeling, *Inf.* funny feeling, *Inf.* feeling in one's bones, suspicion, *Inf.* sneaking suspicion, *Inf.* hunch, intuition; anxiety, misgiving, apprehension, apprehensiveness, boding; dread, fear, ill feeling, chill along the spine, *Sl.* bad vibes.

premonitory, *adj.* forewarning, foretokening, foreshadowing, foreshowing, preindicative, prognostic, predictive, monitory, augural; ominous, portentous, foreboding, bodeful.

preoccupation, *n.* abstraction, raptness, engrossment, engrossing, absorption, absorbing, immersion, immersing; concentration, intensity, pensiveness, musing, preoccupying, fixation, obsession, obsessing, *Inf.* bag, *Sl.* hang-up; obliviousness, oblivion, unawareness, unconsciousness, absent-mindedness, absence of mind, reverie, woolgathering, daydreaming, castle-building; unmindfulness, insensibility, blindness, blinding; distraction, distracting, diversion, diverting, inattentiveness, unattentiveness, inadvertence, inadvertency, unheedfulness, heedlessness.

preoccupied, *adj.* **1.** abstracted, rapt, engrossed, consumed, lost in, absorbed, immersed, wrapped up, *Inf.* into [s.t.], busy, occupied; obsessed, *Sl.* hung up; oblivious, unaware, unconscious, unmindful, insensible, blind; distracted, diverted, distrait, inattentive, unattentive, inadvertent, deaf, unheeding, unheedful, heedless.

2. intent, concentrating, focusing, pensive, cerebrational, thoughtful, thinking, lost in thought, bemused; cogitative, cogitating, deliberative, deliberating, meditative, meditating, contemplative, contemplating, reflective, reflecting; musing, pondering, wondering about, *Archaic.* museful; ruminative, ruminant, ruminating, chewing, chewing one's cud, brooding, mulling over, in a brown study.

3. preempted, co-opted, usurped, appropriated, claimed, spoken for, taken, gone; filled, nonvacant, in use.

preoccupy, *v.* absorb, immerse, engross, obsess, consume, devour, monopolize, keep to oneself, rivet, fix, fixate, arrest, attract, engage, keep one busy, take all one's time, occupy, hold; hold one's attention, distract, divert.

preordain, *v.* **1.** predetermine, predestine, *Obs.* predestinate, foreordain, foreordinate, predecide, preelect, preestablish, foredoom, *Inf.* have in store for; fate, ordain, doom, destine, *Rare.* destinate.

2. designate, dedicate, allot, *Obs.* appoint; mark, earmark, tag, set apart *or* aside; consecrate, devote; reserve, *Brit.* bespeak; plan, project; design, intend, purpose, mean, resolve, determine, set.

preparation, *n.* **1.** preparatory measure, *Inf.* prep, proceeding, provision, step, arrangement, plan; groundwork, spadework, *Inf.* homework; foundation, substructure, base, basis; framework, frame, scaffold, scaffolding; outline, sketch, draft, rough draft, layout, blueprint, diagram.

2. teaching, schooling, learning, book learning, education, formal education, instruction; tutelage, tuition, tutorship, training, grooming, basic training, briefing, familiarization, apprenticeship; experience, background, qualifications.

3. priming, *Inf.* prepping, making ready, readying, getting ready *or* set; setting up, fixing up, arranging, ordering, setting one's house in order; *Sl.* psyching oneself up, *Inf.* getting oneself in gear, revving up one's engines; practice, rehearsal, tuning up.

4. outfitting, accoutering, equipping, furnishing, supplying, providing; fitting out *or* up, rigging up *or* out, decking out, trapping; *All Mil.* arming, forearming, *Sl.* heeling, *Archaic.* harnassing.

5. preparedness, readiness, fitness.

6. preparative, compound, composition, mixture, concoction, product, drug, pharmaceutical, pharmaceutical preparation, *Med.* prescription, medicine medication, medicament.

preparatory, *adj.* preparative, preliminary, prefatory, precursory, prelusive, prelusory, proemial; introductory, inaugural, beginning, opening, initial, initiatory, first; rudimentary, elementary, basic, primary, fundamental; prerequisite, qualifying, college-preparatory, *Inf.* college-prep; preceding, precedent, previous, prevenient, prior, foregoing, anterior, antecedent.

prepare, *v.* **1.** make ready, ready, *Inf.* prep; clear the decks, prepare for, make preparations for, prime, groom, get ready *or* set, *Inf.* square away, *Archaic.* boun; set up, fix up, arrange, order, put things in order, set one's house in order; lay the groundwork, set the stage, take steps, take the necessary steps, make provisions; draw the wagons tight, make all snug, batten down the hatches; *Sl.* psych oneself up, get up one's courage, *Inf.* gear oneself up, *Inf.* get oneself in gear, rev up one's engines, *Literary.* gird one's loins; warm up, rehearse, practice, get into shape *or* condition, whip into shape, tune up, *Music.* noodle; study, review, go over, read over, reread, do one's homework; brief, familiarize, train, teach.

2. outfit, accouter, equip, furnish, supply, provide, purvey; fit, fit out *or* up, rig, rig out *or* up, gear; array, deck, deck out, bedeck, caparison, trap; *All Mil.* arm, forearm, munition, *Sl.* heel, *Archaic.* harness.

3. (*all of a meal*) fix, make, do, cook, bake.

4. manufacture, make, produce, turn out; construct, erect, build, put up; forge, fashion, mold, form, shape, carve, chisel, sculpture; compound, combine, put together, concoct, mix up, whip up, cook up, brew; compose, work up, write up, make up, develop; devise, invent, contrive, fabricate, hatch, come up with, dream up, think up.

prepared, *adj.* **1.** ready, all ready, dressed, ready to go, *Inf.* on deck; set, all set, *Inf.* squared away, in order; set up, fixed *or* fixed up, arranged, in readiness; primed, *Inf.* prepped, briefed, trained; *Sl.* psyched up, *Inf.* in gear, revved up; warmed up, in shape, in condition, in tune, tuned up; equipped, outfitted, accoutered, fitted out, rigged out; *All Mil.* armed, forearmed, *Sl.* heeled, *Archaic.* harnessed.

2. processed, precooked, frozen, made-up, premade, ready-made; ready-to-serve, ready-to-eat.

preparedness, *n.* readiness, fitness, preparation.

preponderance, *n.* **1.** majority, bulk, mass, lion's share, greater part, more than half; prevalence, common occurrence, extensiveness.

2. ascendancy, predomination, primacy, paramountcy, sovereignty, preeminence, superiority, transcendence, greatness, supremacy; influence, sway, weightiness, weight, force, strength, power, upper hand, advantage; dominance, domination, mastery, control, rule, authority, leadership, hegemony.

preponderant, *adj.* **1.** prevalent, prevailing, widespread, extensive, comprehensive, preponderating; major, greater, larger, large, higher.

2. important, *Sl.* big-time, capital, principal, chief, leading, foremost, recognized; ascendant, dominant, predominant, prime, primary, sovereign, paramount, preeminent, superior, great, first-rate, supreme, transcendent, second to none; powerful, influential, weighty, outweighing, forceful, strong; controlling, ruling, authoritative, overruling.

prepossessed, *adj.* biased, warped, slanted, predisposed, partial, prejudiced. See **prejudiced** (*def.* **1**).

prepossessing, *adj.* attractive, pleasing, appealing, charming, engaging, winsome, winning, taking; interesting, fascinating, captivating, enchanting, bewitching, alluring; beautiful, lovely, *Inf.* eye-filling, striking, well-favored, good-looking, handsome; delightful, pleasant, agreeable, likable; memorable, signal, notable; forceful, eloquent, well-spoken.

prepossession, *n.* predilection, liking, predisposition, bias, slant, partiality, prejudice. See **prejudice** (*defs.* **1, 2**).

preposterous, *adj.* **1.** unreasonable, irrational, illogical, meaningless, senseless; incongruous, inconsistent, unconnected, groundless; high-flown, extravagant, extreme, outrageous, excessive, overdone, exaggerated, hyperbolized; incredible, unbelievable, astonishing; unthinkable, out of the question, impossible.

2. foolish, absurd, inane, fatuous, nonsensical, *Inf.* damfool, *Inf.* damfoolish, tomfoolish, *Scot. and North Eng.* glaikit, *Sl.* cockeyed; stupid, unintelligent, mindless, fatuitous, brainless; poppycockish, *Sl.* cockamamie, amphigoric; ridiculous, derisible, risible, laughable, ludicrous, *Sl.* for the birds; comical, funny, farcical, humorous, droll; asinine, anserine, idiotic, *Inf.* moronic, imbecilic; crazy, crazed, *Sl.* kooky, *Scot.* doiled, mad, wild, insane, demented, crackbrained, *Inf.* nutty; *All Sl.* balmy, dippy, batty, cuckoo, buggy, screwy, wacky, goofy, loony.

preposterousness, *n.* **1.** unreasonableness, irrationality, irrationalness, illogic, illogicalness, illogicality, meaninglessness, senselessness; incongruity, inconsistency, groundlessness; extravagance, excess, excessiveness, outrageousness, exaggeration, hyperbole; incredibleness, unbelievability, unthinkableness, impossibility.

2. folly, foolishness, ridiculousness, ridiculosity, ludicrousness, absurdity, absurdness; nonsensicalness, nonsensicality, nonsense, silliness, inanity; idiocy, lunacy, madness, craziness, *Sl.* screwiness; imbecility, stupidity, asininity, idioticalness.

prerequisite, *adj.* **1.** necessary, needful, needed, wanted; essential, indispensable, requisite, unavoidable, necessitous; imperative, demanded, required, called for.

—*n.* **2.** requisite, necessity, necessary, necessaries, need; essential, *Latin. sine qua non*, the essentials; imperative, demand, requisition, requirement, prerequirement, obligation.

3. condition, provision, proviso, stipulation, qualification; specification, terms, *Inf.* fine print, *Inf.* catch.

prerogative, *n.* right, liberty, choice, privilege, rightful power, due, droit, authority; claim, pretension, demand; birthright, advantage, title; authorization, *Law.* prescription, license, legal power, franchise, grant; sanction, vouchsafement, permission, allowance, leave, consent, *Inf.* O.K.; blanket permission, unconditional authority, carte blanche, *Sl.* the run of the place; exemption, exception, immunity.

presage, *n.* **1.** presentiment, foreboding, feeling, vague feeling, *Inf.* funny feeling, *Inf.* feeling in one's bones, suspicion, *Inf.* sneaking suspicion, *Inf.* hunch, intuition; anxiety, misgiving, apprehension, apprehensiveness, boding; dread, fear, ill feeling, chill along the spine, *Sl.* bad vibes.

2. omen, sign, portent, token, foretoken, harbinger; prognostic, prognostication, bodement, prediction, soothsaying, forecast, prophecy, prefigurement, augury, auspice, vaticination, divination; premonition, indication, preindication, forewarning, foreshadowing, handwriting on the wall.

3. foresight, prevision, prescience, foreknowledge, clairvoyance, clairvoyancy, precognition, second sight.

—*v.* **4.** sense, intuit, feel, foresee, have a feeling, *Inf.* have a funny feeling, *Inf.* feel in one's bones.

5. foreshadow, forebode, foretoken, foreshow, prefigure, presignify, preindicate; augur, portend, bode, omen; betoken, signify, mean, indicate, point to.

6. forecast, predict, prognosticate, prophesy, divine, soothsay, vaticinate; foretell, forewarn, threaten, *Rare.* premonish, *Obs.* auspicate.

presbyter, *n.* priest, father, minister, reverend, parson; lay minister, elder, preacher, sermonizer; prelate, bishop; ecclesiastic, clergyman, cleric, churchman. See also **priest, ecclesiastic.**

presbytery, *n.* **1.** (*both collectively*) presbyters, elders; clergy, ministry; holy orders, priesthood, the cloth, the pulpit, the desk.

2. ecclesiastical court, council, tribunal, consistory, (*in some Reformed churches*) classis; chapter, convocation, synod, conclave, diet; committee meeting, conference, session.

3. sanctuary, chancel, altar; sacristry, vestry.

4. *Rom. Cath. Ch.* rectory. See **parsonage.**

prescience, *n.* foreknowledge, clairvoyance, clairvoyancy, precognition, second sight; foresight, prevision; farsightedness, far-seeingness, long-sightedness, circumspection.

prescient, *adj.* clairvoyant, precognitive, precognizant, divinatory, prophetic, vaticinal, oracular, presageful; foresighted, farsighted, farseeing, sagacious, discerning, perceptive, perspicacious, penetrating, shrewd, quick-witted; anticipatory, forward-looking; provident, prudent, cautious, precautious, precautionary.

prescribe, *v.* dictate, impose, set, lay down, lay down the law, *Inf.* call the shots, *Inf.* call the tune, wield one's power *or* authority; exact, demand, require, requisition; constrain, oblige, necessitate; charge, bid, tell, enjoin, direct, instruct; urge, advocate, recommend; decree, ordain, pronounce, proclaim, rule, adjudge, order, command; appoint, authorize, enact, establish, institute, legislate, codify.

prescript, *adj.* **1.** dictated, imposed, laid down; decreed, ordained, ruled, adjudged, ordered, commanded; pronounced, proclaimed, authorized, enacted, established; exacted, demanded, required, imperative, requisite; constrained, obliged, necessitated.

—*n.* **2.** decree, ordinance, edict, *Law.* writ, rescript, assize, prescription; dictate, dictum, order, charge, injunction, directive, direction, command, commandment, instruction; fiat, sanction, mandate, firman; proclamation, pronunciamento, manifesto, ukase; ruling, verdict, judgement, *Law.* award, finding, sentence; rule, regulation, precept, law, canon, enactment, *Law.* statute, act; warrant, authorization.

prescription, *n.* **1.** *Medicine.* (*all usu. in writing*) direction, instruction, bidding, Rx.

2. *Medicine.* medicine, remedy, formula, recipe, receipt.

3. *Law.* right, privilege, prerogative, claim, pretension, due; grant, title.

4. decree, ordinance, edict, *Law.* writ, rescript, assize, prescript. See **prescript** (*def.* **2**).

5. axiom, theorem, maxim, principle; doctrine, ruling, precept, regulation.

presence, *n.* **1.** existence, entity, substantiality, subsistence, life, being; residence, habitation, inhabitancy; attendance, company, accompaniment, companionship.

2. closeness, close proximity, neighborhood, immediate vicinity; proximation, proximity, adjacency, contiguity.

3. poise, ease, self-assurance, confidence, self-confidence, self-possession; dignity of bearing, fine carriage; urbanity, urbaneness, suavity, suaveness, savoir-faire, elegance, polish, refinement.

4. spirit, supernatural being, manifestation, spiritual manifestation, incorporeality; shade, phantasm, eidolon, specter, wraith, revenant, shadow, apparition, ghost.

presence of mind, *n.* alertness, self-possession, aplomb; composure, steadiness, stability, self-restraint, self-control, collectedness; equanimity, calmness, equilibrium, balance; sang-froid, cool, imperturbability; level-headedness, common sense, rationality; sedateness, dispassion, staidness; poise, assurance, confidence, self-assurance, self-confidence, self-command, ability to keep one's head when all about are losing theirs.

present[1], *adj.* **1.** present-day, existing, extant, current; living, alive, still alive; here, at this place, at hand, to hand, nigh, near, nearby, vicinal, about, afloat; attending, in attendance, in this company, among us, remaining, on duty.

—n. **2.** *Usu.* **the present** now, this time, this point, this point in time; this very moment, this very hour, this very minute; this juncture, right now, just now, nowadays, today; the nonce, the time being, this day and age.

present[2], *v.* **1.** give, bestow, donate, contribute; turn over, hand over, confer, award, accord, grant, put at [s.o.'s] disposal; vouchsafe, leave, entrust; allot, apportion, will, endow, furnish, *Law.* bequeath; assign, allocate, mete out, distribute, dispense, dole, dole out, *Inf.* fork out *or* over; hand out, supply, *Inf.* shell out, *Inf.* dish out, pay, tip.

2. proffer, offer, set forth, show, display; evidence, manifest, indicate, demonstrate; sponsor, introduce, show, exhibit, put on display, put on show, bring to notice; put on a show, make a production, bring to the public, put in the public eye; make visible, uncover, disclose, unscreen, raise the curtain on, expose to view, register, introduce.

3. aim, direct, point, run; (*all of firearms*) orient *or* position toward, track towards.

—n. **4.** gift, benefaction, favor, endowment; donation, donative, contribution, offering; tip, gratuity, bonus, prize, premium, giveaway, freebie, benefit, boon; charity, largess, alms, dole, handout; grant, aid, allowance, allotment.

presentable, *adj.* **1.** adequate, suitable, fit; ample, satisfactory, passable, up to scratch, up to the mark, *Inf.* up to par, *Inf.* up to snuff; tolerable, acceptable, all right, good enough, better than nothing, admissible, allowable.

2. well-mannered, well-bred, polite; respectable, decent, unobjectionable, attractive enough; eligible, marriageable, parent-approved.

3. dressed, clothed, covered, *Inf.* decent.

presentation, *n.* **1.** introduction, acquaintance; amenity, civility, politeness, courtesy.

2. exhibition, exhibit, show, display, exposition, presentment; representation, portrayal, performance, enactment; spectacle, panorama, pageant, parade; production, materialization, manifestation, appearance; unveiling, opening, exposure, disclosure, revelation.

3. offering, bestowal, bestowment, giving; offer, offering, proffer, proffering, award, awarding; conferral, investiture, delivery, impartment, communication; proposal, proposition, advance, overture; submission, bid, broaching, posing; motion, suggestion, resolution.

4. gift, present, *Brit.* fairing, oblation, handsel; donation, donative, contribution, benefaction, boon, grace; gratuity, tip, compliment, *Fr. pourboire*, favor, douceur; bonus, extra, premium, bounty; subsidy, allowance, grant; reward, award, prize, trophy; legacy, bequest, bequeathal.

presentiment, *n.* foreboding, premonition, intuition, premonishment, presagement; forethought, prenotion, presage, foretaste; anticipation, expectation, apprehension, misgiving, feeling, *Inf.* hunch, dread; forecast, foreknowledge, prescience, prevision.

presently, *adv.* **1.** soon, shortly, forthwith, in a while, in a little while; anon, *Archaic.* eftsoon, directly, by and by; after a while, after a time, *Inf.* pretty soon, before long, ere long; in due time, at the first chance *or* opportunity, in due course; in no time, without delay, betimes, in a moment, in a minute.

2. now, currently, at present, nowadays, for the nonce; at this moment, at this very moment, at this time, right now, for the time being, at the present time; at this juncture, at this point in time, at this writing, as of now, as one reads this.

preservation, *n.* **1.** maintenance, upkeep, support, sustenance, continuance, upholding; perpetuation, immortalization, eternalization, eternization; continuation, extension, prolongation, lengthening; conservation, reservation, keeping.

2. salvation, saving, sheltering, safekeeping, safeguarding; protection, defense, guarding; storage, custody, watch.

3. retention, keeping, holding, hold, grip, grasp.

4. drying, dehydration, desiccation, dry storage, jerking; curing, corning, smoking, fuming, salting, brining, seasoning; pickling, kippering, marination; refrigeration, freezing, icing, cold storage, quick-freezing, deep-freezing, freeze-drying; canning, *Brit.* tinning, bottling, jarring; embalming, mummification, stuffing, taxidermy.

preserve, *v.* **1.** keep alive, conserve, sustain; reserve, save, spare; keep; keep going, extend, lengthen, perpetuate, prolong; maintain, keep up, continue, uphold.

2. keep safe, save, safeguard, shelter, shield, screen; guard, watch over, protect, defend; cloak, harbor, cover, hide; foster, nurse, doctor, care for, cherish.

3. retain, keep, put aside *or* away, shelve, put away for a rainy day, save, bank; hold, keep hold of, *Inf.* hang on to, keep a firm hold *or* grip on.

4. cure, smoke, smoke-cure, salt, brine, corn; dry, jerk, dehydrate, desiccate, evaporate; pickle, kipper, marinate; freeze, refrigerate, put in the deep freeze, freeze-dry, ice, put on ice; can, *Brit.* tin, put up, bottle, jar; embalm, mummify, stuff; put in formaldehyde.

—n. **5.** jam, jelly, marmalade, confiture, comfit; compote, gelatin, meringue; confection, sweets, candy, sweetmeat.

6. sanctuary, bird sanctuary, reserve, reservation, game reserve, park; domain, enclosure, zoo.

preserver, *n.* **1.** preservative, vinegar, salt, brine; formaldehyde, embalming fluid.

2. savior, defender, protector, saver, safekeeper; keeper, conservator, conservationist; lifesaver, rescuer, lifeguard.

3. life preserver, life jacket, buoy, lifesaver, life ring, life belt, safety belt; lifeline, life rope, life net, safety net; parachute, *Inf.* chute.

preside, *v.* supervise, superintend, watch over, oversee, overlook; direct, control, manage, administrate; regulate, head, lead; command, govern, rule, *Inf.* boss; hold the chair, wield the gavel, officiate, moderate, chair; hold *or* wield authority, be at the head of, *Inf.* be in the driver's seat, *Inf.* be in the saddle, hold the reins, pull the strings, call the shots.

president, *n.* **1.** chief executive, chief of state, head of state, commander-in-chief, first citizen; Mr. President, *Sl.* prez, the man in the White House.

2. director, manager, controller, chief; administrator, executive, leader; superintendent, supervisor, overseer, *Inf.* boss, *Sl.* the man; commander, captain, master, general; principal, headmaster, dean, prefect, provost; premier, prime minister, chancellor, doge, vizier.

3. presider, chairman, moderator; master of ceremonies, *Inf.* emcee, M.C., toastmaster, speaker.

presignify, *v.* foreshadow, prefigure, pretoken, point to, forbode. See **foretell**.

press, *v.* **1.** force, push, drive, ram, shove, elbow; impel, propel, thrust, trundle; cram, jam, crush, pinch.

2. compress, squeeze, condense, clamp; cramp, compact, concentrate, roll into a ball; strain, strangle, constrict, constringe.

3. weigh upon, depress, press down, bear down; let down, force down, thrust down, cast down; lower, push down, detrude, shove down, sink, stuff down.

4. embrace, hug, clasp, cleave, embosom; enfold, snuggle, fondle, caress, pet, nuzzle; press to the bosom, take to the heart, fold in one's arms, throw one's arms around.

5. flatten, make flat, iron, steam, calender, mangle, hot-press; smooth, roll, roll out, bulldoze, plane.

6. beset, torment, assail, besiege; harass, annoy, vex, disquiet, disconcert, worry; plague, afflict, grieve, wound; trouble, irk, aggravate, irritate; rack, grate, grind, fret, gnaw; oppress, tyrannize, persecute, subjugate; saddle, overwhelm, suppress, repress; burden, embarrass, encumber, drag down, strain; drive to the wall, strong-arm, intimidate, cow; grind the heel, rule with an iron fist, ride roughshod over.

7. urge, impel, induce, persuade; incite, move, motivate, provoke, goad, spur; instigate, animate, prick, prod; whip, lash, *Inf.* egg on, hound, sting; energize, electrify, galvanize, actuate, spark, charge: inspire, rouse, arouse, foment, evoke, elicit.

8. hasten, hurry, push, rush, dash; speed, hustle, make haste, scramble, move, scuttle, scurry, scamper; bustle, plunge headlong, work under pressure, work against time, put one's nose to the grindstone, work overtime.

9. importune, entreat, beg, implore, plead, supplicate; bid, petition, appeal, sue, pray; enjoin, exhort, insist, drive; beseech, imprecate, dun, tax; adjure, conjure, invoke, impetrate; nag, pressure, blandish, *Inf.* jawbone.

10. require, demand, requisition; enforce, compel, coerce, constrain; bind, oblige, necessitate; extort, twist from, wrench from, wring from; twist one's arm, tie one down, put the screws on, pin down, bring pressure to bear.

11. impress, draft, conscript, induct; call up, summon, mobilize, levy, recruit, raise; enlist, sign up, sign on, enroll.

12. push forward, advance, forge ahead, progress, drive on; move on, trudge on, drag on, march on, plod on.

13. crowd, throng, crush, mill; swarm, herd, flock, surge, seethe; cluster, conglomerate, huddle, gather round, rally round; merge, converge, gather, meet, *Inf.* gang up.

—*n.* **14.** newspapers, periodicals, newspaperdom, newspaper world, the papers; fourth estate, journalism, Fleet Street, media, broadcasting, broadcast journalism, radio, television, wire services, news service.

15. news reporters, news photographers, newsmen, journalists, reporters, correspondents, gentlemen of the press, columnists.

16. coverage, play, space, time, air time.

17. printing press, printing machine, letter press, linotype press, rotary press, proof press; hand press, flatbed press, web press, platen press, roller press, electrotype press, rotogravure press.

18. pressure, urgency, instance, insistence; provocation, instigation, stimulation, actuation, motivation; incitement, inducement, encouragement, prompting.

19. compulsion, pressure, stress, duress, coercion, force, constraint; enforcement, obligation, necessity; exigency, need, pinch, extremity, crisis.

20. crowd, throng, crush, multitude, mob, pack, *Inf.* heap; swarm, flock, herd, drove, troop; flood, deluge, sea; rabble, bunch, host, horde, army, legion.

21. hustle, bustle, hustle-bustle, hurry, great hurry; hum of business, flurry, fluster, ferment; ado, *Sl.* rat race, *Inf.* much going on, plenty to do, storm.

22. draft, conscription, enrollment, enlistment, call, call-up, summons; impressment, induction, raising; recruitment, muster, mobilization, levy.

press agent, *n.* publicity agent, publicity person, public relations person, P.R. man, P.R. person, flak; publicist, publicizer, propagandist, ballyhooer, ballyhoo artist.

pressing, *adj.* urgent, crucial, exigent, emergent, importunate, imperative, high-priority; demanding, compelling, requiring immediate attention; important, all-important, significant, portentous, of great import; consequential, of great consequence, critical; decisive, determining, pivotal; momentous, climactic, eventful, major, profound; weighty, heavy, ponderous, pregnant, carrying great weight, of substance; grave, serious, severe, acute.

pressure, *n.* **1.** gravity, *Physics.* gravitation; weight, heaviness, force; compression, density, denseness.

2. coercion, constraint, compulsion, force, coaction; duress, obligation; persuasion, inducement, insistence, armtwisting; urgency, provocation, requirement, necessitation, necessity, necessitude, need.

3. stress, tension, strain, heat, drain, drag, charge, tax; burden, *Archaic.* burthen, cross, encumbrance, cumbrance, trouble, vexation; *All Inf.* squeeze, crunch, pinch, push; load, weight, millstone, albatross.

4. oppression, persecution, subjugation, enslavement; harassment, dogging, hounding, tormenting, bullying, intimidation, browbeating; cruelty, severity, harshness, hardness.

5. influence, power, potency, force, strength; control, sway, *Inf.* jawboning, mastery, hold; guidance, leadership, direction.

—*v.* **6.** coerce, constrain, compel, force, drive, press, oblige, hustle, railroad; impel, urge, impress, provoke, instigate, exhort; goad, prod, egg on; influence, act on, play on, work on, *Inf.* jawbone; incite, rouse, arouse; cause, require, exact, necessitate, make; persuade, induce, prevail upon, insist upon; pin [s.o.] down, *Inf.* shove *or* ram down one's throat; apply pressure, *Sl.* lean against *or* on, get on [s.o.'s] back, armtwist, twist [s.o.'s] arm, put the screws on *or* to, *Inf.* strong-arm, put the heat on, squeeze; bribe, blackmail, buy.

7. tyrannize, terrorize, threaten, bulldoze, dragoon; bully, hector, torment, harass, abuse, taunt, tease, bullyrag; intimidate, browbeat, cow, frighten, terrify, petrify.

pressured, *adj.* **1.** tense, harried, full of stress, taxed, tired; burdened, troubled, put-upon, weighted down, dragged down, overworked.

2. oppressed, persecuted, subjugated, enslaved; harassed, tormented, intimidated, browbeaten; bribed, blackmailed, bought.

3. influenced, swayed, persuaded, instigated, provoked; driven, pressed, obliged, hustled, railroaded.

prestidigitation, *n.* **1.** legerdemain, sleight of hand, jugglery, juggling, conjuring, hocus-pocus; magic, trickery, thaumaturgy.

2. deception, deceit, dissimulation, duplicity, dark and crooked ways, evil ways; fraud, cheating, chicane; trumpery, dupery, fraudulence, shenanigan; craft, wiles, finesse, *Inf.* razzle-dazzle, cozenage, double-dealing; chicanery, knavery, *Inf.* hanky-panky, *Sl.* funny business, *Sl.* monkey business.

prestidigitator, *n.* legerdemainist, sleight of hand artist, juggler; magician, trickster, wizard, conjurer; theater artist, theatrical performer, artiste, artist.

prestige, *n.* **1.** influence, authority, *Inf.* clout, weight, sway, *Sl.* pull; ascendancy, supremacy, primacy, predominance; stature, superiority, seniority, rank, importance, significance; eminence, preeminence, prominence, distinction, reputation.

2. notability, primacy, fame, repute, reputation; illustriousness, celebrity, stardom, place in the spotlight, notoriety; singularity, uniqueness, impressiveness, stateliness, majesty, grandeur, dignity.

prestigious, *adj.* **1.** distinguished, eminent, famous, famed, well-known, renowned; illustrious, great, glorious, brilliant, radiant, lustrous; celebrated, honored, exalted, acclaimed, much-touted; peerless, unequalled, matchless, unmatched, unparalleled, nonpareil, *Fr. sans pareil*; unsurpassed, unexcelled, second to none, *Latin. nulli secundus.*

2. extraordinary, unusual, different, uncommon, rare, singular, exceptional, out-of-the-ordinary, *Inf.* one for the books, unique, distinct.

3. notable, noteworthy, remarkable, signal, outstanding, noticeable, marked; memorable, unforgettable, *Sl.* hell of a, special, particular, especial; important, significant, momentous, worthy of notice.

4. striking, impressive, imposing, majestic, grand, august, stately, dignified; awesome, awe-inspiring, lofty, wondrous, marvelous, prodigious; stupendous, amazing, astounding, incredible.

presto, *adv.* **1.** quickly, hastily, speedily, hurriedly; promptly, instantly, straightaway, *Sl.* pronto, in a wink, in an instant, double-quick, *Inf.* like greased lightning, like a shot, like a thunderbolt, *Sl.* like mad, *Sl.* like a bat out of hell; directly, at once, without delay, in less than no time, before one can say "Jack Robinson," before the ink is dry, *Sl.* P.D.Q., *Inf.* lickety-split; swiftly, rapidly, fast, full tilt, as fast as one's legs can carry one; in no time, in no time at all, right away, no sooner said than done, immediately if not sooner.

—adj. **2.** quick, hasty, speedy, fast, brisk; rapid, swift, hurried, express; sudden, instant, immediate.

presumable, *adj.* probable, odds-on, likely, most likely, reasonable; undoubted, indubitable, certain, sure, *Inf.* sure-as-shooting; apparent, expected, anticipated, in the cards; promising, potential, liable, possible; plausible, credible, believable, feasible, practical.

presumably, *adv.* probably, in all probability, everything being equal, all things considered; likely, most likely, in all likelihood, *Inf.* as like as not, on the face of it, to all appearances; reasonably, in a fair way, apparently, expectedly, seemingly; undoubtedly, indubitably, no doubt, doubtless, doubtlessly, unquestionably, with no question, certainly, surely, positively, *Inf.* dollars to doughnuts.

presume, *v.* **1.** assume, suppose, take for granted, presuppose, postulate, posit, predicate, theorize, hypothesize, hypothecate, speculate; suspect, imagine, surmise, conjecture, guess, hazard a guess; believe, fancy, think, think likely, daresay, opine, *Northern U.S.* calculate, *Inf.* allow, conclude, judge, realize; infer, *Inf.* take it, deduce; understand, gather, apprehend, get, *Sl.* dig; divine, intuit.

2. take liberties, overstep, intrude, go too far, encroach, be so bold, *Sl.* come on like gangbusters; venture, dare, stick one's neck out, strike out, surge ahead *or* forward; usurp, arrogate, take over.

presumption, *n.* **1.** assumption, presupposition, predisposition, posit, postulate; belief, conviction, confidence, bias, feeling, gut feeling; expectation, anticipation, hope, trust; inference, deduction, theory, hypothesis, thesis; thought, view, attitude, position, stand; guess, suspicion, conjecture, speculation, surmise.

2. ground, reason, basis, premise, proposition, evidence; probability, likelihood, plausibility, feasibility.

3. presumptuousness, forwardness, self-assurance, self-assertiveness, self-importance, immodesty, vanity, conceit, *Inf.* bigheadedness, *Inf.* swelled-headedness; arrogance, overconfidence, *Sl.* snottiness, nastiness, *Inf.* pushiness, *Inf.* nerve, *Inf.* gall, brass, *Inf.* cheek; brazenness, boldness, chutzpah, audacity, audaciousness, temerity; impertinence, effrontery, insolence, impudence, frowardness, obstinacy, willfulness; imperiousness, lordliness, snobbishness, loftiness, disdain, hauteur.

presumptive, *adj.* **1.** reasonable, plausible, credible, believable; logical, sane, sound, firm; making sense, sensible, holding water.

2. inferred, supposed, believed, deduced; assumed, understood, presumable, hypothetical, theoretical; postulated, postulative, predicated; predicted, predictable, probably, likely, in the cards.

presumptuous, *adj.* **1.** confident, presuming, assuming, convinced, persuaded, satisfied; undoubting, unquestioning, trustful, trusting; expectant, anticipatory, anticipating; assured, positive, sure, cocksure, *Inf.* pretty damned sure, sure in one's own mind; hopeful, sanguine.

2. impertinent, insolent, impudent, saucy, *Inf.* sassy, fresh; smart-alecky, *Sl.* wise, *Sl.* smart-assed, *Sl.* biggety, *Inf.* too big for one's britches, *Inf.* bigheaded, *Inf.* swelled-headed, egotistical; bold, overbold, forward, obtrusive, audacious, brazen; bumptious, self-assertive, *Inf.* pushy, *Inf.* cheeky, nervy, brassy; arrogant, overconfident, overweening, overbearing, haughty; brash, cocky, lippy, mouthy, loud-mouthed; rude, ill-mannered, disrespectful, discourteous; disdainful, snobbish, lordly, imperious, domineering, dictatorial.

presuppose, *v.* suppose, assume, presume, take for granted, premise; postulate, posit, predicate, theorize, hypothesize, hypothecate, speculate; suspect, *Nonstandard.* suspicion, be inclined to think, imagine, expect, surmise, guess; think, deem, opine, *Chiefly Midland and Southern U.S. Inf.* reckon, believe, *Archaic.* trow, fancy, dream; infer, conclude, *Inf.* take it, take it into one's head, jump to conclusions, rush to conclusions; understand, gather, conjecture, divine, intuit.

presupposition, *n.* supposition, assumption, presumption, premise; preconception, prenotion, preconceived notion, prejudice, bias, slant, foregone conclusion; speculation, view, opinion, belief; guess, guesswork, conjecture; surmise, inference, deduction, understanding; thesis, hypothesis, theory, postulate, postulation, axiom.

pretend, *v.* **1.** simulate, dissimulate, fake, feign, sham, malinger, dissemble, act, sail under false colors, make out, *Sl.* make like, *Inf.* let on; fake it, go through the motions, seem; affect, assume, take on, put on, put on an act, posture, play the role of, put on a false front, *Sl.* ham it up.

2. make believe, imagine, fabricate, create, make up, invent, concoct, hatch.

pretended, *adj.* **1.** alleged, so-called, nominal, in name only, ostensible, professed, claimed, purported, avowed.

2. simulated, dissimulated, feigned, fake, faked; counterfeit, unauthentic, unreal, mock, ersatz, sham, spurious, bogus, *Inf.* phony; fictitious, contrived, imaginary, make-believe, trumped-up, created, concocted, fabricated; affected, adopted, put-on, artificial, plastic, unnatural, insincere, pseudo; specious, meretricious, theatrical.

3. reputed, supposed, assumed, presumed, inferred; asserted, asseverated, avered, affirmed.

pretender, *n.* **1.** humbug, humbugger, masquerader, wolf in sheep's clothing, dissembler, hypocrite, pharisee; imposter, fake, *Inf.* faker, fraud, sham, phony; charlatan, quack, empiric, mountebank, *Inf.* shyster; deceiver, bamboozler, hoodwinker, trickster; misleader, bluff, bluffer, *Inf.* fourflusher, deluder, duper; cheat, cheater, defrauder, chiseler, bilker; exploiter, confidence man, *Sl.* con man, *Sl.* rip-off artist, *Sl.* flimflam man, smooth *or* fast talker; sharper, sharpie, shark; liar, prevaricator, fibber.

2. *Often* **pretender to** claimant, claimer, aspirant, seeker, suitor, competitor, rival, candidate.

3. poser, poseur, posturer, attitudinarian; braggart, boaster, *Sl.* blowhard, puffer, *Sl.* gasbag, *Sl.* windbag.

pretense, *n.* **1.** pretending, feigning, faking, simulation; make believe, fantasy, fabrication, concoction, invention, creation; figment, fiction, fable; false show, semblance, appearance, guise, color; disguise, camouflage, masquerade, mask, veil, cloak, cover; mummery, shield, deflection, false front, false colors, obscuration; gloss, varnish, veneer.

2. humbug, hoax, fraud, wile, ruse, sham, *Archaic.* chouse; counterfeit, fake, falsification; deception, delusion, imposition, imposture, artifice, humbuggery; dissemblance, misrepresentation, untruthfulness; falsehood, lie, fib, dodge, blind, feint, shift; swindle, trickery, trick.

3. pretension, pretext, ostensible *or* alleged reason, motive. See **pretext** (*def.* **1**).

4. pretentiousness, show-offishness, peacockishness, pomposity, pompousness, inflation; vaunting, flaunting, affectation, *Brit. Sl.* side; boasting, gasconade, bragging, fanfaronade, braggadocio, bluster, *Sl.* gas, *Sl.* wind, *Sl.* hot air; ostentatiousness, showiness, gaudiness, loudness.

pretentious, *adj.* **1.** alleging, claiming, professing, purporting, avowing; pretending, feigning.

2. pompous, bombastic, inflated, vain, vainglorious, peacockish, show-offish; boastful, bragging, flaunting, rodomontade; egotistical, self-important, self-glorifying, fastuous, arrogant, haughty, puffed-up, *Inf.* highfalutin; stuck-up, conceited, high-and-mighty, *Brit. Sl.* toffee-nosed; complacent, smug; dandified, foppish, *Inf.* la-di-da, preening, mannered, affected.

3. ostentatious, overwrought, overdone, overdecorated, extreme; artificial, surface, specious, doggy; ornate, baroque, rococo, gaudy; high-toned, high-flown, flowery, florid, grandiose, elaborate, spectacular, fancy; orotund, conspicuous, loud, garish, brassy, showy, flashy, flamboyant, glittering, theatrical, *Sl.* grandstand; raw, crude, vulgar, untasteful, tasteless.

preternatural, *adj.* **1.** abnormal, anomalous, anomalistic, unnatural, supranatural; unusual, uncommon, exceptional, singular; fabulous, remarkable, extraordinary, out of the ordinary, out of this world; wondrous, wonderful, marvelous, miraculous, thaumaturgic, thaumaturgical.

2. supernatural, supernormal, hypernormal, preternormal; superhuman, preterhuman; superphysical, hyperphysical.

3. otherworldly, unearthly, supermundane, supramundane, extramundane; spiritual, transcendental, metaphysical; magical, unreal, fey; occult, cabalistic, mystic, mystical; mysterious, arcane, esoteric, unknown; eerie. weird, strange, bizarre, uncanny.

pretext, *n.* **1.** pretense, pretension, ostensible *or* alleged reason, motive; reason, basis, grounds, support, justification, vindication; plea, allegation, defense, apology, rationalization, rationale; claim, assertion, profession, avowal, declaration; excuse, *U.S. Inf.* alibi, explanation, story, cover story, *Inf.* song and dance.

2. subterfuge, evasion, *Sl.* cop-out; cover, cloak, disguise, camouflage, mask; semblance, appearance, show, guise, color.

prettify, *v.* **1.** *Often Disparaging.* pretty, pretty up, make pretty, beautify, make beautiful; dress up, *Sl.* jazz up, liven up, perk up, brighten up; spruce up, smarten up, *Inf.* titivate, *Sl.* spiff up; embellish, trim, garnish, decorate, adorn, deck, bedeck, deck out, array, ornament; polish, burnish, buff, shine; paint, repaint, redo, redecorate, renew, restore.

2. (*usu. of oneself*) dress, primp, prink, prank, preen, *Archaic.* prune, *Sl.* doll up, *Sl.* dude up, dress to the hilt *or* teeth, *Sl.* gussy up.

3. minimize, downplay, de-emphasize, gloss over, explain away, make light *or* little of, brush [s.t.] off.

pretty, *adj.* **1.** pleasing, delightful, pleasant, nice, lovely, appealing, attractive, handsome, canny, *Inf.* eye-catching; pretty as a picture, *Both Chiefly U.S. Inf.* cute, cute as a button; dainty, delicate, minion, graceful, elegant; well-favored, good-looking, nice-looking, fair, *Chiefly Scot.* bonny, becoming, seemly, sightly, *Inf.* eye-filling, comely, pulchritudinous, *Chiefly Literary.* beauteous; beautiful, *Fr. beau* or *belle*, gorgeous, stunning, ravishing, sexy, *Sl.* foxy; shapely, well-shaped, well-proportioned, *Inf.* curvaceous, *Inf.* curvy, voluptuous, *Sl.* stacked, well-endowed, full-bosomed, buxom; fetching, charming, engaging, captivating, enthralling, enchanting, bewitching, fascinating, winsome, winning; alluring, enticing, tempting, seductive, come-hither, inviting.

2. pleasing to the ear, melodious, tuneful, dulcet, sweet-sounding, musical, silvery; velvety, smooth, golden.

3. *Informal.* considerable, fairly large, substantial, sizable, goodly, rather big.

—n. **4.** *Usu.* **pretties** ornaments, jewelry, pretty clothes, pretty things, finery.

—adv. **5.** moderately, reasonably, fairly, passably, adequately, decently, acceptably, satisfactorily, sufficiently.

6. quite, fairly, rather, somewhat; very, really.

7. **sitting pretty** *Slang.* **a.** in a good spot, in an advantageous *or* favorable position, in the catbird seat. **b.** well-to-do, well-off, in clover, *Sl.* on easy street, *Inf.* well-fixed, financially set; prosperous, rich, wealthy, fat, *Inf.* well-heeled, affluent, opulent, flush, moneyed, *Sl.* loaded, *Sl.* in the bucks, *Sl.* rolling in dough.

—v. **8.** pretty up, prettify, make pretty, beautify. See **prettify** (*defs.* **1, 2**).

prevail, *v.* **1.** predominate, reign, rule, hold sway, have force, preponderate; lead, win out, succeed, be successful, be a winner *or* a success, dominate, hold authority, wear the crown, sit on the throne, *Inf.* sit in the driver's seat; wield the scepter, govern, command, have ascendancy, have mastery.

2. triumph, win, be victorious, be the victor, conquer, overcome, defeat; best, checkmate, outmaneuver, gain a victory, carry the day, win out, win one's spurs; ring the bell, gain the palm, take the crown, *Inf.* bring home the bacon.

3. endure, last, continue to exist, persist, be durable, wear well, abide, *Archaic.* bide, stay, remain, hold on, hold one's ground; hold out against, withstand, sustain without yielding, bear, weather, take it, brave it out, *Inf.* hang in there, keep one's head above water, weather the storm.

4. prevail on *or* **upon** persuade, induce, influence, sway, incline, dispose; move, prompt, motivate, stimulate, rouse, inspire; urge, exhort, inportune; bring to bear upon, bear down upon, put the pressure on, press, apply pressure, *Inf.* pressure *or* high-pressure; convince, convert, wean, win *or* win over, bring round *or* around, enlist, make [s.o.] see the light; talk into, sell, sell [s.o.] on, wangle, *Inf.* rope in *or* into, *Sl.* hook, *Sl.* con; wheedle, cajole, coax, sweet-talk.

prevailing, *adj.* **1.** predominant, preponderant, preponderating, dominant, dominating; ruling, regnant, reigning; preeminent, supreme, chief, principal.

2. prevalent, current. See **prevalent**.

3. effective, effectual, telling, moving, affecting, powerful, potent, vigorous, forceful, convincing, persuasive.

prevalence, *n.* **1.** predominance, preponderance, ascendancy. See **predominance**.

2. ubiquity, ubiquitousness, omnipresence, universality, catholicity; pervasiveness, diffusiveness; commonness, currency, popularity, acceptance, favor.

prevalent, *adj.* widespread, extensive, ubiquitous, general, rife, rampant; universal, catholic, world-wide, global, nationwide; generally held, common, commonplace, everyday, conventional, established, usual; present, current, making the rounds, popular, in fashion, in vogue, modern, *Inf.* trendy. See also **prevailing** (*def.* **1**).

prevaricate, *v.* **1.** lie, equivocate, stretch the truth, be untruthful, be a liar, *Inf.* tell a story, deviate from the truth; fib, euphemize, shilly-shally, evade, sidestep; dodge, fence, hedge, beat about the bush; elude, shy, weasel, be evasive, evade the truth, shuffle, shift, parry, beg the question, dissemble; fake, counterfeit, *Inf.* fake it, *Inf.* talk a good game; play a double game, play false, hoodwink; pettifog, quibble, cavil, split hairs, mince words, stickle, trifle.

2. falsify, belie, misrepresent, distort *or* twist the truth, misinform, mislead, construe falsely, put a false construction on, give a false color to; put on, pretend, sham, make-believe, sail under false colors; pervert, distort, strain, warp, twist, slant, color; gild, varnish, gloss, doctor, dress up, embellish, embroider, *Inf.* titivate, *Inf.* talk through one's hat, *Inf.* speak with forked tongue; deceive, lead [s.o.] down *or* up the garden path, throw [s.o.] off the scent, put [s.o.] on a false scent; drag *or* draw a red herring across the trail; disguise *or* mask the truth, conceal *or* hide the truth, cover up, *Inf.* deodorize, *Inf.* whitewash.

3. tell a lie *or* falsehood, fabricate, invent, manufacture, make up, trump up; hatch, concoct, *Inf.* cook up, *Inf.* make out of whole cloth; exaggerate, hyperbolize, inflate, blow up, puff up; magnify, enlarge on, overkill, carry too far, caricature, travesty, burlesque, make a mockery of the truth; slander, defame, libel, calumniate, traduce; perjure oneself, swear falsely, forswear, lie in one's teeth, lie flatly, speak falsely, bear false witness, lie like a trooper, lie like a rug.

prevarication, *n.* **1.** lie, falsehood, untruth, fib, white lie, little white lie, quibble, overrefinement, *Inf.* taradiddle; equivocation, evasion, shuffling; pettifoggery, hairsplitting, caviling; fencing, evasiveness, elusiveness; chicanery, pretense, artfulness, guile, *Inf.* flimflammery.

2. falsity, fiction, falsification, invention, concoction, fabrication; half-truth, stretching *or* distortion *or* perversion of the truth; story, trumped-up story, tale, fairy tale, fable, myth, romance; exaggeration, overstatement, coloring, magnification, enlargement, yarn, *Inf.* tall tale *or* story, *Inf.* cock-and-bull story, *Inf.* shaggy dog story, *Inf.* fish story; nonsense, *Inf.* claptrap.

3. counterfeiting, faking, shamming, falsifying; misrepresentation, corruption, inaccuracy; misconstruction, subterfuge, deceptiveness, false coloring, falseness, deception, slanting, straining, torturing; canard, rumor, hoax, forgery; monstrous lie, the big lie, *Sl.* whopper, *Sl.* barefaced lie; perjury, foreswearing, false swearing, defamation, slander, traducement, calumny, calumniation.

prevaricator, *n.* **1.** liar, fibber, storyteller, taleteller, falsifier, fabricator; dodger, equivocator, shuffler, evader, bluffer, bluff, fake, hypocrite; dissembler, sophist, casuist, quibbler, canter; deceiver, beguiler, seducer.

2. humbug, cheat, cozener, deluder, hoaxer, double-dealer, confidence man, *Sl.* con man; perjurer, false witness.

prevent, *v.* **1.** obstruct, hinder, hamper, block, impede, interrupt, interfere, interpose, intervene; stop, put a stop to, halt, check, arrest, abort, preclude; frustrate, thwart, foil, balk, baffle; restrain, inhibit, repress, constrain; delay, retard, forestall, hold back; oppose, contravene, override; prohibit, proscribe, debar, disallow, veto, taboo.

2. avert, obviate, avoid, nip in the bud, ward off, fend off, stave off; deflect, parry, turn aside, draw off, sidetrack; neutralize, render harmless.

prevention, *n.* **1.** impediment, hindrance, obstacle, block, obstruction, barrier, oppilation, obtrusion, interference; interruption, determent, stoppage, arrest, check; retardation, forestalling; curb, inhibition, restraint, constraint, restriction, constriction; checkmate, deadlock, foreclosure, defeat; forbiddance, prohibition, interdiction, injunction, proscription, preclusion, ban, embargo, veto, taboo.

2. preventive, preventative, prophylactic, shield, safeguard; deterrent, neutralizer, counteragent; remedy, medicine, antidote, vaccine, serum.

preventive, *adj.* **1.** prophylactic, preventative, deterrent; counteractive, neutralizing, shielding, protective.

2. hindering, hampering, impeding, impedimental, obstructive; interfering, intrusive, interruptive; inhibitive, restrictive, constraining.

—*n.* **3.** prophylactic, preventative, prevention, shield, protection, safeguard, deterrent, neutralizer, counteragent; remedy, medicine, antidote, vaccine, serum.

4. hindrance, impediment, obstacle, obstruction, oppilation; barrier, stopper, blockage, blockade, block, *Archaic.* remora; retardation, setback, forestalling, determent, stoppage; curb, restraint, constraint, restriction, inhibition; forbiddance, prohibition, interdiction, injunction, proscription, preclusion, ban, embargo, veto, taboo.

preview, *n.* **1.** prior *or* previous view *or* study.

2. advance showing, private screening, sneak preview, preview of coming attractions; trailer, clip, shots, scenes; foretaste, appetizer, teaser, lure, *Inf.* come-on.

previous, *adj.* **1.** prior, former, earlier, foregone; preceding, antecedent, anterior, precedent, precurrent; erstwhile, ex, onetime, sometime, quondam, whilom; foregoing, aforegoing, forerunning, pre-existent; preliminary, prelusive, precursory, prevenient; fore, once, then; recent, late, last, *Fr. feu*; old, early, ancient, older, elder; latter, aforesaid, aforementioned, above-mentioned, aforenamed, above-named, named, said,

Fr. ci-devant.

2. previous to before, prior to, earlier than, preceding; hereinbefore, hereinabove.

previously, *adv.* **1.** formerly, at one time, once, aforetime; hitherto, thitherto, heretofore, theretofore, ere now, *Archaic.* erst, *Archaic.* erewhile; a while ago, a while back, sometime back; until now, beforetime, then, before, above, ultimo.

2. once upon a time, on the eve of, yesterday, yesteryear, recently; in days of yore, of yore, in days of old, of old, in the past; in times past, back then, long ago, ages ago; in years gone by, ago, one fine day, one fine morning, *Archaic.* agone; since, back when, way back.

prey, *n.* **1.** quarry, game, kill, the hunted; victim, target, objective; dupe, patsy, *Inf.* mark *or* easy mark, sitting duck, *Inf.* easy pickings; trusting soul, *Inf.* babe in the woods.

—*v.* **2.** *Usu.* **prey on** *or* **upon** feed upon, feast upon, gorge upon, devour, eat, consume; fasten upon, catch hold of, grab, nab.

3. victimize, override, trample *or* stamp upon, crush, ride roughshod over, subjugate; coerce, intimidate, *Sl.* strong-arm, bully; bear hard upon, *Inf.* put the screws to, terrorize; fleece, take advantage of, take for a ride, *Inf.* con, *Inf.* flimflam, cheat.

4. pillage, depredate, loot, sack, ransack, freeboot, pirate, privateer; raid, raven, ravage, ravish, despoil; destroy, strip, spoil.

5. oppress, weigh one down, rest hard upon, lie heavy upon, weigh on *or* upon, bear on *or* upon, weigh down, hang like a millstone *or* a dark cloud; encumber, cumber, tax, overburden, burden, strain, worry, vex.

price, *n.* **1.** cost, expense, charge, *Inf.* damages, fee, rate; check, *Inf.* tab, bill, *Fr. addition*; pay, payment, hire, rent, fare, toll, tax, levy, duty, assessment; consideration, compensation, recompense, remuneration; outlay, expenditure; value, worth, amount, figure; valuation, appraisal, quotation, demand, asking price.

2. bounty, reward, *Literary.* guerdon, premium, bonus; prize, honorarium, stipend.

3. threshold of honor, threshold, limit; weakness, susceptibility, chink in one's armor, Achilles heel.

4. consequence, result, penalty, fine, loss, forfeiture, suffering, damage.

5. without price priceless, of incalculable value, precious, treasured, prized, cherished, invaluable. See **priceless**.

—*v.* **6.** value, evaluate, appraise, rate, judge, assess, assay; set the price *or* cost.

priceless, *adj.* without price, beyond price, inestimable, invaluable, incalculable; precious, treasured, prized, cherished; costly, expensive, high priced, high, out-of-sight, dear, costing a fortune; worth its weight in gold, worth a king's ransom; irreplaceable, incomparable, peerless, nonpareil, one-of-a-kind, one-in-a-million, unique.

prick, *n.* **1.** puncture, perforation, hole, pinhole, pock, pit, nick, gouge, groove.

2. sting, smart, prickle, tingle, tickle, ache, pain, hurt, discomfort.

3. point, rowel, spur, barb, barbule, prong, tine, spike.

—*v.* **4.** pierce, puncture, perforate, make a hole in, punch, honeycomb, riddle; stab, knife, lancinate, stick, nick, pink, gore; cut, gash, slit, gride; cut up, lacerate.

5. pain, stab, wound, hurt; affect, afflict, move, touch, cut to the quick, *Inf.* hit home, *Inf.* get *or* get to; turn the knife in the wound, rub it in, sadden, cast down; touch one's heart, touch a chord, tug at the heartstrings, break one's heart; make an impression, make a dent, *Inf.* sink in; melt, soften, mellow, play on.

6. urge, goad, poke, spur, prompt, prod; push, drive, propel, hound, dog, whip, lash; incite, sic, provoke, instigate, actuate, activate, motivate; foment, agitate, stimulate, *Inf.* start something; excite, arouse, rouse, whip up, work up, stir up, enflame, inflame, fire up, kindle, light a fire under, touch off; encourage, exhort, pique, *Sl.* goose, egg on, put up to.

7. sting, prickle, tingle, smart, itch, ache.

prickle, *n.* **1.** point, cusp, spur, barb, barbule, prong, tine, spike, needle, tang, spicule, *Zool.* spiculum, spine, spinule, bristle, acicula; thorn, sticker, brier, *Bot.* apiculus, bur, burr, snag; nettle, bramble, cocklebur.

2. tingle, tingling, gooseflesh, crawly flesh; sting, tickle, smart, prick, formication, *Pathol.* paresthesia.

—*v.* **3.** prick, stick, nick, pink, flick.

4. tingle, sting, smart, itch, twitch, vellicate.

prickly, *adj.* **1.** brambly, briery, thorny; bristly, *Bot.* strigose, *Zool.* barbellate, setigerous, setaceous, setose; spiny, spinous, spinulose, acanthoid, like a porcupine, thistlelike, aciculate; barbed, *Bot., Zool.* muricate, spiculate.

2. troublesome, difficult, hard, tough, arduous, trying; entangled, complicated, intricate, knotty; nettlesome, irksome, tedious, irritating; thorny, touchy, delicate, ticklish, critical.

3. prickling, pricking, smarting, stinging, tingling, tickling, itchy, scratchy.

pride, *n.* **1.** arrogance, haughtiness, hauteur, hoity-toity, *Inf.* uppitiness, *Inf.* toploftiness; hubris, overconfidence, cocksureness, presumption, bumptiousness, overbearingness, overweeningness.

2. conceit, vanity, vainglory, vaingloriousness, bovarism, *Inf.* ego trip, *Inf.* big head; egotism, egoism, self-importance, self-conceit, self-approbation, self-admiration, self-love, self-worship, self-adulation, self-idolization; self-praise, self-glorification, boastfulness, braggadocio, jactation, bluster, fanfaronade, gasconade; complacency, smugness, self-satisfaction, self-content.

3. self-respect, self-esteem, ego, feelings, sensibilities, *Fr. amour propre*; self-image, self-concept, self-identity, identity, picture *or* image of oneself.

4. boast, pride and joy, treasure, jewel, gem; good thing, thing to be desired.

—*v.* **5.** preen, take pride, be proud; glory in, exult in, bask in, wallow in; congratulate oneself, hug oneself, pat oneself on the back.

priest, *n.* **1.** clergyman, cleric, clerical, clerk, ecclesiastic, churchman, minister, divine, man of the cloth, man of God, minister of the gospel, servant of God, cassock, abbé, spiritual father, rabbi, religious, reverend, *Brit.* blackcoat, liturgist, *Rare.* liturge.

2. monastic, monk, friar, brother, celibate, cenobite, conventual, *Eastern Church.* caloyer; prior, abbot, *Eastern Church.* archimandrite.

3. pastor, rector, dean, vicar, *Dial.* dominie, parson, father, padre, curate, curé, chaplain; Levite; presbyter, deacon, lector.

4. pope, pontiff, chief priest, high priest, hierarch, bishop, archbishop, prelate, primate, cardinal, penitentiary; *Hinduism.* Brahman *or* Brahmin, *Tibetan Buddhism.* lama, *Ethiopian Church.* abuna.

5. prophet, diviner, druid, hierophant; theologian, Talmudist, canonist; *Judaism.* scribe; *Class. Myth.* Corybant, (*in ancient Rome*) flamen, (*in ancient Greece*) hierodule.

6. preacher, evangelist, missionary, *Usu. Disparaging.* pulpiteer; sermonizer, sermonist, *Obs. Rare.* sermoneer.

priesthood, *n.* **1.** prelacy, episcopacy; clericality, clericalism, episcopalianism, sacerdotalism, ultramontanism; vocation, call, calling, sacred calling, holy orders.

2. the clergy, the ministry, the cloth, the pulpit, the desk.

priestly, *adj.* clerical, canonical, sacerdotal, prelatic, pastoral, ministerial, ecclesiastic, ultramontane; churchly, priestlike.

prig, *n.* prude, puritan, bluenose; snob, intellectual snob, *Disparaging.* highbrow; pedant, precisionist, purist, formalist; fussbudget, fusspot, *Inf.* fuddy-duddy, carper, caviler, pettifogger, faultfinder, *Inf.* nitpicker.

priggish, *adj.* **1.** prudish, puritanical, bluenosed, overmodest, old-maidish; hidebound, strait-laced, stiff, stiff-necked, strict, severe, formal; snobbish, stilted, *Inf.* high-hat, *Sl.* snooty, *Sl.* snotty; smug, sanctimonious, *Inf.* stuffy; fastidious, punctilious, fussy; censorious, reproachful, condemnatory, disparaging, contemptuous; carping, caviling, pettifogging, faultfinding, *Inf.* nitpicking; pedantic, puristic, formalistic, precisionistic.

2. overnice, precious, précieux, namby-pamby, *Inf.* goody-goody, *Inf.* nice-Nelly, *Brit. Sl.* twee.

priggishness, *n.* **1.** prudery, prudishness, puritanicalness, overmodesty, old-maidishness, Grundyism; hideboundness, strait-lacedness, buckram, stiffness, stiff-neckedness, strictness, severity, formality; snobbery, snobbishness, stiltedness, *Sl.* snootiness, *Sl.* snottiness; smugness, sanctimony, *Inf.* stuffiness; fastidiousness, punctiliousness, fussiness, censoriousness, reproachfulness, contemptuousness; pedantry, purism, formalism, precisionism.

2. overniceness, preciousness, namby-pambyism, *Inf.* goody-goodyism, *Inf.* nice-Nellyism.

prim, *adj.* starched, rigid, stiff, formal, *Inf.* tight; strait-laced, stiff-necked, hidebound, in buckram; prudish, priggish, puritanical, squeamish; exact, exacting, punctilious, fastidious, scrupulous.

primal, *adj.* **1.** primary, prime, initial, initiative, first, premier, opening; pristine, earliest, early.

2. original, aboriginal, autochthonal, autochthonous; primitive, primordial, primigenial; incipient, beginning, germinal, embryonic, embryonal, genetic, genetical, nascent.

3. primeval, archaic, fossil, fossillike, fossilized; ancient, antiquated, antique, oldest, old, aged; prehistoric, preadamic, Noachian, Noachic, Noachical, antediluvian, before the Flood *or* Deluge; eolithic, Paleolithic, Mesolithic, Neolithic.

4. principal, main, major, meat-and-potatoes, central, most important; head, capital, chief, cardinal, paramount; prominent, dominant, predominant, hegemonic, prevailing; crucial, vital, critical, significant, consequential, momentous.

5. fundamental, basic, radical, root, elemental, underlying; essential, indispensable, necessary, needed; elementary, rudimentary, rudimental, inchoate.

primarily, *adv.* **1.** above all, first and foremost, in the first place, to begin with; essentially, in essence, fundamentally, basically, in substance, at heart, at the core, at bottom, *Fr. au fond*; especially, particularly; chiefly, mainly, in the main, mostly, for the most part, principally, predominately, on the whole.

2. at first, at the beginning, in the beginning, originally, initially; from the beginning, from the start, *Inf.* from the word go, *Latin. ab inito, Latin. ab orgine, Latin. ab ovo.*

primary, *adj.* **1.** prime, principal, capital, chief, cardinal, paramount; main, major, meat-and-potatoes, central, head, most important.

2. earliest, pristine, primeval, primal; primitive, primordial, primigenial, aboriginal, autochthonal, autochthonous.

3. original, genetic, genetical, incipient, beginning, nascent, embryonic, embryonal, germinal; initiative, initial, premier, first, opening.

4. basic, fundamental, radical, root, elemental, underlying; introductory, preparatory, proemial; elementary, simple, rudimentary, rudimental, inchoate.

5. immediate, noninterventional; direct, without intermediary, straightforward, not roundabout.

—n. **6.** first, alpha, beginning; original, antecedent, precedent, ancestor, precursor; zenith, acme, summit, pinnacle, peak; eminence, senior, elder, presbyter; principal, chief, head; paramount, overlord, sovereign, ruler.

primate, *n.* **1.** *Eccles.* cardinal, archbishop, metropolitan, bishop, coadjutor, auxiliary, suffragan; prelate, hierarch, high priest, archpriest, *Ethiopian Ch.* abuna, *Eastern Ch.* exarch; patriarch, patriarch of Constantinople, patriarch of Alexandria; pope, pontiff, Holy Father, Vicar of Christ, Supreme Pontiff; official, dignitary, overseer, supervisor; (*both usu. used as titles*) reverence, eminence.

2. mammal, breast-feeder; man, *Homo sapiens*, biped; anthropoid, ape, monkey, simian, gorilla, orang-utan, chimpanzee, *Inf.* chimp, baboon, gibbon; lemur, tarsier, marmoset.

prime, *adj.* **1.** primary, principal. See **primary** (*def.* **1**).

2. supereminent, preeminent, eminent, *Archaic.* egregious, illustrious; distinguished, famous, famed, renowned, celebrated, prominent, well-known; star, sovereign, ruling; ranking, leading, top drawer; predominant, hegemonic, prevailing; senior, elder.

3. valuable, precious, expensive, costly, worth a lot.

4. first-rate, first-class, ace, grade A, tops, topflight, *Inf.* tiptop, *Inf.* topnotch, *Brit. Sl.* top-hole, second to none; quality, select, choice, picked, selected.

5. supreme, superlative, best, highest, top, crowning, acmic, summital; greatest, maximal, nonpareil, unparalleled, matchless, peerless, utmost, uppermost; transcendent, unsurpassed, unapproached; superior, extraordinary, exceptional, excellent, *Inf.* dandy, *Inf.* whiz-bang, *Inf.* crack, *Brit. Sl.* whizzo; outstanding, great, admirable, remarkable, noteworthy.

6. earliest, pristine, primeval, primal; original, genetic, genetical, incipient, beginning, nascent, embryonic, embryonal, germinal; initiative, initial, premier, first, opening; primitive, primordial, primigenial, aboriginal, autocthonal, autochthonous.

7. basic, fundamental. See **primary** (*def.* **4**).

—n. **8.** heyday, efflorescence, flower, full flowering, bloom, blossom, blossoming.

9. maturity, adultness, adulthood, manhood, womanhood.

10. peak, pinnacle, summit, apex, acme, zenith, top, the tops; climax, culmination.

—v. **11.** prepare, prep, break the ice; ready, make *or* get ready, break in; educate, instruct, teach, tutor, coach, train, drill; guide, show; supply, equip, fit out *or* up, *Inf.* beef up.

12. inform, apprise, notify, tell, brief, prompt, *Inf.* cue [s.o.] in, *Inf.* cram, *Sl.* fill in, *Inf.* give [s.o.] the low-down.

primed, *adj.* **1.** ready, ready for anything, ready to go, all ready, good and ready, in readiness, set, all set, prepared, *Inf.* prepped, *Sl.* loaded for bear; in the saddle, booted and spurred, *Inf.* itching *or* dying to get started, *Inf.* rarin' to go, *Inf.* champing at the bit, *Inf.* psyched *or* psyched up; (*both of a firearm*) loaded, cocked.

2. informed, well-informed, versed, well-versed, up-to-date, up on, *Fr. au courant*, abreast of; posted, briefed, familiarized, brought up to date; trained, coached, instructed, taught.

primeval, *adj.* primitive, primal, prehistoric, preadamic, Noachian, Noachic, Noachical, antediluvian, eolithic, Paleolithic, Mesolithic, Neolithic; primary, prime, pristine, early, earliest, initiative, initial, premier, first; primordial, autochthonal, autochthonous, aboriginal, indigenous, endemic, endemical, native, vernacular; archaic, fossil, fossilized, fossillike, antiquated, antique, ancient, aged, oldest, old; original, embryonic, embryonal, genetic, primigenial, etiological.

primitive, *adj.* **1.** primeval, primal, prehistoric, preadamic, Noachian, Noachic, Noachical, antediluvian, eolithic, Paleolithic, Mesolithic, Neolithic, atavistic; early, earliest; original, autochthonal, autochthonous, aboriginal, native, endemic, endemical, indigenous, vernacular.

2. uncivilized, barbaric, savage, barbarous, wild, untamed.

3. quaint, old-fashioned, unmodern; ancient, oldest, immemorial, remote, age-old, old, elderly, aged, antiquated, fossilized, fossillike, archaic.

4. primordial, primigenial, elementary, simple, uncomplicated, plain, natural; pristine, uncorrupted, unsullied; unsophisticated, uncultivated, uncultured, uncouth.

5. crude, unrefined, coarse, rough, unpolished; rudimentary, embryonic, undeveloped.

6. radical, basic, fundamental, elemental, underlying, underived, immediate; essential, requisite, required, necessary, needed, indispensable; innate, connate, congenital, inborn, intrinsic, inbred, genic, genetic, inherent, inherited, hereditary, ingrained, deep-rooted.

7. prime, primary, initial, first.

—n. **8.** antediluvian, prehistoric man, preadamite, cave man, ape-man; autochthon, aboriginal, *Australian Inf.* boong, original, settler, pioneer, *Australian.* bushman.

9. barbarian, savage, wild man.

10. antiquity, antique, relic, fossil, petroglyph.

11. rudiment, fundamental; essential, requisite, requirement, necessity.

primordial, *adj.* **1.** original, primigenial, etiological; seminal, generative, genic, genetic, inherent, inherited, hereditary; elementary, elemental, radical, basic, fundamental, underlying; embryonic, rudimentary; originitive, creative, imaginative, institutive, inventive, formative, initiative.

2. primitive, primal, primary, prime, pristine; early, earliest, initial, first, primeval. See **primeval.**

primp, *v.* **1.** adorn, decorate, ornament, trim, garnish, furbish, embellish, *Archaic.* dight, *Archaic.* ouch; dress, clothe, garb, habit; outfit, fit up, accouter, gear, turn out; array, bedizen, deck, deck out, bedeck, trap.

2. (*all of oneself*) preen, plume, groom; beautify, prettify, *Inf.* titivate, *Inf.* spruce up, *Inf.* doll up, *Inf.* gussy up, *Sl.* trick up *or* out, *Sl.* dude up, *Sl.* swank up, *Sl.* fig out.

princely, *adj.* **1.** liberal, generous, beneficent, bounteous, munificent; magnanimous, big, big-hearted; philanthropic, altruistic, benevolent; open-handed, unstinting, giving; ungrudging, kind, kindhearted, compassionate, gracious; tolerant, indulgent, unprovincial, cosmopolitan, unprejudiced, unbiased, impartial.

2. lavish, profuse, rich, ample, copious, abundant; bountiful, plenteous, plentiful, rife, luxuriant; magnificent, splendid, *Inf.* splendiferous, resplendent; superb, glorious, brilliant, radiant; luxurious, sumptuous, gorgeous, *All Inf.* posh, plush, swank, ritzy.

3. noble, royal, titled, highborn, to the manner born; royal, regal; stately, grand, august, imposing, impressive, awesome; majestic, dignified, imposing, princelike; royal, monarchical, monarchial; of noble blood, of noble rank, of royal blood.

principal, *adj.* **1.** chief, prime, paramount; most important, first, highest, leading; main, major, cardinal, supreme; superlative, best, crowning, acmic, acmatic, summital; greatest, maximal, nonpareil, unparalleled, matchless, peerless; utmost, uppermost, supereminent, preminent; star, sovereign, ruling; prevailing, hegemonic, dominant, predominat; ranking, leading, foremost; definitive, conclusive, determinative; key, vital, crucial, central, essential; strongest, most effective, ultimate.

—n. **2.** chief, head, lead; captain, *Inf.* boss, *Inf.* bossman, *Inf.* kingpin, *Inf.* number one; *Sl.* top dog, *Sl.* honcho *or* head honcho; director, superior, chairman; manager, overseer, supervisor, foreman, *Brit.* gaffer; pacesetter, mover, inspirer, firer, spark, *Inf.* sparkplug; ringleader, bellwether, flagship, *Sl.* the brains.

3. headmaster, dean, school principal, school superintendent; director, college president, chancellor.

4. capital, capital funds, assets, nonliquid funds, savings, reserves, cash reserves; investments, means, working capital, resources, wealth, treasure, trust moneys; backing, *Inf.* seed money.

principality, *n.* **1.** realm, kingdom, domain, dominion; princedom, principate, empery, monarchy; duchy, grandduchy, archduchy, dukedom; earldom, palatinate, province, nation, state.

2. authority, position, power, supreme power, sovereignty; dynasty, regency, prerogative; predominance, rule, reign, hegemony; control, sway, mastery; influence, guidance, leadership; authorization, power, force; jurisdiction, domination, administration.

3. **principalities** *Theology.* archangels, princedoms; celestial attendants, divine messengers, messengers of God; heavenly host, host of heaven, choir invisible, ministering spirits.

principally, *adv.* chiefly, mainly, in the main, mostly, for the most part, predominately, on the whole; essentially, in essence, fundamentally, basically, in substance, at heart, at the core, at bottom, *Fr. au fond*; primarily, above all, first and foremost, in the first place, to begin with; especially, particularly, exceptionally, markedly, signally, notably.

principle, *n.* **1.** rule, law, moral law, golden rule; rule of conduct, rubric, precept; guideline, rule of thumb, basic rule; formula, formulary, method, way; model, standard, criterion, convention, custom, practice; natural law, general truth, universal truth; regulation, ordinance, commandment; mandate, directive, dictum, canon, *Both Rom. Cath. Ch.* bull, encyclical.

2. tenet, maxim, axiom, postulate; truism, truth, self-evident truth; mathematical rule, *Math.* formula, theorem, hypothesis, *Math.* proposition, *Math.* corollary.

3. **principles** code, personal code, moral *or* ethical code; morals, ethics, ethos; standards, platform, ideals, conscience, moral sense, inner monitor, scruples, sense of duty; voice of conscience, that still small voice; morality, probity, uprightness, goodness, rectitude, righteousness; honesty, integrity, honor, character, decency, respectability; responsibility, fidelity, faithfulness, trustworthiness, constancy, loyalty; equity, justice, fair play, fairness, scrupulousness, justness; virtue, piety, purity, innocence, continence, temperance, restraint.

4. order, system, plan, design; discipline, course, routine, program, line; way, manner, mode, process, procedure, *Latin.* *modus operandi,* means, technique, practice.

5. essential quality, essence, element; substance, constituent, germ, seed, heart; rudiment, basic component; substratum, bedrock, basis; stuff, brute matter, constituent material.

6. reason, grounds, motive, rationale, call, motivation; *Inf.* whys, *Inf.* wherefores; basis, impulse, origin genesis.

prink, *v.* **1.** dress *or* dress up, deck *or* deck out, bedeck, bedizen, array, prank; decorate, adorn, ornament, trim, garnish, embellish; prettify, pretty, make pretty, beautify, make beautiful; perk up, brighten up, spruce up, smarten up, make smart, *Inf.* titivate, *Sl.* spiff up, *Sl.* jazz up.

2. (*all of oneself*) dress *or* dress up, deck out, *Sl.* doll up, *Sl.* dude up, dress to the teeth *or* hilt, *Sl.* gussy up; primp, prank, preen, groom, fuss over, *Archaic.* prune.

print, *v.* **1.** reproduce, *Print.* strike off, copy, make a copy of, run off, pull a proof, mimeograph, *Inf.* mimeo, *Trademark.* Xerox, reprint; lithograph, *Print.* offset, electrotype; set, set in print, type-cast, typeset, *Print.* linotype, put *or* send to press, *Print.* put to bed.

2. impress, imprint, indent, mark, stamp, engrave, emboss.

—n. **3.** type, *Print.* face, typeface, lettering, letters, characters; roman type, italics *or* italic type, *Print.* block letter, *Print.* boldface, *Print.* lightface.

4. typescript, printed page, typewriting, letterpress, newsprint.

5. publication, newspaper, magazine, periodical. See **magazine** (*def.* **1**).

6. reproduction, copy, replica, duplicate, facsimile, ectype; lithograph, *Print.* offset, electrotype; carbon copy, carbon, mimeograph, *Inf.* mimeo, *Trademark.* Xerox, reprint; likeness, picture, design, illustration, photograph, *Inf.* photo, snapshot, *Inf.* snap, *Photog.* still.

7. indentation, dent, dint, impression, depression; mark, stamp, seal; imprint, footprint, handprint, thumbprint, fingerprint, smudge.

8. in print a. in printed form, published. **b.** available, on the shelves, in the stores *or* publishing houses.

9. out of print unavailable, not to be found, no longer published, no longer in print.

printer, *n.* pressman, typographer, compositor, typesetter, type-caster, linotyper; master printer, journeyman printer, printer's apprentice, printer's devil, *Print.* devil.

prior[1], *adj.* **1.** former, anterior, earlier; ex, erstwhile, onetime; latter, aforementioned. See **previous** (*def.* **1**).

2. prior to before, earlier than, pervious to. See **previous** (*def.* **2**).

prior[2], *n.* **1.** officer, superior, general, provincial, vicar, abbot; conventual, monk, monastic, cenobite, friar, brother; ecclesiastic, cleric, priest.

2. prioress, abbess, mother superior, mother general, mother vicar.

priority, *n.* **1.** previousness, antecedence, anteriority, foregoing, preceding, precession; anteposition, foreground, forehand, prelude, preface; front, van, the lead; antedating, predating, preexistence.

2. precedence, precedency, seniority, rank, tenure; preference, urgency, top priority, prerogative; authority, weight, moment, influence, consequence, eminence; primacy, preeminence, superiority, supremacy, paramountcy, importance, consequentiality, weightiness.

priory, *n.* monastery, religious house, abbey, cloister, cenoby, friary; convent, nunnery; seminary.

prison, *n.* penitentiary, *Sl.* pen, house of detention, penal institution, state prison, state *or* federal penitentiary, *Sl.* big house, *Sl.* slammer, *Sl.* stir, *Brit. Sl.* college, *Brit. Sl.* porridge; jail, jailhouse, station house, lockup, *Scot.* tolbooth, *Inf.* clink, *U.S. Inf.* calaboose, *Brit. Inf.* bridewell; guardhouse, guardroom, *U.S.* brig; dungeon, black hole, hold, oubliette; *All Sl.* can, cooler, coop, jug, hoosegow, boobyhatch, pokey, *Brit.* choky, *Brit.* quod.

prisoner, *n.* jailbird, convict, *Sl.* con, trusty *or* trustee, *Inf.* lifer, *Sl.* lag, *Sl.* lagger; parolee, *Brit.* (*formerly*) ticket-of-leave man; recidivist, repeat offender, *Inf.* chronic crook.

pristine, *adj.* **1.** primitive, primordial, primigenial; primary, prime, early, earliest, initial, first; incipient, basic, fundamental, elementary, rudimentary, inchoate, simple, uncomplicated; original, autochthonal, autochthonous, aboriginal.

2. natural, plain, pure, clean, unsullied; untarnished, spotless, stainless, unmarred, unblemished, unspoiled, unpolluted; chaste, virginal, virgin, maidenly, maidenish, *Archaic.* honest, untouched; uncorrupted, undefiled, unfallen, moral, virtuous.

privacy, *n.* **1.** privateness, intimacy, intimateness, seclusion, solitude, retreat, retirement; isolation, aloneness, loneness, solitariness, loneliness, remoteness, obscureness, obscurity; aloofness, apartness, separateness, separation; withdrawal, withdrawment, hermitry, hermitship, reclusion, unsociability, unsociableness; independence, independency, self-sufficiency.

2. secrecy, secretness, secretiveness, mysteriousness; reticence, silence, silentness, reservedness, taciturnity, uncommunicativeness; hugger-mugger, concealment, clandestineness, hiddenness, concealedness, confidentiality, confidentialness; covertness, furtiveness, sneakiness, surreptitiousness, slyness, stealthiness, underhandedness.

private, *adj.* **1.** individual, personal, particular, singular, peculiar, special, especial.

2. confidential, strictly confidential, privy, unofficial, off-the-record, not to be quoted, not to be disclosed, not to be made public, *Inf.* hush-hush, highly secret.

3. nonpolitical, nonofficial, nonpublic.

4. secret, secretive, mysterious, hidden, concealed; underground, clandestine, covert, furtive, surreptitious, sly, stealthy, sneaky, sneaking, underhand, underhanded.

5. not open to the public, off-limits, unaccessible, inaccessible, closed; exclusive, restrictive, restricted, limited.

6. alone, solitary, *Fr. seul,* by oneself; secluded, seclusive, withdrawn, retired, sequestered, backwater, isolated; reclusive, hermitic, hermitical, hermitish, hermitlike, shut off, apart; removed, remote, out-of-the-way, off the beaten path *or* track; deserted, lonesome, lonely, forsaken, desolate.

7. intimate, bosom, most personal.

—n. **8.** private soldier, enlisted man, *Mil.* regular, noncommissioned officer, *Inf.* noncom, private first class; G.I., G.I. Joe, Tommy Atkins, Tommy; infantryman, *Inf.* doughboy, foot soldier, *Rare.* footman,

legionnaire, legionary.

9. **in private** privately, secretly, behind closed doors, off-camera. See **privately.**

privateer, *n.* 1. armed ship, pirate ship, pirate, sea rover, corsair.

2. (*all hired or mercenary*) pirate, viking, corsair, buccaneer, freebooter, rapparee; raider, plunderer, marauder, depredator, vandal, looter, rifler.

—*v.* 3. buccaneer, freeboot, pirate, filibuster, waylay; commandeer, hijack.

privately, *adv.* 1. in private, alone, individually, personally, separately, exclusively; confidentially, off-the-record, unofficially; secretly, sub rosa, behind closed doors, off-camera, out of public view, behind the scenes; secludedly, seclusively, in solitude, in retirement, hermitically.

2. secretively, mysteriously, clandestinely, covertly, furtively, surreptitiously; slyly, on the sly, stealthily, sneakily, sneakingly, underhandedly, under the table, through the back door.

privation, *n.* deprivation, want, need, lack; loss, bereavement, hardship, distress, suffering; difficulty, predicament, plight, strait; seizure, confiscation, forfeiture, divestiture, disinheritance, dispossession; poverty, destitution, beggary, pauperism, indigence, mendicancy, mendicity, neediness, necessity.

privilege, *n.* 1. right, prerogative, due, entitlement, birthright; benefit, advantage, authorization, permission, leave, consent, sanction, warrant, allowance; license, power, franchise; liberty, freedom, choice, blanket permission, carte blanche; immunity, exemption, exception, dispensation, indulgence, concession.

—*v.* 2. exempt, free from, excuse, release; except, make an exception, exclude; (*all in reference to something otherwise forbidden*) authorize, empower, license, permit, allow.

privileged, *adj.* 1. favored, entitled, advantaged, unaccountable, not liable; exempt, exempted, immune, excused, released, excepted, granted dispensation; indulged, suffered, accommodated, protected, sheltered, *Inf.* spoiled.

2. allowed, granted, admitted, permitted, free, licensed, enfranchised, chartered, accredited; authorized, empowered, sanctioned, commissioned, charged, entrusted, invested, vested.

3. (*of information*) confidential, off-the-record, not for publication, privy, inside, top-secret, *Inf.* eyes-only. See **privy** (*def.* 3).

privy, *adj.* 1. **privy to** informed of, apprised of, cognizant of, aware of, in on; *Inf.* in the know, *Inf.* wise to, *Inf.* hep to, *Inf.* on to.

2. private, personal, own, close, intimate; individual, particular, singular, peculiar, special, especial; reserved, limited, exclusive, restricted; not open to the public, off-limits, unaccessible, inaccessible, closed.

3. confidential, strictly confidential, off-the-record, not to be quoted, not for release, not to be disclosed, top-secret, *Inf.* hush-hush, *Inf.* eyes-only.

—*n.* 4. outdoor toilet, outhouse, *Chiefly Dial.* jakes, stool, closet, cloaca, *Chiefly New Eng.* necessary, *Brit. Sl.* bogs, latrine, *Sl.* one *or* two-holer, *Euph.* throne; portable toilet, *Trademark.* Johnny-On-The-Spot, *Trademark.* All American Kan, *Trademark.* Port-o-Let, *Trademark.* Port-o-San, *Trademark.* Here's Johnny.

prize[1], *n.* 1. award, trophy, medal, medallion, decoration, blue ribbon, ribbon, riband, citation; honor, laurels, wreath, palm, bay *or* bays, garland, plume, crown; cup, loving cup; mention, honorable mention, consolation prize, booby prize; reward, *Literary.* guerdon, recompense, remuneration, premium; bestowal, endowment, grant, scholarship, fellowship; distinction, glory, honors, high honors; mark *or* badge of distinction, token, favor, *Inf.* plum, *Inf.* feather in one's cap; kudos, accolade, tribute.

2. sweepstakes, jackpot, lottery, stake; windfall, pot at the end of the rainbow, dream come true; take, profit, gain, receipts, winnings, *Inf.* earnings.

3. capture, seizure, spoil, spoils, loot, booty, plunder, pillage, *Archaic.* prey; stolen goods, *Inf.* steal, *Sl.* hot goods, *Sl.* boodle, *Sl.* the take, *Sl.* the goods, *Sl.* swag.

4. treasure, gem, jewel, masterpiece, wonder, godsend, *Inf.* catch, *Inf.* find; *All Inf.* pip, lulu, peach, dandy, jimdandy, honey, dilly, humdinger, corker.

—*adj.* 5. champion, superior, best, best-of-show; outstanding, elect, select, choice, chosen; surpassing, excellent, a cut *or* stroke above; first-rate, blue-ribbon, A-1; the best, masterful, *Inf.* all-around, one-in-a-million.

prize[2], *v.* 1. value, appreciate, esteem, esteem highly, cherish, hold dear, treasure, set a high value on, rate highly, value highly, make much of; revere, reverence, set great store by, attach importance to, regard, think of as special; admire, hold a high opinion of; like, love, care for, be fond of, hold in affection, adore, hold dear, consider precious; praise, extol, exalt, endorse, hail, respect.

2. evaluate, appraise, *Obs.* apprise, assess, assay, valuate; price, set a value on, set a price on, fix the price of.

3. gauge, rate, rank, weigh, measure, *Archaic.* mete, judge, size, *Inf.* size up; arrive at an estimate; (*of value*) compute, calculate, ascertain, determine, figure out, figure, reckon, estimate, guess.

prize fight, *n.* boxing match, match, pugilistic contest, contest in the ring, bout, fight, sparring match; boxing, fisticuffs, sparring.

prize fighter, *n.* boxer, pugilist, fighter, combatant, battler; *Inf.* scrapper, *Sl.* bruiser, *Sl.* slugger, *Sl.* pug, *Sl.* mug, *Sl.* palooka, *Sl.* Joe Palooka; contestant, contender, *Inf.* champ; *Inf.* has-been, *Inf.* punch-drunk bum, *Inf.* stumblebum.

probability, *n.* 1. likelihood, likeliness, liability, law of averages; expectation, outlook, prospect, distinct possibility; appearance of truth, verisimilitude; chance, possibility, mathematical probability, plausibility, aptitude; good chance, eventuality, favorable chance, even chance; odds-on chance, reasonable chance, sporting chance; good prospect, favorable prospect, well-grounded hope, good expectation, great expectation; off chance, outside chance, remote possibility, long shot.

2. believability, credibility, conceivability, thinkability; reasonability, plausibility, feasibility, viability, operability, potentiality.

3. favorite, *Sl.* shoo-in, *Sl.* sure bet, *Sl.* sure thing; *Inf.* front runner, favorite son, best bet.

probable, *adj.* 1. likely, liable, apt; odds-on, favored, to be expected, in the cards, *Inf.* two-to-one, potential, contingent; presumable, presumptive, logical, predictable, foreseeable; well-founded, rational, sound, dependable, reliable; doubtless, indubitable, unquestionable.

2. believable, tenable, plausible, credible, admissible, verisimilar; conceivable, thinkable, colorable, imaginable; reasonable, viable, operable, actuable.

3. apparent, ostensible, supposed, alleged, seeming; declared, shown, exhibited, displayed, avowed, said, as it were.

probably, *adv.* 1. likely, most likely, doubtless, indubitably, unquestionably; in all likelihood, in all probability, *Inf.* like enough, *Inf.* as like as not, *Inf.*

two-to-one, *Inf.* dollars to doughnuts; all things considered, for all practical purposes, to all intents and purposes; possibly, perhaps, maybe, *Archaic.* belike; soundly, rationally, dependably, reliably.
2. credibly, believably, conceivably, plausibly; reasonably, logically, feasibly, viably, tenably.
3. apparently, ostensibly, seemingly, supposedly, allegedly; on the first impression, by all appearances, superficially, externally, as far as can be seen.

probation, *n.* **1.** test, essay; trial, *Inf.* tryout, *Inf.* workout; experiment, test run, dry run, *Inf.* pilot.
2. trial period, test *or* testing period.

probationer, *n.* novice, novitiate, abecedarian, catechumen; postulant; candidate, aspirant.

probe, *v.* **1.** investigate, look into, *Inf.* check out; scrutinize, study, examine thoroughly, go over step by step, go deep into, perscrutate, *Obs., Rare.* perscrute.
2. explore, poke around, feel around, *Sl.* nose around; question, ask questions, query; sound out, feel out, feel the pulse, send up a trial balloon, put *or* throw out a feeler, see which way the wind blows, see how the land lies.
—n. **3.** investigation, examination, study; scrutiny, close inquiry, careful search, exhaustive study, perscrutation; exploration.
4. inquiry, inquest; feeler, pilot balloon, trial balloon, *Fr. ballon d'essai.*

probity, *n.* honesty, uprightness, upstandingness, rectitude; integrity, virtue, principle, scruples, conscientiousness; justice, justness, fairness, open-mindedness, freedom from bias *or* prejudice; honor, goodness, decency, sense of decency, morality, moral fiber; straightness, squareness, square dealing, plain dealing, square shooting, straight shooting; truthfulness, veracity, veraciousness, truth-telling, truth-speaking, truth-loving, truth-dealing.

problem, *n.* **1.** question, vexed question, knot, knotty point, stickler; moot point, bone of contention, point at issue, subject of dispute.
2. enigma, puzzle, riddle, conundrum, mystery, question mark, Chinese puzzle; puzzler, poser, teaser, *Inf.* brain-teaser, *Inf.* hard nut to crack, *Inf.* mind-boggler, *Inf.* stumper, *Inf.* floorer; maze, labyrinth, tangle, intricacy; secret, arcanum, closed *or* sealed book; oracle, dark saying, obscure statement, hidden meaning, riddle of the sphinx.
3. dilemma, quandary, predicament, plight, sorry plight, *Inf.* pickle, *Inf.* pretty pickle, *Inf.* fine kettle of fish, *Inf.* fine how-do-you-do; complication, mess, imbroglio, stew, hornet's nest, Pandora's box, *Inf.* can of worms; difficulty, trouble, affliction; inconvenience, disadvantage, handicap.
4. nuisance, pest, bother, *Inf.* headache, *Inf.* pain, *Sl.* pain in the neck *or* rear, *Sl.* hassle, vexation, annoyance.
—adj. **5.** unmanageable, ungovernable, uncontrollable; unruly, restive, obstreperous; intractable, refractory, recalcitrant, contumacious; incorrigible.

problematic, *adj.* doubtful, dubious, open to doubt, questionable, unconvincing, *Inf.* thin *or* a bit thin, problematical; debatable, disputable, arguable, contestable, controvertible, controversial, moot; implausible, untenable, hard *or* difficult to believe, *Inf.* hard to swallow; suspicious, suspect, in doubt, in question, in dispute; uncertain, unsure, unreliable, undependable, not to be relied *or* depended on *or* upon, untrustworthy, precarious; ambiguous, vague, indeterminate, indefinite; unsettled, undecided, undetermined, unestablished; open, up in the air, in the balance, in suspense.

procedure, *n.* **1.** course, line, plan of action; policy, polity, guidelines; method, methodology, technique, system; attack, tack, approach; way, wise, manner, means, mode, fashion, style, ways and means; wont, custom, practice, praxis, *Latin. modus operandi,* MO; common practice, rule, standard operating procedure, SOP, *Inf.* bit.
2. step, measure, move, maneuver; process, operation, course *or* mode of action; transaction, proceedings.
3. bureaucracy, red tape, rigmarole; routine, rut, groove, beaten path; *Inf.* rat race, treadmill, merry-go-round.

proceed, *v.* **1.** advance, progress, continue, move, move on, move ahead, go, go ahead *or* forward, pass on, get along, come on, wag; roll, roll on, gather head *or* steam, cover ground, make headway, make progress; make one's way, work one's way, press on, push on, forge ahead.
2. take action, take steps *or* measures, act on, do something about, *Sl.* get with it, *Sl.* get on the stick.
3. issue, issue forth, come forth, sally forth; course, run, flow, stream.
4. *Usu.* **proceed from** arise, emanate, spring, stem, come; begin, commence, start, originate; derive, descend; result, ensue, follow, grow out of.
—n. **5.** **proceeds** **a.** result, final *or* end result, outcome, consequence; produce, product, yield, output, crop, harvest. **b.** gross, gross receipts, receipts, handle, returns; gate receipts, gate, box office; revenue, earnings, income; gross profit; total, final tally. **c.** profits, net profit, net, reward, gain, remuneration, *Archaic.* avails, *Inf.* percentage, *Brit. Sl.* get.

proceeding, *n.* **1.** step, measure, move, maneuver; act, deed, doing; operation, process, course *or* mode of action.
2. procedure. See **procedure** (*def.* **1**).
3. **proceedings** the record, records, minutes, transactions, Acta; affairs, matters, concerns, dealings, doings, *Inf.* goings on.

process, *n.* **1.** procedure; operation. See **procedure** (*defs.* **1, 2**).
—v. **2.** prepare, treat, pretreat; refine, smelt; cure, tan; brew, distill, extract; convert, transform, change, change over.
3. handle, deal with, contend with, do with; organize, systemize, systematize; classify, categorize, group, bracket; grade, gradate, rank; screen, sift, sieve.

procession, *n.* **1.** train, cortege, pageant, *Obs.* pomp; parade, march, line, column, file, string; caravan, cavalcade, motorcade; review, promenade, march past; stream, steady stream.
2. series, sequence, continuation, run, course, string; cycle, round, rotation.

proclaim, *v.* **1.** announce, advertise, promulgate, declare, profess, enounce; herald, publish, broadcast, make known; signal, annunciate, knell; cry, blazon, blare, trumpet, bruit; disclose, reveal, divulgate.
2. pronounce, rule, decree, report, ordain.

proclamation, *n.* **1.** announcement, promulgation, pronunciamento, manifesto, statement, formal *or* authoritative statement *or* announcement; declaration, pronouncement, enouncement, profession; notification, notice, formal notice.
2. edict, fiat, decree, dictum, ukase, bull, papal bull, *Rom. Cath. Ch.* encyclical, allocution; command, order, imperative; rule, ruling, law, ordinance.

proclivity, *n.* **1.** inclination, inclining, propensity, leaning, bent, turn, veering, *Biol.* tropism, cast; tendency, tending, bearing, verging, gravitation, drift; proneness, subjectability, aptness, liableness, likeliness, susceptibility, weakness, openness; mind-set, disposition, *Pathol.* diathesis, idiosyncrasy, idiosyncrasis, grain,

Archaic. crasis, temperament, temper, mind, humor, vein.

2. determination, resolve, resolution; penchant, predisposition, predilection, partiality; prejudice, tendentiousness, bias, preference; affinity, attraction, sympathy, liking, fancy, fondness, affection, love, ardor, fervor, zeal, passion; desire, longing, wishing, hankering, craving, itch, avidity; appetite, appetency, relish, taste; voracity, pruriency, concupiscence, lust.

3. aptitude, gift, genius, talent, faculty, readiness, skill.

procrastinate, *v.* **1.** delay, temporize, *Inf.* stall, *U.S. Cong.* filibuster, play for time, gain time, use dilatory tactics, play a waiting game; prolong, protract, retard, slacken, slow down, decelerate; forestall, prevent, stave off, obstruct, block, avoid.

2. defer, put off, postpone, table, shelve, prorogue; adjourn, suspend, respite; waive, put aside, pigeonhole; shunt, push aside, *Inf.* wait on, let stand, put on ice, put in cold storage, put on a back burner, let hang fire, hold in abeyance, keep in a holding pattern, call a time-out.

3. vacillate, hesitate, waver; wait, tarry, linger, dawdle; dally, dillydally, idle, mark time, tread water; lag, *Inf.* drag one's feet, *Inf.* footdrag, poke along; loaf, shirk, *Inf.* goof off, kill *or* waste time, *Inf.* sleep on the job, *Brit. Sl.* scrimshank.

procrastination, *n.* **1.** delay, postponement, deferment, deferral; adjournment, suspension, abeyance, moratorium, prorogation; dilatoriness, prevention, forestallment, forestalling, *Law.* laches; obstruction, blockage, blocking, avoidance, evasion; temporization, play for time, *U.S. Cong.* filibuster *or* filibustering; dilatory tactics, waiting game, time-out.

2. vacillation, hesitation; delaying, dawdling, dalliance, dillydallying, idling, *Inf.* footdragging; shirking, loafing, *Inf.* sleeping on the job; neglect, laxity, disregardance, default, omission.

3. prolongation, protraction, retarding, retardation, shelving, deferring, pigeonholing, waiving; tardiness, lateness, cunctation, slowness.

procrastinator, *n.* delayer, deferrer, postponer, cunctator, temporizer; malingerer, shirker, loafer, *Sl.* goof-off, *Sl.* goldbrick, idler, *Brit. Sl.* scrimshanker, do-nothing, fainéant; neglector, ignorer, disregarder; dodger, evader.

procreate, *v.* **1.** beget, engender, generate, create, conceive, father, sire, give birth to, get; breed, propagate, reproduce, spawn.

2. cause, produce, effect, effectuate, make happen, bring about, bring to pass, give rise to, occasion; begin, originate, initiate, sow the seeds of.

procreation, *n.* **1.** generation, engenderment, genesis, siring, fathering, begetting, giving birth to; propagation, proliferation, multiplication.

2. creation, origination, invention, innovation; formation, formulation, materialization, embodiment; establishment, institution, foundation.

procreative, *adj.* generative, genetic, genesic, progenerative, procreant, propagative, reproductive, life-giving; creative, formative.

procreator, *n.* sire, father, begetter, engenderer; creator, maker, producer, architect.

proctor, *n.* **1.** (*in a university or college*) monitor, teacher's aide, watcher, overseer, supervisor; deputy, surrogate, delegate; procurator, steward; rector, preceptor.

—*v.* **2.** supervise, monitor, oversee, manage, watch over, attend to.

procurable, *adj.* obtainable, acquirable, purchasable, available, securable; attainable, reachable, accessible, getatable.

procuration, *n.* **1.** procurement, acquisition, obtainment. See **procurement** (*defs.* **1, 2**).

2. pandering, pimping. See **procurement** (*def.* **3**).

3. appointment, assignment, designation; commissioning, deputation.

procure, *v.* **1.** obtain, get, acquire, secure, gain, come by, fall into; take possession of, get one's hands on, get a hold of; capture, seize, grasp, net, bag; reap, gather, glean, harvest, garner; buy, purchase, pick up, *Inf.* find, *Scot. Archaic.* coff; attain, achieve, reach, win.

2. hire, rent, rent out, hack, charter; lease, sublease, let, sublet.

3. contrive, manipulate; rig, *Inf.* fix, *Sl.* square, cause, bring about; bribe, suborn; smuggle, run, *U.S.* bootleg; embezzle, *Law.* defalcate, misappropriate, steal, peculate.

4. pander, pimp, solicit, *Sl.* hustle; purvey, supply, furnish, provide.

procurement, *n.* **1.** acquisition, acquirement, obtainment, obtaining, getting, gaining, securing, procuration; takeover, gain, annexation; seizure, appropriation, capture.

2. purchasing, buying, picking up; hire, hiring, renting, rental, lease, leasing.

3. pandering, pimping, soliciting, *Sl.* hustling; whoremongering, whoremastery, white-slaving; prostitution, harlotry, whoredom.

procurer, *n.* pimp, pander, panderer, whoremonger, *Sl.* flesh-peddler, *Sl.* hustler, *U.S. Sl.* sweetman, *Fr. maquereau;* procuress, *Archaic.* bawd, madam; white slaver, smuggler, runner; go-between, intermediary, middleman, agent, solicitor; purveyor, supplier, provider, furnisher.

prod, *v.* **1.** poke, jab, punch, dig; prick, rowel, stick; nudge, elbow, shoulder, butt, boost; push, shove, drive, propel, move, get [s.o.] moving *or* going; press, hurry, hustle, rush, speed, quicken, accelerate.

2. goad, spur, prompt, thrust, give [s.o.] a little encouragement *or* boost *or* shove; incite, provoke, stimulate, motivate, rouse, arouse, actuate; encourage, urge, impel, egg on; agitate, whip up, work up, stir up, wind up, inflame, fire up; nag, harp at, hound, badger, needle; pester, hector, harass, ride; fret, vex, irritate, annoy, aggravate, torment, plague, persecute, *Inf.* drive up the wall; henpeck, pick on, criticize, carp at, complain, cavil, *Yiddish.* kvetch.

—*n.* **3.** poke, jab, dig, finger in the ribs; nudge, elbow, boost, butt, punch, push, shove.

4. goad, poker, stick; spur, prickspur, prick, pricket, rowel, needle.

prodigal, *adj.* **1.** profligate, wasteful, spendthrift, dissipative, squandering, improvident, thriftless; extravagant, immoderate, inordinate, overweening, exorbitant, excessive, unwarranted; munificent, generous, open-handed, free-handed.

2. abundant, abounding, plentiful, plenteous, bountiful, bounteous, copious, ample; profuse, profusive, lavish, overflowing, exuberant, superabundant; exhaustless, boundless, bottomless, limitless, measureless; rich, luxuriant, rank, thriving; replete, rife, flush, teeming, swarming; myriad, multitudinous, numerous, numberless, innumerable.

—*n.* **3.** profligate, wastrel, waster, squanderer; spendthrift, scattergood, *Inf.* high liver, *Inf.* big spender, *Inf.* free spender, spender.

prodigality, *n.* **1.** extravagance, profligacy, waste, wastefulness, squandering, improvidence, thriftlessness; liberality, munificence, generosity, generousness, open-handedness, free-handedness.

2. abundance, plenty, plentitude, bounty, cornucopia,

horn of plenty, endless supply; amplitude, ampleness, fullness, plenteousness, plentifulness, bountifulness, copiousness; richness, exuberance, luxuriance, lavishness.

3. excess, surplus, surfeit, oversupply, overflow, nimiety, superfluity; glut, plethora, overabundance, supersaturation; riot, landslide, bonanza, flood, heap, avalanche, profusion.

4. unrestraint, licentiousness, abandon, wantonness; immoderation, intemperateness, inordinateness, *Obs.* inordinancy; dissipation, overindulgence, incontinence, incontinency, intemperance.

prodigious, *adj.* **1.** tremendous, stupendous, *Inf.* whopping, *Inf.* thumping, huge, enormous, immense; monumental, leviathan, colossal, titanic, gigantic, giant, cyclopean, Brobdingnagian; mammoth, mastodonic, monster, gargantuan, Herculean, mighty; vast, far-reaching, extensive, magnitudinous, sweeping, grand, towering, boundless, unlimited; extraordinary, exceptional, out-of-the-ordinary, unusual; unprecedented, unheard-of, unparalleled, nonpareil, rare, singular, uncommon, *Latin. sui generis*, unique.

2. wonderful, wondrous, marvelous, *Sl.* marvy, fabulous, *Sl.* fab, fantastic, miraculous; terrific, *Sl.* neat, great, *Sl.* swell, *Sl.* super, *Inf.* nifty; admirable, estimable, striking, impressive; amazing, astounding, mystifying, astonishing, flabbergasting, *Sl.* mind-blowing, dumfounding, staggering; remarkable, noteworthy, renowned; superb, excellent, superior, surpassing, preeminent, overwhelming.

3. abnormal, unnatural, supernatural, outlandish, outrageous, monstrous, teratogenic; grotesque, freakish, freaky, anomalous, incongruous; strange, passing strange, *Sl.* wacky, queer, *Inf.* funny, *Sl.* far out, *Sl.* too much, *Sl.* off the wall; peculiar, curious, weird, bizarre; indescribable, beyond description, inexpressible, ineffable, unutterable, unspeakable, unnamable; unbelievable, unimaginable, unthinkable; dreadful, frightful, fearful, terrible, appalling, startling, horrible, horrifying.

prodigy, *n.* **1.** child genius, wonder child, *Ger. Wunderkind*, Mozart, *Sl.* Whiz Kid, *Inf.* quiz kid, Joel Kupperman; genius, *Inf.* natural-born genius, *Inf.* brain, Einstein, *Inf.* wizard, *Inf.* whiz, mental giant, intellect, intellectual; walking encyclopedia *or* dictionary, one with a mind like a steel trap; sage, savant; expert, past master, virtuoso, *Sl.* crackerjack.

2. exemplar, paragon, example, model, role model, champion.

3. wonder, wonderment, marvel, phenomenon, miracle, sensation, *Sl.* stunner; rara avis, *Sl.* rare bird, one of a kind, *Sl.* oner, one in a million, jewel without price, rare gem.

4. freak, mutation, *Biol.* sport, monster, jackalope, curiosity, grotesque, grotesquery, trick of nature, gargoyle; abnormality, anomaly, aberration, peculiarity.

produce, *v.* **1.** cause, make, bring about, bring to pass, set off, give rise to; effect, occasion, generate, engender, sow the seeds of; spark, initiate, start.

2. create, compose, originate, invent; turn out, *Sl.* knock out *or* together, hammer out, *Sl.* slap together; form, formulate, draw up, draft; shape, frame, design, fashion, work out; manufacture, construct, carve, chisel out, weave, fabricate, build.

3. bear, give birth to, give life to, bring forth, bring into the world, bring into being *or* existence, beget; breed, hatch, whelp, drop, throw.

4. provide, supply, furnish, give, yield, render, afford; deliver, come through as promised, perform as desired; propagate, fructify.

5. bring forward, present, set forth; disclose, make plain, reveal; manifest, bring to light, bring before the public; show, display, exhibit, bring out, put on, put before the public.

—n. **6.** yield, product, production, result, outcome, outgrowth, output; crop, harvest, gatherings, gleanings, return, proceeds.

7. vegetables, fruits, greens, *Brit.* green-grocery.

8. offspring, spawn, brood, hatch, issue.

producer, *n.* **1.** creator, grower, maker, builder, fabricator, manufacturer; innovator, initiator, originator; one who gets things done *or* out, worker, laborer, digger, miner, workhorse.

2. director, auteur, manager, stage manager; entrepreneur, impresario; backer, broker for angels, angel.

product, *n.* **1.** production, produce, by-product; output, turnout, goods, offerings; work, handiwork, artifact, representation, symbol, image, creation.

2. result, effect, outcome, fallout, repercussion, echo, reverberation.

production, *n.* **1.** creation, origination, producing, manufacture, fabrication, formation, making, shaping; assembling, assemblage, putting together, execution, construction, building, preparation.

2. output, turnout, goods, offerings; work, handiwork, artifact, by-product. See also **produce** (*def.* **6**).

3. composition, piece; publication, book, volume, tome, novel, story; handicrafts, arts and crafts; painting, work of art, opus, *Fr. oeuvre*; brainchild, invention.

4. exhibition, display, presentation, staging; disclosure, revelation, opening.

5. drama, theatrical performance, play, show, stage show, theater, performance; concert, opera, musical comedy, musical; film, motion picture, moving picture, movie; artistic direction *or* management.

productive, *adj.* **1.** generative, fructificative, fruitive, fruit-bearing; reproductive, propagative, propagatory, propagational, progenitive, multiplicative, regenerative; formative, shaping, constructive, making; creative, inventive, imaginative, resourceful, ingenious; energetic, energetical, vigorous, dynamic, forcible, effective, worth one's salt, worthwhile, valuable, invaluable.

2. fertile, yielding, fruitful, fructiferous, feracious; fecund, prolific, proliferative, proliferous; pregnant, copious, rich, rank, *Rare.* uberous; fructuous, profitable, remunerative, paying, well-paying, fat.

productivity, *n.* **1.** generativity, reproductiveness, progenitiveness, productiveness; creativity, creativeness, inventiveness, imaginativeness, imagination, resourcefulness, ingenuity, originality.

2. fertility, fertileness, fruitfulness, *Rare.* feracity; fecundity, prolificness, prolificalness, prolificacy; copiousness, copiosity, pregnancy, richness, rankness, *Rare.* uberity.

3. output, yield, production.

profanation, *n.* **1.** irreverence, indevoutness, irreligion, impiety, ungodliness, unholiness, profanity, profaning, profaneness; blasphemy, sacrilege, desecration; unrighteousness, unvirtuousness, conscienceless-ness, immorality; godlessness, sinfulness, iniquity, peccancy, wickedness, reprobacy.

2. debasement, degradation, dishonoring, prostitution; defilement, perversion, contamination, infection, vitiation, befoulment, pollution; misuse, ill-usage, misemployment, misapplication; abuse, maltreatment, violation, outrage.

profane, *adj.* **1.** irreverent, indevout, irreligious, infidel, impious, ungodly; secularist, atheistic, free-thinking, disbelieving, unbelieving, faithless; blasphemous, sacrilegious, desecrative; heretical, not-born-again, unsaved, unchristian, impenitent, unrepentant, living in a state of sin, bound for hell; unsaintly, unvirtuous, unrighteous, conscienceless, immoral, reprobate; godless, iniquitous, sinful, peccant, wicked, satanic, diabolic.

2. lay, laic, nonclerical, nonordained, nonministerial; secular, civil; nonreligious, nonecclesiastical, unholy, unhallowed, unconsecrated, unsanctified; mundane, temporal, worldly.

3. heathen, pagan, barbarian, barbarous, uncivilized, savage, brutish, unenlightened, idolatrous; polytheistic, pantheistic, voodooistic.

4. common, mean, low, vile, cheap, base, lewd, depraved, indelicate, gross, trashy, tawdry; odious, low-minded, of the street, indecent, improper, unseemly, shameless, immodest, indecorous; uncouth, coarse, vulgar, obscene, smutty, dirty, off-color, *Inf.* blue; swearing, cursing, maledictive, foul-mouthed, Fescennine, thersitical, blackguardly, scurrilous, ribald, bawdy; unspeakable, unmentionable, unprintable.

—*v.* **5.** desecrate, misuse, misemploy, misapply; abuse, maltreat, violate, ravage, ruin; defile, pervert, corrupt, debase, degrade, prostitute; vitiate, pollute, infect, taint, contaminate, waste.

profanity, *n.* **1.** irreverence, irreligion, impiety, ungodliness, blasphemy, desecration, profanation. See **profanation** (*def.* **1**).

2. malediction, curse, imprecation, damning, damnation, execration, *Archaic.* malison; swearing, cursing, scurrility, ribaldry, billingsgate, double entendre, *Archaic.* bawdry; obscenity, curse word, swearword, oath, expletive, dirty word, four-letter word, *U.S. Inf.* cuss; vulgarism, filth, dirt, smut.

profess, *v.* **1.** pretend to, lay claim to, purport, allege, make a pretense of; make out as if, *Sl.* make like, *Inf.* let on, dissemble, act as if, seem as if; simulate, dissimulate, fake, feign, sham.

2. assert, asseverate, aver, proclaim, declare, predicate; advance, propound, propose, offer, proffer, present, put forward, set forth, broach; emphasize, stress, pronounce, announce, enunciate, state, tell, say, utter; affirm, postulate, protest, claim; admit, avow, own, acknowledge, confess.

professedly, *adv.* **1.** alledgedly, purportedly, ostensibly, supposedly, under the pretext of; pretendedly, falsely, slyly, deceptively, under false pretense.

2. avowedly, admittedly, by open declaration, acknowledgedly, confessedly.

profession, *n.* **1.** vocation, calling, occupation, career, pursuit, lifework; métier, trade, craft, art, skill, job, livelihood, living, work, employment, business; forte, field, line, sphere, specialty; office, post, situation, position, walk of life.

2. declaration, avowal, assertion, asseveration, affirmation, averment; confession, acknowledgement, admittance; avouchment, assurance, guarantee, certification; propounding, protestation, proclamation, predication; deposition, testimony, statement, announcement, enunciation, attestation; vow, oath, pledge.

3. allegation, plea, excuse, pretext, ostensible reason, pretense, pretension.

professional, *adj.* **1.** skilled, knowledgeable, learned, *Inf.* pro; white-collar; experienced, *Fr. au fait*, veteran, seasoned, trained; skillful, adept, dexterous, adroit, deft, facile; accomplished, able, apt, gifted, talented; finished, polished, practiced; expert, proficient, masterful, masterly; topflight, top-drawer, big-league, big-time, *Inf.* topnotch, *Inf.* crack, *Sl.* crackerjack, *Inf.* whiz-bang, *Brit. Sl.* whizzo.

2. efficient, competent, capable, able; hardworking, conscientious, thorough, systematic; prompt, quick, *Sl.* on the ball, on top of everything; practical, realistic, sensible, pragmatic, matter-of-fact, prosaic; businesslike, formal, official, authoritative.

—*n.* **3.** expert, *Inf.* pro, master, proficient, adept, mavin, master hand, *Chiefly Brit. Inf.* dab hand, *Brit. Dial.* dabster; veteran, journeyman, past master, past mistress, old hand, old stager; specialist, authority, connoisseur; (*both of martial arts*) black belt, dan.

4. maestro, virtuoso, talent, genius, prodigy, standout, *Inf.* wizard, *Inf.* whiz, *U.S. Sl.* crackerjack, *Inf.* sharp, *Sl.* shark.

professor, *n.* full professor, associate professor, assistant professor, doctor, *Inf.* prof, visiting professor; teacher, *Inf.* teach, instructor, trainer, coach; fellow, *Brit.* don, tutor, preceptor, preceptress, lecturer, lector, *Brit.* reader; educator, pedagogue, educationalist, *Educ.* methodologist; schoolteacher, schoolmaster, *Chiefly Brit.* master, *Chiefly Scot.* dominie, schoolmistress, schoolmarm; schoolman, scholastic, academician, academe, gownsman; teaching assistant, *Inf.* T.A., graduate assistant.

professorial, *adj.* preceptorial, preceptoral, instructorial, tutorial, pedagogic; educational, educatory, teaching, instructional; didactic, preachy, pedantic, pedagoguish; methodological, academic, academical, scholastic; schoolteacherish, schoolmarmish, disciplinary.

proffer, *v.* **1.** offer, tender, present, hold out, extend; give, donate, volunteer; propose, pose, put forward, set forth, suggest, recommend, advance, propound; submit, set before, put to choice; move, make a motion.

2. approach, proposition, invite, make advances towards, make overtures towards, *Sl.* put the moves on.

—*n.* **3.** offer, proposal, suggestion, recommendation, submission, offering, presentation.

4. proposition, motion, advance, approach, overture, *U.S. Sl.* come-on, invitation, *Chiefly Dial.* invite, *Inf.* bid.

proficiency, *n.* **1.** expertness, expertise, expertism, mastery, authority, excellence, adeptness, address, finesse, facility; adroitness, deftness, dexterousness, dexterity, skillfulness; knowledgeableness, know-how, savoir-faire, cleverness, ingenuity; capability, capableness, ability, ableness, aptness, competence, competency, efficiency; efficacy, effectiveness.

2. forte, strong point, skill, talent, faculty, knack; specialty, strong suit, bailiwick, trademark, stock in trade, *Sl.* bag, *Sl.* thing.

proficient, *adj.* **1.** expert, masterful, masterly, virtuoso, virtuosic, topflight, top-drawer, first-rate, *Inf.* topnotch, ace, *Inf.* crack, *Sl.* crackerjack, *Inf.* whiz-bang, *Brit. Sl.* whizzo; adept, polished, finished, accomplished, versed, practiced, experienced, *Fr. au fait*; skillful, skilled, talented, good at, *Sl.* on the ball; capable, able, competent, efficient, qualified.

—*n.* **2.** adept, expert, master, master hand, *Chiefly Brit. Inf.* dab hand, *Brit. Dial.* dabster, maestro, virtuoso; genius, prodigy, *Inf.* wizard, *Inf.* whiz, talent, *U.S. Sl.* crackerjack, *Sl.* shark, *Inf.* sharp; connoisseur, authority, specialist; professional, *Inf.* pro, journeyman, veteran, past mistress, past master, old hand, old stager.

profile, *n.* **1.** silhouette, side view, outline, shape, cast, form, contour, line, lineaments, delineation, configuration, conformation; features, face, visage, countenance; drawing, sketch, portrait, picture, bust, statue.

2. analysis, study, examination, review, survey.

3. biographical sketch, biography, characterization, character sketch, thumbnail sketch, portrait, vignette.

profit, *n.* **1.** *Usu.* **profits** gain, return, yield, interest; income, revenue, net, bottom line; winnings, proceeds, *Sl.* take, *Sl.* velvet, *Sl.* clean-up, pickings;

remuneration, recompense, reward; surplus, excess, leftover, *Sl.* gravy.
2. advantage, behoof, welfare, interest; benefit, help, aid, service; good, avail, efficacy, use, usefulness, serviceableness; advancement, furtherance, improvement, betterment; increment, augmentation.
—v. **3.** benefit, get, help, serve, avail, bestead, *Archaic.* boot; advance, contribute to, improve, better, further, promote, advantage.
4. avail oneself of, make good use of, make the most of; take advantage of, exploit, use, turn to account, make capital out of, make hay; graft, line one's pockets.
5. *Inf.* clean up, *Inf.* make a killing, *Sl.* make a haul, *Sl.* make a bundle, *Sl.* break the bank.

profitable, *adj.* **1.** remunerative, gainful, rewarding, productive, cost-effective, fructuous, fruitful; lucrative, paying, well-paying, moneymaking, fat, going.
2. beneficial, useful, serviceable, convenient, handy; advantageous, desirable, suitable, appropriate, right; favorable, propitious, opportune, timely; good, worthwhile, valuable, invaluable; helpful, helping, conducive, aidful, aiding.

profitless, *adj.* **1.** unprofitable, gainless, unrewarding, unremunerative, unpaying, thankless; disadvantageous, unhelpful, unbeneficial; worthless, valueless, nugatory, unserviceable, impracticable, inoperative, not worth the money, not worth the powder to blow it up.
2. vain, unavailing, useless, futile, bootless, idle, ineffective, inefficacious, Sisyphean, unsuccessful, *Inf.* no-go, to no avail, to no purpose, for naught; fruitless, unproductive, abortive, barren, sterile, impotent, effete.

profligacy, *n.* **1.** dissoluteness, dissipation, libertinism, lasciviousness, debauchery, dolce vita, profligateness; licentiousness, abandon, unrestraint, wantonness, looseness; lechery, *Pathol.* satyriasis, goatishness, carnality, carnalness, carnalism; eroticism, voluptuousness, voluptuosity, sensuality, sybaritism; obsceneness, lewdness, indecency, dirtiness, indelicacy; degeneracy, depravity, turpitude, corruption, perversion; immorality, evil, sin, sinfulness, vice, wrongdoing.
2. extravagance, prodigality, waste, wastefulness, squandering, improvidence, thriftlessness; liberality, munificence, generosity, open-handedness, free-handedness.
3. abundance, plenty, plenitude, bounty; copiousness, bountifulness, bounteousness, plentifulness, plenteousness; amplitude, ampleness, fullness; richness, exuberance, luxuriance, lavishness, profusion, profuseness; exorbitance, excess, surplus, overabundance.

profligate, *adj.* **1.** dissolute, libertine, rakish, rakehell; disssipated, lascivious, debauched; lecherous, lubricous, *Sl.* horny, satyric, satyrical, satyrlike, goatish, *Archaic.* lickerish; carnal, erotic, voluptuous, sensual, sybaritic; licentious, abandoned, unbridled, unrestrained, loose, wanton, wild; promiscuous, whorish, of easy virtue, unchaste; obscene, lewd, Fescennine, salacious, Cyprian, indecent, dirty, indelicate.
2. degenerate, depraved, corrupt, perverted, vitiated; vicious, foul, vile, base; wicked, iniquitous, nefarious, heinous, flagitious, atrocious; immoral, sinful, peccant, evil-minded, vice-ridden; unregenerate, unredeemable, unprincipled, shameless, unscrupulous, reprobate; shameful, disgraceful, rascally, worthless; notorious, infamous, scandalous, disreputable.
3. prodigal, wasteful, spendthrift, dissipative, squandering, improvident, thriftless; extravagant, immoderate, inordinate, overweening; exorbitant, excessive, unwarranted; profuse, profusive, lavish.
—n. **4.** rake, rakehell, blood, roué, libertine, debauchee, dissipater, *Inf.* rip; voluptuary, sensualist, sybarite, hedonist; reprobate, degenerate, pervert, sodomite; lecher, satyr, satyromaniac; whoremonger, pander, pimp, procurer.
5. wastrel, waster, prodigal, squanderer, spendthrift, scattergood, *Inf.* high liver, *Inf.* big spender, *Inf.* free spender, spender.

profound, *adj.* **1.** wise, sage, sagacious, scholarly, intellectual; learned, erudite, educated, informed, well-read, well-versed, well-posted; knowledgeable, knowing, gnostic; comprehensive, encyclopedic, omniscient, all-knowing; philosophical, thoughtful, reflective, reflecting.
2. intense, extreme, acute, keen, sharp, poignant; piercing, penetrating, cutting, biting, stinging; indelible, deeply felt, deep-felt, strongly felt, keenly felt, heartfelt, *Archaic.* homefelt; moving, heart-moving, heart-rending, heart-breaking, heart-stirring, heart-swelling, soul-stirring; overpowering, overwhelming, overcoming, overmastering.
3. difficult, hard, over one's head, *Inf.* tough; complex, complicated, perplexed, *Inf.* tricky; intricate, involved, tangled, knotty, crabbed; deep, esoteric, recondite, abstruse, abstract, heavy, *Sl.* heavy-duty; impenetrable, incomprehensible, past *or* beyond comprehension, inscrutable, indecipherable; mystic, transcendental, cabalistic; occult, secret, hidden, cryptic, perdu; obscure, unclear, dark, dim, vague, nebulous; mysterious, arcane, inexplicable; puzzling, enigmatic, enigmatical.
4. sunken, sunk, plunging; deep-down, deep-set, deep-laid, deep-lying, deep-sunk, deep-sunken; deep-reaching, down-reaching, deep-going.
5. complete, total, utter, absolute; thorough, thoroughgoing, downright, outright, out-and-out; pronounced, decided, positive, perfect, consummate, *Inf.* regular, *Brit. Inf.* proper; low, low-lying, depressed, abject, desperate, stark.
6. abysmal, yawning, cavernous; bottomless, fathomless, unfathomable, soundless.

profundity, *n.* **1.** depth, deepness, profoundness; abstrusity, abstruseness, reconditeness, abstractness; impenetrability, impenetrableness, incomprehensibility, incomprehensibleness, inscrutability, inscrutableness, unknowableness; mysticity, mysticality, mysticalness, cabalism, occultness; obscurity, nebulousness; obfuscation, obscurantism, *Inf.* mumbo jumbo.
2. difficulty, difficultness, hardness; complexity, complicatedness, *Inf.* trickiness; intricacy, intricateness, tangledness, knottiness, crabbedness.
3. wisdom, wiseness, sagacity, sagaciousness; acumen, astuteness, penetration; erudition, learnedness.
4. abyss, chasm, cavity, pit, hole, hollow, shaft, well, crater, bottomless pit.

profuse, *adj.* **1.** lavish, extravagant, excessive, exorbitant, inordinate, immoderate, profusive, beyond all bounds; uncalled for, unwarranted; extreme, superlative, overblown, overgrown, overmuch; overgenerous, overliberal, overlavish, too much, too many.
2. wasteful, prodigal, profligate, wanton, dissipative; easy come, easy go; intemperate, incontinent, reckless; improvident, spendthrift, unthrifty, thriftless, pound-foolish, penny-wise and pound-foolish.
3. generous, liberal, free, munificent, bounteous, bountiful, unsparing, unstinting, unstinted, stintless; unselfish, openhanded, free-handed; magnanimous, big-hearted, large-hearted, greathearted, openhearted, freehearted.
4. abundant, plentiful, plenteous, plenitudinous, *Inf.* plenty, fat, copious; ample, enough and to spare, enough and then some, more than enough, more than adequate; in quantity *or* quantities, in plenty, in profu-

sion, *Inf.* aplenty, *Inf.* galore.

5. big, large, great, huge, bumper; much, many, numerous, multifarious, multiple, multitudinous, multitudinary, *Inf.* ever so many, *Inf.* dime a dozen; immeasurable, unmeasured, measureless, boundless, without bound, limitless, without limit, innumerable, infinite, without end.

6. abounding, exuberant, superabundant, bursting, overflowing, overspilling, spilling over, running over; rampant, bristling, thick, thick with, teeming, teeming with, swarming with, crawling, crawling with, alive with, *Sl.* lousy with.

7. rife, replete, well-supplied, well-furnished, well-provided, well-stocked; full, filled, abrim, chock-a-block, *Brit. Inf.* chocker, *Inf.* chock-full, jammed, packed, *Inf.* jam-packed, *Archaic.* fraught.

8. rich, luxuriant, luxurious, rank, thriving; fruitful, fertile, fecund, yielding, productive, prolific, proliferous.

profusion, *n.* **1.** abundance, plenitude, bounty, cornucopia, horn of plenty, endless supply, *Scot.* scouth *or* skouth, *Scot. and North Eng.* routh.

2. quantity, quantities, volume, volumes, mass, masses, fund, mine, store; multitude, number, numbers, scores, host, hoard, legion; sea, ocean, oceans, world, worlds, galaxy, great quantities *or* quantity; lot, lots, heap, heaps, mountain, mountains, stack, stacks, pile, piles, load, loads, mess, slew, slews, whole slew, full supply, full measure, good supply, good *or* great deal, quite a little, *Sl.* scads *or* scad, *U.S. Sl.* boodle; *All Inf.* ton, tons, bag, bags, barrel, barrels, gob, gobs, oodles, *Chiefly Brit.* lashings *or* lashing.

3. excess, surplus, surfeit, satiety, oversupply, overflow, nimiety, superfluity; glut, plethora, flood, deluge, overabundance, superabundance, supersaturation; riot, landslide, bonanza.

4. lavishness, extravagance, excessiveness, exorbitance, exorbitancy, inordinateness, *Obs.* inordinacy, immoderacy, immoderateness, profusiveness, profuseness.

5. wastefulness, waste, prodigality, profligacy, profligateness, wantonness, dissipation, dissipativity; intemperance, intemperateness, incontinence, recklessness; improvidence, unthriftiness, thriftlessness.

progenitor, *n.* **1.** ancestor, forefather, forbear, primogenitor, *Archaic.* predecessor; procreator, begetter; patriarch, matriarch, parent, father, mother, sire, dam.

2. predecessor, precursor, forerunner, foregoer, antecedent; original, model, exemplar, prototype, archetype, first, form.

progeny, *n.* descendants, offspring, offshoots, issue, seed, posterity, scions; successors, heirs, heirs apparent; lineage, succession, progeniture, younger *or* rising generation; family, children, *Inf.* kids, sons, daughters, brood; young, spawn, litter, fry; (*all of animals*) kids, calves, lambs, whelps, foals, cubs, pups, puppies, kittens, kitties, chicks, chickens; (*all of plants*) shoots, offsets, *Bot.* runners, *Bot.* stolons, stems, sprouts, sprigs, plantlets, slips, cuttings.

prognosis, *n.* forecast, prediction, prophesy, prognostication. See **prediction**.

prognostic, *adj.* **1.** prophetic, predictive, fatidic, vaticinal, presageful, divinatory, sibylline, precursory, diagnostic.

—*n.* **2.** omen, portent, sign, token, foretoken, harbinger; premonition, preindication, forewarning, foreshadowing, handwriting on the wall, warning, indication.

3. presage, presentiment, foreboding, feeling, vague feeling, *Inf.* funny *or* creepy feeling, *Inf.* feeling in one's bones, intuition, suspicion, *Inf.* sneaking suspicion, *Inf.* hunch; anxiety, misgiving, apprehension.

4. prediction, prognostication, forecast, prophecy, prefigurement; augury, vaticination, divination, auspice.

prognosticate, *v.* **1.** predict, prophesy, forecast. See **predict** (*def.* **1**).

2. foreshadow, presage, portend, forebode. See **predict** (*def.* **2**).

prognostication, *n.* prediction, prophecy, forecast. See **prediction.**

prognosticator, *n.* forecaster, predictor, prophet. See **prophet** (*def.* **1**).

program, *n.* **1.** schedule, agenda, calendar, order of the day, protocol; docket, book, slate, listing, guide; menu, bill of fare, *Fr. carte du jour;* list, card, bill, scroll, rota, *Inf.* line-up, roster, *Baseball.* batting order; playbill, list of players, dramatis personae; prospectus, syllabus, curriculum, synopsis, outline; checklist, check roll, roll.

2. scheme, plan, design, project, proposition; blueprint, sketch, outline, draft, masterplan; method, system, approach, attack, procedure, way; systematization, methodization, schematization, organization.

3. performance, radio show, television show, show, play, production; drama, documentary, docudrama, situation comedy, *Inf.* sitcom, game show, soap opera, melodrama, cartoon show; broadcast, telecast, showing, viewing, concert, symphony, recital.

4. plank, plan, platform, political platform, creed, principles; policy, plan of action, position, course, line; position paper, campaign promises.

—*v.* **5.** schedule, list, *Inf.* line up; arrange, slate, book, empanel, bill; budget, calendar, docket.

6. plan, attack, approach a problem; calculate, project, predetermine, prepare, engineer; blue-print, lay out, map out, plan out; systematize, range, frame, design, set up, work out, formulate, contrive.

progress, *n.* **1.** furtherance, upward movement, rise, promotion, improvement in rank, preferment; move up, graduation, elevation, ascension; ascent, climb, mounting, scaling.

2. breakthrough, step forward, stride, gain, major development; discovery, finding; invention, innovation, creation, production.

3. growth, development, advance, advancement, progression, progressiveness; improvement, strengthening, amendment, betterment, upgrading, amelioration, melioration; purification, perfection; enrichment, fattening, enhancement; repairing, fixing, replacement; recovery, revival; increase, increment, addition, augmentation; enlargement, extension, expansion, spread, swell.

4. movement forward, onward movement, headway; gaining ground, pushing forward, forging ahead; moving along, going forward, pressing on, pushing ahead; inching ahead, edging along.

5. **in progress** going on, under way, being done, *Inf.* in the works, taking place; happening, occurring.

—*v.* **6.** advance, go forward, make headway, (*usu. neg.*) *Inf.* get to first base; move on *or* onward, march *or* step forward, stride ahead; proceed, continue, keep going, press *or* push on, persevere, strive, put one's shoulder to the wheel; get *or* go on, lose no ground, not let the grass grow under one's feet; gain ground, catch up, take the lead, get *or* go ahead, shoot *or* rush ahead, *Inf.* go full steam ahead; push forward, forge *or* move ahead, make way, clear the way; edge *or* inch along, move *or* go along; move upward, climb, scale, mount, ascend, rise.

7. improve, better, perfect, upgrade, amend, ameliorate, meliorate; enhance, enrich, fatten, strengthen; add to, increase, augment, alter, change; enlarge, swell, extend, expand, spread; grow, develop, mature, maturate, ripen, grow up.

8. recuperate, get *or* become better, come around, recover, revive, turn the corner, make a turn for the better; convalesce, become stronger, become healthier.

progression, *n.* **1.** movement forward, onward movement, headway; gaining ground, pushing forward, forging ahead; moving along, going forward, advancement, advance; pressing on, pushing ahead, perseverance; continuance, continuation; inching ahead, edging along; furtherance, upward movement, rise, ascension, elevation; ascent, climb, mounting, scaling.

2. succession, order, sequence, gradation, step; series, cycle, round, catenation, concatenation; course, flow, chain, train.

progressive, *adj.* **1.** reformist, progressivistic, revisional, revisionist, meliorist, gradualistic, Fabian; liberal, liberalistic, left-wing, left of center.

2. progressing, advancing, enlightening; improving, ameliorative, meliorative, mending, bettering.

3. advanced, forward, avant-garde; modern, enlightened, twentieth-century, up-to-the-minute, up-to-date, abreast of the times; dynamic, active, motive.

4. forward-going, forward-moving, ongoing, continuing, profluent; going, moving, running, flowing, fluent, streaming, passing; successive, transitional, successional, consecutive, serial, sequential, catenary.

5. graduated, gradational, hierarchical, calibrated.

6. *Medicine.* increasing, worsening, intensifying, aggravating; extending, spreading, malignant, enlarging.

—*n.* **7.** liberal, progressivist, leftist, left-winger; reformer, reformist, revisionist, gradualist, meliorist, Fabian.

prohibit, *v.* **1.** forbid, interdict, disallow, proscribe, outlaw, taboo, ban; reject, veto, turn thumbs down, nix, nay, deny, kill; quash, smother, subdue, quell; preclude, exclude, shut out, debar, bar, segregate, except, omit, disqualify; ostracize, banish, expel, exile, deport, throw out, kick out, excommunicate, blackball.

2. prevent, make impossible, put out of reach, leave no chance, rule out; stop, put a stop to, *Archaic.* forfend, halt; arrest, check, abort, stay; hinder, obstruct, hamper, block, impede, interrupt, delay; thwart, foil, balk, frustrate; restrain, inhibit, constrain, repress, suppress.

prohibition, *n.* **1.** interdiction, interdict, forbiddance, outlawry; proscription, injunction, disallowance, ban, embargo; rejection, veto, thumbs down, nix, nay, no, denial; exclusion, preclusion, debarment, exception, disqualification, segregation; ostracism, banishment, exile, expulsion, deportation, excommunication.

2. prevention, restriction, constriction, suppression; stoppage, determent, interruption, arrest, check, forstalling, retardation; curb, inhibition, restraint, constraint; checkmate, deadlock, foreclosure; block, hindrance, obstacle, impediment, barrier, interference.

prohibitionist, *n.* teetotaler, nephalist, abstainer, water-drinker, hydropot; temperance advocate, W.C.T.U. member, blue-ribboner, blue-ribbonist, blue-ribbonite, *Inf.* dry, *Chiefly Brit.* pussyfoot; puritan, ascetic; Rechabite, Encratite.

prohibitive, *adj.* preventive, restrictive, constrictive, constraining, restraining, confining; exclusive, preclusive, exceptional; proscriptive, forbidding, inhibitory, prohibitory, interdictive, repressive, suppressive; segregative, selective, separative.

project, *n.* **1.** plan, scheme, design, prospectus; proposal, purpose, intent, hope, desire, aspiration; intention, ambition, resolution, determination, mind; calculation, figuring, planning, strategy; contemplation, conception, idea, cogitation; aim, end, goal, objective, point.

2. undertaking, enterprise, venture, operation, campaign; program, proposition, deal; job, game, task, effort, work; contract, commitment, obligation; engagement, occupation, activity, assignment.

—*v.* **3.** propose, present, lay down, design; plan, plot, scheme, devise, concert; concoct, contrive, conjure up, brew, invent, hatch; contemplate, purpose, intend, destine; aim, drive at, determine.

4. throw, cast, pass, fling, toss, hurl, snap, hike; eject, expel, ejaculate, emit; impel, propel, shoot; discharge, fire, launch, blast off; jaculate, arch, *Archaic.* traject.

5. calculate, predetermine, prearrange, predesign, arrange; take steps, take measures, cut out, mark out a course of action, shape a course, draw up a plan; set forth, draft, outline, delineate, map out, chalk out, block out; predict, preorder, foreordain, foreordinate, forecast, plan ahead.

6. put on, screen, show; flashforward.

7. externalize, actualize, extrapolate, objectify; transfer, transmit, impart.

8. jut out, protrude, stick out, poke out; extend, bulge, obtrude, excurve; overhang, beetle, hang over, impend; swell out, protuberate, bow, embow, vault; distend, belly, bag, pop; round out, balloon, billow; stick up, bristle, stand up, shoot up.

projecting, *adj.* protuberant, protruding, protrusive, salient, outstanding; prominent, eminent, *Bot.* excurrent, protrusile, excrescent; extrusive, extruding, jutting, beetling; overlying, overlapping, overhanging, pendulous, pendent, hanging; bulging, swelling, swollen, convex, bowed; arched, vaulted, excurved.

projection, *n.* **1.** protrusion, jut, overhang, extrusion, excurvation; beetling, jutting, impendence, hang; prominence, eminence, excrescence, tuberosity, gibbosity, salience, convexness, convexity; protuberance, outgrowth, *Anat., Bot.* apophysis, *Archit.* apophyge; bulge, bow, swelling, bell, bump, lump, hump, clump, hunch, bunch, tumescence; blister, bubble, bleb, welt, wart; knob, knurl, knot, gnarl, node, nodulation, nodosity; tooth, fang, thorn, outshoot, spine, needle, quill, bristle; spur, snag, jag, snaggle; peak, crag, horn, arete; extension, jetty, jutty, pier; stud, dowel, peg, pin; lip, ear, flap, loop, dogear; ledge, flange, eaves.

2. externalization, objectification, extrapolation, actualization; ascription, transference, transferral, transmittal.

3. scheme, schema, plan, design, program; intention, intent, purpose, plot; proposal, proposition, resolution, resolve, suggestion, motion, presentation.

4. estimation, estimate, guess, *Inf.* guesstimate, prediction; appraisal, appraisement, appreciation; approximation, calculation, figuring, figure; reckoning, computation.

5. layout, delineation, diagram, outline, map; ground plan, skeleton outline, prospectus, conspectus; elevation, relief map, blueprint, house plan; sketch, draft, drawing, plot, plat, rough copy, copy.

proletariat, *n.* laboring class, working class, commonalty, the common people, commoners, lower classes, humbler classes, rank and file, *Latin. hoc genus omne*; plebians, third estate, bourgeoisie; grass roots, *Inf.* the silent majority, the men in the street, *Jocular.* booboisie, *Both U.S.* Middle America, Main Street U.S.A.; the many, the multitude, the great unnumbered, the populace, *Chiefly Brit.* admass; the masses, the common people, hoi polloi, the vulgus, *Archaic.* the vulgar; low life, dregs, underlings, riffraff, *Contemptuous.* ragtag and bobtail, *Inf.* the great unwashed, the vulgar herd, the rabble, the mob, King Mob, the crowd.

proliferate, *v.* **1.** increase, enlarge, make larger, aggrandize; spread, expand, extend, spread out, grow rife *or* rampant, branch out, *Pathol.* metastasize; widen, thicken, lengthen, prolong, protract; grow, wax, swell, inflate; elevate, raise, boost.

2. multiply, double, duplicate, make twofold, redouble, triple, triplicate, quadruple, quintuple, quintuplicate, sextuple, octuple, decuple, make tenfold, make numerous *or* multitudinous.

3. escalate, step up, give a boost to, *U.S. Sl.* soup up, *Sl.* hop up, *Sl.* jazz up; accelerate, snowball, mushroom; burgeon, shoot up, rise, skyrocket, boom, develop vigorously; thrive, prosper, flourish.

4. propagate, produce, generate, make fruitful *or* prolific *or* fecund, fecundate; reproduce, breed; be prolific, fructify, be fruitful, pullulate, be fertile, breed like a rabbit, bloom, blossom, flower; spring up, sprout.

proliferation, *n.* **1.** increase, augmentation, buildup, enlargement, expansion, extension; magnification, amplification; spread, spreading out, branching out; growth, waxing, swelling, inflation; elevation, raise, boost.

2. multiplication, doubling, duplication, redoubling, tripling, triplication, quadrupling, quadruplication, quintuplication, quintupling, sextupling, septupling, septuplication, octupling, decupling.

3. escalation, acceleration, intensification, concentration; snowballing, mushrooming, skyrocketing; mounting, rising, ascending; upsurge, upswing, shooting up, step-up; burgeoning, flourishing, booming, thriving.

4. propagation, breeding, generation, production; reproduction, procreation, engenderment; fructification, pullulation, fecundation, multiparity.

prolific, *adj.* **1.** fertile, philoprogenitive, yielding, fruitful, fructiferous, fructuous, feracious; fecund, proliferative, proliferous; productive, generative, fructificative, fruitive, fruit-bearing; propagative, propagatory, propagational, multiplicative, regenerative.

2. profuse, abundant, plenteous, *Rare.* uberous, full; exuberant, luxurious, lush, rank, rife, rich, flush, copious, bounteous, rich.

prolix, *adj.* **1.** verbose, wordy, long-winded; tautological, redundant, pleonastic, battological; discursive, digressive, rambling, wandering; circumlocutory, roundabout, circuitous, ambagious; lengthy, very long, extensive, sesquipedalian; extended, drawn out, dragged out, protracted, long-drawn, long-drawn-out, long-spun, spun out, prolonged, prolongated, lengthened, elongated, elongate; profuse, profusive, extravagant, uneconomical; detailed, full of detail, full of verbiage, padded; diffuse, garrulous, talkative, loquacious, voluble; boring, tedious, tiring, dreary, wearisome, monotonous, dry, dry-as-dust, humdrum, prosaic.

2. bombastic, orotund, grandiose, grandiloquent, Johnsonian, Ossianic; flatulent, turgid, plethoric, euphuistic, periphrastic.

prolixity, *n.* verbosity, verboseness, wordiness, long-windedness, verbiage; tautology, redundance, pleonasm, battology; discursiveness, discursion, digression, rambling, maundering, wandering; circumlocution, circuity, ambagiousness, roundaboutness; garrulity, talkativeness, loquaciousness, volubility; tediousness, monotonousness, tiresomeness.

prologue, *n.* **1.** introduction, *Inf.* intro, foreword, preface, preamble, prelude, prelusion, prolegomenon, proem, preliminary, *Sl.* prelim, *Print.* preliminaries; opening, lead, commencement, beginning, start; opening remarks, introductory comments, explanation, explication, exposition; introductory scene, first scene, opening scene, protasis, *Gk. prologos.*

—*v.* **2.** introduce, prefix, premise, prelude, prologize.

prolong, *v.* lengthen, make longer, elongate, prolongate, extend; draw out, stretch, stretch out, spin out, protract, spread out, expand; continue, perpetuate, keep up, string on, carry on, drag on, drag out; maintain, preserve, sustain, keep the ball rolling.

prolongation, *n.* lengthening, elongation, protraction, extension; drawing out, stretching out, spinning out, spreading out, expansion; continuation, perpetuation, stringing on, carrying on, dragging on, dragging out; maintaining, preserving, sustaining, keeping the ball rolling; postponement, deferment, prorogation.

promenade, *n.* **1.** walk, stroll, turn, saunter, airing, ramble; outing, *Inf.* whirl; ambulation, perambulation, peregrination; exercise, stretch, constitutional; march, tramp, hike, trek.

2. parade, public walk, passageway, path, footpath, footway, esplanade; sidewalk, pavement; course, run, lane; arcade, covered path, ambulatory, boardwalk.

3. dance, *U.S. Inf.* prom, ball, cotillion.

—*v.* **4.** stroll, go for a walk, walk, take a walk, stretch one's legs; ambulate, saunter, amble; ramble, wander, roll along; meander, circumambulate, gad about, gallivant, traipse; perambulate, traverse, trek, travel, peregrinate; roam, rove, range, tour.

5. parade, flaunt, display, *Inf.* sport, exhibit, air, flash, make a show of, spotlight, draw attention to, show off.

prominence, *n.* **1.** conspicuousness, noticeableness, outstandingness, salience; pointedness, markedness, poignancy, glaringness, egregiousness, flagrance; singularity, uniqueness, peculiarity, uncommonness, specialness, particularity; distinguishability, unmistakability, identifiability, recognizability, discernibleness; superiority, primacy, precedence, paramountcy, top billing.

2. projection, protuberance, extrusion, outgrowth, outshoot, excurvation, *Anat. Bot.* apophysis, *Archit.* apophyge; jutting, beetling, impendence; bulge, swelling, bell, bump, lump; knob, knurl, knot, burr, snag, jag; eminence, excrescence, tumescence, convexity, gibbosity; peak, crag, precipice, cliff, promontory, point; hill, rise, alp, hillock, monticule, mount; crest, steep, summit, pinnacle, tor; dune, ridge, spine, arete, barrow, comb, mound.

3. note, notability, repute, renown, report, fame; distinction, importance, consequence, greatness, grandness; eminence, preeminence, prestige, glory, dignity, honor, celebrity, popularity; standing, rank, account, regard, name, weight.

prominent, *adj.* **1.** conspicuous, standing out, outstanding; noticeable, salient, showing, pointed, pronounced, well-marked, marked; glaring, striking, telling, egregious, flagrant, arrant; singular, peculiar, unique, special, particular; distinguishable, unmistakable, identifiable, recognizable, discernible; manifest, apparent, evident, obvious, patent, self-evident; principal, chief, important, significant, main, paramount; superior, primary, prime, first.

2. projecting, protruding, protuberant, jutting, protrusive, *Bot.* erumpent; extrusive, beetling, excrescent, tumescent, tumid; bold, raised, embossed, bossed, chased, superimposed, in high relief, in Braille; bulging, swelling, swollen, gibbous, convex, arched, vaulted, excurved; *Inf.* popeyed, *Sl.* bug-eyed, goggled; knotty, knurled, burred, gnarled, nubby, burled, nodular; studded, snagged, pinned, pegged, doweled; edged, flanged, lipped, extended.

3. important, famous, famed, renowned, acclaimed, heralded; leading, eminent, preeminent, distinguished, well-known, celebrated, notable, noted; remarkable, extraordinary, exceptional, noteworthy; estimable, reputable, creditable, prestigious, honorable, noble; memorable, unforgettable, never to be forgotten; illustrious, exalted, splendid, brilliant; popular, respected, well-thought-of, grand.

promiscuity, *n.* **1.** looseness, laxness, libertinism, licentiousness; wantonness, wildness, abandon, wild abandon, lack of restraint, fastness, *Inf.* swinging; sluttishness, slatternliness, whorishness, whoredom, harlotry, *Inf.* sleeping around; disreputableness, dishonorableness, *Sl.* trashiness, *Sl.* cheapness; lustfulness, lasciviousness, carnality, sensuality, *Scot.* cadginess, *Archaic.* lickerishness; lewdness, lecherousness, lubricity, salaciousness, prurience, concupiscence, goatishness, animalism, *Sl.* horniness; unchasteness, unchastity, impurity, impureness, uncleanliness; immorality, moral turpitude, unvirtuousness, unscrupulousness, indecency, immodesty, shamelessness; dissoluteness, debauchery, rakishness, dissipation, profligacy, profligateness, depravity, corruptness.

2. hodgepodge, mishmash, motley, jumble, scramble, menagerie, gallimaufry, farrago.

promiscuous, *adj.* **1.** loose, lax, libertine, licentious, Cyprian, immoderate, intemperate, incontinent; wanton, wild, uninhibited, abandoned, unrestrained, uncurbed, ungoverned, unrestricted, unbridled, fast, *Inf.* swinging; dishonorable, *Sl.* trashy, *Sl.* cheap; sluttish, slutty, slatternly, strumpetlike, whorish, whoring, harlot; lustful, lascivious, carnal, libidinous, sensual, on the make, *Sl.* hot *or* hot for, *Sl.* hot to trot, *Scot.* cadgy, *Archaic.* lickerish; lewd, lecherous, lubricous, salacious, prurient, concupiscent, satyric, satyrlike, goatish, ruttish, animalistic, animal, *Sl.* horny; unvirginal, unvirgin, unvirginlike, unchaste, impure, unclean; shameless, immodest, indecent, unvirtuous, of easy virtue, easy, unscrupulous, unprincipled, unregenerate, unredeemable; dissolute, debauched, rakish, rakehell, rakehelly, dissipated, profligate, depraved, corrupt.

2. hodgepodge, motley, jumbled, scrambled; miscellaneous, heterogeneous, medley, composite, mixed, intermixed, intermingled, mingled, commingled, combined, integrated; divers, diversified, varied, manifold; wholesale, general, inclusive, sweeping, broad, wide, extensive; amorphous, arbitrary, unmethodical, methodless, unsystematic, systemless, unorganized, unarranged; disorderly, disorganized, disordered, unordered, disarranged, disarrayed, deranged; harum-scarum, helter-skelter, higgledy-piggledy, confused, chaotic, incoherent; haphazard, random, uncontrolled, hit-or-miss, irregular, thrown together; messy, sloppy, untidy, unneat.

3. indiscriminate, indiscriminating, indiscriminative, undiscriminating, nondiscriminative, nondiscriminatory, undifferentiating; uncritical, unselective, unchoosy, unparticular, unfussy, unfastidious; careless, disregardful, heedless, thoughtless, mindless; unconscientious, remiss, negligent, neglectful, slack, slipshod, slovenly; perfunctory, cursory, hasty, slapdash, casual, indifferent, lackadaisical, devil-may-care; reckless, rash, precipitate, capricious, irresponsible.

promise, *n.* **1.** pledge, assurance, word, solemn word, word of honor, parole, *Archaic.* troth; vow, oath, sworn statement *or* declaration, testimony; endorsement, signature, written statement, testimonial; attestation, affirmation, profession, avowal, asseveration, avouchment; engagement, betrothal, *Archaic.* plight; marriage contract, marriage bond, marriage vow; obligation, bond, agreement, contract, compact, covenant, pact, *Rare.* paction, treaty; gentleman's agreement, unwritten agreement, understanding; guarantee, guaranty, warrant, warranty, *Law.* covenant of warranty, *Law.* warranty deed, *Obs.* vouch.

2. potential, potency, ability, capacity, capability.

—*v.* **3.** pledge, give one's word *or* solemn word, give one's word of honor, give one's parole, *Inf.* cross one's heart and hope to die; vow, solemnly swear, state on one's honor, swear to, declare *or* state under oath, *Law.* testify; assure, offer assurance, aver, asseverate, affirm, avouch, declare, state, profess; guarantee, warrant, vouch for, attest to, bear witness to, testify to; engage, oblige, obligate, contract, covenant, enter an agreement, make a bargain *or* deal, shake on it; endorse, sign, *Inf.* sign on the dotted line.

4. give hope of, look like, show signs of, seem likely to, be in the cards; indicate, denote, bespeak, signify; betoken, portend, foreshadow, foretoken, augur, presage.

5. plight, affiance, betroth, become engaged, pledge to marry.

promising, *adj.* **1.** full of promise, favorable, auspicious, propitious, bright, sunny, rosy, roseate, inviting; hopeful, positive, optimistic, *Inf.* upbeat, *Inf.* looking up; good, encouraging, enheartening, heartening, reassuring, assuring, cheering, cheerful; happy, fortunate, lucky, prosperous, halcyon.

2. probable, likely, most likely, liable, apt, possible, presumable.

promontory, *n.* headland, foreland, head, point, *Archaic.* ness; bluff, cliff, precipice, overhang, projection; hill, height; spit, tongue, cape, isthmus, peninsula, chersonese.

promote, *v.* **1.** encourage, inspirit, hearten; boost, build up, raise, lift; support, patronize, sanction, back, sustain, uphold, hold up, maintain; improve, strengthen, amend, make better, upgrade, help develop, ameliorate; enrich, enhance, fatten, add to, increase, augment, contribute to, conduce to.

2. help, aid, abet, succor; assist, lend a hand, give a leg up, do a good turn; facilitate, enable, make easy for, clear the way for; benefit, be good to, be of service to; foster, cultivate, nourish, nurture, care for, nurse along, minister.

3. advance, work up to, move up, pass, graduate; improve in rank *or* standing, rise to a higher position, *Inf.* kick upstairs.

4. present, propose, submit, recommend, advocate, speak for; advance, bring up, introduce; call attention to, bring to mind, bring into consideration *or* notice.

5. advertise, publicize, talk up, bill, subserve; announce, blurb, broadcast, make known, publish; declare openly, promulgate, proclaim, herald, trumpet, ballyhoo, beat the drum; push, *Inf.* plug, *Inf.* hype, puff, vaunt; post, display, blazon, placard, circularize; circulate, distribute, propagate, propagandize, spread, disseminate, disperse, scatter.

promoter, *n.* publicist, publicity man *or* agent, press agent, public relations man, P.R. man, *Inf.* flak, spokesman; advertiser, adman, ad writer, copy writer; announcer, broadcaster, blurbist, *Inf.* plugger, pusher, ballyhooer, propagandist; backer, supporter, advocate, proponent, patron; distributer, salesman, saleswoman.

promotion, *n.* **1.** advance, advancement, improvement; graduation, rise, move up, elevation; enhancement, ennoblement, aggrandizement, exaltation; honor, dignity.

2. encouragement, furtherance, boosting; support,

backing, patronage, sanction, countenance; sustainment, upholding, maintenance, upkeep; improvement, strengthening, development, build-up; amendment, betterment, up-grading, amelioration; enrichment, fattening, enhancement; increase, increment, gain, addition, augmentation, contribution.

3. help, aid, abetment, abettal, succor, relief, assistance, a hand; facilitation, enabling, clearing the way for; good deed, benefaction, *Archaic.* benefit, service; fosterage, cultivation, nourishment, nurturing, caring for, nursing along, ministering.

4. presentation, proposal, submittal, recommendation, advocacy, espousal; introduction, bringing up, calling attention to, bringing to mind.

5. advertising, publicity, *Inf.* fanfare, publication, broadcasting; heralding, trumpeting, ballyhooing; propaganda, puffery, *Inf.* hype, *Inf.* promo, hard sell, pushing, *Inf.* plugging; circulation, circularization, distribution, propagation, dissemination, dispersal, dispersion.

6. advertisement, blurb, announcement, statement, broadcast, *Inf.* plug; circular, notice, placard, poster, display; bulletin, bill, handbill, flyer, leaflet, throwaway, broadside.

prompt, *adj.* **1.** immediate, instant, instantaneous; direct, summary, fast; rapid, fleet, meteoric, quick, swift, brisk, expeditious, *Inf.* Johnny-on-the-spot; timely, seasonable, punctual, early, in good time, *Inf.* bright-and-early.

2. ready, willing, ready and willing; prone, apt, inclined, disposed, predisposed; agreeable, compliant, unhesitating, *Inf.* game, *Archaic.* fain, *Sl.* into it; zealous, earnest, fervent, fervid, enthusiastic, anxious, eager, keen, avid, agog, *Sl.* psyched; voluntary, spontaneous, gratuitous, unasked, unsought, unforced.

3. alert, intent, sharp, acute; attentive, observant, vigilant, watchful, alive; bright, wide-awake, on the alert, on the job, on guard, open-eared, open-eyed, on the qui vive, agile, energetic, spry, sprightly, nimble, speedy, mercurial, lively, animate; businesslike, efficient, no-frills, no-nonsense.

—v. **4.** push, press, drive, propel, force, force along, shove; induce, impel, compel, constrain, move; instigate, actuate, initiate, activate, set going, put *or* set in motion.

5. urge, admonish, exhort, advise, counsel; persuade, influence, incline, dispose, predispose, prevail upon, *Inf.* twist [s.o.'s] arm; coax, ply, sway, talk into; tempt, lure, allure, beguile, inveigle, entice, *Obs.* allect.

6. incite, poke, prod, prick, thrust, goad, spur, egg on, encourage, put up to; provoke, foment, agitate, excite, arouse, rouse; whip up, work up, stir up, wind up, fire up, inflame, enflame, enkindle, kindle, touch off; evoke, elicit, call forth, summon up.

7. stimulate, whet, animate, reanimate, invigorate, motivate, inspire; inspirit, rally, awaken, vivify, bestir, enliven, liven up, jolt, jog, shake up; embolden, enhearten, hearten, build up, buck up, boost, boost up; produce, occasion, give rise to, bring about; promote, advance, forward, foster, favor; support, advocate, patronize.

8. (*all of a speaker*) assist, aid, help, rescue, relieve; suggest, hint, put words in [s.o.'s] mouth; *Theat.* cue, remind, feed lines, jog *or* refresh *or* renew the memory, set back on the track.

—n. **9.** stimulus, stimulant, incentive, fillip, provocative, motive; spur, prick, jog, poke, jolt; incitement, inducement, instigation, encouragement, abetment, provocation; dare, taunt, gibe.

10. (*all of a speaker*) assistance, aid, help, relief; suggestion, hint, dictation; *Theat.* cue, reminder, refresher.

prompter, *n.* **1.** *Theat.* playreader; *All Television.* idiot card *or* sheet *or* board, prompter's card, *Trademark.* Teleprompter; reminder, jogger, memorandum, *Inf.* memo.

2. mover, prime mover, impeller, energizer, galvanizer, inducer, actuator, animator, moving spirit; encourager, abettor, inspirer, firer, spark, *Inf.* spark plug; stimulator, gadfly.

3. instigator, inciter, exciter, urger; provoker, *Fr. agent provocateur or provocateur,* catalyst; agitator, fomenter, inflamer, agitprop, firebrand, incendiary; rabble-rouser, rouser, demagogue.

prompting, *n.* **1.** pushing, pressing, driving, propelling, forcing, shoving; inducing, inducement, impelling, compelling, constraining, moving; instigating, instigation, actuating, activation, *Inf.* starting something, *Inf.* looking for trouble.

2. urging, urge, admonishing, admonition, exhorting, exhortation, advising, advisement, counseling, consultation; persuading, persuasion, influencing, influence, disposing, inclining, inclination, prevailing upon, *Inf.* twisting [s.o.'s] arm; coaxing, plying, swaying, talking into, convincing; tempting, luring, alluring, beguiling, beguilement, inveigling, inveiglement, enticing, enticement.

3. inciting, incitement, incitation, poking, prodding, pricking, goading, spurring, egging on, encouraging, encouragement; provoking, provocation, fomenting, fomentation, exciting, excitement, excitation, arousing, rousing; whipping up, stirring up, working up, winding up, firing up, kindling, inflaming, enflaming, inflammation, touching off; evoking, evocation, eliciting, elicitation, calling forth, summoning up.

4. stimulating, stimulation, animating, animation, invigorating, motivating, motivation, inspiring, inspiration; rallying, awakening, vivifying, vivification, bestirring, enlivening, livening up, jolting, jogging, shaking up; emboldening, enheartening, building up, bucking up, boosting, boosting up; inducing, producing, occasioning, giving rise to, bringing about; promoting, advancing, forwarding, fostering, favoring; supporting, advocating, patronizing.

5. (*all of a speaker*) assisting, aiding, helping, rescuing, relieving; suggesting, hinting, putting words in [s.o.'s] mouth; *Theat.* cuing, reminding, putting in mind, jogging *or* refreshing *or* renewing the memory, setting back on the track.

promptness, *n.* punctuality, earliness, promptitude; swiftness, quickness, dispatch, expedition; haste, speed, celerity; readiness, willingness, alacrity, eagerness, zeal, enthusiasm, avidity; liveliness, briskness, sprightliness, alertness, animation.

promulgate, *v.* **1.** proclaim, decree, rule, pronounce, announce, annunciate, declare; report, make public, publicize, advertise, broadcast, disseminate, propagate; herald, cry, blare, blazon, trumpet, bruit, noise abroad; publish, issue, put out, circulate, give out; make known, bring into the open, let out, come out with, disclose, divulge, reveal.

2. set forth, present, teach, instruct, indoctrinate; preach, lecture; propagandize, proselytize; promote, back, advocate, sponsor.

prone, *adj.* **1.** apt, inclined, tending toward, leaning toward, of a mind to; disposed, predisposed, liable, given, ready, subject, likely, incident, *Archaic.* propense; open, susceptible, vulnerable.

2. face downward, prostrate, procumbent; laying flat, horizontal, recumbent, decumbent; accumbent, reclining, lying down, couchant, supine.

3. declivous, declivitous; sloping, slant, slanting, oblique, tilted, inclined, inclining, leaning.

pronounce, *v.* **1.** enunciate, articulate, vocalize, voice, enounce; say, utter, express, breathe, give *or* let out, come out with; (*all of speech*) garble, confuse, mispronounce, clip, *Fig.* butcher, *Fig.* mutilate.

2. affirm, assert, aver, asseverate, avow, avouch; insist, maintain, contend, hold, stand for; propound, propose, put forward; allege, claim, set forth; depose, testify, attest, swear.

3. declare, pronounce, profess, enounce; rule, decree, report, ordain, proclaim, promulgate; order, direct, command, dictate; pass judgment, deliver judgment, sentence, pass sentence.

4. announce, publish, publicize, broadcast, herald, make known; signal, annunciate, knell; cry, blazon, blare, trumpet.

pronounced, *adj.* **1.** conspicuous, prominent, salient, noticeable, notable, in the foreground, *Sl.* sticking *or* hanging out; striking, outstanding, bold, vivid, graphic, in bold *or* high relief; glaring, flagrant, arrant, shocking, egregious, rank, crass, gross.

2. clear, crystal clear, clear as day, *Inf.* clear as the nose on one's face, plain, manifest, lucid; obvious, patent, evident, clear-cut, recognizable, unmistakable, not to be mistaken, plain to see; broad, round; visible, distinct, definite, well-defined, well-marked.

3. decided, positive, perspicuous; unequivocal, unmitigated, unqualified, undisguised, unhidden; outright, out-and-out, downright; absolute, utter, thorough, thoroughgoing, complete, total; perfect, consummate, *Inf.* regular, *Brit. Inf.* proper.

4. articulated, enunciated, vocalized, voiced, spoken, said, uttered.

pronouncement, *n.* **1.** edict, fiat, decree, dictum, ukase, bull, Papal bull, allocution; command, order, imperative; rule, law, ordinance.

2. proclamation, manifesto, prounnunciamento, announcement, promulgation, statement, formal *or* authoritative statement *or* announcement; notice, formal notice, notification; declaration, profession, enouncement; affirmation, averment, asseveration, avowal, avouchment; allegation, accusation, *Latin. ipse dixit;* protest, formal protest.

3. opinion, observation, reflection; comment, remark, statement, utterance, expression, *Inf.* one's two cents' worth, *Sl.* crack; decision, resolution, verdict, judgment, determination, ruling, finding.

4. enunciating, articulating, vocalizing, voicing; saying, uttering, expressing; affirming, asserting, avowing; insisting, maintaining, contending; propounding, proposing; alleging, claiming; declaring, pronouncing, professing; ruling, decreeing, proclaiming, promulgating; ordering, directing, commanding, dictating; announcing, publishing, publicizing.

pronunciation, *n.* articulation, enunciation, utterance, vocalization, voice, voicing, phonation; intonation, inflection, modulation; emphasis, accent, accentuation, stress, syllable stress; elocution, diction, dialect, manner of speaking, mode of expression, speech pattern; delivery, presentation, attack, force of utterance.

proof, *n.* **1.** validation, evidence, verification, proof positive, confirmation, ratification, authentication, *Law.* certification; conclusiveness, certainty, conviction, surety, assurance, guarantee.

2. documentation, document, substantiation, corroboration; support, ground, attestation, testification, certificate, testimony, *Law.* deposition, warrant, *Obs.* vouch; data, facts, information, (*of guilt*) the goods, *Inf.* ammunition, *Sl.* ammo.

3. test, trial, trial run, try-out, probation, *Obs.* assay, *Obs.* essay; checking, examination, inspection, scrutinization.

4. demonstration, manifestation, illustration, display, exhibition, exhibit; indication, sign, signal, token, mark, denotation; *All Printing.* impression, print, blueline, proof sheet, galley proof, galley, revise.

5. validity, validness, soundness, realness; strength, strongness, sturdiness, toughness, stamina, resistance, endurance; impenetrability, imperviousness, invulnerability, invincibility.

—*adj.* **6.** strong, sturdy, tough, sound; impenetrable, impervious, impregnable, invincible; resistant, repellent, tight, (*both of metal*) *Both Trademark.* galvanized, zinc-coated; treated, hardened, steeled, *Metallurgy.* tempered.

7. proven, tested, tried out; examined, checked out, inspected, scrutinized, *Inf.* O.K., all right.

8. firm, steadfast, steady, fixed, unwavering, unswerving, undeviating, unbending, unyielding; resolute, resolved, determined, staunch, stanch, stalwart, hard-line; obstinate, stubborn, obdurate, intransigent.

9. proving, testing, trial, pilot, experimental.

10. quality, top, topnotch, first-class, first-rate, good; standard, true, authentic, genuine, real.

prop, *v.* **1.** support, hold up, uphold, truss, truss up, bear, bear up; brace, bolster, buttress, gird; underprop, underpin, underbrace, bed, base, form the foundation of, underlie; reinforce, restrengthen, crutch, shore up; cradle, pillow, buoy, buoy up, keep afloat.

2. lean against *or* on, stand up against, rest against *or* on, lay against, arrange against; balance against or on, steady *or* stabilize against.

3. sustain, maintain, provide for; feed, victual, provision, board; carry, shoulder, keep up, keep alive; nurse, nourish, nurture.

4. finance, sponsor, patronize, fund, capitalize, subsidize, underwrite, put up the money for, pay for, grubstake, *Inf.* stake, *Inf.* bankroll, *Inf.* angel.

—*n.* **5.** support, beam, horizontal, cross-beam, rafter, joist; vertical, upright, column, post, shaft, pillar, pole, rod, stick; underprop, underpinning, shore, truss, fulcrum, *Archaic.* socle; brace, bracer, bolster, bracket, stay, buttress, shoulder, arm; rope, cable, guywire, guyline, guy; base, basis, foundation, substructure, underbuilding, groundwork, embankment, abutment; stand, sill, bed, bedding.

6. supporter, maintainer, mainstay, sustainer, upholder, *Sl.* meal ticket, *Sl.* sugar daddy; benefactor, benefactress, benefitter, friend, guardian angel, tutelary, tutelor, patron saint, *Inf.* fairy godmother; financer, funder, backer, patron, subsidizer, underwriter, angel, *Inf.* staker, *Inf.* grubstaker; advocate, endorser, second, booster.

propaganda, *n.* **1.** information, publicity, advertising, advertisement, promotion, *Sl.* PR puff; newspeak, agitprop; rumors, lies.

2. doctrine, dogma, creed, principles, teachings, tenets; belief, conviction, opinion, view; religion, persuasion.

3. brainwashing, propagandism, dissemination, teaching, indoctrination, spreading. See **propagandism.**

propagandism, *n.* **1.** propaganda, propagation, promulgation, evangelism, sowing the seeds; dissemination, spreading, transmission, passing on *or* along, circulation; broadcasting, advertizing, advertisement, promotion, pushing, *Sl.* hyping, *Inf.* plugging, talking up, ballyhooing; publicizing, publication, making public *or* known, printing; giving out, distribution, dispersal, diffusion, dispensation.

2. brainwashing, persuasion, convincing, conversion, proselytism; teaching, instruction, indoctrination, introduction; infusion, instillment, instillation, ingraining, implantation, infixion, inculcation, inoculation, imbuement; infection, contamination, tainting.

propagandist, *n.* **1.** propagator, promulgator, disseminator, circulator, spreader; broadcaster, announcer, advertiser, adman, promoter, pusher, *Inf.* plugger, ballyhooer; publicist, publicity man *or* agent, press agent, public-relations man, PR man, *Inf.* flak, spokesman.

2. brainwasher, agitprop, persuader, converter, proselytizer; teacher, instructor, indoctrinator; evangelist, revivalist, missionary.

propagandize, *v.* **1.** propagate, promulgate, sow the seeds of; disseminate, spread, transmit, pass on *or* along, circulate; broadcast, advertise, promote, push, *Inf.* plug, *Sl.* hype, talk up, ballyhoo; publicize, make public, make known, print, publish; give out, give to the world, distribute, dispense, diffuse, disperse.

2. brainwash, persuade, convince, convert, evangelize, proselytize; teach, instruct, indoctrinate, introduce; infuse, instill, ingrain, implant, infix, inculcate, inoculate, imbue; infect, contaminate, taint.

propagate, *v.* **1.** reproduce, multiply, proliferate; breed, procreate, beget, generate; bear, bring forth, deliver, give birth, (*of animals*) drop; hatch, spawn.

2. promulgate, disseminate, spread, transmit; circulate, give out, give to the world, distribute, dispense, diffuse, disperse; dissipate, scatter, sow; broadcast, air, advertise, *Sl.* hype, *Inf.* plug, propagandize; publish, issue, put out; publicize, make public, make known, drag into the open, bring into the open, let out, come out with, tell; proclaim, herald, cry, blare, bandy about, blaze about, blazon, trumpet, bruit, noise abroad.

3. increase, grow, develop, enlarge, wax, become greater *or* larger; extend, distend, stretch, widen, lengthen, heighten.

propagation, *n.* **1.** reproduction, multiplication, increase, proliferation, growth, development; breeding, procreation, begetting, generation; giving birth, parturition, delivery, bringing forth, bearing, (*of animals*) dropping; hatching, laying, spawning.

2. promulgation, dissemination, passing on *or* along, transmission, spreading; circulation, distribution, dispensing, diffusion, dispersion; publication, issuance; reporting, broadcasting, airing, advertisement, *Sl.* hyping, talking up, promotion, propaganda; proclamation, heralding, blaring, blazoning.

propel, *v.* **1.** move, actuate, get going, set in motion, start, launch; drive, impel, urge, press, push, thrust, shove; spur, prod, goad, induce, compel, make, force, *Inf.* pressure *or* high pressure; constrain, oblige, necessitate, require, demand, leave no option *or* choice.

2. project, discharge, eject, shoot, *Sl.* zap; hurl, heave, toss, throw; sling, catapult; precipitate.

propensity, *n.* **1.** inclination, inclining, proclivity; proneness, aptness, liableness, likeliness; subjectability, susceptibility, weakness, openness; tendency, tending, bearing, leaning, bent, turn, veering, *Biol.* tropism, cast, gravitation, drift; mind-set, disposition, *Pathol.* diathesis, temperament, temper, mind, humor, vein, idiosyncrasy, idiosyncrasis, grain, *Archaic.* crasis.

2. penchant, predisposition, predilection, partiality; affinity, attraction, tendentiousness, preference, prejudice, bias; sympathy, liking, fancy, fondness, affection, love, ardor, fervor, zeal, passion; desire, longing, wishing, hankering, craving, relish, appetite, appetency, taste.

3. aptitude, gift, genius, talent, faculty, readiness, skill.

proper, *adj.* **1.** suitable, appropriate, apt, apposite, apropos; fit, fitting, befitting, *Brit. Dial.* gradely, meet, *Fr. comme il faut,* according to Hoyle; expedient, advantageous, advisable; just, right, commensurate, proportionate, equitable, equivalent, correspondent; in character, in keeping, suited, adapted, compatible.

2. seemly, decorous, decent, becoming; tasteful, in good taste, dignified, refined, polished, elegant, genteel; stiff, formal, strict, straight-arrow, fastidious, fussy, finicky, finical.

3. accurate, precise, exact, right, correct; regular, usual, customary, accustomed, normal, routine.

4. own, peculiar, distinctive, individual; innate, natural, indigenous, inherent; belonging, characteristic, representative, specific.

property, *n.* **1.** belongings, effects, personal effects, chattels, possessions, *Inf.* things, *Sl.* stuff, *Sl.* junk; baggage, bag and baggage, gear, paraphernalia, accouterments, appurtenances, appointments, goods; *All Law.* personalty, choses, choses in possession *or* action, choses transitory.

2. means, investments, assets, fortune, capital, worth; income, money, revenue, stock, substance.

3. real estate, realty, land, acreage, grounds; yard, lawn, plot; allodium, estate, demesne, *Law.* messuage.

4. ownership, possession, tenure, hold, proprietorship, lordship, monopoly.

5. quality, attribute, distinction, note, mark, cachet; characteristic, character, feature, trait, trademark, earmark, badge; idiosyncrasy, idiocrasy, singularity; eccentricity, peculiarity, quirk, oddity.

prophecy, *n.* **1.** prognostication, foretelling, prediction; foresight, precognition, foreknowledge, prescience, prevision, presentiment, second sight, clairvoyance.

2. fortunetelling, augury, divination; palmistry, palm-reading, crystal-gazing; horoscopy, astrology, stargazing; dowsing, witching. See also **fortunetelling** and **divination** (*def.* 2).

prophesy, *v.* **1.** foretell, forespeak, augur, *Obs.* auspicate, divine, soothsay, foresee; read *or* interpret signs and omens, read palms *or* tea leaves, tell fortunes, see in the stars; forewarn, *Rare.* premonish; predict, prognosticate, forecast, vaticinate, *Med.* prognose; project, envision, see in the future, see in one's crystal ball; speculate, guess, theorize, hypothesize, conjecture.

2. foreshadow, presage, portend, forebode, bode, foretoken, point to, omen; herald, harbinger, prefigure, signify, indicate, promise, hint at, intimate, tell of, announce, proclaim.

prophet, *n.* **1.** diviner, soothsayer, seer, clairvoyant, oracle, augur, fortuneteller, prognosticator, forecaster, predictor; palmist, Chaldean, astrologer, horoscoper, astromancer, geomancer, (*in ancient Rome*) haruspex; prophetess, sibyl, witch; sorcerer, conjurer, wizard, magician, necromancer.

2. conjecturer, surmiser, guesser, theorizer, theorist, hypothesizer, hypothesist; interpreter, reader, expounder, explainer.

3. spokesman, proclaimer, adherent, follower, preacher, publicist, promoter, booster, pusher.

prophetic, *adj.* **1.** oracular, augural, divinatory, vaticinal, mantic, fatidic, sibyllic; predictive, prognostic, foretelling, forecasting, forewarning; premonitory, significant, meaningful; preindicative, foretokening, foreshowing, foreshadowing.

2. ominous, portentous, foreboding, bodeful, ill-boding, boding, evil; ill-omened, of evil portent; inauspicious, unpropitious, unfavorable, unpromising, unfortunate, unlucky, ill-fated, ill-starred, star-crossed, doomed from the start.

prophylactic, *adj.* **1.** preventive, preventative, protective; sanitary, hygienic.

—*n.* **2.** preventive, preventative, safeguard, guard, shield; counteractant, counteragent, neutralizer, nullifier, offset; remedy, antidote; vaccine, serum.

3. contraceptive; condom, sheath, *Trademark.* Trojan, *Sl.* rubber, *Sl.* skin, *Sl.* raincoat, *Sl.* French letter.

propinquity, *n.* **1.** proximity, approximation, vicinity, nearness, closeness, nighness. See **proximity** (*def.* **1**).

2. kindship, relationship, relation, tie. See **proximity** (*def.* **2**).

3. rapport, affinity, like-mindedness, oneness, unity; sympathy, empathy, identity, fellow feeling, fellowship; accord, agreement, understanding; compatibility, *Sl.* good vibrations *or* vibes.

propitiate, *v.* **1.** conciliate, appease, accommodate, compromise, adjust; yield, submit, surrender, concede, give in, cave in, accede to demands.

2. placate, pacificate, *Archaic.* attemper; assuage, mollify, dulcify, soothe, *Brit., Australian.* dill, *Rare.* lenify.

3. reconcile, bring to terms, make peace, settle differences, defuse, pour oil on troubled waters, *Archaic.* accord.

propitiation, *n.* **1.** conciliation, placation, appeasement; mollification, dulcification, pacification, peacemaking; compromise, concession, adjustment, accommodation; surrender, yielding, submission, acquiescence, accession.

2. satisfaction, recompense, redress, remuneration; reparation, amends, atonement, sop, pacifier; peace offering, olive branch, peace pipe, calumet, white flag; apology, acknowledgment; confession; penance, contrition, breast-beating.

propitiatory, *adj.* conciliatory, placatory, placative, propitiative, appeasing, pacifying, pacificatory, assuaging; accommodating, obliging, deferential, obeisant; reconciliatory, reconciliating, peacemaking, pacific, pacifical, dovish.

propitious, *adj.* **1.** favorable, advantageous, profitable, beneficial, suitable, fit, applicable, conducive; auspicious, promising, benign, reassuring, encouraging; opportune, lucky, timely, fortunate, providential, happy; pleasing, fair, rosy, bonny, looking up.

2. favorably inclined, well-disposed, agreeable, *Sl.* into it; friendly, sympathetic, congenial, understanding, kind; benevolent, beneficent, gracious; merciful, ruthful, compassionate.

proponent, *n.* advocate, enthusiast, backer, patron, promoter, endorser; upholder, abettor, second, seconder; espouser, adherent, propagator, propagandist, favorer, supporter, sustainer, maintainer; exponent, spokesman, defender, champion, justifier, vindicator; pleader, apologist, friend at court, friend in need, friend, well-wisher, sympathizer, *Inf.* angel; partisan, sectary, votary, supporter, moral support.

proportion, *n.* **1.** relationship, ratio, comparative size *or* extent, relative importance *or* significance, relative size *or* extent; correlation, correspondence, agreement, analogy, commensurateness; conformity, congruity, keeping, consistency; symmetry, ideal distribution, uniformity, parallelism, apposition, harmony, regularity, evenness, euphony, grace; arrangement, distribution, balance, adjustment; contrast, opposition, likenesses and differences, comparison, perspective.

2. portion, part, share, division, lot, percentage, commission, *Inf.* cut, *Sl.* whack, *Sl.* rake off; measure, quantity allotted, quota, consignment, allotment, ration, dole, allowance, just degree.

3. proportions dimensions, measurements; size, scope, range, greatness, magnitude, mass, bulk; spread, span, width, breadth, expanse, area, volume, capacity.

—*v.* **4.** regulate, adjust, modulate, arrange, order, balance, poise, equalize, equate; square, true, correct, rectify; harmonize, match; put in proportion, fit, conform, shape.

proportional, *adj.* **1.** corresponding, compatible, harmonious, balanced, well-proportioned, symmetrical, on a proper scale; consistent, agreeing, in accordance with, accordant; comparable, like, analogous, akin, commensurate, equivalent, matching, commensurable, parallel.

2. relative, related, correlated, connective, correspondent, complementary.

proposal, *n.* **1.** recommendation, suggestion, proposition; presentation, offer, proffer; overture, suit, request, invitation, bid.

2. scheme, plan, program, project; prospectus, draft, outline, delineation, sketch; pattern, layout, diagram, plot, projection; policy, line, plan of action, platform; terms, conditions, arrangement.

propose, *v.* **1.** offer, proffer, present, tender, submit, advance, recommend, move, make a motion, offer a resolution, lay *or* bring before, maintain, prefer; court, woo, suit, press one's suit, bid for, make a bid for, make an offer, ask for [s.o.'s] hand, *Inf.* pop the question.

2. suggest, submit, broach, come up with, initiate, launch, open, throw out, offer for what it's worth, bring to [s.o.'s] attention; project, drive at, urge, press, *Inf.* push, offer for consideration.

3. present, introduce, nominate, name, designate, offer in nomination; commend, put up, advance, name for membership *or* office.

4. design, plan, intend, purport, purpose; mean, have every intention, have the best intentions; expect, aim for, aim at, aspire to, set one's sights on, resolve, determine, decide, come to a determination; talk of, dream of, have in mind.

5. state, assert, voice, aver, allege, say, declare; pose, posit, predicate, postulate, propound, put forward, put *or* set forth, lay down.

proposition, *n.* **1.** proposal, recommendation. See **proposal** (*def.* **1**).

2. plan, program, project, scheme. See **proposal** (*def.* **2**).

3. hypothesis, theory, thesis, axiom, postulate; premise, supposition, assumption; statement, declaration, assertion, view, belief.

4. sexual advance *or* overture, improper suggestion, indecent proposal, *Inf.* come-on, *Inf.* the moves.

—*v.* **5.** offer, propose, suggest, recommend; submit, set forth, put, put forward, introduce; present, tender, advance.

6. make sexual advances *or* overtures, make an improper suggestion *or* an indecent proposal, *Inf.* make a pass, *Inf.* come on strong, *Inf.* put the moves on, *Sl.* put the make on.

propound, *v.* advocate, suggest, offer *or* present for consideration. See **propose** (*def.* **5**).

proprietor, *n.* **1.** owner, titleholder, deedholder, landowner, landholder, property owner; propertied *or* landed person, person of property, freeholder, possessor, holder; improprietor, proprietary; master, mistress, landlord, landlady, *Scot.* laird, lord of the manor, mesne lord, feudatory, feoffee; squire, country gentleman, householder.

2. keeper, innkeeper, hotelkeeper, barkeep, permittee, manager, restaurateur.

propriety, *n.* **1.** properness, correctitude, correctness, conformity; decorum, decency, suitability, suitableness, appropriateness, seemliness, becomingness, fitness, congruity.

2. etiquette, protocol, punctilio, good form, the thing to do; politeness, good manners, mannerliness, best behavior; gentility, breeding, gentlemanliness, ladylikeness, dignity, sedateness, respectability; modesty, delicacy, grace, refinement.

3. the proprieties accepted conduct *or* comportment, social code, rules of conduct, formalities, social procedures *or* conduct, social graces, courtliness; formality, formalness, ceremony, ritual; amenities, decencies, civilities, proper thing, what is done, social conventions; time-honored practice, tradition, standing custom *or* practice.

propulsion, *n.* propelling force, impulse, push, thrust, drive; prompting, initiative, motivation, driving force; impetus, impulsion, momentum, power, *Inf.* steam, energy.

prosaic, *adj.* **1.** commonplace, common, ordinary, everyday, workaday, household, usual, routine, par for the course; mediocre, undistinguished, unimpressive, pedestrian, homely, *Inf.* run-of-the-mill; dry, matter-of-fact, sober, unimaginative, tame, flat, lifeless, spiritless; vapid, dull, tedious, tiresome, wearisome; boring, monotonous, humdrum, unvaried; bland, insipid, jejune, uninteresting, uninspiring, unmoving, unentertaining, pointless; trite, cliché, hackneyed, platitudinous, *Inf.* bromidic, stock, familiar, oft-repeated, stereotyped, tautological; stale, tired, thin, threadbare, worn-out, overused, *Inf.* old hat, *Inf.* moth-eaten, *Inf.* warmed over.

2. prosy, prose, prosaical; unrhyming, unrhymed, unmetric, unmetrical, unpoetic, unpoetical.

proscribe, *v.* **1.** damn, doom, condemn, sentence, pass sentence on, censure; restrict, restrain, circumscribe, check.

2. outlaw, forbid, prohibit, interdict, ban, disallow.

3. banish, exile, expatriate, deport, expel; drive away, exclude, excommunicate; blackball, reject, boycott, repudiate; ostracize, taboo, ignore, send to Coventry.

proscription, *n.* **1.** condemnation, damning, dooming, censuring; circumscription, restriction, restraint, interdiction, prohibition, ban, taboo, injunction, outlawry.

2. banishment, exile, expatriation, expulsion, exclusion, excommunication, ejection, eviction, deportation, the punishment of Philip Nolan, repudiation, ostracism.

prosecute, *v.* **1.** *Law.* bring to court *or* trial *or* justice, try; summon, sue, bring suit, prefer charges, arraign, indict; accuse, charge.

2. follow up, carry through, consummate, finish, end, dispose of, see to the end, see [s.t.] through; stick with, persist at, persevere, dog, give one's all.

3. practice, carry on, proceed with, continue, keep one's hand *or* oar in; conduct, exercise, perform, direct, manage; work at, labor at, engage in, deal with, handle, devote oneself to.

proselyte, *n.* convert, new believer, catechumen, neophyte, novice, tyro; disciple, born-again Christian.

proselytize, *v.* proselyte, convert, win over, bring into the fold; persuade, influence, bring pressure on, induce; redeem, save.

prospect, *n.* **1.** *Usu.* **prospects** probability, likelihood, likeliness, liability, outlook for the future; distinct possibility, possibility, chance, good chance, even *or* fair chance; favorable chance, well-grounded hope, great expectation; off chance, outside chance, remote possibility, long shot.

2. anticipation, envisagement, envisionment; expectation, expectancy, thought, hope; intention, design, plan; assumption, presumption, speculation, reckoning, calculation, contemplation.

3. outlook, view, vista, exposure, aspect, scene, scenery, landscape, picture, panorama; spectacle, display, pageant, show.

4. perspective, mental viewpoint, attitude, point of view; position, standpoint, interpretation, side, slant, angle.

5. in prospect in view, in one's eye, on the horizon; in the offing, in store, in the wind, *Inf.* in the cards; under consideration, on the docket, on the table; projected, planned; near, close, at hand, close at hand.

—*v.* **6.** explore, search, check out, take a look at, inspect, survey; investigate, scrutinize, examine, analyze, *Archaic.* indagate; experiment, sample, try.

prospective, *adj.* future, coming, to come, expected, to be expected, intended, planned; in prospect, in view, on the horizon; in the offing, brewing, yet unborn, in the cards, in the wind, in store; pending, impending, imminent, overhanging, approaching, looming, threatening; probable, likely, destined, to be; looked for, hoped for, anticipated, foreseeable, foreseen; at hand, near at hand, close at hand, about to be, next, near, immediate; subsequent, eventual, hereafter, in the near future, forthcoming; potential, possible, imaginable, conceivable, not improbable.

prospectus, *n.* **1.** announcement, notice, notification, report; advertisement, flier, handbill, circular, blurb.

2. plan, outline, design, sketch, draft, *Inf.* roughout; syllabus, synopsis, digest, brief, summary.

prosper, *v.* **1.** succeed, make good, *Brit. Dial.* tadge, fare well, be fortunate, have a streak *or* run of luck; advance, get ahead, go up in the world, progress, make headway, get on *or* along; grow rich, become wealthy, make one's fortune, add to *or* increase one's riches; profit, gain, feather one's nest, line one's pockets, make one's pile, get all the gravy, enrich oneself; be well-off, be well-to-do, be on easy street; lead a charmed life, live a life of luxury *or* ease, live the life of Riley, bask in the sun, live in the clover, live off the fat of the land.

2. thrive, flourish, luxuriate; burgeon, mushroom, boom, spring up, burst forth, grow *or* develop vigorously.

prosperity, *n.* wealth, riches, fortune, affluence, opulence, *Sl.* fat city; prosperousness, good life, life of ease *or* luxury, *Sl.* easy street, *Sl.* life of Riley; bed of roses, *Inf.* velvet, milk and honey; golden age, prime, heyday, boom, palmy *or* halcyon days; zenith, height, peak, culmination, high tide, flood; abundance, plenty, bounty, cornucopia, fat of the land.

prosperous, *adj.* **1.** flourishing, thriving, palmy; successful, glorious, booming, ascendant, in the ascendant, on the rise *or* upswing, prospering, in full swing; growing, mushrooming, burgeoning, waxing, developing vigorously; lush, luxuriant, exuberant, plentiful, abundant, flush, prolific, rank, rife.

2. wealthy, rich, opulent, affluent, halcyon, fat; well-to-do, well-off, *Inf.* well-heeled, *Inf.* like a million dollars *or* bucks; moneyed, *Inf.* in the money, *Sl.* in the bucks, *Sl.* golden, *Sl.* on easy street; very comfortable, on a bed of roses, *Sl.* on velvet, in clover, born with a silver spoon in one's mouth.

3. favorable, propitious, good, timely, opportune, seasonable, advantageous, profitable; helpful, conducive, contributive, expedient; fortunate, lucky, providential, auspicious; optimistic, promising, bright, rosy, roseate, sunny, smiling.

prostitute, *n.* **1.** harlot, whore, demire, slut, hussy, cocotte, demimondaine, loose woman, wanton, fallen woman, woman of ill repute, white slave; lady of the evening, lady of pleasure, woman of the profession, Mrs. Warren, *Fr. fille de joie,* trollop, strumpet, *Archaic.* wench, trull, drab, quean, painted woman, woman of the streets, streetwalker, bar girl, *Inf.* pickup, call girl, Cyprian, *All Sl.* cat, tart, hustler, bim, moll, hooker, floozie, working girl, *Brit. Sl.* bird, *Mexican Sl.* caliente, bitch, broad, chippy.

2. madam, bawd, procuress, pander; paramour, courtesan, mistress, concubine, kept woman, *Sl.* doxy; temptress, siren, seductress, Jezebel, Delilah, flirt, coquette, minx; adventuress, hetaera.

3. hack, hireling, mercenary, exploiter; flunky, henchman, myrmidon; traitor, turncoat, Judas; tool, instrument.

—*v.* **4.** (*usu. of oneself*) debase, devaluate, lower, degrade, demean, belittle; profane, desecrate, defile, soil, dirty; corrupt, pervert, contaminate, mar, spoil, ruin; misuse, abuse, misdirect, misapply, misemploy.

prostitution, *n.* **1.** harlotry, whoredom, streetwalking, Mrs. Warren's profession, the oldest profession; whoremongering, whoremastery, pimping, pandering, procuring, procurement, procuration, hustling.

2. debasement, devaluation, degradation, lowering, demeaning, belittling, belittlement; profanation, profaning, desecration, defilement; perversion, perverting, corruption, corrupting; misuse, abuse, misdirection, misapplication, misemployment.

prostrate, *v.* **1.** (*all of oneself*) fall at [s.o.'s] feet, throw *or* cast oneself at [s.o.'s] feet; bow before, bow down to, bend the knee to, fall on one's knees before; kowtow, bow and scrape, truckle, grovel, crouch, crawl, snivel; eat crow, eat dirt, *Sl.* lick *or* bite the dust.

2. overthrow, overcome, overwhelm, overpower, overmaster; reduce, disarm, paralyze; cast *or* throw down, knock down, bowl down *or* over, floor, *Inf.* deck; fell, level, flatten, precipitate, drop, bring down, bring low, take down; crush, smash, humble, bring [s.o.] to his knees.

3. jade, fag *or* fag out, fatigue, weary, tire, tire out, exhaust, wear down *or* out, *Inf.* tucker out.

—*adj.* **4.** supine, resupine, recumbent, accumbent, decumbent, procumbent, prone; laid low, laid out, stretched out, couchant; flat, flat on one's back.

5. overcome, overwhelmed, overpowered, overmastered, overthrown; smashed, crushed, flattened, humbled, brought to one's knees; reduced, disarmed, paralyzed; impotent, helpless, defenseless, powerless; out of action, out of the fight, off the field, *Fr. hors de combat*; laid up, bedridden, sick abed.

6. exhausted, jaded, fagged *or* fagged out, drained, spent, worn out, played out; tired, dog-tired, dead-tired, dead on one's feet, more dead than alive, tired to death; *Both Inf.* done in, tuckered out; *All Sl.* bushed, whipped, beat, all in, wiped out, pooped, pooped out, too pooped to pop.

7. deferential, obeisant, submissive, compliant, obedient; passive, resigned, accepting, nonresisting; humble, meek, abject; subservient, servile, obsequious; groveling, crawling, kowtowing, cringing, cowering, sniveling.

8. disconsolate, inconsolable, desolate, forlorn, in despair, in the depths *or* bowels of despair; heartbroken, broken-hearted, heartsick, sick at heart, *Sl.* cut up, *Sl.* torn up.

prostration, *n.* **1.** obeisance, kowtow, salaam; crouch, stoop, bow, genuflection; reverence, groveling, crawling, sniveling.

2. lowness, supineness, resupineness, proneness; recumbency, accumbency, decumbence; fall, downfall, collapse; overthrow, upset, upheaval; submissiveness, submission, abjectness.

3. disconsolation, desolation, forlornness, desperation, agony, agony of mind *or* spirit; despair, depths *or* bowels of despair, depth of misery, extremity, *Sl.* the pits; misery, miserableness, wretchedness, woe, bale; broken-heartedness, broken heart, heartache, aching heart, heavy heart.

4. exhaustion, enervation, lassitude, weariness; weakness, feebleness, debility; (*all in reference to health*) breakdown, *Inf.* crackup, nervous breakdown, nervous exhaustion, *Pathol.* neurasthenia.

prosy, *adj.* prose, prosaic, commonplace, ordinary, dull, unimaginative, flat, vapid. See **prosaic** (*defs.* **1, 2**).

protagonist, *n.* **1.** (*all in a drama or literary work*) principal, principal *or* main *or* leading character, agonist, hero, heroine, antihero, antiheroine, nonhero; (*all in a drama or film*) lead, title role, leading man *or* lady.

2. advocate, supporter, upholder, exponent; spokesman, mouthpiece; champion, defender, apologist; admirer, aficionado, *Inf.* fan, *Inf.* buff.

3. (*all of a movement, cause, etc.*) leader, prime mover, moving spirit; bellwether, front runner, pacesetter, pacemaker; standard-bearer, torchbearer; leader of men, charismatic leader, born leader; messiah, savior, (*in Muslim usage*) Mahdi.

protean, *adj.* **1.** variable, changeable, changeful, ever-changing, mutable, permutable, labile, kaleidoscopic; polymorphous, polymorphic, metamorphic, metamorphotic.

2. (*all of an actor*) versatile, *Inf.* all-around, generally capable; resourceful, flexible, adaptable, adjustable; proteiform, many-sided, multifaceted.

protect, *v.* **1.** defend, forfend, *Archaic.* fend, defend tooth and nail, defend to the last man; secure, make safe, safeguard, guard from, guard against; cover, cloak, screen, veil; house, shelter, take in; hide, hide out, conceal; champion, stick up for, *Inf.* go to bat for, take [s.o.'s] side; run interference for, *Sports or Fig.* block for, pick *or* lay a pick for; escort, chaperone, convey, conduct, shepherd, *Inf.* ride shotgun.

2. keep, keep up, preserve, conserve, maintain, sustain; watch, mind, tend, keep an eye on, look after; care for, take care of, take under one's wing; nurse, nurture, foster, cherish; attend, attend to, minister to.

protection, *n.* **1.** preservation, preserval, conservation, care, safekeeping, maintenance, upkeep; safety, security, immunity.

2. defense, guard, safeguard, palladium, shield; bulwark, barrier, wall, buffer; cover, screen, cloak; covert, coverture, hiding place, hideaway; asylum, sanctuary, safehold, safety zone; shelter, refuge, haven, harbor, port in a storm, *Scot. and North Eng.* bield; convoy, escort, bodyguard; charm, good luck *or* lucky charm, talisman, amulet; precaution, preventive measure, measure, step, *Fig.* insurance; steps, measures, steps and measures.

3. patronage, aegis, sponsorship, tutelage, auspices, offices, good offices; ministry, ministration, care, custody, charge, ward, keeping, protectorship, guardianship; support, advocacy, backing, blessing, well-wishes; aid, assistance, help, championship.

4. *Informal.* **a.** protection money, extortion, blackmail, *Inf.* shakedown. **b.** bribe, sop, *Inf.* payoff, *Sl.* payola, *Sl.* hush money, *Sl.* boodle.

5. pass, passport, visa, permit, safe-conduct.

protective, *adj.* preventive, preventative, prophylactic; defensive, defending, shielding, sheltering, screening, protecting, guarding, safeguarding; conservatory, conservative, conserving, preservative, preservatory, preserving; conservational, conservationist; custodial, ministrant, ministering; guardian, tutelar, tutelary; fostering, nurturing, cherishing; watchful, heedful, mindful, vigilant; possessive, jealous, smothering, overbearing.

protector, *n.* defender, champion, paladin, knight in shining armor; tower *or* pillar of strength, rock, rock of Gibraltar, Gibraltar; guardian, patron, benefactor, benefactress, patron saint; familiar spirit, guardian angel, fairy godmother; advocate, apologist, vindicator; keeper, safekeeper, steward, custodian, caretaker, warden, warder, protectress; *Law.* guardian ad litem, *Law.* next friend, *Law.* prochain ami; gamekeeper, gamewarden, ranger; escort, chaperon, governess, duenna; guard, bodyguard.

protest, *n.* **1.** objection, exception, disagreement; demur, demurral, scruple, qualm, compunction; challenge; negation, denial, disclaimer; complaint, grievance, *Inf.* beef, *Inf.* kick, *Sl.* squawk, *Sl.* bitch, peeve, *Inf.* pet peeve, *Inf.* gripe, *Inf.* grouse.

2. demonstration, public demonstration, *Inf.* demo, rally, march, sit-in; walkout, strike, shutdown, closedown, slowdown; boycott.

—*v.* **3.** remonstrate, expostulate, plead, argue; demur, scruple, have qualms *or* scruples, boggle.

4. object to, say no to, dissent, oppose, take issue, take exception, beg to differ; mind, balk at, draw the line at, make one's stand against, stand and be counted against, vote against; complain, put up a fight, not take lying down, fuss, make a fuss over, *Inf.* kick up a fuss, *Inf.* kick, *Inf.* beef, *Inf.* raise hell, *Inf.* cry bloody murder, *Sl.* bitch, *Sl.* squawk; inveigh, censure, denounce; disapprove, disfavor, view with disfavor, frown at *or* upon, not think much of, not take kindly to, *Inf.* take a dim view of.

5. demonstrate, sit in, march, rally; boycott; strike, picket.

6. assert, asseverate, aver, avow, avouch, attest, affirm, assure; declare, announce, annunciate, pronounce, enounce, have one's say, speak one's mind *or* piece; profess, obtest; maintain, contend, argue, insist.

protestation, *n.* **1.** remonstrance, remonstration, expostulation; compunction; objection, dissent, disagreement, nonconcurrence, nonobservance, noncompliance, nonconformance; assertion, asseveration, averment, avowal, avouchment, attestation, affirmation.

2. oath, solemn oath, vow; word, assurance, pledge, guarantee; declaration, pronouncement, announcement, statement, profession; manifesto, proclamation; position, stand, stance.

3. protest; challenge. See **protest** (*def.* **1**).

protocol, *n.* **1.** dipolmatic code; social code, rubric, code of behavior, rules of conduct; rules, regulations, formalities; customs, conventions, standards, manners, decorum, etiquette; conventional practice *or* usage, prevailing form.

2. agreement, contract, compact, pact, covenant, concordat.

prototype, *n.* **1.** original, source, protoplast, *Television.* pilot; model, pattern, paradigm; mold, cast; precedent, lead.

2. illustration, example, classic example, type, archetype, representative, epitome; sample, instance, case, typical case; standard, norm, criterion, rule, touchstone, measure, barometer, yardstick; mirror, exemplar, paragon, ideal, beau ideal, shining example.

protract, *v.* prolong, prolongate, extend, lengthen, elongate, stretch out, spin out, draw out, drag out; continue, perpetuate, sustain, maintain, keep up, keep going, keep alive, dwell on, linger on; develop, expand, enlarge, enlarge upon, amplify; pad, fill out.

protracted, *adj.* extended, prolonged, prolongated, lengthened, drawn-out, long-drawn-out, spun out, dragged-out, strung-out, stretched-out; long, lengthy, overlong, too-long, long-winded, marathon; interminable, unending, never-ending, endless, everlasting, unrelenting; redundant, repetitious, repetitive, battological, pleonastic, tautological, *Inf.* broken-record; padded, filled out.

protrude, *v.* **1.** project, extrude, jut *or* jut out, stick out, poke out; extend, excurve, obtrude, bulge, bilge, protuberate, *Anat.* protract; swell, swell out *or* up, distend, belly, bag, balloon, billow; (*all usu. in reference to the eyes*) pop, goggle, *Inf.* bug; vault, vault over, arch, arch over, bow, embow; beetle, overhang, hang over, *Rare.* impend; stick up, bristle, stand up, shoot up.

2. pout, thrust out *or* forward.

protuberance, *n.* **1.** prominence, eminence, excrescence, gibbosity, tuberosity, convexity.

2. bulge, bow, swelling, bell, bump, lump, hump, tumescence; outgrowth, *Anat., Bot.* apophysis, *Archit.* apophyge; blister, bubble, bleb, pimple, welt, wart; knob, knurl, knot, gnarl, node, nodulation, nodosity; protrusion, projection, jut, overhang, extrusion, excurvation; beetling, jutting, impendence, hang.

protuberant, *adj.* gibbous, bulbous, bulging, bilging, bulging *or* bilging out; swelling, swollen, tumid, turgid, tumescent; distended, bellied, potbellied, bagging; goggled, *Inf.* pop-eyed, *Inf.* bug-eyed, *Sl.* googly-eyed; projecting, protruding, protrusive, salient, bold, outstanding, conspicuous, prominent; eminent, protrusile, excrescent, *Bot.* excurrent; extrusive, jutting, beetling; overlying, overlapping, overhanging, *Rare.* impending; arched, vaulted, bowed, convex, excurved, excurvate; bossed, embossed, chased, raised, superimposed, in relief, in high *or* strong relief.

proud, *adj.* **1.** content, contented, satisfied, gratified, pleased, well-pleased, *Inf.* pleased as punch; glad, delighted, happy, sunny, cheerful; complacent, smug, self-satisfied, self-contented, pleased with oneself, like the cat that swallowed the canary.

2. conceited, self-important, self-esteeming, self-admiring, self-centered, egocentric, narcissistic, *Sl.* stuck *or* hung up on oneself; vain, vainglorious, egotistical, puffed-up, inflated, swollen, swell-headed, *Inf.* big-headed; boastful, bragging, crowing, blustering, *Sl.* full of hot air; cocky, cocksure, bumptious, assertive, self-assertive, self-assured, aggressive, *Inf.* pushy, *Scot.* vaunty.

3. arrogant, fastuous, overbearing, overweening, presumptuous, assuming, *Inf.* too much; contemptuous, disdainful, scornful, derisive, insolent; imperious, lordly, magisterial, high-handed, highfalutin; haughty, snobbish, on one's high horse, high-and-mighty, too good for the rest of us, priggish, *Inf.* high-hat, *Inf.* nose in the air, *Sl.* snooty, *Sl.* snotty, *Sl.* sniffy, *Sl.* stuck-up; supercilious, cavalier, condescending, patronizing, *Inf.* toplofty; aloof, remote, distant, detached, removed, above-it-all; unbending, stiff-necked, unapproachable, forbidding; pompous, pretentious, affected, hoity-toity.

4. creditable, estimable, laudable, admirable, praiseworthy; honorable, righteous, virtuous, high-minded, high-principled, upright, upstanding.

5. noble, sublime, majestic, august, stately; imposing, impressive, commanding, awe-inspiring, *Archaic.* magnific; grand, royal, regal, kingly, princely; elegant, graceful, handsome; magnificent, splendid, *Inf.* splendiferous, resplendent, superb, glorious, brilliant, radiant; luxurious, lavish, sumptuous, gorgeous, *Inf.* out of this world; *All Inf.* posh, plush, swank, ritzy.

6. eminent, distinguished, notable, noteworthy, noted, important; illustrious, worthy, reputable; elevated, exalted.

7. vigorous, full of vigor, spirited, lively, full of life, animated, vivacious, energetic, brisk.

prove, *v.* **1.** establish the truth of, show to be true, bear out, demonstrate, manifest, evince, evidence, give credence to, *Law.* probate; document, back *or* back up, support, uphold, sustain; affirm, confirm, *Inf.* go to show, corroborate, verify, authenticate, validate, substantiate; attest to, certify, bear witness to, witness, testify to, vouch for; *Inf.* put up or shut up, *Inf.* put your money where your mouth is.

2. test, put to the test, put to trial, assay, give a test *or* trial run, try *or* try out, give a tryout; examine, probe, analyze, check *or* check out, go over.

3. show, evidence, demonstrate, manifest, evince, exhibit, display.

4. turn out, come out, result, end up, be found to be.

provenance, *n.* provenience, origin, source; root, taproot, *Bot.* radicle, *Bot.* radix, etiology, derivation, etymon; fountainhead, fount, fountain, head, wellspring, well, spring, rise; base, basis, foundation, fundamental, rudiment, ground.

provender, *n.* **1.** (*all of livestock*) feed, fodder, forage, silage, ensilage, hay, straw, grass; wheat, rye, oats, barley, corn, grain, bran, meal, mash; swill, *Inf.* glop, *Sl.* slop.

2. food, nourishment, nutriment, nurture, aliment, alimentation, pabulum, sustenance, sustentation, subsistence; viands, meat, bread, daily bread, groceries, foodstuffs, solids, edibles, *Inf.* grub, *Sl.* eats, *Sl.* chow, *Chiefly Brit. Sl.* scoff; snack, between-meal-snack, bite, nosh, *Sl.* munchies; victuals, provisions, cheer, rations, commons, comestibles, *Western U.S. Sl.* chuck, *Brit. Sl.* prog; board, fare, meals, mess, menu, table, diet, regimen.

proverb, *n.* maxim, aphorism, apothegm, gnome, adage, *Archaic.* word, *Archaic.* sentence; saw, pithy statement, sententious saying, saying; axiom, precept, prescript, dictum, moral; epigram, witticism, *Fr. jeu d'esprit*, quip, Atticism; cliché, hackneyed phrase, platitude, truism, *Inf.* bromide, commonplace; byword, slogan, motto, catchword, catch phrase.

proverbial, *adj.* axiomatic, self-evident, aphoristic, apothegmatic, apothematical; cliché, trite, hackneyed, platitudinous, *Inf.* bromidic; commonplace, common, ordinary, everyday, familiar; universal, general, well-known, famed, famous, legendary, traditional.

provide, *v.* **1.** furnish, supply, contribute, accommodate, equip, outfit, *Archaic.* dight, *Obs.* appoint; cater, purvey, provision, provender, victual; store, stock, stock up, fill, gird, *Chiefly Scot.* plenish.

2. afford, yield, produce; present, serve, give, afford, accord, donate, award, confer; distribute, administer, deal out, give out, dole out, mete out, *Inf.* hand out, *Inf.* dish out, *Sl.* shell out *Sl.* fork out; grant, tender, proffer, extend, bestow, lavish; endow, endue, invest.

3. allow for, make allowances for, consider, take into consideration, take into account, take account of; prepare for, make provision for, make sure, make sure against, forearm, provide for *or* against a rainy day; take precautions, take steps *or* measures, guard against, keep on the safe side, *Inf.* play safe; set one's house in order; leave nothing to chance, leave no room for error, consider every angle, leave no stone unturned; hedge, hedge one's bets, cut one's losses; clear the decks, batten down the hatches, shorten sail.

4. lay in provisions, lay up stores, lay by, husband one's resources, salt *or* squirrel away.

5. arrange for, make arrangements for; support, maintain, sustain, secure, uphold; care for, take care of, look after, take charge of, take under one's wing, attend *or* minister to; finance, back, sponsor, fund, patronize, provide money *or* capital for, put up the money, grubstake, *Inf.* stake, *Inf.* angel, *Inf.* bankroll.

provided, *conj.* on condition that, in case that, in case, if, if and only if, if it should happen that; in the event that, just in case, in any *or* either case; providing, with the proviso that, on condition, on condition that, with the stipulation *or* understanding, subject to, contingent upon.

providence, *n.* **1.** divine intervention, God's will, predetermination; destiny, fate, fortune, lot, cup, portion, doom; karma, kismit; Fortune's wheel, wheel of fortune, stars, planets, astral influence; chance, mere chance, happenstance, fortuity, serendipity, happy chance; accident, uncertainty, luck, fortune; vicissitudes, ups and downs, fickle finger of fate.

2. foresight, prudence, care, judgment, discretion, discrimination, sagacity, perspicacity, judiciousness, presence of mind; caution, readiness, preparation, precaution, heed, watchfulness, farsightedness, longsightedness, circumspection.

3. economy, husbandry, careful *or* thrifty management, conservation; conserving, saving, economizing; thrift, thriftiness, frugality, frugalness, sparingness, cutting corners, making ends meet; keeping, safekeeping, care.

provident, *adj.* providential, farsighted, long-sighted, sagacious, judicious, thoughtful; prepared, ready, anticipating, equipped, with one's lamps trimmed; precautionary, wary, discreet, precautious, at the ready, in practice *or* shape, ready for anything, *Inf.* all set.

providential, *adj.* **1.** auspicious, propitious, favorable, advantageous, ripe; opportune, seasonable, timely, well-timed, just in time, convenient; encouraging, promising, full of promise; rosy, bright, fair, sunny, golden, benign, benignant.

2. lucky, fortuitous, happy, felicitous, *Scot. and North Eng., Irish Eng.* sonsy, fortunate; favored, blessed, blessed with luck, with God's blessing; granted, bestowed, God-given, given, allowed, accorded, vouchsafed, gratuitous.

provider, *n.* **1.** supporter, sole support, head of the household, breadwinner, *Inf.* one who brings home the bacon, *Inf.* one who puts food on the table.

2. patron, giver, donor, contributor, backer, financer, funder, angel; bestower, *Law.* grantor, imparter, fairy godmother, Lady Bountiful, Santa Claus, *Inf.* sugar daddy, *Inf.* soft touch; philanthropist, do-gooder.

3. supplier, furnisher, procurer, purveyor, provisioner, caterer.

province, *n.* **1.** state, territory, region, area, district, division, zone, section, quarter, estate, pale, lands, demesne; dependency, dominion, realm, domain; arrondissement, canton, department; precinct, constituency, parish, borough, county; city, township, town, village, community; ward, neighborhood.

2. bailiwick, jurisdiction, beat, circuit, round, post, billet, station, berth; assignment, part, job, situation, place; sphere, compass, orbit, locale, locality, *Inf.* neck of the woods; authority, charge, function, capacity, role.

3. discipline, field, specialty, forte, specialization, branch, school, art, science; employment, line, occupation, business, trade, profession, *Inf.* racket, *Inf.*

game, line of business *or* work; walk, walk of life, category, status; area of activity *or* pursuit, calling, lifework, persuasion; scope, latitude, ambit, span; long suit, métier, gift, genius, special genius, endowment.

4. the provinces outlying districts, backwoods, hinterlands, wilds, wilderness, frontier, woods, bush, *Sl.* boondocks, *Sl.* boonies, *Australian.* outback, parts unknown, no man's land; the country, the countryside, small towns, farm country, exurbia, *U.S. Inf.* the sticks, *U.S. Sl.* hicksville.

provincial, *adj.* **1.** regional, sectional, territorial, divisional; local, home, independent; topical, topographic, topographical.

2. rural, bucolic, country, countrified, small-town, *Inf.* one-horse, *Inf.* jerkwater, *Sl.* hick-town, *Sl.* hick; hinterland, backwood *or* backwoods, backwater; hillbilly, hill-country; rustic, downhome, homegrown, domestic; unsophisticated, unpolished, rude, unrefined, gauche, ungraceful, gawky; rough, hayseed, yokelish, clodhopping, clodish, oafish, awkward, boorish, loutish, churlish; untraveled, home-town, ingrown.

3. narrow, insular, locked-in, illiberal, hidebound, purblind, deaf to reason; rigid, inflexible, set in one's ways; stiff-necked, intolerant, narrow-minded, closed-minded, bigoted, prejudiced, partial, one-sided; parochial, creed-bound, dogmatic, opinionated, ex parte, fanatical.

—*n.* **4.** peasant, farmer, country cousin *or* bumpkin, *Sl.* hayseed, *Sl.* rube, *Sl.* hick, *Sl.* hick from Hicksville, *Sl.* okie from Muskogee.

provincialism, *n.* **1.** regionalism, idiom, localism; dialect, patois; local habit *or* custom, idiosyncrasy, trait, characteristic, earmark, distinctive feature, *Inf.* giveaway *or* dead giveaway.

2. narrowness, bias, bent, leaning, colored *or* slanted view, partiality, prepossession, arbitrariness, one-sidedness, jingoism, patriotism, chauvinism, parochialism, cliquishness; illiberality, intolerance.

3. ignorance, unawareness, unenlightenment, benightedness, want *or* lack of knowledge *or* experience; innocence, simplicity, inexperience, greenness; denseness, thickness, stolidness, dumbness.

provision, *n.* **1.** proviso, stipulation, condition, clause, term, specification, given; restriction, limitation, qualification, *Inf.* catch, *Inf.* string, *Inf.* small *or* fine print; reservation, exemption, exception; requisite, prerequisite, obligation.

2. supply, supplying, providing, accouterment, furnishing, furnishment; equipment, equipping, outfitting, fitting out, rigging up; giving, bestowal, endowment, donation, donating; purveyance, purveying, catering, victualing.

3. prearrangement, forearming, prior measures *or* steps, provident steps *or* measures; organization, arrangement; deliberation, predeliberation, calculation, premeditation, preconsideration; adjustment, adaptation.

4. wherewithal, means, resources, material, materials; equipment, equipage, matériel; apparatus, gear, machinery.

5. stock, store, supply, quantity, fund, lot, *Chiefly U.S. Dial.* grist; reserve, reservoir; stockpile, collection, cache, hoard, amassment, accumulation; inventory, supply on hand; resources, wealth, savings, capital, nest egg; abundance, plenty, plenitude, cornucopia; treasure, mine, quarry, well; lode, bed, vein; heap, pile, mass, stack, load.

6. provisions food, foodstuff, provender, edibles, eatables, victuals, *Inf.* vittles, comestibles, viands, board; staples, sustenance, subsistence, *Fig.* bread, *Fig.* daily bread, *Fig.* staff of life; forage, feed, fodder; supplies, stores, rations, groceries, larder, food supply.

—*v.* **7.** cater, purvey, victual, provender; feed, forage; board, sustain.

provisional, *adj.* **1.** temporary, *Latin. pro tempore,* pro tem, interim, transitional, limited; substitute, substitutional, substitutionary; makeshift, impermanent, temporal; incidental, circumstantial.

2. conditional, dependent, contingent, relative, subject to, based on; experimental, speculative, *Inf.* iffy.

3. restrictive, restricted, qualified, with reservations; under restriction, limited, limitative, limiting; stipulatory, provisory, provisionary, probationary, pending, probative.

proviso, *n.* provision, stipulation, condition. See **provision** (*def.* **1**).

provisory, *adj.* provisional, conditional. See **provisional** (*defs.* **2, 3**).

provocation, *n.* **1.** instigating, instigation, actuating, actuation, initiating, initiation, looking for trouble; fomenting, fomentation, agitating, agitation, exciting, excitement, excitation, arousing, rousing, whipping up, working up, stirring up, enflaming, impassioning, enkindling, kindling, firing up, touching off; eliciting, elicitation, evoking, evocation, calling forth, summoning up.

2. inciting, incitement, incitation, poking, prodding, pricking, thrusting, goading, prompting, spurring, egging on, encouraging, encouragement, putting up to; impelling, compelling, constraining, pressing, pushing, moving, forcing, propelling, lashing, driving, hounding; striking, penetrating, penetration, touching to the quick; stimulating, stimulation, animating, animation, reanimation, invigorating, invigoration, motivating, motivation.

3. annoyance, irritation, aggravation, disturbance; insult, affront, offense, sting, wound.

4. stimulus, fillip, motive, incentive, inducement; promotion, furtherance, advance, advancement; temptation, allurement, beguilement, inveiglement, infection, intoxication; poke, prod, prick, thrust, goad, spur, jolt, jog, *Inf.* start of something; impulse, push, urge, drive, itch, desire; dictate, call.

provocative, *adj.* **1.** alluring, inviting, tempting, tantalizing, irresistible; charming, captivating, intriguing, fascinating, entrancing, beguiling, intoxicating, bewitching, enrapturing; attractive, desirable, seductive, sensuous, *Inf.* sexy; ravishing, voluptuous, luxurious.

2. angering, incensing, enraging, infuriating, maddening, outrageous, shocking; exasperating, exacerbating, disquieting, discomposing, distressing, ruffling, chafing, vexing, vexatious, galling, grating; annoying, irritating, aggravating, irksome, fretting, hectoring, nettlesome, nettling, perturbing, tormenting, plaguing, badgering, pestering, persecuting, harassing, besetting; insulting, affronting, offensive, offending, stinging, wounding, molesting, mortifying, humiliating.

3. instigating, instigative, actuating, initiating, generating, starting, causing, effecting, contriving, establishing, creating, instituting; fomenting, agitating, agitative, agitational, exciting, excitant, excitative, excitatory, arousing, rousing, stirring, inflaming, enflaming, enkindling, kindling, impassioned; eliciting, evocative.

4. inciting, incitant, incitive, poking, prodding, pricking, thrusting, goading, prompting, spurring, encouraging; impelling, compelling, constraining, pressing, pushing, moving, forcing, propelling, lashing, driving, hounding; striking, penetrating, disturbing, bitter, caustic, acrimonious, envenomed, venemous, biting, cutting; stimulating, animating, invigorating,

motivating, inspiring, inspirational, rallying, reviving, awakening, enlivening, livening up, vivifying, electrifying, electric.
5. inducing, producing, productive; promoting, furthering, forwarding, fostering, favoring, favorable, advancing.
—*n.* **6.** stimulus, incentive, motive. See **provocation** (*def.* **4**).

provoke, *v.* **1.** anger, incense, huff, enrage, infuriate, madden, outrage, raise [s.o.'s] ire, make [s.o.'s] blood boil; exasperate, exacerbate, defy, disquiet, discompose, distress, ruffle, roil, pique, chafe, vex, gall, envenom, grate, put out, try [s.o.'s] patience, *Sl.* get [s.o.'s] goat; annoy, irritate, aggravate, fret, hector, nettle, disturb, perturb, torment, plague, badger, pester, persecute, harass, beset, bullyrag, get on [s.o.'s] nerves; insult, affront, offend, sting, wound, molest, mortify, humiliate.
2. instigate, actuate, initiate, generate, start, cause, effect, contrive, establish, create, institute, put in motion, sow the seeds of, *Inf.* start something, look for trouble; foment, agitate, excite, arouse, rouse, whip, whip up, work, work up, stir, stir up, wind, wind up, inflame, enflame, impassion, enkindle, kindle, fire, fire up, touch off; elicit, evoke, call forth, summon up.
3. incite, poke, prod, prick, thrust, goad, prompt, spur, egg on, encourage, put up to; impel, compel, constrain, press, push, move, force, propel, lash, drive, hound; strike, penetrate, disturb, touch to the quick; stimulate, animate, whet, reanimate, invigorate, motivate, inspire, inspirit, rally, revive, awaken, wake up, enliven, liven up, vivify, electrify, warm up, shake up; tempt, lure, allure, seduce, tantalize, beguile, inveigle, infect, intoxicate.
4. induce, produce, occasion, give rise to, bring about; promote, further, forward, foster, favor, advance.

prow, *n.* (*all of a ship or boat*) bow, nose, stem, forepart, fore, front.

prowess, *n.* **1.** bravery, courage, valor, valorousness, valiancy, valiance, heroism; stout-heartedness, lionheartedness, iron-heartedness, great-heartedness, high-heartedness; virility, manliness, manfulness, manhood, gallantry, chivalry, chivalrousness, knight-errantry; intrepidity, intrepidness, fearlessness, dauntlessness, awelessness, dreadlessness; boldness, bold-spiritedness, high-spiritedness, daring, derring-do, audacity, audaciousness, rashness; dash, élan, panache, verve, style, flair, bravado; independence, self-reliance, assurance, self-assurance, confidence, self-confidence; pot-valor, pot-valiancy, pot-valiance.
2. fortitude, resoluteness, resolution; indomitableness, indomitability, invincibleness, invincibility; staunchness, steadfastness, stalwartness, doughtiness, sturdiness, stoutness, lustiness, hardiness, hardihood, bulldog courage; strength, force, potency, power, sinew, vigor, energy, vitality, *Archaic.* pith; mettle, pluck, pluckiness, spirit *or* fighting spirit, game; backbone, gumption, blood, heart, nerve, grit, *U.S. Inf.* sand, *Inf.* starch, *Inf.* spunk, *Sl.* guts, *Sl.* gutsiness, *Sl.* moxie.
3. superior ability, skill, martial skill, talent, genius; expertism, expertise, expertness, mastery, authority, control; excellence, adeptness, finesse, facility; adroitness, deftness, dexterousness, dexterity, skillfulness; knowledgeableness, know-how, savoir-faire, cleverness, ingenuity; capability, capableness, aptness, competence, competency, efficiency, proficiency; efficacy, efficaciousness, effectiveness.

prowl, *v.* **1.** rove around, roam around *or* about, range about, wander around; skulk, sneak, slink, steal, move with stealth, tiptoe, *U.S. Sl.* gumshoe, *Inf.* snoop; lurk, hide, lie in wait *or* ambush, lie low, couch.
2. search *or* search for, look for, seek, nose around, range over, scour, scavenge, forage; *Sl.* cat, *Sl.* tomcat; hunt, pursue, chase, hound, dog; stalk, still-hunt, track, trail, follow, shadow, haunt, *Inf.* tail; hunt out *or* down, mouse, track down, trace down, search out, seek out, ferret out.

proximate, *adj.* **1.** preceding, next, following, succeeding, successive, subsequent, sequent, sequential, immediately before *or* after, nearest.
2. close, very near, close by, nearby, in close proximity; vicinal, neighboring, adjacent, next-door, juxtapositioned, juxtaposed; bordering, adjoining, adjoined, abutting, tangential, tangent, contiguous, conjoined, conjoining, connecting, connected.
3. approximate, fairly accurate, not far off, close, *Inf.* warm, *Inf.* hot.
4. forthcoming, imminent, approaching, coming toward, nearing, drawing nigh *or* near; close at hand, at hand, within sight, staring [s.o.] in the face, just about *or* almost here, about to happen, going to happen soon, upon us, momentary, likely to occur at any moment; impending, lying in wait, in store, in the air *or* wind; overhanging, projecting, lowering; threatening, looming, brooding.

proximity, *n.* **1.** proximateness, nearness, closeness, nighness, propinquity; approximation, vicinity, vicinage, neighborhood; contiguity, contiguousness, conterminousness, adjacence, adjacency, juxtaposition, apposition.
2. kinship, relationship, relation, tie; blood tie, family connection; consanguinity, cognation, agnation, enation, common descent.

proxy, *n.* **1.** deputy, vicar, surrogate, substitute, vice-regent, *Govt.* chargé d'affaires ad interim, representative, agent; fill-in, stopgap, makeshift, temporary substitute, *Chiefly Brit.* locum tenens; substitute teacher, *Inf.* sub; alternate, understudy, backup, pinch hitter.
2. authorization, warrant, permit, *Accounting.* voucher.

prude, *n.* prig, *Inf.* bluenose, puritan, old maid, *Inf.* goody-goody, *Inf.* nice Nelly, *Derog.* nun.

prudence, *n.* **1.** caution, cautiousness, care, carefulness; sagacity, practical wisdom, good judgment, common sense, sense, *Inf.* horsesense; presence of mind, cool judgment, perspicacity, shrewdness, acumen, deliberateness, deliberation, consideration, calculation, *Scot.* canniness, *Brit.* pawkiness; discretion, judiciousness, discrimination, circumspection, tact; attention, vigilance, watchfulness, heedfulness, weighing all the possibilities, watching one's step, *Inf.* looking both ways, looking before one leaps; expedience, politicness, *Inf.* cutting one's losses, *Inf.* pulling in one's horns; self-control, steadiness, stability, temperateness, temperance, self-restraint, unexcessiveness, moderation, moderation in all things, sophrosyne.
2. forethought, planning, looking *or* planning ahead, anticipation, taking preventive measures, foresightedness, preparation, forehandedness, providence, provision, foresight, preparedness, precaution, taking a stitch in time, string-saving; economy, thrift, thriftiness, unwastefulness, frugality, husbandry, careful budgeting, watching one's pennies, good management *or* stewardship, economizing, saving.

prudent, *adj.* **1.** sensible, level-headed, judicious, sagacious, sage, discreet, circumspect; thoughtful, reflecting, sapient, sober, sane, moderate, reasonable, rational, sound, full of common sense; cool, wary, heedful, vigilant, advertent, attentive, guarded, chary.

2. careful, cautious, practical, shrewd, discerning, discriminating, selective, calculating, canny, politic, considerate.

3. provident, prudential, forehanded, foreseeing, farsighted, precautious, precautionary, looking *or* planning ahead, saving for a rainy day; prepared, safe, forearmed, well-advised, worldly-wise, wide-awake, seeing beyond the end of one's nose; economical, saving, sparing, thrifty, chary, frugal, parsimonious.

prudery, *n.* coyness, overmodesty; priggishness, puritanicalness. See also **priggishness** (*def.* **1**).

prudish, *adj.* coy, demure, reserved, modest, overmodest; squeamish, queasy; priggish, old-maidish, *Inf., Derog.* nunny. See also **priggish** (*def.* **1**).

prune, *v.* **1.** lop off, crop, top, cut, cut down, cut short; poll, pollard, truncate, detruncate; dock, nip, snip; pare, shave, mow; chop, sever, dissever.

2. thin, thin out, weed, weed out; clear of, rid, remove, detach, amputate; relieve of, disburden, disencumber, unload.

3. curtail, shorten, abbreviate, condense, contract, compact; retrench, cut back on, reduce, diminish.

prurient, *adj.* **1.** lascivious, lewd, lecherous, lubricous, *Archaic.* lickerish, satyric, satyrical, satyrlike, hircine, goatish, ruttish, *Sl.* horny; lustful, randy, *Sl.* hot *or* hot for; concupiscent, libidinous, salacious; fleshly, carnal, sensual, voluptuous, erotic; licentious, loose, Cyprian, wanton, abandoned, incontinent; debauched, rakish, rakehell, dissolute, dissipated, profligate; promiscuous, whorish, of easy virtue, *Sl.* cheap, shameless; depraved, degenerate, perverted, incestuous, masochistic, sadistic, pederastic, coprophilic; immodest, impure, unchaste, unvirtuous.

2. obscene, lurid, blue, pornographic, *Inf.* porno, porn, smutty, *Sl.* raunchy; indecent, offensive, suggestive, vulgar, coarse, gross, crude; dirty, unclean, foul, filthy, vile; foulmouthed, dirty-minded; ribald, scurrilous, irreverent; bawdy, Fescennine.

3. desirous, covetous, avaricious, grasping, rapacious; open-mouthed, hoggish, piggish, swinish; insatiable, insatiate, unquenchable; anxious, breathless, impatient, restless, longing, burning; hungry, craving, esurient.

pry[1], *v.* **1.** inquire, question, query, quiz, ask; examine, interrogate, *Inf.* grill, cross-examine; meddle, interfere, intermeddle, *Brit. Dial.* mell, interlope; intrude, butt in, *U.S. Sl.* horn in, obtrude; impose, interpose, intervene; mind other people's business, *Inf.* nose into, *Inf.* nose around, *Inf.* nose about, *Inf.* stick one's nose in, poke one's nose in, poke *or* stick one's nose where it doesn't belong, *Inf.* kibitz, put one's two cents in, put in one's oar; busybody, have one's finger in every pie, have one's nose in every door.

2. peek, peep, peer, squint at, sneak a look *or* peek; look curiously, look closely *or* narrowly, look hard *or* intently at; inspect, survey, scan; watch, follow with the eye, view, witness; ogle, gape, gawk, crane, gaze at, stare at, goggle, *Inf.* rubber, *Inf.* rubberneck; study, scrutinize, examine.

3. search, seek out, investigate, probe, prowl around, dig, dig into, delve, smell *or* sniff out; explore, look into, *Inf.* snoop, *Inf.* snoop around, spy.

—n. **4.** meddler, intermeddler, quidnunc, busybody, *Inf.* busy, Paul Pry; *Inf.* snoop, *Inf.* snooper, *Inf.* kibitzer, *Australian Sl.* stickybeak; inquisitive, inquirer, questioner, *Inf.* question box, *Inf.* nosy, *Sl.* nosy Parker, *Inf.* nosybody, *Inf.* rubberneck, *Inf.* rubbernecker, Peeping Tom.

pry[2], *v.* **1.** force open, pull open, pull apart, detach; raise, lift, hoist; lever, move, work up, yank.

2. get, obtain, procure; ferret out, worm out, smoke out; fish for, angle for.

3. force, wrest, wring, wrench; extract, dig up, root up, grub up *or* out, uproot, excavate, dredge; drag out, tear out, pull out; separate, disunite, disjoin.

prying, *adj.* **1.** peeking, peeping, peering; inspecting, surveying, scanning; studying, scrutinizing, examining; searching, prowling, investigating; snooping, snoopy, spying, eavesdropping; ogling, gaping, gawking, craning, goggling, *Inf.* rubbernecking; agog, agape, all agog.

2. inquisitive, inquiring, questioning, probing, investigative; curious, eager, eager for knowledge, interested, burning with curiosity, dying to know; intrusive, obtrusive, officious, *Inf.* nosy; meddlesome, interfering, impertinent, persistent, forward.

psalm, *n.* **1.** hymn, paean, alleluia, hallelujah, gloria, doxology, spiritual, religious song, *Eccles.* cantus firmus; chant, plainsong, plainchant, *Both Eccles.* antiphon, antiphony; song of praise, song, melody, tune, air, composition; ode, poem, verse, (*in ancient Greece*) chorus.

—v. **2.** hymn, doxologize, carol, sing the praises of; chant, intone, cantillate, descant, *Archaic.* deacon; praise, laud, exalt, glorify, extol, celebrate.

pseudo, *adj.* counterfeit, fraudulent, imitation, forged, false, fake, faked, *Inf.* phony; not genuine, bogus, spurious, supposititious, bastardly; pretended, feigned, simulated, make-believe, sham, flash; unreal, mock, ersatz, synthetic; artificial, factitious, contrived, *Sl.* hokey, fictitious; assumed, put-on; specious, theatrical, meretricious.

pseudonym, *n.* false name, assumed name, professional name, pen name, nom de plume, *Fr. nom de guerre*, stage name, *Fr. nom de théâtre;* allonym, anonym, alias; familiar name, epithet; nickname, sobriquet, agnomen, cognomen, byname, moniker, handle, *Chiefly Scot.* to-name.

psych, *v. Slang.* **1.** *Usu.* **psych out a.** intimidate, make nervous *or* uncomfortable, put [s.o.] off balance; discompose, upset, unsettle, disturb; agitate, *Inf.* throw into a tizzy; frighten, scare, *Sl.* spook, *Sl.* bug. **b.** understand, comprehend, know what makes [s.o.] tick.

2. *Usu.* **psych up a.** excite, arouse, rouse, move; inspire, stimulate, impress. **b.** persuade, urge, prompt, talk [s.o.] into, goad, prod, push.

3. (*of oneself*) prepare, get ready, *Inf.* get up for, get in the mood for, get in the right frame of mind, change one's attitude; steel oneself, *Literary.* gird one's loins.

psyche, *n.* spirit, life force *or* energy, inner man, essential nature, true being, spiritual principle, vital spirit, pneuma, anima, divine spark, soul; mind, reason, intellect, intelligence, understanding, *Gk. Philos.* nous; self, personality, ego.

psychiatrist, *n.* psychopathologist, psychopathist, psychotherapist, psychoanalyzer, alienist, *Sl.* shrink, *Sl.* headshrinker, *Sl.* couch doctor.

psychic, *adj.* **1.** spiritual, mystical, soulful; psychological, subjective; mental, intellectual, cognitive, cerebral, philosophical, metaphysical.

2. otherworldly, unearthly, supermundane, extramundane; occult, magical, unreal, cabalistic, fey; mysterious, arcane, esoteric, unknown; immaterial, incorporeal, intangible, disembodied, insubstantial, *Archaic.* spiritous; supernatural, supernormal, preternormal, preternatural, superhuman, superphysical, hyperphysical; extrasensory, supersensible, supersensory, supersensual, telepathic, clairvoyant, telekinetic; hallucinatory, spectral, ghostly, phantom; mediumistic, spiritualistic, spiritistic.

psychological, *adj.* **1.** mental, cerebral, psychical, intellectual, of the mind; conceptual, inward, subliminal, subconscious; perceptual, cognitive, prehen-

sive; sensory, percipient, psychometrical, psychometric.
2. emotional, emotive, irrational, *Psychol.* affective; psychic, psychical, subjective, personal.

psychotic, *adj.* **1.** psychopathic, insane, mentally ill; deranged, mad, lunatic, demented, *Latin. non compos mentis;* paranoiac, severely neurotic, neuroasthenic; abnormal, aberrant, exceptional, deviate; unbalanced, disturbed, sick.
—n. **2.** psychopath, *Psychiatry.* psychopathic personality, insane person; lunatic, madman, maniac, bedlamite; schizophrenic, *Sl.* schiz, *Sl.* schizo; paranoiac, manic-depressive, megalomaniac, pyromaniac, psychopathic killer.

puberty, *n.* adolescence, teens, teenage, teen-aged years; pubescence, pubescency, young adulthood; nubility, ripeness, heyday, springtime of life, flower of youth, bloom *or* flower of life.

pubescent, *adj.* **1.** teen-aged, in the teens, adolescent; young, fresh, blooming, budding, new-fledged; nubile, ripe, ready; youthful, inexperienced, tender, green, wet behind the ears; downy-cheeked, untried, underaged, minor.
2. *Botany., Zoology.* downy, hairy, *Bot.* tomentose, *Bot.* villous *or* villose; soft, smooth, silken, silky, satiny, velvety, velutinous.

public, *adj.* **1.** general, common, communal, joint, united, collective; national, nationwide, statewide, countrywide; widespread, universal, world-wide; ecumenical, catholic, extensive, comprehensive; civic, popular, plebeian, proletarian.
2. unrestricted, not private *or* exclusive; unenclosed, available, accessible; unfenced, unbounded, uncircumscribed, shared; free to all, open to the public, of free access; elective, voluntary, unconditional, publicly-financed, tax-supported, tax-dependent, under the public domain; tax-paid, elected, publicly-appointed, serving the voters.
3. open, published, in circulation; known, notorious, recognized; admitted, avowed, widely known; manifest, done in broad daylight; overt, plain, plain to see, apparent, clearly apparent; unconcealed, exposed, clear, clear-cut, plain as day; visible, naked, bald, unhidden; unveiled, unshrouded, uncurtained, unobscured; obvious, patent, palpable, conspicuous; blatant, flagrant, egregious; up front, right out in the open, in front of all the world, for all the world to know, *Inf.* on the front page.
4. prominent, well-known, eminent, famous, celebrated; important, considerable, substantial, named, renowned, illustrious; exalted, respected, credited, honored, consequential, of consequence, of high *or* great reputation *or* repute; influential, weighty, powerful, prestigious, notable; disreputable, infamous, notorious, on the "most wanted" list.
—n. **5.** populace, population, community, citizens, nation, voters, voting public; society, men, women, children; hoi polloi, common people, masses, vulgus, *Archaic.* the vulgar, commonage, demos; proletariat, plebeians, bourgeoisie; the multitude, the many, *Chiefly Brit.* admass; rank and file, *Latin. hoc genus omne, Fr. tout le monde,* everyone; grass roots, *Inf.* the silent majority, the man in the street, *U.S.* Middle America, Main Street USA.
6. clientele, buyers, *Inf.* trade; patrons, patronage, *Inf.* regulars; following, followers, fans, admirers, readers, subscribers, audience.

publication, *n.* **1.** publishing, printing, issuance, production, putting out, putting together; editing, going over, proofreading, binding, manufacture.
2. announcement, pronouncement, advertisement, proclamation; broadcast, airing; disclosure, exposure, exposition, revelation, promulgation, dissemination.
3. edition, issue, copy, printing; magazine, book, serial, review, digest, comic book, funny book, house organ, employee publication; newsmagazine, newsletter; periodical, daily, weekly, monthly, quarterly, almanac, yearbook; newspaper, paper, newspaper of record, journal, bulletin, gazette; tabloid, *Sl.* tab, *Sl.* sheet, *Sl.* yellow journal, *Sl.* rag, scandal sheet, *Sl.* Daily Blat, *Sl.* Daily Bugle; throw-away, give-away, *Dial.* shopper, flier, handbill, circular; monograph, treatise, thesis; *All Sl.* girlie magazine, skin magazine, nudie book, cheesecake *or* beefcake magazine.

publicist, *n.* **1.** press agent, publicity man, agent, public relations man, *Inf.* PR man, *Sl.* flak, *Sl.* hornblower; adman, *Sl.* plugger, *Sl.* ballyhooer, *Sl.* pitchman; advance man, *Inf.* front man.
2. news analyst, commentator, journalist, columnist, editorialist, editorial writer; pressman, critic, political essayist, pamphleteer; political economist, political scientist; correspondent, foreign correspondent.
3. international lawyer, trade lawyer, expert in international law.

publicity, *n.* public notice, spotlight, limelight; promotion, build-up, *Sl.* hype; presentation, broadcast, ventilation, publication, publicness, notoriety; advertisement, advertising, *Inf.* hype, *Sl.* ballyho, puffery, *Sl.* blurb, *Sl.* spot, *Sl.* plug, *Inf.* write-up, *Inf.* spread, *Inf.* press, *Sl.* flak *or* flack, fanfare, *Sl.* hoopla, *Inf.* whoop-de-doo.

publicize, *v.* advertise, spread about, make public, make known; placard, publish, announce, blazon, herald, report, post, promulgate, propagate; give publicity to, air, ventilate, broadcast, circularize, disseminate; play up, glorify, promote, *Inf.* hype, *Inf.* plug, *Inf.* push; *Inf.* drumbeat, *Inf.* beat the drum, put into the limelight, put into the spotlight, offer for sale.

public-spirited, *adj.* unselfish, altruistic, philanthropic; humanitarian, human; charitable, beneficent, bighearted, *Inf.* big, princely, liberal, munificent, magnanimous, open-handed; kind, kind-hearted, compassionate; other-directed, *Psychol.* extroverted, nonegotistic, non-egotistical, non-egocentric; disinterested, tolerant, unprejudiced, unbiased, impartial.

publish, *v.* **1.** issue, produce, print, get out, *Inf.* crank, *Derog.* spew *or* spit out; set forth, put out, come out with; circulate, distribute, dispense, disseminate; sponsor, back.
2. promulgate, proclaim, give out, announce, annunciate; report, make public, publicize, advertise; herald, proclaim, cry, blare, blazon, trumpet, bruit, broadcast, noise abroad, advance, promote.
3. disclose, reveal, declare, divulge; tell, impart, inform, relate, utter, *Archaic.* discover, declare; break the news, let slip, *Inf.* leak; let the cat out of the bag, spill the beans, blow the lid off of, *Inf.* blow, blab; release, *Inf.* break, *Archaic.* divulgate; tattle, betray, blow the whistle, *Sl.* squeal, *Sl.* squeak, *Sl.* rat, *Sl.* fink, *Sl.* stool; expose, uncover, bare, show; bring to light, unearth, exhibit.

publisher, *n.* publishing house, publishing concern, *Inf.* house; printer, newspaperman.

pucker, *v.* **1.** gather, shirr, pleat, ruck, ruffle, draw together; compress, shrink, wither, contract, furrow, squeeze, tighten, purse, knit, crinkle, corrugate, shrivel, wrinkle, crease; muss, rumple, mess up.
—n. **2.** wrinkle, fold, gather, pleat; crumple, tuck, pinch, crinkle, ruck, ruffle, rumple, muss, mess; irregularity, flaw, mistake, error.

puckery, *adj.* **1.** gathered, shirred, pleated, rucked, ruffled, drawn together; compressed, shrunken, withered, contracted, furrowed; squeezed, tightened, knitted, crinkled, corrugated; shriveled, wrinkled, creased, mussed, rumpled, messed up.

2. astringent, acerbic, sour, tart; bitter, acetic, acid, acetous; constringent, contractive.

puckish, *adj.* mischievous, full of mischief, mischiefmaking; prankish, impish, imp-like, pixyish, puckish, elfish, elfin, fey; waggish, naughty, roguish, scampish, arch, *Scot.* hempy; playful, sportive, frolicsome; devilish, trouble-making, unruly, unmanageable, difficult to handle, difficult; annoying, vexatious, exasperating, teasing; obnoxious, *Inf.* pesky, insufferable, nasty.

pudding, *n.* custard, flummery, rennet custard, egg custard, junket, blancmange; soufflé, mousse, mousseline, bombe, *U.S.* pandowdy.

puddle, *n.* **1.** mudpuddle, plash, plashet; pondlet, wallow, slop; standing water, rain runoff, water-pocket.

—*v.* **2.** collect, accumulate, stand; flow together, converge; back up, well up, bubble up.

3. wet, muddy, dirty, soil, spot, bespot, speck, bespeck; smear, smudge, foul, besmear; sully, splatter, splash, blotch, daub, besmirch, besmudge.

pudgy, *adj.* dumpy, thick, thick-set; stumpy, squabby, squat, chunky, stocky, built like a fire-plug; stout, buxom, plump, plumpish, pleasingly plump; rotund, chubby, *Inf.* tubby, *Inf.* paunchy, corpulent, obese, fat, *Esp. Brit.* podgy.

puerile, *adj.* **1.** infantile, infantine, *Inf.* kiddy, *Rare.* childly, babyish; boyish, girlish, youthful, young, juvenile, juvenescent; adolescent, pubescent, immature, underaged, minor, undeveloped, unfledged, unfeathered, jejune; budding, tender, soft, unripe, delicate; inexperienced, green, sophomoric, callow, defenseless; unsophisticated, unwise, inexpert, untried; childlike, innocent, pure, unsullied, uncorrupted, virgin.

2. childish, foolish, silly, asinine; foolheaded, incautious, imprudent, indiscreet; irresponsible, injudicious, unwise, ill-considered, ill-advised, impolitic; impetuous, impulsive, hasty, short-sighted, heedless, foolhardy; headlong, rash, brash, unwary.

3. trivial, trifling, petty, nugatory; frothy, frivolous, shallow; unimportant, inconsequential, immaterial, inconsiderable, insignificant; petty, picayune, measly, paltry; small, minor, slight, meager.

puerility, *n.* **1.** childhood, infancy, babyhood; youth, boyhood, girlhood, adolescence, puberty, immaturity, minority, springtime of life, salad days.

2. dotage, second childhood, senility, *Psychiatry.* puerilism.

3. foolishness, inanity, silliness, absurdity, absurdness, pointlessness, fatuousness, *Archaic.* insipience, folly; senselessness, nonsensicalness, nonsensicality, illogicalness, illogicality; triviality, triflingness, unimportance, inconsequentiality; inconsiderableness, insignificance; superficiality, shallowness, frothiness; vapidity, insipidness, banality, blandness, dullness, *Inf.* blahness.

4. foolery, fooling, tomfoolery, clownery; silly trick, impishness, prank, practical joke, hazing; nonsense, poppycock, amphigory, bosh, drivel, gibberish, balderdash; bathos, farce, sophism.

puff, *n.* **1.** whiff, whiffet, breath, flurry, small cloud; gust, short blast; huff, pant, wind.

2. swelling, lump, protuberance, projection, tuberosity, *Anat.* condyle, protrusion; node, nodule, bulb; growth, excrescence, excretion, *Biol.* auxesis, tubercle; tumescence, intumescence, enlargement; bump, *Inf.* goose egg, hump, buckle, bulge, bubble, balloon, ball; *Pathol.* tumor, *Pathol.* neoplasm, *Pathol.* cyst, *Pathol.* wen, *Pathol.* blain, boil, *Pathol.* carbuncle, inflammation.

3. commendation, recognition, good word, honorable mention; overpraise, overcommendation, overlaudation; publicity, promotion, mention, *Sl.* boost, *Inf.* plug, *Sl.* buildup; *Sl.* hype, *Sl.* blurb, word, advertising.

—*v.* **4.** whiff, breeze; pant, huff, blow, breathe hard, suck wind; wheeze, gasp, gasp for breath, gulp; (*of a locomotive*) chug.

5. smoke, inhale, *Inf.* drag, draw, pull.

6. *Usu.* **puff up** swell, distend, stretch, bloat, balloon, bubble; inflate, *Obs.* sufflate, pump up, expand, dilate, enlarge, amplify, increase, grow.

7. bluster, roister, boast, *Sl.* blow hard, *Sl.* talk big; brag, crow, trumpet, blow one's own horn, toot one's own horn, sing one's own praises; show off, strut, parade, swagger, flaunt.

8. *Usu.* **puff up** magnify, overpraise, overestimate, exaggerate, enhance, color, embroider; eulogize, panegyrize, praise, applaud, laud, extol, exalt, celebrate; compliment, salute, make much of, flatter, *Inf.* slather, overdo it, lay it on.

9. advertise, promote, advance, push, *Inf.* plug, *Inf.* hype; publicize, bill, subserve; announce, blurb, make known, publish; herald, trumpet, ballyhoo, beat the drum.

puffery, *n.* **1.** undue praise, overpraise, overlaudation, overcommendation, overrating, overvaluation; trumpetry, crying out, ringing *or* singing [s.o.'s] praises; inflation, inflating, magnification, magnifying, blowing up; *All Inf.* slathering, overdoing it, laying it on, laying it *or* spreading it on thick, piling it up *or* on; flattery, compliment, salute, praise, laudation; tribute, extolment, exaltation, celebration, glorification; eulogy, eulogization, encomium, panegyric, adulation.

2. publicity, promotion, build-up, *Inf.* hype, advertisement, advertising, *Sl.* ballyhoo, *Sl.* blurb, *Sl.* spot, *Sl.* plug, *Inf.* write-up, *Inf.* spread, *Inf.* press, *Sl.* flak, fanfare, *Sl.* hoopla, *Inf.* whoop-de-doo.

puffy, *adj.* **1.** gusty, blasty, blustery, squally; windy, breezy, airy.

2. short-winded, panting, blowing, out of breath, breathless, winded, blown, exhausted, gasping, wheezing.

3. inflated, *Obs.* sufflated, swollen, distended, turgid, tumid, bulging, bulbous; expanded, dilated, enlarged; bloated, dropsical, edematous; fat, corpulent, pursy, fleshy, rotund, stout, portly; plump, tubby, paunchy, bellied out, bowed out; full, bouncing, round, large, buxom, ample.

4. conceited, self-important, self-esteeming, self-admiring, self-worshiping, self-centered, egocentric, narcissistic, peacockish, *Sl.* stuck *or* hung up on oneself; proud, overproud, overweening, vain, vainglorious, egotistical, swell-headed, *Inf.* big-headed, puffed-up; haughty, supercilious, snobbish, *Sl.* uppity, *Sl.* snooty, *Inf.* nose-in-the-air, high-and-mighty, *Sl.* stuck-up, *Sl.* snotty; smug, complacent, self-satisfied, self-contented; boastful, bragging, crowing, blustering.

5. bombastic, pompous, orotund, fustian, pretentious, ostentatious, flaunting; grandiose, magniloquent, grandiloquent, Johnsonian, Ossianic, sonorous, sesquipedalian; high-sounding, high-flown, lofty, *Inf.* highfalutin, *Inf.* high-hat; extravagant, ranting, mouthy, declamatory; flamboyant, flashy, showy, ornate, ornamental, flowery, florid.

pugilism, *n.* boxing, prize fighting, the art of fisticuffs, fisticuffs, the boxing game.

pugilist, *n.* boxer, fighter, contestant, contender. See **prize fighter**.

pugnacious, *adj.* belligerent, bellicose, combative,

aggressive, antagonistic, hostile; unpeaceful, unpacific, warlike, jingoistic, militant; unfriendly, threatening, contending, battling, fighting; quarrelsome, argumentative, litigious, disputatious, contentious; fractious, irritable, irascible, ill-tempered, disagreeable, discordant.

puke, *v.* vomit, retch, regurgitate, throw up, *Sl.* frow up, heave, spit up, spew up, disgorge; be sick to one's stomach, be nauseated, nauseate, *Inf.* have the throw-ups, get the dry heaves; be seasick, have mal de mer, turn green; *All Sl.* barf, upchuck, toss one's cookies, return one's breakfast, blow lunch.

pulchritude, *n.* beauty, loveliness, comeliness, personableness, attractiveness, *Scot.* bonniness, prettiness, gorgeousness; grace, elegance, delicacy, radiance.

pulchritudinous, *adj.* beautiful, *Literary.* beauteous, comely, fair, fair of face, lovely, pretty, *Scot.* bonny, *Fr. joli*; personable, seemly, sightly, attractive, well-favored, *Sl.* easy on the eyes, *Sl.* not hard to look at, *Inf.* eye-filling, good-looking; shapely, well-proportioned, with an hourglass figure, *Sl.* built, *Sl.* stacked, *Sl.* built like a brick outhouse, *Sl.* zaftig, voluptuous, *Sl.* volumptuous; handsome, elegant, graceful; winsome, engaging, charming, fetching, pleasant; in full bloom, glowing, rosy-cheeked.

pule, *v.* whine, whimper, peep, snivel, mew, meow; cry, weep, sniffle.

pull, *v.* **1.** draw, draft, hale, *Physiol.* adduct; puff, take a puff *or* drag, suck in, inspire, inhale, breathe in, drink in; haul, lug, drag, transport; tow, take in tow, row, lead, *Naut.* warp, *Naut.* kedge; draggle, trail, trawl, troll.

2. tug, yank, snake, hitch, hike; tweak, twitch, nip, twinge, vellicate.

3. tear, rip, rend, tear *or* rip out *or* away *or* apart, disjoint, dismember; strain, stretch, overexert; wrench, sprain, twist.

4. pluck, snatch out, pick out, extract, take *or* pull out *or* off, tear *or* rip out *or* off; wrest, pry out, extort, wring out, exact; remove, withdraw, produce; uproot, root out, deracinate, dig up, weed *or* dig out.

5. strip, pick clean, deplume, displume; unclothe, unsheathe, divest; denude, denudate, bare.

6. attract, magnetize, allure, lure, decoy; invite, entice, interest, catch [s.o.'s] eye, captivate, capture [s.o.'s] fancy, fascinate.

—*n.* **7.** draw, draft, haul, lug, (*of an oar*) stroke; drag, puff, inhalation, breath; tug, yank, hitch; hike; wrest, snatch, grasp, clutch, catch; tweak, twitch, twinge, nip.

8. force, forcefulness, power, pulling power, powerfulness, strength, might, energy, *Inf.* steam; effort, work, exertion, strain; drag, tug, traction; magnetism, magnetic force *or* intensity, gravity, *Physics.* gravitation, *Both Elect.* gauss, oersted; attraction, lure, allurement, enticement, appeal, drawing power; attractiveness, seduction, seductiveness, interest, charm, winsomeness, charisma, *Sp. duende*; influence, authority, authoritativeness, dominance, weight, leverage, hold, sway, *Inf.* muscle, *Inf.* clout.

9. handle, knob, hold, bail, grip, hilt, halt, helve; lever, trigger, crank, shank, shaft, handle bar, *Print.* rounce.

pulp, *n.* **1.** marrow, flesh, pith, succulent part, soft part, heart.

2. mash, mush, squash; paste, pomace, ooze, slush, pap, dough; gluten, gel, gelatin, starch; jelly, curd, batter; poultice, butter, *Fr. Cookery.* pâté; wood pulp, papier-mâché.

3. sensational magagine, thriller, lurid literature; cheap books *or* magazines, *Inf.* yellow journalism, tabloid, coarse *or* vulgar periodicals, *Inf.* girlie magazines, *Inf.* skin books, *Euph.* adult books *or* magazines, *Inf.* dirty books.

pulpit, *n.* **1.** lecturn, platform, rostrum, dias, desk, estrado.

2. the pulpit a. the ministry, the clerical profession, preaching, the cloth, the church, clerical *or* priestly office; pastorate, holy orders, priesthood, cassock, prelacy, hierarchy, episcopacy, presbytery. **b.** clergymen, clergy, clericals, priests; preachers, lay preachers, ecclesiastics, the Fathers, parsons, reverends, *Usu. Disparaging.* pulpiteers, *Inf.* Bible thumpers.

pulpy, *adj.* fleshy, pithy, succulent; pulpous, pulpal, pulplike, pulpaceous; mushy, pappy, squashy, doughy; soft, flabby, spongy, mucid, gelatinous, gluey; semiliquid, viscous, viscid; thick, starchy, loamy, claylike.

pulsate, *v.* beat, tick, throb, pitapat; palpitate, pulse, thump, thrum, pound, drum, reverberate; alternate, undulate, wave, ebb and flow, wash in and out; vibrate, quiver, quaver, tremble; flutter, shiver, twitter, shake, shudder, dance.

pulsating, *adj.* **1.** beating, pulsating, pulsing; palpitating, throbbing, thumping, thrumming, drumming, thudding; vibrating, quavering, wavering, quivering, trembling, shuddering, dancing; (*all of water*) lapping, washing, bathing, undulating, rolling, broiling, churning, breaking, lashing.

2. regular, periodic, recurrent, recurring, alternate; metrical, cadent, pulsatory.

pulsation, *n.* beat, beating, pulse, throb, throbbing, drumming; vibration, quaver, tremor, tremble; flicker, flutter, shudder, quiver; palpitation, pitapat, shake, shiver, twitter, reverberation; undulation, tick-tock, waving, ebbing and flowing, dance, dancing; accent, rhythm, pattern, recurrent beat; riff, vamp, *Inf.* umpapa, stroke.

pulse, *n.* **1.** beat, beating, throb, throbbing; pulsation, oscillation, vibration, stroke; stress, accent, emphasis; time pattern, meter, cadence; systole and diastole.

—*v.* **2.** pulsate, beat, tick, throb, palpitate, thump. See **pulsate**.

pulverize, *v.* **1.** grind, crush, crunch, mortar, comminute, triturate, levigate, powder, granulate, crumble; pound, batter, bray, beat, mash, smash, *Sl.* smush.

2. demolish, ruin, wreck, devastate, ravage; shatter, smash, smash *or* crush to bits, *Sl.* smash *or* crush into smithereens; raze, tear down, rip down *or* apart; crush, stamp out, exterminate, annihilate, kill *or* kill off, put an end to.

3. *Slang.* beat up, defeat, trounce, vanquish, worst; *Inf.* lick, *Sl.* shellac, *Sl.* cream, *Sl.* beat to a pulp.

pumice, *n.* **1.** abrasive, abradant, polish, wax, cleanser; pumice stone, obsidian, volcanic glass, lava.

—*v.* **2.** smooth, rub down; polish, burnish, buff, wax; shine, gloss, luster, brighten, glaze, *Scot. and North. Eng.* sheen; grind, whet, mill, stone, sand, sandpaper, levigate, triturate; abrade, scour, scrub, clean.

pump, *n.* **1.** force pump, lift pump, sump pump, air pump, bicycle pump.

—*v.* **2.** *Usu.* **pump out** force out, push out, drive out; empty, drain, siphon out, draw off *or* out; extract, take out, remove, bail out, clear out; deflate, let the air out.

3. *Usu.* **pump up** inflate, blow up, enlarge, puff out, *Obs.* sufflate, swell, bloat, expand, dilate.

4. drive, force, push, send.

5. question closely, cross-examine, cross-question, interrogate, quiz, *Inf.* grill, catechize, *Chiefly U.S.*

Inf. give [s.o.] the third degree.

pun, *n.* play on words, equivoque, *Rhet.* paronomasia, *Fr. jeu de mots, Fr. calembour,* double-entendre, equivocation; witticism, clever expression, bon mot.

punch[1], *n.* **1.** blow, jab, *Inf.* clip, *U.S. Sl.* biff, box, *Boxing.* left *or* right, uppercut, stroke, knockout, *Sl.* sockdolager; buffet, cuff, *Inf.* bop, strike, hit, knock, thump, *Sl.* sock, bust, *Scot.* dunt, *Scot. and North Eng.* paik; thwack, *Inf.* whack, slap, swat, *Dial.* hit upside the head, smack, *Inf.* clout, *Sl.* conk, *Sl.* bash; beat, *Inf.* whomp, *Inf.* wallop, *Brit. Dial.* douse, *Brit. Dial.* yerk.

—*v.* **2.** jab, *Inf.* clip, box, *Boxing.* throw a left *or* right, take a poke at, uppercut, hit, strike, *Boxing.* knock out, smite; knock, cuff, buffet, thwack, *Inf.* whack, *Dial.* hit [s.o.] upside the head, slap, swat, smack, *Australian.* ding, *Scot.* dunt, *Scot. and North Eng.* paik; *Sl.* nail, *U.S. Sl.* biff, *Inf.* bop, *Inf.* clout, *Inf.* slug, *Inf.* knock [s.o.'s] block off, *Inf.* wallop, *Inf.* crown, *Sl.* conk; *Sl.* bash, *Sl.* belt, *Sl.* smash, *Sl.* sock, *Sl.* plug; *Inf.* trim, *Inf.* thump, *Inf.* lace, *Inf.* lambaste, *Inf.* whale, *Sl.* whomp; beat, batter, pound, lay on, pommel, pummel, pelt, thrash, *Sl.* paste, *Archaic.* belabor.

3. poke, prod, push, elbow, bump, stick, dig into.

punch[2], *n.* **1.** paper punch, hole punch, perforator; awl, *Carpentry.* bradawl, sewing awl, (*in goldsmith work*) puncheon, drill, brace and bit.

—*v.* **2.** perforate, hole, honeycomb, bore, drill, pink, puncture, pierce, riddle.

punctilio, *n.* **1.** fine point, particular, detail, formality, form; nicety, delicacy, subtlety, refinement.

2. convention, rule, standard, usual *or* customary practice, observance, code, custom, usage, manner; decorum, the thing, etiquette, propriety; duty, dictate, ethic, rule of conduct, moral.

3. conformity, rigid adherence, discharge of duty; exactness, exactitude, particularity, strictness, punctiliousness, meticulousness; conscientiousness, fastidiousness, scrupulousness, preciseness, precision; squeamishness, finicalness, finickiness, inflexibility.

punctilious, *adj.* formal, correct, decorus, proper, conventional; strict, rigid, stiff, starched; exact, precise, accurate, close; meticulous, scrupulous, conscientious, careful; particular, finical, finicky, picky, fussy, hard to please; critical, exacting, demanding, painstaking, fastidious; minute, detailed, fine, nice, thorough, searching; scientific, mathematical, severe, rigorous.

punctual, *adj.* **1.** prompt, on time, when expected; timely, seasonable, in good time, early, *Inf.* bright-and-early, well-timed; immediate, instant, instantaneous; rapid, fleet, meteoric, quick, swift, brisk, expeditious, *Inf.* Johnny-on-the-spot; direct, summary, fast.

2. regular, constant, cyclic, steady, systematic, regular as clockwork.

punctuality, *n.* **1.** promptness, promptitude, punctualness; timeliness, seasonableness, earliness; readiness, quickness, alacrity, haste, dispatch, expedition.

2. regularity, constancy, steadiness.

punctuate, *v.* **1.** interrupt, interfere, intrude, obtrude; intersperse, interpose, interpolate, insert, interject, wedge in, put in; cut in, break in, barge in, *Inf.* butt in, *Inf.* horn in, *Inf.* muscle in, *Inf.* chisel in; interspace with, interfuse, incorporate, interweave, interwind; pepper, scatter, sprinkle; talk out of turn, cut short, *Inf.* chip in, *Inf.* chime in, *Inf.* put in one's two-cents worth.

2. emphasize, stress, lay stress *or* emphasis on, give emphasis to, accent; underline, underscore, point up, italicize, call attention to, mark, bring home, press home; feature, highlight, spotlight, play up, give prominence to, bring to the fore, bring into relief, *Inf.* headline, write in gold.

puncture, *n.* **1.** perforating, boring, drilling, punching, pinking, puncturing; piercing, stabbing, lancinating, pricking, sticking; cutting, slitting, splitting, gashing, slashing.

2. hole, perforation, cut, incision, split, gash, scotch, rent, slit, slot; gap, space, interstice, breach, break; opening, orifice, aperture, mouth, vent, eyelet.

—*v.* **3.** perforate, make a hole in, hole, honeycomb, bore, drill, punch, pink; pierce, riddle, stab, lancinate, prick, stick; cut, slit, gash, slash, trepan; penetrate, pass through, transpierce, run through, *Sl.* let the daylight in; impale, transfix, fix, spit, skewer; spike, spear.

pundit, *n.* sage, savant, learned man *or* woman, wise person; expert, authority, scholar; one of the cognoscenti, connoisseur, critic; master, proficient, adept, mavin, master hand; maestro, virtuoso, talent, genius, prodigy, *Inf.* wizard, *Inf.* whiz, *U.S. Sl.* crackerjack, *Sl.* sharp; pantologist, literate, bibliophile, bluestocking, man of letters, *Archaic.* clerk, aesthete; scholar, academician, philosopher, philosophe, theorist, thinker, thinking person; (*all sometimes disparaging*) pedant, highbrow, *Inf.* longhair, *Inf.* know-it-all, *Inf.* walking encyclopedia, bookworm.

pungency, *n.* **1.** acridity, sting, acrid taste *or* smell; sourness, tang, tartness, bitterness, nip, acidity, vinegar; savoriness, spiciness, flavorfulness, pepperiness, saltiness.

2. poignance, pathos, touchingness, patheticalness, piteousness; distressfulness, painfulness, heartbreak, sadness, melancholiness, sorrowfulness, seriousness; evocativeness, emotionalism, intensity, profoundness, keenness, acuteness; forlornness, woefulness, wistfulness.

3. causticity, trenchancy, incisiveness, cuttingness, mordancy; acrimony, acrimoniousness, sharpness, harshness, severity; sarcasm, edge, pointedness; sardonicism, cynicism, contemptuousness.

4. piquancy, provocativeness, stimulation, excitation; spirit, liveliness, electricity, wittiness, ginger, snap.

pungent, *adj.* **1.** (*all usu. of taste or smell*) bitter, biting, acrid; acid, tart, harsh, sour, subacid, acetous, vinegarish, vinegary; acerb, acerbic, acidulous, acidulent, acescent, acidulated; stinging, burning, smarting, irritating.

2. (*all usu. of taste or smell*) seasoned, hot, peppery, spicy, piquant, tangy, tart, salty; strong, highly flavored, flavorful, nippy, saporous, sapid.

3. distressful, distressing, harrowing, heartbreaking, heartrending; sad, unhappy, sorrowful, woeful, tearful, lamentable, mournful, regrettable; poignant, moving, touching; acute, intense, severe; painful, smarting, agonizing, tormenting, torturous, excruciating; grievous, crushing, deplorable, dreadful, brutal; oppressive, burdensome, consuming, racking; ruinous, calamitous, disastrous, tragic.

4. caustic, mordant, acrimonious, bitter, acrid, acidulous, acid, trenchant, cutting, incisive, slashing, scathing; penetrating, piercing, stinging, pricking, nipping, biting; astringent, severe, stern, austere, stringent; harsh, keen, pointed, sharp, sharp-tongued.

5. sarcastic, satirical, ironic, ironical, cynical; double-edged, edged; contemptuous, contumelious, taunting, teasing; scornful, mocking, derisive, derisory, sardonic.

6. witty, keen-witted, quick-witted, attic, clever, brilliant; spirited, lively, sprightly, sparkling, scintillating; stimulating, provocative, tantalizing, stirring; electric, shocking, startling, galvanic; exciting, thrilling, sensational.

punish, *v.* **1.** penalize, discipline, take disciplinary action; sentence, imprison, lock up, *Sl.* send up river, *Sl.* throw the book at, *Inf.* come down hard on, fine, amerce, mulct; correct, admonish, reprove, chasten, chastise; castigate, criticize, scold, rebuke, dress down, *Sl.* chew out, call down, call on the carpet; *Sl.* make it hot for, *Sl.* give [s.o.] the business, *Sl.* fix [s.o.'s] wagon; warm *or* tan [s.o.'s] hide, spank, turn over one's knees; give a demerit, withdraw privileges, rap [s.o.'s] knuckles, slap [s.o.'s] wrist; tar and feather, keelhaul, ride out on a rail, put in the stocks, pillory; scourge, lash, give the cat-o'-nine-tails, flog; hang, execute, *Sl.* send to the chair.

2. cudgel, thrash, *Archaic.* swinge, fustigate; trounce, beat, beat up, *Inf.* lambaste; hurt, bruise, pain; manhandle, knock around, rough up, batter, *Sl.* beat up on, go at, *Sl.* knock silly, *Inf.* thump.

punishable, *adj.* chargeable, impeachable, accusable, indictable; at fault, faulty, in the wrong, culpable; blameworthy, blamable, asking for it, deserving of punishment.

punishment, *n.* **1.** penalty, penalization, discipline; sentence, condemnation, imprisonment, fine, mulct, *Sl.* rap; correction, admonition, chastening, chastisement; castigation, criticism, scolding, dressing down, *Sl.* chewing out, *Inf.* what-for; deserved reward, just deserts, *Inf.* comeuppance; pay, payment, wages; reckoning, judgment.

2. manhandling, maltreatment, beating, trouncing, *Inf.* giving [s.o.] the works; hard work, slave labor, overexertion.

punitive, *adj.* punishing, penalizing, penal, disciplinary, correctional, corrective, castigatory; retaliatory, revengeful, retributive, recriminatory; harsh, severe, bruising, hurtful.

punk, *n.* **1.** *Slang.* **a.** nobody, nonentity, nobody anyone knows, lightweight, small potatoes, small fry, obscurity, *Inf.* a nothing, *Inf.* a big nothing, *Inf.* a zilch, *Inf.* a zero, *Inf.* nebbish. **b.** lowlife, riffraff, good-for-nothing; mischief- *or* trouble-maker, rowdy, hooligan, ruffian, petty criminal, hoodlum, *Inf.* hood, *Inf.* ugly customer, *Inf.* goon, *Inf.* mug, *Inf.* gorilla. **c.** pest, brat, whippersnapper, young whippersnapper, twit; juvenile delinquent, *Inf.* JD; runt, squirt, green kid, new kid on the block, *Brit.* new boy; sonny, sonnyboy, puppy, pup, cub, shaver, shave-tail, *Inf.* runny-nosed *or* snot-nosed kid, rotten kid.

—adj. **2.** *Informal.* worthless, good-for-nothing, trashy, valueless, *Inf.* no-good, *Sl.* NG, *Sl.* strictly NG, *Dial.* no-account; cheap, shoddy, shabby, *Inf.* crummy, *Inf.* cheesy, paltry, poor, common, sorry, sad; insignificant, inconsequential, small-time, *Inf.* one-horse, *Inf.* two-by-four, *Inf.* jerkwater; unimportant, of no importance, *Inf.* no great shakes, inferior, minor, not worth considering, small, *Inf.* dinky, *Inf.* puny; forceless, soft, weak, powerless, *Inf.* weak as a kitten.

punster, *n.* rhymster, rhymer, versemaker, versifier, epigrammatist, whip with words, wag, wit, humorist, quipster.

puny, *adj.* **1.** weak, feeble, delicate, fragile, tender, frail, sickly, poor, thin, runty, undersized, underdeveloped, stunted; starved, underfed, emaciated, undernourished; small, little, pint-sized, bantam, halfpint, dwarfish, pygmy, Lilliputian, miniature, minikin, diminutive, *Inf.* itsy-bitsy-teeny-weeny, tiny, minute; inferior, scrubby, slight; inept, inadequate, impotent, jejune.

2. petty, unimportant, insignificant, trivial, paltry, picayune, niggling, minor; trifling, piddling, fiddling, fribble; inconsequential, inconsiderable, negligible, nugatory, worthless, useless; of minor importance, of little *or* no account, nothing great, no great shakes, *Inf.* no big deal, nothing to write home about.

3. inferior, lower, second-fiddle; ineffectual, fatuous, shallow, superficial.

pup, *n.* puppy, whelp, cub, youngling; baby dog, baby seal; doggy, baby doggy, *Dial.* lil' fella.

pupil, *n.* **1.** student, schoolgirl *or* schoolboy, learner, *Fr. élève*; scholar, *Inf.* grind, *Inf.* bookworm.

2. beginner, novice, tyro, abecedarian, catechumen, neophyte, initiate, probationer, postulant.

3. apprentice, ward, trainee, protégé, disciple, follower, apostle, proselyte; adherent, sectary, admirer, votary, devotee.

puppet, *n.* **1.** marionette, dummy, doll, doll on a string, fantoccino, hand-puppet, finger-puppet, moppet; Howdy-Doody, Charlie McCarthy, Punch, Judy, Punchinello.

2. pawn, instrument, tool, cat's paw, creature, figurehead, *Inf.* front *or* front man, man of straw; hireling, underling, employee, subordinate, assistant, accomplice, henchman, appendage, *Sl.* stooge, yes man, man *or* gal Friday; dupe, *Sl.* pigeon, gull, gudgeon, *Inf.* sucker, patsy; myrmidon, minion, follower, toady, sycophant, hanger-on, ward-heeler; jackal, flunky, lackey, attendant.

purblind, *adj.* **1.** half-blind, partially blind *or* sighted, dim-sighted, weak-eyed, blear-eyed; myopic, near-sighted, short-sighted, nyctalopic *or* night-blind, hemeralopic *or* day-blind.

2. obtuse, unfeeling, tactless, insensitive; imperceptive, unobservant; insentient, impercipient, insensible, undiscerning; unfeeling, cold, cool, withdrawn; thick-skinned, callous, uncaring, unsympathetic; unconscious, unaware, blind, unseeing; unable to see beyond the end of one's nose, wearing blinders *or* blinkers; jaundiced, partial, arbitrary, one-sided, opinionated, prepossessed.

purchasable, *adj.* **1.** available, in stock, on the shelves, for sale, on sale, offered, commercial, commercially developed; obtainable, accessible, to be had.

2. venal, corrupt, dishonest, dishonorable, bribable, approachable, available at a price, *Inf.* on the take; unscrupulous, conscienceless, shameless, having one's price, fixable; corruptible, faithless, going to the highest bidder, crooked, *Inf.* shady.

purchase, *v.* **1.** buy, pick up, pay for, get one's hands on, come by; invest in, put money into; acquire, obtain, get, procure, secure; take possession of, get a hold of; shop for, rent, hire, pay a price for, bargain for, barter for, dicker for.

2. bribe, suborn, pay off, buy off, oil, *Sl.* grease [s.o.'s] palm; fix, *Inf.* rig, *Inf.* square.

3. earn, attain, win, gain, achieve, realize.

—n. **4.** purchasing, buying, acquiring; obtainment, securement, accession; procurement, procural, gaining, getting, *Inf.* getting hold of; buy, acquisition, possession, *Law.* acquest.

5. hold, grasp, grip, gripe, clasp, clutch, clench, clinch; iron grip, tight grip, firm hold; leverage, fulcrumage; footing, foothold, toehold, stand, stance, perch; advantage, lever, support, power, force, play, edge, vantage.

pure, *adj.* **1.** unmixed, unalloyed, unmingled, unadulterated, uncontaminated; genuine, real, natural, unartificial; unspecious, authentic, sterling, simonpure, unsynthetic; fourteen-carat, flawless, faultless, perfect; unvarnished, uncolored, undisguised, unspurious; unfeigned, unassumed, unfaked, uncounterfeited.

2. clean, clear, fair, white, immaculate, snowy; stainless, spotless, unspotted, unsmirched, unbesmirched; unsullied, unsoiled, unpolluted, unblemished, unblotted, unstained; untainted, uncorrupted, undistorted, unmarred; uninfected, germ-free, sterilized, sterile, antiseptic, disinfected; fresh, fit to drink or eat, drinkable, eatable, potable, edible; healthful, uninjurious, wholesome, sanitary, innocuous.

3. sheer, stark, clean, out and out, wholesale, outright, downright, *Inf.* plumb, dead; unmitigated, unqualified, absolute, thorough, veritable; utter, total, consummate, perfect, born, plain, clear, mere.

4. theoretical, abstract, academical; nonobjective, speculative, conjectural, hypothetical, postulational; conceptual, notional, immaterial, metaphysical.

5. guiltless, innocent, uncorrupt, clean, moral, virtuous; decent, delicate, proper, seemly, becoming, decorous; unwanton, undissipated, undissolute, unlicentious; chaste, continent, abstinent, temperate, *Rare.* intemperate; celibate, virgin, vestal, maidenly, immaculate, intact; impeccable, sinless, above suspicion, uncorrupt, undefiled, inculpable, with clean hands.

6. high-principled, honorable, reputable, upright, righteous, uprighteous; honest, good, sincere, worthy, noble; creditable, estimable, full of integrity; ethical, high-minded, truehearted; purehearted, pious, saintly, holy, angelic, divine, godly; religious, devout, reverent, God-fearing, faithful.

7. unaffected, simple, plain, unadorned; tasteful, polished, graceful; refined, formal, classic, restrained, Attic; unornamented, inornate, straightforward; bare, flawless, faultless; euphonic, harmonious, flowing.

8. pure-blooded, purebred, thoroughbred; homozygous, pedigreed, full-blooded.

purebred, *adj.* pure-blooded, full-blooded, blooded, pedigreed, thoroughbred, registered, of good stock.

purely, *adv.* **1.** simply, plainly, forthrightly, directly, straightforwardly, genuinely; sincerely, honestly, truly, verily, bona fide; in truth, in reality, really, intrinsically.

2. merely, only, exclusively, solely.

3. entirely, wholly, totally, fully, thoroughly, completely; integrally, indivisibly, absolutely, utterly, unequivocally, indeed, altogether, all, in all respects; punctiliously, meticulously, consistently, certainly, assuredly; impeccably, spotlessly, unconditionally, in good faith; perfectly, faultlessly, flawlessly.

4. innocently, virtuously, righteously, decently, devoutly, unimpeachably, irreproachably; chastely, cleanly, blamelessly, immaculately, high-mindedly, morally, scrupulously, admirably, uprightly.

purgation, *n.* **1.** purging, cleansing, washing, lavage, ablution, purification, lustration, epuration; catharsis, cleansing away, emotional release, release, freeing, *Psychoanal.* abreaction; riddance, expurgation, bowdlerization, cutting out.

2. justification, vindication, clearing of one's name *or* reputation, destigmatizing, destigmatization, exculpation, compurgation; acquittal, exoneration, absolution; penance, repentance, atonement, clearing of one's conscience.

purgative, *adj.* **1.** purging, cleansing, detergent, detersive, cleaning; laxative, diuretic, evacuant, aperient; purifying, depurative.

—*n.* **2.** purge, physic, laxative, cathartic, aperient, ipecac, castor oil, ricinus oil, salts, dose of salts; purgation, dose, *Med.* catharsis; enema, *Med.* clyster.

purge, *v.* **1.** cleanse, clear, purify, lustrate, clean out, scour out, free from impurity; deterge, mundify, depurate.

2. eject, expel, rout out, weed out, root out, ease *or* freeze out, close the door on, cashier, drum out, get rid of; clear out, sweep out *or* away, clean house, make a clean sweep; depose, overthrow, remove from office, throw off *or* over, cast aside, remove, displace, oust, *Inf.* dump; destroy, do away with, exterminate, liquidate.

3. expurge, expurgate, bowdlerize.

4. exonerate, acquit, exculpate, absolve, vindicate, pardon, excuse, forgive; release, reprieve, free from, free.

5. expiate, destigmatize, remit, grant remission, justify, clear, clear *or* clean the skirts of, clear [s.o.'s] name; exempt, grant immunity, exempt from, grant amnesty to, *Inf.* let off, quash the charge *or* indictment; wipe the slate clean, take the charge *or* record off the books, erase, eradicate.

6. treat, physic, flush out, irrigate, drain; eliminate, evacuate, void, empty *or* empty out, defecate.

—*n.* **7.** purging, cleansing, purgation. See **purgation** (*def.* **1**).

8. deposal, deposition, removal, displacement, ousting, unseating; overthrow, overthrowal, expulsion, excommunication; riddance, ejection, expulsion, liquidation.

9. elimination, evacuation, voidance, defecation.

10. release, freeing, deliverance, suspension; respite, reprieve, discharge.

11. purgative, cathartic. See **purgative** (*defs.* **1, 2**).

purification, *n.* **1.** sanitization, sanitizing, sanitating, depuration, depurating; depollution, depolluting, freshening, deodorizing, decontamination, decontaminating, disinfection, disinfecting, antisepticizing; cleansing, detersion, deterging, mundification, mundifying; cleaning, washing, bathing, lavation, lavage, laving, *Chiefly Scot.* dighting.

2. expurgation, expurgating, purging, defecation, defecating, ridding, *Med.* absterging; elutriation, elutriating, *Both Chem.* edulcoration, edulcorating, winnowing, filtering, filtration, filtrating, straining, sifting, sieving, bolting; clarification, clarifying, clearing, refinement, refining, distillation, distilling, *All Chem.* sublimation, sublimating, rectification, rectifying.

3. absolution, absolving, redemption, redeeming, shriving, lustration, lustrating; exoneration, exonerating, vindication, vindicating, exculpation, exculpating, acquittal, acquitting, amnestying, pardoning, excusing, sublimating, baptism, christening, sanctification, sanctifying, consecration, consecrating, hallowing, blessing, *Both Rom. Cath. Ch.* beatification, beatifying.

purify, *v.* **1.** sanitize, sanitate, depurate; depollute, freshen, deodorize, decontaminate, disinfect, antisepticize; cleanse, deterge, mundify, clean, wash, bathe, lave, *Chiefly Scot.* dight.

2. expurgate, purge, defecate, rid, *Med.* absterge; elutriate, *Chem.* edulcorate, winnow, filter, filtrate, strain, sift, sieve, bolt; clarify, clear, refine, rarefy, distill, *Chem.* sublimate, *Chem.* rectify.

3. absolve, redeem, shrive, lustrate; exonerate, vindicate, exculpate, acquit, amnesty, pardon, excuse, forgive, wipe the slate clean; sublime, baptize, christen; sanctify, consecrate, hallow, bless, *Rom. Cath. Ch.* beatify.

purist, *n.* classicist, Atticist, Hellenist; precisionist, précieux *or* précieuse, blue stocking, *Fr. bas bleu*, formalizer; pedant, stickler, intransigent, dogmatist, positivist, fanatic, *Inf.* diehard, *Inf.* bitterender.

puritan, *n.* pietist, zealot, religionist, fanatic; formalist, precisian, dogmatist; moralist, prude, bluenose, stuffed shirt, pharisee, tartuffe.

puritanical, *adj.* strict, austere, ascetic; severe, precise, strait-laced, anchoritic, abstinent; hyperorthodox, pietistic, formal, dogmatic, zealous, fanatical, puritan, puritanic; narrow, uncompromising, rigid, arbitrary, hide-bound, stiffnecked, stiff.

puritanism, *n.* **1.** hyperorthodoxy, precisianism, dogmatism, zealotry; strictness, severity, grimness, authoritarianism, sternness, intolerance, narrow-mindedness, bigotry.

2. austerity, asceticism, self-denial, rigor, sobriety, abstinence, abstemiousness, mortification, anchoritism, monasticism.

purity, *n.* **1.** genuineness, realness, naturalness, unartificiality; authenticity, realism, naturalism; unadulteratedness, unaffectedness, unspuriousness; flawlessness, faultlessness, perfection; homogeneity, integrity, excellence, *Biol.* homozygosis.

2. cleanness, cleanliness, fairness, immaculateness; spotlessness, stainlessness, taintlessness; unblemishedness, unblottedness, unsoiledness, untarnishedness; sterility, germlessness, antisepticness, asepsis; healthfulness, wholesomeness, salubrity, innocuousness.

3. innocence, guiltlessness, virtue, shame; immaculateness, whiteness, snowiness, cleanness; morality, probity, rectitude, virtuousness, uprightness, uprighteousness; blamelessness, irreproachability, unimpeachability; incorruptibility, clear conscience, clean hands, guilelessness; chastity, abstinence, continence, temperance, temperateness; modesty, pudicity, sinlessness, uncorruptness; celibacy, virginity, intactness, maidenhood.

4. honor, repute, esteem, decency, honesty, integrity; goodness, delicacy, propriety, decorum, seemliness; creditability, ethicalness, trueheartedness; piety, saintliness, sanctity, pureheartedness, holiness, godliness; religiousness, devoutness, devotion, reverence, faithfulness, faith.

5. polish, finish, refinement, classicism; clarity, clearness, felicity; euphony, beauty, gracefulness, concinnity, harmony; tastefulness, unadornment, unornamentation; plainness, simplicity, restraint, bareness; perfection, excellence, distinction.

purlieu, *n.* **1.** outskirts, outposts; perimeter, periphery, fringe; limits, city limits, outer limits; suburbs, outlying districts.

2. **purlieus** environs, environment, surroundings, milieu; vicinity, vicinage, neighborhood, *Inf.* neck of the woods, *Inf.* part of town.

3. sphere, area, orbit, orb, ambit; territory, region, realm, domain; district, quarter, precinct, bailiwick, zone, province; range, compass, pale, locale; circuit, round, beat.

4. haunt, spot, place, rendezvous, meeting place, gathering place, *Inf.* hangout, *Inf.* stomping *or* stamping ground, *Inf.* watering hole, *Chiefly Brit.* local; resort, refuge, retreat, haven, sanctuary, hideout, hideaway, hiding place; nest, lair, den, cave, mew, covert, coverture.

purloin, *v.* **1.** steal, rob, thieve, pilfer, filch, finger, *Inf.* snitch, cabbage, abstract, *Chiefly Brit.* prig, *Brit. Sl.* snaffle, *Euph.* borrow, *Archaic.* nim; peculate, embezzle, *Law.* defalcate, misappropriate; swindle, pocket, mulct, shark; shoplift, palm, *Sl.* boost, walk off *or* away with, make off with, *Euph.* remove; *All Sl.* pinch, hook, swipe, hustle, rip off, frisk, crook, cop, lift.

2. appropriate, expropriate, arrogate, usurp; commandeer, hijack, skyjack; pirate, plagiarize, copy, *Inf.* lift, *Inf.* crib; forge, counterfeit, reproduce illegally.

3. mooch, sponge, scrounge, freeload, scavenge, *Sl.* bum.

purple, *n.* **1.** lilac, lavender, mauve; orchid, plum, violet.

2. eminence, importance, significance; nobility, aristocracy, blue blood, noble birth, silver spoon; majesty, royalty, kingship; the thrown, the crown, the scepter.

—adj. **3.** purplish, perse; lilac, lavender, mauve; orchid, plum, violet.

4. imperial, regal, royal, kingly, queenly, princely; noble, aristocratic, blue-blooded.

5. brilliant, radiant, glorious, superb, splendid, resplendent, *Inf.* splendiferous, magnificent; luxurious, lavish, sumptuous, gorgeous, *Sl.* out-of-this-world; *All Inf.* posh, plush, swank, ritzy.

6. (*all of speech or writing*) ornate, flamboyant, florid, flowery, euphuistic; grandiose, high-sounding, bigsounding; pompous, orotund, grandiloquent, highflown, high-flying; affected, pretentious, stilted, lofty; fulsome, overdrawn, hyperbolic.

purport, *v.* **1.** claim, profess, contend, maintain, hold, allege; assert, aver, asseverate; declare, announce, proclaim; pretend, pretext, feign, put up a false front.

2. imply, implicate, insinuate, infer, intimate, suggest, hint at, import, involve, allude to, connote; mean, indicate, denote, signify, betoken, point to; bespeak, breathe, argue, tell.

—n. **3.** meaning, significance, signification, import, sense; implication, idea, point, drift, tenor, trend; essence, burden, gist, pith, spirit, sum and substance; relevance, pertinence, bearing, relation, reference.

4. purpose, intention, intent, object, design, aim, plan.

purpose, *n.* **1.** reason, point, why, why and wherefore; principle, guiding principle, basis, root; idea, plan, design, proposal, scheme; motive, motivation, mainspring, driving force, cause; rationale, explanation, background, meaning; rationalization, justification, excuse, mitigation, vindication.

2. intention, intent, aim, spirit; objective, object, goal, target, mark, destination, end, end in view *or* mind, ultimate aim, by-end, end-all, be-all; expectation, expected outcome, anticipation, outlook, prospect; aspiration, vision, dream, ideal, wish, hope, desire, desideratum.

3. determination, deliberation, will, volition, decision, mind; resoluteness, resolution, resolve, firmness, steadfastness, single-mindedness; ambition, drive, diligent *or* assiduous pursuit *or* work, diligence, assiduousness, industry; persistence, constancy, perseverance, *Inf.* stick-to-it-iveness, tenacity, intransigence, stubbornness; fervor, ardor, avidity, zeal, enthusiasm, eagerness, intentness, earnestness, devotion, devotedness.

4. subject, topic, theme, thesis, issue, point, subject at hand, subject matter; central *or* main idea, keynote, heart, gist, kernel, core, essence; question, concern, problem, affair, business, study, matter at hand.

5. result, outcome, issue, effect; use, utility, service; advantage, avail, benefit; behoof, enjoyment, happiness, well being, welfare, interest; profit, gain, return, *Obs.* wealth, *Archaic.* weal.

—v. **6.** aim, set one's sights, have an eye to, have in view, steer *or* head for, zero in on, be after; aspire to, dream of, long *or* yearn for; work *or* labor *or* struggle toward, pursue, seek; intend, mean, have in mind, drive at.

7. contemplate, consider, weigh, revolve, turn over in one's mind, meditate on, think about, talk of; plan, design, scheme, devise, calculate; undertake, venture upon, set about, take upon oneself, endeavor, essay, try.

8. *Usu.* **purpose to do [s.t.]** resolve, determine, commit oneself, make a commitment, stand firm, stick to one's guns; conclude, decide upon, settle upon, fix upon, make up one's mind; will, have a mind, elect, choose, prefer, select; mean business, buckle down, get down to work, take the bit in one's mouth; steel oneself, grit one's teeth, set one's jaw.

purposeful, *adj.* **1.** practical, pragmatic, pragmatical, utilitarian, useable, useful, *Obs.* utile; applicatory, workable, serviceable, practicable; realistic,sensible, commonsensical, commonsensible; down-to-earth; longheaded, hard-headed, businesslike, all-business, hard-nosed, unsentimental, *Sl.* nuts and bolts; ambitious, aimful, goal-oriented, far-sighted, farseeing; shrewd, planning, scheming, designing, *Inf.* on the make.

2. determined, strong-willed, decided, decisive, resolved, settled, positive, sure, confirmed, committed, *Law.* peremptory; resolute, firm, steadfast, fixed, set, staunch, stanch, do-or-die, relentless, *Inf.* hellbent; unyielding, unfaltering, unwavering, unflagging; strongminded, intransigent, obdurate, stubborn, obstinate, mulish; constant, persevering, persistent, dogged, pertinacious, tenacious, *Inf.* stick-to-it-ive; diligent, sedulous, assiduous, industrious, hardworking, indefatigable, tireless, untiring; intent, earnest, avid, enthusiastic, energetic, zealous, arduous.

purposeless, *adj.* **1.** objectless, aimless, goalless, visionless, near-sighted, myopic, living for the present; targetless, without destination, wandering, rambling, lost; pointless, idealess, discursive, vacuous, empty.

2. impractical, unrealistic, nonpragmatic, nonpragmatical, nonutilitarian, nonuseable; nonapplicatory, nonworkable, nonserviceable, nonpracticable.

3. reasonless, motiveless, senseless, nonsensical; wanton, unnecessary, uncalled-for.

purposely, *adv.* **1.** intentionally, with intent, deliberately, on purpose, of set purpose; willfully, decidedly, determinedly, resolutely, with presence of mind; volitionally, voluntarily, of one's own free will, of one's own accord, on one's own initiative, on one's own; meditatedly, meditatively, studiously, considerately, thoughtfully; premeditatedly, premeditatingly, with aforethought, predeterminately; preconcertedly, designedly, by design, wittingly, knowingly, with one's eyes wide open; calculatedly, methodically, systematically, in cold blood, dispassionately, coolly, calmly, collectedly, composedly.

2. expressly, just, precisely, exactly; specifically, specially, especially, in particular, with [s.t.] in mind, for just such an occasion, purposively.

purse, *n.* **1.** change purse, wallet, *Fr. porte-monnaie*, moneybag, (*in Scottish Highland costume*) sporran; case, carrying case, tote bag, satchel, sack, pouch, pocket.

2. handbag, bag, pocketbook, shoulder bag, clutch *or* clutch purse, evening bag, disco bag.

3. (*all of money*) present, gift; prize, award, reward.

4. means, resources, capital, finances, income, revenue, profit, gain, lucre, *Sl.* velvet, *Sl.* gravy; wherewithal, funds, money, cash, ready cash, *U.S.* bankroll, cold *or* hard cash, *Inf.* pocket; paper money, bills, greenbacks, dollars, *Sl.* wad; *Sl.* dough, *U.S. Sl.* bucks, *Sl.* shekels, *Sl.* bread; wealth, substance, riches, *Disparaging.* pelf, mammon, affluence, opulence, fortune, millions, billions.

—*v.* **5.** pucker, gather, shirr, pleat, ruck, ruffle, draw together; compress, shrink, shrivel, wither, contract, furrow, squeeze, tighten; knit, crinkle, corrugate, wrinkle, crease, rumple.

pursuance, *n.* (*all of a plan, course or injunction*) following, doing, carrying out, execution, performance, discharge; bringing about, effecting, effectuating, production; fulfillment, completion, achievement, accomplishment, attainment.

pursuant, *adj.* **1.** *Usu.* **pursuant to** proceeding after, succeeding, following, coming after, next after, subsequent to.

2. pursuing, in pursuit, in hot pursuit, hot on the trail of; chasing, hunting, stalking, tracking *or* tracking down, trailing, following, shadowing, *Inf.* tailing.

—*adv.* **3.** *Usu.* **pursuant to** pursuantly, according to, accordingly, in accordance with, in harmony with, in agreement with, in conformity to, conformably; in keeping with, in step *or* tune *or* line with, consistent with, in uniformity with, consonant with, corresponding to, commensurate with.

pursue, *v.* **1.** follow, trail, hunt, hunt down, *Inf.* tail, go after; chase, run after, *Brit.* chevy, seek, tag after; stalk, course, track, trace, run down, give chase to; take off after, give chase, raise the hunt, raise the hue and cry; prowl after, look after, search for, hunt for, cast about for, follow the scent of; dig for, delve for, fish for, angle for, gun for, leave no stone unturned.

2. attend, go with, haunt, wait upon, hang upon, accompany; dog, hound, bedog, stick to, cling to, heel, sit on the tail of; shadow, tread on the heels of, tread behind, go behind, follow in the steps of, follow in one's trail; beset, harass, persecute, harry, oppress.

3. aspire to, desire, seek, push toward; be intent on, quest, contend for, aim for, try to get, have in mind, resolve to; be bent upon, struggle, strive for, try one's best for; woo, court, address, pay attention to, *Sl.* chase after; serenade, pay suit, *Inf.* set one's cap for.

4. proceed, hold to, maintain, follow up; carry on, perform, bring to pass, carry through, bring through, work out; continue, go on with, prolong, protract, push; persist in, persevere in, adhere to, endure, see through, follow out.

5. practice, engage in, carry on, undertake; wage, prosecute, conduct, exercise, ply; apply oneself to, devote oneself to, take on, tackle, take to; go out for, address oneself to, work at, take up, go in for, have a go at; occupy, employ, use.

pursuit, *n.* **1.** chase, hunt, run, hue and cry, foxhunt, *Brit.* chevy, (*in India*) shikar; trailing, pursuance, following, coursing, tracking, tracing; stalking, prowling, seeking, searching; investigation, inquiry, exploration, inquest, probe.

2. quest, grail, goal, aim, mark, objective; destination, end, target, bull's-eye; quarry, quintain, prey, game; intent, intention, purpose, point, end in view; ambition, desire, desideratum, nisus, striving.

3. prosecution, execution, effectuation, fulfillment, perfomance, conduct; prolongation, protraction, continuation, continuance, extension, maintenance, perpetuation.

4. business, work, line of work, line; field, forte, métier; occupation, employment, profession, practice, specialty, trade; calling, vocation, mission; career, undertaking, venture, avocation, pastime; craft, *Sl.* racket, art; livelihood, walk of life, lifework.

purulence, *n.* **1.** suppuration, pussiness, purulency, festering, running, mattering, rankling; abscess, ulcer, ulceration, fester, gathering, *Obs.* apostem, *Archaic.* impostume; canker, lesion, chancre, chancroid, soft chancre, simple chancre; boil, blain, furuncle, furunculus, carbuncle, pustule, pimple, papule, papilla, wen, whelk, *Rare.* bleb, *Archaic.* botch; sore, open *or* running sore, gall, excoriation.

2. pus, matter, purulent matter, *Biol.* humor, *Archaic.* peccant humor *or* matter; discharge, excretion, fluid, *Med.* rheum, *Pathol.* ichor, *Pathol.* sanies, *Pathol.* gleet, *Pathol.* the whites, *Pathol.* leukorrhea.

purulent, *adj.* **1.** suppurating, gathering, festering, mattering, maturating, coming *or* drawing to a head; discharging, excreting, draining, running.

2. ulcerous, ulcerative, ulcerated, festered, furuncular, furunculous, cankerous, cankered; gangrenous, gangrened, morbid, mortified, necrotic, necrosed, sphacelated; contaminated, infested, tainted, septic, bad, peccant.

3. suppurative, suppurated, puslike, *Med.* puruloid, *Pathol.* sanious, *Pathol.* impetiginous, *Pathol.* gleety, *Pathol.* leukorrheal.

purvey, *v.* provide, furnish, supply, render, accommodate, *Archaic.* dight, *Obs.* appoint; gird, ready, prepare, store, stock *or* stock up, fill up, *Chiefly Scot.* plenish; outfit, equip, accouter, fit out *or* up, rig out *or* up, gear.

purview, *n.* **1.** jurisdiction, bailiwick, province; sphere, compass, orbit; area, territory; care, commission, responsibility.

2. understanding, comprehension, apprehension, prehension, ken, mental grasp, *Sl.* savvy; scope, field of vision.

pus, *n.* purulence, purulent matter, *Biol.* humor, *Archaic.* peccant humor *or* matter; suppuration, purulency, pussiness, festering, running, mattering, rankling; discharge, excretion, fluid, *Med.* rheum, *Pathol.* ichor, *Pathol.* sanies, *Pathol.* gleet, *Pathol.* the whites, *Pathol.* leukorrhea.

push, *v.* **1.** propel, move, actuate, get going, set in motion; drive, trundle, wheel, roll; shove, thrust, pole, stick.

2. press forward, make one's way, squeeze through, wedge, *Inf.* elbow *or* shoulder one's way; bulldoze, ram, butt, bunt; crowd, pack, cram, jam; jostle, knock against, bump into, jolt, jog; nudge, poke.

3. impel, urge, spur, prod, goad, induce, compel, make, force, *Inf.* pressure *or* high-pressure; encourage, egg on, motivate, stimulate, inspire, inspirit, embolden; prompt, instigate, rouse; influence, sway, persuade; importune, beg, nag, hound, provoke; demand, leave no option *or* choice.

4. advance, forward, hasten, speed, expedite, railroad; endorse, get *or* stand behind, back, support, advocate, work for; go to bat for, stick up for, uphold.

5. publicize, make known, advertise, promote, boost, *Sl.* plug, *Sl.* hype, *Sl.* ballyhoo, propagandize.

6. press, bear hard upon, constrain, oblige, dragoon, coerce, put on the screws; trouble, beset, agitate, badger, hound, browbeat, plague, harass, harry; pin down, put [s.o.] in a difficult position, drive [s.o.] to the wall, *Inf.* strong-arm.

7. **push off** *Informal.* go away, depart, leave, launch, shove off.

8. **push on** continue, keep on, carry on, forge ahead; put one's shoulder to the wheel, endeavor, keep the ball rolling; persevere, persist, strive, struggle on, not give up, never say die, be undeterred, be undaunted; plod, grub, grind, drudge, labor.

—*n.* **9.** propulsion, impulsion, shove, thrust; jog, jolt, jostle, butt, bunt.

10. vigorous effort, endeavor; onset, onslaught, attack, assault, besetment, hit, strike; rush, charge, blitz, blitzkrieg, storming, raid, foray, sortie, sally, invasion, *Fr. coup de main, Obs.* brunt; bombardment, strafing, air raid, peppering, salvo, fusillade, *Both Mil.* barrage, enfilade, *Navy.* broadside.

11. exigency, exigence, urgency, need, needfulness; insistence, instance, pressure; exigencies, demands, needs, wants, requirements, urgencies, necessities, essentials, requisites; extremity, pinch, contingency; strait, difficulty, rub, trouble, plight; stress, strain.

12. *Informal.* ambition, enterprise, drive, force, striving; energy, vigor, vim, verve; zeal, enthusiasm, eagerness, spirit, get up and go, *Dial.* gimp.

pusher, *n.* **1.** ambitious person, aggressive person, hard worker, *Inf.* human dynamo; *U.S. Inf.* go-getter, *Inf.* hustler, *U.S. Inf.* rustler; salesman, saleswoman.

2. *Slang.* (*in reference to narcotics*) peddler, dealer.

pushing, *adj.* **1.** enterprising, ambitious, go-ahead, driving; aspiring, hoping, scheming, planning, designing, *Inf.* on the make, climbing, goal-oriented; industrious, diligent, devoted, hard-working, assiduous, sedulous, determined; perseverant, persevering, pertinacious, persisting, dogged, tenacious.

2. energetic, vigorous, dynamic, forceful, emphatic, powerful, effective; zealous, ardent, fervent, fervid, avid, earnest, enthusiastic, eager; spirited, full of vim and vigor, active, *Inf.* full of pep, *Inf.* peppy, *Inf.* snappy.

3. aggressive, offensive, invasive, intrusive, meddlesome, officious, incursive; assertive, self-assertive, forward, insistent, peremptory; presumptuous, bumptious, *Inf.* cheeky, nervy, brassy, obnoxious; brash, cocky, lippy, mouthy, loud-mouthed; smart-alecky, *Sl.* wise, *Sl.* smart-assed, *Sl.* biggety, *Inf.* bigheaded.

pushover, *n.* *Slang.* **1.** something easy, *Inf.* snap, *Sl.* cinch, *Sl.* child's play, *Sl.* a breeze, duck soup, piece of cake, *Sl.* a picnic, *Inf.* shoo-in, a sure thing.

2. *Inf.* easy mark *or* prey, *Inf.* lightweight, featherweight, *Sl.* patsy, *Sl.* sap; milquetoast, namby-pamby, *Sl.* pansy, *Sl.* wimp; *All Sl.* schlepp, schlemiel, nebbish, schnook, twirp.

pushy, *adj.* *Informal.* self-assertive, bumptious, obtrusive, obnoxious, brassy, aggressive, pushing. See **pushing** (*def.* 3).

pusillanimity, *n.* timidity, timorousness, cowardice, cowardliness, lily-liveredness, faint-heartedness, weak-heartedness, *Inf.* chicken-heartedness, *Sl.* yellow-belliedness; faint heart, weak knees, white feather, no backbone, a backbone of banana, *Inf.* chicken heart, *Inf.* funk, *Sl.* cold feet, *Sl.* yellow streak; poltroonery, dastardliness, recreancy, cravenness.

pusillanimous, *adj.* timid, timorous, fearful, afraid, afraid of one's own shadow, frightened; unmanly, faint-hearted, weak-hearted, lily-livered, white-livered, having no backbone, with a backbone of banana, *Inf.* chicken-hearted, *Inf.* chicken-livered, *Inf.* pantywaist, *Inf.* yellow, *Sl.* yellow-bellied, *Sl.* candy-assed; cowardly, craven, poltroon, dastardly, base, recreant, *Archaic.* niddering, *Archaic.* caitiff.

puss, *n.* **1.** cat, feline, pussy, pussycat, *Sl.* puttytat, tabby, tabby cat, tomcat, alley cat, grimalkin; kitten, kit, kitty, *Brit. Dial.* kitling, *Archaic.* catling; mouser.

2. woman, lady; girl, maiden, lass; nymph, young thing, wench, *Inf.* baggage, *Australian Inf.* girl-o; *All Sl.* chick, doll, dame, tomato, babe, cutie, skirt, *Brit.* bird.

3. *Slang.* face, visage, physiognomy, *Sl.* mug, *Sl.* pan, *Sl.* kisser.

4. *Slang.* mouth, *Fig.* maw, *Fig.* muzzle, *Sl.* mush, *Sl.* trap, *Sl.* yap, *Sl.* bazoo, *Sl.* gob, *Scot. Sl.* gab.

pussyfoot, *v.* **1.** walk on eggshells, step lightly, tread warily; creep, steal, skulk, slink, prowl, sidle, pad, *U.S. Sl.* gumshoe; worm, worm one's way, inch along.

2. equivocate, prevaricate, hem and haw, blow hot and cold, straddle the fence; dodge, evade, sidestep; beat around *or* about the bush, beg the question, not come to the point, evade the issue.

pustule, *n.* **1.** pimple, papule, papilla, boil, blain, furuncle, furunculus, carbuncle, wen, pock, whelk, *Rare.* bleb, *Archaic.* botch; eruption, inflammation, swelling, rising, lump, bump, wheal; blemish, mark, spot, pockmark, whitehead, *Pathol.* milium, blackhead, *Med.* comedo, *Sl.* zit, *Sl.* woogit, *Sl.* hickey.

2. abscess, ulcer, ulceration, fester, festering, gathering, tubercle, *Obs.* apostem, *Archaic.* impostume; gumboil, parulis, whitlow, agnail, *Ophthalm.* sty; canker, lesion, chancre, chancroid, soft chancre, simple chancre.

put, *v.* **1.** place, pose, set, lay; drop, *Inf.* plop, *Inf.* plunk, *Inf.* plank, plump; park, station, post, stand; plant, implant, imbed; perch, mount, deposit; situate, locate, emplace, position, center; dispose, allocate, install, collocate, spot, pinpoint, fix, pin down; assign, relegate, consign.

2. send, shoot, thrust; pierce, plunge, stick, spear, lance; drive, lunge, stab; force, hammer, pound, hit, knock, whack, bang.

3. throw, toss, fling, chuck, flip, pass; hurl, clap, slap, cast; snap, heave, hike, lob, let fly; shy, catapult.

4. subject, sentence, condemn, convict, doom; commit, consign, send, relegate, reduce.

5. impose, inflict, set, subject to; exact, levy, demand, require, necessitate, oblige; tax, burden, charge, fasten upon; enjoin, force, enforce, dragoon, constrain, leave no alternative; bring, visit upon, yoke with, saddle with; administer, bestow, give, prescribe, dose.

6. set before, pose, posit, advance, forward; propose, propound, predicate, postulate, lay down.

7. express, say, utter, pronounce, announce, proclaim, speak; state, declare, assert, avow, affirm, predicate, voice; aver, asseverate, allege, profess, avouch.

8. convert, turn into, make into, interpret; translate, render, transform, transcribe, transliterate, English, anglicize; say, phrase, put in words, couch, express; formulate, present, style, frame, paragraph.

9. attribute, assign, ascribe, lay on, pin on; impute, attach, apply, fix, place, settle upon, put down; saddle with, blame, charge, credit with, accredit to.

10. impel, incite, urge, prompt, motivate, stimulate, animate; compel, move, shove, push, thrust; actuate, cause, start, forward; whip, lash, spur, drive.

11. invest, put money in, risk, speculate, *Inf.* stake, venture; sink, *Inf.* plunge, tie up money in, pour money in, buy into; finance, fund, financier, *Inf.* bankroll; sponsor, back, *Inf.* angel, put up, support.

12. bet, wager, gamble, risk, chance; take a chance, take a risk, hazard, take a leap in the dark; stake, play, go.

13. estimate, guess, *Inf.* guesstimate, deem, esteem; rate, assess, appraise, evaluate, valuate; place, set, gauge, measure, value; calculate, count, reckon, account, figure; consider, size up, think, prize, regard.

14. assign, detail, delegate, depute, allocate, tell to do; detach, post, commission, empower; appoint, name, designate.

15. put across convey, spell out, communicate, make clear, explain, get across; make oneself understood, make [s.t.] perfectly clear.

16. put away a. discard, throw away, get rid of, rid oneself of, get quit of; *Sl.* dump, *Sl.* ditch, *Inf.* chuck, *Sl.* eighty-six, cast aside; jettison, throw overboard, *Inf.* deep-six. **b.** consume, eat, eat up, ingest, take in, take down; devour, down, get down, tuck in; swallow, gulp, gobble, wolf, bolt, stuff. **c.** institutionalize, confine, commit, consign, remand. **d.** kill, do away with, dispose of, execute, slaughter, gas, hang, electrocute, shoot; put an end to, dispatch, finish, slay, put to sleep; *Sl.* rub out, *Sl.* waste, *Sl.* bump off, *Sl.* wipe out. **e.** save, put by, lay in, store away, lay away; stow away, cache, hide away, bank, file away; repose, reposit, deposit, *Inf.* stick away; put aside, squirrel away, save up, treasure, keep, save for a rainy day.

17. put down a. disparage, deprecate, ridicule, berate, dispraise, disvalue; belittle, denigrate, depreciate, disdain, deride; contemn, despise, hold in contempt, misprize; thumb one's nose at, *Sl.* dump on, sneer at, curl one's lip at. **b.** criticize, knock, disapprove, disfavor, look askance at, frown upon; not take kindly to, turn up one's nose at, take a dim view of; object to, discountenance, take exception, think ill of, think little of. **c.** humiliate, embarrass, mortify, crush; abash, debase, demean, lower, abase; disgrace, shame, make one blush; bring lower, bring down, take down, take down a notch, put a tuck in one's tail; deflate, let down, take the wind out of one's sails. **d.** squelch, suppress, quash, quell, repress; smash, crush, crack down, clamp down; smother, strangle, gag, throttle, suffocate; drown, extinguish, kill. **e.** enter, set down, inscribe, book, log; record, register, tabulate, file, catalog, put in writing; write down, mark down, post, note down, jot down.

18. put forth a. assert, propose, present, put forward; submit, bid, insist, contend; argue, hold, maintain. **b.** issue, emit, bring out, publish; broadcast, advertise, publicize, make known; spread, circulate, propagate, air, broach; write up, break, make public. **c.** exert, use, exercise, *Inf.* put out; apply oneself, endeavor, ply, ply the oar, bear down; tax, strain, stress, sweat blood, buckle down.

19. put in a. interpose, introduce, insert, interpolate, interject, interjaculate; stick in, slip in, throw in, pop in, insinuate, inject, implant. **b.** spend, expend, pass, use, consume, use up; make use of, utilize, exercise; devote, dedicate, give to, consecrate. **c.** induct, inaugurate, install, instate, place in office, invest; enthrone, crown, throne, chair, anoint, ordain, ordinate, initiate.

20. put off a. repel, disgust, offend, revolt; sicken, nauseate, *Sl.* gross out; disconcert, discomfort, distress, dismay. **b.** postpone, delay, put over, defer; table, shelve, adjourn, put on ice; suspend, stay, extend, hold over, lay over, stand over; forestall, hold off on, *Sl.* stall off, play for time.

21. put on a. don, change into, slip into, dress, get dressed; clothe, apparel, cloak, coat, jacket; attire, garb. **b.** feign, fake, assume, dissimulate, dissemble; act, play, playact, make believe, pretend; bluff, put on an act, put up a front; affect, go through the motions, profess; make a show of, let on. **c.** gain, add, increase, grow, fatten, widen, balloon. **d.** exaggerate, overstate, overdo, stretch the truth; hyperbolize, overreach, overdraw, overestimate, carry too far; *Inf.* talk big, make much of, lay it on thick. **e.** produce, present, open a show, mount; perform, stage, dramatize, theatricalize; represent, portray, depict, impersonate. **f.** kid, joke, josh, jest, jape, *Inf.* jolly; tease, banter, haze, chaff, ride; *Sl.* rib, *Sl.* razz, *Inf.* needle, rally, *Sl.* rag. **g.** fool, befool, dupe, gull; make a monkey out of, make a fool of.

22. put out a. extinguish, drown, kill, douse, quench; stamp out, snuff out, rub out, blow out. **b.** publish, issue, print, run, bring out, get out, put forth; publicize, make known, make public, circulate, spread. **c.** annoy, irritate, harass, give [s.o.] a hard time; aggravate, pester, exasperate, irk, vex, perturb, worry; torment, distress, *Sl.* bug. **d.** inconvenience, discommode, incommode, put on the spot; trouble, impose upon, disadvantage, bother, disturb.

23. put through carry through, conclude, wind up, complete, finish; realize, achieve, accomplish, do, compass; put across, finish up, top off, cap; dispose of, dispatch, execute, effect; terminate, end, close, get done, call it a day; *Inf.* pull off, bring off, come through with, carry out, bring through.

24. put up a. can, preserve, *Brit.* tin, jar, bottle,

pot; store, preservatize, conserve. **b.** accommodate, house, quarter, billet, bunk, bed, room; lodge, board, give one room, give one a bed to sleep on. **c.** erect, build, raise, set up, make; construct, put together, create, make up, frame, fabricate; produce, form, shape, fashion. **d.** pay, contribute, ante, *Inf.* kick in, *Inf.* fork over; pledge, posit, stake; come up with, *Inf.* cough up, *Sl.* shell out; post, pawn, hock, put up as collateral; mortgage, bond, put up bail.

25. **put up with** endure, tolerate, suffer, bear, stand; abide, *Inf.* lump, bide, take, stand for; condone, submit to, resign oneself to, accept, make the best of; swallow, stomach, down, brave, brook.

—*adj.* **26.** fixed, set, secure, fastened, tight; stuck, glued, fast, cemented; stationary, motionless, static, still, at ease, at rest.

27. worded, phrased, presented, couched, styled; expressed, said, spoken, formulated.

putative, *adj.* supposed, reputed, assumed, commonly believed, so-called, *Fr. soi-disant*; reported, stated, given, presumed, granted; alleged, presumptive, imputed, acknowledged, accepted, recognized, established, known; fabled, supposititious, pretended.

put-down, *n.* **1.** humiliation, mortification, embarrassment; abashment, debasement, abasement, self-abnegation, self-diminishment, self-abasement; comedown, deflation, letdown; disgrace, shame.

2. gibe, sneer, jeer, fleer; derision, *Inf.* dig, twit, taunt, retort, parting shot; quip, jape, *Inf.* swipe, crack, wisecrack.

put-on, *adj.* **1.** pretended, assumed, meretricious, sham; faked, simulated, *Inf.* phony, spurious, counterfeit, fake; falsified, feigned, colored; artificial, ersatz, unnatural, synthetic, plastic; alloyed, mixed, adulterated.

—*n.* **2.** airs, affectation, show, pretense, front; facade, image, sham, artificiality, airs and graces.

3. mockery, mock, imitation, fake, counterfeit; hoax, swindle, rip-off, cheat, fraud, *Inf.* phony.

4. parody, spoof, farce, take-off; burlesque, caricature, mimicry, harlequinade.

putrefy, *v.* rot, decay, go bad, deteriorate, disintegrate; decompose, addle, spoil, taint, curdle, stale, fust; putresce, stagnate, canker, fester, suppurate, sicken; *Pathol.* sphaculate, *Pathol.* mortify, *Pathol.* gangrene, *Pathol.* necrose.

putrid, *adj.* **1.** rotten, decaying, purulent, decomposed; diseased, saprogenic, gangrenous, bad, *Pathol.* sphaculate, *Pathol.* necrotic, *Pathol.* mortified; rancid, carious, stagnant, maggoty, wormy, worm-eaten; fetid, feculent, polluted, rank, *Archaic.* reechy; stale, sour, mildewy, moldy, fusty, frowzy; addled, curdled, spoiled, tainted, unclean, foul, flyblown, contaminated; fecal, excrementitious, *Physiol.* stercoraceous; putrescent, noxious, noisome, mephitic; ulcerous, suppurating, festering.

2. corrupt, depraved, vile, evil, wicked; foul, base, low, mean, scurvy, abominable, execrable; abhorrent, loathsome, despicable, odious, detestable, nasty, contemptible; malefic, virulent, malignant.

3. offensive, objectionable, bad; disgusting, repulsive, repellent, revolting; nauseating, sickening, filthy, fulsome.

putter, *v.* **1.** busy, fool around, trifle, fool with; fiddle, toy, play, *Inf.* monkey with, *Inf.* mess with; potter, piddle, fidget with, fribble, *Inf.* fiddle-faddle; tinker, dabble, footle, *Sl.* screw around with.

2. loiter, dawdle, diddle, diddle-daddle, dally, dilly-dally; kill time, waste time, beguile, pass time, while away time, bide time, lose time; doodle, lallygag, loll, fritter away time, fool away time; loaf, idle, squander away time, *Inf.* lazy away.

put-upon, *adj.* taken advantage of, imposed upon, put-out, inconvenienced; beset, troubled, disturbed, distressed, bothered, pestered, disquieted; embarrassed, mortified, abashed, chagrined, humiliated.

puzzle, *n.* **1.** acrostic, crossword puzzle; anagram, logogriph, word game; jigsaw puzzle; Chinese puzzle.

2. enigma, mystery, riddle, conundrum, question, question mark; problem, dilemma, quandary, plight, predicament; maze, labyrinth, tangle, knot; secret, arcanum, closed *or* sealed book; oracle, dark saying, obscure statement, hidden meaning, riddle of the sphinx; puzzler, poser, *Inf.* hard nut to crack, *Inf.* brain-teaser, *Inf.* mind-boggler, *Inf.* stumper, *Inf.* floorer.

3. perplexity, bewilderment, confoundment, bafflement, puzzlement, puzzledness; uncertainty, incertitude, confusion, disconcertment.

—*v.* **4.** confuse, bewilder, perplex, nonplus, baffle, confound, mystify, *Inf.* bamboozle, *Inf.* buffalo, *Inf.* stump, *Inf.* stick, *Inf.* beat, *Inf.* lick, *Inf.* get; disconcert, stagger, stun, daze, astonish, astound, dumfound, *Brit. Dial.* boggle, *Inf.* floor, *Inf.* flabbergast, gravel; fuddle, befuddle, muddle, bemuddle, fog, befog, mix up; fool, delude, trick, outwit, hoodwink, bluff, distract.

5. ponder, study, consider, contemplate, meditate, reflect, muse, brood, deliberate, ruminate; ponder over, think over, study over, meditate upon *or* over, reflect upon *or* over, muse over, mull over, brood over, deliberate over *or* upon, puzzle over; think about, cogitate, give thought to; think hard, rack one's brains, *Inf.* sweat *or* stew over.

6. **puzzle out** solve, resolve, figure out, work out, think through *or* out, sort out, reason out, *Inf.* get; crack, decode, decipher, break down, unlock, find the key; untangle, unravel, untie, unriddle, clear up.

puzzled, *adj.* perplexed, mystified, staggered, flustered; bewildered, muddled, baffled, dazzled, dazed, mixed up; confused, confounded, dumfounded, *Sl.* stumped, *Inf.* flummoxed; lost, fogged, in a fog, in a cloud, at a loss.

puzzler, *n.* poser, brain-teaser, brain-twister, stickler; dilemma, mystery, enigma, quandary. See **puzzle** (*def.* **2**).

puzzling, *adj.* **1.** enigmatic, enigmatical, baffling, bewildering, perplexing, confounding, mystifying; inexplicable, unexplainable, insoluble, insolvable, *Obs.* inextricable.

2. mysterious, esoteric, occult, hermetic, hermetical; secret, hidden, concealed, veiled, masked, arcane, cryptic, perdu; obscure, indistinct, indefinite, unclear, shadowy, nebulous, vague; inscrutable, oracular, sphingine, sphinxian, sphinxlike; mystic, mystical, cabalistic; strange, weird, bizarre; odd, curious, peculiar, queer.

3. abstruse, recondite, abstract, heavy, *Sl.* heavy-duty; difficult, hard, over one's head, *Inf.* tough; complex, complicated, perplexed, *Inf.* tricky; intricate, involved, labyrinthine, tangled, knotty, crabbed; impenetrable, unfathomable, incomprehensible, past *or* beyond comprehension *or* understanding, undecipherable.

4. ambiguous, equivocal, discreet, noncommital, secretive, covert, clandestine, under-the-table, under-the-counter; evasive, shifty, circuitous.

pyromaniac, *n.* arsonist, *Inf.* firebug, fire buff, pyrophile, incendiary, fire-setter.

Q

quack¹, *v.* cackle, gaggle, clack, honk.

quack², *n.* **1.** pretender, impostor, masquerader, fake, *Inf.* faker, humbug; mountebank, charlatan, *Inf.* phony; hoaxer, cozener, trickster, cheat, swindler, *Inf.* shyster, sharper; slicker, spieler, knave, rogue, *Inf.* con man, *Inf.* con artist, *Inf.* bunko artist; shammer, bluffer; medicine man, witch doctor, shaman, nostrum peddler, medicaster, quacksalver.

—adj. **2.** fake, *Inf.* phony, false, charlatanish; pseudo, quasi, sham, pretended, fraudulent; affected, assumed, put-on.

quackery, *n.* charlatanism, charlatanry, sciolism, humbuggery, humbug; imposture, trickery, chicanery, knavery, fraudulence; deception, cozenage, delusion, fraud, sham; swindle, hoax, *U.S. Inf.* bunko, defraudment, misrepresentation; sharping, sharking, cheating, duplicity; double-dealing, confidence game, *Inf.* con game, *Inf.* flim-flam game, *Inf.* ripoff.

quaff, *v.* drink, imbibe, *Inf.* swig, *Inf.* pull, *Inf.* take a pull at; drain, wash down, *Inf.* belt, toss off, *Inf.* chug, *Inf.* chug-a-lug; gulp, swallow, guzzle, *Sl.* swill, soak up, drink one's fill; tipple, *Archaic.* bib, tope, bouse, *Archaic.* dram, *Inf.* booze; *Inf.* wet one's whistle, *Inf.* gargle, lap, lap up; drink like a fish, drink hard, drink seriously, *Sl.* knock a few back, *Sl.* dip the beak; *Sl.* scoop a few, *Sl.* liquor up, *Sl.* souse; carouse, wassail, revel.

quaggy, *adj.* **1.** marshy, boggy, fenny, swampy, *Archaic.* marish; miry, quagmiry, sloughy, oozy, muddy, sludgy, mucky; squashy, spongy, paludal, moory; plashy, poachy, slushy, slobby, squishy; soggy, pulpy, mushy, loamy.

2. soft, flabby, flaccid, limp; floppy, supple, ductile, flexible, flexile, whippy; flimsy, pliable, malleable.

quagmire, *n.* **1.** bog, fen, marsh, swamp, quag, morass, *Archaic.* marish; slough, wash, squash, wallow, *Brit.* sough, *Brit. Dial.* sump, *Scot.* moss; mire, quicksand, ooze, mud, muck, sludge; moor, peatbog, flat, mudflat, everglade; swampland, marshland, fenland, forest swamp; bottomland, slobland, moorland.

2. imbroglio, stalemate, checkmate; impasse, cul-de-sac, corner, blind corner; dilemma, quandary, perplexity, intricacy, involvement; meshes, pass, strait, crisis, juncture; muddle, mess, pinch, *Sl.* stew, *Sl.* pickle, *Sl.* jam; *Inf.* scrape, hot water, nonplus, deadlock.

quail, *v.* shrink, recoil, shy, shy away from, pull back, draw back, turn back; flinch, blench, blink, lose heart, *Inf.* funk; wince, quiver, quaver, quake, shake, tremble, shiver in one's shoes, quake in one's boots; start, have cold feet, take fright; hesitate, falter, waver; skulk, cower, cringe, crouch; slink, sneak, worm, weasel out, tuck one's tail between one's legs, think with one's feet; have no heart, have no stomach, show the white feather, knuckle under, *Inf.* chicken out.

quaint, *adj.* **1.** strange, peculiar, unusual, curious, uncommon; unfamiliar, odd, queer, singular, unique; eccentric, pixilated, bizarre, *Sl.* rum; unconventional, unorthodox, outlandish, extraordinary; fanciful, whimsical, fantastic, absurd, preposterous; ridiculous, humorous, ludicrous, droll, funny, funny-looking; weird, offbeat, *Inf.* kooky, *Inf.* off the wall, *Sl.* freaky, *Sl.* wacky.

2. picturesque, old-fashioned, small-town, archaic, antiquated; gothic, rococo, grotesque, baroque, daedal.

quake, *v.* **1.** shake, tremble, shudder; rock, reel, sway, toss, pitch; toss and turn, toss and tumble, pitch and plunge, rock and roll; waver, oscillate, librate, falter; totter, wobble, flounder, stagger; pendulate, tick, tock, tick-tock.

2. quiver, vibrate, quaver; throb, pulsate, palpitate, writhe, squirm, quail; shiver, chill, flutter, flitter, flit, twitch, vellicate.

—n. **3.** earthquake, tremor, trembler, *Chiefly U.S.* temblor, shock; cataclysm, breakup, upheaval, diastrophism, seismic disturbance.

4. agitation, vibration, oscillation; jolt, jog, jar, jostle, jerk, start, stir, succussion; pulsation, palpitation, beat, pitter-patter, pitapat; twitch, vellication, tic, rictus; paroxysm, orgasm, throe, cramp, convulsion, spasm, fit, seizure, *Pathol.* ictus; stroke, apoplexy, heart attack, *Pathol.* coronary thrombosis, *Pathol.* jactation.

5. quiver, quaver, tremble, shudder; shiver, jitter, twitter, ague, *Inf.* shakes, St. Vitus dance; fidget, jiggle, jig, flutter, flitter, flap; rock, reel, roll, lurch, welter; toss, tumble, pitch, swing, sway.

qualification, *n.* **1.** competence, competency, fitness, fittedness, eligibility, preparedness, readiness; proficiency, adeptness, experience, know-how, skillfulness, knowledgeability; capability, capableness, ability, ableness, efficiency; commensurability, satisfactoriness, acceptability, acceptableness; suitability, meetness, adequacy, sufficiency.

2. requirement, requisite, condition; criterion, standard.

3. restriction, restricting, limitation, limiting, regulation, regulating; definition, defining, confinement, confining, narrowing, bounding, boundary; dependence, condition, proviso, provision; modification, alteration, change, adaptation, adjustment.

qualified, *adj.* **1.** capable, able, efficient, *Sl.* on the ball; competent, fit, fitted, equipped, prepared, well-grounded, trained, ready, up to grade; proficient, adept, finished, polished, practiced, experienced, *Fr. au fait*; skilled, skillful, knowledgeable, versed, well-informed, *Inf.* knowing the ropes, *Inf.* knowing one's stuff, *Sl.* knowing one's onions; commensurate, equal to, *Inf.* up to; satisfactory, *Inf.* up to snuff, acceptable; adequate, all right, *Inf.* OK, *Archaic.* sufficient; suitable, suited, fitting, proper, meet.

2. deserving, worthy, eligible; authorized, certified, licensed, warranted, legitimized.

3. restricted, restrictive, qualificatory, regulated, limited, limitative, narrowed, defined; confined, circumscribed, bounded, marked off; conditional, provisional, dependent, contingent; adapted, adjusted, modified, modificative, modificatory, altered, changed.

qualify, *v.* **1.** endow, endue, supply, provide for, fit, fit out, outfit, equip, arm; prepare, condition, ready, get ready; ground, train, instruct, coach, teach, educate; capacitate, enable, empower, delegate, authorize, warrant; certify, license, permit, pass, commission.

2. characterize, describe, designate, distinguish, call, name, repute, regard.

3. restrict, limit, regulate, define; confine, bound, narrow, circumscribe, mark off, make conditions, make exceptions, make provisions; adapt, adjust, affect; modify, alter, change; moderate, temper, mitigate, meliorate; reduce, abate, diminish, lessen, lighten, *Inf.* let up; relieve, assuage, alleviate, ease, modulate, soften, tone down; mollify, appease, pacify, calm, soothe.

4. deserve, be worthy of, meet requirements, be eligible for, pass inspection, pass muster, make the grade, succeed; *Sl.* cut it, *Sl.* hack it; be licensed, be commissioned.

quality, *n.* **1.** characteristic, property, attribute; distinction, note, mark, cachet, feature, trait, grace, virtue; idiosyncrasy, singularity, eccentricity, peculiarity, quirk, oddity; character, nature, kind, grade, sort, condition; complexion, tone, mood, cast; turn, bent, style; detail, particular, point, element; personality, temperament, disposition; tendency, bias, leaning, propensity, proclivity, penchant, proneness, predilection, predisposition, inbred *or* innate attribute, streak; endowment, gift, talent, genius; faculty, knack, ability, capability; specialty, stock in trade, badge, earmark, trademark; forte, *Sl.* bag, *Sl.* thing, *Sl.* trick; strong point *or* suit, talking *or* selling point; merit, asset, advantage.

2. superiority, excellence, *Sl.* class; eminence, preeminence, distinction, greatness, nobility, transcendence; fineness, worth, value; supremacy, perfection, certain something, *Fr. je ne sais quoi*.

3. high station, high degree, high rank; elevated social position, standing, social status; dignity, grandeur, importance, influence; fame, notability; precedence, caste, blue blood.

4. aristocracy, gentry, nobility, patriciate, (*in Britain*) peerage; elite, privileged class, dominant class, ruling class, upper class, the high and mighty, *Inf.* upper crust, gentility; meritocracy, the best and the brightest; high society, *Fr. haut monde*, beau monde, fashionable society; social elite, clique, coterie, jet set, the beautiful people.

qualm, *n.* **1.** compunction, pang of conscience, scruple, remorse, contrition, regret; penitence, repentance, contriteness; sorrow, guilt, shame, embarrassment; self-reproach, self-reproof, self-blame, self-accusation, self-condemnation, self-castigation.

2. misgiving, doubt, question; hesitation, reluctance, unwillingness, disinclination, uncertainty; feeling, odd feeling, bad feeling, *Inf.* funny feeling; *Sl.* bad vibes, uneasiness, apprehensiveness, *Inf.* butterflies, *Sl.* heebie-jeebies, jitters, *Sl.* willies, *Sl.* creeps; apprehension, fear, foreboding, presentiment, premonition, prescience, presage; trepidation, disquiet, care, concern; anxiety, dread, alarm, consternation.

3. sudden sickness, nausea, queasiness; repugnance, disgust, turn, loathing.

quandary, *n.* **1.** predicament, dilemma, crossroads; perplexity, puzzle, enigma, riddle, conundrum, poser; paradox, knot, knotty problem, Gordian knot; imbroglio, intricacy, entanglement, maze; slough, muddle, quagmire, stalemate; dangerous condition *or* situation, plight, extremity; hornet's nest, pretty kettle of fish, straits, jam, hot water; pinch, exigency, emergency, trouble, distress, difficulty.

2. uncertainty, indecision, incertitude; dubiousness, doubtfulness, doubt; perplexity, bewilderment, confusedness; indetermination, vacillation, wavering; insecurity, precariousness.

quantity, *n.* **1.** amount, substance, measurement, measure, extent, strength; weight, content, capacity; total, sum, whole, lot, aggregate, whole deal, whole shebang; large amount, big amount, lots, lots and lots.

2. share, portion, proportion, quota; dose, dosage, allotment, apportionment; dole, allowance, pittance, spoonful, mouthful, armful, handful, dipperful; batch, lot, pinch.

quarrel, *n.* **1.** dispute, discord, wrangle, wrangling, bickering, *Sl.* beef, controversy; contradiction, dissension, variance, difference of opinion; debate, discussion, polemic, logomachy, war of words; contestation, litigation, disputation, argumentation, argument, *Inf.* words; disagreement, squabble, spat, tiff, *Brit. Dial.* fratch; personal conflict, *Inf.* run-in, *Inf.* hassle, *Inf.* barney; falling-out, rupture, break, schism, faction, open variance, feud, vendetta.

2. contention, contest, altercation, conflict, clash, *Law.* chance-medley; *Sl.* blow-up, row, dustup, *Sl.* rhubarb, fracas, fray; uproar, brouhaha, brawl, rumpus, *Inf.* ruckus, breach of the peace; fight, tussle, donnybrook, *Scot. and North Eng.* threap, *Inf.* scrap, *Inf.* set-to; broil, embroilment, imbroglio, *Scot.* sturt, *Scot.* collieshangie; strife, tumult, disturbance, commotion, outbreak, declaration of war; scrimmage, riot, squall, pandemonium.

3. issue, question at issue, battleground, bone of contention, disputed point; apple of discord, *Latin. casus belli*, cause of complaint, objection, root of the trouble.

—*v.* **4.** squabble, altercate, have an altercation; argue, disagree, dispute, spar, have words, *Inf.* pick a crow; fall out, be at loggerheads, be at odds; spat, tiff, quibble, wrangle; differ, contend, break, carry on a vendetta; make something of it, clash, brawl, be at each other's throats; broil, fight, scuffle, conflict, go on the warpath.

5. debate, dissent, have words, raise voices, have a misunderstanding; contend, take issue, object, *Scot.* thraw; carp, find fault, raise a complaint; scold, nag, *Inf.* rip into, *Inf.* tear into, *Inf.* bawl out, *Inf.* lace into, *Inf.* lay out, *Inf.* let have it.

quarrelsome, *adj.* **1.** argumentative, inharmonious, contentious, combative, wranglesome; dissident, dissentient, dissentious; exceptive, controversial, litigious, disputatious, hostile, unpacific, pugnacious, combative; discordant, bellicose, battlesome, belligerent, brawling, turbulent; fiery, hot, hot-headed, hot-tempered; peppery, quick-tempered, *Inf.* quick on the trigger.

2. antagonistic, unfriendly, unamiable, alienating; abrupt, sharp, acrimonious, caustic, sarcastic, biting, thorny; vixenish, shrewish, termagant; fractious, choleric, churlish, captious, contradictory, disagreeable; cantankerous, captious, irascible, irritable; contrary, dyspeptic, bad-tempered, ill-humored; frettish, petulant, peevish, querulous, grouchy; cross, cranky, testy, snappish, *Inf.* ugly, *Inf.* mean, *Inf.* ornery, waspish; touchy, pettish, splenetic, difficult; thin-skinned, cross-grained, quick to take offense.

quarry[1], *n.* **1.** excavation, pit, mine, strip mine.

—*v.* **2.** quarry, mine, strip mine.

quarry[2], *n.* game, hunted animal *or* bird, prey, raven, the hunted, object of the chase, victim, the kill.

quarter, *n.* **1.** one fourth, a fourth part; quarter-hour; one fourth of a year *or* three months; half a semester, quarter term; twenty-five cents, *Sl.* two bits.

2. point, direction, compass point *or* direction.

3. country, region, district, zone, province; area, parts, *Inf.* neck of the woods, part of the country; territory, tract of land, land, terrain; place, locality, section, neighborhood, block.

4. quarters a. lodgings, lodging, lodging place, lodgment, living quarters, quarterage, rooms, accommodations, housing, shelter, roof over one's head, *Inf.* pad, *Inf.* crash pad, *Chiefly Brit. Inf.* diggings, *Brit. Inf.* digs; home, abode, domicile, domicil, residence, residency, dwelling, dwelling place, habitation, habitat, inhabitance, inhabitancy; flat, apartment, tenement, rent, walk-up, cold-water flat, *Brit.* chambers, *Brit.* apartments, *Chiefly Brit.* maisonette; penthouse, townhouse, suite, story, condominium, *Inf.* condo; chamber, room, stall, cell, cabin, compartment; nook, nest, roost, perch; address, location, situation, whereabouts, place. **b.** *Military.* barracks, billet, casern, cantonment, military quarters, *Sl.* the Q.

5. mercy, indulgence, favor, clemency, forgiveness, pardon, grace; mercifulness, compassion, compassionateness, *Latin. misericordia*, pity, humaneness, humanity, leniency, lenity, sparingness, mildness.

—*v.* **6.** quadrisect, cut *or* divide into quarters; cut up, carve, divide into sections, section, split up.

7. board, furnish with lodgings, *Inf.* put up, house, billet, lodge, accommodate, bed, give food and shelter, put a roof over [s.o.'s] head.

8. station, assign, locate, post, place, situate.

9. lodge, take up quarters, take up residence, abide, dwell, live, stay, take root, settle down; make camp, encamp, pitch one's tent, *Inf.* park oneself and one's belongings.

quash[1], *v.* **1.** subdue, suppress, squelch, *Inf.* put the kibosh on, squash, vanquish; quell, quench, stamp out, put down, repress, crush; terminate, put an end to, dissolve, stop; overthrow, overwhelm, overturn, subvert, defeat, conquer, overcome.

2. annihilate, exterminate, extinguish, extirpate, eradicate, obliterate; destroy, demolish, devastate; expunge, efface, wipe out, blot out, erase, delete, cancel, strike out.

quash[2], *v.* **1.** annul, disannul, nullify, declare null and void, render null and void, void, avoid; vacate, vitiate, invalidate, disenact, disestablish; cancel, discharge; supersede, set aside; repeal, revoke, rescind, reverse, abrogate, abolish; discontinue, break off, *Law.* nol-pros, suspend, stop, cease.

2. recant, retract, abjure, unsay, recall; withdraw, take back, undo; renounce, repudiate, deny, disclaim, disown, relinquish, abnegate, disavow; countermand, counterorder, overrule, override; veto, negate.

3. terminate, put an end to, bring to an end, dissolve; discard, dismiss, cast aside.

quasi, *adj.* **1.** resembling, seeming, apparent; partial, part, kind of, sort of, *Inf.* semi; pseudo, pretended, fake.

—*adv.* **2.** seemingly, as it were, apparently; partially, partly, to a certain extent *or* degree.

quaver, *v.* **1.** quiver, vibrate, tremble, shake, shudder, shiver; flicker, flutter, oscillate, fluctuate, vacillate, waver. See **quiver** (*def.* **1**).

2. trill, twitter, warble, yodel.

—*n.* **3.** quiver, quivering, quavering, vibration, trembling, shaking, shuddering, shivering; flickering, fluttering, vacillating, wavering. See **quiver** (*def.* **2**).

4. trill, trilling, twitter, twittering, warble, warbling, yodel, yodeling, *Music.* vibrato, *Music.* tremolo.

quean, *n.* **1.** hussy, *Sl.* broad, brazen woman, *Archaic.* malapert, jade; shrew, harridan, scold, virago, vixen, termagant, *Sl.* bitch.

2. prostitute, harlot, strumpet, whore; slut, slattern, demirep, cocotte, demimondaine, loose woman, wanton, fallen woman, tramp, vamp, white slave; lady of the evening, woman of the profession, Mrs. Warren, *Fr. fille de joie;* trollop, *Archaic.* wench, trull, drab; *All Sl.* tart, hustler, hooker, floozie. See also **prostitute** (*def.* **1**).

queasy, *adj.* **1.** nauseous, nauseated, sick to one's stomach, sick, ill, indisposed; out of sorts, *Sl.* hung over, *Inf.* under the weather, qualmish, *Inf.* woozy, faint, dizzy.

2. nauseating, sickening, disgusting, revolting, repulsive, repellent, *Sl.* gross.

3. uneasy, uncomfortable, conscience-stricken; concerned, worried, anxious, nervous.

4. squeamish, overfastidious, overnice, dainty; overparticular, fussy, finicky, finical.

queen, *n.* **1.** queen consort, queen dowager, queen mother, sultana, infanta; female sovereign *or* monarch, empress, *Hist.* princess, czarina, ranee, maharanee, Her Grace *or* Majesty.

2. movie queen, beauty queen, idol, star; model, paragon, pink, phoenix, ideal, perfection.

queer, *adj.* **1.** unconventional, uncommon, unusual, unique, unorthodox, uncustomary, unwonted, rare; atypical, original, singular, exceptional, individual; unexampled, unparalleled, unprecedented, unfamiliar, uncomfortable; odd, curious, peculiar, offbeat, cranky; incongruous, anomalous, irregular, abnormal, deviate, deviant, *Inf.* funny, *Sl.* rum.

2. quaint, eccentric, droll, comical, fanciful, whimsical, capricious, waggish, *Sl.* balmy, *Chiefly Brit.* barmy; weird, strange, bizarre, freakish, *Sl.* far out; grotesque, ridiculous, ludicrous, absurd, preposterous, outlandish, extravagant, fantastic; remarkable, astonishing, extraordinary; exotic, unreal, unnatural, fey, supernatural, preternatural; nondescript, amorphous, indescribable, unclassifiable.

3. suspicious, suspect, questionable, dubious, doubtful, open to doubt, wrong, not right, *Inf.* shady, *Sl.* fishy; untrustworthy, disreputable, *Inf.* crooked, *Inf.* shifty-eyed.

4. giddy, faint, light-headed, dizzy, reeling, vertiginous; qualmish, uneasy; *All Sl.* blitzed, zonked, spaced, ripped, spent, wrecked, wasted, out of it.

5. crazy, mad, insane, demented, deranged, irrational, unbalanced, unhinged, insensate, brainsick, of unsound mind, out of one's mind *or* head *or* wits, off one's head, mad as a hatter *or* March hare, daft, touched, crackbrained, *Latin. non compos mentis*; crazed, frenzied, frantic, frenetic, wild, delirious, rabid, raving, *Inf.* cracked, *Inf.* dotty, *Inf.* daffy, *Inf.* haywire, *Sl.* over the top; with bats in one's belfry, with a screw loose, with a few buttons missing, not playing with a full deck, with rooms to let; *All Sl.*

schizo, screwy, squirrely, wacko, wacky, nuts, loony, loco, nutty, ape, bananas, bats, batty, bonkers, bughouse, bugs, cuckoo, dippy, mental, off one's rocker, off the wall, out in left field, *Brit.* off one's chump.

6. *Derogatory.* homosexual, *Inf.* gay, *Inf.* bent. See **homosexual** (*def.* **1**).

7. *Slang.* **a.** bad, poor, worthless, useless, defective, faulty; deficient, inferior, second-rate, below par *or* standard. **b.** counterfeit, spurious, fraudulent, forged, bogus, ungenuine, unauthentic, supposititious, apocryphal, colorable, sham, mock, dummy, bastard, quasi, pseudo, so-called, *Inf.* fake, *Sl.* phony.

—*v.* **8.** spoil, ruin, mar, *Fig.* butcher; impair, damage, hurt, harm; bungle, bosh, muff, blunder, foul up, make a mess *or* hash of, *Inf.* butch, *Inf.* flub, *Inf.* gum up the works, *Inf.* bolix, *Sl.* mess up, *Sl.* screw up, *Sl.* louse up, *Sl.* blow, *Sl.* bitch.

9. jeopardize, jeopard, imperil, peril, hazard, threaten, expose, endanger, put in *or* expose to danger; compromise; commit, venture, chance, stake, gamble, dare, take a chance, tempt fortune.

—*n.* **10.** *Derogatory.* homosexual, *Derog.* homo, *Derog.* faggot. See **homosexual** (*def.* **2**).

11. *Slang.* counterfeit money, false *or* bad money, base coin, *Inf.* phony *or* bogus money, *Sl.* green goods.

quell, *v.* **1.** suppress, subdue, abort, extinguish, stamp out; vanquish, conquer, subjugate; overpower, overcome, overwhelm; crush, defeat, worst, beat down, put down, squelch; rout, disperse, scatter.

2. quiet, silence, calm, *Archaic.* becalm, hush, lull, pacify, compose, tranquilize; allay, assuage, alleviate, mitigate, palliate, moderate; soothe, appease, mollify, soften; dull, deaden, blunt; abate, stem, stay.

quench, *v.* **1.** satisfy, satiate, sate, flake, surfeit, glut, saturate, allay; *Sl.* take care of it, *Sl.* hit the spot; have one's fill, have more than enough, have enough for now; gorge, cloy, pall.

2. extinguish, snuff out, put out, *Inf.* douse, *Inf.* dinch, blow out, (*of a light*) turn off, *Sl.* snub out; smother, suffocate, stifle, damp, choke.

3. quash, quell, suppress, squelch, crush, vanquish, overcome, subdue, put down, squelch; nip, nip in the bud, *Inf.* put the kibosh on; overthrow, overturn, overwhelm, subvert, topple, defeat, conquer.

quenchless, *adj.* **1.** insatiable, insatiate, unappeaseable, unquenchable, unsatisfied, unslaked, unsated; hungry, craving, famished; dry, athirst, thirsty, *Dial.* droughty, parched, arid.

2. greedy, desirous, cupidinous, avaricious, avid, esurient; predacious, rapacious, voracious, ravening.

3. inextinguishable, unsmotherable, ever-burning.

querulous, *adj.* **1.** complaining, caviling, faultfinding, carping, censorious, hypercritical; whining, fretful, murmuring, grumbling, lamenting, plaintive; finical, finicky, overparticular, fastidious, fussy, *Inf.* pernickety, overnice, meticulous, squeamish; captious, disputatious, quarrelsome, contentious, fractious; contrary, perverse, *Scot.* thrawn; antagonistic, ill-willed, hostile; unaccommodating, unkindly, unamiable, unfriendly; difficult, exacting, demanding.

2. peevish, ill-humored, touchy, testy, thin-skinned, waspish, petulant; cross, irascible, choleric, ill-tempered, splenetic; crabby, crabbed, cranky, grouchy, grumpy, cantankerous, crotchety, crusty; irritable, out of sorts, snappish, snappy, huffish, huffy, curt, short, impatient; piqued, in a pique, *Archaic.* in a pucker.

3. moody, sulky, dour, gloomy, dyspeptic, sullen, morose; discontented, dissatisfied; injured, wounded, sore, offended, indignant.

query, *n.* **1.** question, interrogatory, inquiry; interrogation, questioning, asking; issue, problem, poser, matter in dispute, question at issue, knotty point; request, demand, desideratum; quandary, dilemma, perplexity, confusion, ambiguity; investigation, inquest, exploration, probe.

2. doubt, uncertainty, hesitation, reservation, indecision, undecidedness, irresolution; incertitude, dubiety, dubiousness, lack of certainty; incredulity, skepticism.

—*v.* **3.** ask, inquire, question, ask questions; quiz, catechize, probe, examine, test; interrogate, *Inf.* grill, pump, cross-examine, *U.S.* give the third degree, interpellate; sound out, ferret out, fish out, nose out; analyze, look into, investigate, scrutinize; examine, survey, probe, fathom.

4. doubt, suspect, mistrust, distrust, have one's doubts, entertain doubts, be uncertain, not know what to think, disbelieve, misbelieve; harbor suspicions, consider questionable, hesitate to believe, *Inf.* smell a rat, *Inf.* take with a grain of salt.

5. dispute, challenge, raise objections, protest, controvert; take exception, object, demur.

quest, *n.* **1.** search, exploration, pursuit; expedition, excursion, journey, voyage; campaign, crusade, mission, pilgrimage, march; chase, hunt, *Brit.* chevy; trailing, pursuance, following, coursing, tracking; stalking, prowling, seeking, searching.

2. goal, aim, mark, objective; destination, end, target, bull's-eye; quarry, quintain, prey, game; intent, intention, purpose, point, end in view; ambition, desire, desideratum, nisus, striving.

—*v.* **3.** *Usu.* **quest for** *or* **after** search for, look for, hunt for, cast about for; delve for, fish for, angle for, leave no stone unturned; chase, run after, seek, stalk.

4. pursue, desire, seek, aspire to, push toward; be intent on, contend for, aim for, have in mind; strive for, try one's best for; crave, covet, beg for.

question, *n.* **1.** query, interrogatory, inquiry; leading question, loaded question.

2. problem, issue, poser, subject of investigation, bone of contention, quodlibet, query; puzzle, enigma, riddle, mystery, conundrum. See **query** (*def.* **1**).

3. doubt, uncertainty, hesitation, query. See **query** (*def.* **2**).

4. **beyond question** beyond doubt, beyond a shadow of a doubt, beyond dispute, past dispute, without doubt, no doubt, doubtless, doubtlessly, undoubtedly, indubitably; undeniably, indisputably, incontestably, incontrovertibly, irrefutably.

5. **call in** *or* **into question** dispute, challenge, entertain doubts, be uncertain, consider questionable, query. See **query** (*defs.* **4, 5**).

6. **in question** **a.** under consideration, under advisement, under examination; before the house, on the docket, on the agenda, on the table, on the floor. **b.** in dispute, at issue; questionable, problematic, debatable.

7. **out of the question** impossible, absurd, ridiculous, unheard of, preposterous; inconceivable, unimaginable, unthinkable, not to be thought of, not to be considered; prohibited, forbidden, unauthorized, unlicensed, banned, *Inf.* no go.

—*v.* **8.** ask, inquire, query; quiz, catechize, probe, examine. See **query** (*def.* **3**).

9. doubt, suspect, mistrust, distrust, have one's doubts, query. See **query** (*defs.* **4, 5**).

questionable, *adj.* **1.** debatable, controversial, polemical, in dispute; subject to discussion, moot, open to question, in question, problematic, problematical, hard to believe, open to doubt, doubtful, dubious, dubitable; uncertain, unsure, unsettled, undecided, borderline; tentative, undetermined, contingent, provisional; discussible, disputable, contestable, arguable, controvertible.

2. ambiguous, equivocal, *Logic.* amphibolous, paradoxical, duplicitous, ironic; two-edged, ambivalent, multi-leveled, figurative, suggestive, symbolic; misleading, left-handed, roundabout, circuitous, ambagious, hedging, weasel-worded; untrustworthy, unreliable, suspicious, *Inf.* fishy, *Inf.* shady.

3. obscure, abstruse, veiled, indefinite, vague, unintelligible, incomprehensible; puzzling, mystifying, mysterious, enigmatic, enigmatical, confusing, perplexing; cryptic, delphic, oracular.

questioner, *n.* **1.** interrogator, inquisitor, interlocutor; inquirer, querist, asker; examiner, investigator, inspector, scrutator, scrutinizer; catechist, quizzer.

2. disbeliever, doubting Thomas, unbeliever, misbeliever, *Turkish. giaour;* skeptic, nullifidian, Pyrrhonist; cynic, nihilist; heathen, pagan, infidel; freethinker, iconoclast, agnostic, atheist, latitudinarian; heretic, recusant; apostate, backslider; rationalist.

queue, *n.* **1.** braid, pigtail, ponytail, cue.

2. line of persons, file, row, cordon, rank, range; string, series, train, chain, concatenation; sequence, succession, progression, order.

—*v.* **3.** line up, get in line, wait in line, fall into line, fall in; arrange, order, group, rank.

quibble, *n.* **1.** equivocation, prevarication, evasion, dodge, elusion, avoidance; shuffling, shifting, hedging, beating around the bush; qualification, compromise, cop out; ambiguity, amphibology, vagueness, indefiniteness, indistinctness, indeterminateness; vacillation, tergiversation; double-speak, double talk, palter, weasel words, sophistry, deception, deceit, speciousness, chicane, chicanery, fraud.

2. pun, play upon words, word play, double-entendre; riddle, puzzle, enigma, conundrum.

3. criticism, objection, complaint, protest; bickering, caviling, *Inf.* nitpicking, pettifogging, splitting hairs, chopping logic, trifling.

—*v.* **4.** doubletalk, *Inf.* talk out both sides of one's mouth, palter; equivocate, prevaricate, *Sl.* waffle, fudge, lie; evade, dodge, elude, weasel out, shuffle; shift, hedge, beat around the bush; mislead, deceive, mystify.

5. cavil, *Inf.* nitpick, pettifog, belabor a point, split hairs, chop logic, trifle, beg the question; bicker, bandy words, moot, sift; squabble, haggle, *Sl.* hassle, *Scot.* argle-bargle.

quibbler, *n.* captious reasoner, caviler, hairsplitter, *Inf.* nitpicker, nag; equivocator, sphinx, Delphic oracle; double-talker; sophist, casuist, *Logic.* parologist; prevaricator, liar, palterer.

quibbling, *adj.* **1.** carping, caviling, pettifogging, hairsplitting, niggling, *Inf.* nitpicking; jesuitical, sophistical, casuistic, *Logic.* paralogistic; critical, hypercritical, captious, censorious, overcritical, faultfinding.

2. prevaricative, prevaricatory, deceptive, misleading; elusive, evasive, enigmatic, double-talking; ambiguous, amphibological, equivocative, equivocal, amphibolous, amphibolic.

quick, *adj.* **1.** prompt, immediate, sudden, instantaneous, expeditious; rapid, speedy, swift, fast, fleet; express, light-footed, nimble-footed, winged; flying, hurried, precipitate, headlong; hasty, cursory, summary, perfunctory.

2. brief, fleeting, momentary, transient, transitory, fugacious; evanescent, ephemeral, elusive, mercurial; temporary, passing, impermanent; perishable, caducous, deciduous.

3. impatient, irascible. See **quick-tempered.**

4. lively, keen, alert, active, vigorous, yare, spanking, energetic; spry, agile, sprightly; snappy, vivacious, animated, spirited, frisky; up-and-coming, wide-awake, go-ahead.

5. adroit, dexterous, deft, skillful, apt, expert, able, adept; facile, handy, nimble-fingered, neat-handed, clever.

6. acute, shrewd, astute. See **quick-witted.**

7. living, live, alive, animate, viable; existing, alive and kicking, breathing.

—*n.* **8.** living persons, the living.

9. vital part, most important part; crux, heart, essence, pith.

10. **cut to the quick** injure deeply, hurt the feelings of, crush, *Fig.* devastate.

quicken, *v.* **1.** accelerate, speed up, hasten, expedite, precipitate; propel, advance, impel, drive, dispatch; hustle, bestir, rush.

2. stimulate, stir up, rouse, incite, kindle, enkindle, fire; arouse, instigate, fan, foment, inspire, whet; press, push, spur, goad, urge, egg on.

3. animate, restore to life, revive, vivify, resuscitate; awaken, energize, vitalize, revitalize, enliven, strengthen; introduce new blood, infuse new life into, restore vigor to; refresh, sharpen, affect, move.

quickly, *adv.* **1.** swiftly, speedily, rapidly, fast; promptly, without delay, with dispatch, expeditiously; posthaste, apace, hotfoot, with celerity, hastily, helter-skelter, pell-mell, hurry-scurry, slapdash, head over heels; abruptly, briskly; hurriedly, headlong, precipitately, full-tilt, at full speed, at full gallop, tantivy, in full sail.

2. immediately, instantaneously, on the spur of the moment, on the spot, on the instant, straightway; presently, directly, forthwith, very soon, *Archaic.* anon, erelong; instantly, in a flash, in a wink, in a zip, in less than no time, in no time, in nothing flat, in no time flat, in short order, in two shakes of a lamb's tail, on the double, *Sl.* pronto; suddenly, overnight.

quickness, *n.* **1.** haste, speed, rapidity, swiftness, celerity, fleetness, velocity, fastness; suddenness, hastiness, abruptness, briskness, speediness; dispatch, promptness, punctuality; brevity, impermanence, transitoriness, transience, ephemerality, ephemeralness, evanescence.

2. animation, liveliness, agility, nimbleness, spryness; energy, vim, dash, élan, spirit, snap; alertness, keenness, alacrity.

quick-tempered, *adj.* impatient, irritable, irascible; high-strung, high-mettled, temperamental, excitable, impulsive, volatile; hot-blooded, hot-tempered, fiery, like tinder, like touchwood; testy, touchy, petulant, snappish, peppery, waspish, shrewish; choleric, splenetic, fretful; bad-tempered, cantankerous, captious, churlish, quarrelsome.

quick-witted, *adj.* acute, keen, shrewd, astute, *Scot. and North Eng.* gleg; intelligent, discerning, perspicacious, brainy, hard-headed, long-headed, far-sighted, penetrating, thoughtful; alert, wide-awake; brilliant, luminous, bright; smart, clever, foxy, ingenious, sharp-witted, sharp as a tack, *Sl.* on the ball, *Inf.* crack, *Sl.* crackerjack, *Inf.* whiz bang, *Brit. Sl.* whizzo; nimble-witted, witty, salty, jocose, jocular, facetious, humorous, waggish.

quiddity, *n.* **1.** haecceity, essence, inner essence, stuff, substance, *Metaphys.* hypostasis.

2. subtlety, subtle distinction, fine *or* thin line, quirk, quodlibet, *Archaic.* quillet; quibble, cavil, quip, trifling nicety.

quidnunc, *n.* gossip, gossipmonger, rumormonger, newsmonger, newshound, scandalmonger, *Sl.* yenta, *Archaic.* flibbertigibbet; meddler, intermeddler, busybody, pry, Paul pry, snoop, *Inf.* snooper, *Inf.* busy, *Inf.* nosy, *Inf.* nosybody, *Inf.* nosy Parker, *Inf.* kibitzer, *Australian Sl.* stickybeak; eavesdropper, Dumbo.

quid pro quo, *Latin.* substitution, exchange, interchange, interplay, one thing for another, something for something; trading, barter, *Inf.* swapping, *Chiefly U.S. Politics.* logrolling, *U.S. Sl.* pork barrel; persiflage, badinage, repartee; retaliation, reprisal, requital, lex talionis, talion, an eye for an eye and a tooth for a tooth; tit for tat, measure for measure, like for like, give and taken, blow for blow, a Roland for an Oliver; a game two can play, battledore and shuttlecock.

quiescence, *n.* **1.** rest, repose, ease; dormancy, hibernation, latency; pause, lull, break, halt, stop; suspension, suspense, standstill; cessation, discontinuance, inaction, inactivity; deferment, postponement, hesitation, hesitancy, delay, wait; interim, interval, intermission, intermittence, intermittency; status quo, waiting period, waiting game.

2. stagnation, inertia, lethargy; immobility, motionlessness, inertness.

3. tranquillity, peace, peacefulness, quiet, quietude, calm, calmness; stillness, silence, hush.

4. drowsiness, sleepiness, somnolence, sleep.

quiescent, *adj.* **1.** still, stock-still, motionless; stationary, inactive, unmoving, immovable, immobile; becalmed.

2. calm, quiet, reposeful, serene, placid, tranquil; unruffled, unagitated, undisturbed, untroubled; pacific, peaceful, restful; silent, noiseless, soundless, hushed.

3. stagnant, sluggish, lifeless, inert, passive, lethargic; torpid, torpescent, dull, sleepy, asleep, sleeping, comatose.

4. suspended, deferred, postponed, abeyant; waiting, hesitating, hesitant, delaying; pausing, resting, stopping, breaking, in abeyance.

quiet[1], *n.* **1.** silence, stillness, hush; soundlessness, noiselessness, quietness, quietude; tranquillity, serenity, placidity, imperturbation, calmness, calm; quiescence, peacefulness, peace; ease, repose, rest.

2. pause, lull, break, halt, standstill, stop; cessation, abatement, discontinuance, suspension, suspense, abeyance; deferment, postponement, delay, wait; interim, interval, intermission, intermittence, intermittency; dormancy, hibernation, latency; status quo, waiting period, waiting game; inaction, inactivity, stagnation, stagnancy; immobility, motionlessness.

3. uncommunicativeness, secretiveness.

quiet[2], *adj.* **1.** calm, passive, peaceable, mild, quiescent; tranquil, reposeful, halcyon, serene, sedate, placid, peaceful, pacific, restful; undisturbed, unruffled, untroubled, unagitated.

2. composed, temperate, sober, grave, unexcitable, unexcited, unperturbed, imperturbable, indifferent, cool, cool-headed; subdued, restrained, moderate, unobtrusive, unobtruding, undemonstrative; taciturn, uncommunicative, reserved, reticent; stoical, unimpassioned, dispassionate, philosophical.

3. still, stock-still, motionless, immovable, immobile; stationary, fixed, unmoved, unmoving, becalmed; stagnant, lifeless, inert; inactive, latent, dormant, dormient.

4. silent, noiseless, soundless, hushed; mute, speechless, mum, voiceless.

5. sleepy, sleeping, slumbering, dozing, somnolent, slumberous; sluggish, lethargic, torpid, torpescent; idle, slothful, lazy, indolent, supine, otiose; listless, languid, lackadaisical.

6. uncommunicated, unrevealed, undisclosed, secret, hushed up.

7. deferred, postponed, suspended, abeyant.

—*v.* **8.** silence, still, shush, hush, *Chiefly Brit.* quieten; lull, calm, tranquilize; pacify, appease, smooth, soothe, compose; repress, suppress, subdue, temper, put down, damp, dampen; chasten, restrain, sober; play down, tone down, *Inf.* soft-pedal; soften, allay, mitigate; ease, assuage, mollify, palliate.

9. moderate, blunt, dull, deaden; decrease, weaken, slacken, lessen, diminish, abate; settle, alleviate, relieve.

10. quell, quench, *Inf.* squelch; muzzle, stifle, muffle, mute; gag, throttle, choke, strangle, smother; stop, arrest, curb, check, stay, cut off, cut short, prevent, forestall, preclude; interrupt, cut in.

quietly, *adv.* **1.** silently, noiselessly, soundlessly; softly, inaudibly, gently; mutely, dumbly, voicelessly, speechlessly; secretly, clandestinely, uncommunicatively, privately, on the sly.

2. modestly, diffidently, humbly; unobtrusively, unostentatiously, unpretentiously, unassumingly; reservedly, demurely, constrainedly.

3. calmly, peaceably, peacefully, pacifically; mildly, meekly, serenely, unexcitedly, composedly, patiently, placidly, sedately, soberly, tranquilly; imperturbably, collectedly, impassively; dispassionately, stoically, indifferently, coolly.

quietude, *n.* **1.** tranquillity, serenity, placidity, calmness, calm; rest, repose, peacefulness, peace, ease; stillness, still, quiescence, quietness, quiet; silence, hush, soundlessness, noiselessness.

2. stagnation, inertia, inactivity, inaction.

3. composure, sang-froid, self-possession, poise, equanimity, self-control, steadiness; self-restraint, stoicism, staidness, sobriety; impassivity, dispassion, coolness, inexcitability.

4. resignation, submission, sufferance, long-suffering; tolerance, toleration, forbearance, longanimity.

quietus, *n.* **1.** finishing stroke, death stroke *or* blow, final blow, *Fr. coup de grâce;* knockout, knockout blow, *Sl.* sockdolager; end-all, ender, clincher, crusher, stopper, topper, windup; last straw, straw that broke the camel's back, *Inf.* kibosh.

2. death, demise, decease; end, finish, finis, finale; final curtain, end of the line, end of one's rope.

3. retirement, withdrawal, hibernation; inactivity, inertia, idleness, stagnation; calm, slumber, rest, repose, sleep, dormancy, quiescence.

quill, *n.* **1.** feather, plume, plumelet, pinion, *Ornithol.* plumule.

2. hollow spine, prick, ray, spine, *Anat., Zool.* spina, *Zool.* shaft, *Zool.* spicule.

3. pen, writing pen, stylus, nib.

quilt, *n.* coverlet, counterpane, bedspread, blanket, bedcover, bedquilt; crazy quilt, patchwork quilt; eiderdown, *U.S.* comforter, puff, *Brit. Inf.* downy, feather bed.

quintessence, *n.* **1.** quiddity, essence, essential part, essentiality, essentialness, suchness, *Metaphys.* hypostasis; extract, elixir; pith, heart, core, soul, marrow, backbone, kernel, gist, sum and substance, sum total; life, lifeblood, spirit, truth, purport, verity; tenor, import, drift, sense, significance.

2. perfect embodiment, perfection, cream, paragon, personification, exemplar, pattern, model, nonpareil, beau ideal, prototype, *Fr. crème de la crème.*

quintet, *n.* quintette, quintuplet, cinquain, fivesome, pentad; group of five singers *or* players, combo, jazz band, rock band.

quip, *n.* **1.** gibe, jape, *Inf.* wisecrack, *Inf.* crack, put-down, barb, *Sl.* zinger, squib, smart-aleck remark.

2. joke, jest, witticism, sally, mot, bon mot, ad-lib; gag, waggery, drollery, one-liner, wheeze, pleasantry; pun, double entendre; epigram, apothegm, gnome, aphorism; repartee, riposte, retort.

3. quibble, evasion, equivocation, sophism, ambiguity; cavil, criticism, niggling, nagging.

—*v.* **4.** gibe, *Inf.* wisecrack, *Inf.* crack wise, put down, slam, let [s.o.] have it, give [s.o.] a piece of one's mind; joke, jest, gag, kid, kid around; ad-lib, pun; quibble, equivocate, shilly-shally, split hairs, talk with forked tongue, talk out of both sides of one's mouth, mince words; pettifog, bicker, carp, cavil, object, niggle; complain, nag, mouth off.

quipster, *n.* giber, *Sl.* wisecracker, *Sl.* wisenheimer, smart aleck, *Sl.* kidder; joker, jester, wag, wit, Goodman Ace, humorist, gagman, gagger, gagster, gag writer; jokesmith; punster, epigrammist, aphorizer; quibbler, niggler, carper, caviler.

quirk, *n.* **1.** idiosyncrasy, idiocrasy, particularity, singularity, rarity; peculiarity, oddity, curiosity, warp; abnormality, aberration, aberrance, aberrancy, freak, anomaly, *Rare.* anomalism; irregularity, variation, deviation, discrepancy, exception; mannerism, habit, behavior, one's own way of doing things, affectation; characteristic, trait, feature, attribute, quality, property; quip, crotchet, whim, whimsy, notion, caprice, flight of fancy, vagary, humor; obsession, infatuation, fixation, mania, craze, passion, fetishism, blind devotion; pet idea, hobby-horse, pet peeve, ax to grind, bee in one's bonnet; monomania, fixed idea, *Fr. idée fixe, Sl.* hang-up.

2. subterfuge, evasion, elusion, avoidance, excuse; equivocation, equivoque, amphibology, ambiguity, double speak, double talk; song and dance, jive, hedging, beating around the bush; quibble, quiddity, subtlety, sophism, sophistry, elenchus, casuistry, *Both Disparaging.* Jesuitism, Jesuitry, *Both Logic.* paralogism, antilogism; shift, dodge, shuffle, fancy footwork, maneuver, move; trick, artifice, stratagem, wile, ruse, chicanery, chicane, sham, make-believe, deception; pretext, pretense, front, disguise, mask, veil.

3. twist, turn, curve, angle; flourish, twirl, coil, spiral, fancy stroke, convolution, contortion.

quisling, *n.* fifth columnist, collaborationist, subversive, conspirator; traitor, Judas, betrayer, renegade, turncoat, deserter.

quit, *v.* **1.** stop, discontinue, desist, *Archaic.* surcease, end; leave off, break off, pause, intermit, suspend, rest; abate, lessen, lull, quiet down, let up, come to a halt *or* standstill; (*of machinery*) *Sl.* conk out; (*all usu. of work*) *Inf.* call it a day, *Inf.* call it quits, *Inf.* shut up shop, *Sl.* knock off, *Brit.* pack it in.

2. depart from, leave, go away from, get away from; take off, flee, fly the coop, *Inf.* skip, take French leave, *Sl.* cut out, *Sl.* vamoose; evacuate, vacate, decamp, emigrate. See also **leave** (*defs.* **1, 2**).

3. abandon, relinquish, abnegate, let go, surrender, concede, yield, submit, *Sl.* throw in the towel *or* sponge; resign, abdicate, give up.

4. repudiate, abjure, reject, disown, renounce; renege, forswear, disavow, disclaim, recant; bail out, bow out, pull out of, *Inf.* back out of, back-pedal, *Inf.* back away from, back off on, *Inf.* cop out, *Sl.* chicken out; apostatize, defect.

5. discard, get rid of, toss off *or* aside, drop, *Inf.* ditch, *Inf.* chuck.

quite, *adv.* **1.** completely, wholly, entirely, totally, fully, altogether; in all, in all respects, with no exception, across the board, from A to Z, *Latin. in toto,* from tip to toe, from head to toe; utterly, thoroughly, positively, absolutely, out and out, perfectly; clean, right, sheer, stark, *Inf.* plumb.

2. actually, truly, really, in reality, in truth, *Archaic.* forsooth, in fact, indeed, *Archaic.* verily, veritably; certainly, assuredly.

3. considerably, noticeably, very, exceedingly, remarkably, surprisingly, excessively; enormously, hugely, vastly, highly.

quittance, *n.* **1.** reward, recompense, *Literary.* guerdon, requital, retribution, repayment; reparation, amends, redress, atonement, expiation; compensation, indemnification, satisfaction; payment, remuneration, reimbursement, defrayal, defrayment, remittance.

2. discharge, release, acquittance, clearance; settlement, liquidation, redemption; receipt, voucher.

quitter, *n.* *Informal.* **1.** defeatist, *Sl.* cop out.

2. shirker, slacker, loafer, malingerer, *Sl.* goldbrick, *Sl.* goof-off, *Brit.* skulker, *Brit. Sl.* scrimshanker; welsher, *Inf.* skip.

3. deserter, runaway, fugitive, truant; turncoat, renegade, backslider.

quiver, *v.* **1.** quaver, vibrate, tremble, shake, shudder, shiver, convulse, tremor, quake; palpitate, pitapat, beat, pulse, pulsate, throb, thump, pound; flicker, flutter, oscillate, fluctuate, vacillate, alternate; waver, wobble, waggle, totter, teeter, teeter-totter; wave *or* sway to and fro, flap, flop, toss, swish, wag, dangle; ripple, wave, undulate, purl; jerk, move, twitch, vellicate, jump, start.

—*n.* **2.** quivering, quaver, quavering, vibration, vibrating, tremble, trembling, shake, shaking; shudder, shuddering, shiver, shivering, tremor, quake, quaking; palpitation, pitapat, beating, pulsing, pulsation, throbbing, thumping, pounding; flicker, flickering, flutter, fluttering, osillation, fluctuation, vacillation, alternation; waver, wavering, wobbling, tottering, teetering, flapping, swaying to and fro, flopping, tossing, swishing, wagging, dangling; ripple, rippling, waving, undulation, purling; jerk, jerking, twitch, twitching, vellication, jump, start.

quivering, *adj.* quivery, quavering, quavery, quaverous, vibrating, trembling, trembly, tremulous, tremulant, shaking, shaky; quaking, quaky, shuddering, shuddery, shivering, shivery; flickering, flickery, fluttering, fluttery, oscillating, oscillatory, vacillating, vacillant, vacillatory, wavering; fluctuating, fluctuant, moving, rippling, ripply, waving, wavy, undulating, undulant, undular, undulatory.

quixotic, *adj.* impractical, impracticable, unrealistic, fanciful, notional; fantastic, visionary, chimerical, rhapsodical, romantic, ideal, utopian; imaginary, whimsical, dreamy, in the clouds; useless, inutile, inefficacious, ineffective, inoperative, unserviceable; starry-eyed, wild, absurd, mad, madcap, crackpot, preposterous, ridiculous; impulsive, rash, temerarious, daredevil, foolhardy, reckless, headlong, precipitate; adventurous, chivalrous, gallant, courageous, doughty; valorous, brave, valiant, heroic.

quixotism, *n.* **1.** impracticability, unrealisticness, fancifulness, romanticism; imagination, invention, whimsy; futility, uselessness, ineffectiveness; knight-errantry, chivalrousness, gallantry, courage, valor; foolhardiness, impulsiveness, rashness, madness, delirium.

2. caprice, whim, quirk, vagary, fancy, *Archaic.* maggot, crotchet, notion; fantasy, illusion, vision, chimera, hallucination; dream, daydream, castle in the air, castle in Spain, *Inf.* pipe dream, reverie, flight of fancy; romance, rhapsody, ideal, Utopia.

quiz, *v.* **1.** test, examine, check up on; catechize, inquisition, shoot questions at [s.o.], pick [s.o.'s] brains.

2. interrogate, question, put to the question, demand an answer; pump, third-degree, put [s.o.] through the third degree, put [s.o.] through the wringer, cross-examine, cross-question, *Inf.* grill, *Inf.* put [s.o.] on the grill, *Inf.* roast, *Inf.* put the pressure on, *Sl.* go *or* work over, *Sl.* put the screws to.

—n. **3.** test, checkup, catechism, set of questions, examination, *Inf.* exam, review; essay test, multiple choice, *Inf.* multiple guess, fill in the blanks, *Inf.* take-home test.

4. catechizing, questioning, querying, quizzing; interrogation, investigation, interpellation, inquisition; cross-examination, third degree, pumping, *Inf.* grilling, *Sl.* the grill.

5. gag, prank, practical joke, joke, jest, jape, caper, trick, hoax, *Inf.* dido, *Sl.* monkeyshine.

quizzical, *adj.* **1.** odd, peculiar, curious, queer, offbeat, cranky, *Inf.* funny; eccentric, quaint, droll, comical, laughable, *Inf.* quirky, *Sl.* squirrely, *Sl.* buggy; fanciful, whimsical, waggish, capricious, notional, *Archaic.* maggoty, crotchety, *Chiefly Brit.* barmy, *Sl.* balmy; deviate, deviant, aberrant, anomalous, irregular, incongruous; strange, weird, bizarre, freakish, *Sl.* freaky, *Sl.* rum, *Sl.* far-out; ridiculous, ludicrous, absurd, outlandish, preposterous; nondescript, amorphous, indescribable, unclassifiable.

2. questioning, puzzled, perplexed, mystified; bewildered, baffled, muddled; confused, confounded, dumfounded; lost, at a loss, in a fog.

3. derisive, derisory, ridiculing, mocking, jeering; insulting, contumelious, taunting, flouting, teasing; sarcastic, sardonic, satirical, parodistic.

quota, *n.* part, proportion, share, portion, apportionment, quantity, quantum; allotment, lot, dole, parcel, percentage, allowance, ration, allocation; quantity required, assignment, measure, goal, product, count, total, tally, aggregate.

quotation, *n.* **1.** quote, citation, reference, allusion, epigraph, passage, line, excerption, excerpt, extract, selection; exemplification, instance, illustration, example, case, case in point, particular, particular instance; repetition, duplication.

2. quoted price, price, bid price, asking price, market price, fixed price, stated value, book value, current *or* going price; rate, charge, cost, expense, worth; valuation, appraisement, estimate, estimation.

quote, *v.* **1.** cite, call to mind, instance, adduce, cite a particular *or* particulars, give an example, cite chapter and verse; repeat, recite, retell, run over, say again, reproduce, duplicate, repeat word for word *or* verbatim; excerpt, extract, select a passage, echo, re-echo, chorus, reflect, parrot; recall, remember, recollect, call to mind, repeat from memory, repeat by heart; proclaim, state.

2. refer to, bring forward, allude to, make reference to, document, substantiate, evidence, exemplify, attest, detail, circumstantiate, establish, note.

3. price, value, evaluate, valuate, set *or* fix a price on, place a value on; demand, charge.

—n. **4.** See **quotation** (*defs.* **1, 2**).

quotidian, *adj.* **1.** daily, diurnal, every day, nightly, once-a-day, one-a-day; regular, habitual, rhythmic, cyclic, periodic, constant.

2. everyday, ordinary, commonplace, run-of-the-mill, day-to-day, workaday; routine, customary, usual, common, wonted.

R

rabbit, *n.* cottontail, cony, *Inf.* bunny, *Inf.* bunny rabbit; jack rabbit, hare, leveret; Peter Rabbit, Peter Cottontail, Easter bunny.

rabble, *n.* **1.** crowd, mob, throng; horde; *Inf.* mob scene, rout, surge.

2. the rabble the common people, commonalty, the masses, the hoi polloi, proletariat, rank and file, commoners, the lower classes, peasantry; trash, riffraff, canaille, doggery, *Inf.* the great unwashed, scum, ragtag and bobtail, flotsam and jetsam, dregs of society, outcasts, vermin.

rabble-rouser, *n.* demagogue, soap-box orator, agitator; inciter, instigator, provoker, fomenter, agitprop, *Sl.* labor baiter, *Fr. agent provocateur;* firebrand, incendiary, rebel, revolutionary, insurgent, insurrectionist, radical; troublemaker, *Sl.* hell-raiser, mischief-maker, stormy petrel, ringleader.

rabid, *adj.* **1.** extreme, extremist, fanatical, perfervid, overzealous, overenthusiastic; unreasonable, irrational.

2. raging, raving, frenzied, frenetic, frantic, wild-eyed, blue in the face; furious, violent, wild, infuriate, maniacal, *Inf.* hog-wild, *Inf.* raving mad, *Inf.* stark raving mad; hysterical, distracted, carried away, beside oneself, like one possessed; amuck, berserk.

3. mad, insane, deranged; *Pathol.* hydrophobic, foaming *or* frothing at the mouth.

race[1], *n.* **1.** footrace, sprint, dash, relay, cross-country, marathon; heat, lap; horse race, steeplechase, handicap; road race, drag race, drag, Grand Prix; road rally *or* rally; soapbox derby; (*motorcycling*) motocross *or* moto-x, (*motorcycling*) enduro; regatta.

2. races derby, sweepstakes; the horses, the ponies, the trotters, the sulkies; the dogs.

3. contest, competition, contention.

4. progress, progression, advance, advancement, onward movement *or* progression.

5. channel, waterway, watercourse, course, chute, flume, sluice, spillway.

6. flow, flux, efflux, outpour, outflow; rush, surge, gush; flood, torrent, river; millstream, millrace, *Chiefly Brit.* raceway.

—*v.* **7.** run, dash, dart, bolt, tear, bowl along, cover ground, make strides; sprint, fly, flit, whiz, whisk; zoom, zip, career, rip, scour, scud, scorch, burn up the road, outstrip the wind, race like the wind, go *or* be off like a shot, *Chiefly Brit.* hare, *Inf.* clip, *Inf.* barrel, *Inf.* pour it on.

8. haste, make haste, speed, hustle, hurry, post, rush, scramble, step lively, double-time, *Inf.* hump it; *All Sl.* get the lead out, step on it, hop on it, get a move on, stir one's stumps.

race[2], *n.* **1.** nation, people, folk; tribe, clan, family.

2. line, bloodline, descent, blood, strain, stirps, breed, extraction; ancestry, parentage, paternity; house.

3. man, mankind, humankind, family of man, humanity, human race, Homo sapiens.

4. class, species, genus; kind, sort, ilk, variety, *Inf.* lot.

racer, *n.* **1.** race horse, mudder, plate horse, quarter horse, trotter, *Inf.* pony, *Horse Racing Sl.* bangtail; greyhound; racing car, stock car, formula-I, dragster, hot rod; runner, sprinter, miler, long-distance runner, cross-country runner, harrier.

2. speeder, flier; *All Inf.* hummer, sizzler, hustler, hell-driver, *Inf.* scorcher, speed demon, speed merchant.

racetrack, *n.* racecourse, raceway, course, oval, (*in ancient Greece and Rome*) hippodrome, (*in Ancient Rome*) circus; the turf, the track; autodrome, speedway, drag strip.

raciness, *n.* (*all of speech or writing*) piquancy, pungency, spiciness, saltiness, race; liveliness, spiritedness, spirit, verve, vigorousness, briskness; suggestiveness, lewdness, indelicacy, ribaldry, *Archaic.* bawdry; earthiness, rawness, coarseness, grossness, crudeness.

racism, *n.* racialism, racial discrimination, discrimination, apartheid, Jim Crowism, white supremacy *or* power; intolerance, bigotry, prejudice, narrow-mindedness, closed-mindedness; anti-Semitism.

racist, *n.* **1.** bigot, intolerant, illiberal, *Inf.* little person, *Sl.* Archie Bunker; anti-Semite.

—*adj.* **2.** prejudiced, bigoted, intolerant, illiberal, closed-minded; anti-Semitic.

rack, *n.* **1.** frame, framing, framework, trestle, arbot, scaffolding, structure; stretcher, form, *Both Textiles.* drawing frame, perch; hanger, clothes *or* hat tree *or* rack, bar, pole, dowel; stand, trivet, grate, grating, holder; crib, cradle, bed, *Naut.* chock; shelf, ledge, counter, row.

2. torture, infliction, pain, hurt, wound, sting, pang; torment, persecution, crucifixion, harassment; affliction, plague, adversity, scourge, curse, visitation, thorn in one's side *or* flesh; agony, misery, suffering, wretchedness, martyrdom; anguish, distress, woe, harrowment, tribulation, trouble, hell.

—*v.* **3.** torture, agonize, excruciate, martyr, put [s.o.] on the rack; pain, hurt, scathe, abuse, maltreat, beat, *Sl.* work [s.o.] over, *Sl.* give [s.o.] the works, *Archaic.* belabor; torment, persecute, crucify, afflict, plague, beleaguer, harass; anguish, distress, grieve, sorrow, rend, tear [s.o.] up, lacerate, put [s.o.] through the wringer; harrow, upset, disturb, toss, agitate, derange, convulse, shake up, rattle, disquiet, discomfit; worry, trouble, *Scot.* fash.

4. wring, wrest, extort, exact; pressure, press, push, exert, work; (*all of one's brains*) search *or* sort through, ransack, beat *or* cudge; think hard, exhaust.

5. strain, stretch, draw, *Archaic.* extenuate; wrench, pull, tear, lacerate, disjoint, throw out; sprain, twist, turn.

racket, *n.* **1.** noise, din, uproar, clamor, hubbub; vociferation, vociferousness, babel, shouting, whooping, bellowing, yelling, roaring, hooting, *Inf.* hollering, squalling, howling, crying, bawling, wailing, shrieking, screeching, shrilling, caterwauling; babbling, chattering, jabbering; hullabaloo, ballyhoo, outcry, bawl, hue and cry, fuss; clangor, clatter, rattle, rattling around, brattle, clanking, jangling, *Inf.* clunking.

2. jollity, jollification, hilarity, frolic, fun, fun and games, gaiety, merriment, conviviality, merrymaking, *Inf.* goings on, *Inf.* whoopee, *Brit. Inf.* mafficking, *Brit.* holiday-making; festivities, partying, revelry, revelment, revels, carousal, wassail, saturnalia, orgy, charivari, *Inf.* shivaree, *Inf.* shindig, *Inf.* do, *Sl.* hot time, *Sl.* bash, *Sl.* wing-ding, *Sl.* blowout; commotion, bedlam, pandemonium, bluster, rumpus, hurly-burly, rowdiness, *Inf.* ruckus; fracas, brawl, donnybrook, free-for-all, beer garden, row, riot, turbulence, turmoil, tumult, disturbance, stir.

3. organized crime, illegal activity, the rackets, gangster *or* mob activities; smuggling, bootlegging, extortion, blackmail, embezzlement, graft, gambling, usury, theft, stealing; trick, scheme, machination, swindling, confidence game, *Sl.* con game, *Brit.* confidence trick, *Inf.* flimflamming.

racketeer, *n.* **1.** gangster, mobster, mafioso, *Sl.* gunsel; desperado, thug, terrorist; tough, *Inf.* toughie, mugger, ruffian, rowdy, hoodlum, *Sl.* hood, *Inf.* goon, hooligan, *Inf.* roughneck, *Inf.* baddy, *Sl.* bad actor, *Sl.* mug, *Australian Sl.* larrikin.

2. extortionist, extortioner, blackmailer, usurer, loan shark, *Sl.* bleeder; smuggler, runner, bootlegger, contrabandist, white slaver; forger, counterfeiter, *Fr. faux-monnayeur, Brit. Inf.* coiner; fence.

3. swindler, fleecer, bilker, rook, trickster, sharper, *Inf.* hawk, card-sharper, bunko steersman, blackleg; confidence man, con artist, flimflam artist, highbinder, thimblerigger, *Brit. Sl.* magsman, *Australian.* spieler; defaulter, *Sl.* welsher; embezzler, peculator, *Law.* defalcator.

4. bandit, hold-up man, *Sl.* stick-up man, armed robber; robber, thief, *Inf.* crook, stealer; criminal, felon, convict, *Sl.* jailbird, parolee, ex-convict, *Inf.* ex-con; recidivist, *Inf.* chronic crook.

5. villain, blackguard, miscreant, malefactor, evildoer, *Inf.* bad guy, *Inf.* no-good.

rackety, *adj.* **1.** noisy, loud, deafening, blatant, blaring, blasting; uproarious, clamorous, clamoring, vociferous, loud-mouthed; thunderous, blustery, blusterous, stentorian, stentorous; clangorous, clattering, rattling, clanking, jangling, *Inf.* clunking; shrill, sharp, piercing, ear-piercing, earsplitting, stridulous, stridulant, stridulatory, strident, harsh, harsh-sounding, cacophonous, discordant, dissonant.

2. hilarious, fun-loving, high-spirited, partying, convivial, jolly, gay, merry; reveling, carousing, winebibbing, saturnalian, drunken, wild, orgiastic; rowdy, raucous, roisterous, boisterous, obstreperous; brawling, unruly, uncontrollable, out of control, riotous, turbulent, pandemonian, pandemonic, chaotic.

racking, *adj.* torturous, torturesome, excruciating, agonizing, scathing; severe, sharp, acute, piercing, poignant; insufferable, unbearable, unendurable, extreme, terrific; painful, abusive, harmful, hurtful, injurious; backbreaking, killing, murderous, laborious, toilsome, operose, exacting, tough, hard; hellish, awful, terrible, horrible, dreadful, bad; anguishing, distressing, distressful, afflictive, harrowing; worrisome, troublesome, oppressive, burdensome, wearing; distressing, disturbing, upsetting, disquieting, discomfiting.

raconteur, *n.* storyteller, anecdotist, relator, narrator, Scheherazade; teller of tales, romancer, spinner of yarns.

racy, *adj.* **1.** suggestive, risqué, off-color, ribald, bawdy; lewd, obscene, pornographic, *Sl.* porno *or* porny, erotic; immodest, indecent, shameless, *Inf.* blue; vulgar, filthy, dirty, smutty, *Sl.* raunchy; gross, coarse, crude, rude, indelicate, tactless.

2. vigorous, lively, alive, full of life, *Inf.* peppy, *Inf.* full of pep, full of vim and vigor, *U.S. Inf.* chipper, sprightly, spry; energetic, dynamic, spirited, mettlesome; animated, vivacious, enthusiastic, buoyant, bouncy.

3. piquant, pungent, strong, forceful, poignant; piercing, biting, sharp, trenchant, keen; stimulating, interesting, intriguing, fascinating, captivating; entertaining, electric, exciting, challenging, galvanizing.

4. flavorful, flavorous, good, tasty, savory; well-seasoned, spicy, tart, tangy, zesty, zestful, snappy, with a kick *or* bite; hot, acid, peppery, curried, spiced *or* highly spiced.

radial, *adj.* spokewise, centrifugal, fanlike, outspread, spread apart, divergent, divaricate, branching, branched.

radiance, *n.* **1.** radiancy, resplendence, splendor, refulgence, brilliance; brightness, light, luminosity, luminance, luminousness, illumination; glow, effulgence, gleam, glare, dazzle; sparkle, luster, glitter, *Archaic.* glister, glisten, sparkle, coruscation, lambency, shimmer.

2. sunniness, warmth, cheeriness, blitheness, gladness, joyfulness, light-heartedness, gaiety.

radiant, *adj.* **1.** shining, bright, sunny, sunshiny; illuminated, alight, lit, lighted; irradiant, lambent, resplendent, brilliant, beaming, beamy; dazzling, vivid, intense, ablaze, aflame, afire; fulgent, effulgent, refulgent; splendid, splendrous, gorgeous, rich, superb, magnificent; lustrous, lucid, lucent, *Rare.* relucent; glowing, aglow, luminous, luminescent, luminiferous, incandescent, phosphorescent; shiny, glossy, gleaming, agleam, glaring; sheenful, sheeny, nitid, polished, burnished; sparkling, scintillating, scintillant, coruscating, twinkling, shimmering; glimmering, aglimmer, glistening, aglisten, *Archaic.* glistering, aglint, glittering, aglitter, rutilant, fulgid.

2. happy, blissful, beatific, pleased, delighted, *Inf.* tickled pink; blithe, blithesome, merry, gay, gleeful; glad, gladsome, joyful, joyous, hopeful, sunny, animated; sparkling, bubbling, bubbly, effervescent; charming, winsome, riant, laughing, smiling, happy as a lark, in good *or* high spirits; buoyant, cheerful, cheery, sprightly, pert, jaunty; airy, light-hearted, jolly, jovial, convivial; mirthful, playful, jocose, frolicsome, jocund, sportive, zestful; excited, enthusiastic, enthused, exhilarated, rhapsodic, rhapsodistic; ecstatic, jubilant, overjoyed, elated, exultant, in seventh heaven; rapturous, enrapt, enraptured, enchanted, entranced, transported, intoxicated.

radiate, *v.* **1.** spoke out, send out, branch out, divaricate, diverge, spread out.

2. irradiate, disseminate, disperse, diffuse, scatter, circulate.

3. glow, beam, scintillate, twinkle, glitter, sparkle, light up.

radical, *adj.* **1.** fundamental, rudimentary, constitutional, basic, basal, basilar, elementary, elemental, primary; main, principal, cardinal; vital, essential, necessary, requisite; supporting, substratal, substrative, underlying; uncompounded, simple, primitive.

2. complete, total, entire, absolute, unmitigated, unqualified, whole, universal, definitive, unabridged, full, plenary, consummate, sheer, utter, perfect, positive, downright, out-and-out; comprehensive, exhaustive, thorough, thoroughgoing, sweeping, solid, all-inclusive, all-embracing; extreme, excessive, immoderate, inordinate, undue, exorbitant, unreasonable, extravagant, intemperate; drastic, severe, stringent, strict, intransigent, exacting; ultra, advanced, overzealous, fanatical, rabid, hysterical, frantic, frenzied, frenetic, raving, possessed.

3. revolutionary, rebellious, rebel, Jacobinic, Jacobinical, insurgent, insurrectionary, seditious, iconoclastic, underground, freethinking, avant-garde, nonconformist, anarchistic, nihilistic; leftist, leftwing, red, pink, *Derog.* pinko, Bolshivistic, Communistic, commie.

4. innate, inherent, intrinsic, indigenous, ingenerate, immanent, indwelling, instinctive, inner, subsistent, deep-seated, ingrained, rooted, implanted, native, natural, organic; inherited, hereditary, inbred, inborn, congenital, connate.

—*n.* **5.** extremist, fanatic, immoderate, ultra, ultraist, zealot, raver, radical reformer, sans-culotte, *Politics.* Jacobin; nihilist, anarchist; avant-gardist, freethinker; rebel, revolutionary, revolutionist, revolter, insurgent, mutineer, firebrand, rioter, iconoclast, fifth columnist, *U.S. Politics.* weatherman, yippie; leftist, leftwinger, leftwing extremist, *Inf.* Wobbly, Communist, Bolshevik, Red, commie, *U.S. Sl.* pink, *U.S. Sl. Derog.* pinko.

radically, *adv.* **1.** fundamentally, rudimentarily, constitutionally, basically, elementarily, elementally, primarily; mainly, principally, chiefly; vitally, essentially, necessarily.

2. completely, totally, entirely, absolutely, without doubt, wholly, consummately, utterly, perfectly, positively, extremely, in the extreme, most, immeasurably, incalculably, indefinitely, infinitely, beyond compare *or* comparison, beyond measure; thoroughly, comprehensively, solidly, unconditionally, unequivocally, downright, dead; excessively, immoderately, inordinately, unduly, exorbitantly, unreasonably, extravagantly, intemperately, beyond all bounds.

3. innately, inherently, intrinsically, indigenously, immanently, instinctively, natively, naturally, organically; congenitally, hereditarily, connately.

radio, *n.* **1.** radiotelegraph, radiotelephone; radio set, receiver, console, cabinet, old stand-up radio, *Jocular.* Marconi, Stromberg-Carlson, *Chiefly Brit.* wireless; crystal set; transistor, portable *or* portable radio, pocket radio; AM-FM radio, CB *or* citizens band radio, police radio, shortwave radio, car radio, clock radio.

—*v.* **2.** radiocast, broadcast, transmit, air, put on the air, shortwave, beam.

radiograph, *n.* x-ray, x-ray photograph, roentgenogram, skiagraph, negative, picture; atinogram.

raffish, *adj.* **1.** vulgar, tasteless, crude, uncouth, gross, coarse, boorish, loutish; unrefined, ill-bred, unmannerly, uncultured, uncultivated, inelegant; tawdry, gaudy, showy, cheap, flashy, garish, meretricious; trashy, common, ignoble, base.

2. disreputable, discreditable, dishonorable, disgraceful; rakish, dissolute, rakehell, dissipated, degenerate; decadent, debauched, depraved, amoral, immoral; profligate, wanton, abandoned, intemperate; ribald, indecent, obscene, scatological, with one's mind in the sewer, foul-mouthed, dirty-mouthed, sewer-mouthed; libertine, licentious, lewd, lecherous, lascivious; libidinous, goatish, like an old goat, randy, *Sl.* horny.

raffle, *n.* lottery, drawing, draw, sweepstake, *Sl.* sweep; game of chance.

raft[1], *n.* **1.** floating platform, float, kelek, pontoon, *Naut.* catamaran.

2. life raft, rowboat.

raft[2], *n.* *Informal.* lot, heap, pile, stack, batch, ton.

rafter, *n.* beam, timber, girder; joist, crossbeam, *Archit.* trave, lintel; support, cantilever.

rag[1], *n.* **1. rags** tattered clothing, tatters, old clothes, castoffs, hand-me-downs, odds and ends.

2. tatter, shred, scrap, fragment, remnant, bit, piece.

rag[2], *v.* *Informal.* **1.** scold, chide, tongue-lash, rate, upbraid, *Sl.* chew out, *Inf.* dress down, *Inf.* jump on; castigate, chastise, berate, censure, reproach, rebuke, reprove, reprimand, reprobate, blame; denounce, take to task, call to account, call down, lecture; admonish, caution, warn, forewarn, put on one's guard.

2. tease, taunt, *Inf.* kid, badinage, chaff, pull [s.o.'s] leg, *Inf.* josh, *Inf.* rib, *Inf.* fun, *Sl.* put [s.o.] on, *Sl.* jive; ridicule, twit, make fun of, poke fun at, scoff at, gibe at, mock, mimic, make game of, sport; trifle with, toy with, play with, make light of; harry, harass, pester, heckle, badger, beset, plague, bother, annoy, irritate; bait, torment, persecute, bully, bullyrag, abuse.

ragamuffin, *n.* **1.** tatterdemalion, scarecrow; beggar, panhandler, guttersnipe; hobo, tramp, vagrant, beachcomber, vagabond, derelict; *Inf.* bum, *Sl.* vag, *Sl.* bo, *Sl.* stiff, *Sl.* bindle stiff, *Sl.* canvasback.

2. orphan, waif, street Arab, gutter urchin, gamin, mudlark.

rage, *n.* **1.** fury, frenzy, madness, hysterics, violence, ferocity, towering *or* burning *or* blind rage; wrath, vials of wrath, passion, fever heat, hot blood; anger, ire, dudgeon, high dudgeon, *Scot.* birse, *Inf.* Irish, *Inf.* dander.

2. fit, tantrum, spasm, paroxysm, seizure, spasm, convulsion, *Chiefly Brit.* wax, *Brit. Inf.* paddywhack, *Sl.* wing-ding; tear, rampage, mad.

3. turbulence, tumult, pandemonium, uproar, chaos, furor, fire and fury, storm, storm and stress.

4. (*all of a violent or uncontrollable nature*) desire, passion; obsession, fixation, *Sl.* hang-up; fascination, infatuation, *Sl.* bug; lust, *Sl.* hots, *Sl.* hot pants.

5. ardor, zeal, zealousness; vehemence, fanaticism; eagerness, enthusiasm, ebullition.

6. fad, craze, mania; vogue, fashion, mode, style; *Sl.* the thing, *Sl.* latest *or* newest thing, *Inf.* last word, *Fr.* *dernier cri.*

—*v.* **7.** rant, rave, rant and rave, roar, bellow, storm, fulminate; bluster, splutter; seethe, sizzle, smolder, boil, stew, simmer, fume, stir, *Inf.* do a slow burn, *Inf.* steam *or* steam up, *Sl.* work oneself up into a sweat *or* lather *or* stew.

8. rampage, tear, go on a rampage *or* tear, run amuck, run wild, run riot, wreak havoc, go berserk, *Sl.* go nuts.

9. explode, *Sl.* blow up, *Sl.* blow one's cool, *Sl.* blow a gasket *or* fuse, *Sl.* blow one's top *or* stack, *Sl.* flip, *Sl.* flip one's wig *or* lid, *Sl.* freak *or* freak out; fly into a passion, *Inf.* fly off the handle, go into hysterics, have a tantrum, have a fit, *Inf.* have a conniption *or* conniption fit, *Inf.* have a cat fit, *Inf.* hit the ceiling *or* roof, *Sl.* have a hemorrhage.

ragged, *adj.* **1.** shabby, seedy, tacky; slovenly, sloppy, unkempt, untidy, dowdy, frumpish, frumpy; scraggly, shaggy; needy, lacking, down-and-out, indigent, poor, impoverished, poverty-stricken.

2. tattered, shredded, worn to shreds *or* pieces, scrappy, *Scot.* duddy; rent, torn, ripped, split out at the seams; worn, frayed, *Inf.* frazzled, raveled, unraveled, threadbare, the worse for wear.

3. jagged, barbed, spurred, spinous, spiny, spiniferous, spinigerous, thorny, bristly, spiculate, pointy, snaggy, studded; notched, notchy, serrated, serrate, serriform, saw-toothed, toothed; craggy, rugged, ridged, rugose, scraggy, nicked, chipped, uneven, irregular.

4. rough, abrasive, scratchy, raspish, grating, scraping, chafing; corroded, fretted, gnawed *or* eaten away, erose, eroded.

5. deteriorated, dilapidated, degenerate, degenerated, degraded, run-down; neglected, abandoned, desolate, forgotten; abused, battered, broken, *Inf.* beat-up.

6. faulty, defective, imperfect, marginal, substandard, inferior; unpolished, unfinished.

7. harsh, grating, strident, stridulous, stridulant, raucous; rasping, stertorous, gritting, griding, scraping, scratchy, scratching; hoarse, croaky, croaking, squawky; screeching, creaky, creaking, screaky, screaking, rusty; clanking, jangling, jarring, twangy, twanging; discordant, dissonant, absonant, cacophonous, disharmonious, unmelodic, unmusical.

raging, *adj.* **1.** enraged, wrathful, wroth, irate, ireful, very angry; incensed, fuming, infuriated, *Rare.* infuriate, furious; inflamed, flaming, flaring, flared up, heated, red-hot, white-hot; distraught, overwrought, upset, feverish, hysterical, irrational; violent, unrestrained, uncontrollable; ranting, raving, storming, foaming at the mouth, rabid, fanatical, frenzied; frantic, crazed, *Pathol.* delirious, mad, *Inf.* wild, out of one's mind, beside oneself.

2. violent, strong, savage, turbulent, wild, rough; roaring, howling, wailing, thundering; stormy, tempestuous, squally, squallish; blustering, blustery, windy, gusty, blowing; ebullient, boiling, foaming, seething.

ragpicker, *n.* ragman; scavenger, garbage collector, trash man, street cleaner; *Chiefly Brit.* rag-and-bone man, junk peddler, rag dealer.

raid, *n.* **1.** attack, assault, onset, onslaught; incursion, invasion, inroad, razzia, irruption; intrusion, encroachment, trespass, (*by police*) *Sl.* bust; foray, charge, thrust, sortie, sally; expedition, operation, encounter, offensive, skirmish.

2. sack, sacking, pillage, plundering, rapine, depredation, spoliation, despoliation, despoilment, *Obs.* direption; ravaging, harrying, marauding, foraging, looting; ravishment, seizure, grab, rape.

—*v.* **3.** assault, attack, assail, rush, storm; fall upon, set upon, pounce upon, strike at, march upon, swoop down upon, descend upon, (*by police*) *Sl.* bust.

4. invade, intrude, encroach, trespass; (*usu. of cattle*) rustle, *Inf.* poach, deerjack.

5. plunder, pillage, loot, forage, sack, rifle, ransack, gut, strip; despoil, desolate, devastate, lay waste, wreak havoc upon.

raider, *n.* **1.** pillager, plunderer, marauder, despoiler, depredator; ransacker, sacker, looter, rifler, forager; invader, attacker, assaulter, assailant.

2. pirate, rover, viking, corsair, buccaneer, privateer; freebooter, rapparee, (*in the Scottish Highlands*) cateran; kidnapper, abductor, rustler, hijacker; predator.

3. highwayman, footpad, *Sl.* yegg *or* yeggman, bandit, *Sp. bandolero, Southwest U.S.* ladrone, *Australian.* bushranger, brigand, picaroon, desperado, outlaw.

4. robber, burglar, thief, stealer, *Inf.* crook.

rail[1], *n.* **1.** horizontal bar, log rail; train *or* railroad track, third rail.

2. railing, balusters, banister, fence. See **railing**.

rail[2], *v.* *Often* **rail at** *or* **against** denounce, inveigh against, declaim against, attack, assail; criticize, condemn, denunciate, arraign, animadvert on *or* upon, reprobate, remonstrate, proscribe; decry, censure, disapprove, belittle, disparage, discredit, depreciate.

railing, *n.* balusters, *Archaic.* balustrade, banister; fence, palisade, paling, barrier; rails, pales, stakes.

raillery, *n.* **1.** banter, badinage, persiflage, pleasantry, frivolity, *Sl.* put-on; joking, jesting, *Inf.* kidding, japing, teasing, *Inf.* ragging; ridicule, satirization, mockery, parody; mimicry, aping, parroting, impersonation.

2. joke, jest, jape, quip, witticism; retort, smart reply *or* answer, *Sl.* comeback.

3. denunciation, diatribe, attack, criticism, condemnation, censure, disapproval, disparagement, depreciation.

railroad, *n.* **1.** track *or* tracks, train tracks, rails, *Railroads.* switchback.

2. rail, line, railway, tramway; funicular *or* funicular railway, cable railway, elevated railroad, el; *Fr. chemin de fer, Sp. ferrocarril, It. ferrovia, Ger. Eisenbahn;* electric railroad, subway, *Brit.* tube, *Chiefly Brit.* underground, metro; rolling stock, cars, boxcars, freight cars, passenger cars, locomotives, engines, *Inf.* iron horse; railroad company, *U.S.* Amtrak *or* National Railroad Passenger Corporation.

—*v.* **3.** (*all via railroad*) transport, ship, convey, carry, take, send, deliver.

4. push through, send through, rush, expedite; speed up, quicken, accelerate, hurry, hasten.

raiment, *n.* *Chiefly Literary.* clothing, clothes, apparel, wearing apparel, attire; garments, vestments, habits, habiliments, *Inf.* gear, *Inf.* toggery, *Inf.* togs, *Inf.* duds, *Sl.* threads, *Sl.* rags; investment, investiture, vesture.

rain, *n.* **1.** precipitation, raindrops; fine *or* light rain, serein, drizzle, sprinkle, *Chiefly Dial.* mizzle, mist; rainfall, cloudburst, rainstorm, shower, sun shower, thundershower, thunderstorm, electrical storm, thundersquall, squall, hurricane; torrent, downpour, heavy rain, driving rain, pouring rain, drenching rain, deluge, *Chiefly Oklahoma and Texas.* gully washer.

2. **rains** rainy season, monsoon *or* monsoon season, wet season, seasonal rainfall.

3. flood, deluge, outpour, outpouring, stream, torrent.

—*v.* **4.** (*all of rain*) fall, come down, pour out, send down; precipitate, shower, rain lightly, drizzle, sprinkle, spit, *Chiefly Dial.* mizzle, mist, drip, leak, weep; pour, rain heavily, rain hard, rain cats and dogs, come down in buckets *or* by the bucketfuls, rain pitchforks, *Sl.* really come down.

5. offer, bestow, give generously, spend, expend, lavish, pour out.

rainbowlike, *adj.* rainbowy, prismatic, prismatical, spectral; many-colored, multicolored, multicolor, polychromatic, polychromic, versicolor, many-hued, pavonine, colorful, brilliant; iridescent, irisated, pearly, opalescent, opaline, nacreous, nacred, *Crystall.* pleochroic; shot, variegated, parti-colored, varied, varicolored, kaleidoscopic.

raincoat, *n.* waterproof coat, *Chiefly Brit.* waterproof, mackintosh, *Brit. Inf.* mac, poncho, rain cape, slicker, southwester *or* sou'wester *or* nor'wester, oilskins; trench coat, Burberry, *Trademark.* London Fog, *Trademark.* Aquascutum.

rainy, *adj.* **1.** raining, pluvial, pluvious, hyetal, showery, showering, stormy; drizzly, drizzling, sprinkling, *Chiefly Dial.* mizzling, dripping, drippy.
2. wet, damp, moist, drenched, soaked.

raise, *v.* **1.** elevate, lift, lift up, loft, move up, thrust up, cast up; heave, hoist, bear up; run up, raise aloft, hold up; upcast, upthrow, upheave, upthrust, uplift, upraise; jack up, jerk up, pull up, hike up, draw up, haul up; pry up, tilt up, lever, prize; fish up, dredge up, bring up.
2. set up, set upright, put back, put up; turn over, right, up-end, stand, stand up, stick up; make vertical, stand on end, put on its feet *or* legs.
3. rouse, stir, arouse, awaken, waken, wake; bestir, start, jostle, ruffle, shake; nudge, budge, poke.
4. build, erect, construct, put up, uprear, set up; fabricate, fashion, model, form, frame, put together.
5. activate, motivate, prompt; effect, produce, cause, occasion, start, begin, actuate; originate, give rise to, put in motion, set going, get going; establish, institute, initiate, launch, inaugurate, commence.
6. cultivate, farm, grow, till, harvest; develop, shepherd, *Archaic.* husband; rear, breed, hatch; parent, mother, father, bring up, nurture, nurse, foster.
7. bring up, introduce, broach, open, present; put forward, bring into question, touch on.
8. restore, bring back to life, raise from the dead; summon up, call up, invoke, conjure up; revive, resuscitate, reanimate.
9. stir up, excite, arouse, instigate, foment, foster; incite, goad, urge, fillip, spur, prompt, prod, provoke; kindle, stimulate, whet, sharpen, electrify, energize; agitate, pique, quicken, inflame, impassion.
10. animate, invigorate, vitalize; gladden, put in a good mood, cheer, cheer up, elate; hearten, encourage, revive, buoy, inspirit, *Inf.* give a lift, raise the spirits; enliven, exhilarate, refresh, regale.
11. advance, elevate, exalt, dignify; honor, aggrandize, ennoble, knight; prefer, promote, *Sl.* kick upstairs; upgrade, improve, better, ameliorate, meliorate; enhance, enrich, amend, mend, reform.
12. collect, assemble, congregate, convene, bring together, gather together, convoke; muster, levy, mobilize, rally; round up, accumulate, amass, mass; scrape together, come up with, get, get together, dig up, rake up.
13. increase, advance, heighten, enlarge, extend, add to, add on; magnify, exaggerate, greaten, hyberbolize; double, redouble, strengthen, reinforce, *Inf.* beef up; *Sl.* soup up, *Sl.* hop up, key up, *Sl.* jazz up; augment, amplify, aggravate, exacerbate, intensify, *Inf.* step up, accelerate; escalate, inflate, *Inf.* hike, boost, *Inf.* jack up, *Inf.* jump up, run up.
14. leaven, expand, rise, ferment; puff up, swell, blow up.
—*n.* **15.** increase, *Inf.* boost, *Inf.* hike, pay raise, *Inf.* up, salary increase.

raison d'être, *n.* reason, reason for being, cause, principle, *Sl.* the name of the game; ultimate cause, primary cause, root, source; inspiration, inducement, motive, incitement; justification, excuse, rationalization, rationale.

rake[1], *n.* **1.** hoe, trowel, spade, scraper, scuffle.
—*v.* **2.** dig, scrape, spade, hoe, break up; comb, hackle, rasp, card; harrow, weed, dibble, delve, pick; smooth, prepare, brush up.
3. gather, draw, cull, pluck, pick, garner, catch; remove, dredge, scrape up, net.
4. **rake in** collect, gather, pull in, stack up, haul in, make a killing; mass, amass, pile up, round up, clean up.
5. search, scour, look for, look all over for, look everywhere for; rifle through, rummage, ransack, comb, hunt through; turn upside down, turn inside out, look high and low, leave no stone unturned.
6. scrape, scratch, graze, kiss, brush, nudge, glance; touch, contact, skin, shave, caress, lick.

rake[2], *n.* roué, profligate, debauchee, lecher, libertine, dissipater, prodigal; playboy, rakehell, blood, *Inf.* rip, *Sl.* swinger, fast man, man about town; womanizer, lady-killer, bedhopper, lover, ladies' man, *Inf.* wolf; adulterer, fornicator, seducer, satyr, goat, old goat, *Sl.* dirty old man, pervert, *Sl.* letch; Don Juan, Lothario, Cassanova.

rake-off, *n.* (*often illicit*) share, cut, slice, piece, take, *Inf.* take-in, kickback; deal, lot, portion; fee, commission, dividend, half.

rakish[1], *adj.* dissolute, profligate, dissipated, wanton, adulterous; prodigal, depraved, debauched, prurient, goatish, satyric; loose, carnal, immoral; lascivious, lecherous, *Archaic.* lickerish, lubricious; libidinous, lustful, libertine, lewd; randy, rammy, *Sl.* horny, ruttish, hot, sexed-up, riggish; woman-crazy, sex-crazy, sex-mad, priapic, lip-licking.

rakish[2], *adj.* smart, dapper, dashing, spruce, debonair; natty, neat, *Chiefly Brit.* trig, sharp; jaunty, breezy, airy, springy, high-stepping; well-groomed, handsome, classy, *Fr.* *soigné*; fine, chic, stylish, fashionable, elegant; dandy, foppish, gay, flashy.

rally[1], *v.* **1.** gather, collect, reorganize, reassemble, regroup; muster, assemble, unite, draw together; mobilize, raise, levy, call up, call to the colors.
2. call together, get together, bring together, assemble, congregate; put together, consolidate, lump together, group, convene, convoke; shepherd, herd, corral, round up; meet, come together, gather, troop; huddle, bunch, cluster, rally around, rally round the flag, crowd.
3. recover, recuperate, pick up, perk up, convalesce; revive, reanimate, rouse; regenerate, rejuvenate, refresh, renew, revivify; improve, mend, get better, get well, regain one's strength; come around, pull through, take a turn for the better, turn the corner; make a comeback, *Inf.* snap out of it, *Inf.* get back in shape, get back on one's feet, bounce back, *Inf.* get back in the swing of things.
4. embolden, encourage, nerve, put heart into, enhearten; inspirit, cheer, lift, raise the spirits, give confidence to; gladden, *Inf.* give a lift, buoy up.
—*n.* **5.** recovery, recuperation, renewal, convalescence, revival; rejuvenation, regeneration, renaissance, rebirth, restoration, rehabilitation; refreshment, reanimation, revivification; comeback, road to recovery, resuscitation, resurgence, resurrection.
6. convocation, convention, assemblage, assembly, gathering, convergence; meeting, mass meeting, pep rally, meet; congregation, concourse, conference.

rally[2], *v.* banter, chaff, tease, twit, josh, taunt; jolly, joke, rail at, *Sl.* rag, *Inf.* ride, *Inf.* needle, dig at, *Inf.* swipe; poke fun at, *Sl.* roast, *Sl.* razz, *Sl.* rib; ridicule, deride, mock, gibe, jeer, fleer; make game of, make fun of, pull [s.o.'s] leg, laugh at.

ram, *n.* **1.** male sheep, tup, *Astron.* Aries.
2. rammer, battering ram, hydraulic ram, pile driver; monkey, tamper, tamping iron, sledgehammer, mallet, mall, piston.
3. iron warship, iron-clad, floating battery, man-of-war; Monitor, Merrimac, Constitution *or* "Old Ironsides".
—*v.* **4.** drive, drive in, force, pound in; hit down, beat, poke, hammer, hammer in, cudgel; force in, cram, crowd, stuff, compress, squeeze; tamp, choke, plug, *Inf.* ramrod.

5. strike, hit, dash against, collide with, run into; butt, batter, bump, crash, clash, buffet, smash, thwack, clip; wham, whack, thump, slam, jolt, telescope; (*of ships*) run against and sink.

ramble, *v.* **1.** wander, wander around, meander; saunter, perambulate, take a walk, go for a walk, stroll, go for a stroll, promenade, hike; amble, amble about, gad, gad about, jaunt; nomadize, peregrinate, flit, traipse; wander off, stray, deviate, detour, go round about; straggle, drift, mosey, shuffle, stumble *or* limp *or* hobble along; range, rove, prowl, float, skip around; follow the wild goose, wander from pillar to post, see the country, *Inf.* hit the road *or* trail.

2. digress, speak discursively, maunder, expatiate; rant, rant on, blather, rave, dwell on, talk aimlessly; gibber, chatter, babble, gabble, run off at the mouth, rattle on, twaddle, go on, go on and on, ramble on; *Inf.* chew [s.o.'s] ear off, *Inf.* bend [s.o.'s] ear, *Inf.* beat about the bush, *Inf.* beat a dead horse, dwell on, harp on, *Inf.* beat a subject to death.

—*n.* **3.** walk, saunter, stroll, constitutional, promenade; perambulation, hike, tramp; jaunt, junket, prowl, circuit; trek, excursion, tour, *Brit.* walkabout, peregrination; deviation, digression, divagation, excursus, detour.

rambler, *n.* roamer, gadabout, traveler; wayfarer, journeyer, tripper, tourist; hiker, trekker, peregrinator; bird of passage, globetrotter, jetsetter, sun-follower; itinerant, *Inf.* corporate gypsy; nomad, arab, gypsy; vagabond, hobo, tramp, stray, beachcomber, ski bum.

rambling, *adj.* **1.** wandering, traveling, roving, itinerant, peripatetic, migratory; vagrant, homeless, nomadic; wayfaring, perambulatory, drifting.

2. straggling, meandering, irregular, uneven, erratic, capricious, fitful; unsystematic, aberrant, circuitous, indirect, zigzagging.

3. discursive, excursive, circumlocutory, circumlocutional, circumlocutionary, circuitous, roundabout, ambagious; diffuse, wordy, long-winded, prolix, verbose; desultory, episodic, rhapsodic; disconnected, disjointed, maundering, periphrastic.

rambunctious, *adj.* **1.** boisterous, agitated, unquiet, restive, hyperactive; rowdy, brawling, disorderly, robustious, riotous, wild; rampageous, reckless, *Sl.* hell-raising; obstreperous, unrestrained, unruly, uncontrolled, uncontrollable, out of hand; ungoverned, unbridled, refractory, recalcitrant; defiant, contumacious, fractious, *Inf.* ornery.

2. noisy, loud, vociferous; rackety, clamorous, clamant, blatant, clangorous; ear-splitting, ear-piercing, ear-rending, deafening, enough to wake the dead.

ramification, *n.* **1.** branching, diverging, forking; configuration, radiation, divergency.

2. branch, bough, limb; sprig, twig, sprout, shoot; scion, spur, arm, spray; offshoot, runner, tendril.

3. outgrowth, consequence, fruit, development, aftermath, eventuation, end; outcome, result, product, effect, upshot; sequel, derivative, implication; complexity, complication, technicality, subtlety.

ramp, *n.* **1.** slope, sloping surface, inclined plane, grade, gradient, incline; acclivity, rise, ascent; declivity, dip, downhill slope; access ramp, approach, entrance *or* exit ramp, on *or* off ramp.

—*v.* **2.** rear, rear *or* rise up, uprear, rise on the hind legs.

3. ramp about, rear up and roar, rear and roar like a lion, tear around, run amuck, go berserk, *Inf.* come on strong, *Inf.* carry on; fly into a passion *or* rage, go into hysterics, *Inf.* throw a fit, *Inf.* have a tantrum *or* temper tantrum, *Inf.* get into a lather *or* dither *or* swivet, *Inf.* race one's motor, *Sl.* blow a gasket; rage, storm, bellow, *Inf.* blow up, *Inf.* explode, *Inf.* blow one's top *or* cool; ramp and rage, rant and rave, tear one's hair.

rampage, *n.* **1.** violent behavior, uncontrollable temper, display of wild temper, wild commotion *or* disturbance *or* agitation, loss of control, amok, running amuck, going berserk.

2. fury, rage, frenzy, passion; furor, turmoil, upset.

—*v.* **3.** rage, storm, rave, rant, roar, carry on, tear about, lose control, display one's anger, vent one's rage.

rampageous, *adj.* violent, uncontrollable, wild, stormy, storming; raging, berserk, running amuck, uncurbed, unchecked, *Inf.* rip-roaring, rampaging, rampant; turbulent, tempestuous, frenzied, frantic, furious, mindless; fierce, savage, ferocious, unruly, out of control, riotous, disorderly, obstreperous, boisterous, rambunctious.

rampancy, *n.* excess, excessiveness, wild unrestraint, extravagance; predominance, proponderance, prevalence; profusion, superabundance, repletion, glut, saturation, rankness.

rampant, *adj.* **1.** raging, furious, wild, frenzied, frantic, enraged, infuriated, *Rare.* infuriate; violent, storming, stormy, towering, turbulent, blustering, tumultuous, tempestuous; fierce, savage, ferocious; disorderly, unruly, ungovernable, outrageous, riotous, chaotic, uncontrollable, uproarious, out of hand, out of control; abandoned, excited.

2. predominant, predominating, regnant, dominant, in the ascendant, in full sway; prevailing, prevalent, widespread, pandemic, epidemic, besetting; unbridled, unchecked, unrestrained, sweeping, wholesale, indiscriminate; excessive, exceeding all bounds, wanton, rank, rife, running wild, far-ranging; profuse, lavish, extravagant, overabundant, copious, prodigal, luxuriant.

3. ramping, rearing, erect, up on the hind legs, bolt upright, raised, upraised, upreared, upright, upstanding; ascending, mounting.

rampart, *n.* embankment, earthwork, fieldwork, parados, gabion, glacis; fortification, breastwork, bulwark, defense, security, guard; barricade, contravallation, outwork, barbican, redan.

ramshackle, *adj.* rickety, shaky, jerry-built, unstable, unsubstantial, thrown together; falling to pieces, crumbled, crumbling; rundown, decrepit, infirm, tottering, nodding to its fall; tumbledown, dilapidated, broken-down, in ruins, derelict, gone to wrack and ruin; the worse for wear, neglected, out of repair.

rancid, *adj.* rank, stinking, evil-smelling, malodorous, reeking, reeking to high heaven, fetid, noxious, *Sl.* yechy; pungent, offensive, foul, noisome, mephitic; putrid, miasmic, rotten; gamy, ripe, high, turned, sour, stale, musty, *Brit. Inf.* frowsty, fusty.

rancor, *n.* resentment, ill will, malice, spite, venom, malevolence, malignity, vindictiveness; hatred, hate, abhorrence, distaste, abomination; animosity, animus, aversion, antipathy, antagonism, enmity, hostility; irritation, dudgeon, indignation, fury, anger, pique; bitterness, acrimony.

rancorous, *adj.* resentful, spiteful, venomous; malicious, malignant, maleficent, malevolent, hateful; vindictive, unforgiving, vengeful, revengeful, retaliatory, out to get [s.o.]; mean, cruel, ruthless, pitiless, merciless, remorseless, implacable; bitter, acrimonious, virulent.

random, *adj.* **1.** haphazard, casual, arbitrary, hit-or-miss, desultory; chance, fortuitous, serendipitous, aleatory, *Inf.* fluky; careless, slapdash, willy-nilly, thrown *or* slapped together, *Inf.* scratch; unarranged, unsystematic, unmethodical, disorganized, orderless, unordered, irregular; unplanned, unconsidered, undesigned, unpremeditated, uncalculated, aimless; stray, incidental, accidental, sporadic, occasional, contingent, adventitious.

—*adv.* **2. at random** haphazardly, casually, arbitrarily; by chance, fortuitously, as it happens, as it chanced, as luck would have it, by a fluke; randomly, incidentally, whichever way the wind blows; unsystematically, irregularly, erratically, indiscriminately, carelessly, aimlessly, purposelessly; fitfully, sporadically, spasmodically, at irregular intervals, off and on, when the mood strikes, when the spirit moves, *Inf.* every now and then, *Inf.* every once in a while.

range, *n.* **1.** reach, sweep, scope, compass, extent, limit; stretch, margin, latitude; stride, span; scale, register, gamut.

2. rank, class, order, race, species, genus; kind, sort, ilk, variety, *Inf.* lot.

3. row, line, file, string, queue; tier, aisle; series, succession, sequence, run.

4. pasture, pasturage, pastureland, grazing ground, grass, grassland, *Scot.* shieling; meadow, meadowland, lea, *Archaic.* mead.

5. mountain range, chain, sierra, massif.

6. stove, cooking stove, gas *or* oil *or* electric stove, oven.

—*v.* **7.** align, line, line up, draw up, rank, order, put *or* set in order.

8. array, marshal, dispose, distribute; place, fix.

9. classify, categorize, group, pigeonhole, bracket; rate, grade, gradate; break down, subdivide; index, digest, catalogue, file.

10. level *or* level out, even up, straighten out *or* up.

11. vary, alternate, fluctuate, vacillate, pass.

12. extend, stretch, stretch out, outstretch, reach, sweep, cover; lie, run, go.

13. traverse, travel over, go *or* pass over; roam, rove, wander, meander, stray, drift, gad *or* gad about, wayfare, gallivant, *Inf.* knock around *or* about.

14. pasture, put *or* turn out to pasture, fodder, feed, grass.

ranger, *n.* **1.** forest ranger, forester, *Brit.* woodman; keeper, warden, warder.

2. commando, shock trooper, storm trooper, *U.S.* Green Beret, *U.S. Navy.* Seal, (*in czarist Russia*) cossack.

3. guerrilla, irregular, bushfighter, *U.S.* bushwhacker.

4. border patrol, Texas Ranger, Mountie.

rangy, *adj.* lank, lanky, gangling, gangly, weedy; long-limbed, long-legged, leggy, *Inf.* all leg *or* legs.

rank[1], *n.* **1.** class, level, stratum, caste; state, station, place, position, standing, status, situation, circumstances; grade, estate, order, range.

2. blood, high birth, nobility, peerage, aristocracy; distinction, eminence, dignity; connection, influence, power, weight, prestige, importance.

3. category, division, section, branch, department; stage, graduation, degree, step; standard, plane.

4. file, line, column, tier, bank; queue, string, thread, swath, procession, train; row, series, sequence.

5. array, alignment, arrangement, classification, organization, assignment.

—*v.* **6.** array, marshal, align, line up, queue up, put in a row, arrange, range.

7. classify, prioritize, dispose, place, group; position, locate, station, establish, set, fix; organize, sort, assort, size; class, type, name, label, tag, ticket, brand; distinguish, rate, grade, graduate; allocate, allot, assign, distribute.

8. outrank, rank above, have supremacy, take precedence; have standing, have weight, be influential, be powerful, be preeminent.

rank[2], *adj.* **1.** exuberant, superabundant, luxuriant, lush, overgrown; tropical, jungly, dense, wild; abundant, profuse, prolific, fructuous, productive, fertile.

2. strong, smelly, rammish, pungent, acrid; malodorous, fetid, reeky, reeking, stinky, stenchful, foul-smelling, strong-smelling, odorous, odiferous; noisome, mephitic, nauseating, sickening, unpleasant, disagreeable; putrid, rancid, rotten, tainted, spoiled, gamy, putrescent, miasmal; offensive, disgusting, repulsive, repellent, revolting.

3. utter, complete, sheer, entire; absolute, out-and-out, downright, thorough, unqualified, unmitigated; flagrant, glaring, egregious, striking, blatant.

4. indecent, immodest, shameless, indecorous, coarse; obscene, vulgar, gross, risqué, off-color, *Inf.* blue; lurid, shocking, abusive, scurrilous, *Archaic.* scurrile, thersitical, profane, foul-mouthed, Fescennine, *Obs.* blackguard; lewd, salacious, pornographic, vile, foul, filthy, dirty, smutty, nasty, scatologic, *Sl.* raunchy.

rank and file, *n.* **1.** commonalty, the public, the general public, citizenry, populace, world-at-large; society, community, commonwealth, state, body politic; stockholders, shareholders, shareholders, participants, membership.

2. proletariat, hoi polloi, the masses, the many, the great unnumbered, multitude, crowd; bourgeoisie, middle classes; lower classes, humbler classes, commoners, peasantry, salt-of-the-earth; low life, dregs, underlings, riff-raff, *Inf.* the great unwashed; mob, rabble, horde, herd, rout.

rankle, *v.* (*all of feelings*) fester, rile, gall, irk, get, get to one, get one's goat; irritate, vex, provoke, pique, annoy, peeve, nettle, chafe, grate, get on [s.o.'s] nerves, *Inf.* aggravate, *Inf.* give [s.o.] a pain, *Inf.* rub [s.o.] the wrong way; torment, plague, bother, fret, exacerbate, exasperate; anger, inflame, enflame, stir, stir up, work up.

ransack, *v.* **1.** search, rummage, rake through, probe, *Brit. Dial.* ripe, look everywhere in; look high and low, turn everything upside down *or* inside out, leave no stone unturned; explore, seek everywhere, look all over, scour, range over, scan, survey; scrutinize, pry, ferret out, nose out, hunt out.

2. pillage, plunder, rob, despoil, *Archaic.* spoil, spoliate; ravage, harry, rape, maraud, devastate, lay waste, depredate; sack, loot, gut, fleece, strip, rifle; pirate, freeboot, privateer, buccaneer.

3. rob, burglarize, burgle, break in; steal, thieve, pilfer, purloin, filch, *Inf.* snitch; help oneself to, make free with, walk off with; *Sl.* rip off, *Sl.* crook.

ransom, *n.* **1.** redemption, buying back, buying *or* paying off; rescue, extrication, restoration, deliverance, delivery; release, freeing, freedom, liberty, liberating, emancipation, manumission; discharge, parole, furlough, probation, acquittal, acquittance, reprieve, stay of execution, exemption; loosing, disenthrallment, unfettering, unbinding, untying, unshackling, unchaining, unbridling, unyoking.

2. price, cost, payment, pay, payoff, *Sl.* take, *Brit. Sl.* get; sum, amount, total.

3. penalty, fine, fee, (*in Anglo-Saxon and Germanic countries*) wergild; compensation, repayment, remuneration, recoupment, indemnity, indemnification, damages, *Law.* solatium; reparation, amends, retribution, restitution, redress, return, settlement; atonement, expatiation, propitiation, peace offering, quittance, requital, satisfaction.

—*v.* **4.** redeem, buy back, pay for, buy *or* pay off; rescue, extricate, restore, get [s.o.] out, deliver, *Theol.* save.

5. release, free, set free *or* loose, loose, get *or* turn loose, let go, set at liberty; liberate, emancipate, manumit; disimprison, disenthrall, unpen, unmew, unfetter, unbind, untie, unmanacle, unhandcuff, unshackle, unchain, unbridle, unyoke, *Archaic.* untruss; acquit, discharge, dismiss, parole, furlough, put on probation; reprieve, grant a stay of execution, exempt, let off *or* out of, *Inf.* let off the hook.

rant, *v.* **1.** orate, speechify, declaim, discourse, expound, expatiate, hold forth, perorate, go on, go on and on; speak, make an address, talk, take to the hustings, soapbox, *Inf.* stump; boast, brag, crow, trumpet, talk big, exaggerate, hyperbolize, tell a fish story, *Sl.* shoot off one's mouth *or* face; lecture, pontificate, preach, sermonize, prelect, hold court; harangue, deliver a diatribe *or* tirade *or* philippic, scold.

2. rave, rant and rave, fume, get all riled *or* worked up, go into a rage *or* hysterics, *Inf.* fly off, *Inf.* fly off the handle, *Sl.* blow one's stack *or* top, *Sl.* blow up, *Sl.* explode; vociferate.

—*n.* **3.** bombast, turgidity, tumidity, flatulence, inflated language, *Archaic.* tympany; rhetoric, heroics, extravagance, pomposity, grandiosity, grandiloquence, magniloquence, sesquipedality, high-flown language; histrionics, theatrics, acting, act, show, display, exhibition; braggadocio, bravado, gasconade, fanfaronade, rodomontade, boasting, bragging, bluster, exaggeration.

4. harangue, tirade, diatribe, philippic, excoriation, vituperation, scolding, *Inf.* talking-to; lecture, sermon, prelection; oration, declamation, discourse, expatiation; speech, address, talk.

rap, *v.* **1.** strike, whack, thwack, bang, hammer, pound; slap, clip, hit, cuff, thump, crack, *Sl.* wham, *Inf.* whop, slam, *Inf.* bonk, *Inf.* biff; punch, *Inf.* bat, wallop, belt, pelt, *Sl.* sock; smite, *Sl.* deck, pommel, flair, *Inf.* clobber, *Inf.* bash; clout, swat, swipe, jab, drub, buffet; box, duke, *Sl.* pop.

2. fillip, flick, snap, flip; chuck, pat, dab, tip; tap, knock.

3. utter, exclaim, emphasize, stress; assert, sing out, voice, call out; ejaculate, vociferate, blurt out, give voice to, cry out.

4. *Slang.* converse, talk, chat, communicate, bandy words; discourse with, *Sl.* shoot the breeze, *Sl.* chew the fat, confabulate, *Inf.* confab, gab, gossip.

5. *Slang.* discuss, talk over, talk about, confer, compare notes; deliberate, sit down with, consult with; comment about, go into, take up, reason out.

—*n.* **6.** blow, cuff, stroke, clip, poke, lick; whack, thwack, slap, hit, bang; punch, pound, belt, *Inf.* bat, wallop, pelt; flap, *Inf.* biff, *Sl.* wham, *Inf.* whop, clout, swat, jab, uppercut; *Sl.* slug, *Inf.* chop, drubbing, *Inf.* bonk.

7. tap, pat, fillip, snap, flick, flip; chuck, tip, dab, tweak.

8. *Informal.* blame, responsibility, account, credit, charge; attribution, acknowledgement, imputation.

9. *Informal.* conviction, judgment, condemnation, damnation; punishment, sentence, death sentence.

10. bum rap *Slang.* frame-up, *Sl.* frame, *Inf.* put-up job, trumped up charge, false charge; directed verdict.

11. take the rap *Slang.* take the blame, accept the responsibility, shoulder the responsibility, *Inf.* take it, do [s.o.'s] time, go to prison for another, play the scapegoat.

rapacious, *adj.* **1.** predatory, predacious, preying, vulturine, raptorial, wolfish, lupine; marauding, plundering, pillaging, looting, piratical; savage, bestial, fierce.

2. ravenous, ravening, voracious, devouring, gluttonous, insatiable, cormorant; greedy, avaricious, grasping, mercenary, acquisitive, covetous.

3. extortionate, exorbitant, usurious, excessive, inordinate, immoderate, extreme; insatiable, insatiate, omnivorous.

rapacity, *n.* **1.** ravenousness, ravening, rapaciousness, craving, voracity, voraciousness, omniverousness.

2. avarice, avariciousness, cupidity, greed, greediness, avidity; graspingness, acquisitiveness, *Inf.* itching palm.

3. extortion, usury, bloodsucking, leeching, sponging.

rape, *n.* **1.** (*all usu. in reference to sexual relations*) assault, attack, violation, molestation, ravishment; defilement, seduction; abuse, maltreatment, ill-usage; deflowering devirgination, *Obs.* constupration, *Obs.* stupration.

2. (*usu. of persons*) abduction, robbery, theft, capture, seizure, kidnapping; impressment, conscription; commandeering, hijacking, skyjacking, air *or* sky piracy.

3. plundering, pillage, despoilment, rapine, spoliation, ravaging, foraging, raid, sacking, depredation.

—*v.* **4.** (*all usu. in reference to sexual relations*) assault, attack, abuse, ill-use, ill-treat, maltreat, *Euph.* take advantage of, *Euph.* have one's way with; ravish, violate, deflower, *Obs.* devirginate, *Obs.* constuprate, *Obs.* stuprate; molest, defile, outrage, desecrate; debauch, seduce, corrupt, pervert.

5. (*usu. of persons*) abduct, carry off, seize, steal, snatch, make off *or* away with; kidnap, seize as hostage, hold for ransom; commandeer, take over by force, hijack, skyjack; usurp, accroach, expropriate, arrogate.

6. plunder, pillage, despoil, *Archaic.* spoil, spoliate, devastate; lay waste, ravage, desolate, wreck havoc upon; raid, sack, loot, forage, maraud, depredate.

rapid, *adj.* quick, swift, fast, fleet, speedy; hurried, winged, express, expeditious, galloping, tantivy, light-footed, light of heel, light-legged, eagle-winged, quick as lightning, swift as an arrow; brisk, lively, spanking, *Music.* mosso, *Music.* allegro; agile, nimble, spry, active, agitated, feverish, bustling; hasty, impetuous, headlong, precipitate, rushing, urgent; prompt, instant, instantaneous, sudden; cursory, fleeting, perfunctory, superficial.

rapidity, *n.* **1.** swiftness, fleetness, fastness, speed, quickness; dispatch, huriedness, expedition, expeditiousness; velocity, acceleration, celerity; instantaneousness, immediateness, urgency, promptness, promptitude; abruptness, suddenness, precipitation; alacrity, agility, nimbleness, briskness, smartness, liveliness, tall stepping.

2. hurry, rush, hustle, bustle, dash, scurry, flurry; haste, helter-skelter, pell-mell, hurry-scurry; run, sprint, gallop, canter, tantivy; clip, spurt; scramble, scuttle, scamper; flight, flying, race.

rapidly, *adv.* **1.** quickly, speedily, swiftly, hurriedly; promptly, instantly, expeditiously, straightway, *Sl.* pronto, in a wink, in an instant, in a jiffy, in a trice, in a flash, double-quick, *Inf.* like greased lightning, like a shot, like a house afire, like blazes, like a thunderbolt, *Sl.* like mad, *Sl.* like a bat out of hell; directly, at once, without delay, in less than no time, before one can say "Jack Robinson," before the ink is dry, *Sl.* P.D.Q., *Inf.* lickety-split; fast, full tilt, full pelt, full gallop, tantivy, by leaps and bounds, hotfoot, at full blast, in high gear, as fast as one's legs can carry one.

2. precipitately, hurriedly, headlong; abruptly, suddenly, unexpectedly; rashly, at half cock, pell-mell, harum-scarum, helter-skelter, head over heels.

rapier, *n.* blade, sword, short *or* small sword, estoc, *Archaic.* tuck; *Fencing.* épée, *Fencing.* foil, *Fencing.* saber; broadsword, claymore, *Archaic.* glaive, Toledo, *Archaic.* bilbo, *Archaic.* brand; cutlass, saber, scimitar, yataghan, falchion, creese, kris, anelace.

rapine, *n.* **1.** plunder, plundering, plunderage, pillage, depredation, spoliation, despoilment, raven, *Obs.* direption; ravaging, harrying, marauding, sacking. *Rare.* sackage, laying waste, devastation, desolation; raid, razzia, foray, foraging, looting; ravishment, seizure, grab, rape; kidnapping, hijacking, skyjacking, air *or* sky piracy, commandeering.

2. brigandage, piracy, buccaneering, freebooting, highway robbery, *Obs.* latrociny, privateering, filibustering, (*usu. of cattle*) *U.S. Inf.* rustling; robbery, theft, thievery, *Law.* larceny.

rapport, *n.* relation, relationship, connection, bond, tie; affinity, compatibility, harmony, agreement, accord, understanding.

rapprochement, *n.* reconciliation, harmonization, settlement, agreement, understanding, entente, accord, détente.

rapscallion, *n.* rascal, rogue, scamp, scapegrace, *Inf.* scalawag; bad *or* naughty boy, mischief-maker, troublemaker, devil, *Inf.* cut-up, prankster, practical joker; cad, churl, louse, bully, ruffian; knave, blackguard, villain, miscreant, picaroon, wretch, dastard, reprobate; cur, dog, *Inf.* hound, *Sl.* lowlife, *Archaic.* caitiff, *Archaic.* coistrel; delinquent, misdemeanant, felon, malefactor, criminal, outlaw; good-for-nothing, *Fr. vaurien,* ne'er-do-well, *Sl.* bum, *Sl.* rip, vagabond, black sheep.

rapt, *adj.* **1.** abstracted, engrossed, lost in, consumed, absorbed, immersed, wrapped up, busy, occupied, obsessed, *Sl.* hung up; preoccupied, intent, concentrating, focusing, pensive, cerebrational, thoughtful, thinking, lost in thought, bemused, musing, *Archaic.* museful; meditative, meditating, contemplative, contemplating, reflective, reflecting.

2. enraptured, enrapt, rapturous, ecstatic, exalted, entranced, ravished; transported, moved, carried away, bewitched, enchanted, fascinated, captivated, spellbound; thrilled, excited, in a quiver, inspired, delighted, delectated, charmed, emoting, emotional; blissful, beatific, joyful, joyous, jubilant, elated, blithe, happy.

rapture, *n.* exaltation, elation, exhilaration, thrill, *Sl.* rush, excitement, excitation; ecstatic joy *or* delight, delectation, enjoyment, fun, pleasure, ravishment; enchantment, bliss, euphoria, transport, seventh heaven, cloud nine; elysium, paradise, heaven, heaven on earth, eden *or* Garden of Eden, utopia; blessedness, beatitude, happiness, gladness, felicity.

rapturous, *adj.* ecstatic, orgasmic, exalted, exhilarated, excited, enthusiastic, thrilled, elated, overjoyed; transported, ravished, enravished, enraptured, overcome; rhapsodic, blissful, in heaven, in seventh heaven, on cloud nine, happy as a clam at high tide; beside oneself, bouncing with joy, delirious, euphoric, *Inf.* high, intoxicated; in orbit, flying, swinging on stars, floating, walking on air; entranced, enchanted, captivated, fascinated, charmed; very happy, delighted, joyful, glad, felicitous, beaming, smiling.

rara avis, *n.* rare bird, rarity, rare person *or* thing, one of a kind; curiosity, oddity, anomaly, aberration, freak, freak of nature; wonder, marvel, miracle, find, discovery; masterpiece, chef d'oeuvre, gem, pearl, flower; nonesuch, nonpareil, ideal, paragon, phoenix, perfection.

rare, *adj.* **1.** uncommon, unusual, uncustomary, unaccustomed, unfamiliar, unwonted, unique; singular, exceptional, out of the ordinary, noteworthy, notable, distinctive, atypical, individual; unexampled, unparalleled, unprecedented, unheard-of, recherché; remarkable, wonderful, marvelous, extraordinary, phenomenal.

2. excellent, fine, superfine, exquisite; outstanding, standout, superior, a cut *or* notch above, preeminent, *Fr. par excellence*; first-rate, first-class, of the first water, *Inf.* A-1 *or* A-one *or* A-number-one; special, choice, of choice, select; incomparable, inimitable, nonpareil, peerless, matchless, second to none, in a class by itself, *Latin. sui generis;* precious, priceless, invaluable.

3. infrequent, few and far between, seldom seen, seldom met with; scattered, scattered *or* spread here and there; sparse, scant, scanty, exiguous, in short supply, at a premium, not to be had, not to be had for love or money, *Inf.* scarcer than hen's teeth.

4. (*all of meat*) undercooked, underdone, red, blue, bloody, *Fr. saignant.*

rarefied, *adj.* **1.** lofty, elevated, exalted, high, prominent, eminent; sublime.

2. exclusive, select, selective, *Inf.* choosy, *Inf.* picky; cliquish, clannish, insular, closed; snobbish, too good for one.

rarely, *adv.* **1.** infrequently, seldom, seldom if ever, very seldom, hardly, hardly ever, scarcely, scarcely ever; not often, on rare occasions, only now and then, only when necessary, once in a great while, *Inf.* once in a blue moon.

2. unusually, uncommonly, uncustomarily; exceptionally, singularly, notably, distinctively, atypically; remarkably, marvelously, wonderfully, extraordinarily, phenomenally.

rarity, *n.* **1.** nonesuch, nonpareil, one of a kind, one in a thousand, *Inf.* one for the books, *Inf.* something to write home about, *Inf.* something else; oddity, curiosity, funny *or* peculiar *or* strange thing, curio, conversation piece; abnormality, anomaly; marvel, wonder, wonderful thing, really something; marvelment, wonderment, gazingstock, *Brit. Dial.* gapeseed.

2. rareness, uncommonness, unusualness, uniqueness, exceptionality; unfamiliarity, unwontedness.

3. infrequency, infrequence, seldomness; irregularity, intermittence, occasionalness, sporadicity; scarcity, scarceness, scantness, fewness.

4. excellence, superiority, eminence, preeminence, distinction, greatness; quality, fineness, worth, value.

5. thinness, tenuousness, tenuity, subtlety, exiguity.

rascal, *n.* **1.** devil, little devil, holy terror, troublemaker, mischief-maker; imp, puck, scamp, wag, minx, bad boy, *Sl.* little bugger, *Fr. enfant terrible, Irish Eng.* spalpeen.

2. knave, rogue, rapscallion, scapegrace, ne'er-do-well, wastrel; villain, miscreant, reprobate, incorrigible; wretch, cur, cad, dog, scoundrel, dastard, blackguard, *Archaic.* bezonian, *Inf.* rat, *Inf.* creep, *Inf.* louse, *Inf.* stinker, *Derog.* bastard, *Derog.* SOB, *Sl.* bum, *Chiefly Brit. Sl.* rotter, *Chiefly Brit. Sl.* bounder, *Brit. Inf.* blighter.

rascality, *n.* **1.** mischievousness, impishness, puckishness, devilishness, scampishness, waggishness.

2. knavery, roguery, roguishness, unscrupulousness, baseness; villainy, miscreancy, reprobacy; churlishness, blackguardism.

3. mischief, pettifoggery, chicanery, shenanigans, hanky-panky, *Sl.* funny business, *Sl.* monkey business, *Sl.* monkeyshines.

rash[1], *adj.* **1.** unduly quick, precipitate, hasty; reckless, careless, heedless, thoughtless, pell-mell, helter-skelter, harum-scarum, head-over-heels, brash, incautious, injudicious, ill-advised, indiscreet, unwary, foolish; abrupt, sudden, unexpected, premature.

2. overbold, bold, impetuous, impulsive, unrestrained, ungoverned, uncontrolled, unchecked, unbridled; feverish, impatient, frantic, impassioned; madcap, madbrained, foolhardy, daredevil, breakneck, adventurous, hot-headed, harebrained, blindfolded; volatile, flighty, frivolous, erratic, fickle, unreliable, irresponsible; wild giddy, dashing, overconfident, rampant, quixotic, punch-drunk; death-defying, devil-may-care, dangerous, ruinous, perilous.

rash², *n.* **1.** skin eruption, breaking-out, *Pathol.* efflorescence; hives; heat rash, prickly heat; diaper rash.

2. eruption, outburst, outbreak, torrent, spate, spurt; multitude, number, large number; series, succession, run, sequence.

rasp, *v.* **1.** scrape, scratch, excoriate, abrade, rub, scour, scrub; grate, shred, file, whet, sand, sandpaper, pumice; grind, mortar, levigate, triturate.

2. irritate, aggravate, exasperate, exacerbate, rub the wrong way; annoy, vex, irk, peeve, gall, nettle; wear on, weary, fatigue, fatigate, tire; tax, strain, burden,

3. grit, gride, clank, jangle, clash; screech, creak, screak, shrill, stridulate; squawk, caw, croak, bray.

—*n.* **4.** scraping, scratching, excoriation, excoriating, abrasion, abrading, rubbing, scouring, scrubbing; grating, shredding, filing, whetting, sanding, sandpapering, pumicing; grinding, mortaring, levigation, levigating, trituration, triturating.

5. grating, grind, scrape, scratching, gride, clank, jangle, clash; screech, creak, screak, stridor, stridulation; squawk, caw, croak, bray.

6. file, grater, shredder, grinder.

rasping, *adj.* harsh, scratchy, gravelly, creaky, discordant. See **grating** (*def.* **2**).

rate¹, *n.* **1.** pay, payment, rent, fare, hire, freightage, towage, truckage, wharfage; percentage, commission, brokerage; duty, tax, capitation, custom, toll, tollage; price, cost, expense, charge, *Commerce.* quotation, *Inf.* damages, fee, dues; expenditure, outlay.

2. pace, velocity, speed, *Inf.* clip, gait, stride, career; tempo, time, meter, measure; progress, movement, motion.

3. rating, distinguishing, classification, evaluation, grade, gradation; sort, kind, type, brand; class, caste, rank, position, station, place, standing, status; value, valuation, worth.

—*v.* **4.** appraise, evaluate, value, price, set the price *or* cost; judge, weigh, gauge, assess, assay; calculate, reckon, compute.

5. distinguish, prioritize, rank, grade, graduate, categorize, pigeonhole; classify, arrange, range, order, dispose, place, group, organize; sort, assort, size; class, type, name, label, tag, ticket, brand.

6. esteem, regard, consider, deem, account, think of.

7. count, figure, be important, carry weight, make a mark; have prestige, be distinguished, have value, have standing; shine, glow, glitter, make a splash.

rate², *v.* scold, tongue-lash, *Inf.* rag, upbraid, *Sl.* chew out, *U.S. Inf.* bawl out, *Inf.* dress down, *Inf.* jump on; castigate, chastise, berate, censure, reproach, rebuke, reprove, reprimand, reprobate, blame; denounce, take to task, call to account, call down, lecture; admonish, caution, warn, forewarn, put on one's guard.

rather, *adv.* **1.** somewhat, in a measure, to a certain extent, slightly, a bit; after a fashion, *Inf.* sort of, *Inf.* kind of, more or less, pretty, quite, very.

2. sooner, more willingly, more readily; preferably, in preference to, instead, in lieu of.

3. more truly, correctly speaking, strictly speaking, to be exact, to be precise.

ratify, *v.* **1.** sanction, accredit, authorize, warrant; approve, homologate, endorse, support, underwrite; sustain, back up, uphold, make good, justify, vindicate; countersign, sign, subscribe, recognize, acknowledge; agree, consent, accede, assent, concur, accord, acquiesce, comply.

2. confirm, corroborate, verify, authenticate, validate, substantiate; bear out, prove, establish, evidence, give credence to; attest, certify, bear witness to, testify, vouch for; affirm, aver, assure, pledge, promise, guarantee, ensure, secure, insure; bind, seal, settle, clinch, clench, secure, fix, make certain *or* sure.

rating¹, *n.* classification, assignment, designation, relegation, consignment; grade, sort, class, rank, rate. See **rate¹** (*def.* 3).

rating², *n.* scolding, chiding, tongue-lashing, *Inf.* ragging, upbraiding, *Sl.* chewing out, *U.S. Inf.* bawling out, *Inf.* dressing down, *Inf.* piece of one's mind; castigation, chastisement, berating, censure, reproach, rebuke, reproof, reprimand, lecture, admonishment.

ratio, *n.* proportion, proportional *or* fractional relationship, *Math.* fraction; relationship, comparative size *or* extent, relativity, correlation, correspondence, balance; percentage, percent, rate per hundred, rate.

ratiocinate, *v.* reason, use logic, use inductive *or* deductive thinking, think logically; deduce, infer, derive, draw a conclusion, syllogize; calculate, put two and two together, rationalize, *Inf.* figure, *U.S. Dial.* reckon, *Sl.* dope out.

ratiocination, *n.* **1.** logic, science of reasoning, reasoning, deductive *or* inductive thinking, syllogization, syllogistic reasoning; *All Logic.* inference, deduction, induction.

2. polemics, argumentation, debate, art of disputation *or* controversy.

ration, *n.* **1.** allowance, allotment, portion, quota, part, provision; share, dole, meed, measure, modicum; proportion, percentage, budget; lot, *Inf.* take, dose, clutch, batch, amount, *Inf.* chunk, helping.

2. rations provisions, supplies, stock, board; provender, victuals, viands, comestibles, eatables, commons.

—*v.* **3.** supply, distribute, deal out, divide, *Inf.* divvy up, split; apportion, mete, dole, allot, give out, measure out; allocate, assign, appoint; disperse, dispense, administer, issue, hand out, pass out.

4. restrict, circumscribe, reserve, mark off, set aside, set off, save, conserve; budget, allowance, schedule.

rational, *adj.* **1.** reasonable, logical, practical, pragmatic, commonsense, commonsensical; sensible, good, right, fair; fit, proper, advisable, well-advised; well-argued, well-grounded, well-founded; plausible, credible, admissible.

2. intelligent, wise, judicious, sagagious, sage; enlightened, just, discriminating; discreet, prudent, circumspect; politic, perspicacious, far-sighted, astute, provident; perceptive, apperceptive, foresighted; understanding, thoughtful, reflective, philosophical.

3. lucid, clearheaded, right-minded, clearminded, cogent, balanced; responsible, sane, *Latin. compos mentis,* sober, sound, right; normal, wholesome, healthy-minded, *Sl.* with it, *Sl.* all there.

4. thinking, cognitive, mental, cerebral; reasoning, intelligent, knowing; ratiocinative, perceiving, percipient, analytic; ideational, conceptual, noetic, sophic, phrenic, noological.

rationale, *n.* theory, account, ground, pretense, pretext, excuse; hypothesis, thesis, exposition; reason,

reason why, why and wherefore, explanation, explication, exegesis, interpretation; allegorization, illustration.

rationalize, *v.* **1.** intellectualize, paralogize, explain away, talk away; invent, make excuses for, construe; justify, vindicate, account for, make acceptable, make allowance for; attribute, ascribe, misapply.

2. reason, deliberate, contemplate, reflect, cerebrate, think, speculate, ratiocinate, cogitate, excogitate; philosophize, logicize, syllogize.

3. clarify, clear up, make clear, explain, explicate, account for; elucidate, spell out, throw light on, shed light on; enlighten, illuminate, illustrate, expound, allegorize, demythologize; show, show how, tell how, demonstrate.

rattle, *v.* **1.** clatter, *Dial.* clutter, racket, din; jangle, clang, clank, clangor, bang; clink, jingle, tinkle; rap, knock, ping.

2. jiggle, jounce, shake, rap.

3. hurtle, bounce, bump, clash, crash, collide.

4. chatter, jabber, cackle, clack, cluck, clatter, gibber, gabble; prate, blab, babble, prattle, *Inf.* spout forth, *Sl.* run off at the mouth, talk a blue streak, *Sl.* yackety-yak.

5. disconcert, faze, confuse, perplex, bewilder; muddle, addle, fluster, put in a dither; disturb, perturb, upset, put off the track, discompose.

—*n.* **6.** clatter, clutter, rattling, racket, rapping, ticktack, knocking, tapping; banging, thumping, crashing, clanking, clank, clanging, clangor, din.

7. noisemaker, clapper, clack, castanets.

rattlebrained, *adj.* rattlepated, addlepated, scatterbrained, giddy, *Inf.* slaphappy, unstable, unsteady, volatile, *Sl.* flaky, fickle; foolish, silly, inane, eccentric, *Sl.* balmy, *Brit. Sl.* barmy; frivolous, flighty, birdbrained; fuzzy, vague, out in left field, out of it, with one's head in the clouds, preoccupied, *Sl.* goofy, *Sl.* wacky; muzzy, confused, flustered, muddled, addled, bewildered, at sea.

rattletrap, *n.* jalopy, wreck, *Sl.* heap, *Inf.* pile of junk, *Inf.* junk, *Inf.* crate, *Inf.* clunker, *Facetious.* flivver, *Sl.* tin lizzie, *Inf.* lemon, *Sl.* bomb, *Sl.* buggy, *Sl.* bucket of bolts, *Inf.* survivor of the demolition derby; car, used car, automobile, auto, vehicle.

raucous, *adj.* strident, shrill, screeching, piercing, ear-piercing; harsh, sharp, grating, rasping, scratching, dissonant, discordant, jarring, twanging; cacophonous, noisy, loud, earsplitting, clamorous, clangorous.

ravage, *n.* **1.** devastation, waste, desolation, destruction, ruin, havoc, damage, wreckage; burning, razing, leveling, demolishing; desecration, defilement, outrage, violation, vandalism; injury, harm, hurt, impairment, loss, scathe; collapse, breakdown.

2. pillage, plunder, plundering, plunderage, rapine, depredation, spoliation, despoliation, despoilment, *Obs.* direption, raven; pillaging, harrying, marauding, sacking, *Rare.* sackage; raid, razzia, foray, inroad; foraging, looting, ravishment, seizure, grab, rape.

3. brigandage, piracy, buccaneering, freebooting, banditry, highway robbery, *Obs.* latrociny; robbery, theft, thievery, stealing.

—*v.* **4.** devastate, lay waste, desolate, ruin, lay in ruins; destroy, level, raze, burn, demolish, shatter, wreck.

5. pillage, plunder, rob, despoil, *Archaic.* spoil, spoliate, *Chiefly Scot.* reive; harry, maraud, rape, ravish; ransack, sack, loot, gut, fleece, strip, rifle, steal.

6. desecrate, defile, outrage, violate; harm, injure, mar, spoil; weaken, enervate, debilitate.

rave, *v.* **1.** talk wildly, ramble, babble, maunder; be delirious, run off.

2. rage, storm, thunder, fulminate, explode, flare up; roar, howl, holler, yell, *Inf.* raise a ruckus, *Sl.* raise Cain, *Sl.* raise hell; lose one's temper, *Sl.* fly off the handle, lose control, *Sl.* flip one's lid *or* wig; bluster, rant, declaim, harangue.

3. praise, praise to the skies, bestow kudos, give a great notice; gush, *Inf.* enthuse, go wild about; cheer, champion, root for, promote.

ravel, *v.* **1.** disentangle, untwist, undo, unroll, take apart; comb, card, separate, divide; loose, unloose, disconnect, disjoin, disengage, untie.

2. tangle, entangle, involve, complicate, make complicated; knot up, intertwine, intertwist, twist; interweave, interlace, snarl, mat, plait; jumble, disorder, mix, muddle.

3. fray, unravel, unweave, shred, wear to shreds, wear to pieces, wear out, wear; tatter, *Inf.* frazzle, waste away.

4. explain, interpret, explicate; simplify, make plain, unfold, delineate, spell out; decipher, unriddle, decode, translate, render intelligible; sift, winnow, figure out, fathom, puzzle out; clarify, clear up, elucidate, resolve, solve; throw *or* shed light on, get the facts on, justify, warrant, account for.

raven, *adj.* black, glossy black, sable, ebony; pitch-black, jet, jet-black; coal-black, inky, nigritudinous; blackish, nigrescent.

ravenous, *adj.* **1.** rapacious, predatory, preying, vulturing, raptorial; wolfish, lupine; marauding, plundering, pillaging, looting, piratical; savage, bestial, fierce.

2. (*usu. in reference to food*) ravening, voracious, devouring, gluttonous, cormorant; edacious; greedy, hoggish, piggish, swinish; insatiable, unquenchable, omnivorous.

ravine, *n.* chasm, gorge, cleft, canyon, abyss, gulf; crevasse, crevice, rift, fissure; defile, pass, *Fr. couloir,* gap, notch, *Chiefly Scot.* linn, dell; gulch, gully, *Sp. arroyo, Sp. barranca,* wadi; gullet, *Brit.* clough, ditch.

raving, *adj.* **1.** delirious, out of one's mind *or* head, incoherent, not oneself, irrational, crazy, *Sl.* cuckoo, *Sl.* off one's rocker; deranged, *Sl.* unglued, unhinged, unstuck, unstrung, *Sl.* haywire, *Sl.* batty, *Sl.* nuts, *Sl.* nutty; raging, frenzied, frantic, frenetic, hysterical, rabid; manic, maniacal, insane, berserk, mad, crazed; overexcited, overwrought, impassioned, extremely agitated, beside oneself, perturbed; furious, in a furor, in a frenzy, out of control, running amuck, wild; demoniac, possessed.

2. *Informal.* extraordinary, out-of-the-ordinary, uncommon, unusual, rare, singular; remarkable, noteworthy, stunning, striking, outstanding, prominent, conspicuous; phenomenal, special, great, signal.

—*n.* **3.** gibberish, babbling, gabble, jabber, sound without meaning.

4. bombast, rodomontade, magniloquence, grandiloquence, pomposity; extravagance, rant, high-flown language.

ravish, *v.* **1.** transport, fill with joy, rejoice, delight, gladden, cheer; enchant, entrance, enrapture, *Literary.* rapture, captivate, bewitch, enthrall, charm; entice, allure, attract; excite, titillate, fascinate, electrify, dazzle.

2. (*all usu. of persons*) abduct, carry off, seize, steal, snatch, make off *or* away with; kidnap, seize as hostage, commandeer, take by force; usurp, accroach.

3. (*all usu. in reference to sexual relations*) rape, assault, attack, abuse, *Euph.* take advantage of, *Euph.* have one's way with; violate, deflower. See **rape** (*def.* **4**).

ravishing, *adj.* entrancing, enchanting, bewitching, captivating, enthralling; alluring, enticing, seductive; spellbinding, dazzling, engaging, intriguing, fascinating; charming, attractive, delightful, pleasing.

ravishment, *n.* **1.** rapture, transport, ecstasy; felicity, bliss, joy, delight, exaltation, delectation; trance, paroxysm, orgasm.

2. (*all usu. of persons*) abduction, robbery, theft, capture, seizure, kidnapping; impressment, conscription.

3. (*all usu. in reference to sexual relations*) rape, assault, attack, violation, molestation. See **rape** (*def.* **1**).

raw, *adj.* **1.** uncooked, fresh; rare, bloody, *Fr. saignant.*

2. natural, organic, unprocessed, unprepared, undressed; crude, rough, uncut, unrefined, unmilled, unground.

3. open, exposed, uncovered, bare; skinned, excoriated.

4. crude, rough, coarse, crass, rude, uncouth; unrefined, uncultured, unsophisticated, unpolished, unfinished; rough-hewn, homespun, homely, earthy; rustic, backwoods, countrified, hick, boorish, churlish, loutish; ignorant, backward, awkward, clumsy, oafish; ill-bred, ill-mannered, unmannerly, impolite, uncivil; indecorous, improper, unseemly, unbecoming, inappropriate, unappropriate.

5. inexperienced, callow, immature, green, unfledged; unsophisticated, naive, innocent, born yesterday, wet behind the ears; untried, untested, new, fresh, young, youthful, tender, in one's salad days; unskilled, untrained, unschooled, untutored, undrilled, undisciplined; unconversant, unversed, unenlightened, uninitiated, uninformed, ignorant; unacquainted, unfamiliar, unaccustomed, unhabituated, unpracticed, unseasoned, uninured.

6. frank, candid, forthright, direct, straightforward; plain, plain-spoken, blunt, bluff, brusque, tactless; outspoken, free-spoken, bold, unreserved, unabashed, uninhibited, unshrinking.

7. damp, wet, chill, chilly, cool, nippy, cold; freezing, freezing cold, ice cold, bitter cold, biting, nipping, numbing, chilling; stinging, penetrating, piercing, sharp, brisk, keen, crisp, snappy, zippy; inclement, bad, disagreeable, unpleasant.

8. undiluted, straight, neat, pure, unadulterated.

9. **in the raw** *Slang.* in the nude, naked, without clothes, *Inf.* in one's birthday suit, without a stitch on, stark-naked, in the buff, *Brit.* starkers.

rawboned, *adj.* gaunt, thin, thin as a reed *or* rail, lean, meager, spare, lank, lanky, gangling, gangly; skinny, too skinny to throw a shadow, skin-and-bones, bony, angular, skeletal; stalky, spindly, spindle-shanked, spindle-legged; scrawny, scraggy, looking like a plucked chicken, weedy; pinched, starved-looking, withered, shriveled, shrunken, wasted, hollow-cheeked, emaciate, emaciated.

ray, *n.* beam, shaft, streak, streamer, pencil; emanation, stream, blaze, flame, radiance, radiation, irradiation; gleam, glitter, patch, spot, speck; glint, glimmer, blink, sparkle, scintilla, twinkle, flicker, spark, flash.

raze, *v.* **1.** tear down, pull down, take down, bring down, break down, throw down, beat down, batter down; cast down, knock down, fling down, hurl down, precipitate, *Inf.* spill, tumble, topple; fell, lay level, prostrate, level, bulldoze, flatten; cut down, chop down, hew down, mow down.

2. demolish, pulverize, wreck, *Sl.* total, knock to pieces, dash to pieces, smash, reduce to nothing; devastate, desolate, lay waste; ravage, work havoc upon, destroy, ruin, *Dial.* ruinate, bring to ruin, lay in ruins; vandalize, waste, *Sl.* trash; undo, unmake, unbuild, dismantle, disassemble, take apart.

3. annihilate, discreate, exterminate, extirpate, extinguish; erase, efface, eradicate, expunge, cancel, obliterate; scrape off, cut off, cut out, excise; blot out, strike out, stamp out, crush out, wipe out, rub out; purge, get rid of, leave no vestige *or* trace of, liquidate, remove, dispose of; terminate, dissolve, bring to an end, put an end to, do away with.

reach, *v.* **1.** stretch out *or* forth; outstretch, extend, hold out, thrust out, stick out.

2. touch, grasp, seize; clutch at, grab at, catch at.

3. attain, gain, accomplish, achieve, make, *Inf.* make it, *Inf.* get there; amount to, come to, run to, measure up to, come up to, *Inf.* stack up to; approach, overtake, keep pace with, rival, correspond, be level with, parallel, match, equal.

4. reach *or* extend to, go as far as, go to, stretch to; touch, neighbor, border on, abut, be contiguous, adjoin, conjoin; penetrate, enter.

5. arrive at, get to, set foot in *or* on, land at *or* on, *Naut.* put in *or* into.

6. span, straddle, take in, hold, encompass.

7. influence, impress, interest, affect, stimulate, quicken, waken, awake, awaken, excite, arouse; touch, move, move to tears; animate, impassion, inspirit.

8. hit, hit the mark, strike, *Inf.* be on target.

9. be heard, register, make an impression, carry; contact, get to, get through to, make oneself heard, communicate, make contact with.

—*n.* **10.** reaching, stretching, going for; stretch, extension, effort, strain, aspiration.

11. purview, scope, compass, range, latitude; authority, jurisdiction, dominion, sway, rule, power, sovereignty; precinct, orbit, circuit, vicinage, proximity; field, zone, territory, sphere, area; capacity, function; grasp, control, grip, hold, influence.

12. extent, span, sweep, swing, expanse, distance, space, room, length, breadth, width; limit, bounds, margin.

react, *v.* **1.** respond, reply, answer, acknowledge; retort, rebut, refute, come back.

2. reciprocate, return, match; retaliate, repay, requite, get back at, come back at, get even.

3. counteract, conflict, oppose, contradict; counterbalance, offset, frustrate, hinder, counterwork.

4. retroact, reverse, back up; recoil, rebound, boomerang, spring back, bounce back, resile.

5. revert, retrovert, backslide, regress, retrogress, relapse, slip *or* sink back, retrograde.

6. recede, retrocede, ebb, withdraw, shy, shy away; retire, draw back, retreat; renege, back-pedal, back down *or* out, do an about face.

7. be moved *or* affected *or* stimulated; become angry *or* sad *or* happy; emote; weep, sob, lament, bewail, cry; scream, shout, cheer, applaud; laugh, chuckle, snort, guffaw; flush, glow, blush; blanch, quake, *Inf.* shiver in one's shoes; thrill, throb, pant, quiver, flutter; jump, start, swoon, faint.

8. (*all in reference to a particular stimulus or circumstance*) act, behave, move, play, comport *or* conduct oneself; proceed, operate, function, work; deal with, cope with, handle.

reaction, *n.* **1.** counteraction, opposition, resistance, recalcitration, renitence, contradiction, antagonism; offset, neutralization, compensation, counterbalance, counterpoise; retroaction, recoil, rebound, ricochet, boomerang, backlash.

2. return, reversion, retroversion, reversal, revulsion; retreat, withdrawal, recession, retrocession; relapse, backslide, regress, regression, retrogression, retrogradation; throwback, atavism.

3. reciprocation, reciprocity, exchange, give-and-take, like for like, tit for tat, measure for measure, quid pro quo; retaliation, reprisal, requital, retribution, vindication, blow for blow, a Roland for an Oliver, an eye for an eye.

4. response, answer, reply, feedback; retort, riposte, counterstroke; result, effect, repercussion, fallout; reflection, echo.

5. (*of politics*) ultraconservatism, extreme rightism, Birchism, Bourbonism.

reactionary, *adj.* **1.** ultraconservative, retrogressive, reversionary, conservative, regressive, unprogressive, obstructionistic, backward.

2. (*all of politics*) extreme rightwing, Birchist, Birchite, Bourbonian, Bourbonic.

3. rigid, unyielding, uncompromising, hardline, diehard.

4. reactive, counteractive. See **reactive** (*def.* **1**).

—*n.* **5.** ultraconservative, conservative, obstructionist; (*all of politics*) rightwinger, Bircher, Bourbon.

reactive, *adj.* **1.** counteractive, conflicting, antagonistic, contrary, reverse, counterclockwise, *Brit.* anticlockwise, *Rare.* retroactive; refluent, crablike, retrogressive, regressive, retrograde.

2. resistant, recalcitrant, die-hard, reactionary, renitent.

3. recoiling, resilient, elastic, springy, *Obs.* repercussive.

read[1], *v.* **1.** peruse, study, go over, review, run over *or* through; pore over, wade through, plunge into, consume, devour, bury oneself in; scrutinize, attend to, pay attention to; go over quickly, thumb through, flip through, scan, skim, glance *or* run the eye over, dip into.

2. interpret, analyze, define, translate; decipher, figure out, deduce, gather, take to mean; discern, perceive, discover; express, explain.

3. foresee, foretell, predict, forecast, prognosticate; prophesy, vaticinate, divine, soothsay, haruspicate.

4. deliver, recite, elocutionize, present; declaim, orate.

5. read for study for, study, go in for, specialize in; major in, minor in.

6. read into a. infer, interpolate, assume; read between the lines, see beneath the surface; interject, insert, place in, add in, drag in, draw in. **b.** misconstrue, misinterpret, see in a false light, see with a jaundiced eye, see more than is there.

read[2], *adj.* learned, versed, well-versed, conversant; at home, familiar, acquainted, easy with; skilled, strong, proficient, master of, grounded, well-grounded, solid.

readable, *adj.* **1.** comprehensible, intelligible, apprehensible, understandable, easily understood; clear, crystal-clear, plain as day.

2. entertaining, engaging, gripping, interesting, stimulating, absorbing, spellbinding; enjoyable, pleasurable, pleasant, pleasing; worthwhile, worth reading; meaningful, pithy, meaty, thought-provoking.

3. legible, decipherable, distinct, clear-cut; fluent, flowing, regular, uniform; painstaking, precise, careful, neat, tidy, orderly, fair.

reader, *n.* **1.** booklover, bibliophage, bibliolator, *Inf.* bookworm, *Sl.* reading nut *or* freak, one who always has his nose in a book; lover of learning *or* knowledge, intellectual, man of letters, bluestocking, *Inf.* egghead; bookman, scholar, student, *Inf.* grind; literate; book club member, magazine subscriber.

2. primer, hornbook, battledore, abecedary, text, textbook, manual.

3. editor, copy editor, copyreader, proofreader, copyholder; first reader, second reader, reviewer; researcher, searcher, browser.

4. elocutionist, reciter, lecturer, lector, prelector.

readily, *adv.* **1.** quickly, promptly, swiftly, apace, speedily, *Sl.* pronto; immediately, at once, instantly; in no time, without delay, right away, straightaway; at short notice, at the drop of a hat, on the spur of the moment, offhand, extempore.

2. easily, without difficulty, swimmingly, with no effort, effortlessly, hands-down, smoothly, with one hand tied behind one's back.

3. willingly, *Archaic.* aptly, in a ready manner, ungrudgingly, graciously, nothing loath, without reluctance; with pleasure, freely, gladly, lief, *Archaic.* fain, with good *or* right good will, with good grace; cheerfully, happily, joyously; with all one's heart, zealously, with open arms, heart and soul.

readiness, *n.* **1.** preparedness, preparation, ripeness, maturation, maturity, fitness; vigilance, alertness, wariness.

2. promptness, promptitude, punctuality; quickness, haste, alacrity, rapidity, dispatch, address.

3. willingness, cheerful consent, agreement, concurrence, affirmation, approval; acquiescence, compliance, acceptance; geniality, cordiality, good will, cheerfulness, gladness; inclination, tendency, propensity, predilection, leaning, bias, turn, bent; enthusiasm, eagerness, avidity, ardor, fervor; pleasure, desire, wish, mind, will.

4. facility, finesse, expertness, proficiency, efficiency; skill, ability, knack; dexterity, adroitness, agility, nimbleness; ingenuity, cleverness, versatility.

reading, *n.* **1.** perusal, study, examination, scrutiny, inspection, survey, review, look-through, scan, browsing, skimming; research, search, quest, inquiry, exploration, studying, *Inf.* grinding, *Inf.* boning, *Inf.* cramming.

2. interpretation, construction, version, conception, impression; apprehension, understanding, consideration; amplification, explanation, explication, illumination, elucidation, analysis; grasp, comprehension, seeing *or* understanding, diagnosis, decipherment, decoding, cracking, unlocking.

3. rendering, recitation, delineation, rendition, representation, declamation; lection, prelection, pericope; lesson, instruction, lecture, homily, sermon.

4. printed matter, print, reading matter, literature, readings; text, edition; assignment, exercise, task, homework.

5. acquirements, enlightenment, attainments, learning, body *or* store of knowledge, scholarship, erudition.

readjust, *v.* adjust again, rearrange, reorganize; accommodate, adapt, readapt, accord; assimilate, integrate, reintegrate; harmonize, reconcile, square; balance, poise, equalize; regulate, fix, set, reset; join, fit together, *Carpentry.* dovetail; put back, replace; return to a former status, reestablish, restore.

ready, *adj.* **1.** prepared, primed, all set, set, in readiness, *Latin. semper paratus, Latin. animis opibusque parati*; in condition, fit, in shape, in practice, on one's toes; up to, equal to; mature, ripe, seasoned; equipped, booted and spurred, fitted out, furnished; in working order, *Inf.* all systems go; in the saddle, in harness, in gear; well-stocked, well-provided, armed.

2. willing, agreeable, *Inf.* game, content, consenting, acquiescent, concurrent, assenting; happy, eager, keen, glad, cheerful, delighted, enthusiastic; gracious, cordial, genial; inclined, disposed, given, prone, predisposed, minded, well-disposed; apt, likely.

3. prompt, punctual, speedy, hasty, quick, alacritous, swift, brisk; expeditious, timely.

4. dexterous, agile, deft, adroit, skillful, expert; nimble-witted, quick-witted, bright, knowing; astute, keen, penetrating, sharp, acute, piercing; attentive, alert, on the qui vive, wide-awake, expectant; perceptive, discerning, percipient, subtle; cunning, clever, shrewd, ingenious, artful; masterly, resourceful, versatile.

5. about to, on the verge of, on the brink of; tending, prone; expectant, waiting; subject, open, liable, endangered, exposed, in danger of.

6. immediately available, on hand, usable, on tap, present, available, on call; handy, accessible, at one's finger tips.

7. psyched *or* psyched up, excited, geared *or* geared for *or* geared up; animated, lively, energetic, alive; anxious, *Inf.* raring to go.

—*v.* **8.** prepare, make ready, arrange, order, organize.

9. psych up, gear up, get up for, get in the mood for, get ready.

ready-made, *adj.* **1.** prefabricated, *Inf.* prefab, preformed, preconstructed; ready-to-wear, ready-prepared, ready-to-use, ready-cooked, ready-mixed; off-the-rack, *Brit.* off-the-peg; no muss no fuss, instant, carry out, take home, to go, self-serve, as is; (*both of food*) frozen, TV.

2. unoriginal, unimaginative, uninspired; conventional, standard, usual, everyday, stock, routine; commonplace, pedestrian, common, ordinary, run-of-the-mill; prosaic, matter-of-fact, dull, stale, tedious, jejune; trite, cliché, stereotyped, hackneyed, bromidic, platitudinous.

real, *adj.* **1.** true, actual, *Brit. Dial.* gradely, *Both Archaic.* sooth, soothfast; factual, unimaginary, unfictitious, true-to-life, realistic; authentic, genuine, *Dial.* sure-enough, bona fide, veritable, valid, confirmed; rightful, legitimate, lawful, just, legal, licit, official.

2. sincere, heartfelt, earnest, fervent; unfeigned, unpretended, unaffected, natural; ingenuous, artless, guileless, unsophisticated, innocent, undeceitful; honest, truthful, veracious.

3. pure, simple, *Inf.* honest-to-goodness, unvarnished, unexaggerated, unembellished; unadulterated, uncorrupted, undistorted, unwarped.

4. existent, physical, corporeal, bodily, substantial, material; tangible, palpable, sensible, perceptible.

—*adv.* **5.** *Informal.* very, truly, really; exceptionally, remarkably, exceedingly, extremely, enormously.

realism, *n.* **1.** practicalness, practicality, practical-mindedness, sober-mindedness, pragmatism; rationality, reasonableness, sensibleness, saneness; worldliness, secularism, materialism; matter-of-factness, down-to-earthness.

2. candor, frankness, forthrightness, straightforwardness, calling a spade a spade, *Sl.* telling it like it is, *Sl.* running it down; plain-speaking, plain-spokenness, downrightness, outrightness, explicitness, unequivocalness.

3. authenticity, genuineness, realness, legitimacy; naturalism, verisimilitude, lifelikeness, literalness.

realistic, *adj.* **1.** practical, practical-minded, pragmatic, sober-minded, unidealistic, unromantic, unsentimental; commonsense, down-to-earth, matter-of-fact, with both feet on the ground; sensible, reasonable, rational; businesslike, no-nonsense, tough-minded, hardheaded, hard-boiled; clear-eyed, nobody's fool, not born yesterday, not wet behind the ears, having been around, ungullible, unfoolable.

2. natural, naturalistic, lifelike, true-to-life, true-to-nature; authentic, real, genuine, true-to-type, true-to-form, veracious, truthful; exact, precise, literal, close, constant, faithful; vivid, graphic, well-drawn.

reality, *n.* **1.** actuality, actualness, realness; actualization, realization, entelechy; truth, verity, *Archaic.* troth, fact, *Archaic.* sooth.

2. physical existence, physicalness, corporeality, corporealness, substantiality, substantialness, materiality, materialness; tangibility, tangibleness, palpability, palpableness.

realization, *n.* **1.** achievement, accomplishment; effectuation, execution, performance, doing; establishment, foundation, formation, organization; completion, consummation, culmination, fulfillment; materialization, coming to be *or* pass.

2. cognizance, recognition, identification, perception; awareness, consciousness, comprehension, apprehension, understanding.

realize, *v.* **1.** understand clearly, comprehend, know, *Sl.* savvy; cognize, be aware of, be cognizant of; get the idea, *Inf.* get it, *Sl.* get into, *Inf.* get through one's head, absorb, take in; grasp, seize, *Inf.* catch on, *Sl.* get the hang of, *Inf.* get the drift of, *Inf.* get a fix on, *Brit.* lay hold of, *Sl.* latch onto; learn, discover, find out, glean; perceive, apprehend, discern, make out; fathom, penetrate, *U.S. Inf.* figure out, *Inf.* psych out, *Inf.* make heads or tails of, *Brit.* twig; recognize, see, see through, see the light, get the picture, read.

2. actualize, make real, make actual; make happen, cause, bring about, effect, effectuate, work out, engineer, produce; bring off, manage, *Sl.* pull off, *Inf.* put over, swing, cut, hack; accomplish, attain, achieve, reach, arrive at, compass; succeed in, make good, *Inf.* make it, fulfill, carry out, follow through, consummate.

3. profit, gain, clear, make, take *or* bring in; make a profit, make money; capitalize on, take advantage of, *Inf.* cash in on.

really, *adv.* **1.** in reality, actually, in actuality, in fact, de facto; in essence, essentially, intrinsically, in truth, truthfully, truly, literally; indeed, verily, as a matter of fact, in point of fact.

2. genuinely, truly, authentically; certainly, surely, assuredly, decidedly; positively, absolutely, categorically, unquestionably, undoubtedly, unequivocally; beyond question, beyond a doubt.

3. virtually, in effect, just about, almost, for the most part, to all intents and purposes, for all practical purposes.

realm, *n.* **1.** kingdom, domain, empire; sultanate, archduchy, duchy, principality, palatinate.

2. region, area, zone, territory; province, precinct, department; district, quarter, section; field, pale, arena; bailiwick, dominion, jurisdiction.

3. specialty, concern, branch *or* field of study, department of knowledge.

reanimate, *v.* **1.** reinvigorate, revitalize, regenerate, rejuvenate, revivify, recharge, rekindle, renew, restore, revive, refresh, resuscitate, breathe *or* put new life into.

2. vivify, energize, galvanize, exhilarate, quicken, animate, stimulate, enliven, inspirit, breathe life into.

reap, *v.* **1.** cut, crop, mow; shear, shave, clip, trim; poll, prune.

2. harvest, glean, gather, gather in, bring in, take in.

3. acquire, get, obtain, procure, secure; realize, come into, come by; win, score.

rear[1], *n.* **1.** back, reverse; end, stern, heel, *Inf.* tag

or tail end, fag end, caboose; (*of the head*) *Anat.* occiput, (*of the neck*) nape, (*of the neck*) scruff.
2. buttocks, rump, posterior, fundament, hindquarters, hinder parts, (*of animals*) croup; (*all of humans*) *Inf.* backside, *Inf.* behind, *Inf.* fanny. See **buttocks.**
3. bring up the rear follow behind, lag behind, come in last, get the booby prize.
rear², *v.* **1.** raise, bring up, parent, nurture, nurse, *Dial.* fetch up; foster, develop, take in hand, bring along, develop, train, educate, instruct; cultivate, breed, groom, fit, form.
2. erect, build, put up, construct, put together, run up, fabricate, fashion, frame, *Inf.* slap together, *Inf.* whomp together, *Inf.* throw together.
3. raise upright, upraise, set up, put *or* stand up, upright, upend, stand on end, set [s.t.] on its feet *or* legs *or* base.
4. elevate, escalate, raise up, loft, hoist, lift, boost, uplift, hold up.
5. rear up, arise, uprise, rise on the hind legs, sit up; stand on tiptoe.
6. *Often* **rear up** bristle, bristle up, get one's back up, *Inf.* see red, *Sl.* get hot under the collar, *Inf.* do a slow burn; let one's anger rise, get one's blood up, *Inf.* get one's dander *or* Irish up, *Inf.* get mad; stiffen up, rise in anger, bridle up, bridle.
7. rise, tower, loom, bulk, command, dominate, rise *or* tower above, look down upon *or* over, overshadow; soar, spire, soar into the clouds.
reason, *n.* **1.** basis, cause, ground, grounds, motive, warrant, occasion, *Obs.* skill; inducement, inspiration, impetus, incentive; mover, prime mover, agent; instigation, incitement, provocation; stimulation, actuation, fomentation.
2. justification, vindication, excuse, explanation, rationalization; reason why, why, underlying reason, why and wherefore, *Inf.* whyfor; pretense, pretext.
3. clarification, illumination, enlightenment, enucleation, elucidation; interpretation, exegesis, exposition, explication; illustration, allegorization, demonstration.
4. intellect, understanding, intelligence, mind, mentality; comprehension, *Gk. Philos.* nous, conception, cognition, recognition, apprehension, intuition; perception, percipience, insight, intellectuality; discernment, perspicacity, penetration, brainpower.
5. sense, good sense, common sense, brains, parts, *Sl.* smarts; reasonableness, rationality, logicalness, sensibleness, sensibility; wisdom, sagacity, shrewdness, astuteness, *Sl.* savvy, keenness; long-headedness, hard-headedness, acuity, quickness, sharpness.
6. premise, logic, thinking, reasoning, understanding; argumentation, argument, contention; analysis, synthesis, epistemology, dialectics; theory, thesis, hypothesis, account.
7. by reason of on account of, because of, due to the fact that, due to, owing to, by virtue of, as a result of.
8. within reason justifiable, reasonable, sensible, rational, in reason; proper, fitting, acceptable, allowable, warrantable, within bounds, within limits.
9. with reason properly, fittingly, accordingly; justifiably, in all reason, just so, logically.
—*v.* **10.** think, logicize, explain, explicate; philosophize, syllogize, analyze, intellectualize; ratiocinate, use reason, use one's head, put on one's thinking cap; cogitate, excogitate, cerebrate, muse; ponder, deliberate, contemplate, reflect, ruminate.
11. discuss, argue, debate, moot, talk over; confer with, exchange views, examine, analyze, review, pass in review; deliberate upon, sit down together, take up with, *Sl.* rap about, *Sl.* kick around; consider, treat, study, deal with, thresh out.
12. deduce, infer, conclude, surmise, generalize, draw conclusions, put two and two together; gather, glean, understand, figure, *Sl.* dope out, come to a conclusion; see, make out, estimate, reckon, find.
13. point out, bring to reason, prevail upon, show, show one the error of his ways; dissuade, talk out of, remonstrate, expostulate, plead with; convince, persuade, coax, urge, move; lead to believe, make one see the light, win over, bring round.
reasonable, *adj.* **1.** logical, practical, pragmatic; sensible, intelligent, rational; judicious, wise, sound, sane; plausible, credible, admissible, tenable; believable, arguable, justifiable, vindicable, maintainable; proper, advisable, suitable, well-advised, commonsense, commonsensical; well-grounded, well-founded, well-argued.
2. moderate, open to reason, conscientious, dispassionate, impersonal; equitable, fair, just, right; straight, sincere, honest, candid; impartial, disinterested, even, aboveboard, square; even-handed, fair-minded, high-minded, upright, ethical; moral, honorable, principled, scrupulous; unbigoted, unbiased, unwarped, uninfluenced, unswayed.
3. inexpensive, moderate, low-priced, modest, conservative, unexcessive, unextravagant; low, cheap, economical, easy, worth the money; manageable, budget, within means, within reason, to fit the pocketbook, low-cost.
4. thinking, reasoning, cogitative, cognitive, mental, cerebral; intelligent, knowing, ratiocinative, percipient, perceiving; analytic, ideational, conceptual, noetic, noological; phrenic, sophic, philosophical.
5. intelligent, wise, sage, sapient, judicious, sagacious; understanding, thoughtful, reflective, philosophical, contemplative; enlightened, just, discriminating, considerate, discerning; discreet, prudent, provident, circumspect; politic, perspicacious, far-sighted, astute, shrewd, keen, sharp; perceptive, apperceptive, percipient, foresighted.
reasoning, *n.* **1.** argumentation, thinking, ratiocination, logic, thought, rationalization, reason, idea; inference, induction, deduction, syllogization, conceptualization; cerebration, ideation, intellectualization, cogitation, excogitation, speculation.
2. premises, reasons, arguments, rationale; proof, argument, contention, case, pros, cons, pros and cons; position, assumption, lemma, supposal, supposition, postulate; theory, hypothesis, exposition, how one sees it; explanation, explication, interpretation, exegesis.
reasonless, *adj.* **1.** illogical, unreasonable, without rhyme or reason, void of reason, unreasoning; unwise, unsound, injudicous, impolitic, imprudent; senseless, irrational, insensible, insensate; unintelligent, unthinking, lackwitted; thoughtless, witless, mindless, brainless, empty-headed; asinine, absurd, ludicrous, preposterous, ridiculous, nonsensical; insane, mad, crazy, lunatic, *Sl.* screwball, *Sl.* screwy, *Sl.* nutty, *Sl.* goofy, *Sl.* wacky.
2. obtuse, dull, stolid, bovine, slow-witted, dull-witted, dim-witted, thick-witted.
reassure, *v.* encourage, hearten, enhearten, cheer, uplift, buck up, buoy up, pat [s.o.] on the back; bolster, support, brace, hold up; nerve, embolden, rally, inspire, inspirit; comfort, give [s.o.] hope, raise [s.o.'s] hopes, hold out hope, yield *or* afford hope; assure, put *or* set at ease, put *or* set [s.o.'s] mind at ease, satisfy [s.o.'s] mind, settle [s.o.'s] doubts.
rebate, *n.* **1.** partial refund, repayment; deduction, reduction, allowance, discount, decrease, markdown, cutback, rollback; percentage, share, cut, slice, *Inf.*

kickback, (*usu. illicit*) rake-off.
—*v.* **2.** refund, repay, pay back, *Sl.* kickback; discount, take off, *Sl.* knock off, mark down; deduct, subtract, allow.

rebel, *n.* **1.** insurgent, insurrectionist, revolutionary, revolutionist, revolter, seditionist; mutineer; agitator, malcontent, anarchist, *U.S.* weatherman; rioter, brawler; traitor, turncoat, Benedict Arnold.
2. apostate, backslider, recusant, schismatic, sectarian, heretic.
—*adj.* **3.** rebellious. See **rebellious** (*def.* **1**).
—*v.* **4.** revolt, mutiny, rise up, rise up in arms, mount the barricades; kick over the traces; riot, run riot, take to the streets.
5. recoil, shrink from, draw *or* pull back *or* away from, turn away from.

rebellion, *n.* **1.** revolt, insurrection, insurgence, insurgency, revolution, uprising, rising, outbreak; mutiny; sedition, subversion, treason; riot, anarchy, civil disorder, mob-law, street-fighting, fighting in the streets, turmoil, chaos; peasant revolt, jacquerie; putsch, coup d'état, overthrow, takeover.
2. resistance, defiance, waywardness; disobedience, willful disobedience, insubordination; nonobservance, noncompliance, nonconformance.

rebellious, *adj.* **1.** insurgent, insurrectionary, revolutionary, rebel, seditious, factious; mutinous; traitorous, treasonable, subversive; lawless, riotous, ungovernable, uncontrollable, out of control, unmanageable.
2. recalcitrant, refractory, contumacious, obstreperous, restive, unruly, wild; defiant, resistant, resistive; incorrigible.

rebirth, *n.* **1.** renaissance, renascence, palingenesis, revival, revivement; new awakening, regeneration, renewal, renewing, new activity *or* growth; resurrection, reviviscence, rejuvenation, rejuvenescence; revivification, reanimation, resumption, restoration, resuscitation.
2. conversion, religious conversion, being born again; baptism, cleansing, purification, purgation, *Psychiatry.* catharsis; reformation, change of heart, change in character *or* behavior, casting off of old ways, putting on the new man, remolding, remodeling.

rebound, *v.* **1.** bound back, spring back, recoil, boomerang, fly back, ricochet, return, return quickly; throw back, cast back, give back; echo, reverberate, resound, resonate, reecho, repeat, ring, ring again.
—*n.* **2.** recoil, reaction, reflex, backlash, return; repercussion, result, reflux, ebb, counteraction, backwash, retroaction; echo, reecho, reverberation, reflection.

rebuff, *n.* **1.** rejection, repulsion, spurning; parry, resistance, check, checkmate; refusal, denial, disallowance, negation, denegation; forbiddance, proscription, *Inf.* no-go, thumbs down; declination, repudiation, renouncement, recantation, renunciation; disinheritance, disinheriting.
2. snub, *Inf.* cut, *Inf.* put-down, slight, cold shoulder, *Inf.* slap in the face; discouragement, *Inf.* dash of cold water, *Inf.* turndown, *Inf.* the brush-off.
—*v.* **3.** check, repel, drive away, reject, fend off, ward off, keep off, stave off, parry; refuse, spurn, turn down, decline, deny, disallow; ignore, slight, disregard; keep at arm's length, keep at a distance, turn one's back on, cold-shoulder; snub, *Inf.* cut, take no note of, look right through [s.o.], freeze [s.o.] out, cut [s.o.] out of the herd; *Inf.* put down, put in one's place, *Sl.* zap, *Inf.* tell [s.o.] where to get off, *Inf.* tell [s.o.] to buzz off, *Inf.* tell [s.o.] to get lost, *Inf.* slam the door in [s.o.'s] face.

rebuke, *v.* **1.** reprove, reproach, reprehend, reprimand, remonstrate with; chide, *Inf.* take to task, find fault with; scold, lecture, censure, call down, *Inf.* call on the carpet, *Inf.* dress down, *Inf.* bawl out, exprobate, objurgate; admonish, give a piece of one's mind, *Inf.* tell [s.o.] a thing or two, *Inf.* tell [s.o.] off, take [s.o.] down a peg.
2. berate, upbraid, castigate, vituperate; flay, *Sl.* give [s.o.] the business, rake [s.o.] over the coals, keelhaul; let [s.o.] have it, let [s.o.] have it right between the eyes, let [s.o.] have it with both barrels, tell [s.o.] where to get off; *All. Sl.* blast, bawl out, yell at, give [s.o.] hell, lay [s.o.] out in lavender, read the riot act.
—*n.* **3.** reproach, remonstration, reproof, reprimand; lecture, *Inf.* a word to the wise, stricture; expostulation, berating, upbraiding, castigation, objurgation, vituperation, censure; scolding, dressing down, tongue-lashing, *Sl.* hell, *Inf.* bawling, admonishment.
4. blame, accusation, accusal, charge; imputation, incrimination, inculpation, *Inf.* pointing the finger.

rebut, *v.* refute, disprove, invalidate, negate, deny; confute, controvert, contradict, prove to be false, prove to the contrary; discredit, belie, deny the efficacy of, give the lie to; expose, show up, show the fallacy of, expose the weak points of; explode, *Inf.* blow sky-high, puncture, *Inf.* shoot full of holes, *Inf.* knock the bottom out of; defeat, overturn, overthrow, throw out, *Inf.* scuttle, squash, *Inf.* squelch, *Inf.* put the kibosh on, *Inf.* shoot down; answer, retort, parry, retaliate, *Inf.* come back, riposte.

rebuttal, *n.* retort, response, answer; counter-argument, counter-statement, formal disproof; parry, riposte, retaliation, *Inf.* comeback; refutation, denial, disproval, disproof; confutation, contradiction, invalidation, negation; discreditation, giving the lie to, exposing, showing up, puncturing.

recalcitrant, *adj.* refractory, unmanageable, unsubmissive, intractable, contumacious, disobedient, insubordinate, difficult; fractious, rebellious, mutinous, unruly; headstrong, willfull, pervicacious, strong-willed, defiant, wayward; perverse, contrary, oppugnant, obstinate, bullheaded, stubborn, pig-headed, mulish; obdurate, unyielding, unbending, inflexible, rigid, cross-grained, immovable, *Inf.* cussed, flinty, stony; opposed, resistant, renitent.

recall, *v.* **1.** recollect, remember, reminisce, muse, look back on, think back to, *Literary.* hark back; call to mind, review, retrace; recognize, place; commemorate; call up, evoke.
2. call back, summon; encore, applaud.
3. revoke, take back, withdraw, retract; countermand, repeal, rescind, veto, overrule, override; annul, nullify, cancel; recant, abjure, disavow, disown, disclaim, deny.
4. revive, revivify, bring back, renew.

recant, *v.* **1.** retract, withdraw, recall, revoke, repeal, reverse; rescind, abrogate, annul, nullify, disannul, void, avoid; countermand, counterorder, overrule, override; veto, negate.
2. disavow, disclaim, disown, deny; renounce, relinquish, repudiate, abjure, forswear, abnegate; unsay, go back on one's word, take back, eat one's words, back-pedal, renege; apostatize, defect, tergiversate, change one's mind.

recantation, *n.* **1.** retraction, palinode, withdrawal, recall, revocation, repeal, reversal; rescinding, rescindment, rescission, abrogation, annulment, nullification, disannulment, voidance, avoidance, *Law.* defeasance; countermand, counterorder, overruling, overriding; veto, negation.
2. disavowal, disclaimer, disclamation, disownment,

disowning, denial; renouncement, renunciation, relinquishment, repudiation, abjuration, forswearing, abnegation; unsaying, going back on one's word, *Cards.* renege; tergiversation, apostasy, defection.

recapitulate, *v.* summarize, sum up; review, run over, go over, reword, restate, repeat, reiterate; recount, enumerate, relate, narrate, recite.

recapture, *v.* capture again, reseize, retake, take back, resume, reclaim, reoccupy; regain, recoup, recover, retrieve, get back, *Law.* replevy, *Law.* replevin, repossess; redeem, rescue, save, ransom, free, liberate.

recede[1], *v.* **1.** go away, move away, retreat, withdraw, leave, retire, retrograde; return, go back, move back, reverse, back up.

2. lessen, diminish, lower, abate, decrease; subside, ebb, retrocede; dwindle, *Inf.* peter out, slacken, let up, wind down, slow down, de-escalate; fall off, taper off, wane, fade away, die out.

3. slope downward, fall away, slant.

4. give in, submit, yield; back down, decline, retract, take back, eat one's words.

recede[2], *v.* cede back, give back, hand over, relinquish, yield, grant.

receipt, *n.* **1.** voucher, acquittance, quittance; sales slip, sales check, sales ticket; ticket, stub, stamp.

2. receipts payment, amount paid, payment received; income, proceeds, gate, handle, *Sl.* take.

3. reception, recipience, acceptance, taking.

4. recipe, list of ingredients, directions, instructions, formula, medical prescription; method, system, means, ways and means, technique.

receive, *v.* **1.** get, come by, realize, succeed to, inherit, come into, fall into; gain, derive, obtain, acquire; take in, harvest, garner, reap, gather, collect, glean; (*all usu. of wages*) earn, make, draw, *Sl.* pull down, gross, clear, net, *Inf.* take home, pocket.

2. be informed of, be notified of, be told, hear; acquire knowledge of, find out about, learn of *or* about, pick up.

3. be burdened with, sustain, endure, bear; experience, undergo, suffer, go *or* pass through; come upon, meet with, encounter, taste.

4. hold, contain, include, comprise, incorporate, embody, enclose, encompass, embrace, cover; admit of, reckon among, number among, count among.

5. (*all of the mind*) take in, apprehend, comprehend, understand, grasp, *Inf.* get it.

6. (*all of guests or visitors*) greet, greet with open arms, embrace, welcome, bid welcome to, give a warm reception to; admit, give entré, give entrance to, let in, show in, lead in, take inside.

7. accept, agree with, embrace, adopt, follow, subscribe to, believe, swear by; take on faith *or* trust, take [s.o.'s] word for it, take for granted.

receiver, *n.* **1.** recipient, beneficiary, legatee, *Law.* donee, *Law.* grantee, *Law.* devisee, *Law.* assignee.

2. receptacle, container, repository. See **receptacle.**

recent, *adj.* fresh, new, new-sprung, late, latest, just out, hot off the presses, red-hot; brand-new, new-model, modernistic, newfangled, new-fashioned; modern, neoteric, latter-day; current, up-to-date, up-to-the-minute, *Sl.* with it, *Sl.* now.

receptacle, *n.* container, vessel, jar, bottle, holder, box, basket, bag, paper bag, plastic bag; catch-all; receiver, repository, bin, hamper, hopper, chamber, reservoir, basin, catch basin; wastepaper basket, wastebasket, circular *or* round file, file thirteen, trash bag, litter bag, trash can; jacket, cover, wrapper, envelope, sheath.

reception, *n.* **1.** receipt, recipience, admission, acceptance, admittance, access, ingress; welcome, greeting, hello.

2. levee, formal party, soiree, social, tea, wedding party; audience, hearing, interview.

receptive, *adj.* **1.** perceptive, sensitive, quick on the uptake, quick-witted, sharp-witted; keen, astute, alert, bright, intelligent, perspicacious, clear-sighted; like a sponge, like a blotter, like a steel trap.

2. open, open-minded, undogmatic, open to suggestion, suggestible, amenable; acceptant, influenceable, persuadable, persuasible; pliant, tractable, flexible, plastic; responsive, willing, interested, involved, engagé.

receptiveness, *n.* perceptiveness, sensitivity, intelligence, quickness, acuity, sharpness, keenness; open-mindedness, openness, accessibility, acceptance, responsiveness; willingness, eagerness, eagerness to listen, interest; suasiveness, pliancy, flexibility.

recess, *n.* **1.** respite, interval, interlude, intermission; rest, relief, breathing spell, breather; time out, playtime, pause, lull, *Inf.* letup, break, coffee break, *Inf.* taking five; day off, long weekend, holiday, vacation.

2. nook, niche, cranny, corner, alcove, bay, bay window, oriel; side altar, chapel.

3. indentation, notch, hiatus, gap, scoop, hole, hollow; gulf, fissure, scission.

4. recesses penetralia, interior, innards, bowels, depths, heart; inner sanctum, sanctuary, asylum, refuge; retreat, *Archaic.* privacy, hideout.

—*v.* **5.** niche, pigeonhole, hide, retreat.

6. rest, *Sl.* knock off, *Inf.* take five, break, take a break, gather at the water cooler, go for coffee, go out to play, call it a day; close up shop, *Inf.* go fishing, vacation; adjourn, adjourn sine die, prorogue.

recession, *n.* **1.** withdrawal, retirement, regression, retrogression; retreat, turning back, reversal, reversion; moving away, receding, going, leaving, departure.

2. indentation, hollow, curvature, obliquity, inclination; nook, niche. See **recess** (*def.* **2**).

3. (*of business*) slump, crisis, depression, hard times, mini-depression, slowdown, downturn; bear market, inflation; stagflation.

recherché, *adj.* special, singular, exceptional, unique, individual, one of a kind; prize, valuable, priceless, invaluable, costly, expensive; rare, scarce, in short supply, not to be found, not to be had, *Inf.* scarcer than hen's teeth; different, unusual, uncommon, out of the ordinary, unfamiliar; exotic, strange, foreign, alien, outland; outlandish, unheard-of, seldom seen, odd, curious, peculiar, weird, *Inf.* way-out; arcane, recondite, little known, esoteric, abtruse, obscure.

recidivism, *n.* repeated relapse, habitual backsliding, chronic repetition; reversion, regression, retrogression, falling back, lapse, deterioration, decline, degeneration, retrogradation, declension.

recipe, *n.* **1.** prescription, Rx, formula, receipt.

2. method, technique, system, way, means, process, procedure.

recipient, *n.* receiver, beneficiary, legatee. See **receiver** (*def.* **1**).

reciprocal, *adj.* **1.** mutual, *Archaic.* commutual, returned, exchanged, interchanged, reciprocative, reciprocatory; retaliative, retaliatory, requited, retributive; alternate, alternated, shared, give-and-take, to-and-fro, back-and-forth, *Inf.* flip-flop.

2. correlative, correspondent, corresponding, interrelated, conforming, equivalent, common, similar, analogous; complementary, complemental, completing.

reciprocate, *v.* **1.** return, give back, respond, respond in kind, return the favor, do the same for [s.o.], *Inf.* scratch [s.o.'s] back, *Chiefly U.S.* logroll; come back, retort, riposte; pay back, retaliate, requite; correspond, complement, complete.

2. interchange, exchange, give and receive, give and take, counterchange; bandy, barter, bargain, swap, dicker.

3. alternate, rotate, switch, shift, shift the burden, share, share the load, take turns.

reciprocation, *n.* **1.** mutuality, interchange, exchange, trade-off, return, give-and-take, *Obs.* counterchange; correspondence, correlation, reciprocity, reciprocality, reciprocalness, *Inf.* backscratching, quid pro quo, tit for tat, *Chiefly U.S.* logrolling.

2. return, repayment, compensation; retaliation, requital, reprisal, retribution, vindication, vengeance, an eye for an eye.

3. bargain, barter, trade, dicker, swap, switch, transfer.

4. transposition, permutation, substitution, commutation; alternation, rotation.

reciprocity, *n.* See **reciprocation** (*def.* **1**).

recital, *n.* **1.** musical performance, musicale, concert, staging; solo performance, solo, one-man show; performance, public performance, presentation, delivery, entertainment, show.

2. recitation, reading, rehearsal, repetition; monologue, soliloquy, speech, talk. See **recitation** (*def.* **1**).

3. narration, narrative, account, report, in-depth report *or* account, chronicle, history, record; relation, communication, sharing, telling, recounting, recapitulation; delineation, circumstantiation, exposition; description, portrayal, characterization, sketch, depiction, picture, picturization, representation, word painting; rendition, version, interpretation. See **narrative** (*defs.* **1-3**).

recitation, *n.* **1.** recital, reciting, reading, solo; monologue, soliloquy, rehearsal, repetition, review, running through *or* over, recapitulation; presentation, delivery, performance, rendition, interpretation; oration, declamation, address, *Speech.* elocution.

2. oral response *or* answer, oral lesson *or* instruction, oral exercise, oral reading, round robin; oral, oral exam *or* examination.

3. memorized piece, something learned by heart, quotation; piece, number, speech, talk, *U.S. Sl.* bit, *Sl.* thing.

recite, *v.* **1.** repeat *or* say from memory *or* by heart, quote, do a recitation, give a recitation *or* recital, give *or* do a reading; repeat, rehearse, review, run through *or* over; present *or* do one's number *or* piece, *U.S. Sl.* present *or* do one's bit *or* thing, give one's spiel; deliver one's speech *or* talk, declaim, orate; perform, give a performance, give one's rendition *or* interpretation *or* version.

2. relate, narrate, recount, tell, tell about, tell the story of, brief [s.o.], fill [s.o.] in; report on, give an account *or* report of, chronicle, make a report; state, utter, articulate, put [s.t.] into words; communicate, convey, impart, relay, pass on, share; detail, circumstantiate, set forth, lay [s.t.] out, delineate; describe, portray, sketch, depict, render, characterize, *Archaic.* limn.

3. enumerate, numerate, number, count off, rattle off, reel off, call off, check off; list, itemize, specify, particularize, name one by one, read one at a time; recapitulate, go over, check over, run over *or* through, review; count up, add up, sum up, tally up, score up, total up, reckon, figure, calculate, compute.

reckless, *adj.* rash, temerarious, heedless, unheeding, careless, thoughtless, regardless, incautious; unmindful, inattentive, unwatchful, unwary, unobservant; mindless, forgetful, scatterbrained, unthinking, *Sl.* spaced *or* spacey; negligent, neglectful, remiss, slack; imprudent, uncircumspect, unwise, injudicious, ill-considered, ill-suited, ill-advised, impolitic; daring, venturous, venturesome, adventurous, daredevil, wild; brash, devil-may-care, madcap, impetuous, headlong, impulsive, hasty, overhasty, breakneck, dangerous, desperate; audacious, bold, fearless; harebrained, foolhardy, foolish, irresponsible, *Inf.* trigger-happy; spontaneous, spur-of-the-moment, unpremeditated, unplanned, sudden, abrupt, precipitate.

reckon, *v.* **1.** calculate, compute, tally, score, figure, give a figure to, put a figure on, quantify; add up, tally up, sum up, total up, figure up.

2. count, enumerate, numerate, number; tell, count off, list, name.

3. consider, regard, esteem, deem, hold, judge, look upon; estimate, value, appraise; rate, rank, class, gauge.

4. *Informal. Chiefly Midland and Southern U.S.* think, opine, be of the opinion, believe, fancy, imagine, presume, daresay, conclude, come to *or* arrive at the conclusion.

5. settle, settle with, settle *or* square accounts, get even *or* quits with, *Sl.* even the score; clear the board, pay old debts.

6. count on *or* upon, depend on, lean on, rely on, figure on, *Inf.* bank on; trust, take on trust, take for granted, be sure of; include, number among.

7. reckon with a. anticipate, contemplate, foresee; take into account *or* consideration, take note *or* notice of, take cognizance of, bear in mind, not lose sight of. **b.** face, treat, handle, cope with, deal with, contend with, do with; face facts, face reality, *Inf.* face the music.

reckoning, *n.* **1.** count, computation, calculation, tally, score, sum, number, amount, *Inf.* bottom line.

2. enumeration, numeration, numbering, tallying, counting.

3. (*all of accounts*) settlement, adjustment, quittance, satisfaction; liquidation, clearance.

4. amount due, bill, check, *Inf.* tab; fee, charge, price; quotation, *Inf.* quote, appraisal; dun, demand for payment.

reclaim, *v.* restore, regenerate, rejuvenate, recondition; recover, regain; redeem, retrieve, rescue, save, salvage; recycle, convert, transform, change, process.

reclamation, *n.* restoration, regeneration, rejuvenation, reconditioning; recovery; redemption, retrieval, rescue, salvation; recycling, conversion, transformation, processing.

recline, *v.* lie *or* lean back; repose, lie down, loll, sprawl, couch, lounge, drape oneself.

recluse, *n.* **1.** hermit, anchorite, anchoret, eremite, solitary, *Islam.* marabout, *Islam.* santon; nun, anchoress, ancress, hermitess, *Obs.* hermitress; troglodyte, cave dweller, incluse; stylite, pillarist, pillar-saint; ascetic, celibate, monk, monastic, holy man.

2. loner, isolate, isolato, solitudinarian, *Inf.* introvert, *Inf.* lone wolf.

—adj. **3.** shut off, set apart, separate, separated, secluded, sequestered, cloistered, reclusive; shut up, immured, troglodytic.

4. isolated, solitary, eremitical, hermitical, anchoritic; alone, estranged alienated, lonely.

5. ascetic, austere, self-disciplined, hermitlike, celibate, puritanical.

reclusion, *n.* **1.** monasticism, anchoritism, eremitism; hermitship, sisterhood, nunhood.
2. retreat, withdrawal, retirement, separation, self-exile; seclusion, aloneness, solitude, privacy, hermitism, hermitry; alienation, estrangement, loneliness.

recogniton, *n.* **1.** identification, reidentification, recollection, remembrance, recall, memory; spotting, placing, detection, discovery.
2. perception, awareness, cognizance, realization, eyeopener; understanding, comprehension, apprehension; knowledge, cognition, sensibility; admission, acceptance, acknowledgment.
3. appreciation, gratitude, honoring, paying respect, singling out.
4. approval, sanction, endorsement, support.

recognize, *v.* **1.** identify, reidentify, *Inf.* spot, *Inf.* peg, *Inf.* nail, *Sl.* make, make out, tell, detect, *Sl.* get a fix on, place; recall, recollect, remember, call to mind.
2. realize, understand, apprehend, perceive, note, mark; acknowledge, *Archaic.* agnize, admit, own, accept, avow, confess, concede, grant, warrant; see, discern, respect, appreciate.
3. give the floor *or* podium to, yield to, give the nod to, call upon, tap, introduce.
4. formally accept, endorse, sanction, approve, support, uphold; put the seal of approval on, validate, ratify.
5. show appreciation *or* gratitude, honor, reward, distinguish, pay respect *or* homage to, signalize, point with pride.

recoil, *v.* **1.** shy, jump, jump back, start; shrink, shrink back, hang back, balk, quail, flinch, wince, blench, cower; falter, give way, lose heart, lose courage.
2. spring back, lash back, fly back, kick back, rebound, resile, reverberate, reflect.
—*n.* **3.** shying, flinching, shrinking; rebound, backlash, reaction, counteraction, kick.

recollect, *v.* **1.** recall, remember, *Archaic.* bethink, call to mind, bring to mind; bring back, evoke; be unable to forget, keep the memory green.
2. meditate, pray, commune, contemplate; concentrate, ponder, mull.

recollected, *adj.* **1.** collected, composed, cool, self-possessed, controlled, in control; calm, placid, peaceful, serene, quiet.
2. remembered, recalled, in mind, brought to mind; not forgotten, unforgotten, still alive, still green.

recollection, *n.* remembering, calling to mind, recall; remembrance, memory, reminiscence, souvenir; mind, mental image, inward eye.

recommend, *v.* **1.** commend, mention favorably, promote; speak well of, put in a good word for, have a good word for; approve, sanction, *Chiefly U.S.* approbate; favor, *Sl.* root for, *Sl.* plug for, *Sl.* tout, cry up; condone, countenance, look with favor on, support, uphold; endorse, second, vouch for, undersign, underwrite, cosign, lend one's name to; OK, back, guarantee, stand up for, *Inf.* stick up for.
2. advise, counsel, guide, instruct, teach; urge, encourage, coax; appeal, bid, remonstrate, admonish, exhort, expostulate; persuade, convince, talk into; dissuade, talk out of.
3. suggest, offer, propose, offer an opinion; forward, advance, pose, propound; prescribe, enjoin, direct, command, order; warn, caution, *Archaic.* monish.
4. promote, enhance, enrich, refine; build up, improve upon, show off to advantage; polish, embellish, furbish.

recommendation, *n.* **1.** letter, letter of recommendation, letter of introduction, reference, referral; voucher, credential, testimonial; good word, favorable mention, honorable mention, blurb, *Inf.* plug; sanction, approval, blessing, say-so, nod of approval; approbation, endorsement.
2. advice, counsel, advocacy; suggestion, proposal, opinion, idea; tip, hint, pointer, word to the wise, *Latin.* *verbium sapienti, Inf.* flea in the ear.
3. direction, order, steer, instruction, guidance, teaching, *Chiefly Brit. Dial.* rede; prescription, charge, command, precept; appeal, enjoiner, bidding, bid; persuasion, urging, encouragement, prompting; injunction, exhortation, remonstrance, admonition, monition; dissuasion, caution, warning.

recompense, *v.* **1.** repay, pay back, reimburse, indemnify, recoup, refund; pay, remunerate, reward, *Literary.* guerdon.
2. make restitution, make amends, requite; compensate, make up for, redress, satisfy; atone, expatiate, make good.
—*n.* **3.** restitution, repayment, reimbursement, compensation, amends; satisfaction, damages, *Law.* solatium, indemnification, recoupment, indemnity; requital, quittance, return, redress; atonement, expiation, reparation, retribution.
4. remuneration, payment, pay, salary, wages, emolument, hire, consideration; earnings, income, revenue; charge, *Hist.* scot, fee, stipend, honorarium; reward, bonus, grant, benefaction; tip, gratuity, douceur; bribe, hush money; commission, percentage, share, brokerage; cut, *Inf.* rake-off, *Inf.* kickback.

reconcile, *v.* **1.** conciliate, resign, let pass, submit to, yield to; accommodate oneself to, accept, condone, overlook; make the best of, not make an issue of, make the most of, rise above; take things as they come, *Inf.* roll with the punches, grin and bear it, shrug it off.
2. bring around, win over, gain the trust of, earn the confidence of; defer to, give in to, make adjustments for; allay, alleviate, *Rare.* lenify, *Archaic.* attemper; pacify, propitiate, placate, appease; assuage, mollify, dulcify, soothe, tranquilize, calm.
3. settle, bring to terms, resolve differences, make peace between; resolve, compromise, adjust, accommodate, compose; reunite, unite, get back together, help to make up; arbitrate, mediate, negotiate, intervene, bridge the gap; restore harmony, smooth, smooth over, harmonize, *Archaic.* accord.
4. mend, patch up, mend fences, heal, remedy; bury the hatchet, put it all behind one, fix up; make up, shake hands, smoke the peace pipe, kiss and make up.

reconciliation, *n.* **1.** conciliation, resignation, acceptance, submission; accommodation, moderation, deference.
2. propitiation, appeasement, placation, pacification, alleviation; mollification, dulcification, tranquilization, peacemaking; relaxation, easing, détente; satisfaction, expiation.
3. compromise, adjustment, regulation, reconcilement; adaptation, coadaptation, attunement, synchronization, coordination; settlement, agreement, resolutions, terms, arrangement, squaring; arbitration, mediation, negotiation, intervention, *Politics.* fence-mending; rapprochement, making up, shaking of hands, understanding.
4. harmony, conformity, peace, amity, accord, concord; compatibility, affinity, cooperation, rapport.

recondite, *adj.* **1.** difficult, hard, over one's head, *Inf.* tough; complex, complicated, perplexing, *Inf.* tricky; intricate, involved, tangled, knotty, crabbed.
2. profound, deep, esoteric, abstruse, abstract; impenetrable, incomprehensible, uncomprehensible, past

or beyond comprehension, unfathomable, unknowable, inscrutable, incognizable, indecipherable, undecipherable, beyond understanding; mystic, mystical, transcendental, cabalistic, supernatural, preternatural, otherworldly, supermundane.

3. occult, secret, hidden, cryptic, perdu, concealed; obscure, dark, dim, vague, nebulous, *Rare.* imperspicuous; mysterious, arcane, inexplicable, unexplainable, insolvable, insoluble, unaccountable, *Obs.* inextricable; enigmatic, enigmatical.

recondition, *v.* repair, mend, restore; doctor, service, overhaul, give new parts; fix, fix up, patch, patch up; correct, adjust, straighten, straighten out *or* up; rectify, remedy, better, amend; make over, remodel, renovate; refinish, resurface, revamp, renew, completely overhaul *or* redo.

reconnaissance, *n.* **1.** reconnoitering, inspection, advance information, observation, exploration, probe; spying, *Inf.* spy work, espionage, scout's report.

2. survey, preliminary survey, scrutiny, scrutinization; preview, examination, analysis; *Inf.* once-over, *Inf.* walkaround, *Inf.* pre-flight check.

reconnoiter, *v.* **1.** survey, probe, spy out, spy on, scout out, *Obs.* picketeer; get a view of, *Sl.* case, *Sl.* stake out, *Inf.* get the lay of the land, *Inf.* see how the land lies.

2. examine, inspect, observe, view, scan; study, size up, *Inf.* check out, take stock of.

reconsider, *v.* reexamine, think over, take under advisement, review, look at again; sleep on, consider overnight, recheck, check again, retrace; revise, view in a new light, think better of, think twice; correct, amend, modify, make over.

reconstruct, *v.* **1.** rebuild, make over, restore, reframe, reassemble; reproduce, remake, refabricate; reform, refashion, remodel, reshape, revamp; reforge, recast, re-create, recompose, redevise, reformulate, redesign; renovate, recondition, regenerate, rehabilitate, reinstate.

2. remember, recall, recollect, review, view in retrospect; call up, recover knowledge of, *Inf.* string *or* piece together events.

record, *v.* **1.** document, enter, post, make an entry of; note, make a note of, write down, write; register, enroll, take down, put down; chronicle, journalize, keep a diary *or* record *or* log; set down for posterity; file, put in the files, docket, list, log; catalogue, itemize, enumerate, score, count up, chalk up.

2. state, say, indicate, go to record, say publicly, affirm.

—n. **3.** journal, record, chronicle, diary, memoir, *Fr. journal intime*; dossier, *Latin. adversaria,* notes; album, scrapbook, memory book; yearbook, almanac, annals; history, chronology, narrative; registry, register, log, logbook, guestbook; inventory, stock list, catalogue; *Lib. Science.* card catalogue, *Lib. Science.* shelf list; ledger, roll, attendance book; schedule, calendar, datebook, daybook; Acta, transactions, minutes.

4. registry, deed, contract, certificate, *Law.* memorandum, *Law.* instrument; bond, indenture, marriage certificate, birth certificate, automobile title; land records, voter list.

5. reputation, life history, past performance, *Inf.* style, track record, book; résumé, work history, employment record; school record, permanent school file, transcript, academic record.

6. police record, list of offenses, criminal life history, history of crime, reputation for crime.

7. memento, keepsake, remembrance, relic, souvenir, token, token of remembrance.

8. recording, photograph record, phonodisc, *Inf.* disc, *Inf.* platter; album, *Trademark.* LP, *Inf.* single; film, tape, cassette, 8-track, videotape, photograph.

9. off the record confidential, unofficial, not for publication *or* circulation; secret, private, privy, restricted, not public, *It. in petto*; not to be disclosed, not to be mentioned, not to be spoken, sub rosa.

—adj. **10.** prime, extreme, ultimate, unbeaten, tops, at the acme *or* zenith, *Latin. ne plus ultra.*

recorder, *n.* **1.** registrar, archivist, annalist, chronicler, prothonotary, chronologist, chronologer, chronographer, chronographist; historian, marker, scorer, scorekeeper; secretary, stenographer, amanuensis, copyist, scribe; clerk, agent, official, administrator.

2. bookkeeper, accountant, certified public accountant, C.P.A., *Both Brit.* chartered accountant, C.A.; auditor; *Insurance.* actuary.

3. tape recorder, recording device, *Inf.* tap, *Inf.* bug.

4. fipple flute, flute, woodwind instrument.

recount, *v.* **1.** relate, rehearse, repeat, review, run over, recapitulate, sum up; chronicle, tell, retell, tell about; report, give a report *or* account of, set forth; articulate, communicate, convey, impart, unfold, render; describe, depict, explain, define, elucidate; detail, specify, give the facts, give the particulars, particularize; flesh out, footnote, annotate.

2. enumerate, list, specify, name, cite; check off, go over, run over, take account *or* stock of; catalogue, mark, count, compute, calculate, reckon; numerate, number, tally, add up, add; poll, call roll, *Inf.* count noses, *Inf.* count the house, poll the delegation.

recoup, *v.* **1.** get back, regain, recover, retrieve. See **recover** (*def.* **1**).

2. reimburse, indemnify, pay back, repay, recompense, compensate for, make up for, come up with the difference, remunerate, requite; make good, redeem, refund, give back, remit; replace, repair, set to rights, correct, set straight, fix *or* fix up, make everything better, amend, emend, remedy, restore; redress, make restitution for, atone, make amends, satisfy, pay off, *Inf.* get out from under.

recourse, *n.* **1.** access, resort, appeal, request, entreaty, prayer; plea, petition, application, solicitation, suit, supplication.

2. resource, reserve, backup, reinforcement; anchor, support, rock, pillar; refuge, asylum, retreat, sanctuary, sanctum, cloister, haven, stronghold, fortress.

recover, *v.* **1.** get back, make back, win back, reobtain, recoup, regain, retrieve, find; recapture, reseize, retake, take back; repossess, replevy, replevin, resume, reclaim, recall.

2. make up for, compensate for, make good. See **recoup** (*def.* **2**).

3. reclaim, save, salvage, rescue, deliver, redeem, ransom; rehabilitate, restore, reestablish, renew, recruit, regenerate; rejuvenate, refresh, come back to life, revive, revivify, revitalize, reanimate; redo, remodel, recondition, remake, make over, renovate, revamp; reform, improve, better, make better, ameliorate, meliorate.

4. recuperate, convalesce, get better *or* well, return to health, heal, mend, be on the mend *or* upswing; rally, regain strength, improve, take a turn for the better, *Inf.* come around; pull through, survive, make it, live, live to see better days; *Inf.* snap *or* come out of it, be oneself again, revive, resuscitate, perk up, liven up, get back on one's feet.

recovery, *n.* **1.** recoupment, regaining, retrieval, finding; recapturing, retaking, repossession, reseizure, *Law.* replevin, resumption, recall.

2. reclamation, saving, salvation, rescue, deliverance, redemption, ransom; rehabilitation, restoration, reestablishment, renewal, recruitment, regeneration, rebirth, palingenesis; revival, revivification, revitalization, reanimation, rejuvenation; reformation, improvement, betterment, amelioration, melioration.

3. recuperation, convalescence, return to health, *Inf.* comeback, survival; rally, turn for the better, resurgence, reactivation.

recreant, *adj.* **1.** cowardly, craven, dastardly, base, *Archaic.* niddering, *Archaic.* caitiff; pusillanimous, timorous, timid, nervous, fearful, afraid, scared, scary, frightened, afraid of one's shadow, cowering; spineless, weak, uncourageous, unmanly, weak-hearted, fainthearted, lily-livered, white-livered, *Sl.* chicken, *Inf.* chickenhearted, *Inf.* chicken-livered, *Inf.* yellow, *Sl.* yellow-bellied, *Sl.* candy-assed, *Inf.* pantywaist, sissy.

2. unfaithful, faithless, disloyal, untrue, false, false-hearted; two-faced, Janus-faced, double-tongued, talking out of both sides of one's mouth, hypocritical, heretical; two-timing, cheating, perfidious, betraying, *Inf.* double-crossing, traitorous, treasonous, treasonable, double-dealing; shifty, crafty, conniving, tricky, dishonest, deceitful, insidious, untrustworthy; apostate, renegade, deserting, defecting; dissident, divergent.

—*n.* **3.** coward, craven, poltroon, dastard, *Archaic.* caitiff, *Archaic.* niddering; yellowbelly, mouse, baby, big baby, crybaby, wheyface; *Inf.* nervous nellie, *Sl.* chicken, *Inf.* fraidy-cat, *Inf.* scaredy-cat; invertebrate, *Inf.* jellyfish, weakling, *Sl.* weak sister, namby-pamby, sissy, milksop, milquetoast, mama's boy, mollycoddle, *Inf.* pantywaist.

4. apostate, renegade, deserter, defector, bolter, turncoat; renouncer, abjurer, repudiator, rejecter, dissenter; heretic, hypocrite, dissembler, dissimulator, deceiver; traitor, betrayer, *Inf.* double-crosser, Judas *or* Judas Iscariot, Brutus, Benedict Arnold, informer, *Sl.* rat; double-dealer, snake in the grass.

re-create, *v.* create anew, make over, remake, reconstruct, rebuild, remodel, refashion, reform, renovate; duplicate, match, echo, double; reproduce, copy, facsimile.

recreate, *v.* **1.** refresh, restore, renew, rejuvenate, regenerate; invigorate, enliven, exhilarate; entertain, divert, occupy, absorb, interest; amuse, cheer, gladden, gratify, tickle, take *or* tickle one's fancy, regale.

2. unwind, relax, rest, put one's feet up; play, sport, disport, be entertained, be diverted, escape; romp, gambol, revel, skylark.

re-creation, *n.* creating anew, remaking, remake, make-over; renovation, reconstruction, reformation, remodeling, rebuilding, refashioning; reproduction, copy, facsimile; duplicate, match, echo, double.

recreation, *n.* **1.** relaxation, rest, easement; refreshment, restoration, renewal, rejuvenation, regeneration; revivification, invigoration, enlivening, exhilaration; dalliance, merrymaking, pleasantry, merriment.

2. pastime, diversion, distraction, entertainment, fun, festivity, après-ski; play, game, sport, exercise; antic, lark, romp, gambol, spree, junket; prank, practical joke, escape, revelry, tomfoolery, skylarking.

recrimination, *n.* countercharge, payment in kind; retaliation, retortion, reprisal, requital, retribution; vengeance, revenge, avengement.

recruit, *n.* **1.** (*all in reference to the military*) inductee, enlistee, draftee, conscript; cadet, plebe; buck private, private, P.F.C., seaman.

2. rookie, fledgling, tenderfoot, greenhorn, neophyte; newcomer, novice, tyro, beginner, initiate, apprentice.

3. supporter, helper, auxiliary; follower, operative, worker.

—*v.* **4.** (*in reference to military service*) draft, impress, press, induct, conscript, conscribe, *Naut.* shanghai, crimp; enlist, *Archaic.* list, muster in, levy; activate, call up, mobilize.

5. furnish, stock, provision, store, provide; equip, arm, fit out, accouter.

6. engage, obtain, acquire, procure, muster, gather up *or* together, *Inf.* round up; enroll, sign up.

7. replenish, replace, reinforce, strengthen, fortify, shore up, buttress; enlarge, augment, increase, *Inf.* beef up.

8. (*of health or strength*) renew, restore, refresh, revive, reinvigorate, regain, rehabilitate; recover, recuperate, convalesce, get well; improve, mend, heal, be on the mend; pull through, survive.

rectangular, *adj.* quadrate, right-angled, angular, *Math.* orthogonic, oblong; square, quadratic, foursquare.

rectify, *v.* **1.** set right, right, square, correct, redress, revise, reform, straighten out; repair, fix, remedy, mend, cure, heal, doctor, minister; better, ameliorate, meliorate, improve, amend, emend.

2. adjust, regulate, straighten, focus, tune in *or* up, attune, fine-tune; bring into line, synchronize, collimate, calibrate, align, balance.

rectitude, *n.* **1.** moral virtue, moral strength, integrity, probity, morality, uprightness; rightness, goodness, virtuousness, righteousness, honorableness; honor, virtue, decency, upstandingness, respectability, good character; veracity, honesty, truthfulness, credibility, guilelessness, scrupulousness; impeccability, unimpeachability, irreproachability, uncorruptness, cleanness; sinlessness, purity, innocence, immaculateness, immaculacy, spotlessness, stainlessness; saintliness, godliness, chastity, pudicity, modesty, unlicentiousness, undissoluteness.

2. correctness, soundness, accuracy, precision, exactness, exactitude; validity, verity, justness, accordance; closeness, nicety, fidelity, faithfulness, literalness.

rector, *n.* **1.** pastor, vicar, dean, chaplain, spiritual director; dignitary, prelate, bishop, monsignor.

2. clergyman, ecclesiastic, churchman, parson, *Dial.* dominie, divine, clerk, clerical, reverend, cassock, servant of God, *Brit.* blackcoat.

3. minister, priest, presbyter, father, confessor, padre, curé, abbé.

4. preacher, evangelist, *Usu. Disparaging.* pulpiteer. See **preacher, evangelist.**

5. theologian, canonist, hierophant. See **theologian.**

rectory, *n.* **1.** parsonage, *Rom. Cath. Ch.* presbytery, pastorate, parish house, church house, manse, vicarage, deanery, *Southern U.S.* pastorium, *Brit. Archaic.* glebe house.

2. *British.* benefice, parsonage, pastorate, episcopate, bishopric, diocese, see, deanery, chaplaincy, curacy.

recumbent, *adj.* **1.** lying down, decumbent, accumbent, reclining, couchant; supine, resupine, flat, lying flat, flat on one's back; prone, procumbent, prostrate; horizontal, stretched out, spread out, spread-eagle, sprawling; resting, leaning, inclined.

2. idle, inactive, at leisure, unoccupied, doing nothing; lounging, lolling, lazy, listless, languid, lackadaisical, apathetic, phlegmatic; sedentary, passive, dull, sluggish; hebetudinous, lethargic, drowsy, sleepy, somnolent, slumberous, torpid, torpescent.

recuperate, *v.* **1.** recover, convalesce, pick up, perk up, rally, recruit; improve, get better, get well, heal, mend, be on the mend, be on the road to recovery, regain one's strength; revive, come back, resurge, resurrect, be on the rise; come around, pull through, come through, take a turn for the better, take a favorable turn; turn the corner, make a comeback, *Inf.* snap out of it, *Inf.* get back on one's feet, *Inf.* bounce back, *Inf.* feel one's oats again; take a fresh *or* new lease on life, come to, get back in shape, return to health.

2. regenerate, rejuvenate, renew, restore, refresh; reanimate, resuscitate, revivify, revive, bring back to life.

recuperative, *adj.* corrective, restorative, revivatory, reviviscent, recuperatory.

recur, *v.* **1.** occur again, re-occur, persist, continue, reappear, persevere; alternate, come in turn, intermit; repeat, return, come and go, *Dial.* come 'round.

2. be remembered, return to the mind, flash across the memory, intrude on one's thoughts; live *or* dwell in memory, haunt one's thoughts, never leave one's mind for long, run through one's mind; be recollected, come back when least expected; trouble, vex, harass, badger, rankle one's thoughts.

recurrent, *adj.* repeated, repetitious, repetitive, persistent, continual, frequent; haunting, incessant, re-echoing, rhythmic, pulsative, pulsating, throbbing, regular as clockwork; renewed, cyclical, periodic, periodical, seasonal, regular; alternate, coming again and again; returning at intervals, intermittent, reappearing, continuous, chronic, remittent, ceaseless; iterative, reiterative, reiterated, habitual, like the beat beat beat of the tom-tom.

red, *adj.* **1.** reddish, crimson, cardinal, *Fr. rouge, Heraldry* gules, carmine, Tyrian; rubescent, rufous, rufescent, rubicund, amaranthine; vinaceous, wine-colored, claret-colored, port-wine; scarlet, ruby, vermilion, vermeil, russet, cherry, cochineal, maroon; murrey, stammel, auburn, Titian; pink, salmon, coral; lobster-red, fire-engine red, beet-red.

2. rosy, roseate, flushed, hot, red-hot, hectic, feverish, fevered, febrile, fiery, burning; blooming, glowing, florid, blowzy; sunburned, burnt, ruddy, red-faced.

3. sanguine, bloody, incarnadine, gory; ensanguined, blood-red, bloodstained, bloodshot.

4. red-haired, redheaded, red-bearded; chestnut, carroty, rusty, brick-red, lateritious; strawberry, strawberry blond, sandy.

5. embarrassed, blushing, flushed, sheepish, red in the face, *Inf.* slapped.

6. radical, revolutionary, revolutionist, left, leftist, left-leaning, extremist, ultra, *U.S. Sl.* pink, *U.S. Sl.* pinko; communist, Soviet, Russian, Bolshevist; Marxist, Leninist, Stalinist, Trotskyist, Maoist.

7. sore, raw, chafed, inflamed, open, blistered; smarting, irritating, burning, fiery; sensitive, tender, tingling, algetic.

—*n.* **8.** redness, reddishness, rubricity, rubicundity, *Heraldry.* gules, *Fr. rouge,* rubor; ruddiness, floridness, floridity, color, rosiness, flush, blush.

9. see red *Informal.* get mad, get angry, madden, rile, become enraged, lash into a fury, become irritated, become exasperated; seethe, boil, explode, burst.

redeem, *v.* **1.** retrieve, regain, buy back, recover, reclaim; repay, make good, pay in full, pay off, cover, make the final payment.

2. ransom, rescue, save, deliver, liberate, emancipate, free, set free, release; extricate, repossess, *Law.* replevy.

3. exchange, change, give in exchange, turn in, cash in, trade in, collect on.

4. regenerate, reform, set straight, *Inf.* get on the straight and narrow; turn from sin, convert, restore, reinstate, rehabilitate; absolve, purge, shrive; intercede for, mediate on behalf of.

5. discharge, make good, be as good as one's word, acquit, satisfy; keep, hold to, obey, adhere to, abide by; see through, be faithful to, keep faith with, meet, perform, carry out, dispatch, execute; complete, realize, consummate, accomplish.

6. recompense, requite, propitiate, compensate; offset, expiate, atone for, make amends for, redress, make restitution, settle.

redeemable, *adj.* exchangeable, good for, worth something; retrievable, restorable, extricable; correctable, curable, improvable, amendable; corrigible, rescuable, salvageable, worth saving.

redeemer, *n.* **1.** ransomer, emancipator, liberator, rescuer, deliverer, freer, manumitter, savior.

2. Redeemer Savior, Our Lord, Jesus Christ. See **Jesus** (*def.* **1**).

redemption, *n.* **1.** repurchase, recovery by payment, restitution, restoration, reinstatement, re-establishment.

2. paying in full, paying off, *Inf.* burning the mortgage.

3. compensation, conciliation, propitiation, expiation, atonement, reparation, amends.

4. retrieval, saving, freeing; liberation, deliverance, emancipation, rescue; release, reprieve, escape.

5. rehabilitation, regeneration, reformation, salvation, rebirth, reconstitution, reclamation, conversion, *Inf.* comeback.

red-handed, *adv.* in the act, in the very act, *Latin. in flagrante delicto, Law.* flagrante delicto, with one's hand in the till, with one's hand in the cookie jar, with one's finger in the pie, *Sl.* with one's pants down, *Sl.* dead to rights; at the scene of the crime.

red-hot, *adj.* **1.** burning, scorching, blistering, sizzling; white-hot; molten.

2. fiery, hot, hot-blooded, impassioned, heated, inflamed, feverish, febrile, flushed; passionate, vehement, fervid, fervent, zealous, intense, ardent; fanatic, perfervid, totally committed, hard-core; excited, anxious, agog, all agog, all hopped-up, *Sl.* psyched *or* psyched-up; enthusiastic, eager, avid, keen, *Sl.* gung-ho.

3. mad, *Inf.* raving mad, *Inf.* stark-raving mad, rabid, foaming *or* frothing at the mouth; raging, raving, frenzied, frenetic, frantic, wild-eyed, blue in the face; furious, violent, wild, infuriate, ferocious, maniacal, *Inf.* hog-wild; hysterical, distracted, carried-away, beside oneself, like one possessed; berserk, amuck, running amuck.

4. brand-new, newest, latest, most-recent, up-to-the-minute; hot off the presses.

redolence, *n.* fragrance, aroma, perfume, essence, scent, incense, bouquet, *Archaic.* flavor; odor, smell, reek.

redolent, *adj.* **1.** fragrant, aromatic, odoriferous, odorous, perfumed, scented, ambrosial, savory, sweet, sweet-smelling.

2. smelly, reeking, malodorous; pungent, strong, sharp, nose-piercing.

3. suggestive, reminiscent, evocative, mindful, remindful.

redoubtable, *adj.* formidable, awesome, aweful, awe-inspiring; terrible, dread, dreadful, fearful, fearsome.

redress, *n.* **1.** amends, reparation, atonement, restitution, restoration, correction, repair; requital, quittance, retribution, satisfaction; compensation, recompense, payment, remuneration, indemnification.

2. improvement, betterment, amelioration, melioration, help, aid, assistance; relief, alleviation, assuagement, mitigation, mollification, appeasement, softening, easing, reduction, lessening; rescue, deliverance, liberation, release, *Law.* acquittal.

—*v.* **3.** rectify, set right, make right, set straight, square, settle, patch up; remedy, heal, repair, mend, fix, fix up, correct, reform, amend; improve, better, ameliorate, meliorate, help *or* aid a situation; relieve, alleviate, assuage, allay, mitigate, mollify, appease, ease, soften, reduce, lessen; readjust, adjust, regulate, put on an even keel; balance, even up, make fair.

4. recompense, repay, compensate for, make it up to [s.o.]; make amends, make reparation *or* restitution, restore, make up for; atone for, expiate, pay for.

red tape, *n.* paperwork, paper pushing, writing, documentation, information-gathering, research; papers, forms, documents, blanks to be filled out; make-work, nonsense, junk, *Inf.* fiddle-faddle, *Inf.* messing *or* playing around, *Sl.* bull, *Sl.* mickey-mouse; bureaucracy, procedure, routine, motions, steps, protocol, etiquette, *Inf.* SOP; ceremony, ceremoniousness, formality, concern with form, propriety, *Inf.* hocus pocus, *Inf.* mumbo jumbo; rigidity, punctilio, attention to detail; officialism, beadledom, redtapism, pettiness, small-mindedness, rigmarole.

reduce, *v.* **1.** decrease, diminish, retrench, subtract, subduct, lessen, shorten, contract, miniaturize; cut, cut into, cut down, cut back, cut short, *Inf.* make a dent in, abridge, abbreviate, *Obs.* breviate; narrow, shrink, compress, buff, dock, crop, clip, shear, trim, pare down, shave, nip; curtail, limit, constrict, restrict, confine, cramp; abstract, synopsize, summarize, condense, digest, brief, epitomize; stub, stunt, truncate; slim down, slenderize, shrivel, wither; *Naut.* reef.

2. mitigate, ease, relax, alleviate, relieve, let up, attenuate, abate, slacken, remit, assuage, mellow, *Obs.* lenify; restrain, harness, bridle, repress, retard, curb, check, temper, modify, moderate; soften, modulate, tone down, turn down, tune down, muffle, mute, quiet, silence, deaden; brake, slow down, throttle down, rein, rein in; blunt, bate, dull; incapacitate, enfeeble, debilitate, break, inactivate, devitalize.

3. degrade, demote, downgrade, lower in rank *or* standing, dismiss *or* remove from office, declass, break *or* strip of rank, disrate, cashier, *Mil.* drum out, *Mil. Sl.* bust, *Inf.* kick upstairs, disbar, defrock *or* unfrock; depose, unseat, dethrone, *Rare.* disenthrone; shame, put to shame, disgrace, dishonor, bring low, ruin, debase, abase, vitiate, lower; humble, humiliate, mortify, *Sl.* put down.

4. belittle, deprecate, disparage, detract, deflate, put in one's place, depreciate, derogate, *Inf.* talk down; minimize, dispraise, underestimate, underrate, underreckon, undervalue, slight, take away from, beggar, extenuate, misprize, think nothing of, set no store by, fail to count on.

5. embarrass, disconcert, chagrin, discomfit, discountenance, abash, confound, perplex, nonplus, confuse.

6. (*all of price*) discount, mark down, cut, slash, cheapen, put on sale; deduct, subtract, drop; relax, ease.

7. subdue, quell, quash, squash, checkmate, *Inf.* squelch, put down, foil, still, stamp out, put out, extinguish; crush, rout, discomfit, overrun, put to flight, conquer, vanquish, surmount, overcome, overpower, overwhelm, *Sl.* wipe the floor with, *Euph.* kill; subjugate, subject, master.

8. dilute, thin, mix, admix, alloy, rarefy, *Inf.* doctor, *Archaic.* extenuate; (*all of alcohol*) weaken, cut, water, water down.

reduction, *n.* **1.** decrease, decreasing, loss, lessening, decline, cutback, rollback, decrement, decrescence, depression; abbreviation, diminution, subtraction, subduction, shortening, condensing, condensation, compressing, compression, contracting, contraction; abridgement, syncope, ellipsis, elision; retrenchment, shrinking, shrinkage, narrowing, cutting down *or* short, cropping, clipping, concision, constricting, constriction; limiting, limitation, restricting, curtailing, curtailment; abstracting, abstraction, summarizing, summarization.

2. mitigation, easing, relaxing, relaxation, alleviating, alleviation, relief, attenuation, abatement, slackening, remission, assuagement; restraint, harnessing, bridling, repressing, repression, retardation, curbing, checking, tempering, temperance, modification, moderation; softening, modulating, toning down, tuning down, turning down, muffling, muting, quieting, silencing, deadening; braking, slowing down, throttling down, reining in; blunting, bating, dulling; incapacitating, incapacitation, enfeebling, debilitating, debility, weakening, weakness.

3. degradation, demotion, deposition. See **degradation** (*def.* **1**).

4. discount, cut, cutrate, deduction, write-off, concession, allowance; depreciation, devaluation; refund, rebate, reimbursement, remuneration, compensation; agio, premium.

5. miniature, copy, model, draft, sketch, abstract, outline, proposal, syllabus, résumé, précis, prospectus, conspectus, compendium, survey, epitome, brief, summary; abridgment, digest, pandect, condensation; synopsis, review, recapitulation.

redundancy, *n.* **1.** repetition, pleonasm, tautology, battology; verbosity, prolixity, verbiage, wordiness, overamplification, windiness, long-windedness.

2. surplus, excess, hypertrophy, glut; superfluity, plethora, excessiveness, uselessness, needlessness, a fifth at bridge, fifth wheel; exaggeration, inflatedness, hyperbole, magnification; superabundance, lavishness, profusion, copiousness, repletion.

redundant, *adj.* **1.** verbose, prolix, wordy, diffuse; tautological, pleonastic, repetitious, reiterating, battological; periphrastic, roundabout, circumlocutory; fustian, bombastic, windy, long-winded.

2. excessive, excess, in excess, hypertrophic, exorbitant; more than enough, more than ample, overmuch, superfluous, *Fr. de trop,* too much, surplus, plethoric; unnecessary, needless, unwarranted, useless, needed like a hole in the head, about as useful as a fifth wheel.

3. superabundant, lavish, profuse, prodigal, bountiful, copious, inexhaustible, replete; exuberant, extravagant, luxuriant; inflated, hyperbolic, exaggerated, inordinate, immoderate.

reduplicate, *v.* double, repeat, duplicate; echo, imitate, ape, iterate, do again; copy, ditto, replicate, facsimile.

reecho, *v.* echo back, echo back and forth, resound, reverberate, resonate; bounce back, repeat again; ring, peal.

reedy, *adj.* **1.** stalky, long, tall, slender, thin, thin as a rail, skinny, slim, wispy.

2. piping, pipy, shrill; windy, airy; silvery, mellifluous, mellow, sweet, musical.

reef, *n.* bar, sand bar, bank, sandbank, shoal, shallows, flat, mud flat, ridge, coral ridge.

reefer, *n.* marijuana cigarette; *All Sl.* joint, jay, jay bar, jay smoke, j.; *All Sl.* stick, tea stick, stick of tea, dope stick, dream stick, stick of gage *or* gauge, gage stick, gage butt; *All Sl.* reefer weed, hointer, spliff.

reek, *n.* **1.** stink, stench, fetor, fetidness, odor, malodor, mephitis; body odor, *Sl.* B.O., halitosis, bad breath.

2. vapor, effluvium, steam, exhaust, fume, mist, fog, cloud.

—*v.* **3.** stink, smell, smell to high heaven, smell like a goat, assault the nostrils, knock out.

4. steam, smoke, vaporize, evaporate, gasify; smoke, treat, cure.

5. perspire, drip, sweat, be soggy; be bloody, be covered with blood.

reel[1], *n.* rotary device, wheel; bobbin, spool, spindle, *Obs.* arbor, holder; pin, axle.

reel[2], *v.* **1.** sway, rock, swing; stagger, stumble, totter, falter, flounder; lurch, pitch, roll, surge; waver, fall back.

2. turn round and round, whirl, twirl, spin, gyrate; turn, rotate, circumrotate, revolve, circumvolve, pivot, pirouette.

refer, *v.* **1.** direct, point, conduct, send, turn; intend, mean, indicate, denote, signify, suggest, connote, have to do with.

2. hand over, submit, yield, deliver, consign, relegate, render; transfer, bestow, entrust, deposit.

3. assign, attribute, put down to, ascribe; arrogate, impute, blame on; trace, accredit to, credit with, account to, chalk up to.

4. relate, correspond with, apply, pertain, belong; involve, connect, touch, take in, cover, encompass.

5. address, appeal to, consult, ask, talk over with, confer with, have recourse; turn to, resort to.

6. mention, speak of, allude to, invoke, bring up; cite, quote, adduce, give as an example; hint at, make mention of, touch on, comment upon, advert to, animadvert upon, make note of, point out; name, specify, indicate, direct attention to, call attention to, bring to one's notice, call to mind.

referee, *n.* **1.** arbiter, arbitress, judge, determiner, decider, adjudicator, *Inf.* ref; moderator, umpire, *Inf.* ump, linesman; arbitrator, negotiator, bargainer, reconciler, peacemaker, *Obs.* arbitrer; go-between, intermediary, mediator, intercessor.

—*v.* **2.** umpire, *Inf.* ump, *Inf.* ref; arbitrate, decide, determine, settle; judge, adjudge, adjudicate, pronounce *or* pass judgment, decree, sentence.

3. mediate, intervene, interpose, step in, come between; negotiate, bargain, bring to terms, parley; intercede, conciliate, placate, reconcile.

reference, *n.* **1.** mention, mentioning, referral, referment; allusion, notice, adducement, quotation, specification; notification, apprising, advisement; hint, suggestion, intimation, inkling, innuendo, implication, insinuation; substantiation, illustration, instance.

2. assignment, attribution, ascription, credit, arrogation, imputation, blame.

3. note, citation, indication, indicator, direction, key.

4. endorsement, affirmation, allegation, voucher; attestation, testimony, evidence, witness; declaration, statement.

5. relation, regard, respect, bearing, consideration, concern; applicability, relevance, pertinence, correlation.

refine, *v.* **1.** purify, rarefy, subtilize; clarify, clear; wash, lave, *Chem.* edulcorate, cleanse, depurate; strain, sift, filter, *Chem.* rectify, elutriate; purge, *Med.* absterge, expurgate, winnow.

2. cultivate, polish, humanize, civilize, subtilize, spiritualize; elevate, uplift, advance, ennoble, sublime, sublimate, sensitize; soften, temper, improve, meliorate, ameliorate.

3. elaborate, perfect, complete, consummate; improve, hone, chisel, sharpen; adjust, regulate, square.

4. ripen, mature, develop; soften, mellow.

5. discriminate, split hairs, cavil, mince, subtilize, quibble, pettifog; prevaricate, equivocate, wiredraw, beg the question, reason in a circle, beat about the bush.

refined, *adj.* **1.** cultivated, polished, cultured, civilized, well-bred, genteel, courtly; finished, fine, urbane; gentlemanly, ladylike, mannerly, polite, courteous; aesthetic, tasteful, in good taste, graceful, delicate, exquisite; noble, gentle, pure; classic, aristocratic, high-class; elevated, ennobled, sublimated, high-minded.

2. pure, purified, rarefied, clarified, distilled, subtilized; purged, cleansed, clean, cleaned, *Chem.* sublimed, *Chem.* sublimated.

3. subtle, exact, precise; meticulous, punctilious, discriminating, fastidious; overscrupulous, overconscientious, overcritical; formal, proper, dainty, strict, overnice; squeamish, fussy, finicking, finicky, finical; hairsplitting, casuistic, pettifogging, quibbling.

refinement, *n.* **1.** fineness, elegance, gentleness, polish, grace, delicacy, beauty; culture, cultivation, civilization; urbanity, urbaneness, suavity, suaveness, sophistication; tastefulness, discrimination; fastidiousness, nicety, finesse; chivalry, gentility, good breeding, breeding; propriety, civility, tact, politeness, good manners, courtesy.

2. purification, subtilization, clarification, distillation; cleaning, cleansing, *Chem.* edulcoration, elutriation; abstersion; *Chem.* sublimation, filtration; lustration, expurgation.

3. improvement, betterment, reform, revision, rectification, amendment, amelioration, melioration; advancement, enhancement, enrichment; progress, development, advance; lift, elevation, rise; perfection, progression.

4. distinction, subtlety, fine point, nuance, nicety, delicacy, punctilio; discrimination, exactness, preciseness, differentiation; fastidiousness, meticulousness, punctiliousness, hairsplitting, casuistry, pettifoggery, quibbling; finicality, finicalness, hypercriticism.

reflect, *v.* **1.** mirror, return, give back, cast back, throw back, send back, rebound; echo, reecho, repeat; copy, imitate, ditto, reproduce; resonate, resound, repercuss, reverberate, reply; flashback, flash.

2. manifest, exhibit, show, evince, display, present, demonstrate, exemplify, illustrate; express, make known, set forth, advertise, publicize, announce, broadcast; parade, show off; expose, air, reveal, lay open, lay bare, bring to light, disclose, unveil, uncover; betray, give away, divulge; indicate, imply, suggest, connote, denote, give evidence of, betoken.

3. meditate, contemplate, muse, ponder, brood, mull over, dwell on, be in a brown study; cogitate, ruminate, chew over, chew one's cud; think about *or* over, be lost in thought, put on one's thinking cap; have one's mind on, wonder about, consider, speculate; review, turn over, weigh, evaluate, study, examine.

4. discredit, throw a bad light on, destroy confidence in, undermine belief in, impair the reputation of; credit, do credit to, strengthen confidence *or* belief in.

reflection, *n.* **1.** mirror, twin, image, *Sl.* spitting image, counterpart, duplicate, clone; imitation, reproduction, copy, replica, replication; representation, semblance, likeness, picture; shadow, outline; echo, reverberation, repercussion; recoil, reaction, reflex, backlash, return, ricochet, backlash.

2. evidence, sign, symbol, token, mark; indication, symptom, syndrome; proof, substantiation, testimony, corroboration, certification.

3. contemplation, contemplating, meditation, thought; consideration, cogitation, rumination, ruminating, brown study, musing, pondering, brooding, mulling over, chewing over, chewing one's cud, wondering; deliberation, deliberating, speculation, speculating, conjecture, conjecturing, lucubration, cerebration.

4. impression, perception, sentiment, feeling, notion, idea, conception; theory, view, opinion, observation, remark, speculation, comment.

5. imputation, attribution, ascription, arrogation, accounting; incrimination, crimination, implication, *Obs., Rare.* accrimination; indictment, blame, censure, reproach, inculpation.

reflective, *adj.* 1. imitative, mirrorlike, repetitive, echoing; resounding, reverberating.

2. contemplative, meditative, meditating, musing, pondering, brooding, mulling over; reflecting, cogitative, cogitating, ruminant, ruminating; pensive, thoughtful, concentrating, intent, abstracted, preoccupied, absorbed, engrossed, rapt in thought, lost in thought, bemused, *Archaic.* museful; dreamy, woolgathering; deliberative, excogitative, lucubrative; philosophical, intellectual, speculative.

reflector, *n.* mirror, looking glass, pier glass, cheval glass, glass, speculum; reverberator, reflecting surface, resonator, sounding board.

reflex, *adj.* 1. reactive, responsive, reflexive; rebounding, boomeranging, recoiling; resilient, elastic, springy, bouncy; knee-jerk, spontaneous, automatic, immediate, involuntary.

2. reflected, mirrored, returned; echoed, echoing, repetitive, reechoed, reechoing, reverberating, reverberant, reverberative, resounding, *Obs.* repercussive.

3. bent, crooked, curved, hooked, hook-shaped, adunc, unciform, *Anat.* hamate, *Biol.* uncinate, *Meteorology.* uncinus.

reform, *n.* 1. improvement, betterment, amelioration, melioration; change, revision, revolutionary *or* major change, step ahead, progress; switch, changeover, conversion; rewrite, remake, reorganization, cleanup, purification, purgation; amendment, emendment, correction, rectification, reparation, renovation, reclamation, recovery; salvation, rescue, deliverance, redemption, ransom.

—*v.* 2. improve, better, make better, ameliorate, meliorate; change, revise, revolutionize, change over, switch, convert; rewrite, redo, refashion, remodel, remake, make over, revamp, reorganize; clean up, purify, purge, cleanse; amend, emend, correct, set straight, straighten out, set to rights, rectify; fix *or* fix up, cure, mend, repair, remedy, renovate, restore; rehabilitate, reclaim, recover, save, salvage, rescue; deliver, redeem, ransom.

3. mend one's ways, be a new man, turn over a new leaf, wipe the slate clean, start anew; make amends, make up for the past, atone for one's sins.

reformatory, *adj.* 1. reformative, reforming, corrective, correcting, emendatory, remedial; restorative, restoring, medicinal, restitutive, restitutory; therapeutic, curative, curing, sanative, sanatory, healing, recuperative, recuperatory.

2. reform school, house of correction, penal institution.

refractory, *adj.* recalcitrant, contumacious, froward, balky, uncooperative, crossgrained, wrongheaded, perverse, contrary, willful, self-willed, stiffnecked, *U.S. Inf.* notionate, *Inf.* cussed, *Archaic.* untoward; obstinate, stubborn, stubborn as a mule, mulish, muleheaded, pigheaded, bullheaded, bullish, headstrong; ungovernable, unmanageable, uncontrollable, difficult, restive, unruly, wayward, fractious, incorrigible.

refrain, *v.* abstain, forbear, desist, restrain, hold back voluntarily; forgo, do without, sacrifice; give up, *Inf.* swear off, quit, leave off; break off, let up, pause; renounce, relinquish, put aside; discontinue, stop, *Sl.* cheese, hold, stay, cease; drop, have done with, let alone, let be, let well enough alone, keep one's hands off, turn aside, resist.

refresh, *v.* 1. renew, revive, revivify, resuscitate, breathe new life into, bring back to life, reanimate; regenerate, rejuvenate, put *or* infuse new blood into, invigorate, reinvigorate, revitalize, energize, give new energy, pick up, exhilarate, *Inf.* hit the spot; strengthen, give new strength to, fortify, brace, reinforce.

2. cheer, cheer up, enliven, liven up, freshen, freshen up, make fresh, perk up, brighten up.

3. freshen, stimulate, jog, prod, prompt, set in motion, activate; motivate, give impetus to, provoke; awaken, reawaken, rouse, arouse, kindle, enkindle, rekindle.

4. restore, repair, renovate, fix *or* fix up, recondition, revamp, redo, redecorate, refurnish, refurbish, do over; repaint, revarnish, rewax, retouch, touch up, brush up, polish up, spruce up, *Sl.* spiff up.

refreshing, *adj.* renewing, reviving, revivifying, resuscitating, reanimating; regenerating, rejuvenating, tonic, invigorating, reinvigorating, revitalizing, energizing, stimulating, exhilarating; thirst-quenching, cooling, like a breath of fresh air; cheering, encouraging, good, pleasant, bright; enlivening, livening, enheartening; strengthening, fortifying, bracing, reinforcing.

refreshment, *n.* 1. food, nutriment, nutrition, pabulum, alimentation, nurture, sustenance, sustenation, subsistence; aliment, viands, meat, bread *or* daily bread, groceries, foodstuffs, solids, edibles, *Inf.* grub, *Sl.* eats, *Sl.* chow, *Chiefly Brit. Sl.* scoff; snack, a little something to eat, bite, nosh, between-meal snack, *Sl.* munchies; victuals, provisions, cheer, provender, rations, commons, comestibles, *Western U.S. Sl.* chuck, *Brit. Sl.* prog.

2. renewal, revival, revivification, revitalization, resuscitation, reanimation; regeneration, rejuvenation, invigoration, reinvigoration, revitalization, stimulation, exhilaration; cheering up, encouragement, enlivening, livening up, enheartening, inspiration; strengthening, fortification, reinforcement.

refrigerate, *v.* put in the refrigerator, keep cold, keep cool, keep in the refrigerator *or* icebox; cool, chill, congeal; put in the freezer, freeze, *Physics.* regelate, keep in the freezer.

refrigeration, *n.* cooling, chilling, congealment, congelation, keeping cold, freezing, *Physics.* regelation.

refrigerator, *n.* 1. icebox, ice chest, *Sl.* fridge, *Sl.* refridge, *Trademark.* Frigidaire; cold storage, cooler, refrigerated room *or* box, refrigerator car.

2. condenser, rectifier.

refuge, *n.* 1. shelter, protection, security, safety, shelter from a storm; custody, keeping, charge, ward, guardianship, preservation, safekeeping; hiding, concealment, seclusion, privacy, retirement; help, aid, support, patronage, defense, championship; guard, escort, convoy.

2. asylum, haven, sanctuary, palladium, sanctum,

sanctum sanctorum, ark; safety zone, harbor, port, port in a storm, *Scot.* bield; retreat, hospice, hermitage, cloister, ashram; mew, cover, covert, coverture, hideout, hiding place, hideaway; corner, dark corner, shade, recess, nook, cranny, niche; stronghold, fortress, fortification, citadel, bastion, keep, safehold, tower, pillar, pillar of strength, rock, rock of ages; nest, lair, den, cave, hole, dugout, abri.

3. resort, recourse, last resort *or* recourse, expedient, provision, stopgap; tactic, stratagem, machination, intrigue; artiface, device, trick, ruse, wile, subterfuge; maneuver, circumvention, dodge, feint, evasion, shift, sleight, juggle; front, facade, sham, blind, screen, smoke screen; pretext, pretense, pretension, loophole, contrivance.

refugee, *n.* **1.** fugitive, runaway, escaper, escapee, émigré, fleer; deserter, bolter, eloper, absconder, *Inf.* skedaddler.

2. foreigner, stranger, alien, displaced person, D.P., outsider, outlander, tramontane; exile, outlaw, wanderer, stateless person, man without a country, Wandering Jew.

refulgent, *adj.* shining, glistening, aglisten, sparkling, glittering, aglitter; bright, sunny, sunshiny, illuminated, alight, lit, lighted, illuminated; irradiant, irradiated, lambent, resplendent, brilliant, beaming, beamy; dazzling, intense, ablaze, aflame, afire, blazing; fulgent, effulgent, splendid, splendrous, gorgeous; radiant, radiative; lustrous, lucid, lucent, *Rare.* relucent; glowing, aglow, luminous, luminescent, luminiferous, incandescent, phosphorescent, nitid, orient; shiny, glossy, gleaming, agleam, glaring; polished, burnished, argent.

refund, *v.* **1.** restore, replace, return, repay, give back, pay back; recompense, compensate, remunerate, reimburse; remit, make compensation, satisfy; adjust, settle, square, square with; make repayment, make amends, redress, make good, make restitution; cover, indemnify, requite, redeem.

—n. **2.** repayment, return, reimbursement, rebate; allowance, percentage, *Inf.* cut; discount.

refurbish, *v.* renovate, revamp, overhaul, recondition, rejuvenate, resurrect, rescue; renew, retouch, restore, remodel, refit, rebuild; repair, put in repair, put in good order, service, treat, mend, patch, *Inf.* fix up; refresh, freshen, face-lift, revive, resuscitate; brighten up, polish up, rub up; clean, spruce up, *Sl.* spiff *or* spiffy up, *Inf.* clean up-fix up-paint up.

refusal, *n.* **1.** denial, nonconsent, withholding, disallowance; disapproval, turndown, veto, thumbs down, nay; negation, dissent, forswearing, abjuration, abnegation, disfavor; unwillingness, noncompliance, declension; regrets, nonacceptance; disclaimer, renouncement, disavowal, repudiation, renunciation, rejection, rebuff, repulse, *Inf.* the big NO.

2. option, preemption, emption, election, choice *or* privilege of refusal.

refuse[1], *v.* **1.** reject, spurn, disdain, say no *or* nay, refuse to consider, refuse point blank, put one's foot down, not budge an inch, not yield an inch, turn thumbs-down, shake one's head at; decline, *Inf.* pass up *or* by, *Inf.* not buy; abstain from, stand aloof from, put behind one, abnegate.

2. deny, forbid, withhold consent, not allow, not permit, turn a deaf ear to, resist entreaty, naysay, *Sl.* nix; not countenance, not hear of, not put up with.

3. repel, rebuff, repulse; bar, prohibit, exclude, slam the door, refuse to have anything to do with, have nothing to do with, turn one's back on, set one's face against, *Inf.* turn down; send back, cast aside; veto, disallow, vote nay, vote in the negative, withhold one's assent, disapprove, frown upon, view with disfavor, discountenance, look askance at, grudge, begrudge, keep back.

4. dodge, shirk, avoid; balk, be unwilling, resist, protest, boggle, demur, stickle, scruple.

refuse[2], *n.* **1.** garbage, rubbish, *Dial.* culch, waste, *Brit.* wastrel, discarded matter; offal, carrion, rot, spoil; offscourings, dregs, draff, grounds, remains, leavings, leftovers; scraps, orts, hogwash, swill; remainder, residue, residuum, scum; scoria, dross, recrement, slag.

2. junk, worthless stuff, *Sl.* dreck, trumpery; trash, riffraff, *Brit. Dial.* raff, litter, chaff; filth, dirt, dust, sweepings; debris, detritus, rubble, stubble, wreckage; fragments, remnants, fag ends, bits and pieces, odds and ends; castoffs, rags, tatters, castaways, rejects, discards.

—adj. **3.** rejected, discarded, cast off, thrown out *or* away; worthless, useless, good-for-nothing, of no real value, nugatory.

refutation, *n.* disproof, invalidation, contradiction; negation, denial, disclaimer, confutation, rebuttal; exposé, exposure, *Inf.* show-up. See **rebuttal**.

refute, *v.* disprove, rebut, contradict, repugn; confute, deny, prove to be false, discredit, belie, give the lie to, expose. See **rebut**.

regain, *v.* **1.** get back, recover, make back, win back, reobtain, recoup, retrieve, find; recapture, reseize, retake, take back; repossess, *Law.* replevy, *Law.* replevin, resume, recall, reclaim; reestablish, reinstate.

2. get back to, reach again, return to, reattain.

regal, *adj.* majestic, kingly, princely, royal, lordly, noble, monarchal, monarchial, monarchical, imperial, magisterial, *Rare.* magistral, sovereign; august, stately, dignified, distingué, distinguished, proud, noble; grand, magnificent, pompous, palatial, splendid, resplendent, marvelous, superb; sublime, elevated, high, lofty, exalted, glorious; awesome, imposing, impressive, striking.

regale, *v.* **1.** banquet, treat, fete, take out; give *or* throw a party for, hold a reception for; honor, do the honors, kill the fatted calf, ring the bell for; toast, salute, drink to, raise *or* tilt glasses to, celebrate.

2. delight, entertain, amuse, divert; humor, indulge, comfort, flatter; please, gratify, warm the heart of, gladden; captivate, fascinate, interest; entrance, bewitch, transport, enchant, enrapture, charm, becharm.

3. feast, dine, wine, wine and dine, partake; gormandize, gorge, engorge, glut, play a good knife and fork; indulge, cram, stuff, eat one's fill, *Sl.* pig out.

regard, *v.* **1.** look, look on *or* upon, view, see, eye, behold, set *or* lay eyes on; witness, see with one's own eyes, sight, catch sight of, descry, glimpse, catch *or* get a glimpse of, spy, espy, *Inf.* get a load of, take a sidelong look; perceive, discover, detect, discern, find, take in, make out; notice, note, mark, be aware of, be conscious of, take notice of, remark, pay attention to, heed, attend, mind; watch, keep an eye on.

2. consider, contemplate, weigh, think over, turn over in one's mind, give thought to, mull over; ponder, *Archaic.* perpend, ruminate, cogitate, meditate on, brood over, muse on; deliberate, reflect upon, put one's mind to, give one's attention to, pay attention to, study, pore over, examine; chew over, think about, kick around, tinker with; *Inf.* take a long, hard look at.

3. esteem, value, appreciate, prize, cherish, hold dear, treasure; honor, revere, reverence, respect, venerate, pay respect to, defer to; admire, think highly of, look up to, hold a high opinion of; like, love, be fond of, hold in affection, adore, care for; commend, speak well of, praise, extol, exalt.

4. concern, relate to, pertain to, appertain to, have to do with; refer to, apply to, mean, go for; affect, touch, bear on *or* upon, have bearing on, be relevant to, be of importance *or* interest to, interest; be connected with, be affiliated with, be involved with.

5. deem, adjudge, judge, think, believe, hold, opine, suppose; estimate, gauge, appraise, rate.

—*n.* **6.** reference, relation, importance, bearing, respect; connection, association, link, tie-in, interconnection, correlation; pertinence, relevancy, applicability, applicableness.

7. aspect, point, particular; item, detail, feature.

8. concern, care, thought, consideration; attention, carefulness, caution, prudence, pains; heed, heedfulness, watchfulness, advertence; alertness, vigilance, circumspection, wariness; awareness, consciousness, mindfulness; study, inquiry, scrutiny; contemplation, reflection, meditation, circumspection.

9. look, glance, glimpse; gaze, leer, stare, come-hither look; glare, glower, scowl, dirty look.

10. sight, espial, first sight; inspection, search, examination, *Inf.* once-over, *Inf.* look-see, *Sl.* gander; survey, sweep, observation, observance, watch; review, overlook, birds-eye view.

11. respect, esteem, favor, estimation, high regard, high opinion; admiration, approval, approbation, appreciation; honor, reverence, veneration; awe, homage, deference.

12. liking, fondness, love, attraction, affinity, soft spot, weakness; infatuation, *Inf.* crush, fancy, *Sl.* shine.

13. regards greetings, salutations, remembrances; best wishes, good wishes, one's best, love, best love; compliments, compliments of the season, commendations, congratulations.

regardful, *adj.* **1.** heedful, attentive, careful, mindful, advertent; prudent, circumspect, thoughtful, *Scot.* canny, provident, precautious; alert, vigilant, ready, on guard, on one's toes, on the qui vive, alive to, all ears, not missing a thing, *Inf.* on the ball *or* stick, quick on the trigger *or* uptake; watchful, wary, chary, awake, wide-awake, open-eyed, all eyes, *Inf.* on the job; observant, aware, interested, curious, intent; fastidious, meticulous, scrupulous, conscientious, exact, accurate, punctilious, particular, precise.

2. deferential, respectful, reverential; ceremonious, courteous, obeisant; faithful, loyal, devoted; obedient, dutiful, compliant, acquiescent, obsequious.

regardless, *adj.* **1.** careless, unmindful, inattentive, inadvertent, unthoughtful, unthinking, nonobservant, disregardful; unwise, imprudent, injudicious, indiscreet, uncircumspect; unwary, incautious, off guard, unguarded, unheeding, heedless; reckless, rash, temerarious; negligent, neglectful, uncaring, remiss, slack, lax, loose; nonchalant, indifferent, blasé, thoughtless, forgetful, absent-minded.

—*adv.* **2.** in any case, at all events, in any event; no matter what, anyhow, anyway, in spite of the fact that, notwithstanding; at any rate, nevertheless, nonetheless.

regency, *n.* regentship, viceroyship, vicereineship; protectorship, protectorate; seneschalship, seneschalsy; caliphship, caliphate; pashaship, pashadom; proxy, surrogation, deputation.

regenerate, *v.* **1.** reform, make a new man of, rehabilitate, moralize; better, improve, amend, uplift, correct, convert, set straight, inspirit; reclaim, redeem, retrieve, save, rescue; turn over a new leaf, see the error *or* folly of one's ways.

2. reconstitute, make over, remake, reconstruct, rebuild; reshape, put in shape, refashion, remodel, recompose, restore; renovate, renew, recondition, put in condition, put in working order; repair, overhaul, mend, patch up, fix, fix up, face-lift, service, refit, do over.

3. revive, reproduce, replace, recreate.

regeneration, *n.* **1.** reformation, rehabilitation, betterment, improvement, uplifting, conversion; reclamation, restoration; redemption, salvation.

2. reconstitution, reconstruction, rebuilding, remodeling, renovation, renewal; repair, mending, overhaul, reconditioning.

3. rebirth, revival, renascence, reproduction, recreation.

regent, *n.* **1.** viceroy, vice-emperor, vice-king, vice-sultan, vice-caliph; vice-queen, vicereine; protector, palatine, khedive, satrap, margrave, burgrave; mandarin, pasha, bey, tetrarch, nabob; minister, commissioner; deputy, agent, proxy, substitute, *Latin. alter ego, Latin. locum tenens,* surrogate; *Inf.* tool, *Inf.* frontman, *Inf.* catspaw.

2. ruler, governor, master, lord, seigneur; controller, dictator, commander, overlord; patriarch, potentate, sovereign, suzerain, monarch; emperor, king, majesty, liege, liege lord; chief, head, principal; autocrat, despot, tyrant, oligarch, dictator.

regime, *n.* government, governance, regimen, system of government; rule, control, command, dominion; reign, administration, direction; guidance, conduct, regulation, management.

regimen, *n.* **1.** diet, *Obs.* dietary, regime; therapy, treatment, medical treatment *or* attention *or* care.

2. rule, reign, sovereignty, sway; government, direction, management, administration, regulation, discipline.

3. method, system, way, means, manner; style, fashion, mode.

regiment, *v.* **1.** discipline, rule with an iron hand *or* fist, hold *or* keep a tight hand upon, keep a tight rein upon, keep [s.o.] in line, run a tight ship; wield authority, crack the whip.

2. methodize, systematize, standardize, organize, regulate, coordinate.

regimentation, *n.* **1.** discipline, strict *or* rigid discipline, strictness, severity, sternness, *Inf.* toughness; tight ship, tight rein, iron hand *or* fist *or* grip.

2. methodization, systematization, standardization, organization, coordination; arrangement, distribution, disposition, disposal, formation.

region, *n.* **1.** area, territory, zone; section, part, portion; site, place, whereabouts, locale, location, spot; plot, plat, lot, tract.

2. district, province, precinct, quarter; department, division.

3. sphere, orbit, orb, ambit; arena, field, pale; realm, domain, dominion; jurisdiction, bailiwick.

regional, *adj.* **1.** territorial, geographical, topographic, zonal.

2. local, localized; sectional, provincial; parochial, insular.

register, *n.* **1.** record, records, ledger, registry, cashbook, journal, bank book, passbook; account book, daybook, record book, books; accounts payable ledger, accounts receivable ledger, balance sheet, cost sheet; score sheet, score card; minutes, proceedings, notes; timesheet, timecard, check sheet, log, logbook; almanac, ephemeris, yearbook, annual; annals, diary, notebook, scrapbook, memory book; archive, chartulary, chancery, public records.

2. roll, roster, list, beadroll, muster, muster roll, poll; list of names, attendance, *Sports.* line-up, *Law.* panel; schedule, datebook, appointment book, calendar, docket; social calendar, program, order of the day, protocol; social register, Who's Who; chronicle, catalogue, inventory; slate, file, index, table of contents; directory, telephone directory, book of names, yellow pages, white pages; scroll, rota, tablet, chronology.

3. range, compass, scale, scope; reach, stretch, carry, sweep; gamut, spectrum, *Music.* diapason.

4. cash register, cashbox, till, check-out.

—*v.* **5.** enter, catalogue, list, write down, put on record, put in writing; put down, jot down, take down, note down, set down; chronicle, minute, record, tape; schedule, *Law.* docket, calendar; post, book, log, insert, inscribe, write in; codify, classify, sort, assort, arrange; tabulate, alphabetize, group.

6. enroll, sign up, enlist, sign on, join, enter, matriculate.

7. indicate, show, read, mark, point; denote, signify, represent.

8. express, show, display, manifest; evince, demonstrate, bespeak; disclose, reveal, divulge, expose; exhibit, evidence.

9. make an impression, have an effect, affect; fall on the ear, get across, sink in, soak in, penetrate, dawn on, *Sl.* hit.

registrar, *n.* recorder, archivist, annalist, chronicler, prothonotary, chronologist, chronologer, chronographer, chronographist; bookkeeper, accountant, certified public accountant, C.P.A., *Both Brit.* chartered accountant, C.A., auditor, *Insurance.* actuary; secretary, clerk, agent, official, administrator.

registration, *n.* **1.** registry, register, recording, record-keeping; enrollment, enlistment, joining, recruitment; matriculation, sign-up, sign-in; cataloguing, itemization, listing, tabulation; booking, inscription, reservation.

2. certificate, document, papers, ticket, permit, license; authority, authorization, certification; affidavit, note, warrant, attestation, deposition.

regress, *v.* **1.** go back, move backward, return, reverse, back up, recede, ebb, retire, fall back, retrocede, withdraw, retreat; retroact, recoil, ricochet, rebound, spring back.

2. revert, retrogress, backslide, relapse, degenerate, decay, retrograde, recidivate; fall away *or* off, decline, wane, subside, sink, fade, fail.

—*n.* **3.** See **regression** (*def.* **1**).

regression, *n.* **1.** reversion, return, regress, reversal, backwardness; relapse, backsliding, retrogradation, retrogression, recidivism, *Obs.* recidivation; *Med.* subsidence.

2. recession, recedence, retrocession, retrocedence, retirement; retreat, withdrawal, drawing back, reflux, ebb, recoil, revulsion.

3. retroaction, repercussion, ricochet, rebound, springing back.

regressive, *adj.* **1.** retrogressive, reversionary, reversional, reactionary, retrograde, reverse, backward, crablike; lapsing, relapsing, backsliding, recidivous, recidivistic, atavistic.

2. receding, recessive, recedent, retrocedent, refluent, ebb.

3. (*of tax rate*) decreasing proportionately, varying inversely.

regret, *v.* **1.** lament, bewail, rue, rue the day; deplore, deprecate, bemoan, repine; weep over, grieve, mourn, keen, pine; fret, be stung by conscience; *Inf.* kick oneself, bite one's tongue, cry over spilt milk; curse one's luck, curse the day, curse one's folly, gnash one's teeth, never forgive oneself, never get over; wish undone, pity oneself, despond.

2. miss, be homesick, long for, want back; feel the loss of, sadly miss, sorely regret; want, desiderate, lack, need; yearn for, pine for, wish for.

—*n.* **3.** remorse, sorrow, sorriness; regretfulness, remorsefulness, contrition, contriteness, shamefulness, shame; lamentation, rue, grief, mournfulness, woe, dole; soul-searching, self-analysis, self-condemnation, self-punishment, self-reproach, self-debasement, self-accusation; discontent, inquietude, disquietude; qualms, pangs, pangs of conscience, twinge of conscience, voice of conscience; disappointment, bitterness, frustration, disillusionment, disillusion, second thoughts; anxiety, worry; wistfulness, nostalgia, homesickness.

regretful, *adj.* **1.** sorrowful, rueful, contrite, sorry, compunctious; conscience-stricken, conscience-smitten, remorseful, repining, regretting, full of regrets; apologetic, repentant, penitent, humbled, abject, sheepish; self-condemning, self-punishing, self-reproachful, self-accusing, self-debasing; ashamed, shameful, shamefaced, *Sl.* bummed out.

2. disgruntled, disappointed, dissatisfied, malcontent; sad, disillusioned, sadder but wiser, bitter; thwarted, balked, foiled, baffled; wistful, nostalgic, homesick.

regrettable, *adj.* deplorable, lamentable, doleful, woeful, sad; unfortunate, unlucky, hapless, pitiable, pitiful; distressful, disheartening, discouraging, depressing; awful, terrible, saddening, moving, affecting; much to be regretted, greatly lamented, too bad, a shame.

regular, *adj.* **1.** usual, normal, natural, commonplace, matter-of-fact; customary, wonted, accustomed, habitual, consuetudinal; conventional, typical, ordinary, archetypal; stock, set, regulation, standard; household, traditional, familiar; universal, popular, current, average, everyday; widespread, prevalent, obtaining, prevailing, predominating.

2. symmetrical, even, uniform, level, orderly; smooth, flat, plane; aligned, balanced, straight, plumb.

3. periodic, fixed, cyclic, seasonal; habitual, recurrent, recurring, repetitive, daily, quotidian; established, prescriptive, accepted, set; frequent, persistent, constant, steadfast; chronic, confirmed, inveterate; incorrigible, fast, deep-rooted.

4. rhythmical, rhythmic, steady, repeated, continual; constant, unchanging, unchanged, unvarying, unvaried; uninterrupted, unintermitting, incessant, ceaseless, unceasing, unremitting; pulsating, vibrating, staccato, machine-gun, automatic.

5. methodical, systematic, controlled, regulated, well-regulated, well-ordered, predictable; orderly, neat, shipshape, tidy; harmonious, businesslike, routine, Fogglike.

6. *Informal.* real, genuine, authentic, bona fide, true, right, veritable.

7. *Informal.* utter, thorough, thoroughgoing, positive, decided; downright, out and out, definitive, outright; perfect, consummate, absolute, unmitigated, unqualified.

—*n.* **8.** habitual customer, client, patron, patronizer.

9. **regulars** *Sports.* starters, first string, first team, varsity.

regularity, *n.* **1.** uniformity, constancy, consistency, order; rhythm, rhythmicity, cadence, even tenor, even pace, even keel; invariability, sameness, evenness, agreement, unity, unison; harmony, concord, concinnity, orderliness, continuity.

2. method, methodicalness, system, rule; habit, custom, tradition, discipline, fixed practice, regular course; routine, monotony, tedium.

regularly, *adv.* **1.** recurrently, habitually, always; seasonally, periodically, cyclically; persistently, constantly, steadfastly, continuously; at fixed intervals, in due order, at stated periods, intermittently.

2. rhythmically, steadily, repeatedly, continually; constantly, incessantly, unceasingly, unchangingly, unvaryingly; uninterruptedly, unintermittently, ceaselessly; day in, day out, everyday, like clockwork.

3. commonly, usually, generally, normally, naturally; customarily, ordinarily, typically, archetypically, traditionally, familiarly, popularly, currently.

regulate, *v.* **1.** control, direct, rule, govern, manage; order, instruct; administer, handle, run, operate, discharge, maintain; overlook, superintend, supervise, look after, have charge of; pilot, steer, guide; arrange, conduct, dispose.

2. adjust, fix, set, establish; equalize, balance, equate, counterbalance, counterpoise; time, coordinate, synchronize.

3. systematize, methodize, systemize, organize; standardize, normalize, centralize; order, discipline, put to rights; marshal, set up, *Inf.* line up; classify, codify, categorize, catalogue; line, align, lay out, sort out.

regulation, *n.* **1.** rule, order, command, commandment, directive, direction, instruction; imperative, ultimatum, dictum, dictate, behest, *Archaic.* hest; act, law, *Latin. lex*, statute, ordinance, ruling, (*pl.*) parietals; formula, formulary, standing order, bylaw; norm, canon, code, convention, standard; edict, decree, fiat, ukase; proclamation, pronouncement, declaration, bull.

2. direction, management, control, administration, governance, government; supervision, superintendence, oversight, eye, auspices, aegis, jurisdiction; arrangement, disposition, conduct, organization; guidance, lead, authority; rule, discipline, regime, reign, regnancy.

3. adjustment, establishment, setting, fixing; coordination, adaptation, synchronization, harmonization; timing, squaring, balancing, balance.

—adj. **4.** standard, regular, stock, mean; accepted, universal.

5. usual, customary, normal, typical, ordinary; accustomed, wonted, habitual, consuetudinal; every day, widespread, popular.

regulatory, *adj.* **1.** directing, directive, managerial, managing, governing, controlling, commanding; guiding, leading, head, regulating; administrative, executive, supervisory, superintendent.

2. reigning, sovereign, chief, leading; ascendant, dominant, predominant, prevalent, prevailing, obtaining.

regurgitate, *v.* **1.** surge back, rush back, flow back, resurge, reflow, back up; ebb, bring back, reissue, regorge.

2. vomit, egest, throw up, *Sl.* puke, *Sl.* barf; heave, *Sl.* upchuck, *Sl.* urp, keck, retch; disgorge, spew, discharge, throw out, belch, burp; expel, ejaculate, debouch, disembogue, shoot out, gush forth, stream out.

3. repeat, retell, recapitulate, say over, redo; reiterate, *Inf.* rehash, quote oneself; restate, go over the same ground.

rehabilitate, *v.* **1.** restore, reclaim, redevelop, recondition, return to normal *or* normalcy; renovate, renew, refurbish, redecorate, brighten up, give a breath of fresh air; repair, fix, fix up, mend, doctor, get back in shape; redintegrate, make whole again, put back together, reconstitute, recompose, reconstruct, rebuild; remedy, rectify, correct, amend.

2. reform, improve, better, ameliorate, meliorate, straighten out *or* up, set straight, put on the straight and narrow; transform, reconvert, change, alter; reorganize, rearrange, readjust, revise, revamp; reeducate, reorient, change one's outlook *or* views, give one's life new meaning; reteach, indoctrinate, brainwash; salvage, save, redeem, convert.

3. reestablish, reinstate, reinstitute, bring back, reinstall, replace; revive, revivify, bring back to life, reinvigorate, refresh, put new life into.

rehabilitation, *n.* **1.** restoration, reclamation, redevelopment, reconditioning, normalization; renovation, renewal, refurbishment; reparation, repair, fixing up, mending, redintegration, reconstruction, rebuilding, reconstitution, recomposition; remediation, correction, amendment, rectification.

2. reformation, improvement, amelioration, melioration; transformation, reconversion, change, alteration; reorganization, rearrangement, readjustment, revision, revampment; reeducation, reorientation, reteaching, indoctrination, brainwashing; salvation, *Theol.* redemption.

3. reestablishment, reinstatement, reinstitution; reinstallation, reinstallment, replacement; revival, revivification, reinvigoration, refreshment.

rehash, *v.* **1.** rework, rephrase, paraphrase, state differently, say in different words, restate, translate; discuss again, retalk, renegotiate, *Inf.* go over the same ground.

—n. **2.** reworking, rewording, translation; interpretation, restatement, *Inf.* rewrite; new version, revival, elucidation, elaboration; repetition, reiteration, same old tune, broken record.

rehearsal, *n.* **1.** drill, exercise, practice, *Inf.* the practice that makes perfect; reading, first reading, read-through, dry run; pre-performance run-through, dress rehearsal, preliminary performance; training, discipline, warm-up, preparation, making ready.

2. repetition, recounting, restatement, reiteration; retelling, recapitulation, the same old story; retold story, twice-told tale; drumming, hammering, dinning, tautology, battology.

rehearse, *v.* **1.** practice, prepare, run through; get ready, *Inf.* walk through, *Inf.* block in, hold a rehearsal; *Inf.* put [s.o.] through his paces, *Inf.* go through one's act.

2. drill, do again and again, train, exercise, discipline; warm up, make ready.

3. relate, recount, repeat; review, run over, sum up; chronicle, tell, tell about; give a report *or* account of, set forth, articulate, communicate, convey, impart, unfold, render; delineate, describe, portray, depict; explain, give the particulars, particularize; recapitulate, *Inf.* go over the same ground, retell, say the same old thing, *Inf.* go around twice; ditto, encore, tautologize, battologize, repeat oneself.

reign, *n.* **1.** reigning years, period of rule, dynasty, time of authority, time on the throne.

2. kingship, crown, regime, regency, suzerainty; authority, sway, administration, governance, government, jurisdiction, direction; leadership, mastery, hegemony, predominance; prerogative; tyranny, dictatorship, despotism, absolutism, mastery; autocracy, monarchy, imperialism; control, command, domination, power, mastery.

—v. **3.** rule, dominate, master, control, govern; command, order, run the show, rule the roost, wear the crown, occupy the throne, (*in India*) raj; be on top, wield the scepter, wield the power, hold sway; govern, supervise, boss, manage, handle, regulate, lead; tyrannize, rule with a rod of iron, rule with an iron hand; oppress, suppress, keep down, subjugate.

4. prevail, predominate, be prevalent, be widespread, be in general use, be universal; be rife, be rampant, be epidemic; be common, be commonplace, be in everyday use; be usual, be ordinary, be customary; be regular *or* standard *or* average; be current, be popular, be in fashion, be in style, be in vogue; be all the rage, be the present trend, *Sl.* be it *or* the thing.

reigning, *adj.* **1.** ruling, commanding, controlling, directing, governing; supreme, head, chief, first, foremost, headmost, premier; main, principal, cardinal, prime, primary, uppermost, most important; dominant, preeminent, preponderant, superior; masterful, authoritarian, authoritative, dictatorial, hegemonic.

2. prevailing, widespread, general, universal; rife, rampant, epidemic; common, commonplace, the norm; popular, in fashion, in style, in vogue, à la mode, all the rage; *Sl.* the thing, *Sl.* the latest thing; fashionable, stylish, modish, *Fr. au courant.*

reimburse, *v.* repay, refund, pay back, make repayment; recompense, compensate, indemnify; pay, remunerate, reward; make restitution, make amends, satisfy, make up for, redress, make good; settle the bill, pay the tariff, settle one's account, *Inf.* square things up, *Inf.* pay the piper.

reimbursement, *n.* **1.** repayment, satisfaction, damages, *Law.* solatium; indemnity, indemnification, recoupment, restitution; penalty, fine; requital, return, redress; amends, expiation, reparation.

2. compensation, payment, pay, repayment, remuneration; salary, wages, *Brit. Sl.* get, emolument, consideration, hire; earnings, charge, fee, honorarium; reward, bonus, tip, gratuity; commission, percentage, share, brokerage.

rein, *n.* **1.** check, curb, restraint, constraint, control, restriction, limitation.

2. **reins** helm, tiller, rudder, wheel; driver's seat, saddle, throne.

3. **draw rein** halt, come to a halt *or* stop, stop, stop dead, come to a dead stop, stop in one's tracks, *Inf.* stop on a dime; put on the brakes, rein in, pull up, bring up, fetch up.

4. **give free rein to** give carte blanche, issue a blank check, give full authority *or* power, give a free hand, leave alone, permit *or* allow anything, give [s.o.] the run of the place; indulge, oblige, yield to, give way to.

—*v.* **5.** check, curb, restrain, constrain, bridle, trammel; retard, delay, detain, hold back; impede, block, obstruct, bar; hinder, hamper; stay, arrest, hold up, hold in check.

6. control, direct, guide, govern.

reinforce, *v.* **1.** strengthen, fortify, bolster, *Inf.* beef up; support, brace, brace up, prop, prop up, hold up, uphold, upbear, buttress; stay, mainstay, undergird; harden, toughen, stiffen, steel.

2. augment, supplement, add to; increase, aggrandize, amplify, enlarge; double, redouble, triple.

reinforcement, *n.* **1.** fortification, strengthening, restrengthening, bolstering, *Inf.* beefing up; augmentation, supplementation, addition; increase, aggrandizement, amplification, enlargement; doubling, redoubling, tripling.

2. support, supporter, prop, brace, stay, mainstay, shore, buttress, flying buttress.

3. *Often* **reinforcements** backup, reserve, reserves, auxiliaries.

reinvigorate, *v.* reanimate, revitalize, regenerate, rejuvenate, rejuvenize, revivify, recharge, rekindle, renew, restore, revive, refresh, resuscitate, breathe *or* put new life into.

reiterate, *v.* repeat over and over, go over and over, belabor, labor, dwell on, harp on, hammer *or* pound away at, hammer *or* pound *or* drive into [s.o.'s] head; thresh *or* thrash out *or* over, *Inf.* rehash, run down; repeat, iterate, ingeminate. See also **repeat** (*def.* **1**).

reiteration, *n.* (*all to an excessive degree*) repetition, iteration, recapitulation, recital, restatement, rehearsal, the same thing all over again, *Inf.* rehash; redundancy, tautology, battology, pleonasm.

reiterative, *adj.* redundant, pleonastic, battological, tautological, *Inf.* broken-record; endless, unending, never-ending, everlasting, unrelenting; repetitive, repetitious, reiterant.

reject, *v.* **1.** refuse, decline, turn down; forbid, veto, disallow, interdict, proscribe, negative, say no to, *Law.* disaffirm; abnegate; turn thumbs down, turn a deaf ear to, brush off, brush aside, *Sl.* kiss off, turn away from, *Inf.* give [s.o.] the bum's rush, leave [s.o.] out in the cold, give [s.o.] the cold shoulder *or* the deep six; dismiss, oust, bump; give [s.o.] the gate *or* the air, show [s.o.] the door, throw [s.o.] to the dogs, send [s.o.] packing.

2. rebuff, slap down, repel, repulse, send away, cast aside; ignore, slight, disregard, shun, neglect, avoid, eschew; have no regard *or* use for, place no value on, set no store by, set at naught; *Sl.* cut [s.o.] dead.

3. renounce, give up, *Inf.* swear off, *Inf.* cut out; disclaim, disavow, forswear; repudiate, (*usu. under oath*) abjure, disown, disinherit; jilt, throw over, turn one's back on, wash one's hands of.

4. abandon, desert, forsake, leave behind; maroon, isolate, banish, relegate, ostracize; discard, throw away, cast off, *Inf.* junk, jettison; remove, exclude, leave out, rule out, pass over, eliminate, *Inf.* scratch; excise, tear out.

5. disbelieve, discredit, disprove, explode; negate, deny, gainsay, contradict, negative.

6. disapprove, disfavor, discountenance; disagree with, demur, take exception to, dispute; object to, protest, challenge, oppose, contravene, controvert; obstruct, thwart, traverse.

7. disdain, scorn, contemn, hold in contempt, disesteem, *Archaic.* disprize; flout, scout, spurn, snap one's fingers at; revile, mock, deride, ridicule, make fun of, scoff at, jeer at, sneer at, gibe, *Fig.* spit upon; abhor, despise, detest, misprize.

8. cast out *or* up, eject, expel; regurgitate, vomit, *Inf.* throw up, *Inf.* upchuck, *Sl.* puke, *Sl.* barf.

—*n.* **9.** **a.** discard, castaway, castoff, *Inf.* throwout, (*of cards*) slough. **b.** second, irregular, *Inf.* markdown, (*pl.*) rejectamenta, leftovers, leavings, spoils, remains; hand-me-downs; (*of persons*) outcast, derelict, dregs, rejectee.

rejection, *n.* **1.** refusal, denial, turndown, declination; forbiddance, veto, disallowance, interdiction, proscription, negation; *Law.* disaffirmation; abnegation.

2. rebuff, repulse, repulsion, repelling, repellence, repellency; *Sl.* brush-off, *Inf.* the cold shoulder, *Inf.* the bum's rush; dismissal, ouster, *Sl.* heave-ho, *Inf.* the gate, the door; disregard, slighting, shunning, spurning, ignoring, neglecting, avoiding, eschewal, eschewing.

3. renunciation, disclamation, disclaimer, disclaiming, disavowal, retraction, recantation; repudiation, (*usu. under oath*) abjuration; disowning, disinheriting, disinheritance.

4. abandonment, desertion, forsaking, banishment, relegation, ostracism; removal, exclusion, omission, elimination, excision.

5. disbelief, unbelief, incredulity; disproving, exploding; negating, denying, contradiction, contradicting.

6. disapproval, disfavor, discountenance; disagreement, demur, demurral, disputing, disputation; objection, protest, challenge; opposition, contravention.

7. disdain, scorn, contempt, disesteem; flouting, scouting, scoffing; reviling, mocking, mockery, deriding, derision, ridicule, ridiculing; jeering, sneering; abhorrence, despising, detesting, detestation, misprizing.

8. ejection, expulsion, regurgitation, vomiting.

9. Dear John letter, rejection slip; blue slip, pink slip, layoff notice.

rejoice, *v.* celebrate, exult, jubilate, triumph, glory, revel, delight in; be glad, be happy, be pleased, be delighted, *Inf.* be tickled *or* tickled pink; be elated, feel elation, be transported with joy, be overjoyed, sing, sing for joy, carol, sound the trumpet, shout hallelujah, shout, yell, cheer, cry out with joy, be inspired; make merry, sport, skip, frolic, dance, hop, jump for joy; glow, luxuriate in, bask in; gloat over, crow, crow about.

rejoicing, *n.* **1.** festivity, celebration, jubilee, thanksgiving; reveling, revelry, merrymaking, feasting; romp, *Inf.* high old time, lark, *Inf.* do, *Inf.* carrying-on.

2. exultation, exultancy, triumph, glory, rapture, transport, ecstasy, joyfulness; jubilation, joyousness, delight, gladness, happiness; excitement, exhilaration, elation, joy, gaiety, merriment, mirth, hilarity; pleasure, amusement, conviviality, sportiveness, revelment; liveliness, jollity, jocundity, joviality, good cheer.

rejoin¹, *v.* **1.** recombine, reconsolidate, reassociate, come *or* get together again, regather, reassemble, reconvene, meet again; reenlist, reenroll, sign up again, reaffiliate, realign with.

2. reunite, bring together again, rematch, recement; heal the breach, restore harmony, patch things up; repair, splice, knot, tie, put *or* piece together.

rejoin², *v.* **1.** reply, rebut, make rebuttal; confute, refute, counterreply, counterclaim, counterchange.

2. answer, make *or* give answer, retort, riposte, parry, *Inf.* come back *or* come back at, *Inf.* come back with a quick *or* snappy answer, *Inf.* snap back; answer *or* talk back; react, respond, answer in kind.

rejoinder, *n.* answer, response, reply, riposte, counterstroke, return, comeback, counterblast; retort, replication, repartee; refutation, contradiction, counterargument; *Law.* surrebuttal, *Law.* surrejoinder, counterstatement, countercharge, counterclaim.

rejuvenate, *v.* restore to youth, turn back the clock *or* the hands of time, dip in the fountain of youth; reanimate, reinvigorate, revitalize, regenerate, rejuvenize, recharge, rekindle, renew, revive, refresh, freshen, resuscitate, put *or* breathe new life into, stir [s.o.'s] blood.

rejuvenation, *n.* **1.** reinvigoration, reanimation, revitalization, regeneration, rejuvenescence, revivification, revival, renewal, resuscitation.

2. rebirth, new birth, renascence; new day, new lease on life, second wind.

relapse, *v.* **1.** (*all in reference to a former state*) fall *or* slip back, revert, *Rare.* retrovert, regress, retrogress; backslide, lapse, recidivate, fall from grace, apostatize.

2. move backward, reverse, recede, retrocede, ebb; decline, deteriorate, weaken, degenerate, wane, sink, slide.

—*n.* **3.** regression, retrogression, reversion, falling back, backset; backsliding, lapse, deterioration, degeneration, retrogradation, recidivism, *Obs.* recidivation; throwback, atavism.

4. retrocession, retirement, retreat, reflux, ebb; decline, setback, fall, downslide, *Inf.* the skids, weakening, sinking, *Inf.* turn for the worse, declination.

5. (*of illness*) return, recurrence, reappearance, recrudescence, metastasis.

relate, *v.* **1.** tell, repeat, recite, recount, rehearse; describe, detail, delineate, particularize, tell about, convey knowledge of, apprise [s.o.] of; narrate, give an account of, set forth, represent, put into words, make known; communicate, mention, announce, divulge, vent, air, broadcast, give news of, disseminate, let fall; tell a story, impart, *Sl.* spiel off; say, speak, utter, give words *or* expression to, emit, pour forth, present; articulate, enunciate, verbalize, give voice to, pronounce, phrase, express; summarize, sum up, recapitulate, *Inf.* recap.

2. connect, associate, ally, link, wed, marry, bind, tie, couple, link with; connect with, be linked with, be associated with, be joined with, be united with.

3. respect, regard, refer to, apply to, belong to, have to do with; pertain to, appertain to, bear upon, have a bearing on, have connection with, *Sl.* tie in with; touch, affect, concern, involve, bring into relation with.

4. relate to identify with, empathize, sympathize; respond, react, understand, comprehend, grasp, assimilate, be in tune with, *Sl.* be hip to, *Sl.* be into, *Sl.* dig, *Sl.* be turned on to; deal with, draw a parallel, compare with; assimilate, project oneself into, experience vicariously, put oneself into another's place *or* shoes, *Inf.* tune in.

related, *adj.* **1.** associated, associative, associate, in association, companionate, fellow, affiliated; correlative, correlated, interrelated, interconnected, interdependent, reciprocal, mutual, *Archaic.* commutual, shared, in common; concomitant, concurrent, attendant, accompanying, accessory, complementary; appended, appendant, adjunctive, adjunct, annexed; auxiliary, ancillary, subsidiary, subordinate.

2. connected, joined, attached, bound, bonded, tied, spliced, lashed, taped; linked, chained, coupled, yoked; coherent, cohered, fused, welded, soldered, glued, cemented, sealed; relative, relevant, germane, applicable, pertinent, appurtenant, to the point; apposite, apt, appropriate, apropos, fitting, meet, suitable.

3. allied, in alliance, united, in union, combined, conjoined, conjoint, joint, in conjunction; coalescent, coalesced, coalitional, leagued, in league, fraternal; amalgamated, federate, federated, confederate, confederated, incorporated, syndicated.

4. kindred, akin, kin, consanguineous, consanguine, agnate, cognate, sib, of the same parentage *or* heritage, having similar roots, of similar descent, *Gram.* paronymous; affinitive, affinal, affined, similar, resemblant, alike, like; comparable, analogous, parallel, corresponding, equivalent, in the same category *or* league; married, wedded, mated, matched, coupled, paired, *Sl.* hitched.

5. narrated, recited, read; recounted, reported, detailed, delineated, chronicled; told, said, uttered; revealed, divulged, disclosed.

relation, *n.* **1.** connection, tie, link, bond, union, liaison; association, relationship, connectedness, relatedness; affiliation, alliance, accord; rapport, affinity, sympathy; interconnection, interdependence, concatenation; dependency, contingency, relativity; similarity, similitude, closeness, nearness, propinquity, approximation, proximation.

2. relations a. intercourse, dealings, *Inf.* doings, affairs, proceedings, *Inf.* truck; state of affairs, state of things, conditions. **b.** sexual intercourse, sex, coitus, coition, copulation, venery; lovemaking, act of love, marriage act; carnal knowledge, sleeping together, cohabitation.

3. kinship, relationship, consanguinity, filiation, apparentation; blood, blood ties, flesh and blood, family ties; ancestry, common ancestry, descent, lineage, patrilineage, matrilineage, parentage; cognation, agnation, enation, affiliation; extraction, stock, breed, stirps; ilk, kind, line, sept.
4. kinsman, clansman, fellow, cognate. See **relative** (*def.* **1**).
5. reference, regard, respect, bearing, concern, interest; pertinence, relevance, applicability; materiality, germaneness, appositeness, relatedness, aptness.
6. narration, recitation, recital, description; depiction, portrayal, delineation, representation; rehearsal, telling, storytelling, recounting; retelling, recapitulation, repetition, summary of the facts.
7. narrative, account, side, report; story, tale, yarn; parable, fable, apologue, folktale, allegory; chronicle, history, record, life story, life, biography.

relative, *n.* **1.** kinsman, kinswoman, relation, consanguinean; tribesman, clansman, countryman, fellow, compatriot; cognate, agnate, enate, affine; father, mother, brother, sister, son, daughter; uncle, aunt, nephew, niece, cousin; grandfather, grandmother, grandson, granddaughter; stepfather, stepmother, stepbrother, stepsister; great-uncle, granduncle, great-aunt, grandaunt; father-in-law, mother-in-law, brother-in-law, sister-in-law, son-in-law, daughter-in-law; next of kin, near relation, kissing kin, kissing cousin; bastard, natural child.
—*adj.* **2.** comparative, correlative, correspondent, proportionate, proportional; analogous, parallel, approximate, proximate, equivalent; near, close, similar, like; comparable, homologous, in common, common to; matchable, commensurate, commensurable.
3. dependent, contingent, subject to; provisory, provisional, liable, conditioned; subordinate, subservient, ancillary, auxiliary, subsidiary, subordinate; accessory, accompanying, complementary, attendant.
4. connected, related, allied, affiliated; correlative, correlated, interrelated, interconnected, interdependent; associated, associative, associate, in association, connective, linking; agnate, enate, cognate, kindred, kin.
5. relevant, pertinent, appurtenant, pertaining, referring; germane, apropos, *Latin. ad rem,* material, applicable; apposite, appropriate, proper, due, meet; apt, fitting, befitting, suitable, suited, congruous, pat; belonging, involving, in point, *Fr. à propos.*

relatively, *adv.* respectively, in respect to, in relation to, in a relative manner, in a like *or* similar manner; comparatively, pertinently, appositely, germanely, apropos of; conditionally, provisionally, contingently.

relax, *v.* **1.** loose, slacken, untighten, relieve tension, *Obs.* slake; relinquish one's grip *or* hold, let go of, release, free, liberate.
2. lessen, diminish, lower, decrease, decline; abate, bate, subside, recede, ebb, lull, quell, slake; flag, wane, fade away, tail off, let down, run down, die down, dwindle, taper off, attenuate.
3. ease up, ease off, *Inf.* let up, slack off *or* up, *Inf.* let up on; go easy, be easy *or* lenient *or* clement, show clemency *or* mercy, forbear, give in; modulate, soften, cushion, milden, mellow, lighten, reduce, weaken, tone down, *Inf.* soft-pedal, downplay; moderate, subdue, chasten, temper, check, curb, take the edge off; mitigate, alleviate, allay, assuage, mollify, dulcify; muffle, hush, quiet, damp, dull, blunt, deaden, *Music.* flatten.
4. calm, tranquilize, quiet, soothe, smooth, pacify; calm down, unwind, unbend, loosen up, hang loose, *Inf.* let oneself go, be oneself, *Inf.* let one's hair down, *Sl.* let it all hang out; be calm, be tranquil, be *or* hold *or* lie still, not move a muscle, be quiet, quiet down, be inactive.
5. rest, repose, lay back, sit back, *Sl.* take it easy, *Sl.* cool it; sit *or* lie down, put one's head down, get off one's feet, *Sl.* rest one's dogs; take a break, take time out, take time to catch one's breath, *Inf.* take a breather, *Inf.* take five; take *or* go on a vacation, take a holiday, take time off, take leave, take a leave of absence, take a sabbatical, enjoy oneself; lounge, lounge around, hang *or* loiter around, loaf, loaf around, lie around, laze, vegetate, *Inf.* lallygag, *Sl.* goof off, *Sl.* gold-brick, *Sl.* sit on one's duff *or* can; idle, be idle, idle *or* while away the hours, twiddle one's thumbs, pass *or* mark *or* kill time, *Sl.* screw around, *Sl.* futz around, *Inf.* fool *or* mess around.
6. linger, tarry, take one's time, take it slow, dawdle, hang back; slow down *or* up, decelerate, wind down, throttle down, put on the brakes, rein in, deescalate, retard; intermit, pause, halt, pull *or* draw *or* hold up, come to a halt, come to a standstill, suspend activity, cease, stop, discontinue, *All Naut.* bring to, lay to, lay up, rest on one's oars.

relaxation, *n.* **1.** rest, repose, taking it easy, leisure, ease; leisure time, free time, spare time, *It. dolce far niente*; break, recess, rest time, time-out, intermission, breather, time to catch one's breath, breathing time *or* spell; vacation, holiday, time off, leave, leave of absence, sabbatical; relief, respite, letup, lull, pause, halt, stay; quiet time, quietude, tranquillity, calm, calmness, peace.
2. abatement, subsidence, recession, flagging, waning, falling off; dwindling, slacking off *or* up, attenuation, tapering off; lessening, diminution, decrement, decrease, lowering, decline, letting down.
3. diversion, pastime, leisure time *or* recreational activity, hobby, avocation; recreation, entertainment, game.
4. loosening, slackening, untightening, *Obs.* slaking.
5. modulation, moderation, softening, cushioning, lightening, reduction; mitigation, alleviation, assuagement, mollification, dulcification; easing up *or* off, leniency, clemency, mercifulness, palliation, extenuation; remission, *Inf.* letting up, forbearance, giving in.

relaxed, *adj.* **1.** loose, loosened, slack, untaut, untightened, let out, *Obs.* slaked; lax, limp, *Dial.* limpsy, flabby, flaccid; hanging, drooping, droopy, bagging, baggy, sagging, saggy, *Inf.* floppy.
2. at ease, taking it easy, taking a break *or* breather, on break, on vacation *or* holiday, on leave *or* sabbatical; at rest, resting, reposeful, still, *Chiefly Brit.* stilly; off one's feet, with one's feet up, lying down, dozing, napping.
3. easygoing, laid-back, *Inf.* loose as a goose, mellow, mild, mild-mannered, mild-tempered, even-tempered; calm, serene, tranquil, placid, cool, composed, collected, peaceful, pacific, at peace *or* ease with oneself, *Inf.* together; carefree, free and easy, devil-may-care, happy-go-lucky, without a care in the world, careless, insouciant, blasé, nonchalant, casual, informal, unceremonious; lackadaisical, listless, languid, languorous, lethargic, lazy, idle, idlish, loafing, laggard, indolent, otiose; sedentary, inactive, comatose.

release, *v.* **1.** set free, loose, set loose, let loose, turn loose, unpen, unmew, disimprison; acquit, exculpate, clear, exonerate, vindicate; dismiss, discharge, let go, let off, *Inf.* let off the hook; exempt, dispense with, relieve of, except from, exclude from, let out of, leave [s.o] out, keep [s.o.] out; free, liberate, enfranchise, affranchise, franchise, manumit, emancipate; deliver, rescue, ransom, redeem, *Theol.* save.
2. disenthrall, unbind, untie, unbridle, unyoke, unfetter, unshackle, unchain, unhandcuff, unmuzzle, *Ar-*

chaic. untruss; unhand, ungrip, let go of; extricate, disengage, disunite, disjoin, disconnect, unpin, dissociate; separate, part, divide, sunder, sever, disintegrate, dissolve, break apart *or* up; loosen, detach, unfix, undo, unfasten, unhook; deregulate, decontrol.

3. announce, advertise, declare, make a statement, proclaim, promulgate, disclose, leak; publish, print, put in the newspaper, broadcast, televise, air; send out, mail out, pass out, hand out, issue, circulate, disseminate, distribute; reveal, unveil, show, display, exhibit; give final approval, give the go-ahead, let fly, let go with.

—*n.* **4.** freedom, freeing, loosing, setting loose, letting loose, turning loose, releasing; acquittal, acquittance, acquitting, compurgation, exculpation, exculpating, clearance, clearing, exoneration, exonerating, vindication, vindicating; dismissal, dismissing, discharge, discharging, letting go, letting off, *Inf.* letting off the hook; exemption, exempting, immunity, impunity, indemnity, exclusion, exception; liberation, liberty, liberating, enfranchisement; deliverance, delivery, delivering, rescue, rescuing, ransom, ransoming, redemption, redeeming, *Both Theol.* salvation, saving.

5. disenthrallment, disenthralling, unfettering, unbinding, untying, unbridling, unyoking, unshackling, unchaining; extrication, extricating, disengagement, disengaging, disuniting, disjoining, disconnection, disconnecting, unpinning, dissociation, dissociating; separation, separating, parting, division, dividing, sundering, severance, severing; loosening, detachment, detaching, undoing, unfastening; deregulation, decontrolling.

6. announcement, declaration, proclamation, statement, promulgation, disclosure, disclosing, leak, leaking; publication, 'publishing, printing, broadcasting, airing; issue, issuance, circulation, dissemination, distribution; revealing, unveiling, showing, display, displaying, exhibition, exhibiting; permission, the rights to, final approval, the go-ahead.

7. control, button, *Electricity.* switch, *Machinery.* regulator.

relegate, *v.* **1.** consign, transfer, send, dispatch, ship, assign, delegate, depute, commission; confide, entrust.

2. attribute, put down to, ascribe, refer; arrogate, impute, credit with, blame on; trace, accredit to, account to, chalk up to.

3. banish, exile, expatriate, proscribe, outlaw, deport, transport; unfrock, excommunicate, disfellow, disenfranchise; oust, eject, cast out, throw out, expel; discharge, drum out, cashier, *Sl.* bounce, *Sl.* dump; ostracize, exclude, shut out, bar, debar, segregate, blacklist; repudiate, disinherit, disown, cast aside; reject, discard, blackball.

relegation, *n.* **1.** consignment, assignment, delegation, deputation, commission; confiding, entrusting, intrusting.

2. attribution, ascription, reference, credit, arrogation, imputation, blame.

3. banishment, exile, proscription, outlawing, expatriation, deportation, transportation; expulsion, ejection, ouster, ousting; excommunication, disfellowship; ostracism, exclusion, barring, removal, separation, segration; repudiation, rejection, abandonment.

relent, *v.* **1.** bend, yield, give, unbend; give way, ground, submit, comply, resign, acquiesce, succumb; face the music, swallow the pill, take it, obey, take it lying down, put up with; not resist, not rock the boat, not make waves, keep the peace; remit, sober down, simmer down, settle down, go out like a lamb.

2. soften, mitigate, reduce, attemper, lenify; slacken, loosen up, relax, let up, go easy on; forbear, have pity on, give quarter, temper the wind to the shorn lamb; subdue, moderate, modulate, weaken; melt, thaw, warm up; repreive, forgive, pardon, grant amnesty.

relentless, *adj.* **1.** unyielding, unrelenting, implacable, unsparing; inexorable, remorseless, unflagging, dogged; undeviating, unswerving, persistent, persevering, undaunted; rigid, stern, strict, harsh, grim, austere; merciless, ruthless, unmerciful, pitiless, unpitying, unforgiving; unmitigable, inflexible, unbendable, resisting, grudging; hard, imperious, obdurate, adamant, adamantine, intransigent; uncompassionate, unfeeling, unsympathetic, intolerant.

2. cruel, inclement, unkind; brutal, rigorous, fell, savage, ferocious; cold-blooded, marble-hearted, cold-hearted, stony-hearted; bloodthirsty, barbarous, ferine, inhuman, heartless, vicious, truculent, devilish.

relevance, *n.* pertinence, appurtenance, germaneness, applicability, application, relatedness, relation, bearing; correspondence, congruence, consistency, comparability, affinity, connection, tie-in; opportuneness, seasonability, timeliness, expedience, expediency, felicity, felicitousness; aptness, fitness, suitability, suitableness, appropriateness, appositeness.

relevant, *adj.* pertinent, pertaining, appurtenant, to the point, germane, apropos, *Latin. ad rem,* material, applicable; at issue, in question; opportune, seasonable, timely, expedient; related, analogous, correspondent, comparable, allied, akin; apposite, appropriate, proper, due, meet; apt, suitable, suited, congruous, fitting, befitting, apposite, well-adapted, pat.

reliable, *adj.* **1.** dependable, trustworthy, honest, upright, honorable, aboveboard, as good as one's word, honest as the day is long, truthful; responsible, principled, conscientious, punctilious, careful; trusty, sure, unfailing, infallible, strong, abiding, steady, firm, *Inf.* all right, *Inf.* O.K.; faithful, true, steadfast, true-blue, devoted, *Inf.* Johnny-on-the-spot.

2. authentic, genuine, real, substantiated, well-grounded, well-founded; authoritative, established, reputable, secure, safe, stable; believable, credible, sound, certain; assured, guaranteed, unquestionable, indisputable, incontestable, indubitable.

reliance, *n.* confidence, trust, faith, belief, dependence; security, sureness, assuredness, surety, positiveness, conviction, certainty.

relic, *n.* **1.** artifact, ancient object, reminder of times past; antique, heirloom; ancient ruins, wreckage, debris, detritus; surviving trace, vestige, impression, sign, evidence, record.

2. relics remains, reliquiae, remainders, what's left; parts, pieces, bits and pieces, fragments, shards.

3. relics corpse, dead body, organic remains, cadaver, *Sl.* stiff, carcass, mummy; bones, skeleton, fossil, petrified remains, petrifactions.

4. souvenir, memento, keepsake, remembrance, reminder of days gone by, something to remember [s.o.] by.

relief, *n.* **1.** alleviation, mitigation, abatement, assuagement, palliation; ease, easement, comfort, solace, consolation, calming; softening, mollification, slackening, loosening, relaxation.

2. deliverance, rescue, release, freeing, liberation, extrication, riddance; assistance, support, strengthening, reinforcement; succor, help, aid, redress, remedy.

3. money, food; welfare, the dole, handout, alms, charity; food stamps, unemployment compensation, *Inf.* unemployment, social security; the public till.

4. break, recess, respite, lull, letup, rest, remission; change of pace, divertissement, diversion; refreshment, relaxation.

5. replacement, successor, follower; substitute, *Inf* sub, stand-in, backup, fill-in, *Theat.* understudy.

6. cure, corrective, remedy, treatment; therapy, medicine, medication, tonic, *Med.* roborant; bracer, stimulant, stimulation, restorative, *Med.* analeptic; sedation, sedative, *Med.* calmative, tranquilizer, palliative, lenitive, *Med.* emollient; painkiller, anodyne, narcotic, opiate, drug, *Med.* analgesic; balm, unguent, ointment, liniment, lotion, embrocation.

relieve, *v.* **1.** alleviate, palliate, mitigate, abate, reduce, lessen; allay, assuage, soothe, calm, pacify, appease, *Med.* abirritate; subdue, quell, slake, quench, ease, salve.

2. comfort, console, solace, rest; minister to, attend, doctor, treat; cure, remedy, correct, redress, restore; freshen, quicken, revitalize, cheer.

3. assist, help, aid, succor; support, subvene, strengthen, reinforce.

4. free, exempt, deliver, liberate, release, extricate, rid, disburden, disembarrass; replace, supplant, dispossess, *Inf.* ease out; substitute for, take over for.

5. vary, shift, modify; break, interrupt, respite, let up on; relax, slacken.

religion, *n.* **1.** set *or* system of religious belief, creed, dogma, doctrine, principles, tenets, canons; theology, divinity, theosophy, dogmatics, doctrinal *or* dogmatic theology.

2. religious belief *or* conviction, faith, persuasion; sect, denomination, church.

3. deism, theism, monotheism, polytheism, pantheism.

religious, *adj.* **1.** theological, doctrinal, dogmatic, dogmatical, orthodox, canonical; denominational, sectarian.

2. devout, pious, godly, holy, saintly, divine, sacred; spiritual, spiritual-minded, reverent, respectful; righteous, morally upright, good, pure, unworldly.

3. faithful, true, loyal, constant, devoted; unfailing, unerring, unswerving, undeviating; conscientious, scrupulous, exact, strict, rigid, rigorous, stern, severe.

relinquish, *v.* **1.** renounce, surrender, *Law.* disclaim, abdicate, resign, *Chiefly Scot.* demit; transfer, hand over, sign away, *Law.* demise, lease, deliver up, turn over to.

2. abandon, forsake, desert, leave behind; depart, quit, go away from, vacate, evacuate, pull out of.

3. discontinue, give up, retire from, put aside, leave off, desist from, stop; forbear, drop, forgo, do *or* go without, waive, lay aside.

4. repudiate, abjure, reject, disown; abnegate, concede, yield, cede.

5. discard, cast off, jettison, throw away, get rid of, rid oneself of, toss out, throw out, *Inf.* ditch, *Inf.* chuck.

6. let go, release, free, set free, liberate; unloose, loosen, untie.

relinquishment, *n.* **1.** renunciation, abnegation, abdication, resignation, *Archaic.* demission; transfer, transferal, transference, ceding, leasing, handing over.

2. recantation, repudiation, disavowal, denial, backpedaling; defection, heresy, apostasy, recreance, recreancy.

relish, *n.* **1.** enjoyment, pleasure, satisfaction, delight, zest, gusto; appreciation, liking, fancy, love, fondness; desire, wish, longing, hankering, craving; partiality, predilection, prejudice, leaning, inclination, preference.

2. flavor, savor, tang, taste, palate.

3. *Cookery.* piccalilli, chili, chili sauce, chow-chow, chutney, pickle; appetizer, hors d'oeuvre, antipasto, starter, canapé.

4. smack, touch, hint, bit, trace, touch, suspicion, soupçon.

—*v.* **5.** enjoy, delight in, take pleasure in; appreciate, approve, *Sl.* dig. *Sl.* get off on, *Sl.* buy, *Sl.* get a kick *or* bang out of; eat up, *Sl.* lick one's chops over.

reluctance, *n.* unwillingness, disinclination, aversion; hesitancy, shrinking, holding back, cautiousness, wariness, carefulness; distaste, disrelish, dislike, prejudice against; obstinacy, recalcitrance, renitency.

reluctant, *adj.* **1.** unwilling, disinclined, indisposed, demurring, loath, averse; hesitant, hanging back, faltering, laggard; cautious, chary, careful, circumspect, wary, leery.

2. opposed, dissenting, oppugnant, antagonistic, antipathetic; contrary, rebellious, resistant, struggling against, recalcitrant, renitent.

rely, *v.* depend, count, bet one's bottom dollar, bank, lean; trust, put faith in, swear by; put one's life in [s.o.'s] hands; be sure of, be certain of.

remain, *v.* **1.** continue, abide, endure, last, perdure, hold up; succeed, prevail; draw out, drag on, be protracted; *Inf.* stay put, *Inf.* stand pat, be immobile, be dormant, not stir, not move, vegetate.

2. stay, wait, rest, tarry, linger, dwell, reside, sojourn, lodge, inhabit; stay at home, keep indoors, be housed; be established at, get a footing, settle down, make one's abode, domesticate, take up one's quarters.

3. survive, endure, outlive, persevere, outlast, remain alive, keep a hold on life.

—*n.* **4.** *Usu.* **remains a.** remnants, leavings, leftovers, residue, balance, rest, remainder; oddments, rummage, odds and ends, fragments, truck, waste, garbage, junk, *Inf.* crap; rejectamenta, discards, throwaways. See also **remainder** (*defs.* **1-6**). **b.** traces, vestiges, semblances. **c.** cadaver, carcass, dead body, *Sl.* stiff.

remainder, *n.* **1.** remnant, residue, residuum, remains, balance, rest; surplus, excess, superfluity, extra, surplusage, redundance, *Commerce.* overage.

2. oddments, rummage, stuff, odds and ends, flotsam, jetsam, pickings; fragment, scrap, shard, truck, junk, *Inf.* crap; rejectamenta, castoffs, throwaways, discards, tares; (*all usu. of food*) leftovers, leavings, orts.

3. waste, wastage, refuse, spoils; offscourings, scourings, sweepings; sawdust, shavings, parings, filings, scrapings, raspings; chuff, stubbles; slag, scum, sprue, dross, sordes, scoriae; (*all of skin*) slough, sheddings, sloughings, scurf, furfur, dandruff.

4. rubbish, trash, garbage, offal, refuse, sewage; swill, slop, hogwash, riffraff, *Brit. Dial.* raff, *Scot.* lave; carrion, bones, skeleton, fossil.

5. ruins, rubble, detritus, debris, litter; cinder, ashes, embers, coal, soot, carbon, dirt, smut; lava, sinter.

6. deposit, sediment, settlings, alluvium, silt; precipitation, condensation.

7. aftermath, consequence, aftergrowth, afterpart, afterglow, outgrowth, afterpart, afterglow, outgrowth; wake, trail, train; suffix, postfix, appendix, postscript, postface, subscript, postlude, epilogue.

8. inheritance, bequest, estate, property; right, entail, claim, title.

remake, *v.* make again, make over, redo, do over, refashion, re-form, reshape, re-create, reproduce; change, change around, revise, alter, modify, rewrite, restyle, rearrange, recompose; change into, convert, transform; reconstruct, rebuild, reconstitute, remodel, revamp; renovate, restore, renew, repair, fix up, repaint, revarnish, spruce up.

remark, *v.* **1.** comment *or* comment upon, mention, speak of, refer to, say in passing; utter, speak, say, express, give one's opinion; verbalize, articulate, put into words, present, put forth, communicate, convey; vocalize, voice, speak up *or* out, come out with, give mouth to, *Sl.* mouth off; state, declare, enunciate, pronounce, allege, assert, aver, asseverate; *Inf.* make a crack, *Inf.* make a wisecrack, give a smart answer, reply, respond.

2. note, take note of, notice; perceive, see, view, observe, watch, look at, regard; heed, pay heed to, pay attention to, mind, mark, make a note of, give some thought to.

3. comment, mention, reference; utterance, saying, thing to say, expression, sentence, phrase, word; statement, declaration, averment, asseveration, pronouncement, enunciation, assertion, allegation.

—n. **4.** remarking, notice, regard, mind, thought, attention, heed, note, observation, perception, percept.

remarkable, *adj.* **1.** extraordinary, unusual, different, uncommon, rare, singular, exceptional, out-of-the-ordinary, *Inf.* one for the books; unique, distinct, peculiar, odd, strange, curious.

2. striking, impressive, imposing, majestic, grand, august, stately, dignified; large, big, substantial, considerable; awesome, awe-inspiring, lofty, wondrous, marvelous, prodigious; stupendous, amazing, astounding, astonishing, surprising, shocking; incredible, *Sl.* unreal, unbelievable, inconceivable, unimaginable, unthinkable, unheard-of; overwhelming, overpowering, indescribable, inexpressible, ineffable, unspeakable, unutterable; fantastic, miraculous, fabulous, *Inf.* great, *Inf.* super, *Inf.* super-duper, superb, splendid, magnificent, wonderful, *Inf.* smashing.

3. superlative, unequaled, matchless, unmatched, unparalleled, nonpareil, *Fr. sans pareil;* unsurpassed, unexcelled, second to none, *Latin. nulli secundus;* unprecedented, a first; unrivaled, incomparable, inimitable; supreme, *Latin. ne plus ultra,* paramount, preeminent, superior, sovereign, transcendent; sublime, consummate, perfect, *Sl.* the living end; best, finest, greatest, highest, prime, select, choicest; excellent, first-rate, of the first order, capital, *Inf.* tiptop, *Inf.* A-1, *Inf.* A number 1, first-class, classic.

4. notable, noteworthy, signal, outstanding, noticeable, marked; memorable, unforgettable, *Sl.* hell of a, special, particular, especial; important, on the map, significant, momentous, meaningful, worthy of notice.

5. conspicuous, obvious, evident, manifest, patent, apparent, ostensible; blatant, bold, overt, obtrusive, flagrant, glaring, egregious; prominent, in bold relief, salient, pronounced, marked; visible, seeable, showing, discernible, perceptible, perceivable; plain, clear, unmistakable, lucid, plain as day, plain as the nose on one's face, distinct, clear-cut, explicit.

remediable, *adj.* curable, medicable, healable, treatable, reparable, mendable; amendable, emendable, rectifiable, correctable, fixable, restorable; recoverable, retrievable, reclaimable, redeemable; corrigible, reformable, improvable.

remedial, *adj.* corrective, reparative, reparatory, mending, restorative, restoring, restitutive, restitutory, recuperative, recuperatory; curative, therapeutic, medicinal, *Rare.* medical, tonic, curing, healing, sanative, sanatory; beneficial, advantageous, helpful, salutary, healthy, healthful, good, good for you, wholesome.

remedy, *n.* **1.** cure, restorative, antidote, counteracter, neutralizer, corrective, preventive, prophylactic, *Med.* specific; cure-all, panacea, elixir, cure for what ails you, cure for all ills, nostrum; medicine, medicament, medication, *Med.* prescription, *Pharm.* drug, pharmaceutical; *Biochem.* antibiotic, bactericide, germicide, antiseptic; sedative, tranquilizer, soporific; analgesic, *Inf.* painkiller, anodyne, anesthetic; antitoxin, serum, vaccine; *Med.* vaccination, inoculation, injection, *Inf.* shot; tonic, *Physiol., Med.* stimulant; poultice, *Med.* pack, *Med.* compress; herb, homeopathic remedy; physic, purgative, cathartic, laxative; healing substance *or* agent, application, *Pharm.* lotion, *Pharm.* ointment, unguent, *Pharm.* inunction, balm, balsam, vulnerary, *Pharm.* cerate; liniment, embrocation, emollient, demulcent, *Med.* abirritant, palliative, alleviative; treatment, remedial treatment, therapy, speech therapy, *Med.* hydrotherapy, physical therapy, psychotherapy, group therapy.

—v. **2.** cure, work a cure, restore to health, make well *or* whole, *Inf.* bring around, put back on one's feet; resuscitate, revive, revivify, reanimate, bring back from death's door; heal, mend, knit, grow back together; treat, doctor, apply remedies to, give medicine to, medicate, drug, dose; physic, relieve, free from pain, ease, lessen, alleviate, palliate, mitigate, assuage, soothe, calm.

3. straighten out, rectify, set to rights; right a wrong, redress, make good, compensate for, make up for, make amends for, atone for, make reparation for, make everything all right *or* better; fix, fix up, repair, restore, set right *or* straight, adjust, regulate, correct, amend, emend; better, make better, improve, ameliorate, meliorate.

4. counteract, antidote, counterbalance, offset, counterpoise, countervail; neutralize, destroy the effect of, undo, reverse; annul, void, nullify, cancel out; remove, destroy, root out.

remember, *v.* **1.** recall, recollect, call to mind, bethink; have at one's fingertips, have at the tip of one's tongue; put one's fingers on [s.t.], place, recognize, reidentify, *Inf.* spot.

2. reminisce, think back, look back, retrospect, return to thoughts of, muse; dwell upon the past, live in the past; commemorate, memorialize.

3. keep in mind, bear in mind, be aware of; review, go over, memorize, have by heart.

4. reward, tip, remunerate, recompense, requite, compensate, *Obs.* gratify.

remembrance, *n.* **1.** memory, recollection, anamnesis, reminiscence, retrospect; thought, glimmering from the past, whisper from the past, something from the dim recesses of the mind, reminder, prompting; recognition, reidentification.

2. calling to mind, retrospection, recollecting, remembering, minding, looking back, reviewing the past, summoning up the past.

3. commemoration, memorial, shrine, testimonial; token, souvenir, keepsake, memento, something to remember one by, token of one's affection.

remind, *v.* cause to remember, put in mind, awake memories of, ring a bell; prompt, cue, throw out a hint, jog the memory, refresh the memory; call up, leave [s.o.] a note.

reminder, *n.* **1.** prompting, cue, hint, intimation, suggestion; clue, glimmer; note, memorandum, *Inf.* memo, string around one's finger; phone call.

2. token, souvenir, keepsake, remembrance. See **remembrance** (*def.* **3**).

reminisce, *v.* remember, recollect, recall, call to mind, bethink; think back, look back, retrospect, return to thoughts of the past, muse, dwell upon the past, live in the past, sentimentalize, be nostalgic.

reminiscence, *n.* **1.** memory, anamnesis, recollection, glimmering from the past, remembrance. See **remembrance** (*def.* **1**).

2. recalling, remembering, thinking back, recollecting, retrospection, reviewing, remembrance of things past, contemplation, reflection; dwelling in the past, living in the past, nostalgia.

reminiscent, *adj.* **1.** *Usu.* **reminiscent of** suggestive of, evocative of, redolent of, expressive of, indicative of.

2. recollective, recollecting, remembering, bethinking, musing; nostalgic, sentimental.

remiss, *adj.* **1.** negligent, delinquent, derelict, *Inf.* asleep at the wheel *or* at the switch *or* on the job; indolent, lazy, slothful, laggard, shiftless, do-nothing, fainéant; slack, loose, lax, sloppy, slipshod, hasty, cursory, perfunctory; dilatory, delaying, procrastinative, cunctatious, cunctatory.

2. neglectful, disregardful, disregarding, disregardant, inattentive, careless, heedless, unheeding; unobservant, unwatchful, inadvertent, unguarded; thoughtless, unthinking, unmindful, forgetful, oblivious, unaware; improvident, imprudent, injudicious; reckless, rash, temerarious, *Obs.* respectless.

remission, *n.* **1.** forwarding, transmission, transmittal, transmitting, sending, dispatch, dispatching, remitting; payment, paying, discharge, discharging; remunerating, reimbursement, reimbursing, compensation, settlement, settling, paying off *or* up, liquidation.

2. pardon, pardoning, amnesty, excuse, excusal, reprieve, reprieving, vindication, vindicating; exoneration, exonerating, freedom, freeing, release, releasing, liberation, emancipation, deliverance, forgiveness, forgiving, absolution, absolving, shriving; condonation, condoning, overlooking, disregarding, disregard, oblivion, forgetting, ignoring.

3. abatement, subsidence, subsiding, recession, receding, ebb, ebbing, lulling, decrease, decreasing, decline, declination, declining, sinking; diminution, diminishing, reduction, reducing, lessening, lightening, attenuation, waning; contraction, contracting, shrinkage, shrinking, dwindling, falling off; relaxation, relaxing, slackening, loosening, easing; mitigation, mitigating, assuagement, assuaging, allaying, alleviation, alleviating, palliation, relieving; quelling, quieting, calming, stilling; mollification, mollifying, moderation, moderating, modification, temperance, tempering, subduing, chastening, softening, weakening; yielding, submission, submitting, giving in, surrender, surrendering, giving up.

4. pause, lull, lapse, interregnum, *Inf.* letup; respite, reprieve, breath, breathing spell, breather, relief, rest, repose, relaxation, recess, inactivity, *Archaic.* bever; interruption, hiatus, break, intermission, *Both Prosody.* mora, caesura; suspension, abeyance, prorogation, deferment, deferral, delay, postponement, protraction, extension, continuation, *Law.* continuance; stemming, checking, cessation, ceasing, desistance, desisting, arrest, stoppage, stopping, halt, standstill, discontinuance, discontinuation, termination.

remit, *v.* **1.** forward, transmit, send, dispatch; pay, make payment, discharge; remunerate, recompense, reimburse, compensate; settle, pay off *or* up, pay in full, liquidate.

2. respite, reprieve, stay, grant a stay of execution, interrupt, stem, check, hold up; arrest, stop, brake, halt, desist, cease; forbear, spare, judge with leniency *or* clemency, be easy on, give a light sentence, refrain, hold back.

3. exonerate, release, free, set free, let off, *Inf.* let off the hook, *Inf.* let out of, liberate, emancipate, deliver, *Obs.* vindicate; exempt, except, make an exception, *Rom. Cath. Ch.* dispense; continue, grant an extension, *Finance.* extend, *Commerce.* indulge; waive, abolish, do away with, cancel, void, nullify, delete, erase, clear the books, wipe the slate clean.

4. pardon, amnesty, excuse, forgive, absolve, shrive, condone, overlook, make allowances for, pass over, wink at; disregard, dispense with, forget, forgive and forget, let bygones be bygones, not give the matter a second thought; ignore, look the other way, pay no attention to.

5. relax, slacken, loosen up, ease up *or* off, grant a breathing spell, *Archaic.* slake; mitigate, assuage, allay, alleviate, relieve, palliate, commute; mollify, moderate, modify, temper, subdue, chasten, soften, weaken, tone down; quell, quiet, tranquilize, calm, soothe, hush, still, deaden; abate, subside, recede, ebb, lull, decrease, decline, sink; diminish, lessen, lighten, attenuate, wane; reduce, contract, shrink, dwindle, fall off; yield, submit, give in, surrender, give up.

6. return, give back, send back, remand; replace, put back, reinstate, make restitution; rectify, redress, make amends, correct, make *or* set *or* put right; restore, recondition, repair, mend, renew, renovate, refurbish; rebuild, reconstruct, reconstitute, remodel, remake, make over, recreate.

7. postpone, defer, prorogue, suspend, intermit, put off, stave off, shelve, reschedule; delay, stall, wait, hold off, procrastinate.

remnant, *n.* **1.** remains, remainder, rest, residue, residuum, balance. See **remainder** (*defs.* **1-6**).

2. little bit, piece, chip, strip, bit, fragment, scrap, shard.

3. trace, vestige, archaism, relic, record; keepsake, souvenir, reminder, remembrance, memento, memorabilia, heirloom, inheritance, trophy.

remonstrance, *n.* **1.** protestation, expostulation, remonstration; objection, dissent, disagreement, nonconcurrence, noncompliance, nonconformance; disapproval, disapprobation, deprecation; reproach, rebuke, reproof, censure, blame; criticism, reprimand, reproval; admonition, warning, caution, exhortation, dissuasion; castigation, chastisement, scolding, berating, upbraiding; *Inf.* talking-to, *Inf.* dressing-down, *Inf.* tongue-lashing.

2. protest, objection, complaint; grievance, *Inf.* beef, *Sl.* squawk, *Sl.* bitch, *Inf.* gripe; negation, denial, disclaimer.

remonstrate, *v.* **1.** expostulate, plead in protest, argue, reason against, object, protest; say no to, dissent, oppose, take issue, take exception, beg to differ; make one's stand against, balk at, draw the line at, stand and be counted against, vote against; put up a fight, not take lying down, fuss, make a fuss over, *Inf.* kick up a fuss, *Inf.* beef, *Inf.* raise hell, *Sl.* bitch, *Sl.* squawk; admonish, warn, forewarn, caution, exhort, put on one's guard; advise, counsel against, *Archaic.* dissuade, *Archaic.* dehort.

2. reproach, rebuke, disapprove of, complain of; inveigh, censure, denounce; upbraid, reproach, reprove, reprehend; castigate, vituperate, reprimand, admonish; chide, scold, carp at, berate, *Inf.* take to task, *Inf.* call on the carpet, *Inf.* dress down; *All Sl.* blast, bawl out, yell at, give [s.o.] hell, lay [s.o.] out in lavender, read the riot act.

remorse, *n.* sorrow, sorriness, contrition, regret, penitence, repentance, contriteness, sackcloth and ashes; compunction, bad conscience, guilt, shame, shamefulness, embarrassment, self-humiliation, self-mortification; self-reproach, self-reproof, self-blame, self-accusation, self-condemnation; lamentation, rue, grief, mournfulness, woe, dole; discontent, inquietude, disquietude; disappointment, bitterness, frustration, disillusionment, disillusion, second thoughts, anxiety, angst, worry.

remorseful, *adj.* sorry, sorrowful, regretful, rueful, contrite, compunctious; conscience-stricken, conscience-smitten, guilt-ridden, repining, regretting, full of regrets; apologetic, repentant, penitent, penitential, atoning, in sackcloth and ashes; humbled, abject, sheepish, embarrassed, chastened; self-condemning, self-punishing, self-reproachful, self-accusing, self-debasing; ashamed, shameful, shamed, shamefaced, *Sl.* bummed out, disturbed, troubled.

remote, *adj.* **1.** distant, removed, far, far-off, faraway, yon, yonder; out-of-the-way, isolated, secluded, sequestered, private; lonely, forsaken, Godforsaken; outlying, inaccessible, unapproachable.

2. foreign, alien, peregrine; tramontane, ultramontane, transalpine; ultramarine, transmarine, transatlantic, transpacific.

3. irrelevant, impertinent, inappropriate, inapt, inapposite, unrelated, unassociated, disassociated, unconnected; extraneous, extrinsic, external, adventitious, ulterior, outside.

4. unlikely, improbable, questionable; inconsiderable, hardly any, not much, not enough to speak of, insignificant.

5. aloof, indifferent, apathetic, unconcerned, disinterested, incurious; detached, uninvolved, distant, unapproachable, unsociable, stand-offish, *Inf.* offish; above all that, cool, haughty, *Inf.* high-hat, icy, frigid.

removal, *n.* **1.** taking off, shedding, casting off, throwing off, dropping; throwing overboard, jettison; divestiture, stripping, uncovering, exposing, baring; undressing, unclothing, undraping, disrobing; exfoliation, *Pathol.* desquamation, peeling off, flaking.

2. disengagement, disentanglement, disburdenment, dissociation, disconnection, unattachment, extrication; disuniting, unbinding, unfastening, untying, undoing, unchaining; detaching, disjoining, uncoupling, loosening, unloosening; dismantling, stripping, tearing off.

3. subtraction, deduction, withdrawal, abstraction, *Rare.* prescission; taking away, rebating, drawing away; lessening, diminishing, shortening, curtailment; excision, cutting off, lopping off, chopping off, cutting out *or* away, *Surg.* ablation; amputation, *Surg.* resection, truncation, detruncation, obtruncation.

4. uprooting, unrooting, pulling out by the roots, pulling up, plucking up, rooting out, deracination; pulling out, drawing out, taking out, raising up *or* out, extraction; unearthing, excavation, digging up *or* out, grubbing up *or* out; weeding out, raking out; drawing forth, bringing out, evocation, education, elicitation.

5. erasure, erasion, cancellation, rubbing out, scrubbing out, scratching out; washing out, sponging out, purging, deterging; deletion, *Print.* dele, editing, editing out; crossing out, blacking out.

6. eradication, extirpation, extermination, annihilation; expunction, obliteration, extinguishment, extinction, effacement, abolition, abolishment; blotting out, striking out, stamping out, crushing out, wiping out.

7. killing, killing off, slaying, slaughter, execution, destruction; murder, finishing off, *Sl.* doing in, *Sl.* zapping, disposing of; assassination, sacrifice, getting rid of, mowing down, putting out of the way, doing away with; massacre, liquidation, decimation.

8. nullification, neutralization, counterpoise, counterbalance, counteraction; offsetting, obviation, prevention, prohibition, deterrent, deterrence, preclusion; cancellation, discharge, negation, invalidation, *Logic.* sublation, disaffirmation.

9. transfer, transferal, transference, transportation, displacement, dislocation, transplantation; translocation, relocation, transshipment, evacuation; seclusion, retreat, retirement.

10. banishment, relegation, sequestration, exile, expatriation, proscription, deportation, excommunication; expelling, ejecting, ejaculating, emitting; casting out, forcing out, dislodgement, eviction, ouster, dispossession; driving out, thrusting out, extrusion, throwing out, *Sl.* bouncing; exclusion, omission, exception, barring, debarment, ostracism, blackballing; segregation, separation, division, isolation, insulation; disowning, repudiation, renunciation, renouncement, divorce.

11. deposition, deposal, ouster, unseating, dethronement, discrownment, unfrocking; dismissal, discharge, laying off, letting go.

remove, *v.* **1.** take off, shed, cast off, throw off, drop, throw overboard, jettison; divest, strip, uncover, expose, lay open, bare; undress, unclothe, undrape, disrobe; disburden, disencumber; exfoliate, *Pathol.* desquamate, peel off, flake.

2. subtract, deduct, rebate, take away; withdraw, draw away, abstract, prescind; lessen, diminish, curtail, shorten; excise, cut off, lop off, chop off, cut out, cut away; amputate, *Surg.* resect, detruncate, truncate, obtruncate.

3. uproot, unroot, pull out by the roots, pull up, pluck up, root out, outroot, deracinate; pull out, draw out, tear out, take out, raise up *or* out, extract; unearth, excavate, dig up *or* out, grub up *or* out; weed out, rake out; draw forth, bring out, evoke, educe, elicit.

4. extricate, disentangle, disengage, disconnect, dissociate, disunite; unbind, unfasten, untie, undo, unchain, unattach; detach, disjoin, uncouple, loosen, unloose; dismantle, strip, tear off.

5. banish, relegate, exile, expatriate, proscribe, deport, maroon, excommunicate; expel, eject, ejaculate, emit; cast out, force out, dislodge, evict, oust, dispossess; drive out, thrust out, extrude, throw out, *Sl.* throw [s.o.] out on his ear, *Sl.* bounce; exclude, except, shut out, shut the door upon, bar, debar, ostracize, blackball; segregate, set apart, set aside, put aside, separate, divide, isolate, insulate; disown, repudiate, renounce, divorce.

6. depose, dethrone, unseat, uncrown, discrown, unfrock; dismiss, discharge, fire, *Sl.* sack, *Sl.* can, lay off, let go.

7. erase, cancel, rub out, scrub out, scratch out; wash out, sponge out, purge, deterge; delete, *Print.* dele, blue-pencil, edit, edit out; cross out, x out, black out, mark off.

8. eradicate, extirpate, exterminate, annihilate; expunge, obliterate, extinguish, efface, abolish; blot out, strike out, stamp out, crush out, wipe out.

9. kill, kill off, slay, slaughter, execute, end, destroy; murder, finish, finish off, *Sl.* do in, *Sl.* zap, dispose of; assassinate, sacrifice, get rid of, mow down, put out of the way, *Inf.* wipe out, do away with; massacre, liquidate, decimate.

10. nullify, neutralize, counterpoise, counterbalance, counteract, offset; render unnecessary, obviate, prevent, deter, preclude, rule out; cancel, discharge, negate, invalidate, *Logic.* sublate, disaffirm.

11. transfer, transport, carry, shift, displace, transplant; translocate, relocate, transship, eloign, evacuate, *Inf.* pull up stakes; sequester, seclude, *Archaic.* sequestrate, retreat, retire; depart, go forth; leave, quit, go one's way, *Inf.* vacate, exit, decamp, debouch.

—n. **12.** subtraction, deduction, withdrawal, drawing away, abstraction; taking off, shedding, casting off, throwing off, uncovering, removal. See **removal** (*defs.* **1, 3**).

13. distance, interval, space, separation; degree, stage, grade, gradation, graduation; step, extent, measure, amount, scope; mark, rung, peg, notch, cut, reach; range, compass, scale, caliber, pitch.

removed, *adj.* **1.** unrelated, unconnected, unassociated, unaffiliated, disconnected, dissociated, detached; disengaged, disjoined, unattached, dislocated; foreign, alien, strange, exotic, outlandish, different, distinct from.

2. aloof, stand-offish, detached, distant, remote, cool, cold, frigid; undemonstrative, unexpansive, unaffable; inaccessible, unapproachable, exclusive; isolated, insular, solitary, solitudinous, apart, separated, separate; alone, independent, secluded, withdrawn, retired; lone, lonely, lonesome.

remunerate, *v.* **1.** pay, fee, recompense, reimburse, repay, indemnify, redress, requite, compensate, satisfy; reward, *Literary.* guerdon, *Obs.* gratify.

2. yield, return, net, profit, benefit.

remuneration, *n.* **1.** payment, pay, compensation, consideration; salary, wages, emolument, earnings, *Brit. Sl.* get; perquisites, *Inf.* perks, fringe benefits, *Inf.* fringes, *Inf.* extras; hire, fee, stipend, honorarium, allowance; returns, interest, yield, gain, profits, proceeds, income, revenue.

2. recompense, repayment, requital, quittance; reparation, indemnification, indemnity, redress; amends, restitution, damages, *Law.* solatium.

3. tip, gratuity, douceur, *Fr. pourboire,* (*in India and Turkey*) baksheesh, remembrance; bribe, boodle, blackmail, hush money; percentage, cut, *Inf.* kickback.

4. payoff, liquidation, discharge, satisfaction, redemption, settlement; remittance.

remunerative, *adj.* profitable, gainful, rewarding, lucrative, fat, big-time; paying, well-paying; valuable, moneymaking, advantageous; worthwhile, well-spent.

renaissance, *n.* renascence, rebirth, reemergence, resurgence, rekindling; revival, renewal, reappearance, rejuvenation, revivication, recrudescence; new birth, new day, new dawn, awakening.

renascent, *adj.* awakening, resurgent, reappearing, regenerative, rejuvenescent; revived, revivified, renewed, rejuvenated, reanimated, resurrected, resuscitated, redivivus, reborn, born-again, awakened.

rend, *v.* **1.** rip up, tear to bits *or* pieces, shred, splinter, reave, break up, chop up, mangle; smash, smash to smithereens, break into a million pieces, shatter.

2. sever, sunder, split, slice, separate, part, divide, dissect, cleave, rive; disunite, disjoin, tear apart; rupture, fracture, crack, snap.

3. harrow, distress, disturb, trouble, worry; pain, hurt, afflict; smite, pierce, stab, wound.

render, *v.* **1.** make, cause, effect, bring about, produce, create.

2. do, perform, practice, carry on *or* out, execute; achieve, accomplish.

3. provide, furnish, give, supply, contribute.

4. exhibit, show, display, manifest.

5. present, proffer, offer, deliver, tender, put up, hand over, hand down.

6. pay, remit, yield, hand out, give tribute; give up, surrender, cede.

7. translate, transcribe, convert, turn into; reword, rephrase, restate; do an exegesis, make intelligible, decipher, decode.

8. represent, depict, picture, portray, illustrate, design.

9. interpret, elucidate, illuminate, shed light on; explain, define, spell out, show the meaning of, plumb, probe.

10. melt, clarify, try out oil, try out.

rendezvous, *n.* **1.** date, appointment, engagement, tryst, assignation, meeting.

2. gathering point *or* place, meeting place; trysting place, place of assignation.

—*v.* **3.** meet, assemble, muster, gather, collect, get together.

rendition, *n.* **1.** translation, metaphrase, interlinear, transliteration, transcription, decipherment, decoding; paraphrase, rewording, restatement; reading, recital, lection.

2. interpretation, exegesis, construction, construe, conception, understanding; representation, depiction, delineation, portrayal, reproduction; version, variation, arrangement, *Music.* transcription, *Fr. rendu;* production, performance, execution, enactment, rendering.

renegade, *n.* **1.** defector, turncoat, recreant, tergiversator, *Archaic.* renegado; deserter, forsaker, abdicator, abdicant; dropout, seceder, quitter, departer, leaver, bolter, runaway; traitor, betrayer, *Inf.* double-crosser, *Inf.* double-dealer, *Sl.* ratter, *Sl.* fink, *Sl.* ratfink; rebel, dissenter, renouncer, abjurer, repudiator, rejector, retractor, recanter; malcontent, seditionist, insurgent, insurrectionist, mutineer, revolter, revolutionary.

2. apostate, heretic, schismatic; nonbeliever, heathen, infidel; backslider, slider, lapser, sinner.

—*adj.* **3.** recreant, defecting, tergiversating, abdicant, abdicative; disloyal, unfaithful, untrue; dissident, divergent, unorthodox; traitorous, *Inf.* double-crossing, *Inf.* double-dealing, perfidious, treacherous, treasonous.

4. apostate, heretical, schismatic; faithless, nonbelieving, heathen, infidel, infidelic; backsliding, lapsing, sinning.

renege, *v.* go back on one's word, cry off, be an Indian giver, default, *Sl.* welsh; back-pedal, backwater, back up; back out, back down, pull out, *Inf.* cop out, *Inf.* weasel out, *Inf.* worm out of, *Inf.* stand down; recant, repudiate, retract, abjure, withdraw, change one's tune; reverse, revoke, rescind, abrogate.

renew, *v.* **1.** resume, recommence, begin *or* start again, start *or* begin all over; make a new beginning, make a fresh start.

2. restore, resupply, restock, replenish, *Scot.* plenish.

3. repeat, reiterate, iterate, recount, recapitulate, ingeminate; redo, do again, do over; reconstruct, remake, reshape, re-create.

4. revive, reestablish, bring back, resurrect.

5. rejuvenate, reinvigorate, revitalize, regenerate, recharge, refresh, resuscitate, put *or* breathe new life into; renovate, recondition, refurbish, rehabilitate, reconstitute, revamp, refit; repair, fix up, put into shape, give a face-lift to.

renewal, *n.* **1.** resumption, recommencement; restoration, replenishment; repetition, reiteration, iteration, recapitulation, gemination; reconstruction, recreation; revivification, resurrection, rejuvenation, reinvigoration, revitalization, regeneration, resuscitation; repair, renovation, refurbishment, rehabilitation, reconstitution, reconditioning.

2. renaissance, renascence, revival, rebirth, new birth, new day, new dawn; fresh start, new beginning, another try; rally, recovery, new lease on life, another chance; (*all of disease*) relapse, lapse, reversal, reverse, setback, recurrence, return.

renounce, *v.* **1.** forgo, do *or* go without, give up, *Inf.* swear off; forswear, avoid, shun, eschew; forbear, desist from, cease, stop; eliminate, discard, jettison, cast aside *or* off; abandon, desert, forsake, leave, quit, throw over, turn one's back on.

2. abdicate, resign, give up claim *or* right to, *Law.* disclaim, lay down, part with, retire from, vacate, abnegate, *Chiefly Scot.* demit; relinquish, let go, deliver up, hand over, turn over; surrender, yield, cede, give way.

3. repudiate, reject, disown, disinherit, wash one's hands of, have nothing further to do with; renege, disavow, deny, retract, disclaim, recant, (*usu. under oath*) abjure; defect, apostatize.

4. refuse, decline, turn down.

renovate, *v.* **1.** repair, renew, recondition, refurbish, rehabilitate, reconstitute, revamp, refit; mend, fix, fix up, patch up, put into shape, give a face-lift to.

2. revive, rejuvenate, rejuvenize, reinvigorate, revitalize, revivify, regenerate, recharge, refresh, resuscitate, resurrect, put *or* breathe new life into.

renovation, *n.* repair, renewal, refurbishment, rehabilitation, reconstitution, reconditioning; revival, revivification, rejuvenation, rejuvenescence, reinvigoration, revitalization, regeneration, resuscitation, resurrection.

renown, *n.* fame, bays, celebrity, stardom, prominence, illustriousness; popularity, vogue, favor; greatness, preeminence, supereminence, superiority, supremacy, primacy, paramountcy; eminence, notability, repute, distinction, note, mark, eminency; standing, station, rank, position; consequence, importance, weight, significance, account; reputation, prestige, dignity, esteem, high regard, admiration, respect; honor, laurels, glory, praise, kudos, éclat, acclamation, acclaim.

renowned, *adj.* famous, famed, celebrated, illustrious, well-known, prominent, notorious, *Inf.* name, *Inf.* big-name, notable, eminent, preeminent, supereminent, peerless, matchless, outstanding, *Archaic.* eximious; honored, honorable, esteemed, respected, revered, venerable, distinguished; important, consequential, great, grand, glorious, brilliant; exalted, acclaimed, much-touted, big-time, on the map, popular, well-liked; reputable, prestigious; immortal, fabled, legendary, historical, memorable.

rent[1], *n.* **1.** fee, hire, price, cost; payment, dues, toll, tariff, tax; profit, return, proceeds.

—*v.* **2.** live in, occupy temporarily; charter, hire, farm, take; lease, let, let out, hire out, farm out, sublet, sublease, underlet, *Law.* demise.

rent[2], *n.* **1.** slit, incision, hole, flaw, split, tear, rip, gash, slash; gap, opening, perforation, puncture; rift, scission, rupture, break, crack, fracture, chap, check; fissure, crevice, crevasse, chink, cleft, chasm, stria, cranny, interstice.

2. division, schism, separation, breach; disunion, discord, dissension.

renunciation, *n.* **1.** relinquishment, abnegation, abdication, resignation, giving up, *Archaic.* demission; transfer, transferal, transference, ceding, cession, handing over; surrender, yielding, renouncement.

2. abandonment, desertion, forsaking, rejection, disowning, disinheriting, turning one's back on, washing one's hands of; neglect, negligence, dereliction, remissness.

3. repudiation, disavowal, denial, recantation, (*usu. under oath*) abjuration, retraction, disclaimer, disclamation, back-pedaling; defection, heresy, apostasy, recreance, recreancy.

4. sacrifice, self-denial, self-restraint, self-control; austerity, abstemiousness, abstinence, abstention, continence, celibacy; forbearance, restraint, moderation, temperance.

reorganize, *v.* rearrange, redo, do over, overhaul, make over, revamp, reconstruct; redistribute, realign, restructure, straighten out, *Inf.* get the kinks out, *Inf.* get rid of the deadwood, *Inf.* shake up, *Inf.* clean house; redevelop, develop, elaborate.

2. re-form, refashion, re-create, remake, revolutionize, change; improve, make better, enhance; rehabilitate, restore, revive, salvage, redeem, resuscitate, *Inf.* dust off; refurbish, touch up, brush up; correct, emend, emendate, revise, edit, rectify, *Inf.* clean up.

repair[1], *v.* **1.** restore, mend, patch *or* patch up, put back together, make good as new; service, fix, fix up, make improvements on, improve, better, ameliorate, meliorate; amend, emend, correct, adjust, align, regulate; recondition, redo, remake, make over, overhaul, rebuild, reconstruct, remodel, revamp, renovate, renew, redecorate; repaint, touch up, brush up, polish up, clean up, spruce up.

2. renew, revive, heal, cure. See **remedy** (*def.* **2**).

3. remedy, redress, right a wrong, make up for, compensate for, make amends for, atone for, make restitution for, satisfy; recoup, reimburse, indemnify, pay back, repay, recompense, come up with the difference, remunerate, requite; pay off, *Inf.* get out from under; make good, redeem, refund, give back, remit.

—*n.* **4.** restoration, mending, patching *or* patching up; servicing, fixing *or* fixing up, improvements, betterment, amelioration, melioration; amendment, emendment, correction, adjustment, alignment; reconditioning, redoing, remaking, making over, overhauling, rebuilding, reconstruction, remodeling, revamping, renovation, *Archaic.* instauration, renewal, redecoration.

5. *Usu.* **repairs** adjustments, corrections; work, service, attention, fixing.

repair[2], *v.* **1.** betake oneself, go, leave for, head for, take off for; hie, hasten, go in haste, speed, hurry.

2. frequent, resort, go often, visit regularly, haunt.

reparable, *adj.* remediable, curable, medicable, healable, treatable, mendable; amendable, emendable, rectifiable, correctable, fixable, restorable; recoverable, retrievable, reclaimable, redeemable; corrigible, reformable, improvable.

reparation, *n.* **1.** redress, amends, atonement, redemption, restitution, expiation; requital, quittance, retribution, satisfaction; compensation, indemnity, indemnification, recompense, solatium; remuneration, payment, repayment, reimbursement, refund, one's money back, recoupment.

2. repair, restoration, renovation, *Archaic.* instauration, renewal. See **repair**[1] (*def.* **4**).

repartee, *n.* **1.** give-and-take, witty conversation, lively exchange, tit for tat, measure for measure, stroke for stroke; badinage, banter, raillery, wordplay, persiflage; joking, jesting, pleasantry, drollery, jocularity, waggery, *Inf.* kidding, *Inf.* kidding back and forth, *Inf.* joshing, *Sl.* funning around.

2. rejoinder, answer, quick answer, response, reply, riposte, counterstroke, return, comeback, *Inf.* snappy comeback; counterblast, blow for blow, a Roland for an Oliver, retort, replication, quip, *Inf.* shot, *Inf.* zinger, *Inf.* a good one.

repast, *n.* **1.** meal, refection, *Inf.* bite to eat; mess, table, board, *Inf.* feed; snack, collation, *Inf.* bite, *Inf.* nosh; square meal, full meal, hearty meal, man-sized meal; feast, banquet, *Inf.* spread, *Inf.* blowout, *Chiefly Brit. Sl.* beanfeast *or* beano.

2. mealtime, dinnertime, lunchtime, suppertime, *U.S. Sl.* chowtime.

repay, *v.* **1.** pay back, reimburse, requite, make requital, compensate, make restitution, make amends, indemnify, make it up to; refund, return, recompense, render, square accounts with, *Inf.* wipe the slate clean,

Inf. get back on the board, *Inf.* get even-steven; reward, reward for favors received, pay back in kind, return the compliment *or* the favor, reciprocate.

2. retaliate, hit back at, get back at, *Inf.* pay off an old score, *Inf.* settle the score, *Inf.* even the score, get even with [s.o.], revenge, avenge; make reprisal, give as good as one gets, pay [s.o.] in his own coin, give [s.o.] a dose of his own medicine, give [s.o.] his just deserts, give [s.o.] his comeuppance.

repayment, *n.* **1.** compensation, remuneration, reimbursement, return, emolument; quittance, requital, reciprocation, recompense, indemnity, indemnification, redress, reparation, restitution, atonement, amends.

2. retaliation, revenge, vengeance, retribution, comeuppance, just deserts; reprisal, measure for measure, tit for tat, *Inf.* a dose of one's own medicine.

repeal, *v.* **1.** revoke, rescind, abrogate; annul, disannul, nullify, abolish, declare null and void, void, make void; quash, invalidate, vacate, set aside; recant, retract, withdraw, disavow, recall, abjure; countermand, counterorder, overrule, override; renege, reverse; terminate, dissolve, do away with, remove, dispense with, cancel, put an end to, throw overboard.

—*n.* **2.** revocation, rescinding, rescission, abrogation, repealing; annulment, disannulment, nullification, abolishment, abolition, voidance, voiding; quashing, invalidation, setting aside; recantation, retraction, withdrawal, disavowal, recall, abjuration, repudiation; countermand, counterorder, overruling, overriding, reversal; termination, dissolution, cancellation, doing away with, removal, putting an end to, throwing overboard.

repeat, *v.* **1.** iterate, reiterate, recite, restate, recapitulate, rehearse, recount, retell, reword, rephrase, paraphrase, ingeminate; rerun, play back, regurgitate, reprise, *Sl.* come again; tautologize, battologize; redo, do over *or* again; hammer *or* beat *or* drive into [s.o.'s] head; hammer away, pound away, dwell on, harp on.

2. reproduce, duplicate, reduplicate, ditto, replicate; echo, reecho, parrot; remake, reconstruct, reshape, recreate, resurrect; ring the changes.

—*n.* **3.** repetition. See **repetition** (*def.* **1**).

4. duplicate, duplication, reduplication, copy, reproduction, *Inf.* ditto; *All Music.* reprise, refrain, repetend.

5. rerun, rebroadcast, replay; encore, repeat performance; playback; retrospective.

repeated, *adj.* **1.** frequent, recurrent; constant, continuous, continual, incessant, steady, ceaseless, endless, unending, unbroken, unremitting.

2. duplicated, reduplicated; doubled, redoubled; iterated, reiterated, twice-told, often-told.

repeatedly, *adv.* frequently, often, oftentimes; recurrently, again and again, over and over, many times over, time and again, time and time again, time after time; day after day, day in, day out, night and day, all the time; constantly, continually, continuously, steadily, incessantly, ceaselessly, on and on, without letup *or* intermission *or* break.

repel, *v.* **1.** drive back, push back, thrust back, ward off, beat back, force back; throw off, check, scotch, repulse, chase away, run off, put to flight, rout, *Inf.* send packing; scatter, disperse, oppose, withstand, make a stand against, *Archaic.* forfend.

2. resist, hold off, fend off, stave off, keep at arm's length, keep at bay, parry, stand off; avert, foil, checkmate, frustrate, contravene, *Inf.* cross, confound, nonplus; rebuff, reject, refuse to deal with, have nothing to do with, spurn, slight, *Inf.* snub, *Inf.* cut, *Inf.* cut dead; give the cold shoulder to, *Inf.* cold-shoulder, scorn, disdain, contemn.

3. revolt, nauseate, sicken, make one vomit *or* puke *or* retch, turn one's stomach, *Sl.* gross out; offend, put off, turn off; appall, disgust, be disgusting, be hateful, be vulgar, fill with loathing, make one's flesh crawl, make one's hair stand on end, *Inf.* give one the creeps; set one against, stick in one's throat *or* craw *or* gullet, go against the grain, set one's teeth on edge, make one shudder, grate on one's nerves, give one goose pimples; vex, irritate, alienate, *Inf.* bug.

repellent, *adj.* **1.** offensive, obnoxious, revolting, repugnant, disgusting, repulsive, abominable, beastly, vile, loathsome, execrable; distasteful, upsetting, off-putting, rebarbative; nauseating, sickening, *Sl.* icky; unbearable, hateful, despicable, detestable, abhorrent; forbidding, frightful, *Inf.* creepy, contemptible, heinous, scurvy, odious; base, low, abject, mean, vile, sordid, *Inf.* crummy.

2. filthy, dirty, tainted, corrupt; rotten, putrid, putrescent, obscene; decaying, putrefactive, fetid; rank, foul-smelling, noisome, fulsome, reeking; slimy, feculent, foul; unsightly, sloppy, gross, unclean, impure.

3. repelling, opposing, oppugnant, resistant, rebellious, unyielding, counterattacking.

repent, *v.* **1.** regret, feel sorry for *or* about, feel contrition for; lament, bewail, rue, rue the day; deplore, deprecate, bemoan, repine; weep over, grieve, mourn, keen, pine; fret, be stung by one's conscience; *Inf.* kick oneself, bite one's tongue, cry over spilt milk; curse one's luck, curse the day, curse one's folly, gnash one's teeth, never forgive oneself, never get over; wish undone, pity oneself, despond.

2. be penitent, do penance, atone for, make up for, make amends for, expiate, compensate for, redress.

repentance, *n.* penitence, sackcloth and ashes, compunction, remorse, remorsefulness, contrition, contriteness, sorrow, sorriness, regret, regretfulness; lamentation, rue, grief, mournfulness, weeping, woe, dole; twinge *or* pang of conscience, voice of conscience, guilt, shame, shamefulness, embarrassment; self-humiliation, self-mortification, self-debasement, self-accusation, self-reproach, self-blame, self-denunciation, self-condemnation, self-punishment.

repentant, *adj.* penitent, penitential, contrite, in sackcloth and ashes, atoning; remorseful, compunctious, regretful, regretting, full of regrets; apologetic, sorry, sorrowful, rueful, mournful, doleful, troubled, disturbed; conscience-stricken, conscience-smitten, guilt-ridden, self-accusing, self-reproachful, self-debasing, self-condemning, self-punishing; chastened, humbled, shamed, ashamed, embarrassed, abject, sheepish.

repercussion, *n.* **1.** effect, consequence, outcome, result, upshot; harvest, fruit, product; aftermath, aftereffect, fallout.

2. impact, reaction; backlash, backwash, kickback; reflex; recoil, rebound.

3. echo, reverberation; report, concussion, shock.

repertory, *n.* **1.** theatrical company, acting company, stock company; company, troupe.

2. store, stock, supply, supply on hand, inventory, repertoire; reserve, reservoir; collection, cache, amassment, stockpile.

3. repository, depository, depot, supply depot, warehouse, storehouse, storeroom, storage.

repetition, *n.* **1.** iteration, gemination, restatement, recitation, recapitulation, rehearsal, recounting, recapping, retelling; reiteration, redundancy, battology, tautology, macrology, the same old story *or* thing, the same thing all over again, reproduction, duplication, reduplication, replication.

2. duplicate. See **repeat** (*defs.* **4, 5**).

repetitive, *adj.* recurrent, recurring, continuous, continual; incessant, constant, ceaseless, endless, unending, never-ending, interminable; monotonous, humdrum, tedious, boring; iterant, reiterant, redundant, tautological, battological, pleonastic.

repine, *v.* **1.** regret, deplore, rue, rue the day; mourn, lament, moan, bemoan, bewail, sigh, *Inf.* sing the blues; reproach oneself, curse one's folly, *Sl.* kick oneself; cry over spilt milk.

2. complain, groan, grumble, moan, *Inf.* grouch, *Inf.* gripe, *Inf.* beef, *Inf.* kick, *Sl.* squawk, *Sl.* bellyache, *Sl.* bitch; fret, fuss, make *or* kick up a fuss, carry on, go on, *Inf.* take on.

replace, *v.* **1.** succeed, supplant, supply, supersede, follow *or* follow after, come after; substitute for, *Inf.* sub for, subrogate, act for, fill in for, fill *or* take the place of, double for, cover for, stand in lieu of, *Inf.* step into [s.o.'s] shoes, *Inf.* fill [s.o.'s] shoes; pinch-hit, fill a vacancy *or* space *or* hole.

2. return, restore, replace, put back; repay, refund, make good, give satisfaction.

replenish, *v.* **1.** refill, reload, recharge; top off, fill to the brim, round out, eke out.

2. supply, provide, furnish; store, stock up, fill up, gird, *Chiefly Scot.* plenish.

replete, *adj.* **1.** full, filled, filled to the brim, full to bursting, abrim, chock-a-block, *Brit. Inf.* chocker, *Inf.* chock-full, jammed, packed, *Inf.* jam-packed, *Archaic.* fraught; profuse, abounding, superabundant, exuberant; bursting, overflowing, spilling over, running over; rife, rampant, thick with, bristling with, teeming with, *Sl.* lousy with.

2. (*all with food*) stuffed, gorged, sated, satiated, surfeited, glutted, jaded, cloyed.

3. complete, stocked-up, well-stocked, well-provided, well-supplied, well-furnished.

repletion, *n.* **1.** fullness, completeness, amplitude, *Rare.* impletion; plenteousness, plentifulness, bountifulness, bounteousness, copiousness; richness, exuberance, luxuriousness, lavishness.

2. overfullness, superabundance, overabundance, plethora, superflux; engorgement, congestion; profusion, more than enough, enough and then some, enough and to spare; surfeit, satiety, glut, excess; overdose, too much of a good thing.

replica, *n.* version, takeoff, imitation, representation, *Inf.* knockoff; image, likeness, reflection, resemblance; model, facsimile, reproduction; copy, carbon copy, duplicate, duplication, *Inf.* dupe, *Inf.* ditto.

replicate, *v.* repeat, do over, do again; reproduce, reduplicate, duplicate, ditto; remake, reconstruct, recreate.

reply, *v.* **1.** answer, respond, acknowledge; retort, rejoin, riposte, return, come back; echo, reecho, resound, reverberate.

—*n.* **2.** answer, response, replication, acknowledgment; retort, rejoinder, riposte, return, repartee, comeback, snappy comeback, barb, zinger; reaction, *Sl.* rise.

3. echo, repercussion, reverberation, report.

report, *n.* **1.** detailed statement, detailing, in-depth account, delineation, circumstantiation, exposition, exposition, explanation, *Archaic.* delation; description, sketch, characterization, portrayal, picturization, representation; account, recounting, telling, sharing, relation, narration, narrative, recital, recitation, recapitulation; reportage, article, piece, column, story, review, critique, exposé, *Inf.* write-up; record, chronicle, annals, history; transcription, transcript, minutes, notes, copy of the proceedings.

2. announcement, statement, speech, public address, broadcast; revelation, disclosure, *Archaic.* divulgation; release, press release, publication, bulletin, notification, notice; note, memorandum, *Inf.* memo, dispatch, communiqué, communication.

3. rumor, grapevine, hearsay, gossip, tittle-tattle, dirt, *Inf.* scuttlebutt, *Fr. oui-dire, Archaic.* bruit; word, news, tidings, latest; information, info, intelligence, *Inf.* inside info, *Sl.* dope, *Sl.* poop.

4. boom, bang, crack, crash, rumble, echo, reverberation, noise, sound; discharge, explosion, detonation, fulmination; shot, blast, gunfire, backfire, thunderclap.

5. report card, academic report, school *or* college file, transcript, grades.

6. paper, position paper, white paper, white book, blue book, dossier; documentary, monograph, treatise thesis, dissertation, study, in-depth look; analysis, discussion, commentary, editorial; findings, conclusion, results, end result, outcome, issue, product; finding, decision, opinion, determination, judgement, verdict, decree, order, final word.

7. repute, reputation, renown, distinction, notability, notoriety, fame, name; regard, esteem, consideration; performance, past performance, track record, history.

—*v.* **8.** relay, pass on, repeat, communicate; inform, advise of, brief, fill [s.o.] in, enlighten; present oneself, show up, be there *or* present, come in *or* around.

9. relate, tell, tell about, recount, put into words, set forth, give an account of; narrate, recite, rehearse, recapitulate, review, go over, run through; describe, detail, sketch, depict, portray, characterize.

10. disclose, reveal, divulge, *Archaic.* divulgate; publicize, make public, circulate, send out, spread *or* pass the word *or* news; state publicly, broadcast, announce, voice, publish, print, put out.

11. give one's position on, tell where one stands, give an accounting, go on record; analyze, critique, discuss, talk about; publish one's results or findings, put out a position paper *or* white paper; reveal one's final decision *or* conclusion, give one's opinion *or* judgment, state the verdict *or* determination.

12. tell on, tattle on, inform on, *Inf.* blab on, *Sl.* squeal on, *Sl.* rat on, *Chiefly Scot.* delate; accuse, charge, make a charge against; go to the authorities *or* police, make a complaint.

13. transcribe, take the minutes, take dictation, take notes, take down, write down, jot down, make a note of; record, keep a record of, put into writing, document, write up, write about *or* on, chronicle, put into the annals.

reporter, *n.* **1.** journalist, newsman, newswoman, newspaperman, newspaperwoman; writer, news writer, newspaper writer, wire reporter, *Facetious.* scribe, pad-and-pencil man; the press, member of the press *or* fourth estate, gentleman of the press, SDX member; *Inf.* newshawk, *Inf.* newshound, *Inf.* newshen, Brenda Starr, Lois Lane; general assignment reporter, G.A., feature writer, beat man; investigator, digger, investigative reporter, Woodstein, Scoop, hatchet man, snoop, snooper; staffer, correspondent, stringer, roving reporter, foreign correspondent, Nellie Bly, Richard Harding Davis; bureau chief, bureau man, legman, district man; rewrite man, rewrite, deskman, editor; sportswriter, sports editor, women's editor, obituary writer, obit man, police reporter, *Sl.* ambulance chaser, financial *or* business editor, outdoors editor; reviewer, drama critic, arts critic, book reviewer; columnist, pundit, Walter Lippman; sob sister, Miss Lonelyhearts; society reporter, gossip col-

umnist, scandalmonger, Walter Winchell.
2. (*of television*) announcer, newscaster, reader, on-camera man, anchorman, co-anchorman; news analyst, news commentator, commentator.
3. photojournalist, news photographer, photog, cameraman, Matthew Brady; crime photographer, Casey, Flash.
4. court reporter, court stenographer, court recorder.

repose, *n.* **1.** rest, sleep, slumber, somnolence, land of Nod, arms of Morpheus, *Inf.* beauty sleep, *Sl.* shut-eye, *Sl.* Z's, *Chiefly Brit. Sl.* Bo-Peep; nap, catnap, nod, snooze, doze, siesta, *Inf.* forty winks.
2. dormancy, latency, idleness, passivity, inaction, inactivity; hibernation, estivation, vegetation; stagnation, stagnancy, inertness, inertia, motionlessness; immobility, lifelessness, inanimateness, inanimation, death.
3. peace, peacefulness, peaceableness; tranquillity, calm, calmness, quiet, quiescence, quietude; stillness, silence, hush.
4. respite, holiday, vacation, time off; recess, break, time-out, breath, breather, breathing time, breathing spell, time to catch one's breath; slackening, abatement, letup, lull; relief, ease, leisure, restfulness, relaxation.
5. composure, poise, serenity, equanimity, equability, self-possession, assurance, aplomb.
—*v.* **6.** rest, be dormant, be latent, be inactive; hibernate, estivate, vegetate, be quiet, be tranquil, be calm, be peaceful, be pacific; be still, lie still, be dead, lie dead.
7. relax, take one's ease, take it easy, do nothing; be idle, idle, be lazy, lazy, laze, loaf, loll, lounge, unwind, unbend; let up, ease up, slack off, take a break, take time out, have a breathing spell, have time to catch one's breath, take a breath, *Inf.* take a breather, *Inf.* take five; pause, wait, hold, stay, remain.

repository, *n.* **1.** receptacle, hold, compartment, bin, container, case, box, holder; drawer, file drawer, file, pigeonhole, cubbyhole; cache, hiding place, secret spot, *Inf.* stash; storeroom, reservoir, repertory, arsenal, magazine, armory, armed car; depot, storehouse, warehouse (*in the Orient*) godown; cabinet, cupboard, pantry, larder, buttery; closet, wardrobe, armoire, bureau, dresser, chest of drawers, chiffonier; safe, vault, safety-deposit box, strongbox, locker, chest, trunk, money chest; coffer, treasury, bank; museum, *Fr musée, It. musèo, Obs.* conservatory, reliquary, shrine.
2. sepulcher, grave, crypt, tomb, catacomb, mausoleum, *Archaic.* sepulture; coffin, pine box, urn; burial ground *or* place, graveyard, cemetery, urnfield.
3. trustee, depositary, steward, guardian, guard, *Law.* fiduciary; treasurer, banker, cashier, bursar, purser, *Rom. Hist.* quaestor; confidant, confidante, intimate, familiar, close *or* dear *or* intimate friend, bosom buddy, a shoulder to cry on, *Latin. fidus Achates.*

reprehend, *v.* find fault with, reprove, rebuke, reproach, reprimand, berate, rate, castigate, chastise; upbraid, dress down, scold, *Inf.* trim, chide, bawl out, *Sl.* chew out, tongue-lash; call to account, bring to book, call on the carpet; talk to, take to task, lecture, admonish, warn; censure, reprobate, criticize, remonstrate, condemn; blame, charge, accuse, impute, indict.

reprehensible, *adj.* reproachable, reprovable, rebukable, condemnable, blameworthy, blamable, censurable; delinquent, felonious, amiss, penitentiary, transgressive; culpable, guilty, criminal, unlawful, illegal, illicit, illegitimate, lawless; sinful, peccant, peccable, erring, errant; wicked, reprobate, iniquitous, nefarious, villainous, heinous, flagitious; shameful, disgraceful, opprobrious, discreditable, disreputable, dishonorable, ignoble; objectionable, unpardonable, unforgivable, inexpiable, indefensible, unjustifiable, inexcusable.

represent, *v.* **1.** exemplify, stand for, symbolize; serve as an example of, be a sample *or* specimem of; illustrate, epitomize, embody, personify, typify; be a case *or* an instance of, give an idea of; be regarded as, be the equivalent of.
2. express, designate, depict, illustrate; delineate, draw, paint, *Archaic.* limn; sketch, trace, reproduce; describe, characterize, define, depict; outline verbally, set forth in words, verbalize; narrate, relate, recite, recount, romance; record, chronicle, preserve for the ages.
3. stand for, replace, act for; be deputy for, be spokesman for, negotiate for, transact business for; substitute for, be ambassador for, be envoy for, be legate *or* messenger for, go in someone's place, act vicariously, be the authorized agent for, have someone's proxy *or* vote.
4. present, produce, bring forward, set forth; bring before the public, put on, put on for the public, display, exhibit, bring out, put on the stage, stage.
5. personate, perform as, portray, impersonate, assume the guise of, appear as, pretend to be; take the part *or* place of, assume the role *or* character of, do a study *or* characterization of, masquerade as, mask oneself as, represent oneself as; ape, take off on, do an impression of, mimic, parody, caricature, burlesque; monkey, parrot, simulate, *Sl.* make like.
6. correspond to, be the equivalent of, mirror, be the counterpart of; copy, duplicate, be a facsimile of, be the parallel of, be analogous to.

representation, *n.* **1.** depiction, illustration, likeness, semblance, similitude, icon, simulacrum, depictment; portrait, painting, drawing, engraving, sketch; photograph, daguerreotype, *Inf.* photo, snapshot, *Inf.* snap, *Inf.* candid; X-ray, radiogram, fluoroscope; image, reflection, shadow, silhouette.
2. facsimile, exact copy, replica, reproduction; reprint, imitation, counterpart, ditto; model, statue, statuette, figurine, bust, head; effigy, waxwork, marionette, puppet, manikin; architect's model, shipbuilder's model, diagram, blueprint, plans.
3. play, skit; drama; burlesque, parody; imitation, impersonation, personification, acting.
4. representatives, delegation, delegates, deputies, embassy, embassy staff, legation; committee, subcommittee; body of delegates, body of deputies.
5. mental image, thought, impression, concept, conception; fancy, romance, illusion; memory, recollection, recall, total recall, *Psychol.* mneme; remembrance, reminiscence, retrospect.
6. Often **representations** description, account, explanation, commentary, version; exposition, unfolding, detailing, elaboration; recital, recitation, rehearsal, history of the events; statement, allegation, positive declaration, formal averment; profession, deposition, thesis; justification, plea, excuse, pretext.
7. vicarship, mandate, deputation, delegation, proxy, commission, warrant, authorization, charge, trust.

representative, *n.* **1.** substitute, stand-in, understudy, factotum, proxy, consignee; agent, attorney, solicitor, spokesman, spokesperson, *Inf.* mouthpiece; commissioner, broker, factor, trustee, regent, vice-regent; lieutenant, steward, surrogate, vicar, clerk, bailiff; diplomat, plenipotentiary, legate, consul, ambassador; attaché, envoy, messenger, nuncio, emissary, negotiator.

2. delegate, elected representative; senator, congressman, congresswoman, assemblyman, assemblywoman, councillor; member of Parliament, M.P.

3. specimen, sample, trial run; typical example, typical instance, case in point; exemplification, illustration, epitome.

—adj. **4.** representing, delegated, deputized, ordained, commissioned; accredited, official, operative, ambassadorial; empowered, authorized, licensed, endorsed; vicarious, substitute, proxy, surrogate.

5. typical, typifying, exemplifying, illustrative, indicative, characteristic; symbolic, emblematic, model, true-to-type, stereotypical, standard; normal, usual, expected, in character.

repress, *v.* **1.** keep under control, control, check, keep in check; arrest, contain, restrain, hold back; harness, bridle, rein in, hold in leash; restrict, fetter, shackle, confine, limit, cramp, constrain; hold in, bottle up, cork up, box up, shut up, seal; block, impede, inhibit, hinder, hamper, deter; detain, keep in, hold, stay; prohibit, forbid, disallow, interdict, prevent, suppress; preclude, obviate, nip in the bud, *Inf.* put the kibosh on.

2. curb, curtail, cut down on, moderate, temper; interrupt, let up, pause, suspend, intermit, *Inf.* bite *or* hold one's tongue; discontinue, stop, cease, halt, terminate, put an end to; drop, have done with, let alone, let be.

3. suppress, keep from, withhold, hide, conceal, bury, reserve, refrain from giving; keep secret, not disclose, *Sl.* clam up; censor, keep back, *Inf.* pull punches, deny, abnegate; mask, cloak, secrete, veil, screen, shroud, camouflage, cover up; squelch, muzzle, muffle, mute, still, tone down, hush up, silence, quiet; smother, stifle, choke, gag.

4. put down, quell, quash, subdue, suppress; squelch, *Inf.* put the kibosh on, squash; overthrow, overturn, overcome, overbear, overwhelm, overpower; subvert, topple, conquer, defeat, vanquish; quench, snuff out, extinguish, kill; stamp out, trample, put out; do away with, remove, dissolve, dispose of, get rid of, eliminate; terminate, stop, put an end to.

5. subjugate, subject, enthrall, enslave, reduce to slavery, hold captive, hold in bondage; dominate, rule, overrule, control, command; master, gain the upper hand, subdue, get the better of; browbeat, intimidate, bully, break, humble; oppress, keep down, tyrannize, domineer, govern despotically; crush, ruin, devastate, defeat, conquer, vanquish.

repression, *n.* **1.** control, restraint, check, curb; blockage, impediment, obstruction, inhibition, hindrance, encumbrance, determent, deterrent, restriction, fettering, shackling, chaining, tethering, harnessing, bridling; constraint, cramp, limitation, confinement, keeping back, suppression; prevention, forbiddance, embargo, interdict, interdiction, prohibition; disallowance, preclusion, obviation.

2. suppression, withholding, hiding, concealing, concealment, burial; censorship, keeping back, denying, denial, abnegation; mask, disguise, cloak, veil, screen, shroud, camouflage, cover-up; muzzling, muffling, muting, stilling, hushing up, quieting, silencing; smothering, stifling, suffocating, suffocation, choking down, gagging.

3. quelling, quashing, putting down, squelching, squashing; overthrow, overturn, subversion; overcoming, conquest, defeat, vanquishment; quenching, extinguishment, killing, stamping *or* snuffing out, putting out, trampling; doing away with, removal, disposal, getting rid of, dissolution; elimination, termination, stoppage, arrestment, putting an end to.

4. subjugation, subjection, enthrallment, enslavement, slavery, captivity, bondage; oppression, ruling with a high *or* iron hand, ruling with a rod of iron; tyranny, *U.S.* (*usu. of politics*) bossism, dictatorship, despotism, sovereignty, supremacy; ascendancy, authority, influence, power, mastery, the whip *or* upper hand; domineeringness, browbeating, intimidating, intimidation; bullying, riding roughshod over, riding herd on.

reprieve, *v.* **1.** respite, remit, stay, grant a stay of execution, let off, *Inf.* let off the hook; continue, grant an extension, *Finance.* extend, *Commerce.* indulge; postpone, defer, prorogue, adjourn, suspend, intermit, lay over, put off, stave off, shelve, table, hold in abeyance, reschedule; delay, stall, wait, hold off, procrastinate; stem, check, hold up.

2. relieve, alleviate, allay, assuage, mitigate, palliate; commute, ease up *or* off, slacken up, loosen up, relax, grant a breathing spell, *Archaic.* slake.

—n. **3.** respite, remission, stay, stay of execution, protraction, extension, continuation, *Law.* continuance; postponement, deferment, deferral, delay, prorogation, suspension, abeyance, adjournment, intermission.

4. relief, alleviation, assuagement, mitigation, palliation; easing up *or* off, slackening up, loosening up, relaxation, hiatus, breather, breathing spell, *Inf.* letup, *Rom. Cath. Ch.* dispensation.

reprimand, *n.* **1.** reproof, reproval, reproach, rebuke, rating; castigation, upbraiding, *Inf.* dressing down, *Inf.* trimming, scolding, *U.S. Inf.* bawling out, tongue-lashing, hell; chastisement, rap on the knuckles, slap on the face; talking-to, lecture, admonishment, warning; condemnation, censure, reprehension, animadversion, criticism, remonstration, remonstrance; disapprobation, disapproval, objection, disparagement, deprecation; denunciation, denouncing, tirade, philippic, execration, invective; objurgation, berating, vituperation, contumely; reprobation, imprecation, fulmination, detraction, derogation; stricture, aspersion, obloquy, traducement, defamation, vilification, vilipending; inveighing, declamation; blame, accusation, imputation, indictment.

—v. **2.** reprove, reproach, rebuke, rate, reprehend, castigate, chastise; upbraid, *Inf.* dress down, *Inf.* trim, scold, chide, *U.S. Inf.* bawl out, *Sl.* chew out, tongue-lash; *Inf.* give [s.o.] a piece of one's mind, *Inf.* tell [s.o.] a thing or two, tell off, tell [s.o.] where to get off, take [s.o.] to task, call down, *Sl.* give [s.o.] the business, give [s.o.] hell, *Sl.* lay [s.o.] out in lavender, *Inf.* rake over the coals, *Inf.* skin alive, *Sl.* pin [s.o.'s] ears back, *Inf.* blast, *Inf.* jump on *or* all over, throw [s.t.] in [s.o.'s] face *or* teeth; call to account, bring to book, call on the carpet, read the riot act; talk to, lecture, admonish, warn; condemn, censure, reprobate, criticize, remonstrate, animadvert on; denounce, denunciate, objurgate, berate, vituperate; blame, charge, accuse, impute, indict; inveigh against, rail against, decry, declaim, run down, fulminate against; lash, vilify, curse, revile, vilipend.

reprint, *n.* new edition, second edition, republication, reissue, reimpression, reproduction; offprint, separate, copy, duplicate, facsimile, replica, *Inf.* ditto.

reprisal, *n.* retaliation, revenge, retribution, redress, paying back, vengeance, vendetta; counterblow, counterattack, recrimination; requital, vindication, satisfaction, compensation, reparation, restitution, indemnification, indemnity, repayment, recompense; tit for tat, *Latin. quid pro quo,* a Roland for an Oliver, blow for a blow, tooth for a tooth, eye for an eye, lex talionis.

reproach, *v.* **1.** find fault with, blame, censure, reprehend, criticize; reprove, rebuke, scold, upbraid, call to account, reprimand. See **reprimand** (*def.* **2**).

2. shame, discredit, dishonor, degrade, abase, debase, vitiate; scandalize, sully, blacken, smirch, besmirch, taint, tarnish, spot, stain, brand, stigmatize, drag through the mud *or* mire.

—*n.* **3.** disapproval, blame, censure, reprehension, criticism; reproof, rebuke, scolding, upbraiding, reprimand. See **reprimand** (*def.* **1**).

4. disgrace, discredit, dishonor, shame, degradation, scandal, debasement, vitiation, ill-repute, ingloriousness; ignominy, infamy, odium, opprobrium; slur, smear, smirch, blot, blot on the escutcheon; stain, taint, tarnish, spot, brand, stigma.

reproachful, *adj.* censuring, reproving, disapproving, admonitory, admonishing, warning, monitory; condemnatory, comminatory, incriminatory, accusatory, damnatory; upbraiding, scolding, abusive, berating; objurgatory, denunciatory, fulminatory; censorious, critical, faultfinding, captious, carping, hypercritical; disparaging, derogatory, depreciatory; vituperative, vilifying, invective, opprobrious; caustic, biting, vitriolic, cutting, trenchant, severe; beetle-browed, sullen, scowling, threatening, ominous, menacing, minatory.

reprobate, *n.* **1.** miscreant, villain, blackguard, knave, wretch, *Archaic.* caitiff; scapegrace, scoundrel, rogue, rascal, *Archaic.* varlet, scamp, *Inf.* scalawag, rapscallion; ne'er-do-well, good-for-nothing, *Fr. vaurien, Sl.* bum; cur, *Sl.* dog, *Inf.* hound, reptile, *Sl.* lowlife, degenerate; profligate, rake, roué, libertine, debauchee; fallen angel, sinner, transgressor, trespasser, offender, culprit; wrongdoer, evildoer, malefactor, malfeasant, misfeasor, *Inf.* scofflaw; lawbreaker, delinquent, juvenile delinquent, misdemeanant, larcenist, larcener, felon, criminal; recidivist, repeat offender, *Inf.* chronic crook; convict, *Sl.* jailbird, parolee, ex-convict, *Inf.* ex-con; outlaw, gangster, mobster, racketeer, mafioso, desperado, terrorist, hijacker, kidnapper; thug, *U.S.* tough, *Inf.* toughie, mugger, ruffian, hoodlum, *Sl.* hood, hooligan, *Chiefly Brit.* rough, *Inf.* roughneck, *Inf.* baddy; thief, *Inf.* crook, swindler, cheat, cheater, defrauder, *Sl.* rip-off artist; mischief-maker, troublemaker, *Inf.* cut-up, *Inf.* hellion, rowdy; devil, hellhound, demon, fiend, monster; recreant, traitor, conspirator, *Inf.* snake in the grass, *Inf.* backstabber, squealer, *Sl.* fink, *Sl.* ratfink.

2. outcast, castaway, pariah, *Sl.* leper, exile.

—*adj.* **3.** depraved, miscreant, debased, degenerate, corrupt, perverted; villainous, cruel, malicious, spiteful, vicious, viperous, reptilian; bad, evil, wicked, nefarious, sinful, sinning, iniquitous, *Archaic.* facinorous; vile, foul, reprehensible, despicable; base, low, mean, unprincipled, unscrupulous; scoundrelly, knavish, roguish, rascally; recreant, *Inf.* back-stabbing, traitorous, treasonous, treacherous; criminal, felonious, delinquent, wrongdoing, evildoing.

4. amoral, immoral, nonmoral, unmoral, profligate, shameless, dissolute, abandoned; irredeemable, irreclaimable, unsaveable, past hope, hopeless, past praying for; out-and-out, through-and-through, complete, unqualified, hard-core, hardened, inveterate, recidivistic, recidivous.

—*v.* **5.** condemn, censure, criticize, blame, reprove, reproach, animadvert upon; disapprove, frown upon, take exception to, disagree, reject.

reproduce, *v.* **1.** copy, duplicate, replicate, clone; make a copy of, run off, print, xerox, mimeograph, *Inf.* mimeo, ditto.

2. remake, make over, re-create, re-form, reshape, refashion; remodel, rebuild, reconstruct, renovate, restore, recondition, overhaul; redo, do over, redecorate, refurbish, renew, face-lift.

3. imitate, pattern *or* model after, do like, follow, follow suit, emulate, parallel, match, approximate; copy, *Inf.* copycat, mimic, mime, ape, monkey, parrot, repeat, reflect, mirror, echo; impersonate, *Sl.* make like, mock, parody, *Inf.* take off, satirize, burlesque, caricature; simulate, assume, represent, take on, affect, put on.

4. counterfeit, forge, fake; plagiarize, *Sl.* lift.

5. reperform, re-act, act *or* perform again, give a repeat performance, encore.

6. propagate, multiply, increase and multiply, proliferate, spawn; breed, procreate, produce, beget, engender, generate; bear, bring forth, deliver, give birth to, mother, father; (*all of animals*) sire, dam, drop, throw, hatch, farrow, foal, calve, whelp, fawn, kitten.

reproduction, *n.* **1.** copy, duplicate, *Inf.* dupe, carbon copy, carbon, *Inf.* ditto, *Trademark.* Xerox, *Trademark.* Mimeograph, *Inf.* mimeo; replica, facsimile, ectype, print, reprint; forged signature, forgery, counterfeit, fake; likeness, image, representation, picture, illustration, photograph, *Inf.* photo, snapshot, *Inf.* snap; twin, identical twin, living *or* very image, double, look-alike, clone, exact match; perfect likeness, *Inf.* spit and image *or* spitting image, chip off the old block, *Sl.* ringer, *Sl.* dead ringer.

2. propagation, multiplication, increase, proliferation; breeding, procreation, production, begetting, generation; giving birth, parturition, delivery, bringing forth, bearing; (*all of animals*) dropping, hatching, laying, spawning.

reproductive, *adj.* progenitive, propagative, proliferative, procreative, productive, generative, conceptive, germinative; sexual, sex.

reproof, *n.* reproval, rebuke, reproach, scolding, censure, reprehension, condemnation, reprimand. See **reprimand** (*def.* **1**).

reprove, *v.* rebuke, reproach, rate, scold, censure, reprehend, condemn, denounce, disapprove, reprimand. See **reprimand** (*def.* **2**).

reptilian, *adj.* **1.** reptiloid, reptilelike; saurian, lizardlike; creeping, *Zool.* reptant, *Zool.* repent.

2. base, vile, mean, low, *Inf.* low-down, contemptible, despicable; obsequious, groveling, slithering, crawling, cringing.

3. treacherous, dangerous, bad, hurtful, harmful, deleterious, pernicious; spiteful, malignant, malevolent, venomous, viperous, viperish.

—*n.* **4.** reptile, saurian, ophidian.

repudiate, *v.* **1.** reject, disavow, forswear, renounce, (*usu. under oath*) abjure, disclaim; recant, retract, recall, unsay; deny, contradict, gainsay.

2. *Law.* disaffirm; nullify, annul, declare null and void, void, invalidate, cancel; abrogate, rescind, revoke; quash, set aside, overrule, veto, override, overturn, reverse, repeal, countermand; set at naught, dissolve, abolish, dismiss.

3. cast off, disown, abandon, discard; wash one's hands of, have nothing further to do with, turn one's back on, *Inf.* have no truck with.

4. disapprove, condemn; oppose, contravene, protest, object, demur, refuse assent, disagree; refute, disprove, confute.

5. ignore, disregard, neglect, slight; flout, spurn, scout, scorn, hold in contempt; evade, dishonor, refuse to honor; transgress, violate, disobey.

repudiation, *n.* **1.** rejection, disavowal, renunciation, renouncement, (*usu. under oath*) abjuration, disclaimer, disclamation; recantation, retraction, recall; tergiversation, defection, apostasy; denial, contradiction, gainsay.

2. nullification, annulment, voidance, cancellation, *Law.* defeasance; abrogation, rescission, rescindment, revocation, veto, repeal; countermand, quashing, setting aside, dismissal, overturn, reversal, *Law.* disaffirmation; abolition, dissolution.

3. discarding, disowning, rejection, disinheriting; ignoring, disregarding, slighting, slight, neglecting, neglect; dishonoring, disobeying, violation, transgression, evasion.

4. disapproval, disagreement, dissent, demur, demurral; protest, objection, opposition, contravention; refutation, disproof, confutation; condemnation, disapprobation, denunciation.

repugnance, *n.* **1.** revulsion, repulsion, nausea, queasiness; obnoxiousness, fulsomeness, noisomeness; distaste, disrelish, disgust, offense.

2. aversion, disapprobation, opposition, objection, rejection, disapproval, disfavor, resistance; reluctance, disinclination, unwillingness, indisposedness, adverseness, inimicalness, inimicality; antagonism, animosity, hostility, antipathy, unfriendliness, dislike, disrelish, hatred, detestation, odium, abhorrence, abomination, loathing, execration, *Fr. bête noire.*

3. contrariety, contrariness, oppugnancy, oppugnation, renitence, recalcitrance, withstandingness, reluctation, resistance; conflict, discordance, inaccordancy, clashing; incompatibility, irreconcilability, irreconcilableness, disharmony, incongruity, disagreement; contradictoriness, inconsistency, discrepancy.

repugnant, *adj.* **1.** fulsome, noisome, obnoxious, rank; revolting, repellent, repulsive; distasteful, disgusting, aversive, offensive, funny as a crutch; objectionable, disagreeable, undesirable, unpleasant; nauseating, nauseous, sickening, unsavory, unpalatable, unappetizing, insipid.

2. averse, loath, objecting, counter; reluctant, disinclined, unwilling, indisposed; adverse, inimical; antagonistic, hostile, antipathetical, unfriendly; hateful, detestable, despicable, heinous, loathsome, odious, abhorrent, abominable.

3. contrary, opposed, oppugnant, at variance; conflicting, incompatible, unconformable, irreconcilable; disharmonious, inharmonious, discordant, inaccordant, clashing, incongruous; contradictory, inconsistent, discrepant; refractory, renitent, recalcitrant, resistant, withstanding.

repulse, *v.* **1.** repel, drive back, drive away, chase out; defeat, overthrow, rout, squelch; thwart, stem, check, frustrate, impede, hinder; resist, defend, oppose, confront, counteract, countervail, make a stand.

2. reject, rebuff, repudiate, spurn, veto, give the cold shoulder to, turn down; refuse, deny, disclaim, disavow; disown, renounce, turn one's back upon.

—*n.* **3.** repelling, repellence, driving back, driving away, chasing out; overthrowing, defeating, routing, squelching; thwarting, stemming, checking; rejecting, rebuffing, repudiating, spurning, turning down; refusing, denying, disowning, renouncing.

4. retroaction, oppugnation, reluctation, disclamation, renunciation.

5. rejection, rebuff, repudiation, discountenance, veto; refusal, recusancy, denial, disclaimer.

repulsion, *n.* **1.** repelling, repellence, driving back, driving away, rejecting, refusing, spurning, denying; repercussion, retroaction, oppugnation, reluctation; disclamation, renunciation.

2. repugnance, disgust, nausea, distaste; aversion, revulsion, antagonism, hostility, animus; odiousness, enmity, abhorrence, abomination, loathing, loathsomeness, detestation, hatred, hate.

repulsive, *adj.* **1.** repugnant, repellent, offensive, revolting; nauseating, nauseous, sickening, disgusting; foul, vile, noisome, fulsome, noxious, mephitic; stinking, malodorous, reeking, fetid, rank, smelling, *Inf.* smelly, *Inf.* stinky; slimy, grimy, gooey, mucky, feculent, turbid; unclean, maggoty, flyblown, wormy, worm-eaten; reeky, excrementitious, *Pathol.* stercoraceous, dung-covered; *Sl.* icky, *Sl.* yukky, *Sl.* ishy, *Sl.* yecchy, *Sl.* ecchy; beastly, dreadful, rotten, horrible; rancid, curdled, sour, bad.

2. obnoxious, objectionable, off-putting, gross, odious, rebarbative; abominable, execrable, loathsome, detestable, despicable, hateful; anathematic, abhorrent, base, contemptible.

3. crude, obscene, pornographic, filthy, dirty, vulgar, foul-mouthed; ugly, homely, plain, ugly as sin, not fit to be seen, homely enough to curdle milk; hideous, horrid, gorgonian, grisly, ghastly; misshapen, malformed, freakish, sideshow; unsightly, frightful, monstrous, grotesque, grim.

4. shameless, disgraceful, low, ignoble, shocking, appalling; unseemly, opprobrious, infamous, discreditable, dishonorable; scandalous, outrageous, reprehensible, disreputable; disagreeable, displeasing, obnoxious, unpleasant, nasty, mean, unsavory.

reputable, *adj.* **1.** honest, aboveboard, legitimate, *Sl.* legit; straight, straightforward, square-dealing, fair and square, on the level, *Sl.* on the up-and-up, uncorrupt; in good repute, in good odor.

2. trustworthy, reliable, dependable; upright, principled, scrupulous, conscientious; righteous, virtuous, noble, good; unimpeachable, irreproachable, above *or* beyond reproach, impeccable.

3. honorable, honored, respectable, respected, estimable, esteemed, worthy, in high favor; renowned, celebrated, noted, recognized; prominent, eminent, outstanding.

4. (*all of usage*) standard, acceptable, good, up to par.

reputation, *n.* **1.** name, repute, *Sl.* rep, face, regard; standing, position, status, station, rank.

2. reputability, respectability, good *or* fair name, good report; estimation, respect, esteem, consideration, honor, laurels, distinction, dignity; illustriousness, fame, bays, renown, vogue, celebrity, famousness, popularity, popular favor, star billing; notability, noteworthiness, notoriety; eminence, prominence, prestige, influence, authority; name to conjure with, big name, importance, consequence, significance, high rank; glory, exaltation, admiration, veneration; halo, *Sl.* wings, radiance, luster; acclamation, acclaim, éclat, celebration, approbation, acknowledgment, recognition.

repute, *n.* **1.** reputation, name; esteem, respect. See **reputation** (*defs.* **1, 2**).

—*v.* **2.** deem, hold, reckon, judge, think, believe, fancy; consider, suppose, view, see; assume, presume, gather.

reputed, *adj.* supposed, supposititious, putative, assumed, presumed; ostensible, apparent, seeming, professed, purported; plausible, reasonable, logical, likely.

request, *n.* **1.** solicitation, entreaty, obsecration, supplication, obtestation, invocation; appeal, petition, suit; plea, pleading, intercession; importunity, adjuration, impetration, imploration; prayer, orison; requisition, behest, demand; application, *Law.* motion, inquiry, interrogation; begging, panhandling, *Sl.* touch, *Sl.* bite; interpellation; invitation, summons, call; proposition, proposal, overture, tender, offer, proffer.

—*v.* **2.** ask for, beg, plead, appeal to, cry for; beseech, entreat, implore, supplicate, obtest; importune, adjure, impetrate; solicit, pass the hat; interpellate, move, petition, pray; put in for, apply for, speak for, *Inf.* have dibs on; demand, insist on, enjoin, command, bid, summon; panhandle, have one's hand out, *Sl.* mooch, cadge, *Sl.* put the bite on, *Sl.* hit [s.o.] up for, *Sl.* put the arm on [s.o.], hustle; proposition, propose, invite, suggest, hint strongly.

require, *v.* **1.** need, want, lack; have need of, stand in need of, be lacking in; not reach, come short of, be found wanting, fall short of the mark, be deficient in, be short of, be caught short, be without; miss, be inadequate, fall down in, be insufficient in.

2. demand, insist upon, urge, press for; direct, order, dictate; dun, exact, call for.

requirement, *n.* **1.** need, necessity, urgent need, dire necessity, imperative; must, must item, essential, *Latin. sine qua non*, indispensable, basic; exigency, essentiality, indispensability.

2. demand, exaction, call, directive; bidding, command, mandate, injunction, charge.

3. requisite, prerequisite, stipulation, provision, proviso, condition, contingency, term, *Inf.* string, *Inf.* catch, *Inf.* rub; reservation, qualification, requisition, constraint, necessitation.

requisite, *adj.* **1.** required, needed, necessary, needful, vital, essential, imperative, necessitative, compulsive, obligatory, binding, incumbent; wanted, called for, indicated, in demand, indispensable.

—*n.* **2.** requirement, need, want; condition, prerequisite. See **requirement** (*defs.* **1, 3**).

requisition, *n.* **1.** demand, call, summons, conscription, draft, injunction, exaction; behest, bidding, command, mandate, beck and call, nod.

2. written order *or* request, authorization, voucher, claim, claim check, ticket, *Inf.* chit.

—*v.* **3.** commandeer, appropriate, take over, take possession of, occupy, take, confiscate, seize, impress, nationalize; request, order, *Inf.* put in for.

requital, *n.* **1.** repayment, satisfaction, amends, reparation, restitution, redress; recompense, return, compensation, consideration, emolument; reward, *Literary.* guerdon, *Archaic.* meed; remuneration, indemnification, indemnity, payment, quittance, acknowledgement, sop, *Inf.* pay-off.

2. retribution, lex talionis, talion, an eye for an eye, measure for measure, tit for tat, nemesis; counterstroke, a Roland for an Oliver, quid pro quo, just deserts; retaliation, revenge, reprisal.

requite, *v.* **1.** repay, satisfy, make repayment for, make amends, make reparation, make restitution; redress, atone for, make good, settle with, reimburse; reciprocate, pay back, recompense, compensate, give consideration *or* compensation for, make return to; remunerate, indemnify, pay, pay off; reward, tip, remember, give a sop to.

2. give in return, even the score, wipe the slate clean, get even with, turn the tables on, return like for like, give tit for tat *or* measure for measure, pay in kind; pay off old scores, avenge a wrong, right a wrong, take revenge, retaliate for, wreak one's vengeance, give a Roland for an Oliver.

rescind, *v.* **1.** repeal, revoke, reverse, abrogate, abolish; annul, disannul, nullify, declare null and void, render null and void, void, avoid; quash, invalidate, vitiate, vacate, disenact, disestablish; cancel, discharge; supersede, set aside.

2. recant, retract, abjure, unsay, withdraw, recall; take back, undo, renege, back-pedal, go back on one's word; renounce, relinquish, abnegate, repudiate, deny, disclaim, disavow; countermand, counterorder, overrule, override; veto, negate.

3. terminate, dissolve, put an end to, bring to an end, do away with; discard, cast aside, cast behind, sweep aside, throw overboard, scatter to the winds, get rid of.

rescission, *n.* **1.** repeal, revocation, reversal, abrogation, abolishment, abolition, rescinding, rescindment; annulment, annulling, disannulment, nullification, voidance, avoidance, *Law.* defeasance; quashing, invalidation, vitiation, *Obs.* vacatur, disenactment, disestablishment, setting aside; cancellation, discharge; suspension, *Law.* nolle prosequi, discontinuance, cessation.

2. recantation, retraction, retractation, abjuration, withdrawal, recall; taking back, undoing, *Cards.* renege; renouncement, renunciation, relinquishment, abnegation, repudiation, denial, disclaimer, disavowal; apostasy, change of mind, tergiversation; countermand, counterorder, overruling, overriding; veto, negation.

3. termination, dissolution, putting an end to, bringing to an end, doing away with.

rescue, *v.* **1.** deliver, ransom, redeem, *Theol.* save; liberate, free, enfranchise, affranchise, franchise, manumit, emancipate; release, loose, let loose, turn loose, set loose, set free, unpen, unmew, disimprison; disenthrall, unfetter, unbind, untie, unbridle, unyoke, unshackle, unchain, unhandcuff, unmuzzle, *Archaic.* untruss; acquit, dismiss, discharge, let go, let out of, let off, *Inf.* let off the hook; absolve, not hold responsible; hold out a hand, come to the aid of, bail out, snatch from danger, form a life line.

—*n.* **2.** deliverance, delivery, delivering, rescuing, ransom, ransoming, redemption, redeeming, *Theol.* salvation, saving; liberation, freedom, freeing, liberty, liberating, enfranchisement, enfranchising, affranchisement, franchisement, franchising, manumitting, manumission, emancipation, emancipating; release, releasing, loosing, disenthrallment, disenthralling, unfettering, unbinding, untying, unbridling, unyoking, unshackling, unchaining; acquittal, acquittance, acquitting, dismissal, dismissing, discharge, discharging.

3. aid, assistance, succor, help, helping hand; intervention, *Latin. deus ex machina,* resolution.

research, *n.* **1.** investigation, inquisition, *Archaic.* indagation, inquiry, study, analysis; fact-finding, legwork; examination, scrutiny, scrutinization, inspection, canvass; exploration, probe, search, quest, pursuit; sifting, going through *or* over, survey, review, checkout, audit; assessment, appraisal, *Sl.* casing.

—*v.* **2.** investigate, probe, explore, search for *or* seek out clues; examine, look into, scrutinize, study, analyze, go over with a fine-tooth comb, inspect, sift through, winnow; track down, ferret out, smell out, nose out, *Inf.* smoke out; inquire into, canvass, see about, check into *or* on *or* up on, *Inf.* give [s.t.] the once-over, *Sl.* check out, *Brit. Sl.* suss out, *U.S. Sl.* case, *Sl.* bird-dog; leave no stone unturned, follow up on leads, bury one's head in the stacks.

resemblance, *n.* **1.** likeness, similarity, semblance, similitude, identicalness, identity, selfsameness; analogy, analogousness, parity, parallelism, correspondence, alikeness; sameness, uniformity, homogeneity, equivalence, equivalency, oneness; comparison, comparability; approximation, nearness, closeness, affinity; agreement, accordance, accord, conformity, concurrence, congruity; repetition, repeat, duplication, iteration.

2. counterpart, complement, correspondent, equivalent, coordinate; analogue, parallel; replica, copy, duplicate, facsimile, faithful copy, reproduction; twin, identical twin, living image, double, look-alike, clone, exact match; perfect likeness, *Inf.* spit and image *or* spitting image, chip off the old block, *Sl.* ringer, *Sl.* dead ringer.

resemble, *v.* be similar to, be like, bear resemblance to, bear likeness to, appear like, seem like, sound like; look like, take after, favor, remind one of, bring to mind; savor *or* smack of, have the earmarks of; approximate, come close to, come near; follow the fashion, swim with the stream; duplicate, parallel, match, follow, correspond; tally, accord with, agree with; copy, echo, mimic, reproduce; simulate, imitate, counterfeit.

resent, *v.* **1.** be offended at, take offense at, take umbrage at; feel displeasure at, be irritated, be annoyed, chafe at; be indignant at, be in a dudgeon over, show indignation at; dislike, view with dissatisfaction, take exception, disagree with; take the wrong way, take amiss, take in bad part; harbor a grudge, never forget *or* forgive, keep the wound open, bear malice, have rankle in the breast, harbor revenge; frown, pout, sulk.

2. be provoked at, be piqued, be in a huff about, be irascible, grouch; be angry, bristle, snarl, growl, show one's teeth, champ at the bit, be impatient; flare up, fly into a rage, lose one's temper, kick up a row; fume, boil with indignation, foam, bluster; scowl, look daggers, look black, glower, lower; bridle, give a dirty look, look with disdain.

resentful, *adj.* bitter, embittered, hostile, revengeful; indignant, irate, ireful, incensed, angry, angered, wrathful, wroth, *Inf.* mad, *Inf.* sore, *Sl.* teed-off, *Sl.* ticked-off, *Sl.* hot, *Sl.* hot under the collar; uptight, in a temper, in a pet, in high dudgeon, in a huff, *Inf.* huffy; annoyed, irritated, peeved, piqued, irked, exasperated, provoked, *Chiefly U.S.* riled, *Inf.* aggravated, *Inf.* miffed.

resentment, *n.* **1.** indignation, offense, umbrage, pique, righteous anger, disgust; anger, ire, wrath, dudgeon, rancor, fury, rage, venomousness; displeasure, disapproval, disapprobation, dissatisfaction, disgruntlement, unhappiness; irritation, annoyance, vexation, exasperation, perturbation, *Inf.* aggravation; virulence, bitterness, gall and wormwood, vindictiveness, vengefulness, vehemence, malice; animosity, invidiousness, hatred, ill feelings, ill will.

2. alienation, disaffection, estrangement, coolness, iciness, aloofness; grouchiness, gruffness, surliness, crabbedness, irritability, petulance, peevishness, irascibility; moodiness, glumness, moroseness, sullenness, sourness, tartness, perverseness, perversity; soreness, wounded pride, mortification; jealousy, envy, suspicion.

reservation, *n.* **1.** qualm, scruple, demur, second thoughts; exception, qualification, proviso, provision, condition, term; grain of salt.

2. *U.S.* reserve, preserve, game preserve, sanctuary; park, national *or* state park, state forest; tract, plot, plat; area, region, zone, territory.

3. booking, advance booking; engagement, preengagement.

reserve, *v.* **1.** husband, hold, withhold, hold back, keep, keep back, conserve, save, save for future use, save for a rainy day; set aside, put aside, put away, lay away, lay by, lay up, stow away, squirrel away, salt away, *Sl.* sock away; store, stockpile, amass, accumulate, pile up.

2. retain, secure; engage, book, charter.

3. earmark, tag, set apart *or* aside; allot, allocate, apportion.

—*n.* **4.** store, stock, supply, supply on hand, inventory; stockpile, accumulation, amassment, backlog; reservoir; nest egg, something to fall back on, something for a rainy day; card up one's sleeve, *Sl.* ace in the hole.

5. reservation, preserve. See **reservation** (*def.* **2**).

6. exception. See **reservation** (*def.* **1**).

7. *Military.* support, backup, reinforcements; auxiliaries, National Guard, home guard.

8. formality, restraint, self-restraint, self-control, undemonstrativeness, unexpansiveness; guardedness, discretion; aloofness, offishness, stand-offishness, unsociability; distance, detachment, remoteness, inaccessibility, unapproachability; coolness, chilliness, coldness, frigidness, iciness.

9. reticence, taciturnity, untalkativeness, uncommunicativeness, unresponsiveness, closed-mouthedness; secrecy, secretiveness.

10. **in reserve** reserved, held back, put aside; in hand; in store, in readiness. See also **reserved** (*def.* **1**).

11. **without reserve** without restraint, frankly, candidly, directly, straightforwardly; plainly, explicitly, unequivocally; freely, outspokenly, uninhibitedly, unabashedly; bluntly, brusquely, tactlessly.

—*adj.* **12.** spare, extra; substitute, alternate, secondary, backup, auxiliary.

reserved, *adj.* **1.** held, retained, taken, engaged, booked, saved, arranged for, *Brit.* bespoken; set apart, put aside, roped off; appointed, slotted, destined.

2. formal, restrained, rigid, stiff, prim, strait-laced, proper, decorous, seemly, sedate, dignified, grave, serious; composed, controlled, constrained, undemonstrative, unresponsive, cool, cold, icy.

3. distant, aloof, pompous, haughty, snobbish, disdainful, condescending, high-hat, stand-offish, *Inf.* offish, unapproachable; withdrawn, quiet, reticent, uncommunicative, taciturn, silent, untalkative, unneighborly, unsocial, unsociable.

4. self-contained, self-reliant, private, guarded, cautious, noncommittal; secretive, close-mouthed, tight-lipped, buttoned-up, mum.

5. retiring, diffident, self-conscious, bashful, timid, shy, modest, coy, demure, backward, *Archaic.* verecund; unassuming, unobtrusive, unpretentious, self-effacing.

reservoir, *n.* **1.** (*all used to contain liquid*) receptacle, chamber; basin, bowl; jug, urn, keg, vat, cask.

2. repository, repertory, depository, depot, supply depot, warehouse, storehouse, storeroom, storage.

3. reserve. See **reserve** (*def.* **4**).

reside, *v.* **1.** live, live at, abide, *Archaic.* bide, dwell, tenant, stay, stay at, remain, sojourn; domicile, domiciliate, establish oneself, take up residence, take up one's abode, inhabit, occupy, settle, settle down, locate, ensconce, make one's home, *Inf.* hang up one's hat; domesticate, cohabit, keep house, set up housekeeping; take *or* strike root, plant oneself, anchor, drop anchor, come to anchor, moor; nest, nestle, perch, roost, squat, burrow, hive; lodge, rent, room, bunk, berth, quarter *or* billet at, put up at, *Inf.* hang out, *Sl.* crash, *Brit.* doss down; camp, camp out, bivouac, pitch one's tent.

2. inhere, be inherent in, be immanent, be ingrained, be innate, be intrinsic, be indigenous, belong, pertain, be a quality of; be comprised in, be contained in, be constituted by, rest, rest in, lie, lie in, lie within, exist, exist in, abide in, be present in, dwell in, indwell, consist in, subsist in, repose in.

residence, *n.* **1.** home, abode, domicile, domicil, dwelling, dwelling place, dwelling home, habitation, habitancy, residency, *Scot. and North Eng.* bigging, *Scot.* howff; lodging, lodgings, lodging place, lodgment, nest, roost, perch; quarters, living quarters, rooms, accommodations, living accommodations, housing, roof over one's head, *Inf.* pad, *Inf.* crash pad, *Chiefly Brit. Inf.* diggings, *Brit. Inf.* digs; apartment, flat, tenement, walk-up, cold-water flat, *Brit.* chambers, *Chiefly Brit.* maisonette; penthouse, townhouse, condominium, *Inf.* condo; mobile home, motor home, camper, trailer, caravan; address, location, situation, place, whereabouts.

2. mansion, palace, palatial *or* stately dwelling, *Fr. hôtel, It. palazzo*, villa, chateau, castle, *Chiefly Brit.* hall, *Brit.* court, *Archit.* folly; manor, manor house, manor home, manor seat, estate, country estate, house in the country, country house, country home, country seat, house and grounds, house and lot, *Brit. Dial.* toft, demesne, *Law.* messuage, plantation, *Sl.* spread; farm, farmstead, farmhold, *Brit.* farmery, grange, *Brit.* croft, *Brit.* homecroft, *Scot. and North Eng.* steading; ranch, rancho, rancheria, hacienda.

3. cottage, cot, bungalow, bower, cabin, *Brit. Dial.* cote, *Scot.* but-and-bend; hut, hutch, shed, shack, shanty, *Scot.* bothy; hovel, hole, hole in the ground, dump, garbage heap, sty, pigsty, pigpen, tumbledown shack, wretched hut, mean dwelling, miserable quarters.

4. hearth, hearthstone, hearth and home, hearthside, fireside, fireplace, chimney corner, *Brit. Dial.* ingle, *Brit. Dial.* ignleside, *Chiefly Brit.* inglenook; household, family, family circle, domestic circle, bosom of one's family, seat of one's affections, home sweet home, *Inf.* place where one's heart is, *Inf.* place where one hangs his hat.

5: habitation, habitancy, inhabitation, inhabitancy, domiciliation, *Law.* commorancy; sojourn, sojournment, sojourning, stay, stay-over, stop, stop-over, stop-off, lay-over.

6. center, center of activity, center of operations, center of authority, central administration, nerve center, base of operations; central office, main office, head office, home office, chief office, executive office; headquarters, HQ, general headquarters, GHQ, corporate headquarters.

resident, *n.* 1. inhabitant, *Archaic.* inhabiter, habitant, occupant, occupier, denizen, resider, residencer, residentiary, dweller, householder, sojourner; indweller, incumbent, inmate; tenant, lodger, boarder, roomer, paying guest, *Sl.* crasher; renter, lessee, leaseholder.

2. settler, homesteader, squatter, cottager, cottier, *Scot.* cotter; villager, townsman, burgher, burgess, oppidan.

3. diplomat, diplomatic agent; minister, envoy, emmisary, legate.

4. intern, house physician, resident physician.

—adj. 5. living, dwelling, abiding, staying, remaining, residing, residentiary, in residence; inhabiting, occupying, settling, locating, ensconcing; nesting, nestling, perching, roosting, squatting; lodging, rooming, bunking, boarding, berthing, *Inf.* hanging out, *Sl.* crashing, *Brit.* dossing down; renting, leasing.

6. inner, internal, intrinsic, inward; implicit, immanent, inherent, indwelling; implanted, ingrained, in fixed, deep-seated; inborn, congenital, innate; indigenous, native, native to, natural, natural to.

residual, *adj.* remaining, leftover, surplus, extra; residuary, spare, over, supplementary, outstanding; excessive, unnecessary, needless, unneeded; overabundant, superabundant, profuse, plethoric; redundant, superfluous, too much, oversufficient, over and above, *Inf.* a bit much, extreme.

residue, *n.* 1. remainder, remains, rest, balance, residual; surplus, extra, excess, superfluity, surplusage, redundance, *Commerce.* overage; overplus, nimiety, overflow, superabundance, overabundance, superflux; overload, more than enough, enough and to spare, enough and then some; surfeit, glut, plethora, profusion.

2. leavings, leftovers, rest, remnants, residuum; oddments, odds and ends, fragments, rummage; rubbage, waste, garbage, junk; offal, refuse, sewage; hogwash, swill, slop, *Scot.* lave; rejectamenta, discards, throwaways, castoffs, jettison, jetsam, flotsam; offscourings, sweepings, shavings, parings, scrapings, filings, leavings, raspings, pomace; slag, dross, scum, scoriae, sordes; detritus, debris, litter, rubble, *Geol.* talus; cinders, ashes, soot, carbon, smut, dirt.

resign, *v.* 1. (*usu. in reference to office or position*) abdicate, renounce, give up, *Law.* disclaim, lay down, part with, retire from, vacate, abnegate, *Chiefly Scot.* demit; relinquish, let go, deliver up, hand over, transfer, turn over; surrender, submit, yield, cede, give way.

2. **resign oneself to** accept, give in, acquiesce, comply, accede, concur, admit, go along with; be reconciled to, tolerate, brook, abide, bear, stand, endure, stomach, bear with, put up with; grin and bear it, lie down and die, take it lying down, *Sl.* lump it; lose hope of, despair of, give up, abandon, quit, *Sl.* pack it in, give up the ship, throw in the towel *or* sponge, cry *or* say uncle.

resignation, *n.* 1. abdication, resigning, renunciation, renouncing, retirement, retiring, abnegation, *Archaic.* demission; relinquishment, abandonment, surrender, yielding, ceding, cession; transfer, transferal, transference, handing over; repudiation, rejection, disowning, disclamation.

2. submission, acquiescence, compliance, obedience; yielding, appeasement, capitulation, surrender; submissiveness, docility, passivity, passiveness, meekness, nonresistance.

3. resignedness, reconciliation, acceptance; patience, forbearance, endurance, toleration, tolerance, sufferance, long-suffering, longanimity.

resigned, *adj.* 1. submissive, passive, unresisting, nonresistant, yielding, docile, obedient; deferential, subservient, meek, humble, mild.

2. acquiescent, complying, compliant; accepting, tolerant, unquestioning, reconciled; patient, long-suffering, forbearing, uncomplaining, unrepining, cheerful, chin-up.

3. stoical, disciplined, composed, collected; unperturbed, unruffled; unperturbable, dispassionate, philosophical.

resilience, *n.* 1. elasticity, springiness, flexibility, suppleness; spring, bounce, give, kick, snap, recoil, rebound; plasticity, ductility, rubberiness, reflexiveness; tensibility, tensileness, extensibility; contractability, contractility, stretchability; adaptability, malleability, adjustableness, movability, responsiveness.

2. buoyancy, lightness, carefreeness, airiness, cheerfulness; liveliness, jauntiness, light-heartedness, breeziness, perkiness.

resilient, *adj.* 1. rebounding, recoiling, springing back; flexible, bendable, pliable, supple, springy, bouncy; tensile, stretchable, extensile, extensible; contractile, contractive; elastic, rubbery, plastic, ductile; malleable, adaptable, yielding, adjustable, responsive.

2. buoyant, irrepressible, recuperative; lively, jaunty, lighthearted, breezy, perky; light, carefree, airy, cheerful.

resist, *v.* 1. withstand, repel, repulse, *Archaic.* reluct; stand fast, make a stand, stand, breast, front, brook; stand at bay, breast the current, weather, not yield an inch, *Inf.* hang in there; stand one's ground, hold the line against; hold out, hold up, bear up.

2. oppose, counteract, neutralize, counterwork, countermine; cancel, militate against, countervail; confront, face, encounter; rebuff, strike back, recalcitrate; beat back, drive back, siege, repress; fight, attack, assail, assault, oppugn, combat; retaliate, strike back, impugn; struggle against, contend with, contest,

battle, antagonize; revolt, rebel, mutiny; overcome, defeat, overpower, stem the tide.

3. stop, check, stem, curb; obstruct, hinder, impede, block; thwart, foil, frustrate, cross, *Scot.* thraw; restrain, restrict, inhibit, bar, interfere; prevent, preclude, prohibit, proscribe; forfend, obviate, override.

4. refrain, avoid, abstain, forbear; desist, refuse, quit, stop; renounce, eschew, swear off, take no part in; check oneself, contain oneself, deny oneself.

resistance, *n.* **1.** withstanding, opposition, contravention, counteraction; repugnance, repulsion, oppugnance, repellence; stand, front, repulse, rebuff; defiance, refusal, oppugnancy, *Rare.* oppugnation; self-preservation, self-defense, protection, defense; recalcitrance, renitency, refractoriousness, obstinacy; rebelliousness, intransigence, stubbornness, contumacy.

2. insurgency, insubordination, mutiny, sedition, insurrection, revolt; uprising, riot, strike; protest, demonstration, boycott; collision, clash, contention, fight, struggle; encounter, confrontation, crossing, combat.

3. impediment, hindrance, obstruction, obstacle; preclusion, prevention, proscription, prohibition, interdiction; frustration, thwarting, inhibition.

resistant, *adj.* **1.** withstanding, repellent, defiant, opposing, antagonistic, counteractive; repugnant, clashing, reactionary, oppugnant, dissident; indomitable, die-hard, intractable, obstreperous; belligerent, bellicose, hostile; insubordinate, rebellious, disobedient; obstinate, stubborn, recalcitrant, renitent, contumacious; restive, recusant, refractory; riotous, wild, ungovernable, unmanageable, unruly, indocile, incorrigible.

2. immovable, unsubmissive, unyielding, uncomplying; obstructive, retardant, reluctant; opposed, at odds, disagreeing, unwilling, averse; intransigent, inflexible, willful, uncompromising, headstrong, stiff-necked.

3. hard, tough, resistive, firm, solid, strong; tight, proof, rigid, stiff; fireproof, asbestine, flame-resistant, flame-retardant, flameproof, rustproof; waterproof, watertight; soundproof, airtight, hermetic, leakproof; bulletproof, armored, shatterproof, bombproof, shellproof; burglarproof, impregnable, foolproof.

resolute, *adj.* **1.** determined, resolved, decided, firm, set, intent, steadfast, stable; earnest, serious, concentrated; iron, adamantine, steely, fast, staunch; confident, self-possessed, self-assured, self-reliant; purposeful, purposive, deliberate, inflexible, strong-willed, grim, strong-minded, stern, bulldog; unwavering, unfaltering, unswerving, unflinching, unhesitating, undeviating; unyielding, unbending; obstinate, obdurate, imperturbable, hard-line.

2. relentless, dogged, steady, constant, inexorable, implacable; plodding, persistent, indefatigable, unflagging, untiring; unchangeable, changeless, unalterable, immutable, irreversible, irrevocable; pertinacious, persevering, tenacious, *Inf.* stick-to-it-ive; single-minded, devoted, dedicated.

3. undaunted, dauntless, unshaken; bold, hardy, game, plucky, spunky, *Inf.* scrappy, gritty, *Sl.* gutsy, *Inf.* hellbent; stout-hearted, indomitable, doughty; spirited, mettlesome, valiant, courageous, gallant, brave; stalwart, lion-hearted, daring, audacious, fearless, unafraid; chivalrous, soldierly, heroic; adventurous, venturesome, enterprising, industrious.

resolution, *n.* **1.** declaration, decree, judgment, opinion; expression, statement, proclamation; conclusion, finding, verdict, sentence, ruling.

2. determination, intent, intention, point, aim; resolve, decision, objective; plan, purpose, ambition, project, idea; aspiration, desire, nisus, desideratum; proposition, proposal, advance, suggestion, prospectus; contemplation, mind, will, thought, dream; mark, pursuit, end, end in view, object in mind, ultimate aim, target, butt, bull's-eye.

3. steadfastness, resoluteness, firmness, fortitude. See **resolve** (*def.* **9**).

4. solution, answer, finding; outcome, upshot, end, point, issue, result, end result; explanation, explication, reason; unraveling, disentanglement, unscrambling, unriddling; sorting out, unspinning, untwisting, unweaving; decoding, decipherment, cracking, interpretation, breaking open.

resolve, *v.* **1.** fix, settle, confirm, seal; determine, decide, make up one's mind; will, purpose, set one's heart on; insist upon, take a stand, take a step; cross the Rubicon, nail one's colors to the mast, keep to one's courses, stick to one's guns, stick fast, stand pat; face, confront, front, meet, beard.

2. calculate, design, plan, project, propose; aspire to, intend, mean, have every intention to, have in mind, have in view, harbor a design; aim for, destine, bid for, pursue, set one's sights on.

3. break up, separate, anatomize, dissect; disintegrate, reduce, dissolve, segment; analyze, break down, divide, subdivide.

4. convert, change, alter, vary, transform, transmute, translate; metamorphose, metabolize, reorganize, reform.

5. explain, solve, answer, interpret; explicate, clear up, unscramble, unriddle, get to, figure out; unspin, untwist, unweave; decipher, decode, crack, break open, unravel; disentangle, untangle, *Sl.* dope out; recognize, realize, make out, detect, see through; uncover, disclose, unearth, hit, *Inf.* hit the nail on the head; prove, establish, identify, ascertain, find out; fathom, plumb, get to the bottom of.

6. dispel, disperse, scatter, dissipate; clear away, drive away, cast off, shake off, shoo; dismiss, put an end to, remove, remove all doubts, banish, expel.

7. settle, reconcile, compose, compromise; fix up, patch up, mend, heal; harmonize, accommodate, adjust, settle amicably.

8. declare, express, state, aver; decide, conclude; settle; ordain, adjudge, decree, enact, order, command; vote on, pass upon, choose to; pass sentence, judge.

—n. **9.** determination, firmness, firmness of purpose, fixity of purpose, resoluteness, resolution; steadfastness, constancy, stability; strength, fortitude, will, will power, iron will; perseverance, tenacity, *Inf.* stick-to-it-iveness, indefatigability; indomitability, relentlessness, inexorability, implacability; obstinacy, obduracy, stubbornness, intransigence; staunchness, steeliness, fastness.

10. zeal, earnestness, vigor, élan, effort; mettle, backbone, courage, intrepidity, grit, *Sl.* guts, *Jocular.* intestinal fortitude, nerve, spunk, sand; self-command, self-possession, self-reliance, self-assurance, self-confidence, self-mastery, aplomb; drive, push, persistence, pertinacity, doggedness; single-mindedness, devotion, dedication; manliness, hardihood, daring, derring-do; enterprise, audacity, valiance, gallantry, chivalry.

11. determination, intention, intent; aspiration, ambition. See **resolution** (*def.* **2**).

resonance, *n.* sonority, sonorousness, fullness, richness, deepness; loudness, thunderousness, plangency, amplification; reverberation, echoing, reechoing; vibration, tremulousness, *Both Music.* vibrator, tremolo; prolongation, sustenance, drawing out, holding.

resonant, *adj.* **1.** resounding, booming, thunderous, loud, powerful, amplified; ringing, singing, tolling, plangent, clangorous; echoing, reechoing, reverberating, reverberant, reverberative, reflected; vibrant, vibrating, vibratory, vibrative, pulsating, tremulous; sustained, prolonged, drawn out, held, long, *All Phonet.* vowellike, vowel, sonorant.

2. sonorous, full-bodied, full, rich; pear-shaped, rounded, round; deep, deep-toned, low, bass, basso, baritone, sepulchral.

resort, *v.* **1.** turn to, look to, ask for help *or* assistance from, use as a recourse; try, try out, experiment with, take to *or* up; employ, use, make use of, take, utilize, exercise, bring into play; return to, end up with, find oneself with.

2. frequent, haunt, repair, visit regularly *or* often, *Sl.* hang out *or* around; patronize, be a regular customer, be a fixture *or* part of the furniture; gather, assemble, collect, meet, come together, unite, hover, swarm, herd, cluster, flock, crowd, throng, converge.

—*n.* **3.** popular spot *or* place, *Sl.* in place, *Sl.* hot spot, *Sl.* watering hole, rendezvous, meeting place; spa, hot *or* mineral springs, *Brit.* watering place, vacation spot *or* place, tourist trap; refuge, retreat, sanctuary, asylum, haven, hideaway, den, lair.

4. recourse, place to turn, source of assistance *or* help, aid, aide, help, helper; alternative, choice, option, possibility, available resource; reserve, backup, reinforcement, last resort.

resound, *v.* **1.** echo, reecho, echo back, echo back and forth, bounce off the walls, reverberate, resonate, ring; fill the air, rend the heavens *or* skies, roar, thunder, rumble, boom, bellow, clang, sound.

2. be famed, be celebrated, be glorified, be exalted, be honored, be extolled, be lauded, be praised.

3. proclaim, trumpet, make known, announce; cry out, yell out, shout, call out, speak out, make oneself heard; voice, vociferate, give mouth to, sound, sing.

resource, *n.* **1.** resort, recourse, backup, reinforcement, support, backing, help, aid; reserve, reserve, source, cache, storehouse, hidden supply, money in the bank, savings account.

2. **resources** collective wealth, natural resources, natural wealth.

3. *Usu.* **resources** assets, property, real estate, goods, possessions, holdings; income, revenue, profits, gains; wealth, money, *U.S. Sl.* bucks, funds, finances, capital, cash, wherewithal, *Fr. de quoi*; effects, estate, personal assets, chattle, belongings; real property, liquid assets, frozen assets, accounts receivable, securities, bonds, stocks, notes, I.O.U.s, equitable assets; inventories, *Commerce.* good will, fixtures, machinery.

4. *Often* **resources** means, ability, capability, capacity, aptitude, mind for, faculty, skill; know-how, knowledge, experience, background, qualifications, prerequisites; good quality, virtue, strength, power, talent, endowment; edge, advantage, plus, strong point, forte, talking point, selling point.

5. inventiveness, ingenuity, ingeniousness, cleverness, resourcefulness, adaptability, adaptableness.

resourceful, *adj.* inventive, ingenious, slick, clever, Daedalian; original, orginative, creative; intelligent, *Inf.* brainy, smart, bright, sharp, quick, quick-witted, keen, acute, astute, *Sl.* on the ball; handy, skillful, deft, dexterous, adept.

respect, *n.* **1.** *Usu.* **in respect** particular, point, detail, matter, feature, way.

2. reference, regard, relation, connection, bearing on.

3. esteem, estimation, high regard, high opinion, admiration; veneration, reverence, awe, adoration, worship; honor, homage, laudation, praise; approval, approbation, appreciation.

4. consideration, thoughtfulness, attentiveness, good will; courtesy, urbanity, etiquette, civility, politeness; deference, submission, acquiescence, compliance.

5. **respects** regards, greetings, salutation, *Archaic.* commendations; remembrances, love, best.

—*v.* **6.** esteem, admire, have a high opinion of, revere, venerate, look up to, think the world of, think highly of, set great store by; approve, commend, take one's hat off to, doff one's cap to; pay homage to, honor, extol, laud, praise, speak well of, applaud; appreciate, enjoy, delight in, prize; love, adore, idolize, worship; wonder at, marvel at, be *or* stand in awe of.

7. show regard, show courtesy, be polite, be considerate, be thoughtful; be formal, stand upon ceremony, observe due decorum; observe, notice, heed, pay attention to, acknowledge, comply with, do the will of, abide by, follow, be faithful to, adhere to, obey; defer to, make obeisance, bow before.

respectability, *n.* **1.** decency, propriety, good taste, decorum, dignity, respectableness; appropriateness, seemliness, fitness, suitability, suitableness, becomingness, etiquette, formality.

2. virtue, goodness, morality; probity, integrity, uprightness, rectitude, honor, principle; honesty, good faith, truthfulness, constancy, loyalty.

3. social standing, rank, status, position; nobility, peerage, aristocracy.

respectable, *adj.* **1.** estimable, worthy, deserving, praiseworthy, laudable, commendable; honorable, honored, admirable, admired, venerable, revered; valuable, valued, esteemed, respected, creditable.

2. reputable, in good repute, unsullied, untainted, undefiled, unmarred, unblemished; trustworthy, reliable, dependable; upright, honest, truthful, aboveboard, principled; unimpeachable, unassailable.

3. proper, decorous, seemly, becoming; well-bred, genteel, refined, polished; decent, modest, chaste, pure, innocent.

4. passable, tolerable, acceptable, adequate, satisfactory, all right, unexceptional; presentable, admissible, fairly good, *Inf.* not that good, not too bad; fair, *Inf.* no great shakes, mediocre, middling, indifferent, average, so-so, *Inf.* nothing to write home *or* brag about; barely adequate, minimal, minimum, lowest acceptable.

5. sizable, good-sized, substantial; considerable, goodly, tidy.

respectful, *adj.* **1.** regardful, considerate, thoughtful, deferential; obedient, dutiful, attentive, obliging, accommodating; civil, cordial, courteous, gracious, ladylike, gentlemanly, mannerly, polite; gentle, well-bred, urbane, suave, chivalrous, chivalric, knightly, gallant; formal, ceremonious, decorous, proper, seemly.

2. submissive, acquiescent, subservient; obeisant, servile, slavish; prostrate, salaaming, kneeling, bowing, curtsying.

respective, *adj.* particular, specific, special, several, separate, individual; corresponding, commensurate; own.

respiration, *n.* breathing, inhalation and exhalation; huffing and puffing, panting, gasping, wheezing; *Pathol.* eupnea; *Pathol.* dyspnea.

respire, *v.* **1.** breathe, breathe in and out, inhale and exhale; pant, gasp, huff and puff, suck wind; wheeze.

2. exhale, expire, breathe out, puff, blow; emit, exhaust, evacuate, let out; sigh, suspire.

respite, *n.* **1.** interval, hiatus, intermission, break, interruption; pause, lull, lapse, interregnum; relief, breath, breather, breathing spell, rest, repose, relaxation, recess, inactivity, *Archaic.* bever; alleviation, assuagement, mitigation, palliation; commutation, easing up *or* off, slackening up, loosening up.

2. remission, reprieve, stay, stay of execution, *Inf.* letup; postponement, suspension, adjournment, abeyance, prorogation; deferment, deferral, delay, extension, protraction, continuation, *Law.* continuance; cessation, desistance, arrest, stoppage, halt, standstill, discontinuance, discontinuation.

—*v.* **3.** relieve, alleviate, allay, assuage, mitigate, palliate; commute, ease up *or* off, slacken up, loosen up, relax, grant a breathing spell, *Archaic.* slake.

4. remit, reprieve, stay, grant a stay of execution, let off, *Inf.* let off the hook; continue, grant an extension, *Finance.* extend, *Commerce.* indulge; postpone, defer, prorogue, adjourn, suspend, intermit, lay over, put off, stave off, shelve, table, hold in abeyance, reschedule; delay, stall, wait, hold off, proscrastinate.

resplendent, *adj.* **1.** brilliant, radiant, irradiant, lambent; dazzling, vivid, intense, ablaze, aflame, afire; fulgent, effulgent, refulgent; shining, bright, illuminated, alight, lit; white, golden, rutilant, aureate; sparkling, scintillating, coruscating, shimmering; aglimmer, glimmering, glistening, aglisten, *Archaic.* glistering, glittering, aglitter.

2. splendid, *Inf.* splendiferous, superb, glorious, divine, marvelous, *Sl.* marvy, wonderful, *Sl.* out-of-this-world.

respond, *v.* **1.** reply, make reply, answer, give answer, field, write back, R.S.V.P., confirm [s.t.]; report back, get back to, send word to, let someone know; retort, come back with, counter with, answer back, talk back, *Inf.* sass, *Inf.* make a wisecrack, *Sl.* give [s.o.] lip; rejoin, make a rejoinder, rebut, make a rebuttal, counterreply, counterclaim.

2. react to, acknowledge, recognize, notice; make a response, signal to, make a gesture, nod, shake one's head, salute, raise one's hand, wave, tip *or* doff one's cap, greet [s.o.]; reciprocate, give in return, return the compliment, smile back, extend the hand, shake hands with; thank, give one's thanks, express gratitude, show appreciation.

3. *Usu.* **respond to** react, be moved, be touched, be reached, be affected; feel with, empathize with, identify with, experience vicariously, understand, *Inf.* tune into, *Sl.* be hip to; sympathize with, feel for, commiserate with, feel pity for, pity; join into, enter into, participate in, engage in, become involved in, show *or* take an interest in, be stimulated by; share in, partake of, be caught up in, become a part of.

4. *Usu.* **respond to** correspond, go with, match, suit, fit in with, complement; agree with, conform to, coincide with, jibe with, tally with, square with, dovetail with, mesh with, *Inf.* gee with; accord, think alike, *Inf.* be on the same wavelength; hit it off, *Inf.* click, *Inf.* work.

response, *n.* **1.** answer, reply, return, respondence, replication, R.S.V.P., confirmation; communication, communiqué, message letter, epistle, note, *Inf.* memorandum, *Inf.* memo.

2. retort, repartee, riposte, rebuttal, counter, *Sl.* comeback, smart remark, back talk, *Inf.* sass, *Inf.* wisecrack, *Sl.* lip, *Sl.* mouth; rejoinder, counterreply, retaliation, counterclaim, counterblast, refutation, *All Law.* surrebuttal, surrejoinder, defense, plea.

3. acknowledgement, recognition, notice, reaction, feedback; signal, gesture, nod, salute, salutation, greeting; thanks, expression of gratitude *or* appreciation; reaction, feeling, emotion, empathy, sympathy, pathos.

responsibility, *n.* **1.** answerability, answerableness, accountability, accountableness, liability, chargeability, amenability.

2. duty, bounden duty, obligation, onus, burden; office, charge, care, custody, trust; jurisdiction, bailiwick, beat; part, role, bit, task.

3. reliability, dependability; responsibleness, trustworthiness, creditability.

4. fault, guilt, blame, blameworthiness, culpability, culpableness, *Scot.* wite; censurability, reprehensibility, reprehensibleness.

responsible, *adj.* **1.** answerable, accountable, liable, amenable, chargeable; in one's hands, on one's shoulders, *Inf.* in one's lap; beholden, obligated, obliged, bound, duty-bound, subject.

2. sane, rational, competent, *Latin. compos mentis*, sensible, sound, stable, reasonable.

3. reliable, dependable, conscientious, hardworking; solvent.

4. moral, ethical, upright, trustworthy, trusty; creditable, honest, faithful.

5. culpable, guilty, blamable, blameworthy; censurable, reprehensible.

6. authoritative, executive, decision-making, administrative.

rest[1], *n.* **1.** sleep, repose, slumber, *Inf.* beauty sleep; nap, catnap, nod, snooze, doze, siesta, *Inf.* forty winks; coma, *Pathol.* sopor, trance, stupor; lethargy, sluggishness, torpor, torpescence; dormancy, hibernation, estivation.

2. pause, halt, stand, hold, stay, stop; recess, break, time-out, breather, breathing time, breathing spell, time to catch one's breath; respite, inaction, inactivity; slackening, abatement, letup, lull; holiday, vacation, time off.

3. interim, interval, interlude, intermission, interstice, intermittence, intermittency; disconnection, disconnectedness, gap, hiatus, interruption, remission, lacuna.

4. cessation, ceasing, suspense, suspension, abeyance, discontinuance; status quo, waiting period, waiting game, holding pattern; impasse, stand-off, deadlock, stalemate.

5. ease, idleness, leisure, relaxation, otiosity, otioseness; loafing, laziness, indolence, vegetation, unemployment; *It. dolce far niente.*

6. still, stillness, silence, hush; quiet, quiescence, quietude, quietness; calmness, calm, tranquillity, peacefulness, peaceableness, peace, placidity, serenity, imperturbation; inertness, inertia, stability; motionless, immobility, fixity.

7. death, demise, decease, final rest, end, quietus; departure, crossing over, release.

8. refuge, shelter, retreat, haven; inn, hotel, motel, lodging place, resting place; camp, encampment, bivouac; home, abode, domain, domicile.

9. support, brace, bracket, prop, shore, stay; buttress, strut, splint, truss; mainstay, cornerstone, *Archit., Civ. Eng.* abutment; pillar, column, pier, *Archit.* pilaster; underpinning, *Archit.* rib, framework, grillage, grid, trellis, lattice; foundation, base, seat; substructure, substruction, substratum, understructure, understratum, *All Archit.* stereobate, socle, plinth; footing, flooring, floor, *Building Trades.* bedding; platform, scaffold, stand; trivet, trestle, sawhorse; sill, shelf, ledge; tie, tie beam, *Brit.* sleeper; footrest, armrest, headrest.

—*v.* **10.** sleep, slumber, repose; *All Sl.* flake out, hit the sack, sack in, sack out, conk off, crash, log Z's, catch some Z's, count sheep, *Brit. Sl.* doss; nap, catnap, take a siesta, *Inf.* catch forty winks; doze, snooze, drowse.

11. retire, refresh oneself, take a rest; lie down, go to bed, recline; be still, be quiet, be tranquil, be calm, be inactive, lie still; relax, take one's ease, take it easy, do nothing; unwind, unbend, laze, lazy, be lazy, idle, be idle, loll, languish; putter, *Brit.* potter, dabble; let up, ease up, slack off, take a break, take time out, have a breathing spell, have time to catch one's breath, take a breath, *Inf.* take a breather, *Inf.* take five; sojourn, visit, vacation, take a vacation, holiday, take a holiday, take time off.

12. stop, stop short, cease, desist, halt; pause, wait, hold, stay, remain, tarry, linger; stand, stand still, come to a stand *or* standstill; discontinue, suspend, interrupt, intermit, pull up, draw up; heave to, anchor, cast anchor, ride at anchor; abide, dwell, roost, perch, sit, sit back.

13. calm, calm down, soothe, smooth, lull, tranquilize; repress, suppress, subdue, compose, sober, quell, damp, dampen, put down; moderate, blunt, dull, deaden; temper, decrease, weaken, slacken, lessen, lighten, diminish, abate; ease, soften, pacify, appease, allay; reconcile, alleviate, relieve, slake, quench; silence, still, shush, hush, put to rest, quiet.

rest², *n.* **1.** remainder, residue, residuum, balance, remains.

2. surplus, excess, surplusage, superfluity, redundance, overplus, *Commerce.* overage.

3. leftovers, leavings, orts; oddments, rummage, stuff, odds and ends, flotsam, jetsam, pickings; fragments, scraps, shards, truck, junk, *Inf.* crap; rejectamenta, castoffs, throwaways, discards.

restaurant, *n.* eating house *or* establishment, *Sl.* eatery, *Sl.* beanery, *Sl.* greasy spoon, *Sl.* hash house; chophouse, steak house; café, brasserie, coffeehouse, coffee shop, tearoom, delicatessen, *Inf.* deli; lunch, luncheonette, lunchroom, lunch counter, lunch bar, buffet, cafeteria, automat; diner, short-order restaurant; snack bar, drive-in *or* drive-in restaurant, fast-food restaurant, hot dog stand, hamburger stand; pizzeria; inn, tavern, taproom, bar, bar and grill, grill room; bistro, rathskeller, night club, cabaret, roadhouse, *Inf.* hot spot, *Inf.* honky-tonk, *Sl.* after-hours joint, *Sl.* rinky-dink.

restful, *adj.* **1.** tranquilizing, calming, *Med.* calmative, sedative, narcotic, opiate; comforting, soothing, relaxing; sleepy, slumberous, slumbering, drowsing, drowsy, oscitant, dozing, dozy, somnolent, soporose, soporous; soporific, hypnotic, somniferous, somnific, somnifacient, sleep-inducing.

2. tranquil, calm, serene, quiet, quiescent, peaceful, peaceable, pacific, reposeful, still; undisturbed, unagitated, untroubled, unstirring; dormant, torpid, languid, lethargic, comatose, sluggish; inactive, idle, sedentary; unconscious, sleeping, anesthetized.

restitution, *n.* **1.** reparation, redress, amends, atonement, redemption, expiation; requital, quittance, retribution, satisfaction; compensation, indemnity, indemnification, recompense, solatium; remuneration, payment, repayment, reimbursement, refund, one's money back; recoupment, recovery, retrieval, reclamation, recapture, retaking, regaining, repossession, *Law.* replevin, apocatastasis, reestablishment, restoration, reinstatement, reinstation, repatriation.

2. restoration, repair, renovation, instauration. See **repair** (*def.* **4**).

restive, *adj.* **1.** restless, uneasy, nervous, unquiet, impatient. See **restless** (*def.* **2**).

2. refractory, fractious, disobedient, recalcitrant, contumacious; undutiful, uncomplying, noncomplying, uncompliant, noncompliant, noncooperative, uncooperative; reluctant, unwilling, disinclined, indisposed, *Archaic.* untoward; cross-grained, perverse, contrary, froward, opposed, *U.S.* balky, balking, dissentient, recusant, resistant, renitent; stubborn, obstinate, pig-headed, mulish, obdurate, headstrong, willful, wayward; intractable, unsubmissive, indocile, disorderly, unruly, bad; incorrigible, reprobate, impossible, unmanageable, ungovernable, uncontrollable; insubordinate, unsubordinate, defiant, rebellious.

restless, *adj.* **1.** moving, moving about, on the move, on the go, in motion; changeable, changing, astatic, unstable, unsettled, at loose ends; migrant, migrating, migratory, nomadic, wandering, rambling, roving, roaming, *Sl.* rolling, traveling, itinerant, peripatetic.

2. restive, uneasy, ill at ease, unquiet, nervous, fretful; discontent, discontented, dissatisfied, unsatisfied, unhappy, *Pathol.* dysphoric; impatient, fidgety, itchy, itching, *Sl.* antsy; jumpy, jittery, edgy, on edge, *Inf.* on pins and needles, on tenterhooks; on a tightrope, on a cliff edge, waiting for the other shoe to drop, waiting for the bomb to go off, waiting for the ax to fall; apprehensive, alarmed, anxious, with one's heart in one's mouth, fearful; skittish, shy, timid, timorous, tremulous, trembling, shaking, shaky.

3. excitable, perturbable, agitable, *Sl.* flappable; high-strung, tense, strained, *Sl.* uptight, keyed up; excited, *Inf.* hyper, worked up, wrought up, *Sl.* in a sweat; agitated, disturbed, upset, perturbed, distressed, troubled, worried, concerned, disquieted, *Archaic.* disquiet; bothered, flustered, ruffled, rattled, shaken, shook up.

4. sleepless, wakeful, insomnious, unrestful, without rest *or* sleep.

restlessness, *n.* restiveness, uneasiness, unquietness, nervousness, nervosity, fretfulness; sleeplessness, wakefulness, insomnia, unrestfulness; discontentedness, dissatisfaction, unhappiness, discontent, *Pathol.* dysphoria; impatience, fidgets, itchiness, *Sl.* ants in one's pants, jitters, *Inf.* butterflies, *Inf.* butterflies in one's stomach, *Sl.* heebie-jeebies, *Sl.* habdabs, *Inf.* whim-whams, *Sl.* willies, *Sl.* creeps, *Inf.* screaming meemies; inquietude, apprehension, alarm, anxiety, anxiousness; concern, worry, trouble, distress, disquiet, upset, agitation, perturbation; unquiet, unrest, commotion, stir, fuss, pother, *Inf.* to-do, flutter, flurry; excitement, fluster, confusion, *Inf.* stew, *Inf.* dither, *Inf.* tizzy, *Sl.* flap; excitability, excitableness, perturbability; hypertension, tension, tenseness, strain.

restoration, *n.* **1.** renewal, revival, reestablishment; reconstruction, repair, renovation, *Archaic.* instauration; resuscitation, reanimation, revivification; reversion, reconversion; resurrection, renaissance, renascence, rebirth, new birth, new life; rejuvenation, rejuvenescence, regeneration, resurgence, resumption.

2. restitution, return, recovery; compensation, replacement, indemnification, amends, repayment.

3. (*all of buildings*) rehabilitation, reconstruction, representation; reproduction, copy, duplication, simulation, imitation.

restore, *v.* **1.** reestablish, put back, replace, reinstate, reinvest, revest, reinstall; rehabilitate, reconstitute, reorganize; convert, reconvert, refit, reinforce, recoup.

2. revive, bring round, bring to, resuscitate; cure, remedy, heal, make whole again, put back on one's feet, minister to, treat, nurse, nurse back to health; revivify, quicken, reanimate, recall to life; vivify, put new life into, warm up *or* over; rekindle, stir the embers, heat the ashes; reinvigorate, refresh, freshen up; stimulate, strengthen, brace, exhilarate, energize.

3. mend, fix, fix up, recondition, put in good repair; retouch, refinish, darn, patch, patch up; cobble, splice, calk; refit, reequip, make good *or* as good as new.

4. give back, return, put back, bring back, send back, replace, hand back; remit, reimburse, compensate, indemnify.

5. rebuild, reconstruct, refashion, recreate; remake, make over, build afresh *or* anew, remodel.

restrain, *v.* **1.** constrain, check, curb, bridle, trammel, rein; delay, detain, retard, hold back *or* up; hamper, impede, inhibit, hinder; bind, tie, tie hand and foot, *Inf.* hogtie; stop, stay, halt, arrest, scotch.

2. control, govern, regulate, harness, moderate, keep within bounds, keep in tow, keep under control, hold in check, *Sl.* keep the lid on; suppress, repress, subdue, contain, smother, stifle, muzzle, bottle up, cork up, *Sl.* sit on it; rein in, put the brakes on, *Inf.* pull up *or* back on, *Inf.* tighten up on.

3. restrict. See **restrict** (*def.* **1**).

restraint, *n.* **1.** check, curb, constraint, stay, stop, arrest; barrier, block, obstacle, bar; hindrance, impediment, deterrent, holdback, stumbling block; hitch, snag, knot, drawback, *Inf.* fly in the ointment.

2. bonds, shackles, manacles, fetters, pinions, gyves, handcuffs, *Inf.* cuffs, *Sl.* bracelets, ball and chain; muzzle, gag; strait jacket.

3. coaction, restriction, obstruction, blockage, stoppage; suppression, repression, stifling, smothering, subduing; delay, retardation.

4. confinement, circumscription, detention; imprisonment, incarceration, durance; bondage, duress, captivity.

5. reserve, formality, undemonstrativeness, unexpansiveness; moderation, prudence, judiciousness, temperateness; equanimity, self-control, self-possession, aplomb, poise, presence of mind, levelheadedness; taste, good taste, discrimination; subtlety.

restrict, *v.* **1.** confine, circumscribe, pen, cage, impound, immure, coop up, wall in, box in, hem in, bottle up; bound, demarcate, delimit, deliminate, mark off, rope off, set *or* mark the boundaries; constrict, narrow, stint, cramp, straiten, limit; qualify, modify, draw the line, lay down the law, condition, set conditions *or* limits.

2. restrain. See **restrain** (*defs.* **1, 2**).

restricted, *adj.* **1.** limited, prescribed, cramped, straitened; confined, circumscribed, bound, bounded.

2. off-limits, out-of-bounds; classified, secret, top-secret, *Inf.* hush-hush, *Inf.* under wraps.

3. private, closed, exclusive, segregated; select, particular, by invitation only.

restriction, *n.* **1.** provision, proviso, clause, stipulation, specification, condition, qualification, qualifier, *Inf.* string, *Inf.* small print; rule, regulation; reservation, exception; check, curb. See also **restraint** (*def.* **1**).

2. confinement, circumscription, limitation; demarcation, delimitation; proscription, prescription, preclusion, exclusion, nonadmission.

3. narrowness, closeness, tightness, straitness, restrictedness; imprisonment, incarceration. See also **restraint** (*def.* **4**).

restrictive, *adj.* **1.** conditional, provisional, provisory, contingent, qualifying, modifying.

2. limitative, limiting, confining, circumscriptive, cramping; stiff, narrow, tight, cramped, straitened; hindering, hampering, inhibiting, inhibitive; restraining, constraining; suppressive, repressive; obstructive, in the way.

3. select, selective, exclusive, exclusory.

result, *n.* **1.** effect, consequence, outcome, denouement, issue, conclusion, end, upshot, event, sequel; aftermath, outgrowth, afterclap, turnout, aftereffect, fallout, backwash, wake; spin-off, side effect, by-product, offshoot; product, harvest, crop, fruit, yield; development, repercussion, reaction, feedback.

2. decision, resolution, resolve, determination; finding, answer, solution, deduction, inference; opinion, judgment, verdict, sentence, *Law.* adjudication, decree.

—*v.* **3.** eventuate, follow, ensue, supervene; proceed, emanate, issue, arise, redound, spring, flow, come, come forth, emerge; evolve, come about, come to pass, befall, *Archaic.* bechance, betide, happen, turn out, occur.

4. resolve, end, conclude, terminate, finish, culminate.

resume, *v.* **1.** take up, go on with, continue, proceed, advance; pick up, pick up where one left off; begin again, recommence, start again, restart, start afresh, start anew, begin at the beginning, renew.

2. take, occupy again; assume again, take back.

résumé, *n.* **1.** summary, epitome, synopsis, abstract, compendium, compilation, digest, conspectus; condensation, abridgment, reduction, compression, abbreviation; analysis, recapitulation; brief, précis; outline, *Fr. apercu,* sketch, review, syllabus, prospectus, *Latin. multum in parvo*; docket, bulletin, *Chiefly Brit.* minute; extracts, fragments, cuttings, analects, clippings, citations.

2. curriculum vitae, vita; biography, *Sl.* bio; work history, work experience.

resurrection, *n.* rising from the dead, reappearance, reincarnation, metempsychosis; revival, revivification, resuscitation, reanimation; rebirth, regeneration, palingenesis; renovation, restoration, renewal, rejuvenescence.

resuscitate, *v.* revive, revivify, quicken, restore to life, bring back from death's door, bring back to life, bring to, bring round; give mouth-to-mouth resuscitation, breathe new life into, restore, reanimate, reinvigorate, refresh; raise from the dead, resurrect.

retain, *v.* **1.** keep possession of, hold, keep, secure, reserve, preserve, save, maintain; keep on, hold onto, *Sl.* hang onto, hold in abeyance, put on the back burner; cling to, stick to, hug, hold fast *or* tight, grasp, clench, clasp, gripe, clutch, grip; detain, keep in custody, keep captive, keep back, hold back, restrain, inhibit, keep from, restrict.

2. continue to use, put to use, put in practice, make use of, practice, keep up on *or* with.

3. keep in mind, remember, recall, recollect, bethink; be aware of, not forget, bear in mind, have in mind, have at one's fingertips; memorize, fix in the mind, impress upon the memory, have by heart, know by rote.

4. engage, hire, employ.

retainer[1], *n.* servant, slave, domestic servant, attendant, servitor; employee, hired help, hired hand, worker, staffer, hireling, menial, clerk, *Inf.* gofer, errand boy, messenger boy, messenger, herald, pursuivant; dependent, subordinate, subject, vassal, liegeman, *Archaic.* yeoman; lackey, *Disparaging.* flunky, male servant, valet, butler, gentleman, manservant, *Archaic.* varlet; footman, *Fr. valet de pied*, groom, equerry, livery; footboy, boy, page, bellboy, bellhop, *Brit.* boots, *Brit.* buttons; female servant, maidservant, handmaid, handmaiden, maid, housemaid, cleaning lady *or* woman, scullery maid.

retainer[2], *n.* retaining fee, preliminary fee, partial payment, down payment, initial payment, first installment; advance, payment up front, deposit.

retaliate, *v.* **1.** return like for like, give tit for tat, give a blow for a blow, give a Roland for an

Oliver, take an eye for an eye and a tooth for a tooth, give measure for measure *or* pound for pound; give [s.o.] a dose *or* taste of his own medicine, pay [s.o.] back in his own coin, pay back in kind, repay, pay back, return the compliment *or* favor, reciprocate, give as good as one gets, do unto others as they do unto you.

2. make reprisal, requite, avenge, revenge, take revenge, wreak revenge, inflict punishment, exact payment, exact one's pound of flesh; hit back at, strike back at, get back *or* get back at, get even with, *Inf.* pay off an old score, *Inf.* settle a score, *Inf.* wipe out an old score; give [s.o.] his just deserts, *U.S. Dial.* give [s.o.] his comeuppance, *Inf.* give [s.o.] what he has coming to him.

retaliation, *n.* reprisal, redress, satisfaction, revenge, vindication, retribution, vengeance; vendetta, feud; requital, repayment, paying back, counterpunch, counterblow, counterstroke, counterattack, counterblast, countercharge, recrimination; tit for tat, *Latin. quid pro quo,* a Roland for an Oliver, blow for a blow, eye for an eye and a tooth for a tooth, measure for measure, pound for pound, lex talionis, talion; dose *or* taste of one's own medicine, just deserts, *Inf.* what's coming to one, *U.S. Inf.* comeuppance.

retard, *v.* make slow, slow down, slow up, *Sl.* hang up, delay; detain, hold back, set back, check, hold in check, restrict, restrain; hinder, hamper, impede, forestall, prohibit, debar; interfere, interrupt, frustrate, thwart, foil, balk, *Inf.* short-circuit; handicap, encumber; clog *or* scotch the wheels, dam up, obstruct, block, stand in the way, inhibit, deter, prevent; arrest, stay, stop, halt.

retardation, *n.* **1.** deceleration, slowing up, lagging, lingering, delaying; delay, postponement, stoppage, suspension; procrastination, stalling, prolongation, protraction.

2. encumbrance, hindrance, impediment, obstacle, obstruction, *Archaic.* remora, oppilation, interference, *Law.* estoppel; restriction, bar, barricade, stop, stopper, block, stumbling block; curb, check, balk, catch, hitch, snag, difficulty.

3. limitation, handicap, incapacity, incapability, inability; slowness, dullness.

retarded, *adj. (all in reference to mental development)* limited, *Rare.* incapacious, deficient, defective, abnormal, subnormal, exceptional; impaired, disabled, unsound, handicapped; slow, dull, unaware.

retch, *v.* gag, keck, dry-heave; vomit, regurgitate, puke, throw up, *Sl.* frow up, heave, spit up, spew up, disgorge; be sick to one's stomach, be nauseated, nauseate, *Inf.* have the throw-ups; be seasick, have mal de mer, turn green; *All Sl.* barf, upchuck, toss one's cookies, return *or* lose one's breakfast, blow lunch, *Sl.* ralph.

retention, *n.* **1.** hold, keeping, safekeeping, maintenance; reservation, withholding; custody, detention, captivity, restriction, restraint, inhibition; grasp, grip, gripe, clasp, embrace, hug.

2. memory, recall, recollection, retentiveness.

reticence, *n.* reserve, taciturnity, quietness, silence, muteness, speechlessness; self-containedness, stand-offishness, uncommunicativeness, unconversableness, unsociability, unsociableness; diffidence, shyness, bashfulness; restraint, unobtrusiveness, undemonstrativeness, unresponsiveness.

reticent, *adj.* reserved, taciturn, quiet, silent, close-mouthed, tight-lipped; mum, mute, speechless; self-contained, stand-offish, unconversable, unconversational, unsociable; retiring, subdued, restrained, moderate, unobtrusive, unobtruding, *Inf.* wallflower; undemonstrative, unresponsive.

retinue, *n.* suite, train, attendance, cortege, entourage, court, following, satellites, *Archaic.* meiny; escort, bodyguard, guard, convoy; personnel, staff, employees, the help, hired help.

retire, *v.* **1.** withdraw, go apart, isolate oneself, secede, separate oneself; rusticate, hibernate, estivate; leave, depart, decamp, take off, go off, go away, abscond; exit, take one's leave; retreat, fall *or* draw back, give way, lose ground, take flight, flee, beat a retreat; recede, retrocede, ebb.

2. go to bed, turn in, call it a day, consult one's pillow, *Sl.* sack in *or* sack out, *Sl.* hit the hay, *Sl.* hit the sack.

3. resign, abdicate; give up work, stop working, cease employment, take early retirement; go on Social Security, collect one's pension, be pensioned; take mandatory retirement, be shelved, be put on the shelf, be superannuated.

4. redeem, call in, recover, reclaim, buy back, pay off.

5. (*of machinery*) discard, throw out, scrap, *Inf.* junk, abandon use of, withdraw from service, disuse.

retired, *adj.* **1.** pensioned, on social security, unemployed; superannuated, shelved, on the shelf, discharged, dismissed, let go, *Fig.* discarded, *Fig.* cast aside; elderly, aged.

2. withdrawn, secluded, sequestered, *Archaic.* sequestrated; isolated, removed, solitary; secret, private, hidden, covert; unfrequented, unvisited, apart, remote, outlying, in a backwater, in the backwoods, out-of-the-way.

retiree, *n.* pensioner, pensionary; senior citizen, *Euph.* golden-ager; oldster, old-timer, veteran, graybeard; sexagenarian, septuagenerian, octogenarian, nonagenarian, centenarian; (*all collectively*) the elderly, the aged, the retired, *Inf.* seniors; *All Fig.* discard, reject, castoff, castaway.

retirement, *n.* **1.** removal, withdrawal; retreat, flight, departure, evacuation, countermarch; reversion, regression, retrogression, recession, retrocession, retrogradation; (*all in reference to employment*) severance, separation, leaving, parting, resignation, abandonment, forsaking, abdication, relinquishment.

2. *All Euph.* the golden years, the golden age, leisure years, retired years, sunset years, evening of life.

3. privacy, seclusion, sequestration; solitude, isolation, loneliness; concealment, obscurity, reclusion, exile, anchoritism, monasticism; aloofness, unsociability, separateness; recess, rest, respite, sabbatical.

4. retreat, hermitage, covert, hideaway; cloister, monastery, abbey, priory; refuge, haven, resort, sanctuary; den, lair, cave, grotto, hibernaculum, hibernacle.

retiring, *adj.* reserved, shy, bashful, diffident, shrinking, timorous, timid, *Archaic.* verecund; modest, unpretentious, demure, coy, humble, unassuming, meek, unobtrusive, unofficious; quiet, untalkative, uncommunicative, taciturn, unsocial, unsociable, reticent, private, self-contained, *Inf.* introverted; withdrawn, in a shell, distant, aloof, unapproachable, stand-offish, *Inf.* offish; solitary, reclusive, eremitic, eremitical, cenobitic.

retort, *v.* **1.** answer, give answer, reply, respond, acknowledge; rejoin, riposte, return, come back, flash back, *Inf.* crack back, *Inf.* shoot back.

2. retaliate, reciprocate, reply in kind, return the compliment, give tit for tat, give measure for measure, give like for like, give a *quid pro quo;* pay [s.o.] in his own coin, *Inf.* give [s.o.] a dose of his own medicine.

3. rebut, contradict, confute, refute, counter, counterclaim.

4. *Inf.* talk back, back-talk, *Inf.* answer back, *Inf.* sass, *Sl.* give [s.o.] lip.

—*n.* 5. answer, reply, response, replication, acknowledgment; rejoinder, return, repartee, sally, comeback, snappy comeback, barb, zinger, *Inf.* backchat; witty reply, quip, mot, bon mot.

6. retaliation, reciprocation, measure for measure, like for like, tit for tat, *Latin.* *quid pro quo*; countermeasure, counterstroke, counterblow, counterattack; *All Law.* surrebuttal, surrebutter, surrejoinder.

7. rebuttal, counterclaim, counterstatement, counterblast.

8. back talk, *Inf.* sass, *Inf.* sauce, *Sl.* lip, *Sl.* mouth.

retouch, *v.* touch up, brush up, furbish; rework, revamp, renovate, refurbish, recondition, refresh.

retract[1], *v.* draw back *or* in, pull back *or* in, withdraw, abduce, *Physiol.* abduct, *Dentistry.* retrude.

retract[2], *v.* 1. disavow, recant, unsay, withdraw, take back, *Inf.* eat *or* swallow one's words; deny, gainsay, renounce, forswear, abjure; repudiate, disclaim disown; back down *or* out of, renege, backtrack, backpedal, shift one's ground, *Inf.* flip-flop, about-face, do an about-face, change one's mind, tergiversate.

2. revoke, annul, disannul, nullify, void, declare null and void, cancel; rescind, recall, repeal, dissolve, abolish, abrogate; reverse, override, overrule, set aside, quash, countermand, counterorder.

retraction, *n.* 1. disavowal, recantation, unsaying, withdrawal, taking back, retractation; palinode; denial, renunciation, abjuration; repudiation, disclaimer, disowning; reversal, *Inf.* flip-flop, backtracking, back-pedaling, tergiversation.

2. revocation, annulment, disannulment, nullification, voidance, cancellation; rescission, repeal, dissolution, abolition, abolishment, abrogation.

retreat, *n.* 1. (*all usu. of armed forces*) strategic withdrawal, countermarch, volte-face, recoil, pullout, rout, evacuation, exodus, stampede, katabasis.

2. departure, flight, hegira, escape, getaway.

3. backing away, reversal, about-face, turnabout, *Inf.* flip-flop, backtracking, back-pedaling, retraction, disavowal.

4. receding, recession, retrocession; ebb, reflux, refluence; falling back, regression, retrogression, relapse, reversion, retrogradation.

5. retirement, withdrawal, seclusion, isolation, solitude, privacy; rustication; concealment, obscurity, exile, separation, reclusion; recess, rest, respite, sabbatical.

6. refuge, haven, asylum, shelter, sanctuary, sanctum sanctorum, ark, covert, hermitage, hideaway; cloister, monastery, friary, abbey, priory, convent, nunnery.

7. cabin, cottage, cot, hut, bungalow, shack, shanty; villa, lodge; den, lair, hibernaculum, hibernacle; nest, aerie, perch, roost; cell, study, library, *Brit.* snuggery.

8. fortress, fastness, stronghold, keep; dugout, bivouac.

—*v.* 9. (*usu. of troops*) recoil, flee, take flight, turn tail, beat a retreat; pull *or* drop back, give way, give *or* lose ground, back away *or* off, fall back.

10. escape, make off, cut and run, make a getaway, get clear of, take to one's heels, show a clean pair of heels, give [s.o.] the slip.

11. depart, leave, go off, withdraw; decamp, evacuate, vacate.

12. recede, slope backward, move back, retrocede, retire, ebb.

retrench, *v.* 1. reduce, decrease, diminish, subtract, subduct, lessen, shorten, contract, cut, cut down, cut short, cut back, abridge, abbreviate, narrow, shrink, compress, *Obs.* breviate, dock, crop, clip, shear, trim, prune, pare down, shave, nip; curtail, limit, tie down, restrict, constrict, confine, cramp; stub, stunt, truncate; slim down, slenderize, shrivel, wither.

2. remove, detach, sever, disever, cleave, cut off, saw off, sunder, separate, rive, rend, tear off, hew, hack, chop, obtruncate, detruncate, lop, lop off; amputate, dislimb, dismember, mutilate.

3. economize, conserve, meet expenses, reduce expenses, manage frugally, cut costs, pinch, pinch pennies, *Inf.* cut corners, make both ends meet, *Inf.* keep one's head above water, *Inf.* tighten one's belt, *Inf.* tighten up on, *Inf.* put the squeeze on, stint; save, scrimp, husband, hoard, reserve, lay by, *Inf.* save for a rainy day, *Sl.* sock away.

retrenchment, *n.* 1. reduction, reducing, decrease, decreasing, diminution, diminishing, subtracting, subduction, subducting, loss, lessening, shortening, contraction, contracting, decline, cutback, rollback, decrement, decrescence, depression, abridgment, abbreviation, shrinkage, shrinking, narrowing, cutting down *or* short, docking, cropping, clipping, shearing, trimming, pruning, shaving, nipping, concision, constriction, constricting; curtailment, curtailing, limitation, limiting, restriction, restricting, confinement, confining.

2. removal, removing, severance, severing, disseverance, disseverment, disseveration, cleavage, cleaving, cutting off, sawing off, sunderance, sundering, separation, separating, riving, rending, tearing off, hewing, hacking, chopping, obtruncation, detruncation, lopping, lopping off; amputation, amputating, dismemberment, dismembering, mutilation, mutilating.

3. economy, economization, economizing, frugality, thrift, thriftiness, prudence, care, stint, meeting of expenses, reduction *or* reducing of expenses, frugal management, cost cutting, cutting of costs, pinching, penny-pinching, pinching of pennies, *Inf.* cutting of corners, cost reduction, reduction *or* reducing of costs, making both ends meet, *Inf.* keeping one's head above water, *Inf.* tightening one's belt, conservation, conserving; savingness, saving, scrimping, husbandry, housewifery, hoarding, reserving, laying by, *Inf.* saving for a rainy day, *Sl.* socking away.

retribution, *n.* 1. requital, reparation, restitution, redress; repayment, satisfaction, atonement, sackcloth and ashes; recompense, return, compensation, payment.

2. punishment, just deserts, condign judgment *or* punishment, what is coming to one; retaliation, revenge, reprisal; lex talionis, talion, an eye for an eye, measure for measure, tit for tat; counterstroke, a Roland for an Oliver, *Latin.* *quid pro quo*.

retrieve, *v.* 1. recover, regain, get back; recoup, win back; retake, take back, recapture; ransom, buy back; reclaim, recycle, salvage.

2. restore, reestablish, reinvest, reinstate, reinstall, rehabilitate; return, replace, put back.

3. redeem, make amends for; repair, remedy, rectify, redress, correct, right, put *or* set right, make good.

4. *Hunting.* (*of hunting dogs*) fetch, bring back.

5. save, rescue, deliver, liberate, free.

retroaction, *n.* 1. counteraction, countermotion, counterblast, repulse, rebuff; boomerang, backlash, reaction, repercussion, reverberation; recoil, rebound, ricochet, reflex, kick, spring; revulsion.

2. opposition, resistance, check, recalcitration,

renitence, renitency.

3. recession, retrocession, reflux, refluence; regression, retrogression, retrogradation.

retroactive, *adj.* **1.** retrospective, ex post facto.

2. See **reactive** (*def.* **1**).

retrocede, *v.* **1.** recede, fall *or* draw back, ebb, shrink, depart, run away; retire, give place, yield, withdraw; retreat, turn back, wheel, put about, veer round, double back, countermarch, turn tail.

2. regress, revert, return, retrograde, lose ground.

retrocession, *n.* **1.** recession, receding, going back, reflux, refluence; retirement, withdrawal, retreat, departure, flight.

2. regression, retrogression, regress, retrogradation, recidivism.

retrograde, *adj.* **1.** moving backward, retreating, retiring, returning, refluent, recessive, retrogressive, regressive, recidivous, recidivistic, atavistic; inverse, reversed, crablike, backward, counterclockwise, *Brit.* anticlockwise.

2. deteriorated, degraded, degenerate, worsened, decayed, blighted, debilitated, weakened, undermined, sapped, on the decline, on the wane, on the downgrade *or* downslide.

—v. **3.** retrogress, regress, revert, reverse; retire, recede, retrocede, ebb; retreat, withdraw, fall *or* turn back, countermarch.

4. decline, deteriorate, degenerate, worsen, lose ground, relapse, backslide, recidivate; decay, wither, wane, fade, fail, go downhill.

retrogress, *v.* decline, degenerate, deteriorate, worsen; revert, regress, reverse, return, recidivate; decay, disintegrate, atrophy, wither, weaken, grow feeble, sink, fall, go downhill, lose ground; withdraw, retreat, retire, back up; ebb, wane, recede, retrocede, retrograde.

retrogression, *n.* **1.** movement backward, retrogradation, regression, regress, recession, retrocession, retroaction; ebb, refluence, reflux; withdrawal, retreat, retirement.

2. *Biol.* retrograde metamorphosis; decline, deterioration, dilapidation, declination, declension, degeneration, degeneracy, reversion, relapse, decadence; senility, caducity, second childhood; impairment, vitiation, pejoration, degradation, depravation.

retrospect, *n.* **1.** (*all of the past*) contemplation, reflection, consideration, meditation, survey, view, overview, review.

2. looking back *or* backward, reconsideration, afterthought, hindsight, Monday morning quarterbacking; recollection, remembrance, recalling, reminding, rememoration, reminiscence, memory, revisualization.

3. **in retrospect** now, today, at this time; reconsidering, on second thought.

retrospective, *adj.* looking backward, directed backward, backward, reflective of the past; *Law.* retroactive, ex post facto.

return, *v.* **1.** go back, revert to, reverse, back up, backtrack; recede, ebb, wane, retreat, turn back; relapse, backslide, regress, fall back, retrograde.

2. come back, recur, reoccur, reappear, recrudesce; revolve, roll around, come round again; retroact, recoil, rebound, boomerang.

3. reciprocate, give back, exchange, requite, recompense, indemnify, recoup, reimburse, refund; repay, pay back, release, give up, restitute, disgorge; retaliate, redress, revenge, avenge, vindicate, get even, get back.

4. replace, restore, put back, send back; reinstate, reinstall, reseat, reestablish, rehabilitate.

5. reply, retort, answer, respond, come back, recriminate, rebut, rejoin, *Law.* surrejoin, *Law.* surrebut; reflect, cast back, repeat, echo, reecho, resound, reverberate, ring.

6. yield, pay back, remunerate, compensate.

7. render, report, announce, pronounce, pass sentence *or* judgment, adjudicate.

—n. **8.** recurrence, repetition, reappearance, renewal, recrudescence; duplication, iteration, reiteration, rehearsal, recapitulation.

9. response, reply, answer, rejoinder, comeback, rebuttal, retort, repartee, riposte, counterstatement, counterblast, countercharge, *Law.* rebutter, *Law.* surrebutter, *Law.* surrejoinder; echo, reverberation, antiphon.

10. gain, profits, revenue, income, proceeds, *Archaic.* avails; yield, interest, increase, rent, earnings; crop, harvest, bounty; advantage, benefit.

11. reciprocation, requital, compensation, consideration, quittance, reward, *Archaic.* meed, *Literary.* guerdon; repayment, reimbursement, indemnification, indemnity, recompense; reparation, restitution, amends, atonement, retribution; retaliation, vindication, redress, quid pro quo.

12. homecoming, arrival, advent, comeback, reentry, repatriation; restoration, rehabilitation, reinvestment, reinstatement.

13. reversion, regression, regress, retrogression, retrogradation, recidivism, atavism.

14. report, financial statement, account.

revamp, *v.* renovate, repair, recondition, refurbish, rehabilitate, refit, overhaul, give a face-lift to, face-lift; mend, fix, fix up, patch up, put into shape.

reveal, *v.* **1.** make known, disclose, divulge, bring out, bring out into the open, bring to light; tell, impart, inform, *Inf.* tip off, relate, utter, declare, state, *Archaic.* discover, break the news; release, report, publish, *Archaic.* divulgate, print; advertise, broadcast, proclaim, announce, herald, trumpet; vociferate, voice, give mouth *or* voice to, air, vent, ventilate, communicate, let be known; disbosom, disembosom, get [s.t.] off one's chest, make a clean breast of [s.t.], unburden oneself, confess, *Sl.* fess up, own up, admit, acknowledge; blurt out, blab, leak, give away, *Inf.* let out, let slip, let the cat out of the bag, spill the beans, *Sl.* blow the lid off; tell everything, *Inf.* give away the whole show, tell all *or* all one knows, *Sl.* spill one's guts, *Sl.* open up; betray, *Inf.* blow the whistle on, *Sl.* pull the plug on, *Inf.* pull the rug out from underneath [s.o.]; tattle, tattletale, tell *or* inform on, *All Sl.* squeal, squeak, rat, fink, stool, peach.

2. lay open, display, exhibit, *Inf.* lay one's cards on the table, tip *or* show one's hand, show, indicate, point out, make manifest; expose, uncover, bare, take the wraps off, unveil, unmask, show up, show one's true colors, come out of the closet, *Inf.* come out; discover, decry, detect, find, uncover, unearth, exhume, dig up, smoke out.

—n. **3.** revelation, disclosure, revealment. See **revelation** (*def.* **1.**).

revel, *v.* **1.** *Usu.* **revel in** delight, rejoice, take great pleasure, like, lóve, *Inf.* adore; enjoy, appreciate, relish, savor, gloat over, feast on, *Inf.* smack the lips; glory, indulge, luxuriate, bask, wallow, swim, bathe; *All Sl.* groove on, get high on, get a kick *or* lift *or* charge *or* bang *or* boot out of.

2. carouse, roister, wassail, make merry, cut loose, let loose, *Inf.* step out, whoop it up, *Sl.* make whoopee; drink, tipple, bouse, *Inf.* booze, *Sl.* hit the bottle *or* booze *or* sauce, *Sl.* souse, *Sl.* scoop a few, *Sl.* knock a few back; go on a spree, make the rounds, *Sl.* tie one on, *Sl.* go on a drunk *or* binge *or* bender *or* hellbender *or* toot *or* tear *or* bat *or* jag, *Sl.* paint the town red, *Sl.* barhop, *Sl.* bar-crawl, *Brit. Sl.* pub-crawl; debauch, dissipate, wanton, sow wild oats, have one's fling; overindulge, overdo, burn the candle at both ends.

—*n.* **3.** revelry, spree, fling, romp, bout, wassail; drinking bout, brannigan, drunk, potation, bouse, guzzle, bacchanal, bacchanalia; *All Sl.* binge, bender, hellbender, toot, tear, bust, jag, bat, barhop, bar-crawl, *Brit.* pub-crawl. See **revelry.**

4. celebration, gala, gala affair, feast, *Sl.* hot time; festival, carnival, jamboree, fete, revels; holiday, red-letter day.

revelation, *n.* **1.** disclosure, reveal, divulgement, eyeopener, surprise, shock; exposure, exposé, exposition, manifestation, showing, exhibition, displaying; uncovering, unmasking, unveiling, baring, laying open; discovery, detection, unearthing, digging up, exhumation; airing, publication, broadcast, report, news release, story, newspaper story; news, tidings, communication, bulletin, communiqué, statement, announcement, proclamation, declaration; telling, leak, giveaway, betrayal, slip *or* slip of the tongue; admission, confession, avowal, acknowledgement.

2. secret, private *or* confidential information; tip, information, *Inf.* info, inside information.

reveler, *n.* **1.** merrymaker, carouser, roisterer, wassailer, rollicker, *Inf.* cut-up; drinker, tippler, toper, bibber, bibbler, *Obs., Rare.* biberon; drunk, drunkard, inebriate, sot, tosspot, *Inf.* guzzler, *Inf.* swiller, *Inf.* sponge, *Sl.* boozer, *Sl.* lush, *Sl.* juicer, *Sl.* elbow-bender. See also **drunk** (*def.* **5**).

2. rake, libertine, debaucher, debauchee, rip, gay deceiver, *Sl.* playboy; hedonist, sensualist, sybarite, pleasure-lover, pleasure-seeker, man of pleasure.

revelry, *n.* merriment, merrymaking, conviviality, cheer, good cheer, jollification, *Inf.* goings on, *Inf.* high jinks, *Sl.* whoopee; orgy, debauch, debauchery, saturnalia; carousal, carouse, carousing, reveling, making merry, high living; drinking, imbibing, tippling, toping, bibition, bibation, bibbing, bibbling, *Rare.* bibbery, *Inf.* boozing, *Inf.* swilling, *Sl.* hitting the bottle *or* booze *or* sauce, *Brit. Sl.* bevying.

revenge, *v.* **1.** make reprisal, requite, avenge, wreak revenge upon, inflict punishment for, exact payment from, exact one's pound of flesh; hit back at, strike back at, get back *or* get back at, get even with, *Inf.* pay off an old score, *Inf.* settle a score, *Inf.* wipe out an old score; give [s.o.] his comeuppance, *Inf.* give [s.o.] what he has coming to him.

2. retaliate, return like for like, give tit for tat, give a blow for a blow, give a Roland for an Oliver, take an eye for an eye and a tooth for a tooth, give measure for measure *or* pound for pound; give [s.o.] a dose *or* taste of his own medicine, pay [s.o.] back in his own coin, pay back in kind, repay, pay back, *Inf.* get, return the compliment *or* favor, reciprocate, give as good as one gets, do unto others as they do unto you.

—*n.* **3.** reprisal, redress, satisfaction, vindication, retribution, vengeance; vendetta, feud; requital, repayment, paying back, counterpunch, counterblow, counterstroke, counterattack, counterblast, countercharge, recrimination; retaliation, tit for tat, *Latin. quid pro quo,* a Roland for an Oliver, blow for blow, eye for an eye and a tooth for a tooth, measure for measure, pound for pound, lex talionis, talion; dose *or* taste of one's own medicine, just deserts, *Inf.* what's coming to one, *U.S. Inf.* comeuppance.

4. vindictiveness, revengefulness, vengefulness, spite, spitefulness; malice, maliciousness, ill will, hate, hatred, venom, animosity, malevolence, malignance, malignancy, rancor, rancorousness; bitterness, resentment, anger, fury, wrath, violence; cruelty, meanness, ruthlessness, mercilessness, pitilessness; relentlessness, implacability, implacableness.

revengeful, *adj.* vindictive,. vengeful, spiteful, malicious, maleficient, malevolent, malignant, malign, rancorous; retributive, retaliative, retaliatory, recriminatory, reciprocal, avenging; envenomed, embittered, bitter, *Inf.* sore, peeved, hurt, offended, indignant, up in arms, ready to fight; angry, mad, furious, infuriate, wrathful; violent, ferocious, fierce, savage, cruel, vicious, venomous, viperous; mean, tough, hard, rigorous, vigorous, severe, rough, harsh; unforgiving, stony-hearted, hard-hearted, cold-hearted, unfeeling, coldblooded; ruthless, remorseless, merciless, pitiless, relentless, unrelenting, implacable, inexorable.

revenue, *n.* **1.** income, receipts, incomings; return, yield, gain, gross, profits, interest, winnings, *Sl.* take, *Sl.* velvet; proceeds, net, *Sl.* clean-up, pickings; salary, wages, emolument, compensation, pay, *Brit. Sl.* get, remuneration, competence; stipend, fee, payment, hire; annuity, pension, subsidy, allowance; livelihood, maintenance, alimony, support.

2. capital, wealth, possessions, substance; funds, cash, finances, money, *Sl.* bread, *Brit. Sl.* rhino; means, wherewithal.

reverberate, *v.* **1.** echo, reecho, resound; sound, report, boom; roll, rumble, thunder.

2. recoil, rebound, bounce *or* bound back, fly *or* spring back, snap back.

reverberation, *n.* echo, echoing, resounding, bounce-back; report, boom, sound, noise; roll, rumble, rumbling.

revere, *v.* **1.** venerate, worship, honor, reverence, adore, idolize; beatify, sanctify, enshrine, consecrate, hallow, bless, glorify, laud, praise, *Archaic.* magnify, sing the praises of, offer sacrifice to, burn candles to, send up incense before.

2. respect, esteem, awe, admire, look up to, put on a pedestal, think highly of, have a high regard for, hero-worship; treasure, cherish, prize, hold dear, make much of, cling to, dote on.

3. do *or* make obeisance, salute, hail, bow the head to, salaam; genuflect, kowtow, bend the knee before, prostrate oneself before, fall down before; defer to, pay tribute *or* homage to, stand on ceremony, observe due decorum, kiss the hem of [s.o.'s] garment, humble oneself before.

reverence, *n.* **1.** veneration, respect, awe, adoration, honor, worship, devotion, homage, fealty; admiration, regard, estimation, esteem; deference, humility; consecration, glorification, *Archaic.* magnification.

2. offering, sacrifice, oblation, libation; prayer, benediction, hosanna, alleluia.

3. obeisance, bow, salaam, salute; genuflection, curtsy, kneeling, kowtow, prostration; respects, devoirs, courtesies.

—*v.* **4.** revere, honor, pay homage to. See **revere** (*defs.* **1, 3**).

reverend, *adj.* **1.** estimable, venerable, honorable, worthy, admirable; admired, respected, esteemed, valued, revered; sacred, holy, hallowed, blessed, consecrated, divine.

2. ordained, in holy orders, of the cloth; clerical, sacerdotal, priestly, hieratic, ministerial, pastoral.

—*n.* **3.** See **clergyman.**

reverent, *adj.* **1.** solemn, awed, respectful, worshipful, ceremonious, decorous, reserved, subdued, proper, grave, serious; deferential, humble, cap-in-hand, submissive; prostrated, obsequious, abject, abased.

2. respectful, reverential, devout, devotional, religious, saintly, godly, God-fearing, believing, pious, *Obs.* sanctimonious, holy, spiritual, otherworldly, heavenly-minded; pure in heart, sanctified, faithful.

reverie, *n.* **1.** daydreaming, fantasizing, woolgathering, musing; meditation, contemplation, introspection; mulling, pondering, pensiveness, thought, deep thought, brown study; preoccupation, absorption, engrossment, absent-mindedness.

2. daydream, *Psychol.* fantasy, flight of fancy, distraction, castles in Spain, castles in the air; trance, daze, dreamland; *Inf.* pipe dream, castle-building, abstraction.

reversal, *n.* **1.** revocation, revokement, repeal, annulment, nullification, voidance, cancellation; dissolution, abrogation, abolition, abolishment; rescission, counterorder; *Law.* overthrow, overturn, upset, rejection.

2. retraction, retractation, withdrawal, recantation, palinode, abjuration; repudiation, renunciation, defection, bolting, going over, apostasy.

3. turnabout, turnaround, about-face, rightabout, volte-face, *Literature.* peripeteia; switch, *Sl.* switcheroo, *Inf.* flip-flop, *Inf.* a 180°; backtracking, back-pedaling; change of heart, second thought, *Inf.* a different tune *or* song; tergiversation.

4. See **reverse** (*def.* 5).

reverse, *adj.* **1.** opposite, contrary, counter, contrasting, polar, antipodal; converse, inverse; antithetic, antithetical, oppositive, adversative.

2. backward, reversed, mirror; inverted, inversed, upside-down, topsy-turvy; transposed, interchanged, turned around, vice versa; palindromical; *Rhet.* hyperbatic.

—*n.* **3.** opposite, contrary, other side of the coin, inverse, converse; counterpart, vis-à-vis; pole, antipode, antithesis; *Print.* verso.

4. back, rear, tail; other side, flip side; extremity, terminus.

5. reversal, upset, check, setback, comedown, fiasco, fizzle, washout, *Inf.* no go, nonsuccess; defeat, repulse, rebuff, rout, beating, overthrow, collapse, downfall, undoing, deathblow.

6. misfortune, mishap, mischance, misadventure, accident, rainy day, humiliation, contretemps; blow, buffet, trouble, blight, curse, harm, hard times; affliction, adversity, trial, ordeal, hardship, visitation, sorrow, scourge, infliction; tragedy, casualty, disaster, calamity, catastrophe.

—*v.* **7.** transpose, invert, turn around *or* inside out *or* upside down *or* topsy-turvy; upset, overturn, tip over, capsize, turn turtle, *Fr. bouleverser*; subvert, undermine, overthrow, upend, unmake, undo, topple, turn the tables; introvert, invaginate, intussuscept.

8. back, back up, backtrack; back down, renege, retract, withdraw, take back, *Inf.* flip-flop, backpedal, recant, renounce, forswear, abjure; repudiate, disclaim, disavow, deny, contradict, gainsay; *Inf.* do an about-face, *Inf.* do a 180°, *Inf.* change one's tune, *Inf.* sing a different tune, *Inf.* shift gears.

9. revoke, annul, disannul, nullify, void, declare null and void, set aside, vacate, recall; abrogate, invalidate, cancel, negate, quash; override, overrule, countermand, counterorder; rescind, repeal, veto, *Law.* disaffirm.

reversion, *n.* **1.** reversing, turning back, inversion; return, ebb, reflux; reaction, retroaction, repercussion, reverberation; recoil, reflex, rebound, boomerang, backlash, ricochet; retrospection.

2. regression, regress, retrogression; lapse, relapse, backslide, falling back, retrogradation, recidivism; degeneration, deterioration, decline, decay; throwback, atavism.

3. reversal, turnabout, about-face, volte-face, switch, *Inf.* flip-flop, *Sl.* switcheroo, *Inf.* a 180°, reconversion, revulsion; backtracking, back-pedaling, change of heart, second thought; retraction, withdrawal, denial, disavowal.

4. recurrence, reappearance, recrudescence; alternation, rotation, coming round; restoration, resumption, resurgence; revival, renascence, renewal.

5. *All Law.* escheat, succession, conveyance, transfer, transference, assignment.

revert, *v.* **1.** return, go back, reverse, back up, backtrack, retreat, *Rare.* retrovert; hark back, resume, readopt.

2. relapse, lapse, regress, retrogress, backslide, retrograde, recidivate, degenerate, decay.

3. recur, reappear, come back, come round, recrudesce; boomerang, backfire, come home to roost.

review, *n.* **1.** critical article, critique, criticism, commentary, editorial; evaluation, rave, *Inf.* pan; dissertation, thesis, essay, theme, discourse, tract, study, treatise.

2. magazine, periodical, quarterly, monthly, biweekly, weekly, annual, yearbook; newspaper, paper, journal, gazette, tabloid, *Sl.* rag; publication.

3. second view, revision, retrospection, reconsideration, reexamination, survey, summation, rundown; study, cogitation, rumination, speculation, meditation, cerebration; rote, recitation, repetition, lucubration.

4. formal examination, official inspection; pageant, spectacle, exhibition, demonstration; exposition, show, array, military display; parade, procession, promenade, cavalcade, file, caravan; gala day, field day, fete.

5. summary, epitome, synopsis, abstract, compendium, symposium, compilation, digest, conspectus; condensation, abridgment, reduction, compression, abbreviation; analysis, recapitulation; résumé, brief, précis; outline, *Fr. aperçu*, sketch, syllabus, prospectus; docket, bulletin, minute; extracts, fragments, cuttings, analects, clippings, citations.

—*v.* **6.** reconsider, reexamine, go over again, look over again, *Sl.* hash over, retrace mentally; study, *Sl.* brush up on, *Sl.* bone up on; digest, weigh, brood over, mull over.

7. inspect formally, survey officially, examine, regard, watch, look over.

8. survey, summarize, abstract, epitomize; skim, restate briefly, recapitulate, reiterate, sum up, run down, run over.

9. critique, criticize, notice critically; comment upon, interpret, explain, explicate; edit, revise, correct.

reviewer, *n.* critic, commentator, essayist, pamphleteer, publicist, writer; editor, censor, arbiter; examiner, analyst, inspector, inquisitor, investigator, scrutinizer; interpreter, expounder, expositer, exponent, explainer, annotator; connoisseur, assessor, evaluator, judge.

revile, *v.* **1.** vituperate, oppugn, assail, abuse, attack, belabor, lash, rail against, inveigh against, *Inf.* sail into, *Inf.* jump down [s.o.'s] throat, *Archaic.* clapperclaw; scold, rate, slate, harangue, rant, tongue-lash, curse, execrate, imprecate, anathematize; upbraid, objurgate, excoriate, lambaste, flay, fulminate against, *Inf.* spout off at; berate, castigate, chastise, censure, criticize, reproach, rebuke, reprove, *Inf.* dress down, *Sl.* strafe, *Sl.* chew out, *Sl.* jump all over.

2. vilify, traduce, asperse, calumniate, impugn, slur,

malign, defame, denigrate, slander, libel, backbite, bespatter, *Sl.* badmouth; denounce, decry, disparage, discredit, depreciate, deprecate, belittle, minimize, run *or* put down, *Inf.* knock; scorn, deride, gibbet, ridicule, mock, lampoon, pasquinade, make fun of.

revilement, *n.* **1.** vituperation, assailment, abuse, attack, belaboring; curse, execration, imprecation, malediction, anathematization; invective, railing, fulmination, upbraiding, objurgation, contumely, berating, scolding, tongue-lashing; censure, reproach, rebuke, reproval.

2. vilification, impugnment, traducement, aspersion, calumniation, calumny, obloquy, slur; maligning, defamation, denigration, slander, libel, *Inf.* backbiting; diatribe, tirade, philippic, denunciation, disparagement, discrediting, depreciation, deprecation, insinuation, belittlement, minimization; scorn, derision, ridicule, mockery.

revise, *v.* **1.** amend, alter, change; correct, rectify, right, straighten out; (*all of opinions, beliefs, etc.*) reconsider, review, reappraise.

2. rewrite, redraft, rework; update, bring up to date; edit, emend, emendate; retouch, revamp, overhaul, doctor, repair.

revision, *n.* **1.** change, alteration, amendment; correction, rectification; review, reassessment, reappraisal, re-evaluation, reconsideration, re-examination, second look; (*all of a written piece*) recension, redation, emendation.

2. rewrite, revised *or* new edition, update.

revival, *n.* **1.** renewal, resumption, recommencement; revivification, resurrection, rejuvenation, rejuvenescence, reinvigoration, revitalization, regeneration, resuscitation, recrudescence.

2. renaissance, renascence, rebirth, new birth, new day, new dawn; fresh start, new beginning, another try; rally, recovery, new lease on life, another chance.

revive, *v.* **1.** reactivate, renew, activate, set in motion, start; incite, instigate.

2. rejuvenate, reanimate, reinvigorate, revitalize, regenerate, recharge, rekindle, renew, refresh, freshen, resuscitate, put *or* breathe new life into.

3. cheer, encourage, hearten, raise [s.o.'s] spirits, *Inf.* set [s.o.] back on his feet *or* legs, *Inf.* give [s.o.] a boost *or* a lift; animate, stimulate, vivify, enliven, invigorate, exhilarate, stir, stir up, stir [s.o.'s] blood, quicken, arouse, breathe life into.

4. refresh [s.o.'s] memory, call *or* bring to mind, call up, summon up, conjure up, evoke.

5. come to, *Inf.* come round *or* around, regain *or* return to consciousness, awaken; come alive, come to life, live again, rise again, rise from the dead; recover, recuperate, rally, pull through, get better *or* well, *Inf.* make a comeback.

6. (*all of a theatrical production*) restage, remount, reproduce.

revocation, *n.* **1.** repeal, rescinding, rescission, abrogation; annulment, disannulment, nullification, abolishment, abolition, avoidance, voidance, *Law.* defeasance; quashing, invalidation, *Obs.* vacatur, disenactment, cancellation, setting aside; suspension, *Law.* nolle prosequi, discontinuance, cessation.

2. recantation, retraction, palinode, abjuration, withdrawal, taking back, recall; renouncement, renunciation, relinquishment, abnegation, repudiation, denial, disclaimer, disavowal; apostasy, defection, tergiversation; countermand, counterorder, reversal, overriding, overruling; veto, negation; termination, dissolution, putting an end to, bringing to an end, doing away with.

revoke, *v.* **1.** rescind, abrogate, repeal; annul, disannul, nullify, abolish, declare null and void, void, make void; quash, invalidate, vacate, disenact, cancel, set aside; veto, negate; reverse, change sides.

2. recant, retract, withdraw; take back, call back, back down, back off, back out of; go back on one's word, unsay, renege, back-pedal, eat one's words; renounce, forswear, abjure, relinquish, repudiate, disclaim, disavow, apostatize; countermand, counterorder, override, overrule; terminate, dissolve, put an end to, bring to an end, do away with, remove, sweep away; discard, disown, dismiss.

revolt, *v.* **1.** rebel, mutiny, rise up, rise up in arms, rise up against, mount the barricades, kick over the traces; riot, run riot, take to the streets; renounce allegiance, break away from, refuse to support; say no, resist, oppose, defy, contradict; protest, dissent, raise one's voice against, confront; violate, infringe, disobey, transgress; secede, desert, defect, bolt.

2. appall, horrify, shock, make the flesh creep; sicken, nauseate, make sick, disgust, turn the stomach; repulse, repel; offend, disturb, distress, go against the grain.

3. abhor, detest, loathe, abominate, execrate; feel horror, shudder at, shrink from, recoil, draw *or* pull back *or* away from, turn away from; dislike, disrelish.

—*n.* **4.** revolution, rebellion, insurrection, uprising, rising. See **revolution** (*def.* **1**).

5. abhorrence, abomination, loathing, detestation, dislike, disaffection; aversion, dispprobation, revulsion, repulsion.

revolting, *adj.* **1.** offensive, repugnant, repulsive, repellent; obnoxious, objectionable, off-putting, gross, odious, rebarbative; abominable, execrable, loathsome, detestable, hateful; anathematic, abhorrent, despicable, base, contemptible; nauseating, nauseous, sickening, foul, vile; noisome, fulsome, mephitic, noxious; stinking, malodorous, reeking, fetid, rank; slimy, grimy, unclean, maggoty, reeky, excrementitious, *Pathol.* stercoraceous; *Sl.* icky, *Sl.* yukky, *Sl.* ishy, *Sl.* yecchy, *Sl.* ecchy; beastly, dreadful, rotten, horrible, rancid, curdled, sour, bad.

2. crude, obscene, pornographic, filthy, dirty, vulgar; ugly, homely, plain, ugly as sin, not fit to be seen, homely enough to curdle milk; hideous, horrid, gorgonian, grisly, ghastly; misshapen, malformed, unsightly, frightful, monstrous, grotesque, grim.

3. rebellious, seditious, mutinous, insurrectionist; insubordinate, defiant, refractory; riotous, revolutionary, dissentient, recusant, ungovernable.

revolution, *n.* **1.** rebellion, revolt, insurrection, insurgence, insurgency, uprising, rising, outbreak, mutiny; sedition, subversion, treason; overthrow, takeover, putsch, coup d'état; riot, anarchy, civil disorder, mob-law, street-fighting, fighting in the streets, turmoil, chaos; peasant revolt, jacquerie.

2. radical change, sea change, alteration, modification, metamorphosis, transformation; innovation, modernization; upset, upheaval, cataclysm.

3. rotation, single turn, whirl, round, reel, spin; full circle, full cycle, 360°; gyration, whirling, turning, revolving; orbit, circular movement, circumgyration, circumrotation.

4. circuit, cycle, round, ambit, run, lap.

revolutionary, *adj.* **1.** rebellious, insurgent, insurrectionary, seditious, factious; mutinous, insubordinate, disobedient; traitorous, treasonable, subversive; lawless, riotous, ungovernable, uncontrollable, out of control, unmanageable.

2. underground, counter-culture, counter-cultural, avant-garde; radical, drastic, thoroughgoing, fundamental, drastic, sweeping; progressive, newfangled,

innovative, experimental.
3. revolving, rotating, circumrotating, gyrating, circumgyrating, whirling, turning, spinning.
—*n.* 4. rebel, insurgent, insurrectionist, sansculotte, revolutionist, revolter, seditionist, mutineer; agitator, malcontent, anarchist, *U.S.* weatherman; rioter, brawler; traitor, turncoat, Benedict Arnold.
5. counter-culturist, radical, extremist; fanatic, zealot.

revolutionize, *v.* change fundamentally, effect radical change, change drastically; break with the past, modernize, innovate; reform, turn over a new leaf; reconstruct, refashion, remodel, recast, reorganize, revamp; transform, alter, change the face of; tamper with, work a change, chop and change; subvert, overthrow.

revolve, *v.* 1. turn around, turn, rotate, wheel, whirl, twirl, reel; spin, gyrate, pirouette, pivot, swivel, swing; circumrotate, circumvolve; orbit, circle.
2. come round again, recur, reoccur, reappear, return.
3. think about, cerebrate, reflect upon, meditate on, speculate on; consider, run over in the mind, mull over, ruminate on, ponder, weigh; study, con.

revolving, *adj.* 1. turning, rotating, rotary, rotative, circumrotatory, circumrotating, wheeling, circumvolving; whirling, twirling, reeling, spinning, gyrating, gyral, gyratory, pirouetting, pivoting, swiveling, swinging.
2. recurring, recurrent, reoccurring; periodical, cyclical.

revulsion, *n.* repugnance, disgust, nausea, queasiness; aversion, abhorrence, repellence, abomination, loathing, execration; hatred, detestation, odium, antipathy, dislike, disrelish, distaste, offense; repulsion, *Sl.* the creeps, shrinking, recoil.

reward, *n.* 1. recompense, payment, return, requital; reparation, quittance, indemnification, indemnity, redress; amends, restitution, damages, *Law.* solatium.
2. remuneration, compensation, pay, payoff, *Fig.* carrot; salary, wages, emolument, allowance; hire, fee, stipend, honorarium.
3. award, prize, honor, tribute, testimonial, compliment, *Literary.* guerdon, *Archaic.* meed; present, benefaction, bounty, premium; bonus, grant, windfall, gain; tip, gratuity, douceur, *Fr. pourboire,* baksheesh, remembrance; bribe, boodle, blackmail, hush money; graft, cut, *Inf.* rake-off, *Inf.* kickback.
4. just deserts, *Inf.* comeuppance, punishment, retribution.
—*v.* 5. remunerate, pay, fee, recompense; reimburse, repay, indemnify, redress, requite, compensate, satisfy, *Obs.* gratify; tip, remember, acknowledge.
6. bribe, suborn, oil, graft, buy off, *Sl.* pay off, cross *or* grease [s.o.'s] palm.

reword, *v.* 1. rephrase, paraphrase, put another way, recast; revise, rewrite, edit, redact, rectify.
2. repeat, reiterate, recapitulate, review, rehash; summarize, explain, interpret, elucidate, gloss; translate, metaphrase.

rhapsodic, *adj.* 1. ecstatic, thrilled, exhilarated, enthusiastic, excited, elated, overjoyed, transported, ravished, overcome, orgasmic; rapturous, blissful, in heaven, in seventh heaven, on cloud nine, happy as a clam at high tide, happy as a pig in mud; beside oneself, bouncing with joy, delirious, in orbit, flying, high, intoxicated, floating, walking on air; delighted, joyful, beaming.
2. unconnected, disconnected, irregular, broken, uneven, erratic.

rhetoric, *n.* 1. eloquence, power of speech, appeal, forcefulness, expressiveness, cogency; elocution, diction, articulation, enunciation, intonation, vocalization, address, delivery; command of words, way with words, *Inf.* gift of gab, *Archaic.* facundity; (*all of speech*) fluency, facility, ease, gracefulness, glibness, slickness, smoothness.
2. bombast, grandiosity, rodomontade, pomposity, orotundity, magniloquence, grandiloquence; oratory, rant, declamation, extravagance, high-flown language, sesquipedality; verbosity, verboseness, wordiness, prolixity, prolixness; tumidity, turgidity, flatulence, inflatedness, *Archaic.* tympany; bravado, braggadocio, gasconade, boasting, *Sl.* hot air.
3. *Disparaging. (all in reference to speech)* technique, form, art; artfulness, cleverness, deftness, ingeniousness, ingenuity, slickness; trickery, hocus-pocus, linguistic legerdemain.

rhetorical, *adj.* 1. eloquent, articulate, well-spoken, silver-tongued, *Archaic.* facund, *Obs.* facundious, Ciceronian; (*all of speech*) poetic, graceful, easy, facile, flowing, fluent, glib, slick, smooth, smooth-tongued.
2. (*all of speech*) expressive, cogent, telling; forceful, emphatic, spirited, vigorous, impassioned, trenchant, vehement, burning; striking, vivid, graphic; effective, persuasive, impressive; concise, succinct, pointed, pithy, meaty.
3. bombastic, bombastical, orotund, fustian, haughty, pretentious, ostentatious, flaunting; grandiose, magniloquent, Johnsonian, Ossianic, sonorous, sesquipedalian; high-sounding, high-flown, lofty, *Inf.* highfalutin, *Inf.* high-hat; inflated, swollen, bloated, turgid, tumid, flatulent, plethoric; euphuistic, periphrastic, extravagant, oratorical, ranting, mouthy, declamatory; flamboyant, flashy, ornate, ornamental, showy, flowery, florid.

rhyme, *n.* 1. verse, poetry, limerick, jingle, versification, *Archaic.* poesy.
2. **rhyme or reason** logic, sense, plan; motive, motivation, casue.

rhythm, *n.* 1. beat, cadence, tempo, pulse, throb; pulsation, cadence, cadency, rhythmicity; beating, throbbing; oscillation, undulation; periodicity, recurrence, reoccurrence, reappearance, intermittence.
2. flow, harmonious flow, movement, regular movement, rhythmic flow, lilt, jingle, swing; balance, proportion, symmetry, order; harmony, equilibrium, concinnity, euphony, right word in the right place.
3. accent, accentuation, stress, emphasis, syllable stress, primary *or* secondary *or* tertiary stress, weak stress; periodic emphasis, rhythmical emphasis, rhythm pattern, *Music.* rhythmical accentuation, *Music.* arsis *or* upbeat, *Music.* thesis *or* downbeat, *Pros.* ictus, prominent pulsation.
4. *Prosody.* meter, measure, numbers, rate; strain, foot; prosody, metrics, *Rare.* orthometry.

rhythmic, *adj.* cadenced, cadent, metrical, metric, measured, tripping; rhythmical, regular, steady, periodic, accentual, recurrent, recurring, seasonal, cyclical; pulsating, pulsing, beating, throbbing, palpitating; balanced, even, symmetrical, symmetric; flowing, fluent, melodious, harmonious; prosodic, prosodical.

ribald, *adj.* 1. vulgar, obscene, lewd, salacious, pornographic; suggestive, risqué, off-color, *Inf.* blue; lecherous, lubricous, goatish, lustful, ruttish, libidinous, concupiscent, carnal, sexy, erotic, sensual, *Archaic.* lickerish; licentious, lascivious, Cyprian, prurient, wanton, loose, libertine, promiscuous, Paphian, unchaste; offensive, disgusting, gross, rank, vile, foul, filthy, dirty, smutty, nasty, scatologic, scatological, *Sl.* raunchy; indecent, distasteful, broad, shameless, immodest, indelicate.

2. immoral, degenerate, dissolute, dissipated, debauched, rakish, profligate, depraved, perverted; coarse, rough, base, baseborn, tatty; inferior, ignoble, raffish, low, lowly, low-class; gauche, uncouth, crass, rude, boorish, loutish, brutish, raw, unmannerly, ill-mannered, uncivil; unrefined, uncultured, ungentlemanly, unladylike, uncultivated, uncivilized.

3. scurrilous, thersitical, blackguardly, profane, foulmouthed, Fescennine, *Obs.* blackguard, *Archaic.* scurrile; abusive, outrageous, affronting, insulting, *Archaic.* affrontive; derisive, scornful, mocking, ridiculing, irreverent.

—*n.* **4.** vulgarian, lecher, dirty old man, Cyprian; libertine, profligate, rake; boor, lout, churl, knave, blackguard, brute, swine.

ribaldry, *n.* **1.** scurrility, scurrilousness, abusiveness, blackguardism, profaneness; indecency, shamelessness, suggestivity, immodesty, indelicacy; offensiveness, grossness, rankness, repulsiveness, repulsivity; vulgarity, vulgarness, obsceneness, lewdness, salaciousness, vileness, foulness, filthiness, nastiness, *Sl.* raunchiness; lecherousness, lubricity, lustfulness, bawdiness, libidinousness, concupiscence, carnality, carnalness, sexiness, sensuality; licentiousness, lasciviousness, wantonness, looseness, promiscuity, promiscuousness.

2. immorality, dissoluteness, dissipation, rakishness; gaucheness, gaucherie, uncouthness, crassness, rudeness, boorishness, brutishness, rawness; ill-breeding, unmannerliness, ill-manneredness, incivility, uncivilness, ungentlemanliness; coarseness, roughness, baseness, commonness, ignobility, raffishness, lowliness.

3. vulgarism, obscenity, salacity, filth, dirt, smut; scurrility, billingsgate, profanity, double entendre, *Archaic.* bawdry; derision, scorn, scoff, jeer, gibe, sneer, mockery, ridicule.

ribbon, *n.* **1.** band, ribband, strip; headband, frontlet, fillet; collar, collarband, neckband, *Inf.* choker; sash, girdle, waistband, cummerbund, cestus, *Archaic.* zone, *Archaic, Poetic.* cincture.

2. ribbons shreds, tatters, strips, odds and ends; mungo, shoddy.

rich, *adj.* **1.** wealthy, affluent, prosperous, opulent, flush, moneyed, well-off, well-to-do, worth a great deal, *Inf.* worth a bundle *or* a pretty penny, *Inf.* well-heeled, *Inf.* made of money, *Inf.* rolling in money *or* dough, *Inf.* loaded, *Sl.* stinking *or* filthy rich, *Sl.* in the money *or* dough *or* chips; comfortable, easy, in easy circumstances, fat, *Inf.* on Easy Street, *Sl.* high on the hog, *Inf.* in clover, *Inf.* on velvet, *Inf.* well-situated, *Inf.* well-fixed, *Brit. Inf.* warm.

2. replete, rife, well-supplied, abundantly supplied, well-stocked, well-provided; abounding, overflowing, overspilling, running over with, bursting; profuse, exuberant, superabundant.

3. valuable, valued; precious, priceless, invaluable, inestimable; exquisite, fine, superfine, superexcellent; outstanding, standout, preeminent, *Fr. par excellence;* special, select, choice, of choice.

4. expensive, costly, dear, high, high-priced, premium-priced, at a premium, priced beyond one's means *or* pocketbook, *Inf.* fancy, *Inf.* stiff, *Inf.* steep; overpriced, exorbitant, inordinate, immoderate, excessive, unreasonable.

5. opulent, lavish, lush, luxurious, sumptuous, splendid, resplendent, *Inf.* splendiferous, superb, gorgeous, magnificent, grand, grandiose.

6. (*all of colors*) deep, strong, intense; vivid, graphic, striking, impressive; brilliant, lustrous, full-toned, bright-hued, high-colored, deep-colored; vibrant, dynamic, gay, bright; gaudy, garish, loud, screaming, *Sl.* jazzy.

7. sonorous, canorous, resonant, full; mellifluous, euphonic, euphonious, harmonious; dulcet, melodic, melodious, silver-toned.

8. redolent, fragrant, aromatic, odoriferous, odorous; perfumed, scented, ambrosial, savory; pungent, strong, sharp, nose-piercing.

9. fruitful, fecund, productive, generative, progenerative, potent; prolific, proliferous, pullulating, multiparous.

10. abundant, plentiful, plenteous, plenitudinous, bountiful, bounteous, copious, unstinted, bumper; ample, more than enough, *Inf.* plenty; immeasurable, unmeasured, inexhaustible, bottomless; much, many, numerous, *Inf.* dime a dozen; in quantity, in plenty, *Inf.* aplenty, *Inf.* galore.

11. *Informal.* **a.** amusing, humorous, comical, funny, *Inf.* rib-tickling; hilarious, too funny for words, *Inf.* priceless, *Inf.* side-splitting. **b.** ridiculous, ludicrous, absurd, nonsensical, *Sl.* screwball, *Sl.* screwy, *Sl.* nutty, *Sl.* wacky.

12. (*all of food*) heavy, creamy, fattening; succulent, juicy, mouth-watering, flavorful, savory; spicy, tangy, piquant.

riches, *n.* affluence, wealth, wealthiness, prosperity, prosperousness; opulence, opulency, comfort, easy circumstances, *Inf.* Easy Street, *Inf.* velvet, *Inf.* clover; gold, treasure, fortune; money, cash, *Sl.* dough, *Sl.* bread, *Sl.* moolah, *Sl.* spondulicks, *Sl.* loot, *Sl.* gravy, *U.S. Sl.* bucks, *U.S. Sl.* big bucks; capital, assets, means, funds, finances, resources, wherewithal; nest egg, *Sl.* cushion, *Sl.* tidy bundle.

richness, *n.* **1.** wealthiness, affluence, opulence, prosperousness. See **riches.**

2. luxuriousness, lushness, lavishness, sumptuousness; splendidness, resplendence, *Inf.* splendiferousness, gorgeousness, magnificence, grandness, grandiosity.

3. vividness, graphicness, intensity, deepness; brilliancy, lustrousness; vibrancy, brightness, gayness; gaudiness, garishness, loudness, *Sl.* jazziness.

4. resonance, sonorousness, canorousness, fullness, orotundity; mellifluousness, euphoniousness, harmoniousness; dulcetness, melodiousness.

5. redolence, fragrance, aromaticity, odorousness, odoriferousness.

6. fruitfulness, fecundity, productiveness, fertility, frugiferousness, fructiferousness; prolificness, proliferousness.

7. plenteousness, plentifulness, bountifulness, bounteousness, copiousness; amplitude, ampleness; abundance, profusion, plenitude, bounty, plenty, cornucopia, horn of plenty, endless supply, *Scot.* scouth, *Scot. and North Eng.* routh.

8. (*all of food*) heaviness, creaminess; succulence, juiciness, flavorfulness, savoriness; spiciness, tanginess, piquancy.

rickety, *adj.* **1.** shaky, unsteady, unstable, unsound, unfixed, unsecure, unsafe, precarious, hanging by a thread; tottering, teetering, doddering.

2. infirm, feeble, frail; withered, wasted, worn-out; unhealthy, in poor health, on the decline, reduced to skin and bones, skeleton-like; crippled, lame, halt; (*all of bones*) brittle, frangible, fragile, breakable.

3. dilapidated, deteriorated, battered, in disrepair, broken-down, tumble-down, ramshackle, seedy, decrepit; old, ancient, on its last legs, the worst for wear, having seen better days.

4. irregular, uncertain, unsure, unpredictable, erratic, fickle, capricious, changeable; sporadic, fitful, desultory, stop-and-go, come-and-go.

ricochet, *n.* **1.** rebound, recoil, reaction, reflex, backlash, return; repercussion, result, counteraction, retroaction; echo, reecho, reverberation, reflection; deflection, glancing off, turning aside, divergence.

—*v.* **2.** rebound, bound back, spring back, recoil, boomerang, fly back, return, return quickly; deflect, glance, glance off, swerve off, bear off, diverge.

rid, *v.* **1.** *Usu.* **rid of** clear, cleanse, purify, clean, depurate, flush, flush out; empty of, deplete, purge, expurgate; weed out, destroy, annihilate, crush, abolish, cut away *or* out, eliminate, *Inf.* stamp out, ban; kill, murder, depose, eject, drive away, evict, throw out.

2. free, disentangle, disencumber, relieve, disembarrass; untie, unknot, loosen, liberate, detach, unfasten, unloose, separate, undo, divorce, unmarry, set asunder.

riddance, *n.* **1.** clearing, clearance, elimination; purging, purgation, *Med.* catharsis; cleaning out, ablution, purification, purifying; censoring, censorship, bowdlerization.

2. deliverance, release, extrication, freeing, liberation, disembarrassment, disencumbrance, relief.

riddle[1], *n.* **1.** puzzle, puzzler, poser, conundrum; code, cryptogram, cryptograph; rhymed puzzle, anagram, logogriph, word game, acrostic, *Trademark.* Double-Crostic, crossword puzzle, *Inf.* crossword, diagramless puzzle, *Inf.* diagramless; charade, guessing game; Chinese puzzle, *Inf.* hard nut to crack, *Inf.* brain teaser, *Inf.* mind-boggler, *Inf.* stumper, *Inf.* floorer.

2. enigma, mystery, secret, arcanum, question, question mark; mysterious person, closed *or* sealed book, *Latin. terra incognita,* unexplored ground *or* territory; oracle, dark saying, riddle of the Sphinx, obscure statement, ambiguity, equivoque; hidden meaning, occult meaning, symbolic meaning, anagoge.

3. dilemma, problem, quandary, plight, predicament, *Inf.* pickle, *Inf.* jam, *Inf.* fix; *Inf.* tight spot, box, bind, double-bind, strait; catch-22, vicious circle, cul-de-sac, dead end, blind alley, impasse, standstill, stalemate, deadlock; difficult choice, *Fr. embarras de choix,* tough question; entanglement, intricacy.

—*v.* **4.** speak enigmatically *or* cryptically.

riddle[2], *v.* **1.** pierce, perforate, fill with holes, fill full of holes; honeycomb, punch; pepper with shot *or* buckshot.

2. screen, sift, separate, filter, strain; refine, winnow, pick, comb, weed, sort through.

3. permeate, pervade, penetrate, fill, diffuse, spread.

ride, *v.* **1.** (*all in reference to animals*) sit on, manage, mount, bestride, perch on, sit on top of; be carried by, be borne along by, travel on.

2. motor, automobile, taxi; tour, travel, journey; float, body surf, *Inf.* surf, *Inf.* catch a wave, *Inf.* hang ten.

3. harass, harry, hector; nag, rag, annoy, tease, provoke, heckle; ridicule, make fun of, deride; browbeat, bother, badger, bait; tyrannize, intimidate, bully, terrorize, torment; push around, pester, plague, persecute, dragoon.

4. ride down overtake, track down, run down, run to ground; catch up with, pursue and capture.

5. ride for a fall live dangerously, take risks, ask for trouble, court disaster; be improvident, be imprudent, not look ahead, gamble foolishly, trust to blind luck, sell short.

6. ride out endure, bear, bear up, weather, suffer; take it, brave it out, *Inf.* tough it out, *Inf.* stick it out, *Sl.* sweat it out; *Inf.* take it on the chin, *Inf.* take it and come back for more; *Inf.* hang in there, *Inf.* stand the gaff; tolerate, brook, withstand; hold, hold on, stand *or* hold one's ground.

—*n.* **7.** excursion, journey, drive, spin, outing, airing; trip, tour, circuit, peregrination, expedition, jaunt, side-trip, little trip; transportation, lift.

8. take for a ride *Slang.* **a.** murder, do in, do away with; execute, *Inf.* execute a contract on, *Sl.* bump off, *Inf.* erase, *Sl.* put cement boots on and take for a swim. **b.** deceive, trick, gull, cozen, dupe; mislead, misinform, misguide; take in, pull the wool over [s.o.'s] eyes; cheat, victimize, defraud; humbug, hoodwink, trick, entrap.

rider, *n.* **1.** equestrian, horseman, horsewoman, equestrienne, jockey; roughrider, bareback rider, breaker, trainer, exercise rider, exercise boy *or* girl; cossack, cavalryman, cowboy; whip, postilion, coachman, reinsman; cabdriver, *Inf.* cabby, hackman, *Inf.* hack; truckdriver, teamster; postrider, dispatch rider, estafette; racecar driver, bicyclist, motorcyclist, snowmobiler, surfer; pilot, copilot, flight engineer; passenger, traveler, commuter.

2. addition, attachment, appendage; amendment, codicil, additional clause; appendix, supplement, suffix, adjunct, affix, addendum; sequel, postscript; small print, catch, *Sl.* hooker.

ridge, *n.* **1.** reef, ledge, saddle, hummock, escarpment, *Geology.* hogback, *Physical Geography.* arete, *Geology.* esker, *Chiefly Brit.* watershed; chain, range, line, file, row, column, string, series, set.

2. crest, *Anat., Zool.* crista, *Anat.* (*of the nose*) bridge, *Bot.* rachis, *Bot., Zool.* carina, *Bot., Zool.* carination, *Bot., Zool.* keel; peak, top, tip, pinnacle, summit, apex, vertex.

3. spine, chine, fin, spinal *or* vertebral column, vertebrae, *Anat.* backbone, *Anat.* spina, *Anat.* dorsum; back, dorse, *Anat.* posterior.

4. rip, cord, wale, welt, wheal, fret, strip, seam, fillet, list; corrugation, crimp, stria, striation, ripple, crinkle, crease, fold, wrinkle; bump, knob, knot, protrusion, projection, protuberance, outgrowth, excrescence.

ridged, *adj.* **1.** crested, cristate, cristated, *Both Bot., Zool.* carinate, carinated, *Anat.* bridgelike; spiny, finlike, ridgelike; peaked, hilly, mountainous.

2. ribbed, corded, cord, corduroy, waled, welted, fretted, seamed; corrugated, fluted, crimped, striated, rippled, ripply, crinkly, creased, wrinkled; bumpy, knobby, knotty.

ridicule, *n.* **1.** derision, mockery, mimicry; satire, black humor, lampoon, sarcasm, irony, cynicism; burlesque, travesty, parody, farce, take-off, caricature, skit, squib; raillery, banter, chaff, badinage, persiflage, sport, joke; ribbing, teasing, making fun of, guying, making game of, poking fun at, making a monkey out of; quizzing, joshing, deviling, kidding, razzing; criticizing, roasting; contempt, disdain, scorn, insult, sneer.

2. taunt, jeer, scoff, gibe, flout, gird, fleer, twit, quip, jape, *Australian.* borak; buffoonery, foolery, practical joke, prank, antic, antics.

—*v.* **3.** deride, mock, bemock, mimic; satirize, burlesque, parody, lampoon, travesty, caricature, cartoon, do a take-off on, squib; rib, tease, make merry, make fun of, make game of, make sport of, make a monkey out of, poke fun at; guy, laugh at, grin at, rag; josh, devil, kid, razz; taunt, jeer, scoff, gibe, flout, gird, fleer, twit, quip, jape, sneer; criticize, roast, pillory; scorn, insult, *Sl.* rank out, ride, show up; make a butt of, haze, make a laughingstock of; snicker, snigger, laugh in *or* up one's sleeve; harass, call names, harry, play tricks on *or* upon; hoot, hiss; disparage, depreciate, belittle, treat with disrespect, vilipend; humiliate, dishonor, disgrace, shame; cheapen, undervalue, detract from; abuse, revile, malign, vilify, traduce.

ridiculous, *adj.* **1.** absurd, inane, pointless, fatuous; nonsensical, senseless, *Inf.* damfool, *Inf.* damfoolish, tomfoolish, foolish, *Scot. and North Eng.* glaikit, *Sl.* cockeyed; poppycockish, *Sl.* cockamamie, amphigoric; asinine, anserine, idiotic, *Inf.* moronic, imbecilic; stupid, unintelligent, mindless, fatuitous, slow, brainless; empty-headed, blank, vacant, vacuous; childish, puerile, green, immature; crazy, crazed, *Sl.* kooky, *Scot.* doiled, mad, wild, insane, demented; daft, *Inf.* daffy, crackbrained, *Inf.* nutty; *All Slang.* balmy, dippy, batty, cuckoo, buggy, screwy, wacky, goofy, loony.

2. comical, farcical, burlesque; satirical, ironical, sarcastic, cynical; derisible, risible, laughable, good for a laugh, ludicrous, *Sl.* for the birds; humorous, funny, too funny for words, droll; waggish, witty, roguish, jocular, jocose, facetious, sportive; diverting, entertaining, mirthful, amusing; sidesplitting, screaming, hilarious, uproarious.

3. unreasonable, irrational, illogical, without rhyme or reason, meaningless; preposterous, extravagant, outrageous, monstrous, outlandish, bombastic, high-flown; eccentric, odd, *Archaic.* antic, out-of-the-way, strange, peculiar, quaint; queer, quizzical, grotesque, bizarre; imaginary, fantastic, fabulous, illusory, illusive, chimerical; incredible, inconceivable, unimaginable, unthinkable; unbelievable, hard to believe, beyond belief, implausible, untenable, unheard-of; doubtful, doubtable, dubitable, questionable.

4. untrue, fallacious, impossible, sophistic, sophistical, incorrect, erroneous; self-contradictory, paradoxical, inconsistent, incongruous.

5. inappropriate, unbecoming, improper, impractical, *Fr. outré,* unwise, ill-considered, ill-suited, ill-advised; egregious, glaring, flagrant, gross, arrant.

rife, *adj.* **1.** prevalent, widespread, extensive, ubiquitous, general, rampant; universal, catholic, worldwide, global, nationwide; generally held, common.

2. present, current, making the rounds, popular, in fashion, in vogue; prevailing, predominant, preponderant, preponderating.

3. plentiful, abundant, plenteous, plenitudinous, bountiful, bounteous, copious; much, many, numerous, multifarious, *Inf.* dime a dozen; in quantity *or* quantities, in plenty, *Inf.* aplenty, *Inf.* galore; profuse, abounding, exuberant, bursting, overflowing, overspilling, running over; rampant, bristling, thick, teeming, teeming with, swarming, alive with.

riffraff, *n.* **1.** the hoi polloi, the rabble, the masses, proletariat, rank and file, commoners, the lower classes, peasantry, the common people, commonalty; trash, canaille, doggery, *Inf.* the great unwashed, scum, ragtag and bobtail, flotsam and jetsam, dregs of society, outcasts, vermin.

2. rubbish, trash, litter, *Brit. Dial.* raff, sweepings, chaff; refuse, *Dial.* culch, garbage, waste, offal; debris, rubble, wreckage.

rifle[1], *n.* carbine, shoulder firearm, shotgun, fowling piece, muzzleloader, repeating rifle, magazine rifle, *Ordn.* breechloader, petronel; musket, blunderbuss, matchlock, harquebus; gun, shooting iron, flintlock, firelock, fusil.

rifle[2], *v.* **1.** ransack, sack, loot, gut, fleece, strip; rob, burglarize, burgle, break in; frisk.

2. plunder, strip bare, pillage, despoil, spoliate; ravage, harry, rape, maraud.

3. steal, thieve, pilfer, purloin, filch, finger, *Inf.* snitch; make free with, walk off with, *Sl.* rip off, *Sl.* crook, *Sl.* lift; shoplift, palm, *Sl.* boost; *Inf.* poach, deerjack, (*of cattle*) rustle.

4. abduct, carry off, seize, capture, run off with, spirit away, steal away; lay hold of, lay hands on.

rifleman, *n.* musketeer, carabineer, fusilier, *Archaic.* firelock; sharpshooter, marksman, jaeger; infantryman, (*in the French army*) chasseur, dragoon, calvalryman, trooper, skirmisher.

rift, *n.* **1.** split, fissure, cleft, *Archaic.* scissure, tear, rent; crevice, schism, cleavage, breach, chink, slit, rip; gap, opening, hole, gulf, cavity; slash, gash, cut; crack, cranny, notch, nick.

2. opening, space, hiatus, lacuna, gap, slot; hole, hollow, cavity, aperture, orifice, ostiole.

3. interruption, intermission, interlude, recess, rest; pause, interval, lapse.

4. altercation, difference, falling out, divergence, variance; parting of the ways, breaking up, breaking off, separation, disunion; discord, dissension, dissent, disagreement, friction, disruption, conflict, contention; dispute, tiff, argument, quarrel, misunderstanding.

—*v.* **5.** split, rend, reave, tear apart; fracture, fragmentize, splinter, shiver, tear, chip, crack; cleave, sunder, sever, disjoint.

rig, *v.* **1.** equip, furnish, supply, provide, purvey, gird, *Archaic.* dight, *Obs.* appoint; outfit, fit out, fit up, fit, turn out, gear, gear up; rig up, rig out, set out, put together.

2. clothe, attire, accouter, array, deck, bedeck, deck out, caparison, trap, adorn, ornament; dress, dress out, habit, robe, gown, drape, bedizen, get up, trick out, *Inf.* duke out, *Inf.* doll up.

3. manipulate, juggle, falsify, fake, trump up, pack, stack; tamper with, doctor, fiddle with, twiddle with, play with, fix; engineer, wheel and deal, maneuver, *Inf.* angle, jockey, *Inf.* finagle, *Inf.* wangle, gerrymander; contrive, plot, scheme, intrigue, machinate, pull the strings.

—*n.* **4.** carriage, equipage, coach and four, coach and six; fourwheeler, barouche, brougham, landau, phaeton, victoria; two-wheeler, chaise, *Chiefly Dial.* shay *or* one hoss shay, sulky, buckboard, horse and wagon, team and wagon; *All Informal.* truck, tractor-trailer, 16-wheeler.

5. outfit, gear, equipment, furnishings, accouterments, appurtenances, appointments; apparatus, fixtures, fittings, paraphernalia, *Inf.* things, *Inf.* stuff, *Inf.* junk; supplies, matériel, materials, wherewithal; harness, trappings, tack, tackle, rigging; belongings, effects; kit, duffel; bags, baggage, bag and baggage, luggage; provisions, supplies.

6. *Informal.* costume, livery, uniform, regalia; garb, habit, dress; raiment, *Inf.* gear, *Inf.* togs, *Sl.* rags, *Sl.* threads, ensemble, outfit, *Inf.* getup.

right, *adj.* **1.** good, just, fair, impartial, equitable, reasonable; righteous, upright, virtuous, moral, ethical; honorable, noble, high-minded, scrupulous, principled, right-minded; honest, *Inf.* square, *Inf.* fair and square, straightforward, aboveboard, open.

2. correct, *Inf.* on the mark, on target, *Inf.* right on, *Sl.* spot on; on the button, on the dot, *Inf.* on the nose, *Sl.* on the beam; unerring, certain, sure, positive, fixed; absolute, unfailing, infallible, inerrable.

3. accurate, exact, precise, close, faithful, strict; flawless, faultless, perfect, defectless, errorless, inerrant; factual, actual, literal, true to life; authentic, real, sound, valid; true, truthful, veracious.

4. sound, normal, rational, sober, sane; lucid, clear, logical, sensible, reasonable; competent, responsible, accountable.

5. healthy, healthful, well, fine, good, in the pink, in good health *or* spirits; fit, trim, in fine fettle, fit as a fiddle; robust, hale, vigorous, hearty, hardy, strong, energetic.
6. straight, in proper order, in good order *or* condition.
7. desirable, preferable, favorable, propitious, auspicious, promising, fortunate, opportune; convenient, suitable, appropriate, advantageous, beneficial; proper, *Fr. comme il faut,* fit, fitting, befitting, meet, apt, correct; seemly, becoming.
8. genuine, authentic, real, actual, true, rightful; lawful, legitimate, legal, licit.
9. dextral, dexter, on the right side, right-hand; right-handed, dexterous.
10. straight, direct, rectilinear, linear, lineal; straight as an arrow, in a beeline, as the crow flies.
—n. **11.** just claim, title, privilege, prerogative; authority, power, liberty, freedom, license; due, birthright, heritage, inheritance.
12. goodness, justness, justice, fairness, impartiality, equity, equitableness, reasonableness; righteousness, uprightness, integrity, virtuousness, virtue, rectitude, morality; honorableness, truth, truthfulness, nobleness, nobility, high-mindedness, scrupulousness, right-mindedness; honesty, honestness, *Inf.* straightforwardness, openness.
13. (*usu. all of property*) interest, concern, portion, share, part, stake; holding, possession, ownership.
14. accuracy, accurateness, exactness, exactitude, precision, preciseness; closeness, fidelity, faithfulness, conformity; truth, veracity, verity, veritableness; fact, actuality, factuality, literalness; authenticity, validity, validness; flawlessness, inerrancy, faultlessness, perfection.
15. correctness, unerringness, inerrableness, infallibleness, unfailingness; absoluteness, certainty, sureness, positiveness, definiteness, fixedness.
16. by rights in fairness, justly, fairly, equitably, honestly.
—adv. **17.** straight, directly; in a straight line, in a beeline, as the crow flies.
18. quite, completely, entirely, totally, wholly, all the way.
19. immediately, promptly, quickly, instantly.
20. exactly, precisely, just.
21. rightfully, lawfully, legitimately, legally, licitly; uprightly, righteously, virtuously, morally, ethically; honorably, nobly, high-mindedly, scrupulously, right-mindedly.
22. correctly, accurately, properly, suitably, fittingly, befittingly, appropriately, aptly.
23. advantageously, beneficially, favorably, well, propitiously, fortunately, auspiciously, opportunely.
24. right and left on every side, from all directions, one after another.
25. right away *or* **off** straight off *or* away, point-blank; immediately, promptly, at once, forthwith, without delay, *Sl.* pronto, instantly, right this minute, on the spot; quickly, swiftly, apace, speedily, summarily, before you can say "Jack Robinson," before you can turn around.
—v. **26.** correct, set right, make right, set *or* make straight, redress, rectify; amend, emend, remedy, straighten out, fix, repair; doctor, cure, mend, touch up; improve, better, ameliorate, meliorate; reform, restore, rehabilitate, readjust; adjust, alter, change, modify.
27. do justice to, avenge, vindicate, take vengeance for; repay, requite, retaliate, get back at, revenge.

righteous, *adj.* **1.** blameless, pure at heart, incorrupt, good, guiltless; virtuous, holy, saintly, unerring, taintless; upright, noble, sterling, faultless; goodly, moral, scrupulous, clean-living; saintly, innocent, angelic, sinless, stainless, unspotted, unsoiled, unsullied; pious, godly, God-fearing, reverent; solemn, devout, religious, believing, heavenly-minded, spiritual; self-righteous, pietistic, smug, sanctimonious, *Inf.* goody-goody.
2. justifiable, equitable, fair, right; rightful, legitimate, reasonable, proper; defensible, supportable, well-founded, well-grounded, suitable.
3. just, honest, trustworthy, reputable, irreproachable, above suspicion; worthy, honorable, exemplary, meritorious, laudable, deserving, commendable, praiseworthy; consecrated, sacred, sanctified.

righteousness, *n.* **1.** blamelessness, goodness, virtuousness, holiness, saintliness, nobleness, honor, reputability, faithfulness; purity, innocence, virtue, honesty, integrity, probity, rectitude, morality, uprightness, incorruptibility, decency; scrupulousness, impeccability, stainlessness; reverence, veneration, devotion, consecration, dedication; piety, sanctity, godliness, devoutness, religiousness; religiosity, sanctimony, sanctimoniousness.
2. justice, fairness, equity, rightfulness, equitability, justness, legitimateness, legitimacy, reasonableness.

rightful, *adj.* **1.** legitimate, legal, licit, lawful; within the law, by law, de jure, legally correct; decreed, ordained, prescribed, mandated; proper, right, correct.
2. valid, genuine, unspurious, real, *Inf.* for real, *Inf.* honest-to-goodness *or* honest-to-gosh; true, authentic, authenticated, *Inf.* true-blue, sincere, unfaked.
3. fair, just, equitable; ethical, proper, moral; good, true, scrupulous; honest, straight, *Inf.* square, *Inf.* fair and square. See also **righteous** (*defs.* **1, 2**).
4. deserved, merited, earned; proper, due, well-deserved, (*of punishment*) condign, fitting, appropriate, apt, suitable, meet.

rigid, *adj.* **1.** stiff, hard, inflexible, unflexible, nonflexible, unbendable, unbending, unyielding; inelastic, unplastic, nonpliant, unmalleable, nonmalleable; tight, tense, taut, *Inf.* stiff as a poker, *Inf.* stiff as a ramrod.
2. fixed, set, firm, immovable, unalterable, unchangeable, unvarying, hard and fast, ironclad; undeviating, unswerving, resolute, steadfast, resolved, determined, tenacious, dogged, persevering, unrelenting, relentless, implacable, inexorable, never-say-die, diehard; hard-core, inveterate, absolute, unqualified, unmitigated.
3. strict, severe, stern, austere, spartan, harsh, *Inf.* hard as nails, tough; uncompromising, inflexible, *Inf.* set in one's ways, narrow-minded, close-minded; ultraconservative, strait-laced, *Sl.* straight, on the straight and narrow; unadaptable, unaccommodating, unconformable, nonconforming, noncompliant, uncompliant, noncooperative, uncooperative; stubborn, obstinate, pig-headed, mulish, obdurate, headstrong, willful.
4. demanding, exacting, rigorous, stringent, close, tight; scientific, mathematical, nice, accurate, exact, precise, literal, to the letter; well-defined, definite, clear-cut; cut and dried, structured, formal.

rigmarole, *n.* **1.** nonsense, falderal, gibberish, babble, babbling, babblement, *Fr. bavardage*; twaddle, twaddling, *Both Brit.* twattle, twattling; blather, blathering, drivel, driveling, drool, drooling; jargon, *Sl.* jive, Greek, *Chiefly Southern U.S.* Choctaw; hocus-pocus, mumbo jumbo, abracadabra, fiddle-dedee; moonshine, gobbledegook, foolish humbug, foam, froth, bunkum *or* buncombe, *Sl.* bunk, *Sl.* blah; flummery, *Inf.* hokum, *Sl.* applesauce, *Sl.* eyewash; rubbish, *Sl.* tripe, refuse, *Dial.* culch, chaff, trash, *Inf.* truck, trumpery; tommyrot, *Inf.* rot, *Sl.* garbage, *Sl.* crap, *Sl.* crock, *Sl.* bull; balderdash, hogwash, swill, *Sl.* horsefeathers; stuff, stuff and nonsense, *Inf.* bosh, *Brit. Inf.* gammon, *Brit. Sl.* tosh; fudge, foolishness, folly, amphigory; footle, *Inf.* malarkey, *Sl.* bushwa, *Sl.* baloney, *Sl.* bilge *or* bilge water, *Sl.* meshugaas, *Scot. and North Eng.* haver; poppycock, *Inf.* fiddle-faddle, *Inf.* piffle, *Inf.* hooey, *Inf.* kibosh, *Inf.* flapdoodle; idle talk, *Inf.* gab, *Sl.* gas, palaver, palavering, palaverment; claptrap, rodomontade, fustian, bombast, rant, *Sl.* hot air; Jabberwocky, jabber, jabbering, prate, prating; patter, pattering, gabble, gabbling; clack, clacking, clatter, clattering, rattling, *Sl.* running off *or* on at the mouth; chatter, chattering, prattle, prattling, chippering, cackle, cackling; chit-chat, chitter-chatter, small talk, *Anglo-Indian.* bukh.

2. elaborate procedure, involved ceremony, pomposity, affectation; red tape, excessive formality, protocol, bureaucracy, complicated routine; bother, pain, annoyance, *Inf.* hassle.

rigor, *n.* **1.** rigorousness, rigorism, strictness, stringency, closeness, tightness; rigidity, rigidness, inflexibility, inflexibleness, unbendingness, stiffness, formality, formalness; severity, severeness, harshness, toughness, roughness, asperity, hardness, sternness, grimness; unyieldingness, relentlessness, unrelentingness, implacability, implacableness, inexorability, inexorableness; domination, iron hand *or* rod, oppression, repression, despotism, tyranny, absolutism, autocracy, dictatorship.

2. austerity, hardship, privation, lack, need; suffering, affliction, trouble, burden.

3. accuracy, accurateness, exactness, exactitude, precision, preciseness, niceness, meticulousness, punctiliousness; scrupulousness, painstakingness, care, carefulness, conscientiousness.

4. (*all of weather or climate*) inclemency, inclementness, severeness, severity, harshness; storminess, cold, coldness, bitterness, wintriness.

rigorous, *adj.* **1.** strict, stringent, severe, stern, austere, spartan, harsh, rough, tough; rigid, hard, inflexible, unflexible, nonflexible, uncompromising; stiff, formal, structured; unbendable, unbending, unyielding, not giving an inch; inelastic, unplastic, nonpliant, unmalleable, nonmalleable; fixed, set, firm, immovable, unalterable, unchangeable, unvarying, hard and fast, ironclad, absolute; undeviating, unswerving, persevering, unrelenting, relentless, implacable, inexorable; remorseless, pitiless, merciless, unsparing, unforgiving, hard-hearted, stony-hearted, cold-hearted; dominating, domineering, controlling, ironhanded, oppressive, repressive, despotic, tyrannical, autocratic, dictatorial.

2. exact, precise, accurate, literal, to the letter, nice, scientific, mathematical; exacting, demanding, close, painstaking, meticulous; difficult, arduous, strenuous, laborious, wearisome, exhausting, trying.

3. (*all of weather or climate*) inclement, bad, stormy, rain, windy; chilly, raw, bitter, biting, cold, nippy, freezing, frigid, arctic, icy, snowy, wintry.

rile, *v.* **1.** irritate, annoy, irk, vex, pique, peeve, nettle, chafe, get on [s.o.'s] nerves, tread on [s.o.'s] toes, *Inf.* aggravate, *Inf.* miff, *Inf.* give [s.o.] a pain, *Inf.* rub [s.o.] the wrong way, *Inf.* get under [s.o.'s] skin, *Inf.* get in [s.o.'s] hair; exasperate, ruffle, disturb, disquiet, discountenance, put out, try [s.o.'s] patience, *Inf.* put [s.o.'s] nose out of joint, get, *Sl.* get [s.o.'s] goat.

2. anger, incense, raise [s.o.'s] ire, get [s.o.'s] back up, *Inf.* get [s.o.'s] Irish *or* dander up, *Inf.* burn [s.o.] up, *Sl.* tick [s.o.] off, *Sl.* tee [s.o.] off.

3. (*all of water, etc.*) muddy, cloud, becloud; agitate, disturb, shake up, stir up, churn up; roil.

rill, *n.* stream, brook, creek, *Dial.* crick, *Dial.* kill, runnel, branch. See **rivulet**.

rim, *n.* **1.** border, perimeter, periphery, edge, skirt, fringe, hem; lip, verge, brink, brim, brow; curb, ledge, sill, threshold; circumference, circuit, compass, ambit, margin, frame, outline; confine *or* confines, bound *or* bounds, limit *or* limits, bourn, pale, extremity, termination, end; city limits, outer limits, outskirts, purlieu, suburbs, *Fr. banlieue*.

—*v.* **2.** edge, skirt, verge, line, hem, frame, bound, margin, marginate.

rind, *n.* peel, skin, integument, tegument, tegman, *Biol.* investment, outer layer, *Bot.* pericarp, *Bot.* epicarp, bark, *Bot.* cortex; hull, husk, shuck, shell, pod, sheath, casing, case; pellicle, membrane, involucre, coating, coat, film; cover, covering, *Anat., Zool.* capsule, crust, incrustation, scale.

ring[1], **1.** band, wedding band, engagement *or* diamond ring, symbol of love; earring, bracelet, armlet, anklet; loop, eye, eyelet; grommet, becket, ferrule, washer.

2. circle, circlet, round, roundlet, roundel, disk, annulus, annulation, hoop, noose, *Archaic.* orb; belt, girdle, girth, sash, waistband, cummerbund, cestus, baldric, *Archaic.* zone, *Poetic.* cincture; wristband, cuff, *Eccles.* maniple, handcuff, manacle; collar, collarband, torque, torc, neckband, necklace; headband, ribbon, frontlet, fillet, hatband, sweatband; crown, wreath, garland, coronet, diadem, halo, corona, aureole, nimbus; circuit, stripe, strip, streak, striation, line, bar, *Archit.* annulet, *Archit.* bandelet, *Archit.* square and rabbet; coil, spiral, whorl, volution.

3. gang, mob, syndicate; bloc, cartel, combination, *Inf.* combine, monopoly, *Commerce.* trust; camorra, camarilla, junto, cabal, confederacy, secret society; sect, faction, order, side, party, (*in China*) tong; coterie, clique, clan, knot, set, *Inf.* crowd, in crowd, *Inf.* bunch; club, society, lodge, guild, fraternity, brotherhood, sorority, sisterhood, sodality, community, school; company, troop, troupe, team, crew, pack; group, league, alliance, union, coalition, confederation, federation, association, affiliation, organization, Bund, *Ger. Verein*.

4. arena, rink, circus, pit, cockpit, lists, *Gk. Antiquity.* palestra; field, track, gridiron, course, turf; gymnasium, auditorium, stage, platform; amphitheater, bowl, coliseum, hippodrome, stadium, bear garden.

—*v.* **5.** encircle, circle, loop, belt, girdle, gird, compass, *Archaic.* orb; circumscribe, circumnavigate, circumambulate, circumvent, span, travel *or* go around; surround, environ, ensphere, encompass, engird, envelop, embrace; enclose, close off, hem in, hedge in, fence in, confine; barricade, blockade, block off.

6. coil, wind, spiral; curl, loop, eddy, gurge; rotate, revolve, whirl, twirl, reel, wheel, spin, gyrate, swivel, pivot, pirouette, circumrotate, circumvolve, turn around.

ring[2], *v.* **1.** toll, peal, chime, ding, dong; jingle, tinkle, clink; clang, jangle, twang; resound, reverberate, echo, reecho, resonate, vibrate, trill.

2. knoll, knell, herald, signal, signalize, annunciate, usher in *or* out, celebrate, commemorate, honor, hymn; sing out, cry out, yell, shout from the rooftops, proclaim, announce, broadcast, advertise, make known; blare, trumpet, bruit, fill the air.

—*n.* **3.** peal, knoll, knell, chime, ding, dong, dingdong, ringing; tintinnabulation, tinkle, jingle, clink; clang, clangor, jangle, twang; sounding, sound, reverberation, resonance, echoing, vibration.

ringed, *adj.* **1.** striped, striated, streaked, annu-

late, annulated, *Archit.* banded.
2. circled, hooped, belted, girded, cinctured, compassed; encircled, encompassed, engirt, begirt, circumscribed, embraced, *Archaic.* orbed; surrounded, enclosed, hemmed in, hedged in, fenced in, confined.
3. ringlike, ring-shaped, disklike, discoid, hoop, hooplike, annular, *Archaic.* orblike; circular, round.

rinse, *v.* **1.** wash, bathe, lave, clean, cleanse, rinse out; shampoo, (*of clothes*) launder, lather, soap, mundify, deterge; absterge, wipe, swab, mop, scrub.
2. wet, sponge, flush, flush out, irrigate, shower, splash, swash, slosh; dip, immerse, submerge, dunk; soak, steep, drench, imbue, saturate.
—*n.* **3.** washing, bathing, lavation, lavage, laving, cleaning, cleansing, ablution; shampoo, shampooing, (*of clothes*) laundering, lathering, soaping, mundifying, deterging; abstersion, absterging, wipe, wiping, swab, swabbing, mopping, scrub, scrubbing.
4. wetting, sponge bath, sponging, flushing, flushing out, irrigation, irrigating, shower, showering, splashing, swashing, sloshing; dip, dipping, immersion, immersing, submersion, submerging, dunk, dunking; soak, soaking, steep, steeping, drench, drenching, imbuement, imbuing, saturation, saturating.
5. wash, bath, rinsing, drench, steep, soak, water, wash water, bath water; suds, foam.
6. tint, dye, preparation, cream rinse.

riot, *n.* **1.** brawl, broil, imbroglio, melee, fray, affray, fracas, free-for-all, donnybrook, scuffle, street fight, *Inf.* rumble, *Inf.* knock-down-drag-out.
2. civil disorder *or* strife, anarchy, mob-law, street-fighting, fighting in the street; revolt, rebellion, insurrection, insurgency, uprising, outbreak; chaos, pandemonium, bedlam; disorder, confusion.
3. uproar, outburst, disturbance, commotion, ado, *Inf.* to-do, bother, pother, stir, fuss, *Inf.* foofaraw; tumult, turbulence; rumpus, *Inf.* ruckus, hubbub, hullaballoo.
4. profligacy, dissipation, indulgence, incontinence, intemperance, licentiousness, libertinsm, debauchery; loose *or* fast *or* high living, life in the fast lane, fastness, looseness, wildness.
5. revelry, carousal, merrymaking, merriment, jollification, *Inf.* high jinks, *Sl.* whoopee; drinking, imbibing, tippling, toping, *Inf.* boozing, *Sl.* painting the town red, *Sl.* barhopping, *Brit. Sl.* pub-crawling *or* doing the pub-crawl.
6. (*all of color*) brilliant display, flourish, flash, splash, show.
—*v.* **7.** fight, brawl, create a disturbance, make trouble, *Inf.* raise hell, *Inf.* raise Cain, *Inf.* raise a ruckus; rage, storm, rampage, go on a rampage, run amuck *or* amok, go berserk; loot, pillage, sack, burn, lay waste.
8. rebel, revolt, rise up, rise up in arms, mount the barricades; kick over the traces; run riot, take to the streets.
9. carouse, revel, wassail, roister, bouse, make merry, cut loose, let loose, step out, *Inf.* live it up, *Inf.* party, whoop it up, *Sl.* make whoopee; go on a spree, make the rounds, *Sl.* tie one on, *Sl.* go on a drunk *or* binge *or* bender *or* toot *or* bust *or* jag, *Sl.* paint the town red, *Sl.* barhop, *Brit. Sl.* pub-crawl; debauch, dissipate, wanton, sow wild oats, have one's fling; overindulge, overdo, burn the candle at both ends, not know when one has had enough, not know when to stop.
10. (*all of vegetables*) luxuriate, flourish, grow rank *or* lush, grow like a weed.

rioter, *n.* rowdy, brawler, tough, hooligan, affrayer, street fighter, street-fighting man; anarchist, malcontent, *U.S.* weatherman, *Fr. frondeur*; agitator, agitprop, troublemaker, instigator, inciter, provoker; demagogue, rabble-rouser; firebrand, incendiary; rebel, revolter, revolutionary, insurrectionist, insurgent, sans-culotte.

riotous, *adj.* **1.** obstreperous, unruly, disorderly, out of order, out of hand, out of control, uncontrollable, ungovernable, unmanageable; wild, rowdy, brawly; turbulent, tumultuous; chaotic, anarchic, lawless, pandemoniac.
2. rebellious, insurgent, insurrectionary, revolutionary, rebel, seditious, factious; mutinous, insubordinate.
3. dissolute, dissipated, debauched, wanton, libertine, licentious, abandoned, rampant; fast, loose, fast-living, free-living; orgiastic, corybantic, saturnalian.
4. boisterous, uproarious, rampageous, rambunctious, roisterous, rollicking, *Inf.* rip-roaring, rough-and-tumble, *Inf.* harum-scarum, *Brit. Inf.* mafficking.
5. *Informal.* hilarious, too funny for words, screaming, *Inf.* rich, *Inf.* priceless, *Inf.* sidesplitting.

rip, *v.* **1.** tear, rend, tear apart, put asunder, shred; cut, slit, slash, lacerate; rupture, separate, sever, dissever, cleave; split, rive, divide, halve, cut in two, quarter; hack, gash, gore, score.
2. tear off, pull off, detach, remove, unfix, disjoin; yank off, pick, withdraw, extract; peel, strip, bark, husk, skin.
3. *Informal.* speed, scuttle, *Inf.* hustle, flee, skip, tear; rush, hurry, gallop, *Inf.* go hellbent for leather, *Inf.* zip; fly, *Inf.* zoom, *Inf.* go like lightning, *Inf.* go like the dickens; clip, bound, cut along, scurry.
4. **rip into** *Informal.* attack, assail, besiege, oppugn; harry, harass, bombard; malign, impugn, vituperate, vilify, vilipend, calumniate, slander, abuse.
5. **rip off** *Slang.* **a.** steal, pilfer, shoplift, thieve, purloin, rob; pocket, snatch, loot, *Sl.* swipe, *Sl.* hock, *Sl.* pinch. **b.** swindle, cheat, humbug, victimize, trick, mislead, deceive; juggle, ensnare, fleece, dupe, cozen; sell, gyp, palm off, hoodwink, bamboozle.
—*n.* **6.** rend, tear, crack; cut, laceration, slit, slash, score; split, fissure, rift, cleavage; severance, breach, rupture, fracture; cleft, break, fault.

ripe, *adj.* **1.** grown, mature, aged, seasoned, well-aged, full-aged, tempered; mellow, ripened, in full bloom, in full flower, out, blooming; full-blown, golden, full, *Anglo-Indian.* pukka, ruddy, soft, fully developed.
2. experienced, seasoned, veteran; responsible, sensible, dependable, reliable; prudent, judicious, sage, wise, sagacious, provident; worldly-wise, worldly, knowing, sophisticated, not born yesterday.
3. advanced, matured, developed; perfect, full, full-fledged, full-scale, full-grown; finished, polished, refined, consummate.
4. prepared, ready, set, primed, all ready, all set, on the mark; fit, good and ready, groomed, coached, *Inf.* prepped; planned, prearranged, well-prepared, provided.
5. auspicious, favorable, propitious, promising; encouraging, timely, opportune, seasonable; golden, bright, felicitous.

ripen, *v.* **1.** age, season, develop, *Dial.* ripe; mature, maturate, bear fruit, come to fruition; mellow, soften, reach maturity; bloom, blossom, flower, *Archaic.* blow, flourish.
2. become, change into, turn into, fall into, slide into, glide into; evolve, transform, develop, grow into, get to be.

riposte, *n.* **1.** retort, rejoinder, return, repartee, sally, comeback, snappy comeback, barb, zinger, *Inf.*

backchat; witty reply, quip, bon mot, mot; answer, reply, response, replication, acknowledgment.

2. retaliation, reciprocation, like for like; countermeasure, counterstroke, counterblow, counterattack.

—v. **3.** retort, rejoin, return, come back, flash back, *Inf.* crack back, *Inf.* shoot back; answer, reply, respond, acknowledge.

4. retaliate, reciprocate, reply in kind, return the compliment, give tit for tat, give like for like, give measure for measure, give a *quid pro quo*; pay [s.o.] in his own coin, *Inf.* give [s.o.] a dose *or* taste of his own medicine.

ripple, *v.* **1.** wave, undulate, purl, ruffle; trill, lap, swash, wash, slap, splash, swish; gurgle, guggle, babble, burble, murmur.

2. ruffle, curl, rumple, crumple, dimple, crinkle; crimp, fret, crisp; fold, ruff, wrinkle, cockle, twill, crease.

—n. **3.** wave, undulation, wavelet, ruffling, riffle, ripplet, rimple; swish, splash, trill, purl, trickle, *Naut.* cat's-paw; babble, burble, gurgle, lap.

rise, *v.* **1.** get up, arise, levitate, ascend, uprise; get on one's feet, leap up, jump up, spring up, bolt up; clamber up, climb up, scale, go up, *Inf.* shin up, *Inf.* shinny up, *Inf.* shimmy up; scramble up, scrabble up, work one's way up, escalade, surmount; upgo, upsurge, upswarm, upheave, upswing.

2. awaken, get up, waken, wake up, get out of bed, *Inf.* rise and shine; greet the day, *Inf.* roll out, *Inf.* turn out, *Sl.* hit the deck; *Sl.* up and at 'em.

3. ascend, move upward, mount, climb; soar, zoom, take off, leave the ground; rocket, skyrocket, jet; kite, float, glide, plane, hang, hover; tower, spire, spiral, rear, stand.

4. slant upward, tilt upward, slope, grade, tip; uprise, go uphill, climb; advance, elevate, heighten, step up, go upstairs; boost, lift, raise, erect.

5. escalate, step up, go up, pick up; skyrocket, *Inf.* sky, loft, go out of sight.

6. spring up, grow, shoot up, sprout; blossom, bud, flower, bloom, burgeon.

7. increase, enlarge, spread, widen, broaden; bloat, swell, wax, balloon, grow, distend; multiply, proliferate, pullulate, boom, breed; intensify, magnify, aggrandize; strengthen, gain strength, steepen; snowball, crescendo, mushroom; accrue, accumulate, add.

8. progress, improve, better; get ahead, make headway, forward; succeed, turn out well, batten, boom; thrive, prosper, bloom, flower; make good, *Inf.* make it, go far, work one's way up, make one's way, *Inf.* get ahead, climb the ladder of success, come out on top; cut a swath, make a breakthrough, set the world on fire, arrive, make the scene.

9. stiffen, horripilate, bristle, stand on end; prickle, stick up, cock up, start up.

10. revolt, rebel, insurrectionize, upheave, overthrow, mutiny, subvert; resist, take up arms, defy, break forth; wage war, strike, take the law into one's hands, mount the barricades; disobey, fly in the face of, refuse, kick over the traces.

11. protrude, project, protuberate, stick out; swell, bulge, blister, nodulate; jut, beetle, hang out, hang over, overhang; impend, extend.

12. occur, happen, take place, come up; come, go, pass, come off, come about, come to pass; crop up, eventuate, ensue, take effect; befall, betide, *Archaic.* bechance.

13. originate, begin, commence, start, be born; issue, proceed, arise, spring from, head; emanate, flow from, come from, exsurge, take rise; break out, erupt, spring up; dawn, usher in, set in, open, initiate, inaugurate; grow out of, come forth, ensue from, stem from, sprout from, come out of, follow from.

14. appear, materialize, come into view, show up, make an appearance, turn up; emerge, arise, manifest, reveal oneself, expose oneself; enter, peep out, come to light, appear on the scene, appear on the horizon, show one's face; loom, break in, *Motion Pictures.* fade in, pop up, flare up, flash.

15. return from the dead, return to life, resurrect, resurge; be born again, live again, revive, come alive, reanimate, revivify, reincarnate, come back.

—v. **16.** ascension, ascent, rising, uprising, upgoing; climb, climbing, mount, mounting, escalade, clamber; takeoff, rocketing, soaring, leaving the ground, zooming, gaining ground *or* altitude; levitation, hanging, hovering.

17. elevation, increase, steepening; gain, expansion, extension, dilation, enlargement, spread; addition, augmentation, aggrandizement; advance, advancement, progression, progress; headway, march, growth, development; increment, accretion, accrual, accumulation; multiplication, proliferation, breeding, pullulation, propagation; intensification, magnification, enhancement; escalation, inflation, uptrend, upping, upturn, upbend; upsweep, upswing, upcurve, upsurge, upgrowth.

18. slope, acclivity, climb, incline, upslope; upgrade, uphill, uplift, upclimb, uprise; ramp, gradient, bank; high ground, upland, highland, knoll, hillock, hill; eminence, prominence, elevation.

19. origin, source, spring, fountain, fount, fountainhead, head, start; beginning, commencement, outset, inception, incipience, opening, dawn; birth, nativity, genesis; onset, outbreak, exordium; debut, coming out, inauguration; prelude, introduction, overture.

20. appearance, materialization, emergence, coming, apparition, arising; incarnation, revelation, presentation, realization, manifestation; avatar, theophany, forthcoming, epiphany; showing, disclosure, uncovering, unfolding, opening, exposure.

21. **give rise to** produce, cause, effect, bring out; bring into being, institute, set afloat; bear, yield, spawn, turn out.

rising, *adj.* **1.** advancing, coming, approaching, nigh; ascending, uprising, mounting, accelerating, increasing; lifting, climbing, soaring, wafted.

—n. **2.** advance, approach, drawing nigh *or* near; ascension, ascent, uplifting, climbing, mounting.

3. uprising, revolt, revolution, rebellion, sedition, insurgence, mutiny, peasant revolt, jacquerie; insurrection, outbreak, outburst, riot; resistance, insubordination, defiance; strike, walkout, sit-down, sit-down strike, sit-in.

4. prominence, eminence, projection, protuberancy, protuberance, protrusion, outcrop; bulge, swelling, hump, tumescence; mound, rise, bump; hill, height, elevation.

risk, *n.* **1.** hazard, peril, danger, jeopardy; endangerment, imperilment, liability, vulnerability, susceptibility, exposure; precariousness, insecurity, unpredictability, uncertainty; chance, big chance, long shot; speculation, plunge, gamble, leap in the dark.

—v. **2.** endanger, expose to danger, hazard, peril, imperil, jeopardize, jeopard, put in jeopardy; menace, threaten; take one's life in one's hands, play with fire, skate on thin ice, walk a tightrope, go up without a parachute.

3. dare, venture, chance, gamble, take a chance; try, attempt, tempt fate, *Sl.* give a whirl, *Inf.* stick one's chin *or* neck out, lay *or* put [s.t.] on the line, put one's head in the lion's mouth; throw caution to the winds,

Sl. go for broke, *Sl.* shoot the works, hazard all; plunge, *Inf.* take a flier, (*both of finance*) speculate, sell short.

risky, *adj.* perilous, dangerous, fraught with danger, chancy, *Sl.* dicey, touch-and-go, jeopardous, *Archaic.* parlous; venturesome, venturous, adventuresome, adventurous, daring, bold, foolhardy, daredevil; treacherous, deceptive, unreliable, untrustworthy; menacing, threatening, minatory, minacious; dubious, uncertain, unpredictable, unsure, *Inf.* iffy, questionable, up in the air; scary, *Sl.* hairy, frightening, disquieting, *Inf.* spooky; precarious, unsound, unsafe, shaky; ticklish, delicate, touchy, thorny, difficult, critical; ominous, inauspicious, unfavorable.

risqué, *adj.* off-color, indelicate, improper, improprietous, indecorous; offensive, unseemly, tasteless, in poor taste, indecent; broad, coarse, earthy, Rabelaisian, crude, rough, unrefined; not fit for mixed company, not fit for delicate ears, not fit to print, unprintable, censorable; racy, salty, spicy, suggestive; smutty, *Sl.* raunchy, *Inf.* blue, obscene, scabrous, Fescennine, salacious, pornographic, X-rated, scatological; gross, ribald, bawdy, lewd, erotic, sexy; shocking, shameless, naughty, wicked, terrible; nasty, nasty-minded, vulgar, dirty, filthy, foul, foulmouthed, disgusting.

rite, *n.* ritual, observance, ceremony, ceremonial, solemnity, solemnization, celebration; public worship, liturgy; exercise, exercises, service, office, performance, duty; custom, practice, habit, form, formality, convention, usage, wont, consuetude; tradition, institution, ordinance, way, prevalence, time-honored practice.

ritz, *n.* **1.** ostentation, ostentatious *or* pretentious display, *Inf.* swank, splash, flourish, flashiness, frills; spectacle, show, parade, pageantry, pomp; pomposity, pompousness, inflation, peacockery, foppery; vaunting, flaunting, affectation; semblance, pretension, pretense; gilding, window dressing, *Inf.* front, veneer.

2. put on the ritz *Slang.* assume airs, *Sl.* put on the dog, put on airs; pose, posture, peacock; do for effect, make a show of.

—*v.* **3.** *Slang.* snub, treat with condescension *or* indifference, turn up one's nose at, not trouble oneself about, *Inf.* cold-shoulder, *Inf.* high-hat; disregard, overlook, slight.

ritzy, *adj.* *Slang.* elegant, high-class, *Sl.* classy, high-toned, *Sl.* tony; posh, luxurious, deluxe, luxury, sumptuous, custom, special; fancy, *Inf.* swank, *Inf.* swanky, *Sl.* swell, *Sl.* snazzy, *Sl.* sharp, *Sl.* sharp as a tack; suave, urbane, sophisticated, chichi, chic, stylish, cosmopolitan; dressy, flashy, elaborate, flowery, showy; ostentatious, decorative, pretentious, overdone, embellished.

rival, *n.* **1.** competitor, vier, opponent, *Rare.* corrival; emulator, challenger, contender, contestant, bidder, aspirant; candidate, participant, entrant; antagonist, adversary, foe, enemy, assailant; opposition, opposer, oppositionist, competition, other side; disputant, controversialist; fighter, battler, jouster, competer, *U.S. Inf.* go-getter.

—*adj.* **2.** competitive, vying, emulative, competing, *Rare.* corrival; striving, emulous, ambitious, aggressive, dog-eat-dog, cutthroat; opposing, contentious, antagonistic, conflicting; combative, ready to fight, competitory.

—*v.* **3.** compete, vie, contend, strive, struggle, fight, grapple, jockey for position; combat, fight, battle, spar, joust, tilt, fence; meet, lock horns, clash, collide, encounter, engage; throw *or* toss one's hat in the ring; contest, oppose, challenge, play against, pit oneself against, try to beat [s.o.] or [s.t.], defend one's title.

4. equal, match, compare with, parallel; outdo, surpass, exceed, overtop, transcend; outclass, outrank, outrate, be superior to; be a cut above, be head and shoulders above, outmatch.

rivalry, *n.* competition, emulation, vying; contest, game, meet, meeting, match, one-on-one, tug of war; contention, challenge, opposition; bout, tournament, encounter, engagement; race, run, run for one's money; strife, struggle, conflict, clash, fight, infighting; *Sl.* rat race, *Inf.* one-upmanship, *Inf.* keeping up with the Joneses.

rive, *v.* **1.** rend, sever, sunder, split, splinter. See **rend** (*defs.* **1, 2**).

2. harrow, distress, injure, wound, tear at, tug at, *Inf.* discombobulate. See **rend** (*def.* **3**).

river, *n.* branch, tributary, reach, estuary, rivulet, freshet; waterway, watercourse, stream, wadi, arroyo, creek, *Dial.* crick; affluent, anabranch, feeder, race, cataract, cascade; flow, current, torrent, flood, spate, rapids, flux, drift; tide, onrush, run, surge, rush, gush; discharge, overflow, burst, storm; eddy, backstream, swirl, countercurrent, backflow, backwash.

rivet, *n.* **1.** bolt, anchor, pin, tack, button.

—*v.* **2.** fasten, secure, fasten securely, bolt down, batten, affix, clinch, pinion; attach, link, clasp, lock, fix, fix firmly, make fast, lock *or* bolt in place, bond.

3. concentrate on, give attention to, focus on, focus attention on, direct one's attention to, study closely, peruse carefully, examine closely; put one's mind on, brood over, be engrossed in, occupy the mind *or* thoughts with; scrutinize, contemplate, regard, watch, be absorbed in, give exclusive attention to; keep the eyes on, stare at, keep in sight, watch unblinkingly.

rivulet, *n.* brook, stream, brooklet, streamlet, creek, *Dial.* crick, *Dial.* kill, rill, rindle, run, runnel, runlet, *Dial.* rundle, *Brit. Dial.* beck, *Brit. Dial.* gill *or* ghyll, *Scot. and North Eng.* sike *or* syke, *Scot. and North Eng.* burn *or* bourn *or* bourne; channel, branch, waterway, watercourse.

road, *n.* **1.** street, thoroughfare, main road, *Inf.* drag, *Brit. Sl.* toby, artery, highroad, roadway; avenue, boulevard, concourse, strip, pavement; lane, drive, terrace, circle, row; alley, by-path, byway, byroad, by-street, side road *or* street.

2. highway, turnpike, pike, toll road, state highway; freeway, *Brit.* clearway, expressway, parkway, causeway, throughway, *U.S. Inf.* interstate; speedway, autobahn, superhighway.

3. way, course, method, means; route, path, avenue, lane; channel, in, entrée, access, approach; admission, admittance, entrance, entry, entryway, inlet, ingress.

4. burn up the road *Slang.* speed, race, fly, drive fast; go like a shot, go hellbent, *Sl.* burn rubber, go like lightning *or* greased lightning, outstrip the wind.

5. on the road driving, cruising, traveling, journeying, on a trip *or* voyage; on tour, on the circuit, on a road trip.

roam, *v.* **1.** wander, stray, range, rove, wend, drift, forage, browse; loiter, dally, dawdle, *Inf.* window-shop, *Inf.* loaf along, *Inf.* lallygag; straggle, prowl, stalk, cruise, shuffle along, pad along, toddle, toddle on; jaunt, traipse, bowl along, gad, gad about, flit, go aimlessly, gallivant; meander, circumambulate, stroll, saunter, perambulate.

2. wander *or* pass over, explore, scout, trek, walk *or* range over, tramp, travel, journey, traverse, cross, pass through; nomadize, peregrinate, tramp through, *Inf.* knock about, go from pillar to post; ramble, jog along, course, trudge, plod on, wend one's way, make one's way.

roar, *v.* **1.** cry, howl, yowl, scream, shriek, wail;

shout, *Inf.* holler, squall, yell, bellow; growl, snarl; vroom.

2. laugh loudly, guffaw, howl with laughter, laugh hysterically.

3. growl, rumble, roll, thunder, clap; blare, sound, resound, boom, bang, crash; blast, explode, fulminate, detonate, blow up.

—n. 4. deep cry, howl, yowl, scream, shriek, wail; shout, *Inf.* holler, yell, bellow; growl, snarl; vroom.

5. rumble, roll, thunder, thunderclap, crash, blare, bang, boom; blast, explosion, fulmination, detonation, blowup.

6. loud laughter, *Inf.* belly laugh, guffaw, hysterical laughter.

roaring, *n.* 1. howling, yowling, shouting, *Inf.* hollering, yelling, bellowing; growling, snarling; rumbling, rolling, thundering; blaring, blasting, sounding, resounding, banging, booming.

—adj. 2. brisk, good, successful, profitable, prosperous, halcyon, halcyonic, halcyonian; booming, flourishing, prospering.

3. noisy, rackety, clamorous, clamoring, boisterous, obstreperous, unruly; disorderly, riotous, uproarious, tumultuous, turbulent, pandemonian, pandemonic, pandemoniac, pandemoniacal.

—adv. 4. very, really, extremely, completely, absolutely.

roast, *n.* 1. bake, cook, broil, grill, barbecue; brown, toast, dry, sun, sun-dry, parch; heat, torrefy, fire, calcine; char, sear, scorch, burn, singe, scald.

2. *Informal.* (*all often in jest*) ridicule, guy, poke fun at *or* of, make fun of, mock, tease, twit, *Inf.* kid; joke, jest, banter, badinage, chaff, *Inf.* josh, *Inf.* rib, *Inf.* fun; taunt, jeer, *Inf.* rag, gibe, scoff, deride; make a laughingstock out of, haze, abuse, humiliate, embarrass, make a fool of; ride, give [s.o.] a hard time, *Inf.* jump on, *Inf.* jump all over, *Sl.* get on [s.o.'s] case; criticize, pick apart, pick to pieces, *Inf.* pick holes in; shoot down, *Inf.* slam, *Inf.* knock, *Inf.* pan, *Sl.* put down, *Sl.* dump on; haul *or* rake over the coals, attack, flay, light into, *Inf.* lace *or* tear *or* rip into, *Sl.* blast, *Sl.* let [s.o.] have it with both barrels; excoriate, denounce, decry, disparage, belittle, depreciate, minimize.

rob, *v.* 1. burglarize, burgle, *Inf.* hold up, *Sl.* stick up, *Sl.* heist, break in; assault, strong-arm, *Inf.* mug, *Sl.* jump, *Sl.* roll.

2. steal, thieve, pilfer, purloin, finger, filch, *Inf.* snitch, cabbage, abstract, *Chiefly Brit.* prig, *Euph.* borrow; peculate, embezzle, misappropriate, pocket, shark; shoplift, *Sl.* boost, walk off *or* away with, *Euph.* remove, help oneself to, make free with; *All Sl.* pinch, hook, swipe, hustle, rip off, frisk, crook, cop, lift.

3. plunder, despoil, *Archaic.* spoil, spoliate, pillage, *Chiefly Scot.* reive; ravage, harry, rape, maraud, devastate, depredate; ransack, sack, loot, gut, fleece, strip, rifle; raid, foray, forage, prey on *or* upon; lay waste, desolate, wreak havoc upon.

4. pirate, freeboot, buccaneer, privateer, filibuster, waylay.

5. swindle, defraud, mulct, shark, cheat, fleece, *Inf.* flimflam, rook, bilk, *Inf.* welsh, *Archaic.* chouse, *Inf.* do out of, *Inf.* gyp, *Inf.* bunko, *Inf.* diddle, *Inf.* take, *Inf.* take [s.o.] for a ride, *Inf.* take [s.o.] to the cleaners, *Sl.* pluck, *Sl.* chisel, *Sl.* clip.

6. victimize, deceive, cozen, dupe, take in, take advantage of, *Inf.* euchre [s.o.] out of [s.t.]; put [s.t.] across *or* over on [s.o.], foist, palm off on, *Inf.* pull a fast one, *Sl.* screw, *Sl.* bag.

7. appropriate, expropriate, arrogate, usurp; commandeer, hijack, skyjack; plagiarize, copy, *Inf.* lift, *Inf.* crib, forge, counterfeit.

8. (*usu. of persons*) abduct, kidnap, *Sl.* snatch, make off with, carry off, rape, seize; (*usu. in reference to military service*) impress, press, conscript, *Naut.* shanghai, crimp.

robber, *n.* 1. burglar, thief, stealer, *Inf.* crook; housebreaker, *Sl.* cracksman, *Brit.* picklock, Raffles, sneak thief, cat burglar, *Inf.* second-story man; *Inf.* hold-up man, *Sl.* stickup man; mugger; safecracker, Jimmy Valentine.

2. petty thief, *Sl.* ripoff, pilferer, filcher, purloiner, shoplifter, *Sl.* ganef; *Psychol.* kleptomaniac; pickpocket, cutpurse, purse-snatcher, *Sl.* dip.

3. highwayman, footpad, *Sl.* yegg or yeggman, bandit, *Sp.* bandolero, *Southwest U.S.* ladrone, *Australian.* bushranger, brigand, picaroon, desperado; outlaw, gangster, criminal, mafioso; thug, ruffian, rogue, (*in India and Burma*) dacoit.

4. pirate, rover, viking, corsair, buccaneer, privateer; freebooter, rapparee, (*in the Scottish Highlands*) cateran; kidnaper, abductor, rustler, hijacker, skyjacker, air *or* sky pirate; predator.

5. poacher, deerjacker; smuggler, contrabandist, runner, bootlegger.

6. pillager, plunderer, marauder, despoiler, depredator, ransacker, sacker, looter, rifler, forager, raider.

7. swindler, fleecer, trickster, bilker, sharper, *Inf.* hawk, cardsharp, bunko steersman, blackleg; confidence man, con artist, flimflam artist, racketeer, highbinder, thimblerigger, *Brit. Sl.* magsman, *Australian.* spieler; defaulter, *Sl.* welsher; embezzler, peculator.

8. forger, counterfeiter, *Brit. Inf.* coiner; plagiarist, plagiarizer, *Inf.* cheater.

robbery, *n.* 1. burglary, theft, *Sl.* heist, break-in; *Inf.* holdup, *Sl.* stickup, *Sl.* hustle, *Inf.* mugging, *Sl.* jumping, *Sl.* rolling.

2. thievery, pilferage, pilfering, *Sl.* swiping, *Sl.* hustling, *Sl.* copping; peculation, embezzlement, misappropriation; purse-snatching, shoplifting, palming, *Sl.* boosting; smuggling, bootlegging.

3. brigandage, piracy, buccaneering, freebooting, banditry, highway robbery, *Obs.* latrociny, privateering, filibustering, *Inf.* (*usu. of cattle*) rustling.

4. plunder, plundering, plunderage, rapine, pillage, depredation, spoliation, despoliation, despoilment, *Obs.* direption, raven *or* ravin; ravaging, harrying, marauding, sacking, *Rare.* sackage, laying waste, devastation, desolation; raid, razzia, foray; foraging, looting, ravishment, seizure, grab, rape.

5. commandeering, hijacking, skyjacking, air *or* sky piracy; (*usu. of persons*) abduction, kidnapping, *Sl.* snatch, capture, impressment, conscription, man-stealing, child-stealing; (*all of animals*) poaching, deerjacking, petnapping, dognapping.

6. expropriation, appropriation, arrogation, usurpation, accroachment, assumption.

7. plagiarism, copying, *Inf.* cribbing, *Inf.* lifting, pirating.

8. dispossession, deprivation, deprival, divestiture, bereavement; confiscation, impoundment.

9. swindle, fraud, flimflam, confidence game, *Inf.* gyp, *Inf.* ripoff, thimblerigging.

robe, *n.* 1. gown, outer garment, vestment, *Archaic.* investment; cap and gown, academicals; pontificals, canonicals, cassock, surplice, scapular, *Eccles.* alb, *Eccles.* dalmatic, *Eccles.* chasuble, *Rom. Cath. Ch.* mantelletta; frock, habit; toga, praetexta, tunic, *Gk. Antiq.* chiton, kimono, sari, djellabah, *Archaic.* stole; cloak, mantle, pallium.

2. bathrobe, housecoat, *Fr. robe-de-chambre*, wrap-

per, dressing gown, peignoir, caftan, lounging robe, muumuu.
3. gown, evening gown, dinner gown *or* dress, long dress, cocktail gown *or* dress, dress, frock, fancy dress.
4. **robes** clothing, clothes, garments, *Archaic.* vesture, apparel, costume, garb, attire; *Chiefly Literary.* raiment, *Chiefly Literary.* vestments, habit, habiliments, *Inf.* gear, *Inf.* toggery, *Inf.* togs, *Inf.* duds, *Sl.* threads, *Sl.* rags; wardrobe, array, accouterment; livery, uniform.
5. blanket, covering, *Fr. couverture*, wrap, lap robe, buffalo robe.
—*v.* 6. gown, drape, enrobe, invest, clothe; vest, garb, attire, apparel, costume, habit, outfit, fit out, rig up *or* out; dress *or* dress up, adorn, *Archaic.* dight, array, bedizen, bedeck, deck out, *Sl.* dude up, *Sl.* swank up.
7. (*all of a robe*) don, put on, change into, slip on *or* into.

robot, *n.* **1.** automaton, mechanical being, mechanical man, machine, computer.
2. puppet, pawn, instrument, tool, cat's-paw, straw man; mouthpiece, figurehead, henchman, hireling; follower, minion, myrmidon.

robust, *adj.* **1.** vigorous, full of vigor, hearty, hardy, hale, hale and hearty, lusty, strong and healthy, bursting with health *or* vigor; energetic, full of energy, lively, full of life, active; sound, healthy, in good health, in good condition, *Inf.* in good shape, fit, physically fit, in fine fettle; stout, staunch, stanch, firm, sturdy, tough, iron, inured, hardened, *Inf.* tough as nails, *Inf.* hard as rock; powerful, potent, mighty, all-powerful, herculean, *Literary.* puissant.
2. stalwart, rugged, hefty, husky, burly, *Scot. and North Eng.* stiff, solid, well-knit; able-bodied, able, athletic, sinewy; muscular, brawny, strapping, huge, gigantic, broad-shouldered, powerfully-built, *Derog.* musclebound.
3. rough, crude, coarse; boisterous, robustious, rambunctious, rollicking, riotous, clamorous, tumultuous, noisy, loud, roaring, uproarious, unrestrained, rampageous, out of hand, out of order.
4. rich, rich-flavored, substantial, full-bodied, flavorful, full of flavor, full-flavored, flavorsome, flavorous, flavory, well-flavored; nutty, fruity, pungent.

rock¹, *n.* **1.** boulder, crag, tor; flint, slate, granite, adamant; stone, pebble; bedrock, shelf, reef.
2. foundation, platform, cornerstone, foundation stone, footing; support, prop, brace; bulwark, rampart, fortress, stronghold; anchor, mainstay, staff, shoulder, security, protection, aid.

rock², *v.* **1.** roll, move to and fro *or* backward and forward, sway, swing, seesaw; undulate, oscillate, wobble, ripple, vibrate.
2. stun, shock, stagger, floor, paralyze, send into a tailspin, *Inf.* throw, overwhelm; astound, atonish, surprise, amaze; bewilder, confuse, daze, stupefy; disturb, perturb, upset, distress, trouble; shake, jar, convulse, rattle, topple.
—*n.* 3. roll, sway, swing, seesaw, bob, undulation, oscillation.

rocket, *n.* **1.** rocket launcher, launching tube *or* mortar, projector tube, firing tube, retrorocket; gun, cannon.
2. capsule, space capsule, space vehicle, spacecraft, spaceship, moonship, mooncraft, rocket ship, module, command module, satellite; missile, bullet, ballistic misile, surface-to-air missile, SAM, surface-to-surface missile, SSM, guided missile, buzz bomb; skyrocket, firework.
—*v.* 3. launch, project, blast off, fire, shoot, shoot off.
4. soar, zoom, climb, ascend, gain altitude; skyrocket, shoot up, take off, fly, disappear into the distance; bullet, tear, *Inf.* zip, *Sl.* highball, streak, flash, tear; go like a shot, go like the wind, go like greased lightning, go like a bat out of hell, go hellbent for leather, go full blast *or* full steam, go full speed ahead; whiz, whish, zing.

rocky¹, *adj.* **1.** stony, pebbly, craggy, boulder-strewn.
2. rocklike, hard, adamant, adamantine, flinty, granitic, impermeable.
3. difficult, arduous, strenuous, laborious; wearisome, exhausting, uphill, trying, demanding; hazardous, perilous, dangerous, chancy, risky, venturesome, adventurous; disquieting, frightening, *Sl.* hairy, scary.
4. firm, solid, unyielding, unbending; stout, determined, resolute, unwavering, unfaltering; steadfast, staunch, constant, steady, sure, dependable, reliable.
5. unfeeling, unemotional, passionless, cold, impassive; apathetic, unsympathetic, uncompassionate, uncaring; indifferent, detached, *Fr. dégagé*, uninvolved; callous, tough, thick-skinned, unaffectable, insusceptible.

rocky², *adj.* **1.** tottering, wobbly, wobbling, teetering, teetering on the brink, swaying, shaky, unsteady, on rubbery legs; giddy, dizzy, light-headed.
2. uncertain, unsure, undetermined, up in the air; vacillating, wavering, going every which way; doubtful, dubious, questionable, *Inf.* iffy.

rococo, *adj.* **1.** ornate, baroque, convoluted, curlicued, intricate, involved; flamboyant, showy, ostentatious, gaudy, florid; sumptuous, elegant, gorgeous; extravagant, overdecorated, excessive, *Fr. outré*, *Sl.* too much; flowery, overblown, pretentious, windy, inflated, bombastic.
2. antiquated, ancient, old, ante-bellum; outmoded, old-fashioned, of another era, from the past, quaint; unstylish, out-of-style, passé, obsolete, bygone.

rod, *n.* **1.** stick, staff, pike, baton, cane, alpenstock, crook, crutch; switch, rattan, crop, quirt; scepter, wand, crosier, standard, caduceus; dowel, shaft, pole, post, stake, picket, stanchion, *Cricket.* stump; bar, rack, bracket, crosspiece, tube.
2. switch, cane, birch, whip, scourge, cat-o'-nine-tails, cat, lash, cowhide, thong; cudgel, truncheon, knout.
3. correction, discipline, punishment, chastisement, castigation, scourge, chastening, reprimand, reproof.
4. domination, suppression, control, grip, grasp, hold, dictatorship, tyranny, despotism, absolutism, imperialism, oppression; rule, authority, sway, dominion, sovereignty, supremacy ascendancy, supreme power; suzerainty, hegemony, lordship, regency, regnancy; command, mastery, jurisdiction.
5. *Slang.* pistol, gun, revolver, *Inf.* 44, *Inf.* six-shooter, *Inf.* shooting iron. See **gun** (*def.* **1**).

rodomontade, *n.* **1.** boasting, bluster, bragging, fanfaronade, gasconade, *Sl.* hot air, *Sl.* bunk; self-approbation, self-praise, vainglory, vainglorious boasting; bravado, braggadocio, bombast, grandiosity, magniloquence, grandiloquence; extravagance, exaggeration, pretension, hyperbole, fustian, rant, blustering rant, claptrap, high-flown language, sesquipedality; puffery, bunkum, flourish, heroics, tumidity, turgidity, flatulence, *Archaic.* tympany, vaporing, gush, balderdash, *Latin. vox et praeterea nihil*, *Sl.* gas.
—*v.* 2. brag, boast, crow, prate, vaunt; draw the longbow, trumpet, blow one's trumpet, toot one's own horn, sing one's own praises; bluster, roister, gasconade; puff, bluff, vapor, *Sl.* blow hard, *Sl.* talk big, be

windy; pat oneself on the back, flatter oneself, glorify oneself, congratulate oneself; exaggerate, overstate, hyperbolize, color, *Sl.* pile it higher and deeper, *Sl.* shovel it, *Sl.* shoot the bull, *Sl.* lay it on thick; rant, cry up, blazon forth.

rogue, *n.* **1.** knave, scapegrace, wastrel, ne'er-do-well, good-for-nothing, good-for-naught; villain, miscreant, reprobate, incorrigible; wretch, churl, cur, cad, dog, scoundrel, dastard, blackguard, *Archaic.* bezonian; *All Inf.* rat, creep, louse, stinker, *Euph.* son of a gun, *Derog.* SOB, *Derog.* bastard; *All Sl.* bum, *Chiefly Brit.* rotter, *Chiefly Brit.* bounder, *Brit.* blighter.

2. mountebank, charlatan, quack, *Archaic.* quacksalver, *Archaic.* empiric; impostor, impersonator, *Sl.* ringer; fraud, fake, *Inf.* faker, carpetbagger, crimp, *Inf.* bunko artist; cheat, deceiver, swindler, confidence man, *Inf.* con man; trickster, fourflusher, snake in the grass, wolf in sheep's clothing.

3. rascal, rapscallion, scamp, devil, imp, wag, puck, troublemaker, mischief-maker, *Irish Eng.* spalpeen.

roguery, *n.* **1.** knavishness, rascality, roguishness, churlishness; villainy, miscreancy, reprobacy, incorrigibleness; blackguardism, currishness, caddishness, dastardliness, quackery, *Archaic.* quacksalvery, mountebankery, charlatanism; imposture, impersonation, fraudulence, fakery, deception.

2. mischievousness, impishness, waggishness, puckishness, devilishness, scampishness.

3. mischief, pettifoggery, chicanery, shenanigans, hanky-panky, *Sl.* funny business, *Sl.* monkey business, *Sl.* monkeyshines; gag, prank, practical joke, joke, jest, jape, caper, trick, hoax, quiz, *Inf.* dido.

roguish, *adj.* **1.** knavish, rascally, scoundrelly, *Obs.* blackguard; villainous, reprobate, recreant, base, vile; unscrupulous, unprincipled, treacherous, perfidious, untrustworthy, unreliable, undependable; dishonest, deceitful, crooked, false, false-hearted, double-dealing, two-timing; shifty, slippery, *Inf.* shady.

2. mischievous, impish, waggish, puckish, elfish, prankish; naughty, scampish, arch, *Scot.* hempy; playful, sportive, full of mischief, fond of mischief, frolicsome.

roil, *v.* **1.** (*all of water, wine, etc.*) agitate, disturb, shake up, stir up, churn up; muddy, cloud, becloud.

2. irritate, annoy, irk, vex, pique, peeve, nettle, chafe, get on [s.o.'s] nerves, tread on [s.o.'s] toes, *Inf.* aggravate, *Inf.* miff, *Inf.* give [s.o.] a pain, *Inf.* rub [s.o.] the wrong way, *Inf.* get under [s.o.'s] skin, rile; exasperate, disquiet, discountenance, put out, try [s.o.'s] patience, *Inf.* put [s.o.'s] nose out of joint, get, *Sl.* get [s.o.'s] goat.

3. provoke, badger, bait, hector, harass, plague, bedevil.

4. anger, incense, raise [s.o.'s] ire, get [s.o.'s] back up, *Inf.* get [s.o.'s] Irish *or* dander up, *Inf.* burn [s.o.] up, *Sl.* tick [s.o.] off, *Sl.* tee [s.o.] off.

roister, *v.* **1.** bluster, puff, harangue, *Sl.* blow *or* blow hard, *Sl.* talk big; strut, swagger, parade, flaunt, show off, *Literary.* plume oneself; throw one's weight around, lord it over [s.o.] , be overbearing, give [s.o.] a hard time, bully, badger.

2. fight, brawl, riot, create a disturbance, make trouble, make a commotion, *Inf.* kick up a fuss, *Inf.* raise hell *or* the devil, *Inf.* raise Cain, *Inf.* raise a rumpus *or* ruckus.

3. carouse, revel, wassail, bouse, make merry, cut loose, let loose, *Brit.* maffick, *Inf.* live it up, *Inf.* party, *Inf.* whoop it up, *Sl.* make whoopee; go on a spree, make the rounds, *Sl.* tie one on, *Sl.* go on a drunk *or* binge *or* bender, *Sl.* paint the town red, *Sl.* barhop, *Brit. Sl.* pub-crawl.

role, *n.* **1.** part, character, characterization, portrayal, personification, impersonation; lines, *Theat.* sides.

2. capacity, position, place, status, situation; function, use, purpose, operation.

roll, *v.* **1.** revolve, rotate, bowl, trundle, troll, tumble, somersault, somerset, turn, go around; (*all of a vessel*) pitch, lurch, haw, swing, toss, rock, incline, sway, lean; spin, gyrate, whirl, pivot, pirouette, wheel, reel, swirl, twirl, twiddle.

2. cart, push, pull, move, convey, transport; drive, ride, float, sail, coast.

3. wave, undulate, ripple, billow, surge; flow, run, stream.

4. thunder, rumble, roar, boom, bellow, fulminate, rend the heavens *or* skies; resound, resonate, reverberate, echo, reecho, bounce back, bounce off the walls, fill the air *or* room; peal, toll, ring, knoll, knell, chime, ding, dong, tinkle, jingle; whir, hum, buzz; sing, trill, vibrate, rattle, quaver, quiver, shake, quake, tremble.

5. *Usu.* **roll out** unroll, flatten, flat, level, level off, even off, grade, symmetrize; smooth, smooth out, spread out, press, iron, mangle; mash, squash, crush, *Sl.* smush.

6. wrap, enwrap, wrap up, enfold, encompass, enwreath, encircle, envelop; sheathe, encase, case, package, enclose; cover, clothe, muffle, swathe, shroud, enshroud.

7. wind, curl, spiral, intort, twist; furl, ball, clew, convolve, intervolve, sinuate, curve, incurvate, roll around *or* up, unflatten; entwine, twine, wreathe, twist *or* wrap around.

—*n.* **8.** scroll, rota, tablet, document; coil, corkscrew, twist, spiral, twirl, whorl, vortex, gyration, convolution, volute, *Bot., Zool.* involution; curl, curlicue, ring, lock, kink, winding, helix, circle, rondure, *Bot.* tendril.

9. roster, register, muster, muster roll, beadroll, attendance; list, *Sports.* line-up, *Law.* panel, slate, ticket, ballot, docket; catalogue, inventory, directory, book of names, atlas, index, yellow pages.

10. spool, reel, bobbin, roller, cylinder; ball, loaf, head, bundle, bunch; dossier, file, package, packet.

11. *Cookery.* bun, scone, biscuit, *Brit.* cookie; bread, pastry, cake, *Inf.* sweet.

12. undulation, wave, waviness, curve, curviness; hilliness, ripple, billow.

13. rumble, thunder, thundering, thunderclap, roar, boom, bellowing, fulmination; reverberation, resonance, echoing, reechoing; drumroll, ratatat, pitapat, pitter-patter; vibration, tremor, rattle, quake, quiver, quaver, shake, trembling, *Both Music.* vibrato, tremolo; whir, hum, buzz, singing.

14. *Slang.* bankroll, money, pocketful of bills, full wallet; bundle, wad, pile.

rollick, *v.* frisk, gambol, romp; party, carouse, revel, make merry. See **romp** (*defs.* **1, 2**).

rollicking, *adj.* jolly, jocose, jaunty, swaggering; frolicsome, sportive, jovial, jocund; playful, frisky, lively, sprightly; merry, blithe, happy, cheerful, spirited; gay, buoyant, free and easy, breezy, airy; spry, vivacious, animated, sparkling, rattling, hearty, waggish.

romance, *n.* **1.** fiction, novel, story, tale, narrative; love story, torrid romance; fairy tale, heroic epic, legend, science fiction, fantasy, Western, spy thriller, *Inf.* thriller; Gothic novel, horror story, ghost story, *Inf.* spine-tingler.

2. invention, concoction, trumped-up story; flight of fancy, fabrication, tall tale, cock-and-bull story, fish story, exaggeration, bosh; equivocation, shift, shiftiness, evasion, half-truth; fib, white lie, misrepresentation, prevarication, falsehood, lie, untruth, falsity.

3. love affair, *Inf.* affair, romantic affair, liasion, dalliance, intrigue; romantic attachment, amour, *Fr. affaire d'amour, Fr. affaire de coeur*; infatuation, fascination, *Inf.* crush, *Inf.* case; courtship, wooing, pursuit, seduction.

4. daydream, reverie, castle-building, quixotism; fancy, fantasy, whimsy, whim, caprice, figment, flight, flight of fancy; notion, vagary, conceit; quirk, crotchet, craziness, crazy notion *or* idea, *Inf.* screwball *or* whacky idea, peculiar notion.

—*v.* **5.** invent, daydream, fantasize; build castles in the air, ride a magic carpet; imagine, envision, see things; speculate, let the mind roam *or* have free rein, give free rein to the imagination.

6. court, woo, address, pay address to, pay suit to; serenade, make love to, *Archaic.* sue; go with, keep company with, go steady with, take out, date, *Brit.* walk out with; make love, make out, pitch woo, bill and coo, *Inf.* neck.

7. curry favor with, flatter, fawn upon, toady to, pander to; *Inf.* soft-soap, *Inf.* honey up, *Inf.* butter *or* grease up, *Inf.* bootlick, *Inf.* apple-polish, *Sl.* brownnose.

romantic, *adj.* **1.** imaginative, original, inventive, creative, poetic; capricious, whimsical, flighty; irresponsible, unstable, unpredictable, quixotic, erratic, irregular, wild; eccentric, odd, strange, bizarre, queer, freakish, freaky; grotesque, mad, wild, crazy; frivolous, unpractical, impractical, impracticable; extravagant, rococo, baroque, showy, ostentatious, Byzantine.

2. unrealistic, starry-eyed, dreamy, head-in-the-clouds, out of touch with reality, *Latin. in nubibus, Sl.* spacy, dreamy; idealistic, perfectionist, philosophical, transcendental; optimistic, hopeful, Panglossian.

3. sentimental, sensitive, tender, tender-hearted, soft, understanding, considerate, sympathetic, compassionate, loving, fond; impressionable, susceptible, maudlin, overemotional; mawkish, saccharine, *Inf.* sticky, *Inf.* sugary, *Inf.* mushy.

4. amorous, ardent, passionate, erotic; lustful, burning, desirous; stimulated, excited, aroused, *Inf.* hot, *Inf.* turned-on; impassioned, fervent, fervid, perfervid; emotional, emotive, excitable.

5. imaginary, fictitious, fabulous, improbable; unreal, fancied, fanciful, fantastic; illusory, visionary, quixotic, shadowy, chimerical; mythical, mythological, legendary; figmental, fictive, notional, abstract; preposterous, far-fetched, *Inf.* far-out, *Inf.* way-out; cloud-built, air-drawn, unsubstantial, impractical; phantasmal, phantasmic, phantasmagorial, phantasmagoric.

—*n.* **6.** romanticist, idealist, dreamer, daydreamer, stargazer, knight errant, Don Quixote; visionary, impractical person, ivory-tower planner, theorist, armchair quarterback; idealist, pursuer of ideals, perfectionist; metaphysicist, philosopher, transcendentalist, spiritualist, ideologist.

romp, *v.* **1.** frisk, gambol, rollick; frolic, caper, cavort, disport oneself gaily; spring, spring about, vault, hop, trip, trip about, trip gaily; bounce, skip, jump around.

2. carouse, revel, tear about, have a fling; celebrate, make merry, have fun.

—*n.* **3.** celebration, good time, party, lark, *Sl.* bash, gala affair, *Inf.* field day; revelry, merrymaking, jollification; drinking bout, brannigan, drunk, potation, compotation; drunken carouse *or* revel, bacchanal, bacchanalia, orgy, debauch, debauchery, saturnalia; cocktail party, happy hour, spree; *All Sl.* binge, bender, hellbender, bust, beer bust, toot, tear.

roof, *n.* **1.** ceiling, top, housetop, roofing, eaves; dome, cupola; canopy, awning, tilt, tester, *Archit.* baldachin.

2. cover, covering, cope, shade, tarpaulin, *Inf.* tarp.

3. dwelling, home, house, abode; cabin, cottage, bower, log house, bungalow, hut, shanty, shack, hovel, lean-to; tent, wigwam, tepee, igloo, (*in Turkey and Iran*) kiosk.

4. hit the roof *Slang.* get angry, rage, storm, rave, *Inf.* see red, *Sl.* get hot under the collar, bridle, reach boiling point; explode, *Inf.* blow up, *Sl.* blow one's top *or* stack, flip one's lid, *Sl.* blow a fuse *or* gasket; *Sl.* throw a fit, *U.S. Inf.* have a conniption, stamp one's foot; lose one's temper, *Inf.* fly off the handle, *Sl.* hit the ceiling, fly into a rage *or* passion.

5. raise the roof *Slang.* **a.** create a loud noise, be noisy, make a racket, *Sl.* raise hell, *Sl.* raise Cain *or* Ned, make an uproar. **b.** complain, gripe, grump, *Sl.* bitch, grumble, *Sl.* squawk *or* holler, *Sl.* bellyache, make a fuss.

rook, *v.* swindle, defraud, mulct, shark, cheat, *Inf.* flimflam, fleece, bilk, *Inf.* welsh, *Inf.* do out of, *Inf.* gyp, *Inf.* bunko, *Inf.* diddle, *Inf.* take, *Inf.* take [s.o.] for a ride, *Inf.* take [s.o.] to the cleaners, *Sl.* pluck, *Sl.* chisel, *Sl.* clip; overcharge, soak, *Sl.* sting, *Inf.* rip off.

room, *n.* **1.** compartment, cubicle; parlor, living room, sitting room, chamber, bedroom, boudoir, dining room, kitchen, bathroom, playroom, recreation room, *Inf.* rec room.

2. rooms lodgings, quarters, a place to stay, a place; residence, abode, dwelling, apartment, habitation.

3. space, expansion, expanse; spaciousness, amplitude, vastness, capaciousness, largeness; open space, free space, clearing, opening; leeway, latitude, margin, swing, play, elbowroom; range, scope, extent, compass, measure.

4. capacity, aptitude, potential, capability, the stuff, *Inf.* what it takes, *U.S. Inf.* the goods; ability, talent, endowment; capableness, readiness.

5. no room to swing a cat very little space, no room to move, a tight squeeze; incommodious, cramped.

—*v.* **6.** lodge, reside, live, abide, dwell; sojourn, stay, bunk, tenant, quarter, take up quarters; settle, plant oneself, put down stakes.

roomy, *adj.* spacious, commodious, capacious, ample, voluminous; large, big, huge, great, vast, extensive; loose, loose-fitting; comfortable, *Inf.* comfy, cozy, livable, habitable, pleasant, *Sl.* cushy; accommodating, convenient, conducive; enough room to swing a cat; broad, expansive, wide, widespread; massive, gigantic, tremendous, mammoth.

roost, *n.* **1.** perch, rest, seat, throne; feeder, pole, rod, bar, tree, branch, twig; nest, aerie, eyrie, rookery, nidus, birdhouse, henhouse, chicken coop, (*of bees*) hive; abode, home, habitat, habitation, domicile, quarters, house.

—*v.* **2.** perch, sit on, rest upon, sun upon; alight on, land on, sit down on, plop down on, squat down on, deposit oneself on, place *or* position oneself on, plant oneself on; situate oneself in, get situated *or* settled in, settle in *or* down in; bivouac, camp, set up camp, set up housekeeping; spend the night, stay over *or* overnight, bed *or* bunk down, put up for the night, sojourn, remain with *or* at, stay with *or* at; live in *or* at, reside in *or* at, dwell in *or* at, inhabit, call [s.t.] home.

root[1], *n.* **1.** *Anat., Zool.* radix, *Bot.* radicle, *Bot.* rootlet, *Bot.* taproot, *Bot.* rhizome, *Bot.* rootstock; *Bot.* tuber, *Bot.* bulb, *Bot.* bulbil, earthnut, groundnut.

2. base, foundation, basis, seat, foot, footing, substructure, lower part, bottom, downside.

3. fundamental, principle, radical, rudiment, basal portion; starting place *or* point, point of departure, takeoff, takeoff point, conception, inception, commencement, start; premise, proposition, presupposition, hypothesis, thesis; reason, rationale, motive, cause, occasion, ground, causation, mainspring, causality, leaven; basic element *or* part, essential part, egg, ovum, germ, nucleus, seed, embryo, bud; grass roots, stem, stock; source, origin, beginning, derivation, rise, fountainhead, font, *Latin. fons et origo*; wellspring, spring, head.

4. roots heritage, country, land, nationality, fatherland, motherland, mother country, native land, native soil, homeland; birthplace, breeding place, cradle, nursery, womb, origin, place of birth, genesis, origination; antecedents, ancestors, predecessors, forefathers, forebears, family, ancestry, lineage, line, extraction, bloodline, descent, strain, stock, race; genealogy, pedigree, family tree; house, ancestral home.

—*v.* **5.** become fixed *or* established, send out roots, get a footing, strike, settle.

6. take root begin to grow, sprout, develop, germinate, flourish, thrive, mushroom, spread, spring up.

7. implant, plant, embed, fix, fasten, graft, insert, establish *or* sink deeply; place, set, put, situate, lay, station, deposit.

8. pull *or* tear *or* dig up, uproot, eradicate, tear out, tear up by the roots, dig out, weed out; extirpate, exterminate, remove, destroy, do away with, abolish.

root[2], *v.* **1.** poke, pry, search *or* poke around, dig, delve, nose around, scrabble, ransack, rummage, rake, rifle; look everywhere, look into every nook and cranny, search every corner, look high and low, *Inf.* beat the bushes.

2. unearth, discover, reveal, uncover, expose, bring to light; search *or* hunt out, pry *or* dig out, ferret *or* hound out, grub up, nose *or* smell *or* sniff out, run to ground *or* earth.

root[3], *v.* **1.** cheer, give a cheer, applaud, hail, give a hand *or* a big hand, cry *or* shout *or* yell for, yell oneself hoarse; huzzah, hurrah, hurray, *Australian, Brit.* barrack.

2. support, lend moral support, cheer on, bolster, boost, encourage; urge on, *Inf.* egg on, goad *or* spur on, pat *or* clap on the back.

rooted, *adj.* **1.** fixed, firm, set, fast, rigid; implanted, embedded, ingrained, deep-rooted, deep-seated, firmly established, firmly planted; inbred, inborn, congenital, ingrafted; fundamental, radical, inherent; established, confirmed, absolute, definite.

2. immovable, stationary, glued, cemented, riveted, locked in place, frozen, immobilized, motionless, stock-still, statuelike.

3. durable, perennial, traditional, long-standing; permanent, chronic, continuous, inveterate; settled, stable, steady, habituated, accustomed, wonted.

rooter, *n.* partisan, *Inf.* fan, *Inf.* loyal fan, *Inf.* booster; supporter, follower, *Inf.* buff, devotee, votary, adherent, enthusiast, admirer, fancier, *Sl.* freak, *Sl.* nut, *Sl.* bug, *Sl.* groupie; promoter, *Inf.* plugger, *Inf.* tout, *Inf.* touter; applauder, clapper, claqueur.

rope, *n.* **1.** cord, line, cable, wire rope, twist; cordage, roping, rigging, sennit, tackle; hawser, halyard, guy, painter, bowline; leader, lead, rein, longe; clothesline.

2. lasso, lariat, riata, bola.

3. noose, hangman's rope, hemp, hempen collar, *Inf.* necktie; halter, cord, garrote.

4. string, chain, thread, belt, band, strip.

5. at the end of one's rope desperate, without hope, in despair; wretched, miserable, disconsolate, careworn, worried; frantic, frenzied, not knowing which way to turn, sick at heart.

6. enough rope latitude, free rein, free hand, elbowroom, range, scope, room, tolerance, margin, swing, play, long rope *or* tether, *Inf.* leeway.

7. know the ropes *Informal.* be knowledgable, be informed, be aware, be familiar, be comfortable, be at home; be in the know, have savvy, know the score, know how to get along *or* by, *Sl.* have the inside dope, *Sl.* know the poop.

—*v.* **8.** tie, bind, fasten, secure, moor, attach, hitch, lash; tether, picket, restrain, curb; tow, pull, pull in; lasso, longe, harness; check, rein in, hold back.

9. rope in *Slang.* take in, dupe, gull, victimize; set a snare for, lay a trap for, bait the hook, spread the toils; delude, entrap, hook, waylay; ensnare, inveigle, lure, tempt, intrigue, sniggle.

ropy, *adj.* **1.** viscid, viscous, mucilaginous, glutinous, gelatinous, mucous, oozy, tacky, sticky, thick, gummy; stringy, thready, threadlike, fibrous, filamentous, filamentary, filar, filiform, fibrillose.

2. tough, wiry, sinewy, leathery, strapping.

roster, *n.* list, rota, roll, beadroll, register; catalog, directory, table, index, inventory, file, record; cadastre, grand list; docket, schedule, agenda, calendar; ticket, slate.

rostrum, *n.* platform, dais, stage; lectern, reading stand; pulpit, ambo, desk; stand, witness stand, witness box; hustings, *Fig.* stump.

rosy, *adj.* **1.** rose-colored, roseate, pink, pinkish-red, salmon, coral; red, rose-red, reddish, cherry, cerise.

2. (*of persons, the cheeks, lips etc.*) ruby, apple-red; rubicund, ruddy, florid; blushing, erubescent, flushed, burning, glowing, blooming; sunburned, windburned, inflamed.

3. promising, full of promise, likely, auspicious, favorable, looking good; encouraging, reassuring, inspiriting, cheering.

4. cheerful, sunny, bright, upbeat, beamish, enthusiastic; positive, optimistic, confident, sanguine, hopeful, full of hope.

rot, *v.* **1.** decay, decompose, putrefy, fester, spoil, go bad; mold, molder, rust; suppurate, *Pathol.* gangrene, *Pathol.* mortify.

2. deteriorate, disintegrate, fall apart, come apart, go to pieces, crumble; degenerate, retrograde.

3. eat away, eat at, erode, wear away, break down, gnaw at the root of, undermine; impair, harm, injure.

4. corrupt, canker, abase, degrade; debase, vitiate, pervert, warp, deprave, demoralize; defile, ruin, deflower; taint, stain, sully, blemish, poison.

—*n.* **5.** decay, decomposition, putrefaction, putrescence, putrescency, spoilage; mold, moldiness, mildew, dry rot, blight; deterioration, dissolution, disintegration; suppuration, purulence, *Pathol.* gangrene, *Pathol.* mortification.

6. corruption, perversion, degradation, debasement, vitiation; decadence, the skids, dissoluteness, degeneracy, degenerateness, demoralization; pollution, contamination.

7. *Informal.* nonsense, tommyrot, twaddle, rubbish, *Sl.* applesauce, *Sl.* baloney, balderdash, hogwash; idiocy, absurdness, craziness.

rotary, *adj.* **1.** rotating, rotational, revolving, turning, vertiginous; gyral, gyratory, gyrating, spinning; vortical, vorticose, vortiginous, whirling; circumrotatory, circumvolutory, circumgyratory.

—*n.* **2.** traffic circle, *Brit.* roundabout.

rotate, *v.* **1.** revolve, turn, spin, twirl, twiddle, *Archaic.* trundle; wheel, swivel, pivot; gyrate, reel, circle, circumvolve, circumrotate; (*all of the hips*) bump, grind, bump and grind.

2. (*all in reference to a job, position, etc.*) replace, switch, move around, exchange, interchange; alternate, change *or* exchange places, trade places, trade off, take turns, *Inf.* swap.

rote, *n.* **1.** routine, fixed routine, mechanical procedure, ritual; habit, rut, groove.

2. by rote from memory, by heart; unthinkingly, without thinking; mechanically, automatically, by remote control.

rotten, *adj.* **1.** putrid, decayed, decomposed, purulent; rancid, carious, maggoty, wormy, worm-eaten; fetid, feculent, rank, *Archaic.* reechy; spoiled, contaminated, tainted, unclean, foul, flyblown; diseased, saprogenic, gangrenous, bad, *Pathol.* sphaculate, *Pathol.* necrotic, *Pathol.* mortified; putrescent, decaying, decomposing, rotting; noxious, noisome, mephitic.

2. corrupt, immoral, unprincipled, unscrupulous, shameless, abandoned, reprobate, miscreant; depraved, wicked, evil, iniquitous, facinorous, nefarious, flagitious, villainous; debased, debauched, demoralized, degenerate, warped, perverted; dissolute, profligate, dissipated, wanton.

3. *Informal.* miserable, wretched, sorry, pitiful, pitiable, pathetic; meager, petty, piddling, *Inf.* measly, paltry, *Inf.* lousy, *Sl.* crummy; unacceptable, unsatisfactory, inadequate, insufficient.

4. despicable, contemptible, beneath contempt, worthy of contempt, detestable, base, base-spirited, mean, mean spirited, vile, low, *Inf.* low-down, *Sl.* low-down-dirty-rotten, *Archaic.* caitiff; loathsome, abominable, disgusting.

rotund, *adj.* **1.** round, rounded, bulbous; globular, global, globelike, globoid; spherical, spheroid; orbic.

2. corpulent, plump, pleasingly *or* pleasantly plump; stout, portly, chubby, pudgy, roly-poly, well-fed, (*of a woman*) buxom, *Inf.* tubby; fat, overweight, obese.

3. sonorous, canorous, full, full-toned, rich, mellow, orotund; resonant, vibrant.

rotundity, *n.* **1.** roundness, roundedness, globularity, globosity; sphericity, sphericalness, orbicularity.

2. corpulence, plumpness, stoutness, *Fr. embonpoint*, portliness, chubbiness, pudginess, roly-poliness, (*of a woman*) buxomness; obesity, fatness, adiposity.

3. sonority, sonorousness, canorousness, fullness, richness, mellowness, orotundity; resonance, vibrancy.

roué, *n.* rake, rakehell, profligate, wanton, blood, debauchee, libertine, *Inf.* rip, *Sl.* swinger; playboy, womanizer, ladies' man, man about town, woman-chaser, *Sl.* skirt-chaser, *Sl.* wolf, *Sl.* lover boy, *Sl.* tomcat, *Sl.* masher, *Sl.* make-out artist, *Sl.* man on the make; philanderer, trifler, dallier, gay dog, gay deceiver, gallant, flirt, *Obs.* coquet, *Inf.* two-timer; Don Juan, Cassanova, Lothario, Romeo, charmer, *Inf.* lady-killer, *Sl.* stud, *Sl.* sheik; *Inf.* sugar daddy.

rough, *adj.* **1.** irregular, uneven, coarse, not smooth, rugged, bumpy, jagged, craggy, scraggy; stony, rocky; stubbled, knotted, nodose, gnarled; wrinkly, rugulose, crinkly, corrugated, scaly; lumpy, nodulous.

2. shaggy, hairy, hirsute, crinose, trichoid; bristly, bristling, *Bot., Zool.* hispid, setaceous, setose, *Bot., Zool.* setulose, setigerous, setiferous, *Bot.* strigose; bushy, unshorn, unshaven, bearded; unkempt, disheveled, disordered; furry, pilose; velvety, *Bot.* villous; tufted, *Bot., Entomol.* crinite; downy, nappy, *Bot., Zool.* pubescent, lanuginose, *Bot., Zool.* tomentose; woolly-haired, ulotrichous, kinky, flocculent, lanate; threadlike, filamentous, *Bot., Zool.* ciliated; feathery, *Zool.* plumate, plumous.

3. violent, disorderly, riotous, berserk, amuck; noisy, boisterous, uproarious, rowdy, rowdyish; frantic, frenzied, rampant; fierce, ferocious, furious, raging, vehement, savage.

4. turbulent, tumultuous, tempestuous, stormy; inclement, wintry, blustery; choppy, agitated.

5. rude, discourteous, impolite, uncivil, unceremonious, unmannerly, bad-mannered, disrespectful, misbehaved; indelicate, uncourtly, ungallant, indecorous; ungentlemanly, unladylike, brash, bold, hoydenish, *Scot.* randy; brazen, barefaced, insolent, impudent, insulting, impertinent, pert, saucy, fresh; sharp, keen, trenchant, acrimonious, caustic, stinging, biting, piercing, stringent, brutal, cruel; bluff, bearish, gruff, inconsiderate, tactless, *Scot. and North Eng.* mislearned, blustering; sulky, morose, sullen, ill-tempered, ill-humored; sarcastic, bitter, virulent, snarling, venomous; grouchy, peevish, petulant, splenetic, thorny, cross; abrupt, blunt, brusque, curt, stern, austere; base, vile, obscene, indecent, ribald, foul mouthed, smutty, low, offensive, vulgar, crude.

6. difficult, unpleasant, hard; austere, severe, demanding; drastic, extreme, brutal.

7. (*of sounds*) discordant, inharmonious, disharmonious, cacophonous; harsh, grating, jarring, strident; raucous, gruff, hoarse, husky.

8. (*of tastes*) tart, astringent, sour, crabbed; acrid, sharp, biting, pungent, bitter, mordant; spicy, peppery.

9. uncouth, uncultured, unrefined, unpolished, uncivilized, incondite; coarse, vulgar, churlish, loutish, barbarous, brutish, wild, savage, gross; ignorant, illiterate, unlearned, untrained, untaught, untutored, uneducated, uncultivated; unskilled, unskillful, clumsy, gauche, crude; countrified, provincial, unfashionable, unsophisticated, homespun, homebred.

10. rough-hewn, crude, unwrought, uncut, unfashioned, unprepared, unprocessed; shapeless, formless, amorphous; incomplete, unfinished, imperfect; not elaborated, vague, sketchy, approximate, inexact; cursory, superficial; rudimentary, preliminary.

—*n.* **11.** unpleasantness, difficulty, trial, tribulation, trouble, hardship.

12. rudiment, crude form, preliminary form, sketch, outline, foundation.

—*adv.* **13.** roughly, violently, harshly, sharply, crudely, coarsely, ungently.

—*v.* **14.** roughen, coarsen, harshen, sharpen, hone.

15. rough up beat, pummel, thrash, manhandle, do violence to.

16. rough out sketch, outline, delineate, block out, mark out, chalk out, demarcate.

roughhouse, *n.* rowdy conduct, rough behavior, horseplay, disorderly play; rowdyism, ruffianism, blackguardism, manhandling; brutality, ferocity, violence, brawling; brute force, barbarity, outrage.

roughneck, *n.* *Informal.* rowdy, ruffian, tough; hoodlum, *Sl.* hood. See **rowdy** (*defs.* 1,2).

roughness, *n.* **1.** coarseness, ruggedness, bumpiness, jaggedness, cragginess, cragginess; stoniness, rockiness; knottedness, nodosity, gnarledness; wrinkledness, nugosity, crinkledness, corrugation; lumpiness; irregularity, unevenness.

2. hairiness, hirsuteness, *Bot., Zool.* hispidity, pilosity; hair, thatch, shock, mat, tangle, shag; whiskers, beard, Vandyke, imperial, goatee, sideburns, muttonchops, mustache; bristle, *Bot.* awn, *Bot., Zool.* setula, vibrissae, *Bot.* arista; crest, tuft; fur, coat, mane, wool.

3. ungentleness, disorderliness, riotousness, noisiness, boisterousness, uproariousness, rowdyism, violence; franticness, frenzy; fierceness, ferocity, ferociousness, fury, rage, vehemence, savageness.

4. turbulence, tumultuousness, tempestuousness, storminess, inclemency, choppiness, agitation.

5. rudeness, discourteousness, impoliteness, incivility, unmannerliness; inconsideration, tactlessness, disrespectfulness, misbehavior; ungraciousness, indecorum, uncourtliness, ungentlemanliness, hoydenism; brashness, boldness, brazenness, insolence, impudence, impertinence, pertness, tartness, sauciness, freshness; gruffness, bluffness, bearishness; grouchiness, crabbedness, surliness, sulkiness, moroseness, peevishness, petulance, sourness, acerbity; abruptness, bluntness, brusqueness, curtness, shortness; harshness, austerity, sternness; raffishness, ribaldry, smuttiness, obscenity.

6. (*of sounds*) discordance, inharmoniousness, dissonance, cacophony; harshness, gratingness, jarringness, stridence; raucousness, gruffness, hoarseness, huskiness.

7. (*of tastes*) unsavoriness, tartness, astringency, sourness; pungency, bitterness, mordancy.

8. uncouthness, coarseness, crudeness, crudity, vulgarity; boorishness, churlishness, loutishness; brutishness, barbarity, savagery, grossness; ignorance, illiteracy; clumsiness, ungainliness, gaucherie.

9. rawness, crudeness; shapelessness, formlessness, amorphism, amorphousness, asymmetry; incompleteness, imperfection; vagueness, sketchiness, approximation, inexactness; cursoriness, superficiality.

round, *adj.* **1.** circular, cycloid, disklike, discoid; ring-shaped, ringlike, ringed, hoop, hooplike, hooped, rotiform, annular; cylindrical, tubular; spherical, spheroidal, spheroid, spheric, spheral, spheroidic, ball-shaped, globelike, globe-shaped, globular, globate, globose, orbed, orblike, orbicular, orbiculate, orbiculated, bulb-shaped, bulbous; balloonlike, bouffant, puffy; elliptical, oval, ovoid, ovate, egg-shaped.

2. curved, rounded, curvilinear, curvilineal, parabolic; arched, arcuate, arcuated, enarched, vaulted, bowed, bow-shaped, crescent-shaped, bent; pear-shaped, pyriform, bell-shaped; curvy, *Inf.* curvaceous, voluptuous, well-shaped, full-figured, voluptuous, fully developed *or* grown, mature; plump, pleasingly plump, hippy, roly-poly, pudgy, *Chiefly Brit.* podgy, potbellied, chubby, chunky, stout, rotund; heavy, overweight, fat, obese, corpulent.

3. ample, generous, liberal, abundant, superabundant, bountiful, bounteous, plentiful, plenteous.

4. complete, entire, total, whole, (*both of numbers*) integer, integral; solid, intact, unbroken, undivided, uncut, unshortened, unabridged, unreduced, undiminished, unlessened.

5. rounded off, approximate, *Inf.* ball-park, rough, close; estimated, *Sl.* guesstimated, guessed.

6. finished, polished, practiced, disciplined, well-developed; perfected, perfect, consummate, crowning, august; ideal, exemplary, model.

7. orotund, pear-shaped, rounded, resonant; sonorous, mellifluous, harmonious.

8. straightforward, straight-shooting, direct, up front; candid, frank, outspoken, blunt; plain, down to earth, simple; ingenuous, artless, guileless, naive, open, honest; aboveboard, square, fair, upright, honorable.

—*n.* **9.** circle, disk, circlet, roundlet, roundel, wheel; ring, hoop, band, annulus, annulation; sphere, globe, ball, orb, bulb, spherule, globule, bead, drop, *Geom.* spheroid; hemisphere, semicircle, half-circle, half-moon, crescent; curve, arch, vault, bow, *Both Geom.* parabola, conic section.

10. cylinder, tube, spool, bobbin, reel, roller; dowel, pole, rung.

11. *Sometimes* **rounds** sequence, chain, catena; succession, progression, procession, train, string; set, collection, bunch; period, session, sitting, bout, spell, turn.

12. *Often* **rounds** circuit, ambit, compass, lap, perambulation; beat, route, routine, course, path, run, track, itinerary; watch, jurisdiction, area, region; trip, journey, travels, voyage, tour.

13. revolution, roll, rotation, circumrotation, orbit, trajectory; circumference, perimeter, outline; spin, circumgyration, whirl, twirl, pirouette, pivot, turn.

—*adv.* **14.** through, throughout, from beginning to end, from start to finish, from first to last, from A to Z, from head to toe, from tip to toe; on all sides, all over, everywhere, everywhere one looks, in all parts *or* every part.

15. around, in a circle *or* ring, circularly, in a circuit; circumferentially, perimetrically, on the outside.

—*prep.* **16.** throughout, through, all over, in all parts of, here and there in; during, over the course of.

17. around, near, nigh, in the vicinity *or* neighborhood *or* area of, close to, not far from; about, approximately, roughly, somewhere in the vicinity *or* neighborhood *or* area of.

—*v.* **18.** curve, incurve, incurvate, camber; bend, arch, bow, *Archit.* embow; take the edge off of, smooth, rub down, polish, buff.

19. *Often* **round off** *or* **out** complement, supplement, implete, fill in *or* out, enrich, enhance, embellish, adorn; bring to completion, complete, finish, conclude, finalize, terminate, close, end; bring to perfection, perfect, refine; consummate, crown, culminate, cap, top off.

20. encircle, encompass, hoop, gird, girdle, engird, belt, ring, span; circumscribe, outline, delineate, demarcate, mark off, define, delimit, stake out; surround, embrace, enclose, environ, rope off, hem *or* hedge *or* fence in, confine; circumvent, entrap, ensnare.

21. circle, compass, revolve *or* rotate around, circumrotate, orbit, circumnavigate, circumambulate, circuit; circulate, make the circuit, make a complete trip.

roundabout, *adj.* winding, turning, twisting, crooked, zigzag, helical, labyrinthine, mazelike; sinuous, serpentine, tortuous, anfractuous; circuitous, indirect, ambagious, circular; circumlocutory, circumlocutional, circumlocutionary, periphrastic, rambling, wandering, meandering, desultory, digressive, excursive, sidetracked, stray; discursive, loose, long-winded, long, drawn-out, never-ending.

rouse, *v.* **1.** arouse, call, summon; actuate, initiate, put in motion; stimulate, animate, reanimate, whet, invigorate, motivate, inspirit, inspire, galvanize, electrify; vivify, rally, revive, enliven, liven up, awaken, shake up, jolt, jog; impel, induce, compel, move, press, drive, stir, fillip; alarm, startle, disturb, impress.

2. incite, provoke, prod, prick, goad, prompt, spur; encourage, urge, abet, egg on, put up to; instigate, stir up, work up, wind up, whip up, hype up, *Inf.* turn on; foment, agitate, suscitate, excite, impassion; fire up, inflame, enflame, enkindle, kindle, touch off, ignite the spark, build a fire under, stir the embers, fan the fire.

3. awaken, awake, wake up, waken, wake, bestir, get up; revive, become conscious, come to, come around, become aware.

rousing, *adj.* 1. lively, animated, spirited, active, brisk; enlivened, invigorated, energetic, energized, vivified, vitalized, inspirited; vigorous, spry, sprightly, *Inf.* peppy, *Inf.* snappy; swift, quick, prompt, alacritous; airy, breezy, jaunty, zestful, sportive; zealous, enthusiastic, fervent, fired up; jumping, hopping, swinging.

2. extraordinary, great, tremendous, remarkable; *All Sl.* whopping, whooping, thumping, thundering, whaling, spanking.

roustabout, *n.* 1. dock-worker, wharf laborer, lumper, dock-walloper, longshoreman, *Naut.* deck hand; stevedore, cargo loader; circus worker.

2. unskilled laborer, common laborer *U.S.* roughneck.

rout[1], *n.* 1. conquest, vanquishment, defeat, subjugation, subdual; drubbing, beating, *Sl.* pasting, *Sl.* shellacking, trouncing; discomfiture, overwhelming, trampling, overcoming, overpowering, overthrow, wipeout, upset; debacle, disorderly flight, complete dispersal, total repulse.

2. rabble, riffraff, ragtag and bobtail, canaille; mob, herd, horde, clamorous multitude.

3. evening party, soiree; ball dance, ridotto.

—*v.* 4. defeat, conquer, vanquish, subdue, subjugate; discomfit, overwhelm, *Sl.* mop *or* wipe the floor with, overrun, trample, *Inf.* run into the ground; crush, overthrow, smash, thrash, trounce, trim, whip, drub, floor; worst, hash, *Sl.* skin, *U.S. Sl.* skunk, *Inf.* lick, *Sl.* cream, *Sl.* shellac, *Sl.* pulverize; break, quash, destroy, *Sl.* zap, clobber, polish off, *Sl.* do in; beat, get the better of, best, upset, upend, *Inf.* whomp; disperse, break up, scatter.

rout[2], *v.* 1. search, rummage, ransack, hunt, rifle through, look through, *Sl.* paw through, explore; turn over, turn inside out, turn upside down, forage; look into, look about for, examine, pry into, poke around for, peer into, snoop around, smell out; shuffle through, sift through.

2. *Usu.* **rout out** find, find out, come across, discover, uncover, unearth; bring up, bring to light, dig up, ferret out; root out, fish out, come up with.

route, *n.* 1. course, itinerary, way, path, road, *Brit. Sl.* toby, pavement; roadway, highway, turnpike, pike, tollroad; freeway, expressway, parkway, causeway, throughway; speedway, autobahn, superhighway, *U.S. Inf.* interstate; main road, highroad, thoroughfare, public road; street, lane, terrace, circle, row; avenue, boulevard, concourse, strip, *Inf.* drag; airway.

2. round, lap, track, beat, ambit, turn, spin, compass; cycle, circuit, circle.

3. **go the route** see [s.t.] through, complete, finish, terminate; achieve, accomplish.

—*v.* 4. chart, map, map out, set the itinerary.

5. forward, send, mail.

routine, *n.* 1. pattern, system, method, way, regular course of procedure, daily routine; rote, treadmill, groove, rut, beaten path; habit, habitude, matter of course, second nature, practice, wont, custom; convention, order, consuetude, observance, regulation, rule, protocol, formality, bureaucratic rigmarole, red tape.

2. act, performance, number, part, bit, *Inf.* shtik.

—*adj.* 3. habitual, customary, accustomed, wonted, regular, daily; ordinary, everyday, usual, typical, conventional; perfunctory, automatic.

rove, *v.* wander about, meander, ramble, straggle, roam, stray, range, drift; move hither and thither, go from pillar to post, cruise, gad about, flit, go aimlessly; *Inf.* knock about, *Sl.* bum around, *Inf.* run around, gallivant, jaunt; walk, stroll, saunter, amble, perambulate, circumambulate, prowl; wander over *or* through, traverse, cross, pass through *or* over, explore, scout, walk *or* range over; traipse, tramp, march, trudge, plod along, wend one's way, make one's way; trek, travel, journey, peregrinate, migrate, nomadize.

rover, *n.* wanderer, roamer, rambler, landloper, adventurer, meanderer, straggler, strayer, gadabout; nomad, Bedouin, nomadic Arab, Kuchi, gypsy, Romany, Bohemian; mover, ambulator, traveler, walker, peregrinator, journeyer, pilgrim, wayfarer, sojourner; voyager, globetrotter, international *or* world traveler, tourist, visitor, sightseer; migrator, trekker, bird of passage, *Sl.* rolling stone, migrant *or* migrant worker, itinerant, peripatetic; *Usu. Disparaging.* Okie, drifter, *Inf.* floater, transient, fly-by-night; vagabond, tramp, vagrant, hobo, *Inf.* bum; runaway, fugitive, *Archaic.* runagate.

row[1], *n.* line, file, queue, column, rank, tier; series, range, chain, string, succession, sequence, concatenation, catena; suite, train, retinue, cortege, cavalcade, procession, parade, *Fr. défilé.*

row[2], *v.* oar, pull, paddle, canoe, kayak.

row[3], *n.* 1. dispute, quarrel, discord, spar, wrangle, bicker, *Obs.* brabble, contention, controversy, disagreement, argument, *Inf.* words, *Scot. and North Eng.* threap; *Inf.* dustup, *U.S. Sl.* rhubarb, squabble, spat, tiff, *Brit. Dial.* fratch, *Inf.* run-in, *Inf.* hassle, *Inf.* barney, falling-out, *Sl.* blow-up; tussle, *Inf.* scrap, *Inf.* set-to, scuffle, broil, embroilment, imbroglio, *Scot.* sturt, *Scot.* collieshangie; struggle, combat, fight, fistfight, fisticuffs, altercation, conflict, strife, clash, *Law.* chance-medley; fray, skirmish, battle, brawl, free-for-all, melee, donnybrook.

2. *Informal.* noise, clamor, din, hubbub, babel, racket; ballyhoo, outcry, bawl, hue and cry, vociferation; uproar, fracas, hullabaloo, clangor, brouhaha, commotion, fuss, stir, disorder, rumpus, *Inf.* ruckus; bedlam, tumult, turmoil, pandemonium, chaos, confusion.

—*v.* 3. quarrel, squabble, altercate, spar, cross swords; argue, debate, dispute, bandy words, have words, *Inf.* pick a crow; disagree, differ, take exception to, contend, contest, make something of it, fall out, clash, be at odds, be at loggerheads; spat, tiff, *Brit. Archaic.* brangle, wrangle, bicker, *Obs.* brabble; fight, brawl, scuffle, tussle, struggle, *Inf.* scrap, battle, go at each other's throats.

rowdy, *n.* 1. ruffian, tough, *Inf.* toughie, thug, mugger, hoodlum, *Sl.* hood, *Sl.* yap, *Inf.* plugugly, *Inf.* goon, hooligan, *Chiefly Brit.* rough, *Inf.* roughneck, *Inf.* baddy, *Sl.* bad actor, *Sl.* gunsel, *Sl.* mug, *Australian Sl.* larrikin, *Brit. Hist.* Mohock, (*in Paris*) apache; terrorist, desperado, gangster, mobster, racketeer, mafioso.

2. brute, bully, brawler, barbarian; savage, vandal, yahoo, *Sl.* ugly customer; scoundrel, knave, wretch, *Archaic.* caitiff; blackguard, villain, hellhound, fiend; rascal, rapscallion, scamp.

—*adj.* 3. disorderly, unruly, rowdyish; unrestrained, abandoned, lawless, libertarian, licentious; rough, coarse, crude, loud, unrefined; barbarous, brutish, savage, vicious, atrocious; roguish, rascally, mischievous.

4. blackguardly, villainous, contemptible, despicable, scurvy, mean, shameful; evil, sinister, unprincipled, corrupt, depraved, reprobate, iniquitous, malicious, nefarious, flagitious; disreputable, raffish, rakish, opprobrious, discreditable; criminal, felonious, fiendish, demonic, demoniacal, devilish.

rowdyism, *n.* **1.** ruffianism, hooliganism, hoodlumism, blackguardism, vandalism; brutality, barbarity, barbarism, atrociousness, savageness, savagery, viciousness; malevolence, villainy, wrongdoing.
2. boisterousness, crudeness, crudity, rudeness, coarseness, vulgarity, commonness; maliciousness, destructiveness, meanness; unruliness, disorderliness, misbehavior, misconduct; lawlessness, abandon, unrestraint.
3. mischief, mischief-making, mischievousness; knavery, knavishness, rascality, roguery; roughhouse, horseplay.
—*v.* **3.** quarrel, squabble, altercate, spar, cross swords; argue, debate, dispute, bandy words, have words, *Inf.* pick a crow; disagree, differ, take exception to, contend, contest, make something of it, fall out, clash, be at odds, be at loggerheads; spat, tiff, *Brit. Archaic.* brangle, wrangle, bicker, *Obs.* brabble; fight, brawl, scuffle, tussle, struggle, *Inf.* scrap, battle, go at each other's throats.

rowdy, *n.* **1.** ruffian, tough, *Inf.* toughie, thug, mugger, hoodlum, *Sl.* hood, *Sl.* yap, *Inf.* plugugly, *Inf.* gon, hooligan, *Chiefly Brit.* rough, *Inf.* roughneck, *Inf.* baddy, *Sl.* bad actor, *Sl.* gunsel, *Sl.* mug, *Australian Sl.* larrikin, *Brit. Hist.* Mohock, (*in Paris*) apache; terrorist, desperado, gangster, mobster, racketeer, mafioso.
2. brute, bully, brawler, barbarian; savage, vandal, yahoo, *Sl.* ugly customer; scoundrel, knave, wretch, *Archaic.* caitiff; blackguard, villain, hellhound, fiend; rascal, rapscallion, scamp.
—*adj.* **3.** disorderly, unruly, rowdyish; unrestrained, abandoned, lawless, libertarian, licentious; rough, coarse, crude, loud, unrefined; barbarous, brutish, savage, vicious, atrocious; roguish, rascally, mischievous.

royal, *adj.* **1.** kingly, queenly, princely, regal, basilic, majestic, august; kinglike, lordly, noble, aristocratic, highborn, patrician, courtly.
2. sovereign, imperial, monarchical, absolute, regnant, paramount, hegemonic, dynastic; authoritative, imperious, despotic, autocratic, dominant, peremptory.
3. imposing, commanding, stately, impressive, grand, magnificent, lofty, elevated, exalted, eminent, sublime.
4. *Informal.* fine, excellent, first-rate, first-class, prime, of the highest order, of the best sort; crack, choice, tiptop.

royalty, *n.* **1.** kingship, queenship, majesty, divine right, sovereignty, primacy, supremacy, suzerainty, dominion, hegemony; authority, command, regnancy, lordship; autocracy, monocracy, imperialism, absolutism, rod of empire, iron sway, domination; Caesarism, czarism, kaiserism.
2. royal family, royal house, royal line; dynasty, monarchy, nobilty, aristocracy.
3. kingliness, regality, imperiality, imperialness; augustness, stateliness, grandeur, preeminence; loftiness, excellence, greatness, nobleness; magnificence, splendor, glamour; prestige, authoritativeness; dignity, honorableness, gallantry, courtliness.
4. share, fee, compensation, return, dividend; remuneration, reimbursement, recompense; percentage, commission, brokerage fee, *Inf.* rake-off, *Inf.* cut; reward, finder's fee.

rub, *v.* **1.** massage, knead, embrocate; stroke, caress, fondle, pet, pat, palm; brush, graze; (*all of horses*) curry, currycomb, groom.
2. polish, buff, burnish, rub down, smooth; abrade, chafe, levigate, triturate; scour, scrub.
3. *Often* **rub off** *or* **out** erase, wipe off, blot out, dissolve, eradicate; expunge, obliterate, wipe out; cancel, delete.
4. **rub out** *Slang.* destroy, do away with, extirpate, exterminate; kill, execute, slaughter, slay. See **murder** (*defs.* **4-6**).
—*n.* **5.** friction, rubbing against, rubbing down, massage, massaging, kneading, embrocation; stroke, stroking, caress, caressing, fondling, petting, patting, palming; (*all of horses*) currying, currycombing, grooming.
6. polishing, buffing, burnishing, smoothing; abrasion, abrading, chafing, grating, rasping; scour, scouring, srub, scrubbing.
7. irritation, aggravation, annoyance, nuisance, chafe, bother, pest, vexation, torment, pain in the neck; hurt, wound, sting, pain; animadversion, criticism, castigation, reproof, reproach, rebuke, scolding; derision, sneer, sarcasm, insult, slight, cut, left-handed compliment, blow to one's pride; gibe, jeer, taunt; affliction, jinx, adversity, plague, scourge.
8. tribulation, trial, botheration; predicament, position, situation, circumstance, plight, fix, pinch, scrape, pickle, stew, mess; mishap, emergency, exigency.
9. obstacle, obstruction, barrier, bar, interference; delay, holdup, hitch; impediment, hindrance, setback, check; difficulty, trouble, problem.
10. abrasion, scrape, scratch, scuff, graze, sore; erosion, fray, *Inf.* frazzle.

rubbish, *n.* **1.** trash, riffraff, *Brit. Dial.* raff, litter, sweepings, chaff; refuse, *Dial.* culch, garbage, waste, offal; debris, detritus, rubble, wreckage; remains, leavings, leftovers, scraps, orts, hogwash, swill; remainder, residue, residuum; scoria, dross, recrement, slag, scum; filth, dirt, dust, offscourings; dregs, fag ends, remnants, fragments, bits and pieces, odds and ends; junk, worthless stuff, *Sl.* dreck, trumpery; castoffs, rags, tatters, castaways, rejects, discards.
2. nonsense, moonshine, gobbledegook; humbug, bunkum, *Sl.* bunk, *Sl.* blah; flummery, *Inf.* hokum, *Sl.* applesauce, *Sl.* eyewash; refuse, *Dial.* culch, *Sl.* ripe, chaff, trash, *Inf.* truck, trumpery; balderdash, tommyrot, *Inf.* rot, *Sl.* garbage, *Sl.* crap, *Sl.* crock, *Sl.* bull; hogwash, swill, *Sl.* horsefeathers, stuff, stuff and nonsense, *Inf.* bosh, *Brit. Inf.* gammon, *Brit. Sl.* tosh; fudge, foolishness, folly, rigamarole, amphigory; footle, *Inf.* malarkey, *Sl.* bushwa, *Sl.* baloney, *Sl.* bilge *or* bilge water, *Sl.* meshugaas, *Scot. and North Eng.* haver; poppycock, *Inf.* fiddle-faddle, *Inf.* piffle, *Inf.* hooey, *Inf.* kibosh, *Inf.* flapdoodle; claptrap, rodomontade, fustian, bombast, rant; idle talk, froth, *Sl.* hot air, *Sl.* gas.

rubbishy, *adj.* trashy, cheap, dirty. See **trashy** (*def.* **2**).

ruddy, *adj.* red, reddish, rubicund, sanguine, rosy; rosy-cheeked, cherry-cheeked; roseate, flushed, blooming, healthy-complexioned; glowing, florid, sunburned, suntanned, burnt, red-faced, beet-red; rufous, rufescent, russet; amaranthine.

rude, *adj.* **1.** discourteous, impolite, uncivil, unceremonious, unmannerly, bad-mannered, disrespectful, misbehaved; indelicate, uncourtly, ungallant, indecorous; ungentlemanly, unladylike, brash, bold, hoydenish, *Scot.* randy; brazen, barefaced, insolent, impudent, insulting, impertinent, pert, saucy, fresh; sharp, keen, trenchant, acrimonious, caustic, stinging, biting, piercing, stringent, brutal, cruel; bluff, bearish, gruff, inconsiderate, tactless, *Scot. and North Eng.* misleared; sulky, morose, sullen, ill-tempered, ill-humored; sarcastic, bitter, virulent, snarling, venomous; grouchy, peevish, petulant, splenetic, thorny, cross; abrupt, blunt, brusque, curt, stern, austere; disdainful, disparaging, derisive, contemptuous, opprobrious, contumelious; base, low, vile, obscene, indecent, ribald, foul-mouthed, smutty, offensive.

2. uncouth, uncultured, unrefined, unpolished, uncivilized, incondite; coarse, vulgar, raffish, plebian; churlish, loutish, barbarous, brutish, wild, savage, gross; ignorant, illiterate, unlearned, untrained, untaught, untutored, uneducated, uncultivated; unskilled, unskillful, clumsy, gauche, crude; countrified, provincial, unfashionable, homespun, homebred.

3. rough, harsh, ungentle; hard, coarse, scratchy, abrasive.

4. rugged, crude, raw, rough, roughly wrought, unwrought, unfasioned; amorphous, shapeless, formless, unformed, unshapely, unhewn, scraggy; unfinished, unshapen, ill-formed, asymmetric, asymmetrical.

5. (*of sounds*) harsh, strident, piercing, ear-splitting; jarring, grating, discordant, inharmonious, cacophonous.

6. artless, inartificial, natural, simple, unadorned, classic.

7. violent, tempestuous, stormy, turbulent, tumultuous, blustering, uproarious; ferocious, savage, fierce, boisterous, riotous; vehement, raging, frenzied, frantic, furious; vigorous, robust, robustious.

rudeness, *n.* 1. discourteousness, impoliteness, incivility, unmannerliness; inconsideration, tactlessness, disrespect, disrespectfulness, misbehavior; ungraciousness, indecorum, uncourtliness, ungentlemanliness, hoydenism; brashness, boldness, brazenness, insolence, impudence, impertinence, pertness, tartness, sauciness, freshness; flippancy, arrogance, cheek, lip, effrontery, presumption; sharpness, keenness, acrimoniousness, causticity; brutality, cruelty; sarcasm, bitterness, virulence, contemptuousness, opprobriousness, derision; gruffness, bluffness, bearishness; grouchiness, crabbedness, surliness, sulkiness, moroseness, peevishness, petulance, sourness, acerbity; abruptness, bluntness, brusqueness, curtness, shortness, harshness, austerity, sternness; raffishness, ribaldry, smuttiness, obscenity.

2. uncouthness, crudeness, crudity, vulgarity; boorishness, churlishness, loutishness; brutishness, barbarity, savagery, grossness; ignorance, illiteracy; clumsiness, ungainliness, gaucherie.

3. roughness, harshness, ungentleness; hardness, coarseness, scratchiness, abrasiveness.

4. rawness, crudeness, roughness; shapelessness, formlessness, amorphism, amorphousness, asymmetry, unshapeliness, misshapenness.

5. (*of sounds*) harshness, stridence, piercingness, earsplittingness; dissonance, discordance, discord, disharmony, cacophony.

6. artlessness, naturalness, rusticity, simpleness, simplicity, plainness, unadornment.

7. violence, tempestuousness, storminess, turbulence, tumultuousness; uproariousness, boisterousness, riotousness; ferocity, fierceness, savageness, vehemence, rage, frenzy, fury; vigor, robustness.

rudiment, *n.* 1. *Usu.* **rudiments** first principles, elements, foundation; mainspring, fountainhead, nucleus, source, spring, font, ultimate cause, *Latin. fons et origo*; prime mover, generator, determinant; beginning, starting point, commencement, first appearance, imperfect form.

2. *Biology.* undeveloped form, arrested form, vestige; embryo, germ, root; egg, ovum, roe, spawn; sperm, semen, milt; foetus.

rudimentary, *adj.* 1. elementary, fundamental, abecedarian, primary, initial; original, primal, primordial, elemental; initiatory, formative, germinal, germinative.

2. undeveloped, immature, incomplete, imperfect, unprepared; premature, unripe, green, raw, crude; inchoate, natal, fetal, embryonic, unhatched, unfledged; vestigial, abortive.

rue, *v.* 1. repent of, regret bitterly, sorrow about, lament, bewail, deplore, bemoan, weep over, grieve; mourn, pine, fret; repent, be stung by conscience, be contrite over, feel shame over, be heartsick about, be conscience-stricken over; curse the day, *Inf.* kick oneself, curse one's folly, wish undone, be despondent about.

—*n.* 2. sorrow, remorse, remorsefulness, regret, regretfulness, contrition, contriteness, shame, shamefulness; lamentation, grief, mournfulness, woe, dole; disquietude, inquietude, pangs *or* twinge of conscience, voice of conscience; qualms, second thoughts.

3. pity, compassion, tenderness, heart; mercy, grace, sympathy, commiseration, consolation, concern; kindliness, tender-heartedness, loving-kindness; charity, benevolence, beneficence.

rueful, *adj.* 1. pitiable, piteous, deplorable, pathetic; miserable, wretched, abject, squalid, stark, dismal, shabby, mean, low, a sad sight, sad to behold.

2. mournful, doleful, dolorous, grieving, plaintive, lamenting; woebegone, full of woe, lugubrious, repining, melancholy, depressed, despondent, *Inf.* down in the dumps, *Inf.* down, cheerless, funereal; regretful, regretting, heartsick, sorry, penitent, repentant, penitential, conscience-stricken, apologetic; humbled, abject, sheepish; self-condemning, self-reproachful, self-accusing, self-castigating, self-debasing; ashamed, shameful, shamefaced, *Sl.* bummed out; sad, disillusioned, sadder but wiser, bitter, chagrined.

ruffian, *n.* 1. thug, tough, *Inf.* toughie, mugger, rowdy, *Inf.* plugugly, hoodlum, *Sl.* hood, *Sl.* yap, *Inf.* goon, hooligan, *Chiefly Brit.* rough, *Inf.* roughneck, *Inf.* baddy, *Sl.* bad actor, *Sl.* gunsel, *Sl.* mug, *Australian Sl.* larrikin, *Brit. Hist.* Mohock, (*in Paris*) apache; terrorist, desperado, mafioso, racketeer, mobster, gangster.

2. highwayman, footpad, *Sl.* yegg *or* yeggman, bandit, *Sp. bandolero*, outlaw, *Southwest U.S.* ladrone, *Australian.* bushranger, bravo, brigand; picaroon, rogue, (*in India and Burma*) dacoit.

3. pirate, rover, viking, corsair, buccaneer, privateer; freebooter, rapparee, (*in the Scottish Highlands*) cateran; pillager, plunderer, marauder, despoiler, depredator; ransacker, sacker, looter, rifler, forager, raider.

4. brute, bully, brawler, barbarian; savage, vandal, yahoo, *Sl.* ugly customer; scoundrel, knave, wretch, blackguard, villain, hellhound, fiend, *Archaic.* caitiff; rascal, rapscallion, scamp.

ruffle, *v.* 1. gather, pucker, plait, shirr, full, rimple, crimp, crisp, smock, flounce.

2. ripple, roil, roughen, stir up, undulate; curl, crumple, crinkle, cockle, crease, fold, ruck; dimple, wimple, corrugate, *Inf.* scrunch up, *Inf.* squish together.

3. disarrange, disorder, derange, rumple, dishevel, entangle, jumble; run the fingers through, *Inf.* tousle, *Inf.* muss *or* muss up, *Inf.* mess *or* mess up; shuffle, riffle, mix up, intermix.

4. annoy, irritate, ruff, exasperate, raise one's dander, madden, get under one's skin, get in one's hair, get on one's nerves; disturb, agitate, upset, unsettle, rattle; disconcert, fluster, chagrin, embarrass, abash, discomfit, confuse, throw into confusion, perturb, stir; rile, disquiet, discompose, *Inf.* shake up; trouble, fret, pique, nettle, gall, chafe; torment, harass, plague, worry.

—*n.* 5. crimping, tucking, gathering, edging, trim, fillet, frill; jabot, ruche, ruching, flounce, ruff, wimple.

6. ripple, undulation, rimple, ruffling; flurry, bustle, stir, swirl, swirling, flutter.

rug, *n.* carpet, floor cover *or* covering, carpeting. wall-to-wall carpeting, indoor-outdoor carpeting; broadloom, drugget, braided rug, hooked rug, rag rug, ingrain, rya; scatter rug, area rug, throw rug, runner; mat, doormat, welcome mat, bathmat.

rugged, *adj.* **1.** (*of terrain or other surfaces*) rough, uneven, heavily wooded, dense, overgrown, bushy; pathless, trackless, impregnable, impassible; steep, rocky, rockstrewn, stony, full of obstacles, unassailable; anfractuous, tortuous; craggy, cragged, jagged, craggy, roughly broken, ragged, bumpy, unlevel, scabrous; stark, sheer, sharp, headlong, precipitous; furrowed, irregular, seamed, wrinkled, weathered, weather-beaten, seasoned; crabbed, gnarled, leathery, corrugated.

2. uncouth, unpolished, blunt, churlish; unruly, unmanagable, unrefined, barbarous.

3. harsh, severe, stern, gruff, dour; unbending, unmalleable, intractile, unyielding, firm; austere, stringent, demanding, strict; challenging, Spartan, exacting; difficult, hard, thorny, arduous, rigorous, onerous, uphill, strenuous, draining.

4. stormy, tempestuous, turbulent, wild, violent, raging; cruel, cutting, piercing, biting, fierce, pitiless, ruthless, savage.

5. strong, tough, hardy, robust, vigorous, hearty, hale, stalwart, sound; stout, substantial, solid, husky, brawny, steely, muscular, mighty, tough as leather, strong as a lion, solid, beefy, burly, lusty; sturdy, staunch, able-bodied, fit; wiry, sinewy, well-knit; hard-working, *Inf.* gritty

ruin, *n.* **1.** devastation, desolation, ravagement, havoc, destruction; dilapidation, ruination, wreck, wreckage, wrack, wrack and ruin; disruption, upheaval; crash, collision, crack-up.

2. overthrow, overturn, subversion, suppression, subdual, conquest; defeat, Waterloo, discomfiture, vanquishment, subjugation.

3. deterioration, decay, waste, breakdown, disintegration, depletion, dissipation, dispersion; collapse, breakup, disorganization, dissolution, undoing, debacle, failure, fiasco.

4. downfall, fall, nemesis, labefaction; failing, shortcoming, flaw, defect; curse, damnation, perdition, doom, fate, destiny, lot.

5. corruption, depravation, perversion, demoralization, vitiation; debasement, degradation; contamination, taint, poison, pollution, defilement; injury, damage, spoilage; scar, defacement, blemish.

6. distress, calamity, affliction, infliction, adversity, hardship, scourge; misfortune, setback, reversal, blow, disaster, catastrophe, cataclysm, accident; straits, difficulty, necessity.

7. loss, privation, deprivation, bereavement; poverty, impoverishment, want, destitution, neediness; impecuniosity, pennilessness, penury, indigence; beggary, mendicity, mendicancy; pauperage, pauperdom; bankruptcy, insolvency; wolf at the door, low water.

8. **ruins** remains, remnants, remainders; wreckage, debris, detritus; refuse, rubbish, waste; husks, chaff; vestige, trace, shadow; relics, reliquiae, fossil.

—*v.* **9.** devastate, demolish, desolate, lay waste, *Dial.* ruinate; ravage, work havoc upon, wreak havoc on, gut, bring to ruin, lay in ruins; wreck, *Sl.* total, knock to pieces, dash to pieces, reduce to nothing; pulverize, crush, smash, squelch, *Sl.* smush, mash; crash, shatter, blast, blow up, batter, break; fracture, splinter, tear, crack, split, rend, tear apart, wrench apart; mutilate, mangle, maim, make mincemeat of; despoil, spoliate, rob, plunder, pillage, sack, ransack; vandalize, waste, *Sl.* trash; undo, unmake, unbuild, dismantle, disassemble, take apart.

10. raze, tear down, pull down, take down, bring down, break down, throw down, beat down, batten down; cast down, knock down, fling down, hurl down, precipitate, *Inf.* spill, tumble, topple; fell, lay level, prostrate, level, floor, bulldoze, flatten; cut down, chop down, hew down, mow down.

11. quash, crush, subdue, quell, stifle, suppress, squelch, vanquish, squash; cut short, shoot down, *Inf.* put the kibosh on, *Inf.* cook one's goose, nip, nip in the bud, scuttle; terminate, check, put an end to, dissolve, stop.

12. subvert, topple, cause the downfall of, upset, *Sl.* put the skids under, defeat, triumph over, conquer; overthrow, overturn, overwhelm, overcome; damn, seal the doom of, curse.

13. extirpate, destroy totally, annihilate, discreate, exterminate, abolish; expunge, obliterate, efface, eradicate, erase, decimate; strike out, blot out, stamp out, crush out, snuff out, wipe out; purge, eliminate, remove, liquidate, get rid of, leave no vestige *or* trace of, cast off, expel; extinguish, put an end to, bring to an end; kill, kill off, slay, slaughter, cut [s.o.'s] throat; murder, finish, finish off, *Sl.* do in, *Sl.* zap, sacrifice.

14. blunder, fail, *Sl.* gum up the works, mess up, *Inf.* rain on, play havoc with, raise havoc with; spoil, *Dial.* butch, botch, *Sl.* cook, *Sl.* louse up, *Sl.* screw up, *Inf.* make a hash of, upset the *or* one's applecart.

15. corrupt, deprave, pervert, demoralize, vitiate; debase, degrade, disgrace, dishonor; taint, poison, pollute, defile; injure, harm, impair, damage, spoil; mar, mark, stain, scar, deface, blemish.

16. undermine, sap, weaken; discredit, invalidate; nullify, neutralize, counteract.

17. deteriorate, decay, waste, break down, disintegrate, disrupt, disorganize; collapse, break up, dissipate, disperse.

18. reduce to poverty, impoverish, bring to want, pauperize, bankrupt; fleece, defraud, swindle.

19. violate, deflower, devirginate, rape, debauch, ravish, ravage; assault, attack, abuse, molest; seduce, betray, deceive, lead astray.

ruination, *n.* **1.** demolition, wiping out, laying waste, gutting, devastation, desolation; destroying, bringing to ruin, laying in ruins; wrecking, knocking to pieces, dashing to pieces, smashing; dismantling, disassembly, taking apart.

2. razing, tearing down, pulling down, taking down, bringing down, breaking down, throwing down, beating down; casting down, knocking down, flinging down, hurling down, precipitating, *Inf.* spilling; felling, leveling, prostration; cutting down, chopping down, hewing down.

3. pulverizing, crushing, squelching, *Sl.* smushing, mashing; crashing, shattering, battering, breaking; fracturing, tearing apart, wrenching apart, cracking, splitting; mutilation, mangling, making mincemeat of.

4. annihilation, discreation, extermination, extirpation, extinguishment, extinction; erasure, erasion, effacement, eradication, expunction, cancellation, obliteration; excising, cutting out, cutting off; blotting out, striking out, stamping out, crushing out, rubbing out; killing, slaying, slaughter; murdering, finishing off, *Sl.* zapping, sacrificing.

5. quashing, crushing, subduing, quelling, suppressing, squelching, vanquishing, squashing; cutting short, shooting down, *Inf.* putting the kibosh on, *Inf.* cooking [s.o.'s] goose, nipping in the bud; termination, checking, putting an end to, stopping.

6. blundering, failing, *Sl.* gumming up the works,

messing up, playing havoc with, raising havoc with; spoiling, *Dial.* butching, botching, *Sl.* lousing up, *Sl.* screwing up, *Inf.* making a hash of, upsetting the applecart.
7. corrupting, perverting, demoralizing, vitiating; debasing, degrading, disgracing, dishonoring; tainting, poisoning, polluting, defiling; injuring, harming, impairing, damaging; marring, marking, staining, scarring, defacing.
8. undermining, sapping, weakening; discreditation, invalidation; nullification, neutralization.
9. deteriorating, decaying, wasting, breaking down, disintegrating, disrupting; collapsing, breaking up, dissipating, dispersing.

ruined, *adj.* **1.** dilapidated, decrepit, in ruins, derelict, gone to wrack and ruin, the worse for wear, weather-beaten, weather-scarred, blasted; blighted, rotting, deteriorated, crumbling, falling down, going to pieces, *Inf.* tottering, nodding to its fall; time-worn, time-scarred, moth-eaten, moss-covered, moldering, gone to pot, *Inf.* gone to the dogs, gone to seed, worsened, on the downgrade, on the decline; *Inf.* down the drain, *Inf.* shot, *Sl.* kaput, *Sl.* cooked, *Sl.* sunk; spoiled, marred, decayed, rotten, damaged, wrecked, ravaged, despoiled, eroded, wasted; mangled, rent, torn, mutilated, vandalized; shattered, smashed, in bits *or* pieces; burned, scorched; *All Inf.* botched, screwed up, fouled up, loused up, snafued, bollixed up, messed up, hashed up.
2. destroyed, devastated, desolated; smashed, crushed, broken, overcome, overthrown, overwhelmed, vanquished, fallen, *Sl.* done in; defeated, undone, *Inf.* done for, finished; worsted, bested, outdone, beaten, put to rout, routed, scattered, *Inf.* licked, *Inf.* whipped, *Inf.* trimmed, *Inf.* trounced.
3. wasted, withered, shriveled, wilted, wizened, dried-up.
4. past hope, beyond recall, irreclaimable, unsalvageable, irreversible, irremediable, irreparable, beyond remedy, lost, gone.
5. insolvent, broken, bankrupt, *Inf.* broke, *Inf.* flat-broke, *Inf.* stone-broke, *Sl.* busted, *Sl.* flat; destitute, in the gutter, *Sl.* on the skids, shabby, seedy, down at the heels, out at the elbows.

ruinuous, *adj.* **1.** devastating, disastrous, destructive, dire, dreadful, calamitous, catastrophic, cataclysmic; wasting, wasteful, ravaging, pulverizing; disruptive, troublesome, distracting, obstreperous, unruly, subversive.
2. extirpative, annihilative, eradicative, obliterative; deadly, fatal, fell, mortal, lethal, *Archaic.* lethiferous; killing, murderous, suicidal, homicidal, slaughterous.
3. injurious, pernicious, deleterious, baneful, mischievous; hurtful, harmful, noxious, noisome; malicious, vicious, wicked, evil, malevolent; detrimental, disadvantageous, damaging; baleful, menacing, malignant, bad; unwholesome, poisonous, toxic, pestilential, pestiferous, virulent.
4. adverse, negative, contrary, contradictory, opposed, opposing, opposite, antithetical, conflicting; disproving, refuting, confuting, discrediting, invalidating; derogatory, disparaging, disapproving; unfavorable, unpropitious, unauspicious; unfriendly, antagonistic, clashing, hostile.
5. fallen into ruin, run-down, weather-beaten, time-worn, worn-out; dilapidated, broken-down, decrepit, tumble-down, antiquated; decayed, crumbling, moldering, rotten, moth-eaten, seedy; rusty, frayed, shabby, threadbare, faded.
6. devastated, desolated, ravaged, destroyed, wrecked, demolished; deteriorated, decayed, wasted, depleted, dissipated, dispersed; collapsed, disorganized, dissolved, undone.
7. corrupted, depraved, perverted, demoralized, vitiated; debased, degraded; contaminated, tainted, poisoned, polluted, defiled; injured, damaged, spoiled, marred, scarred, defaced.
8. deprived, bereaved; impoverished, wanting, destitute, *Inf.* on the rocks, needy; penniless, penurious, indigent; bankrupt, insolvent.

rule, *n.* **1.** principle, tenet, law, precept; regulation, ordinance, bylaw, statute; control, restriction, ban, embargo, prohibition; mandate, commandment, directive, order, court order.
2. standard, guide, guideline; basic rule, *Inf.* rule of the road, formula, formulary, recipe, method, way; model, canon, criterion; natural law, general truth, truth *or* self-evident truth; rubric, doctrine, dogma, belief; mathematical rule, *Math.* formula, theorem, *Math.* proposition, *Math.* corollary; moral law, rule of conduct, code, personal code *or* standards.
3. dominion, reign, government, regulation, direction; command, domination, mastery, sway, authority, control, mastery, power, influence; sovereignty, supremacy, ascendancy; supervision, oversight, leadership; kingship, (*in India*) raj, presidency, chieftaincy, chieftainship, czarism, imperial rule, papal rule; dominance, eminence; tenure of office.
4. usual occurrence, custom, convention, customary practice, habitual practice, wont, routine, matter of course, habit, rut, groove.
5. **as a rule** usually, generally, ordinarily, commonly; habitually, customarily, frequently, often, repeatedly; universally, extensively, almost always; for the most part, in the main, on the whole, mainly; most times, almost every time, on a regular basis.
—*v.* **6.** control, have control of, be in control; boss, call the shots, *Inf.* call the tune; direct, supervise, superintend, oversee; head, lead, manage, administer, have *or* be in charge, preside over; dominate, rule the roost, wear the crown, wield the scepter, wield the power *or* authority, sit on the throne.
7. prevail, be prevalent, predominate, hold sway; preponderate, abound, flourish, thrive, overspread, spread over, be widespread, be universal, be rife, be rampart, be epidemic; be widely-known, be all-pervasive, be all over; endure, last, continue, persist; be current, be fashionable, be popular, be in vogue, be à la mode, be all the rage.
8. decree, deem, judge, adjudge; settle, order, hand down a decision; decide, make a judgment, exercise judicial power.
9. **rule out** eliminate, exclude, dismiss, reject; disregard, ignore, by-pass, overlook; refuse to admit, not put into consideration, not consider eligible *or* worthy, put out of the running.

ruler, *n.* **1.** sovereign, monarch, crowned head, majesty, royal personage, potentate, dynast, king, *Latin. rex;* caesar, czar, kaiser; prince, prince consort, prince regent, regent, viceroy; protector, governor, tetrarch; suzerain, overlord, chief, chieftain, high chief; liege, ethnarch, gerent, caliph, sultan, shah, khan, mogul, mikado, doge, inca, rajah, maharajah, amir, khedive, satrap; pasha, bey, tetrarch, mandarin, hierarch; pharaoh, sachem, sheik, aga, archon.
2. commandant, magistrate, provost; mayor, chancellor, prefect; generalissimo, Lord admiral, commander-in-chief, *Ger. Führer,* duce; patriarch, doyen, superior, senior, ruling elder; leader, cicerone, conductor.

ruling, *n.* **1.** decision, judgment, decree, judicial decision, opinion, official opinion; adjudication, finding, verdict, award, call; determination, resolution, outcome, upshot, result; penalty, sentence.

—*adj.* 2. governing, managing, directing, commanding; presiding, officiating; overseeing, supervising, superintending.

3. main, dominant, predominant; preponderant, preponderating, prevailing; preeminent, prominent, supreme, chief, principal; controlling, determining, strongest.

4. widespread, prevalent, general, universal, rife, rampant, epidemic; common, commonplace, usual, normal, conventional; current, popular, à la mode, modish; all the rage, stylish, up to the minute, the latest thing.

rumble, *v.* 1. thunder, peal, roll, roar, boom; grumble, growl, groan; resound, sound, echo, reecho, reverberate.

—*n.* 2. thunder, roar, bang, boom; grumble, growl, groan, peal; reverberation, roll, rumbling, resonance, *Obs., Rare.* reboation; drumming, barrage, tattoo, cannonade, din.

ruminate, *v.* 1. chew the cud, rechew, remasticate, *Dial.* rechaw; chew, masticate, *Dial.* chaw.

2. meditate, contemplate, cogitate; cerebrate, lucubrate, think, put on one's thinking cap, be abstracted, be lost in thought; concentrate, focus, put one's mind to, have one's mind on; muse, ponder, think about, wonder about; brood, mull over, dwell on, be in a brown study; reflect on, think over, consider, speculate.

rumination, *n.* 1. chewing the cud, remastication; chewing, mastication, *Dial.* chawing.

2. meditation, meditating, contemplation, contemplating, cogitation, cogitating; cerebration, lucubration, thought, thinking, concentration; musing, pondering, thinking about, wondering about, reverie; brooding over, consideration, considering, speculation, speculating.

rummage, *v.* 1. search, hunt, ransack, rifle through, *Sl.* look through, *Sl.* paw through, explore; turn over, turn inside out, turn upside down, disarrange, forage; look into, look about for, examine, pry into, poke around for, peer into, snoop around, smell out; sift through, flip through, shuffle through, winnow; *Sl.* frisk, *Sl.* snatch around for, leave no stone unturned.

2. find, find out, come across, discover, uncover, unearth; bring up, dredge up, root out, fish out, come up with.

—*n.* 3. odds and ends, miscellanea, hodgepodge, mingle-mangle, mishmash; knick-knacks, bric-a-brac, farrago, motley.

4. search, hunt, quest, probe; exploration, examination, scrutinization, investigation, inquiry, inquest; scavenger hunt, forage, house-search, perquisition.

rumor, *n.* 1. report, *Archaic.* bruit, news, tidings, information, word, *Inf.* the good word; *Inf.* the lowdown, gossip, hearsay, grapevine, buzz, word of mouth, talk, *Inf.* scuttlebutt, tittle-tattle; *Sl.* inside info, *Sl.* scoop; canard, hoax, whispering campaign, scandal.

—*v.* 2. gossip, tattle, tell, say, give out, make known, reveal, drop, leak, let fall; fill [s.o.] in, give [s.o.] the lowdown; whisper, breathe, intimate, hint, suggest.

3. (*all of gossip*) bruit, circulate, noise abroad *or* about, broadcast, circulate, spread, disseminate; publish, proclaim, display, blazon, announce.

rump, *n.* 1. buttocks, posterior, loins, breech, hindquarters, (*of a horse*) croup, *Anat.* sacrum, *Zool.* podex, *Zool.* pygidium.

2. (*all of humans*) bottom, seat, *Fr. derrière, Inf.* rear *or* rear end, *Brit. Inf.* bum, *Inf.* backside, *Inf.* butt, *Inf.* duff, *Inf.* tail. See **buttocks.**

rumple, *v.* 1. crumple, wrinkle, crush, crinkle, crankle, cockle, ripple; pucker, purse, crease, crimple, twill, ruck, ruckle; crisp, fold, curl, flounce, rimple, crimp; knit, furrow, ridge, corrugate, shirr.

2. tousle, ruffle, dishevel, muss, disorganize; mess, disarrange, disorder, snarl.

—*n.* 3. crease, fold, ruck, pucker; wrinkle, furrow, ridge, crow's-feet; tuck, pleat, plait, gather, dog-ear, double, lapel; plicature, ply, flexure, flounce, plica; crinkle, crankle, crumple, cockle; ripple, ripplet, wavelet, wave, undulation.

rumpus, *n.* 1. commotion, uproar, fracas, confusion, disturbance; tumult, storm, affray, ado, bedlam, mayhem, *Inf.* shindy, rowdydow, hoo-ha, *Inf.* foofaraw; pother, stir, brouhaha, *Fr. tohu-bohu;* melee, brawl, rough-house, free-for-all, *Sl.* rumble, rout, riot.

2. controversy, quarrel, row, hassle, scrap; tiff, spat, rhubarb, argument, dispute; *Inf.* ruction, *Brit.* barney, *Sl.* knock-down-drag-out; wrangle, dustup, donnybrook, fight, altercation; broil, embroilment, embranglement, words, squabble, squall, imbroglio, tussle, perturbation.

run, *v.* 1. dash, dart, bolt, tear, tear along, bowl along, make time, cover ground, make strides *or* rapid strides; sprint, fly, flit, whiz, whisk; zoom, zip, career, rip, scour, scud, scorch, burn up the road, outstrip the wind, race like the wind, go *or* be off like a shot, *Chiefly Brit.* hare, *Inf.* clip, *Inf.* roar, *Inf.* barrel, *Inf.* pour it on, *Inf.* eat up the road; hasten, make haste, race, speed, accelerate, hustle, hurry, post, rush, scramble, move swiftly, move quickly, step lively, step quickly, double-time, *Inf.* hump *or* hump it; step on it, hop to it, snap to it, *Sl.* get cracking, *Sl.* get the lead out, get a hustle *or* move on, *Sl.* stir one's stumps; jog, trot, canter, lope; scamper, scurry, scoot, trip, skip.

2. flee, abscond, escape, take flight, take to flight, take wing, *Sl.* wing it, *Inf.* beat it, *Inf.* skip out, *Inf.* skedaddle, *Sl.* skidoodle, *Sl.* vamoose; run away, run off, elope, take to one's heels, make a quick exit, *Inf.* take off, *Inf.* clear out, *Inf.* make tracks, *Inf.* cut out, *Inf.* cut and run, *Inf.* fly the coop, *Sl.* split, *Sl.* scram, *Sl.* blow, *Sl.* hightail it, *Sl.* lam *or* take it on the lam; retreat, withdraw, decamp, take oneself off, take French leave, quit the scene, make a getaway, beat a retreat, beat a hasty retreat, run for it, make a run for it, show the heels, show a clean *or* extra-light pair of heels, make a beeline for, *Inf.* take to the woods, *Inf.* head for the hills.

3. go, go by, go *or* pass over, go at, *Scot.* gang; proceed, move, advance, pass, pass on; progress, wend one's way, roll, roll on, continue; migrate, transmigrate, traverse, travel, trek; meander, wander, rove, gad, roam, drift, stray, veer.

4. turn, rotate; slide, slip, glide, pass through.

5. flow, stream, spill, spill into, empty, empty into; issue, issue forth, surge, gush, flood, jet, spurt, spout; leak, leak out, leak into, seep, trickle; overflow, flow over, spill over, well over, brim over, slop, slosh; cataract, cascade.

6. melt, fuse, mold, cast, deliquesce, liquesce, thaw, *Obs.* colliquate; melt down, flux, liquefy, liquate, liquidize, dissolve.

7. spread, spread over, creep, climb, trail, shift, drift; extend, range, reach, sweep, stretch, span, cover, straddle, take in, surround, environ, encompass.

8. operate, function, work, perform, act, *Inf.* tick, *Inf.* percolate; drive, propel, push, force, impel; actuate, turn, mobilize; direct, manage, conduct, maintain, handle, carry on *or* out *or* through; drive, steer, pilot, navigate; manipulate, maneuver, control,

govern, command, order, prescribe, make the rules, lay down the laws, *Inf.* mastermind, *Inf.* pull the strings, *Inf.* call the shots; supervise, superintend, oversee, head, head up, stand over, *Inf.* boss.
9. (*all of animals*) herd, shepherd, tend, ride herd; drive, ride hard, ride into the ground.
10. unravel, come undone, come apart, come apart at the seams; snag, tear, rip.
11. amount, amount to, total, total up to, come to, come up to, add up to, mount up to, run to, run into, *Inf.* tote *or* tote up to, *Inf.* tot *or* tot up to; cost, sell for, bring, bring in, fetch, *Inf.* set one back.
12. incur, amass, accumulate, run up; get, gain, acquire, contract, invite, bring, bring on; fall into, slip into, slide into; increase, raise, advance, extend, enlarge, *Inf.* boost, *Inf.* hike *or* hike up, *Inf.* up, *Inf.* jack up.
13. drive, propel, force, thrust, lash, flog, push, shove, bulldoze, pile drive; impel, compel, press, prod, poke, goad.
14. convey, transport, ship, dispatch, smuggle, sneak, sneak in, bootleg, rustle, poach, shanghai.
15. **run across** come on *or* upon, come across, stumble upon *or* over, hit upon, chance upon, happen upon, find; encounter, meet, meet with, run into, cross the path of, *Inf.* meet up with, *Inf.* come *or* run up against, *Inf.* bump into, *Inf.* run smack into.
16. **run after** pursue, follow, chase, chase after, give chase, make after, prowl after, *Archaic.* prosecute; shadow, haunt, trail, tread on the heels of, dog, hound, *Inf.* tail.
17. **run down** **a.** overturn, strike and fell, overrun, run over, ride down, trample, trample on *or* upon, trample underfoot, ride roughshod over; collide with, crash into, bang into, slam into, ram, bump, strike, knock down, hit and run, bump and run. **b.** track, track down, hunt, hunt down, stalk, trace; capture, catch, apprehend, collar, secure, take prisoner; seize, net, bag, ensnare, entrap, snatch, tackle, pounce upon. **c.** inspect, examine, peruse, view, study, look at, observe, survey, scan, look over, pass over, pore over. **d.** stop, shut off, shut down, break down, close down, give out, die; tire, get tired, weary, grow weary, flag, droop, play out, run out, burn out, *Inf.* peter out, *Sl.* poop out; fail, sink, decline, weaken, languish, slip, fade, wane, go downhill, waste, waste away, wither, wither away, lose strength, fall off, fall away. **e.** badmouth, vilify, defame. See **disparage** (*def.* 3). **f.** discover, find, locate, determine; search out, trace, trace down, track down; hunt out, fish out, ferret out, spy out, smell *or* sniff out, nose out, follow the trail *or* scent of.
18. **run out** end, finish, cease, terminate, conclude, expire, close, come to a close, draw to a close, come to an end, wind up; go out, pass away, be no more, be all over, run its course, *Inf.* have it *or* have its time.
19. **run out of** exhaust, consume, expend, deplete, use up, eat up, finish, finish off.
20. **run out on** *Informal.* abandon, desert, forsake, *Inf.* leave high and dry, *Inf.* leave out in the cold, *Inf.* leave holding the bag, *Inf.* leave in the lurch.
21. **run over** **a.** run down, hit and knock down, knock down, ride over, override, overrun, trample, trample on *or* upon, trample underfoot, ride rougshod over; hit and run, bump and run. **b.** exceed, pass, surpass, transcend, go beyond; overreach, overgo, overpass, overlap, overshoot, overshoot the mark; overflow, flow over, spill, spill over, spill out, slosh, slop, well over, brim over. **c.** repeat, iterate, reiterate, recant, recapitulate, rehearse; reproduce, duplicate, echo, redo, do again, do over, say again, *Sl.* come again; review, rehash, summarize, sum up, go over *or* through, *Inf.* run it down.
—*n.* **22.** dash, sprint, stride, clip, race, career, speed, scud, swoop; burst, burst of speed, spurt; rush, plunge, headlong rush *or* plunge; scoot, scamper, scurry, scuttle.
23. escape, *Archaic.* scape *or* 'scape, flight, departure; running away, bolt, decampment, desertion, abandonment, elopement, absquatulation, French leave, retreat, hasty retreat, *Sl.* disappearing act, *Sl.* skedaddle, *Sl.* skedaddling, *Sl.* scramming; getaway, jailbreak, prisonbreak, *Inf.* break, *Inf.* breakout.
24. pace, running pace; jog, trot, jogtrot, dogtrot; canter; lope, high lope; gallop, hand gallop, full gallop, dead run.
25. trip, quick trip, sojourn, visit, short stay; journey, peregrination, excursion, tour; jaunt, outing, junket; expedition, trek, stalk, hike; walk, stroll, ramble, saunter, promenade, sally, turn, perambulation, constitutional; drive, ride, Sunday drive, *Inf.* whirl, *Inf.* spin, *Inf.* joyride, *Sl.* tool; voyage, cruise, crossing, sail.
26. interval, period, length of time; time, term, duration, while, space; spell, season, round, stretch, fit, *Inf.* go.
27. amount, quantity, make, making, batch, lot, deal, extent, measure, *Inf.* heap, *Inf.* mess; part, portion; number, count, sum; total, whole, sum total, grand total.
28. stream, brook, streamlet, brooklet, creek, *Dial.* crick, *U.S. Dial.* kill, rivulet, rill, rindle, runnel *or* runlet *or Dial.* rundle, *Brit. Dial.* beck, *Brit. Dial.* gill, *Scot. and North Eng.* sike, *Scot. and North Eng.* burn; channel, branch, waterway, watercourse.
29. flow, flux, effluence, efflux, outpour; spate, surge, rush, onrush, outrush, gush, outgush, outburst; flood, inundation, deluge, torrent, river; jet, spout, spurt.
30. average, norm, mean, golden mean, medium, happy medium, balance, midpoint, middle, middle course, middle-of-the-road, *Latin. via media;* rule, generality, par, mainstream, main current, main course; trend, drift, tendency, general tendency, movement, direction, tenor, swing, sign of the times.
31. course, way, procedure, use, usage, order, observance; vogue, mode, fashion; bias, aim, set, leaning, turn, penchant; wont, habit, habitude, attitude; custom, practice, second nature, matter of course, standing procedure, common practice; routine, rut, groove, track, treadmill, rat race, *Inf.* grind, *Inf.* daily grind.
32. command, control, governance, power, rule, reign; freedom, liberty, license, *Archaic.* loose, free reign, free course, free hand, carte blanche; latitude, *Inf.* leeway, room, scope, free scope, long rope *or* tether.
33. deposit, mineral deposit, quarry, ore bed, dike; vein, lode, rich lode, mother lode; mine, gold mine, bonanza, cornucopia, well, fountain, fount.
34. (*all of hosiery*) rip, tear, rent, slash, *Chiefly Brit.* ladder; pull, snag; fray, frazzle.
35. motion, locomotion, passage, advance, progress, forward motion, onward movement; current, tide, drift, flow, flux.
36. continuance, continuation, maintenance, stay, staying power, endurance; permanence, permanency, constancy; persistence, perseverance; extension, prolongation, protraction; currency, popularity, continued popularity.
37. series, sequence, progression, succession, continuum, concatenation, nexus; string, unbroken string, row, set, chain, stream, steady stream.
38. path, pathway, trail, track, beaten path *or* track,

way, runway, footway.

39. pipe, trough, runner, conduit; gutter, drain, eave *or* eaves trough, scupper, *Brit.* sough *or esp. Scot.* sugh; chute, shoot, flume, sluice, spillway.

40. herd, flock, drove, pack, bunch, colony; (*all of birds*) bevy, flight; (*all of fish*) school, shoal; (*all of bees*) swarm, swarming; (*all of insects*) cloud, plague.

41. *Music.* roulade, cadenza, bravura, fioritura, flourish, arpeggio, trill, *Jazz or Rock.* riff.

42. **in the long run** finally, ultimately, in the end; eventually, in time, in due time; after all, all things considered, all things said and done, in the final analysis; generally, in general, on the whole, on the average, mainly, in the main, by and large, for the most part, all in all; virtually, chiefly, mostly.

43. **on the run** *Informal.* **a.** hurriedly, in a hurry, hastily, in haste, with haste *or* all haste, with a rush, in a sweat; quickly, speedily, swiftly. **b.** on the move, on the go, on the fly, on the march, on the wing, on the road, in motion, *Inf.* on the hop *or* jump. **c.** bolting, escaping, running, hiding, fleeing, in flight, *Sl.* on the lam *or* lamming it, *Sl.* hightailing it.

—adj. **44.** melted, molten, fused; liquefied, liquescent, deliquescent, thawed.

runaway, *n.* **1.** fugitive, fleer, escaper, *Archaic.* runagate; deserter, defector, decamper, absconder, *Inf.* skedaddler; escapee, truant, eloper, displaced person, DP, émigré, evacuee; renegade, *Chiefly Australian.* (*of animals*) breakaway, mustang, maverick.

—adj. **2.** escaped, fled, fugitive, at large, flown, out, in flight; wild, renegade, loose, on the loose, *Sl.* on the lam, *Sl.* hot.

3. easy, easily won, *Sl.* pie, *Sl.* cake, easygoing, plain-sailing; cinchy, nothing to it, effortless.

run-down, *adj.* **1.** unhealthy, in poor health, sickly, peaked, with low resistance, languishing, on one's last legs; debilitated, valetudinarian, *Inf.* off one's feed, below par, not oneself, laid low, *Sl.* in a bad way, *Inf.* far gone; weakened, out of condition *or* shape, worn-out, fatigued, drained, exhausted, tired, enervated, spent, *Inf.* used up, *Inf.* pooped, *Inf.* feeling awful.

2. dilapidated, ramshackle, tumbledown, broken-down, decrepit, tottery; in ruins, in a shambles, gone to wrack and ruin, *Inf.* beat-up, *Sl.* slummy, seedy.

3. unwound, wound down, stopped, silent, still, stilled, hushed, mute; not running, not working, out of order, *Inf.* out-of-commission, *Inf.* on the fritz.

rundown, *n.* summary, résumé, conspectus, recapitulation, *Inf.* recap, summation, *Inf.* wrapup, windup, debriefing; sketch, thumbnail sketch, outline, skeleton, highlights, overview; run-through, walk-through, once-over-lightly; rehash, review, brief, briefing, flight plan, game plan, scenario, *Inf.* chalk-talk.

runlet, *n.* stream, brook, streamlet, brooklet, creek, rivulet, rill. See **rivulet**.

runner, *n.* **1.** racer, sprinter, hurdler; miler, long-distance runner, cross-country runner, harrier; track and field man.

2. messenger, messenger-boy, courier, dispatch-bearer, *Brit.* commissionaire, *Brit.* express, *Sl.* gopher.

3. branch, shoot, offshoot; creeper, *Bot.* stolon, *Bot.* flagellum, *Bot.* sarmentum.

run-of-the-mill, *adj.* average, common, ordinary, normal, garden-variety; commonplace, everyday, matter-of-fact, familiar, *Inf.* same old, run-of-the-mine; fair, tolerable, passable, so-so, *Fr. comme ci, comme ça, Sp. así así*; decent, modest, not bad, moderate, betwixt and between; mediocre, middling, second-rate, unimpressive, *Inf.* no great shakes, *Inf.* nothing to get excited about; usual, regular, routine.

runt, *n.* midget, short person, dwarf, pygmy, dandiprat, chit, urchin; punk, *Sl.* shrimp, *Sl.* wart, pipsqueak, half-pint, *Inf.* shortie; elf, Lilliputian, pigwidgeon, manikin, cock sparrow, hop-o'-my-thumb, homunculus; fingerling, dapperling, *Inf.* peewee, gnome, brownie; Humpty Dumpty, Tom Thumb, Thumbelina.

rupture, *n.* **1.** rift, fissure, scissure, fault, flaw, crack, split; fracture, break, burst; disruption, disjunction, breakage, breaking, bursting; severance, cleavage, separation, division; rent, tear, rip, cut, cleft, slit; slash, slice, rime, gap, space; *Pathol.* hernia.

2. breach, falling-out, schism, break; disunion, disunity, division; discord, disagreement, disfavor, disaffection, alienation, estrangement; quarrel, argument, dispute, polemic, altercation, controversy; feud, vendetta; contention, litigation, variance, opposition.

—v. **3.** break, burst, crack, fissure, *Sl.* bust; fracture, split, disrupt, breach, check; rend, separate, disunite, disjoin; part, sunder, put asunder, cleave, divide; break up, snap, tear, cut, rip.

rural, *adj.* **1.** country, countrified, unsophisticated, rough, inurbane, crude, farmerish; bucolic, rustic, agrestic, provincial; pastoral, Arcadian.

2. agricultural, farm, farming, agrarian; agronomical, geoponic, georgic.

ruse, *n.* trick, stratagem, artifice, wile, contrivance; subterfuge, device, blind, sham, dodge; deception, deceit, maneuver, manipulation, machination, move, gambit, coup; feint, sleight, ploy, decoy; chicanery, jugglery, cheat, knavery; tactic, *Sl.* gimmick, red herring, *Inf.* fakement, put-on; game, *Sl.* gig, *Sl.* racket.

rush, *v.* **1.** hasten, *Literary.* haste, hurry, move quickly, lose no time; make haste, *Scot.* swith, *Scot.* whirry, race, scurry, skip, spurt, whisk, run, sprint; press on, push on, shoot, tear, fly, fly on the wings of the wind, outstrip the wind, take wing, take to flight; scour, hustle, bustle, scamper, scuttle, trip, flit; hotfoot, hotfoot it, hightail, hightail it, *Inf.* skeddadle, *Inf.* move on out, *Inf.* move it, be on the run, beat a hasty retreat; whip off, whip away, dash off, run like mad, *Sl.* get cracking, *Sl.* get one's rear in gear, *Sl.* shake a leg, *Sl.* go like a bat out of hell, go *or* run wide open, *Inf.* go like a shot; speed up, put on more speed, step on the gas, *Sl.* step on it, *Sl.* burn up the road, cover ground, *Inf.* burn rubber, *Inf.* scratch off; make strides, do some tall stepping, hie one's way, *Inf.* make it snappy, look alive.

2. accelerate, quicken, advance, precipitate; expedite, dispatch, make short work of; finish quickly, dash off, send through fast.

3. charge, attack, blitzkrieg, blitz, rampage, assault; set upon, pounce upon, descend upon, fall on, open fire upon; light into, *Inf.* lace into, *Inf.* rip into, *Inf.* tear into, *Sl.* zap; beset, besiege, siege, beleaguer, *Inf.* gang up on.

—n. **4.** charge, attack, assault, offensive, onslaught, blitzkrieg, blitz; storming, *Fr. coup de main*, invasion, aggression, incursion, escalade; siege, besiegement, besetment; surge, sudden appearance, ambush; onset, sudden commencement, fast start, abrupt beginning.

5. drive, dash, run, stampede; scramble, mad scramble, race, scurry, push, plunge.

6. haste, harum-scarum, hurry-scurry, pell-mell, helter-skelter; bustle, ado, hubbub; velocity, speed, rapidity, dispatch, celerity; quickness, expedition, promptitude, hastiness; flurry, flutter, turmoil, commotion; stir, whirl, pother, ferment.

—adj. **7.** hasty, quick, rapid, swift, fast, brisk; prompt, expeditious, instantaneous, immediate; hurried, urgent; careless, slapdash, cursory, superficial.

russet, *adj.* reddish-brown, coppery, chestnut, foxy,

hazel, auburn, rust-colored, rusty; yellowish-brown, fawn, cinnamon, tawny; light brown, ecru, beige; brownish-red, rufous, maroon; brickdust-colored, autumnal.

rust, *n.* **1.** oxidation, patination, corrosion; patina, verdigris, aerugo; tarnish, stain, film, incrustation.

—*v.* **2.** oxidize, corrode, erode, wear away; film over, tarnish.

3. deteriorate, go to pot, go to seed, go stale, go downhill, degenerate, decline; fall apart, fall apart at the seams, hit the skids; decay, wither, wither on the vine, rot.

4. erode, eat away, eat at, wear away, gnaw at, undermine; impair, injure, damage, harm; spoil, blight.

rustic, *adj.* **1.** rural, farm, country, agrestic, agrarian, agricultural, agronomical, geoponic, georgic; pastoral, bucolic, bucolical, sylvan, Arcadian.

2. plain, simple, modest, unpretentious, unpretending, unassuming, unaffected, normal, informal; unsophisticated, unpolished, unrefined, uncultured, uncultivated; naive, artless, guileless, ingenuous, candid, open, unsuspecting; coarse, rough, roughcast, roughhewn, linsey-woolsey, inelegant, indelicate; inurbane, backwoods, provincial, countrified, country-bred, country-born, upcountry, from the sticks, yokelish, *Sl.* hickish, *Sl.* rube, *Sl.* hayseed; homespun, homebred, homey, homely, homelike, homish, down-home, (*usu. of thought or philosophy*) cracker-barrel, *Inf.* folksy.

3. uncouth, rude, graceless, lacking in the social graces, unmannerly, ill-mannered, ill-bred, low-bred; crude, vulgar, crass, raw, boorish, churlish; awkward, clumsy, inept, maladroit, heavy-handed, blundering, bungling, gawky, gawkish, ungainly, like a bull in a china shop; loutish, oafish, doltish, lumpish, lumpen, lubberly, cloddish, clodhopping, clownish.

—*n.* **4.** peasant, provincial, country cousin, countryman, hobnail; farmer, plowman, plowboy, chuff, gaffer, swain, kerne, son *or* tiller of the soil, (*in Egypt*) fellah, (*in Russia*) muszhik, (*in Spanish America and Southwestern U.S.*) peon, *Archaic.* hind; yokel, bumpkin, country bumpkin, hawbuck, *Dial.* lumpkin, *Often Disparaging.* hillbilly, *Disparaging.* bogtrotter, *Inf.* chawbacon, *Inf.* cider squeezer, *Sl.* hick, *Sl.* woodhick, *Sl.* rube, *Sl.* hayseed, *Sl.* hoosier, *Fr. Sl. truffe.*

rusticate, *v.* **1.** vacation, vacation in the country, sojourn, sojourn in the country, retire to the country, estivate; retire, go into retirement, retire from the world, abandon *or* forsake the world, seclude oneself, go into seclusion, shut oneself up, hole up, live apart, live alone; drop out *or* opt out of society, drop *or* opt out, *Sl.* cop out.

2. ruralize, go rural, pastoralize, go pastoral, countrify, go country, return to the soil *or* land.

rusticity, *n.* **1.** ruralism, agrarianism, agriculturalism; pastoralism, pastorality, bucolicism, provincialism, provinciality.

2. plainness, simplicity, modesty, unspoiledness, unpretentiousness, unaffectedness, normality, normalcy, informality; unsophisticatedness, unsophistication, lack of polish *or* refinement, unculturedness; naïveté, naïveness, artlessness, guilelessness, ingenuousness, candidness, openness; coarseness, roughness, inelegantness, indelicateness; inurbanity, backwoodsiness, yokelism, *Sl.* hickishness, *Sl.* rubishness; hominess, homeliness, homishness, *Inf.* folksiness.

3. uncouthness, rudeness, gracelessness, unmannerliness, ill-manneredness; crudeness, crassness, rawness, boorishness, churlishness, oafishness; awkwardness, clumsiness, gawkiness, cloddishness, doltishness, loutishness.

rustle, *v.* **1.** swish, whisper, whoosh, susurrate, sibilate; crinkle, tinkle, ripple; swash, plash.

2. move, stir, sway, agitate, flutter, wave, flap.

3. *U.S. Informal.* poach, abduct, plunder, kidnap, pirate; steal, purloin, filch, *Sl.* lift, *Sl.* liberate.

4. **rustle up** *U.S. Informal.* hunt, find, forage, get, gather, assemble, scout out.

—*n.* **5.** whoosh, froufrou, whisper, susurration, susurrus, rustling, crinkling, crinkle, ripple, rippling, swash, plash.

rustling, *adj.* swishing, whooshing, susurrous, susurrant, whispering, sibilant, crinkling, rippling; stirring, waving, swaying.

rusty, *adj.* **1.** oxidized, patinated, aeruginous; corroded, rusted, incrusted, stained, tarnished.

2. rust-colored, reddish; reddish-yellow, reddish-brown, yellowish-red. See **russet**.

3. (*of clothes, drapery, etc.*) faded, shabby, worn, worn thin, worn-out, time-worn, dilapidated, holey, falling apart, coming apart, needing mending *or* patching.

4. impaired, diminished, weak, feeble; below par, unpracticed, out of practice; out of shape, soft, stiff, sluggish, poorly; unalert, *Sl.* without the old pizzazz.

rut, *n.* **1.** furrow, groove, crack, track, cart *or* car path *or* track, slough; hollow, indentation, depression, gouge, stria; gutter, ditch, fosse, trench, channel, canal; wrinkle, line, seam, scar.

2. routine, pattern, system, habit, custom; grind, daily grind, treadmill, assembly line, *Inf.* rat race; dead end, stagnation.

—*v.* **3.** furrow, dig, excavate, scoop out, hollow out, groove.

4. be in heat, be in estrus, *Chiefly Brit.* tup, be sexually excited.

ruthful, *adj.* compassionate, pitiful, merciful; clement, mild, lenient, soft-hearted, kind-hearted, kind; indulgent, forbearing, exorable; forgiving, humane, long-suffering, tolerant; nice, gracious, hospitable; beneficent, benign, benevolent, philanthropic; sympathetic, understanding, empathic; sorrowful, comforting, commiserative, condolatory; obliging, friendly, brotherly, amicable, loving, good.

ruthless, *adj.* merciless, unmerciful, pitiless, unpitying, compassionless, uncompassionate; relentless, unrelenting, remorseless, implacable, inexorable, unsparing, unforgiving; heartless, unfeeling, cold, stony, steely, inflexible, inclement; hard, harsh, severe, stern; fell, grim, dire; adamant, hard-hearted, marble-hearted, adamantine; cruel, vicious, barbarous, inhuman, truculent, rancorous; vindictive, revengeful, vengeful, retaliatory; ferocious, savage, brutal, ferine; malevolent, malign, malignant, maleficent; cutthroat, murderous, bloodthirsty.

ruthlessly, *adv.* heartlessly, mercilessly, pitilessly, unmercifully, unpityingly; relentlessly, remorselessly, inexorably, implacably; with a vengeance, without mercy, spitefully, unforgivingly; unscrupulously, without feeling, without compassion, without compunction; cold-bloodedly, in cold blood, with malice aforethought, deliberately; cruelly, harshly, severely, savagely, brutally, inhumanly, barbarously.

ruthlessness, *n.* mercilessness, pitilessness, heartlessly, unkindness, hard-heartedness; relentlessness, remorselessness, implacability, inexorability, uncompassionateness, unforgivingness; unfeelingness, coldness, inflexibility, hardness, harshness, severeness, severity, grimness, sternness; cruelty, viciousness, barbarity, barbarousness, ferocity, fierceness, savagery, truculence; brutality, brutishness, inhumanity; sadism, masochism; fiendishness, deviltry, diablery.

rutilant, *adj.* glittering, glinting, glimmering, glistening, *Archaic.* glistering; shining, glowing, sparkling, twinkling, scintillating; shimmering, dazzling, bedazzling; flashing, fulgurating, gleaming, glaring, coruscating.

ruttish, *adj.* salacious, lustful, libidinous, libidinal, concupiscent, prurient, randy, *Sl.* horny, *Sl.* hot, *Sl.* hot to trot, *Sl.* with hot pants; passionate, hot-blooded, feverish, steamy, *Sl.* all fired up, in rut, in heat; lecherous, lubricous, satyric, satyrical, satyrlike, goatish, hircine, *Archaic.* lickerish; beastly, bestial, animalistic, swinish; licentious, lascivious, libertine, debauched, dissolute, depraved, dissipated, demoralized, rakish, rakehell; loose, wanton, wild, abandoned, profligate, lost; promiscuous, whorish, impure, of easy virtue, *Inf.* easy; dirty-minded, foul-minded, low-minded, base-minded, with one's mind in the gutter.

S

sable, *adj.* black, jet, jetty, jet-black; pitch, black as pitch, pitch-black, pitch-dark; inky, black as ink; raven, raven-black; coal-black; black *or* dark as night.

sabotage, *n.* **1.** treachery, subversion, treason; impairment, damage, harm, hurt, detriment, mischief, *Brit. Inf.* rattening; disablement, incapacitation.

—*v.* **2.** subvert, undermine, sap, sap the foundations of [s.t.]; hurt, harm, impair, damage; incapacitate, disable; hinder, hamper; cripple, lame, hamstring; spoil, ruin, dash, scotch; wreck, *Inf.* throw a wrench *or* a monkey wrench into the works, *Brit. Inf.* ratten; *All Sl.* bugger, queer, queer the works, gum up *or* screw up the works, foul up.

sac, *n.* baglike structure, pocket, pouch, *Anat., Zool.* bursa, *Anat., Zool.* capsule; vesicle, cyst; bladder, *Anat.* vesica; blister, bleb; *Bot.* cell, *Bot.* theca, *Biol., Anat.* loculus; *Both Anat.* saccule, sacculus; pod, seed vessel, legume, *Bot.* follicle, *Bot.* silique, pericarp, utricle; cuplike part, cavity, *Anat., Zool.* calyx.

saccharine, *adj.* **1.** sweet, sweetened, sugary, sugared, honey, honeyed, sweet as sugar *or* honey; candied, nectared, nectarous, nectareous, nectarean, confectionary; rich, luscious, delicious.

2. oversweet, cloying, sickening, nauseating, syrupy, mawkish, sentimental, maudlin, *Inf.* mushy, *Brit. Sl.* soppy.

sacerdotal, *adj.* priestly, hieratic, hieratical; episcopal, vicarly, prelatic, papal, pontifical, apostolic; pastoral, ministerial, clerical; ecclesiastical, churchly, hierarchic, hierarchical; sacred, divine, holy, consecrated.

sacerdotalism, *n.* hierarchy, hierocracy, hierarchism; prelacy, prelatism, clericalism, episcopacy, papalism, papality, papacy, theocracy; *Usu. Disparaging.* priestcraft.

sack[1], *n.* **1.** bag, pouch, *Midland U.S. and Scot.* poke, *Chiefly Scot.* pocket, *Obs.* budget; pack, packet, satchel; purse, grip, valise, carpetbag; saddlebag, *Southwestern U.S.* alforja; backpack, knapsack, kitbag, haversack, rucksack; gunnysack, gunny-bag, duffel bag; mailbag, mail pouch.

2. *U.S. Slang.* bed, bunk, cot, *Brit.* lair, *Brit. Sl.* kip.

3. *Slang.* discharge, walking papers, *Inf.* bounce, *Sl.* boot, *Sl.* pink slip; *Sl.* the bum's rush, *Sl.* heave-ho.

4. hit the sack *Slang.* go to bed, go to sleep, retire, turn in, bed down, *Sl.* hit the hay, *Sl.* sack out; nap, snooze, *Sl.* conk out.

—*v.* **5.** bag, pocket, pouch.

6. *Slang.* fire, dismiss, put out of a job, let go, lay off, give [s.o.] his walking papers, *Inf.* bounce, *Inf.* give [s.o.] the sack, *Inf.* send down the road, *Sl.* can, *U.S. Govt. Inf.* rif.

sack[2], *v.* **1.** pillage, plunder, rob, despoil, *Archaic.* spoil, spoliate, *Chiefly Scot.* reive; ravage, harry, rape, maraud, depredate; ransack, loot, gut, fleece, strip, rifle, steal; raid, foray, forage, prey on *or* upon; desecrate, defile, outrage, violate.

2. devastate, lay waste, waste; desolate, wreak havoc upon, destroy, damage, ruin, vandalize; burn, level, raze, demolish.

3. pirate, freeboot, buccaneer, privateer, filibuster; burglarize, burgle, break in.

—*n.* **4.** pillage, plunder, plundering, rapine, depredation, spoliation, despoliation, despoilment, *Obs.* direption, raven; ravaging, harrying, marauding, *Archaic.* maraud, sacking, *Rare.* sackage; raid, razzia, foray; foraging, looting, ravishment, seizure, grab, rape.

5. devastation, laying waste, desolation; destruction, ruin, burning, razing, leveling, vandalizing; vandalism, desecration, defilement, outrage, violation.

sackcloth, *n.* **1.** sacking, coarse cloth, stout woven material, burlap, gunny, hopsacking, homespun, fustian, linsey-woolsey.

2. in sackcloth and ashes contrite, sorrowful, repentant, penitent, penitential, atoning; sorry, sorrowful, remorseful, compunctious, regretful, regretting, troubled, disturbed; conscience-stricken, guilt-ridden, self-reproachful; chastened, shamed, embarrassed.

sacrament, *n.* **1.** ritual, rite, liturgy, ceremony, ceremonial, solemnity, observance; sign, symbol, token, mystery.

2. oath, pledge, promise, assurance, word, word of honor, vow, *Archaic.* troth, *Archaic.* plight; contract, compact, covenant, obligation, engagement, agreement.

3. (*often cap.*) the Eucharist, Lord's Supper.

4. (*of Protestant churches*) baptism, Lord's Supper.

5. (*of Roman Catholic and Greek Orthodox churches*) baptism, confirmation, penance, the Eucharist, holy orders, matrimony, extreme unction.

sacred, *adj.* **1.** consecrated, set apart, dedicated, devoted, sanctified; holy, blessed, blest, hallowed; purified, unspotted, clean.

2. religious, spiritual, heavenly, celestial, ethereal, supernal; devotional, ceremonial, ceremonious; ecclesiastical, churchly, church, priestly, hieratic; Biblical, scriptural.

3. divine, godlike, godly, deiform, deified, sainted, heaven-born; venerable, venerated, exalted, supreme.

4. sacrosanct, sacred-cow, inviolable, inviolate, untouchable, inalienable, indefeasible, unimpeachable, unchallengeable; safe, secure, protected, defended, unthreatened; invulnerable, unassailable, impregnable.

sacrifice, *n.* **1.** offering, gift, oblation, *Chiefly Biblical.* corban, libation; immolation, burnt offering, holocaust, human sacrifice, sacrificial slaughter *or* killing, hecatomb.

2. surrender, relinquishment, yielding, ceding, *Law.* waiver; giving up, renunciation, abandonment, discontinuation, cessation, stopping, quitting, desistance, forbearance, abstention, self-sacrifice; loss, destruction, ruin.

—*v.* **3.** offer as a sacrifice, offer up, pour out; immolate, burn, kill, slaughter.

4. surrender, relinquish, yield, cede, resign, *Law.* waive; give up, *Inf.* swear off, renounce, abandon, discontinue, cease, stop, quit; do without, forgo, abstain from, refrain from, forbear, desist.

5. (*of all goods or property*) dispose of, get rid of, sell at any price, sell at a loss, take a loss on, give away, let go, part with.

sacrificial, *adj.* **1.** expiatory, atoning, reparatory, reparative, piacular.

2. sacrificed, immolated, burnt, killed, slaughtered.

sacrilege, *n.* **1.** profanation, profaneness, profanity, cursing, blasphemy, desecration; mockery, irreverence, indevoutness, irreligion, impiety, impiousness, disrespect, disrespectfulness, unrespectfulness; ungodliness, unholiness, unrighteousness, unvirtuousness, immorality, godlessness; sinfulness, iniquity, peccancy, wickedness, reprobacy.

2. violation, defilement, perversion, contamination, infection, befoulment, pollution; vitiation, debasement, degradation, lowering, cheapening, dishonoring, prostitution; abuse, maltreatment, mistreatment, misuse, outrage.

sacrilegious, *adj.* profane, blasphemous, desecrative, disrespectful, unrespectful, heretical; irreverent, indevout, irreligious, infidel, impious, unpious, ungodly; unsaintly, unvirtuous, unrighteous, immoral, reprobate; godless, iniquitous, sinful, sinning, peccant, wicked, evil, perverted, corrupt.

sacrosanct, *adj.* sacred, holy, hallowed, venerated, consecrated, set apart, sanctified, purified; religious, godly, divine, heavenly, celestial; sacred-cow, inviolable, inviolate, untouchable, inalienable, indefeasible, unimpeachable, unchallengeable.

sad, *adj.* **1.** unhappy, dejected, depressed, despondent, crestfallen, chapfallen, downcast, *Inf.* down, *Inf.* low, feeling low, in low spirits, in the doldrums, *Inf.* down in the dumps, *Inf.* down in the mouth; discouraged, disheartened, downhearted, dispirited, *Sl.* bummed *or* bummed out; gloomy, melancholy, blue; sorrowful, mournful, heavy-hearted; inconsolable, disconsolate, crushed, broken, heartbroken, brokenhearted, sick at heart, heartsick; bowed-down, heavy-laden, in the depths *or* bowels of despair, *Sl.* in the pits; wretched, miserable, woebegone.

2. grievous, lamentable, deplorable, rueful, doleful, dolorous; regrettable, unfortunate, infelicitous, unlucky, hapless, *Scot.* donsie; woeful, plaintive, touching, heartbreaking, heartrending, piteous; sore, bitter, sharp, afflictive, oppressive, distressing, painful; pleasureless, joyless, cheerless.

3. sorry, pitiful, pitiable, pathetic; mean, despicable, contemptible, beneath contempt; paltry, petty, piddling, beggarly, scrubby, shabby, *Sl.* crummy.

4. (*all of colors*) dark, black, gray, leaden; drab, dull, dead, lifeless; dismal, dreary, *Literary.* drear, bleak, dingy; somber, grave, heavy, lugubrious, atrabilious, funereal.

sadden, *v.* deject, depress, oppress, *Inf.* get one down, cast down; discourage, dispirit, dishearten, damp, dampen one's spirits, cast a gloom upon, take the heart out of, *Inf.* bring one down, *Sl.* bum one out; sorrow, grieve, aggrieve, anguish, *Inf.* cut up; break one's heart, make one's heart bleed, make one's ribs hurt, bring tears to one's eyes.

saddle, *n.* **1.** seat, perch, roost; sidesaddle, demipique, pad, panel, pillion; packsaddle, *Span. aparejo.*

—*v.* **2.** (*of a horse or other animal*) equip, outfit, accouter; tack up, saddle up, prepare *or* get ready for riding.

3. *Usu.* **saddle with** charge, assign [s.t.] to, invest, impose [s.t.] on, put [s.t.] on; load, load up *or* down, weigh down, weight, cumber, encumber; burden, overload, overburden, overtask; tax, overtax, strain, beset, embarrass, overwhelm; impede, hamper, handicap, cramp; tie [s.o.] down, shackle, oppress.

sadness, *n.* **1.** unhappiness, joylessness, cheerlessness, uncheerfulness; discouragement, disheartenment, downheartedness; dolefulness, grievousness, plaintiveness; gloominess, bleakness; sorrowfulness, wretchedness, miserableness, woefulness.

2. dejection, depression, despondency, gloom, melancholy, melancholia, megrims, the blues, *Inf.* blue devils, low spirits, sinking heart; grief, sorrow, despair, misery, woe, bale, agony, agony of mind *or* spirit; heartache, aching heart, broken heart, heavy heart, bleeding heart.

safe, *adj.* **1.** secure, protected, guarded, sheltered, defended; under lock and key, out of reach, out of harm's way; out of the woods, home free, on home ground, on the ground again; invulnerable, impregnable, unassailable, unconquerable, inexpugnable, unmolestable; bombproof, bulletproof.

2. sound, safe and sound, well, alive and well, hale; uninjured, unhurt, unmolested, unscathed, undamaged, unbroken, intact, in good shape; satisfactory, *Sl.* hunky, *Inf.* OK *or* okay, all right.

3. riskless, unhazardous, in the bag, sure, on solid ground, guaranteed; careful, cautious, wary, chary, circumspect, conservative, on the safe side; unventuresome, unadventurous, timid, not sticking one's neck out, playing the cards close to one's vest *or* chest.

4. dependable, responsible, reliable, unfailing; trusty, trustworthy, faithful, steadfast, true, tried and true, bona fide; honorable, *Sl.* straight-arrow, honest; reputable, scrupulous, on the level, on the up-and-up, upright.

5. harmless, innocuous, innoxious, impotent; powerless, disabled, *Fr. hors de combat*; tame, defanged, nonpoisonous; in custody, locked up, put away.

—*n.* **6.** strongbox, safe-deposit box, safety-deposit box, coffer; cashbox, moneybox, jewelry box *or* case; chest, trunk, locker; vault, crypt, bank, depository, treasury.

safeguard, *n.* **1.** protection, palladium, defense, armor, bulwark, shield, aegis; preventive, precaution, seat belt, safety harness, *Circus.* mechanic, life preserver, water wings; amulet, talisman, charm, lucky piece, rabbit's foot, scarab, four-leaf clover, St. Christopher medal.

2. safe-conduct, passport, pass, *Fr. laissez-passer*, permit, license, ticket.

3. guard, convoy, escort, bodyguard, armed guard, security guard *or* force; guard dog.

—*v.* **4.** guard, protect, shelter, harbor; shield, defend, circle the wagons; secure, fortify, garrison; watch over, escort, ride shotgun, chaperon, convoy; look after, tend, care for, conserve.

safekeeping, *n.* protection, care, charge; guardianship, wardship, tutelage, custody, keeping, trusteeship, patrondom, patronship; watch, surveillance, supervision, superintendence; possession, holding.

safety, *n.* secureness, security, safeness, invulnerability, unassailability; harmlessness, innocuousness; reliability, dependability, reputability; clear sailing, snug harbor, anchorage, shelter, sanctuary.

sag, *v.* **1.** sink down, swag, bend down, list, lean, droop, slump.

2. flag, fail, languish, wilt, weaken, falter, cave in; wither, fade, wane, ebb, die down; weary, *Archaic.* faint, tire.

3. decline, descend, lower, go down, dip, slip; drop, fall, sink; plummet, plunge, tumble, topple, take a header; decrease, diminish, lessen, subside.

—n. **4.** droop, sagging, sinking, bending, bend, *Vet. Pathol.* sway-back, curvature; depression, concavity, cavity, hollow, indentation, scoop.

5. (*of prices*) decline, decrease, lowering, lessening, drop, dip.

saga, *n.* epic, edda, history, *Archaic.* gest, tale; legend, romance, adventure; chronicle, *Fr. roman-fleuve.*

sagacious, *adj.* **1.** shrewd, astute, *Sl.* savvy, keen, clever, canny, subtle, *Inf.* cute, *Archaic.* parlous; calculating, cunning, sly, wily, foxy; acute, sharp, sharp-witted, sharp as a tack; discerning, perspicacious, penetrating, perceptive, percipient, insightful; intelligent, smart, apt, ingenious, bright; agile, quick, quick-witted, nimble-witted; knowledgeable, versed, enlightened, aware, knowing, wide-awake, far-sighted.

2. sage, wise, sapient. See **sage** (*def.* **2**).

sagacity, *n.* sound judgment, clear thinking, prudence, judiciousness, clearheadedness, common sense; acumen, perspicacity, perspicaciousness; astuteness, shrewdness, ingenuity, intelligence, brains, *Inf.* gray matter, *Sl.* smarts; sagaciousness, wisdom, understanding, penetration, perceptiveness, discernment.

sage, *n.* **1.** philosopher, philosophe, theorist, Solomon, *Hinduism.* rishi, *Class. Myth.* Nestor; savant, scholar, pundit, pantologist, rabbi, wise man, learned man; mentor, venerable, oracle; luminary, master, expert, authority.

—adj. **2.** sagacious, wise, sapient, pansophic, pansophical; Solomonic, gash, rational, reasonable, logical; judicious, prudent, politic, discreet, sensible; commonsensical, long-headed, hard-headed, with a good head on one's shoulders.

sail, *n.* **1.** canvas, piece of sailcloth *or* duck, *Naut.* cloth, *Naut.* mainsail, *Naut.* jib, *Naut.* square sail, *Naut.* fore-and-aft sail; (*all of a windmill*) vane, blade, arm, wing.

2. cruise, voyage at sea, crossing, boat trip *or* journey; excursion, outing, pleasure trip, vacation.

3. sailboat, sailing boat, sloop, dory, pinnace, yacht, vessel, craft; ship, schooner, windjammer, galleon, cutter, yawl, *All Naut.* ketch, jack, brigantine, brig, bark.

—v. **4.** boat, cruise, yacht, ride the sea *or* waves, plow the waves, traverse the seas *or* ocean *or* water, *Literary.* ride the bounding main.

5. set sail, hoist *or* raise sail, put to sea, ship out, leave port *or* dock, *Naut.* make sail, *Naut.* raise *or* hoist the blue peter; put off, shove off, push off, take off, set out, embark on a cruise *or* voyage.

6. float, flow, stream, roll, run, steam; coast, drift, move with the wind; glide, slide, glissade, sweep, skate, slip; plane, skim, flit, dart, scud; fly, wing, soar, *Aeronautics.* volplane.

7. pilot, steer, helm, captain, navigate.

sailor, *n.* **1.** mariner, seaman, seafarer, bluejacket, marine, jack-tar, Jacky, *Inf.* windjammer, *Inf.* gob, *Brit. Sl.* matelot, *East Indian.* lascar, *Fr. matelot, Ger. Matrose, Sp. marinero, It. marinaio;* sea dog, shellback, *Inf.* salt, *Inf.* salty dog, *Inf.* water dog, *Inf.* tar, *Sl.* limey, *Rare.* tarpaulin; boatman, boater, yachtsman, yachtswoman, cruiser.

2. skipper, captain, shipmaster, master, old man; first mate, chief mate, first *or* chief officer, *Naut.* mate; helmsman, steersman, pilot, navigator.

3. petty officer, boatswain, bo's'n, bosun, coxswain; crewman, hand, *Naut.* deck hand; midshipman, *Inf.* middy, (*at the U.S. Naval Academy*) plebe *or* pleb, *Both Naut. Disparag.* landlubber, lubber.

saint, *n.* **1.** holy person, canonized person, martyr.

2. founder, sponsor, patron, backer, Maecenas, supporter, promoter; benefactor, helper, philanthropist, well-wisher; guardian, fairy godmother, angel, *Inf.* lifesaver.

saintly, *adj.* holy, godly, pious, pietistic, reverent, God-fearing, devout, devotional, faithful, believing, religious; righteous, moral, upright, right-minded, just, good, virtuous, pure in heart; spiritual, otherworldly, unworldly, innocent, childlike, lamblike, dovelike, saintlike, sainted; perfect, pure, chaste, clean, spotless, unstained, immaculate, sinless; angelic, seraphic, heavenly, heaven-born, celestial, ethereal, supernal; divine, godlike, deiform; blessed, blest.

sake, *n.* **1.** cause, account, interest, behalf, welfare, well-being; concern, consideration, regard, respect; use, avail, advantage, profit, gain, benefit, good.

2. purpose, end, object, objective, view, aim, goal; rationale, reason, intention, intent, plan, design; occasion, motive, inducement, call, prompting.

salable, *adj.* marketable, vendible, merchantable, *Obs. Rare.* merchandisable, commerciable, exchangeable, interchangeable, staple; readily sold, of ready sale, disposable; in demand, sought-after, desirable, desired, wanted, needed, requested, called-for; in vogue, fashionable, *Inf.* in, popular, *Sl.* hot.

salacious, *adj.* **1.** lustful, libidinous, libidinal, concupiscent, prurient, randy, *Sl.* horny, *Sl.* hot; passionate, hot-blooded, steamy, *Sl.* all fired up; lecherous, lubricous, satyric, satyrical, satyrlike, goatish, hircine, *Archaic.* lickerish; ruttish, beastly, bestial, swinish; licentious, lascivious, libertine, debauched, dissolute, dissipated, rakish, rakehell; loose, wanton, wild, profligate, abandoned; promiscuous, whorish, of easy virtue, impure.

2. (*of writings, pictures, etc.*) obscene, pornographic, Fescennine, Cyprian, indecent, indelicate; crude, coarse, gross, fulsome; bawdy, ribald, dirty, smutty, foul, vile, offensive, scurrilous.

salary, *n.* wage, pay, *Brit. Sl.* get, emolument, remuneration, compensation, earnings; payment, hire, stipend, fee, honorarium; perquisites, *Inf.* perks, fringe benefits, *Inf.* fringes, *Inf.* extras; recompense, requital, reward, *Archaic.* meed, *Literary.* guerdon, deserts; returns, interest, yield, gain.

sale, *n.* **1.** selling, vending, vendition, trade, trading, traffic, exchange; bargaining, jobbing; auction, vendue.

2. market, *Com.* outlet, demand; buyers, purchasers, consumers, customers.

3. reduction, cut, discount, markdown, closeout, fire sale; white sale; tag sale, garage sale, yard sale, rummage sale.

4. for sale on the market, on the block, up for sale; available, obtainable, purchasable, at hand, accessible, attainable.

salesperson, *n.* **1.** salesman, shopman, saleswoman, saleslady, salesgirl, shopgirl; clerk, salesclerk, *Sl.* counterjumper; seller, vendor, middleman, agent; traveling salesman, *U.S.* drummer, door-to-door salesman, solicitor; Fuller Brush man, Avon lady.

sales talk, *n.* approach, *Inf.* spiel, *Sl.* pitch, fast talk, hard sell, *Sl.* line, *Inf.* song and dance, *Sl.* bill of goods.

salience, *n.* **1.** prominence, conspicuousness, noticeability; egregiousness, flagrancy, blatancy; singularity, peculiarity, uniqueness; discernibility, obviousness, patency; importance, significance, memorability, unforgettability, eminence, superiority.
2. projection, protuberance, protuberancy, prominence, intumescence, tumescence, swelling, extension; bow, curve, bulge, excurvature, convexity, convexedness; knob, bump, hump.

salient, *adj.* prominent, conspicuous, standing out, outstanding; noticeable, showing, striking, pronounced, well-marked, marked, remarkable; glaring, telling, egregious, flagrant, arrant; singular, peculiar, unique, special, particular; distinguishable, unmistakable, identifiable, recognizable, landmark; discernible, manifest, apparent, evident, obvious, patent, self-evident; principal, chief, important, significant, main, paramount; superior, primary, prime, first; memorable, unforgettable, considerable, imposing, eminent; extraordinary, exceptional, noteworthy.
2. projecting, protruding, protuberant, protrusive, jutting; extrusive, excrescent, tumescent; bold, raised, embossed, chased, superimposed, in high relief, in bold *or* strong relief; bulging, swelling, bowed, arched, bellied, convex.

saline, *adj.* salty, salt, salt-tasting. See **salty** (*def.* **1**).

saliva, *n.* spittle, spit, sputum, slaver, slobber, water, froth, drool, salivation.

sallow, *adj.* pale, wan, pallid, *Obs.* blate, palefaced; anemic, sickly-looking, waxen, pasty, pasty-faced, ashen, ashy, livid; whey-faced, tallow-faced, yellowish, jaundiced-looking, unhealthy-looking, unwholesome-looking; peaked, colorless, drained.

sally, *n.* **1.** sortie, foray, charge, thrust, offensive, drive; raid, attack, assault, onset, onslaught; rush, dash, going forward, onrush, outrush, outflow, efflux, effluence, outpour, outpouring.
2. excursion, expedition, trip, tour, visit, voyage, sail, cruise, junket; outing, airing, jaunt, stroll, ramble, walk, hike, trek, tramp, peregrination, pilgrimage.
3. flight, flash, outburst, outbreak, eruption, flare-up, blowup, explosion; flow, gush, torrent, jet, stream, spurt, spout, burst, discharge.
4. smart remark, *Inf.* wisecrack, *Inf.* crack, witticism, joke, jest, quip, mot, bon mot; retort, reply, rejoinder, return, repartee, *Inf.* backchat, comeback, snappy comeback, barb, zinger.
—*v.* **5.** sortie, raid, foray, charge, attack, assault, assail, storm; rush, surge *or* come *or* sweep forward, thrust *or* drive *or* push forward, take the offensive; fall upon, set upon, pounce upon, strike at, march upon, swoop down on, descend upon *or* on.
6. set out, start off, start out, embark, venture forth; put off, push off, shove off, get underway, set sail, *Naut.* make sail; depart, leave, take leave, go, run *or* move along, be off, be gone, make one's exit, *Sl.* split, *Sl.* cut out, take off, *Sl.* blow this joint *or* pop stand.
7. (*all of things*) issue forth, emanate, proceed, come forth, come out; flow out, pour out, stream out, gush, jet, spurt, spout; break out, erupt, explode, burst out *or* forth.

salmagundi, *n.* **1.** salad, mixed dish, *Italian Cookery.* antipasto; stew, hash, goulash, *Fr. Cookery.* ragout, *Fr. ratatouille,* (*in China, India, etc.*) chow-chow.
2. mixture, blend, intermixture, admixture, compound, composite; conglomeration, Chinese menu, miscellany, miscellanea, omnium-gatherum, menagerie, motley; mélange, medley, olio, potpourri, olla-podrida, combination, *Inf.* combo; pastiche, pasticcio, mosaic, collage, patchwork; mishmash, hodgepodge, *Brit.* hotchpotch, gallimaufry, farrago, jumble, scramble, tangle.

salon, *n.* **1.** reception room, lounge, saloon, drawing room, front room, parlor, sitting room, living room.
2. assembly, meeting, gathering, function, reception; soiree, party, dinner party, tea *or* tea party.
3. hall, exhibition hall, gallery.
4. shop, small shop, boutique.

saloon, *n.* **1.** tavern, brasserie, grill, grillroom, bar and grill, bar, barroom, *Archaic.* dramshop, taproom, alehouse, *Brit.* grogshop, *Brit.* public house, *Brit.* pub, *Brit.* local; rathskeller, *Ger. Ratskeller, Ger. Hofbrauhaus, Ger. Biergarten;* cocktail lounge, bistro, café, cabaret, night club; roadhouse, inn, hotel, hostel, *Ger. Gasthaus; Sl.* gin mill, *Sl.* watering hole, groggery, *Sl.* dive, *U.S.* barrelhouse, *Sl.* honky-tonk, *Sl.* speakeasy, *Sl.* after-hours joint, *U.S. Sl. Obs.* blind tiger *or* pig.
2. salon, drawing room, reception room. See **salon** (*def.* **1**).

salt, *n.* **1.** sodium chloride, table salt, sea salt, rock salt.
2. salts Epsom salts, potassium salts, *Chem., Pharm.* Rochelle salt; purgative, cathartic, laxative.
3. wit, Attic wit, Attic salt, sarcasm, dry humor; spice, spiciness, pepper, piquancy, piquantness, pungency, sharpness, bite; punch, zap, force, zing, zip, liveliness, zest, vigor.
4. *Informal.* old sailor, sea dog, shellback; mariner, seaman, seafarer, *Inf.* tar, bluejacket, Jack, *Inf.* gob, *Sl.* limey, *Brit. Sl.* matelot.
—*v.* **5.** (*all with salt*) season, flavor, cure, kipper, preserve, treat; brine, corn, pickle, souse.
—*adj.* **6.** saline, salty, salted; (*all with salt*) cured, preserved, treated.

salty, *adj.* **1.** saline, salt, salt-tasting, salted, briny, brackish.
2. piquant, pungent, sharp, biting, tart, spicy; zesty, zestful, tangy, well-seasoned, snappy, *Sl.* kicky; lively, hearty, peppy; clever, smart, keen, snappy, witty; interesting, entertaining, exciting, stimulating.
3. racy, risqué, off-color, ribald, bawdy; indecent, *Inf.* blue, vulgar, filthy, dirty, smutty, *Sl.* raunchy; gross, coarse, crude, rude, indelicate, low-class.

salubrious, *adj.* healthful, healthy, salutary, salutiferous, hygienic; nutritious, nourishing, health-giving; invigorating, bracing, stimulating, stimulative, refreshing, tonic, *Med.* roborant.

salutary, *adj.* **1.** healthful, salubrious. See **salubrious.**
2. wholesome, beneficial, good for one; good, useful, advantageous, profitable, gainful, valuable; helpful, serviceable, practical.

salutation, *n.* greeting, salute, hail, ave, hello, how-do-you-do; curtsey, bow, bob, nod; handshake, handclasp; wave; hug, embrace, kiss; genuflection, reverence, homage, obeisance, salaam.

salute, *v.* **1.** address, greet, hello, say hello *or* how do you do; hallo, hail, call to, *Archaic.* gratulate.
2. nod to, tip *or* doff one's hat *or* cap to, wave to, extend one's hand to, shake hands with, give [s.o.] the glad hand, *Inf.* glad-hand, embrace, kiss, kiss on both cheeks; bow to, curtsy to, kiss the hand of, genuflect to, bend to, bend the knee to, salaam, kneel before, fall on one's knees before, throw oneself at the feet of, prostrate oneself before; welcome, receive, give a warm reception; present arms, dip colors, play a fanfare, give a twenty-one-gun salute *or* salvo.
3. honor, pay homage to, pay respects to; recognize, make a tribute to, testimonialize, panegyrize, eulogize.

—*n.* **4.** salutation, address, compellation; greeting, how do you do, hello, hallo, hail, aloha, *Chiefly Dial.* howdy.

5. nod, bob, duck, tipping *or* doffing of one's hat *or* cap, wave; handshake, embrace, kiss, welcome, *Inf.* glad hand; bow, curtsy, genuflection, salaam, kowtow; fanfare, fanfaron, "Ruffles and Flourishes," salvo, twenty-one-gun salute.

6. homage, respects, honoring; recognition, tribute, testimony, testimonial; laudation, commendation, panegyric, encomium, eulogy.

salvage, *n.* **1.** recovery operation, rescue operation; recovery, reclamation, retrieval, rescue, saving, salvation, ransom, redemption; restoration, restitution, reestablishment, regeneration, reconstitution, rejuvenation, revitalization, revivification, renewal; reconditioning, rehabilitating, reparation.

2. salvaged goods *or* parts, scraps, junk; remains, leftovers.

—*v.* **3.** save, rescue, ransom, redeem; reclaim, retrieve, recover; restore, reestablish, regenerate, rejuvenate, revivify, renew; recondition, rehabilitate, repair.

salvation, *n.* **1.** redemption, liberation, deliverance, emancipation; release, reprieve, escape, rescue; retrieval, saving, freeing, extrication, acquittance, acquittal; restoration, restitution, conversion, rebirth, regeneration, reconstitution.

2. protection, preservation, preserval, conservation, caring, safekeeping, exemption; safety, security, immunity.

salve, *n.* **1.** healing ointment, lotion, oil, balm, liniment, unguent, embrocation, demulcent, *Pharm.* cerate; lenitive, *Med.* abirritant, *Med.* emollient.

2. remedy, cure, restorative, antidote, neutralizer; sedative, tranquilizer, *Med.* calmative, narcotic, opiate, drug; soporific, somnifacient, somnific, somniferous; analgesic, *Inf.* painkiller, anodyne, anesthetic; healing substance *or* agent, application; palliative, alleviative.

—*v.* **3.** assuage, mitigate, relieve, ease, alleviate, palliate; moderate, temper, weaken, qualify; abate, lessen, diminish, lower, reduce; mollify, soften, *Rare.* lenify, soothe, *Brit., Australian.* dill, *Archaic.* attemper; pacify, calm, calm down, subdue, compose, comfort; succor, remedy, heal; pour oil on troubled waters.

salvo, *n.* **1.** discharge of artillery, fusillade, *Navy.* broadside, volley; (*with artillery or firearms*) salute; bombardment, cannonade, fireworks; blast, peal, roar, thunder; explosion, eruption, burst.

2. applause, round of applause, cheers, plaudits, hand clapping, *Inf.* hand, cheering, rooting, whistling, stomping; éclat, outcry, outburst.

same, *adj.* **1.** identical, identic, one and the same, consubstantial; the very same, selfsame, one and only, one, exact; ditto, repeat, duplicate, twin.

2. agreeing, corresponding, coincident, coinciding, congruous, matching; interchangeable, exchangeable, transposable; equivalent, equal, coequal, even; reciprocative, reciprocal, mutual; correlative, comparable; similar, alike, like, much the same; synonymous, close, approximate, analogous, near.

3. unchanged, unaltered, unvaried, intact; constant, persistent, steady; changeless, unchanging, unvarying; lasting, enduring, abiding.

4. all the same a. nevertheless, nonetheless, *Archaic.* natheless, anyway, anyhow; regardless, be that as it may, for all that, after all is said and done, in spite of the fact, despite the fact, *Archaic.* withal, notwithstanding; at any rate, in any case, in any event; but, still, still and all, yet, even so, after all; at the same time. **b.** immaterial, of no consequence, inconsequential, unimportant, not worth mentioning *or* talking about, not worth worrying about.

5. just the same a. in the same manner *or* way, the same; in an identical *or* similar way. **b.** nevertheless, nonetheless; notwithstanding, after all is said and done. See (*def.* **4a**).

sameness, *n.* **1.** identity, oneness, selfsameness, identicalness, exactness, exactitude, unity; indistinguishability, *Eccles.* Homoousia, consubstantiality; equivalence, correspondence, coincidence, agreement; congruence, congruency, equality, interchangeability, convertibility.

2. resemblance, likeness, alikeness, similarity, similitude, semblance; closeness, approximation, nearness; synonymy, analogy, accordance, consimilarity.

3. monotony, lack of variety, uniformity, changelessness, tedium, tediousness, routine, predictability; lack of excitement, humdrum, deadness, flatness; iteration, reiteration, repetition, recurrence, redundancy, tautology.

sample, *n.* **1.** specimen, example, *Archaic.* ensample, instance, illustration, representative, exemplification, type; model, pattern, exemplar; sampling, cross section, representation; foretaste, prospect, warning; piece, swatch, scrap; handout, *Sl.* freebie; bite, sup, sip, taste; test, experiment, trial, *Inf.* pilot; demonstration, *Inf.* demo.

—*adj.* **2.** representative, illustrative, representational; typifying, symbolizing, personifying.

—*v.* **3.** test, try, test *or* try out; taste, have a piece *or* sip; try on, try on for size.

sanatorium, *n.* asylum, hospital, *Fr. hôtel-Dieu,* infirmary, sick bay; home, old folk's home, nursing home, convalescent home; rehabilitation center, halfway house; hospice, hospitium, retreat, refuge; sanitarium, health resort, *Chiefly Brit.* watering place, spa; mineral spring, hot *or* warm spring, springs, baths.

sanctified, *adj.* **1.** holy, annointed, *Rom. Cath. Ch.* beatified; consecrated, sacred, blessed, blest, hallowed; enshrined, canonized, glorified, exalted; dedicated, devoted, set apart; pure, cleansed, unsullied, untainted, sinless, spotless; godly, saintly, unworldly, otherworldly, divine, spiritual; devotional, religious, ceremonious; sacrosanct, inviolable, inviolate.

2. sanctimonious, holier-than-thou, self-righteous. See **sanctimonious**.

sanctify, *v.* **1.** consecrate, make holy *or* sacred, bless, hallow, annoint, *Rom. Cath. Ch.* beatify; enshrine, canonize, glorify, exalt; dedicate, devote, set apart.

2. purify, cleanse, make free from sin, wash one's sins away, clear; correct, better, restore, uplift.

3. sanction, ratify, confirm; give sanction to, legitimize, legitimatize; license, warrant, support, defend.

sanctimonious, *adj.* self-righteous, holier-than-thou, simon-pure, *Inf.* goody-goody, *Inf.* too good to be true; pharisaic, pietistic, over-pious, falsely pious; hypocritical, Tartuffian, canting; mealy-mouthed, unctuous, oily.

sanctimony, *n.* pietism, sanctimoniousness, Tartuffery, formalism, hypocrisy, pharisaism, phariseeism; false piety, excessive piety, religiosity; self-righteousness, *Inf.* goody-goodiness, *Inf.* goodiness; cant, lip service, mouth honor, mealy-mouthedness; hollowness, empty ceremony; affectation, pretense, false pretense, bluff; dissimulation, feigning, dissembling, duplicity.

sanction, *n.* **1.** authority, authorization, warrant, warranty, certification, accreditation, legalization, validation; permission, allowance, consent, vouchsafement; license, liberty, leave, imprimatur, carte blanche.

2. countenance, acknowledgement, endorsement, seal *or* stamp of approval, stamp, seal, signet, sigil, cachet; support, backing, advocacy, sponsoring, favor, encouragement.

3. ratification, confirmation, passage, acceptance; affirmative vote, aye, yea, yes, *Inf.* O.K.; approval, approbation, grant; assent, agreement, concurrence, compliance, accedence, acquiescence.

—*v.* 4. authorize, warrant, certify, accredit, license, legalize, validate, notarize, visa; permit, allow, consent to, subscribe to, vouchsafe; commission, empower, entitle, invest, depute, *Eccles.* ordain.

5. countenance, acknowledge, endorse, underwrite, countersign, witness; support, uphold, defend, vouch for, back up, stand behind *or* by; sponsor, advocate, patronize, favor, promote, foster, boost, abet, encourage.

6. ratify, confirm, bind, accept, pass, vote for, say "aye" or "yea"; approve, give one's nod of approval, *Inf.* O.K., *Chiefly U.S.* approbate; agree to, give one's assent, concur with, accede to.

sanctity, *n.* holiness, sanctitude, saintliness, godliness; sacredness, divineness, divinity; religiosity, spirituality, devoutness, piety, religiousness; devotion, dedication, reverence; righteousness, goodness, virtue, virtuousness, purity, chastity, grace.

sanctuary, *n.* 1. holy place, shrine, reliquary, naos, dagoba; sanctum, delubrum, adytum, bethel; altar, tabernacle, holy of holies, sanctum, sanctorum, ark; chancel, *Eccles.* sacrarium, conventicle, chapel, chantry, oratory, prayer house, *Hinduism.* ashram *or* asmara; church, house of worship, house of God, temple, synagogue, *Yiddish.* shul, mosque, pagoda.

2. asylum, refuge, haven, port; shelter, safe-hold, retreat; hideout, hideaway, hiding place, cover, covert, cache, cubbyhole; safety, seclusion, immunity, quarantine.

3. preserve, reserve, reservation, park; wildlife preserve, bird sanctuary, national park, national forest, state forest; Indian reservation, sacred ground.

sand, *n.* 1. gravel, debris, grit, detritus, attritus; grain, grain of sand, granule, speck, bit, brecchia.

2. **sands** beach, shore, seashore, strand; sandbar, sand dune, sand hill, sand pile; desert, waste, Sahara.

3. *U.S. Informal.* pluck, courage, grit, true grit, nerve, *Inf.* backbone; mettle, *Inf.* spunk, *Sl.* guts, chutzpah, toughness, gameness.

—*v.* 4. smooth, sandpaper, emery, file; grind, abrade, pumice, scour, buff; polish, burnish, dress, rub.

sandbank, *n.* shoal, ridge, reef, bar, shallow; sandbar, ford, coral reef; key, cay, atoll, island, isle.

sandy, *adj.* 1. gravelly, gritty, shingly, pebbly; sabulous, arenose, grainy, granular, granulated, *Geol.* psammitic.

2. yellowish-red, saffron, tawny, ocher, ocherous, buff; yellow, yellowish, xanthous, topaz, lutescent, golden; flaxen, blond, tow-headed, dirty blond.

3. unstable, shaky, shifting, vicissitudinous; infirm, unsteady, changeful, changing; unsubstantial, unreliable, precarious, unsafe, unsound, hazardous.

sane, *adj.* 1. rational, normal, right, right-minded, *Latin. compos mentis;* sober, stable, of sound mind, of sound judgment, sound-minded; sound, healthy, wholesome; lucid, cogent, logical, perceiving, discerning; *Sl.* all there, *Sl.* together, *Sl.* having all one's marbles, in possession of one's faculties or senses.

2. sensible, reasonable, intelligent, sapient, sage, sagacious, judicious, understanding; responsible, level-headed, thoughtful, far-sighted; prudent, politic, discriminating, discreet, enlightened; cool-headed, cool, commonsense, commonsensical, pragmatic, practical; fit, advisable, proper; plausible, credible, justifiable, believable; well-founded, well-grounded.

sang-froid, *n.* coolness, calmness, composure, coolheadedness, countenance; self-possession, self-control, self-restraint, presence of mind; poise, equanimity, equilibrium, balance, aplomb; imperturbability, dispassion, dispassionateness, *Inf.* unflappability, unexcitability; nerve, cool, cool under fire, steadiness, unshakableness, steady hand.

sanguinary, *adj.* 1. bloody, gory, ensanguined, sanguine, sanguineous, sanguinolent; bloodshot, bloodstained, blood-drenched, blood-soaked, bloodied.

2. bloodthirsty, murderous, slaughterous, killing, cutthroat, homicidal, fell, grim, brutal, cold-blooded; savage, cruel, barbarous, inhuman, ferocious; harsh, ruthless, remorseless, unmerciful, unpitying, heartless, soulless.

sanguine, *adj.* 1. buoyant, lively, spirited, elated, zestful; hopeful, expectant, anticipatory; confident, optimistic, reassured, assured; happy, blithe, warm, sunny, light-hearted, bright, exultant; enthusiastic, zealous, ardent, fervid.

2. reddish, rubescent, rufescent, rubicund; ruddy, russet, rusty, brick-red, lateritious; red-faced, flushed, glowing, blooming, inflamed, red, feverish; florid, blowzy, sunburned, burnt; salmon, pink, coral, rosy, roseate.

3. bloody, blood-stained, gory, ensanguined. See **sanguinary** (*def.* 1.).

4. red, blood-red, bloodlike, crimson, incarnadine, scarlet, vermilion; vinaceous, claret-colored, wine-colored, port, cherry, amaranthine, murrey; cardinal, carmine, Tyrian, *Heraldry.* gules, ruby, stammel; lobster-red, fire engine-red, beet-red, strawberry.

sanitary, *adj.* 1. clean, cleanly, hygienic, antiseptic, germ-free; sterile, pure, prophylactic, disinfected, decontaminated, aseptic; unpolluted, harmless, innoxious, innocuous, hurtless, uninjurious; uninfected, immunized, uninfectious, vaccinated, inoculated; chlorinated, boiled, pasteurized.

2. healthy, healthful, salutary, salubrious, Hygeian; wholesome, health-promoting, sanitarian; beneficial, benign, good; tonic, refreshing, constitutional, bracing.

sanitation, *n.* 1. hygienics, hygiology, cleanliness, prophylaxis, preventive medicine, preventive dentistry.

2. sterilization, antisepsis, disinfection, chlorination, decontamination; immunization, inoculation, vaccination, pasteurization.

sanity, *n.* 1. mental normality, normalcy, rationality, reason, reasonableness, sense, intelligence; sobriety, coherence, saneness, healthy mind, *Inf.* right mind; balance, level-headedness, sober-mindedness; lucidity, clear-headedness; mental health, mental hygiene; cogency, perspicuity, perspicacity, perceptiveness, astuteness, acuity.

2. judiciousness, sagacity, wisdom, sageness, sapience; practicality, pragmatism, coolness, cool-headedness; common sense, *Inf.* horse sense, prudence, polity, judgment; discrimination, discretion, thoughtfulness.

sap[1], *n.* 1. juice, fluid, life fluid, *Archaic.* lymph; milk, blood, lifeblood, *Class. Myth.* ichor.

2. *Slang.* fool, dupe, gull, gudgeon, *Inf.* chump, *Sl.* schnook, *Sl.* schlemiel, sitting duck, easy mark, *Inf.* sucker, *Sl.* patsy, *U.S. Sl.* fall guy, *Sl.* pushover, *Sl.* jerk.

sap[2], *v.* undermine, weaken, impair, enfeeble, reduce; deplete, exhaust, wear, enervate, drain, bleed, milk, rob; invalidate, debilitate, cripple; destroy, ruin, sabotage, subvert; devastate, despoil, blight.

sapience, *n.* wisdom, sageness, sagacity, sense, common sense, reason, soundness, reasonableness; intelligence, knowledge, genius, judgment; judiciousness, discretion, discrimination, circumspection, prudence, providence; perceptiveness, perception, percipience, perspicacity, perspicuity; discernment, penetration, insight, profundity, depth, deepness; astuteness, acuity, acumen; shrewdness, cleverness, sharpness, smartness, keenness; cunning, mother wit, wit, parts, *Inf.* smarts, *Inf.* brains.

sapient, *adj.* wise, sage, sagacious, sound; sensible, rational, reasonable, knowing, intelligent; philosophical, oracular, enlightened, deep, profound; judicious, discreet, circumspect, discriminating, prudent, provident; penetrating, discerning, perspicacious, perceptive, percipient; astute, apt, keen, sharp, bright, keen-sighted, clear-sighted, clear-headed; clever, brainy, smart, quick-witted, nimble-witted; shrewd, foxy, calculating, sharp-witted; long-headed, far-sighted, long-sighted.

sapless, *adj.* **1.** withered, wizened, shriveled, shrunk, shrunken; juiceless, dry; decayed, dead.

2. insipid, flat, uninteresting, unentertaining, inexpressive, unimaginative, colorless, jejune, *Sl.* blah; unamimated, spiritless, zestless; tame, lifeless, empty, *Sl.* dead, *Sl.* nothing; pointless, impotent, weak, feeble, anemic, limp, namby-pamby; dry-as-dust, prosaic, prosy, arid, barren, sterile; dull, boring, monotonous, tedious, tiresome, *Sl.* a drag; stale, tired, trite, hackneyed, banal, overworked; indistinctive, run-of-the-mill, ordinary, commonplace, average; bland, vapid, thin, watered-down, dilute.

sapling, *n.* **1.** young tree, seedling.

2. young person, youth, youngling, juvenile, girl, boy; sprig, stripling, slip, fledgling; youngster, child, *Inf.* shaver, *Inf.* kid, tot, *U.S. Inf.* tad, urchin.

sappy, *adj.* **1.** succulent, juicy, lush, oozy, seepy; moist, watery, hydrous; sticky, tacky, adhesive, viscous, viscid.

2. energetic, energetical, vigorous, dynamic, electric; active, alive, full of energy, *Inf.* full of pep, *Inf.* peppy, *Inf.* snappy, *Inf.* on one's toes, full of vim and vigor; eager, ready to go, bright-eyed and bushy-tailed; lively, spirited, *Sl.* go-go, full of life, animated, vibrant, vital, vivacious.

3. *Slang.* silly, foolish, corny; sentimental, *Brit. Sl.* soppy, emotional, maudlin, overdone, *Inf.* tear-jerking, *Inf.* mushy; mawkish, insipid, vapid.

sarcasm, *n.* **1.** derision, ridicule, scorn, mockery, jest; satire, irony, cynicism, lampoon, burlesque; contempt, disparagement, disdain, superciliousness, haughtiness, arrogance; criticism, censure, hit, fling, *Inf.* flak, rub, dig; taunt, fleer, gibe, jeer, flout, scoff, sneer, wipe, quip, nip; abuse, contumely, barb, slur, vituperation, aspersion.

2. acrimony, acrimoniousness, causticity, aperity, mordancy, acridness, acridity, pungency, venom, venomousness, venomness; trenchancy, keenness, incisiveness; harshness, sharpness, pointedness; virulence, spite, spitefulness, malice, malicousness, viciousness; astringency, severity, sternness, acerbity, austerity, stringency; peevishness, petulance, *Rare.* petulancy, crabbedness, testiness, touchiness, irascibility, edginess; ill temper, ill-temperedness, short-temperedness, ill humor, ill-humoredness.

sarcastic, *adj.* **1.** sardonic, scornful, mocking, ridiculing, derisive, derisory, Rabelaisian; satirical, ironic, ironical, double-edged, edged, cynical; contemptuous, contumelious, disparaging, sneering, disdainful, supercilious, haughty, arrogant; taunting, teasing, chaffing, gibing, jeering, quizzical, scoffing; critical, captious, faultfinding, carping, caviling, censorious.

2. caustic, mordant, mordacious, acrimonious, bitter, acrid, acidulous, acid, pungent; trenchant, cutting, incisive, slashing, scathing; penetrating, piercing, stinging, pricking, nipping, biting; keen, pointed, sharp, sharp-tongued; astringent, severe, acerb, acerbic, stern, harsh, austere, stringent; spiteful, virulent, malicious, malificent, venomous, vicious, malevolent, malignant; invidious, hateful.

3. insulting, excoriating, denouncing, berating, lashing; abusive, scurrilous, offensive, vituperative; corrosive, corroding, erosive, withering; cruel, mean, brutal; unkind, uncharitable, unbenevolent, uncordial, unamiable, unfriendly.

4. abrupt, brusque, blunt, curt, short, gruff, crusty; peevish, petulant, crabbed, testy, touchy, waspish, irascible, edgy; ill-tempered, ill-humored, ill-natured, short-tempered; hostile, resentful, indignant, piqued, angry; morose, surly, sour, moody.

sardonic, *adj.* scornful, mocking, cynical, contemptuous, contumelious, sneering, disdainful; caustic, mordant, mordacious, acrimonious, bitter, acrid, acidulous, acid, pungent; trenchant, cutting, incisive, slashing, scathing; sarcastic, biting, harsh, keen, pointed, sharp, sharp-tongued; astringent, severe, acerb, acerbic; spiteful, virulent, malicious, malificent, venomous, vicious, malevolent, malignant. See also **sarcastic** (*defs.* **1-4**).

sass, *n.* **1.** *Informal.* impudence, insolence, sauciness, *Inf.* sauce, *Inf.* cheek, *Inf.* sassiness; *Inf.* back talk, *Sl.* lip, *Sl.* mouth, *Sl.* mouthing off, *Sl.* smarting off; discourtesy, rudeness, incivility, impertinence, flippancy, brashness, disrespect, disdain, contempt, derision, *Sl.* freshness, *Sl.* fresh talk; impudent talk, audacity, effrontery, boldness, presumption, brazenness.

—*v.* **2.** *Informal.* be impudent, be insolent, back-talk, talk back, *Inf.* answer back, *Inf.* sauce, *Inf.* give [s.o.] lip, *Inf.* mouth off, *Sl.* get fresh, *Sl.* get smart, *Dial.* sass back; forget one's place, forget oneself, dare, presume, take liberties, make bold, speak out of turn.

Satan, *n.* **1.** Lucifer, Mephistopheles, Beelzebub, Sathan, Sathanas; Moloch, Belial, Clootie, *Scot.* Hornie, *Japanese Myth.* Oni, *Jewish Myth.* Asmodeus; Abaddon, Apollyon, Diabolus, Azazel, *Islamic Myth.* Elbis, Iblis.

2. the Devil, the Evil One, the Wicked One, prince of darkness, prince of sinners, Spirit of Evil, monarch of hell, prince of liars, evil incarnate; Lord of the Flies, Lord of Vermin, the Serpent, the dragon, the goat, seirizzin, the dickens, the deuce; the Adversary, the Tempter, Foul Fiend, the Archfiend, the Archdemon; Old One, Old Bogy, Old Boy, Old Scratch; Old Harry, Old Davy, Nick, Old Nick; *All Scot.* the Auld Ane, the Deil, Auld Clubfoot, Auld Nick.

satanic, *adj.* **1.** diabolic, diabolical, devilish, fiendish, ghoulish; Mephistophelian, demonic, demoniac, demoniacal, demonian, cacodemonic; infernal, hellish.

2. wicked, iniquitous, evil, sinful, odious, *Obs.* scelerous; impious, unholy, ungodly, godless; base, vile, sinister, dire, dark, dreadful, baleful, black; black-hearted, corrupt, depraved, vicious, *Archaic.* facinorous; profligate, immoral, dissolute, vitiated, perverted, perverse; pestilential, malevolent, malicious, malign, maleficent, malefic, fell, venomous; nefarious, flagitious, unspeakable, villainous, heinous; damnable, abominable, execrable, horrible, horrid, hideous, monstrous, atrocious, accursed; hateful, detestable, infamous, despicable, loathsome, abhorrent.

sate, *v.* **1.** fill, satisfy, suffice, satiate. See **satiate** (*def.* **2**).

2. surfeit, overfill, cloy, stuff, saturate, satiate. See **satiate** (*def.* **1.**).

satellite, *n.* **1.** moon.

2. spacecraft, space capsule, unmanned satellite, communications satellite, weather satellite, orbiting observatory, research satellite, relay satellite.

3. follower, disciple, apostle, sectarian, sectary, proselyte, acolyte, votary; aide, aide-de-camp, assistant, lieutenant, minion, subordinate; deputy, second, delegate, agent, surrogate, secondary, helper; partisan, ally, adherent, counselor, advisor, privy councilor; friend, mate, companion, *Inf.* buddy, partner, *Inf.* sidekick, *Inf.* sideman, pal, shadow, appendage, accompanier, auxiliary, appendant; confidante, right-hand man, good right arm, man Friday.

4. henchman, underling, second banana, lackey, flunky, *Sl.* stooge, *Sl.* gofer, *U.S. Sl.* ward heeler, cat's-paw, puppet, tool; hanger-on, barnacle, bur, camp follower, parasite, sponger, groveler, bootlicker, lickspittle, yes man, toadeater, toady, fawner, sycophant, tufthunter, spaniel, apple polisher, wheedler; frontman, strong-arm man, *U.S.* tough, *Inf.* goon.

5. retainer, attendant, dependent, servant, vassal, menial; courtier, carpet knight.

6. satellite nation, protectorate, dependency, possession, territory, domnion, colony, mandate.

satiate, *v.* **1.** surfeit, pall, overfill, overdo, indulge; cloy, glut, englut, stuff, cram, gorge, overfeed, *Sl.* pig out, *Sl.* stuff one's face; saturate, soak, drench, flood, deluge, engulf, inundate; overload, overburden; suffocate, choke, gag, sicken, nauseate, disgust; jade, dull, deaden, weary, exhaust, tire, bore.

2. sate, fill, suffice, content, satisfy, gratify; quench, slake, allay.

satiety, *n.* **1.** fullness, repletion, the point of satisfaction, contentment, gratification, satiation; cloyedness, overfullness, overindulgence; saturation, supersaturation, overflow, flood, deluge, inundation; suffocation, choking, gagging, nausea, disgust; dullness, weariness, exhaustion, boredom.

2. surfeit, excess, oversupply, *Sl.* bellyful, glut, surplus, waste, nimiety; superabundance, overabundance, superfluity, exuberance, too much; abundance, plethora, prodigality.

satiny, *adj.* satinlike, glowing, lustrous, shiny, sheeny; smooth, glossy, glazed, burnished, polished, waxed, varnished; sleek, slick, *Inf.* snaky; slippery, glassy.

satire, *n.* **1.** burlesque, parody, travesty, mocking exaggeration, caricature, cartoon, political cartoon; lampoon, spoof, pasquinade, squib, takeoff, *Inf.* put-down, *Inf.* shot; cut, jibe, fleer, slur; black comedy *or* humor, gallows humor, political humor.

2. irony, sarcasm, ridicule, mockery; disparagement, contempt, acrimony, contumely, scoffing, aspersion, censure, criticism; making fun of, holding [s.o.] up to ridicule, making [s.o.] the butt, tweeking [s.o.'s] nose, sneering, jeering, laughing at, taunting, *Inf.* hitting [s.o.] where it hurts, *Inf.* hitting home *or* hitting the mark.

satirical, *adj.* ironic, Rabelaisian, pungent, trenchant, keen, pointed, sharp, biting, stinging, astringent, ascerbic, tart, cutting, caustic, sarcastic, mordant; sardonic, cynical, dry, bitter; burlesque, farcical, parodic, caricatural, macoronic, Hudibrastic; mocking, derisive, ridiculing, irreverent, flippant, smart, *Inf.* smart-alecky; twitting, taunting, kidding; sneering, chaffing, disparaging, contumelious, abusive, scornful.

satirize, *v.* burlesque, parody, caricature, cartoon, travesty, pasquinade; lampoon, squib, poke fun at, mimic, mock, ridicule, hold up to ridicule, make [s.o.] a laughing stock, make fun *or* sport of, *Inf.* go after, *Inf.* hit at, *Inf.* take off on, *Inf.* do a takeoff of; make [s.o.] the butt of one's humor, prick [s.o.'s] balloon, tweak [s.o.'s] nose; pillory, put [s.o.] on the spit, *Sl.* roast, *Sl.* ride, *Sl.* razz, *Sl.* rag, *Sl.* put down, *Sl.* rank out, *Sl.* run down.

satisfaction, *n.* **1.** fulfillment, gratification, appeasing, assuaging, assuagement, placating.

2. content, contentment, pleasure, enjoyment, joy, delight, happiness, comfort.

3. acceptance, assurance, belief, trust.

4. reparation, compensation, indemnity, recompense, requital; payment, repayment, remuneration, reckoning; amends, atonement, expiation.

satisfactory, *adj.* sufficient, adequate, suitable, fit; up to par, up to scratch, *Inf.* up to snuff; competent, able, capable, commendable, worthy, good, acceptable, all right; fine, okay, O.K., *U.S. Sl.* hunky-dory.

satisfied, *adj.* **1.** content, happy, pleased, smug, like the cat that swallowed the canary.

2. paid in full, requited, compensated, reimbursed.

3. convinced, persuaded, assured; positive, certain, sure.

satisfy, *v.* **1.** please, gratify, gladden, delight; content, appease, assuage, pacify, placate; fulfill, fill, sate, satiate.

2. convince, assure, reassure, persuade, make [s.o.] see the light.

3. answer, solve, resolve, meet; match, equal, confirm.

4. make reparation, atone for, repay, requite; recompense, square up, compensate, reimburse, remunerate, pay, pay back.

5. suffice, do, be enough *or* adequate *or* sufficient, serve; *Inf.* hit the spot *or* bull's-eye, be on target.

saturate, *v.* **1.** soak, drench, wet through, sop, souse, waterlog, suffuse; ret, steep.

2. impregnate, ingrain, infuse, instill; permeate, penetrate, pervade, imbue, shoot through, imbrue; fill, charge, surfeit, glut, sate, satiate.

saturated, *adj.* **1.** soaked, drenched, sopping, soused, waterlogged, sodden, suffused.

2. permeated, pervaded, shot through, riddled; filled, imbued, imbrued, stuffed, crammed, packed; sated, satiated, glutted, cloyed, jaded.

3. (*of colors*) intense, pure, brilliant, prismatic, spectral.

saturnalia, *n.* revelry, merrymaking, revels, frolic; party, partying, wild party, *Sl.* hot time, *Sl.* bash, *Sl.* lollapalooza, *Inf.* clambake; carnival, festivity, festival, feast; bacchanalia, bacchanal, orgy, debauch, carousal, carouse.

saturnine, *adj.* gloomy, glum, dismal, blue, morose, sulky; depressed, discouraged, low-spirited; downhearted, *Inf.* down in the dumps, downcast, dejected, dispirited; sorrowful, sad, unhappy, melancholy, weepy, tearful; pessimistic, hopeless, despairing, despondent; dour, stern, severe, sullen; reserved, taciturn, quiet, silent, withdrawn, apathetic, moody, torpid.

satyr, *n.* letch, libertine, rake, roué, goat, debauchee, debaucher, corrupter, dissipator; playboy, *Inf.* fun-loving boy, *Inf.* rip, *Sl.* swinger; adulterer, *It. cicisbeo,* gigolo, fornicator, seducer, *Inf.* wolf; big lover, *Inf.* lover-boy, *Sl.* make-out artist, *Sl.* swordsman, *Sl.* stud, bed-hopper, philanderer, womanizer, woman chaser, lady-killer, Don Juan, Lothario, Casanova; ravisher, rapist, raper; pincher, feeler, *Sl.* dirty old man, *Sl.* funny uncle, pervert, exhibitionist, *Sl.* flasher.

sauce, *n.* **1.** condiment, dressing, relish, chutney;

seasoning, flavoring.

2. *Informal.* impertinence, impudence, insolence, audacity; boldness, brazenness, freshness, brashness, pertness, sauciness, *Inf.* cheekiness, *Inf.* sassiness, *Inf.* brassiness; *All Inf.* brass, sass, face, cheek, back talk, guff, crust; *All Sl.* gall, nerve, mouth, lip.

3. *U.S. Slang.* liquor, hard liquor, alcohol, spirits, *Inf.* booze, *Inf.* hard stuff, *Sl.* hooch, *Sl.* medicine. See also **intoxicant** (*def.* **3**).

saucy, *adj.* **1.** impertinent, insolent, impudent, audacious, presumptuous, out-of-line; bold, brazen, brazen-faced, brash, fresh, pert, shameless, *Inf.* flip, *Inf.* cheeky, *Inf.* sassy, *Inf.* brassy, *Sl.* wise, *Sl.* mouthy, *Sl.* smart-mouth.

2. (*all of clothing, appearance, etc.*) jaunty, dapper, gay, rakish, brave, *Scot. and North Eng.* braw; showy, ostentatious, gaudy, flash, flashy, show-offish, *Inf.* show-offy.

sauna, *n.* hot-air bath, sudatorium, sudatory, bagnio, Turkish bath, Finnish bath, Swedish bath; bathhouse, bathing house, bath, the baths, *Obs.* stew; (*all in ancient Greece or Rome*) thermae, tepidarium, caldarium.

saunter, *v.* **1.** stroll, promenade, perambulate, amble, ramble, meander, *Inf.* mosey along, *Inf.* breeze along, *Inf.* traipse.

—n. **2.** stroll, promenade, jaunt, walk, amble, ramble, *Inf.* constitutional.

sausage, *n.* salami, peperoni; bologna, *Inf.* baloney, liverwurst, luncheon meat; knackwurst, bratwurst, korv, kielbasa; frankfurter, *Inf.* frank, *U.S.* wiener, *Inf.* weenie, hot dog, *Sl.* dog; Vienna sausage, wienerwurst; blood sausage, blood pudding, black pudding, white pudding; pork sausage, *Brit. Sl.* banger; headcheese.

savage, *adj.* **1.** ferocious, fierce, ruthless, vicious, fell, truculent; untamed, wild, undomesticated, unbroken; feral, ferine, wolfish, lupine, beastly, bestial, *Obs.* belluine; brutal, inhuman, barbarous, barbaric, hellish, Tartarian, Hunnish, Vandalic, Gothic; brutish, murderous, homicidal, slaughterous, bloodthirsty; sadistic, animalistic, cannibalistic, fiendish, ogreish; diabolical, demonic, demoniac, devilish; terrible, harsh, grim, hard, severe; unrelenting, relentless, remorseless, implacable, inexorable, grinding.

2. pitiless, merciless, heartless, unkind, inhumane, *Archaic.* immane; cruel, hard-hearted, stony-hearted, marble-hearted, cold-blooded.

3. gross, rude, coarse, vulgar, rough, rugged; gruff, bearish, boorish, crass, rustic, ill-bred, churlish, clodhopping, *Archaic.* carlish; loutish, doltish, cloddish, oafish; uncivil, unrefined, uncouth, inurbane, unpolished; uncultivated, uncivilized, unmannered, ill-mannered, ungentlemanly, ungentle, uncourtly, inelegant, indelicate.

—n. **4.** brute, barbarian, hellkite; Yahoo, wild man, ogre, monster, troglodyte; Vandal, Goth, Hun, Tartar.

5. boor, rustic, churl, lout, dolt, clod, oaf, *Archaic.* carl; bumpkin, yokel, *Sl.* rube, *Sl.* hick, *Disparaging.* bogtrotter, hobnail, *Inf.* hayseed, kern, yahoo, *Sl.* lug.

savant, *n.* scholar, learned man, giant of learning, colossus of knowledge, mine of information, walking encyclopedia, *Archaic.* clerk; intellectual, intellect, towering intellect; philosopher, thinker, sage, wise man; master, mastermind, mavin, mandarin, pundit; authority, expert, adept.

save¹, *v.* **1.** rescue, come to [s.o.'s] rescue, liberate, free, bail [s.o.] out; redeem, deliver, snatch from the jaws of death; salvage, *Baseball.* (*of a relief pitcher*) put out the fire.

2. protect, safeguard, guard, secure; shield, screen, cover, cloak, veil; keep, keep up, preserve, conserve, maintain, sustain, carry over.

3. reserve, husband, withhold, hold back, hold, hold in reserve, save for future use, save for a rainy day; set aside, put *or* lay aside, put away, lay away, lay by, lay up, stow away, squirrel away, salt away, *Sl.* sock away; store, store up, hoard, stockpile, amass, accumulate, pile up.

4. economize, scrimp, scrape, *Inf.* pinch pennies, *Inf.* tighten one's belt; waste not, want not; cut expenses, cut costs, buy wholesale, buy in bulk *or* quantity.

5. obviate, preclude, prevent, forestall, debar, rule out; keep on the safe side, cover all angles, leave nothing to chance.

save², *prep., conj.* but, except, excepting, except for, with the exception of, saving, *Inf.* outside of; less, minus, leaving out, omitting, barring, not counting, discounting.

saving, *adj.* **1.** rescuing, delivering, freeing, releasing, liberating.

2. protective, protecting, safeguarding; preservative, preserving, maintaining, sustaining, upholding, conservative; restorative.

3. compensating, reparatory, reparative, restitutory; redeeming, redemptory.

4. thrifty, economical, provident, prudent, frugal, careful, sparing, penny-wise, *Inf.* tight.

—n. **5.** economy, thrift, thriftiness, frugality, providence, prudence; conservation, husbandry, management; economizing, scrimping, scraping.

6. reduction, price reduction, price-cut, cut, discount, deduction, *Inf.* rollback; rebate, refund, *Sl.* kickback.

7. reserve, reservoir, supply, stockpile, cache, something to fall back on; card up one's sleeve, *Sl.* ace in the hole.

8. savings capital, assets, funds, finances, resources, reserves, means, wherewithal; nest egg, reserve fund, mad money; kitty, pool, pot.

—prep., conj. **9.** save. See **save²**.

savior, *n.* **1.** messiah, (*in Muslim usage*) Mahdi, redeemer, deliverer; liberator, freer, emancipator, manumitter; champion, knight in shining armor, knight errant; lifesaver.

2. the Savior Jesus Christ, Our Lord, Son of God, Son of man, Lamb of God, King of Kings, Immanuel, Prince of Peace, the Good Shepherd.

savoir-faire, *n.* sophistication, worldliness, savoir-vivre, *Sl.* savvy; culture, cultivation, refinement, polish; finesse, adaptability, skill, adroitness, ability; grace, style, poise; graciousness, mannerliness, manners, good manners, breeding, comity, gentility, social grace; suavity, suaveness, urbanity, smoothness; tact, tactfulness, diplomacy, prudence; discernment, perceptiveness.

savor, *n.* **1.** relish, smack, zest, spice, tang, sapidity, piquancy, taste, flavor; odor, scent, fragrance, smell, aroma, attar, perfume, sachet; redolence, pungency, odoriferousness, bouquet, incense; trail, trace, breath.

2. essence, spirit, soul, nature; aspect, property, characteristic; touch, vein, tone, complexion, color.

3. attraction, magnetism, draw, drawing power; enticement, inducement, fascination, allurement, lure; charm, enchantment, bewitchment; stimulation, excitement, ravishment.

—v. **4.** enjoy fully, enjoy to the hilt, relish, *Sl.* dig, *Sl.* get a kick out of; take pleasure in, be pleased with, take satisfaction in, derive pleasure from; revel in, riot in, *Sl.* groove on; luxuriate in, bask in, indulge in, swim *or* wallow in; feast on, gloat over, *Inf.* smack one's lips over, *Sl.* lick one's chops over, eat up; like,

love, care for, delight in, rejoice in; appreciate, value, cherish, treasure, prize.

5. flavor, season, salt, spice, give zip to, put herbs and spices in, *Inf.* doctor up.

6. *Often* **savor of** smack, have all the earmarks, approximate, resemble, exhibit traces, show influence, show signs, have the hallmark.

7. taste good, be savory, tickle the palate, tickle the taste buds, tempt the appetite, please the palate; appeal, entice, attract, draw in, *Inf.* pull in off the street.

savory, *adj.* delicious, delectable, tasty, dainty, appetizing, luscious, ambrosial, ambrosian; flavorful, epicurean, nectarous, nectarean, sweet, sweet as honey; palatable, toothsome, *Scot.* gustable; piquant, pungent, poignant, spicy, zesty, zestful; tangy, well-seasoned, snappy, with a kick, *Sl.* kicky; fragrant, odoriferous, aromatic, perfumed, scented, sweet-smelling.

saw[1], *n.* **1.** cutting tool, handsaw, hacksaw, circular saw, band saw, keyhole saw, butcher's saw, lumberman's saw.

—*v.* **2.** cut, divide, sever, dissever; split, rend, sunder, dispart, cleave, rive; bisect, halve, quarter, intersect; subdivide, compart, partition, repartition, demarcate.

saw[2], *n.* old saying, saying, sententious saying, pithy statement; maxim, aphorism, apothegm, gnome, mot; proverb, axiom, precept, prescript, dictum, epigram, adage; witticism, *Fr. jeu d'esprit,* quip, Atticism; cliché, hackneyed phrase, platitude, truism, *Inf.* bromide, commonplace; byword, slogan, motto, catchword, catch phrase, *Sl.* catchy phrase, doggerel verse.

saw-toothed, *adj.* serrated, serrulate, *Chiefly Biol.* serrate, serriform; crenate, crenated, crenulate; *Both Bot., Zool.* dentate, denticulate; notched, nicked, jagged, jaggy; sawlike, zigzag, zigzagged, uneven, rough, in-and-out.

say, *v.* **1.** utter, vocalize, pronounce, announce, speak, mouth; word, put in words, phrase, articulate; answer, respond, reply, rejoin, retort; remark, come out with, communicate, convey; state, declare, tell, impart; present, mention, add, put, put before; reveal, let out, divulge, disclose, make known, cry, noise abroad; breathe, whisper, betray.

2. repeat, recite, declaim, orate, deliver, rehearse, render.

3. estimate, predict, predicate, speculate, hypothesize, conjecture, hazard a guess; assume, judge, imagine; promise, imply, give the implication *or* impression that.

4. report, allege, asseverate, aver, avow, avouch; attest, testify, certify, vouch; depose, bear witness, give evidence, give one's word, warrant; profess, claim, purport, pretend; impute, insinuate; cite, name, attribute, assign, ascribe; adduce, advance, bring forward, bring to attention, introduce; offer, propose, plead.

—*n.* **5.** statement, expression, utterance, representation; pronouncement, announcement, dictum, manifesto; recital, recitation, repetition; monologue, soliloquy, speech, talk; pronouncement, assertion, proclamation, predication; averment, avowal, asseveration, assurance, promise, pledge, word, say-so; allegation, affirmation, protestation, profession, acknowledgement.

6. turn, *Inf.* crack, *Inf.* turn at bat, chance to speak, *Sl.* two cents' worth, right to speak; vote, option, prerogative, privilege, influence, weight, sway.

saying, *n.* **1.** saw, maxim, aphorism. See **saw**[2].

2. go without saying be understood, be self-evident, be manifest; be accepted, be matter of course, be clear *or* clear-cut, be plain as day, be plain as the nose on your face; be indubitable, be indisputable, be unquestionable, be an accepted fact.

scabby, *adj.* **1.** crusty, incrusted, scaly, scurfy, furfuraceous, *Pathol.* psoriatic, *Vet. Pathol.* mangy, scabbed, scabrous; broken, chapped, coarse, rough, sloughy, peeling, flaky.

2. *Slang.* mean, nasty, contemptible, scurvy, low, base, vile.

scaffold, *n.* **1.** scaffolding, frame, framework, gantry, skeleton.

2. gallows, drop, gibbet; elevated platform, block, guillotine.

3. raised platform, stage.

scalawag, *n.* *Informal.* scamp, rascal, rogue, rapscallion, scapegrace, scaramouche. See **scamp**.

scale[1], *n.* **1.** squama, scurf, furfur, dandruff, flake; *Anat., Zool., Biol.* plate, *Zool.* scute, *Zool.* shield; lamella, lamina, layer, *Bot.* palea.

2. coat, coating, crust, incrustation, cover, covering.

—*v.* **3.** remove the scales from, flake, scrape *or* scrape off, abrade, cut away, shave.

scale[2], *n.* *Usu.* **scales** weigher, balance, bathroom scales *or* scale, calorie scale, postage scale.

scale[3], *n.* **1.** steps, degrees, gradations, levels, series, succession, progression, sequence; musical scale, decimal scale; hierarchy, pecking order, social scale, caste system, seniority system.

2. ruler, measuring stick, yardstick, gauge.

3. range, gamut, scope, extent, reach, spread, expanse, field.

—*v.* **4.** climb up *or* over, mount, ascend, go up, escalade.

5. *Often* **scale down** reduce, trim, cut down, decrease, lower, lessen.

scaly, *adj.* **1.** scalelike, squamous, squamosal, squamose, squamulose, scurfy, furfuraceous; *Zool.* scutate, lamellate, lamellar.

2. peeling, flaking, flaky.

scamp, *n.* rascal, rogue, rapscallion, scapegrace, *Inf.* scalawag, scaramouche; bad *or* naughty boy, imp, puck, mischief-maker, troublemaker, *Inf.* cut-up, prankster, practical joker; devil, little devil, holy terror, *Fr. enfant terrible, Irish Eng.* spalpeen; cad, churl, *Sl.* louse, bully, ruffian; knave, blackguard, villain, scoundrel, *Archaic.* bezonian, miscreant, picaroon, wretch, dastard, reprobate; cur, dog, *Inf.* hound, *Sl.* lowlife, *Archaic.* caitiff, *Archaic.* coistrel; delinquent, juvenile delinquent, misdemeanant, *Inf.* scofflaw, felon, malefactor, criminal, outlaw; good-for-nothing, *Fr. vaurien,* ne'er-do-well, *Sl.* bum, *Sl.* rip; *Inf.* rat, *Inf.* creep, *Inf.* stinker, *Derog.* bastard, *Derog.* SOB, *Chiefly Brit. Sl.* rotten, *Chiefly Brit. Sl.* bounder, *Brit. Sl.* blighter.

scamper, *v.* **1.** scurry, scoot, race, *Brit.* chevy; hasten, make haste, speed, accelerate, hustle, hurry, post, rush, scramble; move swiftly, move quickly, hie, step lively, step quickly, spank, clip, double-time, *Inf.* hump *or* hump it; jog, trot, canter, lope; run, dash, dart, bolt, tear, tear along, bowl along, make time, cover ground, make strides *or* rapid strides; sprint, fly, flit, whiz, whisk; zoom, zip, career, rip, scour, scud, scorch, burn up the road, outstrip the wind, race like the wind, go *or* be off like a shot, *Chiefly Brit.* hare, *Inf.* roar, *Inf.* barrel, *Inf.* pour it on, *Inf.* eat up the road; take flight, take to flight, take wing, *Inf.* beat it, *Inf.* skip out, *Inf.* skedaddle, *Sl.* skidoodle, *Sl.* vamoose; take off, *Inf.* clear out, *Inf.* make tracks, *Inf.* cut out, *Inf.* fly the coop, *Sl.* split, *Sl.* scram, *Sl.* blow, *Sl.* hightail it; *All Sl.* step on it, hop to it, snap to it, get cracking, get a hustle *or* a move on, stir one's stumps.

2. brattle, skip, hop, jump, trip, gambol, caper, romp, play.

scan, *v.* **1.** examine, study, scrutinize, inspect, sift; anatomize, probe, delve into, research; sound, investigate, search, explore, *Archaic.* indagate; overhaul, check; consider, take stock of, size up.

2. skim, read over, peruse, browse, dip into, have a look at, look over, run over, check over, review; thumb through, flip through, leaf through, look through, glance through.

scandal, *n.* **1.** misdoing, evildoing, wrongdoing, transgression, malefaction, violation, crime, sin, offense, atrocity, delinquency, dereliction, disgraceful action, outrageous *or* flagrant misconduct *or* misbehavior, evil behavior, blameworthy action; political impropriety, unethical conduct; vice, wickedness, baseness, turpitude, depravity, corruption, iniquity, villainy; immodesty, impropriety, impudicity, indecency, lust, carnality, concupiscence, lewdness, lechery, debauchery, libertinism, dissipation.

2. commotion, disturbance, stir, affair, ado, furor, fuss, flurry, turbulence, turmoil, tumult, *Inf.* to-do, uproar, storm, explosion, hubbub, hullabaloo, *Sl.* big stink.

3. disgrace, shame, dishonor, degradation, debasement, ill-repute, disrepute, reproach, ingloriousness; ignominy, infamy, odium, opprobrium, revilement, condemnation; censure, blame, inculpation, railing, commination, invective, curse, denunciation, contumely, malediction, animadversion, imprecation, delation, execration; discredit, disfavor, disrespect, disapproval, disapprobation, obloquy, disesteem, loss of face, fall, downfall, debacle, descent, (*usu. political*) Watergate; humiliation, humble pie, mortification; belittlement, disparagement, deprecation, detraction, deflation, depreciation, devaluation, derogation.

4. slander, libel, calumny, calumniation, misrepresentation, falsehood, lie, untruth, malicious falsehood *or* untruth, traducement; aspersion, imputation, insinuation, innuendo, *Inf.* brickbat, backbiting, malicious gossip, dirt, scandalmongering, abuse, injury, mudslinging; slur, defilement, blot, blot on the escutcheon, smear, smirch, stain, taint, attaint, tarnish, spot, black spot *or* mark, blemish, smudge, brand, stigma, badge of infamy; defamation, denigration, vilification, vituperation, *Inf.* skeleton in the closet, yellow journalism, muckraking.

scandalize, *v.* **1.** shock, outrage, appall, disturb, upset, jar, horrify; insult, affront, offend, raise eyebrows; abuse, injure, ill-treat, maltreat; gall, rankle, cause to stick in [s.o.'s] throat.

2. sicken, nauseate, turn one's stomach, make one sick; repel, revolt, disgust, fill with loathing; shame, disgrace, dishonor, degrade, debase, abase, vitiate.

scandalous, *adj.* **1.** disgraceful, shameful, dishonorable, degraded, inglorious; infamous, ignominious, odious, opprobrious, contemptible, despicable, sordid, detestable; degenerate, depraved, unmentionable, corrupt, reprehensible, debased, abased, vitiated, iniquitous, immoral, profligate; horrible, heinous, vicious, atrocious, flagitious, *Archaic.* facinorous, felonious; base, vile, evil, infernal, sinister, diabolic, sinful, bad, wrong; low, arrant, nefarious, mean, dastardly, villainous, ignoble; denunciatory, damnatory, execrable, deplorable, reproachful, vituperative, invective, fulminating, objurgatory, imprecatory; disreputable, discreditable, disfavorable; belittling, disparaging, deprecatory, derogatory, detracting, deflating, depreciating, devaluating; humiliating, humbling, mortifying.

2. immodest, improper, fulsome, unseemly, unbecoming, indecorous; unworthy, undutiful, delinquent, objectionable, uncommendable, reprovable, peccable, illaudable; shocking, outrageous, notorious, flagrant; indecent, lewd, obscene, perverse, lustful, lascivious, lecherous, licentious.

3. slanderous, libelous, calumnious, calumniatory, traducent, false, untrue, maliciously false *or* untrue, misrepresentative, aspersive, imputative, insinuating, gossiping; abusive, thersitical, hurtful, scurrilous, *Archaic.* scurrile, injurious, contumelious, insulting, backbiting; defiling, sullying, soiling, staining, smearing, smirching, tainting, tarnishing, blemishing, smudging, stigmatizing; defamatory, denigrating, vilifying, vilipenditory.

scanty, *adj.* **1.** scant, skimpy, scrimpy, meager, exiguous, *Scot. and North Eng.* jimp; meanly small, beggarly, paltry, poor, piddling, *Inf.* measly, mere; slight, slender, lean, thin, narrow, puny, stunted; very little, insufficient, inadequate, short, shy; insubstantial, modest, light; nominal, minute, negligible, *Inf.* barely there.

2. sparse, scattered, thinly distributed, few and far between; sporadic, infrequent, spotty, irregular, intermittent.

scapegoat, *n.* victim, butt, *Inf.* the one on the receiving end, object, target, *Chiefly Brit.* Aunt Sally, *Inf.* goat; dupe, gull, cat's paw, *U.S. Sl.* fall guy, *Sl.* patsy, *Inf.* sucker; laughingstock, gazingstock, byword.

scapegrace, *n.* scamp, *Inf.* scalawag, rascal, rogue, rapscallion, scaramouche. See **scamp**.

scar, *n.* **1.** pock, pockmark, *Med.* cicatrix, blemish, old wound, spot; patch, blotch, discoloration, birthmark, nevus; defect, fault, defacement, disfigurement, flaw, cut, crack, scratch; stain, blot, speck, blur, smudge, smirch, smutch, taint; bruise, *Sl.* hickey; brand.

2. trauma, injury, damage; upset, shock, blow, ordeal.

—*v.* **3.** blemish, mark, brand; impair, deface, disfigure, mar, scratch, cut, crack; spot, speckle, stain, blotch, discolor; sully, tarnish, taint.

4. upset, shock, *Psychiatry.* traumatize, hurt, injure, damage.

scarce, *adj.* **1.** scant, scanty, exiguous, unplentiful, in short supply, at a premium, not to be had, not to be had for love or money, *Inf.* scarcer than hen's teeth; meager, skimpy, paltry, too little, not enough, too little, too late; short, low, tight, lean, not abundant; insufficient, deficient, inadequate, lacking, wanting, needful.

2. rare, almost unheard-of, infrequent, occasional, few and far between, seldom seen, seldom met with; uncommon, unusual, unwonted, unique; singular, exceptional, out of the ordinary, noteworthy, notable, distinctive, atypical.

scarcely, *adv.* **1.** barely, hardly, *Dial.* scantly, only just, just, with difficulty, not easily; by a narrow margin, *Inf.* by the skin of one's teeth, by a hair's breadth, by a little bit, by an inch; faintly, dimly, slightly, not quite.

2. probably not, definitely not, certainly not, on no account, on no occasion; ill, little, by no means, noway, nowise, in no way, not at all, not in the least, not a bit.

scarcity, *n.* **1.** lack, dearth, want, need, crying need; insufficiency, inadequacy, deprivation, deficiency; paucity, sparseness, sparsity, scantiness; exiguity, exiguousness, slenderness, thinness, leanness, meagerness, shortage, small number, paltriness; poverty, poorness, indigence, destitution; famine, drought.

2. infrequency, seldomness, rarity, rareness, uncommonness, unusualness, uniqueness.

scare, *v.* **1.** frighten, fright, affright, *Archaic.* affray, alarm, startle, shock; terrify, daunt, strike terror into, terrorize, appall, horrify, dismay; put the fear of God into, intimidate, awe, *Sl.* psych out, cow, threaten, menace; *Sl.* scare the bejeesus out of, *Sl.* scare the pants off, *Sl.* scare the living daylights out of, *Sl.* scare out of one's wits, curl one's hair, make one's hair stand on end, make one's flesh crawl, make one's blood run cold; scare stiff, start, panic, break out in a cold sweat.

2. **scare up** *Informal.* find, get, obtain, secure, gather, collect, raise; round up, dig up, scrape up, scrounge, rustle up, hustle.

—*n.* 3. fright, alarm, shock, start; panic, dither, consternation, nervousness, jitters, shakes; terror, horror, fear, phobia.

scarf, *n.* neckpiece, barb, neckerchief, fichu, muffler, tippet; kerchief, babushka, bandanna, headpiece, headdress, (*in the Middle East*) kaffiyeh; headcloth, wimple, cornet; stole, boa, shawl, throw, prayer shawl, *Judaism.* tallith, (*in Mexico*) rebozo, (*in Latin America*) serape, (*in Asia*) chapan; veil, *Moslem.* yashmak, (*in India*) purdah, (*in Afghanistan*) chadri; ascot, necktie, cravat, four-in-hand.

2. runner, cloth, doily, antimacassar, tidy.

scary, *adj.* hair-raising, terrifying, horrifying, appalling, shocking; daunting, intimidating, threatening, menacing; frightening, goosepimply, creepy, crawly, discomfiting, dismaying, disturbing, *Sl.* hairy, difficult, bad.

scathing, *adj.* severe, harsh, extreme, stern; caustic, vitriolic, mordant, sarcastic, nasty; biting, bitter, acrimonious, acrid, keen, incisive, trenchant; cutting, sharp, tart, pointed, stinging, lacerating, scarifying; critical, denunciatory, excoriating, derisive; virulent, spiteful, hostile, rancorous; harmful, hurtful, injurious, damaging, malignant; searing, burning, scorching, heated, fierce, ferocious, savage.

scatter, *v.* 1. strew, broadcast, sprinkle, sparge, disject, bestrew, disseminate, sow; spread, circulate, diffuse, scatter to the winds; fling, toss, throw.

2. dispel, disperse, dissipate, dissolve, disband, dismiss; separate, break up, drive off, rout, eject, send off.

scatterbrained, *adj.* rattlebrained, harebrained, frivolous, flighty, impractical; irresponsible, *Inf.* slaphappy, *Inf.* dizzy, *Sl.* dippy, *Sl.* screwy, *Sl.* having a screw loose; dreamy, drifty, woolgathering, *Inf.* on another planet, with one's head in the clouds, *Sl.* in the ozone; featherbrained, hairbrained, not all there, missing some marbles, not having all one's buttons, with a mind like a sieve; nonserious, clownish, always kidding; erratic, changeable, mercurial, fickle, volatile.

scavenge, *v.* 1. cleanse, clean up, tidy, sweep up, hose down.

2. search, seek, hunt, prowl, look for, dig for; scrounge, forage, rummage, plunder; rustle up, *Inf.* scare up; *Inf.* sponge, *Sl.* mooch, *Inf.* freeload, *Inf.* bum.

scavenger, *n.* 1. sweeper, street cleaner *or* sweeper, *Anglo-Indian.* bhangi, sanitation engineer, garbage man, garbage collector, trash man.

2. forager, rummager, searcher, seeker, hunter; scrounger, scrounge, *Inf.* sponge, *Inf.* freeloader, *Sl.* moocher, *Sl.* mooch.

scenario, *n.* 1. outline, plot outline, sketch, abstract, summary, capsule, précis, synopsis; idea, concept, scheme, plan; framework, skeleton, *Inf.* bare bones; structure, organization, conception, master plan, floor plan, game plan; review, analysis, rehash, brief.

2. *Motion Pictures.* manuscript, script, working script, shooting script, screenplay, book.

scene, *n.* 1. place, location, site, locale, setting, *Fr. mise en scène;* arena, stage, theater, surroundings; region, locality, sphere; spot, center, focus; milieu, environment, circumstances, background, backdrop, situation.

2. landscape, view, picture, scenery, vista, panorama, prospect; exposure, outlook, perspective; seascape, dreamscape, streetscape.

3. episode, incident, chapter, segment; moment, happening, event, affair; proceeding, business.

4. outburst, eruption, explosion, *Inf.* flare-up, *Inf.* tantrum; upheaval, disturbance, altercation, brouhaha, furor.

5. **make the scene** *U.S. Slang.* go out, go on the town, go where the action is; be on hand, be on deck, be on the scene; participate, become involved *or* interested in, get into, *Sl.* groove on.

scenery, *n.* 1. view, scene, sight, vista, sweep, panorama; landscape, scape, seascape, waterscape, skyscape; (*of a place*) features, characteristics, aspects, phenomena, configuration, lay of the land, general appearance; air, atmosphere, setting, location, background, site.

2. stage setting, set, scene, *Fr. mise en scène; Theat.* drop curtain, scrim; flats, screens, *All Theat.* borders, tormentors, teasers.

scenic, *adj.* panoramic, grand, awe-inspiring, breathtaking, impressive, beautiful, pleasing to the eye; picturesque, pretty as a picture, charming; bucolic, pastoral, rustic, rural, natural, unspoiled, unmarred.

scent, *n.* 1. aroma, fragrance, fragrancy, incense, redolence, redolency, balm, balminess, bouquet; odor, smell; slight trace, hint, wind, whiff; track, trail, spoor.

2. perfume, cologne, eau de Cologne, toilet water, *Ger. kölnisch Wasser, Fr. parfum;* fragrance, essence, extract; attar, scented oil.

3. sense of smell, olfaction, olfactory sense.

—*v.* 4. sniff, smell, detect, discern, perceive, recognize, distinguish.

5. perfume, aromatize, make fragrant, incense, cense.

scepter, *n.* 1. rod, wand, staff, baton, truncheon, fasces.

2. sovereignty, royalty, majesty, reign, royal power *or* authority; empery, dominion, control, domination, rule, command; influence, sway, ascendancy, supremacy, primacy.

schedule, *n.* 1. timetable, train *or* bus *or* flight schedule; agenda, program, plan, itinerary, *Sl.* sked; syllabus, outline; list, listing, slate, record, register, *U.S.* docket; calendar, social calendar, list of appointments.

—*v.* 2. make up *or* out a schedule, write up a schedule, work out a schedule; put on a schedule, write *or* enter in a schedule; register, calendar, slot, slate.

3. plan, arrange, reserve, make reservations, book, make arrangements *or* plans; budget, allot, appropriate, set aside *or* apart, earmark, dedicate, assign.

schematic, *adj.* 1. diagrammatic, diagrammatical, graphic, plotted, charted; illustrative, representational, delineative.

—*n.* 2. diagram, drawing, tracing, blueprint, sketch, delineation; chart, flow chart, graph, line graph; plan, arrangement, layout, design, order; ground plan, floor plan, game plan.

schematize, *v.* organize, arrange, classify, categorize, sort, grade, rank; catalogue, file, collocate, group, codify, put into order; pigeonhole, pinpoint, pin down, tie up loose ends; regulate, methodize, standardize, systematize.

scheme, *n.* 1. plan, design, intent, purpose, intention; objective, end, aim, object; program, project, enterprise; proposal, suggestion, idea, thought; fancy, dream, daydream, vision, air castle, castle in the air, castle in Spain, *Inf.* pie in the sky, *Inf.* brainstorm, *Inf.*

pipe dream.

2. arrangement, order, distribution, systematization, organization, codification; policy, system, course of action; method, strategy, procedure, way, game plan, scenario, process; schedule, *Sl.* sked, agenda, calendar, docket, order of business.

3. diagram, sketch, outline, delineation, design, projection; drawing, blueprint, schema, layout, chart, map; prospectus, syllabus, synopsis, summary, digest, brief.

4. device, ploy, stratagem, maneuver, machination, subterfuge, flimflam, *Inf.* racket, *Sl.* game; contrivance, trick, wile, finesse, ruse, tactic, *Inf.* move; conspiracy, intrigue, complot, cabal, collusion, connivance.

—*v.* **5.** devise, prepare, think out, plot, plan, project, lay *or* form plans, formulate, frame, figure out, design, organize, *Inf.* cook up; imagine, dream up, envision, visualize, spin, contrive, conceive, invent; map out, block out, hit upon; hatch, machinate, maneuver, connive, concoct, complot, cabal, intrigue, wheel and deal, *Inf.* finagle.

scheming, *adj.* **1.** crafty, artful, designing, sly, cunning, *Scot. and North Eng.* pawky, wily; underhanded, conniving, devious, Machiavellian, calculating, intriguing, machinating, maneuvering; slick, slick as a whistle, slippery, slippery as an eel, tricky, unpredictable, foxy, guileful.

2. adroit, resourceful, inventive, ingenious, clever, astute.

schism, *n.* **1.** division, separation, parting of the ways, divergence, variance, splintering, faction; rift, split, break, breaking off *or* up, breach, rupture; cleavage, scission, severance; disunion, disjuncture, disjunction, disconnection, detachment.

2. faction, side, splinter party, contingent, party, group, band, ring, *Inf.* crowd; branch, arm, division, section, sector; sect, cult, denomination, persuasion, faith.

scholar, *n.* **1.** savant, man of letters, learned person, bookman, intellectual, highbrow, *Inf.* egghead, *Inf.* longhair, *Inf.* brain, *Inf.* walking encyclopedia; authority, expert, pundit, luminary; bibliophile, bibliophilist, bookworm; professor, doctor, teacher, pedagogue; pedant, *Inf.* know-it-all.

2. student, pupil, schoolgirl *or* schoolboy, learner, *Fr. élève, Fr. étudiant, Sl.* grind; undergraduate, *U.S. Inf.* coed, graduate student, *Inf.* grad student; *All Educ.* student teacher, practice teacher, pupil teacher, teaching *or* teacher's aide, teaching assistant, *Inf.* T.A., graduate assistant.

scholarly, *adj.* academic, scholastic, intellectual, highbrow, highbrowed, *Inf.* long-haired, intelligent, *Inf.* brainy; studious, bookish, bibliophilistic, bibliophilic; ivory-towerish, pedagoguish, professorial, pedantic, *Inf.* know-it-all; erudite, learned, lettered, punditic, wise, sage, profound, deep; well-versed, knowledgeable, literate, literary, well-read; educated, book-learned, well-educated, well-instructed, well-tutored, well-schooled, well-posted, well-grounded.

scholarship, *n.* **1.** erudition, learning, letters, *Archaic.* literature, book learning, formal education, schooling, preparation, training; skill, know-how, knowledge, wisdom, study, *Usu. Derog.* bookishness; enlightenment, edification, cultivation, culture, refinement.

2. grant, award, endowment, purse, fellowship, assistantship, *Fr. bourse, Fr. boursier.*

3. collective knowledge, lore, learning, wisdom; information, facts, data.

school, *n.* **1.** educational institution, primary school, grammar school, secondary school, high school; institution of higher education *or* learning, college, university, multiversity, *Both Derog.* phrontistery *or* phrontisterion; private school, boarding school, academy, seminary; kindergarten, nursery school, day-care center; (*all within a school*) department, division, faculty, area, discipline, field.

2. style, fashion, manner, tone, character, stamp; method, system, mode; (*used collectively*) followers, disciples, pupils, students, apostles, protégés; adherents, proponents, devotees, votaries, admirers; imitators, copiers, epigones, emulators; successors, heirs, perpetuators.

3. belief, creed, credo, dogma, doctrine, ism; thought, view, opinion, position; sect, denomination, persuasion, faction, party, class, communion, fellowship.

—*adj.* **4.** educational, instructive, informative, didactic; academic, academical, scholastic, instructional, pedagogic, pedagogical.

—*v.* **5.** teach, instruct, tutor, inform, enlighten, edify; train, coach, break in, prepare, ready, prime; exercise, practice, drill, discipline; nurture, foster, nourish, breed, rear, bring up, cultivate, educate, develop, broaden, civilize, humanize; inculcate, instill, infuse, indoctrinate; govern, direct, guide; mold, shape, form; preach, lecture, moralize.

schoolbook, *n.* textbook, text, book, manual, handbook; abecedarium, primer, hornbook, first reader, reader, copybook, grammar *or* grammar book.

schooling, *n.* education, formal education, book learning, teaching, instruction, tuition, tutelage, tutorship; direction, guidance, nurture, breeding, development; preparation, training, discipline, exercise, practice; inculcation, instillment, indoctrination, initiation, introduction; enlightenment, edification, culture, cultivation, refinement.

science, *n.* **1.** body of knowledge, body of facts *or* information, body of laws *or* principles, body of truths *or* verities *or* realities, pantology; discipline, area of study, academic area, area, field, subject; sphere, domain, realm, world; branch, specialization, specialty.

2. physical science, technology, physics, chemistry, biology, geology, geography; social science, sociology, psychology, economics.

3. scholarship, academics, academic pursuit, learning, erudition, philosophy; research, experimentation, trial and error, investigation, discovery.

4. skill, proficiency, expertise, expertness, mastery; adeptness, aptness, finesse; address, application, efficiency; facility, dexterity, deftness; sophistication, know-how, savoir-faire.

scientific, *adj.* **1.** physical, natural, technological, technical, sciential, *Rare.* philosophical.

2. scholarly, academic, learned, erudite, punditic, scientistic.

3. systematic, systematical, orderly, ordered, regular, regulated, controlled; methodical, thorough, painstaking, meticulous; exact, precise, mathematical, mathematic; experimental, empirical, observable, measurable, provable, verifiable, quantitative.

scintilla, *n.* spark, gleam, glimmer; trace, touch, hint, trifle, tinge, suggestion, suspicion, soupcon, tincture, *Archaic.* spice, shadow; modicum, iota, bit, mite, speck, smidgen, *Inf.* smitch; molecule, atom, jot, whit, tittle, straw, pin; dot, point, dab, fleck; particle, moit, mote; fraction, hair, shaving, paring, sliver, shive, splinter, fragment, scrap, snip; morsel, crumb, grain, granule; drop, droplet, dash.

scintillate, *v.* spark, flare, flash; gleam, glare, effulge, fulgurate, coruscate; flame, blaze, burn, conflagrate; streak, stream, beam; glitter, glimmer, glisten,

Archaic. glister, glint; shimmer, shine, flicker, sparkle, twinkle; waver, dance, flutter, fluctuate, oscillate, vacillate; radiate, glow, phosphoresce, incandesce, make radiant; dazzle, bedazzle, blind.

scintillating, *adj.* **1.** sparkling, glittering, twinkling, flickering, flashing, scintillant; shimmering, shimmery, gleaming, resplendent, dazzling, blinding; shining, glimmering, glistening, glistering, lustrous, (*of a gem or pearl*) orient; luminous, lucent, radiant, effulgent, lambent; beamy, bright, brilliant, vivid, nitid; flaming, blazing.

2. lively, stimulating, invigorating, exciting, brisk, spirited, dynamic; vivacious, buyoant, sanguine, effervescent; enthusiastic, hearty, heated.

scion, *n.* **1.** descendent, heir, successor; offspring, issue, child, progeny.

2. shoot, offshoot, twig, branch, stem, cutting, graft; sprout, sprig, spray.

scoff, *n.* **1.** jeer, gibe, sneer, fleer, flout, fling, raillery, chaff; poke, dig, cut, rub, barb; insult, *Inf.* brickbat, aspersion, obloquy, slur, invective, disparagement, defamation; taunt, quip, wisecrack, thrust, skit; boo, hiss, hoot, catcall, cry, *U.S.* raspberry; derision, scorn, mockery, ridicule, sarcasm.

2. laughingstock, gazingstock, joke, byword; butt, victim, *Inf.* the one on the receiving end, object, target, *Chiefly Brit.* Aunt Sally, *Inf.* goat, scapegoat; dupe, gull, gudgeon, cat's-paw, *U.S. Sl.* fall guy, *Sl.* patsy, *Inf.* sucker.

—*v.* **3.** *Often* **scoff at** mock, jeer, gibe, sneer at, fleer at, gird; make light of, dismiss, make fun of, laugh at, spoof, ridicule, knock, deride; taunt, tease, twit, rag, chaff, rib, kid, *Sl.* razz; hiss, boo, hoot at, heckle, rail at, catcall; scorn, flout, contemn, disdain.

scold, *v.* **1.** chide, reprimand, *Inf.* dress down, *Inf.* trim, upbraid, *U.S. Inf.* bawl out, *Sl.* chew out, tongue-lash; reprove, reproach, rebuke, rate, reprehend, castigate; chastise, rap [s.o.'s] knuckles, slap [s.o.'s] wrists; *Inf.* give [s.o.] a piece of one's mind, *Inf.* tell [s.o.] a thing or two, tell off, tell [s.o.] where to get off; take [s.o.] to task, call down, *Inf.* let [s.o.] have it, *Sl.* give [s.o.] the business, give [s.o.] hell, *Sl.* lay [s.o.] out in lavender, *Inf.* rake over the coals, *Inf.* skin alive, *Sl.* pin [s.o.'s] ears back, *Inf.* blast *or* blast off, *Sl.* let [s.o.] have it with both barrels, *Inf.* jump on *or* all over, *Inf.* jump down [s.o.'s] throat, throw [s.t.] in [s.o.'s] face; call to account, bring to book, call on the carpet, read the riot act, lay down the law, lecture, talk to, admonish; *Inf.* come down hard on, *Sl.* light into, *Inf.* rip into, *Inf.* tear into, lace into, *Inf.* sail into, *Inf.* raise the roof; condemn, censure, reprobate, criticize, *Inf.* get down on [s.o.], remonstrate, animadvert on; denounce, denunciate, objurgate, berate, vituperate; blame, charge, accuse, impute, indict; inveigh against, rail against, decry, declaim, run down, fulminate against; lash, vilify, curse, revile, vilipend.

—*n.* **2.** chider, rebuker, castigator, vituperator, reviler; nag, fishwife, *Sl.* battle-ax; hag, crone, harridan beldam; shrew, hellcat, Xanthippe, virago, termagant; fury, tigress, amazon.

scolding, *n.* reprimand, chiding, *Inf.* dressing down, *Inf.* trimming, *U.S. Inf.* bawling-out, tongue-lashing, hell; reproof, reproval, reproach, rebuke, castigation; chastisement, rap on the knuckles, slap on the wrists; talking-to, lecture, admonishment, warning; condemnation, censure, reprehension, animadversion, criticism, remonstration, remonstrance; disapprobation, disapproval, objection, disparagement, deprecation; denunciation, denouncing, tirade, philippic, execration, invective; objurgation, berating, vituperation, contumely; reprobation, imprecation, fulmination, detraction, derogation; stricture, aspersion, obloquy, traducement, defamation, vilification, vilipending; inveighing, declamation; blame, accusation, imputation, indictment.

scoop, *n.* **1.** ladle, spoon, dipper, bailer; shovel, backhoe; (*of a dredge or backhoe*) bucket.

2. hollow, crater, pit, dimple, concavity; hole, cavity, depression, dent.

3. dip, ball, spoonful, ladleful.

4. (*of news stories*) beat, exclusive.

5. *Informal.* inside information, *Sl.* poop, *Inf.* low-down, real story, inside story; facts, information, *Sl.* info, *Brit. Sl.* gen.

—*v.* **6.** ladle, spoon, dip, lade, bail, shovel.

7. hollow out, pit, dent, dig, gouge, excavate.

8. sweep up, gather, haul in, take in.

scope, *n.* **1.** extent, range, reach, compass; depth, width, length, breadth; space, area, expanse, stretch, spread, sweep, span; sphere, orbit, influence, realm.

2. purpose, aim, object, goal, end, target, heart's desire, intent, drift.

scorch, *v.* **1.** char, toast, brown, tan, blacken; blister, sunburn.

2. parch, sear, bake, roast, torrefy, scald, wither, shrivel; heat, singe, burn.

3. excoriate, scathe, denounce, condemn; scarify, flay, lacerate, lash, cut to ribbons, cut up, attack; deride, mock, ridicule; criticize, *Inf.* knock, *Sl.* rap, *Sl.* slam, rake over the coals, *Inf.* blast, *Sl.* let [s.o.] have it; castigate, censure.

4. (*of crops, towns, land*) burn down, set the match to, devastate, raze, destroy, ruin.

scorching, *adj.* **1.** burning, hot, fiery, flaming, sizzling, red-hot, searing, roasting, broiling; sweltering, torrid, hellish, tropical.

2. scathing, caustic, vitriolic, mordant, trenchant, incisive, cutting, sharp; acrimonious, bitter, biting, harsh.

score, *n.* **1.** record of points, reckoning, tally, sum, amount, number, count, computation, calculation.

2. amount due, bill, check, *Inf.* tab; fee, charge, price; dun, demand for payment.

3. notch, nick, groove, nock, hole, gouge; cut, incision, slit, gash, scotch, slash; crenation, crenelation, crenature, crenel; indentation, indent, dent, dint; chip, flaw, defect.

4. scores multitude, host, mass, crowd, throng, crush, *Sl.* mess, horde; drove, bevy, herd, pack, flock, swarm, school, shoal; army, legion, band, team, troop, company, group, party, body.

5. reason, basis, cause, ground, grounds; inducement, inspiration, impetus, incentive; instigation, incitement, provocation.

6. *Informal.* **a.** situation, status, point of progress; story, *Inf.* latest, scoop. **b.** successful move *or* remark, good hit, coup, master stroke; great idea, bright thought; triumph, victory, conquest; knockout, win, *Sl.* killing.

7. settle a score retaliate, return like for like, give tit for tat, give a blow for a blow, give measure for measure *or* pound for pound; give [s.o.] a dose *or* taste of his own medicine, pay [s.o.] back in his own coin, pay back in kind, repay.

—*v.* **8.** make a point, earn a point *or* points; earn, make, get, *Sl.* hit, *Sl.* cop, *Sl.* bag, *Sl.* catch.

9. *Often* **score up** reckon, calculate, compute, tally, figure, give a figure to, put a figure on; add up, tally up, sum up, total up, figure up; count, enumerate, numerate, number.

10. notch, nick, nock, gouge; cut, make a cut in, chip; cut into, incise, slit, split, gash, slash; scrape, scratch, scarify; chisel, carve.

11. berate, censure, criticize, reproach, rebuke, reprove, *Inf.* jump on, *Inf.* dress down; denounce, belittle, minimize, put down, *Inf.* knock.

12. achieve, attain, realize; gain, get, obtain, procure, win, earn, wrest.

scorn, *n.* **1.** disdain, contempt, contemptuousness, scornfulness, contumely, opprobrium; insolence, arrogance, haughtiness; deprecation, disparagement, belittling.

2. derision, sneering, scoffing, jeering, mockery, mocking, taunting, flouting, gibing, twit, hissing, booing, catcall; ridicule, laughter.

—*v.* **3.** disdain, contemn, hold in contempt, revile; misprize, spurn, spit upon, consider beneath oneself, look down one's nose at, curl one's lip at, thumb one's nose at; despise, reproach, deprecate, disparage, belittle, pooh-pooh, look down upon, *Sl.* put down.

4. disregard, slight, snub, shun, cut, *Inf.* high-hat, upstage, give a cold shoulder to, turn up one's nose at, ostracize, rebuff; ignore, sneeze at, have nothing to do with, disown, cut off, disavow, have no use for, wipe one's feet on.

5. deride, ridicule, laugh at, poke fun at, make fun of; mock, jeer at, sneer at, twit, scoff at, taunt, scout, flout, gibe at, hoot at, fleer, boo, hiss, *Sl.* give the Bronx cheer, *Sl.* give the raspberry.

scornful, *adj.* derisive, derisory, mocking, sarcastic, sardonic, ridiculing, Rabelaisian; satirical, ironic, ironical, double-edged, edged, cynical; contemptuous, contumelious, disparaging, sneering, disdainful, supercilious, haughty, arrogant; critical, captious, faultfinding, carping, caviling, censorious; rude, impolite, discourteous; overweening, presumptuous, high-handed, overbearing.

scotch, *v.* **1.** thwart, abort, foil, balk, frustrate; cripple, clip the wings of, hamstring, handicap; undermine, injure, sabotage; obstruct, impede, interfere with, intercept, inhibit, hamper, hinder, *Sl.* screw up, *Inf.* short-circuit; checkmate, outmaneuver; cut the ground from under, throw cold water on, *Sl.* slap down; cancel, nullify, render null and void, neutralize; crush, quash, nip in the bud; defeat, stamp out, destroy.

2. notch, ridge, score; nick, nock, chip, indent; cut, make a cut in, cut into, incise, slit, split; gash, slash, gouge; scrape, scratch, scarify; damage, mark, flaw, mar, hurt, impair, disfigure, mutilate.

—*n.* **3.** score, nick, groove, slit. See **score** (*def.* **3**).

scoundrel, *n.* **1.** villain, miscreant, reprobate, incorrigible; rogue, knave, scapegrace, wastrel, *Archaic.* coistrel, ne'er-do-well, good-for-nothing, good-for-naught; wretch, churl, cur, cad, dog, dastard, blackguard, *Archaic.* bezonian; *All Inf.* rat, creep, fink, ratfink, heel, stinker, *Euph.* son of a gun, *Derog.* SOB, *Derog.* bastard, *Archaic.* whoreson; *All Sl.* bum, *Sl.* louse, *Chiefly Brit.* rotter, *Chiefly Brit.* bounder, *Brit.* blighter, scab.

2. mountebank, charlatan, quack, *Archaic.* quacksalver, *Archaic.* empiric; imposter, impersonator, *Sl.* ringer; fraud, fake, *Inf.* faker, bad actor, carpetbagger, crimp, *Inf.* bunko artist; cheat, deceiver, swindler, confidence man, *Inf.* con man; snake in the grass, wolf in sheep's clothing.

—*adj.* **3.** villainous, reprobate, recreant, base, vile; roguish, knavish, rascally, scoundrelly, *Obs.* blackguard; unscrupulous, unprincipled, treacherous, perfidious, untrustworthy, dishonest, deceitful, crooked, false, false-hearted, double-dealing, two-timing; shifty, slippery, *Inf.* shady.

scour[1], *v.* **1.** scrub, scrub up, rub, abrade; polish, burnish, buff, shine, brighten; wipe, swab, mop, brush; wash, clean, clean up, cleanse, wash up, *Brit.* *Inf.* tub, lave, *Chiefly Scot.* dight.

2. purge, cleanse, clear, purify, lustrate; clean out, *Med.* absterge, free from impurity; deterge, mundify, depurate.

3. eject, expel, rout out, weed out, root out, close the door on, drum out, get rid of, clear out, exterminate, do away with.

scour[2], *v.* **1.** rummage, ransack, rake, comb, turn upside down, turn inside out; look everywhere, look high and low, look in every corner, look all over, look upstairs and downstairs, leave no stone unturned.

2. hurry, move quickly *or* fast, tear along; zip, whiz, dash, scoot; dart, bolt, shoot, fly; *Sl.* go like a bat out of hell, go like a shot, outstrip the wind, go like the wind, scorch the ground, burn up the track.

3. roam, wander, range about, traverse, cross, cover ground.

scourge, *n.* **1.** whip, horsewhip, bullwhip, cowhide, rawhide, thong, strap; flail, lash, switch, cat-o'-nine-tails, cat; flagellum, knout, quirt, *U.S.* blacksnake; bastinado, rod, stick, baton, cane, cudgel, blackjack, club, *Inf.* billy.

2. plague, pestilence, bane, affliction; adversity, evil, curse, misfortune, ill fortune, back luck, hard luck, bitter cup *or* pill; torment, torture, blow, catastrophe, misery, woe; trouble, worry, trial, tribulation; burden, load, heavy load, hardship, cross to bear; vexation, irritation, gall, pain in the neck, thorn in one's side, *Inf.* headache; aggravation, annoyance, nuisance, pest, bother, *Sl.* pill.

—*v.* **3.** whip, horsewhip, cowhide, strap, curry, *Sl.* belt; flail, lash, switch, birch, flog, flagellate; bastinado, baste, cane, cudgel, fustigate; thrash, thresh, spank, paddle, *Inf.* whale, *Inf.* whale the tar out of, *Inf.* whomp, *Inf.* lace, *Inf.* tan [s.o.'s] hide; strike, hit, smite, swat, slap, smack, thwack, *Dial.* hit up side the head; beat, batter, *Inf.* lambaste, *Inf.* thump, *Inf.* wallop, *Inf.* give it to, *Inf.* give [s.o.] the works *or* the business *or* what for, *Inf.* let [s.o.] have it.

4. chasten, castigate, discipline, correct; punish, dole out punishment, give [s.o.] what is coming to him *or* what he deserves, penalize, rap [s.o.'s] knuckles, slap [s.o.'s] wrists.

5. excoriate, objurgate, berate, rate, tongue-lash, fulminate against, lay out in lavender, *Inf.* bawl *or* chew out, *Inf.* jump down [s.o.'s] throat, *Sl.* lay into, *Sl.* strafe, *Archaic.* clapperclaw; chastise, take [s.o.] to task, call on the carpet, *Inf.* dress down, *Inf.* jump on, *Sl.* jump all over; scold, reproach, rebuke, reprove, reprimand, chide; criticize, censure, call down, run *or* put down, *Inf.* slam, *Inf.* knock.

scout[1], *n.* **1.** reconnoiterer, outrider, leader, guide, advance man, avant-courier, spy, bird dog, emissary; advance guard, vanguard, van.

2. Cub Scout, Boy Scout, Eagle Scout; Brownie, Girl Scout, Cadette, Senior Scout.

—*v.* **3.** reconnoiter, *Obs.* pickeer, inspect, observe, study, *U.S. Sl.* case, watch, spy *or* spy on; survey, explore, *Inf.* check out, investigate, examine.

4. *Informal. Usu.* **scout out** *or* **up** seek, search for, look for, look around for, hunt for, cast around for, fish for; find, come up with, hunt down, track down, chase down, search out, ferret out; scare up, rustle up.

scout[2], *v.* flout, contemn, disdain, despise, detest, loathe, misprize, spurn, reject, scorn; revile, abuse, berate, vilify, vilipend, vituperate, objurgate, denounce; disparage, deprecate, depreciate, belittle, decry, minimize; downgrade, *Inf.* knock, *Inf.* pan, *Inf.* put down, pooh-pooh; look down on, spit upon, consider beneath oneself; ridicule, laugh at, mock, make fun of, poke fun at, deride, jeer, scoff.

scowl, *v.* **1.** frown, glower, glare, lower, gloom, look black, look daggers, *Scot.* glunch, *Sl.* give a dirty *or* nasty look, *Sl.* don the hate-mug; look gloomy *or* sullen; threaten, menace.

—*n.* **2.** frown, furled *or* knitted brow; glower, grimace, glare; dirty look.

scraggy, *adj.* **1.** scrawny, thin, thin as a reed *or* rail, weedy, lean, slender, stalky; skinny, too skinny to throw a shadow, skin and bones, gaunt, rawboned, angular, bony, skeletal; meager, spare, lank, lanky, gangly, gangling, spindly, spindle-shanked, spindle-legged; pinched, starved-looking, withered, shriveled, shrunken, wasted, hollow-cheeked, emaciate, emaciated.

2. meager, scanty, scrimpy, skimpy, scant, shy; lacking, wanting, deficient; shallow, superficial, insubstantial, depthless; sketchy, incomplete, inadequate, beggarly, insufficient; very little, paltry, poor, piddling, *Inf.* measly, mere, small, puny, slight; nominal, minute, negligible, nugatory, trifling.

3. jagged, notched, notchy, serrated, serrate, serriform, saw-toothed, toothed; ragged, raw, scraggly, craggy, ridged, rugose, rugged, uneven, irregular, zigzag, zigzagged, pinked.

scramble, *v.* **1.** hurry, move quickly, hasten; rush, lose no time, make haste; race, scurry, spurt, whisk; press on, push on, bustle, scamper, scuttle; flee, hotfoot, hotfoot it, hightail, hightail it, *Inf.* skedaddle, beat a retreat; whip away, run like mad, *Sl.* get cracking, *Sl.* get one's rear in gear, *Inf.* get off the dime, *Sl.* go like a bat out of hell, *Inf.* go like a shot; hustle, step on the gas, *Sl.* step on it, *Sl.* burn up the road, *Sl.* burn rubber, cover ground, *Inf.* make it snappy, look alive.

2. contend, strive, struggle, grapple, jockey for position; participate, enter the lists, throw *or* toss one's hat in the ring; compete, vie, rival, contest, oppose, challenge, play, play against, pit oneself against, try to beat [s.o.'s] time, *Sl.* enter the rat race, keep up with the Joneses.

3. mix, mix up, blend, intermix, combine, mingle, intermingle, commingle; merge, tangle, entangle; disarrange, derange, disorder, disarray, disorganize; jumble, fuddle, *Brit. Sl.* muzz, snarl, *Sl.* ball up; confuse, make incomprehensible, code, encode; intermix, transpose, juggle, switch, dislocate; deliberately befog, obfuscate, becloud, obscure.

—*n.* **4.** struggle, competition, contest, scrimmage, match, one-on-one; bout, encounter; race, run for one's money; contention, challenge, strife, struggle, conflict, clash, fight; infighting, internecine warfare, internal struggle, power play, *Sl.* rat race.

5. upset, imbroglio, disorderly proceedings; muddle, huddle, mess, tumble, jumble, litter, clutter, disarray, disarrangement; pandemonium, bedlam, chaos, anarchy.

scrap[1], *n.* **1.** fragment, bit, part, particle; chip, chink, smithereen, splinter, sliver; snip, snippet, wisp, tatter, corner; morsel, crumb, ort; modicum, iota, whit, mite, dam, tinker's dam, trifle; remnant, fraction, section, segment; snatch, shred, sample, specimen, dose, taste; drip, drab, *Sl.* sniggie.

2. scraps leftovers, remainders, leavings, residue, balance; rejectamenta, discards, throwaways; traces, vestiges, semblances; clues, shards, archaeological bits, *Inf.* pieces of the puzzle.

—*v.* **3.** discard, *Inf.* junk, throw away, reject, eject, toss out, thrust aside, lay aside, cast aside; dismiss from use, have done with, forsake, abandon, jettison, *Sl.* eighty-six, *Sl.* deep-six, *Inf.* sink; dispense with, get rid of, drop.

scrap[2], *n.* **1.** *Informal.* contention, contest, altercation, conflict, clash; row, *Sl.* blowup, *Law.* chance-medley, dustup, *Sl.* rhubarb, fracas, fray; brouhaha, brawl, rumpus, *Inf.* ruckus, tussle; donnybrook, *Inf.* set-to; disagreement, squabble, spat, tiff, *Brit. Dial.* fratch; *Inf.* run-in, *Inf.* hassle, *Inf.* barney, scrape.

—*v.* **2.** *Informal.* fight, clash, brawl, be at each other's throats; broil, fight, scuffle, conflict, war; come to blows, grapple, scrimmage; have at it, *Inf.* lace into each other, *Inf.* sail into each other, quarrel, squabble, have an altercation; argue, disagree, dispute, spar, have words, *Inf.* pick a crow; fall out, *Inf.* engage in a shouting match, spat, tiff, quibble, wrangle; differ, contend, make something of it.

scrape, *v.* **1.** grate, rasp, file, scrape off; strip, decorticate, peel, skin, bark, husk, shuck, excoriate; grind, whet, sand, sandpaper, pumice; abrade, rub off, chafe, graze, scour, scrub; smooth, polish, burnish, buff.

2. scratch, scuff, mar, scar, *Scot.* scart, deface, disfigure, flaw; damage, impair, injure, harm, spoil, ruin; engrave, mark, print, imprint, impress, trace, draw.

3. *Usu.* **scrape up** *or* **together** glean, gather, get *or* bring together, rake *or* take in, garner; acquire, obtain, collect, assemble, muster, marshal; amass, aggregate, agglomerate, accumulate, cumulate, compile; stack, heap *or* pile up, lump together, *Inf.* stash.

4. grate, rasp, grit, gride, clank, jangle; screech, creak, screak, shrill, stridulate, sound off key, jar, clash, set one's teeth on edge; squawk, caw, croak, bray; scratch, crunch, scrunch.

5. bow, salaam, curtsy, genuflect; kowtow, kiss the hem *or* feet, grovel, bow and scrape.

6. get by, barely manage; economize, be frugal *or* thrifty, husband, conserve, *Archaic.* manage.

—*n.* **7.** grate, grating, rasp, rasping, filing, grinding, whetting, sanding, sandpapering, pumicing; stripping, decortication, decorticating, peeling, skinning, excoriation, excoriating; abrasion, abrading, chafe, chafing, graze, grazing, scour, scouring, scrub, scrubbing; polishing, smoothing, burnishing, buffing.

8. bow, salaam, obeisance, curtsy, genuflection, kowtow, groveling, bowing and scraping.

9. gritting, gride, griding, clank, clanking, jangle, jangling; screech, screeching, creak, creaking, screak, screaking, shrilling, stridulation, stridulating; sounding off key, jarring, clash, clashing; squawk, squawking, caw, cawing, croak, croaking, braying; scratch, scratching, crunch, crunching, scrunch, scrunching.

10. abrasion, rub, scuff, graze, scratch, sore.

11. predicament, imbroglio, position, situation, circumstance; dilemma, quandary, entanglement, trouble, difficulty, kettle of fish; plight, fix, pinch, strait, tough *or* tight spot, pickle, stew, mess, muddle.

12. collision, clash, argument, quarrel, embroilment, altercation, squabble, wrangle, brawl, fight, strife; dispute, conflict, contention, controversy, debate; friction, dissension, disagreement, contrariety, difference of opinion.

scratch, *v.* **1.** abrade, skin, bark, scrape, graze; scarify, gash, incise, score, slit; lacerate, cut, claw; mark, scuff.

2. rub, chafe, file; poke at, dig, tear at.

3. rasp, grate, gride, grit, stridulate, screak.

4. erase, rub out, cross out, x out, strike out, *Print.* dele, delete; expunge, excise, eradicate, eliminate, exclude, blot out, obliterate.

5. manage, get along, eke, make do, survive.

—*n.* **6.** abrasion, scrape, scuff; laceration, cut, incision, gash, puncture, wound; line, mark, striation, scar.

7. scrawl. See **scrawl** (*def.* **2**).

8. up to scratch adequate, satisfactory, competent,

able, capable, *Inf.* up to snuff.

scrawl, *v.* **1.** scribble, scrabble, scratch; doodle.

—*n.* **2.** scribble, scrabble, scratch, *Inf.* chicken-scratch, bad hand, cacography.

scrawny, *adj.* lean, thin, spare, scraggy, skinny, lank, lanky; reedy, spindly, stalky, spindle-shanked; gaunt, drawn, emaciated, cadaverous; skeletal, bony, raw-boned, skin and bones.

scream, *v.* **1.** shriek, screech, screak, squeal, shrill, stridulate, *Scot. and North Eng.* skirl; cry out, sing out, pipe up; cry, wail, squall, yowl, squawk, yelp, bay, caterwaul, ululate.

2. roar, howl, hoot and howl, laugh one's head off, laugh until tears run down one's face, *Sl.* yuk it up; roll, roll in the aisles, hold one's sides with laughter.

3. shout, call out, yell, *Inf.* holler, yell bloody murder, shout *or* yell one's head off, bellow, blare; cheer, huzza, hurrah, bravo.

—*n.* **4.** shriek, screech, screak, shrill, stridulation, *Scot. and North Eng.* skirl; cry, squall, squawk, yelp, bay, caterwaul, ululation.

5. shout, yell, calling, *Inf.* holler; roar, howl, vociferation.

6. joker, clown, comedian, *Inf.* card, *Sl.* sketch *or* hot sketch, barrel of laughs, laugh a minute; howl, *Inf.* riot, *Sl.* knee-slapper, *Sl.* thigh-slapper, sidesplitter, *Sl.* panic; joke, *Inf.* funny, *Sl.* a good one.

screen, *n.* **1.** partition, (*in a church*) parclose, divider, room divider, dividing wall, wall, separatrix; barrier, fence, hedge; grate, grating, lattice, latticework; screening, wire mesh, mesh, netting, net; gauze, scrim, cheesecloth, sheer, curtain; shade, window shade, blind, Venetian blind.

2. cover, covering, canopy, awning, shelter; protection, shield, safeguard, guard, buffer, palladium; sunshade, parasol, umbrella.

3. veil, mask, cloak, shroud, mantle, robe; camouflage, disguise, fog, cloud, film, smoke screen; facade, false front, blind, *Inf.* front.

4. sieve, filter, percolator, strainer, strain, colander; riddle, separator, winnow.

—*v.* **5.** shelter, place under cover, canopy; cover, overlay, overspread; blanket, mantle, cloak, clothe, robe, wrap up, muffle; protect, shield, guard, safeguard, keep safe; flank, bulwark, secure, fortify, reinforce; defend, forfend, *Archaic.* fend, *Sports.* block for, run interference for, *Sports.* pick *or* lay a pick for; veil, mask, shroud, hood; camouflage, hedge, disguise, *Inf.* lay down a smoke screen; shadow, cloud, fog, adumbrate, muddy, obscure, obfuscate; hide, conceal, keep secret *or* dark, cover up; bury, ensconce, secrete, cache.

6. sift, filter, strain, percolate, winnow, riddle, separate; filtrate, clean, clarify, purify, refine; sort through, look over, evaluate, interview; rank, order, grade; select out, pick, choose; separate out, weed out, eliminate, get rid of, throw out *or* away, reject.

screw, *n.* **1.** bolt, pin, fastener, screw-bolt, clamp; round-head screw, flat-head screw, oval-head screw, Phillip's-head screw, fillister-head screw, metal screw, lag screw.

2. twist, turn, twirl, gyre, whorl; curl, curlicue, spiral, helix; corkscrew, scroll, whirl, volute.

3. **screws** coercion, pressure, force, compulsion; insistence, duress, obligation, enforcement, necessitation, constraint.

—*v.* **4.** fasten, clamp, batten, rivet; tighten, force.

5. insert, work in, turn, twist, rotate, crank, wamble; snake, wind, corkscrew.

6. distort, knot, deform, gnarl; contort, warp, twist, twist and turn, twirl, turn awry; twine, entwine, twill, serpentine, worm; writhe, convolve, misshape, wrench, wring, wrest; buckle, crumple, crook; grimace, pull *or* make a face, screw up one's face.

7. coerce, compel, impel, force, drive, put the screws on *or* to; threaten, bring pressure to bear, press, hold a gun to [s.o.'s] head *or* a knife to [s.o.'s] throat, twist [s.o.'s] arm; constrain, bully, impress, dragoon, oblige, obligate, necessitate.

8. extort, exact, levy, blackmail; extract, take, *Sl.* shake down, *Sl.* badger; squeeze, wrest, wring, wrench, *Sl.* bleed.

9. *Slang.* cheat, defraud, take advantage of, victimize; con, gull, swindle, humbug, gyp, *Inf.* rip off, bilk, *Inf.* flam; *Inf.* stick, fleece, *Sl.* do in, do out of, cozen, bunco, *Sl.* clip, *Sl.* take, *Sl.* take for all one's worth.

scribble, *v.* **1.** scratch, scrawl, scrabble; doodle, jot.

—*n.* **2.** scrabble, scratch, scrawl, scribbling, illegible writing; poor handwriting, cacography, clumsy hand; hen tracks, hen scratches, chicken scratch, pothooks.

scribe[1], *n.* **1.** penman, inscriber, copyist, copier, transcriber, scrivener; letterer, calligrapher, chirographer; letter writer, pen, penner, *Inf.* pen-pusher, *Inf.* pencil-pusher, *Inf.* scribbler.

2. clerk, record clerk, recorder, notary, registrar, deputy registrar, *Brit.* articled clerk; stenographer, *Inf.* steno, stenotypist, court reporter; prothonotary, tachygrapher; amanuensis, secretary, recording secretary; logographer, annalist, chronicler, memorialist.

3. writer, author, essayist, poet, dramatist, playwright, novelist, short-story writer, *Inf.* hack, ghost writer; inditer, wordsmith, reviser, technical writer, copy writer, compiler; newswriter, newspaperman, journalist, rewriter, rewrite man; columnist, *Sl.* sob sister, reviewer, critic, editorial writer, editorialist.

scribe[2], *v.* mark, groove, scratch, score; incise, engrave, etch, enchase, carve, scrimshaw.

scrimmage, *n.* **1.** struggle, scramble, scuffle, *Inf.* scrap, tangle, fray; fracas, rumpus, *Inf.* ruckus, brawl, affray, brouhaha, melee; dispute, quarrel, contention, run-in; encounter, battle, fight, engagement, conflict; row, free-for-all, Donnybrook, dustup.

2. practice, practice session, warm-up, scramble, match, play; pre-season game, non-league *or* non-conference game; exhibition game.

scrimp, *v.* **1.** economize, conserve, save, be sparing *or* frugal; skimp, pinch pennies, tighten the purse strings, cut corners; be penurious, be parsimonious, be stingy *or* cheap, *Inf.* pinch a penny till it squeaks.

2. restrict, limit severely, dole, stint, pinch, cramp; reduce, curtail, straiten, cut down on, curb; grudge, begrudge, give reluctantly.

scrimpy, *adj.* scanty, meager, skimpy, scant, shy; lacking, wanting, deficient; shallow, superficial, insubstantial, depthless; sketchy, incomplete, inadequate, beggarly, insufficient; very little, paltry, poor, piddling, *Inf.* measly, mere; small, narrow, puny, slight, slender, brief, short; nominal, minute, negligible.

script, *n.* **1.** handwriting, penmanship, style of writing, cursive writing, longhand, *Inf.* fist, *Scot.* hand of writ, chirography; calligraphy, good hand; cacography, bad hand, scribble, scrawl, scratch, henscratch.

2. book, playbook, manuscript, MS, text; scenario, continuity, scene book, scene plot, plot book; working script, shooting script; screenplay, teleplay; part, role, lines; libretto, score, prompt book.

scriptural, *adj.* evangelical, biblical, textual, literal, authoritative, divine, inspired, theopneustic; orthodox, accepted, sound, firm, authentic, canonical, approved, standard; revealed, revelational; apocalyptic, prophetic, prophetical.

Scripture, Scriptures, *n.* **1.** Holy Writ, the Bible, the Good Book, the Word of God, the Holy Scriptures, the Book of Books, Divine Revelation; sacred writings, inspired writings.

2. The Old Testament, the Law, the Law and the Prophets, the Mosaic Law, the Prophets, Hagiographa, Pentateuch, Torah, Hexateuch, Octateuch; Septuagint, Apocrypha; Talmud, Masorah, Gemara.

3. The New Testament, the Gospels, the synoptic Gospels, the Epistles, Pauline epistles, the Acts of the Apostles; the Authorized Version, Douay Version, King James Version, the Vulgate. See also **gospel** (*def.* **1**).

scrounge, *v.* **1.** forage, hunt for, seek out, dig up, ferret out, smell *or* nose out, track down, seek out, *Inf.* scare up, *Inf.* scrape up, pull together; beg, borrow, or steal.

2. borrow, cadge, *Sl.* sponge, chisel, *Sl.* mooch, *Inf.* bum, *Yiddish.* shnorren; parasitize, poach, *Inf.* freeload.

—n. **3.** borrower, cadger, scrounger; parasite, *Inf.* freeloader, leech, *Inf.* sponger *or* sponge, *Sl.* moocher *or* mooch, *Yiddish.* shnorrer.

scrub[1], *v.* **1.** rub, absterge, scour, polish; wipe, swab, mop, brush. See **wash** (*def.* **1**).

2. *Slang.* cancel, discontinue, drop, give up; terminate, stop, end, abort, do away with.

scrub[2], *n.* **1.** brush, brushwood, thicket, copse, *Chiefly Brit.* coppice; bush, jungle, *Canadian.* bush lot.

2. mongrel, *Sl.* mutt, hybrid, half-breed.

3. whippersnapper, *Sl.* twerp, *Sl.* punk; nonentity, cipher, jackstraw, *Inf.* nobody, *Inf.* no-account, *Sl.* nebbish, *Inf.* loser, *Inf.* lightweight.

4. midget, homunculus, Tom Thumb, pygmy, *Inf.* little person, miniature, shrimp, *Inf.* squirt; dwarf, runt, *Inf.* pip-squeak, *Inf.* peewee.

—adj. **5.** midget, shrimplike, undersized, small, miniature; stunted, dwarfed, underdeveloped, immature, runtish.

6. insignificant, inconsequential, inconsequent, unimportant; trifling, petty, trivial, slight, puny; not worth mentioning, not worth speaking of; inferior, second-class, second-rate, *Sl.* two-bit.

7. brushy, thicketed; bushy, jungled.

scrumptious, *adj. Informal.* delectable, delightful, delicious, mouth-watering, *Sl.* more-ish, palatable, savory, tasty; splendid, gorgeous, magnificent, wonderful, *Inf.* terrific, fine; great, *Inf.* nifty, perfect, *Sl.* neat, *Sl.* swell; first-rate, top-drawer, *Sl.* top-shelf.

scrunch, *v.* crush, squash, squish, press, mash, smash, beat down; crumple, rumple, wrinkle, wad up, mat down, mess up; crunch, chew, grind, grate.

scruple, *n.* **1.** qualm, pang, misgiving, distrust, mistrust, suspicion, apprehension; scrupulousness, punctiliousness, meticulousness; conscientiousness, conscience, twinge of conscience, New England conscience, guilt, guilt feeling, point of honor; compunction, uneasiness, hesitation, hesitancy, doubt, dubiety, dubiousness, caution, carefulness, concern; restraint, restriction, circumscription, constraint.

—v. **2.** hesitate, pause, falter, waver, boggle, stick at, beat about the bush; hang back, draw back, recoil, shrink from *or* at; think twice about, ponder, weigh, consider the pros and cons; demur, take exception, object, raise objections, have qualms, stickle, stick at; doubt, distrust, mistrust, look askance at, look down on, be loath, misgive, have misgivings.

scrupulous, *adj.* **1.** principled, right-minded, ethical, moral, conscionable; upright, righteous, just, honorable, upstanding, high-minded; good, sincere, all wool and a yard wide, true, earnest, conscientious; cautious, careful, prudent, politic, discreet, judicious, circumspect.

2. punctilious, formal, correct, decorous, proper, conventional; strict, rigid, stiff, starched; exact, precise, accurate, close; meticulous, particular, finical, finicky, picky, fussy, hard to please; critical, exacting, demanding, painstaking, fastidious; minute, detailed, fine, nice, thorough, searching; scientific, mathematical, severe, rigorous.

scrutinize, *v.* examine, study, peruse, pore, pore over; investigate, search, search into, probe, probe into, *Archaic.* indagate; inspect, survey, observe, look over, eye, *Inf.* eyeball, keep an eye on, *Sl.* give the eye, *Sl.* give the once-over; take a long, hard look; perscrutate, *Obs., Rare.* perscrute, *Obs.* perlustrate, examine thoroughly *or* point by point, go over step by step, make a close study of.

scrutiny, *n.* **1.** examination, study, perusal, perscrutation, *Obs.* perlustration; investigation, probe, inquiry, checkup, *Archaic.* indagation; research, canvass, analysis; survey, overview.

2. surveillance, observation, observance; close study *or* attention.

3. close *or* careful look, *Sl.* the eye, *Sl.* the glad eye, *Sl.* the once-over.

scuffle, *v.* **1.** fight, struggle, tussle, battle, *Sl.* mix it up, *Sl.* go at it; brawl, riot.

2. fuss, flutter, bustle, hurry-scurry, rush about *or* around, tear around, buzz *or* whiz about, dart to and fro, scramble, run around like a chicken with its head cut off.

3. shuffle, shamble, scuff, drag one's feet.

—n. **4.** fight, struggle, tussle, battle, *Inf.* mix-up; brawl, riot, free-for-all, donnybrook, brouhaha, fray, affray, melee, *Inf.* knock-down-drag-out; rumpus, *Inf.* ruckus, streetfight, *Inf.* rumble; snarl, imbroglio; shoving match.

sculptor, *n.* chiseler, carver, stonecarver; sculptress; woodcarver, whittler; framer, forger, shaper, fashioner, designer, artist; worker in marble, worker in stone, worker in bronze, worker in clay.

sculpture, *n.* **1.** statuary, sculpturing, plastic art; stone cutting; wood carving, xylography; scrimshaw.

2. figure, figurine, statue, statuette, bust, *Obs.* monument; marble, bronze; carving; figurehead.

—v. **3.** sculp, sculpt, chisel, cut, carve, tool, block out, rough-hew; shape, fashion, form, model, figure, cast.

scum, *n.* **1.** film, covering, sheet, layer; spume, foam, froth.

2. dregs, lees, settlings, deposit; offscourings, remains, leftovers; remainder, residue, residuum; scoria, dross, recrement, slag; refuse, waste, garbage, discarded matter.

3. rabble, riffraff, canaille, doggery, trash, ragtag and bobtail, flotsam and jetsam, dregs of society, *Inf.* the great unwashed.

scurrility, *n.* **1.** abusiveness, blackguardism, profaneness, scurrilousness; vulgarity, vulgarness, obsceneness, lewdness, salaciousness; grossness, rankness, vileness, foulness, filthiness, nastiness, *Sl.* raunchiness; indecency, immorality, shamelessness, immodesty, impudicity, indelicacy.

2. vituperation, revilement, assailment, belaboring; invective, railing, upbraiding, objurgation, contumely, berating, scolding, tongue-lashing; diatribe, tirade, philippic; derision, scorn, scoff, jeer, gibe, sneer, mockery, ridicule.

3. vulgarism, obscenity, salacity; filth, dirt, smut; ribaldry, billingsgate, profanity, double entendre, *Ar-*

chaic. bawdry; curse word, swearword, oath, dirty word, four-letter word, *U.S. Inf.* cuss.

scurrilous, *adj.* **1.** vituperative, contumelious, objurgatory, objurgative; abusive, outrageous, affronting, insulting, *Archaic.* affrontive; thersitical, blackguardly, profane, foul-mouthed, Fescennine, *Obs.* blackguard, *Archaic.* scurrile; vulgar, obscene, lewd, salacious, pornographic; gross, rank, vile, foul, filthy, dirty, smutty, nasty, scatologic, scatological, *Sl.* raunchy; indecent, broad, shameless, immodest, indelicate.

2. ribald, risqué, off-color, *Inf.* blue; buffoonish, roguish, knavish, waggish; derisive, scornful, mocking, ridiculing, irreverent.

scurry, *v.* **1.** hurry, hasten, make haste, race, speed, hustle, post, rush, scramble, move swiftly *or* quickly, step lively, double-time, *Inf.* hump it *or* hump, *Sl.* step on it, *Sl.* hop to it, *Sl.* get cracking, *Sl.* get the lead out, *Sl.* get a move on, *Sl.* stir one's stumps; run, dash, dart, bolt, tear; sprint, fly, flit, whiz, whisk; zoom, zip, career, rip, scour, scud, scorch, *Chiefly Brit.* hare, *Inf.* clip, *Inf.* barrel; scoot, scamper, trip.

2. fuss, bustle, scuffle. See also **scuffle** (*def.* **2**).

scutcheon, *n.* escutcheon. See **escutcheon** (*def.* **1**).

scuttle¹, *v.* **1.** hurry, scurry. See **scurry** (*defs.* **1, 2**).

—*n.* **2.** quick *or* running pace, run, dead run, gallop, full gallop.

3. dash, sprint, race, clip, career, speed, scud, swoop; burst, burst of speed, spurt; rush, plunge, headlong rush *or* plunge; scoot, scamper, scurry.

scuttle², *v.* **1.** sink, swamp, send to the bottom, send to Davy Jones's locker.

2. abandon, ditch, forsake, desert, quit, leave, give up on; withdraw, back out, pull out, *Inf.* stand down.

3. wreck, ruin, destroy, scotch, *Sl.* dish; do for, undo, do in, *Inf.* fix, *Sl.* put the kibosh on.

scuttlebutt, *n.* *Informal.* rumor, grapevine, See **rumor** (*def.* **1**).

sea, *n.* **1.** ocean, ocean blue, brine, *Inf.* briny, *Inf.* briny deep, *Chiefly Literary.* the deep, deep blue sea, Neptune's kingdom, hydrospace, *Inf.* the drink, *Sl.* the big drink; open ocean *or* sea, *Literary.* main, *Literary.* bounding main, high sea; Neptune, Poseidon, *Naut.* Davy Jones's locker.

2. wave, swell, heave, billow, surge, roller, breaker, *Physics.* undulation.

3. abundance, superabundance, plethora, profusion, flood, spate, *Inf.* lot, *Inf.* raft; ton, mountain, pile, heap, stack, load, slew, mint, million, trillion, *Inf.* zillion; host, army, legion; *Inf.* lots, *Inf.* tons, *Inf.* heaps, *Inf.* oodles, *Inf.* gobs, *Sl.* scads.

4. at sea perplexed, bewildered, baffled, confused, mystified, at a loss, *Inf.* beat; uncertain, unsure, undecided; adrift, astray, lost, disoriented, off the track, out of one's bearings.

seacoast, *n.* seashore, shore, seaside, seaboard, strand, shore, coast, littoral, water's edge; shoreline, coastline, strand line; beach, sands, sand, foreshore, inning, *Fr. plage, Chiefly Brit.* shingle.

seal¹, *n.* **1.** emblem, representation, symbol, badge, insignia, regalia, token, sign, mark; label, monogram, cartouche, signet, stamp, imprint; coat of arms, escutcheon, crest; seal ring, ring, medallion, die.

2. sealant, sealing wax, adhesive, tape, stamp; closure, fastening, fastener, lock, bolt, bar; clasp, catch, snap, hook and eye.

3. assurance, pledge, promise, vow, oath, word of honor; guaranty, guarantee, warrant, warranty, contract, bond, security, surety, confirmation.

—*v.* **4.** affix a seal to, set one's seal to, authorize, sanction, approve, endorse, sign, stamp, *Inf.* O.K.; certify, guarantee, warrant; assure, pledge, promise, vow, give one's word *or* one's word of honor; bind, obligate, engage; ensure, insure, make sure *or* certain, confirm, corroborate, make firm, stabilize, settle, decide; secure, clinch, clench, *Sl.* cinch, complete, consummate.

5. close, fasten shut, secure, bind, lock, bolt, bar; clasp, snap, zip; stop, cork, plug, bung; seal up, board up, fasten *or* batten down.

seal², *n.* fur seal, harbor seal, sea dog, sea lion, sea elephant.

seam, *n.* **1.** suture, commissure, joint, juncture, junction.

2. wrinkle, crow's-foot, line, furrow, ridge; scar, mark, *Med.* cicatrix.

—*v.* **3.** furrow, wrinkle, line, ridge; scar, mark.

seaman, *n.* sailor, mariner, seafarer, bluejacket, marine, jack-tar. See **sailor** (*defs.* **1-3**).

seamstress, *n.* semptress, dressmaker, couturière, tailor, sewer, stitcher; needlewoman, needleworker, needlepointer, embroiderer, crewelworker, lace maker, tatter; knitter, crocheter.

seamy, *adj.* **1.** disagreeable, unpleasant, unpleasing, distasteful, unpalatable, unsavory; disgusting, nauseating, nauseous, sickening, *Sl.* gross, *Sl.* yukky; obnoxious, offensive, objectionable, noisome, nasty, repugnant, repulsive, repelling, repellent, revolting.

2. sordid, low, low-down, dirty, mean, ignoble, base; dishonorable, disreputable, discreditable, disgraceful, shabby, shameful, scandalous, opprobrious; corrupt, depraved, perverted, debased, vitiated, degenerate, miscreant, villainous; vile, bad, foul, rotten, scurvy, contemptible; detestable, despicable, execrable, odious, abominable, abhorrent.

séance, *n.* **1.** divination, mediumistic communication; contact with the spirits, contact with the afterworld, contact with the spirits of the departed.

2. session, sitting, meet, meeting; convocation, congregation, assemblage, congress, get-together, gathering; conclave, audience, consultation, palaver, caucus, *Inf.* powwow, huddle, strategy meeting.

sear, *v.* **1.** burn, singe, toast, brown, broil; overcook, burn to a crisp, scorch, char, cauterize, oxidize.

2. brand, stamp, mark, put one's mark on.

3. harden, steel, toughen, brutalize, make callous, caseharden, inure; dull, blunt, obtund, hebetate; desensitize, stupefy, make insensible.

4. wither, parch, dry, dry up, dry out; dehydrate, exsiccate, desiccate; wilt, shrivel, shrink.

search, *v.* **1.** go through, look through, investigate, hunt through, rummage *or* plow through, scrounge around; explore, examine, frisk; scrutinize, peruse, inspect; sift, sift through, winnow, comb, go through with a finetooth comb; fish for, cast about for; inspect, *Inf.* give the once-over, peer into, probe into, scour; seek, look for, look up, scout out, dig up *or* out; track down, follow the trail, seek clues, leave no stone unturned.

2. search me *Slang.* I don't know, it's hard to tell, that's a mystery, who knows, don't ask me, how should I know, beats me.

—*n.* **3.** examination, perusal, inspection; scrutiny, scrutinization; analysis, research, sifting, close look, *Inf.* once-over, observation, exploration, reconnaissance, reconnoitering, patrol, scouting; hunt, quest, pursuit, chase; tracking, tracking down, looking for, investigation; inquest, inquisition, inquiry, probe, query, questioning.

searching, *adj.* **1.** thorough, thoroughgoing, total, exhaustive, in-depth, A to Z, absolute, complete.

2. penetrating, penetrative, piercing, incisive; observant, aware, regardful; intent, wide-awake, alert, keen, sharp, *Inf.* heads-up; conscious, cognizant, not missing a trick *or* thing; sensitive, knowing, discerning, sentient, comprehending, *Sl.* tuned-in.

3. questioning, inquiring, analytic; inquisitive, curious, eager for knowledge, thirsty for knowledge; research-oriented, scholarly.

seasick, *adj.* nauseous, nauseated, sick to *or* at one's stomach, vomitive, vomitous, *Sl.* barfy; queazy, qualmish, squeamish, *Inf.* green *or* blue around the gills; dizzy, light-headed, vertiginous, faint, unsteady, *Inf.* woozy, *Pathol.* giddy; sick, ill, unwell, under the weather, out of sorts.

seaside, *n.* seacoast, coast, seashore, shore, seaboard. See **seacoast**.

season, *n.* **1.** period, time, spell, space, span, interval, duration; term, tenure, semester, quarter; month, lunation.

—*v.* **2.** spice, salt, pepper; prepare, pickle, marinate, marinade, preserve, corn, brine; cure, kipper, dry, smoke; tincture, tinge, touch up; spruce up, enliven, enhance, improve, heighten, add to, give relish to.

3. mature, maturate, ripen, mellow, improve; condition, prepare, rear, form, prime, nurture, cultivate.

4. habituate, accustom, make used to, make familiar with, familiarize, make routine; harden, toughen, inure, temper, anneal; adapt, acclimate, acclimatize, naturalize, domesticate; break in, train, drill, discipline.

seasonable, *adj.* **1.** springlike, summery, summerly, summerlike, autumny, wintry, winterish.

2. timely, well-timed, felicitous, opportune, right, proper, correct; suitable, appropriate, apt, apropos, apposite, fitting, congruous; befitting, meet, seemly, becoming; characteristic, suit, suited, well-suited, fit; propitious, fortunate, auspicious, providential, convenient, lucky, happy, welcome; expedient, advantageous, favorable, beneficial, profitable, *Archaic.* available; useful, serviceable, handy, good.

seasoned, *adj.* **1.** salty, salted, saline, peppery, peppered; spicy, spiced, tangy, hot, racy, heady, *Inf.* zippy; pungent, poignant, strong, sharp, nippy, piquant; savory, full-bodied, rich.

2. experienced, veteran, established, well-versed, proficient, skilled; adapted, acclimated, acclimatized, naturalized, at home in *or* with, familiar with, conversant with, acquainted with.

3. accustomed, in the habit of, given to, wont to, prone to, in the practice of; habituated, used to, addicted; chronic, inveterate, confirmed, hard-core; hardened, casehardened, hard-boiled, toughened, inured, tempered, annealed.

seasoning, *n.* spice, herb, herbs and spices, flavoring, flavor, extract, vanilla, almond, lemon; salt, pepper, cayenne, chili pepper, horseradish, garlic; cinnamon, nutmeg, ginger, cloves, mace, allspice, peppermint, mint; sage, rosemary, thyme, marjoram, dill, saffron; condiment, dressing, relish, tartar sauce, chutney, ketchup, hot sauce, *Trademark.* Tabasco.

seat, *n.* **1.** chair, couch, sofa, bench, settle, stool, hassock; bleacher, grandstand seat, pew, box, loge, stall; cushion, pillow, squab, *Oriental.* musnud; saddle. See also **bench, chair, sofa, stool**.

2. throne, cathedra, seat of authority, seat of state; office, authority, status, power, position, *Brit.* berth, right, role, situation, station, commission, mission.

3. rump, buttocks, posterior, fundament, hindquarters, bottom, derrière, *Inf.* fanny, *Inf.* rear end, *Brit. Inf.* bum, *Inf.* backside, *Inf.* behind, *Inf.* butt, *Sl.* ass, *Brit. Sl.* arse, *Sl.* tail. See **buttocks**.

4. site, location, whereabouts, locale, region; habitat, habitation, residence, lodging place, domicile; roost, nest, perch, spit, quarters, headquarters; source, origin, root, cause, origination, genesis; fountainhead, cradle, matrix.

5. foundation, base, pedestal, stand, post, footing, bed, foot, substructure.

—*v.* **6.** situate, place, put, deposit, usher, escort, lead, conduct, guide, direct.

7. accommodate, hold, contain, have room for, have capacity for.

8. install, invest, instate, induct, initiate, establish; chair; anoint, enthrone, crown, *Rare.* coronate; ordain, *Obs.* ordinate; swear in, inaugurate.

9. (*of oneself*) sit down, take a seat, perch on, roost on, plop down *or* into [s.t.], *Inf.* take a load off one's feet.

secede, *v.* **1.** sever *or* separate oneself, withdraw, break away from, break with, abandon, forsake; pull out of, drop out of, wash one's hands of, have nothing further to do with, turn one's back on, have no truck with; defect, apostatize, bolt, (*of oneself*) expatriate, repudiate, reject, disavow, forswear, renounce, disclaim.

2. rebel, revolt, mutiny, riot, revolutionize; defy, kick over the traces.

secession, *n.* **1.** withdrawal, separation, breakaway; schism, severance, defection; dissidence, apostasy, bolting, tergiversation; repudiation, rejection, disavowal, renunciation, renouncement, disclamation; abandonment, forsaking, resignation, abdication, relinquishment.

2. rebellion, insurrection, insurgence, insurgency, mutiny, revolution, sedition.

secessionist, *n.* **1.** seceder, separatist, schismatic; denominationalist, factionalist, sectarian; dissenter, nonconformist, protester, protestant.

2. deserter, defector, apostate, turncoat, bolter, *U.S. Hist.* mugwump, convert, repudiator; traitor, betrayer, renegade, recreant, tergiversator, *Sl.* fink.

3. rebel, insurgent, insurrectionist, revolutionary, mutineer, anarchist.

4. *U.S. Hist.* Confederate, *U.S.* States' righter; (*in Communist ideology*) deviationist.

—*adj.* **5.** dissident, nonconformist, independent; breakaway, renegade, turncoat; factious, dissentious, sectarian, factional, partisan; rebellious, mutinous, insurgent, insurrectionary, revolutionary.

seclude, *v.* **1.** isolate, shut off, shut out, keep out, blackball; sequester, sequestrate, quarantine, zone, ghettoize; keep apart, separate, segregate, exclude; circumscribe, encircle, insulate, enisle, cordon off, rope off; maroon, exile, evict, cast out, send away, send into exile, deport, kick out, bar, ban; relegate, banish, excommunicate, ostracize.

2. retire, hide, hide away, hibernate; go into retreat, go into retirement, shut oneself up, drop out; hide out, go into hiding, hole up, *Inf.* lie low, *Sl.* go on the mattress; remove, put away, shelve, set aside, set apart, keep apart; confine, imprison, incarcerate, lock up.

secluded, *adj.* **1.** sheltered, shut in, hidden, shut away; concealed, covered, buried, tucked away, behind the purdah, behind the veil; closed, enclosed, screened, curtained, walled in; private, secret, covert.

2. withdrawn, retired, alone; solitary, hermetic, eremetic, anchoritic, monastic.

3. isolated, insular, quarantined, sequestered, sequestrated, cloistered; confined, ghettoized, zoned in, behind the pale; incarcerated, imprisoned, locked up, in jail; detached, separate, apart, aside; in ambush, *Sl.* on the mattress, behind closed doors.

4. remote, out-of-the-way, off the beaten track,

backwoods, backwater; deserted, forsaken, God-forsaken, abandoned, ghost; unvisited, unfrequented, unexplored; lonely, enisled, marooned, lost, adrift.

seclusion, *n.* **1.** hiding, retreat, hibernation, concealment, cover, secrecy, incognito; retirement, withdrawal.

2. isolation, sequestration, segregation, separation, apartheid; insulation, quarantine, sanitary cordon, *Fr. cordon sanitaire*; detachment, apartness, aloofness; solitude, loneliness, solitariness, aloneness; captivity, confinement, incarceration, detention, house arrest; wraps, purdah, veil, curtain.

3. sanctuary, asylum, retreat, refuge, haven; hideaway, hideout, hiding place, covert, cubbyhole; lair, den, *Sl.* hang-out; aerie, hermitage, cloister.

second[1], *adj.* **1.** secondary, next after the first; next, following, subsequent, consequent, resultant; alternate, other, every other, the next but one.

2. duplicate, copy, replicate, twin; surrogate, fill-in, substitute, double.

—n. **3.** subordinate, subaltern, substitute, stopgap, *Sl.* sub, fill-in; double, understudy, alternate, stand-in; twin, surrogate, copy, alter ego; *Baseball.* pinch hitter, *Baseball.* relief pitcher, *Sports.* second stringer; proxy, agent, representative, succedaneum, delegate, minister; underling, henchman, creature, *Sl.* goon; second fiddle, *Sl.* second banana, second hand.

4. backer, supporter, booster, patron, *Sl.* angel; champion, advocate, promoter, endorser, sympathizer, apologist; assistant, attendant, seconder, helper, aide, abettor; lieutenant, adjutant, aide-de-camp; man Friday, gal Friday, right-hand man, fides Achates, right hand.

—v. **5.** assist, help, aid, abet; support, back, promote, encourage; countenance, give moral support, favor, smile upon; sustain, stand by *or* beside, stick by, defend, side with; further, advance, forward; boost, patronize, sponsor; endorse, advocate, espouse, subscribe to; back up, *Baseball.* pinch hit, go to bat for; stand in, fill in, substitute, *Sl.* sub; stand up for, take up the cudgels for, lend one's support to; fight for, join in, unite with, *Inf.* throw in with, join hands with, enlist under the banner of, come to the aid of.

—adv. **6.** in the second place, secondly, secondarily; next, right after this, coming right up, number two.

second[2], *n.* moment, *Inf.* sec, instant, stroke of time, tick, split second, half a second, *Brit. Inf.* half a mo; twinkling, twink, wink, wink of an eye, bat of an eye, trice, breath, crack; jiffy, jiff, flash, shake, two shakes of a lamb's tail.

secondary, *adj.* **1.** second, next. See **second** (*defs.* **1, 2**).

2. derived, derivative, not primary, indirect; inferential, mediate, implicative.

3. lesser, less, lower, smaller; inferior, minor, junior; auxiliary, ancillary, subsidiary, subordinate, subaltern; accessory, adventitious, adscititious, collateral; inessential, nonessential, unimportant.

4. backup, alternative, alternate, substitute, utility, spare, extra; temporary, provisional, reserve, *Inf.* back-burner.

secondary school, *n.* high school, senior high school, *Inf.* senior high, *Brit.* grammar school, (*in France*) lycee; preparatory school, *Inf.* prep school, *U.S.* private school, *Brit.* public school; academy, boarding school, day school, seminary, institute, finishing school; classical school, Latin school, (*in Germany*) gymnasium; junior high school, *Inf.* junior high, middle school.

second-hand, *adj.* **1.** borrowed, learned, taught, read; acquired, *Sl.* picked-up.

2. used, owned, pre-owned, worn; hand-me-down, not new, old; antique, antiquated, superannuated.

second-rate, *adj.* **1.** mediocre, fair, middling, passable, fair to middling; so-so, *Fr. comme ci, comme ça*; medium, humble, modest, common, commonplace, ordinary, average, everyday.

2. inferior, minor, poor, *Inf.* tacky, shabby, cheap, tinny; second-class, second-best, low-grade, low-quality, low-class; not striking, undistinguished, colorless, neutral, inglorious, inoffensive.

3. unimportant, of no account, *Sl.* two-bit, of no consequence, of no concern, of no interest; of little importance, of no significance, *Inf.* no great shakes, of no importance, low-priority, not worth mentioning, not worth going into, not worth explaining.

secrecy, *n.* concealment, hiding, coverture, burial; privacy, retirement, seclusion, sequestration, solitude, isolation; confidentiality, secretness; stealthiness, stealth, furtiveness, surreptitiousness, clandestineness, covertness; slyness, sneakiness, underhandedness, subterfuge, evasion; reticence, hugger-mugger, quietness, taciturnity, silence, muteness, mystery, secretiveness.

secret, *adj.* **1.** hidden, under wraps, concealed, ensconced, perdu, buried, covered; shrouded, cloaked, veiled, masked, screened, in the dark; incognito, disguised, camouflaged; undercover, *Inf.* closet, underground, clandestine, covert, under one's hat, furtive, backdoor, surreptitious; sly, stealthy, sneaky, sneaking, underhand, underhanded.

2. private, confidential, strictly confidential, *Archaic.* privy, hugger-mugger, *Inf.* hush-hush, unrevealable; unrevealed, undisclosed, unpublished; intimate, bosom, most personal.

3. secretive, close-mouthed, tight-lipped; reticent, quiet, taciturn, silent, mute, uncommunicative.

4. secluded, seclusive, sheltered, withdrawn, retired, sequestered, backwater, isolated, shut off, apart; removed, remote, out-of-the-way, off the beaten track *or* path; deserted, lonesome, lonely, foresaken, desolate.

5. esoteric, obscure, recondite, abstruse; mysterious, arcane, cryptic, cryptographic, occult, mystic; riddling, enigmatic, puzzling.

—n. **6.** confidential matter, private affair, *Latin. arcanum arcanorum*, closed book; skeleton in the closet.

7. mystery, puzzle, riddle, enigma; cabal, intrigue, plot.

8. method, plan, way; formula, recipe.

secretary, *n.* **1.** chronicler, annalist, minutes keeper; scribe, scrivener, penman, *Sl.* quill driver, copyist, transcriber; stenographer, shorthand writer, stenotypist, amanuensis; clerk, notary, file clerk, office worker, typist; bookkeeper, registrar; assistant, aide, helper, right-hand man.

2. desk, writing desk, writing table, escritoire, *Fr. Furniture.* secretaire.

secrete[1], *v.* discharge, emit, excrete, exude, transude, perspire, salivate; drain, seep, ooze, leak, filter, trickle, drip, dribble; send forth, emanate, extrude, *Pathol.* extravasate, send out, give off, expel.

secrete[2], *v.* hide, conceal, cache, cover, ensconce; closet, stow away, store away, file and forget, lock up, seal up, bury, entomb; shroud, enshroud, cloak, veil, mask, curtain, screen, make invisible; dissemble, disguise, camouflage; sequester, seclude, harbor, withdraw.

secretion, *n.* discharge, emission, emanation, excretion, exudation, exudate, transudation, perspiration, salivation, *Pathol.* ptyalism; oozing, leakage, drainage, seepage; trickle, drip, dribble, drop; extrusion,

Pathol. extravasation.

secretive[1], *adj.* reticent, reserved, close, taciturn, quiet, silent, close-mouthed, tight-lipped, uncommunicative, mum, mute, speechless; self-contained, standoffish, unconversable, unconversational, unsociable; clandestine, covert, hole-and-corner, furtive, backdoor, surreptitious; sly, cunning, feline, stealthy, sneaky, sneaking, underhanded, evasive; private, confidential, *Archaic.* privy, cryptic, secret.

secretive[2], *adj.* discharging, emitting, excretive, exudative, transudative, perspiring, salivating, secretory; oozing, leaking, draining, seeping, filtering; trickling, dripping, dribbling.

secretly, *adv.* clandestinely, covertly, furtively, surreptitiously, slyly, on the sly, on the Q.T., behind one's back, stealthily, sneakily, underhandedly; mysteriously, cryptically, enigmatically; privately, confidentially, intimately.

sect, *n.* **1.** religious denomination, religious group, order, religious order; school of thought, cult, ism, affiliation.

2. cabal, faction, schism, side; set, clique, knot, club, coterie.

3. party, group, classification, division, persuasion, interest, class, caste.

sectarian, *adj.* **1.** cultish, cultist, denominational, partisan; narrow, confined, limited; narrow-minded, insular, provincial, bigoted, prejudicial, prejudiced, partial; dogmatic, orthodox, hyperorthodox; absolute, doctrinaire, uncatholic; categorical, creed-bound, hide-bound; fanatic, zealot, eccentric, *Inf.* weird, *Inf.* weirdo.

—*n.* **2.** partisan, true believer, zealot, bigot; extremist, dogmatist, dogmatizer, positivist; fanatic, religious fanatic, political extremist, political fanatic, *Sl.* bug, *Sl.* nut.

section, *n.* **1.** segment, division, portion, part, parcel, fragment, fraction; integral part, component, essential part, factor, element, part and parcel; particular, item, particle, slice, wedge, finger; subdivision, department, compartment, branch; group, subgroup, detail, detachment; clause, subclause, excerpt, extract; domain, province, estate, range, terrain, bailiwick; orb, sphere, compass, circuit, precinct.

—*v.* **2.** cut, split, cleave, rend, sunder; divide, halve, cut in halves; apportion, portion out, assign, allocate, allot, *Inf.* divvy *or* divvy up; distribute, dispense, dole, deal *or* mete *or* parcel out.

3. classify, categorize, catalog, label, segregate, group, grade, rate, sort, assort, dispose.

secular, *adj.* **1.** worldly, nonspiritual, profane, temporal, non-religious, secularistic, mundane; material, carnal; lay, laical, nonclerical, nonecclesiastic, non-church, state, civil.

2. periodic, periodical, recurrent; centenary, once-in-a-lifetime, occuring every hundred years.

—*n.* **3.** layman, laywoman, member of the laity, nonecclesiastic; laypreacher, layreader; churchmember, parishioner, member of the congregation, communicant.

secure, *adj.* **1.** safe, protected, sheltered, defended, fortified; unexposed, immune, unthreatened, unmolested, unimperiled, unhazarded; unperilous, free from danger, not dangerous, vaccinated, inoculated, free; invulnerable, unattackable, unassailable, unexpugnable, impregnable, impenetrable; out of danger, out of harm's way, in the clear, clear, on the safe side, out of the woods; in port, in harbor, at anchor, at home, high and dry, above water; in safety, in security, under shelter; sitting pretty, in the catbird seat, looking good, sitting high, *Sl.* in the bag, home free.

2. firm, stable, fast, immovable, tight, close; steady, sure, sound, proof; sturdy, strong, solid; dependable, reliable, trustworthy, trusty; rooted, planted, fixed, settled; anchored, moored, immobilized; fastened, shut, closed, bound, tied, lashed, sealed, braced.

3. established, fixed, guaranteed, confirmed, clinched; decided, resolved, settled, determined; assured, sure, certain, convinced; confident, positive, definite; conclusive, definitive, proved, proven, demonstrated; well-grounded, well-founded; categorical, unquestioned, absolute, unmistakable, irrefragable, *Inf.* sure-fire; indubitable, undeniable, undoubtable, unquestionable; uncontestable, incontrovertible, irrefutable, unimpeachable.

—*v.* **4.** procure, obtain, get, acquire; gain, earn, win, reap, harvest; purchase, buy; come by, come into, *Inf.* land, *Inf.* nail down; get hold of, *Sl.* grab, get possession of, come into possession of.

5. make sound, make safe, keep sound, uphold, sustain; fortify, strengthen, reinforce, support; garrison, man, arm.

6. attach, fix, affix, tie, stick; fasten, lock, shut, close, make fast; anchor, immobilize, moor, *Naut.* belay; bind, hitch, knot, bend, lash; nail, bolt, screw, tack, staple; brace, hook, tighten, seal; clamp, clasp, rivet, stitch, sew, suture, reeve; thread, lace, brail, trice up; couple, buckle, hasp, button; truss, cinch, gird, string, rope, strap; latch, chain, clinch, tether; bandage, swath, swaddle; weld, fuse, solder; glue, paste, cement; tie down, tie up, pinion, shackle, fetter, tie one's hands, shackle, handcuff, manacle, hobble, cripple.

7. ensure, assure, guarantee, underwrite; make certain, make sure, establish, confirm, authenticate, verify, validate, substantiate; corroborate, endorse, sign, cosign, countersign; seal, stamp, attest; pledge, pawn, hypothecate, *Brit.* pop.

8. protect, guard, safeguard; defend, forfend, shield, barricade, ward, blockade; ensconce, harbor, shelter; preserve, conserve, conservate; take care of, watch over, keep watch over, take charge of; look after, look out for, mind, attend, chaperon, babysit, sit, keep an eye on; cover, house, screen, cloak; escort, flank, support.

security, *n.* **1.** safety, secureness, surety, safeness; invulnerability, impregnability, immunity; unattackability, unassailability, inexpugnability; dependability, reliability, trustiness, trustworthiness; firmness, steadiness, stability, fastness; tightness, closeness, immovability.

2. confidence, assurance, reassurance, conviction; certainty, certitude, sureness, freedom from doubt; trust, faith, faithfulness, reliance, credence, hope; conclusiveness, definitiveness, positiveness, absoluteness, definiteness; irrefutability, incontestability, unimpeachability, incontrovertibility, indubitability, undeniability, irrefragability.

3. protection, defense, strength; bulwark, fortification, rampart, tower of strength, stronghold; bastion, shelter, guard, safeguard, shield, screen, cover; palladium, asylum, refuge, sanctuary, retreat.

4. preservation, self-preservation, safekeeping; protectorship, protectorate, custodianship; auspices, aegis, eye, father's eye, patronage; ward, charge, custody, keep.

5. assurance, guarantee, warrant, warranty; surety, bail, *Law.* replevin, recognizance; collateral, mortgage, *Marine Law.* bottomry, *Law.* escrow; stake, pledge, hostage, pawn; troth, vow, contract, word, word of honor, verbal agreement.

sedan, *n.* automobile, closed automobile, car; passenger car, limousine, *Sl.* limo, touring car.

sedate, *adj.* **1.** calm, quiet, serene, collected, *Inf.* together, self-possessed, unruffled, unperturbed; cool, self-controlled, passionless, impassive, detached, even-tempered, imperturbable, unexcitable, unflappable.

2. staid, proper, decorous, dignified, refined, genteel; stiff, formal, strict, straitlaced, *Inf.* uptight, straight-arrow, fussy; solemn, dreary, dull, *Inf.* deadly; old-fashioned, fusty, extremely conventional, *Inf.* of the old school.

sedative, *adj.* **1.** calming, soothing, lenitive, palliative, assuasive, allaying, alleviative, balsamic, pleasing; anodyne, *Med.* analgesic, anesthetic, pain-killing, deadening, numbing; sleep-inducing, soporific, opiate, narcotic, Lethean, hypnotic.

—n. **2.** opiate, drug, soother, palliative, anodyne, nepenthe; balm, solace, comfort; depressant, tranquilizer, soporific, sleeping pill; analgesic, pain-killer, aspirin; meperidine, *Pharm. Trademark.* Demerol; hypnotic, narcotic, barbiturate, *Sl.* barbs, *Inf.* down *or* downer.

sedentary, *adj.* **1.** immobile, stationary, fixed, unmoving; seated, sitting, *Inf.* sit-down; idle, dormant, static, stagnant, vegetative; unchanging, routine, *Inf.* stay-put, *Inf.* stay-at-home.

2. quiet, calm, tranquil, serene; relaxed, peaceful, reposeful; unruffled, undisturbed.

sediment, *n.* lees, dregs, grounds, deposit, settlings, draff, dunder, *Chem.* sublimate, crystals, *Chem.* precipitate; residue, residuum, remainder, remains, dross, scoria, scum; silt, alluvium, precipitation, deposition, sinter.

sedition, *n.* **1.** incitement, incitement to riot, incitation, instigation, excitation, fomentation, agitation, firing, stirring, stirring-up, whipping-up, rabble-rousing.

2. rebelliousness, mutinousness, defiance, defiance of authority, civil disobedience, passive resistance, insurrectionism, insurgency.

3. insurrection, mutiny, insurgence, rebellion, uprising, civil disorder; sit-in, protest, protest march, demonstration; commotion, disorder, disturbance, excitement, unruliness, restiveness, restlessness, fractiousness.

seditious, *adj.* **1.** dissentious, factious, seditionary; defiant, rebel, insurrectionary, renegade, mutineering, revolutionary; rebellious, mutinous, insurgent, insurrectionist; inflammatory, rabble-rousing.

2. unruly, restive, refractory, insubordinate, disobedient; riotous, tumultuous, turbulent, out of control; lawless, extreme, extremist; treasonable, traitorous, turncoat, subversive; breakaway, secessionist, protestant, separatist, recreant.

seduce, *v.* **1.** lead astray, tempt, lure, inveigle, bewitch, enrapture, enthrall, snare, ensnare, trap, entrap, hook, rope in; blandish, cajole, induce, persuade, *Inf.* sweet-talk; lead down the primrose path, *Sl.* give the come-on, *Sl.* charm the pants off of, *Sl.* put the make on, *Sl.* score with.

2. attract, allure, entice, beguile, captivate, charm; titillate, excite, draw on, magnetize.

3. deflower, ravish, violate, debauch; defile, corrupt, pervert.

seducer, *n.* **1.** flirt, charmer, tempter; playboy, fast man, fancy man, *Inf.* rip, *Sl.* swinger; womanizer, lady killer, bedhopper, chaser, woman chaser, *Inf.* wolf; lover, Don Juan, Lothario, Cassanova, Romeo; philanderer, ladies' man, heartbreaker, skirt chaser, *Inf.* man on the make, *Inf.* make-out artist, gay dog, gay blade, gay deceiver, *Inf.* lover-boy; debaucher, cad, betrayer, defiler, violator, ravisher, satyr, goat, old goat, *Sl.* dirty old man, *Sl.* letch.

2. seductress, siren, Lorelei, temptress, enchantress, beauty; cocotte, Jezebel, loose woman, woman of easy virtue; nymphomaniac, *Sl.* nympho, nymphet; adventuress, demimonde, *Fr. femme fatale, Inf.* man-trap, vampire, *Inf.* vamp; streetwalker, *Inf.* hustler, *Sl.* hooker.

seduction, *n.* **1.** tempting, tantalizing, enticing; coaxing, cajoling, blandishment, wheedling.

2. enticement, allurement, allure, temptation, fascination; invitation, beguilement, inveiglement, tantalization, seducement; lure, bait, snare, trap, forbidden fruit, *Sl.* come-on; honeyed words, *Sl.* soft soap.

seductive, *adj.* tempting, alluring, tantalizing, inviting, appealing, appetizing, mouth-watering, *Sl.* yummy; enchanting, entrancing, bewitching, enravishing, provocative, exciting, *Inf.* sexy, *Inf.* foxy; attractive, engaging, prepossessing, taking, winsome, winning.

sedulous, *adj.* **1.** assiduous, constant, unremitting, continuous, continual, uninterrupted, ongoing, *Inf.* without letup; untiring, tireless, indefatigable, inexhaustible, unfailing, unflagging, undrooping, unfaltering; patient, plodding, determined, resolved, resolute, unswerving, undeviating; persistent, dogged, tenacious, pertinacious, unrelenting, relentless, die-hard, never say die.

2. diligent, industrious, studious, hardworking, working like a dog; zealous, devoted, ardent, fervent, intense; scrupulous, careful, attentive, particular, painstaking, conscientious; busy, occupied, involved, engrossed; busy as a bee, busy as a beaver, bustling, energetic, active, on the go.

see[1], *v.* **1.** perceive, look at, behold, discern; notice, observe, regard, hold in view, have in sight; descry, make out, espy, sight, spot; take in, survey, scan, look upon; scrutinize, read, inspect, examine; distinguish, remark, note, take note *or* notice of; identify, recognize, tell; lay eyes on, keep one's eyes peeled, *Inf.* take a gander, cast an eye upon, *Sl.* get a load of, get an eyeful; ogle, stare, gaze, gape; peek, peep, spy, eye.

2. watch, view, *Sl.* spectate, observe, witness; attend, visit, go to, be at, be present at, look on, *Fr. assister.*

3. understand, know, comprehend, *Scot.* ken; penetrate, fathom, plumb; realize, be cognizant of, be conscious of, be aware of, be acquainted with; apprehend, discern, *Sl.* get the hang of; grasp, *Inf.* get, catch the idea of, get the meaning of, know what one means, *Sl.* get the drift, *Inf.* savvy.

4. visualize, envision, envisage, call up, conjure up, summon up, remember; imagine, conceive, image, picture, draw a picture of, fancy, dream; actualize, objectify, externalize, substantialize.

5. ascertain, learn, find out, determine; discover, root up, ferret out, dig up, uncover, unearth, uproot.

6. meet, speak with, have words with, have a talk with, confer with, consult, meet with; encounter, confront, face, come face to face, sit down with, have a tête-à-tête; come into contact with, come into the presence of, light on *or* upon; receive, welcome, greet; be introduced to, be presented to, become acquainted with, make another's acquaintance.

7. court, pay court, *Archaic.* sue, address, woo; date, go out with, go steady with, step out with, walk out with.

8. undergo, experience, go through, encounter; bear, submit to, stand, weather, suffer, brook, brave; endure, be subjected to, sustain; have experience of, know, taste, test.

9. escort, accompany, usher, lead, take, take [s.o.'s] arm, lead the way, guide; pilot, convoy, steer, drive, walk, bring; attend, watch, wait upon, look after, watch over; flank, cover, screen.

10. consider, think, deliberate, reflect upon, speculate; contemplate, ruminate, muse, meditate; cogitate, ponder, brood over, run over, mull over, turn over, chew over; direct the mind to, occupy oneself with, have in mind, give thought to, wonder about.

11. see about a. investigate, inquire about *or* into, ask about, probe, look into, make inquiries of. **b.** take care of, see to, attend to, look to, advert to; mind, pay attention, give attention to, pay mind to, give a thought to, give heed to; devote oneself to, trouble one's head about, give oneself up to.

12. see through a. last, remain, stay to the end, stay to the very *or* bitter end, see out, ride out; persevere, persist, never say die, stick out, keep at, *Inf.* hang in; make, survive, manage, take. **b.** detect, see the inside of, catch on to, see what is really there; penetrate, see [s.o.'s] true colors, have [s.o.'s] number, be wise to, *Sl.* be hip to, *Sl.* be hep to, be on to, know what one is about.

—interj. **13.** look, lo, behold, lo and behold, *Inf.* looky, *Latin.* *ecce*; attention, look here, *Russian.* *vnimanya*.

14. I told you so, so there, what did I tell you; am I right, see what I mean, put that in your pipe and smoke it.

see[2], *n.* **1.** *Eccles.* (*of a bishop*) diocese, jurisdiction, district, province, territory, episcopate; cathedral, seat, office, authority, miter, chair, cathedra; benefice, *Brit.* incumbency; bishopric, episcopacy, prelacy, prelateship, archbishopric, cardinalship.

2. papacy, pontificate, Holy See, See of Rome, the Vatican, the Papal See, the Apostolic See, the See of Peter.

seed, *n.* **1.** *Bot.* ovule, *Bot.* embryo, *Embryol.* germ, *Bot.* ovum; tuber, bulb, *Bot.* corm.

2. sperm, spermatic fluid, semen, spermatozoa, milt; egg, gamete, germ cell; zygote, fertilized egg, spawn, roe.

3. germ, source, root, origin, cause, provocation; basis, grounds, reason, motive, motivation, motivating factor.

4. progeny, descendants, offspring, offshoots, issue, posterity, scions; successors, heirs, heirs apparent; lineage, succession, progeniture, younger *or* rising generation; family, children, *Inf.* kids, sons, daughters, brood; young, spawn, litter, fry; (*all of animals*) kids, calves, lambs, whelps, foals, cubs, pups, puppies, kittens, kitties, chicks, chickens; (*all of plants*) shoots, offsets, *Bot.* runners, *Bot.* stolons, stems, sprouts, sprigs, plantlets, slips, cuttings.

—v. **5.** (*all of seeds*) scatter, sow, distribute; plant, put in, set in, place in, inset, bury.

seedy, *adj.* **1.** seed-filled, full of seeds.

2. poorly kept, run-down, broken-down, shabby, scruffy; mean, squalid, mangy, wretched, sorry, abject, miserable.

3. shabbily dressed, down-at-heel, unkempt, uncombed, disheveled, messy, untidy, slipshod, sloppy, slovenly; dowdy, frumpy, drab, unattractive.

4. run-down, under the weather, worn-out, drained, tired, wearied, exhausted; ailing, bad, poor, poorly, ill, sick.

5. disreputable, degraded, shoddy, sleazy, *Inf.* no-good, *Sl.* crummy, cheap, *Sl.* lousy.

seek, *v.* **1.** search, look for, pursue, quest, hunt for, go for, follow the trail of; look around for, cast around for, poke around for, probe for, fish for; nose out, ferret out, track down, follow up on; ransack, rummage, check out, leave no stone unturned, scour; follow the trace of, scout out, sniff out; dig for, delve for.

2. investigate, look into, make inquiry, explore; research, look up, inspect, scrutinize; inquire, question, poke into.

3. seek to try to, essay to, attempt to; endeavor, venture upon, undertake, set about, go about, have a go at.

4. desire, covet, want, want with all one's heart, want in the worst way, be dying for; crave, yearn for, long for, hanker for.

5. solicit, ask for, petition for; beg for, plead for; beseech, entreat, implore; angle for, bid for.

seem, *v.* appear, appear like, look like, look as if, look to be, have the look of; sound, sound like, strike one as, have every appearance of, have every indication of, have the earmarks of; evidence, exhibit, show, manifest; be obvious, be patent, be plain, be self-evident, be clear.

seeming, *adj.* **1.** apparent, appearing, ostensible, presumable, *Archaic.* semblable; outward, external, surface, superficial; pretended, feigned, assumed, put-on; likely, probable; possible, conceivable, plausible, specious; supposed, presumed, reputed, inferred; professed, claimed, purported, avowed, alleged, so-called, nominal, in name only.

—n. **2.** appearance, semblance, face value, *Inf.* front, guise, show, false show, pretense, presentment, image; face, outward form, exterior, color.

seemingly, *adv.* apparently, ostensibly, on the face of it; outwardly, superficially, externally, in semblance, in show; presumably, likely, probably, possibly, conceivably, plausibly, speciously; avowedly, professedly, pretendedly, allegedly.

seemly, *adj.* **1.** decorous, decent, proper, becoming; tasteful, in good taste, dignified, refined, polished, elegant, genteel; politic, prudent, discreet, tactful, judicious, diplomatic; conventional, acceptable; unoffensive.

2. suitable, appropriate, apt, apposite, apropos; fit, fitting, befitting, *Brit. Dial.* gradely, meet, *Fr. comme il faut*; expedient, advantageous, advisable; just, right, commensurate, proportionate, equitable, equivalent, correspondent, in character, in keeping; relevant, *Latin. ad rem*, germane, to the point, pertinent; to the purpose, applicable, practicable, feasible; opportune, seasonable, timely, felicitous; suited, adapted, compatible, reasonable; favorable, commodious, convenient.

3. attractive, handsome, well-made, well-proportioned; good-looking, comely, well-favored, goodly, fair, bonny, pretty, beautiful; striking, pleasing, agreeable, charming, enchanting, alluring, engaging, ravishing.

seep, *v.* ooze, trickle, dribble, drizzle, drip; transude, flow *or* pass through, filter, filtrate, strain, percolate, leach; exude, bleed, sweat, weep, drain out, pass out, escape, flow out, issue, emanate.

seepage, *n.* transudation, percolation, filtration; exudation, effluence, outflowing, effusion, ooze, seep; leakage, leak, *Pathol.* defluxion; secretion, transudate, exudate, discharge, sweat, perspiration, blood, sap, juice.

seer, *n.* **1.** observer, onlooker, looker-on, witness, eyewitness, spy; watcher, viewer, spectator, sightseer; gaper, goggler, ogler, *Inf.* rubberneck, *Inf.* sidewalk superintendent, *Inf.* drugstore cowboy; inspector, scrutinizer, examiner.

2. forecaster, predictor, prognosticator, presager, foreteller, foreseer; conjecturer, surmiser, guesser, theorizer, hypothesizer.

3. sage, wise man, Solomon, venerable, mentor, guru, *Class Myth.* Nestor; high priest, rabbi, *Hinduism.* rishi; philosopher, philosophe, theorist, thinker, learned man, pundit.

4. prophet, prophetess, soothsayer, vaticinator, augur, oracle, Cassandra; clairvoyant, diviner, dowser, astromancer, geomancer, (*in ancient Rome*) haruspex, telepathist, mind reader; psychic, parapsychologist, spiritualist, medium, agent, agency; palmist, palm reader, chiromancer, fortune teller, crystal-gazer; stargazer, astrologer, horoscoper, Chaldean; wizard, magician, thaumaturge, magus, theurgist, necromancer, sorcerer, conjurer, Merlin; witch, sibyl, warlock, devil.

seethe, *v.* **1.** steep, marinate, sodden, macerate; soak, saturate, drench, souse, imbue; immerse, submerge, douse, plunge, dip, sink, dunk, duck, *Rare.* immerge, swash, slosh; inundate, drown, flood.

2. stew, braise, brew; boil, simmer, parboil, steam.

3. foam, froth, spume, bubble over, roll, reach the boiling point; surge, swell, rise.

4. smolder, do a slow burn, burn, get hot under the collar; get all worked up, get all excited, *Inf.* take on; get all steamed up, get angry *or* mad, be in a state, boil over, *Inf.* work up a lather; foam at the mouth, rage, rant and rave, make a fuss, *Inf.* carry on, *Sl.* raise Cain, *Sl.* blow one's top.

segment, *n.* **1.** division, portion, section, part, parcel, fragment, fraction; component, integral part, essential part, factor, element, part and parcel; particular, item, particle, slice, wedge, finger; subdivision, department, compartment, branch; group, subgroup, detail, detachment; clause, subclause, excerpt, extract.

—*v.* **2.** separate, split, cleave, rend, sunder, put asunder; divide, halve, cut in halves; anatomize, dismantle, take apart, break up; subdivide, sectionalize, fragment.

segregate, *v.* **1.** separate, set apart, isolate, cut off, insulate, *Med.* quarantine; seclude, keep in solitude, sequester, put in solitary confinement, lock up, pen up; exclude, leave out, ostracize, banish, exile, expatriate, excommunicate, *Inf.* kick out.

2. go apart, go off, withdraw, retire, leave, go away, depart.

segregation, *n.* separation, setting apart, isolation, cutting off, insulation, *Med.* quarantine; imprisonment, solitary confinement, *Sl.* cooler, *Sl.* icebox; seclusion, withdrawal, introversion, retirement, reclusion, self-exile; exclusion, leaving out, ostracism, sequestration, banishment, exile, expatriation, excommunication; racial segregation, discrimination, Jim Crowism, (*in the Republic of South Africa*) apartheid.

seize, *v.* **1.** grasp, take hold of, grip, grab, clasp, handle, embrace.

2. understand, comprehend, absorb, digest; catch the idea, *Inf.* get the hang of, *Sl.* savvy; know, master, fathom, penetrate, cognize; discern, perceive, recognize.

3. steal, rob, purloin, appropriate, abstract, fleece, pocket, *Inf.* snap up, *Sl.* swipe, *Sl.* stick up, *Sl.* pinch, *Inf.* rustle; adopt, annex, pirate, *Sl.* lift, *Inf.* crib, plagiarize, arrogate; plunder, sack, maraud, rifle, pillage, loot; ravish, rape, kidnap, abduct, carry off.

4. confiscate, impound, commandeer, *Law.* sequestrate, *Law.* sequester, *Law.* levy, *Law.* disseize, *Law.* distrain.

5. take into custody, capture, apprehend, bag; arrest, *Inf.* collar, *Inf.* nab, *U.S. Inf.* corral, *Inf.* pick up, *Sl.* bust, *Sl.* pinch; take prisoner, imprison, incarcerate, jail, detain.

seizure, *n.* **1.** forceful possession, grasping, grabbing, snatching; capture, apprehension, interception; appropriation, confiscation, *Law.* sequestration, usurpation; takeover, *Law.* attachment, annexation, acquisition; dispossession, *Law.* disseizin, *Law.* divestment.

2. commandeering, piracy, sky *or* air piracy, hijacking, skyjacking; abduction, rape, kidnapping, *Sl.* snatch, impressment; pillage, plundering, marauding, looting; theft, robbery, stealing.

3. fit, convulsion, *Pathol.* ictus; spasm, paroxysm, throe; apoplexy, stroke, shock; attack, onset, grip.

seldom, *adv.* **1.** infrequently, rarely, very rarely, seldom if ever, hardly, hardly ever, scarcely, scarcely ever; on rare occasions, occasionally, only now and then, once in a great while, *Inf.* once in a blue moon, *Inf.* once in a coon's age.

2. rare, infrequent, occasional, few, scarce.

select, *v.* **1.** choose, pick, hand-pick, pick and choose, *Inf.* pick out *or* on, single out, set apart *or* aside, lay *or* put aside, place to one side; prefer, show preference, favor; decide upon, settle on *or* upon, fix upon, make up one's mind, make one's choice, make a selection, opt *or* opt for; sift, sift out, weed *or* weed out, sieve out, screen, screen out, cut *or* cut out; sort, sort out *or* through; pick over *or* through, separate the wheat from the chaff, separate the sheep from the goats; distinguish, discriminate, differentiate, draw the line.

—*adj.* **2.** preferred, preferable, preferential, favored, favorite; more desirable, better, worthier, superior; choice, prime, best, finest, first-rate, first-class, *Inf.* champion, tiptop, A-1, A number 1; elect, singled out, chosen, hand-picked, elite, cream; exceptional, singular, particular, special, extra-special, unique, rare, uncommon; superb, excellent, superlative, supreme, paramount, preeminent.

3. selective, discriminating, discriminatory, particular, picky, *Inf.* choosy, fussy. See **selective**.

4. exclusive, limited, restricted, restrictive, closed, tight.

selection, *n.* **1.** choosing, picking, hand-picking, singling out, setting apart *or* aside; making up one's mind, settling on, opting for; sifting out, weeding out, screening out, sorting out *or* through, picking over *or* through; separating, separation, distinguishment, discrimination, differentiation, drawing the line.

2. choice, pick, preference, option.

3. pericope, extract, excerpt, piece, passage, quotation, quote, citation.

4. assortment, collection, series, line-up, group, bunch, batch, set, lot.

selective, *adj.* select, discriminating, discriminatory, careful, cautious; particular, picky, *Inf.* choosy, finicky, finical, fastidious, fussy, *Inf.* pernickety; hard to please, critical, hypercritical, overcritical, demanding, overpaticular.

self, *n.* **1.** person, individual, being, human being, entity; ego, the I; mind, psyche, consciousness; soul, spirit.

2. nature, character, individuality, personality, selfhood, selfness.

self-abnegation, *n.* See **self-denial** (*defs.* **1-4**).

self-abuse, *n.* **1.** self-reproach, self-reproof, self-chastisement, self-condemnation.

2. masturbation, self-gratification, self-manipulation, self-stimulation, autoeroticism, manustupration, onanism, self-defilement, *Sl.* playing with oneself.

self-acting, *adj.* automatic, automated, self-moving, self-propelling, self-propelled, self-directing, automotive.

self-assurance, *n.* self-confidence, confidence, assurance, security. See **self-confidence**.

self-assured, *adj.* self-confident, sure of oneself, assured, confident. See **self-confident**.

self-centered, *adj.* egoistic, egoistical, egotistic, egotistical, egocentric, narcissistic, narcistic; self-absorbed, wrapped up in oneself; selfish, self-serving, self-seeking, *Sl.* on the make *or* take, self-aggrandizing; self-indulgent, self-gratifying, self-interested.

self-confidence, *n.* **1.** self-assurance, assurance, confidence, security, self-reliance, self-dependence; self-possession, self-control, equanimity, composure, unflappability, coolness, calmness, collectedness.
2. overconfidence, cocksureness, arrogance, front, haughtiness, self-importance; impudence, effrontery, gall, *Inf.* cheek, insolence, brashness; impertinence, sauciness, *Inf.* sauce, *Inf.* nerve, audacity, boldness; presumption, presumptuousness, *Inf.* face, forwardness, self-assertiveness, chutzpah, assertiveness, aggressiveness, bumptiousness, brazenness, brassiness.

self-confident, *adj.* self-assured, sure of oneself, assured, confident, secure; believing, undoubting, questionless; steady, unwavering, unhesitating, unflinching, unblinking; cocksure, overconfident.

self-conscious, *adj.* self-aware, self-concerned, diffident, shy, bashful, modest, coy, demure, retiring, shrinking, backward; timorous, fearful, timid, apprehensive, insecure, unconfident, hesitant, reluctant, constrained; reserved, reticent, restrained, uncommunicative, unsocial, unsociable; humble, unassuming, unobtrusive, self-effacing; embarrassed, sheepish, blushing, flushed, flushing, redfaced, *Inf.* red; awkward, clumsy, oafish, *Sl.* klutzy.

self-consciousness, *n.* self-awareness, diffidence, shyness, bashfulness, abashment, modesty, coyness, demureness, backwardness; timorousness, timidity, fearfulness, apprehension; insecurity, lack of self-confidence, hesitancy, reluctance, constraint; reserve, reticence, restraint, unsociability; humility, unobtrusiveness, self-effacement; embarrassment, sheepishness; awkwardness, clumsiness.

self-contained, *adj.* **1.** self-reliant. See **self-reliant**.
2. reserved, reticent, taciturn, uncommunicative, closed-mouthed, tight-lipped, mum, silent.
3. self-possessed. See **self-possessed**.

self-control, *n.* **1.** self-restraint, restraint, control, self-discipline. See **self-denial** (*def.* **2**).
2. abstemiousness, abstention, Puritanism, nonindulgence; temperance, moderation, sobriety. See **self-denial** (*def.* **3**).
3. will power, strength of character, moral fiber; endurance, fortitude, forbearance, longanimity; patience, tolerance, resignation; composure, coolness, calmness, collectedness, cool-headedness; sang-froid, presence of mind, self-possession; aplomb, poise, savoir-faire, self-confidence, self-assurance; level-headedness, equanimity, equilibrium, mental balance; constancy, unchangingness, stability, firmness, steadiness; sedateness, imperturbability, imperturbableness, even temper, *Rare.* inexcitability; tranquillity, peace, serenity, placidity, placidness.

self-denial, *n.* **1.** self-abnegation, self-sacrifice, self-immolation, selflessness, unselfishness, self-forgetfulness; self-giving, magnanimity, generosity, altruism.
2. restraint, self-restraint, control, self-control, will power, strength; self-discipline, self-command, self-government, self-mastery, self-conquest; curbing, curb, checking, check.
3. abstemiousness, habitual abstinence, abstention, Puritanism, nonindulgence; temperance, moderation, sobriety, soberness; continence, celibacy, chasteness, chastity, virginity; refrainment, refraining, forbearance, forbearing, desistance, desisting; holding off, resisting, resistance; turning aside from, keeping one's hands off, letting alone; giving up, *Inf.* swearing off, renouncing, renouncement, renunciation.
4. asceticism, self-deprivation, fasting; privation, hardship, affliction, trouble, burden, oppression; suffering, self-abasement, self-effacement, self-mortification; self-abuse, self-flagellation, scourging, whipping, martyrdom.

self-deprecating, *adj.* self-critical, overly modest, humble, unpretentious; unassertive, shrinking, retiring, backward, quiet, constrained, restrained, reserved; self-abnegating, self-abasing, self-effacing, unassuming, unpresuming; diffident, shy, hesitant, reluctant, reticent, bashful, demurring, *Archaic.* verecund; unwilling, timorous, timid, blushing, fading into the wallpaper.

self-esteem, *n.* **1.** self-respect, pride, confidence, confidence in oneself *or* one's abilities, self-assurance, faith in oneself; self-confidence, self-reliance, independence, self-sufficiency, ability to stand on one's own two feet, ability to face oneself squarely.
2. egoism, self-conceit, self-regard, self-importance, self-approbation, self-admiration, self-love, self-worship, self-adulation; conceit, vanity, vainglory, vaingloriousness, bovarism, *Inf.* ego-trip, *Inf.* big head; self-serving, self-consideration, self-interest, self-aggrandizement; self-importance, smugness.

self-evident, *adj.* axiomatic, apodictic, manifestly true, patently true; uncontestable, manifest, certain; apparent, clear, clear-cut, clear as crystal; obvious, plain, visible, distinct, patent, bald-faced, bald, as plain as the nose on one's face; open, overt, unconcealed; inescapable, undeniable, incontrovertible; tangible, definite, explicit, express, plain as day.

self-government, *n.* **1.** home rule, self-rule, political independence; autonomy, freedom, self-determination; democracy, democratic government, republic, republicanism, constitutional rule, constitutionalism.
2. self-control, control, self-restraint, restraint; self-discipline, self-command, self-mastery, self-conquest; abstemiousness, habitual abstinence, abstention, Puritanism, nonindulgence; will power, strength of character, moral fiber.

self-important, *adj.* proud, conceited, egocentric, narcissistic, self-centered, self-admiring, self-esteeming, *Sl.* stuck *or* hung up on oneself; vain, vainglorious, egotistical, puffed-up, inflated, swollen swell-headed, *Inf.* big-headed; arrogant, fastuous, overbearing, overweening, presumptuous, assuming, *Inf.* too-much; haughty, snobbish, on one's high horse, high-and-mighty, too good for the rest of us, priggish, *Inf.* high-hat, *Inf.* nose in the air, *Sl.* snooty, *Sl.* snotty, *Sl.* sniffy, *Sl.* stuck-up. See also **proud** (*defs.* **2, 3**).

self-indulgence, *n.* self-gratification, unrestraint, intemperance, incontinence, immoderation; hedonism, pleasure-seeking, pursuit of pleasure, la dolce vita; wild *or* riotous *or* free *or* fast living, *Inf.* high living, the sporting life; licentiousness, libertinism, debauchery, dissoluteness, dissipation, profligacy; sensuality, sensualism, carnality; gluttony, gormandizing, swinishness; alcoholism, dipsomania, crapulence.

selfish, *adj.* **1.** self-seeking, egotistic, self-centered, egocentric; self-interested, self-indulgent, self-concerned, self-regarding.
2. greedy, avaricious, grasping, acquisitive, *Sl.* grabby, rapacious, hoggish, piggish; covetous, hoarding, possessive; miserly, penurious, parsimonious, grudging, niggardly, churlish; stingy, mean, illiberal, ungenerous, uncharitable, close-fisted, tight-fisted, close, *Inf.* tight, penny-pinching; mercenary, sordid, venal, usurious.

self-possessed, *adj.* calm, collected, composed, cool, *Inf.* cool as a cucumber, *Inf.* together; self-controlled, steady, poised, balanced, level-headed; imperturbable, inexcitable, unflappable, even-tempered, easy-going; nonchalant, at ease, unruffled, untroubled, undisturbed, undismayed, unperturbed, unexcited, unmoved; dispassionate, peaceful, serene, tranquil, sedate.

self-reliant, *adj.* self-sufficient, self-supporting, *Inf.* standing on one's own two feet; independent, self-determined, being one's own man; self-assured, self-confident, sure of oneself; confident, secure, sure, assured.

self-renunciation, *n.* self-denial. See **self-denial** (*defs.* **1-4**).

self-respect, *n.* self-esteem, pride, confidence, belief in one's own worth *or* abilities. See **self-esteem** (*def.* **1**).

self-restraint, *n.* **1.** self-control, control, restraint, self-discipline. See **self-denial** (*def.* **2**).

2. abstemiousness, abstinence, abstention, Puritanism, nonindulgence. See **self-denial** (*def.* **3**).

3. will power, strength of character, moral fiber. See **self-control** (*def.* **3**).

self-righteous, *adj.* sanctimonious, holier-than-thou, simon-pure, *Inf.* goody-goody, *Inf.* too good to be true; pious, over-pious, falsely pious, pietistic, pharisaic; hypocritical, tartuffian, canting; mealy-mouthed, unctuous, oily.

self-sacrifice, *n.* See **self-denial** (*defs.* **1-4**).

self-satisfaction, *n.* ease, peace of mind, contentment, tranquillity, serenity; complacency, smugness, self-content, self-contentedness; egotism, egoism, self-approbation, self-approval, self-admiration, self-love; conceit, vanity, vainglory, bovarism, *Inf.* ego trip, *Inf.* big head.

self-satisfied, *adj.* content, at ease, placid, serene, tranquil; pleased, well-pleased, *Inf.* pleased as punch, glad, delighted; smug, complacent, self-contented, pleased with oneself, proud of oneself, like the cat that swallowed the canary; puffed-up, inflated, swollen, boastful, bragging, crowing, blustering; cock-a-hoop, elated, triumphant, flushed with success.

self-seeking, *n.* **1.** selfishness, self-indulgence, self-gratification, self-satisfaction, self-serving; egoism, self-consideration, self-interest, self-aggrandizement, *Inf.* looking out for number one; personalism, privatism, individualism; personal ambition, careerism, self-advancement.

—*adj.* **2.** selfish, self-serving, self-indulgent, opportunistic, timeserving, ambitious for oneself, careerist; venal, mercenary, fortune-hunting, gold-digging, *Inf.* on the make, *Inf.* on the take.

self-styled, *adj.* would-be, so-called, *Fr. soi-disant*; self-named, self-christened, self-dubbed, self-titled, self-called.

self-willed, *adj.* willful, contrary, *Archaic.* contrarious, contumacious, crossgrained, perverse, wrongheaded, balky, uncooperative; froward, refractory, recalcitrant, querulous, seditious, *Scot.* thrawn, *U.S. Inf.* notionate, *Inf.* cussed, *Archaic.* untoward; wayward, disobedient, intransigent, troublesome, vexatious, difficult; wild, unruly, unmanageable, uncontrollable, ungovernable, restive, incorrigible; obstinate, stubborn, stubborn as a mule, mulish, muleheaded, pigheaded, bullheaded, bullish, headstrong.

sell, *v.* **1.** vend, get [s.o.] to buy *or* purchase, take *or* get money for, liquidate, exchange *or* trade for money, take a profit for, make a transaction on, make a deal *or* bargain on; transfer title to, make over to, negotiate, put up for sale, make available for a price; sell off, auction off, dispose of, get rid of, unload, dump, *Brit.* sell up.

2. trade in, deal in, traffic in, be in the business of; handle, carry, offer for sale, supply, furnish; peddle, vend, hawk, hustle, push, *Inf.* truck; solicit, run for, *Sl.* fence.

3. market, retail, wholesale, go for, be had for, be bought for, be found for; be in demand, be bought, go, go like hotcakes, move.

4. (*all of an idea*) win acceptance *or* approval of, get accepted *or* approved, get [s.t.] through, get [s.t.] across, get support *or* votes for, *Inf.* deliver on; (*all of people*) convince of, persuade of, bring around *or* round, sway, induce; talk [s.o.] into, *Inf.* jawbone, win [s.o.] over, get [s.o.'s] trust *or* confidence.

5. sell out a. be bought up *or* out, be depleted, *Brit.* sell up. **b.** *Informal.* take a bribe, go with the money, do anything for money, prostitute oneself, sell one's soul; go over to *or* join the other side, betray one's cause *or* self, knife [s.o.] in the back.

6. *Informal.* swindle, defraud, cheat, fleece, bilk, pluck, flimflam, diddle, run a confidence game *or* trick on, run a number on, *U.S. Sl.* con, do [s.o.], victimize; palm [s.t.] off on, *Inf.* gyp, *Sl.* rob [s.o.] blind, *Archaic.* chouse out of; fool, dupe, gull, pigeon, cully, take in, get, deceive, delude; hoax, trick, *Sl.* hornswoggle, humbug, cozen, hoodwink, pull the wool over [s.o.'s] eyes, throw dust into [s.o.'s] eyes.

seller, *n.* merchant, retailer, shopkeeper, storekeeper, tradesman, trader, businessman, wholesaler, jobber; salesperson, salesman, saleswoman, saleslady, salesgirl, shopman, shopgirl, salesclerk, clerk, *Sl.* counterjumper; vendor, peddler, hawker, huckster, chandler, sutler, packman, colporteur, auctioneer, *Both Chiefly Brit.* monger, costermonger; traveling salesman, door-to-door salesman, *U.S.* drummer, Fuller Brush man, Avon lady; trafficker, dealer, hustler, supplier, *Sl.* pusher; solicitor, pimp, middleman, broker, runner, *Sl.* fence, *Sl.* duffer.

semblance, *n.* **1.** aspect, appearance, demeanor, mien, air, cast, look; countenance, visage, complexion, feature, face.

2. disguise, camouflage, mask, cloak, incognito; covering, concealment, masquerade; guise, pretense, cover, cover-up; show, veneer, façade, false front, *Inf.* front; deception, trickery, ruse, artifice, dissimulation.

3. image, portrait, statue, effigy, death mask; bust, simulacrum, icon, facsimile; voodoo doll, fetish doll, idol, graven image, totem.

4. apparition, ghost, shade, *Inf.* spook, *Inf.* haunt; shadow, revenant, Doppelgänger, doubleganger; spirit, presence, wraith, *Inf.* thing, fetch, phantom, phantasm, specter; vision, eidolon, sight, spectacle; illusion, chimera, creature of the imagination, phantom of the mind.

seminal, *adj.* **1.** potential, possible, probable, prospective, likely, *Latin. in posse*; undeveloped, yet to be realized, incipient, embryonic, unrealized; full of possibilities, with lots of potential.

2. creative, original, imaginative, ingenious, institutive, individualistic; divergent, unorthodox, unconventional, nonconforming; unimitative, unimitating, unborrowed; prototypal, prototypic, prototypical, exemplary; innovative, fresh, novel, new, unprecedented; singular, special, rare, uncommon, signal, extraordinary, different, unusual, out of the ordinary, unique, *Latin. sui generis*, one of a kind; influential, precedent-setting, first of its kind, landmark.

seminary, *n.* **1.** preparatory school for the priesthood, divinity school, rabbinical school.

2. academy, institute, private school, boarding school, day school, preparatory school, *Inf.* prep school, Latin school, grammar school; finishing school.

3. origin, source, well, cradle, breeding place, hotbed.

send, *v.* **1.** transmit, convey, deliver, direct; broadcast, televise, telecast, telegraph, radio, telegram; forward, pass along, mail, post, ship, remit; consign, intend for, address to.

2. delegate, depute, charge, assign, commission.

3. propel, cast, hurl, fling, let fly; project, shoot; detonate, explode, burst.

4. emit, discharge, give off, exude, ooze, leak.

5. *Slang.* please, delight, transport; excite, *Inf.* turn on; enthrall, put into ecstasy, thrill, titillate.

6. send for summon, call for; muster, call together; summons, subpoena.

7. send forth produce, yield, bear; flower, blossom, fructify; generate, engender, propagate.

8. send packing dismiss, discharge, send away; turn out, send [s.o.] about his business, turn away; banish, oust, expel, cashier; break off with, *Inf.* give [s.o.] the air, *Sl.* give [s.o.] the gate, *Sl.* give [s.o.] the brushoff.

senescent, *adj.* old, aging, getting old; elderly, aged, on *or* up in years, along *or* advanced in years, past one's prime, *Inf.* over the hill, *Derog.* long in the tooth; gray, gray-haired, gray-headed, grizzled; hoary, venerable, patriarchal, heavy with the weight of years; declining, failing, senile, (*of women*) anile, decrepit; superannuated, old as the hills, old as Methuselah.

senile, senescent; declining, failing, failing in mind, losing one's faculties *or* abilities, *Inf.* slipping, no longer in full command; waning, fading, (*of women*) anile; mentally infirm, foolish, decrepit; in one's dotage, in one's second childhood, childish, daft, *Inf.* dotty, feeble-minded, simple; confused, disoriented, forgetful.

senility, *n.* dotage, superannuation, caducity; decrepitude, (*of women*) anility, senescence, failure of mental abilities, loss of one's faculties, waning *or* fading of abilities; foolishness, second childhood, childishness.

senior, *adj.* **1.** older, elder, of greater years, more advanced in age; first-born, primogenitary.

2. higher ranking, ranking, over, above, uppermost, top; superior, chief, leading, preeminent, paramount, foremost, primary, prime, principal.

3. prior to, before; earlier, former, previous, bygone.

—*n.* **4.** elder, superior, master, first-born, primogenitor; parent, forefather, ancestor, forebear, predecessor.

5. chief, ruler, patriarch; dean, elder, statesman; upperclassman.

sensation, *n.* **1.** sense, sense impression, impression, feeling, sentiment; consciousness, awareness, sentience, sensibility, perception, cognizance, apprehension, detection, realization, experience; intuition, inkling, *Inf.* funny feeling, suspicion, *Inf.* sneaking suspicion, *Inf.* hunch; hint, intimation, foreboding, presentiment, premonition; tingle, quiver, throb, palpitation, *Scot.* tabet, *Sl.* rush.

2. excitement, animation, stimulation; commotion, ado, fuss, to-do, hubbub, uproar; agitation, disturbance, perturbation.

sensational, *adj.* **1.** exciting, excitant, excitatory, stimulating, stirring, bracing, rousing, invigorating; thrilling, electrifying, galvanizing, galvanic, spine-tingling, hair-raising, *Inf.* rip-roaring, *Inf.* rip-snorting; emotinal, moving, impelling, compelling, affecting, soul-stirring, heart-stirring, heart-moving.

2. melodramatic, lurid, vivid, *Inf.* scare, *Inf.* yellow; agitating, perturbing, incitant; exaggerated, extravagant, extreme, startling, shocking.

3. good, great, excellent, wonderful, terrific; phenomenal, extraordinary, prodigious, remarkable, wondrous, marvelous, *Inf.* boffo; amazing, astounding, astonishing, miraculous, surpassing belief; fabulous, fantastic, *Sl.* far-out; indescribable, ineffable, mind-boggling, *Sl.* mind-blowing, staggering, breathtaking, *Sl.* stunning; peerless, matchless, unmatched, nonpareil.

sensationalism, *n.* melodrama, luridness, vividness, shock; blood and thunder, blood and guts, yellow journalism; exaggeration, extremity, extravagance; emotionalism, sentimentality, mawkishness, maudlinness, morbidity.

sense, *n.* **1.** sensation, feeling, perception, awareness, *Inf.* living daylights, sensibility; impression, intuition, suspicion. See **sensation** (*def.* **1**).

2. *Usu.* **senses** sanity, mental balance, normality, clearheadedness, coherence, sobriety.

3. appreciation, estimation, recognition, regard.

4. intelligence, aptitude, intellect, mind, mentality, brain, brains, braininess, brain-power, *Inf.* gray matter, *Sl.* smarts, reason, *Gk. Philos.* nus; acumen, discernment, perspicacity, penetration, understanding, sensitivity; astuteness, shrewdness, *Sl.* savvy, keenness, sconce, long-headedness, hard-headedness, levelheadedness, common sense, *Inf.* rhyme or reason; ingenuity, cleverness, aptness; adroitness, deftness, agility, quickness; alertness, brilliance, brightness, acuity, sharpness.

5. meaning, import, spirit, gist, upshot, sum and substance, effect, essence, core, pith, content; intent, purport, tenor, tone, vain, drift; implication, connotation, signification, denotation; message, point; intention, purpose, significance; design, plan, scheme, aim.

—*v.* **6.** intuit, feel, have a feeling, *Inf.* have a funny feeling, *Inf.* feel in one's bones, *Inf.* have a hunch, *Inf.* get *or* have the impression, just know; apprehend, perceive, know, discern, see, note, understand, comprehend, *Brit. Sl.* suss; appreciate, esteem, regard, recognize.

senseless, *adj.* **1.** unconscious, insensible, insentient, comatose; numb, sensationless, feelingless, deadened, insensate; insensible, unaware, unperceiving, undiscerning, inappreciative.

2. foolish, fatuous, silly, asinine, anserine, idiotic, *Inf.* moronic, imbecilic; crazy, crazed, *Sl.* kooky, *Scot.* doled, mad, wild, insane, demented daft, *Inf.* daffy, crackbrained, *Inf.* nutty; peculiar, strange, off, *Sl.* balmy, *Sl.* dippy, *Sl.* batty, *Sl.* cuckoo, *Sl.* screwy, *Sl.* wacky; simple-minded, birdbrained, featherbrained, featherheaded, rattleheaded, rattlebrained, light-minded, half-witted, witless; muddled, muddleheaded, addlepated, addlebrained; stupid, unintelligent, mindless, fatuitous, brainless; harebrained, giddy, mercurial, erratic, unstable, harum-scarum; thoughtless, heedless, careless, reckless, foolhardy, unwary.

3. ridiculous, pointless, nonsensical, *Inf.* damfool, *Inf.* damfoolish, tomfoolish, *Scot. and North Eng.* glaikit, *Sl.* cockeyed; poppycockish, *Sl.* cockamamie, amphigoric; unreasonable, irrational, illogical, meaningless, purposeless, aimless, haphazard, unconnected, groundless; inconsequential, irrelevant, beside the point, immaterial, inapplicable, inappropriate; incongruous, inconsistent.

sensibility, *n.* responsiveness, reactiveness, sentience; consciousness, aliveness, alertness, acuteness; sensitivity, sensitiveness, impressionability, impressibility, receptiveness, receptivity, susceptiveness, susceptivity, susceptibility; feeling, soul, intuition, perception, perceptivity, awareness, insight, insightfulness, appreciation.

sensible, *adj.* **1.** prudent, level-headed, judicious, sagacious, sage, politic, discreet, circumspect; thoughtful, reflective, reflecting, sapient, sober, sane, moderate, cool, cool-headed; reasonable, rational, ratiocinative, logical, analytical, sound, full of common sense; practical, down-to-earth, realistic; far-sighted, shrewd, intelligent, percipient, discerning, discriminating; wary, heedful, careful, well-advised.

2. *Usu.* **sensible of** cognizant, familiar with, acquainted with, *Sl.* wise to, knowledgeable of, understanding; aware, conscious, sentient, alive to, *Archaic.* ware; mindful, regardful, observant, awake, wide-awake.

3. palpable, tangible, tactual, touchable, ponderable, appreciable, non-abstract; incarnate, embodied, corporeal, physical, material, bodily, somatic; concrete, real, solid, substantial, substantive; visible, seeable, observable, beholdable, manifest; discernible, perceptible, detectable, apprehensible, ascertainable, knowable, cognizable, intelligible.

4. plausible, credible, likely, within reason, well-founded, well-grounded; legitimate, equitable, fair, right; suitable, proper, fit, meet, advisable, seasonable, timely.

sensitive, *adj.* **1.** impressionable, susceptible, receptive, susceptive; responsive, reactive, alive to, sentient, sensible, conscious; feeling, intuitive, perceptive, aware, insightful; refined, cultivated, aesthetic.

2. sympathetic, compassionate, concerned, understanding; kind, kindly, kind-hearted, caring, generous; feeling, tender, tender-hearted, warm, gentle.

3. (*all usu. of instruments*) fine, delicate, responsive, subtle, discriminating.

4. oversensitive, hypersensitive, supersensitive, temperamental, thin-skinned, easily hurt, umbrageous; irritable, touchy, ticklish, excitable; huffy, quick-tempered, impatient; quarrelsome, testy, irascible, petulant.

sensitivity, *n.* **1.** impressionability, susceptibility, receptiveness, receptivity, susceptiveness, susceptivity; responsiveness, reactiveness, sentience; sensibility, consciousness, aliveness; feeling, intuition, perception, perceptivity, awareness, insight, insightfulness, soul, sensitiveness.

2. sympathy, compassion, concern, understanding; kindliness, kind-heartedness, caring, generosity; feeling, tenderness, tender-heartedness, warmness, gentleness.

3. (*all usu. of instruments*) fineness, delicacy, responsiveness, subtleness, discrimination; accuracy, precision, exactness; fidelity, faithfulness.

4. oversensitiveness, oversensitivity, hypersensitivity, supersensitivity, temperamentalness; irritability, touchiness, excitability; huffiness, quick temper, impatience; testiness, irascibility, petulance.

sensual, *adj.* **1.** carnal, voluptuous, fleshly, physical, bodily; erotic, sexual, slinky, *Inf.* sexy; lustful, concupiscent, lascivious, libidinous, lubricous, lecherous, *Archaic.* lickerish, *Sl.* horny; satyric, satyrical, satyrlike, goatish, hircine, ruttish; licentious, loose, Cyprian, wanton, abandoned; debauched, rakish, dissolute, dissipated, profligate.

2. lewd, prurient, salacious; unchaste, impure, unclean, indecent, unvirtuous, wayward; offensive, vulgar, coarse, gross, crude; obscene, lurid, blue, pornographic, *Inf.* porno, *Inf.* porn, smutty; dirty, foul, filthy, vile; ribald, scurrilous, Fescennine.

3. earthly, worldly, temporal, mundane, terrestrial; secular, profane, unspiritual; irreligious, irreverent.

sensualist, *n.* voluptuary, *Fr. bon vivant*, epicure, epicurean, hedonist, sybarite, cormorant, *Archaic.* carpet knight; gourmet, gourmand, gastronome, gastronomist; glutton, hog, belly-god, wine bibber; libertine, roué, debauchee, lecher, Paphian, whoremonger, pander; satyr, goat, animalist; seducer, fornicator; Don Juan, Casanova, rake, fast man, Romeo, Lothario.

sensuality, *n.* **1.** carnality, voluptuousness, physicalness, sexuality, *Inf.* sexiness, earthiness; lustfulness, concupiscence, lasciviousness, libidinousness, lecherousness, lewdness, prurience, salaciousness, *Sl.* horniness; animality, bestiality, brutishness, coarseness, grossness.

2. unchasteness, impureness, indecency; offensiveness, vulgarity, crudeness; dirtiness, foulness, filthiness.

3. worldliness, earthliness, temporalness, secularity, profaneness, unspirituality; irreverence, irreligiousness.

sensuous, *adj.* **1.** sensory, sensorial; sensitive, receptive, responsive.

2. rich, luscious, luxurious, sumptuous; deep, intense, affective; (*of music*) Lydian, soft, sweet.

sentence, *n.* **1.** *Law.* **a.** condemnation, decree, ruling, judgment, *Sl.* rap. **b.** punishment, prison term, term, *Sl.* time, *Sl.* stint, *Sl.* stretch, *Sl.* stretch up the river, *Sl.* stretch in the can, *Sl.* vacation.

—*v.* **2.** pass judgment, pronounce sentence, pass sentence on, meet out justice to; doom, condemn, penalize, *Sl.* send to the pokey *or* the lockup, *Sl.* throw in the can, *Sl.* send up, *Sl.* send up the river; commit to prison, *Inf.* lock [s.o.] up and throw the key away.

sententious, *adj.* **1.** pompous, bombastic, fustian, grandiloquent, grandiose, lofty, orotund, stilted; turgid, swollen, inflated, overblown, puffed-up, *Inf.* windy, *Inf.* gassy; magniloquent, high-flown, high-sounding, *Inf.* high-falutin, big-sounding, lexiphanic, *Rare.* grandisonant; overdrawn, strained, affected, put-on.

2. pithy, terse, succinct, concise, compact; epigrammatic, laconic, aphoristic, apothegmatic, short and sweet; capsule, condensed, summary, synoptic, in a nutshell, compendious.

sentiment, *n.* **1.** feeling, attitude; response, reaction, *Inf.* gut reaction.

2. opinion, outlook, view, viewpoint, point of view, slant; notion, idea, thought, conception, estimation, theory; stance, stand, angle, position, posture, thinking, way of thinking; conviction, mind, persuasion.

3. sentimentality, sentimentalism. See **sentimentality**.

sentimental, *adj.* **1.** emotional, feeling, warm, tender, affectionate, loving, soft-hearted, warm-hearted, sympathetic, compassionate; impressionable, sensitive, receptive, responsive.

2. maudlin, melodramatic, mawkish, misty-eyed, dewy-eyed, gushy, *Australian.* soony, *Inf.* drippy, *Sl.* icky; soupy, romantic, with the soul of a shopgirl, *Inf.* mushy, *Inf.* slushy, *Inf.* gloppy, *Sl.* schmaltzy, cow-eyed, salt-eyed; teary, lachrymose, weepy, *Inf.* drippy, choked up, soppy; sloppy, uncontrolled; babyish, namby-pamby, insipid; over-romantic, *Inf.* corny, *Sl.* hokey; affected, *Inf.* bleeding heart; nostalgic, pining, languishing.

sentimentality, *n.* emotionalism, gushiness, mawkishness, maudlinism, maudlinness, sentimentalism; emotiveness, emotivity, play on *or* appeal to the emotions, melodrama, melodramatics, dramatics, theatrics, play-acting; corniness, hokiness, affectation; bathos, mush, *Inf.* glop, treacle, *Sl.* hearts and flowers, *Sl.* schmaltz, *Sl.* goo; *Sl.* sob stuff, *Sl.* sob story.

sentinel, *n.* guard, sentry, picket, patrol, garrison; scout, lookout, watch, watchdog; protector, defender, guardian, guarder, guardsman; custodian, watchman, night watchman.

separate, *v.* **1.** part, divide, space, interspace, space out, set at intervals, set *or* keep apart; disentangle, pull apart, disconnect, disengage, disarticulate, uncouple, unyoke, disunite; intersect, bisect.

2. come between, intervene, interfere, interlope, interpose; split, estrange, alienate, disaffect, set at odds, cause dissension, make hostile, cause to fall out, *Inf.* break up, *Inf.* split apart, *Inf.* stir up trouble, *Sl.* bust up.

3. sunder, cleave, disjoin, disjoint, rive, rend, split; partition, part asunder, dispart, divide into parts, halve, quarter, segment.

4. allot, assign, dispose, apportion, portion, compartmentalize, distribute, parcel out, *Sl.* divvy *or* divvy up; select, pick out, sift out, discriminate; abstract, extract, take out.

5. sort, analyze, break down; cull, glean, winnow, sift, sieve; grade, rank, size; classify, group, subdivide, collocate, codify, type.

6. screen, eliminate, excise, exclude, cut off *or* away; separate the sheep from the goats, separate the men from the boys, separate the wheat from the chaff; discharge, remove, eject, throw out, weed out, discard, expel, cut off *or* out *or* adrift, *Sl.* give the bounce.

7. isolate, single out, segregate, shut off, cut off, sever, sequester, quarantine, wall *or* fence off, cordon *or* seal off, rope off.

8. withdraw, disassociate, leave, depart, pull out, stand apart, *Sl.* split; dissent, dissent from, drop out, secede, *Sl.* quit; fall out, break with, come to a parting of the ways, agree to disagree; part company, split up, disband, scatter, disperse, break up, go separate ways, fan out, spread out; divorce, break up, break up housekeeping.

9. come apart, give, give way, spring open, gape, tear apart, crack, yawn, gap, spread.

10. fork, diverge, branch, branch off, split, divaricate, bifurcate, ramify, radiate, branch out, *Scot.* twine; open, open up, unclench.

—*adj.* 11. sole, unique, singular, only; single, solitary, individual, independent; disparate, divergent; diverse, different, dissimilar, unlike.

12. discrete, disjunct, separated, unrelated, divorced, detached, unjoined; distinct, unconnected, unassociated, disjointed, disjoined, unallied, disconnected, unattached, disengaged, unbound, clear, free.

13. withdrawn, detached, removed, alone, apart; segregated, quarantined, secluded, sequestered, isolated, shut off.

14. asunder, in twos, severed, cut, cloven, cleft, halved, quartered; reft, sundered, split, bisected.

separately, *adv.* singly, one by one, individually, severally, each to each, each; in order, one at a time; independently, distinctly, respectively; particularly, uniquely, exclusively.

separation, *n.* 1. division, partition, subdivision; disjunction, disjointure; dissociation, disassociation, detachment, withdrawal, break, breach, rupture; segmentation, dismemberment, divulsion; disintegration, shattering, fragmentation; disconnection, disengagement, disjointing, cleavage, severence, fracture, split, rend, fission, scission, sunderance; removal, isolation, segregation, apartheid.

2. divorce, divorcement, breakup, *Sl.* bust-up; parting, alienation, estrangement, dissolution, disunion.

3. divergence, dichotomy, bifurcation, bifidity, branching, ramification, fork; line of demarcation, point of departure, cut-off point.

4. fracture, rift, gulf, chasm; break, hiatus, space, interspace, interstice; gap, opening, hole, aperture; gash, slit, crack, slot, crevice, chink.

sepulcher, *n.* tomb, crypt, vault, catacomb, burial chamber *or* pit *or* place, *Archaic.* sepulture; mausoleum, pyramid, (*in ancient Egypt*) mastaba; tumulus, barrow, mound; grave, ossuary, ossuarium, cinerarium, repository, resting place.

sepulchral, *adj.* 1. gravelike, tomblike, tombal, sepultural, cinerary; burial, cemeterial, of *or* for the dead; funeral, funerary, mortuary, exequial, obsequial.

2. funereal, dirgeful, dirgelike, doleful, lugubrious; mournful, woeful, sorrowful, grievous; somber, grave, solemn, long-faced, unhappy, uncheerful, cheerless, sad, melancholy, *Fr. triste*; dreary, depressing, dismal, bleak, heavy, feral; gloomy, lowering, clouded, murky, dusky, dark, Cimmerian, Stygian, black.

3. hollow, hollow-sounding, empty, vacant, blank; toneless, flat, dull, dead, defunctive; cavernous, deep, deep-toned, bass, basso, thunderous, rumbling, echoing, resounding, resonant; ghostly, ghost-like, spectral, eerie, weird, uncanny, *Inf.* spooky, *Inf.* scary.

sequel, *n.* continuation, continuance, follow-up, supplement; sequent, result, end result, consequence, effect, outcome, issue, upshot; aftermath, outgrowth, offshoot, afterclap, turnout, aftereffect, fallout, wake, aftertaste, afterglow.

sequence, *n.* 1. succession, consecution, consecutiveness, successiveness, continuance, continuation, continuousness, continualness, unbrokenness.

2. order, arrangement, organization, classification, categorization.

3. round robin, series, progression, chain, string, concatenation; line, rank, file, queue; row, tier.

sequential, *adj.* successive, consecutive, succeeding, sequacious, next, proximate; following, ensuing, subsequent, consequent, sequent.

sequester, *v.* 1. withdraw, retire, hibernate, drop *or* keep out of sight, seclude oneself, hide *or* conceal oneself, go into hiding, cover one's tracks; lie hid *or* hidden, lie perdu, *Dial.* lie snug *or* close, *Inf.* lie low, *Inf.* hide out, *Sl.* hole up, *Sl.* sit tight.

2. secrete, hide away, ensconce, closet, stow away, store away, file and forget, lock up, seal up.

3. remove, separate, divorce, part, estrange; isolate, alienate, segregate, shut off, cut off *or* out, send to Coventry.

sequestered, *adj.* withdrawn, recluse, secluded, cloistered, shut up *or* in; isolated, cut off, separated, alienated, segregated, in isolation; solitary, in solitude, alone; covert, underground, under cover, in hiding, incommunicado, incognito, hidden, concealed, perdu.

sequestration, *n.* 1. removal, separation, dispatch, dislodgment, displacement; exile, banishment, expatriation, expulsion, excommunication, deportation, transportation; disbarment, ostracism, blackballing, sending to Coventry.

2. retirement, withdrawal, seclusion, isolation, retreat, rustication.

sere, *adj.* dry, *Inf.* bone-dry, arid; parched, burnt, scorched, baked; withered, shriveled, shriveled up, wizened, dried up, shrunk, shrunken; dessicated, dehydrated.

serendipity, *n.* chance, fortuity, fortuitousness, happenstance, hap, mere chance, happy chance; luck, Lady Luck, fortune, Lady *or* Dame Fortune, wheels of fortune *or* chance, heads or tails, roll *or* toss of the dice; accident, coincidence, irony, contingency.

serene, *adj.* 1. tranquil, peaceful, calm, quiet, restful, apollonian, halcyon, *Brit. Dial.* bonny; pastoral, idyllic.

2. collected, composed, self-possessed, cool, *Inf.* cool as a cucumber, *Inf.* together; self-controlled, steady, poised, balanced, level-headed; imperturbable, unflappable, unexcitable, even-tempered, easy-going; nonchalant, at ease, at peace, unruffled, undisturbed, untroubled, undismayed, unperturbed, unexcited, unmoved.

3. clear, cloudless, unclouded, unobscured; fair, bright, sunny, rosy.

serenity, *n.* tranquillity, peacefulness, peace, quiescence, quiet, quietude, quietness, calmness, stillness; peace of mind, ataraxia; imperturbability, unflappability, inexcitability, even-temperedness; composure, self-possession, self-control, self-command, aplomb, sang-froid, poise, repose, *Inf.* cool; presence of mind, level-headedness, cool-headedness, coolness, equability, equanimity, equilibrium.

serf, *n.* **1.** helot, villein, vassal, peon, (*in pre-Norman England*) ceorl, *Obs.* churl.

2. slave, bondman, bond slave, chattel, chattel slave, indentured servant, servant, thrall, *Hist. or Archaic.* theow.

series, *n.* sequence, round robin, succession, run, consecution, concatenation; chain, train, parade, line, string, row, tier, range; round, cycle; progression, procession; catena, catenation, set, suite, suit.

serious, *adj.* **1.** pensive, deep in thought, thoughtful, wrinkle-browed, reflective, meditative; engrossed, absorbed, preoccupied.

2. grave, somber, grim, unsmiling, unlaughing; sedate, staid, dour, severe, stern; solemn, sober, sober as a judge, straight-faced, poker-faced, long-faced.

3. earnest, resolute, firm, definite, decided; sincere, honest, genuine, real, *Inf.* for real; intent, intense, fervent, deep, heartfelt.

4. heavy, weighty, difficult, involved, complex, challenging.

5. important, significant, momentous, of moment, consequential, of consequence, not to be laughed at, no laughing matter; crucial, vital, fateful, life-and-death.

6. critical, acute, bad, dangerous, perilous, hazardous, menacing; scary, fearful, alarming; precarious, touchy, ticklish, touch-and-go.

sermon, *n.* **1.** homily, preaching, *Obs.* predication; lesson, interpretation, exegesis; sermonizing, pulpitry.

2. discourse, disquisition, expatiation, descant; speech, talk, address, oration, peroration, prelection; eulogy, encomium.

3. exhortation, lecture, preachment, moralizing; castigation, remonstrance, reprimand, reproof, dressing down, *Inf.* talking-to.

4. declamation, tirade, harangue, ranting, spouting, diatribe, screed, invective, philippic; bombast, rodomotade.

sermonize, *v.* **1.** preach, homilize, evangelize, predicate, pulpit, *Usu. Disparaging.* preachify, *Scot. and North. Eng.* sough; propagate, disseminate, inculcate, indoctrinate, catechize.

2. discourse, expound, expatiate, descant, prelect, lecture, moralize, criticize, admonish, reprimand, upbraid, castigate, reproach, censure.

3. exhort, advocate, urge, press; decry, denounce, declaim.

serpent, *n.* **1.** snake, viper, pit viper, ophidian, sea snake, *Archaic.* dragon, cockatrice.

2. snake in the grass, traitor, quisling, turncoat, renegade, Benedict Arnold; double-dealer, *Inf.* double-crosser, Judas, betrayer; fifth-columnist, informer, subversive, double agent; spy, company spy, *Sl.* fink, *Sl.* weasel, *Sl.* stool pigeon, *Sl.* stoolie; sneak, cheat, *Inf.* crook, swindler, rascal, knave, rogue; cutie, sharper, sharpie; liar, dissimulator, pretender, *Inf.* phony; worm, *Sl.* lowlife, *Sl.* creep, *Sl.* crumb, *Sl.* crud; villain, blackguard, scoundrel, *Sl.* rat, *Inf.* skunk, cur; *All Sl.* bastard, rotter, putz.

3. Satan, Devil, Beelzebub, fiend, archfiend.

serpentine, *adj.* **1.** slender, svelte, lithe, elongated; wriggly, writhing, squirming, slinky; coiled, convoluted, spiral, (*of a woman*) *Inf.* curvaceous, anguilliform.

2. sinuous, winding, meandering, twisting; curvy, flexuous, curved, tortuous, crooked, bending; circuitous, ambagious, anfractuous, roundabout, devious; loopy, cloverleaf; vermicular, vermiculate, mazelike, labyrinthine.

3. shrewd, wily, cunning, crafty, artful, sly, slick, shifty, tricky, insidious; sharp, astute, canny, keen, clever, smooth, *Inf.* cute; designing, scheming, intriguing, calculating, Machiavellian.

serrate, *adj.* **1.** serrulate, saw-toothed, serrated. See **serrated**.

—*v.* **2.** scallop, pink, jag, tooth, notch, nick, groove, nock.

serrated, *adj.* serrulated, serriform, *Chiefly Biol.* serrate, saw-toothed; crenate, crenelated, crenulate; toothed, *Both Bot., Zool.* dentate, denticulate; notched, nicked, jagged, jaggy, sawlike; zigzag, zigzagged, uneven, rough, in-and-out.

servant, *n.* **1.** domestic, cleaning man, cleaning woman, cleaning lady, charwoman, *Chiefly Brit.* char; housekeeper, *Fr. bonne à tout faire, Brit. Inf.* slavey; factotum, steward, valet, gentleman's gentleman, butler, houseman; maid, upstairs maid, au pair girl, (*in India*) ayah, (*in China*) amah; cook, scullion; handyman, yardman; chauffeur, driver; cupbearer, footman, footboy.

2. employee, assistant, right-hand man, aide, helper, subordinate; girl *or* gal Friday, amanuensis, secretary, stenographer, steno; hireling, hired hand *or* man, hand, help, menial, flunky, lackey; bellhop, bellboy, redcap, porter; messenger, runner, copyboy, page, *Sl.* gofer, myrmidon; waiter, waitress, ganymede; janitor, doorman, concierge.

3. public servant, officeholder, state worker, government worker, servant of the people, minion.

serve, *v.* **1.** wait on *or* upon, wait on hand and foot, attend, minister to, care for, give service, be at [s.o.'s] beck and call; wait on table, waitress, cocktail waitress, give food and drink; offer refreshments, pass out *or* come around with refreshments.

2. (*all of a term of service*) hold, fill, go through, carry out, fulfill, complete.

3. help, render assistance, be of use *or* service, lend a hand, give a leg up, do a good turn, oblige, accommodate; aid, abet, succor, assist, avail, *Archaic.* bestead.

4. be in the service of, work for, be employed at *or* by, have a job with.

5. obey, be dutiful to, pay homage to, pay tribute to, honor, respect, revere, reverence, venerate, bow down to.

6. perform the duties of, do duty as, function as, work as, do the work of.

7. suffice, suit the purpose, serve the purpose, do, *Inf.* fill the bill, fulfill all requirements; be adequate, *Inf.* be O.K., *Inf.* be all right.

8. help, benefit, contribute to, conduce to; further, promote, advance, forward, give a boost; advocate, recommend, push for, *Inf.* plug for, *Inf.* put in a good word for; support, back, stand behind; facilitate, enable, make easy for, clear the way for; foster, cultivate, nourish, nurture, encourage.

9. (*all of desire, needs, wants*) gratify, satisfy, fulfill, content.

service, *n.* **1.** assistance, help, aid, abetment, abettal; good turn, favor, a hand, a leg up, benefit, contribution; boost, promotion, advancement. furtherance, advocacy, recommendation, support, backing.

2. (*all of public services*) supplying, providing, furnishing; supplier, provider, furnisher.

3. system, organization, department, agency, commission, bureau, office.

4. waiting on table, waitressing, cocktail waitressing, serving food and drink.

5. employment, employ, work, job, duty, function, capacity, situation, position, station, place, berth.

6. armed forces, military, army, navy, marines, air force, coast guard.

7. **services** professional services *or* care, public services, utilities, commoditites.

8. ritual, rite, ceremony, sacrament, vows, solemn pledge.

—adj. 9. useful, of service, serviceable. See **serviceable.**

—v. 10. work on *or* do work on, repair, restore, fix *or* fix up; align, straighten out, set straight *or* right, adjust, tune up, fine-tune.

serviceable, *adj.* 1. service, useful, of use *or* service, utilitarian, functional, practical, pragmatic; helpful, beneficial, advantageous, propitious, favorable, valuable, profitable, constructive; instrumental, conducive, contributory, contributive; aidful, aiding, obliging, accommodative, accommodating, helping; available, at-hand, handy, convenient.

2. durable, wearing well, lasting, long-lasting, resistant, rugged, tough, strong.

servile, *adj.* 1. slavish, obsequious, *Obs.* obsequent, subservient, menial, *Obs., Rare.* vernile; submissive, docile, unassertive, compliant, acquiescent, deferential, Tomish, Uncle Tomish, tractable, mealy-mouthed; prostrate, obeisant, on one's knees; groveling, crawling, creeping, crouching, slithering; squirming, cringing, cowering; whining, whimpering, sniveling.

2. sycophantic, sycophantical, sycophantish, fawning, flattering, truckling, wheedling, toadying, toadyish, ingratiating, timeserving, *Sl.* bootlicking, *Sl.* footlicking, *Inf.* apple-polishing, *Sl.* brown-nosing, *Obs., Rare.* blandiloquous; buttery, candied, unctuous, oily, honey-mouthed, smooth-talking, sweet-talking, *Rare.* blandiloquent.

3. abject, humble, poor, meek, lowly, beggarly, beggared; base, base-spirited, mean, mean-spirited, low, vile, ignoble, inglorious, dishonorable, discreditable, disreputable.

4. unoriginal, lacking originality, unimaginative, prosaic, imitative; inflexible, rigid, stiff; (*all in a negative sense*) strict, close, exact, undeviating, direct, strightforward, faithful, literal.

5. opressed, suppressed, kept down, downtrodden, *Archaic.* downtrod; subjugated, in subjection, in bondage, in bonds, in chains, captive, in captivity, enslaved, in slavery, enthralled.

servility, *n.* 1. slavishness, servileness, obsequiousness, obsequence, subservience, *Obs.* vernility; submissiveness, docility, unassertiveness, compliance, acquiescence, deference, obeisance, abjection, abjectness, self-abasement; groveling, crawling, creeping, crouching, slithering; squirming, cringing, cowering; whining, whimpering, sniveling.

2. sycophancy, sycophantism, flattery, fawning, truckling, wheedling, toadyism, toadeating, tufthunting, lip-homage, mouth-honor, unctuousness, *Inf.* soft soap, *Sl.* bootlicking, *Sl.* footlicking, *Inf.* apple-polishing, *Sl.* brown-nosing, *Rare.* blandiloquence, *Obs., Rare.* blandation, *Obs., Rare.* blandiloquy.

servitude, *n.* 1. slavery, enslavement, thralldom, enthrallment, bondage, captivity, impressment; prison, imprisonment, confinement, durance, duress; serfdom, vassalage, villeinage, indentureship, indention; oppression, repression, subjugation, subjection, subordination, domination, yoke, control; compulsion, coercion, constraint, restraint, fetters, shackles, chains, bonds, irons.

2. hard labor, compulsory service, penal servitude.

set, *v.* 1. put, place, position, move into position; situate, locate, localize, plant, mount; deposit, reposit, lay down, plump, rest; land, bring down, bring in, set down; park, station, stick; lodge, quarter; slap, tuck, slip, insert; implant, install, embed; arrange, collocate, deploy, distribute, allocate, array; order, group, assemble.

2. apply, lay, effect, bring about, bring to pass; create, generate, originate, begin, make; bring to bear, bring into effect, execute; give occasion to, give rise to, induce, instigate; prosecute, perform, enact, discharge, dispel; employ, exploit, use, turn, adopt, convert; put, enlist, press, call, draw; exert, exercise.

3. establish, fix, pinpoint, get a fix on; pin down, nail down, narrow down; zero in on, focus on, home in on.

4. post, station, relegate; appoint, detail, delegate, charge, consign; assign, prescribe, schedule, allocate; entrust, repose, invest, commit; destine, fate.

5. value, valuate, evaluate, estimate; price, appraise, rate, rank, gauge; count, reckon, quantify, assess, calculate; compute, *Inf.* size up, set a value *or* price on, measure.

6. determine, establish, fix, specify; stipulate, designate, indicate, select, name; define, limit, delimit, demarcate; mark off, bound, set off, delineate.

7. resolve, decide, settle, conclude, seal; purpose, will, fix upon, insist upon; come to a conclusion, choose, make up one's mind; adjudge, adjudicate, rule; ascertain, confirm, set at rest, agree upon.

8. present, place before, provide, offer; cut, stand up as, pose; afford, supply, furnish, yield, allow.

9. adjust, regulate, collimate, right, true; synchronize, time, coordinate, harmonize; align, balance, line up, equalize, square; orient, gauge, focus; accommodate, adapt, fit, reconcile; arrange, alter, fix.

10. ornament, deck, bedeck, decorate, array; bedizen, bejewel, bedight, grace; embellish, adorn, furbish, brighten.

11. plant, implant, ground, install, place, emplace; pitch, base, put in; put up, invest, vest.

12. direct, level at, fix on, turn; aim, point, bend, train, draw a bead on, hold on; bear, steer, tend, incline, lean; head, verge, go, lead.

13. urge, encourage, goad, motivate; animate, actuate, enkindle, inflame, instigate, foment, incite; rouse, egg on, provoke, fire; enjoin, move, start, excite; quicken, embolden, whet, kindle; exhort, drive, press, push, shove, thrust; impel, propel, lash, whip, spur on, work up; inflict, force, constrain, coerce, dragoon, oblige, necessitate.

14. affix, apply, attach, append, tack on, stick on; seal, stamp, impress, sign, set the seal on, countersign, undersign, cosign; adjoin, annex, tag on.

15. sink, drop, fall, go down, dip, descend; disappear, pass away, die away; decline, wane, ebb, diminish.

16. fix, rigidify, tighten, lock; root, entrench, stabilize, ground; solidify, make firm, stiffen, harden; congeal, gel, jellify, gelatinate; coagulate, conglobate, clot, stick together, cohere; agglomerate, conglomerate, cake, thicken; concrete, cement, granulate, crystallize.

17. (*with* forth, out *or* off) start, begin, commence, go ahead; embark, start out, move out, sally forth, *Inf.* take off, turn to; set sail, unmoor, get underway, put out to sea; venture out, push off, depart, go, leave, exit, quit, *Inf.* hit the road, *Inf.* hit the trail.

18. set about undertake, launch, set out, set to; get going, get a move on, *Inf.* kick off, *Inf.* blast off, *Inf.* jump off; engage in, enter upon, get to, take up; put one's shoulder to the wheel, put one's hand to the plow, put the ball into another's court, put the ball in motion; set in motion, take the first step, make a start, take the plunge, start the ball rolling, put into execution; set on foot, lead off, open, pioneer; break the ice, break gound; start in, plunge in, *Inf.* dive in, *Inf.* pitch in, *Inf.* get down to it, *Inf.* get to it.

19. set apart a. set aside, reserve, earmark, pigeonhole; save, lay away, put away, squirrel away, lay up; keep by, lay by, keep in reserve; store up, bank, treasure up, cache, *Sl.* stash away; collect, accumulate, garner, amass. **b.** distinguish, characterize, mark, mark off; differentiate, set off, *Inf.* keynote, demarcate.

20. set back hinder, impede, obstruct, prevent; retard, delay, throttle, detain, stay; hamstring, cross, foil, block, check; frustrate, thwart, inhibit, counterwork.

21. set down a. record, register, write down, write; list, enroll, sign up, inscribe; enter, put down, docket; insert, mark down, jot down, commit to writing; catalogue, tabulate, codify. **b.** attribute, ascribe, assign, attach; charge, place, pin, put down to; impute, accuse, saddle, father upon, lay at the door of. **c.** humble, humiliate, mortify, put down; bring down, abase, demean, take down; embarrass, meeken, put to shame, discomfit.

22. set forth a. describe, express, give expression to, give utterance to, utter, pronounce; state, affirm, declare, voice, enunciate, articulate, vocalize, verbalize. **b.** submit, offer, broach, present, propose, propound; bring forward, advance, move, make a motion, bid, suggest; predicate, postulate, posit; allege, aver, asseverate, avouch, say. **c.** embark, start out. See **set** (*def.* **17**).

23. set in arrive, begin, come into being, come into existence; arise, rise, dawn; issue forth, burst forth, come forth, break out; crop up, spring up, come up.

24. set off a. ignite, light, touch off, inflame; detonate, explode, fire, *Sl.* blow, blow up. **b.** start out, begin. See **set** (*def.* **17**).

25. set on attack, sic on, put on, go for; aggress, assail, assault, fall on, pounce on; pitch into, strike, fly at.

26. set out a. define, describe, explain, elucidate; detail, specify, fill in the particulars; report, chronicle, relate, tell, narrate, recite, recount; express, pronounce, give an account of; show, expose, reveal, exhibit, display. **b.** start out. See **set** (*def.* **17**).

27. set up a. erect, raise, elevate, put up; construct, assemble, build, put together. **b.** prepare, ready, prearrange, prime, plan, project; devise, block out, form, design; contrive, prescribe, fix. **c.** inaugurate, establish, introduce, usher in; institute, organize, found, lay the foundation, lay the first stone; give rise to, give birth to, engender, create, beget, conceive, father.

—n. **28.** collection, assortment, arrangement, selection; array, order, collocation; disposition, ordering, ordination; group, combination, number, series; succession, progression, run, hierarchy; suite, suit, scale, gamut, service; miscellany, mixture.

29. clump, cluster, bunch, batch, lot, *Bot.* sorus, pack, packet; heap, pile, stack, mass, amassment, accumulation, assemblage; articles, furnishings, fixtures, things, appurtenances; outfit, gear, kit, rig, equipment, *Sl.* stuff, belongings.

30. company, party, society, assembly, crowd; circle, clique, ring, club, cabal, circle; clan, tribe, sect, faction, knot; body, corps, crew, force, team, band, regiment; gathering, congregation, committee, commission; association, league, guild, union, federation, establishment, cadre; squad, troupe, gang, detail, work party, detachment; fraternity, brotherhood, merry men, sorority, sisterhood, sodality; flock, herd, drove, swarm, throng, school, shoal; bevy, covey, gaggle, colony, brood, hatch, *Rare.* eyrie.

31. bearing, carriage, posture, cast, demeanor; turn, pose, poise, port; attitude, air, aspect, countenance, front.

32. bent, inclination, trend, run, tendency; direction, line, aim, way, course; tack, track, bearing, drift, orientation; lay, lie, point, reading, *Survey.* azimuth; fit, hang, fall.

33. apparatus, receiver, radio, *Brit.* wireless, crystal set, transceiver, Citizen's Band radio; television, TV, *Brit.* telly, *Inf.* boob tube, *Inf.* idiot box; console, cabinet.

34. stage set, scene, setting, place, location, mise en scène, decor; scenery, wings, flats, *Theat.* tormentor, screen, *Theat.* backdrop. See **setting** (*def.* **1**).

—adj. **35.** fixed, prescribed, predetermined, prearranged; specified, agreed upon, appointed, ordained; decided, determined, arranged; preestablished, said, aforementioned.

36. customary, regular, stock, normal, usual; conventional, habitual, wonted, accustomed, traditional, consuetudinal; everyday, household, vernacular, vulgar, common, commonplace.

37. rigid, fixed, fast, bound, cemented, welded, soldered; riveted, nailed, fastened, secured, clinched, held; attached, connected, coupled, pinned, clasped, tied; permanent, stationary, motionless, rooted, one of the fixtures; firm, immovable, stable, constant; deep-seated, ingrained, indelible, irremovable; entrenched, vested, prescriptive, inveterate.

38. resolved, determined, decided, intent, resolute; persistent, stubborn, obstinate, bullheaded, immovable, steadfast; hardened, inflexible, obdurate, impervious, hidebound.

39. prepared, ready, primed, fit, ripe; armed, equipped, loaded, cocked; on the qui vive, alert, booted and spurred, ready to go.

setback, *n.* backset, relapse, recurrence; reverse, reversal, undoing, upset, defeat, loss; disappointment, failure, *Inf.* flop, nonsuccess, no go, abortion; check, rebuff, rejection, foil, frustration, thwarting; mishap, misadventure, problem, trouble; stumbling block, block, obstruction, impediment, hindrance, balk; deadlock, checkmate, stalemate.

setting, *n.* **1.** scene, stage setting, set, stage, *Fr. mise en scène*; scenery, *Theat.* backdrop, *Theat. Chiefly Brit.* back-cloth, drop curtain, drop, scrim; flats, screens, *All Theat.* borders, tormentors, teasers.

2. environment, milieu, fabric, framework, arena, theater; surroundings, locality, region, area, sphere, realm; locale, place, location, site; period, time, era, century, decade; background, circumstances, conditions, situation; scenario, setup, layout, lay of the land.

settle, *v.* **1.** appoint, fix, set, define; decide, confirm, conclude; stabilize, make certain, ascertain, ground; organize, coordinate, systematize, methodize; resolve, agree upon, determine, choose, elect; rule, ordain, adjudge, adjudicate.

2. order, bring to order, arrange, compose, set to

rights; align, line up; classify, allocate, segregate, group, assort, screen, sieve; distribute, array, apportion, parcel out, range.

3. pay, disburse, expend, defray; close, discharge, dispose of; adjust, balance, square, liquidate; satisfy, wipe off, clear, acquit oneself of.

4. dwell, abide, reside, remain, live, inhabit, domicile; lodge, locate, encamp, squat, nest, roost; establish oneself, carve a home, set up housekeeping; anchor, put down roots, pitch tent, take *or* strike root, get a footing; set up in business, *Inf.* hang up one's shingle.

5. populate, people, inhabit, occupy, fill; establish, found, colonize, domicile.

6. quiet, become quiescent, subside, recede, abate, become stable; soothe, tranquilize, allay, compose, pacify; quell, calm, still, lull.

7. (*of liquids*) filter, precipitate, purify, clarify, clear.

8. gravitate, sink, incline, droop, sag; descend, drop, plunge, swag; solidify, make firm, harden; coalesce, concentrate, compact, condense, consolidate.

9. reconcile, resolve, harmonize; pacify, make peace, heal, mend, patch; mediate, negotiate, talk out, arbitrate, compromise, *Inf.* bury the hatchet; rectify, regulate, adjust, straighten out, simplify, clear up; disembroil, unravel, disentangle; demonstrate, show, prove, conclude, clinch.

10. alight, land, repose, perch, roost, lodge, sit down.

settlement, *n.* **1.** completion, conclusion, resolution; execution, decision, confirmation, ratification, decision; arbitration, agreement, negotiation; covenant, contract, reckoning, compromise, reciprocal concession, disposition; stabilization, coordination, organization, foundation; appointment, installation, ordination, fixation.

2. colonization, denization, denizenation, naturalization; settling, populating, peopling, founding, forging, clearing, establishing; migration.

3. colony, community, village, post, encampment; satellite, possession, protectorate, dependency, mandate.

4. satisfaction, payment, liquidation, defrayal, defrayment; quittance, recompense, release, acquittance, clearance.

5. reconciliation, conciliation, reapproachment, reunion, propitiation; appeasement, accommodation, placation, mollification.

settler, *n.* colonist, colonizer, pioneer, frontiersman; immigrant, emigré, *Amer. Hist.* redemptioner, outlander; squatter, homesteader, founder, Pilgrim.

setup, *n.* **1.** format, layout, arrangement, organization, configuration; structure, construction, framework, frame; composition, make-up, constitution, *Inf.* getup; form, look, appearance, style.

2. plan, design, scheme; plot, outline, scenario, sketch, draft; procedure, process, implementation.

sever, *v.* **1.** dissever; cut off, chop off, lop off, bob, dock, hack off, hew off, slice off, shear off, scissor; cleave, rive, cut in two *or* apart, split, divide, halve, bisect, bifurcate, *Obs.* dimidiate; separate, break apart, tear *or* rip apart, dissect, disjoint, dismember, dislimb, *Surg.* divulse; partition, subdivide, compart, part, segment, section, quarter.

2. disjoin, dispart, disbond, disunite, disassociate, dissociate, alienate, estrange, split up, divorce, put asunder; disband, break up, disintegrate, fall apart; part, go in separate ways *or* directions, disperse, scatter, spread out.

3. dissolve, break off, abscind, suspend, discontinue, terminate, stop, end, cease, put an end to; disengage oneself from, pull out of, leave, quit; fall off, dwindle, fade away, *Inf.* peter out, die out.

4. discriminate between, distinguish between, make a distinction between, see the difference between; dichotomize, categorize, classify, group.

several, *adj.* **1.** some, a few, a sprinkling of, a handful of, a fistful of, a mouthful of, a pocketful of; not a few, a number of, *Inf.* quite a few.

2. separate, distinct, discrete; single, sole, lone, solitary; different, divergent, diverging, disparate, dissimilar, assorted, various, sundry.

3. respective, own, exclusive, personal, private; individual, particular, specific, certain, chosen; unique, special, characteristic, typical, customary, peculiar.

—*n.* **4.** some, a few, a sprinkling, a handful, a fistful, a mouthful, a pocketful; more than a couple, *Inf.* quite a few, a number.

severance, *n.* **1.** sunderance, chopping *or* cutting off, slicing *or* shearing off, bobbing, docking, lopping off, detachment, *Both Bot.* abstriction, abjunction; cleavage, cleaving, splitting, fissure, scission; division, halving, bisection, bifidity, bifurcation, *Obs.* dimidiation, *Bot.* mitosis; separation, dissection, dismemberment, divulsion; partition, partitionment, segmentation, dichotomy.

2. breach, breaking up, break, split, schism, divorce, disunion, disassociation, disjuncture, *Inf.* split in the ranks; divergence, divarication, alienation, estrangement, *Inf.* parting of the ways; dissolution, abscission, breaking off, suspension, discontinuance, termination, stoppage, ending, cease; disengagement, pulling out, leaving, quitting.

severe, *adj.* **1.** extreme, stringent, strict, harsh, rough; inflexible, uncompromising, unbending, unyielding, obdurate, flinty, rigid; persistent, unremitting, inexorable, implacable, relentless; merciless, pitiless, unfeeling, unsympathetic, inhuman, cruel, brutal, savage; ruthless, cold-blooded, hard-hearted, iron-handed, iron-fisted, iron-hearted; despotic, peremptory; autocratic, tyrannical, abusive, punitive; distressing, agonizing, afflictive, torturous, tormenting, excruciating, racking; painful, insufferable, unbearable, overpowering, overwhelming; stinging, galling, sharp, bitter, caustic; piercing, biting, cutting, incisive, penetrating.

2. serious, sober, sedate, somber, grave; formal, aloof, cold, distant, stiff, tight, stilted; stern, grim, austere, hard, forbidding, strait-laced, puritanical.

3. grave, critical, acute, dire, fatal, mortal; dreadful, fearful, awful, dangerous, risky, hazardous, perilous, *Inf.* hairy; uncertain, touchy, touch-and-go, *Inf.* chancy.

4. simple, plain, modest, bare, blank, stark, Spartan, ascetic; unadorned, untrimmed, unembroidered, unembellished, unornamental, undecked; unfurbished, undecorated, unvarnished, unpainted.

5. inclement, stormy, raging, tempestuous, turbulent; freezing, frigid, frozen; hot, steaming, burning, sweltering; drastic, acute, intense, violent, fierce, furious.

6. exacting, rigorous, tough, demanding, exigent, fastidious, *Rare.* exactive; unsparing, grinding, oppressive, burdensome, grievous, onerous, heavy; difficult, painstaking, close, searching; arduous, laborious, toilsome, operose; trying, troublesome, uphill.

severity, *n.* **1.** harshness, rigor, rigorousness, stringency, asperity, strictness, roughness, extremity; inflexibility, unbendingness, unyieldingness, obdurateness, flintiness; persistence, unremittance, inexorability, implacability, relentlessness; pitilessness, mercilessness, unfeelingness, inhumanity, cruelty, savagery; acrimony, acrimoniousness, acerbity, keenness; ruth-

lessness, cold-bloodedness, hard-heartedness, ironhandedness, peremptoriness, tyrannicalness, abusiveness, punitiveness.
2. seriousness, soberness, sobriety, sedateness, solemnity, staidness, somberness, gravity; formality, aloofness, coldness, stiffness, tightness, stiltedness; sternness, grimness, austerity, hardness, forbiddingness; strait-lacedness, puritanicalness, rigidity, rigidness.
3. simplicity, plainness, modesty, bareness, spareness, blankness, starkness, asceticism; unadornment, undecorousness, unornamentation, unembellishment.
4. inclemency, storminess, temmpestuousness, turbulence; fierceness, furiousness, ferociousness, ferocity, ferity, vehemence, fury, rage; violence, force, might, intensity, sharpness.
5. grievousness, burdensomeness, opressiveness, onerousness, heaviness; toughness, exigency, difficulty, arduousness, laboriousness, toilsomeness, operoseness.
6. exactness, exactitude, accuracy, precision; scrupulousness, meticulousness, fastidiousness.

sew, *v.* stitch, machine stitch, seam, baste, hem; embroider, smock, gather, tuck, pleat; take in, alter, fit; make, *Inf.* whip up, run up; secure, fasten, attach, join, close; repair, fix.

sex, *n.* **1.** gender; kind, sort, persuasion.
2. instinct, drive, appetite; attraction, pull, magnetism, animal magnetism, *Sl.* chemistry, allurement, allure, fascination.
3. facts of life, *Inf.* birds and the bees; coitus, sexual intercourse, coition, copulation, fornication, congress, consummation, commerce, union, conjugation, conjunction; coupling, mating, making love, *Sl.* getting it on, *Sl.* doing it, *Sl.* going to bed.

sexton, *n.* church official, *Archaic.* sacristan, warden, caretaker, janitor, bell-ringer.

sexuality, *n.* **1.** sexual character, femininity, womanhood, masculinity, manhood; sex, gender; heterosexuality, homosexuality, lesbianism, bisexuality, androgyny, hermaphrodism.
2. earthy nature, physical nature, bodily appetite, drive, instinct, animal magnetism; carnality, fleshliness, voluptuousness, physicalness, sensuality, *Inf.* sexiness; lustfulness, concupiscence, lasciviousness, libidinousness, lecherousness, lewdness, prurience, salaciousness, *Sl.* horniness; animality, bestiality, brutishness, coarseness, grossness.

sexy, *adj.* *Informal.* **1.** suggestive, exciting, arousing, sensual, sensuous, sexual, erotic; risqué, ribald, bawdy, bedroom, off-color, indecent, lewd; shameless, immodest, indecorous, unseemly, improper, indelicate, rude; obscene, pornographic, vulgar, foul, filthy, dirty, smutty, *Sl.* raunchy, scatalogical; gross, crude, coarse.
2. attractive, appealing, fascinating, captivating; enticing, alluring, inviting, tempting, seductive, (*of a woman*) foxy; beautiful, lovely, pretty, stunning, *Inf.* eye-filling, striking, zingy; shapely, curvy, *Inf.* curvaceous, voluptuous, *Sl.* built, *Sl.* stacked, *Sl.* busty, beddable; good-looking, handsome, virile.

shabby, *adj.* **1.** worn, shopworn, threadbare, faded; ragged, raggedy, in rags, tattered, frayed; mangy, ratty, scrubby, scruffy.
2. grungy, dingy, dirty, *Inf.* grubby, *Scot.* ourie; impoverished, sorry, down-and-out, down-at-the-heels, out-at-the-heels *or* elbows, the worse for wear.
3. slovenly, disheveled, slipshod, untidy, unkempt, unsightly, frowzy, blowzy, *Inf.* messy, frumpish, draggled, bedraggled, scraggly; ill-dressed, unfashionable, out-of-date, *Inf.* tacky.
4. dilapidated, deteriorated, battered, in disrepair, run-down, broken-down, tumble-down, ramshackle, seedy, *Sl.* crummy, *Sl.* beat-up; squalid, wretched, miserable, abject, slummy, slum-like.
5. mean, stingy, cheap, mingy, tight, tight-fisted, closefisted, miserly, niggardly, niggard, pinchpenny, penny-pinching, grudging, ungenerous, illiberal, beggarly, penurious, parsimonious.
6. base, base-spirited, low, vile, mean-spirited; contemptible, beneath contempt, worthy of contempt, despicable, detestable, odious, opprobrious, infamous, ignominious, sordid, heinous, atrocious, flagitious, abominable, degenerate, depraved, scurvy; ignoble, inglorious, discreditable, disreputable, dishonorable, rascally, villainous; coarse, vulgar, crude, uncouth, ungentlemanly, unhandsome, unbecoming.
7. inferior, mediocre, secondary, second-best, second-rate, third-rate, fourth-rate, substandard, below standard, subpar, below par; inadequate, insufficient, deficient, imperfect; incompetent, unskillful, maladroit; not to be compared *or* mistaken, not comparable, *Inf.* not a patch on it, *Inf.* out of the picture *or* running, *Inf.* not in the same league.

shackle, *n.* **1.** fetter, chain, manacle, handcuff, cuff, gyve, bilboes, trammel; hobble, hamper, restraint.
2. **shackles** **a.** fetters, chains, irons, bonds, pinions, gyves, trammels; manacles, handcuffs, cuffs, *Sl.* bracelets, *Brit. Sl.* darbies. **b.** impediment, hindrance, check, deterrent; obstacle, obstruction, bar, barrier, barricade; stop, block.
—*v.* **3.** fetter, manacle, handcuff, *Sl.* slap the cuffs *or* bracelets on [s.o.], put in irons; chain, enchain, tether, gyve; hobble, truss, bind, tie up, tie hand and foot, *Inf.* hogtie; trammel, entrammel, pinion.
4. restrict, restrain, rein, bridle, constrain; frustrate, thwart, impede, hinder, handicap; bar, obstruct, block, blockade, barricade, stand in the way; stop, stay, halt.

shade, *n.* **1.** darkness, duskiness, dusk, dimness, lightlessness; shadiness, shadowiness; cloudiness, murkiness, murk; gloom, gloominess, somberness, tenebrousness; obscurity, indistinctness, nebulousness, faintness, vagueness.
2. apparition, specter, spirit, soul, vision, phantom, phantasm, eidolon, materialization; ghost, (*in Irish folklore*) banshee, (*in Roman religion*) manes, (*in Roman religion*) lemures *or* larvae, *Inf.* spook.
3. shadow. See **shadow** (*def.* **1**).
4. degree, small *or* slight degree, nuance; hair, hair's-breadth, fraction, fraction of an inch, skin of one's teeth.
5. hint, suggestion, suspicion, intimation, soupçon, trace, tinge; touch, speck, sprinkling, dash; little bit, modicum, iota, grain, scintilla, atom.
6. blind, Venetian blind, window shade; sunshade, parasol, umbrella; cover, covering, canopy, awning, shelter; protection, shield, safeguard.
7. **shades** *Slang.* sunglasses, dark *or* colored glasses *or* lenses, *Inf.* sunspecs.
8. **cast** or **put someone into the shade** surpass, exceed, excel, transcend, trump, overcome, better, *Inf.* go one better; cap, top, overtop; beat, best, worst; overshadow, eclipse, put to shame, *Inf.* show [s.o.] up; outstrip, outdo, outvie, outrival, outclass, outperform, outplay, *Inf.* run rings *or* circles around.
—*v.* **9.** darken, blacken, black, opaque, adumbrate; eclipse, occult, black out, blot out.
10. obscure, obfuscate, cloud, becloud, benight,

bedim, befog; blur, dull, dim; overcast, overcloud.
11. screen, veil, curtain, cloak, shroud, enshroud, *Inf.* cover up; hide, hide away, conceal; disguise, camouflage, mask.

shadow, *n.* **1.** silhouette, adumbration, outline, reflection.
2. shade, shadiness. See **shade** (*def.* **1**).
3. shelter, protection, refuge, asylum, haven, sanctuary, sanctum, safety zone, *Scot.* bield; security, safety, safekeeping, preservation; help, aid, support, defense, championship.
4. hint, suggestion. See **shade** (*def.* **5**).
5. specter, phantom. See **shade** (*def.* **2**).
6. hint, intimation, suggestion, implication, imputation, insinuation, innuendo; inkling, clue, cue, *Sl.* tip-off; signal, sign, omen, portent, foretoken, harbinger; premonition, preindication, forewarning, foreshadowing.
7. (*all falsely assumed*) semblance, aspect, appearance, demeanor, mien, cast, look; show, veneer, front, false front, façade; guise, pretense, cover, cover-up; disguise, camouflage, mask, masquerade; deception, ruse, artifice, subterfuge.
8. influence, sway, domination, preeminence; atmosphere, environment, milieu, medium, condition; background, setting, sphere, element; spirit, tone, tenor, mood, aura, ambience; temper, character; feelings, *Sl.* vibrations, *Sl.* vibes; threat.
9. close friend, constant companion, sidekick, alter ego, other self, *Scot. and North Eng.* marrow, *Sl.* Siamese twin; comrade, chum, crony, *Fr. Inf. copain, U.S. Inf.* buddy *or* bosom buddy, *Inf.* pal, *Obs.* copemate.
10. detective, investigator, private investigator, *Sl.* private eye, *Inf.* sleuth, *Inf.* bird dog, *Inf.* sherlock, *Inf.* tail, *U.S. Sl.* dick, *U.S. Sl.* gumshoe.
—*v.* **11.** shade. See **shade** (*defs.* **9, 10**).
12. follow, trail, trail after, heel, *Inf.* tail, *Sl.* bird-dog; trace, track, stalk; pursue, chase, dog, hound.
13. hint, intimate, suggest, imply, insinuate; signal, signify, mean, betoken, indicate, point to, connote, allude to, advert.
14. portend, forebode, foretoken, foreshadow, foreshow, omen, augur, presage, presignify, preindicate, promise, body forth; warn, forewarn, warn in advance *or* beforehand *or* ahead of time.

shadowy, *adj.* **1.** indistinct, indeterminate, indefinite, vague, nebulous; obscure, unclear, indistinguishable, ill-defined; opaque, dark, murky; dim, faint, feeble, pale, weak.
2. unsubstantial, impalpable, imponderable, intangible, immaterial; ethereal, vaporous, airy, air-built, cloud-built, gossamer, gossamery, gaseous; unreal, dreamlike, illusory, visionary, imaginary, figmental, hallucinatory, chimerical; spectral, ghostly, phantasmal, phantasmagorial, phantom, phantomlike, wraithlike.
3. shady. See **shady** (*def.* **1**).

shady, *adj.* **1.** bowery, bosky, arbory; shaded, arbored.
2. dark, umbrageous, umbral, penumbral, obumbrate, *Archaic.* caliginous.
3. shadowy. See **shadowy** (*defs.* **1, 2**).
4. *Informal.* of dubious character, disreputable, discreditable, dishonorable; dishonest, crooked, underhand, underhanded, not kosher; devious, invidious, shifty, tricky, evasive, slippery.
5. on the shady side of *Informal.* (*all in reference to age*) past, beyond, more than, older than; on the wrong side of, on the other side, on the dark side of.

shaft, *n.* **1.** pole, rod, stick; long handle, helve; bar, beam; staff, flagpole, flagstaff; post, pillar, column, upright, support, stanchion.
2. barb, cutting remark, cut, gibe, sarcastic remark; verbal blow, *Inf.* slam, *Inf.* put-down, *Inf.* knock, slap *or* slap in the face.
3. ray, beam, gleam, patch, spot, pencil, streak.
4. passage, duct, flue, pipe, tube; vertical passageway, elevator shaft, mine shaft, tunnel; well, excavation, hole, pit.

shaggy, *adj.* **1.** hairy, hirsute, crinite, comose, comate, piliferous.
2. untidy, unkempt, messy, disheveled, snarled, tangled, entangled, matted; ragged, rough, coarse.

shake, *v.* **1.** vibrate, rattle, chatter; convulse, commove, twitch, vellicate, toss and turn; shimmy, wiggle, rock, bounce, bob, dance, (*both of dice*) roll, toss; swing, sway, oscillate, wave, roll.
2. tremble, quiver, twitter, trill; pulsate, pulse, throb, palpitate, jump, beat; quaver, quake, shudder, shiver; wriggle, squirm, move around.
3. *Usu.* **shake off** *or* **down** *or* **out** dislodge, disengage, unstick, loosen, loose, free, liberate; knock, bring down *or* out, remove, extricate; fall, fall down, fall out, settle, precipitate; elude, escape, get rid of, rid oneself of, get away from, leave behind, leave in the dust, lose, drop, throw off, slough off, brush off, give the slip.
4. jiggle, joggle, (*of coins*) jingle; jostle, hustle, jounce, jar, jolt, bump, shove, buffet, knock around; jerk, tweak, pluck, twang, flip, flick.
5. waver, falter, wobble, teeter, totter, dodder, shuffle, stagger, stumble, be on the verge of collapse; flutter, flicker, sputter, splutter, skip a beat, beat irregularly; fluctuate, vacillate, vary, shift, go up and down, go back and forth.
6. brandish, wave, flourish; flaunt, vaunt, parade, display, disport, exhibit, show off; swing, wag, dangle, flap, move about; wield, raise, poke, point, stick.
7. *Often* **shake up** churn, churn up, mix up, succuss, (both of water, wine, etc.) roil, *Chiefly U.S.* rile; agitate, unnerve, rattle, perturb, ruffle, flurry, fluster, discompose, disconcert, discomfit, unsettle, disquiet; stir, excite, overcome, overwhelm; confuse, muddle, confound, puzzle, perplex, stupefy, daze, *Inf.* throw, *Inf.* throw for a loop; disturb, trouble, worry, upset, upheave, heave, throw into disorder *or* disarray, throw into a tailspin; affect, touch, hit a nerve, *Inf.* get to.
8. weaken, enervate, infirm, incapacitate, debilitate, impair, wound, harm, hurt, hamstring; undermine, pull the rug out from under; daunt, cause doubt in, deject, discourage, dampen one's spirits, set back on one's heels, pull one up short, *Inf.* take the fight *or* starch out of; cool one off, lower *or* reduce one's enthusiasm, disincline, disaffect, disenchant; scare, frighten, affright, terrorize, chill to the bone, scare to death, petrify; shock, alarm, startle, stun, astonish, abash, take aback, surprise, make one's heart skip a beat *or* stop, *Brit. Sl.* knock.
9. shake down a. condition, break in, put *or* get in shape *or* working order, get the bugs out of, give [s.t.] a workout, put [s.t.] through its paces; take on a trial run, take on a maiden voyage, run through, try out, test, prove. **b. Slang.** blackmail, extort, milk, squeeze, *Inf.* bleed; wrest, wrench, exact, get out of, obtain by force, force out of, extract; coerce, lean on, put the arm on *or* screws to, *Inf.* put the bite *or* squeeze on; threaten, intimidate, bully.
—*n.* **10.** jiggling, joggling, (*of money*) jingling; agitation, churn, mixing, succussion; jounce, jar, jerk, bump, shove, buffet.

11. vibration, rattle, chatter, motion; tremor, twitter, *Both Music.* vibrato, tremolo; tremble, quiver, shudder, shiver; quaver, quake, earthquake; the shakes, convulsion, palsy, twitch, tick, vellication; swing, sway, swivel, oscillation, roll, wave, ripple, wriggle, undulation; palpitation, thrill, jump, pulsation, throb, heartbeat, beat; sputter, splutter, flutter, flicker; wavering, faltering, wobble, teeter, totter, stagger, skip.

12. shock, start, scare, chill, surprise, stun; blow, jolt, wound, hurt; disturbance, upset, disappointment.

13. crack, break, rupture, fracture, fissure, split; hiatus, gap, space, hole, opening, cavity; chink, chip, chap, crevice, cranny; chasm, gorge, canyon.

shakedown, *n.* **1.** extortion, blackmail, badger game, skin game, *Inf.* the squeeze, *Sl.* murphy; milking, wringing, blood-sucking, *Inf.* bleeding; wresting, wrenching, exaction, extraction, obtaining by force; coercion, threat, terrorization, intimidation, bullying.

2. investigation, search, exploration, probe, inquiry; inspection, examination, scrutinization, scrutiny, *Sl.* casing; purge, weeding out, winnowing, removal, elimination, search and destroy mission.

shaky, *adj.* **1.** shaking, chattering; convulsive, twitching, jerky, vellicative; tremulous, tremulant, vibratory, vibrative, vibratile, quivering, twittery, resonant; trembling, quavering, shuddery, shuddering, shivery, shivering; skittish, jumpy, jittery, high-strung, nervous; fearful, afraid, frightened, scared, having cold feet; timid, timorous, easily frightened, cowardly, weak-kneed, lily-livered, *Inf.* yellow, *Sl.* chicken.

2. wobbly, rattly, rattling, wiggly, jiggly, loose, movable, *Inf.* floppy; flimsy, rickety, ramshackle, tumble-down, decrepit, jerry-built, gimcrack, cheap, unsubstantial; teetering, tottery, tottering, staggering, doddering, ready to topple *or* fall down; unsteady, unstable, insecure, unfortified; unsupported, unsound, ungrounded, unfounded, unproven; unreliable, undependable, untrustworthy, not to be counted on; perilous, vulnerable, dangerous, hazardous.

3. tenuous, tentative, up in the air, dubious, questionable, half-hearted; wavering, fluttering, flickering, sputtering, spluttering, faltering, failing, fading; unsure, unconfidant, hesitant, shilly-shallying, irresolute, undecided, uncommitted; fluctuating, vacillating, oscillatory, swinging back and forth, inconstant, variable, irregular, fitful.

shallow, *adj.* **1.** not deep, shoal.

2. superficial, skin-deep, external, outward, on the surface; unprofound, empty, meaningless, without substance; trifling, unimportant, petty, trivial, frivolous.

—*n.* **3.** *Usu.* **shallows** shoal, flat, sandbank, sand bar, shelf.

sham, *n.* **1.** imitation, counterfeit, copy, duplicate, forgery, fake; bastard, two-dollar bill, wooden nickel; substitute, ersatz.

2. impostor, fraud, pretender, make-believe, fake, *Inf.* faker, *Inf.* phony; masquerader, humbug, wolf in sheep's clothing, dissembler, hypocrite, pharisee.

3. cover, slipcover, pillow sham, pillowcase, pillowslip.

—*adj.* **4.** pretended, feigned, simulated, make-believe, fairy-tale, fictitious, made-up, unreal, mock; assumed, put-on, fake, faked, contrived, factitious, *Sl.* hokey; ersatz, artificial, synthetic, plastic; counterfeit, forged, copied, duplicated; fraudulent, fraud, imitation, insincere, ungenuine, unauthentic, false, *Inf.* phony; bogus, spurious, supposititious, pinchbeck, bastardly, *Australian.* bunyip.

—*v.* **5.** counterfeit, make an imitation of, forge, copy, duplicate.

6. pretend, fake, feign, malinger, dissemble, act, simulate, imitate, make believe; affect, assume, put on, take on.

shamble[1], *n.* **shambles a.** slaughterhouse, slaugter-pen, butchery, abattoir, *Obs.* butcher-row. **b.** mess, wreck, disaster area, rathole, dump, garbage pile *or* heap, pigpen, pigsty, *Brit.* piggery, Augean stables, *Inf.* snake pit, mare's nest.

shamble[2], *v.* shuffle, drag one's feet, walk clumsily, hobble, limp, hitch, halt, pause, hesitate; toddle, dodder, falter, move unsteadily, totter.

shame, *n.* **1.** disgrace, dishonor, reproach, degradation, illrepute, bad repute, scandal; baseness, turpitude, debasement, vitiation, ingloriousness; ignominy, infamy, odium, opprobrium, condemnation; slur, imputation, aspersion, defamation, denigration, slander. libel, calumniation, vilification, smear, smirch, blot, blot on the escutcheon; stain, taint, tarnish, black spot *or* mark, blemish, smudge, brand, stigma, *Inf.* skeleton in the closet.

2. discredit, disfavor, disrepute, disrespect, obloquy, disesteem, loss of face; detraction, derogation, devaluation, depreciation, disparagement, belittlement, deprecation.

3. humiliation, mortification, humble pie, humbled pride; (*all of oneself*) guilt, remorse, shamefacedness, feeling of unfitness *or* unworthiness, disgust, hate, abomination, abasement; embarrassment, disconcertment, discomposure, discomfort, confusion, perplexity, abashment, bewilderment; chagrin, pique, vexation, displeasure, dissatisfaction, dislike, disappointment, discontentment.

4. misfortune, ill fortune, bad fortune, adverse fortune, adversity, bad luck, ill luck; calamity, disaster, catastrophe.

5. modesty, propriety, decency, respectability, sensibility, decorum, decorousness, moderation, fitness, appropriateness, honor, virtue, virtuousness, sobriety, pudency, *Rare.* pudicity; innocence, chastity, virginity, purity.

6. put to shame surpass, outdo, outclass, outshine, outstrip, overtop, override, outrun, transcend, excel, exceed, best, beat; overshadow, eclipse, tower over, cast into the shade.

—*v.* **7.** humiliate, humble, mortify, bring down, *Inf.* take *or* bring down a notch *or* peg, *Sl.* put down, make [s.o.] eat humble pie, *Inf.* make [s.o.] eat crow *or* his words, make [s.o.] swallow his pride, make lowly, meeken, chasten, subdue; confuse, abash, perplex, bewilder, confound, nonplus, dumfound; embarrass, put to the blush; vex, chagrin, disappoint, displease, dissatisfy.

8. impel, compel, constrain, induce, prevail upon, insist upon, cause; coerce, drive, force, press, commandeer, push, impress, bully, *Inf.* twist [s.o.'s] arm.

9. disgrace, dishonor, strip of rank *or* honor, degrade, abase, debase, vitiate, reproach; sully, slur, impute, asperse, slander, libel, calumniate, defame, denigrate, scandalize, vilify, blacken, smear, smirch, besmirch, taint, tarnish; stain, spot, smudge, brand, stigmatize, *Sl.* dump on, drag through the mud *or* mire, heap dirt upon.

10. discredit, disfavor, disprove, refute, devaluate, depreciate, lower, reduce, depress; disparage, decry, belittle, deprecate, demean, deflate, detract, derogate.

shamefaced, *adj.* **1.** modest, restrained, reserved; demure, coy; meek, diffident, timid, timorous, shrinking, retiring; shy, blushing, bashful, sheepish.

2. embarrassed, red-faced, put to the blush, made to blush, made to change color; crestfallen, chapfallen, dejected, dispirited, hangdog, *Inf.* sourfaced; abashed, confused, perplexed, confounded, bewildered, dumfounded, nonplused, disconcerted; chagrined, vexed, disappointed, dissatisfied, put out, displeased, discontented; guilty, ashamed, remorseful, regretful, contrite, penitent, conscience-stricken.

3. humiliated, humbled, mortified, meekened, made to eat humble pie; shamed, disgraced, dishonored, reproached; discredited, disfavored, *Sl.* in the doghouse.

shameful, *adj.* humiliating, humbling, mortifying; belittling, deflating, disparaging, derogatory, deprecating, detractive; discreditable, disreputable, disfavorable; censurable, blameworthy, blamable, culpable, chargeable, accusable, impeachable, imputable.

2. disgraceful, dishonorable, degraded, inglorious, deplorable; infamous, ignominious, odious, opprobrious, contemptible, despicable, detestable, execrable, sordid, degenerate, depraved, corrupt, vicious, reprehensible, unmentionable, horrible, horrifying, heinous, atrocious, flagitious, iniquitous, *Archaic.* facinorous; unprincipled, debased, immoral, profligate, base, vile, sinister, infernal, diabolic, evil, sinful, bad, wrong, low, dastardly, arrant, nefarious; mean, villainous, ignoble.

3. libelous, slanderous, defamatory; shocking, scandalous, notorious, flagrant, outrageous; improper, fulsome, unseemly, unbecoming, unworthy, undutiful, delinquent, objectionable, uncommendable, reprovable, peccable, illaudable; indecent, lewd, obscene, perverse.

shameless, *adj.* **1.** immodest, improper, fulsome, unseemly, unbecoming, indecorous, *Archaic.* malapert, shocking, outrageous, scandalous, notorious, flagrant; indecent, lewd, obscene, perverse, lustful, lascivious, lecherous, licentious.

2. audacious, impudent, insolent, presumptuous, bold, bold-faced, brazen, rude, brash, barefaced; fresh, forward, daring, unreserved, flippant, pert, *Inf.* cheeky; unashamed, unabashed, unembarrassed, unblushing.

3. hardened, unprincipled, unconscienced, unscrupulous, qualmless, corrupt, degenerate, depraved, perverted, debased, abased, base, vile, wicked, iniquitous, vicious, evil, sinister; dissipated, dissolute, abandoned, profligate, wanton, debauched.

shanty, *n.* hut, hutch, shack, *Scot.* bothy; cottage, cot, bungalow, bower, cabin, *Brit. Dial.* cote, *Scot.* but-and-ben; hovel, hole, dump, pigpen, pigsty.

shape, *n.* **1.** form, figure, configuration, figuration, conformation, formation, arrangement, format, organization, pattern; contour, outline, lines, profile, silhouette; cut, style, model, pattern; structure, construction, frame, exterior, outward form.

2. phantom, ghost, (*in Irish Folklore*) banshee, *Inf.* spook; phantasm, specter, apparition, vision, shadow, spirit, soul, wraith, eidolon, materialization.

3. guise, likeness, aspect, appearance, look, semblance, image; cover, *Inf.* front, show, pretense, presentment; figure, physique, build; face, countenance, features; air, mien, manner, bearing.

4. condition, state, state of affairs, circumstances, situation, ball game; position, footing, status.

—*v.* **5.** fashion, form, mold, model, pattern; create, design, devise; construct, build, frame; make, put together, produce; cast, block, block out, hammer, chisel, carve, hew, rough-hew, sculpture.

6. organize, assort, sort out; order, arrange, lay out, line up, line, align.

7. adjust, adapt, accommodate, fit, regulate, convert; alter, change, transform, modify.

8. **shape up** **a.** take form, take shape, crystallize, develop, fall in, fall into place, fall into line, come together. **b.** improve, grow better, show improvement, look up, pick up; progress, make headway, gain ground, go forward, come along, go along.

shapeless, *adj.* **1.** formless, unformed, without form, not formed, unshaped, unshapen; embryonic, undeveloped; unhewn, uncarved, rough, unfashioned; misshapen, ill-fashioned, ill-made, distorted, deformed, grotesque, disfigured, ill-proportioned.

2. amorphous, indeterminate, indefinite, vague, nebulous, characterless, nondescript; unorganized, confused, jumbled, chaotic, structureless, unstructured.

shard, *n.* fragment, part, particle, piece; chip, chink, smithereen, splinter, sliver; cut, cutting, paring; scale, flake, shaving, lamina; particle, scrap, bit, snip, snippet, wisp, tatter, corner; morsel, crumb, ort; modicum, iota, whit, mite, trifle, scantling; remnant, fraction, section, segment, remainder; snatch, shred, sample, specimen, dose, taste.

share, *n.* **1.** allotment, allocation, appropriation, consignment, apportionment, allowance, grant; dispensation, donation, ration, pittance, dole, handout; endowment, inheritance; portion, part, division, lot, *Inf.* whack, dividend, helping, serving; percentage, measure, quota, stint; cut, *Sl.* rake off, commission; a piece of the action, a piece of the pie *or* cake.

—*v.* **2.** divide up, *Inf.* divvy up, subdivide, partition, adjust; apportion, allocate, allot, appropriate; ration, measure out, measure off, admeasure; mete out, portion out, divide and assign, parcel out, deal out, dole out; go halves, go fifty-fifty, split the difference, share and share alike, go Dutch treat, go Dutch.

3. *Usu.* **share in** **a.** have a share *or* part in, have a stake in, have a percentage *or* piece of. **b.** take part in, participate, partake of *or* in.

shark, *n.* **1.** swindler, cheat, cheater, fraud, highbinder, confidence man, *Sl.* con man, *Sl.* flimflam man, bunko artist, crook, chiseler; sharper, *Sl.* city slicker, *Inf.* fast talker, *Inf.* hawk. See **swindler.**

2. *Slang.* expert, adept, master, professional, *Inf.* pro, *Inf.* ace, *Inf.* crackerjack, star, *Sl.* no slouch.

—*v.* **3.** steal, cheat, defraud, fleece, rook, gull, *Archaic.* chouse; overcharge, *Sl.* soak, *Inf.* gyp, *Sl.* chisel, *Sl.* gaff, pluck, mulct; victimize, exploit, play on *or* upon, take advantage of, *Inf.* do, *Sl.* burn.

sharp, *adj.* **1.** thin-edged, razor-edged, knife-like; keen, acute, pointed, needle-sharp, edged, cutting, thin; sharp as a bayonet, sharp as a butcher knife.

2. pointed, toothed, dentiform, barbed, cusped, cuspidate, cuspidal; peaked, *Bot.* apiculate, *Bot., Zool.* acuminate; bristly, prickly, echinate, setaceous, spiculate; thorny, spinous; craggy, jagged, angular; notched, serrate; spear-shaped, sword-shaped, *Anat. Zool.* xiphoid, sagittate; tapering, *Bot., Zool.* subulate.

3. abrupt, sudden, rapid; steep, sheer, extreme, acclivitous, vertical, precipitous; stiff, arduous.

4. (*of taste*) pungent, biting, bitter, acid, acrid; keen, acute.

5. (*of noise*) piercing, shrill, strident, harsh; high-pitched, high-toned, ear-splitting.

6. (*of pain*) distressing, cutting, intense, acute, piercing, fierce, extreme; sudden, violent, crucial, critical, severe.

7. bitter, harsh, caustic, cutting, scathing; lashing, virulent, rancorous, galling, acrid, acrimonious; derisory, insulting, excoriating, invidious, mocking, satirical; merciless, brutal, cruel, unkind, hurtful, malicious, spiteful, malignant, mean, venomous, envenomed; curt, brusque, tart, blunt, gruff, abrupt, bearish; ungracious, uncordial, uncivil,

discourteous, impolite, unmannerly, rude.
8. eager, ardent, earnest, perfervid, fervent, zealous, feverish; high-mettled, vehement, animated, spirited, active; ambitious, aspiring, diligent, enterprising, sedulous, unfaltering.
9. alert, vigilant. See **sharp-sighted.**
10. shrewd, intelligent, smart. See **sharp-witted.**
—adv. **11.** keenly, acutely, vividly.
12. abruptly, suddenly, unexpectedly, all of a sudden, at once, on the spur of the moment, without warning.
13. punctually, on time; on the dot, on the nose.
14. vigilantly, watchfully, carefully.
15. briskly, quickly, swiftly, speedily, hastily, hurriedly, rapidly, fast.

sharpen, *v.* put an edge on, make keen, acuminate; point, tip, hone, strop, whet, file, grind, taper.

sharper, *n.* swindler, highbinder, cheat, cheater, fraud, defrauder, confidence man, *Sl.* con man, sharpie. See **swindler.**

sharp-sighted, *adj.* all-observant, vigilant, watchful, wary; wide-awake, broad-awake, wakeful; on the lookout, on the qui vive; circumspect, prudent, alert; lynx-eyed, Argus-eyed, eagle-eyed, hawk-eyed, gimlet-eyed, ferret-eyed; keensighted, quick-sighted.

sharp-witted, *adj.* shrewd, quick-witted, keen, acute, astute, *Scot. and North Eng.* gleg; intelligent, critical, discerning, discriminating, perspicacious, brainy, hard-headed, long-headed, farsighted, penetrating, thoughtful; sagacious, judicious, prudent, wise, sensible, knowing, comprehending, imaginative; alert, wide-awake; brilliant, luminous, bright; smart, clever, foxy, crafty, cunning, calculating, sharp as a tack, *Sl.* on the ball, *Inf.* crack, *Sl.* crackerjack, *Inf.* whiz-bang, *Brit. Sl.* whizzo.

shatter, *v.* **1.** break, break into pieces, smash, *Sl.* smash to smithereens, *Sl.* bust, crash; split, crack, fracture, fragmentize, splinter, shiver.
2. damage, impair, weaken, injure, harm, hurt, do damage to; crush, beat down, drive to one's knees; destroy, demolish, wreck, dash, ruin, *Sl.* total, devastate, wipe out.
3. (*all of ideas or opinions*) weaken, undermine; refute, confute, disprove, rebut, prove wrong.

shave, *v.* **1.** poll, cut off, shear, fleece, remove, retrench; cut away, scrape away, scale, peel, pare, whittle, cut *or* trim down to size; mow, trim, snip off, clip, crop, lop off, dock, prune, cut back.
2. scrape, graze, brush, touch, rub.
—n. **3.** shaving, thin slice, paring, peeling, sliver, shive, piece, bit; scrap, remnant, shred, snip, snippet, cutting; splinter, flake, scale, fragment, shard.

shear, *v.* **1.** cut, shave, fleece, poll, cut off, remove, retrench; trim, clip, snip off, shingle, crop, cut back, lop off, dock, prune.
2. *Usu.* **shear of** strip, deprive, divest, remove, take away, relieve of.
—n. **3.** **shears** large scissors, sewing shears, kitchen shears, pinking shears; clippers, cutters, pruners.

sheath, *n.* scabbard, case, casing, encasement, cover, covering, sheathing; envelope, wrapper, wrapping, *Pharm.* capsule, encapsulation; integument, tegument, outer layer, *Biol.* investment; skin, rind, peel, shell, husk, hull, shuck.

sheathe, *v.* scabbard, sheath, invaginate, reinsert, put back *or* away; case, enclose, encase, encapsule, encapsulate; cover, wrap, enwrap, envelop, enfold, swathe, enswathe.

shed[1], *n.* lean-to, shack, outhouse, shanty, hut, hutch, cote; hovel, sty, pen, stable, barn; booth, stall; garage, hangar; shelter, building, structure; annex, addition.

shed[2], *v.* **1.** pour forth, surge out, stream out, let flow, spill; discharge, exude, impart, release, let fall, give forth, send forth, cast forth; emit, emanate, shine forth, radiate, effuse, spread, dispel, scatter, strew, bestrew, disseminate.
2. resist, repel, repulse, throw off; withstand, hold up against.
3. cast off, slough off, exuviate, molt; exfoliate, defoliate; peel, flake, *Pathol.* desquamate; take off, remove, doff, strip; discard, dispense with, get rid of, drop, abandon.

sheen, *n.* luster, burnish, shine, polish, gloss, glow; gleam, glimmer, glint, glitter, sparkle, twinkle, shimmer; brightness, brilliance, dazzle, radiance, luminousness, lambency, refulgence, effulgence; opalescence, incandescence.

sheepish, *adj.* **1.** embarrassed, ashamed, shamefaced, blushing; bashful, shy, timid, timorous, backward, hesitant, retiring, shrinking, unobtrusive, unostentatious; diffident, abashed, modest, reserved, restrained, self-conscious, unconfident, *Scot. and North Eng.* blate; coy, demure, meek, modest, unassuming.
2. docile, passive, gentle, mild, subdued; manipulatable, manipulable, tractable, malleable, ductile, pliable, pliant, manageable, *Scot.* tawie; compliant, complying, amenable, cooperative, accommodating, agreeable, willing, disposed; nonresistant, obedient, biddable, dutiful, responsive.

sheer[1], *adj.* **1.** transparently thin, diaphanous, translucent, filmy, gossamer, gossamery; naked, clear, crystal, glassy, hyaline.
2. simple, plain, pure, unadulterated, unmixed, unalloyed, unmingled; homogeneous, uniform; elemental, elementary.
3. utter, downright, absolute, unqualified, complete, out-and-out, total, veritable, unconditional, rank.
4. steep, precipitous, bluff, abrupt, sharp, bold, stiff, arduous; perpendicular, vertical, upright, straight up and down; acclivitous, ascending, uphill; declivitous, descending, downhill.
—adv. **5.** clear, completely, quite, totally, entirely.
6. steeply, abruptly, vertically, perpendicularly, precipitously.
—n. **7.** gauze, chiffon, voile, netting; cloud, mist, veil, film.

sheer[2], *v.* **1.** go off course, change the heading, deviate, yaw, stray, drift; swerve, sag, skew; turn, turn aside, cant, twist, shift, bear off, slue, veer; lurch, list, heel, tilt.
—n. **2.** deviation, divergence, swerve, swerving, turning aside, turning; drift, deflection, skew, twist.
3. (*of a ship's hull*) curve, swoop, angle, pitch, warp.

sheet, *n.* **1.** bedsheet, linen, bed linen, bedding, bedclothes, bedclothing, fitted sheet, contour sheet, sheeting.
2. layer, lamina, overlay, surface, covering, coating, coat, blanket; veneer, facing, revetment, facade; patina, plating, plate, film, scale, scum, pellicle, skin, integument; sheathing, wrapping; drop cloth, ground cloth, groundsheet.
3. plate, panel, pane; slab, foil.
4. sail, canvas, mainsail, jib, spinnaker.
5. piece of paper, leaf, folio; page, recto, verso.
6. newspaper, paper, tabloid, *Sl.* tab, *Sl.* scandal sheet, *Sl.* rag; journal, gazette; periodical, daily, weekly, monthly; flyer, circular, throwaway.
7. expanse, stretch, reach, span, range, sweep; field, spread, curtain.

—*v.* **8.** cover, overlay, face, veneer; wrap, envelop, enfold; sheathe, enshroud, swathe, swaddle.

shelf, *n.* **1.** bracket, hob; mantel, mantelpiece; platform, bench, banquette; ledge, protrusion, projection, overhang.

2. sandbank, sand bar, bank, bar, shoal, ridge, reef.

3. put on the shelf *Slang.* postpone, defer, prorogue, delay, suspend, hang up, table, shelve, put aside for the time; put in cold storage, put on ice, put in a holding pattern, put on a back burner.

4. on the shelf *Slang.* inactive, inoperative, nonfunctioning, nonperforming; unused, unoccupied, unbusied, unemployed, useless, worthless, unusable.

shell, *n.* **1.** hard outer covering, hard case, *Anat., Zool.* theca, casing, coat, coating, incrustation, sheathing, sheath; envelope, wrapper, capsule, cloak, jacket; casement, housing, protection; carapace, shield, *Zool.* test, (*pl.*) exuviae; integument, tegument, *Bot.* testa, rind, crust, peel, skin, *Bot.* epicarp; husk, bark, cortex, hull, shuck, chaff; pod, calyx, *Dial.* cod, pericarp; *Bot.* involucre, *Bot.* involucrum, wrapping, *Bot.* investment.

2. cavity, hollow, crater, cup, bowl.

3. framework, frame, structure, outline, skeleton, *Metall.* skull.

4. cartridge, cartouche, canister; cylinder, case, container; reservoir, magazine, cassette.

5. *Military.* projectile, bullet, ball, grenade, canister shot, shot, shrapnel.

—*v.* **6.** husk, shuck, peel, skin, pare, decorticate, excorticate, flay, scale, hull, bark.

7. bombard, bomb, *Brit. Sl.* prang, strafe, torpedo, *Mil.* barrage, fusillade, blitz, blitzkrieg; shoot, fire on, open fire on, pepper, cannonade.

8. come off, detach, separate, split; exfoliate, *Pathol.* desquamate, shed, slough, molt, exuviate, flake.

9. shell out *Slang.* spend, pay out, outlay, *Inf.* lay out, *Sl.* fork out, *Sl.* dish out, ante up, expend, disburse; squander, dissipate, burn up, waste, fritter away.

shelter, *n.* **1.** refuge, asylum, haven, sanctuary, sanctum, sanctum sanctorum, safety zone, harbor, port, port in a storm, *Scot.* bield; retreat, hospice, hermitage, cloister, ashram; nest, lain, den, cave, hole, dugout, abri; mew, cover, covert, coverture, hideout, hiding place, hideaway; corner, dark corner, shade, recess, nook, cranny, niche; stronghold, fortress, fortification, citadel, bastion, keep, safehold, tower, pillar, tower *or* pillar of strength, rock, rock of ages.

2. protection, security, safety, shelter from a storm; custody, keeping, charge, ward, guardianship, preservation, safekeeping; hiding, concealment, seclusion, privacy, retirement; help, aid, support, patronage, defense, championship; guard, escort, convoy.

3. immunity, diplomatic immunity, legislative *or* congressional immunity, impunity, indemnity, exemption, exception; privilege, *Politics.* executive privilege, prerogative, right, liberty, freedom, dispensation, special privilege, special favor; reprieve, pardon, amnesty, sparing.

4. home, abode, domicile, residence, residency, dwelling, dwelling place, dwelling home, habitation, inhabitance, inhabitancy, *Scot. and North Eng.* bigging, *Scot.* howff; housing, rooms, accommodations, roof over one's head, *Inf.* pad, *Inf.* crash pad, *Chiefly Brit. Inf.* diggings, *Brit. Inf.* digs; hearth, hearthstone, hearthside, hearth and home, fireside, fireplace, chimney corner, *Brit. Dial.* ingle, *Brit. Dial.* ingleside, *Chiefly Brit.* inglenook; homestead, household, family, family circle, domestic circle, bosom of one's family, seat of one's affections, home sweet home, *Inf.* place where one hangs his hat.

—*v.* **5.** house, give shelter to, lodge, provide lodging *or* lodgings *or* lodgment for, put up, take in, have as a guest *or* lodger, roof, provide with a roof; quarter, provide quarters for, billet, bed, bunk, berth.

6. guard, safeguard, protect, keep, secure, make safe; defend, champion, help, aid, keep from harm, take under one's wing, *Inf.* go to bat for, *Inf.* ride shotgun for, escort; hide, conceal, shield, screen, cover, cloak, *Archaic.* shroud; harbor, haven.

7. take *or* seek shelter, take *or* seek refuge, take *or* seek sanctuary; find shelter, find refuge, find sanctuary; retire, hole up, seclude oneself, shut oneself up; hide, hide out, conceal oneself, lie hidden, lie perdu, lie snug *or* close, *Inf.* lie low; couch, skulk, steal, lurk.

shelve, *v.* **1.** (*all on a shelf*) arrange, group, space, align, line up, set out, fix; place, put, set.

2. put off *or* aside, shunt, put on the shelf, lay aside, table, pigeonhole; sleep on, waive, dispense with, put aside for the time. See **shelf** (*def.* **3**).

3. dismiss, retire, lay off; fire, put out of a job, let go, give [s.o.] his walking papers, drop, deselect, send packing, *Inf.* bounce, *Inf.* sack, *Inf.* give [s.o.] the sack, *Inf.* send down the road, *U.S. Govt. Inf.* rif, *Sl.* can.

shenanigan, *n.* *Usu.* **shenanigans** *Informal.* tomfoolery, antics, *Sl.* monkeyshines, *Sl.* monkeybusiness; mischief, prankishness, *Inf.* hanky-panky, *Scot. and North Eng.* daffing; prank, antic, caper, escapade, trick, practical joke, roguish trick, *Fr.* *espièglerie;* fooling, foolery, horseplay, skylarking; clowning, clownery, clownishness, zanyism; buffoonery, buffoonism, buffoonishness, harlequinade; joking, jesting, jocosity, jocoseness, jocularity, waggishness, waggery, drollery; levity, frivolity, silliness.

shepherd, *n.* **1.** herder, herdsman, sheepherder.

2. protector, defender, guardian, guard, guarder, guardsman.

3. clergyman, minister, priest, rabbi, parson, servant of God, man of the cloth; confessor, spiritual director, shepherd of souls; preacher, evangelist, missionary, spreader of the Word.

4. the Shepherd Jesus Christ. See **Jesus Christ.**

—*v.* **5.** guard, protect, watch over, look after, see after; stand guard over, police, secure, defend; shield, shelter, screen; preserve, save, conserve; escort, conduct, convoy, ride shotgun.

shibboleth, *n.* **1.** badge, trademark, earmark, hallmark, symptom, mark; idiosyncrasy, idiocrasy, affectation, quirk, twist, eccentricity, peculiarity, singularity; characteristic, quality, trait; style, manner, mannerism, way.

2. catchword, catch phrase, buzz word, byword, saying, motto, slogan, battle cry, red flag, trigger word; signal, cue, cue word; watchword, password, formula, pet phrase, cliché; tag, epithet, name.

shield, *n.* **1.** buckler, pavis, pelta, *Class. Myth.* aegis, *Rom. Religion.* ancile, piece of armor.

2. protection, defense, guard, safeguard; protector, guardian, guardian angel, watchman, watchdog, sentry, sentinel.

—*v.* **3.** protect, run interference, defend, guard, shelter, screen; hide, conceal, cover, shroud, ensconce, bury, tuck away, keep out of sight.

shift, *v.* **1.** change direction, *Naut.* tack; move from one person to another, pass; move around, swerve around, get by, get around, outmaneuver.

2. *Usu.* **shift for** manage by oneself, make it on one's own, stand on one's own two feet, paddle one's own canoe, fend for oneself, take care of oneself, go it alone; get along, make do, get by, scrape by *or* along.

3. change gears, downshift.

4. change, exchange, make an exchange, commute, transpose, interchange, switch, swap, trade *or* trade in, substitute, replace.

5. transfer, relocate, move, send from one place to another, reassign; move around, rearrange, change around, change the place *or* position of, alter, vary.

—n. **6.** change, change of direction; maneuver, move, swerve; transfer, relocation, reassignment; rearrangement, alteration, variation.

7. spell of work, stint.

8. expedient, device, contrivance, resource, resort; plan, scheme, strategy, strategem, *Inf.* wrinkle, artifice, trick, *Inf.* flimflam, ruse, wile, trap; subterfuge, blind, *Inf.* dodge, fetch; feint, deception, sleight, move, evasion, shuffle.

9. change, exchange, commutation, transposition, interchange, switch, swap, trade *or* trade-in, substitution, replacement.

shiftless, *adj.* inefficient, lazy, idle, indolent, slothful, fainéant, do-nothing, otiose; unindustrious, unenterprising, unambitious, nonaggressive; listless, *Dial.* limpsy, lackadaisical, insouciant, pococurante, easygoing, *Sl.* laid-back; slack, lax, careless, negligent, neglectful, remiss, derelict; worthless, good-for-nothing, ne'er-do-well.

shifty, *adj.* **1.** tricky, crafty, artful, cunning, sly, wily, subtle, foxy, sly as a fox, *Scot. and North Eng.* pawky; shrewd, *Archaic.* parlous, sharp, astute, wary, *Inf.* cagey; evasive, elusive, hard to catch, slippery, smooth, slick; insidious, guileful, disingenuous, scheming, plotting, designing, calculating, contriving; deceptive, deceitful, crooked, dishonest, underhanded, *Inf.* left-handed; false, false-hearted, double-dealing, two-faced, Janus-faced.

2. resourceful, clever, ingenious, inventive, Daedalian.

shilly-shally, *v.* **1.** vacillate, yo-yo, seesaw, teeter-totter; waver, be indecisive, be irresolute, hesitate, hem and haw; go back and forth, fluctuate, oscillate, alternate, blow hot and cold, tergiversate, straddle the fence.

—n. **2.** irresolution, indecision, undecisiveness, uncertainty, hesitation, hesitancy, hemming and hawing, wavering; vacillation, fluctuation, oscillation, alternation, blowing hot and cold, tergiversation, fence-straddling, fence-sitting.

—adj. **3.** shilly-shallying, irresolute, undecided, uncertain, unsure, hesitant, hesitating, wavering; vacillating, fluctuating, oscillating, alternating, blowing hot and cold, tergiversating, sitting on *or* straddling the fence.

shimmer, *v.* **1.** glow, gleam faintly, shine; luminesce, incandesce, phosphoresce, make radiant *or* lustrous; illuminate, illumine, *Archaic.* illume, *Obs.* enlumine; brighten, light up, cast light upon, make brilliant *or* luminous; radiate, irradiate, effulge; shine forth, beam, stream.

2. glint, glimmer, glisten, *Archaic.* glister, glitter, twinkle, sparkle; spark, scintillate, flame; flash, fulgurate, gleam, coruscate, glare; flicker, flutter, flare *or* flare up, waver, sway; quiver, shiver, ripple; oscillate, vacillate, fluctuate, move to and fro; quaver, shake, quake, tremble, twitter, shudder; undulate, vibrate, pulsate, throb; jerk, twitch, vellicate, jump.

—n. **3.** glow, afterglow, faint gleam *or* glare, shine; luster, iridescence, incandescence, phosphorescence, radiance; brilliance, illumination, luminosity, luminance; refulgence, refulgency, refulgentness, effulgence; beam, ray, shaft, streak, patch, subdued *or* tremulous light.

4. glint, glimmer, glistening, glistering; twinkling, glittering, sparkling, unsteady light; flame, spark, scintilla, scintillation; flash, fulguration, gleam, coruscation, glare; flickering, fluttering, flaring, wavering, swaying; quivering, shivering, rippling; oscillation, oscillating, vacillation, vacillating, fluctuation, fluctuating, movement to and fro; quavering, shaking, quaking, trembling, twittering, shuddering; undulation, vibration, vibrating, pulsation, pulsating, throbbing; jerking, twitching, vellication, jumping.

shine, *v.* **1.** glow, radiate, irradiate, illuminate; glare, beam, gleam, gloze, streak, flash, coruscate, fulgurate; light, light up, luminesce, incandesce, phosphoresce; glimmer, glitter, shimmer, flicker, twinkle; sparkle, glint, glisten, *Archaic.* glister, dazzle; flare, spark, flutter, scintillate; flame, blaze, burn.

2. (*all of people*) radiate, glow, look healthy, bloom; look good, look like a million dollars, take the breath away.

3. excel, tower above, be head and shoulders above, dominate; be conspicuous, stand out, stand out in the crowd; outshine, throw into the shade, eclipse, shadow.

4. polish, wax, buff, burnish, rub down; gloss, luster, brighten, glaze, *Scot. and North Eng.* sheen; scour, scrub, clean.

5. **shine up to** *Slang.* attempt to impress [s.o.], curry favor, *Inf.* run after, make up to, play up to, *Sl.* suck up to; fawn upon, fall all over, throw oneself at the feet of, kowtow; get on the good *or* right side of.

—n. **6.** radiance, brightness, vividness, intensity, richness; splendor, resplendence, brilliance, effulgence, refulgency; illumination, flash, glare, beam, ray; shimmer, flicker, twinkle, glitter, glimmer, sparkle, glint, glistening.

7. luster, gloss, sheen, shimmer; polish, glaze.

8. *Informal.* prank, caper, escapade, trick, antic, joke, practical joke, shenanigan, lark.

9. **come rain or shine** no matter what, whatever may happen, come what may, whatever the cost *or* risk, without fail, come hell or high water, if worst comes to worst, live or die, sink or swim.

10. **take a shine to** *U.S. Informal.* take a liking to, like, take to, have a fancy for, *Inf.* cotton to, fancy, want to get to know better.

shiny, *adj.* glossy, glowing, lustrous, nitid, gleaming, agleam, sheenful, sheeny, burnished, polished, waxed; glassy, glistening, aglisten, shining, silken, smooth, sleek, satiny; bright, radiant, irradiant, effulgent, lambent, resplendent, beaming, beamy, beamish; dazzling, fulgent, glimmering, aglimmer; sparkling, scintillating, scintillant, coruscating, shimmering, glittering, fulgid, rutilant.

ship, *n.* **1.** liner, steamer, ferry, ark, *Inf.* windjammer; slipper, schooner, galleon, cutter, *Naut.* ketch, *Naut.* brigantine, *Naut.* brig, *Naut.* bark, *Naut.* barkentine; freighter, merchantman, carrack, barge, whaler, *Eastern U.S.* smack; vessel, tartan, junk, man-of-war, caravel; argosy, merchant ship, corsair; *Naut.* galley, *Naut.* galleass, galiot, *Class. Hist.* trireme; *Naut.* catamaran, float, raft; yacht, houseboat, packet, sailboat, sloop, dory, pinnace.

—v. **2.** freight, barge, ferry, boat; transport, convey, carry, dispatch, send; cart, haul, move, bear, transplant, transmit.

3. *Informal.* send packing, send off, get rid of, send away.

4. embark, set sail, ship out, take off.

shirk, *v.* **1.** (*all of work, responsibility, etc.*) evade, avoid, run from, dodge, whiffle, side-step, elude, weasel out; shrink from, *Inf.* funk, blench at, blink at; sneak off, sneak out the back way, make oneself scarce, take off, take a walk; play truant, stay out, skip, *Sl.* cut, *Sl.* bag, shuffle off to Buffalo; get out of, slip out of, slide out of, sneak out of, *Inf.* pass the buck.

2. malinger, call in sick, feign illness; loaf, *Sl.* goldbrick, *Sl.* goof off, *Brit.* skulk, *Sl.* mess *or* fool around, *Sl.* screw around; slack, lie down on the job, *Brit. Sl.* scrimshank, cop out; look busy, *Inf.* boondoggle, feign interest, *Sl.* featherbed, *Sl.* dog it; procrastinate, put off; neglect, close one's eyes to, ignore; default, abandon, leave undone.

—*n.* **3.** shirker, malingerer. See **shirker.**

shirker, *n.* shirk, malingerer, *Brit.* skulker, *Brit. Sl.* scrimshanker, *Inf.* soldier, *Inf.* goldbricker, *Brit. Sl.* skiver, clock watcher, *Sl.* goof-off, *Inf.* boondoggler; slacker, procrastinator, idler, layabout, loafer, fainéant, trifler, Micawber; avoider, evader, deserter, absconder; truant, absentee, dodger, defaulter, neglector; sponger, sponge, *Sl.* schnorrer, *Inf.* deadbeat.

shiver[1], *v.* **1.** tremble, quiver, quaver, quake, shake, shudder, twitter; vibrate, rattle, chatter; convulse, commove, vellicate, twitch; flutter, splutter; shimmy, wiggle; pulsate, pulse, throb, palpitate.

—*n.* **2.** tremble, quiver, shudder; quaver, quake; sputter, splutter, flutter, flicker.

3. *Usu.* **the shivers** the shakes, chills, *Inf.* the creeps, goose pimples, goose bumps.

shiver[2], *v.* **1.** break into pieces, splinter, split, split up, shatter, explode, rupture, blast; fragment, chip, crumble, crack off; chisel, whittle, hew.

—*n.* **2.** splinter, sliver, shive, shaving, flake; slice, rasher, *Brit. Dial.* collop; fragment, shard, snip, snippet; piece, cantle, corner.

shivery[1], *adj.* shuddering, shivering, trembling, quivering, quavering, quaking, shaking, twittering; vibrating, rattling, chattering; convulsing, vellicating, twitching; fluttering, spluttering; shimmying, wiggling; pulsating, pulsing, throbbing, palpitating.

shivery[2], *adj.* brittle, breakable, fragile, frangible, smashable, splintery, shattery, (*of wood*) brash; crumbly, friable, pulverulent, pulverable, pulverizable, powdery, triturable.

shock[1], *n.* **1.** blow, jar, jolt, turn, start, staggering blow; impact, brunt, clash, collision, crash, *Inf.* crack-up, *Inf.* smash-up, *Inf.* crunch; appulse, bump, encounter, jostle, jounce, brush, bounce, jerk; assault, attack, offense, insult.

2. agitation, perturbation, disturbance, distress; conflict, upset, turmoil; setback, comedown, check; surprise, amazement, astonishment, dismay; horror, fear, repulsion, revulsion.

3. earthquake, quake, vibration, shaking, quaking, tremor; explosion, blowup, detonation, blast, burst, shock wave, shock force; eruption, outburst, torrent, rush; disaster, calamity, catastrophe, cataclysm.

5. traumatism, trauma, state of shock, prostration, stupor, stupefaction; paralysis, stroke, concussion, breakdown, collapse; shell shock, battle fatigue.

5. startler, shocker, bolt out of the blue, thunderbolt, thunderclap, bomb, bombshell, blockbuster, earthshaker, eyeopener, revelation, *Inf.* switch, *Inf.* kicker, *Inf.* joker, *Inf.* kick in the teeth.

—*v.* **6.** stagger, bowl over, take one's breath away, boggle, boggle the mind, strike dumb, dumfound, overwhelm, bewilder, give a turn, confound, *Inf.* flabbergast; paralyze, stupefy, electrify, galvanize; revolt, repel, horrify, appall, make one's hair stand on end, make one's blood curdle *or* run cold, freeze the blood; jar, jolt, stun, shake, shake up, throw off, throw off balance, *Inf.* discombobulate; disgust, scandalize, raise eyebrows, offend; surprise, astonish, astound, startle; disturb, upset, perturb, stir, agitate; disquiet, discompose, unsettle, catch unprepared, catch off-guard, *Sl.* curl one's hair.

shock[2], *n.* **1.** bunch, stand, cluster, clump, tussock, hassock, stack, cock, rick, sheaf, mow, *Brit.* stook.

2. thatch, mass, pile, mop, mane, crop; tuft, hank, lock, knot, forelock, cowlick.

shocking, *adj.* **1.** surprising, astonishing, startling, astounding, electrifying, striking, amazing; unexpected, sudden, without notice *or* warning, like a bolt from the blue, incredible, breath-taking, stunning, paralyzing, stupefying, mind-boggling, *Inf.* mind-blowing.

2. horrifying, abominable, terrible, horrible, frightful, appalling, monstrous, awful; grisly, abhorrent, hideous, ghastly; fearful, direful, dreadful, horrid, horrific, dire, *Inf.* god-awful.

3. disgusting, offensive, outrageous, disgraceful, reprehensible, odious, revolting, obnoxious, repugnant, loathsome, repulsive; scandalous, lamentable, in poor taste, vulgar, shameless, intolerable, out of line, insufferable, unheard-of.

shoddy, *n.* **1.** imitation, imposter, dummy, pinchbeck, junk, plastic, tinsel, tickytacky, brummagem, bastard, whited *or* painted sepulcher; sham, deception, hoax, mockery, mock, make-believe, *Inf.* put-on, *Inf.* whitewash job; forgery, counterfeit, spurious article, fraud, *Inf.* fake, *Inf.* phony; cheat, swindle, *Inf.* flam, *Inf.* flimflam, *Sl.* rip-off, *Sl.* gyp, *Sl.* sell.

2. pretense, pretension, false pretense, simulation, dissimulation, dissemblance, dissembling, feigning; hypocrisy, insincerity, mere show, bluff, false front *or* appearance, façade, *Inf.* front, quackery, charlatanism, charlatanry; claptrap, humbug, humbuggery, cant, bunkum, *Sl.* bunk, moonshine, eyewash, hogwash, *Inf.* bosh, *Inf.* gammon, *Sl.* hooey, *Sl.* hoke *or* hokum, *Sl.* bull, *Sl.* baloney; deceit, dishonesty, fraudulence, fraudulency, *Inf.* fakery; trick, artifice, stratagem, deception, disguise.

—*adj.* **3.** imitation, artificial, sham, mock, pinchbeck, brummagem, bastard, quasi, pseudo, feigned, simulated, pretended; plastic, tawdry, tinsel, *Sl.* tickytacky; meretricious, pretentious, showy, gaudy, flashy, flash; deceptive, tricky, specious, misleading, colorable, sophisticated, sophisticate; spurious, bogus, counterfeit, illegitimate, forged, false, fraudulent, fictitious, trumped-up, *Inf.* fake, *Inf.* phony.

shoe, *n.* **1.** footwear, footgear, sandal, slipper, oxford, brogue, brogan, blucher, sabot; buskin, chopine, balmoral, boot; loafer, moccasin, bootee; clog, pump, *Trademark.* Mary Janes; house slipper, scuff, mule; tennis shoe, sneak, sneakers; clodhoppers, *Sl.* gunboats, dancing slippers, ballerinas, spikes, *Inf.* highheels, *Inf.* lowheels, *Inf.* flats.

2. fill [s.o.'s] shoes substitute for, *Inf.* sub for, fill in for, double for, stand *or* sit in for, *Inf.* pinch-hit, *Inf.* cover for; replace, supplant, supersede, succeed, take the place of, step into the shoes of.

3. ferrule, plate, cap, rim, boot, brake, runner, drag, skid.

shoemaker, *n.* bootmaker, booter, cobbler, shoe builder, crispin, *Scot. and North Eng.* souter.

shoestring, *n.* **1.** shoelace, lace, tie, thong, fastener, *Archaic.* latchet.

2. pittance, trifling amount, a string and a prayer, little bit, tight budget, next to nothing, mere subsistence, small change, nickles and dimes, pennies, scratch, *Sl.* peanuts, *Sl.* chicken feed, *Sl.* small potatoes; slave wages, meager earnings, barely enough to scrape *or* get by on, not enough to live on; mite, modicum, barely anything.

shoot, *v.* **1.** hit, wound, hurt, harm, damage, injure; shoot down, bring down, drop, fell; riddle, *Sl.* pump full of lead, *Sl.* zap, pick off; kill, slay, *Sl.* knock off, *Sl.* snuff out.

2. send forth, discharge, fire *or* fire off, let fly, let off, eject; project, propel, throw, cast, sling, fling, toss, heave, chuck, catapult, launch.
3. fire at *or* on, shoot at, snipe at, aim at, draw *or* get a bead on; open fire, bombard, shell, pepper, pelt, blitz, barrage, *Sl.* blast.
4. direct, send, throw, flash.
5. hunt, stalk, course, chase, pursue.
6. move suddenly, start, spring, leap, spurt, dash ahead, pass; dart, whisk, whiz, tear, rush, fly; bound, run, sprint, race, speed, hie, hasten, hurry, post; scoot, scud, scuttle, *Inf.* skedaddle.
7. variegate, diversify, streak, stripe, striate, interweave.
8. *Often* **shoot out** reach out, stretch out, stick out, put out, throw out.
9. put forth buds *or* shoots, burgeon, sprout, germinate, pullulate, come up *or* forth, spring up, arise; grow, develop, flourish, thrive, luxuriate, mushroom, boom.
10. detonate, explode, set off, *Obs.* detonize.
11. extend, jut out, project, protrude, bulge out, stick out.
12. flow through, permeate, pervade, penetrate, pierce, pass through.
13. **shoot at** *or* **for** *Informal.* strive toward *or* for, try for, aim for, set one's sights on.
—*n.* **14.** (*all of plants*) bud, burgeon, sprout, sprig; stem, twig, small branch; offshoot, *Bot.* runner, *Bot.* stolon, *Bot.* sucker; scion, cutting, slip, *Hort.* graft.

shop, *n.* **1.** small store, retail store, shoeshop, *Sl.* headshop, boutique, clothing store; department.
2. workshop, studio, atelier.
3. plant, factory, business, office.
—*v.* **4.** window-shop, look to buy, be in the market for, search *or* hunt for.

shore[1], *n.* **1.** seashore, seaside, beach, strand, seacoast, coast, seaboard; foreshore, waterside, bank, *Fr. rive, Archaic.* rivage; margin, border, edge, brink, *Archaic.* brim.
2. land, dry land, ground.

shore[2], *n.* **1.** support, prop, strut, brace, buttress, stay, underpinning, reinforcement.
—*v.* **2.** *Usu.* **shore up** support, hold up, prop up, underpin, reinforce, strengthen, brace, buttress.

short, *adj.* **1.** little, small, *Chiefly Scot.* wee, miniature, miniscule, minikin, diminutive, *Scot.* cutly; tiny, elfin, bantam, slight, (*of women*) petite, Lilliputian, *Inf.* Tom Thumb, *Sl.* pint-sized, *Sl.* pocket-sized, *Sl.* sawed-off, *Sl.* knee-high to a grasshopper, dwarfish, runty, runtish, pygmy; atomic, amoebic; squat, stunted, stubby, dumpy, truncated, (*of trees or shrubbery*) pollard.
2. momentary, temporary, impermanent. See **short-lived.**
3. concise, succinct, brief, to the point, short-winded, straightforward, direct, pointed, emphatic; abbreviated, abridged, compressed, summarized, thumbnail, condensed, curtailed, curtate, contracted, *Obs.* breviate; compact, lean, bare, close, neat; comprehensive, summary, synoptic, *Inf.* meaty; pithy, sententious, epigrammatic, crisp, precise, exact, gnomic; laconic, terse, elliptical, breviloquent, *Rare.* pauciloquent.
4. curt, sharp, abrupt. See **short-tempered.**
5. inadequate, insufficient, lacking, wanting, in arrears, short-handed, missing, shy; meager, sparse, scanty, unplentiful, scarce, tight, slender, slim, lean, thin, scraggy; below standard, poor, low, deficient, defective, failed.
6. *Cookery.* (*all of pastry*) crumbly, flaky, crusty, crispy.
7. (*all of metals*) brittle, friable, breakable, fragile, frangible, fissile, shivery.
8. *Chiefly Brit.* (*all of whiskey*) undiluted, unmixed, uncut, straight, straight-up.
9. *Ceramics.* stiff, hard, rigid, inflexible, unpliable, unpliant, impliant, inelastic, inductile; brittle, friable, fissile, shivery.
10. **short and sweet** pleasantly *or* appropriately brief, concise, succinct, direct, straightforward; apt, appropriate, pertinent, to the point.
11. **short of** **a.** less than, inferior to. **b.** poor, deficient, lacking, wanting, missing. **c.** excluding, disregarding, not counting, leaving out; besides, other than, apart from, aside from.
—*adv.* **12.** abruptly, suddenly, all of a sudden, unexpectedly, without warning, out of the blue; instantly, hastily, posthaste, quickly, swiftly, rapidly, fast, hurriedly, forthwith.
13. briefly, concisely, succinctly, directly, pointedly; curtly, sharply, tersely, tartly, rudely, brusquely, gruffly.
14. not far enough, this side of, on the near side of; prematurely, precipitately, beforehand, too soon, too early, too hastily; inopportunely, untimely.
15. **cut short** terminate, stop, stop short, stop in the midst of, arrest, halt, cut off; interrupt, interfere, intermit, interpose, cut in on, break in upon, butt in.
16. **sell short** *Informal.* disparage, deprecate, demean, belittle, deflate, derogate, detract, depreciate, devaluate, talk down, put down; underestimate, dispraise, minimize, slight, underrate, undervalue, underreckon, beggar, extenuate, misprize, think nothing of, set no store by, fail to count on.
—*n.* **17.** gist, essence, sum and substance, long and short; effect, drift, sense, spirit, import, tenor, purport, significance, implication, burden; pith, core, heart, marrow, main point, essential part.
18. **shorts** **a.** bermudas, short pants, culottes, *Inf.* cut-offs, *Inf.* short shorts, hot pants. **b.** underpants, underwear, underdrawers, drawers, briefs, *Sl.* skivvies, *Sl.* undies, *Trademark.* BVDs, *Trademark.* Fruit of the Looms, trunks, boxer shorts, jockey shorts, *Brit.* y-fronts, *Brit.* knickers; panties, bloomers. **c.** knickerbockers, knickers, breeches, knee breeches, *Brit.* plus-fours, *Inf.* trousers, clamdiggers. **d.** (*all of manufacturing or cutting processes*) remnants, remainders, debris, scraps, fragments, shavings, chips, parings; discards, discharge, refuse, waste, garbage.
19. *Motion Pictures.* short subject, documentary, travelogue, cartoon; preview, trailer.
20. deficiency, insufficiency, deficit. See **shortage.**
21. *Chiefly Brit.* (*all of whiskey*) shot, jigger, gill, measure, single, *Sl.* a finger or two, *Sl.* nip, *Sl.* quick one.
22. **in short** **a.** in summary, in conclusion, *Inf.* in a nutshell, all in all, in all, in the final analysis. **b.** in brief, in a word, in a few words, to put it briefly, to be brief, for shortness sake, to come to the point, to cut the matter short, to make a long story short.

shortage, *n.* deficiency, deficit, insufficiency, scarcity, sparsity, sparseness, straitness, scantiness, scantness, rareness; dearth, shortfall, lack, paucity, poorness, short, short supply, limitation, stint, meagerness, absence, emptiness, inanition, drought, famine, poverty, indigence, want, need; failure, inadequacy, (*of liquors or grains*) ullage.

shortcoming, *n.* failing, failure, deficiency, defect, frailty; weakness, liability, drawback, weak point, infirmity; flaw, imperfection, fault, foible.

shorten, *v.* **1.** abbreviate, condense, compress,

abridge, narrow, shrink, *Obs.* breviate; abstract, synopsize, summarize, digest, brief, epitomize.
2. reduce, lessen, decrease, contract, dock, curtail, limit, restrict; cut, cut down, cut short, retrench, crop, clip, shear, trim, prune, lop, pare down, (*of trees or shrubbery*) pollard; (*all of clothing*) hem, take up, take in, alter.

shorthand, *n.* **1.** stenography, phonography, (*in ancient Greece and Rome*) tachygraphy, *Obs.* brachygraphy; cryptography; pasigraphy.
2. *Figurative.* code, cipher, symbols, *Obs.* polygraphy.

short-lived, *adj.* momentary, temporary, of brief duration, impermanent, mortal, unenduring, brief, fleeting, passing, fading, transitory, transient, fugacious, caducous, deciduous, *Both Med.* monohemerous, monemerous; evanescent, ephemeral, mercurial, volatile, perishable, precarious; quick, fast, swift, sudden, brisk, fleet, meteoric; cursory, hurried, hasty.

shortly, *adv.* **1.** soon, presently, anon, directly, before long, *Inf.* before you know it, by and by, in a short while, in a little while.
2. briefly, concisely, succinctly, directly, pointedly.
3. abruptly, curtly, sharply, tersely; testily, tartly, rudely, brusquely, gruffly.

short-sighted, *adj.* **1.** myopic, purblind, near-sighted; weak-eyed, dim-eyed, mope-eyed, lazy-eyed; weak-sighted, dim-sighted, partially-sighted, half-blind.
2. unthinking, thoughtless, unmindful, heedless, regardless; reckless, rash, brash, headlong, pell-mell, precipitate, incautious, unwary, improvident; inattentive, unobservant, unwatchful, careless, negligent, neglectful, uncircumspect, imprudent, *Inf.* unable to see beyond the end of one's nose; impolitic, injudicious, ill-advised, ill-considered.

short-tempered, *adj.* curt, sharp, abrupt, short-spoken, rudely brief; cutting, biting, sarcastic, acute, keen; caustic, acrimonious, virulent, mordant, trenchant, sullen, tart, petulant, sour, splenetic, choleric, acetose; testy, edgy, touchy, grouchy, irascible, short-fused, crabbed, crabby, peevish, snapping, snarling, growling, bearish, currish, waspish; brusque, brash, gruff, peppery, surly, crusty, thorny; unmannerly, discourteous, rude, impolite, ungraceful; stern, austere.

short-winded, *adj.* **1.** breathless, out of breath, short of breath, pursy, winded; panting, huffing, puffing, gasping, heaving; wheezing, (*usu of horses*) broken-winded, *Pathol.* dyspneal.
2. concise, succinct, brief, to the point, short and sweet; direct, pointed, emphatic, straightforward; pithy, sententious, epigrammatic, crisp, precise, exact, gnomic; laconic, terse, elliptical, breviloquent, *Rare.* pauciloquent.

shorty, shortie, *n.* *Informal.* **1.** midget, dwarf, homunculus, *Chiefly Scot.* wee fellow *or* lad, little man; pygmy, manikin, Tom Thumb, Lilliputian, dapperling, fingerling, chit, cock-sparrow, hop-o'-my-thumb, *Obs.* pigwidgin *or* pigwidgeon, *Archaic.* dandiprat; shrimp, runt, *Inf.* peewee, *Inf.* squirt, *Inf.* pip-squeak, *Inf.* half pint, small fry.
2. bed jacket, hospital smock, apron; miniskirt, hot pants; nightgown, negligee, peignoir, *Inf.* nightie, *Inf.* baby dolls; jacket, *Brit.* jerkin, bomber jacket, waistcoat.
—adj. **3.** (*all of clothing*) abbreviated, short, slight, scanty, meager, *Inf.* barely there.

shot¹, *n.* **1.** crack, report, discharge; blast, explosion, detonation; bang, boom, burst, eruption, crash.
2. ball, Minié ball, pellet, bullet, slug; missile, projectile, ammunition, *Inf.* ammo; cannonball; *Archaic.* grapeshot, *Archaic.* grape.
3. marksman, sharpshooter, rifleman, bersagliere; good shot, crack shot, dead shot, *Sl.* deadeye.
4. attempt, effort, endeavor, go, try, *Inf.* the old college try, *Inf.* stab, *Inf.* crack, *Inf.* whack.
5. comment, remark, statement, utterance, word, pot shot, *Sl.* cheap shot, *Sl.* low blow.
6. guess, conjecture, supposition, assumption, presumption, hypothesis, postulate, See also **shot** (*def.* **15**).
7. injection, booster, booster shot, inoculation, vaccine, vaccination; dose, overdose, *Sl.* fix, *Sl.* hit, *Sl.* bang.
8. (*all of liquor*) drink, nip, spot, tot, jigger, *Inf.* finger or two; sip, sup, *Inf.* swig, *Inf.* swill, *Inf.* pull, *Inf.* snort, *Inf.* jolt; swallow, *Inf.* slug, *Inf.* guzzle, *Inf.* gargle.
9. photograph, *Inf.* photo, picture, snapshot, *Inf.* snap, *Inf.* candid.
10. wager, gamble, bet, risk, hazard, chance; venture, speculation, *Inf.* flier, *Inf.* plunge, *Brit. Inf.* birl; pot luck, blind bargain, sight-unseen transaction, pig in a poke.
11. **by a long shot** **a.** far and away, by far, by a great deal; indubitably, undoubtedly, unquestionably, incontestably, without doubt *or* question, *Inf.* in everybody's book. **b.** by no means, under no circumstances, on no account, not in the least, not at all, never, noway, nowise, *Inf.* nohow, *Sl.* forget it; nowhere near, not nearly.
12. **call the shots** *Slang.* direct, administer, dispose, make decisions, run the show, quarterback, *Inf.* call the plays; dominate, domineer, boss, ride herd on; control, regulate, rule, rule the roost; be in command, be in control, be in the driver's seat *or* saddle, be at the helm, have the upper hand, hold all the cards, *Inf.* wear the pants *or* trousers.
13. **like a shot** like a flash, with the speed of light, *Inf.* like greased lightning, *Inf.* like a house afire; instantly, instantaneously, immediately; quickly, hastily, hurriedly; swiftly, speedily.
14. **shot in the arm** *Slang.* stimulus, incentive, impetus, fillip, provocative, motive, whet; incitement, inducement, instigation, excitement, provocation, motivation, encouragement.
15. **shot in the dark** *Slang.* wild guess, random, guess, pot shot, *Sl.* guesstimate. See also **shot** (*def.* **6**).

shot², *adj.* **1.** (*all of textiles*) variegated, varicolored, multicolored, many-colored.
2. ruined, wrecked, beyond repair; dead, defunct; spent, exhausted, worn-out, *Inf.* used-up; *All Sl.* sunk, cooked, kaput, fini, done in, done for, SOL.

shoulder, *n.* **1.** projection, protuberance, protrusion, prominence, salient, abutment; shelf, shelve, ledge, sill, hob, mantel, mantelpiece.
2. **put one's shoulder to the wheel** strive, endeavor, apply oneself, exert oneself; set to work, roll up one's sleeves, get busy, *Inf.* buckle down, *Inf.* knuckle down.
3. **rub shoulders with** hobnob with, mingle with, mix with, associate with, keep company with, touch elbows with, *Inf.* take up with, *Inf.* hang around *or* out with, *Inf.* pal around with.
4. **shoulder to shoulder** jointly, together, cooperatively, in cooperation, in partnership; side by side, arm in arm, cheek by jowl, back to back, hand in hand; in unison, in close harmony, in company with.
5. **straight from the shoulder** directly, straightforwardly, frankly, candidly, man-to-man, heart-to-heart; plainly, explicitly, unequivocally, unambiguously; freely, boldly, outspokenly, unabashedly, uninhibitedly; bluntly, bluffly, brusquely, tactlessly.
—v. **6.** push, shove, jostle, See **shove** (*def.* **2**).
7. carry, take up, bear; support, maintain, sustain, brace, prop, uphold, hold up, keep up; bolster, rein-

force, strengthen.

8. assume responsibility, take *or* accept responsibility, take upon oneself, commit oneself.

shout, *v.* **1.** yell, yelp, yap, bray, bay, bellow, howl, roar, scream, *Inf.* holler; vociferate, cry out, call out, sing out, *Sl.* belt out; cry aloud, cry at the top of one's lungs *or* voice, rend the air, awake the dead; cheer, root, huzzah, *Australian., Brit.* barrack.

2. clamor, make *or* raise a clamor, make a racket, kick up a racket, make an uproar, raise the roof, raise Cain, whoop it up.

—n. **3.** cry, call, yell, yelp, yap, bay, bray, bellow, howl; outcry, exclamation, ejaculation, outburst, burst, blurt; cheer, hurrah, huzzah, whoop, *Inf.* holler, *Inf.* whoop and holler; battle cry, war cry, war whoop, rallying cry; hunting cry, *Chiefly Brit.* tallyho, *Fox Hunting.* huic, *Fox Hunting, Rare.* yoicks.

4. clamor, racket, din, noise, clangor, clap; hue and cry, vociferation, flap, uproar, hullaballoo, hubbub, ballyhoo.

shove, *v.* **1.** push, propel, move; thrust, pole, stick; drive, trundle, wheel, roll.

2. jostle, jolt, jog, shoulder, bump into, knock against; press forward, make one's way, squeeze through, wedge, elbow, elbow one's way, fight one's way, force one's way; butt, bunt, ram, bulldoze; crowd, pack, cram, jam; nudge, poke.

3. shove off a. put to sea, put off *or* out, push off, get under way, hoist the blue peter. **b.** *Slang.* depart, leave, go, go away, go off, *Inf.* buzz off, *Inf.* take off, *Inf.* clear out, *Sl.* split, *Sl.* scram, *Sl.* beat it, *Sl.* vamoose.

—n. **4.** jostle, jog, jolt, butt, bunt; push, thrust; impulsion, propulsion.

shovel, *n.* **1.** spade, scoop, spud, trowel.

2. power shovel, steam shovel, bulldozer, *Sl.* dozer, *Trademark.* Caterpillar, *Sl.* Cat; backhoe; snowplow, plow.

—v. **3.** dig, dig up, spade, spud, scoop, scoop up; excavate; gouge, furrow, trench, groove.

show, *v.* **1.** exhibit, display, present, demonstrate, set forth, offer; put in plain sight, bare, lay bare, unveil, unscreen, uncover, undrape.

2. indicate, express, manifest, make plain *or* clear; expose, reveal, betray, give away; evince, evidence, exemplify, *Scot. and North Eng.* kithe; produce, bring forward, bring out, roll out, *Inf.* trot out.

3. escort, usher, conduct, pilot, steer, guide, lead, direct; chaperon, matronize, accompany; attend, assist, aid.

4. explain, define, interpret, explicate, expound, point out; simplify, make plain, unfold, put across, spell out; clarify, elucidate, clear up, resolve, solve; illustrate, throw *or* shed light on; describe, account for, give the facts, tell the whole story.

5. prove, authenticate, document, substantiate; verify, corroborate, confirm; certify, uphold, validate, bear out.

6. inform, tell, express, state; teach, instruct, tutor, indoctrinate; give an idea of, let [s.o.] in on.

7. be visible, appear, be in view, be seen; come into view, come in sight, become visible; arise, crop up, loom up.

8. show off flaunt, parade, brandish; make a big deal, *Sl.* showboat; be vain, be ostentatious; swagger, strut, strut one's stuff, peacock; pose, posture, grandstand, swank; put on airs, give oneself airs, *Inf.* put up a front, *Sl.* dog it, *Sl.* hotdog, *Sl.* put on the dog; talk big, name-drop, boast, gasconade, *Inf.* go on about [s.t.].

9. show up a. expose, reveal, give away. See **show** (*defs.* **1, 2**). **b.** appear, look, strike one as, come across. **c.** *Informal.* come, arrive, land; get here, pull in, *Sl.* make it. **d.** *Informal.* outdo, outshine, outdazzle, outglitter, upstage; overshadow, tower above, eclipse, dwarf.

—n. **10.** display, exhibition, array, arrangement, presentation, demonstration; manifestation, evincement, disclosure, revelation, exposure, uncovering.

11. ostentation, pretension, pretense, ritz, splash; blazon, spectacle, parade, pageant, pageantry, ceremony; pomp, magnificence, grandeur, splendor, glitter, pizzazz, flourish; affectation, airs, *Sl.* dog, pretentiousness, artificiality, affectedness; theatricality, histrionics, melodramatics; foppery, peacockery, dandyism, flaunting.

12. appearance, posture, stance, stand; bearing, presence, carriage, demeanor, port; mien, look, visage, countenance; cast, attitude, air.

13. indication, trace, tinge, spark, flash, glimmer, whisper, vestige; mark, evidence, track, trail, scent, symptom; sign, cue, clue; intimation, hint, suggestion, suspicion, inkling, implication; idea, notion; taste, touch.

14. theatrical performance, production, presentation, *Music.* gig; premiere, matinée; exhibition, exhibit, showing, exposition.

15. *Informal.* chance, opportunity, try.

16. run the show manage, take charge of, direct, command, govern, rule; oversee, regulate, supervise, head; dominate, hold the reins, be in charge.

17. steal the show usurp credit, be the main attraction, be the center of attraction, get all the attention; stand out, be the best.

showdown, *n.* confrontation, face-off; settlement, crisis, climax, turning point; contest, battle, encounter, conflict.

shower, *n.* **1.** sprinkle, sprinkling, mist, misting, drizzle, drizzling, *Chiefly Dial.* mizzling, spatter, spattering, sparge, sparging, spit, spitting, flurry; raindrops, rainfall, rain shower, wet.

2. spray, hail, torrent, pouring, downpour, cloudburst, *Archaic.* aspersion; barrage, volley, bombardment, salvo.

3. abundance, plenty; profusion, flood, deluge, gush, overflow, plethora, effusiveness, surplus, excess, nimiety, superabundance, superfluity; bounty, copiousness, opulence, lavishment, lavishness, extravagance, prodigality.

4. party, bridal shower, baby shower.

5. douse, dousing, rinse, rinsing, shower bath; bath, wash, washing, cleaning.

6. sprinkler, sprayer, sparger, nozzle, shower head, shower stall.

—v. **7.** wet, rinse, douse, drench; bathe, wash, clean.

8. spray, hail, snow, spit, sparge; barrage, bombard, volley; fall, descend.

9. snow under, drown, flood, deluge, gush, overflow; inundate, whelm, overwhelm, teem; lavish, indulge.

10. sprinkle, drizzle, mist, *Chiefly Dial.* mizzle, spatter, flurry, *Scot.* dribble, trickle, rain.

show-off, *n.* **1.** exhibitionist, extrovert, *Sl.* grandstander, *Sl.* hot dog, *Sl.* hotshot, *Sl.* show-boat; dandy, fop, clotheshorse, coxcomb, peacock.

2. snob, name-dropper, prig, high-hatter.

3. blusterer, swaggerer, strutter, gascon, fanfaron, trumpeter, tooter; blowhard, windbag, blatherskite, *Sl.* gas bag, *Sl.* big-mouth; bluffer, humbug, four-flusher; loudmouth, braggart, braggadocio, brag, coaster, *Sl.* bullshooter, Thraso, Rodomonte.

showy, *adj.* **1.** flamboyant, ornate, elaborate, involved, *Music.* bravura; fancy, florid, flowery, highwrought; conspicuous, striking, imposing, obvious.

2. ostentatious, fastuous, pretentious, doggy, affected; over-wrought, overdone, extreme, frilly, overdecorated; artificial, surface, specious; glittering, theatrical, *Sl.* grandstand.

3. gaudy, garish, flashy, *Sl.* flash, loud, bold, hard, *Inf.* honky-tonk; tawdry, meretricious, cheap, dimestore, tinselly, gimcrack, trashy, *Inf.* chintzy, *Inf.* tacky, *Sl.* rinky-dink; tasteless, in bad taste, indelicate, crude, vulgar.

shred, *n.* **1.** bit, scrap, fragment, chip; splinter, sliver, snip, snippet; wisp, rag, tatter, corner; strip, slip, band, ribbon, shaving, filament; remnant, fraction, segment, snatch; modicum, iota, whit; mite, micron, molecule, atom, trace; speck, fly speck, grain, hair; scintilla, straw, cent, farthing.

—*v.* **2.** cut up, tear up, reduce to shreds; strip, rip, rip up, splinter, pound to shreds *or* splinters, shatter; grate, pulverize, powder, atomize, demolish.

shrew, *n.* virago, termagant, harpy, fury; vixen, spitfire, she-wolf, hell-cat, tigress; haridan, witch, orgress, old cat, brimstone; hag, crone, beldam, *Sl.* bitch; nag, *Inf.* biddy, *Inf.* old biddy; scold, common scold, fish wife; grouch, crab, grumbler; henpecker, fault-finder, rebuker, reviler, vituperator, chider, castigator, Xanthippe; complainer, caviler, whiner, *Yiddish.* kevtch, pest, *Sl.* pain in the neck, *Sl.* pain, *Sl.* old bag.

shrewd, *adj.* **1.** astute, acute, sharp, keen, *Archaic.* parlous, sharp as a tack; apt, agile, quick, ready, able, adept, proficient; discerning, discriminating, perceptive, perspicacious, *Inf.* cagey; wise, sagacious, intelligent, clever, smart, bright, luminous; ingenious, resourceful, inventive, creative, Daedalian.

2. artful, slick, quick-witted, cunning; canny, subtle, crafty, sly, wily, foxy; guileful, devious, deceitful, dishonest, crooked, unscrupulous; slippery, stealthy, tricky, scheming, designing, intriguing; circuitous, shifty, insidious; perfidious, treacherous, Machiavellian; expedient, oportunistic.

shrewish, *adj.* ill-humored, cranky, grumbling, petulant, peevish, whining, grouchy; continually complaining, full of complaints, nitpicking; castigating, vituperating, rebuking, nagging, scolding, chiding, fault-finding; quarrelsome, contentious, vixenish; termagant, volcanic, peppery, hot-tempered, discordant; fractious, polemical, unpeaceful, troublesome, troublemaking; pugnacious, argumentative, litigious, disputatious; obstreperous, refractory, contrary, perverse, pesky; blatant, blustering, loudmouthed, vociferous, brawling.

shriek, *n.* **1.** scream, shrill, screech, screak, *Scot. and North Eng.* skirl, squeal, squawk; cry, shout, whoop, *Inf.* holler, squall, yell.

—*v.* **2.** scream, shrill, screech, screak, *Scot. and North Eng.* skirl, squeal, squawk; cry, shout, whoop, *Inf.* holler, squall, yell.

shrill, *adj.* **1.** high-pitched, high, piercing, sharp, keen, acute; screechy, shrieky, ear-piercing, harsh, stridulous; loud, ear-splitting, intense, strong, forceful.

—*v.* **2.** shriek, scream, screech, screak. See **shriek** (*def.* **2**).

—*n.* **3.** shriek, scream, screech, screak. See **shriek** (*def.* **1**).

shrine, *n.* reliquary, repository, receptacle; tomb, sepulcher, burial chamber, mausoleum, aedicule; monument, cenotaph, (*in Buddist countries*) tope, stupa; church, temple, tabernacle, *Archaic.* fane, sanctuary, *Rom. Hist.* sacrarium, sacred *or* holy place.

shrink, *v.* **1.** draw back, shy away, recoil, start back; back away, move back, retreat, retire, withdraw; balk, hesitate; wince, flinch, cringe.

2. contract, narrow, shorten, constrict, lessen in size, become smaller *or* reduced; shrivel *or* shrivel up, pucker *or* pucker up, purse, wrinkle, buckle, fold *or* fold up, wither, dry up; decrease, diminish, reduce, dwindle, decline, drop *or* fall off.

shrinkage, *n.* shrink, contraction, constriction, narrowing, shortening; reduction, diminution, decrease, depreciation, lessening, dwindling, decline; loss, waste.

shrive, *v.* **1.** (*all of sinners*) impose penance on, penalize, punish, sentence.

2. (*all of penitents*) absolve, grant absolution, pardon, forgive, remit, excuse.

3. confess, make confession, do penance, declare one's sins, be penitent, repent; plead guilty, own up *or* to.

shrivel, *v.* shrink, contract, pucker, wrinkle; wither, dry up, desiccate, dehydrate; decline, fade, waste away. See also **shrink** (*def.* **2**).

shroud, *n.* **1.** winding sheet, sheet, wrap, wrapper, cerecloth, cloth, cerements, graveclothes.

2. cover, covering, pall, cloak, mantle, blanket, cloud; veil, screen, shield, mask, hood.

—*v.* **3.** (*all for burial*) enshroud, wrap, enwrap, sheet, cover, clothe.

4. cover, hide, conceal, shield, veil, keep dark; screen, curtain, shade, cloak, mask, hood, disguise, camouflage.

shrubbery, *n.* bushes, foundation plantings, plantings, hedges, hedging; underbrush, brushwood, thicket, brake, *Brit.* bracken, copse, *Chiefly Brit.* coppice.

shrug, *v.* **1.** show disdain, show indifference; toss one's head, turn aside.

2. shrug off disregard, overlook, ignore, take no notice of, close the eyes to, wink at; not trouble about, dismiss from one's thoughts, gloss over, pass over, let pass; minimize, make light of, sneeze at, de-emphasize, underplay, *Inf.* play down; (*all of illness*) throw off, weather, have a light case of, recover quickly from, bear well.

shudder, *v.* **1.** shiver, tremble, quiver, quaver, quake, shake, twitter; vibrate, rattle, chatter; convulse, commove, vellicate, twitch; flutter, splutter; shimmy, wiggle; pulsate, pulse, throb, palpitate.

—*n.* **2.** tremble, quiver, shiver; quaver, quake; vibration, convulsion; spasm, paroxysm, jerking, twitching, jerking; agitation, disquietude.

shuffle, *v.* **1.** shamble, scuff the feet, scrape, scrape along; drag, lag, linger, falter, flag; hobble, limp, hitch, scuttle.

2. hedge, equivocate, evade, elude, *Inf.* waffle; dodge, fence, shift, shy, parry; quibble, pettifog, beg the question, split hairs, beat around the bush; mislead, throw off the scent *or* trail, draw a red herring across the trail; distort, pervert, mince the truth, color, gloss over, refine, whitewash, clean up; lie, prevaricate, cavil.

3. intermix, interfile, intersperse, interchange; shift, shift about, shift around; tangle, entangle, jumble; mess, muss, clutter, litter, strew about; scatter, turn upside-down, turn topsy-turvy; disarrange, disorganize, discompose, displace; upset, dishevel, complicate, *Inf.* screw up, botch, muddle, *Sl.* muck up.

4. shuffle off a. thrust aside, put aside, cast aside; get rid of, discard, trade off. **b.** drag off, move slowly, move reluctantly; inch away, drag one's heels, *Inf.* mosey along.

—*n.* **5.** dragging gait, limp, hobble, hitch, stagger,

toddle.

6. evasion, evasive, trick, blind, guise, artifice, subterfuge; dodge, side-step, shift, feint, circumlocution, ruse; cloak, mask, sham, pretext, subtlety; prevarication, fib, white lie, distortion of the facts, circumvention; ambiguity, quirk, jesuitism, quibble, verbal retreat, backing down, reneging, *Sl.* welshing.

shun, *v.* eschew, avoid, steer clear of; have nothing to do with, refuse to touch with a 10-foot pole; abstain from, refrain from, forgo, forbear; shirk, evade, get out of, elude, keep one's distance, shrink from, shy away from, recoil, back away from, run away from, escape, flee from, keep out of the way of; snub, give [s.o.] the cold shoulder, *Inf.* cold-shoulder; spurn, rebuff, disdain, ignore, turn up one's nose at, disregard, turn away from.

shut, *v.* **1.** close, close up, close off, seal, seal up, seal off, occlude, obturate; lock, padlock, bolt, latch.

2. block, obstruct, occlude, barricade, blockade, stand in the way; stop, stay, arrest; clog, choke, congest, jam; impede, hinder, get in the way.

3. confine; imprison. See **shut** (*defs.* **7, 10a**).

4. bar. See **shut** (*def.* **9a**).

5. shut up shop, close shop, close down, close up, shutter, put up the shutters; close for the night, *Inf.* call it a day, lay off, *Inf.* knock off.

6. shut down *Informal.* discontinue, suspend, cease, halt, stop, drop, break off, leave off; strike, call a strike, go out on strike, walk out, stage a walk out.

7. shut in confine, enclose, keep in, quarantine, isolate; restrict, restrain, constrain, astrict, bind; circumscribe, hem in, pen in, fence, pale, picket, corral.

8. shut off a. turn off, close off, switch off, kill, cut. **b.** isolate, separate, part, divorce, estrange; alienate, segregate, sequester, cut off *or* out, send to Coventry.

9. shut out a. bar, exclude, omit, except, leave out, spurn, ostracize; reject, repudiate, debar, lock out, blackball; exile, banish, relegate, excommunicate, outlaw. **b.** hide, conceal, screen, veil, cover, *Inf.* cover up.

10. shut up a. cage, coop, coop up, box in, bottle up; jail, imprison, incarcerate, immure, intern, embar, clap up, *Sl.* jug, *Sl.* lag. **b.** *Informal.* be silent, keep one's mouth shut, hold one's tongue, keep still *or* quiet, seal one's lips, keep mum, *Sl.* keep one's trap *or* yap shut, *Sl.* dummy up, *Sl.* clam up, *Sl.* put the lid on, *Sl.* button one's lip. **c.** *Informal.* silence, put to silence, hush, shush, quiet, still; gag, muzzle, stifle, *Sl.* put the kibosh on.

—adj. **11.** closed, closed-up, closed-tight, shut tight; locked, latched, bolted, fixed, fastened, fast, secure.

shut-in, *adj.* **1.** house-bound, confined, *Inf.* confined to quarters, incarcerated, captive of one's surroundings; enclosed, hemmed in, kept in; cooped up, immured, locked up, shut away; constricted, restricted, helpless, laid up, bedridden, disabled, crippled, paralyzed, paralytic.

2. *Psychiatry.* introverted, solitary, inner-directed, private, withdrawn, isolated, catatonic.

—n. **3.** invalid, sickly person, infirm person, convalescent, valetudinarian; chronically ill person, severely handicapped person, cripple.

shutter, *n.* blind, shade, roman shade, venetian blind, storm shutter, vertical blind, roll-up blind.

shuttle, *v.* alternate, alternate between, pass back and forth, go back and forth between, shuttlecock, zigzag, trade off between, *Inf.* coast-hop, commute.

shy[1], *adj.* **1.** bashful, diffident, retiring, reserved, backward, unconfident, *Archaic.* verecund, *Scot. and North Eng.* blate; shrinking, withdrawn, distant, *Inf.* introverted, unsocial, unsociable; modest, meek, demure, coy; self-conscious, constrained; sheepish, shamefaced, blushing, embarrassed.

2. timid, timorous, tremulous, fearful, afraid, scared; apprehensive, anxious, nervous; cowardly, uncourageous.

3. reluctant, loath, averse, disinclined, indisposed; wary, heedful, cautious, careful, chary, leery, gingerly; suspicious, distrustful, cynical; precautious, prudent, circumspect, politic, guarded, noncommittal, evasive, discreet; demurring, grudging, unwilling, dissenting, opposing, adverse.

4. deficient, indebted, in debt, in arrears, behind, *Inf.* short.

5. (*all of plants and animals*) barren, unfruitful, infecund, unproductive, sterile, infertile, *Bot.* acarpous; scant, skimpy, meager, unprolific.

6. fight shy of avoid, evade, shy away from, elude, dodge, shun; escape, save oneself from, keep away from, steer clear of, balk at, sidestep, get around.

—v. **7.** start, jerk, draw back, recoil, take alarm, boggle; dodge, duck, dart, swerve, blench, flinch, quail; blink, *Inf.* bat, wince; react, rebound, spring back.

8. shrink, cower, cringe, *Inf.* get cold feet; waver, falter, hesitate, demur, scruple, stickle; avoid, evade, retreat.

—n. **9.** start, jerk, duck, dodge, flinch; wince, blink; recoil, reaction, rebound, springing back.

shy, *v.* **1.** cast, toss, pitch, fling, sling, flip, jerk, flirt, cant, dart, chuck, bowl, hurl, shoot, throw, propel.

—n. **2.** cast, toss, pitch, fling, flip, jerk, cant, chuck, sling, hurl, shot, heave, throw.

shyness, *n.* diffidence, self-consciousness, timidity, timorousness, hesitation, constraint; embarrassment, abashment, discomfort, uneasiness; modesty, reserve, demureness, coyness.

sibilant, *adj.* hissing, sibilous, sibilatory; wheezy, whispery, whistling

sibilate, *v.* hiss, lisp, rasp; wheeze, whistle, whiffle, whisper.

sibyl, *n.* prophetess, predictor, forecaster; medium, soothsayer, augur, diviner, oracle; fortune teller, crystal-gazer, pythoness, palmist, witch, sorceress; *Gk. Myth.* Pythia, *Gk. Myth.* Delphian sibyl; *Class. Myth.* Cassandra.

sick, *adj.* **1.** ill, ailing, unwell, unhealthy, sickly, delicate; indisposed, laid up, bedridden, infirm, valetudinarian, confined, shut-in; hurt, afflicted, injured, lame, disabled, crippled; not up to snuff, *Inf.* out of sorts, *Inf.* under the weather, on the sick list, *Inf.* down with the bug, *Sl.* off one's feed. See also **sickly** (*def.* **2**).

2. nauseated, queasy, *Sl.* barfy, sick to one's stomach, squeamish, qualmish, *Inf.* green around the gills; seasick, airsick, carsick.

3. sorrowful, grieving, suffering; troubled, miserable, wretched, heavy-laden, burdened, stricken; heartsick, heart-broken, sick at heart, pining, languishing.

4. shocked, repelled, offended, disturbed, revolted, appalled; upset, perturbed, annoyed, put out.

5. *Often* **sick of** tired, sick and tired, glutted, sated, cloyed, jaded, surfeited, satiated; *Inf.* fed up, *Inf.* fed *or* had it up to here.

6. deranged, mentally unsound, psychotic, severely neurotic, unbalanced, disturbed.

7. gruesome, sadistic, ghoulish, morbid; macabre, grotesque; frightful, shocking, repulsive; strange, bizarre, odd.

8. *Informal.* disgusted, chagrined, annoyed, *Inf.* put out, *Sl.* turned off.

sicken, *v.* **1.** nauseate, turn one's stomach, make one's gorge rise; make sick, infect, afflict, poison; debilitate, enervate, weaken, enfeeble, devitalize; impair, injure, wound, cripple, incapacitate; derange, craze, madden, disorder.

2. revolt, disgust, offend, repel, shock, appall, dismay; rankle, gall, annoy, irk, *Sl.* bug; weary, tire, cloy, surfeit, satiate, glut, jade.

3. take *or* fall sick, take *or* fall ill, take to one's bed; ail, come down with [s.t.], *Inf.* get the bug, *Inf.* have the mulligrubs; weaken, waste, fade, fail; droop, flag, pine.

sickening, *adj.* nauseating, nauseous, noisome, fulsome; distasteful, unpalatable, inedible, uneatable, *Sl.* stomach-turning; repulsive, offensive, disgusting, loathsome, detestable; revolting, off-putting, nasty, unpleasant, disagreeable; gross, vile, foul.

sickly, *adj.* **1.** sick, ailing, unwell. See **sick** (*def.* **1**).

2. unhealthy, chronically ill, *Pathol.* cachectic, frail, delicate; feeble, puny, weak, drooping, anemic, rundown, washed out; diseased, morbid; pale, wan, pallid, peaked, ashen, haggard, emaciated, gaunt, cadaverous; (*all in reference to illness*) susceptible, vulnerable, with no resistance.

3. mawkish, maudlin, sickening, sentimental; soupy, soppy, mushy.

sickness, *n.* **1.** disease, pathology, morbidity, distemper, *Pathol.* affection, *Pathol.* idiopathy; infection, virus, *Inf.* bug, *Inf.* mulligrubs; ailment, malady, disorder, complaint, illness, affliction, indisposition; ill health, unhealthiness, unsoundness, *Pathol.* cachexia; delicate constitution, frailty, delicacy, weakness; disability, handicap, impairment, injury, invalidism, valitudinarianism; mental disorder, derangement, neurosis, psychosis, madness, insanity.

2. nausea, queasines, upset stomach, indigestion, *Inf.* throw-ups, *Inf.* collywobbles; vomiting, throwing up, *Inf.* upchucking; sea *or* air *or* car *or* motion sickness.

side, *n.* **1.** border, edge, rim, margin, fringe, verge, brink, brim, skirt, flank.

2. phase, aspect, facet, angle, *Inf.* slant, *Inf.* twist; vantage point, standpoint, point of view, viewpoint, view.

3. (*all of a city*) quarter, section, division, precinct, part, part of town, neighborhood.

4. team, squad, string, (*in baseball*) nine, (*in basketball*) five, (*in American football* or *soccer*) eleven; party, faction, sect, caucus, wing, splinter group; interest, camp.

5. side by side jointly, conjointly, together, cooperatively, in cooperation, in partnership; shoulder to shoulder, arm in arm, hand in glove, cheek by jowl, back to back, hand in hand; in unison, in close harmony, *Latin. pari passu.*

—*adj.* **6.** lateral, flanking, bordering, skirting.

7. oblique, indirect; sidelong, sideways, sidewise, sidewards.

8. secondary, subordinate, auxiliary; incidental, extrinsic, extraneous, nonessential, adventitious; parenthetical, tangential, by-the-way; negligible, unimportant, of little *or* small *or* no importance, inconsequential, of little *or* no consequence, insignificant, inconsiderable, inappreciable.

—*v.* **9. side with** join, join with, unite with, go in with, *Inf.* go along with, *Inf.* throw in with, *Inf.* team up with, *Inf.* sink *or* swim with.

side-step, *v.* **1.** step aside, move off to the side; sidle, edge, skew, veer, go sideways, *Scot and North Eng.* sklent.

2. evade, avoid, dodge, *Inf.* duck, shun, steer clear of; hedge, equivocate, prevaricate, hem and haw, pussyfoot, *Inf.* waffle, *Inf.* weasel.

sidewalk, *n.* pavement, walk, *Inf.* byway, *Brit.* footpath, *Brit.* footway; promenade, esplanade, almeda, mall.

sideways, *adv.* obliquely, indirectly; sidewise, sidewards, sidelong, edgeways, edgewise; askew, asquint, awry, askant; laterally, off to the side, to one side, on the side of.

siege, *n.* **1.** blockade, besiegement, beleaguerment, investment, encirclement, envelopment, cutting off of supply lines.

—*v.* **2.** besiege, lay siege to, invest, contain, confine, cordon off; blockade; surround, encircle, encompass, hedge in, pen in, shut in, box in, bottle up.

sieve, *n.* **1.** strainer, sifter, filter, riddle, colander; screen, grate, grating.

—*v.* **2.** sift, strain. See **sift** (*def.* **1**).

sift, *v.* **1.** strain, sieve, riddle, bolt, filter, screen, pan, rack; separate, winnow.

2. scatter, sprinkle, spread.

3. examine, look into, scrutinize, question, search, investigate; study, analyze, test, review; ransack, rummage.

sigh, *v.* **1.** exhale, expire, breathe out, aspirate, *Chiefly Literary.* suspire; moan, sob, whine, wail; sough, rustle.

2. lament for, mourn for, grieve for, weep for; bemoan, bewail.

—*n.* **3.** deep breath, *Scot. and North Eng.* sough, *Chiefly Literary.* suspiration, whisper, exhalation; murmur, hiss, susurration, susurrus, rustle; sob, wail, moan, whine.

sight, *n.* **1.** vision, eyesight, eyes.

2. range *or* field of vision, eyeshot, eyereach, ken, view; gaze, look; inspection, scrutiny.

3. glimpse, brief look, look, glance, *Fr. aperçu, Scot.* glisk, *Fr. coup d'oeil, Inf.* once-over, *Inf.* looksee, *Sl.* gander, peek, peep.

4. judgment, opinion, observation, estimation, point of view; feeling, impression, perception.

5. spectacle, curiosity, rarity, nonesuch; marvel, wonder, miracle, phenomenon; quite a thing, really something, one for the books, something to write home about.

6. *Chiefly Dialect.* a great deal, lots, a lot, tons, loads, heaps, piles, slews.

7. sighthole, peep sight, open sight, telescopic sight, bead.

8. at first sight a. at the first glimpse, at once, at the first blush, on the spot. **b.** apparently, ostensibly, to all appearances, to the eye, on the surface, on the face of it.

9. catch sight of see, get a glimpse of, *Sl.* get a load of, take in, look on *or* upon, set *or* lay eyes on, see with one's own eyes; glance, look quickly *or* briefly, cast a brief look at.

10. not by a long sight *Informal.* probably not, hardly, not likely; definitely not, no way, not in a million years.

11. out of sight a. beyond range of vision, out of range, imperceptible, unseeable, sightless; remote, far away, in the distance. **b.** beyond reason, unreasonable, unconscionable; preposterous, outrageous, ridiculous, absurd; out of the question, not worth considering *or* talking about. **c.** exorbitant, expensive, extravagant, inordinate, immoderate. **d.** *Slang.* extraordinary, *Sl.* far out, unreal, outrageous, neat, *Sl.* cool, out of the ordinary.

—*v.* **12.** see, view, behold, catch sight of, look at, *Inf.* lay eyes on, *Inf.* eyeball, *Sl.* lamp; observe, witness, look on, survey, scan; scrutinize, inspect, pour over, peer at; stare at, goggle, gawk at, ogle.

13. glimpse, glance, catch sight of. See **sight** (*def.* **9**).

14. aim, take aim, *Inf.* draw a bead on, aim at.

sightless, *adj.* **1.** blind, visionless, unsighted, unseeing, eyeless, stone-blind, amaurotic; purblind, partially sighted, blear-eyed, *Opthalmol.* hemeralopic, *Opthalmol.* nyctalopic.

2. invisible, imperceivable, imperceptible, indiscernible, indistinguishable, unseeable; unnoticeable, unapparent; unseen, unbeheld.

sightseer, *n.* tourist, *Sl.* Kodak carrier, traveler, excursionist, globe-trotter; bystander, onlooker, observer, sidewalk superintendent; gawker, *Sl.* rubberneck, *Brit. Dial.* gapeseed.

sign, *n.* **1.** token, representation, signification; indication, mark, index, measurement; trademark, brand, monogram, initials, stamp, badge, emblem, ensign, device, scepter, logotype, *Print.* logo; slogan, theme song, watchword, password, countersign, grip; shibboleth, earmark, peculiarity, idiosyncrasy, trait, characteristic, feature, symptom, dead giveaway, sure sign.

2. symbol, notation, cipher, code, cryptogram, abbreviation, shorthand, *Both Music.* note, signature; ideogram, ideograph, hieroglyphic, hieroglyph, figure, letter, grapheme, phonogram; name, denomination, designation, denotation, label, word.

3. signal, cue, tip, *Sl.* high sign, *Sl.* tip-off; gesture, gesticulation, gest, motion, movement, action, wigwag; glance, look, wink, beckon, nod, wave.

4. placard, nameplate, nametag, shingle, *Journalism,* masthead; poster, public notice, bulletin, bill, broadside, broadsheet, announcement, advertisement, *Fr. affiche*; billboard, signboard; pointer, reference, arrow, *Both Print.* fist, hand; marker, guidepost, directional marker, milepost, milestone, landmark, seamark, beacon.

5. manifestation, evidence, shred of evidence, (*of God*) miracle, marvel, *Archaic.* prodigy; trace, track, spoor, path, wake, footprint, fingerprint, dactylogram, hide nor hair; intimation, touch, tinge, speck, dash, bit, suspicion, soupçon, nuance, whisper; suggestion, clue, key, inkling, idea; smell, sniff, scent, odor, aroma, taste, flavor; vestige, remnant, remains, relic, telltale, scar, *Med.* cicatrix; reminder, memento, souvenir.

6. omen, augury, portent, warning, prognostic, presage, foreshadowing, prefigurement, prefiguration, foreboding, boding, prognostication, auspice, handwriting on the wall; presentiment, premonition, dream, prescience, foreknowledge, feeling in one's bones; prophecy, vaticination, prediction, forecast, hint, *Inf.* tipoff.

—*v.* **7.** autograph, initial, write one's name on the dotted line, put one's John Henry *or* John Hancock on [s.t.], inscribe, write on, letter, character, engrave; undersign, subscribe, underwrite, countersign, cosign for, witness, endorse; notarize, certify, validate, authenticate, seal, stamp, visa, *Inf.* O.K., approve.

8. **sign on** *or* **up** **a.** register, enlist, enroll, get on the list, put one's name on the list; join, join up, become a member of; contract with, sign a contract with; go to work for, hire on with. **b.** put under contract, indenture, take into one's employ, put to work, put on the payroll, hire, employ, engage, retain, take into service, secure the services of; recruit, appoint, get, take on, bring aboard, *Inf.* take on board; apprentice, give [s.o.] a chance, try [s.o.] out.

9. indicate, show, point to, add up to, argue, make a case for; signify, mark, note, signalize, specify; symbolize, represent, refer to, stand for, betoken, typify, embody; name, denominate, designate; mean, denote, purport, import, connote, convey, carry; imply, suggest, intimate, hint at, allude to, bring to mind.

10. portend, omen, augur, bode, presage, foreshadow, *Archaic.* bespeak; prophesy, prognosticate, foretell.

11. signal, flag, semaphore, *Naut.* wigwag; gesture, gesticulate, motion, cross oneself, make the sign of the cross; beckon, wave, wiggle *or* wag *or* crook one's finger, nod, *Inf.* give the nod, wink, give [s.o.] a knowing glance, give thumbs up to, give thumbs down to, *Sl.* give the high sign *or* O.K.

12. **sign away** waive, forgo, dispense with, remit, quit *or* abandon claim to; give away, part with, say goodbye to, relinquish, release, give up, surrender, sacrifice, *Chiefly Scot.* demit; dispose of, get rid of, wash one's hands of, throw away, throw out the window.

13. **sign over** consign, entrust [s.t.] with [s.o.], give to [s.o.] for safekeeping; transfer, negotiate, make over, hand over, turn over, deliver, *Law.* assign; sell, vend, peddle off, auction off.

signal, *n.* **1.** sign, marker, guidepost, milepost, milestone, landmark, seamark; beacon, light, flag, warning light, caution light, flare, rocket; monitor, pilot, gauge, meter, instrument; alert, warning, siren, whistle, alarm, *Archaic.* alarum, horn, toot, tocsin, bell; cry, call, yell, scream.

2. gesture, gesticulation, *Sl.* high sign; cue, tip, *Sl.* tip-off. See **sign** (*def.* **3**).

3. password, watchword, countersign, grip; convention, *Cards.* play.

4. impetus, stimulus, fillip, spur, goad, prick; incentive, motive, reason, cause.

5. token, symbol; indication, mark. See **sign** (*def.* **1**).

—*adj.* **6.** indicative, marking; directional, signaling, semaphoric, semaphorical; pilot, guiding, lead; warning, caution, admonitory, *Biol.* sematic.

7. significant, historic, landmark, important, meaningful, momentous, weighty, big, consequential; outstanding, extraordinary, extraordinaire, glorious, grand, fantastic, fabulous, splendid, *Inf.* super, *Sl.* bang-up; unparalleled, nonpareil, unequaled, unprecedented; striking, impressive, breathtaking, brilliant; unbelievable, amazing, astonishing, *Inf.* unreal; notable, noteworthy, remarkable, unforgettable; exceptional, special, unusual, uncommon, unfamiliar, out of the ordinary, unheard of; rare, unique, singular, one of a kind. See also **significant** (*def.* **1**).

—*v.* **8.** gesture, gesticulate, *Inf.* fugle. See **sign** (*def.* **11**).

9. communicate, express, speak, transmit, send, convey; semaphore, flag, *Naut.* wigwag; give away, tip [s.o.] off, *Inf.* telegraph, *Inf.* broadcast.

10. alert, warn, alarm, sound an alarm *or* siren *or* whistle, honk one's horn, ring a bell, scream *or* yell *or* cry out at; flash a light, light a flare, put on one's flashers, send up a rocket, shine a beacon. See also **sign** (*def.* **10**).

signature, **n.** **1.** autograph, hand, inscription, *Inf.* John Hancock, *Inf.* John Henry; symbol, mark, cross, X; trademark, brand, emblem, logo, seal, stamp; name, label, *Sl.* handle, *Sl.* moniker. See **sign** (*defs.* **1, 2**).

2. signing, endorsement, countersignature, subscription, underwriting; notarization, certification, validation, authentication; approval, acceptance, ratification, seal, stamp of approval, *Inf.* O.K.

significance, *n.* **1.** consequence, moment, matter, interest, consideration, concern, *Archaic.* concernment, significancy; account, value, materiality; priority, precedence, press, urgency, emergentness; gravity, graveness, seriousness, solemnity; importance, weight, weightiness, heaviness, substance, size; eminence, prominence, distinction, high standing, standing, rank, high rank *or* position, elevation; influence, sway, power, powerfulness, force; note, notability, mark; merit, worth, high caliber.

2. import, purport, signification; portent, implication, intimation, underlying meaning; meaning, sense, content, gist, essence, main idea, sum and substance, core, pith; drift, vein, tenor, theme, idea, thought, spirit; moral, lesson, message, point, intent, intention, purpose, objective, aim, goal.

significant, *adj.* **1.** consequential, of great consequence, momentous, eventful, fateful, historic, landmark; vital, crucial, essential, valuable, necessary; critical, decisive, material; priority, urgent, emergent, exigent, pressing; grave, serious, sober, solemn; important, of great import, portentous; weighty, carrying great weight, heavy, ponderous, substantial, sizable; big, big-time, great, large, on the map; major, main, principal, prime, primary, chief, leading, foremost; outstanding, emiment, prominent, high-ranking, high-level, top-level; notable, of note, noteworthy, remarkable, of merit, meritorious, worthy; influential, well-connected, powerful.

2. meaningful, fraught with meaning, pregnant, pithy, of substance, deep, profound; suggestive, meaning, significative; indicative, symptomatic, diagnostic, *Med.* diacritic; prognostic, prognosticative, prognosticatory, prophetic, presageful; portentous, ominous, premonitory, warning, foreboding, boding; allusive, connotative, inferential, implicative, implicational; denotative, denominative, designative, representational, symbolic.

3. expressive, telling, informative, communicative, revealing, demonstrative, exhibitive, pointed, forceful, effective; signal, knowing, understood, conventional, agreed upon; inside, esoteric, private, personal; secret, furtive, surreptitious, stolen, covert, clandestine.

signification, *n.* **1.** meaning, sense, content; import, purport, essence. See **significance** (*def.* **2**).

2. indication, showing, pointing out; denotation, acceptation, designation, denomination, naming; symbolization, signing, signaling, representation; implication, connotation, allusion, reference; intimation, suggestion.

significative, *adj.* **1.** indicative, signaling, semaphoric, communicative; symbolic, representational, denotative, designative, denominative, naming, specifying, specific.

2. suggestive, expressive, meaning; meaningful, pregnant, pithy. See **significant** (*def.* **2**).

signify, *v.* **1.** signal, sign, flag, semaphore, *Naut.* wigwag; convey, impart, get *or* put across, make known; transmit, send, pass on *or* along, *Inf.* telegraph, *Inf.* broadcast; communicate, express, relate, speak, tell of *or* about, voice, utter, breathe; announce, proclaim, declare, pronounce, come out with, blurt out; disclose, reveal, divulge, bring out, lay open.

2. represent, symbolize; denote, mean; imply, suggest; indicate, point to; portend, omen. See **sign** (*defs.* **9, 10**).

3. be significant, import, be of importance, leave one's *or* its mark; weigh, carry weight, matter, count, be of consequence, make a difference; amount to something, warrant consideration *or* attention, deserve merit.

silence, *n.* **1.** stillness, still, hush; noiselessness, soundlessness, quiet, quietness, quietude, *Chiefly Irish.* whist, *Sl.* q.t.; peace, peacefulness, peaceableness, calm, calmness, placidity, serenity, tranquility, rest, repose.

2. muteness, *Psychiatry.* mutism, speechlessness, dumbness, *Pathol.* aphonia, voicelessness, wordlessness, tonguelessness; incommunicativeness, inexpression, tacitness; dumfounderment, amazement, astonishment.

3. reticence, taciturnity, uncommunicativeness, reserve, reservation; bashfulness, shyness, meekness, timidity, timorousness, diffidence; modesty, constraint, unassertiveness.

4. oblivion, obscurity, privacy; adumbration, shade, darkness.

5. secrecy, secretiveness, suppression, repression, concealment, delitescence, delitescency; stealth, furtiveness, evasion.

—*v.* **6.** still, shush, hush, quiet, *Chiefly Brit.* quieten; lull, calm, tranquilize; pacify, appease, dulcify, propitiate, reconcile, smooth, soothe, compose; play down, tone down, *Inf.* soft-pedal; soften, allay, mitigate; ease, assuage, mollify, palliate.

7. moderate, blunt, dull, deaden; temper, decrease, weaken, slacken, lessen, lighten, diminish, abate; settle, alleviate, relieve, slake, quench.

8. repress, suppress, subdue, inhibit, quell, quash, put down, damp, dampen; chasten, restrain, sober; stifle, gag, mute, muffle, smother, *Inf.* squelch; talk down, *Inf.* squash, *Inf.* shut up, *Sl.* slap down; muzzle, throttle, choke, strangle; stop, arrest, curb, check, stay, cut off, cut short, prevent, forestall, preclude, put an end to; kill, slay, murder; interrupt, cut in.

—*interj.* **9.** be silent, be quiet, be still, quiet, sh, shush, hush, not another word, hold your tongue, whist, hist; *All Sl.* pipe down, shut your mouth, turn it off, can it, shut up, *Sl.* soft.

silent, *adj.* **1.** soundless, quiet, still, stock-still, *Chiefly Literary.* stilly, noiseless, hushed, inaudible, deathlike; calm, tranquil, sedate, placid, peaceful, pacific, peaceable, reposeful; unruffled, unagitated, undisturbed, untroubled; even, flat, smooth; muffled, muted, dampened, stifled, echoless.

2. speechless, mute, dumb, voiceless, wordless, tongueless; mum.

3. taciturn, reticent, reserved, tight-lipped, close-mouthed, close, uncommunicative, unvocal, nonvocal; tongue-tied, bashful, shy, timid, timorous, diffident; modest, retiring, unassertive.

4. unspoken, tacit, understood, implicit; implied, hinted at, suggested, intimated, insinuated; unsaid, unexpressed, unstated, undeclared, unuttered, unarticulated, unmentioned; uninformative, uninformatory, uninstructive, unenlightening, unelucidating, unelucidative; inferred, derived, concluded.

5. inactive, quiescent, passive, idle, dormant, dormient, latent; unstirring, reposing, resting, slumbering, hibernating, estivating, (*of land*) fallow; inert, inanimate, lifeless, dead.

6. not sounded, unvoiced, unpronounced, unvocalized, unintoned, *Phonet.* aphonic, *Phonet.* surd.

silhouette, *n.* outline, delineation, contour, profile; form, shape, figure, configuration, conformation; perimeter, circumference, periphery; shadow, shadowgraph, radiograph, skiagraph.

silken, *adj.* silklike, silky, sericeous; soft, agreeable to the touch, luxurious, elegant; delicate, fragile, diaphanous, finely textured, smooth, sleek.

silly, *adj.* **1.** absurd, inane, pointless, fatuous; foolish, *Inf.* damfool, *Inf.* damfoolish, senseless, nonsensical, *Scot. and North Eng.* glaikit, tomfoolish,

Sl. cockeyed; poppycockish, *Sl.* cockamamie, amphigoric; ridiculous, derisible, risible, laughable, ludicrous, *Sl.* for the birds; comical, funny, farcical, humorous, droll; asinine, anserine, idiotic, *Inf.* moronic, imbecilic; childish, puerile, green, immature; crazy, crazed, *Scot.* doiled, *Sl.* kooky, mad, wild, insane, demented; daft, *Inf.* daffy, crackbrained, *Inf.* nutty; peculiar, strange, odd, *All Sl.* balmy, dippy, batty, cuckoo, buggy, screwy, wacky, goofy, loony.

2. weak-minded, simple, simple-minded, birdbrained; featherheaded, featherbrained, rattleheaded, rattlebrained; light-minded, light-headed, *Inf.* dizzy, trifling, *Inf.* footling, frivolous; muddled, muddleheaded, addlebrained, addlepated; absent-minded, scatterbrained, confused, bemused; feeble-minded, deficient, subnormal, retarded; dull, vapid, *Inf.* dopey, insensate, *Inf.* dumb; dull-witted, dim-witted, slow-witted, half-witted, witless, unwitty; harebrained, giddy, mercurial, reckless, erratic, unstable, harum-scarum; stupid, unintelligent, mindless, fatuitous, brainless, slow; dense, thick, thickheaded, thick-skulled, thick-witted, obtuse, stolid, lumpish, blunt; blockheaded, boneheaded, blockish, doltish; empty-headed, blank, vacant, vacuous.

3. unreasonable, irrational, illogical, meaningless; preposterous, extravagant, excessive; haphazard, aimless, driftless, unconnected, groundless; irrelevant, inconsequential, purposeless; thoughtless, careless, short-sighted, unwary, unheeding, heedless; inappropriate, inept, improper, incongruous, inconsistent; imprudent, indiscreet, foolhardy, irresponsible; unwise, ill-considered, ill-suited, ill-advised, injudicious.

4. *Informal.* stunned, dazed, dazzled, in a daze, knocked silly; stupefied, numb, benumbed.

—n. **5.** fool, ninny, nincompoop; simpleton, idiot, imbecile, *Inf.* moron, nitwit, half-wit, goose; scatterbrain, rattlebrain, harebrain, dolt, dunce, dullard, dope, *Inf.* dummy; blockhead, bonehead, *Sl.* dumbhead, *Sl.* lunkhead, *Inf.* knucklehead, *Sl.* stupidhead.

silver-tongued, *adj.* **1.** eloquent, articulate, well-spoken, *Archaic.* facund, *Obs.*. facundious, Ciceronian; oratorical, rhetorical, declamatory; (*all of speech*) poetic, graceful, easy, facile, flowing, fluent, glib, slick, smooth, smooth-tongued.

2. persuasive, convincing, impressive, effective; suasive, inducive, compelling, impelling; (*all of speech*) forceful, emphatic, spirited, vigorous, impassioned.

silvery, *adj.* **1.** shining, shiny, lustrous, sheeny, burnished, polished; bright, brilliant, radiant, lambent, refulgent; gleaming, glittering, coruscating, glistening, shimmering.

2. (*all of sound*) clear, ringing, clarion; dulcet, melodious, musical; sweet, mellifluous, mellifluent, euphonious.

similar, *adj.* resembling, nearly alike; like, same, much the same, suchlike; kindred, allied, akin; connatural, congeneric, consanguineous; corresponding, correspondent, comparable, conformable, agreeing; analogous, parallel, equivalent.

similarity, *n.* resemblance, similitude, likeness; agreement, concordance, equivalence, coincidence; comparability, correspondence, congruity, conformability; analogy, approximation, parallel; homogeneity, uniformity, consistency.

simile, *n.* analogy, parallel, comparison, similitude.

similitude, *n.* **1.** resemblance, likeness, similarity; agreement, concordance, equivalence, coincidence, comparability, correspondence, congruity, conformability.

2. counterpart, match, image, semblance; representation, depiction, portrayal, delineation; reproduction, likeness, duplicate, reflection, simulacrum; model, replica, copy, facsimile; snapshot, photograph; sketch, portrait, profile; picture, tableau, study, drawing, print; icon, effigy, statue.

3. parable, allegory, fable, apologue, myth; simile, analogy, parallel, comparison.

simmer, *v.* **1.** bubble, boil gently, seethe, stew, poach, cook.

2. be excited, be agitated, be tense, be feverish, be angry, fume, chafe.

simper, *v.* smile, giggle, titter, snigger, snicker, *Inf.* tee-hee; grin, smirk, grimace, mouth, *Sl.* mug, *Archaic.* mow, make a face.

simple, *adj.* **1.** easy, facile, effortless, like falling off a log, *Inf.* hands down, *Sl.* no sweat, *Inf.* soft, *Sl.* cushy, *Music.* semplice, *Scot.* eath; *Inf.* a snap, *Inf.* a breeze, *Sl.* cinchy, *Sl.* a cinch; understandable, comprehensible, intelligible, clear, lucid; obvious, evident, unmistakable; uncomplicated, uninvolved, manageable, wieldly, controllable.

2. plain, homely, shirtsleeve, down-home, informal, casual, unceremonious; natural, unaffected, unpretentious, unpretending; modest, unassuming.

3. attic, classic, clean, neat, trim; unembellished, unadorned, unarrayed, untrimmed, undecorated.

4. fundamental, basic, basal, radical, root, underlying; rudimentary, rudimental, inchoate, imperfect, undeveloped; introductory, preparatory, proemial, preliminary, prefatory; embryonic, embryonal, germinal, genetic, genetical, nascent, incipient, beginning.

5. single, uncombined, uncompounded, uncomplex, simplex; pure, unalloyed, unmixed, unblended; sole, only, alone, mere; bare, scarce, deficient, insufficient.

6. guileless, artless, uncontrived, candid, open, aboveboard, true-dealing; undissembling, undissembled, uncorrupted, unbought; sincere, honest, true, decent, fair, equitable, righteous, upright; straightforward, *Inf.* square, direct, unevasive, frank, blunt; unconditional, unqualified, absolute; ingenuous, naïve, credulous, credent, believing, trusting, trustful, gullible; innocent, childlike, wholesome, unsophisticated, green, rustic.

7. ordinary, common, commonplace, prosaic, plebian, household, everyday, of the garden variety; mediocre, middling, average; humble, subservient, subordinate, lowly, inferior, meek; mean, low, base; insignificant, unimportant, inconsequential, trivial, trifling, paltry.

8. ignorant, unknowing, unknowledgeable, unaware; unlearned, unversed, uneducated, untutored, untaught; stupid, witless, brainless, unintelligent, feeble-minded, feeble, *Inf.* dumb, *Inf.* moronic, *Sl.* dopey; duncish, duncical, doltish, cloddish, oafish, blockheaded, boneheaded, thickskulled, *Sl.* lunkheaded; obtuse, dense, bovine, dull, dull-witted, *Sl.* dim-witted; retarded, slow, purblind, limited.

9. simple-minded, senseless, nonsensical, foolish, idiotic, imbecilic, imbecile, absurd, asinine, fatuous, *Sl.* loony; silly, inane, pointless, *Inf.* nutty, *Sl.* goofy; featherbrained, scatterbrained, rattlebrained, rattleheaded; irrational, insensate, illogical, unreasoning, unreasonable, *Sl.* wacky.

—n. **10.** ignoramus, idiot, imbecile, halfwit; fool, simpleton. See **simpleton** (*defs.* **1, 2**).

simpleton, *n.* **1.** ignoramus, idiot, imbecile, half-wit, loon, *Inf.* moron, *Inf.* dummy, *Sl.* dope; dunce, dullard, dolt, clod, oaf; blockhead, bonehead, dunderhead, dunderpate, loggerhead, *Inf.* lightweight, numskull, *Sl.* dim-wit, *Sl.* lug, *Sl.* lunkhead, *Sl.* cottagehead, *Inf.* stupid, *Sl.* stupe.

2. fool, simple, Simple Simon, *Sl.* simp; nincompoop, ninny, ninnyhammer, goose, jackass, ass, donkey; featherbrain, scatterbrain, rattlehead, mooncalf, *Inf.* coot, *Sl.* jerk; dupe, gull, greenhorn, *Inf.* jay.

simplicity, *n.* **1.** clearness, lucidity, limpidity; perceptibility, distinctness, obviousness, explicitness, conspicuousness, salience, unmistakableness; clarity, cognizability, intelligibility, penetrability, decipherability, legibility.

2. plainness, modesty, bareness, spareness, blankness, starkness, severity, asceticism; unadornment, austereness, unornamentation, unembellishment.

3. artlessness, openness, open-heartedness, ingenuousness, guilelessness, sincerity, genuineness, undeceptiveness, undeceitfulness; candor, candidness, frankness, forthrightness, straightforwardness, calling a spade a spade, *Sl.* telling it like it is; naturalness, unaffectedness, unpretentiousness; naïveté, naïveness, simple-mindedness, innocence; unsophisticatedness, greenness, rawness, unworldliness; trustfulness, unsuspiciousness, unwariness, unguardedness.

4. unskillfulness, inexpertness, uncleverness, undeftness, unfacileness; ungiftedness, untalentedness, dullness, slowness.

simplify, *v.* make plainer, decipher, unravel, disentangle, make intelligible, translate; paraphrase, summarize, explain, clarify, clear up; abridge, cut down, condense, shorten; pare down, get down to bare essentials; make easier, spoon-feed.

simply, *adv.* **1.** easily, clearly, distinctly, plainly, intelligibly, lucidly, legibly; obviously, evidently, conspicuously, unmistakably, transparently.

2. sincerely, artlessly, openly, ingenuously, guilelessly, genuinely, undeceptively, undeceitfully; naturally, unaffectedly, unpretentiously; naively, innocently, unsophisticatedly, unaffectedly.

3. merely, only, solely, purely; wholly, absolutely, completely, fully, entirely; totally, nothing short of, unqualifiedly, utterly; categorically, unconditionally, unreservedly, implicitly; positively, certainly, veritably, unquestionably, unequivocably, unambiguously.

4. foolishly, unwisely, imprudently, incautiously, injudiciously; heedlessly, thoughtlessly, carelessly.

simulacrum, *n.* **1.** superficial likeness, semblance, similarity, similitude; resemblance, likeness, counterpart, match, duplicate, double, twin, Doppleganger.

2. image, representation, effigy, icon, depiction, portrayal; reproduction, reflection, model, replica, copy, facsimile; snapshot, *Inf.* snap, photograph, *Inf.* photo; sketch, portrait, profile, study, life study, picture.

simulate, *v.* feign, pretend, make believe, malinger, playact, act; put on airs, assume airs, posture, do for effect; impersonate, personate, pose as, pretend to be, pass oneself off as, sail under false colors; ape, imitate, parrot, mimic, mime, *Sl.* make like; mirror, reflect, echo, take on the appearance of; copy, affect, do like, follow suit; duplicate, reproduce, parallel; parody, caricature, burlesque, travesty, mock, sham, counterfeit.

simultaneous, *adj.* concomitant, concurrent, coincident, parallel, collateral, side-by-side; contemporaneous, coinstantaneous, synchronal, synchronous, isochronal, isochronous; coexistent, coexisting, contemporary, coeval, coetaneous; conterminous, coterminous, coextensive.

sin, *n.* **1.** transgression, trespass, violation; impiety, impiousness, profaneness, profanity, profanation, blasphemy; desecration, sacrilege, irreverence, irreligiousness; deviltry, ungodliness, godlessness; nefariousness, flagitiousness, heinousness, vileness, viciousness.

2. sinfulness, wrong, wickedness, vice, bad, badness, baseness, foulness, meanness; immorality, iniquity, evil, wrong; error, guilt, obduracy, hardhardedness; unregeneracy, impenitence, incorrigibility; maleficence, malignancy, malevolence, malignity, rancor, maliciousness; atrocity, outrage, abomination.

3. offense, fault, crime, infraction, criminal infraction, violation; infringement, misdeed, dereliction, slip, lapse, omission; shortcoming, peccadillo, foible, malefaction, delinquency, law breaking, felony, misdemeanor.

—*v.* **4.** transgress, trespass, offend, desecrate, profane, defile, debase; go astray, fall from grace; break the law, fault, commit a sin *or* crime; make a mistake, go wrong, slip up, lapse, trip, stray from the straight and narrow, misbehave; go to pot, go to hell, go to hell in a handbasket; be degraded, sink to the depths; sin against, injure, hurt, harm, wound, damage, wrong, malign.

sincere, *adj.* **1.** open, open-hearted, ingenuous, guileless, artless, undeceptive, undeceitful, undeceiving, unfeigning, undissembling, undissimulating; aboveboard, open and aboveboard, up front, out front, no-nonsense, *Sl.* on the level, *Sl.* up and up *or* on the up and up; upright, upstanding, straight, square, fair and square, square-dealing, plain-dealing, square-shooting, straight-shooting; honest, trustworthy, *Inf.* trusty, uncorrupt, uncorrupted, *Inf.* O.K.

2. candid, frank, forthright, foursquare, straightforward, straight-from-the-shoulder; plain, plain-spoken, plain-speaking, downright, outright, explicit, unequivocal, unambiguous, undisguised, *Inf.* straight-out, *Inf.* flat-footed, *Inf.* matter-of-fact; genuine, real, true, truehearted, heartfelt, veracious, bona fide, all wool and a yard wide; natural, unaffected, uncontrived, unassuming, inartificial, unvarnished, unpretentious, unpretending.

3. earnest, fervent, fervid, serious, dedicated, resolute, single-hearted, single-minded, wholehearted.

sincerity, *n.* **1.** openness, openheartedness, ingenuousness, guilelessness, artlessness, undeceptiveness, undeceitfulness; uprightness, honorableness, straightness, squareness, square-dealing, plain-dealing, square-shooting, straight-shooting; honesty, trustworthiness, *Inf.* trustiness, uncorruptedness.

2. candor, candidness, frankness, forthrightness, straightforwardness, calling a spade a spade, *Sl.* telling it like it is; plain-speaking, plain-spokenness, downrightness, outrightness, explicitness, unequivocalness; genuineness, trueness, truheartedness; naturalness, unaffectedness, inartificiality, inartificialness, unpretentiousness.

3. earnestness, ferventness, fervidness, seriousness, dedication, resolution, single-heartedness, single-mindedness, wholeheartedness.

sinecure, *n.* soft job, *Sl.* cushy job, *Sl.* patronage plum, *Sl.* political plum, *Sl.* plum, *Sl.* pork barrel, *Sl.* gravy train, *Inf.* boondoggle; child's play, *Sl.* snap, *Sl.* cinch, *Inf.* picnic.

sinew, *n.* **1.** tendon, ligament, *Anat.* ligamentum; thew, muscle.

2. *Often* **sinews** strength, vigor, vitality, driving spirit, power, might, brawn, force; lustiness, energy, resilience, stamina; robustness, muscle, *Sl.* beef, potency; grit, nerve, courage, *Sl.* guts, iron, *Literary.* puissance.

sinewy, *adj.* **1.** strong, powerful, mighty; muscular, stout, strapping, robust, athletically-built, wiry; virile, lusty, vigorous, burly, brawny; herculean, able-bodied, stalwart, doughty, Atlantean.

2. tough, firm, resilient, hardened, toughened, weathered; adamantine, steely, steady, constant, unwavering, steadfast, indomitable, inexorable; determined, resolute, staunch.

3. stringy, fibrous, fibroid, filamentous, filamentary, tensile, springy, elastic, ropy, cord-like, corded.

4. (*of language, style, etc.*) vigorous, forceful, dynamic, energetic; virile, lusty, strong, robust, mighty, powerful; potent, effective, gripping; intensive, vehement, emphatic.

sinful, *adj.* **1.** wicked, evil, iniquitous, peccable, wrong, *Archaic.* facinorous, *Obs.* scelerate, *Obs.* scelerous; bad, base, vile, odious, obnoxious; black-hearted, villainous, sinister, ignoble; nefarious, flagitious, heinous, infamous, *Rare.* nefast; opprobrious, shameful, disgraceful, ignominious; criminal, reprehensible, blameworthy, guilty; unregenerate, unrepentant, impenitent, obdurate, incorrigible.

2. ungodly, godless, unholy, impious, profane; damnable, accursed, demonic, devilish, satanic; blasphemous, irreligious, irreverent, sacrilegious; transgressive, peccant, erring; immoral, dissolute, dissipated, abandoned, profligate, reprobate; debauched, debased, degenerate, corrupt, depraved, defiled; wanton, unchaste, impure, unclean, carnal, incontinent.

sing, *v.* **1.** vocalize, carol, trill, warble, lilt, flute, chirp, croon, pipe, quaver; hymn, serenade, lullaby, melodize, *Sl.* belt out, *Inf.* deliver, *Inf.* render; chant, intone, cantillate.

2. tell about, praise, laud, extol; emblazon, sound the praises of, sing the praises of, cry up, *Archaic.* magnify; eulogize, panegyrize, glorify; exalt, pay tribute to, pay homage to, honor, crown; celebrate, acclaim, applaud.

3. *Slang.* inform, betray, *Inf.* tell on, tell tales out of school, *Inf.* blow the whistle on, turn in; *All Sl.* fink, peach, stool, rat, rat on, squeal, squeak, snitch; *All Sl.* finger, put the finger on, name names, sell [s.o.] down the river, weasel; disclose, divulge, let slip, leak, *Sl.* spill the beans, *Sl.* blow the lid off, let it all out.

4. sing out *Informal.* shout, cry, cry out, yodel, yell, yelp, bray, bellow; make outcry, exclaim, burst out, blurt out; cheer, whoop, *Inf.* holler, *Inf.* whoop and holler.

—n. **5.** song fest, song festival, song jamboree, community sing, hootenanny; battle of song, service of song, carol service, choral service, madrigal party.

singe, *v.* char, toast, grill; sear, roast, torrefy, shrivel, burn, cauterize; brown, tan, blacken, blister, sunburn.

singer, *n.* **1.** vocalist, warbler, crooner, soloist, *Inf.* lead, choir member, choir boy, choir girl; chorus member, chorus boy, chorus girl, gleeclub member; chorister, precentor, chanter, hymner, caroler, church choir member, cantor; opera singer, diva, prima donna; band singer, *Inf.* pop singer, chantress, chanteuse, *Fr. cantatrice,* blues singer; *All Inf.* songbird, wren, thrush, nightingale, philomel, lark, canary.

2. poet, bard, minstrel, wandering minstrel, jongleur, troubadour, ballad singer, streetsinger, Meistersinger, minnesinger.

3. songbird, singing bird, songster; warbler, nightingale, *Poetic.* philomel; lark, ringdove, cuckoo, thrush, *Brit. Chiefly Poetic.* mavis, canary, song sparrow, oriole, mockingbird.

single, *adj.* **1.** one only, only, *Sl.* one-shot, sole, unique, singular; lone, isolated, solitary, exclusive, separate, alone; particular, individual, personal, special; distinct, lonely, different, distinctive, extraordinary, uncommon, rare; detached, disconnected, disjoined.

2. unmarried, unwed, unwedded, spouseless, mateless; bachelorly, wifeless, celibate, monkish, monastic, misogynous; spinsterish, old-maidish, virginal, maidenly, husbandless; widowed, divorced, separated, misogamous.

3. (*as in combat*) one against one, one-on-one, one-to-one, single-handed, going it alone; unaided, unaccompanied, unassisted.

4. one-piece, simple, elementary, unmixed; indivisible, united, unified, integral, irreducible; uniform, standard, straight, clear.

5. sincere, genuine, real, heartfelt, frank, candid; unreserved, open, open-hearted; honest, forthright straightforward, guileless, unfeigning, undisguised; true, true-blue, faithful, loyal, constant, devoted; undivided, single-minded, single-hearted, wholehearted; strong, pure, intense, concentrated, unadulterated, undimmed; solid, mighty, firm, staunch, steady, steadfast; unfailing, unwavering, unfaltering, unswerving, undeviating.

—v. **6.** *Usu.* **single out** pick, choose, select, opt for, elect, decide on, prefer; set apart, separate, segregate, isolate; winnow, cull, glean.

—n. **7.** individual, singleton, *Sl.* oner, one-of-a-kind.

8. bachelor, *Inf.* bach, misogynist, confirmed bachelor, divorcé, widower, grass widower, playboy; miss, spinster, old maid, maiden lady, bachelor girl *or* woman, career girl *or* woman, divorcée, widow, grass widow; unwed mother, (*usu. pl.*) parents without partners, misogamist.

singly, *adv.* **1.** separately, individually, lonelily, in isolation, alone, apart; exclusively, particularly, specially, distinctly, purely; single-handed, single-handedly.

2. one at a time, one by one, in order, in line, in succession, successively.

singular, *adj.* **1.** exceptional, *Inf.* terrific, wonderful, wondrous, impressive, *Inf.* super, unparalleled, nonpareil, incomparable; extraordinary, remarkable, noteworthy, notable, outstanding, striking, conspicuous, eminent, prominent; amazing, astonishing, astounding; uncommon, rare, special, signal; important, significant, distinctive, of consequence.

2. unusual, different, divergent, deviant, preposterous, outlandish; strange, odd, peculiar, curious, queer, quaint, bizarre; eccentric, *Inf.* dotty, erratic, weird, wild, fantastic, *Sl.* far out, *Fr. outré, Sl.* flipped out; abnormal, atypical.

3. unique, sole, only, one-of-a-kind. See **single** (*def.* 1).

singularity, *n.* **1.** extraordinariness, uncommonness, strangeness, rareness, rarity; conspicuousness, prominence, significance; queerness, weirdness, preposterousness, outlandishness, *Sl.* kookiness, freakishness.

2. peculiarity, eccentricity, oddity, quirk, crotchet, whim, maggot; idiosyncrasy, individuality; abnormality, aberration, deviation, warp, kink, twist.

sinister, *adj.* **1.** ominous, inauspicious, unpropitious, portentous, ill-omened, sinistrous, foreboding, fateful, direful; menacing, minatory, minacious, threatening; dangerous, perilous, hazardous; treacherous, perfidious, untrustworthy.

2. bad, base, vile, nefarious, low, low-down, foul, vicious, without any redeeming qualities; mean, underhanded, sneaky, furtive, covert, crafty, sly, insidious; contemptible, abominable, odious, despicable, reprehensible, damnable, accursed; evil, wicked, diabolic, fiendish, devilish, satanic; baleful, malicious, malign, maleficent, malefic, harmful, injurious, pernicious, destructive; immoral, sinful, iniquitous, depraved, degraded, corrupt; cruel, fell, lacking the milk of human kindness, heinous, villainous, infamous, scoundrelly, unscrupulous.

3. unfortunate, ill-starred, unlucky, hapless, untoward, unfavorable; disastrous, ruinous, calamitous; woeful, lamentable, unhappy, sad, terrible, deplorable, regrettable.

4. left-handed, sinistral, *Scot.* car, on the left, left, port, *Naut.* larboard.

sink, *v.* **1.** fall, drop, descend, go down; hang heavily, swag; subside, recede, retrocede, ebb; fall back, lapse, relapse; slope, dip, slant, lean, list, cant, tilt, incline.

2. settle, precipitate, gravitate, hit bottom; become submerged, capsize, drown, founder; plunge, immerse, engulf, souse, douse, inundate, submerge, submerse, vail, drown; *Naut.* scuttle.

3. collapse, fall in, cave in, become sunken *or* concave; slump, fall down, slip; feint, swoon; despond, despair.

4. decline, fail, weaken, languish; droop, sag, flag, wither, wilt; deteriorate, worsen, regress, retrogress, backslide, revert; degenerate, go downhill, *All Sl.* go to seed, go to pot, go to the dogs, hit the skids.

5. reduce, lower, depress; devaluate, depreciate, degrade, debase, abase; decrease, diminish, lessen, drop off, swindle, wane.

6. abate, moderate, alleviate; soften, tone down, temper, modulate, quiet, turn down.

7. put down, bury, mire, plant, lay, drive; hollow out, dig, bore, drill, excavate.

8. destroy, ruin, cause the downfall of, be the ruin of; devastate, demolish, vanquish, overcome; *Sl.* put the skids under, seal the doom of; pauperize, bankrupt, impoverish, *Sl.* break.

9. (*usu. in reference to a sum of money*) invest, risk, venture, put down, put out; lose, *Sl.* blow, be out, be set back; go bankrupt, go under, go broke.

10. *Usu.* **sink in** *or* **into** enter, pierce, penetrate, reach, permeate; become known *or* understood, become engrossed *or* absorbed.

11. suppress, conceal, hide, mask, disguise; ignore, slight, refuse to notice, take no note *or* heed of; omit, drop, dismiss, cast aside, *Inf.* give a miss, *Inf.* give a go-by, turn one's back on, not bother with.

—n. **12.** basin, washbasin, washbowl, commode, *Eccles.* piscina; water receptacle, tub, washtub.

13. swamp, marsh, *Brit.* fen, bog; sinkhole, swallow hole, swallow, cesspool, polluted pond; hole, dip, cavity, depression, hollow, crater.

14. den of iniquity, hellhole, *Inf.* dive, *Sl.* joint; tenderloin, Alsatia; red light district, Storyville, Combat Zone; skid row, the Bowery.

15. drain, sewer, gutter, cloaca; ditch, trench, conduit, culvert; channel, race, waterway, watercourse.

sinker, *n.* **1.** plummet, plumb bob, plumb, bob, weight, lead.

2. deadweight; nonswimmer; unseaworthy vessel; *Sl.* doughnut, *Sl.* muffin, *Sl.* biscuit.

sinless, *adj.* pure, immaculate, stainless, spotless; uncorrupted, undefiled, untainted, unspotted, unsullied, unsoiled, unblemished, unmarred, untarnished; faultless, sterling, perfect, saintly, without fault; innocent, guiltless, free from guilt, clear, *Sl.* clean; blameless, inculpable, unblamable, uncensurable, unimpeachable, irreproachable, above reproach, above suspicion, like Caesar's wife.

sinner, *n.* transgressor, trespasser, wrongdoer, evildoer, malefactor, offender, culprit; delinquent, juvenile delinquent, misdemeanant, *Inf.* scofflaw, lawbreaker, *Law.* malfeasant, *Law.* misfeasor; felon, criminal, *Sl.* chronic crook, recidivist, backslider.

sinuosity, *n.* winding, sinuation, sinus, curve, incurvature, incurvation, excurvature, excurvation; bend, flexure, turn, crook, tortuosity, flexuosity, anfractuosity; spiral, helix, corkscrew, twirl, convolution, *Zool.* volute, whorl, curl, curlicue; labyrinth, maze.

sinuous, *adj.* **1.** winding, sinuate, flexuous, flexuose, anfractuous, serpentine, tortuous, crooked, zigzag; curving, curved, curvy, curvilinear, twisting, twisted, turning, bending, bent; spiral, helical, spiraling, twining, convoluted, volute, coiled, tortile; curled, curling, curly, kinky; labyrinthine, mazelike, mazy, intricate, complicated.

2. indirect, devious, roundabout, circuitous, ambagious, circumlocutory; oblique, backhanded, unclear, ambiguous.

sip, *v.* **1.** sup, taste, sample, drink bit by bit, lap up, suck up, *Sl.* slurp.

—n. **2.** taste, sample, drop, lick, thimbleful, sup, mouthful, spoonful; drink, dram, nip, draught, swallow, *Inf.* swig.

siren, *n.* **1.** seductress, temptress, enchantress, vamp, vampire, sexpot, *Fr. femme fatale, Inf.* mantrap; Circe, Lorelei, *Class. Myth.* Parthenope.

—adj. **2.** seductive, beguiling, enchanting, enrapturing, enravishing, bewitching; captivating, fascinating, spellbinding, intriguing; tempting, alluring, luring, inviting, tantalizing, irresistible; Circean, Parthenopian, sirenic.

sister, *n.* **1.** sibling, *Inf.* sis, *Inf.* sissy.

2. nun, conventual, clergywoman, *Fr. religieuse,* bride of Christ; Mother Superior; abbess, prioress.

3. *British.* nurse, registered nurse, RN, head nurse, *Brit.* nursing sister.

4. *Informal.* (*all used in direct address*) miss, woman, madam, ma'am, lady, *Scot.* hen, *Inf.* toots, *Sl.* kid, *Sl.* doll, *Sl.* baby, *Sl.* cutie.

sit, *v.* **1.** seat oneself, be seated, *Sl.* take a load off one's feet, plop down; squat, crouch, hunker down, perch, roost; straddle, sit astride, bestride, bestraddle; repose, lean, recline, loll, lounge, sprawl; (*all of a hen*) brood, incubate, cover, nest, hatch.

2. settle, situate, place, position, locate, put, establish, deposit; seat, usher, escort, lead, conduct, guide, introduce.

3. be situated, be located; occupy, dwell, reside, inhabit; sojourn, abide, stay, lodge, bide.

4. remain quiet, rest, abide, repose, relax, be quiescent; pause, mark time, be at a standstill, not stir; refrain, forbear, abstain, cease, stop; idle, stagnate, vegetate, lie fallow; lie dormant, slumber, sleep, be inert, be latent.

5. correspond, harmonize, befit, go well with, conform to, accord, agree.

6. reign, fill an office, officiate, preside, chair; superintend, supervise, govern, direct, rule, manage, administer.

7. (*of an assembly*) be convened, meet, gather, join, unite, assemble.

8. babysit, supervise, superintend, mind; care for, tend, take care of, watch over, be responsible for, look out for *or* after.

9. accommodate, lodge, hold, contain, have room for, have capacity for.

site, *n.* position, placement, arrangement, placing, disposition; place, location, locality, locale, whereabouts, setting, milieu, scene; environment, surroundings, purlieus; neighborhood, vicinity, environs, precincts; territory, district, area, region, province, station; ground, plot of ground, plot, lot, spot.

sit-in, *n.* protest, demonstration, public demonstration, *Inf.* demo, rally, march; strike, sit-down strike, shutdown, closedown, slowdown.

situate, *v.* place, position, locate, put, set, deposit;

settle, install, ensconce, lodge, nest; plant, *Inf.* plunk, park.

situation, *n.* **1.** location, position, place, site. See **site.**

2. condition, case, plight, predicament, *Inf.* kettle of fish, *Inf.* how-do-you-do; circumstances, state of affairs, state, *Inf.* ball game; the lay of the land, the picture.

3. standing, footing, status, estate, class, caste; level, degree, grade, rank; lot, fate, luck, portion, cup.

size, *n.* **1.** proportions, dimensions, measurements; density, thickness, magnitude, bulk, mass, largeness; quantity, volume, weight; extent, amount, range, scope; expanse, area, square footage.

2. condition, circumstance, state, state of affairs, situation, *Inf.* ball game.

—*v.* **3.** *Usu.* **size up** appraise, judge, assess, assay, evaluate, valuate; gauge, rate, rank, measure; estimate, reckon, guess, *Inf.* guesstimate.

skeleton, *n.* **1.** bone structure, bones, anatomy; backbone, spine, shine, vertebrae.

2. framework, frame, structure, shape; beams, rafters, girders; shell, chassis, hull; support, scaffold, scaffolding, platform.

3. scarecrow, bag of bones, *Fig.* cadaver; long *or* tall drink of water, Jack Sprat.

4. outline, sketch, scenario, layout, design; blueprint, diagram, plan, draft, rough draft; cast, mold, die.

skeptic, *n.* questioner, doubter, man *or* woman from Missouri, doubting Thomas; disbeliever, nonconformist, dissenter, freethinker, agnostic, unbeliever, nullifidian; scoffer, cynic, Pyrrhonist, minimifidian; defeatist, pessimist.

skeptical, *adj.* distrustful, mistrustful, suspicious; questioning, doubting, doubtful, dubious, wondering; disbelieving, unbelieving, incredulous, cynical, minimifidian; pessimistic, defeatist; apprehensive, uncertain, fearful, afraid.

skepticism, *n.* doubt, distrust, mistrust, suspicion; disbelief, incredulity, incredulousness; cynicism, negativism, defeatism, defeatist attitude, pessimism; unbelief, agnosticism, Pyrrhonism, minimifidianism.

sketch, *n.* **1.** preliminary drawing, study, draft, rough outline; representation, delineation, configuration, diagram; design, blueprint, scenario.

2. summary, epitome, synopsis, abstract, compendium, digest, conspectus; condensation, abridgment, reduction, compression, abbreviation; analysis, recapitulation; résumé, brief, précis; outline, aperçu, review, syllabus, prospectus; docket, bulletin, minute; extracts, fragments, cuttings, analects, clippings, citations.

3. short play, skit, charade, act, routine, scene, depiction, interlude, pantomime, characterization; lampoon, take-off.

—*v.* **4.** outline, design, contour, draft, trace; block out, mark out, chalk out, rough out; portray, depict, picture; scratch, limn, stencil, pencil, demarcate, delineate.

5. summarize, sum up, give a brief accounting of.

sketchy, *adj.* **1.** rough, preliminary, provisional, preparatory, initial; rough-hewn, crude; unfinished, unexecuted, unrefined, unpolished.

2. imperfect, incomplete, defective, deficient; superficial, slight, shallow, skindeep; cursory, touch-and-go, brief, short, slipshod, careless, *Sl.* half-ass; meager, insufficient, skimpy, scrimpy, scanty, light, modest, inconsiderable, insignificant, inadequate; inexact, ill-defined, vague, indistinct, fuzzy.

skew, *v.* **1.** turn aside, bend *or* move aside, deflect, shift, swerve, sheer, turn, veer, deviate, diverge, curve, bend, twist.

2. squint, look obliquely, look askance, glance sidewise.

3. oblique, slant, slope, tilt, incline.

4. misrepresent, belie, misquote, misstate, misrender, misreport, misread, misconstrue, misinterpret, misunderstand; distort, pervert, falsify, twist, *Scot.* thraw, change, tamper with; slant, bias, color, varnish; embroider, embellish, add to, dress up; exaggerate, stretch, overdraw, strain.

—*n.* **5.** swerve, deflection, shift, sheer, turn, veer, deviation, divergence, divergency; curve, curvature, bend, twist; slant, slope, tilt, pitch, angle, incline.

skid, *v.* **1.** slide, coast, glide, skim, skate, ski, sled, toboggan, glissade.

2. check, brake, retard, slow up *or* down, stop, halt, arrest.

3. slide, slip, sideslip; turn, veer, swerve, sheer; go out of control.

skiff, *n.* small boat, dinghy, cockle, rowboat, caïque; canoe, piragua, pirogue, dugout, kayak, shell, sampan; sailboat, *Trademark.* Sunfish, *Trademark.* Sailfish, *Naut.* jolly boat, catboat *or* cat, *Naut.* catamaran.

skill, *n.* **1.** ability, faculty, talent, gift, forte; competence, competency, efficiency, efficacy, adequacy, sufficiency; capableness, readiness, technique, execution, know-how, savoir-faire.

2. expertise, expertness, excellence, mastery; proficiency, adeptness, knack, finesse, address, ingenuity, subtlety; dexterity, adroitness, facility, artistry, felicity, ambidexterity, deftness, skillfulness, handiness.

3. trade, industrial art, craft, handicraft, art; vocation, calling, line, occupation, profession, métier.

skillful, *adj.* **1.** proficient, adept, skilled, good at, finished, polished; dexterous, adroit, deft, facile, ambidexterous, handy, neat, *Brit. Dial.* feat; expert, masterful, masterly, veteran, professional, *Fr. au fair;* top-flight, top-drawer, first-rate, *Inf.* topnotch, ace, *Inf.* crack, *Sl.* crackerjack, *Sl.* hotshot, *Sl.* on the ball, *Inf.* whiz-bang, *Brit. Sl.* whizzo.

2. talented, gifted, endowed, apt, clever; conversant, learned, *Archaic.* studied, versed, knowledgeable; practiced, accomplished, experienced; able, capable, competent, efficient, adequate, sufficient, qualified, trained.

skim, *v.* **1.** cream, despumate; take up, remove, take off, scoop off *or* up.

2. glide, move over lightly, fly, skate, slide, coast.

3. brush, touch, scrape, graze, shave.

4. skip, throw, bounce, ricochet.

5. scan, glance at, read quickly, flip through the pages, dip into, look through quickly, spot-check; go *or* run through, *Inf.* breeze through.

6. cover, overspread, overlay, coat, film.

skimp, *v.* **1.** scrimp, pinch pennies, cut corners; economize, conserve, save, be sparing *or* frugal; be penurious, be parsimonious, be stingy *or* cheap, *Inf.* pinch a penny till it squeaks.

2. restrict, limit serverly, dole, stint, pinch, cramp; reduce, curtail, straiten, cut down on, take shortcuts, curb, grudge, begrudge, give reluctantly.

3. scamp, run through, dash off, do work negligently, perform hurriedly *or* hastily.

skimpy, *adj.* **1.** scanty, meager, scrimpy, scant, shy; lacking, wanting, deficient; shallow, superficial, insubstantial, depthless; sketchy, incomplete, inadequate, beggarly, insufficient; very little, paltry, poor, piddling, *Inf.* measly, mere; small, narrow, puny, slight, slender, brief, short; nominal, minute, negligible.

2. stingy, niggardly, *Rare.* illiberal, parsimonious, cheeseparing, penurious; miserly, skinflinty, mean, tight, tight-fisted, close-fisted, cheap, *Sl.* chintzy, moneygrubbing, grasping; scrimping, penny-pinching, grudging, begrudging, ungenerous, stinting; thrifty, frugal, sparing, chary; economical, prudent, saving, penny-wise.

skin, *n.* **1.** integument, epidermis, cuticle, scarfskin, *Anat.* corium, derma, cutis; hide, pelt, jacket, fleece, fell, fur, leather, vellum, shagreen; slough, *Pathol.* desquamation, exuviae.

2. rind, peel, *Bot.* epicarp, hull, bark, cortex, shell, husk; cover, covering, pod, case, *Anat., Zool.* theca, sheath, *Zool.* lorica, *Bot.* colerhiza; pellicle, membrane, involucre, *Anat.* aponeurosis; coating, coat, layer, overlay, lamina, veneer; film, crust, incrustation.

3. wineskin, pouch, container.

4. by the skin of one's teeth *Informal.* just barely, barely, hardly, scarcely, *Dial.* scantly, only just, just; by a hair's breadth, by a narrow margin, by a little bit, by an inch.

5. get under one's skin *Slang.* **a.** irritate, nettle, chafe, gall, grate, rub the wrong way, irk, vex; bother, upset, disturb. **b.** affect deeply, penetrate, move, touch, impress, excite, inspire.

—*v.* **6.** peel, pare, decorticate, excorticate, flay, scale, hull, bark; pod, shell, husk, shuck; strip, denude, excoriate, exfoliate; scalp, shave, lay bare, uncover, unwrap, remove, strip off.

7. scrape, abrade, graze, cut, hurt.

8. skin alive *Informal.* scold, chide, upbraid, *Inf.* dress down, *Sl.* chew out, tongue-lash, *Inf.* come down hard on, *Inf.* rip into; reprimand, reprove, reproach, rate, reprehend, castigate.

skin-deep, *adj.* shallow, superficial, external, outward, on the surface, surface; artificial, plastic, pseudo, fake; unprofound, empty, meaningless, unsubstantial; trifling, unimportant, insignificant, petty, trivial, frivolous, slight.

skinflint, *n.* miser, niggard, *Sl.* skin, *Sl.* cheapskate, *Inf.* piker, muckworm, *Sl.* screw; penny pincher, pinchpenny, lickpenny, *Inf.* tightwad; cheeseparer, hoarder, save-all, *Scot.* carl; scrooge, Harpagon, money-grubber, harpy; curmudgeon, churl, hunks.

skinny, *adj.* **1.** lean, slender, lank, thin, thin as a rail, attenuate; bony, lanky, gangling, gangly, *Inf.* weedy; gaunt, haggard, emaciated, meager, spare, scrawny, fleshless; scraggy, spindly, spindle-shanked, skeletal, bare-boned, raw-boned, skin and bones, twiggy; hollow-cheeked, pinched, withered, wizened, shriveled, shrunken, wasted; underfed, undernourished, half-famished, half-starved.

2. integumentary, epidermal, epidermic, cuticular, cutaneous, membranous; skinlike, epidermoid, dermatoid, dermoid.

skip, *v.* **1.** spring, jump, bound, hop, leap, leapfrog; romp, caper, gambol, frisk, prance, curvet, buck, buckjump, sport.

2. omit, except, exclude, leave out; miss, give a miss, fail to mention; overlook, pass over, ignore, disregard, pay no attention to; neglect, forget, forget about, not think of, let slip, let slide, let go, *Sl.* let ride, leave undone, not trouble oneself with; eschew, avoid, shun, shirk, steer clear of, be absent from, absent oneself from, cut.

3. ricochet, bounce; skate, skim, glide, coast; scud, shoot, *Inf.* scoot, spank, fly, flit.

—*n.* **4.** spring, jump, leap, bound, hop, saltation; buck, buckjump, gambol, frisk, romp, caper, prance.

5. omission, exception, exclusion, noninclusion, preclusion; disregard, ignoring, overlooking, passing over, preterition; oversight, miss, *Inf.* go-by, inadvertence; gap, break, hiatus, lacuna, interval; mistake, error, fault, flaw, slip, *Inf.* slip-up, *Inf.* miscue.

skipper, *n.* sea captain, seaman, mariner; captain commander, leader, master, boss; pilot, guide, conductor.

skirmish, *n.* argument, altercation, dispute, tilt, row quarrel, *Inf.* ruction, squabble, dustup, spat, tiff, *Brit. Dial.* fratch; encounter, meeting, engagement, confrontation, showdown; fight, battle, rencounter, struggle, conflict, scrimmage, tussle, bout, donnybrook, *Scot.* sturt, *Inf.* scrap, *Inf.* run-in; action, combat, brush, fray, affray; melee, fracas, uproar, brouhaha, free-for-all.

skirt, *n.* **1.** kilt, dirndl, crinoline, *Scot. and North Eng.* jupe, (*in Tahiti*) lava-lava, (*in Tahiti*) pareu; miniskirt, midiskirt, maxiskirt; *All Inf.* mini, midi, maxi.

2. *Usu.* **skirts** outskirts, outposts, outer limits, outlying districts; purlieu, perimeter, periphery, fringe; limits, city limits; suburbs, *Sl.* burbs, *Sl.* shruburbs.

3. *Slang.* woman, lady; girl, maiden, lass, miss, *Irish Eng.* colleen; nymph, slip, wench, young thing; *All Sl.* doll, chick, piece, gal, dame, tomato, *Brit.* bird.

—*v.* **4.** border, edge, verge, line, flank; rim, hem; frame, march, bound, margin, marginate.

5. adjoin, abut, impinge upon; neighbor, side, lie next to; touch, reach, meet, butt, impinge, kiss.

6. circle, circumnavigate, circumambulate, go *or* pass around.

7. evade, avoid, dodge, sidestep, steer clear of, *Inf.* duck; hedge, equivocate, prevaricate, pussyfoot, hem and haw, *Inf.* waffle, *Inf.* weasel; beat around the bush, not come to the point, beg the question.

skittish, *adj.* **1.** jumpy, startlish, *Sl.* trigger-happy; excitable, high-strung, high-spirited; nervous, (*of hunting dogs, horses, etc.*) gun-shy.

2. restless, restive, unquiet, fidgety, fretful, *Inf.* having ants in one's pants, *Sl.* antsy, *Sl.* antsy-pantsy.

3. fickle, capricious, flighty, moody, changeable, changeful, ever-changing, mutable, permutable, variable; uncertain, unpredictable, irregular, fitful, spasmodic, desultory, stop-and-go, come-and-go.

4. shy, shrinking, bashful, timid, diffident, mousy, self-conscious; coy, demure, prim.

skulk, *v.* **1.** lurk, couch, lie in wait, lie in ambush, lie low, *Inf.* lay for.

2. slink, steal, sidle, prowl, pad, pussyfoot, creep, *U.S. Sl.* gumshoe.

3. *British.* shirk, malinger, loaf, *Sl.* goof off, *Sl.* goldbrick; slack, lie down on the job, *Brit. Sl.* scrimshank; look busy, *Inf.* boondoggle, *Sl.* featherbed, *Sl.* dog it.

—*n.* **4.** shirker, slacker. See **shirker**.

sky, *n.* **1.** upper atmosphere, the void, outer space.

2. heavens, heaven, firmament, empyrean, vault of heaven, *Chiefly Literary.* welkin, ether, hyaline; the blue, the blue yonder, azure, deep blue, cerulean.

3. out of a clear blue sky abruptly, suddenly, rapidly; unexpectedly, without warning *or* notice, out of the blue.

4. to the skies extravagantly, excessively, profusely; highly, a great deal.

slab, *n.* thick slice, hunk, piece, chunk, wad; plank, board, puncheon.

slack, *adj.* **1.** loose, not tight, not taut, not rigid *or* firm, lax, hanging, drooping, droopy, bagging, baggy, sagging, saggy, flapping, *Inf.* floppy; limp, *Dial.* limpsy, flabby, flaccid; relaxed, flexible, pliant.

2. remiss, negligent, neglectful, delinquent, *Inf.* asleep at the wheel *or* switch, *Inf.* asleep on the job;

unorganized, slapdash, slipshod, offhand, *Inf.* harum-scarum; disorderly, sloppy, untidy, *Inf.* messy; unthinking, thoughtless, inattentive, absent-minded, forgetful; reckless, imprudent, unwary, heedless; unguarded, unmindful, uncircumspect.

3. indolent, lazy, idle, otiose, fainéant, do-nothing, shiftless; procrastinative, dilatory, cunctatious, cunctatory; dronish, slothful, sluggardly, laggard; sluggish, lethargic, listless; apathetic, indifferent, unconcerned, insouciant, nonchalant.

4. slow, slow-moving, slow-paced; not busy, inactive, quiet, peaceful; gentle, easy; creeping, crawling.

—*n.* **5.** decrease, diminution, reduction, lessening, diminishing, decrement, abatement, cutback; subsidence, ebb, recession; decline, downturn, drop-off, fall-off, declension, decrescence, wane; falling off, dwindling, dying out.

—*v.* **6.** shirk, lie down on the job, *Brit. Sl.* scrimshank, cop out; neglect, close one's eyes to, ignore; abandon, leave undone; (*all of work, duty, etc.*) evade, avoid, run from, dodge, whiffle, sidestep, elude, weasel out.

7. *Often* **slack up** relax, let up, slacken, remit; relieve, ease, soften, mollify, lighten; lower, turn down, tone down, quiet, still, soft-pedal, *Both Music, Acoustics.* damp, dampen; subside, ebb, recede, retrocede; dwindle, *Inf.* peter out; wind down, slow down, deescalate; fall off, taper off, wane, fade away, die out.

8. *Often* **slack off** *or* **out** loosen, slacken, untighten, relieve tension, *Obs.* slake; relax, ease up *or* off.

slacken, *v.* **1.** relax, loosen, lessen, ease, soften; mitigate, moderate, abate; weaken, attenuate; diminish, reduce, decrease.

2. slow down, drop off, taper off, wane, dwindle, *Inf.* peter out, slack up, let up.

3. retard, delay, decelerate; arrest, check, stem, stay; deescalate, wind down, bring to an end *or* close.

slacker, *n.* shirker, shirk, malingerer, *Brit.* skulker, *Brit. Sl.* scrimshanker, *Inf.* soldier, *Inf.* goldbricker, *Brit. Sl.* skiver, clock watcher, *Sl.* goof-off, *Inf.* boondoggler; procrastinator, dallier, dawdler, idler, layabout, loafer, fainéant, trifler, Micawber; avoider, *Sl.* welsher, evader, *Inf.* funker, *Sl.* bum; deserter, absconder; truant, absentee, dodger, defaulter, neglector; sponger, sponge, *Sl.* schnorrer, *Inf.* deadbeat.

slake, *v.* **1.** satisfy, sate, satiate, gratify, indulge; allay, appease, pacify, dulcify, relieve, ease, assuage, salve, *Rare.* lenify, mitigate; quench, extinguish, check, curb, quell, still, stem, stay; hush, quiet, calm, tranquilize; dull, deaden, obtund, blunt, take the edge off of; subdue, tame, mollify; alleviate, palliate.

2. cool, chill, refresh, freshen; brace, stimulate, quicken, fortify; restore, revive, revivify, reinvigorate.

3. abate, lessen, slacken, decrease, diminish, reduce; weaken, dilute, minimize; damp, dampen, put a damper on, cast a pall over; moderate, temper.

slam, *v.* **1.** shut forcefully, close noisily; heave, hurl, fling.

2. smash, shatter, dash, crash, *Brit. Dial.* pash; strike, smack, beat, batter, hit, ram, smite; bang, clap, slap, *Inf.* swat, thwack, whack.

3. *Informal.* criticize, attack, flay, light into, *Inf.* lace into, *Inf.* pan, shoot down, *Sl.* blast; vilify, malign, run down, put down.

—*n.* **4.** blow, smack, hit, knock, whack, thwack, dash, smash, clap, *Inf.* swat.

5. loud noise *or* sound, crash, crashing, banging.

6. *Informal.* criticism, *Inf.* brickbat, *Inf.* swipe; censure, reproof, reproach, condemnation, derogation, denunciation, disparagement.

slander, *n.* **1.** defamation, denigration, vilification, vituperation; scandal, *Inf.* skeleton in the closet; censure, reproach, denunciation, curse, malediction, railing, invective, commination, *Archaic.* exprobration; shame, disgrace, dishonor, ill-repute, obloquy, loss of face; belittlement, disparagement, deprecation, detraction, deflation, depreciation, derogation, devaluation; humiliation, humble pie, mortification.

2. calumny, libel, false report, misrepresentation, yellow journalism; traducement, falsehood, lie, untruth, aspersion, imputation, insinuation, *Inf.* brickbat, innuendo; abuse, injury, maliciousness, stricture, backbiting, *Archaic.* malison; slur, blot, blot on the escutcheon, smear, smirch, taint, attaint, stain, tarnish, spot, black spot *or* mark, blemish, smudge, brand, stigma.

—*v.* **3.** defame, vilify, vilipend, denigrate, vituperate, scandalize, run down, berate, impugn, revile, *Obs.* avile, malign, gibbet, criticize, pull to pieces, *Sl.* do a hatchet job on, give a bad name, speak ill of, speak evil of, sneer at, lampoon, pasquinade, muckrake; denounce, rail, curse, execrate, damn, imprecate, *Obs.* exprobrate, anathematize, censure, cry down, reproach; disgrace, dishonor, shame, debase, vitiate, degrade, discredit, disprove, disfavor; belittle, disparage, detract, decry, deprecate, depreciate, derogate, devaluate, deflate; humiliate, humble, mortify, *Sl.* put down.

4. calumniate, libel, asperse, impute, traduce, falsify, accuse falsely, misrepresent, belie; injure, abuse, assail, stab, insult, backbite, *Sl.* badmouth, engage in personalities; slur, sully, defile, smear, smirch, besmirch, soil, blacken, tarnish, taint, stain, smudge, blemish, spot, brand, stigmatize, drag through the mud *or* mire, heap dirt upon, fling dirt, throw mud on, *Sl.* dump on.

slang, *n.* **1.** lingo, colloquialism, vernacularism, vernacular, vocabulary; provincialism, regionalism, localism; vulgarism, barbarism; Americanism, Anglicism, Briticism, Gallicism; journalese, newspaperese, legalese, medicalese, officialese, collegese, newspeak.

2. argot, jargon, cant, shoptalk; jabber, gibber, gibberish, mumbo-jumbo, palaver, gobbledygook; thieves' Latin, pig Latin, peddlers' French, St. Giles' Greek.

slant, *v.* **1.** slope, lean, incline, tilt, pitch, dip; bend, bias, shift, shelve, cant, list, keel; skew, curve, veer, swerve; deviate, diverge, angle off, bear off, bevel, sheer.

2. bias, bend, twist, screw, wrest, garble; distort, misrepresent, misreport, falsify; misquote, misrender, misconstrue, misinterpret; color, *Inf.* stretch, doctor, varnish, embellish, embroider.

—*n.* **3.** slope, slanting, incline, inclination; pitch, obliquity, obliqueness, skewness, wryness; deflection, divergence, divagation, deviation; lean, leaning, angle, bias, bevel, bezel; tilt, sway, tip, cant, rake; grade, ramp, scarp, side; angularity, *All Geol.* syncline, anticline, anacline, catacline.

4. bias, one-sidedness, partiality, leaning, prejudice, tendency; distortion, misrepresentation, misinterpretation, misrendering, falsification; misreading, perversion, misconstruction, misusage, misquotation.

5. viewpoint, point of view, standpoint, stance, position; opinion, view, judgment, idea, impression, notion; approach, turn, bent, proclivity; attitude, aspect, angle, light.

slanting, *adj.* sloping, oblique, slanted, inclined, tilted, atilt; leaning, stooping, canting, listing, diagonal; abaxial, plagihedral, rhomboidal, cater-cornered, *Brit.* wonky, *Brit.* skew-whiff; askew, skew, aslant, awry, wry, askant, asquint; biased, warped, shelvy, tipsy; *All Geol.* synclinal, anticlinal, anaclinal, cataclinal; acclivous, declivous, uphill, downhill.

slap, *n.* **1.** blow, smack, buff, rap, spank, flap,

clap, crack; stripe, cut, whack, thwack, hit, bang; *Inf.* swat, clip, *Inf.* biff, *Inf.* bat, *Inf.* belt, *Inf.* clout; *Sl.* sock, *Sl.* slug, *Sl.* shot; swipe, cuff, wallop, jab; poke, buffet, *Sl.* whop, *Sl.* bash, knock.

2. gibe, jeer, quip, cut, fleer; rebuke, remark, retort, *Inf.* dig, twit, taunt; shot, thrust, *Sl.* crack, short answer, *Brit.* barracking.

—*v.* **3.** strike, hit, smack, pound; bang, whack, thwack, flap, rap, spank, crack; box, cuff, jab, wallop, buffet, swipe; *Inf.* clobber, *Inf.* swat, clip, zap, *Inf.* biff; *Sl.* sock, *Sl.* deck, *Sl.* drub, *Sl.* slug; *Inf.* belt, *Inf.* bat, *Inf.* clout.

4. dash, fling, plump, drop, *Inf.* plop; cast, thrust, hurl, clap, throw, toss.

slapdash, *adj.* careless, disorderly, untidy, thoughtless; casual, cursory, perfunctory, lax, slack; unmindful, negligent, unthinking, rash; hasty, speedy, snap, passing, hurried; offhand, last-minute, slap-bang; slipshod, messy, slovenly, slatternly, sloppy; slapped together, thrown together.

slaphappy, *adj. Informal.* **1.** punch-drunk, befuddled, confused, mixed-up, *Sl.* out of it, *Sl.* spacey.

2. foolish, silly, giddy, *Inf.* dizzy, giggly, giggling, laughing.

slash, *v.* **1.** cut, gash, score, hack; nick, jag, notch, scotch, blaze, incise; crenellate, pink, mill, knurl; slice, slit, split, cleave, halve; saw, butcher, ax, sever, chop, hew; rig, tear, rive, rend, break, sunder; scar, mutilate, lacerate, mangle, haggle; swipe, bayonet, knife, saber.

2. lash, whip, scourge, knout, flog, horsewhip, flagellate; switch, birch, cat, lambaste, baste, beat; flail, lace, thresh.

3. reduce, curtail, abridge, abbreviate, trim, devalue; lower, drop, cut, halve, mark down, come down; plunge, dive, plummet, fall, slump, cool off, relax.

—*n.* **4.** stroke, sweep, swipe, coup; blow, jab, drive, plunge.

5. cut, wound, gash, score, laceration; incision, nick, notch, jab, scotch; crenation, crenelation, serration; slice, slit, split, rent; rip, tear, break, rupture; cleft, fissure, crack.

6. curtailment, reduction, abridgment, lowering; markdown, price cut, cut, cheapening, drop, devaluation; plunge, dive, plummet, fall.

7. stroke, line, score, streak, stripe, strip; bar, band, striation, dash, hairline; underline, underscore, hachure, hatching.

8. diagonal, virgule, *Heraldry.* bend, slant, oblique, transverse.

slattern, *n.* **1.** drab, draggletail, slut, trollop, *Sl.* slob, dowdy, frump, slovenly woman.

2. tramp, hussy, wanton, loose *or* fallen woman, woman of ill repute; harlot, strumpet, prostitute, whore, *U.S. Sl.* tart, streetwalker, *Sl.* hustler, *Sl.* hooker, lady of the evening.

slatternly, *adj.* **1.** untidy, bedraggled, draggletailed, disheveled, disorderly, messy, sloppy, slovenly, slipshod, careless; shabby, frumpish, frumpy, dowdy, drab.

2. sluttish, *Inf.* loose, promiscuous, wanton, unrestrained, dissolute, licentious, immoral, bad.

slaughter, *n.* **1.** (*all of animals*) killing, butchering, chopping, cutting, carving; trimming, slicing, dismembering, mincing; abattage.

2. murder, homicide, manslaughter, assassination, slaying, killing; bloodshed, bloodletting, butchery, death by violence, brutal *or* bloody murder, murder most foul, foul murder, violent murder; mutilation, disembowelment, dismemberment.

3. carnage, massacre, wholesale butchery, random *or* indiscriminate butchery, general butchery; wholesale killing, hecatomb, mass murder, mass homicide, mass slaying, mass execution, mass destruction; bloodbath, effusion of blood, fusillade of blood, noyade, *Rare.* internecion, *Rare.* trucidation, decimation, annihilation, extermination, liquidation, pogrom, genocide.

—*v.* **4.** (*all of animals*) butcher, cut, hack, chop, carve, slice, trim; dress, prepare.

5. butcher, cut to pieces, maul, savage, hew, hack, hack to pieces, chop, chop to pieces, mow down, mutilate, tear limb from limb, dismember, disembowel, wade in blood, give no quarter, show no mercy, run amuck, go berserk; kill, murder, slay, cut down, do to death, execute, put to death, put to the sword, destroy, shed *or* spill blood, assassinate.

6. massacre, kill off, decimate, destroy a great number, annihilate, exterminate, eliminate, liquidate, obliterate, eradicate, erase, blot out.

7. trounce, trample, thrash, defeat thoroughly *or* utterly, rout, overwhelm, discomfit, humble, tread *or* trample underfoot, vanquish, conquer; crush, break, smash.

slaughtered, *adj.* **1.** butchered, cut to pieces, hewn, hacked, chopped to pieces, mutilated, torn limb from limb, dismembered, disemboweled; killed, murdered, slain, cut down, done to death, executed, put to death, put to the sword, destroyed, assassinated.

2. massacred, decimated, annihilated, exterminated, eliminated, liquidated, obliterated, eradicated, erased, blotted out.

3. trounced, trampled, thrashed, defeated thoroughly *or* utterly, routed, overwhelmed, overpowered, humbled, vanquished, conquered; crushed, broken, smashed.

slaughterhouse, *n.* slaughter-pen, butchery, abattoir, shambles, *Obs.* butcher-row.

slave, *n.* **1.** bond servant, bondman, indentured servant, serf, helot, hierodule, odalisque.

2. drudge, hack, fag, menial worker, laborer, toiler, workhorse.

3. addict, alcoholic, *Inf.* workaholic.

—*v.* **4.** work like a slave, drudge, grub, grind, work one's fingers to the bone; work hard, labor, toil, moil, work like a Trojan, work like a horse; sweat, struggle, *Sl.* kill oneself, work day and night, burn the midnight oil, burn the candle on both ends.

5. enslave, hold in bondage, enthrall, subjugate, reduce to slavery.

slaver, *v.* **1.** slobber, slabber, drool, drip saliva, drivel.

2. fawn *or* fawn upon, toady *or* toady to, truckle *or* truckle to, toadeat, *Sl.* fall all over.

slavery, *n.* **1.** enslavement, thralldom, enthrallment, bondage, captivity, impressment; servitude, hard labor, compulsory service, penal servitude; prison, imprisonment, confinement, durance, duress; serfdom, vassalage, villeinage, indentureship, indention; oppression, repression, subjugation, subjection, subordination, domination, yoke, control; compulsion, coercion, constraint, restraint, fetters, shackles, chains, bonds, irons.

2. labor, toil, travail, moil, drudgery, grind, hard work *or* toil; exertion, effort, strain, struggle, laboriousness.

slavish, *adj.* **1.** servile, subservient, subject, menial, enslaved, in bonds *or* bondage, in harness; submissive, docile, subdued, restrained, resigned, compliant, deferential, tractable, mealy-mouthed, obsequious, *Obs.* obsequent, *Obs., Rare.* vernile; abject, humble, poor, meek, lowly, downtrodden; prostrate, obeisant, on one's knees.

2. sycophantic, sycophantical, sycophantish, fawning,

flattering, toadyish, toadying, truckling, ingratiating, honey-mouthed, unctuous, *Sl.* bootlicking, *Sl.* footlicking, *Sl.* brown-nosing; groveling, crawling, crouching, slithering; squirming, cringing, cowering; whining, whimpering, sniveling.

3. base, base-spirited, mean, mean-spirited, low, vile, ignoble, inglorious, dishonorable, discreditable, disreputable.

4. unoriginal, without *or* lacking originality, unimaginative, prosaic, imitative; inflexible, rigid, stiff; (*all in a negative sense*) strict, close, exact, undeviating, direct, straightforward, faithful, literal.

slay, *v.* 1. kill, murder, assassinate, shoot, put to death, execute; dispose of, get rid of, *Sl.* do in, *Sl.* waste, *Sl.* rub out, *Sl.* bump *or* knock off. See **murder** (*def.* 4).

2. destroy, ruin, demolish, wreck, *Sl.* total; extinguish, annihilate, wipe out, obliterate, eradicate, extirpate. See **murder** (*def.* 7).

sleazy, *adj.* thin, flimsy, unsubstantial, pasteboard, jerry-built; inferior, *Sl.* schlock, gimcrack, *Inf.* dimestore, *Inf.* tacky, *Inf.* ticky-tacky; cheap, poor, poor-quality, *Sl.* chintzy, *Sl.* cheesy, *Sl.* crummy, junky, trashy; shabby, shoddy, tatty, sorry, run-down; low, mean, base, contemptible, dirty.

sled, *n.* bobsled, toboggan, jumper; sledge, sleigh, dray, *U.S. and Canada.* pung, cutter.

sleek[1] *adj.* 1. smooth, glossy, shiny, lustrous, satiny, silken, silky; rubbed, buffed, burnished, polished, shined, varnished, waxed.

2. well-fed, well-groomed, brushed, combed, tended; clean, neat, tidy, trim, spruce.

3. smooth, slick, suave, oily, unctuous, smug; honeyed, flattering, ingratiating.

sleek[2] *v.* sleeken, make sleek, smooth, slick; make glossy *or* lustrous, polish, burnish, shine, buff, varnish, wax.

sleep, *v.* 1. rest, repose, slumber, *All Sl.* flake out, sack in, sack out, hit the sack, conk off, crash, log Z's, catch some Z's, count sheep, *Brit. Sl.* doss; nap, catnap, take a siesta, *Inf.* catch forty winks; doze, drowse, nod off, drop off, *Inf.* snooze; oversleep, sleep late, sleep in.

2. retire, refresh oneself, take a rest; lie down, recline, go to bed, *Inf.* turn in.

3. be still, be quiet, be tranquil, be calm, be inactive, lie still; hibernate, estivate, vegetate; lie dormant, be latent, be quiescent.

4. be inattentive, be unwary, let one's mind wander; be asleep at the wheel *or* the switch; be caught unawares *or* offguard.

5. **sleep over** sojourn, visit, stay at.

—n. 6. rest, repose, slumber, land of Nod, arms of Morpheus, *Inf.* beauty sleep, *Sl.* shut-eye, *Sl.* Z's, *Chiefly Brit. Sl.* Bo-Peep; nap, catnap, nod, snooze, doze, siesta, *Inf.* forty winks.

7. coma, *Pathol.* sopor, trance, faint, swoon, blackout, stupor.

8. torpor, torpidity, torpidness, sluggishness, lethargy, lassitude; dormancy, latency, hibernation, estivation.

9. lifelessness, inanimateness, inanimation, death.

sleepiness, *n.* 1. drowsiness, tiredness, slumberousness, somnolence, somnolency, oscitance, oscitancy, (*in the Middle East*) kef; hypnosis, hypnotism.

2. sluggishness, languor, lassitude, lethargy, torpor, torpidity, torpidness, comatoseness, comatosity.

3. quietness, quietude, quiescence, quiet, inactivity, inaction, passivity, idleness, stillness; dormancy, latency, hibernation, estivation.

sleeping, *n.* 1. slumber, repose. See **sleep** (*def.* 6).

—adj. 2. asleep, sound asleep, *Med.* soporose, soporous; resting, reposing, slumbering, dozing, drowsing, *Inf.* snoozing, somnolent; napping, catnapping; oversleeping, late-sleeping.

3. dormant, inactive, passive, idle, quiescent, quiet, calm, becalmed; hibernating, estivating, vegetating.

4. inattentive, heedless, unmindful; unobservant, unwatchful, unaware; wandering, daydreaming, musing, staring into space; off guard, off on cloud nine, with one's head in the clouds, a million miles away.

sleeplessness, *n.* wakefulness, restlessness, insomnia, insomnolence; vigil, vigilance, vigilantness, alertness, watchfulness.

sleepwalking, *n.* 1. somnambulism, somnambulation.

—adj. 2. somnambulant, somnambulistic.

sleepy, *adj.* 1. drowsy, tired, dozy, half asleep, nodding, slumberous, slumbery, somnolent, oscitant; weary, faint, fatigued, exhausted, *Sl.* beat, *Sl.* pooped.

2. languid, languorous, lazy; sluggish, torpid, lethargic, comatose.

3. quiet, inactive, passive, idle, still; dormant, sleeping, asleep, latent, hibernating, estivating, (*of land*) fallow.

4. soporific, somniferous, somnific, somnifacient, sleep-inducing; narcotic, sedative, opiate; hypnotic, mesmeric.

sleigh, *n.* See **sled.**

sleight, *n.* 1. skill, proficiency, efficiency, facility, knack; deftness, adeptness, handiness, readiness, adroitness; cleverness, ingeniousness, wit, inventiveness, artistry.

2. artifice, stratagem, intrigue, maneuver, gambit, ploy, expedient; trick, hoax, ruse, wile, scheme, device, *Sl.* gimmick; underhandedness, surreptitiousness, deception, hocus-pocus.

3. cunning, guile, craft, slyness, sneakiness, furtiveness, shiftiness, insidiousness; artfulness, subtlety, shrewdness, sharpness, foxiness.

sleight of hand, *n.* legerdemain, prestidigitation, conjuration, hocus-pocus; magic, thaumaturgy, jugglery, trickery, feint, manipulation; shell game, thimblerig, thimblerigging, cardsharping, dealing from the bottom of the deck, stacking the deck; pulling rabbits out of hats *or* silver dollars out of thin air; trompel'oeil.

slender, *adj.* 1. slim, thin, thin as a rail, reedy, stalky, twiggy, like a pipestem, narrow, narrow as an arrow; spare, lanky, lean; slight, wispy.

2. gracile, willowy, svelte, lissome, lithe, sylphic, sylphlike; wasp-waisted, with an hourglass figure, snake-hipped.

3. meager, exiguous, scant. See **slim** (*def.* 3).

4. unconvincing, flimsy; unpromising, inauspicious; limited, restricted; uncertain, unfounded, lightweight.

5. (*of sound*) weak, faint, feeble, pallid; fragile, frail, delicate, fine, attenuated, airy, light, ethereal.

slice, *n.* 1. slab, wedge, hunk, chunk, cut, piece, *Brit. Dial.* collop, (*of bacon*) rasher; layer, shaving, paring, sliver.

2. part, portion, share, allotment, proportion, segment; division, section, fraction, fragment.

—v. 3. cut through, split, skive, sever, part, separate; cleave, knife, carve; split up, divide, segment; pare, peel, whittle.

slick, *adj.* 1. glossy, sleek, shiny, lustrous, shining, satiny, silken; smooth, smooth as glass, glazed, lacquered; bare, smooth as a billiard bail *or* baby's bottom.

2. suave, urbane, *Sl.* with it, sophisticated, worldly,

Ivy League; elegant, refined, cultured, smooth-spoken, well-spoken, well-bred; polite, unfailingly polite, courtly, gracious, agreeable, disarming, proper, decorous; affected, *Inf.* la-di-da, pretentious; ingratiating, smarmy, unctuous, smug.

3. sly, shrewd, cunning, crafty, wily, sharp, sharp-witted; calculating, designing, manipulative; subtle, insidious, Byzantine, devious.

4. ingenious, clever, bright, brilliant, inventive, resourceful, creative, imaginative, *Inf.* nifty.

5. slippery, oily, glassy, greasy, lubricated, soapy.

6. (*of art or literature*) glib, fluent, *Sl.* Madison Avenue, *Sl.* Mad Av; superficial, shallow, surface, two-dimensional, without depth; popular, *Inf.* pop, lowbrow, unintellectual, hack, second-rate; trivial, frothy, kitschy, slight, thin, lightweight, *Inf.* half-baked; inferior, mediocre, trashy, rubbishy, *Sl.* schlock, worthless; vulgar, coarse, tasteless, fulsome, *Sl.* for the birds.

7. *Slang.* wonderful, remarkable, noteworthy, notable; extraordinary, exceptional, *Inf.* terrific, great, amazing, *Sl.* A-OK, *Inf.* a bit of all right; first-rate, *Sl.* top-hole, top-drawer, *Sl.* top-shelf, *Inf.* A-one, perfect, first-class, *Sl.* super.

slide, *v.* **1.** glide, plane, skate, skim, glissade, ski; coast, toboggan, sled, roll down, snowball; slither, fall, bounce down, slink, wriggle; skid, sideslip, tumble.

2. slip, move, pass, lapse, decline.

3. push, nudge, shove, shoot; hand over, pass along.

4. **let slide** forget, neglect, ignore, drop, abandon, not give a thought to; pay no mind to, let ride.

—*n.* **5.** chute, trough, tube, shaft, conveyor.

slight, *adj.* **1.** small, little, tiny, *Inf.* teeny, smallish, diminutive; miniature, pocket-sized, bantam, *Inf.* baby, *Inf.* baby-sized, small-scale; wee, *Inf.* dinky, puny, *Inf.* pint-sized, short, *Inf.* half-pint.

2. slender, slim, thin, light; delicate, minikin, (*of a woman*), petite, gracile; lean, dapper, narrow, filamentous, filiform.

3. infinitesimal, minute, microscopic, molecular; inappreciable, imperceptible, imponderable, indiscernible; intangible, impalpable, subtle, fine, evanescent.

4. petty, minor, unimportant, insignificant, immaterial, irrelevant, not vital, neither here nor there; negligible, unsubstantial, insubstantial, inconsiderable, of no consequence, inconsequential, unnotable, unnoted; trivial, trifling, paltry, nugatory, worthless.

5. superficial, shallow, depthless, pointless, skin-deep; empty, vacuous, hollow, void; inane, fatuous, silly, airy, ridiculous, foolish, fatuitous; frivolous, frothy.

6. frail, feeble, fragile, flimsy, sleazy; weak, faint, *Dial.* pindling, enervated; attenuated, tenuous, weakened.

7. breakable, frangible; jerry-built, unsteady, undependable, defective; precarious, unstable, insecure; rickety, tottering, tottery, unsteady, *Chiefly U.S.* teetery.

8. tolerable, fair, passable, mediocre, moderate, modest; below *or* under the mark, below *or* under par, insufficient, not enough, deficient; inadequate, scanty, meager, sparse, skimpy, poor, weak, lame.

—*v.* **9.** snub, cut, turn one's back upon, turn up one's nose at, *Inf.* high-hat. See **snub** (*def.* **1**).

10. insult, affront, *Sl.* put down, *Sl.* cut up, give offense to. See **snub** (*def.* **2**).

11. embarrass, disconcert, abash, mortify, *Inf.* gross out, upset; confuse, fluster, ruffle, discountenance, distract, discompose, confound.

12. scamp, slur over, touch upon, pass over lightly, skim the surface; do negligently, do haphazardly, do heedlessly, do carelessly, do superficially, do perfunctorily; skim over, slip over, skip over, trifle with; play with, toy with, *Inf.* mess *or* fool around; dash off, knock off, toss off *or* out; slough off, cut corners, cut a corner, fribble away; forget, neglect, overlook.

—*n.* **13.** snub, cold shoulder, coldness, indifference. See **snub** (*def.* **5**).

14. affront, insult, slur, dig, barb. See **snub** (*def.* **6**).

15. rudeness, disrespect, ill-treatment. See **snub** (*def.* **7**).

slighting, *adj.* **1.** offensive, insulting, *Archaic.* affrontive, disparaging, denouncing, derogatory, depreciating; disdainful, contemptuous, contemning, contemnible, supercilious, contumelious, scouting, flouting; scornful, derisive, jeering, ridiculing, mocking, scoffing; twitting, gibing, taunting, fleering; hissing, booing, catcalling.

2. abusive, vilifying, vituperative, impugnable, traducing, slurring, calumnious; blasphemous, scurrilous, irreverent, sarcastic; profane, ribald, foulmouthed, obscene, vulgar; maligning, defamatory, denigrating, slanderous, libelous; injurious, harmful, damaging, invidious; vexatious, provoking, aggravating, incensing, inflammatory, exasperating, teasing, distressing; irritating, chafing, disturbing, annoying, displeasing.

3. rude, impolite, disrespectful, discourteous, uncourteous, uncivil, incivil, dishonorable; insincere, indirect, backhand, backhanded; impertinent, insolent, flippant, impudent, fresh, saucy, bold, *Archaic.* malapert; ill-mannered, ill-bred, ill-behaved, unrefined; surly, bad-tempered, ill-tempered; obnoxious, objectionable, odious.

4. snobby, cold, cool, icy, arrogant, haughty, exclusive; indifferent, aloof, neglectful; humiliating, belittling; shameful, disgraceful, opprobrious, degrading, ignominious; blunt, gruff, brusque, harsh, acrimonious; caustic, cutting, trenchant; overbearing, obtrusive.

slim, *adj.* **1.** slender, thin, gracile; spare, slight, lean; lithe, svelte, willowy, slinky.

2. poor, inferior, second-rate, third-rate; inadequate, unsuitable, unacceptable, unsatisfactory; sorry, sad, pitiful, pathetic.

3. small, inconsiderable, insignificant, meager, scanty; trifling, piddling, petty; puny, paltry, *Inf.* measly, *Inf.* chintzy, *Inf.* skimpy, *Inf.* rotten, *Sl.* lousy, *Sl.* crummy.

—*v.* **4.** slenderize, thin down; reduce, lose weight, take off weight, shed pounds.

slime, *n.* mud, muck, ooze, sludge, *Inf.* glop, *Inf.* gunk, *Sl.* guck, *Inf.* goo, *Sl.* goop; slush, slosh, mush, squash, mess, slop, swill, *Irish.* slob.

slimy, *adj.* **1.** muddy, mucky, miry, oozy, sludgy, *Sl.* gloppy, *Inf.* gunky, *Inf.* gooey, *Sl.* goopy; messy, sloppy, slushy, sloshy, mushy, soft, spongy, squashy, squishy, splashy, plashy; marshy, marshlike, *Archaic.* marish, boggy, boggish, swampy, swampish, moory, poachy, paludal, fenny, quaggy, quagmiry, sloughy.

2. foul, vile, noxious, obnoxious, offensive, sickening, disgusting, nauseating, loathsome, repulsive; putrid, rotten, decayed, bad, off.

3. despicable, contemptible, beneath contempt, base, hateful.

sling, *n.* **1.** slingshot, catapult, mortar, arbalest, trebuchet.

2. bandage, strap, band, loop; support, brace.

—*v.* **3.** fling, flirt, heave, jerk, cant, shoot, fire; propel, project, jaculate, catapult; cast, throw, toss,

dart, shy, chuck, pitch, dash, let fly, send, launch.
4. suspend, hang, swing, dangle.

slink, *v.* skulk. See **skulk** (*def.* **2**).

slip[1], *v.* **1.** glide, slide, flow, move smoothly, *Dance.* glissade; slither, slink, sneak, skulk, lurk, prowl, creep, *U.S. Sl.* gumshoe; worm, wiggle, wriggle; steal away, slip out *or* off, escape, get away, flee, run off; evade, elude, dodge, get clear of, break away.
2. pass, elapse, go by, flit *or* fly by, drift by, be lost.
3. fall, fall down, stumble, lose one's footing, go down, take a spill; tumble, skid, trip, sideslip, dive, go head over heels.
4. (*all of knots*) untie, unfasten, unbind, untangle, unsnarl, undo.
5. err, blunder, slip up, miscalculate, misjudge, misreckon, mistake; fumble, boggle, botch *or* botch up, *Sl.* screw up.
6. decline, depreciate, fall off, drop off, lower, decrease, slump; deteriorate, go downhill, degenerate, regress, backslide, retrogress; flag, sink, droop, fail, wane.
7. don, put on; doff, take off, shed, slough off.
8. neglect, miss, omit, bypass; overlook, disregard, slight.
9. **slip [s.t.] over on [s.o.]** deceive, defraud, trick, delude, take in, pull the wool over [s.o.'s] eyes.
—n. **10.** fall, trip, stumble, spill, skid; slide, glide, *Dance.* glissade.
11. mistake, error, oversight, omission, inadvertence, *Inf.* slip-up; indiscretion, impropriety, faux pas, gaffe, gaucherie; blunder, *Sl.* boo-boo, *Sl.* goof, *Sl.* boner, slip of the lip *or* tongue *or* pen, Freudian slip, *Radio & TV. Sl.* blooper; sin, transgression, offense, trespass.
12. decline, downturn, diminution, lessing, lowering, fall-off, downtrend, downslide, downswing, slump, nosedive; depreciation, falling-off, drop-off, dip, decrease, recession; dwindling, deterioration, degeneration, regression, retrogression, retrogradation.

slip[2], *n.* **1.** scion, cutting, offshoot, sprout, sprig, spray; runner, *Bot.* sarmentum; switch, twig, branch.
2. strip, slat, splinter, sliver, shiver, shred, fragment.
3. paper, notepaper, note; permission slip, pass, admission, papers, certificate, stub, card.
4. underdress, undergarment, underwear, lingerie; underskirt, petticoat, half-slip; undershirt, chemise, camisole.

slipper, *n.* pump, mule, sandal, moccasin; house shoe, bedroom slipper, loafer, slip-on; dancing pump, ballet slipper, opera pump; zori, *Sl.* flip-flop; clog, wooden shoe, *Trademark.* Dr. Scholls.

slipperiness, *n.* **1.** oiliness, lubricity, greasiness, slitheriness; smoothness, sleekness, glassiness, glossiness, iciness; soapiness, waxiness, butteriness, unctuousness; sliminess, mucosity.
2. shiftiness, trickiness, deceitfulness; foxiness, craftiness, cunning, snakiness; slickness, dishonesty, *Inf.* shadiness, close-dealing, sharp trading.
3. unreliability, undependability, unfaithfulness, faithlessness, disloyalty, unsteadfastness; capriciousness, whimsicality, fancifulness, flightiness; changeability, variability, mutability; moodiness, unpredictability, mercuriality, unaccountability.
4. unsteadiness, insecurity, unsafeness; precariousness, danger, peril, hazard; ticklishness, risk, chance, speculation; unsureness, totteriness, shakiness, criticalness, unsoundness, *Inf.* chanciness.

slippery, *adj.* **1.** slick, oily, greasy; smooth, sleek, glassy, glossy, skiddy, icy; soapy, waxed, buttery, unctuous, lubricated, lubricous, mucous, synovial.
2. hard to grasp, hard to hold, transient, transitory, passing; temporal, ephemeral, fleeting, momentary; fragile, evanescent, vanishing, disappearing; provisional, intermediate, temporary, impermanent, perishable, short-lived.
3. shifty, tricky, deceitful; two-faced, Janus-faced, foxy, crafty, cunning, reptilian, snaky; slick, dishonest, *Inf.* shady; double-dealing, treacherous, perfidious, faithless, disloyal; unreliable, undependable, untrustworthy, fly-by-night.
4. unstable, unsteady, insecure, unsafe; precarious, dangerous, perilous, hazardous; ticklish, risky, chancy, *Sl.* hairy; speculative, unsure, built on sand, tottery, shaky; critical, unsound, hanging by a thread, trembling in the balance, needing but a shove.

slipshod, *adj.* last-minute, slap-bang, careless, hurried. See **slapdash.**

slip-up, *n.* *Informal.* mistake, error, human error, *Inf.* miscue; blunder, botch, bungle, fumble, flub, muff; leak, slip, slip of the tongue *or* pen; faux pas, gaffe, indiscretion, breach of etiquette, offense, peccadillo; oversight, omission, miss, *Inf.* go-by; inadvertence, loose thread, (*pl.*) paralipomena; *All Sl.* pratfall, fool mistake, foul-up, louse-up, screw-up, boner, boo-boo, boot, goof, blooper, clinker, clunker.

slit, *v.* **1.** cut, slice, slash, gash, incise, pierce, lance; sever, abscind, split, carve, cleave, sunder; rend, rive, tear, rip; snip, clip, scissor; divide, section, apportion; disjoin, disunite, dismember.
—n. **2.** cut, gash, slash, cleft, rift, trench; incision, groove, opening, aperture, indentation; wound, laceration; nick, tear, rip, split.

sliver, *n.* splinter, shive, fragment, segment, chip, whittling, shaving, flake, filament; shred, bit, scrap, snip, snippet; snatch, modicum, iota, whit; mite, micron, molecule, trace.

slobber, *v.* slaver, slabber, drool, water at the mouth, drivel, dribble, drip saliva; sputter, splutter.

slogan, *n.* motto, byword, catchword, catch phrase, battle cry, buzz word, red flag, watch word, shibboleth, test word, pet phrase; expression, saying, phrase; sign, logo, *Journalism.* masthead.

slop, *v.* **1.** spill, splash, splatter, spatter; wash over, slosh over, slosh around, swish around, swash around.
—n. **2.** swill, hogwash; kitchen refuse, garbage, rubbish, waste, offscourings, scraps, orts, leavings, leftovers.
3. *Often* **slops** dirty water, dish water, liquid refuse.
4. liquid mud, muck, mire, *Sl.* guck, slime, sludge, ooze.

slope, *v.* **1.** slant, oblique, skew, fall obliquely, angle, bevel, pitch, grade, bank; ascend, rise; descend, drop *or* drop off, dip, sag, sink; list, lean, tip, tilt, cant, heel, *Naut.* careen.
—n. **2.** inclination, slant, bevel, pitch, grade, angle, skew, tilt, cant; ramp, inclined plane, bank, hillside, hill, mount, acclivity, ascent, rise; declivity, downward slope *or* slant, *Scot. and North Eng.* brae, decline, declension, descent, downgrade; drop, fall, dip, sag.
3. *Usu.* **slopes** hills, foothills, bluffs, mountains.

sloping, *adj.* oblique, slanted, diagonal. See **slanting.**

sloppy, *adj.* **1.** muddy, oozy, slimy, *Sl.* gucky; slushy, sloshy, wet, watery, sodden, soggy, plashy; slippery, *Inf.* slippy.
2. splashed, splashy, spotty, spotted, soiled, stained, splattered, spattered.

3. overly emotional, gushy, *Inf.* mushy, oversentimental, *Inf.* gooey.
4. careless, loose, lax, slack, slipshod; hugger-mugger, haphazard, slapdash, hasty, offhand.
5. untidy, dowdy, frumpy, frumpish; messy, disorderly, disheveled, uncombed, unkempt, tangled; slovenly, frowzy, slatternly, bedraggled, draggletailed, sluttish; unclean, piggish, dirty, grimy, grubby, filthy, *Sl.* grungy; scruffy, shabby, down-at-the-heels, rundown, sleazy, *Sl.* raunchy.

slot, *n.* slit, crack, hole, keyhole, opening, aperture; depression, groove, notch.

sloth, *n.* **1.** slothfulness, acedia, laziness, idleness, indolence, faineance, do-nothingness, otiosity; unindustriousness, unenterprisingness, unambitiousness, want *or* lack of ambition *or* enterprise, nonaggressiveness; listlessness, *Dial.* limpsiness, lackadaisicalness, insouciance, pococurantism; shiftlessness, worthlessness, good-for-nothingness; slackness, laxity, remissness, negligence, neglectfulness, carelessness.
2. inertia, inactivity, stagnation, torpor, torpidness, torpidity, supineness, passiveness, passivity; sluggishness, lumpishness, lethargy, phlegm, heaviness, dullness, languidness, languor, hebetudinousness, lentitudinousness.

slothful, *adj.* **1.** lazy, idle, indolent, sluggard, sluggardly, fainéant, do-nothing, otiose; unindustrious, unenterprising, unambitious, nonaggressive; listless, *Dial.* limpsy, lackadaisical, insouciant, pococurante, easy-going; slack, lax, remiss, negligent, neglectful, careless; shiftless, worthless, good-for-nothing, ne'er-do-well.
2. slow-moving, slow-going, creeping, crawling, *Inf.* poky; lingering, loitering, lagging, dilly-dallying, dallying, laggard, foot-dragging; inert, inactive, stagnant, torpid, supine, passive; sluggish, lumpish, lethargic, phlegmatic, heavy, dull, languid, languorous, hebetudinous, lentitudinous.

slouch, *v.* **1.** slump, hunch, stoop, droop, bend; shuffle, shamble, lumber, drag.
—*n.* **2.** crouch, slump; droop, bend; shuffle, shamble, hobble.
3. lout, dolt, oaf, clod, clodhopper, gawk, looby, lubber, *Chiefly Scot.* cuddy, *Inf.* lummox, *Sl.* klutz, *Sl.* galoot; bungler, bumbler, fumbler, botcher, blunderer, boggler, *Inf.* stumblebum, *Inf.* duffer, *Sl.* slob; churl, curmudgeon, barbarian, yahoo, *Chiefly Scot.* tyke, *Brit. Sl.* mucker.
4. *Informal.* sluggard, lazybones, lazy person, slugabed, Oblomov, good-for-nothing, idler, loafer, lounger, lingerer, *Sl.* bum; malingerer, shirker, *Sl.* drugstore cowboy.

sloven, *n.* slattern, drab, draggletail, slut, trollop, *Sl.* slob, dowd, frump, *Sl.* pig, slovenly person, *Sl.* mess.

slovenly, *adj.* **1.** untidy, unclean, unkempt, draggletailed, bedraggled, *Inf.* messy, *Inf.* sloppy; frumpish, frumpy, dowdy, *Inf.* tacky; disheveled, *Inf.* mussed up, messed up, rumpled, tousled, *Chiefly Scot. Dial.* toused; shabby, dirty, blowzy, slatternly, sluttish.
2. slipshod, careless, disorderly, slapdash; offhand, last-minute, slap-bang; slapped together, thrown together; casual, cursory, perfunctory, lax, slack; unmindful, unthinking, thoughtless; negligent, careless, loose.

slow, *adj.* **1.** not rapid, snail-like, going at a snail's pace, tortoise-like, slower than molasses in January, crawling, plodding, shuffling; dawdling, lagging, lallygagging; hesitant, faltering, pausing, hanging back.
2. gradual, moderate, leisurely, unhurried, slow-paced; inchmeal, imperceptible; measured, paced, methodical, deliberate.
3. sluggish, lagging, laggard, sluggardly; dallying, dillydallying, idling; dilatory, procrastinating, postponing, deferring; lackadaisical, indolent, slothful, otiose.
4. dull, unintelligent, witless, slow-witted, dull-witted, stolid, obtuse, crass, Boeotian, bovine, blockish, lumpish; dense, thick-headed, *Inf.* thick, stupid, *Australian Inf.* dill, *Scot. and North Eng.* dowf; backward, doltish, *Sl.* birdbrained, simple; empty-headed, vacuous; unimaginative, undiscerning.
5. slack, not busy, inactive, unhurried, quiet, peaceful; gentle, easy, unpressured; creeping, crawling.
6. dragging, draggy, protracted, lengthened, spun-out, drawn-out, prolonged, never-ending, interminable, dragged-out.
7. behind the times, unprogressive, conservative, backward, *Sl.* not with it, *Sl.* square.
8. dull, uninteresting, tedious, tiresome, boring, boresome, wearisome, *Sl.* dead, dry, dry-as-dust; uneventful, humdrum, monotonous, ordinary.
9. *Usu.* **slow to** reluctant, disinclined, unwilling, half-hearted, loath, hesitant, hesitating.
—*v.* **10.** *Often* **slow up** *or* **down** retard, *Sl.* hang up, delay; detain, hold back, set back, check, hold in check, restrict, restrain; put the brakes on, reduce speed, take it easy, relax.
11. *Often* **slow down** subside, slack, ebb, recede, retrocede; dwindle, peter out; wind down, deescalate; fall off, taper off, wane, fade away, die out.

sludge, *n.* mud, muck, mire, ooze, slime, *Inf.* glop, *Inf.* gunk, *Sl.* guck, *Inf.* goo, *Sl.* goop; slush, slosh, mush, squash, slop, swill, *Irish.* slob.

sluggish, *adj.* slow, slow-moving, slow-going, snail-paced, snail-like, moving at a snail's pace, crawling, creeping, *Inf.* poky; inert, inactive, stagnant, torpid, supine; lumpish, lethargic, phlegmatic, heavy, dull, languid, languorous, hebetudinous, lentitudinous; sleepy, drowsy, somnolent, slumberous, yawny.

sluggishness, *n.* **1.** languor, languidness, laggardness, *Archaic.* languishment; inertia, inactivity, stagnation, torpor, supineness, *Archaic.* lenitude, (*in the Middle East*) kef; lifelessness, inanimateness, inanimation, spiritlessness, listlessness, apathy, indifference, *Inf.* the blahs; phlegm, lethargy, heaviness, lumpishness, dullness, hebetudinousness; somnolence, sleepiness, drowsiness, doziness.
2. laziness, idleness, indolence, sloth, slothfulness, acedia, faineance, otiosity, do-nothingness; unindustriousness, unenterprisingness, unambitiousness, want *or* lack of ambition *or* enterprise, nonaggressiveness; lackadaisicalness, insouciance, pococurantism; shiftlessness, worthlessness, good-for-nothingness.

slum, *n.* *Usu.* **slums** warren, ghetto, shanty town, (*in Jamaica*) Trenchtown, Hell's Kitchen, hell's half-acre, Hooverville, skid row, *Inf.* rookeries.

slumber, *v.* **1.** doze, drowse, nap, catnap, take a nap, take a siesta, nod off, drop off, *Inf.* snooze, *Inf.* snatch *or* catch forty winks, *Inf.* catch some shut-eye, *Sl.* zizz, *Brit. Sl.* doss; sleep, count sheep, rest in the arms of Morpheus, visit the sandman, go to the land of Nod, *Sl.* log Z's, *Sl.* catch some Z's, *Sl.* saw logs *or* wood.
—*n.* **2.** sleep, repose, the arms of Morpheus, land of Nod, slumberland, dreamland, *Inf.* beddy-bye, *Sl.* shut-eye.
3. nap, cat nap, siesta, *Inf.* snooze, *Inf.* forty winks.
4. abeyance, dormancy, suspense, suspended animation.

slumberous, *adj.* **1.** sleepy, half-asleep, asleep on one's feet, heavy with sleep, heavy-eyed; somnolent, drowsy, dozy, groggy, *Sl.* dopey; yawny, oscitant, nodding, nodding-off, ready for bed.

2. inert, inactive, dormant, static, latent, abeyant, in abeyance *or* suspense; sluggish, torpid, stagnant; calm, still, quiet, quiescent.

3. soporific, somniferous, sleep-inducing, sleep-producing; narcotic.

slump, *v.* **1.** sink, subside, go down, get bogged down; collapse, cave in, give way; sag, droop.

2. decrease, depreciate, devaluate, drop, reach a new low; fall, plunge, plummet, dive, nosedive, go into a tailspin, *Inf.* come a cropper, *Inf.* take a header.

3. deteriorate, degenerate, decline, worsen, take a turn for the worse, go from bad to worse, slip, slide; go downhill, go to pieces, *Inf.* go to pot, *Inf.* go to the dogs, *Sl.* hit the skids; fail, lapse, weaken, retrogress, retrograde, let oneself go.

4. slouch, hunch; bow, bend, stoop.

—n. **5.** decrease, depreciation, devaluation; decline, deterioration, degeneration, vitiation, atrophy; lapse, retrogression, retrogradation, regression.

6. descent, fall, downturn, downtrend, downslide, downswing; plunge, drop-off, nosedive, tailspin, *Inf.* header.

7. depression, recession, slowdown, dry spell, hard times, *Sl.* bust.

slur, *v.* **1.** slight, gloss over, minimize; omit, miss, give a miss, fail to mention; overlook, pass over, skip, jump; ignore, disregard, dismiss, pay no attention to.

2. garble, drawl, elide; mumble, lisp, sputter.

3. calumniate, slander, libel, traduce, misrepresent; insinuate, impute, cast aspersions; sully, stain, soil, blacken, blemish, smudge, stigmatize, drag through the mud *or* mire, heap dirt upon, throw mud on, *Sl.* dump on.

4. defame, denigrate, vituperate, vilify, vilipend, scandalize, run down, revile, malign, give a bad name to, speak ill of, cut to pieces, *Sl.* do a hatchet job on; disparage, detract, derogate, deprecate, *Sl.* put down.

—n. **5.** insult, slight, *Sl.* put-down; aspersion, imputation, innuendo, insinuation, reflection, *Inf.* brickbat; calumny, slander, libel, false accusation, misrepresentation, falsehood, lie, untruth.

6. disgrace, stigma, brand, blot, blot on the escutcheon, smear, smirch, stain, spot, black spot *or* mark.

slush, *n.* **1.** slosh, melting snow.

2. slime, muck. See **slime**.

3. bathos, sentimentality, oversentimentality, mawkishness, maudlinness, cloyingness, mushiness, soppiness, *Inf.* slushiness; bleeding heart, namby-pamby, mush, *Inf.* goo, *Inf.* schmaltz, *Sl.* hearts and flowers.

slut, *n.* **1.** slattern, drab, trollop, sloven, draggletail; frump, dowdy; hag.

2. prostitute, harlot, whore, hussy, loose woman, wanton, fallen woman, woman of ill repute, lady of the evening; trull, quean, painted woman, streetwalker, bar girl, *Inf.* pick-up, *All Sl.* tart, hooker, floozie, working girl. See also **prostitute** (*def.* **1**).

3. bitch, female dog.

sly, *adj.* **1.** cunning, crafty, wily, artful, subtle, foxy, *Sl.* crazy like a fox, *Scot. and North Eng.* pawky; shrewd, astute, canny, sharp, knowing, *Inf.* cagey.

2. covert, clandestine, undercover, stealthy, surreptitious, feline, back-alley, *Canon Law.* subreptitious; secret, hugger-mugger, hole-and-corner, closed-door, closet; furtive, underhand, underhanded, *Inf.* under the table *or* counter, back-room, sneaky, sneaking; devious, insidious, guileful, disingenuous, scheming, plotting, designing; tricky, crooked, dishonest, unethical, dishonorable, *Inf.* left-hand; shifty, slippery, *Inf.* shady.

3. roguish, impish, puckish, waggish, elfish, prankish, mischievous; naughty, scampish, arch, *Scot.* hempy; playful, sportive, frolicsome, full *or* fond of mischief.

—n. **4. on the sly** undercover, covertly, clandestinely, stealthily, surreptitiously, slyly, *Scot.* stownlins, *Scot. and North Eng.* pawkily; in secret, secretively, *Inf.* under the table *or* counter, *Sl.* on the quiet, *Sl.* on the Q.T.; furtively, underhandedly, sneakily, behind [s.o.'s] back, like a thief in the night.

smack[1], *n.* **1.** taste, flavor, savor; sniff, scent, tang, tincture, pungency, aroma; relish, sapor, sapidity; essence, character, zest, piquancy, poignancy.

2. trace, hint, idea, tinge, suspicion, soupçon; touch, speck, sprinkling, dusting, dash.

3. mouthful, bite, morsel, tidbit; chew, *Dial.* chaw, bit, crumb, grain; thimbleful, spoonful, ounce, dollop, splash; shot, *Inf.* swig, *Sl.* hit, *Sl.* slug, drop, dot, driblet; *Inf.* little taste, sample, test bite *or* slice, sampling.

—v. **4.** *Usu.* **smack of** resemble, be similar to, be like, bear resemblance to; appear like, seem like, sound like; look like, take after, favor, remind one of, bring to mind; have the earmarks of, have the stamp of, have the hallmark of; approximate, come close to, come near to; follow the fashion of, parallel, follow, correspond to; accord with, copy, simulate, imitate, counterfeit.

smack[2], *v.* **1.** strike, slap, hit, smite, thwack; cuff, buffet, knock, punch, box; *Inf.* clout, *Inf.* slug, *Inf.* whack, *Inf.* knock [s.o.'s] block off, *Inf.* crown, *Sl.* bash, *Sl.* bop, *Sl.* plug, *Sl.* belt, *Sl.* sock; beat, batter, pound, lay on, *Sl.* lay into; pommel, pummel, pelt, *Sl.* paste.

2. drive, hit hard, impel, push forward; slam, hammer, pound, bang, tap smartly, drive in *or* home, *Inf.* send home.

—n. **3.** blow, hit, bastinado, punch, *Inf.* wallop, *Inf.* whomp; thwack, slap, *Inf.* clout.

4. *Informal.* kiss, loud kiss, *Inf.* buss, *Inf.* smooch, osculation; salute, accolade, handkiss.

—adv. **5.** *Informal.* directly, straight, *Inf.* smack-dab, plumb.

small, *adj.* **1.** little, tiny, teeny, pint-sized; wee, mini, short, *Inf.* sawed-off, snub; *Inf.* teeny-weeny, *Inf.* itty-bitty, *Inf.* itsy-bitsy, *Inf.* itty, *Inf.* eensy-weensy; Lilliputian, elfin, like Tom Thumb, pygmy, dwarf, *Inf.* peewee; baby, bantam, diminutive, (*of a woman*) petite, minikin; midget, miniature, miniscule, minute, atomic; puny, runty, stunted, bonsaied, dwarfed, scrubby, shrunken.

2. thin, slender, slight, dainty, slim, lean, spare, gracile; narrow as an arrow, thin as six o'clock, slender as a thread, thin as a reed, reed-like; tapered, indented, narrow, drawn out, fine-drawn, attenuated; narrowish, isthmian, narrow-gauged, like a needle's eye.

3. brief, limited, abbreviated; curt, compact, condensed, terse, succinct, laconic, clipped, concise.

4. insufficient, inadequate, wanting, skimpy, scanty, scant; meager, *Inf.* dinky, exiguous; too little, too small, piddling, not enough; unsatisfactory, unequal to the need *or* demand, incommensurate; nominal, negligible, *Inf.* measly, mere, beggarly, poor.

5. unimportant, trifling, minor, secondary; nugatory, inconsequential, insignificant, inappreciable; not vital, immaterial, obscure, unknown, unnoticed; lesser, subordinate, lower, second-fiddle; subsidiary, ancillary, second-class, third-class, small-time, minor-league, bush, bush-league; small-town, one-horse, *Sl.* two-bit, *Sl.* tinhorn, *Sl.* small potatoes, small-fry; *Sl.* mickey-mouse, baby, small-time, *Sl.* rinky-dink, *Inf.* no great shakes, *Dial.* no account; (*all of a business*) small-scale, private, individual, owner-run, mom-and-pop.

6. humble, modest, unpretentious, plain; common, commonplace, ordinary, humdrum; simple, poor, plebian, low-ranking, inferior; homely, homespun, unrefined, vulgar, ill-bred, lowbred, uncouth; shabby, scruffy, *Inf.* slumy, slum-like, scrubby; low, ignoble, inglorious, base; ignominious, sordid, squalid.

7. mean, petty, stingy, parsimonious; niggardly, cheap, selfish, grudging, penny-pinching, stinting, begrudging, uncharitable, illiberal, unaltruistic; tight, miserly, carking, skin-flinty; penurious, tight-fisted, close, close-fisted, Scrooge-like, *Inf.* yankee.

8. limited, insular, parochial, provincial, uncatholic, *Sociol.* ethnocentric, limited in one's horizons *or* scope; biased, prejudiced, bigoted; one-sided, opinionated, close-minded; ultra-conservative, rigid, creed-bound; prim, puritanical, *Inf.* stuffy.

9. weak, diluted, dilute; watery, thinned, reduced, insipid, wishy-washy; (*all of sound or the voice*) gentle, soft, low, light, faint, whispering; quiet, delicate, hushed, indistinct; murmuring, subdued, muted, muffled, stifled, barely audible.

10. **feel small** be mortified, be chagrined, be humiliated; be discomforted, *Inf.* be put down, be disconcerted, be discomposed; be brought down, be degraded; be redfaced, be sheepish, be ashamed, be shamefaced, be hangdog; feel like a failure, feel like two cents, *Inf.* feel like a goose.

—*n.* **11.** common people, the meek, the meek and the small; the masses, hoi polloi, the vulgus; proletariat, plebians, the multitude, the many; the rank and file, *Contemptuous.* ragtag and bobtail, the vulgar herd, the poor, the great unwashed, the underprivileged.

smart, *v.* **1.** sting, prick, prickle, bite, nip, pinch, pierce, stab; gripe, burn, chafe, itch, rasp, grate, gall; hurt, pain, ache, throb, tingle.

2. injure, offend, aggrieve, grieve, sorrow, cut to the quick, cut to the heart, wound the feelings; disturb, distress, annoy, irritate, nettle, aggravate, rub the wrong way, vex; rile, rankle, roil, irk.

3. regret, feel shame *or* remorse, be stung with remorse, feel chagrin; lament, deplore, rue.

—*adj.* **4.** sharp, keen, stinging, poignant, sore, painful; hard, resounding, severe, rough, harsh, stiff; vigorous, swift, brisk, fast, sudden.

5. cutting, trenchant, scathing, derisive, derisory, insulting; curt, rude, crusty, abrupt, brusque, gruff; tart, bitter, acrid, acrimonious, rancorous; lashing, malicious, malevolent, venomous, envenomed, spiteful, maleficent.

6. energetic, lively, alive, full of life, vivid, spirited, animated; eager, alert, active, spry, quick, agile, jaunty, perky; breezy, buoyant, airy; jocund, sportive, hearty, merry, cheery; earnest, enthusiastic, fervent, ardent, heated, zealous.

7. apt, adroit, ingenious, deft; alert, wide-awake, bright, brilliant, acute, sharp-witted, sharp as a tack; intelligent, quick-witted, ready; sagacious, sage, wise, sapient, sapiential; rational, logical, reasonable, common-sensical, having a good head on one's shoulders; judicious, prudent, sensible; able, capable, competent.

8. perspicacious, discerning, long-headed, penetrating, perceptive, percipient, insightful; gifted, talented, well-endowed, intellectual, brainy; educated, learned, well-schooled, instructed; erudite, knowledgeable, versed, well-read, aware, *Sl.* hip, knowing, *Fr. au fair;* ace, topflight, top-drawer, first-rate, *Inf.* topnotch.

9. astute, shrewd, *Sl.* savvy, hard-headed, subtle; cunning, foxy, artful, politic, wily, crafty, sly, calculating.

10. clever, witty, nimble-witted; whimsical, droll, humorous, funny, jocose, jocular; effective, masterly, forcible, stirring, vigorous, racy; pointed, barbed, trenchant.

11. spruce, trim, neat, *Brit.* trig, well-groomed; fashionable, elegant, soigné, chic, up-to-the-minute, modish, *Sl.* hip; natty, *Sl.* spiffy, *Inf.* snappy, *Sl.* classy, *Inf.* nifty; rakish, saucy, dashing, dandy, dapper, showy.

—*n.* **12.** sting, bite, nip, pinch, sharp pain; ache, gnawing pain, burn, sore, pang, twinge, tingle.

13. pain, sorrow, woe, grievance, worry; torment, torture, agony; shame, remorse, embarrassment, mortification.

14. injury, offense, cut, blow, shock; aggravation, gall, vexation, fret; oppression, load, burden, cross, curse, bitter pill, trial; blight, canker.

smarten, *v. Usu.* **smarten up** **1.** spruce up, make trim, groom; shine, polish, *Sl.* spiff up; order, arrange, organize, tidy; beautify, embellish, embroider, ornament, set off, deck out.

2. enlighten, inform, educate, school, instruct, sophisticate, *Sl.* wise [s.o.] up, clue [s.o.] in; disabuse, disillusion, open [s.o.'s] eyes, put [s.o.] wise, burst [s.o.'s] bubble.

3. *All Sl.* get wise, get with it, shape up, whip oneself into shape, get on the stick.

smash, *v.* **1.** break, shatter, shiver, splinter; pulverize, comminute, triturate, crumble, disintegrate, crunch; dash, crash, batter, strike, beat, hit, crack; plunge, hurtle, fling, hurl; jar, jolt.

2. defeat, disappoint, disillusion, disenchant; frustrate, thwart, foil, balk; hinder, hamper, impede, interfere, interrupt.

3. overthrow, destroy, ruin, devastate, ravage; vanquish, master, overmaster, overcome, overpower, subdue, subjugate, overwhelm, rout, discomfit, confound; quash, suppress, put down.

—*n.* **4.** smashing, shattering, shivering, splintering, breaking; dashing, crashing, crushing, mashing, crumbling; beating, drubbing.

5. blow, hit, slap, smack, thwack; collision, crack-up, wreck, crash; impact, jolt, shake, *Dial.* shog.

6. collapse, destruction, demolition; ruin, ravage, waste, havoc, desolation; catastrophe, debacle, disaster; overthrow, defeat, rout, undoing, vanquishment.

7. bankruptcy, failure, going under, financial ruin *or* disaster.

smear, *v.* **1.** spread, daub, bedaub, besmear, *Inf.* slap on; cover, coat.

2. stain, spot, dirty, soil, smudge, begrime; spatter, splatter, splash.

3. sully, villify, tarnish, blacken, taint; defame, scandalize, denigrate, vituperate, vilipend; slander, libel, calumniate, slur, defile; brand, stigmatize, drag through the mud *or* mire.

4. *Slang.* defeat, overwhelm, drub, shellac, *Sl.* cream, *Sl.* wipe the floor with.

—*n.* **5.** stain, spot, smudge, smirch, patch, daub, splotch, *Sl.* splot; blot, taint, attaint.

6. slur, slander, libel, false accusation; aspersion, reflection, imputation, insinuation, innuendo; vilification, defamation, calumny.

smell, *v.* **1.** scent, nose, get a whiff of, sniff, snuff; inhale, breathe in.

2. perceive, detect, discern; intuit, sense, feel, suspect.

3. reek, stink, smell to high heaven, smell like a goat, assault the nostrils, *Inf.* knock out.

—*n.* **4.** olfaction, smelling.

5. odor, smell, scent; aroma, fragrance, perfume,

redolence, odoriferousness; bouquet, savor, trace, breath, whiff; stink, stench, fetor, fetidness, malodor, mephitis.

smelly, *adj.* fetid, reeky, reeking, stinky, stinking, stenchful, foul-smelling, ill-smelling, strong-smelling, malodorous; noisome, mephitic, foul, rank, offensive, disgusting, nauseating; putrid, rancid, rotten, tainted, spoiled, strong, game, miasmal, miasmatic.

smile, *v.* **1.** beam, grin, laugh; grin from ear to ear, grin like a Cheshire cat; simper, smirk, snicker, fleer, grimace, mouth, *Sl.* mug, *Archaic.* mow.

2. *Often* **smile on** *or* **upon** regard with favor, look favorably on, shine upon, bless, grace; favor, support, encourage, countenance.

—*n.* **3.** grin, laugh; simper, smirk, grimace, fleer, snicker.

4. blessing, benediction, good graces; favor, support, encouragement, countenance.

smirch, *v.* **1.** dirty, soil, smut, stain, discolor; spot, smudge, begrime, besmear, smear, besmirch, defile; draggle, bedraggle, splash, spatter, muddy *Inf.* slop up, *Inf.* foul up, foul, befoul.

2. discredit, disfavor, derogate, disprove, depreciate, devaluate; demean, belittle, disparage, decry, deprecate, deflate; disgrace, shame, dishonor, degrade, abase, debase, vitiate, reproach; impute, slur, asperse, vilify, brand, stigmatize; damage, mar, blot, sully, blacken, tarnish, taint, attaint, *Sl.* dump on, drag through the mud *or* mire, heap dirt upon; slander, calumniate, libel, denigrate, defame, give a bad name, *Sl.* do a hatchet job on.

—*n.* **3.** stain, blot, smut, smutch, spot, smudge, blotch, splotch; smear, blur, taint, blemish, flaw; mark, brand, stigma, bad name; imputation, slur, aspersion, vilification.

smirk, *v.* mouth, *Sl.* mug, *Archaic.* mow, grimace, make a face, grin, smile; giggle, titter, snigger, snicker, te-hee, simper.

smite, *v.* **1.** hit, strike, smack, thwack, slap, *Australian.* ding; cuff, buffet, knock, punch, box, sandbag, *Scot.* dunt, *Scot and North Eng.* paik, *Inf.* clout, *Inf.* slug, *Inf.* whack; *Inf.* knock [s.o.'s] block off, *Inf.* wallop, *Inf.* crown, *Sl.* conk, *Dial.* hit [s.o.] upside the head, *Sl.* bash, *Sl.* plug, *U.S. Sl.* biff, *Sl.* bop, *Sl.* belt, *Sl.* sock; beat, pound, lay on, pommel, pummel, pelt, *Sl.* paste, *Sl.* lay into, *Sl.* let [s.o.] have it, *Archaic.* belabor; thrash, flog, lash, switch, birch, scourge, whip, strap, thresh, flail, spank, *Inf.* tan [s.o.'s] hide; *Inf.* trim, *Inf.* thump, *Inf.* lace, *Inf.* lambaste, *Inf.* whale, *Sl.* whomp; cudgel, fustigate, bludgeon, cane, bastinado, club, hammer.

2. attack, assail, fall upon, bombard, storm; beset, beseige, beleaguer; destroy, demolish, wipe out, pulverize, wreck, *Sl.* total, knock to pieces; raze, gut, fell, prostrate, level; pull down, tear down, cast down, knock down; shatter, crash, smash, batter, break; blast, blow up, devastate, desolate, lay waste.

3. enamor, captivate, enthrall, enrapture, bewitch, ensorcell, infatuate, charm, allure, fascinate, enchant, sweep off one's feet, *Sl.* snow.

smitten, *adj.* **1.** struck, slapped, smacked; cuffed, knocked, punched, *Inf.* slugged, *Inf.* whacked, pounded, thrashed.

2. stricken, afflicted, beset, plagued, burdened, overburdened, crushed; troubled, worried, distressed, grieved; haunted, bothered, harassed, hounded, roiled, galled, irked, vexed.

3. enamored, captivated, enthralled, enraptured, bewitched, ensorcelled, infatuated, charmed, allured, attracted, fascinated, enchanted; in love, head over heels in love, swept off one's feet, *Sl.* snowed, gaga, *Sl.* stuck on, *Inf.* sweet on.

smog, *n.* haze, fog, smaze, gauze, dirty air, dirty fog, brume; pollution, air pollution, particulate.

smoke, *n.* **1.** gas, fume, smog, smaze, *Dial.* drisk; exhaust, effluvium, pollution; soot, smut, carbon, coke, reek, *Brit. Dial.* coom.

2. vapor, mist, brume, fog, gauze, film, cloud; smolder, smudge, smooch.

3. cigarette, *Sl.* cig, *Sl.* butt, *Sl.* weed, *Sl.* fag; cigar, stogie, *Sl.* stinker, cheroot.

—*v.* **4.** fume, smolder, steam, vaporize, fog, befog; emit, give off, reek, exhaust, vent, send out.

5. puff, draw, inhale, *Inf.* drag, pull; exhale, blow, toke, *Sl.* take a hit.

6. fumigate, disinfect, sterilize; perfume, aromatize, cense.

7. cure, dry, smoke-dry.

8. darken, blacken, black; cloud, nubilate, mist, fog, haze; blot, blotch, smear, smirch, smutch, smudge; sully, grime, dim, muddy, dirty, tarnish.

smokestack, *n.* stack, chimney, smokeshaft; flue, pipe, shaft, stovepipe, tube, funnel.

smoky, *adj.* **1.** hazy, foggy, smoggy, brumous, *Archaic.* caliginous; grimy, sooty, murky, bleary; smutchy, dirty, dingy, smirched, smutty, blotchy, blackened, begrimed; gray, mat, dim.

2. fumy, fuming, fuliginous, steamy, steaming, smoking, reeky, reeking, miasmal; misty, drizzly, spraylike.

3. cloudy, frosty, filmy, semitransparent, semipellucid, opaque, unclear; nebulous, nubilous, shadowy, blurry, blurred.

smolder, *v.* **1.** burn, smoke, fume, reek, sizzle, simmer.

2. seethe, boil, boil over, fire up, reach the boiling point; simmer, stew, foam; rankle, fester, stagnate; chafe, bristle, fret, rave, rant, bluster, *Inf.* carry on, burn up, breathe fire; *Inf.* steam, *Inf.* get steamed up, *Inf.* get hot under the collar, *Inf.* see red.

smooth, *adj.* **1.** glassy, glossy, polished, varnished, burnished; sleek, silky, satiny, velvet, fine; delicate, filmy, gossamery, attentuated; greasy, buttery, slippery, slick, icy, oily.

2. even, level, plane, horizontal, flush; flat, unrough, unruffled, unwrinkled; jointless, gapless, seamless.

3. clean-shaven, smooth-shaven, bald, hairless, *Zool., Bot.* glabrous, tonsured, depilated; bare, naked, barren, coverless.

4. easy, facile, plain, simple, effortless, light; uniform, even, regular, steady; constant, stable, consistent, unchanging, unvarying; unvaried, eventless, uneventful, businesslike, monotonous; ceaseless, incessant, unstopped; uninterrupted, unbroken, continuous, unintermittent; flowing, fluent, liquid; rhythmical, harmonious, methodical, orderly, well-ordered, systematic, routine, unaltered.

5. untroubled, unagitated, undisturbed, unperturbed, unruffled, composed, collected, cool; calm, placid, still, quiescent, sedate; serene, pacific, peaceful, reposeful, restful; equable, peaceable, quiet, mild, moderate, gentle, meek; level-headed, poised, self-possessed, even-tenored, even-tempered; inexcitable, unirritable, impassive, nonchalant, unworried, unmoved.

6. elegant, polished, refined; graceful, tripping, measured, flowing, fluent; eloquent, pleasing, articulate, well-spoken, silver-tongued, smooth-tongued; glib, facund.

7. pleasant, agreeable, felicitous; polite, courteous, courtly, mannerly, courierly; suave, soigné, sophisticated, urbane, civil.

8. fawning, flattering, blandishing, insinuating; adulatory, honey-tongued, mealymouthed, smarmy, gushing; fulsome, slimy, oily, unctuous; obsequious, sycophantic, toadyish, insincere, *Sl.* soapy, *Inf.* soft-soaping.

9. crafty, cunning, shrewd, canny, wily, *Inf.* cagey; Machiavellian, politic, sophistical, tactical, scheming, slick, designing, strategic; clever, shifty, sly, foxy, stealthy, sneaky, resourceful, tricky, subtle.

10. gentle, soft, honey, sweet, dulcet, soothing; mellifluous, mellow, golden, molten-golden; euphonious, metrical, lyric, musical; silvery, tuneful, mellisonant.

—*v.* **11.** plane, level, even, align, planish; flatten, roll, steamroll, bulldoze; press, iron, mangle, calender; raze, lay, fell; pare, shave, mow, sheer, poll; dress, smooth out, equalize; scrape, abrade, rub down, scour, grind; buff, sand, sandpaper, pumice, file; furbish, burnish, glaze, slick, gloss; wax, lubricate, oil, grease, finish, varnish.

12. ready, prepare, prime; facilitate, ease, clear, clear the way, make way, expedite, quicken; pave, help, aid, help along, open the way, open the door; grease, grease the wheels, soap, lubricate; lighten, disembarrass, disencumber, unhamper, disburden, free up.

13. polish, refine, harmonize; correct, cultivate, civilize; temper, soften, perfect, mellow; improve, ameliorate, meliorate, better.

14. tranquilize, calm, soothe, compose, moderate; assuage, mollify, allay, mitigate, alleviate; modulate, attemper, temper; soften, appease, pacify, propitiate, placate, conciliate; hush, lull, still, quiet, rock, cradle; dulcify, lenify, quell, subdue, pour oil on troubled waters, pour balm on, take the sting out of.

15. gloss over, extenuate, apologize, excuse, palliate; whitewash, varnish, dress up, cloak.

smooth-spoken, *adj.* **1.** gentle, soft-spoken, subtle; silver-tongued, persuasive, suasive, eloquent, moving, winning; fluent, flowing, smooth, suave; dulcet, agreeable, pleasant, sweet, mellifluent, mellifluous.

2. glib, slick, fast-talking; oily, unctuous, suave; talkative, garrulous, voluble; possessed of the gift of gab.

smother, *v.* **1.** stifle, suffocate, asphyxiate, choke to death; strangle, burke, garrotte, throttle, *Sl.* scrag.

2. extinguish, damp, dampen, deaden, put out, snuff out, stamp out.

3. muffle, dull, soften, tone down; mute, silence, still hush, quiet.

4. envelop, cover, shroud, blanket, wrap, enwrap, enshroud, surround; pile with, heap with, load with, shower with.

5. suppress, repress, choke back *or* down, hold back; conceal, hide, veil, mask, disguise, cloak, cover up; put down, quash, quell, crush, squash, squelch.

smudge, *n.* **1.** dirty mark, smut, smear, smutch, blur, streak; stain, blot, taint, blemish, spot, smirch, blotch, splotch.

—*v.* **2.** smear, blur, streak, smutch, smut; dirty, sully, soil, stain, spot, smirch, discolor, blacken; begrime, besmear, besmirch, defile, daub, mar, blemish.

smug, *adj.* **1.** conceited, self-important, vain, proud, overproud; overconfident, cocksure, too sure of oneself, *Inf.* riding for a fall; self-satisfied, content, complacent.

2. trim, neat, dapper, smart, spruce, natty; well-groomed, smooth, sleek, glossy.

smuggle, *v.* (*all illegally*) import, bring in, sneak in; export, send out, take out, sneak out; transport, run, convey, traffic, *U.S.* bootleg.

smuggler, *n.* contrabandist, runner, *U.S.* bootlegger, *U.S. Inf.* rumrunner, (*of drugs*) *Sl.* mule.

smut, *n.* **1.** soot, ashes, filth, grime, dirt; dirty mark, smudge, smear, smutch. See **smudge** (*def.* **1**).

2. obscenity, *Sl.* raunch, pornography, *Inf.* porn.

—*v.* **3.** soil, smudge, smear, streak, smutch. See **smudge** (*def.* **2**).

smutty, *adj.* **1.** dirty, sooty, unclean, grimy, *Sl.* grungy, filthy, muddied, dirt-encrusted; soiled, sullied, stained, spotted, smudged, smeared, streaked, smutched, smirched; begrimed, besmeared, besmirched, bedaubed.

2. indecent, obscene, suggestive, risqué, racy, off-color, dirty; vulgar, ribald, bawdy, gross, low, *Sl.* gutter, coarse, earthy, rude, crude, offensive, tasteless; pornographic, blue, *Sl.* raunchy, salacious, lewd; lascivious, lustful, concupiscent, prurient, libidinous, *Archaic.* lickerish, perverted; wanton, loose, promiscuous, libertine, dissolute, profligate, immoral, shameless.

snack, *n.* **1.** nosh, bite, bite to eat, between-meal snack, light *or* small meal, light lunch; canapé, hors d'oeuvre, appetizer, tidbit, morsel, nibbles *or* nibblies, *Sl.* munchies.

—*v.* **2.** nosh, nibble, *Sl.* munch *or* munch out, eat between meals, pop [s.t.] into one's mouth, sneak [s.t.] to eat, eat on the sly.

snag, *n.* **1.** concealed log, projection, prominence.

2. impediment, hindrance, encumbrance, obstacle, obstruction, stumbling block, road block; knot, hitch, curb, bit, tether; inhibition, restriction, determent, damper, restraint; bar, barrier, block, counteraction, embargo, stricture, blockade; opposition, objection, discouragement, difficulty, drawback, disadvantage; problem, catch, complication, intricacy, Gordian knot; delay, hang-up, snarl, tangle, bottleneck, red tape, interference, setback, drag.

snake, *n.* **1.** serpent, viper, pit viper, ophidian, sea snake, *Archaic.* dragon, cockatrice.

2. snake in the grass, traitor, quisling, turncoat, renegade, Benedict Arnold; double-dealer, *Inf.* double-crosser, betrayer, Judas; fifth-columnist, informer, subversive, double agent; spy, company spy, *Sl.* fink, *Sl.* weasel, *Sl.* stool; pigeon, *Sl.* stoolie; swindler, *Sl.* con artist, *Sl.* con man, *Inf.* flimflammer; seducer, perverter, wolf in sheep's clothing, beguiler; intriguer, Machiavelli, Rasputin, *Sl.* string-puller, power behind the throne, maneuverer, contriver, schemer, plotter.

snaky, *adj.* **1.** serpentine, anguine, colubrine; snake-infested, snake-ridden.

2. twisting, winding, sinuous. See **serpentine** (*def.* **2**).

3. venomous, poisonous, toxic, baneful, virulent; malignant, malicious, malevolent; noxious, pernicious, injurious, destructive; spiteful, vicious, acrimonious; treacherous, treasonous, faithless, traitorous, perfidious, disloyal, two-faced; untrustworthy, sneaky, sly, cunning; insidious, subtle, beguiling; deceitful, guileful, underhanded, furtive, slippery.

snap, *v.* **1.** crack, crackle, crepitate, decrepitate, pop; click, clink.

2. catch, hook, pin, clasp, secure; link, couple, clinch.

3. break, fracture, fragmentize, splinter, shiver, chip; separate, cleave, sunder, disjoint, sever.

4. sparkle, flash, twinkle, dance; glow, radiate.

5. *Often* **snap at** bite, nip, gnash, growl at, lunge at; attack, lash out at, loose one's temper, *Inf.* fly off the handle; be abrupt, be short, be brusque, be curt.

6. *Usu.* **snap up** *or* **off** seize, take, grab, nab, pluck hook, pounce upon, swoop down on.

7. **snap out of it** *Informal.* recover, get over, come around, revive; pull oneself together, get a hold *or* a grip on oneself; perk up, cheer up, liven up.

—*n.* **8.** crack, crackle, pop; click, clink, clank.

9. catch, fastener, coupler, copula, hook, pin, clasp.

10. *Informal.* briskness, vigor, energy, vitality, get

up and go; animation, liveliness, sprightliness, vivacity, spirit; dash, élan, zest, verve, flair, panache, zing; bounce, sparkle, *Inf.* zip, *Inf.* pep, *Sl.* oomph.

11. bite, nip, champ, chomp; grab, seizure.

12. spell, wave, period, interval, time.

snappish, *adj.* **1.** irritable, testy, touchy, petulant, irascible, prickly; high strung, hot-tempered, hot-blooded, thin-skinned, quick-tempered, quick, hasty, trigger-happy; peevish, huffish, waspish, raspy, peppery, fretful; huffy, edgy, on edge.

2. grumpy, cranky, grouchy, crotchety, churlish, bearish; gruff, cantankerous, impatient, crabby; splenetic, choleric, dyspeptic, moody, temperamental, out of sorts; cross, crusty, crabbed, ill-tempered, ill-humored, sharp, tart, acerbic; curt, abrupt, brusque, short, snappy.

snare, *n.* **1.** trap, gin, springe, *Archaic.* trepan, deadfall, pitfall; noose; net, seine, meshes.

—*v.* **2.** trap, entangle, enmesh, *Archaic.* trepan; inveigle, take in, hoodwink, ensnare. See **ensnare**.

snarl¹, *v.* **1.** growl, gnarl, gnar, bark; menace, threaten.

2. snap at, lash out at, loose one's temper, *Inf.* fly off the handle, *Inf.* flare up, bite [s.o.'s] head off.

—*n.* **3.** growl, bark.

snarl², *n.* **1.** tangle, knot, snag, jam; kink, twist, coil; network, web, webwork; wilderness, jungle, labyrinth, maze.

2. entanglement, complication, problem, perplexity, puzzle, Gordian knot; hitch, snag, catch; complexity, intricacy, difficulty, involvement, imbroglio; predicament, fix, *Inf.* pickle, tight spot, plight, quandary, dilemma; trouble, muddle, mix up, *Sl.* snafu, *Sl.* foul-up, *Inf.* mess, *Inf.* a heap of trouble; obstruction, obstacle, quagmire, quicksand.

—*v.* **3.** tangle, entangle, ravel, knot, jam; kink, twist, coil, interweave, interlace.

4. *Often* **snarl up** confuse, scramble, mix up, disorder, dishevel, tousle, jumble, muddle, fuddle, *Sl.* muzz, *Sl.* ball up; complicate, make difficult, make obscure; perplex, bewilder, baffle, nonplus, puzzle, mystify.

snatch, *v.* **1.** *Usu.* **snatch at** grab at *or* for, make a grab at, grasp at *or* for, grope for, clutch at, catch at, claw at, reach for, pursue; grapple for, scramble for, wrestle for, fight over; handle, feel, pick at, play with.

2. grab, pluck, pull, whisk, jerk, yank, *Inf.* snap up, *Inf.* nip; grip, gripe, grasp, clasp, clutch, clench; seize, catch, catch hold of, lay hold of, lay hands on, latch onto, fasten upon, get, *Inf.* get one's fingers *or* hands on; hook, snag, make off with, walk away with, carry off; apprehend, capture, arrest, take into custody, take prisoner, bag, *Inf.* pick up, *Inf.* collar, *Inf.* nab, *U.S. Inf.* corral, *Sl.* bust, *Sl.* pinch; clinch, secure, lock up, tie up, wrap up, *Inf.* cinch, *Sl.* sew up, *Sl.* have in the bag, *Sl.* put on ice; imprison, incarcerate, jail.

3. take, take over, take for oneself, assume, appropriate, expropriate, confiscate, impound, usurp, misappropriate, arrogate, *Law.* sequester, *Law.* sequestrate, *Law.* levy, *Law.* disseize, *Law.* distrain; commandeer, hijack, skyjack, pirate, take by force; steal, rob, purloin, fleece, pocket, *Sl.* swipe, *Sl.* pinch; abstract, plagiarize, borrow, *Inf.* crib, *Sl.* lift.

4. *Usu.* **snatch from** rescue, save, ransom, liberate, deliver, redeem; pull [s.t.] out, turn [s.t.] around, salvage, wrest, extract.

5. *Slang.* kidnap, petnap, dognap, abduct, rape, hold as hostage *or* for ransom.

—*n.* **6.** scrap, shred, remnant, tatter, fragment, splinter, chunk, chink, chip, smithereen; snip, snippet, slice, sliver, shaving, rasher; piece, corner, cantle, fraction, section, segment, part, portion, ration; bit, particle, morsel, crumb, ort, wisp, drib, drab, *Sl.* sniggie; sample, specimen, dose, taste, mouthful, handful, few, some; whip, iota, speck, grain, modicum, moiety, mite, micron, molecule, atom, trace.

7. spell, fit, stroke, brief period; outburst, outbreak, explosion, eruption, furor.

sneak, *v.* **1.** skulk, slink, steal, sidle, prowl, pad, pussyfoot, walk on eggshells, creep, *U.S. Sl.* gumshoe.

2. *Informal.* grab, *Inf.* catch, slip in, work in, fit in.

—*n.* **3.** snake in the grass, skulker, sneaker; scoundrel, dastard, craven, poltroon, *Archaic.* caitiff.

4. *Informal.* French leave, stealthy departure, *Obs.* steath; quick exit, hasty retreat.

5. sneaks *Informal.* sneakers, tennis shoes, gym shoes, boat shoes, *Brit.* plimsolls, *Inf.* high tops, *Sl.* jimmies; *All Trademark.* Converse, *Sl.* Cons, Keds *or* Pro-keds, P.F. Flyers, Pumas, Adidas, Top-Siders.

sneaking, *adj.* **1.** furtive, underhand, underhanded, sneaky; covert, clandestine, sly, undercover, stealthy, surreptitious, feline, back-alley, back-door.

2. devious, insidious, disingenuous, guileful; tricky, crooked, dishonest, shifty, slippery, *Inf.* shady, *Inf.* left-hand; unethical, dishonorable, unscrupulous, unprincipled, double-dealing, two-faced, deceitful; contemptible, beneath contempt, despicable, base, vile.

3. secret, private, hidden, concealed, veiled, *Inf.* covered-up, suppressed; unconfessed, unavowed, unadmitted, .unvoiced, unrevealed, undivulged, undisclosed, unexpressed, intuitive, innate, inherent.

sneer, *v.* **1.** fleer, look askance; smirk, snicker, curl one's lip.

2. scoff, gibe, mock, jeer, twit, taunt, hoot, laugh in [s.o.'s] face, *Sl.* knock, *Sl.* dig; scorn, hold up to scorn, revile, ridicule, deride, contemn, hold in contempt, despise; snort, sniff, turn up one's nose at, thumb one's nose at, spit upon, *Inf.* sneeze at.

—*n.* **3.** fleer, smirk, snicker, sardonic grin; snort, sniff; gibe, jeer, taunt, twit, wisecrack, *Inf.* brickbat, *Sl.* dig; insult, slight, offense, slap in the face.

sneeze, *v.* **1. sneeze at** *Informal.* make light of, laugh off, wink at, ridicule, mock; scoff at, disregard, pay no attention to, be indifferent *or* apathetic toward; ignore, dismiss, reject, brush off; scorn, disdain, look down one's nose at, sniff at.

—*n.* **2.** sternutation, achoo, kerchoo.

snicker, *v.* snigger, laugh under one's breath *or* to oneself, laugh up *or* in one's sleeve, chuckle, show one's amusement; te-hee, titter, giggle, cackle, chirp, chirrup; laugh at, mock, make fun of; smirk, grin, smile at, simper, mouth, *Sl.* mug, *Archaic.* mow; sneer, curl one's lip at, make a face.

sniff, *v.* **1.** snuff, snuffle, inhale, breathe in, take in air, whiff; sniffle, snivel.

2. smell, smell in the air, get a whiff of, perceive *or* detect the aroma *or* odor of, catch the scent of; smell out, trace, track, trail.

3. sniff at turn one's nose up at, scoff at, flout, disdain, scorn, treat with contempt, contemn; look down one's nose at, look down upon, consider beneath oneself, condescend to, *Inf.* high-hat; snub, slight, ignore, pay no attention to, disregard; rebuff, reject, spurn, scout.

snip, *v.* **1.** cut, snick, nick, slit, incise, cut into, gash, slash.

2. clip, trim, crop, prune, cut back; remove, cut off, lop off, dock, chop off.

—*n.* **3.** small cut, nick, snick, slit, incision, gash, slash.

4. small piece, slice, bit, snippet, cutting; scrap, tatter, fragment, remnant, shred, snatch, fritter; morsel, crumb, taste, sample, mouthful, bite, thimbleful, sip, sup; grain, granule, fleck, speck, touch, trifle, mite, smidgen, *Inf.* smitch, jot, dot, dab.

snippy, *adj.* **1.** *Informal.* sharp, snappy, snappish, curt; short, short-spoken, abrupt, brusque; rude, uncivil, impolite; condescending, patronizing, haughty.

2. scrappy, fragmentary, disconnected, broken.

snivel, *v.* **1.** snuffle, sniffle, sniff, snuff.

2. weep, blubber, cry, sob, boohoo, whine, whimper, mewl, pule.

3. run at the nose, drip at the nose, *Inf.* have a runny *or* running nose, *Inf.* have the sniffles.

—n. **4.** whining, whimpering, mewling, puling, crying, tears, weeping, blubbering, sobbing; pretended weeping, crocodile tears, false *or* stage tears.

5. sniff, snuff, sniffle, snuffle.

6. mucus, phlegm, *Inf.* snot.

snob, *n.* *Inf.* snoot, *Inf.* stuffed shirt, *Sl.* stiff-neck, social climber, condescending *or* pretentious person; egotist, egoist, *Inf.* swellhead, braggart, boaster, *Inf.* phony, show-off.

snobbery, *n.* snobbishness, snobbiness, snobbism, condescension, condescendence, patronage; conceit, conceitedness, *Inf.* uppishness, *Inf.* snootiness, *Inf.* snottiness; arrogance, high horse, haughtiness, hauteur, cavalierness, cavalierism; contemptuousness, contempt, disdainfulness, disdain, scornfulness, scorn, superciliousness, *Inf.* sniffiness; loftiness, lordliness, pompousness, pomposity, stuffiness, pretentiousness, pretension, airs, affectation; pride, proudness, vaingloriousness, vainglory, vanity, vainness, *Inf.* swellheadedness, puffiness, inflatedness; self-importance, egocentricity, egocentrism, narcissism, self-love, self-esteem, self-admiration, self-worship; self-centeredness, self-conceit, egoism, egotism, boastfulness, braggartism, bragging; overconfidence, cockiness, cocksureness, smugness, complacency, self-satisfaction.

snobbish, *adj.* snobby, conceited, *Inf.* stuck-up, condescending, patronizing, *Inf.* uppity, *Inf.* uppish, *Inf.* snotty, *Inf.* snooty; arrogant, *Inf.* up on one's high horse, haughty, cavalier, cavalierly, contemptuous, disdainful, scornful, supercilious, sniffish, *Inf.* sniffy; *Inf.* high-hat, above-it-all, lofty, lordly, high and mighty, pompous, high-flown, pretentious, *Inf.* highfalutin, hoity-toity, stuffy; proud, prideful, overproud, vainglorious, vain, stuck on oneself, *Inf.* swellheaded, *Inf.* bigheaded, puffy, puffed up, inflated; self-important, egocentric, narcissistic, self-loving, self-esteeming, self-admiring, self-worshiping; self-centered, egoistic, egoistical, egotistical, egotistic; overconfident, cocky, cocksure, too sure of oneself, *Inf.* riding for a fall, smug, complacent, self-satisfied; boastful, braggart, bragging, crowing, *Scot.* vaunty, peacockish, show-offish.

snore, *v.* *All Sl.* saw wood, saw logs saw gourds.

snort, *v.* **1.** grunt, honk, oink; sniff, snuffle; chortle, snicker.

—n. **2.** grunt, honk; chortle, snicker.

3. *Slang.* (*all of liquor*) drink, shot, nip, spot, tot, jigger, *Inf.* finger or two; sip, sup, *Inf.* swig, *Inf.* swill, *Inf.* pull, *Inf.* jolt, *Inf.* a quickie *or* quick one; swallow, *Inf.* slug, *Inf.* guzzle, *Inf.* gargle.

snow, *n.* **1.** snowfall, blanket of snow; blizzard, snowstorm, snow squall; flurry, snow flurries.

2. *Slang.* **a.** cocaine, *Sl.* coke, *Sl.* C, *Sl.* blow, *Brit. Sl.* charlie. **b.** heroin, *Sl.* H, *Sl.* horse, *Sl.* smack, *Sl.* scag, *Sl.* junk.

—v. **3.** *Slang.* **a.** amaze, astonish, astound, awe, stagger, boggle, make one's head swim, take one's breath away, overpower, *Inf.* bowl over, *Sl.* knock out, *Sl.* blow away, *Sl.* blow one's mind. **b.** deceive, dupe, trick, hoax, gull, beguile, pigeon, humbug, take in, hoodwink, pull the wool over [s.o.'s] eyes, *Inf.* bamboozle, *Sl.* hornswoggle.

4. snow under *Slang.* (*all with work, correspondence, etc.*) overwhelm, inundate, engulf, swamp, submerge, drown, flood.

snub, *v.* **1.** slight, turn one's back upon, *U.S. Sl.* brush off, turn up one's nose at, *Sl.* ritz, *Inf.* high-hat; cut, give the cold shoulder to, *Inf.* cold-shoulder, *Inf.* put the freeze on, look coldly upon; keep at arm's length, avoid, shun, stand *or* hold aloof; make light of, take no account of; pay no attention *or* regard to, sneeze at; overlook, disregard, ignore, take no notice of, blink *or* wink at, neglect, forget; push aside, set aside, let pass; gloss over, pass by *or* over, skip *or* skim over, pass up, give [s.o.] the go-by; omit, cut out; reject, rebuff, slam the door in [s.o.'s] face; not trouble oneself about, dismiss from one's thoughts *or* mind, leave out of consideration; exclude, keep out.

2. insult, affront, *Sl.* put down, *Sl.* cut up, give offense to, disoblige; call names, *Sl.* rank out, fling dirt at, slap in the face; denounce, decry, disparage, discredit, vilipend, depreciate, minimize; disdain, contemn, scout, flout; scorn, spurn, deride, misprize, jeer, ridicule, mock, scoff, laugh in *or* up one's sleeve at; burlesque, lampoon, make a fool of, guy, twit, gibe at, taunt, fleer; heckle, hoot, hiss, catcall, boo; abuse, wrong, vilify, impugn, traduce, slur, calumniate; blaspheme, profane, take [s.o.'s] name in vain; malign, defame, denigrate, slander, libel, *Inf.* backbite; humiliate, belittle, put to shame, disgrace, degrade; offend, injure, hurt, hurt the feelings of, harm, ill-treat, smart, wound, damage.

3. embarrass, disconcert, abash, mortify, *Inf.* gross out, upset; confuse, fluster, ruffle, discountenance, distract, discompose, confound.

4. check, arrest, bridle, rein, stop, curb; squelch, squash, quash, *Inf.* put the kibosh on, *Inf.* kibosh, nip, nip in the bud; curtail, shorten, abbreviate, cut short, cut off short, clip; reprove, rebuke, reprimand, censure; admonish, reprehend, upbraid, chide, put [s.o.] in his place; oppose, cross, rebuff, repel, withstand.

—n. **5.** slight, cold shoulder, coldness, indifference, neglect, disregard, ignoring, the go-by; inattention, nonobservance, oversight, omission; rejection, denial, repulse; rebuff, short answer, hard words, tartness, acerbity, acrimony; rebuke, reproof, reprimand, chiding, reproach.

6. affront, insult, slur, dig, barb, *Sl.* cut, spurn, *Sl.* put-down, slap in the face; abuse, contumely, contempt, disdain, scorn; repudiation, disparagement, belittlement, depreciation; derision, ridicule, sarcasm, mockery, scoffing, sneering; flout, gibe, jeer, taunt, fling, quip; hoot, hiss, catcall, sibilation; obscenity, vulgarity, blasphemy, profanity, scurrility.

7. rudeness, disrespect, ill-treatment; offense, indignity, discourtesy, uncourteousness, incivility, dishonor, outrage; humiliation, degradation, abasement, mortification; provocation, kick in the pants, vexation, irritation, annoyance.

—adj. **8.** snubby, snubbed, pug-nosed, turned-up; blunt, stumpy, thickset, stocky, stodgy.

snug, *adj.* **1.** cozy, intimate, comfortable, *Inf.* comfy, *Scot.* canny, homey, homelike, lived-in; easeful, restful, relaxing; quiet, peaceful, tranquil, serene, pleasant, cheery, enjoyable; warm, friendly, inviting; informal, casual, easy, simple.

2. (*of a ship*) trim, spruce, trig, neat, tidy, shipshape, well-ordered, orderly.

3. (*of clothing*) tight, too small, close-fitting; skin-tight, revealing, indecent.

4. small, smallish, compact; protected, safe, secure, out of the wind.

5. smug, complacent, self-satisfied; exclusive, snobbish, clannish, cliquish, select, narrow.

6. goodly, adequate, ample, sufficient; good, excellent, nice, satisfactory, pleasing.

7. secret, private, covert, secluded, isolated; concealed, hidden, well-hidden; unknown, unseen, camouflaged, screened off.

snuggle, *v.* nestle, cuddle, nuzzle, snug; curl up, scrunch up; squeeze together, hug, embrace; bundle, lie together.

so, *adv.* **1.** thus, thus and so, in this way, in this fashion, in this manner.

2. like that, that way, in that state *or* condition.

3. very, extremely, considerably, *Inf.* damn well, *Inf.* terrifically, extraordinarily, enormously; very greatly, a lot, lots.

4. therefore, for this *or* that reason, hence; consequently, resultingly, that being the case, that being so, because of that, on that account.

5. certainly, indeed, truly, absolutely, positively, definitely.

6. also, too, additionally, likewise, correspondingly, similarly, in like manner.

—adj. **7.** true, positive, confirmed, factual, real, actual, *Inf.* for real; correct, accurate, truthful.

soak, *v.* **1.** saturate, drench, imbrue, immerse, souse, sop, wet, wet down; steep, seethe, marinate, ret.

2. permeate, pervade, riddle, infuse, penetrate, imbue, charge.

3. soak through seep, leak, drip, dampen; infiltrate, pass through, come through.

soapy, *adj.* lathery, sudsy, foamy, frothy, bubbly, saponaceous.

soar, *v.* **1.** fly, take wing, wing one's way, take off, take to the air, volitate; sail, zoom, cruise, coast, sweep, skim, *Inf.* kite; glide, plane, volplane, sailplane; float, hover, drift, hang, poise, float in the air.

2. ascend, climb, rise, mount, tower, spire, *Archaic.* aspire, spiral, loom.

sob, *v.* weep, cry, shed tears, boohoo; bawl, blubber, whimper, mewl, snivel, sniffle; moan, wail, ululate; lament, mourn, bewail, keen.

sober, *adj.* **1.** not intoxicated *or* drunk, temperate, teetotal, *Inf.* sworn off, *Sl.* on the wagon *or* water wagon, *Brit.* on the water cart; prohibitionary, *U.S.* dry, blue-ribbon.

2. abstemious, habitually abstinent, nonindulgent; moderate, self-restrained, self-controlled; continent, celibate, chaste, virginal, virgin, pure; puritanical, puritan-like, austere, strict, severe; refraining, forbearing, desisting, self-depriving, self-mortifying; ascetic, self-denying, self-abnegating.

3. serious, earnest, solemn, formal; sedate, staid, reserved, dignified; poised, self-confident, self-assured, self-possessed; composed, cool, calm, collected, coolheaded; level-headed, equanimous, balanced; unruffled, imperturbable, unflustered, reposed, at ease; tranquil, peaceful, content, quiet, serene.

4. grave, crucial, decisive, vital, important, consequential; significant, considered, concerned, responsible; momentous, weighty, heavy, ponderous, massive; great, large, enormous, huge; vast, immense, magnitudinous, extensive; deep, profound, intense.

5. subdued, quiet, soft, softened, mellow, toned down; gray, grayish, grayed, neutral; dull, dreary, mousy, drab; somber, dark, sad, gloomy, dun, heavy, leaden.

6. plain, simple, unexaggerated, unembroidered, unvarnished, unadorned, unembellished; unornamented, undecked, ungarnished, unenriched; pure, unadulterated, chaste, unaffected, unpretentious, wholesome; dull, tedious, prosaic, unimaginative, boring; hard, harsh, severe, cold, realistic, practical; solid, substantial, firm, sound, real, tangible.

7. sane, lucid, clear, rational, reasonable, sensible; well-founded, well-grounded, well-advised, logical, objective, proper, correct; just, right, fair, humane, equitable, impartial, judicious, moderate; well-considered, level-headed, prudent, provident, circumspect, politic.

—v. **8.** sober up, *Inf.* dry out, detoxify, make *or* become sober.

9. make pensive *or* serious, cause to reflect, make [s.o.] stop and think, give [s.o.] pause, *Inf.* shake [s.o.] up; quiet, subdue, calm down, pacify.

sobriety, *n.* **1.** soberness, teetotalism, nephalism, abstinence; prohibition, blue-ribbonism; Rechabitism.

2. temperance, moderation, self-restraint, self-control; refrainment, forbearance, desistance; abstention, nonindulgence, abstemiousness; continence, celibacy, fasting; Puritanism, austerity, self-mortification, self-deprivation; asceticism, self-denial, self-abnegation.

3. seriousness, earnestness, solemnity, solemnness; sedateness, staidness, dignity, formality, formalness, reserve; poise, self-confidence, assurance, self-possession; composure, self-control, coolness, cool-headedness, level-headedness; calmness, equanimity, equilibrium, imperturbability, imperturbableness, tranquillity, serenity.

4. gravity, cruciality, decisiveness, vitalness, import, importance, consequence; significance, consideration, concern, moment, momentousness; weight, responsibility, ponderousness, massiveness; greatness, largeness, enormity, enormousness; vastness, immensity, immenseness, magnitude, scope, extent; depth, profundity, profoundness, intensity, intenseness.

sobriquet, *n.* nickname, agnomen, cognomen, byname, moniker, handle; familiar name, pet name, diminutive, epithet, *Chiefly Scot.* to-name.

sociability, *n.* **1.** gregariousness, friendliness, amicability, congeniality, *Ger. Gemütlichkeit*, neighborliness, companionability; affability, approachableness, accessibility, communicativeness, talkativeness, chattiness; easiness, openness, unreservedness, familiarity, easygoingness; amiability, pleasantness, goodnaturedness; agreeableness, willingness, amenableness, considerateness; graciousness, geniality, politeness, cordiality, courteousness.

2. friendship, intimacy, closeness, mutual trust; fellowship, fraternization, partnership, colleagueship, cooperation.

sociable, *adj.* friendly, gregarious, outgoing, extroverted, social; affable, approachable, accessible, communicative, conversational, conversable, chatty, *Inf.* gabby, *Inf.* gossipy, talkative; familiar, folksy, *Inf.* chummy, *Inf.* cozy, intimate; amiable, amicable, congenial, neighborly, hospitable, genial, cordial, gracious; companionable, brotherly, sisterly, kindly, warm-hearted; hearty, hail-fellow-well-met, convivial, jovial, agreeable, pleasant.

social, *adj.* **1.** friendly, companionable, affable, amiable, convivial, outgoing, sociable. See **sociable**.

2. community, communal, societal, human; collective, popular, widespread, common; civic, civil, municipal, city, urban.

socialize, *v.* get together, *Sl.* party, hang out, fraternize, band together; talk, chat, *Sl.* chew the fat *or* rag, *Inf.* gab, gossip; mix, mingle, rub elbows, rub shoulders, mill; associate with, hobnob with, consort with, keep company with, *Inf.* run around with, hang around with, pal around with, chum around with; keep open house, keep the latchstring out, keep the welcome mat out, have the door always open.

society, *n.* **1.** association, consociation, club, circle, band, group; community, congregation, assembly, body; affiliation, fraternity, brotherhood, sisterhood; alliance, federation, league; guild, union.

2. humanity, the human race, humankind, mankind, people, the world, *Fr. monde*; the public, the general public, the commonwealth, the body politic; the community.

3. company, companionship, friendship, camaraderie, fellowship.

4. high society, *Fr. haut monde, Inf.* upper crust; upper classes, nobility, peerage, aristocracy, gentility; the privileged classes, the rich, the elite.

sod, *n.* **1.** clump *or* chunk of turf, *Scot.* divot.

2. turf, sward, greensward; lawn, grass, grass court, green, grounds, mall, parkland, park; pasture, meadow, grassland, hayfield, field, *Archaic.* glebe.

sodden, *adj.* **1.** soggy, soppy, sopping, sopping *or* wringing wet, wet, dripping; oozy, leaking, seepy, seeping; humid, damp, dank, moist, soupy, clammy, sweaty, muggy, steamy; soaked, drenched, saturated, soused, waterlogged; drowned, flooded, inundated, covered with water, under water; imbued, imbrued, infused, permeated, steeped, marinated, soaked through; bloated, swollen, puffy, distended, blown up; macerated, decomposing, disintegrating, falling apart.

2. spongy, marshy, paludal, boggy, swampy, quaggy, miry, slimy, muddy, lutose; soft, mushy, squashy, squishy, pulpy, flabby, fleshy, fat, thick, succulent, *Bot.* uliginous; watery, thin, pappy, paplike, runny; doughy, gummy, tacky, sticky, viscid, gluey, gluelike, glutinous, *Inf.* gooey; lumpy, pasty, starchy, heavy, indigestible, unhealthful.

3. solemn, staid, somber, sober, stodgy; ponderous, laborious, labored, tedious, tiresome, tiring, wearisome; dull, dry, dry-as-dust, prosaic, uninteresting, boring, boresome, humdrum, monotonous, dead; expressionless, vapid, vacant, empty; bland, tasteless, insipid, jejune, pallid, *Sl.* nothing, *Sl.* blah, *Sl.* for the birds; dull-witted, stolid, doltish, loutish, lumpish, blockish, bovine, *Inf.* thick; stupid, slow-witted, *Inf.* dumb, retarded.

4. spiritless, lifeless, unanimated; heavy, leaden, torpid, listless, lethargic, phlegmatic, sluggish, languid, lazy, oscitant, drowsy; stationary, static, stagnant, standing, dormant, still, motionless, inactive, inert.

sofa, *n.* couch, divan, lounge, ottoman, *U.S.* davenport; love seat, settee, causeuse; studio couch, sleep sofa, day bed, *Trademark.* Castro convertible; téte-à-téte, siamoise, vis-à-vis; sectional.

soft, *adj.* **1.** plushlike, plushed, squashy, squishy, mushy, spongy; pulpy, pulpal, pulpous, pulplike, pulpaceous, overripe, overmature; pappy, paplike, mashed, softened; thin, watery, runny, liquid; loamy, friable, crumbly; marshy, paludal, boggy, swampy, quaggy, miry, slimy; doughy, pasty, starchy, *Inf.* gooey; fleshy, flabby, fat.

2. pliable, pliant, malleable, ductile, flexible, flexile, flexuous, bendable; extensile, extensible, tractile, tractable, stretchable; plastic, shapable, moldable, fictile, lithe, supple; jellylike, gelatinous, semiliquid; limp, flaccid, unfirm, slack, unstiff, unstiffened, unstarched, starchless, *Both Dial.* limpsy, limsey; flimsy, unsound, unstable, unsubstantial, rickety, jerry-built.

3. smooth, silky, silken, silklike, satiny, velvety, creamy, like a baby's bottom; agreeable to the touch, touchable, kissable; fuzzy, downy, fleecy, furry.

4. comfortable, *Inf.* comfy, commodious, snug, cozy, warm, *Inf.* homey; relaxing, restful, reposeful; peaceful, pacific, irenic, tranquil, sedative, sleepinducing; soothing, calm, low-key, laid back; pleasant, pleasing, pleasurable, agreeable, favorable, not hard to get used to, easy to take; heavenly, exquisite, delightful, enjoyable, gratifying, welcome, ingratiating, inviting, attractive; lenitive, palliative, alleviative, mitigative, assuasive, healing, balsamic, demulcent.

5. subdued, mellow, muted, understated; low, faint, quiet; (*of sound*) whispered, murmured, hushed, stifled, inaudible, imperceptible; (*of music*) easy-listening, dinner, turned down; melodious, mellifluous, dulcet, sweet; (*of color*) pale, pastel, light; dusty, grayish, soft-toned; matte, mat, dull; (*of light*) diffuse, indirect, low intensity, on the low beam; dim, dimmed, turned low, shaded.

6. (*of lines*) curvilinear, curvilineal, rounded, curved, curvaceous; loose, flowing, fluid; blended, shaded, blurred, blurry; bleary, bleared, fuzzy, hazy, foggy, adumbrated, obscure, indistinct, ill-defined, unclear, vague, ambiguous.

7. gentle, light, calm, zephyr-like, slight; mild, fair, moderate, temperate, genial, even; balmy, springlike, halcyon, halcyonian, warm, summery, estival.

8. lenient, clement, humane, merciful, reasonable; forgiving, pardoning, tolerant, forbearing, restrained; indulgent, permissive, liberal, lax, loose, nondisciplinary; amenable, obliging, compliant, capitulative, acquiescent, yielding, giving in, submissive, deferential, meek, docile, tame.

9. sensitive, tender, gentle, sweet, mild as a dove, gentle as a lamb *or* kitten, even-tempered, equable; gentle-hearted, kind-hearted, benign, kind, kindly, nice, gracious, *Fr. gentil*; tender-hearted, affectionate, warm, loving; compassionate, sympathetic, sympathizing, understanding, considerate, responsive, commiserative; pitying, piteous, ruthful, bleeding-heart.

10. sentimental, romantic, emotional; maudlin, mawkish, mushy, slushy; teary, weepy, lachrymose, *Inf.* drippy, *Brit. Sl.* soppy, *Sl.* schmaltzy; flowery, sweet, sickening, cloying; pathetic, poignant, doe-eyed, calf-eyed.

11. delicate, fragile, untough, unhardened; dainty, unvirile, unmanful, unmannish, sissyish, petticoat, effeminate, femine, womanish, muliebral; nonmuscular, puny, wispy, slight, skinny, thin; frail, weak, weakly, faint, feeble, unfit, out of condition *or* shape; enfeebled, sickly, infirm, debilitated, shaky, *Scot.* shilpit; thin-skinned, super-sensitive, babyish, puerile, childish, sniveling, blubbering; sinewless, pithless, namby-pamby, spineless, nerveless, characterless, *Sl.* gutless; weak-kneed, wishy-washy, chicken-hearted, lily-livered, timid, timorous, *Sl.* chicken, *Sl.* candy-assed; impotent, powerless, impuissant, helpless, strengthless, ineffective.

12. *Informal.* easy, simple, easy *or* simple as pie, easy *or* simple as 1, 2, 3; a pushover, a piece of cake, *Inf.* a snap, *Sl.* a cinch, *Sl.* cinchy, *Sl.* cushy, *Sl.* a breeze, *Sl.* a picnic, *Sl.* duck soup, *Sl.* child's play, *Sl.* no sweat; easygoing, leisurely, of leisure, relaxed; carefree, untroubled, unplagued, rosy, rose-colored, sunny; affluent, luxurious, plush, prosperous, well-to-do, of the rich, Park Avenue.

soften, *v.* **1.** melt, mellow, touch, move, affect; gentle, meeken, disarm, unman, unnerve, emasculate; win over, conciliate.

2. mollify, tame, smooth down; relax, loosen, slacken; pacify, calm, compose, tranquilize, lull, soothe; appease, *Archaic.* attemper, placate, dulcify.

3. mitigate, abate, reduce, diminish, lessen, weaken; alleviate, palliate, allay, assuage, *Rare.* lenify; ease, relieve, cushion, lighten, temper, moderate.

4. muffle, deaden, mute, still, quiet, soft-pedal; lower, turn down, tone down; throttle, silence, stifle, *Both Music., Acoustics.* damp, dampen.

5. relent, give in, acquiesce, yield, give way, bend; accede, agree, assent, consent, concur, *Inf.* come round; relax, ease up, let up.

soggy, *adj.* **1.** soppy, sopping *or* wringing *or* dripping wet; soaked, drenched, saturate. See **sodden** (*def.* **1**).

2. heavy, doughy, pasty; pulpy, mushy, soft. See **sodden** (*def.* **2**).

3. dull, dry, uninteresting; dull-witted, stolid, *Inf.* thick; torpid, phlegmatic, spiritless. See **sodden** (*defs.* **3, 4**).

soil[1], *n.* **1.** ground, earth, *Archaic.* glebe, turf, marl, loam, humus; clay, dirt, dust.

2. country, land, region; property, premises.

soil[2], *v.* **1.** dirty, stain, spot, maculate, smudge, muddy, sully; splash, spatter, *Inf.* slop up, *Inf.* foul up; bedraggle, draggle, begrime, besmear, smear, smirch, besmirch; foul, befoul; blacken, tarnish.

2. defile, pollute, taint, poison; smear, blot, blur; contaminate, make impure; sully, dishonor, disgrace, asperse; deprecate, defame, denigrate.

—n. **3.** dirt, mud, mire, muck, sludge, slush, sediment, silt; filth, refuse, trash, garbage, slop; sewage, dregs, lees, slime; decay, rot, offal, foul matter.

4. manure, fertilizer; excrement, waste matter, waste, feculence, dung, muck, ordure, guano, animal droppings, coprolites, coproliths.

sojourn, *v.* **1.** (*all temporarily*) live, reside, abide; tarry, stop over, visit; rest, repose, vacation, take the air.

—n. **2.** (*all temporary*) dwelling, residence, visit, stopover, stay; pause, respite, halt; holiday, vacation, rest, relaxation, repose.

solace, *n.* **1.** comfort, balm, consolation, condolence, soothing words; succor, relief, aid, help, support; encouragement, enheartenment, cheer.

—v. **2.** comfort, console, condole; cheer, encourage, enhearten, hearten, reassure, bolster, inspirit, *Inf.* buck up, *Inf.* pat [s.o.] on the back, *Inf.* give [s.o.] a lift *or* boost.

3. (*all of pain, sorrow, etc.*) soothe, mitigate, alleviate, ameliorate, meliorate, soften, assuage, allay; relieve, disburden, lighten [s.o.'s] load *or* burden.

soldier, *n.* **1.** brave, warrior, fighter, fighting man, man-of-arms, man-at-arms; infantryman, common soldier, cannon fodder, GI *or* GI Joe, *U.S. Sl.* grunt, *U.S. Marine Sl.* leatherneck, *U.S. Sl.* gyrene, *Brit.* Tommy, *Scot.* Jock, *Fr. poilu, Inf.* doughboy; intrepid *or* fearless warrior, lion, tiger, bulldog, gamecock, fighting cock.

2. hero, champion, paladin, knight; stalwart, gallant, valiant, cavalier, chevalier; a man, brave man, man of courage *or* mettle.

3. *Informal.* shirker, malingerer, *Inf.* goldbricker, *Sl.* goof-off, *Sl.* boondoggler; idler, loafer, layabout. See also **shirker**.

—v. **4.** bear arms; serve, serve one's country *or* flag, do one's duty, fulfull one's military obligation; go to war, see action *or* combat, see active duty.

5. *Informal.* shirk, malinger, *Sl.* goldbrick, *Sl.* goof off, *Brit.* skulk; slack off, lie down on the job, *Brit. Sl.* scrimshank. See also **shirk** (*def.* **2**).

soldierly, *adj.* **1.** martial, military, military-minded, soldierlike; brave, courageous, valiant, valorous; stout, stalwart, staunch, doughty; mettlesome, plucky, spirited, game, red-blooded.

2. militant, warlike, aggressive; bellicose, belligerent, combative, pugnacious, truculent, full of fight, *Sl.* scrappy.

sole, *adj.* **1.** single, only, one and only, lone, one-shot; exclusive, separate, individual, personal, particular, distinct; detached, disconnected, disjoined, *Zool., Bot.* azygous.

2. unique, singular, one-of-a-kind, nonpareil, unparalleled, unequaled, matchless; unexcelled, unsurpassed, unbeatable, untoppable, beyond *or* past compare, one-in-a-million; select, choice, rare, uncommon, distinctive, extraordinary, special, different.

3. lonely, lonesome, alone, solo, all all alone; solitary, apart, separated, isolated, insular, standing alone *or* apart; companionless, friendless, unaccompanied, unescorted; alienated, estranged, withdrawn.

solecism, *n.* **1.** (*of grammar*) substandard use, incorrectness, misusage, faulty syntax, misconstruction, anacoluthon; barbarism, corruption, cacology; malapropism, spoonerism.

2. gaffe, gaucherie, faux pas, stupidity, impropriety, indiscretion, indelicacy, discourtesy.

3. error, mistake, blunder, slip, fumble, lapse, misstep, *Sports.* miscue, *Inf.* bobble, *Inf.* slip-up; *All Sl.* boo-boo, boner, goof, blooper, pratfall.

solemn, *adj.* **1.** grave, *Archaic.* sage, sober, sedate, staid; mirthless, unsmiling, long-faced; gloomy, somber, saturnine, glum, grim, frowning, beetle-browed, severe, stern; thoughtful, pensive, contemplative, reserved, taciturn.

2. impressive, thought-provoking, moving, stirring, striking, piercing, heart-rending, disturbing; awe-inspiring, awesome, imposing, august, stately, grand, majestic; profound, significant, momentous.

3. serious, earnest, sincere, true, honest, genuine, real, heartfelt; feeling, intense, fervent, unfrivolous; explicit, express, definite.

4. ceremonious, ceremonial, ritualistic, formal, reserved, dignified, standing on dignity.

5. reverential, devotional, sacred, holy, divine; liturgical, sacramental.

solemnity, *n.* **1.** gravity, seriousness, earnestness, staidness, sobriety; intensity, urgency; gloominess, thoughtfulness; impressiveness, stateliness, grandeur, majesty, momentousness, importance, consequence.

2. solemnities observance, ceremonial, formalities, ceremonies, celebration, rite, ritual, proceedings.

solicit, *v.* **1.** ask *or* ask for, request, apply for, seek *or* seek for; solicit votes, canvass, campaign, *Inf.* stump; call upon, appeal to, implore, beseech, entreat, plead, beg, *Brit. Inf.* prig, pray, crave; petition, supplicate, obtest, adjure, conjure, *Rare.* sue; urge, press, importune, insist, demand.

2. accost, approach, come up to on the street, tout; *Sl.* hustle, pimp, pander; lure, invite, attract, *U.S. Inf.* bark, entice, tempt, woo; bring in, obtain, get, procure, find, drum up, create, make.

solicitor, *n.* asker, requester, petitionary, petitioner, suppliant, supplicant, suitor; canvasser, campaigner, *Inf.* stumper; tout, *Inf.* touter, *Chiefly U.S. Inf.* barker; *Sl.* hustler, pimp, pander, procurer; salesman, door-to-door salesman, traveling salesman, *U.S.* drummer.

solicitous, *adj.* **1.** anxious, overanxious, concerned, overconcerned, nervous, worried; uneasy, uncomfortable, disquieted, *Archaic.* disquiet; apprehensive, overapprehensive, fearful, afraid; alarmed, troubled, bothered, disturbed, agitated, perturbed, upset.

2. desirous, earnest, eager, eager to please, overeager, zealous, enthusiastic, fervent, fervid, ardent, intense, avid, keen; persistent, importunate, importune, pushing, *Inf.* pushy; ambitious, aspiring, itchy, itching, longing, wishing, wanting, aching.

3. particular, scrupulous, painstaking, conscientious,

hard-working, thorough; careful, mindful, thoughtful, regardful, heedful, attentive.

solicitude, *n.* **1.** concern, care, thought, regard, consideration; anxiety, overconcern, nervousness, worry, inquietude; uneasiness, disquietude, disquiet, apprehension, fearfulness, fear, alarm.

2. overanxiety, overanxiousness, eagerness, overeagerness, desire, desirousness; zealousness, zeal, enthusiasm, ardor, intensity, fervor, fervidness, earnestness; effusion, gush, smothering, shower of attention, hovering.

solid, *adj.* **1.** cubic, three-dimensional.

2. block, unbroken, in a row; one-piece, monadic, unipartite.

3. dense, thick, compact, close, firm, hard; impenetrable, impervious, impermeable, nonporous; proof, resistant, hermetic; indissoluble, insoluble, infusible; integral, irreducible, indivisible, inseparable, impartible, infrangible; condensed, compressed, compacted; frozen, crystallized, crystalline, solidified; thickened, inspissate, clotted, grumous, congealed, coagulated, curdled, jelled; cohesive, coherent.

4. crowded, serried, clustered, congested, concentrated, massed, amassed; jammed, packed, *Inf.* jampacked, crammed, chock-a-block, *Inf.* chock-full, *Brit. Inf.* chocker, standing room only, SRO, *Inf.* like sardines in a can; teeming, swarming, bristling, swollen, full to bursting.

5. substantial, ponderable, tangible, palpable; bulky, heavy, hefty, massive, ponderous.

6. sound, stable, sturdy, stout, rugged, tough, well-built, well-constructed, well-put-together; durable, lasting, long-lasting, made to last, enduring; fast, secure, fixed, riveted, set.

7. continuous, uninterrupted, unrelieved, unremitting, constant; serial, sequential, successive.

8. whole, entire, complete, intact.

9. real, genuine, authentic, bona fide, *Australian.* dinkum, *Sl.* honest-to-God; sterling, twenty-four carat; pure, unalloyed, unmixed, uncut, unadulterated; unsynthetic, inartificial.

10. (*all of arguments, ideas, etc.*) good, valid, logical, reasonable, well-founded, well-grounded; cogent, weighty, authoritative; concrete, convincing, rational; irrefutable, indisputable, indubitable, incontrovertible, incontestable, unquestionable, undeniable.

11. sober-minded, down to earth, with both feet on the ground, sensible, level-headed; law-abiding, straight-arrow, straight.

12. trustworthy, *Inf.* trusty, dependable, reliable, to be depended *or* relied upon, sure, tried and true, true-blue; constant, steadfast, stalwart, faithful.

13. financially sound, solvent, credit-worthy, above-water, out of the red, in the black, in good standing.

14. strong, mighty, powerful, potent, forceful, forcible; vigorous, energetic, dynamic.

15. unanimous, consentient, consentaneous, with one voice; united, undivided, consolidated, at one, of a piece; concurrent, concordant, accordant, in accord, in agreement, in unison, like-minded, of one mind, of the same mind.

16. *Slang.* excellent, fine; *All Sl.* swell, great, cool, tuff, far out, out of sight, gear, fab, crackerjack, jim-dandy, boss, marvy, *Australian.* bonzer.

solidarity, *n.* **1.** stability, firmness, soundness; reliability, trustworthiness; strength, power; integrity, completeness, wholeness, totality, entirety.

2. unanimity, consentaneity, singleness of purpose, like-mindedness, mutuality; union, unity, concurrence, concordance, concord, accordance, accord, fellowship, fellow feeling; joint *or* mutual interest *or* concern, community of interests; team spirit, esprit de corps camaraderie.

solidify, *v.* **1.** harden, concrete, cake, crystallize, compress, set; coagulate, congeal, clot, gel, gelatinize, jell, jelly, jellify, thicken, inspissate, *Obs.* incrassate; curdle, curd, *Scot. and North Central U.S.* lopper, *Pathol.* caseate.

2. consolidate, combine, join, join forces, unite, league, ally, confederate, *Inf.* hitch horses, pool interests; incorporate, amalgamate, merge, fuse, syndicate.

solitary, *adj.* **1.** alone, unattended, companionless,*Scot.* waff; sole, single, lone, individual; apart, separate, cut off; deserted, abandoned, outcast, derelict, forlorn, forsaken.

2. by oneself, unassisted, unaided, single-handed.

3. one, only, exclusive, unique, freakish, unrepeated; unparalleled, unequaled, unmatched, nonpareil.

4. unfrequented, secluded, hidden, lonely, isolated, private, remote, solitudinous; recluse, sequestered, cloistered, set apart; cut off, desolate, out-of-the-way, unvisited, in a backwater.

5. antisocial, unsocial, unsociable, estranged, alienated, friendless; retiring, withdrawn, reclusive, *Inf.* introverted; hermitlike, hermitical, monastic, monachal, eremitical, eremitic, anchoritic, stylitic.

—n. **6.** recluse, hermit, eremite, anchorite, stylite, pillarist; cenobite, monk, monastic; troglodyte, cave dweller, incluse.

7. loner, *Inf.* lone wolf, isolate, isolator, *Inf.* introvert.

solitude, *n.* **1.** seclusion, retirement, privacy, isolation, solitariness, aloneness; reclusion, reclusiveness, hermitry.

2. remoteness, separateness, separation, loneliness; unsociability, withdrawal, introversion.

3. desert, waste, wilderness, wasteland; desolation, vast expanse, emptiness.

solution, *n.* **1.** resolution, finding out, discovery; denouement, revelation, revealing, unraveling, deciphering; clarification, definition, unfolding, unfoldment.

2. answer, explanation; key, secret, clue, signification, meaning; accounting, reason, justification, vindication; rationalization, elucidation, explication, exegesis, *Fr. éclaircissement.*

3. emulsion, suspension, mixture, infusion.

solvable, *adj.* explainable, resolvable, decipherable, penetrable, ascertainable; understandable, intelligible, interpretable; capable of clarification, lending itself to solution.

solve, *v.* work out, figure out, resolve, find the answer; crack, disentangle, untangle, unravel, unriddle; translate, decode, unlock, find the key; penetrate, fathom, get at; clear up, explain, interpret, elucidate, make clear, make plain, unfold; justify, account for.

solvent, *adj.* financially responsible, credit-worthy, reliable, sound, solid, responsible; *Inf.* out of the hole, *Inf.* in the black, *Inf.* out of the red, debt-free, on an even financial keel.

somber, *adj.* **1.** dark, dusky, shadowy, dim, cloudy, gray, leaden, black, Cimmerian; drab, dull, dead, lifeless, dingy, bleak; gloomy, dismal, dreary, *Literary.* drear; murky, inky, pitchy.

2. depressing, depressive, melancholy, mournful, doleful, dolorous, dispiriting, disheartening; heavy, lugubrious, atrabilious, funereal, morbid.

3. grave, serious, sober, staid, sedate, solemn; grim, grim-visaged, grim-faced, stone-faced.

somebody, *pron.* **1.** one, someone.

—n. **2.** personage, dignitary, notable, *Inf.* VIP; person of note *or* consequence, public figure, famous

or well-known person, household name, *Inf.* name, *Inf.* big name; celebrity, *Sl.* celeb, star, superstar; luminary, worthy, pillar of society; standout, heavyweight, *Sl.* heavy, *Inf.* head honcho, *Inf.* biggest frog in the pond; magnate, mogul, baron, nabob, pooh bah, panjandrum, *Sl.* high-muck-a-muck, *Inf.* bigwig; *All Sl.* big shot, big gun, big wheel, big cheese, big noise, big-time operator, BTO. See also **personage** (*def.* **1**).

somehow, *adv.* someway, in some way, in one way or another, by some means, by some means or other, somehow or other; no matter how, by fair means or foul, by hook or by crook, *Sl.* come hell or high water.

sometime, *adv.* **1.** someday, one day, one of these days, one fine day *or* morning, sooner or later, somewhen; in time, in due time, in the fullness of time, in the long run, when all is said and done, eventually, ultimately; in the future, at a future time *or* date, by and by, *Inf.* in the sweet by and by; soon, before long, *Inf.* before you know it.

—adj. **2.** former, erstwhile, late, previous, onetime, past, recent, quondam.

sometimes, *adv.* occasionally, on occasion, at times, from time to time, now and then, now and again, off and on, once in a while, every so often.

somewhat, *adv.* to some extent, to a certain extent, to a degree, to some degree, in some measure, more or less, *Inf.* sort of, *Inf.* kind of; quite, rather, pretty; fairly, reasonably, moderately, mildly; comparatively, relatively; passably, tolerably; in part, partly, partially; a little, a bit, slightly.

somnambulism, *n.* sleepwalking, noctambulism, *Rare.* nightwalking; somnambulation, noctambulation.

somnambulist, *n.* sleepwalker, noctambulist, noctambule, somnambule, somnambulator, *Rare.* nightwalker.

somnolence, *n.* sleepiness, drowsiness, doziness, grogginess, slumberousness, *Sl.* dopiness; oscitancy.

somnolent, *adj.* **1.** sleepy, half-asleep, asleep on one's feet, heavy with sleep, heavy-eyed; slumberous, drowsy, dozy, groggy, *Sl.* dopey; yawny, oscitant, nodding, nodding-off, ready for bed.

2. soporific, somniferous, sleep-inducing, sleep-producing; narcotic.

son, *n.* **1.** male child, boy, chip off the old block.

2. (*all used as forms of address*) lad, laddie, sonny, sonny boy, young man, *Inf.* kid, *Inf.* junior, *Sl.* bub, *Sl.* punk.

song, *n.* **1.** melody, tune, air, lyric, ditty, strain; chant, round, chanty, descant; chorus, anthem, paean, cantata; madrigal, canzone, round, solo, duet, trio; vocal music, vocalization, *Inf.* pop tune, ballad, canzonet; art song, *Ger. Lied,* love song, torch song, blues; drinking song, scolion; serenade, lullaby; dirge, psalm, hymn; spiritual, folk song, *Ger. Volkslied.*

2. verse, versification, poetry, lay, rhyme; meter, number, versecraft; rondeau, rondel, roundelay; rhapsody, idyll, dithyramb, ode, sonnet, triolet, ballade, villanella; elegy; jingle, doggerel.

3. warble, chirping, pipe, whistle, trill; clamor, din, racket, outcry.

songster, *n.* **1.** singer, vocalist, warbler, crooner, soloist. See **singer** (*def.* **1**).

2. poet, bard, minstrel, wandering minstrel, jongleur, troubadour, ballad singer, streetsinger, Meistersinger, minnesinger. See also **poet**.

3. songbird, singing bird, warbler. See **singer** (*def.* **3**).

sonority, *n.* sonorousness, fullness, richness, deepness; loudness, thunderousness, clamor, plangency, amplification; reverberation, resonance, echoing, re-echoing; vibration, tremulousness, *Both Music.* vibrato, tremolo.

sonorous, *adj.* **1.** (*all of sound*) resonant, loud, resounding, booming, thunderous, powerful, amplified; ringing, tolling, plangent, clangorous; echoing, re-echoing, reverberating, reverberant, reberative, reflected; vibrant, vibrating, vibratory, vibrative; pulsating, tremulous; sustained, prolonged, drawn-out, held, long; rich, full, full-bodied, pear-shaped, rounded, round; deep, deep-toned, low, bass, basso, baritone, sepulchral.

2. grandiloquent, high-flown, bombastic, bombastical; pompous, orotund, fustian, haughty, pretentious, ostentatious, flaunting, grandiose; magniloquent, Johnsonian, Ossianic, Ciceronian, sesquipedalian; high-sounding, lofty, *Inf.* highfalutin, *Inf.* high-hat; inflated, swollen, bloated; flatulent, turgid, plethoric; impressive, euphuistic, periphrastic; extravagant, ranting, declamatory.

soon, *adv.* **1.** before long, shortly, within a short period; presently, anon, at an early date, betimes; erelong, in good time, in due time; *Inf.* any old day now, *Inf.* any minute, in the near future, before you know it.

2. promptly, quickly, directly, speedily, as soon as possible, A.S.A.P., at the first opportunity; forthwith, apace, by return mail *or* post; without delay, expeditiously, straightway, punctually, with dispatch, at once, before one can say "Jack Robinson;" immediately, *Fr. tout de suite,* instantaneously, on the spot, lickity-split, in a wink, in no time, in less than no time, in nothing flat; in short order, on the double, *Sl.* pronto, in two shakes of a lamb's tail, overnight, in the twinkling of an eye.

3. lief, fain, freely, readily, willingly; graciously, with delight, happily, gladly.

4. sooner or later eventually, finally, ultimately, in the end; at last, at the final whistle, at the showdown, when all is said and done; at some time, in the course of time, in time, in the long run; inevitably, inescapably, automatically, unequivocally, absolutely, as a foregone conclusion; indubitably, inescapably, like the approach of doom; fixedly, ineluctably, inevasibly, ineludibly; for certain, *Inf.* for sure, surely, surely as death, surely as death and taxes.

soothe, *v.* **1.** tranquilize, pacify, quiet, sober; placate, conciliate, calm, compose, still, hush; subdue, tame, settle; relieve, ease, heal, comfort, console, solace; relax, refresh, restore; cheer, hearten, gladden, reassure.

2. mitigate, moderate, temper, lessen, reduce; assuage, *Rare.* lenify, salve, allay, alleviate, palliate; appease, *Archaic.* attemper, mollify, soften, dulcify; lull, smooth, put to rest, *Brit., Australian.* dill; quench, slake, blunt, take the edge off of; dull, deaden.

soothsayer, *n.* **1.** forecaster, predictor, seer, augur; druid, sibyl, diviner, divinator; fortune teller, crystal-gazer, palmist; geomancer, hauruspice, haruspex; python, pythoness, prophet, prophetess; oracle, *Gk. Myth.* Pythia *or* the Delphian sibyl, *Class. Myth.* Cassandra, *Gk. Myth.* sphinx, *Bible.* Witch of Endor, *Celtic and Arthurian Legend.* Morgan le Fay, *Gk. Myth.* Tiresias.

2. astrologer, psychic, sorcerer, witch doctor; weather prophet, weather forecaster, weatherman, weathergirl, meteorologist.

sooty, *adj.* **1.** (*all with soot*) blackened, smirched, besmirched, soiled, dirtied, sullied, stained, smudged; begrimed, besmeared, smeared; smutchy, grimy, dirty.

2. black, pitch-black, coal-black, jet, jetty; ebony, ebon, raven, sable; inky, pitchy; blackish, nigrescent, dusty, swarthy.

sophism, *n.* See **sophistry**.

sophist, *n.* **1.** casuist, paralogist, paralogican, Jesuit, circuitous reasoner *or* arguer; quibbler, specious arguer, equivocator, *Sl.* waffler, fudger; liar, prevaricator, dissembler, deceiver, caviler; evader, dodger, *Inf.* weasel; hedger, doubletalker, backtracker, back-pedaler; tergiversator, vacillator; quack, charlatan, *Inf.* fake.

2. scholar, savant, man of letters, learned person; sage, philosopher, intellectual, highbrow, *Inf.* egghead, *Inf.* brain, *Inf.* walking encyclopedia; authority, expert, pundit.

sophistic, *adj.* fallacious, false, unsound, faulty, flawed, imperfect, *Inf.* full of holes; inaccurate, specious, spurious, erroneous, mistaken, incorrect, *Logic.* paralogistic; quibbling, casuistical, subtle, captious, jesuitic, jesuitical, sophisticated; illogical, irrational, *Sl.* cockeyed, *Sl.* cockamamie; unfounded, baseless, ungrounded, groundless; untenable, invalid.

sophisticate, *n.* **1.** man *or* woman of the world, man about town, playboy, city boy, cosmopolite, cosmopolitan, citizen of the world, world traveler; connoisseur, gourmet, one of impeccable taste, one who knows his way around, one who's been around.

—*v.* **2.** indoctrinate in the ways of the world, open [s.o.'s] eyes, show around, expose to harsh reality; disillusion, rob of one's illusions, disenchant; educate, cultivate, refine, take the rough edges off.

3. mislead, misguide, misdirect, delude, deceive; pervert, corrupt, adulterate, debase, defile; distort, garble, misinterpret, misstate, warp, stretch, twist, falsify, doctor.

4. quibble, equivocate, lead around Robin Hood's barn, beat around the bush, doubletalk, beg the question; palter, parry, sidestep, split hairs, cavil, fence, tergiversate.

sophisticated, *adj.* **1.** worldly-wise, knowing, knowledgeable, in the know, *Sl.* hip, *Sl.* hep, *Sl.* cool, *Sl.* with it; slick, suave, urbane, citified, worldly, cosmopolitan, at home anywhere; polished, refined, cultured, educated, Ivy League; elegant, stylish, chichi; in society, very social, jet-set, *Sl.* swinging; realistic, practical, hard-headed, hard-boiled; experienced, seasoned, inured, not born yesterday, not easily surprised *or* shocked, nobody's fool; blasé, unimpressed, unimpressionable, jaded, world-weary.

2. high-toned, highbrow, intellectual, epicurean, gourmet.

3. deceptive, misleading, deceiving, delusive, fallacious, specious; unsound, faulty, *Inf.* phony, counterfeit, traveling under false colors, two-faced, bogus, sham.

4. (*of processes and machinery*) complicated, complex, intricate, multifaceted; advanced, very modern, latest, highly developed, fancy, excellent.

sophistication, *n.* **1.** worldliness, knowledgeableness, knowledgeability, wide experience; urbanity, suaveness, suavity, tact, savoir-faire; polish, finesse, refinement, knowing what fork to use, culture; elegance, savoir-vivre, style, graciousness; good taste, tastefulness, discrimination, discernment, awareness; civility, decorum, gentility; politeness, politesse, graciousness, poise; adaptability, practicality, hard-headedness, knowing which way the wind blows *or* which side one's bread is buttered on.

2. debasement, degradation, corruption, perversion, defilement, prostitution; impairment, vitiation, spoliation, ruination.

3. quibble, equivocation, sophism. See **sophistry**.

sophistry, *n.* sophism, philosophism, casuistry, jesuitism, illogicality, irrationality, elenchus; fallacy, *Logic.* paralogism, *Logic.* antilogism; subterfuge, feint, dodge, stratagem; subtlety, quibble, cavil; misrepresentation, untruth, equivocation, deception, prevarication.

soporific, *adj.* **1.** somniferous, somnific, somnifacient, sleep-inducing; narcotic, sedative, opiate, soothing, balmy; hypnotic, mesmeric.

2. sleepy, drowsy, tired, dozy, half-asleep, yawning, nodding, slumberous, slumbery, somnolent, oscitant; weary, faint, fatigued, exhausted, *Sl.* beat, *Sl.* pooped; sluggish, torpid, lethargic, *Med.* soporose, comatose.

—*n.* **3.** sedative, sleep-inducer, sleeping potion *or* pill; anesthetic, narcotic, somnifacient.

soppy, *adj.* **1.** sodden, soggy, sopping *or* wringing *or* dripping wet; soaked, drenched, saturated. See **sodden** (*defs.* **1, 2**).

2. rainy, pluvial, pluvious, *Meteorology.* precipitative, raining cats and dogs, coming down in buckets; rain-drenched, watery, puddly, flooded, drowned, inundated, covered with water; slushy, splashy, plashy, sloppy, messy, muddy; drizzly, misty, foggy, vaporous; dreary, cloudy, dismal, bleak, grey, grim, *Scot. and North Eng.* dowel, *Literary.* drear; humid, damp, dank, moist, soupy, clammy, sweaty, muggy, steamy.

3. *British Slang.* teary, weepy, lachrymose, *Inf.* drippy; maudlin, mawkish, soft, mushy, slushy, *Sl.* schmaltzy; flowery, sickening, cloying; sentimental, romantic, emotional; pathetic, poignant, doe-eyed, calf-eyed.

sorcerer, *n.* witch, necromancer, wizard, diabolist, demonologist, warlock; magician, thaumaturgist, theurgist, enchanter, charmer; medicine man, witch doctor, obi doctor, voodooist, shaman; diviner, soothsayer, seer, exorcist, exorciser.

sorcery, *n.* **1.** black magic, witchcraft, witchery, sortilege; magic, wonder-working, wizardry, necromancy, thaumaturgy, theurgy; black art, voodoo, hoodoo, obiism *or* obeahism; deviltry *or* devilry, demonolatry, diabolism, Satanism; supernaturalness, mysticism, spiritualism, occultness, psychomancy, fetishism; ritual, rite, apotropaism, magical ceremony, voodooism, exorcism.

2. spell, rune, *Scot.* cantrip, jinx, hex, evil eye, negative influence; charm, incantation, invocation, evocation, conjuration, conjuring; enchantment, bewitchment, bedevilment; fascination, obsession, possession, trance, hypnosis, hypnotism, mesmerism.

sordid, *adj.* **1.** filthy, dirty, foul, unclean, unwashed, slimy, mucky, feculent, fecal; impure, offensive, fulsome; defiled, polluted, tainted; musty, smelly, rotten, fetid, gone bad, fly-blown, maggoty, putrid, purulent, *Sl.* cruddy; soiled, stained, grimy, smeared, sooty, begrimed.

2. poor, destitute, impoverished, poverty-stricken, down-and-out, seamy, seedy; squalid, wretched, shabby, back-alley; deteriorated, ramshackle, dingy, *Sl.* slummy, uncared-for; piggish, sloppy, sleazy.

3. ignoble, mean, petty; base, vile, low, low-down; degraded, debased, abased, disgraceful, shameful; dishonorable, ignominious, infamous; execrable, detestable, abominable, abhorrent; scurvy, rotten, *Inf.* lousy; vulgar, indecent, crude, coarse, boorish, loutish, obnoxious; depraved, gross, bad.

4. selfish, greedy, avaricious, grasping, *Sl.* grabby, rapacious, hoggish, piggish; miserly, penurious, parsimonious, grudging, niggardly, churlish; stingy, mean, illiberal, ungenerous, uncharitable, closefisted, tightfisted, close, *Inf.* tight, penny-pinching; mercenary, venal, usurious.

sore, *adj.* **1.** painful, tender, sensitive, raw; smarting, stinging, burning, inflamed; irritated, ulcerated, ulcerous; hurting, in pain, aching, achy, bruised, injured, wounded; ailing, unwell, ill, sick.

2. aggrieved, grieved, sorrowful, pained, suffering, sad, mournful; distressed, troubled, unhappy; agonized, tormented, tortured; offended, stung, hurt.

3. painful, distressing, grievous, harrowing, afflictive, troublesome; depressing, heavy, oppressive, burdensome; unbearable, intolerable, insufferable; tormenting, torturous, cruel, violent; cutting, harsh, sharp, poignant; severe, acute, dire.

4. *Informal.* annoyed, irritated, peeved, vexed. See **angry** (*def.* **2**).

5. irritating, annoying, vexing, irksome, provocative; offensive, disturbing, disconcerting; embarrassing, awkward, ticklish, touchy, delicate, unmentionable; difficult, troublesome, spiny, thorny; entangled, knotty, intricate, exacting.

—*n.* **6.** wound, hurt, injure, swelling, inflammation, *Pathol.* blain; ulcer, ulceration, *Pathol.* canker, *Pathol.* carbunkle, boil, pimple, pustule, abscess, fester; bruise, abrasion, scrape, cut, laceration; pain, ache, pang, twinge, gripe, burn, smart.

7. annoyance, irritation, vexation, exasperation; nuisance, bother, pest, thorn in the side *or* flesh, *Sl.* hassle; burden, load, trial, ordeal, tribulation; sorrow, grief, woe, distress; blight, plague, pestilence, scourge.

sorrow, *n.* **1.** grief, sadness, *Archaic.* dole, woe, ruth, heartache, heartbreak; misery, *Archaic.* bale, dolor, anguish; ache, hurt, pain, suffering; torture, torment, agony; bereavement, mourning; woefulness, wretchedness, heaviness of heart, desolation, dejection, depression, oppression; disconsolateness, unhappiness, infelicity.

2. repentance, contrition, penitence, regret, rue, remorse, compunction.

3. distress, affliction, grievance, trouble, worry, vexation; plight, strait, predicament, sea of troubles, difficulty, rub; burden, load, albatross, cross, onus, crown of thorns, bitter pill, millstone around one's neck; cares, pressure, stress, strain; trial, travail, tribulation, curse, ordeal, infliction.

4. misfortune, adversity, mischance, reverse; hindrance, handicap, impediment; hard luck, ill luck, bad luck, bad fortune, hard times, evil days; hardship, privation, austerity, pinch, extremity; disaster, calamity, catastrophe, evil; blight, cancer, canker, scourge, pestilence.

5. lament, lamentation, jeremiad, cry, wail, weep, ululation, weeping and wailing and gnashing of teeth; keen, threnody, dirge, (*in Scotland and Ireland*) coronach.

—*v.* **6.** grieve, mourn, pine, weep; bewail, bemoan, lament; despond, despair, lose heart, droop, languish, sink.

7. rue, regret, repine, deplore; take to heart, lay to heart.

sorrowful, *adj.* **1.** sad, unhappy, dejected, depressed, despondent, crestfallen, chapfallen, downcast, *Inf.* down, *Inf.* low, feeling low, in low spirits, in the doldrums, *Inf.* down in the dumps, *Inf.* down in the mouth; discouraged, disheartened, downhearted, dispirited, *Sl.* bummed *or* bummed out; gloomy, melancholy, blue; inconsolable, disconsolate, heavyhearted, crushed, broken, heartbroken, brokenhearted, sick at heart, heartsick; wretched, miserable, woebegone; bowed-down, heavy-laden, in the depths *or* bowels of despair, *Sl.* in the pits.

2. plaintive, mournful, sighful, full of pathos; wistful, longing, yearning; wailing, ululating, crying, moaning, weeping; heart-rending, moving, affecting, touching; doleful, rueful; pitiful, piteous, pathetic; elegiac, dirgelike, dirgeful.

3. grievous, lamentable, unfortunate, deplorable, regrettable, infelicitous, unlucky, hapless, *Scot.* donsie; sore, bitter, sharp, afflictive, oppressive, distressing, painful; difficult, wearying, trying, tiring, wearing, wearisome; irksome, troublesome, bothersome; sinister, perverse, black.

sorry, *adj.* **1.** remorseful, regretful, rueful, contrite, compunctious; conscience-stricken, conscience-smitten, guilt-ridden, repining, regretting, full of regrets; apologetic, repentant, penitent, pentitential, atoning, in sackcloth and ashes; humbled, abject, sheepish, embarrassed, chastened; ashamed, shameful, shamed, shamefaced, *Sl.* bummed out, disturbed, troubled.

2. sympathetic, understanding, commiserative, commiserating, empathetic, pitying, full of pity.

3. miserable, wretched, pitiful, pitiable, piteous, *Inf.* lousy, *Sl.* rotten; adverse, difficult, troublesome, hard, trying; star-crossed, ill-starred, evil-starred, unlucky, luckless, unfortunate, hapless; tragic, ruinous, fatal, dire, black, grievous, joyless, grim, stark, bleak; abject, sordid.

4. sorrowful, dejected, depressed, despondent, crestfallen, downcast. See **sorrowful** (*def.* **1**).

5. melancholy, dismal, disheartening, depressing, dreary, somber, dark, gloomy; solemn, wailful, sepulchral, funereal, melancholic, plaintive; threnodic, dirgelike, dirgeful, epicedial, elegiac; pathetic, touching, heartrending, heartbreaking.

6. destitute, indigent, poverty-stricken, abject, needy, wanting, lacking, beggared, beggarly; poor, underprivileged, disadvantaged, deprived, bereft, *Inf.* hard-up; impoverished, ruined, down-and-out, down at the heels, out at the elbows, *Sl.* busted, *Sl.* broke.

sort, *n.* **1.** kind, class, category, genre, order; lot, style, manner, cast, mold, stamp, brand, kidney; grain, make, mark; color, stripe, streak, feather, vein; nature, aspect, character; group, set, suit, variety, genus, species, phylum, subgenus, subspecies, strain; race, breed, people, fold; clan, family, tribe, brood, ilk, kin, stock, stirps.

2. manner, fashion, way, method, mode; custom, pattern, style.

3. **of sorts** **a.** adequate, passable, acceptable, tolerable, admissable, *Inf.* not that good, not bad, not too bad, mediocre. **b.** of one sort or another, undistinguished, unexceptional, unnotable, modest; neutral, bland, *Sl.* ho-hum, *Sl.* blah.

4. **out of sorts** **a.** in low spirits, depressed, dejected, downcast, *Inf.* down, *Inf.* down in the dumps; unhappy, cheerless, gloomy, under a cloud; melancholy, mopey, *Inf.* down in the mouth, *Sl.* off one's feed, *Sl.* bummed out. **b.** indisposed, ill, sick, sickly, sickened, ailing, valetudinarian; in a bad way, on the sick list, *Inf.* under the weather, not up to snuff; unhealthy, unsound, unwell. **c.** irritable, testy, touchy, snappish, petulant, irascible; grumpy, cranky, grouchy, crotchety; gruff, impatient, crabby, cross, crabbed; moody, temperamental; ill-tempered, ill-humored.

5. **sort of** *Informal.* somewhat, rather, to some extent, to a certain extent, to a degree, to some degree, in some measure, more or less, *Inf.* kind of; fairly, reasonably, moderately, mildly; in part, partly, partially; a little, a bit, slightly.

—*v.* **6.** classify, categorize, arrange, order, put in order, class; assort, organize, systemize, systematize, methodize; lay out, line up, align; tidy, neaten; catalogue, index, list; sort out, separate, divide, subdivide.

sortie, *n.* **1.** sally, foray, charge, thrust, offensive, drive; raid, attack, assault, onset, onslaught; rush, dash, coming forward, issuance, coming out, onrush, outrush, outflow, efflux, effluence, outpour, outpouring.

—*v.* **2.** sally *or* sally forth, raid, foray, charge, attack, assault, assail, storm; rush, surge *or* come *or* sweep forward, thrust *or* drive *or* push forward, take the offensive; fall upon, set upon, pounce upon, strike at, march upon, swoop down upon, descend on *or* upon.

so-so, *adj.* **1.** mediocre, indifferent, *Fr. comme ci, comme ça;* fair, fair to middling, betwixt and between, *Inf.* no great shakes, *Inf.* nothing to write home *or* brag about; undistinguished, unexceptional, unnotable, modest, of sorts, of a sort; neutral, bland, insipid, uninspiring, unmoving, *Sl.* ho-hum, *Sl.* blah.

2. average, middling, moderate, medium; adequate, passable, acceptable, tolerable; respectable, presentable, admissible, fairly good, *Inf.* not that bad, not too bad.

—*adv.* **3.** middling, moderately, fairly, passably, adequately, tolerably, sufficiently, satisfactorily.

sot, *n.* drunkard, drunk, inebriate, soak, tosspot, toper, winebibber, bibber, bibbler, *Obs., Rare.* biberon, *U.S. Inf.* barfly; alcoholic, chronic alcoholic *or* drunk, dipsomaniac; drinker, hard drinker, serious drinker, problem drinker; tippler, guzzler, swiller, *Inf.* lovepot; *All Sl.* soaker, sponge, boozer, boozehound, lush, souse, rummy, wino, alky, dipso, juicehead, juicer, hooch hound, gin hound, swillbelly, swillpot, stew, stewbum, elbow-bender, elbow-crooker.

sough, *v.* **1.** sigh, whisper, moan, rustle, murmur, sing, whistle, shriek, wail, rush, roar.

—*n.* **2.** sigh, sighing, whisper, whispering, moan, moaning, rustle, rustling, murmur, murmuring; singing, whistling, shrieking; wailing, rushing, roaring.

soul, *n.* **1.** spirit, animating principle, vital spirit, pneuma, breath of life, anima, life; consciousness, psyche, mind, intellect, *Gk. Philos.* nous; reason, understanding, intelligence; self, ego, inner self, true being.

2. ghost, wraith, disembodied spirit, presence, *Gk. and Rom. Religion.* shade, specter, apparition, phantom, eidolon.

3. heart, center of emotion, seat of feelings *or* sentiments.

4. human being, human, being, person, mortal, life, creature, member of the human race, Adamite; individual, entity, personage, personality, persona; living soul, spirit; world soul, anima mundi, Weltgist.

5. essential part, essence, quiddity, quintessence, substance, sum and substance; marrow, pith, heart of the matter, crux, gist, *Inf.* nub, meat, nitty-gritty; core, inner core, heart, center, nucleus, kernel; base, bottom, root.

6. embodiment, incarnation, personification.

7. *Informal.* negritude, Blackness, intense sensitivity, emotional fervor, feeling.

—*adj.* **8.** *Informal.* Black, Negro; earthy, intense, soulful, *Trademark.* Motown.

soulful, *adj.* emotional, moving, deep, *Sl.* heavy, intense, meaningful, expressive.

sound[1], *n.* **1.** noise, utterance, sonance; tone, note, chord, music.

2. outcry, vociferation, clamor, din, hubbub, racket; shout, whoop, yell, roar; blare, blast, bang, rumble, jingle, tinkle, peal, ring, toll; clatter, clink, clank, creak, grate. See also **noise** (*def.* **1, 3-6**).

3. quality, cast, color, coloring, tenor, drift.

4. earshot, earreach, hearing, hearing distance.

—*v.* **5.** ring, chime, clang, ding-dong, peal, knell, toll; tinkle, clink, clank; rumble, thunder, boom; reverberate, resonate, resound, echo.

6. seem, appear, appear like, look like, look as if, look to be, have the look of; strike one as, have every appearance of, have every indication of, have the earmarks of, sound like.

7. pronounce, enunciate, articulate, phonate, vocalize, voice, utter, express; vociferate, shout, bawl, cry; declare, announce, annunciate, broadcast, herald, blare, blazon, trumpet, noise abroad.

sound[2], *adj.* **1.** healthy, fit, fit as a fiddle, physically-fit, in good condition, in fine fettle, *Inf.* in shape, *Inf.* in good *or* fine shape, *Inf.* in fine *or* high feather, *Inf.* in fine whack, *Inf.* in the pink, *Brit. Dial.* bonny; well, in good health, rosy-cheeked, glowing, blooming; ruddy, vigorous, full of vigor, hale, hearty, hale and hearty, robust, lusty, strong and healthy, bursting with health *or* vigor *or* life.

2. intact, unimpaired, undamaged, unharmed, uninjured, unscathed, unmutilated, undecayed, inviolate; whole, unbroken, as good as new, faultless, flawless, defectless; well-built, well-constructed, built to last, solid, firm, sturdy, strong, rugged, tough, durable, resistant.

3. solvent, having good credit, secure, in the black; well-off, well-situated, well-to-do.

4. rational, practical, pragmatic, commonsense, commonsensical, reasonable, logical, sensible; competent, reliable, dependable, good, fair; fit, proper, advisable, well-advised; well-argued, well-grounded, well-founded; valid, believable, credible, plausible.

5. lucid, clearheaded, right-minded, clear-minded, cogent, balanced, level-headed, stable; responsible, sober, sane, *Latin. compos mentis,* right; normal, wholesome, healthy-minded, *Sl.* together, *Sl.* with it, *Sl.* all there; intelligent, wise, judicious, sagacious, sage; discreet, prudent, circumspect; politic, perspicacious, farsighted, astute, provident; perceptive, apperceptive, foresighted; understanding, thoughtful, reflective, philosophical.

6. upright, upstanding, ethical, moral, virtuous; honest, truthful, aboveboard, trustworthy, honorable; loyal, steadfast, faithful, true, constant.

sound[3], *v.* **1.** fathom, plumb, measure, test.

2. dive, plunge, go to the bottom, submerge.

3. *Often* **sound out** check out, see how the land lies, feel out; look into, explore, investigate, probe, seek information, examine.

sound[4], *n.* inlet, arm, loch, fjord, *Chiefly Scot.* firth; bay, harbor, cove, gulf, bight; estuary, mouth, *Dial.* creek.

soundless[1], *adj.* silent, quiet, noiseless, echoless; hushed, calm, still, deathlike; inaudible, muffled, stifled, muted, dampened.

soundless[2], *adj.* deep, unfathomable, fathomless, plumbless, immeasurable, abyssal, abysmal, bottomless; unmeasured, unfathomed, unsounded.

soup, *n.* broth, stock, bouillon, consommé, julienne; bisque, purée, pottage, *U.S.* chowder, bouillabaisse, jumbo, mulligatawny; borscht, vichyssoise, gazpacho.

sour, *adj.* **1.** acid, tart, subacid, acetous, vinegarish, vinegary; acerb, acerbic, acidulous, acidulent, acescent, acidulated; fermented, turned, bad, spoiled, rancid, curdled, clabbered.

2. unpleasant, bitter, nasty, disagreeable, unlikable, undesirable; distasteful, unappetizing, unpalatable, unsavory; offensive, repulsive, repugnant, odious, disgusting.

3. harsh, severe, austere, stringent, stern, brusque; caustic, mordant, acrimonious, stinging; trenchant, cutting, incisive, scathing, penetrating, biting; keen, sharp, sharp-tongued; spiteful, virulent, venemous, vitriolic, rancorous; splenetic, choleric, waspish, irritable, testy, touchy, edgy, on edge, snappy, snappish, huffy, huffish; peevish, petulant, crabbed, crabby, grouchy, grumpy; surly, churlish, ill-tempered, ill-natured, ill-humored, crusty, sullen, morose.

—*v.* **4.** ferment, acidify, spoil, go bad, turn, curdle, clabber; acerbate, acidulate.

5. embitter, envenom, disillusion, disenchant.

source, *n.* **1.** origin, provenience, provenance; beginning, commencement, genesis, dawn, dawning; incipience, inception, start, outset; germ, seed, nucleus, embryo; root, taproot, *Bot.* radicle, *Bot.* radix; derivation, ancestry, extraction; matrix, womb, cradle, hotbed; fountainhead, fount, fountain, head, wellspring, well, spring; basis, base, foundation, ground; cause, reason, occasion.

2. informant, appriser, adviser, notifier, *Inf.* tipster, *Inf.* horse's mouth, *Sl.* Deep Throat; reference, authority, citation, documentation, footnote, note.

souse, *v.* **1.** immerse, plunge, dip, submerge, duck, dunk, sink; soak, steep, swash, slosh; drench, douse, imbue, saturate; flood, inundate, drown.

2. pickle, marinade, brine, corn.

3. *Slang.* intoxicate, inebriate, besot, *Sl.* put under the table; stupefy, befuddle, fuddle, muddle.

souvenir, *n.* memento, remembrance, remembrancer, keepsake, memorial; record, relic, vestige; trophy, token, reminder; *(pl.)* memorabilia.

sovereign, *n.* **1.** ruler, monarch, rex, king, crowned head, queen; potentate, dynast, majesty, royal personage; empress, emperor, czar, kaiser; autocrat, monocrat, autarch, overlord; dictator, tyrant, despot; absolute ruler, supreme master.

—*adj.* **2.** royal, kingly, queenly, princely, regal, basilic, majestic, august; kinglike, lordly, noble, aristocratic, patrician.

3. imperial, monarchical, absolute, imperious, despotic, autocratic; regnant, ruling, governing; paramount, hegemonic, dominant, predominant, superior, supreme, highest; leading, top-rank, ranking, chief, principal; preeminent, utmost, uppermost, cardinal, peerless, *Sl.* number one.

sovereignty, *n.* **1.** dominion, supremacy, primacy, preeminence, sway, hegemony; reign, royalty, suzerainty, empery, *(in India)* raj; kingship, lordship, mastership, leadership, seignority; authority, jurisdiction, power, *Inf.* say *or* say-so; rule, command, mastery, control, domination; hold, grasp, grip, clutches.

2. autonomy, autarchy, self-government, self-rule, home rule; independence, freedom, liberty, self-determination, self-direction.

3. territory, region, area, country, kingdom, domain. See **domain** (*def.* **1**).

sow, *v.* **1.** scatter, disperse, strew, bestrew; broadcast, disseminate, spread, circulate, distribute, propagate; publicize, make known, give out, pass the word around, blaze about, hawk, rumor, bruit.

2. foment, sow the seeds of, provoke, incite, instigate, actuate, brew; stir up, work up, ignite, touch off; stir the embers, fan the fire; promote, foster, further, forward, advance.

3. sprinkle, besprinkle, bedew; scatter, litter.

space, *n.* **1.** expanse, extension, expansion, spaciousness, vastness, immensity, largeness, greatness, amplitude, capaciousness; capacity, volume, proportions, dimensions, size; breadth, width, depth, broadness, wideness, height, length; stretch, spread, reach, span, scope, sweep, range, compass, measure; room, area, acreage, land, open country; personal space, elbowroom, leeway, latitude, margin, swing, play; surface space *or* area.

2. air, plenum, atmosphere; heavens, sky, firmament, aerosphere, ether; vault *or* canopy of heaven, celestial sphere, the blue, *Inf.* wild blue yonder; empty space, vacuum, void; outer space, infinity; universe, cosmos, macrocosm.

3. seat, berth, place, spot, reserved seat.

4. separation, break, crevice, schism, rift, breach; gap, opening, chasm, abyss, gulf; hole, hollow, cavity, crater.

5. *(all of time)* extent, stretch, period, interval, interspace, interstice; span, spell, a while; season, stage; age, era, epoch.

6. break, interruption, pause, lapse; intermission, interlude, recess, rest, respite; hiatus, lacuna, gap, omission.

—*v.* **7.** arrange, range, line up, order, array, rank, align; interspace, put a space between, set apart, put distance between, place *or* set at intervals.

spacious, *adj.* **1.** roomy, commodious, capacious, ample, enough room to swing a cat; voluminous, large, big, sizable, huge, great, vast, immense; extensive, far-flung, expansive, broad, wide; massive, gigantic, enormous, tremendous, mammoth, gargantuan; *(all of clothes)* loose, loose-fitting, oversized, outsized.

2. broad, widespread, wide-ranging, far-reaching, extensive, in-depth, comprehensive, universal, all-inclusive.

span, *v.* extend across *or* over, bridge, reach across, stretch across; cross, traverse, go over, pass over, arch over; join, conjoin, connect, unite, link, tie.

spangle, *n.* **1.** sequin, bright spot, bead.

—*v.* **2.** *(all with spangles)* decorate, adorn, ornament, dress *or* dress up, embellish, *Sl.* jazz up.

3. glitter, sparkle, shine, shimmer, twinkle, scintillate, catch the light, glint, flash, gleam, coruscate.

spank¹, *v.* slap, smack, *Inf.* paddywhack, rap; take over one's knee, *Inf.* lick, *Inf.* give [s.o.] a licking *or* good licking, give [s.o.] a hiding, *Inf.* tan [s.o.'s] hide, warm [s.o.'s] bottom, fix [s.o.'s] wagon *or* little red wagon, take [s.o.] out to the woodshed; thwack, *Inf.* whack, beat, *Inf.* whale, thrash, beat the tar out of; paddle, switch, birch, strap; box [s.o.'s] ears, *Dial.* hit upside the head; punish, show who's boss, *Sl.* give [s.o.] what for.

spank², *v.* rush, run, haste, speed, hie, career, *Inf.* scoot, scamper, scurry; dart, dash, shoot, tear, sprint, race, charge; fly, outstrip the wind; whip along, zoom, whoosh, whiz, *Sl.* zing, *Sl.* smoke, *Inf.* zip, *Inf.* hightail it; hustle, get a move on, cover ground; bolt, *Inf.* skedaddle, run like a scared rabbit, *Sl.* beat it out fast, *Sl.* make tracks; gallop, trot, come up from behind, run like Secretariat *or* Man o'War; go hellbent for leather *or* election, go like a bat out of hell, go like a shot, go like lightning *or* greased lightning; *All Inf.* tear up the road, put the pedal on the floor, floor it, step on the gas, gun it, rev it, burn rubber.

spanking, *adj.* **1.** rushing, tearing, shooting, racing, dashing, zooming.

2. quick, quick as an arrow, fast, rapid, speedy, swift, like greased lightning, winged.

3. snappy, smart, lively, brisk; crisp, invigorating, bracing, like a tonic; whipping, churning, turbulent, stormy, windy, blowy, blustery; breezy, airy, rippling.

spare, *v.* **1.** save, leave uninjured, leave alone, live and let live; free, liberate, redeem, rescue.

2. be considerate of, prevent, forestall, deliver from; *(all with* against *or* from) safeguard, protect, guard, shield, defend, shelter.

3. withhold, forbear, hold back, not use; omit, delete, cancel, forget, avoid, neglect; stop, cease, halt, stay, hold.

4. afford, manage, handle, eke out; part with, relinquish, give, lend, supply, yield, provide.

5. dispense with, do without, get along without, manage without; give away, give up, let go, forgo, sacrifice, forsake, drop.

6. be meager, skimp, scrimp, hold back, husband, limit; hoard, keep, retain, conserve, lay up, set aside; economize.

—*adj.* **7.** reserve, extra, on hand, substitute, supplementary, auxiliary.

8. excessive, in excess, superfluous, surplus, left over, unneeded, unnecessary; abundant, plentiful, plenteous, copious; free, unoccupied, unscheduled, not spoken for, unconsumed.

9. restricted, constricted, stringent, strict; meager, frugal, skimpy, limited.

10. *(of a person)* lean, thin, lanky, lank, skinny, gangling, rawboned, without an extra ounce of fat, all skin and bones.

11. economical, parsimonious, penurious. See **sparing** (*def.* **1**).

sparing, *adj.* **1.** economical, frugal, thrifty, saving, knowing the value of a dollar; penurious, parsimonious, *Inf.* tight, *Inf.* tight-fisted, close, close fisted; stingy, niggardly, miserly, skinflinty, Scroogelike, having the first nickel one ever made; cheap, mean, grudging; chary, cautious, careful, wary, watchful, leery.

2. lenient, tolerant, permissive, indulgent, forbearing; easy, tender, soft, soft-hearted, kindhearted, kindly, kind, full of the milk of human kindness; merciful, benignant, clement, forgiving, sympathetic, understanding, compassionate.

spark[1], *n.* **1.** scintilla, sparkling, sparkle, flicker. See also **sparkle** (*def.* **1**).

2. bit, trace, touch, hint, trifle, tinge, suggestion, suspicion, shadow; gleam, glimmer, sparkling, glint; mite, speck, smidgen, iota, molecule, atom, jot, whit, tittle; dot, point, dab, fleck, speck; minimum, pittance, modicum, driblet.

3. life, liveliness, animation, vivacity, spirit; dash, zest, verve, zing; fire, warmth, glow, dazzle; sprightliness, airiness, buoyancy, ebullience; vigor, vim, vitality, energy; exuberance, enthusiasm, dynamism; pungency, flavor, *Inf.* punch, *Inf.* kick, spice.

—*v.* **4.** ignite, take fire, catch fire; *(of engines)* start, start up, turn over.

5. *Informal.* kindle, enkindle, stimulate, animate, reanimate, whet, invigorate; motivate, inspirit, inspire, galvanize, electrify; energize activiate, rally, revive, enliven; push, press, drive, propel; promote, advance, *Inf.* sparkplug.

spark[2], *n.* **1.** fop, dandy, coxcomb, Beau Brummel, fancy Dan, popinjay; fashion plate, exquisite, fashionable, swell, blade.

2. lover, beau, infatuate, swain, wooer, courter, Romeo; suitor, gallant, amorist.

3. beauty, belle, siren, seductress, charmer, enchantress, *Fr. femme fatale.*

sparkle, *v.* **1.** spark, light, scintillate, flame, blaze, burn; shine, twinkle, flicker, blink, wink, flutter; quiver, shiver, ripple; shimmer, dance, dazzle, bedazzle; glisten, *Archaic.* glister, glitter, glint, glimmer; gleam, glare, effulge, shine forth, beam, streak; flash, flare, fulgurate, coruscate; radiate, glow, incandesce, phosphoresce; illuminate, illumine, *Archaic.* illume.

2. effervesce, bubble, burble; foam, froth, fizz, fizzle, hiss, sputter; pop, snap; spume, spew forth.

3. caper, romp, frolic, make merry, be vivacious *or* lively; effervesce, bubble, rejoice, delight, laugh, show excitement; exhibit happiness, exult, be in good *or* high spirits, be the life of the party; play, disport, dance, be lively *or* spirited.

—*n.* **4.** spark, sparkling, scintilla, scintillation; flame, flaming, lambency, flare, flaring; flash, flashing, streak, streaking, gleam, gleaming; glare, glaring, coruscation, fulguration.

5. glint, glinting, glimmer, glimmering; glistening, *Archaic.* glistering, glittering; shining, twinkle, twinkling, flicker, flickering; flutter, fluttering, quivering, shivering, ripple, rippling, shimmer, shimmering, dancing, dazzling, dazzle; bedazzling, bedazzlement, splendor, resplendence; brilliance, lambency, radiance, irradiance, radiation; brightness, gleam, gleaming, glare, glaring, blare, blaring; refulgence, refulgency, effulgence; illumination, luminosity, luminousness, lucidity; luster, shine, gloss, polish, burnish, sheen, nitidity; glow, incandescence, phosphorescence, iridescence, opalescence.

6. liveliness, vivacity, brilliance, effervescence, bubbling; blithesomeness, airiness, breeziness, buoyancy; high spirits, good spirits, gaiety, merriment, lightheartedness; gladsomeness, joyousness, jubilation, cheerfulness, levity; hilarity, mirth, mirthfulness, elation; jocundity, joviality, conviviality, jollity; jauntiness, sprightliness, pertness, friskiness, playfulness, sportiveness; energy, spirit, élan, dash, ardor, passion, zeal, gusto; vigor, briskness, alacrity; eagerness, animation, *Inf.* ginger, enthusiasm; exhilaration, ebullience, excitement, ecstasy, thrill, *Inf.* rush, tingling.

sparse, *adj.* scanty, meager, slim, slight, poor; scattered, widely dispersed, thinly distributed, few and far between; sporadic, infrequent, spotty, irregular, intermittent; insufficient, inadequate, in short supply, hard to come by.

Spartan, *adj.* **1.** austere, severe, harsh, strict; stern, grim, forbidding, rigid; rigorous, hard, demanding, laborious, Herculean, difficult.

2. disciplined, controlled, self-controlled, restrained, self-restrained; self-mortifying, ascetic, self-denying, self-abnegating; abstemious, puritanical, puritanlike, abstinent.

3. brave, courageous, valiant, valorous, heroic, stout-hearted; virile, manly, soldierly, bold, bold-spirited, daring, *Inf.* nervy; firm, resolute, stalwart, doughty, sturdy, hardy; indomitable, redoubtable, formidable; dauntless, undaunted, intrepid, fearless, unafraid; unblenching, unwavering, unfaltering, unbending, unyielding.

spasm, *n.* **1.** fit, convulsion, paroxysm, *Pathol.* eclampsia, *Pathol.* tetanus, throe, qualm, *Pathol.* jactation; attack, seizure, epilepsy, spell, stroke, *Pathol.* ictus, tantrum; cramp, charley horse, contraction, orgasm.

2. outburst, explosion, eruption; tempestuousness, turbulence, boisterousness, rage, fume, fury, *Inf.* conniption, *Inf.* cat fit; raving, hysterics, delirium, *Pathol.* calenture, tarantism; violent emotion, emotional upheaval.

spasmodic, *adj.* **1.** spasmodical, *Pathol.* spastic, convulsive, twitchy, hitchy, jerky, paroxysmal, vellicative.

2. intermittent, fitful, irregular, snatchy, sporadic, random, *Pathol.* arrhythmic; recurring, recurrent, remittent, on-again-off-again, on-and-off, hot-and-cold, alternate, alternating; periodic, cyclic, cyclical, seasonal; rhythmic, pulsating, punctuated; discontinuous, broken, interrupted, broken off, disconnected.

3. excitable, nervous, high-strung, emotional, skittish; inflammatory, volcanic, explosive, ebullient, stormy, tempestuous, turbulent; frantic, frenzied, rabid, hysterical, delirious; impulsive, uncontrollable, uncontrolled, irrepressible.

spat, *n.* **1.** quarrel, disagreement, squabble, tiff, *Brit. Dial.* fratch; personal conflict, *Inf.* run-in, *Inf.* hassle, *Inf.* barney; falling-out, rupture, open variance; dispute, wrangle, bickering, controversy, difference of opinion.

2. slap, blow, smack, buff, spank, flap, clap, crack; whack, thwack, hit, bang; *Inf.* swat, clip, *Inf.* biff, *Inf.* bat, *Inf.* belt, *Inf.* clout; *Sl.* sock, *Sl.* slug, *Sl.* shot; swipe, cuff, jab; buffet, *Sl.* whop, bash.

—*v.* **3.** squabble, altercate, quarrel; argue, disagree, dispute, spar, have words, *Inf.* pick a crow; fall out, tiff, quibble, wrangle; differ, contend, clash, raise voices, take issue, object.

4. spatter, splash. See **spatter.**

5. slap, smack, hit, whack, thwack, rap, spank, *Inf.* swat, clip, *Inf.* bat, *Inf.* clout.

spatter, *v.* splash, besplash, slosh, swash, plash, dabble; sprinkle, besprinkle, spat, sparge, dot, speckle, spangle; scatter, strew, bestrew; spray, shower, spread, diffuse; dash, beat, batter, hit, strike; splutter, fly in all directions; bespatter, splotch, spot; smear, besmear, daub.

spawn, *n.* **1.** *Usu. Disparaging.* progeny, offspring, offshoots, descendents, posterity, issue, seed; family, children, *Inf.* kids, sons, daughters, brood; young, litter, fry.

—*v.* **2.** give birth to, bring into the world, bring forth, have, bear, produce; procreate, generate, engender, beget, father, mother, sire, dam; give rise to, bring into being, give life to, call into existence, cause to exist; create, compose, make up, originate, invent, conceive of, think up, *Inf.* dream up, *Inf.* hatch.

3. reproduce, breed, propagate, multiply, increase and multiply, proliferate, spread.

speak, *v.* **1.** converse, talk, discuss, chat, chitchat, confabulate, *Inf.* confab, coze, pass the time of day, *Brit. Dial.* tell, *Sl.* yap, *Sl.* rap, *Sl.* chin, *Sl.* chew the fat *or* the rag, *Sl.* shoot the breeze, *Sl.* bull.

2. communicate, inform, advise, apprise, notify, give notice to, give word to, mention to, point out, bring to [s.o.'s] attention, let know, have one to know, give one to understand, enlighten, clue in, *Inf.* open [s.o.'s] eyes; convey, relate, put across, get across; disclose, reveal, divulge, bring out, make known, lay open.

3. say, utter, express, breathe, whisper, give *or* let out, come out with, blurt out; speak up, speak out, open one's mouth, *Inf.* pipe up; *(of a dog)* bark.

4. articulate, enunciate, enounce, pronounce, voice, vocalize.

5. discourse, make a speech, give a talk, deliver an address, address, soapbox, platform; declaim, hold forth, orate, lecture, sermonize, preach, pontificate; harangue, rant, out-herod Herod, *Inf.* spout; spiel, *Australian Sl.* spruik.

6. signify, import, point to, give a token *or* sign of, betoken, bespeak; show, demonstrate, display, evince, exhibit, manifest, betray, give away; indicate, imply, intimate; mean, denote, connote, suggest, purport.

7. **so to speak** as it were, in a manner of speaking; figuratively speaking, metaphorically speaking.

8. **speak for** represent, act for, act in behalf of, intercede for; defend, advocate, support, uphold, contend for, *Inf.* stick up for, *Inf.* stand up for; recommend, put in a good word for.

9. **speak out** proclaim, announce, herald; have one's way, take the floor; affirm, assert, aver, asseverate, avow, avouch, declare, protest.

10. **speak well of** commend, speak highly of, describe in glowing terms *or* colors, have a good word for; promote, cry up, puff, sing the praises of, *Inf.* boost, *Sl.* tout, *Sl.* plug, *Sl.* hype.

speaker, *n.* **1.** orator, soapbox orator, stump orator, speechmaker, public speaker, spellbinder; keynoter; haranguer, declaimer, ranter, *Inf.* spouter, *Inf.* spieler, *Inf.* tub-thumper, *Sl.* jawsmith; demagogue, rabble-rouser.

2. loudspeaker. See **loudspeaker.**

spear, *n.* **1.** lance, javelin, pike, halberd, trident, harpoon.

—*v.* **2.** pierce, transpierce, penetrate; stab, gore, gouge, lance, lancinate, spike, run through, *Sl.* let the daylight in; impale, transfix, fix, spit, skewer, *Sl.* shish kebab.

spearhead, *n.* **1.** vanguard, van, advance guard, cutting edge, point; forefront, avant-garde.

—*v.* **2.** lead, lead off, lead the way, blaze the trail, pioneer, take the first step, take the initiative, take the lead, break the ice.

special, *adj.* **1.** especial, particular, specific, certain, distinct; distinctive, individual, singular, signal, one of a kind; different, unusual, uncommon, rare, unique; out-of-the-ordinary, unconventional, unorthodox, novel, new; peculiar, idiosyncratic, strange, curious, odd, bizarre, queer, weird.

2. specific, exact, precise, explicit, definite, express, pointed, strict.

3. important, significant, memorable, momentous, great; earthshaking, pressing, urgent, of the utmost importance; foremost, predominant, primary, paramount, chief, principal, prime; distinguished, notable, noteworthy, noted, remarkable; eminent, respected, prominent, outstanding; well-known, famous, famed, renowned, illustrious, celebrated.

4. secret, confidential, personal, private; exclusive, restricted, limited, select, elite.

5. extraordinary, extraordinaire, exceptional, spectacular, incredible, unbelievable, *Inf.* unreal, *Sl.* mind-blowing, overwhelming, astounding, astonishing, amazing; unparalleled, unprecedented, unequaled, peerless, matchless, unrivaled, inimitable, incomparable; striking, magnificient, impressive, breath-taking, glorious, grand, sublime, miraculous, wondrous, wonderful, fantastic, fabulous, superb, excellent, marvelous; *All Inf.* terrific, super, super-duper, far-out, too good for words, out of this world; *All Sl.* the greatest, too much, out of sight.

6. great, good, dear; close, intimate, bosom, *Sl.* tight, fast; devoted, true, tried and true, staunch, loyal, steadfast, faithful, constant.

specialist, *n.* expert, authority, connoisseur; master, maestro, proficient, adept, master hand; professional, *Inf.* pro, veteran, old hand, old stager, past master.

specialty, *n.* **1.** specialization, field of study, major, concentration; forte, strength, *Inf.* what one does best, line, sphere; *Inf.* baby, *Inf.* cup of tea, *Sl.* bag, *Sl.* thing; line of work, métier, trade, craft; talent, gift, genuis, ability, skill.

2. house special, feature, featured item, soup of the day.

3. peculiarity, idiosyncrasy, idiocrasy, eccentricity, mannerism, habit, quirk; characteristic, trait, quality, property, attribute, part; feature, distinction, mark, earmark, hallmark, stamp. See also **pecularity** (*defs.* **1, 4**).

species, *n.* **1.** class, sort, kind, kidney, variety, type, genre; genus, subgenus, category, subcategory, division, subdivision, section, branch; classification, group, grouping, set, suit; make, cast, cut, mold, form, style, manner; grain, feather, tone, color, stripe; name, brand, designation, description, denomination.

2. **the species** the human race, mankind, flesh, Homo

sapiens, humanity, humankind.

specific, *adj.* **1.** exact, precise, pointed; made for, aimed for, directed toward, appropriate for, right for, good for; only good for *or* with, only effective on *or* with, only works on; pertinent to, apposite to, bearing upon, regarding, in respect to; symptomatic, diagnostic, signal, signaling, indicative, marking, designative, *Med.* diacritic.

2. explicit, express, well-defined, defined, definitive, delineated, detailed, stated, spelled *or* written out; circumscribed, conditional, qualified, restricted, limited, bounded; plain, obvious, manifest; clear, clear-cut, unambiguous, unequivocal, indisputable.

3. specified, established, fixed, set, determined, determinate, decided upon; unalterable; particular, certain, definite; distinct, distinguished, different, discrete, separate, distinguishable, identifiable.

4. special, especial, singular, unique, one of a kind, original; own, various, diverse, chosen; characteristic, typical, usual, normal, customary, regular, expected; intrinsic, innate, inherent, inborn, concomitant, accompanying, side, found with *or* in, occuring with *or* in; peculiar, quirkish, idiosyncratic, idiocratic, idiocratical; unduplicated, unmatched, uncommon, unusual, unconventional, rare; strange, odd, curious, outlandish, freakish.

specification, *n.* **1.** itemization, listing, list, checklist, enumeration, numeration, inventory; register, roll, attendance, muster, muster roll, roster, beadroll; catalog, index, table of contents, directory.

2. description, detailing, sketch, depiction, picture, portrayal, portraiture; delineation, outline, syllabus, reading list, program, schedule, agenda, slate, docket, *Sports.* line-up; articulation, recitation, report, detailed statement; clarification, explanation, exposition.

3. particular, particularity, item, specific, *Inf.* spec; detail, feature, aspect, component, ingredient, element; article, point, line item; number, entry, note; consideration, condition, stipulation, requirement, qualification, restriction.

specify, *v.* **1.** itemize, enumerate, number, numerate, list, name *or* mention one by one *or* one at a time *or* individually, name, mention, cite, call off, call roll, poll; identify, indicate, point out, designate; catalog, make a list of, count, account for, take stock of, take account of, check off, go over, run over *or* through; analyze, differentiate, distinguish among, rank; determine, ascertain, decide on, select, choose, pick, appoint, assign.

2. detail, spell out, delineate, outline, set out; articulate, make clear, clarify, explain, express *or* give one's thoughts *or* feelings on, speak of, make known, bring out.

3. define, establish, determine, fix, set, lay down, prescribe; characterize, depict, describe, paint, portray, represent, render, illustrate, exemplify; distinguish, make distinctive, set apart *or* off; label, brand, tag, call, term, denominate, name, christen, baptize, entitle; style, stylize, fashion, design, lay out, plan.

4. qualify, restrict, delimit, limit, set limits *or* boundaries, bound, mark out *or* off, circumscribe, demarcate; stipulate, condition, make stipulations *or* conditions, require, insist upon, list requirements *or* qualifications, *Law.* provide; arrange for, agree upon, contract upon.

specimen, *n.* sample, example, exemplar, instance, *Archaic.* ensample; specific, case, case in point, *Inf.* for instance, typical situation, illustration, exemplification;; representative, exponent, *Biol.* type; sampling, taste, bite, sip, look, peek, idea; piece, cutting, slip, scion, swatch; (*in medicine, microbiology, etc.*) slide, *Biol.* culture.

specious, *adj.* plausible, possible, conceivable, believable, likely, probable, tenable; seeming, apparent, appearing, ostensible, presumable, *Archaic.* semblable; supposed, presumed, reputed, inferred; professed, claimed, purported, avowed, alleged, so-called, nominal, in name only; deceptive, misleading, fallacious, sophistic, casuistic, *Both Logic.* paralogical, paralogistic; false, untrue, unveracious.

speck, *n.* **1.** fleck, spot, dot, point, mark, flaw, blemish, stain; freckle, speckle; dab, daub, smudge, smutch.

2. bit, mite, smidgen, *Inf.* smitch, iota, molecule, atom, jot, whit, tittle, *Metric System.* micron; spark, scintilla, gleam, glimmer; trace, touch, hint, trifle, tinge, suggestion, suspicion, tincture, *Archaic.* spice, shadow; minimum, pittance, modicum, driblet, dribble; particle, moit, mote, grain, granule, crumb.

spectacle, *n.* **1.** picture, vision, sight, panorama, phantasmagoria; show, showing, display, exhibition, scene; phenomenon, event, incident, curiosity; wonder, marvel, prodigy, revelation, sign; sensation, splash.

2. demonstration, presentation, exhibit, unveiling, airing; stage show, staging, production, performance, revue, extravaganza; light show, sound and light show, *Fr. son et lumière;* retrospective; exposition, *Inf.* expo, fair, festival; pageant, parade.

3. spectacles eyeglasses, glasses, *Inf.* specs; horn-rims, wire-rims, granny glasses; sunglasses, *Sl.* shades, aviators; pince-nez, lorgnette, opera glasses, lorgnon, monocle, eyeglass; goggles, blinkers; contact lenses, contacts, lenses, hard lenses, soft lenses.

spectacular, *adj.* scenic, panoramic, picturesque; striking, impressive, staggering, breath-taking, magnificent, grand; wondrous, extraordinary, remarkable, phenomenal; vivid, brilliant, *Sl.* stunning, smashing, gorgeous, sumptuous; superb, splendid, glorious, divine, terrific, *Sl.* terrif, sensational, exceptional, marvelous, *Sl.* marvy, wonderful, *Sl.* super, *Inf.* super-duper, gee-whiz; fabulous, fantastic, *Sl.* far-out, out of this world; thrilling, daring; dramatic, theatrical, stagy, operatic, melodramatic, histrionic; decorative, ornamental, elaborate, showy, ostentatious.

spectator, *n.* watcher, viewer, beholder, gazer, gaper, gawker; theatergoer; moviegoer, patron, attender; sightseer, tourist, *Inf.* rubberneck; bystander, onlooker, observer, witness, eyewitness; passer-by, looker-on, *Inf.* sidewalk superintendent.

specter, *n.* apparition, ghost, shade, shadow, manes, revenant, Doppelgänger, doubleganger; spirit, presence, wraith, fetch, banshee; phantom, phantasm, *Inf.* spook; fairy, fay, sprite, elf, Puck, Robin Goodfellow; vision, eidolon, sight, image, hallucination, spectacle; ignis fatuus, friar's lantern, will-o'-the-wisp; illusion, chimera, figment of the imagination, phantom of the mind; hobgoblin, goblin, (*in German folklore*) kobold, bogy, bogle, bugbear, bugaboo; imp, ghoul, evil spirit, demon.

speculate, *v.* **1.** meditate, think, reflect, cogitate, excogitate, rationalize, intellectualize; deliberate, put on one's thinking cap, contemplate, ponder; study, muse, mull over, ruminate; digest, think over, ponder over, brood over; reflect over, reflect on, turn over in the mind; weigh, evaluate, take under advisement, sleep on, reconsider, reexamine.

2. conjecture, guess, surmise, suppose, theorize; believe, think, fancy, imagine; infer, take it, assume, *Archaic.* trow, presuppose, presume, premise, take for granted; postulate, posit, predicate, hypothesize, hypothecate; consider, conceive; judge, deem, conclude, deduce.

3. trade, exchange, buy and sell; venture, gamble, sport, *Inf.* plunge, buy low and sell high, sell short, buy futures, *Inf.* play the market.

speculation, *n.* **1.** thinking, thought, reflection, meditation, contemplation; musing, pondering, brooding, mulling over, dwelling on; cogitating, cogitation, excogitating, excogitation; rumination, ruminating, chewing over, chewing one's cud; putting on one's thinking cap, cerebrating, cerebration, lucubration, brainwork, headwork; wondering, considering, weighing, evaluating, studying, examination.

2. inference, deduction, judgment, conclusion; conviction, persuasion, position; conjecture, surmise, guess, *Sl.* shot in the dark; impression, *Inf.* hunch, assumption, supposition, presupposition, premise, presumption; hypothesis, thesis, postulate, postulation; theory, guesswork, augury, forecast, prediction; suspicion, inkling, feeling, intuition, divination.

3. venture, trading, exchanging, buying and selling; gambling, sporting, *Inf.* playing the market.

speculative, *adj.* **1.** deliberative, cogitative, rational, reasoning, intellectual, ideational; abstract, ideal, notional, imaginary, philosophical; analytic, experimental.

2. theoretical, academic, hypothetical, supposititious, suppositional, conjectural; presumptive, assumptive, postulational, empirical, projected, trial-and-error; probative, tentative, provisional, controvertible, unproven, vague, indefinite, undemonstrated, unconfirmed; questionable, debatable, contestable; dubious, doubtful, improbable, unreliable; uncertain, undetermined, hard to believe, problematic.

speech, *n.* **1.** talking, speaking; communication, conversation, discussion, dialogue, colloquy, parley.

2. utterance, remark, comment; declaration, statement, avowal, assertion, asseveration, averment; observation, aside, mention, mutter.

3. talk, oration, after-dinner speech, address, declamation; sermon, allocution, homily, lecture, discourse; harangue, diatribe, tirade, philippic; sales pitch, spiel, pep talk.

4. language, dialect, tongue, patois, *Inf.* lingo, argot, cant; vernacular, idiom, parlance; regionalism, colloquialism; gobbledegook.

5. elocution, diction, enunciation, accent, brogue, inflection, intonation.

speechless, *adj.* **1.** dumbstruck, dumbstricken, struck dumb, dumfounded, *Inf.* choked up, wordless; tongue-tied, inarticulate, unable to get a word out; shocked, amazed, astounded, *Inf.* floored, paralyzed; thunderstruck, confounded, dazed, nonplused.

2. voiceless, unvoiced, unspoken, unuttered, unexpressed, unsaid; tacit, implied, implicit; quiet, silent.

3. dumb, mute, unspeaking, voiceless, soundless, *Sl.* m.o.s.

speed, *n.* **1.** rapidity, haste, hurry, hurriedness, celerity, velocity, speediness; alacrity, promptness, dispatch; swiftness, fleetness, quickness, fastness, expeditiousness, precipitousness.

—*v.* **2.** further, forward, expedite, promote, advance; nudge ahead, get moving, get on the road, boost, give a boost to, give a leg up; back, assist, aid, support, pull strings for, facilitate.

3. rush, run, haste, scamper, *Inf.* scoot, scurry, hie, career; dash, dart, shoot, tear, sprint, race, charge; fly, go like the wind, outstrip the wind; whip along, spank, zoom, whoosh, whiz, *Sl.* zing, *Sl.* smoke, *Inf.* zip, *Sl.* make it snappy, *Inf.* hightail it; hustle, cover ground, streak; bolt, *Inf.* skedaddle, run like a scared rabbit, *Sl.* vamoose, decamp, *Sl.* make tracks; gallop, trot, *Sl.* put the heat on; *Inf.* go hellbent for leather *or* election, go at breakneck speed, go like a bat out of hell, go like a shot, go like lightning *or* greased lightning; *Inf.* tear up the road, *Sl.* barrel, *Inf.* floor it, *Inf.* gun it.

4. drive too fast, exceed the speed limit, *Sl.* have a heavy foot, disobey the rules of the road *or* highway signs.

5. speed up accelerate, hurry up, quicken, hasten, precipitate, get moving *or* going, get a move on, shake a leg, step on the gas, *Inf.* rev up.

speedy, *adj.* **1.** fast, hasty, rapid, swift, fleet, fleet of foot, winged; hurried, precipitate, *Inf.* hellbent, high-speed; nimble, agile, snappy, spanking.

2. prompt, punctual, expeditious, quick; early, *Sl.* in jig time, in good time, *Sl.* P.D.Q., immediate, instant, without delay, as soon as possible.

spell[1], *v.* **1.** orthographize, name *or* say the letters, write the letters, write out.

2. signify, mean, amount to, add up to, promise, look like; signal, indicate, point to; denote, bespeak, stand for, symbolize, represent; portend, augur, presage, omen.

3. spell out specify, make explicit, clarify, make clear *or* plain, leave no doubt.

spell[2], *n.* **1.** charm, rune, *Scot.* cantrip; incantation, chant, invocation, conjuration.

2. enchantment, bewitchment, bedevilment; mesmerism, hypnotism, obsession; captivation, possession, entrancement, enthrallment; rapture, transport, esctasy.

3. fascination, irresistible influence, magnetism, draw, pull; allure, allurement, charm, appeal, engagingness, attraction; enticement, lure, temptation, tantalization, seducement; beguilement, wiles, cajolery, blandishment, inducement, persuasion.

spell[3], *n.* **1.** period, course, run, round, turn, bout, fit; shift, stint, tour, watch; term, time, prison term, *Sl.* stretch.

2. (*all of time*) space, extent, stretch, span, period, time, interval, interspace, interstice.

—*v.* **3.** relieve, take over for, replace, substitute for, *Inf.* sub for.

spellbind, *v.* cast a spell on *or* over, put under a spell, bewitch, ensorcell, charm, seduce; hex, hoodoo, cast an evil spell on *or* over; enchant, entrance, mesmerize, *Archaic.* magnetize, hypnotize; fascinate, captivate, enthrall, enrapture, transport, overpower; catch, snare, ensnare, trap, entrap, *Sl.* hook.

spellbound, *adj.* enchanted, entranced, mesmerized, *Archaic.* magnetized, hypnotized; fascinated, captivated, enthralled, enraptured, rapt, transported, overpowered, *Sl.* hooked; under a spell, bewitched, ensorcelled, charmed; speechless, agape, dumbstruck, amazed, astonished.

spend, *v.* **1.** pay out, disburse, expend, outlay, *Inf.* lay out, *Sl.* fork out, *Sl.* shell out, *Sl.* dish out, ante up; misspend, squander, dissipate, throw away, waste, throw good money after bad, pour down the drain, burn up, go *or* run through; lavish, slather, *Sl.* hang the expense, splurge, play the profligate *or* prodigal, throw money around, spend money like water, spend like a drunken sailor, spend money as if it grew on trees *or* were going out of style.

2. employ, give, put in, use, apply, devote.

3. (*all of time*) pass, while away, fill, occupy, take up, use up, eat up, swallow up; kill, fritter *or* fool away, misuse, waste, lose, *Sl.* blow.

4. use up, consume, take; exhaust, wear out, *Sl.* burn out; impoverish, deplete, drain, empty; finish *or* finish off, *Sl.* polish off, *Sl.* knock off, dispose of.

spendthrift, *n.* **1.** prodigal, profligate, wastrel, waster, squanderer; scattergood, spender, *Inf.* big spender, *Inf.* free spender, *Inf.* high liver.

—*adj.* **2.** prodigal, profligate, wasteful, extravagant; dissipative, squandering, improvident, thriftless; munificent, generous, open-handed, free-handed.

spent, *adj.* used up, consumed, emptied, drained, depleted; exhausted, prostrate, prostrated, worn-out, jaded, *Sl.* burned-out; played out, *U.S. Inf.* tuckered out, *Inf.* beat, beaten, *Inf.* done for, *Inf.* done in; fatigued, tired, wearied, weary, fagged out, *Inf.* bushed; on one's last legs, ready to drop, half-dead, more dead than alive; weak, weakened, feeble, enfeebled, faint, emasculate, emasculated.

spew, *v.* **1.** disgorge, spit out, vomit, vomit forth; regurgitate, throw up, heave, be sick, puke, retch, *Sl.* barf, *Sl.* upchuck, *Sl.* blow lunch.

2. gush, issue, spout, spurt; emit, send forth, eject, discharge.

sphere, *n.* **1.** globe, ball, orb, round, globoid; globule, spherule, spheroid, oval.

2. planet, moon, star, luminary, heavenly *or* celestial body, orb.

3. field, domain, realm, district; territory, province, bailiwick, bounds, department; environment, habitat, medium, element; beat, jurisdiction, precinct; office, function, responsibility.

4. discipline, specialization, forte, specialty, expertise, *Sl.* bag, *Sl.* thing, *Inf.* cup of tea.

5. rank, class, level, stratum, caste; state, station, place, position, standing, status, situation, circumstances; grade, estate, order, range.

spherical, *adj.* globular, global, globulous, globe-shaped, globate, globoid, globose, globelike; spheroid, spheroidal, sphery, spheral, orbicular, orbiculate, round, rounded, rotund, bulbous, bulb-shaped; oval, ovate, oviform, ovoid, egg-shaped; elliptical, ellipsoidal, circular, cyclindrical, cyclindroid; bell-shaped, campanulate; pear-shaped, pyriform.

spice, *n.* **1.** seasoning, herb, relish, condiment, flavoring, flavor; salt, pepper, cayenne, chili pepper, horseradish, garlic. See **seasoning.**

2. piquancy, spiciness, pungency, poignancy, sharpness; zest, relish, tang, *Inf.* twang; bite, sting, edge, race, zip, *Sl.* kick, *Sl.* punch, *Inf.* ginger; acidity, keenness, hotness, pepperiness, snappiness.

3. appeal, interest, charm, glamor, witchery, provocativeness, invitingness, bewitchery, winning ways; fascination, stimulation, provocation, attraction; liveliness, spirit, vigor, vim.

—*v.* **4.** season, salt, pepper; spruce up, enliven, enhance, improve, heighten, add to, give relish to.

spicy, *adj.* **1.** seasoned, spiced, tangy, tart, hot, burning, racy, heady, *Inf.* zippy, peppery, curried; strong, sharp, nippy; savory, full-bodied, rich; zesty, zestful, well-seasoned, snappy, with a kick; sweet, sweet and sour.

2. aromatic, fragrant, sweet-smelling, scented, balmy, redolent, odorous, odoriferous.

3. piquant, pungent, sharp, biting, poignant; harsh, rough, gamy, caustic; strong, astringent, mordant, piercing, stinging, acerb, cutting, acrid.

4. risqué, suggestive, off-color, indelicate, improper, indecorous; offensive, unseemly, tasteless, in poor taste, indecent, racy; not fit for delicate ears, bawdy, sexy.

5. *Informal.* lively, spirited, vigorous, peppy, full of pep, full of vim and vigor; brisk, crisp, hearty, buoyant, enthusiastic; sharp, clever, keen, quick-witted, fast, quick.

spigot, *n.* **1.** peg, spill, spile; plug, stopper, stopple, cork, bung; wedge, wad, packing, stuffing; *Dentistry.* dowel.

2. faucet, tap, valve, cock, petcock, stopcock.

spike, *n.* **1.** nail, skewer, rivet, bolt, pin, peg, treenail, dowel, toggle; stake, pike; stud, prong, projection.

—*v.* **2.** pierce, impale, penetrate, prick, stick, spit, pike, lance.

3. frustrate, foil, check, stay, halt, end; thwart, balk, circumvent, hinder, obstruct, deter; defeat, checkmate, beat, eliminate, stamp out, crush, destroy, eradicate; nullify, cancel, annul, void.

4. discard, throw out *or* away *or* overboard, jettison, *Sl.* deep-six, *Inf.* put in *or* relegate to the circular file, file; eliminate, *Sl.* kill, scotch; forget, drop, lose.

spill, *v.* **1.** pour, pour out; overflow, run over, well over, brim over; slosh, slop.

2. *Slang.* reveal, divulge, disclose, make known, *Inf.* leak; confess, turn state's evidence, *Sl.* rat, *Sl.* squeal, *Sl.* sing, *Sl.* spill the beans, *Sl.* spill one's guts.

—*n.* **3.** *Informal.* fall, tumble, *Inf.* cropper, *Inf.* header, *Sl.* flop.

spin, *v.* **1.** revolve, rotate, turn, twirl, whirl, *Archaic.* trundle; gyrate, reel, circle, circumvolve, circumrotate; wheel, swivel, pivot, pirouette.

2. develop, evolve, unfold; narrate, tell, relate, recount; produce, fabricate, invent, concoct, make up.

3. protract, prolong, prolongate, extend, lengthen, elongate, stretch out, draw out, drag out; continue, perpetuate, sustain, maintain, keep up, keep going, keep alive, dwell on, linger on; expand, enlarge, enlarge upon, amplify; pad, fill out.

—*n.* **4.** ride, drive, Sunday drive, *Inf.* joy ride, *Inf.* whirl, *Sl.* tool; (*all usu. in a motor vehicle*) trip, quick trip, run, journey, peregrination, excursion, tour; jaunt, outing, junket.

spine, *n.* **1.** backbone, spinal column, vertebrae, *Anat.* spina, *Anat.* dorsum, (*of animals*) chine, (*of animals*) ridge, *Bot.* rachis.

2. resolution, determination, firmness; fortitude, hardihood, pluckiness, gameness; pluck, mettle, grit, stamina, *Inf.* intestinal fortitude, *Inf.* spunk, *Sl.* guts, *Sl.* moxie.

spineless, *adj.* **1.** *Zool.* invertebrate; limp, flaccid, lax, slack, infirm; rubbery.

2. weak, weak-willed, feeble, without a will of one's own; irresolute, indecisive, infirm of purpose, wishy-washy.

3. pusillanimous, timid, timorous, fearful, afraid, afraid of one's own shadow; unmanly, fainthearted, weakhearted, lily-livered, white-livered, without backbone, with a backbone of banana, *Inf.* chicken-hearted, *Inf.* chicken-livered, *Inf.* pantywaist, *Inf.* yellow, *Inf.* yellow-bellied, *Sl.* candy-assed.

spiny, *adj.* **1.** spiniferous, spinous, *Chiefly Biol.* spinose, spiculose, *Zool., Bot.* spiculate, acanthoid; thorny, briery, thistly, prickly.

2. spinelike; pointed, spiked, barbed, tined, pronged, horned.

3. troublesome, difficult, hard to handle.

spiral, *n.* **1.** helix, volute, gyre, spire; coil, curl, curlicue, ringlet, corkscrew, whorl.

—*adj.* **2.** helical, volute, coiled, corkscrew, turbinate, turbinal, cochleate.

—*v.* **3.** wind, twist, twine, twist and turn, sinuate; swirl, sworl, whirl; wreathe.

4. (*all of prices, costs, etc.*) increase, rise, mount, ascend, go up; accelerate, soar, skyrocket.

spire, *n.* **1.** steeple, belfry, *Archit.* flèche.

2. peak, pinnacle, tip, point, top, tiptop, apex, acme, vertex; crown, crest, summit.

3. sprout, shoot, spear, blade, *Bot.* acrospire.

spirit, *n.* **1.** animating principle, vital spirit,

pneuma, breath of life, anima, life; consciousness, soul, psyche; mind, intellect, *Gk. Philos.* nous; reason, understanding, intelligence; heart, self, ego, inner self.
2. incorporeality, immateriality, insubstantiality, spirituality; impalpability, intangibility.
3. apparition, phantom, eidolon, shadow, presence; wraith, shade, manes, revenant, ghost, specter, *Inf.* spook; fairy, sprite, elf; angel, devil, demon, ghoul; imp, goblin, hobgoblin, *Obs.* bugbear; (*in Irish folklore*) banshee.
4. motivating force, impulse, urge; dominant character, prevailing tendency, genius; complexion, cast, characteristic, quality; ethos; essence, quintessence, quiddity, embodiment; sense, root, reality, truth; meat, pith, marrow, core.
5. meaning, intent, aim, purport; implication, intimation, suggestion, underlying message, signification, significance; sense, gist, tenor, drift, nature; purpose, intention, animus.
6. (*cap.*) God, Divinity; the Holy Spirit, the Holy Ghost, the Spirit of Truth, the Spirit of Love; the Sanctifier, the Comforter, the Paraclete, the Dove; the third person of the Trinity.
7. *Often* **spirits** feelings, sentiments, mood, humor, temper, grain; disposition, affection, temperament, constitution, make-up; outlook, attitude, frame *or* turn of mind; vein, stripe, streak, tone, cast, hue; tendency, propensity, proclivity, predisposition.
8. valor, courage, bravery, fearlessness, dauntlessness; mettle, pluck, backbone, grit, *U.S. Inf.* sand, *Inf.* spunk, *Sl.* guts; firmness, resoluteness, vigor, stoutness, manfulness, stout-heartedness; audacity, boldness, daring; doughtiness, gameness, feistiness.
9. enthusiasm, eagerness, zeal; ardor, fervor, fire, passion; energy, enterprise; liveliness, vivacity, animation, glow, warmth; dash, élan, *It. brio,* zest, verve, style, flair, panache; spice, pungency, piquancy.
10. esprit de corps, fellowship, togetherness, fellow feeling; cohesiveness, communality, oneness, unity; allegiance, devotion, attachment, adherence, bond.
11. **spirits** alcohol, whiskey, liquor, grog, *Sl.* hard stuff; *Inf.* firewater, *Sl.* booze, *Sl.* hooch.
—*v.* **12.** animate, inspirit, enliven; inspire, embolden, enhearten, encourage; stimulate, arouse, incite, urge on, goad, stir, kindle; activate, quicken, waken; vivify, vitalize, invigorate.
13. carry off, abduct, capture, seize; steal away, make *or* run off with; kidnap, *Sl.* snatch.

spirited, *adj.* **1.** animated, lively, vivacious, energetic, active, alive; forceful, dynamic, vigorous; sparkling, glowing, dazzling, bright, brilliant, vivid, florid, *Music.* bravura; sprightly, airy, brisk, breezy, buoyant; effervescent, bubbling, bubbly, ebullient.
2. courageous, valiant, valorous, brave, heroic, lionhearted; high-spirited, mettlesome, game, plucky, feisty, gritty, *Inf.* spunky; hearty, stout-hearted, stout, stalwart; resolute, determined, tenacious.
3. ardent, fervent, heated, zealous, passionate; enthusiastic, eager, avid, earnest, keen; fiery, volatile, excitable, high-strung; hasty, quick-tempered, impetuous, vehement, violent.

spiritless, *adj.* **1.** listless, languid, droopy, mopey, mopish; exanimate, torpid, sluggish, phlegmatic, lethargic, *Inf.* dopey, heavy; lifeless, inanimate; inert, inactive, stagnant; lazy, oscitant, drowsy, *Sl.* out of it.
2. indifferent, uncaring, unmoved, unconcerned, uninterested; passionless, cold, dead.
3. colorless, pallid, pale, wan, wishy-washy, anemic, ashen; flat, mat, lackluster, lusterless, dull, dingy, washed-out.
4. tedious, tiresome, boring, boresome, wearisome, uninteresting, dry, dry-as-dust; bland, insipid, vapid, empty, inane, jejune, *Sl.* for the birds, *Sl.* nothing, *Sl.* blah; monotonous, humdrum, prosaic, matter-of-fact.

spiritual, *adj.* **1.** incorporeal, insubstantial, asomatous, bodiless, nonmaterial, immaterial; unearthly, unworldly, extramundane, ultramundane, unreal; ethereal, impalpable, intangible; psychical, spectral, ghostly, supernatural; occult, mystic, mystical, transcendental, metaphysical.
2. spiritual-minded, devout, devoted, pious, godly, God-fearing, God-loving, religious; humble, worshipful, reverent, reverential, venerative; righteous, moral, virtuous, good, right-minded, clean-minded, pure in spirit, pure of heart; holy, saintly, angelic, Christly, Christlike.
3. ecclesiastical, churchly, nonsecular; clerical, cleric, ministerial, pastoral; priestly, sacerdotal, prelatic, episcopal; sacred, heavenly, celestial, supernal, devotional.

spirituality, *n.* **1.** incorporeality, incorporeity, immateriality, insubstantiality, bodilessness; intangibility, impalpability, imponderability; otherworldliness, unworldliness, unearthliness; ghostliness, shadowiness.
2. piety, piousness, prayerfulness, devoutness, devotion, religiousness, fear of God; sanctity, saintliness, holiness, godliness; spiritual-mindedness; virtuousness, righteousness.

spit¹, *v.* **1.** expectorate, hawk, spew, slobber, salivate, drivel, drool, dribble, froth, slaver, slabber, sputter, splutter.
2. jeer, hiss, sneer, scoff, slur, flout, *Sl.* razz; snort, curl one's lip, *Sl.* give the raspberry *or* Bronx cheer, hoot, rail; revile, taunt, gibe, ridicule; traduce, vilify, denegrate, disparage, decry, calumniate, deride, contemn.
3. fall, precipitate, shower, sprinkle, drizzle.
—*n.* **4.** spittle, drool, sputum, saliva, slobber, expectoration.
5. **spit and image** *Informal.* exact likeness, counterpart, copy, duplicate, duplication, *Inf.* ditto; chip off the old block, the very image, the spitting image, mirror image, twin, clone.

spit², *n.* **1.** turnspit, rotisserie, roasting rod, grill; skewer, pin rod.
2. point, projection, promontory; tongue, cape, reach, strip, head, peninsula, land's end, *Inf.* jumping off place.
—*v.* **3.** impale, transfix, bore, pink, spike, spear; puncture, stab, stick, prick, pierce, penetrate, transpierce, pass through *or* into, enter; perforate, make a hole through, punch, lancinate, gore.

spite, *n.* **1.** malice, malignity, malignance, malevolence, maliciousness, venom, ill will; animosity, antagonism, hostility, evil, evil eye; resentment, envy, jealousy, covetousness, cupidity.
2. grudge, hate, hatred, aversion, detestation, antipathy, contempt, abhorrence, loathing, odium, enmity, ill feeling; choler, acerbity, acrimony, bitterness, gall, bile, spleen, virulence, invidiousness, viciousness.
3. pique, anger, ire, wrath, dudgeon; vengeance, revengefulness, feud, bad blood.
4. **in spite of** despite, notwithstanding, regardless of; despite the fact that, although, albeit, even if, even so, for all that, even though, though; in the face of, disregarding, in disregard of, in defiance of, flying in the face of; overcoming, ignoring, in the teeth of, counter to, in the face of; disobeying, in conflict with, flouting, *Fr. malgré.*
—*v.* **5.** injure, hurt, harm, abuse, attack, misuse; maltreat, inflict injury on, wound, *Sl.* shaft, *Sl.* do a

job on, *Sl.* let [s.o.] have it.

6. annoy, bother, pester, hector, harass, *Sl.* bug, *Sl.* hassle, *Sl.* drive [s.o.] up the wall, hound, dog, nag, pick on, pick at, *Sl.* ride, *Inf.* give [s.o.] a bad *or* hard time.

7. vex, offend, irritate, irk, pique; provoke, peeve, nettle, chafe, get on [s.o.'s] nerves, *Inf.* give [s.o.] a pain, *Inf.* rub [s.o.] the wrong way, *Inf.* get under [s.o.'s] skin.

spiteful, *adj.* vengeful, revengeful, unforgiving, vindictive, retributive, retaliative, retaliatory, recriminatory, out to get even, avenging; mean, cruel, malevolent, malicious, *Archaic.* despiteous; wanton, malignant, maleficent, malefic; antagonistic, ill-disposed, hostile, unkindly; obnoxious, hateful, invidious; rancorous, bitter, embittered, acrimonious; sardonic, venomous, envenomed, acerb; demoniac, diabolic, evil-minded, fell; vicious, harsh, cold-blooded, cold-hearted, pitiless, unfeeling, merciless.

spittle, *n.* See **spit**[1] (*def.* **4**).

splash, *v.* **1.** spatter, spat, bespatter, sprinkle, besprinkle; sparge; splotch, spot, smudge, smear, besmear, daub; dot, speckle, spangle; splatter, besplash, slosh, swash, swish, plash, dabble.

2. spray, shower, spread, diffuse, disperse; splutter, fly in all directions; scatter, strew, bestrew.

3. dash, beat, batter, buffet, plop, hit, strike, smack; break, surge, wash; heave, hurl.

—*n.* **4.** rush, gush, flush; spurt, jet, squirt; splatter, swash; spatter, spray, sprinkle.

5. spot, splotch, blot, blotch, macula, maculation; smear, smudge, daub, smirch, smutch; mark, stain, blemish, discoloration; blur, mackle, macule.

6. patch, dash; stream, streak, ray, beam; stroke, line, touch, daub.

7. blazon, spectacle, parade, pageant, pageantry, ceremony; ostentation, pretension, pretense, ritz; pomp, grandeur, splendor, glitter, flourish, pizzazz; affectation, airs, *Sl.* dog, pretentiousness, artificiality; theatricality, histrionics, melodramatics; foppery, peacockery, dandyism, flaunting.

spleen, *n.* **1.** petulance, peevishness, pettishness, *Rare.* petulancy; ill-humoredness, ill humor, touchiness, testiness, waspishness, querulousness, carpingness; irascibleness, irascibility, biliousness, cholericness; ill-temperedness, bad temper, crabbiness, crabbedness, crankiness, grouchiness, grumpiness, cantankerousness, crotchetiness; irritableness, irritability, snappiness, snappishness, huffiness, huffishness, curtness, shortness, impatience; moodiness, sulkiness, sullenness, dourness, gloominess, moroseness.

2. acrimony, acrimoniousness, causticity, asperity, mordancy, acridness, acridity, venom, venomousness, venomness; astringency, severity, sternness, acerbity, harshness, sharpness, sourness, acidulousness, bitterness, tartness; virulence, spite, spitefulness, malice, maliciousness, viciousness.

splendid, *adj.* **1.** gorgeous, dazzling, showy, pompous, splendorous; magnificent, imposing, palatial, stately, august, majestic; sumptuous, luxurious, plush, deluxe, *Inf.* posh, *Inf.* swank, *Inf.* ritzy; regal, royal, imperial, kingly, princely, lordly, magisterial; commanding, awe-inspiring, inspiring, *Archaic.* magnific; ornate, resplendent, glittering, adorned, flashing, aureate; elegant, graceful, handsome, beautiful, *Scot.* wally, *Inf.* eye-filling.

2. distinguished, glorious, illustrious, eminent, brilliant, notable, noted, *Archaic.* eximious; renowned, famous, celebrated, revered, honorable, venerable, respectable, respected; noble, lordly, exalted, lofty, sublime, high, elevated; remarkable, conspicuous, prominent, preeminent; fabled, legendary, storied, memorable; immortable, deathless, unfading.

3. admirable, outstanding, superior, grand, superb, supreme; fine, exemplary, virtuous, exceptional, standout, striking; prime, best, sterling, select, choice, nonpareil, classic, peerless, matchless, sovereign, superlative, first-class, *Australian Sl.* bosker, *Scot. and North Eng.* braw; creditable, estimable, commendable, meritorious, deserving, worthy; praiseworthy, noteworthy, laudable, honorable.

4. excellent, good, very good, really good, fine, great; marvelous, wonderful, *Brit. Sl.* ripping, *Inf.* smashing, *Sl.* bang-up, extraordinary; capital, *Inf.* tiptop, *Northwest U.S. and Canada.* skookum, *Inf.* A-1, *Inf.* A number 1; fantastic, terrific, stupendous, *Australian Sl.* bonzer; *Inf.* super, *Inf.* neat, *Sl.* keen, *Sl.* boss, *Sl.* tuff, *Sl.* bad, *Sl.* wild, *Sl.* cool, *Inf.* dandy, *Inf.* jim-dandy, *Sl.* swell; *Sl.* solid, *Sl.* far-out, *Sl.* out of sight, *Sl.* way-out, *Sl.* magic.

splendor, *n.* **1.** magnificence, impressiveness, imposingness, grandiosity; gorgeousness, *Jocular.* gorgeosity, exquisiteness, superbness, splendidness, *Inf.* splendiferousness; show, dash, display, parade, spectacle; pomp, grandeur, pageant, ceremony, state; elegance, beauty, stateliness, handsomeness, majesty; luxury, luxuriousness, sumptuousness, lavishness, richness; *All Inf.* poshness, plushness, swankness, ritziness.

2. glory, distinction, eminence, renown, prestige, illustriousness; repute, reputation, celebrity, report, mark, fame, name; esteem, honor, respect, credit; nobleness, nobility, loftiness, resplendence, blaze of glory; importance, consequence, significance, moment, gravity, weight.

3. preeminence, sublimity, superiority, supremacy, paramountcy; excellence, greatness, grandness, exaltation, transcendence; worth, value, merit; wonder, marvel.

4. brightness, brilliance, radiance, irradiance; luster, sheen, glitter, gleam, gloss, shimmer, shine; dazzle, refulgence, light, fire, blaze; luminosity, luminousness, effulgence, nitency, lambency.

splenetic, *adj.* **1.** irritable, peevish, petulant, choleric, splenetical; cantankerous, irascible, iracund, surly, crabbed, crabby; unfriendly, ill-natured, brusque, peppery, crusty, grumpy, grouchy, dyspeptic, bearish, snappish, snarling; cross, feisty, huffy, cranky; bilious, testy, touchy, ill-tempered, bad-tempered, quick-tempered, short-tempered; argumentative, quarrelsome, fractious, contentious, disagreeable, *Inf.* ornery, *Inf.* bitchy, *Inf.* ugly, *Dial.* evil; uncivil, sharp, abrupt, curt, short, terse, blunt, rough, rude.

2. spiteful, revengeful, vindictive, vengeful; malicious, maleficient, malevolent, rancorous; acrimonious, caustic, virulent, mordant, trenchant, venomous, envenomed. See also **spiteful.**

splice, *v.* **1.** interweave, braid, knit, twist; intertwine, intertwist, interlace, interknit; join, unite, connect, tie, bind, conjoin, fix; fasten, *Naut.* bend, knot, yoke, link, belt, cinch; dovetail, miter, weld, rabbet; mortise, overlap, graft.

—*n.* **2.** union, juncture, joining, bond, tie, joint, link, fastener; connection, liaison, tie-up, knotting, knot; linkage, linking, fastening.

splinter, *n.* **1.** sliver, fragment, piece, shiver, bit, shard, stinger; spill, spall, *Brit. Dial.* spale; paring, chip, shaving, shred, slip; *All Collective.* flinders, *Inf.* smithers, smithereens.

—*v.* **2.** split, break up, break into pieces, chip, spall; separate, part, fragment, segment; crumble, disintegrate, shatter; atomize, pulverize, break into smithereens.

split, *v.* **1.** divide, separate, break, break up, part, disjoin, disjoint, break asunder; rive, halve, bisect, cut in two, partition, dichotomize, *Obs.* dimidiate; sever, dissever, rend, abscind, sunder; dissect, anatomize, divorce, disband, go separate ways, fan out, spread out; pull apart, disconnect, disarticulate, disengage, unclench, detach; fork, branch, bifurcate, ramify, radiate.

2. chop, cut, hew, cleave, carve; slice, lop, whack, cut off; hack, dismember, mangle, slash, slit, gash, score; break, *Sl.* bust, fracture, rupture, snap, crack.

3. rend, burst, tear, rip, break apart, open, dehisce, come apart, give way; disjoin, loose, unloose, loosen, undo, untie, unbind; splinter, shatter, spall, fragment; gape, yawn, gap, spread.

4. alienate, isolate, set apart, estrange, disunite; set against, set at odds, come between; disaffect, make hostile, *Inf.* stir up trouble, cause dissension.

5. share, apportion, portion, divide, *Inf.* divvy, dispose; partition, subdivide, carve up, demarcate, segregate; distribute, deal, dole, parcel out, allot, allocate; disperse, dispense, assign, detail.

6. *Slang.* depart, leave, take off, quit, exit; vacate, check out, be off, take leave, push off, shove off, go forth.

—n. **7.** crack, fissure, tear, rip, rift, cleft; slot, interstice, interspace, chink, cranny; gap, hiatus, opening, aperture, orifice; chasm, gulf, crevice, crevasse, check, chap; slit, slash, score, gash; furrow, ridge, channel, groove, sucus, *Archaic.* scissure; fission, partition, section; fork, bifurcation, ramification, bifidity, *Obs.* dimidiation.

8. break, breach, rupture, separation, severance, sunderance, cleavage; schism, difference, dissension, dichotomy; disjunction, disconnection, disengagement, disunion, divulsion; interruption, disjunction, divarication; division, subdivision, partition, scission; dissolution, parting, alienation, detachment, withdrawal; segregation, isolation, fragmentation, compartmentalization; breakup, divorce, divorcement, *Sl.* crack-up.

—adj. **9.** parted, broken, ruptured, cleft, cloven, riven, reft; halved, dimidiate, bisected; slit, rent, cut, torn, cracked, dehiscent.

10. divided, disunited, parted, divorced, asunder; alienated, estranged, poles apart; detached, apart, withdrawn, isolated.

splotch, *n.* **1.** blotch, patch, blob, glob, splash; spot, blot, ink stain, stain, soil, mark, dirty spot, smudge, smutch, smear, smirch.

—v. **2.** splash, splatter, spatter, bespatter, splutter; blotch, spot, blot, stain, soil, sully, dirty; mark, smudge, smutch, smear, besmear, bedaub, smirch, besmirch.

splurge, *v.* **1.** indulge, go all out, *Inf.* go whole hog, *Sl.* shoot the works, go overboard, go off the deep end.

2. show off, make a splash, *Inf.* cut a dash, be ostentatious, flaunt, parade, make a big deal, *Sl.* showboat.

3. lavish, spend extravagantly, slather, *Sl.* hang the expense, play the profligate *or* prodigal; throw money around, spend money like water, spend like a drunken sailor, spend money as if it grew on trees, spend money as if it were going out of style; squander, dissipate, throw away, burn up, waste, *Sl.* blow, pour down the drain.

—n. **4.** spree, shopping spree; indulgence, indulgency, extravagance; display, show, splash.

spoil, *v.* **1.** damage, harm, hurt, injure, impair, disable; disfigure, scar, deface, deform; mar, blemish, blight, tarnish.

2. destroy, crack, break, demolish; ruin, wreck, queer, vandalize, trash, *Sl.* cook, *Inf.* upset the *or* [s.o.'s] applecart.

3. pamper, indulge, lavish, gratify; dote on, coddle, baby, overprotect; corrupt, pervert.

4. defile, debase, vitiate; foul, befoul, soil, sully, blacken, smear, smudge, stain.

5. botch, bungle, mess up, butcher, *Dial.* butch, hash *or* hash up *or* make a hash of, make sad work of, *Sl.* bitch *or* bitch up, *Sl.* screw *or* screw up, *Sl.* gum up the works, *Sl.* louse up.

6. decompose, decay, rot, addle, putrefy; go bad, sour, turn; mold, mildew.

7. spoiling for eager, desirous of, longing for, hungry, craving, *Inf.* looking for, *Inf.* after, *Inf.* out to get.

—n. **8.** *Often* **spoils** booty, *Archaic.* boot, loot, plunder, pillage, *Archaic.* prey, *Scot. Obs.* reif; stolen goods, *Inf.* steal, *Sl.* hot goods, *Sl.* boodle, *Sl.* the take, *Sl.* the goods, *Sl.* swag.

9. *Usu.* **spoils** *Chiefly U.S.* political patronage, sinecures, *Sl.* plums; emoluments, advantages, perquisites, *Inf.* perks.

10. *Usu.* **spoils** prize, winnings, reward, recompense; profits, earnings, wages, salary; gain, grab, pickings, takings, *Inf.* haul.

11. *Usu.* **spoils** valuables, treasures, gifts; possessions, purchases, goods; riches, hoardings, savings; stock, cache.

12. *Usu.* **spoils** waste, refuse, offscourings, scourings, sweepings; rubbish, trash, garbage, slag, sprue, dross, sordes; dregs, draff, sediment, settlings deposit, lees, grounds; residue, remainder, rest, left overs; cinders, ashes, embers, soot, smut; *Chem.* precipitate.

spoilage, *n.* **1.** (*usu. used in reference to foodstuffs*) decomposition, decay, putrefaction, putrescence; putrefying, rotting, addling, souring; mold, mildew; disintegration, dissolution, deterioration.

2. damaged goods, discount goods, markdowns, seconds, factory rejects, irregulars.

3. residue, rest, leftovers, dregs; rubbish, trash, garbage.

spoken, *adj.* oral, vocal, vocalized, voiced, sounded, intoned; pronounced, enunciated, articulated; uttered, said, told, recited, stated, expressed, declared; verbal, word of mouth, parol, nuncupative, viva-voce; unwritten, unrecorded, undocumented.

spokesman, *n.* **1.** mouthpiece, voice, spokeswomen, spokesperson; public relations man, P.R. person, press agent, ad man, copywriter; mediator, intermediator, intermediary, intercessor, interceder, intermedium, medium, go-between, messenger, middleman; negotiator, arbitrator, umpire, referee; interagent, agent, proxy, surrogate, stand-in, representative, *Inf.* rep, delegate, elected official, appointed official, minister, diplomat; advocate, espouser, propagandist, activist, champion, defender, backer; attorney, defense attorney, prosecuting attorney, prosecutor, lawyer, counselor-at-law, counselor, counsel, councilor, barrister, solicitor; pleader, apologist, friend of the court, *Law.* amicus curiae; instrument, tool, operative, puppet, cat's- paw, front.

2. speechmaker, addresser, *Inf.* stumper, reciter; orator, declaimer, rhetorician, *Speech.* elocutionist; spellbinder, silver-tongued devil, smooth talker, salesman, saleswoman; speaker, keynoter, valedictorian, salutatorian; chairman, chairwoman, chair, (*of a jury*) foreman, prolocutor, moderator, interlocutor, emcee, host, announcer, broadcaster, anchorman, reader; lecturer, preacher, sermonizer, Boanerges, expositor, expounder; haranguer, ranter, talker, *Inf.* spouter, *Inf.* spieler, *Sl.* jawsmith.

spoliate, *v.* **1.** plunder, rob, despoil, *Archaic.* spoil, pillage, *Chiefly Scot.* reive; ravage, harry, rape, maraud, depredate; ransack, sack, loot, gut, fleece, strip, rifle; raid, foray, forage, prey on *or* upon.

2. devastate, lay waste, desolate, wreak havoc upon; destroy, ruin, lay in ruins, blast, wreck; demolish, raze, level, obliterate, annihilate, extirpate.

spoliation, *n.* **1.** pillage, plunder, plundering, rapine, depredation, despoliation, despoilment, *Obs.* direption, raven; ravaging, pillaging, harrying, marauding, sacking, *Rare.* sackage; raid, foray, razzia, inroad; foraging, looting, ravishment, seizure, grab, rape.

2. devastation, ravage, waste, desolation, destruction, ruin, havoc, damage, wreckage; burning, razing, leveling, demolishing; desecration, defilement, outrage, violation, vandelism.

3. vandalizing, injuring, damaging, disabling, harming, marring; hurt, impairment, disablement.

4. defilement, debasement, vitiation; fouling, befouling, soiling, blackening, smearing, staining.

sponge, *n.* **1.** *Informal. parasite, Inf.* sponger, scrounge *or* scrounger, *Sl.* mooch *or* moocher. See **sponger.**

—*v.* **2.** wipe, wipe off *or* up, rub, clean, clean off *or* up, wash *or* wash off, rinse *or* rinse off, swab, mop *or* mop up.

3. *Often* **sponge out** wipe out, efface, expunge, obliterate, blot out; erase, rub out, cancel, delete, cross out, scratch out, x out, black out, mark off, bluepencil, *Print.* dele.

4. *Often* **sponge up** take up, pick up, soak up, sop up, absorb, take in, suck up *or* in, drink in.

5. *Often* **sponge off** *or* **on** *Informal.* scrounge, *Sl.* mooch, *Sl.* bum *or* bum off, *Yiddish.* shnorren, borrow, cadge, *Inf.* four-flush; take advantage of, impose on *or* upon, parasitize, live off of, *Inf.* freeload.

sponger, *n. Informal.* parasite, *Inf.* sponge, scrounge *or* scrounger, *Sl.* mooch *or* moocher, *Yiddish.* schnorrer, *Inf.* freeloader; borrower, cadger, *Inf.* four-flusher, *Sl.* bum, beggar, *Inf.* panhandler; leech, hanger-on, barnacle, bur, appendage; courtier, minion, follower, attendant, satellite; flunky, lackey, yes man, jackal, spaniel, bootlick, bootlicker, footlicker, lickspit, lickspittle; kowtower, *Contemptuous.* Uncle Tom, *Sl.* oreo, cringer, groveler, sniveler; sycophant, toady, toadeater, tufthunter, fawner, fawning flatterer, truckler; flatterer, wheedler, puffer, backslapper, timeserver, *Inf.* apple-polisher, *Sl.* brown-nose, *Sl.* brown-noser, *Sl.* brownie, *Obs., Rare.* blander, *Archaic.* pickthank.

spongy, *adj.* **1.** light, lightweight; porous, holey, sievelike, loose, incompact; yielding, compressible, flexible, resilient, springy.

2. absorbent, absorbing, bibulous; soft, mushy, squashy, pulpy, pithy, *Bot.* fleshy; squishy, wet, damp, moist, oozy; plashy, marshy, boggish, boggy, quaggy, swampy.

sponsor, *n.* **1.** patron, (*of the arts*) Maecenas, financer, angel, subsidizer; guarantor, warrantor, endorser, ensurer, co-signer; supporter, upholder, champion, advocate, promoter, advertiser, *Inf.* pusher; proponent, favorer, partisan, sympathizer, well-wisher.

2. godfather, godmother, godparent.

—*v.* **3.** answer for, speak for; promise, assure, guarantee, warrant, attest to, vouch for; *Inf.* go to bat for, *Inf.* stick up for, take [s.o.'s] side *or* part, stand by, *Inf.* stick by; aid, support, back, finance, subsidize, uphold, maintain, sustain, endorse, smile upon; promote, further, advance, give a boost, forward, *Inf.* push for, advocate, recommend.

spontaneity, *n.* **1.** spontaneousness, naturalness, instinctiveness, intuitiveness; instinct, tendency, urge; involuntariness, reflexiveness.

2. freedom, openness, effortlessness, unrestraint, lawlessness, abandon; enthusiasm, spirit, élan, animation; verve, dash, life, vigor, ardor, zest.

3. immediateness, directness, extemporaneousness, extemporaneity, extemporariness; impulsiveness, impetuosity, rashness.

4. self-determination, self-activity, self-propulsion; independence, initiative.

spontaneous, *adj.* **1.** natural, instinctive, unconscious, intuitive, *Sl.* gut, *Sl.* seat-of-the-pants; reflex, reflexive, involuntary, automatic, mechanical; compulsive, uncontrollable, irresistible; impulsive, impetuous, blind, rash, snap.

2. free, open, effortless; voluntary, willing, unrestrained; unconstrained, unforced, uncompelled; unprompted, unbidden, unasked for, unrequested, gratuitous.

3. unpremeditated, unplanned, unstudied, unprepared, unrehearsed; immediate, offhand, extemporaneous, extempore, extemporary, extemporized, spur-of-the-moment, on-the-spot, ad-lib, impromptu, *Inf.* off-the-cuff; unwitting, unknowing, unthinking, unguarded, unintentional.

4. self-acting, self-induced, independent; self-directing, self-moving, self-determined; self-initiated, self-generating, *Biol.* parthenogenic.

5. (*usu. of vegetation*) uncultivated, wild, in a natural state, native, unadorned; untended, untouched, overrun, overgrown; dense, lush, luxuriant, rank, flourishing.

spoon, *n.* **1.** teaspoon, tablespoon, measuring spoon, soupspoon, dessert spoon, grapefruit spoon, serving spoon, iced tea spoon, slotted spoon, wooden spoon; ladle, dipper, scoop.

2. spoonful, teaspoonful, tablespoonful, scoopful.

spoon-feed, *v.* **1.** hand-feed, feed by hand, feed with a spoon.

2. pamper, coddle, mollycoddle, cocker, cosset, baby; indulge, cater to, wait on hand and foot, overindulge, spoil, *Sl.* spoil rotten.

sporadic, *adj.* **1.** sporadical, occasional, chance, random, irregular, uneven, spotty, intermittent, periodic; fitful, spasmodic, spasmodical, erratic, up-and-down; infrequent, unfrequent, seldom, scarce, few; rare, unusual, uncommon, exceptional, uncustomary, unhabitual, unwonted; sparse, scattered, strewn, dispersed, widely distributed, spread out, few and far between.

2. isolated, separate, disconnected, unconnected, unassociated, disjoined, disunited, disjunct; distinct, individual, different, disparate; single, solitary, lone.

sport, *n.* **1.** game, contest, tournament, competition, athletic event; athletics, sports, exercise.

2. recreation, play, pastime, amusement, entertainment; diversion, divertissement, distraction, relaxation; pleasure, enjoyment, delight, gaiety, cheer, good fun, *Brit.* beer and skittles, *Inf.* fun and games, *Sl.* jollies; merriment, merrymaking, revelry, jollification, joviality, *Inf.* whoopee; tomfoolery, skylarking, *Sl.* monkey business, *Sl.* high jinks, antics.

3. fun, jest, jesting, joke, joking, waggery, drollery, mirth; trifling, badinage, banter, raillery, persiflage; ridicule, mockery, scoffing, derision, insult, slur, disparagement, detraction.

4. laughingstock, gazingstock, byword, butt, fool, everybody's fool, ass, fair game, *Inf.* goat, *Brit. Sl.* mug; dupe, gudgeon, *Brit. Dial.* cull, *Archaic.* cully, *Inf.* chump, *Sl.* sap, *Sl.* schnook, *Sl.* schlemiel, *Sl.* boob; greenhorn, sitting duck, easy *or* soft mark, easy *or* soft target, *Inf.* sucker, *Inf.* cinch, *Sl.* patsy, *U.S. Sl.* fall guy, *Sl.* softie, *Sl.* soft touch, *Sl.* pushover; victim, pawn, puppet, tool, instrument, cat's-paw, creature, minion, dummy, *Sl.* stooge.

—*v.* **5.** amuse onself, have fun, while away time, play, disport; frolic, frisk, gambol, skip, trip, dance about, jump about, romp, rollick, lark; cavort, caper, cut capers, curvet; have a good time *or* a good old time, make merry, revel, carouse, wassail, roister, whoop it up, *Inf.* make whoopee.

6. dally, trifle, toy, treat lightly, make light with; potter, putter, smatter, tinker, fiddle, tamper with, *Inf.* fool with; play upon, take advantage of.

7. clown, clown around, play the clown; horse around, fool around, kid around, *Inf.* cut up; joke, jest, fool, tease, *Inf.* josh, *Inf.* kid, *Inf.* put [s.o.] on, *Inf.* pull [s.o.'s] leg; banter, chaff, poke fun at, rally, twit; taunt, jeer, gibe, mock, ridicule, make fun of, laugh at; satirize, lampoon, parody, caricature, travesty, burlesque, *Inf.* roast; scoff at, fleer, scout, flout, deride, disparage.

8. *Informal.* show off, show, display, exhibit, wear.

sportive, *adj.* **1.** playful, gamesome, (*in musical directions*) scherzando; frolicsome, full of fun, fun-loving; spirited, high-spirited, frisky, coltish, skittish, *Inf.* full of beans, *Inf.* feeling one's oats; kittenish, romping; sprightly, lively, jaunty, debonair; sparkling, buoyant, light-hearted, airy, blithe, blithesome, whimsical; merry, gay, sunny, riant, cheerful, gleeful, jocular, jocose, jovial; jesting, joking, full of mischief, mischievous, scampish, devilish, impish, elfish; waggish, prankish, tricksy.

2. athletic, gymnastic, acrobatic, *Gk. Antiq.* agonistic, *Gk. Antiq.* palaestral.

sportsmanship, *n.* **1.** skillfullness, expertness, mastership, mastery, proficiency; dexterity, dexterousness, adroitness, nimbleness, facility, ability.

2. fair play, honesty, justice, fairness; scrupulosity, probity, rectitude, uprightness, integrity, self-control, honorableness; courtesy, politeness, good will.

spot, *n.* **1.** mark, dot, point, speck, speckle, fleck, flyspeck, mote, moit, particle; dab, daub, maculation, smudge, smirch, smutch, blur; defect, fault, defacement, disfigurement; patch, blotch, splotch, dapple, mottle, discoloration, birthmark, nevus; blemish, blot, flaw, taint, stain, tarnish, stigma, brand.

2. pimple, pustule, papule, papilla, boil, blain, wen, whelk, *Archaic.* botch; pock, pockmark, pit, whitehead, blackhead, *Sl.* zit.

3. place, location, position, niche; site, locality, locale; scene, scene of the crime, setting, *Law.* venue; bearings, latitude and longitude; region, area, section, quarter, zone, neighborhood.

4. on the spot without delay, quickly, posthaste, before one can say "Jack Robinson," in a flash; straightway, immediately, at once, instantly, this instant, right now, right away.

—*v.* **5.** stain, dirty, soil, muddy, sully, dab, daub, blot, smudge, smutch; sprinkle, spray, sparge, splash, spatter, *Inf.* slop up; bedraggle, begrime, besmear, smear, smirch, besmirch, defile, foul, befoul; mar, injure, damage, blemish, tarnish, blacken, taint, stigmatize, brand.

6. mark, dot, speckle, speck, fleck; dapple, mottle, diversify, variegate, color; strew, bestrew, stud.

7. *Informal.* detect, descry, espy, observe, spy, see, discern, make out; recognize, identify.

8. place, situate, lay, set down, set, station, position, locate; settle, fix, plant, establish, install; stand, rest, seat.

spotless, *adj.* **1.** unspotted, speckless, clean, unsoiled, white, snowy, immaculate; cleansed, washed, bathed, laundered, scrubbed, wiped, scoured; polished, dusted, swept, vacuumed, whisked; tidy, well-groomed, well-kept, spick-and-span.

2. pure, unstained, stainless, untarnished, unsullied, unblemished; perfect, flawless, faultless; virgin, virginal, untouched, unadulterated, unspoiled, untainted; unpolluted, uncontaminated, sanitized, disinfected, antisepticized, deodorized.

spotlight, *n.* **1.** floodlight, flood, arc light, arc, footlight, *Inf.* foot, klieg light, *Inf.* spot; searchlight; flashlight, *Brit.* torch.

2. limelight, public eye *or* consciousness, glare of public attention, glare, daylight, bright light; fame, notoriety; publicity; currency, popularity; attention, interest, observation.

—*v.* **3.** light, light up, lighten, illuminate; shine light upon, shed light upon, cast *or* throw light upon; floodlight, flood *or* bathe with light.

4. feature, highlight, play up, set off, give prominence to, bring to the fore, bring into relief; star, *Inf.* headline; emphasize, stress, lay stress *or* emphasis upon, give emphasis to, punctuate, accent, accentuate; underscore, underline, italicize, point up, call attention to, mark; intensify, deepen, heighten.

spotted, *adj.* **1.** speckled, specked, flecked, freckled, spotty; marked, dotted, punctate, ocellated; blotchy, splotchy, uneven, macular; pimpled, pocked; dappled, mottled, flea-bitten, pied, piebald, pinto; particolored, variegated, diversified.

2. sullied, dirty, unclean, soiled, stained, discolored, smudged, smutched; unwashed, grimy, filthy, muddied, bedraggled, smeared, besmeared, smirchy; blemished, tarnished, flawed, marred, injured, defiled, spoiled, ruined.

spotty, *adj.* **1.** marked, speckled, dotted, blotchy, variegated, spotted. See **spotted** (*def.* **1**).

2. irregular, uneven, rough, ununiform; unmethodical, methodless, inconsistent, desultory, orderless, unsystematic; disarranged, disordered, confused; rambling, wandering, straying, roving; inconstant, erratic, eccentric, capricious, spasmodic, fitful.

spouse, *n.* husband *or* wife, common-law husband *or* wife, *Inf.* better half, consort, companion, marital partner, partner, (*former*) ex, yokefellow, yokemate; married man, benedict, bridegroom, groom, *Inf.* hubbie, *Sl.* old man, *Archaic.* goodman; married woman, wedded wife, bride, housewife, woman, lady, matron, *Amer. Ind.* squaw, wife of one's bosom, *Law.* feme, *Law.* feme covert, concubine, *Inf.* missis, *Inf.* little woman, *Humorous.* rib, *Sl.* old lady *or* woman, *Scot. Inf.* wifey, *Archaic.* goodwife *or* goody. See **partner** (*def.* **3**).

spout, *v.* **1.** spurt, squirt, gush, jet, spray; surge, flow, stream, pour; spurt, spit, spew, eject, discharge, debouch, disgorge, disembogue, pour out, *Geol.* extravasate.

2. *Informal.* declaim, orate, *Australian Sl.* spruik, rant, rant and rave; harangue, soapbox, speechify, sermonize, preach, spiel; hold forth, run off at the mouth, go on and on, ramble on, maunder.

—*n.* **3.** nozzle, nose, lip, rose, jet; waterspout, gargoyle, drain, outlet, duct; chute, pipe, tube, sluice, trough, conduit.

4. stream, rivulet, runoff; spillage, overflow; geyser, jet, spurt, squirt; spray, fountain, *Inf.* spritz, gush, rush.

sprawl, *v.* **1.** stretch out, spraddle, straddle, loll, lounge, *Brit. Dial.* lollop; lie around, recline, repose, supinate; droop, slump, flop, slouch.

2. branch out, flare, splay, spill over; spread, straggle, ramble, wander, trail, draggle, meander, wind.

3. scramble, crawl, creep, scrabble; scuttle, hitch, hobble, jerk, shuffle, shamble.

—*n.* 4. spread, stretch, *Sl.* skimble-scamble, growth, outgrowth; expansion, extension, widening, broadening; branching out, spreading out, dispersion, dispersal.

spray[1], *n.* 1. sprinkle, sprinkling, shower; mist, drizzle, *Dial.* mizzle; fountain, jet, splash, plash, spatter, splatter, hail; spindrift, foam, froth, spume; effervescence, fizz.

2. sprinkler, sprinkling can, sprayer, rose, nozzle, atomizer, vaporizer, evaporator.

—*v.* 3. scatter, disperse, disseminate, sow, sprinkle, spatter; fusillade, barrage, shotgun; shower, drizzle, jet, splatter, spout, gush, splash, dash.

spray[2], *n.* bough, branch, sprig; nosegay, posy, bouquet, floral arrangement, May basket, corsage, blossoms; chaplet, wreath, garland, festoon; (*all of flowers, twigs, etc.*) cluster, bunch, sheath.

spread, *v.* 1. *Often* **spread out** stretch, extend, enlarge, widen, broaden, augment, aggrandize, amplify; stretch out, draw out, lengthen, elongate, protract, prolongate, drag out; expand, dilate, distend, swell, bloat; grow, develop, increase, advance, multiply, mushroom, branch out; deepen, heighten, wax, intensify, escalate, accelerate; sprawl, overdevelop, overgrow, become a cancer; travel, transfer, move around, *Pathol.* metastasize.

2. *Often* **spread out** stretch out, open out, unfurl, uncurl, uncoil, unroll, unfold, untwist; open up, bloom, flower; display, exhibit, show, present; produce, reveal, unveil, uncover.

3. *Often* **spread out** disseminate, distribute, send out, dispense, give out, pass out, hand out, circulate; broadcast, air, televise, publish, publicize, make public; promulgate, propagate, spread around, teach, preach, tell of *or* about, give to the world; advertise, trumpet, blazon, herald, blaze about, hawk, announce; recite, repeat, bruit, bandy about, rumor; disperse, scatter, strew, bestrew, cast, throw out, sow; shed, radiate, shine, effuse, throw off, give forth; diffuse, circumfuse, dissipate, dispel.

4. array, arrange, set up, organize, order; put things on *or* around, situate, position, posit, locate, dispose; lay out, set out, (*both of a table*) set, lay.

5. apply, put on, daub on, lay on, smooth on, paint on, rub on, smear on; pour on, plaster on, go heavy with, be generous with, *Inf.* slather, *Sl.* slop on, *Sl.* pile on.

6. *Usu.* **spread [s.t.] over** cover, overspread, overlay; blanket, mantle, cloak, wrap up, enwrap, bundle up, muffle up, swaddle; shelter, canopy, house, protect; shield, screen, veil, curtain, shroud; coat, film, layer, carpet, pave, plaster, parget, incrust; plate, gild, enamel, lacquer, paint, varnish, wash; glaze, ice, top off, sugar-coat, candy, spatter, sprinkle, asperse, bespatter, fleck, dot; wash over, overflow, overrun, engulf, inundate, flood, submerge, drown, smother.

7. separate, part, come apart, come undone *or* unglued; force apart, take apart, fold *or* bend back, hold open *or* down, pin *or* tack back *or* down; unfasten, undo, open; flatten out, flatten, make flush, level; smush, mash, squash, crush, pound down.

—*n.* 8. expansion, extension, enlargement, augmentation, magnification, aggrandizement; widening, broadening, dilation, dilatation, distension, swelling, bloating, tumefaction, *Physiol.* diastole; growth, propagation, multiplication, increase, increment, development, advance, advancement, inflation, mushrooming; deepening, heightening, waxing, intensification, escalation; transmission, transference, communication, contagion, movement, *Pathol.* metastasis; sprawl, invasion, blight, cancer; stretching out, branching out, spreading out; dissemination, dispersion, dispersal, *Mil.* deployment; circumfusion, broadcasting, aspersion, effusion, radiation; diffusion, dissipation.

9. elasticity, stretchability, extensibility, tensibility, tensileness, springiness, dilatability; rubberiness, plasticity, ductility, flexibility, suppleness, resilience.

10. expanse, extent, distance, breadth, broadness, width, wideness, depth, deepness, length, height; size, gauge, dimensions, measurements, proportions, volume, capacity; space, area, region, territory, district, stretch, reach, compass, radius, orbit, swing, sweep, play; limit, margin, bound, boundary; period, term, length of time, time, duration, longevity.

11. bedspread, bedcover, counterpane, coverlet; comforter, eiderdown, quilt, cover, blanket; throw, slipcover, top, protection, covering, tablecloth, cloth; mantle, cloak, shawl, robe, wrap; veil, mantilla, hood, cowl, scarf, kerchief.

12. butter, margarine, oleo, peanut butter, apple butter; jelly, jam, gelatin, marmalade, preserve, conserve, confiture, comfit, compote; topping, sauce, gravy; coating, icing, glaze, meringue; screen, lotion, oil, emulsion, cosmetic, make-up.

13. layout, array, arrangement, organization, setup; full-page ad, two-page ad, double truck, centerfold, *Journalism.* center spread.

14. *Informal.* table, board, fare, menu, diet, bill of fare, table d'hôte; meal, repast, collation, feast, banquet, *Inf.* feed.

15. *Informal.* place, piece of property *or* land *or* real estate, plantation; farm, farmplace, farmstead, *Archaic.* farmhold, *Brit.* farmery, ranch, rancho, rancheria, hacienda, manor, manor farm; home, homestead, *Both Brit.* croft, homecroft, *Scot. and North Eng.* steading.

spree, *n.* 1. frolic, outing, romp, lark, gambol, rollick, frisk; escapade, antic, adventure; celebration, gala affair, wing-ding, *Inf.* get-together, *Irish.* hooley; merrymaking, revelry, jollification, *Inf.* goings on.

2. fling, bout, carouse, carousal, revel, wassail; drinking bout, drunk, brannigan, bouse, guzzle, drunken carouse *or* revel, potation, compotation, bacchanal, bacchanalia; *Inf.* binge, *Inf.* booze, *Sl.* bender, *Sl.* hellbender, *Sl.* bust, *Sl.* drunk, *Sl.* toot, *Sl.* tear, *Sl.* jag, *Sl.* bat, *Sl.* barhop, *Sl.* bar-crawl, *Brit. Sl.* pub-crawl; orgy, debauch, debauchery, saturnalia.

sprig, *n.* 1. spray, nosegay. See **spray**[2].

2. twig, stem, branch, bough; shoot, sucker, offshoot, spur, switch, sprout, scion, cutting; leafstalk, *Bot.* petiole.

3. youth, young fellow, young one, youngster, *Dial.* young'un, juvenile; boy, chap, young buck, lad, *Scot.* laddie, pup, kid, sonny, junior.

sprightliness, *n.* liveliness, vivacity, animation; dynamism, energy, *Inf.* get up and go, briskness, vitality; spark, fire, warmth, dash, élan, spirit, spiritedness; eagerness, enthusiasm, exhilaration, sanguineness, cheerfulness, optimism; airiness, buoyancy, effervescence, sparkle; sportiveness, playfulness; gaiety, jollity, joviality.

sprightly, *adj.* brisk, frisky, spry, nimble, agile, quick, *Dial.* peart, yare, *Scot. and North Eng.* crouse; dynamic, animated, spirited, flushed, go-go, mettlesome; vivacious, gay, jocund, breezy, buoyant, sanguine; effervescent, *Inf.* peppy, *Inf.* chipper, *Inf.* snappy; enthusiastic, excited, hearty, zealous; rollicking, playful, gamesome, frolicsome, sportive; jocular, jocose, joking, jesting, waggish; cheerful, mirthful, jolly, blithe, blithesome; elated, ecstatic, joyful, jubilant; light-hearted, debonair, jaunty, lively, airy, spry.

spring, *v.* **1.** leap, jump, bound, vault, hop, skip.
2. appear, come into view, uprise, come to light; come up, crop up, *Inf.* pop up, *Inf.* come out of nowhere.
3. recoil, rebound, resile, bound *or* bounce back, snap back, fly back, kick back, kick.
4. shoot, dart, fly, start.
5. begin, start, commence, come into being, come into existence; arise, rise, dawn, see the light of day, take birth.
6. originate, proceed, emerge, emanate, issue, flow, effuse, stream forth; grow, develop, evolve, wax; sprout, burgeon, shoot up; break out, burst forth.
7. derive, come from, stem from, grow out of, descend from, result from, issue from, be the effect of.
8. bend, warp, buckle; contort, twist, crook, wrench.
9. split, crack, part, come apart, come undone, come unstuck, come unglued; fracture, rupture, open up, fly open *or* apart.
10. (*all suddenly or without warning*) disclose, reveal, divulge, bring out; pop, surprise [s.o.] with.
—*n.* **11.** leap, jump, bound, vault, hop, skip.
12. resilience, resiliency, elasticity, tensility, flexibility; buoyancy, springiness; give, snap, stretch, stretchiness, stretchability.
13. split, crack, fissure, rent, separation, cleft; bend, warp, buckling.
14. fount, fountain, fountainhead, *Archaic.* font; well, wellhead, headwater, headspring, springhead.
15. source, origin, provenience, provenance, root; starting point, square one, base, foundation, fundamental, rudiment, ground; wellspring, mainspring.
16. bloom, blossom, flower; youth, prime, prime of life.
17. coil, spiral, helix, volute, gyre, spire.
18. springtime, springtide, Maytime, Maytide, Eastertide, seedtime.

springy, *adj.* bouncy, buoyant; youthful; elastic, resilient, flexible, stretchable, stretchy, extensile, extensible, protrusible.

sprinkle, *v.* **1.** hail, splash, sparge, spit, spatter, dabble, dribble, trickle; barrage, volley, bombard.
2. disperse, spread, disburse, scatter, asperse, diverge; distribute, broadcast, spray, throw; disseminate, diffuse, strew, bestrew.
3. suffuse, overspread, dust, powder, *Cookery.* dredge; overlay, screen, coat, cover; stipple, dapple, speckle, mottle; dot, spot, fleck, speck, maculate, bespatter.
4. intersperse, insert among, diversify, variegate, vary.
5. shower, drizzle, mist, *Chiefly Dial.* mizzle, flurry, rain.
—*n.* **6.** showering, drizzling, misting, *Chiefly Dial.* mizzling, sprinkling; dribbling, trickling, sparge, sparging, spit, spitting, spew, spewing; barrage, volley, bombardment.
7. dispersion, dispersing, spreading, disbursement, disbursing, scatter, scattering, aspersion, aspersing; distribution, distributing; broadcast, broadcasting, spraying, throwing, dissemination, disseminating, diffusion, diffusing; strewing, bestrewing.
8. diversification, diversifying, variegation, variegating, variation, varying, interspersion, interspersing, interjection, interjecting, insertion, inserting.
9. **sprinkles** jimmies, shots, sprinklies.
10. shower, drizzle, mist, *Chiefly Dial.* mizzle, *Scot.* dribble, rain, wet.
11. dash, pinch, smattering. See **sprinkling.**

sprinkling, *n.* scattering, sprinkle, dribble, driblet, trickle, drop, droplet; few, modicum, smattering, handful, fistful; dash, pinch, tinge, scantling, touch, bit; trace, suspicion, soupcon.

sprite, *n.* fairy, fay, pixy, peri, sylph, nymph, dryad; nix, nixie, kelpie; goblin, gremlin, brownie; imp, demon; Puck, Oberon, Mab, Titania, Tinker Bell; elf, leprechaun, troll, gnome, kobold; (*pl.*) wee folk, little folk, little people.

sprout, *v.* **1.** burgeon, bud, begin to grow, come up, germinate, pullulate, put forth, shoot out *or* up; bloom, blossom, flower, open, bear fruit, fructify; flourish, luxuriate.
2. grow, develop, proliferate, wax, multiply; accelerate, quicken, snowball, mushroom; increase, escalate, expand, spread.
—*n.* **3.** new growth, bud, burgeon, shoot, sprig; stem, twig, small branch; offshoot, *Bot.* runner, *Bot.* stolon, *Bot.* sucker; scion, cutting, slip, *Hort.* graft.

spruce, *adj.* **1.** trim, neat, dapper, looking as if one just stepped out of a bandbox, smart, natty, chic, *Inf.* slick, *Sl.* spiffy, sleek; tidy, orderly, well-ordered, in good order, shipshape, *Chiefly Dial.* tight, *Chiefly Brit.* trig, *Inf.* neat as a pin, regular, in place, spick-and-span.
—*v.* **2.** *Usu.* **spruce up** neaten, tidy, tidy up, straighten up *or* out, pick up, clean, clean up; groom, trim, put in trim, *Brit. Dial.* trig up *or* out; arrange, order, put in order; primp, prink, trick up *or* out, deck out, *Inf.* do up, *Inf.* fig out.

spry, *adj.* active, energetic, energetical, vibrant, full of verve; vital, lively, full of life, *Inf.* snappy, *Inf.* full of pep, *Inf.* peppy, *Inf.* full of get up and go, *Chiefly U.S. Inf.* chipper; vivacious, sprightly, sprightful, jumping, hopping, swinging, animated, spirited, *Sl.* go-go; vigorous, hearty, brisk; nimble, agile, lithe, light and quick; light-footed, nimble-footed; playful, sportive, frisky, gamesome, frolicsome.

spume, *v.* **1.** *Often* **spume forth** eject, discharge, emit, send forth; gush, issue, spout, spurt.
2. foam, froth, cream, lather, soap; boil over, bubble, fizzle, effervesce.
—*n.* **3.** foam, head, froth, lather, suds; spray, mist, spindrift, spoondrift, surf; fizz, fizzle, effervescence, sparkle.

spunk, *n.* **1.** *Informal.* pluck, mettle, mettlesomeness, spirit, pluckiness, gameness, nerve, chutzpah, backbone, gumption, heart, blood, marrow, *Archaic.* pith, stamina, *Inf.* toughness, grit, true grit, *Inf.* starch, *U.S. Inf.* sand, *Inf.* spunkiness, *Sl.* guts, *Sl.* gutsiness, *Sl.* moxie; high-spiritedness, daring, derring-do, bravado, élan, dash, panache.
2. tinder, touchwood, punk, amadou.

spur, *n.* **1.** rowel, goad, prick, point, prod.
2. stimulus, stimulant, incentive, fillip, provocative, motive; jolt, jog, poke, lash, whip; incitement, inducement, instigation, encouragement, abetment, provocation, egging on, putting up to; dare, taunt, gibe.
3. *Ornithology.* horny process, horn, promontory, knob, gnarl, knot.
4. spike, prong, tooth, gaff, spit, cusp, tip; tine, spine, quill, barb, barbule, barblet, prickle, nib, neb, spicule.
5. shoot, scion, spear, stem, twig, branch, stunted branch, ramification; snag, projection, burgeon, bud, sprout.
6. **on the spur of the moment** impulsively, impetuously, precipitately, without thinking, unthinkingly, thoughtlessly, recklessly, rashly, brashly, incautiously, headlong, pell-mell, helter-skelter; suddenly, all of a sudden, abruptly, unexpectedly, out of the blue, without warning, all at once, slap, *Inf.* slap-

bang.

—*v.* **7.** prick, poke, stick, goad, prod, prompt, thrust, jog, jolt; push, drive, press, propel, hound, whip, lash, flog; speed, speed up, accelerate, hurry, hasten, quicken, *Obs.* festinate.

8. incite, provoke, actuate, instigate, set in motion, look for trouble, *Inf.* start something; foment, agitate, excite, arouse, rouse, whip up, work up, stir up, wind up, inflame, enflame, kindle, touch off; stimulate, animate, whet, reanimate, enliven, liven up, vivify, bestir; boost, embolden, build up; encourage, egg on, urge on.

9. wound, strike, cut, lacerate, gash, slash, slice; pierce, puncture, stab, lancinate, spike, spit, impale, penetrate, slit.

10. gallop, race, sprint, whisk, bolt, dart, fly, post, dash, clap spurs, ride hard, tear along, cover ground, burn up the road, fly like *or* race with the wind.

11. make haste, proceed hurriedly, make strides *or* rapid strides, make time, open up, *Inf.* move out; press forward, press on, push on, carry on, plunge ahead.

spurious, *adj.* **1.** counterfeit, fraudulent, imitation, fake, *Inf.* phony, forged; not genuine, bogus, supposititious, bastardly, *Australian.* bunyip; unreal, false, insincere, mock, ersatz, synthetic; pretended, feigned, simulated, sham, make-believe; artifical, factitious, contrived, *Sl.* hokey, fictitious; put-on, pseudo; specious, meretricious, theatrical.

2. bastard, illegitimate, misbegotten, baseborn, unlawfully begotten, out-of-wedlock.

spurn, *v.* **1.** reject, refuse, repudiate, turn away, cast out, cast aside, turn down, *Sl.* give thumbs down to, slam the door in [s.o.'s] face; scorn, slur, rebuff, disregard, ignore, snub; brush off, cut, *Inf.* give [s.o.] the cold shoulder, *Inf.* cold-shoulder, *Inf.* give [s.o.] the go-by; refuse to associate with, not have anything to do with, not want any part of, turn one's back upon, wash one's hands of.

2. despise, disdain, contemn, scout, hold in contempt; sneer at, sneeze at, curl one's lip at, look down upon, look down one's nose at, turn one's nose up at, spit upon.

—*n.* **3.** rejection, repudiation, refusal; disregard, *Inf.* the go-by, *Inf.* the cold shoulder.

4. contumely, contempt, disdain, scorn; derision, ridicule, mockery, raillery, jeering, sneering, scoffing.

5. kick, boot.

spurt, *v.* **1.** spout, squirt, shoot out *or* up, spray, project; gush, jet, spring, burst forth, well forth *or* up *or* out; surge, swell, swash; pour, effuse, stream, flow, issue, emanate; emerge, come out, debouch, disembogue.

2. have a burst of energy, accelerate, increase one's speed, double-time, *Inf.* pour it on, *Sl.* step on it; race, race like the wind, sprint, fly, flit, whiz, whisk; speed, zoom, zip, career, rip, scour, scud, *Inf.* scorch, *Sl.* burn up the road, *Chiefly Brit.* hare, *Inf.* clip, *Inf.* barrel.

3. disgorge, spit out, expel, eject, discharge, emit, send forth; vomit, regurgitate, throw up, spit up, heave, be *or* get sick, puke, *Sl.* retch, *Sl.* barf, *Sl.* upchuck, *Sl.* blow lunch.

—*n.* **4.** gush, outgush, spate, squirt, shoot, spray, projection; gust, blast, explosion; jet, spring, fountain, geyser, well, outwell, flood; ebullition, outrush, outpour, outpouring, efflux, outflux, effluence, effusion; outstream, stream, flow, tide, emanation; surge, swell, swash.

5. burst, burst of energy, sprint, rush, spree, spell *or* period of increased activity, flash *or* moment of increased activity, impulse, spell *or* moment of inspiration, *Sl.* tear; acceleration, increase, increment, heightening, raise.

6. outburst, outbreak, eruption; burst of emotion, profusion, profusiveness, exuberance, bubbling over, enthusiasm, excitement; flare-up, blowup, temper tantrum, fit.

sputter, *v.* **1.** splutter, spew, discharge, spume, froth, foam; spit *or* spit out, emit, eject, shoot forth, come out; fly in all directions, spatter, spat, splatter, splash; spray, shower, diffuse, disperse, scatter, strew.

2. stammer, stutter, speak thickly, talk rapidly *or* incoherently, gibber, jabber, *Inf.* gibber-jabber.

spy, *n.* **1.** operative, secret agent, intelligence agent, undercover agent, *Inf.* spook, *Fr. espion, Sl.* 007, FBI agent, G-man, CIA agent; double agent, informer, informant, *Horse Racing.* tout; detective, investigator, private detective *or* investigator, *Sl.* private eye, *Inf.* sherlock, *U.S. Sl.* gumshoe, *Inf.* sleuth, *U.S. Sl.* dick; shadow, *Inf.* tail; scout, reconnoiterer.

—*v.* **2.** *Often* **spy on** *or* **upon** watch secretly, observe, scout, reconnoiter, *Inf.* check out, *Sl.* case; keep an eye on, shadow, follow, *Inf.* tail.

3. search for, seek, look for; scan, search, survey; explore, range *or* go over, scour, leave no stone unturned; examine closely, scrutinize, go over with a fine-tooth comb, inspect; investigate, *Inf.* check out, look into, probe.

4. discover, detect, find *or* find out, determine, figure out, come up with; hit upon *or* on, stumble upon, fall upon, come upon, light on *or* upon; trace *or* trace down, track down, *Inf.* scout out, ferret out, nose out, hunt down *or* out; root out, dig up, unearth, disinter, uncover, bring to light, smoke out, expose.

5. espy, catch sight of, glimpse, catch a glimpse of; sight, *Inf.* spot, recognize, identify; descry, make out, discern; see, view, set *or* lay eyes on, *Sl.* get a load of, notice, note, remark.

squab, *adj.* **1.** fat, obese, corpulent, overweight, portly, pursy, *Scot.* fodgel; dumpy, stumpy, stubby, squat, squatty, squabby; chunky, lumpy, lumpish.

2. chubby, tubby, pudgy, *Chiefly Brit.* podgy, plump; round, rounded-out, rotund; fleshy, filled-out, well-fed, bouncing; ample, substantial, full.

3. stout, stodgy, thick, thickset; heavy, heavyset, stocky; beefy, brawny, burly, sturdy.

squabble, *v.* **1.** quarrel, row, altercate, spar, cross swords; argue, debate, dispute, bandy words, have words, *Inf.* pick a crow; disagree, differ, take exception to, contend, contest, make something of it, fall out, clash, be at odds, be at loggerheads; fight, spat, tiff, *Brit. Archaic.* brangle, wrangle, jangle, bicker, *Obs.* brabble.

—*n.* **2.** quarrel, dispute, row, spar, wrangle, jangle, *Obs.* brabble; contention, controversy, disagreement, difference of opinion, argument, *Inf.* words, *Scot. and North Eng.* threap, *Brit. Archaic.* brangle; spat, tiff, *Brit. Dial.* fratch, *Inf.* run-in, *Inf.* hassle, *Inf.* barney, falling-out, *Sl.* blow-up; broil, embroilment, imbroglio, *Inf.* set-to, *Scot.* sturt, *Scot.* collieshangie; fight, brannigan, altercation, conflict, clash, *Inf.* dustup, *U.S. Sl.* rhubarb.

squad, *n.* company, platoon, squadron, troop, force, unit, section, *Inf.* outfit; band, *Theat.* troupe, crew, gang, pack; group, set, cluster, knot, cohort; party, league, alliance, federation.

squalid, *adj.* **1.** foul, filthy, mucky, feculent, slimy, smutty, grungy, dingy, mangy, ratty; dirty, grubby, soiled, unclean, unwashed, *Rare.* immund, *Scot.* ourie; repulsive, offensive, rank, reeking, odious, horrid, nasty.

2. abject, miserable, wretched, stark, sordid, slummy, slum-like, poverty-stricken; poor, impoverished, sorry, down-and-out, degraded, depressed, decayed; neglected, uncared-for, dilapidated, ramshackle, battered, in disrepair, rundown, broken-down, tumbledown, seedy, *Sl.* crummy, *Sl.* beat-up.

squall[1], *n.* **1.** strong wind, gale, gust, blast, blow; windstorm, storm, tempest, hurricane, barat.

2. disturbance, commotion, excitement, furor, agitation, disruption; turmoil, tumult, turbulence, hurly-burly; disorder, chaos, confusion, upheaval, unrest, disquiet; trouble, fuss, fuss and feathers, bother, pother, *Inf.* to-do, *Inf.* foofaraw.

—*v.* **3.** blow, bluster, gust, storm, rage.

squall[2], *v.* **1.** cry, weep, wail, sob, bawl; cry out, scream, shriek, yell, shout, *Inf.* holler, yowl, howl.

—*n.* **2.** crying, weeping, wailing, sobbing, bawling; crying out, screaming, shrieking, yelling, shouting, *Inf.* hollering, yowling, howling.

squalor, *n.* misery, miserableness, poverty, wretchedness, squalidness, squalidity; sordidness, abjectness, abjection, slumminess, starkness; filth, dirt, foulness, vileness, fulsomeness, feculence, scumminess, muckiness, sliminess, smuttiness, grunginess, dinginess, griminess, grubbiness, uncleanliness, uncleanness, filthiness, dirtiness, *Rare.* immundity, *Obs.* immundicity; repulsiveness, offensiveness, rankness, odorousness, nastiness.

squander, *v.* misspend, misuse, waste, dissipate, go *or* run through, *Sl.* blow; (*all of time*) kill, fritter *or* fool away, lose; spend recklessly, play ducks and drakes with, throw away, burn up, *Sl.* shoot one's wad, pour down the drain, throw good money after bad; throw money around, spend money like water, spend like a drunken sailor, spend money as if it grew on trees *or* as if it were going out of style; splurge, lavish, slather, *Sl.* hang the expense, play the profligate, *or* prodigal.

square, *n.* **1.** quadrate, rectangle, *Rare.* tetragon; block, cube.

2. try square, T-square, measure, ruler, straightedge, set square, carpenter's square.

3. plaza, place, park, piazza, forum, rialto; town green, green, town common, common, marketplace, market, public square, (*in ancient Greece*) agora; block, city block; tract, section, close, enclave, enclosure, quadrangle, *Inf.* quad.

4. *Slang.* conformer, conventionalist, traditionalist, conformist, *Inf.* middle-class type; classicist, formalist, precisianist, *Inf.* longhair, *Inf.* dodo, *Inf.* fuddy-duddy, *Inf.* mossback.

—*v.* **5.** quadrate, cube, dice; block out, mark off, measure off; set at right angles, line up.

6. (*of the shoulders or back*) straighten, straighten up, set, throw back; stiffen, tense, make rigid.

7. true, true up, render true, plumb, make plumb; regulate, adjust, set, try, fix, rectify, resolve; equalize, flatten, smooth, even off *or* out, align, coordinate; fit, tailor, measure, proportion; put in order, order, neaten, put to rights, right, set right; settle, arrange, unravel, disentangle.

8. *Often* **square with** adapt, reconcile, synchronize, *Inf.* sync; compose, harmonize, coordinate, balance, compensate; agree, accord, suit, correspond, conform, accommodate, comport with, be congruous, comply; adjust to, trim to, cut to, gear to, key to, be in tune, be in unison; combine, team, match, tally, dovetail, *Inf.* jibe, wash; fit together, integrate; prove, conclude, clinch.

9. pacify, make peace, come to terms, patch up, mend; clear up, solve, heal, bridge over, mediate, negotiate.

10. *Often* **square up** pay off, settle, settle up, pay in full, *Inf.* pay up; discharge, liquidate, honor; settle with, settle *or* square accounts, square oneself with, get square with; atone, make restitution, satisfy, meet one's obligations, make good, make up for, *Inf.* square things; even the score, pay old debts, clear the board, *Inf.* ante up, *Inf.* pay one's dues, *Inf.* wipe the slate clean; recompense, pay back, repay, reimburse, compensate.

11. *Slang.* bribe, suborn, fix, rig; purchase, *Inf.* buy, *Inf.* buy off, corrupt, tamper with.

12. **square off** take a stance, toe the mark, *Inf.* assume the position; be at the ready, be on guard, be ready to fight, prepare to do battle, make ready, stand toe to toe, wait for the bell, take the measure of [s.o.]; confront, come face to face, face, challenge, defy; disagree, conflict, collide, come to blows, take exception, offer resistance, show fight, take one's stand.

—*adj.* **13.** angular, cornered, right-angled, sharp-angled; sharp, neat, folded, tucked in, boxed.

14. quadrangular, foursquare, cubic, cubiform, cube-shaped, rectangular; cubed, diced, boxy.

15. equal, on a par, commensurate, proportionate, measured, uniform; consistent, accordant, harmonious; counterpoised, counterbalancing, equiponderating.

16. straight, level, even, true, exact, precise, absolute; accurate, close, faithful, correct, right, justified; specific, strict, on the line.

17. corresponding, balanced, poised, parallel, symmetrical; appropriate, suitable, meet, fit, satisfactory, well-balanced.

18. paid off *or* up, *Inf.* quits, *Inf.* even-steven, *Inf.* in the black, *Inf.* out of the red, *Inf.* on the board, *Inf.* having a clean slate.

19. *Informal.* just, fair, honest, fair and square, on the up-and-up, on the level, on the square, *Inf.* straight-arrow; as it should be, right and proper, fit, fitting; even, even-handed, fair-minded, sporting, square-dealing, *Inf.* square-shooting, honest as the day is long.

20. *Informal.* straightforward, direct, unequivocal, plain-spoken, explicit, undeceptive, undeceiving, *Inf.* straight-out; open, open and aboveboard, bona fide, downright, straight, guileless, trustworthy, reliable, dependable, tried and true, *Inf.* salt of the earth, *Inf.* straight as a die.

21. *Slang.* conventional, conservative, conformist, orthodox, traditionalistic, formalistic, precisianistic, stiff-necked, strait-laced, *Inf.* stiff as a board, *Inf.* stiff, *Inf.* stuffy, *Inf.* uptight; trite, banal, unoriginal, *Inf.* corny; stock, set, commonplace, hackneyed, stale, musty, dull, boring, predictable, unimaginative, *Inf.* not hip, *Inf.* not with it, *Inf.* out of it, *Sl.* for the birds.

squash, *v.* **1.** crush, mash, pulp, macerate, masticate; press, squeeze, squeeze the life out of, *Sl.* squeeze the bejeesus out of; press flat, flatten, compress, condense, reduce, decrease; smash, pulverize, beat, pound, *Dial.* squish, *Sl.* squooze.

2. crowd, crowd in, compact, cram in *or* together, scrunch, cramp, constrict, jam, pack, jam *or* pack together.

3. suppress, put down, quash, hold down, keep down; prostrate, vanquish, overcome, overpower, conquer, overwhelm, mow down, sink, swamp; oppress, persecute, repress, *Inf.* put the lid on, smother, stifle, extinguish, strangle, choke off, gag, muzzle; subdue, quell, squelch, scotch, nip in the bud, *Sl.* pull the plug on, clamp down on, *Sl.* put the kibosh on, put a damper on; engulf, submerge, make mincemeat of, put through the mill *or* the wringer, erase, blot out, trample in the dust; put [s.o.] in his place, *Inf.* sit on, *Sl.* jump on, *Inf.*

crack down on, *Sl.* slap down.

4. *Informal.* silence, strike dumb, cut [s.o.] short, refute, confound, nonplus, put down, bring down, take down, *Inf.* take down a peg or two; dumfound, disconcert, intimidate, upset, embarrass, humiliate, mortify; shatter, cut to the quick, flatten with a word, *Inf.* floor, *Inf.* step on, *Inf.* squash like a bug, *Sl.* dump on; take [s.o.'s] breath away, deflate, prick [s.o.'s] balloon, take the wind out of [s.o.'s] sails, put to shame, browbeat, ride roughshod over.

squashy, *adj.* **1.** pulpy, pithy, *Bot.* fleshy, pulpous, pulpal, pulplike, pulpaceous; mushy, pappy, succulent, juicy.

2. spongy, squishy, soft, wet, damp, moist, oozy; plashy, marshy, boggish, boggy, quaggy, swampy.

squat, *v.* **1.** crouch, sit on one's haunches *or* heels, hunker, hunker down, bend, bend down, stoop, hunch, hunch over.

2. cringe, cower, shrink, lie low, crawl, creep.

3. settle, take up residence, set up housekeeping, establish oneself, put down roots; locate, encamp, pitch tent; inhabit, dwell, abide, reside.

—adj. **4.** short, stubby, stubbed, stumpy, dumpy, squabbish, squabby, squatty; chunky, thick, thickset, broad, stocky, stout, stodgy; fleshy, filled-out, plump, chubby, tubby, pudgy; fat, portly, pursy.

5. crouching, stooping, bending, hunching.

squawk, *v.* **1.** cry, call, cackle, screech, screak, shriek, scream, scold, hoot, ululate, whoop, yawp.

2. *Slang.* complain, grouse, yowl, howl, yap, *Sl.* bellyache, *Sl.* bitch; bellow, roar, *Sl.* holler.

—n. **3.** cry, call, screech, screak, shriek, scream, hoot, ululation, stridor, squall, caterwaul, blare, keen.

4. *Slang.* complaint, protest, whine, wail, howl, outcry, yammer, *Sl.* beef, *Sl.* kick, *Sl.* gripe, *Sl.* bellyache.

squeak, *n.* **1.** creak, scrape, screech, twang, whine; squeal, shriek, screak, scream, yelp, yip, yowl.

—v. **2.** squeal, shriek, screak, scream, yelp, yip, yowl; pule, whine, whimper, squall, cry, cry out.

3. squeak by squeeze by, just make it, have a near miss, graze *or* brush by, scrape by, have a close call, escape by the skin of one's teeth.

squeal, *n.* **1.** See **squeak** (*def.* **1**).

—v. **2.** See **squeak** (*def.* **2**).

3. *Slang.* inform, tell on, tell tales, *Inf.* tell tales out of school, *Inf.* snitch, *Inf.* blow the whistle on, *Inf.* shoot one's mouth off, *Inf.* let the cat out of the bag, blab; *Inf.* turn in; *All Sl.* fink, peach, stool, rat, rat on, put the finger on, finger, name names, sell [s.o.] down the river, sing, weasel.

squeamish, *adj.* **1.** prudish, modest, overmodest, coy, demure, shy, reserved; prim, proper, priggish, old-maidish, *Inf., Derog.* nunny.

2. dainty, delicate, finical, finicky, fussy, *Inf.* fuddy-duddy, *Inf.* pernickety; particular, overparticular, picky, *Inf.* choosy; fastidious, hard to please, critical, demanding, exacting, difficult; overcritical, hypercritical, overdemanding, overexacting; meticulous, careful, painstaking, minute, detailed, circumstantial, fine, nice, thorough.

3. easily nauseated *or* disgusted, queasy, qualmish.

squeeze, *v.* **1.** compress, pinch, tweak, crush, squash, *Dial.* squish; compact, press together, force together, constrict, constringe, astringe, tighten, contract, condense, concentrate, consolidate; shorten, reduce, retrench, curtail, cut down, cut back, cut off, cut short; decrease, diminish, subtract, subduct, narrow, bridge; abbreviate, abridge, abstract, summarize, digest, epitomize, brief, synopsize.

2. wring, twist, extract the juice from, crush.

3. thrust, push, shove, press, wedge, pack, ram, force, jam, crowd, stuff, cramp, *Obs.* constipate.

4. hug, embrace, take into one's arms, clasp, press to one's bosom, embosom, enfold, *Sl.* clinch; clasp *or* shake hands, clutch, grasp, hold onto, grip.

5. *Informal.* extort, wrest, wrench, tear from, wring, extract; blackmail, milk, *Inf.* bleed, get out of, pry out, obtain by force; shake down, *Inf.* put the bite *or* shake on, put the arm on [s.o.], *Sl.* lean on *or* against, put the screws to [s.o.].

6. *Usu.* **squeeze through** press forward, make one's way, wedge, slip through, *Inf.* elbow *or* shoulder one's way, shove *or* push through, fight one's way through.

—n. **7.** compression, pinching, pressing together, constriction, constringency; crowding, crushing, packing, cramming, ramming, stuffing, wedging, cramping; condensation, condensing, concentration, consolidation, compaction, compacting; shortage, shortening, reduction, reducing, retrenchment, contraction, contracting; curtailment, cut, cutting down *or* back, cutting short; decrease, diminution, subtraction, subduction, narrowing, bridging; abbreviation, abridging, abstracting, summarizing, digesting, epitomizing, synopsizing.

8. hug, embrace, clasp, tight hold, *Sl.* clinch, bear hug; handclasp, handshake, grasp, grip, clutch.

9. small quantity, drip, drop, droplet, particle, pinch, bit, dab, spot, mite, speck, dash.

10. *Informal.* coercion, force, extortion, blackmail, shakedown, exaction; wrenching, wringing, extraction, elicitation, milking, *Inf.* bleeding.

squelch, *v.* **1.** squash, crush down, mash, smash, smush, ram, crunch, *Dial.* squish, strike *or* press forcefully; pulp, masticate, knead; pulverize, granulate, powder; stamp on, fall on, trample on; squeeze, compress, compact, flatten; stuff, cram, crowd, overcrowd, pack.

2. subdue, put down, quell, quash, suppress, repress; overthrow, subvert, overpower, overcome, overwhelm; conquer, vanquish, defeat, topple, cause the downfall of; extinguish, quench, snuff out, kill, stamp out, put out; smother, stifle, strangle, choke; terminate, dissolve, stop, cut short; check, *Inf.* put the kibosh on, put the lid on, sit on *or* upon, sit down on, crack down on, clamp down on, shoot down, slap down, smack down; keep down, hold down, keep under; silence, still, hush, shush, muffle, muzzle, quiet; deflate, take the wind out of [s.o.'s] sails, *Inf.* settle [s.o.'s] hash, take down a peg or two, humiliate.

3. squish, swish, swash, whish, slosh, plash, splash, slush, splotch.

—n. **4.** pulp, mash, mush, pap, paste, squash.

5. squish, swish, swash, whish, slosh, plash, splash, slush, splotch.

6. quelling, quashing, suppression, repression; overthrow, subversion, vanquishment, defeat; termination, dissolution, check; extinguishment, extinction, quenching, killing, smothering, stifling.

7. *Informal.* retort, riposte, barb, *Sl.* put-down, comeback, rejoinder, quip, sally.

squint, *v.* **1.** skew, look askance, look sidewise, glance obliquely, look out of the corner of one's eye; look out of half-closed eyes, peer, peek, peep; blink, wink, nictitate.

2. *Usu.* **squint toward** *or* **at** refer to indirectly, allude to, infer, imply, intimate, insinuate, suggest, hint; tend toward, incline toward, lean toward, be prone to, be prejudiced toward.

—n. **3.** *Informal.* glance, side glance, brief *or* quick look.

4. indirect reference, allusion, inference, implication,

intimation, innuendo, insinuation, suggestion, hint.
5. inclination, tendency, leaning, penchant, proneness, bent, propensity, proclivity, predilection, prejudice, bias.

squire, *n.* **1.** (*in England*) country gentleman, landowner, landholder, landed proprietor.
2. attendant, servant, servitor, *Archaic.* yeoman, retainer, (*in the Middle Ages*) esquire; valet, man, gentleman, manservant, *Archaic.* varlet, *Fr. valet de chambre, Fr. valet de pied;* lackey, flunky, liveried servant, footman, footboy, page, *Brit.* boots, *Brit.* buttons.
3. date, partner, companion, accompanier, escort, cavalier, beau, suitor, gallant, boyfriend.
—v. **4.** attend, esquire, wait on *or* upon, serve, assist, aid; usher, conduct, pilot, steer, guide, lead, direct.
5. escort, go with, accompany, companion; date, take out, *Inf.* go out with.

squirm, *v.* wriggle, wiggle, writhe, twist; turn, move, shift.

squirt, *v.* **1.** eject, ejaculate, emit, discharge, release, expel, spew out; shoot out, spurt, spout, jet, gush, rush, surge; effuse, flow out, run out, pour out, stream out, cascade, fall; issue, come out *or* forth, emanate, well forth.
2. wet, splash, plash, splatter, bespatter, spatter, spray, shower, sprinkle, besprinkle, sparge.
—n. **3.** spurt, jet, stream, flow, spray, fountain; outflow, outpour, outpouring, rush, gush; issuance, emanation, afflux, flux, efflux, effluence.
4. syringe, douche; spray gun, sprayer, atomizer, plant mister, sprinkler.
5. *Informal.* pip-squeak, *Sl.* twerp, *Sl.* punk.

stab, *v.* **1.** pierce, puncture, lancinate, prick, stick, cut, slit, gash, slash, slice, trepan; penetrate, enter, pass through, transpierce, run through, *Sl.* let the daylight in; impale, transfix, fix, spit, skewer; spike, spear, pike; knife, bayonet; lance, pink, lacerate, perforate, gouge, gore; thrust, drive, plunge, bury, jab, poke, strike, hit.
2. wound, hurt, pain, violate, attack, injure; grieve, aggrieve, distress, afflict, trouble, discomfort.
3. stab [s.o.] in the back *Slang.* betray, reveal [s.o.'s] secrets, break faith with, *Inf.* double-cross, let down, sell *or* sell out, play false, go over to the enemy; backbite, be two-faced, play Judas, give the Judas kiss, slander, vilify, *Sl.* badmouth, *Sl.* knife.
—n. **4.** thrust, blow, jab, pass, stroke, lunge, punch, poke; pink, prick, hit, coup.
5. wound, laceration, trauma, gash, slash, slit, nick, tear, rent; scratch, cut, incision, puncture.
6. *Informal.* try, attempt, effort, plunge, flyer, risk, chance, *Inf.* whirl.
7. pang, twinge, ache, pain, shooting *or* piercing pain; throe, throb, spasm; kink, stitch, crick.
8. stab in the back *Slang.* betrayal, Judas kiss, kiss of death, double-dealing, duplicity, *Inf.* double cross.

stability, *n.* **1.** fixedness, permanence, solidity, solidness, fixity, immovability, stableness; rest, repose, immobility, inertia, dormancy, inaction, inactivity, quiescence; balance, equilibrium, steadiness.
2. changelessness, unchangeableness, immutability; abidingness, endurance, maintenance, perseverance, pursuance, perpetuation; continuity, unity, similarity, uniformity; continuance, duration, prolongation.
3. steadfastness, reliability, dependability, constancy, steadiness; resolution, resoluteness, determination, perseverance, persistence; tenacity, adherence, devotion, *Inf.* stick-to-it-iveness; resolve, poise, aplomb, decisiveness, purposiveness; grit, mettle, will, pluck, *Inf.* sand, backbone, hardiness of spirit; obstinateness, obstinacy, doggedness, stubbornness, *Inf.* cussedness, inflexibility, intransigence; obdurateness, contumacy, contumaciousness.

stabilize, *v.* **1.** steady, immobilize, make fast, secure, strengthen, fortify; fix, attach, fasten, clinch; anchor, moor, ground, root; establish, define, set, settle.
2. maintain, sustain, support, preserve, conserve, retain, uphold, keep up; prolong, perpetuate, protract, continue, extend, carry on.

stable, *adj.* **1.** firm, steady, fixed, fast; sound, solid, stout, sturdy, staunch, substantial; established, riveted, moored, anchored; immovable, still, inert, quiescent, motionless, statuelike, stationary.
2. enduring, abiding, lasting, continuing, permanent; long-lived, long-lasting, longstanding, longevous; constant, valid, secure, durable, rooted, grounded, deep-rooted, deep-seated, well-founded, well-grounded; immutable, unchangeable, unchanging, indissoluble, perdurable, unalterable, invariable, irrevocable, irreversible; persistent, chronic, continual; perpetual, endless, unceasing, everlasting.
3. steadfast, unwavering, unfaltering, undeviating, unswerving, steady, uniform; reliable, dependable, faithful, true; resolute, determined, serious, decided, undaunted, indomitable; persevering, industrious, sedulous; persistent, relentless, enduring, patient, plodding, untiring, unflagging, unwearied, indefatigable; tenacious, strong-willed, grim, settled, unshrinking; game, plucky, gritty; obstinate, stubborn, *Inf.* cussed, uncompromising, unbending, unyielding, inflexible, inexorable, obdurate, contumacious.
4. balanced, well-balanced, sane, mentally sound, *Latin. compos mentis;* reasonable, sensible, reliable, competent, dependable, responsible, accountable; even-tempered, equable, undisturbable, unirritable, dispassionate, placid, calm, cool, inexcitable; self-controlled, self-possessed.

stack, *n.* **1.** haystack, mow, rick, shock, *Scot. and North Eng.* rickle, cock.
2. heap, pile, mass, accumulation, bulk, drift; hoard, store, stock, stockpile, supply; deposit, mound, bank, hillock, hill, mountain; packet, bale, bundle, load, barrow, cartload, wagonload, carload, cargo.
3. collection, amassment, assemblage, aggregation; concentration, pyramid, agglomeration, conglomeration, cluster, congeries; clump, bunch, batch; rouleau.
4. smokestack, chimney, funnel, flue, vertical duct *or* vent.
5. *Informal.* abundance, bounty, volume, plenty; quantitive, profusion, *Inf.* lots, *Inf.* raft, storm, shower, ocean, sea, world; multitude, throng, array, legion, crowd; numbers, scores, pack, host, swarm, mob.
6. *Informal.* hoard, store, quite a little, considerable, deal, great deal; peck, *Inf.* lots, mess, *Inf.* load, *Sl.* pot, mint, *Inf.* oodles, *Inf.* tons; chunk, *Sl.* wad, lump, *Inf.* hunk, gob, *Sl.* scad, *Inf.* slew.
7. *Slang.* **blow one's stack** *Sl.* blow one's top, *Inf.* lose one's cool, *Sl.* sound off.
—v. **8.** accumulate, heap, pile, pile up, roll up, pack, compile, amass, cumulate; hoard, squirrel away, load up, stow away.
9. gather, glean, take in, pull in, harvest, reap, collect; garner, store up, stock up, lay by, lay up, lay in, *Inf.* stash away, reserve, set aside; save, save up.

stadium, *n.* arena, bowl, circus, hippodrome, amphitheater, theater, coliseum, colosseum; park, ball park, field, playing field, athletic field; football field, gridiron, *Chiefly Brit.* pitch.

staff, *n.* **1.** stick, rod, pole, cane, crutch, stave, crook; walking stick, supplejack, alpenstock, *Chiefly*

Irish Eng. shillelagh.

2. baton, wand, truncheon, rod of authority; mace, scepter, crosier, verge, fasces, *Class. Myth.* caduceus.

3. personnel, employees, hired help, the help; gang, crew.

—*v.* **4.** (*all with personnel*) equip, furnish, supply, provide, man.

stage, *n.* **1.** level, echelon, stratum; place, position, station, status, standing, rank.

2. platform, rostrum, dais, podium, pulpit, estrade, scaffold, *Inf.* soapbox, *Fig.* stump; thrust stage, picture-frame stage, proscenium stage, (*in ancient Greek and Roman theater*) scene.

3. the stage show business, *Inf.* show biz; drama, the theater, the footlights, the boards.

4. site, scene of action, arena, field, ground; setting, milieu, background, backdrop, locale, frame, *Fr. mise en scène.*

5. juncture, point, period, time, moment, hour, day, season.

—*v.* **6.** present, produce, mount, put on; block, block out; act, perform.

stagger, *v.* **1.** reel, sway, rock; teeter, totter, teeter-totter, wobble; lurch, pitch, *Brit. Dial.* stoit.

2. falter, waver, hesitate, pause, hang back; demur, boggle, think twice, have second thoughts; hem and haw, blow hot and cold, shilly-shally, be of two minds, not know one's own mind, be unable to make up one's mind, be betwixt and between; vacillate, fluctuate, vary, seesaw.

3. shock, startle, stun, gravel, shake, jar, jolt, give one a turn, take aback; astonish, amaze, astound, take one's breath away, make one's head swim, overwhelm, *Inf.* flabbergast, *Inf.* bowl over, *Inf.* snow, *Sl.* blow one's mind, *Sl.* blow away; dumfound, confound, nonplus, bewilder, discompose, stupefy, strike dumb, *Inf.* flummox.

4. alternate; zigzag.

staging, *n.* **1.** (*all of a drama*) production, presentation, mounting, performance; stage management, *Fr. mise en scène.*

2. scaffolding, framework, grid, skeleton.

stagnant, *adj.* **1.** foul, stale, flat; dirty, filthy, polluted; putrid, putrescent, putrefied.

2. sluggish, leaden, phlegmatic, lymphatic, lethargic, torpid, torporific, torpescent; idle, passive, supine, inactive, lazy; dull, listless, languid, lackadaisical.

3. motionless, quiet, quiescent, still, stock-still, unstirring, unmoving, immovable, immobile; undisturbed, latent, dormant, dormient, reposing, resting, sleepy, sleeping; inert, lifeless, dead; stationary, fixed, static; becalmed.

stagnate, *v.* **1.** rot, decompose, decay, spoil, putrefy; fester, suppurate, *Pathol.* maturate; deteriorate, degenerate, decline, worsen, go to seed, go to pot; smell, stink, reek; stale, sour.

2. idle, lie idle, slumber, loaf, vegetate, rest; languish, laze, lazy, loll, *Inf.* bum, *Inf.* bum around; trifle *or* fritter *or* fool *or* while away one's time, twiddle one's thumbs, let the grass grow under one's feet; lag, tarry, linger, loiter, hang back.

3. stop, cease, desist, halt; stand, come to a standstill, lie *or* stand still, remain motionless; pause, wait, hesitate; procrastinate, defer, postpone, delay; stall, suspend, mark time, hang fire.

4. abate, slacken, *Inf.* slack off, *Inf.* let up.

stagy, *adj.* **1.** theatrical, dramatic, dramaturgical; scenic; operatic; thespian, histrionic, Roscian.

2. artificial, unnatural, forced; melodramatic, overdone, overacted, *Sl.* hammy; ostentatious, pretentious, affected, la-di-da.

staid, *adj.* grave, serious, somber, sober, sedate, solemn; quiet, pensive, introspective, thoughtful; settled, steady-going, steady, sober-minded, sobersided, serious-minded; proper, formal, rigid, stiff, starched, prim, *Inf.* stuffy, *Inf.* tight, *Sl., Derog.* nunny.

stain, *n.* **1.** discoloration, spot, speck, mark, maculation, dot; patch, blotch, splotch, daub; smudge, smutch, smut, smirch, smear, blur; soil, dirt; flaw, imperfection, defacement, disfigurement, fault, defect.

2. blemish, taint, attaint, blot, blot on the escutcheon, tarnish; brand, stigma, shame, disgrace, dishonor, *Inf.* black eye.

3. dye, color, coloring, pigment, tint, *Obs.* tincture, *Chem.* reagent.

—*v.* **4.** spot, soil, dirty, sully, smudge, smutch, smirch, besmirch; blotch, splotch, mark, speckle, maculate, ink; daub, bedaub, spatter, bespatter, sprinkle, splash, plash, draggle, drabble, *Archaic.* daggle; smear, slime, muck, bemire; discolor, rust, oxidize.

5. blemish, tarnish, blacken, blot; mar, damage, injure, hurt, spoil; brand, stigmatize, *Sl.* dump on, drag through the mud *or* mire, heap dirt upon; impute, slur, asperse, vilify, scandalize; slander, calumniate, libel, denigrate, defame; disgrace, shame, dishonor, degrade, abase, debase, vitiate; corrupt, defile, contaminate, taint, pollute, foul.

6. dye, color, tint; imbue, imbrue.

stake[1], *n.* **1.** pale, picket, palisade, spike, pike, stick; post, upright, column, pillar, standard; rod, bar, peg, pin.

2. the stake death by fire *or* burning, auto-da-fé.

—*v.* **3.** *Often* **stake out** *or* **off** mark, demarcate, define, outline, delineate, determine; limit, delimit, circumscribe, bound; possess, claim, reserve.

4. separate, close off, enclose, hem in, shut in, close in; pen, pen in, fence in, corral, *Archaic.* pound, impound, cage, confine; immure, wall in, imprison, embar, cloister; encompass, surround, girdle, picket.

5. support, brace, prop, stay, hold up.

6. tether, fetter, picket, hitch, tie, fasten; lash, moor, secure, make fast.

stake[2], *n.* **1.** wager, bet; ante, pot, jackpot; chance, long shot, *Sl.* shot in the dark, risk, hazard, *Obs.* venture.

2. investment, share, interest, concern, involvement.

3. *Often* **stakes** prizes, award, reward, winnings, purse, trophy; gain, profit, *Sl.* take, returns; spoils, plunder, loot, booty.

4. at stake risked, at risk, gambled, invested; endangered, in danger, in jeopardy; involved, implicated, concerned, in question.

—*v.* **5.** bet, put up collateral, put money on; gamble, wager, lay a wager, *Obs.* impone, *Brit.* punt; risk, take a chance, venture, hazard, jeopardize, imperil, endanger.

stale, *adj.* **1.** unfresh, wilted, limp, withered, moldy; dry, hardened, hard; tasteless, savorless, bland, insipid, vapid, flat; sour, turned, spoiled; stuffy, musty, fusty, frowzy, close.

2. hackneyed, banal, trite, overdone, *Inf.* bromidic, platitudinous, *Inf.* corny; tired, thin, threadbare, shopworn, worn-out, played out, *Inf.* old hat, old, moth-eaten, warmed-over; unimaginative, unoriginal, insipid, uninspired; prosaic, prosy, dull, tedious, uninteresting, matter-of-fact; conventional, humdrum, commonplace, stock, overused, familiar, stereotyped; simple, fatuous, inane, feeble, wishy-washy.

3. weary, bored, vigorless, effete; uninitiative, uneffective, unproductive, useless.

stalemate, *n.* **1.** deadlock, impasse, standstill; qui-

etus, deathblow; halt, stop, stoppage, full stop, dead stop; stand, stay, check, checkmate, mate; blockage, block; stand-off, tie, draw, dead heat.
2. dilemma, perplexity, nonplus; predicament, hole, *Inf.* fix, corner; dead end, blind alley, cul-de-sac.
3. defeat, overthrow, rout, vanquishment; collapse, fall, downfall.
—v. **4.** stop, halt, cease; deadlock, bring to a standstill; stand, stay, curb, check, checkmate; forestall, preclude, obviate, intercept; block, blockade, bar, debar; thwart, trump.
5. prostrate, paralyze, incapacitate, disable, render helpless, make ineffective; undermine, spike, *Inf.* put the kibosh on.
6. hinder, impede, obstruct, clog, trammel; cramp, bind, shackle, inhibit; corner, run *or* drive into a corner, drive *or* push to the wall, *Inf.* tree.
7. confuse, confound, perplex, bewilder, stump, embarrass, nonplus, *Inf.* flummox.

stalk[1], *n.* **1.** stem, trunk, caudex, culm, haulm, cane, calamus, quill, *Bot.* caulis, *Bot.* caulicle, *Bot.* axis; shaft, shank, spike, spindle, pivot, swivel, axle.
2. leafstalk, *Bot.* stipe, *Bot.* petiole, *Bot.* petiolule, *Biol.* pedicle, *Bot.* pedicel, *Both Bot., Zool.* peduncle, footstalk, *Both Bot.* funicle, funiculus, *Bot.* gynophore; twig, branch, arm, leg, neck, support.

stalk[2], *v.* **1.** pursue, chase, give chase, course, Brit. chevy, (*in India*) shikar, follow close *or* hot on [s.o.'s] heels *or* trail; hunt, track down, track, trail, still-hunt, follow, shadow, haunt, *Inf.* tail; hound, *Sl.* bird-dog, dog, scent, hawk, pigstick, smell out; approach, sneak *or* creep up on, surprise, ambush.
2. march, goose-step, tramp, stamp, flounce, *Dial.* traipse; strut, swagger, prance, peacock; hike, foot, hoof, stump; stride, walk, step, tread, pace.
—n. **3.** hunt, tracking, *Inf.* still hunt, *Inf.* tailing; chase, pursuit, course, coursing, *Brit.* chevy, (*in India*) shikar, *Archaic.* venery; hawking, falconry, *Brit.* beagling.
4. march, goose step, slow march; strut, prance, swagger; stride, walk, gait, step, pace.

stall[1], *n.* **1.** crib, booth, cage, cell, bay, carrel, carol; quarters, chamber, room, roomette, apartment, enclosure, *Theater.* box; compartment, cubicle, pigeonhole, cubbyhole, cubby, niche, nook, alcove, corner; partition, section, part, division; closet, locker, *Brit.* lockup; parking space *or* place, slot, garage; slip, *Naut.* anchorage, *Naut.* moorage, *Naut.* quayage; dressing room, shower, bathroom, toilet, privy.
2. corral, pen, coop, hutch, cote, fold, sty, pigpen; stable, barn, cowshed, shed, lean-to, outbuilding, outhouse; house, home, shelter, protection, roof.
3. booth, stand, cart, table, counter.
—v. **4.** pen, cage, coop, sty, corral, fence in, picket; quarter, room, house, shelter, shed, sleep, bed down; place, put, situate, locate, set up; park, garage, *Naut.* moor, *Naut.* dock, *Naut.* anchor, *Naut.* tie up; enclose, shut in, immure, wall in, lock up, confine, imprison, jail, incarcerate.
5. (*of a motor or vehicle*) flood, choke, kill; halt, stop, bring *or* come to a stop, bring *or* come to a standstill *or* a stand; give out, die, *Sl.* conk out; get stuck, stick, get caught; bog down, mire, swamp, get sucked in, sink into; slide, spin one's wheels, go nowhere, make no progress.

stall[2], *n.* **1.** *Informal.* delay, dilatory tactic *or* maneuver, *Inf.* footdragging, *U.S.* filibuster, *Brit.* stonewalling; subterfuge, wile, ruse, Trojan horse; artifice, trick, stratagem, maneuver, move; pretext, pretense, deception, deceit, *Obs.* cog.
—v. **2.** delay, go into a holding pattern, slow down, dally, dillydally, dawdle, linger, lag, loiter, poke along, *Both Inf.* drag one's feet, footdrag; beat around the bush, skirt *or* evade the issue, hem and haw, haw, mutter, mumble, hum, *Inf.* give [s.o.] the run-around, *Scot. and North Eng.* haver, *Brit. Dial.* mammer; play for *or* gain time, kill time, eat up *or* consume time, use up time, waste time, *U.S.* filibuster, *Brit.* stonewall; stave off, put *or* hold off, keep busy *or* occupied, send on a wild-goose chase.

stalwart, *adj.* **1.** stout, sturdy, rugged, hefty, husky, burly, *Scot. and North Eng.* stiff, solid, iron, *Inf.* tough as nails, *Inf.* hard as rock; able-bodied, able, athletic, sinewy, well-knit; muscular, muscled, well-muscled, full-muscled, brawny, strapping, broad-shouldered, powerfully built, *Derog.* musclebound, herculean; powerful, mighty, *Literary.* puissant.
2. robust, vigorous, full of vigor, hearty, hale, hale and hearty, hardy, lusty, strong and healthy, bursting with health *or* vigor; sound, healthy, in good health, fit, physically fit, in fine fettle, in good condition, *Inf.* in good shape, *Inf.* in shape.
3. brave, courageous, valiant, valorous, intrepid, indomitable, heroic, manly, manful, brave and strong, *Archaic.* stalworth; stout-hearted, lionhearted, ironhearted, great-hearted, strong-willed; bold, daring, audacious, adventurous, fearless, aweless, dauntless, dreadless; mettlesome, gritty, plucky, game, spirited, red-blooded, defiant, *Inf.* spunky.
4. firm, steadfast, staunch, tenacious; uncompromising, unyielding, inexorable, intransigent; resolute, resolved, determined, decided, settled, fixed; unflinching, unswerving, unwavering, undeviating, unshrinking, unbending, unfaltering, unhesitating; persevering, pertinacious, relentless, implacable, stubborn, indefatigable, tireless, persistent, unflagging, unwearied, enduring, staminal; true, faithful, constant, steady, stable, unshaken, undaunted.
—n. **5.** hero, heroine, paladin, valliant, gallant, good soldier, trouper, a man; strong man, tower *or* pillar of strength.
6. support, supporter, mainstay, maintainer, sustainer, upholder, *Inf.* stand-by, *Inf.* old faithful *or* reliable; regular, loyalist, partisan, party man, party member, party faithful.

stamina, *n.* endurance, staying power, *Inf.* stick-to-it-iveness, *Inf.* stick-at-it-iveness; fortitude, intestinal fortitude, inner strength, *Sl.* guts, *Sl.* gutsiness; courage, pluck, spirit, mettle, *U.S. Inf.* sand; vigor, vitality, energy, *Inf.* steam, *Inf.* starch, *Inf.* punch, *Inf.* kick, *Inf.* zip; resistance, health, soundness, staunchness, lustiness, heartiness, vigorousness, robustness, haleness, fitness, able-bodiedness; strength, might, power, *Literary.* puissance, force, *Archaic.* pith; sturdiness, stalwartness, ruggedness, toughness, steeliness.

stammer, *v.* **1.** stutter; pause, hesitate, falter, stumble, speak haltingly; mutter, mumble.
—n. **2.** stutter, speech impediment; stuttered utterance.

stamp, *v.* **1.** (*all with the foot*) strike, beat, pound, crush, mash, squash, *Dial.* squish; step on, *Inf.* stomp, tread on, tramp on, trample.
2. *Usu.* **stamp out** put out, extinguish, snuff out, kill; suppress, subdue, quell, quash, put down, squelch, scotch, repress, *Inf.* put the kibosh on, nip in the bud; eliminate, abolish, get rid of, terminate, put an end to, dissolve; annihilate, exterminate, extirpate, eradicate, obliterate.
3. grind, crush, crunch, mortar, comminute, triturate, levigate, powder, granulate, crumble; pulverize, pound, batter, bray, beat, mash, smash, *Sl.* smush.
4. imprint, print, engrave, emboss, inscribe; initial, monogram, sign, seal, mark, label.

5. characterize, distinguish, reveal, show to be; brand, name, designate, denominate, dub; style, term, label, tag, nickname.
6. tread, tramp, *Sl.* tromp, *Inf.* stomp.
—*n.* **7.** postage stamp, trading stamp, *Trademark.* S & H Green Stamps.
8. die, block, plate, intaglio, mold, *Print.* matrix, punch; seal ring, ring, seal, medallion.
9. design, pattern, legend, inscription, engraving; print, imprint, impression, mark.
10. seal, official seal, emblem, representation, symbol, badge, insignia, regalia; coat of arms, escutcheon, crest; label, monogram, cartouche, signet, initials, signature, mark, sign.
11. label, brand, trademark, logo; tag, earmark, hallmark.
12. character, sort, kind, kidney, variety, type, genre; make, cast, cut, mold, form, style, manner; grain, feather, tone, color, stripe; name, brand, designation, description, denomination; species, class, classification, group, grouping.
13. pestle, stamper, crusher, pulverizer, pounder, mallet, hammer.

stampede, *n.* **1.** rush, dash, race, run, flight, rout, *Chiefly Australian.* breakaway, panic, scattering.
—*v.* **2.** scatter, flee, rout, rush, dash, race, *Inf.* tear off, take flight, take to one's heels, panic.

stand, *v.* **1.** rise, rise to one's feet, get up; remain upright, hold oneself erect, be vertical.
2. set upright, place on end, upend; set, position, place, put.
3. (*usu. imperative*) halt, stop, pause, come to a halt *or* standstill.
4. last, continue on, continue to exist, persist, perdure; endure, be steadfast, be constant, be permanent; be durable, wear, wear well, stand up.
5. remain, remain in force, obtain, be the case, hold, hold good; abide, stay.
6. face, encounter, meet, meet with; undergo, experience, submit to.
7. withstand, endure, resist, tolerate, brave, breast, suffer; bear, weather, hold out against, cope with, handle.
8. stand by a. uphold, support, defend, stand *or* stick up for, go to bat for, take the side of, stand behind. **b.** adhere to, affirm, stick with; repeat, reiterate; stick to one's guns. **c.** wait, hold on, tarry, bide one's time; be patient.
9. stand for a. represent, symbolize, exemplify, illustrate; embody, personify, typify, epitomize; be the equivalent of, be regarded as. **b.** advocate, favor, countenance, support, back, second; champion, defend, sponsor, promote; speak in favor of, argue for, uphold; subscribe to, take the side of, fall in with, lend one's name to, take up *or* espouse the cause of. **c.** *Informal.* allow, permit, sanction, put up with, hear of, countenance, approve of; tolerate, suffer, brook, abide, acquiesce in; swallow, stomach, digest, pocket; condone, forgive, overlook.
10. stand out a. project, protrude, jut out, stick out, poke out; extend, bulge, obtrude, excurve; overhang, beetle. **b.** be conspicuous, be prominent, be noticeable; be extraordinary, be singular.
11. stand up to confront, meet boldly, defy, face in defiance; question, dispute, challenge, oppugn.
—*n.* **12.** stance, posture, carriage, bearing, port.
13. defensive effort, resistance, opposition, withstanding, counteraction; repulsion, repulse, front, rebuff; defiance, refusal, oppugnancy.
14. policy, position, line; attitude, point of view, viewpoint, way of seeing things; principle, doctrine, belief, assertion, contention; feeling, sentiment, way of thinking, opinion, philosophy; plan, plan of action, *Inf.* game plan, strategy.
15. station, post; place, location, locale, spot, site, ground.
16. platform, dais, pulpit, rostrum, podium, lecturn, stage; reviewing stand, gallery, box; witness stand, *Chiefly Brit.* witness box.
17. stands grandstand; bleachers, box seats, *Inf.* boxes, clubhouse.
18. table, counter, stall, booth, display case; rack, frame, shelf, bracket, support.
19. grove, copse, *Chiefly Brit.* coppice, thicket, brake, *Brit.* spinney, covert, pinery, *Southwestern U.S.* chapparal; orchard, orangery; wood, woods, woodland.
20. performance, show; engagement, appearance; run, stay, stopover.

standard, *n.* **1.** model, pattern, example, paradigm, exemplar, ideal, beau ideal, mirror, paragon; prototype, archetype; rule, principle, canon, law, guideline, rule of thumb, regulation, precept, order; gauge, yardstick, scale, guide, touchstone, measure, criterion; axiom, fundamental.
2. par, norm, normal, average, mean, median; grade, level, degree, rank.
3. flag, ensign, oriflamme, banner, pennant, pennon, streamer, (*collectively*) bunting; gonfalon, guidon, labarum, vexillum; jack, union jack, *Brit.* Union Jack, *Both U.S.* Stars and Stripes, Old Glory; *France.* tricolor; emblem, insignia.
4. upright, stanchion, pier, footing, platform, base, support; column, post, pillar.
—*adj.* **5.** recognized, accepted, approved, orthodox, official; definitive, classic, authoritative; established, dependable, sure, reliable.
6. usual, customary, consuetudinary, wonted, habitual; regular, stock, set, normal, expected, traditional; common, commonplace, familiar, ordinary, conventional; required, *Fr. de rigueur;* universal, widespread, prevalent, popular.

standard-bearer, *n.* leader, ringleader, bellwether, fugleman; commander, chief, commander-in-chief, head; boss, person in charge, the one who calls the shots; torchbearer, leading light, pacemaker, pacesetter; very important person, *Inf.* VIP, *Sl.* top dog; party leader, party boss, party chairman, sachem; campaigner, *Inf.* war-horse; candidate, party choice, office seeker, office holder, governor, president.

standardize, *v.* make uniform, regulate, systematize, stabilize, normalize, equalize, homogenize; cut to size, cut to a pattern, cut from the same cloth.

stand-by, *n.* **1.** supporter, adherent, backer, booster, promoter; fan, admirer, votary, disciple, partisan, well-wisher, champion; friend, alter ego, bosom buddy, confidant, confidante; sidekick, buddy, *Fr. copain, Inf.* pal, chum, comrade.
2. stalwart, mainstay, *Inf.* shoulders, *Inf.* old faithful.
3. substitute, fill-in, backup; understudy, replacement, alternate, second.

stand-in, *n.* **1.** (*of motion pictures*) stunt man, stunt girl, double.
2. substitute, sub, succedaneum, replacement, alternate, backup, fill-in; agent, proxy, surrogate, secondary, deputy, chargé d'affaires; understudy, stand-by, second; pinch hitter, designated hitter, relief pitcher, pinch runner.

standing, *n.* **1.** rank, status, place, position, estate, station, footing; caste, class; order, echelon,

level, stratum, grade; situation, condition, circumstance, state.
2. reputation, reputability, repute, good *or* high repute, good name, good odor, credit.
3. duration, pe*r*manence, longevity, continuance; endurance, durability, lastingness, abidingness.
—adj. **4.** erect, upright, plumb, perpendicular, vertical, stand-up, straight-up-and-down, *Heraldry.* rampant.
5. still, static, stagnant; stationary, immobile, fixed; motionless, unmoving.
6. continuous, continual, constant, steady, unbroken, uninterrupted, ongoing; unrelieved, unremitting; perpetual, lasting, long-lasting, permanent.
7. customary, conventional, habitual, usual, regular; received, approved, accepted, admitted, recognized.
8. idle, unused, out of use, unemployed.

stand-off, *n.* **1.** reserve, aloofness, coolness, coldness; unfriendliness, unsociableness, unneighborliness; remoteness, inaccessibleness, unapproachableness.
2. tie, tied score, draw; dead heat, photo finish; deadlock, stalemate.
3. counterbalance, counterweight, counterpoise, equipoise, offset.
—adj. **4.** aloof, reserved, stand-offish, *Inf.* offish; cool, cold, icy, frigid, frosty; withdrawn, distant, removed, remote, detached; inaccessible, unapproachable, Olympian; unfriendly, unamiable, unsociable, unneighborly; unexpansive, undemonstrative, unaffable, uncongenial.

standpoint, *n.* **1.** vantage point, seat, post, station, distance, footing; lookout, overlook, observatory, observation post *or* point, watchtower.
2. position, stance, where one stands *or* sits; angle, slant, side, light, frame of reference; attitude, outlook, opinion, point of view, viewpoint, view, perspective; mind, frame of mind, dispostion; idea, belief, conviction, mind-set, *Sl.* hang-up.

standstill, *n.* **1.** cessation, arrest, end, stop, stoppage; halt, desistance, termination, abruption, full stop, dead stop, deadlock, stalemate, impasse; stand, stand-off, tie, draw; check, checkmate, mate.
2. pause, rest, respite, lull, lapse, *Inf.* letup; recess, adjournment, time-out; breath, breather, breathing spell, spell, breathing space; wait, waiting period; hold, holdup, holding pattern, status quo; reprieve, stay, moratorium.
3. interruption, discontinuance, suspension; deferral, deferment, postponement, abeyance, prorogation; gap, hiatus, break, interstice; interval, interlude, interim; intermission.

staple, *n.* **1.** (*all principal or basic*) commodity, product, raw material, resource.
2. *Often* **staples** basics, fundamentals, necessities, essentials; stock items, goods, vendibles, salables.
3. (*all principal or basic*) item, thing, feature, element, part; substance, body, bulk, mass, *Archaic.* heft, main part, chief ingredient.
—adj. **4.** chief, primary, prominent, principal, main, foremost, leading; basic, fundamental, radical, essential, indispensable, necessary, important, vital, sustentatitve, supporting; established, proved; marketable, merchantable, salable, vendible, popular, in demand.

star, *n.* **1.** heavenly body, celestial body, *Astron.* nova, *Archaic.* lamp, luminary; orb, planet, *Astron.* planetoid, *Astron.* asteroid; falling star, shooting star, meteor, *Astron.* meteoroid, meteorite, comet.
2. destiny, fate, kismet, predestination, *Brit.* cup of tea; luck, fortune, lot, doom; plight, state, condition, situation, estate, status.
3. pentagram, pentalpha, pentacle; asterisk, mark, check, tick.
4. celebrity, *Sl.* celeb, somebody, name, *Inf.* big name, toast of the town, superstar; personage, dignitary, *Inf.* VIP, *Inf.* bigwig, *Sl.* big shot, *Sl.* biggie, *Sl.* big wheel, *Sl.* big chesse.
5. principal, lead, leading lady, leading man, hero, heroine, *Theat.Sl.* headliner; diva, prima donna.
—adj. **6.** celebrated, renowned, well-known, prominent, famous, illustrious; chief, main, principal, leading, first; preeminent, superior, distinguished, peerless, matchless, supreme, sublime, transcendent; incomparable, inimitable, unrivaled, unsurpassed, unmatched, unequaled, unparalleled; utmost, topmost, top, foremost; paramount, surpassing, reigning, ruling; brilliant, great, glorious, exalted, prized.
—v. **7.** spangle, bead, stud, bejewel; decorate, adorn, ornament, dress *or* dress up, embellish, *Sl.* jazz up.
8. feature, present, introduce; advance, promote.
9. asterisk, mark, check, tick, indicate, note.
10. shine, be brilliant; be prominent, be distinguished, be important; appear, be presented.

starch, *n.* **1.** formality, ceremony, stiffness, rigidity, inflexibility; primness, propriety, prudery, *Sl.* uptightness; etiquette, manners, decorum, convenance; strictness, exactness, exactitude, punctilio, punctiliousness, precision, preciseness, fastidiousness, meticulousness.
2. *Informal.* vigor, energy, vitality, birr, stamina, get up and go; grit, pluck; intensity, force, boldness, courage, *Sl.* guts, nerve.

stare, *v.* **1.** gaze, gape, gawk, goggle, *Inf.* rubberneck, *Inf.* rubber; eye, *Inf.* eyeball, ogle, stare at; keep an eye on, watch.
2. be conspicuous, catch the eye, stand out, be prominent, project, stick out; glare, be vivid, be ostentatious; loom, beetle, jut.
3. (*all of hair, feathers, etc.*) bristle, stand on end, stick up.
—v. **4.** empty gaze, blank look, fixed look; gaping, gawking, goggling, ogling.

stark, *adj.* **1.** sheer, utter, downright, absolute, unqualified, unmitigated, arrant, thorough, pure, perfect; complete, entire, out-and-out, outright, total, veritable, unconditional; rank, gross, glaring, flagrant, conspicuous; clear, evident, patent, unmistakable, obvious, plain; mere.
2. harsh, grim, dreary, drear, gray; desolate, barren, bare, vacant, abandoned, empty; arid, desert; wasted, laid waste, ravaged, destroyed; exhausted, depleted, worn, unfertile.
3. simple, severe, austere, spartan, puritanical, ascetic; unadorned, undecorated, unfurnished, unfurbished.
4. stiff, rigid, hard, inflexible, nonflexible, unbendable, unbending, inelastic, unplastic, nonpliant, unpliable, unmalleable; tight, tense, taut, *Inf.* stiff as a poker, *Inf.* stiff as a ramod; cold, dead, *Inf.* stiff as a board, petrified, ossified.
—adv. **5.** utterly, absolutely, downright, out-and-out, outright, all-out, straight-out; through and through, backward and forward, *Sl.* all the way, to the nth degree, grossly, quite; completely, entirely, wholly, totally, thoroughly, fully, altogether; unqualifiedly, unconditionally, unreservedly, unequivocally, unambiguously, clearly and simply, plain, plainly; clearly, obviously, evidently.

starlike, *adj.* **1.** stellate, stelliform, stellular, star-shaped, astral, starry; radiate.
2. shining, bright, brilliant, illuminated, alight, light,

lit, lighted; white, aureate, radiant, irradiant, lambent, resplendent, beaming, beamy; dazzling, fulgent, effulgent, refulgent; aglow, glowing, luminous, luminescent, luminiferous, incandescent; sparkling, scintillating, scintillant, coruscating, twinkling, shimmering; glimmering, aglimmer, glittering, aglitter.

starry, *adj.* **1.** star-spangled, bespangled, star-studded, full of stars.

2. stellar, sidereal; celestial, empyreal, empyrean, heavenly, astonomical, uranic; planetary, asteroidal.

3. stellate, star-shaped, starlike. See **starlike** (*def.* **1.**).

4. shining, bright, alight, radiant, twinkling, glittering, starlike. See **starlike** (*def.* **2.**).

start, *v.* **1.** depart, start out, set off, embark; *Inf.* take off, *Inf.* jump off, *Inf.* kick off, *Inf.* blast off, become airborne; *Inf.* hit the trail *or* road *or* pavement, sally forth, push off, set sail.

2. commence, begin, go ahead, go ahead with, undertake; turn to, *Inf.* buckle down, get going on [s.t.], set about doing [s.t.], take steps toward, start in on; plunge in, *Inf.* pitch in, *Inf.* roll up one's sleeves; *Inf.* dive in, *Inf.* dive in headfirst, *Inf.* get one's feet wet, *Inf.* get down to business, *Inf.* get down to it, *Inf.* get to it, *Inf.* get around to it; *Inf.* buckle down, *Inf.* put one's hand to the plow, *Inf.* put one's shoulder to the wheel, *Inf.* get the show on the road, *Inf.* get off the dime, *Sl.* get off one's duff.

3. appear, emerge, rise, rise up, dawn, be created, come into existence, come to be, have birth, be born, first see the light of day; be developed, be invented, come into being; issue forth, come forth, burst forth, break out; spring out, spring forth, loom up; sprout, mushroom, pop up, crop out, crop up; come into view, enter the picture, come into play, become a factor; issue, gush, rush, stream, spurt, shoot, jet, squirt, well, well out.

4. spring, dart, move; jump out, leap out, bound out, leap out from cover; jerk, twitch, blink, shy, draw back, recoil; quail, cower, blench, flinch, wince, shrink; lurch, bounce, convulse, be shaken, be taken aback, be frightened, *Inf.* jump out of one's skin.

5. protrude, project, extrude, jut *or* jut out, stick out, poke out; extend, excurve, obtrude, bulge, protuberate, *Anat.* protract; swell out, swell, (*all usu. in reference to the eyes*) dilate, pop, goggle, open wide, *Inf.* bug, *Inf.* bug out, stare, nearly start from their sockets.

6. slip, slip out, come loose, come unloosed, work loose; become disengaged, come unnailed *or* unscrewed, work out; come unhinged, become unseated; divide, separate, drop off *or* out.

7. begin the race *or* contest, be among the contestants, be a contender, be entered; enter the lists, join in, compete, be part of the field, *Sl.* make the scene.

8. set moving, set into motion, propel, give impulse to, activate, (*of engines*) turn over, crank up, *Inf.* gear up; propel, launch, push forward, push; poke, prod, goad, shove, *Inf.* wind up; encourage, back, second, *Inf.* get behind, prompt, urge, promote, aid; endorse, sponsor, finance, subsidize, set up, befriend, patronize.

9. establish, found, insitute, actuate, implement, instigate, set in motion; intiate, *Inf.* start the ball rolling, take the first step, take the initiative, take the plunge, make a start, break the ice; open, pioneer, lead off; inaugurate, set up, organize, originate; break ground, lay the foundation, lay the cornerstone; introduce, broach, usher in; create, beget, engender, father, conceive, give birth to.

—*n.* **10.** beginning, outset, onset, commencement; outbreak, dawn, conception, birth, genesis, exordium, *Inf.* kickoff, *Inf.* takeoff, *Inf.* blast-off, *Inf.* getaway; leaving, exodus, sailing, departure.

11. rise, arising, beginnings, emergence, incipience, nascence, infancy, creation, inception; origin, source, first cause; starting line *or* point, square one; foundation, fountainhead, wellspring, spring, mainspring.

12. impulse, signal, *Inf.* send-off, *Inf.* starting gun; initiation, actuation, institution; introduction, establishment, origination, organization, founding, foundation.

13. jerk, twitch, jump, leap, bound, vault; startle, surprise, jar, jolt, *Inf.* turn.

14. head start, lead, advantage, advance, odds, *Inf.* good break; superiority, precedence, antecedence, *Inf.* jump, *Inf.* edge, *Inf.* drop *or* draw, *Inf.* inside track, *Inf.* good post position; upper hand, whip hand.

15. chance, opportunity, opening, *Inf.* break; support, financing, backing, introductions, sponsorship; interest, encouragement, patronage, guidance; favor, aid, assistance.

startle, *v.* **1.** dismay, disturb, agitate, shake up, perturb, unsettle, discompose, upset, jolt, jar; surprise, come up behind, sneak up on, take aback, take off one's guard; astonish, astound, amaze, boggle, overwhelm, overcome; stun, shock, scare, frighten, fright, affright, *Archaic.* affray, alarm; intimidate, daunt, *Inf.* faze, awe, overawe, put the fear of God into; terrify, strike terror into, terrorize, appall, horrify; scare stiff, *Sl.* scare the living daylights out of, *Sl.* scare the bejeesus out of, *Sl.* scare the pants off, *Inf.* scare out of one's wits, curl one's hair, make one's hair stand on end, make one's flesh crawl, make one's blood run cold.

2. start, jump, blink, flinch, wince; draw back, recoil, shy away from, shrink, quail, blench, cower.

starvation, *n.* extreme hunger, famine, inanition; exhaustion, depletion, deprivation, need, want, lack, emptiness.

starve, *v.* **1.** die, perish, starve to death, *Archaic.* famish.

2. go hungry, go without food, fast, suffer from hunger, hunger, be hungry, be famished, crave food, be ravenous, *Inf.* lick one's chops.

3. *Usu.* **starve for** want, hunger for, long for, pine for, yearn for, *Inf.* hanker for, have a yen for; itch for, ache for, be hurting for, be dying for, burn for, die for; covet, crave, thirst for *or* after, lust after, pant after, *Sl.* have the hots for, desire, gasp after.

starveling, *adj.* **1.** starving, very hungry, famished, dying for food; undernourished, underfed, ill-fed; starved-looking, pinched, withered, shriveled, wizened; emaciate, emaciated, wasted, attenuated, *Pathol.* tabetic, *Pathol.* tabid; thin, thin as a reed *or* rail, skinny, too skinny to throw a shadow, lean, meager, gaunt, mere skin and bones, skeletal, bony, rawboned, fleshless; scrawny, scraggy, spindly, spindle-shanked, spindle-legged, gangly, gangling.

2. poor, second-rate, second-class, inferior, substandard, *Sl.* cheesy, flimsy, *Inf.* no-good, bad, cheap; pitiful, pathetic, sorry, shabby, beggarly, seedy, *Sl.* crummy, *Sl.* crappy, run-down, sleazy.

state, *n.* **1.** condition, stage, phase; situation, circumstance, state of affairs; form, shape.

2. predicament, scrape, plight, quandary, dilemma, fix, corner, pinch, *Inf.* pickle.

3. standing, rank, status, place, position, estate, station, place, footing; caste, class; order, echelon, level, stratum, grade.

4. grandeur, splendor, brilliance, glory, magnificence, style; dignity, gravity, solemnity.

5. country, nation; commonwealth, republic; *Political Science.* body politic, people; land, realm,

dominion, kingdom.
—*adj.* **6.** governmental, national, federal, official.
7. ceremonial, formal, solemn, celebratory; ceremonious, dignified, stately, imposing, impressive, majestic.
—*v.* **8.** declare, aver, assert, asseverate, affirm, avow, avouch, set down, lay down, speak up *or* out, have one's say; maintain, contend, have, hold, insist, submit; allege, profess, claim; swear, predicate, attest, testify; certify, validate, ratify, confirm.
9. announce, annunciate, publish, broadcast, herald, cry, blare, blazon, trumpet; pronounce, rule, decree, proclaim, promulgate.
10. disclose, divulge, tell, give out, come out with, let out, make known, manifest, reveal.

stated, *adj.* **1.** settled, fixed, set, defined; decided, confirmed, concluded; resolved, agreed upon, determined, chosen; ruled, ordained, adjudged, adjudicated.
2. authorized, warranted, sanctioned, approved, allowed; certified, licensed, accredited, validated, authenticated; authentic, valid, verified, documented.
3. official, authoritative, from the top, *Latin. ex cathedra, Sl.* from the horse's mouth; imperative, commanded, directed, ordered, prescribed.

stately, *adj.* august, dignified, distingué, distinguished, proud; grand, magnificent, pompous, palatial, splendid, resplendent, marvelous, superb; majestic, regal, kingly, princely, royal, lordly, noble, monarchal, monarchial, monarchical, imperial, magisterial, *Rare.* magistral; sublime, elevated, high, lofty, exalted, glorious; awesome, imposing, impressive, striking.

statement, *n.* **1.** declaration, announcement, annunciation, publication; averment, asseveration, assertion, say-so, affirmation, avowal, avouchment; testimony, evidence; revelation, disclosure, divulgement, manifestation.
2. proclamation, pronouncement, manifesto, pronunciamento, promulgation; notice, formal notice, notification.
3. *Commerce.* bill, invoice, check, charge, tally, *Inf.* tab, reckoning; account, record.

static, *adj.* **1.** stationary, motionless, unmoving. See **stationary** (*def.* **1**).
2. changeless, unvarying, constant. See **stationary** (*def.* **3**).
3. abeyant, resting, at rest, dormant, reposing; torpid, stagnant, lifeless, dead.

station, *n.* **1.** place, stand, spot, point; site, scene of the crime, scene, setting, *Law.* venue; position, locus, location, bearings, longitude and latitude, locale, whereabouts, hereabouts, *Latin. locus sigili,* L.S., *Latin. locus in quo;* point of reference, reference point, lookout, outlook, view, angle, slant, respect, *Survey.* set-up; perspective, point of view, viewpoint, way of looking at things, way of thinking, philosophy.
2. stop, stopping place, destination, end of the line, terminus, terminal; depot, *Fr. gare, Ger. Bahnhof;* bus station, train *or* railroad station, airport, port, dock.
3. headquarters, base of operations, central *or* administrative office, office, bureau, *U.S. Army.* command post; seat, center, hub; station house, police station, fire station, firehouse, fire hall, *U.S. Army.* armory.
4. status, standing, class, caste, rank; estate, situation, circumstances, condition, state; degree, order, grade, gradation, stage, level, step, rung; importance, distinction, prominence, elevation, prestige, dignity, eminence, precedence.
5. post, berth, billet, slot, assignment, appointment, commission, sinecure; place of duty, placement, *Mil.* duty, disposition, booth, (*of banks*) window, cage, (*of restaurants*) table, service area; office, department, division, section, branch, category; zone, territory, realm, province, district, parish, precinct, neighborhood, *Journalism.* beat; capacity, role, function, work, activity; duty, responsibility, task, chore, operation, mission, purpose; job, occupation, profession, career, trade, business, livelihood; field, scope, sphere, compass, arena, bailiwick, speciality, métier, line, *Sl.* thing, *Sl.* bag; vocation, calling, pursuit.

stationary, *adj.* **1.** motionless, unmoving, at a standstill, stock-still, *Chiefly Literary.* stilly, dead-still, frozen, still as a statue, statuelike; inactive, inert, sedentary, quiescent; stiff, rigid.
2. fixed, rooted, riveted, set, fast, secure, moored, anchored, stuck, planted, grounded, stable; immovable, immobile, static; permanent, settled.
3. changeless, immutable, unchangeable, invariable, unalterable; undeviating, unfaltering, unwavering, steadfast, reliable, dependable; constant, solid, stable, steady.

statue, *n.* representation, likeness, image, icon; bust, portrait bust, head, figure; sculpture, effigy, acrolith, *Obs.* monument, *Gk. Antiquity.* xoanon; carving, wood carving, casting, bronze, waxwork, wax figure, (*collectively*) statuary; figurine, statuette; colossus, equestrian statue, caryatid, figurehead; Statue of Liberty, Venus de Milo.

statuesque, *adj.* majestic, stately, imposing, impressive, magnificent, splendid, noble; dignified, formal, august, lofty, regal; towering, colossal, great, grand; graceful, elegant, attractive, comely, handsome, beautiful; well-proportioned, symmetrical, harmonious.

stature, *n.* **1.** height, length, tallness, size, elevation, altitude, measurement.
2. status, rank, degree; standing, position, posture, condition, station, state, place; importance, import, consequence, eminence, prominence, prestige, estimation.

status, *n.* **1.** position, posture, standing, station, stature, place; rank, level, grade, class, degree; importance, consequence, significance; reputation, repute, name, character, consideration, estimation.
2. condition, state, state of affairs, circumstances, situation, case; shape, form, mode, appearance, looks, aspect, tenor, air, health.

staunch, *adj.* **1.** firm, steadfast, unflinching, unswerving, unwavering, undeviating, unshrinking, unbending, unbowing, unfaltering, unhestitating; constant, dedicated, devoted, true, faithful, sure, dependable, reliable, steady, stable; unshaken, undaunted, undismayed, unalarmed.
2. resolute, resolved, tenacious, inexorable, inflexible, uncompromising, unyielding, intransigent, adamantine, adamant, determined, decided, fixed, settled; persevering, pertinacious, relentless, unrelenting, implacable; indefatigable, tireless, untiring, unflagging, unwearying, unwearied, weariless; plucky, gritty, game, mettlesome, spirited, red-blooded, *Inf.* spunky.
3. sound, sturdy, stout, solid, substantial, well-built, well-constructed, well-made; heavy, tough, hard, durable, lasting, long-lasting, made to last; rugged, hefty, husky, burly, *Scot and North Eng.* stiff; able-bodied, able, athletic, sinewy, well-knit; muscular, muscled, well-muscled, full-muscled, brawny, strapping, broad-shouldered, powerfully built; healthy, in good health, fit, physically fit, in good condition, *Inf.* in good shape, *Inf.* in shape.
4. watertight, waterproof, moistureproof, dampproof, impermeable, unporous, nonporous, im-

passable, unpassable, impenetrable; sealed, hermetically sealed, airtight; water-repellent, water-resistant, impervious, imperviable; *Naut.* seaworthy.

stave, *n.* **1.** slat, stay, lath, rib, board; staff, crook, walking stick, alpenstock, pikestaff, cane; stick, branch, club, cudgel; rod, wand, baton; pole, shaft, beam, upright, standard; pale, paling, stake, post, picket.

—v. **2.** break in, crush, put a hole in, cave in, pound in, push in, press in, indent.

3. break, break to pieces, *Inf.* break into smithereens, smash, splinter, shiver, fracture; rip *or* tear apart, rive, split, rend, cleave; hack up, chop up.

4. beat, bastinado, cudgel, cane, birch, club; lay on, strike, attack, set on; whack, thump, buffet, batter, pound, pommel; trounce, *Inf.* lambaste, scourge, thrash.

5. stave off **a.** ward *or* fend off, evade, avert, duck, dodge; avoid, shun, side-step, fence, parry, deflect, keep at bay *or* at arm's length; repel, repulse, rebuff, shove back *or* off, turn aside. **b.** forestall, prevent, hinder, obviate, deter, preclude; put off, delay, postpone, defer; intercept, inhibit, stop, halt, obstruct, block, trip up; thwart, foil, frustrate, scotch, spike, end.

stay[1], *v.* **1.** remain, dwell, live, reside, sojourn, lodge, abide, inhabit, cohabit; establish oneself, pitch tent, settle, anchor, put down stakes, plant oneself.

2. continue, keep, remain, maintain, sustain, *Inf.* stand pat, be stable, be permanent.

3. *Usu.* **stay with** endure, persist, persevere, perdure, last; abide, remain, continue, survive, hold on, go on, be constant, be steadfast, *Inf.* stick it out; cling to, cleave to, hold to, remain through *or* during, weather; see it through, die in harness.

4. wait, linger, delay, pause, tarry; loiter, hover, lag, dawdle, loaf, trifle; mark time, take time, let the grass grow under one's feet.

5. restrain, constrain, arrest, prevent, check, curb, rein in; hamper, obstruct, block, retard, foil, impede, hinder, deter, thwart, scotch, frustrate, *Inf.* put the kibosh on.

6. suppress, quell, stop, halt, put down, *Inf.* squelch, *Inf.* sit on, nip in the bud, prostrate; destroy, overpower, overturn, overcome, vanquish; crush, smash, rout, upset, discomfit; put an end to, deal a deathblow to, bring to naught, break the neck *or* back of, stamp *or* trample out, make short work of; undermine, deadlock, checkmate, bring to a standstill.

7. adjourn, recess, suspend, postpone, delay, put off, interrupt, intermit; take a break, shut up shop, take time out.

8. appease, satisfy, allay, reduce, alleviate; pacify, tranquilize, compose, comfort, soothe, calm, quiet, lull, settle, stop, put at rest.

—n. **9.** stop, halt, standstill; intermission, break, suspension, interval, interlude; pause, stoppage, cessation, discontinuance, desistance; rest, respite, *Inf.* letup, lull, reprieve, breathing spell, wait, lapse, recess, *Inf.* time out.

10. sojourn, stopover, visit, residency, habitation; rest, repose, pause, vacation, holiday.

11. *Informal.* staying power, endurance, stick-to-itiveness, perseverance.

stay[2], *n.* **1.** support, brace, prop, underprop, base, fulcrum, *Archit.* socle; abutment, truss, frame; bolster, bracket, mainstay, buttress, shoulder, reinforcement; beam, girder, rafter, lintel; post, pillar, upright, shaft, stanchion, strut.

—v. **2.** bear, bear up, hold, hold up, truss; prop, prop up, brace, bolster, buttress, gird, mainstay, shoulder, shore, reinforce, strengthen; underlie, underprop, underpin, underbrace, bed, embase, be at the bottom of, form the foundation of.

3. sustain, maintain, foster, keep, keep up; succor, relieve, comfort; cheer, inspirit, reassure, give *or* raise [s.o.'s] hope, yield *or* afford hope, hold out *or* justify [s.o.'s] hopes, raise [s.o.'s] hopes *or* expectations; encourage, enhearten, hearten, embolden, pat [s.o.] on the back, *Inf.* buck up.

steadfast, *adj.* **1.** steady, direct, fixed, intent, undistracted, unbroken; keen, piercing, penetrating; searching, questioning; rapt, enraptured, engrossed, absorbed; thoughtful, attentive.

2. constant, dedicated, devoted, true, faithful, sure, dependable, reliable, steady, stable, unshaken, undaunted; unflinching, unswerving, unwavering, undeviating, unshrinking, unbending, unfaltering, unhesitating.

3. resolute, resolved, tenacious, inexorable, inflexible, uncompromising, unyielding, intransigent, determined, decided, fixed, settled; persevering, pertinacious, relentless, implacable, indefatigable, obstinate, stubborn, insistent, persistent, tireless, unflagging, unwearied, untiring, unwearying; mettlesome, gritty, plucky, game, spirited, red-blooded, defiant, *Inf.* spunky.

4. infixed, ingrained, implanted, rooted, deep-rooted, deep-seated, deep-set, well-founded, well-grounded, long-established, well-established, firmly established; durable, of long duration, long-lived, long-lasting, longstanding, remaining, staying, continuing, enduring, lasting, abiding; perpetual, constant, indissoluble; settled, proved, irrefutable, unchangeable, immutable, unalterable.

5. firm, solid, grounded, stable, substantial, secure, fast, *Inf.* solid as a rock; riveted, moored, anchored, planted, fixed, irremovable, immovable, unmovable; immobile, stationary, static, frozen, stiff, rigid, inflexible, changeless, unchanging.

steady, *adj.* **1.** stable, solid, substantial, stout, sound; poised, balanced, offset, counterbalanced, counterpoised.

2. (*all of movement*) even, regular, rhythmic, rhythmical; metronomic, metronomical.

3. uniform, changeless, unchanging, unvarying, invariable, undeviating, the same; continuous, continual, nonstop, ceaseless, unceasing, perpetual, persistent, twenty-four hour, round-the-clock, unintermittent, undying; unending, endless, never-ending, unremitting, unrelieved, unbroken.

4. constant, chronic, inveterate, habitual; frequent, recurrent; faithful, longstanding.

5. calm, collected, composed, cool, *Inf.* cool as a cucumber, *Inf.* together; self-possessed, self-controlled, poised; imperturbable, inexcitable, unflappable, even-tempered, easygoing; dispassionate, peaceful, serene, tranquil.

6. direct, fixed. See **steadfast** (*def.* **1**).

7. steadfast; resolute. See **steadfast** (*defs.* **2, 3**).

8. sensible, rational, steady-going, level-headed, down-to-earth, *Fr. terre à terre,* having both feet on the ground; staid, settled, somber, sober, sober-minded, sobersided, serious-minded, serious.

—interj. **9.** be calm, calm down, take it easy, control yourself, pull yourself together, get a grip on yourself, *Sl.* cool it.

—n. **10.** sweetheart, *Inf.* sweetie, *Scot.* jo, honey; girlfriend, girl, best girl, *Sl.* sweet patootie; boyfriend, beau.

—v. **11.** stabilize, settle, fix; balance, poise; counterbalance, offset.

12. compose oneself, control oneself, calm down, settle down, cool off, *Inf.* simmer down; get hold of oneself, take oneself in hand; come to one's senses, see things in proper perspective.

steal, *v.* **1.** rob, thieve, pilfer, purloin, finger, filch, *Inf.* snitch, cabbage, abstract, *Chiefly Brit.* prig, *Euph.* borrow, *Archaic.* nim; peculate, embezzle, *Law.* defalcate, misappropriate; swindle, pocket, mulct, shark; shoplift, palm, *Sl.* boost, walk off *or* away with, *Euph.* remove; *All Sl.* heist, pinch, hook, swipe, hustle, rip off, frisk, crook, cop, lift.

2. appropriate, expropriate, arrogate, usurp; commandeer, hijack, skyjack; pirate, plagiarize, copy, *Inf.* lift, *Inf.* crib, forge, counterfeit.

3. (*usu. of persons*) abduct, kidnap, *Sl.* snatch, make off with, carry off, rape, seize; (*usu. in reference to military service*) impress, press, conscript, *Naut.* shanghai, crimp.

4. plunder, despoil, pillage, ravage, harry, ransack, sack, loot, gut, fleece, strip, rifle.

5. pirate, freeboot, buccaneer, privateer, filibuster.

6. *Inf.* poach, deerjack; smuggle, bootleg, *Inf.* sneak [s.t.] in.

7. scrounge, *Sl.* freeload, *Sl.* mooch, *Inf.* sponge, scavenge, *Sl.* bum.

8. sneak, prowl, lurk, couch, skulk, *U.S. Sl.* gumshoe; slink, worm, slide, slither; slip, tiptoe, pussyfoot.

9. pass, go by, elapse, lapse, fly, flit, glide, drift, flow; slide, creep.

—*n.* **10.** *Informal.* theft, stealage, pilferage. See **stealing** (*def.* **1**).

11. *Informal.* booty, loot, spoils. See **plunder** (*def.* 5).

12. *Informal.* bargain, good deal, good buy, *Inf.* buy, *Inf.* giveaway.

stealing, *n.* **1.** robbery, theft, thievery, pilferage, pilfering, filching, *Sl.* swiping, *Sl.* hustling, *Sl.* copping; peculation, embezzlement, *Law.* defalcation, misappropriation; shoplifting, palming, *Sl.* boosting; *Psychol.* kleptomania; smuggling, bootlegging; burglary, breaking and entering, *Law.* larceny, safe-cracking; purse-snatching, *U.S. Inf.* mugging, *Sl.* jumping.

2. expropriation, appropriation, arrogation, usurpation, accroachment, assumption; plagiarism, copying, *Inf.* cribbing, *Inf.* lifting; dispossession, deprivation, deprival, divestiture, bereavement.

3. commandeering, hijacking, skyjacking, air *or* sky piracy; (*usu. of persons*) kidnapping, capture, seizure, rape, impressment, conscription, manstealing, child-stealing; (*all of animals*) poaching, deerjacking, petnapping, dognapping, (*of cattle*) rustling.

4. stealings loot, booty. See **plunder** (*def.* 5).

stealth, *n.* furtiveness, surreptitiousness, clandestineness, covertness, stealthiness; slyness, sneakiness, *Inf.* shadiness; underhand dealing, *Inf.* shady operation.

stealthy, *adj.* covert, clandestine, surreptitious, undercover, underground, back-alley; sly, furtive, sneaky, sneaking, underhand, underhanded, *Inf.* under the table *or* counter, backroom, backstairs; secret, hugger-mugger, hole-and-corner, closed-door, closet; shifty, slippery, *Inf.* shady.

steam, *n.* **1.** vapor, condensation, mist, haze, fog, cloud, fume, smoke; moisture, dampness, wetness; vaporescence, exhalation.

2. blow off steam *Slang.* get excited, rant and rave, holler, yell, scream and holler; let oneself go, revel, roister, cut loose, let loose, *Sl.* party, whoop it up; *Sl.* let it all hang out; give vent to one's feelings.

—*v.* **3.** vaporize, volatilize, *Chem.* sublime, *Chem.* sublimate, moisturize, gasify; distill, concentrate, purify.

4. steam up mist, bemist, fog, befog; dim, blur, cloud.

5. rush, race, dart, dash, sprint; tear, *Inf.* rip, charge; speed, spank, haste, hurry, hie; zip, whoosh, chug, sail, skim, slide, glide.

steamy, *adj.* **1.** vaporous, gaseous, volatile, fumy.

2. misty, hazy, fogged, befogged, dim, bedimmed, beclouded, cloudy, obscure, blurred.

3. hot and humid, muggy, sticky, damp, moist, wet, dank, like a Turkish bath *or* sauna, dripping, sodden, soppy, sweaty; sweltering, sultry, close, like the Black Hole of Calcutta; steaming, broiling, boiling, roasting.

steel, *n.* **1.** blade, razor, knife; sword, saber, *Japanese.* aikuchi, Excalibur, cutlass; rapier, foil, épée; scimitar, bayonet, cold steel; dirk, stiletto, dagger.

—*v.* **2.** brace, fortify, shore up, invigorate, *Inf.* beef up; toughen, nerve, screw one's courage to the sticking point; harden, harden one's heart, inure, stiffen.

steely, *adj.* **1.** gray, steel, blue-gray, steel-gray, iron-gray.

2. strong, like tempered steel, sturdy, mighty, iron-hard, tough, stout, rugged; stalwart, determined, resolute, intrepid, undaunted; inflexible, unyielding, unbending, rigid, stiff, adamant, adamantine; firm, solid as a rock, hard, hardened, hard as nails, flinty.

steep¹, *adj.* **1.** sheer, abrupt, precipitous, sudden, high, upright, plumb, sharp, bold, bluff, arduous; perpendicular, vertical; declivitous, descending; acclivitous, ascending.

—*n.* **2.** height, elevation, rise, hill, acclivity; cliff, bluff, crag, alp, escarpment, pinnacle, crest, palisade.

steep², *v.* **1.** soak, seethe, brew, ret, let sit *or* stand; marinate, marinade, pickle, souse, brine.

2. saturate, imbue, submerge, submerse, immerse, *Rare.* immerge; souse, douse, drench, sop, wet, wet down.

3. flood, inundate, overspread, suffuse, engulf, surround, submerge, cover, overflow; pile, load, stuff, fill, glut; imbue, impregnate, imbrue, infuse, tincture; infiltrate, permeate, penetrate, pervade.

steeple, *n.* spire, tower, turret, minaret, belfry, bell tower, campanile, *Archit.* cupola, *Archit.* dome.

steer, *v.* **1.** guide, pilot, drive, fly, navigate; run, operate, work, handle; conduct, lead, direct, control, manage, boss; be in charge of, have direction of, be in control of, be in the driver's seat, be at the wheel.

2. steer clear of keep *or* stay away from, shun, avoid, eschew, evade, dodge.

—*n.* **3.** *Informal.* tip, suggestion, lead, bit *or* piece of advice, helpful hint, idea.

steersman, *n.* helmsman, wheelman, coxswain, navigator, pilot, co-pilot; driver, conductor, motorman, chauffeur, back-seat driver; airplane pilot, aviator, *Inf.* birdman, flier, avigator, aeronaut.

stellar, *adj.* **1.** astral, sidereal; starry, stelliferous, star-filled.

2. star-shaped, stellate, stellated, stellular, starlike, sphery; bright, brilliant, dazzling, shining, glowing, twinkling, sparkling.

3. leading, chief, main, principal, primary, prime, first, foremost.

stem¹, *n.* **1.** stalk, trunk, caudex, culm, *Brit.* haulm, cane, colamus, quill, *Bot.* caulis, *Bot.* caulicle, *Bot.* axis; leafstalk, *Bot.* petiole, *Bot.* petiolule, *Biol.* pedicle, *Bot.* pedicel, *Both Bot., Zool.* footstalk, peduncle, *Both Bot.* funicle, funiculus, *Bot.* gynophore; bine, tendril, runner, *Bot.* sormentum, *Bot.* rootlet; arm, leg, neck; support, stay, mainstay, staff; shaft, shank, spike, rod, bar, *Mach.* arbor; peg, pin, thill, link, connector.

2. spindle, swivel, pilot, axle, winder, turner, turnbuckle, screw; handle, holder.

3. stock, strain, line, lineage, bloodline, blood, race; genealogy, pedigree, family tree, ancestry, parentage, family, tribe, people, clan, *Anthrop.* gens; heritage, origin, birth, background, extraction, descent.

—*v.* 4. *Usu.* **stem from** arise, rise, spring, issue, emanate, flow, come, proceed; root, sprout, bud, grow, evolve, develop, burgeon; germinate, originate, start, commence, begin; descend, derive, follow, ensue, result, be generated by, be brought about by, be bred by, be caused by, be based *or* grounded on.

stem², *v.* 1. stop, arrest, stay, stall, bring to a halt *or* standstill; put a stop *or* an end to, terminate, end, quash, quell, squash, *Inf.* put the kibosh on; check, nip in the bud; curb, control, limit, circumscribe, restrict, contain, *Law.* enjoin; restrain, hold back, repress, constrain, suppress, hold in, pull back on, hold the reins on; retard, slow down, cut back on, diminish, decrease, reduce, lessen, curtail, abridge, cut short.

2. dam, dam up, plug, plug up, stop, stop up, bung, cork, stopple, spile, (*in blasting*) tamp, *Surg.* tampon; stuff up, fill up, pack, *Obs.* constipate; close off, shut off, cut off, caulk, seal off; stanch, bind, put a tourniquet on, stop the flow, stop the leak; block, obstruct, jam up, clog up, choke; prevent, bar, debar, forbid, proscribe, *Law.* estop; hinder, hamper, inhibit, oppilate, impede, handicap.

stem³, *v.* breast, push through, inch through, move through, advance against, make headway against, gain ground against, make strides against, make progress against; surmount, rise above, prevail over, win over, beat; confront, meet, face; repel, fend off, beat back, thwart, ward off; oppose, defend against, hold one's ground against, hold off, keep at bay; withstand, stand up against, hold up against; outlast, survive, endure, last out, come through.

stench, *n.* stink, fetor, malodor, rancidity, foul odor, strong *or* gamy smell, body odor, *Inf.* B.O.; halitosis, bad breath, mephitis, miasma, effluvium, fume, taint; fetidness, fetidity, malodorousness, stinkiness, smelliness; gaminess, rancidness, putrescence, putrescency, putridness, putridity, rottenness; rankness, noisomeness, foulness.

stenographer, *n.* stenographist, shorthand writer, stenotypist, phonographer, phonographist, tachygraph, tachygrapher, tachygraphist; secretary, amanuensis; scribe, scrivener, *Sl.* quill driver, copyist, transcriber, transcriptionist; chronicler, annalist, minutes keeper.

stenography, *n.* shorthand, Gregg shorthand, speed writing, stenotype, phonography, tachygraphy.

stentorian, *adj.* (*all in reference to sound*) stentorious, thunderous, thundering, booming, roaring, trumpetlike, deafening, ear-splitting; powerful, strong, big, orotund, resonant, vibrant, rich, full, sonorous, full-throated; deep, guttural, throaty, husky; deep-toned, heavy, low, alto, bass, baritone.

step, *n.* 1. footstep, stride, pace, military pace.

2. footfall, tread, tramp, pad; clip-clop, clippety-clop, hoofbeat.

3. footprint, footmark, print, track; trail, spoor, vestige, imprint.

4. gait, walk, bearing, carriage; shuffle, hobble; mincing step; goose step; roll, swagger; hop, skip; gallop, canter, trot.

5. **steps** course, path, way, route; passage, travels, journey, trip.

6. move, proceeding, act, action, measure; period, point, stage, installment, phase; deed, effort, exploit, stroke.

7. mark, rank, degree, grade, level, rung.

8. short distance, stone's throw, earshot, spitting distance.

9. (*in reference to movement*) pattern, design, configuration, shape, structure, rhythm.

—*v.* 10. move, go, advance, proceed; walk, ambulate, perambulate, foot, stride, pace, hoof it; stroll saunter, amble; slog, plod, trudge; (*all usu. of horses*) race, run, sprint, gallop, trot; cover ground, travel spurt, scamper, scurry, hustle, scoot; bolt, dart, fly bound, outrun one's shadow.

11. **step on** tread, stamp, tramp, trample; press, tap, kick, treadle.

stepping stone, *n.* toehold, foothold, good grounding; rung on *or* up the ladder, leg up; lift, boost, assist, aid, help, support, assistance, hand, push; way, route, passageway, bridge, link, connection, tie; vehicle, means; opportunity, good chance, open sesame, door, opening.

stereotype, *n.* 1. convention, set form; tradition, custom; pattern, groove, rut, routine; habit, wont, one's old way.

2. banality, hackneyed phrase, conventionalism, cliché.

—*v.* 3. class, classify, generalize, categorize, pigeonhole, *Sl.* peg, *Sl.* button down, *Inf.* put [s.o.] *or* [s.t.] down as, *Sl.* have [s.o.'s] number, prejudge; identify, label, type, typecast; designate, denominate, style, tag, term, name, call, dub; brand, mark, stigmatize.

stereotyped, *adj.* conventional, humdrum, commonplace, stock, familiar; hackneyed, banal, trite, overdone, *Inf.* bromidic, platitudinous, *Inf.* corny; tired, thin, threadbare, shopworn, worn-out, played out, *Inf.* old hat, moth-eaten, warmed-over; unimaginative, unoriginal, stale, insipid, uninspired.

sterile, *adj.* 1. pure, sterilized, harmless, uninfected, disinfected, germfree, sanitary, aseptic, uncontaminated, unpolluted, antiseptic.

2. unfruitful, fruitless, unproductive, unyielding; childless, barren, abortive, fallow, infecund, infertile, unprolific, *Bot.* acarpous, impotent, effete; empty, bare, arid, dry, dead.

3. useless, futile, vain, idle, unavailing, bootless; ineffectual, ineffective, inefficacious, inadequate, inoperative, unserviceable, impracticable; worthless, valueless, meritless, nugatory; unprofitable, profitless, unremunerative, unrewarding, unpaying, gainless; unsuccessful, *Inf.* no-go, to no avail, to no purpose, for naught.

sterility, *n.* 1. purity, harmlessness, uninfectiousness, asepticism, cleanliness.

2. childlessness, barrenness, infertility, unprolificness, infecundity, *Med.* agenesis, impotence, effeteness.

3. unproductiveness, unyieldingness, unfruitfulness, fruitlessness; exhaustion, depletion, impoverishment; meagerness, scarcity, poverty, emptiness; dryness, aridity, baldness, nakedness, bareness, waste, desolation, death.

4. ineffectiveness, ineffectualness, inefficacy, inadequacy, inefficiency, incompetence, ineptness; uselessness, inutility, worthlessness, valuelessness, meritlessness, nugacity; futility, bootlessness, unavailingness, idleness; unprofitableness, profitlessness, nonsuccess, failure, defeat.

sterilize, *v.* 1. purify, disinfect, fumigate, cleanse, depurate, *Med., Bacteriol.* autoclave.

2. asexualize, geld, *Sl.* cut, spay, *Inf.* fix, castrate, (*of fowl*) caponize, neuter, alter; unman, emasculate, eunuchize; *Surg.* vasectomize.

sterling, *adj.* 1. genuine, pure, unadulterated, unmingled, unalloyed; priceless, precious, exquisite; perfect, flawless.

2. excellent, exceptional, superior, standout, outstanding, striking; superlative, supreme, transcendent, sovereign, the best; matchless, peerless, nonpareil, perfect, classic, first-class; choice, prime, select, very good, *Australian Sl.* bosker, *Scot. and North Eng.* braw; fine, admirable, worthy, estimable, notable.

3. first-rate, *Inf.* tiptop, *Inf.* A-1, *Inf.* A number 1; extraordinary, very remarkable, *Sl.* bang-up, *Inf.* smashing, wonderful, splendid.

stern¹, *adj.* **1.** strict, demanding, exacting, stringent, critical, unsparing, unremitting, rigid, harsh, severe, rigorous, hard; firm, steadfast, determined, resolute, resolved; uncompromising, adamant, relentless, unrelenting, inflexible, immovable, obdurate, recalcitrant, unyielding, hardlined, inexorable, implacable, unbending, flinty; obstinate, stubborn, willful; unsympathetic, unfeeling, hard-hearted, hard-boiled, ruthless, pitiless, unkind, unmerciful, inclement, cold-blooded, cold, cruel.

2. overbearing, coercive, ironhanded, ironfisted, dictatorial, imperious, peremptory, tyrannical, despotic, autocratic; excessive, extreme, drastic, Draconian, exigent, extortionate, arbitrary, unreasonable.

3. austere, stark, grave, sober, somber; stiff, ascetic, Spartan, strait-laced, puritanical; sour, vinegary, acetous; grim, forbidding, dour, gaunt, frowning, saturnine, gloomy, taciturn; fierce, rough, craggy; ungentle, gruff, churlish, crabbed, surly, rude, crusty; brusque, short, curt, blunt, bluff.

4. formidable, laborious, rugged, toilsome, difficult, burdensome, Herculean, operose; irksome, distressing, painful, afflictive.

5. sharp, biting, piercing, trenchant, acrid, stinging, acerbic, caustic, mordant, cutting, virulent, bitter, venomous.

stern², *n.* **1.** (*both of a ship*) afterpart, poop; rear, back, tail, end, heel, caboose.

2. *Informal.* See **buttocks**.

3. from stem to stern fore and aft, from head to foot *or* toe, from head to tail, from top to bottom, from cover to cover, from A to Z, *Brit.* from A to Zed; completely, totally, all the way through, throughout; comprehensively, thoroughly, backward and forward, inside out, from the ground up, soundly, solidly.

stew, *v.* **1.** simmer, seethe, boil; fricasse.

2. *Informal.* fret, fuss, worry, agonize, torture oneself, writhe, lose sleep over, toss and turn, stay awake nights; pout, frown, sulk, brood over, mope; chafe, fume, burn, sizzle, smolder, stir, *Inf.* do a slow burn, *Inf.* steam up, *Sl.* work oneself up into a sweat *or* lather.

3. swelter, perspire, sweat, *Sl.* sweat bullets *or* blood, drip with sweat.

—n. **4.** ragout, salmi, salmagundi, slumgullion, hash, mash, fricasse, paella, bouillabaisse, *U.S.* chowder, olio, olla-podrida, *Sp. olla,* (*in China, India, etc.*) chow-chow, *U.S. Sl.* mulligan.

5. *Informal.* fuss, fluster, flurry, dither, twitter, fret, bother, pother, *Inf.* tizzy, *Archaic.* pucker.

steward, *n.* **1.** fiduciary, guardian, *Brit.* warden; trustee, keeper, custodian, caretaker, curator.

2. majordomo, butler, housekeeper, maître d'hôtel, chamberlain, (*in the middle ages*) seneschal, head *or* chief servant; (*in Great Britain*) bailiff, *Scot.* factor.

3. hostess, stewardess, waitress; waiter.

stick¹, *n.* **1.** branch, limb, stem, bough, spray, switch, twig; shoot, sprout, runner, tendril, scion.

2. kindling, fagot, tinder; firewood, brush, brushwood, driftwood.

3. rod, wand, baton, staff, pike, pole; scepter, crosier, crook, standard, caduceus; walking stick, alpenstock, cane, crutch.

4. club, birch, whip, scourge, cat-o'-nine-tails, cat, lash, cowhide, thong; cudgel, truncheon, knout, bludgeon, bastinado, blackjack, billy club, billy, *Chiefly Irish Eng.* shillelagh, mace.

5. sliver, splinter, shive, fragment; chip, whittling, shaving, flake.

6. on the stick alert, wide-awake, aware, *Inf.* heads-up, *Inf.* on the ball; moving, active, bustling, hustling, on the go, on the move; busy, astir, up and doing, up and about; smart bright, keen, sharp, quick.

7. the sticks *U.S. Informal.* rural districts, provinces, backwater, country, countryside, *Sl.* boondocks, *Sl.* boonies, *Australian.* outback; backwoods, hinterlands, back country, woods, bush, *Sl.* the bushes; no man's land, the middle of nowhere.

stick², *v.* **1.** pierce, puncture, penetrate, transfix; pass through *or* into, transpierce, spear, stab, lancinate; prick, pink, spike, spit, impale, gore, run through; perforate, punch, honeycomb, riddle; thrust in *or* into, tunnel, bore, drill, enter.

2. place, set, lay, put, posit; position, plant, locate, situate; drop, plunk, plop.

3. fasten, attach, make adhere, join, unite; glue, agglutinate, paste, cement, size, gum; tape, scotchtape, pin, tack, nail; weld, solder, fuse; coalesce, cohere.

4. confuse, puzzle, bewilder, perplex, nonplus; baffle, mystify, stump, *Inf.* bamboozle, *Inf.* buffalo; stun, daze, confound, stupefy.

5. hold, cleave, cling, stay, adhere; adhere to, hold on to, hang on to, clench, clutch, clasp, grip, grasp; comply with, abide by, fulfill; observe, respect, acknowledge; obey, follow, heed, mind.

6. be embedded, be mired, be bogged down; be hindered, be impeded, be checked; be stationary, be stopped.

7. persist, persevere, stand firm, stand fast, be resolute; be unyielding, stick to one's guns, insist, hold one's ground; never say die, not give up the ship, go down fighting, *Inf.* keep the faith, die trying *or* in harness *or* with one's boots on; be tenacious, hold fast, not take no for an answer, brook no denial.

8. *Usu.* **stick out** extend, project, protrude, jut out, poke out, stand out; bulge, obtrude, excurve; overhang, beetle, hang over, impend; swell out, protuberate, bow, embow; distend, belly, swell, round out, balloon, billow.

9. stick at scruple, stickle, demur, hesitate; waver, doubt, pause, falter; hang back, draw back, recoil, shrink from *or* at, balk at.

10. stick by *or* **to** be loyal *or* faithful *or* constant; stand by, stay with through thick and thin *or* through fair times and foul.

11. stick [s.t.] out endure, put up with, see through, see through to the end, stay until the last gun is fired; take it, brave it out, *Inf.* tough it out, *Inf.* hang in *or* hang in there, *Sl.* sweat it out.

12. stick up for defend, go to bat for, speak in behalf of *or* up for, stand up for, fight for, take up the cudgels for; guard, protect, safeguard, screen, shield; support, bolster, sustain.

stickle, *v.* **1.** haggle, higgle, wrangle, bicker, dicker, *Sl.* hassle, *Scot.* argle-bargle, *Scot.* sturt, *Scot. and North Eng.* threap, *Scot. and North Eng.* prig; hold out, stand out, stick to one's guns, not yield an inch, *Inf.* stand pat.

2. demur, scruple, boggle, have qualms; balk at, stick at, hesitate, hang back, falter, pause, think twice, have second thoughts, fight shy of.

stickler, *n.* **1.** perfectionist, precisionist, *Inf.* nit-picker; fussbudget, fusspot, *Inf.* fuddy-duddy; mule, diehard, intransigent, *Inf.* standpat *or* standpatter; martinet, disciplinarian.

2. problem, puzzler, poser, teaser, *Inf.* brain-teaser, *Inf.* hard nut to crack, *Inf.* mind-boggler, *Inf.* stumper, *Inf.* floorer; puzzle, enigma, riddle, conundrum, mystery, Chinese puzzle.

sticky, *adj.* **1.** adhesive, adherent, tacky; gluey, glutinous, gummy; viscid, viscous, viscoid.

2. (*all of the weather*) hot and humid, muggy, close, sultry, dank, *Rare.* madid.

3. awkward, tricky, ticklish, delicate, *Sl.* hairy, precarious, touch-and-go, *Dial.* kittle, being easier said than done.

stiff, *adj.* **1.** rigid, firm, unpliable, inflexible, unmalleable, unbending, unyielding, resistant; impervious, impenetrable, impregnable, repelling, unassailable, rugged; brittle, crisp, dried-out, *Inf.* stiff as a board.

2. (*all of a person or animal*) unlimber, not supple, unbendable, arthritic, rheumatic, gouty, *Inf.* creaky, *Inf.* frozen, *Inf.* musclebound, *Inf.* out of shape.

3. (*all of a beverage*) strong, potent, alcoholic; fermented, corned, turned; overpowering, *Sl.* pickling, *Sl.* packing a wallop, enough to grow hair on one's chest *or* on a cueball.

4. resolute, unyielding, taut; determined, decided, set, set upon, resolved, confirmed; staunch, authoritative, authoritarian, autocratic; stubborn, intractable, obstinate, pertinacious, hard-line, obdurate, intransigent; unrelenting, unflagging, dogged, indomitable, relentless, inexorable, plodding; tenacious, gritty, *Inf.* hellbent, *Inf.* stick-to-it-ive.

5. consistent, unchanging, steady, stable, balanced, even, constant; unchangeable, unalterable, changeless, immutable, invariable; irrevocable, irreversible, indissoluble, irrepealable; abiding, enduring, durable, deep-rooted, deep-seated, longstanding; steadfast, unwavering, unswerving, unflinching, unfaltering, undeviating, unhesitating, true.

6. strong, forceful, powerful, fresh, spanking, vigorous, steady, pounding; keen, brisk, intense, persistent, gusty, gusting, howling, smacking.

7. formal, unrelaxed, reserved, constrained, restrained, *Sl.* uptight, starched, strait-laced; prim, priggish, prudish, puritanical, old-fashioned, old-school; strict, rigid, exact, precise, punctilious, stuffy, proper, decorous, ceremonial, ritualistic; elaborate, *Sl.* veddy-veddy proper; elegant, pretentious, pompous; cold, chilly, unfriendly; unreceptive, exclusive, snobbish, standoffish, *Inf.* offish, aloof.

8. gauche, awkward, ungraceful, graceless, clumsy, inelegant; gawky, bumbling, maladroit; all-thumbs, having two left feet, unhandy, unskillful, inept, bunglesome, bungling, *Inf.* klutzy; ungainly, lumbering, lubberly, like a bull in a china shop; unpolished, unmannered, uncouth; unrefined, cloddish, coarse; provincial, unsophisticated, *Inf.* hick, *Inf.* off the farm, *Inf.* country, *Inf.* not with it.

9. laborious, difficult, hard, fatiguing, arduous, strenuous, heavy, toilsome; uphill, full of obstacles, Herculean, *Inf.* wicked, *Inf.* rough, *Inf.* tough, *Inf.* nasty; rigorous, exacting, painstaking, challenging; tedious, unmitigating, seemingly endless, infinite; tiresome, boring, *Inf.* deadly, *Inf.* a drag; knotty, complicated, complex, involved; trying, deep, profound.

10. severe, harsh, stringent; unsparing, punitive, to the full extent of the law; inclement, merciless, avenging, revengeful; ruthless, vindictive, oppressive, cruel; excessive, unusually great *or* heavy, unwarranted; immoderate, extravagant, undue.

11. thick, solid, solidified, close, compressed, pressed, dense, compact, condensed; flinty, stony, steely, concrete, petrified, ossified, hardened, lithoid, marblelike, granitelike; substantial, stout, fixed, stable, sound; set, tight, secure, fast; tough, horny.

—n. **12.** *Slang.* **a.** corpse, body, dead body; **b.** prude, prig, priggish person, puritan; snob, *Inf.* bluenose, pedant, precisionist, purist, formalist; fussbudget, fusspot, *Inf.* fuddy-duddy, *Inf.* old biddy, *Inf.* biddy; pettifogger, *Inf.* nitpicker, stickler, *Inf.* stick-in-the-mud. **c.** miser, niggard, skinflint, *Sl.* skin, *Sl.* cheapskate, *Inf.* piker, muckworm, *Sl.* cheap screw, pennypincher, pinch-penny. **d.** drunkard, drunk, inebriate, sot, soak, tippler; tosspot, toper, barfly; alcoholic, chronic alcoholic *or* drunk, dipsomaniac; hard drinker, serious drinker; *All Inf.* guzzler, swiller, soaker, sponge, lovepot; *All Sl.* boozer, boozehound, lush, souse, rummy, wino, alkie, juicehead, hooch hound, gin hound, swillbelly, swillpot, stew, stewbum, elbow-bender.

13. *Slang.* **a.** fellow, individual, chap, guy, duffer, gaffer, *Inf.* customer, *Brit. Sl.* cove, *Sp. hombre,* codger. **b.** laborer, worker, working man, *Inf.* working stiff; day laborer, field hand, manual laborer, blue-collar worker; hired man, drudge, coolie, peon, plodder, proletarian.

stiffen, *v.* **1.** harden, make stiff, starch; callous, indurate, temper, cement, fix; *All Cooking.* beat, whip, gelatinize, ossify, petrify, *Archaic.* lapidify, turn to stone, fossilize; vitrify, crystallize; freeze, clot, jell, congeal.

2. brace, brace oneself, prepare oneself; anticipate, hold oneself in readiness, forearm, arm, *Inf.* square one's shoulders, steel oneself, gird one's loins.

stiff-necked, *adj.* **1.** pertinacious, stubborn, *Inf.* ornery; pigheaded, bullheaded, mulish, stubborn as a mule; unyielding, intractable, obdurate, obstinate, *Inf.* hard-headed, *Inf.* boneheaded; inflexible, unbending, adamant, adamantine; rigid, stony, fixed; unswerving, undeviating, uncompromising, relentless, unrelenting, unshrinking, stern; perverse, headstrong, self-willed, pervicacious; refractory, contrary, intransigent; unmanageable, ungovernable, immovable, unshakeable; persistent, insistent, tenacious, bulldog.

2. opinionated, bigoted, intolerant, illiberal, close-minded, narrow, narrow-minded, limited; unreceptive, prejudiced, biased, warped, twisted, partial, one-sided.

stifle, *v.* **1.** smother, suffocate, asphyxiate, choke; strangle, burke, garrotte, throttle, *Sl.* scrag.

2. check, restrain, hold back, keep back, control, limit, circumscribe, restrict; prevent, preclude, make impossible; curb, repress, constrain, contain, suppress, hold in, withhold; still, hush, silence, mute; conceal, keep to oneself.

3. put a stop *or* an end to, terminate, end, quash, quell, squash, *Inf.* put the kibosh on, nip in the bud; stop, arrest, stay, bring to a standstill; annihilate, destroy, extinguish.

4. gasp, gag, suffocate, smother, be breathless.

stigma, *n.* mark of disgrace, slur, loss of reputation, disparagement, depreciation, defamation; blemish, blotch, smudge, smirch, smutch, taint; mark, spot, blot, blot on the escutcheon, demerit, stain; imputation, false accusation, calumniation, slander, *Law.* libel; shame, disgrace, dishonor, *Inf.* black eye.

stigmatize, *v.* **1.** disgrace, discredit, ruin [s.o.'s] reputation; spot, blot, stain, blemish, blotch, smudge, smirch, smutch, taint, spoil, sully, dirty; slur, disparage, depreciate, defame; charge, *Law.* impute, accuse falsely, calumniate, slander, *Law.* libel.

2. brand, tattoo; label, ticket, tag.

still, *adj.* **1.** motionless, unstirring, unmoving, inert, immovable, immobile, becalmed, stock-still, *Chiefly Literary.* stilly; stationary, stable, fixed, static;

stagnant, inactive, passive; idle, sedentary; quiescent, quiet, calm, halcyon, serene, tranquil, sedate, mild, placid; peaceful, pacific, peaceable, reposeful; unruffled, unagitated, undisturbed, untroubled; even, flat, smooth.

2. silent, noiseless, soundless, inaudible; mute, dumb, speechless, mum, voiceless.

3. subdued, hushed, muted, low; gentle, soft, softened; murmuring, murmured, whispering, whispered, susurrant; feeble, weak, faint, dim.

4. reposing, resting, at rest, slumbering; latent, dormant, dormient, hibernating, (*of land*) fallow; delayed, suspended, deferred, postponed, abeyant.

—*n.* **5.** stillness, silence, hush; calmness, calm, tranquillity, peacefulness, peace; quiet, quietude.

—*adv.* **6.** at this time, at that time, as previously, yet; up to this time, up to that time, as yet; to this day, even now; until now.

7. subsequently, even then, nevertheless, regardless; in addition, even, yet.

—*conj.* **8.** and yet, but yet, even so; for all that, in any event, in any case; however, nevertheless, notwithstanding.

9. still and all *U.S.* nonetheless, nevertheless, *Inf.* anyway.

—*v.* **10.** silence, shush, hush, quiet, *Chiefly Brit.* quieten; lull, calm, tranquilize; pacify, appease, dulcify, propitiate, reconcile, smooth, soothe, compose; play down, tone down, *Inf.* soft-pedal; soften, allay, mitigate; ease, assuage, mollify, palliate.

11. moderate, blunt, dull, deaden; temper, decrease, weaken, slacken, lessen, lighten, diminish, abate; settle, alleviate, relieve, slake, quench.

12. repress, suppress, subdue, inhibit, quell, quash, put down, damp, dampen; chasten, restrain, sober; stifle, gag, mute, muffle, smother, *Inf.* squelch; talk down, *Inf.* squash, *Inf.* shut up, interrupt, cut in, *Sl.* slap down; muzzle, throttle, choke, strangle; stop, arrest, curb, check, stay, cut off, cut short, prevent, forestall, preclude, put an end to; kill, slay, murder.

stilted, *adj.* pompous, inflated, bombastic, turgid, high-sounding, high-flown; overblown, swollen, tumid, pedantic; starched, *Inf.* stuffy, prim, priggish; formal, forced, labored, stiff, wooden; affected, mannered, feigned, put-on; stately, dignified, august, ceremonious.

stimulant, *n.* **1.** *Physiology.* excitant, quickener, *Med.* psychic energizer, anti-depressant; *Biochem.* epinephrine, *Biochem.* adrenaline, adrenin, *Chem., Pharm.* caffeine; amphetamine, amphetamine sulfate, *Sl.* white cross, *Sl.* black beauty; *Pharm., Trademark.* Benzedrine, *Sl.* bennie *or* benzie; *Pharm., Trademark.* Dexedrine, *Sl.* dexie, *Sl.* heart, *Sl.* football; *Pharm., Trademark.* Dexamyl, *Sl.* purple heart; *Pharm., Trademark.* Methedrine, *Sl.* meth, *Sl.* speed, *Sl.* up per, *Sl.* pep pill, *Sl.* crystal *or* crystal meth, *Sl.* businessman's trip; *Pharm.* amyl nitrate, cocaine, *Sl.* coke, *Sl.* C, *Sl.* snow, *Chiefly Brit. Sl.* charlie.

2. alcoholic beverage *or* liquor, drink, liquor, spirits, intoxicant, inebriant, the bottle, the cup, *Inf.* pick-me-up *or* pick up; tonic, cordial, *Inf.* bracer, *Med.* roborant; coffee, espresso, tea, cocoa.

3. stimulus, incentive, impetus, fillip, provocative, motive; goad, spur, prick, prod, poke, jog, jolt; impulse, urge, drive, push, itch; dictate, call; encouragement, abetment, provocation, egging on, putting up to; dare, taunt, gibe; temptation, enticement, allurement, beguilement, inveiglement, persuasion.

stimulate, *v.* **1.** incite, instigate, provoke, urge, goad, spur, prompt, prod, prick, poke, thrust, nettle, needle, egg on, put up to; foment, agitate, suscitate, actuate, excite, arouse, rouse, activate, stir up, hype up, work up, wind up, whip up, lash into a fury, inflame, fire, fire up, enkindle, kindle, fan, touch off.

2. animate, reanimate, whet, invigorate, motivate, *Inf.* spark, *Inf.* psych up, *Inf.* turn on; inspire, inspirit, electrify, galvanize, rally, revive, alert, vivify, bestir, awaken, waken, wake up; enliven, liven up, shake up, sting, jolt, jog.

3. encourage, abet, embolden, nerve, boost, build up, buck up, pluck up; induce, impel, compel, constrain, press, move, force, force along; hustle, drive, propel, hound, whip, lash, flog; persuade, influence, dispose, prevail upon, sway, ply, coax, wheedle; tempt, lure, inveigle, beguile.

stimulus, *n.* **1.** incentive, impetus, fillip, provocative, motive, whet, *Sl.* shot in the arm; goad, prick, prod, poke, spur, jog, jolt, lash, whip, sting; impulse, urge, drive, push, itch; dictate, call; incitement, inducement, instigation, excitement, provocation, motivation, oestrus; encouragement, abetment, egging on, putting up to; dare, taunt, gibe; enticement, temptation, allurement, beguilement, inveiglement, persuasion.

2. *Physiology.* excitant, quickener. See **stimulant** (*def.* **1**).

sting, *v.* **1.** prick, nettle, bite, nip, snip, pinch; prick, stick, stab, pierce, wound, envenom; smart, burn, chafe, grate, rasp, gall, irritate; gripe, grind, gnaw.

2. hurt, pain, injure, cut to the quick, excruciate, rack, wring; grieve, aggrieve, distress, afflict, harrow, anguish, agonize, torment, torture.

3. goad, prod, spur, prompt; push, drive, propel, motivate, move; incite, provoke, agitate, excite, arouse, rouse, whip up, work up, stir up, enflame, inflame, fire up, kindle, touch off; exasperate, exacerbate, ruffle, roil, aggravate.

4. *Slang.* cheat, overcharge, *Sl.* soak; gull, fleece, swindle, mulct, *Inf.* gyp.

—*n.* **5.** prick, prickle, bite, nip, pinch; injury, wound, cut, scratch, puncture, stab; sore, burn; smart, pain, hurt, tingling, tingle.

6. shock, blow, stroke; bane, curse, poison, venom, worm, canker, blight, scourge; affliction, torment, torture, agony, anguish, grievance, woe, distress; trial, tribulation, bitter cup *or* pill, cross, load, burden; bitterness, wormwood, gall and wormwood; rub, irritation, vexation, thorn in one's flesh *or* side.

7. goad, stimulus, stimulant, incentive, motive; spur, incitement, inducement, instigation, provocation, egging on.

stingy, *adj.* **1.** niggardly, miserly, parsimonious, carking, skinflinty; penurious, mean, tight, tight-fisted, close-fisted; cheap, *Sl.* chintzy, moneygrubbing, grasping, *Rare.* illiberal, cheeseparing; scrimping, penny-pinching, grudging, begrudging, ungenerous, stinting; thrifty, frugal, sparing, chary; economical, prudent, saving, penny-wise.

2. scanty, meager, skimpy, scrimpy, scant; meanly small, beggarly, paltry, poor, piddling, *Inf.* measly, mere; slight, slender, narrow, puny, very little; insufficient, inadequate, short, shy; insubstantial, nominal, minute, negligible.

stink, *v.* **1.** reek, smell, smell to high heaven, smell like a goat, assault the nostrils, *Inf.* knock out.

2. be in disrepute, be in disgrace, have a bad name, have one's name be mud, have a blot on one's escutcheon *or* record, lose caste *or* face.

—*n.* **3.** stench, fetor, malodor, rancidity, foul odor, strong *or* gamy smell, body odor, *Inf.* B.O.; halitosis, bad breath, mephitis, miasma, effluvium, fume, taint; fetidness, fetidity, malodorousness, smelliness, stinkiness; gaminess, rancidness, putrescence, putrescency, putridness, putridity, rottenness; rankness, noisomeness, foulness.

4. *Slang.* fuss, to-do, commotion, hubbub, brouhaha, uproar, turmoil, disturbance, upset; scandal, crisis.

stinking, *adj.* **1.** fetid, reeking, reeky, stenchful, smelly, foul-smelling, ill-smelling, strong-smelling, malodorous, stinking; noisome, mephitic, foul, rank, offensive, disgusting, nauseating; putrid, rancid, rotten, tainted, spoiled, strong, game, miasmal, miasmatic.

2. *Slang.* drunk, *Inf.* boozed, *Sl.* soused, *Sl.* plastered, *Sl.* smashed, *Sl.* bombed, *Sl.* wasted; in one's cups, intoxicated, inebriated.

3. *Slang.* very rich, wealthy, flush, *Sl.* loaded, made of money, rolling in riches *or* dough.

4. contemptible, despicable, sorry, wretched; disgusting, vile, mean, base, low, obnoxious.

stint, *v.* **1.** limit, set limits to, restrict, circumscribe, confine; restrain, constrain, bind, inhibit; define, fix, set; prohibit, proscribe.

2. scrimp, economize, conserve, save, be sparing *or* frugal; dole, pinch, cramp, straiten, cut down on, curb; skimp, pinch pennies, tighten the purse strings, tighten one's belt, cut corners; be penurious, be parsimonious, be stingy *or* cheap, *Inf.* pinch a penny till it squeaks.

—n. **3.** limitation, restriction, constraint, restraint, check, curb, control; condition, qualification, reservation, exception.

4. allotment, lot, portion, part, piece, piece of the pie, helping, measure, dose; share, ration, quota, allowance, sum, pittance.

5. chore, task, job, work; routine, exercise, turn; assignment, duty, obligation, charge, care, responsibility.

stipend, *n.* **1.** salary, pay, earnings, wages, hire; remuneration, recompense, remittance, reward, emolument.

2. allowance, honorarium, provision, viaticum, allotment, quarterage, subvention; grant, fellowship, scholarship, assistantship, subsidy, bounty; pension, annuity, *Law.* alimony, payment, support, maintenance.

stipple, *v.* dot, dab, dapple, paint, tattoo; spot, maculate, bespot, mottle, blotch, splotch; daub, bedaub, fleck, speck; spatter, speckle, bespeckle, freckle, sprinkle, spangle.

stipulate, *v.* **1.** specify, determine, fix, designate, indicate; stickle for, contend for, insist upon, make a point of, condition, *Inf.* have a catch; qualify, set conditions, attach a condition, limit, set terms; require, demand, warrant, render, provide.

2. agree to, bargain for, contract, compact, covenant; promise, pledge, guarantee, insure, assure, certify; arrange, underwrite, give, settle, engage.

stipulation, *n.* condition, prerequisite, essential, specification, given, *Fr. donnée;* demand, requirement, must, *Latin. sine qua non;* obligation, agreement, article, arrangement, convention; promise, term, part of the bargain, *Inf.* string, *Inf.* catch, fine print; provision, clause, proviso, qualification, contingency.

stir, *v.* **1.** mix, commix, intermix, scramble; blend, mingle, commingle, intermingle; fuse, merge, amalgamate; beat, whip, churn.

2. move, budge, act; trouble oneself, move an inch, exert oneself, make an effort, lift a finger; shift, change positions, roll, go, move over, slide, pass.

3. flutter, flicker, jiggle, twitch, itch; rustle, agitate, disturb, perturb, upset, trouble; vibrate, palpitate, pulsate, throb, go pit-a-pat; shake, jog, joggle, quiver, quaver, quake; shudder, tremble, dance.

4. bestir, move about, mill about, be up and about, be up and doing; bustle, hustle, flit, flutter, step lively, shake a leg; scramble, whirl, rush, buzz about, dart to and fro; push, *Sl.* get down to it, *Inf.* go all out, *Inf.* get moving, *Sl.* get a move on.

5. *Usu.* **stir up** rouse, awaken, waken, wake up, shake up; revive, resuscitate, rekindle, enliven, vitalize, invigorate.

6. *Usu.* **stir up** incite, instigate, prompt, actuate, motivate; arouse, foment, provoke, stimulate, start, encourage; goad, spur, prick, whip, lash, urge, nag; drive, egg on, forward, impel, propel, poke.

7. affect, excite, quicken, whet, infect, infuse, thrill; animate, galvanize, electrify, start, energize; inspire, inspirit, touch, move; enflame, enthuse, pique, exhilarate; jolt, boost, jostle, vivify; kindle, startle, fan; disquiet, discompose; work up, impassion, impress.

—n. **8.** movement, hustle, activity, action, motion, militancy; bustle, perturbation, flurry, agitation, disturbance; tremble, tremor, flutter, flicker; quiver, quaver, shake, shudder, quake; pulsation, palpitation, throb, twitch.

9. excitement, commotion, disorder, ado, confusion, to-do; fuss, pother, fidget, bother; hurly-burly, hubbub, bubble, *Inf.* flap, hullabaloo, stew, fluster; outburst, uproar, upheaval, convulsion, tumult, turbulence, turmoil, storm; ferment, furor, ebullition, fever, fervor, rush, flush, frenzy.

10. rustle, susurration, susurrus, breath; murmur, sigh, whisper, hush, rush; hum, buzz, whizz, sibilation.

11. impulse, sensation, feeling, impression; thrill, awakening, excitation, stimulation, upsurge, passion; flutter, twitter, palpitation, titillation, tingle, throb.

stirring, *adj.* **1.** rousing, moving, stimulating, provocative; gripping, telling, dramatic, melodramatic, forceful, eloquent; exciting, thrilling, heady, breathtaking, *Sl.* mind-blowing, intoxicating, exhilarating; electric, galvanic, energizing, charged; impassioned, glowing, fiery, burning, passionate; impressive, imposing, awe-inspiring, inspiring; majestic, sublime, grand, august, overwhelming, overpowering.

2. moving, active, busy, eventful; bustling, lively, excited, spirited, ebullient, effervescent; animated, sprightly, brisk, alacritous, spry; *Inf.* peppy, *Inf.* snappy, perky, energetic, vivacious; astir, afoot, alive, full of pep, full of go; full of vim, vigor, and vitality.

stitch, *n.* **1.** tuck, *Surg.* suture; loop, piece of thread *or* floss *or* yarn.

2. embroidery *or* crewel stitch, cross-stitch, French knot; knitting *or* crochet stitch, purl, stockinet; pattern, design, decoration, ornamentation, adornment.

3. thread, strip, shred, tatter, scrap, snatch, remnant; piece, article, any clothing *or* clothes; bit, speck, atom, iota, whit, jot, tittle, particle; trace, hint, speck, *Inf.* smidgen, *Inf.* smitch; any, no, zero; anything, nothing, *Sl.* zilch.

4. pang, twinge, pain, sharp pain, stabbing pain, shooting pain; twitch, spasm, *Pathol.* tic douloureux, *Pathol.* neuralgia; crick, kink, pinch.

—v. **5.** sew, suture, loop up, baste, seam, sew together, machine stitch; take a tuck in, tuck, smock, gather, pleat; make, run up, *Inf.* whip up; turn up, hem, take in, alter, fit, tailor; sew up, mend, repair, fix; embroider, cross-stitch, do crewel *or* crewelwork, knit, purl, crochet, tat, do needlework *or* needlepoint; decorate, put a design on, ornament, adorn.

6. secure, close up, close; fasten, hook, attach, clasp; link, join, couple, connect; staple, rivet, clip, pin, tack.

stock, *n.* **1.** supply, store, stockpile, inventory; quantity, fund, lot, bunch, heap, pile, mass, stack, load, *Chiefly U.S. Dial.* grist; assortment, range, selection, variety; collection, accumulation, amassment, aggregate, *Obs.* commodity; reserve, reservoir, backlog, nest egg, hoard; treasure, mine, quarry, well;

storeroom, stockroom, storehouse, warehouse, magazine, pantry, larder, repository, cache.

2. provisions, supplies, stores, rations, goods, dry goods, provender; groceries, produce, food, foodstuff, edibles, eatables, comestibles, viands, victuals, *Inf.* vittles, bread and butter; forage, fodder, feed, grain, hay, silage, ensilage; wares, commodities, products, items, articles, things; stock in trade, merchandise, vendibles, salables, assets, capital, investment.

3. livestock, animals, domestic *or* farm animals; cattle, cows, neat, *Archaic.* kine; horses, sheep, goats, pigs, chickens.

4. trunk, treetrunk, base of a tree, bottom, foundation; stalk, stem, caudex, culm, *Brit.* haulm, cane, calamus, quill, *Bot.* caulis, *Bot.* caulicle, *Bot.* axis; leafstalk, *Bot.* stipe, *Bot.* petiole, *Bot.* pedicle, *Bot.* pedicel, *Both Bot., Zool.* peduncle, footstalk, *Both Bot.* funicle, funiculus, *Bot.* gynophore.

5. species, breed, genus, subgenus, class, *Biol.* phylum; denomination, name, classification, category, subcategory, division, subdivision, section, branch; type, kind, sort, genre, *Both Genetics.* genotype, phenotype; brand, make, cast, cut, mold, form, style, manner; grain, feather, tone, color, stripe.

6. race, people, *Both Sociol.* ethnic group, ethnos; dynasty, house, family, clan, sept, relatives, flesh and blood, kind, *Anthropol.* gens; lineage, line of descent, descent, genealogy, pedigree, bloodline, family, ancestry, parentage, heritage, background, extraction.

7. progenitor, primogenitor, forefather, ancestor, forebear, *Archaic.* predecessor; patriarch, father, procreator, begettor; founder, originator, source; forerunner, precursor, foregoer, antecedent; prototype, archetype, first form, original; model, pattern, paradigm, exemplar, *Television.* pilot.

8. haft, hilt, helve, lug, withe, handle, grip, hold, grasp, command, pull; spindle, swivel, pivot; shaft, shank, butt, end; frame, framework, skeleton, body, chassis, hull, shell, main *or* principal part, bulk, mass, majority, most.

9. stump, tree stump, log; stub, (*of a tail*) dock, wooden leg, *Inf.* peg, artificial limb, prosthesis.

10. blockhead, numskull, bonehead, knucklehead, lunkhead, *Inf.* woodenhead; dunce, dope, thickhead, *Inf.* stupid, *Sl.* dumbbell, *Inf.* dummy; lout, clod, oaf, boor, *Inf.* lummox, looby, *Sl.* meathead, *Sl.* klutz; dullard, dolt, dunderhead, ignoramus, *Inf.* chump; lamebrain, half-wit, lightweight, idiot, moron, imbecile, cretin, retardate, *Sl.* retard; fool, tomfool, nincompoop, ninny, simpleton, *Sl.* sap, *Sl.* dingbat, *Sl.* ding-a-ling, *Sl.* meatball, *Sl.* boob, *Sl.* booby, *Sl.* noodle, *Sl.* nudnick, *Sl.* blubberhead.

11. dummy, mannequin, model, effigy; carcass, corpse, cadaver, dead body, *Sl.* stiff; thing, *Sl.* block of wood, *Sl.* piece of furniture, *Sl.* dead wood, *Both. Theat.* property, prop.

12. upright, column, pillar, post, standard, pier, caryatid, telamon, atlas, verticle, support, *Chiefly Dial.* stob, *Both Naut.* mast, spar; spine, backbone, chine; pole, spoke, rod, pin, spindle; pile, pylon, spike, stake; support, footing, base.

13. raw material, resource, stuff; material, fabric, cloth, substance; *Both Printing, Publishing.* paper, newsprint.

14. *Cookery.* broth, bouillon, consommé, soup; liquid, juice, gravy, blood; concentrate, essence, heart, quintessence; foundation, base, basic *or* main ingredient.

15. shoot, offshoot, *Bot.* rhizome, *Bot.* rootstalk, *Bot.* rootstock, *Bot.* rootlet; runner, creeper, *Bot.* stolen, *Bot.* sarmentum, *Bot.* flagellum.

16. collar, collaret, neckcloth, neckpiece, dickey, gorget, wimple; ruff, rabato, ruche, bertha, boa; neckerchief, kerchief, scarf, ascot, cravat, tie, bowtie; necklace, choker, neckband, ribbon.

—*adj.* **17.** staple, basic, fundamental, regular, regularly *or* always in stock *or* in supply *or* on hand, permanent, easy to find; essential, necessary, needed, required, indispensable, important, vital, sustenative; standard, classic, recognized, established, acknowledged, accepted, approved, official, authoritative; customary, consuetudinary, normal, usual, traditional, conventional, expected, familiar; most important, primary, prime, principal, main, chief, leading, foremost, biggest; most popular, highly requested, in demand.

18. common, ordinary, average, *Inf.* plain old, garden-variety, *Inf.* dime-a-dozen, run-of-the-mill, run-of-the-mine, pedestrian; commonplace, everyday, household, G.I.; oft-repeated, oft-met, often heard, *Inf.* same old; banal, hackneyed, trite, stale, overused, overworked, worn out, old, tired.

—*v.* **19.** supply, provision, ration, provender, fill up; equip, furnish, outfit, gear, accouter, prepare, ready, get ready, make ready; handle, keep, provide, offer, deal in, trade, sell, market; store, store up, lay in, stock up on, accumulate, amass, heap up, pile up, stack up, gather, collect, buy up; save, reserve, put away, *Inf.* salt away, retain, hold, hoard; cache, stow away, *Sl.* stash; provide for a rainy day, build a nest egg, feather one's nest; put up, can, salt down, preserve, conserve; refrigerate, put on ice, bottle, jar, *Brit.* tin.

stocking, *n.* *Often* **stockings** hose, hosiery, nylons, pantyhose, fishnets, opaques, *Archaic.* stock; tights, leotards, leg warmers, leggings, gaiters, puttees, gambodos; sock, Argyle, footie, *Trademark.* Ped, anklet, knee sock, knee highs, over-the-calf hose, thigh highs; slipper sock, mukluk, slipper, footwear.

stock-still, *adj.* **1.** motionless, inert, unmoving, still, *Chiefly Literary.* stilly; stationary, fixed, immobile, immovable, static.

2. inactive, idle, passive, dormant, dormient, latent; unstirring, stagnant, becalmed; inanimate, lifeless, dead.

stocky, *adj.* heavy-set, thick-set, thick, stodgy; solid, stout, sturdy, burly, beefy, *Scot. and North Eng.* stiff, *Inf.* chunky; squat, stubby, *Inf.* stumpy.

stodgy, *adj.* **1.** dull, dull as dishwater, uninteresting, boring, boresome, tedious, tiresome, wearisome, dreary, dry, dry-as-dust, *Sl.* dead, *Sl.* deadly; flat, bland, insipid, vapid, jejune, *Sl.* for the birds, *Sl.* nothing, *Sl.* blah; ponderous, elephantine; stiff, wooden; prosaic, commonplace, humdrum, monotonous, uneventful.

2. (*all of food*) heavy, dense, thick, indigestible.

3. stocky. See **stocky**.

4. old-fashioned, old-fogyish, stuffy, behind the times, *Inf.* fuddy-duddy, *Sl.* out of it.

5. awkward, clumsy, cloddish, clodhopping, loutish, oafish, lumpish, lumpen; graceless, inelegant, like a bull in a china shop.

stoical, *adj.* impassive, dispassionate, passionless, unimpassioned, stolid, stoic; indifferent, apathetic, uninterested; cool, self-disciplined, self-possessed, self-controlled; imperturbable, inexcitable, unflappable; enduring, long-suffering, forbearing, patient, patient as Job.

stoicism, *n.* self-control, self-discipline; dispassion, inexcitability, imperturbability, unflappability; strength, fortitude, endurance, sufferance; patience, forbearance, longanimity, long-suffering, *Archaic.* long-sufferance.

stolid, *adj.* unemotional, impassive, dispassionate,

unimpassioned, stoical, stoic; indifferent, disinterested, apathetic; dull, obtuse, thick, thick-witted, dense.

stomach, *n.* **1.** belly, abdomen, *Inf.* tummy, gut, *Sl.* breadbasket, *Brit. Inf.* little Mary, *Scot. and North Eng.* wame; paunch, potbelly, *Inf.* bay window, *Inf.* corporation, *Sl.* pot, *Sl.* beerbelly, *Sl.* spare tire.

2. colonic cavity, intestinal cavity, visceral cavity, *Anat., Zool.* venter, ventral region, ventricle, ventricular cavity, *Anat.* epigastrium; pouch, (*of birds*) gizzard, (*of birds*) crop, craw, maw, ingluvies, (*of birds*) proventriculus, (*both of ruminating animals*) first stomach, rumen; intestines, bowels, colons, (*of swine*) chitterlings; innards, inwards, insides, vitals, viscera, (*of animals*) entrails, *Inf.* gizzard, *Sl.* guts.

3. appetite, appetence, appetency, hunger, thirst, craving, gluttony, *Pathol.* bulimia; relish, gusto, zest, eagerness, hankering, yearning, longing; lust, *Sl.* letch.

4. desire, liking, fondness, weakness, fancy, *Inf.* mind, pleasure, preference; tendency, leaning, bent, inclination, favoritism, bias; partiality, predilection, disposition, predisposition, proclivity, propensity.

—v. **5.** endure, tolerate, bear, bear with, *Archaic.* forbear, suffer, abide, *Inf.* take, *Inf.* stand, *Inf.* swallow, put up with, pocket; be content with, reconcile oneself to, resign oneself to.

6. permit, allow, allow for, make allowance for, be lenient toward, admit, countenance.

7. forgive, pardon, excuse, condone, let pass; overlook, blink at, wink at, close the eyes to, shut the eyes to; ignore, disregard, pass over.

stone, *n.* **1.** pebble, lapillus, rock, boulder; flint, slate, granite, adamant; crag, tor; gravel, lava, scoria; shale, bluestone, sandstone.

2. slab, flagstone, paving stone, cobblestone, building stone, cornerstone; monolith, obelisk.

3. precious stone, gem, jewel, *Sl.* rock, *Sl.* ice, bijou, brilliant, birthstone.

4. pit, seed, kernel, nut, *Bot.* endocarp, pip.

5. gravestone, tombstone, headstone, footstone; marker, tablet, memorial stone, monument, stela, cenotaph.

6. grindstone, whetstone, millstone, hone.

—v. **7.** lapidate, pelt, stone to death.

8. sharpen, whet, polish, hone, smooth, scour, grind, abrade, grate.

stony, *adj.* **1.** rocky, rock-strewn, rock-ribbed, pebbly, *Brit.* shingly, gravelly, gritty, cobbled; rough, jagged, bumpy.

2. lithic, hard, adamantine, adamant, granite, marble, rock-hard; petrified, ossified, hardened; craggy, flinty, impervious, impenetrable.

3. unfeeling, uncaring, bloodless, iron-hearted, unsympathetic; callous, indurate, insensible, insensitive; indifferent, aloof, dispassionate, uninvolved, haughty, austere; hard-boiled, unsentimental, tough, heartless, unmoved, unstirred; cold-hearted, cold, cool, icy, frigid; merciless, pitiless, ruthless, unrelenting, unforgiving; cruel, severe, stern, harsh, cold-blooded, unkind, hard-hearted; obdurate, obstinate, stubborn, unyielding, unbending, inflexible, rigid, steely; iron-jawed, persevering, determined.

4. motionless, unmoving, calm, unflickering, unwavering, still; rigid, fixed, staring, staring-down, glaring; deadpan, poker-faced, unreadable, indecipherable, unknowable, sphinxlike, sphingine, enigmatic, puzzling; expressionless, vacant, empty, blank, without depth *or* feeling; withering, scathing, searing.

5. petrifying stupefying, paralyzing, unnerving, numbing, dumfounding, overwhelming; bloodcurdling, blood-chilling, hair-raising, shivery; terrifying, frightful, frightening, scary, horrible, nightmarish; amazing, astounding, astonishing, stunning.

stool, *n.* **1.** footstool, hassock, ottoman, taboret; stepstool, folding stool, campstool, milking stool; seat, bench, cricket; kneeler, prie-dieu, faldstool.

2. decoy, bait, lure, come-on, trick; trap, snare, springe.

3. toilet, commode; privy, cloaca, latrine, outhouse, backhouse; bathroom, washroom, lavatory, *Brit.* water closet.

4. feces, fecal matter, feculence, excrement, excreta, bowel movement; dung, ordure, manure, *Obs.* stercoration.

5. window sill *or* ledge, apron, casement.

stoop¹, *v.* **1.** bend, lean, crook; bow, curtsy, salaam, kowtow, genuflect; crouch, squat, hunker, hunch, *Sl.* scrooch down, kneel; slouch, slump, droop, nod, flag, sag, sink; duck, bob, dip, dive.

2. condescend, lower *or* humble oneself, deign; assent, consent, submit, yield, give in, acquiesce, concede.

—n. **3.** slouch, slump, droop, sag; *Vet. Pathol.* swayback; bow, curtsy, salaam, genuflection, kowtow, cowering; crouch, squat; duck, bob, dip.

4. condescension, deigning, debasement, abasement, comedown; humbling, humility, self-deprecation, overmodesty, self-abnegation; yielding, submission, acquiescence.

stoop², *n.* porch, portico, *Hawaiian. lanai,* veranda, *Chiefly New Eng. and Southern U.S.* piazza, front *or* back step *or* steps; patio, terrace, *Fr. terrasse.*

stop, *v.* **1.** discontinue, quit, cease from, leave off, *Inf.* drop, abandon; desist from, forbear, *Inf.* cut out, *Sl.* can, *Sl.* cheese, *Brit. Sl.* nark it; withdraw from, have done with; (*all of work*) *Inf.* call it quits, call it a day, shut up shop, *Inf.* knock off; finish, complete, culminate, consummate.

2. pause, desist, cease, halt, quit, *Sl.* hold the phone, *Archaic.* surcease; slow down, hold one's horses, come to a standstill, (*of a car*) pull up *or* over, (*of a ship*) lie to; come to an end, conclude, draw to a close, lapse, break off, wind up, run out, run its course; rest, wait, linger, tarry, idle.

3. terminate, close, end, stay, put an end to; lay to rest, make an end of; silence, quiet, still; quell, squelch, subdue, put down, squash, scotch; lower the boom, crack down on, quash, put the kibosh on; arrest, check, cut short, interrupt, nip in the bud, throttle, *Archaic.* stanch; defeat, discomfit, rout, smash, crush, destroy, overpower, master.

4. intercept, cut off, choke off, shut off; withhold, refuse, deny; retain, hold back.

5. restrain, repress, suppress, curb, rein in, constrain; hamper, impede, thwart, foil, frustrate, checkmate, deadlock; hinder, delay, retard, detain, prevent, *Inf.* tie up; deter, stall, postpone.

6. block, bar, obstruct, clog, barricade, blockade, occlude; stifle, muzzle, choke, stem; close, stuff, cram, ram, dam, oppilate; caulk, seal, plug, bung, cork.

7. stop by a. visit, pay a visit, pay a call, stop in *or* over, drop in *or* over. **b.** remain, lodge, sojourn, put up at, lay over, stop off, *Inf.* stay *or* sleep over.

—n. **8.** cessation, arrest, end, stay, standstill, halt, desistance, termination, abruption; intermission, interlude, interval, abeyance, break, *Inf.* letup; interruption, disruption, discontinuance, discontinuation, discontinuity; delay, hold back.

9. sojourn, stay, visit; stop-off, stopover, layover; rest, respite, vacation, *Brit.* holiday.

10. station, depot, terminal, terminus, station house; rest area, roadstop, truck stop, *Brit.* layover.

11. closing up, closure, shutting off, *U.S. Parl. Proc.* cloture; blocking, filling up, stoppage, oppilation, blockage, occlusion, *Pathol.* embolism; obstruction, *Pathol.* infarction.

12. barricade, obstacle, impediment, hindrance, barrier, ban, block, *Law.* estoppel; ban, prohibition, proscription, disallowance, embargo, injunction, enjoining, curb, crackdown; prevention, debarment, preclusion; repression, suppression, quashing, squelch, *Inf.* kibosh; trammel, restraint, constraint, bridle, shackle, restriction; dam, snag, catch.

13. plug, stopper, stopple, cork, bung, tampion; *Med.* obstruent; peg, spill, spile, *Dentistry.* dowel; tap, spigot, cock, stopcock, faucet, valve; governor; pledget, *Surg.* tent, packing, wadding, stuffing, *Med.* tampon; *Engraving.* dossil.

stopcock, *n.* tap, spigot, cock, petcock; faucet, valve.

stopgap, *n.* **1.** makeshift, temporary, substitute, fill-in; alternate, alternative, replacement; improvisation, contrivance, make-do arrangement; last resort, *Fr. pis aller.*

—adj. **2.** temporary, makeshift, juryrigged, provisional, tentative, stand-by; emergency, improvised, contrived, unrehearsed, unprepared, unplanned; ersatz, artificial, impermanent; haphazard, thrown-together.

stopover, *n.* brief stop, short visit, layover. See **stop** (*def.* 9).

stoppage, *n.* **1.** arrest, halt, standstill; termination, ending, completion, finish, conclusion, close, desinence; discontinuance, ceasing, stay, end, quitting, desisting, desistance.

2. intermission, pause, cease, rest, break, *Inf.* breather, lull, respite, *Inf.* letup, recess, leaving off; suspension, interruption, discontinuation, abeyance, remission; (*usu. of work*) slowdown, layoff, job action, shutdown.

3. blockage, hindrance, obstruction, obstacle, impediment, barrier; snarl, snag, *Inf.* tie-up; prevention, debarment, preclusion; repression, suppression, check.

storage, *n.* **1.** stowage, storage space *or* room; space, area, accommodation, content; capacity, volume, extent.

2. storehouse, storeroom, warehouse. See **storehouse.**

store, *n.* **1.** shop, market, mart, establishment; department store, supermarket, outlet, emporium; co-op, thrift shop; mom and pop store, five-and-ten; drug store, pharmacy, apothecary; liquor store, package store, *Brit.* off-license, *U.S. Mil.* Class Six.

2. booth, counter, stall; concession, franchise, business.

3. accumulation, heap, pile, mass, cumulation; hoard, stock, stockpile, supply, fund; treasure, holdings, savings, *Inf.* loot; commodities, staples, wares, goods, provision; assets, inventory, stock in trade; reserve, capital, backlog, nest egg; effects, assortment; cache, deposit, reservoir.

4. abundance, bounty, volume, plenty; quantity, profusion, *Inf.* lots, *Inf.* raft; numbers, scores, multiplicity, richness, plenitude; superfluity, plethora.

5. in store a. in readiness, in reserve, kept back. **b.** about to happen, coming, at hand, imminent; approaching, impending, destined.

6. set *or* **lay store by** have a high regard for, value, esteem, prize, appreciate, credit; count on, depend on, rely on; trust in, have faith in, pin one's faith on, swear by, bank on.

—v. **7.** accumulate, heap up, pile, pile up, roll up, stack up; collect, gather, assemble, mass, aggregate, bring together; amass, cumulate, agglomerate.

8. supply, provision, garner, store up, stock up, lay by, lay up, lay in, *Inf.* stash away, reserve, put aside, set aside; save up, save; hoard, squirrel away, load up, stow away; deposit, keep, hold, preserve; conserve, retain, husband; cache, warehouse; feather one's nest, *Inf.* salt down *or* away.

9. keep, keep well, hold, hold up, *Inf.* last forever.

storehouse, *n.* warehouse, depository, depot, repository; granary, silo, elevator, barn, garner; storeroom, loft, attic, cellar, stockroom; closet, cabinet, locker; safe, crib, vault, bunker; store, reservoir; cache, bank, coffer, treasury; hold; armory, arsenal, magazine.

storied[1], *adj.* celebrated, honored, sung; famed, famous, renowned, well-known, remembered; traditional, legendary, mythical, fabled; chronicled, epic, Homeric, historical, historied.

storied[2], *adj.* leveled, layered, floored, tiered.

storm, *n.* **1.** tempest, squall, barat, williwaw; rainstorm, cloudburst, deluge, downpour, torrent, *Chiefly Oklahoma and Texas.* gully washer; rainfall shower, sun shower, thundershower, thunderstorm, electrical storm, thundersquall, hailstorm; windstorm, gale, gust, blast, blow, big blow, wind, heavy winds, monsoon, levanter; hurricane, typhoon, tornado, whirlwind, *U.S.* twister, cyclone, tropical *or* extratropical cyclone, *Philippines.* baguio, *Central America.* cordonazo, *Australia.* willy-willy; duststorm, duster, sirocco, harmattan, sandstorm, simoom, samiel; blizzard, northeaster, snowstorm, snow squall, snow flurry, snow, snowfall.

2. assault, attack, offensive, rush, onslaught, onset; raid, foray, sortie, sally; invasion, aggression, incursion, escalade; siege, besiegement, besetment, investment; blitz, blitzkrieg, storming, *Obs.* brunt; bombardment, strafe, air raid.

3. discharge, cannonade, *Navy.* broadside, volley, salvo, fusillade, *Both Mil.* barrage, enfilade; spray, shower, rain, deluge.

4. violent disturbance, disruption, disorder, outbreak, breach of the peace; tumult, turmoil, turbulence, hurly-burly, upheaval; unrest, disquiet, excitement, commotion, imbroglio, confusion, chaos, furor, agitation; bustle, stir, *Inf.* to-do, bother, pother, fuss, fuss and feathers, *Sl.* flap, *Inf.* stew, *Sl.* hoo-ha, trouble; fight, fisticuffs, scuffle, tussle, *Inf.* set-to, *Inf.* scrap; combat, battle, skirmish, fray, clash, struggle, conflict, embroilment; broil, brawl, donnybrook, free-for-all, melee; riot, demonstration, manifestation, protest, protest march, sit-in, strike, picketing; rebellion, insurrection, insubordination, mutiny, revolt, uprising, revolution, sedition, insurgency.

5. outburst, burst, eruption, explosion; fit, tantrum *or* temper tantrum; outpour, outpouring, effusion, gush.

6. storm in a teacup tempest in a teapot, much ado about nothing, mountain out of a molehill.

—v. **7.** squall, rage, blow, bluster, gust, howl, roar; rain, shower, pour, rain cats and dogs, come down in buckets, rain pitchforks; snow, hail, sleet, thunder, thunder and lightning.

8. rage, rant, rave, rant and rave, roar, bellow, thunder; explode, *Sl.* blow up, throw a fit *or* tantrum, *Inf.* fly off the handle, *Sl.* blow one's top *or* stack, lose one's temper, fly into a passion; *Sl.* raise hell, *Sl.* raise the roof, *Inf.* carry on, protest, object, complain angrily; seethe, sizzle, smolder, boil, stew, simmer, fume.

9. attack, assault, raid, charge, rush, sally *or* sally forth, sortie, invade; set upon, *Inf.* go at, descend upon, fall upon; assail, beset, besiege, siege, beleaguer; blitz, blitzkrieg, bombard, strafe, fusillade, broadside, *Mil.* enfilade; fire on, open fire on, pelt, pepper, barrage.

10. rush angrily *or* headlong, charge, tear, stamp, *Inf.* stomp, stalk, stride, flounce.

stormy, *adj.* **1.** tempestuous, violent, wild, procellous, turbulent, squally; windy, gusty, blustery, blusterous, howling, roaring, raging; rainy, damp, raw, sleety, snowy, icy, cold; bad, foul, inclement; bleak, gray, overcast, threatening.

2. violent, fierce, intense, impassioned, inflamed, fiery, strong, vehement; loud, noisy, boisterous, raving, ranting; angry, irate, wrathful, furious, mad, boiling, raging; excited, agitated, wrought up, worked up, frantic, frenzied, frenetic, feverish, beside oneself, out of control.

story[1], *n.* **1.** narration, tale, account, recital, chronicle, history; fable, myth, fairy tale, epic, saga, *Archaic.* gest; parable, allegory, apologue; anecdote, incident, joke, *Inf.* yarn, tall tale, *Sl.* fish *or* war story, *Sl.* megillah; fiction, fictitious tale.

2. narrative, novel, romance, novella, novelette, short story; drama, play, teleplay, script, episode; adventure story, mystery story, *Inf.* mystery, detective story, *Inf.* whodunit, thriller, tale of suspense; science fiction, *Sl.* sci-fi, speculative fiction; horse opera, *Inf.* Western, soap opera, dime novel.

3. story line, plot, plot development; events, episodes, series of incidents.

4. statement, allegation; rumor, gossip, scandal, hearsay.

5. *Informal.* lie, fib, falsehood; alibi, excuse.

6. report, news, news article *or* item, piece, exposé, copy; scoop, *Both Journalism.* exclusive, beat; dispatch, aviso; word, information, intelligence, tidings.

7. memoirs, biography, *Inf.* bio, autobiography, life; experiences, confessions, fortunes, adventures.

story[2], *n.* floor, level, tier, stage, deck, stratum; *It.* piano nobile, mezzanine, *Archit.* entresol.

storyteller, *n.* **1.** taleteller, teller of tales, *Inf.* yarnspinner *or* spinner of yarns, fabler, fabulist; narrator, relator, recounter, reporter; describer, delineator, outliner; author, novelist, writer, romancer, historian, biographer; anecdotist, raconteur.

2. *Informal.* fibber, liar, fabricator, prevaricator, falsifier, *Psychiatry.* mythomaniac.

stout, *adj.* **1.** thick, thickset. heavy, heavy-set, stocky; fat, obese, corpulent, overweight, portly, pursy, *Scot.* fodgel; fleshy, filled-out, well-fed, bouncing; ample, substantial, full, big, large; bulky, hulky, hulking.

2. beefy, brawny, burly, husky, sturdy, well-built, herculean, strapping, *Brit. Inf.* chopping; muscular, hefty, able-bodied, rugged, athletic, solid, seasoned; hardy, manly, virile, masculine; tough, powerful, mighty, *Literary.* puissant.

3. bold, brave, unafraid, fearless. See **stout-hearted** (*def.* **1**).

4. determined, strong-willed, resolute, firm. See **stout-hearted** (*def.* **2**).

5. loyal, faithful, devoted, dedicated, staunch; patient, plodding, sedulous, assiduous, untiring, unflagging, unfaltering; durable, enduring, lasting.

6. healthy, fit, sound; vigorous, staminal, robust, lusty; youthful, fresh.

—*n.* **7.** ale, malt liquor, porter, porter's ale, brew.

stout-hearted, *adj.* **1.** brave, courageous, valiant, valorous, heroic, heroical, hero-like, lion-hearted, ironhearted, great-hearted; intrepid, fearless, dauntless, dreadless, aweless, nervy, *Sl.* gutsy, unafraid, unblenching, unblenched, undaunted, unalarmed, undismayed, unappalled; bold, bold-spirited, high-spirited, daring, dashing, adventurous; audacious, reckless.

2. firm, resolute, resolved, determined, staunch, steadfast, stalwart, *Archaic.* stalworth, doughty, sturdy, hardy; indomitable, redoubtable, invincible, unconquerable, unyielding, unbending, unbowing, unshrinking, unfaltering, unhesitating, unswerving, unwavering, undeviating; mettlesome, plucky, gritty, game, red-blooded, spirited, *Inf.* spunky.

stove, *n.* range, oven, microwave oven, toaster oven; kiln, furnace, incinerator, reverberatory, forge, fireplace; heater, electric heater, gas heater, infrared heater; heated chamber *or* box, firebox.

stow, *v.* **1.** pack, stuff, crowd, cram, tuck, wedge; reposit, deposit, warehouse, garner; store, hoard, save, *Inf.* salt away *or* down; squirrel away, load up, save up, feather one's nest; stock up, lay by, lay up, lay in.

2. (*all of a place or receptacle*) contain, hold, receive, take in, admit, carry, seat; accommodate, have capacity for, be capable of holding.

3. *Often* **stow away** hide, conceal, secrete, ensconce, closet, cache, bury, *Sl.* stash.

straddle, *v.* **1.** bestride, bestraddle, get astride of, stand *or* sit astride; sit *or* stand with legs apart.

2. *Informal.* refrain from committing oneself, be noncommittal, waffle, hedge, sit on the fence; be vague *or* indefinite *or* ambiguous, equivocate, *Inf.* talk out of both sides of one's mouth, doubletalk, skirt the issue, fence, hem and haw, beat around the bush.

strafe, *v.* **1.** bombard, bomb, *Brit. Sl.* prang, shell, torpedo, *Mil.* barrage, fusillade, blitz, blitzkrieg; shoot, fire on, open fire on, pepper, cannonade.

2. *Slang.* **a.** punish, penalize, retaliate, settle *or* square accounts with, discipline. **b.** reprimand, scold, censure, admonish, reproach, upbraid.

straggle, *v.* **1.** stray, wander off, digress, deviate; detour, go round about.

2. ramble, wander, wander around, meander; amble, amble about, gad, gad about, jaunt; nomadize, peregrinate, flit, traipse; drift, mosey, shuffle, stumble *or* limp *or* hobble along; range, rove, prowl, skip around; follow the wild goose, wander from pillar to post, see the country.

straggly, *adj.* **1.** straggling, straying, irregular, uneven, erratic, fitful; unsystematic, unmethodical, circuitous, indirect, zigzagging, zigzag.

2. rambling, wandering, traveling, roving, itinerant, peripatetic, migratory; vagrant, nomadic; wayfaring, perambulatory, drifting, aimless, undirected, helter-skelter.

straight, *adj.* **1.** direct, uncurved, undeviating, unswerving, unbent, unbowed; linear, lineal, in a line; straightaway, straightforward, straight-lined, straight as an arrow, dead straight.

2. level, even, flat, smooth, horizontal; perfect, true, right, just right, *Inf.* O.K., *Inf.* all right, *Brit. Sl.* bang on.

3. frank, candid. See **straightforward** (*def.* **3**).

4. upright, upstanding, honest, honorable, aboveboard; virtuous, moral, righteous, right-minded; law-abiding, straight-arrow, conventional, conformist, conservative, *Inf.* square. See also **straightforward** (*defs.* **5, 6**).

5. *Informal.* (*all in reference to information, reports, etc.*) reliable, trustworthy, trusty, dependable, to be depended *or* relied upon, tried and true; authentic, from the horse's mouth.

6. (*all of ideas, arguments, etc.*) right, correct, veracious; sound, valid, sensible, good, sober, well-founded, well-grounded.

7. orderly, in order *or* proper order, neat, tidy, shipshape, spruce, straightened-out, *Inf.* fixed-up, in place.

8. continuous, running, nonstop, round the clock, twenty-four hour, unintermittent; unbroken, uninterrupted, successive, consecutive.

9. *U.S.* thoroughgoing, through and through, complete, total, full; categorical, unconditional, unreserved, unmitigated, unqualified; absolute, sheer, utter, out-and-out, outright, downright, *U.S. Inf.* straight-out; perfect, proper, veritable, born, *Inf.* plumb, *Inf.* regular.

10. unmodified, unaltered; uncut, unadulterated, unmixed, undiluted, unwatered; pure, unmingled, unblended, alloyed, uncombined, unsophisticated.

11. *Slang.* heterosexual, normal.

—adv. **12.** directly, straightly, in a straight line, *Inf.* down the pipe, *Inf.* down the alley, *Inf.* in the groove. See also **straightforward** (*def.* **7**).

13. square, squarely, flush, right; plumb, plump, *Inf.* smack-dab.

14. frankly, candidly, forthrightly, straightforwardly; plainly, explicitly, unequivocally, undisguisedly, in plain words *or* English, with no nonsense, all joking aside; outspokenly, freely, boldly, unreservedly, unabashedly, uninhibitedly, with no holds barred, with no punches pulled.

15. honestly, honorably, justly, fairly, equitably, aboveboard; virtuously, righteously, morally; by the book, along the straight and narrow.

16. **straight off** straightaway. See **straightaway** (*def.* **2**).

straightaway, *adj.* **1.** straight. See **straight** (*def.* **1**).
—adv. **2.** immediately, *Inf.* immediately if not sooner, now, right now, right away, at once, this minute *or* instant, summarily, forthwith, without delay *or* further delay, without further ado, straightway, *Sl.* pronto, *Sl.* PDQ; promptly, on the spot, right off, right off the bat, straight off, then and there.

straighten, *v.* **1.** adjust, correct, rectify, right, square, set *or* put straight; unbend, uncurl, unkink, (*of hair*) conk; unsnarl, untangle, disentangle.

2. *Usu.* **straighten out** mend one's ways, turn over a new leaf, reform oneself, take to *or* follow the straight and narrow, *Inf.* go straight.

3. *Usu.* **straighten up** order, put *or* set in order, arrange, tidy *or* tidy up, neaten, put in trim, police, pick up, clean up, *Inf.* fix up, *Inf.* spruce up.

straightforward, *adj.* **1.** steady, steadfast, fixed, inflexible; undeviating, unveering, unswerving, unbending, unflinching; keen, intent, unbroken, undistracted; piercing, penetrating, probing, searching.

2. direct, straight, straightaway, linear, lineal, rectilinear, rectilineal; even, true, unbent, unturned, undistorted.

3. candid, frank, forthright, foursquare, straight-from-the-shoulder, man-to-man, heart-to-heart; plain, plain-spoken, plain-speaking, shirt-sleeve, downright, outright, explicit, unequivocal, unambiguous, undisguised, *Inf.* flat-footed, *Inf.* matter-of-fact; outspoken, free-spoken, free-speaking, free, unreticent, bold, unreserved, unrestrained, unconstrained, unchecked, unabashed, uninhibited, unshrinking; blunt, bluff, brusque, tactless.

4. open, open and sincere, open-hearted, genuine, transparent; guileless, ingenuous, sincere, artless, naive, simple, undeceptive, undeceitful, undeceiving, undissembling.

5. aboveboard, open and aboveboard, legitimate, *Sl.* legit, sound, up front, up and up, on the up and up, on the level, no-nonsense; straight, square, fair and square, square-dealing, square-shooting, straight-shooting, shirt-sleeve; honest, trustworthy, *Inf.* trusty, uncorrupt, uncorrupted, faithful, *Inf.* O.K.; honorable, reputable, creditable, estimable; right, rightful, lawful, licit.

6. just, fair, impartial, equitable, objective, balanced, even, even-handed, *Inf.* level; unbiased, nonbiased, unprejudiced, nonprejudiced, nonprejudicial, unprepossessed, unjaundiced, open-minded.

—adv. **7.** direct, directly, right, straight, straightforwards, straightly, straight ahead, dead ahead; unswervingly, unveeringly, undeviatingly; in a direct *or* straight line, in a line for, in line with, *Inf.* in a beeline, *Inf.* as the crow flies, *Inf.* straight as an arrow.

strain[1], *v.* **1.** tighten, draw tight *or* taut, stretch, extend, elongate, distend.

2. exert to the utmost, sharpen, whet, hone, make keen, sensitize; rack the brain, peel the eye, squint, listen hard, cock the ear, keep one's ears open.

3. sprain, wrench, wrick, twist, dislocate, injure, hurt, damage; impair, weaken, exhaust, tire, fatigue.

4. distort, warp, falsify, garble, pervert, stretch too far, change; exaggerate, hyperbolize.

5. force, drive, tax, overtax, burden, overburden; push to the limit, make ineffectual, negate, nullify; overreach, overshoot, overstep, impose upon, go *or* carry too far, overdo it.

6. draw off, rack, filter, percolate, sieve, bolt, screen, riddle; sift, winnow, refine, purify; pan, separate; drain, ooze, seep, trickle, flow.

7. clasp, hold, enfold, envelop, hug, embrace; press, squeeze, clutch, grasp, seize.

8. pull, tug, heave, haul; try hard, make a supreme effort, struggle, strive; labor, toil, moil, drudge, grub, grind; overwork, work night and day, *Inf.* go all out, *Inf.* give it one's all, drive oneself, push oneself, burn the midnight oil, burn the candle at both ends; work one's fingers to the bone, work like a dog, slave away, work like a slave, *Inf.* put one's back into it, keep one's shoulder to the wheel, keep one's nose to the grindstone; be under stress, be under pressure, be tense.

—n. **9.** force, weight, heft; pull, stretch, draw, traction, tensity, tautness; extension, distension, elongation.

10. effort, exertion, struggle, laboriousness, plodding, *Inf.* plugging, pegging; industry, industriousness, operoseness, diligence; labor, toil, travail, sweat of one's brow, moil, drudgery, grind.

11. distortion, falsification, garbling, perversion, changing, warping; exaggeration, hyperbole, overstatement.

12. sprain, wrench, twist, dislocation, injury, damage; impairment, weakening, exhaustion, fatigue.

13. pressure, stress, tension, heat, drain, drag, charge, tax; burden, *Archaic.* burthen, cross, encumbrance, cumbrance, trouble, vexation; load, millstone, albatross; *All Inf.* squeeze, crunch, pinch, push.

14. (*all of language*) flow, stream, rush, burst, outburst, outpour, outpouring, deluge, torrent.

15. *Music.* theme, melody, tune, air; aria, song, descant, lay, ballad, carol; ditty, canzonet, cavatina, arietta.

16. stanza, verse, canto, passage *or* piece of poetry.

17. style, manner, tone, tenor, timbre, quality, cast, complexion; temper, humor, mood, spirit, vein; temperament, disposition, nature, character.

strain[2], *n.* **1.** family, dynasty, house, clan, tribe, race, people; stock, stirps; offspring, young, children, progeny, seed, issue; successors, succession.

2. ancestry, ancestral line, lineage, descent, parentage, birth, derivation, extraction, filiation; heritage, background, past, history, roots; breed, bloodline, pedigree, stem, branch.

3. disposition, temperament, temper, grain; trait, characteristic; tendency, inclination, proclivity, propensity; proneness, subjectability, susceptibility, weakness, openness.

4. vein, streak, trace, mark, vesture; sign, indication, manifestation, evidence.

5. variety, kind, sort, type, description.

strained, *adj.* forced, unnatural, artificial, plastic, false, *Sl.* phony, insincere; overdone, stagy, theatrical, far-fetched, catachrestic; affected, stilted, *Inf.* put-on, feigned, pretended; studied, labored, laborious, calculated, mannered; self-conscious, stiff, formal, ceremonious.

strainer, *n.* sieve, tamis, tammy, sifter, filter, screen, riddle; colander, steamer.

strait, *n.* **1.** *Often* **straits** narrows, inlet, gut, arm.

2. *Often* **straits** predicament, *Inf.* pickle, dilemma, plight, *Sl.* hot seat, hot spot, hot water, stew; impasse, dead end, crisis, crux, hitch, rub, bind; quandary, perplexity, imbroglio, intricacy, entanglement, maze; slough, muddle, quagmire; problem, trouble, distress, difficulty, *All Inf.* clutch, jam, scrape, corner, hole, box, mess, pretty kettle of fish, fine how-do-you-do *or* how-de-do, pretty state of affairs, pretty pass, *Sl.* screw-up.

straiten, *v.* **1.** pauperize, impoverish, break, bankrupt, ruin; distress, embarrass, press, corner, *Inf.* drive to the wall, *Inf.* have on the ropes, *Inf.* have between a rock and a hard place; trouble, bother, harry, vex, annoy; persecute, plague, harass, oppress; afflict, perturb, disturb; encumber, overburden, overload, tax, strain.

2. limit, restrict, confine, keep within bounds, keep on a budget, *Inf.* keep on a short leash *or* rein; curb, restrain, shackle, bridle, trammel, bind, stay, hold in check; cut down, cut back, watch; impede, hinder, hamper, tie one's hands; frustrate, thwart, clip one's wings.

straitened, *adj.* **1.** poor, destitute, poverty-stricken, impoverished, penurious, impecunious, beggared, pauperized, penniless, indigent, needy, necessitous, bad off, badly off; pinched, *Inf.* strapped, *Inf.* up against it, *Inf.* on one's uppers, *Inf.* hard up; financially embarrassed, out of cash, out-of-pocket, *Inf.* short, *Brit. Sl.* skint, *All Inf.* broke, dead broke, flat broke, stone broke; bankrupt, ruined, wiped out, *Inf.* on the rocks, insolvent, overdrawn, in the red.

2. distressed, *Inf.* at the end of one's rope, *Inf.* between a rock and a hard place, between Scylla and Charybdis, in a sea of difficulties *or* troubles; in a precarious situation, in jeopardy, *Inf.* out on a limb, *Inf.* up a creek, *Inf.* up a creek without a paddle; encumbered, overburdened, overloaded; taxed, overtaxed, strained, close to breakdown; afflicted, perturbed, disturbed, troubled, worried, bothered, harried, vexed, perplexed.

strait-laced, *adj.* puritanical, puritan, prudish, nicenelly, moralistic, strict, austere, ascetic; severe, precise, abstinent, abstemious; stiff, stiff-necked, rigid, arbitrary, narrow, uncompromising; priggish, overmodest, old-maidish, old-fashioned, of the old school; formal, stilted, *Inf.* stuffy, fussy, fusty; prim, proper, overscrupulous, blue-nosed; sanctimonious, moralizing, self-righteous, holier-than-thou, *Inf.* goody-goody; pharisaic, unctuous, tartuffian.

strand¹, *v.* **1.** shore, ground, run ashore *or* aground; beach, shipwreck, wreck, maroon, *Inf.* pile up, cast away.

2. leave, abandon, desert, quit, give up; leave alone, leave high and dry, turn one's back on, leave in the lurch, forsake.

—n. **3.** shore, coast, beach, seaside, seashore, seacoast; littoral, plage, *Fr. côte,* sands; bank, brink, *Archaic.* brim, ground, margin, embankment, edge; waterside, waterfront, *Archaic.* rivage, foreshore, loom of the land.

strand², *n.* **1.** rope, cord, cordage, string, yarn, twine; cable, line, wire, catgut, lace; braid, twist, ligament.

2. fiber, filament, thread; hair, cilium, lash, capillament, whisker, antenna.

3. tress, lock, wisp, curl, flock, bang, plait, quiff; elflock, lovelock, forelock, cowlick; pigtail, pony-tail.

—v. **4.** plait, braid, weave, twist, twine; entwine, intertwine, interlace, interweave, intertwist, twirl.

strange, *adj.* **1.** unusual, uncommon, unconventional, unorthodox, uncustomary, unwonted, rare; atypical, original, singular, exceptional, individual; deviate, deviant, aberrant, anomalous, anomalistic, abnormal, irregular; unexampled, unparalleled, unprecedented; odd, oddish, peculiar, curious, queer, offbeat, quizzical, cranky, incongruous, *Inf.* funny, *Inf.* off-center; quaint, eccentric, idiosyncratic, *Inf.* quirky, *Inf.* kinky; droll, comical, laughable, flaky, *Sl.* wacky, *Sl.* squirrelly, *Sl.* buggy, *Sl.* screwy, *Sl.* balmy, *Chiefly Brit.* barmy, *Sl.* off the wall; weird, bizarre, erratic, freakish, grotesque, *Inf.* freaky, *Sl.* rum, *Sl.* far-out; extraordinary, egregious, remarkable, astonishing, *Scot. and North Eng.* unco; fantastic, incredible, inconceivable; fey, supernatural, preternatural, out of this world.

2. estranged, alienated, disaffected, separated, separate, apart, segregated, sequestered, shut off; isolated, alone, solitary, insular, lonely, friendless, companionless; nervous, troubled, rattled, discomposed, restless, on edge, constrained, uneasy, ill-at-ease, uncomfortable; lost, overwhelmed, disoriented, confused, bewildered, befuddled, perplexed, puzzled, baffled, nonplused, confounded, mystified.

3. unfamiliar, uncomfortable; remote, distant, far-off; foreign, alien, exotic, tramontane, transmontane, barbarian, *Scot.* fremd; extraneous, external, exterior, exoteric, ulterior, outside, outland, outlandish.

4. new, fresh, novel, unique, different, dissimilar, disparate, unlike, diverse, divergent; unknown, unheard of, untried, unsuspected, unperceived, unprecedented, never encountered, hitherto unknown; virgin, unspoiled, undiscovered, unexplored.

5. unaccustomed to, inexperienced in *or* at, unfamiliar with, unacquainted with, a stranger to, a novice at; ignorant, uninformed, unenlightened, uninitiated, unversed; raw, green, rookie, amateurish, unskilled, unpracticed, unseasoned, unconversant, unused to, new to, uninured, unhabituated.

6. aloof, reserved, detached, remote, removed, unsocial, uncommunicative; shy, bashful, diffident, meek, reticent, demure, demuring, shrinking, withdrawn, introverted, retiring; timid, reluctant, evasive, skittish, fearful, afraid, *Inf.* scared, uncourageous, cowardly, shamefaced; distrustful, suspicious, guarded, on guard, wary, chary, leery; cautious, careful, circumspect, precautious, prudent, noncommital.

stranger, *n.* **1.** nonacquaintance; unknown person, John *or* Jane Doe.

2. newcomer, new arrival, immigrant, emigrant, Johnny-come-lately, *Inf.* new kid in town; alien, foreigner, outlander, outlier, tramontane, barbarian; guest, visitor, incomer, *Inf.* out-of-towner; entrant, novitiate, tenderfoot, greenhorn; interloper, intruder, obtruder, crasher, gate-crasher, trespasser, squatter; uninvited, unwanted, undesired, undesirable.

3. outsider, odd man out, loner, maverick; nonmember, uninitiated, uninformed.

strangle, *v.* **1.** choke, throttle, squeeze, garrote, strangulate, bowstring, burke; stifle, suffocate, smother, gag, asphyxiate.

2. suppress, subdue, check, inhibit; repress, hold back, muzzle, restrain, restrict, curb; obstruct, clog, block, stop up, cramp, plug, cork; congest, constrict, close, occlude.

strap, *n.* **1.** band, strip, cord, string; thong, lash, tie, leash, strop; belt, cordon, braid, baldric; girdle, sash, waistband, cummerbund, *Archaic.* zone, cestus; ligature, ligament, tendon, bond, link, nexus; withe, fascia, copula, vinculum.

—*v.* **2.** secure, fasten, tether, lash, leash; bind, tie, truss, pinion, moor; bandage, band.

3. sharpen, strop, edge, whet.

4. beat, flog, whip, lash, scourge, flagellate; flail, lace, thrash, belt, horsewhip.

strapping, *adj.* **1.** muscular, brawny, broad-shouldered, powerfully-built, musclebound; stalwart, rugged, hefty, husky, solid, well-knit; ablebodied, able, athletic, sinewy.

2. robust, vigorous, full of vigor, hearty, hardy, hale, hale and hearty, lusty, strong and healthy, bursting with health *or* vigor; sound, healthy, in good health, in good condition, *Inf.* in good shape, fit, physically fit, in fine fettle; stout, staunch, firm, sturdy, burly, *Scot. and North Eng.* stiff, tough, iron, *Inf.* tough as nails, *Inf.* hard as rock; powerful, potent, mighty, all-powerful, herculean, *Literary.* puissant.

3. *Informal.* huge, gigantic, large, whopping, big, titanic, massive, tremendous.

stratagem, *n.* scheme, plot, artifice, wile, subterfuge, trick, trickery, ruse; maneuver, machination, gambit, ploy; device, tactic, trap, snare, deception, feint, intrigue, conspiracy, cabal.

strategic, *adj.* **1.** tactical, calculated, plotted, laid out, planned ahead, well-thought-out, outlined, arranged, devised; skillful, adroit, clever, smart, shrewd, sharp; wise, prudent, politic; wily, cunning, sly.

2. important, significant, momentous, essential; pivotal, crucial, decisive, key, vital; fundamental, integral, basic.

strategy, *n.* **1.** generalship, military science, martial art, tactics, logistics.

2. plan, *Inf.* game plan, master plan, *Inf.* scenario, outline, diagram, schema, blueprint; program, schedule, organization, management; scheme, plot, design, arrangement, method; policy, game, intent, approach.

stratum, *n.* **1.** layer, bed, tier, stage, table; lamina, plate, sheet, coat, streak, plane; seam, vein, lode.

2. level, degree, grade, gradation; status, standing, station, class.

straw, *n.* **1.** stalk, *Bot.* petiole, spear, blade, spire, shoot, stem, reed, fiber, sprig.

2. hay, fodder; silage, ensilage; chaff.

3. trifle, least bit, pin, fig, bean, hill of beans; tinker's dam, damn, *Inf.* darn; hoot, hoot in hell; continental, sou, cent, two cents, red cent, farthing, brass farthing; *Sl.* diddly-poo, *Sl.* poop; speck, flyspeck, iota, jot, tittle.

stray, *v.* **1.** wander, roam, meander, straggle, ramble, rove; range, nomadize, drift, live like a gypsy; stroll, amble, *Inf.* mosey, saunter, prowl; peregrinate, travel about, traverse.

2. deviate, go off course, swerve, veer, sheer, go astray; err, sin, transgress, go down the garden path *or* primrose path, take the path of least resistance.

3. digress, divagate, go off on a tangent, get off the subject *or* track, forget oneself, forget what one is talking about, get lost, lose oneself.

—*n.* **4.** homeless *or* friendless animal, homeless *or* friendless person, waif, *Brit.* wastrel, foundling, orphan; poor little lamb, little black sheep, *Southwestern U.S.* maverick, *Western U.S.* dogie, range horse; cowboy, lonesome cowboy; migrant worker, *Inf.* Okie; nomad, Kuchi, Bedouin, gypsy, vagabond, hobo, knight of the road, tramp; ski bum, beachcomber, bird of passage.

5. renegade, apostate, deserter, runaway, fugitive, backslider.

—*adj.* **6.** lost, gone astray, abandoned, deserted, derelict, unclaimed; vagrant, vagabond, wandering, vagarious, roaming.

7. incidental, occasional, random, chance, wanton, accidental; separate, apart, unconnected, isolated, single, singular; unexpected, unanticipated, aberrant, freak, odd, out of the way, capricious.

streak, *n.* **1.** band, strip, bar, streaking; stripe, striation, line, mark; stroke, dash, rule, score.

2. layer, stratum, ledge, level, bed; vein, seam, plane, lode.

3. bolt, flash, fulguration, lightning, ray, thunderbolt, *Archaic.* levin; beam, flare, coruscation, burst; glint, glance, glister.

4. admixture, nature, spirit, characteristic, property, temperament; strain, vein, stripe, feather; idiosyncrasy, twist, turn, bent, individuality.

5. *U.S. Informal.* spell, period, time, stage, duration; run, term, bout, space, span, lapse, snap.

—*v.* **6.** mark, striate, band, stripe, furrow; variegate, rainbow, motley, tessellate; smudge, stain, smirch, smutch, soil.

7. flash, fulgurate, coruscate, glance, flare; beam, glint, glister, light.

8. run, rush, dash, tear, race, sprint; scurry, hurry, hasten, fly, flee, fly like a bird; scud, scour, scoot, trip, pace; zip, zoom, speed, go like lightning, sweep, swoop; bound, clip, post, gallop, hie, *Inf.* go like a shot, *Inf.* go hellbent for leather, fly on the wings of the wind, outstrip the wind.

stream, *n.* **1.** river, freshet, *U.S. Dial.* kill, brook, creek, *Dial.* crick; streamlet, rivulet, rill, run, runnel, runlet; channel, watercourse, waterway, artificial waterway, canal, sluice, wadi, arroyo; branch, tributary, feeder, affluent, confluent; estuary, inlet, reach, arm, fjord.

2. current, *Geol.* race, drift, course; flow, flux, tide, inflow, flood, outflow, ebb; undercurrent, undertow, underset, riptide.

3. flow, afflux, issuance, emanation, flux, outflow, outrush, outpour, outpouring, efflux, effluence; rush, onrush, surge, flood, torrent, gush; jet, bolt, spurt, squirt, spout, spring, fountain, geyser; cascade, cataract, waterfall, falls, rapids.

4. air current, wind current; electrical current.

5. (*all of light*) beam, ray, shaft, trail, pencil, streak, gleam, glimmer.

6. continuous flow, torrent, rush, outpour, outpouring, gush, effusion, flood, deluge; succession, battery, barrage, volley, outburst, burst.

—*v.* **7.** flow *or* flow from, flow out, issue, emanate, come from, well out *or* forth; run, roll, course, slide, glide, move, pass, proceed, drift, go along; fall, cascade, pour out *or* forth, spill, effuse, shed, let fall *or* drop; flood, overflow, brim over, well over, run over, spill over; rush, gush, surge, spurt, spout, jet, ejaculate, squirt, shoot out.

8. (*all of light*) shine, gleam, beam; come in, flood in, pour in.

9. file, parade, walk, march, roll, move, proceed.

10. wave, stir, move to and fro, flutter, blow; float outward, extend, waft; flap, sway, swing, hang.

streamer, *n.* **1.** flag, pennant, pennon, banderole, bannerol, burgee, bunting, jack, banner, banneret.

2. ribbon, hair ribbon, feather.

streamlet, *n.* brook, brooklet, stream, creek, *Dial.* crick, *U.S. Dial.* kill, rivulet, rill, rindle, run, runnel, *Brit. Dial.* beck, *Brit. Dial.* gill, *Scot. and North Eng.*

sike, *Scot. and North Eng.* burn; channel, waterway, watercourse; branch, offshoot, tributary.

street, *n.* **1.** public road, thoroughfare, main road, *Inf.* drag, artery, highroad, roadway; avenue, boulevard, concourse, strip, pavement; lane, drive, terrace, circle, row.

2. walk, walkway, sidewalk, path, pathway; passage, passageway, alley, by-path, byway, crosscut, short cut; by-road, by-street, side road *or* street.

3. highway, turnpike, pike, tollroad, state highway; freeway, expressway, parkway, causeway, throughway, *U.S. Inf.* interstate; speedway, autobahn, superhighway.

4. residents, locals, inhabitants, occupants, dwellers; neighborhood, quarter, district, section, precinct.

streetwalker, *n.* prostitute, harlot, whore, woman of the streets; lady of the evening, woman of the profession, Mrs. Warren, call girl, *Fr. fille de joie;* strumpet, trollop, *Archaic.* wench, trull, drab, quean, painted woman, bar girl, *Inf.* pick-up; slut, hussy, cocotte, demimondaine, loose woman, wanton, fallen woman, woman of ill repute, white slave; *All Sl.* cat, tart, hustler, bim, moll, hooker, floozie, working girl, *Brit. Sl.* bird, *Mexican Sl.* caliente, bitch, broad, chippy. See also **prostitute** (*def.* **1**).

strength, *n.* **1.** muscular power, power, muscles, muscularity, brute force, might, mightiness, brawn, brawniness, thews, *Inf.* huskiness, *Inf.* heftiness, *Inf.* beefiness, burliness, sinewiness; force, forcefulness, dint, *Literary.* puissance; vigor, lustiness, *Archaic.* lustihood, vitality, energy, dynamism; hardiness, sturdiness, robustness, stoutness, toughness, steeliness; sinew, sinews, resilience, resiliency.

2. courage, fortitude, intrepidity, backbone, firmness; pluck, grit, will power, nerve, *Sl.* guts, *Sl.* gutsiness, *Inf.* intestinal fortitude; tenacity, pertinacity, perseverance, resoluteness, persistence; determination, red-bloodedness, full-bloodedness, doughtiness, *Inf.* stick-to-it-iveness; boldness, gameness, *Inf.* spunk.

3. greatness, magnitude, immensity, largeness, bigness, enormity; sway, control, dominance; seriousness, gravity, import, urgency.

4. efficacy, effectiveness, efficiency, potency, potence; weight, substance, pith, solidity; cogency, incisiveness; validity, soundness, stability; reliability, dependability, trustworthiness.

5. durability, durableness, toughness, hardness, callosity; solidity, impregnability, impenetrability, imperviousness; resistance, renitency; imperishability, incorruptibility.

6. intensity, intentness, concentration; fullness, richness; fervor, ardor, fervency, warmth, glow, fire, heat; excitement, enthusiasm, eagerness, keenness; animation, *Inf.* punch, *Inf.* pep, *Inf.* ginger; clarity, clearness, brightness, vividness; pungency, sharpness.

7. mainstay, chief support; refuge, security, foundation, base.

8. **on the strength of** on the basis of, based on, relying on.

strengthen, *v.* **1.** make strong *or* stronger, give strength to, fortify; renew, restore, reinforce; energize, vitalize, invigorate; nourish, build up, promote; nerve, brace, steel; indurate, harden; buttress, prop up, shore up.

2. substantiate, back up, give body to, authenticate, validate, confirm.

3. intensify, heighten, enhance, aggravate, exaggerate, magnify; give a boost to, step up, *Inf.* jazz up.

4. gain strength, grow stronger; recuperate, recover, improve, revive; perk up, come around, rally; convalesce, get well, mend, heal.

strenuous, *adj.* **1.** active, vigorous, energetic, energetical, vibrant, vital, dynamic; ardent, intense, acute, keen; forceful, strong.

2. industrious, assiduous, diligent, sedulous; enterprising, aggressive, pushing; unflagging, unfailing, untiring, tireless, indefatigable; persistent, persevering, dogged, tenacious; constant, unremitting, steady.

3. laborious, toilsome, toilful, difficult, uphill, tough, hard; heavy, burdensome, hefty, weighty; arduous, straining, exertive, vigorous; tiring, wearisome, tedious; labored, heavy, difficult, strained, forced.

stress, *n.* **1.** emphasis, accent, accentuation, italics, underscoring, underlining; significance, consequence, consideration, moment, import, concern, note, mark; importance, primacy, priority, preeminence, distinction, prestige; value, worth, merit, virtue; weight, gravity, seriousness, solemnity; urgency, imperativeness, exigency, press, pinch, high pressure; affirmation, assurance, averment.

2. *Phonetics.* accent, accentuation, syllable stress, primary *or* secondary *or* tertiary stress, weak stress; attack, delivery, force of utterance.

3. *Prosody.* ictus, metrical stress, cadence, beat, rhythm; rhythmic pattern, rhythmical emphasis, rhythmical accentuation.

4. strain, straining, tension, tensity, physical tension *or* pressure; stretch, extension, distension, elongation, protraction; pull, draw, haul, tug; force, thrust, push, shove, heave.

5. pain, distress, grief, suffering; stress and strain, rigor, stress of life, vicissitude, care, heat; nervous strain *or* tension, mental strain *or* pressure, worry, anxiety; psychological stress, frustration, conflict, trauma; overexertion, overstraining, overstress; stresssfulness, tenseness, tautness.

—v. **6.** emphasize, lay stress *or* emphasis upon, give emphasis to, punctuate, accent; underline, underscore, point up, italicize, call attention to, mark, bring home, press home; feature, spotlight, highlight, play up, give promience to, bring to the fore, bring into relief, *Inf.* headline; intensify, strengthen, deepen, heighten.

7. insist upon, reassert, reaffirm, repeat; belabor, rub in, harp on, dwell on, hammer away, pound away; dramatize, overemphasize, overstress, overaccentuate, make a mountain out of a molehill, make a big thing out of nothing, make a federal case out of [s.t.].

8. drive, whip, flog, force, run, run into the ground; harass, bull, bulldoze; tire, fatigue, weary, fag; exhaust, enervate, prostrate, bleed white; tax, burden, oppress, press, bear, bear upon; overwork, overtax, overtask, overstrain.

9. tense, stretch; pull, tug, haul; push, shove, heave.

stretch, *v.* **1.** extend, draw out, pull, tense, tauten; lengthen, elongate; widen, broaden; expand, enlarge, increase, amplify, aggrandize; distend, dilate, puff up, blow up, balloon, inflate.

2. offer, proffer, hold out, reach out, reach forth.

3. spread, sweep, range, cover, take in, encompass, span.

4. strain, overstrain, overstretch, overextend, overdraw; tax, overtax, burden, overburden, overwork, overtask, push to the limit, push too far.

5. recline, lie down, sprawl, loll, lounge.

—n. **6.** range, reach, compass, extent, scope, sweep, measure, distance, length and breadth.

7. period, term, tenure, spell, run, fit, interval, bout; tour, tour of duty, *Inf.* hitch.

8. elasticity, resilience, resiliency, tensility, give, snap; extensibility, stretchability, stretchiness, protrusibility.

—adj. **9.** elastic, resilient, stretchable, extensible, extensile, protrusible.

stretcher, *n.* litter, pallet.

strew, *v.* **1.** scatter, sprinkle, spread, diffuse, sow, disperse, distribute, bestrew.

2. broadcast, propagate, promulgate, publish; advertise, bruit, pass the word around, disseminate.

stricken, *adj.* **1.** wounded, smitten, hit, struck, hurt, injured, laid low.

2. beset, afflicted, plagued, tormented, persecuted; tortured, torn, harrowed, wracked, agonized.

3. overcome, overwhelmed, crushed, broken, undone, *Inf.* done in; demoralized, inconsolable, disconsolate, desolate; heartsick, sick at heart, heartbroken, broken-hearted, sorrow-stricken, grief-stricken.

strict, *adj.* **1.** narrow, rigid, rigorous, stringent, harsh, illiberal; hard, hard and fast, adamant, inflexible, inexorable, unyielding, uncompromising, hard-nosed.

2. exact, exacting, precise, accurate, faithful, literal; scrupulous, meticulous, conscientious, religious, particular, fussy, fastidious, punctilious.

3. close, careful, detailed, minute, microscopic.

4. abolute, perfect, total, utter, complete.

5. orthodox, fundamentalist, purist, hidebound, creedbound.

6. stern, severe, austere, dour, grim, strait-laced, *Inf.* tough.

stricture, *n.* **1.** criticism, hostile *or* adverse criticism, bad press, *Inf.* flak; thrust, *Inf.* hit, *Inf.* knock, *Inf.* slam, *Inf.* rap, *Inf.* swipe, *Sl.* shot; animadversion, derogation, aspersion, imputation.

2. (*all of a bodily duct or passage*) contraction, constriction, compression, strangulation.

3. restriction, limitation, astriction; check, curb, control, constraint, restraint, hindrance.

stride, *v.* **1.** step, walk, pace, take long steps, take giant steps; pass over *or* across, straddle.

—n. **2.** long *or* giant step, footstep, pace, military pace; striding gait *or* walk.

strident, *adj.* stridulous, stridulant, stridulatory, harsh, raucous, rough, grating, grinding, creaking, jarring; sour, out of tune, untuneful, unmelodious, unmusical, dissonant, discordant, absonant, unharmonious, cacophonous, clashing; shrill, acute, sharp, ear-piercing; guttural, throaty, husky, gravelly, hoarse, gruff; scratchy, scratching, raspy, rasping, croaking, *Sl.* froggy.

strife, *n.* **1.** conflict, discord, disaccord, dissension, friction, variance, opposition; bad *or* hard feelings, hostility, antagonism, antipathy, bad blood, ill will, hatred.

2. disagreement, difference of opinion, imbroglio, contention, controversy, altercation, embroilment; argument, *Inf.* words, quarrel, dispute, squabble, row, spar, wrangle, jangle, *Scot.* sturt, *Scot.* collieshangie, *Obs.* brabble, *Scot. and North Eng.* threap, *Brit. Archaic.* brangle; spat, tiff, *Brit. Dial.* fratch, *Inf.* run-in, *Inf.* hassle, *Inf.* barney, falling-out, *Sl.* blow-up; fight, fisticuffs, scuffle, tussle, *Inf.* set-to, *Inf.* scrap, struggle; hand-to-hand combat, combat, battle, skirmish, fray; brannigan, broil, brawl, donnybrook, free-for-all, melee, *Inf.* dustup, *U.S. Sl.* rhubarb.

3. competition, contest, rivalry; match, game, regatta, meet, joust, duel, tug of war; debate, battle of wits; tournament, tourney, bout, round, encounter, engagement, *Fr. concours,* athletic event; race, run, dash, sprint; trial, heat, scrimmage; run-off, sudden death, showdown; sweepstakes, derby, handicap, steeplechase; Olympics, (*in ancient Greece*) agon, decathlon, pentathlon, marathon, (*in ancient Greece*) agonistics.

strike, *v.* **1.** hit, smite, thwack, slap, smack, *Australian.* ding; cuff, buffet, knock, punch, box, sandbag, *Scot.* dunt, *Scot. and North. Eng.* paik, *Inf.* clout, *Inf.* slug, *Inf.* whack, *Inf.* knock [s.o.'s] block off, *Inf.* wallop, *Inf.* crown, *Sl.* conk, *Dial.* hit [s.o.] up side the head, *Sl.* belt, *Sl.* bash, *Sl.* plug, *Sl.* sock, *U.S. Sl.* biff, *Sl.* bop; beat, batter, pound, lay on, pommel, pummel, pelt, *Sl.* paste, *Sl.* lay into, *Sl.* let [s.o.] have it, *Archaic.* belabor; thrash, flog, lash, switch, birch, scourge, flagellate, whip, horsewhip, curry, strap, thresh, flail, cowhide, spank, *Brit. Dial.* yerk, *Inf.* tan [s.o.'s] hide, *Inf.* trim, *Inf.* thump, *Inf.* lace, *Inf.* lambaste, *Inf.* whale, *Sl.* whomp; cudgel, fustigate, bludgeon, baste, cane, bastinado, club, hammer, sledge-hammer; tap, rap, fillip.

2. attack, charge, storm, rush, set upon, assail, assault; fell, drop, sink, bring down, shoot, send to the mark, make a bull's-eye, *Sl.* zap, *Sl.* blast; drive, bat, propel.

3. thrust, shove, push, plunge, lunge, force; stab, pierce, dagger, spear, javelin, harpoon.

4. ignite, light, kindle, enkindle, inflame, flame, fire, set on fire; spark, light up, glow, flare, flame, burn, blaze.

5. collide with, impact, crash against, smash into, dash against, jolt, jar, bang into *or* against; bump, knock into, clap together, percuss, run into, meet head-on, impinge upon *or* against.

6. impress, arouse *or* pique one's interest, catch one's eye; accord, please, appeal to, delight, tickle, gratify; suit, fit, befit.

7. come upon, light *or* fall upon, happen *or* chance upon, blunder upon, meet with, *Inf.* dig; find, discover, uncover, unearth, ferret out, dig up, learn of *or* about; detect, descry, notice, espy, perceive, discern, *Inf.* spot, *Sl.* pick up; pitch on *or* upon, think of, get into one's head, come up with, dream up, hatch, concoct.

8. root, take root, put down roots, take hold, settle, plant, *Rare.* implant.

9. reach, attain, gain, achieve, arrive at; compromise, find a balance, find a median, determine a middle ground.

10. take apart, undo; pull down, take down, knock down, *Inf.* level.

11. level, smooth, plane, even, flatten, strickle.

12. *Usu.* **strike out** delete, cross out, mark through; efface, erase, rub out, blot out, wipe out *or* away, obliterate, remove all traces of; cancel, stamp out, void, annul, invalidate.

13. (*all of coins, medals, etc.*) coin, mint, stamp, punch out, cut, form, make; impress, imprint, print.

14. (*all of clocks*) ding, ring, clang; sound, go off, cuckoo; resound, resonate.

15. *Often* **strike down** afflict, distress, plague; disease, make sick *or* ill, harm, impair, damage, injure, hurt, wound, cripple, mame; kill, slay, slaughter, murder, massacre, deal a deathblow; annihilate, destroy, ruin, blight.

16. terrify, terrorize, frighten, instill fear, scare to death; overwhelm, move, affect, have an effect on, influence, make an impact *or* impression on, leave a mark on; induce, cause, effect, bring about, create, produce.

17. assume, adopt, take on; imitate, copy, mimic, reproduce; affect, feign.

18. agree *or* settle on, reach accord, make a settlement; approve, sanction, ratify, confirm.

19. walk out, walk off the job, quit *or* stop working, sit down on the job, picket.

—n. **20.** hit, hitting, smiting, thwack, slap, slapping, smack, smacking; cuff, buffet, knock, punch, box, *Inf.* whacking, knockout, *Both Boxing.* left, right, *Inf.* whack, *Inf.* wallop, *Inf.* whomp, *Inf.* clout,

plug, *Sl.* bop, *Sl.* sock; blow, bastinado, *Scot.* dunt, *Scot. and North. England.* paik, *Both Brit. Dial.* yerk, douse, *Sl.* conk, *Sl.* bash, *U.S. Sl.* biff, *Sl.* bop; beating, battering, pounding, pommeling, pummeling, pelting, going over, *Sl.* pasting; thrash, thrashing, flogging, lashing, flagellation, whipping, spanking, *Inf.* tanning; cudgeling, fustigation, bludgeoning, basting, flogging, clubbing, hammering.

21. collision, impact, crash, clash, bang; bump, thud, thump.

22. walkout, sit-down, work stoppage, job action, wildcat *or* outlaw strike, slow-down, go-slow, sick-out.

striking, *adj.* **1.** impressive, imposing, majestic, grand, august, awesome, awe-inspiring; wondrous, marvelous, stupendous, amazing, astounding, incredible; miraculous, fabulous, exceptional, out-of-the-ordinary, unusual, singular, unique; extraordinary, excellent, magnificent, *Inf.* great, superb, *Sl.* bang-up, *Inf.* smashing; splendid, wonderful, brilliant, dazzling, *Brit. Sl.* ripping.

2. noticeable, conspicuous, obvious, evident; effective, forceful, impactful; blatant, obtrusive, flagrant, glaring, egregious; overt, visible, prominent, unconcealed, plain, unmistakable; clear, lucid, plain as day, plain as the nose on one's face, distinct, clear-cut, explicit.

3. attractive, good-looking, stunning, beautiful, gorgeous; handsome, comely, well-favored, well-groomed.

string, *n.* **1.** cord, line, cable, rope, yarn, twine; thread, lace, catgut; braid, twist, ligament, strand, tendon; fiber, filament, tendril; chord, wire, gut, bowstring, piano wire; ribbon, strap, strip, thong.

2. necklace, rivière, band, strand, beads; gorget, carcanet, chaplet.

3. series, chain, range, concatenation, catenation, cantena; row, file, tier, column, queue, line, single file, Indian file; procession, train, stream, parade, cavalcade, motorcade, cortege, caravan, coffle.

4. strings *Informal.* limitations, conditions, qualifications, contingencies, stipulations; prerequisites, requirements, musts; terms, *Inf.* catches, *Sl.* hookers, fine print; provisions, provisos, articles, conventions, clauses.

—*v.* **5.** tie, bind, lash, leash, moor; fasten, secure, batten, pinion; tether, grapple, truss, strap, hitch, clinch.

6. link, concatenate, chain, string together, run together; connect, join, catenate; loop, hook, ring.

7. arrange, align, range, row, line, line up; file, rank, array, dispose, order; pose, marshal, set in line, deploy, enfilade.

8. suspend, sling, hang, drape, decorate, trim; adorn, ornament, festoon, garnish, array, deck, bedeck, embellish.

9. string along take in, deceive, bluff, fool, dupe, cozen; put [s.t.] over on, slip one over on, *Sl.* hornswoggle, trick, bamboozle; gull, pigeon, *Sl.* snow, *Sl.* buffalo, humbug, play [s.o.] false.

10. string out stretch, extend, elongate, outstretch, outreach, reach out; prolong, lengthen, protract, draw out, continue; stretch out, spin out, run out, let out.

11. string up hang, noose, gibbet, neck, lynch; *Inf.* stretch, *Inf.* scrag, *Sl.* let [s.o.] dangle, *Sl.* make [s.o.] swing.

stringent, *adj.* **1.** strict, severe, harsh, rigorous, tight, exacting, demanding, tough, rough; rigid, stiff, hard, inflexible, unflexible, uncompromising; unbendable, unbending, unyielding, not giving an inch; fixed, set, firm, immovable, unalterable, unchangeable, unvarying, hard and fast, ironclad, absolute; oppressive, repressive, despotic, tyrannical, autocratic, dictatorial.

2. compelling, urgent, pressing, imperative, exigent, taking priority *or* precedence, requiring immediate attention; important, of the utmost importance, crucial, vital, life-and-death.

3. convincing, cogent, good, persuasive, suasive, moving, winning, impressive; effective, forcible, strong, forceful, powerful, influential, weighty.

stringy, *adj.* **1.** fibrous, sinewy, ropy, wiry, thready, threadlike; ligamental, filamentary, tough, leathery, gristly, *Inf.* chewy.

2. ropy, mucous, albuminous, *Vulgar.* snotty; gluey, pasty, tacky, gooey, *Archaic.* sizy; glutinous, mucilaginous, synovial, gumbo, viscous, gelatinous.

strip[1], *v.* **1.** peel, pare, skin, excoriate, decorticate, excorticate, flay, scale, bark; hull, shell, husk, shuck; uncover, expose, lay open, bare, denude.

2. remove, take off, cast off, throw off, drip; shed, exfoliate, *Pathol.* desquamate, slough, molt, exuviate, flake off, peel off, scale.

3. deprive, deprive of, take away, take from; dispossess, *Law.* disseize, expropriate, confiscate, seize.

4. clear out, empty *or* empty out, clean out; dismantle, disfurnish.

5. rob, burglarize, burgle, *Sl.* rip off, steal, take *or* take away, walk off *or* away with; plunder, despoil, *Archaic.* spoil, spoliate, pillage, *Chiefly Scot.* reive; ransack, rifle, sack, loot, gut.

6. undress, disrobe, undrape, unclothe, *Inf.* peel, doff, shed, cast *or* throw off, *Sl.* drop one's drawers, *Sl.* drop trow, strip down to nothing, striptease.

strip[2], *n.* **1.** narrow piece, band, stripe, belt, cord, cordon, braid, thong, ribbon, frontlet, fillet. See **stripe[1]**(def. **2**).

2. comic strip, cartoon, comics, *U.S.* funnies.

stripe[1], *n.* **1.** band, bar, tricolor, tiger-stripe, zebra-stripe, striation; furrow, ridge, stria, *Archit.* strix, flute; streak, streaking, lineation, delineation; line, dash, stroke, score, scratch; rule, mark, slash, hatching, hachure.

2. strip, braid, tape, ribbon, fillet, string; chevron, insignia, eagle, wings; belt, cordon, girdle, sash, *Archaic.* zone, waistband.

3. layer, seam, vein, lode; stratum, level, ledge, bed, plane.

4. style, sort, kind, variety, brand, line; ilk, set, lot, character, description, nature, *Inf.* like *or* likes; species, genus, family, race, strain, blood, breed; stamp, form, mold, cast, make; persuasion, manner, type, color, feather, kidney, grain; aspect, grade, classification, order, degree.

—*v.* **5.** striate, bar, blaze, streak, line; hatch, score, rule; variegate, seam, band, vein, marble.

stripe[2], *n.* lash, stroke, whip, cut, whack, smack, blow; lacing, beating, flogging, flagellation, thrashing, scourging.

striped, *adj.* banded, streaked, streaky, stripy; variegated, striated, striate; listed, veined, brindle, brindled, brinded, *Zool.* strigose.

stripling, *n.* youth, juvenile, minor, young man *or* fellow, youngling, teen-ager, teen *or* teener, pre-teen, hobbledehoy, schoolboy; youngster, lad, boy, *Fr. garcon, Scot.* laddie, *Inf.* laddo, *Irish Eng.* gossoon; child, young one, *Dial.* young'un, *Inf.* kid, *U.S. Inf.* tad, *Inf.* shaver *or* little shaver; master, son, *Inf.* sonny, *Inf.* sonnyboy; chip off the old block, junior; whippersnapper, brat; urchin, street urchin, gamin.

strive, *v.* **1.** aspire to, aim for, set one's sights on, shoot for *or* at, *Sl.* buck for; venture, essay, seek to, set out to, drive at, go about; undertake, take in hand, take upon oneself, try one's hand at; try, try hard, attempt, make an effort, endeavor, work at, tackle; do one's best, do all one can, *Sl.* shoot one's bolt, do all that lies within one, *Inf.* go all out, knock oneself out, *Inf.* give it one's all, *Inf.* bend over backwards, *Sl.* do it up brown.

2. work hard, toil, labor, moil, grudge, grub, grind; work one's fingers to the bone, slave *or* slave away, work like a slave, work like a Trojan, *Inf.* put one's back into it, *Sl.* kill oneself; work day and night, burn the midnight oil, burn the candle at both ends; sweat, *Sl.* beat one's brains out, strain oneself.

3. compete, contend with; fight, battle, tussle, skirmish, struggle. See **struggle** (def. **1**).

stroke, *n.* **1.** blow, hit, slam, buffet, cut, uppercut; jab, punch, belt, chop, crack, clip, sock, smack, whack, *Sl.* paste, *Sl.* kerpow, thwack, *Inf.* wallop, swat, *Inf.* lick; rap, tap, slap, cuff, knock, pounding.

2. (*of a bell*) striking, peal, ringing, tolling, toll; knell, reverberation, dong, ding-dong, clank, clang, clash, crash, bong, gong, boom; tintinnabulation, tinkle, jingle.

3. (*of the heart*) throb, thump, pulsation, palpitation, beat, pumping, vibration, rhythm, murmur.

4. attack, seizure, paroxysm, spasm, fit, collapse; apoplexy, paralysis; embolism, thrombosis, cerebral vascular accident, CVA, aneurysm; sunstroke, *Pathol.* ictus, insolation, siriasis, thermic fever, heatstroke, heat prostration.

5. (*of a pen, brush, etc.*) line, mark, marking; dash, serif; quick movement, lining, underlining, scratch, writing.

6. touch, style, hand, guiding hand, mastery; inspiration, work.

7. piece, bit, particle, iota, slice, part, portion; act, measure, degree.

8. feat, accomplishment, attainment, achievement; doing, action, performance, stunt, move.

9. happening, occurrence, occasion, event, happenstance, chance.

—*v.* **10.** rub, caress, pat, *Yiddish.* glet, massage, palpate, touch, finger, pet, gentle; soothe, placate, mollify, appease, calm.

stroll, *v.* **1.** saunter, perambulate, amble, ramble, take a walk, go for a walk; stretch one's legs, take the air, get some fresh air; stray, meander, dawdle along, *Inf.* mosey *or* mosey along, straggle.

2. wander, rove, roam, range, tramp, hike; tour, travel, journey, jaunt, peregrinate, traverse.

—*n.* **3.** walk, saunter, amble, perambulation, constitutional; airing, turn; ramble, excursion, hike.

strong, *adj.* **1.** mighty, powerful, strong as a bull *or* horse *or* moose *or* lion, Herculean, Atlantean, *Sl.* packing a punch *or* wallop, *Archaic.* potential; muscular, sinewy, wiry, brawny, strapping, well-built, athletic, musclebound; sturdy as an ox, burly, stout, stocky, *Inf.* husky, *Inf.* hefty, *Inf.* beefy; tough, hard-nosed, hard-fisted, rugged, hardy, outdoorsy, (*of plants*) cold-weather; virile, robust, red-blooded, hearty, hale.

2. keen, sharp, clear; astute, perspicacious, insightful, discerning; capable, able, competent, good, efficient, quick, ready; well-versed, well-read, knowledgeable.

3. ethical, morally sound, of strong moral fiber; valiant, stalwart, like the rock of Gibraltar; courageous, brave, stout-hearted, heroic.

4. great, major, important; weighty, carrying a lot of weight, *Inf.* carrying clout; recognized, influential, effective, effectual, efficacious.

5. impressive, eloquent, poignant, gripping, moving, touching; persuasive, suasive, winning, compelling, irresistible, convincing, believable; forceful, forcible, cogent, incisive, well-presented, well-written, *Literary.* puissant; conclusive, decisive, determining, final.

6. strong-voiced, full, resonant, resounding, loud.

7. secure, sound, healthy, salubrious; financially sound *or* secure, wealthy, rich, well-off, well-heeled; well-supplied, well-stocked, complete.

8. heavily fortified, well-fortified, armed to the teeth; well-defended, well-protected, impregnable, impenetrable, invulnerable, inviolable, unassailable; invincible, unconquerable, indomitable, unsubduable, unbeatable.

9. sturdy, durable, heavy-duty, cast-iron, substantial; endurant, enduring, long-lasting, lasting, permanent, fixed, mordant; sound, solid, solid as a rock; well-made, well-constructed, well-built, built on a solid foundation.

10. firm, resolute, unyielding, unbending, unchangeable; confirmed, decided, positive, unequivocal; doctrinaire, opinionated, dogmatic, rigid, stiff, inflexible; strong-willed, strong-minded, willful, stubborn, obstinate, recalcitrant, with a mind of one's own, hard-headed; emphatic, insistent, vehement.

11. intent, earnest, dedicated; fierce, fervent, fervid, perfervid, rabid; zealous, enthusiastic, eager, spirited, *Inf.* gung-ho; loyal, steadfast, true-blue, died in the wool, staunch, die-hard; thorough-going, through and through, all the way, total, 100 percent.

12. diligent, sedulous, assiduous, strenuous, arduous, untiring, tireless; dynamic, vigorous, energetic, active.

13. vivid, graphic, stark; distinct, clear-cut, definite, pronounced, marked; notable, remarkable, unbelievable, incredible, amazing, astounding.

14. intense, deep, bright; glaring, brilliant, radiant, gleaming, glowing, luminous; severe, harsh, cruel, mean, nasty; mordant, caustic, pointed, cutting, biting, sarcastic.

15. concentrated, intensified, pure, (*of coffee*) black; stimulating, exhilarating, bracing, astringent; intoxicating, quickening, heady; provocative, overwhelming; potent, penetrating, sharp, acute; tart, acrid, bitter, sour, vinegary, acidic, acetous, mordacious, stingy, stinging, nippy, biting; pungent, piquant, spicy, highly seasoned, peppery, hot, fiery; rich, flavorful, savory, tasty, racy.

16. heavy, overdone; aromatic, fragrant, odoriferous; smelly, stinky, rank, gamey; putrid, foul, vile, awful, terrible, gross, bad; disgusting, sickening, nauseating, offensive.

strongbox, *n.* safe, safe-deposit box, safety-deposit box, lockbox, vault, locker; cashbox, coin box, cash register, till; coffer, jewelry box, casket, chest, treasury.

stronghold, *n.* **1.** fort, fortress, fortification, citadel, bulwark, bastion, rampart, castle, château; donjon, keep, redoubt, stockade, tower, *Archaic.* hold.

2. hotbed, center, headquarters, haven, refuge.

structure, *n.* **1.** building, construction, erection, superstructure, skyscraper, pile, edifice, fabric; house, apartment building, office *or* office biulding, hotel, motel; lodge, shelter, cabin, cottage; shack, shanty, shed, lean-to.

2. form, shape, configuration, figuration, conformation, formation; construction, construct, frame, framework, exterior, outward form; figure, physique, build, skeletal structure; arrangement, disposition, organization, order, system, *Inf.* shebang; infrastructure, fabric, contexture, constitution, make-up, composition, design, pattern.

struggle, *v.* **1.** contend, wrestle, grapple, tussle, scuffle; battle, fight, combat, war, wage war, skirmish; join battle with, set to, engage, encounter; clash, joust, tilt at, duel, cross swords with, fence; spar, brawl, scrap, box, fall to blows; compete, vie, rival, contest; oppose, challenge, pit oneself against, play against, take on, face; dispute, debate, argue, wrangle, altercate, squabble, quarrel, spat.

2. endeavor, labor, try hard, do one's best, do all one can *or* that lies within one, *Sl.* do it up brown, set at [s.t.] with a will; work hard, burn the midnight oil, burn the candle at both ends, work day and night, work like a Trojan, keep one's shoulder to the wheel; beat one's head against a wall, fight a losing battle, get nowhere fast; try, make an effort, take pains, bestir oneself; attempt, tackle, take on, essay, undertake, work at, go about; seek to, venture, make a bold push.

—*n.* **3.** labor, work, toil, travail, sweat of one's brow, moil, drudgery; exertion, effort, strain, laboriousness, plodding, *Inf.* plugging, pegging; industry, industriousness, operoseness, diligence; endeavor, striving, try, attempt, essay, effort, nisus, conatus.

4. contention, conflict, strife, hostilities, combat, war; fight, clash, skirmish, battle; fray, affray, fracas, melee, brawl, scuffle, tussle, tug of war; set-to, scrap, fisticuffs, slugfest; rivalry, competition; wrangle, broil, quarrel, feud.

5. task, chore, *Inf.* hassle, *Sl.* drag; grind, *Inf.* rat race; bother, worry, trouble, trial.

strumpet, *n.* **1.** harlot, whore, prostitute; hussy, slut, slattern, demirep, cocotte, demimondaine, loose woman, wanton, fallen woman, tramp, vamp, white slave; lady of the evening, woman of the profession, Mrs. Warren, *Fr. fille de joie;* trollop, *Archaic.* wench, trull, drab, quean, painted woman, woman of the streets, streetwalker, bar girl, *Inf.* pick-up, call girl, Cyprian, *All Sl.* cat, tart, hustler, bim, moll, hooker, floozie, working girl, *Brit. Sl.* bird, *Mexican Sl.* caliente.

2. madam, bawd, procuress, pander.

3. paramour, courtesan, mistress, concubine, kept woman, *Sl.* doxy.

4. temptress, siren, seductress, *Fr. femme fatale,* Jezebel, Delilah; flirt, coquette, minx; adventuress, hetaera.

strut, *v.* swagger, peacock, prance, parade, promenade; flourish, flaunt, show off, throw out one's chest, put on airs; flounce, *U.S. Inf.* sashay, mince.

stub, *n.* **1.** end, butt, tail, tail end, remains; dock, stump.

2. ticket, receipt, *Chiefly Brit.* counterfoil.

stubbed, *adj.* **1.** stumpy, snubby, dumpy, squabby, short, squat, squatty, stubby; chunky, thick, thickset, broad, stocky, stout, stodgy; plump, chubby, tubby, pudgy, fleshy.

2. blunt, dull, worn down.

stubborn, *adj.* **1.** obstinate, mulish, muleheaded, stubborn as a mule, pigheaded, bullheaded, bullish, headstrong; willful, self-willed, strong-willed, contrary, perverse, wrongheaded, cross-grained; balky, uncooperative, froward, refractory, rusty, recalcitrant, contumacious, *U.S. Inf.* notionate, *Inf.* cussed, *Archaic.* untoward; ungovernable, unmanageable, uncontrollable, difficult, restive, unruly, wayward, fractious, incorrigible.

2. inflexible, immovable, adamant, adamantine, diehard, stiff-necked, set, set in one's ways, *Inf.* hard-core, *Inf.* hard-shell, hard-nosed; inexorable, implacable, intransigent, intractable, uncompromising, unbending, unwavering, unyielding; unmalleable, unpersuadable, uninfluenceable, unswayable, unpliable; persistent, persevering, pertinacious, tenacious, dogged, bulldogged, relentless, unrelenting, single-minded.

stubby, *adj.* **1.** blunt, dull, worn down.

2. stumpy, short, squat, stubbed. See **stubbed** (def. **1**).

3. bristly, stubbled, stubbly, rough.

student, *n.* **1.** pupil, schoolgirl, schoolboy, learner, educatee, *Fr. élève;* collegian, undergraduate, coed; scholar, intellectual, *Inf.* bookworm, *Inf.* grind, *Sl.* squid.

2. beginner, novice, tyro, abecedarian, catechumen, neophyte, initiate, probationer, postulant.

3. apprentice, ward, trainee, protegé, disciple, follower, apostle, proselyte; adherent, sectary, admirer, votary, devotee.

4. observer, spectator; commentator, reviewer, critic, interpreter, analyst; examiner, investigator.

studied, *adj.* **1.** deliberate, premeditated, preconceived, predetermined; calculated, contrived, forced, unnatural, artificial, plastic, *Sl.* phony, *Inf.* put-on, feigned; affected, mannered, precious, recherché; strained, labored, laborious, self-conscious, stiff, stilted, formal, ceremonious; overdone, elaborate, stagy, theatrical.

2. considered, well-considered, pondered, contemplated, meditated, carefully weighed; planned, well-laid-out, well-arranged, well-thought-out, thoughtful; careful, thorough.

studious, *adj.* **1.** diligent, industrious, sedulous, hard-working; busy, busy as a bee *or* beaver, active, employed, engaged, occupied, hard at it; intent, intense, concentrated, steady, earnest, zealous; assiduous, painstaking, thorough, thorough-going; persistent, pertinacious, dogged, plodding, slogging, plugging; persevering, unremitting, unrelaxing, unfaltering, untiring, tireless, indefatigable.

2. scholarly, academic, intellectual, cerebral; erudite, cultured, lettered, literary, bookish.

3. considered, well-considered, well-thought-out, planned, studied. See **studied** (def. **2**).

study, *n.* **1.** reading, review, reviewing, learning, taking in, absorption, memorization; concentration, intentness, attentiveness, application, endeavor, effort, enterprise, work, hard work; industry, industriousness, sedulousness, assiduity, plodding, *Inf.* plugging, pegging, *Inf.* grinding; thought, reflection, mulling, pondering, contemplation, rumination, deliberation, speculation, consideration; attention, observance, observation, notice, note, regard.

2. research, investigation, inquiry, exploration; examination, scrutiny, inspection, probe, dissection; analysis, interpretation, explanation, elucidation; treatise, thesis, text, survey, *Civ. Eng.* reconnaissance.

3. subject, field, area, branch of knowledge.

4. reverie, woolgathering, musing; meditation, introspection, pensiveness, brown study; preoccupation, absorption, engrossment, absent-mindedness, abstraction.

5. library, reading room, den; office, workroom, studio; schoolroom, study hall.

—*v.* **6.** apply oneself, endeavor, work, work hard, *Sl.* crack a book, *Inf.* hit the books; learn, con, memorize, get by heart, learn by rote, *Inf.* grind, *Brit. Sl.* muzz, *Brit. Sl.* swot, *Sl.* pull an allnighter, burn the midnight oil, *Inf.* cram; slog, toil, drudge; review, go over, *Inf.* bone up; peruse, pore over, read, scan, skim, glance at, dip into; take up, occupy oneself with.

7. consider, deliberate, excogitate, take to heart, *Archaic.* perpend; revolve, turn over, weigh, evaluate; cogitate, reflect, ruminate, chew over, chew one's cud, be in a brown study; meditate, muse, ponder, brood, mull over; think, think about *or* over, cerebrate, put on one's thinking cap, be abstracted, be lost in thought.

8. contemplate, watch, keep an eye on, keep a vigil, rivet one's eyes upon, stare at, gaze at, view, look at, observe, regard; attend, pay attention to, heed; survey, reconnoiter, scrutinize, scan, examine, inspect, dissect.

stuff, *n.* **1.** matter, material, substance, fabric, building blocks.

2. belongings, personal belongings, effects, personal effects, personal estate, personal possessions, chattels, properties, *Inf.* things, *Sl.* junk; baggage, bag and baggage, gear, impedimenta, dunnage, luggage, kit, duffel; *Law.* choses, *Law.* choses in action *or* possession, *Law.* choses transitory, *Law.* personalty; paraphernalia, accouterments, appurtenances, appointments, appendages, accessories, trappings; goods, goods and chattels, movables, movable articles, furniture.

3. essence, inner essence, quiddity, haecceity.

4. waste, rubbish, trash, litter, chaff, refuse, *Dial.* culch, *Brit. Dial.* raff.

5. nonsense, stuff and nonsense, twaddle, poppycock, humbug, bunkum, *Sl.* bunk, *Sl.* blah; balderdash, tommyrot, *Inf.* rot, *Sl.* crap, *Sl.* crock, *Sl.* bull; hogwash, *Sl.* horsefeathers, *Sl.* bosh, *Brit. Sl.* tosh; footle, *Inf.* malarkey, *Sl.* bushwa, *Sl.* baloney, *Sl.* bilge water, *Sl.* meshugaas; claptrap, *Inf.* fiddle-faddle, *Inf.* piffle, *Inf.* flapdoodle; idle talk, *Sl.* hot air, *Sl.* gas. See also **nonsense** (def. **2**).

6. *Informal.* trade, occupation, profession, job; field, sphere, area; facts, information, data.

—*v.* **7.** crowd, cram, pack, press, jam, *Inf.* jampack.

8. line, pad; wad, fill.

9. gorge, engorge, glut, guttle, gluttonize, gormandize, make a pig *or* hog of oneself.

10. thrust in, drive in, ram in, shove in, push in, wedge in, run in, force in.

11. stop, stop up, obstruct, cork, bung, stanch, spile, plug, choke, block.

stuffing, *n.* **1.** filling, filler, padding, packing, wadding.

2. dressing, *Cookery.* forcemeat, *Cookery.* farcemeat *or* farce.

3. *Informal.* insides, internals, inwards, *Inf.* innards, *Sl.* guts.

stuffy, *adj.* **1.** close, poorly ventilated, ill-ventilated; airless, stifling, suffocating, sultry, oppressive; stale, musty, moldy, mildewy, fusty, frowzy, *Brit. Inf.* frowsty.

2. dull, dull as dishwater, uninteresting, boring, boresome, tedious, tiresome, wearisome, *Inf.* ho-hum; dry, dry-as-dust, *Sl.* deadly, *Sl.* dead; flat, bland, insipid, vapid, jejune, *Sl.* for the birds, *Sl.* nothing, *Sl.* blah; ponderous, elephantine, wooden.

3. pompous, self-important, impressed with oneself, pedantic; puffed up, inflated, swollen; proud, conceited, egocentric, narcissistic, self-centered, self-admiring, self-esteeming, *Sl.* stuck *or* hung up on oneself; haughty, snobbish, on one's high horse, high-and-mighty, too good for the rest of us, *Inf.* high-hat, *Inf.* nose-in-the-air, *Sl.* snooty, *Sl.* snotty, *Sl.* sniffy, *Sl.* stuck-up.

4. stodgy, old-fashioned, old-fogyish, *Inf.* fuddy-duddy; rigid, stiff, starched, stiff-necked, *Inf.* uptight; prudish, nice-nelly, priggish, prim, prim and proper, proper, puritanical, old-maidish; conservative, strait-laced, *Inf.* straight, *Inf.* square.

stultify, *v.* **1.** smother, stifle, suffocate, muzzle, strangle; suppress, repress, frustrate, thwart; neutralize, nullify, negate, cancel, annul, invalidate, *Sl.* nip in the bud, *Sl.* put the kibosh on.

2. make a fool of, *Sl.* make a monkey of, *Brit. Sl.* make a mug of, *Sl.* put [s.o.] on, *Sl.* play for a sucker.

stumble, *v.* **1.** trip, fall, fall down, fall flat on one's face, tumble, take a spill, *Inf.* take a header, *Inf.* come a cropper; stagger, lurch, pitch, careen, *Brit. Dial.* stoit.

2. err, make a mistake, blunder, bungle, botch, muff, flub, fumble, *Inf.* slip up, *Inf.* drop the ball, *Inf.* put one's foot in one's mouth, *Inf.* put one's foot in it, *Sl.* goof, *Sl.* make *or* pull a boner, *Sl.* make a boo-boo, *Sl.* commit a no-no, *Sl.* boot one *or* it.

3. falter, hesitate, waver, hover, hang back, pause; demur, balk, boggle, scruple, have qualms, think twice, have second thoughts; hem and haw, blow hot and cold, shilly-shally, be of two minds, be unable to make up one's mind, not know one's own mind.

4. **stumble upon** chance upon, happen upon, come across, hit upon, find, discover, locate; encounter, meet, run across *or* into, cross the path of, *Inf.* meet up with, *Inf.* come *or* run up against, *Inf.* bump into, *Inf.* run smack into.

stumbling block, *n.* obstacle, obstruction, block, impediment, hindrance, barrier, bar; difficulty, hurdle; snag, hitch, catch, drawback, rub, fly in the ointment, *Inf.* joker, *Inf.* one small problem.

stump, *n.* **1.** trunk, stem, stalk; remnant, remains; stub, end, butt, tail end, tail, dock.

2. heavy footfall *or* footstep, clump, clunk, thud, thump; tramp, stomping, lumbering.

3. hustings, campaign trail, rubber-chicken circuit; podium, dais, speaker's platform.

—*v.* **4.** truncate, shorten, lop *or* lop off, cut off, dock, amputate; crop, poll, clip, snip, trim, prune, pollard; chop down, hack, hew, fell.

5. nonplus, render at a loss, perplex, puzzle, confuse, confound, baffle, bewilder, mystify; embarrass, disconcert, perturb, ruffle; outwit, trick, surprise.

6. clump, clomp, clunk, peg, hobble, limp; stomp, stamp, trudge, lumber, plod.

7. *Informal.* campaign, whistle-stop, take to the stump *or* hustings, run, run hard; kiss babies, shake hands, ring doorbells, visit factory gates, work the crowds; electioneer, canvass, round up votes, count votes.

stun, *v.* **1.** deaden, numb, benumb, anesthetize, knock out, *Euph.* put to sleep; *All Sl.* KO, kayo, lay out, coldcock.

2. shock, startle, gravel, jar, jolt, shake, shake up, give one a turn, take aback, *Inf.* discombobulate; hit like a ton of bricks, daze, bedaze, strike dumb, stupefy, paralyze, freeze; terrify, frighten out of one's wits *or* senses, *Sl.* scare stiff.

3. amaze, astound, astonish, take one's breath away, make one's head swim, overwhelm, overpower, *Inf.* flabbergast, *Inf.* bowl over, *Inf.* snow, *Sl.* blow away, *Sl.* blow one's mind; dumfound, confound, nonplus, bewilder, discompose, *Inf.* flummox.

stunning, *adj.* **1.** astonishing, astounding, amazing, extraordinary, out of the ordinary, incredible, unbelievable; marvelous, wonderful, wondrous, fabulous, prodigious, miraculous; sensational, spectacular; startling, shocking, staggering, jolting, jarring, eye-opening; overwhelming, overpowering, mind-boggling, *Sl.* mind-blowing; confounding, bewildering, stupefying, paralyzing; petrifying, terrifying, frightening.

2. dazzling, resplendent, brilliant, foudroyant, gorgeous, glorious, ravishing, divine, sublime, *Sl.* devastating, *Sl.* killing; splendid, capital, grand, magnificent, superb, exquisite, *Sl.* out of this world; beautiful, lovely, fetching.

stunt[1], *v.* **1.** dwarf, stop, slow, check, arrest, abort, hinder, hamper, impede; curb, restrain, restrict, confine, delimit, cramp.

—*n.* **2.** hindrance, impediment, dwarfing, check, curb, restraint, confinement, delimitation.

3. dwarf, midget, pygmy, runt, shrimp, homunculus, *Archaic.* atomy, bantam.

stunt², *n.* feat, trick, exploit, tour de force; deed, act, action, doing, *Archaic.* gest.

stupefaction, *n.* **1.** stupor. See **stupor** (*def.* **2**).

2. amazement, astonishment, astoundment; wonder, wonderment, breathless wonder, awe; bewilderment, confoundment, perplexity, bafflement.

stupefied, *adj.* **1.** numb, numbed, benumbed, deadened; comatose, in a coma *or* stupor, senseless, insensible, unconscious, oblivious, out, out cold, dead to the world, knocked out, anesthetized, *Euph.* asleep; drugged, doped; *All Sl.* blitzed, stoned, out of it, in the ozone, in another zone, spaced *or* spaced out, in outer space, lost in space.

2. stunned, dazed, bedazed, dazzled; amazed, astonished, astounded, *Inf.* flabbergasted; breathless, awestruck, thunderstruck, unable to believe one's eyes; bewildered, confounded, dumfounded, struck dumb; petrified, paralyzed, frozen, scared to death, *Sl.* scared stiff.

stupefy, *v.* **1.** stun, benumb; drug, narcotize, *Sl.* dope up. See also **stun** (*def.* **1**).

2. daze; amaze. See **stun** (*defs.* **2, 3**).

stupendous, *adj.* **1.** amazing, astounding, astonishing, miraculous, surpassing belief; wondrous, wonderful, remarkable, marvelous, extraordinary, out of the ordinary, *Sl.* out of this world, phenomenal; fabulous, fantastic, *Sl.* far-out; staggering, breath-taking, *Sl.* stunning; indescribable, ineffable, mind-boggling, *Sl.* mind-blowing.

2. immense, colossal, vast, prodigious, huge, gigantic, *Sl.* gigundo, titanic, enormous, massive, monstrous, mighty.

stupid, *adj.* **1.** dull-witted, *Inf.* dumb, unintelligent, fatuitous, insensate, *Brit. Inf.* gormless; empty-headed, brainless, mindless, *Rare.* insulse; dull, *Sl.* lamebrained, slow, *Inf.* dopey, *Inf.* dill, oxlike; unthinking, unreasoning, incogitant; dim-witted, slow-witted, half-witted, fat-witted, thick-witted, beef-witted, witless, unwitty; imbecilic, *Inf.* moronic, retarded, subnormal, deficient; dense, thick, duncish, obtuse, bovine, *Inf.* cretinous, stolid, Boeotian; lumpish, oafish, cloddish, boorish, blunt, crass, tactless; addlepated, addlebrained, addleheaded, muddled, muddleheaded; doltish, blockish, asslike, blockheaded, dunderheaded, noodle-headed; boneheaded, wooden-headed, thickheaded, thickskulled; obstinate, stubborn, intractable, mulish, bullish, bullheaded, obdurate, unyielding, unbending.

2. simple-minded, simple, bird-brained, weak-minded, weak-headed, feeble-minded; harebrained, light-minded, light-headed, giddy, mercurial; absent-minded, scatterbrained, confused, bemused; featherheaded, featherbrained, rattleheaded, rattlebrained; childish, puerile, immature; naive, simple, unsophisticated, gullible, green.

3. foolish, silly, absurd, inane, *Sl.* cuckoo, fatuous; pointless, futile, profitless, fruitless; senseless, nonsensical, *Inf.* damfool, crackbrained, *Scot.* doiled, *Sl.* cockeyed, *Scot. and North Eng.* glaikit; ridiculous, laughable, risible, derisible, ludicrous, *Sl.* for the birds; asinine, anserine, idiotic, idiotical; frivolous, frothy, superficial, undiscriminating.

4. unreasonable, irrational, illogical, meaningless; preposterous, extravagant, excessive; unrealistic, half-baked; haphazard, aimless, driftless, unconnected, groundless; irrelevant, inconsequential, purposeless; inappropriate, inept, improper, incongruous, inconsistent; imprudent, indiscreet; unwise, ill-considered, ill-suited, ill-advised, injudicious; heedless, unheeding, short-sighted, careless, unwary; foolhardy, reckless, irresponsible, rash, harum-scarum.

5. vapid, insipid, *Brit. Dial.* wearish, banal, bland, tame; prosaic, humdrum, unimaginative, uninteresting, ordinary, commonplace; tedious, boring, monotonous, wearing, tiring, tiresome; empty, void, vacuous, blank, unoccupied.

6. stupefied, numb, benumbed; comatose, insensible, impassive, unconscious, semiconscious; inanimate, insensate; stunned, dazed, dazzled, in a daze, knocked silly; spiritless, lifeless, inert, torpid, lethargic; sluggish, groggy, drugged, punchy; soporific, slumberous, somnolent; lazy, lackadaisical, fainéant.

—*n.* **7.** *Informal.* imbecile, mooncalf, *Inf.* moron; fool, saphead, Simple Simon, noodle, *Inf.* jay, *Sl.* jerk, goose; simpleton, nincompoop, silly billy, driveler; dimwit, nitwit, half-wit, featherbrain; scatterbrain, rattlehead, rattlepate, rattlebrain; dope, booby, *Sl.* lamebrain, *Inf.* dummy, *Sl.* dumb-bell, *Sl.* dumbhead; dolt, *Inf.* cretin, dunce, clod, oaf; ignoramus, know-nothing, lowbrow, illiterate.

stupidity, *n.* **1.** dull-wittedness, *Inf.* dumbness, unintelligence, fatuity, insensateness, bêtise; imbecility, *Inf.* moronism, *Inf.* moronity, retardation, subnormality; empty-headedness, brainlessness, mindlessness; dullness, *Inf.* dopiness, witlessness, unwittiness; vapidity, insipidness, insipidity, banality, blandness; emptiness, voidness, vacancy, vacuity, blankness.

2. denseness, density, obtuseness, bovinity, stolidness; lumpishness, oafishness, cloddishness, boorishness; doltishness, blockheadedness, thickheadedness; obstinateness, obstinacy, stubbornness, bullheadedness; bluntness, crassness, tactlessness.

3. simple-mindedness, feeble-mindedness; childishness, puerility, immaturity; naivité, simplicity, unsophistication, gullibility.

4. unreasonableness, irrationality, illogicalness, illogicality, meaninglessness; irrelevance, inconsequentiality, insignificance, nugacity, triviality; inappropriateness, ineptness, ineptitude, improperness, incongruousness, incongruity, inconsistency; imprudence, indiscretion, heedlessness, carelessness, unwariness, foolhardiness, recklessness, irresponsibility, rashness.

5. absurdity, absurdness, foolishness, folly, silliness, inanity, fatuousness; pointlessness, senselessness, futility, fruitlessness; ridiculousness, ridiculosity, laughableness, ludicrousness, asininity, idiocy, idioticalness; superficiality, frothiness, frivolousness.

6. nonsense, nonsensicality, nonsensicalness, fiddle-faddle; amphigory, poppycock, bosh, balderdash; twaddle, babble, babblement, prattle, blather, gabble.

stupor, *n.* **1.** coma, *Pathol.* sopor; daze, trance, dream state.

2. numbness, unfeelingness, deadness, stupefaction; unconsciousness, senselessness, insensibility, obliviousness; torpor, inertness, supineness; lassitude, listlessness, lethargy, sluggishness, languor, lifelessness, *Inf.* dopiness; apathy, indifference, unresponsiveness, dullness, phlegm.

sturdy, *adj.* **1.** stalwart, stout, rugged, hefty, husky, burly, iron, solid, tough, yeomanly, *Scot.* buirdly, *Scot. and North Eng.* stiff, *Inf.* tough as nails, *Inf.* hard as rock; muscular, muscled, well-muscled, full-muscled, strong, brawny, strapping, broad-shouldered, powerfully-built, herculean, musclebound; powerful, mighty, *Literary.* puissant; able, able-bodied, athletic, sinewy, well-knit; robust, vigorous, full of vigor, hardy, hearty, hale and hearty, hale, lusty, strong and healthy, bursting with health *or* vigor; sound, healthy, in good health, fit, physically fit, in fine fettle, in good condition, *Inf.* in good shape, *Inf.* in shape.

2. sound, stout, solid, substantial, well-built, well-made, well-constructed; hard, heavy, tough, durable, long-lasting, lasting, made to last.

3. firm, staunch, steadfast, doughty, tenacious; uncompromising, unyielding, inexorable, intransigent; resolute, resolved, determined, decided, fixed; unflinching, unswerving, unwavering, undeviating, unshrinking, unbending, unfaltering, unhesitating; stubborn, obstinate, pertinacious; indefatigable, tireless, untiring, unflagging, unwearying, enduring, staminal; indomitable, invincible, unconquerable, defiant, resistant, resisting; mettlesome, plucky, gritty, game, spirited, red-blooded, *Inf.* spunky.

4. brave, courageous, valiant, valorous, heroic, herolike, stout-hearted, ironhearted, lionhearted, greathearted, *Archaic.* stalworth; virile, manly, manful, masculine, gallant, chivalrous, chivalric; intrepid, fearless, dauntless, aweless, dreadless, undaunted, unalarmed, undismayed, unappalled, unblenched; bold, daring, dashing, audacious, adventurous, bold-spirited, high-spirited.

stutter, *v.* **1.** stammer, pause, hesitate, falter, stumble, speak haltingly.

—*n.* **2.** stammer, speech impediment *or* defect.

sty, *n.* **1.** pigpen, pigsty, *Chiefly Brit.* piggery.

2. hole, hovel, pesthole, *Sl.* dump, *Sl.* dive, *Sl.* flop house; slum, warren, rookery; sink, sewer, cesspool.

style, *n.* **1.** mode, manner, *Archaic.* guise, method, taste; system, approach, way; type, kind, sort; fashion, cut, line, design, pattern; form, shape, texture, quality.

2. fashion, *Brit.* twig, mode, vogue, look; trend, rage, fad, craze, latest thing; practice, custom, general tendency.

3. stylishness, smartness, nattiness, spruceness, dapperness, trimness, neatness; fashionableness, modishness, chic, elegance; dressiness, flashiness, *Sl.* snazziness, *Sl.* sharpness; flair, panache, pizzazz, dash; fanciness, *Sl.* ritziness, *Inf.* swankiness, luxuriousness, *Sl.* class; polish, grace, refinement, culture; sophistication, cosmopolitanism, urbanity, urbaneness, suavity, suaveness.

4. tone, spirit, strain, vein; character, *Obs.* tenor, characteristic, condition; spirit, feeling, mood, temper; mark, stamp, brand, seal, touch.

5. phraseology, wording, phrasing, expression; language, words, vocabulary, dialect, speech.

—*v.* **6.** name, call, address, denominate, designate; term, tag, label, dub.

7. design, fashion, make, do; sketch, outline, draft, plan, delineate, trace out, block out.

stylish, *adj.* **1.** fashionable, smart, natty, spruce, dapper, trim; chic, modish, a-go-go, in the very latest style; in vogue, à la mode, in fashion, in style; popular, in, *Sl.* in the groove, all the rage; up-to-date, current, modern, mod, new; up-to-the-minute, *Inf.* trendy, *Sl.* cool, *Inf.* nifty, *Sl.* neat, *Sl.* hip, *Sl.* hep.

2. elegant, high-class, *Sl.* classy, high-toned, *Sl.* tony; silk-stocking, posh, luxurious, *Sl.* ritzy, fancy, *Inf.* swank, *Inf.* swanky, *Sl.* swell; dressy, flashy, *Sl.* snazzy, *Sl.* sharp, *Sl.* sharp as a tack; suave, urbane, sophisticated, chi-chi, cosmopolitan.

stylist, *n.* **1.** craftsman, purist, classicist; writer, author; speaker, orator; artist.

2. couturier, couturière, fashion designer, designer; interior decorator, decorator, room designer.

stylize, *v.* formalize, conventionalize, ritualize, ceremonialize, solemnize; shape, pattern, design, form, arrange, fashion, frame, block out.

suave, *adj.* urbane, sophisticated, worldly; courteous, polite, civil, fair-spoken, smooth-spoken; pleasant, agreeable, easy to get along with, tactful, diplomatic; smooth, bland, untroublesome; nonchalant, unexcitable, casual. See also **slick** (*def.* **2**).

subaltern, *adj.* **1.** subordinate, junior, lower, inferior. See **subordinate** (*def.* **1**).

—*n.* **2.** subordinate, underling, inferior, subject. See **subordinate** (*def.* **3**).

subconscious, *adj.* **1.** suppressed, repressed, hidden, unconscious, latent, *Inf.* Freudian; deep, inmost, innermost, inner, deep-rooted, underlying, *Psychol.* subliminal.

—*n.* **2.** subconsciousness, inner self, unconscious, unconsciousness; collective unconscious.

subdivision, *n.* **1.** division, subcategory, category, subgenus, genus, *Biol.* phylum, subclass, class, subgroup, group, subspecies, species, *Biol.* suborder, *Biol.* order, *Biol.* subfamily, *Biol.* family.

2. portion, piece, share, part, section, subsection, segment, subsegment.

subdue, *v.* **1.** conquer, vanquish, subjugate, oppress; rout, discomfit, put to flight, overwhelm, overrun, trample, crush, overthrow; smash, thrash, trim, whip, drub, floor, bow; *Inf.* skin alive, *Inf.* settle [s.o.'s] hash, worst, defeat.

2. master, overpower, overcome, surmount, triumph over, get the better of; control, subject to one's will, dominate, gain the upper hand over, browbeat, overawe, intimidate; humble, bring down, have at one's beck and call, have eating out of one's hand, *Inf.* have wrapped around one's little finger; captivate, charm, enthrall, ensnare, capture, tame, break, bend, reduce, break in, discipline, gentle, domesticate, *Obs.* domesticize; repress, suppress, put down, quell, restrain, check, curb, choke, smother, inhibit; muzzle, bridle, harness, rein, rein in, hold back, keep down, hold *or* keep in check.

3. reduce, moderate, temper, soften, mellow, tone down, muffle, silence, mute, quiet, dull, soft-pedal.

4. allay, alleviate, palliate, mollify, assuage, salve, relieve, dulcify; appease, pacify, soothe, still, ease, calm, gentle; mitigate, reduce, abate, slacken, slake, *Obs.* lenify; blunt, dull, cushion, tranquilize, deaden, kill; remedy, ameliorate.

subdued, *adj.* **1.** quiet, hushed, mute; calm, peaceful, tranquil, sedate, composed, collected, reserved, solemn, grave, somber, sober, unperturbed, unagitated.

2. controlled, repressed, restrained, inhibited, smothered, bridled, muzzled, held in check.

3. unresponsive, undemonstrative, unimpassioned, unemotional, inactive, passive, dull, dead, lifeless, spiritless.

4. reduced, lowered, muted, toned down; subtle, refined, finely shaded, tasteful.

subject, *n.* **1.** topic, subject matter, matter, theme, angle; gist, meaning, substance, point, *Inf.* nub, heart; text, thesis, proposition; plot, plot line, story; motif, leitmotif.

2. branch of knowledge *or* study, discipline, course, study, course of study.

3. motive, cause, ground, rationale, reason, basis, source; peg, occasion, instance, factor; provocation, inducement, instigation.

4. liege, dependent, retainer.

5. citizen, national, allegiant, inhabitant, resident, taxpayer, voter.

6. puppet, satellite, cat's-paw, tool, instrument, *Sl.* stooge; underling, subordinate, follower, handmaid; chattel, thrall, slave, bondman, bondmaid, vassal, serf.

7. patient, case, client; examinee, testee, *Inf.* guinea pig.

—*adj.* **8.** dependent, subservient, subordinate, inferior, under [s.o.'s] thumb, not able to call one's soul one's own, at [s.o.'s] beck and call; servile, slavish, subjugated, crushed, abject; puppetlike, satellite, vassal; controlled, manipulated, dominated, ruled; powerless, impotent, unable to stand on one's own two feet;

downtrodden, oppressed, voiceless, without any say.

9. allegiant, loyal, faithful, obedient, respectful; obeisant, deferential, reverential.

10. open, exposed, naked, vulnerable, in danger of; susceptible, pregnable, assailable.

11. conditional, depending, contingent, at [s.o.'s] pleasure, provisional.

12. liable, prone to, sensitive to, susceptive, apt to, likely to.

—*v.* **13.** conquer, quell, subdue, subjugate, subordinate, bring to one's knees, master, dominate, rule; enslave, enthrall, capture; tame, break, bend to one's will, lead by the nose, use as a doormat, humble, crush, keep down.

14. lay open, expose, make vulnerable; treat, put through, give, deal, deliver, administer.

subjection, *n.* **1.** quelling, crushing, trampling, defeating, subduing, conquering, enslaving, breaking, humbling, humiliating; domination, subjugation, mastery, control.

2. thrall, thralldom, bondage, captivity, slavery, servitude; chains, shackles, manacles, fetters; enslavement, vassalage, peonage; dependence, powerlessness, weakness, humiliation, abasement.

subjective, *adj.* **1.** nonobjective, mental, internal, in the mind's eye, subconscious, intellectual.

2. individual, personal, biased, prejudiced, idiosyncratic.

3. egocentric, self-centered, selfish, self-interested, egoistic, self-serving; wrapped up in oneself, narcissistic, introverted, self-conscious; bigoted, illiberal; self-confident, self-assured, self-satisfied.

4. intrinsic, inherent, essential, substantial, integral, material, fundamental.

subjugate, *v.* **1.** master, overcome, overpower, overbear, overwhelm; conquer, vanquish, rout, defeat, beat; reduce, subdue, quash, quell, suppress; squash, trample on, beat down, put down, crush, bring [s.o.] to his knees; humble, bring down, humiliate; tame, discipline, break, break in, bring to heel, put under the yoke.

2. enslave, enthrall, subject, hold in bondage, hold captive, make chattel of; fetter, chain, enchain, shackle; command, dominate, domineer, overrule, rule, sway, tyrannize; oppress, tread on, walk on, sit on, keep under; colonize, annex.

sublimate, *v.* **1.** channel, redirect, turn, shift, transfer, divert; change, alter, convert, transform, transmute.

2. elevate, ennoble, greaten; exalt, heighten, lift, uplift; raise, boost, aggrandize, magnify.

3. clean, cleanse, purify, refine; expurgate, purge, bowdlerize, clear, spiritualize.

sublime, *adj.* **1.** elevated, lofty, exalted, noble, high; eminent, dignified, solemn, ennobled; glorified, beatified, sanctified, canonized, deified, apostheosized; distinguished, renowned, celebrated, lauded, famed, famous; prominent, preeminent, notable, noted, respected; estimable, creditable, meritorious, laudable, righteous, virtuous; principled, high-minded, admirable, honorable, good, magnanimous.

2. inspiring, awe-inspiring, soul-subduing, majestic, imposing, humbling; impressive, breath-taking, *Sl.* mind-blowing, *Inf.* out of this world; magnificent, grand, august, stately, princely, kingly, regal; gorgeous, superb, resplendent, splendid; fabulous, marvelous, wondrous, remarkable, stupendous, tremendous; overwhelming, overpowering, dramatic, sensational; heavenly, divine, splendrous, amazing; glamorous, beautiful, Junoesque, goddess-like, dazzling.

3. outstanding, great, excellent, fantastic; supreme, big, superb; perfect, ideal, consummate, pure; matchless, peerless, capital, paramount; superior, first-rate, first-class, exemplary; classic, sterling, choice, prime, best, select; irreproachable, impeccable, stainless, spotless, blameless, infallible.

—*n.* **4.** perfection, ideal, beau ideal, quintessence; paragon, model, example; crown, peak, apex, acme, pinnacle, zenith; height, summit, the highest, supremacy, *Inf.* tops.

sublimity, *n.* loftiness, elevation, exaltation, nobility; magnificence, glory, majesty, stateliness; dignity, eminence, preeminence, esteem, prominence; excellence, greatness, grandness; grandeur, pomp, circumstance.

submerge, *v.* **1.** sink, submerse, put under, bathe; dip, *Inf.* dunk, duck, push under, douse, wet; immerse, baptize, souse.

2. plunge, plummet, dive, descend, founder; go down, go under, go below, go to the bottom; sound, fathom, plumb.

3. inundate, drown, bury, engulf, overwhelm, whelm; flood, deluge, waterlog, swamp; soak, drench, saturate, rinse.

submerged, *adj.* **1.** underwater, undersea, submarine, subaqueous, subaquatic, below the surface; submersed, immersed, sunk, sunken, buried, engulfed, on the bottom; drowned, flooded, inundated, below, under.

2. hidden, unseen, concealed, cloaked, veiled; shrouded, unknown, untold, unsolved, indecipherable; impenetrable, enigmatic, arcane, recondite, hieroglyphic, puzzling.

submission, *n.* **1.** yielding, giving in, submitting, surrender, subjection, capitulation; compliance, conformity, acquiescence, abidance, acceptance; obedience, allegiance, observance; reverence, deference, respect.

2. submissiveness, conformability, adaptability, complaisance; malleability, tractability, biddableness, pliancy; meekness, timidity, gentleness, passiveness, docility, unassertiveness.

3. subservience, obsequiousness, servility, ingratiation, prostration, obeisance, abasement; truckling, bowing, scraping, fawning, cowering, cringing, crawling, toadying, *Inf.* bootlicking; self-effacement, self-surrender, self-abasement.

submissive, *adj.* **1.** acquiescent, yielding, compliant, pliant, malleable; flexible, accommodating, amenable, agreeable, adapting, adaptable; dutiful, faithful, respectful, deferential, capitulating; willing, assenting, complying, obliging, obedient, obeying; tractable, manageable, nonresisting, unassertive, docile, timid; patient, gentle, meek, passive, subdued.

2. subservient, servile, obsequious, ingratiating, obeisant, prostrate, *Archaic.* sequacious; truckling, bowing, scraping, fawning, cowering, cringing, crawling, toadying, toadyish, *Inf.* bootlicking, self-effacing, self-surrendering, self-abasing.

submit, *v.* **1.** yield, surrender, give in, give way to; capitulate, succumb to, fall, bite the dust, lay down arms, raise the white flag, cry *or* say uncle; resign oneself, acquiesce, throw in the towel, give up the ship, cease the struggle, grin and bear it.

2. obey, observe, comply with, acknowledge, respect; adhere to, abide by, conform to; get into line, toe *or* mark the line, keep in step, walk the chalk mark *or* line; acquiesce in, consent to, agree to; grant, accede, concur, accept.

3. defer to, be regulated by, be governed by, be subject to; stoop, bend to, bow to, truckle to, humble oneself to, bend the knee to, knuckle under, do [s.o.'s] bidding, *Inf.* jump through hoops.

4. refer, present, hand in, turn in, apply, enter, address, appeal.

5. propose, offer, proffer, tender; suggest, advance, present, introduce, put forward, put forth, volunteer, move, bid.

subnormal, *adj.* **1.** inferior, low, too low, under the required level, insufficient, inadequate; below par, below normal, less than average, not up to standards, not up to snuff, second-rate, low-grade; shoddy, slipshod, rickety, cheap, dime-store, bargain-basement, *Inf.* junky, *U.S. Inf.* cheesy, *Brit. Sl.* humpty; bad, awful, terrible, abysmal, wretched, miserable, sorry, dismal, *Inf.* lousy, *Sl.* crappy; shabby, sleazy, seedy, raunchy, squalid, grubstreet.

2. retarded, slow, dull, dull-witted, dim-witted, feeble-minded, weak-minded, of low intelligence, unintelligent, stupid, imbecilic, moronic, *Inf.* dumb; half-witted, not all there, deficient, lacking, unsound, incompetent, infirm, senile, *Inf.* dotty; psychologically *or* emotionally disturbed, maladjusted, unbalanced, neurotic, psychotic; abnormal, aberrant.

subordinate, *adj.* **1.** subaltern, junior, lower, inferior, second-class, less than, below, under; subservient, subject, dependent.

2. secondary, auxiliary, accessory, ancillary, subsidiary.

—*n.* **3.** subaltern, junior, underling, inferior, second fiddle; hireling, employee, hired hand *or* help; dependent, subject, vassal, servant, slave, serf.

subordination, *n.* **1.** inferiority, lesser standing, inferior status, secondary position, second fiddle; lowliness, subservience, subserviency.

2. servility, slavishness, submissiveness, docility, unassertiveness; obsequiousness, abjection, obeisance, prostration; self-abasement, groveling, crawling, creeping, crouching.

sub rosa, *adv.* confidentially, in confidence, just between you and me, just between the two of us, just between you and me and the lamppost, entre nous, *Latin.* *inter nos*; off the record, unofficially; secretly, in secret, softly, sotto voce, in a whispered voice, in a hush-hush manner; privately, in private, aside, alone, exclusively; behind closed doors, *Law.* in camera, out of view, off-camera, in seclusion; obscurely, reconditely, occultly, mysteriously; covertly, clandestinely, surreptitiously, furtively; on the sly, stealthily, sneakily, sneakingly, underhandedly, under-the-table, under-the-counter, through the back door, illicitly, illegally.

subscribe, *v.* **1.** sign up for, sign on the dotted line, sign for, contract for, enter into a contract for; promise to pay for *or* purchase, make a pledge to, promise to contribute *or* give to; take, accept, assume, undertake, take on responsibility for.

2. buy, purchase, pay for, make payment for, remit; buy into, invest in, put money into; contribute toward, make a contribution toward, chip in for, go in on, donate [s.t.] to, make a donation to, give [s.t.] to.

3. sign for, cosign for, countersign for, underwrite; attest to, testify to, advocate, recommend, guarantee; endorse, back up, second, stand behind *or* by, befriend, help, aid.

3. sign for, cosign for, countersign for, underwrite; attest to, testify to, advocate, recommend, guarantee; endorse, back up, second, stand behind *or* by, befriend, help, aid.

4. assent to, give one's assent to, agree to, say "yes" to, consent to, give one's consent for, give permission for, give approval for, approve a request for, authorize, *Inf.* O.K., *Inf.* give the green light *or* go-ahead on; sanction, condone, countenance, give one's blessing to, approve of, go for; allow, permit, tolerate, brook, stand for, put up with, take; believe in, have faith in, have confidence in, trust, *Inf.* put stock in, *Inf.* buy, *Inf.* swallow; accustom oneself to, get used to, reconcile oneself to.

subscription, *n.* **1.** payment, remission, amount paid, price, cost; money, grant, grant-in-aid, subvention, subsidy, stipend, pension, alimony, subsistence allowance; endowment, contribution, oblation, donation, charity, alms; gratuity, tip, gift, present, bounty, largess.

2. purchase agreement, agreement to buy, contract; pledge, obligation, responsibility, investment.

3. outstanding pledges, amount due *or* owed, income from a drive; fund, collection, offering, *Eccles.* offertory.

4. signing, signing on the dotted line, signature; countersignature, underwriting, endorseent, guarantee.

5. postscript, P.S., afterthought, afterword, epilogue, colophon; postfix, suffix, affix; attached signature, autograph, hand, inscription, *Inf.* John Hancock, *Inf.* John Henry; attachment, addendum, appendage, tag, supplement, codicil, appendix, rider, addition, amendment.

6. approval, vote of approval, yes *or* aye vote, ratification, stamp of approval, seal, authorization, *Inf.* O.K.; assent, nod, consent, permission, *Inf.* the green light, *Inf.* the go-ahead; sanction, countenance, blessing, condonation; agreement with, acceptance of, belief in, faith in, trust in, confidence in.

subsequent, *adj.* following, ensuing, succeeding, next, coming, to come, future; successive, consecutive, sequent, sequential, consequent, sequacious.

subserve, *v.* promote, encourage, foster, cultivate, nourish, nurture, help develop; advance, further, help along, bolster, boost, recommend, advocate, speak in favor of, push for, *Inf.* plug *or* put in a plug for; patronize, support, endorse, sanction, back, finance; conduce to, contribute to, add to, improve, strengthen, better, upgrade, ameliorate, meliorate, enhance, enrich, fatten, augment; help *or* help out, lend a hand, give a helping hand, give a leg up, do a good turn, aid, assist, succor; be of service to, be of some use to, be useful to, benefit, serve [s.o.'s] purposes, do some good for; enable, empower, make possible, pave the way, facilitate, facilitate matters, make things easier for, grease the wheels, soap the way.

subservient, *adj.* **1.** subordinate, subaltern, junior, lower; secondary, auxiliary, accessory, ancillary, subsidiary; inferior, second-class, less than, below, under; dependent, subject, under [s.o.'s] thumb.

2. servile, obsequious, *Obs.* obsequent, submissive; docile, tractable, manageable, unassertive, compliant, obedient, deferential, yielding; truckling, obeisant, prostrate, on one's hands and knees; slavish, groveling, cringing, cowering, crawling; sycophantic, sycophantical, sycophantish, fawning, flattering, toadyish, toadying; unctuous, oily, ingratiating, *Sl.* bootlicking, *Sl.* footlicking, *Sl.* brown-nosing, *Inf.* apple-polishing.

3. useful, instrumental, valuable, beneficial, advantageous, favorable, good; helpful, aidful, contributory, contributive, conducive.

subside, *v.* **1.** sink down, sink back, descend, lower, decline; settle, precipitate, gravitate; recede, retrocede, retire, fall back, draw back; lapse, sag, droop, dip, slump, fall off, fail.

2. abate, moderate, let up, mitigate, intermit; quiet down, calm down, *Sl.* simmer down, lull, diminish, lessen, slacken, remit; wane, ebb, taper off, fade away, die out, dwindle, *Inf.* peter out; approach an end, come to a close, be on the way out, obsolesce, be on the wane.

subsidiary, *adj.* **1.** auxiliary, additional, supplemental, supplementary, complementing, reserve, extra; accessory, ancillary; tributary, contributory; helping, assisting, assistant, adjuvant, aiding, abetting, ministrant; ministerial, instrumental.

2. subordinate, subaltern, secondary, junior; lower, inferior, second-class, less than, below, under; subservient, subject, dependent.

subsidize, *v.* **1.** support, finance, maintain, back; fund, sponsor, pay the bill, foot the bill, *Inf.* pick up the tab; aid, help, assist; stake, sink into, invest, *Sl.* angel, set up, bankroll, underwrite.

2. buy over, bribe, purchase, suborn, secure, tip; oil, *Sl.* grease, *Sl.* grease [s.o.'s] palm, throw a sop to; facilitate, speed, expedite, help along.

subsidy, *n.* aid, grant, provision, subvention; allotment, allowance, expense account, viaticum, honorarium, stipend; backing, contribution, gift, award, sponsorship; fellowship, scholarship, assistantship, financial aid, grant-in-aid, state aid, federal aid; pension, annuity, *Law.* alimony, bounty; subsistence, maintenance, support, help; price support, subsidization, write-off, tax exemption, tax break; welfare, dole, public assistance, relief, poor relief; pecuniary assistance, economic aid, foreign aid.

subsist, *v.* **1.** exist, be, live, breathe, draw breath, respire.

2. remain, stay alive, endure; last, continue, stay, survive, persist, hold; abide, bide, fare, run, wear; perdure, keep on, go on, maintain, *Sl.* hang in there; scrape by, eke out, keep body and soul together, *Sl.* get along, *Sl.* get by, make out; cope, keep one's head above water, keep afloat, make ends meet.

3. maintain, support, sustain, keep; feed, nourish, nurture, provide, supply; keep alive, preserve, keep going.

4. *Usu.* **subsist in** reside, dwell, lie in, inhabit; inform, consist in, inhere in; stand, obtain, hold, prevail, be present.

subsistence, *n.* **1.** existence, being, *Latin. esse*, living; actuality, reality, factuality, substantiality, materiality.

2. endurance, duration, continuance, persistence; abidingness, lastingness, preservation, survival, maintenance.

3. support, keep, maintenance, board, room and board, bed and board; upkeep, accommodation, sustenance, sustainment, provision; nourishment, nutriment, nurture, food; daily bread, bread, manna, rations, aliment, bread and water; means, living, livelihood.

substance, *n.* **1.** matter, material, stuff, medium, fabric; building blocks, sum and substance, stock; body, something, element, mass; meat, marrow, flesh and blood.

2. reality, actuality, realness, factuality, hypostatization; materiality, substantiality, substantialness, corporeality, corporeity, ponderability; concreteness, palpability, tangibility, physicality.

3. essence, essentiality, being, essential part, quiddity, haecceity, quintessence, *Metaphys.* hypostasis; principle, entity, suchness, essentialness; essential, fundamental, gravamen, main point, *Latin. sine qua non*, vital element, necessary condition; gist, meat, sum total, soul, core; crux, heart, *Inf.* nub, kernel; keystone, cornerstone, quoin, mainstay.

4. subject, subject matter, theme, thesis, motif; focus, topic, content, purport, text; point, issue, question, case, concern, interest.

5. solidity, density, firmness, stoutness, strength; steadiness, soundness, stability, durability.

6. consistency, body, thickness, stiffness, density, denseness, compactness; cohesion, viscosity, viscidity.

7. meaning, significance, signification, purport, intent, intention; gist, essence, spirit, pith; sense, drift, tenor, tone, vein; denotation, connotation, sense, idea; import, importance, gravity, weight, consequence, moment.

8. in substance a. substantially, essentially, in essence, *Latin. per se*; fundamentally, basically, at heart, at bottom, *Fr. au fond.* **b.** actually, really, in reality, truly; in truth, truthfully, to tell the truth, veritably, verily; in point of fact, as a matter of fact, in fact, in effect, for all practical purposes, as it were, *Fr. au fait.*

substantial, *adj.* **1.** considerable, significant, sizable, major, big, great, grand; large, goodly, tidy, healthy, *Inf.* tall; *Inf.* big-league, *Inf.* major-league, *Inf.* pro, *Inf.* heavyweight, *Inf.* big-time; consequential, weighty, momentous, bulky; notable, noteworthy, marked.

2. real, actual, physical; material, corporeal, incarnate, bodily, somatic, fleshly; palpable, tangible, ponderable, concrete; temporal, earthly, secular; hypostatic, hylic, hylozoistic, materialistic; appreciable, sensible, substantive.

3. firm, strong, solid, hard; stout, massive, big; stable, sound, steady, steadfast, staunch; fast, secure, close; durable, lasting, perdurable, longstanding.

4. compact, dense, tight, thick, packed; concentrated, crowded, jammed, crammed; close-set, thickset, heavy, serried; impenetrable, impermeable, imporous, solid.

5. wealthy, prosperous, well-to-do, rich; flush, flourishing, thriving, affluent; influential, prestigious, powerful, forceful; landed, propertied, moneyed, well-heeled; responsible, solvent, independent, unindebted.

6. essential, fundamental, basic, constitutional, basal, primal; necessary, vital, indispensable, imperative; material, serious, grave, grievous; important, significant, valuable.

7. valid, true, veritable, genuine, authentic; existent, substantive, factual, *Latin. de facto*; positive, absolute, undeniable, reliable, plain, authoritative.

substantiality, *n.* actuality, reality, corporeality, physicality. See **substance** (*def.* **2**).

substantiate, *v.* **1.** prove, establish, demonstrate, ascertain; manifest, evidence, show clearly, document; validate, authenticate, confirm, verify, certify; corroborate, bear out, support, sustain, back up, uphold, vindicate, justify, circumstantiate; vouch for, warrant, guarantee, avouch, attest to, swear to, testify to, endorse.

2. materialize, embody, incarnate, reify, solidify; actualize, realize, externalize, exteriorize, hypostatize.

3. strengthen, breathe life into, flesh out, invigorate, animate; reinforce, bolster, build up.

substantiation, *n.* **1.** proof, documentation, validation, authentication, confirmation, verification, certification; corroboration, vindication, circumstantiation, endorsing; establishment, acknowledgment, avowal, acceptance.

2. embodiment, reification, realization, actualization; animation, strengthening.

substitute, *n.* **1.** sub, succedaneum, replacement, alternate, backup, relief, fill-in; agent, proxy, dummy, surrogate, secondary, deputy, vicar, *Chiefly Brit.* locum tenens, regent, chargé d'affaires; understudy, stand-by, double, stand-in, *Sl.* ringer, imitation, copy, fake, second, changeling; pinch hitter, designated hitter, relief pitcher, pinch runner, second string *or* team, bench warmer; scapegoat, whipping boy.

—*v.* **2.** replace, relieve, sub, fill in, back up, *Inf.* cover, do duty for; stand in, understudy, take the place of, double for, pinch-hit; supersede, supplant; *Sl.* take the rap for.

3. subrogate, surrogate, deputize, delegate; change, interchange.

substitution, *n.* replacement, relief, supersession, supplanting, subrogation, surrogation; deputation, delegation, exchange.

substratum, *n.* base, basis, foundation, footing, groundwork, substructure, substruction, understructure; frame, underlayer, floor, bed.

substructure, *n.* foundation, groundwork, underbuilding, understructure, substruction; basement, cellar, subcellar; base, bottom, underlayer, floor, bed, rest, frame, *Naut.* keel.

subterfuge, *n.* device, contrivance, expedient, *Inf.* dodge, fetch, blind; manuever, feint, deception, sleight, coup, blow, stroke; artifice, stratagem, trick, deceit, wile, ruse, Trojan horse; fake, sham, hoax, swindle, shuck, fraud; shift, move, evasion, shuffle; prevarication, untruth, lie, fib, falsehood; intrigue, plot, plan, scheme, strategy, machination; conspiracy, complot, cabal.

subterranean, *adj.* 1. underground, hypogeal, hypogeous, subterrestrial; below the surface, buried, sunk.

2. hidden, secret, sub rosa, under wraps; concealed, ensconced, shrouded, cloaked, veiled, masked, screened, in the dark; undercover, clandestine, covert, under one's hat, furtive, backdoor, surreptitious; sly, stealthy, sneaky, sneaking, underhand, underhanded.

subtilize, *v.* 1. elevate, sublimate, exalt, heighten, uplift, magnify, ennoble, raise up.

2. sharpen, intensify, deepen, enhance, whet, pique; quicken, accelerate, inflame, increase, augment.

3. refine, rarefy, attenuate, thin out; volatilize, etherealize.

4. discriminate, split hairs, quibble, cavil, pettifog; evade, equivocate, beat about the bush, reason in a circle, beg the question; varnish, gloss over.

subtle, *adj.* 1. thin, tenuous, slender, slight, attenuated; filmy, diaphonous, sheer, gossamer, gossamery, silken, transparent; ethereal, volatile, light, buoyant, floating, unsubstantial, imponderous; rarefied, refined, sublimated.

2. delicate, fine, nice, intricate, elegant, exquisite; not obvious, faint, mysterious.

3. astute, acute, keen, shrewd, sagacious, discerning, penetrating, discriminating, deep, profound.

4. crafty, cunning, wily, foxy, sly, artful, tricky; insidious, strategic, designing, casuistic, Machiavellian, jesuitical; insinuating, shifty, deceptive, crooked, underhand, stealthy.

5. clever, ingenious, expert, skillful, adroit, dexterous, deft, *Fr. au fait*; quick, apt, *Brit. Dial.* feat, slick, smart, crackerjack; proficient, masterly, accomplished, versed, experienced, finished, neathanded, fine-fingered, artistic, sophisticated, resourceful.

subtlety, *n.* 1. thinness, slenderness, slightness, attentuation; sheerness, transparency, silkiness; lightness, airiness, etherealness, buoyancy, unsubstantiality.

2. delicacy, fineness, nicety, intricacy, elegance, exquisiteness; rareness, refinement, rarefaction.

3. astuteness, acuteness, keenness, shrewdness, sharpness, acumen; sagaciousness, discernment, discrimination, depth, profundity.

4. craftiness, cunning, slyness, guile, artfulness; insidiousness, stratagem, intrigue, casuistry, Machiavellianism, *Disparaging.* jesuitism, deception, artifice.

5. cleverness, ingenuity, expertness, skillfulness, adroitness, dexterity, deftness; proficiency, mastery, accomplishment, resourcefulness.

subtract, *v.* 1. withdraw, take away, abstract, remove, take out, take from, *Archaic.* subduct.

2. deduct, discount, take off, *Inf.* lop off, *Sl.* knock off.

subtraction, *n.* deduction, removal, withdrawal, abstraction, *Archaic.* subduction, taking away; diminution, lessening, abridgment, reduction.

suburb, *n.* 1. outlying district *or* region, faubourg, purlieu, *Sl.* shruburb, bedroom community; environs, outskirts, *Sl.* burbs, *Fr. banlieue*; neighborhood, *Fr. alentours*, vicinity, vicinage, area, surrounding area.

2. edge, fringe, periphery, perimeter, border, boundary, frontier; confines, limits, bounds, pale.

subvention, *n.* grant, award, gift, provision, bounty. See **subsidy**.

subversion, *n.* 1. overthrow, overturn, defeat, conquest, vanquishment; upset, disruption, upheaval, revolution, coup d'état; supplantation, ouster, replacement, displacement; disestablishment, deposition; espionage, treason, sabotage, incendiarism, sedition.

2. demolition, pulverization, destruction, breakup; devastation, desolation, ravagement, despoilment, ruin, ruination, waste; obliteration, annihilation, extinguishment, extinction, expunction, abolition, abolishment; extirpation, discreation, eradication, extermination; blotting out, striking out, stamping out, crushing out, wiping out.

3. corruption, depravation, warping, perversion, demoralization, vitiation; debasement, degradation, demeaning; contamination, tainting, pollution, defilement; injury, marring, damage, spoilage.

4. undermining, sapping, weakening; discrediting, invalidation; nullification, neutralization, counteraction.

subversive, *adj.* 1. insurrectionary, seditionary, seditious, insurgent, incendiary; treasonous, traitorous; revolutionary, underground.

2. overpowering, overwhelming, upsetting; disruptive, riotous, calamitous, disastrous, cataclysmic, catastrophic; destructive, destroying, ravaging, wasting, ruinous, ruining; demolishing, demolitionary, devastating, desolating, shattering.

3. undermining, weakening, demoralizing, invalidating, nullifying, neutralizing.

—*n.* 4. saboteur, insurrectionary; insurgent, fifth column, fifth columnist; traitor, Trojan Horse; sympathizer, collaborator, collaborationist; seditionary, incendiary; radical, revolutionary, rebel.

subvert, *v.* 1. overthrow, overturn, overpower, topple, defeat, conquer, vanquish, oust; upset, overwhelm, turn upside down, invert, disrupt, upheave; supplant, replace, displace; disestablish; depose, dethrone, unseat, remove from office, uncrown, discrown, unfrock.

2. demolish, wipe out, pulverize, wreck, *Sl.* total, destroy; obliterate, annihilate, extinguish, expunge, abolish; extirpate, eradicate, exterminate; blot out, strike out, stamp out, crush out, devastate, desolate, lay waste; ravage, despoil, work havoc upon, ruin, *Dial.* ruinate; raze, fell, level; shatter, crash, smash, batter, break; pull down, tear down, take down, bring down, break down, throw down, cast down, beat down, knock down, undo.

3. corrupt, deprave, warp, pervert, demoralize, vitiate; debase, reduce, lower, degrade, demean; contaminate, taint, poison, pollute, defile; injure, mar, damage, spoil, spot, mark, stain; scar, deface, blemish.

4. undermine, sap, weaken; discredit, invalidate; nullify, neutralize, counteract.

subway, *n.* underground railroad, underground, *Inf.* tube, metro, BMT, IRT, MTA; el.

succeed, *v.* **1.** turn out well, *Inf.* pan out, work out; reach *or* get to first base, get off the ground, *Sl.* fly.

2. accomplish, do, carry out *or* through, complete, fulfill, realize; achieve, attain, reach, arrive at; succeed in, manage, bring off, *Sl.* pull off, *Inf.* put over, *U.S. Sl.* swing it, *Inf.* cut it *or* cut the mustard, *U.S. Sl.* hack it.

3. attain success, make good, make it, *Inf.* arrive; thrive, prosper, grow, flourish, fare well, *Brit. Dial.* fadge; advance, get ahead, *Inf.* go places, go *or* come up in the world, rise in the world, climb the ladder of success, progress, make headway, get on *or* along; pass, *Inf.* make the grade, *Inf.* pass muster, *U.S. Sl.* come through, come through with flying colors; triumph *or* triumph over, win, win out over, be victorious, prevail *or* prevail over, conquer; win one's spurs, earn one's wings; impress favorably, make a hit, make a splash, *Inf.* go over big; be fortunate, *Inf.* luck out, have a streak *or* run of luck; strike it rich, strike oil *or* gold, make it big, hit the jackpot, *Inf.* hit the bull's-eye; grow rich, become wealthy, make one's fortune *or* pile; be well-off, be on easy street, be comfortable *or* set, lead a life of luxury *or* ease, live the life of Riley.

4. *Often* **succeed to** accede to, inherit, come into, enter upon, assume, take on *or* over, replace, take the place of, supersede, supplant.

5. come after, come next, follow, follow after, ensue, supervene.

succeeding, *adj.* subsequent, following, ensuing, next, coming. See **subsequent.**

success, *n.* attainment, accomplishment, achievement; hit, *Inf.* smash, *Sl.* sockeroo, sensation, winner, best seller; box-office hit, sellout, *Theat.* boff, *Sl.* boffo *or* boffola; triumph, victory, *Inf.* ten-strike, *Inf.* grand slam; coup, stroke of genius, tour de force, master stroke, *Fr. coup de maître*; stroke *or* piece of luck, good fortune; prosperity, prosperousness, good life, life of ease *or* luxury, *Sl.* easy street, *Sl.* life of Riley; money, wealth, riches, fortune, affluence, opulence, *Sl.* fat city; fame, celebrity, renown, widespread and high repute.

successful, *adj.* prosperous, flourishing, thriving, prospering, going, booming, growing, mushrooming, burgeoning; profitable, remunerative, gainful, rewarding, productive, cost-effective, fructuous, fruitful; lucrative, paying, well-paying, moneymaking; best-selling, *Sl.* boffo, *Sl.* socko, impressive, winning, triumphant, victorious; important, big, great, famous, famed, renowned, well-known, known the world over, rising, *U.S.* up-and-coming, advancing, aggressive, *Sl.* hotshot; succeeding, out in front, at the head of the pack, leading, ahead of the game, on top, *Sl.* on top of the heap *or* pile, *Inf.* on top of the world, in the catbird seat, *Sl.* sitting pretty; well-to-do, well-off, *Inf.* well-heeled, wealthy, rich, opulent, affluent, fat; moneyed, *Inf.* in the money, flush, *Sl.* loaded, *Sl.* in the bucks, *Sl.* rolling in dough; very comfortable, financially set, *Inf.* well-fixed, in clover, *Sl.* on easy street, on a bed of roses, *Sl.* in velvet.

succession, *n.* **1.** order, sequence, consecution, progression, gradation, step; series, procession, following, consecutiveness, suite; cycle, round, rotation, turn, catenation, concatenation; course, flow, run, chain, train; continuity, continuousness, continuance, extension, prolongation.

2. (*usu. of an office, title, or position*) accession, inheritance, assumption, taking on *or* over; entering upon, arrival at, advent to; elevation, promotion, rise, coming to, reaching, attainment; induction, installation, initiation, inauguration, investiture, crowning.

3. dynasty, ancestral line, ancestry, lineage, descent, extraction, derivation, filiation; heritage, birth, birthright, family, stock; pedigree, bloodline, strain, race; descendants, offspring, children, progeny, issue, seed, posterity, future generations.

successive, *adj.* **1.** consecutive, serial, seriate, seriatum, in a series, one after the other, in a row, side by side; back to back, uninterrupted, without a break, unbroken, continuous, nonstop; in sequence, step-by-step, progressive, regular, in order, orderly, ordinal, 1-2-3, consequent, logical; direct, lineal, in a line.

2. next, next in line, sequential, sequent, succeeding, subsequent, following, ensuing; adjacent, next-door, neighboring, bordering, contiguous, adjoining, attached; immediate, closest, nearest, proximate.

successor, *n.* **1.** heir, inheritor, heritor, heir apparent, heir at law, heiress, heritress, inheritrix; coheir, coheiress, joint heir, *Law.* parcener; follower, *Inf.* next in line; replacement, substitute; beneficiary, recipient, receiver, devisee, legatee, *Law.* reversioner; *Law.* donee.

2. dispossessor, supplanter, usurper.

3. descendant, scion, offspring; children, progeny, brood, spawn, issue, seed, posterity, future generations.

succinct, *adj.* **1.** concise, brief, short, written in a few well-chosen words, short and sweet, tight, neat; terse, pithy, meaty, epigrammatic, sententious; direct, straightforward, to the point, pointed; cryptic, shorthand, coded; clipped, cut short, Yankee, abrupt; curt, brusque, crisp, military, brisk, fast.

2. compact, capsule, condensed, compressed, compendious, synoptic, summary, summarized; abridged, abbreviated, shortened, curtailed, pocket-sized, traveling.

succor, *n.* **1.** aid, assistance, help, a helping hand, support, reinforcement; relief, a rest, a break, a breather; ministration, ministry, treatment, therapy; care, tender loving care, TLC, comfort, consolation, solace, a lift, a boost, a shot in the arm.

2. lifesaver, savior, rescuer, the cavalry; aid, aide, aider, abettor, helper, helpmate, helpmeet, assistant, auxiliary, coadjutor, coadjutress, coadjutrix, coadjutant, right hand, right-hand man, gal *or* man Friday, *Mil.* aide-de-camp; relief, reinforcement, substitute, *Inf.* sub, backup, fill-in, stand-in, replacement; pain-reliever, succorer, ministrant, nurse, doctor, therapist; comforter, consoler, solacer, shoulder to cry on; friend, friend in need, ally, supporter, good Samaritan, *Inf.* fairy godmother.

—*v.* **3.** aid, come to [s.o.'s] aid, render assistance to, assist, help out, help, lend a helping hand, support, back up, reinforce; come to [s.o.'s] rescue, rescue [s.o.] from [s.t.], save, liberate, deliver; disburden, relieve, give [s.o.] a rest, give [s.o.] a break, fill in for, substitute for, take [s.o.'s] place, take over for, replace; care for, take care of, attend to, minister to, nurse, doctor, treat.

succulent, *adj.* **1.** juicy, full of juice, sappy, dripping; soft, doughy, spongy, pappy, mushy; (*all of plants*) fleshy, pithy, pulpy, pulpous, pulpal, pulplike, pulpaceous.

2. rich, rich in vitamins and minerals, nutritious, nutritive, nourishing, good for you, healthy, healthful, salubrious.

succumb, *v.* **1.** yield, give way, submit, give in, admit, concede; surrender, give up, capitulate, admit defeat, cry *or* say uncle, throw in the towel *or* sponge, lay down one's arms, strike one's colors; draw in one's horns, put one's tail between one's legs, retreat, back off *or* down, withdraw, retire.

2. deteriorate, worsen, go downhill, fail, go under *or* down; die, expire, decease, perish, *Sl.* bite the dust, *Sl.* kick the bucket, *Sl.* kick in; give up the ghost, breathe one's last, draw one's last breath, *Sl.* croak; pass away *or* on, go the way of all flesh, pay the debt of nature, pay Charon, *Sl.* cash in, *Sl.* cash in one's chips, *Sl.* turn up one's toes; go to one's reward, go to one's resting place, go to one's last home, go the happy hunting ground, leave this world, *Euph.* go west.

such, *adj.* of that kind, of that sort, of that type, suchlike; like, similar, akin, kindred; corresponding, resembling, representing.

suck, *v.* **1.** (*all in reference to or by means of the mouth*) draw into, take in; pull at, extract; dissolve, absorb.

2. ingest, eat, mouth; drink, sip, quaff, imbibe.

3. suck in *Slang.* deceive, mislead, misinform; cozen, dupe, gull, defraud; bamboozle, hoodwink, *Sl.* hornswoggle. See **deceive**.

4. suck up to *Slang.* toady to, fawn upon, *Sl.* fall all over, *Sl.* brown-nose, *Inf.* apple-polish, lick [s.o.'s] boots. See **toady** (*def.* **2**).

sucker, *n.* *Informal.* dupe, gull, gudgeon, *Inf.* chump, *Sl.* sap, *Sl.* schnook, *Sl.* boob; greenhorn, sitting duck, easy *or* soft mark *or* target, *Inf.* cinch, *Sl.* patsy, *Sl.* pigeon, *U.S. Sl.* fall guy, *Sl.* softie *or* soft touch, *Sl.* pushover; laughingstock, butt, fair game, fool, everybody's fool, *Inf.* goat.

suckle, *v.* **1.** nurse, give suck, breast-feed, feed at the breast.

2. nurture, nourish, sustain, provide for, care for, take care of, tend; parent, foster, bring up, rear, raise.

sudden, *adj.* **1.** unexpected, unforeseen, unanticipated, unlooked-for, unannounced, without warning; prompt, expeditious, instant, instantaneous, immediate.

2. rapid, meteoric, quick, swift, fleet, speedy; abrupt, brisk, hasty; hurried, precipitate, feverish, headlong; fleeting, brief, short-lived, momentary, ephemeral, transient.

suddenly, *adv.* **1.** unexpectedly, out of the blue, all of a sudden, abruptly, at once, on the spur of the moment, without warning; forthwith, promptly, expeditiously, with dispatch; instantly, instantaneously, *Sl.* P.D.Q., immediately; presto, at short notice, straightway, apace, posthaste, hotfoot.

2. rapidly, quickly, overnight; swiftly, speedily, briskly; hastily, hurriedly, precipitately, headlong, feverishly, pell-mell, helter-skelter.

3. fleetingly, briefly, momentarily, in an instant, in a flash, in a jiffy, in no time, in a trice, in the twinkling of an eye, *Inf.* before one can say "Jack Robinson."

suds, *n.* **1.** foam, lather, froth, spume, spray, spindrift, surf; bubbles, head, *Brit. Inf.* barm.

2. *Slang.* beer, ale, malt liquor, *Inf.* brew.

sue, *v.* **1.** prosecute, bring to court *or* trial *or* justice, try; summon, bring suit, prefer charges, arraign, indict; accuse, charge.

2. petition, request, solicit, address; apply to, appeal to, call on *or* upon; beg for, pray for, plead for; supplicate, implore, entreat, adjure, obtest; beseech, obsecrate, imprecate, impetrate, importune.

suffer, *v.* **1.** feel pain, ache, hurt, agonize; groan, moan, gasp; smart, twinge, convulse, writhe; sweat, bear the cross, wince, bleed; grieve, lament; droop, languish, pine, despair; break down, give way.

2. undergo, endure, experience, sustain, bear, go through, pass through; encounter, live out, meet with, taste, fare; support, weather, forbear, *Chiefly Scot.* thole, *Scot. and North Eng.* dree; take it, brave it out, *Inf.* tough it out, *Inf.* stick it out, *Sl.* sweat it out, *Inf.* go through the mill, *Inf.* take it on the chin; *Inf.* hang in, *Inf.* keep the faith, keep one's chin up, *Sl.* stand the gaff; take one's punishment, reap the whirlwind.

3. tolerate, withstand, take patiently, brook, submit to, abide, stand, put up with; swallow, digest, stomach, pocket.

4. let, permit, admit, allow; concede, vouchsafe, accord, oblige, acquiesce; grant, privilege, authorize, sanction; empower, give license to, give leave to; favor, humor, indulge, connive at, wink at, close the eyes to, stretch a point.

sufferance, *n.* **1.** tolerance, toleration, forbearance; permission, authorization, tacit allowance, concession, connivance, laxity, laissez faire; favor, indulgence, grace; license, leave, liberty, freedom; scope, latitude, play, range, rope, free rein.

2. endurance, stoicism, long-suffering, patience, abidingness, submission; equanimity, composure, tranquillity, sang-froid, calmness, coolness, placidity, imperturbation, command, self-control, self-possession, self-restraint; sobriety, gravity, staidness.

sufferer, *n.* tolerator, endurer, stoic; victim, martyr, shorn lamb; patient, case, invalid, cripple; convalescent; hypochondriac, valetudinarian.

suffering, *n.* **1.** discomfort, distress, misery, *Obs.* pathos, anguish, *Archaic.* misease; torment, torture, agony, affliction; ache, hurt, pang, pain; twinge, nip, pinch, smart; soreness, throbbing, shooting, cramp, stitch; seizure, spasm, throe, paroxysm, convulsion.

2. grief, *Archaic.* teen, woe, sorrow, dolor, heavy heart, heartache; worry, fret, care, concern, solicitude, anxiety; ordeal, trial, tribulation, trouble; burden, load; blow, shock.

3. endurance, patience, sufferance, tolerance, toleration, forbearance, sustainment; stoicism, resignation, resignedness, acceptance; long-suffering, longanimity.

suffice, *v.* be enough, be adequate, be sufficient, pass muster; do, serve, satisfy, answer; please, gratify, appease, content, assuage, pacify, placate; fulfill, fill, sate, satiate; saturate, quench, slake; *Inf.* hit the spot *or* bull's-eye, do the trick, be on target.

sufficiency, *n.* **1.** adequacy, adequateness, sufficientness; enough, no less, no more and no less; satisfaction, satisfactoriness, acceptability, tolerableness, contentment; completeness, thoroughness, extensiveness.

2. plenty, amplitude, abundance, copiousness, plenitude, plenteousness, profusion; repletion, surfeit, satiety, fill.

sufficient, *adj.* **1.** enough, adequate, ample, abundant; plenteous, plentiful, *Inf.* plenty, *Archaic.* enow; suitable, commensurate, proportionate, equivalent, equal.

2. satisfactory, up to scratch, *Inf.* up to snuff, passable, tolerable; presentable, admissible, allowable; fairly good, *Inf.* not that bad, not too bad, pretty good.

suffix, *n.* **1.** ending, postfix, *Gram.* termination; affix, addition, appendage, subjoinder, postscript, tag; appendix, codicil, adjunct, supplement, addendum, amendment, rider.

—*v.* **2.** postfix, affix, tag on, tack on; add on, append, subjoin, supplement, amend.

suffocate, *v.* **1.** asphyxiate, smother, stifle, burke; choke, strangle, strangulate, throttle, garrote, bowstring.

2. suppress, quell, put down, subdue, overcome; extinquish, dampen, *Inf.* douse, snuff out.

suffocation, *n.* **1.** asphyxiation, smothering, stifling, burking; choking, strangulation, throttling, (*in India*) thuggee, garroting.

2. suppression, quelling, subduing, overcoming; extinguishment, dampening, *Inf.* dousing, snuffing out.

suffrage, *n.* franchise, right to vote, ballot; determination, voice, say, choice, option.

suffuse, *v.* overspread, cover, mantle; bathe, color, dye, tint, tincture; imbue, imbrue, permeate, infiltrate, transfuse, diffuse, infuse, steep, soak, saturate.

sugar, *n.* *Chem.* sucrose, *Chem.* saccharose, *Chem.* glucose, *Chem.* dextrose, *Chem.* fructose, *Chem.* levulose, *Chem.* lactose, *Chem.* maltose; muscovado, turbinado sugar, raw sugar, brown sugar, confectioner's sugar, granulated sugar, refined sugar; *Chem.* saccharin, *Trademark.* Crystallose.

sugary, *adj.* **1.** sweet, sweetened, honeyed, honey, confectionary; sugared, candied, nectared, nectareous, nectarean, saccharine; rich, delicious, cloying, sickening.
2. dulcet, mellifluous, mellifluent, sweet-sounding, melodious; soothing, pleasant, agreeable.
3. flattering, cajoling, blandishing, syrupy, sickeningly sweet, *Inf.* buttery, sugar-coated; ingratiating, ingratiatory, smooth-tongued, smooth, suave, unctuous.

suggest, *v.* **1.** mention, bring up, propose, introduce, submit, offer, proffer; put forward, advance, propound, *Inf.* toss *or* throw out; counsel, advise, offer an opinion, recommend, advocate.
2. intimate, hint, imply, insinuate, lead one to believe, *Inf.* give one to understand, *Inf.* put a bug *or* flea in one's ear.

suggestion, *n.* **1.** idea, thought, proposal, proposition; advice, counsel, opinion, recommendation; word to the wise, tip, pointer, helpful hint, *Inf.* steer *or* steer in the right direction; implication, insinuation, intimation, innuendo, *Rhet.* paralipsis.
2. slight trace, hint, touch, tinge, shade, suspicion, soupçon, sprinkling, dash.

suggestive, *adj.* **1.** indicative of, redolent of, reminiscent of, remindful of.
2. provocative, provoking, stimulative, stimulating, evocative, evoking.
3. indecent, obscene, risqué, racy, off-color, dirty, smutty; vulgar, ribald, bawdy, gross, low, *Sl.* gutter, coarse, earthy, rude, crude, offensive, tasteless; pornographic, blue, *Sl.* raunchy, salacious, lewd.

suicidal, *adj.* **1.** self-destructive, despondent, dangerously depressed.
2. lethal, deadly, Kamikaze; dangerous, full of risk, too risky, hazardous, perilous, unsafe; reckless, wanton, wild, desperate, madcap, daring, death-defying, foolhardy, harebrained; impetuous, headlong, breakneck, rash, temerarious.

suicide, *n.* **1.** self-murder, self-destruction, felo-de-se; self-immolation, hara-kiri, seppuku, suttee, *Sl.* brodie.
2. self-murderer, self-killer, self-executioner.
—*v.* **3.** kill oneself, *Sl.* take a brodie, *Sl.* take a dive, *Sl.* take the gas, *Sl.* take a powder, *Sl.* do oneself in, *Sl.* pack it in.

suit, *n.* **1.** set of clothes, matched outfit, outfit, ensemble; costume, *Inf.* getup, *Inf.* rig; turnout, best clothes, best bib and tucker, *Inf.* Sunday clothes, *Inf.* Sunday best, *Inf.* Sunday-go-to-meeting clothes, *Sl.* heavy threads, *Sl.* glad rags; business suit, grey flannel suit, Brooks Brothers uniform; tuxedo, *Inf.* tails; uniform, livery, regimentals.
2. courtship, addresses, attentions; wooing, pursuit, courting, court; *Sl.* the make.
3. lawsuit, case, action at law; trial, process, litigation, proceeding, cause, judicial contest.
4. petition, entreaty, request, requisition, application, address; supplication, obsecration, obtestation, impetration, solicitation, invocation, adjuration, imploration, beseechment, *Eccles.* rogation; plea, prayer, orison, appeal.
5. follow suit comply, go along, concur; be conventional, be regular, run with the herd *or* pack, swim with the current, follow the crowd, follow the fashion; copy, imitate, emulate, do like, parallel, model after, copycat; mimic, ape, monkey, parrot, mirror, echo.
—*v.* **6.** adapt, fashion, shape, proportion, remodel; conform, accommodate, comply, fit, adjust, modify.
7. satisfy, fill one's needs, please, content, gratify, gladden, charm, cheer, delight, *Inf.* tickle pink, *Inf.* suit to a T; do one's heart good, *Inf.* hit the spot, delectate.
8. array, dress, garb, clothe, vest, attire, apparel, habit, *Sl.* dude up, robe, costume; equip, furnish, *Obs.* appoint; gird, ready, prepare; *All Mil.* arm, forearm, *Sl.* heel, *Archaic.* harness; deck, deck out, bedeck, caparison, trap, adorn, dress out, decorate.
9. conform to, befit, become, be seemly, be fitted to, be suitable to *or* for; get along, be compatible, *Inf.* hit it off; correspond, harmonize, tally, mesh, fit, agree with, accord with, square, match.

suitability, *n.* **1.** appropriateness, aptness, appositeness, fitness, meetness; seemliness, decorum, decency, propriety; justness, rightness, commensurateness, equitability, equivalence.
2. relevance, relevancy, pertinence, germaneness; applicability, practicability, feasibility, usefulness, acceptability; opportuneness, seasonableness, timeliness, felicitousness.
3. compatibility, consistency, congruence, congruousness, congruity, harmoniousness, harmony, consonance; commodiousness, agreeableness, convenience; expediency, expedience, advantageousness, advisability.
4. aptitude, capability, competence, competency; predilection, talent, gift, faculty; proclivity, bent, leaning.

suitable, *adj.* **1.** appropriate, apt, apposite, apropos; fit, fitting, befitting, idoneous, *Brit. Dial.* gradely, meet, *Fr. comme il faut*, expedient; just, right, commensurate, proportionate, equitable, equivalent, correspondent, in character, in keeping; proper, becoming, seemly, decorous, decent; relevant, *Latin. ad rem,* germane, to the point, pertinent, pat.
2. suited, adapted, *Inf.* cut out for, compatible, consistent; congruent, congruous, harmonious, consonant, accordant, agreeing, conformable; agreeable, congenial, likely, acceptable, reasonable; favorable, commodious, convenient; opportune, seasonable, timely, felicitous; to the purpose, useful, applicable, practicable, feasible.
3. worthy, qualified, eligible, deserving; deserved, merited, earned, due, (*of punishment*) condign.

suitcase, *n.* valise, traveling bag, overnight bag, duffel bag, carpetbag, bag, grip, gripsack, carryall, *Chiefly Brit.* portmanteau.

suite, *n.* **1.** set, series, suit, *Inf.* kit, *Inf.* outfit.
2. apartment, flat, penthouse, town-house.
3. retinue, train, attendance, cortege, entourage, court, following, satellites, *Archaic.* meiny; escort, guard, bodyguards, convoy.

suitor, *n.* **1.** lover, wooer, admirer, secret admirer, infatuate, paramour; beau, swain, inamorato, gallant, *It. cicisbeo*; boyfriend, gentleman friend, *Inf.* steady, *Inf.* fellow, *Inf.* flame, *Brit. Inf.* follower.
2. petitioner, solicitor, suppliant, supplicant, beseecher; applicant, bidder, solicitant; claimant, complainant, plaintiff, appellant, party.

sulk, *v.* **1.** mope, pout, make *or* pull a long face, hang the lip, look sullen, be out of sorts *or* humor, be put out.
—*n.* **2.** bad *or* ill mood, bad *or* ill temper; grumpiness, *Inf.* mulligrubs; pout, blue funk, snit, pique.

sulkiness, *n.* sullenness. See **sullenness** (*defs.* **1-3**).

sulky, *adj.* sullen. See **sullen** (*defs.* **1-3**).

sullen, *adj.* **1.** cross, angry, peeved, miffed, in a bad *or* ugly mood, out of humor, *Inf.* sore, *Inf.* mad, *Sl.* hot, *Sl.* ticked-off, *Sl.* teed off; scowling, frowning, glowering, beetle-browed, black-browed.

2. sulky, morose, mumpish, glum; resentful, bitter, embittered, rankled; acrimonious, acerb, acerbic, choleric, splenetic, dyspeptic, bilious; ill-tempered, bad-tempered, ill-natured, temperamental; irritable, irascible, petulant, peevish, cranky, touch, tetchy; surly, churlish, crusty, *Inf.* mean, *Inf.* ornery; grumpy, grouchy, crabby.

3. gloomy, depressing, cheerless, somber, mournful, doleful, dolorous; cloudy, clouded, overcast; dismal, dreary, *Literary.* drear, bleak, grim, funereal, lugubrious; dark, black, saturnine.

4. slow, slow-moving, slow-going, sluggish, stagnant.

sullenness, *n.* **1.** crossness, angriness, anger; ill *or* bad temper, ill *or* bad humor, ill *or* bad mood, sulk, sulks.

2. sulkiness, moroseness, mumpishness, glumness, moodiness; resentfulness, bitterness, embitteredness; acrimoniousness, acerbity, choler, spleen, bile, gall; irritableness, irritability, irascibleness, irascibility, petulance, peevishness, crankiness, touchiness, tetchiness; surliness, churlishness, crustiness, *Inf.* meanness, *Inf.* orneriness, *Inf.* bitchiness; grouchiness, grumpiness, crabbiness, crabbedness.

3. gloominess, gloom, cheerlessness, somberness, mournfulness, dolefulness, dolorousness, dolor; cloudiness; dismalness, dreariness, bleakness, grimness, lugubriousness; darkness, blackness.

4. slowness, sluggishness, stagnancy.

sully, *v.* **1.** soil, stain, spot, blemish, maculate, smudge, smear, besmear; begrime, bedraggle, draggle; mar, spoil, ruin; contaminate, pollute, adulterate.

2. defile, disgrace, dishonor, dirty; defame, denigrate, vilify, scandalize, revile, malign; stigmatize, drag through the mud *or* mire, throw mud upon, heap dirt upon, *Sl.* dump on.

sultriness, *n.* **1.** humidity, mugginess, *Inf.* stickiness.

2. sensualness, sensuality, sensuousness, sexiness, animal magnetism, voluptuousness; luxuriousness.

sultry, *adj.* **1.** hot and humid, humid, muggy, sweltering, *Inf.* sticky, *Archaic.* madid; oppressive, suffocating, stifling, close.

2. sensual, sexy, voluptuous, luxurious; alluring, enticing, seductive, tempting.

sum, *n.* **1.** aggregate, total, sum total, grand total, answer; gross amount, gross, bottom line, total cost *or* price; gross income, receipts, proceeds, *Inf.* take; tale, tally, score, final score, end result, outcome.

2. amount, quantity, count, measure, just so much, *Scot. and North Eng.* feck; mass, pile, stack, wad, *Sl.* heap, *Sl.* mess.

3. addition problem, *Math.* additive group, problem, *Math.* arithmetic equation.

4. whole, whole *or* entire thing, entire amount, entirety, entire, totality, ensemble; lot, *Inf.* whole kit and caboodle, *Sl.* whole lot *or* bunch *or* mess, whole shebang, whole shooting match *or* works, whole ball of wax; everything, be-all and end-all, beginning and end, Alpha and Omega, all there is *or* that exists, it.

5. sum and substance, content, meaning, message, point; main *or* central idea *or* thought, pith, substance, gist, crux, heart, soul, backbone, core, kernel, center, nucleus; essence, quintessence, quiddity, elixir, suchness, *Latin. sine qua non.*

6. summary, summation, synopsis, compendium; abstract, précis, résumé, epitome; condensation, digest, brief, concise *or* brief form, abridgement, *Chiefly Brit.* minute; syllabus, outline, sketch, quick look, glance, *Fr. aperçu;* summing-up, recapitulation, review, rehash, rundown, wrap-up; overview, survey, conspectus, prospectus.

—v. **7.** *Often* **sum up** add up, add, total up, total, tot up, tot, foot up, cast up, come up with *or* get the answer; count up, count, tally up, tally, score up, score, (*on a cash register*) ring up, enumerate, numerate, cipher; calculate, compute, figure up, reckon, ascertain, estimate.

8. *Often* **sum up** summarize, synopsize, capitulate, encapsulate, capsule, epitomize, put in a nutshell; recapitulate, rehash, review, run *or* go *or* skim over, wrap up; condense, concentrate, consolidate, brief, digest, abridge, abbreviate, shorten; outline, survey, sketch, give a glance *or* look *or* peek at.

9. *Usu.* **sum to** *or* **into** amount to, add up to, total up to, count up to, number in, reckon up to; approximate, near, reach, come to, be; run to, mount up to, climb to, rise to, soar to.

summarily, *adv.* **1.** promptly, forthwith, immediately, instantly, instantaneously, *Sl.* P.D.Q., directly, straightaway, without delay, right off the bat; with dispatch, *Archaic.* presently, *Inf.* in a jiffy, in a trice, *Inf.* in a mo *or* sec, at once, right now; quickly, speedily, swiftly, briskly, expeditiously, apace; readily, at short notice, on the spot; curtly, tersely, peremptorily; suddenly, abruptly, precipitately, headlong, extempore, on the spur of the moment; shortly, soon, *Archaic.* anon.

2. concisely, succinctly, straightforwardly, emphatically, pointedly; condensedly, compressedly, contractedly, abridgedly; compactly, closely, neatly; compendiously, comprehensively, synoptically; pithily, sententiously, epigrammatically, crisply, precisely, exactly, gnomically; laconically, elliptically, economically, breviloquently; in brief, in short, in a word. See also **brief** (*def.* **10**).

summarize, *v.* **1.** abstract, epitomize, sum up, encapsulate, capsule, wrap up, synopsize, brief; digest, survey, outline, sketch, skim over; review, recapitulate, rehash, go over, run over, run down.

2. condense, compress, concentrate, consolidate, compact; contract, abbreviate, abridge, shorten, reduce, cut down, cut short, cut back.

summary, *n.* **1.** abstract, synopsis, compendium, survey, précis, conspectus, prospectus; digest, epitome, brief, outline, capitulation, enumeration, sketch; review, recapitulation, résumé, summation, rehash, fill-in, rundown, wrap-up, roundup.

—adj. **2.** concise, succinct, brief, to the point, short and sweet, short, straightforward, direct, pointed, emphatic; abbreviated, abridged, shortened, condensed, compressed, summarized, thumbnail, curtailed, curtate, contracted, *Obs.* breviate; compact, compendious, packed, lean, close, neat; comprehensive, synoptic, synoptical, *Inf.* meaty; pithy, sententious, epigrammatic, crisp, precise, exact, gnomic; laconic, elliptical, breviloquent, *Rare.* pauciloquent.

3. direct, prompt, immediate, instant, instantaneous; fast, rapid, fleet, quick, brisk, swift, speedy, meteoric, expeditious; hasty, cursory, hurried; curt, terse, short, peremptory, abrupt, sudden.

summer, *n.* **1.** summertime, daylight-saving time, *Astron.* (*in the northern hemisphere*) summer solstice; summer break, school vacation, end of school, vacation time, vacation, *Chiefly Brit.* holiday; dog days, hot *or* warm weather, sunny *or* bright weather, beach weather.

2. heyday, prime, acme, zenith; efflorescence, flowering, blossoming, fructification, bloom, blossom, pink.

—*adj.* **3.** summery, summerlike, summerly, estival; warm-weather, seasonal, seasonable; vacation, *Chiefly Brit.* holiday.

4. sunny, sunshiny, bright, warm, hot, baking, sultry, sweltering, humid, muggy, sticky, close.

—*v.* **5.** spend the summer, estivate, go *or* repair to for the summer, have a summer home *or* beach cottage in; pass the summer, relax, rest, retire.

summerhouse, *n.* **1.** parkhouse, gardenhouse, pavilion, gazebo, (*in Turkey and Iran*) kiosk; pergola, arbor, bower, trellis, lattice, leafy shelter; grotto, alcove, recess; greenhouse, conservatory.

2. retreat, refuge, haven, shelter, hermitage; asylum, resort, sanctuary, ark, covert, hideaway, mew.

summit, *n.* **1.** apex, vertex, apogee, crest, heights, pinnacle, peak, spire, point, tip, tiptop; top, cap, crown, headpiece, head.

2. prime, heyday, bloom, full flower; ideal, aspiration, goal, aim, objective.

3. acme, zenith, maximum, climax, culmination, crowning point, *Latin. ne plus ultra*; meridian, sublimity, supremacy, best, finest, perfection, consummation; extreme, utmost, uttermost, *U.S. Slang.* the most, *U.S. Slang.* the greatest.

4. top level, high echelon, highest grade *or* rank.

summon, *v.* **1.** call, call upon, ask, invite, signal; bid, tell, request, ask for, call for; command, order, direct, require, adjure, charge, instruct, stipulate, demand, exact.

2. convoke, convene, muster, assemble, call together, convocate.

3. call to witness, command to appear, serve with a writ, *Law.* arraign, *Law.* subpoena, cite.

4. *Often* **summon up a.** rouse, arouse, call up, provoke, call into action; excite, work oneself up, nerve oneself, get up steam; muster up, gather up; impassion, inspire, set astir; awaken, wake up. **b.** recall, recollect, remember, revive; conjure up, call up, bring to mind, refresh the memory, fan the embers, rekindle; retrace, review, look back upon, keep in mind.

summons, *n.* **1.** signal, alarm, tocsin; invocation, invitation, bidding, calling, call, appeal, notice, notification, request.

2. order, dictate, dictation, dictum, instruction, direction, directive, behest, *Archaic.* hest, imperative; exaction, imposition, requirement, demand, requisition, assignment; commandment, precept, prescript, prescription, enjoinment, ordainment; mandate, decree, edict, proclamation.

3. warrant, authorization, citation, *All Law.* writ, subpoena, habeas corpus, arraignment.

sumptuous, *adj.* expensive, costly, dear, high-priced, exorbitant, extravagant; valuable, precious, priceless, inestimable; rich, opulent, lavish, magnificent, splendid, luxurious, gorgeous; dazzling, showy, splendorous; imposing, palatial, stately, august, majestic; plush, deluxe, *Inf.* posh, *Inf.* swank, *Inf.* ritzy; regal, royal, imperial, kingly, princely; awe-inspiring, inspiring, *Archaic.* magnific; elegant, graceful, handsome, beautiful, *Scot.* wally, *Inf.* eye-filling; lordly, exalted, lofty, sublime, high, elevated; remarkable, grand, conspicuous, superb, supreme, prominent, preeminent.

sun, *n.* **1.** luminary, source of light, star of day, *Archaic.* daystar, heaven's bright light, *Inf.* old sol, *Literary.* Phoebus; orb, sphere, fireball, ball of fire; Helios, Sol, Hyperion, Mithras, Ra, Shamash, Utu; *Meteorol.* parhelion, star.

2. sunshine, sunlight, daylight. See **sunshine** (*defs.* **1-4**).

sunburned, *adj.* **1.** inflamed, burned, blistery, peeling; red, reddened, ruddy, crimson, scarlet; windburned, chapped.

2. tan, bronzed, sun-tanned, brown, brown as a berry.

sunder, *v.* separate, part, divide, divorce, split, cleave, sever, dissever, rupture; partition, halve, bisect, quarter, section; rive, rend, *Obs.* dimidiate, bifurcate; disconnect, disjoin, dissociate, disassociate; cut *or* chop apart, cut in two, hack, slash.

sundry, *adj.* various, varied, variegated, diversified, diverse, heterogeneous, assorted; divers, several, manifold, multifarious, multifaceted, many; dissimilar, separate, individual, different.

sunk, *adj.* *Slang.* done for, washed-up, beyond help; ruined, demolished, kaput; bankrupt, on the rocks; had it.

sunken, *adj.* **1.** submerged, submersed, immersed, engulfed, inundated; drowned, capsized, foundered, *Naut.* scuttled.

2. settled, compacted, buried, mired, planted, laid; lowered, at a lower level, below ground.

3. hollow, depressed, indented, concave; incurvate, incurving; cup-shaped, calathiform, *Bot., Zool.* cyathiform.

sunless, *adj.* **1.** dark, *Literary.* darkling, unlighted, tenebrous; black, black as pitch, inky-black, pitchy, Cimmerian, like Erebus, dark as a well; nightlike, dim, darksome, darkish, dusky, subfuscous, murky; hazy, misty, *Archaic.* caliginous, cloudy, overcast, gray, nebulose, foggy, shadowy, shaded, umbrageous.

2. gloomy, Stygian, bleak, dismal, somber, grim, glum; dreary, *Literary.* drear, sad, depressing, funereal; cheerless, joyless, unsmiling, unhappy, mirthless.

sunlight, *n.* sunshine, brightness, happiness, cheer. See **sunshine** (*defs.* **1-4**).

sunny, *adj.* **1.** sunshiny, sunbeamy, sunlit, well-lighted, bright, streaming with light *or* sunshine; shining, blazing, glowing; golden, clear, pleasant, radiant; cloudless, without a cloud in the sky *or* on the horizon, unclouded, clement, mild; summery, like a day in July, tropical.

2. cheery, cheerful, joyous, gay, blithe, jovial, jocund; happy, mirthful, jolly, genial, warm, warm-hearted; bubbly, ebullient, buoyant, light-hearted; smiling, laughing, dancing, singing, songful, with a song on one's lips; optimistic, hopeful, hoping for the best; bright-eyed, bright-eyed and bushy-tailed.

sunrise, *n.* **1.** sunup, dawn, dawning, dawn's early light, crack of dawn *or* day, daybreak, morning, morn; beginning of a new day, rosy-fingered dawn, cockcrow, first blush of day, peep of day, gold of the day, Aurora, Eos; twilight, crepuscule.

2. morning watch, dogwatch, sunrise watch, *Journalism.* lobster trick, *Journalism.* bulldog trick, *Eccles.* matins, small hours, wee hours.

3. beginning, opening, start, initiation, inauguration, kickoff; genesis, commencement, aurora, fresh start, new start.

sunset, *n.* **1.** nightfall, close of day, sundown, evenfall; twilight, crepuscule, candlelight; evening, eve, eventide, *Archaic.* even, *Archaic.* evensong; dusk, *Literary.* gloaming, *Archaic.* glooming.

2. children's hour, cocktail time, happy hour, curfew, *Inf.* shank of the evening.

3. culmination, finish, finis, finale, end, conclusion, termination; homestretch, last round *or* lap *or* stage, final act, final curtain, curtain; waning days, golden years, sunset years; last inning, bottom of the ninth.

sunshade, *n.* **1.** sun hat, sunbonnet, sun helmet, pith helmet, topee; kibbutz hat, kerchief, kaffiyeh; goggles, dark glasses, sunglasses, *Sl.* shades, smoked glasses, eyeshade, eyeshield, visor; tarpaulin, *Inf.* tarp,

covering, canvas, tent; summerhouse, gazebo, pavilion, beach house, cabana, summer kitchen; shutter, blind, shade, curtain, screen, venetian blind, jalousie.
2. awning, tilt, canopy, baldachin.
3. parasol, umbrella, beach umbrella.

sunshine, *n.* **1.** sunlight, sun, light, daylight, light of day, direct light, *Inf.* yellow, *Inf.* yellow stuff, broad daylight, midday sun, noon sun; sunbeam, ray of sunshine.
2. brightness, radiance, sunniness, warmth; brilliance, luminosity, luminance, illumination; glow, glare, dazzle, gleam; sparkle, luster, glitter, *Archaic.* glister, glisten, coruscation, lambency, shimmer.
3. cheerfulness, cheeriness, happiness, bliss, blitheness, gladness, gaiety, joy, joyfulness; light-heartedness, good spirits, merriness, joviality, jocundity; laughter, smile, bluebird of happiness.
4. cheer, good cheer, encouragement, approval, inspiration; comfort, balm, ease, calm; bright prospects, clear skies, clear sailing, light at the end of the tunnel.

sup, *v.* **1.** sip, taste, sample, drink bit by bit; *Inf.* wet *or* moisten one's whistle, take a drop, lap *or* lap up, suck up, *Sl.* slurp.
—n. **2.** sip, taste, sample, drop, lick, thimbleful, mouthful, spoonful; drink, dram, nip, draught, swallow, *Inf.* swig.

superable, *adj.* surmountable, conquerable, vincible, beatable. See **surmountable**.

superabound, *v.* **1.** overabound, overstep, overstride, overleap, overjump, know no bounds; exceed, excel, outstrip, transcend, surpass, overpass, pass beyond, leave behind.
2. overflow, flow over, overspill, spill over, run over, well over; overrun, run riot, run rampant, overgrow, overspread, spread over, be all over, meet one at every turn; infest, plague, beset; swarm, swarm with, teem, teem with, crawl, crawl with, creep, creep with, bristle, bristle with, pullulate.
3. overwhelm, overcome, overpower; choke, smother, suffocate; mount, mount up, pile up; flood, deluge, inundate, drench, engulf, swamp, submerge, whelm, sweep; sate, surfeit, gorge, glut, stuff.

superabundance, *n.* **1.** overabundance, overfullness, overprofusion, overplentifulness, overplenteousness, overplenty, superflux; superfluity, superfluousness, oversufficiency, supererogation, redundance, redundancy; repletion, engorgement, congestion, surcharge; profusion, more than enough, enough and to spare, enough and then some.
2. surplus, surfeit, satiety, glut, plethora, excess, overflow, overspill; flood, deluge, inundation, spate, avalanche, landslide, riot, drug on *or* in the market, supersaturation; oversupply, overmeasure, overload, overburden; overdose, too much of a good thing.

superabundant, *adj.* **1.** overabundant, plethoric, overfull, overprofuse, overplentiful, overplenteous, overplenty, oversufficient, overmuch; overflowing, flowing over, overspilling, spilling over, running over, welling over; rampant, bristling, thick, thick with, teeming, teeming with, swarming, swarming with, crawling, crawling with, creeping with, alive with, *Sl.* lousy with, pullulating.
2. lavish, lush, rank, extravagant, excessive, profuse, profusive, exorbitant, inordinate, immoderate, beyond all bounds; uncalled-for, unwarranted, needless, unnecessary; overgenerous, overliberal, overbounteous, overbountiful, overlavish; too much, too many.
3. wasteful, prodigal, profligate, wanton, dissipative; intemperate, improvident, incontinent.

superannuated, *adj.* **1.** retired, pensioned, *Inf.* put *or* let out to pasture; too old to work, *Inf.* over the hill, past one's prime; aged, elderly, old, on *or* up in years, along *or* advanced in years; senile, (*of women*) anile, decrepit, senescent, infirm.
2. antiquated, old-fashioned, *Inf.* old hat, passé, outdated, out-of-date, outworn, outmoded, out of style, out; obsolete, obsolescent, archaic, out of use, no longer used; dated, vintage, antique, ancient.

superb, *adj.* **1.** fine, admirable, worthy, estimable, notable, noteworthy, distinguished; creditable, commendable, exemplary, meritorious, deserving, praiseworthy, laudable; excellent, first-rate, of the first water, top-drawer, *Inf.* topnotch, crackerjack, *Brit. Sl.* whizzo; choice, prime, select, *Inf.* tiptop, *Inf.* A-1, *Inf.* A number 1, *Northwest U.S. and Canada.* skookum, *Australian Sl.* bosker, *Scot. and North Eng.* braw.
2. superlative, matchless, peerless, nonpareil, perfect, sterling, classic; extraordinary, very remarkable, *Sl.* bang-up, *Brit. Sl.* spot on, *Brit. Sl.* bang on, exceptional, superior, standout, outstanding, striking; superfine, superexcellent, marvelous, *Sl.* marvy, wondrous, wonderful, *Inf.* smashing, magnificent, splendid, *Inf.* splendiferous, glorious, divine, sensational.
3. resplendent, dazzling, radiant, brilliant, glittering; incredible, unbelievable, amazing, astounding, astonishing, miraculous, surpassing belief, breath-taking, *Sl.* stunning, staggering, mind-boggling, *Sl.* mind-blowing; really good, fantastic, fabulous, terrific, *Sl.* terif, stupendous; *Inf.* out of this world, *Sl.* unreal, *Sl.* out of sight, *Sl.* far-out, *Sl.* way-out, *Sl.* keen, *Sl.* boss, *Sl.* solid, *Sl.* magic; very good, capital, swell, *Inf.* great, *Inf.* super, *Inf.* super-duper, *Brit. Sl.* ripping, *Sl.* tuff, *Sl.* bad, *Sl.* cool, *Inf.* dandy, *Inf.* jim-dandy, *Inf.* bully.
4. luxurious, lavish, deluxe, plush, rich, sumptuous, *Inf.* posh, *Inf.* swank, *or* swanky, *Inf.* ritzy; elegant, fancy, ornate, gorgeous, beautiful; costly, expensive, precious, valuable.
5. majestic, august, stately, grand, noble, sublime; palatial, imposing, impressive, commanding, awe-inspiring, *Archaic.* magnific; royal, regal, kingly, princely, imperial.

supercilious, *adj.* arrogant, *Inf.* up on one's high horse, haughty, cavalier, cavalierly, insolent, contemptuous, disdainful, scornful, sniffish, *Inf.* sniffy; snobbish, snobby, conceited, *Inf.* stuck-up, condescending, patronizing, *Inf.* uppity, *Inf.* uppish, *Inf.* snotty, *Sl.* snooty, *Inf.* with one's nose in the air, *Inf.* high-hat; above-it-all, lofty, lordly, high and mighty, pompous, high-flown, pretentious, *Inf.* highfalutin, hoity-toity, stuffy; proud, prideful, overproud, vainglorious, vain, stuck on oneself, *Inf.* swell-headed, *Inf.* bigheaded, puffy, puffed up, inflated; self-important, egocentric, narcissistic, self-loving, self-esteeming, self-admiring, self-worshipping; self-centered, egoistic, egoistical, egotistical, egotistic; overconfident, cocky, overweening, overbearing, domineering, dominating, *or* bossy, imperious, magisterial, dictatorial.

superficial, *adj.* **1.** surface, exterior, external, outer, outside, extrinsic, outward.
2. shallow, skin-deep, cosmetic; slick, glossy, glib, facile, smooth; unprofound, empty, meaningless, without substance, insubstantial; insignificant, unimportant, trifling, trivial, petty, frivolous.
3. apparent, seeming, ostensible, presumable, *Archaic.* semblable; avowed, alleged, so-called, nominal, in name only; specious, plausible, possible; deceptive, misleading, fallacious, sophistic, casuistic, *Logic.* paralogical.
4. cursory, slapdash, hasty, hurried, inattentive, careless.

superficies, *n.* exterior, outside, façade, appearance, surface. See **surface**.

superfluity, *n.* **1.** excessiveness, redundancy, redundance, superfluousness; immoderacy, immoderateness, extravagance, extravagancy, exuberance, lavishness, lushness, rankness, profuseness, profusiveness; inordinateness, *Obs.* inordinacy, exorbitance, exorbitancy, fulsomeness; overliberality, overliberalness, overgenerosity, overgenerousness, overlavishness.

2. needlessness, unnecessariness, unwarrantedness; unessentiality, inessentiality, nonessentiality, extraneousness, dispensability, dispensableness, gratuitousness; uselessness, worthlessness, valuelessness.

3. superabundance, spare, extra, remainder, residual; overflow, spillover, runoff; surplus, surfeit, glut. See also **superabundance** (*defs.* **1, 2**).

4. luxury, finery, frill *or* frills, frillery, frilliness, frills and furbelows.

superfluous, *adj.* **1.** excessive, in excess, excess, redundant, supererogatory, supererogative; immoderate, extravagant, exuberant, lavish, profuse, profusive; inordinate, exorbitant, fulsome, beyond all bounds; extreme, in extreme, superlative, overblown, overgrown, overmuch; overliberal, overgenerous, overlavish, too much, too many.

2. superabundant, overabundant, plethoric, overfull, overflowing, flowing over, overspilling, spilling over, running over, welling over; extra, spare, surplus, residuary; over and above, more than enough, more than adequate, more than one needs, enough and to spare, enough and then some.

3. unnecessary, unneeded, needless, uncalled-for, unwarranted, unrequired; unessential, inessential, nonessential, extraneous, dispensable, gratuitous; useless, of no use, worthless, valueless, *Inf.* no go.

superhuman, *adj.* **1.** supernatural, preternatural, preterhuman, paranormal, otherworldly, extraterrestrial, supermundane, hyperphysical; divine, godlike, transcendent, almighty, omnipotent, all-knowing, omniscient, supernal, supreme, lofty, exalted.

2. herculean, courageous, brave, valiant, valorous, heroic; daring, death-defying; extraordinary, unheard-of, unexplainable, unbelievable, amazing, phenomenal, miraculous.

superimpose, *v.* place on *or* over, lay on *or* over, set on *or* over, superpose; bring in, add, superinduce; cover, face, coat, veneer, plate, pave.

superintend, *v.* oversee, administer, direct, manage, run, look after, supervise. See **supervise**.

superintendence, *n.* oversight, direction, management, control, guidance, care, supervision. See **supervision**.

superintendent, *n.* **1.** overseer, director, manager, boss, administrator, advisor, supervisor. See **supervisor**.

2. rent collector, *Inf.* super; doorkeeper, doorman, (*esp. in France*) concierge; elevator man; janitor, custodian, maintenance man.

superior, *adj.* **1.** excellent, first-rate, of the first order, capital, *Inf.* tiptop, *Inf.* jim-dandy, *Inf.* A-1, *Inf.* A number 1; extraordinary, *Sl.* bang-up, very remarkable, *Sl.* bang-up, *Inf.* smashing, marvelous, wonderful, splendid, *Brit. Sl.* ripping; *Inf.* great, *Inf.* super, *Sl.* tuff.

2. exceptional, standout, outstanding, striking; superlative, supreme, transcendent, sovereign, high-class, the best; matchless, peerless, nonpareil, perfect, sterling, classic, first-class; choice, prime, select, very good, *Australian Sl.* bosker, *Scot. and North Eng.* braw; fine, admirable, *Inf.* topnotch, *Inf.* of the first water, worthy, estimable, notable, noteworthy.

3. pretentious, snobby, condescending, *Inf.* holier-than-thou, sanctimonious.

—*n.* **4.** standout, heavyweight, *Sl.* heavy, biggest frog in the pond, *Inf.* honch, lion, toast of the town; executive, higher-up, (*collectively*) brass; personage, dignitary, *Archaic.* dignity, notable, very important person, *Inf.* V.I.P.; person of note *or* consequence, well-known figure, celebrity, *Sl.* celeb, somebody.

5. supervisor, manager, foreman, boss. See **supervisor**.

superiority, *n.* **1.** excellence, superexcellence, perfection, extraordinariness, superlativeness, magnificence; peerlessness, matchlessness; incomparability, inimitability, virtuosity; eminence, importance, top billing; greatness, prominence, mark, note; sublimity, regard, renown, prestige, grandeur, glory.

2. preeminence, dominance, predominance, control, power, dominion, domination; pull, sway, hold, prevalence; preponderancy, paramountcy, primacy, prepollence; ascendancy, supremacy, sovereignty, mastery; priority, seniority, command, hegemony; advantage, vantage, *Inf.* edge; vantage ground, superior *or* strategic position.

superlative, *adj.* **1.** supreme, paramount, preeminent, superior, transcendent; uppermost, best, greatest, finest, prime, choicest; unexcelled, second to none, *Latin. nulli secundus*; matchless, peerless, unequalled, unparalleled, nonpareil, *Fr. sans pareil*, incomparable, inimitable, unrivaled; perfect, ultimate, *Sl.* the living end.

2. excellent, sterling, classic, first-class; first-rate, of the first order, capital, *Inf.* tiptop, *Inf.* A-1, *Inf.* A number 1; exceptional, extreme, outstanding, out of the ordinary, unusual, singular, unique; extraordinary, *Inf.* out of this world, *Inf.* fantastic, *Inf.* terrific, great, *Inf.* super, superb, *Sl.* bang-up, *Inf.* smashing; splendid, wonderful, brilliant, dazzling, *Brit. Sl.* ripping.

3. exaggerated, bombastic, high-sounding, high-flown, inflated, overblown, turgid, tumid; pretentious, pompous, grandiose, fustian, magniloquent, grandiloquent, sonorous; ornate, flowery, euphuistic, rhetorical, stilted, declamatory, pedantic.

—*n.* **4.** summit, apogee, pinnacle, zenith; maximum, utmost, uttermost, topmost.

supernal, *adj.* **1.** heavenly, divine, godly, sublime, celestial, supernatural; ethereal, paradisiacal, Elysian, Edenic, Arcadian, Olympian, utopian; angelic, seraphic, cherubic, saintly, blessed, blest, holy, hallowed; majestic, splendorous, blissful, glorious, golden, ambrosial.

2. lofty, honorable, venerable, revered, respected; dignified, distingué, stately, august; sublime, exalted, magnificent, imposing, imperious; lordly, noble, kingly, queenly, imperial, princely, magisterial.

supernatural, *adj.* **1.** supernormal, hypernormal, preternormal; superhuman, preterhuman; superphysical, hyperphysical; abnormal, anomalous, anomalistic, unnatural, supranatural; unusual, exceptional, singular.

2. divine, almighty, omnipotent, all-powerful; godly, godlike; Olympian; celestial, heavenly, sublime, supernal; transcendent, *Theol.* immanent.

3. preternatural, fabulous, remarkable, extraordinary, out of the ordinary, out of this world; wondrous, wonderful, marvelous, miraculous, thaumaturgic; sensational, phenomenal, *Inf.* fantastic, incredible, unbelievable.

4. otherworldly, unearthly, supermundane, supramundane, extramundane; metaphysical, spiritual; spectral, astral, ethereal, ghostly, phantom, phantomlike, wraithlike; magical, unreal, fey; bewitched, enchanted, haunted, *Inf.* spooky; occult, cabalistic, mystic, mystical, transcendental; mysterious, arcane, eso-

teric, unknown; eerie, weird, strange, uncanny, bizarre.
5. impenetrable, incomprehensible, uncomprehensible, inapprehensible, past *or* beyond comprehension *or* understanding, unknowable, incognizable, incognoscible, unfathomable, inscrutable; unaccountable, inexplicable, unexplainable, indescribable, ineffable, unutterable, unspeakable.
—*n.* **6.** supernaturalism, supranaturalism, preternaturalism, transcendentalism; unearthliness, otherworldliness, eerieness; the occult, the mystical, the supersensible.

supersede, *v.* **1.** supplant, displace, succeed; oust, subvert, cut out, expel; dethrone, unseat, take over, usurp; replace, take the place of, change places with; substitute for, act for, fill in for, relieve, pinch-hit, stand in the stead of, stand in the shoes of, represent.
2. void, *Law.* avoid, declare *or* render null and void, annul, nullify, disannul; quash, invalidate, vitiate, vacate, disenact, disestablish; cancel, discharge, set aside, neutralize; suspend, *Law.* nol-pros, stop, cease, discontinue, break off; countermand, counterorder, overrule, override; negate, veto.
3. revoke, rescind, abrogate, reverse, repeal, abolish; recant, retract, withdraw, take back, undo, unmake, recall; renounce, relinquish, repudiate, abjure, forswear, abnegate; disavow, disclaim, disown, deny.
4. discard, dismiss, cast aside, abandon, throw out, dispose of; obsolesce, put into disuse, shelve, table, obviate, render unnecessary.

superstition, *n.* **1.** blind belief, warped notion, fallacy, mare's nest; illusion, delusion, mote in the eye; prejudice, prepossession, fanaticism; irrational fear, belief in omens, obsession; myth, fable, old wives' tale.
2. evil eye, *It. male occhio*; hobgoblin, bogy; werewolf, *Fr. loup-garou*; amulet, talisman, charm, periapt.
3. sorcery, occult art, black magic, necromancy, powwow, witchcraft, black art, thaumaturgy, demonology, diablerie, fetishism, voodoo, hoodoo, shamanism, vampirism; conjuration, incantation, abracadabra, hocus-pocus, mumbo jumbo.

superstitious, *adj.* ungrounded, groundless, unreal, unsubstantial, untrue, false, refuted, disproven; apocryphal, fallacious, erroneous; illusory, delusive; magical, incantatory; fetishistic, talismanic; fearful, apprehensive, obsessed, fanatical, zealous.

supervise, *v.* oversee, administer, orchestrate, quarterback, *Inf.* call the plays, run the show; make the decisions, dispose, direct, pilot, steer, guide, advise; see to, look after, watch over, protect, care for, be in custody of; manage, superintend, run, operate, be on duty, handle; boss, be master over, dominate, domineer, ride herd on, *Inf.* keep tabs on; command, take charge, wield one's power *or* authority; preside over, control, have control over, regulate, rule, govern, be on top of, be master of; be in command, be in the driver's seat *or* saddle, wear the pants *or* trousers, *Inf.* be where the buck stops.

supervision, *n.* oversight, direction, management, regulation, control, command, superintendence; ministration, ministry, administration, government, governance; dominion, jurisdiction; guidance, pilotage, tutelage, surveillance, watchful care; care, custody, charge, keeping, ward, hands; auspices, protection, protectorship, guardianship, stewardship, patronage.

supervisor, *n.* overseer, director, manager, line manager, foreman, fugleman, *Inf.* super; overlooker, overman, headman, boss, *Inf.* bossman, *U.S. Inf.* straw boss, gang boss, *Sl.* the man, *Inf.* honcho, *Inf.* head honcho, *Brit.* gaffer; pilot, skipper, helmsman, man at the wheel; master, commander, overlord, taskmaster; administrator, executive, bureaucrat, functionary, official, marshal, officer, inspector; president, head, headmaster, chief, principal; governor, regent, dean, chairman, chairwoman, chairperson; provost, monitor, proctor, captain; guide, advisor, counselor.

supine, *adj.* **1.** prone, prostrate, flat, flat on one's back, horizontal; accumbent, recumbent, decumbent, procumbent, couchant; abed, sprawling, lounging, lolling, spread, laid out, reclining, reposing, lying.
2. inactive, passive, inert, motionless, lifeless, exanimate, inanimate, stationary; indolent, idle, otiose, lazy, inattentive; indifferent, apathetic, uninterested, unconcerned, unfeeling, lethargic, incurious; sluggish, slothful, torpid, languid, lumpish, insensible; listless, lackadaisical, nonchalant, vegetative, phlegmatic; sleeping, quiescent, dormant, nonactive; unresisting, resigned, nonopposing, nonresistant, nonactivist, do-nothing, laissez-faire.

supper, *n.* repast, meal, evening meal; dinner, *Fr. dîner*, buffet dinner, TV dinner; collation, refection, spread.

supplant, *v.* **1.** displace, remove, supersede, succeed, step into the shoes of; unseat, unload, crowd out, dethrone, eject, expel, fire, bump, oust; depose, drive out, turn out, dismiss.
2. exchange, substitute, commute, subrogate, interchange, swap, trade; replace, double for, fill in for, *Inf.* sub for, act for; stand in for, do duty for, do time for; take the rap, take the blame, *Sl.* be the goat; take the place of, take over for, ghost, understudy for; relieve, pinch-hit, pinch-run.

supple, *adj.* **1.** pliant, flexible, pliable, bendable; elastic, extensible, stretchable; ductile, tractile, plastic, flexuous, flexile; whippy, springy, nonrigid, giving, fictile.
2. limber, lithe, lissom, lithesome, *Archaic.* lithy; willowy, loose-limbed, double-jointed.
3. compliant, yielding, submissive, passive, unresistant; complaisant, acquiescent, docile, tame.
4. adaptable, malleable, adjustable, movable, changeable, resilient; responsive, accepting, receptive; agreeable, amenable, willing, easy, well-disposed.

supplement, *n.* **1.** addition, enlargement, supplementation, extension, annexation, *Rare.* annexment, annex, wing; appendage, appurtenance, appurtenant, adjunct, ancilla, appanage, attachment; complement, completer, accessory, accompaniment, concomitant, concurrent, attendant, counterpart, corollary, correlative, *Astron.* comes; additive, reinforcement, fortification, fortifier, strengthener; support, buttress, prop; accession, increase, raise, increment, gain, augmentation, bonus.
2. appendix, addendum, codicil, rider, *Law.* allonge; epilogue, postscript, p.s., P.S., subjoinder, subjunction, suffix, postfix, endpiece, tailpiece, tag; updating, yearbook; amendment, modification, change, correction.
3. (*all of newspapers*) extra, special *or* added feature, magazine section, special section, advertising supplement; comic section, funny papers, funnies, comics, comic strips; insert; follow-up, follow, sidebar, shirttail.
—*v.* **4.** complement, complete, accompany, top off; augment, enlarge, extend, add on *or* to, increase; reinforce, strengthen, fortify, support, subsidize.
5. compensate for, make up for, fill a gap *or* need; upgrade, bring up to par *or* standard, boost, lift, raise.

supplementary, *adj.* **1.** additional, additory, added, appended, attached, annexed, suffixed, supplemental, codicillary; complementary, accompanying, attendant, accessory, accessorial, concomitant, concurrent; suppletory, compensatory, upgrading, boosting.
2. auxiliary, adjunct, ancillary, supportive, contributory; subsidiary, subordinate, secondary, incidental;

extra, spare, fresh, new, reserved; further, other, more, another; excess, peripheral, extraneous, outside, adscititious, supervenient, adventitious; unessential, unnecessary, irrelevant.

—*n.* **3.** auxiliary, aide, helper, assistant, ancilla, coadjutor, coadjutress, affiliate; subordinate, underling, small fry, *Inf.* small potatoes, *Sl.* stooge.

4. addition, supplement, supplementation, enlargement, extension, annexation, *Rare.* annexment, annex, wing; complement, completer, accessory, accompaniment, concomitant, concurrent, attendant, counterpart, corollary, correlative, *Astron.* comes; appendage, appurtenance, appurtenant, adjunct, appanage, attachment; additive, reinforcement, fortification, fortifier, strengthener.

suppliant, *adj.* **1.** supplicant, supplicating, supplicatory; asking, petitioning, precatory, entreating, suing, beseeching, praying, imploring, imprecatory; begging, mendicant, solicitous, importunate; hat in hand, on bended knee, looking for a handout.

—*n.* **2.** petitioner, petitionist, postulant, solicitor; suitor, beseecher, pleader; applicant, bidder, solicitant; candidate, aspirant, seeker; claimant, complainant, plaintiff, appellant, party; beggar, cadger, *Inf.* panhandler, beadsman, mendicant, almsman, *Scot.* gaberlunzie; moocher, *Inf.* sponger, *Inf.* sponge, *Sl.* schnorrer, parasite, leech, hanger-on, user.

supplicate, *v.* **1.** pray, implore, entreat, bid, ask, ask for; apply for, seek, request, call upon; appeal to, beseech, plead, beg, *Brit. Inf.* prig, crave; petition, solicit, obtest, adjure, conjure, *Rare.* sue; urge, press, importune, insist.

2. seek alms, *Inf.* panhandle, pass the hat *or* cup *or* plate, go from door to door; hustle, *Sl.* bum, use, impose on, mooch off, sponge off, live off, cadge, *Scot.* sorn.

supplication, *n.* entreaty, petition, suit, request; requisition, application, overture, address; obsecration, obtestation, impetration, solicitation, invocation, adjuration, imploration; begging, beseechment, *Eccles.* rogation; plea, prayer, orison, appeal, entreaty, humble address; mooching, *Inf.* panhandling, *Sl.* bumming, cadging, hustling, imposing; passing the hat *or* cup, going from door to door, seeking alms *or* charity.

supplicatory, *adj.* suppliant, petitionary, precatory, obtestative, importunate. See **suppliant** (*def.* **1**).

supply, *v.* **1.** provide, furnish, outfit, equip, accommodate, *Archaic.* dight, *Obs.* appoint; cater, purvey, victual, provision, provender, feed, forage; store, stock, stock up, fill up, gird, *Chiefly Scot.* plenish.

2. render, give, contribute, afford, avail; oblige, favor; present, serve, yield; distribute, administer, deal out, give out, dole out, mete out, *Inf.* hand out, *Inf.* dish out, *Sl.* shell out, *Sl.* fork out; grant, tender, proffer, extend, bestow, lavish; endow, endue *or* indue, invest.

3. replenish, refill; satisfy, fulfill, make good; make up, compensate for.

4. substitute for, *Inf.* sub for, subrogate, stand *or* sit in for, fill in for, fill the place of, stand in lieu of; fill a vacancy *or* space *or* hole, pinch-hit.

—*n.* **5.** provision, providing, accouterment, furnishing, furnishment, supplying; equipment, equipage, outfitting, fitting out; purveyance, provisioning, catering, victualing; replenishment, replenishing, resupply, resupplying, refilling.

6. stock, store, quantity, fund, lot, *Chiefly U.S. Dial.* grist; reserve, reservoir; stockpile, collection, cache, hoard, amassment, accumulation; inventory, supply on hand; resources, savings, nest egg; abundance, plenty, plenitude, cornucopia; treasure, mine, quarry, well; lode, bed, vein; heap, pile, mass, stack, load.

7. *Usu.* **supplies** provisions, stores, rations, groceries, provender, larder, food supply; material, materials, matériel; wherewithal, means.

support, *v.* **1.** bear, bear up, upbear, hold, hold up, uphold, truss, truss up; prop, prop up, brace, bolster, bolster up, buttress, gird, stay, mainstay; carry, shoulder, keep up, crutch, shore, shore up, reinforce, restrengthen; bed, embed, base, be at the bottom of, form the foundation of, underlie, underprop, underpin, underbrace; cradle, pillow; buoy, buoy up, keep afloat.

2. suffer, bear, tolerate, stomach, brook, abide, *Archaic.* bide, put up with, *Inf.* stand *or* stand for, *Inf.* lump *or* lump it, *Inf.* love it or leave it; endure, persevere, withstand, brave, accept, resign oneself to, take what comes, hold out, *Inf.* stick *or* stick it out, *Sl.* hang in *or* hang in there *or* hang tough; undergo, experience, submit to.

3. succor, relieve, comfort, condole, sympathize; cheer, inspire, inspirit, assure, reassure, give *or* raise hope, yield *or* afford hope, hold out *or* justify hope, raise one's hopes *or* expectations.

4. maintain, sustain, nurse, nourish, nurture, cherish, foster, mother; provide *or* provide for, keep, keep alive, care for, take care of, look after, take charge *or* under one's wing, see after, see *or* look to, *Inf.* look *or* watch out for; watch, mind, tend, keep an eye on, watch over, keep watch over.

5. finance, pay for, subsidize, underwrite, fund, sponsor, capitalize, provide money for, put up the money for, set up, meet the expense, *Inf.* foot the bill, *Inf.* bankroll, *Inf.* pick up the check *or* tab, *Inf.* stake, grubstake, *Inf.* angel.

6. encourage, abet, further, forward, uphold, back, second; help, aid, assist, oblige, accommodate, lend oneself to; hearten, enhearten, embolden, pat [s.o.] on the back, *Inf.* buck up *or* brace up.

7. advocate, promote, patronize, espouse, sanction, countenance, recommend, commend, speak well *or* highly *or* warmly of, have *or* put in a good word for, puff, *Sl.* plug, *Sl.* tout, *Sl.* hype, sing the praises of; fall in with, join oneself to, associate oneself with, lend one's name to, take the part of, take up *or* espouse *or* adopt the cause of; speak for, contend for, argue for, stand up for, side with *or* take sides with, stand behind; shield, protect, defend, champion, take up the cudgels for, *Inf.* stick up for, *Inf.* run interference for, *Fig.* block for, *Inf.* go to bat for.

8. confirm, affirm, verify, validate, certify, authenticate, accredit, attest, vouch for, swear to, warrant, guarantee, endorse, ratify; corroborate, circumstantiate, substantiate, bear out, make good.

—*n.* **9.** prop, underprop, base, fulcrum, *Archit.* socle, abutment, truss, frame; basis, bed, bedding, sill, substructure, foundation, underbuilding, underpinning, groundwork, embankment; brace, bracer, bolster, bracket, stay, mainstay, buttress, shoulder, reinforcement; beam, crossbeam, joist, rafter, girder, lintel, arm; post, pillar, column, upright, shaft, pole, shore, strut, stanchion; rope, cable, guy, guywire, guyline.

10. maintenance, sustenance, subsistence, sustainment, sustentation, upkeep, keep, provision, living, livelihood; nurture, nourishment, nutriment, alimentation, mothering, tender loving care, *Inf.* TLC; provisions, stores, necessities, food, victuals, aliment, meat, bread, daily bread; economic *or* price support, subsidy, subsidization, subvention, compensation, dole, *Brit. Sl.* brew, welfare, relief, charity, handout; bounty, means; alimony.

11. advocate, patron, patronizer, sympathizer, backer, champion, endorser, upholder, maintainer, sustainer, bearer, carrier, sanctioner, approver; subsidizer, underwriter, benefactor, benefactress, angel, financer.

12. backing, approval, approbation, advocacy, encouragement, countenance, favor, espousal, patronage, promotion, blessing, grace, sponsorship, auspices, good offices, kind regard; fosterage, furtherance, advancement, advance, advantage, welfare; help, aid, assistance, helping hand, lift, boost; relief, succor, championship, protection, friendship.

13. helper, aide, assistant, attendant, subsidiary, ancilla, auxiliary, second, right hand, right-hand man, acolyte, deputy; partner, ally, comrade, colleague, associate, consociate, companion, helpmate, helpmeet, co-worker, consort, confrere, sidekick, crony, *Inf.* buddy, *Chiefly Brit.* mate; cooperator, collaborator, contributor, participant, participator.

supportable, *adj.* **1.** tolerable, endurable, sufferable, bearable, abidable, acceptable, maintainable, excusable.

2. tenable, defensible, vindicable, provable, demonstrable, confirmable, sustainable, apodictic, evincible, checkable, attestable, verifiable, validatable, substantiable, establishable, authenticable.

supporter, *n.* **1.** prop, base, fulcrum, socle, truss; brace, bracer, bolster, buttress, bracket, stay, shoulder, reinforcement. See also **support** (*def.* **9**).

2. maintainer, sustainer, upholder, advocate, backer, second, abettor, patron, endorser, promoter; champion, defender, apologist, exponent, protagonist, friend in *or* at court, mediator, intercessor, paraclete; adherent, follower, partisan, mainstay, stalwart, sectary, votary, rooter, booster, aficionado, devotee, admirer, lover, *Inf.* fan, *Inf.* buff; encourager, favorer, well-wisher, sympathizer.

3. financer, funder, subsidizer, underwriter, angel, *Inf.* staker, grubstaker, *Sl.* meal ticket; benefactor, benefactress, benefiter, friend in deed, guardian angel, tutelary, patron saint, *Inf.* fairy godmother.

4. ally, partner, comrade, comrade in arms, colleague, associate, consociate, companion, helpmate, helpmeet, co-worker, copartner, co-aid, consort, confrere, sidekick, crony, *Inf.* buddy, *Chiefly Brit.* mate; accomplice, accessory *or Chiefly Law.* accessary, *Law.* principal, confederate, partner in crime.

5. athletic supporter, jockstrap, jock; G-string; garter; brassiere, bandeau, *Inf.* bra, *Sl.* over-the-shoulder-boulder-holder; girdle, corset, foundation garment, garter belt; suspender, suspenders, pair of suspenders, *Chiefly Dial.* gallus.

supportive, *adj.* encouraging, reassuring, understanding, sympathetic; well-disposed, ready to help, helpful, aidful; behind [s.o.], in back of [s.o.], on [s.o.'s] side.

suppose, *v.* **1.** assume, take for granted, presume, presuppose, postulate, posit, predicate, theorize, hypothesize, hypothecate, speculate; suspect, imagine, surmise, conjecture, guess, reckon, hazard a guess; believe, fancy, think, think likely, daresay, opine, *Northern U.S.* calculate, *Inf.* allow, conclude, judge, realize; infer, *Inf.* take it, deduce; understand, gather, apprehend, get, *Sl.* dig; divine, intuit.

2. imply, presuppose, require logically.

supposed, *adj.* **1.** hypothetical, theoretical; imagined, imaginary, made-up, invented.

2. assumed, presumed, presupposed, taken for granted; accepted, believed, thought; professed, purported, rumored, said to be, claimed, so-called.

supposition, *n.* presumption, assumption, presupposition, posit, postulate, premise; inference, deduction, conclusion, theory, hypothesis, thesis; belief, conviction, persuasion, tenet, opinion, view, viewpoint, position, stand, attitude, feeling, gut feeling; idea, notion, thought, suspicion, *Sl.* sneaking suspicion *or* feeling, *Inf.* hunch; guesswork, guess, educated guess, *Sl.* shot in the dark, *Sl.* stab, wild shot *or* guess, conjecture, speculation, surmise.

suppress, *v.* **1.** restrain, curb, harness, check, stop, arrest; block, impede, inhibit, hinder, hamper, deter, halt; restrict, confine, limit, cramp; preclude, obviate, nip in the bud, *Inf.* put the kibosh on; prohibit, forbid, interdict, prevent.

2. extinguish, quench, snuff out, kill, stamp out, put out; do away with, remove, leave no vestige *or* trace of; eliminate, put an end to, get rid of, dispose of; quell, squelch, crush, vanquish, squash; overthrow, overturn, overwhelm, overpower, subvert, topple, defeat, conquer.

3. obliterate, annihilate, extinguish, expunge, extirpate, discreate, eradicate, exterminate; blot out, strike out, stamp out, crush out.

4. keep secret, conceal, hide, bury, withhold; mask, cloak, secrete, veil, screen, shroud, keep dark, camouflage, disguise; squelch, muzzle, muffle, mute, still, tone down, hush up, silence, quiet; repress, hold in *or* back, keep down, smother, stifle, choke, gag.

5. censor, erase, rub out, efface, scrape out, scratch out; delete, *Print.* dele, blue-pencil, edit, edit out; cross out, x out, cancel, black out, mark off; wash out, sponge off *or* away; excise, cut, cut out, expurgate.

6. abolish, nullify, quash, invalidate; cancel, discharge, set aside; counterorder, countermand, overrule, override.

suppression, *n.* **1.** restraint, curb, harness, check, stoppage, arrest; blockage, impediment, obstruction, inhibition, hindrance, determent, deterrent; restriction, confinement, limitation; preclusion, obviation; prohibition, forbiddance, interdiction, prevention, repression.

2. extinguishment, extinction, quenching; removal, elimination, putting an end to, getting rid of, disposing of; termination, dissolution; quelling, subdual, squelching, crushing, squashing, vanquishment; overthrow, overturn, conquest, subversion, defeat.

3. obliteration, annihilation, expunction, extirpation, discreation, eradication, extermination, destruction; blotting out, striking out, stamping out, crushing out.

4. concealment, hiding, keeping in the dark, withholding; masking, cloaking, veiling, screening, camouflage, disguise; silencing, quieting, holding back, keeping quiet.

5. censorship, erasure, deletion, editing; crossing out, cancellation, blacking out, marking off; excision, cutting, cutting out, expurgation.

6. abolition, abolishment, nullification, quashing, invalidation; cancellation, discharge, setting aside; overruling, overriding, repeal, veto.

suppurate, *v.* fester, gather, matter, maturate, ripen, come *or* draw to a head; run, drain, discharge, excrete, rankle, weep.

suppuration, *n.* **1.** festering, gathering, mattering, maturating, ripening, coming *or* drawing to a head; discharging, excreting, running, draining, weeping, rankling.

2. pus, pussiness, purulence, purulency, purulent matter, *Biol.* humor, *Archaic.* peccant humor *or* matter; discharge, excretion, fluid, *Med.* rheum, *Pathol.* ichor, *Pathol.* sanies, *Pathol.* gleet, *Pathol.* the whites, *Pathol.* leukorrhea.

supremacy, *n.* **1.** paramountcy, preeminence, preponderance, preponderancy, superiority, ascendance, ascendancy, transcendence, transcendency; primacy, superlativeness, excellence, capitalness, sublimeness; peerlessness, matchlessness, incomparability, incomparableness, inimitableness, inimitability.

2. sovereignty, principality, scepter, reign, regnancy, rule, monarchy; hegemony, leadership, chieftainship, chieftaincy, captainship, captaincy, headship; mastery, mastership, predominance, predomination, dominance, dominancy, domination, dominion, control, authority, power; omnipotence, almightiness.

supreme, *adj.* **1.** paramount, preeminent, superior, ascendant, transcendent, *Latin. facile princeps*; foremost, first, primary, leading; chief, main, capital, principal, cardinal, head; sovereign, monarchal, monarchic, monarchical, overruling, ruling, reigning, regnant; predominant, dominant, hegemonic, hegemonical, omnipotent, all-powerful, almighty, supernal.

2. uppermost, topmost, highest, soaring, top, tiptop; summital, apical, apogean, crowning; best, finest, prime, choicest, superlative, unexcelled, second to none; excellent, ace, first-rate, top-grade, top-drawer, topnotch, top-dog, *Inf.* A-one, *Sl.* crackerjack; peerless, matchless, incomparable, inimitable, unrivaled, unequaled, unparelleled, nonpareil, *Fr. sans pareil*; sublime, masterful, masterly, consummate, perfect, unbounded, unlimited, limitless, boundless.

3. greatest, maximal, maximum, max., most, utmost, uttermost; extreme, exceptional, extraordinary, out of the ordinary, outstanding, remarkable, notable, *Sl.* hell of a.

4. ultimate, endmost, last, *Fr. dernier*; final, ending, finishing, terminal, terminating, concluding, culminating, culminant; sunset, twilight, fading, waning.

surcease, *n.* **1.** cessation, discontinuance, expiration, abruption, breaking off, adjournment, stoppage, halt, standstill; ending, end, termination, finish, conclusion, close, desinence, windup, completion.

—v. **2.** come to an end, end, conclude, terminate, close, wind up *or* down, complete, finish *or* finish off, bring to an end, put an end to, make an end of; cease, stop, halt, discontinue, adjourn, break off, cut, cut short, drop, ring down the curtain.

sure, *adj.* **1.** certain, definite, positive, absolute, categorical; conclusive, definitive, decisive, well-grounded, well-founded, proven, demonstrated, incontestable, apodictic, irrefragible, irrefutable, incontrovertible; unquestionable, unquestioned, beyond question, indisputable, undisputed, indubitable, doubtless, undoubted; undeniable, unimpeachable, unqualified, unmitigated; authoritative, final, telling, irresistible; firsthand, eyewitness.

2. confident, decided, determined, settled, assured, reassured; convinced, persuaded, satisfied, *Inf.* sold; positive, free from doubt, dogmatic, cocksure; undoubting, undoubtable, unhesitating, unwavering, undeviating, unfaltering, unshaken.

3. reliable, trustworthy, trusty, dependable, faithful, loyal; tested, tried, tried and true, certified, guaranteed, insured, attested, documented.

4. firm, stable, sound, steady, secure, good; fixed, close, tight, fast, constant; strong, solid, substantial; steadfast, changeless, unchanging, invariable, unalterable; well-founded, settled, rooted, unshakable; sealed, bound tied, lashed, planted, anchored.

5. unfailing, infallible, inerrable; unerring, never-slipping, impeccable; *Inf.* sure-fire, foolproof, *Sl.* goof-proof.

6. inevitable, unavoidable, inescapable, inevasible, ineluctable; inexorable, unstoppable, irrevocable, unpreventable, irresistible; set, *Sl.* in the bag, cinched, fixed, established, *Sl.* on ice, clinched.

7. destined, fated, bound, fateful, doomed; foreordained, predestined, prearranged, *Inf.* in the cards, out of one's hands.

surely, *adv.* **1.** firmly, confidently, securely; surefootedly, unerringly, unswervingly, undeviatingly, unhesitatingly, unfalteringly, unwaveringly; steadily, determinedly, doggedly.

2. undoubtedly, indubitably, doubtless, doubtlessly; unquestionably, positively, absolutely, unequivocally, beyond question, beyond a doubt, beyond the shadow of a doubt; certainly, decidedly, definitely, assuredly.

3. inevitably, unavoidably, inescapably, unfailingly; unalterably, invariably, inexorably.

—interj. **4.** yes, OK, of course, certainly, *Archaic.* certes, to be sure, by all means, *Sl.* yup, *Sl.* yessir, *Sl.* yessiree.

surety, *n.* **1.** security, indemnity, assurance, insurance, guarantee, pledge, warranty, warrant; bond, bail, *Law.* replevin, *Law.* escrow, *Marine Law.* bottomry; gage, earnest, stake, deposit, money in advance, collateral; hostage, pawn, hock; contract, vow, troth, word, word of honor, verbal agreement.

2. sponsor, guarantor, warrantor, insurer, mortgagor, bondsman, bailsman; godparent, godfather, godmother; cosigner, countersigner; guardian, trustee, custodian, warder.

3. certainty, certitude, sureness, freedom from doubt; confidence, assurance, reassurance, self-assurance, assuredness; conviction, belief, confidence, reliance, trust; positiveness, dogmatism, unshakableness.

4. absoluteness, unequivocalness, unquestionableness, indisputability, unmistakability; indubitability, doubtlessness, incontrovertibility, irrefutability, irrefragibility, incontestability; definiteness, conclusiveness, definitiveness, unimpeachability.

5. secureness, security, safety, safeness, invulnerability, impregnability; dependability, reliability, trustworthiness, trustiness; stability, firmness, steadfastness, steadiness.

surf, *n.* waves, rollers, whitecaps, white horses; billows, swells, surge, rise, welling up; breakers, beachcombers, combers; tide, influx, flowing in; ocean *or* sea spray, foam, spindrift, spume; tidemark, residue, scum.

surface, *n.* exterior, superficies, outside, externals, superficiality; veneer, façade, appearance, aspect, face; integument, skin, covering, shell, carapace; superstratum, finish, coat, coating, crust, top.

surfeit, *n.* **1.** excess, surplus, oversupply, glut, nimiety, *Sl.* bellyful, overdose, too much; superabundance, overabundance, exuberance, superfluity, waste; supersaturation, saturation, flood, deluge, inundation, overflow, avalanche; copiousness, profuseness, profusion, luxuriance, lavishness; abundance, plethora, prodigality.

2. fullness, repletion, satiation, satiety; cloyedness, overfullness, overindulgence; disgust, revulsion, nausea.

—v. **3.** satiate, pall, overfill, overdo, indulge; cloy, glut, englut, stuff, cram, gorge, overfeed, overeat, *Sl.* pig out, *Sl.* munch out, *Sl.* stuff one's face; saturate, soak, drench, flood, deluge, engulf, inundate; overload, overburden, overwhelm; suffocate, choke, gag, sicken, nauseate, disgust; jade, dull, deaden, weary, exhaust, tire, bore.

surge, *n.* **1.** gush, rush, stream, flow, efflux, effusion, outpouring; upsurge, rise, ascension, upsweep, upcurve, uptrend, ungrowth, upgoing; increase, acceleration, inflation, escalation, intensification; takeoff, rocketing, soaring, skyrocketing.

2. swell, welling up; billow, wave, roller, whitecap, white horse, breaker, beachcomber, comber; sea, ocean, tide, influx.

—v. **3.** billow, swell, well forth, bulge; gush, rush,

pour, stream, flow; rise, ascend, mount, climb, come up; heave, rise and fall, go up and down, ebb and flow, oscillate, undulate, wave; rock, roll, turn, toss, storm.

surly, *adj.* **1.** cantankerous, irascible, iracund, obnoxious, crabbed, choleric, brusque, peppery, crusty; grumpy, grouchy, crotchety, dyspeptic, thorny, bearish, snarling, growling; cross, feisty, huffy, sulky, sullen, bilious, cranky, peevish, irritable; testy, touchy, tetchy, ill-tempered, bad-tempered, short-tempered, ill-humored, ill-natured; fractious, quarrelsome, disagreeable, *Inf.* ornery, *Inf.* mean, *Inf.* bitchy, *Inf.* ugly; caustic, mordant, mordacious, sarcastic, insulting, biting; sharp, uncivil, rough, harsh; curt, short, terse, blunt.

2. unfriendly, unsociable, inhospitable, unamiable, unaffable; hostile, antagonistic, adverse, averse, contrary, oppugnant, inimical; anti, against, *Sl.* agin, down on.

3. gloomy, depressing, cheerless, mournful, doleful, dolorous; dismal, dreary, bleak, grim, funereal, lugubrious; dark, black, sinister, heavy, malign, malignant, malevolent; threatening, menacing, lowering, looming.

surmise, *v.* **1.** imagine, suppose, presume, infer, suspect, guess, conjecture; assume, understand, gather, deduce, conclude, reckon, deem, feel, opine, be of the opinion, daresay.

—n. **2.** matter of conjecture, open question; possibility, likelihood, probability.

3. idea, thought, belief, opinion; inference, assumption, presumption, supposition, supposal.

4. guess, conjecture, hypothesis, postulate, *Inf.* hunch, *Inf.* stab, *Inf.* shot, *Inf.* shot in the dark.

surmount, *v.* **1.** climb, climb over, ascend, scale, mount, clear, vault.

2. overcome, conquer, triumph over, prevail over, get the better of, beat, *Inf.* lick; survive, pull through, make it, weather the storm.

3. top, overtop, tower above, rise above; overlook, command, dominate.

4. top off, cap, crown, crest.

surmountable, *adj.* superable, capable of being overcome, conquerable, vincible, beatable; achievable, attainable, obtainable, within reach, reachable, realizable.

surname, *n.* **1.** last name, family name, proper name, cognomen; patronymic, metronymic, matronymic; maiden name.

2. epithet, appellative, byword, label, tag; nickname, pet name, sobriquet, *Sl.* handle, *Sl.* moniker; appellation, designation, name, title, honorific, style.

surpass, *v.* **1.** exceed, pass, pass *or* go beyond, *Sl.* one-up, break the record, *Inf.* go over the top; transcend, leave behind, leave in the dust; prevail over, take precedence over, supersede.

2. excel, better, *Inf.* go one better, trump; walk off *or* away with, take the cake *or* prize; outstrip, outdo, outvie, outrival, outclass, outshine, outperform, outplay, *Inf.* run rings *or* circles around; cap, top, overtop; beat, best, worst; overshadow, throw *or* cast into the shade, eclipse, put to shame, shame, *Inf.* show [s.o.] up; outrun, outpace, outdistance, distance; overtake, overhaul, overpass, lap, shoot ahead of, get ahead of.

surpassing, *adj.* transcendent, transcending, exceeding, excelling, outstripping, eclipsing; extraordinary, out of the ordinary, rare; superior, better, finer, greater, a cut *or* stroke *or* notch above; outstanding, standout, preeminent, *Fr. par excellence*; incomparable, inimitable, nonpareil, peerless, matchless, second to none, in a class by itself, *Latin. sui generis;* unequaled, unmatched, unrivaled, unsurpassed, unparalleled.

surplus, *n.* **1.** surfeit, superabundance, plethora, glut, satiety, excess; flood, deluge, inundation, spate, avalanche, landslide, riot, drug on *or* in the market, supersaturation; oversupply, overmeasure, overabundance, overload; overdose, too much of a good thing.

2. remainder, remnants, residue, residuum, remains, balance, rest.

—adj. **3.** extra, space, unused; remaining, surviving, unconsumed; excess, superfluous, redundant.

surprise, *v.* **1.** astonish, amaze, astound, stun, *Inf.* flabbergast, *Inf.* snow, *Sl.* blow away, *Sl.* blow one's mind; overwhelm, overpower, *Inf.* bowl over, *Inf.* floor, *Inf.* knock *or* throw one for a loop, *Inf.* set back on one's heels; hit like a ton of bricks, *Inf.* hit between the eyes.

2. take by surprise, take unawares, catch off-guard, catch napping; catch red-handed, catch in the act, catch *in flagrante delicto*, *Sl.* catch with one's pants down, *Sl.* catch dead to rights.

3. ambush, *U.S.* bushwhack, *Inf.* jump; pounce upon, fall upon, descend upon, swoop down upon; come out of nowhere, drop from the clouds, come like a bolt from the blue; blitz.

4. pop, spring [s.t.] on [s.o.].

—n. **5.** bolt from the blue, bombshell, shocker, blow; eyeopener, revelation; ace in the hole, card *or* ace up one's sleeve.

6. amazement, astonishment, astoundment, marvelment, wonder, wonderment, breathless wonder, awe.

7. marvel, phenomenon, prodigy, miracle, rarity, portent, sensation, *Sl.* stunner.

8. surprise attack, *Inf.* sneak attack, Pearl Harbor.

surprising, *adj.* **1.** amazing, astounding, astonishing, extraordinary, out of the ordinary, incredible; unusual, uncommon, unwonted, unfamiliar.

2. unexpected, unforeseen, unanticipated, unlooked-for; sudden, like a bolt from the blue; stunning, foudroyant, jolting, jarring.

surrealistic, *adj.* bizarre, weird, erratic, freakish, grotesque, *Inf.* freaky, *Sl.* rum, *Sl.* far-out; dadaistic, absurd, phantasmagoric, nightmarish, Kafkaesque; strange, unusual, uncommon, unconventional, unorthodox, uncustomary; irregular, odd, oddish, peculiar, curious, queer, extraordinary, fantastic, incredible, inconceivable; fey, supernatural, preternatural, out of this world.

surrender, *v.* **1.** yield, deliver up, turn over, hand in, part with; render, remit; release, let go of, quit one's hold on, yield control of; relinquish, renounce, forsake, forgo, *Law.* disclaim; abdicate, resign, *Chiefly Scot.* demit; transfer, give over, cede, make over, convey, sign away, waive, *Law.* demise.

2. give oneself up, turn oneself in, throw oneself at the mercy of, *Inf.* hands-up.

3. lose hope of, despair of, give up, abandon, quit, *Sl.* pack it in, give up the ship, cry quits, cry craven, throw up one's hands, throw in the sponge *or* the towel; resign oneself to, grin and bear it, lie down and die.

4. capitulate, submit, succumb to; fall, bite the dust, lay down arms, raise the white flag; acquiesce, comply, accede, give in, cry *or* say uncle; concede, back down, eat crow, eat humble pie, retract, recant, eat one's words; truckle, defer to, kneel to, bend *or* bow before, fall at [s.o.'s] feet.

—n. **5.** capitulation, submission, yielding; acquiescence, compliance, accedence, concession, nonresistance; homage, prostration, deference.

6. relinquishment, renunciation, abnegation, abdication, resignation, *Archaic.* demission; transfer, transferal, transference, *Law.* conveyance, ceding, leasing, handing over; release, quittance, acquittance, abandonment.

surreptitious, *adj.* **1.** clandestine, covert, undercover, stealthy, feline, nighttime, back-alley, backstreet, CIA-type, Watergate, *Canon Law.* subreptitious; collusive, conspirative, conspiratory, furtive, underhand, underhanded, *Inf.* under the counter, backroom, sneaky, sneaking, sly, foxy, vulpine, crafty, cunning; unethical, dishonorable, illegal, unlawful, unauthorized, *Canon Law.* obreptitious.

2. secret, secretive, hugger-mugger, dark, closed, unpublic, not open to the public, private, confidential, closed-door, closet, *Archaic.* privy; hidden, concealed, ensconced, shrouded, cloaked, disguised, veiled, masked, screened, in the dark; undisclosed, unrevealed, unpublicized, silent; mysterious, arcane, intriguing.

surreptitiously, *adv.* **1.** clandestinely, covertly, under cover, stealthily, under the table *or* counter; collusively, conspiratorily, furtively, underhandedly, sneakily, craftily, cunningly, slyly, on the sly, behind one's back, behind the scenes; unethically, dishonorably, illegally, unlawfully, fraudulently.

2. secretly, privately, in private, behind closed doors, confidentially, sub rosa; silently, mysteriously, in the dark; in a whisper, aside.

surrogate, *n.* **1.** agent, proxy, secondary, deputy, delegate, vicar, chargé d'affaires, regent, viceroy; representative, envoy, emissary, ambassador, consul; pinch runner, pinch hitter, designated hitter, relief pitcher; substitute teacher, sub.

2. replacement, succedaneum, alternate, backup, relief, fill-in, *Chiefly Brit.* locum tenens; understudy, stand-by, double, stand-in, *Sl.* ringer, dummy, imitation, copy, fake, changeling; benchwarmer, second team *or* string; scapegoat, whipping boy.

surround, *v.* **1.** enclose, enwrap, enfold, envelop, encase, encompass, environ, ensphere, circumfuse, encircle, circle, circumscribe, compass, belt.

2. circumvent, begird, engird, encincture, gird, girdle, confine, fence in, pen in, hedge in, hem in; circumvallate, beset, besiege, entrap, ensnare, blockade.

—n. **3.** perimeter, circle, box, square; girdle, belt, border, fence, wall, confine, boundary, frontier; enclosure, encasement, case, surrounding, covering, coating, coat; envelopment, envelope, wrapping, wrap, integument, *Bot.* testa, shell, skin.

surrounding, *n.* **1.** perimeter, enclosure, belt, border. See **surround** (*def.* **3**).

2. surroundings environs, neighborhood, vicinity, vicinage, region, area, locale, district, section; environment, habitat, setting, *Fr. mise en scène,* scene, entourage, milieu, ambience, background; suburbs, faubourgs, outskirts.

3. enclosing, enwrapping, enfoldment, enfolding, envelopment, enveloping, encasement, encasing; encompassment, encompassing, begirding, encirclement, encircling, circumscription, circumscribing, environing, circumambience, encincture, encincturing, circumvallating, besetment, besetting, hemming in.

—adj. **4.** enclosing, enwrapping, enfolding, enveloping, encasing, integumentary; encompassing, girdling, begirding, circumfluent, circumventive, circumventing; encircling, circling, circumscribing, circumjacent, circumambient, ambient, environing, circumvallating, besetting, hemming in.

5. environmental, vicinal, regional, sectional, local; neighboring, next-door, adjoining, conjoining, connecting, attached; adjacent, juxtapositional, juxtaposed, next to, proximate, bordering; contiguous, abutting, meeting, tangential, tangent, touching, *Obs.* attingent; near, nearby, close, close-by, nigh.

surveillance, *n.* **1.** watch, observation, espial; reconnaissance, probe, espionage, spying, police observation, *Sl.* stakeout; examination, visual examination, study, scrutiny, perusal, review, overview, survey; exploration, observing, noticing, seeing, looking, watching, viewing, witnessing, eyeing; notice, note, attention, inspection, regard.

2. supervision, care, careful attention; monitering, regulation, control, management, administration, superintendence; direction, government, command, leadership; oversight, stewardship, charge, conduct, guidance, treatment.

survey, *v.* **1.** appraise, take stock of, assess; take the measure of, size, size up, judge; ascertain, determine, figure, figure out; reckon, calculate, compute, estimate, *Inf.* check, *Inf.* check out.

2. scan, observe, scrutinize, regard, contemplate; consider, review, study, examine, investigate; inspect, pore over, peruse, take a close *or* careful look; take note *or* cognizance of, cast an eye over, *Inf.* give the once-over.

3. watch, keep an eye on, keep in sight *or* view; reconnoiter, keep under observation, *Sl.* case, scout, scout out, stake out, spy upon; follow, monitor, *Inf.* keep tabs on; keep watch, be watchful; notice, note, take note of.

4. delineate, delimit, measure, calibrate; graph, lay out, chart, map, map out, trace, pace off, make a map *or* survey of.

—n. **5.** examination, perusal, inspection, scrutiny, scrutinization, *Sl.* look-see, *Inf.* shopping trip; close observation *or* watch, investigation, inquisition, inquiry; study, analysis, research, exploration, probe, search; sifting, going through *or* over, review, checkout, audit; assessment, appraisal, *Inf.* once-over.

6. report, statement, detailing, in-depth account; review, recounting, recapitulation, *Inf.* rehash; overview, précis, abstract, summary, digest, condensation.

survival, *n.* **1.** endurance, subsistence, maintenance, nourishment, nurture, sustenance, sustentation; living, livelihood; lasting, staying, enduring, going on through thick and thin, continuing through the ages, continuance.

—adj. **2.** lifesaving, life-giving, emergency; sustaining, maintaining, supporting, nurturing, nourishing.

survive, *v.* **1.** outlive, outlast, outwear; remain, remain alive, live on, subsist, endure; last, continue, abide, *Archaic.* bide, be extant.

2. live, persist, get through, succeed, win over, live through; weather the storm, stand fast, hold one's footing, hold one's ground; keep body and soul together.

susceptibility, *n.* **1.** vulnerability, defenselessness, pregnability, weakness, weak spot, exposed area, chink in one's armor, loophole; subjectability, proneness, liability, predisposition, tendency to get, inclination, propensity, leaning, proclivity; predilection, partiality, affinity, liking, sweet tooth, *Inf.* thing for; sympathy, affection, fondness, soft spot, understanding.

2. openness, amenability, amenableness, receptiveness, responsiveness, sensitivity, sensibility, susceptivity, susceptiveness; impressibility, impressibleness, impressionability, impressionableness; gullibility, dupability, credulousness, naiveté, innocence.

susceptible, *adj.* **1.** *Usu.* **susceptible of** *or* **to** open to, receptive to, amenable to, susceptive to; responsive to, sensitive to, alive to; easily hurt, thin-skinned, tender; easily excited *or* upset, excitable, high-strung, emotional; willing to listen to, accessible, reachable; influenceable, impressible, impressionable, likely to be taken in by *or* fall for; gullible, dupable, easily deceived; credulous, wide-eyed, naive, innocent, innocent as a newborn babe, born yesterday, wet behind the ears.

2. *Usu.* **susceptible to** vulnerable to, defenseless

against, pregnable, unable to endure *or* tolerate *or* stand; subject, given to, disposed to, likely to get, liable to; prone to, predisposed to, inclined toward, lean ing toward.

suspect, *v.* **1.** doubt, disbelieve, be skeptical *or* suspicious, distrust, mistrust; harbor suspicions, *Inf.* smell a rat, smell something rotten, have one's doubts, not bet on.

2. surmise, guess, hazard a guess, conjecture, infer; imagine, fancy, think, opine, theorize, believe, wonder; suppose, postulate, assume, presume, hypothesize; divine, have a sneaking suspicion, intuit, have a clue.

—adj. **3.** open to *or* under suspicion, suspicious, questionable, not believed, not trusted, doubted; sneaky, furtive, shady, hiding something.

suspend, *v.* **1.** hang, put up, depend, dangle, sling, drop, fall.

2. hold off, withhold, postpone, defer, delay, retard, put off; table, shelve, pigeonhole, put on the back burner; carry over, keep pending, continue, keep on ice; procrastinate, lallygag, fiddle around, dally.

3. stop, put a stop to, halt, stay, quit, cease, end, bring to an end; hold up, arrest, detain, stall, check, cut short; lift, intermit, remove, rescind; pretermit, interrupt, break off, discontinue.

4. debar, shut out, exclude, eliminate, blackball, reject; expel, dismiss, throw out, *Inf.* bounce, eject, evict; unseat, *Law.* disbar, unfrock, discharge, send packing.

suspended, *adj.* **1.** hanging, dependent, depending, pendent, pendulous, dangling, drooping.

2. postponed, put off, delayed, held up, withheld; tabled, shelved, continued; up in the air, in suspense, undecided, unfinished, unresolved, unsettled, pending, on ice.

3. inactive, in mothballs, in wraps; discontinued, not in force, out of action.

suspenders, *n.* *Chiefly Dial.* galluses, *Brit.* braces, *Brit.* sock suspenders, garters; support.

suspense, *n.* **1.** excitement, anticipation, expectation; uncertainty, incertitude, unsureness, doubt, doubtfulness, dubitation, dubiety, dubiousness, dubiosity; indefiniteness, ambiguity, ambiguousness, vagueness, haziness, fogginess.

2. indecision, indecisiveness, irresolution, irresoluteness, wavering, hesitancy, hesitation; unsettledness, ambivalence, double-mindedness, mixed feelings; fence-sitting, fence-straddling, tergiversation, shilly-shally, vacillation, oscillation, fluctuation, blowing hot and cold.

3. suspension, interruption, discontinuance, discontinuation. See **suspension.**

suspension, *n.* interruption, discontinuance, abeyance, suspense; cessation, stop, stoppage, stopping, halt; surcease, abruption, breaking off, severance, sunderance, disconnection, temporary dismissal; adjournment, postponement, deferment, delay; stay, reprieve, respite; intermission, interval, interim, interlude, interregnum, *Sports.* half time; pause, break, pause *or* break in the action, time-out, hiatus, lacuna, gap; recess, rest, rest period, breather, lull, *Inf.* letup, remission; truce, cease-fire, armistice.

suspicion, *n.* **1.** distrust, mistrust, credibility gap, lack of confidence *or* trust; doubt, doubtfulness, dubitation, dubiety, dubiousness, dubiosity; disbelief, unbelief, incredulity, incredulousness; watchfulness, wariness, leeriness, shyness; hesitation, uncertainty, misgiving, qualm, question, second thought, funny feeling, *Sl.* bad vibes.

2. notion, idea, thought, feeling, gut feeling, *Sl.* sneaking suspicion *or* feeling, *Inf.* hunch; supposition, conjecture, guess, piece of guesswork, speculation, surmise; inference, deduction, conclusion.

3. suggestion, trace, soupçon, taste, flavor; inkling, hint, touch, tinge, shade, bit, sprinkling, dash, dab.

suspicious, *adj.* **1.** questionable, open to question *or* doubt, debatable, doubtful, dubious, shaky; untrustworthy, shady, suspect, suspected, under suspicion; odd, peculiar, strange, queer, *Inf.* funny, *Sl.* funny-looking.

2. distrustful, mistrustful, skeptical, doubting, disbelieving, unbelieving, from Missouri, incredulous; watchful, wary, leery, chary, shy; hesitant, hesitating, uncertain, unsure, wondering, questioning; qualmish, uneasy, nervous, anxious, apprehensive, fearful.

sustain, *v.* **1.** carry, support, hold, hold up, uphold; truss, shoulder, buttress, brace, shore up, underprop, underpin, underset, reinforce; bear, bolster, strengthen.

2. undergo, experience, suffer, endure, tolerate, hold out; brook, submit to, abide, stand, withstand; brave, weather, carry on under, labor under.

3. maintain, continue, prolong, keep alive, keep intact; preserve, keep up, save from decay, conserve; nurture, nourish, feed, provide for, tend; cherish, foster, nurse, rear, raise, strengthen.

4. establish, ratify, sanction, accredit; authorize, warrant, justify, vindicate, confirm, corroborate, verify, authenticate, validate, substantiate; bear out, prove, establish, evidence, give credence to; attest, attest to, certify, bear witness to, testify, vouch for.

sustenance, *n.* **1.** nourishment, food, nutriment, nurture, nutrition, pabulum, subsistence; aliment, viands, meat, bread *or* daily bread; groceries, foodstuffs, solids, edibles, *Inf.* grub, *Sl.* eats, *Sl.* chow, *Chiefly Brit. Sl.* scoff; snack, between-meal snack, bite, bite to eat, nosh, *Sl.* munchies; victuals, provisions, cheer, provender, rations, commons, comestibles, *Western U.S. Sl.* chuck, *Brit. Sl.* prog; board, fare, meals, mess, menu, table, diet, regimen.

2. livelihood, living, maintenance, subsistence, keep, upkeep, support, sustainment, sustentation, necessaries, provision; board and lodging, room and board.

suzerain, *n.* sovereign, monarch, majesty, crowned head, king, potentate, dynast; lord, lord and master, overlord, master, chief, ruler, tyrant, dictator; prince, emperor, rajah, czar, caesar, kaiser, *Fr. roi, Latin. rex,* sheik, khan.

suzerainty, *n.* sovereignty, dominion, supremacy, primacy, preeminence, sway, hegemony; reign, royalty, empery, (*in India*) raj; kingship, lordship, mastership, leadership, seigniory; authority, jurisdiction, power, *Inf.* say *or* say-so; rule, command, mastery, control, domination; hold, grasp, grip, clutches.

svelte, *adj.* slender, lithe, lithesome, lissome, thin, slim, lean; willowy, wasp-waisted, hourglass, sylphlike, slinky, foxy; shapely, clean-limbed, lanky, arrowy; delicate, graceful, fine, elegant.

swab, *n.* **1.** swob, mop; sponge, cotton, cloth.

—v. **2.** swob, mop *or* mop up, clean *or* clean up, wipe up *or* off, absterge, sponge, wash, rinse *or* rinse off, scrub, scour, rub.

swaddle, *v.* bind, wrap, wrap up, enwrap, confine, bundle up, muffle up, swathe, roll up, bandage; enfold, envelop, encircle, enclose; clothe, drape, cover, shroud.

swagger, *v.* **1.** strut, swash, prance, flourish, parade, march, step out.

2. boast, brag, gasconade, crow, *Australian.* skite, draw the long bow, vaunt, trumpet; blow one's own horn, sing one's own praises, *Inf.* tout oneself, pat oneself on the back, flatter oneself, congratulate oneself; bluster, roister, puff, *Sl.* blow hard, *Sl.* talk big, *Sl.* shoot the bull, *Sl.* lay it on thick, tell fish stories; show off, *Inf.* put on the dog, act like a big shot, bluff;

splutter, sputter, rant, bully.

—*n.* **3.** swashbuckling, vainglory, pomp, ostentation, show, display, parade; bluster, gasconade, braggadocio, brag, boastfulness, fanfaronade, *Sl.* hot air; arrogance, haughtiness, snobbishness, *Inf.* snootiness, *Inf.* highfalutin manner, pomposity.

swaggerer, *n.* **1.** swashbuckler, swasher, strutter, blusterer, *Brit. Sl.* bucko, bully, cock of the walk; snob, dandy, prig, coxcomb, fop; braggart, braggadocio, gascon, boaster, fanfaron, *Sl.* blowhard, *Sl.* gasbag, *Sl.* hot-air artist; blatherskite, *Sl.* windbag, *Sl.* bigmouth, loud-mouth.

swain, *n.* **1.** lover, suitor, beau, inamorato, gallant, admirer, adorer, idolizer; boyfriend, young man, Romeo, flame, fiancé, intended.

2. country boy, country cousin, yokel, rustic, *Archaic.* hind, country bumpkin, clodhopper, bogtrotter, *Inf.* hayseed, *Inf.* hick, *Sl.* rube.

swallow, *v.* **1.** gulp, guzzle, digest, engorge; eat, sup, down, *Archaic.* manducate; pop, drop; bolt, snap up, wolf down, dispatch, put down *or* away; drink, imbibe, quaff, belt, swill, swig; tipple, tope, toss off, throw back, knock back, *Sl.* chug-a-lug; ingest, intake, take in, suck up, tuck away.

2. *Usu.* **swallow up** absorb, assimilate, engross, soak up, mop up; engulf, swamp, overwhelm, whelm, flood, inundate; consume, devour, ingurgitate, ingulf.

3. *Informal.* accept, take, take the bait, lap up, suck up; take for granted, take on faith, believe anything; fall for, swallow whole, swallow hook, line and sinker, be a sucker for; take one's word, *Sl.* buy, *Inf.* take as gospel truth, trust, take stock in, credit.

4. put up with, tolerate, bear, grin and bear it, suffer, live with; stomach, stand, abide, take, pocket; brook, brave, endure; ignore, disregard, turn a blind eye to.

—*n.* **5.** gulp, *Physiol.* deglutition, ingestion, imbibition; ingurgitation, engorgement; consumption, absorption, assimilation; eating, drinking.

6. mouthful, bite, nibble, munch, snap, cud, tidbit, gobbet, *Sl.* gob, bolus; spoonful, sippet, driblet, dose; drink, draught, shot, dram, belt, *Inf.* swig, *Sl.* swill; sip, nip, suck, *Inf.* pull, *Inf.* chug; tot, *Sl.* snort, *Sl.* slurp, *Sl.* guzzle.

swamp, *n.* **1.** marsh, bog, fen, morass, quagmire, quag, *Archaic.* marish; mire, quicksand, mud, muck, ooze, sludge; sough, slough, *Brit. Dial.* sump, *Scot.* moss, wash, squash, wallow; flat, mud flat, everglade, peat bog, moor, *Chiefly Brit.* moorland; bottom land, swampland, fenland, marshland, forest swamp.

—*v.* **2.** flood, inundate, deluge, pour down, teem, stream; drench, soak, saturate, douse; splash, wet, water, hose; wash out, mop, swab, bathe.

3. overwhelm, whelm, engulf, swallow up; oversupply, abound, flush; overburden, overcharge, overweigh, oppress, prostrate; stagger, bow, crush, overload, overtax, weigh down.

4. immerse, submerge, submerse, drown, plunge in, sink in.

swampy, *adj.* marshy, quaggy, boggy, fenny, *Archaic.* marish; mucky, sludgy, muddy, oozy, miry, quagmiry, sloughy; paludal, moory, squashy, spongy; poachy, plashy, slobby, squishy, slushy; soggy, pulpy, mushy, loamy, soft; soaking, watery, *Archaic.* irriguous.

swanky, *adj. Informal.* **1.** stylish, smart, chic, fashionable, swank; dashing, dashy, showy, splashy; ostentatious, garish, gaudy.

2. luxurious, lavish, sumptuous, grand, elegant, rich, plush, *Inf.* posh, *Sl.* ritzy, *Sl.* snazzy; fancy, custom, special, deluxe, luxury; magnificent, gorgeous, beautiful, resplendent, splendid, *Inf.* splendiferous, brilliant.

swap, *v.* exchange, trade, barter, substitute; switch, transpose, invert, commute, permute; interchange, bandy, give and take.

sward, *n.* grass, turf, sod, artificial grass, *Trademark.* Astroturf; greensward, grassplot, patch of grass, green, grassy land; lawn, grounds, gardens, grassland, field, meadow, *Archaic.* mead; village green, common, quadrangle, *Inf.* quad, mall, park.

swarm, *n.* **1.** hive, horde, host, multitude, crowd, throng, mob; drove, herd, pack, flock, cloud, gaggle, bevy, covey, flight, school, shoal; band, company, group, body, assemblage, assembly, aggregation; congregation, gathering, concentration, huddle, bunch, cluster, knot; mass, concourse, confluence, conflux, convergence; congestion, jam, crush, press, rush, stream, flood, deluge.

—*v.* **2.** throng, crowd, herd, group, cluster, huddle, concentrate, bunch up *or* together; mass, congregate, gather, agglomerate; flock together, surge, stream; convene, forgather, converge, come together, meet.

3. *Usu.* **swarm with** abound, teem with, pullulate, burst with, bristle with, be alive with, crawl with; overflow, overspill, overbrim, superabound, exuberate, know no bounds; throng with, crowd with, jam, pack, stuff, fill.

4. overrun, run riot *or* wild, overspread, overgrow, infest, plague, beset.

swarthy, *adj.* dark-colored, swart, *Archaic.* swarth, dark-complexioned, dark-complected, dark-skinned, dark, dusky; black-skinned, black, ebony, sable, jet-black, coal-black, pitch-black, *Inf.* black as tar, raven; blackish, nigrescent; brown-skinned, brown, brown-colored, chocolate, tawny, olive-skinned; Black, Negro, Negroid, African, Ethiopian, Arab.

swashbuckler, *n.* soldier of fortune, musketeer, soldier, adventurer, daredevil, hotspur; swordsman, duelist, fencer; Errol Flynn, Douglas Fairbanks, Jr.

swatch, *n.* sample, patch, specimen; example, copy; scrap, remnant; piece, bit, portion, fragment, chunk, cut, clipping.

swathe, *v.* **1.** bind, wrap, bundle up, bandage, swaddle. See **swaddle**.

—*n.* **2.** bandage, swaddle, wrapping, covering, dressing, gauze; bind, tie.

sway, *v.* **1.** swing, oscillate, rock, move back and forth *or* to and fro, librate, undulate, wave, vibrate; nod, wobble, flicker; sheer off, *Naut.* jibe, teeter, reel, totter.

2. incline, bend, lean, tend, swerve, veer, tilt; slip, slide, slope, slant, yaw, deviate, stray.

3. fluctuate, vacillate, waver; equivocate, *Sl.* waffle, hesitate.

4. jiggle, agitate, convulse, shake, nudge, push, jolt.

5. influence, impress, touch, move, stir, strike; persuade, talk into, win over, bring around, convince, induce, bias, predispose; urge, spur, stimulate, impel, prompt.

—*n.* **6.** swaying, swinging, oscillation, vibration, libration, undulation; fluctuation, vacillation, hesitation; incline, bend, tilt; slant, bias, prejudice, onesidedness, partiality, predisposition, predilection, close-mindedness.

7. rule, dominion, authority, mastery, iron hand; influence, control, command, leadership, guidance, direction; domination, power, hands, palm of one's hand, charge; ascendancy, supremacy, reach, scope, range, grasp, grip, clutches.

swear, *v.* **1.** take an oath, swear on the Bible, swear on a stack of Bibles, swear by all that's holy, say before God.

2. vow, pledge, promise, solemnly promise; give one's word, say on Scout's honor, pledge one's honor, cross one's heart and hope to die; affirm, asseverate, avow, aver, attest, declare, assert, state flat out; own, acknowledge, profess, admit, confess.

3. testify, testify under oath, give evidence, witness, bear witness to, depose, depone; sign an affidavit; tell the truth, the whole truth and nothing but the truth.

4. curse, *Inf.* cuss, blaspheme, take the name of the Lord in vain; use profanity, be profane *or* sacrilegious *or* irreverent; swear like a stevedore *or* muleteer *or* trooper, *Inf.* cuss a blue streak, turn the air blue, be foul-mouthed; imprecate, damn, curse in every language one knows, curse up hill and down dale, execrate, anathematize, denunciate, *Sl.* badmouth.

5. swear by a. *Informal.* rely on, depend on, have confidence in, trust, trust implicitly, believe in, count on; guarantee, avouch, vouch for, stake one's life on; respect, admire, reverence, worship, venerate. **b.** know, know for certain, be sure, be positive, *Inf.* be one-thousand percent sure; confirm, substantiate, document, demonstrate, prove, warrant.

sweat, *v.* **1.** perspire, *Obs.* sudate; swelter, drip with sweat, *Sl.* sweat bullets.

2. execrate, exude, transude, ooze; distill, condense.

3. *Informal.* drudge, work hard, grind, grub, toil, moil, plod, slog, peg, *Inf.* plug along, *Brit. Sl.* swot; slave, sweat and slave, *Inf.* scratch, *Inf.* hustle; work like a slave, work like a coal miner, work like a horse, *Inf.* work one's head off, *Brit. Archaic.* swink.

4. *Informal.* fret, fuss, worry, agonize, torture oneself, writhe, lose sleep over, toss and turn, stay awake nights, *Inf.* stew.

5. sweat [s.t.] out *Slang.* **a.** endure, last, hold up *or* out, see [s.t.] through, never say die, never give up, *Inf.* stick it out, *Inf.* go the distance, *Inf.* hang tough. **b.** strive, struggle, endeavor, strain, exert oneself, *Sl.* sweat blood.

—n. **6.** perspiration, sudoresis, *Med.* diaphoresis, *Obs.* sudation, *Latin. sudor;* body odor, BO.

7. *Informal.* drudgery, toil, moil, travail, hard work, slave labor, slavery; manual labor, spadework, backbreaking, work, *Brit. Sl.* swot.

8. *Informal.* fuss, fluster, flurry, dither, twitter, fret, bother, pother, *Inf.* stew, *Inf.* lather, *Inf.* tizzy, *Archaic.* pucker.

sweaty, *adj.* **1.** clammy, *Inf.* sticky; soaked, dripping with sweat; perspiring, sudoriferous, sudoriparous, sudorific.

2. laborious, strenuous, toilsome, arduous, operose, oppressive, onerous, backbreaking, uphill; hard, difficult, rough, tough.

sweep, *v.* **1.** *Often* **sweep away** *or* **out** whisk, brush, vacuum; clean, clean up, spruce up, tidy up, clear out, remove the dirt from; dust, wipe, swipe, swab, mop, scrub.

2. force, push, drive, blow, drift, carry, move; draw, pull, stroke, paint; clear, open, make a path through.

3. pan, scour, comb, winnow, sift through, rout through, search through; drag across, flow along, stream along, trail over, pass over; graze, brush against, rub against, glance, touch, hit; shave, skim, scrape, chafe, abrade.

4. curve, round, arch, bow, bend, *Archit.* embow; compass, go *or* move around *or* round, lap, circle, circuit, circumambulate, surround, encircle, encompass; extend, range, stretch, reach, go; span, cover, include, comprise.

5. *Usu.* **sweep along** *or* **through** scurry, hurry, rush, run, haste, hasten, career, hie, hightail it, scamper, *Inf.* skedaddle; dash, dart, shoot, tear, sprint, race, fly, go like the wind, streak, bolt; whip along, spank, zoom, whoosh, whiz, go like lightning, *Sl.* zing, *Sl.* zip, *Sl.* smoke; swoop down upon, blitz, charge, rampage, tear, stampede, rip.

—n. **6.** stroke, swipe, move, movement, motion, action.

7. drive, thrust, push; swoop, fell swoop, blow, attack, blitz; charge, rampage, stampede.

8. curvature, curvation, roundness, roundedness, bending, flexure; incurvation, incurvature, arcuation, *Pathol.* cyrtosis; curve, bend, arch, arc, vault, *Archit.* extrados; incurve, camber, crescent, lunule, lune, menscus, half-moon, horseshoe, *U.S.* oxbow; lap, round, turn, loop, circle, circuit, cycle, orbit, revolution.

9. compass, swing, scope, range, breadth, width; reach, stretch, spread, span, extent, area; space, room, play, elbowroom.

sweeping, *adj.* **1.** broad, wide, widespread, extensive, expansive, far-reaching, panoramic, bird's-eye, *Inf.* wall-to-wall; inclusive, inclusory, nonexclusive, unlimited, indiscriminate; general, universal, worldwide, pandemic, all-embracing, catholic, ecumenical; umbrella, blanket, comprehensive, all-inclusive, liberal; encyclopedic, voluminous, exhaustive.

2. (*of the outcome of a contest*) overwhelming, decisive, final; complete, total, full, thorough, thoroughgoing, out-and-out, outright, sheer; absolute, plenary, unconditional, unqualified.

—n. **3. sweepings** dirt, dust, offscourings, filth, ashes, cinders; leavings, remains, residue, scum, scoria, slag, dross; leftovers, orts, crumbs, bits and pieces, shreds, fragments, odds and ends, junk, rummage; litter, debris, rubbish, rubble, refuse, trash, throwaways.

sweet, *adj.* **1.** sugary, sweetened, honeyed, honey, honey-sweet, confectionary; candied, nectared, nectareous, nectarean, saccharine.

2. fresh, pure, refreshing, wholesome, clean; appetizing, flavorous, flavorsome, delicious; good, tasty, palatable, delectable, saporous.

3. sweet-sounding, mellifluous, dulcet, melodious. See **sweet-sounding.**

4. fragrant, perfumed, sweet-smelling. See **sweet-scented.**

5. pleasing, pleasant, pleasurable, enjoyable, to one's liking, to one's fancy, to one's taste.

6. amiable, gracious, likeable, pleasant, good-natured, *Scot. and North Eng., Irish Eng.* sonsy; congenial, *Scot.* couthie, *Ger. gemütlich*, complaisant; gracious, genial, polite, cordial, courteous, accommodating; amicable, friendly, neighborly, sociable.

7. appealing, attractive, comely, beautiful, elegant; bewitching, entrancing, charming, captivating, seductive, glamorous, alluring.

8. dear, beloved, dearest, loved, precious, treasured, cherished, valued, prized; favorite, pet, favored, darling.

9. sentimental, treacly, sickening, cloying; syrupy, sickeningly sweet, *Inf.* buttery; overdone, cutesy, too nice.

10. sweet on *Informal.* infatuated with, in love with, taken with, *Sl.* stuck on, gone on, keen on *or* about, wild about, mad about, head over heels in love with.

sweeten, *v.* **1.** make sweet, dulcify; candy, sugar, sugar-coat; mull.

2. soften, make mild, milden, mellow; make tender, make kind; mollify, pacify, appease, soothe, solace; alleviate, relieve, mitigate, palliate, allay, solace, assuage, ease, abate; temper, moderate.

3. purify, cleanse, disinfect, *Chem.* edulcorate; freshen, deodorize; ventilate, aerate, air.

sweetheart, *n.* sweet, sweetie, *Archaic.* leman, *Sl.* sweet patootie, *Sl.* tootsie, *Sl.* tootsy-wootsy, *Fr. petit chou, Fr. chou-chou, Fr. poulet, Fr. ma petite;* honey, *Inf.* honeybun, *Inf.* sugar, *Inf.* sugar pie, darling, beloved, dear, dear one, dearest; heartthrob, heart's desire, truelove, love of one's life, one and only, one's all; lover, paramour, *Fr. intime*, sex partner, bedmate, admirer, *Inf.* boyfriend, girl friend; suitor, beau, swain, inamorato, Romeo, wooer; betrothed, intended, *Inf.* steady, fiancé, fiancée; mistress, *Sl.* moll, best girl, ladylove, inamorata; turtledove, angel; spark, *Inf.* flame; goddess, Venus, Aphrodite; *Sl.* sweet mama, sugar daddy.

sweetmeat, *n.* confection, confiture, confectionary, candy, sweet, sweets; bonbon, fondant, comfit, sugarplum, sugar candy; taffy, butterscotch, praline, peanut brittle; fudge, cream, nougat, toffee, caramel, chocolate; mint, peppermint, kiss, lollipop, sucker; dainty, tidbit; pastry, pie, cake, patisserie, tart, puff.

sweetness, *n.* **1.** sugariness, honeyedness, saccharinity.

2. freshness, pureness, refreshingness, wholesomeness, cleanness; goodness, tastiness, saporosity, flavorfulness.

3. sweet-soundingness, melodiousness, mellifluence, mellifluousness, melody, harmony, dulcetness, euphoniousness, euphony, canorousness; softness, mellowness.

4. sweet-smellingness, sweet-scentedness, redolence, fragrance, odorousness, odoriferousness, balminess, perfume, bouquet.

5. pleasantness, agreeableness, amiableness, amiability; mildness, gentleness, kindliness, tenderness, lovableness; graciousness, generosity, selflessness.

6. loveliness, fairness, comeliness, prettiness; beauty, handsomeness, attractiveness; charm, winsomeness.

sweet-scented, *adj.* fragrant, aromatic, sweet, sweet-smelling, odoriferous, odorous; redolent, balmy, ambrosial, perfumed, scented.

sweet-sounding, *adj.* musical, dulcet, mellifluous, mellifluent, mellisonant, canorous, melodious; soothing, mellow, pleasant, agreeable; flowing, euphonic, euphonious, harmonious, symphonious; graceful, rhythmical; easy, soft, golden, silvery, silver-toned; clear, clear as a bell; singing, songful, lyric.

sweet-tempered, *adj.* kind, kindly, cordial, amiable, amicable, good-natured, well-disposed; neighborly, friendly, nice, genial, hospitable, affable; well-meaning, well-intentioned, sympathetic, sympathizing, warm, affectionate, commiserating; considerate, understanding, thoughtful; helpful, obliging, accommodating; good, benevolent, benign, benignant, benificent; mild, gentle, tender, *Fr. gentil*; compassionate, loving, decent, human; gracious, generous, charitable, bounteous, giving; warm-hearted, kindhearted, tender-hearted, soft-hearted; pleasant, likeable, expansive, *Scot. and North Eng., Irish Eng.* sonsy.

swell, *v.* **1.** dilate, expand, extend, spread, outspread, spread out; distend, inflate, bloat, puff out, blow up, dome; intumesce, tumefy; fill out, fatten; lengthen, elongate, stretch.

2. increase, enlarge, magnify, amplify, augment; wax, grow larger, rise, well up; intensify, escalate, step up, accelerate, snowball, mushroom.

3. protrude, project, extrude, jut *or* jut out, stick out, poke out; extend, excurse, obtrude, bulge, bilge, protuberate, *Anat.* protract; belly, bag, balloon, billow.

4. strut, swagger, peacock, prance, parade, promenade; ride a high horse, swashbuckle, bluster; flourish, flaunt, show off, throw out one's chest, put on airs, be arrogant, be insolent; flounce, *U.S. Inf.* sashay, mince.

—n. **5.** dilation, enlargement, widening, thickening, broadening, dilatation; lengthening, expansion, extension, spread; distention, inflation, swelling, bloating, intumescence, tumefaction, turgescence, turgidness, turgidity.

6. protuberance, prominence, eminence, excrescence, gibbosity, tuberosity, convexity; bulge, bow, bell, bump, lump, hump; knob, knurl, knot, node, nodulation, nodosity; protrusion, projection, jut, extrusion, excurvation; beetling, jutting, impendence, overhang.

7. hill, incline, acclivity, slope, *Scot. and North Eng.* brae, rise; grade, gradient, climb, ramp, hillside, upgrade.

8. increase, magnification, amplification, crescendo; intensification, concentration, exaggeration, deepening, heightening.

9. *Slang.* **a.** dandy, fop, coxcomb, *Sl.* peacock, Beau Brummell, fancy Dan; clotheshorse, prettyboy; jack-a-dandy, blade, gay blade, *Chiefly Brit.* blood, buck; gallant, lady-killer, ladies' man. **b.** aristocrat, silk-stocking, blue blood; dignitary, celebrity, notable, social lion.

—adj. **10.** *Slang.* (*all usu. of things*) stylish, modish, fashionable, chic, smart, newfangled; elegant, recherché, grand, luxurious, deluxe, high-toned.

11. (*all of persons*) aristocratic, silk-stocking, blue-blooded; distingué, of high standing; poised, genteel, refined, polished, gentlemanly, urbane, suave.

12. first-rate, excellent, first-class, jim-dandy, top-flight, superior, of the highest grade.

swelter, *v.* perspire profusely, sweat, be dripping wet, be bathed with sweat; be oppressed with heat, be overcome by heat, languish, wilt; be flushed, be hot, *Inf.* be dying from the heat; bake, fry, cook, broil, roast; simmer, boil, steam.

sweltering, *adj.* humid, hot and humid, sultry, *Inf.* close, sticky, clammy, muggy, moist, damp; stuffy, stifling, suffocating, oppressive; sudorific, *Med.* diaphoretic; hot, torrid, roasting, baking, broiling; steamy, dank, misty; tropical, drizzly, rainy.

swerve, *v.* **1.** turn aside, twist, shift. See **sheer** (*def.* **1**).

2. move, budge, turn, push, jog, joggle, stir, sway.

—n. **3.** deflection, deviation, swerving. See **sheer** (*def.* **2**).

swift, *adj.* **1.** quick, fast, fleet, speedy; hurried, rapid, winged, express, expeditious, galloping, tantivy, light of heel, eagle-winged, quick as lightning, swift as an arrow; brisk, lively, agile, light-footed, nimble, spry, active, agitated, feverish, bustling; hasty, impetuous, headlong, precipitate, rash, rushing, urgent; prompt, instant, instantaneous, sudden; cursory, fleeting, superficial, perfunctory.

2. ready, eager, alert, prompt, responsive; bright, intent, ardent, fervent, earnest, avid, zealous.

swiftly, *adv.* **1.** quickly, *Sl.* P.D.Q., speedily, fleetly, rapidly, hurriedly; promptly, instantly, expeditiously, straightaway, *Sl.* pronto, in a wink, in an instant, *Inf.* in a jiffy, in a trice, in a flash, double-quick, *Inf.* like greased lightning, like a shot, like a house afire, like blazes, like a thunderbolt, *Sl.* like mad, *Sl.* like a bat out of hell; directly, at once, without delay, in less than no time, before one can say "Jack Robinson," before the ink is dry, *Inf.* lickety-split; fast, full tilt, full pelt, full gallop, tantivy, by leaps and bounds, hotfoot, at full blast, in high gear, as fast as one's legs can carry one.

2. precipitately, hurriedly, headlong; abruptly, suddenly, unexpectedly; rashly, at half cock, pell-mell, harum-scarum, helter-skelter, head over heels.

3. nimbly, agilely, spryly, sprightily, actively, trippingly.

swiftness, *n.* **1.** quickness, fleetness, fastness, speed, rapidity; dispatch, hurriedness, expedition, expeditiousness; velocity, acceleration, celerity; instantaneousness, immediateness, urgency, promptness, promptitude; briskness, abruptness, suddenness, smartness, preciptiation.

2. hurry, rush, hustle, bustle, dash, scurry, flurry; haste, pell-mell, hurry-scurry; run, sprint, gallop, canter, tantivy; spurt, clip; scramble, scuttle, scamper.

3. alacrity, agility, nimbleness, liveliness, sprightliness, tall stepping.

swill, *n.* **1.** slop, hogwash, scraps, orts; garbage, refuse, *Dial.* culch, rubbish, waste, offal; dregs, remains, offscourings.

2. deep draught, guzzle, gulp, swig, drink, dose.

—v. **3.** guzzle, toss off, drink quickly, *Sl.* chug-a-lug, *Sl.* chug; swig, drink down, quaff, *All Inf.* put it down *or* away, soak it up, take it in, pack away *or* down, tuck it in; drain, empty, finish, finish off, *Sl.* knock off, *Sl.* polish off, *Sl.* take care of, *Sl.* do a job on, *Sl.* do in; consume, swallow up, gulp *or* gulp down.

swim, *v.* **1.** float, tread water, dog-paddle, scull, crawl; skinny-dip; be buoyed up; skim, glide.

2. be immersed, be steeped in, be drenched in; be inundated, be flooded, be soaked, be doused.

3. be dizzy, be giddy, feel light-headed, have a whirling sensation.

swimmingly, *adv.* easily, effortlessly, with ease, with no trouble at all, without difficulty, readily, handily, hands down, without even trying, with one's eyes closed, no hands, single-handed, with one hand tied behind one's back; smoothly, skillfully, facilely, dexterously, adroitly; with great success, successfully, with flying colors, triumphantly, beyond all expectation, beyond one's wildest dreams; as good luck would have it, luckily, fortunately, propitiously, auspiciously.

swindle, *v.* **1.** cheat, defraud, fleece, rook, *Sl.* clip, gull, *Archaic.* chouse; overcharge, *Sl.* soak, *Inf.* gyp, *Sl.* take [s.o.] to the cleaners, *Sl.* chisel, *Sl.* gaff, pluck, mulct; victimize, exploit, play on *or* upon, take advantage of, *Inf.* diddle, *Inf.* do, do out of, *Sl.* burn; delude, deceive, beguile, mislead, *Inf.* take [s.o.] for a ride, hoodwink; pull the wool over [s.o.'s] eyes, cozen, bluff, take in, bamboozle, bilk, *Sl.* hornswoggle, cully, *Inf.* buffalo, *Inf.* finagle, *Sl.* con, pull a fast one, *Inf.* flimflam, *Sl.* flam, *Sl.* sting, *Sl.* screw, *Sl.* put across; trick, thimblerig, spoof, outwit, *Inf.* euchre out, jockey, overreach, circumvent, get around, put one over on, fob [s.t.] off on [s.o.].

—n. **2.** fraud, sharp practice, trickery, thimblerigging, double-dealing, skin game, cozenage, *Law.* barratry, *Canon. Law.* obreption, *Scots Law.* subreption, *Archaic.* covin; chicanery, knavery, *Inf.* hanky-panky, *Inf.* racket, the old army game, *Sl.* monkey business, *Sl.* funny business; imposture, imposition, humbug.

3. wile, ruse, sham, shuck, trick, deception, chicane, hoax, subterfuge, artifice, stratagem, *Sl.* scam, *Scot.* brogue; cheat, *Sl.* gyp, *Inf.* ripoff; dirty deal, dirty trick.

swindler, *n.* **1.** highbinder, cheat, cheater, fraud, defrauder, confidence man, *Sl.* con man, *Sl.* flimflam man, bunko artist, crook, chiseler; sharper, sharpie, *Sl.* city slicker, *Inf.* fast talker, *Inf.* hawk, shark, bilk, bilker, diddler; duper, hoaxer, humbugger; rook, fleecer, gyp, gypper; embezzler, peculator, *Law.* defalcator, defaulter, *Sl.* welsher, thief, robber; rackateer, thimblerigger, criminal, lawbreaker.

2. fake, faker, phony, humbug, trickster, inveigler, bamboozler, dissembler, bluff, pettifogger; deceiver, deluder, beguiler, hoodwinker; impostor, masquerader, pretender, mountebank, hypocrite, charlatan, *Inf.* quack; adventurer, rogue, picaroon, rascal, wolf in sheep's clothing, knave, scoundrel, *Sl.* fourflusher, villain.

swine, *n.* **1.** hog, pig, sow, barrow; razorback, boar, wart hog, peccary, babirusa; porker, grunter, tusker, oinker; piggy, piglet, pigling, hogling, shoat.

2. brute, animal, wolf, monster, savage; masher, lecher, libertine, pervert, dirty old man; worm, cur, hound, louse, vermin; cad, *Brit.* blighter, *Chiefly Brit. Sl.* bounder, scab, fink, skunk, *Sl.* bastard; pimp, pander.

3. sensualist, sybarite, voluptuary, hedonist, pleasure-seeker; gourmand, epicure.

4. slob, pig, sloppy Joe, sloven, mudlark, wallower; lout, litterer, litterbug; frump, schlep, drab, draggletail; slattern, trollop, slut.

swing, *v.* **1.** sway, oscillate, pendulate, librate; vacillate, rock, move back and forth *or* backward and forward, lurch, yaw; wag, wave, waver, waggle, *Naut.* jibe; wobble, bob, dangle, hang; seesaw, teeter-totter, ebb and flow, come and go, wibble-wabble; hitch and hike, zigzag, wigwag, pass and repass.

2. curve, veer, turn, lead, steer; lean, go, warp, head, point; wind, crook, arch, hook; circle, encircle, bow, twist.

3. *Usu.* **swing around** whirl, spin, swivel, turn about, turn around; make a U-turn, *Sl.* pop *or* hang a U, *Sl.* bang a U-ie, turn on a dime; put about, heel, turn on one's heel, pivot; wheel, pirouette, gyrate, round, rotate, wamble.

4. shuffle, flounder, vary, alternate, equivocate; shift, blow hot and cold, straddle the fence; tergiversate, quibble, dodge, evade; beat around the bush, hem and haw, beg the question.

5. direct, incline, drive, guide, bias, bend; influence, prevail upon, sway, work upon, move; persuade, win over, talk over; change, alter, vary, transform, convert, modify; engineer, manage, put through, *Sl.* put over, carry, *Inf.* negotiate.

—n. **6.** oscillation, vibration, vacillation; fluctuation, libration, vibratility, nutation; pendulation, wag, waggle, wave; rock, lurch, reel, roll; to and fro, flux and reflux, coming and going, *Fr. va-et-vient*, ebb and flow, ups and downs, teeter-totter.

7. sweep, scope, range, play, carry; compass, reach, stretch, extent, radius; way, room, latitude, leeway, elbowroom, headroom; margin, space, clearance; freedom of action, free scope, no holds barred, free hand; carte blanche, blank check, free play.

8. rhythm, movement, beat, pulse; regularity, periodicity, meter, cadence, lilt; measure, number *or* numbers, metrics, pattern.

9. progression, course, curve, drift, current, stream, tide; trend, the way things go, the way the wind blows, the way it is; set, line, run, tack, track.

10. **in full swing** *Informal.* in operation, in business, going, moving, open, *Inf.* cooking, hopping, underway, under sail; at full steam, in high *or* fourth gear, on the go, on the run, on the move, on the fly.

swinish, *adj.* **1.** hoggish, piggish, porcine, *Jocular.* porky.

2. gross, coarse, churlish, beastly, animalistic, animal, brute; raffish, low, smutty, base, broad; licentious, lascivious, lewd, lecherous.

3. sensual, voluptuous, pleasure-seeking, self-seeking, hedonist; sybaritic, luxurious, epicurean; carnal, fleshly, physical, earthy.

4. slobby, slovenly, slatternly, unclean, filthy, dirty; sluttish, slatternly, blowzy, frowzy; unkempt, untidy, *Inf.* messy, mussy, *Inf.* sloppy, shabby, scraggly; scruffy, *Sl.* grungy, grubby, unwashed, slimy.

5. voracious, ravenous, rapacious, edacious, gluttonous; crapulous, omnivorous, insatiable, glutting, gorging, overfed.

swirl, *v.* **1.** whirl, eddy, gurge; swish around, move around, stir around, churn, agitate; circulate, rotate, turn, circumrotate, revolve, circumrevolve, circle, move in a circle, gyrate, spin around.

2. twist, spin, coil, spiral, convolute, convolve, roll, curl, furl, involute; incurve, curve; reel, wind, wind around, unwind.

—n. **3.** whirl, eddy, whirlpool, gurge, maelstrom; circulation, rotation, turn, circumrotation, revolution, circumvolution, volution, circling; moving around, gyration, gyre, spin, spinning.

4. twist, coil, turbination, spiral, helix, corkscrew, twirl, convolution, *Zool.* volute, whorl, curl, curlicue.

5. curve, incurvation, incurvature, excurvature, excurvation; sinuosity, winding, sinuation, sinus; bend, flexure, turn, crook, tortuosity, flexuosity, anfractuosity.

6. confusion, disorder, disarray, confusedness, jumble, mess; stir, commotion, fuss, fuss and feathers, *Inf.* to-do, bustle, flurry, excitement, agitation, unrest; disturbance, trouble, upheaval, turmoil, tumult, turbulence, storm, tempest.

swish, *v.* **1.** whish, whoosh, whiz, whistle, hiss, sibilate, whir, hum, buzz.

2. rustle, swoosh, sough, sigh, whisper, murmur.

3. swirl around, move around, stir around, agitate, swash around; splash, swash, dash against, wash, lap.

4. flourish, brandish, wave, swing, whisk.

5. take off, cut off, *Inf.* whack off, lop off, chop off, hack off, slice off.

6. flog, whip, switch. See **switch** (*def.* **4**).

—n. **7.** whish, whishing, whoosh, whooshing, whiz, whizzing, whistle, whistling, hiss, hissing, sibilation; whir, whirring, hum, humming, buzz, buzzing, rushing sound; rustle, rustling, susurrus, swoosh, swooshing, sough, soughing, sigh, sighing, whisper, whispering, susurration, murmur, murmuring.

8. switch, stick, rod. See **switch** (*def.* **1**).

switch, *n.* **1.** rod, stick, swish, birch *or* birch rod, withe, willow twig, *Chiefly Brit.* osier; whip, lash, scourge, strap, belt, thong, rawhide, cat, cat-o'-nine-tails.

2. (*all of plants*) shoot, bud, burgeon, sprout, sprig; stem, twig, small branch; offshoot, *Bot.* runner, *Bot.* stolon, *Bot.* sucker; scion, cutting, slip, *Hort.* graft.

3. change, change of direction, new tack, shift; turn, maneuver, swerve, sheer, deviation, divergence, detour; move, transfer, relocation, reassignment; reversal, *Inf.* flip-flop, U-turn *Sl.* U-ie, about-face, turnabout, turnaround, 360 degree turn, pirouette.

—v. **4.** hit, strike, beat, whip, *Southern U.S.* whup, thrash, lash, swish, birch, scourge, flagellate, horsewhip; curry, strap, thresh, flail, cowhide, spank, *Brit. Dial.* yerk, *Inf.* tan [s.o.'s] hide.

5. cast, throw, whisk, swing, sweep, move, wave, flourish, brandish, swish.

6. exchange, change, replace, substitute, swap, trade, barter; interchange, transpose, invert, commute, permute.

7. turn, veer, curve, bend, bear off, go off; swerve, shift, sheer, divert, deviate, detour, make a detour, go around; change course *or* direction, tack, *Naut.* jibe; reverse, *Inf.* flip-flop, about-face, do a turnaround *or* turnabout, make a U-turn, *Sl.* pull a U-ie.

8. move back and forth *or* up and down, wag, wave.

swivel, *n.* **1.** pivot, spindle, reel, spool, bobbin, gimbal; fulcrum, axis, axle; thole, tholepin, pin, pintle.

—v. **2.** turn, pivot, swing around, circle, twist, revolve, rotate, pirouette.

swollen, *adj.* **1.** enlarged, tumid, tumescent, turgid, inflated, *Obs.* sufflated, distended, expanded, dilated, *Pathol., Bot.* hypertrophied; bloated, puffed up *or* out, puffy, *Pathol.* dropsical, *Pathol.* edematous, *Pathol.* edematose; full, filled, stuffed, overfilled, overstuffed, bulging; fat, corpulent, pursy, stout, portly, fleshy, plump, tubby, paunchy, bellied out, bowed out, round, rotund.

2. bombastic, bombastical, pompous, orotund, fustian, pretentious, overinflated, overblown; grandiose, magniloquent, grandiloquent, Johnsonian, Ossianic, sonorous, sesquipedalian; high-sounding, high-flown, lofty, *Inf.* highfalutin; eloquent, rhetorical, oratorical, declamatory, mouthy, ranting, extravagant; ostentatious, flaunting, showy, flamboyant, flashy, ornate, ornamental, flowery, florid, euphuistic.

swoon, *v.* **1.** faint, lose consciousness, pass out, black out; limpen, go limp, crumple, succumb, give in *or* way, keel over, fall over, drop, collapse, *Sl.* conk out, faint dead away.

—n. **2.** faint, unconsciousness, blackout, fainting spell, *Pathol.* syncope, *Chiefly Scot.* dwalm.

swoop, *v.* **1.** *Often* **swoop down** *or* **on** sweep down, glide *or* fly downward, descend, dip, plunge, dive, nose-dive, plummet; drop down on, come down on *or* upon, fall upon, pounce *or* pounce on; lunge at, leap at, spring at, jump at; attack, go at *or* for, have at, come at, make a move towards.

2. *Often* **swoop up** *or* **away** take *or* take up, lift *or* lift up, scoop up, pick up; seize, clutch, grab, snatch *or* snatch up, capture, *Inf.* nab.

—n. **3.** descent, dive, nose dive, plunge, dip, drop.

sword, *n.* **1.** blade, trusty blade, steel, cold steel; cutlass, saber, rapier, broadsword, claymore, anelace, schiavone.

2. war, combat, strife, violence; carnage, massacre, butchery, slaughter; military force *or* power; brute force.

3. cross swords a. fight, battle, do battle, engage in combat; struggle, tussle, scuffle, have it out; spar, exchange blows, engage in fisticuffs, *Inf.* slug it out, *Sl.* duke it out. **b.** argue, contend, dispute, disagree, contest, controvert, lock horns; wrangle, haggle, higgle, bicker, *Scot.* argle-bargle, *Sl.* hassle.

4. put to the sword execute, put to death; kill, slay, murder; butcher, slaughter, massacre; cut to pieces, hew, hack, hack to pieces, chop, chop to pieces.

sword-shaped, *adj.* swordlike, *Biol.* ensiform, *Bot.* ensate, *Bot.* gladiate, *Anat., Zool.* xiphoid.

swordsman, *n.* swordplayer, swordman, swashbuckler, *Fr. sabreur*; fencer, *Fencing.* foilsman.

sybarite, *n.* sensualist, voluptuary, pleasure-seeker, hedonist, epicure, epicurean, *Fr. bon vivant, Archaic.* carpet knight, *Sl.* cake eater; gourmet, gourmand, gastronome, gastronomist; glutton, cormorant, hog, pig, swine, belly-god; libertine, roué, rake, rakehell, rip, debauchee, playboy, *Sl.* swinger, *Sl.* lounge lizard.

sybaritic, *adj.* hedonistic, self-indulgent, epicurean, pleasure-seeking, pleasure-bent, luxury-loving; voluptuous, sensual, sensuous; debauched, dissolute, dissipated; luxurious, elegant, posh, sumptuous, grand, fine, refined.

sycophancy, *n.* **1.** flattery, fawning, truckling, wheedling, toadeating, toadyism, tufthunting, sycophantism, lip-homage, mouth-honor, unctuousness, *Inf.* soft soap, *Sl.* bootlicking, *Sl.* footlicking, kowtow, *Sl.* apple-polishing, *Sl.* brown-nosing, *Rare.* blandiloquence, *Obs.* blanding, *Obs., Rare.* blandation, *Obs., Rare.* blandiloquy.

2. slavishness, servility, obsequiousness, obsequence, subservience, *Obs.* vernility; submissiveness, docility, unassertiveness, compliance, acquiescence, deference, tractability, tractableness; prostration, obeisance, abjection, abjectness, self-abasement; groveling, crawling, crouching, slithering; squirming, cringing, cowering; whining, whimpering, sniveling.

sycophant, *n.* toady, toadeater, fawner, flatterer, truckler, tufthunter, courtier, wheedler, puffer, backslapper, backscratcher, timeserver, *Sl.* apple polisher, *Sl.* brown-nose, *Sl.* brown-noser, *Sl.* brownie, *Obs., Rare.* blander, *Archaic.* pickthank; parasite, leech, sponge, sponger, hanger-on; flunky, lackey, *Inf.* yes man, jackal, spaniel, bootlick, bootlicker, footlicker, lickspit, lickspittle, kowtower, Uncle Tom, *Sl.* oreo, cringer, groveler, sniveler; puppet, slave, dupe, instrument, tool, cat's-paw, rubber stamp, doormat, footstool, *Sl.* stooge.

sycophantic, *adj.* **1.** fawning, flattering, truckling, wheedling, toadying, toadyish, ingratiating, timeserving, sycophantical *or* sycophantish, *Sl.* bootlicking, *Sl.* footlicking, *Sl.* apple-polishing, *Sl.* brown-nosing, *Obs.* blanding, *Obs., Rare.* blandiloquous; buttery, candied, unctuous, honey-mouthed, sweet-talking, *Rare.* blandiloquent.

2. slavish, servile, obsequious, *Obs.* obsequent, subservient, menial, *Obs., Rare.* vernile; submissive, docile, unassertive, compliant, acquiescent, deferential, tractable, mealy-mouthed; prostrate, kowtowing, obeisant, on one's knees; abject, base, mean, beggarly, beggared; groveling, crawling, crouching, slithering; squirming, cringing, cowering; whining, whimpering, sniveling.

syllabus, *n.* summary, epitome, synopsis, abstract, compendium, compilation, digest, conspectus; condensation, abridgment, reduction, compression, abbreviation; analysis, recapitulation; résumé, brief, précis; outline, aperçu, sketch, review, prospectus; docket, bulletin, *Chiefly Brit.* minute; extracts, fragments, analects, clippings, citations.

sylvan, *adj.* **1.** woody, woodsy, bosky, forested, arboreous; forestal, forestial, forestlike; shady, shaded, umbrageous, bowery, leafy; treelike, arboreal, arborescent; rustic, bucolic, scenic; wild, uncultivated.

—n. **2.** rustic, peasant, provincial, backwoodsman, yokel, bumpkin.

3. dryad, hamadryad, deity, nymph; faun; Pan, Silvanus.

symbol, *n.* **1.** emblem, representation, insignia, regalia, token, sign, badge, totem; character, glyph, ideogram, ideograph, hieroglyphic, hieroglyph, figure, letter, phonogram; trademark, brand, monogram, stamp, initials, badge, ensign, logotype, *Print.* logo; watchword, password, countersign, grip, shibboleth; earmark, peculiarity, idiosyncrasy, trait, characteristic, feature, dead giveaway, *Sl.* tip-off, sure sign; notation, cipher, code, cryptogram, abbreviation, shorthand, *Both Music.* note, signature; arms, crest, coat of arms, escutcheon, armorial, bearings, epaulet, chevron, stripes, *Mil. Sl.* scrambled eggs; flag, pennant, standard, banner, oriflamme.

2. talisman, charm, amulet, periapt, phylactery, fetish, voodoo; charm, good-luck charm, lucky piece, rabbit's foot; mascot; hoodoo, love charm, scarab; swastika, gammadion; crucifix, cross, rood.

3. metaphor, figure of speech, *Rhet.* trope; simile, similitude, correlation, likeness; imagery, personification, figurativeness, metonymy; allegory, allegorization, apologue, anagoge, parable, fable.

symbolic, *adj.* **1.** representative, characteristic, typical, indicative, illustrative, token, emblematic; distinguishing, differentiative, distinctive, discriminative, diacritical.

2. metaphorical, figurative, allegorical; suggestive, indicative, indicant, denotative, allusive.

3. cabalistic, mystical, occult; esoteric, hermetic, supernatural, transcendental; mysterious, secret, arcane, mystic.

symbolize, *v.* represent, signify, token, stand for, exemplify, serve as an example of, be a sample *or* specimen of; illustrate, epitomize, embody, personify, typify; correspond to, be the equivalent of, mirror, be the counterpart of, be analogous to; indicate, show, point to, add up to; mean, denote, purport, import, connote, convey; imply, suggest, bring to mind.

symmetrical, *adj.* well-proportioned, proportional, balanced, well-balanced, eurhythmic; isomerous, isometric, *Biol.* actinomorphic, isogonal; harmonious, concinnous, congruous, consonant, concordant, congruent, consistent; parallel, corresponding, even, equal, commensurate, coextensive; regular, uniform, orderly, well-ordered, well-arranged, tidy; euphonious, cadenced, rhythmic, patterned; graceful, well-formed, well-made, shapely, classic, Praxitelean, acropolitan.

symmetry, *n.* **1.** regularity, uniformity, evenness, sameness, similarity, parallelism; consonance, congruence, consistency, correspondence, conformity, agreement.

2. harmony, concinnity, balance, poise, proportion, eurhythmy, congruity, appropriateness, fitness; orderliness, order, tidiness; euphony, grace, gracefulness, elegance, cadence, rhythm; beauty, comeliness, pleasingness, agreeableness, attractiveness.

sympathetic, *adj.* **1.** compassionate, commiserative, pitying, ruthful, concerned, caring, solicitous; sorrowful, tearful, heartbroken, grief-stricken, moved, touched; comforting, supportive, consoling; affectionate, loving, fond, with a heart as big as all outdoors, generous, big-hearted; humane, kind, kindly, kindhearted, good-natured, warm-hearted, warm, charitable; gentle, tender, good, considerate, thoughtful, patient; understanding, empathetic, interested.

2. congenial, simpatico, in rapport with, *Fr. en rapport,* compatible, easy to get along with, agreeable, pleasant; close, intimate, friendly, neighborly, brotherly, sisterly.

3. approving, supporting, backing, on the side of, pro; favorable, appreciative, commendatory, approbatory, laudatory, admiring.

sympathize, *v.* **1.** get along, hit it off, complement each other, harmonize; go hand in hand, have rapport, understand each other, relate, be close to; see eye to eye, *Inf.* be on the same wavelength, agree, accord, correspond, correlate.

2. pity, feel sorry for, feel for; have one's heart go out to, have one's heart bleed for, cry for, weep for, mourn with, grieve with, be moved *or* touched; commiserate, console, comfort, solace; ease, assuage, lend a shoulder, be a shoulder.

3. approve, like, admire, value, esteem, favor; back, encourage, side with, second; applaud, commend, praise; nod assent, endorse, *Inf.* O.K., *Inf.* give the O.K. *or* go-ahead, signal thumbs-up.

sympathizer, *n.* **1.** commiserator, comforter, condoler, soother, shoulder, wailing wall; friend in need, helping hand, good Samaritan, real *or* true friend.

2. well-wisher, partisan, advocate, backer, second, booster; fan, adherent, disciple; collaborator, cooperationist, ally.

sympathy, *n.* **1.** harmony, agreement, accord, concert, rapport; concord, concordance, congruity, consonance, conformance, correspondence; bond, link, tie, union, unity; correlation, mutuality, reciprocity, congeniality, compatibility, closeness, familiarity, intimacy, mutual attraction; similarity, likeness, affinity, sameness, similitude; communion, fellowship, brotherhood, sisterliness, friendship, camaraderie.

2. compassion, commiseration, ruth, heart, pity, concern, care, solicitousness; condolence, tears, sorrow, consolation, comfort, solace; affection, love, agape, brotherly *or* sisterly love; humanity, humaneness, responsiveness, kindness, kindliness, benevolence; considerateness, thoughtfulness, patience, consideration; fellow feeling, understanding, empathy, getting into somebody else's skin, walking in somebody else's shoes; mercy, mercifulness, clemency, tenderness, tender-heartedness, warm-heartedness, warmth, gentleness, benignity, charity.

3. approval, assent, nod, *Inf.* O.K., *Inf.* okay, endorsement, sanction, approbation, go-ahead, thumbs up; consent, acquiescence, concurrence; favor, esteem, good will, well-wishing, high regard; encouragement, assistance, backing, patronage, cooperation; appreciation, admiration, commendation, applause, plaudits, praise, kudos.

symphonious, *adj.* **1.** harmonious, in harmony, euphonious, symphonic, homophonic, monodic; assonant, unisonous, unisonant, unisonal, *Music.* isotonic; tuneful, in tune; musical, melodic, melodious, ariose, pleasant-sounding, pleasant to the ear; resonant, chiming.

2. concordant, accordant, consonant, agreeing, in agreement, in accord, correspondent, corresponding, in correspondence; concurrent, concurring, consentient, consentaneous; unanimous, in unison, as one, in rapport, of the same mind, of one mind, like-minded, single-minded.

symphony, *n.* **1.** piece, opus; sonata, concerto, fantasia; tone poem, symphonic poem, symphonic ode; classical music, concert music, symphonic music, *Inf.* longhair music.

2. orchestra, symphony orchestra, Philharmonic.

3. concert, pop *or* pops concert; performance, show, recital.

4. concord, concordance, accord, accordance, consonance, consonancy; agreement, consensus, correspondence, correspondency, congruity, congruence, congruousness.

5. harmony, harmoniousness, *Obs.* concent, euphony, homophony, monody, *Rare.* unisonance, *Obs.* consort; *Music.* polyphony, *Music.* counterpoint; tune, melody, diapason; chord, resonance, chime, chiming, attunement; chorus, one voice, single voice.

symposium, *n.* **1.** conference, panel discussion, round table; debate, parley, colloquy, powwow, *Fr. pourparler*, confabulation; congress, synod, convocation, assembly.

2. compendium, compilation, abstract, review, survey, summary, epitome, synopsis; dissertation, treatise, discourse, tract, thesis, essay, theme.

3. (*in ancient Greece and Rome*) revel, festival, party, fete; saturnalia, jollification, wassail, carousal, gala.

symptom, *n.* **1.** characteristic, feature, trait, earmark, specific, peculiarity; manifestation, evidence, diagnostic, index, means of identifying *or* recognizing, proof; accompaniment, concomitant, side effect; syndrome, pattern, picture, image.

2. sign, sure sign, dead giveaway, mark, symbol, representation, indication; signal, marker, warning, red light, cue, tip, notice, *Sl.* tip-off.

symptomatic, *adj.* *Often* **symptomatic of** characteristic, emblematic, token, symbolic, syndromic; diagnostic, specific, special, peculiar, idiosyncratic, *Med.* diacritic; signalizing, signaling, significant, marking, indicating, indicative, suggestive, meaningful, denotative; valuable, crucial, vital, essential, necessary.

synchronism, *n.* simultaneity, simultaneousness, coinstantaneousness, isochronism, *Inf.* sync; concurrence, concurrency, concomitance, concomitancy, coincidence; coexistence, coexistency, coevality, contemporaneousness, contemporaneity, contemporariness, coetaneity, coetaneousness; coextension, conterminousness.

synchronous, *adj.* simultaneous, coinstantaneous, synchronal, *Inf.* in sync, isochronal, isochronous; concurrent, concomitant, parallel, coincident; coexistent, coexisting, contemporary, contemporaneous, coeval, coetaneous; conterminous, coterminous, coextensive.

syndicate, *n.* **1.** cartel, trust, monopoly, pool; merger, consolidating company, holding company, joint concern, joint-stock company, chain, chain of stores; guild, firm, house, partnership; cooperative, collaboration, pool, co-op, *Inf.* combine; alliance, entente, coalition, confederation; commune, grange, society, fraternity, (*of organized crime*) family.

—*v.* **2.** associate, affiliate, ally, marry, wed; bond, weld, fuse, yoke, bind, tie together; connect, join, link, chain, attach; couple, mate, partner, match *or* pair up, bring together; unite, conjoin, coalesce, league, club; merge, join forces, federate, confederate, incorporate; amalgamate, conglomerate, agglomerate; synthesize, consolidate, coordinate, put together.

synergetic, *adj.* cooperative, coactive, collaborative, collaborating, coordinated, interactive, interactional, interacting, symbiotic, synergistic, consentient, consentaneous; mutual, joint, concurrent, concerted, coadjuvant; helpful, helping, accommodative, accommodating; simpatico, congenial, *Inf.* on the same wavelength.

synonymous, *adj.* equivalent, equal, even, parallel, twin, corresponding; same, similar, like, alike, identical, exact; correlative, comparable, exchangeable, transposable; reciprocative, reciprocal.

synopsis, *n.* **1.** outline, sketch, abstract, general view, précis, conspectus, prospectus; digest, survey, brief, epitome, pandect; review, recapitulation, résumé, summation, rehash, fill-in, rundown, wrap-up; condensation, compression, contraction, abridgment, abbreviation, extract, excerpt.

2. compendium, syllabus, *Chiefly Brit.* minute, bulletin; capitulation, enumeration; chart, diagram, delineation.

3. summary, plot summary, story line, plot line, analysis, *Trademark.* Monarch Notes, notes; gist, essence, sum and substance, long and short, effect, drift, sense, spirit, import, tenor, purport, significance, implication, burden; pith, core, heart, marrow, main point, essential part.

synopsize, *v.* **1.** summarize, abstract, epitomize, sum up, wrap up, encapsulate, capsule, brief; digest, survey, outline, sketch, skim over; review, recapitulate, rehash, go over, run over, run down.

2. condense, compress, concentrate, consolidate, compact; contract, abbreviate, abridge, shorten, reduce, cut, cut down, cut short, cut back, tighten.

synoptic, *adj.* comprehensive, compendious, synoptical, encapsulating, encompassing; pithy, *Inf.* meaty, substantive.

synthesis, *n.* **1.** combination, union, unification, integration, incorporation, amalgamation, consolidation, fusion, coalescence, syncretism.

2. amalgam, alloy, mixture, admixture, blend, composite, compound.

synthesize, *v.* coalesce, merge, fuse, blend; combine, join, unite, unify; amalgamate, incorporate, consolidate, integrate, embody.

synthetic, *adj.* imitation, sham, mock, pseudo, ersatz; artificial, ungenuine, unauthentic, make-believe, bogus, spurious, fake, *Inf.* phony; plastic, tinsel, pinchbeck, brummagem; unnatural, man-made, test-tube; feigned, faked, simulated, put-on, pretended, counterfeited, affected.

syrupy, *adj.* **1.** sweet, honeyed, honey, molasses-like, treacly; sugary, candied, saccharine, cloying, *Archaic.* luscious; thick, viscous, viscid, *Inf.* gooey, *Inf.* gunky, sticky.

2. mawkish, sentimental, maudlin; sickening, nauseating, sickeningly sweet; oversweet, overdone, overromantic, overemotional, melodramatic; *Inf.* mushy, *Inf.* slushy, *Sl.* kissy-face.

system, *n.* **1.** order, organization, arrangement, disposition, structure, setup, layout, line-up.

2. process, procedure, method, methodology, technique; attack, tack, approach; way, wise, means, mode, fashion, style, ways and means; wont, custom, practice, praxis, *Latin. modus operandi*, M.O.; common practice, rule, standard operating procedure, SOP, *Inf.* bit; policy, polity, guidelines.

3. course, line, plan of action, plan, scheme, design, program; pattern, outline, delineation.

4. cosmos, universe, world, all creation.

systematic, *adj.* methodical, regular, steady, businesslike, routine, like clockwork; orderly, well-ordered, well-arranged, well-organized, well-regulated; formal, planned, well-planned, blocked-out, *Inf.* all worked out.

systematize, *v.* order, put *or* set in order, organize, arrange; regulate, regularize, methodize, standardize, systemize, normalize.

T

tab, *n.* **1.** flap, lap, lappet; strap, loop, ring, appendage; projection, ear, handle.
2. tag, label, mark, marker, indicator; price tag, sticker, ticket, docket, stamp.
3. *Informal.* bill, check, *Scot.* lawing, *Sl.* score; statement, manifest, *Fr. addition*; account, tally, count, reckoning.

tabby, *n.* **1.** old maid, spinster, lone woman, bachelor girl, *Fr. femme sole*; unmarried woman, single woman, maid.
2. gossip, tattler, magpie, *Sl.* yenta; newsmonger, gossipmonger, rumormonger; talebearer, tattletale, telltale, taleteller; busybody, quidnunc, meddler, gossip columnist.
—adj. **3.** striped, brindled, banded, streaked, stripy, streaky; listed, striated, variegated, *Zool.* strigose.

table, *n.* **1.** plane, horizontal, level, flat; ledge, platform, shelf, sill, mantle, shoulder, *Archit.* corbel.
2. plateau, plain, flatland, flats. See **tableland**.
3. stand, counter, bar, buffet, sideboard; desk, writing table, secretary; bench, workbench, worktable; card table, folding table, coffee table, tea table; trivet.
4. slab, sheet, plate, lamina; desk top, pool table, slate; board, plank, slat, tablet.
5. chart, graph, scheme, design, plan; schema, blueprint, draft, diagram.
6. index, census, code, tabulation, itemization, inventory, syllabus; list, table of contents, contents, synopsis; register, schedule, catalogue, file, digest.
—v. **7.** lay aside, defer, hold off; postpone, shelve, put off, delay, pass to the order of the day; put on the shelf, *Inf.* put on ice, put in mothballs, pigeonhole, *Inf.* sideline; suspend, stay, hold up, lay over.

tableau, *n.* **1.** painting, picture, picturization, depiction, delineation, representation, portrayal, illustration; scene, view, scape, diorama, cyclorama, panorama, montage.
2. sight, spectacle, striking scene, eyeopener; pageant, *Fr. tableau vivant*.

tableland, *n.* plateau, mesa, table, upland, highland; elevated plain, bench, berm; flatland, flats, plain, steppe.

tablet, *n.* **1.** pad, scratch pad, writing pad, notebook, spiral notebook, memorandum book.
2. slab; slat, plank.
3. stone, tombstone, gravestone, headstone, memorial.
4. lozenge, pill, capsule, *Pharm.* troche, *Pharm., Trademark.* Tabloid, *Pharm., Vet. Med.* bolus.

taboo, *adj.* **1.** (*among the peoples of the South Pacific*) inviolable, inviolate, sacred, sacrosanct, untouchable.
2. prohibited, banned, proscribed, vetoed; forbidden, *Ger. verboten*, unallowed, unpermissible.
—n. **3.** prohibition, proscription, forbiddance, interdiction, disallowance.
4. ostracism, exclusion, blackballing.
—v. **5.** prohibit, proscribe, interdict, forbid; rule out, ban, disallow, veto.
6. bar, exclude, ostracize, shut out, leave out, keep out, send to Coventry, blackball.

tabulate, *v.* tabularize, systematize, systemize, chart, graph; line up, line, arrange, range, order, dispose, place, group; rank, rate, grade, graduate; organize, sort *or* sort out, assort, class, classify, categorize, pigeonhole, *Sl.* peg; catalog, inventory, index, list, file, codify, alphabetize.

tacit, *adj.* **1.** silent, quiet, close-mouthed, tight-lipped, unspeaking; speechless, voiceless, mute, mum.
2. understood, implied, implicit, *Inf.* inferred; unstated, undeclared, unexpressed, unmentioned, unsaid, unvoiced, unspoken.

taciturn, *adj.* **1.** reticent, uncommunicative, unconversable, unconversational, untalkative; quiet, silent, close-mouthed, reserved, shy; tight-lipped, tacit, speechless, voiceless, mum, mute; distant, aloof, stand-offish, unsociable, antisocial, antisocialistic.
2. dour, stern, sullen, gloomy, sluggish, saturnine.

taciturnity, *n.* **1.** reticence, uncommunicativeness, unconversableness, reserve, shyness; quietness, silence, silentness, tacitness, speechlessness, voicelessness, muteness; distantness, aloofness, stand-offishness, unsociability, unsociableness.
2. dourness, sternness, sullenness, gloom, gloominess; sluggishness, saturnineness, saturninity.

tack[1], *n.* **1.** nail, rivet, brad, cleat, staple; pin, peg, dowel, skewer; spike, bolt, toggle, cotter, cotter pin, treenail, trunnel, thole *or* tholepin; thumbtack, *Brit.* drawing pin, carpet tack, roofing tack; stitch, baste, lace; safety pin, straight pin, snap, button; catch, clamp, hook, grappler, holdfast, latch, loop.
2. direction, way, route, heading, bearing, trajectory, *Naut.* leeway, course; road, path, pathway, trail, track; run, cut, channel.
3. zigzag, *Naut.* jibe, deviation, yaw, *Aeron.* drift; divergence, by-pass, detour, alteration, change, swerve, sheer, switch, shunt, divagation, sidling, *Navig.* driftage, *Navig.* windage; declination, divarication.
4. set, aim, tendency, inclination, bent, tenor; ap-

proach, attack, method, procedure, practice, line, line *or* course of action.

5. harness, equipment, equipage, gear, fittings, outfit, kit, tackle, rigging, apparatus, rig, appointments.

—v. **6.** fasten, pin, attach, fix, pin on *or* down; nail, rivet, bolt, screw, skewer, peg, staple, toggle; lace, tie, hitch, bind, clinch, knit, splice, sew, stitch, baste; hook, snap, button, buckle, zipper, *Inf.* zip; brace, truss, wire; join, unite, combine, couple, yoke, bracket, tether.

7. *Often* **tack on** append, annex, affix; add on *or* onto, tag, tag on, *Inf.* slap on, *Inf.* hitch on; prefix, suffix, subjoin, adjoin, conjoin; ornament, decorate.

8. zigzag, *Naut.* jibe, yaw, warp, chop, shunt, chop and change; proceed to windward, go about, heel; wander, stray, divagate.

9. swerve, sheer, turn, shift, change course, turn a corner; deviate, veer, diverge, go through a change of heart, switch sides, make a turnabout, do an about-face, come about, come round *or* around; modify, adapt, alter, transform, go through a sea change.

tack[2], *n.* fare, food, nutriment, aliment, viands, edibles, bread; victuals, provisions, rations, commons, comestibles; meals, board, sustenance, nourishment; diet, regimen, menu, table.

tackle, *n.* **1.** equipment, gear, outfit, rig, *Archaic.* tackling; apparatus, accourterments, trappings, traps, appointments, fittings; paraphernalia, impedimenta, luggage, baggage, matériel; tools, implements, instruments.

2. rigging, cordage, cording, ropework, roping, ship's ropes.

3. crane, derrick, halyard, crab, lift, hoist, gantry crane; winch, pulley, windlass, capstan.

—v. **4.** undertake, attempt, endeavor, engage in, go about, set to work, get busy at, roll up one's sleeves, plunge into, *Inf.* knuckle down to, *Inf.* get on the job, *Inf.* get going, *Inf.* have a go at, *Inf.* make a try, *Inf.* give a try, *Inf.* give it the old college try, *Sl.* get cracking, *Sl.* get at it; pursue, devote *or* apply oneself to, take in hand, work at, put one's shoulder to the wheel, bend an oar; set about, begin, enter upon, start at, embark upon, turn one's hand to, take up, *Inf.* go in *or* out for, *Inf.* have a fling at, *Inf.* take a crack at.

5. deal with, come to grips with, take on, approach, face, face up to, stand up to, address oneself to, take the bull by the horns, get down to cases, *Inf.* tear *or* wade *or* sail into.

tacky[1], *adj.* adhesive, adherent, sticky, gluey, gummy, gummous; viscous, viscid, glutinous, syrupy, ropy, stringy; moist, damp, dampish, humid, dank, clammy, slimy, *Inf.* gooey.

tacky[2], *adj.* **1.** *Informal.* bedraggled, draggled, draggletailed, scraggly, unkempt; unsightly, untidy, careless, slipshod, slovenly, scruffy, seedy, *Inf.* messy, *Inf.* sloppy, *Inf.* grubby; shabby, shoddy, chintzy, ratty, tatty, dowdy, frowzy, blowzy, frumpy, frazzled.

2. garish, gaudy, flashy, showy, loud, screaming, shrieking, blinding, overbright; brazen, shameless, obtrusive, vulgar, crude, tawdry, meretricious.

tact, *n.* diplomacy, savoir-faire, *Inf.* savvy, poise, polish, finish, *Inf.* class, grace, style, finesse; taste, discrimination, refinement; perception, sensitivity, awareness, discernment, discretion; sagacity, shrewdness, cleverness, acumen; prudence, judiciousness, sense, good *or* common sense; skill, adroitness, dexterousness, dexterity.

tactful, *adj.* diplomatic, politic, discreet, prudent; judicious, shrewd, sagacious, perspicacious; sensitive, perceptive, keen, sharp; adroit, skillful, clever; smooth, urbane, suave, civil, mannerly, polished, gracious; considerate, cautious, careful.

tactic, *n.* **1. tactics** strategems, strategics, moves, maneuvers, military operation, *Mil.* campaign; generalship, military science, martial art; logistics, engineering, orchestration, coordination, masterminding; management, conducting, direction, *Inf.* quarterbacking, superintendence, supervision, oversight, handling, running, execution.

2. strategy, plan, battle plan, *Inf.* game plan, master plan, *Sl.* scenario, outline, diagram, schema, chart, blueprint; program, schedule, timetable; scheme, plot, design, format, organization, arrangement; method, means, ways and means; policy, game, intent, approach.

—adj. **3.** tactical, tactful, skillful, adroit, clever, artful, adept.

tactician, *n.* strategist, military strategist, mastermind; planner, plotter, schemer, intriguer, conspirer, conspirator, conspiratress; maneuverer, *Sl.* operator, manipulator; diplomat, ambassador; politician, campaigner, campaign manager; manager, engineer, orchestrator, coordinator, director, supervisor, overseer, *Inf.* quarterback.

tactile, *adj.* tactual, touchable, tangible, palpable, material, corporeal, substantial.

tactless, *adj.* undiplomatic, impolitic, inexpedient, injudicious, imprudent, unwise, ill-advised, inadvisable, unadvisable; ill-considered, hasty, rash, impetuous, brash, brashy, impertinent, impudent; inappropriate, malapropos, gauche, maladroit; ill-suited, unsuitable, unmeet, unbecoming, unseemly, improper, unladylike, ungentlemanly; blundering, clumsy, uncouth, awkward, *Sl.* klutzy, embarrassing, bunglesome, unskillful, inept, stupid, *Inf.* dumb; frank, candid, outspoken, direct, straightforward, plain-spoken, blunt, to the point; brusque, abrupt, short, sharp, gruff; thoughless, inconsiderate, rude, impolite, uncivil, discourteous, disrespectful; offensive, disagreeable, unpleasant, unkind, unnice.

tag, *n.* **1.** tab, stub, flap, lap, lappet, loop, ear; ticket, sticker, docket, price tag.

2. tatter, snip, snippet, rag, remnant, shred; sliver, slip, fragment, clipping, particle.

3. end, tail end, tail, butt, dock; fag end, tip, stub, stump, nib, extremity.

4. postscript, sequel, addendum, supplement, suffix; appendix, postfix, postlude, epilogue, codicil, rider, colophon; refrain, chorus; curtain line, conclusion, last words, parting shot; trailer, tail, queue, train, tailpiece, afterpiece.

5. epithet, label, name, byword, *Sl.* handle, *Sl.* moniker; appellation, appellative, designation, title, honorific.

6. cliché, catch phrase, stock phrase, hackneyed expression, banality, *Inf.* old song; prosaicism, platitude, bromide, *Inf.* chestnut.

—v. **7.** ticket, mark, earmark, label, attach, tab, give a citation.

8. append, add on, affix, postfix, suffix, adjoin, fasten on; annex, *Inf.* tack on, attach, *Inf.* hitch on, *Inf.* slap on.

9. label, dub, name, call, nickname, term, style; identify, title, entitle, *Archaic.* clepe; christen, baptize, address.

10. follow, pursue, shadow, trail, *Inf.* tail, *Sl.* tailgate; tread close upon, tread upon the heels of, hang on the skirts of; hound, dog, chase, heel.

tail, *n.* **1.** brush, scut, dock, *Hunting.* flag, *Anat., Zool.* cauda.

2. hinder part, rear appendage, tailpiece, rear; tail fin, flipper, rudder, stabilizer; (*both of coins*) reverse, flip side.

3. extremity, tip, nib, end; conclusion, termination, tag *or* fag end; stub, remnant, remainder, leftover.
4. *Informal.* See **buttocks** and **rump** (*defs.* **1, 2**).
5. queue, line; retinue, train, suite, cortege, entourage, following, escort; wake, trail, track.
6. (*all of hair*) braid, pigtail, tress, ponytail.
7. *Informal.* See **detective**.
8. **tails.** See **cutaway**.
9. **turn tail** run away, flee, retreat, escape, take off, cut and run, hightail it, take to one's heels, *Inf.* skedaddle.
—*v.* **10.** *Usu.* **tail into** fade away, wane, die out, trail off; merge into, blend, become; dwindle, fall off.
11. *Informal.* follow, trail, shadow, spy on, stay with, stay on top of, keep an eye on; dog, bedog, tag after.
12. terminate, come after, trail behind.

tailor, *n.* garment maker, couturier, couturière, dressmaker, modiste, costumer, costumier, seamstress, semptress, sewer, stitcher; needlewoman, needleworker, needlepointer, embroiderer, crewelworker, lace maker, tatter; knitter, crocheter.

taint, *n.* **1.** trace, touch, suggestion, drop, bit, dab, spot, speck, fleck, dot; stain, discoloration, blemish, maculation, scar, *Med.* cicatrix, pit, pock, pockmark; flaw, imperfection, defacement, disfigurement, fault, defect; blotch, patch, splotch; dirty *or* black mark, soil, *Obs.* sully, smudge, smutch, smut, smirch, smear, streak, blur.
2. infection, contamination, pollution, poisoning, contagion, septicity; dirtying, sullying, befoulment; corruption, perversion, defilement, vitiation, lowering, debasement, adulteration, weakening, degradation; dissipation, depravity, depravation, debauchery, debauchment.
3. dishonor, discredit, disgrace, *Inf.* black eye, shame, stigma, brand; blemish, attaint, blot, blot on the escutcheon, tarnish.
—*v.* **4.** contaminate, infect, poison, adulterate, blight, canker, envenom, empoison; defile, befoul, pollute, dirty, foul, begrime, make unclean; soil, sully, tarnish, stain, spot, smudge, smutch, smut, smirch, besmirch, smear, besmear, streak, blotch, splotch; *Inf.* muck up, *Inf.* mess up, litter, strew, *Inf.* junk up, spoil, ruin; maculate, mark *or* mark up, blemish, deface, disfigure, mar, damage, harm, injure, hurt, bruise, blacken; vitiate, lower, abase, debase, degrade, devalue, deprave, corrupt, pervert; desecrate, profane, unhallow, violate, despoil, abuse, misuse, ill-use.
5. brand, stigmatize, *Sl.* dump on, drag through the mud *or* mire, heap dirt upon; impute, slur, asperse, vilify, scandalize; slander, calumniate, libel, denigrate, defame; disgrace, shame, dishonor.

take, *v.* **1.** acquire, secure, get, obtain, gain, procure, come by, *Sl.* cop; catch, seize, capture; hold, grasp, grip, clasp, embrace; garner, harvest, gather, glean; reach, attain, achieve, win; receive, accept, react *or* respond to; have, possess, experience, feel.
2. pick, hand-pick, select, choose, single out, set apart; prefer, favor, opt for; make one's choice *or* decision, decide *or* settle upon.
3. derive, stem from, come from, originate with, hail from; extract, quote, cite, excerpt.
4. ingest, swallow, eat, drink, consume; devour, gobble up, gulp down, bolt, wolf, *Inf.* put away; snack, nosh, nibble.
5. use, utilize, make use of, avail oneself of.
6. undergo, endure, bear, go through, pass through; tolerate, brook, abide, stand, withstand, put up with; swallow, stomach, digest, pocket.
7. carry off, remove, appropriate; steal, rob, purloin, pilfer, abstract, fleece, *Sl.* swipe, *Sl.* pinch; shoplift; palm, *Sl.* boost, walk off with, *Sl.* crook, *Sl.* cop, *Sl.* rip off; pirate, *Sl.* lift, *Inf.* crib, plagiarize; confiscate, impound, commandeer, arrogate, usurp, expropriate, accroach; peculate, embezzle, misappropriate, *Law.* defalcate.
8. kill, destroy, put to death; liquidate, erase, obliterate, blot *or* wipe out, carry off, finish off; annihilate, exterminate, massacre, decimate.
9. *Usu.* **take away** *or* **off** subtract, deduct, withdraw, remove, *Archaic.* subduct; discount, *Inf.* lop off, *Sl.* knock off, reduce; take from, devalue, devaluate, lessen, weaken, diminish.
10. carry, *Inf.* tote, bear, bring, deliver, transmit; convey, transport; conduct, escort, guide, usher, lead.
11. clear, negotiate, get over *or* around, hurdle; vault *or* leap *or* spring *or* bound over; make it over.
12. captivate, charm, attract, fascinate; delight, enchant, enthrall, enrapture, bewitch; lure, snare, ensnare; dazzle, transport, mesmerize, hypnotize; hold [s.o.'s] attention, entertain, divert, amuse.
13. require, call for, need, have need for, demand, insist upon, want.
14. occupy, fill, fill up, use up, consume.
15. act, perform, do, execute; operate, work, take effect, be effective, be efficacious; *Inf.* do the trick.
16. study, pursue, practice, learn, take up; school oneself in, steep oneself in, apply oneself to, occupy oneself with; prepare for a career in.
17. grasp, understand, comprehend, apprehend, get; realize, perceive, know.
18. assume, undertake, adopt, enter upon, begin, set about, attend to; take upon oneself, accept, take responsibility for.
19. *Often* **take it** presume, understand, gather, infer, deduce; suppose, guess, surmise, deem, reckon, suspect; imagine, believe, fancy, think.
20. **take after** resemble, look like, favor, remind one of, be the spit and image *or* spitting image of, be a chip off the old block; be like, bear resemblance to, be out of the same mold *or* cut from the same cloth, be brothers under the skin; echo, reflect, mirror, image, copy.
21. **take off after** follow, chase, give chase, pursue, run *or* fly after, make after, *Brit.* chevy; hound, dog, bedog; stalk, course, track, run down.
22. **take back a.** repossess, re-claim; accept back, welcome, forgive, forgive and forget. **b.** exchange, return, bring back; trade, swap, switch; get one's money back. **c.** remind, put in mind of, awake *or* call up memories of, make nostalgic. **d.** retract, recant, unsay, disavow, *Inf.* eat *or* swallow one's words; deny, gainsay, repudiate, disclaim; back down, renege, backtrack, back-pedal, *Inf.* flip-flop.
23. **take down a.** lower, let down, depress, drop; let sink, vail, dip. **b.** dismantle, disassemble, take apart, tear down; raze, level, demolish, destroy, fell. **c.** record, write down, put in *or* commit to writing; set down, chronicle, document, make a note *or* memorandum of. **d.** humble, humiliate, mortify, shame, disgrace; degrade, debase, abase; discredit, devalue, detract; belittle, demean, deprecate, disparage.
24. **take in a.** admit, let in, open the door to, give access *or* entrée to. **b.** lodge, board, house, quarter, billet, accommodate. **c.** include, encompass, embrace, contain, comprise, cover. **d.** grasp, comprehend; assimilate, absorb. **e.** deceive, trick, cheat, defraud; cozen, dupe, gull, pull the wool over [s.o.'s] eyes, bamboozle, hoodwink, *Sl.* hornswoggle; bilk, swindle, overcharge, mulct, *Sl.* soak, *Sl.* clip. **f.** observe, notice, note; see, perceive, pick up, *Inf.* catch; not miss a trick *or* thing.

25. take it out of *Informal.* **a.** exhaust, drain, enervate, tire, fatigue, weary; wind, fag, *Inf.* tucker, *Inf.* bush, *Sl.* poop out. **b.** penalize, punish; exact payment, extort, wrest, wrench, wring, milk, bleed, squeeze.

26. take on a. hire, employ, engage, retain, contract with, secure the services of, enlist, *Inf.* take on board. **b.** undertake, assume. See **take** (*def.* **18**). **c.** challenge, face, pit oneself against, contend against, oppose, rival, compete with, vie with. **d.** overreact, emote, overplay, overact; get excited *or* all excited, *Inf.* get in a stir *or* tizzy *or* dither; blow one's top, *Sl.* lose one's cool, *Sl.* go bonkers *or* bananas *or* ape.

27. take up a. occupy, cover, extend over; overlay, overspread, blanket, mantle, canopy, carpet. **b.** consume, use up, absorb, expend; wipe out, destroy, kill. **c.** continue, resume, pick up, go on with; begin again *or* anew, recommence. **d.** lift, hoist; raise, elevate, upraise, set upright, upright.

—*n.* **28.** taking, grasping, grabbing; seizure, appropriation, obtainment, procurement, acquisition.

29. *Slang.* profits, gain, revenue, income, return; winnings, proceeds, *Sl.* velvet, *Sl.* clean-up; surplus, excess, leftover, *Sl.* gravy, net, bottom line; booty, plunder, *Sl.* swag.

30. on the take *Slang.* acquisitive, greedy, grasping, avaricious, covetous; venal, mercenary, opportunistic, *Inf.* on the make; self-seeking, self-serving, self-aggrandizing.

takeoff, *n.* **1.** taking off, ascent, climbing, mounting, rising, soaring, flying; spiraling, increase, escalation, augmentation.

2. starting point, starting line, starting gate, starting gun; threshold, square one, starting out, outset, beginning, *Inf.* kickoff, *Inf.* blast-off, face-off.

3. burlesque, parody, amphigory, spoof, *Sl.* put-on, *Brit.* send-up; satire, lampoon, pasquinade; caricature, mockery, travesty; imitation, apery, mimicry.

taking, *adj.* captivating, winning, engaging, winsome, charming, pleasing, delightful; attractive, appealing, *Inf.* fetching, agreeable, likeable, prepossessing, intriguing, beguiling, enticing, tempting; irresistible, lovable, compelling, enchanting, bewitching, entrancing, *Inf.* cute, *Inf.* cute as a bug's ear.

tale, *n.* **1.** story, narration, account, recital, chronicle, history; fable, myth, fairy tale; epic, saga, *Archaic.* gest; parable, allegory, apologue; anecdote, incident, joke; *Inf.* yarn, tall story, *Sl.* fish *or* war story, *Sl.* megillah, *Inf.* song and dance, sob story, *Sl.* snow job; fiction, fictitious tale, invention.

2. narrative, novel, romance, novella, novelette, short story, *Fr. conte*; drama, play, teleplay, script, episode; adventure story, mystery story, *Inf.* mystery, detective story, *Inf.* whodunit, thriller, tale of suspense; science fiction, *Sl.* sci-fi, speculative fiction; horse opera, *Inf.* Western, soap opera, dime novel.

3. statement, allegation; rumor, canard, gossip, tittle-tattle; hearsay, talk, report, *Inf.* scuttlebutt, *Inf.* scoop.

4. lie, fib, falsehood, falsification, falsity, untruth; fabrication, *Inf.* story, misrepresentation, cock-and-bull story, *Inf.* whopper; alibi, excuse.

5. enumeration, numbering, count, tally, score, reckoning; calculation, computation.

talebearer, *n.* gossip, gossipmonger, rumormonger, scandalmonger, tattletale, tattler, *Inf.* blabbermouth, *Sl.* big mouth; telltale, busybody, snooper, troublemaker, meddler, informer, quidnunc.

talent, *n.* **1.** gift, faculty, endowment, genius, facility, flair, bent, turn, knack, forte, strong point, dowry; aptitude, intelligence, mother wit, ingenuity, cleverness, aptness, mind for.

2. ability, ableness, capacity, capability, capableness, potential, potentiality, potency, power; skill, skillfulness, dexterity, adroitness, address, efficiency, deftness, know-how, savoir-faire; proficiency, expertness, mastery, *Sl.* a lot on the ball.

3. star, *Inf.* superstar, *Inf.* wizard, *Inf.* whiz, *U.S. Slang.* crackerjack, *Sl.* shark; expert, master, master hand, maestro, virtuoso, prodigy, *Inf.* sharp.

talented, *adj.* gifted, well-endowed, intelligent, apt, smart, ingenious, brilliant, clever; artistic, skillful, skilled, dexterous, adroit, deft, *Brit. Dial.* feat; expert, masterful, masterly, *Fr. au fait;* topflight, top-drawer, first-rate, *Inf.* topnotch, ace, *Inf.* crack, *Sl.* crackerjack, *Sl.* on the ball, *Inf.* whiz-bang, *Brit. Sl.* whizzo; able, capable, competent, proficient, adept, good at, accomplished, finished, polished.

talisman, *n.* **1.** amulet, periapt, charm, fetish, abraxas, phylactery; scarab, swastika, rabbit's foot, lucky horseshoe, lucky coin *or* piece, *Brit.* merrythought; magic ring, magic stone, sacred ring.

talk, *v.* **1.** communicate, converse, exchange ideas, *Sl.* rap *or* rap with, speak with *or* to, have a talk *or* little talk with; consult, confer *or* confer with, check with, parley, *Archaic.* parle, palaver, discuss, talk over, consider.

2. gossip, buzz, tell secrets *or* confidences, *Inf.* blab, circulate *or* spread rumors, *Sl.* dish the dirt; talk behind [s.o.'s] back, whisper, breathe.

3. chatter, jabber, prattle, cackle, gibber, gibber-jabber; babble, prate, tattle, twaddle, *Brit.* twattle; patter, gabble, blather, drivel; mumble, mutter, stammer, stutter, splutter, sputter, *Sl.* spit out; chat, chitchat, chitter-chatter, chaffer, bandy words, *Sl.* chin, confabulate, *Inf.* confab, coze, pass the time of day; talk idly, visit, *Sl.* shoot the breeze, *Sl.* chew the fat *or* rag, *Sl.* jaw, *Sl.* gas, *Inf.* gab, *Sl.* bull *or* shoot the bull; palaver, clack, clatter, *Sl.* yap, *Sl.* yak, *Sl.* yackety-yak, *Sl.* schmooze; rattle, rattle on, go on, *Inf.* bend [s.o.'s] ear off, *Sl.* run off *or* on at the mouth, *Sl.* have diarrhea of the mouth; be loquacious *or* talkative, ramble *or* ramble on, maunder, digress, go off on a tangent.

4. open one's mouth, speak, articulate, enunciate, enounce, pronounce, voice, give voice *or* mouth to, vocalize, put in words; express, express one's opinion, speak up, pipe up, speak out, speak one's piece, *Inf.* put in one's two cents worth, speak one's mind, say what's on one's mind; air, vent, ventilate.

5. discourse, make a speech, give a talk, deliver an address, address, soapbox, platform; declaim, hold forth, orate, lecture, sermonize, preach, pontificate; harangue, rant, out-herod Herod; rhapsodize, gush, *Inf.* spout, *Australian Sl.* spruik.

6. disclose, reveal, divulge, give out, come out with, blurt out, let slip *or* drop, let out, spill; *Inf.* put one's foot in one's mouth.

7. express, utter, say, state, declare, proclaim; recount, relate, convey, put *or* get across; tell, inform, advise, notify, give word to, let [s.o.] know, bring to [s.o.'s] attention, point out, enlighten, clue [s.o.] in, *Inf.* tip off, give one to understand.

8. talk back back-talk, *Inf.* sass, *Dial.* sass back, *Inf.* answer back, *Inf.* sauce, *Inf.* give [s.o.] lip, *Inf.* give [s.o.] mouth, *Sl.* get fresh, *Sl.* get smart.

9. talk big *Informal.* brag, boast, crow, vaunt, toot one's own horn, *Sl.* mouth off, *Sl.* shoot off one's mouth; exaggerate, *Sl.* pile it higher and deeper, *Sl.* lay it on thick.

10. talk down a. outtalk, outdo. **b.** belittle, disparage, depreciate, deprecate, minimize, *Sl.* put down, *Inf.* knock, *Inf.* pan, criticize.

11. talk up promote, push for, *Inf.* plug, *Sl.* hype up, ballyhoo, beat the drum, advertise, publicize.

—*n.* **12.** conversation, dialogue, chat, tête-à-tête, coze, causerie, confabulation, *Inf.* confab, discussion, *Inf.* chin session, *Sl.* rap *or* rap session, *Sl.* bull session.

13. speech, lecture, address, oration, allocution, declamation; discourse, dissertation, recitation, oral report, *Fr. exposé*; sermon, tirade, harangue, rant, denunciation; sales talk, sales pitch, *Inf.* spiel.

14. conference, consulatation, parley, palaver, meeting, *Inf.* powwow, *Fr. pourparler.*

15. gossip, buzzing, blab, blabbing; rumor, grapevine, *Inf.* scuttlebutt, hearsay, *Fr. ouï-dire*, report, *Archaic.* bruit; an earful, *Sl.* dope, *Inf.* inside info, *Sl.* poop, tittle-tattle; scandal, dirt, whispering campaign, mudslinging.

16. small talk, chatter, chitchat, chitter-chatter, *Inf.* gab, idle talk, *Sl.* schmooze, *Scot.* clishmaclaver, *Sl.* yak *or* yakking, *Sl.* yackety-yak, *Sl.* hot air, *Sl.* gas, *Sl.* bull; prate, prattle, clack, babble, *Fr. bavardage*, rattle, *Brit.* natter; badinage, persiflage, banter, raillery.

17. language, speech, dialect, *Inf.* lingo, *Linguistics.* idiolect; jargon, cant, argot, slang; patois, brogue, accent.

talkative, *adj.* talky, loquacious, garrulous, multiloquous, long-tongued, *Inf.* big-mouthed, *Sl.* all jaw; conversational, voluble, fluent, glib, *Inf.* blessed with *or* possessed of the gift of gab; chatty, gabby, gossipy, *Sl.* blabby, *Sl.* gassy, *Sl.* windy; effusive, gushy, profuse, exuberant, unreserved, unrestrained; wordy, verbose, prolix, long-winded, longiloquent; discursive, digressive, rambling, maundering.

talker, *n.* **1.** speaker, orator, soapbox orator, stump orator, speechmaker, public speaker, spellbinder; main speaker, keynoter; haranguer, speechifier, declaimer, ranter, *Inf.* spouter, *Inf.* spieler, *Inf.* tubthumper, *Sl.* jawsmith; demagogue, rabble-rouser.

2. chatterbox, jabberer, gabbler, blatherskite, *Sl.* windbag, *Sl.* windjammer, *Inf.* hot-air artist; blabber, blabbermouth, blab, gusher; gossip, gossipmonger, newsmonger, scandalmonger; tattler, tattletale, telltale, talebearer, informer; noisy chatterer, palaverer, magpie, popinjay, *Inf.* jay; prattler, babbler, prater, twaddler, *Brit.* twattler, driveler; patterer, patterist, rattlebrain, rattlepate; braggart, bragger, boaster, gascon, vaunter.

tall, *adj.* **1.** high, lofty, towering, skyscraping, sky-high, elevated, beetling; aerial, alpine, cloud-capped, heaven-kissing.

2. giant, big, statuesque, large, sizable; rangy, lanky, *Inf.* gangling, long-legged, leggy, *Inf.* way up there, *Inf.* full-grown.

3. *Informal.* **a.** exaggerated, incredible, preposterous, hard to believe, overblown. **b.** unreasonable, excessive, overdone, inflated, exorbitant. **c.** grandiloquent, magniloquent, grandiose, bombastic, pompous, highfalutin, vainglorious, pretentious, plethoric.

tally, *n.* **1.** count, enumeration, reckoning; sum, score, amount, total, *Inf.* bottom line; inventory, record, invoice, catalog; list, register, roster, roll; census, poll; check list, itemization.

2. notch, mark, stroke, dash, slash.

3. label, ticket, tab, stub, voucher; stamp, sticker.

—*v.* **4.** register, record, enter, enroll, post; list, itemize, tabulate, catalog, inventory.

5. count, enumerate, number, tell; compute, calculate, add up, total up, figure, *Inf.* tote *or* tot up.

6. agree, accord, correspond, coincide, match, *Inf.* jibe, *Inf.* check; conform, comply, concur, fit.

tame, *adj.* **1.** domesticated, tamed, broken, broken to harness, *Sl.* busted; trained, housebroken; (*all of wild animals*) gentle, fearless, unafraid.

2. docile, submissive, tractable, unresisting; meek, subdued, in harness, henpecked, tied to [s.o.'s] apron strings, under [s.o.'s] thumb, at [s.o.'s] beck and call.

3. dull, uninteresting, flat, insipid, inane, vapid, *Sl.* nothing, *Sl.* blah, *Sl.* for the birds; tedious, boring, boresome, dry, dry-as-dust, spiritless, lifeless, *Sl.* dead; commonplace, run-of-the-mill, *Inf.* old hat.

4. weak, pusillanimous, timorous, timid, fearful, afraid of one's own shadow; unmanly, faint-hearted, weak-hearted, lily-livered, with a backbone of banana, *Inf.* chicken-livered, *Inf.* pantywaist, *Inf.* yellow, *Sl.* yellow-bellied, *Sl.* candy-assed.

—*v.* **5.** domesticate, gentle, break, *Sl.* bust; subdue, master, overcome; train, housebreak.

6. soften, tone down, moderate, modulate, mitigate, temper, lighten, ease up on; mollify, ameliorate, assuage; calm, stabilize, tranquilize, pacify.

7. harness, control, get under control, put to use.

tamper, *v.* **1.** meddle with, monkey *or* monkey around with, *Inf.* fool *or* fool around with, *Inf.* mess *or* mess around with; manipulte, maneuver, juggle, pull strings; rig, set up, falsify, fake; load, stack, salt, salt a mine, *Sl.* plant.

2. corrupt, adulterate, contaminate, pollute, debase, taint, *Inf.* doctor, (*of drugs or alcohol*) cut, *Sl.* spike.

tan, *v.* **1.** convert to leather, steep *or* soak in tanbark *or* tannin *or* tannic acid; lie in the sun, sunbathe, weather.

2. brown, embrown, turn brown, toast, darken.

3. *Informal.* spank, thrash thresh, *Inf.* whale the tar out of, *Brit. Dial.* yerk; whip, horsewhip, curry, strap, cowhide, *Inf.* leather, *Sl.* belt; lash, switch, birch, scourge, flagellate, flog, *Inf.* lace; beat; *Inf.* whale, *Inf.* thump, *Inf.* lambaste, *Inf.* trim, *Sl.* lay into, *Sl.* let [s.o.] have it, *Sl.* whomp.

—*adj.* **4.** golden brown, bronze, bronzed, bronzy, copper, coppery, brown, brown a a berry, suntanned; light brown, ecru, khaki, drab; yellowish-brown, sienna, brownish-yellow, fulvous, beige, fawn, tawny.

tandem, *adv.* one in front of the other, one behind *or* after the other; in single file, in a row *or* line *or* queue, Indian file.

tang, *n.* **1.** piquancy, pungency, poignancy, sharpness; zest, zip, race, snappiness, life, *Inf.* twang, *Sl.* kick, *Sl.* punch, *Inf.* ginger; spice, spiciness, relish, hotness, pepperiness; bite, nip, sting, edge, mordancy, astringency, acerbity, asperity; acidity, sourness, harshness, roughness.

2. taste, flavor, aftertaste; touch, dab, smack, trace, hint, suggestion, soupçon.

tangent, *adj.* touching, contiguous, in contact, contactual, tangential, *Geom.* (*of a curve*) osculatory, *Both Obs.* attingent, attiguous; meeting, coming together, convergent, converging, intersecting, concurrent, overlapping; abutting, bordering, neighboring, conterminous; adjacent, juxtapositional, juxtaposed, adjoining, up against one another; proximate, next-door, nearest, closest, immediate.

tangential, *adj.* **1.** touching, contiguous, contactual, tangental. See **tangent.**

2. slightly connected *or* related, just *or* barely touching, just *or* barely grazing, lambent.

3. off on *or* at a tangent, divergent, diverging, digressive, discursive; rambling, meandering, wandering, drifting, roving, straying; off the topic, unrelated, irrelevant, nongermane, unconnected, disconnected, beside the point.

tangible, *adj.* **1.** touchable, palpable, tactile; perceivable, perceptible, sensible, ponderable, appreciable; material, materiate, physical, substantial, substantive; corporeal, corporal, bodily, somatic, incarnate, embodied, *Philos.* hylomorphic; nonspectral, nonspiritual, of this world; nonimaginary, nonillusional, nonchimerical, existing outside the mind; existent, real, real live, actual.

2. solid, concrete, nonabstract, hard, well-documented, supported; definite, well-defined, distinct, well-marked, unmistakable, unambiguous; ascertainable, salient, discernible, noticeable, detectable, recognizable, identifiable; overt, displayed, evident, evidential, self-evident, apparent, seeable, visible, obvious, patent; plain, clear, clear-cut, intelligible, cognizable, comprehensible, comprehendible.

tangle, *v.* **1.** snarl, ravel, knot, mat, entangle; kink, twist, intertwist; intertwine, interlace, interweave; disorder, disarrange, muss, mess, dishevel, shuffle, ruffle, rumple, tousle; complicate, confuse, jumble, scramble, *Sl.* ball up, muddle; jam, tie up, delay.

2. snare, ensnare, *Archaic.* trepan, net, enmesh, trap, entrap.

3. *Informal.* argue, quibble, cavil; contend, dispute, disagree, contest, controvert, spar, cross swords, lock horns; fight, wrangle, bicker, haggle, *Sl.* hassle, *Scot.* argle-bargle.

—*n.* **4.** snarl, knot, snag, jam, entanglement, tanglement; kink, twist, coil; network, web, webwork.

5. jumple, heap, mass, agglomeration, bunch, mess, huddle, disorder, disarrangement, disarray; complexity, complication, confusion, mix-up; scramble, jungle, wilderness, bewilderment, hodgepodge, *Brit.* hotchpotch; mishmash, muddle, fuddle, tumble.

6. *Informal.* argument, disagreement, contention, altercation, conflict, dispute, controversy, discord, clash, *Inf.* hassle, *Inf.* barney; quarrel, row, squabble, dustup, spat, tiff, *Brit. Dial.* fratch, *Brit. Dial.* fratching.

tangled, *adj.* **1.** snarled, raveled, knotty, knotted, entangled; interlaced, interwoven, intertwined, twisted; jumbled up, scrambled, mixed-up, chaotic; jammed, tied-up.

2. intricate, complex, complicated, involved; arduous, difficult, thorny, trying, tough, *Inf.* tough to figure, *Inf.* nasty.

tank, *n.* **1.** cistern, vat, boiler; well, sump; vessel, receptacle; aquarium, bowl.

2. pool, pond, millpond, lake, *Scot.* loch, *Irish Eng.* lough, tarn, *Chiefly Brit. Dial.* mere.

3. *Military.* combat vehicle, armored car.

tantalize, *v.* **1.** allure, entice, bait, intrigue, beguile, inveigle, tempt, seduce, ensorcell, bewitch, enchant; captivate, fascinate, charm, spellbind; entrance, enrapture, transport, enravish, transfix; titillate, tickle, interest, delight; arouse, rouse, incite, whet, stimulate, make one's mouth water; induce, persuade, prevail upon, bribe, suborn; attract, appeal, draw, magnetize, hypnotize, sway, mesmerize.

2. torment, torture, plague, frustrate, disappoint.

tantamount, *adj.* equivalent, equal, synonymous, commensurate, equiparent; identical, indistinguishable, alike, homogeneous, of a piece, of a kind; interchangeable, all one, all the same, much the same, comparable to; correspondent, analogous, correlative, correlated.

tantrum, *n.* outburst, outbreak, eruption, burst, flare-up, explosion, blowup; pet, fume, temper, rage, fury, agitation, *Archaic.* pucker; fit, convulsion, spasm, seizure, attack, paroxysm.

tap¹, *v.* **1.** slap, pat, dab, rap, peck; touch, poke, knock, shove, push, nudge; cuff, spank, box, buffet, smack, whack, thwack, hit, *Inf.* clip, crack; strike, slam, punch, *Sl.* sock; bat, flap.

—*n.* **2.** slap, pat, dab, rap, peck; cuff, box, buffet, punch, *Inf.* clip, *Sl.* sock; stroke, crack, blow, smack, whack, thwack; flap, *Inf.* bat; ping, patter, spatter, rapping, rat-a-tat.

tap², *n.* **1.** spigot, faucet, cock, petcock, valve; seacock, sea valve, sea connection; plug, bung, stopper, stopple, spile, peg, spout.

—*v.* **2.** (*of liquid*) draw off, drain, bleed, siphon off, let run off; broach, draw, decant.

3. summon up, call forth; use, utilize; open up, draw from, exploit; dig into, reach into, probe, explore, penetrate, pierce.

4. wiretap, *Sl.* bug, listen in, eavesdrop, eavesdrop electronically; tape, record, get on tape.

tape, *n.* **1.** strip, fillet, band, stripe, *Naut.* ribband, roll, strap, belt; ribbon, string, thread; cellophane tape, *Trademark.* Scotch tape, adhesive tape, masking tape; tape measure, tapeline; ticker tape.

—*v.* **2.** wrap, bind, seal, scotch-tape, mend, fasten.

taper, *v.* **1.** narrow, thin, diminish, come to a point, contract, constrict, compress.

2. **taper off** diminish, decrease, *Inf.* peter out, ebb, wane, fade, dwindle; lessen, attenuate, slacken, let up, abate, bate; dissipate, blow away, evanesce, go up in smoke, evaporate, melt; weaken, fail, falter, slow down, slow down to a crawl; shrink, wither, wither on the vine, die away, tail, tail off; decline, droop, sag, wilt, drop, drop off, plummet, plunge, fall, fall off, slump; reduce, curtail, cut down, retrench, abridge, lower, shorten, snip off.

tapered, *adj.* tapering, narrowed, dwindling, pointed, flamelike, candlelike, cusped, cuspidal, cuspidate; wedge-shaped, cuneiform, cuneate, triangular, *Bot., Zool.* mucronate, *Bot.* aculeate; fusiform, spindle-shaped, needlelike; conic, pyramidal, peaked, barbed.

tar, *n.* pitch, maltha, bitumen, asphalt, gilsonite, uintaite, uintahite; resin, rosin, colophony, gum, lac.

tardiness, *n.* lateness, slowness, dilatoriness, cunctation, *Inf.* pokiness; sluggishness, indolence, sloth, inertia, laziness, torpor; lethargy, languor; dawdling, fiddling around, *Sl.* screwing around, frittering away one's time; reluctance, hesitation, procrastination, putting off, temporizing, dragging one's feet; remissness, negligence, slackness, thoughtlessness; delay, deferment, postponement, prorogation.

tardy, *adj.* **1.** late, behind time, unpunctual, overdue, behind schedule, belated, behindhand, never on time, eleventh-hour, last-minute; delayed, long delayed, retarded, *Inf.* hung up, *Inf.* held up; put off, deferred, postponed.

2. slow, leisurely, slower than molasses in January, phlegmatic, listless, unmoving; snaillike, *Inf.* poky, lazy, lackadaisical, indolent; sluggish, slothful, sluggardly, lethargic, languid, torpid, droopy, half-asleep.

3. reluctant, dilatory, hesitating, vacillating, procrastinating, holding back, marking time, foot-dragging.

target, *n.* **1.** mark, bull's-eye, circle, point, quintain; objective, object, aim, goal, destination; intent, intention, purpose, idea; quarry, prey, game, pursuit.

2. butt, *Inf.* goat, laughingstock, stock, April fool; fool, game, victim, monkey, *Brit. Sl.* mug; jestingstock, gazingstock, jest, joke.

3. buckler, shield, *Archaic.* targe, *Class. Myth.* aegis; pavis, pelta, ancile.

tariff, *n.* levy, toll, duty, impost, excise. See **tax** (*def.* **1.**).

tarnish, *v.* **1.** dull, discolor, oxidize, rust; dim, mat, fade, erode, corrode, blur; tinge, wash out, decolorize, achromatize, etiolate, blanch, blench.

2. stain, sully, dirty, soil, blemish, taint; spot,

maculate, streak, smudge, smirch, besmirch, begrime; ink, speck, fleck, speckle, mark; daub, bedaub, dab, spatter, bespatter, draggle, drabble, splash, plash; blot, blotch, splotch.

3. blacken, slur, defame, dishonor, disgrace, shame; mar, injure, damage, spoil, hurt; brand, stigmatize, taint, drag through the mud, *Sl.* dump on; denigrate, vilify, abase, debase, degrade; calumniate, asperse, libel, slander, scandalize, impute; vitiate, pollute, corrupt, contaminate, foul.

—n. **4.** discoloration, decoloration, oxidation; patination, corrosion, erosion, fading, blur, etiolation.

5. stain, blemish, blot, patch, taint, attaint; smudge, smutch, smut, smirch, smear, splash, streak, spatter; splotch, blotch, daub, dot, spot, maculation, macula; fleck, speck, speckle, dab; flaw, disfigurement, defacement, mar.

6. stigma, brand, taint; disgrace, shame, dishonor, reproach; blot on the escutcheon, *Inf.* black eye, black mark, mark, badge of infamy; defilement, ignominy, odium, obloquy, turpitude; derogation, disparagement, infamy, ingloriousness; discredit, disesteem, disrepute, ill repute, bad name.

tarry, *v.* **1.** remain, stay, sojourn, abide; continue, stop, rest; dwell, reside, live, bide, house, take up quarters, pitch tent, settle, anchor, put down stakes, plant oneself, be established.

2. delay, linger, loiter, dawdle, lag, dally, be tardy, hang back, stay behind; *Inf.* stall, temporize, retard, procrastinate; postpone, suspend, prorogue, table, shelve; protract, prolong, take one's time, bide one's time.

3. wait, pause, cool one's heels, *Obs.* attend; await, expect, watch for, look for.

tart[1], *adj.* **1.** sharp, sour, acid, acerb, acerbic; acidulous, acescent, acetous, vinegary; acrid, bitter, pungent, harsh, piquant, unripe.

2. caustic, cutting, mordant, biting, acrimonious; trenchant, incisive, piercing, pricking, scathing, burning, nipping, stinging; pointed, sharp, sharp-tongued, edged, barbed, double-edged; keen, stringent, astringent, severe; sarcastic, satiric, sardonic, ironic, cynical, derisive; abusive, corrosive, unkind, cruel; mocking, taunting, teasing, contumelious; spiteful, venomous, malicious, malignant, vicious.

3. peevish, testy, irascible, crabbed, petulant; snappish, waspish, cross-tempered, ill-tempered; surly, curt, grouchy, churlish, brusque; splenetic, morose, sullen, perverse.

tart[2], *n.* **1.** pie, pastry, turnover, puff, Danish pastry, French pastry, patisserie; quiche, strudel, baklava, blintz, éclair.

2. hussy, drab, jade, slut, strumpet, *Sl.* chippy, trollop, doxy, wanton; bitch, witch, quean, demirep, demimondaine; harlot, whore, prostitute, hustler, streetwalker, courtesan; lady of the night, woman of easy viture, woman of ill repute.

tartness, *n.* **1.** sharpness, sourness, acidity, acridness, acerbity; pungency, piquancy, bitterness, acidulousness, harshness.

2. acrimony, causticity, asperity, mordancy, astringency, trenchancy; severity, harshness, austerity, sternness; spite, spitefulness, virulence, malice, abusiveness, corrosiveness, unkindness, cruelty; malevolence, malignity, scorn; sarcasm, cynicism, irony, satire; derision, mockery, contumely.

3. snappishness, testiness, waspishness, curtness, ill humor, ill temper; petulance, crustiness, dourness, spleen, moroseness; captiousness, churlishness, brusqueness; moodiness, surliness, gruffness, grouchiness, sullenness.

task, *n.* **1.** duty, job, chore, odd job, work, devoir; assignment, lesson, exercise, homework; commission, mission, engagement, errand, quest.

2. labor, toil, drudgery, work, strain; difficulty, travail, tribulation, trial, passion; sweat, fag, grind, grindstone, treadmill; test, test of strength, tall order, tough assignment, Augean stables, Herculean task; hard work, backbreaking work, uphill work, donkeywork, manual labor, spadework.

3. **take to task** call to account, blame, inculpate, incriminate, recriminate; impute, indict, charge, cite; censure, tax, reprove, reproach, bring to book; decry, denounce, denunciate, contemn, reprehend.

—v. **4.** strain, load, burden, charge, weigh down, break the back of; encumber, cumber, tax, overload, overtask, overtax; oppress, drive, grind, crush, push too far; exhaust, tire, wear, wear out, weary, fag.

taskmaster, *n.* **1.** martinet, disciplinarian, master; oppressor, tyrant, despot, slave driver, Simon Legree; inquisitor.

2. supervisor, overseer, overlooker, surveyor; superintendent, director, manager, inspector; boss, foreman, fugleman; monitor, proctor.

taste, *v.* **1.** savor, relish, smack, *Inf.* smack one's lips, degust, degustate, sip, nibble at, try.

2. experience, meet, encounter, come up against, undergo; partake of, participate in, assay.

3. (*all in reference to flavor*) perceive, distinguish, differentiate, discern, discriminate.

—n. **4.** gustation, degustation, libation.

5. flavor, savor, sapor, spice, tang, sapidity, piquancy; flavorfulness, savoriness, palatability.

6. morsel, grain, bit, *Scot., Irish Eng.* stime, bite, mouthful, sample; sip, nip, drop, dribble; touch, dash, hint, suggestion, suspicion, soupçon, trace, tinge, shade.

7. appetite, hunger, thirst, craving, hankering, yearning, longing; relish, palate, sweet tooth; zest, gusto, *Fr. goût,* preference, partiality, bias, keenness; affinity, liking, affection, fondness, love; penchant; attraction, disposition, predisposition, predilection, propensity, proclivity.

8. discernment, acumen, perception; discrimination, finesse, judgement; cultivation, culture, fine feeling, refinement, polish, grace, elegance, stylishness, ton, bon ton, polish, finish; rhythm, balance, symmetry, proportion.

9. style, mode, fashion, manner, form.

10. custom, conventionality; correctness, propriety, restraint, tactfulness, politeness, politesse, delicacy, nicety.

tasteful, *adj.* tactful, restrained, polite; correct, appropriate, fitting, fit, proper, *Fr. comme il faut,* decorous; cultivated, cultured, refined, elegant, polished, finished; charming, graceful, dainty; discriminative, aesthetic, artistic; harmonious, symmetrical, balanced, proportional.

tasteless, *adj.* **1.** unflavorful, flavorless, unflavored, savorless, vapid, insipid, *Fr. fade,* dead; flat, stale, unpalatable, unsavory, unappetizing; weak, thin, watery, watered-down.

2. dull, uninteresting, jejune, commonplace, prosaic, run-of-the-mill; boring, wearisome, tiresome, monotonous, humdrum, drab, heavy.

3. tactless, inappropriate, unproper, improper, unfitting, impolite, rude; uncultivated, unrefined, gauche; boorish, churlish, coarse, gross, crude, vulgar; meretricious, tawdry, loud, garish, gawdy, flashy, showy; *Inf.* tacky, *Sl.* schlock, cheap, trashy.

tasty, *adj.* **1.** good-tasting, savory, savorous, sapid, palatable, toothsome, *Scot,* gustable; flavorful, flavorsome, flavorous, appetizing, relishable; delicious, *Sl.* yummy, mouth-watering, luscious, scrumptious, delectable, good enough to eat, finger-lickin' good; ambrosial, ambrosian, like the food of the gods, *Fr. délicieux*; succulent, juicy, rich; nectarous, nectarean, sweet, honeyed; piquant, pungent, spicy, tart; epicurean, gourmet.

2. *Informal.* tactful, appropriate, decorous; cultivated, refined, discriminative, tasteful. See **tasteful.**

tatter, *n.* **1.** rag, shred, scrap, piece, bit.

2. tatters rags, castoffs, old clothes; scraps, shreds, patches, shreds and patches.

tatterdemalion, *n.* ragamuffin, scarecrow; beggar, panhandler, guttersnipe; hobo, tramp, vagrant, beachcomber, vagabond, derelict, *Inf.* bum, *Sl.* vag, *Sl.* bo, *Sl.* stiff, *Sl.* bindle stiff, *Sl.* canvasback; waif, street Arab, gutter urchin, gamin, mudlark.

tattle, *v.* **1.** blab, blurt out, gush, *Inf.* spout; let slip, reveal, divulge secrets; tattletale, tell on, inform on, *Inf.* snitch on, *Sl.* squeal on, *Sl.* rat on, *Sl.* fink on.

2. gossip, tittle-tattle, buzz, talk idly, *Sl.* shoot the breeze, *Inf.* gab, *Sl.* gas, *Sl.* bull *or* shoot the bull; palaver, clack, clatter, rattle, *Sl.* run off *or* on at the mouth; be loquacious *or* talkative, ramble, maunder.

3. chatter, chipper, prate, prattle, cackle; babble, gibber, *Sl.* gibber-jabber, jargon; jabber, gabble, patter; twaddle, *Brit.* twattle, blather, drivel; chit-chat, chitter-chatter, chaffer, bandy words.

—*n.* **4.** tattling, blabbing, bleating, blurting out, gushing, *Inf.* spouting; revealing *or* divulging secrets, gossiping; telling on, telling tales, informing on, *Inf.* snitching on, *Sl.* squealing on, *Sl.* ratting on, *Sl.* finking on.

5. gossip, tittle-tattle, *Inf.* scuttlebutt, idle talk, *Inf.* gab, *Sl.* gas, *Sl.* shooting the bull, *Sl.* shooting the breeze; small talk, *Anglo-Ingian.* bukh, chit-chat, chitter-chatter; palaver, palavering, palaverment; clack, clacking, clatter, clattering, rattling, *Sl.* running off *or* on at the mouth; rambling, maundering.

6. chatter, chattering, chippering, prattle, prattling, cackle, cackling; patter, pattering, gabble, gabbling, jabber, jabbering, Jabberwocky; prate, prating, twaddle, twaddling, *Both Brit.* twattle, twattling; babble, babbling, babblement, gibber, gibbering, gibberish, blather, blathering, drivel, driveling.

tattler, *n.* telltale, tattletale, talebearer, *Brit. Sl.* sneak; informer, *Sl.* squealer, *Sl.* fink, *Sl.* rat, *Sl.* ratfink, *Sl.* stool pigeon; blabber, blabbermouth, sieve, gossip, busybody, rumormonger, excessive talker; jabberer, chatterer, gabbler, blatherskite, *Sl.* windbag, *Sl.* windjammer, *Inf.* hot-air artist.

tattoo, *n.* **1.** signal, summons, call, call to arms.

2. pulse, pulsation, beat, rhythm; patter, pitter-patter, pitapat, ratatat; paradiddle; pant, panting, throb, throbbing.

taunt, *v.* **1.** reproach, censure, unbraid, rebuke, berate, *Sl.* rank out.

2. twit, jeer, sneer, fleer, gibe, chaff, rally, *Inf.* roast, pluck [s.o.] by the beard, *Inf.* dig, *Sl.* razz; mock, flaunt, poke fun at, make fun of, call names; lampoon, burlesque, satirize; tease, kid, harass, ride, get on [s.o.'s] back, torment, *Sl.* bug, *Sl.* rag, *Sl.* hassle; slap, *Inf.* swipe, *Inf.* slam; ridicule, deride, revile, scorn, hold up to scorn; insult, offend, affront, slap [s.o.] in the face.

—*n.* **3.** gibe, skit, jeer, sneer, *Inf.* dig; insult, slap in the face; cut, *Inf.* brickbat, *Sl.* put-down; boo, hoot, catcall, *Sl.* raspberry, *Sl.* Bronx cheer.

4. derision, mockery, ridicule, raillery, sarcasm, fighting words; contumely, contempt, scurrility, scorn.

taut, *adj.* **1.** tense, drawn tight, tight, strained; unrelaxed, under a strain, *Inf.* uptight.

2. tidy, neat, trim, in trim, shipshape, spruce, smart, snug, in order, orderly.

tautological, *adj.* pleonastic, battological, redundant; reiterative, repetitious, repetitive; wordy, verbose, prolix, long-winded, *Sl.* gassy, *Sl.* windy.

tautology, *n.* pleonasm, battology, redundancy; reiteration, repetition, repetitiousness, repetitiveness, wordiness, prolixity, verbosity, long-windedness, *Sl.* windiness, *Sl.* gassiness.

tavern, *n.* **1.** bar, barroom, taproom, saloon, alehouse, *Brit.* public house, *Brit.* pub; bar and grill, grill, grill room, brasserie; cocktail lounge, bistro, cabaret, nightclub; *All Sl.* beer-joint, gin mill, watering hole, dive, barrelhouse, honky-tonk, speakeasy, after-hours joint, *U.S. Obs.* blind tiger *or* pig.

2. inn, hostel, hostelry, hotel, motel, *Fr. auberge, Sl.* flophouse; hospice, traveler's rest, roadhouse, caravansary.

tawdry, *adj.* meretricious, showy, flashy, *Sl.* flash; gaudy, loud, garish, *Inf.* tacky, screaming; cheap, brummagem, tinsel, plastic, *Sl.* rinky-dink.

tawny, *adj.* yellow-brown, yellowish-brown, brownish-yellow, khaki, fawn, fulvous, raw sienna; tan, light brown, ecru.

tax, *n.* **1.** duty, impost, levy, payment, surtax, surcharge; tribute, contribution, capitation; tariff, charge, exaction, taxation, scot; excise, custom, *Brit.* cess, octroi; fee, dues, toll, rate, rating, assessment; poll tax, property tax, income tax, sales tax, tithe, tenth, Peter's pence.

2. charge, duty, burden, obligation, demand, responsibility; weight, onus, *Archaic.* bale, strain; encumbrance, imposition, exertion.

—*v.* **3.** levy, toll, charge, excise, subject to duty; assess, rate, appraise; impose, lay on, put on, fix, inflict; exact, demand, require; wring, squeeze, wrest, pinch.

4. burden, charge, weigh down, load, saddle; encumber, cumber, task, strain; overload, overburden, overtask, overtax; overwork, overdo, wear out, exhaust, fag, push too far; fatigue, tire, weary, prostrate, knock out; wind, whack, jade; oppress, drive, push, flog, whip; grind, crush, trample.

5. censure, reprove, rebuke, asperse, declaim against; decry, reprehend, disparage, contemn; accuse, charge, indict, arraign, impeach; impute, ascribe, cite, blame.

taxable, *adj.* subject to tax, dutiable, leviable tithable, exactable, assessable, *Brit.* ratable.

taxicab, *n.* taxi, cab, hackney, *Inf.* hack, *Trademark.* Checker, *Trademark.* Yellow Cab; carriage *or* coach for hire, fiacre, hansom *or* hansom cab, *Brit.* fly; (*both in Japan, the Philippines*) jinrikisha, rickshaw.

teach, *v.* **1.** instruct, tutor, school, educate, inform, enlighten, edify; question, catechize, drill, beat into, cram; indoctrinate, inculcate, instill, infuse; train, coach, initiate, ground, prepare, ready; counsel, advise, guide, preach, lecture, moralize, sermonize; admonish, reprimand, warn.

2. explain, illustrate, clarify, clear up, elucidate, spell out; interpret, explicate, annotate, gloss; expound, propound, hold forth; indicate, show, show how, demonstrate; describe, point out, tell; acquaint with, familiarize with, introduce to, apprise of.

3. propagate, dissenminate, spread, propagandize; promulgate, make known, broadcast, announce, publish.

teachable, *adj.* **1.** docile, trainable, tractable, manageable, pliable; obedient, compliant, conformable;

amenable, agreeable, disposed, ready; submissive, acquiescent, meek, gentle, timid.

2. understandable, apprehensible, comprehensible, intelligible; learnable, graspable, knowable, cognoscible; evident, obvious, clear, lucid, simple, easy.

3. bright, smart, able, clever; quick, keen, sharp, alert; astute, perceptive, discerning; curious, inquisitive, questioning; scholarly, studious, diligent, conscientious, industrious, assiduous; zealous, intent, eager, enthusiastic.

teacher, *n.* **1.** instructor, trainer, coach; educator, pedagogue, educationist, *Educ.* methodologist; schoolteacher, schoolmaster, *Chiefly Scot.* dominie, schoolmistress, schoolmarm; professor, doctor, master, tutor, fellow, *Brit.* don, preceptor, lector, lecturer, *Brit.* reader; schoolman, scholastic, academician, academe, gownsman.

2. mentor, counselor, advisor; guide, cicerone, docent; explainer, explicator, expositor, expounder; interpreter, (*in the Orient*) dragoman; annotator, glosser.

3. indoctrinator, inculcator, informer, informant, demonstrator; exponent, propagator, propagandist, missionary, apostle; preacher, moralizer, sermonizer; parson, minister, rabbi, priest; mystagogue, catechist, catechizer, *Hinduism.* guru.

4. exemplar, example, pattern, model; ideal, idol, paragon.

teaching, *n.* **1.** instruction, education, tuition, tutelage; grounding, initiation, preparation, schooling, training; inculcation, indoctrination, discipline.

2. explanation, illustration, explication, example; interpretation, elucidation, annotation; exposition, demonstration, communication.

3. disquisition, discourse, prelection, recitation; homily, sermon, preaching, sermonizing; lecture, reading, lesson.

5. *Usu.* **teachings** doctrine, dogma, precept, principle, tenet; belief, creed, credo, opinion, persuasion; rule, rubric, canon, law; rudiment, element.

4. pedagogics, pedagogy, didactics. See **pedagogy** (*def.* **2**).

team, *n.* **1.** crew, company, squad, gang, shift, *Fr. équipe;* corps, group, band, troupe, party; set, matched pair, duo.

2. (*all of draft animals*) pair, span, yoke, tandem, four-in-hand; rig, equipage, carriage and horses.

teamwork, *n.* cooperation, collaboration, combined *or* joint action *or* effort coaction, interaction, pulling together, pooling or resources; mutual cooperation, reciprocity, reciprocation, *Chiefly U.S.* logrolling; complicity, collusion, conspiracy; coordination, synergy, unison, harmony, concert, concord, concerted *or* concurrent action *or* effort.

tear[1], *n.* **1.** teardrop, drop, droplet, bead, globule. —*v.* **2.** (*all of the eyes*) water, well *or* fill up with tears, get moist *or* dewy *or* teary; secrete tears, shed tears, weep, gush, overflow.

tear[2], *v.* **1.** rip, rend, reave, rive, pull apart; shred, rip *or* pull to shreds *or* pieces, tear up, put asunder, destroy.

2. wrench, wrest, extract, yank off, pull off, detach, tear off; peel, strip, bark, husk, skin, unwrap, undo; snatch, grab, grasp, pull at, pick at.

3. divide, split, disrupt, rupture, turn upside down *or* topsy-turvy, cause an upheaval; (*of oneself*) separate, remove, absent, take one's leave, depart, leave, get away from; upset, distress, harrow, worry, torture, torment, tear [s.o.] up, pull at [s.o.'s] heartstrings.

4. wound, injure, hurt, pain; stab, pierce, lancinate, knife, cut, gash, slash, slit, gore, score; lacerate, mangle, hack up, cut to pieces, tear limb from limb, disjoint, dismember, dissect, anatomize, vivisect.

5. come apart, come apart at the seams, rip *or* split open, burst open, dehisce; make *or* leave a hole, fall apart, disintegrate.

6. rampage, rip, dart, dash, shoot, bolt, whiz, *Inf.* zoom, *Inf.* zip, *Inf.* go like lightning *or* the wind, *Inf.* go like the dickens; speed, sprint, race, hie, hasten, fly, flit, run, gallop, burn up the road, rush, hurry, scurry, scramble, bustle, *Inf.* hustle; scoot, scud, scuttle, flee, *Inf.* skedaddle, make tracks.

—*n.* **7.** rip, rent, split, fissure, rift, fault, clevage, cleft, severance, break, breach, rupture, fracture; cut, slit, slash, gore, gash, score, stab, laceration; wound, injury, hurt, *Slang.* boo-boo.

8. rampage, fury, rage, storm, ranting and raving, tantrum, fit, hysterics, passion; flare-up, outburst, explosion, blowup, fulmination; flurry, burst, spurt, gush, outpouring, effusion; dash, dart, rush, hurry, scurry, scramble.

9. *Slang.* spree, lark, fling, escapade, antic, adventure, *Inf.* bout, *Inf.* binge, *Sl.* bust, *Sl.* bender, *Sl.* hellbender, *Sl.* jag, *Sl.* toot, *Sl.* bat; gambol, frolic, rollick, romp, frisk; party, wing-ding, fun time, celebration, merrymaking, revelry, jollification, *Irish.* hooley; orgy, debauch, saturnalia; carousal, carouse, revel, wassail, guzzle, bouse, brannigan, potation, compotation, *Inf.* booze, *Sl.* drunk, *Sl.* barhop, *Sl.* bar-crawl, *Brit. Sl.* pub-crawl.

tearful, *adj.* **1.** lachrymose, lachrymal, lachrymatory, teary, *Inf.* weepy; watery, dewy-eyed, on the verge of *or* close to tears, ready to cry *or* burst into tears *or* break down; weeping, crying, wailing, sobbing, blubbering, sniveling, whimpering; dissolved in tears, inconsolable, heartbroken, broken-hearted, crushed; unhappy, melancholy, blue, gloomy, depressed, dejected, *Inf.* down in the dumps.

2. sad, saddening, sorrowful, woeful, distressing, dismaying, lamentable, mournful; dolorous, lugubrious, funereal, elegaic, dirgeful, epicedial, epicedian, threnodial, black; pitiful, piteous, pathetic, heartrending, heartbreaking, poignant, plaintive, moving, touching, affecting, emotional; maudlin, mawkish, sentimental, romantic, soft, mushy, slushy, sickening, cloying, *Inf.* drippy, *Sl.* schmaltzy, *Brit. Sl.* soppy.

tease, *v.* **1.** torment, bedevil, harass, bother, pester, *Sl.* bug, *Sl.* hassle, *Sl.* drive [s.o.] nuts *or* crazy *or* bananas; irritate, annoy, vex, provoke, pique, *Inf.* aggravate, *Inf.* give [s.o.] a pain; pick on, be on [s.o.'s] back, *Sl.* ride.

2. kid, spoof, clown around, fool around, pull [s.o.'s] leg, *Inf.* put [s.o.] on, *Inf.* give [s.o.] a hard time, *Inf.* needle, *Inf.* rib, *Inf.* josh, *Sl.* jive, *Sl.* get a rise out of [s.o.]; taunt, twit, tweak, gibe, chaff, rally, pluck by the beard, *Inf.* roast, *Inf.* dig, *Sl.* razz, *Sl.* rag; mock, make fun of, poke fun at, call [s.o.] names.

teat, *n.* nipple, tit, titty, *Chiefly Dial.* pap, (*of animals*) dug, *Anat.* mammilla, papilla; pacifier, sugar-tit.

technical, *adj.* **1.** specialized, involved, intricate, complicated, detailed; precise, strict, exact, literal.

2. skilled in, familiar with, conversant with, at home in, versed in, practiced in, experienced in, trained in; competent in, proficient at, adept in, able, cabable, efficient.

technician, *adj.* specialist, authority, expert, proficient, adept, mavin, master hand, *Chiefly Brit. Inf.* dab hand, *Brit. Dial.* dabster; maestro, virtuoso, talent, genius, prodigy, standout, *Inf.* wizard, *Inf.* whiz, *U.S. Sl.* crackerjack, *Sl.* shark, *Inf.* sharp; professional, *Inf.* pro, veteran, journeyman, past master, past mistress, old hand, old stager.

technique, *n.* **1.** manner, method, way, means, wise, fashion, mode, style; system, approach, attack, procedure, course, tack, line; mode of operation, *Latin. modus operandi, Inf.* MO, manner of working; habit, custom, pattern, routine, order, standard operating procedure, *Inf.* SOP.

2. methodology, procedures, methods.

3. technical skill, apitude, ability, faculty, talent, gift, genius, endowment, facility; flair, bent, turn, knack, way, touch; skillfulness, dexterity, dexterousness, adroitness, address, deftness; qualifications, experience, knowledge, know-how; competence, competency, capableness, adeptness, proficiency, savoir-faire; mastery, expertness, expertise, efficiency, efficacy.

tedious, *adj.* dull, boring, boresome, tiresome, wearisome, wearying, tiring, wearing; long, lengthy, drawn out, dragged out, prolonged, long-drawn; long-winded, prolix, wordy, verbose, windy; monotonous, unvarying, unchanging, undeviating, repetitious, soporific, sleep-inducing; uneventful, humdrum, routine, uniform, all the same, unvaried, undiversified; tasteless, bland, insipid, jejune, flat, vapid, *Sl.* blah; uninteresting, ho-hum, *Sl.* dead, dry, dry-as-dust, unexciting, uninspiring, dreary, drab, *Scot. and North Eng.* dree; ponderous, heavy, weighty, burdensome, cumbersome.

tediousness, *n.* tedium, monotony, monotonousness, boredom, ennui, dullness, humdrum, stuffiness. See **tedium.**

tedium, *n.* tediousness, monotony, monotonousness, routine, fixed routine, rut, groove, fixed schedule; lack of variety, changelessness, uniformity, sameness, selfsameness; repetition, iteration, reiteration, recurrence, redundancy; boredom, ennui, *U.S. Sl.* the blahs, low spirits, doldrums, malaise; dullness, lack of excitement, uneventfulness, humdrum, stuffiness, wearisomeness; prosaicness, prosiness, triteness, platitudiousness, banality, ordinariness, commonness, commonplaceness; tastelessness, blandness, insipidity, insipidness, jejuneness, jejunity, flatness, vapidity, vapidness; dryness, *Sl.* deadness, drabness, dreariness.

teem[1], *v. Usu.* **teem with** abound, swarm *or* swarm with, pullulate, burst with, bristle with, be alive with, crawl with, be rife with; be stocked with, be full of, be filled *or* stuffed with, be crowded *or* overcrowded with, be jammed *or* packed with; overflow with, overspill with, brim *or* overbrim with, superabound with, exuberate with; be overun with *or* by, be overspread with *or* by, be overgrown with, be infested with; be prolific, be fertile, be productive, increase, multiply, proliferate.

teem[2], *v.* empty *or* empty out, void, egest, *Physiol.* evacuate, clear out; pour out *or* forth, discharge, emit, eject, send forth *or* out, expel, excrete.

teeming, *adj.* **1.** *Usu.* **teeming with** abounding, swarming with, bursting with, bristling with, alive with, crawling with, *Sl.* lousy with; stocked with, full *or* filled with, stuffed with, crowded *or* overcrowded with, jammed with, packed with; jam-packed, filled to the brim *or* hilt, *Inf.* filled to the gills, filled to overflowing; overflowing with, overspilling with, brimming *or* overbrimming with, superabounding with; overrun with, overspread with, overgrown with, infested with.

2. prolific, fertile, philoprogenitive, yielding, fruitful, fructuous, feracious; fecund, proliferative, proliferous; productive, generative, fructificative, fruitive, fruit-bearing, fructiferous; propagative, propagatory, propagational, multiplicative, regenerative; profuse, abundant, superabundant, plenteous, *Rare.* uberous; exuberant, luxurious, lush, rank, rife, rich, flush, copious, bounteous, rich.

teen-age, *adj.* teen, teen-aged; young, youthful, juvenile, juvenescent; pubescent, adolescent, minor, under legal age.

teen-ager, *n.* teen, teener, teenybopper, teeny; youth, juvenile, adolescent, minor.

teeter, *v.* **1.** seesaw, move *or* bob up and down, pitch; oscillate, vibrate, librate; fluctuate, vacillate, dither.

2. stagger, totter, rock, reel, sway, *Dial.* wamble, roll; wobble, waggle, waddle, waver, zigzag; flap, flop, lurch, jerk, hunch, hitch, lumber; tip, tilt, lean, sag, bend.

teetotaler, *n.* nondrinker, abstainer, nephalist, water-drinker, hydropot; temperance advocate, W.C.T.U. member, prohibitionist, *Inf.* dry, blue-ribbonist, blue-ribbonite, blue-ribboner, *Chiefly Brit.* pussyfoot; puritan, ascetic; Rechabite, Encratite.

teetotalism, *n.* See **temperance** (*def.* **2**).

telegram, *n.* telegraph, wire, cable, cablegram, *Inf.* telex; lettergram, night letter, day letter, singing telegram; radiogram, radiotelegram, *Rare.* marconigram; dispatch, message, *Trademark.* Mailgram; bulletin, flash.

telegraph, *n.* **1.** ticker, stock ticker, news ticker, Telex, teleprinter, wire; radiotelegraph, wireless, marconigraph.

—*v.* **2.** wire, cable, send by wire, send collect, send press collect; flash, radio.

telepathy, *n.* mental telepathy, ESP, extrasensory perception, psychometry, mind reading, thought transference; clairvoyance, second sight, reading [s.o.] like a book, having eyes in the back of one's head.

telephone, *n.* **1.** phone, line, party line, *Sl.* horn; pay telephone, dial *or* push-button telephone, wall *or* desk telephone, videophone.

—*v.* **2.** phone, call, give *or* put in a call, call up, ring, ring up, *Inf.* buzz, *Inf.* give a buzz, dial, *Sl.* get on the horn; call long distance, make a long distance *or* l.d. call, *Chiefly Brit.* make a trunk call, call station-to-station *or* person-to-person, call collect, reverse the charges; give a wake-up call.

telescope, *n.* **1.** scope, glass, spyglass; field glasses, binoculars, opera glasses; periscope, microscope.

—*v.* **2.** shorten, abbreviate, truncate, cut, cut short; condense, reduce, boil, boil down, abstract, capsulize, summarize, brief, synopsize, abridge; compact, compress, contract, tighten, make tight; consolidate, squeeze together, jam together, slide into each other.

television, *n.* **1.** broadcast, telecast, *Sl.* videocast, airing.

2. TV, television set, TV set, video, *Sl.* tube, *Sl.* boob tube, *Sl.* idiot box, *Sl.* box, *Sl.* box in the living room, *Brit. Inf.* telly, small silver screen, cable TV; console, cabinet, set.

tell, *v.* **1.** narrate, relate, report, recount, rehearse, recite; describe, portray, depict, detail, explain; delineate, sketch, picture, paint; romance.

2. vociferate, voice, give mouth *or* voice to, air, vent, ventilate, communicate, let be known; impart, inform, *Inf.* tip off, utter, declare, *Archaic.* discover, break the news; reveal, make known, disclose, divulge, bring out, bring out into the open, bring to light; release, break, report, publish, *Archaic.* divulgate, print; advertise, broadcast, proclaim, announce, herald, trumpet.

3. disbosom, disembosom, get [s.t.] off one's chest, make a clean breast of [s.t.], unburden oneself, confess, *Sl.* fess up, own up, admit, acknowledge; blurt out, blab, leak, give away, *Inf.* let out, let slip, let the cat out of bag, spill the beans, *Sl.* blow the lid off; *Inf.* give away the whole show, *Sl.* spill one's guts, *Sl.* open up; betray, *Inf.* blow the whistle on, *Sl.* pull the plug on, *Inf.* pull the rug out from underneath [s.o.]; tattle, tattletale, *All Sl.* squeal, squeak, rat, fink, stool, peach.

4. discern, make out, espy, perceive; recognize, identify.

5. command, order, direct, charge, adjure, instruct, dictate; require, demand, lay down the law, give orders, determine; bid, request.

6. count, enumerate, number; compute, reckon, calculate, tally, cast, sum up, estimate.

7. weigh, carry weight, have force, be influential.

telling, *adj.* **1.** effective, striking, forceful, cogent, convincing, authoritative, weighty; important, of great import, portentous; influential, forcible, potent, powerful, *Literary.* puissant, clear, plain, certain, sure, positive, definite, evident, luculent; valid, sound, believable, proving, conclusive, unanswerable; persuasive, suasory, efficacious.

2. revealing, expressive, suggestive, telltale. See **telltale** *(def.* **3**).

telltale, *n.* **1.** tattler, talebearer, whisperer; gossip, gossipper, gossipmonger, newsmonger, rumormonger, scandalmonger; loud mouth, *Inf.* blabbermouth, *Sl.* big mouth; *Sl.* yenta, tabby, cat; quidnunc, busybody, Paul Pry, snoop, meddler, *Australian.* stickybeak, eavesdropper.

2. giveaway, hint, clue, tip, inkling, *Sl.* tip-off, cue; omen, foreshadowing, warning, signal, sign.

—*adj.* **3.** revealing, revelatory, *Inf.* giveaway, expressive, informative, communicative, demonstrative, exhibitive; suggestive, meaning, meaningful, significant, significative, indicative, symptomatic.

temerity, *n.* **1.** foolhardiness, rashness, recklessness, incautiousness, carelessness, heedlessness; impetuosity, impetuousness, hot-headedness, impulsiveness; imprudence, improvidence, indiscretion, injudiciousness; audacity, boldness, courage, bravery, valor, hardihood, resoluteness, stalwartness; daring, derring-do, venturesomeness, adventurousness, fearlessness, intrepidity; backbone, grit, nerve, mettle, spirit, pluck, *Inf.* spunk, *Inf.* starch, *Inf.* guts.

2. effrontery, impudence, *Inf.* cheek, *Inf.* brass, gall, bumptiousness; forwardness, *Sl.* chutzpah, assertiveness, *Inf.* pushiness; presumption, presumptuousness, insolence, impertinence; brazenness, brassiness, sauciness, rudeness, *Sl.* mouth, *Sl.* lip.

temper, *n.* **1.** disposition, temperament, constitution, state *or* frame of mind, mood, spirits, humor; nature, condition, vein, tone, tenor, grain, type, character, spirit.

2. ill humor, petulance, peevishness, irritability, huffishness, churlishness, surliness; sulks, sulkiness, moroseness, sullenness; irascibility, volatility, explosiveness, *Inf.* short fuse, *Inf.* low boiling point; impatience, excitabilty, hotheadedness, hot-bloodedness.

3. tantrum, fit, outburst, pet, *Brit. Inf.* paddywhack; discomposure, disorder, agitation; perturbation, vexation, annoyance, irritation, exasperation; pique, dudgeon, umbrage, tiff; anger, *Inf.* dander, passion, ire, choler, wrath, indignation; resentment, spleen, bile, animus; animosity, hostility, acrimony, asperity, bitterness, virulence, gall, rancor; acerbity, harshness.

4. composure, coolness, *Inf.* cool, sang-froid; poise, self-control, self-possession, equanimity, equableness, level-headedness.

—*v.* **5.** moderate, mitigate, abate, reduce, diminish, lessen, weaken; alleviate, palliate, allay, assuage; appease, soothe, *Archaic.* attemper, relieve, ease; soften, tone down, slacken, remit, relax, lighten, cushion; modify, qualify, adapt, adjust, suit.

6. mold, knead, shape, fashion, form.

7. toughen, anneal, harden,indurate; strengthen, fortify, steel.

temperament, *n.* **1.** disposition, mettle, nature, humor, spirit, temper, grain, mood, vein; outlook, mind-set, fame of mind; character, make-up, inner man, qualities, constitution, idiosyncrasy.

2. inclination, bent, bias, leaning, tendency, turn, direction; predisposition, *Pathol.* diathesis, subjectability, liability, proclivity, propensity; readiness, willingness, weakness; predilection, liking, affection, penchant, appetite.

temperamental, *adj.* **1.** distinctive, individual, special, unique, singular, particular; idiosyncratic, peculiar, eccentric.

2. moody, irritable, ill-humored, snappish, snappy, huffish, huffy, curt, short, impatient; high-strung, nervous, sensitive; touchy, testy, thin-skinned, waspish, peevish, petulant; irascible, choleric, ill-tempered; crabby, crabbed, cranky, grouchy, grumpy, cantankerous, crotchety, crusty.

3. constitutional, inherent, innate, inborn, congenital; deep-rooted, ingrained.

temperance, *n.* **1.** moderation, self-restraint, self-control; refrainment, forbearance, desistance; abstention, nonindulgence, abstemiousness; continence, celibacy, fasting; Puritanism, austerity, self-mortification, self-deprivation; asceticism, self-denial, self-abnegation.

2. teetotalism, nephalism, abstinence, sobriety, soberness; prohibition, blue-ribbonism; Rechabitism.

temperate, *adj.* **1.** moderate, self-restrained, self-controlled, self-disciplined; self-possessed, in control, self-assured, self-confident, poised; composed, cool, calm, collected, cool-headed; level-headed, equanimous, balanced; sane, lucid, clear, rational, reasonable, sensible; unruffled, imperturbable, unflustered, reposed, at ease; tranquil, peaceful, content, serene; subdued, quiet, soft, mellow, toned down.

2. abstemious, habitually abstinent, nonindulgent; fasting, dieting; continent, celibate, chaste, virginal, virgin; refraining, forbearing, desisting, self-depriving, self-mortifying; puritanical, puritanlike, austere, strict, severe; ascetic, self-denying, self-abnegating, self-sacrificing.

3. teetotal, sober, not intoxicated *or* drunk, *Inf.* sworn off, *Sl.* on the wagon *or* water wagon, *Brit.* on the water cart; prohibitionary, *U.S.* dry, blue-ribbon.

4. clement, fair, mild, gentle, pleasant; good, nice, warm, sunny; genial, balmy, soft, soothing; cool, comfortable, refreshing; calm, peaceful, tranquil, halcyon.

tempest, *n.* **1.** violent storm, squall, barat, williwaw; hurricane, typhoon, tornado, whirlwind, *U.S.* twister, cyclone; thunderstorm, thundersquall, windstorm; blizzard, northeaster, snowstorm; duststorm, duster, sirocco, harmattan, sandstorm, simoon, samiel.

2. disturbance, disruption, disorder, outbreak, breach of the peace; tumult, turmoil, turbulence, hurly-burly, upheaval; unrest, disquiet, excitement, commotion, imbroglio, confusion, chaos, furor, agitation.

tempestuous, *adj.* **1.** stormy, violent, wild, procellous, turbulent, squally; windy, gusty, blustery, blusterous, howling, roaring, raging.

2. fierce, intense, impassioned, inflamed, fiery, strong, vehement; loud, noisy, boisterous, raving, ranting; wrathful, furious; frantic, worked-up, wrought-up, frenzied, frenetic, feverish, out of control.

temple, *n.* church, house of worship, house of God, synagogue, *Yiddish.* shul, mosque, pagoda; holy place, sanctuary, delubrum, shrine, naos, dagoba; holy of holies, sanctum sanctorum, ark; chancel, *Eccles.* sacrarium, conventicle, chapel, chantry, oratory, prayer house, *Hinduism.* ashram *or* asmara; cathedral, *It. duomo,* basilica; joss house; ziggurat.

tempo, *n.* **1.** time, meter, measure; rate, pace, velocity, speed, *Inf.* clip, gait, stride, career; progress, movement, motion.

2. rhythm, beat, pulse, throb; pulsation, cadence, cadency, rhythmicity; periodicity, recurrence, reoccurrence, intermittence.

temporal, *adj.* **1.** secular, nonspiritual, profane, nonreligious, secularistic, mundane; lay, laical, nonclerical, nonecclesiastic, nonchurch; material, carnal, mortal; earthly, worldly, of this world, terrene, terrestrial, telluric, sublunar, sublunary.

2. temporary, passing, impermanent. See **temporary** (*def.* **1**).

temporarily, *adj.* **1.** fleetingly, flittingly, flickeringly, transiently; quickly, swiftly; briefly, shortly, for the moment, for the minute, for a short time; momentarily, for a while, for a little while, for a short spate.

2. for the meantime, in the interim, in the intervening time, *Fr. en attendant;* for the time being, pro tem, for now, for the nonce.

temporary, *adj.* **1.** passing, impermanent, transient, unenduring, perishable, mortal; transitory, ephemeral, fleeting, flitting, evanescent, fading, fugacious; here today and gone tomorrow, fly-by-night, fugitive, flash-in-the-pan; brief, short, short-termed, short-lived, momentary, soon past.

2. makeshift, juryrigged, stopgap, stand-by, reserve, backup, *Inf.* make-do, *Inf.* band-aid, utility, pinch; provisional, spare, provisory, ad hoc.

temporize, *v.* **1.** procrastinate, delay, pause, hang back; wait, play a waiting game, hesitate, *Inf.* drag one's feet, *Inf.* footdrag, put off, gain time, play for time, sleep on it; hold off, hold [s.t.] up, lay [s.t.] over, refrain from further action, let the matter stand; vacillate, waver, hover, debate, deliberate, think twice about; equivocate, evade, hedge, fence, quibble; *Inf.* stall, stave off, *U.S.* filibuster; detain, retard, hold back, set back.

2. tarry, linger, lag, drag, loiter, idle, trifle, dally, dillydally, dawdle, poke along; waste time, twiddle one's thumbs, sleep on the job; shirk, dodge, hedge, quit, *Sl.* welsh, malinger.

3. accommodate, agree, give in, back off, *Inf.* back down, trim, yield, *Rare.* stoop; politick, politicize, act the timeserver, bide one's time, look after one's own interests, feather one's nest, *Inf.* take care of number one, know which side one's bread is buttered on.

4. compromise, effect a compromise, come to terms with; yield to circumstances, comply with occasions, fall in with current opinion, fall in step, come into line.

temporizer, *n.* **1.** delayer, postponer, procrastinator, cunctator; shirker, dodger, hedger, quitter, *Sl.* welsher, malingerer.

2. waster, wastrel, prodigal, good-for-nothng, do-nothing, Micawber, *U. S.* bum; idler, trifler, fainéant; drifter, loafer, tramp.

3. trickster, schemer, shuffler, intriguer, fox, *Obs.* sly-boots.

4. opportunist, timeserver, self-seeker, trimmer, profiteer, jobber; worldling, fortune hunter.

tempt, *v.* **1.** entice, allure, seduce, lure; fascinate, engage, infatuate, carry away, enamor; excite, titillate, magnetize, draw; beguile, captivate, charm, attract, appeal; enthrall, enrapture, bewitch, ensorcel; tease, whet the appetite, tickle.

2. induce, persuade, cajole, coax, *Inf.* sweet-talk; blandish, lead down the primrose path, suck in; inveigle, prevail upon, move, prompt; influence, sway, bring, carry, lead; hypnotize, mesmerize, make.

3. provoke, instigate, goad, prick, spur; dare, put to the test, *Sl.* play chicken with; invite, incite, bait, court, woo, flirt; solicit, summon, beckon, fetch; seek, ask for, look for, play with.

temptation, *n.* **1.** enticement, allurement, seduction, seducement; fascination, tantalization, captivation; beguilement, enthrallment, enchantment, bewitchment, bewitchery, ensorcellment, entrancement.

2. cajoling, inducement, persuasion, coaxing; blandishment, inveiglement, swaying; provocation, instigaton, dare; invitation, incitation, flirtation, summoning beckoning.

3. lure, bait, decoy, trap, snare, song of the sirens; heart's desire, desire, hope, desideratum; forbidden fruit, plum, golden apple; honeyed words, *Sl.* come-on.

tempter, *n.* **1.** enticer, seducer, charmer, enchanter, tantalizer, teaser; seductress, enchantress, sorceress, temptress, *Fr. femme fatale,* flirt, coquette, vamp; flatterer, deceiver, inveigler, blandisher, fascinator; Siren, Lorelei, Circe; vampire, Pied Piper of Hamelin.

2. Satan, Lucifer, Beelzebub, Mephistopheles; the devil, the Evil One, the Prince of Darkness, the Archfiend.

tempting, *adj.* **1.** inviting, alluring, attractive; enchanting, bewitching, witching, enthralling, charming, entrancing, enravishing; provocative, exciting, fascinating, captivatng; titillating, irresistible, intriguing, appealing; exquisite, ravishing, voluptuous, sensuous; seductive, enticing, *Inf.* foxy, *Inf.* sexy; engaging, winning, taking, fetching, winsome, prepossessing.

2. appetizing, mouth-watering, luscious, savory, delectable, delicious, toothsome, flavorsome, succulent.

tenable, *adj.* **1.** maintainable, sustainable, supportable, justifiable, defensible, defendable, impregnable, invulnerable, invincible; irrefutable, indisputable, incontestable, unarguable, unattackable, unassailable, unassaultable, unquestionable, undeniable, indubitable, sure, certain; ironclad, strong, solid, secure, safe, sound, safe and sound, on safe *or* sure ground, solidly based; cogent, logical, rational, reasonable, sensible; plausible, believable, credible, acceptable, conceivable, imaginable, thinkable, possible, within the realm of possibility.

2. holdable, tenantable, leasable, rentable, occupiable, habitable, livable, usable; unoccupied, available, open vacant, untaken, *Inf.* up for grabs.

tenacious, *adj.* **1.** adhesive, clinging; holding fast, keeping a firm hold; cohesive, tough; viscous, viscid, sticky, mucilaginous, glutinous, gummy.

2. retentive, retaining, unforgetful, unforgetting; grasping, recollective.

3. steadfast, determined, resolute, purposeful, strong-minded, strong-willed; persistent, pertinacious, unfaltering, undeviating, unswerving, unshaken; unchangeable, unalterable, uncompromising, unyielding, inflexible, intransigent; obstinate, stubborn, dogged, mulish, *Inf.* cussed, pigheaded, stiff-necked, perverse; opinionated, bigoted, prejudiced, biased, partisan, dogmatic; grim, set, hard-set, hard-bitten; arbitrary, relentless, inexorable, adamantine; obdurate, refractory, contumacious.

tenacity, *n.* **1.** tenaciousness, adhesiveness, adhesion, cohesiveness, toughness, strength, resilience; viscousness, viscidity, glutinousness, stickiness, gumminess, mucilaginousness.

2. retentivity, retentiveness, retention; readiness of memory, grasp, grip, remembrance, recollection, reminiscence, retrospection.

3. steadfastness, persistence, perseverance; continuance, endurance, abidingness, patience; stamina, indefatigableness, backbone, courage, grit, *Inf.* sand, pluck, *Sl.* guts; application, zeal, ambition, devotion, diligence, pursuance, sedulity, sedulousness, *Inf.* stick-to-it-iveness; resolve, determination, purposefulness, purposiveness, decisiveness, pertinacity.

4. stubborness, mulishness, doggedness, *Inf.* cussedness, inflexibility; insistence, insistency, intransigence, intransigency, obstinacy, obstinateness; obdurateness, contumacy, contumaciousness; intolerance, bigotry, bias, partisanship, prejudice, narrow-mindedness, perversity.

tenancy, *n.* **1.** holding, possession, possessorship; freehold, householdership, title, ownership, proprietorship, proprietary, demesne, *Law.* domain, *Archaic.* aught; tenantry, renting, leasing, lesseeship, leasehold, interest, share, *Finance.* stock; occupancy, occupation, residence, residency, inhabitance, inhabitancy, inhabitation, habitation, habitancy, domiciliation, *Law.* commorancy; lodgement, lodging, billeting, quartering; sojourn, visit, stay, stop, stopover, stop-off, layover.

2. tenure, length of residence; incumbency, term of office, time in office, length of service.

3. position, post, office, place, billet, slot, *Brit.* berth; appointment, assignment, commission, sinecure, job.

tenant, *n.* **1.** lessee, leaseholder, renter, roomer, lodger, paying guest; tenant farmer, métayer, sharecropper; sojourner, guest, houseguest, house-sitter; occupant, occupier, resident, resider, residencer, residentiary, addressee, inhabitant, habitant, *Archaic.* inhabiter; holder, possessor, shareholder, boxholder, landholder, householder, owner; homesteader, squatter, settler, cottager, cottier, *Scot.* cotter.

—*v.* **2.** lease, rent, pay for room and board.

3. *Usu.* **tenant in** inhabit, occupy, reside in, dwell in, live in, room *or* lodge in; hold, possess, own.

tend[1], *v.* be disposed, be inclined, have a tendency, show a tendency, trend, lean, point to, look to; verge, bend, incline, gravitate toward, be directed, be bound for; bear, head, aim, lead, steer toward, make for; conduce, contribute, predispose, influence.

tend[2], *v.* attend to, care for, serve, wait on, pander to, minister to; watch over, guard, keep, protect, take care of; accommodate, oblige, favor; help, aid, assist, abet, succor, relieve, comfort, give solace; nurse, nurture, doctor.

tendency, *n.* **1.** inclination, disposition, proclivity, propensity, leaning, bent, turn, cast, inclining, *Biol.* tropism; tending, bearing, verging, gravitation, drift; proneness, subjectability, aptness, liableness, likeliness, susceptibility.

2. penchant, predisposition, predilection, partiality; prejudice, tendentiousness, bias, preference; affinity, attraction; appetite, appetency, relish.

tender[1], *adj.* **1.** unfibrous, butterlike, crushable, soft, silken.

2. weak, delicate, feeble, frail, frail as a reed, unsturdy, slight, infirm; shaky, tottery, precarious, uncertain, unstable; poor, sickly, unwell, unhealthy, unsound, weakly; wretched, pitiful, pitiable, piteous.

3. immature, inexperienced, callow, unripe, unseasoned, undeveloped, uninitiated, untrained; raw, green, young, wet behind the ears, youthful, juvenile; impressionable, pliable, plastic.

4. subdued, muted, softened, toned down, pastel; subtle, fine, quiet, tame, mellow, mild.

5. gentle, light, smooth, easy, lambent; sensitive, sympathetic, warm.

6. tender-hearted, kind, compassionate. See **tender-hearted.**

7. affectionate, cordial, friendly, amiable, pleasant, agreeable; loving, amatory, amorous, fond, adoring, devoted; melting, emotional, sentimental, romantic.

8. sensitive, sore, easily pained, smarting, painful, hurting; aching, throbbing, red, inflamed, irritated.

9. ticklish, touchy, difficult, arduous, risky, dangerous; knotty, involved, complicated, complex, perplexing, baffling, troublesome.

tender[2], *v.* **1.** present, proffer, offer; propose, suggest, recommend, put forward, hold out, extend; volunteer, give up, cede, yield; pose, set forth, advance, propound; submit, set before; bid, proposition, make overtures, make advances.

—*n.* **2.** offer, proffer, proposal, proposition, offering, presentation; recommendation, suggestion, advice, submission; overture, invitation, bid.

3. payment, recompense, compensation; legal tender, currency, money, monies, specie, coin, cash, bills, notes, bank notes, dollars, *Sl.* spondulicks.

tender[3], *n.* **1.** caretaker, watcher, watchman, night watchman, watchdog, lookout, observer; sitter, babysitter, house-sitter.

2. dinghy, dispatch boat, launch, pilot boat, tugboat, tug, lighter; jollyboat, rowboat, motorboat, outboard, runabout, skiff, scow, dory, gig.

tenderfoot, *n.* **1.** novice, tyro, beginner, neophyte, youngling, freshman, abecedarian; learner, student, pupil, disciple; intern, apprentice, trainee, probationer; fledgling, cub, recruit, raw recruit, rookie, entrant, initiate, novitiate, catechumen.

2. newcomer, *Dial.* newie; immigrant, greenhorn, settler, pioneer, homesteader; new kid, new kid on the block.

tender-hearted, *adj.* soft-hearted, responsive, sensitive, feeling, perceptive, understanding, thoughtful, considerate, outgoing; sympathetic, compassionate, pitying, ruthful, concerned, caring, solicitous, moved, touched; comforting, consoling, supportive; generous, magnanimous, big-hearted, with a heart as big as all outdoors; humane, kind, kindly, kindhearted, soft, gentle, good; good-natured, warm-hearted, warm, merciful, charitable, giving; open, open-hearted, benevolent, benignant; close, friendly, neighborly, helpful.

tenderness, *n.* **1.** immaturity, callowness, rawness, greenness, youth, youthfulness.

2. delicacy, softness, subtlety, fineness, mellowness.

3. tender-heartedness, soft-heartedness, responsiveness, sensitivity, susceptibility, feeling, perception, understanding, thoughtfulness, consideration; sympathy, compassion, pity, ruth, concern, solicitousness; generosity, magnanimity, big-heartedness, charity, good-heartedness, mercy; humaneness, humanity, humanitarianism, decency, niceness, goodness; kindness, gentleness, kindliness, warm-heartedness, kind-heartedness; openness, open-heartedness, forthrightness, selflessness, unselfishness.

4. affection, love, fondness, friendliness; warmth, ardor, devotion, adoration; intimacy, closeness, protectiveness.

5. trickiness, touchiness, ticklishnss; problem, trouble, snag, difficulty; danger, peril, risk, hazard.

tenement, *n.* **1.** dwelling, dwelling house, house, lodge, home, place where one hangs one's hat; abode, habitation, residence, domicile, boarding house.

2. tenement house, apartment house, warren, *Inf.* rookery, *Sl.* dump, slum; flophouse, *Sl.* fleabag, *Brit.* *Sl.* doss house.

3. apartment, flat, *Chiefly Brit.* diggings, *Chiefly Brit.* digs, quarters, lodgings, room, rooms, *Chiefly Brit.* maisonette, *Sl.* pad; cold-water flat, railroad flat, walk-up apartment, studio apartment, studio, penthouse, duplex.

tenet, n. belief, position, conviction, persuasion; assumption, presumpton, supposition; view, opinion, judgment; theory, thesis, hypothesis, postulation; faith, article of faith, creed, credo, ideology; principle, maxim, precept, canon, axiom, basic, fundamental, rule; doctrine, dogma.

tenor, *n.* **1.** purport, intent, meaning, tone, vein; implication, connotation, significance, signification; sense, import, spirit, gist, essence, core, pith; idea, point, burden, argument, sum and substance; intention, purpose, object, design, aim.

2. drift, tendency, direction, bias, trend; course, gravitation, bearing; inclination, bent, leaning, proclivity, propensity, penchant; impulse, drive, impetus, driving force; pressure, push, current, flow, run, movement, motion.

tense, *adj.* **1.** taut, tight, drawn tight; rigid, stiff, inelastic, uplastic, inflexible, unbending, unyielding.

2. nervous, high-strung, strained, under a strain, *Sl.* uptight, keyed up, wound up, choked up; worked-up, wrought-up, agitated, flustered, upset, bothered, perturbed; distressed, troubled, worried, concerned, disquieted; anxious, unquiet, fretful, restless, impatient, fidgety, itchy, itching, *Sl.* antsy; jumpy, jittery, edgy, on edge, *Inf.* on pins and needles, on tenterhooks; on a tightrope, on a cliff edge, waiting for the other shoe to drop, waiting for the ax to fall, waiting for the bomb to go off; uneasy, apprehensive, alarmed, with one's heart in one's mouth, fearful; frightened, scared, afraid; skittish, shy, timid, timorous; trembling, shaky, shaking.

—*v.* **3.** tighten, strain, draw tight, pull taut; stretch, extend, elongate, distend.

4. frighten, scare, affright, panic; choke, choke [s.o.] up, make nervous, key up, put on edge; disturb, distres, agitate, upset, dismay.

tension, *n.* **1.** tautness, tightness; extension, distension, elongation; pull, tug, yank, strain; stretch, draw, traction, tensity.

2. anxiety, uneasiness, disquiet, disquietude, inquietude, fretfulness; worry, trouble, concern, vexation; pressure, stress, heat, burden, cross, encumbrance, cumbrance; nervousness, ants, *Inf.* butterflies, *Sl.* heebie-jeebies, *Sl.* habdabs; excitement, agitation, perturbation; suspense, anticipation, expectation, apprehension, fear.

tent, *n.* wigwam, tepee, yurt, canvas, circus tent, (*in the circus*) *Inf.* big top, (*in the circus*) *Inf.* menagerie tent, pavilion, *Chiefly Brit.* marquee, pup tent, camping tent; baldachin, canopy, awning; booth, *Hebrew.* sukkah, lean-to.

tentative, *adj.* **1.** experimental, probative, probatory, exploratory; probationary, on probation, temporary, on trial, under examination *or* consideration: trial, test, pilot; untried, unproven, in the trial stages, unperfected; questionable, doubtful; hypothetical, speculative, theoretical.

2. unsure, uncertain, doubtful, hesitant; indecisive, wavering, faltering, wobbling, shilly-shallying, hedgy, undecided; provisional, contingent, dependent, *Inf.* iffy.

tenterhook, *n.* **1.** bent nail, hook, hanger.

2. on tenterhooks apprehensive, uneasy, anxious, qualmish, worried, alarmed, concerned; nervous, *Sl.* uptight, queasy, jittery, skittish, jumpy; on edge, edgy, on a cliff edge, on a tightrope, waiting for the ax to fall *or* for the other shoe to drop *or* for the bomb to go off.

See also **tense** (*def.* **2**).

tenuity, *n.* **1.** tenuousness, flimsiness. See **tenuousness.**

2. slenderness, thinness, fineness, leanness; gracility, gracileness, delicateness, delicacy; frailty, frailness, fragility, fragileness; sheerness, diaphaneity, diaphanousness; lightness, etherealness, airiness, unsubstaniality; refinement, subtlety, rareness; rarefaction, attenuation, etherealization, spiritualization, volatilization, vaporization.

tenuous, *adj.* **1.** thin, slender, attenuated, rare, rarefied; fine, airy, light, ethereal, frail, fragile, delicate, gossamer, gossamery.

2. unsubstantial, weak, flimsy; of little *or* no significance *or* importance, insignificant, unimportant, inconsequential; trivial, trifling, negligible, paltry, petty, niggling; doubtful, dubious, questionable, uncertain.

3. vague, general, nebulous, hazy; indefinite, ill-defined, unspecific, undetailed; sketchy, partial, unconvincing.

tenuousness, n. shakiness, insecurity, precariousness, *Sl.* hairiness; uncertainty, indefiniteness, doubtfulness, dubiousness; vagueness, haziness, nebulousness, fuzziness; weakness, flimsiness, insubstantiality. See also **tenuity** (*def.* **2**).

tenure, *n.* **1.** holding, possessing, possession, retention, *Law.* seizin; tenancy, tenantry, renting, leasing; occupancy, occupation, residence, residency, inhabitance, inhabitancy, inhabitation, habitation, habitancy, domiciliation, *Law.* commorancy.

2. incumbency, term of office, time in office, length of service; length of residence, stay, sojourn, visit, stop, stopover, stop-off, layover.

3. permanent status, permanency, permanence; job security, guarantee of continued employment.

tergiversate, *v.* **1.** vacillate, shilly-shally, seesaw, *Inf.* flip-flop, blow hot and cold, waver; shift, hedge, fence, beat around the bush; equivocate, prevaricate, quibble, *Inf.* waffle, fudge, palter, lie; evade, dodge, elude, weasel out, shuffle; qualify, trim, modify, compromise; double-talk, *Inf.* talk out of both sides of one's mouth, *Inf.* straddle, hold with the hare but run with the hounds; backtrack, back-pedal, sidetrack, mislead, deceive, mystify, dissemble.

2. turn renegade *or* traitor, change loyalties, shift ground; veer round, do an about-face, reverse oneself; renege, back out, bail out, bow out, *Sl.* cop out, *Inf.* crawfish; defect, abandon allegiance, desert, change sides, break faith, go over, bolt, apostatize.

term, *n.* **1.** word, vocable, phrase, locution, expression; name, designation, denomination, appellation, title.

2. period, eon, era, epoch, age, time, days, years; space, spell, snap, interval, stretch, span, stage, duration, date; season, cycle.

3. reign, rule, presidency, administration, ministry, incumbency.

4. semester, session, course; sentence.

5. terms a. conditions, provisions, provisos, stipulations, demands; articles, clauses, particulars, points, qualifications; premises, assumptions, suppositions. **b.** footing, standing, relations.

—*v.* **6.** call, name, designate, christen, baptize, style, dub, entitle, *Archaic.* clepe; label, tag, define.

termagant, *n.* virago, shrew, harpy, fury; vixen, spitfire, she-wolf, hell-cat, tigress; haridan, witch, ogress, old cat, brimstone, *Inf.* battle-ax; gorgon, hag, crone, beldam, *Sl.* bitch; nag, *Inf.* biddy, *Inf.* old biddy; scold, common scold, fishwife; grouch, crab, grumbler; henpecker, faultfinder, rebuker, reviler, vituperator, chider, castigator, Xanthippe.

terminal, *adj.* **1.** ending, bounding, limiting, bordering, boundary, restraining, confining, restrictive; fixed, clear-cut, determinate, definite.

2. terminating, closing, concluding, ultimate, final; fatal, deadly, mortal, lethal, *Archaic.* lethiferous.

—n. **3.** end, boundary, terminus, termination; limit, bound, border, edge, verge, bourn, mete, frontier, march; extremity, utmost extent, apex, pinnacle, summit, *Latin. ne plus ultra.*

terminate, *v.* **1.** end, complete, conclude, bring to an end, abort; finish, close, (*in radio and T.V.*) sign off, discontinue, cease, drop; expire, run out, lapse, wind up; accomplish, achieve, consummate.

2. bound spatially, form the extremity of, set bounds to; define, delimit, limit, demarcate; circumscribe, encompass, confine.

termination, *n.* **1.** end, conclusion, close, cessation; completion, consummation, accomplishment, achievement; finish, ending, finis, windup, denouement, *Rhet.* peroration, epilogue, fall of the curtain, lights out.

2. boundary, limit, terminal. See **terminal** (*def.* **3**).

terminology, *n.* nomenclature, terms, language, vocabulary; wording, phrasing, phraseology, locution; jargon, *Inf.* lingo, argot, cant; bureaucratese, journalese, newspaperese, businessese, shoptalk, Washingtonese, Pentagonese, officialese, newspeak, educationese, cinemaese, legalese, medicalese.

terminus, *n.* **1.** end, extremity, furthermost part, terminal; pole, point, nib, tip, top, head, horn; limitation, bound, boundary, limit, pale, bourn; border, confine, margin; acme, apogee, ultimate, utmost, uttermost, extreme.

2. goal, objective, aim, target, mark.

terrestrial, *adj.* **1.** earthly, terrene, tellurian, telluric, *Archaic.* earthy; earthbound, sublunary, subastral, *Bot., Zool.* geophilous; *Class. Myth.* chthonic *or* chthonian.

2. mundane, worldly, temporal, subcelestial; secular, profane.

terrible, *adj.* **1.** unbearable, unendurable, intolerable, insufferable, more than flesh and blood can bear, *Inf.* too much; extreme, severe, harsh, rough, grim.

2. odious, obnoxious, abominable, abhorrent, loathsome, hateful, despicable, detestable, contemptible; disgusting, repugnant, repulsive, revolting, gross; foul, filthy, vile, *Inf.* lousy, *Inf.* rotten.

3. formidable, redoubtable, awesome, awe-inspiring, awful; dread, dreadful, dire, fell; fearful, frightful, horrifying, terrifying, *Inf.* terrific, harrowing; horrible, horrific, horrid, horrendous, unspeakable; hideous, gruesome, grisly, macabre.

terrific, *adj.* **1.** *Informal.* superb, splendid, sensational, exceptional, *Sl.* terrif; marvelous, *Sl.* marvy, *Sl.* far-out, *Inf.* out of this world; wonderful, smashing, superfine, superexcellent, *Inf.* super-duper, *Sl.* super, *Australian,* bonzer; great, excellent, first-class, outstanding, standout, superior, *Inf.* A-1 *or* A-one *or* A number one, *Sl.* bang-up, *Brit. Sl.* bang on, *Brit. Sl.* spot-on.

2. *Informal.* intense, extreme, tremendous, *Inf.* whacking, *Inf.* thumping, *Inf.* rousing.

3. *Informal.* terrible. See **terrible** *(def.* **3**).

terrified, *adj.* horrified, horror-struck, terror-stricken, awe-struck; frightened out of one's wits *or* skin, scared to death, *Sl.* scared stiff; petrified, paralyzed, frozen, stupefied, stunned; unnerved, unmanned, undone, unstrung, *Sl.* spooked.

terrify, *v.* terrorize, fill with terror, consternate, *Chiefly Scot.* fley, *Archaic.* affright; scare to death, *Sl.* scare stiff, *Inf.* scare *or* frighten out of one's wits *or* senses; stun, paralyze, petrify, freeze, strike dumb, put one's heart in one's mouth; appall, shock, horrify, curdle one's blood, make one's blood run cold, make one's hair stand on end, make one's flesh creep, send chills *or* shivers up one's spine.

territorial, *adj.* **1.** geographical, topographic; regional, sectional, zonal.

2. local, localized, insular, provincial, parochial, topical.

territory, *n.* **1.** area, region, zone; district, precinct, quarter; neighborhood, purlieu, vicinity, vicinage, *Inf.* neck of the woods, *Sl.* turf, *Sl.* home turf *or* ground.

2. state, county, canton, shire, department.

3. orbit, orb, ambit, sphere; field, pale, arena, realm, domain; bailiwick, jurisdiction.

terror, *n.* **1.** fear, fright, *Archaic.* affright, horror; dread, awe, consternation, dismay, fear and trembling; panic.

2. *Informal.* hellion, *Inf.* holy terror, *Inf.* spitfire; hoodlum, *Sl.* hood, tough, *Inf.* ugly customer, *Inf.* plugugly; devil, demon, brute, fiend; beast, monster, mad dog.

terrorism, *n.* **1.** piracy, brigandage, banditry; buccaneering, freebooting, privateerng, filibustering.

2. commandeering, hijacking, skyjacking, air *or* sky piracy; abduction, kidnapping, *Sl.* snatch, capturing, holding hostage; impressment, conscription, manstealing.

3. incendiarism, arson, fire-bombing, bomb planting.

4. intimidation, bullying, browbeating, threatening; tyranny, despotism; coercion, pressure, armtwisting, extortion, blackmail.

terrorist, *n.* **1.** desperado, gunman, gangster, criminal, mafioso, (*in Paris*) apache; thug, tough, mugger, ruffian, rowdy, hoodlum, *Sl.* hood, *Inf.* goon, hooligan, roughneck, *Inf.* baddy, *Australian Sl.* larrikin, *Brit. Hist.* Mohock.

2. highwayman, footpad, *Sl.* yegg *or* yeggman, bandit, *Sp. bandolero,* outlaw, *Southwest U.S.* ladrone, *Australian.* bushranger, brigand; picaroon, rogue, (*in India and Burma*) dacoit.

3. revolutionary, insurgent, rebel, subversive; nihilist, anarchist, destroyer, radical, *Derog.* Bolshevik; incendiary, arsonist.

4. abductor, kidnapper; hijacker, skyjacker, sky *or* air priate; assassin, bravo, murderer.

5. pirate, rover, viking, corsair, buccaneer, privateer; freebooter, rapparee, (*in the Scottish highlands*) cateran; pillager, plunderer, marauder, despoiler, depredator, ransacker, sacker, looter, rifler, forager, raider.

6. malefactor, miscreant, villain, hellhound, fiend, knave, blackguard; lawbreaker, felon, cutthroat, murderer, robber, thief.

7. bully, browbeater, hector, intimidator, *Sl.* bulldozer, *Inf.* terror; coercer, dictator, despot, tyrant.

terrorize, *v.* **1.** terrify. See **terrify.**

2. dominate, rule with an iron hand *or* fist, oppress, beat down, tread *or* trample underfoot; intimidate, cow, overawe, put in bodily fear; menace, threaten; bully, dragoon, coerce, *Inf.* strong-arm, *Inf.* bulldoze, ride roughshod over; daunt, unman, unnerve.

terse, *adj.* laconic, elliptical, short-winded, breviloquent, *Rare.* pauciloquent, sparing of words; concise, succinct, brief, to the point, short and sweet; compact, concentrated, close, neat, lean, compendious, packed, *Inf.* meaty; pithy, sententious, epigrammatic, crisp, precise, exact, gnomic; straightforward, direct, emphatic, trenchant, mordant, mordacious; curt, short, clipped, bluff, brusque, blunt.

test, *n.* **1.** trial, essay, attempt, try, *Inf.* crack; tryout, dry run, audition; feeler, trial balloon.

2. examination, exam, checkup, check-out; scrutiny, scrutinization, inspection, close observation; investigation, study, analysis; exploration, probe, search.

3. quiz, interrogation, the third degree, cross-examination, cross-questioning, *Inf.* grilling, catechism; questionnaire, set of questions, flyer; inquiry, inquest, inquisition; day of reckoning, moment of truth.

4. criterion, touchstone, standard, measure, model, pattern.

—v. **5.** assay, try, try out, experiment with, subject to trial, (*of ideas, plans, etc.*) *Inf.* bounce off [s.o.]; put to the test, prove, put to trial; check, double-check, cross-check, check out; feel one's way, fumble, grope.

6. examine, analyze, inspect, scrutinize; investigate, probe, explore; sound, fathom, plumb; evaluate, assess, appraise, judge.

7. interrogate, give [s.o.] the third degree, cross-examine, cross-question, *Inf.* grill, pump; sound out, quiz, question closely, catechize, *Inf.* put through the paces.

testament, *n.* **1.** *Law.* will, last will and testament, *Law.* devise, *Law.* legacy, *Law.* bequest.

2. (*between God and man*) covenant; Old Testament, New Testament, Scriptures, the Bible.

testify, *v.* **1.** attest, witness, bear witness, evidence, offer evidence, depone; depose, certify, certificate, warrant; document, circumstantiate, manifest, show, demonstrate; confirm, prove, bear out, verify, validate, establish, authenticate, corroborate, substantiate, sustain, uphold, vindicate; endorse, vouch for, support, back up, stand behind *or* by.

2. swear to, state under oath, allege, plead; vow, give one's solemn word *or* promise, pledge, state on one's honor, promise; avouch, asseverate, assure, offer assurance, affirm.

3. declare, protest, assert, profess; avow, own, acknowledge, admit, confess to; proclaim, speak out for, announce, make known.

testimonial, *n.* **1.** recommendation, letter, letter of recommendation, reference, referral, voucher, credential; citation, commendation; good word, favorable mention, honorable mention, blurb, *Inf.* plug; sanction, approval, approbation, endorsement.

2. memorial, remembrance, memento, souvenir; trophy, medal, ribbon.

testimony, *n.* **1.** evidence, information, witness, attestation, sworn statement, statement, document, *Law.* affidavit, *Law.* deposition, *Law.* exemplification; documentation, circumstantiation, demonstration; corroboration, substantiation, support, ground; certification, certificate, *Law.* acknowledgement, confirmation, proof, verification, validation, establishment, authentication.

2. declaration, proclamation, announcement, protestation, testification; asseveration, averment, avouchment, affirmation, assertion, profession; avowal, acknowledgment, admission, owning up, confession.

testiness, *n.* irritability, petulance, snappishness, irascibility, touchiness, tetchiness, prickliness; peevishness, waspishness, raspiness, fretfulness, edginess, nervousness; excitability, fieriness, inflammability; grouchiness, crankiness, crabbedness, grumpiness, cantankerousness, huffiness, crabbiness; churlishness, bearishness, crotchetiness, gruffness; spleen, choler, moodiness, ill nature, ill humor, ill temper; crossness, crustiness, sharpness, asperity, tartness, acerbity; resentfulness, chip on the shoulder, fractiousness, captiousness, querulousness, contentiousness.

testy, *adj.* touchy, irritable, tetchy, snappish, petulant, irascible; peevish, huffish, waspish, raspy, peppery, fretful; huffy, edgy, on edge; grumpy, cranky, grouchy, snarling, crotchety, churlish, bearish; gruff, cantankerous, impatient, crabby; splenetic, choleric, dyspeptic, moody, sullen, temperamental, out of sorts; cross, crusty, crabbed, ill-tempered, ill-humored; excitable, fiery, inflammable, hasty, quick, trigger-happy; high-strung, hot-tempered, hot-blooded, thin-skinned, quick-tempered; sharp, sharp-tongued, tart, acerbic; fractious, quarrelsome, querulous, contentious, resentful, captious; currish, shrewish, vixenish.

tête-à-tête, *n.* **1.** private conversation, pillow talk, talk, dialogue, duologue, interview; chat, coze, causerie, confabulation, *Inf.* confab, discussion, *Sl.* rap, *Sl.* schmooze.

—adv. **2.** in private, privately, behind closed doors, *Law.* in camera, secretly, in secret; confidentially, entre nous; vis-à-vis, face-to-face, side by side.

tether, *n.* **1.** cord, chain, rope, tie, thong, line, lead, leash.

2. supply line, cable, connection, link, *Anat.* umbilical cord.

—v. **3.** tie *or* tie up, chain, rope, bind, lash, leash, fasten, secure, stake, picket.

text, *n.* **1.** matter, contents, body, main body, subject matter, printed matter; words, context, wording, wordage, phrasing, choice of words.

2. subject, theme, topic, motif; concern, focus, point, issue, case, idea, question; gist, essence, meat, substance.

3. textbook, reference book, manual, primer, hornbook, schoolbook; grammar, reader, speller, workbook, exercise book.

texture, *n.* **1.** weave, weaving, nap, pile, tissue, fabric; grain, surface, make, denier, feel, touch, granulation; fiber, woof, warp and woof, tooth; contexture, intertexture, crossing, intertwinement, interlacement; mesh, net, web, meshwork, network, webwork; weft, cloth, stuff, warpage, weftage.

2. structure, build, frame, make; make-up, constitution, composition, arrangement, organization; fabrication, formation, set-up, *Inf.* get-up, format.

thank, *v.* **1.** acknowledge, be grateful, give thanks, offer thanks, show one's appreciation, tender thanks; recognize, credit; appreciate, tip, requite, reward, return; repay, recompense, return a favor.

—n. **2. thanks** acknowledgement, credit, cognizance, recognition; thanksgiving, hearty thanks, grace, grace before *or* after meals, *Brit.* grace before *or* after meat; benediction, paean, hymn, praises, Te Deum, tribute; reward, recompense, requital, tip, thank-offering.

3. thanks thank you, I thank you, many thanks, much obliged, much appreciated, I appreciate it, *Obs.* gramercy; thank you kindly, *Chiefly Dial.* thankee, *Brit. Sl.* ta; *Fr. merci, Fr. merci bien* or *beaucoup, Ger. danke, Ger. danke schön, Sp. gracias, It. grazie, Russ. spasibo.*

4. thanks to owing to, because of, due to, due to the fact that; by reason of, as a result of, as, through, since.

thankful, *adj.* grateful, appreciative, obliged; indebted, beholden, under obligation; mindful, gratified, pleased, contented; blessing, praising.

thankfulness, *n.* gratitude, gratefulness, appreciation, appreciativeness, thanks; sense of obligation, beholdenness, obligedness, indebtedness; regard, regards, wishes; acknowledgement, recognition, credit.

thankless, *adj.* **1.** unappreciated, unrewarded, unrewarding, unacknowledged; unrequited, unreturned, unavowed; vain, in vain, useless, for nothing, forgotten.

2. ungrateful, unthankful, unappreciative, *Archaic.* ingrate; unmindful, heedless, inconsiderate, unthinking.

thaw, *v.* **1.** melt, soften, dissolve, liquefy, liquidize, turn into water, liquesce, deliquesce, melt away, leave nothing but a puddle; puddle, flow, stream, run.

2. *Sometimes* **thaw out** defrost, unfreeze, deice, take out of the freezer; warm up, heat up, put in the oven, put in front of the fire.

3. relax, loosen up, become more responsive, let oneself go, *Sl.* go with the flow; bend, give quarter, give an inch, give ground, yield, relent, forbear, give in, submit, acquiesce; break the ice, get [s.t.] going, get the juices flowing.

—n. **4.** melting, melt, ice-out, spring thaw; spring, warm weather, warmth.

theater, *n.* **1.** playhouse, odeum, auditorium, hall, lyceum; arena, colloseum, amphitheater; opera house, opera, music hall, concert hall; cabaret, night club, dinner theather; summer theater, strawhat theater; regional theater, repertory theater.

2. movie theater, movie palace, cinema, kino, *Brit.* picture house *or* palace, first-run house, second-run house; drive-in *or* drive-in theater.

3. audience, *Archaic.* auditory, congregation, house, gallery, *Inf.* peanut gallery.

4. troupe, company, theatrical *or* acting company, repertory company, stock company.

5. **the theater** drama, dramaturgy, dramatic art, dramatic performance, histrionic *or* thespian art; show business, *Inf.* show biz; the stage, the boards.

6. field of operations, seat *or* theater of war; scene *or* place of action.

theatrical, *adj.* **1.** dramatic, dramaturgic, dramaturgical, theatric; scenic, stagy; operatic; histrionic, histrionical, thespian, Roscian, *Sl.* ham *or* hammy, *Sl.* actressy.

2. affected, mannered, unnatural, forced, campy; artificial, false, insincere, put-on, *Inf.* fake, *Sl.* phony; overdone, overacted, overwrought; emotive, emotionalistic, overemotional, melodramatic; sensational, spectacular, *Sl.* grandstand.

3. pompous, bombastic, turgid, orotund, grandiloquent, stilted, self-important.

theft, *n.* **1.** stealing, thievery, pilferage, pilfering, *Sl.* swiping, *Sl.* hustling, *Sl.* copping; peculation, embezzlement, misappropriation; shoflifting, palming, *Sl.* boosting; purse-snatching; smuggling, bootlegging.

2. burglary, robbery, *Law.* larceny, *Sl.* heist; break-in, *U.S. Inf.* hold-up, *U.S. Sl.* stick-up, *Inf.* mugging.

3. expropriation, appropriation, arrogation, usurpation, accroachment, assumption; plagiarism, copying, *Inf.* cribbing, *Inf.* lifting.

4. dispossession, deprivation, deprival, divestiture, bereavement.

5. commandeering, hijacking, skyjacking, air *or* sky piracy; (*all usu. of persons*) kidnapping, capture, seizure, rape, impressment, conscription, man-stealing, child-stealing; (*all of animals*) poaching, deerjacking, petnapping, dognapping, (*of cattle*) rustling.

6. brigandage, piracy, buccaneering, freebooting, banditry, highway robbery, *Obs.* latrociny, privateering, filibustering.

7. swindle, fraud, flimflam, confidence game, thimblerigging, *Inf.* gyp, *Sl.* ripoff.

8. plunder, plundering, plunderage, rapine, pillage, depredation, spolation, despoliation, despoilment, *Obs.* direption, raven.

theme, *n.* **1.** topic, subject, subject matter, matter *or* issue at hand, topic under discussion *or* on the floor *or* up for debate, proposition, question, problem, argument; text, sum and substance, major *or* greater part *or* portion; keynote, main idea, gist, meaning; idea, concept, notion, point.

2. essay, composition, paper, manuscript; story, piece, article, *Sl.* thing; exposition, think piece, commentary, editorial; review, opinion, interpretation, critique, criticism; study, monograph, research paper, thesis, dissertation, disquisition, discourse, treatise, tract, tractate, homily.

3. motif, leitmotif, strain, melody, recurrent pattern; mood, tone, air, *Archaic.* tune.

then, *adv.* **1.** at that time, on that occasion, thereat, at that moment *or* minute *or* second *or* instant; instantaneously, right then, immediately, at once; at the same time, at the same time as, concurrently with, together with, along with.

2. thereupon, immediately following that, right after that; soon afterward, after that, afterwards; next, next on the agenda, moving right along, following that, subsequent to that, subsequently, at a subsequent time, later, at a later time; finally, in conclusion, at the end, to top it off.

3. therewith, in addition, besides, still, else, more; on top of that, as a bonus, to boot, on the side; also, too, yet again, as well, moreover, furthermore, further, additionally; on the other hand, however, but, but also, but remember *or* don't forget.

4. in that case, since *or* seeing that *or* if that's the case, in which case, that being the case, that being so, if *or* since *or* seeing as that's what happened; under those situations *or* this situation, accordingly, taking that into consideration.

5. so, therefore, thus, ergo; for this *or* that reason, on that account, because of that *or* this; consequently, as a consequence *or* result, resultingly, hence, thereafter, thence.

thence, *adv.* **1.** from there, therefrom, from a certain place *or* source.

2. since then, ever since, thenceforth, thenceforward, thereafter, thereinafter.

3. therefore, thus, so, ergo, that being the case, in that case. See **then** (*defs.* **4, 5**).

theologian, *n.* **1.** divine, religious scholar, hierophant, hierologist, theologist, *Rare.* theologician, *Derog.* theologaster; exegete, textualist; canonist, decretist; patrist; rabbi, Talmudist, Talmudic scholar; Christian philosopher, Church Father, Doctor of the Church.

2. divinity student, *U.S. Inf.* theologue, *Rom. Cath. Ch.* scholastic.

theological, *adj.* **1.** doctrinal, dogmatic, dogmatical, canonical, ecclesiastical, rabbinical, theologic, hierologic, heirological, hagiological.

2. Biblical, Scriptural, evangelical, textual, textuary; isagogic, exegetic, hermeneutic, hermeneutical.

3. apostolic, patristic, patristical, prophetic, prophetical.

4. divine, religious, sacred, spiritual, holy.

5. mystical, theosophical, theosophic.

theology, *n.* **1.** divinity, religion, hierology, hagiography, hagiology, *Rare.* theologics; theosophy; patrology, patristics; rabbinism.

2. Scripture, the Gospel, revelation, theopneusty; Torah, Talmud; isogogics, exegesis, exegetics, hermeneutics.

3. canon law, dogmatics, dogma, doctrine, teaching; homiletics, preaching.

4. creed, credo, belief, tenet, *Inf.* philosophy of life

theorem, *n.* **1.** theoretical proposition *or* statement, hypothesis, theory, thesis, postulate; question, problem, moot point.

2. rule, law, dictum, axiom, assumption; idea, concept, belief, method.

theoretical, *adj.* theoretic, pure, unapplied, abstract, impractical, unrealistic; ideal, ideational, ideological, academic, doctrinaire; hypothetical, conjectural, notional, speculatory, moot, postulatory, assumed, suppositive, supposititious, suppositional, putative, presumptive.

theorist, *n.* theoretician, theorizer, speculator, hypothesist, hypothesizer, philosopher, doctrinaire, ideologist; dreamer, woolgatherer.

theorize, *v.* hypothesize, speculate, conjecture, propose, posit, predicate, put forth; assume, suppose, presume, presuppose; impute to, ascribe to, assign as cause, derive from, account for; divine, guess, suspect, fancy.

theory, *n.* **1.** hypothesis, conjecture, speculation, surmise, thesis, theorem; assumption, presumption, supposition, postulate; ascription, attribution, imputation; divination, guesswork, shot, intuition.

2. system of principles, science, school; philosophy, doctrine, pandect, dogma; idea, concept.

therapeutic, *adj.* therapeutical, curative, medicinal, medical, curing, healing, sanative, sanatory; remedial, corrective, reparative, reparatory; mending, restorative, restoring, recuperative, recuperatory; beneficial, advantageous, helpful, salutary, salutiferous, healthy, good, wholesome.

therapy, *n.* treatment, remedial treatment, allopathy, homeopathy; hydropathy, hydrotherapy; preventive treatment, *Med.* prophylaxis; speech therapy, physical therapy, P.T., physiotherapy, massage, occupational therapy, O.T.; psychotherapy, group therapy.

there, *adv.* in that place, at that place, thereat; to that place, into that place, thither, thitherward, to *or* toward that point; over there, yonder, *Chiefly Dial.* yon, *Archaic.* yond, over yonder; at that point; in that matter, in that respect.

thereabouts, *adv.* **1.** about that time, near that time, around that time, approximately that time; about then *or* there, near then *or* there, around then *or* there, approximately then *or* there; about that place, near that place, around that place, by that place, thereby.

2. about that number, about that amount, about that much; nearly, almost, about, circa; roughly, approximately, in round numbers.

thereafter, *adv.* afterwards, afterward, after, after that, then, next, subsequently, thereupon; in after times, latterly, later, ultimately, posteriorly, ensuingly; thence, thenceforth.

therefore, *adv.* consequently, as a result, in which case, hence, whence, thence, wherefore, ergo, accordingly, so, then, thus; for that reason, for which reason, on that account, on account of, because of, due to, owing to.

thermal, *adj.* thermic, thermogenic, calorific; lukewarm, warm, heated, hot, sudorific, *Med.* diaphoretic.

thesaurus, *n.* **1.** dictionary, lexicon, wordbook, synonymy, synonym finder, crossword puzzle dictionary; encyclopedia, cyclopedia.

2. storehouse, warehouse, *Brit.* pantechnican; depository, treasury, cache, vault, repository, receptacle; arsenal, armory.

thesis, *n.* **1.** proposition, argument, side, opinion, view, belief; theory, theorem, hypothesis, idea, supposition, assumption, premise, conjecture, axiom, postulate; statement, declaration, assertion, allegation, charge; question, topic under discussion *or* on the floor *or* up for debate, moot point.

2. theme, topic, subject, area *or* field of inquiry; concept, conceit, notion; keynote, main idea, gist, meaning, point.

3. research paper, study, investigation, dissertation, master's thesis; monograph, disquisition, discourse, treatise, tract, tractate, homily.

thespian, *adj.* **1.** histrionic, histrionical, Roscian, *Sl.* ham *or* hammy, *Sl.* actressy; dramatic, dramaturgic, dramaturgical, theatrical, theatric, tragic; scenic, stagy; operatic.

—*n.* **2.** actor, actress, player, playactor, stage player, stage performer, performer, role player, trouper; theatrician, histrio, histrion, *Archaic.* histrionic, Roscian, *Sl.* ham; personator, impersonator.

thew, *n.* **1.** *Usu.* **thews** muscle, sinew, tendon, *Anat.* ligament.

2. **thews** physical strength, brawn, beef, muscle, physique, musculature; *Inf.* huskiness, *Inf.* heftiness, *Inf.* beefiness, burliness, brawniness, muscularity, sinewiness; hardness, firmness, solidness; power, potency, might, *Literary.* puissance; energy, vigor, vitality; activeness, athleticism, manliness, virility, able-bodiedness.

thick, *adj.* **1.** broad, wide, beamy; large, big, ample, bulky, solid.

2. close-packed, close, dense, gross, heavy, crowded, serried; impenetrable, impermeable, impassable, thickset; compact, tight, compressed, condensed, consolidated.

3. abundant, plentiful, plenteous, numerous, *Inf.* aplenty; full, filled, *Inf.* chock-full, jammed, packed, *Inf.* jam-packed, crammed, stuffed; rife, replete, abounding, overflowing, running *or* spilling over, bristling; teeming with, swarming with, crawling with, alive with, *Sl.* lousy with, thick with.

4. profound, deep, mysterious; intense, extreme, acute, excessive.

5. husky, hoarse, dry, scratching, cracked; harsh, rough, raucous, gruff, raspy, gravelly, grating; guttural, throaty, raspy; indistinct, unclear, blurred, muffled, inarticulate, confused.

6. viscous, viscid, glutinous, ropy, mucilaginous; inspissated, *Pharm.* incrassated; clotted, grumous, curdled, coagulated; gelatinous, congealed, jellified, jelled, jellied, set.

7. turbid, roily, roiled, muddy, sedimentous, feculent.

8. misty, foggy, nubilous, vaporous, soupy, murky, obscure; hazy, smoky, smazy, smoggy, polluted.

9. *Informal.* chummy, clubby, inseparable, hob-and-nob, hand and glove, *Sl.* buddy-buddy, *Sl.* palsy-walsy, *Inf.* thick as thieves; well-acquainted, familiar, close, *Scot.* pack, dear, intimate, confidential, bosom; friendly, comradely, brotherly, sisterly.

10. stupid, unintelligent, dull-witted, dull, slow, *Sl.* lamebrained, *Inf.* dopey, *Inf.* dill, oxlike; duncish, obtuse, bovine, *Inf.* cretinous, stolid, Boeotian; empty-headed, brainless, dim-witted, slow-witted, half-witted, fat-witted, beef-witted, thick-witted; boneheaded, wooden-headed, doltish, blockheaded, blockish, imbecilic, *Inf.* moronic.

thicken, *v.* **1.** inspissate, condense, *Pharm.* incrassate; gelatinize, congeal, jell, jellify, jelly, set, solidify, harden; curdle, clabber, coagulate, clot, cake.

2. grow more intense, intensify, deepen, become intricate, become complex.

thicket, *n.* copse, *Chiefly Brit.* coppice, *Brit.* spinney, small wood, grove, bosket, *Archaic.* bosk, brake, canebrake; brushwood, *Southwestern U.S.* chaparral, underbrush, undergrowth, *Hunting.* covert; scrub, shrubbery, hedges; bush, jungle.

thickhead, *n.* blockhead, dunce, lunkhead, bonehead, knucklehead, fathead, pinhead, numskull; fool, tomfool, dope, nincompoop, ninny, lightweight; oaf, boor, lout, dolt, dullard, *Inf.* chump, lummox, looby, *Sl.* klutz; idiot, simpleton, half-wit, lamebrain, pinbrain, moron, cretin, imbecile; *All Sl.* chump, sap, dumbbell, dingbat, ding-a-ling, meatball, meathead, jerk, booby, boob, noodle, blubberhead, nudnik, schmuck, schlemiel, *U.S.* schmo.

thickheaded, *adj.* stupid, unintelligent, dull-witted, duncish, obtuse, *Inf.* cretinous, half-witted, dense, thick. See **thick** (*def.* **10**).

thickness, *n.* **1.** denseness, density, body, bulk, bulkiness, heaviness, weight; measure, width, breadth, diameter; consolidation, compactness, closeness, crowdedness.

2. inspissation, condensation; viscosity, viscidity, glutinousness; coagulation, congelation, jellification, gelatinization, solidification.

3. layer, stratum, ply, sheet.

thickset, *adj.* **1.** dense, close-packed, crowded. See **thick** (*def.* **2**).

2. stocky, heavyset, thick, solid, stodgy; stout, sturdy, burly, beefy, brawny; squat, stubby, *Inf.* stumpy.

thickskinned, *adj.* **1.** pachydermatous, elephantine, hippopotamic, rhinocerotic.

2. callous, tough, obdurate, hardened, hard, hardboiled, steeled; inured, casehardened; insensitive, insensate, numb, unfeeling, insentient, insensible.

thief, *n.* **1.** pilferer, filcher, *Sl.* ripoff *or* rip-off artist, purloiner, stealer, *Inf.* crook, *Sl.* ganef; shoplifter, pickpocket, cutpurse, purse-snatcher, lightfingered Louie, *Sl.* dip; *Psychol.* kleptomaniac.

2. burglar, robber, housebreaker, *Sl.* cracksman, picklock, Raffles, sneak thief, cat burglar, *Inf.* secondstory man; *Inf.* hold-up man, *Sl.* stick-up man, mugger; safecracker, Jimmy Valentine.

3. swindler, fleecer, bilker, rook, trickster, sharper, *Inf.* hawk, cardsharper, bunko steersman, blackleg; confidence man, con artist, flimflam artist, racketeer, highbinder, thimblerigger, *Brit. Sl.* magsman, *Australian.* spieler; defaulter, *Sl.* welsher; embezzler, peculator.

4. highwayman, footpad, *Sl.* yegg *or* yeggman, bandit, *Sp. bandolero, Southwest U.S.* ladrone, *Australian.* bushranger, brigand, picaroon, desperado; outlaw, gangster, criminal, mafioso; thug, ruffian, rogue, (*in India and Burma*) dacoit.

5. kidnapper, abductor, rustler; hijacker, skyjacker, air *or* sky pirate; pirate, rover, viking, corsair, privateer, buccaneer; marauder, freebooter, (*in the Scottish Highlands*) cateran.

6. poacher, deerjacker; smuggler, contrabandist, runner, bootlegger; fence.

7. extortioner, extortionist, blackmailer; usurer, loan shark, *Sl.* bleeder.

8. forger, counterfeiter, *Brit. Inf.* coiner; plagiarist, plagiarizer, *Inf.* cheater, *Inf.* copier.

thieve, *v.* **1.** steal, rob, pilfer, purloin, finger, filch, *Inf.* snitch, cabbage, abstract, *Chiefly Brit.* prig, *Euph.* borrow; peculate, embezzle, misappropriate; shoplift, *Sl.* boost, walk off *or* away with; burglarize, burgle, break in; *All Sl.* heist, pinch, hook, swipe, hustle, rip off, frisk, crook, cop, lift.

2. appropriate, expropriate, arrogate, usurp; commandeer, hijack, skyjack; pirate, plagiarize, copy, *Inf.* lift, *Inf.* crib, forge; counterfeit, *Brit. Inf.* coin.

3. (*usu. of persons*) abduct, kidnap, *Sl.* snatch, make off with, carry off, rape, seize; (*usu. in reference to military service*) impress, press, conscript, *Naut.* shanghai, crimp.

4. swindle, defraud, cheat, fleece, *Inf.* flimflam, rook, bilk, *Inf.* welsh, *Archaic.* chouse, *Inf.* do out of, *Inf.* gyp, *Inf.* bunko, *Inf.* diddle, *Inf.* take, *Inf.* take [s.o.] for a ride, take [s.o.] to the cleaners, *Sl.* pluck, *Sl.* chisel, *Sl.* clip.

5. victimize, take in, take advantage of, *Inf.* euchre out of, put across *or* over on, foist, palm off on, *Sl.* con, *Sl.* screw, *Sl.* bag.

6. plunder, despoil, spoliate, pillage, ravage, harry, ransack, sack, loot, gut, fleece, strip, rifle; pirate, freeboot, buccaneer, privateer, filibuster.

7. poach, deerjack; smuggle, bootleg, *Inf.* sneak [s.t.] in.

8. mooch, sponge, scrounge, freeload.

thievery, *n.* **1.** stealing, pilferage, pilfering, filching, purloinging, theft, thieving, *Inf.* snitching, *Law.* larceny, *Sl.* swiping, *Sl.* copping; shoplifting, palming, *Sl.* boosting; purse-snatching.

2. peculation, embezzlement, misappropriation; swindling, defrauding, bilking, fleecing, sharking, *Sl.* conning, thimblerigging, cardsharping, *Sl.* hustling; fraud, swindle, confidence game.

3. extortion, usury, blackmail, shakedown, bloodsucking, leeching, rapacity.

4. forgery, counterfeiting; plagiarism, pirating, *Inf.* copying.

5. robbery, burglary, *Inf.* hold-up, *Sl.* stick-up, *Inf.* mugging, break-in; breaking and entering, safecracking, second-story work.

6. brigandage, piracy, buccaneering, freebooting, banditry, highway robbery, *Obs.* latrociny, privateering, filibustering, *U.S. Inf.* (*usu. of cattle*) rustling.

7. plundering, plunderage, rapine, pillage, depredation, spoliation, despoliation, despoilment, *Obs.* direption; ravaging, harrying, marauding, sacking, *Rare.* sackage, laying waste, devastation, desolation; raid, razzia, foray; foraging, looting, ravishment, seizure, grab, rape.

8. commandeering, hijacking, skyjacking, air *or* sky piracy; (*usu. of persons*) abduction, kidnapping, *Sl.* snatch, capture, impressment, conscription, manstealing, child-stealing; (*all of animals*) poaching, deerjacking, petnapping, dognapping.

9. expropriation, appropriation, arrogation, usurpation, accroachment, assumption; dispossession, deprivation, deprival, divestiture, bereavement.

10. thievishness, *Psychol.* kleptomania; (*among animals*) cleptobiosis, lestobiosis.

thievish, *adj.* **1.** light-fingered, sticky-fingered, *Rare.* kleptic, *Humorous.* furacious; thieving, pilfering; piratical, plundering, pillaging, marauding; preying, predatory, predatious, rapacious.

2. stealthy, furtive, clandestine, surreptitious, secretive; sneaking, slippery, sly, evasive.

3. dishonest, fraudulent, underhand, underhanded; unprincipled, unscrupulous, crooked, corrupt.

thievishness, *n.* **1.** *Psychol.* kleptomania, *Humorous.* furacity *or* furaciousness; *All Inf.* sticky fingers, light fingers, itching palm.

2. rapacity, rapaciousness, ravenousness, ravening; greed, avarice, avariciousness, acquisitiveness.

3. dishonesty, fraudulence, underhandedness; knavery, roguery, villainy, unscrupulousness; corruptibility, bribability, venality.

thimbleful, *adj.* capful, spoonful, teaspoonful, mouthful, swallow, sip, sup, drop, droplet; dab, dot, spot, bit, bite, mite, pinch, dash, trifle; touch, tinge, trace, suspicion, soupçon, suggestion; morsel, piece, fragment, scrap, crumb, grain, granule, particle, moit, mote; speck, fleck, smidgen, *Inf.* smitch, jot, whit, iota; minimum, pittance, modicum, driblet.

thin, *adj.* **1.** thinnish, lean, spare, attenuate, attenuated; narrow, slender, slim, gracile, svelte, lithe, graceful; slight, wispy, wisplike; skinny, twiggy, thin as a reed *or* rail, narrow as an arrow, thin as six o'clock, slender as a thread, too skinny to throw a shadow, skin-and-bones, fleshless; gaunt, lank, lanky, bony, rawboned, skeletal; spindly, spindle-legged, spindle-shanked, *Sl.* chicken-legged, gangling, gangly, weedy; scrawny, scraggy, looking like a plucked chicken; scrubby, puny, runty, undersized, undergrown, small, stunted; light, underweight, undernourished, underfed, half-starved, starved-looking; hollow-cheeked, pinched, withered, shriveled, shrunken, wasted, emaciate, emaciated.

2. sparse, scattered, thinly distributed, widely dispersed, infrequent, few and far between; insufficient, inadequate, in short supply, hard to come by.

3. watery, waterish, diluted, dilute, watered-down; rarefied, rare, not dense.

4. scant, scarce, unplentiful, unplenteous; scanty, poor, deficient, lacking, wanting; little, small, paltry, piddling, meager, mere.

5. flimsy, insubstantial, unsubstantial, weak, feeble, frail, fragile; diaphanous, airy, sheer, light, translucent, transparent, see-through; delicate, fine, silken, silky, chiffon, gossamer, gauzy, filmy, cobwebby.

6. weak, small, tiny; gentle, soft, low, quiet, hushed, indistinct, unclear, faint, feeble; subdued, muted, muffled, barely audible, murmuring, whispering.

—*v.* **7.** *Often* **thin out** *or* **down** dilute, weaken, attenuate, extenuate, rarefy; mix, adulterate, *Inf.* water *or* water down, (*of alchol or drugs*) *Inf.* cut; eliminate, weed out, remove, get rid of; prune, trim, cut back.

8. *Often* **thin out** *or* **down** *or* **off** decrease, lessen, become smaller; dissipate, disperse, scatter, disappear.

thing, *n.* **1.** object, article, something, anything, it; substance, element, solid, stuff; lump of matter, matter, lump, blob; constituent, component, ingredient, building block; unit, monad, particle; entity, being, organism, creature, animal; indescribable something, *Fr. je ne sais quoi*; substantiality, materiality, individuality, corporeity, corporeality, hyle; physicality, embodiment, incarnation.

2. item, gadget, device, contrivance, mechanism, apparatus, *Fr. quelque chose*, bird in the hand; widget, hickey, what's-its-name, gimmick; *All Inf.* doohickey, dingus, dojigger, jigger, dofunny, do-hinkey, dowhackey; gizmo, fandangle, flumadiddle; contraption, whachamacallit, thingumajig, thingum, thingumabob, thingumadoodle, *Australian.* doover.

3. things matters, affairs, relations; business, concerns, work; doings, dealings, works, proceedings, operations, goings-on.

4. circumstance, situation, state of affairs, turn of events, course of events, conditions; fact, phenomenon, experience, matter, case; event, occurrence, incident, doing; happening, hap, episode, occasion.

5. action, deed, act, performance, feat; turn, exploit, move, coup, blow, stroke; adventure, proceeding, undertaking, endeavor, effort; accomplishment, achievement, doing, enterprise, measure, step.

6. particular, detail, instance, particularity, factor; item, point, special point, element, facet, minor detail, incidental detail, minutia; respect, feature, regard, aspect, reference, bearing, look.

7. aim, objective, goal, object, point, idea, purpose; intent, intention, design, scheme; end purpose, end in view, ultimate aim; implication, meaningfulness, significance, purport; ambition, view, desideration.

8. things a. utensils, tools, implements, articles, equipment; impedimenta, oddments, paraphernalia. **b.** belongings, possessions, effects, *Law.* choses, property; bags, baggage, luggage; goods, gear, kit, stuff, tackle, outfit; chattels, appurtenances, furnishings, parcels; accouterments, fittings, fixtures; equipage, *Law.* personalty. **c.** clothes, clothing, dress, raiment, wear, habit; wardrobe, *Inf.* togs, *Inf.* toggery, *Inf.* duds, *Inf.* threads, *Sl.* getup, rig, *Brit.* fig; garments, apparel, array, costume, attire; vestment, vesture, rigging, trappings, finery.

9. chore, task, job, duty, odd job; charge, assignment, detail, commission; errand, mission, project, service; homework, busywork, housework, yardwork, spadework, make-work.

10. *Informal.* quirk, phobia, *Fr. idée fixe*, superstition; fixation, obsession, crotchet; fear, mania, paranoia; dislike, aversion, distaste, loathing; terror, horror, abomination, consternation, trepidation.

11. *Slang.* liking, fancy, predilection, predisposition, preference, *Inf.* weakness; taste, bent, prejudice, partiality; inclination, tendency, leaning; *Sl.* bag, *Inf.* cup of tea.

think, *v.* **1.** conceive, imagine, image, picture; ideate, form an image of, think of, dream up; dream, envisage, visualize, make up, conjure, feature; concoct, hatch, brew, fabricate, fashion, form, formulate.

2. meditate, ponder, reason, deliberate; reflect, muse, brood, mull over, turn over in one's mind; wander about, chew one's cud, think about, kick around, tinker with, toy with, flirt with the idea; mentalize, cerebrate, chew over, be in a brown study, put on one's thinking cap, be lost in thought, lucubrate; cogitate, excogitate, cudgel one's brains, rack one's brains, use one's head; concentrate on, focus on, take to heart, *Archaic.* perpend; analyze, examine, review, turn over, revolve, weigh; study, con, evaluate, give attention to.

3. recollect, bear in mind, remember, recall, recall to mind; think back to, pass in review, retrace; call to mind, reminisce, bethink, carry one's thoughts back.

4. believe, opine, fancy, consider; suppose, conjecture, presume, assume, *Archaic.* trow, *Archaic.* ween; hold, maintain, esteem; surmise, speculate, daresay, suspect; judge, deduce, infer, conclude; hypothesize, theorize, posit, postulate.

5. consider, regard, view, look upon; acknowledge, deem, recognize; feel, divine, intuit; see, perceive, understand, comprehend, apprehend, reckon; value, estimate, gauge, appraise, assess, rate, prize.

6. intend, purpose, have in mind, have in view, mean; aim, project, arrange, plan, compass; propose, design, calculate, premeditate, determine, destine.

7. think better of reconsider, change one's mind, think twice, think over; reexamine, review, recheck, look at again, take under advisement, view in a new light.

8. think up devise, contrive, improvise, come up with; invent, create, originate; design, scheme, construct, frame, draft; coin, mint, neologize, neoterize.

thinkable, *adj.* **1.** conceivable, imaginable, cogitable; supposable, picturable, visualizable, fanciable; cognizable, cognoscible, apprehensible, knowable.

2. likely, possible, probable, presumable; believable, credible, plausible, tenable, reasonable.

thinker, *n.* philosopher, philosophe, idea man, theorist; sage, Solomon, *Hinduism.* rishi, *Class. Myth.* Nestor; savant, scholar, pundit, pantologist, rabbi, wise man, learned man, man of learning; wizard, *Inf.*

brain; mentor, master, mastermind, luminary, expert, authority; bookworm, bibliophile, highbrow, (*collectively*) intelligentsia.

thinking, *adj.* **1.** rational, reasoning, reasonable, sensible, cerebral; logical, practical, pragmatic; intelligent, knowing, ratiocinative, percipient, perceiving; analytic, ideational, philosophical, sophic; speculative, imaginative.

2. reflective, contemplative, cogitative, cogitating, meditative, meditating, musing, pondering; reflecting, ruminant, ruminating, introspective; pensive, thoughtful, concentrating, preoccupied, engrossed, rapt in thought, lost in thought, bemused, *Archaic.* museful; deliberative, excogitative, lucubratory, studious; conscientious, careful.

—n. **3.** reasoning, rationcination, rationalization, intellectualization; cerebration, brainwork, headwork, ideation, cogitation, excogitation; train of thought, association of ideas.

4. thought, logic, reason, judgment; opinion, conjecture, belief, view; conviction, persuasion.

5. contemplation, contemplating, meditation, consideration, rumination, ruminating, brown study, musing, pondering, brooding, mulling over, chewing over, chewing one's cud, wondering; deliberation, deliberating, speculation, speculating, conjecturing.

thinness, *n.* **1.** leanness, spareness, attenuation, skinniness; narrowness, slenderness, slimness, gracility, gracileness, slightness; gauntness, lankness, lankiness, boniness; scrawniness, scragginess, scrubbiness, puniness, runtiness, smallness.

2. sparseness, sparcity, scantness, scareness, scarcity, infrequency, infrequence; scantiness, paucity, insufficiency, inadequacy, inadequateness.

3. flimsiness, insubstantiality, unsubstantiality, weakness, feebleness, frailty, frailness, fragility, fragileness; diaphaneity, diaphanousness, airiness, sheerness, lightness; delicateness, delicacy, fineness, silkiness, gauziness, filminess; translucence, translucency, transparency, transparence, transparentness.

thin-skinned, *adj.* sensitive, oversensitive, hypersensitive, supersensitive, easily offended; touchy, temperamental, moody; testy, irritable, tetchy, snappish, petulant, irascible; sulky, sullen, resentful; humorless, grumpy, morose; prudish, prim, squeamish, queasy.

thirst, *n.* **1.** thirstiness, *Med.* polydipsia; dryness, parchedness, dehydration, desiccation.

2. craving, strong desire, eagerness, avidity, lust, lustfulness; desirousness, appetency, appetite, hunger, ravenousness, voracity, voraciousness; rapacity, rapaciousness, greed, greediness, cupidity, avarice, graspingness; longing, wish, wishing, desideration, want, wanting; yearning, hope, hoping, pining, sighing; hankering, *Inf.* yen, *Sl.* itch, *Sl.* the hots; fancy, fancying, coveting, covetousness.

—v. **3.** feel thirst, be thirsty, crave [s.t.] to drink; be dry, be parched, be dehydrated, be desiccated.

4. desire, crave, hunger for, have a strong desire for; lust after, burn for, pant for, be wild *or* mad about, *Sl.* have the hots for, *Inf.* letch after; wish for, long for, desiderate, want; yearn for, hope for, care for, pine for, sign for; hanker after, have a yen for, covet, fancy, have a fancy for, have an eye to, set one's heart on.

thirsty, *adj.* **1.** athirst, craving [s.t.] to drink; needing moisture, dry, droughty, parched, dehydrated, desiccated.

2. desirous, desiring, eager, avid, fain, longing, yearning, desiderative, hankering for, *Sl.* itching for; burning *or* burning for, *Sl.* hot for, lusting after, *Inf.* dying for; greedy, craving, appetitive, hungry, ravenous, voracious, omnivorous; covetous, avaricious, rapacious.

thong, *n.* strip, belt, strap, lash; cord, tie, rope, tether.

thorn, *n.* **1.** prickle, *Inf.* prickler, point, barb, barbule, spike, spicule, *Zool.* spiculum, spine, spinule, bristle, acicula; sticker, brier, *Bot.* apiculus, bur, burr, snag; nettle, bramble, cocklebur.

2. **thorn in one's flesh** *or* **side** pain in the neck, annoyance, nuisance, trouble, irritation, vexation; curse, torment, plague.

thorny, *adj.* **1.** prickly, brambly, briery; bristly, *Bot.* strigose, *Zool.* barbellate, setigerous, setaceous, setose; spiny, spinous, spinulose, acanthoid, like a porcupine, thistlelike, aciculate; spiky, barbed, *Bot., Zool.* muricate, spiculate.

2. thornlike, pointed, pointy, sharp, piercing.

3. painful, trying, difficult, hard, tough, rough, arduous; troublesome, bothersome, annoying, irritating, vexatious, irksome, nettlesome.

4. entangled, tangled, complicated, complex, intricate, involved, knotty; controversial, touchy, delicate, ticklish, critical.

thorough, *adj.* **1.** in-depth, *Inf.* all-out, leaving no stone unturned, top to bottom, stem to stern, head to toe *or* foot, A to Z, exhaustive; extensive, widespread, sweeping, all-inclusive, all-embracing, all-encompassing, universal, world-wide, global.

2. painstaking, careful, meticulous, particular, scrupulous, conscientious; punctilious, precise, exact, accurate, close, fine, nice, scientific, methodical.

3. total, entire, perfect, complete, *Chiefly Brit. Inf.* proper; out-and-out, unqualified, utter, sheer, thoroughgoing, absolute, unmitigated, downright, arrant; drastic, extreme, radical.

thoroughbred, *adj.* **1.** (*all usu. of animals*) purebred, pedigreed, highbred; pure, full-blooded, of unmixed race *or* stock.

2. high-spirited, mettlesome, high-strung, fiery, proud, headstrong, willful; courageous, bold, valiant, brave, daring, fearless, plucky, spunky; eager, fervent, zealous, avid, passionate.

3. elegant, graceful, *Scot.* genty, genteel, gentle, aristocratic, silk-stocking, patrician, noble, blueblooded; well-bred, refined, polished, finished, cultivated; polite, civil, civilized, courteous, mannerly, well-mannered, well-trained; gracious, ladylike, ladyish, fine, delicate; courtly, gentlemanly, gentlemanlike, chivalrous, chivalric, gallant, cavalier; debonair, charming, urbane, suave, sophisticated, cosmopolitan, worldly; fashionable, stylish, à la mode, modish, high-toned, *Sl.* tony, high-class, *Sl.* classy.

thoroughfare, *n.* **1.** throughway, road, street, avenue, boulevard, concourse, strip; main road, *Inf.* drag, *Brit. Sl.* toby, artery, highroad, roadway; highway, turnpike, pike, tollroad, state highway; freeway, *Brit.* clearway, expressway, parkway, causeway, *U. S. Inf.* interstate; speedway, autobahn, superhighway.

2. way, passage, passageway, alley, alleyway; bypath, byway, crosscut, shortcut; path, pathway, footpath, *Brit.* footway, towpath, bike path, bikeway; trail, track, walk, walkway, crosswalk.

3. strait, channel, canal, conduit, aqueduct, waterway, seaway; river, tributary, estuary.

thoroughly, *adv.* **1.** exhaustively, extensively, universally; from top to bottom, from stem to stern, from head to toe *or* foot, from A to Z, backwards and forwards.

2. completely, downright, entirely, absolutely, positively, most definitely, extremely, dead, *Sl.* stone; unreservedly, *Inf.* whole hog, to the full, to the hilt, *Sl.* like mad, *Sl.* like crazy.

though, *conj.* **1.** in spite of the fact that, despite the fact that, notwithstanding that, albeit, howbeit, although, even though.

2. even if, granting that, conceding that, allowing that, admitting that.

—adv. **3.** however, but, yet, still, even so, be that as it may, for all of that, nonetheless, nevertheless, all the same; rather, on the other hand, at the same time.

thought, *n.* **1.** conception, concept, idea, conceit; imagination, notion, whim, whimsy, vagary, crotchet, fancy.

2. cerebration, cerebrating, thinking, brainwork, headwork, lucubration; concentration, concentrating, focusing, having one's mind on, reflection, reflecting; cogitation, cogitating, meditation, meditating, contemplation, contemplating, musing, pondering; speculation, speculating, wondering about, consideration, deliberation, deliberating, excogitation; rumination, ruminating, chewing, mulling, brooding, brown study; recollection, recall, memory, remembrancy, reminiscence, retrospection, review.

3. intelligence, sense, *Gk. Philos.* nous, reason, understanding, imagination; intellect, aptitude, mind, brains, brainpower, *Inf.* gray matter, *Sl.* smarts.

4. intention, aim, destination, purpose, project; design, plan, plot, scheme.

5. expectation, expectancy, prospect, potential, probability; anticipation, hope, aspiration, dream, vision.

6. consideration, thoughtfulness, carefulness; kindness, kindliness, kindheartedness, compassion, compassionateness, tenderness, sympathy; benevolence, good will, beneficence, charitableness; attention, attentiveness, mindfulness, heedfulness; care, concern, solicitude, solicitousness; regard, respect, deference, esteem, homage, honor, reverence, veneration.

7. judgement, conclusion, estimation, appraisal, assessment, calculation; theory, hypothesis, supposition, assumption, surmise, conjecture, guess; opinion, view, apprehension, position, stand, posture; attitude, sentiment, feeling, belief, tenet, conviction.

8. touch, tinge, trace, soupçon, suspicion, hint, suggestion; bit, speck, taste, dash, pinch, sprinkle, sprinkling; thimbleful, trifle, little.

thoughtful, *adj.* **1.** pensive, musing, pondering, *Archaic.* museful; cerebrational, thinking, absorbed, immersed, engrossed, lost in thought, bemused, rapt in thought; intent, concentrating, focusing, ruminative, ruminant, ruminating, chewing, chewing one's cud, brooding, mulling over.

2. profound, deep, serious, grave, momentous; pithy, meaty, substantial, considerable, weighty, heavy.

3. careful, cautious, circumspect, circumspective; canny, prudent, discreet; chary, wary, guarded, watchful, vigilant; attentive, mindful, heedful, concerned, solicitous.

4. considerate, kind, kindly, kindhearted, compassionate, tender, sympathetic; benevolent, beneficent, charitable; respectful, regardful, deferential, reverent.

thoughtless, *adj.* **1.** careless, heedless, unheeding, unmindful, regardless, disregardful, negligent, neglectful, remiss; inadvertent, inattentive, unobservent, unobserving; inconsiderate, insensible, incogitant, unthinking, forgetful, oblivious; tactless, untactful, undiplomatic, unsolicitous.

2. reckless, rash, precipitate, headlong, foolhardy; unreasoning, unreflecting, unreflective; ill-advised, ill-considered, unwise, imprudent, injudicious, impolitic, indiscreet, improvident.

3. scatterbrained, harebrained, lamebrained, flighty, giddy, dizzy, *Inf.* gaga; vacuous, empty, blank, vacant, empty-headed, with rooms to let.

4. foolish, *Inf.* fool, *Inf.* tomfool, stupid, dumb, senseless, witless, brainless, asinine, idiotic, moronic, crazy, insane, mad; *All Sl.* nutty, wacky, daffy, loony, screwy, screwball, batty.

thoughtlessness, *n.* **1.** carelessness, heedlessness, unmindfulness, regardlessness, disregardfulness, negligence, neglectfulness, remissness; inadvertence, inattentiveness, unobservance; inconsiderateness, inconsideration, insensibility, unthinkingness, forgetfulness, obliviousness; tactlessness, untactfulness, unsolicitousness.

2. recklessness, rashness, precipitousness, foolhardiness; imprudence, injudiciousness, indiscretion, improvidence.

3. flightiness, giddiness, dizziness; vacuousness, emptiness, empty-headedness, blankness.

4. foolishness, stupidity, senselessness, witlessness, brainlessness; asininity, idiocy, moronism, craziness, insanity, madness; *All Sl.* nuttiness, screwiness, looniness, daffiness, wackiness, battiness.

thrall, *n.* **1.** slave, bondsman, bond slave, chattel slave, chattel, indentured servant, *Hist. or Archaic.* theow; bondswoman, bondmaid.

2. thralldom. See **thralldom.**

thralldom, *n.* slavery, servitude, subjection, subjugation, enslavement, enthrallment, thrall; captivity, bondage, bond service, indentureship.

thrash, *v.* **1.** flog, lash, switch, birch, scourge, flagellate, whip, horsewhip, curry, strap, thresh, flail, cowhide, spank, *Inf.* tan [s.o.'s] hide, *Inf.* trim, *Inf.* thump, *Inf.* lace, *Inf.* lambaste, *Inf.* whale, *Sl.* whump; beat, batter, pound, pommel, pummel, baste, pelt, lay on, *Sl.* paste, *Archaic.* belabor; punch, smite, hit, strike, thwack, slap, smack, *Australian.* ding, *Scot. and North Eng.* paik; cuff, buffet, sandbag, box, *Inf.* clout, *Inf.* slug, *Inf.* whack, *Inf.* knock [s.o.'s] block off, *Inf.* crown, *Inf.* wallop, *Sl.* belt, *Sl.* sock, *Sl.* plug, *U.S. Sl.* biff, *Sl.* loop; cudgel, fustigate, cane, bastinado.

2. trounce, rout, vanquish, defeat, worse, *Inf.* lick, *Sl.* shellac, *Sl.* pulverize; conquer, overthrow, overpower, overwhelm, master; quash, crush, trample, destroy, do for, *Sl.* do in.

3. thresh, flail.

4. toss and turn, fling oneself about; jerk, jump, twitch; pitch, rock, roll, sway.

—n. **5.** beating, battering, pounding, pommeling, pummeling, pelting, going over, *Sl.* pasting; thrashing, flogging, basting, lashing, whipping, spanking, *Inf.* tanning, smacking, slapping, *Inf.* whacking.

6. blow, bastindo, *Scot.* dunt, *Scot and North Eng.* paik, punch, beat, box, *Inf.* wallop, *Brit. Dial.* douse, *U. S. Sl.* biff, *Sl.* bop; cuff, strike, hit, slap, smack, *Inf.* clout.

thread, *n.* **1.** cord, string, yarn, twine, twist, piping; cable, wire; fiber, filament, fibril.

2. strand, line, seam, strip, chain, tape; wisp, hair; queue, file, row; stream, jet.

3. theme, subject, subject matter, thesis, motif; story line, plot; train of thought.

—v. **4.** string, *Naut.* reeve, braid.

5. pervade, permeate, penetrate, imbue, suffuse, fill; connect, unite, link, tie together, merge, fuse, inosculate.

6. wind, meander, loop, twine, twist, stray, straggle; push through, squeeze through, shoulder through.

threadbare, *adj.* **1.** worn, worn to a thread, worn out, shopworn, (*of a tire*) bald, napless, moth-eaten, frayed, ragged; raveled, holey, in need of patches; faded; marred, damaged.

2. meager, slim, thin, lean, slight, insubstantial,

small; scanty, skimpy, inadequate, trifling, negligible, piddling; poor, empty, unfulfilling, unsatisfying, dissatisfying.

3. hackneyed, banal, trite, overdone, *Inf.* bromidic, platitudinous, *Inf.* corny; tired, played out, *Inf.* old-hat, old as the hills, warmed-over; unimaginative, unoriginal, stale, insipid, jejune, uninspired; prosaic, prosy, dull, boring, *Sl.* ho-hum, uninteresting, tedious, monotonous, dry, dry-as-dust; conventional, matter-of-fact, humdrum, commonplace, ordinary, workaday, wonted; stock, familiar, stereotyped.

4. shabby, dingy, sorry, wretched; seedy, disheveled, slovenly, unkempt, slatternly, untidy; forlorn, desolate, dreary, dismal, sad, pathetic, pitiful; impecunious, penniless, destitute, *Inf.* on one's uppers, in bad *or* tough shape.

threadlike, *adj.* thready, fibrous, filamentous, fibriform, piliform, fibrillar, fibrilliform; stringy, wiry, ropy, attenuated, drawn out; fine, thin, slender, narrow; winding, twisting, meandering, circuitous, tortuous, sinuous.

threat, *n.* **1.** warning, intimidation, commination, caution, caveat, alarm, *Archaic.* alarum, notice, word to the wise, saber-rattling.

2. menace, danger, peril, risk, hazard, jeopardy; time bomb, bomb, sleeping volcano, sword of Damocles, quicksand.

3. omen, forewarning, foreboding, portent, evil portent, premonition; bird of ill omen, Cassandra, handwriting on the wall, gathering clouds, clouds on the horizon, brewing storm.

threaten, *v.* **1.** menace, endanger, imperil, frighten, scare, terrify, alarm, fill with unease; warn, put on one's guard, caution, give fair warning, *Inf.* tip off, comminate; intimidate, daunt, terrorize, cow; browbeat, bully, thunder at, yell at, fulminate, read the riot act; snarl, growl, rattle one's sabers, bark; lower, glower, scowl.

2. tower over, hang over, beetle; impend, loom, be imminent; portend, bode, forebode, presage, forewarn; augur, foreshadow, be in the air, be in the offing.

threatening, *adj.* menacing, frightening, terrifying, intimidating, minacious; dangerous, perilous, hazardous, risky, chancy; looming, imminent, in the air, in the offing, in the wings, pending, impending, portending, boding, foreboding, ominous, lowering.

threnody, *n.* dirge, requiem, funeral song, burial hymn, threnode, *Rom. Cath. Ch.* trenal, *Dies Irae;* elegy, lament, lamentation, keen, epicedium, monody, ululation, jeremaid, *Scot., Irish.* coronach.

thresh, *v.* **1.** thrash, flail, separate the grain from the chaff; gin, seed, pit, remove the seeds from.

2. flog, lash, switch, birch, scourge, flagellate, *Inf.* lace; whip, horsewhip, curry, strap, cowhide, *Inf.* tan [s.o.'s] hide; cane, bastinado, cudgel, fustigate; spank, paddle, beat [s.o.'s] bottom; beat, batter, pommel, pummel, pelt, lay on, baste, *Inf.* lambaste, *Inf.* thump, *Inf.* trim, *Inf.* whale, *Inf.* whale the tar out of, *Sl.* whump, *Sl.* paste, *Archaic.* belabor.

3. thresh out *or* **over** work out, settle, *Inf.* iron out; discuss, talk over, haggle, dicker, *Inf.* hash out, *Sl.* hassle out; go over, go through, review, *Sl.* hash over; debate, moot, *Inf.* kick around.

—*n.* **4.** thrash, thrashing, threshing, flogging, lashing, whipping, spanking, *Inf.* tanning; beating, battering, pounding, pommeling, pummeling, pelting, going over, basting, *Sl.* pasting.

threshold, *n.* **1.** doorsill, sill, groundsill, groundsel, ground beam, ground plate; doorway, door, portal, hatch, *Fr. porte;* gate, gateway, postern; stile, turnstile, wicket; entrance, entryway, entry, entrée, inlet, ingress, approach, opening.

2. entry level, starting point, square one, zero, bottom; top, head, foreward, preface, prologue, preamble, prelude, overture, beginning, start, commencement, outset, brink, edge, verge; onset, outbreak, down, debut, conception, birth, genesis, exordium, *Inf.* kick-off, *Inf.* jump-off, *Inf.* take-off, *Inf.* blast-off, *Inf.* send-off; origin, source, beginnings, incipience, nascence, infancy.

thrice, *adv.* **1.** three times, on three occasions, in three ways.

2. threefold, trebly, triply, three times as, to the third degree *or* power, multiplied by three.

3. much, greatly, highly; well, amply, fully, liberally, abundantly, lavishly, bountifully, profusely, copiously, plenteously, without stint, as much *or* often as one could want *or* hope for, to one's heart's content; very much, very, extremely, radically, drastically, to the nth degree; awfully, terribly, damned, danged, *U. S. Inf.* darned, *Sl.* almighty; too much, too often, far too much *or* often, more than necessary, overly; exceedingly, excessively, inordinately, abnormally, unusually, uncommonly; exorbitantly, outrageously, *Both Chiefly U.S. Inf.* all-fired, all-firedly.

thrift, *n.* economy, husbandry, thrifty management, conservation, prevention of waste; conserving, saving, economizing; thriftiness, frugality, frugalness, sparingness; scrimping, skimping, penny-pinching, cutting corners, tightening one's belt, making ends meet; parsimony, parsimoniousness, penuriousness; miserliness, niggardliness, stinginess, tightness, tight-fistedness, closefistedness, cheapness.

thriftless, *adj.* wasteful, prodigal, profligate, spendthrift, dissipative, squandering, improvident, penny-wise and pound-foolish, unthrifty, unfrugal; extravagant, immoderate, inordinate, lavish; inefficient, imprudent, negligent.

thrifty, *adj.* **1.** frugal, economical, economizing, saving, sparing, chary; provident, prudent, careful, forehanded, unwasteful, conservative, conservant, conservational; scrimping, penny-pinching, parsimonious, penurious; miserly, niggardly, stingy, tight, stinting, tight-fisted, closefisted, cheap.

2. successful, prosperous, thriving, prospering; profitable, gainful, rewarding, productive, cost-effective, fructuous, fruitful; lucrative, paying, well-paying, moneymaking, remunerative.

3. flourishing, booming, *Inf.* going strong; growing, waxing, developing, burgeoning, mushrooming; (*of vegetation*) luxuriant, lush, rank, prolific, rife.

thrill, *v.* **1.** excite, stimulate, sensitize, *Inf.* turn on; inspirit, inspire, *Inf.* spark, reanimate, galvanize, electrify; touch, impress, strike, rivet the attention; penetrate, pierce, touch to the quick; tickle, titillate, kindle, fire; stir, move, rouse, arouse, awaken, *Sl.* send; agitate, incite, impassion, work up.

2. please, *Inf.* tickle pink, gladden, elate, delight; possess, intoxicate, enrapture, overpower, overwhelm, enthrall, charm.

—*n.* **3.** tingling sensation, tingle, tingling, quivering, tremor, vibration, chills, goose flesh, flutter, twitter; throb, palpitation, pulsation.

4. excitement, excitation, electrification, galvanization; titillation, *Inf.* kick, *Inf.* charge, *Sl.* buzz, *Sl.* bang, *Sl.* gas, *Sl.* boot; pleasurable feeling, emotional appeal, (*pl.*) jollies; enravishment, magnetism, intoxication, entrancement.

thrilling, *adj.* **1.** exciting, electrifying, galvanizing, galvanic, spine-tingling, hair-raising, *Inf.* far-out, *Inf.* rip-roaring, *Inf.* rip-snorting; stimulating, stirring, bracing, rousing, inspiring, invigorating, excitant, excitative, excitatory; moving, impelling, compelling, affecting, soul-stirring, heart-moving; overpowering, overwhelming, overcoming, startling, astonishing, *Sl.* mind-boggling, *Sl.* mind-blowing, *Sl.* trippy, kicky.

2. quivering, quavering, vibrating, trembling, trembly, tremulous, tremulant, shaking, shaky; quaking, quaky, shuddering, shuddery, shivering, shivery.

thrive, *v.* **1.** prosper, succeed, make good, *Brit. Dial.* fadge, fare well, be fortunate, have a streak *or* run of luck; advance, get ahead, go up in the world, progress, make headway, get on *or* along; grow rich, become wealthy, make one's fortune, add to *or* increase one's riches; profit, gain, feather one's nest, line one's pockets, make one's pile, get all the gravy, enrich oneself; be well-off, be well-to-do, be on easy street; lead a charmed life, live a life of luxury *or* ease, live the life of Riley, bask in the sun, live in the clover, live off the fat of the land.

2. flourish, luxuriate, burgeon, mushroom, boom, spring up, burst forth, develop vigorously; grow, wax, sprout, bud, germinate, pullulate, shoot up; bloom, blossom, flower, bear fruit, fructify; mature, maturate, ripen.

thriving, *adj.* **1.** prosperous, wealthy, rich, opulent, affluent, halcyon, fat; well-to-to, well-off, *Inf.* well-heeled, *Inf.* in the money, *Sl.* in the bucks, *Sl.* golden, *Sl.* on easy street; very comfortable, on a bed of roses, *Sl.* on velvet, in clover, born with a silver spoon in one's mouth.

2. growing, sprouting, budding, blooming, blossoming, flowering; mushrooming, burgeoning, waxing, developing vigorously; lush, luxuriant, exuberant, plentiful, abundant, flush, prolific, rank, rife; flourishing, palmy, successful, glorious; booming, ascendant, on the rise *or* upswing, prospering, in full swing.

throat, *n.* **1.** gullet, gorge, esophagus, *Archaic.* weasand.

2. cut someone's throat do [s.o.] wrong, *Sl.* do [s.o.] dirty, *Sl.* stab [s.o.] in the back; injure, hurt, harm.

3. jump down someone's throat *Slang.* berate, tongue-lash, yell at, *Inf.* dress down, *Inf.* jump all over, *Inf.* come down on, *Sl.* bawl out, *Sl.* chew out, *Sl.* rank out, *Sl.* jack up, *Sl.* tell [s.o.] where to get off, *Sl.* give [s.o.] what-for.

4. ram [s.t.] down someone's throat *Informal.* impel, compel, force, make, coerce, dragoon, bully, *Inf.* steamroller, *Inf.* bulldoze, *Inf.* strong-arm; pressure, put the pressure on, *Inf.* lean on, *Inf.* squeeze, *Inf.* put the screws on *or* to, *Inf.* twist [s.o.'s] arm.

5. stick in one's throat exacerbate, embitter, envenom, gall, rankle, acerbate, sour, poison, stick in one's craw.

throb, *v.* **1.** beat, pulse, pulsate, palpitate, pound, pant, go pitapat.

—n. **2.** beat, throbbing, pulse, pulsation, palpitation, pitter-patter, pitapat.

throe, *n.* **1.** spasm, paroxysm, convulsion; fit, seizure, stroke, attack, *Pathol.* ictus.

2. pang, pain, shooting pain, sharp *or* piercing pain.

3. throes a. agony, torture, excruciation; grief, distress, suffering, anguish. **b.** turmoil, tumult, turbulence, storm, storm and stress, hurly-burly; disorder, chaos, confusion, pandemonium; upheaval, disruption, cataclysm.

throne, *n.* **1.** royal seat, seat of state, seat of power, (*in India*) musnud, *Anglo-Indian.* gaddi.

2. sovereign, ruler, emperor, king, queen.

3. sovereignty, rule, command, reign, dominion, sway, hegemony, mastery.

throng, *n.* **1.** crowd, horde, mass, host, assemblage, gathering; mob scene; herd, pack, swarm, flock, drove, bevy.

—v. **2.** crowd, swarm, flock, herd, cluster, muster, gather, concentrate, mass, bunch up; flock together, surge, stream.

3. shove, shoulder, jostle, push, press forward, make one's way, fight one's way, elbow one's way, work one's way, *Inf.* pile in, *Inf.* stumble over one another.

4. pack, jam, cram, cramp, squeeze, *Inf.* jam-pack; lump together, compress, congest, bunch, bundle, serry, *Inf.* pack as tight as sardines.

throttle, *n.* **1.** choke, throttler, gas pedal, *Auto.* accelerator.

2. windpipe, *Anat., Zool.* trachea; gullet, throat, esophagus.

—v. **3.** strangle, choke, garrote, strangulate, bowstring, gibbet, hang; stifle, suffocate, smother, asphyxiate, burke; kill, murder, do away with, get rid of.

4. gas, muzzle, mute, still, silence, keep [s.o.] quiet; compress, squeeze, tighten, put pressure on, put a tourniquet on; cut off, shut off, seal off, close off, occlude; obstruct, block, stop up, clog, plug, cork, congest; check, stop, arrest; curb, impede, inhibit, cramp.

through, *prep.* **1.** into and out of, inside, under, out of; past, by, beyond, to the other *or* far side of, outside of; between, among, amongst, mongst, *Both Archaic.* betwixt, 'twixt; admidst, amid, midst, mid; within, in, inside, along, beside, across, over.

2. during, for the duration of, throughout, over the distance of, until the end *or* finish of, until the finale *or* completion of; up to and including, including, inclusive of.

3. *Usu.* **through with a.** finished with, done with, at the end of, at the completion *or* termination of. **b.** at the end of one's rope with.

4. by means of, by vitrue of, by way of, by, via, under the aegis *or* auspices of, through the agency *or* aid of, per; because of, by reason of, on account of, due to, owing to, for; as a consequence of, as a result of.

—adv. **5.** all the way, to the end of the line; straight, directly, right; nonstop, without a stop *or* interruption.

6. from one end to the other, from beginning to end, from top to bottom, fron stem to stern, from head to toe *or* foot, cap-a-pie, from A to Z, completely, thoroughly.

7. to the end, to the completion *or* termination, to a successful *or* favorable completion.

8. get through finish, complete, terminate, end; accomplish, do; survive, endure, make it.

9. pull through recover, come out of [s.t.], get better, get well.

—adj. **10.** nonstop, direct, straight; limited access, express, rapid, fast, quick.

11. finished, done; completed, ended, terminated.

throughout, *prep.* **1.** all over, all around *or* about, in every corner *or* part of, everywhere in; all among, among all, in-between all.

2. all the way through, all through, through; all during, during, for the duration of.

—adv. **3.** everywhere, everyplace, all over, all around, in every nook and cranny, in every corner, everywhere under the sun, *Latin. ubique;* far and wide, widely, in every direction, extensively, to the ends of the earth, to the far reaches of the earth.

4. all the time *or* while, for the duration until [s.t.] is over, until the finish *or* finale *or* end *or* completion.

5. from one end to the other, from beginning to end, from top to bottom. See **through** (*def.* **6**).

throw, *v.* **1.** hurl, sling, toss, cast, fling, dash, pitch, *Inf.* chuck, *Brit. Dial.* slat, *Scot., Australian.* ding; jettison, jaculate, shy, hurtle, pitchfork; launch, send, deliver, impel, propel, project, plunge, precipitate.

2. fell, floor, throw down, bring to the ground, prostrate; vanquish, defeat, drub, discomfit, rout; subjugate, overcome, overthrow, overpower, beat hollow, worst; make [s.o.] bite the dust, trample underfoot, roll in the dust.

3. throw off a. eject, expel, evict, drive off, cast off; abandon, lay aside, ostracize, renounce, reject, repudiate; deport, relegate, banish; dismiss, strike off the roll, turn out, bundle out, sack, fire, send packing. **b.** deceive, misdirect, mislead, misrepresent, misinform, misguide, misstate; bewilder, mystify, *Sl.* flummox, confuse, confound, beguile, delude; put on a false scent, draw a red herring across the trail.

4. throw up a. abandon, desert, give up, relinquish; resign, abdicate, renounce, abjure. **b.** vomit, retch, puke, spew, keck, (*of babies*) *Inf.* spit up, *Inf.* heave *or* heave up, *Sl.* barf, *Sl.* lose *or* spill one's cookies; void, emit, excrete, egest, eject, ejaculate, eruct, eructate.

—*n.* **5.** cast, fling, pitch, toss, shuck, heave, sling, hurtle, hurl, dart, pelt, jerk, bolt, tilt, shot, shy; ejection, ejaculation, discharge, propulsion, precipitation.

6. *Informal.* venture, chance, gamble, wager, bet, risk, fortune, hazard, stake; attempt, try, shot.

7. scarf, muffler, comforter; shawl, stole, boa; yashmak, veil, mantilla, burnous cloak.

8. blanket, afghan, cover, counterpane, coverlet, eiderdown, quilt, *U.S.* comforter.

thrum, *v.* pick, strum, twang, play; finger, pluck, fingerpick.

thrust, *v.* **1.** push, stove, drive, propel, impel; advance, forward, urge forward, power, actuate; hurl, clap, chuck, throw, fling, toss; plump, plank, plop, slap; boost, start, prod, set going, press.

2. stab, pierce, lunge, plunge; pass, cut, feint, jab; pole, stick, jam, cram.

3. force, press forward, make one's way, *Inf.* elbow *or* shoulder one's way; squeeze through, wedge, charge; ram, bulldoze, butt, shunt, batter; pile drive, bump, run against; jog, jolt, jostle, joggle, poke, nudge.

4. thrust in break in, intrude, obtrude, irrupt, interpose; interlope, burst in, muscle in, crash in; invade, encroach, infringe, intevene, come between; charge in, *Inf.* butt in, *Inf.* horn in, *Inf.* barge in, cut in; crowd in, press in, squeeze in, rush in.

5. thrust upon force upon, push upon, urge upon, press upon; make to do, ram down one's throat, impose, enforce, coerce, twist one's arm, oblige, necessitate, constrain.

—*n.* **6.** push, drive, shove, butt, bunt, shunt; propulsion, impulsion, boost, momentum, impetus; acceleration, pickup, motive power, driving force, steam.

7. lunge, stab, dig, press, punch; prod, poke, nudge, bump, jog, jolt, joggle; jab, feint.

8. attack, assault, offensive, charge; onset, onslaught, besetment, outbreak, irruption, incursion; strike, raid, hit, blitz, blitzkreig; foray, sortie, sally, invasion, *Obs.* brunt, *Fr. coup de main;* siege, besiegement, beleaguerment; air raid, air strike, lightning attack.

thud, *n.* thump, knock, *Sl.* clunk, *Sl.* pow, *Sl.* kerpow, wham, rap, clap, smack, thwack, whack.

thug, *n.* **1.** desperado, terrorist, gunman, gangster, criminal, mafioso, (*in Paris*) apache; tough, mugger, ruffian, rowdy, hoodlum, *Sl.* hood, hooligan, *Chiefly Brit.* rough, *Inf.* roughneck, *Inf.* goon, *Inf.* baddy, *Australian Sl.* larrikin, *Brit. Hist.* Mohock.

2. robber, highwayman, footpad, *Sl.* yegg *or* yeggman, bandit, *Sp. bandolero,* outlaw, *Southwest U. S.* ladrone, *Australian.* bushranger, bravo, brigand; picaroon, rogue, (*in India and Burma*) dacoit.

3. assassin, murderer, killer, slayer, sniper; strangler, cutthroat, garroter; liquidator, *Euph.* silencer, *Euph.* dispatcher: *All U.S. Sl.* gun, hired gun, hit man, hatchet man, triggerman, torpedo.

thumb, *n.* **1.** pollex, *Fr. pouce.*

—*v.* **2.** (*of a book*) skim, scan, run through, glance at *or* over, browse, leaf through, riffle through.

3. hitchhike, hitch, thumb *or* hook *or* bum a ride, get a lift.

thump, *n.* **1.** blow, knock, rap, *Sl.* sock, *Sl.* bop, slap, rap, thwack, smack, whack.

2. thud, wham, *Sl.* pow, *Sl.* kerpow, *Sl.* clunk.

—*v.* **3.** beat, cudgel, club, bastinado, bat, cane, birch, switch; hit, strike, thwack, whack, smack, *Sl.* bop, wham, *Inf.* slug; pommel, drub, batter, beat up.

4. pound, trudge, tread, slog, plod.

thumping, *adj.* **1.** resounding, echoing, banging, clanging; dull, heavy.

2. *Informal.* huge, colossal, enormous, great, immense, tremendous; gigantic, giant, gargantuan, mammoth, titanic; monumental, towering, impressive, fantastic; exceptional, unusual, extraordinary, striking, uncommon, singular, *Inf.* terrific, wonderful; *All Inf.* whacking, whopping, walloping, thundering, super-duper.

thunder, *n.* **1.** thundering, thundercrack, thunderclap; rumbling, rumble, roll, boom, roar, loud noise; crack, crash, blast; detonation, explosion, discharge.

—*v.* **2.** rumble, roll, boom, resound, reverberate; crash, crack, blast; detonate, explode, discharge.

3. fulminate against, denounce, denunciate, imprecate, curse, execrate, swear at; threaten, menace, intimidate; bellow, roar, shout, yell; bark, snarl, growl.

thunderbolt, *n.* **1.** thunderstroke, thunderclap, thundercrack; fulguration, lightning, lightning bolt.

2. blow, shock, surprise, eyeopener, bolt out of the blue.

thunderstruck, *adj.* dumfounded, astounded, astonished, amazed, *Inf.* flabbergasted, taken aback, floored, *Inf.* bowled over, open-mouthed, agape; stunned, shocked, startled, surprised, disconcerted, dazed, speechless, dumb, numb, paralyzed, frozen, petrified, incapacitated, aghast; confused, disoriented, baffled, confounded, nonplused, perplexed, bewildered, *Inf.* flummoxed; *Inf.* shaken, *Sl.* shook, *Inf.* caught up short, *Inf.* caught off guard, *Inf.* thrown for a loss, *Sl.* knocked for a loop.

thus, *adv.* **1.** in this way, in this fashion, in this manner, in this wise, as follows, so, *Latin. sic,* thus and so.

2. therefore, consequently, as a result, in which case, hence, whence, thence, wherefore, ergo, accordingly, then, taking that into consideration; that being so, for that reason, on that account.

3. as an example, for example, for instance.

thwack, *v.* **1.** hit, strike, smite, *Inf.* whack, smack, slap, *Australian.* ding; cuff, buffet, knock, punch, box, *Scot.* dunt, *Inf.* slug, *Inf.* wallop, *Inf.* crown, *Sl.* conk, *Dial.* hit [s.o.] upside the head, *Sl.* bash, *Sl.* plug, *Sl.* belt; beat, batter, pound, lay on, pommel, pummel, pelt, *Sl.* paste, *Sl.* lay into, *Sl.* let [s.o.] have it, *Archaic.* belabor; spank, *Brit. Dial.* yerk, *Inf.* tan [s.o.'s] hide, *Inf.* trim, *Inf.* thump, *Inf.* lace, *Inf.* lambaste, *Inf.* whale, *Sl.* whomp; rap, fillip, cane.

—*n.* **2.** hit, strike, *Inf.* whack, smack, slap, *Inf.* clout; blow, *Archaic.* dint, stroke, bastinado, punch, box, knockout, *Inf.* wallop, *Inf.* whomp, *Inf.* thump, *Sl.* conk, *Sl.* bash, *U.S. Sl.* biff, *Sl.* bop; rap, tap, fillip, cuff, buffet, box on the ear.

thwart, *v.* **1.** frustrate, foil, balk, check, stop, abort; oppose, cross, contravene, *Scot.* thraw; defeat, undo, outmaneuver; prevent, preclude, obstruct, block, circumvent; intercept, interpose, intervene, interfere, impede, hinder, hamper; spoil, mar, blight, scotch, *Sl.* screw up, *Inf.* short-circuit; restrain, restrict, inhibit; detain, delay, retard, forestall; nullify, obviate, cancel, render null and void, neutralize.

2. baffle, confound, confuse, puzzle, nonplus, perplex, outwit, disconcert, stymie, *Inf.* tree, *Inf.* discombobulate; damp, dishearten, disable, cripple, clip the wings of, take the wind out of one's sails, take down a peg, pull off one's high horse; disturb, trouble, plague, badger; mortify, embarrass.

tic, *n. Pathology.* twitch, *Med.* spasm, jerk, *All Pathol.* tic douloureux, facial neuralgia, trifacial neuralgia, trigeminal neuralgia.

tick, *n.* **1.** click, tap, tapping, beat, striking, ticktock, ticking; pulsating, throbbing, pounding, drumming, rataplan; rapping, ratatat, rat-a-tat-tat.

2. check, mark, dot, *Print.* bullet, line, stroke, scratch; notch, nick, blaze.

—*v.* **3.** ticktock, click, tap, beat, strike, pulsate, sound.

ticket, *n.* **1.** admission, certificate, season ticket, *Sl.* pasteboard, pass, *Fr. laissez-passer,* stub, coupon, tessera; free pass, *Inf.* freebie, *Sl.* Annie Oakley, *Sl.* twofer; token, transfer, fare.

2. label, tag, price tag, tally, badge, press badge, delegate badge, card; identification tag, I.D., dog tag, credentials.

3. slate, ballot, roster, line-up.

tickle, *v.* **1.** titillate, titivate, stroke, pet, twiddle.

2. gratify, please, content, refresh, delight, tickle pink, tickle to death; enchant, captivate, thrill, excite, fascinate, charm; strike one's fancy, tickle one's fancy, interest, intrigue, arouse, stimulate.

3. amuse, entertain, cheer, gladden, brighten, exhilarate, divert; raise a laugh *or* smile, regale, *Sl.* fracture, *Sl.* knock out, *Sl.* slay, tickle one's funny bone.

ticklish, *adj.* **1.** delicate, tender, fragile, slippery, awkward; difficult, tough, hard, arduous; complex, intricate, complicated, knotty, thorny; puzzling, troubling, troublesome, perplexing, full of unanswered questions, enigmatic, tough to figure; risky, dangerous, perilous, hazardous, threatening.

2. touchy, thin-skinned, oversensitive, hypersensitive, supersensitive, easily offended; temperamental, moody, up and down; testy, irritable, cranky, edgy, prickly, tetchy, snappish; petulant, peevish, irascible, grumpy.

3. unstable, unsteady, rickety, tottery, wobbly, teetering; upsettable, easily capsized; uncertain, unpredictable, untrustworthy, unreliable, unsound.

tide, *n.* **1.** tidewater, tide race; rip tide, neap tide, high tide, low tide, ebb tide, flood tide.

2. tidal flow, stream, current; flow, outflow, flux; inflow.

3. drift, direction, aim, set, turn, tendency, bent, tenor, run.

4. turn the tide reverse, alter, change, turn the tables, *Sl.* put the shoe on the other foot.

—*v.* **5. tide over a.** assist, aid, help, help out, keep [s.o.'s] head above water. **b.** survive, pull *or* come through, live through, endure, weather, weather the storm, last, hold up, land on one's feet.

tidiness, *n.* neatness, trimness, orderliness, spruceness, *Chiefly Brit.* trigness; good trim, *Inf.* good shape, *Inf.* apple-pie order; methodicalness, systematicness.

tidings, *n.* news, word, notification, advice; good news, glad tidings; bad news; information, *Inf.* lowdown, *Inf.* scoop, *Sl.* dope, *Sl.* poop; talk, rumor, buzz, whisper, *Inf.* scuttlebutt, *Inf.* hearsay, *Archaic.* bruit.

tidy, *adj.* **1.** neat, trim, in trim, ordered, orderly, in order, *Inf.* in apple-pie order, snug, *Chiefly Dial.* tight, *Chiefly Brit.* trig, *Fr. en règle*; spruce, shipshape, *Naut.* shipshape and Bristol fashion, spick-and-span.

2. organized, well-organized, systematic, methodical.

3. acceptable, passable, tolerable, fair, fairish, goodish, pretty good, not bad, not half bad, all right *or* O.K.; decent, respectable; adequate, satisfactory, sufficient.

4. *Informal.* considerable, sizable, good-sized, *Inf.* man-sized, goodly; large, big, ample, substantial, *Sl.* healthy.

—*v.* **5.** neaten, put in trim, straighten, straighten up *or* out, *Inf.* fix up, *Inf.* spruce up; order, put *or* set in order, arrange; police, pick up, clean up.

tie, *v.* **1.** tie up, hogtie, truss, wrap *or* wrap up, ligate, bandage *or* bandage up; fasten, attach, join, connect, link, yoke, unite, wed, couple, hook together, splice; bind, secure, strap, moor, fix firmly, make fast; fitch, tether, stake, picket, rope, lash, chain.

2. make a bow, knot, make a knot.

3. confine, restrict, clip one's wings, limit, curb, curtail; hem in, hedge in, tie down, cramp, crimp, astrict, constrain, restrain.

4. bind, oblige, obligate, engage, commit, pledge, promise, give one's word, vow.

5. (*all of a contest*) equal, parallel, be even with, be neck and neck, come out even, divide the honors.

6. tie in connect, be connected, be consistent, fit *or* fit in.

7. tie up a. wrap *or* wrap up, truss, bind, fasten, secure. See **tie** (*def.* **1**). **b.** hinder, hamper, impede, interfere, get in the way, interrupt; frustrate, thwart, foil, balk, *Inf.* short-circuit; handicap, encumber, clog *or* scotch the wheels, *Sl.* gum up the works; retard, slow down, set *or* put back, defer, delay, stay, filibuster, postpone, put off. **c.** arrest, stop, halt, bring to a stop *or* halt. **d.** be busy, be occupied, be engaged.

—*n.* **8.** string, cord, cordon, ribbon, braid, thong; strip, piece of cloth, bandage, ligature, band; shoelace, lace, *Archaic.* latchet, strap; rope, tether, lead, line, leash.

9. necktie, cravat, bow tie, ascot, scarf, neckerchief, *Obs.* neckcloth.

10. bow, hair bow, knot.

11. fastener, fastening, hook, catch, clip, snap, hook and eye, button; latch, lock, padlock, bar, bolt, hasp; pin, buckle, agraffe; clamp, vise, brace; link, bond, vinculum, nexus; binder, holder, connector, copula, yoke, harness; nail, dowel, tack, thumbtack, thumbscrew, screw, clincher, rivet, staple, holdfast, peg, spike; chain *or* chains, fetters, chackles, trammels, manacles, handcuffs, leg irons.

12. bond, connection, relationship, friendship, business acquaintanceship, liaison, affiliation; kinship, blood relation, consanguinity, propinquity; responsibility, obligation, duty, devoir; engagement, pledge, promise, commitment, vow, one's word.

13. tie game, tie match *or* contest, draw, stand-off.

tier, *n.* **1.** row, rank, line.

2. story, floor, level, *Fr. étage*; layer, stratum, stratificaton; band, belt, zone; ridge, *Geol.* esker.

tie-up, *n.* **1.** slow-up, slowdown, delay, retardation; stoppage, blockage, clog, congestion, jam, logjam, traffic jam, bottleneck, *Fr. embouteillage, C.B. Radio.* parking lot.

2. involvement, connection, association, implication, entanglement, tanglement, enmeshment.

tiff, *n.* **1.** quarrel, dispute, row, spar, wrangle, jangle, bicker, *Obs.* brabble; contention, controversy, disagreement, difference of opinion, argument, *Inf.* words, *Inf.* miff, *Scot. and North Eng.* threap; squabble, spat, *Inf.* dustup, *U.S. Sl.* rhubarb, *Brit. Dial.* fratch, *Inf.* run-in, *Inf.* hassle, *Inf.* barney, falling-out, *Sl.* blowup; tussle, *Inf.* scrap, *Inf.* set-to, scuffle, broil, embroilment, imbroglio, fight, *Scot.* sturt, *Scot.* collieshangie.

2. huff, bad mood, ill humor, fume; fit, tantrum *or* temper tantrum, pet; temper, irritation, agitation, snit, *Inf.* stew.

—v. **3.** quarrel, row, squabble, altercate, spar, cross swords; argue, debate, dispute, bandy words, have words, *Inf.* pick a crow; disagree, differ, take exception to, contend, contest, make something of it, fall out, clash, be at odds, be at loggerheads; spat, *Brit. Archaic.* brangle, wrangle, jangle, bicker, *Obs.* brabble, fight.

tight, *adj.* **1.** fixed, fastened, fast, secure, secured, clinched, made fast, set, sound; stable, stationary, unmovable, immovable, irremovable.

2. taut, tense, strained, rigid, stiff; unrelaxed, under a strain, *Inf.* uptight.

3. snug, close-fitting, form-fitting, skin-tight; close, near, compact, compacted, constricted, confined, cramped, compressed, restricted, limited.

4. difficult, touchy, sticky, delicate, ticklish, tricky, precarious; dangerous, perilous, hazardous.

5. impervious, imperviable, impenetrable; impermeable, unporous, nonporous, watertight, waterproof, leakproof; proof, resistant, hermetic, hermetically sealed; closed, shut, sealed.

6. concise, succinct, terse, pithy, epigrammatic; cryptic, laconic, to the point, pointed, direct, straightforward, clear-cut; sharp, incisive, keen, trenchant.

7. *Informal.* close, even, neck and neck, *U.S. Inf.* nip and tuck, nose to nose, shoulder to shoulder.

8. *Informal.* stingy, tight-fisted, parsimonious. See **tight-fisted.**

9. *Slang.* drunk, intoxicated, inebriated; *All Inf.* boozy, lit, lit up, lit to the gills, illuminated, half seas over, three *or* four sheets to the wind, under the sauce, off-color, high, high as a kite, feeling good, feeling no pain, out of it, out-cold, out, under the table.

tighten, *v.* **1.** squeeze, compress, compact, press together, force together, crush, constrict, contract, constringe, choke.

2. secure, anchor, make fast, fasten; lace up, tie up.

3. stiffen, rigidify, tense; tauten, take up the slack.

tight-fisted, *adj.* stingy, niggardly, miserly, parsimonious, carking, skinflinty; penurious, mean, tight, closefisted; cheap, *Sl.* chintzy, moneygrubbing, grasping, *Rare.* illiberal, cheeseparing; scrimping, penny-pinching, grudging, begrudging, ungenerous, stinting; thrifty, frugal, sparing, chary; economical, prudent, saving, penny-wise.

tight-lipped, *adj.* quiet, silent, close-mouthed; tacit, speechless, voiceless, mum, mute; taciturn, reserved, shy, reticent, uncommunicative, unconversable, unconversational, untalkative; secretive, stand-offish, unsociable; laconic, terse, short, brief.

tights, *n.* leotard, *Trademark.* Danskin, leggings; stockings, pantyhose, hosiery, hose; fishnets, opaques.

tightwad, *n. Informal.* miser, niggard, skinflint, *Sl.* skin, *Sl.* cheapskate, *Inf.* piker, muckworm, *Sl.* screw; penny pincher, pinchpenny, lickpenny, cheeseparer, hoarder, save-all, *Scot.* carl; scrooge, Harpagon, money-grubber, harpy; curmudgeon, churl, hunks.

till[1], *prep.* **1.** until, up to the time of, up to, to, down to; before, sooner than, earlier than, prior to, previous to.

—conj. **2.** up to the time when, until; before.

till[2], *v.* cultivate, dress, farm, work, work the land, labor; harrow, weed, delve, dibble; plow, hoe, dig, scrape, spade, rake; sow, plant, seed; fertilize, manure, compost.

till[3], *n.* drawer, compartment, container, receptacle, repository, bin; coffer, box, cashbox, strongbox, safe; cash register, register; treasury, *Eccles.* bursary, thesaurus, depository; kitty, petty cash.

tillable, *adj.* arable, plowable, farmable, cultivable, cultivatable; fertile, fruitful, productive, prolific, fecund.

tillage, *n.* farming, husbandry, agriculture, geoponics, agronomics, agronomy; cultivation, gardening; plowing, harrowing.

tiller[1], *n.* farmer, granger, husbandman, *Brit.* yeoman, plowman, plower; agriculturist, agronomist; cultivator, gardener.

tiller[2], *n.* shoot, sprout, *Bot.* sucker; sapling, seedling.

tilt[1], *v.* **1.** lean, tip, list, cant, heel, *Naut.* careen, lurch; slope, slant, oblique, fall obliquely, skew, angle, bevel, pitch, grade, bank; ascend, rise; descend, drop *or* drop off, dip, sag, sink.

2. *Usu.* **tilt at** rush at, charge; oppose, contest, contend; joust, tourney, break a lance with, run a tilt *or* a tilt at.

—n. **3.** slope, inclination, slant, bevel, pitch, grade, gradient, angle, skew, cant; ramp, inclined plane, bank, hillside, hill, mount, acclivity, ascent, rise; declivity, downward slope *or* slant, *Scot. and North Eng.* brae, decline, declension, descent, downgrade; drop, fall, dip, sag.

4. joust, tournament, tourney; contest, encounter, engagement, match, meeting; test, trial; scrimmage, skirmish.

5. dispute, quarrel; squabble, spat, tiff. See **tiff** (*def.* **1**).

tilt[2], *n.* awning, canopy, *Archit.* baldachin, marquee; covering, cover, tent.

timber, *n.* **1.** wood, lumber; kindling, firewood.

2. spar, beam, pole, mast.

—interj. **3.** look out, look out below, heads up, watch out *or* it, gardyloo, duck.

timbre, *n.* **1.** *Acoustics, Phonetics.* voice quality, voice, tone of voice, tone; frequency, resonance.

2. *Music.* tone color, tone quality, tonality, quality of sound, color, coloring, clang color *or* tint, *Ger. Klangfarbe*; ring, clang, resonance.

time, *n.* **1.** chronology; duration.

2. point, juncture, moment, instant, hour, day; period, spell, span, stretch, while, tide, term, tenure; interval, interim, intermission, interregnum, interruption, interlude, pause, break, hiatus; turn, shift, watch; tour, tour of duy, enlistment, *Inf.* hitch.

3. *Often* **times** era, epoch, age, date, season.

4. ease, leisure, leisure time, convenience; freedom, free time, spare time, odd moments.

5. chance, opportunity, opening, occasion; good chance, fair field, good time, high time, golden opportunity.

6. tempo, beat, rhythm; measure, meter.

7. **ahead of time** early, *Inf.* bright and early, *Scot.* timeous; beforetime, beforehand; in good time, with time to spare.

8. at one time a. once, once upon a time, time was; back when, in the past; previously, formerly, hitherto, heretofore. **b.** at once, at the same time, simultaneously, concurrently, at one and the same time, together, all together.

9. at the same time nonetheless, nevertheless, be that as it may, however that may be, however, still, yet, but, even so, just the same, all the same.

10. at times occasionally, from time to time. See **time** (*def.* 13).

11. behind the times old-fashioned, out of fashion, out of style, out, *Sl.* out of it, out of date, dated, obsolete, passé; of the old school.

12. for the time being for now, for the present; temporarily, *Latin. pro tempore,* pro tem; meanwhile, meantime, in the meantime, till then.

13. from time to time occasionally, on occasion, at times, at intervals, now and then, once in a while, sometimes, *Inf.* every so often.

14. in good time a. on time. See **time** (*def.* **20a**). **b.** ahead of time. See **time** (*def.* 7).

15. in no time in short order, in a second, in an instant, in a trice, in a flash, in the twinkling of an eye, *Inf.* in a jiffy, *Inf.* in two shakes *or* half a shake of a lamb's tail, *Inf.* before you can say "Jack Robinson," *Inf.* in nothing flat; quickly, speedily, swiftly, forthwith, summarily, with dispatch, expeditiously, apace, *Sl.* PDQ.

16. in time a. in good time, early enough, soon enough, with time to spare; just in time, not a minute too soon, just under the wire, in the nick of time, *Facetious.* in the nickel of dime, *Fr. à point.* **b.** in the future, in due time, by and by, *Inf.* in the sweet by-and-by, someday, sometime, one of these days, one fine day *or* morning; sooner or later, eventually, ultimately, in the long run, when all is said and done.

17. kill time consume *or* pass *or* spend time; beguile the time, while away the time, amuse oneself; waste time, fool *or* fritter *or* idle away time.

18. make time a. cover ground, make strides *or* rapid strides, make headway. **b.** *Slang.* woo, court, pay court to, pay suit to, address, *Inf.* spark, *Inf.* court and spark, *Sl.* hustle, *Sl.* put a move on, *Sl.* put *or* slap the make on.

19. many a time frequently, often, oftentimes, as often as not, often enough, most often, many times; habitually, regularly, routinely, commonly.

20. on time a. punctually, precisely, sharp, exact, in good time, to the minute, *Inf.* on the dot. **b.** on credit, on account, on trust, *Chiefly Brit. Inf.* on tick, *Inf.* on the cuff; on the installment plan, in installments, *Brit.* on hire-purchase, *Brit. Sl.* on h.p., *Brit. Sl.* on the never-never; on terms, on easy terms.

21. pass the time of day converse, talk, speak, chat, chitchat, confabulate, *Inf.* confab, coze, *Brit. Dial.* tell, *Sl.* rap, *Sl.* chin, *Sl.* chew the fat *or* rag, *Sl.* shoot the breeze *or* bull, *Sl.* bull.

22. take one's time dawdle, dally, dillydally, shilly-shally, linger, loiter, delay, tarry, drag one's feet, *Inf.* lallygag, *Inf.* take one's own sweet time, *Sl.* goof off *or* around.

23. take time by the forelock seize the day, *Latin. carpe diem,* take the bull by the horns, make one's move, make hay while the sun shines, *Inf.* make hay, strike while the iron is hot; make the most of the situation, take advantage of the situation, turn [s.t.] to account, cash in on [s.t.], capitalize on [s.t.], exploit.

24. time after time again and again, time and again, time and time again, over and over, over and over again, many times over, repeatedly, recurrently.

25. time and time again over and over. See **time** (*def.* 24).

26. time of one's life *Informal.* good time, great time, *Inf.* high time, *Inf.* good old time, *Inf.* a whale of a time, *Sl.* one helluva time; great fun, *Sl.* ball, *Sl.* blast.

—*v.* **27.** schedule, fix *or* set a time.

28. record time, *Inf.* clock.

29. regulate, adjust, set, synchronize, *Inf.* put in sync.

30. keep time, mark time, measure time, count.

timeless, *adj.* everlasting, eternal, *Literary.* sempiternal, *Archaic.* eterne; perpetual, endless, unending, never-ending; ageless, deathless, dateless, immortal, undying, amaranthine, immemorial.

timely, *adj.* **1.** opportune, seasonable, well-timed, *Scot.* timeous; auspicious, propitious, ripe, favorable; fortunate, lucky, happy, felicitous, convenient.

—*adv.* **2.** opportunely, seasonably, *Scot.* timeously; aupiciously, propitiously; in good time; just in time, in the nick of time, none too soon, at the eleventh hour.

timepiece, *n.* **1.** timer, chronometer, chronoscope, chronograph, *Trademark.* Chronotron; metronome.

2. clock, clock watch, *Horol.* repeater, timekeeper, *Sl.* ticker; watch, wrist watch, pocket watch; hourglass; sundial, horologue; water clock, clepsydra.

timeserver, *n.* opportunist, self-seeker, gold digger, fortune hunter, *Fig.* soldier of fortune, *Obs.* timepleaser; double-dealer, double-crosser, snake in the grass; weathercock, chameleon, trimmer, temporizer; toady, toadeater, sycophant, tufthunter, bootlicker, *Inf.* apple-polisher, *Sl.* brown-noser.

timeserving, *adj.* selfish, self-seeking, self-serving, self-indulgent; opportunistic, careerist, ambitious for oneself, *Inf.* looking out for number one, *Obs.* timepleasing; venal, mercenary, fortune-hunting, gold-digging, *Inf.* on the make, *Inf.* on the take, *Inf.* on the hustle; untrustworthy, false-hearted, treacherous, perfidious, double-dealing, double-crossing, *Sl.* back-stabbing; obsequious, servile, slavish, subservient.

timeworn, *adj.* **1.** ancient, aged, archaic, antique, old; worn, the worse for wear, time-scarred, weathered, battered, *Inf.* beat-up; ragged, dog-eared, moth-eaten; shabby, seedy, run-down; dilapidated, decrepit, ramshackle, tumbledown, broken-down, crumbling.

2. antiquated, dated, out of date, out, passé, obsolete, *Inf.* old-hat; trite, hackneyed, worn thin, stale, outworn, overused.

timid, *adj.* **1.** timorous, pusillanimous, fearful, fearsome, afraid, afraid of one's own shadow, frightened, scared, *Inf.* chicken, *Inf.* shaking in one's boots; unmanly, faint-hearted, weak-hearted, lily-livered, white-livered, having no backbone, with a backbone of banana, *Inf.* chicken-hearted, *Inf.* chicken-livered, *Inf.* pantywaist, *Inf.* yellow, *Sl.* yellow-bellied, *Sl.* candy-assed; cowardly, craven, dastardly, *Archaic.* niddering, *Archaic.* caitiff.

2. shy, bashful, diffident, coy, demure, retiring, shrinking, sheepish, blushing, poor in spirit, *Archaic.* verecund.

timidity, *n.* **1.** timorousness, pusillanimity, fearfulness, fearsomeness, lily-liveredness, faint-heartedness, weak-heartedness, *Inf.* chicken-heartedness, *Inf.* chicken-liveredness, *Sl.* yellow-belliedness; cowardice, cowardliness, dastardliness, poltroonery, cravenness; faint heart, weak knees, white feather, no backbone, a backbone of banana, *Inf.* chicken heart, *Inf.* funk, *Sl.* cold feet, *Sl.* yellow streak.

2. shyness, bashfulness, diffidence, demureness, coyness, sheepishness, *Archaic.* verecundity.

tincture, *n.* **1.** infusion, insinuation, injection, imbuement, imbruement, instillation, inculcation, impregnation, implantation, infiltration; intermixture, strain, vein, streak, element.

2. tint, coloring, shade. See **tinge** (*def.* **3**).

3. trace, hint, suggestion; flavor, scent, smell; touch, smack, smattering, dash See **tinge** (*defs.* **4, 5**).

—*v.* **4.** tint, color, tone. See **tinge** (*aef.* **1**).

5. lace, streak, interweave, intermix, intermingle, shoot through with, inject; infuse, imbue, imbrue, instill, ingrain, inculcate, impregnate, implant; infiltrate, suffuse, permeate.

tinder, *n.* kindling, fagot, touchwood, punk, amadou; shavings, twigs, brushwood, brush, peat, buffalo chips, leaves, paper, newspaper; firewood, wood, logs, *Southern U.S.* lightwood; combustible, fuel, lighter fluid, kerosine, gasoline; charcoal, coal.

tine, *n.* prong, projection, tooth, fang, *Anat., Zool., Bot.* cusp; spike, nail, spine, needle, quill, bristle, thorn, outshoot, *Zool.* spiculum.

tinge, *v.* **1.** tint, tincture, color, tone; dye, stain, wash, paint.

2. flavor, season, spice, add [s.t.] to; scent, give [s.t.] a smell *or* fragrance *or* aroma.

—*n.* **3.** tint, tincture, tinct, coloring, hue, shade, tone, cast; stain, dye, wash, paint.

4. trace, hint, suggestion, suspicion, soupçon, nuance; flavor, taste, relish; scent, sniff, whiff, smell, aroma, odor.

5. touch, *U.S. Inf.* tad, trifle, *Both Inf.* smidgen, smitch; smack, dab, bit, little bit, nip, speck; spot, smattering, sprinkling, dash, pinch, drop, driblet.

tingle, *v.* **1.** prickle, tickle, creep, crawl, sting, smart, itch; shiver, quiver, quake, shake, palpitate, have tremors, have goose pimples, *Sl.* have the tremblies; prick, scratch.

—*n.* **2.** excitement, thrill, agitation, *Sl.* tremblies; quiver, tremor, shiver, shiver up one's spine, shudder; pins and needles, *Sl.* pricklies, formication, *Pathol.* paresthesia, itchiness, itch, scratchiness; numbness, stupor, chill, goose flesh *or* bumps *or* pimples.

tinker, *n.* **1.** itinerant; mender, fixer, patcher, repairman, *Sl.* Mr. *or* Miss Fixit, serviceman; jack-of-all-trades, mechanic, troubleshooter, mechanical wizard *or* genius, Swiss clockmaker.

2. bungler, *Sl.* klutz, botcher, *Sl.* screw-up, *Sl.* screw-up artist; lout, oaf, *Sl.* lunkhead.

—*v.* **3.** mend, repair, patch, touch up, doctor, fix; restore, renovate, put in working order, put back in shape, make like new.

4. bungle, botch, spoil, mar, damage, hack, break; mess up, *Sl.* screw up, *Sl.* louse up, *Sl.* foul up.

5. putter, fiddle around, *Inf.* diddle, dawdle; fool around, *Inf.* monkey around; trifle, fribble, toy with, play with.

tinkle, *n.* jingle, ring, ding, chime, peal; clink, clank, jangle; toll, knell, sound; murmur, susurrus, whisper, plash, lap.

tinsel, *n.* **1.** spangle, clinquant, metallic yarn.

2. ostentation, show, gilding, frippery, affectation, *Archaic.* frounce; falseness, unreality, make-believe, pinchbeck, sham, hypocrisy; pretentiousness, *Sl.* dog, airs, artificiality, pretension; pomp, glitter, display, spectacle; ornateness, flamboyance, gaudiness, garishness, floridity; frivolity, triviality, insignificance, meaninglessness, unimportance, hollowness, shallowness.

—*adj.* **3.** ostentatious, showy, gaudy, garish, flashy, flamboyant; clinquant, glittering, sparkling, ornate; loud, conspicuous, glaring; tawdry, meretricious, *Inf.* honky-tonk, cheap, slick, second-rate, dime-store; trashy, gimcrack, *Inf.* chintzy, *Inf.* tacky, *Sl.* rinky-dink, tasteless, indelicate, unsubtle; pretentious, affected, artificial, surface, skin-deep; imitation, fake, false, pinchbeck, *Inf.* phony, counterfeit, sham; shallow, hollow, frivolous, trivial, insignificant, unimportant; meaningless, worthless, valueless, insubstantial, aimless.

tint, *n.* **1.** hue, shade, tone, cast. See **tinge** (*def.* **3**).

2. pastel, soft *or* delicate color, subtle *or* subdued *or* muted color, light *or* pale *or* faint color.

3. dye, hair coloring, wash, solution, *Chem.* aniline dye, *Obs.* taint; coloring, colorant, pigment, stain.

—*v.* **4.** (*all of hair*) color, darken, frost, streak, lighten, bleach; (*all with color*) imbue, ingrain, infuse, instill, impregnate, imbrue, suffuse; tinge, tincture, color.

tintinnabulation, *n.* ring, ringing, ding, ding-dong, chime, peal, clang, clangor; reverberation, resounding, *Sl.* bong; jingle, tinkle.

tiny, *adj.* little, very small, diminutive, miniature, vest-pocket, bantam, baby, wee, *Inf.* teeny; microscopic, animalcular, invisible to the naked eye, atomlike; like a hop-o'-my-thumb *or* Tom Thumb, *Inf.* pint-size, dwarfish, *Med.* nanoid, dwarf, midget, pygmy, *Inf.* peewee, elfin, Lilliputian; petite, minikin, dainty, delicate; puny, runty, stunted, shrunken, *Inf.* sawed-off, snub; minute, infinitesimal, miniscule; minor, paltry, not worth mentioning, insignificant, inconsequential, unimportant, slight, trifling; *All Baby Talk.* teeny-weeny, teensy-weensy, eensy-weensy, itty-bitty. itsy-bitsy.

tip[1], *n.* **1.** point, nib, neb, beak, cusp, cuspid; sprout, shoot, *Bot.* apiculus; cap, crown, head, cover; apogee, extremity, terminal, terminus.

2. top, summit, apex, vertex, zenith, acme, meridian, tiptop; pinnacle, peak, crest, heights; spire, steeple, cupola, loft, aerie.

3. insert, inset, addition, tip-in, tip-on.

—*v.* **4.** crown, cap, top, pinnacle, surmount, *Brit.* nib; sharpen, acuminate, whet, *Metalworking.* point.

5. nip, pinch, break off; snip, prune, clip, crop, trim, poll, pollard, cut, lop off.

tip[2], *v.* **1.** tilt, lean, list, slant, cant, incline.

2. upset, overturn, overthrow, topple, subvert, capsize; turn over, turn upside down, turn turtle, turn topsy-turvy.

3. fall over, keel over, topple over, tumble over, tip over.

—*n.* **4.** incline, inclination, slope, slant, cant, rake, bias, tilt.

tip[3], *n.* **1.** gratuity, consideration, fee, lagniappe, baksheesh, *Fr. pourboire.*

2. hint, suggestion, *Inf.* pointer, *Sl.* steer; advice, piece *or* word of advice, counsel, admonition, word to the wise; clue, *Inf.* tip-off, *Inf.* bug *or* flea in the ear; warning, forewarning, caution.

—*v.* **3.** **tip off** *Informal.* **a.** inform, tell, apprise, let know, have one to know, give one to understand, enlighten, notify, acquaint, *Inf.* clue in, *Inf.* let [s.o.] in on [s.t.], *Inf.* tout after [s.t.], *Sl.* put [s.o.] on to [s.t.]. **b.** forewarn, precaution, prewarn, *Rare.* premonish; alert, warn, give fair warning, put on guard, put on the qui vive, *Sl.* give the high sign to; caution, admonish, advise, say a word to the wise, *Inf.* put a bug in [s.o.'s] ear.

tipple, *v.* **1.** (*all of alcoholic beverages*) drink, tope, bouse, *Inf.* booze, bibble, nip, *Archaic.* dram; drink like a fish, drink hard, drink seriously; get drunk, *Sl.* get plastered *or* pickled, *Brit. Sl.* get bevied; *All Inf.*

gargle, wet or moisten one's whistle, take a drop, chug, chug-a-lug, lap, lap up, commune with the spirits, drown one's sorrows; *All Sl.* hit the bottle *or* booze *or* sauce, knock a few back, liquor up, souse, dip the beak, exercise *or* crook *or* bend *or* raise the elbow.

—n. **2.** intoxicant, alcoholic beverage, drink, potation; liquor, alcohol, spirits, John Barleycorn, the demon rum, *Inf.* booze, *Inf.* hard stuff, *Sl.* hooch, *Sl.* red-eye, *Sl.* medicine; *Sl.* rot-gut, *Sl.* poison, *Sl.* blue ruin; moonshine, firewater, *Sl.* mountain dew, *Sl.* white lightning; mixed drink, cocktail, highball, *Inf.* chaser; the bottle, the cup, the cup that cheers; parting cup, stirrup cup, *Scot.* doch-an-dorrach, *Scot.* wee doch-an-dorrach.

tippler, *n.* drunk, drunkard, sot, soak, toper, tosspot, bibber, bibbler, *Obs. Rare.* biberon, barfly; alcoholic, chronic alcoholic *or* drunk *or* drunkard, dipsomaniac; drinker, hard drinker, serious drinker, problem drinker; *All Inf.* guzzler, swiller, soaker, sponge, lovepot; *All Sl.* boozer, boozehound, lush, souse, rummy, wino, alky, juicehead, juicer, hooch hound, gin hound, swillbelly, swillpot, stew, stewbum, elbow-bender, elbow-crooker.

tipsy, *adj.* **1.** intoxicated, inebriated, inebriate, inebrious, bibacious, crapulent, crapulous; drunk, drunken, sodden, besotted, sottish, awash, *Literary.* in one's cups; under the influence, under the weather; grogged, *Archaic.* groggy, fuddled, muddled, obfuscated, woozy, bleary-eyed, pie-eyed, glassy-eyed; merry, happy, gay, jolly; maudlin.

2. *All Inf.* boozy, tight, lit, lit-up, lit to the gills, illuminated, liquored-up; half seas over, three *or* four sheets to the wind, under the sauce, off-color; pickled, lathered, high; mellow, with a jag on, feeling good, feeling no pain. See also **drunk** (*def.* **2**).

3. *All Sl.* loaded, lubricated, oiled, well-oiled, stewed, tanked, *Brit.* pissed, *Brit.* bevied; primed, gassed, bombed, woozled; crocked, cocked, half-cocked, cockeyed, canned, potted. See also **drunk** (*def.* **3**).

tirade, *n.* diatribe, invective, philippic, screed, curse, jeremiad, vituperation, denunciation, commination, stream of abuse, bitter harangue, verbal onslaught; contumely, billingsgate, condemnation, censure, obloquy, vilification, scurrility; curse, *Archaic.* malison, imprecation, execration, malediction; reproof, rebuke, reprimand, reprehension, objurgation, rating, upbraiding, *Inf.* tongue-lashing, *Sl.* dressing-down, *Sl.* bawling-out, *Sl.* chewing-out, castigation.

tire, *v.* **1.** fatigue, fatigate, weary, drain, wear out, tire out; exhaust, enervate, lethargize; wind, fag, *Inf.* tucker, *Inf.* bush, *Inf.* take it out of, *Sl.* poop, *Sl.* poop out, *Sl.* knock out; burn out, do in, burn the candle at both ends, overwork, overtax; prostrate, debilitate, disable, devitalize.

2. bore, bore stiff, bore to tears, bore to death, set *or* send one to sleep; trouble, bother, wear on, annoy, irritate, irk, exasperate, tax [s.o.'s] patience, *Inf.* get.

tired, *adj.* **1.** fatigued, weary, wearied, worn out, *Inf.* tuckered out, *Inf.* bushed, fagged, fagged out, played out, burned out, wiped out, spent, *Archaic.* forspent; exhausted, *Sl.* dead, dead on one's feet, dead tired, *Inf.* dog-tired, tired out; overtired, done in, all in, ready to drop; drowsy, sleepy, half-asleep, groggy, *Sl.* dopey, *Sl.* drugged; *All Sl.* shot, beat, pooped, pooped out, (*with* have) had it.

2. *Usu.* **tired of** bored with *or* of, sick of, sick and tired of; *Inf.* fed up, *Inf.* fed up to the teeth, *Inf.* fed *or* had it up to here, *Sl.* fed to the gills.

3. bored, world-weary, life-weary, jaded, blasé.

4. stale, worn, hackneyed, commonplace, cliché; trite, platitudinous, *Inf.* bromidic.

tiresome, *adj.* **1.** wearisome, wearying, wearing, fagging, fatiguing, tiring; arduous, laborious, operose, toilsome, uphill; boring, boresome, tedious, monotonous, humdrum, repetitious, routine, unvaried; dull, flat, dead, bland, insipid, *Sl.* blah, *Sl.* ho-hum; uninteresting, uninspiring, unexciting, dry-as-dust, sawdusty; mediocre, *Inf.* nothing to write home about, *Sl.* nothing; long-winded, prolix, windy, wordy, drawn out, dragged out, long-drawn.

2. annoying, vexatious, vexing, irksome, irritating, *Inf.* aggravating; exasperating, trying, bothersome, pestering, *Inf.* pesky, *Inf.* pestiferous, hectoring, harassing; troubling, troublesome, worrying, worrisome.

tissue, *n.* **1.** gause, gossamer, chiffon, Georgette, crepe de Chine, silk, faille; mesh, net, netting, lace, webbing; fabric, cloth, textile.

2. web, network, reticulation, plexus, nexus; interweaving, combination, assemblage, collection, set, accumulation, mass, conglomeration.

3. parchment, onion skin, tissue paper.

titanic, *adj.* huge, gigantic, gargantuan, enormous, *Archaic.* enorm, immense, great, prodigious, herculean; vast, massive, large-scale, mammoth, jumbo, colossal, monumental, monstrous, gigantean, cyclopean, Brobdingnagian; towering, staggering, mountainous, stupendous, tremendous, *Sl.* humongous; elephantine, hippopotamic, leviathan, dinosaurian; *All Inf.* whopping, roaring, spanking, walloping, strapping.

tit for tat, revenge, retaliation, requital, counterblow, counterstroke, countercharge; *Latin. quid pro quo,* a Roland for an Oliver, blow for a blow, eye for an eye, tooth for a tooth, measure for measure, pound for pound, lex talonis, talion; dose *or* taste of one's own medicine, just deserts, *Inf.* what's coming to one, *U.S. Inf.* comeuppance.

titillate, *v.* **1.** tickle, titivate, stroke lightly, pet, twiddle; massage, knead, manipulate.

2. excite, thrill, arouse, turn on, stimulate; strike one's fancy, tickle one's fancy, interest, intrigue; captivate, fascinate, entrance, charm; attract, allure, tempt, seduce, enchant, transport.

3. delight, please, refresh, tickle pink, tickle to death; amuse, entertain, exhilarate, tickle one's funny bone.

titillation, *n.* **1.** tickling, titivating, stroking, petting, massaging, rubbing, kneading, manipulation, handling.

2. excitement, thrill, arousal, stimulation; captivation, fascination, entrancement, enchantment; amusement, entertainment, exhilaration; *Both Sl.* kicks, jollies.

title, *n.* **1.** book name, story name, cover inscription, subtitle; headline, head, banner, banner head *or* line, streamer; heading, subheading, subhead, lemma; caption, rubric, legend, inscription, *Journalism.* cutline, *Motion Pictures.* subtitle.

2. name, denomination, designation, *Both Grammar.* nominative, noun; appellation, compellation, honorific, form of address, term of respect; given name, Christian name, praenomen, family name, last name, surname, patronymic, metronymic; nickname, sobriquet, cognomen, agnomen, pet name, diminutive; by-name, byword, appellative, epithet, style, trade name, trademark, *Sl.* handle, *Sl.* moniker; label, tag, *Computer Tech.* address; pseudonym, anonym, allonym, alias, assumed name, *Fr. nom de guerre,* pen name, nom de plume, stage name, *Fr. nom de théâtre.*

3. deed, title deed, proof of ownership, documentation, document, legal paper, instrument; ownership, proprietorship, possessorship, possession, holding, tenure, demesne, *Law.* domain, *Archaic.* aught; interest, concern, stake, share.

4. grounds, good reason, due cause, *Law.* cause; right, just claim, droit; birthright, due, privilege, prerogative; license, freedom, liberty; immunity, exemption, impunity.

—*v.* **5.** name, nickname, dub, entitle, christen, baptize, surname; denominate, designate, identify, *Archaic.* clepe, *Archaic.* nominate; call, address; label, tag, term, style, stereotype.

titter, *v.* snicker, snigger, laugh under one's breath *or* to oneself, laugh up *or* in one's sleeve, chuckle, show one's amusement; te-hee, giggle, cackle, chirp, chirrup; laugh at, mock; smirk, grin, smile at, simper, mouth, *Sl.* mug, *Archaic.* mow; sneer, curl one's lip at.

tittle-tattle, *n.* **1.** gossip, *Inf.* scuttlebutt, hearsay, *Fr. ouï-dire*, report, *Archaic.* bruit; *Sl.* dope, *Inf.* inside info, *Sl.* poop; prattle, idle talk, *Sl.* schmooze, small talk, palaver, *Scot.* clishmaclaver; chat, chitchat, *Sl.* yackety-yak, *Sl.* yak, twaddle, blather.

—*v.* **2.** tattle, *Inf.* blab, gossip, rumor, bruit, *Scot.* clishmaclaver, spread stories; prattle, prate, palaver; chatter, chat, chitchat, *Sl.* yak, *Sl.* schmooze; gibber, blather, gabble, run off at the mouth, *Sl.* jaw, shoot the breeze.

titular, *adj.* **1.** naming, denominative, designative, designatory, identifying, labeling, *Gram.* nominative; appellative, compellative, honorific, honorifical, titulary; sobriquetical, cognominal, epithetic, epithetical.

2. named, dubbed, labeled, tagged, called, *Archaic.* yclept *or* clept, *Archaic.* hight; titled, noble, royal, regal, blue-blooded, highborn, aristocratic, patrician, silk-stocking; official, high-level, high-ranking, big.

3. nominal, in title *or* name only, so-called, self-called, self-christened, self-styled, *Fr. soi-disant*; empty, powerless, token, (*of governments*) puppet; formal, ex officio; honorary, *Latin. honoris causa.*

—*n.* **4.** official, magistrate, officebearer, officeholder, officer, pooh bah, *Brit.* placeman, *Rare.* officiary; dignitary, VIP, big shot, big man, heavy, *Inf.* brass, *Inf.* bigwig; noble, nobleman, noblewoman, gentleman, gentlewoman; king, prince, czar, emperor, sheik, khan, rajah, maharajah; grand duke, archduke, lord, milord, peer, duke, marquis, *Hist.* margrave, earl, count, viscount, baron; grandee, magnifico, don, hidalgo; baronet, lordling, *Scot. Hist.* thane, princeling, princekin, princelet; seigneur, feudal lord, *Japanese Hist.* daimyo, signior, signor; squire, *Scot.* laird, *Russian Hist.* boyar, (*in medieval Germany*) landgrave; knight, cavalier, *Fr. Hist.* chevalier, *Hist.* banneret, armiger; queen, sovereign queen, princess, czarina, empress, maharanee, maharani, rani, lady, milady, dame, begum, margravine, shahzadi; duchess, archduchess, grand duchess, countess, viscountess, baroness, marchioness, peeress.

5. eponym, who [s.o.] is named after.

toady, *n.* **1.** sycophant, toadeater, fawner, flatterer, fawning flatterer, truckler, tufthunter, courtier, wheedler, puffer, backslapper, backscratcher, timeserver, *Inf.* apple polisher, *Sl.* brown-nose, *Sl.* brownnoser, *Sl.* brownie, *Obs., Rare.* blander, *Archaic.* pickthank; parasite, leech, *Inf.* sponge *or* sponger, hanger-on; flunky, lackey, *Inf.* yes man, jackal, spaniel, bootlick, bootlicker, lickspit, lickspittle, kowtower, *U.S.* Uncle Tom, *U.S. Sl.* oreo, cringer, groveler, sniveler; puppet, slave, dupe, instrument, tool, cat's-paw, rubber-stamp, doormat, footstool, *Sl.* stooge.

—*v.* **2.** fawn, fawn upon, *Sl.* fall all over, truckle, truckle to, toady to, wheedle, puff, puff up, inflate, *Sl.* suck up to, *Sl.* play up to, *Inf.* apple-polish, *Sl.* brownnose, *Sl.* get brownie points; lick [s.o.'s] shoes, lick *or* kiss [s.o.'s] feet, *Inf.* be a yes man to, *Inf.* bootlick; kowtow, bow, bow and scrape, stoop, kneel, fall on one's knees, prostrate oneself; grovel, crawl, creep, crouch, slither; cringe, cower, squirm.

toadyish, *adj.* **1.** sycophantic, sycophantical, sycophantish, fawning, flattering, truckling, wheedling, toadying; ingratiating, timeserving, *Inf.* bootlicking, *Sl.* apple-polishing, *Sl.* brown-nosing, *Obs., Rare.* blandiloquous; buttery, candied, unctuous, oily, honey-mouthed, smooth-tongued, smooth-talking, sweet-talking, *Rare* blandiloquent.

2. slavish, servile, obsequious, *Obs.* obsequent, subservient, menial, *Obs., Rare.* vernile; submissive, docile, unassertive, compliant, tractable, acquiescent, deferential, mealy-mouthed, *U.S.* Tomish *or* Uncle Tomish; prostrate, obeisant, on one's knees; abject, base, mean, beggarly, beggared; groveling, crawling, creeping, crouching, sneaking, slithering; squirming, cringing, cowering; whining, whimpering, sniveling.

toadyism, *n.* **1.** sycophancy, sycophantism, flattery, fawning, truckling, wheedling, toadeating, tufthunting, lip-homage, mouth-honor, unctuousness, *Inf.* soft soap, *Inf.* bootlicking, *Inf.* apple-polishing, *Sl.* brown-nosing, *Rare.* blandiloquence, *Obs., Rare.* blandation, *Obs., Rare.* blandiloquy.

2. slavishness, servility, obsequiousness, subservience, *Obs.* vernility; submissiveness, docility, unassertiveness, compliance, acquiescence, deference, tractability, tractableness; prostration, obeisance, abjection, abjectness, self-abasement; groveling, crawling, creeping, crouching, slithering; squirming, cringing, cowering; whining, whimpering, sniveling.

to-and-fro, *adv., adj.* **1.** back-and-forth, side-to-side, up-and-down, in-and-out, zigzag, seesaw, this way and that; alternating, reciprocal.

—*n.* **2.** alternation, coming and going, ebb and flow, flux and reflux, systole and diastole; seesawing, teetering, teeter-tottering.

toast[1], *v.* heat *or* heat up, warm *or* warm up, brown, cook lightly, grill, roast.

toast[2], *n.* **1.** salutation, pledge health; cheers, cheerio, skoal, your health, *Fr. santé, Fr. salut, Latin. prosit, Hebrew. l'chayim, Yiddish.* mazel tov; happy days, good luck, *Inf.* here's looking at you, *Sl.* here's mud in your eye, *Inf.* bottoms up, *Sl.* down the hatch.

—*v.* **2.** propose a toast, pledge; drink a toast, drink to [s.o.'s] health, clink glasses.

toastmaster, *n.* symposiarch, master *or* mistress of ceremonies, *Inf.* emcee, *Inf.* M.C.; host, hostess, introducer; raconteur, storyteller, anecdotist; joker, jokester, quipster; moderator, interlocutor, coordinator, facilitator; chairman, chairwoman, chairperson, chair.

tocsin, *n.* signal, alarm bell, alarm, alert, warning *or* alarm gun, fire alarm, siren, whistle, horn, foghorn, *Archaic.* alarum; red light, red flag, danger signal, yellow light *or* flag, flashing light; cry of distress, call for help, SOS, May Day.

today, *n.* **1.** this present day, this very day.

2. the present, now, this moment, this time, this age, this period, this era.

—*adv.* **3.** on this present day, on this very day, *Fr. aujourd'hui, Ger. heute.*

4. at the present time, in these days, in this day and age.

toddle, *v.* dodder, falter, wobble, move unsteadily; hobble, limp, hitch, halt, pause, hesitate; totter, *Chiefly U.S.* teeter, *Chiefly U.S.* teeter-totter, sway.

to-do, *n. Informal.* ado, bustle, hustle and bustle, hustle, flurry, flutter, buzzing *or* flitting about, scurry, hurry-scurry, running around, doing, *Sometimes Facetious.* do; busyness, stir, activity, action, motion, movement; fuss, fuss and feathers, bother, pother, trouble; much ado about nothing, tempest in a teapot, storm in a teacup, *Inf.* foofaraw, *Sl.* flap, *Inf.* stew; confusion, excitement, furor, commotion, hubbub, noise; agitation, *Archaic.* pucker, tempest, storm, disquiet, unrest; disturbance, tumult, turmoil, tumultousness, uproar, hurly-burly, hurly, brouhaha.

together, *adv.* **1.** in unison, in concert, all at once, all together, en masse, as a group, *Fr. ensemble, Ger. zusammen.*

2. collectively, conjointly, *Inf.* put together.

3. simultaneously, at the same time, in the same breath, *Fr. en même temps*; synchronously, contemporaneously, concurrently, concomitantly, coincidentally, coincidently.

4. without interruption, in succession, successively, consecutively, in a row.

5. in cooperation, conjointly, shoulder to shoulder, side by side, arm in arm, hand in hand, hand in glove, closely.

6. reciprocally, mutally.

—adj. **7.** *Slang.* (*of persons*) well-balanced, well-adjusted; sensible, level-headed, commonsensical, down-to-earth.

toil[1], *n.* **1.** labor, travail, sweat of one's brow, *Inf.* elbow grease; moil, drudgery, grind, menial work; hard work, hard labor, slavery; exertion, effort, strain, struggle, laboriousness, plodding, *Inf.* plugging, pegging; industry, industriousness, operoseness, diligence.

—v. **2.** work *or* work hard, slog, moil, drudge, grub, grind, put one's shoulder to the wheel, put one's nose to the grindstone; work one's fingers to the bone, slave *or* slave away, work like a slave, work like a dog, work like a Trojan, *Sl.* kill oneself; work day and night, burn the midnight oil, burn the candle at both ends, overdo, overwork, overexert oneself; sweat, struggle, *Sl.* beat one's brains out; peg away at, *Inf.* plug away at, *Inf.* hack away at, hammer away at; plod along, keep trying, persevere; force oneself, push oneself, strain oneself, exert oneself, make an effort, work at, apply oneself to.

toil[2], *n.* **1.** net, snare, springe, gin, trap; mousetrap, lobster pot.

2. *Usu.* **toils** trap, snare, pitfall, stumbling block; difficulty, problem, trouble *or* troubles, trials and tribulations.

toiler, *n.* worker, hand, workman, moiler, laborer, hack, drudge, fag; blue-collar worker, unskilled laborer, day laborer, manual laborer, *Inf.* hardhat, *Disparaging.* (*in the southern U.S.*) redneck; mechanic, longshoreman, stevedore, miner *or* mine worker, bricklayer, construction worker, *Brit. Inf.* navvy; employee, help, hired hand, hireling; servant, domestic servant *or* domestic, menial; working man *or* woman *or* girl, wage earner, breadwinner; skilled laborer, white-collar worker, professional.

toilet, *n.* **1.** flush toilet, *Naut.* head, *Sl.* john, *Sl.* johnny, *Sl.* can, *Sl.* crapper, *Circus.* donicker, hopper, *Sl.* throne, potty, latrine, Turkish toilet, *Euph.* facilities; urinal, *Fr. pissoir.*

2. bathroom, *Euph.* basement, water closet, *Chiefly Brit.* w.c., closet, *Brit.* ablutions, *Chiefly Brit.* convenience, *Chiefly New Eng.* necessary, *Facetious.* reading room, *Brit. Sl.* loo; rest room, comfort station, men's room, *Sl.* gents, boys' *or* little boys' room, women's *or* ladies' room, *Sl.* ladies, girls' *or* little girls' room; privy, outhouse, backhouse, stool, cloaca, *Chiefly Dial.* jakes, *Brit. Sl.* bogs, *Sl.* one- *or* two-holer.

3. dressing room, powder room, lounge, lavatory, *Fr. lavabo,* washroom.

4. dressing, bathing, *Circus.* crumb-up, wash-up, manicure, hairdressing, coiffure, apparel, dress, costume, attire, *Inf.* duds, garb, *Archaic.* vesture, *Chiefly Literary.* raiment.

toilsome, *adj.* laborious, arduous, difficult, *Sl.* bitchy, hard, tough; herculean, strenuous, rugged; onerous, burdensome, backbreaking, uphill; fatiguing, tiring, wearying, wearisome, wearing, taxing, enervating, draining, exhausting; troublesome, irksome.

token, *n.* **1.** symbol, representation, sign, emblem, *Archaic.* recognizance, badge; indication, mark, augury, manifestation, expression, evidence, testimony, proof, indicia.

2. memento, souvenir, keepsake, reminder, remembrance, memorial.

—adj. **3.** symbolic, representative, emblematic.

4. perfunctory, superficial, hasty, heedless, thoughtless, without thought *or* concern; indifferent, impassive, apathetic, unenthusiastic; minimal, slight, small, little.

tolerable, *adj.* **1.** endurable, sufferable, brookable, supportable, acceptable, *Obs. Rare.* abidable; permissible, allowable; experienceable.

2. mediocre, middling, average, so-so, ordinary, indifferent, run-of-the-mill, garden-variety, household; second-rate, secondary, inferior; adequate, satisfactory, respectable; passable, innocuous, decent; pretty good, not too bad, good enough.

tolerance, *n.* **1.** freedom from bigotry, lack of prejudice, liberal spirit, democratic spirit, dispassion, open-mindedness, receptivity; mercy, lenity, indulgence, clemency, quarter; benevolence, charity, good will, philanthropy, altruism, kindliness, brotherly love, benignity, humanity, fellow feeling, sympathy, bonhomie.

2. endurance, toleration, sufferance, forbearance, sustainment, abidingness; patience, stoicism, resignation, resignedness, acceptance; long-suffering, longanimity.

tolerant, *adj.* unprejudiced, unbigoted, liberal, undogmatic, broad-minded, open-minded, catholic, latitudinarian; level-headed, imperturable, dispassionate, moderate, philosophical; merciful, lenient, indulgent, accepting, clement; benevolent, humanitarian, humane, large-hearted, magnanimous, sympathetic, charitable, kindly, considerate, altruistic, philanthropic; patient, forbearing, abiding, enduring, long-suffering, uncomplaining; meek, soft, gentle, submissive, easy-going, complaisant.

tolerate, *v.* **1.** permit, admit, allow, countenance; recognize, accord, oblige, gratify, indulge; sanction, concede, warrant, vouchsafe, approve; favor, give quarter, show mercy, spare the vanquished; disregard, overlook, condone, ignore, wink at; be lax, be lenient, hold a loose rein, give carte blanche to, *Inf.* keep hands off.

2. endure, take, suffer, bear; take patiently, brook, submit to, abide, stand, withstand, put up with; swallow, digest, stomach, pocket; make the best of, carry on, keep one's countenance, put a good face on, grin and bear it.

3. *Med.* (*of drugs*) withstand, endure, resist the action of.

toleration, *n.* **1.** forbearance, sufferance, endurance; allowance, permission, concession, license, franchise, enfranchisement; clemency, lenity, lenience, quarter; laxity, freedom, tolerance, independence, liberty; scope, play, range, rope, latitute, free rein, free stage; laissez faire.

2. open-mindedness, liberality, liberalism, catholicity; impartiality, disinterest, absence of prejudice, freedom from bigotry; magnanimity, largeness of mind, high-mindedness; benevolence, mercy, compassion, altruism, fellow feeling; philanthropy, humanitarianism, humaneness, humanity, good will; benignity, brotherly love, bonhomie, milk of human kindness; generosity, consideration, considerateness.

toll[1], *v.* strike, sound, ring, ring the knell, knell, peal.

toll[2], *n.* payment, recompense; assessment, exaction, fee, dues, charge; rate, tribute, duty, tax, levy, tariff, impost.

tomb, *n.* **1.** grave, resting place, sepulcher, crypt, catacombs, vault, burial chamber, shrine, reliquary.

2. pyramid, mastaba, dolmen, cromlech; cerotaph, memorial.

tomboy, *n.* gamine, hoyden, romp, minx, imp, urchin, whippersnapper; schoolgirl, *Inf.* filly.

tome, *n.* volume, book, opus, magnum opus, heavy *or* learned book; reference book, dictionary, encyclopedia, compendium.

tomfoolery, *n.* **1.** antic, antics, caper, *Inf.* shenanigans, *Sl.* monkeyshines, *Sl.* monkey business; mockery, farce, mummery; mischief, prankishness, *Inf.* hanky-panky, *Scot. and North Eng.* daffing; prank, escapade, trick, practical joke, roguish trick, *Fr. espièglerie*; fooling, foolery, horseplay, frolic, spree, lark, skylarking; clownery, clownishness, zanyism; buffoonery, buffoonism, buffoonishness, harlequinade; joking, jesting, jocosity, jocoseness, jocularity, waggishness, waggery, drollery; levity, frivolity, facetiousness; silliness, childishness, immaturity, puerility, juvenility.

2. absurdity, inanity, pointlessness, fatuity, fatuousness, foolishness, folly; senselessness, meaninglessness, nonsense, *Archaic.* insipience; unreasonableness, irrationality, illogic, illogicality; extravagance, preposterousness; asininity, idiocy, imbecility, *Inf.* moronism, stupidity, bêtise; craziness, *Sl.* kookiness, madness, insanity; peculiarity, strangeness, oddity, *Sl.* screwiness, *Sl.* goofiness.

tommyrot, *n.* **1.** nonsense, falderal, gibberish, Jabberwocky; babble, babbling, babblement, *Fr. bavardage;* twaddle, twaddling, *Both Brit.* twattle, twattling; blather, blathering, drivel, driveling, drool, drooling; hocus-pocus, mumbo jumbo, fiddle-de-dee; moonshine, gobbledegook, foolish humbug, foam, froth, bunkum, *Sl.* bunk, *U.S. Sl.* blah; flummery, *Inf.* hokum, *Sl.* applesauce, *Sl.* eyewash; rubbish, *Sl.* tripe, refuse, *Dial.* culch, chaff, trash, *Inf.* truck; trumpery, *Inf.* rot, *Sl.* garbage, *Sl.* crap, *Sl.* crock, *Sl.* bull; balderdash, hogwash, swill, *Sl.* horsefeathers; stuff, stuff and nonsense, *Inf.* bosh, *Brit. Inf.* gammon, *Brit. Sl.* tosh.

2. utter foolishness, fudge, folly, rigmarole, amphigory; footle, *Inf.* malarkey, *Sl.* bushwa, *Sl.* baloney, *Sl.* bilge *or* bilge water, *Sl.* meshugaas, *Scot. and North Eng.* haver; poppycock, *Inf.* fiddle-faddle, *Inf.* piffle, *Inf.* hooey, *Inf.* kibosh, *Inf.* flapdoodle; idle talk, *Inf.* gab, *Sl.* gas, palaver, palavering, palaverment; claptrap, rodomontade, fustian, bombast, rant, *Sl.* hot air; jabber, jabbering, prate, prating; patter, pattering, gabble, gabbling; clack, clacking, clatter, clattering, rattling, *Sl.* running off *or* on at the mouth; chatter, chattering, prattle, prattling, chippering, cackle, cackling; chitchat, chitter-chatter, small talk, *Anglo-Indian.* bukh.

tone, *n.* **1.** sound, noise, note, voice, sonance; pitch, frequency.

2. timbre, tonality, tone color, tone quality, sound quality, color, coloring, *Music.* clang color *or* tint, *Music, Ger. Klangfarbe;* ring, clang, resonance; sonority, sonorousness, richness, fullness, deepness; tonelessness, monotone.

3. strain, lilt, tune, jingle, flow, harmonious flow, rhythmic flow, movement, swing, speech tune *or* melody.

4. intonation, modulation, inflection, phrasing, suspension; pitch, pitch accent, pitch pattern, intonation pattern *or* contour; voice quality, voice, tone of voice; elocution, diction, speech pattern, manner of speaking, mode of expression; cadence, beat, rhythm, tempo, pulse, throb.

5. regional accent, foreign accent, dialect, regional dialect, *Brit.* Received Standard *or* public school accent; drawl, twang, burr, brogue, broad accent *or* speech.

6. accent, accentuation, emphasis, stress, syllable stress; delivery, presentation, attack, force of utterance.

7. hue, tint, shade, tinge; value, chroma, color quality, purity; prevailing color, coloring, color, key, dye, cast, complexion; saturation; variety of color.

8. *Physiology.* **a.** tension, firmness, soundness, sturdiness. **b.** health, healthiness, vigor, vigorousness; vitality, energy, fitness, strength. **c.** elasticity, resilience, resiliency, healthy sensitivity.

9. spirit, character, mood, tenor, quality; humor, disposition, frame *or* state of mind, temperament, temper; frame, mold, grain, vein, stripe, streak, stamp, brand; state, condition, trim, fiber, fettle, kilter.

10. mode, manner, way, wise, technique, approach, method, system; style, fashion, form; shape, turn, habit, tendency.

11. ethos, climate, intellectual *or* spiritual climate, trend *or* sign of the times, spirit of the age *or* times, *Ger. Zeitgeist;* trend, set, course, current, main current, mainstream, drift, general tendency *or* drift; line, direction, swing, bearing, course of events, way the wind blows, way things go; (*all of a place*) atmosphere, ambience, aura, air, climate, milieu, feel, feeling, sense.

12. style, distinction, elegance, *Inf.* class; appearance, mein, demeanor, guise; carriage, poise, presence.

—*v.* **13.** sound, chime, ring, peal, knell, toll, tintinnabulate; gong, ding, dong, dingdong; clang, clank.

14. change, modify, alter, vary, diversify; adapt, accommodate, fit, accord, adjust, regulate, qualify.

15. tone down a. *Painting.* subdue, darken, shade, shadow, overshadow, dim; pale, whiten, fade, wash out; bleach, blanch, decolorize, achromatize, etiolate. **b.** moderate, temper, season, restrain, constrain, keep within bounds; relax, mitigate, alleviate, assuage, palliate, let up, take the edge off, take the bite *or* string out, *Sl.* take the heat off, *Sl.* lay off; modulate, soften, quiet, turn *or* tune down, cut down; mute, deaden, damp, dampen, soft-pedal.

16. tone up a. furbish, freshen, freshen up, vamp, retouch, touch up, brush up, spruce, spruce up, brighten up; polish, polish up, *Inf.* shine *or* shine up. **b.** tune, tune up, attune, put in tune *or* trim *or* shape *or* working order; limber, limber up, *Inf.* shape up, get into shape *or* condition.

tongue, *n.* **1.** organ of taste, lingua; *Bot., Zool.* ligula.

2. language, speech, dialect, parlance, idiolect; mother tongue, native tongue, native language, parent language; vernacular, common speech; verbal expression, use of words, voice, ability to speak; slang, idiom, vulgarism, colloquialism, vernacularism; jargon, *Ing.* lingo, argot; jabber, gibberish, gibber, gobbledygook, empty talk; prattle, mumbo jumbo, palaver, patter.

3. diction, talk, accent, tone, expression, utterance, vocalization; manner of speaking, locution; phrasing, wording, terminology, phraseology, vocabulary.

4. *Often* **tongues** glossolalia, gift of speaking in tongues.

5. find one's tongue recover one's poise, find the

right words, think what to say, say what one means.

6. hold one's tongue be silent, keep silent, keep one's mouth shut, muzzle oneself, not breathe a word, say nothing, keep mum, not utter a word; refuse comment, save one's breath; keep one's own counsel, not open one's mouth.

7. slip of the tongue mistake in speaking, slip, Freudian slip, wrong *or* bad *or* false move, blunder, faux pas, gaffe, stupidity, indiscretion.

8. tongue in cheek *or* **with tongue in cheek** in fun, in just, in play; kiddingly, jokingly, jestingly, facetiously; mockingly, insincerely, sarastically, ironically.

tongue-tied, *adj.* **1.** speechless, dumbstruck, dumbstricken, struck dumb, dumfounded, *Inf.* choked up, wordless; inarticulate, *Pathol.* aphasic, unable to get a word out; shocked, amazed, astounded, *Inf.* floored, paralyzed, at a loss for words.

2. quiet, silent, close-mouthed, tight-lipped, voiceless, mum, mute; taciturn, reserved, bashful, shy, reticent; uncommunicative, unconversable, unconversational, untalkative.

tonic, *n.* **1.** medicine, *Med.* roborant, *Med.* analeptic, restorative, cordial, ptisan, *Inf.* bracer; invigorant, stimulant, pickup.

2. refresher, boost, *Inf.* pick-me-up, *Inf.* picker-upper, *Inf.* upper, *Inf.* shot in the arm, *Inf.* ego trip; pep talk, build-up, inspiration, uplifting, incentive.

—adj. **3.** invigorating, stimulating, animating, enlivening, vivifying, vitalizing, bracing, invigorative; energizing, fortifying, strengthening; restorative, restoring, remedial, curative, analeptic; healthful, healthy, *Med.* euthropic, salubrious, salutary, salutiferous, wholesome.

too, *adj.* **1.** in addition, additionally, also, besides, as well, to boot, ditto, as well as; furthermore, further, over and above, moreover, more than that; together with that, therewithal, *Archaic.* thereto; along with, together with, in conjunction with, conjointly.

2. extremely, excessively, inordinately, immoderately; exorbitantly, unduly, unreasonably; overmuch, overly, too much, *Inf.* too-too, beyond what is fitting.

tool, *n.* **1.** implement, instrument, utensil, apparatus, device, contrivance, invention; gadget, dohickey, hickey, *Inf.* contraption, *Sl.* gimmick; aid, convenience, *Archaic.* conveniency, time-saver; appliance, mechanism, machine, automaton, robot.

2. vehicle, channel, agency, instrumentality, means, way, ways and means, wherewithal; agent, medium, intermediary, middleman, go-between, broker, *Chiefly Brit.* factor, *Sl.* ten-percenter; cat's-paw, pawn, puppet, creature; jackal, flunky, lackey, attendant, peon, servant, handmaid, menial; minion, follower, toady, sycophant, *Inf.* yes man; hireling, underling, assistant, henchman, *Sl.* stooge; dummy, dupe, *Sl.* pigeon, gull, gudgeon, *Inf.* sucker.

tooth, *n.* **1.** fang, tusk, tush; denticle, denticulation.

2. projection, point, tip, tang, barb, spine, spike, spur, nib, dent, snag, jab; sprocket, ratchet, cog.

3. liking, taste, relish, *Inf.* sweet tooth; predilection, partiality, weakness.

4. by the skin of one's teeth barely, just barely, only just, narrowly.

5. long in the tooth past one's prime, *Inf.* over the hill, *Inf.* having seen better days; old, elderly, aged, ancient, at an advanced age.

6. show one's teeth snarl, snap, growl, spit; bristle, bridle, get one's back up, raise one's hackles.

7. to the teeth fully, completely, entirely, *Sl.* to the nines, *Sl.* to kill.

tooth and nail, with all one's might *or* strength, with might and main, hammer and tongs, heart and soul, *Latin. vie et armis, Archaic.* amain; fiercely, ferociously, savagely, violently, with a vengeance; frantically, frenziedly, furiously, wildly, madly, with abandon.

tooth-shaped, *adj.* odontoid, dentoid, dentiform, cuspidate, cuspidal, cuspal, toothlike.

toothsome, *adj.* **1.** palatable, tasty, good-tasting, savory, savorous, sapid; flavorable, flavorous, flavorsome, appetizing, relishable; delicious, *Sl.* yummy, mouth-watering, luscious, scrumptious, delectable, finger-lickin' good; ambrosial, ambrosian, *Archaic.* gustable, *Fr. délicieux*; piquant, pungent, spicy, sweet, honeyed, nectarous, nectareous.

2. agreeable, pleasing, enjoyable, satisfying; desirable, attractive.

3. voluptuous, curvy, curvaceous, shapely; *Sl.* built, *Sl.* stacked, *Sl.* busty; alluring, *Inf.* sexy, beautiful.

top, *n.* **1.** apex, vertex, summit, apogee, *Latin. ne plus ultra;* pinnacle, peak, crest, heights; tiptop, tip, point, spire.

2. crown, *Anat.* corona, headpiece, cap; steeple, belfry, cupola, loft, aerie; roof, ceiling, overlay, screen, lid; *All Archit.* cornice, entablature, epistyle, architrave, pediment, cover, covering.

3. stem, stalk, shoot, sprout, nib, neb, *Bot.* apiculus.

4. beginning, start, first, outset, onset, commencement, inception, genesis; head, first place *or* position, lead; front, forefront, vanguard, van, advance.

5. leader, pilot, guide, director, conductor; captain, chief, commander, president, chairman, chairwoman, master, headmaster, *Educ.* dean, *Eccles.* superior; supervisor, superintendent, manager, foreman, boss, taskmaster, *Inf.* top dog, *Sl.* big shot.

6. acme, zenith, climax, culmination, meridian, maximum, crowning point, *Med.* fastigum; sublimity, supremacy, perfection, consummation; prime, best, finest, utmost, uttermost, extreme, *U.S. Sl.* the most, *U.S. Sl.* the greatest.

—adj. **7.** summital, apical, highest, uppermost, topmost, tiptop, apogeal, apogean; upper, lofty, supernal, transcendent; culminating, culminant, climactic, climactical, crowning.

8. best, finest, prime, choicest, greatest, maximal, utmost, uttermost; superlative, superior, excellent, ace, first-rate, top-grade, top-drawer, topnotch, top-dog, *Sl.* crackerjack; sublime, supreme, consummate, perfect; peerless, imcomparable, unequaled, second to none, nonpareil, unparalleled, *Fr. sans pareil.*

9. foremost, preeminent, paramount, first, leading; chief, principal, head, ruling, sovereign; main, major, dominant.

—v. **10.** cap, crown, sit atop *or* on, pinnacle, tip, *Brit.* nib; climb, mount, ascend, scale; reach, gain, achieve, attain, accede, arrive at, get to.

11. exceed, go beyond, rise above *or* over; excel, surpass, transcend, eclipse, overshadow, outdo, outstrip, outshine; best, better, beat, win over, prevail over; clear, surmount, overtop, pass over, hurdle, vault, ride over, leap *or* jump over.

12. replenish, refill, fill up, resupply, refresh, freshen; top-dress, manure, fertilize, enrich, feed.

13. crop, trim, prune, snip, clip, poll, pollard, lop *or* cut off; nip, pinch, break off.

topcoat, *n.* overcoat, ulster, greatcoat, surcoat, surtout, trench coat, mackintosh.

tope, *v.* (*all of alcoholic beverages*) drink, tipple, bouse, *Inf.* booze, bibble, nip, *Archaic.* dram; drink like a fish, drink hard, drink seriously; get drunk, *Sl.* get plastered *or* pickled *or* looped, *Brit. Sl.* get bevied; *All Inf.* gargle, wet *or* moisten one's whistle, take a drop, chug, chug-a-lug, lap, lap up, commune with the spirits, drown one's sorrows; *All Sl.* hit the sauce *or* bottle *or* booze, knock a few back, liquor up, souse, dip the beak, exercise *or* crook *or* bend *or* raise the elbow; carouse, revel, wassail, go on a spree, *Sl.* go on a binge *or* bender *or* hellbender *or* tear *or* toot *or* bat *or* jag, *Sl.* tie one on, *Sl.* barhop, *Sl.* bar-crawl, *Brit. Sl.* pub-crawl.

toper, *n.* drunk, drunkard, sot, soak, tippler, tosspot, bibber, bibbler, *Obs., Rare.* biberon, barfly; alcoholic, chronic alcoholic *or* drunk *or* drunkard, dipsomaniac; drinker, hard drinker, serious drinker, problem drinker; *All Inf.* guzzler, swiller, soaker, sponge, lovepot; *All Sl.* boozer, boozehound, lush, souse, rummy, wino, alky, juicehead, juicer, hooch hound, gin hound, swillbelly, swillpot, stew, stewbum, elbow-bender, elbow-crooker.

topic, *n.* **1.** subject, matter *or* issue at hand; question, topic under discussion *or* on the floor *or* up for debate, moot point.

2. subject matter, area of study, field of inquiry; theme, keynote, main *or* central idea, point; concept, conceit, notion, idea; hypothesis, theory, theorem, supposition, assumption, premise, conjecture, axiom, postulate; proposition, argument, opinion, view, belief; assertion, statement, declaration, allegation, charge.

topical, *adj.* **1.** current, *Sl.* now, immediate, up-to-date, in the newspaper, in *or* on the news; of widespread interest, widely-known, well-known, commonly known, familiar, popular; circulated, in circulation, talked-of, talked-about, on everyone's lips *or* tongue, in everyone's mouth, all over town.

2. thematic, thematical.

3. local, of local interest, provincial, parochial; regional, territorial, county, district, town, city, neighborhood.

topmost, *adj.* uppermost, top, tiptop, highest, apical, culminant, consummate, maximum, ultimate; greatest, foremost, headmost, head, chief; preeminent, paramount, supreme.

topple, *v.* **1.** pitch, lurch, stagger; collapse, fall, fall down, fall over, come tumbling down, tumble down; keel over, tip over.

2. upset, knock down *or* over, push over; drop, fell, precipitate, floor, *Sl.* deck, *Inf.* bowl over.

3. subvert, overthrow, overturn, throw down *or* over.

topsy-turvy, *adv.* **1.** upside down, wrong side up bottom side up, bottom up; head over heels.

2. in reverse, backwards, *Sl.* ass-backwards, *Sl.* arsy-varsy.

3. helter-skelter, pell-mell, hurry-scurry, harum-scarum; higgledy-piggledy, hugger-mugger, *Inf.* willy-nilly, *Inf.* every which way; in confusion, in disorder, in disarray, in a jumble, in a tumble, in a muddle, in a mess, all over the place; here, there, and everywhere.

—adj. **4.** reverse, inverted, transposed, turned around, wrong-way around, back-to-front.

5. confused, chaotic, muddled, jumbled; disorderly, disordered, disarranged, deranged; unorganized, disorganized.

—n. **6.** inversion, reversion, reversal, transposition.

7. confusion, disorder, chaos, turmoil, moil, pandemonium, bedlam, topsy-turvydom.

torch, *n.* **1.** brand, firebrand, link, cresset, flambeau, *Archaic.* lamp.

2. carry the torch for *Slang.* pine, yearn for, long for, languish for, ache for, sign for, wish for; love, be desperately in love, *Sl.* have it bad, *Sl.* have a crush on [s.o.].

torment, *v.* **1.** agonize, excruciate, torture, rack, martyr, crucify; pain, hurt, scathe, lacerate, wring, put someone through the wringer; persecute, abuse, beat, *Archaic.* belabor.

2. anguish, distress, harrow, worry, trouble, disturb, *Scot.* fash; afflict, plague, vex, annoy, beleaguer, harass, harry, hector, badger, hound, bother, pester, *Brit.* chevy; exasperate, aggravate, irritate, gall, rub, chafe, roil, *Chiefly U.S.* rile, *Inf.* drive up the wall; provoke, needle, nettle, bullyrag, tease, *Brit.* rag.

3. perturb, upset, derange, agitate, convulse, toss, rattle, shake up, stir up; confuse, addle, muddle, *Inf.* drive crazy; unnerve, discompose, ruffle, fluster, disconcert, discomfit, disquiet, *Inf.* faze.

—n. **4.** agony, misery, suffering, wretchedness, martyrdom; pain, hurt, wound, sting, pang; anguish, distress, woe, tribulation, trouble, hell.

5. torture, infliction, rack, lancination; atrocity, aggrievement, outrage, wrong.

6. affliction, plague, adversity, scourge, curse, thorn; irritation, aggravation, vexation, annoyancy, thorn in one's flesh *or* side; nuisance, rub, chafe, bother, pest, pain in the neck.

tornado, *n.* cyclone, windstorm, storm, gale, gust, squall, blast, simoom, samiel, sirocco, whirlwind; hurricane, typhoon, tempest, twister, waterspout; monsoon.

torpid, *adj.* **1.** sluggish, stagnant, slow, slow-moving, slow-going, snail-paced, moving at a snail's pace, *Inf.* poky.

2. lethargic, phlegmatic, heavy, dull, languid, languorous, hebetudinous, lentitudinous, *Sl.* dopey; listless, spiritless, passive, apathetic; indolent, otiose, lazy, idle, slothful, fainéant; lackadaisical, insouciant, pococurante, *Dial.* limpsy.

3. inactive, supine, dormant, dormient, latent, sleeping, resting; inert, lifeless, inanimate, dead.

torpor, *n.* **1.** inactivity, inertia, stagnation, supineness, *Archaic.* lentitude, (*in the Middle East*) kef; lifelessness, inanimateness, inanimation, deadness.

2. dormancy, dormience, latency; sleepiness, slumber, drowsiness, doziness, somnolence.

3. lethargy, phlegm, heaviness, dullness, sluggishness, languor, languidness, languorousness, laggardness, *Archaic.* languishment; listlessness, spiritlessness, passiveness, apathy, indifference, *Inf.* the blahs.

4. laziness, idleness, indolence, sloth, slothfulness, acedia, fainéance, otiosity; insouciance, lackadaisicalness, pococurantism.

torrent, *n.* **1.** strong current, rapids, white water; flood, deluge, inundation, alluvion; freshet, flash flood, spate; overflow, spillover; cataract, waterfall, cascade; cloudburst, downpour; gullywasher, *Inf.* gullywhomper, monsoon.

2. stream, flow, rush, flush, outpour, outpouring, gush, effusion; succession, battery, barrage, volley, outburst, burst.

torrid, *adj.* **1.** tropical, hot, sultry, humid, steamy, steaming, muggy; sweltry, sweltering, blistering, parching, arid; boiling, sizzling, blazing, scorching; stifling, ovenlike, baking, burning, roasting; fiery, calescent, piping hot, red-hot.

2. ardent, passionate, impassioned, fervent, fervid, perfervid, inflamed, kindled; lusty, lustful, amorous, amatory, erotic, sexual.

tortuosity, *n.* **1.** crookedness, twistedness, anfractuosity, sinuousness, tortuousness; sinuosity, curve, bend, turn, crook, twist, convolution; maze, labyrinth.

2. indirectness, circuitousness, ambagiousness, evasiveness, unstraightforwardness; deviousness, dishonesty, deceitfulness, underhandedness, surreptitiousness.

tortuous, *adj.* **1.** twisting, winding, anfractuous, flexuous, sinuous, sinuate, undulating, serpentine, snaky, vermiculate, zigzag; turning, meandering, curvilinear, curved, curvy; spiraling, circling, convoluted, volute; tortile, twisted, crooked, bent; mazy, mazelike, labyrinthine; complicated, involved, difficult.

2. indirect, roundabout, circuitous, ambagious, evasive, unstraightforward; devious, dishonest, crooked, *Inf.* shady, left-handed, backhand, backhanded; deceitful, fraudulent, guileful, insidious, sharp, slippery, shifty, tricky; two-faced, Janus-faced, double-tongued, false-hearted.

torture, *n.* **1.** persecution, persecuting, excruciation, torment, tormenting, torturing, martyrdom, crucifixion, crucifying; punishment, punishing, castigation; abuse, beating, flagellation, flagging, lashing, whipping; molestation, mistreatment, maltreatment, ill-treatment.

2. agony, misery, suffering, wretchedness; pain, hurt, wound, sting, pang; anguish, distress, woe, harrowment, tribulation, trouble, hell.

3. torture, infliction, rack, lancination; affliction, plague, adversity, scourge, curse, thorn; atrocity, aggrievement, outrage, wrong.

—v. **4.** agonize, excruciate, rack, put someone on the rack, martyr, crucify; pain, hurt, scathe, lacerate, put someone through the wringer; torment, persecute, abuse, beat, *Sl.* work over, *Sl.* give someone the works, *Archaic.* belabor; anguish, distress, grieve, afflict, plague, harrow, rend, worry, trouble, disturb, *Scot.* fash.

5. wring, wrest, pry out, force out, exact, extract, *Law.* extort.

6. contort, deform, disfigure, misshape, cripple; gnarl, convolute, twist, writhe, wrench, turn, bend, draw out of shape.

7. pervert, distort, garble, misrepresent, misrender, misinterpret, misstate, falsify; travesty, butcher, slaughter, murder; corrupt, adulterate, bastardize, vitiate, debase, contaminate, pollute; caricature, burlesque, exaggerate, minimize.

toss, *v.* **1.** throw, chuck, pitch, fling, cant, dart, flirt, shy; cast, hurl, put, heave; dash, sling, let fly, send, launch; propel, project, jaculate, catapault.

2. jerk, jolt, joggle, jostle, shake; agitate, disturb, upset, disquiet, discompose.

3. rock, sway, roll, undulate; lurch, plunge; flap, wave.

4. turn over, be restless, toss and turn; squirm, writhe, wriggle.

total, *adj.* **1.** whole, entire, integral, complete; aggregate, collective, combined, composite; full, plenary; comprehensive, universal, inclusive, all-inclusive, all-embracing; extensive, extended, widespread.

2. thorough, exhaustive, in-depth, A to Z, *Brit.* A to Zed, *Brit. Dial.* gradely; absolute, dyed-in-the-wool, full-fledged, *Inf.* teetotal, complete; utter, gross, rank, sheer, radical, sweeping; unqualified, unmodified, uncompromised, unconditional, unreserved, unmitigated; unequivocal, clear, unambiguous, explicit, express; outright, downright, out-and-out, straight-out, all-out, across-the-board.

—n. **3.** sum, sum total, accumulation, amount, entire amount, gross amount; aggregate, ensemble, *Fr. tout ensemble,* assemblage, collection, collective, mass, lump.

4. all, alpha and omega, beginning and end, length and breadth, totality. See **totality.**

—v. **5.** add up, sum up, figure up, compute, cipher, reckon, count, calculate, tot up, (*on a cash register*) ring up, enumerate, numerate.

6. amount to, number, reach, come to, mount up to, *Inf.* comprise.

7. *Slang.* destroy, demolish. See **destroy** (*def.* **1**) and **demolish** (*def.* **2**).

totalitarian, *adj.* authoritarian, autocratic, monocratic; tyrannical, despotic, oppressive, iron-handed, fascist, fascistic, Nazi; dictatorial, absolute, unlimited, unrestricted, arbitrary, omnipotent, all-powerful.

totalitarianism, *n.* authoritarianism, autocracy, monocracy, dictatorship, absolutism; tyranny, despotism, oppression, iron hand, iron fist, iron rule, absolute control *or* power; fascism, Nazism, Hitlerism.

totality, *n.* **1.** entirety, entireness, wholeness, completeness, allness; integrity, integrality, fullness, plenitude; comprehensiveness, universality, *Rare.* omnitude, inclusiveness.

2. all, the whole, alpha and omega, beginning and end, length and breadth; everything, everybody.

totem, *n.* effigy, icon, figure, image, representation, *Archaic.* recognizance; emblem, badge, insignia, regalia, token; symbol, sign, mark, indicium.

totter, *v.* **1.** shuffle, shamble, limp, hobble, poke along; plod, slog, slug, trudge. See also **teeter** (*def.* **2**).

2. sway, rock, waver, wobble, bob; flutter, tremble, dodder, shake, shimmy, quake, quiver, shiver, shudder; (*of flame or light*) flicker, gutter.

touch, *v.* **1.** feel, finger, thumb, palm; hold, pick up, handle, manipulate, twiddle, trifle with, play with; palpate, poke around in; examine *or* investigate *or* study with the hands, stroke, caress, pet, fondle, paw, *Sl.* feel up, *Yiddish.* glet; massage, knead, rub, press; pat, tap, tamp, rap; strike, hit, bop, conk, thump; poke, jab, elbow, hit; swat, whack, smack, *Inf.* lay a finger *or* a hand on.

2. meet, be *or* come up against, be in *or* come into contact with, be contiguous with, conjoin, adjoin, abut, border on, neighbor; graze, brush *or* rub up against, sweep against *or* across, scrape *or* drag against *or* upon; press up against, bump into, glance, crash into, collide with, impinge upon.

3. attain, reach, arrive at, make it to, get up to, come up to, get to, achieve, gain; measure up to, match, parallel, equal, be on a par with, be on equal footing with, *Inf.* stack up to; compare with, be a match for, be any comparison with, hold a candle to, be in the same class as, rival; approach, be compared with, come near, get close to, be as good as, be mentioned in the same breath as.

4. dab, dot, bedaub, spot, blot; dapple, speckle, bespeckle; mark, leave a mark on, leave a trace of; color, tinge, tincture, tint, tone; lace, interweave, intersperse.

5. touch down land, make a landing, alight, hit ground, come into port *or* shore, drop anchor, splash down, set down, pancake, belly-flop, *Aeron.* belly-land; stop, make a stop, come to a stop *or* rest, make a pit stop; arrive, reach one's destination, get there, reach the end of one's journey; touch base, drop by *or* in, call on *or* up *or* in, keep in contact with, write to, talk to, visit.

6. affect, have an effect *or* impact on, influence, impress, make an impression; imbue, fill, inject with, instill with, ingrain with, inculcate with, indoctrinate with; inspire, inspirit, infect with, rouse, fire up, get all fired up, charge up, arouse, impassion, excite, stimulate.

7. reach, get through to, make contact with, get one's message to, make oneself heard, register with, make a dent in; strike a chord *or* familiar chord in, come home to, *Inf.* hit home, *Inf.* sink in; move, stir, tug at the heartstrings of, play *or* work *or* act on *or* upon one's emotions, soften, melt; strike a nerve in, agitate, upset, perturb, nettle, disturb, shake, rattle, ruffle, disquiet; jolt, jar, shock, *Inf.* throw [s.o.] for a loop; sting, hurt, injure, grieve, cut to the quick, pierce, smite, *Inf.* hit [s.o.] where it hurts.

8. have anything to do with, be associated with, be a part of *or* party to; get *or* go near, get within ten yards of, go in the same room with, have [s.t.] in the house; use, utilize, employ, take, even try, *Sl.* mess with, *Sl.* mess around with.

9. *Usu.* **touch on** *or* **upon** treat, cover, deal with, go into; write about, speak of, talk about; mention, make mention of, remark on, comment upon, make a remark about, point out in passing; bring up, trot out, bring into the picture *or* discussion, go over, review; refer to, allude to, cite, quote.

10. pertain to, appertain to, be pertinent to, bear upon, have a bearing on, have reference to, regard, respect, have to do with; be on the subject *or* topic of, be in the area *or* field of, apply to, belong to, go with, go along with, fall *or* come under the category of; relate to, be connected *or* linked with, have a connection with, fit in with, be appropriate to *or* for, go, *Sl.* tie in with; concern, make a difference to, matter to, be important *or* significant to, be of importance *or* significance to, have meaning for, be of interest to, apply to, go for, have any connection with or relation to.

11. touch off a. initiate, begin, start, start off, *Inf.* kick off; set in motion, be the impetus *or* instigation for, motivate. **b.** set off, actuate, trigger, ignite, light, inflame, *Inf.* set the match to. **c.** invoke, bring to mind, bring back *or* up, help [s.o.] recall *or* remember, refresh [s.o.'s] memory.

12. touch up (*of a painting, photograph, etc.*) improve, better, enhance, spruce up, brush up, polish up, perfect, put the finishing touches on, culminate, top off; fix, fix up, patch up, repair, cure, heal, doctor, make corrections in, straighten out, rectify; cover up defects in, refurbish, give a face-lift to, disguise, gloss over, whitewash; amend, modify, change, rework, redo, revamp, rearrange; refine, revise, rewrite, edit, emend, emendate.

—n. **13.** fingering, thumbing, palming; holding, handling, manipulation, twiddling; stroking, petting, caressing, fondling, pawing, *Sl.* feeling up; palpation, massaging, kneading, rubbing, pressing.

14. contact, taction, tangency, contiguousness, contiguity; abuttal, abutment, adjacency, juxtaposition; connection, conjunction, juncture, junction.

15. tactility, tactile sense, sense of touch *or* feeling, feel; feeling, sensation.

16. feel, feeling, denier, granulation, grain, texture, weave; structure, make composition, make-up; finish, coating, surface, veneer, outside.

17. technique, approach, attack, tack, procedure, routine, system, mode of operation, *Inf.* MO, *Latin. modus operandi;* style, way, manner, bedside manner, manner of working; sensitivity, sensitiveness, intuition, sixth sense, perceptivity, perception, insight, understanding.

18. dexterity, adroitness, right-handedness, deftness, slight, slight of hand, legerdemain; facility, skillfulness, neatness, felicity, finesse; skill, knack, faculty, ability, talent, gift, flair, genius, art, trick.

19. stroke, pat, tap, tamp, rap; swat, whack, smack, poke, jab, *Inf.* swipe; strike, hit, blow.

20. tad, dab, smack; bit, dash, smattering; trace, hit, suggestion; cast, coloring, tincture. See **tinge** (*defs.* **3, 5**).

21. stroke, brush, line, jot, dash; detail, little thing, last addition.

22. action, movement, motion, operation, quality *or* level of performance *or* functioning *or* execution; springiness, quickness, ability to respond *or* react quickly, *Mach.* responsiveness; precision, fineness, detailing, subtleness, subtlety.

touchable, *adj.* **1.** tangible, tactile, palpable, holdable, handleable, manipulable, manipulatable; material, materiate, physical, substantial, substantive, perceptible, perceivable, sensible, appreciable; corporeal, corporal, bodily, somatic, somatologic, somatological; incarnate, embodied, *Philos.* hylomorphic.

2. strokable, petable, caressable; massageable, kneadable; kissable, tender, soft, smooth, silky, silken, silklike, satiny, velvety, creamy, like a baby's bottom; fuzzy, downy, fleecy, furry.

touch-and-go, *adj.* **1.** hasty, helter-skelter, precipitate, rash; sketchy, superficial, slight, skimming the surface; desultory, disconnected, random, erratic, mercurial, inconstant, wavering, indecisive; fitful, spasmodic, jumpy, flighty, wayward, fluttery.

2. risky, dangerous, hazardous, perilous; frightening, *Sl.* hairy, scary, terrifying, hair-raising, making one's hair stand on end, nerve-racking; precarious, uncertain, unsure, suspenseful, cliff-hanging, like the perils of Pauline, hanging by a thread, on slippery ground; ticklish, touchy, delicate, critical.

touched, *adj.* **1.** moved, stirred, jarred, shook, struck; affected, impressed, influenced, melted, softened, seized with; disturbed, distressed, troubled, perturbed, upset.

2. daft, *Inf.* daffy, unbalanced, *Inf.* unglued, *Inf.* half-baked, *Brit. Sl.* bonkers, unhinged, distracted; dazed, moon-struck, possessed, infatuated; brainsick, *Sl.* kooky, *Sl.* meshuga; insane, crazy, crazed, mad, lunatic, lunatical, demented, deranged; of unsound mind, *Latin. non compos mentis,* mentally ill; *All Sl.* balmy, dippy, batty, bats, cuckoo, buggy, bughouse, bugs, screwy, wacky, wacko, goofy, loony, squirrelly, bananas, nuts, nutty, nutty as a fruitcake.

3. odd, peculiar, queer, bizarre, strange, anomalous, *Chiefly Brit. Inf.* potty, *Inf.* dotty, *Inf.* crackpot; abnormal, aberrant, irregular, deviant, perverse.

touchiness, *adj.* **1.** tetchiness, testiness, irritability, edginess, snappishness, nervousness; irascibility, cholericness, petulance, *Rare.* petulancy; grouchiness, grumpiness, crankiness, crabbiness, crotchetiness, crossness, crabbedness; churlishness, surliness, cantankerousness, crustiness, gruffness, bearishness, currishness; quick temper, excitability, inflammability, fieriness, pepperiness; temperamentalness, moodiness, spleen, choler, bad *or* ill temper *or* disposition, ill humor *or* nature; contentiousness, querulousness, fractiousness, captiousness.

2. hypersensitivity, supersensitivity, oversensitivity, oversensitiveness, sensitivity, sensitiveness, sensitive disposition *or* nature; peevishness, huffishness, huffiness, waspishness, raspiness, fretfulness; chip on the shoulder, resentfulness, bitterness; jealousy, envy, low self-esteem, *Psychiatry.* inferiority complex.

touching, *adv.* **1.** affecting, effective, moving, stirring, soul-stirring, heart-moving, heart-swelling, emotive; impressive, striking, breath-taking, thrilling, exciting, rousing, stimulating, stimulative; poignant, tender, plaintive; heartrending, heartbreaking, sad, distressing, pathetic, pitiful, pitiable.

2. tangent, tangential, contiguous, in contact, contactual, *Geom.* (*of a curve*) osculatory, *Both Obs.* attingent, attiguous; meeting, coming together, convergent, converging, intersecting, concurrent, overlapping; abutting, bordering, neighboring, conterminous, sharing a common border; adjacent, juxtapositional, juxtaposed, adjoining, up against one another.

—prep. **3.** regarding, in *or* with regard to, as regards, anent, respecting, with respect to, with reference to; in reference to, referring to, concerning, about, dealing with; relating to, in relation to, relative to, connected *or* associated with.

touchstone, *n.* **1.** norm, standard, criterion; measure, gauge, scale, yardstick; reference point, point of reference, bench mark; acid test, proof, test, try-out, trial, *Obs.* assay; guideline, rule of thumb, guide, *Eccles.* formulary.

2. ideal, exemplar, example, paradigm; model, pattern, prototype, archetype.

touchy, *adj.* **1.** testy, irritable, tetchy, snappish, petulant, irascible; peevish, huffish, waspish, raspy, peppery, fretful; huffy, edgy, on edge; grumpy, cranky, grouchy, snarling, crotchety, churlish, bearish; gruff, cantankerous, impatient, crabby; splenetic, choleric, dyspeptic, moody, temperamental, out of sorts; high-strung, hot-tempered, hot-blooded, quick-tempered; cross, crusty, crabbed, ill-tempered, ill-humored; fractious, quarrelsome, querulous, contentious, resentful, disputatious, captious; currish, shrewish, vixenish; cynical, perverse, spiteful.

2. thin-skinned, sensitive, oversensitive, hypersensitive, supersensitive, easily offended.

3. precarious, risky, riskful, full of risk, chancy, *Brit. Inf.* dicy, hazardous; ticklish, tricky, delicate, *Dial.* kittle; touch-and-go, uncertain, unsure, unpredictable, unsafe, unsound, unstable, unsteady, shaky, unsecure.

tough, *adj.* **1.** strong, durable, firm, hard, rigid, solid; resisting, resistant, lasting, enduring; substantial, sound, well-built.

2. leathery, chewy, gristly, coriaceous; stringy, cartilaginous, fibrous, sinewy, wiry, ropy.

3. brawny, muscular, musclebound, athletic, strapping, thickset, burly; robust, vigorous, virile, lusty, manly; powerful, *Literary.* puissant, herculean, Atlantean.

4. sturdy, hardy, hearty, stout, seasoned; rugged, stalwart, rigorous, *Inf.* hard as nails; doughty, plucky, mettlesome, *Inf.* gritty, intrepid, *Inf.* nervy.

5. unyielding, obdurate, obstinate, stubborn, inflexible, mulish; rigid, stiff-necked, stony, stern, passionless, unfeeling; unsentimental, unsympathetic, hard-boiled, *Sl.* hard-nosed, two-fisted; callous, icy, cold, cool.

6. hard, difficult, formidable, unfathomable, insoluble; arduous, laborious, uphill, exacting; troublesome, irksome, thorny, knotty, crabbed; baffling, trying, puzzling, ticklish; perplexing, involved, intricate, complicated.

7. vigorous, severe, violent, intense, keen, acute; grave, serious, dire, dreadful; furious, ferocious fierce, wild, heavy, woolly, rigorous, raging, frantic, frenzied.

8. *U.S.* rough, vicious, rowdyish; unruly, rambunctious, disorderly, refractory; boisterous, riotous, noisy, uproarious.

—n. **9.** *U.S.* ruffian, rowdy, roughneck, *Inf.* hard guy, *Inf.* tough guy; *Inf.* toughie, bully, animal, gorilla; hoodlum, thug, hooligan.

toughen, *v.* harden, firm, caseharden, indurate; temper, anneal, steel, nerve; stiffen, strengthen, tighten, rigidify; brace, buttress, shore up, *Inf.* beef up; fortify, reinforce, gird.

toupee, *n.* wig, periwig, peruke, hairpiece, *Sl.* rug, *Sl.* carpet; false hair, *Brit. Inf.* jasey, merkin.

tour, *n.* **1.** trip, excursion, run, junket, pleasure trip, sightseeing trip; journey, voyage, sail, passage, round trip; itinerary, peregrination, trek, pilgrimage, hadj; safari, expedition, shoot, stalk; jaunt, airing, outing, ride, drive; ramble, walk, promenade, stroll, perambulation, amble.

2. round, circuit, ambit, circle, cycle, orbit; beat, round, lap, loop, turn; course, track, route, run.

—v. **3.** travel, sightsee, visit; go on the road, *Inf.* hit the trail, campaign; cruise, voyage, sail, *Inf.* globetrot; peregrinate, wayfare, jaunt, trek.

tourist, *n.* visitor, *Inf.* out-of-towner, foreign visitor, sightseer, *Inf.* rubberneck; traveler, voyager, journeyer, excursionist, *Brit. Inf.* tripper, globetrotter, world traveler, jet setter.

tousled, *adj.* disheveled, rumpled, mussed *or* mussed up, messed up, unkempt, blowzy; windblown, uncombed, *Inf.* every which way; disordered, disarranged, disarrayed, untidy, messy, sloppy, slovenly, slatternly.

tout, *v.* *Informal.* **1.** solicit, ask *or* ask for, request, apply for, seek *or* seek for; call upon, appeal to, implore, beseech, entreat, plead, beg, *Brit. Inf.* prig, pray, crave; petition, supplicate, obtest, adjure, conjure, *Rare.* sue; urge, press, importune, insist, demand; accost, approach, come up to on the street, *Sl.* hustle.

2. praise, laud, extol, cry up, talk up; boast of *or* about, brag about, vaunt; blow up, magnify, exaggerate, *Inf.* crack up, *Inf.* make out, make bigger than life, puff up, enlarge, aggrandize, *Inf.* blow all out of proportion; belaud, make much of, lionize; glorify, exalt, idolize, idealize, put on a pedestal; eulogize, panegyrize, praise to high heaven; acclaim, cheer, celebrate, congratulate, *Archaic.* gratulate; applaud, clap; compliment, flatter, *Inf.* pat on the back, hand it to [s.o.], give [s.o.] credit.

3. give a tip on, *Inf.* tip [s.o.] off, give [s.o.] inside information, *Inf.* give [s.o.] inside info, give [s.o.] the word, *Inf.* give [s.o.] the low-down, *Inf.* give [s.o.] the scoop, *Sl.* give [s.o.] the dope.

4. watch, spy on, keep an eye on; investigate, *Inf.* check out, *Sl.* case.

tow, *v.* drag, pull, haul, tug, yank, lug, trail, trawl; transport, convey, *Inf.* tote, carry.

toward, *prep.* **1.** towards, in the direction of, on the road to, on the way to; straight for, in a line with.

2. for, in order to get *or* obtain, in order to attain.

3. in the area of, in the vicinity of, near, near to, close to; turned to, facing.

4. shortly before, just before, right before, soon before, close to; near *or* near to, near about, nearly, nigh; almost, about, just about, not quite, practically; approximately, roughly.

5. with respect to, as regards, in *or* with regard to, anent, regarding, concerning, in reference to, apropos of, about.

—adj. **6.** imminent, impending, near *or* close at hand, just about *or* almost here, about to happen, going to happen soon, likely to occur at any moment, momentary, upon us.

7. going on, happening, in progress, afoot, astir.

8. propitious, favorable, auspicious, opportune, apt, appropriate, timely, seasonable, good, right, perfect, lucky, fortunate, providential; promising, bright, roseate, rosy, encouraging, looking up, optimistic, *Inf.* upbeat.

tower, *n.* **1.** minaret, obelisk, pagoda, pyramid; steeple, spire, *Archit.* flèche, turret, *Fr. tourelle;* campanile, belltower, belfry; cupola, dome, onion dome; column, pillar, shaft; skyscraper, high rise.

2. citadel, fortress, bastille, fortification, acropolis, castle, stronghold, refuge; prison, dungeon, keep, fastness.

—*v.* **3.** reach high, stand high; uprise, rear; mount, soar, ascend; surmount, overtop.

4. *Usu.* **tower above** surpass, exceed, transcend, leave behind, leave in the dust; prevail over, take precedence over, supercede; excel, better, be head and shoulders above, be several cuts above; outstrip, outdo, outvie, outperform, outclass, outshine, *Inf.* run rings *or* circles around; cap, top, overtop; overshadow, throw *or* cast into the shade, eclipse, put to shame, *Inf.* show [s.o.] up.

towering, *adj.* **1.** high, tall, lofty, elevated, alpine, mountainous, skyscraping, sky-high, heaven-kissing; enormous, prodigious, gigantic, Brobdingnagian, titanic, colossal, monumental.

2. surpassing, transcendent, exceeding, excelling, outstripping, eclipsing; extraordinary, out of the ordinary, rare; superior, better, finer, greater, head and shoulders above, a cut *or* stroke above; outstanding, standout, preeminent; incomparable, inimitable, nonpareil, peerless, matchless, second to none, in a class by itself, *Latin. sui generis*; unequaled, unmatched, unrivaled, unsurpassed, unparalleled.

3. intense, violent, vehement, passionate, frenzied, frantic; consuming, burning, flaming, blazing, flaring; strong, fierce, severe; powerful, potent, mighty.

4. inordinate, excessive, immoderate, extravagant, beyond all measure; unrestrained, unlimited, intemperate; unreasonable, disproportionate, undue, uncalled-for, unwarranted, unneeded, unnecessary; exorbitant, extreme, too much, unconscionable, outrageous, preposterous.

town, *n.* **1.** municipality, township, borough, village, *Inf.* burg, (*in Scotland*) burgh, hamlet, *Archaic.* thorp, *Archaic.* wick; settlement, (*in South Africa*) kraal, (*in Spanish America*) pueblo.

2. city, metropolis; downtown, center, shopping area, shopping center, mall; business district, rialto, exchange, mart.

townsman, *n.* oppidan, inhabitant, native, citizen, burgher, villager; dweller, resident, local; fellow townsman, hometown boy, compatriot, *Sl.* paisano.

toxic, *adj.* **1.** poisonous, venomous, virulent, (*in prescriptions*) venenosus, morbific; fell, baneful, mephitic, viperous, *Rare.* virose, *Archaic.* veneose; pestilential, pestiferous, infective, infectious, pestilent, contaminative, contagious, leprous, septic.

2. deadly, lethal, fatal, mortal, mortiferous, *Archaic.* lethiferous; pernicious, dangerous, deleterious, destructive, ruinous; harmful, injurious, nocuous, noxious, malicious, malign; unhealthful, unhealthy, insalubrious, unhygienic, unsanitary.

toxin, *n.* poison, toxicant, venom, miasma; pathogen, virus, bacterium, bacillus, pollutant, contaminant; contamination, infection, pollution, virulence; bane, wolfsbane, henbane, hemlock, arsenic, belladonna, deadly nightshade, strychnine, curare.

toy, *n.* **1.** plaything, doll, *Baby Talk.* dolly, puppet, marionette, teddy bear; hobbyhorse, rocking horse; top, whirligig, teetotum; ball; jack-in-the-box.

2. trifle, triviality, small matter, nothing, nothing at all, no big thing, no big deal, tinker's dam.

3. trinket, bauble, knickknack, gimcrack, gewgaw, kickshaw, bagatelle, whim-wham, (*pl.*) frippery.

—*adj.* **4.** play, miniature; imitation, make-believe fake.

—*v.* **5.** play, play around, sport, disport, amuse oneself; horse around, *Sl.* fool around, *Inf.* fool with; trifle, potter, putter, smatter, tinker, fiddle.

6. act idly, dawdle, dally, dillydally, shilly-shally, loiter, linger, take one's time, take one's own sweet time, *Inf.* lallygag; delay, kill time, waste time, while away the time *or* hours.

7. dally, flirt, make light with, sow one's wild oats; caress, cuddle, coddle, pet, *Sl.* canoodle; nuzzle, make love, bill and coo, *Inf.* spoon, *Inf.* neck, *Inf.* smooch, *Sl.* make out.

trace, *n.* **1.** mark, sign, token, indication, remains, vestige; evidence, clue, intimation, key, *Inf.* lead.

2. touch, hint, suggestion, suspicion, soupçon, inkling; streak, shade, tinge, taint, tincture; dash, trifle, bit, jot, iota.

3. **traces** footprints, prints, footmarks, footsteps; tracks, imprints, impressions.

4. track, wake, path, tail, train, queue; scent, whiff, spoor, *Fr. piste;* record, contrail, vapor trail.

5. sketch, drawing, tracing, delineation, rubbing; design, line drawing, cartoon; image, picture, copy, representation, reproduction, portrait; diagram, map, graph.

6. **kick over the traces** defy, rebel, rise, rise up against, mutiny, disobey; throw off, kick off, thrust off, shuck off; riot, revolt, resist.

—*v.* **7.** follow, track, trail, tail, shadow; course, give chase to, (*in India*) shikar, ride to hounds; stalk, hunt, chase, go after, *Brit.* chevy; dog, hound, tread on the heels of, come close on.

8. find out, discover, uncover, unearth, disclose, reveal; ascertain, determine, get, hit; seek out, search out, look for, lay one's hands on; turn up, dig up, root up; detect, come upon *or* across, run into, *Inf.* spot.

9. draw, sketch, draft, outline; copy, reproduce, stencil, hatch; delineate, line, block out, rough out, chalk out, *Archaic.* limn; represent, depict, portray, figure; diagram, map, chart, graph.

track, *n.* **1.** line, railroad track, railway; way, road, roadway, course, strip; path, beaten path, trail, pathway; footpath, footway, walk, sidewalk, bridle path, bicycle path, towpath; byway, crosscut, short cut, by-path; centerstrip, median, mall, island; passage, passageway, alley, aisle, lane.

2. rut, wheel rut, groove, well-worn groove, jog trot; furrow, channel, cutting, cut; gutter, ditch, trench, fosse.

3. line, route, course, tack, way; trajectory, traject, flight path, ambit, orbit; beat, round, walk, itinerary, tour; sea lane, trade route, artery, air lane; loop, lap, turn.

4. **tracks** footprints, footmarks. See **trace** (*def.* **3**).

5. wake, path, tail, trailer, train. See **trace** (*def.* **4**).

6. **keep track of** follow, keep informed of, keep up on, watch, monitor, oversee, keep a record of.

7. **off the track** astray, adrift, wide of the mark, on the wrong scent, off, afield; wandering, away from the path, lost, at sea; on a tangent, digressing.

—*v.* **8.** follow, trail, tail, shadow, pursue. See **trace** (*def.* **7**.).

9. traverse, go through, pass through, go across, range; range over, travel over, cover, peregrinate; sweep, scout, patrol, reconnoiter.

10. **track down** hunt down, *Inf.* run down, run to earth, look after; nose out, ferret out, mouse, fish out, scour out; worm out, smell out, sniff out.

tract[1], *n.* region, stretch, expanse, area; district, territory, zone, section; plat, lot, plot, patch, parcel, piece of land, site; field, square, quadrant, quarter, yard, close; space, spot, scene, part.

tract[2], *n.* treatise, eassy, disquisition, thesis, dissertation; homily, sermon, lecture, discourse, descant; monograph, article, critique, study; pamphlet, leaflet, booklet, brochure.

tractable, *adj.* **1.** docile, tame, dutiful, obedient;

yielding, submissive, willing, amenable, complaisant; manageable, governable, guidable, leadable.

2. malleable, handleable, pliable, flexible; plastic, ductile, tractile, fictile, adaptable; extensile, stretchable, bendable.

trade, *n.* **1.** commerce, traffic, buying and selling, barter, truck; dealing, transaction, exchange, swap, interchange, reciprocity; business, marketing, merchandising, mercantilism, commercialism; bargaining, negotiating, negotiation.

2. craft, skill, métier, line of work, line; occupation, vocation, profession, career, calling, pursuit, lifework; business, enterprise; employment, job, livelihood, living, work.

—v. **3.** buy and sell, do business, merchandise, transact, deal; sell, traffic, truck, peddle, vend; negotiate, bargain, barter, haggle, *Scot.* argle-bargle, higgle, chaffer, dicker, bandy, *Inf.* beat down.

4. exchange, swap, switch, interchange, substitute; reciprocate, return.

trademark, *n.* brand, stamp, label, name; identification, tab, tag, earmark, hallmark; symbol, sign, representation, seal, marker; logo, logotype; insignia, ensign, sigil, signet, badge, crest, emblem; motto, catch phrase.

trader, *n.* merchant, businessman, salesman, traveling salesman, *U.S.* drummer, dealer; seller, wholesaler, jobber, *Chiefly Brit.* monger; vendor, chandler, sutler, packman, colporteur, *Brit.* chapman, hawker, huckster, *Chiefly Brit.* costermonger; trafficker, middleman, (*in stolen goods*) *Sl.* fence, *Sl.* duffer; retailer, storekeeper, shopkeeper, shopman.

tradition, *n.* folklore, lore, oral history, unwritten law; custom, practice, way, fashion, procedure, policy, rule, use; habit, convention, wont, praxis, usage, observance, habitude, second nature; consuetude, *Law.* presciption, routine, course; conventionality, matter of course, conventionalism, formality, form.

traditional, *adj.* handed down, unwritten, oral, traditive; old, historic, ancestral, familial; customary, accustomed, habitual, set, fixed, inveterate, rooted, established, consuetudinary, confirmed; usual, wonted, regular, daily, routine, normal, natural; ordinary, conventional, everyday, commonplace; general, prevailing, prevalent, common, frequent; well-known, popular, favorite, household; stock, well-worn.

traduce, *v.* **1.** malign, defame, calumniate, slander, libel, misrepresent, lie about; vilify, asperse, cast aspersions on, denigrate, speak ill of, slur, smear, give a bad name, backbite, *Sl.* badmouth; defile, vitiate, blacken, bespatter, besmirch, soil, sully, stain, smudge, blemish, tarnish, taint, drag through the mud *or* mire, heap dirt upon, fling dirt upon.

2. impugn, impeach, attack, injure, hurt, damage, harm; assail, revile, berate, vituperate, rail against, inveigh against, oppugn, censure, criticize, pull to pieces, tear apart, *Sl.* do a hatchet job on; denounce, decry, disparage, discredit, vilipend, impute, depreciate, deprecate, derogate, belittle, minimize, run *or* put down, *Inf.* knock.

traducer, *n.* **1.** maligner, defamer, calumniator, slanderer, libeler, misrepresenter, liar, *Inf.* hatchet man; vilifier, asperser, denigrator, smearer, backbiter; defiler, vitiator, blackener, besmircher, mud *or* dirt flinger.

2. impugner, impeacher, attacker, assailant; vituperator, reviler, oppugner, censurer, critic, carper, faultfinder; denouncer, decrier, disparager, vilipender, imputer, depreciator, deprecator, belittler, minimizer.

traffic, *n.* **1.** movement, transportation, transport, transit, conveyance, freight.

2. commerce, buying and selling, business, barter, truck, exchange, trade. See **trade** (*def.* **1**).

3. smuggling, bootlegging, rumrunning, drug *or* dope dealing, drug *or* dope peddling.

—v. **4.** buy and sell, merchandise, deal, truck, bargain, trade, See **trade** (*def.* **3**).

5. smuggle, bootleg, deal drugs, push drugs.

tragedy, *n.* **1.** tragic drama, buskin; drama, play, *Fr. tragédie, Fr. comi-tragédie.*

2. calamity, catastrophe, disaster; blow, heavy *or* nasty *or* staggering blow, shock; adversity, misfortune, stroke of ill *or* bad luck *or* fortune, bitter pill *or* cup, setback, *Inf.* comedown, reversal, reverse, *Literature.* peripeteia; mishap, mischance, miscarriage, misadventure, *Scot and North Eng.* mishanter; accident, casualty, glitch; wreck, shipwreck, crash, car crash, collision, smash-up, crack-up, pileup; natural disaster, act of God, fire, flood, earthquake, tornado, hurricane.

tragic, *adj.* **1.** pathetic, pathetical, pitiful, pitiable, piteous, lamentable, deplorable, miserable, wretched; touching, moving, disturbing, distressing, upsetting.

2. melancholy, sad, unhappy, doleful, sorrowful; mournful, lachrymose, grievous, dolorous, lugubrious; morose, gloomy, dismal, funereal, cheerless, forlorn; despondent, hopeless.

3. tragical, calamitous, catastrophic, disastrous, ruinous, fatal, deadly; destructive, destroying, devastating, crushing; dire, dreadful, terrible, awful, horrible, shocking, appalling; unlucky, luckless, unfortunate, hapless, ill-fated, ill-starred, star-crossed; inauspicious, unpropitious, unfavorable, unprovidential, untoward.

trail, *v.* **1.** drag, draw, draw along, haul, hale, pull along; tag along, trawl, tow, tug, lug, train.

2. follow, pursue, trace, hunt, track down. See **trace** (*def.* **7**).

3. draw out, prolong, stretch out, protract; extend, lengthen, drag on *or* out, elongate, expand; spin out, linger on, continue.

4. hang down, dangle, depend, pend; droop, sag, swag; swing, flap, daggle, drabble; bob, ripple, flutter; wave, stream from, float from, flow.

5. *Usu.* **trail off** wander off, drift off, fall off, go off; fade, fade out, disappear, *Inf.* fizzle out.

6. drop behind, fall behind, lag, bring up the rear: hang back, straggle, linger behind, dawdle; *All Sports.* be losing, be behind, be down.

7. creep, crawl, slide, glide; steal, sneak, worm along, inch along, slink.

—n. **8.** path, track, way, course; beaten path, bridle path, towpath, bicycle path; footpath, pathway, footway, horse-track, garden path; walkway, walk, sidewalk, aisle, catwalk; by-path, byway, shortcut, crosscut; pass, passage, passageway, lane, alley.

9. track, scent, smell, whiff, spoor, *Fr. piste;* wake, tail, train, queue, trailer, tab, afterpart; aftermath, aftereffect, afterclap, aftercrop, aftergrowth.

10. puff of smoke, stream of dust, cloud of dust; whir, whoosh, flurry.

train, *n.* **1.** order, sequence, consecution, succession, progression, gradation; procession, following, consecutiveness; series, chain, linkage, catenation, concatenation; course, flow, run; continuity, continuousness, continuance, extension, prolongation.

2. parade, cavalcade, *Fr. défilé,* retinue, convoy, line, file, column, queue; suite, attendance, cortege, entourage, court; following, satellites, *Archaic.* meiny, escort, bodyguard, guard; personnel, staff, *Inf.* hangers-on.

3. trail, stream, track, path; wake, wash, backwash, backflow, aftermath.

4. *Railroads.* rail, *Baby Talk.* choo-choo, Amtrak, electric train, steam train, elevated train, el, subway; passenger train, rolling stock, *Trademark.* Pullman, *Sl.* sleeper, wagon-lit, Orient Express; coach, day coach, local, *Sl.* milk train, *Sl.* owl train; commuter train, bankers' express, *Sl.* bankers, express, non-stop; campaign train; freight train, piggyback train.

—*v.* **5.** discipline, drill, coach, exercise; instruct, teach, tutor, give lessons, school, edify; inform, enlighten, inculcate, indoctrinate; ground, prepare, prime, qualify; rear, bring up, form, guide; accustom, familiarize, habituate, toughen, harden, inure; break in, put through the paces.

6. aim, point, direct, draw *or* get a bead on, sight, set one's sights on, focus, zero in on; position, mark, peg, level.

training, *n.* instruction, teaching, education, tuition, tutelage; grounding, coaching, drilling, discipline; direction, guidance, nurture, breeding, development, rearing; inculcation, indoctrination, initiation; preparation, schooling, apprenticeship; learning, knowledge, information, skill.

trait, *n.* **1.** characteristic, quality, feature, attribute, property; idiosyncrasy, idiocrasy, peculiarity, specialty, singularity, mannerism, quirk; particular, particularity, distinguishing mark, sign, badge, trademark, earmark, hallmark, symptom, mark.

2. trace, suggestion, suspicion, soupcon; taste, touch, tinge, shade; sprinkling, dash, dab, bit.

traitor, *n.* **1.** betrayer, *Inf.* double-crosser *Inf.* double-dealer, *Sl.* two-timer; Judas, Brutus, Catilinarian; double agent, fifth columnist, quisling, Benedict Arnold; snake in the grass, snake, back-stabber; informer, squealer, tattler, *Sl.* ratter, *Sl.* fink, *Sl.* ratfink, *Sl.* stool pigeon *or* stoolie.

2. renegade, *Archaic.* renegado, apostate, turncoat; defector, bolter, seceder, dissenter; deserter, forsaker, dropout, quitter, *Sl.* cop-out.

3. seditionist, insurgent, insurrectionist, mutineer; revolter, revolutionary, rebel.

traitorous, *adj.* **1.** perfidious, disloyal, treacherous, faithless, false, untrue, unfaithful; deceitful, dishonest, insidious, false-hearted, knavish; double-dealing, back-stabbing, dissembling, Janus-faced, two-faced, hypocritical; conniving, sneaking, scheming, designing, shifty, sneaky; unscrupulous, dishonorable, unconscionable, corrupt.

2. treasonable, treasonous, seditious, seditionary; subversive, mutinous, insurgent, insurrectionist, insurrectionary; rebel, rebellious, renegade, turncoat; revolutionary, underground, lawless, anarchistic.

trammel, *n.* *Usu.* **trammels 1.** restraint, constraint, check, curb, barrier, block, obstacle, bar; hindrance, impediment, deterrent, holdback, stumbling block; hitch, snag, knot, drawback, *Inf.* fly in the ointment.

2. fetters, manacles, bonds, shackles, pinions, gyves, handcuff, *Inf.* cuffs, *Sl.* bracelets, ball and chain; muzzle, gag; straight jacket; halter, yoke, harness.

3. confinement, circumscription, detention; imprisonment, incarceration, durance; bondage, duress, captivity, custody.

—*v.* **4.** restrict, restrain, rein, bridle, constrain; frustrate, thwart, impede, hinder, handicap; bar, obstruct, block, blockade, barricade; stop, halt, stay; inhibit, hold back.

5. fetter, manacle, handcuff, cuff, *Sl.* slap the cuffs *or* bracelets on [s.o.], put in irons; chain, enchain, tether, gyve; hobble, truss, bind, tie, tie up, tie hand and foot; entrammel, pinion.

6. entangle, ensnare, enmesh, entrap, snag, catch, net.

tramp, *v.* **1.** tread *or* walk heavily, trudge, march, plod, plow, mush; hoof, stump; walk, step, pace, shuffle, stride.

2. *Usu.* **tramp on** *or* **upon** trample, stamp, stomp, step on, tread on, squash, crush, *Dial.* squish.

3. hike, trek, traipse, saunter; ramble, rove, roam, range; wander, nomadize, peregrinate, travel, journey; straggle, stray, gad about, flit, meander.

—*n.* **4.** resounding footfall, heavy tread, firm walk, trudge, plodding; stamping, stomp, stomping, trampling.

5. hike, trek, perambulation, peregrination; shuffle, saunter, stroll, walk; trudge, march.

6. vagabond, *Archaic.* runagate, vagrant, hobo, *Chiefly U.S. Inf.* boomer, *Australian.* swagman, beachcomber, derelict, street Arab, *Inf.* bum, *Sl.* vag, *Sl.* bo, *Sl.* stiff, *Sl.* bindle stiff, *Sl.* canvas back; panhandler, *Yiddish.* shnorrer, down-and-outer; migrant worker, *Usu. Disparaging.* Okie, itinerant, drifter, *Inf.* floater, transient, fly-by-night; wanderer, roamer, rover, rambler, strayer, straggler, gadabout; migrator, bird of passage, *Sl.* rolling stone; gypsy, nomad.

7. loose woman, bimbo, slut, hussy, cocotte, harlot, whore, demirep, wanton, fallen woman, woman of ill repute; lady of the evening, lady of pleasure, woman of the profession, Mrs. Warren, trollop, strumpet, *Archaic.* wench, trull, drab, quean, painted woman, woman of the streets, streetwalker, bar girl, *Inf.* pickup, *All Sl.* cat, tart, hustler, bim, moll, hooker, floozie, working girl, *Brit. Sl.* bird.

trample, *v.* **1.** tramp, tread *or* step heavily, trudge. See **tramp** (*def.* **1**).

2. *Usu.* **trample on** *or* **upon** *or* **over** tread roughly, tramp on, stamp. See **tramp** (*def.* **2**).

3. *Usu.* **trample on** *or* **upon** *or* **over** violate, hurt, do violence to; infringe on, encroach on, trench on *or* upon; run over, ride over, ride roughshod over; domineer, bully, hector, intimidate, browbeat.

4. defy, disregard, treat with scorn, set at naught, fling to the winds, fly in the face of; transgress, break.

5. *Usu.* **trample out** extinguish, put out; conquer, defeat, vanquish, rout; grind under foot, overpower.

trance, *n.* **1.** half-conscious state, dazed condition, half-aware and half-asleep state, suspended animation.

2. stupor, daze, dream state, hypnotic state; coma, *Pathol.* sopor, sleep, deep sleep, slumber; numbness, stupefaction, *Pathol.* catalepsy; drowsiness, sleepiness, lethargy, torpor.

3. mental absorption, abstraction, preoccupation, brown study, deep musing, *Inf.* another world; daydreaming, woolgathering.

tranquil, *adj.* **1.** serene, placid, restful, reposeful, peaceful, halcyon; still, calm, motionless, smooth, undisturbed, unagitated, quiet; windless, waveless, stormless; stationary, becalmed.

2. composed, *Inf.* together, self-possessed; cool, cool-headed, self-controlled, passionless, impassive, dispassionate; easy-going, relaxed, even-tempered, imperturbable, unexcitable, unflappable; unexcited, unmoved, unperturbed, unruffled; sedate, staid, undemonstrative, unemotional, stoical, philosophical.

tranquilize, *v.* **1.** calm, soothe, quiet, still, hush; allay, assuage, mollify, soften; compose, console, solace, comfort; pacify, smoothe, settle, *Inf.* cool [s.o.] off; sedate, opiate, stupefy, narcotize, dull, deaden; relax, loosen [s.o.] up.

2. placate, give a sop to; defuse, depoliticize, devolatilize; mediate, reconcile, reunite.

tranquillity, *n.* **1.** calm, calmness, motionlessness, stillness, quietness, quietude; serenity, sereneness, placidity, placidness; repose, reposefulness, rest, restfulness, peace, peacefulness, harmony, harmoniousness; ataraxia.

2. composure, self-possession, coolness, dispassion; equanimity, poise, sang-froid; steadiness, self-control, level-headedness.

transact, *v.* carry on, conduct, practice, prosecute, perpetrate; carry out, perform, enact, exercise, execute, do, discharge, dispatch; accomplish, realize, achieve, work, negotiate; settle, complete, conclude; treat, handle, deal with, manage, regulate, administer.

transaction, *n.* **1.** perpetration, prosecution, commission; performance, enactment, execution, discharge, dispatch, effectuation, realization, accomplishment, achievement, implementation; negotiation, settlement, arrangement, deal, bargain, agreement; conclusion, completion; treatment, handling, management, administration, regulation.

2. proceeding, action, passage, operation; process, procedure, method, way.

3. **transactions** the record, records, minutes, proceedings, Acta; affairs, matters, concerns, dealings, doings, *Inf.* goings-on.

transcend, *v.* **1.** rise above, exceed, overpass, overstep, go beyond, overleap, outdistance; transgress, trespass.

2. excel, surpass, be superior, outrival, outrank, outstrip, outvie, outdo; overshadow, eclipse, throw into the shade; overtop, *Inf.* take the cake, beat hollow, outshine, prevail, predominate, take precedence.

transcendence, *n.* excellence, superiority, supereminence, supremacy, predominance, preeminence; ascendency, preponderancy, prevalence, paramountcy; advantage, authority, influence, prestige.

transcendent, *adj.* **1.** exceeding, surpassing, magnificent, extraordinary, unparalleled, unrivaled, unequaled, matchless, unsurpassed, incomparable, unique; superior, supreme, consummate, supereminent; paramount, foremost, utmost, principal, second to none.

2. abstract, speculative, recondite, abstruse; unintelligible, indefinite, vague, obscure, indistinct, puzzling, hidden; intangible, impalpable, intuitive, innate; thin, rarefield, attenuated; mysterious, mystical, mystic, occult; transcendental, preternatural, supernatural, otherworldly, transmundane.

transcribe, *v.* **1.** copy, reproduce, duplicate, *Inf.* dupe, replicate; engross, write out.

2. translate, transliterate, render, interpret.

transcriber, *n.* copier, copyist, engrosser, *Judaism.* sopher; scribe, scrivener, amanuensis, secretary, clerk, recorder, penman; translator, transliterator, interpreter.

transcript, *n.* **1.** copy, reproduction, replication, duplicate, duplication, *Inf.* dupe, *Inf.* ditto; engrossment, transcription, apograph; tape recording, tape; carbon copy, carbon; photostat, *Inf.* stat, *Trademark.* Xerox.

2. translation, transliteration, interpretation, rendition, rendering, version.

transfer, *v.* **1.** convey, move, remove, take, carry, transport, cart, haul, deliver, send, forward, transmit; mail, post, ship, freight, truck.

2. transmit, hand down, pass on *or* along; delegate, assign, devolve, shift responsibility, *U. S. Inf.* pass the buck; turn over, *Law.* attorn, hand over, give over; cede, grant, deed, convey, make over, sign over; lease, rent *or* rent out, let, sublet, sublease, *Law.* demise, sell; give, give away, dispose of, bestow; leave, will, *Law.* devise.

3. remove oneself, move, shift, change location, relocate, transplant, displace, move *or* send from one place to another.

—*n.* **4.** transference, transferal, removal, change of residence, move, shift, relocation, transplantation, displacement; passsage, transmission, transmittance, transportation, conveyance, transit, shipment, freightage, truckage.

5. transferee, transfer student.

6. conveyance, *Law.* deed, *Law.* grant, cession, lease; disposition, devisal, bestowal, gift, disposal, sale; *Law.* will, *Law.* bequest, *Law.* bequeathal, *Law.* bequeathment, *Law.* devise.

transferable, *adj.* negotiable, transmissible, transmittable; communicable, contagious, catching, infectious.

transfiguration, *n.* transfigurement, transformation, change, modification. See **transformation.**

transfigure, *v.* transform, transmute, change, alter. See **transform.**

transfix, *v.* **1.** impale, pierce, transpierce, stab, prick, stick; puncture, perforate, bore; penetrate, tap, broach, open up; pink, spear, spike, spit, skewer; run through, gut, disembowel, eviscerate.

2. fasten, attach, affix, fix; pin, tack, nail, bolt, hasp.

3. rivet, make motionless, astound, stun; electrify, galvanize; captivate, possess, bewitch, ensorcel, enchant; fascinate, intrigue, absorb, mesmerize, hypnotize.

transform, *v.* metamorphose, transmute, transfigure, renew, change, *Obs.* transpose; convert, make into, change into, translate, turn into, alchemize, transubstantiate, transmogrify; alter, modify, permute, mutate, permutate; transshape, remodel, redo, remake, make *or* do over, re-form, remold, recast, reconstruct, rebuild, restyle; revolutionize, reorganize, reorder, rearrange.

transformation, *n.* change, modification, permutation, mutation; conversion, metamorphosis, evolution, transfiguration, transfigurement, transmutation, *Obs.* transposition; translation, transubstantiation, alchemy, transmogrification; revolution, radical change, reorganization, reordering, rearrangement.

transgress, *v.* **1.** pass over, overpass, overstep, go beyond, exceed; intrude, encroach, trespass, invade.

2. break, infringe, breach, infract, commit a breach *or* an infraction, violate, disobey, defy, contravene; ignore, disregard, neglect, disdain, scorn; fail to notice, take no note of, let slip *or* slide, forget, shirk, slight.

3. *Usu.* **transgress against** sin, err, deviate from the path of virtue, take a wrong course; go astray, fall from grace, go to the devil; make a mistake, go wrong, slip up, lapse, trip, stray from the straight and narrow, misbehave; go to pot, go to hell, go to hell in a handbasket; offend, sin against, injure, hurt, harm, wound, wrong, malign.

transgression, *n.* **1.** encroachment, trespassing, invasion, intrusion; overstepping, exceeding; infringement, breach, infraction, violation, disobedience, defiance, contravention; ignoring, disregard, neglect.

2. sin, offense, crime, evil deed, wrong; fault, error, misdeed, dereliction, slip, lapse, omission; shortcoming, peccadillo, malefaction, peccancy; delinquency, breaking of the law, felony, misdemeanor.

transgressor, *n.* trespasser, wrongdoer, sinner, evildoer, malefactor, offender, culprit; delinquent, juvenile delinguent, misdemeanant, *Inf.* scofflaw, lawbreaker, *Law.* malfeasant, *Law.* misfeasor; hooligan, rascal, ruffian, hoodlum; felon, criminal, *Inf.* chronic crook, recidivist, backslider.

transience, *n.* impermanence, transitoriness, temporariness, temporalness; brevity, briefness, shortness, momentariness, ephemeralness, evanescence, volatility, fugacity, fugitiveness; mortality, perishability, corruptibility, unendurability, nonpermanence; mutability, changeableness, changefulness, alterability, variableness, permutability, inconstancy; unstableness, unfixedness, unsteadiness, unsettledness.

transient, *adj.* transitory, impermanent, temporary, temporal, fly-by-night; brief, short, short-lived, momentary, here today and gone tomorrow; ephemeral, evanescent, volatile, passing, fleeting, meteoric; fugitive, fugacious, fading, flitting, vanishing; caducous, perishable, mortal, corruptible, unendurable, unenduring, nonpermanent; mutable, changeable, changeful, alterable, variable, permutable, inconstant; unstable, labile, unfixed, unsteady, unsettled.

transit, *n.* **1.** passage, passing, traverse, crossing; movement, progress, motion, going; transition, change, becoming, turning into, conversion; switch, shift, change-over; assimilation, assumption, naturalization, acclimatization; flight, migration, transmigration, emigration, immigration, deportation; journey, voyage.

2. conveyance, transportation, transport, *Chiefy Brit.* carriage; carrying, portage, cartage, haulage, shipment, ferriage, freightage, truckage; transference, transfer, transferal; transmission, transmittance, sending.

transition, *n.* movement, passage, passing, progress; motion, saltation, jump, leap; switch, shift, shifting, change-over; change, gradation, becoming, turning into, conversion, transformation, transmutation, metastasis; alteration, modulation, modification.

transitional, *adj.* changing, developmental, becoming, transitionary; provisional, temporary, impermanent, nonpermanent, passing; unstable, labile, unfixed, unsettled.

transitory, *adj.* impermanent, temporary, short-lived, ephemeral, fleeting, unenduring, transient. See **transient.**

translate, *v.* **1.** transliterate, transcribe, render, interpret; paraphrase, reword.

2. explain, elucidate, clear up, make clear, spell out, *Inf.* put in plain words *or* English.

3. transform, transmute, transmogrify, transfigure, transubstantiate, metamorphose; convert, alter, change; remold, remodel, recast, reconstruct.

4. transfer, transport, convey, forward, remove, move; send, dispatch, ship.

translation, *n.* **1.** transliteration, transcription, interpretation.

2. version, rendition, rendering, transcript; paraphrase.

3. transformation, transmutation, transmogrification, transfiguration, transubstantiation, metamorphosis, *Obs.* transposition; conversion, alteration, change; reconstruction, remodeling.

4. transferal, transference, transportation, conveyance, removal; explanation, elucidation.

translator, *n.* linguist, polygot; interpreter, interpolator, exegete, oneirocritic; metaphrast, paraphrast, paraphraser.

translucent, *adj.* **1.** limpid, lucent, pellucid, translucid, diaphanous.

2. intelligible, understandable, comprehensible; lucid, luculent, clear, crystal-clear, plain, distinct.

transmigration, *n.* **1.** migration, transhumance, emigration, passage, trek, journey, peregrination, pilgrimage; trip, tour, excursion, jaunt, junket, expedition, sally.

2. metempsychosis, reincarnation, rebirth, *Hindu Myth.* avatar.

transmission, *n.* **1.** transfer, transference, transferal, move, shift, relocation, transplantation, displacement; passage, transmittance, transmittal, transportation, conveyance, transit, shipment; sending, forwarding.

2. communication, impartation, impartment; handing down, passing on, sharing.

transmit, *v.* **1.** send, convey, deliver, direct, forward; mail, post, ship, remit; transfer, move, take, carry, transport, cart, haul.

2. communicate, impart, hand down, pass on, share, transfuse; diffuse, disseminate, spread; offer, proffer, extend, tender, present; infuse, suffuse, imbue, instill.

3. broadcast, televise, telecast, telegraph, radio, telegram.

4. bequeath, devise, leave to, hand down, endow; cede, grant.

transmute, *v.* transform, metamorphose, convert, change, alter. See **transform.**

transparency, *n.* **1.** transparence, clearness, pellucidity, pellucidness, lucidity, lucidness, limpidity, limpidness, crystallinity, diaphanousness; sheerness, glassiness, transpicuousness; translucency, translucence, lucency, *Rare.* lucence, translucidness, translucidity, mistiness, frostiness.

2. frankness, candidness, forthrightness, simplicity, honesty, directness, straightforwardness, openness; plainness, explicitness, unequivocalness; obviousness, unambiguity, unmistakability.

transparent, *adj.* **1.** clear, pellucid, lucid, limpid, crystalline, diaphanous; sheer, see-through, gauzy; silken, glassy, transpicuous, hyaline; translucent, lucent, translucid, misty, frosted; cloudless, unclouded.

2. frank, candid, forthright, direct, straightforward, open; plain, plain-spoken, explicit, unequivocal, *Inf.* flat-footed; guileless, ingenuous, artless, naïve, simple, undeceptive, undeceiving, undeceitful, undissembling; aboveboard, up front, on the level, on the up and up, no-nonsense.

3. obvious, patent, manifest, distinct, undisguised, unambiguous, perspicuous, unmistakable; clear-cut, crystal-clear, as plain as day, as plain as the nose on one's face; evident, apparent, visible, noticeable, perceptible, discernible; express, avowed.

transpire, *v.* **1.** happen, take place, occur, come to pass, come about, come, *Archaic.* hap, *Inf.* come off, befall, supervene, betide, chance, *Archaic.* bechance, *Archaic.* arrive; intervene, crop up; become, come into being, appear, fall, materialize, take effect; result, eventuate, turn out, prove; ensue, issue, arise.

2. emit, exude, emanate, exhale; transude, excrete; perspire, sweat, *Obs.* sudate; smoke, steam, vaporize, evaporate, fume, volatilize.

3. be revealed, become known, come to light, get abroad, be made public.

transplant, *v.* replant, repot; *Surg.* graft; transfer, relocate, displace, shift.

transport, *v.* **1.** carry, convey, *Inf.* tote; haul, cart, lug; move, shift, transfer, take, deliver, give, bring, fetch, get, go get; transmit, forward, send; mail, post, ship, freight, truck.

2. enrapture, entrance, enchant, fascinate, captivate, charm, bewitch, spellbind, mesmerize, hypnotize, enthrall; overpower, overwhelm, overcome; overjoy, ravish, thrill, delight, electrify, send chills up and down the spine, *Sl.* give [s.o.] a rush; excite, *Sl.* send, put into ectasy, *Sl.* blow [s.o.'s] mind, *Sl.* turn [s.o.] on.

3. banish, exile, deport, send away, force *or* drive out, expatriate.

—*n.* **4.** conveyance, transportation, transit, ship-

ment, freightage, truckage. See **transportation** (*def.* **1**).
5. truck, bus, ship, cargo ship, troopship, freighter, merchantman, lighter, barge.
6. rapture, ecstasy, exaltation, elation, exhilaration, thrill, *Sl.* rush, excitement, excitation; ecstatic joy *or* delight, delectation, enjoyment, fun, pleasure, ravishment; enchantment, bliss, euphoria, seventh heaven, cloud nine; elysium, paradise, heaven, heaven on earth, Eden *or* Garden of Eden, utopia; blessedness, beatitude, happiness, gladness, felicity.

transportation, *n.* **1.** conveyance, transport, transit, movement, *Chiefly Brit.* carriage; carrying, portage, cartage, haulage; shipment, ferriage, freightage, truckage; transference, transfer, transferal; transmission, transmittance, sending.
2. truck, bus, cargo ship. See **transport** (*def.* **5**).
3. fare, fee, payment, charge, cost, price.
4. banishment, deportation, expatriation, expulsion, exile.

transpose, *v.* interchange, metathesize, substitute, exchange, commute, invert, reverse, switch, swap, trade, change, convert; rearrange, shift, move, transfer.

transude, *v.* ooze, seep, exude, effuse; sweat, perspire, *Pathol.* extravasate; percolate, filter, strain.

transverse, *adj.* **1.** cross, horizontal, thwart, transversal; diagonal, oblique, catercornered, *U. S. Inf.* kitty-cornered.
—n. **2.** crosspiece, crossbeam, crossbar, traverse.

transvestite, *n.* cross-dresser, *Sl.* drag queen; deviant; fetishist.

trap[1], *n.* **1.** pitfall, deadfall; snare, gin, net; mine, booby trap, man-trap.
2. device, ploy, artifice, stratagem, wile, subterfuge, ruse, trick, *Archaic.* trepan; lure, decoy, bait, hook, *Sl.* come-on; ambush, ambuscade, *Obs.* ambuscado.
3. *Slang.* mouth, *Fig.* muzzle; *All Sl.* mug, mush, kisser, bazoo, gob, *Scot.* gab.
—v. **4.** snare, ensnare, gin, enmesh, entrap, *Archaic.* trepan; net, bag, sack, take, catch; booby-trap.
5. ambush, *U. S.* bushwhack, outmaneuver, bring to bay; outwit, outsmart; deceive, beguile, trick, hoax, dupe, take in; lure, inveigle, entice, draw on, *Sl.* suck in, *Sl.* rope in; decoy, bait, bait the hook.

trap[2], *n.* **1. traps** *Informal.* belongings, personal belongings, effects, personal possessions, *Inf.* things, *Sl.* stuff, *Sl.* junk; baggage, bag and baggage, gear, impedimenta, dunnage, luggage, kit, duffel.
—v. **2.** caparison, outfit, fit up, fit, rig up, rig, turn out, gear; equip, furnish, supply, *Obs.* appoint; deck, deck out, bedeck, adorn, array, ornament, bedizen.

trapped, *adj.* cornered, in a corner, up against the wall, with one's back to the wall, at bay, *Inf.* treed, *Inf.* up a tree; in a predicament, *Inf.* in a fix *or* tight spot, *Inf.* in a mess *or* jam, *Inf.* in hot water, *Inf.* in the hole, *Inf.* on the spot, *Inf.* over a barrel, *Inf.* on the ropes, *Inf.* behind the eight ball, *Inf.* up the creek, *Inf.* up the creek without a paddle.

trappings, *n.* **1.** (*all of a sumptuous nature*) equipment, equipage, apparatus, gear, accouterments, appurtenances, appointments; fixtures, fittings, habiliments, *Inf.* things; outfit, turnout, rig; finery, frippery, adornment, ornamentation, decoration.
2. apparel, wearing apparel, clothing, clothes, dress, attire, wear; raiment, garments, vestments, *Inf.* toggery, *Inf.* togs, *Inf.* duds, *Sl.* threads, *Sl.* rags.
3. caparison, housings, trapping; harness, tack, tackle, rigging.

trash, *n.* **1.** rubbish, riffraff, *Brit. Dial.* raff, litter, sweepings, chaff; refuse, *Dial.* culch, garbage, waste, offal; debris, detritus, rubble, wreckage; remains, leavings, leftovers, scraps, orts, hogwash, swill; remainder, residue, residuum; scoria, dross, recrement, slag, scum; filth, dirt, dust, offscourings; dregs, fag ends, remnants, bits and pieces, odds and ends; fragments, twigs, splinters, flinders, chips, slivers, shavings; junk, worthless stuff, *Sl.* dreck, trumpery; cast-offs, rags, tatters, castaways, rejects, discards.
2. nonsense, moonshine, gobbledegook; humbug, bunkum, *Sl.* bunk, *U.S. Sl.* blah; flummery, *Inf.* hokum, *Sl.* applesauce, *Sl.* eyewash; refuse, *Dial.* culch, rubbish, *Sl.* tripe, chaff, *Inf.* truck, trumpery; balderdash, tommyrot, *Inf.* rot, *Sl.* garbage, *Sl.* crap, *Sl.* crock, *Sl.* bull; hogwash, swill, *Sl.* horsefeathers, stuff, stuff and nonsense, *Inf.* bosh, *Brit. Inf.* gammon, *Brit. Sl.* tosh; fudge, foolishness, folly, rigmarole, amphigory; footle, *Inf.* malarkey, *Sl.* bushwa, *Sl.* baloney, *Sl.* bilge *or* bilge water, *Sl.* meshugaas, *Scot. and North Eng.* haver; poppycock, *Inf.* fiddle-faddle, *Inf.* piffle, *Inf.* hooey, *Inf.* kibosh, *Inf.* flapdoodle; claptrap, rodomontade, fustian, bombast, rant; idle talk, froth, foam, *Sl.* hot air, *Sl.* gas.
3. riffraff, rabble, canaille, scum, ragtag and bobtail, flotsam and jetsam; vagrant, vagabond, drifter, tramp, hobo, *U.S.* bum; loafer, idler, good-for-nothing, *Fr. vaurien;* beggar, ragamuffin, tatterdemalion; outcast, castaway, dregs of society, vermin; rascal, rogue, knave, scoundrel; tramp, slut, whore.

trashy, *adj.* **1.** worthless, valueless, good-for-nothing, not worth a straw; meritless, nugatory, of no real value; useless, inutile, catchpenny, unavailing, bootless, frivolous, fribbling, futile; silly, inane, twaddling; petty, *Inf.* picayune, niggling, inconsequential, superficial, shallow; trifling, trivial, insignificant, immaterial, unimportant, twopenny, *Sl.* two-bit, *Sl.* two-by-four; small, puny, little, slight, of no moment; inconsiderable, inappreciable, imperceptible; very little, paltry, nominal, minute, negligible; piddling, meager, mere, *Inf.* measly.
2. rubbishy, *Sl.* schlock, poor, base, mean, commonplace; shoddy, shabby, beggarly, scrubby, wretched; sorry, weak, feeble; flimsy, light, airy; second-rate, mediocre, inferior; brummagem, showy, pretentious, ostentatious, flashy, gaudy, garish, meretricious, tawdry; vulgar, dirty, cheap, obscene.

trauma, *n.* **1.** *Pathology.* **a.** injury, wound, hurt, lesion. **b.** traumatism.
2. *Psychiatry.* shock, shocker, blow, bombshell, jolt; upset, disturbance, agitation, turmoil; pain, anguish, suffering.

travail, *n.* **1.** toil, labor, work, drudgery, *Chiefly Brit.* fag, moil; sweat of one's brow, effort, struggle, exertion, pains, trouble, care; grind, rat race, treadmill, slavery, slave labor, bondage, serfdom; working in a sweatshop *or* the salt mines.
2. anguish, angst, torment, agony, torture, misery, distress, despair, sorrow; pain, ache, suffering, pang, twinge, hurt; hardship, deprivation, adversity.
3. childbirth, parturition, lying-in, accouchement, confinement, labor, labor pains.
—v. **4.** be in labor, go into labor; give birth, lie in, be confined.

travel, *v.* **1.** journey, voyage, take a trip, tour, junket; see the world, *Inf.* globetrot, take a slow boat to China, shuffle off to Buffalo; hit the road *or* trail, cruise, sail, ride the bounding main, fly, jet, drive, motor, thumb, hitchhike, hitch, *Fr. faire l'auto-stop;* roam, *Sl.* truck, wander, peregrinate, gad about; see the sights, sigthtsee, *Inf.* rubberneck, take a tour, take a charter trip; trek, migrate, emigrate, *Sl.* go on a long shlep; traverse, cross, cover, cover ground.
2. proceed, advance, wag, go, *Sl.* mogate, move,

move along, wend.

3. **travel with** consort, associate, *Inf.* pal around, know, socialize, mingle, fraternize, hobnob; drink with, *Sl.* swing with, *Sl.* hang out.

—*n.* 4. **travels** journey, trip, tour, peregrination, wanderings, junket; trek, migration; pilgrimage, hadj, *Hebrew. aliyah.*

5. passage, traverse, transit, movement, advancement.

traveler, *n.* wayfarer, voyager, peregrinator; rambler, rover, roamer, Wandering Jew; adventurer, landloper, explorer, soldier of fortune, *Inf.* boomer, cowboy; trekker, hiker, backpacker; excursionist, sight-seer, *Inf.* rubbernecker, tourist, *Sl.* jet-setter; astronaut, cosmonaut, seaman, sailor, sea captain; bird of passage, migrant, nomad, Kuchi, Bedouin; hobo, vagant, hitchhiker, hitcher; traveling salesman, commercial traveler, tinker, itinerant.

traveling, *adj.* peripatetic, itinerant, wandering, roaming, roving, on the move, on the go; gallivanting, gadding, flitting, moving, mobile, restless, not tied down, unsettled, nomadic, migratory; living out of a suitcase, itchy-footed, always ready to pick up and go.

traverse, *v.* 1. pass over, move over, travel over, tour, fare; range, ply, wander, roam, track; cover, sweep, peregrinate; tramp, trek, ramble, march, walk; sail, voyage, cruise, navigate, make a passage; ford, cross, overpass, cut across.

2. cross, go across, intersect, lie across; extend across, stretch across, bridge, connect, bring together; transverse, intercross, crisscross, crossbar.

3. examine, consider, contemplate, observe, look into; review, pass in review, look over, take stock of, make note of, audit; inspect, scan, scour, reconnoiter.

4. obstruct, hinder, impede, thwart, foil, balk; interfere with, retard, frustrate; oppose, counter, contravene, counteract.

5. deny, contradict, counter, controvert; gainsay, negate, reject, disavow, disclaim, dispute, challenge, contest, call into question; impugn, rebut, go against, oppugn, take issue with, join issue with.

—*n.* 6. crossbar, crosspiece, transverse, transversal, transcept, crossarm; whiffletree, whippletree, swingletree, singletree, doubletree.

—*adj.* 7. transverse, cross, crossing, horizontal, oblique.

travesty, *n.* 1. burlesque, satire, take-off, parody, caricature, lampoon, wicked imitation; mockery, ridicule; exaggeration, hyperbole.

2. distortion, poor imitation, misrepresentation, falsification, slander; grotesquery, monstrosity, abortion, atrocity; debasement, corruption, perversion, botch.

—*v.* 3. burlesque, parody, satirize, lampoon, take off, caricature; mock, ridicule, twit, *Inf.* rag, laugh at, deride; mimic, ape, imitate, copy.

4. distort, misrepresent, falsify; debase, corrupt, pervert; deform, twist, warp, garble; mar, damage, ruin, destroy.

tray, *n.* platter, salver, server, waiter, serving tray, lazy Susan, *Archaic.* trencher, flat container *or* receptacle; coaster, dish, plate, ashtray.

treacherous, *adj.* 1. traitorous, perfidious, disloyal; treasonable, treasonous, subversive. See **traitorous** (*defs.* **1, 2**).

2. deceptive, deceiving, misleading; deceitful, false, untrustworthy, unreliable; dodgy, shifty, wily, reptilian, snaky, evasive, slippery, elusive; specious, bogus, sham, counterfeit, pseudo, mock.

3. precarious, uncertain, unsure, unstable, unsafe, unsound; insecure, infirm, unsteady, shaky, rickety, tottery; ticklish, tricky, delicate, touch-and-go.

4. dangerous, fraught with danger, perilous, *Archaic.* parlous; hazardous, risky, riskful, chancy, dicey, *Sl.* hairy; open, exposed, vulnerable, assailable, defenseless; threatening, dire, menacing, ominous, alarming, minacious.

treachery, *n.* treason, betrayal, violation of faith; treasonableness, traitorousness, bad faith, disloyalty, unloyalty, perfidy, perfidiousness, faithlessness, unfaithfulness, recreance, recreancy; infidelity, *Sl.* two-timing, cheating, double-dealing, falseness, hypocrisy, dissimulation; deceitfulness, deceit, guile, guilefulness, duplicity, deception; fraud, chicanery, trickery, foul play; *Inf.* double cross, Judas kiss, stab in the back.

tread, *v.* 1. step, walk, hoof it, ambulate, stump; tramp, trudge, march, plod, plow, mush, shuffle; pace, stride, strut; perambulate, stroll, trek.

2. trample, tramp on *or* upon, stamp, stomp, step on, squash, crush, *Dial.* squish.

3. oppress, violate, do violence to, hurt; infringe on, trench on *or* upon; run over, ride over, ride roughshod over; domineer, bully, hector, intimidate, browbeat; subjugate, master, conquer.

4. **tread on [s.o.'s] toes** offend, affront, insult; step on the toes of, *Inf.* put [s.o.] off, displease, pique, *Inf.* miff, disgruntle; vex, annoy, incense, exasperate, distress; irk, rankle, roil, *Chiefly U.S.* rile, rattle, ruffle.

—*n.* 5. step, footstep, footfall, walk; plodding, stamping, stomp, stomping, trampling.

treason, *n.* high treason, betrayal, treachery, *Inf.* double cross, Judas kiss, stab in the back; sedition, subversion, undermining, corruption; mutiny, insubordination; insurrection, rebellion, revolt, revolution, insurgence, insurgency, uprising, outbreak, riot, anarchy. See also **treachery.**

treasonable, *adj.* 1. treasonous, seditious, subversive, insurrectionary. See **traitorous** (*def.* **2**).

2. traitorous, perfidious, disloyal, treacherous. See **traitorous** (*def.* **1**).

treasure, *n.* 1. riches, wealth, fortune; savings, hoardings, hoard, store, stock, reserve, cache; capital, assets, funds, means, resources, wherewithal; nest egg, *Sl.* cushion, *Sl.* tidy bundle; bullion, gold, silver, precious gems; money, cash, *Sl.* dough, *Sl.* bread, *Sl.* moolah, *Sl.* spondulicks, *Sl.* loot, *Sl.* gravy, *U.S. Sl.* bucks, *U.S. Sl.* big bucks, *Sl.* wampum, *Sl.* mazuma, *Sl.* simoleons, *Sl.* shekels.

2. prize, pride, pride and joy; gem, jewel; *Inf.* find, *Inf.* catch.

—*v.* 3. keep in memory, bear in mind, retain in the mind, hold in the thoughts, cherish the memory of, keep up the memory of, keep the memory alive, keep fresh in the mind.

4. prize, value, esteem, cherish, hold dear, set a high value on, rate highly, value highly, make much of; revere, reverence, set great store by, attach importance to, regard, think of as special; like, love, care for, adore, consider precious.

5. hoard, store up, stock up, lay by, lay up, lay in; cache, squirrel away, load up, stow away, *Inf.* stash away, reserve, set aside, reposit, husband; save, save up, bank; accumulate, collect, heap up, pile up.

treasurer, *n.* bursar, purser, controller, holder *or* keeper of the purse strings, receiver of moneys, *Rom. Hist.* quaestor, cash-keeper; cashier, teller; banker, financier; depositary; minister of finance, (*in Britain*) Chancellor of the Exchequer.

treasury, *n.* 1. exchequer, fisc, *Eccles.* bursary; depository, thesaurus, chache, vault, repository, receptacle, arsenal.

2. funds, revenue, securities, shares, stocks, bonds;

capital, assets, finances, resources; money, currency, wherewithal; holdings, savings.

3. coffer, strongbox, chest, money-box, till, safe.

4. collection, anthology, compilation, corpus; store, stock; series, assortment, array.

treat, *v.* **1.** behave towards, act towards, conduct oneself towards, do by; deal with, handle, cope with, face; contend with, manage, use, wield.

2. doctor, practice medicine, attend, intern, minister, nurse, care for; prescribe for, medicate, operate; heal, cure, remedy; bandage, strap, plaster, dress; massage, rub, bathe.

3. discuss, take up, deal with, handle, write up; consider, examine, investigate, analyze, study, dissert; discourse, dissertate, touch upon, write upon, go into; comment upon, review, survey, critique, criticize; annotate, interpret.

4. subject, process, prepare.

5. entertain, regale, refresh, be hospitable to; dine, wine and dine, feast; divert, amuse, pleasure, humor, cheer, gratify, satisfy.

6. buy, pay for, pick up the check *or* tab, pay the bill; stand treat, stand drinks, set up, *Inf.* stand to, *Inf.* foot the bill; subsidize, bear the expense, finance, fund, defray.

7. negotiate, make terms, covenant, parley, confer; bargain, higgle, haggle, give and take; engage, contract, agree, stipulate, settle.

—n. **8.** morsel, tidbit, delicacy, goody, kickshaw, *Fr. bonne bouche*; candy, bonbon, taffy, lollipop, sucker, sugarplum; dessert, cake, tart, pie, pudding, jello, ice cream, sundae; nectar, ambrosia, manna.

9. entertainment, regalement, regale, snack; refreshment, refection, feast, banquet, round; meal, repast, *Inf.* spread, *Sl.* feed, table, collation, junket; party, fete, supper, dinner, luncheon, brunch, breakfast; picnic, garden party.

treatise, *n.* discourse, disquisition, treatment, exposition, discussion; tract, thesis, essay, dissertation, tractate; examination, investigation, study; article, paper, monograph, composition, term paper, research paper; criticism, critique, commentary, review, editorial; sermon, screed, homily, descant; excursus, memoir, publication, work; brochure, pamphlet, leaflet.

treatment, *n.* **1.** handling, manipulation, usage, application; utilization, practice, exercise; dealing, way, procedure, process.

2. management, execution, direction, guidance; conduct, care, stewardship.

3. processing, process, preparation, pretreatment; adjustment, modification, qualification, adaptation.

4. therapy, care, therapeutics, nursing, first aid; medication, curative measures, hospitalization.

treaty, *n.* agreement, covenant, compact, bargain, deal, indenture; pact, *Rare.* paction, bond, convention, concordat, international agreement; league, alliance, cartel, conspiracy, collusion; accord, concord, concordance; mutual pledge, mutual understanding, exchange of vows, gentlemen's agreement, promise, word; cease-fire, truce, entente, entente cordiale, détente.

tree, *n.* **1.** plant, shrub, stock, pollard, *Fr. arbre*, *Ger. Baum*; seedling, sapling; evergreen, conifer; fruit tree, timber tree, hardwood tree, softwood tree.

2. gallows, gibbet, drop, cross, hanging tree, gallows tree.

3. family tree, line of descent, descent. See **lineage**.

—v. **4.** *Informal.* drive up a tree, stump, back into a corner, corner, force one to the wall; chase up a tree, *Inf.* have one on the ropes, *Inf.* put one in a hole, nail.

treelike, *adj.* arboreal, arborescent, arboreous, dendroid, dendritic, dendriform, tree-shaped; branched, branchlike, ramose, ramous, ramiform.

trek, *v.* **1.** travel, journey, traverse, pass over; migrate, emigrate, immigrate, transmigrate; peregrinate, roam, wander, range; tramp, march, hike, trudge, plod, rove.

—n. **2.** journey, trip, voyage, sail; migration, passage, transmigration, immigration; exodus, flight, emigration, odyssey, expatriation; expedition, mission, pilgrimmage, hadj; tramp, march, hike.

trellis, *n.* lattice, grille, grid, fret, wattle; grate, grating, reticule; network, reticulation; latticework, grillwork, trelliswork, webwork, meshwork; interlacement, intertwinement, lacework, lacery, texture.

tremble, *v.* shake, quake, quiver, quaver, shudder, shiver; twitter, trill, quail, jitter; teeter, totter, dodder, fidget; shake like a leaf, quake in one's boots, quiver like a rabbit; pulsate, pulse, throb, palpitate, beat, pitapat; vibrate, oscillate, librate, rock; rattle, chatter, flutter, flitter, flit, chill; vellicate, twitch, convulse, commove; wiggle, waggle, waver, shimmy; jingle, jiggle, jangle, joggle.

tremendous, *adj.* **1.** *Informal.* great, huge, grand, vast, gigantic, monstrous; enormous, large, massive, mighty, colossal, prodigious; gargantuan, towering, titanic, mammoth, elephantine, immense, giant.

2. loud, crashing, deafening, earsplitting; booming, thundering, resounding, rolling, roaring; pealing, window-rattling, crashing, enough to wake the dead.

3. dreadful, terrifying, frightening, direful; horrendous, horrible, terrible, monstrous, atrocious; ghastly, grisly, unspeakable, gruesome, outrageous, shocking; harrowing, alarming, distressing, rending, fearsome, formidable, awful.

4. *Informal.* extraordinary, remarkable, marvelous, out of the ordinary, astonishing, astounding, amazing; fantastic, fabulous, *Sl.* fantabulous, *Sl.* far-out, mind-boggling, *Sl.* mind-blowing, supercalifragilisticexpialidocious; wondrous, wonderful, miraculous; unusual, rare, unique, singular, uncommon; stunning, breathtaking, staggering, phenomenal.

5. inordinate, excessive, extreme, preposterous; immoderate, extravagant, exorbitant, exaggerated; unreasonable, intemperate, gross, unbounded; copious, profuse, overflowing, overmuch, lavish.

tremor, *n.* **1.** shaking, shudder, shiver, quaver, quiver; palpitation, pulsation, pulse, throb, beat, sputter, flutter, pitter-patter, pitapat; vellication, swing, ripple, jolt, jerk; vibration, oscillation, libration, shake, rock; agitation, chatter, rattle, twitter, jitter; jingling, joggling, jiggling; palsy, twitch, tic, rictus, convulsion, the shakes, St. Vitus dance; throe, orgasm, paroxysm, spasm, fit, seizure, *Pathol.* jactation.

2. quake, earthquake, shock, trembler, *U.S.* temblor, seismic disturbance, *Geol.* diastrophism.

tremulous, *adj.* **1.** trembling, shaking, quivering, quaking, quavering, shuddering, shivering; quaky, shaky, trembly, tremulant, quivery, quavery, shuddery; rattling, chattering, vibratory, vibrative, twittering, oscillatory; spasmodic, jerky, convulsive.

2. timorous, timid, easily frightened, diffident, fainthearted; cowardly, craven, pusillanimous, *Inf.* yellow, weak-kneed, lily-livered; fearful, frightened, afraid, scared, *Archaic.* affrighted; skittish, jumpy, edgy, on edge, jittery, nervous, high-strung, panicky, panic-stricken; apprehensive, anxious, alarmed, tense, uneasy, disquieted.

trench, *n.* **1.** excavation, cut, ditch, furrow, ridge, sulcation; fosse, moat, dike; passage, duct, course, conduit, adit; sewer, trough, gutter, channel, canal, groove, *Brit.* kennel, watercourse

2. fortification, defense, shelter, abri, outwork, hole; *Fort.* scarp, *Fort.* escarp, sap, sunken fence, ha-ha; pit, foxhole, dugout, pill box, *Mil.* hedgehog, bunker, nest; *All Fort.* work, redan, redoubt, breastwork, earthwork, groundwork.

—v. **3.** furrow, groove, ridge, slot, ditch; dig out, excavate, shovel, scoop, gouge, delve; burrow, tunnel, mine, bore.

4. fortify, bulwark, barricade, fix, establish; solidify, brace, buttress, shore up.

5. trench on *or* **upon a.** encroach, ingress, infiltrate, make inroads; trespass, infringe, impinge, invade; overstep, intrude, obtrude, overrun. **b.** verge on, come close to, border on, near, approach, approximate.

trenchant, *adj.* **1.** incisive, keen, acute, pointed; caustic, cutting, strident; sharp, biting, stringent, pungent; razor-edged, sharp-edged, knife-edged; sarcastic, poignant, piercing, penetrating; tart, acrid, acrimonious, bitter; mordant, acid, acerbic, acidulous, mordacious.

2. vigorous, effective, energetic, intense, strenuous; emphatic, powerful, forcible, vehement, vibrant, dynamic, strong; driving, telling, striking; impassioned, spirited, cogent, expressive.

3. clear-cut, distinct, well-defined, salient; explicit, graphic, vivid; realistic, true-to-life, depictive.

trend, *n.* **1.** tendency, drift, course, bent, career, progress; inclination, bearing, heading, orientation; tack, set, aim, way, track; stream, swing, sweep, current; tenor, tone, spirit.

2. style, vogue, fashion, taste, mode; look, thing, *Inf.* swim, *Inf.* go; fad, rage, craze.

—v. **3.** tend, drift, incline, lean; set, veer, bend, head, point, go; verge, bear, turn, direct; dispose, bias, warp, swing toward, heel; curve, shift, swerve, tack.

trepidation, *n.* **1.** perturbation, alarm, agitation, consternation; fright, fear, panic, dread, terror, funk; unrest, disquietude, inquietude, discomposure, nervousness, stage fright; malaise, unease, jumpiness, stir, fidgetiness; angst, fear and trembling, anxiety, apprehension, apprehensiveness, *Inf.* butterflies; misgiving, qualm, uncertainty, mistrust, cold feet; creeps, chills, *Sl.* willies, *Sl.* jimjams, cold sweat, goosebumps, icy fingers, sinking stomach; dither, tizzy, *Inf.* foofaraw, fluster, fret, bother, pother.

2. trembling, tremor, shake, jolt, jar, jerk, quake; vibration, quivering, quavering, quaking, quiver, quaver; shaking, succussion, oscillation, vellication, shudder, shimmy; tossing, *Pathol.* jactation, the shakes, the jitters, shivers, spasm; pitter-patter, pitapat, twitter.

trespass, *n.* **1.** encroachment, entrenchment, infringement, intrusion, invasion; imposition, obtrusion.

2. wrong, wrongdoing, evildoing, sin, offense; transgression, violation, infraction, breach; crime, misdemeanor, felony; error, mistake, misdeed, misstep.

—v. **3.** encroach, entrench, trench on *or* upon, infringe, intrude, invade, *Chiefly Brit.* poach; impose, obtrude.

4. offend, wrong, sin; violate, transgress.

trespasser, *n.* **1.** encroacher, intruder, interloper, infiltrator, invader, *Chiefly Brit.* poacher; unwelcome guest, *Inf.* gate-crasher.

2. wrongdoer, evildoer, offender, sinner; transgressor, violator; delinquent; criminal, felon, malefactor, malfeasant.

tress, *n.* *Usu.* **tresses** locks, curls, ringlets.

trial, *n.* **1.** hearing, inquisition, inquiry; investigation, examination, review, scrutiny; study, analysis.

2. experimentation, trial and error, hit and miss, process of elimination; test procedure, operation, *Inf.* pilot.

3. attempt, effort, essay, endeavor, undertaking; *All Inf.* try, go, shot, fling, whirl; *All Sl.* crack, whack, lick, stab.

4. proof, proof positive, verification, confirmation, corroboration, substantiation, authentication.

5. test, experiment, venture, tryout, *Inf.* workout, dry run, trial run, road test; audition, rehearsal.

6. probation, trial period, test *or* testing period.

7. engagement, encounter, meet, match, contest.

8. adversity, hardship, misfortune, tribulation, trouble; pain, distress, suffering; grief, woe, sorror, heartache; hard times, heavy weather; bad luck, hard luck, *Inf.* tough *or* rotten *or* lousy luck, *Brit.* hard lines; bad *or* ill fortune.

9. affliction, visitation, curse, blight; shock, blow, bolt from the blue, *Psychiatry.* trauma; reverse, reversal, setback, check; ordeal; load, burden, weight, heavy load *or* burden, cross, cross to bear; inconvenience, disadvantage, handicap.

10. nuisance, pest, bother, *Inf.* headache, *Inf.* pain, *Sl.* pain in the neck *or* rear, *Sl.* hassle; annoyance, vexation, irritant, bur, thorn in the side *or* flesh; bane, gadfly, buttonholer.

—adj. **11.** experimental, tentative, hypothetical, probationary, pending, on approval; exploratory, pilot, under examination *or* consideration, provisional, untried; under observation, under the microscope, in the spotlight, on trial.

triangular, *adj.* **1.** three-cornered, tricorn, tricornered, trigonous, trigonal, triquetrous, three-sided, trilateral; deltoid, cuneiform, wedge-shaped, arrowheaded.

2. triple, treble, threefold, threesome, three-ply.

tribe, *n.* **1.** family, dynasty, house, clan, sept, (*in ancient Greece*) phyle; race, strain, stock, breed, bloodline, pedigree, stem, branch, stirps.

2. class, species, sort, kind, kidney, variety, type, genre; genus, subgenus, category, subcategory, division, subdivision, section; classification, group, grouping, set.

3. company, group, *Inf.* bunch, number.

tribulation, *n.* hardship, affliction, trouble, distress, heartache, pain, suffering, *Archaic.* bale, misery, wretchedness, agony, torture, torment; trial, ordeal, hard *or* bad *or* difficult time; adversity, misfortune, stroke of ill *or* bad luck *or* fortune, bitter cup *or* pill; cross, burden, weight, *Inf.* albatross, load, heavy load *or* burden; tragedy, calamity, catastrophe, disaster, blow, heavy *or* nasty *or* staggering blow, shock.

tribunal, *n.* **1.** court, bench, bar, judiciary, judicature, judicatory; forum, chancery; assizes, trial, session; Areopagus, King's Bench, Queen's Bench; Star Chamber, Inquisition.

2. dais, platform, rostrum; judgment seat.

tributary, *n.* **1.** branch, anabranch, feeder, affluent, confluent; stream, river, freshet, *U.S. Dial.* kill, gill, brook, *Scot. and North Eng.* burn, creek, *Dial.* crick; streamlet, brooklet, rivulet, rill, rillet, run, runnel, runlet.

—adj. **2.** contributory, contributing, helping, assisting, adjuvant, aiding, abetting; supportive, helpful, assistive, cooperative; auxiliary, subsidiary, additional, supplementary, reserve, extra; accessory, ancillary, secondary.

3. subordinate, inferior, second-class, less than, below, under; subject, subjected, dominated, controlled, enslaved, under one's thumb, subservient.

tribute, *n.* **1.** recognition, acclaim, acclamation, homage, honor, glorification, exaltation; commendation, celebration, congratulation, *Archaic.* gratulation, paean, laud; praise, extolment, laudation, kudos, *Archaic.* magnification; eulogy, eulogium, panegyric, encomium, citation; testimonial, declaration, announcement, oration.

2. (*all exacted*) contribution, offering, gift, donation; tax, duty, impost, levy, payment, surtax, surcharge; tariff, charge, exaction, taxation, scot; excise, custom, *Brit.* cess, octroi; rent, fee, dues, toll, rate, rating, assessment; capitation, poll tax, property tax, tithe, tenth, Peter's pence.

trice, *n.* very short time, instant, second, *Inf.* sec, moment, minute; twinkling, twinkling of an eye, *Fr. coup d'oeil*, flash, flash of lightning, jiffy, *Inf.* jiff, two shakes of a lamb's tail, before you can say "Jack Robinson"; breath, crack, burst, flick, *Inf.* whipstitch.

trick, *n.* **1.** artifice, stratagem, finesse, ruse, wile, Trojan horse, deceit; intrigue, plot, plan, tactic, scheme, strategy, machination; conspiracy, complot, cabal; device, contrivance, expedient, *Inf.* dodge, fetch, subterfuge, blind; trap, snare, *Inf.* catch, *Inf.* hooker; manuever, feint, deception, *Obs.* cog, sleight, coup, blow, stroke; shift, move, evasion, shuffle; fake, sham, hoax, swindle, *Archaic.* chouse, *Inf.* bunko, shuck; fraud, imposture, imposition, put-on, *Law.* covin, humbug, *Inf.* flimflam, *Inf.* flam; *All Sl.* gimmick, line, hype.

2. prank, caper, stunt, *Scot.* brogue; mischief, practical joke, *Fr. boutade,* spoof; antics, *Inf.* shenanigans, tomfoolery, *Sl.* monkeyshines, buffoonery, gambado, frolic, *Inf.* dido, horseplay; romp, gambol, sport, game, jest.

3. art, craft, technique, knack, skill, ability.

4. sleight of hand, legerdemain, hocus-pocus, prestidigitation, jugglery.

5. trait, characteristic, singularity, mannerism, idiosyncrasy, eccentricity, quirk, crotchet, habit.

—*v.* **6.** outwit, outmanuever, hoodwink, bamboozle, overreach, trip up; delude, deceive, take in, throw dust in [s.o.'s] eyes, pull the wool over [s.o.'s] eyes, *Inf.* slip [s.t.] over on, *Inf.* slip *or* pass one over on; mislead, misinform, misguide, sail under false colors; dupe, cully, gull, cozen, defraud, cheat; rook, victimize, bilk, swindle, *Inf.* finagle, cog, *Archaic.* chouse, *Sl.* take, *Sl.* snooker; pass off, palm off, impose upon, pull a fast one on, *Inf.* throw a curve; humbug, gammon, bluff, juggle, have [s.t.] up one's sleeve, *Inf.* flimflam; trap, entrap, snare, ensnare, enmesh; beguile, seduce, bait, decoy; lead on, take [s.o.] for a ride, *Inf.* fake [s.o.] out, *Inf.* rope [s.o.] in, *Inf.* string along; betray, play false, double-cross, two-time, *Sl.* shaft, *Sl.* cross [s.o.] up; *All Inf.* jive, fast-talk, flam, hype, buffalo, bulldoze; *All Sl.* con, snow, suck *or* sucker in, murphy.

7. *Often* **trick out** *or* **up** deck out, bedizen, *Archaic.* bedight, prink, dress up, array, attire; adorn, beautify, enhance; decorate, embellish, enrich, ornament, garnish.

trickery, *n.* deceit, guile, artifice, craft, craftiness, shrewdness, wiliness, slyness, circumvention; artfulness, subtlety, finesse, *Inf.* razzle-dazzle, *Sl.* jive, *Sl.* hype; shiftiness, evasiveness, slipperiness; duplicity, double-dealing, cozenage, dark and crooked ways, evil ways; fraud, imposture, imposition, hoax, quackery, charlatanry; feigning, dissimulation, hypocrisy; jugglery, trumpery, dupery, hocus-pocus, shenanigan; deception, chicane, chicanery, knavery, *Inf.* hanky-panky, *Sl.* funny business, *Sl.* monkey business; intrigue, conspiracy, collusion; treachery, betrayal, tergiversation, disloyalty.

trickle, *v.* trill, flow gently, plash, spill over, well out; drip, drop, fall in drops, dribble; sprinkle, drizzle; leak, ooze, exude, transude, seep, filter, distill, percolate.

trickster, *n.* **1.** deceiver, deluder, hoodwinker, beguiler, inveigler, bamboozler, dissembler, bluff, pettifogger; fake, faker, phony, humbug; imposter, masquerader, pretender, mountebank, hypocrite, charlatan, *Inf.* quack; adventurer, rogue, picaroon, rascal, wolf in sheep's clothing, knave, scoundrel, *Sl.* four-flusher, villain.

2. swindler, cheat, cheater, fraud, defrauder, confidence man, *Sl.* con man, *Sl.* flim-flam man, bunko artist, crook, chiseler; sharper, sharpie, *Sl.* city slicker, *Inf.* fast talker, *Inf.* hawk, shark, bilk, bilker, diddler; duper, hoaxer, humbugger; rook, fleecer, gyp, gypper.

3. conjurer, illusionist, sleight-of-hand artist, legerdemainist, magician; juggler, archimage, *Archaic.* mage, Houdini, escape artist.

tried, *adj.* tried out, tested, put through one's *or* its paces, put to the test *or* through the wringer; time-tested, having stood the test of time, put to the acid test; tried and true, true, proven, proved, sure, certain, *Inf.* all-right, *Inf.* O.K.; dependable, reliable, safe, trusty, trustworthy, reputable; established, well-known, used all the time, favorite.

trifle, *n.* **1.** bagatelle, bauble, trinket, knickknack, *Inf.* doodad; gimcrack, gewgaw, whimwham, piece of junk; toy, plaything, dalliance, frivolity.

2. triviality, no great matter, no big thing, technicality; unimportant *or* inconsequential thing *or* matter, nothing to worry *or* get upset over, something of no concern, insignificancy, bêtise, inessential, nothing, nothing at all, *Inf.* fiddle-faddle.

3. pittance, piddling sum, small amount, little something, *Inf.* nothing much; the least *or* slightest amount *or* bit, anything, row *or* hill of beans, tinker's dam, straw, fig, peppercorn, *Inf.* bean; dime, nickel, penny, cent, plug nickel, continental, *U.S. Inf.* red cent; the paper it is printed on.

4. little, bit, little *or* tiny bit, driblet, drop, smidgen, *Inf.* smitch, *Inf.* tad; touch, dab, dash, pinch, handful; sprinkling; mouthful, sip, sup, taste, nip, bite; speck, crumb, mite, jot, whit, tittle, particle, iota, molecule, atom; tinge, tincture, trace, hint, suggestion, suspicion, soupçon.

—*v.* **5.** *Usu.* **trifle with** deal with lightly, make light of, take lightly, pass off as nothing, think nothing of; slight, shortchange, overlook, pass over, leave out, omit, ignore; be frivolous about *or* with, make sport of, laugh off, joke about, play, toy, dally, amuse oneself, *Inf.* frivol; fiddle, tinker, mess, fool, *Inf.* fiddle-faddle; handle, finger, paw, put one's hands all over.

6. talk idly, gossip, chitchat, chatter, engage in small talk, talk about nothing; palaver, prattle, prate, rattle *or* babble on, talk and talk and talk, go on about nothing.

7. putter around, fiddle around, tinker around, play around, mess around, niggle, finick, *Inf.* fool around; goof off, dillydally, hang around, loiter, lay around, twiddle one's thumbs, dawdle, do nothing.

8. *Usu.* **trifle away** fritter, fribble, *Inf.* diddle; idle, pass, while; waste, use up, loose.

trifling, *adj.* **1.** unimportant, trivial, fiddling, insignificant, signifying nothing, inconsequential; not worth mentioning, of little import, of no moment, *Inf.* no-account, not worth a fig *or* a hill of beans, *Sl.* two-bit, *Sl.* two-by-four, *Inf.* penny-ante.

2. worthless, valueless, useless, gimcrack; small, low, nominal, *Inf.* picayune; miniscule, inconsiderable, tiny, infinitesimal, minute; inadequate, paltry, petty, piddling.

3. frivolous, shallow, superficial, light, meaningless, without depth; idle, silly, inane, asinine, foolish.

trim, *v.* **1.** clip, snip, nip, prune, pare; cut, bob, crop, shingle; shear, shave, fleece, pollard, poll, scalp, cut down to the quick; neaten, even up; shape, form, fashion, sculpt, sculp, sculpture.

2. *Often* **trim off** dock, bobtail, lop, chop, hack, cut off, saw off; remove, detach, amputate, cut out *or* away, eliminate.

3. fit, cut down, cut down to size, taper, tailor, hem, (*both of clothing*) take in, let out; pare down, plane, shave, whittle, chisel, carve, hew, scrape *or* sand down; reduce, diminish, decrease, cut back, retrench; shorten, truncate, abridge, abbreviate, cut short, curtail, *Rare.* obtruncate; digest, abstract, epitomize, summarize, brief, synopsize, boil down, condense, contract, compress, concentrate, put in a nutshell.

4. amend, revise, restyle, recast, remold, remodel; edit, blue-pencil, emend, emendate; adjust, modify, make fit *or* conform, make adjustments *or* changes in; shift, redistribute, rearrange, realign, reorganize, reorder, permutate; regulate, symmetrize, equalize, balance, level, coordinate.

5. edge, border, purfle, purl, fringe, befringe; embroider, bead, spangle, bespangel, stud, bestud, beset; bind, cover; decorate, adorn, embellish, ornament, garnish, festoon, *Archaic.* ouch, *Archaic.* dight; furbish, prink, prank, dress up, deck out, deck, bedeck, bedizen, trap out, accouter, attire, caparison; beautify, prettify, fix up, *Inf.* pretty up, *Inf.* spruce up, *Inf.* trick up, *Inf.* gussy up; brighten up, perk up, color, blazon, emblazon.

6. *Informal.* **a.** rebuke, reprove, reproach, reprehend, scold, chide, reprimand; admonish, call down, call on the carpet, take [s.o.] to task, rap [s.o.'s] knuckles, slap [s.o.'s] wrists. **b.** spank, tan [s.o.'s] hide, thrash, flog, lash, switch, birch, scourge; *Inf.* lambaste, *Inf.* lace, *Inf.* thump, *Inf.* whale, *Sl.* whump, *Sl.* beat the tar out of, beat, batter, pummel. **c.** trounce, rout, beat by a mile, win by a landslide, *Inf.* whip, *Inf.* wallop, *Sl.* cream, *Sl.* pulverize, *Sl.* kill; vanquish, conquer, defeat, beat out, worst, win over.

7. be noncommittal, say nothing one way or the other, be vague *or* ambiguous; dodge, duck, fudge, shuffle, waffle, skirt the issue, fence, hem and haw, halt, weasel, doubletalk, palter, beat around the bush; walk a tightrope, tightrope, straddle the fence, *Inf.* talk out of both side's of one's mouth, play both ends against the middle; be politic, be diplomatic *or* tactful, watch one's every step, proceed cautiously *or* with caution, be careful, walk softly; hedge, play it safe, cover one's bets.

—*n.* **8.** good shape *or* condition, proper adjustment, good working order, *Inf.* apple-pie order; trimness, spruceness, orderliness, organization, neatness, tidiness, *Chiefly Brit.* trigness.

9. trimming, edging, fringe, lace, rickrack, ribbon, braid, binding; embroidery, filigree, ornament, frill, flourish, flounce, furbelow, garnish, dressing, window dressing; decoration, ornamentation, ornament, adornment, embellishment; gingerbread, frippery, folderol, fuss, trappings, *Sl.* jazz, *Sl.* flash; spangle, sequins, tinsel, trinket, clinquant, bauble, gimcrack, gewgaw, trifle, *Inf.* doodad, *Inf.* fandangle, *Archaic.* ouch.

10. cut, clip, snip, pruning, paring; haircut, style, shaping, bob, crop, shingle, crewcut, summer cut.

11. clippings, cuttings, snip, snippet, shavings, sawdust; parings, peeling, sliver, shive, shard, thin slice *or* piece, shred, splinter; bit, scrap, fragment, remnant.

—*adj.* **12.** shipshape, orderly, in order, in place, well-organized, well-arranged, *Inf.* in apple-pie order; spruce, trig, neat, tidy, minion, well-groomed, well-kept, well-maintained; smart, sharp, dapper, natty, jaunty, nifty, nobby, well-dressed, well-turned-out, *Sl.* spiffy, *Scot. and North Eng.* braw; compact, condensed, concentrated, short and sweet, in a nutshell, in summary form, succinct.

13. fit, in good condition *or* shape, fit as a fiddle, in fine fettle, physically fit, ready for action; sleek, streamlined, clean, smooth; svelte, lithe, lithesome, lissome, willowy, slim, slender, thin, slight; lean, lanky, arrowy, solid, sinewy, all muscle, muscular, athletic.

trinity, *n.* **1. Trinity** Blessed Trinity, Holy Trinity, Trine, Triune, Triune Godhead; Father, Son and Holy Ghost.

2. triad, triple, triplex, trine, tern, ternary, ternion, trio, triplets, Three Musketeers; triunity, troika, triumvirate, triarchy; triangle, eternal triangle, threesome, *Fr. ménage à trois; Astron.* Triangulum; triplet, trilogy, *Pros., Music.* tercet, *Music.* mordent, *Music.* triple fugue, *Chiefly Bridge.* tripleton, *Piquet.* tierce; triple play, three-base hit, triple crown, *Sports.* triple header.

3. triplicity, trilaterality, triangularity, threefold nature, *Music.* ternary form.

trinket, *n.* ornament, decoration, adornment; pretty, tinsel, spangle, clinquant, jewel, bijou; knickknack; souvenir, memento, keepsake, token; bauble, plaything, toy, thing, *Inf.* doodad; bagatelle, gimcrack, geegaw, whim-wham; triviality, trifling, pittance, row *or* hill of beans, tinker's dam, straw, fig.

trip, *n.* **1.** journey, voyage, cruise, excursion, tour, jaunt, junket; passage, circuit, transit, crossing, sail, grand tour, round trip; expedition, trek, safari, shoot, stalk; outing, ride, drive, run, *Inf.* hop; walk, stroll, hike, promenade, ramble; errand, mission, pilgrimage, hadj.

2. stumble, misstep, drop, fall, tumble; spill, sprawl, *Sl.* flop, *Inf.* pratfall, *Inf.* header; dive, plunge, slip, slide, loss of balance, lurch, pitch.

3. mistake, error, blunder, slip, *Inf.* slip-up, bad move, faux pas; lapse, oversight, *Inf.* miscue, slip of the tongue, *Latin. lapsus linguae*, slip of the pen, Freudian slip; *Inf.* fluff, *Inf.* flub, *Inf.* muff, *Sl.* boner, *Sl.* blooper; malapropism, spoonerism, gaff, solecism, Irish bull, bull, indiscretion; bungle, botch, mispronunciation, missaying, misstatement, misspelling, misquotation; *All Sl.* goof, boot, foozle, screw-up, foul-up.

—*v.* **4.** stumble, fall, fall over, fall down, misstep; lose one's footing, slip, tumble, *Inf.* take a pratfall; pitch, lurch, topple, plunge, dive; spill, sprawl, *Sl.* flop, spread-eagle; stagger, totter, tilt, list, flounder; fall flat on one's face, *Inf.* take a header, *Inf.* come a cropper, precipitate oneself.

5. err, make a mistake, slip, slip up; bungle, blunder, misspeak, *Brit.* duff, *Brit.* drop a brick; misreckon, miscalculate, misjudge; misquote, misstate, missay, mispronounce, misspell; miscue, *Inf.* muff, *Inf.* fluff, *Inf.* flub, *Sl.* blow; *Sl.* goof, *Sl.* screw up, *Sl.* foul up, *Sl.* pull a boner.

6. trap, catch, catch up, sniggle, noose; inveigle, entangle, snare, hook; fool, deceive, gull, *Inf.* bamboozle, *Inf.* hoodwink; outwit, outsmart, outmaneuver, overreach, trick, catch one in his own lies.

7. dance, hop, skip, prance, cavort, bound, gambol; waltz, one-step, two-step, *Sl.* hoof, foot, trip the light fantastic; *Sl.* boogie, *Sl.* cut a rug, *Sl.* shake one's booties; shake, shimmy, twist, shuffle, roll; foxtrot, rumba, tango, polka.

triple, *adj.* **1.** treble, threefold, threesome, ternate, ternary, trinary, trinal, trine, triadic; tripartite, triparted, three-part, tri-state, three-piece, three-ply, three-layer, trifocal, *Genetics.* trisomic, *Bot.* trispermous, *Chem.* triatomic, *Chem.* trivalent; three-way, three-phase, tricyclic, three-time.

2. triform, triformed, tricolor, tricolored, three-color, three-flavor; three-sided, trilateral, triangular, *Geom.* trihedral; three-cornered, tricorned, tricorn, tri-cornered, trigonous, trigonal, triquetrous, triradiate; tricuspid, tricuspidal, tridental, tridentate, trident; trifid, trifurcate, trifurcated, three-forked, trilobate, trifoliate, tridactyl, three-toed, tripodal, tripodic, three-legged, *Bot., Zool.* trilocular.

3. triplex, in triplicate, *Biol.* triploid; tripled.

—*n.* **4.** triad, trinity, triplex, trine. See also **trinity** (*def.* **2**).

—*v.* **5.** treble, triplicate, increase threefold.

tripping, *adj.* **1.** light, light-footed, light-legged, light of heel; agile, nimble-footed, spry; quick, brisk, fast, fleet, swift, rapid; flying, winged; frisky, spirited.

2. graceful, fluent, flowing, rhythmic.

trite, *adj.* hackneyed, overdone, overused; banal, *Inf.* bromidic, platitudinous, proverbial, *Inf.* corny; out-of-date, old, antiquated, ancient, archaic, obsolete; tired, thin, threadbare, stale, shopworn, worn-out, played out, *Inf.* old hat, moth-eaten, warmed-over; unimaginative, unoriginal, uninspired; dull, insipid, tedious, tiresome, wearisome; routine, habitual, everyday, customary; regular, run-of-the-mill, ordinary; prosaic, prosy, matter-of-fact; conventional, traditional, humdrum, commonplace, common, well-known, stock, familiar, stereotyped; simple, fatuous, inane, feeble, wishy-washy.

triumph, *n.* **1.** conquest, victory, win, walkaway, walkover, *Sl.* pushover, *Sl.* picnic; feat, coup, feather in one's cap; *Inf.* ten-strike, *Inf.* grand slam; *Sl.* killing, *Sl.* smash; stroke of genius, tour de force, master-stroke, *Fr. coup de maître;* success, attainment, accomplishment, achievement, palm; mastery, ascendancy, advantage, upper hand; hit, *Inf.* smash, *Sl.* sockeroo, sensation.

2. jubilation, exultation, jubilance, jubilancy; celebration, rejoicing; glory, laurels, acclamation, citation, parade, flourish, fanfare.

—*v.* **3.** win, be victorious, be the victor, win hands down; gain a victory, carry the day, win one's spurs; ring the bell, gain the palm, take the crown, *Inf.* bring home the bacon, take the prize, come off with flying colors.

4. prevail, hold out against, withstand, sustain without yielding, keep one's head above water, weather the storm; surmount an obstacle, make headway.

5. defeat, conquer, subdue, overwhelm, overcome, vanquish, subjugate; best, checkmate, beat, surpass, outwit, outmaster, outmaneuver; dominate, hold authority, wear the crown, sit on the throne, *Inf.* sit in the driver's seat; command, have ascendancy, have mastery.

6. succeed, meet with success, win out, be successful, be a winner *or* success, score a success; accomplish, bring off.

7. rejoice, celebrate, exult, glory, jubilate, revel, delight in; leap for joy, fling up one's cap, hurrah; brag, gloat, swagger.

triumphant, *adj.* victorious, successful, winning; succeeding, out in front, at the head of the pack, leading, ahead of the game, on top, *Sl.* on top of the heap *or* pile, *Inf.* on top of the world, in the catbird seat, *Sl.* sitting pretty; unbeaten, undefeated; crowned, laurel-wreathed, palm-bearing, trophy-winning, prize-holding, bay-wreathed, garlanded.

trivia, *n.* useless information, minor details, details, minutiae, trifles, trivialities, inconsequentia.

trivial, *adj.* insignificant, unimportant, of minor importance, of little *or* no import, negligible, nugatory, inappreciable, inconsiderable, inconsequential, of no consequence; small, light, flimsy, slim; minor, puny, dinky, piddling, *Inf.* rinky-dink; small-time, one-horse, bush, *Sl.* two-bit, *Inf.* penny-ante, lightweight, *Sl.* small-potatoes, small fry, *Sl.* mickey-mouse; inapplicable, irrelevant, immaterial, unessential; unportentous, unmomentous, of no matter *or* concern, of little *or* no account, of no moment, of no great weight; *Inf.* no great shakes, not worth mentioning, not worth speaking of, not worth thinking *or* worrying about, good-for-nothing, not worth a rap *or* a straw; trifling, *Inf.* picayune, pimping, fiddling, paltry, petty, niggling; insubstantial, unsubstantial, shallow, frivolous, foolish, nonsensical.

triviality, *n.* **1.** trifle, trifling, something of little importance, no great matter, no big thing, small *or* little matter, technicality; unimportant *or* inconsequential thing, nothing to worry *or* get upset over, something of no concern, insignificant, insignificancy, bêtise, inessential, nothing, nothing at all, *Inf.* fiddle-faddle; nothing to write home about, mere nothing, nothing to boast about.

2. insignificancy, tinker's dam, flash in the pan, nine days' wonder; trumpery, bagatelle, froth, feather, farthing; drop in the bucket.

troglodyte, *n.* **1.** cave man, ape-man, pithecanthrope, prehistoric man, Cro-Magnon, preadamite, antediluvian; primitive, autochthon, aboriginal, *Australian Inf.* boong.

2. hermit, recluse, incluse, eremite, solitary, anchorite, anchoress; pariah, outcast, outsider.

3. yokel, country bumpkin, rustic, *Inf.* hick, *Sl.* rube; unsophisticate, innocent, ingénue, mere child, babe in the woods.

4. barbarian, Goth, savage, wild man, brute, animal; ruffian, hooligan, rowdy, bully, Neanderthal; cad, churl, boor; guttersnipe, *Brit. Sl.* mucker.

troll[1], *v.* **1.** sing, roll out, warble, croon; carol, trill, rival the birds, lilt; chant, intone.

2. fish, angle, bob, jig; dap, bib, cast.

troll[2], *n.* gnome, leprechaun, dwarf, Rumpelstiltskin; goblin, hobgoblin, hob, fairy, gremlin, imp, sprite, nix, nixie; elf, brownie, kobold, pixie; troglodyte, cave dweller; monster, ogre, fiend, demon, ghoul; giant, titan.

trollop, *n.* **1.** slattern, slut, drab, sloven, draggletail; frump, dowdy; hag.

2. prostitute, harlot, whore, hussy, wanton, loose woman, fallen woman, woman of the streets, streetwalker, trull, quean, painted woman, bar girl, *Inf.* pick-up, *All Sl.* tart, cat, hooker, floozie, working girl. See **prostitute** (*def.* **1**).

troop, *n.* **1.** band, assemblage, company, troupe, group; outfit, corps, squad, team, crew; gang, bunch, pack, circle, clique, set; club, society, association, fraternity, brotherhood, fellowship, sodality, guild, organization, federation; league, confederation, alliance, tribe.

2. multitude, crowd, throng, horde, crush, jam, mass, legion, host, mob; a great many, lots, a lot, piles, *Inf.* heaps, bags, *Inf.* gobs, barrels, tons, a bunch, passel; scores, numbers, *Inf.* scillions, *Inf.* zillions, *Inf.* jillions, *Inf.* oodles; river, torrent, flood, sea, ocean, world.

3. herd, flock, pack, drove, bevy, gaggle, swarm, school, shoal.

4. troops militia, military, soldiery, soldiers, ranks, men, officers; army, military force, cavalry, infantry.

—*v.* **5.** flock together, assemble, convene, muster, mass, gather, collect; unite, confederate, ally, league together, band together, team up, join forces *or* hands, join together, link up; affiliate, associate, hobnob, fraternize; commingle, mingle, get together, consolidate.

6. throng, crowd, swarm; stream, surge, swell; jam, squeeze, bunch, pack, bundle.

7. walk, hike, march, slog; parade, step smartly.

trooper, *n.* **1.** cavalry man, horseman, horse soldier, Cossack, hussar, spahi, uhlan; mounted policeman, Royal Canadian Mounted Police, *Inf.* Mountie; state trooper, state policeman, *Inf.* state cop, *Sl.* Smokey Bear.

2. like a trooper enthusiastically, earnestly, wholeheartedly, zealously, *Inf.* like mad *or* like crazy; energetically, vigorously, with a vengeance, *Inf.* hammer and tongs, with might and main, *Inf.* to beat the band, *Sl.* up a storm.

trophy, *n.* **1.** spoils, booty, loot, plunder, pillage, take, *Inf.* haul.

2. prize, award, honor, medal, ribbon, badge; citation, encomium, kudos; laurels, bays, palm, wreath.

3. memento, reminder, remembrance, remembrancer, souvenir, keepsake, memorial; record, relic, vestige, token.

tropical, *adj.* **1.** warm, hot and humid, muggy, sticky, sultry, steaming, close, damp, soppy, boiling, sweltering; oppressive, heavy; sunny, blazing, broiling, baking, roasting, burning, torrid.

2. metaphorical, allegorical, anagogical, parabolic; similar, comparable.

trouble, *v.* **1.** worry, alarm, upset, agitate, shake up, distress, concern; perturb, disturb, disquiet, discompose, discountenance, fluster, flutter, flurry, distract, unsettle, put out; confuse, bewilder, baffle, perplex, confound.

2. inconvenience, burden, cumber; impose upon, encroach upon, discommode, incommode, put [s.o.] to the trouble, *Inf.* make [s.o.] go out of his way; take the trouble, go to the trouble.

3. afflict, oppress, weigh heavily upon; grieve, aggrieve, sorrow, embitter; anguish, break [s.o.'s] heart, make [s.o.'s] heart bleed, *Inf.* cut up; weaken, debilitate, enervate, enfeeble; disable, invalid, incapacitate, cripple.

4. bother, pester, hector, harass, bedevil, *Sl.* bug, *Sl.* hassle, *Sl.* drive [s.o.] nuts *or* crazy *or* bananas, *Sl.* drive [s.o.] up a wall; plague, fret, torment; hound, dog, nag, pick on, be on [s.o.'s] back, *Inf.* give [s.o.] a hard time, *Sl.* ride; irritate, annoy, vex, irk, provoke, nettle, get on [s.o.'s] nerves, *Inf.* aggravate, *Inf.* get under [s.o.'s] skin, *Inf.* get in [s.o.'s] hair; exasperate, ruffle, try [s.o.'s] patience, *Inf.* grate on [s.o.'s] nerves.

—n. **5.** annoyance, harassment, vexation, irritation, *Inf.* aggravation; bother, inconvenience, imposition, obtrusion, intrusion.

6. adversity, misfortune; pain, distress, suffering; grief, woe, sorrow, heartache, anguish; hard times, heavy weather; bad luck, hard luck, *Inf.* tough *or* rotten luck, *Brit.* hard lines; bad *or* ill fortune; hard time, *Inf.* a bad scene, *Inf.* mess, *Inf.* fix, *Inf.* jam, *Inf.* hot water; devil to pay.

7. disorder, confusion, chaos, bedlam, pandemonium; turmoil, moil, turbulence; civil disorder *or* strife, anarchy, mob-law, street-fighting, fighting in the streets; revolt, rebellion, insurrection, insurgency, uprising, outbreak.

8. ill health, poor health, unhealthiness, sickliness, feebleness, frailty; debility, enervation, infirmity, unsoundness.

9. worry, concern, *Scot.* fash, alarm, distress; anxiety, trepidation, uneasiness, fear and trembling; agitation, disquiet, unrest, disturbance, excitement, distraction.

10. trial, tribulation, ordeal; affliction, visitation, curse, blight; shock, shocker, blow, jolt, bolt from the blue, *Psychiatry.* trauma; reverse, reversal, check, setback, comedown, bringdown, bitter pill; load, burden, weight, heavy load *or* burden, cross, cross to bear; inconvenience, difficulty, disadvantage, handicap.

11. nuisance, pest, *Inf.* headache, *Inf.* pain, *Sl.* pain in the neck *or* rear, *Sl.* hassle; gadfly, buttonholer, *Sl.* nudnik; nag, pesterer, harasser, heckler, badgerer.

12. in trouble (*all out of wedlock*) pregnant, with child, childing, in a delicate condition, *Inf.* expecting, *Inf.* in the family way, *U.S. Sl.* knocked-up.

troublemaker, *n.* stormy petrel, mischief-maker, malcontent, *Fr. frondeur*; gadfly, buttonholer, consumer advocate, Nader raider; instigator, inciter, agitator, provoker, agitprop, fomenter; incendiary, firebrand; rabble-rouser, demagogue; rioter, hooligan, brawler, tough, affrayer, street-fighting man, street fighter, rowdy; meddler, intermeddler, busybody, interloper, marplot, *Sl.* buttinsky; gossip, gossipmonger, scandalmonger.

troubleshooter, *n.* **1.** diplomat, negotiator, mediator, arbitrator, make-peace, peacemaker.

2. repairman, serviceman, trouble man, mender, fixer, *Inf.* Mr. Fixit.

troublesome, *adj.* **1.** vexatious, bothersome, pestering, *Inf.* pesky, *Inf.* pestiferous, hectoring, harassing; hounding, dogging, nagging, tormenting, persecuting; troubling, thorny, fretful, worrisome, worrying, *Archaic. except Dial.* plaguey; confusing, confounding, disconcerting, bewildering, perplexing; puzzling, enigmatic, baffling.

2. laborious, arduous, strenuous, uphill, hard, difficult; burdensome, onerous, oppressive.

trough, *n.* **1.** manger, feedbox, box.

2. channel, flume, conduit, duct, *Civ. Eng.* aqueduct, canal; chute, shoot, gutter, eaves-trough, open tube; drain, sewer, cloaca, culvert; trench, ditch, moat, fosse, *Brit.* sough; furrow, groove, race, rut, chase; depression, hollow, hole, cut, track.

trounce, *v.* **1.** beat, thrash, flog, *Inf.* lambaste, *Archaic.* belabor, pound, batter, pummel, hit soundly, *Inf.* whale; *Inf.* give it to, *Sl.* let [s.o.] have it, *Sl.* sock it to, *Sl.* give [s.o.] the business, *Sl.* work [s.o.] over, *Sl.* give [s.o.] the works.

2. punish, chastise, discipline, castigate.

3. defeat, vanquish, worst, beat *or* beat out, *Inf.* trim; *Inf.* whip, drub, *Inf.* whump, *Inf.* wallop, *Sl.* clobber, beat by a mile *or* country mile, win by a landslide, *U.S. Sl.* skunk; beat up, *Inf.* lick, *Sl.* shellac, *Sl.* cream, *Sl.* kill; flatten, prostrate, knock out, k.o.; pulverize, maul, *Sl.* beat to a pulp, *Sl.* beat into the ground, *Sl.* beat the tar out of, *Sl.* make mincemeat of, *Inf.* punch out, *Inf.* punch [s.o.'s] face in, *Sl.* knock [s.o.'s] block off, *Sl.* beat [s.o.'s] brains out.

trousers, *n.* pants, drawers, slacks, ducks, *Brit. Inf.* strides, *Brit. Sl.* bags; breeches, knee breeches, *Inf.* britches, knickers, knickerbockers, plus fours, (*among Scottish Highlanders*) trews, *Scot. and North Eng.* breeks; pantalets, pantaloons, bloomers; overalls, chaps, chaparajos; palazzo pants, (*in the Orient*) pajamas, harem pants; pegtops, *Sl.* drainpipes, straightlegs; bell-bottoms, hip-huggers, flares; jeans, bluejeans, dungarees, denims, *Trademark.* Levi's; chinos, khakis, fatigues, whites, tweeds, flannels, corduroys, *Inf.* cords, *Sl.* whistle britches; clam diggers, pedal pushers; shorts, bermuda shorts, bermudas, walking shorts, (*in Bavaria*) lederhosen, *Inf.* cut-offs.

truant, *n.* **1.** absentee, dodger, defaulter, neglector;

avoider, evader, draft dodger, deserter, absconder; shirker, shirk, malingerer, *Brit.* skulker, *Brit. Sl.* scrimshanker, *Inf.* soldier, *Inf.* goldbricker, *Brit. Sl.* skiver, clock watcher, *Sl.* goof-off, *Inf.* boondoggler; slacker, procrastinator, do-nothing, layabout, loafer, idler, fainéant, *Inf.* lazybones, sluggard.

—*adj.* **2.** absent without permission, skipping school, skipping, cutting, *Inf.* playing hooky, AWOL, absent without leave.

3. neglectful, negligent, remiss, derelict, slack, lax, careless; lazy, idle, indolent, slothful, fainéant, do-nothing, otiose, shiftless.

truce, *n.* **1.** cease-fire, armistice, suspension of hostilities.

2. treaty, agreement, compact, pact, *Rare.* paction.

3. respite, reprieve, relief, freedom; rest, break, breather, lull, *Inf.* letup, remission.

truck[1], *n.* **1.** pickup *or* pickup truck, panel truck, van, moving van, *Trademark.* U-Haul; camion, trailer truck, *C.B. Radio.* eighteen-wheeler, *Inf.* rig, semitrailer, *Inf.* semi.

2. hand truck, wheelbarrow, barrow, handbarrow.

—*v.* **3.** (*all by truck*) transport, convey, transfer, carry, haul, deliver, ship, freight.

truck[2], *n.* **1.** odds and ends, leftovers, remnants; trinkets, bagatelles, trifles.

2. *Informal.* trash, rubbish, *Sl.* tripe, trumpery, nonsense; bunkum, *Sl.* bunk, tommyrot, *Inf.* rot, *Sl.* garbage, *Sl.* crap, *Sl.* crook, *Sl.* bull.

3. barter, trade, business, traffic, commerce, buying and selling; transaction, exchange, bargaining, negotiation, dealing.

—*v.* **4.** exchange, trade, barter, swap, swop; bargain, deal, traffic, dicker, haggle, *Scot.* argle-bargle, higgle, chaffer, negotiate.

truckle, *v.* **1.** kowtow, bow, bow before, bow to, bow and scrape, bend, bend before, stoop, crouch; kneel, kneel before, fall on one's knees before, prostrate oneself before; grovel, crawl, creep, creep before, slither; cringe, cower, squirm; whine, whimper, snivel; (*all in an obsequious or slavish manner*) submit to, yield to, succumb to, defer to, give up, give in, draw in one's horns, *Inf.* throw in the towel, *Inf.* knuckle under, comply, take, accept, acquiesce, *Inf.* swallow it, *Inf.* take it lying down.

2. toady, toady to, fawn, fawn upon, *Sl.* fall all over, wheedle, slaver, puff, puff up, inflate, blow up, *Sl.* suck up to, *Sl.* shine up to, *Sl.* play up to, *Inf.* apple-polish, *Sl.* butter-up, *Sl.* brown-nose, *Sl.* earn brownie points; lickspittle, lick [s.o.'s] shoes, lick *or* kiss [s.o.'s] feet, *Inf.* be a yes man to, agree to anything, *Sl.* bootlick, court, pay court to, curry favor, dance attendance upon.

truculent, *adj.* **1.** fierce, cruel, ferocious, fell, ruthless; rancorous, stern, grim, dire; brutal, savage, feral, ferine; vicious, barbarous, inhuman, subhuman; murderous, slaughterous, bloodthirsty, sadistic, Hunnish, Tartarean, Vandalic, Gothic.

2. harsh, scathing, scorching, burning, stinging; vitriolic, slashing, biting, bitter, acrimonious; strident, severe, rough, mordant, trenchant, cutting.

3. hostile, aggressive, antagonistic; belligerent, bellicose, warlike, pugnacious; militant, combative, *Sl.* scrappy, contentious; militaristic, warmongering, jingoistic.

trudge, *v.* **1.** walk, tramp, march, plod, *Inf.* plug; drag, lumber, shuffle, *Inf.* galumph, *Inf.* stodge, traipse; chug, stump, *Sl.* schlepp, *Inf.* mosey, poke along; crawl along, inch along, creep, worm; limp, hobble; waddle, stagger, drag one's feet; flag, lag, trail behind, bring up the rear.

—*n.* **2.** tramp, march, mush, *Sl.* schlepp; crawl, walk, snail's pace, turtle's pace, *Jocular.* turtles' stampede.

true, *adj.* **1.** factual, actual, real, *Obs.* veritable, *Brit. Dial.* gradely, *Both Archaic.* sooth, soothfast; unimaginary, unfictitious, authentic, genuine, valid, sound, just, confirmed; sincere, earnest, truthful, veracious; literal, true to life, realistic, credible, believable, natural; honest, faithful, close, strict; pure, unadulterated, unexaggerated, unvarnished, unembellished.

2. loyal, faithful, allegiant, *Scot.* leal, true-hearted; steadfast, fast, steady, steady-going, unchanging, constant, incorruptible; staunch, true-blue, yeomanly, unwavering, unswerving, firm, stable, solid; supportive, devoted, pledged, dedicated, patriotic; dutiful, obedient.

3. reliable, trusted, dependable, good, trustworthy, trusty, tried and true; true to one's word, as good as one's word; unbought, unbribed, uncorrupted.

4. exact, precise, accurate, correct, unerring, *Inf.* on the mark, on target, on the money, *Inf.* right on, *Sl.* spot on; on the button, on the dot, *Inf.* on the nose, *Sl.* on the beam.

5. proper, right, straight, such as it should be.

6. rightful, just, lawful, legitimate, legal, licit, official, bona fide.

7. certain, sure, positive, definite; unfailing, infallible, inerrable, absolute.

—*adv.* **8.** truly, truthfully, honestly, sincerely; frankly, candidly, freely, straightforwardly, openly.

9. come true be realized, be fulfilled, be actualized, become a reality; happen, occur, come to pass.

—*v.* **10.** adjust, regulate, fine-tune, tune in; fix, straighten, align; correct, rectify, set right.

true-blue, *adj.* **1.** loyal, faithful, reliable, true. See **true** (*defs.* **2, 3**).

truehearted, *adj.* **1.** faithful, loyal, true-blue, true, trustworthy, trusty, tried and true; reliable, dependable, stalwart, staunch, unwavering, unswerving, firm, stable; generous, good-hearted, kindly, without a mean bone in one's body.

2. sincere, open, open-hearted, candid, frank, forthright, straightforward; genuine, real, true, veracious, all wool and a yard wide; natural, unaffected, uncontrived, unpretentious, without airs; honest, honest as the day is long, aboveboard, up front, out front, *Sl.* on the level, *Sl.* on the up and up; straight, square, square-shooting, square-dealing, straight-shooting, fair and square; undeceiving, unfeigning, undissembling, like an open book.

truelove, *n.* **1.** sweetheart, sweet, sweetie, love, beloved, love of one's life; darling, dear, dear one, dearest, honey, *Inf.* honeybun, *Inf.* sugar, *Inf.* sugar pie; heartthrob, heart's desire, one and only; lover, paramour, *Fr. intime*, *Inf.* boyfriend, girl friend; beau, swain, inamorato, Romeo, fiancé; best girl, steady girl, fiancée, inamorata; betrothed, intended; turtledove, angel, *Sl.* sweet patootie, *Sl.* tootsy-wootsy, *Fr. petit chou.*

2. friend, friend to all, *Inf.* good guy, *Inf.* nice guy, *Inf.* brick, prince of a fellow, gem.

truism, *n.* axiom, truth, verity, fact; commonplace, cliché, platitude, bromide; aphorism, apothegm, gnome, maxim.

trull, *n.* strumpet, harlot, whore, prostitute; hussy, slut, slattern; demirep, demimondaine, fallen woman, loose woman, wanton. See **prostitute** (*def.* **1**).

truly, *adv.* **1.** really, in reality, actually, in actuality, in fact, de facto, in essence, essentially, intrinsically, in truth, truthfully.

2. genuinely, authentically, verifiably; certainly,

surely, assuredly, decidedly; positively, absolutely, categorically, unquestionably, undoubtedly, unequivocally; beyond question, beyond a doubt, beyond the shadow of a doubt.

3. exactly, precisely, strictly, literally; accurately, correctly, rightly; justly, properly, duly; legitimately, lawfully, by right, rightfully, validly.

4. sincerely, earnestly, honestly, candidly, frankly, openly.

5. indeed, verily, of course, no doubt, aye, yea, amen, so be it.

trump, *v.* **1.** excel, surpass, outstrip, outdo, outperform, outwit, outfox; beat, defeat, checkmate, vanquish, drub, *Inf.* wallop; top, best, worst, overpower, overcome; get the better of, better, get the upper hand, prevail, nose out, win.

2. trump up fabricate, invent, make out of whole cloth, concoct, cook up; hatch, create, conceive; frame, devise, scheme, make up, fake, contrive.

trumpery, *n.* **1.** rubbish, trash, riffraff, *Brit. Dial.* raff, litter, chaff; refuse, *Dial.* culch, garbage, waste, debris, detritus, rubble, wreckage; junk, worthless stuff, *Sl.* dreck; bits and pieces, odds and ends, fag ends, remnants; castoffs, rags, tatters, castaways, rejects, discards.

2. nonsense, falderal, gibberish, Jabberwocky; babble, babbling, babblement, *Fr. bavardage*; twaddle, twaddling, *Both Brit.* twattle, twattling; blather, blathering, drivel, driveling, drool, drooling; jargon, *Sl.* jive; gobbledegook, foolish humbug, foam, froth, bunkum, *Sl.* bunk, *U.S. Sl.* blah; balderdash, hogwash, swill, *Sl.* horsefeathers; stuff, stuff and nonsense, fudge, foolishness.

—adj. **3.** trifling, trivial, insignificant, immaterial, unimportant, twopenny, *Sl.* two-bit, *Sl.* two-by-four; small, puny, little, slight, of no moment.

4. rubbishy, trashy, *Sl.* schlock, poor, base, mean, commonplace; shoddy, shabby, beggarly, scrubby, wretched; worry, second-rate, mediocre, inferior; brummagem, showy, pretentious, ostentatious; flashy, gaudy, garish, meretricious, tawdry; vulgar, cheap, obscene.

trumpet, *n.* **1.** wind instrument, horn, bugle, clarion.

2. wind musician, trumpeter, horn player, bugler.

3. honk, blare, blast, blat. clarion.

—v. **4.** honk, blare, blast, blat, blow, bray, bay, bellow.

5. proclaim, announce, herald, promulgate, bruit, noise abroad; cry out, thunder, shout from the housetops.

truncate, *v.* **1.** shorten, cut short, cut down, retrench, crop, lop, (*both of trees or shrubbery*) poll, pollard; abbreviate, abridge, condense; abstract, summarize, digest, epitomize.

—adj. **2.** truncated, shortened, cut short, cut down, retrenched, reduced, cropped, lopped, polled; abbreviated, abridged, condensed; abstracted, summarized, digested, epitomized.

trundle, *v.* **1.** roll, wheel, push.

—n. **2.** small wheel, roller, caster.

trunk, *n.* **1.** tree trunk, stem, stalk, *Bot.* bole.

2. chest, hope chest, ice chest, coffer, casket, box, cardboard box, storage box, crate, carton; luggage, baggage, suitcase; footlocker, locker, strongbox, safe, repository; container, receptacle, hamper, basket.

3. torso, body; framework, chassis.

4. trunks shorts, gym shorts, athletic shorts, swimming trunks; underwear, *Sl.* skivvies, boxer shorts, jockey shorts.

truss, *v.* tie *or* tie up, bind *or* bind up, hogtie, wrap *or* wrap up, ligate, bandage *or* bandage up; fasten, attach, join, connect, link, yoke, unite, wed, couple, hook together, splice; secure, moor, fix firmly, make fast; hitch, tether, stake, picket, rope, strap, lash, chain.

trust, *n.* **1.** confidence, faith, certitude, certainty, belief, conviction, assurance; reliance, dependence; security, sureness, assuredness, surety, positiveness.

2. hope, hopefulness, optimism, expectation, anticipation.

3. credit, credibility, trustworthiness, faithfulness, reliability, dependability, solvency.

4. charge, custody, keeping, care, guardianship, ward, wardship, protection, *Law.* trusteeship; keep, safekeeping; tutelage, guidance, chaperonage, supervision, superintendence, surveillance, watchful eye, direction, control.

5. responsibility, commitment, engagement, obligation, devoir, duty; mission, assignment, charge, office, commission.

—v. **6.** *Usu.* **trust in** *or* **to** rely on *or* upon, depend on, count on *or* upon, have confidence in, have faith in; set store by, *Inf.* put *or* take stock in, swear by, believe in; believe one's eyes, believe one's ears; put *or* place confidence in, put one's trust in, pin one's faith on *or* upon, put one's hope in.

7. have confidence, be optimistic, be hopeful, hope, expect, anticipate, look forward to, plan on.

8. believe, take on faith, take [s.o.'s] word for [s.t.], accept, *Sl.* buy, *Inf.* swallow.

9. entrust, consign, turn over, make over, sign over; commit, put into the hands of, commend, give over; delegate, invest, assign, depute, empower.

trustee, *n.* fiduciary, depositary, agent, administrator, executor, executrix; guardian, keeper, caretaker, custodian; member of the board, director, officer.

trusting, *adj.* believing, undoubting, trustful, unsuspecting, unquestioning; confiding, confident, sure, certain, convinced, positive, having no doubts, without a doubt in one's mind; naïve, simple, gullible, credulous; incautious, careless.

trustworthiness, *n.* **1.** trustiness, reliability, reliableness, dependability, dependableness, responsibility, responsibleness; credibility, credibleness, believability, believableness; trueness, loyalty, loyalness, faithfulness, true-heartedness; allegiance, patriotism, devotion, dedication.

2. steadfastness, steadiness, unchangingness, constancy, abidingness, lastingness, enduringness, permanence; staunchness, unswervingness, firmness, resoluteness; stability, stableness, solidity, solidness, strength, incorruptibility, incorruptibleness.

3. honesty, honestness, frankness, openness, candor, straightforwardness, bluntness; truthfulness, veracity, veraciousness, sincerity, sincereness, earnestness; uprightness, integrity, probity, righteousness, honorableness, upstandingness; right-mindedness, uncorruptedness, goodness, virtuousness, virtue; ethicalness, ethicality, morality, rightness, conscionableness.

trustworthy, *adj.* **1.** reliable, dependable, responsible, *Scot. and North Eng.* sicker; trusted, trusty, tried and true, *Inf.* all right, *Inf.* O.K.; credible, believable, true to one's word, as good as one's word; true, loyal, faithful, allegiant, *Scot.* leal, true-hearted; steadfast, fast, steady, steady-going; unchanging, constant, abiding, lasting, enduring, permanent; staunch, true-blue, yeomanly, unwavering, unswerving; firm, resolute, stable, solid, strong, incorruptible; supportive, devoted, pledged, patriotic, dedicated; dutiful, obedient.

2. honest, frank, free, open, aboveboard; candid, straightforward, straight, *Inf.* square, blunt, plainspoken; truthful, veracious, sincere, earnest; upright, righteous, honorable, upstanding; principled, right-minded, uncorrupt, good, virtuous; unbought, unbribed, ethical, moral, conscionable.

truth, *n.* **1.** reality, actuality, *Archaic.* sooth; gospel, gospel truth, naked truth, unvarnished truth, *Sl.* straight goods; facts, *Inf.* low-down, *Inf.* scoop, story; inside information, intelligence.

2. verity, *Archaic.* troth, factuality, factualness; actualness, realness, authenticity, genuineness; validity, validness, soundness.

3. fact, certainty, certitude; principle, rule, law, fundamental, canon; *Math.* proposition, theorem.

4. faithfulness, honesty, closeness, strictness.

5. honesty, uprightness, integrity, righteousness, honorableness, upstandingness; truthfulness, sincerity, sincereness, veracity, veraciousness; openness, *Inf.* straightforwardness, candor, frankness.

6. truism, platitude, self-evident truth, axiom; cliché, banality, trite saying; proverb, maxim, adage, saw, aphorism, gnome, apothegm; byword, dictum, precept, motto, mot, epigram.

7. accuracy, trueness, precision, exactness, veracity.

8. in truth in reality, in fact, actually, really, truthfully, as a matter of fact.

truthful, *adj.* **1.** honest, veracious, sincere, earnest; upright, righteous, honorable, upstanding; ethical, proper, moral, conscionable; principled, high-minded, noble, right-minded, uncorrupt; ingenuous, artless, guileless, unsophisticated; frank, straight, *Inf.* square, free, open, aboveboard; candid, straightforward, up front, blunt, plain-spoken.

2. factual, literal, true-to-life, realistic, credible, believable, natural; accurate, exact, precise, faithful, close, strict; pure, unadulterated, unexaggerated, unvarnished, unembellished.

3. actual, real, *Obs.* veritable, *Brit. Dial.* gradely, *Both Archaic.* sooth, soothfast; authentic, genuine, valid, sound, just, confirmed; unimaginary, unfictitious, not false.

try, *v.* **1.** attempt, essay, endeavor, undertake, try one's hand at, venture, seek, aim; strive, make an effort, struggle, push, break one's neck, bend over backward, knock oneself out, *Inf.* do one's damnedest; *All Inf.* have a go at, take a crack *or* shot at, give [s.t.] the old college try, give [s.t.] a go.

2. test, experiment with, assay, prove; examine, look over, inspect, scrutinize, analyze, assess, evaluate; judge, consider, think about; sample, taste, feel, partake of, experience.

3. tax, drain, sap, strain, weary, tire; trouble, bother, distress; vex, irk, annoy, bug, pester, *Sl.* drive up the wall; torment, anguish, rack, pain.

—n. **4.** attempt, effort, endeavor, struggle, essay, crack, shot, stab, fling, turn, go; trial, testing, chance, opportunity.

trying, *adj.* **1.** annoying, irksome, bothersome, troublesome, troubling, fretful, worrisome; irritating, aggravating, disquieting, exacerbating; disturbing, perturbing, vexing; nasty, unpleasant, disagreeable; maddening, infuriating, frustrating.

2. difficult, hard, arduous, tough, rough, tough-sledding, uphill; wearying, tiring, fatiguing, exhausting, enervating; racking, devastating, demoralizing, dispiriting.

tryst, *n.* rendezvous, assignation, date; engagement, appointment, meeting, secret meeting, arrangement.

tub, *n.* **1.** bathtub, bath, *Fr. bain*, balneary; (*for babies*) *Trademark.* Bathinette.

2. bucket, pail, receptacle, vessel, firkin; basin, bowl; barrel, hogshead, puncheon, tun, butt, cask, rundlet, keg, vat.

tube, *n.* **1.** cylinder, pipette, pipe, hose, line, connector, worm, spout; outlet, inlet, passage, channel; duct, main, conduit, shaft, tunnel, canal, trough, shoot.

2. windpipe, *Anat., Zool.* trachea, *Anat.* bronchus, *Anat.* bronchiole.

3. *Informal.* subway, underground, train, metro.

tuck, *v.* **1.** insert, put into, stick *or* thrust *or* shove *or* push in, *Inf.* stuff, *Inf.* stuff in, *Inf.* cram *or* pack in; implant, embed, impact; put away, hide, stow, tuck away.

2. fold, fold up, gather, double, *Sl.* scrunch, *Sl.* scrunch up; fold over *or* down, dog-ear, infold; crinkle, ruck, ruffle, pucker, crease; braid, plait, weave; pleat, take in; finish, bind, bind off, hem, *Surg.* plicate.

3. pull in *or* down, fold under, straighten, neaten, put right; tighten, smooth, make flat *or* neat *or* tight.

4. cover, cover snugly, blanket, wrap, incase, envelop, enwrap, muffle, swaddle, swathe, sheathe, roll up in, shroud.

—n. **5.** fold, crease, pucker, pleat, gather, pinch; pucker, ruffle, crinkle, crumple, cockle; plait, lap, overlap, lappet, flap, doubling, edging, binding; flexure, plication *or* plicature.

tuft, *n.* **1.** bunch, cluster, clump, thatch, batch, wisp; brush, pompon, plume, tassel, feather, *Ornith.* plumule; knot, topknot, knob, crest, scalp lock, elf lock, pompadour, shock, forelock, cowlick, mop.

2. thicket, copse, grove, *Chiefly Brit.* coppice, *Brit.* spinney, small wood, bosket, *Archaic.* bosk, brake, canebrake; brushwood, bush, scrub, scrub growth, *U.S.* chaparral, underbrush, undergrowth, shrubbery, hedges, bushes; truss, *Bot.* raceme, *Bot.* panicle; bouquet, posy; fagot, bundle; fascicle.

tug, *v.* **1.** pull, pull at, draw *or* draw up, hitch *or* hitch up, hike *or* hike up; jerk, wrench, wring, wrest, *Inf.* yank; twitch, pluck, pick at, grab *or* snatch at, tweak, pinch, joggle.

2. drag, haul, draft, heave, *Inf.* lug; toil, strain, strive, exert oneself, *Inf.* sweat, *Inf.* sweat and strain, give one's all, exert oneself, labor, struggle, wrestle, do one's utmost, *Inf.* do one's darndest; work with a will, try, endeavor, slave, grind, drudge, grub, plod, *Inf.* plug away.

3. tow, drag *or* draw along, take in tow, pull after, trawl, troll, trail, draggle, train.

—n. **4.** pull, haul, strain, effort, stress, toil, labor, work; contest, exercise; jerk, twitch, wrench, *Inf.* yank.

tuition, *n.* **1.** tutorage, cost per pupil, cost per credit hour, charge, fee, price, cost, *Inf.* damage *or* damages, *Inf.* tab; expense, outlay, disbursement; exaction.

2. teaching, instruction, tutelage; education, edification, elucidation; training, qualification, schooling; discipline, guidance, direction, preparation, experience, exposure; practice, drill, tutorship, *Inf.* spoon-feeding.

tumble, *v.* **1.** fall down, fall end over end, pitch, pitch forward, precipitate oneself, fall headlong, go down, *Inf.* take a spill, *Inf.* take a flyer *or* a header *or* a pratfall; slip, stagger, totter, falter, lose one's footing, lose one's equilibrium, *Inf.* flop, *Inf.* flop down, *Sl.* take a flop; come a cropper, fall on one's face, *Sl.* fall on one's keester; roll end over end, go head over heels, go tail over teakettle, somersault, flip, backflip, do a flip, flip over.

2. pitch, pitch about, toss, heave, wallow, founder, *Inf.* wallop; flounder, reel, lurch, capsize, turn turtle, pitch and plunge, thrash about, careen, roll, rock.

3. *Usu.* **tumble over** stumble, trip, bumble, blunder, fall over, fumble, sprawl, *Inf.* spread-eagle.

4. fail, decline, drop, plunge, plummet, dive, crash, slide, slump, skid, go downhill, drop off, tend downward; collapse, topple, go to the wall, *Inf.* wash out, *Inf.* bite the dust.

5. overthrow, overturn, upend, topple, bring low *or* down, pull *or* haul down.

6. *Informal. Usu.* **tumble to** understand, become aware, comprehend, grasp the situation, see the light, *Inf.* catch on, *Inf.* get on to, *Inf.* get wise to.

7. disorder, disarray, derange, disarrange, mess up, dishevel, ruffle, tousle, tangle, entangle; jumble, scramble, rifle through, disturb, rumple, snarl up; scatter, spill, upset, toss about.

—n. **8.** fall, stumble, slip, trip, skid, sprawl; somersault, flip, *Inf.* cropper, *Inf.* header, *Inf.* spill, *Inf.* pratfall, *Sl.* nosedive, *Sl.* tailspin, *Sl.* flop, *Sl.* floperoo.

9. collapse, crash, comedown, downfall, dive, plunge, drop; failure, defeat.

10. disorder, disarray, mess, heap, pile, jumble, scramble, hodgepodge, welter, mishmash, clutter, unholy mess; confusion, chaos.

tumble-down, *adj.* dilapidated, ramshackle, ruined, in ruins, broken-down, gone to wrack and ruin; in disrepair, rundown, *Sl.* sleazy; fallen to pieces, crumbled, crumbling, ready to fall; decrepit, tottering, unstable, shaky; untrustworthy, insecure, unsafe.

tumbler, *n.* **1.** acrobat, gymnast, somersaulter, high vaulter; trampoliner, trampolinist; circus performer *or* artist; contortionist, posture-master; athlete.

2. cup, drinking cup, drinking vessel, glass, beaker, dipper; shot glass, jigger.

tumefaction, *n.* swelling, bloating, puffing, distention; enlargement, growth, dilatation, dilation, turgescency.

tumefy, *v.* swell, distend, bloat, protuberate, puff *or* blow up, become larger, fill out, grow, enlarge; inflate, increase, dilate.

tumid, *adj.* **1.** swollen, enlarged, bloated, puffed up *or* out, puffy, *Pathol.* dropsical, *Pathol.* edematous, *Pathol.* edematose, *Bot., Entomol.* incrassate; tumescent, turgid, inflated, *Obs.* sufflated, distended, expanded, dilated, *Pathol., Bot.* hypertrophied; full, filled, stuffed, overfilled, overstuffed.

2. bombastic, pompous, orotund, fustian, pretentious, overinflated, overblown, flatulent, plethoric; grandiose, magniloquent, grandiloquent, Johnsonian, Ossianic, sonorous, sesquipedalian; high-sounding, high-flown, lofty, *Inf.* highfalutin; rhetorical, oratorical, declamatory, ranting, extravagant; ostentatious, flamboyant, ornate, flowery, florid.

3. bulging, protuberant, gibbous, bulbous, bilging, bulging *or* bilging out; projecting, protruding, protrusive, conspicuous, prominent, protrusile; excrescent, *Bot.* excurrent; extrusive, jutting; overlapping, overhanging; convex, excurved, excurvate.

tumor, *n.* swelling, protuberance, tumefaction, intumescence, excrescence, *Pathol.* tubercle, *Pathol.* polyp; neoplasm, growth; malignancy, cancer, *Pathol.* melanoma, *Pathol.* sarcoma.

tumult, *n.* **1.** uproar, disorder, rabblement, turmoil, commotion, turbulence, ferment; hubbub, furor, fury, rampage, confusion, ado, *Inf.* to-do; din, racket, outcry, clamor, clangor, blare, noise, shouting; confusion, chaos, pandemonium, babel, bedlam.

2. riot, upheaval, brawl, free-for-all, brouhaha, donnybrook, *Inf.* ruckus, rumpus, affray; row, broil, fray, fight, melee; breach of peace, disturbing the peace, rending the air; hue and cry, protest, strike; uprising, insurrection, revolt, rebellion, mutiny.

3. agitation, perturbation, disquiet, disturbance; excitement, frenzy, hysteria, rage; discomposure, restlessness, jitters, *Sl.* jimjams, restiveness.

tumultuous, *adj.* **1.** uproarious, tempestuous, stormy, turbulent; explosive, volcanic, unpredictable, uncertain; wild, untamed, raging, fierce, savage, unrestrained, no-holds-barred.

2. noisy, clamorous, clangorous, loud, stentorian, ear-shattering, ear-splitting, blaring; clattering, shrieking, screaming, hollering, yelling; brawling, wrangling, fighting; disorderly, ungovernable, uncontrollable, unruly; boisterous, rowdy, roistering.

3. disturbed, distraught, agitated, uneasy, upset, bothered, troubled; beside oneself, *Inf.* in a tizzy *or* dither, in a turmoil; anxious, *Inf.* in a sweat, impatient, frantic, restless, restive; excited, frenzied, hysterical, rabid, manic, maniacal; furious, mad as a wet hen; fretful, roiled, ruffled, exasperated.

tune, *n.* **1.** melody, air, aria, song, ditty, strain, lay; chant, plainsong, hymn, anthem, dirge, chanson, lied, ballad, *Inf.* pop tune, folk song, carol, lullaby.

2. unison, harmony, concert, agreement, accord, consonance, correspondence, concord, accordance, conformity, congruity; harmoniousness, euphony, symphony, tunefulness, melodiousness.

3. **change one's tune** change one's mind, reverse one's views, have a change of heart, take a different tack; back-pedal, backtrack, about-face, *Inf.* flip-flop.

—v. **4.** *Often* **tune up** adjust, *Archaic.* attune, synchronize, coordinate, align, regulate, set, put in proper condition; warm up, *Music.* noodle, prepare, ready, prime.

5. harmonize, bring into harmony, attune, bring into accord *or* agreement.

6. **tune in** *Slang.* listen, pay attention.

7. **tune out** *Slang. Sl.* space out, *Inf.* turn *or* shut *or* switch off, pay no mind *or* attention.

tuneful, *adj.* melodious, melodic, musical, lyrical, lyric, canorous; harmonious, euphonic, euphonious, symphonious, *Music.* symphonic; sweet-sounding, mellifluous, mellifluent, dulcet, pleasant, agreeable, light, tripping; silvery, silver-toned, clear as a bell, ringing, resonant; rhythmical, rhythmic, flowing, smooth, velvety, golden, mellow, rich.

tunnel, *n.* **1.** underground, underground passageway, subterranean passage, *Mil.* mine; underpass, *Chiefly Brit.* subway, *C.B. Radio.* hole in the wall.

2. (*all of mines*) gallery, corridor, *Mining.* drift, *Mining.* crosscut.

3. (*both of animals*) burrow, hole.

—v. **4.** (*all of a tunnel*) construct, build, make, cut; excavate, dig, burrow, mine.

turban, *n.* headdress, head covering, headgear, head scarf, scarf, bandanna, (*in India*) pugree, tarboosh; toque, cloche.

turbid, *adj.* **1.** unclear, clouded, cloudy, opaque, nontransparent, murky, muddy, muddied; dirty, filthy, unclean, impure, polluted, befouled, foul, feculent.

2. thick, dense, soupy, *Inf.* thick as pea soup, heavy, concentrated, condensed.

3. confused, disjointed, disconnected, incoherent, unclear, indistinct, fuzzy, hazy, foggy, blurry, blurred; muddled, mixed-up, jumbled, disorganized, unorderly, disorderly, deranged; disturbed, troubled, agitated, unsettled.

turbulence, *n.* **1.** agitation, perturbation, excitement. See **tumult** (*def.* 3).

2. violence, storminess, tempestuousness, uproar, squall; commotion, confusion, chaos, pandemonium, bedlam, rampage, racket; fury, frenzy, rage; cataclysm, convulsion, eruption, outburst, explosion; noise, hubbub, sound and fury; fracas, brawling, wrangling.

3. disorder, anarchy, disarray, disruption, discord,

disharmony; untidiness, roughness, choppiness; fuss, bustle, stir, *Inf.* to-do, ado; mess, messiness, disorganization, mix-up, imbroglio; explosiveness, perilousness.

turbulent, *adj.* **1.** disturbed, agitated, upset. See **tumultuous** (*def.* **3**).

2. disordered, confused, mixed-up, untidy, tumultuous; choppy, irregular, shifting, mercurial, undependable; upside-down, *Sl.* out of whack, *Inf.* out of kilter, *Sl.* screwed-up; clamorous, clangorous, noisy, rowdy; explosive, volcanic, dangerous, perilous, uncertain, unpredictable.

3. violent, stormy, tempestuous, wroth, rampagious, uproarious; aggressive, combative, offensive, militant, pugnacious, bellicose, belligerent, hostile, with a chip on one's shoulder; obstreperous, boisterous, roistering; unbridled, raging, furious, rampant, fierce, wild, untamed, savage, unrestrained, no-holds-barred; disorderly, ungovernable, uncontrollable, unruly; fighting, brawling, wrangling, up in arms, angry, ready to fight; pushing, *Inf.* pushy, forward, forceful, bold, assertive.

turf, *n.* **1.** grass, sod, sward, greensward, artificial grass, *Trademark.* Astroturf; lawn, grassplot, patch of grass, green, grassy land.

2. *Slang.* territory, *Sl.* home ground, *Sports.* home field; neighborhood, block, street, backyard, *Inf.* stamping ground.

3. the turf a. race track, *Sports.* track, racecourse. **b.** horse racing, racing.

turgid, *adj.* See **tumid.** (*defs.* **1, 2**).

turgidity, *n.* **1.** swelling, bloatedness, puffiness, turgescence, tumidity, intumescence, tumefaction, ballooning; distention, expansion, extension, enlargement; dilation, dilatation, inflation, *Pathol.* aneurysm, *Pathol.* varix.

2. bombast, grandiosity, rodomontade, pomposity, orotundity, magniloquence, grandiloquence; oratory, rant, declamation, extravagance, highflown language, sesquipedality; verbosity, verboseness, wordiness, prolixity, prolixness; flatulence, inflatedness, *Archaic.* tympany; bravado, braggadocio, gasconade, boasting, *Sl.* hot air.

turmoil, *n.* **1.** tumult, tumultousness, uproar, uproariousness, pandemonium, chaos; agitation, unrest, ferment, *Archaic.* pucker, disquiet, disturbance, upheaval, storm, tempest, disorder, confusion, imbroglio; hurly-burly, hurly, brouhaha, commotion, stir, furor, hubbub, noise, racket, din, clamor; excitement, *Inf.* lather, fuss, fuss and feathers, bother, pother, trouble, *Inf.* to-do, ado; storm in a teacup, tempest in a teapot, much ado about nothing, *Inf.* foofaraw, *Sl.* hoo-ha; upset, *Inf.* dither, *Inf.* tizzy, *Inf.* stew, *Sl.* flap.

2. fight, fisticuffs, scuffle, tussle, *Inf.* set-to, *Inf.* scrap; combat, battle, skirmish, fray, clash, struggle, conflict, embroilment; broil, brawl, donnybrook, free-for-all, melee; riot, demonstration, protest, protest march, sit-in, strike, picketing; violence, rebellion, insurrection, insubordination, mutiny, revolt, outbreak, uprising, revolution, sedition, insurgency, insurgence.

turn, *v.* **1.** rotate, spin, revolve, *Archaic.* trundle; swivel, pivot, wheel, caracole; roll, rev, twirl, twiddle, crank; reel, circumvolve, circumrotate, gyre; gyrate, circle, whirl, circumduct; swirl, eddy, circulate, move in circles, go round; (*of the hips*) bump, grind.

2. change, alter, shift, move, divaricate; diverge, deviate, divagate, detour; sheer, change course, veer; veer off, angle off, shoot off, sidetrack, shunt, rechannel.

3. reverse, invert, interchange, transpose, transplace; turn over, flip over, turn topsy-turvy, subvert; retrovert, retroflex, back, turn back, reverse the course of; wheel around, veer around, swing around, turn about, turn on one's heels, make a U-turn, *Sl.* pop *or* bang a U-ie; flip, tip, turn upside down, topple, tilt, upturn; introvert, evert, turn inside out, fold, invaginate, intusscept.

4. change, convert, resolve, modify, permute, mutate; vary, permutate, reorganize, reorder, adjust, revolutionize; restyle, remodel, recast, reconstruct; reform, refashion, redo, rebuild, recondition, make over; transshape, transform, transmute, transfigure; metamorphose, transubstantiate, transmogrify.

5. nauseate, sicken, unsettle, turn one's stomach, make one sick; offend, repulse, revolt, pall, make one's gorge rise; undo, unhinge, derange, disorder, upset.

6. put, apply, address, use, put to use, engage, employ; fit, adapt, suit, modify, regulate, maneuver; practice, exercise, bring into play, ply, bring into effect, bring to bear; actualize, carry out, effect, put into practice.

7. pass around, go around, round, turn the corner, make a turn, round the bend, double a point, round a point.

8. persuade, prejudice, color, influence, affect; partialize, bias, warp, incline; move, sway, induce, prevail upon, alter the belief of, change the opinion of.

9. decay, rot, spoil, putrefy, molder; curdle, sour, work, lopper, clabber, curd; go bad, reek, taint, stink, smell to high heaven, addle, stagnate.

10. aim, direct, point, head; incline, bend, bear, set, fix, lay; train, zero in, level; steer, lead, conduct, pilot; orient, position, put on the right track, *Chiefly Scot.* airt; lean.

11. avert, turn away, turn aside, ward off, parry; deflect, divert, shunt; countercheck, block, block the way; stave off, fend off, *Archaic.* forfend, check, foil; prevent, thwart, frustrate, balk.

12. shape, form, mold, cast, fashion, construct, formulate; express, style, couch, word, voice, verbalize; term, write, put, say.

13. curve, bend, swerve, flex; arch, arc, bow, vault, camber, *Archit.* embow; round, circle, circumscribe; crook, hook, inflect; twist, wind, curl, coil, spiral; loop, wreathe, twine; meander, zigzag, insinuate, worm, snake.

14. wrench, twist, contort, sprain, wrick; dislocate, tear, rupture; pull, jerk, catch, disjoint, overturn.

15. defect, go over, change sides, apostatize, desert, break faith; tergiversate, change loyalties, do an about-face; renounce, repudiate, cast off, forgo, abandon, forsake; turn renegade, go back on one's word, recant, hold with the hare but run with the hounds, renege, welsh.

16. put about, tack, cant, slue; swing, warp, veer, yaw; jibe, gybe, jib, haul, change course.

17. turn against a. revolt, rebel, mutiny, rise against; oppose, fly in the face of, rise in arms, kick against, kick over the traces; dissent, protest, disagree, say no, demonstrate against; disobey, defy, spurn, repugn. **b.** betray, sell, sell out, play false, play Judas; stab in the back, trick, be false-hearted to, give the Judas kiss to.

18. turn back a. retrace, go back, return. **b.** resist, drive back, beat back, repel, repulse, rebuff.

19. turn down a. lessen, reduce, diminish, lower, decrease; dull, mute, soften, hush, quiet, muffle, stifle. **b.** refuse, reject, decline, deny, veto, turn thumbs down; disapprove, reprobate, dismiss, disallow, discredit; spurn, repudiate, refuse to listen to, ignore.

20. turn in a. submit, hand in, tender, put forward, give; pass in, deliver, hand over, return, give back. **b.** inform on, deliver up, *Sl.* squeal on, rat on, tell on, *Inf.* blow the whistle on; finger, put the finger on, fink on, betray, *Sl.* snitch on, tattle; bear witness against, testify against, *Brit.* turn queen's evidence, turn state's evidence. **c.** retire, go to bed, bed, flop; repair, withdraw, call it a day, roll in, pile in; bid goodnight, say one's prayers, *Sl.* hit the sack, *Sl.* hit the hay, consult one's pillow.

21. turn into a. drive into, walk into, pull into, steer into, come into. **b.** become, get, get to be, grow, turn out to be, go, wax, come, run; be changed into, be converted into, undergo a change, change into, pass into.

22. turn on a. open, start, cause to flow, unstop, unseal; tap, throw open, tear open. **b.** switch on, flick on, plug in, flip on. **c.** activate, start, impel, stimulate, energize. **d.** *Slang.* excite, thrill, titillate, arouse, impassion; inspirit, inspire, touch, penetrate, work up; delight, gladden, *Inf.* tickle pink, elate.

23. turn out a. produce, yield, bear, give, afford; make, put out, bring out, fabricate, manufacture. **b.** drive out, expel, dismiss, oust, discharge; boot out, bounce, bump, ax; can, fire, kick out, cashier, terminate. **c.** result, issue, arise, emanate, spring, proceed; ensue, supervene, follow from, flow from, stem, take rise. **d.** eventuate, become, come to be, grow to be, get to be; come about, end up, *Inf.* pan out. **e.** *Informal.* be present at, appear, *Sl.* make the scene, show up, show; attend, go to, come to, be at; come, make an appearance, arrive.

24. turn over a. consider, reflect, ponder, wonder about, muse; contemplate, brood, mull over, ruminate, think about. **b.** transfer, give, hand over, commend, entrust, consign, commit, relegate. **c.** topple, upturn, flip, capsize, overturn, overthrow, upset, subvert; overset, knock over, keel over, bottom up, tip over, push over, turn turtle; overthrow, inverse, *Fr. bouleverser.*

25. turn tail retreat, move back, recoil, turn and run, cut and run; run away, flee, fly, show a light pair of heels; dance the back step, bolt, take to one's heels, think with one's legs.

26. turn to a. resort, have recourse to, appeal to, call upon, apply to. **b.** work at, attend to, devote, dedicate, give wholly to; buckle down, knuckle down, resign oneself to, give oneself up to, attach oneself to. **c.** change to, become, convert to.

27. turn to account take advantage of, profit from, make the most of, make the best of; obtain a return from, realize a profit from, reap the fruits of, reap the benefits of; capitalize on, make money on, turn to gold.

28. turn up a. fold up, upturn, pleat, plait, double, lap; tuck, ruck. **b.** till, plow, cultivate, turn over. **c.** uncover, find, unearth, discover, dig up; detect, spot, hit upon, come across. **d.** intensify, increase, raise, make louder, amplify. **e.** happen, occur, take place, come to pass. **f.** appear, arrive, present itself, manifest itself; show, show up, make an appearance, put in an appearance; come to notice, emerge, come into view, come to light; uprise, rise, arise, dawn; loom up, creep up, pop up, crop up, enter the picture, meet the eye; burst forth, break forth, come forth, drop from the clouds.

29. turn upon depend upon, hang on, hinge on, turn on, swing on; be contingent upon, be conditional, be subject to.

—*n.* **30.** movement, rotation, revolution, circle; gyration, circumvolution, circumgyration, circumrotation; circuit, cycle, round, circulation; wheel, gyre, roll, reel, turbination; twirl, whirl, spin, eddy, whirlpool, whirligig, pirouette; convolution, *Anat.* gyrus.

31. reversal, inversion, reversement, reversion; return, revulsion, reverse; retrogression, retroversion, turnabout, flip-flop, about-face, volte-face; change of heart, changeabout, rightabout, turnaround.

32. change, alteration, variation, difference, fluctuation, vicissitude; deviation, divergence, shift, switch, qualification; modification, adjustment, modulation, adaptation; transformation, transfiguration, metamorphosis, conversion; transmogrification, transubstantiation, transmutation, mutation, permutation.

33. renewal, revival, improvement, amelioration, betterment, change for the better; worsening, deterioration, change for the worse, relapse.

34. time, opportunity, chance; say, move, hand; *Sl.* crack, *Sl.* go, *Sl.* shot, *Sl.* whack, *Baseball.* at bat; shift, tour, tour of duty, trick, watch; spell, stint, period, cycle.

35. bend, curve, swerve, slue, skew, lurch; bow, arch, arc, vault, *Archit.* extrados; incurve, camber, crescent, lune, half-moon; veer, warp, bias, sweep, sheer, yaw, tack; twist, serpentine, winding, meander, curvature; flexure, incurvation, U-turn, horseshoe, *U.S.* oxbow; hook, crook, angle, corner, dogleg; hairpin turn, zigzag, *Chiefly Scot.* wimple; *Geom.* parabola, *Geom.* ellipse, *Geom.* epicycloid; deflection, double, divarication, divagation, deviation.

36. style, form, mode, manner; guise, phase, makeup; cast, fashion, mold, shape, cut, stamp, type; set, build, make; conformation, configuration, frame, format, construction.

37. bent, tendency, aptitude, flair, aptness; inclination, proclivity, propensity, proneness; penchant, capacity, felicity, affinity, partiality; liking, favor, predilection, predisposition; gift, knack, genius, talent, faculty; head, eye, ear, hand.

38. deed, act, action; service, favor, mercy, courtesy, good deed, grace; kindness, benefaction, benefit; boon; disservice, ill turn, hurt, harm, wrong, injury.

39. juncture, crossroads, turning point, crisis, crunch, turn of the tide; contingency, exigency, emergency; pinch, *Inf.* clutch, strait, pass, extremity; zero hour, moment of truth.

40. walk, hike, stroll, amble, tramp; jaunt, promenade, constitutional, stretch; march, traipse, ramble, airing; ride, spin, whirl, drive.

41. by turns alternately, one after the other, one after another, every other, every second; successively, consecutively, reciprocally, back and forth.

42. in turn in succession, in order, in rotation, in sequence; like dominoes, in a string, down the line.

43. take turns alternate, change places, trade places, trade off; rotate, switch, exchange, interchange, *Inf.* swap; reciprocate, change off, change back and forth, *Sports.* platoon.

44. turn and turnabout alternation, rotation, reciprocity, exchange, *Inf.* backscratching, give-and-take, like for like, tit for tat, quid pro quo, measure for measure; retaliation, reprisal, requital, retribution, vindication, blow for blow, a Roland for an Oliver, revenge, vengeance, an eye for an eye.

turnabout, *n.* reversal, turnaround, aboutface, rightabout, volte-face, switch, *Sl.* switcheroo, *Inf.* flip-flop, *Inf.* a 180°; backtracking, backpedaling; change of heart, second thought, *Inf.* a different tune *or* song.

turncoat, *n.* **1.** renegade, *Archaic.* renegado, deserter, apostate, defector, bolter, seceder; forsaker, dropout, quitter, *Sl.* cop-out.

2. traitor, betrayer, *Inf.* double-crosser, *Inf.* double-dealer, *Sl.* two-timer, *Sl.* cheat *or* cheater; Judas, Brutus, Catilinarian; double agent, fifth columnist, quisling, Benedict Arnold; snake in the grass, snake, backstabber; informer, *Sl.* squealer, tattler, tattletale, telltale, talebearer, *Sl.* ratter, *Sl.* fink, *Sl.* ratfink, *Sl.* stool pigeon *or* stoolie.

turning point, *n.* crossroads, crisis, juncture, conjuncture, critical period, climacteric; point of no return, Rubicon; decisive point, climax, moment of truth, moment of decision, *Inf.* zero hour.

turnkey, *n.* jailer, *Chiefly Brit.* warder, jailkeeper, keeper, guard, *Sl.* screw, *Sl.* bull; warden, *Brit.* governor.

turnout, *n.* **1.** assembly, gathering, collection, amassment, assemblage, number, aggregation, roundup, showing; meeting, meet, rally; crowd, throng, mob; convergence, confluence, cumulation, concourse; party, group, body, circle, knot, bunch, gang, crew, company, troupe, troop, band; flock, pack, herd, swarm; audience, spectators, viewers, watchers, listeners, hearers, attenders, attendants, house; congregation, community, flock; conclave, convocation, muster, mobilization, convention, congress; foregathering, conjunction, coalescence.

2. output, production, product, gross national product, GNP; aggregate, total, quota, limit; batch, amount, lot; bulk, volume, mass.

3. outfit, equipment, equipage, gear, trappings, appointments, fittings.

4. style, fashion, vogue, mode, guise, appearance, *Inf.* getup; make, kind, sort, pattern, cut, *Inf.* cut of one's jib.

turnpike, *n.* pike, tollroad, highway *or* state highway, *U.S. Inf.* interstate; freeway, *Brit.* clearway, expressway, parkway, causeway, throughway; speedway, autobahn, superhighway; main road, highroad, thoroughfare, public road, roadway; street, terrace, circle, row; avenue, boulevard, strip, *Inf.* drag.

turpitude, *n.* **1.** depravity, corruption, corruptness, corruptedness, perversion, depravation; demoralization, deterioration, corrosion, degradation, debasement, abasement, vitiation, degeneration, degeneracy, degenerateness; adulteration, pollution, contamination, defilement, desecration, violation; unchastity, unchasteness, impurity, uncleanness; foulness, baseness, vileness, badness; criminality, wickedness, sinfulness, evil, evilness, iniquitousness, nefariousness; iniquity, sin, evil-doing, wrongdoing, crime.

2. immorality, vice, dissoluteness, profligacy, profligateness, licentiousness, license; lechery, debauchery, debauchment, intemperance, libertinism, prostitution; animalism, carnality, sensuality, lustfulness, lust; libidinousness, lewdness, lecherousness, prurience, pruriency; obscenity, indecency, vulgarity, low-mindedness.

turret, *n.* tower, *Fr. tourelle*; steeple, spire. See **tower** (*def.* **1**).

tussle, *v.* **1.** scuffle, wrestle, *Inf.* scrap, struggle, go at each other's throats, do battle, fight, brawl, fisticuff.

—n. **2.** scuffle, *Inf.* scrap, *Inf.* set-to, *Inf.* boxing *or* wrestling match; strife, contention, combat, struggle; fight, fistfight, fisticuffs, altercation, conflict, clash; fray, skirmish, battle, broil, brawl, free-for-all, donnybrook, melee, hand-to-hand fight.

tutelage, *n.* **1.** guardianship, keeping, care, ward, wardship, protection, safekeeping, *Law.* trusteeship; chaperonage, supervision, surveillance, watchful eye; guidance, direction, control.

2. instruction, teaching, education, tuition, tutorage; grounding, initiation, preparation, schooling, training; inculcation, indoctrination, brainwashing, discipline.

3. pupilage, apprenticeship.

tutelary, *adj.* tutelar, guardian, guarding, protective, protecting, patron, patronal, patronly.

tutor, *n.* **1.** private instructor *or* teacher, preceptor, guru, mentor; trainer, coach; professor, schoolteacher, schoolmaster, schoolmistress.

—v. **2.** instruct, teach, school, educate, inform, enlighten, edify; indoctrinate, brainwash, inculcate, instill, infuse; train, coach, initiate, ground, prepare, ready; guide, direct, control, discipline.

3. care for, take care of, keep, protect; supervise, watch *or* watch over, keep an eye on, baby-sit.

tuxedo, *n.* dinner clothes, dinner jacket, semiformal wear, black tie, *Inf.* tux, *Sl.* monkey suit, *Sl.* soup-and-fish. See also **cutaway**.

twaddle, *n.* **1.** blather, blathering, twaddling, *Brit.* twattle, *Brit.* twattling; drivel, nonsense, moonshine, *Fr. bavardage*, gobbledegook, humbug, flummery, *Sl.* bunk, rubbish, *Inf.* rot, *Sl.* garbage, *Sl.* horsefeathers; balderdash, hogwash, stuff and nonsense, *Inf.* bosh, *Brit. Sl.* tosh, fudge, foolishness, rigmarole; poppycock, *Inf.* fiddle-faddle, *Inf.* piffle, *Inf.* kibosh, *Inf.* flapdoodle.

2. babble, babbling, babblement, prattle, prattling, prate, prating; gibber, gibbering, gibberish, jabber, jabbering, Jabberwocky, *Sl.* gibber-jabbering; chatter, chattering, cackle, cackling; chit-chat, small talk, gossip, tittle-tattle, *Inf.* scuttlebutt, buzz, idle talk, *Inf.* gab, *Sl.* bull; palaver, claptrap, *Sl.* hot air, *Sl.* gas.

—v. **3.** prate, *Brit.* twattle, babble, blather, drivel; talk nonsense, *Inf.* talk through one's hat; jabber, gibber, *Sl.* gibber-jabber, jargon; chatter, chipper, prattle, cackle; chit-chat, chitter-chatter, chaffer, bandy words; talk idly, *Sl.* shoot the breeze, *Sl.* gas, *Sl.* gab, *Sl.* bull *or* shoot the bull; gossip, tittle-tattle, *Inf.* spout, *Sl.* run off *or* on at the mouth.

twang, *v.* **1.** twangle, resound, reverberate, ring; jingle, tinkle, clink, chink, chime, ding.

2. pluck, pick, strum.

—n. **3.** sharp *or* ringing sound, shrillness, stridence, stridency; reverberation, resonance; dissonance, cacophony.

4. nasalization, nasal tone, nasality.

tweak, *v.* pinch, twitch, *Obs.* twinge; twist, squeeze; pull, jerk, grip, nip.

twiddle, *v.* **1.** fiddle with, fidget with, fuss with, fool with, toy with, play with, finger, manipulate; trifle, *Inf.* mess around, *Inf.* monkey around; twirl, twist.

2. twiddle one's thumbs do nothing, be idle, sit back, not lift a finger, while away the time, mark time; shirk, malinger, *Sl.* goof off, *Brit. Inf.* scrimshank.

twig, *n.* small branch, offshoot, shoot, ramification, limb, stem, withe; sucker, spur; switch, stick; runner, tendril, sarmentum; sprout, spring; leafstalk, *Bot.* petiole.

twilight, *n.* **1.** dusk, crepuscule, *Literary.* gloaming; late afternoon, *Inf.* shank of the evening, evening, *Brit. Dial.* cockshut, eventide, evenfall, eve, *Archaic.* even, *Archaic.* evensong, *Archaic.* vesper, sundown, sunset, moonrise, day's end, decline of day, edge of night, edge of darkness, nightfall; half light, faint light.

—adj. **2.** crepuscular, dim, obscure, faint, pale; dusky, shadowy, shady, umbrageous, dark, darkish, darksome, unlit, unilluminated, *Literary.* darkling; gloomy, somber, *Archaic.* sombrous, lowering, tenebrous.

twin, *n.* **1.** counterpart, complement, correspondent; duplicate, double, clone, equivalent, equal; match, mate; alter ego, second self, best friend; companion, brother *or* sister.

—adj. **2.** similar, cognate, Siamese, congeneric, congenerous, kindred, connatural; fellow, like, alike, of a piece, akin to, of a kind; corresponding, correspondent, analogous, comparable, parallel, homologous, matching; identical, same, one and the same, selfsame.

3. double, doubled, duplex, duplicate, two, *Archaic.* twain, *Bot.* bijugate, *Bot.* binate, binary, *Algebra.* binominal; geminate, geminated, coupled, *Bot.* didymous, paired, conjugate, matched; dualistic, dual, twofold.

twine, *n.* **1.** cord, cable, rope, string, wire, yarn; twist, plait, braid.

2. convolution, coil, spiral, helix, spire, volute, whorl, *Bot.* tendril.

3. knot, tangle, snarl.

—v. **4.** interwind, interweave, interlace, intertwine; entwine, weave, lace, knit, splice; plait, pleach, braid.

5. wreathe, encircle, circle, surround, wrap, enwrap.

6. meander, snake, worm, twist and turn, twist, turn, wind, zigzag.

twinge, *n.* **1.** sharp pain, prick, stab, smart; gripe, cramp, spasm, twitch, stitch, crick, kink, tic; ache, throb, tingle.

2. pang, qualm, mental pain, scruple, misgiving; hesitation, hesitancy, recoil, shrinking; uneasiness, discomfort, malaise.

—v. **3.** pinch, bite, gripe, twitch, nip; smart, sting, shoot, stab, lancinate, grind, chafe, gnaw; hurt, pain, ache, throb, tingle.

twinkle, *v.* **1.** glint, glimmer, glitter, glisten, *Archaic.* glister; shine, sparkle, light, spark, scintillate; flicker, blink, wink, flutter; quiver, shiver, ripple; shimmer, dance, dazzle, bedazzle; flash, flare, fulgurate, gleam, glare, coruscate; illuminte, illumine, *Archaic.* illume; glow, radiate, incandesce, phosphoresce; brighten, light up, become luminous *or* radiant; effulge, shine forth, beam.

2. flutter, stir, dart, dartle, spring, move quickly; glint, flash, streak; whisk, skim, glide; flit, flirt, dance, fly, wing; waver, vacillate, oscillate, fluctuate.

—n. **3.** glint, glimmer, glistening, glistering, glittering; shining, sparkling, sparkle, spark, scintillation, scintilla; flickering, flicker, fluttering, flutter, quivering, quiver, shivering, shiver, rippling, ripple; shimmering, shimmer, dancing, dazzling, dazzle, bedazzling; flash, flare, fulguration, gleam, gleaming, glare, glaring, coruscation; illumination, glow, glowing, radiance, incancescence, phosphorescence, iridescence.

4. twinkling, instant, breath, second, split second; moment, minute, trice, flash, *Inf.* jiffy; blink, *Inf.* bat, wink, eyewink, wink of an eye, *Fr. coup d'oeil*; twinkling of an eye, *Inf.* bat of an eye, two shakes of a lamb's tail.

twinkling, *n.* **1.** glinting, glimmering, sparkling. See **twinkle** (*def.* 3).

2. instant, second, moment. See **twinkle** (*def.* 4).

twirl, *v.* **1.** spin, revolve, rotate, whirl, gyrate; pivot, wheel, turn on one's heel, pirouette; twiddle.

—n. **2.** spin, twist, turn, whirl.

3. coil, helix, spiral, spire, volute, whorl, convolution.

twist, *v.* **1.** twine, entwine, weave, lace, knit, splice; plait, pleach, braid; intertwine, interwind, interweave, interlace.

2. circle, encircle, surround, wrap, enwrap, wreathe.

3. sprain, wrench, turn, wrick, throw out of joint.

4. contort, distort, screw, screw up, make a face, grimace; pout, stick out one's lower lip, *Fr. faire la moue.*

5. pervert, warp, garble, *Fig.* mutilate, *Fig.* butcher, *Scot.* thraw; bias, slant, color, varnish, gild; whitewash, gloss, gloss over, *Inf.* fudge; misconstrue, misconstruct, misinterpret, mistranslate, misrender, misreport, miscite; misquote, misstate, lie, miscolor, misrepresent, falsify.

6. curl, coil, spiral, convolute, twirl, whirl, whorl.

7. meander, snake, worm, twist and turn, turn, wind, zigzag; curve, swerve, veer, deviate, slue.

8. writhe, wriggle, wiggle, squirm, *Sl.* have ants in one's pants.

9. rotate, revolve, spin, *Archaic.* trundle; wheel, swivel, pivot, pirouette, turn on one's heel; gyrate, reel, circumvolve, circumrotate; (*all of the hips*) bump, grind, bump and grind.

—n. **10.** curve, bow, bend, turn, bias, warp, veer, swerve, slue, skew; hook, crook, angle, dogleg, hairpin turn, *Sl.* dead man's turn; meander, zigzag, *Chiefly Scot.* wimple.

11. twine, cord, cable, rope, string, wire, yarn; plait, braid.

12. perversion, distortion; misconstruction, misinterpretation, mistranslation, misquotation, miscitation, misstatement; miscoloration, misrepresentation, falsification, subreption; eisegesis.

13. eccentricity, idiosyncrasy, idiocrasy, mannerism, quirk, hobby-horse; oddity, peculiarity, curiosity; irregularity, incongruity, variation, abnormality, difference, variance, inconsistency; quip, crotchet, maggot, whim, caprice, flight of fancy.

14. kink, crick, hitch, pinch, tweak, stab, stitch, stitch in the side, *Inf.* charley horse.

twister, *n.* *U.S. Informal.* tornado, whirlwind, cyclone, (*in the Philippines*) baguio.

twit, *v.* **1.** taunt, tweak, gibe, chaff, rally, pluck by the beard, *Inf.* roast, *Inf.* dig, *Sl.* razz, *Sl.* rag; mock, make fun of, poke fun at, call [s.o.] names; lampoon, burlesque, satirize; ridicule, deride, revile, contemn, scorn, hold up to scorn; tease, kid, pull [s.o.'s] leg, *Inf.* put [s.o.] on, *Inf.* give [s.o.] a hard time, *Inf.* needle, *Inf.* rib, *Inf.* josh, *Sl.* jive, *Sl.* get a rise out of [s.o.].

2. reproach, upbraid, censure, rebuke, berate, *Sl.* rank out, *Sl.* dress down, *Sl.* jump down [s.o.'s] throat.

—n. **3.** taunt, gibe, skit, jeer, sneer, *Inf.* dig; cut, *Inf.* brickbat, *Sl.* put down; boo, hoot, hiss, catcall, *Sl.* raspberry, *Sl.* bronx cheer.

twitch, *v.* **1.** tug, pull, yank, pluck, vellicate, snatch; joggle, jolt, hitch, jar, jiggle, jounce, bounce; shake, agitate, churn; pinch, bite, nip, tweak, twist, wrench.

2. jerk, jump, move spasmodically; quiver, quaver, shiver, wriggle, wiggle, squirm.

3. hurt, pain, ache, twinge, smart, sting, gripe; tingle, throb, pulsate, beat, palpitate, go pitapat.

—n. **4.** tic, spasm, vellication, contraction; quiver, quaver, shake, tremor; throb, palpitation, pulsation; throe, paroxysm, convulsion.

5. pull, tug, jerk, yank; tweak, pinch, nip, twist, wrench.

6. ache, pain, twinge, pang, stab, lancination.

twitter, *v.* **1.** trill, warble, whistle, sing; chirp, chirrup, tweet, cheep, peep; shrill, stridulate, crow, caw, coo.

2. chatter, jabber, prattle, cackle, gibber, *Sl.* gibberjabber; babble, prate, twaddle, *Brit.* twattle, patter, gabble; chit-chat, chitter-chatter, chaffer.

3. be in a flutter, tremble, be excited, be agitated,

Inf. be in a tizzy, *Inf.* be in a dither, be wrought up; fuss, fidget.

—*n.* **4.** trill, warble, whistle, song, call, cry, coo; chirp, chirrup, tweet, cheep, peep; stridulation.

5. flutter, *Inf.* tizzy, *Inf.* dither, excitement, agitation, *Inf.* stew, ferment.

two, *n.* pair, twosome, brace, set, couple, couplet, doublet, *Archaic.* twain; yoke, span, team; binary.

two-faced, *adj.* hypocritical, double-tongued, double-faced, Janus-faced; deceitful, insincere, disingenuous, false, mendacious, untruthful, hollow; dishonest, underhanded, untrustworthy, crooked, knavish; wily, tricky, designing, scheming, guileful, double-dealing; artful, crafty, Machiavellian, cunning, sly, snaky, foxy; subtle, insidious, collusive, circumventive, prevaricative; misleading, fallacious, sophistical, casuistic, deceptive; evasive, dodgy, elusive, slippery, shifty; perfidious, treacherous, traitorous, Punic, treasonable.

twofold, *adj.* binary, *Algebra.* binomial; double, dual, dualistic, duplex, duplicate; geminate, twin, coupled; biform.

two-sided, *adj.* **1.** bilateral, bifacial, bihedral.

2. split, divided, *Sl.* schizo.

tycoon, *n.* magnate, big businessman, businessman, enterpriser, financier, enterpreneur; industrialist, captain of industry, baron, *Inf.* robber baron, *Inf.* wheeler-dealer; top executive, business leader; director, manager, *Sl.* honcho, *Sl.* top dog, *Sl.* Mr. Big, *All Inf.* big shot, big-wig, big brass, big wheel, big cheese, big-timer, big-time operator.

type, *n.* **1.** kind, sort, form, stamp; class, classification, group, category, order, genre; set, suit, suite; genus, species, phylum, division, subgenus, subspecies, subdivision; kin, ilk, family, brood, tribe, clan; strain, sept, breed, stock, variety, brand; sex, gender, race, marital status, religion, creed, sexual orientation, nationality.

2. style, character, nature, temperament, temper, disposition, humor; form, structure, make, designation, description, number, denomination, case, voice; habit, persuasion, bent, inclination, leaning, *Inf.* the like *or* likes of; lot, manner, cast, mold, kidney; grain, vein, mark, color, stripe, streak, feather.

3. specimen, example, representative, exemplar, pilot; instance, case, sample, *Archaic.* ensample.

4. pattern, model, standard, norm; rule, criterion, precedent; mirror, paradigm, epitome, quintessence; prototype, archetype, urtext, original; benchmark, touchstone, normative.

5. print, stamp, typeface, face, font, typecase; character, letter, capital, *Inf.* cap, upper case, majuscule, *Inf.* small cap, lower case, minuscule; italic, boldface, roman.

6. symbol, prefiguration, token, foretoken, image, sign, sure sign; signum, augury, omen, prognostic, portent, presignification, indication, symptom; foreshadow, shadow, shadowing, adumbration.

—*v.* **7.** typewrite; *Inf.* hammer away at the typewriter, *Sl.* bang *or* knock out, *Sl.* hunt and peck.

8. typecast, cast, grade, sort, stereotype; classify, class, categorize, order.

typhoon, *n.* cyclone, hurricane, monsoon, storm, tropical storm; tornado, twister, whirlwind, squall, samiel, simoom; tempest, gale, blast, blow, williwaw; *Philippines.* baguio, *Central America.* cordanazo, *Australian.* willy-willy.

typical, *adj.* **1.** representative, illustrative, paradigmatic, classic, quintessential; suggestive, evidential, symptomatic, implicative; exemplary, sample, pilot, experimental, model, true to type, true to form; characteristic, distinctive, indicatory, indicative; demonstrative, denotative, connotative; distinguishing, differentiative, discriminative, diacritical.

2. symbolic, emblematical, typal, epitomical; particular, specific, special, figural, idiosyncratic, peculiar, singular; categorical, classificational, taxonomical, divisional, subdivisional.

3. normal, ordinary, regular, standard, stock, household, regulation; usual, general, natural, common, commonplace, run-of-the-mill; customary, normative, conventional, habitual, to be expected, *Inf.* par for the course.

typify, *v.* **1.** exemplify, represent, stand for, serve as an example, instance; signify, denote, indicate, mean, token, connote; imply, evince, suggest, evidence, mark, manifest; illustrate, epitomize, personify, embody; be a case *or* instance of, give an idea of, point to.

2. symbolize, portend, foretell, prophesy, shadow; prefigure, augur, bode, betoken; presage, foreshadow, *Archaic.* bespeak.

tyrannical, *adj.* tyrannous, despotic, despotical, autocratic, iron-handed; arbitrary, high-handed, overweening, overbearing, dictatorial, domineering, authoritarian, imperious, peremptory, high-and-mighty, lordly, majesterial; heavy-handed, oppressive, harsh, strict, severe, hard, tough, rigorous, demanding, exacting; cruel, cold-blooded, barbarous, brutal, brutish, savage, inhuman; ruthless, merciless, pitiless, heartless, unfeeling, hard-hearted, cold-hearted; relentless, unrelenting, inexorable, implacable, inflexible, unmovable, unyielding.

tyrannize, *v.* rule despotically, rule with a rod of iron, rule with an iron hand; dominate, domineer, have the upper *or* whip hand, wield the power *or* scepter; boss *or* boss around, dictate to, order around, tell [s.o.] what to do, lay down the law, call the shots *or* plays; browbeat, intimidate, bully, ride roughshod over, trample, ride herd on, *Inf.* step on *or* step all over, *Inf.* use [s.o.] for a doormat, mistreat, maltreat, abuse; overlord, lord it over, oppress, suppress, repress, keep down *or* under, keep under one's thumb; force, coerce, compel, constrain, *Sl.* put the screws to; break, humble, crush, overpower, overcome, overwhelm, get the better of; subdue, subjugate, subject, subordinate, enthrall, enslave, reduce to slavery, hold captive, hold in bondage.

tyranny, *n.* **1.** despotism, dictatorship, supremacy, sovereignty, absolute power, unlimited authority, complete control, domination; iron hand *or* fist, iron rod, iron rule; oppression, repression, suppression.

2. absolutism, totalitarianism, autocracy, monocracy, one-man rule, one-party rule; czarism, Caesarism, kaiserism, Stalinism, imperialism; *U.S.* (*of politics*) bossism.

3. severity, severeness, harshness, strictness, hardness, rigorousness, toughness; cruelty, brutality, inhumanity, inhumanness; ruthlessness, mercilessness, pitilessness, relentlessness, inexorability, inexorableness, implacability, implacableness.

tyrant, *n.* despot, autocrat, dictator, oppressor; monocrat, autarch, absolute *or* supreme ruler, monarch, sovereign, emperor, king; lord, master, overlord; taskmaster, slave driver, martinet, Simon Legree.

tyro, *n.* beginner, abecedarian, novice, novitiate, neophyte, catechumen, tenderfoot, *Sl.* greenhorn; rookie, recruit, raw recruit, newcomer, new member, entrant, freshman, plebe, initiate; learner, pupil, student, protégé, disciple, follower; apprentice, trainee, probationer, intern, *Educ.* student teacher.

U

ubiquitous, *adj.* omnipresent, everywhere, everpresent; universal, catholic, world-wide, in all places, all over; far and wide, right and left, hither and yon, throughout the length and breadth of the land; here, there, and everywhere; under the sun, from pole to pole, the world over, at all points of the compass, on the face of the earth, to the four winds, in all climes, throughout the world.

ubiquity, *n.* omnipresence, ubiquitousness, universality, catholicity; pervasion, pervasiveness, diffusion, diffusiveness, dispersion, dispersal.

uglify, *v.* distort, deform, misshape, twist, turn awry, wrench; mangle, wring, wrest, writhe; contort, gnarl, screw, knot, warp; grimace, snarl, pout, screw up one's face, mow, make a face; disfigure, mutilate, deface, mar, blemish, scar.

ugly, *adj.* **1.** ill-favored, bad-looking, *Inf.* not much to look at, *Inf.* short on looks, *Inf.* not much for looks, *Sl.* hard *or* rough on the eyes; homely, plain, plain-featured, plain-looking; unattractive, unlovely, unpretty, unhandsome, unbeautiful, uncomely; hard-featured, hard-favored; unshapely, unsightly; distorted, deformed, misshapen, twisted, contorted; disfigured, mutilated, defaced, marred, blemished.

2. disagreeable, unpleasant, unpleasing, displeasing, distasteful, objectionable; nauseating, nauseous, sickening, disgusting, noisome, *Sl.* yukky, *Sl.* gross; loathsome, revolting, repulsive, repelling, repellent; repugnant, offensive, obnoxious, shocking, nasty; ignoble, base, low, low-down, dishonorable, disgraceful, shameful, opprobrious; corrupt, depraved, perverted, debased, vile, sordid, bad, foul, rotten, black; scurvy, contemptible, despicable, execrable, abominable, odious, heinous, detestable; cruel, brutal, terrible, awful, *Inf.* god-awful, horrible.

3. ominous, portentous, ill-omened, inauspicious, unpropitious, unfavorable, unpromising, ill-fated, ill-starred, star-crossed.

4. mean, hostile, currish, snarling, curmudgeonly, churlish, irascible; cross, surly, ill-natured, bad-tempered, sour, spiteful; crabbed, crabby, cantankerous, crotchety.

5. (*esp. of natural phenomena*) stormy, tempestuous, violent, wild, procellous, turbulent, squally; howling, roaring, raging, threatening.

ulcer, *n.* **1.** abscess, ulceration, *Pathol.* noma, fester, festering, gathering, gumboil, *Pathol.* parulis, tubercle, *Obs.* apostem, *Obs.* apostemation, *Archaic.* impostume; canker, lesion, chancre, chancroid, simple chancre, soft chancre; boil, blain, *Pathol.* furuncle, carbuncle, pustule, pimple, papule, papilla, pock, wen, whelk, *Rare.* bleb, *Archaic.* botch; sore, open *or* running sore, eruption, gall, excoriation; whitlow, agnail.

2. bane, curse, blight, scourge; plague, pestilence, infestation; cancer, disease; poison, venom; corruption, corrosion, moth and rust, worm in the apple *or* rose; torment, plight, woe, affliction, infliction, worry, grievance; pest, annoyance, vexation, fret, thorn, thorn in one's side, nettle; provocation, offense, sting.

ulcerate, *v.* **1.** canker, *Pathol.* sphacelate, suppurate, *Inf.* rankle; infect, blight, contaminate, pollute, poison, taint; corrupt, degenerate, debase, defile.

2. corrode, erode, deteriorate, wear away, destroy slowly; eat, eat away, eat into, gnaw, gnaw into, gnaw away, nibble away.

ulcerous, *adj.* cankerous, cankered, ulcerative, ulcerated, festering, festered, *Both Pathol.* furuncular, furunculous, suppurating, suppurative; gangrenous, gangrened, mortified, morbid, *Pathol.* necrotic, *Pathol.* necrosed, *Pathol.* sphacelated; diseased, pathological; contaminated, infected, tainted, poisoned, septic, bad.

ulterior, *adj.* **1.** concealed, hidden, secret, unseen, obscured; unexpressed, undisclosed, unrevealed, undivulged.

2. outside, exterior, external; remote, far, faraway, far-off, distant; overseas, transmontane, ultramontane.

ultimate, *adj.* **1.** furthest, furthermost, farthest, remotest, most distant; outmost, outermost, uttermost, extreme; last, hindmost, hindermost, rear, rearmost.

2. maximum, most, utmost; supreme, superlative, paramount, maximal, max., greatest; highest, uppermost, upper, topmost, top, tiptop, summital, apical.

3. final, concluding, completing, terminating, ending, finishing; terminal, endmost, *Inf.* tail-end; conclusive, decisive, determinate, definitive; eventual, unavoidable, inevitable.

4. basic, fundamental, radical, basilar, basal; meat-and-potatoes, elementary, primary, *Inf.* gut; underlying, substrative, substratal; intrinsic, innate, inherent; essential, nitty-gritty, indispensable, necessary, vital, sustentative, supporting.

ultra, *adj.* **1.** extreme, radical, drastic, complete, total, thorough; sheer, utter, downright, out-and-out, unqualified, unmitigated, arrant; excessive, extravagant, exorbitant, outrageous, inordinate, undue, unnecessary, uncalled-for, disproportionate; egregious, flagrant, glaring; outstanding, notable, extraordinary, out of the ordinary, exceptional, remarkable; unusual, offbeat, exotic, bizarre, *Inf.* way-out, *Sl.* far-out.

—*n.* **2.** extremist, radical, revolutionary, immoderate, sans-culotte, *Politics.* Jacobin, ultraist; zealot, fanatic, raver, *Sl.* crazy; nonconformist, dissenter, heretic; leftist, left-winger, Communist, *Derog. Sl.* commie, Bolshevik, Red, *Sl.* pinko, pink, *Inf.* Wobbly; reactionary, rightest, right-winger, ultraconservative, *Inf.* hard-hat; diehard, *Inf.* bitterender; Bircher, Bourbon, Hunker, Tory.

ultraism, *n.* radicalism, extremism, immoderation, fanaticism, zealotry; die-hardism, ultraconservatism.

ultramodern, *adj.* futuristic, ahead of its time, *Inf.* years *or* miles ahead, *Sl.* ultra-ultra, *Sl.* far-out, *Inf.* way-out; modernistic, avant-garde, advanced, progressive, forward-looking.

ultramundane, *adj.* **1.** extraterrestrial, extramundane, transmundane, supermundane, otherworldly, unworldly, unearthly.

2. supernatural, supranatural, preternatural; spiritual, mystic, transcendental; occult, arcane.

ultranationalism, *n.* superpatriotism, overpatriotism, jingoism, chauvinism; my country right or wrong.

ululate, *v.* **1.** howl, bay; hoot.

2. wail, moan, groan, keen; lament, mourn, bewail; cry, weep, shed tears, sob; bawl, blubber, mewl, pule.

umbra, *n.* **1.** shade, shadow, shadiness, shadowiness; dark, darkness, lightlessness, dimness, semi-dark, semi-darkness, half-light, twilight, crepuscule, dusk, duskiness; cloudiness, murkiness, murk, gloom, gloominess, somberness, tenebrousness, obscurity, obscureness.

2. ghost, phantom, phantasm, apparition, eidolon, image, materialization; specter, shade, spirit, *Inf.* spook, (*in Irish folklore*) banshee, *Rom. Religion.* manes, *Rom. Religion.* lemures, *Rom. Antiq.* larvae.

umbrage, *n.* **1.** offense, pain, hurt, ache; displeasure, irritation, annoyance, vexation, pique, chagrin, exasperation, *Inf.* aggravation; indignation, huff, tiff, fume, *Inf.* slow burn; resentment, grudge, bitterness.

2. foliage, leafage, arbor.

umbrella, *n.* parasol, sunshade, beach umbrella, *Fr. parapluie, Brit. Sl.* brolly, *Brit. Facetious.* gamp, *Inf.* bumbershoot.

umpire, *n.* **1.** referee, *Inf.* ref, *Inf.* ump, linesman; moderator, arbiter, arbitress, *Chiefly Scot.* overman, judge, determiner, decider, adjudicator; arbitrator, negotiator, bargainer, reconciler, peacemaker, *Obs.* arbitrer; go-between, intermediary, middleman, mediator, intercessor.

—*v.* **2.** referee, *Inf.* ref, *Inf.* ump, *Sports.* call; arbitrate, decide, determine, settle; judge, adjudge, adjudicate, pass *or* pronounce judgement, decree, sentence.

unable, *adj.* incapable, *Obs.* uncapable, unequal to, not equal to, not up to; powerless, impotent, impuissant, forceless, useless; incompetent, unproficient, no good, inefficient, inefficacious, ineffective, inoperative; unfit, unqualified, unfitted, unsuitable; inept, inapt, unskilled; not up to par, not making the grade, *Inf.* not cutting the mustard, *Inf.* not up to snuff.

unabridged, *adj.* **1.** unshortened, unreduced, uncut, unexpurgated; complete, entire, whole, intact.

2. comprehensive, inclusive, inclusory, all-inclusive, all-encompassing, encyclopedic, exhaustive, thorough, blanket, umbrella; extensive, expansive, broad, widespread, sweeping, far-reaching, universal, world-wide; voluminous, large, big, sizable, substantial.

unaccommodated, *adj.* **1.** not adapted, unadapted, unsuited, ill-suited, unfit; not right, incongruous, at odds, discordant, dissonant; incompatible, mismatched; uncomfortable, awkward, ill-at-ease.

2. without shelter *or* rooms, unsettled, homeless, out in the cold, stranded.

3. unsatisfied, dissatisfied, unfulfilled, discontented, displeased; unhappy, grumbling, unsmiling, *Inf.* sore, irritated, vexed.

unaccompanied, *adj.* lone, alone, solo, unescorted, unattended, *Inf.* stag, companionless, without a partner; on one's own, solitary, separate, apart, single; lonely, lonesome, all by one's lonesome; *Music.* a cappella.

unaccomplished, *adj.* **1.** undone, uncompleted, unfinished, incomplete, half-done; in abeyance, postponed, deferred, put off.

2. inexpert, unskilled, unskillful, amateur, dilettante; uncultivated, uncultured, unrefined, rough; ignorant, unlearned, untutored, unlettered, uneducated; blundering, gauche, without finesse, undiscriminating.

unaccountable, *adj.* **1.** unresponsible, irresponsible, unanswerable, unliable, unsubject; immune, exempt, free, clear, in the clear.

2. inexplicable, unexplainable, insoluble, insolvable, unsolvable, *Obs.* inextricable; impenetrable, incomprehensible, uncomprehensible, inapprehensible, past *or* beyond comprehension *or* understanding; unknowable, incognizable, incognoscible, unfathomable, indecipherable, undecipherable, undiscoverable.

3. mysterious, inscrutable, oracular, sphinxlike; odd, peculiar, curious, queer, offbeat; weird, bizarre, strange.

4. unusual, uncommon, unwonted, unorthodox; atypical, original, singular, individual; abnormal, irregular, aberrant, deviate, deviant, anomalous; fantastic, wondrous, wonderful, miraculous; extraordinary, remarkable, egregious, astonishing, mystic, mystical, cabalistic, transcendental, supernatural, preternatural, otherworldly.

unaccustomed, *adj.* **1.** unusual, unfamiliar, unwonted, unexpected, totally unexpected, unanticipated, out of the ordinary, extraordinary, exceptional; special, remarkable, different, peculiar, distinct; rare, singular, uncommon, unique, once-in-a-lifetime, once-in-a-blue-moon; unheard-of, unprecedented, surprising, amazing, astonishing; incredible, unbelievable.

2. not used to, not ready for, not up to; uninitiated, unpracticed, inexperienced; green, raw, wet behind the ears, *Facetious.* green behind the ears; amateurish, ignorant, naïve.

unadvised, *adj.* **1.** uninformed, unknowing, unaware, unsuspecting; ignorant, blissfully ignorant, naïve, wide-eyed, innocent, like a babe in the woods; misled, misinformed, *Inf.* given a bum steer.

2. ill-advised, imprudent, indiscreet, injudicious, not thought out, unplanned; rash, headlong, bold, hasty, precipitate, precipitous, madcap; impulsive, impetuous, harum-scarum, reckless, foolhardy, venturous, venturesome, devil-may-care; incautious, unwary, careless, heedless, not paying attention, paying no mind.

unaffected[1], *adj.* genuine, real, sincere, candid, frank, open, honest, true, true-blue; straightforward, up front, direct, straight-from-the-shoulder, plain, simple, like an open book; guileless, artless, naïve, ingenuous, unsophisticated, unspoiled, unpretentious, without airs, down-to-earth, homely, unpretending.

unaffected[2], *adj.* unchanged, unaltered, unstirred, unmoved, untouched; unimpressed, unconcerned, uncaring, stoic, stolid, impassive; immutable, changeless; remote, aloof, icy, cold, chilly, bloodless, unemotional, cold-hearted, stony, unfeeling.

unanimity, *n.* unison, concert, accord, chorus, concord, agreement; harmony, unity, union, alliance, consensus, one mind, consent; uniformity, concinnity, consentience, consonancy, consonance, consentaneity; like-mindedness, rapport, sympathy, communion, mutual understanding, confluence of minds; concurrence, accordance, *Latin. consensus omnium;* consistency, congruence, correspondence, coincidence.

unanimous, *adj.* agreed, concordant, accordant, like-minded; in complete accord, in agreement, of one mind, in harmony, at one, of a piece, with one voice; united, concerted, consentient, consentaneous, solid; harmonious, consonant, assonant, uniform, congruous.

unanswerable, *adj.* **1.** unresolvable, undiscoverable, undetectible, insoluble; unascertainable, unverifiable, unconfirmable, untraceable; unexplainable, inexplicable, undecipherable.

2. irrefutable, unarguable, undeniable, incontestable; incontrovertible, unquestionable, indubitable, irrefragable; conclusive, unimpeachable, absolute, positive, definite, unappealable, indisputable.

3. unaccountable, unliable, unreponsible, irresponsible; immune, exempt, unsubject.

unapproachable, *adj.* **1.** remote, out-of-the-way, distant, untouchable, faraway; unreachable, beyond reach, out of reach, godforsaken, forbidding; inaccessible, unattainable, unobtainable, *Inf.* ungettable.

2. unbeatable, unsurpassable, unimitable, incomparable; peerless, matchless, unsurpassed, unexcelled; unequaled, unrivaled, unparalleled, unmatched; without equal, beyond compare, in a class by itself, *Latin. sui generis, Latin. nulli secundus,* second to none; paramount, supreme, foremost, quintessential, preeminent, transcendant, superexcellent.

3. aloof, stand-offish, *Inf.* offish, *Inf.* uncome-at-able; cool, frigid, reticent, unsociable; seclusive, withdrawn, introverted.

unapt, *adj.* **1.** unfit, unsuitable, out of character, out of keeping; unappropriate, inapposite, malapropos, out of place, inapplicable; unfitted, unsuited, ill-adapted, incompatible, uncongenial; improper, unbefitting, unmeet, incorrect, unseemly, indecorous, out of order, imprudent, impolitic; inopportune, unseasonable, untimely, ill-timed, awkward; uncalled-for, impertinent, unwarranted, irrelevant, nongermane, unrelated, neither here nor there.

2. unlikely, improbable, inconceivable, hardly; loath, averse, reluctant, unwilling, disinclined, not prone.

3. slow, dull, cloddish, lumbering, oafish, *Inf.* klutzy; bovine, stolid, dull-witted, blockheaded; incompetent, inept, maladroit, incapable; left-handed, unskillful, inefficient, clumsy, undeft, awkward, graceless; undexterous, *Inf.* butterfingered, *Inf.* all thumbs, unadept.

unarm, *v.* disarm, deprive *or* relieve of weapons *or* arms, make [s.o.] put down his weapon, take [s.o.'s] gun away, frisk; disable, incapacitate, render defenseless *or* helpless *or* powerless, cripple, hamstring.

unarmed, *adj.* **1.** weaponless, without arms, not carrying a gun *or* weapon; unprotected, unshielded, unguarded, unarmored, uncovered, insecure, unsafe; undefended, defenseless, vulnerable, open, exposed, open to attack, attackable, assaultable, assailable, pregnable, susceptible; powerless, helpless, weak.

2. clawless, unclawed, declawed; thornless, scaleless.

unassuming, *adj.* modest, unarrogant, unconceited, unvain; self-effacing, humble, self-humbling, content to stay in the background; low-key, restrained, unpresuming, unpresumptive; retiring, demure, reserved reticent, diffident, shy; simple, quiet, plain, homely, down-to-earth, prosaic; unpretentious, informal, casual, homey, comfortable, unaffected, natural, genuine, ingenuous, *Inf.* regular, *Inf.* O.K., my *or* our kind of; unostentatious, unpompous, unshowy, unobtrusive; unambitious, unaspiring, unaggressive, unassertive; mild, lamblike, docile, meek, submissive.

unattached, *adj.* **1.** unconnected, disconnected, disjoined, detached, apart, separate; unfastened, unlocked, unhooked, unlatched, unhasped, unclasped, unpinned, unbuttoned, unbuckled, undone; untied, unhitched, unleashed, untethered, unchained, unshackled, on the loose, at liberty, at large, scot-free, off the hook; loose, adrift, floating, in suspension.

2. independent, unaffiliated, unassociated, autonomous, autonomic, on one's own, self-sustained, self-supported, self-employed, in business for oneself; self-reliant, self-governing, self-ruling, self-legislating, self-controlled, noncolonial, allodial; freethinking, unorthodox, heterodox, heretic, heretical, iconoclastic; rationalistic, materialistic, positivistic.

3. single, unmarried, unwed, unwedded, spouseless, mateless, husbandless; old-maidish, spinsterish, wifeless, bachelorly; widowed, divorced, separated, misogamic; unengaged, unbetrothed, unpromised, unplighted, uncommitted, unspoken for, datable; heart-free, heart-whole, foot-loose and fancy-free; free, available, untaken, unaccompanied, unescorted, without a date; alone, lone, by oneself, lonely, friendless, without a friend in the world.

unattended, *adj.* **1.** without an audience, sparsely attended, playing to an empty house, unappreciated.

2. unaccompanied, not associated with, off the beaten track.

3. lone, alone, solo, unescorted, *Inf.* stag, without a partner, companionless; on one's own, solitary, separate, apart, single; lonely, lonesome, all by one's lonesome.

4. not cared for, unwatched, untended, left alone, left to fend for oneself; ignored, neglected, disregarded, forgotten, forsaken, abandoned.

5. unheeded, overlooked; out of sight, out of mind; undone, slighted, passed by *or* over, cast aside, filed away, shelved, pigeonholed, postponed, deferred.

unauthorized, *adj.* uncertified, unaccredited, unlicensed, *Eccles.* unordained; unofficial, unapproved, unsanctioned, uncountenanced, wildcat; unwarranted, unpermitted, unallowed, outlawed, prohibited, banned, forbidden, proscribed, interdicted, *Fr. défendu, Ger. verboten*; illegal, unlawful, illicit, unconstitutional, illegitimate, *Sl.* illegit, criminal, wrong, bad, *Law.* felonious; backdoor, under-the-counter, under-the-table, underhand, underhanded, black-market, contraband; secret, secretive, hush-hush, furtive, sneaky, covert, clandestine, concealed.

unavailing, *adj.* vain, futile, useless, bootless, ineffective, inefficacious, Sisyphean; unsuccessful, *Inf.* no go, to no avail, to no purpose, for naught; fruitless, unproductive, abortive, barren, sterile, impotent, effete; worthless, valueless, unserviceable, impracticable, inoperative, invalid; unprofitable, profitless, gainless, unrewarding, unremunerative, unpaying, thankless.

unavoidable, *adj.* inescapable, ineludible, inevasible, ineluctible; inexorable, unpreventable, irresistible, irrevocable, indefeasible; compulsory, required, obligatory, imperative, ordained; inevitable, bound to happen *or* come, impending, just around the corner, just a moment away; predestined, destined, fated, uncontrollable, out of one's hands, *Inf.* in the cards, *Inf.* in the stars; predetermined, determined, decided, settled, fixed, firm, unalterable, unchangeable; certain, definite, sure, as sure as death *or* as death and taxes, *Inf.* for sure; assured, secured, clinched, *Inf.* in the bag; obvious, evident, plain, clear, undeniable, indubitable, unquestionable, incontestable, indisputable, irrefutable, apodictic, incontrovertible.

unaware, *adj.* unknowing, ignorant, unenlightened, incognizant, unacquainted; unconscious, insensible; off one's guard, napping, asleep; blinded, oblivious,

Inf. out of it, *Sl.* out to lunch, *Inf.* unhip; unwarned, unadvised, in the dark, uninformed, uninitiated, unapprised; heedless, unmindful, inattentive; unwary, unanticipative, unprepared, unsuspecting; stupid, dull, dull-witted, witless, slow.

unawares, *adv.* **1.** unknowingly, ignorantly, unwittingly, unaware, unconsciously, unthinkingly; accidentally, unintentionally, undesignedly, without design, by accident, by mistake, mistakenly; inadvertently, inattentively, unguardedly, off guard, in an unguarded moment.

2. suddenly, unexpectedly, without warning *or* notice, abruptly, by surprise, like a bolt from the blue, like a thief in the night.

unbalance, *v.* **1.** throw out of balance, upset, turn the scale, shift the weight, turn topsy-turvy, topple, capsize, overturn; warp, distort.

2. derange, craze, madden, *Obs.* dement, *Archaic.* bedlamize, distemper; drive insane, drive crazy, drive mad, drive wild; disorder, unsettle, distract, unhinge; enrage, frenzy, excite, inflame.

—n. **3.** imbalance, unsteadiness, instability, shakiness, precariousness.

unbalanced, *adj.* **1.** lopsided, unsymmetrical, asymmetrical, unequalized, uneven, unequal, disproportioned, disproportionate, irregular; top-heavy, bottom-heavy, overbalanced; topsy-turvy, disordered, upset; unballasted, unsteady, unstable, insecure, unfortified, unsupported, shaky, wobbly, jiggly.

2. unsound, unreliable, undependable, untrustworthy; unwise, imprudent, injudicious.

3. one-sided, partial, inequitable, unjust, unfair; biased, prejudiced, prepossessed, close-minded, narrow-minded, jaundiced, intolerant, bigoted, partisan, illiberal.

4. deranged, insane, crazy, crazed, mad, lunatic, lunatical, demented; of unsound mind, *Latin. non compos mentis*, mentally ill; daft, *Inf.* daffy, touched, *Inf.* unglued, *Inf.* half-baked, *Brit. Sl.* bonkers, unhinged, distracted; out of one's head *or* mind *or* senses *or* wits, not all there, *Sl.* loco, *Scot.* redwood.

unbar, *v.* open, open up, unlock, unbolt, unfasten, unhitch, undo.

unbearable, *adj.* intolerable, insufferable, insupportable, unendurable, more than flesh and blood can bear, enough to provoke a saint, enough to try the patience of Job, enough to drive one mad, *Inf.* too much.

unbecoming, *adj.* unsuitable, inappropriate, inapt, inapposite, unfit, infelicitous, out of place, out of line, out of keeping, out of character; improper, indecorous, unseemly, indelicate, unladylike, ungentlemanly, ungenteel, inelegant; vulgar, tasteless, in bad taste, offensive; undignified, beneath one's dignity, infra dig, *Latin. infra dignitatem;* (*all of apparel*) unattractive, unsightly, unflattering, not doing one justice.

unbelief, *n.* incredulity, skepticism, Pyrrhonism; doubt, question, misdoubt, mistrust, distrust, disbelief; nonbelief, atheism, faithlessness, infidelity; agnosticism, nullifidianism, minimifidianism; heathenism, paganism, gentilism.

unbeliever, *n.* skeptic, Pyrrhonist; doubter, doubting Thomas, agnostic, nullifidian, minimifidian, disbeliever; nonbeliever, nihilist, atheist, infidel, heretic; heathen, pagan, gentile.

unbelieving, *adj.* **1.** skeptical, incredulous, doubting, full of doubt, disbelieving, nonbelieving, *Sl.* from Missouri; suspicious, mistrustful, distrustful.

2. agnostic, Pyrrhonistic; atheist, infidel, faithless; heathen, pagan, gentile, unconverted.

unbend, *v.* **1.** relax, loosen, loose, slacken, untighten, relieve tension, *Obs.* slake; let go of, release, free, liberate; ease up, ease off, *Inf.* let up, slack off *or* up, *Inf.* let up on.

2. straighten, uncurl, uncoil, unkink; unsnarl, untangle, disentangle; adjust, correct, rectify, right, square, set *or* put straight.

3. calm down, unwind, loosen up, hang loose, *Inf.* let oneself go, be oneself, *Inf.* let one's hair down, *Sl.* let it all hang out; lay back, sit back, *Sl.* take it easy, *Sl.* cool it.

unbending, *adj.* **1.** rigid, stiff, tense, unpliable, inflexible, inelastic, unmalleable, unyielding, resistant; unlimber, not supple, arthritic, rheumatic, gouty, *Inf.* creaky, musclebound; brittle, crisp, dried-out, *Inf.* stiff as a board; hard, wooden, petrified, ossified, frozen.

2. resolute, determined, decided, set, resolved; stubborn, intractable, obstinate, pertinacious, hard-line, obdurate, intransigent, uncompromising; unrelenting, unflagging, dogged, relentless, inexorable; tenacious, gritty, *Inf.* hellbent, *Inf.* stick-to-it-ive.

unbent, *adj.* **1.** unbowed, uncurved, unhunched; straight, direct, undeviating, unswerving; linear, lineal, in a line; straightaway, straightlined, straight as an arrow, virgate; vertical, square, plumb.

2. undefeated, unbeaten, standing, surviving.

unbiased, *adj.* fair, fair-minded, unprejudiced, unjaundiced, unbigoted, impartial, uncolored, *Inf.* colorblind; undistorted, unwarped, unswayed, uninfluenced, unbought; disinterested, dispassionate, detached, neutral; even-handed, equitable, just, *Inf.* square, objective, independent; open, open-minded, broad-minded, tolerant.

unbidden, *adj.* **1.** spontaneous, unrestrained, free, unprompted, voluntary, willing; unconstrained, unforced, uncompelled, unordered, uncommanded; optional, discretionary.

2. unasked, uninvited, unwanted, unwelcome; unrequested, unsolicited, unsought after, unwished-for.

unbind, *v.* **1.** release, disenthrall, extricate, free, liberate; set free, loose, set loose, let loose, turn loose, let go, unpen, unmew, disimprison; acquit, exculpate, clear, exonerate, vindicate; let go, dismiss, discharge, let off, *Inf.* let off the hook; emancipate, manumit, enfranchise, affranchise, franchise; deliver, rescue, ransom, redeem, *Theol.* save.

2. untie, unfetter, unshackle, unchain, unhandcuff, unbridle, unyoke, unmuzzle, *Archaic.* untruss; loosen, unfasten, unhook, undo, unfix, detach; disengage, disunite, disjoin, disconnect, unpin, unstick, unglue; separate, part, divide, sunder, sever, disintegrate, dissolve, break apart *or* up.

unblinking, *adj.* **1.** unemotional, nerveless, strong-nerved, calm, inexcitable; unfaltering, unwavering, steady, cool, calm and collected, steady-handed, unquivering, unshaking, unshaky, sure, without batting an eye.

2. forthright, direct, forward, straightforward, unreserved, without mincing matters; blunt, abrupt, open, artless, sincere; downright, point-blank, to the point.

3. fearless, unfearing, unafraid, unfrightened, unshy, undiffident; undaunted, unintimidated, confident, sure, undismayed; unflinching, unshrinking, unblenching, uncringing.

4. attentive, awake, alert, on the alert, on the qui vive; watchful, on guard, with open eyes, on the lookout, all eyes and ears; unsleeping, unwinking, unnodding, on one's toes, ready, prompt, prepared.

unborn, *adj.* **1.** future, to come, still to appear, latter, henceforward; that will be, coming, eventual, hereafter, subsequent.

2. undelivered, unhatched, unlaid, undropped, in utero; unbegotten, unmade, unconceived, uncreated, unproduced.

unbosom, *v.* disclose, reveal, bare, divulge, expose,

spill; lay bare, let one's hair down, show one's hand *or* cards, disburden, unburden; admit, acknowledge, make a clean breast, get it off one's chest, *Sl.* get it out of one's system, *Sl.* come clean, unburden one's conscience, go to confession; confess, confide, intimate, let [s.o.] in on the secret; uncover, unveil, uncloak.

unbound, *adj.* free, unattached, loose, at liberty; untied, unfastened, detached, uncommitted, uninvolved, divorced; unchained, unfettered, unshackled, untrammeled, ungagged, unmuzzled; unhooked, unbuttoned, unsnapped, unlatched, unzipped.

unbounded, *adj.* **1.** unlimited, boundless, limitless, illimitable; immense, vast, immeasurable, unmeasured; infinite, interminable, endless, indeterminate.

2. unconditional, termless, all-inclusive, all-embracing; undetermined, arbitrary, full, plenary.

3. unrestrained, uncontrolled, unconfined, unrestricted; uncurbed, unchecked, unreined, uninhibited, unrepressed; immoderate, rampant, unruly, unreserved, out of hand; abandoned, free, loose, wild, unsuppressed; intemperate, prodigal, wanton, irrepressible; unconstrained, unbridled, unhindered, unimpeded, unobstructed; excessive, extravagant, lavish, exorbitant, unconscionable.

unbridled, *adj.* unrestrained, unconstrained, uncontrolled, unchecked. See **unbounded** (*def.* **3**).

unbroken, *adj.* **1.** whole, intact, solid, complete; entire, total, uncut, integral; undivided, unabridged, unreduced; all, inviolate, indissoluble, inclusive, indivisible.

2. uninterrupted, continuous, successive, progressive; ceaseless, unremitting, endless, incessant, constant, nonstop, marathon; perpetual, eternal, unceasing, unending, everlasting, perennial.

3. untamed, undomesticated, wild, savage, unsubdued; feral, ferine, maverick.

4. undisturbed, calm, placid, unruffled, still; quiet, peaceful, pacific, tranquil; untroubled, serene, halcyon, restful.

5. unimpaired, unharmed, unhurt, unmarred, sound, fast, undamaged; firm, strong, sturdy, lasting, resistant, rugged, well-built, durable, tough.

unburden, *v.* **1.** unload, disburden, empty, unpack, unlade, unfreight; dump, off-load, discharge; relieve, lighten, ease the load, alleviate; disencumber, disembarrass, unballast, unweight, unship, break bulk; take a load off [s.o.'s] mind, set at ease, make one breathe easier, set one's mind at ease.

2. disclose, reveal, bare; confide, confess. See **unbosom**.

uncalled-for, *adj.* **1.** superfluous, overdone, overwrought, undue, supererogatory, redundant; unwanted, unrequired, unneeded, unnecessary, nonessential; gratuitous, unwarranted, unjustified, expletive.

2. unsought, unasked, uninvited, unsolicited, unrequested; unprompted, unwished, unwelcome; voluntary, free, offered, proffered, volunteer, discretionary.

3. immoderate, excessive, exorbitant; prodigal, lavish, profuse, extravagant; intemperate, unrestrained, overweening, unbridled; unreasonable, unconscionable, outrageous, exaggerated.

4. improper, inappropriate, unmeet, unworthy; unjustified, unearned, undeserved, unmerited, unfair, unjust; wrong, wrongful, unlawful; impertinent, rude, fresh, flippant; disrespectful, *Sl.* nervy, brash, sassy, pert, impudent.

uncanny, *adj.* **1.** extraordinary, remarkable, wonderful, marvelous, noteworthy; astounding, astonishing, amazing, fabulous, fantastic, tremendous, stupendous; exceptional, supernormal, uncommon, unheard-of; unbelievable, incredible, unimaginable, striking, *Sl.* magic; unexampled, singular, prodigious, inspired, divine.

2. strange, mysterious, odd, spooky, queer, *Scot.* unco; preternatural, weird, eerie, creepy, unearthly, ghostly; unnatural, awesome, awful, awe-inspiring, dreadful; bizarre, macabre, unreal, spectral, phantomlike.

unceremonious, *adj.* **1.** informal, without ritual; simple, natural, easy, free, open, casual, relaxed, lax.

2. abrupt, blunt, brusque, curt, clipped, short; quick, brief, hasty, cursory, summary, superficial, hurried, slight; rude, impolite, uncivil, discourteous, unmannerly, bad-mannered, ill-bred, disrespectful, misbehaved; inconsiderate, tactless; indelicate, uncourtly, ungallant, indecorous, ungracious, unpolished, ungenteel, unrefined, ungentlemanly, unladylike; rough, coarse, vulgar, crude, boorish, churlish, gruff.

uncertain, *adj.* **1.** unpredictable, unforeseeable; unaccountable, undeterminable, unascertainable, undivinable, incalculable; casual, haphazard, random, arbitrary, hit-or-miss; chance, fortuitous, serendipitous, aleatory, *Inf.* fluky.

2. ambivalent, undecided, unresolved, unsure, betwixt and between, of two minds, at loose ends, sitting on *or* straddling a fence; fluctuating, oscillating, oscillatory, wavering, hovering; debating, considering, weighing both sides; skeptical, unconvinced, questioning, suspicious, mistrustful, distrustful, untrustful.

3. irresolute, indecisive, infirm of purpose, wishy-washy; hesitant, hesitating, pausing, halting, hanging back, faltering, dallying, dillydallying; equivocating, hedging one's bets, covering *or* touching all bases, seesawing, shilly-shallying; insecure, unassured, unconfident, unsure of oneself; reserved, constrained, restrained, demurring.

4. indefinite, undetermined, unsettled, unestablished, unfixed, up in the air, open, touch-and-go, borderline, hanging in the balance, *Sl.* up for grabs; unproven, undemonstrated, unconfirmed, in suspense, in question, in dispute, at issue; unknown, undiscovered; debatable, contestable, arguable, moot, suspect, open to question *or* doubt; provisional, tentative, pending, contingent, conditional; speculative, conjectural, assumptive, presumptive; theoretical, hypothetical, notional, postulational; problematic, problematical.

5. indistinct, indeterminate, undefined, ill-defined, ill-marked; vague, nebulous, obscure, unclear, *Rare.* imperspicuous; shadowy, hazy, fuzzy, foggy, blurry, blurred, unfocused, out of focus; mysterious, arcane, cryptic; abstract, recondite, abstruse; enigmatic, enigmatical, puzzling, baffling, bewildering, confounding; impenetrable, unfathomable, inscrutable.

6. inconsistent, variable, changeable, changeful, ever-changing, mutable, permutable, protean, vicissitudinous; mercurial, volatile, impetuous, impulsive; fickle, capricious, wayward, skittish, flighty, moody; transient, rambling, roving, wandering.

7. dubious, doubtful, questionable, ambiguous; inconstant, unreliable, undependable, untrustworthy, unsteadfast; treacherous, slippery, shifty, timeserving.

8. chancy, risky, riskful, full of risk, *Inf.* iffy, *Brit. Inf.* dicey; delicate, ticklish, *Inf.* tricky, *Inf.* sticky; dangerous, perilous, hazardous, *Sl.* hairy; unsafe, unsound, unfixed, unstable, unsteady, shaky, wobbling, teetering, tottering, hanging by a thread, trembling in the balance.

9. irregular, intermittent, erratic, sporadic, unmethodical, immethodical, methodless, unsystematic, systemless, *Inf.* on again, off again; spasmodic, fitful, desultory, stop-and-go, come-and-go, coming and going; (*all of light*) dim, faint, pale, poor, inadequate, feeble.

uncertainty, *n.* **1.** doubt, doubtfulness, dubiousness, dubiety, skepticism; unsureness, hesitancy, hesitation; caution, wariness, tentativeness; suspicion, suspiciousness, diffidence, misgiving, distrust, mistrust.

2. guess, piece of guesswork; borderline case, touch-and-go situation; contingency; tossup, open question, undecided issue; gamble, risk, leap *or* shot in the dark, pig in a poke; blind bargain, sight-unseen transaction.

3. unpredictability, unpredictableness, unforeseeableness, unaccountability, unaccountableness; randomness, haphazardness, casualness, arbitrariness; chance, fortuity, fortuitousness, happenstance, serendipity, luck, fortune.

4. ambivalence, equivocation, equivocalness, equivocality, equivocacy, fence-sitting, mugwumpery; fluctuation, vacillation, oscillation, shilly-shally; fluctuating, wavering, shilly-shallying, blowing hot and cold.

5. irresolution, irresoluteness, indecision, indecisiveness, undecidedness, unsureness, indetermination, infirmity of purpose; insecurity, unassuredness, lack of confidence; confusion, perplexity, bewilderment, bafflement, puzzlement.

6. indefiniteness, unsettledness; question, questionableness; suspense, state of suspense; theoreticalness, hypotheticalness, problematicalness; speculation, conjecture, assumption, presumption.

7. indistinctness, indeterminateness, indeterminacy; obscurity, vagueness, nebulousness, unclearness, ambiguity, ambiguousness; impenetrability, impenetrableness, inscrutableness, inscrutability.

8. inconsistency, variableness, variability, changeableness, changeability, mutability; fickleness, capriciousness, whimsicality, waywardness, skittishness; inconstancy, unreliability, unreliableness, undependability, untrustworthiness; treacherousness, slipperiness, shiftiness.

9. riskiness, *Inf.* chanciness, *Brit. Inf.* diceyness; delicacy, ticklishness, touchiness, *Inf.* trickiness, *Inf.* stickiness; dangerousness, hazardousness, perilousness, precariousness, *Sl.* hairiness; danger, peril; instability, unstableness, unsteadiness, shakiness; unsoundness, unsafeness.

10. irregularity, intermittence, erraticism, sporadicalness, sporadicity, sporadism, unmethodicalness, methodlessness, unsystematicalness, systemlessness; fitfulness, desultoriness, spasmodism.

unchain, *v.* free, release, disenthrall, extricate, liberate. See **unbind** (*def.* **1**).

unchangeable, *adj.* **1.** immutable, changeless, unalterable, incommutable, invariable; stable, stationary, firm, fixed, sound, solid, balanced; dependable, reliable, steady, steadfast; permanent, established, confirmed, inveterate, strong, deep-rooted, entrenched, ingrained.

2. enduring, abiding, lasting, persisting; indestructible, imperishable, perdurable, inextinguishable, indissoluble; perpetual, unfading, incorruptible, undecaying, amaranthine, perennial; deathless, undying, immortal, eternal, *Archaic.* eterne, everlasting.

uncharitable, *adj.* unkind, unchristian, uncompassionate, remorseless, insensitive, unfeeling, unconcerned; ungenerous, mean-spirited, petty, small-minded, narrow-minded, selfish, unaccommodating, unforgiving; cold, cool, unfriendly, distant; harsh, severe, austere, stern, rough, stark, stringent; unsparing, unremitting, inexorable, implacable, uncompromising, unbending, inflexible, obdurate; ruthless, merciless, pitiless, cruel, brutal, savage; hard-boiled, cold-blooded, hard-hearted, ironhanded, ironfisted, ironhearted; despotic, inquisitorial, tyrannical, abusive, punitive; distressing, tormenting, biting, cutting.

unchaste, *adj.* impure, unvirtuous, unvirgin, unvirginal, defiled; loose, Cyprian, promiscuous, wanton, immodest, shameless; corrupted, debased, lowered, degraded, vitiated, degenerate, base, low; indecent, obscene, perverted, depraved, evil, vile, sinful, wicked; dissolute, licentious, libertine, profligate, incontinent, unrestrained, *Pathol.* nymphomaniacal, *Pathol.* satyrical; lascivious, lewd, lecherous, lubricous, *Archaic.* lickerish, hircine, *Sl.* horny; lustful, randy, *Sl.* hot *or* hot for; concupiscent, prurient, libidinous, salacious; fleshly, carnal, sensual, voluptuous, erotic; immoral, amoral.

uncivil, *adj.* **1.** rude, discourteous, impolite, unceremonious, unmannerly, bad-mannered, ill-bred, disrespectful, misbehaved; indelicate, uncourtly, ungallant, indecorous, ungracious; ungentlemanly, unladylike, brash, bold, hoydenish, *Scot.* randy; brazen, barefaced, insolent, impudent, insulting, impertinent, pert, saucy, fresh; bluff, surly, sullen, bearish, gruff; inconsiderate, tactless, *Scot. and North Eng.* misleared; abrupt, blunt, brusque, curt, clipped, short.

2. uncivilized, uncultured, unrefined, unpolished, incondite. See **uncivilized.**

uncivilized, *adj.* barbarous, barbarian, unenlightened, primitive; uncultured, unrefined, unpolished, incondite; uncouth, coarse, vulgar, raffish, plebian; churlish, loutish, brutish, wild, savage, gross; ignorant, illiterate, unlearned, untrained, untaught, untutored, uneducated, uncultivated, unskilled, unskillful; clumsy, gauche, crude; countrified, provincial, unfashionable, homespun, homebred.

unclean, *ajd.* **1.** dirty, filthy, polluted, fouled, befouled, unwashed, soiled, sooty, grimy, begrimed, smoky, sullied, maculated; muddied, miry, dirt-encrusted; stained, smeared, smirched; impure, tainted, infected, poisoned, adulterated, *Inf.* mucky, *Inf.* mucked up, littered, litter-strewn, *Inf.* junked up.

2. defiled, contaminated, vitiated, spoiled, corrupted; malodorous, mephitic, rank, putrid, odious, noxious, noisome; slimy, scummy, sludgy, *Inf.* gloppy, *Inf.* gunky; unhygienic, unsanitary, insanitary, morbific, pathogenic, pestiferous, feculent, ordurous; unhealthy, unhealthful, unwholesome.

3. obscene, indecent, suggestive, off-color, bawdy, smutty, prurient, salacious, risqué, ribald, pornographic, blue, *Sl.* raunchy; lewd, lascivious, perverted, lecherous, libidinous, licentious, lustful, *Archaic.* lickerish; coarse, concupiscent, carnal, unchaste, unvirtuous.

uncloak, *v.* **1.** uncover, bare, unveil, unsheathe, discase, uncase; divest, strip, undress, unrobe, disrobe, denude, denudate.

2. bring to light, bring out, make known, reveal, disclose, divulge; expose, present to view, exhibit, display, show, evince, demonstrate, indicate, make manifest; take the wraps off, unveil, unscreen, unmask, show up; produce, hold up to view, lay open.

unclothe, *v.* strip, undress, unrobe, disrobe; denude, denudate, make naked; uncover, bare, lay bare, expose, reveal; unveil, uncloak, unsheathe, undrape, unscreen; discase, uncase.

uncomfortable, *adj.* **1.** embarrassing, discomforting, discomposing, disturbing, distressing, disconcerting, upsetting; unpleasant, disagreeable, painful, hard, rough, difficult, trying, nerve-racking; irritating, irksome, annoying, troublesome, bothersome.

2. uneasy, ill-at-ease, nervous, tense, stressful, strained, *Sl.* uptight, keyed up, tensed up; upset, disturbed, bothered, perturbed, distressed, troubled, worried, concerned, disquieted, *Archaic.* disquiet; unquiet, fretful, restless, impatient, fidgety, itchy, itching, *Sl.* antsy; jumpy, jittery, edgy, on edge, *Inf.* on pins and needles, on tenterhooks; on a tightrope, on a cliff edge, waiting for the other shoe to drop, waiting for the ax to fall, waiting for the bomb to go off; apprehensive, alarmed, anxious, with one's heart in one's mouth, fearful.

uncommitted, *adj.* unpledged, unpromised, unplighted, unengaged, unbetrothed, free, available; footloose and fancy-free, unattached, unbound, unmarried, single, independent; undecided, straddling the fence, on neither side, neutral.

uncommon, *adj.* **1.** unusual, rare, unwonted, uncustomary, unfamiliar, out-of-the-way; scarce, infrequent, occasional, few, few and far between; unique, one of a kind, special, singular, individual, distinctive, different, exotic, recherché; out-of-the-ordinary, unconventional, unorthodox, novel, new; atypical, irregular, aberrant, abnormal, anomalous; peculiar, eccentric, idiosyncratic, strange, curious, odd, bizarre, queer, weird, freakish, freaky.

2. extraordinary, exceptional, remarkable, outstanding, standout, distinctive, noteworthy, notable; unheard-of, unprecedented, unexampled, unparalleled, unequaled, peerless, matchless, unrivaled, inimitable, incomparable; unsurpassed, second to none, supreme, superior, transcendent, the best, superlative, of the first water.

uncommonly, *adv.* **1.** unusually, highly, extremely, inordinately; outrageously, incredibly, unbelievably, amazingly.

2. specially, especially, particularly, exceptionally, singularly; outstandingly, strikingly, remarkably, extraordinarily, marvelously.

3. rarely, very rarely, infrequently, seldom, seldom if ever, hardly, hardly ever, scarcely, scarcely ever; on rare occasions, occasionally, only now and then, once in a great while, *Inf.* once in a blue moon, *Inf.* once in a coon's age.

uncommunicative, *adj.* taciturn, reserved, shy, reticent, unconversable, unconversational, untalkative; quiet, silent, close-mouthed, tight-lipped, tacit, unspoken, speechless, voiceless, mum, mute; distant, aloof, stand-offish, unsociable, antisocial, antisocialistic; laconic, concise, succinct, to the point, terse, short, brief, pithy.

uncompromising, *adj.* **1.** rigid, stiff, hard, inflexible, unflexible, nonflexible, unbendable, unbending, unyielding, hard-line; fixed, set, firm, immovable, unalterable, unchangeable, unvarying, hard-and-fast, ironclad, absolute, resolved, determined, tenacious, dogged, persevering, unrelenting, relentless, implacable, inexorable, never-say-die, die-hard; hardcore, inveterate, absolute, unqualified, unmitigated.

2. strict, severe, stern, austere, Spartan, harsh, *Inf.* hard as nails, tough; rigid, *Inf.* set in one's ways, narrow-minded, close-minded; ultraconservative, strait-laced, *Sl.* straight, on the straight and narrow; unadaptable, unaccommodating, unconformable, nonconforming, noncompliant, uncompliant, noncooperative, uncooperative; stubborn, obstinate, pigheaded, mulish, obdurate, headstrong, willful.

unconcern, *n.* indifference, insouciance, apathy, disinterest, disinterestedness; aloofness, distantness, remoteness, haughtiness, being above it all, *Inf.* not giving a damn, *Sl.* not caring a fig *or* a hoot in hell; nonchalance, pococurantism, lukewarmness, coolness, frigidity; impassiveness, impassibility, dispassion, dispassionateness, passionlessness; passiveness, listlessness, languor, inattentiveness, obliviousness, preoccupation, spiritlessness; insensitivity, insensibility, lack of sympathy *or* compassion; stoniness, stoicism, callousness, hardness, hard-heartedness, obdurateness.

unconcerned, *adj.* **1.** uninterested, indifferent, apathetic, uninvolved, *Fr.* dégagé, disinterested; distant, aloof, remote, removed, haughty, above it all; impassive, impassible, unemotional, dispassionate, passionless; unexcited, nonchalant, pococurante, perfunctory; lukewarm, Laodicean, cool, cold, chilly, icy, frigid; listless, torpid, languid, phlegmatic, dull, half-dead; inattentive, preoccupied, oblivious, in a world of one's own, out of touch; bored, half-awake, nodding, in a reverie, drifting in and out, with one's head in the clouds.

2. unworried, unanxious, untroubled, insouciant; carefree, blithe, without a care in the world; uncaring, unpitying, unsympathetic, unsolicitous, unmoved, untouched, unstirred, unaffected; thick-skinned, callous, insensible, insensitive, unfeeling, hard, hard-hearted, obdurate; impenetrable, unimpressionable, unreachable, stoical, stolid, stony, with a heart of stone *or* ice; flinty, steely, sharp, cruel; inconsiderate, thoughtless, casual, unthinking, heedless, impatient; selfish, egoistic, self-centered.

unconditional, *adj.* unqualified, categorical, positive, absolute, unconditioned, unrestricted, unreserved; complete, total, downright, flat, outright, out-and-out, straight-out, all-out, across-the-board; decisive, certain, veritable, unequivocal, conclusive, sure; emphatic, definite, marked, confirmed, authoritative; incontrovertible, indubitable, demonstrable, demonstrated; settled, fixed, decided, pronounced, indisputable, unmistakable, inescapable, undisputed, incontestable, apodictic.

unconformity, *n.* incongruity, inappropriateness, inaptness, inappositeness, unsuitability, unfitness; impropriety, unseemliness, indecorum; disharmony, disparity, divergence, diversity, difference, dissimilarity; inconsistency, contradiction, contrariety; discrepancy, disagreement, conflict; noncompliance, deviation, aberration, anomaly, abnormality.

unconnected, *adj.* **1.** disjoined, separate, disunited, divorced, parted, severed, unattached, detached.

2. disjointed, disconnected, rambling, diffuse, jumpy, sprawling, wordy, verbose; unrelated, not tied together, without a theme, not unified; incoherent, illogical, nonsensical, meaningless; confused, helter-skelter, disordered, disorderly, hit-or-miss, haphazard, messy, inchoate, disorganized.

unconscionable, *adj.* **1.** unscrupulous, unprincipled, unethical, amoral, immoral, shameless; corrupt, perverse, evil, wicked.

2. unwarranted, uncalled-for, unfair, unfounded, groundless; unreasonable, inordinate, immoderate, undue, exorbitant, drastic, extreme, outrageous; inexcusable, unpardonable, indefensible, unforgivable; unjustifiable, unwarrantable.

3. extortionate, excessive, extravagant, preposterous, prohibitive; *All Inf.* steep, stiff, fancy, high, out of this world.

unconscious, *adj.* **1.** senseless, insentient, oblivious, blacked-out, out, dead to the world, *Inf.* out cold, *Inf.* out like a light, *Sl.* cold; asleep, fast *or* sound asleep, sleeping, *Inf.* sleeping like a log, in the land of Nod, in the arms of Morpheus, *Sl.* flaked-out; *All Sl.* coldcocked, laid-out, KO'd, kayoed.

2. (*all of a person's feelings, etc.*) unaware, insensible, insensitive, incognizant, unknowing, blind to, deaf to, lost to.

3. inanimate, inorganic; mineral.

4. instinctive, subliminal, innate, inherent; involuntary, reflex, automatic, *Sl.* gut; inadvertent, unwitting, unthinking; unintentional, unpremeditated, unplanned, unstudied, indeliberate, accidental, chance.

uncontrollable, *adj.* **1.** ungovernable, unmanageable, unruly, restive, wild, out of control, out of hand;

recalcitrant, contumacious, refractory, intractable, incorrigible.

2. mad, rabid, delirious, distracted, carried away, like one possessed, beside oneself; wild, frenzied, frenetic, frantic, raving, raging, berserk, amok.

unconventional, *adj.* uncommon, unusual, unorthodox, uncustomary, unwonted, rare, unique, out-of-the-ordinary; original, atypical, singular, individual; unexampled, unparalleled, unfamiliar, uncomfortable; eccentric, peculiar, offbeat, curious, queer, odd, oddish, quizzical, cranky, uncouth, *Inf.* funny, *Inf.* kinky; idiosyncratic, *Inf.* quirky, *Sl.* flaky, *Sl.* balmy, *Chiefly Brit.* barmy; strange, weird, bizarre, freakish, *Sl.* freaky, grotesque, *Sl.* rum, *Sl.* far-out; deviant, aberrant, wayward, erratic, anomalous, abnormal, irregular.

uncoordinated, *adj.* clumsy, awkward, ungraceful, ungainly, *Sl.* un-co; oafish, doltish, cloddish, lumbering, clodhopping, heavy-footed, lubberly, lumpish, hulking, bovine; unhandy, inept, bungling, bumbling, blundering, clownish; unskillful, left-handed, maladroit, bunglesome, ambisinister, like a bull in a china shop, *Inf.* all thumbs, *Inf.* butterfingered, *Inf.* klutzy.

uncouth, *adj.* **1.** uncivil, unmannerly, ill-mannered, ill-bred; discourteous, impolite, disrespectful, unceremonious; rude, brash, bold, hoydenish, *Scot.* randy; vulgar, coarse, boorish, raffish, churlish; gross, crude; improper, unseemly, unbecoming, indecorous, indelicate, ungenteel, uncourtly, ungracious; undignified, beneath one's dignity, infra dig, *Latin. infra dignitatem*, ungentlemanly, unladylike.

2. uncivilized, uncultured, uncultivated, unrefined, unpolished, unsophisticated, unworldly, incondite; countrified, country-bred, country-born, upcountry, backwoods, provincial, inurbane, yokelish, *Sl.* hickish, *Sl.* rube, *Sl.* hayseed, *Sl.* from the sticks, *Sl.* from the boondocks *or* boonies; awkward, clumsy, gauche, ungainly, ungraceful, graceless, inelegant.

3. unconventional, uncommon, unusual, unfamiliar; odd, outlandish, curious, peculiar; strange, weird, bizarre. See also **unconventional.**

uncover, *v.* **1.** expose, bare, lay bare, take the wraps off, unwrap, unveil, unmask, unsheathe, uncase, discase; open, uncork, unstop; divest, strip, undress, unclothe, undrape, uncloak; discover, descry, detect, find, unearth, exhume, dig up, smoke out.

2. reveal, make known, disclose, divulge, bring out, bring out into the open, bring to light; tell, impart, inform, communicate, let [s.t.] be known.

3. remove one's hat, uncap, unbonnet, doff one's cap, tip one's hat.

uncritical, *adj.* undifferentiating, undiscriminating, indiscriminate, indiscriminative, promiscuous, unjudging; unselective, unparticular; unthinking, unthoughtful, unreflecting, unaware, unperceptive, obtuse, dense, dull; ignorant, uninformed, unenlightened, unschooled, uneducated; unscholarly, half-baked, *Sl.* half-ass, mediocre, casual, hit-or-miss; superficial, surface, shallow, slick, glossy, glib, facile, smooth; unprofound, empty, meaningless, insubstantial.

unction, *n.* **1.** anointing, oiling, lubrication, *Eccles.* chrism.

2. balm, salve, ointment, unguent, oil, lotion, lubricant; liniment, embrocation, emollient, demulcent, *Med.* abirritant, palliative.

3. (*all affected in speech*) earnestness, fervor, ardor, passion, emotion, feeling, warmth; spirit, verve, zest, enthusiasm, gusto, zeal, eagerness; power, force, vehemence; persuasion, inducement, smoothness.

unctuous, *adj.* **1.** oily, oleaginous, greasy, greased, lubricated, lubricous, unguentary, unguinous, slippery, slithery; buttery, butraceous; soapy, saponaceous, waxy.

2. smooth, suave, urbane; glib, fluent, smooth-talking, honey-tongued; ingratiating, flattering, sycophantic, obsequious, fawning, servile; insincere, hypocritical, dissembling, mealy-mouthed; self-righteous, cantish, moralistic, pious, pietistic, smug, complaisant; fervent, fervid, ardent, gushy.

undamaged, *adj.* unharmed, uninjured, unhurt, unscathed, scatheless, unimpaired, unbroken, undefaced, undisfigured, unmarred, unspotted; sound, safe and sound, alive and well, well, in good shape *or* condition, all right, *Inf.* O.K., *Inf.* okey dokey *or* okle dokle, *Sl.* hunky; intact, in one piece, whole, in perfect condition; unscratched, untouched, unaffected, home free; unspoiled, unruined, unblemished, untainted, unsullied, undefiled.

undaunted, *adj.* **1.** undismayed, unalarmed, unappalled, unflinching, unfaltering, unblenched, unblenching, unswerving, undeterred, not put off; resolute, stalwart, steadfast, inflexible, firm, tenacious, persevering, persistent, unflagging, unrelenting, indomitable, indefatigable.

2. intrepid, bold, audacious, stout-hearted, lion-hearted, valiant, heroic; valorous, dauntless, brave, courageous, mettlesome, manful; high-spirited, spirited, doughty, hardy, plucky, game, gritty, *Inf.* spunky.

undeceive, *v.* unbeguile, disabuse, be honest *or* truthful with, bring [s.t.] out into the open, lay [s.t.] all out; give [s.o.] the facts, give [s.o.] the real *or* true story, lay it on [s.o.], give it to [s.o.] straight, shoot straight from the hip, pull no punches; set [s.o.] straight *or* right, correct, help [s.o.] see the light; disillusion, disillusionize, shatter [s.o.'s] illusion, burst [s.o.'s] bubble, disenchant, open [s.o.'s] eyes, wake [s.o.] up, snap [s.o.] out of it; make [s.o.] grow up, tell [s.o.] how things really are.

undecided, *adj.* **1.** unsettled, unresolved, yet to be decided, up in the air, pending, in suspense; open, open to debate, debatable, arguable, problematic, problematical, questionable, disputable, contestable, controvertible, moot; undetermined, indeterminate, unfixed, unset, undefined, indefinite, a big question mark; unknown, unproven, unestablished, unascertained, unconfirmed, undemonstrated, experimental.

2. unsure, uncertain, doubtful, dubious, at loose ends; ambivalent, of two minds, double-minded, on the fence, betwixt and between, mugwumpish, mugwumpian; divided, torn, in a dilemma; hesitant, indecisive, irresolute, shilly-shallying, wishy-washy, infirm of purpose; vacillating, wavering, tergiversatory, changeful, changeable, variable, blowing hot and cold; fickle, mercurial, capricious, unreliable, undependable.

undecipherable, *adj.* **1.** illegible, unreadable, indecipherable; unclear, *Inf.* clear as mud, indistinct, indistinguishable, undistinguishable, unrecognizable; blotted, blurred, smudged; (*all of writing*) cramped, squeezed, squeezed together, pinched; run-on, run together, strung together; deleted, erased, effaced, eradicated, wiped *or* rubbed out, blotted out

2. hieroglyphic, hieroglyphical, cryptographic, cryptographical, *Obs.* steganographic.

3. secret, hidden, concealed, veiled, cryptic, perdu; impenetrable, incomprehensible, uncomprehensible, unfathomable, inscrutable, unknowable, incognizable, incognoscible; abstruse, recondite, esoteric, abstract, heavy, *Inf.* heavy-duty.

4. difficult, hard, *Inf.* tough; complex, complicated, perplexed, *Inf.* tricky; intricate, involved, tangled, knotty, crabbed; obscure, dim, dark, vague, nebulous,

Rare. imperspicuous; puzzling, baffling, enigmatic, enigmatical; mysterious, arcane, inexplicable, unexplainable, insolvable, insoluble, unaccountable, inextricable.

undefended, *adj.* **1.** defenseless, unprotected, unguarded, unsheltered; unfortified, unarmed, weaponless, weak, helpless, powerless, impotent; insecure, unsafe, dangerous, perilous, precarious.

2. vulnerable, expugnable, uncovered, exposed, naked, wide open; open to attack, pregnable, penetrable, invadable, attackable, assaultable, assailable.

undefiled, *adj.* **1.** pure, clean, clear, fair, white, immaculate, snowy; stainless, spotless, unspotted, unsmirched, unbesmirched; unsullied, unsoiled, unpolluted, unblemished, unblotted, unstained; untainted, uncorrupted, undistorted, unmarred; uninfected, germ-free, sterilized, sterile, antiseptic, disinfected; fresh, fit to drink *or* eat, drinkable, eatable, potable, edible; healthful, uninjurious, wholesome, sanitary, innocuous.

2. guiltless, innocent, uncorrupt, clean, moral; virtuous, decent, delicate, proper, seemly; unwanton, undissipated, undissolute, unlicentious; chaste, continent, abstinent, temperate, *Rare.* intemperate; celibate, virgin, vestal, maidenly, immaculate, intact; impeccable, sinless, above suspicion, inculpable, with clean hands; flawless, faultless.

3. high-principled, upright, righteous, uprighteous; honest, good, sincere; creditable, full of integrity, ethical, high-minded, purehearted, saintly, holy, angelic, divine, godly.

4. unaffected, simple, plain, unornamented, unadorned; tasteful, polished, graceful, refined.

undefined, *adj.* **1.** indefinite, indistinct, impalpable, tenuous; vague, obscure, dim, hazy, nebulous, shadowy, blurred, clouded, veiled; amorphous, formless, shifting, changeable; uncertain, unsure.

2. unexplained, unclear, open to question, unspecified, unspecific, indeterminate, inexact, imprecise; puzzling, perplexing, baffling, mysterious, enigmatic; abstruse, recondite, esoteric, cryptic.

undemonstrative, *adj.* **1.** unresponsive, uncommunicative, unaffectionate, distant, aloof; unexcitable, unemotional, unmoved, unstirred, unperturbed, unsusceptible, unimpressionable, unimpressible; apathetic, phlegmatic, listless, languid; lukewarm, neutral, nonchalant, indifferent; sedate, self-controlled, sober, staid, stoical, philosophical; reserved, shy, demure; calm, composed, poised, quiet, unruffled, placid, stiff, formal, *Inf.* tight, *Sl.* uptight.

2. insensitive, unfeeling, uncompassionate, uncaring, heartless; unkind, pitiless, hard-hearted, cold-hearted, marble-hearted, stony-hearted; impervious, stony, steely, flinty; hardened, obdurate, callous, thick-skinned; unimpassioned, untouched, indurate, inured.

undeniable, *adj.* incontestable, indisputable, incontrovertible, irrefragable, irrefutable, unquestionable, beyond question, admitting of no question *or* doubt, indubitable, beyond a shadow of a doubt, apodictic; *Law.* peremptory, inappealable; conclusive, decisive, definite, definitive, solid, fixed, final; impregnable, invincible, unassailable, insuperable, undefeatable, unbeatable; certain, sure, *Inf.* for-sure, secure, positive; authoritative, unimpeachable, infallible, absolute; proven, demonstrated, established, well-founded.

undependable, *adj.* **1.** unreliable, untrustworthy, untrusty, trustless; irresponsible, fly-by-night, dishonest, disreputable, untruthful; dubitable, doubtful, unauthentic, questionable, disputable, contestable, refutable, unconvincing; uncertain, unassured, inaccurate, implausible, untenable, unbelievable.

2. inconstant, fickle, changeable, flighty, faddish; inconsistent, wishy-washy, indecisive, irresolute, erratic, labile; vacillating, wavering, fluctuating, mercurial, volatile; unpredictable, variable, vicissitudinous; impulsive, impetuous.

3. unsound, unsafe, unsure, infirm, insecure; unsteady, unstable, unsolid, insubstantial, ungrounded; shaky, rickety, shifty, shifting, slippery; dangerous, perilous, hazardous, risky; treacherous, tottery, rocky, uncertain.

under, *prep.* **1.** beneath, below, underneath, *Dial.* neath; further down, lower down, lower than.

2. submerged in, immersed in, sunk in, drowned in; engulfed by, inundated by.

3. subordinate to, inferior to, secondary to, subservient to, subject to; lesser than, lower than, smaller than, cheaper than; at the foot of, under the heel of, at [s.o.'s] mercy, at [s.o.'s] beck and call, in [s.o.'s] clutches, in [s.o.'s] hands.

4. backed by, supported by, sponsored by, brought to one by, funded by, financed by; guarded by, guided by, fostered by, under the care of; under the auspices of, under the aegis of, under the eyes of.

—adv. **5.** beneath, below, underneath, *Dial.* neath; subjacent, on the bottom, on the ground; underground, belowground, belowdecks, downstairs, *Chiefly Brit.* below stairs; underwater, submerged, immersed; underfoot.

6. below, short, less, behind, down; shy of, short of, this side of.

—adj. **7.** lower, lowest, nether, subjacent; underwater, submarine, subaqueous, subterranean, submerged.

8. junior, younger, secondary, auxiliary, subordinate, cadet, lower; subaltern, subsidiary, underling, ancillary.

9. unconscious, hypnotized, mesmerized, out; senseless, comatose, insensible, numb, asleep, sleeping.

underbrush, *n.* undergrowth, underwood, underbush; brush, brushwood, scrub, bush, shrubs, brambles, briers, brier patch, vegetation, *Brit.* bracken; thicket, brake, copse, *Chiefly Brit.* coppice, boscage.

underclothes, *n.* underwear, underclothing, undergarments, underthings, underdress, underpinnings, undies, *Facetious.* unmentionables, *Sl.* skivvies. See **underwear.**

undercover, *adj.* secret, hidden, concealed, secluded, screened, masked, veiled, cloaked, shrouded, ensconced, under wraps, behind the curtain *or* closed doors, in the dark; private, nonpublic, hush-hush, confidential, closed-door, closet, *Archaic.* privy; undisclosed, unrevealed, untold; covert, spy, intelligence, CIA, FBI; clandestine, underground, surreptitious, furtive, stealthy, sly, hugger-mugger, sneaky, underhand, underhanded.

undercurrent, *n.* **1.** undertow, underset, riptide, crosscurrent, countercurrent.

2. undertone, overtone; hidden tendency, drift, trend; implication, suggestion, connotation, hint, murmur; latency, hidden feeling; atmosphere, tenor, aura, flavor.

undercut, *v.* **1.** cut out, cut away, gouge out, scoop out, hollow out; excavate, undermine, mine.

2. undersell, undercharge, underprice, sell cheaply; sacrifice, sell at a loss.

underdog, *n.* **1.** loser, weaker party, dark horse, out-of-towner, second-rater, also-ran.

2. victim, prey, *Inf.* little fellow, *Sl.* stooge, *U.S. Sl.* fall guy, scapegoat.

underestimate, *v.* undervalue, underrate, rate too low, sell short, hold for naught, hold cheap, misprize;

misjudge, miscalculate; disprize, hold in disrespect, look down on, set no store by; sneeze at, spit upon, *Inf.* look down one's nose at; despise, scorn, contemn, be contemptuous of, disdain; feel contempt for, hold in contempt, revile, depreciate, disparage, *Inf.* put down, ridicule, discredit, poke fun at; belittle, minimize, talk down.

underfoot, *adv.* under the feet, beneath one's feet, on the ground; underneath, under, down, below, on the underside.

undergo, *v.* **1.** experience, go through, pass through; encounter, live through, live out, meet with, meet, taste.

2. endure, bear, sustain, tolerate, take patiently, suffer through, brook, submit to, brave; abide, stand, withstand, put up with, weather; permit, allow, suffer; swallow, stomach, pocket, digest.

underground, *adv.* **1.** subterraneously, subterraneanly, by *or* through a tunnel *or* underpass, by subway *or* the metro; under *or* in the ground, in a cave.

2. secretly, in secret, privately, in private, in a hush-hush manner, sub rosa, out of view, behind closed doors, in seclusion; covertly, clandestinely, surreptitiously, furtively, stealthily, on the sly, sneakily, sneakingly; underhandedly, under-the-table, under-the-counter, through the back door, illicitly, illegally, unlawfully.

—adj. **3.** subterranean, subterrestrial, hypogeal, hypogeous, belowground, below the surface of the earth; buried, sunken, covered with dirt *or* earth.

4. secret, undercover, hidden; covert, clandestine, surreptitious; underhand, underhanded, backdoor, under-the-table, under-the-counter. See **undercover.**

—n. **5.** underworld, hell, abode of the dead, nether regions; Hades, Sheol, Orcus, Dis, Avernus.

6. tunnel, underpass, subterranean passage *or* passageway, *CB Radio.* hole in the wall; (*both of mines*) gallery, corridor, *Mining.* drift, *Mining.* crosscut; subterrane, mine, cave, burrow, hole, pit; grave, tomb, sepulcher, hypogeum, crypt, vault.

7. resistance, opposition, guerillas; subversives, insurrectionaries, insurgents, seditionaries, incendiaries, saboteurs, fifth column, fifth columnists; revolutionaries, radicals, extremists, terrorists, *U.S.* Weathermen.

8. *Chiefly British.* subway, underground railroad, metro, *Inf.* tube; MTA, BMT, IRT.

undergrowth, *n.* **1.** underbrush, underwood, underbush; brush, brushwood, scrub. See **underbrush.**

2. down, fluff, fuzz, peach fuzz, baby feathers, underlayer, *Zool.* undercoat, *Bot., Zool.* pubescence, *Biol.* lanugo, *Bot.* tomentum; pelage, fur, feathers, plumage, wool, hair.

underhanded, *adj.* **1.** dirty, unfair, below-the-belt, against the rules, underhand, *Inf.* left-handed; deceitful, treacherous, perfidious, double-dealing, two-timing; dishonest, immoral, sinful, bad, wrong, wrongful, unconscionable, unscrupulous, dishonorable; corrupt, misfeasant, malfeasant, crooked, under-the-table, under-the-counter, (*of politics*) backroom, shady; unauthorized, illicit, illegal, unlawful, criminal, felonious, bootleg; sneaky, clandestine, surreptitious, hugger-mugger, undercover, stealthy, furtive, covert, secret; insidious, shifty, guileful, artful, Machiavellian, scheming, crafty, designing, plotting, calculating, sharp, slippery, cunning, wily, foxy, snaky.

2. undermanned, understaffed, short-handed, short a hand *or* worker, short of workers.

underlay, *v.* undergird, underprop, underbrace, underpin, underset; brace, prop, prop up, shore up, bolster up, support, stay; reinforce, bolster, strengthen.

underlie, *v.* form the foundation of, be at the bottom of, be the basis of; support, sustain, maintain, bolster, bear, upbear, bear up, uphold, hold up, hold, See also **underlay**.

underline, *v.* underscore. See **underscore**.

underling, *n.* subordinate, subaltern, understrapper, junior, nonentity, *Inf.* low man on the totem pole; servant, menial, lackey, *Contemptuous.* flunky; minion, creature, puppet, slave, dupe, instrument, tool, cat's-paw, rubber-stamp, doormat, footstool, *Sl.* stooge; yes man, jackal, spaniel, bootlicker, lickspittle; parasite, leech, sponger, hanger-on.

undermine, *v.* **1.** tunnel, excavate, burrow, dig, mine.

2. subvert, sap, sap the foundations of [s.t.]; sabotage, wreck, *Inf.* throw a wrench *or* monkey wrench into the works, *Brit. Inf.* ratten, *Sl.* bugger, *Sl.* queer, *Sl.* queer the works, *Sl.* gum up *or* screw up the works, *Sl.* foul up.

3. (*all by stealth or treachery*) injure, hurt, harm, impair, damage, incapacitate, disable; spoil, ruin, dash, scotch.

underneath, *prep.* **1.** below, under, beneath, *Dial.* neath, at the bottom of, at the foot *or* base of.

2. subordinate to, at the beck and call of, under the heel of.

—n. **3.** bottom, bottom side, underside.

underprivileged, *adj.* disadvantaged, deprived, in want, in need, beggared, pauperized; on welfare, on relief, *Brit.* on the dole, *Brit. Sl.* on the brew; needy, necessitous, indigent, impoverished, impecunious, penurious, distressed, in reduced, circumstances, in straitened circumstances, in narrow straits, in dire straits; poor, ill-off, *Inf.* hard up, unable to make ends meet, unable to keep the wolf from the door; destitute, poverty-stricken, penniless, without a penny, without a sou, down-and-out.

underscore, *v.* emphasize, stress, lay stress *or* emphasis upon, give emphasis to, punctuate, accent, accentuate; underline, italicize, point up, call attention to, mark, bring home, press home; feature, highlight, spotlight, play up, give prominence to, bring to the fore, bring into relief, *Inf.* headline; intensify, strengthen, heighten, deepen.

undersea, *adj.* underwater, submarine, subaqueous. See also **underwater**.

undersell, *v.* **1.** undercut; underprice, undercharge, sacrifice, sell at a loss, sell wholesale.

2. soft sell, play down, understate.

undersized, *adj.* **1.** underdeveloped, atrophied, stunted, truncated, stubby, squat, undersize; dwarfish, runtish, runty, pygmy, *Med.* nanoid; short, little, small, *Chiefly Scot.* wee, miniscule, minikin, diminutive, *Scot.* cutly, tiny, elfin, bantam, slight; *All Sl.* pint-sized, pocket-sized, sawed-off, knee-high to a grasshopper.

2. skinny, scrawny, scraggy, gaunt, lank; rawboned, bony, skin and bones; underweight; undernourished, underfed, starved; emaciated, wasted, wizened.

understand, *v.* **1.** comprehend, fathom, penetrate, learn, savvy, glean, get the idea, *Inf.* get it, *Sl.* get into, *Inf.* get through one's head, *U.S. Inf.* figure out, *Inf.* psych out; grasp, seize, *Inf.* catch on, *Sl.* get the hang of, *Inf.* get the drift of, *Inf.* get a fix on, *Brit.* lay hold of, *Sl.* latch onto; perceive, apprehend, discern, make out, *Inf.* make heads or tails of, *Brit.* twig; recognize, see, see through, see the light, get the picture, read, read [s.o.] like a book, read [s.o.'s] mind.

2. know, cognize, be acquainted with, be familiar with, have knowledge of, *Inf.* know the ropes, *Inf.* pick up; be cognizant of, be conscious of, be aware of, be in the know; master, feel comfortable with, be conversant with.

3. assimilate, absorb, digest, take in, appreciate.
4. gather, hear, learn of, get word, hear of, get wind of.
5. believe, opine, think, fancy, take it, conceive; infer, surmise, conjecture, conclude, take to mean; presume, suppose, estimate, figure, *Inf., Dial.* reckon; assume, daresay, venture to say, take for granted; interpret, construe, deduce, reason.
6. empathize with, show compassion for, commiserate, pity; sympathize with, be in sympathy with; tolerate, accept.

understanding, *n.* **1.** comprehension, cognition, cognizance, consciousness; knowledge, realization, awareness; grasp, hold, handle, *Inf.* fix; interpretation, conception, idea, view, approach.
2. intelligence, intellect, *Gk. Philos.* nous, intellectuality, aptitude; mind, mentality, brain, brains, *Inf.* gray matter, brainpower, reason, sense.
3. acumen, perspicacity, astuteness, penetration; discernment, apperception, apprehension, perception, percipience, insight, enlightenment, intuition, *Obs.* skill; keenness, shrewdness, savvy; sagacity, sageness, wisdom, sapience, sapiency, *Archaic.* counsel.
4. conversance, acquaintance, intimacy, familiarity; proficiency, skillfulness, dexterity, adroitness, deftness, know-how, savoir-faire; capableness, adeptness, address, efficiency; competence, competency, mastery, expertness.
5. agreement, arrangement, covenant, bargain, compact, pact, concordat, entente, contract; accordance, settlement, reconciliation, conciliation, alliance, treaty, truce; cooperation, tolerability, acquiescence.
—*adj.* **6.** empathic, compassionate, commiserative; merciful, clement, forbearing, lenient, forgiving; feeling, tender, kind, considerate, thoughtful; sympathetic, condolent; tolerant, accepting, patient.
7. intelligent, brilliant, incisive; proficient, adroit, adept, deft, skillful, masterful, expert; competent, capable, comprehensive, thorough.

understate, *v.* de-emphasize, downplay, play down, *Inf.* soft-pedal, make light *or* little of, minimize, reduce the importance of, not do justice to.

understudy, *n.* double, substitute, sub, stand-in, fill-in, replacement, alternate, backup, pinch hitter.

undertake, *v.* **1.** take on *or* upon oneself, put on oneself, assume, accept, shoulder, take *or* assume responsibility for, take in charge, bear the burden of; enter upon, begin, start, commence, set about, embark on, venture upon; tackle, endeavor, try, attempt, essay, try one's hand at, *Inf.* have a go at, *Inf.* give [s.t.] a go, give [s.t.] a whirl, take a shot at, *Inf.* take a crack at; strive, bend over backward, knock oneself out, do one's best, *Inf.* do one's damnedest, make every effort.
2. promise, pledge, agree to, give one's word *or* solemn word, give one's word of honor, give one's parole, *Inf.* cross one's heart and hope to die; vow, solemnly swear, state on one's honor, swear to, declare *or* state under oath, *Law.* testify; assure, offer assurance, aver, asseverate, affirm, avouch, declare, state, profess; guarantee, warrant, vouch for, attest to, bear witness to, testify to; engage, oblige, obligate, contract, covenant, enter an agreement, make a bargain *or* deal, shake on it; endorse, sign, *Inf.* sign on the dotted line.

undertaker, *n.* mortician, funeral director, embalmer; *Euph.* grief therapist.

undertaking, *n.* **1.** project, enterprise, venture, operation, campaign; program, proposition, deal; job, game, task, effort, work; contract, commitment, obligation, commission, assignment; pursuit, quest, search.
2. promise, pledge, assurance, word, solemn word, word of honor, parole, *Archaic.* troth; vow, oath, sworn statement *or* declaration, testimony; endorsement, signature, written statement, testimonial; attestation, affirmation, profession, avowal, asseveration, avouchment; engagement, betrothal, *Archaic.* plight; marriage contract, marriage bond, marriage vow; obligation, bond, agreement, contract, compact, covenant, pact, *Rare.* paction, treaty; gentlemen's agreement, unwritten agreement, understanding; guarantee, guaranty, warrant, warranty, *Law.* covenant of warranty, *Law.* warranty deed, *Obs.* vouch.

undertone, *n.* **1.** murmur, murmuration, whisper, breath, sigh; susurration, susurrus, rustle; low tone, hum, whir, whirring, purr, purring, vibration.
2. undercurrent, undermeaning, subsense; connotation, suggestion, implication, signification, insinuation; nuance, touch, trace, tinge, tint, inkling, intimation; odor, scent, taste, flavor; inference, supposition, coloration; meaning, sense, significance, purport, import.

undervalue, *v.* underestimate, underrate, rate too low, sell short, hold for naught, hold cheap, misprize; misjudge, miscalculate; disprize, hold in disrespect, look down on, set no store by; sneeze at, spit upon, *Inf.* look down one's nose at; despise, scorn, contemn, be contemptuous of, disdain; feel contempt for, hold in contempt, revile, depreciate, disparage, *Inf.* put down, ridicule, discredit, poke fun at; belittle, minimize, talk down.

underwater, *adj.* submarine, subaqueous, undersea; submerged, submersed, sunken.

underwear, *n.* underclothes, underclothing, undergarments, underthings, underdress, underpinnings, *Inf.* undies, *Facetious.* unmentionables, *Sl.* skivvies, *Both Brit.* small clothes, smalls; lingerie, teddies, dainties, things, finery, fine washables; flannels, underflannels, long *or* thermal underwear, *Sl.* long johns; underpants, pants, underdrawers, drawers; panties, bloomers, knickers, bikinis, G-strings; undershorts, shorts, boxer shorts, boxers, briefs, *Trademark.* Jockeys, *Trademark.* BVDs, *Brit.* Y-fronts, jockstrap, athletic supporter; undershirt, T-shirt, *Both Brit.* undervest, vest, *Sl.* skivvy shirt; bra, brassiere, uplift; slip, half-slip, camisole, petticoat, underskirt, chemise, shimmy, shift, hoop, hoopskirt; girdle, corset, corselete, panty girdle, garter belt, *Chiefly Brit.* stays.

underweight, *adj.* skinny, skin-and-bones, fleshless, gaunt, bony, rawboned, skeletal; spindly, spindle-shanked, twiggy, gangling, scrawny, scraggy, undersized; undernourished, underfed, half-starved, starved-looking; hollow-cheeked, pinched, shrunken, wasted, emaciate, emaciated.

underworld, *n.* **1.** criminal element of society, the mob, the Mafia, the syndicate, organized crime; dregs of society, scum of the earth, riffraff, rabble, *Contemptuous.* ragtag and bobtail.
2. abode of the dead, nether regions, grave, hell; Sheol, Hades, Orcus, Dis, Avernus.

underwrite, *v.* **1.** sign, countersign, co-sign, endorse, initial, put one's name to; mark, letter, inscribe, engrave, character, stamp, seal.
2. subscribe to, agree to, consent, accede, approve, sanction, *Inf.* O.K.; concur with, confirm, ratify, corroborate, verify, validate, certify.
3. guarantee, back; subsidize, aid, sponsor, promote, maintain, uphold, support, keep.

undesirable, *adj.* unattractive, uninviting, disagreeable, unpopular; objectionable, indecorous, unseemly, unbecoming, unbefitting, out of place; unfit, unsuitable, inappropriate; unallowable, ineligible, unadvisable, uncommendable, unpraiseworthy, unsatisfactory; inadmissible, unacceptable, untenable, unfeasible, indefensible, unjustifiable; detrimental, disadvantageous, harmful, hurtful, injurious.

undigested, *adj.* **1.** (*all of food*) unbroken down, undissolved, untransformed; unabsorbed, unassimilated, *Rare.* indigested.

2. not understood, uncomprehended, unabsorbed, untaken in; unpondered, unthought over, uncontemplated, unmediated upon *or* on.

undignified, *adj.* improper, indecorous, unseemly, indelicate, inelegant, unladylike, ungentlemanly, ungenteel; infra dig, *Latin. infra dignitatem*, beneath one's dignity; vulgar, offensive, tasteless, in bad taste; unbecoming, unsuitable, inappropriate, inapt, inapposite, unfit, infelicitous, out of place, out of line, out of keeping, out of character.

undiscerning, *adj.* inattentive, unobservant, unmindful, thoughtless, regardless, unheeding, heedless, careless, negligent, neglectful; unthinking, unthoughtful, unreflecting, unperceptive, unaware; undifferentiating, undiscriminating, indiscriminate, indiscriminative, unjudging, uncritical, unselective, unparticular; ignorant, unlettered, uneducated, unschooled, uninformed, unenlightened; uncomprehending, slow-witted, slow, purblind, thick, obtuse, dense, dull, blunt, unintelligent, stupid, simple.

undisciplined, *adj.* **1.** untrained, unprepared, unskilled, unaccomplished, raw, green, inexperienced, unpracticed; uneducated, unschooled, untutored, untaught, uninstructed.

2. unorganized, unsystematic, unmethodical; undependable, unreliable, not to be counted on, untrustworthy; erratic, unpredictable, changeable, inconstant, fickle, whimsical, flighty, mercurical, capricious, wayward; uncontrolled, unrestrained, wild, unruly, disobedient, willful.

undismayed, *adj.* **1.** undaunted, unalarmed, unappalled, unflinching. See **undaunted** (*def.* **1**).

2. intrepid, bold, audacious, lionhearted, valiant, brave. See **undaunted** (*def.* **2**).

undisputed, *adj.* uncontested, unchallenged, unquestioned, undoubted, accepted, recognized, acknowledged; certain, sure, *Inf.* for-sure, absolute, positive; unmistakable, obvious, evident, explicit, unequivocal, clear, clear-cut; indisputable, undisputable, undoubtable, indubitable, unquestionable, beyond question, beyond a shadow of a doubt; apodictic, incontestable, incontrovertible, irrefutable, irrefragable, undeniable, inescapable; conclusive, decisive, definite, definitive, final, inappealable, *Law.* peremptory.

undistinguished, *adj.* common, ordinary, plain, simple, homespun, commonplace, run-of-the-mill, pedestrian; middle-class, bourgeois, philistine, stereotypical; plebeian, provincial, *Inf.* down-home, informal; unexceptional, unimpressive, mediocre, so-so, indifferent, *Inf.* nothing special, *Inf.* nothing to write home about, *Sl.* no big deal, *Sl.* no great shakes; indistinctive, insignificant, unimportant, nameless, lowly, humble, unknown, obscure; unnoticed, unnoticeable, inconspicuous, unobvious, hidden, obscured.

undivided, *adj.* whole, together, *Inf.* in one piece, intact, complete, entire; unseparated, solid, unbroken uncut, unsevered, unsplit, uncleft, uncloven.

undo, *v.* **1.** annul, nullify, disannul, disestablish declare null and void, make void, quash, abolish; repeal, revoke, retract, rescind, abrogate; reverse, countermand, cancel, *Law.* nol-pros; invalidate, vacate, vitiate; do away with, cut out, remove, put an end to, terminate, make an end of, dispense with, eliminate, obviate; offset, counterbalance, counteract, neutralize; thwart, frustrate.

2. destroy, devastate, desolate, lay waste; ravage, work *or* wreak havoc upon, ruin, *Dial.* ruinate, bring to ruin, bring to naught, lay in ruins; fell, prostrate, level, raze, wreck, *Sl.* total, smash, shatter; annihilate, eradicate, expunge, extirpate, obliterate; overthrow, overturn, overwhelm, overcome, topple, defeat, conquer, cause the downfall of; crush, subdue, quell, suppress, squelch, vanquish, squash.

3. loosen, unfasten, unhook, unbutton, unsnap, unlace, untie, unfix, detach; unbind, unfetter, unshackle, unchain, unbridle; release, loose, free; disengage, disunite, disjoin, disconnect, unpin, unstick, unglue; separate, part, divide, sunder, sever, break apart; unmake, unbuild, dismantle, disassemble, take apart.

4. open, tear open, unwrap, uncover.

undoing, *n.* **1.** ruin, ruination, destruction, bane, downfall; defeat, overthrow, overturn, labefaction; collapse, debacle, breakdown, breakup; drop, fall, descent, crash, smash; debasement, abasement, degradation; shame, disgrace, humiliation, mortification.

2. catastrophe, disaster, calamity; misfortune, trouble, affliction, woe, grief, sorrow; trial, ordeal, visitation, curse, blight.

undone[1], *adj.* unaccomplished, not carried out, unexecuted, unfulfilled, not done; incomplete, unfinished; omitted, overlooked, skipped, missed, passed over; unattended to, postponed, shelved, ignored, forgotten, neglected, uncared for.

undone[2], *adj.* ruined, destroyed, wiped out, wrecked, smashed, shattered; overcome, defenseless, helpless, paralyzed, crippled, disabled; weighed down, burdened, crushed, prostrate, *Inf.* broken; daunted, distressed, discouraged, crestfallen, broken-hearted, heartsick, *Inf.* broken-up; dejected, downcast, *Inf.* down, downhearted, *Inf.* low, depressed.

undoubted, *adj.* undisputed, uncontested, unchallenged, unquestioned, accepted, recognized, acknowledged. See **undisputed**.

undoubtedly, *adv.* indubitably, doubtless, doubtlessly, unquestionably; positively, absolutely, certainly, with certainty, decidedly, definitely, assuredly; unqualifiedly, categorically, undeniably, incontrovertibly, unmistakably; beyond question, beyond a doubt, beyond a shadow of a doubt.

undress, *v.* **1.** disrobe, undrape, unclothe, nakedize, *Inf.* peel, doff, shed, cast *or* throw off, *Sl.* drop one's drawers, *Sl.* drop trow, strip, strip down to nothing.

2. uncover, unveil, expose, bare, show, reveal, bring to light, disclose, make known.

—*n.* **3.** dishabille, negligee; informality, carelessness, disarray, sloppiness.

undue, *adj.* **1.** unwarranted, unjustified, gratuitous, expletive, at another's expense; unearned, unmerited, undeserved; inappropriate, unmeet, improper, objectionable, in bad taste; unsuitable, unapt, unbecoming, unseemly; imprudent, ill-advised, indiscreet.

2. superfluous, redundant, supererogatory, uncalled-for; unneeded, unnecessary, nonessential, unrequired; excessive, over and above, immoderate, exorbitant; lavish, profuse, prodigal, supernumerary, overmuch, *Fr. de trop*; inordinate, fulsome, overflowing, overweening.

undulate, *v.* ripple, roll, cockle, wrinkle, popple, porpoise; comb, surge, heave, swell, rise, rise and fall; wave, flap, billow, wag, wigwag, stream, trail.

undying, *adj.* deathless, immortal, perpetual, eternal, *Literary.* sempiternal; unending, never-ending, neverdying; unceasing, ceaseless, incessant, invariable; permanent, imperishable, indestructible, undestroyable, lasting; incorruptible, inextinguishable, ineradicable, ineffaceable; unremitting, steady, unwavering, persistent; continuing, abiding, sustained, staying, fadeless, unfading, never-fading; untiring, constant, undiminished, unwearied, indefatigable.

unearth, *v.* **1.** dig up, exhume, excavate, grub up, dredge up; mine, quarry, pull out, root out, deracinate; disinter; unbury, untomb, disentomb, unsepulcher.

2. uncover, discover, find, come across, hit upon; bring to light, expose, reveal, disclose; turn up, root up, ferret out; divulge, make manifest, evidence.

unearthly, *adj.* **1.** otherworldly, psychical, psychic, spiritual, spiritistic, astral; extramundane, supersensory, discarnate, bodiless; incorporeal, asomatous, immaterial, imponderable; extraterrestrial, transmundane, unworldly, supernal; occult, transcendental, supramundane, preterhuman, pretersensual; supernatural, unnatural, preternatural, hypernormal.

2. ghostly, spectral, numinous, deathly; weird, strange, uncanny, eldritch, eerie, macabre; haunted, ghosted, nightmarish, hag-ridden; creepy, spooky, *Scot.* unco, bizarre, unreal, mysterious; funny, queer, curious, peculiar, *Brit. Sl.* rum, *Inf.* kooky, *Sl.* oddball.

3. out-of-the-ordinary, extreme, ungodly, unreasonable; outrageous, undue, uncalled-for, preposterous; unheard-of, unfamiliar, abnormal, unusual, unconventional.

uneasy, *adj.* uncomfortable, restless, disturbed, perturbed, troubled, discomposed, restive; fidgety, edgy, on edge, jumpy, jittery, nervous; anxious, apprehensive, tense, queasy; upset, flustered, *Inf.* in a stew, agitated, unquiet, all of a flutter, all of a twitter; stirred up, ruffled, flurried, on pins and needles, *Sl.* all hot and bothered; put out, rattled, disquieted, ill-at-ease.

uneducated, *adj.* **1.** ignorant, illiterate, unlettered, uninstructed, untaught, unschooled, untutored, undisciplined, unlearned; green, raw, wide-eyed, innocent; inexperienced, unaccomplished.

2. unaware, unacquainted, unconversant, unapprised, uninformed, uninitiated, unenlightened, unread; unknowing, unwitting, blind, nescient, in the dark, knowing nothing, *Sl.* out of it.

3. uncultivated, unrefined, rude, crude, uncultured, lowbrow; superficial, shallow, sciolistic, unscholarly, half-baked.

unembellished, *adj.* unadorned, unornamented, unvarnished, inelegant, unostentatious; basic, bare, pure, severe, stark, austere; lean, spare, Spartan; uncolored, colorless, monotonous, uninteresting, dull; unfinished, raw, unrefined, rough, unpainted; plain, simple, modest, humble, unaffected, unpretentious, unpretending, unassuming; nondescript, prosaic, matter-of-fact; ordinary, common, commonplace, usual, familiar, everyday, workday, workaday, household-variety, garden-variety; (*of music*) straight-ahead, unexperimental.

unemotional, *adj.* unexcitable, unmoved, unstirred, unkindled, unperturbed, unsusceptible, unimpressionable, unimpressible; apathetic, phlegmatic, listless, languid; lukewarm, neutral, nonchalant, indifferent; sedate, self-controlled, sober, staid, stoical, philosophical; stiff, formal, *Inf.* tight, *Sl.* uptight; reserved, shy, demure; calm, composed, poised, quiet, unruffled, placid; undemonstrative, unresponsive, unaffectionate, distant, aloof; cool, cold, frigid; impervious, stony, steely, flinty; hardened, obdurate, callous, thickskinned; unimpassioned, untouched, indurate, inured.

unemployed, *adj.* **1.** out of work, jobless, workless, laid off, out of a job; idle, inactive, unoccupied, unbusied; free, at liberty, at leisure, leisured, *Inf.* off.

2. inoperative, nonfunctioning, nonperforming; unapplied, unexercised, unused, *Sl.* on the shelf.

3. latent, untapped, unrealized.

unending, *adj.* **1.** endless, never-ending, interminable, perpetual; ceaseless, unceasing, incessant, nonstop, marathon; unimpeded, uninterrupted, continual, continuous, unbroken; unremitting, relentless, persistent; untiring, unwavering, unfaltering, undiminished.

2. enduring, lasting, abiding, eternal, everlasting, *Literary.* sempiternal, aeonian, perennial; immutable, invariable, constant, fixed, stable, durable, steady, permanent.

unendurable, *adj.* unbearable, intolerable, insufferable, insupportable, more than flesh and blood can bear, enough to provoke a saint, enough to drive one mad, enough to try the patience of Job, *Inf.* too much.

unenthusiastic, *adj.* indifferent, apathetic, uninterested, nonchalant, blasé, pococurante; unimpressed, unmoved, unstirred, unresponsive; neutral, lukewarm, unconcerned, uncaring; unexcitable, unemotional, sedate, self-controlled, staid, stoical, philosophical; distant, aloof, cool, cold, frigid; hardened, obdurate, callous, thickskinned, inured.

unequal, *adj.* **1.** different, differing, dissimilar, disparate, unlike, unmatched, unidentical; not uniform, varying, variant, variable; incongruous, incompatible, inharmonious.

2. *Often* **unequal to** inadequate, insufficient, incommensurate, found wanting, not up to, deficient, lacking, wanting, too little, not enough.

3. unbalanced, lopsided, unsymmetrical, asymmetrical, unequalized, uneven, disproportioned, disproportionate, irregular; top-heavy, bottom-heavy, overbalanced.

4. unfair, not equitable, unjust, one-sided; biased, prejudiced, bigoted, partisan, partial.

unequaled, *adj.* **1.** matchless, peerless, unparalleled, unmatched, unrivaled, without equal, *Fr. sans pareil*; incomparable, inimitable, unmatchable; unsurpassed, unapproachable, beyond compare; consummate, perfect, transcendent, quintessential, superlative, impeccable; sterling, gilt-edged, precious, golden; rare, priceless, unique, one of a kind.

2. supreme, greatest, chief, foremost, first, great; best, best ever, champion, *Australian.* bonzer, top, A-1; top-notch, topflight, tiptop, first-rate, first-class, front-rank; elite, choice, select; paramount, second to none, *Latin. nulli secundus*, dominant; prime, cardinal, preeminent.

unequivocal, *adj.* **1.** unambiguous, clear, clear-cut, crystal-clear, unmistakable, unquestionable, incontrovertible; undeniable, irrefutable, irrefragable, indubitable, infallible, unchallenged, incontestable, apodictic, indisputable; evident, plain, obvious, palpable, manifest, apparent, distinct, well-defined; official, confirmed, authoritative.

2. absolute, determinate, certain, veritable, explicit, express; unqualified, categorical, unconditional, unconditioned, unreserved, unrestricted, unlimited, total; outright, downright, out-and-out, straight-out, all-out; direct, straightforward, straight-from-the-shoulder; blunt, bluff, brusque, point-blank.

3. conclusive, sure, confident, settled, fixed, definite, definitive, decided, decisive, pronounced; unavoidable, inescapable.

unerring, *adj.* **1.** certain, sure, positive, definite, fixed; absolute, unfailing, sure-footed, infallible, inerrable; correct, right, *Inf.* on the mark, on target, *Inf.* right on, *Sl.* spot on; on the button, on the dot, *Inf.* on the nose, *Sl.* on the beam.

2. exact, precise, accurate, close, faithful, strict; flawless, faultless, perfect, defectless, errorless, inerrant; factual, actual, literal, true to life; authentic, real, sound, valid; true, truthful, veracious.

unessential, *adj.* **1.** unnecessary, unneeded, needless, superfluous, redundant, expendable, dispensable, unrequired, uncalled-for, unasked-for, gratuitous;

negligible, unimportant, of little *or* small importance, of no importance, of no great importance, inconsequential, of little *or* no consequence, insignificant, of no significance, inconsiderable, inappreciable, of no concern, of no matter, of no account; irrelevant, immaterial, inapplicable, inapt, unconnected, inapposite, inconsequent, beside the point *or* mark, beside the question, off the subject.

2. extrinsic, extrinsical, extraneous, external, incidental, adventitious; extra, additional, supplementary, supplemental, adscititious; subsidiary, subordinate, secondary, accessory, collateral; circumstantial, contingent, conditional, provisional, dependent.

3. meager, paltry, puny; petty, trivial, trifling; little, small, minute, *Sl.* dinky; bush-league, *Inf.* small-time, *Sl.* two-bit, *Sl.* small potatoes.

—n. **4.** nonessential, inessential, accidental; secondary, subsidiary, auxiliary, supplement; appendage, appurtenance, addition, addendum.

unethical, *adj.* unprincipled, immoral, unconscionable, unscrupulous, unprofessional; wrong, illegal, unlawful, lawless, illegitimate; dishonest, deceitful, crooked, under-the-table; foul, unsportsmanlike, below-the-belt, *Sl.* dirty, underhand, underhanded; questionable, *Inf.* shady; bad, sinful, dishonorable, disreputable, discreditable; perverted, warped, debauched; corrupt, depraved, reprobate, unredeemable; wicked, evil, iniquitous; unfair, unjust, inequitable; mean, vicious, unkind, uncompassionate.

uneven, *adj.* **1.** rough, rugged, hubbly, not level, not flat; coarse, unsmooth, unpolished, rough-hewn, rough-grained; jagged, broken, abrupt; gnarled, lumpy.

2. irregular, varying, not uniform; dissimilar, differing, unmatched, unequal, odd.

3. unfair, not equitable, one-sided; (*usu. racially*) imbalanced.

4. unbalanced, asymmetrical, not parallel, lopsided, ill-matched, top-heavy.

uneventful, *adj.* monotonous, humdrum, routine, smooth, unvaried, undiversified, all the same, uniform; usual, customary, normal, average, expected, regular; standard, cut-and-dried, unexceptional; dull, tedious, tiresome, boring, boresome, wearisome; prosaic, prosy, matter-of-fact, uninteresting, unimpressive, ho-hum, *Sl.* dead, dry, dry-as-dust, unexciting, uninspiring, dreary, heavy; ordinary, run-of-the-mill, common, commonplace, everyday, familiar, conventional; unvarying, unchanging, undeviating, repetitious; banausic, mechanical, practical.

unexacting, *adj.* **1.** easygoing, relaxed, *Inf.* laid-back, casual, placid, cool, unruffled, *Inf.* together; calm, carefree, unconcerned, careless, nonchalant, happy-go-lucky, cheerful; unconfined, unconfining, unconstraining, unrestricting.

2. patient, tolerant, understanding, uncritical, accepting; loose, lax, soft; unstrict, undemanding, nonrestrictive; permissive, lenient, overpermissive, overindulgent, easy, *Inf.* wishy-washy, weak.

unexampled, *adj.* unprecedented, unparalleled, unequaled, unmatched, unheard-of; unusual, uncommon, unique, incomparable, one of a kind, special, singular, individual, distinctive, different, recherché; out-of-the-ordinary, unconventional, unorthodox, novel, new; rare, unwonted, uncustomary, unfamiliar, out-of-the-way; atypical, anomalous; first, original, premier; archetypal, prototypal, prototypical, prototypic.

unexceptional, *adj.* **1.** ordinary, usual, conventional, regular, average; typical, general, prevalent, common; familiar, known, everyday, standard, *Inf.* G.I.; commonplace, run-of-the-mill, household, garden-variety, stereotypical, workaday; undistinguished, insignificant, second-rate, third-rate; unimpressive, so-so, humdrum, mediocre, *Inf.* dime-a-dozen, *Sl.* cotton-picking, *Sl.* no great shakes; inconsequential, of little *or* small *or* no importance, trivial, piddling, *Inf.* bush-league *or* minor-league, *Sl.* small potatoes, *Sl.* small-time, *Sl.* two-bit.

2. flat, categorical, absolute, inflexible, dogmatic, rigid; closed, sealed, final.

3. unexceptionable, unobjectionable, acceptable, admissible, agreeable, passable, good enough, *Inf.* O.K., *Inf.* all right; faultless, flawless, unblemished, spotless; commendable, creditable, praiseworthy, laudable, meritorious; unimpeachable, irreproachable, irreprehensible, inculpable, above suspicion.

unexpected, *adj.* unforeseen, unanticipated, unlooked-for, unpredicted; sudden, abrupt, precipitate; surprising, astonishing, startling; unwonted, unusual, unpredictable, accidental, undesigned, unintentional, unintended, unpurposed, fortuitous, extemporaneous; untimely, unseasonable, out of the blue.

unexpressive, *adj.* expressionless, impassive, inscrutable, deadpan, *Inf.* poker-faced; blank, vacant, empty; passionless, inanimate, unemotional, cold; apathetic, indifferent, unresponsive, unfeeling; bland, inane, insipid, jejune, dead, lifeless, spiritless, flat, *Sl.* blah, *Sl.* nothing.

unfailing, *adj.* **1.** certain, sure, *Inf.* surefire, tried and true; dependable, reliable, to be depended *or* relied upon, trustworthy, trusty, as good as one's word; loyal, faithful, constant, true, true-blue; steady, steadfast, staunch, solid; unfading, lasting, enduring, abiding, perpetual.

2. inexhaustible, exhaustless, limitless, unlimited, boundless, unbounded, measureless, immeasurable, innumerable, numberless, countless, infinite.

3. infallible, unerring, inerrable, incapable of error.

unfair, *adj.* **1.** unjust, inequitable, unequal, uneven, unbalanced, one-sided; partial, partisan, prejudiced, interested, undispassionate, prepossessed, biased, warped, jaundiced.

2. unrightful, wrongful, wrong; undue, undeserved, unmerited, unwarranted, uncalled-for; unreasonable, unconscionable, unjustifiable, unwarrantable; disproportionate, out of proportion, excessive, extreme, inordinate, immoderate, drastic.

3. foul, unsportsmanlike, unsporting, below-the-belt, *Sl.* dirty; underhand, dishonest, dishonorable, deceitful, crooked; unscrupulous, unprincipled, unconscientious.

unfaithful, *adj.* **1.** disloyal, false, false-hearted, perfidious, traitorous, treacherous; faithless, inconstant, unsteady, unsteadfast, untrustworthy, undependable, unreliable, not to be depended *or* relied upon; recreant, renegade, apostate, backsliding; adulterous, *Inf.* two-timing.

2. inaccurate, inexact, imprecise, unprecise; faulty, flawed, defective; incomplete, unfinished, sketchy, patchy; incorrect, wrong, erroneous, untrue, fallacious.

3. insincere, disingenuous, uncandid, hypocritical, two-faced, Janus-faced, double-dealing, mendacious, timeserving; insidious, artful, cunning, shifty, slippery; dishonest, dishonorable, deceitful, crooked; unscrupulous, unprincipled, unconscientious.

unfaltering, *adj.* untiring, unfailing, unflagging, unbending; tireless, indefatigable, dogged, pertinacious, persistent, persevering, tenacious, zealous, relentless, sedulous, assiduous; constant, steady, steadfast, staunch, unwavering, unswerving, undeviating, unhesitating, resolute, resolved, firm, determined; indomitable, inexorable, intransigent, inflexible, obstinate, unyielding.

unfamiliar, *adj.* **1.** unacquainted, unconversant, unversed, unused to, a stranger to; unpracticed, unskilled; ignorant, unenlightened, uninformed, uninitiated; inexperienced, raw, green, unseasoned, wet behind the ears.

2. new, newfangled, novel, original; different, unconventional, unusual, uncommon, unorthodox, unique, out of the ordinary; unaccustomed, uncustomary, unwonted; unknown, unheard-of, unexampled, unparalleled; strange, weird, bizarre, *Sl.* freaky, *Sl.* rum, *Sl.* far-out; eccentric, offbeat, quizzical, odd, oddish, *Sl.* oddball, cranky, curious, queer, *Inf.* funny, *Inf.* kinky.

3. unexplored, uncharted, uninvestigated.

unfashionable, *adj.* **1.** out-of-fashion, out-of-style, out, not in, tacky; outworn, timeworn, outmoded, outdated, dated, out-of-date, behind-the-times; obsolete, extinct, dead, defunct, passé, *Inf.* old-hat, *Inf.* back-number; obsolescent, on the way out.

2. unorthodox, unconventional, improper, not done, not kosher, *Brit.* not cricket, *Sl.* not on.

unfasten, *v.* detach, free, separate, undo, open, loose, disjoint; set free, part, sever, cut, let go; unlace, untie, unlash, untether, unloose; unhitch, unbutton, unhasp, unfix, unlock, unlatch, unhook, unlink, unzipper; loosen, release, unharness, unshackle, unfetter, unchain, unpinion, unhandcuff; unbar, unpin, unbolt, unbuckle; disengage, cut off, cut adrift, cast off, unmoor.

unfathomable, *adj.* **1.** impenetrable, incomprehensible, past *or* beyond comprehension, unknowable, inscrutable, incognizable, indecipherable, undecipherable, beyond understanding; profound, deep, esoteric, recondite, abstruse, abstract, heavy, *Sl.* heavy-duty; mystic, mystical, cabalistic, supernatural; occult, cryptic, perdu, secret, hidden, concealed, shrouded; obscure, vague, dim, dark, nebulous, *Rare.* imperspicuous; mysterious, arcane, inexplicable, unexplainable, insolvable, insoluble, unaccountable, inextricable; puzzling, enigmatic, enigmatical.

2. bottomless, soundless, unsounded, fathomless, unfathomed, plumbless, unplumbed, measureless, unmeasured; abysmal, cavernous, plunging; deepsea, deep as the sea *or* ocean, deep as a well.

unfavorable, *adj.* **1.** contrary, adverse, antagonistic, hostile, opposing, opposed; antithetical, counter, converse, contradictory; inimical, negatory, discordant, counteracting, conflicting, contrasting.

2. unpropitious, inauspicious, unlucky, unpromising, untoward, ill, bad, foul; ominous, threatening, lowering, gloomy, dark; menacing, portentous, ill-boding, ill-starred, sinister, ill-omened, ill-fated, doomed; infelicitous, untimely, inopportune, cross, unseasonable.

3. unfortunate, unlucky, disadvantageous, unhappy; noxious, inhibitive, discouraging, disserviceable; detrimental, objectionable, discommodious, undesirable; inconvenient, inexpedient, inapt, inadvisable, unwise.

unfeeling, *adj.* **1.** insensible, insensate, numb, sensationless, feelingless; senseless, insentient, unperceiving; anesthetized, drugged, sedated, paralyzed, dazed, in shock; dead, unconscious, out, under, lifeless.

2. callous, cold, unsympathetic, hard-hearted, hard; insensitive, thickskinned, unimpressionable, unemotional; casehardened, hardened, hard-boiled, indurate, hard-nosed; uncaring, indifferent, obdurate, impervious, unconcerned; pitiless, merciless, ruthless, adamantine, inhuman, cold-hearted; stiff, tough, stern, harsh, unforgiving; unsparing, unmerciful, uncompassionate, untouched; unmoved, unimpressible, stony, flinty, hard-bitten, emotionless.

unfeigned, *adj.* sincere, genuine, earnest, natural, unaffected, unpretended; heartfelt, truthful, candid, frank, straightforward, forward, square; honest, veracious, undeceitful, right, up front; aboveboard, straight-from-the-shoulder, all wool and a yard wide; open-hearted, uncorrupted, forthright, undissembling; guileless, artless, innocent, naive, unsophisticated, ingenuous, simple; pure, plain, direct, unreserved, blunt, outspoken, open.

unfinished, *adj.* **1.** incomplete, uncompleted, deficient, lacking, wanting, imperfect; inchoate, rough, sketchy, crude, raw, undeveloped, insufficient, inadequate, half-baked, *U.S. Sl.* half-cocked, *Sl.* half-assed.

2. undone, unexecuted, unaccomplished, unfulfilled, not carried out; unattended to, postponed, shelved; ignored, omitted, overlooked, skipped, missed; forgotten, neglected, not taken care of.

3. unpainted, unvarnished, unstained; untouched, unchanged, natural.

unfit, *adj.* **1.** unsuitable, unsuited, ill-suited, inappropriate, undue, unfitting, unbefitting, unmeet, unseemly; malapropos, inapt, unapt, inapplicable, inapposite, irrelevant, ungermane, nongermane, unpertinent, off the mark, beside the point *or* question; improper, impertinent, out of place, uncalled-for, objectionable; unseasonable, untimely, ill-timed, inopportune, improvident, inexpedient; imprudent, unwise, ill-advised, inadvisable, injudicious, foolish.

2. unqualified, ineligible, unprepared, unready, unequipped, ill-equiped, not cut out for; deficient, lacking, inadequate, insufficient; unskilled, untrained, undisciplined, undeveloped, raw, crude; incompetent, inept, incapable, unable, *Sl.* half-assed; inefficient, ineffectual, ineffective, useless, no good.

3. in poor condition *or* shape, out of shape, flabby; debilitated, incapacitated, infirm, decrepit, *Inf.* dotty; enervated, enervate, weak, *Pathol.* asthenic; exhausted, spent, tired, not up to; frail, delicate, puny, weakly, sickly, anemic, unhealthy, ailing, *Scot.* shilpit.
—*v.* **4.** disqualify, make ineligible, put [s.o.] out of the running, eliminate; disable, incapacitate, debilitate, impair, hamstring, cripple, lame, maim, injure, harm, hurt; enfeeble, weaken, enervate, sap, deplete, wear down *or* out, exhaust, fatigue, tire, tire out, *Sl.* poop *or* poop out.

unfix, *v.* undo, separate, unhook, unclasp, unlatch. See **unfasten.**

unflagging, *adj.* unfailing, untiring, tireless, indefatigable, unswerving, unwavering, undeviating, unbending, unfaltering, unremitting; determined, decided, resolute, resolved, firm, steady, steadfast, purposeful; staunch, constant, persevering, persistent; sedulous, intent, earnest, fixed; game, plucky, spunky, *Inf.* scrappy; dogged, tenacious, gritty, relentless, unrelenting, *Inf.* hellbent, do-or-die; unhesitating, unflinching, unyielding, indomitable; obstinate, bulldog, stubborn.

unflinching, *adj.* unshrinking, unfaltering, unshaken, unwavering, unflagging, unswerving, undeviating; firm, resolute, resolved, determined, staunch, steadfast, stalwart, *Archaic.* stalworth; grim, unrelenting, relentless, indefatigable, dogged, pertinacious, tenacious, constant, fixed; indomitable, redoubtable, invincible, unconquerable, unyielding, unbending, unbowing; brave, fearless, dauntless, dreadless, unafraid, unblenching, undaunted; mettlesome, *Sl.* gutsy, plucky, gritty.

unfold, *v.* **1.** open, unbend, unwind, unfurl, unroll, uncoil, undo; extend, spread out, expand, straighten, stretch out.

2. display, set forth, present, exhibit, show, uncover, air, demonstrate; manifest, bare, reveal, expose, disclose; hold up to view, bring to light, unveil, uncloak, undrape; publish, publicize, post.

3. explain, define, interpret, explicate, expound, comment on, point out; simplify, make plain, delineate, put across, spell out, get across; decipher, decode, render intelligible, untangle, unravel; clarify, elucidate, clear up, resolve.

4. develop, grow, evolve, fill out, increase, expand, wax, become greater *or* larger; mature, maturate, ripen; bloom, blossom, flower, bear fruit, fructify; sprout, germinate, bud, shoot.

unforeseen, *adj.* unexpected, unanticipated, unlooked-for, unpredicted. See **unexpected.**

unforgivable, *adj.* inexcusable, unpardonable, uncondonable, irremissible, unexpiable, unatonable, inexonerable; unwarrantable, unjustifiable, unvindicable, unexculpable; indefensible, undefendable, untenable; reprehensible, deplorable, contemptible, despicable, condemnable, censurable, blameworthy; outrageous, scandalous, shameful, disgraceful, ignoble, vile, abject, low; heinous, grievous, ghastly, horrible, terrible, awful, atrocious, abominable, abhorrent, odious, *Brit.* beastly.

unfortunate, *adj.* **1.** unlucky, luckless, out of luck, down on one's luck, hapless, *Inf.* jinxed, born under an evil star, cursed; unsuccessful, unprosperous, fortuneless, poor, wretched, unblessed, hopeless; unhappy, woebegone, pathetic, forlorn, pitiable, miserable.

2. untoward, unfavorable, unpromising, adverse, ill, contrary, unpropitious, inauspicious; untimely, inopportune, unseasonable, disadvantageous; ill-fated, ill-starred, star-crossed, ill-omened, doomed; ill-boding, ominous, sinister, hostile, threatening, portentous, menacing, malign, minatory.

3. deplorable, lamentable, regrettable, distressing, upsetting, disturbing, *Inf.* too bad; afflicting, tormenting, troublesome; unforeseeable, tragic, calamitous, heinous, outrageous, grievous, disastrous; somber, solemn, grave, heavy, oppressive.

unfounded, *adj.* unsupported, ungrounded, groundless, unsound, unbased, baseless, without basis, idle, vain; unattested, unevidenced, unproven, uncorroborated, unsubstantiated, unauthorized, unestablished; conjectural, speculative, suppositional, hypothetical, academic, academical, theoretical, imaginary, illusory; unsubstantial, tenuous, faulty, erroneous, apocryphal.

unfriendly, *adj.* **1.** aloof, distant, cool, cold, unamicable, unamiable, uncongenial, *Scot.* fremd; unsociable, unneighborly, inhospitable, unaccommodating, ungracious; unkind, unkindly, unsympathetic, ill-disposed, antipathetic; hostile, antagonistic, aggressive, belligerent, bellicose; mean, crabbed, peevish, snappish, disagreeable; ugly, spiteful, surly, sour, malicious, malevolent; combative, contentious, fractious, quarrelsome, disputatious; estranged, on the outs, not on speaking terms.

2. inimical, harmful, unfavorable, unpropitious, inauspicious; lowering, bleak, threatening.

unfruitful, *adj.* unprofitable, unremunerative, ungainful, unrewarding; unyielding, unproductive, unfructuous, fruitless, infertile, infecund, barren, sterile; exhausted, depleted, worn out, used up, poor, impoverished, fallow.

ungainly, *adj.* **1.** awkward, clumsy, ungraceful; unhandy, inept, inexpert, unskillful, maladroit, bumbling, clownish, bungling, bunglesome, blundering; ambisinister, left-handed, *Inf.* all thumbs, *Inf.* butterfingered, *Sl.* klutzy, like a bull in a china shop; oafish, cloddish, lumbering, heavy-footed, lubberly, bovine, lumpish; stiff, wooden, stodgy, stolid, heavy, unwieldy, bulky, big, hulking.

2. coarse, rough, unpolished, unsophisticated, rustic, backwoods, *Inf.* hick, uncouth, rude, boorish, crude; crass, gross, insensitive, inconsiderate, thoughtless, tactless, gauche.

ungodly, *adj.* **1.** irreligious, unreligious, nonreligious, atheistic, disbelieving, unbelieving, nonbelieving, godless, nonspiritual; infidel, infidelic, heathenish, heathen, pagan, paganistic, unenlightened; agnostic, skeptical, doubting, questioning, Pyrrhonistic, nihilistic.

2. impious, irreverent, disrespectful, unrespectful; heretical, iconoclastic, antireligious, antichristian; sacrilegious, blasphemous, profane, cursing, swearing; bad, evil, sinful, wicked, black-hearted, sinister, iniquitous, *Archaic.* facinorous, *Obs.* scelerous; nefarious, villainous, flagitious, heinous; vile, foul, mean, base, low, dirty, odious, obnoxious; abominable, atrocious, execrable, hideous, grisly, gruesome, unspeakable; maleficient, malefic, malevolent, evil-minded; demonic, demoniac, diabolic, devilish, fiendish, satanic, hellish, infernal.

3. perfidious, treacherous, insidious, traitorous, back-stabbing; unscrupulous, unprincipled, crooked, dishonest; unregenerate, unrepentant, impenitent, obdurate, incorrigible, reprobate; degenerate, corrupt, depraved, *Rare.* turpid; immoral, amoral, nonmoral, dissolute, profligate, reprobate, dissipated; opprobrious, disgraceful, shameful; contemptible, scurvy, abhorrent, loathsome, hateful, detestable, despicable, revolting, repulsive, repugnant, disgusting.

4. *Informal.* dreadful, insufferable, unbearable, intolerable; appalling, shocking, outrageous, awful, god-awful, terrible, horrible, horrid, horrendous, monstrous, frightful; nasty, unkind, disagreeable, unpleasant, *Chiefly Brit. Inf.* beastly, mean, cruel.

ungovernable, *adj.* uncontrollable, unmanageable, irrepressible, unrestrainable, wild, out of control, out of hand; unruly, intractable, disobedient, recalcitrant, obstinate, stubborn, refractory, restive; incorrigible, hopeless, lost, reprobate.

ungracious, *adj.* **1.** rude, discourteous, impolite, uncivil, unceremonious, unmannerly, bad-mannered, ill-bred, disrespectful, misbehaved; indelicate, uncourtly, ungallant, indecorous; ungentlemanly, unladylike, brash, bold, hoydenish, *Scot.* randy; brazen, barefaced, insolent, impudent, insulting, impertinent, pert, saucy, fresh; bluff, surly, sullen, bearish, gruff; inconsiderate, tactless, *Scot. and North Eng.* misleared; abrupt, blunt, brusque, curt, clipped, short; rough, crude, boorish, churlish, loutish, vulgar, coarse.

2. thankless, unpopular, unacceptable, unpalatable; uninviting, undesirable, unenviable; unrewarding, unrequited; unavowed, unacknowledged, unremembered, forgotten.

ungrateful, *adj.* **1.** unthankful, thankless, unappreciative, biting the hand that feeds you; impolite, rude, uncivil.

2. unpleasant, disagreeable, distasteful, repellent, repugnant, repulsive, disgusting.

unguarded, *adj.* **1.** unprotected, unarmored, unshielded, unfortified, defenseless, exposed, uncovered; vulnerable, pregnable, assailable, open to attack; guardless, unwatched, unpatrolled, undefended; weaponless, unarmed.

2. open, open and sincere, frank, candid, openhearted, genuine; guileless, ingenuous, artless, naive, simple, undeceptive, undeceiving, undeceitful, undissembling; honest, aboveboard, open and aboveboard, up front, on the level, on the up and up, no-nonsense.

3. careless, incautious, uncautious, headless,

unheeding, inattentive, inadvertent, unmindful, mindless, unthinking; unwary, unchary, unwatchful, nonobservant, unobservant, unvigilant; off one's guard, sleeping, asleep on the job, napping, daydreaming, looking out the window, staring into space, lost in thought, *Sl.* out to lunch; uncircumspect, indiscreet, imprudent, injudicious, unwise, ill-considered, ill-advised; foolish, foolhardy, irresponsible, reckless, rash, temerarious, harebrained, hasty, impetuous, impulsive, brash; thoughtless, inconsiderate, tactless, untactful.

unguent, *n.* ointment, salve, unguentum, *Pharm.* inunction; balm, liniment, nard, lotion, emollient, demulcent, embrocation; cream, cold cream, pomade, brilliantine.

unhallowed, *adj.* **1.** unconsecrated, unblessed, unsanctified; unpurified, unholy, impious, impure; irreligious, infidel, ungodly, fleshly; unsacred, unregenerate, reprobate; blasphemous, sacrilegious, profane.

2. wicked, sinful, godless, evil, irreverent; damnable, devilish, demonic, satanic, fiendish, infernal; dark, iniquitous, nefarious, vile, base; accursed, cursed, damned, condemned; corrupt, depraved, polluted, immoral, shameful; foul, black, bad, heinous.

unhappy, *adj.* **1.** sad, disconsolate, dejected, depressed, despondent, melancholic; forlorn, woeful, woebegone, *Obs.* baleful, downhearted, heartsick, broken-hearted, crestfallen, crushed, broken; blue, heavy-hearted, long-faced, somber, heavy, glum; low-spirited, disheartened, discouraged, *Inf.* broken-up, *Inf.* cut-up, cast down, *Sl.* bummed-out; desolate, despairing, hopeless, worried, afflicted, grieved, stricken, heavy-laden; mournful, sorrowful, dolorous, doleful, lachrymose, inconsolable; tearful, rueful, joyless, cheerless, grief-stricken; forlorn, chapfallen, pessimistic, plaintive, downcast, unmanned, *Inf.* down in the mouth.

2. unfortunate, unlucky, hapless, luckless, unprosperous, out of luck; unblessed, hopeless, wretched, cursed, accursed, crossed; ill-starred, ill-fated, star-crossed, born under an evil star; jinxed, hoodooed, Jonahesque, under a cloud, born with a wooden ladle in one's mouth; balked, thwarted, jilted, victimized, dashed, foiled; bereft, poor, unsuccessful, impoverished, born on the wrong side of the tracks.

3. unfavorable, inauspicious, unpropitious, unlucky, unpromising; ill-omened, ill-boding, ill, foul, sinister, bad, malign; ominous, menacing, threatening, minacious, lowering, looming; unseasonable, untimely, inopportune, disadvantageous; discouraging, indisposed, opposed, antagonistic, inhibitive.

4. infelicitous, unsuitable, inappropriate, inapt, malapropos; incorrect, out of place, awkward, injudicious; inapposite, unadvisable, ill-advised, impertinent, unwise; unbefitting, indecorous, unbecoming; inexpedient, foolish, inept, out of keeping.

unharmed, *adj.* unhurt, unimpaired, uninjured, undamaged, unscathed, unburned; unmarred, unmarked, undefaced, unscarred, unscratched; intact, inviolate, virgin, unspoiled; untouched, unmolested, safe, sound, out of danger, on the safe side; whole, entire, perfect, undeformed, in perfect condition, without a scratch.

unhealthy, *adj.* **1.** sick, sickly, unsound, in poor health; ill, unwell, ailing, *Inf.* poorly, indisposed, *Inf.* under the weather; afflicted, weak, feeble, frail, delicate, fragile, debilitated; infirm, drooping, withered, worn-out, enervated, spent, played out, helpless, exhausted; decrepit, failing, senile, impotent; on the decline, reduced to skin and bones, skeleton-like, cadaverous; diseased, invalid, valetudinary, bedridden, impaired, in the hospital, hospitalized.

2. noxious, unwholesome, insalubrious, deleterious, baneful, detrimental; injurious, damaging, hurtful, harmful; bad for, unsalutary, unhealthful, peccant, virulent; fell, unfavorable, ruinous, destructive; malignant, malign, malevolent, maleficent; corrosive, corrupting, corruptive, pernicious; unhygienic, unsanitary, malnutritious, unnourishing; toxic, septic, poisonous, pestilential, morbiferous, morbific.

3. bad, degrading, corrupting, demoralizing, polluting; foul, evil, dirty, filthy, vitiating, sinful; contaminating, sickening, unfavorable, baneful; corrupt, offensive, mean, base, degenerate, shameful.

unheard-of, *adj.* **1.** unknown, unfamiliar, unexplained, unidentified; untouched, unexplored, uncharted, unrevealed, undiscovered, untapped; obscure, little-known, unnoted, unremarked, nameless; unrenowned, unsung, unhonored, uncelebrated, unfamed; undistinguished, unpopular, inglorious.

2. unprecedented, unexampled, new, novel, exceptional; original, unique, uncommon, unusual, singular; unordinary, out of the ordinary, offbeat, off the beaten track; surprising, unexpected, undreamed-of, freakish, recherché; unaccustomed, unwonted, never before encountered, improbable; unmatched, unparalleled, matchless, incomparable, unequaled; extraordinary, remarkable, sensational, marvelous, fabulous, fantastic, stupendous, tremendous, terrific.

unheeded, *adj.* ignored, disregarded, overlooked, neglected; unnoticed, unnoted, unobserved, unseen, unperceived; unminded, unobeyed, unfollowed, untaken.

unheralded, *adj.* untrumpeted, unannounced, unproclaimed, unadvertised, unpublicized, unpublished, unbroadcast; unexpected, unanticipated, unlooked-for, unforeseen, unpredicted, unprophesied; out of the blue *or* nowhere, sudden, abrupt, precipitate, surprise, sneak. See also **unsung.**

unhesitating, *adj.* **1.** prompt, ready, immediate, intant, instantaneous, without delay; confident, assured, sure, certain, positive; believing, undoubting, unreserved, implicit, unquestioning, wholehearted.

2. unfaltering. See **unfaltering.**

unhinge, *v.* **1.** detach, disconnect, disengage, disjoin, separate, sever, cleave, part; remove, take away; open wide, split open.

2. unbalance, derange, distemper; make crazy *or* mad *or* insane, drive wild, drive out of one's mind, push over the brink, *Sl.* make [s.o.] crackers *or* bonkers; madden, craze, *Archaic.* bedlamize, *Obs.* dement; obsess, possess; disorient, confuse, confound, *Inf.* throw, overcome, *Inf.* flabbergast, *Inf.* slay, distract; perplex, bewilder, nonplus, *Sl.* blow one's mind, *Sl.* knock for a loop, knock over; upset, drive up the wall, agitate, *Sl.* drive nutty, perturb; disconcert, bother, trouble, disturb, distress; fluster, unnerve, shake, worry, rattle, abash, discompose; astound, astonish, stun, leave speechless.

3. unsettle, change, fluctuate, vary, alter, modify, mutate; disorder, disarrange, disarray, mess up, disorganize; tip over, turn topsy-turvy, move, stir; entangle, snarl, jumble, muddle, muddy.

unhoped-for, *adj.* unexpected, undreamed-of, beyond one's wildest hopes *or* dreams, like a dream come true; unanticipated, unlooked-for, unpredicted, unforeseen; surprising, out of the blue, astonishing, startling, astounding; unwonted, unusual, unpredictable; undesigned, unplanned, unintentional, unintended, unpurposed, extemporaneous; fortuitous, lucky, happy, serendipitous.

unhurried, *adj.* leisurely, leisured, slow, slow-moving, slow-going, deliberate; lingering, loitering, puttering, dillydallying, dawdling, *Inf.* poky, tortoise-like, snail-like, slow-paced; slow and steady, easy, easy-going, loose, loose as a goose, slack, lax; indolent, idle, otiose, slower than molasses in January, lazy; inactive, sluggish, torpid, inert, lethargic, listless, phlegmatic.

unidentified, *adj.* **1.** nameless, unknown, undefined, unidentifiable; unexplained, unfamiliar, unheard-of, strange, mysterious, occult, supernatural; unfathomed, unapprehended, perplexing, enigmatic, puzzling, inexplicable.

2. unrevealed, undivulged, secret, sub rosa, silent, confidential, anonymous, anon., incognito; unnamed, faceless, in the background, disguised, masked, veiled, camouflaged, unspecified, undesignated; obscure, concealed, hidden, in the dark, unseen, out of view, out of the limelight.

unification, *n.* union, junction, merger, fusion, alliance, amalgamation, coalescence, coalition, confederacy; association, confederation, consolidation, corporation; fraternization, getting together; unity, oneness, synthesis.

uniform, *adj.* **1.** consistent, unalterable, invariable, unchangeable; formalized, patterned, unvaried, homogeneous; regulated, standard, established, orderly, ordered, regimented, measured; agreeing, accordant, concordant, compatible, congruous, consonant, harmonious, conformable.

2. unvarying, same, similar, equivalent, identical, selfsame, exact, undiversified, unvariegated, of a sameness, alike, like, as like as two peas in a pod.

3. repetitious, repeated, recurrent, reiterative; usual, normal, customary, wonted, accustomed, habitual; analogous, parallel, symmetrical, correspondent, corresponding, related, akin, comparable, true to type.

4. regular, even, equable, undeviating, unvarying, unmoving, unchanging, constant, invariant; monotonous, flat, dull, plodding, day-in-day-out; predictable, foreseen, expected, unsurprising, certain, sure, as sure as death and taxes; colorless, toneless, drab, dun, tedious, boring, singsong, droning.

5. systematic, methodical, fixed, set; firm, fast, solid, steady, stable; permanent, abiding, enduring, immutable, incommutable, changeless, irreversible; perpetual, endless, unending, never-ending, interminable, everlasting; ceaseless, incessant, unceasing, nonstop, unbroken, uninterrupted; continual, continuous, unremitting, relentless, persistent.

—n. **6.** suit, dress, costume, livery, habit, garb; regalia, trappings.

uniformity, *n.* **1.** sameness, similarity, similitude, equality, equivalency; regularity, symmetry, evenness, homogeneity; order, system; constancy, invariability, stableness, firmness; permanence, lastingness; immutability, unalterability, unchangeability, invariability.

2. conformity, conformance, congruity, correspondence, agreement, consonance, accord, accordance; concord, concordance, harmony, compatibility; consistency, coherence, fitness, appropriateness.

3. monotony, dullness, drabness, deadness, flatness; routine, fixed routine, rut, groove, fixed schedule, treadmill; tedium, tediousness, wearisomeness, boredom, ennui, dreariness, stuffiness; changelessness, lack of variety, same old story, same old thing; iteration, reiteration, repetition, recurrence, redundancy, tautology.

unify, *v.* unite, bring together, fuse, meld, wed, marry, join, merge; link up, combine, coalesce, blend, amalgamate, commingle; confederate, federate.

unimaginable, *adj.* unthinkable, inconceivable, incredible, unbelievable, incogitable; impossible, implausible, out of the question, contrary to reason, unlikely; fantastic, absurd, unheard-of, undreamed-of, unthought-of; preposterous, ludicrous, outlandish, *Sl.* mind-boggling, *Sl.* mind-blowing.

unimaginative, *adj.* uninspired, dull, unremarkable, mediocre; unoriginal, commonplace, everyday, usual, trite, stock, matter-of-fact; hackneyed, stale, dead, platitudinous, tiresome, humdrum, monotonous; vapid, barren, lifeless, flat, dreary; tame, pedestrian, prosaic, literal, unpoetical, dry; unromantic, unembellished, unimpassioned, uninteresting, mundane; ordinary, common, tedious, prosy; insipid, tasteless, bland.

unimpassioned, *adj.* **1.** dispassionate, unemotional, unexcitable, imperturbable, unflappable; unruffled, unstirred, undisturbed, unexcited, unperturbed, untroubled, unflustered; collected, cool, calm, possessed, composed, controlled, cool-headed; impassive, undemonstrative, staid, sedate, philosophical; objective, deliberate, prudent, moderate, temperate; even-tempered, sane, poised, level-headed, reasonable, rational; impartial, unprejudiced, unbiased, fair; judicious, enlightened, circumspect.

2. unresponsive, unpassionate, unemotional, unfeeling, unsympathetic; cold, unloving, self-absorbed, out of touch; untouchable, unimpressible, hard, obtuse, thick, dull.

unimpeachable, *adj.* irreproachable, irreprehensible, blameless, irreprovable, inculpable; faultless, flawless, impeccable, errorless, stainless, spotless; perfect, correct, peerless, matchless, infallible, indefectible, consummate, ideal; unquestionable, unchallengeable, above reproach, like Caesar's wife; unassailable, unexceptionable, unattackable; honest, ethical, principled, respectable, creditable, estimable, honorable, moral; unobjectionable, inappealable, irrefutable, unconfutable, unquestionable, uncontestable, undeniable, admitting of no dispute.

unimpeded, *adj.* unhampered, unchecked, unblocked, unconstrained, unhindered, untrammeled; unstopped, unobstructed, unclogged, free, open, clear, clean; unencumbered, unhandicapped, free-sailing, smooth-sailing; unrestricted, unconfined, unbound, uninhibited, unrestrained, anything goes, no-holds-barred; freehand, full, unqualified, no strings, to one's heart's content.

unimportant, *adj.* insignificant, inconsequential, inconsiderable, of no consequence, of little *or* minor importance; unmomentous, of no matter *or* concern, of little *or* no account, of no great weight, of no moment; nonessential, trifling, immaterial, picayune, piddling, nugatory, negligible; slight, little, worthless, meaningless, inferior, light, trivial; not worth mentioning, not worth speaking of, *Inf.* no great shakes, not worth worrying about; petty, insubstantial, dinky, *Sl.* mickey mouse; two-by-four, bush-league, *Inf.* one-horse, *Inf.* small-time, *Sl.* two-bit; second-rate, uninfluential, small-fry, nondescript, *Inf.* penny ante.

unimposing, *adj.* **1.** unimpressive, unnoteworthy, humble, meager, unimportant, insignificant; little, slight, inconsequential, dinky, puny, inconsiderable; mediocre, so-so, inferior, worthless, nugatory; minor, second-rate, third-rate, ineffectual; obscure, of no account, beneath notice, secondary, peripheral.

2. easy, simple, undemanding, uncomplicated, effortless; facile, not difficult, plain-sailing, nothing to it; unburdensome, light, clear, like taking candy from a baby, like shooting fish in a barrel; *Inf.* soft, *Inf.* cushy, easy as pie, simple as ABC.

uninformed, *adj.* ignorant, unenlightened, unaware, incognizant, unintelligent; uninstructed, untaught, unlearned, uneducated, unschooled, unlettered, unversed, unconversant; unacquainted, a stranger to, uninitiated; unwarned, unadvised, unapprised, in the dark, nescient, *Inf.* out of it, *Sl.* out to lunch; green, young, inexperienced, raw.

uninhabited, *adj.* untenanted, tenantless, unoccupied, unpopulated, unpeopled, depopulated; deserted, abandoned, ghost, necropolitan; desolate, forsaken, godforsaken, isolated; lifeless, lone, lonely, solitary; unfrequented, unvisited, unsettled; vacant, empty, barren, waste.

uninhibited, *adj.* **1.** relaxed, informal, unceremonious, casual, familiar, free and easy; unreserved, unconstrained, unrepressed, hang-loose, free; natural, artless, ingenuous; open, candid, frank, up front, sincere, outspoken, free-spoken.

2. unimpeded, unhampered, unchecked, unblocked, unhindered. See **unimpeded.**

3. lax, loose, intemperate, immoderate, incontinent; startling, shocking, outrageous.

unintelligent, *adj.* **1.** stupid, dull-witted, *Inf.* dumb, fatuitous, insensate, *Brit. Inf.* gormless; empty-headed, brainless, mindless, *Rare.* insulse; dull, *Sl.* lamebrained, slow, *Inf.* dopey, *Inf.* dill, oxloke; unthinking, unreasoning, incognitant; dim-witted, slow-witted, half-witted, fat-witted, thick-witted, beef-witted, witless, unwitty; imbecilic, *Inf.* moronic, retarded, subnormal, deficient; dense, thick, obtuse, bovine.

2. unenlightened, uninformed, ignorant, unaware, incognizant. See **uninformed.**

unintelligible, *adj.* **1.** incomprehensible, uncomprehensible, inapprehensible, indecipherable, undecipherable, ununderstandable, Greek to one; meaningless, incoherent, inarticulate, jumbled, muddled.

2. mysterious, arcane, inexplicable, unexplainable, insolvable, insoluble, unaccountable; puzzling, enigmatic, enigmatical; occult, cryptic, perdu, secret, hidden; obscure, vague, nebulous; mystic, mystical, transcendental, cabalistic, supernatural; unknowable, incognizable, unfathomable, inscrutable.

unintentional, *adj.* accidental, unintended, inadvertent, unpremeditated, unplanned, undesigned, uncalculated, indeliberate; unconscious, involuntary, reflex, automatic, *Sl.* gut; unwitting, unthinking; spontaneous, unexpected, unforeseen, unanticipated, unlooked-for; chance, adventitious, fortuitous, serendipitous, *Inf.* fluky.

uninterested, *adj.* **1.** unconcerned, indifferent, blasé, apathetic, uninvolved, *Fr.* dégagé, disinterested; distant, aloof, remote, removed, *Sl.* turned-off, above it all; impassive, impassible, unemotional, dispassionate, passionless; unexcited, nonchalant, pococurante, perfunctory; lukewarm, Laodicean, cool; cold, chilly, icy, frigid; uncaring, unsympathetic, unsolicitous, unmoved, untouched, unstirred, unaffected; impenetrable, unimpressionable, unimpressible.

2. inattentive, preoccupied, oblivious, in a world of one's own, out of touch; bored, half-awake, drifting in and out, with one's head in the clouds.

uninteresting, *adj.* unexciting, dull, boring, unfunny, unamusing, unentertaining, unenjoyable; wearisome, tiresome, monotonous, humdrum, tedious, uneventful; dreary, drab, slow, colorless, without distinction; flat, tasteless, vapid, insipid, jejune, stale; lifeless, tame, barren, arid, *Sl.* blah; weak, lean, characterless, bloodless; unimaginative, pedestrian, prosaic, prosy, dry, unpoetical, unromantic; unrewarding, unsatisfying, ungratifying; average, undistinctive, everyday, ordinary, common, commonplace, usual; hackneyed, cliché, stock, literal; unmoving, unimpassioned, uninspiring.

uninvited, *adj.* **1.** unbidden, uncalled for, unasked; unsought, unbesought, unsolicited, unrequested; gratuitous, free, complimentary.

2. unwelcome, unwanted, unwished, undesired, unasked-for.

uninviting, *adj.* untempting, unappealing, undesirable, unattractive; disagreeable, unpleasant, unpleasing, distasteful; unpalatable, unsavory, untoothsome, unappetizing, nauseating, nauseous, sickening; disgusting, noisome, *Sl.* yukky, *Sl.* gross; repugnant, offensive, obnoxious, shocking, nasty; repulsive, repelling, repellent, revolting, objectionable.

union, *n.* **1.** unity, unitedness, oneness, singleness, coalescence, *Bot.* homogeny; uniformity, homogeneity, homogeneousness, sameness, conformity, consistency; agreement, consentaneity, consentaneousness, consensus, union, unanimity, accordance, accord; concord, concordance, concert, harmony, harmoniousness, rapport; compatability, congruity, congruousness, meeting, keeping, step, line; fusion, coherence, coherency, cohesion, connection, connectedness, *Genetics.* linkage, *Zool., Bot.* coadunation.

2. compound, composite, hybrid, mongrel, amalgam, alloy, *Chem.* levigation; composition, synthesis, consolidation, mosaic; mixture, mix, conglomeration, agglomeration, combine, blend, homogenization.

3. association, alliance, league, coalition, union, guild, consortium, syndication, conspiracy, cabal; company, partnership, joint concern, corporation, merger, monopoly, trust, alignment, bloc, cartel; society, organization, party, camorra; congregation, assemblage, assembly, convention, meeting, group, gathering, band, ring, gang, team, troop; community, circle, club, fraternity, brotherhood, lodge, clan, clique, fellowship.

4. marriage, matrimony, wedlock, wedding, espousing; coitus, intercourse, copulation, mating, coupling, sexual relationship, physical relationship; fornication, adultery, liaison, affair.

5. graft, splice, joint, seam, articulation; conjuncture, junction, juncture, intersection; confluence, convergence, concourse.

unique, *adj.* **1.** sole, single, solitary, only, lone; one and only, *Zool., Bot.* azygous, exclusive, individual; unrepeated, odd, absolute; first and last, only begotten, one of a kind, in a class by itself, *Latin. sui generis.*

2. unequaled, unparalleled, peerless, incomparable, matchless; unexampled, inimitable, nonpareil, unapproached, unrivaled, unmatched; unexcelled, unsurpassed, without equal, beyond compare, second to none, *Latin. nulli secundus.*

3. rare, strange, singular, uncommon, infrequent, seldom-met, few and far between; peculiar, distinctive, special, exceptional, particular, marked, quintessential; unheard-of, different, novel, new, original, unfamiliar.

unit, *n.* **1.** element, component, constituent, member, part, item, piece, section, segment, portion.

2. measure, quantity, unit of measure, module.

unite, *v.* **1.** combine, mix, commix, admix, conglomerate, agglomerate; amalgamate, blend, homogenize; commingle, mingle, intermingle, intermix, lump together.

2. join, bond, fuse, weld, glue, cohere, stick together, hold together; yoke, bind, tie together; connect, link, chain, attach, inosculate; mate, couple, partner, twin, pair *or* match up.

3. marry, tie the knot, make man and wife; *Sl.* splice, *Archaic.* husband; wed, join in holy wedlock *or* matrimony.

4. associate, affiliate, ally; coalesce, league, club; team, band, herd, pool, merge; syndicate, federate, confederate, incorporate.

5. cooperate, work *or* act together, concert, harmonize, act in concert *or* harmony; join forces, pull together, cast one's lot with, stand shoulder to shoulder, work side by side.

6. unify, bring *or* draw together, make close, grow together, ankylose, become one; solidify, consolidate, congeal, gel, strengthen.

unity, *n.* 1. oneness, singleness, singularity, individuality, union, wholeness, congruity, congruousness; homogeneity, homogeneousness, identicalness, identity, sameness, uniformity; alikeness, similarity, similitude, likeness, resemblance, semblance; closeness, comparableness, comparability, analogy, analogousness; equivalence, parity, correspondence, correlation, parallelism.

2. harmony, agreement, like-mindedness, compatibility, accord, accordance, concord, concordance, concurrence, assent; unanimity, unanimousness, consentaneity, consentaneousness, consensus, one voice, concert, togetherness; amity, love, friendship, brotherhood, fellowship, comradeship, fraternity; congeniality, cordiality, amicableness, amiability, amiableness, good will, good feeling; affinity, rapport, understanding, sympathy.

universal, *adj.* 1. general, generic, all-inclusive, all-embracing, comprehensive, world-wide, widespread, common, preponderant, ubiquitous, omnipresent; catholic, ecumenical.

2. unlimited, limitless, infinite, unmeasurable, measureless, unbounded, boundless, uncircumscribed, endless.

universality, *n.* 1. world-wideness, ubiquity, ubiquitousness, comprehensiveness, all-inclusiveness; predominance, prevalence; catholicity, ecumenicity.

2. generality, generalization, abstraction; principle, general rule, general law.

3. completeness, entirety, wholeness, whole, totality.

universally, *adv.* without exception, always, in all cases, in every instance, uniformly, invariably; comprehensively; everywhere, ubiquitously.

universe, *n.* 1. cosmos, macrocosm, whole creation, heavens, empyrean, firmament, sky, vault *or* canopy of heaven; plenum, space, boundlessness, interminability, illimitability, endlessness.

2. whole world, wide world, length and breadth of the land, land, terra, earth, four corners of the earth; globe, sphere.

3. mankind, man, Homo sapiens, humankind, womankind, the human race; humanity, society, persons, people.

4. sphere, orbit, milieu, circle; province, realm, domain; walk, bailiwick, beat, round, compass, range, span; territory, quarter, region, neighborhood; zone, field, premises, vicinity, vicinage.

university, *n.* 1. graduate school, postgraduate school, specialized school, professional school; multiversity, *Derog.* education factory; institution of higher learning *or* education, college, liberal arts college, four-year college.

2. academia, academe, the groves of academe; the halls of ivy, college life, college years.

unjust, *adj.* 1. unfair, inequitable, unequal, uneven, unbalanced, one-sided; partial, partisan, prejudiced, uninterested, undispassionate, prepossessed, biased; warped, jaundiced.

2. unrightful, wrongful, wrong; undue, undeserved, unmerited, unwarranted, uncalled-for; unreasonable, unconscionable, unjustifiable, unwarrantable; disproportionate, out of proportion, excessive, inordinate, immoderate, extreme.

unjustifiable, *adj.* 1. unwarrantable, indefensible, untenable; inexcusable, unforgivable, unpardonable, irremissible, inexpiable; impeachable, condemnable, reprehensible, censurable, blameworthy, culpable.

2. groundless, ungrounded, unfounded, unsupported, baseless, unbased, without basis, idle, vain; unattested, unevidenced, unproven, unsubstantiated, uncorroborated, unauthorized, unestablished; unsubstantial, tenuous, weak, flimsy; unsound, invalid, fallacious, faulty, erroneous, wrong, incorrect; illogical, unlogical, senseless, irrational; unreasonable, excessive, immoderate, exorbitant, extravagant, outrageous, preposterous, absurd, ridiculous.

unkempt, *adj.* 1. disheveled, messy, messed up, mussed *or* mussed up, rumpled, tousled, blowzy, uncombed, windblown, every which way; untidy, shaggy, disordered, disarranged, disarrayed; ungroomed, sloppy, slovenly, frowzy, slatternly, sluttish, dirty, unclean, draggletailed, scruffy, shabby.

2. rough, coarse, unpolished, unsophisticated, rustic, backwoods, *Inf.* hick, ungainly, uncouth, rude, boorish, crude; crass, gross, insensitive, inconsiderate, thoughtless, tactless, gauche.

unkind, *adj.* 1. unbenign, unbenignant, kindless, unkindly, unchristianly, unchristianlike, unchristian; inconsiderate, unthoughtful, insensitive; uncharitable, inhospitable, unamiable, unfriendly; nasty, mean, mean-spirited, cruel; spiteful, malignant, malicious, malevolent, maleficent; sinister, fiendish, diabolical, hellish, infernal.

2. severe, harsh, unmerciful, merciless, pitiless, ruthless, uncompassionate, unsympathetic, unpitying, unforgiving; unlenient, unsparing, relentless, unrelenting, unyielding, not giving an inch, rigid, inflexible, unflexible, nonflexible, unbending; stern, austere, grim; callous, hard, hardened, hard-hearted, heartless, stony-hearted, flinty, cold, cold-blooded; remorseless, unfeeling, uncaring, unconcerned, unresponsive, indifferent.

unknown, *adj.* 1. unfamiliar, strange, foreign, alien, peregrine; new, novel, never experienced before, virgin.

2. unexplored, untracked, untraversed, untraveled; uninvestigated, unstudied, unresearched, untraced; unheard-of, undiscovered, unnoticed, unseen; unfamous, unrenowned, renownless, unillustrious, undistinguished, uneminent; anonymous, anonymal, nameless, innominate.

3. unrevealed, undisclosed, untold, withheld, to be announced; secret, hidden, concealed, hermetic, hermetical; obscure, dark, occult, esoteric; mysterious, arcane, cryptic, puzzling, inscrutable, insolvable, insoluble, enigmatic, enigmatical.

4. unascertained, undetermined, unmeasured, uncounted, uncalculated, indeterminate, unestablished, unfixed, undefined, unset, unsettled, undecided, up in the air; unidentified, x, unnamed, unlabeled, undesignated, uncategorized, neither fish nor fowl.

—*n.* 5. virgin soil, unexplored territory *or* ground, *Latin. terra incognita*; unknown factor *or* quantity, x; secret, arcanum, closed *or* sealed book; enigma, mystery, question, question mark, puzzle, riddle, conundrum; unknowable, deep *or* profound secret, mystery *or* mysteries, unsolved mystery *or* puzzle, sphinx.

unlamented, *adj.* unmourned, ungrieved, unbemoaned, unbewailed, unwept; unregretted, undeplored; unmissed, unbeloved, unloved.

unlawful, *adj.* 1. illegal, illicit, unconstitutional, against the law, *Sl.* illegit; criminal, felonious, larcenous; contraband, black-market, under-the-counter, under-the-table; unlicensed, uncertified, unaccredited, unrecognized; unwarranted, unauthorized, unapproved, unsanctioned, uncountenanced, unofficial, wildcat; outlawed, prohibited, banned, proscribed, forbidden, interdicted, *Fr. défendu, Ger. verboten.*

2. illegitimate, born out of wedlock, baseborn, misbegotten, misbegot, spurious; fatherless, unfathered, bastard; adulterine, adulterous, *Inf.* love; natural, common-law.

unlike, *adj.* **1.** different, dissimilar, unalike, unidentical, nonidentical, (*of twins*) fraternal; bearing no resemblance whatsoever, as different as night and day; distinct, distinguishable, disparate, contradistinct, contrastive, contrary; diverse, divergent, variant, very far apart; incongruous, inconsonant, inharmonious, discordant, incompatible, ill-matched; unequal, nonequivalent, uncomparable, incommensurable, incommensurate, like apples and oranges, two completely different things.

—prep. **2.** different from, dissimilar to, bearing no resemblance to; distinct from, distinguishable from, in direct contrast to.

3. uncharacteristic of, atypical of, untypical of; unusual for, something new for, abnormal for, peculiar for, strange for; out of the ordinary for, extraordinary for, remarkable for.

unlikelihood, *n.* improbability, unlikeliness, a ghost of *or* a Chinaman's chance, small *or* little chance, poor prospect, remote possibility, long shot, long odds; doubtfulness, dubiousness, questionableness, questionability; implausibility, incredibility, incredibleness, unbelievability, unbelievableness; unthinkability, unthinkableness, unimaginableness, inconceivableness, inconceivability.

unlikely, *adj.* **1.** improbable, not likely to happen, highly unlikely; having little chance, having a Chinaman's *or* a ghost of a chance, remote, slight, faint; doubtful, dubious, contrary to expectation; implausible, incredible, unbelievable, *Inf.* fishy; inconceivable, unthinkable, unimaginable, out of the question.

2. unpromising, unfavorable, unpropitious, inauspicious, ominous, ill-omened, foreboding, ill-boding, ill-starred, doomed; questionable, highly questionable, uncertain, unsure.

unlimited, *adj.* **1.** unrestricted, unconstrained, unstinted, unchecked, uncircumscribed, unconfined; uncontrolled, unrestrained, unhampered, unhindered, untrammeled, unfettered.

2. limitless, illimitable, boundless, unbounded, shoreless; immense, vast, great, extensive; incalculable, undetermined, indeterminate, indefinite, undefined; immeasurable, measureless, beyond measure, innumerable, numberless, myriad, countless, untold, uncounted; infinite, endless, without end, unending, never-ending, interminable, inexhaustible; unceasing, constant, uninterrupted, perpetual, eternal; enduring, everlasting, permanent.

3. unqualified, unconditional, absolute, full, total, complete, entire, plenary; unquestioned, arbitrary, despotic, tyrannical.

unload, *v.* **1.** remove cargo *or* freight, *Naut.* break bulk, unlade, unburden, disburden; empty, dump, jettison, fling away, discard, dispose of, cast off; unship, discharge; unpack; transfer.

2. disencumber, lighten one's load, relieve, alleviate; free, extricate, disengage, disembarrass, disentangle, unsnarl, disembroil; ease, set at ease, set one's mind at ease *or* rest, take a load off one's mind, uplift, buoy up.

unlock, *v.* open, give access to, unbolt, unlatch, unbar, spring, jimmy; unfasten, undo, unhasp, unpin, unbind, untie; release, disengage, free; disconnect, disjoin, separate, part, divide.

unlooked-for, *adj.* unforeseen, unexpected, unanticipated, unhoped-for, unpredicted, unthought of; sudden, abrupt, precipitate, out-of-the-blue; surprise, surprising, astonishing, startling; unwonted, unusual, unpredictable; accidental, undesigned, unintentional, unintended, unpurposed; fortuitous, chance, incidental; untimely, unseasonable.

unloved, *adj.* loveless, lovelorn, unbeloved, unendeared, uncherished, unvalued, unappreciated; unwanted, unpopular; forsaken, rejected, jilted; unlamented, undeplored, unmourned, unmissed; uncared-for, disliked, abhorred, disrelished, detested, hated, despised, loathed.

unlucky, *adj.* **1.** luckless, out of luck, down on one's luck, hapless, unfortunate, *Scot.* donsie, *Scot.* warchancy, *Inf.* jinxed, cursed; born under an evil star, born under a bad sign, ill-fated, ill-starred, star-crossed, ill-omened, doomed; unsuccessful, unprosperous, fortuneless, poor, wretched, hopeless, unblessed; thwarted, foiled; unhappy, woebegone, pathetic, forlorn, pitiable, miserable.

2. untoward, unfavorable, unpromising, adverse, ill, contrary, unpropitious, inauspicious; infelicitous, untimely, inopportune, unseasonable, disadvantageous; ill-boding, ominous, sinister, hostile, threatening, portentous, menacing, minatory; malign, baleful, baneful.

unmake, *v.* **1.** undo, take apart, take to pieces, unbuild, dismantle, disassemble; tear apart, destroy, knock down, raze, pull down, bring down, take down; demolish, wreck, wipe out, ruin, devastate, desolate, work havoc upon; pulverize, atomize, smash, crash, reduce to rubble, *Sl.* total, gut; blow up, blast, bomb, smash to smithereens, disintegrate.

2. depose, unseat, dethrone, remove from office, uncrown, defrock, unfrock; expel, eject, kick out, oust, dismiss, discharge, disbar, dispossess; *Inf.* fire, *Sl.* get rid of, *Sl.* give the boot, *Sl.* can, *Sl.* turn out, *Sl.* bounce; demote, lower, reduce, downgrade, declass; take down a peg, humble, strip of rank, *Mil. Sl.* bust, disrate, *Mil.* drum out.

3. change, alter, convert, change one's opinion, redecide, reconsider; reform, recast, restyle, reshape; shift, veer, reverse, invert, transform; modify, adjust, turn, transpose.

unman, *v.* **1.** break down, wear down, dishearten, discourage, demoralize; depress, dispirit, dismay, sink, push down; weaken, enfeeble, devitalize, enervate, unbrace; unnerve, daunt, intimidate, rattle, unstring, shake; undermine, unstrengthen, sap, lay low; break, subdue, overwhelm, conquer, bend, suppress, bring [s.o.] to his knees, humble, overcome.

2. emasculate, castrate, effeminize, eunuchize; desex, desexualize, demasculinize, sterilize; asexualize, geld, alter, *Inf.* fix, neuter.

unmanageable, *adj.* **1.** unruly, refractory, ungovernable, uncontrollable, difficult; recalcitrant, froward, contumacious, uncooperative, balky, obstreperous; willful, self-willed, stubborn, unyielding, inflexible; perverse, contrary, wrong-headed, cross-grained, *Archaic.* untoward, intractable; unsubmissive, indocile, wayward, lawless, rebellious; irrepressible, wild, out of hand, beyond control, resistant, defiant; restive, fractious, incorrigible.

2. unwieldy, unmaneuverable, uncomfortable, inconvenient, awkward; cumbersome, hulky, bulky, ponderous, incommodious; (*of hair*) unruly, straggly, disheveled, stringy, uncombable.

unmanly, *adj.* **1.** weak, enfeebled, frail, fragile, feeble, delicate, soft; timid, timorous, fearful, afraid, fainthearted, lily-livered, *Inf.* mousy; cowardly, pusillanimous, craven, *Inf.* yellow, weak-kneed, *Sl.* chicken; daunted, intimidated, *Inf.* funky, panicky, afraid of one's shadow, *Inf.* chicken-hearted, pigeon-hearted.

2. womanish, effeminate, feminine, sissy, sissified, sissyish; prissy, *Sl.* pansyish, overemotional, milksoppy, namby-pamby, *Sl.* faggy; voluptuous, Lydian, luxury-loving.

unmannerly, *adj.* impolite, discourteous, disrespectful, bad-mannered, misbehaved; uncivil, unceremonious, ungracious, inelegant, ungentle; ungentlemanly, unladylike, ungallant, uncourtly; indecorous, unseemly, indelicate; crude, coarse, rude, rough, vulgar, boorish, uncouth, unrefined; offensive, loutish, brutish, barbarous, churlish, incondite; brash, blunt, brusque, gruff, tactless, inconsiderate; impudent, insolent, fresh, impertinent, brazen, *Inf.* snippy, short; curt, bluff, bearish, harsh.

unmarried, *adj.* single, unwed, unwedded; celibate, virgin, maiden; spouseless, husbandless, wifeless, bachelor, old-maid, spinster; uncommitted, unpledged, unpromised, unplighted, unengaged, unbetrothed; unattached, unbound, free, available, footloose and fancy-free.

unmask, *v.* expose, unveil, uncloak, uncover, bare, take the wraps off; show up, show one's true colors, *Inf.* come out of the closet, *Inf.* come out; disclose, reveal, make known, bring out into the open, bring to light; discover, decry, detect, find, unearth, exhume, disinter, dig up, smoke out.

unmelodious, *adj.* untuneful, unmusical, tuneless; out of tune, out of step, out of key, off-key, off beat, off-pitch, *Music Inf.* sour, *Music.* flat, *Music.* sharp; inharmonious, unharmonious, inharmonic, dissonant, discordant, absonant, cacophonous, cacophonic; harsh, jarring, strident, stridulous, stridulant, raucous, grating, creaking, scratchy, raspy, rasping.

unmentionable, *adj.* **1.** unspeakable, unutterable, ineffable, unfit *or* inappropriate for public conversation; dirty, foul, filthy, obscene, *Inf.* gutter, indecent, immodest, unladylike, ungentlemanly; disgraceful, dishonorable, disreputable, discreditable, unrespectful, shameful, scandalous, shocking, appalling.

2. unmentionables *Facetious.* undergarments, underwear, underclothes, underclothing, undies. See **underwear.**

unmerciful, *adj.* **1.** merciless, pitiless, unpitying, unforgiving, uncompassionate; cruel, heartless, hardhearted, cold-hearted, flinty, stony-hearted, cold-blooded; unfeeling, insensitive, unsensitive, indifferent, uncaring, unconcerned, unsympathetic, callous, hardened; hard, harsh, tough, rough, severe, strict, stern; rigid, inflexible, unflexible, nonflexible, unbending, unyielding, not giving an inch; unappeasable, implacable, inexorable, relentless, unrelenting, remorseless, ruthless; inhuman, brutal, brutish, vicious, savage, barbarous.

2. excessive, *Sl.* too much, immoderate, inordinate, extreme; unreasonable, exorbitant, incredible, unbelievable, outrageous, *Sl.* unreal.

unmindful, *adj.* unaware, unconscious, oblivious, blind, indifferent; forgetful, absent-minded, scatterbrained, distracted; careless, neglectful, negligent, derelict, remiss, slack, lax; off one's guard, sleeping, asleep on the job, napping, daydreaming, looking out the window, staring into space, lost in thought, *Sl.* out to lunch; unwary, unchary, unwatchful, nonobservant, unobservant, unvigilant, unguarded; incautious, uncautious, heedless, unheeding, inattentive, inadvertent, mindless, unthinking; uncircumspect, indiscreet, imprudent, injudicious, unwise, ill-considered, ill-advised; foolish, foolhardy, irresponsible, reckless, rash, temerarious, harebrained, hasty, impetuous, impulsive, brash; thoughtless, inconsiderate, tactless, untactful.

unmistakable, *adj.* evident, obvious, patent, apparent, plain, plain as day, plain as the nose on one's face; self-evident, manifest, manifestative, standing to reason, *Fr. en évidence*; explicit, unequivocal, unambiguous, precise, exact, specific, strict; clear, clear as crystal, crystal-clear, clear-cut, distinct, well-defined, vivid, graphic; visible, pronounced, conspicuous, sticking out like a sore thumb, prominent, outstanding, striking, blatant, glaring, flagrant, *Sl.* flaming; bald, overt, open, unconcealed, unhidden, exposed, out in the open; outright, *Inf.* bald-faced, downright, complete, total, out-and-out, categorical, unqualified, unconditional, unmitigated; absolute, utter, sheer, stark, arrant, rank, *Inf.* plumb, *Brit.* proper, *Inf.* regular; undisputed, uncontested, unchallenged, unquestioned, undoubted, accepted, recognized, acknowledged; certain, sure, *Inf.* for-sure, positive; indisputable, undisputable, undoubtable, indubitable, unquestionable, beyond question, beyond a shadow of a doubt.

unmitigated, *adj.* **1.** unlessened, untempered, unmoderated, unmodified, unabated, undiminished; unrestrained, unbridled, untamed, unmollified, unreduced; oppressive, severe, harsh, relentless, intense; rigid, unbending, austere, grim.

2. unqualified, categorical, unconditional, absolute, thorough, rank, veritable; sheer, utter, pure, clean, stark, clear, born, plain; outright, downright, out-and-out, straight-out, all-out, across-the-board, *Inf.* plumb, dead; unrestricted, unlimited, total, complete, consummate, perfect.

unmotivated, *adj.* **1.** unprovoked, unelicited, unasked-for, uncalled-for; illogical, senseless, without rhyme or reason, unreasonable, unjustifiable, unwarranted, groundless, ungrounded.

2. uninterested, incurious, indifferent, apathetic, bored, *Sl.* blah; lazy, unindustrious, unenterprising, unambitious, *Inf.* laid-back; idle, indolent, do-nothing; shiftless, good-for-nothing, ne'er-do-well.

unmoved, *adj.* **1.** unaffected, untouched, undisturbed, unstirred, dry-eyed, unsympathetic; unimpressed, unconcerned, indifferent, uncaring, apathetic; cool, aloof, distant, removed; stoical, stolid, impassive, unfeeling, unemotional, cold-hearted, cold, icy, bloodless, soulless; insensible, impervious, deaf and blind to, stony, stern, grim; stony-hearted, with a heart of stone, hard-hearted, hardened, indurated, callous, thickskinned; cruel, ruthless, pitiless, heartless, merciless, unforgiving; harsh, severe, unsparing, relentless, unrelenting, inexorable, implacable.

2. firm, steadfast, unshaken, unwavering, unswerving, unflinching; determined, resolute, decided, resolved, staunch.

unnatural, *adj.* **1.** irregular, anomalous, exceptional, uncommon; aberrant, abnormal, perverse; peculiar, foreign, odd, unusual, eccentric; unseemly, unbefitting, unbecoming, improper.

2. strange, preternatural, uncanny; monstrous, freakish, queer, grotesque, bizarre; outlandish, extraordinary, unique, fantastic, whimsical; rare, wild, astonishing, unaccountable, out-of-the-way, unheard-of, unwonted.

3. inhuman, heartless, cruel, evil, brutal; cold, callous, unfeeling, insentient, soulless, unforgiving; hardened, impervious, unimpressible, untouched; stony, flinty, indurated, marblehearted; indifferent, unconcerned, uncaring; passionless, cold-blooded, frigid, aloof, disdainful; pitiless, unpitying, remorseless, relentless; ruthless, savage, hostile.

4. artificial, affected, mannered, theatrical, stagy; stiff, stilted, constrained; assumed, feigned, simulated, labored, forced, insincere, self-conscious.

unnecessary, *adj.* needless, uncalled-for, gratuitous, unneeded, unrequired, unwanted; unessential, nonessential, useless, dispensible, expendable; irrelevant, extraneous; superfluous, redundant, supererogatory, *Fr. de trop,* excess, in excess, spare; tautological, pleonastic, expletive, excessive, over and above.

unnerve, *v.* discourage, unman, dishearten, dispirit, demoralize; deject, deflate, *Inf.* take the wind out of one's sails; disconcert, discompose, unsettle, discomfit, abash; unsettle, agitate, disquiet, perturb, ruffle, rattle, fluster; upset, trouble, worry, *Inf.* shake up, *Sl.* psych out, intimidate; dismay, daunt, *Inf.* faze, *Inf.* throw off balance, *Inf.* throw for a loss, stun, stupefy.

unobtrusive, *adj.* low-key, restrained, unpresuming, unpresumptive; unpretentious, informal, inconspicuous, casual, homey, comfortable, *Inf.* comfy; unaffected, natural, genuine, ingenuous, *Inf.* regular, *Inf.* O.K.; unostentatious, unpompous, unshowy; unassuming, modest, unarrogant, unconceited, unvain; humble, self-effacing, self-humbling, content to stay in the background; retiring, shy, demure, reserved, reticent, diffident; simple, quiet, plain, homely, down-to-earth; unaggressive, unassertive, docile, mild, meek, submissive.

unoccupied, *adj.* **1.** untenanted, tenantless, vacant, empty; unclaimed, available, *Inf.* up for grabs. **2.** uninhabited, unpopulated, unpeopled, depopulated; deserted, abandoned; desolate, forsaken, godforsaken; lifeless, lone, lonely, solitary; unfrequented, unvisited, unsettled. **3.** unbusied, idle, inactive; loafing, resting, do-nothing; at liberty, at leisure, leisured, *Inf.* off; unemployed, out of work, uninvolved.

unorganized, *adj.* **1.** disorganized, unmethodical, unsystematic, unsystematized, unclassified, unarranged; indiscriminate, promiscuous, haphazard, random, irregular, disjointed; casual, aimless, pell-mell, helter-skelter. **2.** disorderly, confused, chaotic, all mixed-up, upside down, *Inf.* topsy-turvy; at sixes and sevens, muddled, jumbled, hugger-mugger, scrambled, tangled; disordered, out of order, out of place, disarranged, in disarray, deranged; untidy, cluttered, messy, disheveled, *Inf.* mussed up, messed up, ruffled up, rumpled; careless, slipshod, poor; unready, unprepared, *Inf.* like a chicken with its head cut off.

unorthodox, *adj.* **1.** heterodox, heretical, infidelic; unscriptural, uncanonical, unofficial, unauthoritative. **2.** unconventional, uncommon, unusual, uncustomary, unwonted, out of the ordinary; unconforming, nonconforming, unobservant, nonobservant; deviant, deviative, divergent, aberrant; anomalous, abnormal, irregular, heteroclite.

unpalatable, *adj.* unsavory, savorless, untoothsome, unappetizing, nauseating, nauseous, sickening; bitter, sour, rancid, turned; uninviting, undesirable, unattractive, disagreeable, unpleasant, unpleasing, displeasing, distasteful; inedible, uneatable, undelectable; disgusting, noisome, *Sl.* yukky, *Sl.* gross; repugnant, offensive, obnoxious, shocking, nasty; repulsive, repelling, repellent, revolting, objectionable.

unparalleled, *adj.* unequaled, matchless, peerless, unmatched, unexcelled, unrivaled, without equal, *Fr. sans pareil*; incomparable, inimitable, unmatchable; unsurpassed, unapproachable, beyond compare; unprecedented, unexampled, unheard-of; unique, one of a kind, special, singular, distinctive, rare, unusual; supreme, superior, greatest, chief, foremost, best, champion, *Australian.* bonzer, second to none, of the first water; consummate, transcendent, quintessential, superlative.

unpardonable, *adj.* **1.** inexcusable, unforgivable, uncondonable, irremissible, unexpiable, unatonable, inexonerable; unwarrantable, unjustifiable, unvindicable, unexculpable; indefensible, undefendable. **2.** reprehensible, deplorable, contemptible, despicable, condemnable, censurable, blameworthy; outrageous, scandalous, shameful, disgraceful, ignoble, vile, abject, low; heinous, grievous, ghastly, horrible, atrocious, abominable, abhorrent, odious, *Brit.* beastly.

unpertubed, *adj.* calm, steady, composed, peaceful, tranquil, serene, pacific; unruffled, unflustered, undisturbed, unstirred, unexcited, unagitated; imperturbable, unexcitable, *Sl.* unflappable; cool, cool-headed, *Inf.* cool as a cucumber; possessed, controlled, in control, unimpassioned; level-headed, poised, balanced, stable, reasonable; even-tempered, placid, untroubled, *Inf.* hang-loose; impassive, staid, stoical, sedate, philosophical, solemn, serious.

unpleasant, *adj.* **1.** displeasing, annoying, irritating, irksome, bothersome, vexatious, provoking; pestering, *Inf.* pesky, *Inf.* pestiferous; troublesome, rough, thorny, fretful, worrisome, worrying, *Dial.* plaguy; nettlesome, nettling, *Inf.* aggravating, disturbing, perturbing, ruffling, disquieting. **2.** disagreeable, distasteful, unpleasing, unpalatable, unappetizing, brackish, unsavory; nauseating, sickening, disgusting, noisome, *Sl.* yukky, seamy, *Sl.* gross, stinking to high heaven; repugnant, offensive, obnoxious, nasty; repulsive, repelling, repellent, revolting, objectionable; abominable, odious, heinous, detestable, hateful; boring, monotonous, flat, tiresome, wearisome. **3.** offensive, Augean, rank, foul, smelly, reeking, stinking, mephitic, putrid, rancid, sour; shocking, distressing, appalling, insulting; bad, rotten, *Inf.* awful, poor, mean; cutting, scathing.

unpolished, *adj.* **1.** rough, rough-hewn, rude, crude; coarse, gross, vulgar, loutish, boorish, ill-bred, brought up in a barn; gauche, awkward, uncouth, ungainly; disadvantaged, from the wrong side of the tracks. **2.** uncultured, uncultivated, unrefined, unlettered, uneducated, unschooled, untutored, ignorant; tasteless, uncivilized, unsophisticated, countrified, rustic, agrestic, rural, bumpkinish, cloddish, doltish; inelegant, undignified, ungraceful, lacking in the social graces, like a diamond in the rough, rough-and-ready, graceless; loud, big-mouthed, discourteous, unmannerly, incondite; offensive, blunt, short, gruff, uncivil, impolite, brusque, curt, tactless, undiplomatic; sloppy, slatternly, slovenly, messy, cheap, slipshod.

unpopular, *adj.* disliked, unliked, unloved, undesired, uncared-for; friendless, without a friend in the world, lonely, alone in the world; uncourted, uncoveted, not sought out, like a wallflower; unwanted, unwelcome, rejected, rebuffed, unaccepted; disapproved, turned down, looked down on, disdained, unacceptable; unattractive, undesirable, offensive, objectionable, obnoxious; ignored, *Inf.* cold-shouldered, snubbed, slighted, neglected; out in the cold, out of things, on the outs, out of favor, in bad odor, not in the swim, left on the sidelines; tolerated, merely tolerated, *Sl.* treated like a hound dog.

unprecedented, *adj.* unexampled, unparalleled, unequaled, unmatched, unheard-of; unusual, uncommon, unique, incomparable, one of a kind, special, singular, individual, distinctive, different, recherché; out-of-the-ordinary, unconventional, unorthodox, novel, new; rare, unwonted, uncustomary, unfamiliar, out-of-the-way; atypical, anomalous; first, original, premier; archetypal, prototypal, prototypical, prototypic.

unpredictable, *adj.* unforeseeable, undivinable, unknown, impossible to predict *or* tell; questionable, *Inf.* iffy, doubtful, dubious, in doubt; uncertain, *Inf.* fluky, unsure, undecided, up in the air, in the balance; indefinite, vague, obscure, hazy; erratic, fickle, capricious, whimsical, vicissitudinous, mercurial, changeable, impulsive, impetuous; undependable, unreliable, wavering, veering; chance, aleatory, accidental, unexpected, unanticipated, unguessed-at, unhoped-for, undreamed-of.

unprejudiced, *adj.* impartial, unbiased, fair, just, open-minded, broad-minded; uninfluenced, unswayed, unjaundiced, unbigoted, color-blind; broad, wide, latitudinarian, unparochial, unprovincial, catholic; even-handed, objective, equitable, disinterested, detached; dispassionate, neutral, indifferent, unprepossessed, third-party, independent; impersonal, unimpassioned, judicial; unopinionated, undogmatic, liberal, unhidebound.

unpremeditated, *adj.* unstudied, undeliberated, unthought-out; unplanned, unplotted, unarranged, undesigned, unschemed, uncontrived; unintentional, unintended, unpurposive, undeliberate; unconscious, involuntary, automatic, immediate, instinctive, natural; unprepared, extemporaneous, extempore, impromptu, ad-lib, improvised, improvisational, improvisatory, off-the-cuff, off-the-top, shooting-from-the-hip, offhand; spontaneous, spur-of-the-moment, on-the-spot; impulsive, impetuous, madcap, hasty, rash, devil-may-care, reckless, blind.

unprepared, *adj.* **1.** unready, *Inf.* caught short, caught napping, taken off guard, surprised, caught by surprise, taken aback, dumfounded, abashed; disorganized, at sixes and sevens, not set up, confused, jumbled, muddled.

2. untrained, unskilled, ignorant, green, raw, new to, innocent as a baby; inexperienced, unseasoned, unpracticed, unqualified.

3. unfinished, uncompleted, incomplete, just started, inchoate; half-baked, undeveloped, *Sl.* half-assed, half-cocked, ill-prepared, ill-considered, not thought out, unplanned.

4. extemporaneous, ad-lib, off-the-cuff, informal, casual, random.

unpretentious, *adj.* simple, modest, unaffected, humble, unpretending; plain, open, direct, unassuming, straightforward, candid; unartificial, natural, unfeigning, honest; unembellished, unornamented, undecorated, ungarnished, untrimmed, unadorned; unsophisticated, unostentatious, undistinguished, simple, homely; unambitious, unaspiring, unimposing, unobtrusive; artless, homespun, native, unspoiled.

unprincipled, *adj.* dishonest, deceitful, tricky, dissembling, unscrupulous; unconscionable, unethical, unprofessional, amoral, immoral, shameless; corrupt, crooked, underhand, underhanded, bad, wicked; knavish, roguish, scoundrelly, blackguardly, villainous; dishonorable, false-hearted, untrustworthy, faithless, false; treacherous, perfidious, unloyal, disloyal; sinister, devious, shifty, *Inf.* shady, not kosher; unfair, unjust, inequitable, wrongful, felonious; collusive, hypocritical, two-faced, double-tongued, Janus-faced.

unproductive, *adj.* **1.** fruitless, unfruitful, unyielding, issueless; childless, sterile, barren, abortive, infecund, unprolific, fallow, *Bot.* acarpous, impotent, effete; dead, dry, arid.

2. useless, futile, vain, idle, unavailing, bootless; ineffectual, ineffective, inefficacious, inadequate, inoperative, unserviceable, impracticable; worthless, valueless, meritless, nugatory; unprofitable, profitless, unremunerative, unrewarding, unpaying, gainless; unsuccessful, *Inf.* no-go, to no avail, to no purpose, for naught.

unprofessional, *adj.* **1.** improper, undignified, unseemly, indecorous, unbefitting; unscholarly, unacademic; unfitting, unworthy; unethical, unprincipled, transgressive, unfaithful, dutiless; uncanonical, negligent, neglectful, lax, noncompliant, disobedient.

2. amateurish, unbusinesslike, untrained, untutored, unaccomplished, unschooled, unskilled; inexperienced, unpracticed, unseasoned, unconversant; incompetent, bungling, sloppy, careless, unmeticulous, ungraceful; second-rate, inferior, bush-league, *Sl.* bush, poor, a poor excuse for, shoddy.

unpromising, *adj.* unfavorable, unpropitious, inauspicious, sinister; dark, dim, black, gloomy, dreary; dire, threatening, ominous, minacious, menacing; discouraging, not encouraging, adverse, infelicitous; ill-boding, ill-starred, fateful, bodeful, portentous; bad, evil, lowering, looming, *Archaic.* untoward, baleful; hopeless, not likely, unlikely, dubitable, doubtful, *Sl.* fat chance.

unprompted, *adj.* **1.** spontaneous, snap, offhand; unasked, unsought, unbidden, unsolicited; volunteer, free, gratuitous, uninvited, offered, proffered; voluntary, freely given, unforced, uncompelled, uncoerced; willing, *Archaic.* willful, self-determined, self-acting, independent.

2. impulsive, natural, unpremeditated, unthinking, unwitting; unstudied, involuntary, instinctive, unconscious.

unprotected, *adj.* vulnerable, pregnable, defenseless, unfortified, unshielded, open; unsheltered, undefended, unmanned, insecure, open to attack, attackable, assailable; unguarded, unarmed, weaponless; exposed, naked, bare, unflanked, uncovered; aidless, helpless, unattended, unwatched, guardless; surmountable, conquerable, vincible, weak, expugnable, *Inf.* beatable; unscreened, unfenced, ungarrisoned; nonimmune, susceptible, unvaccinated, liable; uninsured, unguaranteed.

unqualified, *adj.* **1.** unfit, incompetent, unsuited, inadequate; ineligible, 4-F, ill-fitted, incapable, unable; ill-qualified, unequipped, not up to, *Inf.* not cut out for, not equal to; unready, unprepared, unadapted.

2. unmitigated, unrestricted, unconditioned, unlimited, without reservation; unconditional, uncircumscribed, categorical, unreserved, without strings, no strings attached; unmodified, unbounded, full, across-the-board, blanket.

3. complete, absolute, utter, thorough, downright, out-and-out, pure and simple; outright, perfect, consummate, *Dial.* flat-out; clear, unequivocal, unmistakable, positive, definitive, *the*; pure, sheer, *Inf.* plumb, wholesale, through and through.

unquestionable, *adj.* **1.** indisputable, undeniable, indubitable, irrefutable, unconfutable; uncontestable, incontrovertible, irrefragable, inappealable, unrefutable; certain, sure, beyond all question, beyond a shadow of a doubt, admitting of no dispute; clear, manifest, patent, evident, self-evident, unmistakable, obvious; conclusive, definitive, authoritative, positive, absolute, definite, decided; doubtless, questionless, undisputed, unchallenged, undoubted, uncontroverted, real.

2. unexceptionable, unobjectionable, unimpeachable, unassailable, unattackable, unimpugnable; irreproachable, irreprehensible, irreprovable, above reproach, above criticism; impeccable, faultless, flawless, spotless, ideal, errorless; uncensurable, unblamable, unblameworthy, blameless.

unravel, *v.* **1.** disentangle, untangle, unweave, unroll, uncurl, undo; unsnarl, untwist, untwine, disentwine; separate, comb out, card, part, unscramble, straighten out; untie, unbind, uncoil, unwind, unfurl, unknot.

2. solve, resolve, figure out, clear up, work out decode, decipher, interpret, crack, break; unriddle, puzzle out, get to the bottom of, fathom, plumb; get, hit, *Sl.* dope out, answer, explain; make out, see through, define; have, unlock, pick the lock, find the key to.

unreal, *adj.* **1.** imaginary, fanciful, fantastic, fabulous; illusory, delusory, deceptive, deceiving; visionary, chimerical, unactual, unsubstantial, airy; phantasmal, phantasmagorical, spectral; imagined, fancied, all in the mind, figmental, dreamy, dreamlike, with one's head in the clouds; immaterial, nonexistent, unrealistic, incorporeal, intangible.

2. sham, fake, false, ungenuine, spurious, artificial, suppositious, fictitious; unauthentic, counterfeit, *Sl.* phony, mock, pseudo, make-believe; seeming, ostensible, misleading, fallacious, fraudulent; bastard, dummy, ersatz, factitious, assumed, pretended.

3. *Slang.* wonderful, marvelous, terrific, great, excellent; fine, *Sl.* neat, *Sl.* swell, fantastic, really good.

unrealistic, *adj.* **1.** impractical, infeasible, impracticable, unworkable, undoable; unreasonable, irrational, illogical, half-baked, *Sl.* half-assed; academic, theoretical, speculative, hypothetical, abstract; ivory-towerish, ivory-towered, idealistic, visionary, romantic, sentimental, starry-eyed; quixotic, fanciful, chimerical, imaginary, dream-world, illusory, delusory; improbable, unlikely, fantastic, wild, absurd, crazy, crackpot, *Inf.* off the wall; silly, foolish, asinine, stupid, dumb.

2. unlifelike, unreal, nonrealistic, unauthentic, unauthentical, nonauthentic, nonauthentical, ungenuine, nongenuine, unnatural, nonnatural, unnaturalistic, nonnaturalistic; fictitious, fictional, made-up, storybook, movie, TV.

unreasonable, *adj.* **1.** irrational, senseless, illogical, without reason, without rhyme or reason; foolish. silly, childish, unintelligent; unwise, unsensible, unreflective, witless, mindless, thoughtless; insensate, reckless, injudicious, indiscreet, imprudent; shortsighted, myopic, undiscerning, unperceiving; moronic, idiotic, *Sl.* dumb, stupid, fatuous; crazy, mad, brainless, imbecilic, *Sl.* dippy, *Sl.* batty, *Sl.* balmy, *Sl.* wacky, *Sl.* goofy.

2. arbitrary, temperamental, whimsical, capricious, notional, fanciful; harebrained, quirky, moody; discretionary, willful, nonrational, self-willed; inconsistent, erratic, crotchety, bumptious.

3. preposterous, absurd, ludicrous, ridiculous, nonsensical; meaningless, unscientific, sophistical, unsound; fallacious, groundless, invalid, fallible; unthinkable, inconceivable, out of the question, impossible; incredible, unbelievable, implausible, untenable; doubtable, doubtful, dubitable, questionable.

4. excessive, immoderate, exorbitant, extravagant, *Sl.* all outdoors; undue, extortionate, unconscionable, unfair, unjust, overpriced; overmuch, uncalled-for, outrageous, inordinate; prohibitive, out of bounds, out of sight.

unrefined, *adj.* **1.** unpurified, coarse, crude, raw, unfinished, unpolished.

2. uncultured, vulgar, unsophisticated, inelegant. See **unpolished** (*defs.* **1, 2**).

unregenerate, *adj.* **1.** unrenewed, not born again, unsaved; unconverted, unconvinced, unpersuaded; godless, ungodly, irreligious, nonbelieving, unbelieving, disbelieving, atheistic; infidelic, infidel, heathenish, heathen, paganistic, pagan; antireligious, antichristian, impious, irreverent, sacrilegious, blasphemous, profane. See **unrepentant.**

2. persistent, dogged, unrelenting; adamant, adamantine, obdurate, stubborn, unyielding, unbending, inflexible, like a stone wall; obstinate, mulish, diehard.

3. unreformed, unrehabilitated, unchanged, reprobate, incorrigible, recidivistic, recidivous, inveterate, hard-core, hardened; irredeemable, unredeemable, irreclaimable, unreclaimable, unsaveable, undeliverable, past hope, hopeless, past praying for, lost, fallen; sinful, sinning, amoral, nonmoral, unmoral, immoral, bad, wicked, evil, miscreant, iniquitous; shameless, wanton, profligate, dissolute, debased, degenerate.

unrelated, *adj.* **1.** different, dissimilar, unlike, unalike, unaffinitive; entirely *or* completely *or* totally different, contradistinct, contrastive, contrary, as different as day and night; distinct, separate, discrete; disparate, divergent, diverse, deviant, variant, very far apart; discrepant, inconsistent, incongruous, inharmonious, inconsonant, discordant, dissonant, incompatible; unanalogous, noncorresponding, noncorrespondent, nonequivalent, unequal, incommensurable, incommensurate, like apples and oranges.

2. unconnected, noncognate, nonaffinitive, irrelative, unrelative, nonrelative, nonrelated; irrelevant, inapposite, nongermane, impertinent, beside the point *or* mark *or* question, *Inf.* off base, *Inf.* off the beam; inapplicable, inappropriate, malapropos; extraneous, foreign, alien, immaterial, insignificant, inconsequential, neither here nor there.

unrelenting, *adj.* **1.** relentless, implacable, inexorable, remorseless, ruthless. See **relentless** (*def.* **1**).

2. unremitting, unabating, unslackening; continuous, continual, unbroken, constant, steadfast, steady; incessant, ceaseless, endless, unending, inexhaustible, unfailing, perpetual.

unreliable, *adj.* **1.** undependable, irresponsible, fly-by-night, disreputable, untrustworthy, untrusty; questionable, dubitable, controvertible, doubtful, open to question; contestable, refutable, impeachable; unassured, uncertain, unconvincing, untenable, implausible.

2. fickle, flighty, wishy-washy, mercurial, volatile; faithless, shifting, changeable, inconstant, inconsistent; indecisive, irresolute, vacillating, wavering, variable, erratic; capricious, whimsical, moonish, fitful, frivolous, impetuous, impulsive.

unrepentant, *adj.* impenitent, unrepenting, refusing forgiveness; uncontrite, remorseless, feeling no remorse. See **unregenerate.**

unreserved, *adj.* **1.** without reservation, unqualified, unrestricted, unmitigated, absolute; complete, full, entire, total, unconditional; unlimited, unbounded, unmeasured, limitless, boundless.

2. outspoken, free, free-spoken, free-speaking, unreticent, bold, unrestrained, unconstrained, unchecked, unabashed, uninhibited, unshrinking; plain, plain-speaking, blunt, point-blank, to the point; frank, candid, forthright, direct, straightforward, straight-from-the-shoulder, man-to-man, heart-to-heart; open, open and sincere, open-hearted, genuine; guileless, ingenuous, artless, naive, simple, undeceptive, undeceiving, undeceitful, undissembling; aboveboard, open and aboveboard, up front, on the level, honest, truthful.

unresolved, *adj.* unsettled, undecided, yet to be decided, up in the air, *Inf.* iffy, pending, in suspense; unanswered, unsolved, unfinished, incomplete, uncomplete; open, open to debate, debatable, arguable, problematic, problematical, questionable, open to question, disputable, contestable, controvertible, moot; undetermined, indeterminate, unfixed, unset, undefined, indefinite, inconclusive, uncertain, unsure, a big question mark; unknown, unproven, unestablished, unascertained, unconfirmed, unsubstantiated, uncorroborated, undemonstrated, experimental, tentative.

unrest, *n.* **1.** disquiet, disquietude, inquietude, unquietness, uneasiness, unease, restlessness; fretfulness, distress, worry, concern; anxiety, anguish, angst, fear, dread, foreboding; nervousness, ants, *Inf.* butterflies, *Inf.* butterflies in one's stomach, *Sl.* heebie-jeebies, *Sl.* hab-dabs, *Sl.* creeps.

2. dissatisfaction, discontentment, dissent, dissension, discord, strife, animosity, hostility; rebellion, uprising, turbulence, storm; agitation, upset, turmoil, tumult, commotion, excitement.

unrestrained, *adj.* **1.** free, unbound, untied, unchained, unshackled, unfettered, untrammeled; unimpeded, unhampered, unbridled, uncurbed, unmuzzled; unhindered, uncircumscribed, unchecked, unsuppressed; unrestricted, unlimited, unbounded, limitless, boundless.

2. unreserved, unconstrained, natural, artless, ingenuous; open, uninhibited, unrepressed; outspoken, free-spoken, free-speaking, unreticent, bold; plain, plain-speaking, blunt, point-blank; frank, candid, forthright, direct, straightforward, straight-from-the-shoulder; overfamiliar, presumptuous, assuming, forward, aggressive, *Inf.* pushy, assertive; impudent, cocky, brash, audacious.

3. wild, fast and loose, riotous, rampageous, boisterous, spirited, lively; morally loose, wanton, licentious, debauched, dissipated, dissolute, profligate, promiscuous; indecent, immoral, improper; intemperate, immoderate, incontinent.

unrestricted, *adj.* **1.** free, unbound, unlimited; unhindered, uncircumscribed, unchecked, unsuppressed; unregulated, ungoverned, freewheeling, laissez-faire, no-holds-barred, catch-as-catch-can; unlimited, unbounded, unmeasured, limitless, boundless. See also **unrestrained** (*def.* **1**).

2. absolute, categorical, complete, unmitigated, unqualified, unconditional, unconditioned, no-strings-attached; unreserved, without reservation, full, entire, total.

unrighteous, *adj.* **1.** evil, wicked, sinful, iniquitous, *Archaic.* facinorous, *Obs.* scelerous; nefarious, villainous, flagitious, heinous, infamous, *Rare.* nefast; black-hearted, sinister, arrant, ignoble; bad, base, vile, foul, low, mean, odious, obnoxious; maleficent, malefic, malevolent, evil-minded; demonic, demoniac, diabolic, devilish, fiendish, satanic; immoral, dissolute, profligate, reprobate, degenerate; disgraceful, shameful, contemptible.

2. inequitable, unjust, unfair, partial, not equitable; biased, prejudiced, close-minded, narrow-minded, intolerant, bigoted, one-sided, partisan; wrongful, wrong, iniquitous; unlawful, illegitimate, illegal; unjustifiable, indefensible, unwarrantable, unreasonable, unconscionable.

ınrivaled, *adj.* unparalleled, unequaled, matchless peerless, unmatched. See **unparalleled.**

ınruffled, *adj.* **1.** calm, steady, composed, peaceful, tranquil, serene, pacific; unflustered, unperturbed, undisturbed, unstirred, unexcited, unagitated; imperturbable, unexcitable, unflappable; cool, coolheaded, balanced, *Inf.* cool as a cucumber; possessed, controlled, unimpassioned; level-headed, poised, even-tempered, staid; stolid, impassive, stoical, sedate, philosophical, solemn, serious.

2. unwrinkled, unmussed, smooth, ironed, pressed; flat, regular, unbroken, uncreased.

nruly, *adj.* ungovernable, unmanageable, uncontrollable, refractory, intractable; lawless, riotous, disorderly, turbulent: disobedient, mutinous, insubordinate; unrestrained, rampant, unreined, undisciplined, unbridled, wildcat; wild, out of hand, beyond control, out of control, irrepressible; contumacious, uncooperative, forward, recalcitrant, *Dial.* breachy; obstreperous, *Inf.* ornery, rampageous, *Brit. Dial.* randy; defiant, restive, rebellious, resistant.

unsafe, *adj.* **1.** dangerous, fraught with danger, perilous, hazardous, jeopardous, *Archaic.* parlous, treacherous; threatening, menacing, minatory, minacious, ominous, sinister; risky, chancy, uncertain, *Sl.* hairy, *Chiefly Scot.* unchancy, *Sl.* dicey, touch-and-go; touchy, ticklish, critical, thorny.

2. insecure, shaky, wobbly, wobbling, unsteady, unstable, decrepit; unsound, unreliable, untrustworthy, *Scot.* unsicker; weak, frail, flimsy, unsubstantial, precarious, built on sand; tottering, teetering, rickety, hanging by a thread.

3. vulnerable, open, susceptible, assailable, unprotected, defenseless; exposed, unsheltered, unshielded, ill-protected, unguarded; endangered, in danger, expugnable, not out of the woods; between the devil and the deep blue sea, between Scylla and Charybdis.

unsaid, *adj.* unspoken, unpronounced, unuttered, unvoiced, tacit; unstated, undeclared, unexpressed, unmentioned, unbreathed, untold, untalked-of; assumed, understood, implied, implicit, meant, suggested, hinted, inferred; held back, held in, kept back, kept in, suppressed, unrevealed.

unsanitary, *adj.* unhealthy, unhealthful, unhygienic, unantiseptic, germ-ridden, germ-infested; unwashed, unclean, unpurified, impure; noxious, unwholesome, insalubrious; toxic, septic, poisonous, pestilential, morbific, morbifical, morbic; foul, dirty, filthy, contaminating, polluted, soiled, tainted.

unsatisfactory, *adj.* **1.** inadequate, insufficient, too little, not enough; incomplete, deficient, lacking, wanting, needing.

2. unsuitable, inappropriate, unfit, unbefitting; imperfect, defective, flawed, faulty, not up to par, poor; unworthy, unacceptable, inadmissible; undesirable, objectionable, troublesome; inconvenient, incommodious, disadvantageous; mediocre, inferior, disappointing, *Australian.* crook, displeasing, no good, not good enough, incommensurate, not equal to.

unsavory, *adj.* **1.** tasteless, unflavorful, flavorless, unflavored, vapid, insipid, *Fr. fade,* dead; flat, stale, weak, thin, watery, watered-down.

2. unpalatable, savorless, untoothsome, unappetizing, undelectable, nauseating, nauseous, sickening; bitter, sour, rancid, turned; inedible, uneatable; disgusting, *Sl.* crummy, *Sl.* yukky, *Sl.* gross.

3. uninviting, undesirable, disagreeable, unpleasant, unpleasing, displeasing, unattractive.

4. objectionable, offensive, repugnant, obnoxious, shocking, nasty; repulsive, repelling, repellent, revolting, objectionable; coarse, gross, crude, vulgar, boorish, churlish; tactless, improper, rude.

unsay, *v.* recant, retract, take back, withdraw, *Inf.* eat one's words, *Inf.* back down; apologize; revoke, repudiate, renounce; disavow, deny, disclaim, *Inf.* sing a different tune.

unscathed, *adj.* unharmed, uninjured, unimpaired, unhurt; unburned, undamaged, safe, sound, in perfect condition, with a whole skin, without a scratch: unscratched, untouched, unscarred, unmarked, scatheless.

unscrupulous, *adj.* unprincipled, unconscionable, unethical, conscienceless, unconscientious, amoral, immoral, shameless; corrupt, corrupted, perverse, perverted, evil, wicked; dishonest, dishonorable, deceitful, crooked; insidious, artful, cunning, shifty, slippery; insincere, disingenuous, two-faced, Janus-faced, double-dealing, timeserving, mendacious; disloyal, false, false-hearted, perfidious, treacherous; unfaithful, faithless, untrustworthy, undependable, unreliable, *Inf.* two-timing.

unseasonable, *adj.* **1.** out of season, unseasonal.

2. untimely, ill-timed, mistimed, anachronous; premature, immature, abortive. See **untimely.**

unseat, *v.* **1.** unsaddle, unhorse, dismount, throw.

2. depose, oust, remove, dethrone, *Rare.* disenthrone; disbar, unfrock; dismiss *or* remove from office, strip *or* break of rank, disrate, cashier, *Mil.* drum out, *Mil. Sl.* bust; liquidate, purge; overthrow, subvert; retire, pension off, superannuate, *Inf.* put out to pasture, *Inf.* kick upstairs.

unseemly, *adj.* **1.** unbecoming, indecorous, improper, unladylike, ungentlemanly, ungenteel, unmannerly, uncivil, impolite; undignified, unrefined, unpolished, inelegant, indelicate; impolitic, imprudent, indiscreet, tactless, injudicious.

2. crude, coarse, vulgar, uncouth, crass, gross, rude, churlish, loutish, boorish; distasteful, shameful, disgraceful, discreditable, disreputable, reprehensible; indecent, offensive, lewd, in poor taste, obscene.

3. inappropriate, inapt, inapposite, unmeet, unfitting, unbefitting; unwarranted, uncalled-for, out of place, out of keeping; inopportune, ill-timed, unseasonable, untimely, infelicitous; unfavorable, incommodious, inconvenient, uncongenial, unlikely; unsuitable, unsuited, unfit, ill-adapted, incompatible; inexpedient, inadvisable, impractical, inapplicable, unfeasible.

unselfish, *adj.* liberal, free, generous, open-handed, unsparing, unstinting, ungrudging; altruistic, charitable, philanthropic, humanitarian; noble, high-minded, magnanimous, munificent, great-hearted; disinterested, unbiased, unprejudiced, even-handed, fair, just, impartial, nonpartisan.

unsettle, *v.* **1.** disturb, perturb, bother, trouble, upset, fluster, flutter, flurry, ruffle, rattle; agitate, shake, shake up, discompose, disconcert, discomfit; confuse, disorient, *Inf.* throw, *Inf.* discombobulate; unnerve, unman, unstring, unhinge, *Sl.* psych *or* psych out, *Sl.* spook, *Sl.* give one the creeps *or* willies *or* heebie-jeebies; stun, shock, rock, jolt, jar, bring one up short, *Inf.* give one a turn, *Sl.* throw one for a loop.

2. disorganize, disorder, put *or* throw into disorder, disarrange, derange.

unsettled, *adj.* **1.** unorganized, disorganized, disordered, disorderly, in disorder, in disarray, disarranged; deranged, discomposed, upset.

2. transient, itinerant, vagrant, *Archaic.* vagrom, vagabond, migratory, nomadic, wandering, roving.

3. uneasy, anxious, tense, *Inf.* on pins and needles; restless, restive, fidgety; disturbed, perturbed, flustered, ruffled, rattled, thrown; in a dither, *Inf.* in a tizzy, *Inf.* in a stew, *Inf.* in a lather; agitated, shaken, *Sl.* shook, *Sl.* all shook up; confused, disoriented, mixed-up, *Inf.* discombobulated.

4. unstable, unsteady, shaky, insecure, infirm; irresolute, indecisive, undecided, of two minds, ambivalent; equivocating, seesawing, wavering, oscillating, betwixt and between, blowing hot and cold; hesitant, hesitating, shilly-shallying; weak-willed, wishy-washy, spineless, infirm of purpose.

5. uninhabited, unpopulated, unpeopled, unoccupied; desolate, barren, forsaken.

6. undetermined, indeterminate, indefinite, uncertain, unsure, at loose ends; unresolved, unestablished, unproved, undemonstrated; moot, debatable, arguable, contestable, disputable; doubtful, dubious, questionable, open to doubt *or* question.

7. pending, open, in suspense, in the balance, *Inf.* up in the air, *Inf.* up for grabs; tentative, contingent, conditional; payable, outstanding, owing, in arrears.

8. inconstant, variable, changeable, changeful, ever-changing, protean, mutable, permutable, alterable; vacillating, fluctuating, irregular, erratic, inconsistent, unreliable, undependable, desultory; fickle, capricious, moody.

unsex, *v.* **1.** asexualize, castrate, neuter, alter, ovariectomize, oophorectomize; (*of horses*) geld, (*of female animals*) spay, (*of fowl*) capon, (*of animals*) *New England.* deacon, *Inf.* fix, *Inf.* cut.

2. emasculate, unman, effeminize, womanize; eunuchize.

unsheltered, *adj.* unprotected, unshielded, uncovered, unscreened; exposed, open, out in the open; vulnerable, pregnable.

unshrinking, *adj.* unflinching. See **unflinching.**

unsightly, *adj.* unattractive, uncomely, unpretty, unlovely, unbeautiful, inelegant, unhandsome, homely; disagreeable, distasteful, offensive, unpleasant; ugly, hideous, horrid, horrible; repulsive, repellent, repugnant, revolting; untidy, unkempt, *Inf.* messy, *Inf.* sloppy; frowzy, blowzy, frumpish, sluttish, slatternly.

unskillful, *adj.* maladroit, inept, unhandy, inexpert, *Fr. inhabile*; unskilled, untrained, untaught, undrilled, undisciplined, inexperienced, amateurish; unapt, unfit, unqualified, incapable, incompetent; awkward, clumsy, gauche, fumbling, bumbling, bungling, all thumbs, butterfingered, left-handed, ambisinister, *Sl.* klutzy; oafish, doltish, cloddish, clodhopping, lubberly, lumbering, loutish.

unsociable, *adj.* unfriendly, unamiable, unaffable, uncongenial, unamicable; unneighborly, unaccommodating, ungracious, disagreeable; hostile, inimical, ill-natured, ill-disposed; solitary, misanthropic; withdrawn, retiring, reticent, shy, uncommunicative; aloof, distant, detached, remote, removed; cool, cold, icy, frigid, frosty.

unsolicited, *adj.* unsought, unbesought, unrequested, unrequired, undemanded, unasked, uncalled-for; unwanted, undesired, uninvited, unwelcome; voluntary, volunteered, freewill, spontaneous, unforced; free, gratuitous, gratis.

unsophisticated, *adj.* **1.** naive, simple, simple-minded, innocent, childlike, like a newborn babe; undeveloped, unworldly, not wise to the world, green, raw, born yesterday, wet behind the ears; unsuspecting, unsuspicious, unwary, unguarded, trusting, trustful; guileless, artless, ingenuous, sincere.

2. uncouth, uncivilized, inurbane, uncultured, uncultivated, unrefined, unpolished, philistine; awkward, clumsy, gauche, ungraceful, graceless, boorish, oafish, cloddish; coarse, rough, roughcast, rough-hewn, *Inf.* linsey-woolsey, inelegant, incondite; countrified, country-bred, country-born, upcountry, backwoods, provincial, yokelish, *Sl.* hickish, *Sl.* rube, *Sl.* hayseed, *Sl.* from the sticks, *Sl.* from the boonies *or* boondocks; ignorant, unaware, *Inf.* not with it, *Inf.* out of it, *Inf.* square, *Sl.* unhip, *Sl.* icky.

3. homespun, homebred, homey, homely, homelike, homish, down-home, (*usu. of thought or philosophy*) cracker-barrel, *Scot.* raploch, *Yiddish.* heimish, *Inf.* folksy; plain, modest, unpretentious, unpretending, unaffected, unassuming, normal, informal.

4. unadulterated, unmixed, undiluted, uncut, uncorrupted, uncontaminated, straight; pure, one-hundred percent, solid, sterling, twenty-four carat; genuine, authentic, real, true, bona fide.

unsound, *adj.* **1.** diseased, in poor health, unhealthy, infirm, decrepit, sick, sickly, ailing, ill, unwell; pathological, morbid, afflicted, affected, infected; laid up, off one's feed, indisposed; deranged, abnormal, unbalanced, unhinged; demented, crazy, mad, insane, *Sl.* nuts; mentally deficient *or* retarded, feeble-minded, simple, dim-witted, incompetent.

2. decayed, unwholesome, rotten, full of dry rot, crumbling, disintegrated; impaired, imperfect, defective, marred, flawed, blemished, broken, disfigured, mutilated.

3. shaky, wobbly, tottery, unsteady, unstable, rickety, flimsy; in disrepair, in need of repair, broken-down; precarious, dangerous, unreliable, unsafe, unsubstantial.

4. fallacious, illogical, *Logic.* paralogistic, faulty, flawed, *Sl.* cockeyed; unfounded, ungrounded, groundless, untenable, invalid; false, untrue, not true, erroneous, mistaken, incorrect, *Sl.* all wet, all wrong, deceptive.

5. (*of sleep*) fragile, light, unquiet, uneasy, unpeaceful, troubled, fitful, restless; tossing, tossing and turning.

6. without adequate backing, in debt, indebted, encumbered, insolvent, in the red; bankrupt, *Inf.* on the rocks, ruined; one step ahead of the bill collector, struggling to keep the wolf from the door; hardscrabble, low-profit.

unsparing, *adj.* **1.** liberal, profuse, lavish, rich, ample, copious, abundant; bountiful, plentiful, luxuriant; extensive, broad, wide, far-reaching, wide-ranging; wholesale, sweeping, large-scale; ungrudging, giving, unstinting, unstinted, open-handed; generous, beneficent, munificent, magnanimous, big-hearted; excessive, immoderate, extravagant, extreme, inordinate, outrageous; ballooning, inflated, mushrooming, spreading, widespread; unbounded, limitless, unrestricted; vast, huge, enormous, gigantic, giant, titanic, colossal, mammoth, gargantuan; total, full, free, unqualified, unchecked, unending.

2. unmerciful, merciless, unrelenting, relentless, unremitting, inexorable, implacable, uncompromising, unbending, inflexible, obdurate; pitiless, ruthless, cruel, harsh, uncompassionate, unfeeling; severe, rigorous, grim, austere, stern, stark, stringent; hard-hearted, hard-boiled, cold, cold-blooded, iron-handed, iron-fisted, iron-hearted; diligent, assiduous, persevering, untiring, dogged, leaving no stone unturned; persistent, determined, obstinate, adamant.

unspeakable, *adj.* **1.** unutterable, inexpressible, ineffable, beyond words, incommunicable; indescribable, undescribable, undefinable, unnamable; dumfounding, overwhelming, stupefying, striking, stunning, stirring, wonderful; unimaginable, unbelievable, incredible, unheard-of; fantastic, extraordinary, singular, signal.

2. bad, awful, horrible, too horrible for words, terrible, horrid, ugly, *Sl.* yukky, disgusting; low, base, vile, despicable, contemptible, loathsome, odious, abhorrent, hateful; slimy, foul, dirty, rotten, putrid, stinky, mean; offensive, objectionable, deplorable, repulsive, repellent, repugnant, revolting, nauseating, rank, sickening; unmentionable, unfit, improper, unallowable.

unspoiled, *adj.* **1.** perfect, as good as new, like new, in mint condition, in good shape, in good condition, in great shape, in A-one condition; sound, whole, fine, excellent; undamaged, unmarred, unharmed, unscratched, unstained, unspotted.

2. innocent, wholesome, fresh, young in outlook, open, simple, free; sweet, agreeable, pleasant, amiable, friendly; natural, plain, pure, pristine, clean, unsullied; uncorrupted, untouched, undefiled, unfallen, virtuous, moral; spotless, stainless, unblemished, unpolluted; chaste, virginal, maidenly.

unspoken, *adj.* **1.** tacit, assumed, understood, implied, implicit; unstated, undeclared, unexpressed. See **unsaid**.

2. silent, mute, mum, unspeaking, tight-lipped, close-mouthed, quiet, not talking, voiceless, wordless, speechless, dumfounded.

unstable, *adj.* **1.** unsteady, not fixed, astatic, unsettled, insecure; tottery, shaky, wobbly, tippy; teetering, faltering, stumbling, staggering; precarious, labile; unpredictable, risky, hazardous, perilous; on the brink, swaying, shifting.

2. inconstant, unsteadfast, changeable, variable, mutable, permutable; fickle, capricious, moody, volatile, mercurial, flighty, giddy; inconsistent, indecisive, irresolute, indefinite, vacillating, fluctuating, wavering, tergiversating, blowing hot and cold; undependable, fly-by-night, untrustworthy, unreliable, faithless; desultory, stop-and-go, come-and-go.

3. eccentric, erratic, peculiar, queer, odd; irrational, *Sl.* goofy, *Sl.* wacky, *Sl.* nutty, *Sl.* far out, *Sl.* spacey; deranged, unbalanced, unhinged, *Sl.* unglued, unstrung.

4. irregular, jumpy, choppy, spasmodic; jerky, fitful, spastic.

unstrung, *adj.* weakened, enervated, spent, drained, emptied; worn out, played out, exhausted, fatigued, wrung out; quivering, shaky, like a bowl of Jello, shaking like a leaf, unsteady; agitated, perturbed, troubled, disturbed; unnerved, unmanned, shaken, flustered, upset, discouraged, frustrated, *Inf.* discombobulated; disconcerted, discomposed, bewildered, *Inf.* fazed, confounded, distracted; unbalanced, unhinged, *Sl.* unglued, disoriented, deranged.

unstuck, *adj.* **1.** unfastened, unattached, unfixed, unglued, apart at the seams; unsnapped, unhooked, undone, loosened, loose, freed, free, opened, open; unplugged, unclogged, unstopped, uncorked, unjammed.

2. chaotic, disorganized, disordered, out of order, disarranged, deranged, unarranged; confused, in disarray, incoherent, incohesive; jumbled, helter-skelter, higgledy-piggledy, harum-scarum, topsy-turvy, skimble-scamble, *Sl.* arsy-varsy.

unstudied, *adj.* **1.** unpremeditated, unlabored, natural, normal, unaffected; spontaneous, impromptu, extemporaneous, extempore, offhand, offhanded, *U.S. Inf.* off-the-cuff, informal, casual; unpretentious, without airs, *Inf.* down-home, unassuming, modest, simple.

2. unversed, unread, ignorant, unknowledgeable, unknowing, unenlightened, uninformed; uneducated, unschooled, unlearned, untutored, untaught, uninstructed; undisciplined, untrained, raw, green, inexperienced; unskilled, inexpert, inefficient, incompetent, unqualified; amateur, unprofessional, nonprofessional.

unsubstantial, *adj.* **1.** insubstantial, fanciful, fancied, imaginary, imagined, chimerical, unreal, visionary, quixotic; airy, vaporous, wild, idle, empty; fantastic, make-believe, mythical, fairy-tale, fictitious, made-up; illusory, illusive, delusive, false, hallucinatory, phantom, phantasmal, spectral, ghostly; intangible, impalpable, immaterial, incorporeal, disembodied, bodiless.

2. paltry, inadequate, insufficient, meager, mere, small, puny, dinky, *Sl.* lousy, *Sl.* crummy; insignificant, unimportant, of little *or* no import, negligible, nugatory, inconsiderable, inconsequential; trivial, trifling, petty, niggling, minor, piddling, *Inf.* picayune.

3. flimsy, tenuous, poor, worry, weak, lame; shallow, superficial, cursory; ungrounded, groundless, unfounded, unsupported, unbased, baseless; illogical, unlogical, unsound, fallacious, erroneous, faulty, *Inf.* full of holes, untenable; feeble, frail, fragile, slight, thin, watery, watered-down; delicate, dainty, light, fine, sheer, diaphanous, ethereal, gauzy, gossamer, cobwebby; cheap, *Sl.* cheesy, inferior, *Inf.* no-good, useless, worthless, rickety, jerry-built; jury-rigged, makeshift, stopgap.

unsubstantiated, *adj.* unconfirmed, uncorroborated, unproven, unevidenced, unestablished, undemonstrated, experimental, tentative; debatable, questionable, open to debate *or* question, disputable, arguable, contestable, controvertible, moot; doubtful, dubious, dubitable, uncertain, unsure, indefinite, inconclusive.

unsuccessful, *adj.* **1.** vain, futile, useless, unavailing, bootless; ineffectual, inefficacious, nugatory, worthless, inutile; fruitless, unproductive, abortive, stillborn, barren, sterile, impotent; unprofitable, unremunerative, ungainful, losing.
2. unfortunate, unprosperous, fortuneless, poor, bereft, infelicitous, unhappy; unlucky, luckless, hapless, ill-starred, ill-fated, under a cloud; victimized, jinxed, unblest, cursed; thwarted, scotched, foiled, crossed, frustrated, balked, stultified.

unsuitable, *adj.* **1.** inappropriate, inapt, inapposite, unfitting, unbefitting, unmeet; unsuited, unfit, ill-adapted, incompatible, uncongenial; incongruous, inconsistent, out of keeping, out of place, out of character; disproportionate, inequitable.
2. inexpedient, disadvantageous, inadvisable; impractical, inapplicable, useless, no good, unfeasible; inopportune, unseasonable, untimely, infelicitous; irrelevant, nongermane, impertinent.
3. unseemly, unbecoming, indecorous, improper; unladylike, ungentlemanly, ungenteel, impolite; impolitic, imprudent, indiscreet, tactless, injudicious.

unsung, *adj.* unacclaimed, uncheered, unapplauded, unhailed; uncelebrated, unglorified, unexalted, unhonored, unmemorialized; unpraised, unlauded, unextolled; unacknowledged, unrecognized, unnoted, unnoticed; unrenowned, renownless, unfamous, unillustrious, uneminent, undistinguished, *Archaic.* inglorious; unknown, anonymous, anonymal, nameless, innominate, unnamed, unidentified; unheard of, obscure, inconspicuous, background; inconsequential, insignificant, unimportant.

unsure, *adj.* **1.** uncertain, unconvinced, dubious, doubtful, skeptical, suspicious, distrustful; ambivalent, of two minds, betwixt and between, on the fence; undecided, up in the air; irresolute, indecisive, infirm of purpose, wishy-washy. See **uncertain** (*defs.* **2, 3**).
2. unconfident, lacking in confidence, unassured, insecure, unsure of oneself, self-distrustful, self-distrusting; diffident, self-conscious, bashful, shy, timid; retiring, demure, reserved, holding back, constrained, restrained.

unsurpassed, *adj.* unexcelled, second to none, unrivaled, peerless, matchless, nonpareil, unparalleled, unequaled, incomparable, inimitable, *Fr. sans pareil*; superlative, consummate, best, finest, choicest, greatest; supreme, paramount, ascendant, transcendent, highest, uppermost, topmost, top, tiptop, *Latin. facile princeps*; preeminent, foremost, first, primary, prime, leading; predominate, dominant, hegemonic, hegemonical.

unsuspecting, *adj.* unaware, off guard, napping, asleep; unprepared, unanticipative, unwarned, uninformed, unapprised; oblivious, unconscious, insensible, unmindful, paying no attention, inattentive, heedless; unsuspicious, unsuspectful, trustful, trusting, overtrustful; overcredulous, credulous, believing, gullible, *Obs.* cullible, easily deceived *or* taken in, deceivable, dupable, unexploitable; naive, ingenuous, wide-eyed, innocent; green, inexperienced, unsophisticated, ignorant.

unsymmetrical, *adj.* asymmetric, asymmetrical, unsymmetrized; nonparallel, unanalogous, noncorresponding, noncorrespondent, inconsistent, discrepant; lopsided, one-sided, unbalanced, unmatched, disproportionate, out of proportion, uneven, irregular, unequalized, unequal.

unsympathetic, *adj.* **1.** uncompassionate, compassionless, ruthless, pitiless, unpitying, uncommiserative, uncommisserating, unsympathizing; uncaring, unfeeling, unemotional, soulless; unconcerned, indifferent, unresponsive, apathetic, untouched, unmoved; callous, thickskinned, insensitive, heartless, cold-hearted, cold-blooded, cold, cold as a fish, frigid; hard-hearted, stony-hearted, flinty, impervious; inconsiderate, unthoughtful, unkind, unkindly, kindless, unbenign, unbenignant, uncharitable, unfriendly, inhospitable, unchristianly, unchristianlike, unchristian; mean, cruel, inhuman, unmerciful, merciless, unsparing.
2. unfavorable toward, disapproving of, having strong feelings against; opposed to, against, contra, con.
3. incongruous, inharmonious, inconsonant, discordant, dissonant; uncomplementary, mismatched, mismated, ill-suited, unsuited to each other, on different wavelengths; uncongenial, incompatible, unable to get along.

unsystematic, *adj.* unorganized, unordered, unmethodical, unsystematical, unsystematized; uncategorized, unclassified, ungrouped; irregular, random, haphazard, indiscriminate, promiscuous, aimless, pell-mell, helter-skelter; disorganized, disorderly, disordered, disarranged, in disarray, deranged, confused, chaotic; hodgepodge, jumbled, muddled, scrambled, tangled, mixed up; unneat, untidy, messy, messed up, *Inf.* mussed up, in a mess; unkempt, slovenly, sloppy.

untarnished, *adj.* scoured, polished, shining, bright; clean, unsoiled, unspotted, spotless, immaculate; unblemished, pure, unstained, stainless, perfect, flawless, faultless; virgin, untouched, unadulterated, unspoiled, untainted; unpolluted, uncontaminated, undefiled, undebased, unsullied, unfouled; uncorrupted, guiltless, innocent, sinless, chaste, vestal, virginal, lily-white.

untenable, *adj.* indefensible, insupportable, unarguable, unmaintainable, unsustainable, undefendable, refutable; weak, flawed, faulty, specious, implausible; illogical, groundless, baseless, unreasonable, *Both Logic.* paralogical, paralogistic; contestable, debatable, moot, questionable; impeachable, unacceptable, inadmissible.

unthinkable, *adj.* **1.** inconceivable, unimaginable, incomprehensible, incredible, implausible, incogitable; unbelievable, contrary to reason, unheard-of, undreamed-of, unthought-of, hard *or* difficult to believe, beyond belief; wondrous, wonderful, miraculous, fabulous, fantastic, *Sl.* mind-blowing, *Sl.* mind-boggling; strange, passing strange.
2. impossible, out of the question, improbable, unlikely, hopeless, *Sl.* no go, *Sl.* fat chance; illogical, absurd, preposterous, ridiculous, ludicrous.

unthinking, *adj.* **1.** thoughtless, inconsiderate, incogitant, tactless, discourteous, uncivil, rude; senseless, mindless, witless, stupid, foolish, inane; unwise, imprudent, injudicious, indiscreet; inattentive, inadvertent, unmindful, nonobservant, disregardful; uncircumspect, incautious, off guard, unguarded, unheeding, heedless, unreflective; regardless, neglectful, negligent, irresponsible; improvident, careless, reckless, harebrained, rash, temerarious.
2. unreflecting, unthoughtful, unintellectual; unreasoning, irrational, blind; mechanical, automatic, instinctive, spontaneous, involuntary, impulsive; unconscious, oblivious; empty, blank, vacuous.

untidy, *adj.* unkempt, disheveled, sloppy, slovenly, slatternly, frowzy, bedraggled; messy, disorderly, helter-skelter, littered, littery; disordered, disarranged, disorganized, at sixes and sevens; confused, muddled, turbid; macaronic, jumbled, topsy-turvy, every which way; chaotic, entangled, snarled up.

untie, *v.* **1.** unfasten, undo, disconnect, disjoin, disunite, disengage; unbind, unlace, unstring, *Archaic.* untruss; unknot, unravel, untwine.

2. release, loose, disenthrall, extricate, free, liberate; set free, set loose, let loose, turn loose, let go, unpen, unmew, disimprison.

3. resolve, settle, solve, figure out, puzzle out, unpuzzle, unriddle, unconfound; find the key, unlock, decipher, decode, *Inf.* crack; explain, explicate, clear up, make clear *or* plain; straighten out, unsnarl, disembroil, untangle, disentangle; penetrate, fathom, understand.

untimely, *adj.* unseasonable, ill-timed, mistimed, anachronous; premature, immature, abortive; inconvenient, inopportune, unfortunate, inapt, malapropos, inexpedient, inapposite, inappropriate; awkward, unsuitable, unbecoming, unbefitting, indecorous, improper, imprudent; infelicitous; out of season, out of place, out of tune, out of keeping; irrelevant, inapplicable.

untiring, *adj.* indefatigable, unwearying, unfailing, unfaltering; determined, persevering, relentless, unflagging. See **unflagging.**

untold, *adj.* **1.** unrelated, unnarrated, unrecounted; unmentioned, unstated, unsaid, unspoken, unexpressed; unimparted, unrevealed, undivulged, undisclosed, unreported, unpublished; unknown, secret, private, hidden.

2. uncounted, unnumbered, unenumerated, unnumerated, countless, innumerable, numberless, myriad, uncountable, more than one can count; infinite, limitless, unlimited, boundless, unbounded, endless, unending, inexhaustible; immeasurable, measureless, incalculable, incomputable, unreckonable, unreckoned, uncomputed, uncomputable, unfathomable, fathomless, undeterminable, undetermined, indeterminite, indefinite; many, numerous, numerous as grains of sand on the seashore, numerous as stars in the Milky Way, very many, *Inf.* a lot, *Inf.* umpteen, *Sl.* skaty-eight, *Sl.* forty-'leven, *Inf.* more than one could shake a stick at.

3. inexpressible, unspeakable, indescribable, undescribable, unutterable; unimaginable, unthinkable, inconceivable.

untouched, *adj.* **1.** unhandled; untouched by human hands.

2. unexplored, unvisited, undiscovered, unknown, unmapped, uncharted.

3. uneaten, undrunk, unsampled, untasted; unconsumed, unused, left over.

4. unchanged, pristine, natural, as God intended, as nature intended; unsullied, pure, virginal, virgin; new, brand-new, unused, never used, mint; perfect, flawless, faultless, untarnished, unblemished, untainted, unsullied, unspotted, spotless, stainless, unstained, unmarred, undisfigured, undefaced, unmarked; unruined, unspoiled, undefiled, unpolluted, undirtied, uncontaminated, unadulterated; pure, fresh, clean.

5. undamaged, unharmed, uninjured, unhurt, unscathed, scatheless, unimpaired, unbroken; intact, in one piece, safe and sound, whole, in perfect *or* mint condition, unscratched, without a scratch.

6. unaffected, unmoved, undisturbed, unstirred, dry-eyed, unsympathetic; unimpressed, unconcerned, indifferent, uncaring, apathetic; stoical, stolid, impassive, unfeeling, unemotional, cold-hearted, icy, bloodless, soulless; insensitive, insensible, unresponsive.

7. untouched upon, untreated, unmentioned, undiscussed, undescribed, undepicted; omitted, neglected, overlooked, left out.

untoward, *adj.* **1.** unfavorable, adverse, cross, contrary, hostile, unfriendly, negative, bad; infelicitous, inappropriate, inopportune, untimely, unseasonable; unpropitious, inauspicious, ominous, threatening, foreboding, menacing, portentous; sinister, evil, black, dark, bleak, unpromising; unfortunate, unlucky, ill-starred, ill-fated, ill-omened, star-crossed, doomed.

2. improper, inappropriate, inapt, inapposite, unmeet, unfitting, unbefitting, unfit, unsuitable, unsuited, unfeasible, incorrect; unwarranted, uncalled-for, out of place, out of keeping; unseemly, unbecoming, indecorous, indecent, unladylike, ungentlemanly, ungenteel, impolite, rude; undignified, unrefined, unpolished, inelegant, indelicate; impolitic, imprudent, indiscreet, tactless, untactful, injudicious; *Inf.* out-of-the-way, *Inf.* off-key, out-of-bounds, out-of-line, out-of-order.

untrained, *adj.* untaught, untutored, uninstructed, unschooled, uneducated, unlearned; unknowledgeable, unknowing, unenlightened, uninformed; undisciplined, raw, green, inexperienced, unprepared, unpracticed; unskilled, inexpert, inefficient, incompetent, unqualified; amateurish, amateur, unprofessional, nonprofessional.

untroubled, *adj.* calm, collected, composed, *Inf.* together; cool, *Inf.* cool as a cucumber, cool-headed, even-tempered, equanimous, poised, balanced, steady; level-headed, reasonable, rational, sensible; possessed, self-possessed, controlled, self-controlled, in control, passionless, impassive, dispassionate; imperturbable, unperturbable, inexcitable, *Sl.* unflappable; unruffled, unflustered, undisturbed, unstirred, unexcited, unagitated, unperturbed, unmoved, unbothered; easy-going, relaxed, *Inf.* hang-loose, *Inf.* mellow, *Inf.* laid-back; peaceful, tranquil, serene, pacific, placid, smooth; unemotional, undemonstrative, stoic, stoical, philosophical.

untrue, *adj.* **1.** faithless, unfaithful, disloyal, unloyal, false; treasonous, traitorous, treacherous, perfidious; two-faced, Janus-faced, hypocritical, double-tongued, deceitful, untrustworthy, dishonorable, false-hearted; double-dealing, recreant, underhanded, shifty, tricky; disingenuous, insincere, conniving, Machiavellian, artful, sly, wily, cunning; crooked, duplicitous, false-principled, double; dishonest, quackish, charlatanish, ambidextrous.

2. erroneous, false, wrong, incorrect, inaccurate, mistaken; imprecise, inexact, not right, amiss, unfactual; fallacious, faulty, flawed, contradictory, erring, in error; all wrong, wide of the mark, astray, *Inf.* off base; illogical, unfounded, unsound, perverse, errant, aberrant; deviant, distorted, perverted, *Sl.* cockeyed; off key, out of tune, off pitch; out of line, out of plumb, off, out of square, wide.

3. fake, fraudulent, counterfeit, mock, ersatz, sham, make-believe; imitation, forged, faked, *Inf.* phony, bogus, spurious, unreal.

untrustworthy, *adj.* **1.** disreputable, dishonest, undependable, untrusty, deceitful, questionable. See **unreliable** (*def.* **1**).

2. changeable, fickle, variable. See **unreliable** (*def.* **2**).

untruth, *n.* **1.** untruthfulness, inveracity, falsity, lying, mendacity, truthlessness; erroneousness, fallaciousness, untrueness, misrepresentation; prevarication, perjury, dissimulation; sophistry, casuistry, jesuitism, subtlety, subreption; deceitfulness, deception, duplicity, fraudulence, equivocation.

2. lie, prevarication, fib, falsehood, fabrication, fiction; distortion, perversion, coloring, misstatement, misrepresentation, falsification; fable, myth, figment, canard, invention, concoction; story, tale, yarn, *Inf.* tall tale, cock and bull story, *Inf.* fish story; white lie, half-truth, *Inf.* taradiddle, *Inf.* flam; dirty lie, monstrous lie, barefaced lie; hoax, humbug, deception, trick, *Inf.* flimflam.

3. error, flaw, deviancy, fault, sin; inaccuracy, mistake, misprint, misquotation, misstatement, misstep, slip; deviation, heresy, misinterpretation, heterodoxy.

untruthful, *adj.* mendacious, lying, fibbing, unveracious; dishonest, deceitful, insincere, uncandid, disingenuous; collusive, *Law.* covinous; dissembling, deceiving, hypocritical, two-faced, pharisaical; perjured, forsworn, prevaricative; misleading, circuitous, hedging, shifty; evasive, ambiguous, equivocal, suspicious; untrustworthy, unreliable, undependable, untrusty, trustless, irresponsible, fly-by-night.

unused, *adj.* **1.** unemployed, unutilized, untried, unapplied, unexercised; unconsumed, unspent, surplus, remanent, remaining, left, leftover; extra, spare, reserve, in hand, in reserve; in abeyance, waived, put aside, suspended; saved, held back, taken out.

2. untouched, unhandled, unfelt; new, original, firsthand, fresh; pristine, virgin, maiden, untrodden, unbeaten; intact, whole, full, unopened, unbroken.

3. unpracticed, unfamiliar, unaccustomed, unacquainted; inexperienced, unseasoned, unversed, unhabituated. See **unaccustomed** (*def.* **2**).

unusual, *adj.* uncommon, unordinary, extraordinary, out of the ordinary, unheard-of; remarkable, strange, odd, peculiar, queer, curious; rare, scarce, infrequent, seldom met with, few and far between; singular, unique, *Latin. sui generis*; new, novel, unfamiliar, unthought-of, undreamed-of, unexpected, surprising; unexampled, unprecedented, uncustomary, unwonted; irregular, funny, bizarre, freakish, offbeat, off the beaten track, *Sl.* off the wall; outlandish, outrageous, oddball, out of this world, out of the pale; unorthodox, unnatural, unconventional.

unutterable, *adj.* **1.** unpronounceable, unsayable, unmouthable, hard to get out, tongue-twisting, tongue-tripping; foreign, alien, strange.

2. ineffable, indescribable, beyond words. See **unspeakable** (*def.* **1**).

unvarnished, *adj.* **1.** plain, clear, straightforward, simple, true, bare, naked, overt; unadorned, unembellished, unfurbished, undecorated, unornamented, untrimmed, undecked, undressed; pure, pure and simple, direct, inartificial, unsophisticated, unpretentious, unaffected; natural, genuine, undisguised, unpretended; undissembling, artless, unfeigning, guileless; sincere, honest, frank, outspoken, straight, open.

2. unfinished, uncoated, unenameled, unwaxed, unpolished; unbuffed, unburnished, unshined, unglossed.

unveil, *v.* reveal, open, lay open, expose, uncover, unwrap, undrape, bare; disclose, divulge, make known, bring to light, bring out into the open.

unverified, *adj.* unconfirmed, unsubstantiated, uncorroborated, unauthenticated; unsettled, undetermined, undeterminate, indefinite, uncertain, unsure; unproven, unestablished, undemonstrated; groundless, ungrounded, unfounded; moot, debatable, arguable, contestable, disputable.

unversed, *adj.* unfamiliar, unacquainted, unconversant, unused to, a stranger to; unpracticed, unskilled, untrained; ignorant, unenlightened, untaught, untutored; uninformed, uninitiated; inexperienced, raw, green, unseasoned, wet behind the ears; uneducated, unschooled, uninstructed, unlettered.

unwanted, *adj.* unwelcome, uninvited, undesired, undesirable; unsolicited, unasked, undemanded, unrequested, unsought, unbesought, uncalled-for; rejected, outcast, ostracized, estranged, excluded, blacklisted, blackballed; unpleasant, distasteful, unenjoyable. thankless; unmourned, unlamented.

unwarranted, *adj.* uncalled-for. See **uncalled-for** (*defs.* **1, 3, 4**).

unwary, *adj.* incautious, rash, reckless, precipitate, headlong; heedless, unheeding, careless, disregardful, regardless, thoughtless, unthinking, unmindful, mindless, witless, unreflecting; indiscreet, imprudent, unwise, improvident; impulsive, unguarded, unwatchful, unobservant, uncircumspect; unsophisticated, unwordly, not wise to the world, innocent, naïve, childlike, like *or* innocent as a newborn babe; gullible, credulous, easily taken in.

unwavering, *adj.* unfaltering. See **unfaltering.**

unwell, *adj.* ill, ailing, indisposed, afflicted, sick, *Inf.* sick as a dog, *Inf.* under the weather, *Inf.* out of sorts, *Inf.* not feeling oneself, *Sl.* off one's feed; in poor health, poorly, unhealthy; sickly, pale, pallid, wan, sallow; anemic, washed-out, seedy, run-down; invalid, valetudinarian, valetudinary; laid up, prostrate, flat on one's back, hospitalized, *Brit.* in hospital.

unwholesome, *adj.* **1.** unhealthful, insalubrious, insalutary; pernicious, injurious, deleterious, harmful, hurtful, destructive; noxious, noisome, toxic, septic, poisonous; unhygienic, unsanitary, germ-ridden, dirty, filthy, foul.

2. demoralizing, depraving, degrading, corrupting, perverting; unscrupulous, unprincipled, conscienceless, immoral, amoral, evil, wicked, sinful, bad.

3. unhealthy, sickly, pale, pallid, pasty, anemic, *Inf.* white as a ghost *or* sheet.

unwieldy, *adj.* unmanageable, unhandy, hard to handle, awkward, clumsy, ungainly; bulky, substantial, large, massive, huge; heavy, hefty, ponderous, cumbrous, cumbersome, weighty.

unwilling, *adj.* **1.** reluctant, averse, loath, disinclined, indisposed, not in the mood, *Sl.* not psyched, *Sl.* not into it; opposed, against, disagreeing, unconsenting, at odds; involuntary, forced, against one's will.

2. obstinate, stubborn, uncooperative, indocile, uncompliant, inacquiescent; recalcitrant, refractory, contumacious, obstreperous; contrary, perverse, cross-grained, wrong-headed, backward.

unwind, *v.* **1.** undo, loosen, loose, release; unravel, uncoil, unfurl, unroll, uncurl, unreel; disentwine, untwine, untwist, disentangle, unwrap, disengage, separate.

2. relax, wind down, calm down, quiet down, be quiet; loosen up, let up, hang loose, *Inf.* let oneself go, *Inf.* let one's hair down; lay back, sit back, *Sl.* take it easy; slow down, take a break, take time out, *Inf.* take a breather.

unwise, *adj.* **1.** imprudent, incautious, indiscreet, irresponsible, injudicious; ill-considered, ill-suited, ill-advised, impolitic; impetuous, impulsive, short-sighted, heedless, unheeding; foolhardy, headlong, rash, unwary; irresponsible, thoughtless, careless, reckless.

2. unreasonable, irrational, illogical; haphazard, aimless, unconnected, groundless; inappropriate, inapplicable, inept; incongruous, inconsistent.

3. foolish, absurd, inane, pointless, fatuous; senseless, nonsensical; ridiculous, derisible, ludicrous, *Sl.* for the birds; asinine, anserine, idiotic, *Inf.* moronic, imbecilic; harebrained, giddy, mercurial, reckless, unstable, harum-scarum; stupid, unintelligent, mindless, fatuitous, brainless, slow; blockheaded, boneheaded, empty-headed.

unwitting, *adj.* **1.** unaware, unknowing, ignorant, unenlightened, incognizant, unacquainted, uninitiated; oblivious, blinded, *Inf.* out of it, *Sl.* out to lunch, *Inf.* unhip; uninformed, in the dark, unapprised, unadvised, unwarned; unconscious, insensible; unwary, unprepared, unsuspecting; stupid, dull, dull-witted, witless.

2. unintentional, accidental, unintended, inadvertent, unpremeditated, unplanned, undesigned, uncalculated, indeliberate; spontaneous, automatic, involuntary, reflex; thoughtless, unthinking, unconscious, unmeant; chance, adventitious, *Inf.* fluky.

unwonted, *adj.* uncommon, unusual, uncustomary, unfamiliar, unique, rare, novel; singular, exceptional, out of the ordinary, atypical, individual; unheard-of, unexampled, unprecedented; infrequent, few and far between, seldom seen, seldom met with; extraordinary, noteworthy, remarkable; unconventional, irregular, unorthodox, anomalous; odd, strange, queer, eccentric, abnormal, peculiar, curious, freakish, bizarre, offbeat.

unwordly, *adj.* **1.** spiritual-minded, spiritual, spiritualistic, spiritistic, religious, *Theosophy.* astral; metaphysical, transcendental, philosophical, abstract, unconcrete, notional, conceptual, ideational, ideaistic; unmaterial, nonmaterial, immaterial, nonphysical, nonbodily; unmaterialistic, nonmaterialistic.

2. naive, inexperienced, raw, green, wet behind the ears, uninitiated, uninitiate; natural, untouched, unaffected, unspoiled, unjaded; unsophisticated, unwise, *Inf.* unhip, *Inf.* out of it; unenlightened, uninformed, uneducated, untaught, unstudied, unversed, unconversant, ignorant; parochial, provincial, small town, country, *Inf.* hick, *Inf.* from the sticks.

3 unearthly, otherworldly, extraterrestrial, extramundane, transmundane; ethereal, spectral, ghostly, wraithlike, eerie, weird, uncanny; supernatural, supramundane, preternatural, preterhuman, pretersensual; supersensory, occult, psychic, psychical.

unworthy, *adj.* **1.** inferior, worthless, small-time, bush-league, *Sl.* bush, *Sl.* two-bit; insignificant, unimportant, petty, puny, small, paltry, lowly, menial, *U.S. Sl.* cotton-pickin'; bad, awful, *Inf.* lousy, *Sl.* crappy, low grade, cheap, *Inf.* junky, *U.S. Sl.* cheesy; lightweight, amateurish, unprofessional, incompetent, not up to par *or* snuff, mediocre.

2. uncommendable, unpraiseworthy, illaudable, reprehensible, blameworthy, objectionable; dishonorable, ignoble, discreditable, disgraceful, shameful.

3. *Often* **unworthy of** unsuitable, inappropriate, unmeet, unfitting, unbefitting, inapposite, inapt; beneath the dignity of, unsuited for, unfit for, ill-adapted, incompatible; out of character, out of place, out of keeping, inconsistent, incongruous.

4. undeserving, unmeriting, unearned; inadequate, unqualified; ineligible, disqualified.

unyielding, *adj.* **1.** unbending, inflexible, inductile, stiff; rigid, firm, hard, adamantine; implastic, inelastic, wooden, petrified, ossified; set, fixed, immobile, immovable, unchangeable.

2. unrelieved, relentless, implacable; stark, hard-core; uncompromising, hard-line, get-tough.

3. steadfast, resolute, staunch, constant, unwavering, unfaltering, steady; undaunted, indomitable; determined, persistent, tenacious, persevering, sedulous, untiring, unflagging; loyal, faithful, zealous, true; strong-willed, decisive, strong, stern; firm, unshaken, undeviating, unswerving, unchanging, enduring; set, fixed, settled, stable, immovable.

4. unmanageable, intractable, refractory, uncontrollable, unruly, ungovernable, disobedient; unmalleable, uncompliant, unamenable, unobliging, unimpressible, uninfluenced, opinionated, bigoted, unreasonable; obdurate, recalcitrant, adamant, unbending, inflexible, intransigent; headstrong, peverse, stubborn, mulish, bullheaded, pigheaded, bulletheaded, resistant, obstinate, willful, pervicacious, pertinacious, renitent.

5. (*of land or soil*) unproductive, unfruitful, sterile, barren, dry, arid, desert, infecund, unprolific.

upbeat, *adj.* optimistic, positive, promising, looking up, favorable, hopeful; uplifting, encouraging, heartening, fortifying, vivifying; cheery, cheerful, sunny; happy, blithe, blithesome, light-hearted, lightsome, buoyant; *Inf.* up-tempo, *Inf.* knee-slapping.

upbraid, *v.* **1.** scold, *U.S. Inf.* bawl out, *Sl.* chew out, tongue-lash, *Inf.* dress down, *Inf.* trim, *Inf.* fix [s.o.'s] little red wagon; reprove, reproach, rebuke, rate, reprehend, castigate, chastise, reprimand; *Inf.* give [s.o.] a piece of one's mind, *Inf.* tell [s.o.] a thing or two, tell off, tell [s.o.] where to get off, take [s.o.] to task, call down, give [s.o.] hell, *Sl.* lay [s.o.] out in lavender, *Inf.* rake over the coals, *Inf.* skin alive, *Sl.* pin [s.o.'s] ears back, *Inf.* blast, *Inf.* jump on *or* all over.

2. condemn, censure, reprobate, criticize, remonstrate, animadvert on; denounce, denunciate, objurgate, berate, vituperate; blame, charge, accuse, impute, indict; inveigh against, rail against, decry, run down, fulminate against; lash, vilify, curse, revile, vilipend.

upgrade, *n.* **1.** incline, rise, slope, acclivity, assent, climb, unslope; uphill, upclimb, uplift, uprise; ramp, gradient, bank, hill.

—*v.* **2.** improve, better, ameliorate; reform, rehabilitate, restore, correct; repair, fix up, touch up, refurbish, furbish.

upheaval, *n.* **1.** earthquake, quake, volcano, eruption, explosion, blowup.

2. violent change, cataclysm, disruption, confusion, disorder, chaos; disquiet, unrest, furor, outburst, outbreak, *Sl.* big stink; debacle, breakdown, collapse, overthrow.

upheave, *v.* **1.** lift, hoist, boost, pull up, heave; elevate, raise, raise up, upraise, uplift; cast up, thrust up, hold up, uphold, raise high, loft, bear aloft.

2. erupt, explode, blow up *or* out, burst, shoot up; force up, buckle, bulge; shake, quake, rock, toss.

3. cause chaos, confuse, disrupt, unsettle, change.

uphill, *adv.* **1.** up, upwards, upward; skyward, heavenward.

—*adj.* **2.** ascending, climbing, mounting, rising, uprising, acclivitous, acclivous.

3. elevated, raised, lofty, prominent, towering, high, skyhigh, skyscraping.

4. laborious, arduous, strenuous, toilsome, rugged, rough, tough, difficult; heavy, hefty, burdensome, onerous, oppressive, backbreaking, punishing, killing, grueling; operose, herculean.

uphold, *v.* **1.** raise, upraise, raise up, lift, uplift, lift up, elevate, upcast, cast up, upthrow, throw up, rise, rear, uprear, hoist, uphoist, hoist up, boost.

2. support, bear, bear up, hold, hold up, uphold, truss, truss up, prop, prop up, brace, bolster, bolster up, buttress, gird, gird up, stay, mainstay, carry, shoulder, keep up, crutch, shore, shore up, reinforce; underlie, underprop, underpin, underbrace.

3. advocate, promote, patronize, espouse, sanction, countenance, recommend, commend; support, back, second, endorse, maintain, sustain; help, aid, assist; defend, protect, champion, guard, stand by; corroborate, substantiate, bear out, make good; justify, vindicate.

upkeep, *n.* **1.** maintenance, preservation, conservation, safekeeping; sustenance, sustainment, subsistence, support, keep.

2. operating costs, costs, outlay, running expenses, expenses, overhead.

uplift, *v.* **1.** raise, upraise, rear, elevate, erect; lift, hoist, heave, upheave.

2. improve, better, meliorate, ameliorate, mend, amend; enrich, enhance, further, foster; rehabilitate, restore, refurbish, upgrade.

3. exalt, ennoble, dignify, promote; glorify, beatify, canonize, deify, apotheosize, put on a pedestal.

—*n.* **4.** elevation, upheaval, erection, rearing, raising, lifting.

5. betterment, improvement, melioration, amelioration, amendment; enrichment, enhancement; edification, enlightenment, education; civilization, cultivation; advancement, furtherance; rehabilitation.

6. exaltation, ennoblement, promotion; glorification, beatification, canonization, deification, apotheosis.

upper, *adj.* **1.** higher, loftier, more elevated; ahead, over, above.

2. superior, greater, ranking; surpassing, exceeding, transcendent, preeminent, supreme, ascendant, predominant.

upper-class, *adj.* aristocratic, patrician, blue-blooded, silk-stocking; noble, highborn, well-born, gentle, genteel, well-bred; above-average, superior, topflight, first-rate, *Inf.* topnotch; high-level, top-drawer; high-class, elegant, fancy, luxurious, deluxe, sumptuous, posh, *Inf.* swank, *Inf.* swanky, *Sl.* ritzy.

upper hand, *n.* the whip hand, the driver's seat, advantage, *Inf.* edge, the catbird seat; control, command, rule, mastery, domination, dominance; power, authority, influence, sway; ascendancy, primacy, superiority, supremacy, sovereignty.

uppermost, *adj.* **1.** upmost, highest, loftiest, most elevated.

2. greatest, best, topmost, *Inf.* tiptop, apical, culminant, comsummate, maximum, ultimate; paramount, surpreme, transcendent, preeminent, superior, surpassing, exceeding, ascendant; predominant, dominant, leading, top, foremost, principal, main, major, cardinal, prime, primary, chief, sovereign, head, headmost.

upright, *adj.* **1.** erect, bolt upright, stright-up, stright up and down, up and down; vertical, plumb, perpendicular, *Math.* normal; standing, standing-up, stand-up, rearing, *Heraldry.* rampant; upraised, upreared, uplifted, upended.

2. honest, upstanding, incorruptible, uncorrupt, uncorrupted; ethical, moral, principled, high-principled, high-minded, noble-minded; virtuous, righteous, uprighteous, right, good, decent, clean; honorable, reputable, creditable, estimable, noble, worthy, sterling; law-abiding, law-loving, stright-arrow.

3. just, fair, impartial, equitable, objective, balanced, even, even-handed, *Inf.* level; straight, square, fair and square, foursquare, square-dealing, plain-dealing, square-shooting, straight-shooting; rightful, proper, right and proper, fit; aboveboard, open and aboveboard, out front, up front, on the level, up and up, on the up and up.

—*n.* **4.** pole, post, prop, column, pillar, shaft, stanchion; newel, newel post, banister, baluster, *Carpentry, Furniture.* stile; pier, pile, piling.

—*adv.* **5.** erectly, vertically, uprightly, upstandingly, up; perpendicularly, plumb, up and down, stright up and down; bolt upright, at attention, on one's feet *or* legs, *Inf.* on one's hind legs; endwise, endways, on end.

—*v.* **6.** erect, rear, uprear, raise, upraise, raise *or* pitch *or* lift up, uplift, elevate, pitch, set up; raise *or* rear *or* heave aloft, upheave; stand up, stand on end, upend; set on one's feet *or* legs.

uprise, *v.* **1.** get up, arise, rise, get to one's feet, scramble up, leap up, jump up, spring up, bolt up; awaken, waken, wake up, get out of bed, *Inf.* rise and shine, *Sl.* up and at 'em; greet the day, *Inf.* roll out, *Inf.* turn out, *Sl.* hit the deck.

2. rise up, revolt, rebel, insurrectionize, upheave, overthrow, mutiny, subvert; resist, take up arms, defy, break forth; wage war, strike, take the law into one's hands, mount the barricades; disobey, fly in the face of, refuse, kick over the traces.

3. ascend, mount, climb, move upward; go uphill, slope upward, slant upward, grade, tip.

uprising, *n.* **1.** rebellion, revolt, insurrection, insurgence, insurgency, revolution, outbreak, rising; mutiny; sedition, subversion, treason; riot, anarchy, civil disorder, mob law, street-fighting, fighting in the streets, turmoil, chaos, confusion, upheaval; peasant revolt, jacquerie; putsch, coup d'état, overthrow, takeover.

2. incline, slope, acclivity, ascent, climb, rise; upgrade, upslope, uphill, uplift, upclimb, uprise; ramp, gradient, bank, hill

uproar, *n.* clamor, brouhaha, hoo-ha, hubbub, hullabaloo, din, racket, clatter, outburst, *Inf.* blowup; commotion, *Sl.* hoopla, hurly-burly, pother, row, *Inf.* to-do, disturbance, disruption, public sensation; turmoil, tumult, broil, brawl, affray, struggle, conflict; pandemonium, bedlam, free-for-all, fracas, rumpus, scramble, scuffle, *Inf.* ruckus; turbulence, disorder, agitation, furor, frenzy, stir, ado, fuss, tempest in a teapot.

uproarious, *adj.* **1.** tumultuous, turbulent, pandemonian, pandemonic, riotous; disorderly, confused, excited, frenzied, rampageous, tempestuous, wild; noisy, rackety, clamorous, clamoring, boisterous, obstreperous, blustery, resounding, deafening, earsplitting; loud-mouthed, vociferous, roaring, bellowing.

2. very funny, screamingly funny, hysterical, hilarious, a laugh riot, a riot, sidesplitting, *Inf.* killing, *Inf.* too much, *Inf.* too much for words, *Inf.* too funny for words.

uproot, *v.* **1.** extirpate, unroot, pull out by the roots, pull up, pluck up, root out, outroot, deracinate; pull out, draw out, tear out, take out, extract; excise, cut, cut out; unearth, excavate, dig up *or* out, grub up *or* out, weed out.

2. destroy, eradicate, annihilate, obliterate; wipe out, eliminate, stamp out, snuff out, crush out; devastate, demolish, ravage, ruin, *Dial.* ruinate, raze.

upset, *v.* **1.** overturn, turn over, overset, throw over, push over, knock over *or* down; upend, tip over, capsize, keel *or* keel over, turn topsy-turvy, turn upside down, invert, reverse; topple, tumble, precipitate, *Inf.* spill.

2. perturb, disquiet, discompose, discountenance, agitate, ruffle, fluster, flutter, flurry, distract, unsettle, put out; unnerve, unman, disconcert, *Inf.* faze, daunt, dismay, *Inf.* throw off balance; shock, jolt, jar, rattle, pull one up short; trouble, worry, scare, frighten, *Inf.* shake up, unhinge, traumatize, *Inf.* give [s.o.] fits, freak out, alarm, stun; anger, infuriate; sadden, grieve, bring to tears, make [s.o.] cry.

3. put out of order, mess up, dishevel, turn topsy-turvy; scatter, strew about, litter; disarrange, jumble, muddle, mix up, shuffle, confuse, disorganize; spoil, *Sl.* gum up the works, *Inf.* discombobulate, *Inf.* rock the boat, *Inf.* make waves.

4. defeat, beat, rout, discomfit, worst, thrash, *Inf.* whip, *Sl.* cream, *Sl.* shellac; overthrow, vanquish, conquer, triumph over, win out *or* out over, *Inf.* beat out, be victorious over, get the better of, displace, depose; destroy, crush, trounce, *Inf.* stomp, trample, ruin, demolish; quash, quell, squash, squelch.

—adj. **5.** overturned, turned over, knocked over *or* down; capsized, tipped over, upside down, topsy-turvy, inverted, reversed; toppled, tumbled, *Inf.* spilled.

6. disordered, disarranged, disorganized, at sixes and sevens; confused, muddled, macaronic, jumbled, *Inf.* every which way; chaotic, entangled, snarled up; messy, disorderly, helter-skelter, littered, littery; untidy, unkempt, disheveled, slovenly, slatternly, sloppy.

7. perturbed, disquieted, discomposed, discountenanced, ruffled, agitated, flustered, unsettled, distracted; unnerved, unmanned, disconcerted, *Inf.* fazed, daunted, dismayed, *Inf.* thrown off balance; distressed, disturbed, troubled, worried, frightened, scared, afraid; traumatized, *Sl.* freaked out, beside oneself, frantic, hysterical, unhinged; furious, angry, mad, *Inf.* fit to be tied, *Inf.* blue in the face; sad, tearfull, broken-hearted, grief-stricken.

upshot, *n.* **1.** result, effect, consequence, outcome, eventuation, denouement, issue, conclusion, end, end result, *Inf.* payoff, consummation; outgrowth, afterclap, turnout, aftereffect, fallout, backwash, wake; spin-off, side effect, by-product, offshoot; product, harvest, crop, fruit, yield; development, repercussion, reaction, feedback.

2. gist, nitty-gritty, heart of the matter, marrow, pith, crux; point, central *or* main idea, keynot, focus, focal point; substance, meat, essence, quiddity, quintessence, sum and substance; keystone, fundamental principle.

upside down, **1.** inverted, upturned, wrong side up, bottom *or* keel upwards, botton side up, bottom up; turned over, overturned, on one's head.

2. topsy-turvy, helter-skelter, confused, chaotic, muddled, jumbled; disorderly, disordered, disarranged, deranged; unorganized, disorganized; upset, intidy, messy, *Inf.* mussed, disheveled; routed, overthrown.

3. in complete disorder, in disarray, in a jumble, all over the place, *Inf.* every which way; here, there, and everywhere.

upstanding, *adj.* **1.** stand-up, standing-up, standing, rearing, *Heraldry.* rampant; upraised, upreared, uplifted, upended; vertical, plumb, perpendicular, *Math.* normal; erect, tall and erect, bolt upright, straight-up, straight up and down, up and down.

2. vigorous, energetic, dynamic, active; robust, hearty, hale, hale and hearty, hardy, strong and healthy, bursting with health and vigor; sound, healthy, in good health, fit, physically fit, in good condition, in fine fettle, *Inf.* in good shape, *Inf.* in shape; stout, staunch, stalwart, firm, sturdy, tough.

3. honest, upright, incorruptible, See **upright** (*def.* **2.**).

4. candid, frank, forthright, foursquare, straightforward, direct; open, open and sincere, open-hearted, ingenuous, guileless, artless, sincere, genuine, undeceptive, undeceitful, undeceiving, undissembling, undissimulating; aboveboard, open and aboveboard, out front, up front, on the level, up and up, on the up and up, no-nonsense.

upstart, *n.* **1.** nouveau riche, arrivé, arriviste, newly rich, social climber, status seeker, snob; *Sl.* pig in clover, *Inf.* codfish aristocrat; parvenu, *Brit. Sl.* bounder, would-be; nobody, impostor, intruder, pretender.

—adj. **2.** nouveau riche, newly-rich, risen from the ranks; baseborn, earthborn, common; pretentious, precocious, presumptuous, *Sl.* cocky, obtrusive; bluffing, pretending, feigning; forward, brash, brazen, *Sl.* brassy, *Sl.* cheeky, arrogant, audacious.

—v. **3.** start up, spring up; be surprised *or* startled, be given a start.

upswing, *n.* **1.** improvement, upgrade, advancement, betterment, advance; change, change for the better, progress, progression; *Inf.* pickup, recovery, revival, *Inf.* up, *Inf.* comeback.

2. upsurge, upturn, step-up; acceleration, escalation, skyrocketing; increase, elevation, raise, boost, rise.

uptake, *n.* understanding, comprehension, apprehension; perspicacity, keenness, acuteness, acuity; insight, perception, intuition, sensitivity; perceptiveness, perspicaciousness; cleverness, shrewdness, ingenuity, ingeniousness.

up-to-date, *adj.* **1.** current, present, now-passing, happening, occurring, ongoing, going on, prevalent, prevailing, present-day; recent, newly-come, late, latest; just out, hot off the press, up-to-the-minute, most-recent, fresh, new, *Sl.* now, *Sl.* today.

2. modern, the latest thing, new-fashioned, new-minted, new-coined, fresh from the factory; fashionable, in fashion, in style, stylish, in vogue, in the swim, all the rage, modish, popular; swinging, à la mode, *Fr. au courant,* right-on, with it, switched on; newest, neoteric, newest of the new; *All Sl.* trendy, in, in thing, the latest, now, hip, hep, mod, in the groove.

upturn, *v.* **1.** disorder, disarrange, discompose, derange, upheave; confuse, upset, dishevel, turn topsy-turvy; jumble, clutter, muss, mess.

2. lift, lift up, uplift, raise, raise up, upraise; tilt, cast, hold up, uphold, raise high.

—n. **3.** upswing, improvement, advancement; upsurge, increase, boost. See **upswing** (*defs.* **1, 2.**).

upward, *adv.* **1.** up, upwards, straight up, skyward, heavenward, starward, to the stars, to the skies, into the wild blue yonder; upstream, upriver, uplong; uphill, to the top, *Scot.* upwith; upstairs, abovestairs, *Dial.* up steps; northward, up north; uptown.

2. *Often* **upwards of** more, above, beyond, over; over and above, in addition, additionally, besides, further.

—adj. **3.** ascending, rising, mounting, upgoing, uprising; uphill, upsloping, acclivitous, climbing, scandent; ascendant, aspiring, on the rise, in the ascendant.

urban, *adj.* city, cityish, citified, town, townish, oppidan, burghal; metropolitan, municipal, civic; built-up, urbanized.

urbane, *adj.* polished, suave, debonair, charming, gracious; elegant, courtly, refined, finished, cultivated; polite, civil, courteous, tactful, diplomatic; agreeable, complaisant, affable, amenable; civilized, mannerly, well-mannered, well-trained; decorous, formal, proper, *Fr. comme il faut,* correct; gentlemanly, gentlemanlike, chivalrous, chivalric, gallant, cavalier; sophisticated, cosmopolitan, worldly; fashionable, stylish, à la mode, modish, high-toned, *Sl.* tony, in vogue, *Inf.* trendy, up-to-date; high-class, *Sl.* classy, *Inf.* swank, *Sl.* swell.

urbanity, *n.* **1.** polish, finesse, suavity, debonairness, chivalry, gallantry, graciousness, charm; refinement, culture, gentility, gentlemanliness, courtliness; elegance, grace, *Sl.* class, style, smartness; sophistication, cosmopolitanism, worldliness.

2. courtesy, courteousness, politeness, politesse, civility; mannerliness, decorousness, formalness, formality, properness; tact, tactfulness, savoir-faire, diplomacy; agreeability, agreeableness, amenability, amenableness, complaisance; deference, affability, affableness, mildness, softness, gentleness, blandness.

3. urbanities civilities, amenities, courtesies, graces; customs, conventions, etiquette, punctilios, fine points; decorum, proprieties, good manners, good breeding, bon ton, good form.

urchin, *n.* imp, brat, bad boy, little monkey, whippersnapper; *Inf.* shaver, *Brit. Inf.* nipper, kid, gamin, *Fr. enfant terrible;* delinquent, juvenile delinquent, punk, *Inf.* smart aleck, toughie, bully, *Sl.* snot-nosed kid; waif, stray, street Arab, mudlark; guttersnipe, ragamuffin, tatterdemalian.

urge, *v.* **1.** push, drive, propel, force, force along, boost, shove, catapult; speed, speed up, accelerate, whip, whip on, lash, flog; hasten, hurry, hustle, *Inf.* hustle up, quicken, expedite, precipitate.

2. impel, constrain, move, press, induce; incite, instigate, actuate, provoke, foment, poke, prod, prick, thrust, goad, prompt, spur, egg on; excite, arouse, agitate, rouse, inflame, fire, fire up, stir, stir up, wind up, *Inf.* psych up; encourage, boost, enhearten, hearten, reassure, assure, cheer, root, bear up, buoy, buoy up, embolden, nerve, build up, buck up; stimulate, animate, whet, invigorate, motivate, inspire, inspirit, rally, awaken, vivify, bestir, enliven, liven up, jolt, jog.

3. persuade, induce, incline, dispose, influence, prevail upon, coax, ply, sway, talk into; exhort, advise, counsel, suggest, admonish, remonstrate, expostulate; sue, demand, request, solicit, claim, postulate; entreat, importune, appeal to, apply to, adjure, impetrate, obsecrate, invoke, conjure; implore, plead, beseech, supplicate, obtest; pray, crave, beg.

4. allege, assert, vow, avow, vouch, avouch, predicate, swear, assure; insist, uphold, sustain, maintain, contend, aver, vindicate, propound; profess, pronounce, claim, testify, depose, protest, proclaim, declare.

5. support, advocate, recommend, back, endorse, sanction, patronize, approve, countenance; promote, further, forward, advance, favor, foster; help, aid, abet, assist, second, defend, champion, succor, relieve, lend oneself to.

—*n.* **6.** impulse, drive, force, push, dictate, desire, itch; propensity, proclivity, penchant; reason, rationale, motive.

7. impulsion, stimulation, stimulus, incentive, motivation, inspiration, fillip, *Sl.* shot in the arm; incitement, inducement, provocation, instigation, actuation, prompting, urging, goad, spur, prick, press, prod, jolt, jog; excitement, arousal.

8. persuasion, inclination, disposal, influence, coaxing, lying, swaying, talking into; exhortation, advice, counsel, suggestion, admonition, remonstration, remonstrance, expostulation; demand, request, solicitation, claim, postulation; entreaty, appeal, adjuration, imprecation, obsecration, invocation, conjuration; imploration, pleading, beseeching, supplication, obtestation, prayer, praying, craving, begging.

9. support, advocacy, recommendation, backing, endorsement, sanction, patronage, approval, approbation, countenance; promotion, furtherance, forwarding, advance, advancement, favor; help, aid, assistance, abetting, defense, championship, succor, relief.

urgency, *n.* imperativeness, imperative, pressingness, exigency, instancy; extremity, dire necessity, stress, press, matter of life and death, pinch; compulsion, needfulness, indispensability, necessitousness; crisis, emergency, juncture; gravity, importance, necessity; demandingness, importunateness, insistence, pressure.

urgent, *adj.* **1.** imperative, exigent, crucial, critical; important, serious, grave, severe; compelling, demanding, pressing, instant, high-priority; vital, necessitous, necessary, primary, obligatory, compulsory; requisite, indispensable, essential.

2. crying, importunate, clamorous, insistent, pertinacious; forceful, pushing, clamant, loud; earnest, solicitous, begging, pleading.

urn, *n.* **1.** vase, bowl, crock, amphora, vessel, pot; ewer, cruse, bottle, pitcher, jug, decanter, flask, jar; funeral urn, cinerarium, ossuary, cinerary urn, bone pot.

2. samovar, teapot, coffeepot, coffee maker, percolator.

usage, *n.* **1.** custom, practice, habit, tradition, way; form, formality, convention, matter of course, observance; routine, course, manner, method, procedure, policy, rule; wont, habitude, consuetude, praxis; fashion, mode, common practice, the way it's done, way of doing things, prescription, folkway.

2. treatment, handling, management, way of dealing, maneuvering; conduct, running, operation, manipulation, control, administration.

3. manner of speaking, manner, speech, diction, language, parole, talk; idiom, parlance, phraseology, dialect, ideolect; expression, locution, wording, word, utterance, turn of expression, phrasing.

4. employment, application, exercise, practice. See **use** (*def.* 7).

use, *v.* **1.** employ, make use of, utilize, apply; ply, wield, operate, manipulate, maneuver; handle, practice, exercise, exert, bring to bear, bring into play, play; occupy, put into service, have the use of.

2. avail oneself of, make the most of, take up, convert to use, get the best out of, put to use; turn to account, profit by, capitalize, make play with; resort to, have recourse to, betake oneself to, fall back on, make do with, press into service; turn to, run to, recur to, *Inf.* take to, refer to; take advantage of, benefit by, make good use of, put to advantage, reap the benefit of, *Inf.* make hay.

3. exploit, take advantage of, abuse, manipulate, misuse; play upon, impose upon, trade upon, walk all over [s.o.]; bleed, drain, suck dry, milk; play for a sucker, presume upon, use for one's own ends, work upon.

4. spend, expend, consume, pass, devote, occupy; give, take, take up, fill; dedicate, consecrate, put, make, bestow.

5. use up exhaust, consume, deplete, run through, go through; waste, fritter away, squander, throw away, gamble away; lose, pour down the drain, spill, diddle away, fribble away, fool away; finish off, gobble up, swallow, absorb, drain.

6. used to accustomed to, in the habit of, wont to, given to, prone to; in the practice *or* custom of, addicted to; would, did; familiar with, acquainted with, adapted to, familiar with; inured to, tempered to, toughened to, hardened to.

—*n.* **7.** employment, exercise, practice, usage, application, utilization, *Archaic.* usance; operation, manipulation, maneuvering, management, working, handling; exploitation, treatment, wear, wear and tear; abhibition, disposal, administration, conversion.

8. power, right, privilege, usufruct, enjoyment, usage; grant, prerogative, license, libertv.

9. advantage, benefit, profit, interest, behalf, behoof; service, help, avail, convenience, good; support, office, benefaction.

10. usefulness, applicability, serviceability, convertibility. See **utility** (*def.* 1).

11. occasion, need, purpose, reason, cause; call, motive, basis, point, ground.

12. form, practice, common practice, custom. See **usage** (*def.* 1).

useful, *adj.* **1.** serviceable, advantageous, helpful, aidful, good for; applicable, employable, usable, functional, utilitarian; of service, of use, of help; availing, commodious, convenient, instrumental, conducive; worthwhile, gainful, profitable, rewarding; contributory, giving, productive, paying, valuable, beneficial.

2. efficacious, effective, expedient, operative, effectual; practical, pragmatic, handy. See **utilitarian.**

useless, *adj.* **1.** purposeless, vain, futile, idle, bootless, unavailing, Sisyphean, ineffective, ineffectual, inefficacious; fruitless, unproductive, abortive, barren, sterile, impotent, effete; unprofitable, profitless, unsuccessful, to no purpose, to no avail, for naught.

2. worthless, inutile, valueless, nugatory, trifling, trivial, inane, inessential, inconsequential, unimportant, frivolous, superfluous; inadequate, inoperative, inefficient, unserviceable, impracticable, *Inf.* no go, no good, *Sl.* on the shelf.

usher, *n.* **1.** escort, usherette, guide, pilot, steerer, leader, conductor, director.

2. doorkeeper, butler, gatekeeper, *Rom. Cath. Ch.* ostiary, porter, concierge; *Sl.* bouncer.

—v. **3.** escort, guide, pilot, steer, lead, see in *or* out, bring in, take out; conduct, direct, show in *or* out, show the way; accompany, companion, keep [s.o.] company, go along with, *Archaic.* company.

4. present, announce, give notice of, herald, bring *or* give tidings of, *Inf.* ring in; inaugurate, initiate, begin, start, ring up the curtain on; launch, get going *or* moving, get under way; induct, institute, install.

usual, *adj.* **1.** habitual, accustomed, customary, routine, normal; established, set, prescribed, time-honored, traditional; regulation, formal, stock, standard; conventional, general, prevailing, prevalent, common, frequent; popular, favorite, natural, wonted, consuetudinary; fixed, rooted, confirmed, daily; repeated, known, well-known, expected, predictable, unvaried.

2. typical, average, everyday, ordinary, common; stereotypical, run-of-the-mill, commonplace, garden-variety, workaday, workday; household, vernacular, colloquial, cliché; middle-class, unexceptional, unremarkable, run-of-the-mine; trite, hackneyed, mediocre, worn-out, prosaic; oft-repeated, platitudinous, humdrum, monotonous, threadbare; philistine, plebeian, bourgeois, vulgar.

usually, *adv.* **1.** ordinarily, generally, commonly, normally, regularly; by and large, generally speaking, as a matter of course, as a rule, all in all; in the main, mostly, mainly, for the most part, on the whole, predominantly, taking all things together.

2. customarily, routinely, habitually, repeatedly; frequently, often, many times, most often, many a time, oftentimes; conventionally, as is usual, as is the custom; by force of habit, inveterately, persistently, chronically.

usurer, *n.* extortionist, loan shark, Shylock, shyster; moneylender, moneymonger, loaner, lender; parasite, *Sl.* bleeder, *Sl.* milker; financier, creditor, banker.

usurp, *v.* **1.** take over, expropriate, seize, commandeer, take possession of, appropriate, lay claim to, arrogate, assume; wrest from, take from, accroach; help oneself to, make free with.

2. encroach, move in on, trespass, infringe; make inroads, ease [s.o.] out, dispossess; supplant, supersede, take the place of; upstage, steal [s.o.'s] thunder, steal the show *or* the spotlight.

3. misappropriate, steal, pirate, plagiarize, copy, *Inf.* lift, *Euph.* borrow; rob, despoil, thieve; snatch, capture, walk off with.

usurpation, *n.* **1.** forceful seizure, expropriation, takeover, appropriation, confiscation, impoundment; arrogation, accroachment, assumption, usurping.

2. encroachment, infringement, inroads, trespass; dispossession, deposition, dislodgment, displacement, removal.

3. misappropriation, theft, thievery, stealing, robbery; plagiarism, piracy, pirating.

utensil, *n.* instrument, tool, implement, device, apparatus, contrivance; knife, fork, spoon, chopstick; container, vessel, receptacle, holder, dish.

utilitarian, *adj.* practical, pragmatic, effectual, effective, efficacious, expedient; functional, handy, good, usable, utilizable; operable, convertible, adaptable; workable, made for, to the purpose, suitable.

utility, *n.* **1.** usefulness, usability, use, applicability, serviceability, convertibility, adaptability; advantageousness, helpfulness, aidfulness, profitability; advantage, benefit, profit, value, worth, merit; service, good, efficacy, effectiveness, beneficialness, favorableness; convenience, point, avail; practicality, practicability, functionalism, utilitarianism.

—adj. **2.** reserve, backup, dummy, substitute, alternate; spare, temporary, secondary, provisional, makeshift.

3. handy, *Inf.* all-around, multipurpose, utilitarian, functional; adaptable, serviceable, commodious.

utilize, *v.* exercise, practice, employ, put to use, make use of; avail oneself of, have recourse to, resort to. See **use** (*defs.* **1, 2**).

utmost, *adj.* **1.** maximum, maximal, greatest, most, uttermost; supreme, paramount, superlative; highest, uppermost, upper, topmost, top, tiptop; summital, apical, apogeal, apogean; meridian, meridional, climactic, climactical, crowning, culminating, culminant.

2. farthest, remotest, outermost, outlying, outer, extreme; endmost, ultimate, terminal, last, final, marginal, peripheral.

—n. **3.** maximum, max, most, uttermost, extreme, the nth degree, *Math.* extremum; apex, vertex, apogee, acme, zenith, *Latin. ne plus ultra;* summit, pinnacle, peak, height, top, tip, tiptop.

4. best, finest, prime, *U.S. Sl.* the most, *U.S. Sl.* the greatest, *Sl.* the tops; hardest, *Inf.* damnedest, *Inf.* darnedest.

5. extremity, farthest point, outer limit, horizon, the end of the earth; limit, ambit, bound, boundary, border, frontier; periphery, margin, edge, rim, brim, brow, lip, ridge, verge, brink; ultimate, end, finale, termination, terminal, terminus.

utopia, *n.* paradise, Garden of Eden, Eden, heaven on earth, the best of all possible worlds; Shangri-la, El Dorado, Erewhon; castle in the air, air castle, castle in Spain.

utopian, *adj.* **1.** idealistic, perfect, ideal, *Inf.* dream, pie-in-the-sky; fantasy, imaginary, imagined, fanciful, fancied, chimerical, unreal, illusory, visionary, quixotic; airy, vaporous, unsubstantial, insubstantial, wild, idle; fictitious, made-up, make-believe, fairy-tale, mythical, fantastic; romantic, impractical, unpractical, unrealistic, infeasible, unfeasible, inoperable, unworkable; unattainable, unrealizable, unfulfillable.

—n. **2.** idealist, Don Quixote, dreamer, daydreamer, visionary, fantast, romantic, romanticist.

utter[1] *v.* **1.** say, speak, tell, pronounce, express; articulate, verbalize, voice, vocalize, enounce; give voice, give forth, let out, emit, raise; enunciate, *Phonetics.* phonate, put in words, formulate, present; whisper, breathe, sigh, mutter, murmur; exclaim, sing, chant, yell, scream, squeal, yelp, bark, growl, snap; vent, air, out with, break, ventilate.

2. reveal, divulge, make known, disclose, impart; communicate, convey, divulgate, broadcast; blazon, trumpet, noise about, blare, bruit about; declare, proclaim, announce, issue, assert, asseverate, nuncupate; publicize, circulate, post, placard, advertise, spread, pass, give publicity to, give to the world.

utter[2], *adj.* absolute, complete, total, thorough; downright, out-and-out, pure and simple, unequivocal; unmitigated, unqualified, unconditional, categorical, unmodified, unbounded; rank, flagrant, egregious, shocking, arrant, glaring, striking; sheer, stark, pure, *Inf.* plumb, through and through; positive, definite, consummate, perfect, outright, *Brit.* proper; clean, plain, *Inf.* regular, born, dyed-in-the-wool; wholesale, all-out, *Sl.* whole-hog, across-the-board, overwhelming, comprehensive.

utterance, *n.* **1.** expression, articulation, verbalization, vocalization, enunciation; telling, announcement, mention, delivery; saying, assertion, asseveration, declaration, proclamation, annunciation; communication, pronouncement, averment, affirmation, indication.

2. remark, word, comment, opinion, statement; question, answer, interjection, exclamation, greeting, address, *Inf.* shot; *Inf.* two-cents' worth, riposte, *Sl.* crack, parting shot.

3. cry, outcry, ejaculation, acclamation, call, calling; sigh, whisper, purr, murmur; squeak, caw, meow, coo, peep, cheep, chirp; moo, whinny, bleat, baa, oink; bark, yelp, growl, caterwaul, bray, neigh; hoot, whoop, squawk, yell, yowl, shout; holler, bellow, boo, roar, howl, skirl, screech, scream.

uttermost, *adj., n.* See **utmost.**

V

vacancy, *n.* **1.** emptiness, void, vacuum, vacuity, vacuousness; gap, hiatus, aperture, interstice; opening, space, breach; foramen, orifice, mouth; fissure, chink, cleft, crack, crevice, cranny; hollow, cavity, hole, pore; chasm, crater.
2. (*all used in reference to availability*) opportunity, chance; position, office, job, slot; apartment, flat, room, quarters, rental.
3. vacuity, inanity, blankness, fatuity. See **vacuity** (*def.* **4**).

vacant, *adj.* **1.** empty, void, without contents, unfilled, hollow, depleted, exhausted, *Scot. and North Eng.* toom; devoid of, destitute of, without, out of, short of, lacking, wanting, bereft of.
2. unoccupied, untenanted, tenantless, uninhabited, unfurnished, bare; abandoned, deserted, unclaimed, available, *Inf.* up for grabs.
3. unused, unutilized, not in use, disengaged; idle, leisure, free, spare, extra.
4. unemployed, loafing, indolent, lazy, shiftless, do-nothing, fainéant; undirected, purposeless, meaningless, unfulfilled.
5. blank, expressionless, inexpressive, deadpan, poker-faced, stupid; vacuous, inane, fatuous, foolish, silly; thoughtless, unthinking, unreflecting, unreasoning, brainless; dull, dense, unintelligent.

vacate, *v.* **1.** make empty *or* vacant, leave unoccupied, evacuate; abandon, surrender, desert, quit, depart from.
2. abdicate, resign, renounce, give up claim *or* right to, lay down, retire from, *Chiefly Scot.* demit; relinquish, let go, deliver up, hand over, turn over, cede, transfer, give way to.
3. repudiate, *Law.* disaffirm; nullify, annul, declare null and void, void, invalidate, cancel; abrogate, rescind, recall, revoke; quash, set aside, overrule, veto, override, overturn, reverse, countermand; set at naught, dissolve, abolish, dismiss.
4. *Informal.* depart, leave, go away, be off, *Sl.* split, *Sl.* cut out, *Brit. Sl.* bugger off.

vacation, *n.* **1.** recess, holiday, time off, pause, rest, break, *Inf.* breather, respite; furlough, leave, rest and recuperation, R & R; freedom, release, suspension; interruption, discontinuation, interim, interval, intermission.
2. trip, excursion, jaunt, cruise, voyage, hike, backpack; estivation.
—*v.* **3.** travel, sightsee, motor, explore, visit, spend the summer, estivate, *Chiefly Brit.* holiday.

vacationer, *n.* vacationist, holidayer; traveler, voyager, excursionist, *Brit. Inf.* tripper, tourist, sightseer; backpacker, camper, hiker; transient, summer resident, estivator.

vacillate, *v.* **1.** shilly-shally, tergiversate, seesaw, *Inf.* flip-flop, *Inf.* yo-yo; oscillate, fluctuate, go back and forth, blow hot and cold, keep changing one's mind; dither, waver, falter, hesitate, pause, be irresolute, be indecisive, straddle the fence, run with the hare and hunt with the hounds, play both ends against the middle; equivocate, hedge, hem and haw, not give a straight answer, beat around the bush, pussyfoot.
2. sway, rock, reel, stagger, totter, *Chiefly U.S.* teeter, *Chiefly U.S.* teeter-totter, wobble.
3. swing, wave, wag, move back and forth, vibrate, flutter, undulate, ripple.

vacillating, *adj.* **1.** vacillant, vacillatory, indecisive, irresolute, unresolved, unsettled, uncertain, undecided, ambivalent, of two minds; of mixed feelings; wavering, dithering, faltering, hesitating, hesitant, wishy-washy; oscillating, fluctuating, going back and forth, blowing hot and cold, betwixt and between, shilly-shally, shilly-shallying, tergiversating, sitting on *or* straddling the fence; off-again on-again, changeable, fickle, capricious, whimsical, erratic, up-and-down.
2. swaying, moving back and forth, rocking, reeling, staggering, tottering, *Chiefly U.S.* teetering, *Chiefly U.S.* teeter-tottering, wobbling.

vacillation, *n.* **1.** indecision, indecisiveness, shilly-shally, shilly-shallying, tergiversation, fence-sitting, fence-straddling; irresolution, irresoluteness, uncertainty, incertitude, unsureness, infirmity of purpose, unsettledness, ambivalence, double-mindedness, mixed feelings; wavering, hesitation, hesitancy, faltering, oscillation, fluctuation, going back and forth, blowing hot and cold; changeableness, fickleness, capriciousness, whimsicality, whimsicalness, erraticism.
2. swaying, moving back and forth, vibration, rise and fall, rising and falling, ebb and flow, flux and reflux; unsteady movement, rocking, reeling, staggering, tottering, *Chiefly U.S.* teetering, *Chiefly U.S.* teeter-tottering, wobbling.

vacuity, *n.* **1.** vacancy, emptiness, void, voidness, vacuum, vacuousness; nothingness, nihility.
2. absence, lack, want, deficiency; need, privation, deprivation, dearth.
3. hollowness, meaninglessness, purposelessness, goallessness; boredom, ennui, tedium, dreariness, dullness, wearisomeness; flatness, stagnation, sameness, monotony.
4. inanity, fatuity, silliness, asininity; unintelligence, stupidity, brainlessness, foolishness, empty-

headedness, idiocy, imbecility; blankness, incognizance, unawareness, reverie, daydream; dreaminess, woolgathering, absent-mindedness, abstraction, distraction, preoccupation.

vacuous, *adj.* See **vacant** (*defs.* **1, 4, 5**).

vacuum, *n.* **1.** emptiness, void, space devoid of air. **2.** vacuum cleaner, sweeper, carpet sweeper, electric broom, *Trademark.* Hoover.
—*v.* **3.** sweep, clean, do the housecleaning; pick up, tidy up.

vagabond, *adj.* **1.** nomadic, vagrant, Bohemian, gypsy; wandering, roaming, roving, rambling, straying, straggling; moving, ambulant, traveling, peregrinating, journeying; migrating, migrant, migratory, itinerant, peripatetic, drifting, floating, *Sl.* rolling; transient, transitory, temporary, fly-by-night.
2. unsettled, carefree, untied, uncommitted; loose, lax, wanton, dissolute, promiscuous; disreputable, worthless, shiftless, good-for-nothing.
—*n.* **3.** tramp, vagrant, *Archaic.* runagate, hobo, *Chiefly U.S. Inf.* boomer, *Australian.* swagman, beachcomber, derelict, street Arab; *Inf.* bum, *Sl.* vag, *Sl.* bo, *Sl.* stiff, *Sl.* bindle stiff, *Sl.* canvas back; panhandler, *Yiddish.* schnorrer, down-and-outer; migrant worker, itinerant, *Usu. Disparaging.* Okie, drifter, *Inf.* floater, transient, fly-by-night; wanderer, roamer, rover, rambler, strayer, straggler, gadabout; migrator, bird of passage, *Sl.* rolling stone; gypsy, nomad; outcast, pariah, castaway.
4. rogue, picaro, knave, scapegrace, wastrel, ne'er-do-well, good-for-nothing, good-for-naught; villain, miscreant, reprobate, incorrigible; rascal, rapscallion, scamp, devil, troublemaker; libertine, rake, wanton, debauchee.

vagary, *n.* caprice, notion, crank, impulse, extravagant idea, brain wave, brainstorm; whim, whimsy, fancy, humor, crotchet, *Archaic.* maggot; idiosyncrasy, idiocrasy, peculiarity, eccentricity, quirk, oddity; erraticism, turn, twist, fit.

vagrancy, *n.* nomadism, peripateticism, vagabondism, Bohemianism, hoboism; itinerancy, wandering, roaming, roving, rambling, wayfaring, drifting, gallivanting, gadding, *Dial.* traipsing, *Australian.* swagging, *Sl.* bumming.

vagrant, *n.* **1.** tramp, vagabond, nomad, *Archaic.* runagate, hobo. See **vagabond** (*def.* **3**).
—*adj.* **2.** nomadic, vagabond, Bohemian, gypsy; wandering, roaming, roving. See **vagabond** (*defs.* **1, 2**).

vague, *adj.* **1.** imprecise, inexact, undefinite, not explicit, not straightforward, unspecific, nonspecific; ambiguous, equivocal, dubious, questionable, *Inf.* neither fish nor fowl.
2. indistinct, indeterminate, undefined, ill-defined, undistinguishable; inaudible, muffled, low, mumbled, muttered, unintelligible; faint, dim, weak, feeble, imperceptible, faraway; pale, faded, undecipherable.
3. obscure, nebulous, unclear, *Rare.* imperspicuous; shadowy, hazy, fuzzy, foggy, blurry, blurred, bleary, out of focus, unfocused; cloudy, opaque, filmy, misty, obfuscated, veiled.
4. uncertain, indefinite, undetermined, unsettled, unfixed, up in the air, open, touch-and-go, borderline; unproven, undemonstrated, in question; speculative, conjectural, assumptive.
5. abstract, recondite, abstruse; enigmatic, enigmatical, puzzling, baffling, bewildering, confounding; mysterious, arcane, cryptic; paradoxical, unfathomable, impenetrable, incomprehensible, confused, doubtful, uncertain.
6. undecided, wishy-washy, hesitant, hesitating; vacillating, wavering, inconstant, fluctuating, shilly-shallying, on the fence.

vagueness, *n.* **1.** impreciseness, inexactness, inexactitude, unspecificity, nonspecificity; ambiguity equivocality, equivocalness, equivocation; dubiousness, doubtfulnes, questionableness; indefiniteness abstractness, abstruseness, reconditeness; incomprehensibility, impenetrableness, confusion.
2. indistinctness, indeterminateness, undistinguishableness, unintelligibility; faintness, dimness, paleness, weakness, feebleness, imperceptibleness, undecipherableness.
3. obscurity, nebulousness, unclearness, unclarity; haziness, fuzziness, fogginess, blurriness, blurredness, bleariness; cloudiness, opaqueness, filminess, mistiness, smokiness, obfuscation.
4. undecidedness, uncertainty, wishy-washiness, hesitance, hesitancy; vacillation, wavering, inconstance, inconstancy, fluctuating, fluctuation, shilly-shallying, fence-sitting.

vain, *adj.* **1.** worthless, nugatory, trivial, insignificant, trifling, unimportant, inessential, valueless, meritless, good-for-nothing; empty, hollow, idle, inane, vapid; inadequate, unserviceable; unsubstantial, unreal, false, baseless, delusive, unfounded; shadowy, dreamy, chimerical, imaginary, mythical, legendary, fictitious, notional; fanciful, fabulous, whimsical, figmental, visionary; high-flown, vaporous, frothy, airspun, romantic, idealistic.
2. conceited, haughty, proud, boastful, *Scot.* vaunty, arrogant, vainglorious; pompous, supercilious, disdainful, insolent, imperious, lordly, magisterial; inflated, puffed up, uppish, high-and-mighty, high-handed, high-toned, on one's high horse, *Inf.* stuck-up, *Inf.* uppity; affected, pretentious, bombastic, presumptuous, overweening; ostentatious, showy, dandyish, foppish, dudish, swaggering, cocky; egotistical, self-complacent, self-satisfied, self-admiring, self-confident, self-flattering.
3. futile, useless, unavailing, bootless, ineffective, inefficacious; fruitless, unproductive, abortive, barren, sterile, impotent; unprofitable, profitless, unsuccessful; for naught, for nothing, to no purpose, to no avail.

vainglorious, *adj.* conceited, haughty, proud, boastful, *Scot.* vaunty, arrogant, braggart. See **vain** (*def.* **2**).

vainglory, *n.* **1.** pride, vanity, boasting, bragging, rodomontade; haughtiness, airs, cheekiness, insolence, arrogance, lordliness, pomposity, pompousness; egotism, self-glorification, self-laudation, self-approbation, self-gratulation, self-applause, *Fr. amour-propre.*
2. ostentation, ostentatiousness, pretention, pretentiousness, pomp, show, affectation, showiness, showing off; swaggering, strut, flourish, dash, swank; foppishness, dandyism.

vainly, *adv.* in vain, futilely, uselessly, unavailingly, to no avail, bootlessly; ineffectually, inefficaciously, unsuccessfully, unprofitably; fruitlessly, unproductively, abortively.

vale, *n.* dale, dell, coulee, glen, valley. See **valley**.

valet, *n.* manservant, man, servant, *Archaic.* groom, *Fr. valet de chambre*; butler, steward, cupbearer; lackey, footservant, footman, *Contemptuous.* flunky; page, *Chiefly Brit.* buttons, squire, pursuivant, *Brit.* boots.

valetudinarian, *n.* **1.** invalid, sickly person, infirm person, convalescent, shut-in, valetudinary; patient, inpatient, outpatient, case; sufferer, carrier, cripple, incurable, victim; hypochondriac, *Pathol.* neurasthenic, malingerer.
—*adj.* **2.** invalid, sick, sickly, infirm, unwell, ill, ailing; weak, weakly, feeble, enfeebled, frail, helpless,

debilitated; exhausted, prostrate, *Pathol.* neurasthenic; unhealthy, diseased, morbose, unsound, under doctor's care; indisposed, confined, laid up, bedridden; handicapped, palsied, crippled, disabled, lame; paralyzed, paralytic, *Pathol.* paretic; tubercular, consumptive; senescent, senile, doting, decrepit; flagging, dropping, moribund, dying.

valiant, *adj.* **1.** brave, courageous, valorous, heroic, hero-like, stout-hearted, lionhearted, great-hearted; virile, manly, manful, gallant, chivalrous, chivalric; intrepid, fearless, unafraid, dauntless, dreadless, aweless, nervy, *Sl.* gutsy, unblenching, unblenched, undaunted, undismayed, unappalled, unalarmed; bold, bold-spirited, daring, dashing, adventurous, audacious, rash, reckless; assured, self-assured, self-reliant, confident; pot-valorous, pot-valiant.

2. firm, resolute, indomitable, unconquerable, invincible, staunch, steadfast, stalwart, *Archaic.* stalworth, doughty, sturdy, hardy; unflinching, unyielding, unswerving, unwavering, undeviating, unshrinking, unfaltering, unhesitating, unbending; mettlesome, plucky, gritty, game, spirited, red-blooded, *Inf.* spunky.

3. worthy, deserving, deserved, due, right, rightful, just, equitable; fit, fitting, befitting, suitable, appropriate, proper, seemly, becoming.

4. excellent, exemplary, sterling; admirable, praiseworthy, meritorious, commendable, laudable, estimable; honest, honorable, noble, reliable, trustworthy, reputable, respectable; upright, righteous, virtuous, good, decent, incorruptible, irreproachable.

valid, *adj.* **1.** sound, solid, well-grounded, well-founded, reasonable, logical; factual, accurate, correct, truthful, veracious, *Obs.* veritable; warrantable, certifiable, authorizable; justifiable, vindicable, excusable, explainable, explicable, accountable.

2. just, equitable, fair, impartial, objective, unbiased; upright, honest, scrupulous; right, proper, appropriate, apt, fitting, meet.

3. effective, effectual, efficacious, forceful, forcible, powerful, potent, *Literary.* puissant, vigorous, strong; cogent, persuasive, convincing, believable, credible; conclusive, decisive, determining, definitive, final; substantiative, corroborative, corroboratory, sustaining.

4. authoritative, official, certified, licensed, accredited, validated, notarized, attested, endorsed; substantiated, documented, circumstantiated; scientific, tested, proven, verified, authenticated, confirmed, demonstrated, established, probative, probatory, (*of wills*) *Law.* probated; substantial, substantive, material, weighty, heavy, grave; significant, consequential, momentous, important; pertinent, apposite, to the point, applicable, relevant, related, relative, germane.

5. lawful, legal, licit, contitutional, statutory, by the book; sanctioned, authorized, warranted, approved, countenanced; defendable, supportable, provable, sustainable; obligatory, binding, contractual; legitimate, vested, rightful, real, actual, true, authentic, genuine, *Inf.* kosher.

validate, *v.* **1.** verify, prove, establish; authenticate, document, circumstantiate, (*of wills*) *Law.* probate; confirm, substantiate, corroborate, sustain, uphold, support, back up.

2. legalize, legitimize, legitimatize, conform to the law, codify, make acceptable; legislate, enact, ordain, ratify, enter into the books; contitute, charter, institute, formalize, set up.

3. authorize, warrant, license, certify, notarize, visa; accredit, qualify, invest, empower, enable, entitle, capacitate; sanction, approve, give one's nod of approval, countenance; allow, permit, consent to, accept, agree to, vouchsafe, *Chiefly U.S.* approbate, *Inf.* O.K.; endorse, attest *or* testify to, give one's stamp *or* seal of approval, set one's seal to, seal.

validity, *n.* **1.** effectiveness, effectivity, effectualness, effectuality, efficaciousness; potency, *Literary.* puissance, force, forcefulness, forcibleness, power, powerfulness, strength, vigor, vigorousness; substantialness, substantiality, substantiveness, materialness, weightiness, heaviness, graveness; significance, consequence, moment, momentousness, import, importance; cogency, persuasiveness, convincibility, convincingness, credibility, credibleness, believability, believableness; pertinence, pertinency, relevance, relevancy, relatedness, germaneness, appositeness, applicability.

2. verifiableness, verifiability, provability, provableness, authenticity, genuineness; accuracy, correctness, factualness, factuality, veracity, veraciousness, trueness.

3. legality, lawfulness, legitimacy, legitimateness, constitutionality; soundness, solidity, solidness, reasonableness, logicalness, logicality; authority, officialness, warrant, sanction.

valise, *n.* traveling bag, overnight bag, bag, case, suitcase, luggage, *Chiefly Brit.* portmanteau, Gladstone bag; attaché case, brief case, duffel bag, grip, carpetbag; vanity case, vanity bag, cosmetic bag.

valley, *n.* river basin, bottoms, dale, *Scot.* strath; dell, vale, coulee, *Brit. Dial.* clough, (*in England*) combe; glen, dingle, *Brit. Dial.* gill; cleft, ravine, gully, defile, gap; depression, hollow, concavity.

valor, *n.* **1.** courage, bravery, valorousness, valiancy, valiance, heroism, prowess, stout-heartedness, lionhe rtedness, great-heartedness; virility, manliness, manfulness, manhood, gallantry, chivalry, chivalrousness; intrepidity, intrepidness, fearlessness, dauntlessness, awelessness, dreadlessness; boldness, bold-spiritedness, high-spiritedness, daring, derring-do, audacity, audaciousness, rashness, recklessness; dash, élan, panache, bravado; assurance, self-assurance, self-reliance, confidence, self-confidence; pot-valor, pot-valiancy, pot-valiance.

2. fortitude, endurance, tenacity, determination, will, will power; firmness, resolution, resoluteness, indomitableness, indomitability, invincibleness, invincibility, staunchness, steadfastness, stalwartness, doughtiness, sturdiness, hardiness, hardihood, bulldog courage; mettle, pluck, pluckiness, spirit, backbone, gumption, blood, heart, nerve, grit, *U.S. Inf.* sand, *Inf.* starch, *Inf.* spunk, *Sl.* guts, *Sl.* moxie.

valorous, *adj.* brave, courageous, valiant, heroic. See **valiant** (*defs.* **1, 2**).

valuable, *adj.* **1.** costly, worth a lot, expensive, high-priced, priceless, beyond one's means; rare, precious, antique, select, choice, elite; fine, superfine, exquisite, dainty; lavish, extravagant, sumptuous, rich; superior, superlative, supreme, prize; extraordinary, special, uncommon, scarce.

2. estimable, admirable, commendable, worthy of respect, revered, venerated; held dear, guarded, kept, memorable, dear, beloved, cherished; favorite, valued, prized.

3. important, serviceable, useful; beneficial, helpful, advantageous, profitable, gainful.

—*n.* **4.** *Usu.* **valuables** jewelry, jewels, gems, silver, gold; heirlooms, family treasures, treasures, prizes, acquisitions.

value, *n.* **1.** worth, merit, use, usefulness, utility; advantage, benefit, gain, profit, avail, good; importance, consideration, consequence, significance, moment, weight.

2. monetary worth, face value; cost, price, market

price, asking price, going price, selling price, charge, expense; rate of exchange, exchange; valuation, appraisal, assessment, evaluation.

3. import, meaning, significance, signification, sense; secondary meaning, connotation, implication; intent, intention, purpose, purport, point.

4. values ideals, standards, morals, principles; customs, institutions, *Sociol.* mores.

—*v.* **5.** assess, appraise, evaluate, valuate, estimate *or* determine the value of, rate, set a value on, price, fix *or* set the price of.

6. prize, appreciate, esteem, regard highly, hold in high regard, have a high opinion of, think highly of; respect, set great store by, admire, look up to, revere, venerate, worship, idolize, put on a pedestal; like, be fond of, love, adore, cherish, hold dear, consider precious; treasure, set a high value on, rate highly, make much of.

valued, *adj.* **1.** prized, esteemed, highly regarded, respected, well-respected, admired, looked up to; liked, well-liked, loved, much loved, adored, cherished, treasured; revered, venerated, worshipped, idolized.

2. assessed, appraised, evaluated, valuated, estimated, calculated; fixed, set, priced.

valueless, *adj.* **1.** worthless, of no value *or* worth, good-for-nothing, *Inf.* of no earthly use *or* good, *Inf.* not worth a damn, *Inf.* not worth a tinker's dam, not worth a straw *or* a fig *or* a continental; not worth having *or* keeping; nugatory, trifling, trivial, petty, inconsequential, minor, insignificant, unimportant, frivolous, superfluous, unnecessary, inessential.

2. useless, unuseful, futile, inutile, vain, wasted, idle; bootless, unavailing, of no avail, Sisyphean, ineffective, ineffectual, inefficacious; fruitless, unproductive, unprofitable, pointless, silly, inane.

vamp[1], *v.* patch *or* patch up, repair, mend, remedy, fix *or* fix up, doctor *or* doctor up; put back together, put back in one piece, restore, rehabilitate, make good as new; sew *or* sew up, stitch, reinforce; recondition, refashion, reconstruct, revamp.

vamp[2], *v.* seduce, persuade, tempt, lure; beguile, charm, captivate, hypnotize; flirt, wink at, cast sheep's eyes at, play fast and loose.

vampire, *n.* **1.** Dracula, lamia, ghoul, fiend.

2. extortionist, extortioner, bloodsucker, usurer; vulture, harpy, *Inf.* gold digger.

3. vamp, siren, seductress, *Fr. femme fatale*, temptress, enchantress; flirt, coquette.

van, *n.* truck, motor truck, *Brit.* lorry, dray; bus; moving van, *Trademark.* U-Haul, trailer, camper; vehicle, wagon, wain, car.

vandal, *n.* **1.** ransacker, sacker, marauder, pillager, plunderer, looter, raider, robber; destroyer, demolisher, desolator, despoiler; wrecker, mutilator; barbarian, Hun.

2. hoodlum, *Sl.* hood, hooligan, tough, ruffian, *Sl.* punk, rowdy, delinquent, juvenile delinquent, *Sl.* j.d.

vanguard, *n.* **1.** advance guard, van, front line, *Mil.* front.

2. forefront, cutting edge, avant-garde; leaders, pioneers, trailblazers, groundbreakers, innovators; pacesetters, pacemakers, trend-setters.

vanish, *v.* **1.** disappear, leave no trace, dematerialize, disappear from sight, disappear from the face of the earth, disappear into thin air, be lost to sight; be swallowed up, go down the drain, go by the board; evaporate, dissipate, disperse, volatilize, vaporize; fade, evanesce, fade away, melt away, dissolve, *Sl.* go poof; recede, recede from view, retrocede, ebb, wane; withdraw, retire, retreat, repair; depart, leave, go, go away, quit, vacate; flit away, fly away, *Brit. Sl.* mizzle, up and go, take wing, *Sl.* vamoose, *Jocular.* absquatulate, decamp.

2. pass away, cease to exist, die out, cease to be, pass on, die, expire, perish; be no more, come to an end, become extinct, pass into oblivion, become obsolete.

vanity, *n.* **1.** egotism, conceit, conceitedness, self-conceit, overweening pride, self-pride, self-love, narcissism, self-admiration, self-worship, *Inf.* me-ism, self-approbation, self-glorification, self-importance, swelled-headedness, vainglory, vaingloriousness, superciliousness; smugness, complacency, self-satisfaction.

2. arrogance, haughtiness, airs, hauteur; pretension, pretentiousness, pomposity, affected manners *or* ways, *Inf.* highfalutin' ways, affectation; ostentation, show, display, pomp, pageantry, glitter, showiness, flourish, fanfare, parade, array, fanfaronade, *Inf.* putting on the dog, *Inf.* getting on one's high horse; high notions, *Inf.* putting one's nose in the air; boasting, boastfulness, braggadocio, crowing, gloating, swagger, dash, panache; bumptiousness, bombast, bravado, shamelessness, brazenness, *Inf.* nerve, *Inf.* gall; foppishness, foppery, dandyism, coxcombry, frippery, frills and furbelows.

3. hollowness, worthlessness, emptiness, vacuity; fruitlessness, uselessness, futility, pointlessness, inanity, fatuity, vapidity; folly, foolishness, frivolity, ridiculousness; triviality, triflingness, nugacity; absurdity, meaninglessness, purposelessness, fecklessness; sham, unreality, unsubstantialness, lack of substance, nothingness, delusion.

vanquish, *v.* **1.** conquer, defeat, subdue, subjugate; rout, put to rout, discomfit, overwhelm, overrun, trample, *Inf.* run into the ground, *Sl.* mop *or* wipe the floor with; crush, overthrow, smash, thrash, trounce, trim, whip, drub, floor, *Inf.* whup, *Sl.* trash, *Sl.* beat to a frazzle, *Sl.* beat the pants off of; break, quell, quench, quash, destroy, clobber, *Sl.* zap, *Inf.* polish off, *Sl.* do in; beat, get the better of, best, upset, upend, *Inf.* whomp.

2. master, overpower, overcome, surmount, drive to the wall, take by storm, get the upper hand over, prevail over; outdistance, surpass, outwit, outmaneuver, outdo; circumvent, foil, checkmate, confound, baffle; triumph over, humble, bring down; dispel, scatter, disperse, dissipate.

3. thwart, check, stop, put a stop *or* an end to, terminate, end, *Inf.* put the kibosh on, nip in the bud; prevent, bar, block, obstruct.

vantage, *n.* **1.** See **vantage point** (*defs.* **1, 2**).

2. advantage, superiority, predominance, dominance, ascendancy, supremacy; importance, prestige, upper hand, whip hand, edge; leverage, authority, influence, sway, *Sl.* pull, *Sl.* drag, *Sl.* say, *Sl.* clout; force, power, strength, command, weight; favor, *Inf.* odds, *Inf.* inside track, *Inf.* head *or* running start, *Inf.* ace in the hole *or* up one's sleeve, *Sl.* jump, *Sl.* drop.

vantage point, *n.* **1.** viewpoint, standpoint, position, outlook, angle, perspective, way of seeing things; perch, aerie, spot, position; lookout, clear view, *Inf.* ringside seat, *Inf.* catbird seat.

2. height, eminence, upland, highland, high ground, elevation, hill, promontory, summit, crest, ridge.

vapid, *adj.* **1.** insipid, flat, lifeless, flavorless, colorless, jejune, *Sl.* blah; tasteless, bland, *Fr. fade*; unsavory, unappetizing, unpalatable; thin, watery, watered-down, wishy-washy.

2. dull, dull as dishwater, tedious, tiresome, prosaic, mundane; boring, monotonous, humdrum, wearisome, *Sl.* a drag; trite, tired, undistinctive, run-of-the-mill; spiritless, unanimated, zestless, sapless, *Sl.* dead, *Sl.* nothing; uninteresting, unentertaining, inexpressive, unimaginative.

vapor, *n.* **1.** fog, mist, cloud, haze, film, pollution, smog; steam, smoke, fume; gas, ether, miasma; breath, exhalation, emanation, *Archaic.* halitus.

2. fantasy, fancy, vagary, dream, daydream, *Inf.* pipe dream; whimsy, rhapsody, romance, invention, imagination; figment, delusion, chimera, vision, mirage, myth; phantom, ghost, illusion, apparition, *Spiritualism.* ectoplasm.

—*v.* **3.** vaporize, steam, smoke, fume, give off, send out, puff, blow, emit; exhale, transpire, expel, let out, expire; outpour, spew; evaporate, melt away, disappear, vanish, go up in a puff of smoke; volatilize, etherealize.

4. brag, bluster, boast, vaunt, flourish, put on airs, puff, preen, blow one's own horn, swagger, talk big, gasconade; glory, exult, crow, trumpet, gloat; talk nonsense, talk through one's hat, *Sl.* gas, *Sl.* throw the bull; run off at the mouth, prattle, blather, blabber, babble, jabber, carry on, go on.

vaporization, *n.* **1.** evaporation, distillation, vaporescence, volatilization, gasification; steaming, clouding, fogging, misting, filming; fumigating, fumigation, vaporizing.

vaporize, *v.* **1.** volatilize, distill, gasify, *Chem.* etherify; etherealize.

2. steam, boil, mist, haze, smoke, fume; evaporate, disappear, vanish, dissolve.

3. brag, boast, advertise oneself, blow one's own horn, pat oneself on the back, vaunt, flourish, gasconade, puff, vapor. See **vapor** (*def.* **4**).

vaporous, *adj.* **1.** gaseous, gasiform, pneumatic, aeriform, vapory, vaporish, vaporlike, vaporific, vaporescent, volatile, *Archaic.* halituous; fumy, fumelike, exhalant, breathy; steamy, foggy, misty, brumous, humid, murky, *Sl.* soupy; hazy, cloudy, beclouded, overcast, gray, smoky; clouded, unclear, indistinct, ambiguous, dim, obscure, dark.

2. diaphonous, aery, aerial, ethereal, etherous, gossamery, gossamer, wispy; thin, tenuous, rare, rarefied, subtle, abstract, esoteric, recondite; vague, indefinite, notional, flimsy, unsubstantial, half-baked, *Sl.* half-assed; fanciful, imaginary, chimerical, dreamy, illusive, illusory, unreal, fantastic; unreliable, undependable, uncertain, questionable, dubious, doubtful, suspect, *Sl.* fishy.

variable, *adj.* **1.** changeable, changeful, changing, chameleonic, chameleonlike, protean, varying, variational, variant, variative; vicissitudinary, vicissitudinous, fluctuating, fluctuant, vacillating, vacillatory, vacillant, wavering, shilly-shallying; moody, emotional, mercurial, capricious, lightsome; fickle, skittish, faddish, flighty, blowing hot and cold, on again-off again, unreliable, undependable; inconstant, unsteady, unstable, irregular, random, intermittent.

2. alterable, modifiable, permutable, mutable, transformable, transmutable; commutative, substitutive, exchangeable, interchangeable, convertible, reversible.

3. varied, diversified, diverse. See **various** (*defs.* **1, 2**).

4. multicolored, many-faceted, many-sided. See **variegated** (*def.* **1**).

variance, *n.* **1.** variability, variableness; diversity, variety, disparateness, heterogeneity, heterogeneousness. See **variety** (*def.* **1**).

2. difference, differential, departure, deviation; discrepancy, disparity, incongruity, contrariety.

3. disagreement, difference of opinion, misunderstanding, falling out, sixes and sevens; dissent, dissension, dissidence, disaccord, discord, jangle, clash, conflict, strife, antagonism; contention, controversy, dispute, contest, debate; altercation, quarrel, argument, wrangle, squabble, spat, tiff, miff, set-to, row, broil, *Inf.* scrap; feud, vendetta, rivalry; division, schism, faction, rupture, break, breach.

variation, *n.* **1.** changeability, fluctuation, vacillation, vicissitude, ups and downs.

2. change, transformation, conversion, metamorphosis, transfiguration, transubstantiation, transmogrification, transmutation, permutation; alteration, modification, modulation, inflection; transposition, metathesis, transition, revolution, reversal, turnaround, turnabout, *Inf.* flip-flop, *Sl.* a 180°.

3. diversification, variegation, variety. See **variegation.**

4. departure, variant, descant; innovation, something new *or* different, change of pace; difference, deviation, divergence.

variegate, *v.* streak, stripe, striate, fleck, dapple, dot, spot, mottle, checker, diaper, sprinkle; color, stain, marble, marbelize; diversify, change, transform, alter, modify.

variegated, *adj.* **1.** multicolored, polychromatic, polychromic, of many colors *or* shades *or* hues, versicolor, multicolor; prismatic, prismatical, spectral, rainbowy, rainbowlike, colorful, brilliant; pavonine; iridescent, pearly, opalescent, opaline, nacreous, nacred, *Crystall.* pleochroic; shot, varicolored, kaleidoscopic, parti-colored; marble, marbled, marbly, marmoreal, marmorean, motley, streaked, striated, striate, striped, tabby; banded, belted, barred, lined, veined, *Zool.* fasciate; piebald, pied, (*esp. of horses*) skewbald, dappled, brindled, spotted, spotty, mottled, speckled, flecked, salt-and-pepper; checked, checkered, tesellated, plaid, tartan.

2. varied, diversified, diverse, various. See **various** (*def.* **1**).

variegation, *n.* streakedness, striation, stripedness, varied coloration; spottedness, spottiness, mottle, mottlement, diversification; iridescence, opalescence.

variety, *n.* **1.** difference, dissimilarity, unlikeness, dissimilitude, contrast, disagreement, confliction, discordance; contrariety, opposition, contradiction, contradistinction, oppositeness, contrariness, adverseness; inconsistency, discrepancy, inconformity, nonconformity; disparity, inequality, imparity, imbalance, incongruity, incompatibility; variation, variance, divergence, deviation; diversity, diversification, multiplicity, multifariousness.

2. assortment, collection, mixture, intermixture, mélange, miscellany, medley, motley, potpourri, olio, olla-podrida, omnium-gatherum; salmagundi, stew, ragout, goulash, hash; conglomeration, hodgepodge, jumble, farrago, gallimaufry, Chinese menu; mixed bag, patchwork, pastiche; heterogeneity, heterogeneousness, multiformity.

3. kind, type, class, category, classification, genre, order, sort; division, subdivision, suborder; group, set, suit; genus, species, phylum, subgenus, subspecies, strain, sept; lot, style, cast, mold, stamp, brand, kidney; grain, make, mark, cue; race, breed, people, folk; description, designation, denomination, number.

various, *adj.* **1.** diverse, unlike, different, dissimilar, varying; multiform, diversiform, diversified, varied, variant, manifold, divergent, differing; miscellaneous, motley, heterogeneous, mixed, assorted, variegated.

2. numerous, many, abundant, several, multiplex, multiple; several, some, not a few; manifold, multifold, multifarious, omnifarious; assorted, heterogeneous, motley, varied; sundry, divers, miscellaneous.

3. distinct, unidentical, nonidentical; separate, individual, not the same, unequal; another, other.

varnish, *n.* **1.** lacquer, glaze, veneer, enamel, japan, stain, shellac; transparent coating, facing, protective layer, wash; mastic, rosin, colophony, resin, lac; gloss, shine, polish, luster.

2. facade, front, camouflage, mask, disguise; pretense, masquerade, deceptive show, show, surface, semblance, false appearance; speciousness, tinsel, sham.

3. explanation, apology, annotation; contrivance, concoction, cover-up, white lie, whitewashing, *Inf.* song and dance.

—*v.* **4.** shellac, lacquer, enamel, glaze; polish, shine, give a shine to, stain, veneer.

5. embellish, adorn, decorate, ornament; elaborate, array, deck, deck out, trap, trap out; emblazon, blazon, bedaub, gild.

6. mask, veil, disguise; smooth over, cover up, slick over; color, falsify, alter, doctor up; explain away, excuse, gloss over, gloze, whitewash, extenuate, palliate; apologize, play down, downplay, soft-pedal.

vary, *v.* **1.** alter, modify, change, diversify; permute, modulate, mutate, inflect; convert, transform, metamorphose, transfigure, transmute, transmorgify; revolutionize, transshape, remodel, remold, recast, reconstruct, restyle; shift, reorganize, reorder, permutate.

2. deviate, veer, shift; diverge, depart, deflect; swerve, bend; differ, disagree, contrast, be unlike.

3. alternate, adjust, correlate, change in succession; fluctuate, vacillate.

vase, *n.* vessel, urn, lachrymatory, lachrymal, *Gk. and Rom. Antiq.* amphora, jar; container, receptacle, cruse, canister; jug, pitcher, ewer; carafe, bottle, decanter.

vast, *adj.* **1.** immense, extensive, broad, wide, expansive, *Archaic.* vasty, *Archaic.* immane; voluminous, bulky, capacious, massive; huge, enormous, *Archaic.* enorm, large, big, prodigious; stupendous, great, towering, staggering, tremendous, *Sl.* humongous, *Sl.* hulking; titanic, cyclopean, Atlantean, Brobdingnagian; colossal, mammoth, gigantic, monstrous, monumental, jumbo; elephantine, hippopotamic, leviathan, behemoth, dinosaurian, megatherian.

2. immeasurable, boundless, illimitable, unlimited, uncircumscribed, unbounded, limitless, shoreless; endless, interminable, infinite, inexhaustible, neverending; incalculable, measureless, fathomless, unfathomable, undeterminable, indeterminate.

vat, *n.* container, tank, caldron, cask, barrel, hogshead, puncheon, tun, butt, rundlet, keg; bucket, tub, pail, receptacle, vessel, firkin; basin, bowl.

vault[1], *n.* **1.** arch, span; bow, bend, curve, arc, camber, *Archit.* cove.

2. underground chamber, cellar, basement; hold, keep; storeroom, strong room, depository, repository, repertory; bank vault; safe, strongbox, safety-deposit box, cashbox; money chest, coffer.

3. crypt, tomb, sepulcher, mausoleum, burial chamber.

—*v.* **4.** arch, bow, bend, curve, camber; overarch, arch over, span, bridge.

vault[2], *v.* leap, spring, jump, bound, hop, curvet; hurdle, clear, leap *or* jump *or* vault over; pole-vault.

vaulted, *adj.* arched, curved, bowed, embowed, cambered, fornicated.

vaulting, *adj.* exaggerated, overblown, puffed-up, inflated; overambitious, high-flown, high-flying, *Inf.* highfalutin.

vaunt, *v.* **1.** boast of, brag about, crow about, make much of, *Inf.* make a big thing about; celebrate, emblazon, trumpet, blow one's own horn; exaggerate, overstate, hyperbolize, *Sl.* shoot the bull, *Sl.* lay it on thick, *Sl.* pile it higher and deeper.

—*n.* **2.** boast; brag, braggadocio, rodomontade, fanfaronade, gasconade, *Sl.* big talk, *Sl.* hot air, *Sl.* gas, *Sl.* bull.

vaunter, *n.* braggart, braggadocio, brag, boaster, gascon, fanfaron, Rodomonte, Thraso, *Latin. miles gloriosus*; *All Sl.* blowhard, windbag, gasbag, loud *or* big mouth, hot-air merchant *or* artist.

veer, *v.* shift, turn, change course, change direction; deviate, diverge, swerve; jibe, tack, yaw, slue; turn about, wheel, swing; sidestep, *Brit.* jib, step aside, shy; bend, curve, sheer, bear off, heel; warp, skew, bias, twist, crook, dogleg; go off, glance off, edge off; change about, alter, chop, chop and change.

veering, *n.* deviation, divergence, deflection, declination, divagation; swerve, shift, turn, change; drift, swing, curve, bend, jibe, tack, yaw; warp, twist, chop, sheer, sweep; glance, crook, bias, skew, slant.

vegetable, *n.* **1.** plant, green, legume; produce, truck.

—*adj.* **2.** vegetative, vegetal, herbal, herbaceous, leguminous; plantlike, botanic, verdurous, vegetarian.

3. inert, inanimate, stagnant, dormant, paralyzed, comatose; motionless, stationary, immobile, static; unthinking, mindless, brainless, nonintellectual; quiescent, supine, leaden, inactive, logy; lethargic, otiose, idle, passive, languid; do-nothing, slack, lazy, indolent, sluggish; dull, stupid.

vegetate, *v.* **1.** grow, sprout, shoot up, bud, burgeon, burst forth; germinate, root, take root, put forth; luxuriate, flourish, flower, bloom, effloresce, leaf; pullulate, develop, blow, swell, overgrow.

2. exist, stagnate, do nothing, idle, hang fire; hibernate, estivate, rusticate; lounge, loaf, lazy around, waste time, cool one's heels; languish, drowse, doze, sit back; sit on the sidelines, *Sl.* warm the bench, twiddle one's thumbs, not stir, not budge; rest, coast, drift, lay back, be inactive.

vegetation, *n.* **1.** plant life, flora, herbage, foliage, leafage, frondescence, umbrage; shrubbery, greenery, verdure, flowerage, vegetable life, plants.

2. passivity, inertia, motionlessness, inactivity, inanimation; mindlessness, brainlessness, unthinkingness; brain death, coma; stagnancy, dormancy, immobility, stasis, paralysis; idleness, indolence, sluggishness, otiosity, torpor, lethargy, languor, inaction.

vehemence, *n.* **1.** ardor, fervor, fervency, zeal, eagerness, verve, enthusiasm, élan, ebullience, exuberance, zest, vim, vigor, spirit; gusto, relish, zing, punch, pep; heart, soul, intensity, heartiness, dash; effervescence, flurry, animation, *Fr. empressement*, abandon; wholeheartedness, intentness, earnestness, devotion, seriousness, devoutness, sincerity.

2. fury, frenzy, passion, impetuosity, wildness; warmth, fire, flame, heat, feverishness; furor, rage, violence, ferment, excitability, fieriness; madness, transport, ecstasy; tempestuousness, storminess, turbulence, tumult; fierceness, keenness, savagery, roughness, rigor, harshness; virulence, acerbity, acrimony, acuteness, venom.

vehement, *adj.* **1.** ardent, fervid, zealous, impassioned, fervent; earnest, intent, keen, eager, enthusiastic; animated, excited, perfervid, ebullient, exuberant, zestful; spirited, vigorous, peppy, *Sl.* gung-ho; hearty, lusty, passionate, hot-blooded, hot, breathless; *Sl.* steamed up about, *Sl.* all hopped about, *Sl.* ape about, *Sl.* wild about, *Sl.* crazy about; intense, high-pressure, forceful, vibrant, vivid; heady, racy, potent, lively, snappy.

2. furious, frenzied, frenetic, feverish, frantic, fast

and furious; burning, fiery, blazing, raging, warm, steaming; impetuous, impulsive, wild, abandoned; stormy, turbulent, tempestuous, violent, volcanic; explosive, eruptive, mad, raving, storming; overexcited, transported, beside oneself, orgiastic, orgasmic, wild-eyed, running amuck.

3. fierce, rigorous, strenuous, strong, intense; virulent, venomous, savage, rough, ferocious; acerbic, acrimonious, acute, mordant, trenchant, cutting, biting, bitter; unmitigated, unsubdued, drastic, severe, *Inf.* tough.

vehicle, *n.* **1.** conveyance carrier, conveyor, transportation, transporter.

2. automobile, car, *Sl.* wheels, jeep, bus, truck; tractor, tank, half-track; cart, wagon, carriage, sulky, stagecoach; bicycle, motorcycle, *Inf.* bike, moped; train, trolley, streetcar; sled, sleigh. See also **car** (*defs.* **1-3**); **carriage** (*def.* **1**); **train** (*def.* **4**); and **sled**.

3. channel, route, way, conduit, passage; medium, means, agency, instrument, method, organ, tool; means to an end, access, entranceway, entryway.

veil, *n.* **1.** purdah, yashmak, chadri; kerchief, head covering, scarf, mantilla.

2. cover, covering, concealment, screen, curtain, shade, film, mantle, cloak, blanket, shroud, canopy; fog, haze, cloud, shadow.

3. mask, masquerade, disguise, camouflage; guise, semblance, appearance, façade, face, false front, front, window dressing, show; pretense, deceit, hypocrisy, deception, artifice, blind, subterfuge; dissimulation, dissemblance, falsification, trickery.

—v. **4.** obscure, dim, shade, becloud, cloud, eclipse, adumbrate, obfuscate; cover, envelop, screen, cloak, curtain, muffle, shield, mantle; conceal, hide, secrete.

5. disguise, camouflage, mask, cover up, cover over; deceive, dissemble, dissimulate, misrepresent, falsify; gloss over, varnish, put a false face *or* front on.

vein, *n.* **1.** blood vessel, artery, aorta, *Anat.* vena, *Anat.* vena cava, venule, *Anat.* capillary; *Bot., Zool.* nervure.

2. lode, seam, stratum, bed, mine.

3. channel, watercourse, underground stream.

4. streak, stripe, thread, string, line, marking, marbling, stria, striation; groove, furrow, sulcus; ridge.

5. temper, mood, disposition, turn of mind, humor, complexion; temperament, character, inclination, bent, tendency; appearance, way, manner, style, cast, quality, strain, grain; type, kind, sort, ilk.

—v. **6.** streak, stripe, striate, line, marble; score, slash, ridge, furrow, groove; snake, wind, thread, twist, curve, twine, meander.

velocity, *n.* **1.** swiftness, speed, precipitation, precipitousness; celerity, rapidity, speediness, alacrity, fleetness, fastness, quickness, briskness; promptness, expeditiousness; rate of speed, miles per hour, mph, revolutions per minute, rpm.

velvet, *n.* **1.** velour, velveteen, waleless corduroy, duvetyn, plush.

2. *Slang.* winnings, prize money, *Sl.* loot, booty, prize; clear gain *or* profit, *Sl.* gravy, yield, return.

—adj. **3.** velveteen, velour, velveted; velvetlike, smooth, soft, velutinous, thick, deep.

venal, *adj.* open to bribery, bribeable, corruptible, corrupt; purchasable, buyable; mercenary, *Obs.* vendible, self-seeking, selfish, greedy, covetous, avaricious, grasping, rapacious.

vend, *v.* **1.** sell, peddle, hawk, huckster, *Sl.* push, retail, market, go door-to-door, sell on commission, *Inf.* try to make a buck *or* dollar; tout one's goods, show one's wares, offer for sale; dispose of, *Inf.* get rid of, *Inf.* unload, *Inf.* dump.

2. publish, print, give utterance to, give voice to, make known, make public, report.

vendetta, *n.* feud, blood feud; warfare, war, conflict, contention, rivalry, infighting; antagonism, hostilities, enmity, acrimony, bitterness, ill will, bad blood.

vendor, *n.* seller, salesman, traveling salesman, door-to-door salesman, Fuller Brush man, Avon lady, colporteur, Bible salesman; street vendor, peddler, hawker, huckster, cheap-jack; pushcart entrepreneur, monger, dealer, trader, merchant, (*formerly*) sutler.

vendue, *n.* auction, public auction, auction sale, outcry, *Scot. and North Eng.* roup; garage sale, tag sale, rummage sale.

veneer, *n.* **1.** facing, casing, covering, sheath; jacket, wrapper; coat.

2. façade, front, false front, show, mere show, outward display; pretension, ostentation, pomposity; glitter, finery, frippery.

—v. **3.** overlay, overspread, laminate; paint, coat; varnish, lacquer, gild, glaze.

4. whitewash, gloss, gloss over, color, prettify; dissemble, disguise, conceal, mask, screen.

venerable, *adj.* **1.** time-honored, honored, revered, respected, hallowed, venerated, esteemed; august, illustrious, eminent.

2. aged, ancient, archaic, old, *Inf.* old as the hills; hoary, gray.

venerate, *v.* hallow, revere, reverence, honor; esteem, admire, look up to, think highly of; fear, dread, hold in awe; adore, idolize, hero-worship, worship, worship the ground [s.o.] stands on, worship the grass [s.o.] walks on, put on a pedestal.

veneration, *n.* **1.** homage, devotion; admiration, estimation; adoration, idolization, worship, hero worship, lionization.

2. awe, fear, dread; reverence, deference, respect.

vengeance, *n.* **1.** revenge, sweet revenge, retribution, requital, revanche; avengement; retaliation, settling a score, an eye for an eye, blood for blood, blow for blow, a Roland for an Oliver, like for like, measure for measure, tit for tat, *Latin. quid pro quo.*

2. reprisal, countermeasure, counterblow, counterstroke.

3. with a vengeance a. violently, vehemently, furiously, fiercely, wildly, *Inf.* like mad, hammer and tongs, tooth and nail. **b.** greatly; utterly, extremely, to the extreme. **c.** to the full, to the limit, to the utmost, all the way, all out, *Brit.* flat out, *Inf.* with no holds barred.

vengeful, *adj.* **1.** vindictive, revengeful, spiteful; unforgiving, unappeasable, irreconcilable, intractable, implacable, inexorable; revanchist.

2. retaliatory, retributive, recriminatory, avenging; punitive.

venial, *adj.* pardonable, forgivable, excusable; allowable, tolerable; slight, minor, insignificant, trifling, petty.

venom, *n.* **1.** poison, toxin, toxicant, virus.

2. spite, spitefulness, rancor, ill will, evil intent; choler, pique, ire, acerbity, acrimony, bitterness; gall, bile, spleen, virulence, invidiousness, envy, resentment, grudge, ill feeling; malice, maliciousness, malignity, malevolence, animosity, antagonism, hostility, evil eye, hate, hatred, detestation, abhorrence, enmity; wrath, anger, dudgeon, bad blood.

venomous, *adj.* **1.** poisonous, virulent, envenomed, deadly, toxic, lethal, fatal; noxious, harmful, hurtful, injurious, mischievous, detrimental, deleterious, unwholesome, unhealthy; destructive, ruinous, pernicious, baleful.

2. hostile, resentful, indignant, piqued, angry; spiteful, malicious, vicious; malevolent, malignant, malign, ill-disposed; antagonistic, rancorous, abusive, corrosive; morose, surly, sullen, moody; aggressive, warlike, belligerent, bellicose; ferocious, brutal, feral, ferine; adverse, opposed, opposing.

3. acrimoniousness, caustic, mordant, bitter, acrid, pungent; astringent, acerb, acerbic, severe, stern, austere, stringent; harsh, sharp, sour, acidulous, acid, tart; trenchant, keen, cutting, scathing, sarcastic, satiric, ironic, ironical; peevish, petulant, crabbed, testy, touchy, irascible, edgy; ill-tempered, ill-humored, short-tempered.

vent[1], *n.* opening, outlet, aperture, hole, airhole, blowhole, spiracle; mouth, orifice, window, porthole, oriel; passage, duct, flue, chimney, smokestack.

vent[2], *n.* **1.** expression, airing, verbalization, utterance, enunciation; announcement, proclamation, declaration, pronouncement; communication, informing, mentioning, telling, revelation; explanation, definition, explication, description.

—*v.* **2.** express, air, verbalize, utter, enunciate; blab, blurt out, announce, proclaim declare, pronounce; communicate, inform, mention, say, tell, reveal, expose, *Archaic.* divulgate, publish, publicize, make public, disseminate, make known, broadcast.

3. emit, discharge, expel, ejaculate, pour forth, outpour, send forth, release, emanate, send out, give off; squirt, spout, shoot, jet; spill out, gush, disembogue, cast forth, throw out, extrude, eject.

ventilate, *v.* **1.** air, aerate, aerify, oxygenate; fan, winnow, circulate through, blow on, air-condition, air-cool; refresh, revivify, cool, freshen, purify.

2. present, bring up, open up for discussion, discuss; go over, review, look at, talk over *or* about, treat, deal with.

3. broach, suggest, mention; propose, offer, proffer, pose; introduce, submit, present, set forth, put before; throw out, advance; utter, vent, express, declare. See **vent**[2] (*def.* **2**).

ventilation, *n.* **1.** air, airing, aerification, oxygen; circulation, cross breeze, breeze, draft; air conditioning.

2. expression, utterance, announcement, declaration, vent. See **vent**[2] (*def.* **1**).

3. discussion, exchange of ideas, *Sl.* rap, *Sl.* rap session, *Sl.* bull session.

venture, *n.* **1.** risky undertaking, enterprise, experiment, adventure, mission; speculation, plunge, gamble, leap in the dark; chance, big chance, long shot.

—*v.* **2.** risk, endanger, expose to danger, hazard, peril, imperil, jeopardize, jeopard, put in jeopardy; take one's life in one's hands, play with fire, skate on thin ice, walk a tightrope, go up without a parachute.

3. dare, chance, gamble, wager, bet, take a chance; try, attempt, tempt fate, *Sl.* give a whirl, *Inf.* stick one's chin *or* neck out, lay *or* put [s.t.] on the line, put one's head in the lion's mouth; throw caution to the winds, *Sl.* go for broke, *Sl.* shoot the works, hazard all; plunge, *Inf.* take a flier, (*both of finance*) speculate, sell short.

4. presume, make bold, take the liberty; broach, offer, proffer, advance, put forward, propound, tender, move, make a motion.

venturesome, *adj.* **1.** adventurous, adventuresome, enterprising, daring, bold, audacious; doughty, courageous, gallant, chivalrous; valorous, valiant, brave, heroic; undaunted, dauntless, intrepid, fearless; game, spirited, plucky, *Inf.* spunky, of sporting blood; daredevil, temerarious, reckless, foolhardy, rash.

2. hazardous, risky, dangerous, perilous, jeopardous; uncertain, chancy, unsafe, shaky, slippery, precarious, *Archaic.* parlous.

veracious, *adj.* **1.** truthful, honest, sincere, earnest; upright, righteous, honorable, upstanding; ethical, proper, moral, conscionable; principled, high-minded, noble, right-minded, uncorrupt; ingenuous, artless, guileless, unsophisticated; frank, straight, *Inf.* square, free, open, aboveboard; candid, straightforward, up front, blunt, plain-spoken.

2. factual, literal, true-to-life, realistic, credible, believable, natural; accurate, exact, precise, faithful, close, strict; pure, unadulterated, unexaggerated, unvarnished, unembellished.

3. actual, real, *Obs.* veritable, *Brit. Dial.* gradely, *Both Archaic.* sooth, soothfast; authentic, genuine, valid, sound, just, confirmed; unimaginary, unfictitious.

veracity, *n.* **1.** truthfulness, honesty, honestness, veraciousness; frankness, openness, candor, candidness, straightforwardness, plainness, bluntness; ingenuousness, artlessness, guilelessness, naiveté.

2. sincerity, sincereness, earnestness; uprightness, integrity, probity, righteousness, honorableness, upstandingness; ethicalness, ethicality, morality, rightness, conscionableness, uncorruptedness.

3. accuracy, faithfulness, honesty, closeness, strictness, literalness; factuality, factualness, actuality, actualness, reality, realness, authenticity, genuineness; truth, vaidity, validness, soundness, credibility, credibleness, believability, believableness.

4. accuracy, accurateness, correctness, exactness, exactitude, precision, preciseness.

5. a truth, verity, *Archaic.* troth; fact, certainty, certitude; principle, rule, axiom, law, fundamental, canon; theorem, *Math.* proposition.

veranda, *n.* porch, stoop; piazza, portico, gallery, galilee, vestibule, loggia; solarium, sun porch; patio.

verbal, *adj.* **1.** lexical, vocabulary, word; linguistic, lingual, language, speech, dialectic.

2. oral, vocal, spoken, expressed, said, uttered; articulated, pronounced, enunciated, enunciative, enunciatory; conversational, colloquial, informal; unwritten, word-of-mouth, vive-voce.

3. verbatim, word for word, literal, letter-for-letter, line-for-line, *Fr. mot à mot*. See **verbatim** (*def.* **2**).

verbalist, *n.* **1.** rhetorician, rhetor, public speaker, speechmaker, declaimer, *Speech.* elocutionist; writer, author, authoress, novelist, poet, man of letters, editor, editress; linguist, lexicologist, lexicographer, semanticist, semasiologicist, etymologist, *Archaic.* glossologist, *Brit.* philologist, *Brit.* philologer, *Rare.* linguistician, *Obs.* glottologist; grammarian, morphologist, dialectologist, phonetician, phonologist.

2. big talker, *Sl.* bullshooter, blowhard, blusterer, braggart, blatherskite, bag of hot air, *Sl.* windbag, *Sl.* gasbag, *Sl.* big mouth, *Sl.* loud mouth.

verbatim, *adv.* **1.** word for word, *Fr. mot à mot*, line for line, literally, letter for letter, literatim, *Latin. verbatim et literatim*; exactly, precisely, accurately, closely, faithfully, honestly, strictly, to a hair, to the letter; in the strict sense of the word, strictly speaking, in plain English, simply, plainly.

—*adj.* **2.** word-for-word, *Fr. mot à mot*, line-for-line, literally, letter-for-letter, literatim, *Latin. verbatim et literatim*; exact, precise, accurate, close, faithful, honest, strict, undeviating; explicit, express, unambiguous, clear, unequivocal.

verbiage, *n.* **1.** verbosity, verbality, verbalism, wordiness, prolixity, long-windedness, longiloquence, multiloquence. See **verbosity** (*def.* **1**).

2. wording, phraseology, phrasing, manner of expression; command of the language, way with words, feel for words, word sense, *Ger. Sprachgefühl, Archaic.* facundity; style, delivery, rhetoric, oratory; diction, elocution, locution; vocabulary, word choice, terminology; usage, grammar, syntax, word order, *Linguistics.* prosody; language, speaking, speech, speech pattern, parlance, tongue, *Inf.* lingo, *Inf.* talk; idiom, dialect, jargon, argot, cant, patois, *Linguistics.* idiolect.

verbose, *adj.* wordy, prolix, loquacious, long-winded, longiloquent, multiloquent, multiloquous, voluble, effusive, fluent; talkative, glib, long-tongued, *Inf.* blessed with the gift of gab, mouthy, *Inf.* big-mouthed, *Sl.* all jaw, *Sl.* gassy, windy; chattering, chatty, gibbering, babbling, blabbering, blathering, jabbering, gabby; discursive, digressive, rambling, roving, meandering, wandering, aimless, pointless; periphrastic, pleonastic, tautological, repetitive, redundant, superfluous, profuse; circumlocutory, ambagious, circuitous, roundabout; plethoric, turgid, overblown, inflated, flatulent, tumid, swollen, bloated; magniloquent, grandiloquent, rhetorical, orotund, sonorous; bombastical; extravagant, euphuistic, florid, flowery, highflown, pretentious, pompous, high-sounding, *Inf.* highfalutin, *Inf.* high-hat.

verbosity, *n.* **1.** wordiness, verbality, verbalism, verbiage, prolixity, prolixness, loquacity, loquaciousness, long-windedness, longiloquence, multiloquence; overtalkativeness, talkativeness, glibness, loose tongue, *Inf.* gabbiness, *Inf.* gift of gab, *Inf.* windiness, *Inf.* gassiness, *Inf.* big mouth; magniloquence, grandiloquence, orotundity, sesquipedality, sesquipedaleanism, sesquipedalism.

2. discursiveness, digressiveness, circumlocution, ambagiousness, circuitousness, roundaboutness; periphrasis, periphrase, pleonasm, tautology, repetitiveness, redundancy, superfluousness, superfluity, profuseness, *Inf.* circumbendibus, *Archaic.* ambages.

3. turgidity, turgidness, turgescence, turgescency, tumidity, flatulence, inflatedness, *Archaic.* tympany; bombast, rodomontade, grandiosity, pomposity, extravagance, highflown language, floweriness, floridness.

verdancy, *n.* **1.** greenness, viridity, verdure, *Bot.* virescence, grassiness.

2. unsophisticatedness, unsophistication, simpleness, simplicity, artlessness, ingenuousness, guilelessness, naïveté, naïveness, innocence; youthfulness, tenderness, immaturity, immatureness, callowness, freshness, salad days; inexperience, rawness, inexpertness, ignorance.

verdant, *adj.* **1.** verdurous, green, grassy, grass-covered, plant-covered.

2. green-colored, greenish, viridescent, virescent, emerald, bluish-green, greenish-blue, grue, aqua, aquamarine, sea-green, grass-green, olive-green, pea-green, glaucous.

3. unsophisticated, simple, artless, ingenuous, guileless, naïve, innocent; young, youthful, tender, immature, callow, fresh, *Inf.* wet behind the ears, in one's salad days; inexperienced, raw, undisciplined, untrained, unpracticed, inexpert, unskilled, unlearned, unversed, ignorant.

verdict, *n.* decision, final decision, judgment, adjudition, *Law.* award, *Sports.* call; determination, resolution, settlement, arbitration, arbitrament; finding, conclusion, *Law.* opinion, ruling, *Law.* sentence, decree, edict, order, command.

verdure, *n.* **1.** grass, green vegetation, herbage, pasturage, pasture, grassland, grassy land, meadow, *Archaic.* mead, field; green, sward, greensward, turf, sod, artificial grass, *Trademark.* Astroturf; greenery, green foliage, leafage, *Eng. Forest Law.* vert.

2. greenness, verdancy, viridity, *Bot.* virescence.

3. freshness, vigor, vitality, healthy, growth, exuberance, luxuriance, lushness.

verge[1], *n.* **1.** edge, border, margin, rim, lip; curb, curbstone, ledge, sill; brink, brim, brow, hem, fringe, periphery, perimeter, skirt; bound *or* bounds, confines, limit *or* limits, city limits, outer limits; butting, abuttal, bourn, pale, extremity, termination, end; boundary, boundary line, border line, frontier, frontier line, partition line, line of demarcation, line.

2. brink, breaking point, threshold.

3. rod, wand, staff, scepter, baton, truncheon, mace, crosier, *Class. Myth.* caduceus.

verge[2], *v.* incline, tend to *or* toward, bear, lean to *or* toward; list, tip, tilt, cant, heel, *Naut.* careen; slope, slant, obique, skew, angle, bevel, pitch, grade, bank; descend, drop *or* drop off, dip, sag, fall, gravitate, sink.

verification, *n.* **1.** confirmation, substantiation, corroboration, establishment, proof; assurance, affirmation, asseveration, averment, certification; attestation, deposition, avouchment; authentication, validation, ratification, endorsement; support, strengthening, reinforcement.

2. certificate, warranty, guarantee, guaranty, voucher; testimonial, testimony, *Archaic.* testimonium; evidence, proof, word, statement, affidavit, instrument in proof.

verify, *v.* **1.** prove, confirm, substantiate, bear out, corroborate; give credence to, establish, fix, make certain, clinch, clench; attest, certify, evidence, go to show, affirm, assure, aver; vouch for, support, sustain, bear witness to, identify, testify, depose, document, demonstrate.

2. authenticate, validate, endorse, accredit, warrant; guarantee, underwrite, countersign, back up; vindicate, justify, make good, uphold; ratify, acknowledge, recognize.

verisimilitude, *n.* **1.** genuineness, authenticity, realness; realism, naturalism, lifelikeness; literalness.

2. probability, likelihood, likeliness; credibility, plausibility.

veritable, *adj.* **1.** real, actual, factual, genuine, authentic, bona fide, legitimate.

2. absolute, positive, certain, sure, definite; unquestionable, indisputable, indubitable, undeniable.

verity, *n.* **1.** truth, *Archaic.* troth, reality, actuality, *Archaic.* sooth; gospel, gospel truth, naked truth, unvarnished truth, *Sl.* straight goods; facts, *Inf.* lowdown, *Inf.* scoop, story; inside information, intelligence.

2. factuality, factualness, actualness; realness, authenticity, genuineness; validity, validness, soundness.

3. fact, certainty, certitude; principle, rule, law, fundamental, canon; theorem, *Math.* proposition.

vermin, *n.* **1.** lice, cooties, *Dial.* varmints.

2. scoundrel, dog, cur, reptile, swine, snake, snake in the grass, *Inf.* bad egg.

3. riffraff, rabble, ruck, rout, canaille, scum, scum of the earth, dregs *or* offscourings of society, *Contemptuous.* ragtag and bobtail.

vernacular, *adj.* **1.** native, natal, indigenous, autochthonous; endemic, local, localized, topical.

2. informal, everyday, ordinary, familiar, unliterary; colloquial, conversational, spoken; substandard, nonstandard.

3. common, commonplace, general, average, public, popular, *Sl.* pop; middlebrow, middle-class, bourgeois, *Inf.* straight, *Sl.* plastic; vulgar, lowbrow, plebeian.

—n. **4.** native speech, mother tongue, language;

living language; plain speech, plain English, everyday language; spoken language, colloquial speech *or* language, conversational English; vulgar tongue, common speech; substandard speech *or* language, nonstandard speech *or* language.

5. jargon, cant, patois, patter, *Inf.* lingo; argot, slang; gibberish, gobbledegook, mumbo jumbo; shoptalk, officialese, legalese, journalese, businessese, business English.

versatile, *adj.* **1.** all-around, multifaceted, many-sided, protean, adaptable, plastic; handy, clever, resourceful, ingenious; multipurpose, all-purpose.

2. variable, changeable, changeful, mutable, permutable; inconstant, unstable, unsteady; fickle, capricious, moody.

verse, *n.* **1.** stanza, strophe, *Prosody.* stave, canto, stich, line; couplet, *Prosody.* triplet, *Prosody.* tercet, quatrain.

2. poem, lyric, sonnet, villanelle, ode, *Class. Prosody.* epode; rondelet, pastoral, idyll, eclogue, bucolic; rhyme, limerick, jingle, doggerel; ditty, song, lay, ballad.

3. poetry, *Archaic.* poesy, versification; metrical composition, meter, numbers.

versed, *adj.* **1.** learned, cultured, literate, lettered, well-read; educated, well-educated, well-schooled, well-instructed, well-tutored, well-trained, well-posted, well-grounded; knowledgeable, well-informed, aware, cognizant; appreciative, appreciatory, appreciating, sensible, enlightened, sophisticated, *Sl.* savvy; acquainted, familiar, conversant, intimate, up; erudite, punditic, wise, sage, scholarly.

2. experienced, practiced, accomplished, polished, *Fr. au fait*; veteran, professional, *Inf.* knowing the ropes; skilled, skillful, adept, proficient; expert, master, masterful, masterly.

version, *n.* **1.** rendition, translation, metaphrase, interlinear, transliteration, decipherment; paraphrase, rewording, restatement; reading, lection.

2. story, account, interpretation, exegesis, construction, construe, conception, understanding, impression; representation, depiction, delineation, portrayal, reproduction; variation, arrangement, *Music.* transcription, *Fr. rendu*; production, performance, execution, enactment, rendering.

3. form, variant, copy, reproduction.

vertex, *n.* summit, apex, apogee, crest, peak, spire, point, tip, tiptop; top, cap, crown, headpiece, head, loft, aerie; acme, zenith, meridian, pinnacle, heights.

vertical, *adj.* **1.** perpendicular, on end, upright, at right angles to, right-angular, at 90 degrees to; plumb, straight, straight-up-and-down, up and down; bolt upright, standing, standing upright, erect.

2. steep, sharp, sheer, precipitous, abrupt, bold, craggy, high.

vertiginous, *adj.* **1.** whirling, spinning, gyrating, wheeling, rotary, rotatory, circumrotatory.

2. dizzy, light-headed, *Inf.* whoozy, *Pathol.* giddy, reeling.

verve, *n.* **1.** enthusiasm, vigor, force, energy, briskness, *Inf.* snap; life, esprit, spirit, élan, dash; ardor, fervor, passion, emotion, feeling; warmth, glow, fire.

2. vivaciousness, vivacity, liveliness, animation, *It. brio*; abandon, exuberance, vitality; zest, gusto, relish, appetite, savor; bounce, zing, spice, *Sl.* oomph; flourish, flair, style, panache, *Inf.* pizzazz.

very, *adv.* **1.** extremely, exceedingly, *Inf.* terribly, quite, *Brit. Inf.* jolly; remarkably, notably, highly, supremely, *Inf.* awfully, *Dial.* right, damned, *Inf.* damn, danged, *U.S. Inf.* darned, *Sl.* hell of a; exceptionally, extraordinarily, unusually, uncommonly, abnormally; absolutely, altogether, entirely, thoroughly, decidedly, unquestionably, unequivocally, downright, totally, completely, *Sl.* stone; hugely, vastly, enormously, greatly, more than.

2. excessively, unduly, inordinately, disproportionately, to a degree, *Sl.* almighty; extravagantly, immoderately, intemperately, overindulgently, uncontrollably, unrestrainably; exorbitantly, to the nth degree, outrageously, drastically, radically; profoundly, deeply, zealously, rabidly, fanatically, *Both Chiefly U.S. Inf.* all-fired, all-firedly.

—*adj.* **3.** perfect, appropriate, fitting, just right, just, precise, exact, express.

4. sheer, utter, simple, plain, pure, unadulterated, unmixed, unalloyed, unmingled; sole, single, mere.

5. actual, real, true, genuine, authentic, *Dial.* sure-enough, simon-pure; bona fide, veritable, *Sl.* real live, *Inf.* honest-to-goodness, *Inf.* kosher.

vessel, *n.* **1.** craft, boat, ship, packet, ark; freighter, cargo ship, commercial ship, merchantman; collier, tanker, oil tanker, liner, ocean liner; flagship, galleon, carrack, clipper, *Naut.* bark, *Naut.* brig, *Naut.* brigantine, *Naut.* galley, *Class. Hist.* trireme; warship, battleship, corvette; yawl, *Naut.* ketch, *Naut.* schooner, junk, felucca, sloop, cutter, *Naut.* knockabout; ferry, ferryboat, tug, tugboat; houseboat, barge, flatboat, scow; steamer, steamship, steamboat; lighter, *Naut.* pram; whaleboat, whaler, trawler, fishing boat, *Eastern U.S.* smack; sailboat, sailer, *Inf.* windjammer, day sailer, pinnance, catboat, *Naut.* catamaran; yacht, pleasure boat, cruiser, cabin cruiser; motorboat, speedboat, hydroplane, hydrofoil; rowboat, skiff, shallop, dinghy, tender, lifeboat, cockboat, cockleboat, *Naut.* cockleshell, launch, scull, shell, caique, *Naut.* gig, dory, *Chiefly Brit.* punt, sampan, gondola; canoe, kayak, dugout.

2. hollow utensil, container, canister, metal box, can, receptacle; jar, crock, pot; bottle, jug, decanter, carafe, flagon, pitcher; bowl, tankard, stein, mug, beaker, cup, glass, tumbler, goblet, chalice; vase, urn, lachrymatory; barrel, keg, cask, hogshead; pail, bucket, tub, vat, cauldron, kettle, boiler.

vest, *n.* **1.** *Chiefly Brit.* waistcoat, jerkin, sleeveless jacket, doublet; dickey, vestee.

—*v.* **2.** clothe, dress, robe, attire, apparel, garb, array, habit; dress up, deck out, *Inf.* doll up, *Inf.* gussy up, *Sl.* dude up, *Sl.* swank up, *Sl.* trick up.

3. invest, endow, endue, give, grant, confer, bestow.

vested, *adj.* **1.** permanent, invariable, fixed, set, stable, constant; inalienable, unrevokable, unrepealable, unannullable.

2. (*all by law*) protected, garanteed, insured, warranted, established, authorized, sanctioned, legalized.

3. clothed, robed, dressed, outfitted, habited, garbed, arrayed.

vestibule, *n.* entrance hall, lobby, foyer, parlor, locutorium; antechamber, anteroom, waiting room, lounge, reception room, outer room, outer office; passage, hall, entrance, entranceway, *Archit.* narthex, propylaeum, propylon, entrance porch, loggia.

vestige, *n.* **1.** trace, mark, sign, token, indication; scent, whiff, spoor; imprint, impression, track, print, footprint, handprint, fingerprint; fossil, petrifaction, remains, reliquiae, relics, fragments, remaining parts *or* pieces, surviving evidence; scar, *Med.* cicatrix, psychological scar, trauma.

2. hint, suggestion, touch, tinge, suspicion, soupçon, inkling; drop, dab, bit, jot, iota, dash, trifle.

vestment, *n.* **1.** *Usu.* **vestments** *Chiefly Literary.* clothing, clothes, garb, attire, apparel, wearing apparel, wear; garments, raiment, habiliments, habits, *Inf.* toggery, *Inf.* togs, *Inf.* duds, *Inf.* gear.

2. canonicals, pontificals, pontificalia, robes, liturgical garments, episcopal vestments, *Inf.* clericals; cloth, habit, ceremonial attire.
3. cover, covering, outer covering; shroud, veil, curtain, drape, shield, screen; hood, cowl, cowling; coat, cloak.

veteran, *n.* **1.** old hand, old stager, trouper, *Inf.* old pro, past master, past mistress; old man, *Inf.* old timer, old soldier, *Inf.* war-horse; senior, senior member, dean, doyen.
2. expert, master, maestro, master hand; professional, journeyman, specialist, authority.
—*adj.* 3. experienced, *Fr. au fait,* prepared, trained, primed; knowledgeable, versed, practiced, accomplished, finished, polished; skilled, skillful, adept, apt, adroit, dexterous, deft, facile; expert, proficient, masterful, masterly, professional, *Inf.* pro; topflight, topdrawer, *Inf.* topnotch, *Inf.* crack, ace.
4. mature, ripened, seasoned, salted; weather-hardened, toughened, inured, battle-scarred, *Inf.* through the mill, *Inf.* through the wringer; sophisticated, knowing, *Sl.* in the know, worldly, wordly-wise, *Sl.* wise, *Inf.* been around, initiated.

veto, *n.* **1.** rejection, thumbs down, nix, nay, no, denial; prohibition, interdiction, interdict, forbiddance, outlawry; proscription, injunction, disallowance, ban, taboo, embargo; preclusion, prevention, restriction, constriction; stoppage, arrest, check, forestalling; refusal, nonconsent.
—*v.* 2. reject, turn thumbs down, *Sl.* nix, nay, nyet, deny, kill; vote down, refuse consent, turn down; quash, smother, subdue, quell; prohibit, forbid, interdict, disallow, proscribe, outlaw, taboo, ban; preclude, prevent, make impossible, rule out; stop, put a stop to, *Archaic.* forfend.

vex, *v.* **1.** anger, incense, irk, raise [s.o.'s] ire, *Inf.* burn [s.o.] up, *Sl.* tick [s.o.] off, *Sl.* tee [s.o.] off; enrage, madden, infuriate, make [s.o.'s] blood boil, *Inf.* make [s.o.] see red; exacerbate, acerbate, envenom, embitter, rankle, gall.
2. irritate, annoy, pique, provoke, peeve, nettle, chafe, *Chiefly U.S.* rile, *Inf.* aggravate, *Inf.* miff, *Inf.* give [s.o.] a pain, *Inf.* get under [s.o.'s] skin, *Inf.* get in [s.o.'s] hair; exasperate, ruffle, roil, disturb, perturb, disquiet, discompose, discountenance, put out, try [s.o.'s] patience, get, *Sl.* get [s.o.'s] goat.
3. bother, pester, hector, harass, *Sl.* bug, *Sl.* hassle, *Sl.* drive [s.o.] nuts *or* crazy *or* bananas, *Sl.* drive [s.o.] up the wall; hound, dog, nag, *Sl.* ride, *Inf.* give [s.o.] a bad *or* hard time; bedevil, torment, tease, taunt, tweak, mock, bully, bullyrag, persecute; trouble, plague, fret, worry, *Scot.* thraw, *Scot.* fash.
4. (*all with vigor or at great length*) discuss, debate, moot, bandy words *or* opinions; canvass, talk over, go over, *Sl.* kick *or* knock around; dispute, contend, argue, wrangle, haggle, *Scot.* argle-bargle.

vexation, *n.* **1.** provocation, fomentation, incitement, incitation, instigation, excitation, agitation, inflammation, deliberate aggravation; provoking, fomenting, inciting, instigating, agitating, inflaming; infuriation, enragement; infuriating, enraging, angering, vexing.
2. irritation, annoyance, exasperation; nettling, ruffling, disturbing, disquieting; bothering, pestering, hectoring, harassing, *Sl.* bugging; hounding, dogging, nagging, *Sl.* riding; tormenting, teasing, taunting, persecuting, bullying.
3. displeasure, discontent, discontentment, dissatisfaction, disapproval, disapprobation; anger, ire, dudgeon, high dudgeon, pique.
4. irritant, nuisance, pest, bother, problem, trouble, bur, thorn in the flesh *or* side, pea in the shoe, salt in the wound, *Inf.* headache, *Inf.* pain, *Sl.* pain in the neck, *Sl.* hassle.

vexatious, *adj.* **1.** bothersome, pestering, *Inf.* pesky, *Inf.* pestiferous, hectoring, harassing; hounding, dogging, nagging, tormenting, persecuting; troublesome, troubling, thorny, fretful, worrisome, worrying, *Archaic. except Dial.* plaguy.
2. irritating, annoying, provoking, peeving, nettling, chafing, *Inf.* aggravating; disturbing, perturbing, ruffling, disquieting, vexing.
3. invidious, hateful, offensive, objectionable, obnoxious, odious; intolerable, unbearable, too much, *Inf.* a bit much.
4. angering, incensing, irksome, irking; maddening, infuriating, enraging; exacerbating, acerbating, embittering, rankling, galling.
5. disordered, in disorder, in disarray, disorganized, disarranged; chaotic, confused, jumbled, muddled, higgledy-piggledy, mixed-up, *Inf.* helter-skelter, *Inf.* bollixed-up, *Sl.* fouled-up, snafu.

vexed, *adj.* **1.** irritated, annoyed, irked, piqued, peeved, nettled, chafed, *Chiefly U.S.* riled, *Inf.* aggravated, *Inf.* miffed; ruffled, roiled, disturbed, disquieted, discomposed, perturbed, discountenanced; exasperated, fed up, sick and tired.
2. bothered, pestered, hectored, harassed, badgered, *Sl.* bugged; troubled, plagued, fretful, beset, worried; tormented, bedeviled, teased, taunted, tweaked, mocked, bullied, persecuted.
3. angry, angered, irate, incensed, mad, *Inf.* sore, hot and bothered, *Sl.* hot, *Sl.* hot under the collar, *Sl.* ticked-off, *Sl.* teed-off; furious, infuriated, enraged, maddened, livid, hopping mad, *Inf.* boiling mad, *Sl.* mad as a wet hen, *Sl.* madder than hell; galled, embittered, exacerbated, acerbate, envenomed, rankled.
4. disputed, in dispute, contested, in contention, debated; controversial, polemic, polemical; moot, questioned, doubted.

via, *prep.* by way of; by means of, by, through.

vial, *n.* glass vessel, small bottle; flask, test tube, *Med.* ampule; carafe, decanter, flagon.

viands, *n.* delicacies, dainties, *Class. Myth.* ambrosia; food, nutriment, nourishment, nutrition, pabulum, sustenance, subsistence; aliment, foodstuffs, edibles; victuals, provisions, cheer, provender, commons, comestibles; board, fare, menu, diet, refreshment.

vibrant, *adj.* **1.** vibrating, vibratory, vibratile, oscillating, oscillatory, swinging, librating, libratory, seesawing, wigwagging, moving to and fro; wobbling, teetering, reeling; undulating, swaying; fluctuating, vacillating, pendulous, wavering, teeter-tottering.
2. resonant, resounding, thunderous; ringing, tolling, plangent, clangorous; echoing, reechoing, reverberating, reverberant, reverberative, reflected; thundering, rumbling, booming.
3. pulsating, pulsatory, trembling, shaking, quaking, quivering, quavering; throbbing, palpitating, beating.
4. energetic, energetical, vigorous, dynamic, electric; active, alive, full of energy, *Inf.* full of pep, *Inf.* peppy, full of vim and vigor; lively, spirited, full of life, animated, vital; sprightly, spry, *Chiefly U.S. Inf.* chipper; eager, ready to go, bright-eyed and bushy-tailed.

vibrate, *v.* **1.** oscillate, move to fro, swing, move backward and forward, librate, move from side to side, ebb and flow, seesaw, wigwag; wobble, teeter, reel; undulate, wave, sway; fluctuate, vacillate, waver, vary, yo-yo, teeter-totter.
2. tremble, shake, quake, quiver, quaver, shudder, shiver; twitter, quail, jitter; pulsate, pulse, throb, palpitate, beat, pitapat.

3. resound, reverberate, resonate, ring, echo, re-echo, echo back, bounce off the walls; fill the air, roar, thunder, rumble, boom, bellow.

vibration, *n.* **1.** oscillation, swinging, libration, ebb and flow, flux and reflux, to and fro; undulation, sway; fluctuation, vacillation, wavering.

2. pulsation, shake, shiver, tremble, trembling, dither; palpitation, throb, throbbing, beat, beating, pulsing; earthquake, convulsion.

3. resonance, reverberation; thunder, rumble, roar, boom, clangor, roll.

4. vibrations *Slang.* feelings, *Sl.* vibes, sensations.

vicar, *n.* **1.** deputy rector, assistant pastor, *Chiefly Brit.* locum tenens; clergyman, cleric, churchman, ecclesiastic; priest, minister, parson, reverend, *Brit.* blackcoat.

2. substitute, surrogate, proxy; deputy, lieutenant, vice-regent, representative; emissary, delegate; plenipotentiary.

vicarious, *adj.* **1.** secondhand, indirect; imagined, mental, empathetic, sympathetic; aesthetic, artistic; imaginary, fantasized; surrogate, by proxy, at one remove.

2. delegated, deputed, commissioned; vice, acting; substitute, substitutional, substitutive.

vice, *n.* **1.** sin, sinfulness, wrong, wickedness, badness, baseness, foulness, meanness; immorality, iniquity, evil; transgression, misdeed, error, offense, violation.

2. fault, defect, flaw, imperfection, *Sl.* bug; frailty, weakness, weak point, infirmity, foible, shortcoming, limitation, failing, failure, deficiency.

3. impurity, unchasitiy, licentiousness, incontinence, dissipation, venery, fornication, carnality; debauchery, lewdness, lasciviousness, *Archaic.* venery.

vice versa, conversely, reversely, inversely; contrariwise, in exchange, on the other hand, the other way around; on *or* to the contrary, just the opposite *or* reverse.

vicinity, *n.* **1.** neighborhood, vicinage, purlieus, nearby area *or* region, *Inf.* neck of the woods; precincts, setting, scene; environs, *Fr. banlieue, Fr. alentours,* surroundings, cirumjacencies, outskirts, suburbs, faubourg, periphery.

2. proximity, proximateness, nearness, closeness, nighness, propinquity, contiguity, adjacence, adjacency.

vicious, *adj.* **1.** degenerate, depraved, corrupt, perverted, vitiated; foul, vile, base, bad, low, mean, odious; wicked, evil, iniquitous, nefarious, heinous, flagitious; immoral, sinful, peccant, evil-minded, vice-ridden; unregenerate, unredeemable, unprincipled, shameless, unscrupulous, reprobate; shameful, disgraceful, worthless; notorious, infamous, scandalous, disreputable; abominable, execrable, horrible, horrid, atrocious, grievous.

2. profligate, dissolute, libertine, rakish, rakehell; dissipated, lascivious, debauched; lecherous, lubricous, satyrlike, goatish; licentious, unrestrained, loose, wild.

3. reprehensible, reproachable, reprovable, condemnable, blameworthy, blamable, censurable; culpable, guilty, criminal, unlawful, illegal, illicit, illegitimate, lawless; objectionable, unpardonable, unjustifiable, inexcusable; delinquent, wrong, felonious, transgressive.

4. malicious, malevolent, malign, malignant, maleficent, malefic, *Archaic.* despiteous; hostile, antagonistic, obnoxious, ill-natured, surly; rancorous, bitter, embittered, caustic, acrimonious, sardonic, sarcastic, venomous, venomed, acerb; spiteful, hateful, invidious, ill-willed, ill-disposed, catty, *Sl.* bitchy, revengeful, vindictive.

5. savage, ferocious, cat-and-dog, dog-eat-dog, fierce, ruthless, fell, truculent; brutal, inhuman, barbarous, barbaric, hellish; sadistic, animalistic, fiendish; terrible, harsh, grim, hard, severe; unrelenting, relentless, implacable, inexorable, grinding.

vicissitude, *n.* **1.** change, mutation, permutation, modification, transformation, metamorphosis; variation, variance, difference, divergence, deviation.

2. alternation, shifting, vacillation, fluctuation, interchange; rotation, reversal, turn-about, turnaround, revolution, turning upside down, turning topsy-turvy.

3. vicissitudes inconstancy, instability, uncertainty, unpredictability, erraticism, mercuriality, shiftiness, choppiness; fickleness, chanciness, fortuitousness, *Inf.* flukiness; ups and downs, ins and outs, ebb and flow, roller coaster, shifting sands, kaleidoscope.

victim, *n.* **1.** sufferer, injured one *or* party, receiver, *Archaic.* patient.

2. dupe, gull, *Inf.* sucker, *Sl.* sap, *Brit. Dial.* cull, gudgeon, *Sl.* poor fish, *Inf.* chump, *Sl.* schnook, *Sl.* schlemiel, winner of the booby prize; easy *or* soft mark *or* target, mark, sitting duck, *Inf.* patsy, *Sl.* pigeon, *Sl.* fall guy, *Sl.* soft touch, *Sl.* pushover; laughing stock, butt, fair game, fool, everybody's fool, April fool, *Fr. poisson d'avril, Inf.* goat.

3. sacrifice, sacrificial lamb, scapegoat, human sacrifice, offering, martyr; prey, quarry.

victimize, *v.* **1.** stalk, prey on, hunt out, pursue, run down, go after; injure, hurt, harm, damage, do harm to, destroy, ruin.

2. exploit, use, take advantage of; dupe, swindle, cheat, *Inf.* diddle, gull, *Sl.* con; defraud, delude, mislead, beguile, pull the wool over the eyes of, throw dust in the eyes of, *Inf.* frame, betray, deceive, fool, make a fool of; rook, bilk, cog, *Sl.* take, *Sl.* snooker; hoodwink, trick, outwit, outfox, outsmart, bamboozle; humbug, *Inf.* fast-talk, *Inf.* flimflam, *Inf.* buffalo, *Sl.* snow, *Sl.* suck *or* sucker in, *Sl.* murphy, *Sl.* shaft.

3. sacrifice, slay, lay on the altar, throw to the wolves.

victor, *n.* conqueror, subduer, subjugator, vanquisher; master, hero, vindicator; winner, champion, *Inf.* number one; pennant winner, prize winner.

victorious, *adj.* conquering, triumphant, winning, successful; exultant, jubilant, on top, home free.

victory, *n.* conquest, triumph, win, walkaway; success, superiority, *Chiefly Scot.* gree, mastery; winning, gaining, excelling, taking the top spot *or* prize; subjugation, subdual, vanquishment, crushing, quelling, whip hand, upper hand.

victuals, *n.* food supplies, provisions, rations, food, viands, edibles, eatables, foodstuffs, *Inf.* grub, *Sl.* eats; nourishment, nutriment, sustenance, aliment; meal, square meal, repast, refreshment, fare, spread, table, mess, *Sl.* chow; board, *Sl.* three squares; feed, provender, forage, fodder.

vie, *v.* **1.** strive for, endeavor, make an attempt, fight *or* struggle for; compete against *or* with, contend, contest; meet, challenge.

2. emulate, equal, rival, challenge comparison.

view, *n.* **1.** sight, eyesight, vision; range *or* field of vision, eyeshot, eyereach, ken.

2. prospect, outlook, scene, vista, panorama, spectacle; landscape, seascape, cityscape, tableau.

3. contemplation, observation, study; survey, examination, inspection, scrutiny.

4. eye, regard, aim, intent, intention, design, purpose, object, objective, end.

5. opinion, belief, judgment; conception, concept, conceit; conviction, mind, persuasion, thinking, way of thinking; tenet, doctrine, dogma, principle, doxy, creed, precept.

6. supposition, theory, speculation, guess, two cents' worth; surmise, conjecture, premise, estimation, assessment, valuation; sentiment, feeling, apprehension; perception, image, impression, notion, idea; attitude, viewpoint, point of view, perspective; stand, standpoint, stance, position, vantage, vantage point, angle, posture.

—*v.* 7.watch, *Sl.* spectate, observe, witness; see, behold, catch sight of, *Inf.* lay eyes on, *Sl.* lamp; perceive, look at, discern, notice, regard, hold in view, have in sight; take in, survey, scan, look upon; scrutinize, read, inspect, pour over, peer at, examine, *Sl.* check out; cast an eye on, *Sl.* get a load of, *Inf.* take a gander, get an eyefull; peek, peep, spy, eye.

8. consider, contemplate, weigh, think over, turn over in one's mind, give thought to, mull over; ponder, *Archaic.* perpend, ruminate, cogitate, meditate on, muse on; delineate, reflect upon, revolve, put one's mind to, give one's attention to, think about.

viewpoint, *n.* attitude, sentiment, feeling, frame of mind, posture; opinion, view, point of view, stand, stance; position, angle, slant, perspective, standpoint, vantage point, vantage.

vigil, *n.* **1.** sleeplessness, wakefulness, insomnia.

2. watch, watch and ward, lookout; wake; *Inf.* stakeout; sharp eye, eagle eye, sleepless eye, *Inf.* peeled eye.

vigilance, *n.* watchfulness, surveillance, observation; guard, guardedness, wariness; caution, precaution, forethought, prudence, circumspection; alertness, keenness, attentiveness; wakefulness, sleeplessness.

vigilant, *adj.* **1.** watchful, on the watch, on the lookout; attentive, observant, sharp-eyed, eagle-eyed, hawk-eyed, Argus-eyed, all eyes and ears, alert, on the alert, on the qui vive, on one's toes, *Inf.* on the job; awake, wide-awake, sleepless, unsleeping, unnodding, *Inf.* with eyes peeled.

2. wary, chary, careful, cautious, circumspect, prudent, mindful, heedful; guarded, on one's guard.

vignette, *n.* **1.** design, small illustration, *Print.* headpiece, *Print.* tailpiece; engraving, print, drawing, illumination; picture, view.

2. literary sketch, delineation, skit; anecdote, narrative, short tale *or* yarn; instance, illustration.

vigor, *n.* **1.** strength, power, potency, virility, force, birr, *Literary.* puissance; stamina, endurance, staying power, mettle, pluck, sap, pith, nerve, steel, *Inf.* spunk, *Inf.* starch, *Sl.* moxie; health, healthiness, haleness, soundness, heartiness, robustness, vigorousness, hardiness, sturdiness; forcefulness, forcibleness.

2. vitality, vivacity, energy, trenchancy, go, get up and go, zing, liveliness, spryness, sprightliness, briskness, *Inf.* zip, *Inf.* pep, *Inf.* punch, *Inf.* bounce, *Inf.* snap, *Sl.* pizzazz, *Sl.* oomph, *Brit. Sl.* stingo.

3. spirit, enthusiasm, eagerness, ebullience, animation, vim, sparkle, keenness, *Dial.* gimp, *Chiefly Scot.* smeddum; zeal, verve, ardor, fervor, élan, dash, fire, vehemence, intensity.

vigorous, *adj.* **1.** energetic, full of energy, dynamic, strenuous, active, trenchant; quick, brisk, spry, sprightly, *Scot. and North Eng.* yauld, *Inf.* bouncing, *Inf.* zippy, *Inf.* peppy, *Sl.* go-go; vivacious, lively, full of life, glowing, sparkling, spanking, zingy, bold, sharp.

2. robust, hearty, hardy, hale, hale and hearty, lusty, strong and healthy, bursting with health *or* vigor; sound, healthy, in good health, fit, physically fit, in good condition, in fine fettle, *Inf.* in good shape, *Inf.* in shape; stout, staunch, stalwart, firm, sturdy, tough.

3. powerful, potent, mighty, forceful, forcible, irresistible, emphatic, aggressive; spirited, mettlesome, steadfast, resolute, doughty, plucky, *Inf.* spunky; eager, enthusiastic, ebullient, keen, *Sl.* psyched; zealous, ardent, fervid, fervent, vehement, impassioned, burning, intense.

4. effective, valid, biting, pointed, to the point; incisive, telling, cogent; graphic, vivid, striking, pithy, meaty.

vigorously, *adv.* **1.** energetically, dynamically, with might and main, hammer and tongs, with a vengeance, like a trooper, *Inf.* to beat the band, *Sl.* up a storm; strenuously, actively, trenchantly; quickly, briskly, spryly, sprightly, sprightfully, *Inf.* zippily, *Inf.* peppily, *Sl.* like mad, *Sl.* like crazy; vivaciously, glowingly, spankingly, zingily, boldly, sharply.

2. robustly, heartily, hardily, lustily; soundly, healthily; stoutly, staunchly, stanchly, stalwartly, firmly, sturdily, toughly.

3. powerfully, potently, mightily, forcefully, forcibly, irresistibly, emphatically, aggressively; spiritedly, steadfastly, resolutely, doughtily, pluckily, *Inf.* spunkily; eagerly, enthusiastically, keenly; zealously, ardently, fervidly, fervently, vehemently, intensely.

4. effectively, validly, bitingly, pointedly; incisively, tellingly, cogently; graphically, vividly, strikingly, pithily, meatily.

vile, *adj.* **1.** base, low, mean, sordid, bad; execrable, abominable, horrible, horrid, gruesome, monstrous, atrocious; dreadful, terrible, dire, grim, dark, black, baleful; accursed, cursed, damnable, damned; demonic, demoniac, diabolic, devilish, satanic, fiendish, hellish.

2. offensive, unpleasant, objectionable, obnoxious, disagreeable; abhorrent, loathsome, odious, hateful, detestable, despicable; contemptible, scurvy, insufferable; opprobrious, reproachful, blameworthy, contemptuous.

3. repulsive, repellent, revolting, repugnant, nauseous, nauseating; foul-smelling, rank, stinking, smelling, reeking, *Rare.* nidorous; fetid, feculent, graveolent, noisome, mephitic, malodorous; disgusting, distasteful, sickening, noxious, fulsome; musty, fusty, moldy; rotten, rancid, tainted, putrescent, putrid, putrefactive; slimy, grimy, excrementitious, fecal, *Physiol.* stercoraceous.

4. depraved, debased, wicked, evil, iniquitous, sinful; debauched, degenerate, immoral, dissolute, dissipated, abandoned, profligate, reprobate; corrupt, black-hearted, ignoble, sinister, evil-minded; nefarious, flagitious, villainous, heinous, *Rare.* nefast.

5. obscene, coarse, vulgar, crude; profane, maledictory, blasphemous; smutty, foulmouthed, scatalogical, filthy, dirty, pornographic, Fescennine; bawdy, ribald, off-color, suggestive, unseemly, indelicate, indecorous; lascivious, lecherous, lewd, licentious, *Archaic.* lickerish, lubricous, lustful.

6. poor, wretched, sorry, abject, squalid, destitute; miserable, dismal, abysmal, dreary, *Literary.* drear; beggarly, shabby, scrubby, seedy, sleazy, abased.

7. menial, lowly, servile, slavish, subservient; groveling, sniveling, cowering, cringing.

8. paltry, trivial, trifling, petty, slight, little, feeble; insignificant, inconsiderable, inappreciable, nugatory, worthless, trumpery; meager, scanty, measly, piddling, niggling, scrimpy, skimpy; niggardly, miserly, cheap, catchpenny.

vileness, *n.* **1.** baseness, meanness, viciousness, lowness, badness; sordidness, ignobility, foulness, sinisterness, darkness, black-heartedness; balefulness, dreadfulness, direness, direfulness, grimness; wickedness, iniquity, nefariousness, flagitiousness, heinousness; sinfulness, ungodliness, profanity, blasphemy; abomination, outrage, enormity, atrocity; criminality, feloniousness, lawlessness; perfidy, treachery, recreancy; villainy, knavery, roguery, rascality.

2. offensiveness, objectionableness, obnoxiousness, disagreeableness; loathsomeness, odiousness, odium, hatefulness, despicability, despicableness, detestability; contemptibility, insufferableness, scurviness; opprobrium, ignominy, disgrace, obloquy; infamy, notoriety, disrepute, disreputableness.

3. repulsiveness, repugnance, disgust, repellence, distastefulness; rankness, smelliness, fetidness, fetidity, nauseousness, *Rare.* nidor, feculence, *Obs.* graveolence; noisomeness, mephitis, malodorousness, noxiousness, fulsomeness.

4. depravity, turpitude, degradation, depravation, debauchery; debasement, vitiation, corruption, pollution, defilement; profligacy, reprobacy, reprobateness, degeneracy, dissipation, dissolution; immorality, obliquity, unchastity; wantonness, salaciousness, salacity, prurience; carnality, bestiality, perversity; lasciviousness, lechery, lewdness, licentiousness, lubricity, lustfulness, *Archaic.* venery; obscenity, coarseness, vulgarity, crudity, grossness; smuttiness, filthiness, dirtiness; ribaldry, *Archaic.* bawdry; unseemliness, indecorum.

5. wretchedness, misery, abjectness; squalor, shabbiness, seediness, abasement; dreariness, dismalness, miserableness; beggary, poverty, destitution; servility, menialness, lowliness, subservience.

6. paltriness, triviality, trivialness, pettiness; insignificance, inconsequentiality, inconsiderableness, worthlessness; meagerness, scantiness, skimpiness.

vilify, *v.* **1.** defame, denigrate, vituperate, vilipend, scandalize, run down; berate, impugn, revile, blackguard, malign, gibbet, criticize, pull to pieces, *Sl.* do a hatchet job on, give a bad name, speak ill of, speak evil of, sneer at, ridicule, contemn, despise, scorn, spurn, muckrake; denounce, fulminate, rail, curse, execrate, damn, imprecate, *Obs.* exprobrate, anathematize, censure, cry down, reproach.

2. shame, disgrace, dishonor, debase, vitiate, degrade, discredit; belittle, detract, decry, deprecate, disparage, deflate, depreciate, devaluate, derogate; humiliate, humble, mortify, *Sl.* put down.

3. slander, libel, calumniate, traduce, falsify, accuse falsely, misrepresent, belie, asperse, impute, insinuate; injure, abuse, stab, assail, insult, *Sl.* badmouth, backbite, engage in personalities; slur, sully, defile, smear, smirch, besmirch, soil, blacken, stain, tarnish, taint, smudge, blemish, spot, brand, stigmatize, drag through the mud *or* mire, heap dirt upon, fling dirt, throw mud on, *Sl.* dump on *or* all over.

villa, *n.* **1.** estate, country estate, country home, country seat, country house, rural mansion, hacienda, manor, manor house, manor seat.

2. mansion, palace, palatial residence, palatial house, stately residence, kingly residence, kingly house, great house, castle, chateau, *Fr. hôtel, It. palazzo, Chiefly Brit.* hall, *Brit.* court, *Archaic.* folly.

village, *n.* community, dorp, hamlet, *Scot., Irish.* clachan, *Archaic.* thorp, *Archaic.* wick; settlement, *India.* bustee, (*in South Africa*) kraal, (*in Spanish America*) pueblo, (*in Malay-speaking lands*) kampong; town, municipality, township, burough, *Inf.* burg.

villain, *n.* **1.** scoundrel, knave, blackguard, wretch, dastard, reprobate, cur, dog, *Inf.* hound, *Sl.* lowlife, *Archaic.* caitiff, *Archaic.* coistrel; bad guy *or* man, *Inf.* baddy, *Sl.* the heavy, Iago; snake, viper, reptile, snake in the rass, evildoer, fiend, hellhound, miscreant, devil; rogue, cad, churl, *Sl.* louse, *Sl.* stinker, *Sl.* rat, *Sl.* creep, *Sl.* jerk, *Sl.* bastard, *Sl.* SOB, *Obs.* stinkard; hoodlum, hooligan, bully, ruffian, brute, abuser, roughneck, delinquent, *Inf.* gallows bird; good-for-nothing, ne'er-do-well, black sheep, *Inf.* rip, *Sl.* bum, *Chiefly Brit.* wastrel, *Chiefly Brit. Sl.* rotter, *Chiefly Brit. Sl.* bounder, *Brit. Sl.* blighter; rascal, scamp, scalawag, rapscallion, scapegrace, troublemaker.

2. traitor, renegade, betrayer, Judas, recreant; deceiver, dissembler, bamboozler, *Inf.* four-flusher; cheat, cheater, trickster, sharper, fox, sly fox, shark, *Inf.* shyster, *Sl.* con man, *Inf.* flimflamer; crook, *U. S. Sl.* chiseler, swindler, bilker, *Inf.* diddler; criminal, felon, outlaw; murderer, assassin, cutthroat.

villainous, *adj.* **1.** evil, sinful, wicked, iniquitous, *Archaic.* facinorous, *Obs.* scelerous; nefarious, flagitious, heinous, infamous, notorious, *Rare.* nefast; monstrous, atrocious, horrible; black-hearted, sinister, arrant, ignoble; base, vile, foul, low, mean, odious, obnoxious.

2. unscrupulous, unprincipled, crooked, dishonorable; perfidious, treacherous, traitorous, faithless; blackguardly, scoundrelly, thievish, ruffianly; knavish, rascally, roguish, scampish; criminal, reprehensible, felonious, lawless; unregenerate, unrepentant, incorrigible; degenerate, corrupt, *Rare.* turpid, depraved; immoral, dissolute, profligate, reprobate, dissipated; opprobrious, disgraceful, shameful.

3. abominable, damnable, execrable, accursed, cursed; revolting, repulsive, repellent, repugnant, offensive; abhorrent, loathsome, hateful, detestable, despicable; malicious, rancorous, venomous, virulent, baneful; pernicious, baleful, fell, menacing, malignant, malign; malevolent, maleficent, malefic, ill-intentioned, evil-minded; demonic, demoniac, diabolic, satanic, devilish.

villainy, *n.* **1.** knavery, roguery, rascality, miscreancy, delinquency; iniquity, sin, sinfulness, deviltry; evil, vice, crime, improbity; nefariousness, flagitiousness, heinousness, infamy; vileness, viciousness, badness, baseness, foulness, meanness; atrocity, outrage, abomination, enormity, flagrancy; perfidy, treachery, foul play, dishonesty; unregeneracy, impenitence.

2. depravity, turpitude, degradation, degeneracy, corruption, pollution, profligacy, reprobacy, reprobateness, immorality, obliquity, debauchery.

vim, *n.* vitality, liveliness, vigor, vigorousness, energy, get up and go, *Inf.* pep, *Sl.* stingo; zeal, verve, enthusiasm, eagerness, spirit, ebullience, effervescence, bubbliness, sparkle, *Inf.* bounce, *Dial.* gimp, *Chiefly Scot.* smeddum; trenchancy, briskness, *Inf.* zip, *Inf.* snap, *Sl.* pizzazz; power, potency, force, kick, *Inf.* punch, *Sl.* oomph, *Literary.* puissance.

vindicate, *v.* **1.** acquit, clear, clear [s.o.'s] name, exonerate, exculpate, prove *or* declare innocent, uphold innocence, pronounce not guilty; remove guilt, free from blame, absolve.

2. justify, show just cause, warrant, authorize; substantiate, prove, verify, corroborate, confirm, bear out; extenuate, palliate, explain, rationalize, tell one's story, apologize, make excuses, *Inf.* alibi, *Inf.* do a song and dance.

3. defend, champion, fight for, plead for, stick up for, stand up for; support, uphold, sustain, bolster up, back, maintain, assert; advocate, vouch, second, stand by.

4. claim, lay claim to, file a claim for, allege ownership, declare oneself entitled to, assert one's right to, *Law.* deraign; demand, requisition, request, ask for.

5. avenge, revenge, *Archaic.* venge; retaliate, requite, take vengeance for, get back at, take an eye for an eye, pay [s.o.] back, repay, give [s.o.] his due, give [s.o.]

what he asks for.

vindication, *n.* **1.** acquittal, acquittance, acquitting, compurgation, exculpation, exculpating, proof *or* declaration of innocence, removal of guilt, freedom from blame, absolution, absolving; exoneration, exonerating, redress, righting, setting *or* putting right.

2. justification, reason, plea, basis, grounds, authorization, warrant, sanction; substantiation, substantiating, proof, proving, evidence, verification, verifying, voucher, corroboration, corroborating, confirmation, confirming; defense, defending, support, supporting, upholding, sustaining, maintenance, maintaining, assertion, asserting, *Law.* deraignment; advocacy, advocating, *Obs.* vouch; explanation, explaining, story, argument, allegation, claim, *Law.* rejoinder, rationalization, excuse, apology, apologia, extenuation, extenuating, palliation, palliating, *Law.* demurrer, *Law.* rebutter, *Law.* essoin, *Inf.* song and dance, *U. S. Inf.* alibi.

3. revenge, vengeance, avenging, retaliation, retaliating, reprisal, requital, requiting, an eye for an eye and a tooth for a tooth; retribution, payment, payoff, repayment.

vindicatory, *adj.* **1.** exculpatory, exculpating, acquitting, compurgatory, exonerative, exonerating, vindicative, vindicating, absolutory, absolvent, absolving, excusatory, excusing; justificatory, justificative, justifying, extenuatory, extenuating, mitigative, mitigating, palliative, palliating.

2. punitive, punitory, punishing, disciplinary, castigative, castigatory, castigating, chastising; mean, harsh, severe, cruel, brutal; merciless, pitiless, remorseless, hard-hearted, stony-hearted, compassionless, unremissive, relentless, unrelenting, inexorable.

3. retributive, retributory, requiting, retaliatory. See **vindictive.**

vindictive, *adj.* vengeful, revengeful, avenging, vindicatory, vindicative; retributive, retributory, requiting, retaliatory, retaliative; spiteful, rancorous, venomous, malevolent, malicious, malignant, antagonistic, hostile, resentful, ill-disposed; unforgiving, grudge-bearing, implacable, unconciliative, unconciliatory, unreconcilable, unreconciling.

vintage, *adj.* **1.** quality, choice, select, best, superior, good.

2. aged, seasoned, mature, ripe, mellow.

3. old-fashioned, old-fangled, old-time, bygone, past; antique, old, antiquated, archaic, outdated, obsolete.

violate, *v.* **1.** break, breach, infract, contravene, infringe, transgress; disobey, ignore, shun, disregard, reject, repudiate; trespass, offend, *Rare.* misdemean, misbehave.

2. disturb, disrupt, interrupt, upset, agitate, disorder, unsettle, trouble; rend, shatter, crack, crash, destroy; interfere, intrude, *Sl.* butt in, encroach on.

3. break through, burst through, invade, run roughshod over, trample; rupture, fracture, split.

4. desecrate, profane, defile, blaspheme, treat sacrilegiously *or* irreverently; debase, degrade, befoul, vitiate, spoil, mar; lay waste, plunder, pillage, despoil, desolate, depredate; corrupt, deprave, pervert.

5. rape, ravish, attack, assault, take by force, force; dishonor, deflower, ruin, ravage; molest, defile, outrage, debauch, seduce; abuse, ill-use, ill-treat, victimize.

violation, *n.* **1.** infringement, infringing, encroachment, encroaching; disturbing, disrupting, disruption, interruption; desolation, destruction.

2. breach, infraction, transgression, trespass, contravention; illegality, delinquency, offense, misbehavior, misdemeanor, felony, crime, sin; disobedience, opposition; dereliction, negligence, evasion.

3. desecration, profanation, blasphemy, sacrilege, defilement; corruption, perversion, degradation, debasement, adulteration; plunder, pillage, rapine, spoliation .

4. rape, ravishment, assault, attack, molestation, seduction; abuse, maltreatment, ill usage, deflowering, dishonoring, ruin, ruination, victimization.

5. (*all of meaning or fact*) distortion, garbling, twisting, warping, alteration, changing; misinterpretation, misrepresentation, misunderstanding.

violence, *n.* **1.** force, brute force, might, mightiness, power, strength; turbulence, storminess, tempestuousness, tumultuousness, boisterousness, bluster; roughness, destructiveness, barbarity; brutality, cruelty, savagery, ferocity, ferociousness, fierceness; severity, harshness, rigor.

2. cataclysm, convulsion, eruption, outburst, explosion, blast, paroxysm, earthquake; uproar, upheaval, commotion, confusion, chaos, babel, bedlam, racket, rampage; sound and fury, blood and thunder, hubbub, fracas, *Inf.* ruckus, rumpus, riot, brawling; fire, heat, blaze; storm, squall, howling; disorder, anarchy, disruption, disarray.

3. frenzy, fury, furiousness, furor, rage, anger; madness, hysteria, wildness, dementedness, craziness; impetuosity, impulsiveness, rashness; vehemence, ardor, passion, fieriness; intensity, excessiveness, acuteness, sharpness, keenness.

4. injury, harm, damage, wrong, injustice; havoc, outrage, rape, desecration, profanation.

violent, *adj.* **1.** strong, powerful, mighty, potent, forceful, great; uncontrolled, unrestrained, untamed, unbridled, savage; stormy, tempestuous, turbulent, wroth, rampageous; roaring, howling, raging, storming, shrieking; explosvie, volcanic, dangerous, perilous, dreadful.

2. destructive, ruinous, dire, disastrous, calamitous, catastrophic, cataclysmic; devastating, wasting, ravaging; injurious, harmful, hurtful, damaging, detrimental; deleterious, baneful, pernicious; deadly, fell, fatal, lethal, killing, murderous; cruel, raw, brutal, barbarous, bloodthirsty, brutish, beastly, inhuman; ruthless, pitiless, merciless, relentless, implacable; wild, crazed, uncontrollable, ungovernable, like a wild bull, seeing red, rough, *Brit. Dial.* lungeous; disorderly, clamorous, knock-down-drag-out, tumultuous, rowdy, roisterous.

3. severe, extreme, excessive, harsh, intense; unremitting, inexorable, persistent, unyielding; distressing, agonizing, torturous, tormenting, excruciating, racking, painful; unbearable, overpowering, overwhelming; stinging, piercing, biting, penetrating; acute, keen, sharp, exquisite, poignant; extraordinary, abnormal, unnatural, unusual; rigorous, stern, grim, hard, forbidding, draconian, drastic.

4. vehement, ardent, impassioned, fervid, fervent, intent, excited, perfervid; burning, fiery, blazing, hot, red-hot; raving, mad, wild-eyed, running amuck, irrational, insane; lusty, passionate, stirred up, on fire.

5. furious, frenzied, frenetic, feverish, frantic, fast and furious; impetuous, impulsive, headstrong, headlong, rash, unheeding, unthinking; fierce, ferocious, daring, *Inf.* hellbent.

viper, *n.* **1.** scoundrel, villain, rogue, knave, good-for-nothing; wretch, cur, churl, *Sl.* stinker, *Obs.* stinkard, *Inf.* heel, cad; blackguard, rascal, scamp, devil; wretch, worm, *Sl.* no-goodnik, *Sl.* lowlife, *Inf.* bum, degenerate; rotter, *Chiefly Brit.* bounder, scum, *Sl.* bastard, *Sl.* son of a bitch, *Sl.* SOB, *Archaic.* whoreson; *All Sl.* crumb, momzer, shmuck, putz, rat.

2. traitor, betrayer, snake, snake in the grass, *Inf.* double-crosser, *Inf.* double-dealer, backstabber, *Sl.* two-timer, Judas; quisling, turncoat, renegade, Benedict Arnold; fifth columnist, informer, subversive, double agent; conspirator, collaborator, Catilinarian, Brutus; spy, company spy, *Sl.* fink, *Sl.* rat-fink, *Sl.* weasel, *Sl.* stool pigeon *or* stoolie, squealer, tattler, *Sl.* ratter; liar, prevaricator, hypocrite, pharisee; deceiver, cheat, swindler; dissembler, wolf in sheep's clothing.

viperous, *adj.* venomous, virulent, poisonous, baneful, deadly, lethal; malignant, malicious, malign, vicious; villainous, scoundrelly, unscrupulous, low, base, mean, churlish; malevolent, maleficent, devilish, demonic; rancorous, spiteful, vindictive, revengeful, vengeful; hateful, contemptible, despicable, abhorrent.

virago, *n.* shrew, *Sl.* battle-ax, termagant, fishwife, Xanthippe; harpy, fury, vixen, tartar, spitfire, she-wolf, hell-cat, *Sl.* bitch; harridan, hag, beldam, crone, witch; scold, nag, *Inf.* biddy, *Inf.* old biddy, *Sl.* old bag.

virgin, *n.* **1.** vestal, maid, maiden, lass, girl, damsel; unmarried woman, *Inf.* bachelor girl, old maid, spinster; bachelor, misogamist, misogynist; celibate, priest, monk, brother; nun, sister, *Fr. religieuse.*

—adj. **2.** virginal, vestal, chaste, *Archaic.* honest, pure, maidenly, maidenish *or* maidish; virtuous, good, innocent, modest, prudish; angelic, saintly, faultless, sinless.

3. untouched, undefiled, unused, uncorrupted, unsullied, unsoiled; decent, clean, wholesome; fresh, pristine, immaculate, snowy; spotless, unblemished, stainless, unstained, untainted, untarnished; pure, unadulterated, unchanged; unalloyed,

4. celibate, single, unmarried, unwed; spouseless, wifeless, husbandless, widowed.

5. first, initial, original; earliest, oldest, premier; maiden, pristine, primordial.

6. unaware, unconscious, insensible, unsuspecting, unanticipative; unknowing, incognizant, ignorant, in the dark, blindfolded, uninformed, unenlightened, uninitiated, unacquainted, unversed; unexperienced, unexposed, sheltered, protected.

virginity, *n.* **1.** chastity, chasteness, virtue, virtuousness, goodness; innocence, innocency, modesty, *Rare.* pudicity; purity, pureness, untouchedness, uncorruptedness; freshness, cleanness, spotlessness, stainlessness, immaculateness, immaculacy.

2. celibacy, maidenhood *or* maidhood, *Obs.* pucelage; singleness, bachelorhood, spinsterhood, unmarried state, *Euph.* single blessedness.

virile, *adj.* **1.** manly, masculine, manful, manlike, he-man, macho; potent, hairy-chested, *Inf.* two-fisted, broad-shouldered.

2. vigorous, lusty, strong, powerful, hardy, robust; mighty, hale, hearty, stout, rugged, red-blooded; burly, thickset, athletic, well-built, well-knit, muscular, brawny, strapping, husky, sturdy, sinewy, wiry.

3. energetic, dynamic, forceful, forcible, spirited; tough, rough, plucky, spunky, doughty, nervy; daring, audacious, mettlesome, fearless, undaunted; dashing, bold, venturesome, valiant, courageous; intrepid, valorous, gallant, chivalrous, heroic, soldierly.

virility, *n.* **1.** masculinity, maleness, manfulness, manliness, manhood; machismo, sexiness, animal magnetism; potency, manly vigor, virileness.

2. vigor, lustiness, hardiness, vitality, robustness, power, force, thews, might, main; strength, powerfulness, brawn, huskiness, muscularity, ruggedness, sturdiness; heftiness, burliness, stoutness, haleness, heartiness.

3. toughness, roughness, mettle, pluck, game, spunk, grit; doughtiness, nerve, stamina, *Sl.* guts, intestinal fortitude, backbone, sand; courage, valor, bravery, intrepidity, fearlessness, dauntlessness; gallantry, heroism, chivalry, daring, derring-do; audacity, boldness, mettlesomeness, soldierliness.

virtual, *adj.* practical, essential, substantial, effective, in effect, functioning as, operating as; tantamount to, equivalent to, equal to; implied, implicit, unstated.

virtually, *adj.* almost, *Inf.* most, for the most part, just about; as good as, practically, for all practical purposes, in effect, substantially, essentially, in essence, to all intents and purposes; nearly, near, next to, well-nigh, nigh, nigh upon *or* onto; close to, in the neighborhood *or* vicinity of, nearing, approaching, toward, verging on, bordering on; all but, not quite, barely, hardly, scarcely.

virtue, *n.* **1.** goodness, righteousness, morality, moral excellence, ethicalness; uprightness, rectitude, probity, integrity, honesty; worth, honor, decency, respectability, character; high-mindedness, upstandingness, nobility, scrupulousness; justness, fairness, fair play, justice, equity; fidelity, faithfulness, loyalty, constancy, trustworthiness, responsibility; grace, merit, worthiness, credit, quality, fortitude, temperance, piety, faith, hope, charity.

2. chastity, virginity, purity, *Rare.* pudicity; immaculateness, spotlessness, stainlessness, innocence, cleanness; sinlessness, guiltlessness, incorruption, impeccability; modesty, decency, continence.

3. power, efficacy, effectiveness, force, potency, might, *Literary.* puissance; energy, strength, cogency, effect, dint; charge, push, drive, vehemence; validity, effectuality, productivity, efficaciousness.

4. **by virtue of** by reason of, because of, on account of, in view of, on the score of; due to, thanks to, owing to, by dint of, as a result of.

virtuosity, *n.* mastery, skill, brilliance, musicianship; craftsmanship, craft, artistry, art, artfulness, workmanship; wizardry, command, bravura, pyrotechnics, razzle-dazzle; expertise, prowess, professionalism, mastership; excellence, incomparability, inimitability, superiority, preeminence.

virtuoso, *n.* **1.** maestro, expert, talent, genius, prodigy, standout, *Inf.* wizard, *Inf.* whiz, *U. S. Sl.* crackerjack, *Sl.* sharp, *Sl.* shark; master, proficient, adept, mavin, master hand, *Chiefly Brit. Inf.* dab hand, *Brit. Dial.* dabster; specialist, authority, conoisseur; (*both of martial arts*) black belt, dan; professional, *Inf.* pro, journeyman, veteran, past master, past mistress, old hand, old stager.

—adj. **2.** virtuosic, masterful, masterly, expert; topflight, top-drawer, *Inf.* topnotch, *Inf.* crack, *Sl.* crackerjack, *Sl.* on the ball, *Inf.* whiz-bang, *Brit. Sl.* whizzo; finished, polished, accomplished, practiced; experienced, *Fr. au fait,* professional, *Inf.* pro, veteran; adept, knowledgeale, skillful, talented, skilled, dextrous, adroit, deft, facile.

3. excellent, first-rate, capital, *Inf.* tip-top, *Inf.* A-1, *Inf.* A number 1; exceptional, superior, standout, outstanding, striking; superlative, matchless, peerless, nonpareil, perfect, sterling, classic, first-class; remarkable, wonderful, marvelous, extraordinary.

virtuous, *adj.* **1.** moral, ethical, upright, good, righteous, upstanding; honest, honorable, decent, noble, high-minded, high-principled; fair, just, fair-minded, scrupulous, square; responsible, trustworthy, constant, loyal, faithful; veracious, truthful, aboveboard, straightforward; creditable, laudable, estimable, commendable; meritorious, praiseworthy, worthy; right-minded; dutiful, equitable, correct; saintly, angelic, holy, godly, seraphic.

2. chaste, pure, virgin, virginal, vestal, immaculate; clean, innocent, spotless, sinless, guiltless, uncorrupted; undefiled, unstained, unsullied, unfallen, unerring; decent, modest, continent.

virulence, *n.* **1.** poisonousness, venomousness, venomness, toxicity, deadliness, virulency; lethality, fatalness; noxiousness, harmfulness, hurtfulness, injuriousness, detrimentalness, detrimentality, deleteriousness, unwholesomeness, unhealthiness; destructiveness, ruinousness, perniciousness, balefulness.

2. hostility, resentment, indignation, pique, anger; spite, malice, rancor; antagonism, malevolence, malignity; aggression, belligerence, bellicosity.

3. acrimony, acrimoniousness, causticity, asperity, mordancy, acridness, acridity, pungency; astringency, severity, sternness, acerbity, austerity, stringency; harshness, sharpness, sourness, acidulousness, acidity, bitterness, tartness, trenchancy, keenness, sarcasm, satire, irony; peevishness, petulance, *Rare.* petulancy, crabbedness, tetchiness, touchiness, irascibility, edginess; ill temper, ill-temperedness, short-temperedness, ill humor, ill-humoredness.

virulent, *adj.* **1.** poisonous, venomous, envenomed, toxic, deadly, lethal, fatal; noxious, harmful, hurtful, injurious, mischievous, detrimental, deleterious, unwholesome, unhealthy; destructive, ruinous, pernicious, baleful; malignant, cancerous; (*all of disease*) infective, infectious, contagious, catching.

2. hostile, resentful, indignant, piqued, angry; spiteful, malicious, venomous, vicious; antagonistic, malevolent, malignant, malign, ill-disposed, rancorous; abusive, corrosive; morose, surly, sullen, moody; adverse, opposed, opposing; aggressive, warlike, belligerent, bellicose.

3. acrimonious, caustic, mordant, bitter, acrid, pungent; astringent, acerb, acerbic, severe, stern, austere, stringent; harsh, sharp, sour, acidulous, acid, tart; trenchant, keen, sarcastic, satiric, ironic, ironical; peevish, petulant, crabbed, testy, touchy, irascible, edgy; ill-tempered, ill-humored, short-tempered.

visage, *n.* **1.** face, countenance, physiognomy; *All Sl.* mug, kisser, puss, pan, map, phiz.

2. looks, features, lineaments; mien, demeanor, complexion, cast, turn; aspect, appearance, *Inf.* cut of one's jib.

vis-à-vis, *adv., adj.* **1.** face to face, eye to eye, *Inf.* eyeball to eyeball, nose to nose, head to head.

—prep. **2.** in relation to, in comparison with, compared with *or* to, in contrast to, contrasted with.

3. facing, opposite, across, against, over against.

viscera, *n.,pl.* body organs, internal organs, internals; intestines, bowels, colons, (*of swine*) chitterlings, (*of animals*) entrails; insides, inwards, *Inf.* innards, *Sl.* guts; vitals, vital organs, vital parts.

visceral, *adj.* **1.** intestinal, abdominal, splanchnic.

2. instinctive, intuitive, emotional, *Sl.* gut; spontaneous, immediate.

3. physical, bodily; earthy, crude, coarse, base.

viscosity, *n.* thickness, stickines, adhesiveness, tackiness, glueyness, mucilaginousness, viscidity; stodginess, slabbiness, heaviness, glutinousness; syrupiness, gumminess, mucosity, gelatinousness, *Physical Chem.* colloidality, jelliedness, yolkiness, albuminousness, glairiness; sliminess, *Inf.* gooeyness, gloppiness, *Sl.* ickiness; inspisation, incrassation, clabbering, lumpiness, curdling; ropiness, stringiness.

viscous, *adj.* thick, sticky, adhesive, tacky, gluey, mucilaginous, viscid; stodgy, glutinous, thickened, heavy, clotted; syrupy, treacly, molasses-like; gummy, gummous, mucous, *Archaic.* pituitous; albuminous, yolky, gelatinous, jellied, glairy; stringy, ropy, *Vulgar.* snotty; clabbered, curdled, lumpy, inspissate; gloppy, *Inf.* gooey, *Sl.* icky, *Sl.* yecchy, *Sl.* ishy.

visibility, *n.* perceptibility, perceivability, seeability, discernibleness, visibleness, observability; plainness, distinctness, definiteness, clearness, clarity.

visible, *adj.* **1.** perceptible, perceivable, discernible, seeable, visual.

2. apparent, evident, self-evident, palpable; noticeable, observable, recognizable; manifest, clear, clear-cut, crystal-clear, open, plain, plain as day; obvious, patent, unmistakable; unhidden, unconcealed, undisguised.

3. conspicuous, salient, prominent, in high relief, *Inf.* plain as the nose on one's face; distinct, well-defined, in sight, in full view, before one's eyes, under one's nose; glaring, *Inf.* sticking *or* hanging out.

vision, *n.* **1.** sight, eyesight; perception, perspicacity, penetration, discernment, insight.

2. dream, *Sl.* trip, chimera, figment, figment of the imagination, illusion, delusion; mirage, hallucination, Fata Morgana, optical illusion, trick of the eyesight.

3. apparition, materialization, specter, shade, shadow, spirit, soul, revenant, wraith, eidolon, phantom, phantasm, phantasma; ghost, (*in Irish Folklore*) banshee, *Inf.* spook; nightmare, incubus, succubus.

4. conception, conceptualization, visualization, envisioning, objectification; anticipation, expectation; mental image, mental picture.

visionary, *adj.* **1.** impractical, unrealistic, unworkable, unfeasible, theoretical, academic, impracticable; utopian, idealistic, romantic, quixotic, starry-eyed, dewy-eyed; pie-in-the-sky, wish-fulfilling.

2. unreal, imaginary, imagined, illusory, delusory, phantasmagoric, phantasmagorial; chimerical, fanciful, fancied, figmental, figmentary; phantasmal, spiritual, spectral, apparitional, ghostly, wraithlike.

—n. **3.** mystic; seer, prophet.

4. dreamer, daydreamer, woolgatherer, castlebuilder, fantast, *Obs.* fantastico; idealist, romantic, romanticist, Don Quixote; escapist, wishful thinker; enthusiast, zealot.

visit, *v.* **1.** call on *or* upon, look in on, look [s.o.] up, see; come around, come by, stop in *or* by, *Inf.* pop in.

2. come *or* go to, attend, *Sl.* make the scene; appear, turn up, show up, make or put in an appearance, show one's face.

3. take in, *Inf.* do, *Inf.* catch.

4. afflict, assail, attack, smite, come upon, fall *or* descend upon; scourge, agonize, harrow, torture; (*all usu. in reference to punishment*) inflict, wreak, bring down upon.

5. converse, talk, chat, chitchat, confabulate, *Inf.* confab, coze, pass the time of day, while away the time, *Brit. Dial.* tell, *Sl.* rap, *Sl.* chin, *Sl.* chew the fat *or* rag, *Sl.* shoot the breeze *or* bull, *Sl.* bull; talk *or* speak with, have a talk *or* little talk with, commune *or* communicate with.

—n. **6.** call, social call; stay, sojourn, stop, stopover, stop-off; conversation, talk, colloquy, chat, chitchat, little talk, *Sl.* rap, *Sl.* rap session.

visitation, *n.* **1.** (*all usu. unpleasant*) event, occurrence, happening, incident, episode, occasion, turn of events; experience, *Sl.* bad trip, *Sl.* bummer.

2. affliction, infliction, bane, blight, curse, scourge, plague, pestilence; shock, blow, heavy *or* nasty *or* staggering blow, buffet, stroke, stroke of ill luck *or* fortune; disaster, tragedy, calamity, catastrophe, cataclysm.

3. (*all of a supernatural being*) appearance, materialization, incarnation, *Spiritualism.* manifestation; coming, arrival.

4. inspection, examination, scrutiny, perusal, review, study.

visitor, *n.* caller, visitant, company, guest; uninvited guest, *Inf.* gate-crasher; pilgrim, tourist; habitué, regular, patron, frequenter, attender.

vista, *n.* view, outlook, *Chiefly Brit.* lookout, prospect, scene, sight; horizon; scenery; panorama; bird's-eye view.

visual, *adj.* **1.** seeing, optic, optical, ocular.

2. visible. See **visible** (*def. 1*).

visualize, *v.* picture, envision; imagine, conceive, fancy; contemplate, consider, conjure up, envisage, picture in the mind's eye.

vital, *adj.* **1.** life-giving, life-preserving, life-sustaining; invigorating, invigorative, vitalizing, animating, quickening, vivifying; reanimating, reviving, restoring, rejuvenating, resurrecting.

2. vivacious, lively, animated, spirited; vigorous, forceful, brisk, dynamic, powerful, intense; zesty, zestful, eager, enthusiastic.

3. critical, crucial, life-and-death, life-or-death; focal, axial, pivotal, central; principal, paramount, preeminent, dominant; leading, main, key, chief, cardinal; important, significant.

4. essential, necessary, needed, indispensable; mandatory, compulsory, requisite, required; imperative, urgent.

5. deadly, lethal, fatal, fateful.

vitality, *n.* life, animation, energy, vigor; stamina, sturdiness, hardiness, power, strength, endurance; liveliness, spirit, spiritedness, exuberance, vivacity, intensity, zeal; *All Inf.* bounce, zing, pep, pizzazz, sparkle, get up and go; *Sl.* oomph, *Brit. Sl.* stingo.

vitalize, *v.* animate, vivify, quicken, inform, inspirit; stimulte, arouse, awaken, inspire, invigorate, energize; charge, fire, kindle, enkindle, liven, enliven; fortify, strengthen, reinforce, brace, buttress, stay; resurrect, revive, reinvigorate, resuscitate, refresh, renew, replenish, rejuvenate; save, revamp, renovate, make over, mend, amend, restore.

vitals, *n.* vital organs, internal organs, viscera. See **viscera.**

vitiate, *v.* **1.** impair, reduce, degrade, devaluate, depreciate, deteriorate, depress, lower; adulterate, pollute, contaminate, spoil, mar, taint; infect, poison; alloy, dilute, weaken, mix, admix, thin, make impure, tamper with, *Inf.* doctor, (*usu. of drugs or alcohol*) *Sl.* cut; foul, befoul, soil, sully, stain, blacken, tarnish, smear, smirch, besmirch, smudge, spatter, bespatter.

2. debase, abase, pervert, corrupt, rot, canker, blight, vulgarize, defile, deprave, demoralize; desecrate, debauch, render unclean.

3. invalidate, void, cancel, annul, nullify, retract, repeal, rescind, countermand, revoke, withdraw, abolish, abrogate, quash, suppress; erase, expunge, delete, efface, wipe out, strike *or* blot out, obliterate; undo, overthrow, undermine, destroy.

vitiated, *adj.* **1.** impaired, reduced, devaluated, deteriorated, depreciated, lowered, fallen; adulterated, polluted, contaminated, spoiled, marred, tainted, infected, poisoned; diluted, weakened, mixed, thinned, impure, *Inf.* doctored, (*usu. of alcohol or drugs*) *Sl.* cut; fouled, befouled, soiled, sullied, stained, blackened, tarnished, smeared, smirched, besmirched, smudged, spattered, bespattered.

2. debased, abased, base, vile, perverted, perverse, corrupted, corrupt, rotten, vulgarized, defiled, depraved, demoralized, desecrated, debauched.

3. invalidated, voided, canceled, annulled, nullified, withdrawn, repealed, revoked, retracted, abolished, abrogated, suppressed; erased, deleted, effaced, obliterated; undone, overthrown, destroyed, undermined.

vitiation, *n.* **1.** impairment, reduction, devaluation, deterioration, depreciation, lowering, descent, fall, detriment; adulteration, pollution, contamination, infection, dilution, poisoning.

2. debasement, abasement, degradation, degeneration, decadence; corruption, perversion, vulgarization, defilement; depravation, demoralization, desecration, debauchment.

3. invalidation, voidance, cancellation, annulment, nullification; withdrawal, repeal, retraction, revocation, abolition, abrogation, suppression; erasure, deletion, effacement, undoing, overthrow, destruction, obliteration.

vitreous, *adv.* glassy, glasslike, hyaline, vitric, vitriform; clear, crystal clear, crystal, crystalline, transparent, transpicuous, translucent, lucid, pellucid, limpid; mirrorlike, reflective, refelecting, gleaming, shiny, shining, glossy, lustrous; smooth, slick, icelike, icy; hard, brittle, breakable, frangible, fragile.

vitriolic, *adj.* **1.** caustic, acrimonious, mordant, mordacious, bitter, acrid, acidulous, acid, pungent; trenchant, cutting, incisive, slashing, scathing; keen, pointed, sharp, sharp-tongued; penetrating, piercing, stinging, pricking, nipping, biting; astringent, severe, acerb, acerbic, stern, harsh, austere, stringent; spiteful, virulent, malicious, maleficent, venomous, vicious, malevolent,malignant; invidious, hateful.

2. sarcastic, sardonic, scornful, mocking, ridiculing, derisive, derisory, Rabelaisian; satirical, ironic, ironical, double-edged, edged, cynical; contemptuous, contumelious, disparaging, sneering, disdainful, supercilious, haughty, arrogant; taunting, teasing, chaffing, gibing, jeering, scoffing; critical, captious, censorious, carping, faultfinding, hypercritical.

vituperate, *v.* **1.** censure, find fault with, slate, dispraise, reprove, reproach, reprobate, cry down, run down, *Inf.* dress down, disapprove, frown upon; inculpate, blame, incriminate, criminate, take to task, call to account; condemn, denounce, rate, objurgate, reprehend, imprecate, fulminate, revile, execrate, rail, damn, curse, animadvert, anathematize, comminate, delate, *Obs.* exprobrate; belittle, disparage, detract, deprecate, depreciate, devaluate, derogate, deflate, decry; humiliate, humble, mortify.

2. berate, upbraid, reprimand, castigate, chasten, chastise, scold, chide, rebuke; contemn, ridicule, scorn, spurn, despise, sneer at.

3. defame, vilify, denigrate, vilipend, scandalize, impugn, blackguard, malign, gibbet, pull to pieces, *Sl.* do a hatchet job on, give a bad name, speak ill of, speak evil of; slander, libel, calumniate, traduce, falsify, accuse falsely, misrepresent, belie, impute, asperse, insinuate; injure, abuse, insult, backbite, *Sl.* badmouth, engage in personalities.

vituperation, *n.* **1.** castigation, chastisement, scolding, chiding, upbraiding, *Inf.* dressing down, reprimand, admonition, lecture, expostulation, *Chiefly Brit. Inf.* jobation, slap in the face, *Inf.* rap on the knuckles; philippic, diatribe, tirade; defamation, denigration, vilification, scandal; slander, libel, calumny, calumniation, misrepresentation, false report, falsehood, lie, untruth, malicious falsehood *or* untruth, aspersion, imputation, insinuation, innuendo, *Inf.* brickbat; abuse, injury, insult, backbiting, mudslinging, *Sl.* badmouthing.

2. denunciation, condemnation, invective, revilement, reproach, contumely, malediction, railing, curse, imprecation, fulmination, rebuke, remonstration, delation, *Archaic.* exprobration, objurgation, reprehension, reproof, reprobatrion, disapproval, disapprobation; censure, blame, inculpation, incrimination, crimination, implication, *Obs., Rare.* accrimination, impeachment, indictment.

3. shame, disgrace, dishonor, disrepute, ill repute, obloquy, loss of face; belittlement, disparagement, deprecation, derogation, deflation, depreciation, devaluation, detraction; humiliation, humble pie, mortification.

vituperative, *adj.* **1.** censorious, reproachful, denunciatory, damnatory, objurgatory, imprecatory, fulminatory, execratory, animadversional, comminatory, *Obs.* exprobratory; abusive, injurious, harsh, virulent, scurrilous, withering, caustic, corrosive; contemptuous, insulting, sarcastic, satirical, sardonic, cutting, sharp-tongued, belittling, disparaging, deprecatory, detractory, derogatory, depreciating, devaluating, deflating; humiliating, humbling, mortifying.

2. defamatory, denigrating, vilipenditory, scandalous, malign; slanderous, libelous, calumnious, calumniatory, false, misrepresentative, imputative, aspersive, insinuating.

vituperator, *n.* **1.** censurer, reviler, castigator, inveigher, reprover, disapprover, censor; denouncer, railer, curser, execrator, imprecator, anathematizer, critic; defamer, vilifier, vilipender, denigrator, scandalizer, impugner, asperser, backbiter, maligner, evilspeaker, carper, caviler, *Inf.* knocker, lampooner, satirist, muckraker, hack; belittler, disparager, deprecator, detractor, derogator, depreciator.

2. slanderer, libeler, calumniator, traducer, falsifier, liar; mudslinger, dirt-flinger.

vivacious, *adj.* lively, full of life, animated, full of pep, *Inf.* full of get up and go, alive, vivid, (*of a woman*) buxom; frisky, spirited, high-spirited, full of spirit, brisk; chipper, jaunty, sprightly, buoyant, breezy, gay, merry, cheerful, jovial, jolly, mirthful; bright, bubbly, effervescent, ebullient, blithe, light-hearted; playful, sportive, gamesome, frolicsome.

vivacity, *n.* liveliness, animation, *Inf.* pep, *Inf.* zip, *Inf.* snap, *Inf.* pizzaz, get up and go; vigor, vigorousness, energy; friskiness, spiritedness, high-spiritedness, chipperness, joviality, cheer, good cheer, cheerfulness, light-heartedness; brightness, sunniness, effervescence; playfulness, sportiveness, gamesomeness, frolicsomeness; high spirits, good spirits, animal spirits.

viva voce, orally, vocally, verbally, by word of mouth.

vivid, *adj.* **1.** bright, brilliant, resplendent, splendid, intense, radiant, dazzling, glittering; refulgent, effulgent, fulgurant, fulgent, fulgid, *Archaic.* fulgorous; lustrous, lucid, luscent, nitid.

2. vivacious. See **vivacious.**

3. realistic, lifelike, true to life; striking, telling, graphic, picturesque, impressive, dramatic.

4. visible, perceptible, perceivable, discernible, seeable, visual; apparent, evident, manifest, clear, crystalclear; conspicuous, salient, prominent, impossible to miss *or* overlook; distinct, well-defined, well-marked.

vividness, *n.* **1.** brilliance, brightness, resplendence, intensity, radiance; refulgence, effulgence, *Archaic.* fulgor; lustrousness, lucidity, nitidity.

2. vivacity. See **vivacity.**

3. realism, lifelikeness; graphicalness, picturesqueness, strikingness, tellingness, impressiveness.

4. visibility, perceptibility, perceivability, discernibleness; apparentness, manifestness, clearness; conspicuousness, salience, prominence; distinctness.

vivify, *v.* animate, quicken, vitalize, energize, galvanize, invigorate; enliven, liven up, inspirit, stimulate, arouse, fire; brighten, encourage, buoy, sharpen, accentuate.

vixen, *n.* shrew, virago, termagant, harpy, tartar, fury, spitfire, Xanthippe; hag, beldam, quean, old crone, *Inf.* catamaran, *Sl.* battle-ax, *Sl.* bitch.

vocabulary, *n.* **1.** lexicon, word stock, word inventory; language, dialect, idiom, *Inf.* lingo, *Linguistics.* idiolect; patois, jargon, cant, argot, slang, vernacular.

2. dictionary, wordbook, *Ger. Worterbuch,* glossary, thesaurus, synonym dictionary, *Fr. dictionnaire.*

vocal, *adj.* **1.** voiced, vocalized, spoken, uttered, oral, expressed, articulated, put into words.

2. vociferous, loud, loud-mouthed, noisy. See **vociferous.**

vocalist, *n.* **1.** singer, melodist, warbler, crooner, soloist, *Inf.* lead; choir member, choir boy *or* girl, chorus member, chorus boy *or* girl, glee club member; chorister, precentor, chanter, hymner, caroler, cantor; opera singer, diva, prima donna; band singer, *Inf.* pop singer, chantress, chanteuse, *It. cantatrice,* blues singer; *All Inf.* songbird, wren, thrush, nightingale, *Poetic.* philomel, lark, canary.

2. lyric poet, minstrel, wandering minstrel, jongleur, troubadour, ballad singer, street singer, *Brit.* busker; Meistersinger, mastersinger, minnesinger.

3. songbird, singing bird, songster, warbler.

vocation, *n.* profession, calling, occupation, walk of life, career, pursuit, lifework; métier, trade, craft, art, skill, job, livelihood, living, work, employment, business; forte, field, subject *or* subject area, line, sphere, specialty, *Sl.* thing, *Sl.* bag, *Inf.* cup of tea; position, situation, office, post.

vociferate, *v.* shout, shout out, bellow, *Inf.* holler, yell, whoop, hoot, boo, hiss, catcall; scream, shriek, screech, cry out, yowl, *Scot. and North Eng.* skirl; cry, squall, bawl, wail, boo-hoo, bray, yelp, moan, groan, howl, caterwaul, ululate; rant, rant and rave, fume, go on, make a fuss *or* to-do *or* commotion, *Inf.* make a ruckus, *Sl.* raise a stink; clamor, din, roar, thunder, blare, make a racket.

vociferation, *n.* clamor, babel, uproar, roar, ballyhoo, shouting, yelling, *Inf.* hollering; din, racket, pandemonium; outcry, hue, hue and cry, hullabaloo, fuss, *Inf.* to-do, *Inf.* ruckus; brawl, fracas, squabble, wrangle, fight, argument, quarrel, row, bicker.

vociferous, *adj.* clamorous, clamant, uproarious, vociferant; shouting, yelling, bellowing, yammering, *Inf.* hollering, *Sl.* yapping, screaming, shrieking, screeching; loud-mouthed, bombastic, blustering, boanergean, *Sl.* big-mouthed; stentorian, stentorious, loud-voiced, big-voiced, voiceful, clarion-voiced, resonant, sonorous; noisy, rackety, loud, loud-sounding, thundering, reverberant, resounding; blatant, blaring, deafening, head-splitting, ear-splitting, ear-piercing, piercing.

vogue, *n.* **1.** fashion, style, design, look, mode, manner of dress, *Brit.* twig; practice, custom, convention, tendency, leaning, taste; trend, fad, thing, rage, craze, last word, latest thing, *Fr. dernier cri.*

2. popularity, prevalence, currency, fashionableness, stylishness, modishness; acceptance, esteem, favor.

voice, *n.* **1.** language; sound, music, cry, call.

2. tone, tonality, timbre, tone of voice, voice quality, tone color *or* quality, ring, sound; intonation, inflection, accent, pronunciation, enunciation, articulation, diction, elocution; brogue, burr, drawl, twang; speech pattern, cadence, rhythm, beat, tempo; dialect, tongue, *Linguistics.* idiolect.

3. expression, verbalization, utterance; airing, ventilation, sounding.

4. vote, choice, option, preference, say, chance to speak, *Inf.* turn at bat, *Inf.* crack; comment, opinion, view, feeling, *Sl.* two cents' worth.

5. mouthpiece, speaker, press agent, public relations *or* PR man; forum, publication, newspaper, paper, journal, magazine, periodical, bulletin, *Inf.* sheet, *Inf.* rag; vehicle, medium, agency, organ, tool, instrument, device.

—*v.* **6.** say, speak, give utterance *or* voice to, verbalize, put into words, mouth, talk about, mention, touch on; express, state, relate, tell, communicate, convey; reveal, disclose, divulge, make known, bring out *or* forward, come out with, blurt out; declare, proclaim, assert, announce, pronounce, broadcast, publish, spread, bruit, rumor, shout [s.t.] from the rooftops; opine, express one's opinion *or* feelings on, express oneself, say a word *or* something about, comment on, editorialize; give vent to, get [s.t.] off one's chest, ventilate, air.

voiceless, *adj.* **1.** mute, speechless, wordless, dumb, *Pathol.* aphonic, nonverbal, signed, finger-spelled, signaled, gestured, gestural, motioned.

2. silent, mum, still, quiet, not saying a word, with one's mouth shut, *Archaic.* hush; taciturn, tight-lipped, close-mouthed, uncommunicative, reticent, reserved, shy, timid, tongue-tied.

3. unexpressed, untold, uncommunicated, unuttered, nonverbalized, not put into words; undivulged, undisclosed, unrevealed, unpublished; secret, private, hidden.

4. voteless, without a vote, unfranchised, disfranchised, disenfranchised.

void, *adj.* **1.** legally ineffectual *or* unenforceable, not binding, nonviable; null and void, invalid, disestablished, cancelled.

2. ineffectual, inoperative, not in force, worthless, inconsequential, null; futile, ineffective, idle, unavailing, vain, nugatory, useless, inutile, bootless; senseless, inane, inept, foolish.

3. devoid of, destitute of, deprived of, lacking, wanting, without; nonexistent, unexisting, inexistent, nonsubsistent; minus, missing, negative, omitted.

4. empty, without contents, unfilled, unsupplied; blank, free, clear, bare; hollow, vacuous; vacant, unoccupied, deserted, forsaken, uninhabited, desolate, waste, tenantless.

—*n.* **5.** emptiness, empty space, vacancy, vacuity, vacuum, blank.

6. gap, opening, break, hole; hollow, cavity, abyss, chasm.

7. naught, nothing, zero, cipher, nil, *Latin. nihil, Sl.* nix, *Sl.* goose egg.

—*v.* **8.** annul, nullify, disannul, declare null and void, render null and void, avoid; quash, invalidate, vitiate, vacate, neutralize, disenact, disestablish; cancel, discharge; supersede, set aside; repeal, revoke, rescind, reverse, abrogate, abolish; suspend, *Law.* nol-pros, stop, discontinue, break off.

9. recant, retract, abjure, withdraw, recall; renounce, repudiate, relinquish, abnegate, deny, disclaim; take back, undo, renege; countermand, counterorder, overrule, override; veto, negate.

10. eject, expel, emit; discharge, egest, defecate, urinate, pass; empty, evacuate, vacate; purge, clear; throw out, send out, pour out.

volatile, *adj.* **1.** evaporative, evaporable, vaporizing, vaporous, vaporizable, vaporlike, vaporish, vaporable, vaporific, vaporescent, *Archaic.* halituous; gaseous, gasiform, aeriform.

2. explosive, volcanic, eruptive; charged, tense, explosible, explodable; fiery, heated, hotheaded, inflammatory.

3. flighty, changeful, capricious, whimsical, impulsive; fickle, skittish, inconstant, moonish, changeable, variable, faddish; mercurial, undependable, unsteady, unstable; giddy, frivolous, flyaway, erratic, irregular, fitful, spasmodic, uneven.

4. fleeting, passing, flitting, flying, unenduring, here today-gone tomorrow; transient, transitory, temporary, impermanent; brief, short-lived, momentary; ephemeral, evanescent, vanishing.

volatility, *n.* **1.** vaporability, vaporizability, evaporability; evaporableness, vaporousness, vaporiness, vaporosity; gaseousness.

2. explosiveness, fieriness, tension.

3. flightiness, changefulness, capriciousness, whimsicality, impulsiveness, fickleness, inconstancy, moonishness, changeableness, variability; mercurialness, unsteadiness, instability; giddiness, irregularity, fitfulness, unevenness.

4. transience, transitoriness, temporariness, impermanence; briefness, shortness, momentariness; evanescence, ephemerality, frailty, caducity.

volition, *n.* choice, option; discretion, will, free will; determination, *Psychol.* conation, intent, resolution, decision; preference, wish, desire, taste, pleasure, velleity.

volley, *n.* **1.** barrage, bombardment, cannonade. shelling, battery, broadside, enfilade, cross fire, assault, salvo, fusillade; barrier of fire, wall of fire.

2. report, boom, bang, crack, crash, rumble, echo, reverberation, noise, sound; discharge, explosion, detonation, fulmination; shot, blast, gunfire, backfire, thunderclap; outbreak, storm, shower, emission.

volubility, *n.* talkativeness, overtalkativeness, garrulity, garrulousness, glibness, *Inf.* gabbiness, loose tongue, *Inf.* gift of gab, *Inf.* windiness, *Inf.* gassiness, *Inf.* big mouth; verbosity, wordiness, verbality, verbalism, verbiage, prolixity, prolixness, loquacity, loquaciousness, long-windedness, longiloquence, multiloquence; magniloquence, grandiloquence, orotundity; fluency, eloquence; discursiveness, digressiveness, circumlocution, ambagiousness, circuitousness, roundaboutness; bravado, braggadocio, gasconade, boasting, *Sl.* hot air, *Sl.* gas.

voluble, *adj.* talkative, talky, loquacious, garrulous, multiloquous, long-tongued, *Inf.* big-mouthed, *Sl.* all jaw; fluent, glib, *Inf.* blessed with *or* possessed of the gift of gab; conversational, chatty, gabby, gossipy, *Sl.* blabby, *Sl.* gassy, *Sl.* windy; wordy, verbose, prolix, long-winded, longiloquent; effusive, gushy, profuse, exuberant, unrestrained; discursive, digressive, rambling, maundering; circumlocutory, ambagious, circuitous, roundabout; plethoric, turgid, overblown, inflated, flatulent, tumid, swollen.

volume, *n.* **1.** tome, book, work, publication, opus.

2. bulk, measure, measurement, amplitude, dimensions, size, capacity; bigness, vastness.

3. mass, abundance, bounty, plenty; quantity, profusion, *Inf.* raft, storm, shower, ocean, sea, world.

4. total, sum, sum total; whole, totality, entirety, aggregate; gross, net, summation; number, amount, gross amount, *Sl.* whole bit.

5. loudness, sound, register, amplification.

voluminous, *adj.* **1.** large, spacious, roomy, capacious, commodious; broad, expansive, wide, extensive, widespread; vast, immense, amplitudinous; huge, big, great, massive, gigantic, tremendous, mammoth, colossal, giant, elephantine, monstrous, stupendous.

2. plentiful, plenteous, plenitudinous, bountiful, bounteous, abundant, fat, copious; immeasurable, unmeasured, inexhaustible, bottomless; much, many, numerous; in quantity, in plenty, *Inf.* aplenty, *Inf.* galore.

3. profuse, abounding, overflowing, overspilling, running over, exuberant, superabundant; rich, lavish, luxuriant, liberal, handsome.

voluntarily, *adv.* **1.** freely, gratuitously, gratis, without being asked, spontaneously; of one's own free will, of one's own accord, of one's volition, on one's own, independently, autonomously.

2. intentionally, on purpose, purposefully, deliberately, premeditatedly.

3. optionally, electively, by preference, by choice.

voluntary, *adj.* **1.** volitional, volitionary, volitive; intentional, intended, on purpose, purposeful, deliberate; designed, preplanned, planned, premeditated, prepense, willful.

2. free, gratuitous, gratis, unasked, unbidden, unrequested, unsolicited; spontaneous, unpremeditated; uncompelled, unforced, unconstrained, unobliged, unobligated; unimpelled, undriven, unurged, unpushed.

3. optional, unmandatory, elective, unrequired.

volunteer, *n.* **1.** unpaid worker, *Sl.* candy striper, missionary, Peace Corps worker, do-gooder.

—v. **2.** offer one's services, put oneself at [s.o.'s] disposal, present *or* proffer oneself, come *or* step forward, not wait to be asked, need no invitation.

3. (*all without being asked*) give, present, bestow, grant, confer; offer, proffer, tender, extend, hold out, hand over *or* in; submit, propound, propose, put forward, advance; say, tell, communicate; perform, do.

voluptuary, *n.* **1.** hedonist, sybarite, sensualist; pleasure seeker, *Fr. bon vivant, Inf.* high liver, *Sl.* swinger, *Sl.* swinging single, playgirl, *Sl.* party girl, playboy, ladies' man, gallant; debauchee, roué, rake, profligate, libertine, Don Juan, Casanova; indulger, epicurean, epicure, connoisseur, gourmet, gastronome, gourmand; glutton, *Inf.* pig, *Sl.* belly-god, winebibber, heavy drinker, *Inf.* boozer.

—adj. **2.** hedonistic, voluptuous, sensualistic. See **voluptuous** (*def.* **1**).

voluptuous, *adj.* **1.** hedonistic, hedonic, hedonist; indulgent, self-indulgent; voluptuary, sybaritic, sybaritical, sensualistic.

2. carnal, sensual, fleshly, bodily, physical, animal, animalistic, sexual, erotic; lustful, concupiscent, *Sl.* horny, lascivious, libidinous, lecherous, goatish, lewd, prurient, salacious; libertine, profligate, dissolute, licentious, loose, wanton, lubricous, promiscuous, amoral, immoral, dissolute, rakish, debauched.

3. pleasing, delightful, attractive, desirable, toothsome; appealing, tempting, inviting, enticing, alluring, seductive, come-hither, provocative, *Inf.* sexy, *Sl.* foxy; beautiful, lovely, *Inf.* eye-catching, pretty, *Chiefly U.S. Inf.* cute, stunning, striking, gorgeous, ravishing, *Inf.* eye-filling; shapely, well-shaped, well-proportioned, *Inf.* curvaceous, *Inf.* curvy, *Sl.* stacked, *Sl.* built, *Sl.* busty, well-endowed, full-bosomed, buxom; good-looking, handsome, virile, manly; soft, sensuous, (*of music*) Lydian.

voluptuousness, *n.* **1.** hedonism, sybaritism, voluptuosity; pleasure-seeking, pursuit of pleasure, la dolce vita, wild *or* riotous *or* free living, *Inf.* high living, *Sl.* partying, *Sl.* swinging; indulgence, self-indulgence, overindulgence, intemperance, gluttony, gulosity.

2. carnality, carnalness, carnalism, sexual desire, sexual appetite, lust, lustfulness, *Sl.* horniness, concupiscence; lasciviousness, libidinousness, lecherousness, goatishness, lewdness, prurience, pruriency, salaciousness, salacity; libertinage, libertinism, profligacy, profligateness, dissoluteness, rakishness, licentiousness, looseness, wantonness, promiscuousness, promiscuity, amorality, immorality, debauchery.

3. pleasingness, delight, delightfulness, attractiveness, desirability, desirableness, toothsomeness; appealingness, temptingness, invitingness, enticingness, alluringness, seductiveness; charm, appeal, sex appeal, allure; animal magnetism, sexiness, sexuality, sensuality, sensualness; shapeliness, buxomness; handsomeness, virility, manliness; beauty, *Sl.* foxiness, loveliness, prettiness, *Chiefly U.S. Inf.* cuteness, strikingness, gorgeousness.

vomit, *v.* **1.** regurgitate, throw up, bring up, puke *or* puke up, heave, spit up, spew up, disgorge, regorge; retch, gag, cough up, keck, dry-heave; be sick to one's stomach, be nauseated, nauseate, *Inf.* have the throw-ups; be seasick, have mal de mer, turn green; *All Sl.* barf, upchuck, toss one's cookies, return *or* lose one's breakfast, blow lunch, ralph *or* talk to ralph.

2. eject, send out *or* forth, belch, give forth, eruct; issue, come up *or* forth.

—n. **3.** puke, *Inf.* throw-up, *Inf.* spit-up.

voodoo, *n.* sorcery, witchcraft, witchery, incantation, magic; necromancy, thaumaturgy, theurgy; black magic, black art, hoodoo, obiism *or* obeahism, conjure, root work; deviltry *or* devilry, demonology, demonaltry, diabolism; supernaturalness, shamanism, mysticism, spiritualism, occultness; ritual, rite, apotropaism, magical ceremony, hocus-pocus, mumbo jumbo.

voracious, *adj.* **1.** ravenous, ravening, devouring, gluttonous, gormandizing, cormorant, edacious; open-mouthed, hoggish, piggish, swinish, gross.

2. insatiable, insatiate, unquenchable, omnivorous; desirous, greedy, cupidinous, avaricious, esurient; grasping, acquisitive, *Sl.* grabby, predacious, rapacious.

3. enthusiastic, avid, ardent, fervent, eager, *Inf.* all fired up, *Inf.* psyched *or* psyched up, *Sl.* hopped up, *Sl.* ape; keen, anxious, *Inf.* wild, breathless, impatient, thirsty, athirst; ambitious, aspiring, hungry, craving; earnest, wholehearted, devoted; zealous, agog, passionate, *Inf.* gung-ho, *Inf.* rah-rah; possessed, fanatic, fanatical, *Sl.* hung up, rabid, mad.

voracity, *n.* **1.** ravenousness, voraciousness, gluttony, edacity, edaciousness, open-mouthedness, hoggishness, piggishness, swinishness, crapulousness; insatiability, insatiateness, omnivorousness, gulosity, *Pathol.* polyphagia.

2. desire, desriousness, covetousness, greed, graspingness, acquisitiveness, *Sl.* grabbiness, avariciousness, rapacity, rapaciousness; eagerness, cupidity, avidity, yearning, craving; keenness, itch, itching, appetite, stomach, *U.S. Dial.* big eye, appetence; anxiousness, breathlessness, impatience, longing, thirst; ardor, zeal, fervency, passion, mania; hankering, aspiration, hunger, lust, ambition, ambitiousness.

vortex, *n.* **1.** whirlpool, maelstrom, gurge, swirl, whirl; eddy, countercurrent, counterflow, undercurrent, undertow.

2. whirlwind, dust devil, dust whirl, tourbillion; tornado, twister, cyclone, typhoon; simoom, samiel; tempest, storm.

votary, *n.* **1.** cenobite, conventual, monastic, celibate, religious, contemplative, *Archaic.* cloisterer; monk, *Tibetan Buddhism.* lama, *Islam.* marabout, *Eastern Ch.* caloyer, *Hinduism.* ashramite; nun, sister, virgin, maiden, bride of Christ.

2. follower, disciple, champion, adherent; zealot, partisan, bigot, fanatic; visionary, cultist; believer, religionist, pietist.

3. enthusiast, fan, devotee, aficionado, *Inf.* buff, *Inf.* hound, *Sl.* bug, *Sl.* nut; addict, *Inf.* fiend, *Sl.* junkie, *Sl.* freak, *Sl.* head.

vote, *n.* **1.** ballot, voting ticket, *Brit.* voting paper, voting ball; show of hands, yeas and nays, count, roll call.

2. voice, say, *Chiefly Brit.* plumper; suffrage, franchise; referendum, election, poll, plebiscite, voting;

placet, *Inf.* the go-ahead; vox populi, mandate.

voter, *n.* balloter, ballot-caster, elector, constituent; citizen, freeman, taxpayer.

vouch, *v.* **1.** *Usu.* **vouch for** endorse, support, back up, stand behind *or* by; sponsor, countersign, witness, sign for, answer for, subscribe, undersign, cosign.

2. *Often* **vouch for** guarantee, ensure, secure, *Finance.* bond, *Law.* mortgage; insure, indemnify, underwrite; assure, offer assurance, avow, asseverate, vow, give one's solemn word *or* promise, state on one's honor, pledge, swear to, state under oath, *Inf.* promise.

3. *Often* **vouch for** certify, certificate, warrant, confirm, verify, validate, authenticate; attest to, testify to, avouch, affirm, assert, declare, state emphatically, say for certain *or* sure; corroborate, substantiate, sustain, uphold; prove, document, establish, manifest, show, demonstrate; depose, bear witness, evidence, offer evidence.

4. adduce, cite, quote, draw on, invoke.

voucher, *n.* **1.** receipt, acknowledgement, chit, slip; note, promissory note, IOU; document, paper.

2. surety, *Law.* security, collateral, earnest, *Law.* earnest money, deposit, pawn, gage, bail, *Insurance.* bond, *Law.* mortgage, *Law.* mortgage bond, *Law.* bail bond, *Rare.* hostage; guarantee, warrant, warranty, *Law.* covenant of warranty, *Law.* warranty deed, contract, compact, covenant, obligation, engagement, agreement, gentlemen's agreement, handshake, bargain, deal, pact, convention, treaty; insurance, indemnity, protection, *Insurance.* coverage; pledge, promise, assurance, word, word of honor, oath, sworn statement, *Archaic.* plight; endorsement, testimonial, attestation, recommendation.

3. guarantor, guarantee, ensurer, warrantor, sponsor, bonder, *Law.* bondsman, *Law.* bondswoman; endorser, attester, patron, supporter, backer; insurer, indemnitor, underwriter, *Insurance.* coverer.

vouchsafe, *v.* **1.** grant, condescend to grant, deign to give, give, bestow, confer, accord, impart, award, present.

2. allow, permit, let; approve of, go along with, agree to, accede to, assent to, consent to; acquiesce, yield, submit to, comply with; tolerate, suffer, bear with.

vow, *n.* **1.** pledge, promise, assurance, word, solemn word, word of honor, parole, *Archaic.* troth; oath, sworn statement *or* declaration, testimony; attestation, affirmation, profession, avowal, asseveration, avouchment; engagement, betrothal, *Archaic.* plight; marriage contract, marriage bond, marriage vow; obligation, bond, agreement, contract; gentleman's agreement, unwritten agreement.

—*v.* **2.** pledge, promise, give one's word *or* solemn word, give one's word of honor, give one's parole, *Inf.* cross one's heart and hope to die; solemnly swear, state on one's honor, swear to, declare *or* state under oath; assure, offer assurance, aver, asseverate, affirm, avouch, declare, state, profess.

voyage, *n.* **1.** cruise, crossing, passage by sea, circumnavigation; journey, trip, expedition, trek, safari; travels, globe-trotting, wayfaring, peregrination, wandering, roving, roaming; flight.

—*v.* **2.** cruise, sail, fly, jet; travel, journey, roam, rove, peregrinate, itinerate, wayfare, travel the open road; take *or* make a trip, tour, globe-trot, go abroad, go overseas, see the world.

voyager, *n.* cruiser, traveler, pilgrim, wayfarer, peregrinator; rambler, rover, roamer, Wandering Jew; adventurer, landloper, explorer, soldier of fortune, *Inf.* boomer, cowboy; astronaut, cosmonaut, seaman, sailor, sea captain; bird of passage, migrant, nomad.

voyeur, *n.* peeper, Peeping Tom, peeker; breather; fetishist, pervert.

vulgar, *adj.* **1.** ignorant, uninformed, unaware, unsophisticated, artless; unlearned, uneducated, untaught, unversed, unlettered, illiterate; ill-bred, unbred, untrained; unrefined, uncultured, ungentlemanly, unladylike, uncultivated, uncivilized; gauche, uncouth, crude, crass, rude, boorish, loutish, brutish, raw, unmannerly, ill-mannered, uncivil; coarse, rough, base, baseborn, tatty; inferior, ignoble, raffish, low, lowly, low-class, humble, untitled.

2. indecent, broad, immodest, shameless, indelicate, indecorous, inelegant; improper, unseemly, unacceptable, tawdry, *Inf.* tacky; gross, rank, repulsive, offensive, disgusting, distasteful, risqué, suggestive, off-color, *Inf.* blue; outrageous, lurid, sensational, scurrilous, blackguardly, thersitical, profane, foul-mouthed, Fescennine, *Obs.* blackguard, *Archaic.* scurrile.

3. obscene, lewd, salacious, pornographic, vile, foul, filthy, dirty, smutty, nasty, scatologic, scatological, *Sl.* raunchy; lecherous, lubricous, goatish, lustful, libidinous, concupiscent, carnal, sexy, sensual, *Archaic.* lickerish; licentious, lascivious, Cyprian, prurient, wanton, loose, libertine, promiscuous, Paphian, unchaste; immoral, degenerate, dissolute, dissipated, debauched, rakish, profligate, depraved, perverted.

4. proletarian, plebeian, provincial, peasantlike, of the masses, working-class, blue-collar; (*all of language*) vernacular, colloquial, spoken.

5. popular, current, in vogue, all the rage; prevalent, rife, widespread, general, universal; conventional, conforming, philistine, bourgeois.

6. ordinary, undistinguished, plain, homespun; common, average, usual, commonplace, household, everyday; banal, trite, platitudinous, hackneyed, overused, stale, tired.

vulgarian, *n.* parvenu, upstart, snob, *Fr. nouveau riche*; Boetian, philistine, barbarian; swine, boor, lout, brute, churl, knave, blackguard; clodhopper, bumpkin, yokel, rustic, clown, peasant, illiterate.

vulgarism, *n.* **1.** indecency, obsceneness, grossness. See **vulgarity** (*defs.* **1, 2**).

2. obscenity, ribaldry, profanity. See **vulgarity** (*def.* **3**).

vulgarity, *n.* **1.** ignorance, unsophistication, unawareness, naïveté, naïveness; gaucheness, gaucherie, uncouthness, crassness, rudeness, boorishness, brutishness, rawness; ill breeding, unmannerliness; ill-manneredness, incivility, uncivilness, ungentlemanliness; coarseness, roughness, baseness, commonness, ignobility, raffishness, inferiority, lowliness, humbleness.

2. indecency, indecorum, indecorousness, indelicacy; impropriety, unseemliness, tawdriness; grossness, rankness, repulsiveness, repulsivity, offensiveness, suggestivity; abusiveness, scurrilousness, blackguardism, profaneness.

3. obsceneness, vulgarness, lewdness, salaciousness, vileness, foulness, filthiness, nastiness, *Sl.* raunchiness; lecherousness, lubricity, lustfulness, bawdiness, libidinousness, concupiscence, carnality, carnalness, sexiness, sensuality; licentiousness, lasciviousness, wantonness, looseness, promiscuity, prominscuousness; immorality, dissoluteness, dissipation, rakishness, shamelessness.

4. obscenity, salacity, pornography, vulgarism, filth, dirt, smut; scurrility, ribaldry, billingsgate, profanity, double entendre, *Archaic.* bawdry; curse word, swearword, dirty word, four-letter word, *U.S. Inf.* cuss, expletive.

vulgus, *n.* the masses, the common people, commonalty, the working class, the lower class, the huddled masses, the multitude, the mob, the populace; the common man, the man in the street; peasants, proletariat, rank and file, plebians, the hoi polloi; rabble, scum, the great unwashed, riffraff, ragtag and bobtail.

vulnerable, *adj.* **1.** unprotected, unguarded, unshielded, accessible, assailable; defenseless, uncovered, exposed, naked, wide open; weak, helpless, powerless, impotent; tender, sensitive, thin-skinned, easily hurt; innocent, wide-eyed, naïve, born yesterday, wet behind the ears.
2. susceptible to, unable to tolerate *or* withstand; subject to, given to, disposed to, likely to get, liable to; prone to, predisposed to, inclined toward, leaning toward.
3. open to attack, pregnable, penetrable, invadable, attackable, unresistant; precarious, risky, dangerous, hazardous, *U.S. Inf.* out on a limb.

W

wad, *n.* **1.** lump, mass, ball, plug, *Dial.* chaw; hunk, chunk, block, *Sl.* gob, mouthful.
2. bankroll, roll of money, roll, *Sl.* pile; thousands, millions, mint, *Sl.* load of money, *Sl.* lots of bucks *or* dough.
3. wads scads, oodles, lots, piles, heaps; a good deal, slew, *Sl.* load, raft, *Sl.* mess, *Sl.* gobs, pack, batch.

waddle, *v.* toddle, paddle, wag, duckwalk, shuffle; wobble, waggle, stagger, swing, sway, bob, wiggle, *Scot.* wamble.

wade, *v.* **1.** walk through water, ford, traverse, cross; paddle, play in water, bathe, dip, splash about.
2. wade into start in, enter in, set to, go to it, *Sl.* get with it; set to work, buckle down, knuckle down, *Inf.* tackle, attack; plunge into, pitch into, dive into, *Inf.* tear into, *Sl.* get cracking, *Inf.* jump into.
3. wade through study, read, peruse, pore over, lucubrate; plug away, hammer away, pound away; drudge, grind, toil, plod, peg, fag.

wafer, *n.* disk, cracker, biscuit, tablet, snap; host, Eucharist.

waffle, *v.* equivocate, tergiversate, shuffle, beat around the bush, straddle the fence; dodge, hedge, evade the truth, evade the issue, not come to the point, mince the truth, fudge; side-step, hem and haw, *Inf.* weasel, duck; euphemize, subtilize, prevaricate.

waft, *v.* float, drift, ride high, whisk, glide, be buoyed up; whiff, blow, puff, huff, whiffle.

wag, *v.* **1.** pendulate, sway, swing, waggle, wiggle, *Inf.* diddle; wobble, bobble, bob, nod, wave, flutter; fluctuate, oscillate, wigwag; flap, flit, flicker, flip, beat; shake, rock, jerk, twitch, vellicate; jiggle, sputter, waver, dance, undulate; swish, switch, vacillate, quiver; wriggle, squirm, turn, writhe.
—n. **2.** shake, wobble, wiggle, waggle; switch, swish, flick, flutter, wave, swing, sway; vellication, jerk, oscillation, jiggle, flicker; waver, quiver, bob, bobble, beat, flap.
3. wit, humorist, jester, joker, comic, comedian; jokester, banterer, wisecracker, droll, life of the party; farcer, buffoon, scaramouche, *Inf.* cutup, harlequin, merry-andrew; punner, epigrammatist, caricaturist, *Fr. bel esprit*.

wage, *n.* **1.** *Usu.* **wages** salary, pay, emolument, remuneration, compensation, earnings, *Brit. Sl.* get; payment, hire, stipend, fee, honorarium; perquisites, *Inf.* perks, fringe benefits, *Inf.* benefits, *Inf.* fringes, *Inf.* extras.
2. *Usu.* **wages** recompense, requital, quittance; reward, *Archaic.* meed, *Literary.* guerdon, deserts; returns, interest, yield, gain.
—v. **3.** carry on, engage in, set about, carry out, execute; undertake, take up, embark upon, devote oneself to; conduct, practice.

wager, *n.* **1.** bet, gamble, stake, collateral, security, surety, guaranty, pledge, *Poker.* ante; chance, risk, throw *or* toss of the dice, spin of the wheel, *Inf.* flier, pig in a poke, long shot, *Inf.* toss-up, *Sl.* shot in the dark; speculation, uncertainty, hazard, venture, undertaking.
—v. **2.** bet, gamble, make a bet, lay a wager, *Brit.* punt; put money on, lay odds, (*in dice games*) shoot, stake, put up, put up collateral, *Poker.* ante, *Obs.* impone, *Obs.* wage; play for money, play the lottery, enter the sweepstakes, shoot craps, play poker; chance, take a chance, cast lots, risk, run a risk, speculate, take a long shot, hazard, stick one's neck out, *Inf.* risk it, *Inf.* chance it.

waggish, *adj.* roguish, puckish, elfish, impish, scampish, mischievous, full of mischief, naughty, bad, arch, *Scot.* hempy; prankish, tricksy, playful, sportive, clowning, joking, jesting, teasing; witty, quick-witted, nimble-witted, keen-witted, clever, salty, droll, amusing, entertaining, diverting, whimsical, light; jocular, jocose, jolly, jovial, merry, good-humored, mirthful, *Inf.* fun; humorous, funny, comical, risible, facetious, *Archaic.* facete, tongue-in-cheek, unserious; hilarious, hysterical, ridiculous, laughable, riotous, side-splitting, knee-slapping, a laugh, *Sl.* riot, *Sl.* a scream, *Sl.* a gas.

wagon, *n.* carriage, tilbury, buggy, tumbrel, gig, dogcart, curricle, *Chiefly Brit.* trap; dumpcart, tipcart, barrow, handbarrow, wheelbarrow; handcart, truck, handtruck, pushcart, dart, dray.

waif, *n.* stray, homeless animal *or* person, street Arab, gutter urchin, ragamuffin, mudlark, poor little lamb, little lost lamb, gamin, parentless child, orphan, *Western U.S.* dogie; foundling, abandoned infant, castaway, outcast, pariah, *Chiefly Brit.* wastrel; vagabond, vagrant, beachcomber, tramp, hobo, bum, tatterdemalion, *Sl.* bag lady, *Australian.* sundowner; wanderer, nomad, gypsy, peripatetic, itinerant, *Inf.* floater.

wail, *v.* **1.** lament, bewail, bemoan, moan, mourn over, cry; keen, ululate, groan, bawl, *Inf.* yawp; whine, whimper, mewl, pule, snivel, sob, weep, boohoo; howl, squall, *Brit. Dial.* yawl, yowl, bay, *Hunting.* quest; yell, scream, caterwaul.
—n. **2.** moan, groan, lament, keen, cry, sob, whine, whimper; ululation, boohoo, *Fr. cri de coeur*, bawl, *Inf.* yawp, caterwaul, yowl, howl, yell; crying, weeping, lamentation; dirge, threnody, requiem.

wait, *v.* **1.** stay, rest, remain, abide; linger, loiter, tarry; await, wait for, *Dial.* wait on; stand by, *Inf.*

hang around *or* about, *Inf.* stick around; pause, hesitate, hover, hold back, hang back, bide one's time; hold one's horses, *Inf.* sit tight, *Sl.* sweat it out, *Sl.* sweat blood *or* bullets; stand in line, line up, *Chiefly Brit.* queue *or* queue up.

2. await, anticipate, expect, look forward to, count on *or* upon, have in prospect; watch for *or* watch out for, look for *or* look out for; be ready, *Inf.* be psyched for *or* be psyched up for; be on the lookout, keep a sharp eye *or* lookout; lie in ambush, set a trap for.

3. delay, postpone, defer, put off, hold off *or* up on, lay [s.t.] over, refrain *or* abstain from, let [s.t.] hang fire, put [s.t.] on ice *or* on a back burner; play a waiting game; adjourn, suspend, recess; table, shelve, pigeonhole, prorogue.

4. procrastinate, temporize, *U.S. Congress.* filibuster; *Inf.* stall, drag one's feet, *Inf.* footdrag; dally, dillydally, dawdle, poke along, kill *or* waste time; linger, loiter.

5. be in readiness, be available; make available, reserve, hold, set aside; waitlist.

6. wait on a. serve, service, attend to, attend, minister to. **b.** tend table, serve table, wait table; *Inf.* waitress. **c.** supply, furnish, provide, accommodate. **d.** wait for. See (*def.* **1**).

7. wait up a. stay up, stay awake, keep vigil. **b.** stop, halt, stop in one's tracks, slow down, slow up, go easy.

—*n.* **8.** delay, holdup, holding pattern; halt, stop, stoppage; discontinuation, suspension, abeyance, cessation, moratorium, prorogation; postponement, deferment, deferral.

9. interval, interruption, hiatus, recess; respite, break, pause, rest, time-out, breath, breather, breathing spell; waiting period, interim, intermission.

waiter, *n.* **1.** steward, butler, servant, servitor, (*in India and the Orient*) boy, attendant; server, checker, cashier.

2. headwaiter, host, maître d'hôtel, *Inf.* maître d'; sommelier, wine steward, cupbearer, Ganymede, Hebe; bartender, *Fr.* (*usu. in direct address*) *garçon*; carhop, *Sl.* hasher, *Sl.* hash-slinger; busboy; waitress, hostess, maid, cook.

3. tray, salver, platter, *Archaic.* trencher.

waiting room, *n.* **1.** vestibule, foyer, lobby, entranceway, entryway, entrance hall, entrance, entry; anteroom, antechamber, antehall; hall, hallway, passageway, corridor.

2. reception room, reception hall, receiving room, receiving area; holding room, detention room.

3. lounge, sitting room, smoking room, parlor, side parlor, living room.

waive, *v.* **1.** relinquish, renounce, *Law.* disclaim; forsake, abandon, surrender, yield, give up, turn over, transfer, cede, sign away, *Law.* demise.

2. forgo, abstain, refrain, do *or* go without, sacrifice, eliminate; shun, avoid, eschew, pass up; turn down, decline, refuse.

3. defer, postpone, delay, put off, shelve, table, prorogue; hold in abeyance, hang fire, put on ice *or* in cold storage, put on a back burner.

4. overlook, neglect, ignore, take no note of, dispense with, disregard; dismiss, put aside, pass over, gloss over, let ride, let stand.

wake¹, *v.* **1.** awaken, awake, waken, get up; rouse, arouse, stir, budge; come to, come around, become conscious, sit up, come alive.

2. animate, stimulate, activate, get [s.o.] going; arouse, enliven, vivify; whet, kindle, fire, ignite, stir up, work up; excite, inspirit, quicken; spur, prod, incite, goad; resuscitate, reanimate, revivify, bring to life; key up, whip into a lather, whip up, move.

—*n.* **3.** watch, vigil, deathwatch, *Obs.* pervigilation, *Eccles.* pernoctation.

wake², *n.* **1.** track, path, train, trail; wash, backwash, course, line; spoor, scent, trace.

2. in the wake of a. as a result of, because of, due to, owing to; by virtue of, in view of, on account of. **b.** succeeding, following, after, ensuing, subsequent, consequent.

wakeful, *adj.* **1.** sleepless, awake, insomnious, restless; slumberless, wide-awake, unsleeping, insomnolent, insomniac; waking, astir, up and about, conscious.

2. watchful, vigilant, on the qui vive, on the alert, alert, on the lookout; open-eyed, wide-eyed, alive to, aware, sharp; wary, cautious, attentive, unblinking, unwinking, unnodding; observant, on guard, all eyes and ears, *Inf.* with one's eyes peeled; mindful, heedful, regardful, prudent, discreet, precautious, circumspect, chary.

wakefulness, *n.* **1.** sleeplessness, slumberlessness, insomnia, insomnolence; restlessness, want of sleep, tossing and turning; consciousness, awareness, awakening, wake, sentience.

2. watchfulness, vigilance, alertness, attentiveness, wariness; readiness, promptness, keenness, sharpness, acuity; circumspection, precaution, caution, prudence, chariness, carefulness, cautiousness; regardfulness, mindfulness; surveillance, observance, watch, vigil, lookout, guard.

walk, *v.* **1.** step, ambulate, perambulate, stride, pace, tread; foot it, *Sl.* hoof it, pad, ride shanks' mare, go by shanks' mare, *Chiefly Scot.* shank; stroll, saunter, amble; slog, trudge, plod; shamble, shuffle, *Inf.* galumph; lurch, stagger, wobble, waddle; sidle, slink, mince, tiptoe; move, go, advance, proceed, wend.

2. stretch one's legs, take a walk, take a turn, take one's constitutional, promenade, traipse; peregrinate, hike, tramp; march, troop, parade; wander, roam, rove, gad, meander, ramble.

—*n.* **3.** stroll, ramble, amble, saunter, promenade; constitutional, airing; hike, tramp, march.

4. gait, pace, step, bearing, carriage; comportment, deportment.

5. line of work, trade, métier, profession, vocation, occupation, career, calling; activity, pursuit; field, arena, area, sphere; department, province, position, place, course.

6. path, pathway, footpath, trail; promenade, esplanade; sidewalk, *Chiefly Brit.* pavement, *Fr. trottoir.*

walker, *n.* hiker, tramper, backpacker, peregrinator, wayfarer, peripatetic; perambulator, ambulator, pedestrian; tramp, hobo, vagabond, knight of the road, itinerant, tinker, nomad.

walking stick, *n.* cane, Malacca cane, alpenstock, stick, crutch; staff, rod, crosier, crook, shepherd's crook.

walkout, *n.* strike, sit-down, work stoppage, job action, wildcat *or* outlaw strike, slowdown, *Inf.* go-slow, sick-out; protest, dissent; uprising, revolt, rebellion, riot.

walkover, *n.* easy victory, walkaway, a sure thing, *Inf.* shoo-in, pushover; something easy, *Sl.* cinch, *Inf.* snap, *Sl.* child's play, *Sl.* a breeze, duck soup, piece of cake, *Sl.* a picnic.

wall, *n.* **1.** partition, separator, divider, room divider, screen, division; brattice, *Civil Eng.* bulkhead; fence, paling, stone wall; embankment, dike, levee, sea wall; dividing wall, *Biol.* septum, membrane.

2. *Usu.* **walls** fortification, protection, enclosure, enceinte; *Fort.* rampart, *Fort.* bulwark, barricade, *Fort.* stockade; *Fort.* breastwork, *Fort.* fieldwork, bunker.

3. obstruction, barrier, block, impediment, obstacle,

Archaic. remora; stop, stopper.

wallet, *n.* billfold, *Chiefly Brit.* notecase; card case, credit-card case, card carrier; pocketbook, purse, change-purse, *Fr. porte-monnaie.*

wallow, *v.* **1.** roll around, splash around, swim; welter, tumble, writhe.

2. luxuriate, indulge oneself, bask; delight, revel, relish, enjoy, take pleasure *or* satisfaction in; savor, appreciate, like, love, fancy, *Sl.* dig, take to; *Sl.* get a bang *or* kick *or* boot out of, *Sl.* get high on.

3. flounder, stagger, lurch, roll, pitch, waver, teeter; waddle, stumble, limp, falter.

4. billow, surge, swell, puff, rise; float, waft.

wan, *adj.* **1.** pale, ashen, ashy, pallid, colorless; white, white as a sheet, bloodless, ghostly, pasty, sallow.

2. tired, worn, weary; unhealthy, sickly, haggard, gaunt, ghastly, thin, emaciated, hollow-cheeked; unhappy, sad, *Fr. triste*, melancholy, mournful, sorrowful, miserable, desolate.

3. weak, sorry, unforceful; ineffectual, useless, futile, unavailing, vain, bootless, profitless; nonproductive, fruitless, hollow, unsuccessful; inept, unskillful, clumsy.

wand, *n.* **1.** rod, baton, stick, staff; scepter, mace.

2. shoot, offshoot, sprig, branch, twig, sprout; tendril, reed.

wander, *v.* **1.** stray, roam, ramble, rove, meander, straggle; range, nomadize, drift, live like a gypsy; stroll, amble, *Inf.* mosey, saunter, prowl, *Sl.* mooch; peregrinate, travel about, traverse, itinerate.

2. deviate, go off course, swerve, veer, sheer, go astray; digress, divagate, go off on a tangent.

3. speak incoherently, rave, be crazed, go off one's head, be delirious; ramble, rhapsodize, drivel, moon.

wanderer, *n.* rambler, roamer, rover, strayer, straggler, gadabout; traveler, wayfarer, voyager, peregrinator; adventurer, landloper, explorer, soldier of fortune, *Inf.* boomer, cowboy; trekker, hiker, backpacker; excursionist, sight-seer, *Inf.* rubbernecker, tourist; bird of passage, migrant, nomad, Kuchi, Bedouin, gypsy, Bohemian; hobo, vagrant, vagabond, *Archaic.* runagate, *Australian.* swagman, beachcomber, derelict, street Arab; *Inf.* bum, *Sl.* vag, *Sl.* bo, *Sl.* stiff, *Sl.* bindle stiff, *Sl.* canvas back; migrant worker, itinerant, *Usu. Disparaging.* Okie, drifter, *Inf.* floater, transient, fly-by-night, *Sl.* rolling stone.

wandering, *adj.* **1.** rambling, roving, roaming, itinerant, peripatetic, migratory, migrant, migratory; vagrant, vagabond, homeless, nomadic, gypsy, Bohemian; wayfaring, perambulatory, drifting; journeying, traveling.

2. straggling, meandering, winding, zigzagging; circuitous, ambagious, indirect, roundabout; discursive, excursive, circumlocutory, circumlocutional.

wane, *v.* **1.** decline, decrease, diminish; abate, let up, taper off, subside, ebb; fade away, evanesce, vanish, die out; approach an end, come to a close, *Inf.* peter out, wind down; obsolesce, be on the way out; dwindle, shrink, contract; shrivel, wither, deteriorate, degenerate; waste away, melt away, deliquesce; weaken, languish, flag, droop, sink, fall, die.

—n. **2.** decrease, diminution, decrescence, falling off, fall-off, decline, downgrade; abatement, subsidence, ebb, recession.

3. weakening, failing, failure, decay, wasting; deterioration, degeneration, declension, declination, retrogradation; dying, ending, termination.

4. on the wane decreasing, decrescent, diminishing, fading, dying; obsolescent, on the way out.

wangle, *v. Informal.* arrange, fix, machinate, manage, *Inf.* finagle, work, maneuver, bring off, *Sl.* pull off, *U.S. Inf.* swing; manipulate, pull strings *or* wires, influence, throw one's weight around; weasel [s.t.] out of [s.o.], get [s.t.] out of [s.o.].

want, *v.* **1.** desire, wish *or* wish for, long for, desiderate; yearn for, hope for, care for, pine for, sigh for; hanker after, have a yen for, covet, fancy, have a fancy for; have an eye to, be attracted to, have a mind to, have at heart, be bent upon, set one's heart on, ask for the moon; crave, hunger for, thirst for, lust after, burn for, *Inf.* be wild *or* mad about, *Sl.* have the hots for.

2. need, require, necessitate, demand, call for, have occasion for, have need of; lack, not suffice, be inadequate *or* insufficient, stand *or* be in need of, be without, miss; be deficient in, be short of, *Inf.* be shy, be absent, be missing *or* lacking, be devoid of, be empty of, be bereft of, be deprived of.

3. feel inclined, feel like, wish, prefer, feel prone to.

—n. **4.** need, exigency, requirement, demand, request, requisite, prerequisite, necessity; desire, wish, hope, craving, appetite.

5. absence, lack, default, dearth; deficiency, inadequacy, inadequateness, insufficiency, shortness, smallness, paucity, scarcity, scarceness, scantiness, shortage.

6. neediness, poverty, destitution, privation, penury, indigence; impecuniousness, impecuniosity, pennilessness, pauperism, beggary, mendicancy; insolvency, bankruptcy, straits, extremity, difficulty.

wanting, *adj.* **1.** in want of, lacking, needing, in need of, short *or* short of, *Inf.* shy; absent, missing, out of, destitute of, empty of, void of, devoid of, deprived of, bereft of, bankrupt of, unpossessed of, shorn of, stripped of, divested of.

2. deficient, incomplete, limited, unfinished, partial, sketchy, patchy; imperfect, defective, flawed, faulty, unsound, damaged, impaired; inferior, mediocre, so-so, *Inf.* leaving something to be desired, second-rate; inadequate, incommensurate, unsatisfactory, unacceptable, not good enough, not up to par, not up to snuff; disappointing, poor, sorry, *Inf.* no-good, bad, *Sl.* lousy, *Sl.* crummy, careless, shoddy, shabby, sloppy, half-baked, *Sl.* half-assed.

—prep. **3.** lacking, without, sans; less, minus.

wanton, *adj.* **1.** malicious, spiteful, vicious, cruel, malevolent; unjustifiable, groundless, needless, unnecessary; unmotivated, uncalled-for, unprovoked, gratuitous.

2. deliberate, willful, calculated; headstrong, froward, perverse, contrary, refractory, intractable, unmanageable, fractious, wayward, unruly.

3. careless, disregardful, mindless; reckless, rash, precipitate, hasty, heedless; inconsiderate, irresponsible, devil-may-care; thoughtless, capricious, arbitrary.

4. lewd, lecherous, lubricous, satyric, satyrlike, goatish, ruttish, *Sl.* horny; lustful, randy, *Sl.* hot *or* hot for, *Scot.* cadgey; concupiscent, prurient, libidinous, salacious; carnal, sensual, voluptuous, erotic; licentious, loose, Cyprian, abandoned, incontinent, intemperate; debauched, rakish, rakehell, dissolute, dissipated, profligate; promiscuous, whorish, of easy virtue, *Sl.* cheap, shameless; immodest, impure, unchaste, unvirtuous.

5. luxurious, opulent, sumptuous, costly, rich, posh, lavish, extravagant.

—n. **6.** profligate, rake, rakehell, roué, libertine, debauchee, dissipater, *Inf.* rip; voluptuary, sensualist, sybarite, hedonist; reprobate, degenerate, pervert, sodomite, bugger; lecher, satyr, *Pathol.* satyromaniac; philanderer, lover, lover boy, seducer, playboy, womanizer, wencher, *Sl.* stud, Don Juan, Casanova, Lo-

thario; whoremonger, pander, pimp, procurer.
7. hussy, harlot, whore, demirep, slut, Jezebel, cocotte, demimondaine, *Inf.* pick-up, *Pathol.* nymphomaniac, *Sl.* bitch, *Sl.* broad, *Sl.* chippy; prostitute, lady of the evening, woman of the profession, *Fr. fille de joie*, trollop, strumpet, *Archaic.* wench, trull, drab, quean, painted woman, woman of the streets, streetwalker, bar girl, call girl, *Sl.* cat, *Sl.* tart, *Sl.* hustler, *Sl.* bim, *Sl.* moll, *Sl.* hooker, *Sl.* floozie, *Brit. Sl.* bird, *Mexican Sl.* caliente; paramour, courtesan, mistress, concubine, kept woman, *Sl.* doxy; flirt, light-o'-love, coquette, minx.
—*v.* **8.** dissipate, debauch, indulge, pursue pleasure, live fast, be dissolute; be promiscuous, wench, whore, *Sl.* sleep around, lecher, *Sl.* letch.
9. squander, waste, misspend, fritter away, be prodigal.

wantonness, *n.* licentiousness, looseness, dissoluteness, dissipation, profligacy, debauchery, rakishness; lechery, lubricity, lust, libidinousness, salaciousness, salacity, promiscuity; abandon, unrestraint, self-indulgence, intemperance, incontinence.

war, *n.* **1.** combat, warfare, fighting, hostilities; clash, conflict, struggle, strife, contention; battle, contest, bout, skirmish, action, brush; collision, engagement, encounter, rencounter; fight, donnybrook, duel, joust, tilt; confrontation, showdown; uprising, resistance; dissension, brawl, affray, fray, tussle, scuffle.
2. slaughter, carnage, bloodshed, massacre, butchery; death, destruction, holocaust.
3. hostility, antagonism, animus, ill will, bad blood, ill feeling; enmity, hatred, hate, odium; malevolence, maliciousness, malice.
—*v.* **4.** wage war, do combat, engage in hostilities; struggle, contend, battle, combat, fight, clash, skirmish, conflict; joust, tilt, duel, cross swords with.
5. militate against, go against, side against, contend against; contradict, belie, counter; rebuff, spurn, foil, counteract; countervail, counterpoise, cancel out, annul; antagonize, oppose, counterattack, oppugn, resist.
6. disagree, differ, fail to agree, disaccord, be at variance, be at odds, be on the outs; think differently, stand in opposition, diverge; argue, quarrel, dispute, spar, have words, fall out; bicker, wrangle, debate, take issue with.

ward, *v.* **1.** *Usu.* **ward off** repel, drive back, push back, thrust back, beat back, force back; throw off, check, scotch, repulse, chase away, run off, put to flight, rout, *Inf.* send packing; scatter, disperse.
2. oppose, withstand, make a stand against; resist, hold off, fend off, stave off, keep at bay, keep at arm's length, parry; avert, avoid, deflect, turn aside; foil, checkmate, frustrate, contravene, *Inf.* cross, confound, nonplus; rebuff, reject, spurn, slight.

warden, *n.* **1.** custodian, keeper, guardian, caretaker; guard, warder, watchman, watchdog; conservator, protector, preserver, defender.
2. steward, curator, overseer, superintendent, *Inf.* super; janitor, concierge, maintenance man.

ware, *n.* *Usu.* **wares** merchandise, goods, commodities, vendibles, produce, stock in trade, stock, staples, supplies; dry goods, yard goods, foodstuffs, hardware; cargo, freight.

warehouse, *n.* storehouse, depository, depot, repository; hold, storeroom, stockroom; loft, attic, cellar, closet, cabinet; vault, bunker; armory, arsenal, magazine.

warfare, *n.* See **war** (*def.* **1**).

warlike, *adj.* **1.** militant, militaristic, aggressive, hawkish; bellicose, belligerent, combative, pugnacious, truculent, full of fight, *Sl.* scrappy; hostile, antagonistic.
2. martial, military, military-minded, soldierly, soldierlike; armed, under arms, armed to the teeth, sword in hand, in battle array, *Archaic.* battailous.

warlock, *n.* **1.** sorcerer, wizard, male witch, conjurer, magician, *Archaic.* mage; shaman, witch doctor, root doctor, medicine man; exorcist.
2. seer, soothsayer, oracle, fortuneteller, palmist, necromancer, thaumaturgist; augur, diviner, dowser, (*in ancient Rome*) haruspice.

warm, *adj.* **1.** tepid, lukewarm, heated; toasty, *Inf.* roasty-toasty, snug, comfortable, cozy.
2. fervid, fervent, zealous, ardent, vehement; emotional, passionate, impassioned, warm-blooded, hotheaded, impetuous.
3. friendly, on friendly terms, on good terms, on a first-name basis; intimate, familiar, close, *Inf.* tight, *Inf.* thick, *Inf.* thick as thieves, *Inf.* like two peas in a pod.
4. cordial, genial, hearty, hospitable, amiable, receptive, open-hearted; enthusiastic, ebullient, effusive, gushing, glowing; earnest, sincere, heartfelt.
5. irritated, annoyed, vexed, piqued, peeved, *Inf.* miffed, *Inf.* aggravated; exasperated, ruffled, discomposed, disturbed; irate, angry, *Sl.* hot, *Sl.* hot under the collar, *Sl.* all riled up, *Sl.* ticked-off, *Sl.* teed-off.
6. lively, full of life, animated, *Inf.* full of pep, *Inf.* full of get up and go; energetic, vigorous, full of vigor; vivacious, vivid, frisky, brisk.
7. *Informal.* unpleasant, unenjoyable, uncomfortable; strained, tense, heated, volatile, explosive.
—*v.* **8.** heat, heat up, mull, tepefy; reheat, warm over.
9. animate, vivify, invigorate, inspirit, rouse, arouse, waken, wake up, stir; incite, foment, agitate, fire up.
10. **warm up** **a.** prepare, practice, drill, *Music.* noodle; train, loosen up, *Inf.* get loose, exercise. **b.** intensify, heighten, deepen, worsen.

warmed-over, *adj.* **1.** reheated, recooked.
2. stale, tired, musty; hackneyed, trite, timeworn, shopworn, worn thin; cut-and-dried, prosaic, unimaginative; banal, stock, familiar, common, commonplace, back-number, *Inf.* old hat; unoriginal, derivative.

warmth, *n.* **1.** fervor, fervidity, ardor, vehemence; zeal, enthusiasm, ebullience; passion, passionateness, impetuousness, warm-bloodedness, hot-headedness.
2. friendliness, cordiality, geniality, heartiness, hospitableness, amiableness, receptiveness, open-heartedness; earnestness, sincerity, genuineness.
3. intimacy, familiarity, closeness, *Inf.* tightness.
4. (*all to a slight degree*) irritation, annoyance, vexation, pique, *Inf.* aggravation; anger, dudgeon.

warn, *v.* **1.** precaution, caution, forewarn, prewarn, *Rare.* premonish; alert, put [s.o.] on the alert, put [s.o.] on guard, put [s.o.] on the qui vive, *Sl.* give [s.o.] the high sign; give notice, give prior notice, give fair warning, read the riot act.
2. remonstrate, expostulate, urge, admonish, *Archaic.* monish, exhort; counsel, advise, say a word to the wise, *Inf.* put a bug in [s.o.'s] ear.
3. notify, inform, tell, apprise, let [s.o.] know, have one to know, give one to understand, enlighten, acquaint, *Inf.* tip off, *Inf.* clue in, *Inf.* let [s.o.] in on [s.t.], *Sl.* put [s.o.] wise, *Sl.* put [s.o.] on to [s.t.].

warning, *n.* **1.** caution, admonition, monition, advice, counsel; expostulation, remonstration.
2. omen, portent, sign, indication, token, foretoken, harbinger; premonition, preindication, forewarning, foreshadowing, handwriting on the wall; augury, prog-

nostication, prediction, prophecy, prefigurement.
3. tip, piece of advice, word to the wise; clue, *Inf.* tip-off, *Inf.* bug *or* flea in the ear.
4. alert, signal, tocsin, alarm; notice, notification, fair warning; threat; nod, nudge, wink, kick, *Sl.* high sign.

warp, *v.* **1.** bend out of shape, bend, twist, turn, wrench; contort, misshape, deform.
2. swerve, curve, veer, deviate, slue.
3. bias, prejudice, jaundice, poison; prepossess, influence, sway, predispose.
4. pervert, distort, misconstruct, misrender, misreport, miscite, misstate, misquote; lie, belie, falsify, misrepresent; color, slant, varnish, gild.
—*n.* **5.** curve, bow, bend, turn, bias, veer, swerve, slue, skew; hook, crook, angle; meander, zigzag, deviation, variation, *Chiefly Scot.* wimple.
6. bias, prejudice, prepossession; bent, proclivity, propensity, tendency; quirk, idiosyncrasy, idiocrasy, mannerism, hobby-horse; oddity, peculiarity, irregularity, incongruity, inconsistency.

warrant, *n.* **1.** authorization, authority, right; permission, allowance, consent, sanction, approval, vouchsafement, *Inf.* O.K.; certification, accreditation, legalization, validation; license, liberty, imprimatur, carte blanche; charter, commission, entitlement, empowerment, warranty.
2. justification, grounds, reason, cause, basis.
3. guarantee, *Law.* certification, *Obs.* vouch; contract, covenant, compact, obligation, *Law.* covenant of warranty, *Law.* warranty deed.
4. certificate, credential, entitlement, document, paper; statement, evidence, *Law.* affidavit, *Law.* deposition; permit, license, pass, *Law.* writ; fiat, edict, decree, decretal, order, command, mandate, summons, *Law.* subpoena, *Law.* injunction.
5. receipt, voucher, acknowledgement, chit, slip.
—*v.* **6.** authorize, invest, empower, enable, entitle, commission, depute, *Eccles.* ordain; certify, accredit, license, legalize, validate, notarize, visa; permit, allow, consent to, subscribe to, vouchsafe; sanction, approve, give one's nod of approval, countenance, acknowledge, *Inf.* O.K., *Chiefly U.S.* approbate.
7. justify, excuse, explain, account for, defend, offer grounds for, be a reason *or* an argument for; require, demand, necessitate, call for.
8. guarantee, pledge, plight, vow, give one's solemn word *or* promise, state on one's honor, swear to, *Inf.* promise; assure, offer assurance, insure, see to it; endorse, vouch for, support, uphold, back up, stand behind *or* by, attest *or* testify to, give testimonial to, recommend, give one's stamp *or* seal of approval.

warrantable, *adj.* **1.** authorizable, permissible, allowable, admissible, lawful, legal, legitimate, *Inf.* kosher, certifiable, qualified, charterable, investable, *Eccles.* ordainable.
2. sanctionable, approvable, acceptable; endorsable, attestable, recommendable.
3. justifiable, vindicable, excusable, explainable, explicable, accountable; defendable, supportable, reasonable, logical, sound, well-founded, valid, right, *Inf.* O.K.
4. insurable, securable, *Insurance.* coverable.

warrior, *n.* **1.** brave, soldier, fighter, fighting man, man-of-arms, man-at-arms; infantryman, doughboy, common soldier, cannon fodder, GI *or* GI Joe, *U.S. Sl.* grunt, *U.S. Marine Sl.* leatherneck, *U.S. Sl.* gyrene, *Brit.* Tommy, *Scot.* Jock, *Fr. poilu*; intrepid *or* fearless warrior, lion, tiger, bulldog, gamecock, fighting cock; mercenary, soldier of fortune, dog soldier.
2. hero, champion, paladin, knight; stalwart, gallant, valiant, cavalier; a man, a real man, brave man, man of courage *or* mettle.
3. struggler, battler, fighter; die-hard, trouper.

warship, *n.* man-of-war, war vessel, ship of war; ship of the line, line-of-battle ship, corvette; battleship, *Inf.* battlewagon, cruiser, dreadnought; destroyer; gunboat; P.T. boat; aircraft carrier, carrier, *U.S. Navy Sl.* flattop; submarine, submersible, U-boat.

wary, *adj.* **1.** chary, careful, cautious, circumspect, prudent, mindful, heedful; guarded, on one's guard; leery, apprehensive, distrustful, suspicious, *Inf.* cagey.
2. vigilant, watchful, *Archaic.* ware, on the watch, on the lookout; attentive, observant, sharp-eyed, hawk-eyed, eagle-eyed, Argus-eyed, all eyes and ears; alert, on the alert, on the qui vive, on one's toes, *Inf.* heads-up, awake, wide-awake, sleepless, unsleeping, unnodding, *Inf.* with one's eyes peeled.

wash, *v.* **1.** clean, clean up, bathe, *Brit. Inf.* tub, lave, cleanse, wash up, scrub up, *Chiefly Scot.* dight; deterge, launder, do the laundry; shampoo, lather, soap; scrub, brush, swab, mop; soak, shower, douse, rinse, flush, sponge, douche; absterge, scour, wipe.
2. cleanse, chasten; baptize, christen, sprinkle, besprinkle, asperse, anoint; immerse, submerge, dunk, *Archaic.* dip.
3. moisten, dampen, dew, bedew, humidify, mist; wet, irrigate, soak, imbue, drench, saturate.
4. splash, swash, dash, break against, beat against, thrash against; roll, lap, undulate, surge, swell, wave, ripple; rush, flow, run, sweep; wear, rub, polish, smooth, level, flatten; consume, deteriorate, waste, abrade, erode, wash away; channel, cut through, groove, cleave, excavate, penetrate.
5. carry, move, drive, convey, transport; deliver, bring, propel, throw, deposit.
6. purify, depurate, purge, expurgate, defecate, mundify, lustrate; elutriate, decant, filter, strain, sieve, sift, *Chem.* edulcorate.
7. (*all with color*) coat, film, glaze, gloss, suffuse, overspread, overlay.
8. hold up, *Inf.* hold water, carry weight, stand up, stand *or* bear the test.
—*n.* **9.** cleaning, bath, bathing, *Both Brit. Inf.* tub, tubbing; lavage, lavation, cleansing, ablution, wash up, washing; deterging, laundering, shampoo, shampooing, lather, lathering, soaping; scrub, scrubbing, brushing, swabbing, mopping; shower, showering, douse, dousing, rinse, rinsing, flush, flushing; sponge bath, sponging, douche, douching, dip, dipping; abstersion, absterging, scour, scouring, wipe, wiping.
10. laundry, washing, dirty clothes *or* linen, *Sl.* socks and jocks.
11. flow, flowing, sweep, sweeping, running; splash, splashing, dashing, beat, beating, thrashing; sea, roll, rolling, lapping, undulation, undulating, surf, breaker, breaking, surgement, surging, swell, swelling, wave, waving, ripple, rippling, wake.
12. rinse, lotion, cold cream, cosmetic, toiletry, cologne, toilet water; emulsion, application, preparation, embrocation, liniment, salve, *Med.* emollient; tint, tinge, dye.
13. antiseptic, disinfectant, *Med.* irrigator, medicine, medicament, remedy; purgative, cathartic.
14. erosion, wearing away, washout, landslide.
15. marsh, fen, bog, swamp, slough, morass, mire, quagmire, *Brit. Dial.* sump.
16. stream, streamlet, brook, rill, rivulet, runnel, creek, run, channel; pool, pond, inlet, estuary, backwater, tidewater; gully, ditch, gutter, ravine.
17. layer, coat, film, glaze, floss, gelatin; suffusion, spread, overspread, overlay, screen, cover; calcimine,

whitewash, washing, stain, varnish; gilding, gold leaf.
18. slosh, swill, *Brit. Inf.* swipes, hogwash, slops, mess; mash, wort.
—adj. **19.** washable, launderable, wash and wear; preshrunk, shrink-resistant, *Trademark.* Sanforized; nonbleeding, bled, faded.

washed-out, *adj.* **1.** faded, bleached, blanched, etiolated; colorless, lusterless, lackluster, dull, dead, drab, flat, mat.
2. *Informal.* **a.** exhausted, spent, drained, *Sl.* bushed, *Sl.* pooped, *Sl.* beat, *Sl.* all in; dead-tired, dog-tired, bone-weary, dead one one's feet; tired out, worn out, played out, *Inf.* fagged out, *Inf.* tuckered out, *Inf.* knocked out, *Inf.* wiped out, *Inf.* pooped out, *Sl.* too pooped to pop. **b.** wan, pale, pallid, anemic; haggard, drawn, tired-looking, tired-eyed.

washed-up, *adj. Informal.* through, finished, *Sl.* fini, *Sl.* done for, *Sl.* kaput, *Sl.* shot, *Sl.* SOL; over, all over, *Sl.* all up.

waspish, *adj.* **1.** resentful, spiteful, peevish, petulant, querulous; touchy, testy, tetchy, thin-skinned, prickly, sensitive, oversensitive, hypersensitive, quick to take offense.
2. irritable, irascible, cranky, cross, cantankerous, feisty, huffish; splenetic, crusty, peppery; grouchy, crabby, grumpy, *Inf.* bitchy; ill-tempered, bad-tempered, temperamental, short-tempered, ill-humored, ill-natured, *Inf.* mean, *Inf.* ornery.

wassail, *n.* **1.** toast, pledge, salute, salutation, cheer.
2. drinking bout, brannigan, drunk, potation, compotation, bouse, guzzle, drunken carouse *or* revel, bacchanal, bacchanalia; spree, fling, bout, romp, carouse, carousal, revel; *All Sl.* binge, bender, hellbender, bust, toot, tear, bat, jag, barhop, bar-crawl, *Brit.* pub-crawl.
3. celebration, gala, gala affair, *Inf.* shindig, *Sl.* hot time.
—v. **4.** carouse, revel, roister, make merry, cut loose, let loose, *Inf.* step out, whoop it up, *Sl.* make whoopee; drink, tipple, tope, bouse, *Inf.* booze, *Sl.* hit the bottle *or* booze *or* sauce, *Sl.* souse, *Sl.* scoop a few, *Sl.* knock a few back; go on a spree, make the rounds, *Sl.* tie one on, *Sl.* go on a drunk *or* binge *or* bender, *Sl.* paint the town red, *Sl.* barhop, *Sl.* bar-crawl, *Brit. Sl.* pub-crawl; debauch, dissipate, wanton, sow wild oats; overindulge, overdo, burn the candle at both ends.
5. toast, drink a toast to, drink to, pledge, drink *or* pledge the health of.

waste, *v.* **1.** squander, fritter away, fool away, dissipate, lose, misuse, misspend; expend, consume, use up, drain, exhaust, deplete; throw away, burn up, run through, go through, *Sl.* blow; disperse, scatter, spill, muddle away; splurge, lavish, play the profligate, *Sl.* hang the expense; misapply, misemploy, overdraw, impoverish, spend recklessly; throw money away, spend money like water, throw good money after bad, play ducks and drakes with, spend money as if it grew on trees *or* were going out of style; (*of time*) kill, while away, pass.
2. wear away, erode, dwindle, eat away, gnaw away; reduce, diminish, decrease, lessen, lower, cut, cut back, shorten; ablate, corrode, wash away, rub away, disintegrate.
3. deteriorate, degenerate, worsen, regress; decline, fall, slip, go downhill, run down; decay, wither, atrophy, wear out, crumble, molder; fag, wilt, pine, languish, shrivel, shrink; emaciate, weaken, enfeeble, macerate, break down; perish, wane, ebb, die, subside, slump, slide; dry up, wizen, fade, droop, run to seed.
4. destroy, devastate, ruin, lay waste, demolish, wreck; ravage, pillage, plunder, sack, spoil, spoliate, despoil; sack, loot, gut, strip, ransack, rifle; maraud, rape, harry, *Chiefly Scot.* reive, raid; wreak havoc upon, overrun, shatter, smash, crush, fell; annihilate, eradicate, extirpate, blast, bow up, raze.
—n. **5.** dissipation, prodigality, squandering, misuse, consumption, overconsumption; depletion, exhaustion, draining, loss; misapplication, misemployment, abuse, neglect; lavishness, extravagance, indulgence, dissoluteness, profligacy; unthriftiness, improvidence, overspending, liberality; overindulgence, crapulousness, gluttony, abandonment.
6. impairment, weakening, degeneration, deterioration, regression; decay, emaciation, consumption, wastage, atrophy; diminution, lessening, lowering, decline, fall; ablation, corrosion, erosion, deliquescence; decrease, reduction, shortening, cut; wear, wear and tear, weathering; dilapidation, disintegration, decomposition, breakup, oxidation, spoilage.
7. devastation, destruction, ruin, desolation, ravage, havoc; wreckage, annihilation, eradication, obliteration, extirpation, extermination; ravishment, despoliation, spoliation, depredation, plunder, pillage, sack; ruination, demolition, razing, burning, leveling.
8. desert, wasteland, wilderness, emptiness, vastness; barrens, heath, dust bowl, salt flat, wilds, bush.
9. rubbish, trash, refuse, spilth, garbage, *Chiefly Brit.* wastrel, leavings, leftovers, remnants, residue, scraps, litter; scourings, offscourings, sweepings, wash, hogwash, slops; scum, dross, dregs, draff, slag, sediment, grounds, lees; alluvium, detritus, debris, deposits, *Geol.* diluvium; orts, odds and ends, rags, ends, ruins, butts, fag ends, stumps; shavings, parings, sawdust, chaff, filings; ashes, cinders, soot, smut, culm.
10. wastes excrement, feces, waste matter, excreta, droppings; dung, ordure, discharges, guano, egesta.
—adj. **11.** wild, desolate, barren, desert, arid; uninhabited, bare, empty, void, vacant, deserted, ghostly, ruined, destroyed, wrecked, ravaged, gutted; depopulated, unpeopled, unoccupied, solitary, lonely; dead, lifeless, fallow, unproductive, unfertile, infecund, sterile, unfruitful; stripped, desolated, spoiled, dismal, cheerless, bleak, dreary.
12. leftover, unused, useless, superfluous, extra, worthless, unserviceable, *Archaic.* losel; unnecessary, needless, of no use, unhelpful, unbeneficial, unprofitable.

wasted, *adj.* **1.** dissipated, dissolute, intemperate, incontinent, self-indulgent; abandoned, wanton, profligate, debauched.
2. spent, consumed, used up, finished, exhausted, depleted; drained, emptied, gone, worn away, eaten up, burnt up; dried up, desiccated, sucked dry, dry, sere, fruitless, fallow, barren, sterile; (*all with reference to drugs or alcohol*) *Sl.* burned-out, *Sl.* wrecked, *Sl.* zapped, *Sl.* zonked.
3. wizened, gaunt, emaciated, shrunken, atrophied; withered, shriveled; skeletal, cadaverous, worn to the bones, corpse-like; deathly, wan, pallid, pale, washed-out.

wasteful, *adj.* prodigal, lavish, extravagant, profligate, spendthrift, thriftless, overindulgent, overliberal; profuse, excessive, improvident, too free, overgenerous, free-handed; unthrifty, free and easy, easy come, easy go, penny-wise and pound-foolish; immoderate, squandering, overlavish, dissipative.

wastrel, *n.* spendthrift, waster, spender, big spender, squanderer; prodigal, prodigal son, scattergood, rounder.

watch, *v.* **1.** look, observe, view, regard, see; look at, take in, gaze at, look on, *Inf.* spectate, eye, ogle, gape, stare at; notice, perceive, espy, detect, descry, sight; contemplate, behold, inspect, make note of, take stock of, scrutinize; survey, scan, examine, pore over, *Inf.* size up; mark, remark, glimpse, glance; look after, keep an eye on, follow, *Inf.* keep tabs on, keep in sight, hold in view, spy upon, reconnoiter.

2. take care, be careful, be attentive, watch out, pay attention, heed; be on guard, be on the lookout, *Inf.* keep one's eyes peeled, keep one's eyes open; be watchful, be on the alert, be vigilant, keep one's ears to the ground, look lively, keep one's eye on the ball.

3. keep watch, stand guard, keep watch and ward, mount guard; patrol, police, go on one's beat; secure, preserve, safeguard.

4. guard, watch over, protect, keep, shelter, cover; mind, tend, oversee, superintend, look over, overlook; foster, shepherd, nurse, mother, attend, minister; chaperon, escort, accompany, convoy, conduct; look after, see after, take care of, care for, *Inf.* baby-sit, *Inf.* sit for.

5. watch for look for, wait for, await, wait upon; watch out for, look forward to, anticipate, expect, count on, reckon on, be ready for, have in prospect.

—*n.* **6.** observation, regard, consideration, contemplation, *Inf.* the eye; inspection, scrutiny, survey, study, observance, examination, overview; surveillance, view, oversight.

7. guard, lookout, watch and ward, sharp eye, watching; vigilance, watchfulness, watchful eye, weather eye; monitoring, guardedness, attention, alertness, attentiveness, wariness; vigil, wake, *Eccles.* pernoctation, *Obs.* pervigilation; custody, safeguard, safekeeping, stewardship, guardianship, charge, supervision.

8. timepiece, wrist watch, clock, pocket watch, stopwatch, chronometer, chronograph; timekeeper, timer, *Inf.* ticker; horologe, sundial, calendar watch.

9. sentry, sentinel, guard, patrolman. See **watchman.**

watchful, *adj.* wary. See **wary** (*defs.* **1, 2**).

watchman, *n.* guard, custodian, night watchman; protector, defender, guardian, guarder, guardsman; watch, sentinel, sentry, picket, patrol, garrison; jailer, warder, warden, keeper, turnkey, *Sl.* screw, *Sl.* bull; scout, lookout, watchdog.

watchword, *n.* password, *Fr. mot de passe, Fr. passe-parole,* shibboleth, test word; keyword, open sesame; slogan, motto, byword, catchword, catch phrase, battle cry, rallying cry, buzz word; countersign, sign, signal.

water, *n.* **1.** H_2O, *Facetious.* Adam's ale, *Chiefly Pharm.* aqua, *Fr. eau;* tap water, bottled water, distilled water, mineral water, soda water, Seltzer water; branch water, ditchwater, *Western U.S.* ditch.

2. rain, dew, condensation, moisture; tears; perspiration, sweat, urine, *Anat., Zool.* amniotic fluid; saliva, spit, spittle, slaver; fluid, exudation, *Old Physiol.* humor.

—*v.* **3.** sprinkle, besprinkle, sparge, moisten, damp, dampen, bedew; hose, spray, water down; wet, splash, douse, slosh; drench, steep, saturate, sodden, imbue; irrigate, flood, deluge, inundate.

4. *Often* **water down** dilute, weaken, thin, rarefy, soften; mix, adulterate, (*of alcohol or drugs*) cut.

waterfall, *n.* cascade, cataract, sault, *Chiefly Scot.* linn, chute, falls; Niagara Falls.

water nymph, *n.* water sprite, undine, water spirit, (*in Scottish legends*) kelpie; naiad, Nereid, *Class. Myth.* Thetis, Lorelei, Oceanid; mermaid, sea-maid, *Class. Myth.* siren, sea nymph, nymph.

watery, *adj.* **1.** aqueous, liquid, liquefied, serous, fluid, hydrous.

2. sodden, soggy, soppy, sopping, sopping wet, wet; oozy, leaking, seepy, seeping; damp, dank, moist, overmoist; soaked, drenched, saturated, soused, waterlogged; boggy, swampy, quaggy, miry, marshy, spongy; soft, mushy, squashy, squishy.

3. runny, thin, pappy, paplike; diluted, weak, adulterated, thinned, mixed, (*of alcohol or drugs*) cut, (*of liquor*) *Scot.* shilpit; tasteless, flavorless, vapid, insipid, bland, *Sl.* blah; flat, dull, tame, washy, uninteresting, jejune.

4. tearful, teary, lachrymose, weeping, weepy, crying; mournful, sad, sorrowful.

wave, *n.* **1.** ripple, riffle, wavelet; comber, beachcomber, breaker, sea, (*collectively*) surf, whitecap, white horse; tsunami, tidal wave, rogue wave, bore; heave, swell.

2. welling up, surge, sweep, ground swell, rush, billow; gush, rush, flow, stream; upsurge, rise, ascension, soaring.

3. trend, drift, movement, tendency, current, undercurrent; general sentiment *or* opinion, consensus.

4. undulation, curve, curl, squiggle, twist.

—*v.* **5.** undulate, ripple, ruffle, wrinkle; rise and fall, ebb and flow, oscillate, fluctuate; flutter, flap, sway, rock, swing, wag, waggle, wigwag; curve, meander, zigzag; bend, incline, toss, shake.

waver, *v.* **1.** sway, wag, flutter, flap, move to and fro, oscillate, librate, vibrate; undulate, wave, ripple, wrinkle.

2. flicker, quiver, (*of flame*) gutter; quaver, tremble, shake, quake; weaken, fade, fail, die, ebb.

3. hesitate, falter, pause, be irresolute *or* indecisive, show doubt; vacillate, fluctuate, whiffle, blow hot and cold, alternate, shilly-shally, tergiversate, *Inf.* flip-flop, seesaw; equivocate, hedge, hem and haw, beat around the bush, pussyfoot, waffle.

4. totter, reel, rock, *Dial.* wamble, stagger, roll; wobble, shake, teeter, stagger; tip, tilt, lean, sag, bend; lurch, stumble, topple.

wavering, *adj.* **1.** vacillating, indecisive, irresolute, uncertain, undecided, unsure; ambivalent, of two minds, of mixed feelings; hesitant, wishy-washy, uncommitted, holding back, dubious; fluctuating, oscillating, alternating, blowing hot and cold, unable to make up one's mind; shilly-shallying, tergiversating, equivocating, stalling for time.

2. swaying, fluttering, flapping; tottering, reeling, staggering, rocking; unsteady, infirm, unreliable, rickety.

wavy, *adj.* undulating, curvy, curling, squiggly, twisting; rippled, wrinkled, ridged, furrowed, grooved; tortuous, curving, winding, sinuous, serpentine, snaky.

wax, *v.* increase, grow, develop, enlarge, magnify, amplify; lengthen, widen, broaden, extend; build up, accelerate, spread, mushroom, swell, expand, blow up, inflate, balloon.

way, *n.* **1.** method, manner, mode, fashion, wise; process, procedure, system, *Latin. modus operandi, Inf.* MO; technique, formula, means; policy, rule, convention, wont, custom.

2. nature, personality, temperament, character, disposition; characteristic, trait, attribute, property, idiosyncrasy, idiocrasy; peculiarity, mannerism, quirk.

3. direction, route, course, path; track, road, roadway, avenue, lane; passage, passageway, channel, access.

4. give way a. collapse, cave in, tumble down, crumple, fall down; crumble, disintegrate, fall into pieces. **b.** yield, surrender, acquiesce, accede; acknowledge, concede.

wayfarer, *n.* traveler, voyager, journeyer, excursionist, *Brit. Inf.* tripper, trekker; globe-trotter, sightseer, tourist; wanderer, roamer, rover, meanderer, landloper, adventurer; gadabout, gallivanter; nomad, gypsy, Bedouin, Kuchi; walker, hiker, tramper. See also **walker.**

wayfaring, *adj.* hiking, on the open road, peregrinating, peripatetic; journeying, traveling, itinerant, rambling, roving, roaming; gypsy, nomadic; on the move, on the go, restless, with sand in one's shoes, with wanderlust.

waylay, *v.* ambush, ambuscade, lie in wait; lurk, skulk; entrap, ensnare, decoy, lure.

way-out, *adj. Informal.* **1.** advanced, progressive, avant-garde, forward-looking, ahead of its time; original, novel, unique, new; imaginative, creative, unconventional, unorthodox, *Inf.* far-out; modern, ultramodern, modernistic; exploratory, experimental, innovative, ground-breaking, precedent-setting.

2. bizzare, strange, odd, unusual, uncommon; abnormal, irregular, deviant, aberrant, erratic; queer, peculiar, curious, singular, offbeat; quaint, eccentric, weird, freakish, outlandish; freaky, *Inf.* kinky, *Sl.* flaky, *Sl.* off the wall.

3. esoteric, exotic, foreign; different, strange, glamorous, exciting.

wayward, *adj.* **1.** disobedient, willful, self-willed, contrary, perverse, wrong-headed, cross-grained, balky, uncooperative, froward, refractory, recalcitrant, contumacious; ungovernable, unmanageable, uncontrollable, difficult, restive, unruly, fractious, incorrigible; stubborn, mulish, pigheaded, bullheaded, headstrong; obstinate, inflexible, immovable, adamant, set, set in one's ways; persistent, persevering, pertinacious, bulldogged, dogged, relentless, single-minded.

2. capricious, whimsical, fanciful, impulsive; fickle, inconstant, changeable, changeful, variable; flighty, mercurial, independable, unsteady, unstable; fitful, erratic, irregular, uneven; wavering, deviating, straying.

weak, *adj.* **1.** frail, fragile, breakable, delicate; unstable, unsteady, unsubstantial; flimsy, jerry-built, gimcrack, rickety, ramshackle, dilapidated, falling apart *or* down, tumble-down, decayed, rotten.

2. feeble, puny, nonmuscular, nonathletic, enervated, enervate, anemic, *Pathol.* atonic, *Pathol.* asthenic, *Pathol.* neurasthenic; dropping, languid, languishing, limp, flagging, *Dial.* limpsy, tired, worn-out, about to drop, exhausted, spent, effete; ailing, indisposed, infirm, sickly, weakly, valetudinarian, in poor health, unwell, unhealthy, debilitated, invalid, bedridden; faltering, shaky, doddering, tottering, trembling, senile, anile, decrepit, *Inf.* dotty; the worse for wear, declining, failing, on one's last legs, going downhill, on the way out, fading, sinking, dying.

3. impotent, impuissant, powerless, helpless; ineffective, ineffectual, inefficacious, inefficient, incapable, incompetent, inept, inapt, feckless; unavailing, futile, inutile, useless, hopeless, bootless, nugatory, good for nothing.

4. trifling, trivial, insignificant, meager, mere, piddling, paltry, niggling, worthless, *Archaic.* seely; inadequate, insufficient, deficient, wanting, lacking, short.

5. lame, shallow, childish, puerile, sophomoric, superficial, vapid, empty, half-baked, *Sl.* half-assed, *Sl.* for the birds; unconvincing, untenable, unbelievable, inconclusive; loose, lax, illogical; unsound, ungrounded, unsupported, unsustained; poor, inferior, unsatisfactory, not up to snuff *or* par; careless, slipshod, shoddy, sloppy, miserable, *Inf.* lousy.

6. weak-minded, feeble-minded, dim-witted, soft *or* weak in the head, balmy, *Brit.* barmy, *Inf.* daffy; dull-witted, slow-witted, retarded, imbecilic, moronic, unintelligent, stupid, *Inf.* dumb; simple-minded, simple, foolish, silly, idiotic, asinine. See also **feeble-minded.**

7. irresolute, wishy-washy, shilly-shallying, tergiversating, indecisive, noncommittal, hedging, mealy-mouthed, weasel-worded; spineless, weak-kneed, lily-livered, white-livered, faint-hearted, *Inf.* chicken-hearted, *Inf.* chicken-livered, *Inf.* yellow, *Sl.* yellow-bellied, *Sl.* candy-assed; timorous, craven, timid, meek, pusillanimous; sissyish, effeminate, unmanly, womanish, *Inf.* pantywaist, *Sl.* old-womanish.

8. faint, low, whispered, muffled, stifled, barely detectable, imperceptible, inaudible, distant, faraway; soft, gentle, dulcet, muted; dim, pale, dull, faded, washed out; slight, slim, thin, slender, tiny, small, wee, bit *or* ghost of a; vague, ambiguous, nebulous, indistinct, unclear, blurred, blurry, hazy, foggy, obscure.

9. thin, watery, runny, watered-down, diluted, cut, stretched, attenuated, (*of liquor*) *Scot.* shilpit; pappy, paplike, milk-and-water, soppy, sodden; insipid, jejune, pallid, *Sl.* nothing, *Sl.* blah; bland, tasteless, unappetizing, unsavory, flavorless, inedible; flat, stale, dead, *Fr. fade.*

weaken, *v.* **1.** enfeeble, debilitate, enervate, devitalize; exhaust, deplete, sap, impoverish; tire, strain, fatigue, *Inf.* take it out of [s.o.], unnerve, unman, emasculate, effeminize.

2. impair, invalidate, incapacitate, cripple, handicap, undermine; dilute, adulterate, debase, water, water down, *Inf.* cut; thin, attenuate; lessen, diminish, lower, reduce, minimize.

3. tire, languish, fail, fade, decline; wane, droop, faint, flag, drop; totter, shake, dodder, crumble; (*all usu. of health*) lose ground, take a turn for the worse, go downhill; (*all usu. of psychological or emotional health*) crack, let go, break down, come apart at the seams.

4. relent, give in, acquiesce, yield, give way, bend, soften; accede, agree, assent, consent, concur, *Inf.* come round; relax, ease up, let up.

weakling, *n.* featherweight, *Inf.* lightweight, baby, small fry; loser, Walter Mitty, *Sl.* sad sack, *Sl.* doormat, *Sl.* pushover, *Sl.* patsy, *Sl.* schnook, *Sl.* easy mark; *Inf.* jellyfish, *Sl.* nebbish, *Sl.* weak sister, *Sl.* weak stick, *Sl.* schlepp, *Sl.* schlemiel; namby-pamby, milquetoast, milksop, sop, mollycoddle, mother's *or* mama's boy, Little Lord Fauntleroy, *Sl.* sap, *Sl.* wimp, *Sl.* twirp, *Sl.* nerd, *Sl.* twit; softy, sissy, effeminate, woman, *Inf.* pantywaist, *Sl.* cream puff, *Sl.* pansy, *Sl.* wimp, *Sl.* old woman; big baby, crybaby, mouse, *Sl.* fraidy-cat, *Sl.* scaredy-cat; coward, poltroon, *Archaic.* caitiff, dastard, *Inf.* chicken.

weakness, *n.* **1.** feebleness, puniness, frailty, frailness, fragility, fragileness, delicateness, delicacy; impotence, impuissance, powerlessness, helplessness, incapacity, inability, incapability, ineptness, ineptitude; exhaustion, enervation, lack of strength, anemia, *Pathol.* adynamia, *Pathol.* asthenia, *Pathol.* neurasthenia, *Pathol.* atony, *Pathol.* atonicity; debility, infirmity, disability, valetudinarianism, unhealthfulness, invalidness, decrepitude, senility, *Pathol.* cachexia.

2. flaw, fault, chink *or* hole in one's armor, weak spot, Achilles heel, underbelly; loophole, way out, lapse, deficiency, defect, imperfection, mar, blemish, blotch, mark against [s.o.]; foible, shortcoming, failing, handicap; vulnerability, vulnerableness, liability, susceptibility, susceptibleness, openness.

3. fondness, liking, affection, love, passion, *Fr. amour*; fancy, appreciation, eye, taste, appetite, sweet tooth; tenderness, soft spot, special place in one's heart, partiality, preference, predisposition, leaning, inclination, proneness, propensity; penchant, desire, longing, yearning.

wealth, *n.* **1.** riches, means, wherewithal, assets, resources, reserves; funds, money, *Sl.* gelt, *Sl.* mazuma; monies, cash, capital; plenty, treasure, fortune, *Sl.* bread, *Sl.* dough, *Sl.* moolah, *Sl.* loot, *Sl.* gravy, *Sl.* bucks, *Sl.* big bucks, blue-chip stocks, gilt-edged securities *or* bonds; affluence, richness, prosperity, opulence, easy circumstances; nest egg, *Sl.* cushion, *Sl.* tidy bundle, nice sum.

2. abundance, heap, pile, mass, ton, great deal; profusion, bounty, plenitude, plenteousness, bountifulness, copiousness, amplitude; cornucopia, bottomless well, treasury, gold mine, mine.

3. fruitfulness, productivity, fertility, fecundity, proliferousness, fructiferousness.

wealthy, *adj.* **1.** rich, affluent, prosperous, moneyed, well-off, well-to-do, forehanded, silk-stocking; worth a great deal, *Inf.* worth a bundle, in the money, *Sl.* in the bucks, in the chips, *Sl.* loaded, made of money, *Inf.* rolling in dough; in clover, *Sl.* on easy street, in easy circumstances, comfortable, *Inf.* not hurting, *Inf.* in velvet; with money to burn, *Sl.* stinking, *Sl.* stinking *or* filthy rich, weighed down by diamonds; with the key to the bank, sitting on top of a gold mine, with an oil well in one's backyard; doing nicely, not having to work, clipping coupons, well-fixed, well-situated, *Inf.* well-heeled; born with a silver spoon in one's mouth, to the manner born; parvenu, newly rich, *Fr. nouveau riche.*

2. opulent, sumptuous, elegant, luxurious, lavish, splendid, glittering, magnificent.

3. abundant, ample, replete, rife, well-supplied; abounding, overflowing, full of, running over with, profuse.

wear, *v.* **1.** dress in, don, put on, slip into *or* on, get into, step into; display, show off, parade, flaunt, flourish, *Inf.* sport; bear, carry, exhibit, show, manifest, evince, reveal; assume, adopt.

2. impair, deteriorate, degenerate, worsen, canker, spoil; damage, harm, hurt, injure, ravage, ruin, destroy; corrode, fret, gnaw, eat out *or* away, consume, devour.

3. abrade, rub, rub down, chafe, fray, *Inf.* frazzle; file, grind, whet, sand, sandpaper, pumice; grate, rasp, scour, scrape, excoriate; erode, wash away, waste away, wear down *or* away; channel, gutter, groove, rut, furrow; waste, spend, use up; diminish, lessen, dwindle, shrink, decrease, reduce; abate, subside, ebb, wane.

4. fatigue, fatigate, tire, weary, overweary; bore, jade, exasperate, irritate, irk, vex, annoy; tax, overtax, strain, burden, overburden, overload, overtask, overwork, overwear; debilitate, enfeeble, weaken, enervate, sap, drain; deplete, wear out, exhaust, prostrate.

5. (*all of time*) pass, kill, wile away, dawdle away, piddle away, idle away.

6. last, endure, hold up, survive, continue, perdure, prove durable.

—*n.* **7.** donning, wearing; use, usefulness, utility, utilization, exercise, employment; adhibition, application, appliance, service, serviceability, serviceableness.

8. clothing, clothes, wearables, garments, garb, dress, costume; apparel, attire, *Both Chiefly Literary.* raiment, vestments; habiliment, habit.

9. deterioration, wear and tear, wearing, wearing down *or* away, wasting away, atrophy, degeneration; worsening, depreciation, dilapidation, decomposition; abrasion, friction, rubbing down, chafing, fraying, grating, rasping, grinding, whetting, filing, scouring, scraping, excoriation; corrosion, gnawing, eating out *or* away, consumption; erosion, detrition, attrition, diminution, diminishing, dwindling, lessening, decrease, reduction.

weariness, *n.* fatigue, tiredness, exhaustion; drowsiness, heaviness, sleepiness; lassitude, lethargy, languor, listlessness, sluggishness; debility, enervation, prostration; ennui, boredom, tedium.

wearisome, *adj.* **1.** wearying, tiring, fatiguing; exhausting, back-breaking, difficult.

2. boring, tedious, monotonous, humdrum, repetitious, routine, unvaried; dull, flat, dead, bland, insipid, *Sl.* blah, *Sl.* ho-hum, *Sl.* nothing; uninteresting, uninspiring, unexciting, dry, dry-as-dust.

weary, *adj.* **1.** tired, fatigued, worn-out, wearied, *Sl.* pooped, *Inf.* tuckered out, *Inf.* bushed; fagged, fagged out, played out, burned out, wiped out, spent; exhausted, *Sl.* dead, dead on one's feet, dead tired, *Inf.* dog-tired, all tired out; overtired, done in, all in, ready to drop, *Sl.* shot, *Sl.* beat; run-down, washed-out.

2. bored, world-weary, life-weary, jaded, hardened, inured; blasé, indifferent, uninterested, listless, lethargic, spiritless.

weasel, *v.* *Often* **weasel out** get out of, *Inf.* worm out of, sneak out of, shuffle out of, *Sl.* sleaze out of; evade, get by *or* around, avoid, dodge, duck, fudge; hedge, fence, not commit oneself, equivocate, double-talk, waffle, beat around the bush, skirt the issue, not give a straight answer, hem and haw, beg the question.

weasel-worded, *adj.* evasive, hedging, mealy-mouthed, noncommital, equivocal, ambiguous, vague; indirect, circuitous, roundabout, circumlocutory, periphrastic; misleading, deceiving, deceptive, tricky, full of small *or* fine print, catchy; subtle, oversubtle, sophistical, casuistic, casuistical; elusive, smooth, clever, slippery, shifty, dodgy.

weather, *n.* **1.** atmospheric conditions, temperature, *Inf.* temp, relative humidity, barometric pressure; climate, *Literary.* clime.

2. strong *or* heavy wind, windstorm, blow, gale, hurricane; storm, thunderstorm, rainstorm, snowstorm.

3. **under the weather** *Informal.* **a.** ill, ailing, sick, *Inf.* nauseous, nauseated, sick to one's stomach, queasy. **b.** crapulous, crapulent, *Sl.* hung-over.

4. dry, season, expose to the elements.

5. discolor, bleach; disintegrate, deteriorate, crumble, fall apart, rot *or* rot out, rust *or* rust out, *Chem.* oxidize.

6. bear up against, endure, stand, withstand, resist; surmount, rise above, overcome, get the better of; weather *or* ride out the storm, keep one's head above water, *Inf.* tough it out, *Inf.* hang in there; come through, pull through, survive, live through, make it back alive *or* in one piece, come back safe and sound; make it, come through with flying colors, land on one's feet.

weatherman, *n.* meteorologist, climatologist, weather prophet, forecaster *or* weather forecaster.

weather vane, *n.* **1.** weathercock, cock, wind vane, vane.

2. barometer, indicator, pointer, indicant, predictor, forecaster; indication, sign, omen, augury, token; herald, forerunner, harbinger; hint, clue, idea.

weave, *v.* **1.** interlace, intertwine, interwind, lace, twine, interweave, interwork, work in *or* together; intertwist, twist together, entwist, entwine, braid, plait, plat; interknit, knit together, join, combine, interlink, interlock, engage, fit together; merge, dovetail, mesh, splice.

2. make *or* make up, create, compose, form, design, fabricate, construct, build.

3. zigzag, crisscross, go in and out; move from side to side, sway.

web, *n.* **1.** cobweb, spider's web, trap, snare, ensnarement, entrapment; mesh, net, network; interlacement, entwinement, intertwinement; lace, lattice, latticework, braiding.

—*v.* 2. envelop, cover, surround, enclose; snare, ensnare, entrap, trap, capture, catch, hook.

wed, *v.* 1. marry, wive, espouse, tie the knot, take the plunge, say one's vows, say "I do," walk down the aisle, become man and wife, *Sl.* splice, *Sl.* hitch up with, *Archaic.* husband; lead [s.o.] to the altar, walk [s.o.] down the aisle, give away; hook up, join in holy wedlock *or* matrimony, *Sl.* hitch.

2. mate, couple, partner, twin, pair up, match up; unite, join, bond, fuse, weld, glue, cohere, stick together, put together; yoke, bind, tie together; connect, link, chain; unify, bring *or* draw together, make close; associate, affiliate, ally; coalesce, league, club; team, band, herd, pool, merge.

3. combine, mix, commix, admix, conglomerate, agglomerate; amalgamate, blend, homogenize; compound, alloy, *Chem.* levigate, commingle, mingle, intermingle, intermix, lump together.

wedding, *n.* 1. marriage, nuptials, marriage *or* wedding ceremony, matrimony, holy matrimony, bridal, *Class Myth.* Nymphaea, spousals, espousals, (*among the ancient Romans*) confarreation; wedlock, holy wedlock, marital union *or* bond, nuptial tie *or* knot.

2. union, alliance, affiliation, association, merger, liaison, *Inf.* hook-up, *Sl.* tie-up; unification, incorporation, amalgamation, consolidation, integration.

weekly, *adj.* 1. hebdomadal, hebdomadary, *Fr. hebdomadaire, Ger. wöchentlich, Sp. semanal, It. settimanale.*

—*adv.* 2. by the week, once a week, every week, hebdomadally.

—*n.* 3. periodical, magazine, publication, newspaper.

weep, *v.* cry, shed tears, boohoo, sob; bawl, blubber, whimper, mewl, pule, whine, snivel; moan, wail, groan, keen, ululate; lament, mourn, bewail, bemoan, grieve.

weepy, *adj.* tearful, teary, lachrymose; close to tears, ready to cry *or* break down, on the verge of tears, with brimming *or* overflowing eyes; melting, giving way, ready to burst into tears, breaking down; weeping, crying, sobbing, blubbering, sniveling.

weigh, *v.* 1. put on the scales, try in the balance, balance, determine the heaviness of; *Inf.* tip the balance, *Inf.* tip the scales at; measure, gauge, quantify.

2. consider, contemplate, think over, turn over in one's mind, give thought to, mull over; ponder, *Archaic.* perpend, ruminate, cogitate, meditate on, brood over, muse on; deliberate, reflect upon, put one's mind to, give one's attention to, pay attention to, study, pore over, examine; think about, kick around, toy with, flirt with.

3. heed, mark, note, observe, take stock; bear in mind, take into account, factor in, take into consideration, keep in view.

4. have importance *or* consequence, carry weight, have influence, count, tell; be influential, work upon; bias, incline, persuade.

5. **weigh down a.** weight, load, load with, tax; encumber, cumber, hamper, handicap; strain, overload, overburden, overtax. **b.** burden, depress, trouble, distress, worry, torment, afflict, oppress; try, vex, perturb, disturb.

weight, *n.* 1. heaviness, heft, heftiness, weightiness, ponderousness, ponderosity, gravity; pounds, tonnage, pressure; mass, density, volume, size; bulk, bulkiness, largeness, bigness, amplitude.

2. load, burden, onus, cross, millstone, albatross; duty, charge, obligation, responsibility, tax; strain, encumbrance, impediment, hindrance, handicap; trouble, care, anxiety, worry; hardship, difficulty, affliction, oppression; trial, tribulation, ordeal; woe, grief, misery, sorrow, *Archaic.* bale.

3. importance, significance, consequence, matter, value, concern, *Archaic.* concernment; moment, weightiness, substance, greatness, magnitude, force; graveness, seriousness, solemnity; influence, power, force, strength, pressure; effect, impact, clout; sway, mastery, hold.

4. **carry weight** have importance *or* meaning, be significant; influence, affect, sway, bias, incline; act on, play on, work on, effect; move, impel, motivate, actuate; persuade, *Inf.* jawbone, rouse, arouse, instigate.

5. **pull one's weight** do one's fair share, do one's part, cooperate.

6. **throw one's weight around** swing one's weight, *Inf.* pull strings, *Inf.* pull rank, *Inf.* pull wires; *Sl.* be a big shot, *Inf.* boss [s.o.] around.

—*v.* 7. weight down, load, add weight to, tax. See **weigh** (*def.* **5a**).

8. bias, slant; handicap, give a handicap, make allowances.

weighty, *adj.* 1. heavy, hefty, bulky, substantial, dense, ample; big, large, huge, gigantic, titantic, enormous, massive, ponderous, prodigious, mammoth, mighty, colossal, immense; unwieldy, cumbrous, cumbersome, awkward, unmanageable.

2. troublesome, burdensome, onerous, oppressive, back-breaking; troubling, thorny, worrisome, worrying; vexatious, bothersome, pestering.

3. important, significant, portentous, of great import; consequential, of great consequence, critical, decisive; momentous, heavy, ponderous, pregnant, carrying great weight, of substance; grave, solemn, sober; crucial, urgent, emergent, exigent, pressing, importunate, imperative.

4. influential, persuasive, powerful, potent, *Literary.* puissant, forceful, forcible; effective, effectual, telling, cogent; controlling, leading, guiding.

weird, *adj.* 1. supernatural, preternatural, uncanny, unearthly, eerie, spooky, ghostly; cryptic, esoteric, arcane, occult, perdu; inexplicable, unexplainable, insolvable, unaccountable; puzzling, bewildering, perplexing, enigmatic, enigmatical, mystifying; mysterious, mystic, mystical, transcendental, cabalistic.

2. strange, bizarre, fantastic, fabulous, outlandish; phantasmagoric, nightmarish, Kafkaesque; irrational, mad, wild, crazy; odd, queer, eccentric, peculiar, freakish, grotesque.

welcome, *interj.* 1. greetings, salutations, hello, hullo, hi, hey *or* heigh, how are you, *Inf.* how ya doin, what's new.

—*n.* 2. greeting, salutation, salute, salaam, hail; hearty reception, *Inf.* glad hand, open door, welcome mat.

—*v.* 3. greet, address, salute, hail, flag, wave to, *Inf.* give [s.o.] the glad hand; nod to, smile at, wink at, tip the hat to, doff the cap to; shake hands, squeeze *or* pump the hand, *Sl.* press flesh.

4. receive, meet, usher in, show in, call in.

—*adj.* 5. agreeable, pleasing, to one's liking, to one's fancy, to one's taste, after one's own heart; refreshing, comfortable, enticing; gladly received.

welfare, *n.* 1. well-being, prosperity, happiness, felicity, health, good health, soundness, heartiness, vigor, *Archaic.* weal; well, success, fortune, good fortune, luck, good luck; prosperousness, affluence, wealth; comfort, contentment, satisfaction, ease, pleasure, gladness.

2. advantage, good, benefit, behoof, interest; profit, gain.

3. public assistance, financial aid, the dole; Social

Security, Medicare, Medicaid, food stamps; unemployment compensation, *Inf.* unemployment.

well[1], *adv.* **1.** prosperously, profitably, advantageously, beneficially; fortunately, happily, auspiciously.

2. commendably, worthily, laudably, meritoriously; excellently, superbly, splendidly, *Inf.* famously, in fine fashion, with flying colors.

3. satisfactorily, considerably, adequately; sufficiently, enough, O.K.

4. thoroughly, soundly, backwards and forwards, inside out; intimately, personally; carefully, conscientiously, attentively.

5. properly, correctly, rightly, suitably; civilly, nicely, politely.

6. undoubtedly, certainly, unquestionably; obviously, plainly, clearly.

—adj. **7.** healthy, sound, in fine fettle, fit, physically fit, in good health; fine, ruddy, vigorous, hale, hearty, hale and hearty, robust, bursting with health.

8. satisfactory, fine, acceptable, O.K.; prosperous, flourishing, thriving, palmy, successful; promising, bright, fortunate, auspicious.

well[2], *n.* **1.** spring, wellhead, headspring, springhead; fountainhead, fountain, fount, *Archaic.* font; wellspring, reservoir, source, mine; hotbed.

2. pit, shaft, crater, abyss, crevasse; depression, hollow, concavity.

—v. **3.** spring, gush, flow, stream, run, ooze, trickle; pour forth, issue, emanate; surge, swell, rush forth; spurt, spout, jet; flood, overflow, brim over, spill over *or* out; emit, send forth, eject.

well-balanced, *adj.* **1.** sensible, sane, rational, reasonable; prudent, judicious, circumspect, thoughtful; sober, moderate, cool, cool-headed, level-headed; sound, commonsense, commonsensical, practical, down-to-earth, realistic; intelligent, discerning, discriminating; (*both of personality*) well-adjusted, *Sl.* together.

2. symmetrical, well-proportioned, proportional, balanced; harmonious, concinnous, congruous; orderly, well-ordered, well-arranged, classic, apollonian; graceful, well-formed, well-made.

3. varied, diversified; motley, mixed, heterogeneous.

well-being, *n.* See **welfare** (*def.* **1**).

well-born, *adj.* highborn, aristocratic, patrician, blueblooded, silk-stocking; noble, gentle, genteel; royal, princely, kingly, titled.

well-bred, *adj.* **1.** well-brought-up, well-trained, well-mannered, well-behaved, highbred; polite, civil, mannerly, courteous; gracious, ladylike, ladyish, courtly, gentlemanly, gentlemanlike; debonair, charming, chivalrous, chivalric, gallant, cavalier.

2. refined, cultivated, polished, finished; elegant, graceful, *Scot.* genty, genteel, fine, delicate, exquisite; urbane, suave, sophisticated, cosmopolitan, worldly.

3. (*all of animals*) thoroughbred, pedigreed, purebred.

well-defined, *adj.* clear, clear-cut, unmistakable, conspicuous, salient, obvious, evident; defined, distinct, discernible, recognizable, well-marked, vivid, graphic; unhidden, undisguised, unconcealed; perceptible, distinguishable, visible, audible; sharp, clean, uncluttered, unblurred.

well-established, *adj.* **1.** fixed, set, rooted, grounded, ingrained, entrenched, inveterate; long-established, established, longstanding, of long standing, traditional; venerable, time-honored, hallowed, immemorial.

2. stable, steady, sound, sturdy; dependable, reliable, trustworthy.

3. chronic, habitual, confirmed, inured, hardened, hard-core, die-hard; unchangeable, immovable, incorrigible, irrevocable, irreversible.

well-groomed, *adj.* clean-cut, clean, spruce, dapper, smart, natty, trim, *Sl.* nifty; clean-shaven, smooth-shaven, manicured, combed, coiffured; well-dressed, chic, *Sl.* spiffy; primped up, prinked up, *Sl.* duded up; neat, meticulous, fastidious, without a hair out of place.

well-known, *adj.* **1.** familiar, known, common, everyday, household, usual, established; customary, conventional, traditional, wonted, habitual; commonplace, trite, stock, hackneyed.

2. famous, famed, renowned, celebrated, prominent, *Inf.* big-name *or* name; touted, big-time, popular, on everyone's lips; noted, notable, eminent, preeminent, illustrious, great; immortal, fabled, storied, legendary, historical.

well-nigh, *adv.* nearly, next to, just about. See **almost**.

well-off, *adj.* wealthy, rich, affluent, prosperous, moneyed, well-to-do. See **wealthy** (*def.* **1**).

well-thought-of, *adj.* esteemed, respected, admired, highly regarded; venerable, distinguished, honored, exalted, acclaimed; looked-up-to, revered, venerated; prized, valued, valuable.

welt, *n.* **1.** ridge, wale, lump, bump, *Inf.* goose egg; contusion, bruise, black-and-blue mark *or* spot; scar, mark.

2. blow, beating, *Sl.* sock, slap, *Inf.* whomp, bang, *Inf.* whack, smack, rap.

welter, *v.* **1.** roll, toss, tumble; heave, surge, swell, billow; wallow, writhe, tumble about.

2. be entangled *or* snarled, get snarled up, flounder, lose one's way, get bogged down, get mired, get over one's head.

—n. **3.** jumble, muddle, tangle, mishmash, hodgepodge; jigsaw puzzle, mosaic, pastiche, collage, patchwork, crazy quilt; clutter, mess, farrago, medley, gallimaufry, mixture, olio, potpourri.

4. commotion, stir, furor, hubbub, turmoil, tumultuousness, tumult, uproar, chaos, bedlam; upheaval, disorder, disturbance, confusion, disquiet; noise, clamor, clangor, racket, din, sound and fury; ferment, unrest, agitation, excitement; convulsion, paroxysm; storm, tempest, whirlwind, winds; outbreak, uprising, riot, brawling, wildness.

wench, *n.* **1.** peasant girl, country lass, woman rustic; working girl, maid, serving woman.

2. *Archaic.* strumpet, prostitute, harlot.

—v. **3.** womanize, whore, wanton, *Sl.* sleep around, lecher, *Sl.* letch.

wet, *adj.* **1.** dampened, damped, moistened; moist, damp; soaked, drenched, wringing wet, wet through, saturated; soppy, sopping, dripping, sodden, soggy.

2. misty, foggy, vaporous, dewy; drizzling, showery, rainy; pouring, monsoonal, raining cats and dogs.

3. watery, watered, aqueous; sloppy, spongy, muddy.

4. dank, humid, muggy, clammy, steamy, sweaty.

—n. **5.** moisture, dampness, water, wetness, moistness; dew, seepage, condensation, steam, vapor.

6. rain, shower, cloudburst, downpour, deluge; mist, fog, drizzle, *Chiefly Dial.* mizzle.

—v. **7.** moisten, damp, humidify, dampen; soak, drench, saturate; splash, hose down, sprinkle, irrigate, water; wash, bathe; steep, ret, dip.

8. (*of animals and children*) urinate, *Sl.* pee, *Baby Talk.* peepee; void, egest.

whale, *n.* **1.** leviathan, cetacean, Moby Dick; white whale, beluga, blue whale, sulpher-bottom, sperm whale, finback, rorqual, humpback; sea monster.

2. *Slang.* enormity, colossus, titan, giant, mammoth, *Inf.* jumbo.

wharf, *n.* pier, quay, dock, dockage, landing, marina, basin, (*in the Far East*) bund; jetty, jutty, mole, breakwater.

wheedle, *v.* coax, cajole, beguile, charm, inveigle; persuade, win over, palaver, induce, move, influence; invite, lure, entice, wile; encourage, urge, entreat, importune, implore; blandish, flatter, *Inf.* sweet-talk, *Inf.* soft-soap, butter up, *Inf.* butter, *Inf.* honey up; humor, jolly, pamper, pander to, cater to, truckle to, mollify, appease; fawn on, play up to, curry favor with, court.

wheel, *n.* **1.** circular frame, disk, round, roundlet, roundel, circle; ring, band, hoop, cordon, annulus; caster, roller; cylinder, drum; trolley.

2. *Informal.* bicycle, cycle, *Inf.* bike, tricycle, velocipede, unicycle, tandem.

3. turn, movement, rotation, revolution; gyration, circumvolution, circumgyration, circumrotation; circuit, circulation; gyre, roll, reel, turbination; twirl, whirl, spin, whirligig, pirouette.

—v. **4.** turn, rotate, spin, revolve, trundle; swivel, pivot, caracole; reel, circumvolve, circumrotate, gyre; gyrate, circle, whirl, circumduct; swirl, eddy, circulate, move in circles, go round.

5. roll, trundle, push, move, convey.

6. *Often* **wheel about** *or* **around** turn around, turn about, turn on one's heels; veer around, swing around, make a U-turn, *Sl.* pop *or* bang a U-ie; reverse.

whereabouts, *n.* vicinity, vicinage, environs, purlieus, neighborhood, area; location, site, place, position, situation, locale, locality; spot, point, latitude and longitude.

whereas, *conj.* because, since, as, inasmuch as, forasmuch as; due to the fact that, in view of the fact that, it being the case that, seeing that, considering that; while on the contrary, while, although, though, even though.

wherewithal, *n.* means, supplies, resources, reserves, funds; money, cash, dollars, *Sl.* bucks, *Sl.* dough, *Sl.* bread, *Sl.* loot, *Sl.* gelt, lucre, *Sl.* moolah, *Sl.* spondulicks, *Sl.* mazuma; price, price of the ticket; ability, talent, competence, essentials, goods, *Sl.* meal ticket.

whet, *v.* **1.** sharpen, point, hone, strop, edge, put an edge on, taper; grind, mill, stone, file, rasp; smooth, abrade, rub, scrape.

2. stimulate, acuminate, awaken, arouse, rouse, stir; quicken, energize, inspire, kindle, fire; titillate, excite, fillip, prick, spur; tempt, appeal to, allure, provoke, incite, instigate.

—n. **3.** sharpening, pointing, honing, stropping, tapering; grinding, whetting, milling, stoning, file, filing, rasp, rasping, smoothing, abrasion, abrading, rub, rubbing, scrape, scraping.

4. stimulation, stimulating, acumination, acuminating, awakening, arousing, rousing, stirring; quickening, energizing, inspiring, kindling; titillation, titillating, exciting, prick, pricking, spur, spurring; tempting, appealing to, allurement, alluring.

5. stimulus, stimulant, stimulator, fillip, spur; tempter, allurement, incentive; provocation, incitement, instigator; appetizer, hors d'oeuvre, canapé, *Hawaiian.* pupu.

whiff, *n.* **1.** puff, whiffet, breath, breeze, stir, movement; gust, blast, blow.

2. trace, sniff, hint, soupçon, suspicion; slight odor *or* scent *or* aroma.

3. pop, snap, flicker, sputter, crackle, shot, spark.

—v. **4.** puff, blow, waft, breeze.

5. sniff, inhale, smoke, drag, draw, pull, (*of drugs*) snort; gulp, gasp.

while, *n.* **1.** period, spell, time, interval, space of time, space; meantime.

—conj. **2.** during the time, in the meantime, at the time, when; as long as, *Chiefly Brit.* whilst.

3. although, though, albeit, even if *or* though, notwithstanding; inasmuch as, because, since.

—v. **4.** idle, loll, loaf, lounge, laze, nod; dillydally, loiter, *Inf.* lallygag.

whim, *n.* **1.** notion, fancy, chimera, crank, caprice, crotchet, *Archaic.* maggot; weird idea, crazy notion, *Sl.* kooky notion; impulse, *Inf.* brain wave, *Inf.* brainstorm, inspiration, great idea; desire, yearning, wish, dream; craze, obsession, passion; inclination, bent, mind.

2. whimsy, whimsicality, humor, frivolity; eccentricity, *Sl.* kookiness, *Sl.* nuttiness; capriciousness, fickleness, erraticism, volatility; quirk of mind, oddness, twist.

whimper, *v.* cry, sniffle, snuffle, snivel, pule, choke up; tear, sob, weep, blubber, boohoo; whine, moan, groan, wail, keen.

whimsical, *adj.* **1.** capricious, notional, fanciful, impulsive; freakish, weird, *Sl.* nutty, *Sl.* kooky, eccentric, peculiar; prankish, pixyish, mischievous, playful; humorous, absurd, funny, laughable, preposterous, extravagant.

2. erratic, fitful, fluctuating, wavering; flighty, frivolous, fickle, changeable, vacillating, mutable, volatile, mercurial; unpredictable; inconsistent, inconstant, unstable, unsteady.

whine, *v.* **1.** whimper, moan, sniffle, cry. See **whimper**.

2. complain, grumble, crab, *Inf.* gripe, *Sl.* grouse, *Sl.* bellyache; nag, *Sl.* kvetch, *Inf.* yammer, cavil, carp, *Inf.* nitpick, criticize; fret, fume, fuss, raise a fuss, *Sl.* kick, *Sl.* squawk, *Sl.* beef, *Sl.* bitch; lament, bewail, deplore, sigh, throw up one's hands; find fault, pick holes in, be dissatisfied.

—n. **3.** moan, groan, wail, whimper, lament; complaint, grumble, *Inf.* gripe, peeve; disapproval, dissatisfaction, objection, criticism, cavil, quibble; *All Sl.* squawk, bellyache, beef, stink.

whip, *v.* **1.** lash, switch, birch, scourge, flog, flagellate; horsewhip, cowhide, curry, strap, flail, *Sl.* belt; spank, thrash, thresh, *Inf.* trim, *Inf.* lace, *Inf.* tan [s.o.'s] hide, *Inf.* whale, *Inf.* whale the tar out of, *Brit. Dial.* yerk; strike, hit, smite, thwack, smack, slap, swat, *Inf.* whack, *Dial.* hit [s.o.] upside the head, *Inf.* lambaste, *Inf.* thump; beat, buffet, pummel, cuff, knock, punch, punch out, box, sandbag, *Inf.* wallop, *Inf.* clout, *Inf.* slug, *Sl.* knock around *or* about, *Sl.* bop, *Sl.* whomp, *Scot. and North Eng.* paik, *Australian.* ding, *Scot.* dunt; *Sl.* lay into, *Sl.* give it to, *Sl.* give [s.o.] what for, *Sl.* let [s.o.] have it, *Sl.* give [s.o.] the business, *Sl.* give [s.o.] the works, *Sl.* work [s.o.] over, give [s.o.] a going-over.

2. drive, push, propel, hound; prick, poke, stick, rowel, spur, prompt, prod; provoke, instigate, incite, actuate; foment, agitate, excite, arouse, rouse, whip up, work up, stir up, wind up, enflame, fire up, kindle, touch off; encourage, urge, egg on.

3. punish, castigate, correct, discipline, teach [s.o.] a lesson, teach [s.o.] right from wrong, teach [s.o.] how to behave, *Sl.* show [s.o.]; chastise, berate, scold, chide, tongue-lash, rate, harangue, upbraid, objurgate, excoriate, fulminate against; criticize, reproach, rebuke, reprove, *Inf.* jump on, *Inf.* dress down, *Inf.* slam, *Sl.* jump all over, *Sl.* chew out, *Inf.* bawl out, *Sl.* strafe.

4. *Informal.* beat, defeat, top, outdo, outstrip, *Inf.* lick, *Inf.* get the better of, *Sl.* beat out; overcome, overthrow, overpower, conquer, prevail over, master, subdue, quell, thwart, check, stop, stop [s.o.] dead in his tracks, bring to a halt; trounce, *Sl.* shellac, *Sl.*

cream, *Sl.* pulverize, *Sl.* skunk; crush, trample, quash, destroy, do for, *Sl.* do in.

5. *Often* **whip out** pull, yank, yerk, whisk, flick; show, display, exhibit, present.

6. *Often* **whip into** go into, move into; begin, start, turn on.

7. *Usu.* **whip around, into,** *or* **off** whisk, flit, bustle, scurry, scramble, hurry, rush, *Inf.* hustle; tear, rip, dart, dash, rampage, zoom, *Inf.* zip; speed, sprint, race, run, hie, fly, shoot, bolt, whiz, *Inf.* go like lightning *or* the wind *or* the dickens *or* a house afire; scoot, scud, scuttle, make tracks, flee, *Inf.* skedaddle.

—n. **8.** lash, knout, scourge, flagellum, bullwhip, cat-o'-nine-tails, cat, cowhide, rawhide, quirt, *U.S.* blacksnake.

9. lash, swat, whack, thwack, swipe, slap, *Inf.* lick, *Sl.* zinger, *Sl.* smackeroo; strike, stroke, hit, buffet, cuff, knock, blow, *Inf.* wallop, *Inf.* sock, *Inf.* whop; stroke, motion, move, fell swoop.

whipping, *n.* lashing, birching, switching, flogging, scourging, flagellation, strapping, *Inf.* lacing, *Inf.* trimming, *Sl.* belting; spanking, thrashing, threshing, thrash, *Inf.* tanning, *Inf.* whacking; smack, smacking, slap, slapping, swat; beating, battering, pounding, pummeling, pelting, *Sl.* pasting, *Sl.* the business, *Sl.* the works, going-over, *Sl.* what for; chastisement, punishment, disciplining, correction, medicine.

whirl, *v.* **1.** spin, gyrate, reel, rotate, pivot, pirouette, twirl, twiddle, swivel; turn, revolve, wheel, roll, somersault, flip-flop; wheel around, swing around, turn around, about-face, do a 180°; circle, circumvolve, circumrotate.

—n. **2.** rotation, spin, gyration, pivot, pirouette, twirl; turn, somersault, roll, flip-flop; revolution, circuit, circumgyration, circumrotation, round, lap, ambit, orbit, full circle *or* cycle, 360°; turn, about-face, 180°.

3. round, series, cycle, chain, sequence, succession, progression, train, string, set, bunch, cluster, *Sl.* whole slew; whirlwind, flurry, flutter, rush.

4. fling, stab, shot, crack, go, try, attempt, essay; trial, trial run, testing, tryout, chance, opportunity, break.

5. whirlpool, maelstrom, swirl, gurge, eddy; vortex, whirlwind, dust devil, dust whirl; tornado, twister, cyclone, typhoon, simoom, samiel; whirlabout, whirligig, gyroscope, top, propeller, whirling dervish; merry-go-round, carousel.

whirlpool, *n.* vortex, maelstrom, gurge, swirl, whirl; eddy, countercurrent, counterflow, undercurrent, undertow.

whiskey, *n.* alcohol, liquor, spirits, *Inf.* booze, *Sl.* hard stuff; rye, Scotch, bourbon; corn, corn liquor, sour mash; moonshine, shine, home brew, *Sl.* sneaky pete; mountain dew, John Barleycorn, little brown jug, *Scot.* barley-bree; tiger milk, *Inf.* firewater, *U.S.* redeye, *All Sl.* rotgut, blue-ruin, hooch, sauce, juice, medicine.

whisper, *v.* **1.** murmur, breathe, sigh, *Literary.* suspire; mutter, mumble; sibilate, hiss, rustle, sough; buzz, hum, drone.

2. divulge, disclose, reveal; intimate, hint, insinuate; rumor, bruit, tell, breathe a word, blab, gossip, *Inf.* open one's mouth.

—n. **3.** undertone, hushed tones, *Inf.* hiss-hiss; murmur, sigh, suspiration, sibilation, sibilance, hiss; rustle, rustling, swishing, swish, susurrus, susurration; drone, buzz, hum.

whit, *n.* particle, bit, jot, tittle, iota; mite, speck, smidgen, *Inf.* smitch, spot, dot, dab; hair, shaving, paring, moit, sliver; morsel, crumb, grain; little, touch, trifle, hint, tinge, tincture; shadow, trace, suggestion, suspicion; scintilla, spark, twinkle.

white, *adj.* **1.** snowy, snow-white, niveous, ivory, creamy; milky, milk-white, opalescent, opaline, pearly, nacreous; marble, marmoreal; chalky, chalk-white, cretaceous; whitish, albescent; white-hot, candent.

2. light-skinned, Caucasoid, Caucasian.

3. pallid, pale, peaked, wan, ashen; pasty, sallow, waxen; sickly, faint, drained, bloodless, anemic; ghastly, deathlike, cadaverous.

4. colorless, lackluster, dull, dingy, dun, hueless, *Optics.* achromatic; bland, nondescript, vanilla, insipid; uncolorful, ordinary, *Sl.* blah.

5. silvery, gray, smoky, hoary, *Rare.* hoar, gray-haired, white-haired, (*of plants*) canescent; grizzled, grizzly.

6. pure, unsullied, unstained, stainless, spotless; immaculate, virtuous, undefiled, chaste, innocent, virginal.

whiten, *v.* **1.** blanch, bleach, pale, gray, wash out; etiolate, achromatize, decolor, decolorize; dim, fade, cloud, grow dull, lose luster *or* brightness.

2. blench, go white, pale, grow pale, become pallid, *Archaic.* wan; droop, flag, sag, faint, sink to the floor, *Inf.* pass out, swoon, black out, *Inf.* keel over.

whitewash, *v.* **1.** calcimine, whiten, *Archaic.* white; paint over, coat, cover.

2. cover up, gild, color, varnish, gloss over, smooth over, veneer; sweeten, sugar-coat, candy-coat, dulcify; lighten, soften, lessen, diminish, moderate, temper, qualify; palliate, extenuate, minimize, make light of, soft-pedal, tone down, play down, downplay; justify, excuse, rationalize, apologize for, make allowances for.

whiz, *v.* **1.** whir, burr, hum, buzz, hiss, whistle; rustle, swish; fizzle, sizzle.

2. rush, race, tear, fly, fly on the wings of the wind, outstrip the wind, zoom, *Inf.* zip; whisk, flit, shoot, dart, skim; scurry, scud, scuttle, scamper.

whole, *adj.* **1.** entire, full, total, plenary, integral, complete, round, aggregate; comprehensive, universal, inclusive, all-inclusive, all-embracing; extensive, extended, widespread; full, filled, pregnant.

2. solid, unbroken, unsevered, uncut, unshorn, unshortened, unabridged, all in one, unitary; undivided, indiscrete, indivisible, undividable, indiscerptible, inseparable; undiminished, unlessened, unreduced, unabated.

3. sound, indissoluble, intact, hale, hearty, in one piece; healthy, vigorous, robust, strong, recovered, well; unimpaired, undamaged, unharmed, uninjured, unscathed, unmutilated, undecayed, inviolate; pure, unmixed, unmingled, unblended, unalloyed; faultless, flawless, defectless; unblemished, spotless, unspotted, stainless, taintless, untainted, unsullied, unsoiled.

4. self-contained, self-supporting, autonomous, independent; well-rounded, all-sided, fully realized, consummate, enlightened.

5. thorough, thoroughgoing, exhaustive, in-depth, A to Z, *Brit.* A to Zed, *Brit. Dial.* gradely; absolute, dyed-in-the-wool, full-fledged, complete; utter, gross, rank, sheer, radical, sweeping; outright, downright, out-and-out, straight-out, all-out, across-the-board; unqualified, unmodified, uncompromised, unconditional, unconditioned, unreserved, unmitigated; unrestricted, unlimited, unhampered, unimpeded, unbounded; unequivocal, clear, unambiguous, explicit, express.

6. out of whole cloth fictitious, untrue, false, unreal, fanciful; imaginary, imagined, invented, improvised, created, feigned, fabricated.

—n. **7.** aggregate, collective, ensemble, *Fr. tout ensemble*, assemblage, unit; all, alpha and omega, beginning and end, length and breadth; entire amount,

sum total, gross amount.

8. totality, fullness, universality, integrity, wholeness. See **wholeness** (*def.* **1**).

9. as a whole a. all together, in a body, en masse. **b.** all in all, in the main, all things included, all things considered, altogether.

10. on *or* **upon the whole** in general, as a rule, usually, as a whole.

wholehearted, *adj.* hearty, warm-hearted, cordial, affectionate, open, unreserved; sincere, genuine, real, heartfelt; earnest, fervent, fervid, serious, dedicated, devoted, resolute, single-hearted, single-minded; enthusiastic, eager, zealous, ardent, energetic, spirited, high-spirited.

wholeness, *n.* **1.** completeness, totality, allness, entirety, entireness; comprehensiveness, universality, *Rare.* omnitude, inclusiveness; integrity, integrality, fullness, plenitude; undividedness, indivisibility; thoroughness, utterness, absoluteness; clearness, explicitness.

2. intactness, soundness, solidarity, solidity; haleness, heartiness, healthiness, vigorousness, robustness, strongness; faultlessness, flawlessness, pureness, innocence, chasteness.

3. self-containedness, autonomy, independence; consummation, enlightenment.

wholesome, *adj.* **1.** salutary, salubrious, salutiferous, healthful, hygienic, sanitary; beneficial, helpful, healing, strengthening, *Med.* roborant; good, good for one, nutritious, nourishing, health-giving; invigorating, bracing, stimulating, refreshing, tonic.

2. healthy, fit, sound, in good condition, in fine fettle, *Inf.* in the pink, *Brit. Dial.* bonny; well, in good health; ruddy, vigorous, full of vigor, hale, hearty, hale and hearty, robust, lusty, strong and healthy.

3. clean-cut, all-American, *Sl.* straight, square, goody-goody.

wholly, *adv.* **1.** entirely, all, completely, purely; totally, stone, perfectly, plenarily, fully; comprehensively, universally, inclusively; aggregately, collectively; as a whole, in all, all in all, in the main, *Latin. in toto*; lock, stock, and barrel; *Inf.* hook, line, and sinker; bag and baggage; nothing short of, 100%, every whit, every inch, to the nth degree; in a body, en masse, all together.

2. thoroughly, from the ground up, to a nicety, extensively, throughout; through and through, backward and forward; in all respects, in every respect, from first to last, from head to foot, cap-a-pie, from top to toe, from A to Z, *Brit.* from A to Zed; utterly, grossly, root and branch, quite, absolutely, altogether; fundamentally, actually, really, truly, verily, essentially, radically; unqualifiedly, unconditionally, unmitigatedly, unreservedly; enthusiastically, heart and soul, whole hog, *Sl.* all the way, *Sl.* like mad, *Sl.* like crazy.

3. unequivocally, positively, clearly, unambiguously, explicitly, expressly; categorically, flatly, downright, out-and-out, outright, all-out, straight-out.

whoop, *n.* **1.** cry, outcry, scream, shout, yell, shriek, *Inf.* holler; bellow, roar, squall, war cry, hoot, battle cry; hallo, halloo, tallyho, *Fox Hunting.* huic, screech, squeal, caterwaul, yelp, bark, yammer, yap; vociferation, ejaculation, exclamation, clamor, hue and cry; cheer, hurrah, huzzah, bravo, rah.

—*v.* **2.** cry, yell, shout, bellow, roar, *Inf.* holler; scream, shriek, screech, squeal, yelp, bark, yap, yammer; howl, yowl, bawl, yawp, caterwaul; cheer, hurrah, rah, hollo, halloo, tallyho, *Fox Hunting.* huic; clamor, raise the hue and cry, cry out, sing out, vociferate, exclaim, ejaculate, call out.

3. whoop it up *Slang.* celebrate, raise Cain, *Sl.* raise hell, *Sl.* raise the roof; let go, let loose, kick up one's heels, make merry, roister, revel; jump up and down, carry on, *Brit. Inf.* maffick, raise a din, kick up dust, raise a hullabaloo, make a racket, make an uproar.

whore, *n.* **1.** hussy, slut, demirep, cocotte, demimondaine, loose woman, fallen woman, wanton, tramp, vamp, white slave, *Sl.* bitch, *Sl.* broad, *Sl.* chippy; harlot, woman of ill repute, prostitute, lady of the evening, woman of the profession, Mrs. Warren, *Fr. fille de joie*; trollop, strumpet, *Archaic.* wench, trull, drab, quean, painted woman, woman of the streets, streetwalker, bar girl, call girl, Cyprian, *All Sl.* cat, tart, hustler, bim, moll, hooker, floozie, working girl, *Brit. Sl.* bird, *Mexican Sl.* caliente.

2. madam, bawd, procuress, pander.

3. paramour, courtesan, mistress, concubine, kept woman, *Sl.* doxy.

4. temptress, siren, seductress, *Fr. femme fatale*; Jezebel, Delilah; flirt, coquette, minx; adventuress, hetaera.

—*v.* **5.** wench, womanize, wanton, *Sl.* sleep around, lecher, *Sl.* letch.

whoremonger, *n.* **1.** libertine, debauchee, dissipater, *Inf.* rip; profligate, rake, rakehell, roué; lecher, *Sl.* letch, satyr, *Pathol.* satyromaniac; voluptuary, sensualist, sybarite, hedonist; reprobate, degenerate, pervert, sadist, masochist; womanizer, wencher, playboy, gigolo, *Sl.* stud, *Sl.* tomcat.

2. pander, procurer, pimp, go-between, *U.S. Sl.* sweetman.

whorl, *n.* spiral, *Bot., Zool.* verticil, coil, curl, helix, volute; convolution, volution, corkscrew, whirl, vortex; circumvolution, roll, ringlet, curlicue; scallop, escallop, twist, twirl, swirl.

wicked, *adj.* **1.** evil, sinful, peccable, iniquitous, wrong, *Archaic.* facinorous, *Obs.* scelerous; bad, base, vile, gross, low, mean, odious, obnoxious; black-hearted, villainous, sinister, ignoble; nefarious, flagitious, heinous, infamous, *Rare.* nefast; dark, black, dire, grim, dreadful; execrable, abominable, horrible, horrid, hideous, gruesome, monstrous, atrocious.

2. abhorrent, loathsome, hateful, detestable, despicable; opprobrious, disgraceful, shameful, dishonorable, ignominious; criminal, reprehensible, blameworthy, guilty; felonious, lawless, illicit, unlawful, illegal, knavish, rascally, blackguardly, dastardly; unregenerate, unrepentant, incorrigible, perverted, perverse.

3. unholy, impious, impure, ungodly, godless, profane; unhallowed, unblest, unsanctified, unconsecrated; sacrilegious, blasphemous, irreligious, irreverent, unrighteous, unprincipled; damnable, diabolic, diabolical, devilish, demonic, demoniac, demoniacal, cacodemonic; satanic, Mephistophelian, fiendish, ghoulish, infernal, hellish, accursed.

4. immoral, dissolute, dissipated, abandoned, profligate, reprobate; debauched, debased, degenerate, corrupt, depraved, evil-minded; lewd, lecherous, lascivious, lustful, libidinous, licentious, *Archaic.* lickerish; salacious, prurient, carnal, wanton, unchaste; concupiscent, promiscuous, incestuous, adulterous, sodomitical, pederastic; bestial, satyric, ruttish; obscene, indecent, scatological, smutty, pornographic; bawdy, ribald, coarse, unseemly, filthy, vulgar, crude.

5. revolting, repulsive, repugnant, foul, rotten; nauseous, nauseating, offensive, outrageous; pestilential, pernicious, deleterious, baneful, pestiferous, noxious, baleful; fell, menacing, malicious, malignant, malign; maleficent, malefic, malevolent.

6. impish, mischievous, elfish, prankish; vexatious, troublesome, naughty, annoying.

7. severe, harsh, grave; awful, formidable, dire; bitter, biting, racking, tearing, gnawing.

8. ill-natured, ill-tempered, cantankerous, crabby,

crabbed, sour, crusty; morose, sulky, surly, churlish, sullen; irascible, irritable, petulant, cross, testy.

9. dangerous, perilous, hazardous, treacherous, unsafe; risky, chancy.

10. *Slang.* masterly, expert, skillful, proficient; deft, adept, adroit, dexterous; excellent, superior, superlative, admirable, outstanding.

wickedness, *n.* **1.** iniquity, evil, vice, improbity, sin, sinfulness, deviltry, ungodliness, godlessness; irreverence, impiety, irreligiousness; nefariousness, flagitiousness, heinousness; vileness, viciousness, badness, baseness, foulness, meanness; opprobrium, ignominy, disgrace, infamy; atrocity, outrage, abomination, enormity; crime, malefaction, wrongdoing, feloniousness, lawlessness; unregeneracy, impenitence, incorribility; maleficence, malignancy; malevolence, malignity, rancor, maliciousness; perfidy, treachery, foul play; villainy, knavery, rascality, delinquency.

2. depravity, turpitude, degradation, degeneracy, corruption, pollution; profligacy, reprobacy, reprobateness, immorality, obliquity; immodesty, impudicity, indecency; debauchery, lewdness, lasciviousness, licentiousness, lust, lustfulness, *Archaic.* venery; salacity, salaciousness, prurience, wantonness, carnality; unchastity, promiscuity, concupiscence; perversity, bestiality; obscenity, profanity, *Archaic.* bawdry, ribaldry, vulgarity.

wide, *adj.* **1.** broad, extensive, expansive, expanded, distended; large, beamy, hippy, thick, hippopotamic; outspread, spread out, splay; broad-beamed, broad-sterned, massive, broad-ribbed; ample, capacious, roomy, spacious, commodious; full, outstretched, extended, open to the full extent.

2. vast, immense, far-reaching, sweeping; amplitudinous, voluminous, large; large-scale, far-ranging, wide-ranging, widespread, diffuse, wide-stretching; latitudinarian, catholic, encyclopedic, all-embracing, comprehensive, ecumenical, composite; of great scope, general, compendious, inclusive.

—adv. **3.** astray, aside, off, away, abroad, afield; wide of the mark, off course, off the track, off the right path.

wide-awake, *adj.* **1.** fully awake, open-eyed, up and about, up.

2. watchful, vigilant, alert, observant, on the lookout; aware, wary, on the job, attentive; sleepless, unblinking, unsleeping, unnodding; keen, astute, sharp, quick, smart, bright; clear-witted, quick-witted, nimble, alive, *Inf.* on one's toes, *Sl.* on the ball.

widen, *v.* broaden, expand, extend, distend, spread *or* spread out, splay; stretch, heighten, lengthen, elongate; enlarge, make greater *or* bigger *or* larger, aggrandize, *Chiefly Literary.* greaten; increase, augment, add to, supplement.

widget, *n.* gadget, device, hickey; *All Inf.* contraption, whachamacallit, thingumajig, thingumabob, thing, doohickey, do-hinkey, dingus, doodad, gismo, fandangle, *Australian.* doover.

width, *n.* **1.** breadth, wideness, broadness, thickness; diameter, radius, caliber, bore; stretch, spread, reach, span; section, piece.

2. extent, magnitude, measure, degree, quantity, amount, fullness; capacity, gauge, volume, proportions, dimensions, size; scope, range, reach, compass, swing, sweep.

3. expanse, space, extension, expansion; spaciousness, extensiveness, amplitude, vastness, immensity, largeness, roominess.

wield, *v.* **1.** exercise, use, utilize, make use of, employ; hold, have, control, handle, manipulate, manage.
2. raise, lift, hold up, flash; brandish, flourish, wave, swing, shake.

wife, *n.* mate, spouse, consort, helpmate, helpmeet, soul mate, *Sl. Facetious.* better half; bride, wedded wife, woman, lady, rib, squaw, *Inf.* missis, *Inf.* old lady, *Inf.* the little woman, woman *or* lady of the house.

wig, *n.* peruke, periwig, powdered wig, Georgian wig, *Brit. Inf.* jasey; partial wig, toupee, *Sl.* rug, *Sl.* carpet, hairpiece, fall, switch; false hair, merkin.

wiggle, *v.* **1.** wriggle, move from side to side, move around, squirm, writhe, twist; wiggle *or* move one's hips, swivel one's hips, shake, shimmy, (*both in dance*) grind, bump and grind.

2. wobble, waggle, shake, quiver, move, jerk, twitch.

wild, *adj.* **1.** undomesticated, untamed, feral, ferine, (*of animals*) *Law.* ferae naturae, unbroken; uncultivated, native, natural.

2. uninhabited, empty, barren, waste; desolate, forsaken, godforsaken, isolated, lifeless; unsettled, unvisited, unfrequented.

3. uncivilized, barbarous, barbarian, unenlightened, primitive; uncultured, unrefined, unpolished; uncouth, coarse, vulgar, raffish; churlish, loutish, brutish, savage, gross; ignorant, unlearned, untrained, untaught, uneducated; clumsy, gauche, unmannerly.

4. violent, furious, forceful, mighty, strong; stormy, tempestuous, turbulent, rampageous; explosive, volcanic, dangerous, perilous, dreadful; devastating, wasting, ravaging; destructive, ruinous, disastrous, catastrophic.

5. frantic, frenzied, hysterical, at one's wit's end; distraught, distracted, *Inf.* in a dither, *Inf.* in a tizzy, upset, extremely agitated; furious, in a furor, beside oneself, out of control, delirious; berserk, *Offensive.* Asiatic, crazy, insane, crazed, mad, stark raving mad, unglued, unhinged, maniac, maniacal; raving, raging, rabid, foaming at the mouth; uncontrollable, ungovernable, like a wild bull.

6. undisciplined, unruly, disobedient, misbehaving; unmanageable, intractable, uncontrollable; rebellious, mutinous, lawless; rough, rough-and-tumble, rowdy, rowdyish, boisterous, noisy; tumultuous, riotous, uproarious, turbulent.

7. unrestrained, unbridled, untrammeled; uncurbed, unmuzzled, unimpeded, unshackled, unfettered; unchecked, unsuppressed, unconstrained, unrestricted.

8. morally loose, wanton, licentious, debauched, dissipated, dissolute, profligate, promiscuous; indecent, immoral, improper; intemperate, immoderate, incontinent.

9. imprudent, impracticable, exceeding the bounds of reason, careless, reckless, madcap; extravagant, unreasonable, outrageous, preposterous; foolhardy, headlong, hazardous; rash, hot-headed, brash, unwary, unguarded.

10. disorderly, disordered, deranged; untidy, messy, disheveled, *Inf.* mussed up, messed up, ruffled up, rumpled, tousled, *Chiefly Scot. Dial.* toused; unkempt, slovenly, sloppy, shoddy; at sixes and sevens, muddled, hugger-mugger.

11. *Informal.* enthusiastic, eager, *Inf.* up for, *Inf.* hog-wild, *U.S. Sl.* ape, psyched, excited, looking forward to.

12. **run wild a.** grow unchecked, grow every which way. **b.** run riot, go on a rampage, go berserk, cut loose, create a disturbance, make a commotion, *Inf.* raise a rumpus.

13. *Often* **wilds** wilderness, desert, the wild. See **wilderness.**

wilderness, *n.* **1.** wasteland, waste, wild *or* wilds, desert, tundra, barrens, no man's land; emptiness, vastness, expanse.

2. forest, woods, woodland, timberland; unexplored *or* uncharted territory; undeveloped land.

3. bewilderment, maze, labyrinth, confusion; tangle, snarl, jumble, jungle, muddle, disorder; combination, mixture, miscellany, mélange, conglomeration, hodgepodge.

wile, *n.* **1.** artifice, stratagem, contrivance, device, subterfuge, expedient; trick, ruse, snare, trap; maneuver, move; scheme, plot, plan, design, *Inf.* game *or* little game; machinations.

2. wiles cunning, craft, slyness, foxiness, artfulness, wiliness, guile, subtlety, shrewdness.

3. chicanery, trickery, jobbery, *Inf.* hanky-panky; deception, deceit, duplicity, fraud, double-dealing.

will, *n.* **1.** volition, choice, option; free will, discretion; intent, intention, *Psychol.* conation.

2. wish, desire, velleity; preference, disposition, inclination, mind, fancy; pleasure, taste.

3. purpose, purposefulness, determination, determinedness, resolve, resolution, firmness, firmness of purpose, decision, will power; commitment, total commitment, earnestness, seriousness, single-mindedness; iron will, moral fiber, grit, sand, pluck, mettle, *Inf.* backbone, *Inf.* spunk, *Sl.* moxie.

4. *Law.* testament, last will and testament.

5. at will **a.** at one's pleasure, at one's discretion, ad libitum, ad lib; as one wishes, as one thinks best, in one's own way. **b.** at one's disposal, at one's command, at one's service, at one's beck and call.

—*v.* **6.** determine, cause, effect, bring about, impose one's will; ordain, decree, enjoin; order, command, dictate, prescribe.

7. decide, choose to, have a mind to, see fit, think fit, think best; resolve, settle, purpose, make up one's mind.

8. bequeath, devise, leave, settle upon; hand down, pass down.

willful, *adj.* **1.** deliberate, intentional, intended; premeditated, prepense, planned, calculated; voluntary, volitional, discretional, unforced, self-determined.

2. obstinate, stubborn, stubborn as a mule, mulish, pigheaded, bullheaded; obdurate, intransigent, inflexible, adamant, unyielding, uncompromising; contrary, perverse, pervicacious, wrong-headed, wayward, self-willed.

willing, *adj.* **1.** inclined, disposed, minded, of a mind, in the mood, *Archaic.* fain; ready, *Inf.* game, desirous, well-disposed; nothing loath, unreluctant, unaverse, ungrudging.

2. enthusiastic, eager, avid, agog, all agog; impatient, anxious, burning to, dying to; content, happy, pleased, *Sl.* psyched; ready and willing, prompt, quick.

3. compliant, agreeable, favorable, cooperative; acquiescent, agreeing, consenting, assenting; amenable, docile, tractable; obedient, dutiful.

willingly, *adv.* freely, of one's own free will, of one's own accord, by choice, voluntarily, spontaneously; cheerfully, happily, gladly, with pleasure; unreluctantly, ungrudgingly, without hesitation, nothing loath; agreeably, compliantly, favorably, *Archaic.* fain; readily, quickly, promptly, *Inf.* at the drop of a hat; enthusiastically, eagerly, avidly, with relish, with zest.

willingness, *n.* eagerness, enthusiasm, avidity; promptness, readiness, quickness, *Inf.* gameness, alacrity; desirousness, good will, favorableness; fervor, fervidity, zeal.

willowy, *adj.* lithe, lithesome, *Archaic.* lithy, lissome, supple, limber, flexible, flexile, pliant, ductile, fictile, bendable; loose-limbed, loose; gracile, slender, svelte, sylphic, sylphlike; slim, reedy, thin, stalky, twiggy, skinny, nothing but skin and bones; lanky, lean, long-limbed, long-legged; graceful, fluent, fluid, smooth, easy, facile.

wilt, *v.* wither, become limp, lose freshness, droop, sag, bend, flop, slump, sink, drop, dip, lean over *or* down, hang down *or* low, bow, nod, stoop, slouch; weaken, lose strength *or* energy, languish, *Dial.* dwine, flag, fade, faint, melt; shrivel, shrink, dry up *or* out, loose moisture; dwindle, ebb, fade away *or* out, fall off, melt away, diminish, lessen, lower, decline, fall; fail, deteriorate, degenerate, waste away, atrophy; molder, decay, rot.

wily, *adj.* **1.** cunning, crafty, artful, sly, subtle, foxy, *Sl.* crazy like a fox, *Scot. and North Eng.* pawky; shrewd, astute, canny, sharp, knowing, *Inf.* cagey.

2. shifty, slippery, slick, smooth, tricky, fast; insidious, guileful, disingenuous, scheming, plotting, designing, calculating, contriving; deceitful, crooked, dishonest, underhanded, left-handed, *Inf.* shady; treacherous, perfidious, false, false-hearted, double-dealing, *Inf.* two-timing, two-faced, Janus-faced.

win, *v.* **1.** finish first, come out first, come out ahead, take, sweep; triumph, conquer, vanquish, prevail over, succeed, carry the day, gain the prize; overwhelm, overcome, overpower, subdue; score a success, gain a victory, take by storm, walk away with, waltz off with, *Inf.* bring home the bacon, carry off the palm, *Inf.* win out, carry.

2. gain, get, reach, touch, make; score, earn, pull down, catch, take, capture; acquire, obtain, procure, secure; achieve, attain, *Inf.* nail down, net, bag, sack; reap, harvest, come into, come by, collect, glean; accomplish, realize, effect; pick up, reclaim, recover.

3. win over persuade, convert, convince, induce, influence, sway; predispose, incline, bring, carry, lead; bring around, draw over, gain, prevail upon; talk into, *Inf.* sell, *Sl.* hook, *Sl.* twist [s.o.'s] arm.

—*n.* **4.** victory, winning, triumph, success, conquest; mastery, subdual, vanquishment, besting.

wince, *v.* flinch, start, blench, quail, startle, shrink; recoil, cringe, blink, draw back, *Inf.* funk; grimace, writhe, squirm, shudder, shiver, quiver, quake; tremble, shy, fight shy of, falter, boggle, stickle.

wind¹, *n.* **1.** air, breeze, zephyr, stream of air, current of air, draft; puff, breath of air, wiffet, sough; inflow, indraft, inspiration, inrush; waft, gentle wind, light air, sea breeze, *Naut.* cat's-paw.

2. gust, blast, squall, gale, flurry, flaw, windflaw, blow; northeaster, nor'easter, northwester, nor'wester, southeaster, sou'easter, southwester, sou'wester; east wind, west wind, levanter, levanto, gregale, mistral, kite-wind, bise; trade wind, doldrums, prevailing wind; tempest, storm, equinoctial, hurricane, typhoon, williwaw; snowstorm, blizzard, snow squall; sirocco, *Sp. leveche*, dust storm, sandstorm, haboob; cyclone, tornado, *Australian.* willy-willy, twister, *Sp. baguio*, whirlwind, eddy.

3. flatulence, flatus, flatuosity, gas; crepitation, *Sl., Vulgar.* fart, *Med.* borborygmus, windiness.

4. empty talk, babble, claptrap, hot air, twaddle, *Sl.* bull, humbug; swagger, boasting, brag, fustian, rodomontade, braggadocio; nonsense, balderdash, falderal, stuff and nonsense, twiddle-twaddle; hogwash, *Inf.* rot, *Sl.* baloney, *Inf.* flapdoodle, *Inf.* hooey; blabber, *Inf.* gibble-gabble, prattle, gibberish.

5. hint, intimation, suggestion, insinuation, inkling; innuendo, information, intelligence, report, news, notice.

wind², *v.* **1.** bend, turn, curve, swerve, loop, crook, hook; meander, zigzag, change course, deviate, warp; tack, heel, yaw, slew, haul, jibe, cast, break, veer, swing; twist and turn, contort, snake, worm, convolute, flow around; wander, rove, *Chiefly Scot.* wimple, wend.

2. coil, curl, round, wreathe, twine, whirl, twirl, swirl, corkscrew; convolve, twist, involve, roll, reel, whorl; scallop, intwist, intort, sinuate, kink, crimp.

3. wind up a. crank, hoist up, turn, set, cock, prepare. **b.** conclude, bring to an end, end, finish up, get done, terminate; round off, top off, close up, get through, put the finishing touches on, resolve. **c.** excite, stir up, fluster, flurry, agitate; perturb, ruffle, disconcert, discompose.

windfall, *n.* unexpected gain, piece of good luck *or* fortune, stroke of fortune, godsend, manna from heaven, boon, blessing, treasure-trove; bonanza, prize, jackpot, strike, hit.

winding, *n.* **1.** twist, tortuosity, meander, curvature, undulation, wave; coil, whorl, sinuosity, anfractuosity, convolution, labyrinth, maze; turn, flexure, incurvation, U-turn, horseshoe, *U.S.* oxbow; hook, crook, angle, corner, dogleg; bend, curve, swerve, slue, slew; veer, warp, bias, sweep, sheer, yaw, tack; deflection.

2. coiling, twisting; folding, wrapping, tying, roping.

—adj. **3.** sinuous, anfractuous, turning, twisting, coiling, twining; serpentine, snaky, tortuous, vermiculate; circuitous, meandering, indirect; roundabout, ambagious, flexuous, curvy, curved; spiral, spiraling, circling, convoluted, volute, coiled; twisted, crooked, bent; mazy, mazelike, labyrinthine.

window, *n.* opening, aperture, ventilator, *Scot.* winnock, *Archit.* fenestra, *Archit.* fenestella; casement, dormer, oriel, bay window, transom, fanlight, lattice, skylight; porthole, port, bull's-eye; (*all of fortification*) embrasure, loophole, crenal.

windup, *n.* end, close, finish, completion, finale, conclusion, terminus, termination, *Inf.* payoff; climax, culmination, consummation, denouement, resolution; epilogue, *Music.* postlude; end *or* final result, outcome, final event *or* scene, last act, bitter end, finis, curtain, final curtain, *Sl.* curtains, lights out, catastrophe.

windy, *adj.* **1.** breezy, blowy, blowing, blustery, blusterous; drafty, gusty, gusting, blasty, flawy; stormy, squallish, cyclonic, turbulent, tempestuous, violent.

2. unsubstantial, empty, worthless, useless, meaningless, senseless.

3. verbose, wordy, prolix, loquacious, long-winded, longiloquent, multiloquent, multiloquous, voluble, effusive, fluent; talkative, glib, long-tongued, mouthy, *Inf.* big-mouthed, *Sl.* all jaw, *Sl.* gassy; magniloquent, grandiloquent, orotund, bombastic, bombastical, high-flown.

wing, *n.* **1.** pinion, pennon, ala, *Fr. aile*; pataguim; *Inf.* arm.

2. appendage, attachment, sidepiece; extension, ell, addition, annex.

3. flying, flight, volitation.

4. on the wing flying, in flight, in the air.

5. under one's wing under one's protection *or* care *or* patronage, sheltered, cloistered, protected.

—v. **6.** (*all in the wing or arm*) hit, hurt, harm, injure, wound, disable, cripple.

7. fly, glide, soar, travel through the air.

8. wing it *Slang.* improvise, extemporize, play it by ear, ad-lib.

winged, *adj.* **1.** alar, alate, alated; winglike, wing-shaped, pterygoid.

2. swift, quick, fast, fleet, fleet afoot, speedy; rapid, tantivy, hurried, hasty, express, expeditious; eagle-winged, quick as lightening, swift as an arrow, faster than a speeding bullet.

3. elevated, lofty, high, soaring; inspired, inspirational, inspirative, inspiring; exalted, grand, glorious, noble, sublime.

4. (*all of the wing or arm*) hit, hurt, harmed, injured, wounded, disabled, crippled.

wink, *v.* **1.** nictitate, blink.

2. twinkle, shine, sparkle, glitter, glimmer, glint, glisten, *Archaic.* glister; scintillate, coruscate, gleam, flash, fulgurate.

3. wink at ignore, overlook, shut one's eyes to, disregard, pretend not to notice, tolerate, put up with; condone, let [s.t.] go, let [s.t.] ride, let [s.t.] slide, let [s.t.] pass.

—n. **4.** nictitation, blink; tic.

5. twinkle, sparkle, glitter, glint, glimmer, glisten, *Archaic.* glister; scintillation, coruscation, gleam, flash, fulguration.

6. bit, iota, jot, whit, particle.

7. hint, signal, sign, *Inf.* high sign; *Inf.* glad eye, *Sl.* come-on.

winner, *n.* **1.** victor, champion, *Inf.* champ, world champion, *Inf.* number one; pennant winner, prize winner; bearer of the palm, wearer of the laurel.

2. *Slang. Sl.* humdinger, *Inf.* beaut, *Sl.* lulu, *Sl.* lollapalooza, *Inf.* dilly, *Sl.* doosy, *Inf.* ripsnorter, *Sl.* corker, *Sl.* pip; *Sl.* something, *Sl.* something else *or* something else again, *Sl.* hot stuff, *Inf.* knockout; *Sl.* daisy, *Inf.* dandy, *Inf.* honey, *Sl.* dream.

winning, *n.* **1.** win, victory, triumph, success. See **win** (*def.* **4**).

2. winnings velvet, booty, spoils, prize money.

—adj. **3.** victorious, conquering, triumphant, exultant, jubilant, on top, successful; undefeated, unbeaten.

4. charming, engaging, pleasing, attractive, winsome. See **winsome.**

winnow, *v.* **1.** sift, strain, sieve, riddle, bolt, filter, screen, pan, rack; separate, differentiate, distinguish, divide, part; sort out, weed out, separate the men from the boys *or* the sheep from the goats *or* the wheat from the chaff, thresh; select, choose, pick, cull.

2. drive *or* drive away, blow *or* blow away; blow upon, fan.

winsome, *adj.* winning, engaging, taking, charming; pleasing, delightful, delectable, enjoyable; sweet, agreeable, likable; lovely, pretty, fair, handsome, prepossessing, beautiful, exquisite; graceful, elegant, refined.

wintry, *adj.* **1.** hibernal, hiemal, brumal; cold, freezing, frigid, ice-cold, shiveringly cold; icy, frosty, snowy; arctic, glacial, hyperboreal, Siberian; inclement, stormy, blizzardly, windy; bitter, nippy, sharp, piercing, biting, cutting, brisk; severe, rigorous, hard, cruel.

2. bleak, desolate, stark; cheerless, gloomy, dismal, dreary, depressing; discouraging, unpromising, somber, melancholy; dark, gray, overcast, sullen, lowering.

wipe, *v.* **1.** rub, stroke, swipe; clean, cleanse, scrub, swab, mop; scour, smooth; dry.

2. wipe out destroy, demolish, raze, rub out; obliterate, erase, blot out, eradicate, eliminate, exterminate; extinguish, annihilate, extirpate; rub into the ground, trample; do away with, send to kingdom come; beat, trounce, vanquish.

wiry, *adj.* **1.** stiff, rigid, bristly, prickly, stubby, thorny.

2. lean and sinewy, strong, powerful, tough, muscular; hard, hardened, in fighting shape, in trim; spare, lank, without an ounce of fat, all muscle.

wisdom, *n.* **1.** sagacity, sageness, sapience, penetration, perceptiveness, discernment; sound judgment, clear thinking, clearheadedness, common sense, rationality; understanding, intelligence, brains, *Inf.* gray matter, *Sl.* smarts; judiciousness, judgment, perspicacity, perspicaciousness, acumen; reason, sense, *Inf.* horse sense, astuteness, perspicuity; intellectuality, prescience, depth, reach of thought, wit, mother wit; long-headedness, shrewdness, foresight, providence, prudence.

2. learning, erudition, knowledge, enlightenment; scholarship, education, attainment.

wise[1], *adj.* **1.** sagacious, sage, intelligent, discerning, penetrating, perceptive; perspicacious, percipient, insightful, sapient, long-headed, shrewd; smart, rational, reasonable, gash, judicious, politic, prudent, discreet, commonsensical; sensible, sound, sane, well-balanced, balanced; bright, brilliant, sharp-witted, quick-witted, competent, capable; gifted, talented, well-endowed, brainy, sapiential.

2. educated, learned, enlightened, instructed, well-schooled; well-read, versed, knowledgeable, erudite; philosophical, Solomonic, pansophic, deep, profound; knowing, lettered, scholarly, deep-thinking, bookish.

3. *Slang.* informed, *Sl.* hip, *Sl.* hep, *Sl.* in the know, knowing, up on; posted, briefed, instructed, up-to-date, *Fr. au courant.*

4. advisable, well-advised, expedient, politic; fit, seeming, proper, meet, decorous; judicious, commendable, desirable, fitting, befitting; strategic, safe, diplomatic, calculated, careful, tactful, well-thought-out.

5. *Slang.* impudent, insolent, impertinent, saucy, fresh, pert; disrespectful, rude, *Inf.* smart, *Inf.* smart-alecky, *Inf.* cocky, *Dial.* sassy.

wise[2], *n.* way, manner, fashion, mode, method, procedure, course; approach, attack, technique.

wiseacre, *n.* smart aleck, wise guy, *Sl.* smartie, *Sl.* smartie pants, wisenheimer, know-it-all, *Sl.* wise ass, *Sl.* smart ass; witling, *Sl.* punk, wise fool.

wise man, *n.* sage, philosopher, philosophe, scholar, savant, pundit, learned man; Solomon, Solon, *Hinduism.* rishi, *Class Myth.* Nestor; oracle, authority, expert; venerable, wise old man, rabbi, pantologist, theorist; guru, mandarin, mahatma, thinker, doctor; elder statesman, elder, luminary, *Archaic.* illuminate.

wish, *v.* **1.** desire, long for, desiderate, want; yearn for, hope for, care for, pine for, sigh for; hanker after, have a yen for, covet, fancy, have a fancy for; have an eye to, be attracted to, have a mind to, have at heart, be bent upon; be inclined towards, be prone to, be predisposed towards, prefer; aspire to, set one's heart on; crave, hunger, thirst, relish; burn for, *Inf.* be wild *or* mad about, *Sl.* have the hots for, *Inf.* letch after.

—n. **2.** desire, longing, wishing, desideration, want, wanting; yearning, hope, hoping, pining, sighing; hankering, *Inf.* yen, *Sl.* itch, fondness, liking, fancy; eagerness, ardor, craving, keenness. avidity, passion; appetency, appetite, thirst, hunger; predilection, inclination, preference, predisposal, predisposition, bent, leaning, disposition; mind, will, whim.

wishful, *adj.* desirous, desiring, longing, yearning, hankering, desiderative; wishing, pining, hoping, hopeful, in hopes, expectant, anticipative, anticipatory, optimistic.

wishy-washy, *adj.* **1.** weak, thin, watery, runny, watered-down, diluted, cut, stretched, attenuated, (*of liquor*) *Scot.* shilpit; pappy, paplike, milk-and-water, soppy, sodden; insipid, jejune, pallid, *Sl.* nothing, *Sl.* blah; bland, tasteless, flavorless, flat, stale, dead, *Fr. fade.*

2. irresolute, shilly-shallying, tergiversating, indecisive, noncommittal; vacillating, fluctuating, going back and forth, blowing hot and cold, sitting on *or* straddling the fence; off-again on-again, wavering, of mixed feelings; unsettled, uncertain, undecided, of two minds; edging, mealy-mouthed, weasel-worded; spineless, milquetoast, weak-kneed, white-livered.

wistful, *adj.* **1.** melancholy, yearning, longing, desirous, wishful; sorrowful, sad, heartsick, forlorn, woeful, woebegone, disconsolate, dismal, triste; sulky, moody, gloomy, glum, somber, sullen; dispirited, cheerless, joyless.

2. pensive, dreaming, dreamy, dreamful, in a reverie; daydreaming, in a trance, absent-minded; thoughtful, thinking, absorbed, immersed, engrossed, lost in thought, preoccupied, bemused, *Archaic.* museful; contemplative, contemplating, introspective, meditative, meditating, musing, pondering, reflective; ruminative, ruminant, ruminating, brooding, serious, in a brown study.

wit[1], *n.* **1.** humor, facetiousness, drollery, funniness, wittiness, cleverness, piquancy, quickness; jocularity, waggishness.

2. badinage, persiflage, repartee, quip, wisecrack, saying, sarcasm; irony, satire, burlesque, parody, caricature, travesty; witticism, Atticism, bon mot, jest, jocosity, joke; pun, wordplay, play on words, spoonerism, double entendre; raillery, banter, joshing; buffoonery, playfulness.

3. humorist, lampoonist, parodist; jokester, joker, comic, comedian, comedienne, slapstick artist, *Fr. farceur,* droll fellow, funny person, *Both Inf.* card, character; wag, reparteeist, banterer, *Inf.* wisecracker, punster; zany, madcap, *Inf.* cutup, antic; mummer, mimer, mimic.

4. intelligence, brains, braininess, *Sl.* smarts; sagacity, sageness, wisdom, sapience, sapiency; acumen, discernment, perspicacity, penetration; perception, percipience, insight; astuteness, shrewdness, savvy, keenness, long-headedness, hard-headedness, common sense; ingenuity, cleverness, aptness, quickness; brilliance, acuity, sharpness.

wit[2], **to wit** namely, *Latin. videlicit,* viz.; that is to say, that is, *Latin. id est,* i.e.; specifically, explicitly, scilicet; for example, for instance, as a case in point, as an illustration.

witch, *n.* **1.** sorceress, hex, enchantress, *Archaic.* wight, Circe; dowser, diviner, pythoness, sibyl; prophetess, soothsayer, fortuneteller, seer, clairvoyant, medium.

2. hag, crone, beldam, *Sl.* old bat; fury, battle-ax, fishwife, gorgon, harridan, ogress; hellcat, harpy, shrew, virago, vixen, nag, *Sl.* bitch, Xanthippe.

witchcraft, *n.* **1.** sorcery, magic, sortilege; necromancy, black magic, black art, thaumaturgy, theurgy, wonder-working, wizardry; voodoo, hoodoo, obi; deviltry, demonolatry, diabolism, Satanism; supernaturalism, shamanism, psychomancy, occultism, spiritualism; apotropaism, fetishism, magical ceremony, incantation, conjuration.

2. magical influence, witchery, spell, hex; fascination, charm, allure, enticement, captivation; enchantment, entrancement, enravishment; appeal, attraction, draw, pull, magnetism.

withdraw, *v.* **1.** draw back *or* in, pull back *or* in, retract, abduce, *Physiol.* abduct, *Dentistry.* retrude; shrink back, recoil, start; take back, take off, recall; remove, subtract; move back, retire, recede, ebb, retrocede.

2. recant, disavow, unsay, disclaim, *Inf.* eat *or* swallow one's words; renege, back down *or* out of, bow out, bail out, pull out of, *Inf.* back away from *or* off on, *Inf.* cop out, *Sl.* fink out; back-pedal, shift one's ground, *Inf.* flip-flop, about-face, do an about-face, change one's mind, tergiversate; apostatize, defect.

3. revoke, annul, disannul, nullify, void, declare null and void, cancel; rescind, repeal, dissolve, abolish, abrogate; reverse, override, overrule, set aside, quash, countermand, counterorder.

4. go apart, isolate oneself, secede, separate oneself; (*all through drugs*) *Sl.* freak out, tune out, turn off; rusticate, hibernate, estivate; leave, depart, decamp, take off, go off, go away, exit, take one's leave.

5. retreat, pull out, fall *or* draw back, give way, lose ground, take flight, flee, beat a retreat.

6. abdicate, resign; surrender, yield, hand over; bow out, drop out.

7. *Often* **withdraw from** (*usu. of drugs*) abandon, give up, forgo, do *or* go without, stop using, quit, quit cold, go cold turkey, take the cure.

withdrawal, *n.* **1.** departure, leaving, going away, setting out *or* off; takeoff, embarkation, sailing; exit, leave, parting, separation; leave-taking, farewell, adieu, good-by, congé.

2. flight, escape, running off *or* away, *Sl.* splitting; pullout, retreat, retirement, removal, evacuation, withdrawment, countermarch.

3. recession, retrocession; reversion, regression, retrogression, retrogradation; secession, separation, severance.

4. resignation, abandonment, forsaking, abdication, relinquishment; defection, apostasy; yielding, surrender, bowing out, dropping out.

5. privacy, seclusion, sequestration; solitude, isolation, concealment, obscurity, reclusion, exile, anchoritism, monasticism; *All Inf.* copping out, tuning out, turning off.

6. retraction, retractation, disavowal, recantation, unsaying, taking back; renunciation, (*usu. under oath*) abjuration.

7. revocation, annulment, disannulment, nullification, voidance, cancellation; rescission, repeal, dissolution, abolishment, abrogation.

8. *Drug Culture.* deprivation, absence, lack, want, need; delirium tremens, *Inf.* the d.t.'s, trembling, tremors, the shakes; perspiration, sweating, cold sweat, the sweats; depression, dejection, despondency.

withdrawn, *adj.* **1.** retiring, shrinking, in a shell, *Inf.* introverted, distant, aloof, unapproachable, stand-offish, *Inf.* offish; shy, reserved, bashful, diffident, modest, timorous, timid, *Archaic.* verecund; reticent, taciturn, untalkative, uncommunicative, quiet, unsocial, unsociable, private, self-contained; modest, meek, self-conscious; unconfident, backward, apprehensive, fearful; solitary, reclusive, eremetic, eremitical, cenobitic.

2. recalled, called in, off the market, out of circulation.

wither, *v.* dry up *or* out, shrivel, shrivel up, wrinkle, pucker, buckle; shrink, contract, constrict, narrow; become limp, droop, sag; dwindle, fade away, fail. See also **wilt.**

withhold, *v.* **1.** hold back, restrain, curb, check, keep in check, arrest, contain; control, keep under control, harness, bridle, rein in, hold in, leash; restrict, fetter, shackle; confine, limit, cramp, constrain; hold in, bottle up, cork up, box up, shut up, seal; block, impede, inhibit, hinder, hamper, deter; detain, keep in, hold, stay; prohibit, forbid, disallow, interdict, prevent, suppress.

2. keep from, hide, conceal, bury, reserve, refrain from giving; keep secret, not disclose, *Sl.* clam up; censor, repress, keep back, *Inf.* pull punches, deny, abnegate; mask, cloak, secrete, veil, screen, shroud, camouflage, cover up; squelch, muzzle, muffle, mute, still, tone down, hush up, silence, quiet; smother, stifle, choke, gag.

within, *adv.* **1.** inside, interiorly, internally, inwardly.

2. indoors, within doors, in the house, under shelter, at home.

—prep. **3.** inside, in, enclosed by; into.

4. not farther than, in the compass of, not exceeding, not beyond, not extending past, no more than, not above.

5. in sight of, in reach of, in the bounds *or* limits of, in the field *or* sphere of.

without, *prep.* **1.** not with, with no, unaccompanied by; in the absence of, sans, lacking, short of, wanting, in want of, less, requiring; destitute of, deprived of, in need of.

2. free from, unburdened by, unencumbered by, not having, in default of; exclusive of, excluding, independent of; outside of, out of.

3. beyond, past, apart, away, out of range.

—adv. **4.** outside, externally, outwardly, exteriorly.

5. outdoors, out-of-doors, *Archaic.* withoutdoors; in the open air, in the fresh air, alfresco.

withstand, *v.* **1.** oppose, resist, offer resistance, stand up to, stand against, hold out against; defy, challenge, confront, breast, face, encounter; stand fast, stand firm, hold one's ground, hold the fort, stick to one's guns, show a bold front, show fight, put up a fight; stand off, thwart, impede, hold off, repulse, repel.

2. endure, stand, tolerate, bear; put up with, take, weather, brave.

witness, *n.* **1.** testimony, attestation, *Law.* deposition, statement, disclosure, evidence, testification; declaration, assertion, allegation; profession, word, affidavit, sworn statement; proof, facts, data.

2. testifier, *Law.* deponent, attestant.

3. eyewitness, looker-on, observer, viewer, spectator, onlooker; watcher, beholder, bystander, passer-by.

—v. **4.** testify, give testimony *or* evidence, depose, bear witness; speak, speak up, speak out; swear, vouch for, bear out, confirm, verify, substantiate.

5. attest, certify, endorse, warrant, certificate, document, circumstantiate.

6. attend, be present at; stand up for *or* with, sponsor.

7. see, observe, view, behold; notice, note, mark, take cognizance of, take in; look on, watch, follow, *Inf.* get a load of, *Inf.* get an eyeful of, *Sl.* check out.

witticism, *n.* **1.** witty remark, clever *or* bright saying, flash of wit, bon mot, *Sl.* one-liner, *Sl.* a good one; quip, jest, joke, *Sl.* gag; pun, play on words, conceit, crank, epigram; gibe, jab, poke, cut, fling, *Inf.* wisecrack, *Sl.* crack, *Sl.* shot, *Sl.* dig, *Sl.* zinger; sally, comeback, retort, answer, quick answer, riposte.

2. banter, *Inf.* josh, raillery, badinage, persiflage, repartee, wordplay, chaff, *Inf.* kidding, *Inf.* kidding back and forth.

witty, *adj.* clever, original, well-turned, scintillating; penetrating, sharp, quick, smart, bright; waggish, droll, amusing, humorous, piquant, salty, racy; comical, mirthful, gay; funny, full of fun, jolly, jocular, jocose; comic, farcical, *Sl.* smart-mouthed, *Sl.* wise.

wizard, *n.* **1.** sorcerer, necromancer, diabolist, demonologist, warlock, witch; magician, *Archaic.* mage, magus, Merlin, thaumaturgist, theurgist, enchanter, charmer; medicine man, witch doctor, obi doctor, root doctor, voodooist, voodoo, shaman;

dowser, geomancer, diviner; soothsayer, prophet, augur, oracle, seer, clairvoyant; exorcist, exorciser.

2. *Informal.* expert, adept, pundit, authority, master, virtuoso, *Inf.* whiz, *Sl.* crackerjack.

wizened, *adj.* withered, shriveled, shrunken, wrinkled, dried-up, dry, sere; wilted, faded, wasted; desiccated, dehydrated.

wobble, *v.* **1.** tip, tilt, lean, incline; teeter, seesaw, totter, rock, waggle, waddle; shake, tremble, dodder, quaver, quiver, quake; stagger, shuffle.

2. vacillate, waver, dither, fluctuate.

woe, *n.* **1.** misery, wretchedness, grief, anguish, agony of mind *or* spirit, bitterness, *Archaic.* bale; sorrow, sadness, infelicity, unhappiness, dolor, heartache, heartbreak, broken heart, broken-heartedness, heartsickness, heavy heart; desolation, bereavement, prostration, extremity, depths of misery; despair, disconsolateness, despondency, depression, gloom, melancholy, melancholia; anxiety, angst, worry, fret, solicitude, concern, cark, care; agony, torture, torment, pain.

2. trial, tribulation, ordeal, load, burden; trouble, adversity, misfortune, affliction, suffering, distress, oppression, mortification; blow, shock, stab, pang, throe; disaster, calamity, catastrophe.

woebegone, *adj.* **1.** miserable, wretched, woeful, *Archaic.* woesome, forlorn, *Obs.* baleful, heartsick, downhearted, broken-hearted, heartbroken, crushed, broken, desolate, despairing; worried, anxious, afflicted, stricken, heavy-laden; down, disconsolate, dejected, depressed, despondent, melancholic, gloomy, dismal, lugubrious, funereal; somber, glum, low-spirited, disheartened, discouraged, *Inf.* broken-up, *Inf.* cut-up, *Sl.* bummed-out *or* bummed; sad, unhappy, infelicitous, sorrowful, doleful, dolorous, dolorific, dreary, *Literary.* drear, grieved, mournful, tearful, teary; lachrymose, comfortless, joyless, cheerless.

2. downcast, cast down, crestfallen, chapfallen, hangdog, long-faced, down in the mouth.

woeful, *adj.* **1.** wretched, miserable, abject, *Archaic.* woesome, forlorn, *Obs.* baleful; bitter, dreary, *Literary.* drear, gloomy, harsh, severe, stark, oppressive, onerous; dreadful, grievous, tragic, ruinous, disastrous, calamitous, catastrophic; painful, excrutiating, racking; pitiful, pitiable, piteous, pathetic, pathetical, sorrowful, heartrending, heartbreaking; plaintive, sad, saddening, distressing, depressing, disheartening; lamentable, regrettable, deplorable, rueful.

2. down, disconsolate, dejected, depressed, despondent, melancholic, woebegone. See **woebegone** (*def.* **1**).

woman, *n.* **1.** female, she, lady, *Scot.* cummer, member of the gentle sex *or* fair sex; girl, maid, maiden, lass, lassie, miss, *Irish, Eng.* colleen; *Inf.* gal, *Inf.* petticoat, *Sl.* skirt, wench, *Sl.* dame, *Sl.* broad, *Sl.* chick, *Inf.* number, *Inf.* baggage; dowager, matron, spinster, old maid, hag, crone.

2. wife, spouse, mate, consort, helpmate, *Sl. Facetious.* better half. See **wife.**

3. beloved, darling, sweetie, sweetheart, ladylove, flame, inamorata, lover; mistress, paramour, courtesan, concubine, *Sl.* doxy, odalisque, kept woman.

4. female attendant, handmaiden, lady-in-waiting, abigail, maidservant, *Archaic.* ancilla; housekeeper, maid, chief maid, female servant, cleaning lady, *Inf.* help.

woman-hater, *n.* misogynist, *Psychiatry.* gynephobe.

womanhood, *n.* **1.** muliebrity, female maturity, matronhood, wifehood; femininity, feminineness, femineity, womanliness, wifeliness, matronliness.

2. women, womenfolk, the female sex, the fair sex, the gentle sex.

womanish, *adj.* **1.** womanly, womanlike, muliebral, ladylike. See **womanly.**

2. effeminate, emasculate, unmasculine, unmanly, unvirile; milksoppy, effete, weak; sissy, sissyish, *Sl.* faggy.

womanly, *adj.* womanlike, muliebral, gynecoid, feministic; mature, matronly, ladylike, refined, genteel; feminine, soft, delicate, gentle, tender, sympathetic, motherly.

womb, *n.* **1.** uterus, *Law.* venter, *Archaic.* matrix.

2. beginning, origin, source, starting point, place of issue; base, basis, foundation, derivation; wellspring, lifeblood, fount, fountain, fountainhead; seed, germ, taproot; family, house, line, lineage, stock, stem.

3. inside, interior, recess, recesses, penetralia, depth, depths; hold, cavity, vault.

wonder, *v.* **1.** muse, meditate, ponder, reflect, deliberate, cogitate, think about; speculate, conjecture, theorize; question, query, doubt; puzzle over.

2. marvel *or* marvel at, stare, gape, gawk, goggle, look *or* stand aghast *or* agog, not know what to make of [s.t.], rub one's eyes, not believe one's eyes *or* ears.

—*n.* **3.** phenomenon, marvel, wonderful thing, amazing thing, quite a thing, really something, *Sl.* phenom; miracle, prodigy; sight, spectacle, eye-opener, *Sl.* stunner, *Sl.* mind-boggler, *Sl.* mind-blower, *Sl.* trip; curiosity, nonesuch, gazingstock, *Brit. Dial.* gapeseed; rarity, nonpareil, one of a kind, one in a thousand; *All Inf.* one for the books, something to brag about, something to shout about, something to write home about.

4. surprise, astonishment, astoundment, amazement; awe, wonderment; bewilderment.

wonderful, *adj.* **1.** marvelous, extraordinary, phenomenal, prodigious, remarkable, *Australian.* bonzer; striking, awesome, awe-inspiring, wondrous; stupendous, amazing, astounding, astonishing, surprising; incredible, *Sl.* unreal, unbelievable, unheard-of, unprecedented.

2. fantastic, miraculous, fabulous, *Inf.* great, *Inf.* super, *Inf.* super-duper, *Sl.* tuff, *Sl.* bad, *Sl.* cool, *Inf.* dandy, *Inf.* jim-dandy; superb, splendid, magnificient, brilliant, dazzling, *Sl.* bang-up, *Inf.* smashing, *Brit. Sl.* ripping; excellent, first-rate, capital, *Inf.* tiptop, *Inf.* A-1, *Inf.* A number 1, first-class, classic.

wont, *n.* custom, convention, consuetude, observance, tradition; use, usage; habit, routine; practice, praxis, way.

wonted, *adj.* **1.** accustomed, habituated, used to, *Archaic.* wont; given to, in the habit of, addicted to, *Sl.* hooked on.

2. customary, conventional, familiar; usual, regular; habitual, routine.

woo, *v.* **1.** court, pay court to, make love to, serenade, *Inf.* spark, *Inf.* court and spark, *Sl.* hustle, *Sl.* make time, *Sl.* put *or* slap the make on, *Sl.* put a move on; pursue, chase, chase after, set one's cap for.

2. (*all in reference to consequences*) invite, incur, contract, bring down, bring on.

3. address, solicit, supplicate, petition, call upon, apply to, invoke; implore, entreat, beg, appeal to; importune, press, urge.

wood, *n.* **1.** timber, lumber; firewood, kindling, fuel.

2. *Usu.* **woods** forest, woodland, timberland, weald, wild, wilderness; grove, thicket, copse, *Chiefly Brit.* coppice, *Archaic.* holt, *Archaic.* bosk.

3. **out of the woods** secure, safe, safe and sound; out of danger, past the danger zone, out of harm's way *or* reach, in safety, in the clear, *Inf.* home free.

—*adj.* **4.** wooden. See **wooden** (*def.* **1**).

wooded, *adj.* forested, timbered; sylvan, arboreous, woodsy, bosky.

wooden, *adj.* **1.** wood, woody; ligneous, ligniform, xyloid.

2. stiff, *Inf.* stiff as a board, rigid; stolid, stodgy, stuffy; awkward, clumsy, ungainly, gauche.

3. dull, dull-witted, thick-witted, dim-witted, slow-witted, dim; obtuse, dense, *Inf.* thick; bovine, doltish, oafish; stupid, witless, *Inf.* dead from the neck up, *Inf.* dead between the ears.

4. expressionless, inexpressive, impassive; blank, empty, vacant; glassy; spiritless, unanimated, lifeless.

wooer, *n.* suitor, lover, admirer, secret admirer, infatuate, paramour; beau, swain, inamorato, gallant, *It. cicisbeo*; boyfriend, gentleman friend, *Inf.* steady, *Inf.* fellow, *Inf.* flame, *Brit. Inf.* follower.

wool, *n.* **1.** fleece; yarn.

2. all wool and a yard wide genuine, sincere, real, true, truehearted; faithful, constant, true-blue, *Inf.* trusty; good, excellent.

3. dyed-in-the-wool inveterate, confirmed, inured, hardened, hard-core, die-hard.

4. pull the wool over [s.o.] eyes trick, deceive, fool, hoodwink, humbug, bamboozle, put one over on, take in.

woolgathering, *n.* daydreaming, dreaming, castle-building, stargazing, *Inf.* mooning; absent-mindedness, absence of mind, inattentiveness; abstraction, abstractedness, preoccupation, distraction, engrossment, bemusement.

woolly, *adj.* **1.** lanate, lanose, flocculent, flocky, *Bot.* floccose.

2. hairy, pubescent, *Bot., Entomol.* tomentose, *Bot.* villous.

3. downy, fleecy, fleecelike, soft, smooth, lanuginose, velvety, velutinous; fluffy, feathery, furry, nappy, shaggy.

4. *Informal.* rough, rowdyish, coarse, unrefined, rugged, unpolished, rough-hewn; vigorous, spirited, robust, lusty, dynamic.

5. fuzzy, indistinct, unclear, ill-defined; confused, muddled, disorganized, chaotic.

word, *n.* **1.** term, name, expression; ideogram, hieroglyphic, *Linguistics.* morpheme, etymon; symbol, representation, sign.

2. words a. talk, speech, rambling, chatter, *Fr. bavardage,* chitchat, patter, babble. **b.** quarrel, spat, wrangle, argument, squabble, tiff, debate, angry discussion.

3. assurance, promise, pledge, solemn word, word of honor, parole; warrant, guarantee, guaranty; oath, vow; handshake.

4. news, tidings, report, communication, notice; communiqué, message, account, recital; information, data, facts, *Brit. Sl.* gen, intelligence; lowdown, *Sl.* info, *Sl.* poop, dirt, dope, inside story, *Sl.* scoop.

5. order, command, dictate, dictum, instruction, direction, directive, behest, ultimatum; commandment, will, prescript, prescription, ordainment; rule, law, edict, mandate, proclamation, pronunciamento; admonition, injunction, charge, exhortation, bidding.

6. the Word Scriptures, Holy Scripture, Bible, Holy Writ, Word of God; Gospel, Holy Gospel, gospel or message of Christ.

—*v.* **7.** express, phrase, put, say, utter; describe, designate, term, style.

word-for-word, *adj.* verbatim, *Fr. mot à mot,* line-for-line, literally, letter-for-letter, literatim, *Latin. verbatim et literatim;* exact, precise, accurate, close, faithful, honest, strict, undeviating; explicit, express, unambiguous, clear, unequivocal.

wordiness, *n.* verbosity, verbiage, loquacity, garrulity, talkativeness, prolixity, long-windedness; glibness, *Inf.* gabbiness, *Inf.* gift of gab, *Inf.* windiness, *Sl.* gassiness, *Sl.* big mouth; circumlocution, digressiveness, discursiveness, ambagiousness, circuitousness; repetitiveness, tautology, redundancy, padding, profuseness; running off at the mouth, diarrhea of the mouth, going on and on, talking nonstop, *Sl.* yackety-yak, *Sl.* gas, chatter.

wordplay, *n.* **1.** repartee, give-and-take, lively exchange, riposte, *Inf.* snappy comeback; quip, *Inf.* zinger, *Inf.* a good one; banter, badinage, persiflage; drollery, waggery, jest, *Inf.* kidding, *Inf.* kidding back and forth, *Inf.* joshing, *Sl.* funning around; witticism, bon mot.

2. pun, double entendre, equivoque, *Rhet.* paronomasia, *Fr. jeu de mots,* equivocation; anagram, acrostic, word square, crossword puzzle; spoonerism, malapropism, Irish bull, Pig Latin, macaronics; clerihew, limerick, patchwork verse; palindrome, pangram, rhopalic, univocalic, stinky pinky.

wordy, *adj.* verbose, loquacious, garrulous, talkative, prolix, voluble, *Inf.* big-mouthed, *Sl.* gassy, *Sl.* windy; chatty, *Inf.* gabby, babbling, jabbering, blabbering, blathering; long-winded, discursive, digressive, maundering; unsuccinct, unterse, rambling; pleonastic, redundant, tautological, repetitive; padded, protracted, spun out; droning, never-ending, interminable.

work, *n.* **1.** labor, toil, exertion, effort, endeavor, exercise; travail, drudgery, slavery, sweat, moil, grind; handwork, spadework, legwork; industry, diligence, trouble, pains; stress, strain, *Inf.* elbow grease; discipline, drill, workout, exercising, exercitation, training.

2. task, undertaking, job, stint, chore; duty, charge, assignment, commission, exercise, homework; errand, odd job, piece of work, mission, service, call.

3. employment, occupation, business, office, job, livelihood, vocation, profession; trade, handicraft, craft, line, art; field, métier, career, calling, walk of life; pursuit, function, role, position, capacity; situation, *Inf.* gig, station, place, post, engagement.

4. deed, performance, act, action, doing, function, working; operation, movement, maneuver, stunt, turn; exploit, feat, achievement, accomplishment, coup, move, stroke; transaction, enterprise, undertaking, production.

5. product, fruit, by-product, end product, creation, child, offspring; oeuvre, opus, opuscule, masterpiece, masterwork, *Fr. chef d'oeuvre, Latin. magnum opus*; invention, concoction, coinage, composition; artifact, handicraft, production, turnout; issue, harvest, outgrowth, effect, result, outcome.

6. works factory, plant, mill, foundry, shop, workshop, *Fr. usine;* assembly plant, manufactory, metalworks, steelworks, saltworks, waterworks; sawmill, flour mill, tannery, smithery, cannery, pottery, bindery, brewery, winery, refinery, armory, arsenal.

7. works working parts, inside parts, *Sl.* guts, insides, inner mechanisms, *Inf.* innards; internals, vitals, what makes a thing tick, viscera, belly, heart, bowels.

8. at work a. on the job, at the shop, working, on duty, walking one's beat. **b.** in action, in operation, in progress, on the fire, in force, in the works.

9. out of work unemployed, jobless, out of a job, disengaged, in the bread line, in the unemployment line; available, free, idle, at liberty.

—*v.* **10.** labor, toil, moil, drudge, grind, work

one's fingers to the bone; slave away, grub, sweat, peg away at, push oneself; exert oneself, be busy, be industrious, exercise, practice, make efforts; fag, work away at, strain oneself, keep trying, spare no effort, take pains; ply the oar, set one's shoulder to the wheel, *Inf.* knock oneself out, keep one's nose to the grindstone, *Sl.* kill oneself, struggle, *Sl.* beat one's brains out; do double duty, do one's utmost, do one's best, strain one's nerve, force oneself, *Inf.* plug away at; plod along, strive, contend, vie, endeavor.

11. be employed, earn one's livelihood, ply one's trade, occupy oneself with, have a job, hold down a job; follow a trade, do business, practice a profession.

12. operate, run, function, go, act, perform, *Inf.* fly; have effect, play, have influence; carry on, get on, move.

13. use, manage, ply, wield, handle, maneuver, manipulate; make go, conduct, deal with, drive, direct, steer; utilize, employ, turn to account, put to use, adhibit, bring into play; apply, treat, take care of, see to.

14. effect, accomplish, cause, make, do, bring about; produce, effectuate, realize, fulfill, attain; engender, beget, bring to effect, implement, put through, carry off, *Inf.* bring off, *Inf.* pull off; enact, execute, compass, discharge, dispatch, take care of.

15. influence, persuade, induce, sway, bend, turn, move; incline, predispose, affect, lead, bias; wear down, bend to one's will, make oneself felt, soften up.

16. **work in** put in, enter, insert, inject, interpose, introduce; edge in, wedge in, move in, foist in, worm in; implant, interpolate, interject, sandwich in, stick in.

17. **work off** dispose of, lose, undo, get off; exercise, sweat off, run off, walk off.

18. **work on** coax, wheedle, cajole, pester, nag, *Sl.* bug; press, importune, urge, *Inf.* pressure, blandish, dun, push.

19. **work out** **a.** resolve, solve, figure out, unriddle, clear up; crack, decode, decipher, unlock; get, do, answer, find out, puzzle out, *Sl.* dope out. **b.** add up to, amount to, come to, total up to, be in all, mount to, extend to. **c.** develop, elaborate, evolve, progress; expand, enlarge, go into, detail, enter into. **d.** drill, train, exercise, practice; discipline, prepare, prime, break in.

20. **work up** excite, stir, rouse, move, incite; whet, spur, quicken, enkindle, inflame, fire up, prompt, impel, instigate, stimulate, foment, animate, arouse.

worker, *n.* **1.** doer, performer, practitioner, operator, actor; agent, operative, perpetrator, executor.

2. laborer, workman, workwoman, workingman, workingwoman, working girl, employee; manual laborer, toiler, moiler; artisan, craftsman, smith, wright, maker, handicraftsman, tradesman; mechanic, master, journeyman, apprentice; jobholder, blue-collar worker, white-collar worker, wage earner, breadwinner, proletarian; hand, hireling, *Brit.* navvy, common laborer, day laborer; menial, flunky, fag, *Sl.* working stiff; slave, serf, peon, coolie, migrant worker, grubber, plodder, drudge, hack; busy bee, workhorse, hustler, workaholic.

working, *n.* **1.** operation, action, process, conduct, activity, doing, performance, execution.

2. shaping, molding, modeling.

—adj. **3.** operating, functioning, going, running.

workmanship, *n.* **1.** craftmanship, art, artistry, style, style, technique; craft, skill, skillfulness, dexterity, adroitness, expertness, expertise, mastery, masterfulness; talent, genius, gift, knack, flair, touch.

2. work, handiwork, handicraft.

workout, *n.* warm-up, trial *or* practice session, scrimmage; exercise, drill, calisthenics, gymnastics, aerobics, slimnastics.

workshop, *n.* **1.** shop, workroom, atelier, studio, loft; garage, plant, mill, factory, *Archaic.* manufactory. See also **work** (*def.* **6**).

2. seminar, discussion group, class.

world, *n.* **1.** earth, globe, sphere, planet, biosphere, terrene, terra, *Fr. terre,* four corners of the earth, *Fr. monde.*

2. mankind, humanity, humankind, the human race, the race of man; people, all the peoples of the world, the whole world, the wide world, the world at large; the general public, everyone, everybody, *Inf.* every Tom, Dick and Harry.

3. society, social milieu *or* circle, high society, *Fr. haut monde,* beau monde, fashionable world.

4. class, group, division, section, sector, part.

5. sphere, realm, domain, kingdom, province, department, field.

6. universe, cosmos, macrocosm, all creation, heavens and the earth, heavens, empyrean, firmament, sky, vault *or* canopy of heaven, plenum, space.

7. heavenly body, orb, moon, *Astron.* satellite, planet, sun, star.

8. **for all the world** **a.** for anything in the world, for anything, for everything in the world, for everything, no matter what, *Inf.* no way, never. **b.** in every respect, in every way, precisely, exactly, just like.

9. **out of this world,** *Informal.* exceptional, great, wonderful, marvelous, fantastic, incredible, unbelievable, *Sl.* mind-blowing, *Sl.* out of sight, *Sl.* far-out.

worldly, *adj.* **1.** earthly, terrestrial, terrene, temporal, mundane; natural, human, carnal, fleshly, corporeal, physical, material; secular, secularistic, nonspiritual, unspiritual, ungodly, profane, nonreligious, unreligious, irreligious; lay, laic, laical, nonclerical, nonecclesiastic, nonecclesiastical, non-church, civil.

2. worldly-minded, materialistic, greedy, avaricious, covetous, grasping, ambitious, power-hungry; pleasure-loving, hedonist, hedonistic, sybaritic, sybaritical.

3. worldly-wise, sophisticated, cosmopolitan, urbane. See **worldly-wise.**

worldly-wise, *adj.* sophisticated, cosmopolitan, *Sl.* cosmo, urbane; knowing, *Sl.* wise, wise in the ways of the world, *Sl.* been around; worldly, *Fr. au courant, Sl.* hip, *Sl.* cool, *Sl.* with it.

world-wide, *adj.* universal, global, international; all-embracing, all-encompassing, all-inclusive, catholic, ecumenical, pandemic, general; extensive, widespread, far-reaching, wide-ranging.

wormlike, *adj.* **1.** vermiform, vermicular, vermiculate, worm-shaped; sinuous, winding, tortuous; crawling, creeping, slithering, sneaking, worming.

2. groveling, servile, slavish, subservient; kowtowing, bowing, bending, crouching, stooping; cringing, cowering, squirming; sycophantic, toadyish, truckling, *Sl.* bootlicking, *Sl.* footlicking, *Inf.* apple-polishing.

worn, *adj.* **1.** worn-out, time-worn, decrepit; deteriorated, decadent, decayed; fallen apart, broken up, disintegrated, decomposed; dilapidated, broken-down, gone to wrack and ruin; in disrepair, unimproved, sleazy, *Sl.* grungy, *Sl.* beat-up, *Inf.* shot, run-down; tumble-down, falling to pieces, crumbled, rickety, shaky; moth-eaten, mildewed, moldy, moldering; threadbare, worn to a thread, faded, rusty, dingy.

2. exhausted, tired, tired out, *Inf.* dog-tired, dead tired, *Sl.* dead, dead on one's feet; overtired, done in, all in, ready to drop; fatigued, weary, worn out, *Inf.* tuckered out, *Inf.* bushed, fagged, fagged out, played out, spent, *Archaic.* forspent; *All Sl.* beat, pooped, pooped out, (*with have*) had it.

worried, *adj.* anxious, distressed, disturbed, troubled, carking, concerned, solicitous; uneasy, ill-at-ease, disquieted, unquiet, fretful, restless, itching; nervous, *Sl.* antsy, *Inf.* on pins and needles, on tenterhooks; on edge, perturbed, worked *or* wrought up; watchful, apprehensive, *Inf.* with one's heart in one's mouth, fearful, afraid; anguished, pained, suffering, tormented, tortured.

worry, *v.* **1.** fret, agonize, lose sleep over, *Inf.* stew, writhe, stay awake nights, *Inf.* get grey hair, *Sl.* sweat, *Sl.* sweat blood, feel uneasy, *Archaic.* cark, be anxious, be tied up in knots, be afraid; fidget, fuss, be restive; lose heart, despond, despair, be heavy-hearted; mope over, grieve over, take to heart, brood over; borrow trouble, be pessimistic; be apprehensive, have prey on the mind.

2. harass, harry, *Inf.* hassle, plague, torture, torment, persecute, trouble; bother, disturb, shake, ruffle, fluster; hector, pester, badger, belabor, *Archaic.* haggle; annoy, nettle, irk, gall, peeve; distract, distress, discompose, confuse, confound; embarrass, mortify, chagrin.

—*n.* **3.** anxiety, uneasiness, disquiet, disquietude, inquietude, cark, fretfulness; trouble, concern, care, solicitude; nervousness, ants, *Inf.* butterflies, *Inf.* butterflies in one's stomach, *Sl.* heebie-jeebies, *Sl.* habdabs; misgiving, presentiment, foreboding; apprehension, fear, fear and trembling, dread, angst; anguish, pain, suffering, torment, torture; plague, hornet's nest, sore subject, thorn in the flesh.

worsen, *v.* **1.** deteriorate, degenerate, decline, sink, take a turn for the worse, slip, slide; go downhill, go to pieces, go to ruin, *Inf.* go to pot, *Inf.* go to the dogs, *Sl.* go *or* run to seed, *Sl.* hit the skids; fall, fail, lapse, weaken, retrogress, retrograde, let oneself go; disintegrate, crumble, break up, fall apart; erode, ablate, wear away, weather; decay, decompose, crumble into dust.

2. aggravate, exacerbate, intensify, heighten, increase.

worship, *n.* **1.** adoration, veneration, reverence, homage; praise, glorification, blessing, exaltation, magnification; honor, respect, esteem, admiration; extolment, laudation, eulogization, panegyrization; deference, bowing down before, genuflection, kneeling before; supplication, invocation, prayer, orison; adulation, incense, idolatry, idolization, deification, apotheosis, hero-worship.

2. religious ceremony, divine service, services, church service, church, temple; prayer meeting, matins, vespers, evensong; Eucharist, Mass, High Mass, Low Mass, Holy Communion.

—*v.* **3.** praise, glorify, exalt, magnify; extol, laud, eulogize, panegyrize; pay homage to, do service to, burn candles to, burn incense before; bow down before, kiss the feet of, prostrate oneself, fall at the feet of, genuflect before, kneel before; give thanks, say grace, say the blessing; supplicate, invoke, pray to, beseech, entreat; pray, commune with God, attend services, go to Mass, go to church, go to meeting, go to temple.

4. revere, reverence, venerate, honor, esteem, respect, admire; look up to, put on a pedestal, lionize, defer to; adulate, idolatrize, idolize, deify, apotheosize; cherish, treasure, love, adore, dote on.

worshiper, *n.* churchgoer, communicant, celebrant; believer, convert, cultist, theist, Pietist; devotee, votary, follower, *Inf.* fan, *Inf.* buff; idolator, idolizer, fanatic, groupie, *Sl.* nut, *Sl.* freak, *Sl.* bug; admirer, adorer, glorifier, extoller, praiser.

worst, *v.* defeat, beat, best, get the better of, upset, upend, *Inf.* whomp; hash, *Sl.* skin, *U.S. Sl.* skunk, *Inf.* settle [s.o.'s] hash, *Inf.* lick, *Sl.* cream, *Sl.* shellac, *Sl.* pulverize; crush, overthrow, smash, thrash, trounce, trim, whip, drub, floor, break, quell, quench, quash, destroy, *Sl.* zap, clobber, polish off, *Sl.* do in; conquer, vanquish, subdue, subjugate, oppress; rout, discomfit, overwhelm, *Sl.* mop *or* wipe the floor with; overrun, trample, *Inf.* run into the ground.

worth, *n.* **1.** merit, excellence, quality, superiority, *Sl.* class; character, integrity, probity, uprightness, respectability; honor, virtue, goodness, trustworthiness; eminence, preeminence, distinction, greatness, nobility, transcendence; fineness, perfection, certain something, *Fr. je ne sais quoi.*

2. usefulness, use, utility; advantage, benefit, gain, profit, avail, good, service, help, aid; importance, consideration, consequence, significance, moment, weight.

3. value, valuation, appraisal, assessment, evaluation, estimation; cost, price, market price, asking price, charge, expense.

worthless, *adj.* **1.** valueless, nugatory, bastardly, meritless, inutile; inadequate, unserviceable, impracticable, inefficient; frivolous, trivial, inessential, inconsequential, unimportant, superfluous, petty; empty, idle, inane, paltry, *Dial.* footy; trashy, shabby, *Inf.* cheesy, sleazy, flimsy, jerry-built, *U.S. Sl.* cottonpickin', not worth a straw *or* a continental; showy, gaudy, glittering, tinsel, tin, superficial.

2. vain, bootless, futile, unavailing, useless, Sisyphean, ineffective, inefficacious; fruitless, unproductive, abortive, barren, sterile, impotent, effete; unprofitable, profitless, unsuccessful, to no purpose, to no avail, for naught.

3. vile, base, depraved, no-good, *Inf.* no-account; despicable, *Archaic.* lurdan, contemptible, abject; corrupt, vicious, wicked, blackguardly, rascally.

worthy, *adj.* **1.** deserving, meritorious, estimable, praiseworthy, laudable, commendable, *Brit. Dial.* gradely, admirable, creditable, acceptable, good enough; suitable, fit, seemly, proper, decorous; appropriate, apt, apposite, apropos; meet, due, right, just, fitting, befitting.

2. virtuous, moral, upright, good, righteous, honest, decent; noble, sterling, excellent, exemplary, matchless; reputable, trustworthy, reliable; of great integrity, incorruptible, irreproachable, unimpeachable, blameless.

—*n.* **3.** eminence, notable, dignitary, personage, official, *Inf.* VIP; potentate, mogul, magnate, *Sl.* big gun, *Sl.* big cheese, *Sl.* big shot; *Inf.* bigwig, *Sl.* biggie, *Inf.* heavyweight, *Sl.* heavy, *Inf.* name, *Sl.* somebody, *Sl.* something, *Sl.* high-muck-a-muck.

would-be, *adj.* assumed, put-on, self-styled, *Fr. soi-disant*, supposed, pretended; feigned, simulated, make-believe, sham, flash; pseudo, counterfeit, bogus, spurious, supposititious.

wound, *n.* **1.** injury, hurt, damage, harm, trauma; cut, stab, slash, puncture, tear, laceration, gash; bruise, contusion, sore, lesion, abrasion, scrape, bump, *Sl.* boo-boo.

2. shock, blow, nasty *or* cruel blow, *Sl.* low blow; insult, mortification, embarrassment; distress, hurt, pang, ache, heartache, throb, wrench; pain, grief, anguish, torture, torment.

—*v.* **3.** injure, hurt, harm, damage, traumatize; cut, lacerate, tear, rend; slit, slash, gash, scratch, *Inf.* cut up; stab, stick, pierce, puncture.

4. wrong, do wrong, do wrong by, aggrieve, sting, *Sl.* burn; grieve, hurt [s.o.'s] feelings, pain, afflict, distress, punish, cut to the quick *or* the heart, touch a sore spot, touch a raw nerve, *Sl.* hit [s.o.] where he lives, *Sl.* step on [s.o.'s] toes *or* corns; offend, insult, affront, give offense *or* injury, make [s.o.] feel small.

wraith, *n.* ghost, specter, fetch, shade, spirit, revenant, haunt; apparition, phantom, phantasm.

wrangle, *v.* **1.** argue, dispute, quarrel, argufy, bicker, squabble, have an altercation; row, brawl, contend, differ, fall out, clash, be at odds, be at loggerheads; fight, spat, tiff, *Brit. Archaic.* brangle, jangle, *Obs.* brabble; differ, haggle, spar, have words, disagree.

—n. **2.** argument, dispute, quarrel, bickering, *Sl.* beef, controversy; contestation, litigation, disputation, *Inf.* words; squabble, spat, tiff, *Brit. Dial.* fratch; conflict, *Inf.* run-in, *Inf.* hassle, *Inf.* barney, *Sl.* blowup; row, *Inf.* dustup, *Sl.* rhubarb, uproar, brouhaha, brawl, rumpus, *Inf.* ruckus; fight, tussle, donnybrook, *Inf.* scrap, *Inf.* set-to; broil, embroilment, imbroglio, *Scot.* sturt, *Scot.* collieshangie.

wrap, *v.* **1.** enfold, envelop, enwrap, encase, enclose, sheathe, cover; muffle, bundle up, swathe, swaddle, shroud, enshroud; secure, tuck in, tuck up.

2. package, parcel, pack, do up, wrap up, gift-wrap; box, case, bundle, truss, bale, tie up.

—n. **3.** coat, jacket, windbreaker, ulster, carcoat, duster, tabard; cape, cloak, opera cloak *or* cape, pelisse; mantle, mantua, manta, palla; shawl, stole, poncho, serape; afghan, burnoose, caftan; mackinaw, parka, peacoat, pea jacket, reefer, sack coat, smock; raincoat, slicker, sou'wester, trench coat.

wrapper, *n.* **1.** covering, cover, casing, jacket, capsule, pod, shell; container, envelope, case; sheath, shroud; bandage, binding.

2. robe, bathrobe, kimono, housecoat, brunch coat; dressing gown, lounging robe; negligee, peignoir.

wrap-up, *n.* **1.** final report, summary, review, recapitulation, summation, rehash, fill-in, rundown, roundup, *Inf.* mop-up, *Inf.* windup; abstract, synopsis, compendium, survey, précis, conspectus; digest, epitome, brief, capitulation.

2. conclusion, end, ending, termination, *Inf.* the last word, *Inf.* the last chapter, the final curtain, *Inf.* firing of the last shot, lights out, finis.

wrath, *n.* **1.** anger, ire, dudgeon, high dudgeon, *Scot.* birse; passion, hot blood, fever heat; rage, towering *or* blind *or* burning rage, frenzy, madness, violence, ferocity.

2. resentment, bitter resentment, bitterness, embitterment, exacerbation, hard feelings; choler, spleen, gall, bile, ill *or* bad humor, ill *or* bad temper; enmity, animosity, ill will, ill *or* bad feeling, bad blood; virulence, acrimony, acerbity.

3. vengeance, revenge, avengement, sweet revenge; punishment, just reward.

wrathful, *adj.* **1.** irate, ireful, angry, wroth, incensed; enraged, raging, fuming, infuriated, *Rare.* infuriate, furious; inflamed, flaming, flaring, flared up, heated, red-hot, white-hot; distraught, overwrought, upset, feverish, hysterical, irrational; violent, unrestrained, uncontrollable; ranting, raving, storming, foaming at the mouth, rabid, fanatical, frenzied; frantic, crazed, *Pathol.* delirious, mad, *Inf.* wild, out of one's mind, beside oneself.

2. peeved, annoyed, vexed, irritated; piqued, chafed, galled, riled, nettled; offended, affronted, displeased, indignant; worked up, stirred up, kindled, enkindled; passionate, impassioned, impassionate, overexcited.

3. irritable, cross, surly, snappish, petulant, peevish; testy, choleric, touchy, huffy, peppery; splenetic, spleenful, bilious, cranky, ill-tempered, bad-tempered; irascible, quick-tempered, short-tempered, *Inf.* short-fused; quarrelsome, contentious, belligerent, pugnacious, bellicose; volatile, volcanic, explosive, hot-tempered, hot-headed, fiery, inflammable.

wreath, *n.* **1.** garland, coronal, *Literary.* anadem, festoon, lei, chaplet; diadem, coronet.

2. circle, loop, ring; curl, spiral, coil.

wreathe, *v.* **1.** adorn, garland, festoon, decorate, embellish; laurel.

2. twist, wind, coil, spiral, snake, curl; twine, entwine, weave.

3. encircle, circle, ring, surround; envelop, enfold, wrap, enwrap, hug, embrace.

wreck, *n.* **1.** wrack, mess, total ruin, ruin, havoc; pileup, accident, smash-up, crack-up, chain accident, collision; shipwreck, *Naut.* derelict; flotsam and jetsam, wreckage, debris, detritus, ruins, fragments, relics, pieces, remains.

2. destruction, devastation, desolation, ravagement, ruination; demolition, pulverization, razing, leveling, pulling down, tearing down; smashing, shattering, crashing, cracking; disintegration, deterioration, decay; quashing, quelling, stifling, suppression; shooting down, cutting short, nipping in the bud; annihilation, extermination, obliteration, cancellation, termination, end, downfall.

—v. **3.** shipwreck, scuttle, run aground, run into the rocks, sink, capsize, founder.

4. devastate, demolish, desolate, ruin, destroy; smash, (*of a car*) *Sl.* total, knock to pieces, reduce to nothing, shatter, *Inf.* break into smithereens; blast, blow up, explode, dynamite, put the torch to; raze, tear down, pull down, knock down, dismantle, disassemble; vandalize, waste, *Sl.* trash; bulldoze, flatten, level, take the wrecker's ball to, gut.

5. quash, crush, subdue, quell, stifle, squelch, put down; defeat, upset, upset the applecart; annihilate, exterminate, eradicate, expunge, obliterate; blot out, erase, rub out, cancel, eliminate, do away with; mess up, *Inf.* rain on, play havoc with, spoil, *Sl.* screw up, *Inf.* make a hash of, botch, *Sl.* louse up, *Sl.* gum up the works, throw a monkey wrench into the works; kill, finish, extinguish, put out, snuff; liquidate, slay, get rid of, expel, throw out; terminate, conclude, finish, put an end to, bring to an end, end, write finis to.

6. collide, crash, smash up, crack up; go up in smoke, come to naught, end with a whimper, come to grief.

wrench, *v.* **1.** twist, turn, pull, jerk, yank, tug, force, tear, rip.

2. strain, wrick, overstrain, sprain, throw out of joint.

3. distress, hurt, trouble, perturb, harrow; tug *or* yank at one's heartstrings, break one's heart, cut to the heart, make one's heart bleed, cut to the quick; affect, touch, move, stir; pain, sadden, wound, dishearten, depress; afflict, bother, worry, torment, torture.

4. wrest, extract, pry out, pull out, pluck out, wring from, withdraw, distill; draw out, elicit, evoke, educe.

—n. **5.** twist, yank, jerk, jolt, tug, pull; strain, sprain.

6. heartache, tug of the heartstrings, pang, throe; pain, hurt, ache, stab in the heart, agony; heartbreak, sorrow, grief, anguish, sadness, despair, desolation, sense of loss.

7. distortion, garbling, perversion, misconstruction, misinterpretation, misrepresentation, mistranslation; falsification, coloring, false coloring, false meaning, slant.

wrestle, *v.* **1.** clinch, grab, *Dial.* rassle, squeeze, press, throw, throw to the mat.

2. grapple, tussle, scuffle, fight, battle; tackle, dive at, tilt at, joust; struggle, contend, pit oneself against, play against, take on, come to grips with, face, face up to; go all out, do one's best *or* damnedest, knock oneself out, labor, work like a Trojan, work at, work like a stevedore; take pains, persevere, persist, be assiduous,

Inf. plug at *or* ahead, knuckle down.

—*n.* **3.** struggle, fight, battle; labor, work, travail, effort, strain, laboriousness; diligence, perseverance, persistence, assiduousness.

wretch, *n.* **1.** unfortunate, miserable *or* poor being *or* creature, poor devil, pilgarlic, sad case, *Sl.* sad sack, *Chiefly Brit. Sl.* poor bugger; victim, sufferer, prey, shorn lamb, martyr, scapegoat; outcast, misfit, pariah; ragamuffin, *Sl.* raggy, tatterdemalion, pauper, beggar; vagabond, tramp, *Inf.* bum, hobo.

2. scoundrel, knave, blackguard, varlet, rascal, rogue, rapscallion, scalawag, scullion, scapegrace, wastrel, ne'er-do-well, *Archaic.* bezonian, *Archaic.* caitiff, *Archaic.* whoreson; miscreant, reprobate, renegade, wrongdoer, delinquent, black sheep; criminal, villain, ruffian, thug, culprit, malefactor, felon; rake, debauchee, libertine, wanton, lecher; beast, cur, hound, viper, skunk, polecat; *All Inf.* jerk, creep, louse, rat, stinker, bad egg; *All Sl.* bum, mucker, bastard, SOB; *All Brit. Sl.* rotter, bounder, blighter.

wretched, *adj.* **1.** forlorn, woeful, woebegone, careworn, heartsick, sick at heart, downhearted, brokenhearted, heartbroken, crushed, broken, heavy-laden, afflicted, desolate, despairing, dismal, despondent; down, disconsolate, dejected, depressed, melancholic, gloomy, disheartened, spiritless, *Inf.* broken-up, *Inf.* cut-up, *Sl.* bummed-out *or* bummed; sad, unhappy, infelicitous, sorrowful, doleful, dolorous, dolorific, dreary, *Literary.* drear, grieved, mournful, tearful, teary, lachrymose; comfortless, cheerless, joyless.

2. miserable, sorry, poor, pitiful, pitiable, piteous, *Inf.* lousy, *Sl.* rotten; adverse, troublesome, difficult, hard, trying; star-crossed, ill-starred, evil-starred, unlucky, unfortunate, hapless; tragic, ruinous, fatal, dire, black, grievous, grim; abject, stark, sordid, slummy, slum-like, poverty-stricken.

3. contemptible, beneath contempt, worthy of contempt, despicable, detestable, base, base-spirited, mean, mean-spirited, low, vile, paltry, *Archaic.* caitiff.

4. worthless, useless, pathetic, *Chiefly Dial.* footy, not worth mentioning, not worth a rap *or* straw *or* damn, not worth a nickel *or* dime.

wriggle, *v.* **1.** squirm, writhe, wiggle, twist and turn, *Inf.* have ants in one's pants.

2. worm, snake, slink.

wriggly, *adj.* **1.** wiggly, wiggling, wriggling, writhing, twisting, twisting and turning, squirming, *Sl.* antsy *or* antsy-pantsy.

2. evasive, shifty, slippery, hard to pin down, *Inf.* cagey.

wring, *v.* **1.** twist, wrench, wrest; force from, wrench from, rend from, tear from, rip from.

2. squeeze, extract, put through the wringer.

3. blackmail, exact, *Law.* extort, *Sl.* shake down, *Sl.* bleed.

4. torment, torture, agonize, harrow, excruciate, rack; rend, stab, pierce, wound.

wrinkle, *n.* **1.** fold, crease, crimp, gather, pucker; corrugation, furrow, ridge, *Chiefly Scot.* wimple; line, crow's foot.

—*v.* **2.** crease, crimp, gather, pucker; corrugate, fold, furrow; pleat; knit, pucker; crumple, crinkle.

wrinkled, *adj.* creased, folded, furrowed, ridged, gathered, puckered; corrugated, lined, puckered; crinkled, crinkly, crumpled, wrinkly.

write, *v.* **1.** inscribe, *Rare.* scribe, pen, put pen to paper, commit to paper; jot down, dash off; scrawl, scribble, scrabble, scratch.

2. draft, draw up, write up *or* out; lucubrate.

3. author, compose, indite; poeticize, poetize, versify, rhyme, sing; pamphletize, pamphleteer.

4. correspond, communicate, epistolize, *Inf.* drop [s.o.] a line *or* note.

5. write down **a.** record, register, note, make a note of; transcribe, list, catalogue. **b.** disparage, deprecate, derogate, detract, decry, belittle; injure, hurt, harm, damage, *Sl.* do [s.o.] dirty.

6. write off **a.** cancel, annul, cross out, rule out, sponge out, blot *or* wipe out; erase, expunge, eradicate. **b.** disregard, think nothing of, forget about, lay by the wayside, *Inf.* shelve, *Sl.* put in the circular file, *Sl.* eighty-six. **c.** *Law.* amortize, pay off, pay up, settle, liquidate.

writer, *n.* **1.** penman, penner, *Sl.* pen-pusher, *Sl.* ink-slinger, *Sl.* ink-spiller, *Sl.* quill-driver; author, composer, creative writer, wordsmith, word painter; hack, scribbler, *Inf.* word-slinger, *Inf.* potboiler, *Chiefly Brit. Archaic.* penny-a-liner.

2. journalist, newsman, newspaperman, *Brit.* pressman, *Archaic.* gazetteer, gentleman *or* representative of the press, member of the fourth estate; reporter, *Journalism.* leg man, newshound, newshawk, newshen, newsmonger; correspondent, contributor, stringer, paragrapher, *Brit.* paragraphist; columnist, gossip columnist, sob sister, scandalmonger, dirt-dealer; critic, reviewer; editor, contributing editor, editorialist, *Brit.* leader writer; newswriter.

3. scribe, scrivener, amanuensis, secretary, clerk, recorder; copier, copyist, engrosser, transcriber, *Judaism.* sopher.

4. scenarist, script writer, movie writer, playwright, dramaturgist; prosaist; paraphrast, paraphraser; ironist, satirist, parodist; mythmaker; magazinist.

writhe, *v.* **1.** squirm, twist about, thrash, flail, wriggle, twist and turn.

2. contort, distort, warp, bend out of shape; misshape, deform.

writing, *n.* **1.** handwriting, penmanship, script, manuscript, longhand, *Inf.* fist, *Scot.* hand of writ, chirography; calligraphy, good hand, Palmer method; cacography, bad hand, scribble, scrabble, scrawl, scratch, chickenscratch.

2. work, piece, composition; publication, book, volume, tome, opus; article, review, critique, editorial.

3. letter, epistle, note, *Inf.* line, missive, correspondence; memorandum, memo, *Chiefly Brit.* chit.

4. writing on the wall omen, sign, portent, indication, preindication, warning.

wrong, *adj.* **1.** bad, immoral, sinful, peccant, wrongful; unlawful, illegal, lawless, illicit, law-breaking, illegitimate, *Inf.* illegit, criminal, felonious, larcenous, delinquent; dishonest, corrupt, crooked, malfeasant, misfeasant, degenerate, depraved, *Sl.* sick; reprehensible, shameful, disgraceful, dishonorable, opprobrious, blameworthy; vile, sordid, foul, base, low, dirty, filthy, scurvy, rotten, wretched, miserable; evil, wicked, iniquitous, nefarious, sinister, dark, black, villainous, evil-minded, nasty, black-hearted, malicious, vicious, spiteful, malevolent, devilish, diabolic, diabolical, satanic, demoniac, demoniacal, Mephistophelian; fiendish, hellish, infernal, Stygian; heinous, atrocious, terrible, awful, horrible, horrid, dreadful, *Inf.* god-awful; abominable, despicable, detestable, contemptible, hateful, odious.

2. erroneous, incorrect, inaccurate, inexact, imprecise; amiss, mistaken, off, *Inf.* off base, *Inf.* off target, *Inf.* off the beam, on the wrong track, *Inf.* barking up the wrong tree; way off, *Inf.* off by a mile, not even close, *Sl.* out in left field, *Sl.* at sea, *Inf.* cold, all wrong, dead wrong; unsound, illogical, irrational, ungrounded, groundless, unfounded, twisted, *Sl.* cock-eyed, *Sl.* screwy; crazy, *Sl.* all wet, full of beans *or* prunes, *Sl.* full of hot air, *Sl.* full of it, *Sl.* nuts, *Sl.* whacko, *Sl.*

cuckoo.

3. wrong-headed, misguided, unwise, imprudent. See **wrong-headed** (*def.* **1**).

4. improper, indecorous, unseemly, unbecoming, unladylike, ungentlemanly, ungentlemanlike; malapropos, inappropriate, inapt, unsuitable, unsuited, unfit, ill-adapted, incompatible, out of keeping, inapposite, inapplicable, irrelevant, out of place; unwarranted, uncalled for, way out of line.

—*n.* **5.** misdeed, misdoing, malefaction, wrongdoing, *Inf.* no-no; immoral act, sin, moral offense, vice, lapse from virtue, unrighteousness, depravity; mistake, error, misstep, blunder, bungle, flub, muff, dereliction, slip, lapse, oversight, omission, *Inf.* slip-up, *Sl.* screw-up, *Sl.* boot, *Sl.* louse-up, *Sl.* E *or* the big E; transgression, trespass, offense, infraction, violation; crime, criminal act, felony, misdemeanor, delinquency, *Law.* tort, malfeasance, *Chiefly Law.* malversation, dirty pool, corruption; bad, bad *or* naughty thing, evil, wickedness, iniquity, something awful; atrocity, horror, outrage, monstrosity, enormity.

6. impropriety, indiscretion, gaucherie, faux pas, misconduct, terrible thing, absurdity, *All Sl.* boo-boo, boner, goof, blooper, clinker, clunker, dumb trick, fool mistake.

—*adv.* **7.** awry, amiss, athwart, astray, *Scot. and North Eng.* agley; out of whack, out of order, on the blink.

8. wrongly, erroneously; injuriously, harmfully, perversely; unfairly, unjustly, inequitably.

—*v.* **9.** abuse, misuse, ill-use, maltreat, mistreat, ill-treat, aggrieve, *Inf.* shaft, *Inf.* give [s.o.] the shaft, *Sl.* do [s.o.] dirty *or* dirt, *Sl.* kick [s.o.] around *or* in the teeth, *Sl.* do [s.o.] wrong; oppress, persecute, keep [s.o.] down; exploit, use, take advantage of, walk all over, impose upon; defraud, cheat, trick, *Inf.* flimflam, *U.S. Sl.* con.

10. transgress, trespass, offend, desecrate, profane, defile, debase, prostitute; malign, slur, impugn, traduce, asperse, vilify, defame, slander, libel, bespatter, make [s.o.'s] name mud; denigrate, belittle, minimize, insult, run *or* put down, *Inf.* knock, *Sl.* bad-mouth; ridicule, mock, scorn, deride, make fun of, laugh at.

wrongdoer, *n.* malefactor, evildoer, transgressor, trespasser, sinner, offender, culprit; lawbreaker, *Inf.* scofflaw, criminal, delinquent, juvenile delinquent, *Sl.* JD, felon, larcener, larcenist, misdemeanant, *Law.* malfeasant, *Law.* misfeasor; convict, reprobate, recidivist, *Inf.* chronic crook, *Sl.* jailbird; gangster, hoodlum, mobster, racketeer, mafioso, desperado, *Sl.* hood; miscreant, villain, blackguard, scapegrace, knave, rogue, rascal, wretch, scamp, scoundrel, rapscallion, *Inf.* scalawag, *Sl.* no-good, *Sl.* bad guy, *Archaic.* caitiff, *Archaic.* varlet.

wrong-headed, *adj.* **1.** misguided, unwise, imprudent, injudicious; ill-considered, ill-judged, ill-advised, ill-contrived, ill-devised, using *or* showing poor judgment; impolitic, inexpedient, infelicitous, disadvantageous, unfavorable, the worst possible; unintelligent, stupid, *Inf.* dumb, *Inf.* dopey.

2. stubborn, stubborn as a mule, obstinate, recalcitrant, mulish, pig-headed, bullheaded, headstrong, willful, self-willed, opinionated, adamant; contrary, perverse, froward, unaccommodating, contumacious, cross-grained, *Inf.* ornery, refractory, intransigent, intractable, *Scot.* thrawn.

wroth, *adj.* **1.** angry, irate, wrathful. See **wrathful** (*def.* **1**).

2. stormy, violent, strong, savage, tempestuous, turbulent, wild, rough; threatening, restless, agitated, foaming, boiling, seething; raging, howling, roaring; windy, blustering, blustery, gusty, blowing, squally, squallish.

wrought-up, *adj.* excited, wound-up, worked-up, beside oneself, stirred-up, stimulated, energized, electrified, hyped-up, *Sl.* psyched; whipped-up, aroused, inflamed, fired-up, fiery; impassioned, enthused, fervid, fervent, zealous, in a fever pitch, red-hot; overwrought, keyed-up, nervous, high-strung, edgy, on edge, tense, uneasy, restless, restive, fidgety, skittish; frantic, frenzied, wild, hysterical, delirious, feverish, *Brit. Sl.* bonkers, *Sl.* out of one's skull *or* gourd; agitated, disturbed, upset, discomposed, disconcerted, ruffled, flustered, fluttered, in a dither, *Inf.* hot and bothered; irritated, annoyed, nettled, perturbed, exasperated, aggravated, vexed; angry, mad, irate, furious, fuming, raging, *Inf.* hot, *Inf.* hot under the collar, *Inf.* hopped up.

wry, *adj.* **1.** lopsided, one-sided, crooked, askew, awry, twisted, distorted; tilted, inclined, aslant, to one side, sideways, off-center, uneven, unsymmetrical, asymmetric, asymmetrical.

2. devious, misdirected, astray.

3. contrary, perverse, wrong-headed, cross-grained. See **wrong-headed** (*def.* **2**).

4. distorted, taken out of context, twisted, warped, perverted, garbled; misstated, misquoted, misrendered, misreported, misrepresented; misread, misinterpreted, misconstrued, misapprehended, misunderstood.

5. ironic, amusing, droll, witty, dry.

X

x, *n.* **1.** unknown, unknown factor *or* quantity, variable; question, big question, question mark, riddle, conundrum, puzzle, sphinx; mystery, obscurity, arcanum, secret, occult; mystery man, ghostly figure, faceless person, invisible man; unexplored territory, *Latin. terra incognita.*

—adj. **2.** experimental, pilot, trial, hypothetical, drawing-board, in the trial stages; untested, untried, ready for the shakedown; new, novel, exploratory.

—v. **3.** (*on a ballot, examination etc.*) choose, opt, select, name, pick one's choice, check, single out; vote for, cast a vote, elect, prefer, mark one's preference; mark, signify, indicate.

4. delete, cross out, strike out *or* over, scratch, blue-pencil, *Print.* dele, *Inf.* bleep; expunge, expurgate, bowdlerize, abridge, edit, cut, slash, butcher, kill; erase, blot out, rub out, take out, knock out.

Xanthippe, *n.* shrew, virago, *Sl.* battle-ax, termagant, fishwife; harpy, fury, Tartar, she-wolf, *Sl.* bitch; harridan, hag, beldam, crone, witch; scold, nag, *Inf.* biddy, *Inf.* old biddy, *Sl.* old hag.

xanthous, *adj.* yellow, yellowish, golden, honey, daffodil, jonquil, saffron, topaz, canary yellow.

xenophobic, *adj.* **1.** fearing foreigners *or* strangers, nationalist, nationalistic, jingoistic, chauvinistic; isolationist; racist, anti-Semitic.

2. parochial, provincial, regional, regionalistic, small-town, microcultural, *Sociol.* ethnocentric, insular; limited, confined, illiberal, uncatholic; narrow, narrow-minded, small-minded.

3. shy, bashful, unconfident, self-conscious; withdrawn, distant, *Inf.* introverted, unsocial, unsociable; timid, fearful, apprehensive, anxious; unaggressive, unassertive.

xerox, *v.* *Trademark.* **1.** copy, reproduce, duplicate, replicate, double, triplicate; mimeo, mimeograph, ditto, photostat, print, photograph.

—n. *Informal.* **2.** copy, dulicate, carbon, ditto, photostat.

x-ray, *n.* Roentgen ray, *Brit.* radiogram; skiagraph, radiograph, shadowgraph, roentgenogram, roentgenograph.

xylophone, *n.* marimba, vibraharp, *Inf.* vibes.

Y

yacht, *n.* **1.** pleasure boat, cruising vessel *or* craft, cruiser, cabin cruiser; sailboat, sailer, *Inf.* windjammer, motorboat, speedboat; racing boat, racer.
—*v.* **2.** sail, voyage, journey, travel, race.

yahoo, *n.* brute, savage, ruffian, barbarian; lout, churl, boor, bumpkin, yokel; philistine, low-brow, bourgeois, *Fr. parvenu,* upstart, *Fr. arriviste, Brit. Sl.* bounder, *Brit. Sl.* mucker; peasant, *Sl.* rube, cad.

yak, *v. Slang.* chatter, babble, gab, prattle, twaddle; gibble-gabble, gibber, jabber, *Sl.* yackety-yak, blather, palaver; spout off, shoot off one's mouth, *Sl.* flap one's gums, ramble on, talk on, go on and on, *Sl.* run off at the mouth.

yammer, *v.* **1.** whine, complain, groan, moan, snivel, blubber; whimper, pule, mewl, wail, cry, bawl; gripe, grumble, murmur, mutter, squawk, *Inf.* beef, *Sl.* bellyache.
2. growl, clamor, howl, yelp, bark, bellow, roar. See **yell.**

yank, *v.* jerk, pull, tug, pluck, *Dial.* yerk; wrench, twitch, snatch, jog.

yap, *v.* yelp, bark, *Inf.* holler, bellow, roar; caterwaul, bray, neigh, moo, bleat, croak, snort, oink; cackle, hoot, quack, caw, clack, crow, gabble. See **yell.**

yard, *n.* grounds, park; dooryard, garden, *Brit.* croft, *Law.* curtilage; courtyard, court, quadrangle, *Inf.* quad, *Brit. Dial.* close, garth *or* cloister garth, bailey; compound, enclosure, confine; pound, run, fold, pen, coop, chicken yard; barnyard, farmyard; stockyard, paddock, corral, kraal.

yardstick, *n.* **1.** measure, ruler, measuring stick.
2. standard, gauge, scale, guide, touchstone, criterion; guideline, rule of thumb, regulation, benchmark; model, pattern, example, paradigm; exemplar, ideal, beau ideal, paragon.

yarn, *n.* **1.** thread, fiber, strand.
2. *Informal.* tale, story, tall story, *Sl.* fish *or* war story, *Sl.* megilla, *Inf.* song and dance, sob story, *Sl.* snow job; fiction, fictitious tale, invention; fib, falsehood, fabrication, cock-and-bull story, *Inf.* whopper.

yaw *v.* **1.** deviate, go off course, change course, change direction, veer, shift, *Naut.* jibe, tack, slue; turn about, wheel, swing; bend, curve, sheer, heel, bear off; wobble, turn, warp, skew, bias, twist, dogleg; change about, alter, chop, chop and change.
—*n.* **2.** deviation, divergence, deflection, veering; swerve, shift, *Naut.* jibe, turn, change; drift, swing, curve, bend, tack; warp, chop, sheer, sweep; bias, skew, slant.

year, *n.* **1.** session, period, space, term, spell, span, stretch.
2. years a. age, lifetime, life span; generation, duration, stage of life. **b.** old age, agedness, oldness, elderliness; senescence, senectitude, second childhood, senility, anility, caducity, dotage, decrepitude. **c.** time, long time, aeon, chiliad, millenium, century, decade.
3. year in and year out regularly, continuously, over and over again, without a break; unfailingly, unchangingly, everlastingly, interminably, endlessly, never-endingly.

yearn, *v.* desire, wish for, long for, set one's heart on, desiderate, want; hope for, care for, pine for, sigh for; hanker after, have a yen for, covet, fancy, have a fancy for; have an eye to, be attracted to, have a mind to, have at heart, be bent upon; be inclined towards, be predisposed towards, prefer; crave, hunger, thirst, relish; lust after, burn for, *Inf.* be wild *or* mad about, *Sl.* have the hots for, *Inf.* letch after.

yearning, *n.* desire, longing, desideration, wish, wishing; hope, hoping, pining, sighing; hankering, *Inf.* yen, *Sl.* itch, *Sl.* itching; aspiration, emulation, ambition; fancy, fancying, coveting, covetousness, eagerness, ardor, craving; appetency, appetite, hunger, thirst, ravenousness; rapaciousness, voracity, voraciousness; avidity, greed, greediness, avarice; mania, craze, rage; passion, obsession, fixation.

yeast, *n.* **1.** ferment, mold, bacteria, leaven, mother, *Brit. Inf.* barm; pepsin, enzyme.
2. foam, head, froth, spume, lather, suds, bubbles; foaminess, frothiness, spumescence.
3. agitation, state of unrest, confusion, stew, brouhaha, fuss, *Inf.* to-do, turmoil, hubbub, commotion, tumult, *Inf.* a can of worms.
—*v.* **4.** ferment, leaven, rise; work, turn, foam, bubble, effervesce.

yeasty, *adj.* **1.** fermenting, fermentative, barmy, frothy, foamy, spumous, spumy, spumescent, lathery.
2. exuberant, ebullient, high-spirited, exhilarated, buoyant, bouncy; animated, effervescent, enthused, enthusiastic, irrepressible; zestful, energetic, lively.
3. frivolous, trivial, trifling, fribbling, nugatory, niggling, *Inf.* piddling; unimportant, insignificant, inconsiderable, petty, paltry; light, airy, frothy, slight, flimsy.
4. agitated, excited, stirred-up, wound-up, whipped-up; frantic, frenzied, mad; unsettled, ruffled, flustered; impassioned, fired-up.

yell, *v.* shout, clamor, cry out, scream, *Inf.* holler; exclaim, ejaculate, blast out, blurt out, sing out; shriek, screech, squall, hoot, ululate, squeal, whoop; bark, bellow, roar, yelp, yip, yawl, blare; howl, yowl, yammer;

hollo, halloo, *Fox Hunting.* huic, give cry, raise the hue and cry; cheer, rah, call out, hurrah, huzzah; vociferate, shout at the top of one's voice, rend the air, strain the throat.

yellow, *adj.* **1.** golden, gold, aureate, aurific, gilt; honey, xanthous, xanthic, butter, gambogian, quince yellow, zinc yellow, primrose; saffron, daffodil, topaz, banana, jonquil, cadmium yellow, canary yellow; lemon, citron, lutescent, luteous; tawny, amber, ocherous, ochery, buff, fulvous, fallow, ecru; blond, flaxen, yellowish, sandy, straw-colored, stramineous.

2. jaundiced, *Pathol.* icteric, sallow, xanthodermatous.

3. Mongolian, Mongoloid, Oriental, Asiatic; Chinese, Vietnamese, Cambodian, Thai, Laotian, Siamese.

4. *Informal.* cowardly, craven, pusillanimous, *Inf.* mousy, *Sl.* chicken; timid, timorous, fearful, afraid, frightened; faint-hearted, weak-kneed, lily-livered, *Inf.* chicken-hearted, pigeon-hearted; unmanly, cringing, groveling, slinking, sniveling, sneaking; panicky, *Inf.* funky, daunted, intimidated, afraid of one's shadow.

5. (*of journalism*) sensational, lurid, sordid, blood-and-thunder; scandal-mongering, muckraking; melodramatic, Barnumesque.

yelp, *v.* cry, bark, scream, shout, *Inf.* holler, whoop. See **yell**.

yen, *n.* *Informal.* **1.** desire, longing, craving, yearning, hankering, *Sl.* itching, *Sl.* itch. See **yearning**.
—*v.* **2.** yearn, set one's heart on, desire, wish for, have a yen for. See **yearn**.

yeomanly, *adj.* loyal, faithful, allegiant, true, true-hearted; devoted, pledged, patriotic, dedicated; steadfast, staunch, true-blue, fast, unwavering, unswerving, firm, stable, solid.

yes, *adv.* **1.** aye, ay, yea, affirmative; *Fr. oui, Sp. si, Ger. ja, Russ. da; Inf.* yeah, *Sl.* yah, *Sl.* yep, *Sl.* yup, *Sl.* uh-huh, *Sl.* youza; yes sir, *Inf.* yes sirree, *Inf.* yes sirreebob, yes ma'am; O.K., all right, right, *Brit. Inf.* righto, *Inf.* alrighty; of course, sure, by all means, be my guest; as you say, good, very well, *Sl.* right on, naturally, *Brit.* hear, hear; true, quite so, just so, why yes, indeed, *Inf.* indeedy, yes indeed; certainly, certes, surely, absolutely, precisely, exactly; really, truly, *Brit.* rather, to be sure, why not, assuredly, *Fr. mais oui*; granted, acknowledged, received, *Inf.* roger; amen, so be it, it is so, you bet, *Sl.* you bet your life, *Sl.* you bet your booties *or* boots.
—*n.* **2.** assent, O.K., affirmation, aye, oui, yea; agreement, acquiescence, consent, acceptance; nod of agreement, nod, thumbs up; approval, sanction, authorization, approbation; ratification, endorsement; allowance, permission, warrant, *Inf.* green light, *Inf.* go-ahead.

yes man, *n.* sycophant, lickspittle, toady, toadeater, tufthunter, fawning flatterer, truckler; flatterer, backslapper, backscratcher, timeserver, *Inf.* apple-polisher, *Sl.* brown-nose *or* brown-noser, *Sl.* brownie, *Obs., Rare.* blander, *Archaic.* pickthank; parasite, leech, *Inf.* sponge *or* sponger, hanger-on; courtier, attendant, flunky, lackey; jackal, spaniel, bootlick, bootlicker, footlicker, lickspit; kowtower, *Contemptuous.* Uncle Tom, *Sl.* oreo, cringer, groveler, sniveler.

yet, *adv.* **1.** at the present time, at the moment; until now, up until now, up to now, up to the present time, as yet, thus far, hitherto.

2. just now, right now, so soon.

3. in addition, additionally, moreover, too, also, besides, as well, to boot, ditto; and, plus, as well as; furthermore, further, over and above, above and beyond, more than that.

4. nevertheless, nonetheless, *Archaic.* natheless, however, howbeit, anyway, anyhow; regardless, be that as it may, for all that, after all is said and done, in spite of the fact, despite the fact, *Archaic.* withal, notwithstanding; all *or* just the same, at any rate, in any case, in any event; but, still, still and all, even so, after all; on the other hand, on the contrary, at the same time.
—*conj.* **5.** though, although, even though, nevertheless, but.

yield, *v.* **1.** produce, give forth, bear, bring forth, give birth to; blossom, flower, bear fruit, fructify; breed, spawn, conceive, beget, engender, reproduce; cause, give rise to; give, furnish, supply; impart, bestow, confer, impart, afford; render, return, fetch, bring in, net, earn, pay, pay back.

2. surrender, deliver up, turn over, hand in, part with; remit; release, let go, relinquish, renounce, forsake, forgo, *Law.* disclaim; abdicate, resign, *Chiefly Scot.* demit; transfer, give over, cede, waive, *Law.* demise.

3. lose hope of, despair of, give up, abandon, quit, *Sl.* pack it in, give up the ship, cry quits, cry craven, throw up one's hands, throw in the sponge *or* the towel; resign oneself to, grin and bear it, lie down and die, *Sl.* lump it.

4. capitulate, submit, succumb to; fall, bite the dust, lay down arms, raise the white flag; acquiesce, comply, accede, give in, cry *or* say uncle; concede, back down, retract, recant; defer, truckle, give place, give precedence; concur, agree, admit, accept, allow, go along with.

5. bend, flex, bow, *Inf.* cave in; relax, stretch; relent, mellow, soften, melt, thaw, dissolve.
—*n.* **6.** crop, harvest, reaping, produce, fruit; product, result, effect, output, fallout; returns, proceeds, gain, net, earnings, receipts; premium, interest.

yielding, *adj.* **1.** submissive, docile, tractable; compliant, obedient, manageable; amenable, complaisant, obliging, agreeable; timid, gentle, meek; deferential, subservient, obsequious, *Archaic.* sequacious, truckling.

2. flexible, pliable, pliant, limber, supple; soft, softened, unresistant; plastic, moldable, fictile, ductile, malleable, impressible; waxy, clayey, argillaceous, doughy, pulpy; flabby, flaccid, spongy, resilient; elastic, extensible, tractile.

3. (*of a crop, soil, etc.*) productive, fertile, fecund, fructuous, profitable; prolific, luxuriant, fruitful, fructiferous; bounteous, plenteous, teeming; workable, cultivable, arable.

yoke, *n.* **1.** harness, collar, frame, oxbow and bar; hitch, link, bond, tie, knot; coupler, coupling, connective; fastening, connection, attachment.

2. (*of draft animals*) pair, brace, span, team, couple.
—*v.* **3.** harness, hitch, attach; fasten, join, connect, unite, bracket, couple, link, concatenate; tie, bond, lash, buckle, chain.

yokel, *n.* rustic, peasant, provincial, country cousin, countryman, hobnail; farmer, plowman, plowboy, chuff, swain, gaffer, *Archaic.* kern, son *or* tiller of the soil, (*in Egypt*) fellah, (*in Russia*) muzhik, (*in Spanish America and Southwestern U.S.*) peon, *Archaic.* hind; bumpkin, country bumpkin, hawbuck, *Dial.* lumpkin, hillbilly, bogtrotter, *Inf.* chawbacon, *Inf.* cider squeezer, *Sl.* hick, *Sl.* woodhick, *Sl.* rube, *Sl.* hayseed, *Sl.* hoosier, *Fr. Sl. truffe*.

yonder, *adj.* **1.** more distant, farther, further; remote, far-off, faraway, yon; ultramontane, transalpine, tramontane, overseas, transatlantic, transmarine; antipodean, inaccessible, out-of-the-way, unapproachable.
—*adv.* **2.** over there, at a distance, yon, thither, thitherward, farther, further; far away, far-off, away,

off, beyond; abroad, over the horizon, overseas, over the hills and far away, out of range, out of the sphere of.

young, *adj.* **1.** youthful, in one's salad days; adolescent, teen-aged, in the teens, pubescent, underage, minor; sophomoric, juvenile, childish, *Sl.* kiddish, *Inf.* like a kid, boyish, girlish, puerile, infantile; callow, immature, inexperienced, green, wet behind the ears; unsophisticated, uninitiated, naïve, innocent, childlike; undeveloped, unformed, unripe; fresh, blooming, bright-eyed, rosy-cheeked, budding, growing, unfledged, newfledged, baby; baby-faced, beardless, smooth-cheeked, downy-cheeked.

2. active, vigorous, enthusiastic, keen; hopeful, sanguine, optimistic, confident, idealistic; cheerful, laughing, buoyant, light-hearted.

3. early, new, newer, recent, unheard-of.

youth, *n.* **1.** childhood, early life, salad days, boyhood, girlhood; adolescence, teens, teenage, teen years, pubescence; minority, nonage; heyday, springtime of life, bloom *or* flower of life, golden season of life, dayspring of life; immaturity, growing time, growing up; juniority, pupilage, wardship.

2. girlishness, boyishness, youthfulness, puerility, juvenescence, juvenility; freshness, vigor, light-heartedness.

3. adolescent, teenager, teen, juvenile, minor; youngster, youngling, young one, child, *Sl.* spring chicken; girl, schoolgirl, lass, lassie, mademoiselle, maiden, maid, slip, sprite, sprig; boy, schoolboy, young man, (*in ancient Greece*) ephebe, scion, lad, junior, cadet, stripling, fledgling, sapling, whelp, whippersnapper; puppy, cub, kitten, chit, chick, *Inf.* small fry, *Inf.* shaver, tyke, *Inf.* kid.

youthful, *adj.* young, adolescent, childish, callow, innocent, fresh, bright-eyed, buoyant, optimistic, cheerful. See **young** (*defs.* **1, 2**).

yowl, *v.* **1.** howl, bay, bark; bellow, bray; yelp, yawl, yap; cry, wail, caterwaul, *Scot.* greet, ululate.

—*n.* **2.** howl, bay, bark; bellow, bray; cry, wail, lament, ululation.

yule, *n.* Christmas, Christmastime, Christmastide, yuletide, Noel, Advent.

yummy, *adj. Informal.* **1.** flavorful, flavorsome, savory, mouth-watering, appetizing, toothsome, tasty, *Chiefly Scot.* gusty; delicious, delectable, delightful, *Inf.* scrumptious, ambrosial.

2. (*all usu. in reference to clothing, ornamentation, etc.*) luxurious, gorgeous, glamorous, glorious, resplendent, splendid, divine; fine, elegant, exquisite.

Z

zaftig, *adj.* **1.** (*all of a woman*) plump, chubby, rotund, rounded, well-fed, well-nourished, full-blown, blooming, lusty; buxom, full-bosomed, bosomy, *Inf.* busty, *Sl.* top-heavy, *Fr. avec beaucoup de monde au balcon*; steatopygous, *Sl.* broad-beamed, *Sl.* broad in the beam, *Sl.* beamy; well-proportioned, shapely, well-shaped; with a nice *or* gorgeous figure, with an hourglass figure, *Sl.* stacked, *Sl.* well-stacked, *Sl.* built, *Sl.* built like a brick outhouse, curvy, *Inf.* curvaceous, callipygian, well-rounded; voluptuous, attractive, appealing, lovely, comely, gorgeous, beautiful, sensational, *Inf.* sexy, seductive, provocative, suggestive, inspirational, giving a fellow ideas; stimulating, exciting, arousing, tempting.

2. appetizing, mouth-watering, juicy, delicious, ripe, well-ripened, inviting; palatable, tasty, *Inf.* scrumptious, *Inf.* yummy, delectable.

zaniness, *n.* clownishness, zanyism, clowning, clownery; buffoonery, buffoonism, buffoonishness, harlequinade; joking, jesting, jocosity, jocoseness, waggishness, waggery, drollery; levity, frivolity, facetiousness; silliness, childishness, prankishness; foolery, absurdity, inanity, fatuousness, foolishness, folly; craziness, *Sl.* kookiness, madness, *Sl.* screwiness, *Sl.* goofiness.

zany, *adj.* **1.** comical, comic, nonsensical, absurd, ludicrous, ridiculous; amusing, laughable, risible, hilarious, silly, inane, foolish; crazy, daft, *Inf.* daffy, *Chiefly Brit. Inf.* potty, *Inf.* crackpot; *All Sl.* balmy, dippy, batty, bats, cuckoo, buggy, bughouse, bugs, screwy, wacky, wacko, goofy, loony, nutty.

2. jocund, merry, mirthful, jovial, jolly; gay, frolicsome, sportive, playful, prankish, frivolous, puckish, flippant.

zap, *v. Slang.* **1.** kill, slay, murder, assassinate, do to death; liquidate, erase, blot out, get rid of; put away *or* out of the way, carry off, remove, dispatch; silence, finish, finish off, do for, fix, settle, lay out *or* low, *Inf.* put the kibosh on; shoot, shoot down, riddle, *Sl.* blow [s.o.'s] brains out, *Sl.* pump *or* fill full of lead; *All Sl.* off, hit, waste, croak, eighty-six, take off, rub out, snuff out, bump off, knock off, polish off, give [s.o.] the works *or* business; *All Euph.* send west, take [s.o.] for a ride, put [s.o.] out of his misery.

2. defeat, conquer, vanquish, rout, discomfit; overcome, overthrow, crush, thrash, trounce, whip, drub, floor; best, worst, outwit, outmaneuver.

3. hit, strike, smite, slap, punch, *Sl.* sock, smack, cuff; beat, *Sl.* belt, pommel, pelt, *Sl.* let [s.o.] have it.

zeal, *n.* **1.** ardor, fervor; fervency; devotion, devotedness; feverishness, passion, fire, glow, warmth.

2. enthusiasm, eagerness, earnestness, keenness, intentness, intensity, excitement; vigor, force, energy, determination, vehemence; relish, gusto, delight, enjoyment; elation, rapture, ecstasy, transport.

3. exuberance, ebullience, vitality, animation, spirit, spiritedness; life, buoyancy, bounce, zest, verve, zing, *Sl.* oomph.

4. fanaticism, zealotry. See **zealotry** (*defs.* **1, 2**).

zealot, *n.* **1.** fanatic, enthusiast, energumen; partisan, bigot, sectarian; extremist, radical.

2. devotee, votary, champion, disciple; fan, aficionado, *Inf.* buff, *Sl.* nut; addict, *Inf.* fiend, *Sl.* junkie, *Sl.* freak; promoter, supporter, booster, *Inf.* pusher.

zealotry, *n.* **1.** fanaticism, single-mindedness, obsession, monomania; feverishness, passion, frenzy, hysteria, insanity.

2. dogmatism, bigotry, intolerance, close-mindedness, narrow-mindedness; prejudice, bias, partiality.

zealous, *adj.* fervent, earnest, eager, enthusiastic, excited; ardent, *Inf.* gung-ho, impassioned, passionate; fervid, perfervid, feverish, rabid, monomaniacal; vigorous, vehement, forceful, energetic; determined, persistent, dogged, tenacious; devoted, devout, religious, pious.

zenith, *n.* **1.** summit, vertex, apex, apogee, peak, pinnacle, spire, point, tip, tiptop; top, crown, cap, head, headpiece.

2. acme, meridian, climax, culmination, crowning point, *Latin. ne plus ultra*; sublimity, supremacy, consummation, perfection; best, finest, utmost, uttermost, extreme, *U.S. Sl.* the greatest, *U.S. Sl.* the most; prime, heyday, bloom, full flower, flowering, blossom, efflorescence.

zero, *n.* **1.** nothing, naught, aught, nil, *Sl.* nix, *Sl.* zilch, *Tennis.* love; cipher, *Inf.* goose egg; absolutely nothing, nothing at all, *Brit. Sl.* sweet Fanny Adams *or* sweet F.A.

2. nobody, nullity, nonentity, *Inf.* nebbish, *Inf.* pipsqueak, twerp; jackstraw, man of straw, lay figure.

3. nadir, lowest point; bottom, rock bottom.

—*v.* **4.** **zero in on** pinpoint, home in on, fix, get a fix on.

zest, *n.* **1.** relish, spice, tang, flavor, seasoning, savor; twang, zing, zip, *Inf.* pizzazz, *Inf.* ginger, edge; pungency, piquancy, bite.

2. gusto, élan, animation, zestfulness; life, spirit, zip, *Sl.* oomph, *Sl.* kick; glow, warmth, soul; vivacity, *Fr. joie de vivre*, liveliness, lustiness, robustness; alacrity, delight, joy, gaiety, spiritedness; exuberance, exhilaration, elation, heartiness.

zestful, *adj.* **1.** piquant, pungent, spicy, nippy;

hot, peppery; tasty, toothsome, savory, delicious, luscious.

2. vivacious, vivid, frisky, brisk, hearty, zesty; energetic, vigorous, *Inf.* full of pep, *Inf.* peppy, *Inf.* full of get up and go; lively, full of life, animated, invigorated; exuberant, *Inf.* full of beans, *Inf.* feeling one's oats.

zigzag, *adj.* staggered, angled, forked, crooked, askew, abrupt; serpentine, sinuous, meandering, circuitous, anfractuous, roundabout, devious; mazy, labyrinthine.

zing, *n.* **1.** enthusiasm, animation, vitality, vim, gusto. See **zest** (*defs.* **1, 2**).

—*v.* **2.** whiz, buzz, zip, streak, fly. See **zoom**.

zip, *n.* **1.** vigor, vim, energy, vitality, life, spirit; relish, gusto, zing. See **zest** (*defs.* **1, 2**).

—*v.* **2.** *Informal.* speed, rush, fly, jet, streak, barrel. See **zoom**.

zombie, *n.* **1.** walking dead, walking corpse; *Psychiatry.* catatoniac.

2. *Slang.* dullard, dolt, *Inf.* deadhead, *Sl.* dummkopf; loggerhead, thickhead, *Sl.* dodo, *Sl.* dope, *Sl.* dumbbell; numskull, bonehead, dunderhead, chucklehead, *Sl.* lunkhead; oaf, lubber, *Sl.* goon; lamebrain, *Sl.* dimwit, nitwit, half-wit; nincompoop, ninnyhammer, *Sl.* yo-yo.

3. *Slang.* robot, automaton, mechanical man; somnambulist.

zone, *n.* area, region, district, quarter; locality, section, territory, realm, domain, province; department, precinct, bailiwick; tract, stretch, terrain, field; expanse, sweep, reach, surface; arena, ring, sphere, circle, orbit; latitude, hemisphere, climate, clime; locale, location, spot, place, part, situation.

zoo, *n.* **1.** zoological garden, menagerie, *Ger. Tiergarten, Fr. jardin zoologique*, park.

2. *Informal.* madhouse, bedlam, chaos, confusion, three-ring circus; disorder, disarray.

zoom, *v.* buzz, whiz, zing, streak, tear, rip; sweep, speed, clip, flit, breeze, outstrip the wind; soar, fly, jet, zip, shoot; speed, race, *Inf.* eat up the road, *Inf.* tear up the track, *Sl.* burn, *Sl.* sizzle, *Sl.* move; rush, put on steam, go all out, *Inf.* pour it on, *Inf.* barrel, hurtle, bolt; *Inf.* run like mad, ride hellbent for leather, run like a scared rabbit, *Sl.* go like a bat out of hell, go like lightning *or* greased lightning.

zzz, *v.* *Slang.* snore, *Sl.* log z's, *Sl.* saw wood, *Sl.* saw logs, *Sl.* saw gourds, snort, wheeze, buzz; nap, snooze, doze, drowse, nod off, catch forty winks; call it a day, turn in, retire, *Sl.* hit the hay *or* the sack, *Baby Talk.* go nighty-night *or* beddy-bye.